PRINCIPLES OF CORPORATE FINANCE

The McGraw-Hill/Irwin Series in Finance, Insurance, and Real Estate

Stephen A. Ross, Franco Modigliani Professor of Finance and Economics,
Sloan School of Management, Massachusetts Institute of Technology, Consulting Editor

PRINCIPLES OF CORPORATE FINANCE

SEVENTH EDITION

RICHARD A. BREALEY

Emeritus Professor of Finance
London Business School

STEWART C. MYERS

Gordon Y Billard Professor of Finance
Sloan School of Management
Massachusetts Institute of Technology

Tata McGraw-Hill Publishing Company Limited

NEW DELHI

McGraw-Hill Offices

New Delhi New York St Louis San Francisco Auckland Bogotá Caracas
Kuala Lumpur Lisbon London Madrid Mexico City Milan Montreal
San Juan Santiago Singapore Sydney Tokyo Toronto

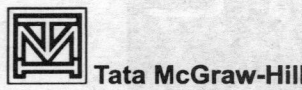
Tata McGraw-Hill

PRINCIPLES OF CORPORATE FINANCE

Tata McGraw-Hill Edition

Tenth reprint 2006
RQZYCRXKDLYXR

Reprinted in India by arrangement with The McGraw-Hill Companies
Inc., New York

Sales territories: India, Pakistan, Nepal, Bangladesh, Sri Lanka and Bhutan

Library of Congress Cataloging-in-Publication Data

Brealey, Richard A.
    Principles of corporate finance / Richard A. Brealey, Stewart C. Myers.—7th ed.
      p. cm.— (The McGraw-Hill/ Irwin series in finance, insurance, and real estate)
    Includes bibliographical references and index
    ISBN 0-07-246766-5 (alk. paper) —ISBN 0-07-115144-3 (international: alk paper)
    1. Corporation—Finance. I. Myers, Stewart C. II. Title. III. Series
    HG4026 .B667 2003
    658.15—dc21   2002069248

ISBN 0-07-052907-8 (book only)

Published by Tata McGraw-Hill Publishing Company Limited,
7 West Patel Nagar, New Delhi 110 008, and printed at
Pashupati Printers Pvt. Ltd., Delhi 110 095

To Our Parents

ABOUT THE AUTHORS

RICHARD A. BREALEY

Emeritus Professor of Finance at the London Business School. He is the former president of the European Finance Association and a former director of the American Finance Association. He is a fellow of the British Academy and has served as a special advisor to the Governor of the Bank of England and director of a number of financial institutions. Other books written by Professor Brealey include *Introduction to Risk and Return from Common Stocks.*

STEWART C. MYERS

Gordon Y Billard Professor of Finance at MIT's Sloan School of Management. He is past president of the American Finance Association and a research associate of the National Bureau of Economic Research. His research has focused on financing decisions, valuation methods, the cost of capital, and financial aspects of government regulation of business. Dr. Myers is a director of The Brattle Group, Inc., and is active as a financial consultant.

"FINANCE IN THE NEWS" BOXES

Timely, relevant news articles from financial publications appear in several chapters throughout the text. Aimed at bringing real life to the classroom, these boxes provide insight into the business world today.

FINANCE IN THE NEWS

THE DIVIDEND CUT HEARD 'ROUND THE WORLD

On May 9, 1994, FPL Group, the parent company of Florida Power & Light Company, announced a 32 percent reduction in its quarterly dividend payout, from 62 cents per share to 42 cents. In its announcement, FPL did its best to spell out to investors why it had taken such an unusual step. It stressed that it had studied the situation carefully and that, given the prospect of increased competition in the electric utility industry, the company's

FPL's substitution of stock repurchases for dividends was also designed to increase the company's financial flexibility in preparation for a new era of heightened competition among utilities. Although much of the cash savings from the dividend cut would be returned to shareholders in the form of stock repurchases, the rest would be used to retire debt and so reduce the company's leverage ratio. This deleveraging was intended to pre-

PART INTRODUCTIONS

New introductions have been added to each part explaining links between different concepts. They include real-world examples that provide motivation for the chapters that follow.

PART ONE

VALUE

IN 2001, DUPONT announced plans to build a new production line at its plant in Richmond, Virginia. The $50 million ... would increase DuPont's ...

thought that the new plant would be worth more than it cost. But that raises an obvious question, ...

NEW AND ENHANCED PEDAGOGY

In this edition of *Principles of Corporate Finance*, we've included several more features to help students succeed in learning the fundamental concepts of financial management.

STANDARD & POOR'S INTEGRATION

Now included in the end-of-chapter material are problems directly incorporating the Educational Version of Market Insight, a service based on Standard & Poor's renowned Compustat database. These problems provide you with an easy method of including current real-world data into your course.

assump...

STANDARD & POOR'S

16. Look up Hawaiian Electric Co. (HI) on the Standard & Poor's Market Insight website (www.mhhe.com/edumarketinsight). Hawaiian Electric was one of the companies in Table 4.2. That table was constructed in 2001.
   a. What is the company's dividend yield? How has it changed since 2001?
   b. Table 4.2 projected growth of 2.6 percent. How fast have the company's dividends and EPS actually grown since 2001?
   c. Calculate a sustainable growth rate for the company based on its five-year average return on equity (ROE) and plowback ratio.
   d. Given this updated information, would you modify the cost-of-equity estimate given in Table 4.2? Explain.

STANDARD & POOR'S

17. Browse through the companies in the Standard & Poor's Market Insight website (www.mhhe.com/edumarketinsight). Find three or four companies for which the earnings-price ratio reported on the website drastically *understates* the market capi-...

EXCEL SPREADSHEET EXERCISES

New to this edition, each chapter includes several problems, noted by an icon , that are tied to a financial analysis spreadsheet found on the Student CD that is packaged with the text. This feature allows students to enhance their knowledge and use of spreadsheets.

13. Borghia Pharmaceuticals has $1 million allocated for capital expenditures. Which of the following projects should the company accept to stay within the $1 million budget? How much does the budget limit cost the company in terms of its market value? The opportunity cost of capital for each project is 11 percent.

Project	Investment ($ thousands)	NPV ($ thousands)	IRR (%)
1	300	66	17.2
2	200	−4	10.7
3	250	43	16.6
4	100	14	12.1
5	100	7	11.8
	350	63	18.0
	400		

MINI-CASES

To enhance the concepts discussed within a chapter, several mini-cases are included so students can apply their knowledge to typical real-world scenarios.

MINI-CASE

Vegetron's CFO Calls Again

(The first episode of this story was presented in Section 5.1.)

Later that afternoon, Vegetron's CFO bursts into your office in a state of anxious confusion. The problem, he explains, is a last-minute proposal for a change in the design of the fermentation tanks that Vegetron will build to extract hydrated zirconium from a stockpile of powdered ore. The CFO has brought a printout (Table 5.1) of the forecasted revenues, costs, income, and book rates of return for the standard, low-temperature design. Vegetron's engineers have just proposed an alternative high-temperature design that will extract most of the hydrated zirconium over a shorter period, five instead of seven years. The forecasts for the high-temperature method are given in Table 5.2.[16]

TABLE 5.1

Income statement and book rates of return for high-temperature...

	Year				
	1	2	3	4	5
1. Revenue	180	180	180	180	180

mhhe.com/bm7e

PART WEBSITES

In today's world the Internet provides students and instructors with a useful and powerful tool. Relevant websites are provided at the end of each part for ease in referencing the best sites for financial data and information.

PART SIX RELATED WEBSITES

The Chicago Board site contains explanations of options markets and lots of data:

www.cboe.com

There are a number of good options sites, many of which provide data and calculators for Black–Scholes values and implied standard deviations:

www.cfo.com

www.fintools.net/options/optcalc.html
(very good calculators)

www.numa.com

...scentral.com

www.schaffersresearch.com/stock/calculator.asp

Two sites devoted to real options are:

www.real-options.com

www.puc-rio.br/marco.ind

Examples of journals specializing in options and other derivatives include:

www.appliedderivatives.com

www.erivativesreview.com

www.futuresmag.com

GLOBAL INDEX

Because many concepts in financial management are relevant around the world, the international coverage in the text has been enhanced and updated. To make this information easier to access, a Global Index was created for this edition.

PREFACE

This book describes the theory and practice of corporate finance. We hardly need to explain why financial managers should master the practical aspects of their job, but we should spell out why down-to-earth, red-blooded managers need to bother with theory.

Managers learn from experience how to cope with routine problems. But the best managers are also able to respond to change. To do this you need more than time-honored rules of thumb; you must understand *why* companies and financial markets behave the way they do. In other words, you need a *theory* of finance.

Does that sound intimidating? It shouldn't. Good theory helps you grasp what is going on in the world around you. It helps you to ask the right questions when times change and new problems must be analyzed. It also tells you what things you do *not* need to worry about. Throughout this book we show how managers use financial theory to solve practical problems.

Of course, the theory presented in this book is not perfect and complete—no theory is. There are some famous controversies in which financial economists cannot agree on what firms ought to do. We have not glossed over these controversies. We set out the main arguments for each side and tell you where we stand.

Once understood, good theory is common sense. Therefore we have tried to present it at a common-sense level, and we have avoided proofs and heavy mathematics. There are no ironclad prerequisites for reading this book except algebra and the English language. An elementary knowledge of accounting, statistics, and microeconomics is helpful, however.

CHANGES IN THE SEVENTH EDITION

This book is written for students of financial management. For many readers, it is their first look at the world of finance. Therefore in each edition we strive to make the book simpler, clearer, and more fun to read. But the book is also used as a reference and guide by practicing managers around the world. Therefore we also strive to make each new edition more comprehensive and authoritative.

We believe this edition is better for both the student and the practicing manager. Here are some of the major changes:

We have streamlined and simplified the exposition of major concepts, with special attention to Chapters 1 through 12, where the fundamental concepts of valuation, risk and return, and capital budgeting are introduced. In these chapters we cover only the most basic institutional material. At the same time we have rewritten Chapter 14 as a free-standing introduction to the nature of the corporation, to the major sources of corporate financing, and to financial markets and institutions. Some readers will turn first to Chapter 14 to see the contexts in which financial decisions are made.

We have also expanded coverage of important topics. For example, real options are now introduced in Chapter 10—you don't have to master option-pricing theory in order to grasp what real options are and why they are important. Later in the book, after Chapter 20 (Understanding Options) and Chapter 21 (Valuing Options), there is a brand-new Chapter 22 on real options, which covers valuation methods and a range of practical applications.

Other examples of expanded coverage include behavioral finance (Chapter 13) and new international evidence on the market-risk premium (Chapter 7). We have also reorganized the chapters on financial planning and working capital management. In fact we have revised and updated every chapter in the book.

This edition's international coverage is expanded and woven into the rest of the text. For example, international investment decisions are now introduced in Chapter 6, right alongside domestic investment decisions. Likewise the cost of capital for international investments is discussed in Chapter 9, and international differences in security issue procedures are reviewed in Chapter 15. Chapter 34 looks at some of the international differences in financial architecture and ownership. There is, however, a separate chapter on international risk management, which covers foreign exchange rates and markets, political risk, and the valuation of capital investments in different currencies. There is also a new international index.

The seventh edition is much more Web-friendly than the sixth. Web references are highlighted in the text, and an annotated list of useful websites has been added to each part of the book.

Of course, as every first-grader knows, it is easier to add than to subtract, but we have pruned judiciously. Some readers of the sixth edition may miss a favorite example or special topic. But new readers should find that the main themes of corporate finance come through with less clutter.

MAKING LEARNING EASIER

Each chapter of the book includes an introductory preview, a summary, and an annotated list of suggestions for further reading. There is a quick and easy quiz, a number of practice questions, and a few challenge questions. Many questions use financial data on actual companies accessible by the reader through Standard & Poor's Educational Version of Market Insight. In total there are now over a thousand end-of-chapter questions. All the questions refer to material in the same order as it occurs in the chapter. Answers to the quiz questions may be found at the end of the book, along with a glossary and tables for calculating present values and pricing options.

We have expanded and revised the mini-cases and added specific questions for each mini-case to guide the case analysis. Answers to the mini-cases are available to instructors on this book's website (**www.mhhe.com/bm7e**).

Parts 1 to 3 of the book are concerned with valuation and the investment decision, Parts 4 to 8 with long-term financing and risk management. Part 9 focuses on financial planning and short-term financial decisions. Part 10 looks at mergers and corporate control and Part 11 concludes. We realize that many teachers will prefer a different sequence of topics. Therefore, we have ensured that the text is modular, so that topics can be introduced in a variety of orders. For example, there will be no difficulty in reading the material on financial statement analysis and short-term decisions before the chapters on valuation and capital investment.

We should mention two matters of style now to prevent confusion later. First, the most important financial terms are set out in boldface type the first time they appear; less important but useful terms are given in italics. Second, most algebraic symbols representing dollar values are shown as capital letters. Other symbols are generally lowercase letters. Thus the symbol for a dividend payment is "DIV," and the symbol for a percentage rate of return is "r."

SUPPLEMENTS

In this edition, we have gone to great lengths to ensure that our supplements are equal in quality and authority to the text itself.

Instructor's Manual
ISBN 0072467886

The Instructor's Manual was extensively revised and updated by C. R. Krishnaswamy of Western Michigan University. It contains an overview of each chapter, teaching tips, learning objectives, challenge areas, key terms, and an annotated outline that provides references to the PowerPoint slides.

Test Bank
ISBN 0072468025

The Test Bank was also updated by C. R. Krishnaswamy, who included well over 1,000 new multiple-choice and short answer/discussion questions based on the revisions of the authors. The level of difficulty is varied throughout, using a label of easy, medium, or difficult.

PowerPoint Presentation System

Matt Will of the University of Indianapolis prepared the PowerPoint Presentation System, which contains exhibits, outlines, key points, and summaries in a visually stimulating collection of slides. Found on the Student CD-ROM, the Instructor's CD-ROM, and our website, the slides can be edited, printed, or rearranged in any way to fit the needs of your course.

Financial Analysis Spreadsheet Templates (F.A.S.T.)

Mike Griffin of KMT Software created the templates in Excel. They correlate with specific concepts in the text and allow students to work through financial problems and gain experience using spreadsheets. Each template is tied to a specific problem in the text.

Solutions Manual
ISBN 0072468009

The Solutions Manual, prepared by Bruce Swensen, Adelphi University, contains solutions to all practice questions and challenge questions found at the end of each chapter. Thoroughly checked for accuracy, this supplement is available to be purchased by your students.

Study Guide
ISBN 0072468017

The new Study Guide was carefully revised by V. Sivarama Krishnan of Cameron University and contains useful and interesting keys to learning. It includes an introduction to each chapter, key concepts, examples, exercises and solutions, and a complete chapter summary.

Videos
ISBN 0072467967

The McGraw-Hill/Irwin Finance Video Series is a complete video library designed to bring added points of discussion to your class. Within this professionally developed series, you will find examples of how real businesses face today's hottest topics, like mergers and acquisitions, going public, and careers in finance.

Student CD-ROM

Packaged with each text is a CD-ROM for students that contains many features designed to enhance the classroom experience. Three learning modules from the new Finance Tutor Series are included on the CD: Time Value of Money Tutor, Stock and Bond Valuation

Tutor, and Capital Budgeting Tutor. In each module, students answer questions and solve problems that not only assess their general understanding of the subject but also their ability to apply that understanding in real-world business contexts. In "Practice Mode," students learn as they go by receiving indepth feedback on each response before proceeding to the next question. Even better, the program anticipates common misunderstandings, such as incorrect calculations or assumptions, and then provides feedback only to the student making that specific mistake. Students who want to assess their current knowledge may select "Test Mode," where they read an extensive evaluation report after they have completed the test.

Also included are the PowerPoint presentation system, Financial Analysis Spreadsheet Templates (F.A.S.T.), video clips from our Finance Video Series, and many useful Web links.

Instructor's CD-ROM
ISBN 0072467959

We have compiled many of our instructor supplements in electronic format on a CD-ROM designed to assist with class preparation. The CD-ROM includes the Instructor's Manual, the Solutions Manual, a computerized Test Bank, PowerPoint slides, video clips, and Web links.

Online Learning Center
(www.mhhe.com/bm7e)

This site contains information about the book and the authors, as well as teaching and learning materials for the instructor and the student, including:

PageOut: The Course Website Development Center and PageOut Lite
www.pageout.net

This Web page generation software, free to adopters, is designed for professors just beginning to explore website options. In just a few minutes, even the most novice computer user can have a course website.

Simply type your material into the template provided and PageOut Lite instantly converts it to HTML—a universal Web language. Next, choose your favorite of three easy-to-navigate designs and your Web home page is created, complete with online syllabus, lecture notes, and bookmarks. You can even include a separate instructor page and an assignment page.

PageOut offers enhanced point-and-click features including a Syllabus Page that applies real-world links to original text material, an automated grade book, and a discussion board where instructors and their students can exchange questions and post announcements.

ACKNOWLEDGMENTS

We have a long list of people to thank for their helpful criticism of earlier editions and for assistance in preparing this one. They include Aleijda de Cazenove Balsan, John Cox, Kedrum Garrison, Robert Pindyck, and Gretchen Slemmons at MIT; Stefania Uccheddu at London Business School; Lynda Borucki, Marjorie Fischer, Larry Kolbe, James A. Read, Jr., and Bente Villadsen at The Brattle Group, Inc.; John Stonier at Airbus Industries; and Alex Triantis at the University of Maryland. We would also like to thank all those at McGraw-Hill/Irwin who worked on the book, including Steve Patterson, Publisher; Rhonda Seelinger, Executive Marketing Manager; Sarah Ebel, Senior Developmental Editor; Jean Lou Hess, Senior Project Manager; Keith McPherson, Design Director; Joyce Chappetto, Supplement Coordinator; and Michael McCormick, Senior Production Supervisor.

We want to express our appreciation to those instructors whose insightful comments and suggestions were invaluable to us during this revision:

Noyan Arsen *Koc University*
Penny Belk *Loughborough University*
Eric Benrud *University of Baltimore*
Peter Berman *University of New Haven*
Jean Canil *University of Adelaide*
Robert Everett *Johns Hopkins University*

Winfried Hallerbach *Erasmus University, Rotterdam*
Milton Harris *University of Chicago*
Mark Griffiths *Thunderbird, American School of International Management*
Jarl Kallberg *NYU, Stern School of Business*
Steve Kaplan *University of Chicago*
Ken Kim *University of Wisconsin—Milwaukee*
C. R. Krishnaswamy *Western Michigan University*
Ravi Jaganathan *Northwestern University*
David Lovatt *University of East Anglia*
Joe Messina *San Francisco State University*
Dag Michalson *BI, Oslo*
Peter Moles *University of Edinburgh*
Claus Parum *Copenhagen Business School*
Narendar V. Rao *Northeastern University*
Tom Rietz *University of Iowa*
Robert Ritchey *Texas Tech University*
Mo Rodriguez *Texas Christian University*
John Rozycki *Drake University*
Brad Scott *Webster University*
Bernell Stone *Brigham Young University*

Shrinivasan Sundaram *Ball State University*
Avanidhar Subrahmanyam *UCLA*
Stephen Todd *Loyola University—Chicago*
David Vang *St. Thomas University*
John Wald *Rutgers University*
Jill Wetmore *Saginaw Valley State University*
Matt Will *Johns Hopkins University*
Art Wilson *George Washington University*

This list is almost surely incomplete. We know how much we owe to our colleagues at the London Business School and MIT's Sloan School of Management. In many cases, the ideas that appear in this book are as much their ideas as ours. Finally, we record the continuing thanks due to our wives, Diana and Maureen, who were unaware when they married us that they were also marrying *The Principles of Corporate Finance.*

Richard A. Brealey
Stewart C. Myers

BRIEF CONTENTS

CONTENTS

VALUE

IN 2001, DUPONT announced plans to build a new production line at its plant in Richmond, Virginia. The $50 million investment would increase DuPont's output of Kevlar high-strength fiber by 15 percent. Meanwhile, in New Orleans Procter & Gamble had started work on a 100,000 square foot facility to produce Folger's coffee. This was expected to open in 2002 at a cost of $100 million.

What was special about these two developments? The answer is "nothing." We cite them because they are typical of the investments in new products and equipment that U.S. companies are making every day.

Presumably, DuPont and Procter & Gamble decided to undertake the investments because they thought that the new plant would be worth more than it cost. But that raises an obvious question. How can firms calculate what an investment is worth when its returns may stretch 10, 20, or more years into the future?

This is the topic of Part One. Chapter 1 sets the scene by showing how businesses are organized and the role that the financial manager plays in evaluating investments and finding money to pay for them. Chapter 2 starts to build a theory of value. By the end of Chapter 6, you should be able to tackle a standard investment decision such as those faced by DuPont or Procter & Gamble.

FINANCE AND THE FINANCIAL MANAGER

THIS BOOK IS about financial decisions made by corporations. We should start by saying what these decisions are and why they are important.

Corporations face two broad financial questions: What investments should the firm make? and How should it pay for those investments? The first question involves spending money; the second involves raising it.

The secret of success in financial management is to increase value. That is a simple statement, but not very helpful. It is like advising an investor in the stock market to "Buy low, sell high." The problem is how to do it.

There may be a few activities in which one can read a textbook and then do it, but financial management is not one of them. That is why finance is worth studying. Who wants to work in a field where there is no room for judgment, experience, creativity, and a pinch of luck? Although this book cannot supply any of these items, it does present the concepts and information on which good financial decisions are based, and it shows you how to use the tools of the trade of finance.

We start in this chapter by explaining what a corporation is and introducing you to the responsibilities of its financial managers. We will distinguish *real assets* from *financial assets* and *capital investment decisions* from *financing decisions.* We stress the importance of financial markets, both national and international, to the financial manager.

Finance is about money and markets, but it is also about people. The success of a corporation depends on how well it harnesses everyone to work to a common end. The financial manager must appreciate the conflicting objectives often encountered in financial management. Resolving conflicts is particularly difficult when people have different information. This is an important theme which runs through to the last chapter of this book. In this chapter we will start with some definitions and examples.

 ## 1.1 WHAT IS A CORPORATION?

Not all businesses are corporations. Small ventures can be owned and managed by a single individual. These are called *sole proprietorships.* In other cases several people may join to own and manage a *partnership.*[1] However, this book is about *corporate* finance. So we need to explain what a **corporation** is.

Almost all large and medium-sized businesses are organized as corporations. For example, General Motors, Bank of America, Microsoft, and General Electric are corporations. So are overseas businesses, such as British Petroleum, Unilever, Nestlé, Volkswagen, and Sony. In each case the firm is owned by stockholders who hold shares in the business.

When a corporation is first established, its shares may all be held by a small group of investors, perhaps the company's managers and a few backers. In this case the shares are not publicly traded and the company is *closely held.* Eventually, when the firm grows and new shares are issued to raise additional capital, its shares will be widely traded. Such corporations are known as *public companies.*

---

[1] Many professional businesses, such as accounting and legal firms, are partnerships. Most large investment banks started as partnerships, but eventually these companies and their financing needs grew too large for them to continue in this form. Goldman Sachs, the last of the leading investment-bank partnerships, issued shares and became a public corporation in 1998.

Most well-known corporations in the United States are public companies. In many other countries, it's common for large companies to remain in private hands.

By organizing as a corporation, a business can attract a wide variety of investors. Some may hold only a single share worth a few dollars, cast only a single vote, and receive a tiny proportion of profits and dividends. Shareholders may also include giant pension funds and insurance companies whose investment may run to millions of shares and hundreds of millions of dollars, and who are entitled to a correspondingly large number of votes and proportion of profits and dividends.

Although the stockholders own the corporation, they do not manage it. Instead, they vote to elect a *board of directors*. Some of these directors may be drawn from top management, but others are non-executive directors, who are not employed by the firm. The board of directors represents the shareholders. It appoints top management and is supposed to ensure that managers act in the shareholders' best interests.

This *separation of ownership and management* gives corporations permanence.[2] Even if managers quit or are dismissed and replaced, the corporation can survive, and today's stockholders can sell all their shares to new investors without disrupting the operations of the business.

Unlike partnerships and sole proprietorships, corporations have **limited liability,** which means that stockholders cannot be held personally responsible for the firm's debts. If, say, General Motors were to fail, no one could demand that its shareholders put up more money to pay off its debts. The most a stockholder can lose is the amount he or she has invested.

Although a corporation is owned by its stockholders, it is legally distinct from them. It is based on *articles of incorporation* that set out the purpose of the business, how many shares can be issued, the number of directors to be appointed, and so on. These articles must conform to the laws of the state in which the business is incorporated.[3] For many legal purposes, the corporation is considered as a resident of its state. As a legal "person," it can borrow or lend money, and it can sue or be sued. It pays its own taxes (but it cannot vote!).

Because the corporation is distinct from its shareholders, it can do things that partnerships and sole proprietorships cannot. For example, it can raise money by selling new shares to investors and it can buy those shares back. One corporation can make a takeover bid for another and then merge the two businesses.

There are also some *disadvantages* to organizing as a corporation. Managing a corporation's legal machinery and communicating with shareholders can be time-consuming and costly. Furthermore, in the United States there is an important tax drawback. Because the corporation is a separate legal entity, it is taxed separately. So corporations pay tax on their profits, and, in addition, shareholders pay tax on any dividends that they receive from the company. The United States is unusual in this respect. To avoid taxing the same income twice, most other countries give shareholders at least some credit for the tax that the company has already paid.[4]

---

[2]Corporations can be immortal but the law requires partnerships to have a definite end. A partnership agreement must specify an ending date or a procedure for wrapping up the partnership's affairs. A sole proprietorship also will have an end because the proprietor is mortal.

[3]Delaware has a well-developed and supportive system of corporate law. Even though they may do little business in that state, a high proportion of United States corporations are incorporated in Delaware.

[4]Or companies may pay a lower rate of tax on profits paid out as dividends.

1.2 THE ROLE OF THE FINANCIAL MANAGER

To carry on business, corporations need an almost endless variety of **real assets.** Many of these assets are tangible, such as machinery, factories, and offices; others are intangible, such as technical expertise, trademarks, and patents. All of them need to be paid for. To obtain the necessary money, the corporation sells claims on its real assets and on the cash those assets will generate. These claims are called **financial assets** or **securities.** For example, if the company borrows money from the bank, the bank gets a written promise that the money will be repaid with interest. Thus the bank trades cash for a financial asset. Financial assets include not only bank loans but also shares of stock, bonds, and a dizzying variety of specialized securities.[5]

The financial manager stands between the firm's operations and the **financial (or capital) markets,** where investors hold the financial assets issued by the firm.[6] The financial manager's role is illustrated in Figure 1.1, which traces the flow of cash from investors to the firm and back to investors again. The flow starts when the firm sells securities to raise cash (arrow 1 in the figure). The cash is used to purchase real assets used in the firm's operations (arrow 2). Later, if the firm does well, the real assets generate cash inflows which more than repay the initial investment (arrow 3). Finally, the cash is either reinvested (arrow 4a) or returned to the investors who purchased the original security issue (arrow 4b). Of course, the choice between arrows 4a and 4b is not completely free. For example, if a bank lends money at stage 1, the bank has to be repaid the money plus interest at stage 4b.

Our diagram takes us back to the financial manager's two basic questions. First, what real assets should the firm invest in? Second, how should the cash for the investment be raised? The answer to the first question is the firm's **investment,** or **capital budgeting, decision.** The answer to the second is the firm's **financing decision.**

Capital investment and financing decisions are typically *separated*, that is, analyzed independently. When an investment opportunity or "project" is identified, the financial manager first asks whether the project is worth more than the capital required to undertake it. If the answer is yes, he or she then considers how the project should be financed.

But the separation of investment and financing decisions does *not* mean that the financial manager can forget about investors and financial markets when analyzing capital investment projects. As we will see in the next chapter, the fundamental financial objective of the firm is to maximize the value of the cash invested in the firm by its stockholders. Look again at Figure 1.1. Stockholders are happy to contribute cash at arrow 1 only if the decisions made at arrow 2 generate at least adequate returns at arrow 3. "Adequate" means returns at least equal to the returns available to investors outside the firm in financial markets. If your firm's projects consistently generate *in*adequate returns, your shareholders will want their money back.

Financial managers of large corporations also need to be men and women of the world. They must decide not only *which* assets their firm should invest in but also *where* those assets should be located. Take Nestlé, for example. It is a Swiss company, but only a small proportion of its production takes place in Switzerland. Its 520 or so

---

[5]We review these securities in Chapters 14 and 25.

[6]You will hear financial managers use the terms *financial markets* and *capital markets* almost synonymously. But *capital markets* are, strictly speaking, the source of long-term financing only. Short-term financing comes from the *money market*. "Short-term" means less than one year. We use the term *financial markets* to refer to all sources of financing.

FIGURE 1.1

Flow of cash between financial markets and the firm's operations. Key: (1) Cash raised by selling financial assets to investors; (2) cash invested in the firm's operations and used to purchase real assets; (3) cash generated by the firm's operations; (4a) cash reinvested; (4b) cash returned to investors.

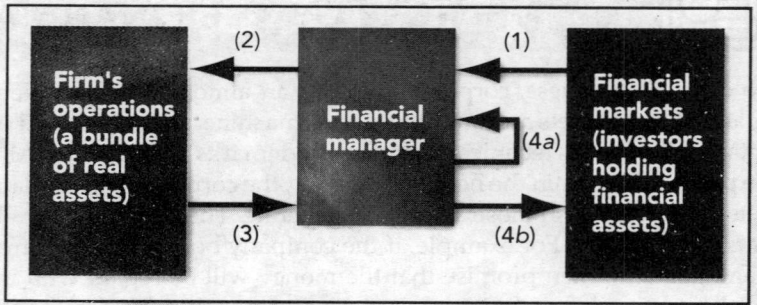

factories are located in 82 countries. Nestlé's managers must therefore know how to evaluate investments in countries with different currencies, interest rates, inflation rates, and tax systems.

The financial markets in which the firm raises money are likewise international. The stockholders of large corporations are scattered around the globe. Shares are traded around the clock in New York, London, Tokyo, and other financial centers. Bonds and bank loans move easily across national borders. A corporation that needs to raise cash doesn't have to borrow from its hometown bank. Day-to-day cash management also becomes a complex task for firms that produce or sell in different countries. For example, think of the problems that Nestlé's financial managers face in keeping track of the cash receipts and payments in 82 countries.

We admit that Nestlé is unusual, but few financial managers can close their eyes to international financial issues. So throughout the book we will pay attention to differences in financial systems and examine the problems of investing and raising money internationally.

 ## 1.3 WHO IS THE FINANCIAL MANAGER?

In this book we will use the term *financial manager* to refer to anyone responsible for a significant investment or financing decision. But only in the smallest firms is a single person responsible for all the decisions discussed in this book. In most cases, responsibility is dispersed. Top management is of course continuously involved in financial decisions. But the engineer who designs a new production facility is also involved: The design determines the kind of real assets the firm will hold. The marketing manager who commits to a major advertising campaign is also making an important investment decision. The campaign is an investment in an intangible asset that is expected to pay off in future sales and earnings.

Nevertheless there are some managers who specialize in finance. Their roles are summarized in Figure 1.2. The **treasurer** is responsible for looking after the firm's cash, raising new capital, and maintaining relationships with banks, stockholders, and other investors who hold the firm's securities.

For small firms, the treasurer is likely to be the only financial executive. Larger corporations also have a **controller,** who prepares the financial statements, manages the firm's internal accounting, and looks after its tax obligations. You can see that the treasurer and controller have different functions: The treasurer's main responsibility is to obtain and manage the firm's capital, whereas the controller ensures that the money is used efficiently.

FIGURE 1.2

Senior financial managers in large corporations.

Still larger firms usually appoint a **chief financial officer (CFO)** to oversee both the treasurer's and the controller's work. The CFO is deeply involved in financial policy and corporate planning. Often he or she will have general managerial responsibilities beyond strictly financial issues and may also be a member of the board of directors.

The controller or CFO is responsible for organizing and supervising the capital budgeting process. However, major capital investment projects are so closely tied to plans for product development, production, and marketing that managers from these areas are inevitably drawn into planning and analyzing the projects. If the firm has staff members specializing in corporate planning, they too are naturally involved in capital budgeting.

Because of the importance of many financial issues, ultimate decisions often rest by law or by custom with the board of directors. For example, only the board has the legal power to declare a dividend or to sanction a public issue of securities. Boards usually delegate decisions for small or medium-sized investment outlays, but the authority to approve large investments is almost never delegated.

 ## 1.4 SEPARATION OF OWNERSHIP AND MANAGEMENT

In large businesses separation of ownership and management is a practical necessity. Major corporations may have hundreds of thousands of shareholders. There is no way for all of them to be actively involved in management: It would be like running New York City through a series of town meetings for all its citizens. Authority has to be delegated to managers.

The separation of ownership and management has clear advantages. It allows share ownership to change without interfering with the operation of the business. It allows the firm to hire professional managers. But it also brings problems if the managers' and owners' objectives differ. You can see the danger: Rather than attending to the wishes of shareholders, managers may seek a more leisurely or luxurious working lifestyle; they may shun unpopular decisions, or they may attempt to build an empire with their shareholders' money.

Such conflicts between shareholders' and managers' objectives create *principal–agent problems.* The shareholders are the principals; the managers are their agents. Shareholders want management to increase the value of the firm, but managers may have their own axes to grind or nests to feather. **Agency costs** are incurred when (1) managers do not attempt to maximize firm value and (2) shareholders incur costs to monitor the managers and influence their actions. Of course, there are no costs when the shareholders are also the managers. That is one of the advantages of a sole proprietorship. Owner–managers have no conflicts of interest.

Conflicts between shareholders and managers are not the only principal–agent problems that the financial manager is likely to encounter. For example, just as shareholders need to encourage managers to work for the shareholders' interests, so senior management needs to think about how to motivate everyone else in the company. In this case senior management are the principals and junior management and other employees are their agents.

Agency costs can also arise in financing. In normal times, the banks and bondholders who lend the company money are united with the shareholders in wanting the company to prosper, but when the firm gets into trouble, this unity of purpose can break down. At such times decisive action may be necessary to rescue the firm, but lenders are concerned to get their money back and are reluctant to see the firm making risky changes that could imperil the safety of their loans. Squabbles may even break out between different lenders as they see the company heading for possible bankruptcy and jostle for a better place in the queue of creditors.

Think of the company's overall value as a pie that is divided among a number of claimants. These include the management and the shareholders, as well as the company's workforce and the banks and investors who have bought the company's debt. The government is a claimant too, since it gets to tax corporate profits.

All these claimants are bound together in a complex web of contracts and understandings. For example, when banks lend money to the firm, they insist on a formal contract stating the rate of interest and repayment dates, perhaps placing restrictions on dividends or additional borrowing. But you can't devise written rules to cover every possible future event. So written contracts are incomplete and need to be supplemented by understandings and by arrangements that help to align the interests of the various parties.

Principal–agent problems would be easier to resolve if everyone had the same information. That is rarely the case in finance. Managers, shareholders, and lenders may all have different information about the value of a real or financial asset, and it may be many years before all the information is revealed. Financial managers need to recognize these *information asymmetries* and find ways to reassure investors that there are no nasty surprises on the way.

Here is one example. Suppose you are the financial manager of a company that has been newly formed to develop and bring to market a drug for the cure of toetitis. At a meeting with potential investors you present the results of clinical trials, show upbeat reports by an independent market research company, and forecast profits amply sufficient to justify further investment. But the potential investors are still worried that you may know more than they do. What can you do to convince them that you are telling the truth? Just saying "Trust me" won't do the trick. Perhaps you need to *signal* your integrity by putting your money where your mouth is. For example, investors are likely to have more confidence in your plans if they see that you and the other managers have large personal stakes in the new

Differences in information	Different objectives
Stock prices and returns (13)	Managers vs. stockholders (2, 12, 33, 34)
Issues of shares and other securities (15, 18, 23)	Top management vs. operating management (12)
Dividends (16)	Stockholders vs. banks and other lenders (18)
Financing (18)	

FIGURE 1.3

Differences in objectives and information can complicate financial decisions. We address these issues at several points in this book (chapter numbers in parentheses).

enterprise. Therefore your decision to invest your own money can provide information to investors about the true prospects of the firm.

In later chapters we will look more carefully at how corporations tackle the problems created by differences in objectives and information. Figure 1.3 summarizes the main issues and signposts the chapters where they receive most attention.

 ## 1.5 TOPICS COVERED IN THIS BOOK

We have mentioned how financial managers separate investment and financing decisions: Investment decisions typically precede financing decisions. That is also how we have organized this book. Parts 1 through 3 are almost entirely devoted to different aspects of the investment decision. The first topic is how to value assets, the second is the link between risk and value, and the third is the management of the capital investment process. Our discussion of these topics occupies Chapters 2 through 12.

As you work through these chapters, you may have some basic questions about financing. For example, What does it mean to say that a corporation has "issued shares"? How much of the cash contributed at arrow 1 in Figure 1.1 comes from shareholders and how much from borrowing? What types of debt securities do firms actually issue? Who actually buys the firm's shares and debt—individual investors or financial institutions? What are those institutions and what role do they play in corporate finance and the broader economy? Chapter 14, "An Overview of Corporate Financing," covers these and a variety of similar questions. This chapter stands on its own bottom—it does not rest on previous chapters. You can read it any time the fancy strikes. You may wish to read it now.

Chapter 14 is one of three in Part 4, which begins the analysis of corporate financing decisions. Chapter 13 reviews the evidence on the *efficient markets* hypothesis, which states that security prices observed in financial markets accurately reflect underlying values and the information available to investors. Chapter 15 describes how debt and equity securities are issued.

Part 5 continues the analysis of the financing decision, covering dividend policy and the mix of debt and equity financing. We will describe what happens when firms land in financial distress because of poor operating performance or excessive borrowing. We will also consider how financing decisions may affect decisions about the firm's investment projects.

Part 6 introduces options. Options are too advanced for Chapter 1, but by Chapter 20 you'll have no difficulty. Investors can trade options on stocks, bonds, currencies, and commodities. Financial managers find options lurking in *real* assets—that is, *real options*—and in the securities the firms may issue. Having mastered options, we proceed in Part 7 to a much closer look at the many varieties of long-term debt financing.

An important part of the financial manager's job is to judge which risks the firm should take on and which can be eliminated. Part 8 looks at risk management, both domestically and internationally.

Part 9 covers financial planning and short-term financial management. We address a variety of practical topics, including short- and longer-term forecasting, channels for short-term borrowing or investment, management of cash and marketable securities, and management of accounts receivable (money lent by the firm to its customers).

Part 10 looks at mergers and acquisitions and, more generally, at the control and governance of the firm. We also discuss how companies in different countries are structured to provide the right incentives for management and the right degree of control by outside investors.

Part 11 is our conclusion. It also discusses some of the things that we *don't* know about finance. If you can be the first to solve any of these puzzles, you will be justifiably famous.

SUMMARY

In Chapter 2 we will begin with the most basic concepts of asset valuation. However, we should first sum up the principal points made in this introductory chapter.

Large businesses are usually organized as corporations. Corporations have three important features. First, they are legally distinct from their owners and pay their own taxes. Second, corporations provide limited liability, which means that the stockholders who own the corporation cannot be held responsible for the firm's debts. Third, the owners of a corporation are not usually the managers.

The overall task of the financial manager can be broken down into (1) the investment, or capital budgeting, decision and (2) the financing decision. In other words, the firm has to decide (1) what real assets to buy and (2) how to raise the necessary cash.

In small companies there is often only one financial executive, the treasurer. However, most companies have both a treasurer and a controller. The treasurer's job is to obtain and manage the company's financing, while the controller's job is to confirm that the money is used correctly. In large firms there is also a chief financial officer or CFO.

Shareholders want managers to increase the value of the company's stock. Managers may have different objectives. This potential conflict of interest is termed a principal–agent problem. Any loss of value that results from such conflicts is termed an agency cost. Of course there may be other conflicts of interest. For example, the interests of the shareholders may sometimes conflict with those of the firm's banks and bondholders. These and other agency problems become more complicated when agents have more or better information than the principals.

The financial manager plays on an international stage and must understand how international financial markets operate and how to evaluate overseas investments. We discuss international corporate finance at many different points in the chapters that follow.

Financial managers read *The Wall Street Journal (WSJ)*, *The Financial Times (FT)*, or both daily. You should too. *The Financial Times* is published in Britain, but there is a North American edition. *The New York Times* and a few other big-city newspapers have good business and financial sections, but they are no substitute for the *WSJ* or *FT*. The business and financial sections of most United States dailies are, except for local news, nearly worthless for the financial manager.

The Economist, Business Week, Forbes, and *Fortune* contain useful financial sections, and there are several magazines that specialize in finance. These include *Euromoney, Corporate Finance, Journal of Applied Corporate Finance, Risk,* and *CFO Magazine*. This list does not include research journals such as the *Journal of Finance, Journal of Financial Economics, Review of Financial Studies,* and *Financial Management*. In the following chapters we give specific references to pertinent research.

FURTHER READING

QUIZ

1. Read the following passage: "Companies usually buy (*a*) assets. These include both tangible assets such as (*b*) and intangible assets such as (*c*). In order to pay for these assets, they sell (*d*) assets such as (*e*). The decision about which assets to buy is usually termed the (*f*) or (*g*) decision. The decision about how to raise the money is usually termed the (*h*) decision." Now fit each of the following terms into the most appropriate space: *financing, real, bonds, investment, executive airplanes, financial, capital budgeting, brand names.*

2. Vocabulary test. Explain the differences between:
   a. Real and financial assets.
   b. Capital budgeting and financing decisions.
   c. Closely held and public corporations.
   d. Limited and unlimited liability.
   e. Corporation and partnership.

3. Which of the following are real assets, and which are financial?
   a. A share of stock.
   b. A personal IOU.
   c. A trademark.
   d. A factory.
   e. Undeveloped land.
   f. The balance in the firm's checking account.
   g. An experienced and hardworking sales force.
   h. A corporate bond.

4. What are the main *disadvantages* of the corporate form of organization?

5. Which of the following statements more accurately describe the treasurer than the controller?
   a. Likely to be the only financial executive in small firms.
   b. Monitors capital expenditures to make sure that they are not misappropriated.
   c. Responsible for investing the firm's spare cash.
   d. Responsible for arranging any issue of common stock.
   e. Responsible for the company's tax affairs.

6. Which of the following statements always apply to corporations?
   a. Unlimited liability.
   b. Limited life.
   c. Ownership can be transferred without affecting operations.
   d. Managers can be fired with no effect on ownership.
   e. Shares must be widely traded.

7. In most large corporations, ownership and management are separated. What are the main implications of this separation?

8. What are agency costs and what causes them?

CHAPTER TWO

PRESENT VALUE AND THE OPPORTUNITY COST OF CAPITAL

COMPANIES INVEST IN a variety of real assets. These include tangible assets such as plant and machinery and intangible assets such as management contracts and patents. The object of the investment, or capital budgeting, decision is to find real assets that are worth more than they cost. In this chapter we will take the first, most basic steps toward understanding how assets are valued.

There are a few cases in which it is not that difficult to estimate asset values. In real estate, for example, you can hire a professional appraiser to do it for you. Suppose you own a warehouse. The odds are that your appraiser's estimate of its value will be within a few percent of what the building would actually sell for.[1] After all, there is continuous activity in the real estate market, and the appraiser's stock-in-trade is knowledge of the prices at which similar properties have recently changed hands. Thus the problem of valuing real estate is simplified by the existence of an active market in which all kinds of properties are bought and sold. For many purposes no formal theory of value is needed. We can take the market's word for it.

But we need to go deeper than that. First, it is important to know how asset values are reached in an active market. Even if you can take the appraiser's word for it, it is important to understand *why* that warehouse is worth, say, $250,000 and not a higher or lower figure. Second, the market for most corporate assets is pretty thin. Look in the classified advertisements in *The Wall Street Journal:* It is not often that you see a blast furnace for sale.

Companies are always searching for assets that are worth more to them than to others. That warehouse is worth more to you if you can manage it better than others. But in that case, looking at the price of similar buildings will not tell you what the warehouse is worth under your management. You need to know how asset values are determined. In other words, you need a theory of value.

This chapter takes the first, most basic steps to develop that theory. We lead off with a simple numerical example: Should you invest to build a new office building in the hope of selling it at a profit next year? Finance theory endorses investment if net present value is positive, that is, if the new building's value *today* exceeds the required investment. It turns out that net present value is positive in this example, because the rate of return on investment exceeds the opportunity cost of capital.

So this chapter's first task is to define and explain net present value, rate of return, and opportunity cost of capital. The second task is to explain why financial managers search so assiduously for investments with positive net present values. Is increased value today the *only* possible financial objective? And what does "value" mean for a corporation?

Here we will come to the fundamental objective of corporate finance: maximizing the current market value of the firm's outstanding shares. We will explain why *all* shareholders should endorse this objective, and why the objective overrides other plausible goals, such as "maximizing profits."

Finally, we turn to the *managers'* objectives and discuss some of the mechanisms that help to align the managers' and stockholders' interests. We ask whether attempts to increase shareholder value need be at the expense of workers, customers, or the community at large.

In this chapter, we will stick to the simplest problems to make basic ideas clear. Readers with a taste for more complication will find plenty to satisfy them in later chapters.

---

[1]Needless to say, there are some properties that appraisers find nearly impossible to value—for example, nobody knows the potential selling price of the Taj Mahal or the Parthenon or Windsor Castle.

2.1 INTRODUCTION TO PRESENT VALUE

Your warehouse has burned down, fortunately without injury to you or your employees, leaving you with a vacant lot worth $50,000 and a check for $200,000 from the fire insurance company. You consider rebuilding, but your real estate adviser suggests putting up an office building instead. The construction cost would be $300,000, and there would also be the cost of the land, which might otherwise be sold for $50,000. On the other hand, your adviser foresees a shortage of office space and predicts that a year from now the new building would fetch $400,000 if you sold it. Thus you would be investing $350,000 now in the expectation of realizing $400,000 a year hence. You should go ahead if the **present value (PV)** of the expected $400,000 payoff is greater than the investment of $350,000. Therefore, you need to ask, What is the value today of $400,000 to be received one year from now, and is that present value greater than $350,000?

Calculating Present Value

The present value of $400,000 one year from now must be less than $400,000. After all, *a dollar today is worth more than a dollar tomorrow,* because the dollar today can be invested to start earning interest immediately. This is the first basic principle of finance. Thus, the present value of a delayed payoff may be found by multiplying the payoff by a **discount factor** which is less than 1. (If the discount factor were more than 1, a dollar today would be worth *less* than a dollar tomorrow.) If C_1 denotes the expected payoff at period 1 (one year hence), then

$$\text{Present value (PV)} = \text{discount factor} \times C_1$$

This discount factor is the value today of $1 received in the future. It is usually expressed as the reciprocal of 1 plus a *rate of return:*

$$\text{Discount factor} = \frac{1}{1 + r}$$

The rate of return r is the reward that investors demand for accepting delayed payment.

Now we can value the real estate investment, assuming for the moment that the $400,000 payoff is a sure thing. The office building is not the only way to obtain $400,000 a year from now. You could invest in United States government securities maturing in a year. Suppose these securities offer 7 percent interest. How much would you have to invest in them in order to receive $400,000 at the end of the year? That's easy: You would have to invest $400,000/1.07, which is $373,832.[2] Therefore, at an interest rate of 7 percent, the present value of $400,000 one year from now is $373,832.

Let's assume that, as soon as you've committed the land and begun construction on the building, you decide to sell your project. How much could you sell it for? That's another easy question. Since the property will be worth $400,000 in a year, investors would be willing to pay $373,832 for it today. That's what it would

---

[2]Let's check this. If you invest $373,832 at 7 percent, at the end of the year you get back your initial investment plus interest of .07 $\times$ 373,832 = $26,168. The total sum you receive is 373,832 + 26,168 = $400,000. Note that 373,832 $\times$ 1.07 = $400,000.

cost them to get a $400,000 payoff from investing in government securities. Of course, you could always sell your property for less, but why sell for less than the market will bear? The $373,832 present value is the only feasible price that satisfies both buyer and seller. Therefore, the present value of the property is also its market price.

To calculate present value, we discount expected payoffs by the rate of return offered by equivalent investment alternatives in the capital market. This rate of return is often referred to as the **discount rate, hurdle rate,** or **opportunity cost of capital.** It is called the *opportunity cost* because it is the return foregone by investing in the project rather than investing in securities. In our example the opportunity cost was 7 percent. Present value was obtained by dividing $400,000 by 1.07:

$$PV = \text{discount factor} \times C_1 = \frac{1}{1 + r} \times C_1 = \frac{400,000}{1.07} = \$373,832$$

Net Present Value

The building is worth $373,832, but this does not mean that you are $373,832 better off. You committed $350,000, and therefore your **net present value (NPV)** is $23,832. Net present value is found by subtracting the required investment:

$$NPV = PV - \text{required investment} = 373,832 - 350,000 = \$23,832$$

In other words, your office development is worth more than it costs—it makes a *net* contribution to value. The formula for calculating NPV can be written as

$$NPV = C_0 + \frac{C_1}{1 + r}$$

remembering that C_0, the cash flow at time 0 (that is, today), will usually be a negative number. In other words, C_0 is an investment and therefore a cash *outflow*. In our example, $C_0 = -\$350,000$.

A Comment on Risk and Present Value

We made one unrealistic assumption in our discussion of the office development: Your real estate adviser cannot be *certain* about future values of office buildings. The $400,000 represents the best *forecast*, but it is not a sure thing.

If the future value of the building is risky, our calculation of NPV is wrong. Investors could achieve $400,000 with certainty by buying $373,832 worth of United States government securities, so they would not buy your building for that amount. You would have to cut your asking price to attract investors' interest.

Here we can invoke a second basic financial principle: *A safe dollar is worth more than a risky one.* Most investors avoid risk when they can do so without sacrificing return. However, the concepts of present value and the opportunity cost of capital still make sense for risky investments. It is still proper to discount the payoff by the rate of return offered by an equivalent investment. But we have to think of *expected* payoffs and the *expected* rates of return on other investments.[3]

---

[3]We define "expected" more carefully in Chapter 9. For now think of expected payoff as a realistic forecast, neither optimistic nor pessimistic. Forecasts of expected payoffs are correct on average.

Not all investments are equally risky. The office development is more risky than a government security but less risky than a start-up biotech venture. Suppose you believe the project is as risky as investment in the stock market and that stock market investments are forecasted to return 12 percent. Then 12 percent becomes the appropriate opportunity cost of capital. That is what you are giving up by not investing in equally risky securities. Now recompute NPV:

$$PV = \frac{400,000}{1.12} = \$357,143$$
$$NPV = PV - 350,000 = \$7,143$$

If other investors agree with your forecast of a $400,000 payoff and your assessment of its risk, then your property ought to be worth $357,143 once construction is underway. If you tried to sell it for more, there would be no takers, because the property would then offer an expected rate of return lower than the 12 percent available in the stock market. The office building still makes a net contribution to value, but it is much smaller than our earlier calculations indicated.

The value of the office building depends on the timing of the cash flows and their uncertainty. The $400,000 payoff would be worth exactly that if it could be realized instantaneously. If the office building is as risk-free as government securities, the one-year delay reduces value to $373,832. If the building is as risky as investment in the stock market, then uncertainty further reduces value by $16,689 to $357,143.

Unfortunately, adjusting asset values for time and uncertainty is often more complicated than our example suggests. Therefore, we will take the two effects separately. For the most part, we will dodge the problem of risk in Chapters 2 through 6, either by treating all cash flows as if they were known with certainty or by talking about expected cash flows and expected rates of return without worrying how risk is defined or measured. Then in Chapter 7 we will turn to the problem of understanding how financial markets cope with risk.

Present Values and Rates of Return

We have decided that construction of the office building is a smart thing to do, since it is worth more than it costs—it has a positive net present value. To calculate how much it is worth, we worked out how much one would need to pay to achieve the same payoff by investing directly in securities. The project's present value is equal to its future income discounted at the rate of return offered by these securities.

We can say this in another way: Our property venture is worth undertaking because its rate of return exceeds the cost of capital. The rate of return on the investment in the office building is simply the profit as a proportion of the initial outlay:

$$Return = \frac{profit}{investment} = \frac{400,000 - 350,000}{350,000} = .143, \text{ about } 14\%$$

The cost of capital is once again the return foregone by *not* investing in securities. If the office building is as risky as investing in the stock market, the return foregone is 12 percent. Since the 14 percent return on the office building exceeds the 12 percent opportunity cost, you should go ahead with the project.

Here then we have two equivalent decision rules for capital investment:[4]

- *Net present value rule.* Accept investments that have positive net present values.
- *Rate-of-return rule.* Accept investments that offer rates of return in excess of their opportunity costs of capital.[5]

The Opportunity Cost of Capital

The opportunity cost of capital is such an important concept that we will give one more example. You are offered the following opportunity: Invest $100,000 today, and, depending on the state of the economy at the end of the year, you will receive one of the following payoffs:

Slump	Normal	Boom
$80,000	$110,000	$140,000

You reject the optimistic (boom) and the pessimistic (slump) forecasts. That gives an expected payoff of $C_1 = 110,000$,[6] a 10 percent return on the $100,000 investment. But what's the right discount rate?

You search for a common stock with the same risk as the investment. Stock X turns out to be a perfect match. X's price next year, given a normal economy, is forecasted at $110. The stock price will be higher in a boom and lower in a slump, but to the same degrees as your investment ($140 in a boom and $80 in a slump). You conclude that the risks of stock X and your investment are identical.

Stock X's current price is $95.65. It offers an expected rate of return of 15 percent:

$$\text{Expected return} = \frac{\text{expected profit}}{\text{investment}} = \frac{110 - 95.65}{95.65} = .15, \text{ or } 15\%$$

This is the expected return that you are giving up by investing in the project rather than the stock market. In other words, it is the project's opportunity cost of capital.

To value the project, discount the expected cash flow by the opportunity cost of capital:

$$PV = \frac{110,000}{1.15} = \$95,650$$

This is the amount it would cost investors in the stock market to buy an expected cash flow of $110,000. (They could do so by buying 1,000 shares of stock X.) It is, therefore, also the sum that investors would be prepared to pay you for your project.

To calculate net present value, deduct the initial investment:

$$\text{NPV} = 95,650 - 100,000 = -\$4,350$$

---

[4]You might check for yourself that these are equivalent rules. In other words, if the return 50,000/350,000 is greater than r, then the net present value $- 350,000 + [400,000/(1 + r)]$ *must* be greater than 0.

[5]The two rules can conflict when there are cash flows in more than two periods. We address this problem in Chapter 5.

[6]We are assuming that the probabilities of slump and boom are equal, so that the expected (average) outcome is $110,000. For example, suppose the slump, normal, and boom probabilities are all 1/3. Then the expected payoff $C_1 = (80,000 + 110,000 + 140,000)/3 = \$110.000$.

The project is worth $4,350 less than it costs. It is *not* worth undertaking.

Notice that you come to the same conclusion if you compare the expected project return with the cost of capital:

$$\text{Expected return on project} = \frac{\text{expected profit}}{\text{investment}}$$

$$= \frac{110,000 - 100,000}{100,000} = .10, \text{ or } 10\%$$

The 10 percent expected return on the project is less than the 15 percent return investors could expect to earn by investing in the stock market, so the project is not worthwhile.

Of course in real life it's impossible to restrict the future states of the economy to just "slump," "normal," and "boom." We have also simplified by assuming a perfect match between the payoffs of 1,000 shares of stock X and the payoffs to the investment project. The main point of the example does carry through to real life, however. Remember this: The opportunity cost of capital for an investment project is the expected rate of return demanded by investors in common stocks or other securities subject to the same risks as the project. When you discount the project's expected cash flow at its opportunity cost of capital, the resulting present value is the amount investors (including your own company's shareholders) would be willing to pay for the project. Any time you find and launch a positive-NPV project (a project with present value exceeding its required cash outlay) you have made your company's stockholders better off.

A Source of Confusion

Here is a possible source of confusion. Suppose a banker approaches. "Your company is a fine and safe business with few debts," she says. "My bank will lend you the $100,000 that you need for the project at 8 percent." Does that mean that the cost of capital for the project is 8 percent? If so, the project would be above water, with PV at 8 percent = 110,000/1.08 = $101,852 and NPV = 101,852 − 100,000 = +$1,852.

That can't be right. First, the interest rate on the loan has nothing to do with the risk of the project: It reflects the good health of your existing business. Second, whether you take the loan or not, you still face the choice between the project, which offers an expected return of only 10 percent, or the equally risky stock, which gives an expected return of 15 percent. A financial manager who borrows at 8 percent and invests at 10 percent is not smart, but stupid, if the company or its shareholders can borrow at 8 percent and buy an equally risky investment offering 15 percent. That is why the 15 percent expected return on the stock is the opportunity cost of capital for the project.

2.2 FOUNDATIONS OF THE NET PRESENT VALUE RULE

So far our discussion of net present value has been rather casual. Increasing value *sounds* like a sensible objective for a company, but it is more than just a rule of thumb. You need to understand why the NPV rule makes sense and why managers look to the bond and stock markets to find the opportunity cost of capital.

In the previous example there was just one person (you) making 100 percent of the investment and receiving 100 percent of the payoffs from the new office building. In corporations, investments are made on behalf of thousands of shareholders with varying risk tolerances and preferences for present versus future income. Could a positive-NPV project for Ms. Smith be a negative-NPV proposition for Mr. Jones? Could they find it impossible to agree on the objective of maximizing the market value of the firm?

The answer to both questions is no; Smith and Jones will always agree if both have access to capital markets. We will demonstrate this result with a simple example.

How Capital Markets Reconcile Preferences for Current vs. Future Consumption

Suppose that you can look forward to a stream of income from your job. Unless you have some way of storing or anticipating this income, you will be compelled to consume it as it arrives. This could be inconvenient or worse. If the bulk of your income comes late in life, the result could be hunger now and gluttony later. This is where the capital market comes in. The capital market allows trade between dollars today and dollars in the future. You can therefore eat moderately both now and in the future.

We will now illustrate how the existence of a well-functioning capital market allows investors with different time patterns of income and desired consumption to agree on whether investment projects should be undertaken. Suppose that there are two investors with different preferences. A is an ant, who wishes to save for the future; G is a grasshopper, who would prefer to spend all his wealth on some ephemeral frolic, taking no heed of tomorrow. Now suppose that each is confronted with an identical opportunity—to buy a share in a $350,000 office building that will produce a sure-fire $400,000 at the end of the year, a return of about 14 percent. The interest rate is 7 percent. A and G can borrow or lend in the capital market at this rate.

A would clearly be happy to invest in the office building. Every hundred dollars that she invests in the office building allows her to spend $114 at the end of the year, while a hundred dollars invested in the capital market would enable her to spend only $107.

But what about G, who wants money now, not in one year's time? Would he prefer to forego the investment opportunity and spend today the cash that he has in hand? Not as long as the capital market allows individuals to borrow as well as to lend. Every hundred dollars that G invests in the office building brings in $114 at the end of the year. Any bank, knowing that G could look forward to this sure-fire income, would be prepared to lend him $114/1.07 = $106.54 today. Thus, instead of spending $100 today, G can spend $106.54 if he invests in the office building and then borrows against his future income.

This is illustrated in Figure 2.1. The horizontal axis shows the number of dollars that can be spent today; the vertical axis shows spending next year. Suppose that the ant and the grasshopper both start with an initial sum of $100. If they invest the entire $100 in the capital market, they will be able to spend 100×1.07 = $107 at the end of the year. The straight line joining these two points (the innermost line in the figure) shows the combinations of current and future consumption that can be achieved by investing none, part, or all of the cash at the 7 percent rate offered in the capital market. (The interest rate determines the slope of this line.) Any other point along the line could be achieved by spending

FIGURE 2.1

The grasshopper (G) wants consumption now. The ant (A) wants to wait. But each is happy to invest. A prefers to invest at 14 percent, moving up the burgundy arrow, rather than at the 7 percent interest rate. G invests and then borrows at 7 percent, thereby transforming $100 into $106.54 of immediate consumption. Because of the investment, G has $114 next year to pay off the loan. The investment's NPV is 106.54 − 100 = +6.54.

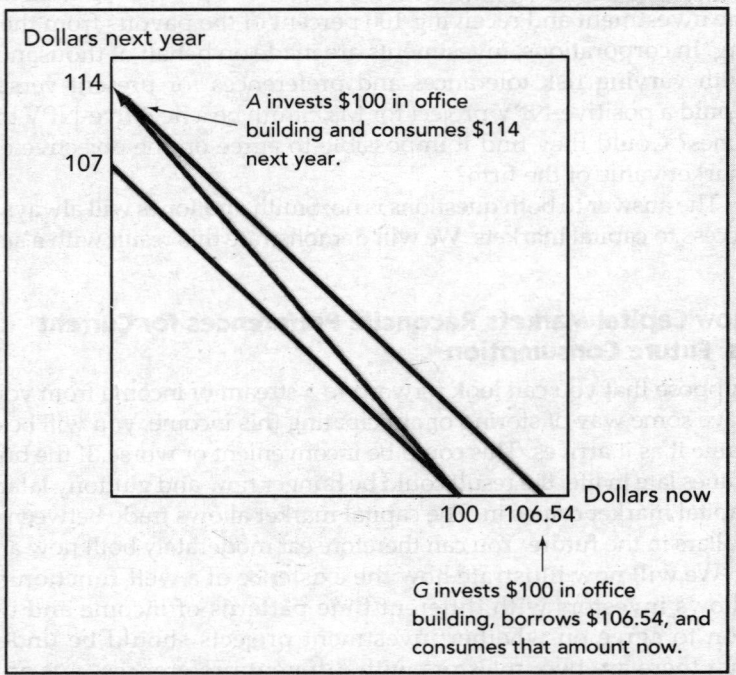

part of the $100 today and investing the balance.[7] For example, one could choose to spend $50 today and $53.50 next year. However, A and G would each reject such a balanced consumption schedule.

The burgundy arrow in Figure 2.1 shows the payoff to investing $100 in a share of your office project. The rate of return is 14 percent, so $100 today transmutes to $114 next year.

The sloping line on the right in Figure 2.1 (the outermost line in the figure) shows how A's and G's spending plans are enhanced if they can choose to invest their $100 in the office building. A, who is content to spend nothing today, can invest $100 in the building and spend $114 at the end of the year. G, the spendthrift, also invests $100 in the office building but borrows 114/1.07 = $106.54 against the future income. Of course, neither is limited to these spending plans. In fact, the right-hand sloping line shows all the combinations of current and future expenditure that an investor could achieve from investing $100 in the office building and borrowing against some fraction of the future income.

You can see from Figure 2.1 that the present value of A's and G's share in the office building is $106.54. The *net* present value is $6.54. This is the distance be-

---

[7]The exact balance between present and future consumption that each individual will choose depends on personal preferences. Readers who are familiar with economic theory will recognize that the choice can be represented by superimposing an indifference map for each individual. The preferred combination is the point of tangency between the interest-rate line and the individual's indifference curve. In other words, each individual will borrow or lend until 1 plus the interest rate equals the marginal rate of time preference (i.e., the slope of the indifference curve). A more formal graphical analysis of investment and the choice between present and future consumption is on the Brealey–Myers website at **www://mhhe.com/bm/7e.**

tween the $106.54 present value and the $100 initial investment: Despite their different tastes, both A and G are better off by investing in the office block and then using the capital markets to achieve the desired balance between consumption today and consumption at the end of the year. In fact, in coming to their investment decision, both would be happy to follow the two equivalent rules that we proposed so casually at the end of Section 2.1. The two rules can be restated as follows:

- *Net present value rule.* Invest in any project with a positive net present value. This is the difference between the discounted, or present, value of the future cash flow and the amount of the initial investment.
- *Rate-of-return rule.* Invest as long as the return on the investment exceeds the rate of return on equivalent investments in the capital market.

What happens if the interest rate is not 7 percent but 14.3 percent? In this case the office building would have zero NPV:

$$NPV = 400,000/1.143 - 350,000 = \$0$$

Also, the return on the project would be $400,000/350,000 - 1 = .143$, or 14.3 percent, exactly equal to the rate of interest in the capital market. In this case our two rules would say that the project is on a knife edge. Investors should not care whether the firm undertakes it or not.

It is easy to see that with a 14.3 percent interest rate neither A nor G would gain anything by investing in the office building. A could spend exactly the same amount at the end of the year, regardless of whether she invests her money in the office building or in the capital market. Equally, there is no advantage in G investing in an office block to earn 14.3 percent and at the same time borrowing at 14.3 percent. He might just as well spend whatever cash he has on hand.

In our example the ant and the grasshopper placed an identical value on the office building and were happy to share in its construction. They agreed because they faced identical borrowing and lending opportunities. Whenever firms discount cash flows at capital market rates, they are implicitly assuming that their shareholders have free and equal access to competitive capital markets.

It is easy to see how our net present value rule would be damaged if we did not have such a well-functioning capital market. For example, suppose that G could not borrow against future income or that it was prohibitively costly for him to do so. In that case he might well prefer to spend his cash today rather than invest it in an office building and have to wait until the end of the year before he could start spending. If A and G were shareholders in the same enterprise, there would be no simple way for the manager to reconcile their different objectives.

No one believes unreservedly that capital markets are perfectly competitive. Later in this book we will discuss several cases in which differences in taxation, transaction costs, and other imperfections must be taken into account in financial decision making. However, we will also discuss research which indicates that, in general, capital markets function fairly well. That is one good reason for relying on net present value as a corporate objective. Another good reason is that net present value makes common sense; we will see that it gives obviously silly answers less frequently than its major competitors. But for now, having glimpsed the problems of imperfect markets, we shall, like an economist in a shipwreck, simply *assume* our life jacket and swim safely to shore.

2.3 A FUNDAMENTAL RESULT

Our justification of the present value rule was restricted to two periods and to a certain cash flow. However, the rule also makes sense for uncertain cash flows that extend far into the future. The argument goes like this:

1. A financial manager should act in the interests of the firm's owners, its stockholders. Each stockholder wants three things:
   a. To be as rich as possible, that is, to maximize current wealth.
   b. To transform that wealth into whatever time pattern of consumption he or she desires.
   c. To choose the risk characteristics of that consumption plan.

2. But stockholders do not need the financial manager's help to achieve the best time pattern of consumption. They can do that on their own, providing they have free access to competitive capital markets. They can also choose the risk characteristics of their consumption plan by investing in more or less risky securities.

3. How then can the financial manager help the firm's stockholders? There is only one way: by increasing the market value of each stockholder's stake in the firm. The way to do that is to seize all investment opportunities that have a positive net present value.

Despite the fact that shareholders have different preferences, they are unanimous in the amount that they want to invest in real assets. This means that they can cooperate in the same enterprise and can safely delegate operation of that enterprise to professional managers. These managers do not need to know anything about the tastes of their shareholders and should not consult their own tastes. Their task is to maximize net present value. If they succeed, they can rest assured that they have acted in the best interest of their shareholders.

This gives us the fundamental condition for successful operation of a modern capitalist economy. Separation of ownership and control is essential for most corporations, so authority to manage has to be delegated. It is good to know that managers can all be given one simple instruction: Maximize net present value.

Other Corporate Goals

Sometimes you hear managers speak as if the corporation has other goals. For example, they may say that their job is to maximize profits. That sounds reasonable. After all, don't shareholders prefer to own a profitable company rather than an unprofitable one? But taken literally, profit maximization doesn't make sense as a corporate objective. Here are three reasons:

1. "Maximizing profits" leaves open the question, Which year's profits? Shareholders might not want a manager to increase next year's profits at the expense of profits in later years.

2. A company may be able to increase future profits by cutting its dividend and investing the cash. That is not in the shareholders' interest if the company earns only a low return on the investment.

3. Different accountants may calculate profits in different ways. So you may find that a decision which improves profits in one accountant's eyes will reduce them in the eyes of another.

2.4 *DO* MANAGERS REALLY LOOK AFTER THE INTERESTS OF SHAREHOLDERS?

We have explained that managers can best serve the interests of shareholders by investing in projects with a positive net present value. But this takes us back to the principal–agent problem highlighted in the first chapter. How can shareholders (the principals) ensure that management (their agents) don't simply look after their own interests? Shareholders can't spend their lives watching managers to check that they are not shirking or maximizing the value of their *own* wealth. However, there are several institutional arrangements that help to ensure that the shareholders' pockets are close to the managers' heart.

A company's board of directors is elected by the shareholders and is supposed to represent them. Boards of directors are sometimes portrayed as passive stooges who always champion the incumbent management. But when company performance starts to slide and managers do not offer a credible recovery plan, boards do act. In recent years the chief executives of Eastman Kodak, General Motors, Xerox, Lucent, Ford Motor, Sunbeam, and Lands End were all forced to step aside when each company's profitability deteriorated and the need for new strategies became clear.

If shareholders believe that the corporation is underperforming and that the board of directors is not sufficiently aggressive in holding the managers to task, they can try to replace the board in the next election. If they succeed, the new board will appoint a new management team. But these attempts to vote in a new board are expensive and rarely successful. Thus dissidents do not usually stand and fight but sell their shares instead.

Selling, however, can send a powerful message. If enough shareholders bail out, the stock price tumbles. This damages top management's reputation and compensation. Part of the top managers' paychecks comes from bonuses tied to the company's earnings or from stock options, which pay off if the stock price rises but are worthless if the price falls below a stated threshold. This should motivate managers to increase earnings and the stock price.

If managers and directors do not maximize value, there is always the threat of a hostile takeover. The further a company's stock price falls, due to lax management or wrong-headed policies, the easier it is for another company or group of investors to buy up a majority of the shares. The old management team is then likely to find themselves out on the street and their place is taken by a fresh team prepared to make the changes needed to realize the company's value.

These arrangements ensure that few managers at the top of major United States corporations are lazy or inattentive to stockholders' interests. On the contrary, the pressure to perform can be intense.

2.5 *SHOULD* MANAGERS LOOK AFTER THE INTERESTS OF SHAREHOLDERS?

We have described managers as the agents of the shareholders. But perhaps this begs the question, Is it *desirable* for managers to act in the selfish interests of their shareholders? Does a focus on enriching the shareholders mean that managers must act as greedy mercenaries riding roughshod over the weak and helpless? Do they not have wider obligations to their employees, customers, suppliers, and the communities in which the firm is located?[8]

Most of this book is devoted to financial policies that increase a firm's value. None of these policies requires gallops over the weak and helpless. In most instances there is little conflict between doing well (maximizing value) and doing good. Profitable firms are those with satisfied customers and loyal employees; firms with dissatisfied customers and a disgruntled workforce are more likely to have declining profits and a low share price.

Of course, ethical issues do arise in business as in other walks of life, and therefore when we say that the objective of the firm is to maximize shareholder wealth, we do not mean that anything goes. In part, the law deters managers from making blatantly dishonest decisions, but most managers are not simply concerned with observing the letter of the law or with keeping to written contracts. In business and finance, as in other day-to-day affairs, there are unwritten, implicit rules of behavior. To work efficiently together, we need to trust each other. Thus huge financial deals are regularly completed on a handshake, and each side knows that the other will not renege later if things turn sour.[9] Whenever anything happens to weaken this trust, we are all a little worse off.[10]

In many financial transactions, one party has more information than the other. It can be difficult to be sure of the quality of the asset or service that you are buying. This opens up plenty of opportunities for financial sharp practice and outright fraud, and, because the activities of scoundrels are more entertaining than those of honest people, airport bookstores are packed with accounts of financial fraudsters.

The response of honest firms is to distinguish themselves by building long-term relationships with their customers and establishing a name for fair dealing and financial integrity. Major banks and securities firms know that their most valuable asset is their reputation. They emphasize their long history and responsible behavior. When something happens to undermine that reputation, the costs can be enormous.

Consider the Salomon Brothers bidding scandal in 1991.[11] A Salomon trader tried to evade rules limiting the firm's participation in auctions of U.S. Treasury bonds by submitting bids in the names of the company's customers without the customers' knowledge. When this was discovered, Salomon settled the case by paying almost $200 million in fines and establishing a $100 million fund for payments of claims from civil lawsuits. Yet the value of Salomon Brothers stock fell by

---

[8]Some managers, anxious not to offend any group of stakeholders, have denied that they are maximizing profits or value. We are reminded of a survey of businesspeople that inquired whether they attempted to maximize profits. They indignantly rejected the notion, objecting that their responsibilities went far beyond the narrow, selfish profit motive. But when the question was reformulated and they were asked whether they could increase profits by raising or lowering their selling price, they replied that neither change would do so. The survey is cited in G. J. Stigler, *The Theory of Price*, 3rd ed. (New York: Macmillan Company, 1966).

[9]In U.S. law, a contract can be valid even if it is not written down. Of course documentation is prudent, but contracts are enforced if it can be shown that the parties reached a clear understanding and agreement. For example, in 1984, the top management of Getty Oil gave verbal agreement to a merger offer with Pennzoil. Then Texaco arrived with a higher bid and won the prize. Pennzoil sued—and won—arguing that Texaco had broken up a valid contract.

[10]For a discussion of this issue, see A. Schleifer and L. H. Summers, "Breach of Trust in Corporate Takeovers," *Corporate Takeovers: Causes and Consequences* (Chicago: University of Chicago Press, 1988).

[11]This discussion is based on Clifford W. Smith, Jr., "Economics and Ethics: The Case of Salomon Brothers," *Journal of Applied Corporate Finance* 5 (Summer 1992), pp. 23–28.

far more than \$300 million. In fact the price dropped by about a third, representing a \$1.5 billion decline in the company's market value.

Why did the value of Salomon Brothers drop so dramatically? Largely because investors were worried that Salomon would lose business from customers that now distrusted the company. The damage to Salomon's reputation was far greater than the explicit costs of the scandal and was hundreds or thousands of times more costly than the potential gains Salomon could have reaped from the illegal trades.

In this chapter we have introduced the concept of present value as a way of valuing assets. Calculating present value is easy. Just discount future cash flow by an appropriate rate r, usually called the *opportunity cost of capital*, or hurdle rate:

$$\text{Present value (PV)} = \frac{C_1}{1 + r}$$

Net present value is present value plus any immediate cash flow:

$$\text{Net present value (NPV)} = C_0 + \frac{C_1}{1 + r}$$

Remember that C_0 is negative if the immediate cash flow is an investment, that is, if it is a cash outflow.

The discount rate is determined by rates of return prevailing in capital markets. If the future cash flow is absolutely safe, then the discount rate is the interest rate on safe securities such as United States government debt. If the size of the future cash flow is uncertain, then the expected cash flow should be discounted at the expected rate of return offered by equivalent-risk securities. We will talk more about risk and the cost of capital in Chapters 7 through 9.

Cash flows are discounted for two simple reasons: first, because a dollar today is worth more than a dollar tomorrow, and second, because a safe dollar is worth more than a risky one. Formulas for PV and NPV are numerical expressions of these ideas. The capital market is the market where safe and risky future cash flows are traded. That is why we look to rates of return prevailing in the capital markets to determine how much to discount for time and risk. By calculating the present value of an asset, we are in effect estimating how much people will pay for it if they have the alternative of investing in the capital markets.

The concept of net present value allows efficient separation of ownership and management of the corporation. A manager who invests only in assets with positive net present values serves the best interests of each one of the firm's owners, regardless of differences in their wealth and tastes. This is made possible by the existence of the capital market which allows each shareholder to construct a personal investment plan that is custom tailored to his or her own requirements. For example, there is no need for the firm to arrange its investment policy to obtain a sequence of cash flows that matches its shareholders' preferred time patterns of consumption. The shareholders can shift funds forward or back over time perfectly well on their own, provided they have free access to competitive capital markets. In fact, their plan for consumption over time is limited by only two things: their personal wealth (or lack of it) and the interest rate at which they can borrow or lend. The financial manager cannot affect the interest rate but can increase stockholders' wealth. The way to do so is to invest in assets having positive net present values.

There are several institutional arrangements which help to ensure that managers pay close attention to the value of the firm:

- Managers' actions are subject to the scrutiny of the board of directors.
- Shirkers are likely to find that they are ousted by more energetic managers. This competition may arise within the firm, but poorly performing companies are also more likely to be taken over. That sort of takeover typically brings in a fresh management team.
- Managers are spurred on by incentive schemes, such as stock options, which pay off big if shareholders gain but are valueless if they do not.

Managers who focus on shareholder value need not neglect their wider obligations to the community. Managers play fair by employees, customers, and suppliers partly because they know that it is for the common good, but partly because they know that their firm's most valuable asset is its reputation. Of course, ethical issues do arise in financial management and, whenever unscrupulous managers abuse their position, we all trust each other a little less.

FURTHER READING

The pioneering works on the net present value rule are:

I. Fisher: *The Theory of Interest*, Augustus M. Kelley, Publishers. New York, 1965. Reprinted from the 1930 edition.

J. Hirshleifer: "On the Theory of Optimal Investment Decision," *Journal of Political Economy*, 66:329–352 (August 1958).

For a more rigorous textbook treatment of the subject, we suggest:

E. F. Fama and M. H. Miller: *The Theory of Finance*, Holt, Rinehart and Winston. New York, 1972.

If you would like to dig deeper into the question of how managers can be motivated to maximize shareholder wealth, we suggest:

M. C. Jensen and W. H. Meckling: "Theory of the Firm: Managerial Behavior, Agency Costs, and Ownership Structure," *Journal of Financial Economics*, 3:305–360 (October 1976).

E. F. Fama: "Agency Problems and the Theory of the Firm," *Journal of Political Economy*, 88:288–307 (April 1980).

QUIZ

1. C_0 is the initial cash flow on an investment, and C_1 is the cash flow at the end of one year. The symbol r is the discount rate.
   a. Is C_0 usually positive or negative?
   b. What is the formula for the present value of the investment?
   c. What is the formula for the net present value?
   d. The symbol r is often termed the *opportunity cost of capital*. Why?
   e. If the investment is risk-free, what is the appropriate measure of r?

2. If the present value of $150 paid at the end of one year is $130, what is the one-year discount factor? What is the discount rate?

3. Calculate the one-year discount factor DF_1 for discount rates of (a) 10 percent, (b) 20 percent, and (c) 30 percent.

4. A merchant pays $100,000 for a load of grain and is certain that it can be resold at the end of one year for $132,000.
   a. What is the return on this investment?
   b. If this return is *lower* than the rate of interest, does the investment have a positive or a negative NPV?
   c. If the rate of interest is 10 percent, what is the PV of the investment?
   d. What is the NPV?

5. What is the net present value rule? What is the rate of return rule? Do the two rules give the same answer?

6. Define the opportunity cost of capital. How in principle would you find the opportunity cost of capital for a risk-free asset? For a risky asset?

7. Look back to the numerical example graphed in Figure 2.1. Suppose the interest rate is 20 percent. What would the ant (*A*) and grasshopper (*G*) do? Would they invest in the office building? Would they borrow or lend? Suppose each starts with $100. How much and when would each consume?

8. We can imagine the financial manager doing several things on behalf of the firm's stockholders. For example, the manager might:
   a. Make shareholders as wealthy as possible by investing in real assets with positive NPVs.
   b. Modify the firm's investment plan to help shareholders achieve a particular time pattern of consumption.
   c. Choose high- or low-risk assets to match shareholders' risk preferences.
   d. Help balance shareholders' checkbooks.

   But in well-functioning capital markets, shareholders will vote for *only one* of these goals. Which one? Why?

9. Why would one expect managers to act in shareholders' interests? Give some reasons.

10. After the Salomon Brothers bidding scandal, the aggregate value of the company's stock dropped by far more than it paid in fines and settlements of lawsuits. Why?

PRACTICE QUESTIONS

1. Write down the formulas for an investment's NPV and rate of return. Prove that NPV is positive *only* if the rate of return exceeds the opportunity cost of capital.

2. What is the net present value of a *firm's* investment in a U.S. Treasury security yielding 5 percent and maturing in one year? *Hint:* What is the opportunity cost of capital? Ignore taxes.

3. A parcel of land costs $500,000. For an additional $800,000 you can build a motel on the property. The land and motel should be worth $1,500,000 next year. Suppose that common stocks with the same risk as this investment offer a 10 percent expected return. Would you construct the motel? Why or why not?

4. Calculate the NPV and rate of return for each of the following investments. The opportunity cost of capital is 20 percent for all four investments.

Investment	Initial Cash Flow, C_0	Cash Flow in Year 1, C_1
1	−10,000	+18,000
2	−5,000	+9,000
3	−5,000	+5,700
4	−2,000	+4,000

EXCEL

a. Which investment is most valuable?

b. Suppose each investment would require use of the same parcel of land. Therefore you can take only one. Which one? *Hint:* What is the firm's objective: to earn a high rate of return or to increase firm value?

5. In Section 2.1, we analyzed the possible construction of an office building on a plot of land appraised at $50,000. We concluded that this investment had a positive NPV of $7,143 at a discount rate of 12 percent.

   Suppose E. Coli Associates, a firm of genetic engineers, offers to purchase the land for $60,000, $30,000 paid immediately and $30,000 after one year. United States government securities maturing in one year yield 7 percent.

   a. Assume E. Coli is sure to pay the second $30,000 installment. Should you take its offer or start on the office building? Explain.

   b. Suppose you are *not* sure E. Coli will pay. You observe that other investors demand a 10 percent return on their loans to E. Coli. Assume that the other investors have correctly assessed the risks that E. Coli will not be able to pay. Should you accept E. Coli's offer?

6. Explain why the discount rate equals the *opportunity* cost of capital.

7. Norman Gerrymander has just received a $2 million bequest. How should he invest it? There are four immediate alternatives.

   a. Investment in one-year U.S. government securities yielding 5 percent.

   b. A loan to Norman's nephew Gerald, who has for years aspired to open a big Cajun restaurant in Duluth. Gerald had arranged a one-year bank loan for $900,000, at 10 percent, but asks for a loan from Norman at 7 percent.

   c. Investment in the stock market. The expected rate of return is 12 percent.

   d. Investment in local real estate, which Norman judges is about as risky as the stock market. The opportunity at hand would cost $1 million and is forecasted to be worth $1.1 million after one year.

   Which of these investments have positive NPVs? Which would you advise Norman to take?

8. Show that your answers to Practice Question 7 are consistent with the rate of return rule for investment decisions.

9. Take another look at investment opportunity (d) in Practice Question 7. Suppose a bank offers Norman a $600,000 personal loan at 8 percent. (Norman is a long-time customer of the bank and has an excellent credit history.) Suppose Norman borrows the money, invests $1 million in real estate opportunity (d) and puts the rest of his money in opportunity (c), the stock market. Is this a smart move? Explain.

10. Respond to the following comments.

    a. "My company's cost of capital is the rate we pay to the bank when we borrow money."

    b. "Net present value is just theory. It has no practical relevance. We maximize profits. That's what shareholders really want."

    c. "It's no good just telling me to maximize my stock price. I can easily take a short view and maximize today's price. What I would prefer is to keep it on a gently rising trend."

11. Ms. Smith is retired and depends on her investments for retirement income. Mr. Jones is a young executive who wants to save for the future. They are both stockholders in Airbus, which is investing over $12 billion to develop the A380, a new super-jumbo airliner. This investment's payoff is many years in the future. Assume the investment is positive-NPV for Mr. Jones. Explain why it should also be positive-NPV for Ms. Smith.

12. Answer this question by drawing graphs like Figure 2.1. Casper Milktoast has $200,000 available to support consumption in periods 0 (now) and 1 (next year). He

wants to consume *exactly* the same amount in each period. The interest rate is 8 percent. There is no risk.

a. How much should he invest, and how much can he consume in each period?

b. Suppose Casper is given an opportunity to invest up to $200,000 at 10 percent risk-free. The interest rate stays at 8 percent. What should he do, and how much can he consume in each period?

c. What is the NPV of the opportunity in (b)?

13. We said that maximizing value makes sense only if we assume well-functioning capital markets. What does "well-functioning" mean? Can you think of circumstances in which maximizing value would not be in all shareholders' interests?

14. Why is a reputation for honesty and fair business practice important to the financial value of the corporation?

CHALLENGE QUESTIONS

1. It is sometimes argued that the NPV criterion is appropriate for corporations but not for governments. First, governments must consider the time preferences of the community as a whole rather than those of a few wealthy investors. Second, governments must have a longer horizon than individuals, for governments are the guardians of future generations. What do you think?

2. In Figure 2.2, the sloping line represents the opportunities for investment in the capital market and the solid curved line represents the opportunities for investment in plant and machinery. The company's only asset at present is $2.6 million in cash.

a. What is the interest rate?

b. How much should the company invest in plant and machinery?

c. How much will this investment be worth next year?

d. What is the average rate of return on the investment?

e. What is the marginal rate of return?

f. What is the PV of this investment?

g. What is the NPV of this investment?

h. What is the total PV of the company?

i. How much will the individual consume today?

j. How much will he or she consume tomorrow?

FIGURE 2.2

See Challenge Question 2.

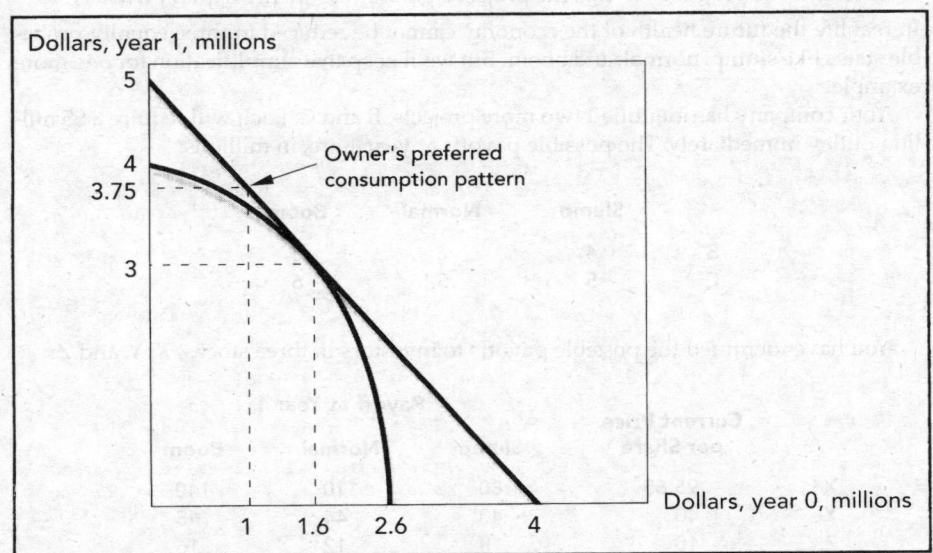

3. Draw a figure like Figure 2.1 to represent the following situation.
   a. A firm starts out with $10 million in cash.
   b. The rate of interest r is 10 percent.
   c. To maximize NPV the firm invests today $6 million in real assets. This leaves $4 million which can be paid out to the shareholders.
   d. The NPV of the investment is $2 million.

   When you have finished, answer the following questions:

   e. How much cash is the firm going to receive in year 1 from its investment?
   f. What is the marginal return from the firm's investment?
   g. What is the PV of the shareholders' investment after the firm has announced its investment plan?
   h. Suppose shareholders want to spend $6 million today. How can they do this?
   i. How much will they then have to spend next year? Show this on your drawing.

4. For an outlay of $8 million you can purchase a tanker load of bucolic acid delivered in Rotterdam one year hence. Unfortunately the net cash flow from selling the tanker load will be very sensitive to the growth rate of the world economy:

Slump	Normal	Boom
$8 million	$12 million	$16 million

   a. What is the expected cash flow? Assume the three outcomes for the economy are equally likely.
   b. What is the expected rate of return on the investment in the project?
   c. One share of stock Z is selling for $10. The stock has the following payoffs after one year:

Slump	Normal	Boom
$8	$12	$16

   Calculate the expected rate of return offered by stock Z. Explain why this is the opportunity cost of capital for your bucolic acid project.
   d. Calculate the project's NPV. Is the project a good investment? Explain why.

5. In real life the future health of the economy cannot be reduced to three equally probable states like slump, normal, and boom. But we'll keep that simplification for one more example.

   Your company has identified two more projects, B and C. Each will require a $5 million outlay immediately. The possible payoffs at year 1 are, in millions:

	Slump	Normal	Boom
B	4	6	8
C	5	5.5	6

   You have identified the possible payoffs to investors in three stocks, X, Y, and Z:

	Current Price per Share	Payoff at Year 1		
		Slump	Normal	Boom
X	95.65	80	110	140
Y	40	40	44	48
Z	10	8	12	16

a. What are the expected cash inflows of projects B and C?

b. What are the expected rates of return offered by stocks X, Y, and Z?

c. What are the opportunity costs of capital for projects B and C? *Hint:* Calculate the percentage differences, slump versus normal and boom versus normal, for stocks X, Y, and Z. Match up to the percentage differences in B's and C's payoffs.

d. What are the NPVs of projects B and C?

e. Suppose B and C are launched and $5 million is invested in each. How much will they add to the total market value of your company's shares?

CHAPTER THREE

HOW TO

CALCULATE

PRESENT VALUES

IN CHAPTER 2 we learned how to work out the value of an asset that produces cash exactly one year from now. But we did not explain how to value assets that produce cash two years from now or in several future years. That is the first task for this chapter. We will then have a look at some shortcut methods for calculating present values and at some specialized present value formulas. In particular we will show how to value an investment that makes a steady stream of payments forever (a *perpetuity*) and one that produces a steady stream for a limited period (an *annuity*). We will also look at investments that produce a steadily growing stream of payments.

The term *interest rate* sounds straightforward enough, but we will see that it can be defined in various ways. We will first explain the distinction between *compound interest* and *simple interest*. Then we will discuss the difference between the nominal interest rate and the real interest rate. This difference arises because the purchasing power of interest income is reduced by inflation.

By then you will deserve some payoff for the mental investment you have made in learning about present values. Therefore, we will try out the concept on bonds. In Chapter 4 we will look at the valuation of common stocks, and after that we will tackle the firm's capital investment decisions at a practical level of detail.

 ## 3.1 VALUING LONG-LIVED ASSETS

Do you remember how to calculate the present value (PV) of an asset that produces a cash flow (C_1) one year from now?

$$PV = DF_1 \times C_1 = \frac{C_1}{1 + r_1}$$

The discount factor for the year-1 cash flow is DF_1, and r_1 is the opportunity cost of investing your money for one year. Suppose you will receive a certain cash inflow of \$100 next year ($C_1 = 100$) and the rate of interest on one-year U.S. Treasury notes is 7 percent ($r_1 = .07$). Then present value equals

$$PV = \frac{C_1}{1 + r_1} = \frac{100}{1.07} = \$93.46$$

The present value of a cash flow two years hence can be written in a similar way as

$$PV = DF_2 \times C_2 = \frac{C_2}{(1 + r_2)^2}$$

C_2 is the year-2 cash flow, DF_2 is the discount factor for the year-2 cash flow, and r_2 is the annual rate of interest on money invested for two years. Suppose you get another cash flow of \$100 in year 2 ($C_2 = 100$). The rate of interest on two-year Treasury notes is 7.7 percent per year ($r_2 = .077$); this means that a dollar invested in two-year notes will grow to $1.077^2 = \$1.16$ by the end of two years. The present value of your year-2 cash flow equals

$$PV = \frac{C_2}{(1 + r_2)^2} = \frac{100}{(1.077)^2} = \$86.21$$

Valuing Cash Flows in Several Periods

One of the nice things about present values is that they are all expressed in current dollars—so that you can add them up. In other words, the present value of cash flow $A + B$ is equal to the present value of cash flow A plus the present value of cash flow B. This happy result has important implications for investments that produce cash flows in several periods.

We calculated above the value of an asset that produces a cash flow of C_1 in year 1, and we calculated the value of another asset that produces a cash flow of C_2 in year 2. Following our additivity rule, we can write down the value of an asset that produces cash flows in *each* year. It is simply

$$PV = \frac{C_1}{1 + r_1} + \frac{C_2}{(1 + r_2)^2}$$

We can obviously continue in this way to find the present value of an extended stream of cash flows:

$$PV = \frac{C_1}{1 + r_1} + \frac{C_2}{(1 + r_2)^2} + \frac{C_3}{(1 + r_3)^3} + \cdots$$

This is called the **discounted cash flow** (or **DCF**) formula. A shorthand way to write it is

$$PV = \sum \frac{C_t}{(1 + r_t)^t}$$

where Σ refers to the sum of the series. To find the *net* present value (NPV) we add the (usually negative) initial cash flow, just as in Chapter 2:

$$NPV = C_0 + PV = C_0 + \sum \frac{C_t}{(1 + r_t)^t}$$

Why the Discount Factor Declines as Futurity Increases— And a Digression on Money Machines

If a dollar tomorrow is worth less than a dollar today, one might suspect that a dollar the day after tomorrow should be worth even less. In other words, the discount factor DF_2 should be less than the discount factor DF_1. But is this *necessarily* so, when there is a different interest rate r_t for each period?

Suppose r_1 is 20 percent and r_2 is 7 percent. Then

$$DF_1 = \frac{1}{1.20} = .83$$

$$DF_2 = \frac{1}{(1.07)^2} = .87$$

Apparently the dollar received the day after tomorrow is *not* necessarily worth less than the dollar received tomorrow.

But there is something wrong with this example. Anyone who could borrow and lend at these interest rates could become a millionaire overnight. Let us see how such a "money machine" would work. Suppose the first person to spot the opportunity is Hermione Kraft. Ms. Kraft first lends $1,000 for one year at 20 percent. That is an attractive enough return, but she notices that there is a way to earn an *immediate* profit on her investment and be ready to play the game again. She reasons as follows. Next year she will have $1,200 which can be reinvested for a further year. Although she does not know what interest rates will be at that time, she does know that she can always put the money in a checking account and be sure of having $1,200 at the end of year 2. Her next step, therefore, is to go to her bank and borrow the present value of this $1,200. At 7 percent interest this present value is

$$PV = \frac{1200}{(1.07)^2} = \$1,048$$

Thus Ms. Kraft invests $1,000, borrows back $1,048, and walks away with a profit of $48. If that does not sound like very much, remember that the game can be played again immediately, this time with $1,048. In fact it would take Ms. Kraft only 147 plays to become a millionaire (before taxes).[1]

Of course this story is completely fanciful. Such an opportunity would not last long in capital markets like ours. Any bank that would allow you to lend for one year at 20 percent and borrow for two years at 7 percent would soon be wiped out by a rush of small investors hoping to become millionaires and a rush of millionaires hoping to become billionaires. There are, however, two lessons to our story. The first is that a dollar tomorrow *cannot* be worth less than a dollar the day after tomorrow. In other words, the value of a dollar received at the end of one year (DF_1) must be greater than the value of a dollar received at the end of two years (DF_2). There must be some extra gain[2] from lending for two periods rather than one: $(1 + r_2)^2$ must be greater than $1 + r_1$.

Our second lesson is a more general one and can be summed up by the precept "There is no such thing as a money machine."[3] In well-functioning capital markets, any potential money machine will be eliminated almost instantaneously by investors who try to take advantage of it. Therefore, beware of self-styled experts who offer you a chance to participate in a sure thing.

Later in the book we will invoke the *absence* of money machines to prove several useful properties about security prices. That is, we will make statements like "The prices of securities X and Y must be in the following relationship—otherwise there would be a money machine and capital markets would not be in equilibrium."

Ruling out money machines does not require that interest rates be the same for each future period. This relationship between the interest rate and the maturity of the cash flow is called the **term structure of interest rates.** We are going to look at term structure in Chapter 24, but for now we will finesse the issue by assuming that the term structure is "flat"—in other words, the interest rate is the same regardless of the date of the cash flow. This means that we can replace the series of interest rates $r_1, r_2, \ldots, r_t$, etc., with a single rate r and that we can write the present value formula as

$$PV = \frac{C_1}{1 + r} + \frac{C_2}{(1 + r)^2} + \cdots$$

---

[1]That is, $1,000 \times (1.04813)^{147} = \$1,002,000$.

[2]The extra return for lending two years rather than one is often referred to as a *forward rate of return.* Our rule says that the forward rate cannot be negative.

[3]The technical term for money machine is *arbitrage.* There are no opportunities for arbitrage in well-functioning capital markets.

Calculating PVs and NPVs

You have some bad news about your office building venture (the one described at the start of Chapter 2). The contractor says that construction will take two years instead of one and requests payment on the following schedule:

1. A $100,000 down payment now. (Note that the land, worth $50,000, must also be committed now.)
2. A $100,000 progress payment after one year.
3. A final payment of $100,000 when the building is ready for occupancy at the end of the second year.

Your real estate adviser maintains that despite the delay the building will be worth $400,000 when completed.

All this yields a new set of cash-flow forecasts:

Period	t = 0	t = 1	t = 2
Land	−50,000		
Construction	−100,000	−100,000	−100,000
Payoff			+400,000
Total	$C_0 = -150,000$	$C_1 = -100,000$	$C_2 = +300,000$

If the interest rate is 7 percent, then NPV is

$$NPV = C_0 + \frac{C_1}{1 + r} + \frac{C_2}{(1 + r)^2}$$

$$= -150,000 - \frac{100,000}{1.07} + \frac{300,000}{(1.07)^2}$$

Table 3.1 calculates NPV step by step. The calculations require just a few keystrokes on an electronic calculator. Real problems can be much more complicated, however, so financial managers usually turn to calculators especially programmed for present value calculations or to spreadsheet programs on personal computers. In some cases it can be convenient to look up discount factors in present value tables like Appendix Table 1 at the end of this book.

Fortunately the news about your office venture is not all bad. The contractor is willing to accept a delayed payment; this means that the present value of the contractor's fee is less than before. This partly offsets the delay in the payoff. As Table 3.1 shows,

TABLE 3.1

Present value worksheet.

Period	Discount Factor	Cash Flow	Present Value
0	1.0	−150,000	−150,000
1	$\frac{1}{1.07} = .935$	−100,000	−93,500
2	$\frac{1}{(1.07)^2} = .873$	+300,000	+261,900
			Total = NPV = $18,400

the net present value is $18,400—not a substantial decrease from the $23,800 calculated in Chapter 2. Since the net present value is positive, you should still go ahead.[4]

 **3.2 LOOKING FOR SHORTCUTS—
PERPETUITIES AND ANNUITIES**

Sometimes there are shortcuts that make it easy to calculate present values. Let us look at some examples.

Among the securities that have been issued by the British government are so-called **perpetuities.** These are bonds that the government is under no obligation to repay but that offer a fixed income for each year to perpetuity. The annual rate of return on a perpetuity is equal to the promised annual payment divided by the present value:

$$\text{Return} = \frac{\text{cash flow}}{\text{present value}}$$

$$r = \frac{C}{\text{PV}}$$

We can obviously twist this around and find the present value of a perpetuity given the discount rate r and the cash payment C. For example, suppose that some worthy person wishes to endow a chair in finance at a business school with the initial payment occurring at the end of the first year. If the rate of interest is 10 percent and if the aim is to provide $100,000 a year in perpetuity, the amount that must be set aside today is[5]

$$\text{Present value of perpetuity} = \frac{C}{r} = \frac{100,000}{.10} = \$1,000,000$$

How to Value Growing Perpetuities

Suppose now that our benefactor suddenly recollects that no allowance has been made for growth in salaries, which will probably average about 4 percent a year starting in year 1. Therefore, instead of providing $100,000 a year in perpetuity, the benefactor must provide $100,000 in year 1, 1.04 × $100,000 in year 2, and so on. If

---

[4]We assume the cash flows are safe. If they are risky forecasts, the opportunity cost of capital could be higher, say 12 percent. NPV at 12 percent is just about zero.

[5]You can check this by writing down the present value formula

$$\text{PV} = \frac{C}{1 + r} + \frac{C}{(1 + r)^2} + \frac{C}{(1 + r)^3} + \cdots$$

Now let $C/(1 + r) = a$ and $1/(1 + r) = x$. Then we have (1) $\text{PV} = a(1 + x + x^2 + \cdots)$.
Multiplying both sides by x, we have (2) $\text{PV}x = a(x + x^2 + \cdots)$.
Subtracting (2) from (1) gives us $\text{PV}(1 - x) = a$. Therefore, substituting for a and x,

$$\text{PV}\left(1 - \frac{1}{1 + r}\right) = \frac{C}{1 + r}$$

Multiplying both sides by $(1 + r)$ and rearranging gives

$$\text{PV} = \frac{C}{r}$$

we call the growth rate in salaries g, we can write down the present value of this stream of cash flows as follows:

$$PV = \frac{C_1}{1 + r} + \frac{C_2}{(1 + r)^2} + \frac{C_3}{(1 + r)^3} + \cdots$$

$$= \frac{C_1}{1 + r} + \frac{C_1(1 + g)}{(1 + r)^2} + \frac{C_1(1 + g)^2}{(1 + r)^3} + \cdots$$

Fortunately, there is a simple formula for the sum of this geometric series.[6] If we assume that r is greater than g, our clumsy-looking calculation simplifies to

$$\text{Present value of growing perpetuity} = \frac{C_1}{r - g}$$

Therefore, if our benefactor wants to provide perpetually an annual sum that keeps pace with the growth rate in salaries, the amount that must be set aside today is

$$PV = \frac{C_1}{r - g} = \frac{100,000}{.10 - .04} = \$1,666,667$$

How to Value Annuities

An **annuity** is an asset that pays a fixed sum each year for a specified number of years. The equal-payment house mortgage or installment credit agreement are common examples of annuities.

Figure 3.1 illustrates a simple trick for valuing annuities. The first row represents a perpetuity that produces a cash flow of C in each year beginning in year 1. It has a present value of

$$PV = \frac{C}{r}$$

FIGURE 3.1

An annuity that makes payments in each of years 1 to t is equal to the difference between two perpetuities.

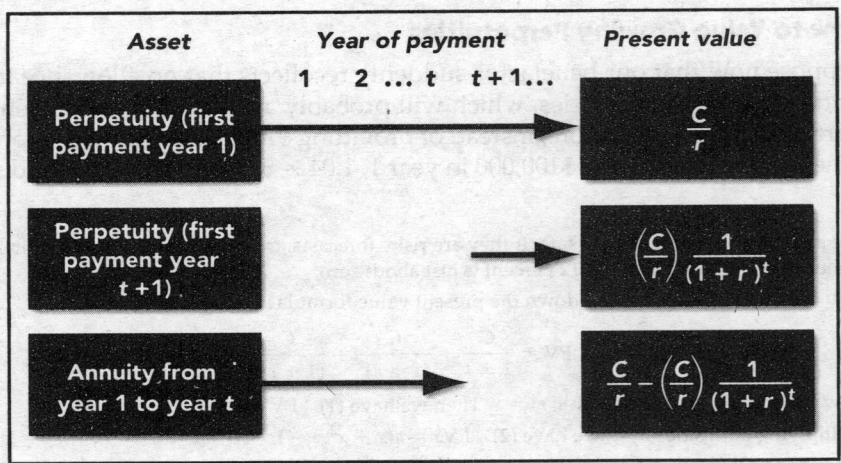

Asset	Year of payment 1 2 ... t t+1...	Present value
Perpetuity (first payment year 1)		$\frac{C}{r}$
Perpetuity (first payment year t +1)		$\left(\frac{C}{r}\right)\frac{1}{(1 + r)^t}$
Annuity from year 1 to year t		$\frac{C}{r} - \left(\frac{C}{r}\right)\frac{1}{(1 + r)^t}$

---

[6]We need to calculate the sum of an infinite geometric series $PV = a(1 + x + x^2 + \cdots)$ where $a = C_1/(1 + r)$ and $x = (1 + g)/(1 + r)$. In footnote 5 we showed that the sum of such a series is $a/(1 - x)$. Substituting for a and x in this formula,

$$PV = \frac{C_1}{r - g}$$

The second row represents a second *perpetuity* that produces a cash flow of C in each year *beginning in year t + 1*. It *will* have a present value of C/r in year t and it therefore has a present value today of

$$PV = \frac{C}{r(1 + r)^t}$$

Both perpetuities provide a cash flow from year t + 1 onward. The only difference between the two perpetuities is that the first one *also* provides a cash flow in each of the years 1 through t. In other words, the difference between the two perpetuities is an annuity of C for t years. The present value of this annuity is, therefore, the difference between the values of the two perpetuities:

$$\text{Present value of annuity} = C\left[\frac{1}{r} - \frac{1}{r(1 + r)^t}\right]$$

The expression in brackets is the *annuity factor,* which is the present value at discount rate r of an annuity of $1 paid at the end of each of t periods.[7]

Suppose, for example, that our benefactor begins to vacillate and wonders what it would cost to endow a chair providing $100,000 a year for only 20 years. The answer calculated from our formula is

$$PV = 100,000\left[\frac{1}{.10} - \frac{1}{.10(1.10)^{20}}\right] = 100,000 \times 8.514 = \$851,400$$

Alternatively, we can simply look up the answer in the annuity table in the Appendix at the end of the book (Appendix Table 3). This table gives the present value of a dollar to be received in each of t periods. In our example t = 20 and the interest rate r = .10, and therefore we look at the twentieth number from the top in the *10 percent* column. It is 8.514. Multiply 8.514 by $100,000, and we have our answer, $851,400.

Remember that the annuity formula assumes that the first payment occurs one period hence. If the first cash payment occurs immediately, we would need to discount each cash flow by one less year. So the present value would be increased by the multiple (1 + r). For example, if our benefactor were prepared to make 20 annual payments *starting immediately*, the value would be $851,400 × 1.10 = $936,540. An annuity offering an immediate payment is known as an *annuity due*.

---

[7]Again we can work this out from first principles. We need to calculate the sum of the finite geometric series (1) $PV = a(1 + x + x^2 + \cdots + x^{t-1})$,

where $a = C/(1 + r)$ and $x = 1/(1 + r)$.

Multiplying both sides by x, we have (2) $PVx = a(x + x^2 + \cdots + x^t)$.

Subtracting (2) from (1) gives us $PV(1 - x) = a(1 - x^t)$.

Therefore, substituting for a and x,

$$PV\left(1 - \frac{1}{1 + r}\right) = C\left[\frac{1}{1 + r} - \frac{1}{(1 + r)^{t+1}}\right]$$

Multiplying both sides by (1 + r) and rearranging gives

$$PV = C\left[\frac{1}{r} - \frac{1}{r(1 + r)^t}\right]$$

You should always be on the lookout for ways in which you can use these formulas to make life easier. For example, we sometimes need to calculate how much a series of annual payments earning a fixed annual interest rate would amass to by the end of t periods. In this case it is easiest to calculate the *present* value, and then multiply it by $(1 + r)^t$ to find the future value.[8] Thus suppose our benefactor wished to know how much wealth $100,000 would produce if it were invested each year instead of being given to those no-good academics. The answer would be

$$\text{Future value} = \text{PV} \times 1.10^{20} = \$851,400 \times 6.727 = \$5.73 \text{ million}$$

How did we know that 1.10^{20} was 6.727? Easy—we just looked it up in Appendix Table 2 at the end of the book: "Future Value of $1 at the End of t Periods."

 ## 3.3 COMPOUND INTEREST AND PRESENT VALUES

There is an important distinction between **compound interest** and **simple interest**. When money is invested at compound interest, each interest payment is reinvested to earn more interest in subsequent periods. In contrast, the opportunity to earn interest on interest is not provided by an investment that pays only simple interest.

Table 3.2 compares the growth of $100 invested at compound versus simple interest. Notice that in the simple interest case, *the interest is paid only on the initial in-*

	Simple Interest				Compound Interest			
Year	Starting Balance	+	Interest	=	Ending Balance	Starting Balance	+	Ending Interest	=	Balance
1	100	+	10	=	110	100	+	10	=	110
2	110	+	10	=	120	110	+	11	=	121
3	120	+	10	=	130	121	+	12.1	=	133.1
4	130	+	10	=	140	133.1	+	13.3	=	146.4
10	190	+	10	=	200	236	+	24	=	259
20	290	+	10	=	300	612	+	61	=	673
50	590	+	10	=	600	10,672	+	1,067	=	11,739
100	1,090	+	10	=	1,100	1,252,783	+	125,278	=	1,378,061
200	2,090	+	10	=	2,100	17,264,116,042	+	1,726,411,604	=	18,990,527,646
226	2,350	+	10	=	2,360	205,756,782,755	+	20,575,678,275	=	226,332,461,030

TABLE 3.2

Value of $100 invested at 10 percent simple and compound interest.

---

[8]For example, suppose you receive a cash flow of C in year 6. If you invest this cash flow at an interest rate of r, you will have by year 10 an investment worth $C(1 + r)^4$. You can get the same answer by calculating the *present value* of the cash flow $\text{PV} = C/(1 + r)^6$ and then working out how much you would have by year 10 if you invested this sum today:

$$\text{Future value} = \text{PV}(1 + r)^{10} = \frac{C}{(1 + r)^6} \times (1 + r)^{10} = C(1 + r)^4$$

FIGURE 3.2

Compound interest versus simple interest. The top two ascending lines show the growth of $100 invested at simple and compound interest. The longer the funds are invested, the greater the advantage with compound interest. The bottom line shows that $38.55 must be invested now to obtain $100 after 10 periods. Conversely, the present value of $100 to be received after 10 years is $38.55.

vestment of $100. Your wealth therefore increases by just $10 a year. In the compound interest case, you earn 10 percent on your initial investment in the first year, which gives you a balance at the end of the year of $100 \times 1.10 = \$110$. Then in the second year you earn 10 percent on this $110, which gives you a balance at the end of the second year of $100 \times 1.10^2 = \$121$.

Table 3.2 shows that the difference between simple and compound interest is nil for a one-period investment, trivial for a two-period investment, but overwhelming for an investment of 20 years or more. A sum of $100 invested during the American Revolution and earning compound interest of 10 percent a year would now be worth over $226 billion. If only your ancestors could have put away a few cents.

The two top lines in Figure 3.2 compare the results of investing $100 at 10 percent simple interest and at 10 percent compound interest. It looks as if the rate of growth is constant under simple interest and accelerates under compound interest. However, this is an optical illusion. We know that under compound interest our wealth grows at a *constant* rate of 10 percent. Figure 3.3 is in fact a more useful presentation. Here the numbers are plotted on a semilogarithmic scale and the constant compound growth rates show up as straight lines.

Problems in finance almost always involve compound interest rather than simple interest, and therefore financial people always assume that you are talking about compound interest unless you specify otherwise. Discounting is a process of compound interest. Some people find it intuitively helpful to replace the question, What is the present value of $100 to be received 10 years from now, if the opportunity cost of capital is 10 percent? with the question, How much would I have to invest now in order to receive $100 after 10 years, given an interest rate of 10 percent? The answer to the first question is

$$PV = \frac{100}{(1.10)^{10}} = \$38.55$$

FIGURE 3.3

The same story as Figure 3.2, except that the vertical scale is logarithmic. A constant compound rate of growth means a straight ascending line. This graph makes clear that the growth rate of funds invested at simple interest actually *declines* as time passes.

And the answer to the second question is

$$\text{Investment} \times (1.10)^{10} = \$100$$

$$\text{Investment} = \frac{100}{(1.10)^{10}} = \$38.55$$

The bottom lines in Figures 3.2 and 3.3 show the growth path of an initial investment of $38.55 to its terminal value of $100. One can think of discounting as traveling *back* along the bottom line, from future value to present value.

A Note on Compounding Intervals

So far we have implicitly assumed that each cash flow occurs at the end of the year. This is sometimes the case. For example, in France and Germany most corporations pay interest on their bonds annually. However, in the United States and Britain most pay interest semiannually. In these countries, the investor can earn an additional six months' interest on the first payment, so that an investment of $100 in a bond that paid interest of 10 percent per annum compounded semiannually would amount to $105 after the first six months, and by the end of the year it would amount to $1.05^2 \times 100 = \$110.25$. In other words, 10 percent compounded semiannually is equivalent to 10.25 percent compounded annually.

Let's take another example. Suppose a bank makes automobile loans requiring monthly payments at an *annual percentage rate (APR)* of 6 percent per year. What does that mean, and what is the true rate of interest on the loans?

With monthly payments, the bank charges one-twelfth of the APR in each month, that is, $6/12 = .5$ percent. Because the monthly return is compounded, the bank actually earns more than 6 percent per year. Suppose that the bank starts with $10 million of automobile loans outstanding. This investment grows to $10 × 1.005 = $10.05 million after month 1, to $10 × 1.005^2 = $10.10025 million after month 2, and to $10 × 1.005^{12} = $10.61678 million after 12 months.[9] Thus the bank is quoting a 6 percent APR but actually earns 6.1678 percent if interest payments are made monthly.[10]

In general, an investment of $1 at a rate of r per annum compounded m times a year amounts by the end of the year to $[1 + (r/m)]^m$, and the equivalent annually compounded rate of interest is $[1 + (r/m)]^m - 1$.

Continuous Compounding   The attractions to the investor of more frequent payments did not escape the attention of the savings and loan companies in the 1960s and 1970s. Their rate of interest on deposits was traditionally stated as an annually compounded rate. The government used to stipulate a maximum annual rate of interest that could be paid but made no mention of the compounding interval. When interest ceilings began to pinch, savings and loan companies changed progressively to semiannual and then to monthly compounding. Therefore the equivalent annually compounded rate of interest increased first to $[1 + (r/2)]^2 - 1$ and then to $[1 + (r/12)]^{12} - 1$.

Eventually one company quoted a **continuously compounded rate,** so that payments were assumed to be spread evenly and continuously throughout the year. In terms of our formula, this is equivalent to letting m approach infinity.[11] This might seem like a lot of calculations for the savings and loan companies. Fortunately, however, someone remembered high school algebra and pointed out that as m approaches infinity $[1 + (r/m)]^m$ approaches $(2.718)^r$. The figure 2.718—or e, as it is called—is simply the base for natural logarithms.

One dollar invested at a continuously compounded rate of r will, therefore, grow to $e^r = (2.718)^r$ by the end of the first year. By the end of t years it will grow to $e^{rt} = (2.718)^{rt}$. Appendix Table 4 at the end of the book is a table of values of e^{rt}. Let us practice using it.

Example 1   Suppose you invest $1 at a continuously compounded rate of 11 percent ($r = .11$) for one year ($t = 1$). The end-year value is $e^{.11}$, which you can see from the second row of Appendix Table 4 is $1.116. In other words, investing at 11 percent a year *continuously* compounded is exactly the same as investing at 11.6 percent a year *annually* compounded.

Example 2   Suppose you invest $1 at a continuously compounded rate of 11 percent ($r = .11$) for two years ($t = 2$). The final value of the investment is $e^{rt} = e^{.22}$. You can see from the third row of Appendix Table 4 that $e^{.22}$ is $1.246.

---

[9]Individual borrowers gradually pay off their loans. We are assuming that the aggregate amount loaned by the bank to all its customers stays constant at $10 million.

[10]Unfortunately, U.S. truth-in-lending laws require lenders to quote interest rates for most types of consumer loans as APRs rather than true annual rates.

[11]When we talk about *continuous* payments, we are pretending that money can be dispensed in a continuous stream like water out of a faucet. One can never quite do this. For example, instead of paying out $100,000 every year, our benefactor could pay out $100 every 8¾ hours or $1 every 5¼ minutes or 1 cent every 3⅙ seconds but could not pay it out *continuously*. Financial managers *pretend* that payments are continuous rather than hourly, daily, or weekly because (1) it simplifies the calculations, and (2) it gives a *very* close approximation to the NPV of frequent payments.

There is a particular value to continuous compounding in capital budgeting, where it may often be more reasonable to assume that a cash flow is spread evenly over the year than that it occurs at the year's end. It is easy to adapt our previous formulas to handle this. For example, suppose that we wish to compute the present value of a perpetuity of C dollars a year. We already know that if the payment is made at the end of the year, we divide the payment by the *annually* compounded rate of r:

$$PV = \frac{C}{r}$$

If the same total payment is made in an even stream throughout the year, we use the same formula but substitute the *continuously* compounded rate.

Example 3 Suppose the annually compounded rate is 18.5 percent. The present value of a $100 perpetuity, with each cash flow received at the end of the year, is $100/.185 = \$540.54$. If the cash flow is received continuously, we must divide $100 by 17 percent, because 17 percent continuously compounded is equivalent to 18.5 percent annually compounded ($e^{.17} = 1.185$). The present value of the continuous cash flow stream is $100/.17 = \$588.24$.

For any other continuous payments, we can always use our formula for valuing annuities. For instance, suppose that our philanthropist has thought more seriously and decided to found a home for elderly donkeys, which will cost $100,000 a year, starting immediately, and spread evenly over 20 years. Previously, we used the annually compounded rate of 10 percent; now we must use the continuously compounded rate of $r = 9.53$ percent ($e^{.0953} = 1.10$). To cover such an expenditure, then, our philanthropist needs to set aside the following sum:[12]

$$PV = C\left(\frac{1}{r} - \frac{1}{r} \times \frac{1}{e^{rt}}\right)$$

$$= 100,000\left(\frac{1}{.0953} - \frac{1}{.0953} \times \frac{1}{6.727}\right) = 100,000 \times 8.932 = \$893,200$$

Alternatively, we could have cut these calculations short by using Appendix Table 5. This shows that, if the annually compounded return is 10 percent, then $1 a year spread over 20 years is worth $8.932.

If you look back at our earlier discussion of annuities, you will notice that the present value of $100,000 paid at the *end* of each of the 20 years was $851,400.

---

[12]Remember that an annuity is simply the difference between a perpetuity received today and a perpetuity received in year t. A continuous stream of C dollars a year in perpetuity is worth C/r, where r is the continuously compounded rate. Our annuity, then, is worth

$$PV = \frac{C}{r} - \text{present value of } \frac{C}{r} \text{ received in year } t$$

Since r is the continuously compounded rate, C/r received in year t is worth $(C/r) \times (1/e^{rt})$ today. Our annuity formula is therefore

$$PV = \frac{C}{r} - \frac{C}{r} \times \frac{1}{e^{rt}}$$

sometimes written as

$$\frac{C}{r}(1 - e^{-rt})$$

Therefore, it costs the philanthropist $41,800—or 5 percent—more to provide a continuous payment stream.

Often in finance we need only a ballpark estimate of present value. An error of 5 percent in a present value calculation may be perfectly acceptable. In such cases it doesn't usually matter whether we assume that cash flows occur at the end of the year or in a continuous stream. At other times precision matters, and we do need to worry about the exact frequency of the cash flows.

 3.4 NOMINAL AND REAL RATES OF INTEREST

If you invest $1,000 in a bank deposit offering an interest rate of 10 percent, the bank promises to pay you $1,100 at the end of the year. But it makes no promises about what the $1,100 will buy. That will depend on the rate of inflation over the year. If the prices of goods and services increase by more than 10 percent, you have lost ground in terms of the goods that you can buy.

Several indexes are used to track the general level of prices. The best known is the Consumer Price Index, or CPI, which measures the number of dollars that it takes to pay for a typical family's purchases. The change in the CPI from one year to the next measures the rate of inflation. Figure 3.4 shows the rate of inflation in the United

FIGURE 3.4

Annual rates of inflation in the United States from 1926 to 2000.

Source: Ibbotson Associates, Inc., *Stocks, Bonds, Bills, and Inflation*, 2001 Yearbook, Chicago, 2001.

States since 1926. During the Great Depression there was actual *de*flation; prices of goods on average fell. Inflation touched a peak just after World War II, when it reached 18 percent. This figure, however, pales into insignificance compared with inflation in Yugoslavia in 1993, which at its peak was almost 60 percent *a day*.

Economists sometimes talk about current, or nominal, dollars versus constant, or real, dollars. For example, the *nominal* cash flow from your one-year bank deposit is $1,100. But suppose prices of goods rise over the year by 6 percent; then each dollar will buy you 6 percent less goods next year than it does today. So at the end of the year $1,100 will buy the same quantity of goods as $1,100/1.06 = $1,037.74 today. The nominal payoff on the deposit is $1,100, but the *real* payoff is only $1,037.74.

The general formula for converting nominal cash flows at a future period t to real cash flows is

$$\text{Real cash flow} = \frac{\text{nominal cash flow}}{(1 + \text{inflation rate})^t}$$

For example, if you were to invest that $1,000 for 20 years at 10 percent, your future nominal payoff would be $1,000 \times 1.1^{20} = \$6,727.50$, but with an inflation rate of 6 percent a year, the real value of that payoff would be $6,727.50/1.06^{20} = \$2,097.67$. In other words, you will have roughly six times as many dollars as you have today, but you will be able to buy only twice as many goods.

When the bank quotes you a 10 percent interest rate, it is quoting a nominal interest rate. The rate tells you how rapidly your money will grow:

Invest Current Dollars		Receive Period-1 Dollars	Result
1,000	→	1,100	10% *nominal* rate of return

However, with an inflation rate of 6 percent you are only 3.774 percent better off at the end of the year than at the start:

Invest Current Dollars		Expected Real Value of Period-1 Receipts	Result
1,000	→	1,037.74	3.774% expected *real* rate of return

Thus, we could say, "The bank account offers a 10 percent nominal rate of return," or "It offers a 3.774 percent expected real rate of return." Note that the nominal rate is certain but the real rate is only expected. The actual real rate cannot be calculated until the end of the year arrives and the inflation rate is known.

The 10 percent nominal rate of return, with 6 percent inflation, translates into a 3.774 percent real rate of return. The formula for calculating the real rate of return is

$$1 + r_{\text{nominal}} = (1 + r_{\text{real}})(1 + \text{inflation rate})$$

$$= 1 + r_{\text{real}} + \text{inflation rate} + (r_{\text{real}})(\text{inflation rate})$$

In our example,

$$1.10 = 1.03774 \times 1.06$$

3.5 USING PRESENT VALUE FORMULAS TO VALUE BONDS

When governments or companies borrow money, they often do so by issuing bonds. A bond is simply a long-term debt. If you own a bond, you receive a fixed set of cash payoffs: Each year until the bond matures, you collect an interest payment; then at maturity, you also get back the face value of the bond. The face value of the bond is known as the *principal*. Therefore, when the bond matures, the government pays you principal and interest.

If you want to buy or sell a bond, you simply contact a bond dealer, who will quote a price at which he or she is prepared to buy or sell. Suppose, for example, that in June 2001 you invested in a 7 percent 2006 U.S. Treasury bond. The bond has a coupon rate of 7 percent and a face value of $1,000. This means that each year until 2006 you will receive an interest payment of .07 × 1,000 = $70. The bond matures in May 2006. At that time the Treasury pays you the final $70 interest, plus the $1,000 face value. So the cash flows from owning the bond are as follows:

Cash Flows ($)				
2002	2003	2004	2005	2006
70	70	70	70	1,070

What is the present value of these payoffs? To determine that, we need to look at the return provided by similar securities. Other medium-term U.S. Treasury bonds in the summer of 2001 offered a return of about 4.8 percent. That is what investors were giving up when they bought the 7 percent Treasury bonds. Therefore to value the 7 percent bonds, we need to discount the cash flows at 4.8 percent:

$$PV = \frac{70}{1.048} + \frac{70}{(1.048)^2} + \frac{70}{(1.048)^3} + \frac{70}{(1.048)^4} + \frac{1070}{(1.048)^5} = 1,095.78$$

Bond prices are usually expressed as a percentage of the face value. Thus, we can say that our 7 percent Treasury bond is worth $1,095.78, or 109.578 percent.

You may have noticed a shortcut way to value the Treasury bond. The bond is like a package of two investments: The first investment consists of five annual coupon payments of $70 each, and the second investment is the payment of the $1,000 face value at maturity. Therefore, you can use the annuity formula to value the coupon payments and add on the present value of the final payment:

$$PV(\text{bond}) = PV(\text{coupon payments}) + PV(\text{final payment})$$
$$= (\text{coupon} \times \text{five-year annuity factor}) +$$
$$(\text{final payment} \times \text{discount factor})$$
$$= 70\left[\frac{1}{.048} - \frac{1}{.048(1.048)^5}\right] + \frac{1000}{1.048^5} = 304.75 + 791.03 = 1095.78$$

Any Treasury bond can be valued as a package of an annuity (the coupon payments) and a single payment (the repayment of the face value).

Rather than asking the value of the bond, we could have phrased our question the other way around: If the price of the bond is $1,095.78, what return do investors expect? In that case, we need to find the value of r that solves the following equation:

$$1095.78 = \frac{70}{1 + r} + \frac{70}{(1 + r)^2} + \frac{70}{(1 + r)^3} + \frac{70}{(1 + r)^4} + \frac{1070}{(1 + r)^5}$$

The rate r is often called the bond's **yield to maturity.** In our case r is 4.8 percent. If you discount the cash flows at 4.8 percent, you arrive at the bond's price of $1,095.78. The only *general* procedure for calculating the yield to maturity is trial and error, but spreadsheet programs or specially programmed electronic calculators will usually do the trick.

You may have noticed that the formula that we used for calculating the present value of 7 percent Treasury bonds was slightly different from the general present value formula that we developed in Section 3.1, where we allowed r_1, the rate of return offered by the capital market on one-year investments, to differ from r_2, the rate of return offered on two-year investments. Then we finessed this problem by assuming that r_1 was the same as r_2. In valuing our Treasury bond, we again assume that investors use the same rate to discount cash flows occurring in different years. That does not matter as long as the term structure is flat, with short-term rates approximately the same as long-term rates. But when the term structure is not flat, professional bond investors discount each cash flow at a different rate. There will be more about that in Chapter 24.

What Happens When Interest Rates Change?

Interest rates fluctuate. In 1945 United States government bonds were yielding less than 2 percent, but by 1981 yields were a touch under 15 percent. International differences in interest rates can be even more dramatic. As we write this in the summer of 2001, short-term interest rates in Japan are less than .2 percent, while in Turkey they are over 60 percent.[13]

How do changes in interest rates affect bond prices? If bond yields in the United States fell to 2 percent, the price of our 7 percent Treasuries would rise to

$$PV = \frac{70}{1.02} + \frac{70}{(1.02)^2} + \frac{70}{(1.02)^3} + \frac{70}{(1.02)^4} + \frac{1070}{(1.02)^5} = \$1,235.67$$

If yields jumped to 10 percent, the price would fall to

$$PV = \frac{70}{1.10} + \frac{70}{(1.10)^2} + \frac{70}{(1.10)^3} + \frac{70}{(1.10)^4} + \frac{1070}{(1.10)^5} = \$886.28$$

Not surprisingly, the higher the interest rate that investors demand, the less that they will be prepared to pay for the bond.

Some bonds are more affected than others by a change in the interest rate. The effect is greatest when the cash flows on the bond last for many years. The effect is trivial if the bond matures tomorrow.

Compounding Intervals and Bond Prices

In calculating the value of the 7 percent Treasury bonds, we made two approximations. First, we assumed that interest payments occurred annually. In practice,

---

[13]Early in 2001 the Turkish overnight rate exceeded 20,000 percent.

most U.S. bonds make coupon payments *semiannually,* so that instead of receiving $70 every year, an investor holding 7 percent bonds would receive $35 every *half* year. Second, yields on U.S. bonds are usually quoted as semiannually compounded yields. In other words, if the semiannually compounded yield is quoted as 4.8 percent, the yield over six months is $4.8/2 = 2.4$ percent.

Now we can recalculate the value of the 7 percent Treasury bonds, recognizing that there are 10 six-month coupon payments of $35 and a final payment of the $1,000 face value:

$$PV = \frac{35}{1.024} + \frac{35}{(1.024)^2} + \cdots + \frac{35}{(1.024)^9} + \frac{1035}{(1.024)^{10}} = \$1,096.77$$

The difficult thing in any present value exercise is to set up the problem correctly. Once you have done that, you must be able to do the calculations, but they are not difficult. Now that you have worked through this chapter, all you should need is a little practice.

The basic present value formula for an asset that pays off in several periods is the following obvious extension of our one-period formula:

$$PV = \frac{C_1}{1 + r_1} + \frac{C_2}{(1 + r_2)^2} + \cdots$$

You can always work out any present value using this formula, but when the interest rates are the same for each maturity, there may be some shortcuts that can reduce the tedium. We looked at three such cases. The first is an asset that pays C dollars a year in perpetuity. Its present value is simply

$$PV = \frac{C}{r}$$

The second is an asset whose payments increase at a steady rate g in perpetuity. Its present value is

$$PV = \frac{C_1}{r - g}$$

The third is an annuity that pays C dollars a year for t years. To find its present value we take the difference between the values of two perpetuities:

$$PV = C\left[\frac{1}{r} - \frac{1}{r(1 + r)^t}\right]$$

Our next step was to show that discounting is a process of compound interest. Present value is the amount that we would have to invest now at compound interest r in order to produce the cash flows C_1, C_2, etc. When someone offers to lend us a dollar at an annual rate of r, we should always check how frequently the interest is to be compounded. If the compounding interval is annual, we will have to repay $(1 + r)^t$ dollars; on the other hand, if the compounding period is continuous, we will have to repay 2.718^{rt} (or, as it is usually expressed, e^{rt}) dollars. In capital budgeting we often assume that the cash flows occur at the end of each year, and therefore we discount them at an annually compounded rate of interest.

SUMMARY

Sometimes, however, it may be better to assume that they are spread evenly over the year; in this case we must make use of continuous compounding.

It is important to distinguish between *nominal* cash flows (the actual number of dollars that you will pay or receive) and *real* cash flows, which are adjusted for inflation. Similarly, an investment may promise a high *nominal* interest rate, but, if inflation is also high, the *real* interest rate may be low or even negative.

We concluded the chapter by applying discounted cash flow techniques to value United States government bonds with fixed annual coupons.

We introduced in this chapter two very important ideas which we will come across several times again. The first is that you can add present values: If your formula for the present value of A + B is not the same as your formula for the present value of A plus the present value of B, you have made a mistake. The second is the notion that there is no such thing as a money machine: If you think you have found one, go back and check your calculations.

FURTHER READING

The material in this chapter should cover all you need to know about the mathematics of discounting; but if you wish to dig deeper, there are a number of books on the subject. Try, for example:

R. Cissell, H. Cissell, and D. C. Flaspohler: *The Mathematics of Finance*, 8th ed., Houghton Mifflin Company, Boston, 1990.

QUIZ

1. At an interest rate of 12 percent, the six-year discount factor is .507. How many dollars is $.507 worth in six years if invested at 12 percent?

2. If the PV of $139 is $125, what is the discount factor?

3. If the eight-year discount factor is .285, what is the PV of $596 received in eight years?

4. If the cost of capital is 9 percent, what is the PV of $374 paid in year 9?

5. A project produces the following cash flows:

Year	Flow
1	432
2	137
3	797

If the cost of capital is 15 percent, what is the project's PV?

6. If you invest $100 at an interest rate of 15 percent, how much will you have at the end of eight years?

7. An investment costs $1,548 and pays $138 in perpetuity. If the interest rate is 9 percent, what is the NPV?

8. A common stock will pay a cash dividend of $4 next year. After that, the dividends are expected to increase indefinitely at 4 percent per year. If the discount rate is 14 percent, what is the PV of the stream of dividend payments?

9. You win a lottery with a prize of $1.5 million. Unfortunately the prize is paid in 10 annual installments. The first payment is next year. How much is the prize really worth? The discount rate is 8 percent.

10. Do not use the Appendix tables for these questions. The interest rate is 10 percent.
    a. What is the PV of an asset that pays $1 a year in perpetuity?
    b. The value of an asset that appreciates at 10 percent per annum approximately doubles in seven years. What is the approximate PV of an asset that pays $1 a year in perpetuity beginning in year 8?
    c. What is the approximate PV of an asset that pays $1 a year for each of the next seven years?
    d. A piece of land produces an income that grows by 5 percent per annum. If the first year's flow is $10,000, what is the value of the land?

11. Use the Appendix tables at the end of the book for each of the following calculations:
    a. The cost of a new automobile is $10,000. If the interest rate is 5 percent, how much would you have to set aside now to provide this sum in five years?
    b. You have to pay $12,000 a year in school fees at the end of each of the next six years. If the interest rate is 8 percent, how much do you need to set aside today to cover these bills?
    c. You have invested $60,476 at 8 percent. After paying the above school fees, how much would remain at the end of the six years?

12. You have the opportunity to invest in the Belgravian Republic at 25 percent interest. The inflation rate is 21 percent. What is the real rate of interest?

13. The continuously compounded interest rate is 12 percent.
    a. You invest $1,000 at this rate. What is the investment worth after five years?
    b. What is the PV of $5 million to be received in eight years?
    c. What is the PV of a continuous stream of cash flows, amounting to $2,000 per year, starting immediately and continuing for 15 years?

14. You are quoted an interest rate of 6 percent on an investment of $10 million. What is the value of your investment after four years if the interest rate is compounded:
    a. Annually, b. monthly, or c. continuously?

15. Suppose the interest rate on five-year U.S. government bonds falls to 4.0 percent. Recalculate the value of the 7 percent bond maturing in 2006. (See Section 3.5.)

16. What is meant by a bond's yield to maturity and how is it calculated?

PRACTICE QUESTIONS

1. Use the *discount factors* shown in Appendix Table 1 at the end of the book to calculate the PV of $100 received in:
   a. Year 10 (at a discount rate of 1 percent).
   b. Year 10 (at a discount rate of 13 percent).
   c. Year 15 (at a discount rate of 25 percent).
   d. Each of years 1 through 3 (at a discount rate of 12 percent).

2. Use the *annuity factors* shown in Appendix Table 3 to calculate the PV of $100 in each of:
   a. Years 1 through 20 (at a discount rate of 23 percent).
   b. Years 1 through 5 (at a discount rate of 3 percent).
   c. Years 3 through 12 (at a discount rate of 9 percent).

3. a. If the one-year discount factor is .88, what is the one-year interest rate?
   b. If the two-year interest rate is 10.5 percent, what is the two-year discount factor?
   c. Given these one- and two-year discount factors, calculate the two-year annuity factor.
   d. If the PV of $10 a year for three years is $24.49, what is the three-year annuity factor?
   e. From your answers to (c) and (d), calculate the three-year discount factor.

4. A factory costs $800,000. You reckon that it will produce an inflow after operating costs of $170,000 a year for 10 years. If the opportunity cost of capital is 14 percent, what is the net present value of the factory? What will the factory be worth at the end of five years?

5. Harold Filbert is 30 years of age and his salary next year will be $20,000. Harold forecasts that his salary will increase at a steady rate of 5 percent per annum until his retirement at age 60.
   a. If the discount rate is 8 percent, what is the PV of these future salary payments?
   b. If Harold saves 5 percent of his salary each year and invests these savings at an interest rate of 8 percent, how much will he have saved by age 60?
   c. If Harold plans to spend these savings in even amounts over the subsequent 20 years, how much can he spend each year?

6. A factory costs $400,000. You reckon that it will produce an inflow after operating costs of $100,000 in year 1, $200,000 in year 2, and $300,000 in year 3. The opportunity cost of capital is 12 percent. Draw up a worksheet like that shown in Table 3.1 and use tables to calculate the NPV.

7. Halcyon Lines is considering the purchase of a new bulk carrier for $8 million. The forecasted revenues are $5 million a year and operating costs are $4 million. A major refit costing $2 million will be required after both the fifth and tenth years. After 15 years, the ship is expected to be sold for scrap at $1.5 million. If the discount rate is 8 percent, what is the ship's NPV?

8. As winner of a breakfast cereal competition, you can choose one of the following prizes:
   a. $100,000 now.
   b. $180,000 at the end of five years.
   c. $11,400 a year forever.
   d. $19,000 for each of 10 years.
   e. $6,500 next year and increasing thereafter by 5 percent a year forever.

   If the interest rate is 12 percent, which is the most valuable prize?

9. Refer back to the story of Ms. Kraft in Section 3.1.
   a. If the one-year interest rate were 25 percent, how many plays would Ms. Kraft require to become a millionaire? (*Hint:* You may find it easier to use a calculator and a little trial and error.)
   b. What does the story of Ms. Kraft imply about the relationship between the one-year discount factor, DF_1, and the two-year discount factor, DF_2?

10. Siegfried Basset is 65 years of age and has a life expectancy of 12 more years. He wishes to invest $20,000 in an annuity that will make a level payment at the end of each year until his death. If the interest rate is 8 percent, what income can Mr. Basset expect to receive each year?

11. James and Helen Turnip are saving to buy a boat at the end of five years. If the boat costs $20,000 and they can earn 10 percent a year on their savings, how much do they need to put aside at the end of years 1 through 5?

12. Kangaroo Autos is offering free credit on a new $10,000 car. You pay $1,000 down and then $300 a month for the next 30 months. Turtle Motors next door does not offer free credit but will give you $1,000 off the list price. If the rate of interest is 10 percent a year, which company is offering the better deal?

13. Recalculate the NPV of the office building venture in Section 3.1 at interest rates of 5, 10, and 15 percent. Plot the points on a graph with NPV on the vertical axis and the discount rates on the horizontal axis. At what discount rate (approximately) would the project have zero NPV? Check your answer.

14. **a.** How much will an investment of $100 be worth at the end of 10 years if invested at 15 percent a year simple interest?
    b. How much will it be worth if invested at 15 percent a year compound interest?
    c. How long will it take your investment to double its value at 15 percent compound interest?

15. You own an oil pipeline which will generate a $2 million cash return over the coming year. The pipeline's operating costs are negligible, and it is expected to last for a very long time. Unfortunately, the volume of oil shipped is declining, and cash flows are expected to decline by 4 percent per year. The discount rate is 10 percent.
    a. What is the PV of the pipeline's cash flows if its cash flows are assumed to last forever?
    b. What is the PV of the cash flows if the pipeline is scrapped after 20 years?
    [*Hint for part (b):* Start with your answer to part (a), then subtract the present value of a declining perpetuity starting in year 21. Note that the forecasted cash flow for year 21 will be much less than the cash flow for year 1.]

16. If the interest rate is 7 percent, what is the value of the following three investments?
    a. An investment that offers you $100 a year in perpetuity with the payment at the *end* of each year.
    b. A similar investment with the payment at the *beginning* of each year.
    c. A similar investment with the payment spread evenly over each year.

17. Refer back to Section 3.2. If the rate of interest is 8 percent rather than 10 percent, how much would our benefactor need to set aside to provide each of the following?
    a. $100,000 at the end of each year in perpetuity.
    b. A perpetuity that pays $100,000 at the end of the first year and that grows at 4 percent a year.
    c. $100,000 at the end of each year for 20 years.
    d. $100,000 a year spread evenly over 20 years.

18. For an investment of $1,000 today, the Tiburon Finance Company is offering to pay you $1,600 at the end of 8 years. What is the annually compounded rate of interest? What is the continuously compounded rate of interest?

19. How much will you have at the end of 20 years if you invest $100 today at 15 percent *annually* compounded? How much will you have if you invest at 15 percent *continuously* compounded?

20. You have just read an advertisement stating, "Pay us $100 a year for 10 years and we will pay you $100 a year thereafter in perpetuity." If this is a fair deal, what is the rate of interest?

21. Which would you prefer?
    a. An investment paying interest of 12 percent compounded annually.
    b. An investment paying interest of 11.7 percent compounded semiannually.
    c. An investment paying 11.5 percent compounded continuously.

    Work out the value of each of these investments after 1, 5, and 20 years.

22. Fill in the blanks in the following table:

Nominal Interest Rate (%)	Inflation Rate (%)	Real Interest Rate (%)
6	1	—
—	10	12
9	—	3

23. Sometimes real rates of return are calculated by *subtracting* the rate of inflation from the nominal rate. This rule of thumb is a good approximation if the inflation rate is low. How big is the error from using this rule of thumb to calculate real rates of return in the following cases?

Nominal Rate (%)	Inflation Rate (%)
6	2
9	5
21	10
70	50

24. In 1880 five aboriginal trackers were each promised the equivalent of 100 Australian dollars for helping to capture the notorious outlaw Ned Kelley. In 1993 the granddaughters of two of the trackers claimed that this reward had not been paid. The prime minister of Victoria stated that, if this was true, the government would be happy to pay the $100. However, the granddaughters also claimed that they were entitled to compound interest. How much was each entitled to if the interest rate was 5 percent? What if it was 10 percent?

25. A leasing contract calls for an immediate payment of $100,000 and nine subsequent $100,000 semiannual payments at six-month intervals. What is the PV of these payments if the *annual* discount rate is 8 percent?

26. A famous quarterback just signed a $15 million contract providing $3 million a year for five years. A less famous receiver signed a $14 million five-year contract providing $4 million now and $2 million a year for five years. Who is better paid? The interest rate is 10 percent.

27. In August 1994 *The Wall Street Journal* reported that the winner of the Massachusetts State Lottery prize had the misfortune to be both bankrupt and in prison for fraud. The prize was $9,420,713, to be paid in 19 equal annual installments. (There were 20 installments, but the winner had already received the first payment.) The bankruptcy court judge ruled that the prize should be sold off to the highest bidder and the proceeds used to pay off the creditors. **a.** If the interest rate was 8 percent, how much would you have been prepared to bid for the prize? **b.** Enhance Reinsurance Company was reported to have offered $4.2 million. Use Appendix Table 3 to find (approximately) the return that the company was looking for.

28. You estimate that by the time you retire in 35 years, you will have accumulated savings of $2 million. If the interest rate is 8 percent and you live 15 years after retirement, what annual level of expenditure will those savings support?

   Unfortunately, inflation will eat into the value of your retirement income. Assume a 4 percent inflation rate and work out a spending program for your retirement that will allow you to maintain a level *real* expenditure during retirement.

29. You are considering the purchase of an apartment complex that will generate a net cash flow of $400,000 per year. You normally demand a 10 percent rate of return on such investments. Future cash flows are expected to grow with inflation at 4 percent per year. How much would you be willing to pay for the complex if it:
   a. Will produce cash flows forever?
   b. Will have to be torn down in 20 years? Assume that the site will be worth
      $5 million at that time net of demolition costs. (The $5 million includes 20 years' inflation.)

   Now calculate the real discount rate corresponding to the 10 percent nominal rate. Redo the calculations for parts (a) and (b) using real cash flows. (Your answers should not change.)

30. Vernal Pool, a self-employed herpetologist, wants to put aside a fixed fraction of her annual income as savings for retirement. Ms. Pool is now 40 years old and makes $40,000 a year. She expects her income to increase by 2 percentage points over inflation (e.g., 4 percent inflation means a 6 percent increase in income). She wants to accumulate $500,000 in real terms to retire at age 70. What fraction of her income does she need to set aside? Assume her retirement funds are conservatively invested at an expected real rate of return of 5 percent a year. Ignore taxes.

31. At the end of June 2001, the yield to maturity on U.S. government bonds maturing in 2006 was about 4.8 percent. Value a bond with a 6 percent coupon maturing in June 2006. The bond's face value is $10,000. Assume annual coupon payments and annual compounding. How does your answer change with semiannual coupons and a semiannual discount rate of 2.4 percent?

32. Refer again to Practice Question 31. How would the bond's value change if interest rates fell to 3.5 percent per year?

33. A two-year bond pays a coupon rate of 10 percent and a face value of $1,000. (In other words, the bond pays interest of $100 per year, and its principal of $1,000 is paid off in year 2.) If the bond sells for $960, what is its approximate yield to maturity? *Hint:* This requires some trial-and-error calculations.

CHALLENGE QUESTIONS

1. Here are two useful rules of thumb. The "Rule of 72" says that with discrete compounding the time it takes for an investment to double in value is roughly 72/interest rate (in percent). The "Rule of 69" says that with continuous compounding the time that it takes to double is *exactly* 69.3/interest rate (in percent).
   a. If the annually compounded interest rate is 12 percent, use the Rule of 72 to calculate roughly how long it takes before your money doubles. Now work it out exactly.
   b. Can you prove the Rule of 69?

2. Use a spreadsheet program to construct your own set of annuity tables.

3. An oil well now produces 100,000 barrels per year. The well will produce for 18 years more, but production will decline by 4 percent per year. Oil prices, however, will increase by 2 percent per year. The discount rate is 8 percent. What is the PV of the well's production if today's price is $14 per barrel?

4. Derive the formula for a growing (or declining) annuity.

5. Calculate the real cash flows on the 7 percent U.S. Treasury bond (see Section 3.5) assuming annual interest payments and an inflation rate of 2 percent. Now show that by discounting these real cash flows at the real interest rate you get the same PV that you get when you discount the nominal cash flows at the nominal interest rate.

6. Use a spreadsheet program to construct a set of bond tables that shows the present value of a bond given the coupon rate, maturity, and yield to maturity. Assume that coupon payments are semiannual and yields are compounded semiannually.

MINI-CASE

The Jones Family, Incorporated

The Scene: Early evening in an ordinary family room in Manhattan. Modern furniture, with old copies of *The Wall Street Journal* and the *Financial Times* scattered around. Autographed photos of Alan Greenspan and George Soros are prominently displayed. A picture window reveals a distant view of lights on the Hudson River. John Jones sits at a computer terminal, glumly sipping a glass of chardonnay and trading Japanese yen over the Internet. His wife Marsha enters.

Marsha: Hi, honey. Glad to be home. Lousy day on the trading floor, though. Dullsville. No volume. But I did manage to hedge next year's production from our copper mine. I couldn't get a good quote on the right package of futures contracts, so I arranged a commodity swap.

John doesn't reply.

Marsha: John, what's wrong? Have you been buying yen again? That's been a losing trade for weeks.

John: Well, yes. I shouldn't have gone to Goldman Sachs's foreign exchange brunch. But I've got to get out of the house somehow. I'm cooped up here all day calculating covariances and efficient risk-return tradeoffs while you're out trading commodity futures. You get all the glamour and excitement.

Marsha: Don't worry dear, it will be over soon. We only recalculate our most efficient common stock portfolio once a quarter. Then you can go back to leveraged leases.

John: You trade, and I do all the worrying. Now there's a rumor that our leasing company is going to get a hostile takeover bid. I knew the debt ratio was too low, and you forgot to put on the poison pill. And now you've made a negative-NPV investment!

Marsha: What investment?

John: Two more oil wells in that old field in Ohio. You spent $500,000! The wells only produce 20 barrels of crude oil per day.

Marsha: That's 20 barrels day in, day out. There are 365 days in a year, dear.

John and Marsha's teenage son Johnny bursts into the room.

Johnny: Hi, Dad! Hi, Mom! Guess what? I've made the junior varsity derivatives team! That means I can go on the field trip to the Chicago Board Options Exchange. *(Pauses.)* What's wrong?

John: Your mother has made another negative-NPV investment. More oil wells.

Johnny: That's OK, Dad. Mom told me about it. I was going to do an NPV calculation yesterday, but my corporate finance teacher asked me to calculate default probabilities for a sample of junk bonds for Friday's class.

   (Grabs a financial calculator from his backpack.) Let's see: 20 barrels per day times $15 per barrel times 365 days per year . . . that's $109,500 per year.

John: That's $109,500 *this* year. Production's been declining at 5 percent every year.

Marsha: On the other hand, our energy consultants project increasing oil prices. If they increase with inflation, price per barrel should climb by roughly 2.5 percent per year. The wells cost next to nothing to operate, and they should keep pumping for 10 more years at least.

Johnny: I'll calculate NPV after I finish with the default probabilities. Is a 9 percent nominal cost of capital OK?

Marsha: Sure, Johnny.

John: *(Takes a deep breath and stands up.)* Anyway, how about a nice family dinner? I've reserved our usual table at the Four Seasons.

Everyone exits.

Announcer: Were the oil wells really negative-NPV? Will John and Marsha have to fight a hostile takeover? Will Johnny's derivatives team use Black-Scholes or the binomial method? Find out in the next episode of The Jones Family, Incorporated.

You may not aspire to the Jones family's way of life, but you will learn about all their activities, from futures contracts to binomial option pricing, later in this book. Meanwhile, you may wish to replicate Johnny's NPV analysis.

Questions

1. Forecast future cash flows, taking account of the decline in production and the (partially) offsetting forecasted increase in oil prices. How long does production have to continue for the oil wells to be a positive-NPV investment? You can ignore taxes and other possible complications.

CHAPTER FOUR

THE VALUE OF COMMON STOCKS

WE SHOULD WARN you that being a financial expert has its occupational hazards. One is being cornered at cocktail parties by people who are eager to explain their system for making creamy profits by investing in common stocks. Fortunately, these bores go into temporary hibernation whenever the market goes down.

We may exaggerate the perils of the trade. The point is that there is no easy way to ensure superior investment performance. Later in the book we will show that changes in security prices are fundamentally unpredictable and that this result is a natural consequence of well-functioning capital markets. Therefore, in this chapter, when we propose to use the concept of present value to price common stocks, we are not promising you a key to investment success; we simply believe that the idea can help you to understand why some investments are priced higher than others.

Why should you care? If you want to know the value of a firm's stock, why can't you look up the stock price in the newspaper? Unfortunately, that is not always possible. For example, you may be the founder of a successful business. You currently own all the shares but are thinking of going public by selling off shares to other investors. You and your advisers need to estimate the price at which those shares can be sold. Or suppose that Establishment Industries is proposing to sell its concatenator division to another company. It needs to figure out the market value of this division.

There is also another, deeper reason why managers need to understand how shares are valued. We have stated that a firm which acts in its shareholders' interest should accept those investments which increase the value of their stake in the firm. But in order to do this, it is necessary to understand what determines the shares' value.

We start the chapter with a brief look at how shares are traded. Then we explain the basic principles of share valuation. We look at the fundamental difference between growth stocks and income stocks and the significance of earnings per share and price–earnings multiples. Finally, we discuss some of the special problems managers and investors encounter when they calculate the present values of entire businesses.

A word of caution before we proceed. Everybody knows that common stocks are risky and that some are more risky than others. Therefore, investors will not commit funds to stocks unless the expected rates of return are commensurate with the risks. But we say next to nothing in this chapter about the linkages between risk and expected return. A more careful treatment of risk starts in Chapter 7.

 ## 4.1 HOW COMMON STOCKS ARE TRADED

There are 9.9 billion shares of General Electric (GE), and at last count these shares were owned by about 2.1 million shareholders. They included large pension funds and insurance companies that each own several million shares, as well as individuals who own a handful of shares. If you owned one GE share, you would own .000002 percent of the company and have a claim on the same tiny fraction of GE's profits. Of course, the more shares you own, the larger your "share" of the company.

If GE wishes to raise additional capital, it may do so by either borrowing or selling new shares to investors. Sales of new shares to raise new capital are said to occur in the *primary market*. But most trades in GE shares take place in existing shares, which investors buy from each other. These trades do not raise new capital for the firm. This market for secondhand shares is known as the *secondary market*. The principal secondary marketplace for GE shares is the New York Stock Exchange

(NYSE).[1] This is the largest stock exchange in the world and trades, on an average day, 1 billion shares in some 2,900 companies.

Suppose that you are the head trader for a pension fund that wishes to buy 100,000 GE shares. You contact your broker, who then relays the order to the floor of the NYSE. Trading in each stock is the responsibility of a *specialist*, who keeps a record of orders to buy and sell. When your order arrives, the specialist will check this record to see if an investor is prepared to sell at your price. Alternatively, the specialist may be able to get you a better deal from one of the brokers who is gathered around or may sell you some of his or her own stock. If no one is prepared to sell at your price, the specialist will make a note of your order and execute it as soon as possible.

The NYSE is not the only stock market in the United States. For example, many stocks are traded *over the counter* by a network of dealers, who display the prices at which they are prepared to trade on a system of computer terminals known as NASDAQ (National Association of Securities Dealers Automated Quotations System). If you like the price that you see on the NASDAQ screen, you simply call the dealer and strike a bargain.

The prices at which stocks trade are summarized in the daily press. Here, for example, is how *The Wall Street Journal* recorded the day's trading in GE on July 2, 2001:

YTD % Chg	52 Weeks		Stock (SYM)	Div	Yld %	PE	Vol 100s	Last	Net Chg
	Hi	Lo							
+4.7	60.50	36.42	General Electric (GE)	.64	1.3	38	215287	50.20	+1.45

You can see that on this day investors traded a total of 215,287 × 100 = 21,528,700 shares of GE stock. By the close of the day the stock traded at $50.20 a share, up $1.45 from the day before. The stock had increased by 4.7 percent from the start of 2001. Since there were about 9.9 billion shares of GE outstanding, investors were placing a total value on the stock of $497 billion.

Buying stocks is a risky occupation. Over the previous year, GE stock traded as high as $60.50, but at one point dropped to $36.42. An unfortunate investor who bought at the 52-week high and sold at the low would have lost 40 percent of his or her investment. Of course, you don't come across such people at cocktail parties; they either keep quiet or aren't invited.

The Wall Street Journal also provides three other facts about GE's stock. GE pays an annual dividend of $.64 a share, the dividend yield on the stock is 1.3 percent, and the ratio of the stock price to earnings (P/E ratio) is 38. We will explain shortly why investors pay attention to these figures.

4.2 HOW COMMON STOCKS ARE VALUED

Think back to the last chapter, where we described how to value future cash flows. The discounted-cash-flow (DCF) formula for the present value of a stock is just the same as it is for the present value of any other asset. We just discount the cash flows

---

[1]GE shares are also traded on a number of overseas exchanges.

by the return that can be earned in the capital market on securities of comparable risk. Shareholders receive cash from the company in the form of a stream of dividends. So

$$PV(\text{stock}) = PV(\text{expected future dividends})$$

At first sight this statement may seem surprising. When investors buy stocks, they usually expect to receive a dividend, but they also hope to make a capital gain. Why does our formula for present value say nothing about capital gains? As we now explain, there is no inconsistency.

Today's Price

The cash payoff to owners of common stocks comes in two forms: (1) cash dividends and (2) capital gains or losses. Suppose that the current price of a share is P_0, that the expected price at the end of a year is P_1, and that the expected dividend per share is DIV_1. The rate of return that investors expect from this share over the next year is defined as the expected dividend per share DIV_1 plus the expected price appreciation per share $P_1 - P_0$, all divided by the price at the start of the year P_0:

$$\text{Expected return} = r = \frac{DIV_1 + P_1 - P_0}{P_0}$$

This expected return is often called the **market capitalization rate.**

Suppose Fledgling Electronics stock is selling for $100 a share ($P_0 = 100$). Investors expect a $5 cash dividend over the next year ($DIV_1 = 5$). They also expect the stock to sell for $110 a year hence ($P_1 = 110$). Then the expected return to the stockholders is 15 percent:

$$r = \frac{5 + 110 - 100}{100} = .15, \text{ or } 15\%$$

On the other hand, if you are given investors' forecasts of dividend and price and the expected return offered by other equally risky stocks, you can predict today's price:

$$\text{Price} = P_0 = \frac{DIV_1 + P_1}{1 + r}$$

For Fledgling Electronics $DIV_1 = 5$ and $P_1 = 110$. If r, the expected return on securities in the same risk class as Fledgling, is 15 percent, then today's price should be $100:

$$P_0 = \frac{5 + 110}{1.15} = \$100$$

How do we know that $100 is the right price? Because no other price could survive in competitive capital markets. What if P_0 were above $100? Then Fledgling stock would offer an expected rate of return that was *lower* than other securities of equivalent risk. Investors would shift their capital to the other securities and in the process would force down the price of Fledgling stock. If P_0 were less than $100, the process would reverse. Fledgling's stock would offer a higher rate of return than comparable securities. In that case, investors would rush to buy, forcing the price up to $100.

The general conclusion is that at each point in time *all securities in an equivalent risk class are priced to offer the same expected return*. This is a condition for equilibrium in well-functioning capital markets. It is also common sense.

But What Determines Next Year's Price?

We have managed to explain today's stock price P_0 in terms of the dividend DIV_1 and the expected price next year P_1. Future stock prices are not easy things to forecast directly. But think about what determines next year's price. If our price formula holds now, it ought to hold then as well:

$$P_1 = \frac{DIV_2 + P_2}{1 + r}$$

That is, a year from now investors will be looking out at dividends in year 2 and price at the end of year 2. Thus we can forecast P_1 by forecasting DIV_2 and P_2, and we can express P_0 in terms of DIV_1, DIV_2, and P_2:

$$P_0 = \frac{1}{1 + r}(DIV_1 + P_1) = \frac{1}{1 + r}\left(DIV_1 + \frac{DIV_2 + P_2}{1 + r}\right) = \frac{DIV_1}{1 + r} + \frac{DIV_2 + P_2}{(1 + r)^2}$$

Take Fledgling Electronics. A plausible explanation why investors expect its stock price to rise by the end of the first year is that they expect higher dividends and still more capital gains in the second. For example, suppose that they are looking today for dividends of $5.50 in year 2 and a subsequent price of $121. That would imply a price at the end of year 1 of

$$P_1 = \frac{5.50 + 121}{1.15} = \$110$$

Today's price can then be computed either from our original formula

$$P_0 = \frac{DIV_1 + P_1}{1 + r} = \frac{5.00 + 110}{1.15} = \$100$$

or from our expanded formula

$$P_0 = \frac{DIV_1}{1 + r} + \frac{DIV_2 + P_2}{(1 + r)^2} = \frac{5.00}{1.15} + \frac{5.50 + 121}{(1.15)^2} = \$100$$

We have succeeded in relating today's price to the forecasted dividends for two years (DIV_1 and DIV_2) plus the forecasted price at the end of the *second* year (P_2). You will probably not be surprised to learn that we could go on to replace P_2 by $(DIV_3 + P_3)/(1 + r)$ and relate today's price to the forecasted dividends for three years (DIV_1, DIV_2, and DIV_3) plus the forecasted price at the end of the *third* year (P_3). In fact we can look as far out into the future as we like, removing P's as we go. Let us call this final period H. This gives us a general stock price formula:

$$P_0 = \frac{DIV_1}{1 + r} + \frac{DIV_2}{(1 + r)^2} + \cdots + \frac{DIV_H + P_H}{(1 + r)^H}$$

$$= \sum_{t=1}^{H} \frac{DIV_t}{(1 + r)^t} + \frac{P_H}{(1 + r)^H}$$

The expression $\sum_{t=1}^{H}$ simply means the sum of the discounted dividends from year 1 to year H.

| Horizon Period (H) | Expected Future Values | | Present Values | | |
	Dividend (DIV_t)	Price (P_t)	Cumulative Dividends	Future Price	Total
0	—	100	—	—	100
1	5.00	110	4.35	95.65	100
2	5.50	121	8.51	91.49	100
3	6.05	133.10	12.48	87.52	100
4	6.66	146.41	16.29	83.71	100
10	11.79	259.37	35.89	64.11	100
20	30.58	672.75	58.89	41.11	100
50	533.59	11,739.09	89.17	10.83	100
100	62,639.15	1,378,061.23	98.83	1.17	100

TABLE 4.1

Applying the stock valuation formula to fledgling electronics.

Assumptions:
1. Dividends increase at 10 percent per year, compounded.
2. Capitalization rate is 15 percent.

FIGURE 4.1

As your horizon recedes, the present value of the future price (shaded area) declines but the present value of the stream of dividends (unshaded area) increases. The *total* present value (future price and dividends) remains the same.

Table 4.1 continues the Fledgling Electronics example for various time horizons, assuming that the dividends are expected to increase at a steady 10 percent compound rate. The expected price P_t increases at the same rate each year. Each line in the table represents an application of our general formula for a different value of H. Figure 4.1 provides a graphical representation of the table. Each column shows the present value of the dividends up to the time horizon and the present value of the price at the horizon. As the horizon recedes, the dividend stream accounts for an increasing proportion of present value, but the *total* present value of dividends plus terminal price always equals $100.

How far out could we look? In principle the horizon period H could be infinitely distant. Common stocks do not expire of old age. Barring such corporate hazards as bankruptcy or acquisition, they are immortal. As H approaches infinity, the present value of the terminal price ought to approach zero, as it does in the final column of Figure 4.1. We can, therefore, forget about the terminal price entirely and express today's price as the present value of a perpetual stream of cash dividends. This is usually written as

$$P_0 = \sum_{t=1}^{\infty} \frac{DIV_t}{(1 + r)^t}$$

where ∞ indicates infinity.

This discounted-cash-flow (DCF) formula for the present value of a stock is just the same as it is for the present value of any other asset. We just discount the cash flows—in this case the dividend stream—by the return that can be earned in the capital market on securities of comparable risk. Some find the DCF formula implausible because it seems to ignore capital gains. But we know that the formula was *derived* from the assumption that price in any period is determined by expected dividends *and* capital gains over the next period.

Notice that it is *not* correct to say that the value of a share is equal to the sum of the discounted stream of earnings per share. Earnings are generally larger than dividends because part of those earnings is reinvested in new plant, equipment, and working capital. Discounting earnings would recognize the rewards of that investment (a higher *future* dividend) but not the sacrifice (a lower dividend *today*). The correct formulation states that share value is equal to the discounted stream of dividends per share.

4.3 A SIMPLE WAY TO ESTIMATE THE CAPITALIZATION RATE

In Chapter 3 we encountered some simplified versions of the basic present value formula. Let us see whether they offer any insights into stock values. Suppose, for example, that we forecast a constant growth rate for a company's dividends. This does not preclude year-to-year deviations from the trend: It means only that *expected* dividends grow at a constant rate. Such an investment would be just another example of the growing perpetuity that we helped our fickle philanthropist to evaluate in the last chapter. To find its present value we must divide the annual cash payment by the difference between the discount rate and the growth rate:

$$P_0 = \frac{DIV_1}{r - g}$$

Remember that we can use this formula only when g, the anticipated growth rate, is less than r, the discount rate. As g approaches r, the stock price becomes infinite. Obviously r must be greater than g if growth really is perpetual.

Our growing perpetuity formula explains P_0 in terms of next year's expected dividend DIV_1, the projected growth trend g, and the expected rate of return on other securities of comparable risk r. Alternatively, the formula can be used to obtain an estimate of r from DIV_1, P_0, and g:

$$r = \frac{DIV_1}{P_0} + g$$

The market capitalization rate equals the **dividend yield** (DIV_1/P_0) plus the expected rate of growth in dividends (g).

These two formulas are much easier to work with than the general statement that "price equals the present value of expected future dividends."[2] Here is a practical example.

Using the DCF Model to Set Gas and Electricity Prices

The prices charged by local electric and gas utilities are regulated by state commissions. The regulators try to keep consumer prices down but are supposed to allow the utilities to earn a fair rate of return. But what is fair? It is usually interpreted as r, the market capitalization rate for the firm's common stock. That is, the fair rate of return on equity for a public utility ought to be the rate offered by securities that have the same risk as the utility's common stock.[3]

Small variations in estimates of this return can have a substantial effect on the prices charged to the customers and on the firm's profits. So both utilities and regulators devote considerable resources to estimating r. They call r the **cost of equity capital.** Utilities are mature, stable companies which ought to offer tailor-made cases for application of the constant-growth DCF formula.[4]

Suppose you wished to estimate the cost of equity for Pinnacle West Corp. in May 2001, when its stock was selling for about $49 per share. Dividend payments for the next year were expected to be $1.60 a share. Thus it was a simple matter to calculate the first half of the DCF formula:

$$\text{Dividend yield} = \frac{DIV_1}{P_0} = \frac{1.60}{49} = .033, \text{ or } 3.3\%$$

The hard part was estimating g, the expected rate of dividend growth. One option was to consult the views of security analysts who study the prospects for each company. Analysts are rarely prepared to stick their necks out by forecasting dividends to kingdom come, but they often forecast growth rates over the next five years, and these estimates may provide an indication of the expected long-run growth path. In the case of Pinnacle West, analysts in 2001 were forecasting an

[2]These formulas were first developed in 1938 by Williams and were rediscovered by Gordon and Shapiro. See J. B. Williams, *The Theory of Investment Value* (Cambridge, Mass.: Harvard University Press, 1938); and M. J. Gordon and E. Shapiro, "Capital Equipment Analysis: The Required Rate of Profit," *Management Science* 3 (October 1956), pp. 102–110.

[3]This is the accepted interpretation of the U.S. Supreme Court's directive in 1944 that "the returns to the equity owner [of a regulated business] should be commensurate with returns on investments in other enterprises having corresponding risks." *Federal Power Commission v. Hope Natural Gas Company*, 302 U.S. 591 at 603.

[4]There are many exceptions to this statement. For example, Pacific Gas & Electric (PG&E), which serves northern California, used to be a mature, stable company until the California energy crisis of 2000 sent wholesale electric prices sky-high. PG&E was not allowed to pass these price increases on to retail customers. The company lost more than $3.5 billion in 2000 and was forced to declare bankruptcy in 2001. PG&E is no longer a suitable subject for the constant-growth DCF formula.

annual growth of 6.6 percent.[5] This, together with the dividend yield, gave an estimate of the cost of equity capital:

$$r = \frac{DIV_1}{P_0} + g = .033 + .066 = .099, \text{ or } 9.9\%$$

An alternative approach to estimating long-run growth starts with the **payout ratio,** the ratio of dividends to earnings per share (EPS). For Pinnacle, this was forecasted at 43 percent. In other words, each year the company was plowing back into the business about 57 percent of earnings per share:

$$\text{Plowback ratio} = 1 - \text{payout ratio} = 1 - \frac{DIV}{EPS} = 1 - .43 = .57$$

Also, Pinnacle's ratio of earnings per share to book equity per share was about 11 percent. This is its **return on equity,** or **ROE:**

$$\text{Return on equity} = ROE = \frac{EPS}{\text{book equity per share}} = .11$$

If Pinnacle earns 11 percent of book equity and reinvests 57 percent of that, then book equity will increase by .57 × .11 = .063, or 6.3 percent. Earnings and dividends per share will also increase by 6.3 percent:

$$\text{Dividend growth rate} = g = \text{plowback ratio} \times ROE = .57 \times .11 = .063$$

That gives a second estimate of the market capitalization rate:

$$r = \frac{DIV_1}{P_0} + g = .033 + .063 = .096, \text{ or } 9.6\%$$

Although this estimate of the market capitalization rate for Pinnacle stock seems reasonable enough, there are obvious dangers in analyzing any single firm's stock with the constant-growth DCF formula. First, the underlying assumption of regular future growth is at best an approximation. Second, even if it is an acceptable approximation, errors inevitably creep into the estimate of g. Thus our two methods for calculating the cost of equity give similar answers. That was a lucky chance; different methods can sometimes give very different answers.

Remember, Pinnacle's cost of equity is not its personal property. In well-functioning capital markets investors capitalize the dividends of all securities in Pinnacle's risk class at exactly the same rate. But any estimate of r for a single common stock is "noisy" and subject to error. Good practice does not put too much weight on single-company cost-of-equity estimates. It collects samples of similar companies, estimates r for each, and takes an average. The average gives a more reliable benchmark for decision making.

Table 4.2 shows DCF cost-of-equity estimates for Pinnacle West and 10 other electric utilities in May 2001. These utilities are all stable, mature companies for which the constant-growth DCF formula *ought* to work. Notice the variation in the cost-of-equity estimates. Some of the variation may reflect differences in the risk, but some is just noise. The average estimate is 10.7 percent.

---

[5]In this calculation we're assuming that earnings and dividends are forecasted to grow forever at the same rate g. We'll show how to relax this assumption later in this chapter. The growth rate was based on the average earnings growth forecasted by Value Line and IBES. IBES compiles and averages forecasts made by security analysts. Value Line publishes its own analysts' forecasts

	Stock Price, P_0	Dividend, DIV_1	Dividend Yield, DIV_1/P_0	Growth Rate, g	Cost of Equity, $r = DIV_1/P_0 + g$
American Corp.	$41.71	$2.64	6.3%	3.8%	10.1%
CH Energy Corp.	43.85	2.20	5.0	2.0	7.0
CLECO Corp.	46.00	.92	2.0	8.8	10.8
DPL, Inc.	30.27	1.03	3.4	9.6	13.0
Hawaiian Electric	36.69	2.54	6.9	2.6	9.5
Idacorp	39.42	1.97	5.0	5.7	10.7
Pinnacle West	49.16	1.60	3.3	6.6	9.9
Potomac Electric	22.00	1.75	8.0	5.7	13.7
Puget Energy	23.49	1.93	8.2	4.8	13.0
TECO Energy	31.38	1.44	4.6	7.7	12.3
UIL Holdings	48.21	2.93	6.1	1.9	8.0
				Average	10.7%

TABLE 4.2

DCF cost-of-equity estimates for electric utilities in 2001.

Source: The Brattle Group, Inc.

Figure 4.2 shows DCF costs of equity estimated at six-month intervals for a sample of electric utilities over a seven-year period. The burgundy line indicates the median cost-of-equity estimates, which seem to lie about 3 percentage points above the 10-year Treasury bond yield. The dots show the scatter of individual estimates. Again, most of this scatter is probably noise.

Some Warnings about Constant-Growth Formulas

The simple constant-growth DCF formula is an extremely useful rule of thumb, but no more than that. Naive trust in the formula has led many financial analysts to silly conclusions.

We have stressed the difficulty of estimating r by analysis of one stock only. Try to use a large sample of equivalent-risk securities. Even that may not work, but at least it gives the analyst a fighting chance, because the inevitable errors in estimating r for a single security tend to balance out across a broad sample.

In addition, resist the temptation to apply the formula to firms having high current rates of growth. Such growth can rarely be sustained indefinitely, but the constant-growth DCF formula assumes it can. This erroneous assumption leads to an overestimate of r.

Consider Growth-Tech, Inc., a firm with $DIV_1 = \$.50$ and $P_0 = \$50$. The firm has plowed back 80 percent of earnings and has had a return on equity (ROE) of 25 percent. This means that *in the past*

$$\text{Dividend growth rate} = \text{plowback ratio} \times \text{ROE} = .80 \times .25 = .20$$

The temptation is to assume that the future long-term growth rate g also equals .20. This would imply

$$r = \frac{.50}{50.00} + .20 = .21$$

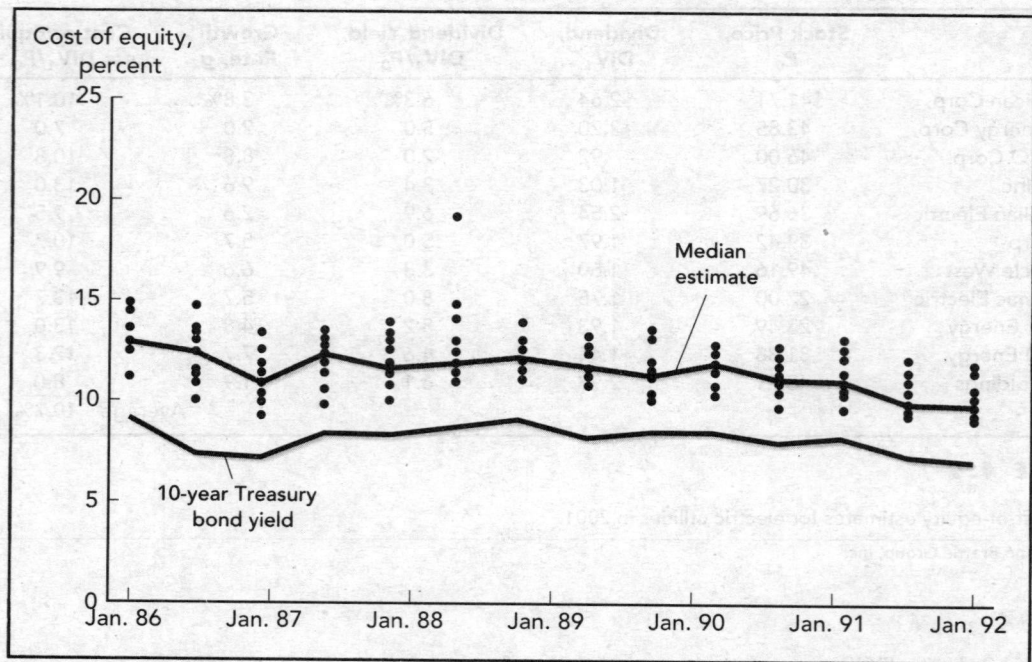

FIGURE 4.2

DCF cost-of-equity estimates for a sample of 17 utilities. The median estimates (burgundy line) track long-term interest rates fairly well. (The blue line is the 10-year Treasury yield.) The dots show the scatter of the cost-of-equity estimates for individual companies.

Source: S. C. Myers and L. S. Borucki, "Discounted Cash Flow Estimates of the Cost of Equity Capital—A Case Study," *Financial Markets, Institutions and Instruments* 3 (August 1994), pp. 9–45.

But this is silly. No firm can continue growing at 20 percent per year forever, except possibly under extreme inflationary conditions. Eventually, profitability will fall and the firm will respond by investing less.

In real life the return on equity will decline gradually over time, but for simplicity let's assume it suddenly drops to 16 percent at year 3 and the firm responds by plowing back only 50 percent of earnings. Then g drops to $.50(.16) = .08$.

Table 4.3 shows what's going on. Growth-Tech starts year 1 with assets of $10.00. It earns $2.50, pays out 50 cents as dividends, and plows back $2. Thus it starts year 2 with assets of $10 + 2 = $12. After another year at the same ROE and payout, it starts year 3 with assets of $14.40. However, ROE drops to .16, and the firm earns only $2.30. Dividends go up to $1.15, because the payout ratio increases, but the firm has only $1.15 to plow back. Therefore subsequent growth in earnings and dividends drops to 8 percent.

Now we can use our general DCF formula to find the capitalization rate r:

$$P_0 = \frac{DIV_1}{1 + r} + \frac{DIV_2}{(1 + r)^2} + \frac{DIV_3 + P_3}{(1 + r)^3}$$

Investors in year 3 will view Growth-Tech as offering 8 percent per year dividend growth. We will apply the constant-growth formula:

	Year			
	1	**2**	**3**	**4**
Book equity	10.00	12.00	14.40	15.55
Earnings per share, EPS	2.50	3.00	2.30	2.49
Return on equity, ROE	.25	.25	.16	.16
Payout ratio	.20	.20	.50	.50
Dividends per share, DIV	.50	.60	1.15	1.24
Growth rate of dividends (%)	—	20	92	8

TABLE 4.3

Forecasted earnings and dividends for Growth-Tech. Note the changes in year 3: ROE and earnings drop, but payout ratio increases, causing a big jump in dividends. However, subsequent growth in earnings and dividends falls to 8 percent per year. Note that the increase in equity equals the earnings not paid out as dividends.

$$P_3 = \frac{DIV_4}{r - .08}$$

$$P_0 = \frac{DIV_1}{1 + r} + \frac{DIV_2}{(1 + r)^2} + \frac{DIV_3}{(1 + r)^3} + \frac{1}{(1 + r)^3} \frac{DIV_4}{r - .08}$$

$$= \frac{.50}{1 + r} + \frac{.60}{(1 + r)^2} + \frac{1.15}{(1 + r)^3} + \frac{1}{(1 + r)^3} \frac{1.24}{r - .08}$$

We have to use trial and error to find the value of r that makes P_0 equal $50. It turns out that the r implicit in these more realistic forecasts is approximately .099, quite a difference from our "constant-growth" estimate of .21.

DCF Valuation with Varying Growth Rates

Our present value calculations for Growth-Tech used a *two-stage* DCF valuation model. In the first stage (years 1 and 2), Growth-Tech is highly profitable (ROE = 25 percent), and it plows back 80 percent of earnings. Book equity, earnings, and dividends increase by 20 percent per year. In the second stage, starting in year 3, profitability and plowback decline, and earnings settle into long-term growth at 8 percent. Dividends jump up to $1.15 in year 3, and then also grow at 8 percent.

Growth rates can vary for many reasons. Sometimes growth is high in the short run not because the firm is unusually profitable, but because it is recovering from an episode of *low* profitability. Table 4.4 displays projected earnings and dividends for Phoenix.com, which is gradually regaining financial health after a near melt-down. The company's equity is growing at a moderate 4 percent. ROE in year 1 is only 4 percent, however, so Phoenix has to reinvest all its earnings, leaving no cash for dividends. As profitability increases in years 2 and 3, an increasing dividend can be paid. Finally, starting in year 4, Phoenix settles into steady-state growth, with equity, earnings, and dividends all increasing at 4 percent per year.

Assume the cost of equity is 10 percent. Then Phoenix shares should be worth $9.13 per share:

$$P_0 = \underbrace{\frac{0}{1.1} + \frac{.31}{(1.1)^2} + \frac{.65}{(1.1)^3}}_{\text{PV (first-stage dividends)}} + \underbrace{\frac{1}{(1.1)^3} \frac{.67}{(.10 - .04)}}_{\text{PV (second-stage dividends)}} = \$9.13$$

We could go on to three- or even four-stage valuation models—but you get the idea. Two warnings, however. First, it's almost always worthwhile to lay out a simple

TABLE 4.4

Forecasted earnings and dividends for Phoenix.com. The company can initiate and increase dividends as profitability (ROE) recovers. Note that the increase in book equity equals the earnings not paid out as dividends.

	Year			
	1	2	3	4
Book equity	10.00	10.40	10.82	11.25
Earnings per share, EPS	.40	.73	1.08	1.12
Return on equity, ROE	.04	.07	.10	.10
Dividends per share, DIV	0	.31	.65	.67
Growth rate of dividends (%)	—	—	110	4

spreadsheet, like Table 4.3 or 4.4, to assure that your dividend projections are consistent with the company's earnings and the investments required to grow. Second, do not use DCF valuation formulas to test whether the market is correct in its assessment of a stock's value. If your estimate of the value is different from that of the market, it is probably because you have used poor dividend forecasts. Remember what we said at the beginning of this chapter about simple ways of making money on the stock market: There aren't any.

 ## 4.4 THE LINK BETWEEN STOCK PRICE AND EARNINGS PER SHARE

Investors often use the terms *growth stocks* and *income stocks.* They buy growth stocks primarily for the expectation of capital gains, and they are interested in the future growth of earnings rather than in next year's dividends. On the other hand, they buy income stocks primarily for the cash dividends. Let us see whether these distinctions make sense.

Imagine first the case of a company that does not grow at all. It does not plow back any earnings and simply produces a constant stream of dividends. Its stock would resemble the perpetual bond described in the last chapter. Remember that the return on a perpetuity is equal to the yearly cash flow divided by the present value. The expected return on our share would thus be equal to the yearly dividend divided by the share price (i.e., the dividend yield). Since all the earnings are paid out as dividends, the expected return is also equal to the earnings per share divided by the share price (i.e., the earnings–price ratio). For example, if the dividend is $10 a share and the stock price is $100, we have

$$\text{Expected return} = \text{dividend yield} = \text{earnings–price ratio}$$
$$= \frac{DIV_1}{P_0} \qquad = \frac{EPS_1}{P_0}$$
$$= \frac{10.00}{100} \qquad = .10$$

The price equals

$$P_0 = \frac{DIV_1}{r} = \frac{EPS_1}{r} = \frac{10.00}{.10} = 100$$

The expected return for *growing* firms can *also* equal the earnings–price ratio. The key is whether earnings are reinvested to provide a return equal to the market capitalization rate. For example, suppose our monotonous company suddenly hears of an opportunity to invest $10 a share next year. This would mean no dividend at $t = 1$. However, the company expects that in each subsequent year the project would earn $1 per share, so that the dividend could be increased to $11 a share.

Let us assume that this investment opportunity has about the same risk as the existing business. Then we can discount its cash flow at the 10 percent rate to find its net present value at year 1:

$$\text{Net present value per share at year 1} = -10 + \frac{1}{.10} = 0$$

Thus the investment opportunity will make no contribution to the company's value. Its prospective return is equal to the opportunity cost of capital.

What effect will the decision to undertake the project have on the company's share price? Clearly none. The reduction in value caused by the nil dividend in year 1 is exactly offset by the increase in value caused by the extra dividends in later years. Therefore, once again the market capitalization rate equals the earnings–price ratio:

$$r = \frac{EPS_1}{P_0} = \frac{10}{100} = .10$$

Table 4.5 repeats our example for different assumptions about the cash flow generated by the new project. Note that the earnings–price ratio, measured in terms of EPS_1, next year's expected earnings, equals the market capitalization rate (r) *only* when the new project's NPV = 0. This is an extremely important point—managers frequently make poor financial decisions because they confuse earnings–price ratios with the market capitalization rate.

In general, we can think of stock price as the capitalized value of average earnings under a no-growth policy, plus **PVGO**, the **present value of growth opportunities:**

$$P_0 = \frac{EPS_1}{r} + PVGO$$

Project Rate of Return	Incremental Cash Flow, C	Project NPV in Year 1*	Project's Impact on Share Price in Year 0†	Share Price in Year 0, P_0	$\frac{EPS_1}{P_0}$	r
.05	$ .50	−$ 5.00	−$ 4.55	$ 95.45	.105	.10
.10	1.00	0	0	100.00	.10	.10
.15	1.50	+ 5.00	+ 4.55	104.55	.096	.10
.20	2.00	+ 10.00	+ 9.09	109.09	.092	.10
.25	2.50	+ 15.00	+ 13.64	113.64	.088	.10

TABLE 4.5

Effect on stock price of investing an additional $10 in year 1 at different rates of return. Notice that the earnings–price ratio overestimates r when the project has negative NPV and underestimates it when the project has positive NPV.

*Project costs $10.00 ($EPS_1$). NPV = −10 + C/r, where r = .10.
†NPV is calculated at year 1. To find the impact on P_0, discount for one year at r = .10.

The earnings–price ratio, therefore, equals

$$\frac{EPS}{P_0} = r\left(1 - \frac{PVGO}{P_0}\right)$$

It will underestimate r if PVGO is positive and overestimate it if PVGO is negative. The latter case is less likely, since firms are rarely *forced* to take projects with negative net present values.

Calculating the Present Value of Growth Opportunities for Fledgling Electronics

In our last example both dividends and earnings were expected to grow, but this growth made no net contribution to the stock price. The stock was in this sense an "income stock." Be careful not to equate firm performance with the growth in earnings per share. A company that reinvests earnings at below the market capitalization rate may increase earnings but will certainly reduce the share value.

Now let us turn to that well-known *growth stock*, Fledgling Electronics. You may remember that Fledgling's market capitalization rate, r, is 15 percent. The company is expected to pay a dividend of \$5 in the first year, and thereafter the dividend is predicted to increase indefinitely by 10 percent a year. We can, therefore, use the simplified constant-growth formula to work out Fledgling's price:

$$P_0 = \frac{DIV_1}{r - g} = \frac{5}{.15 - .10} = \$100$$

Suppose that Fledgling has earnings per share of \$8.33. Its payout ratio is then

$$\text{Payout ratio} = \frac{DIV_1}{EPS_1} = \frac{5.00}{8.33} = .6$$

In other words, the company is plowing back $1 - .6$, or 40 percent of earnings. Suppose also that Fledgling's ratio of earnings to book equity is ROE = .25. This explains the growth rate of 10 percent:

$$\text{Growth rate} = g = \text{plowback ratio} \times \text{ROE} = .4 \times .25 = .10$$

The capitalized value of Fledgling's earnings per share if it had a no-growth policy would be

$$\frac{EPS_1}{r} = \frac{8.33}{.15} = \$55.56$$

But we know that the value of Fledgling stock is \$100. The difference of \$44.44 must be the amount that investors are paying for growth opportunities. Let's see if we can explain that figure.

Each year Fledgling plows back 40 percent of its earnings into new assets. In the first year Fledgling invests \$3.33 at a permanent 25 percent return on equity. Thus the cash generated by this investment is $.25 \times 3.33 = \$.83$ per year starting at $t = 2$. The net present value of the investment as of $t = 1$ is

$$NPV_1 = -3.33 + \frac{.83}{.15} = \$2.22$$

Everything is the same in year 2 except that Fledgling will invest $3.67, 10 percent more than in year 1 (remember $g = .10$). Therefore at $t = 2$ an investment is made with a net present value of

$$NPV_2 = -3.33 \times 1.10 + \frac{.83 \times 1.10}{.15} = \$2.44$$

Thus the payoff to the owners of Fledgling Electronics stock can be represented as the sum of (1) a level stream of earnings, which could be paid out as cash dividends if the firm did not grow, and (2) a set of tickets, one for each future year, representing the opportunity to make investments having positive NPVs. We know that the first component of the value of the share is

$$\text{Present value of level stream of earnings} = \frac{EPS_1}{r} = \frac{8.33}{.15} = \$55.56$$

The first ticket is worth $2.22 in $t = 1$, the second is worth $2.22 \times 1.10 = \$2.44$ in $t = 2$, the third is worth $2.44 \times 1.10 = \$2.69$ in $t = 3$. These are the forecasted cash values of the tickets. We know how to value a stream of future cash values that grows at 10 percent per year: Use the constant-growth DCF formula, replacing the forecasted dividends with forecasted ticket values:

$$\text{Present value of growth opportunities} = \text{PVGO} = \frac{NPV_1}{r - g} = \frac{2.22}{.15 - .10} = \$44.44$$

Now everything checks:

$$\begin{aligned}
\text{Share price} &= \text{present value of level stream of earnings} \\
&\quad + \text{present value of growth opportunities} \\
&= \frac{EPS_1}{r} + \text{PVGO} \\
&= \$55.56 + \$44.44 \\
&= \$100
\end{aligned}$$

Why is Fledgling Electronics a growth stock? Not because it is expanding at 10 percent per year. It is a growth stock because the net present value of its future investments accounts for a significant fraction (about 44 percent) of the stock's price.

Stock prices today reflect investors' expectations of future operating *and investment* performance. Growth stocks sell at high price–earnings ratios because investors are willing to pay now for expected superior returns on investments that have not yet been made.[6]

Some Examples of Growth Opportunities?

Stocks like Microsoft, Dell Computer, and Wal-Mart are often described as growth stocks, while those of mature firms like Kellogg, Weyerhaeuser, and Exxon Mobil are regarded as income stocks. Let us check it out. The first column of Table 4.6

---

[6]Michael Eisner, the chairman of Walt Disney Productions, made the point this way: "In school you had to take the test and then be graded. Now we're getting graded, and we haven't taken the test." This was in late 1985, when Disney stock was selling at nearly 20 times earnings. See Kathleen K. Wiegner, "The Tinker Bell Principle," *Forbes* (December 2, 1985), p. 102.

Stock	Stock Price, P_0 (October 2001)	EPS*	Cost of Equity, $r^\dagger$	PVGO $= P_0 - EPS/r$	PVGO, percent of Stock Price
Income stocks:					
Chubb	$77.35	$4.90	.088	$21.67	28
Exxon Mobil	42.29	2.13	.072	12.71	30
Kellogg	29.00	1.42	.056	3.64	13
Weyerhaeuser	50.45	3.21	.128	25.37	50
Growth stocks:					
Amazon.com	8.88	.30	.24	10.13	114
Dell Computer	23.66	.76	.22	20.20	85
Microsoft	56.38	1.88	.184	46.16	82
Wal-Mart	52.90	1.70	.112	37.72	71

TABLE 4.6

Estimated PVGOs.

*EPS is defined as the average earnings under a no-growth policy. As an estimate of EPS, we used the forecasted earnings per share for 2002. Source: MSN Money (moneycentral.msn.com).

†The market capitalization rate was estimated using the capital asset pricing model. We describe this model and how to use it in Sections 8.2 and 9.2. For this example, we used a market risk premium of 8 percent and a risk-free interest rate of 4 percent.

shows the stock price for each of these companies in October 2001. The remaining columns estimate PVGO as a proportion of the stock price.

Remember, if there are no growth opportunities, present value equals the average future earnings from existing assets discounted at the market capitalization rate. We used analysts' forecasts for 2002 as a measure of the earning power of existing assets. You can see that most of the value of the growth stocks comes from PVGO, that is, from investors' expectations that the companies will be able to earn more than the cost of capital on their future investments. However, Weyerhaeuser, though usually regarded as an income stock, does pretty well on the PVGO scale. But the most striking growth stock is Amazon.com. Its earnings have been consistently negative, so its PVGO accounts for *more than 100 percent* of its stock price. None of the company's value can be based on its current earnings. The value comes entirely from future earnings and the NPV of its future investments.[7]

Some companies have such extensive growth opportunities that they prefer to pay no dividends for long periods of time. For example, up to the time that we wrote this chapter, "glamour stocks" such as Microsoft and Dell Computer had never paid a dividend, because any cash paid out to investors would have meant either slower growth or raising capital by some other means. Investors were happy to forgo immediate cash dividends in exchange for increasing earnings and the expectation of high dividends some time in the future.

---

[7]However, Amazon's reported earnings probably understate its earnings potential. Amazon is growing very rapidly, and some of the investments necessary to finance that growth are written off as expenses, thus reducing current income. Absent these "investment expenses," Amazon's current income would probably be positive. We discuss the problems encountered in measuring earnings and profitability in Chapter 12.

What Do Price–Earnings Ratios Mean?

The **price–earnings ratio** is part of the everyday vocabulary of investors in the stock market. People casually refer to a stock as "selling at a high P/E." You can look up P/Es in stock quotations given in the newspaper. (However, the newspaper gives the ratio of current price to the most recent earnings. Investors are more concerned with price relative to *future* earnings.) Unfortunately, some financial analysts are confused about what price–earnings ratios really signify and often use the ratios in odd ways.

Should the financial manager celebrate if the firm's stock sells at a high P/E? The answer is usually yes. The high P/E shows that investors think that the firm has good growth opportunities (high PVGO), that its earnings are relatively safe and deserve a low capitalization rate (low *r*), or both. However, firms can have high price–earnings ratios not because price is high but because earnings are low. A firm which earns *nothing* (EPS = 0) in a particular period will have an *infinite* P/E as long as its shares retain any value at all.

Are relative P/Es helpful in evaluating stocks? Sometimes. Suppose you own stock in a family corporation whose shares are not actively traded. What are those shares worth? A decent estimate is possible if you can find traded firms that have roughly the same profitability, risks, and growth opportunities as your firm. Multiply your firm's earnings per share by the P/E of the counterpart firms.

Does a high P/E indicate a low market capitalization rate? No. There is *no* reliable association between a stock's price–earnings ratio and the capitalization rate *r*. The ratio of EPS to P_0 measures *r* only if PVGO = 0 and only if reported EPS is the average future earnings the firm could generate under a no-growth policy. Another reason P/Es are hard to interpret is that the figure for earnings depends on the accounting procedures for calculating revenues and costs. We will discuss the potential biases in accounting earnings in Chapter 12.

4.5 VALUING A BUSINESS BY DISCOUNTED CASH FLOW

Investors routinely buy and sell shares of common stock. Companies frequently buy and sell entire businesses. In 2001, for example, when Diageo sold its Pillsbury operation to General Mills for $10.4 billion, you can be sure that both companies burned a lot of midnight oil to make sure that the deal was fairly priced.

Do the discounted-cash-flow formulas we presented in this chapter work for entire businesses as well as for shares of common stock? Sure: It doesn't matter whether you forecast dividends per share or the total free cash flow of a business. Value today always equals future cash flow discounted at the opportunity cost of capital.

Valuing the Concatenator Business

Rumor has it that Establishment Industries is interested in buying your company's concatenator manufacturing operation. Your company is willing to sell if it can get the full value of this rapidly growing business. The problem is to figure out what its true present value is.

Table 4.7 gives a forecast of **free cash flow** (FCF) for the concatenator business. Free cash flow is the amount of cash that a firm can pay out to investors after paying for

	Year									
	1	2	3	4	5	6	7	8	9	10
Asset value	10.00	12.00	14.40	17.28	20.74	23.43	26.47	28.05	29.73	31.51
Earnings	1.20	1.44	1.73	2.07	2.49	2.81	3.18	3.36	3.57	3.78
Investment	2.00	2.40	2.88	3.46	2.69	3.04	1.59	1.68	1.78	1.89
Free cash flow	−.80	−.96	−1.15	−1.39	−.20	−.23	1.59	1.68	1.79	1.89
Earnings growth from previous period (%)	20	20	20	20	20	13	13	6	6	6

TABLE 4.7

Forecasts of free cash flow, in $ millions, for the Concatenator Manufacturing Division. Rapid expansion in years 1–6 means that free cash flow is negative, because required additional investment outstrips earnings. Free cash flow turns positive when growth slows down after year 6.

Notes:
1. Starting asset value is $10 million. Assets required for the business grow at 20 percent per year to year 4, at 13 percent in years 5 and 6, and at 6 percent afterward.
2. Profitability (earnings/asset values) is constant at 12 percent.
3. Free cash flow equals earnings minus net investment. Net investment equals total capital expenditures less depreciation. Note that earnings are also calculated net of depreciation.

all investments necessary for growth. As we will see, free cash flow can be negative for rapidly growing businesses.

Table 4.7 is similar to Table 4.3, which forecasted earnings and dividends per share for Growth-Tech, based on assumptions about Growth-Tech's equity per share, return on equity, and the growth of its business. For the concatenator business, we also have assumptions about assets, profitability—in this case, after-tax operating earnings relative to assets—and growth. Growth starts out at a rapid 20 percent per year, then falls in two steps to a moderate 6 percent rate for the long run. The growth rate determines the net additional investment required to expand assets, and the profitability rate determines the earnings thrown off by the business.[8]

Free cash flow, the next to last line in Table 4.7, is negative in years 1 through 6. The concatenator business is paying a negative dividend to the parent company; it is absorbing more cash than it is throwing off.

Is that a bad sign? Not really: The business is running a cash deficit not because it is unprofitable, but because it is growing so fast. Rapid growth is good news, not bad, so long as the business is earning more than the opportunity cost of capital. Your company, or Establishment Industries, will be happy to invest an extra $800,000 in the concatenator business next year, so long as the business offers a superior rate of return.

Valuation Format

The value of a business is usually computed as the discounted value of free cash flows out to a *valuation horizon (H)*, plus the forecasted value of the business at the horizon, also discounted back to present value. That is,

---

[8]Table 4.7 shows *net* investment, which is total investment less depreciation. We are assuming that investment for replacement of existing assets is covered by depreciation and that net investment is devoted to growth.

$$PV = \underbrace{\frac{FCF_1}{1 + r} + \frac{FCF_2}{(1 + r)^2} + \cdots + \frac{FCF_H}{(1 + r)^H}}_{\text{PV(free cash flow)}} + \underbrace{\frac{PV_H}{(1 + r)^H}}_{\text{PV(horizon value)}}$$

Of course, the concatenator business will continue after the horizon, but it's not practical to forecast free cash flow year by year to infinity. PV_H stands in for free cash flow in periods $H + 1, H + 2$, etc.

Valuation horizons are often chosen arbitrarily. Sometimes the boss tells everybody to use 10 years because that's a round number. We will try year 6, because growth of the concatenator business seems to settle down to a long-run trend after year 7.

Estimating Horizon Value

There are several common formulas or rules of thumb for estimating horizon value. First, let us try the constant-growth DCF formula. This requires free cash flow for year 7, which we have from Table 4.7, a long-run growth rate, which appears to be 6 percent, and a discount rate, which some high-priced consultant has told us is 10 percent. Therefore,

$$PV(\text{horizon value}) = \frac{1}{(1.1)^6}\left(\frac{1.59}{.10 - .06}\right) = 22.4$$

The present value of the near-term free cash flows is

$$PV(\text{cash flows}) = -\frac{.80}{1.1} - \frac{.96}{(1.1)^2} - \frac{1.15}{(1.1)^3} - \frac{1.39}{(1.1)^4} - \frac{.20}{(1.1)^5} - \frac{.23}{(1.1)^6}$$
$$= -3.6$$

and, therefore, the present value of the business is

$$PV(\text{business}) = PV(\text{free cash flow}) + PV(\text{horizon value})$$
$$= -3.6 \qquad\qquad + 22.4$$
$$= \$18.8 \text{ million}$$

Now, are we done? Well, the mechanics of this calculation are perfect. But doesn't it make you just a little nervous to find that 119 percent of the value of the business rests on the horizon value? Moreover, a little checking shows that the horizon value can change dramatically in response to apparently minor changes in assumptions. For example, if the long-run growth rate is 8 percent rather than 6 percent, the value of the business increases from \$18.8 to \$26.3 million.[9]

In other words, it's easy for a discounted-cash-flow business valuation to be mechanically perfect and practically wrong. Smart financial managers try to check their results by calculating horizon value in several different ways.

Horizon Value Based on P/E Ratios   Suppose you can observe stock prices for mature manufacturing companies whose scale, risk, and growth prospects today

---

[9]If long-run growth is 8 rather than 6 percent, an extra 2 percent of period-7 assets will have to be plowed back into the concatenator business. This reduces free cash flow by \$.53 to \$1.06 million. So,

$$PV(\text{horizon value}) = \frac{1}{(1.1)^6}\left(\frac{1.06}{.10 - .08}\right) = \$29.9$$
$$PV(\text{business}) = -3.6 + 29.9 = \$26.3 \text{ million}$$

roughly match those projected for the concatenator business in year 6. Suppose further that these companies tend to sell at price–earnings ratios of about 11. Then you could reasonably guess that the price–earnings ratio of a mature concatenator operation will likewise be 11. That implies:

$$PV(\text{horizon value}) = \frac{1}{(1.1)^6}(11 \times 3.18) = 19.7$$

$$PV(\text{business}) = -3.6 + 19.7 = \$16.1 \text{ million}$$

Horizon Value Based on Market–Book Ratios   Suppose also that the market–book ratios of the sample of mature manufacturing companies tend to cluster around 1.4. (The market–book ratio is just the ratio of stock price to book value per share.) If the concatenator business market–book ratio is 1.4 in year 6,

$$PV(\text{horizon value}) = \frac{1}{(1.1)^6}(1.4 \times 23.43) = 18.5$$

$$PV(\text{business}) = -3.6 + 18.5 = \$14.9 \text{ million}$$

It's easy to poke holes in these last two calculations. Book value, for example, often is a poor measure of the true value of a company's assets. It can fall far behind actual asset values when there is rapid inflation, and it often entirely misses important intangible assets, such as your patents for concatenator design. Earnings may also be biased by inflation and a long list of arbitrary accounting choices. Finally, you never know when you have found a sample of truly similar companies.

But remember, the purpose of discounted cash flow is to estimate market value—to estimate what investors would pay for a stock or business. When you can *observe* what they actually pay for similar companies, that's valuable evidence. Try to figure out a way to use it. One way to use it is through valuation rules of thumb, based on price–earnings or market–book ratios. A rule of thumb, artfully employed, sometimes beats a complex discounted-cash-flow calculation hands down.

A Further Reality Check

Here is another approach to valuing a business. It is based on what you have learned about price–earnings ratios and the present value of growth opportunities.

Suppose the valuation horizon is set not by looking for the first year of stable growth, but by asking when the industry is likely to settle into competitive equilibrium. You might go to the operating manager most familiar with the concatenator business and ask:

> Sooner or later you and your competitors will be on an equal footing when it comes to major new investments. You may still be earning a superior return on your core business, but you will find that introductions of new products or attempts to expand sales of existing products trigger intense resistance from competitors who are just about as smart and efficient as you are. Give a realistic assessment of when that time will come.

"That time" is the horizon after which PVGO, the net present value of subsequent growth opportunities, is zero. After all, PVGO is positive only when investments can be expected to earn more than the cost of capital. When your competition catches up, that happy prospect disappears.[10]

---

[10]We cover this point in more detail in Chapter 11.

We know that present value in any period equals the capitalized value of next period's earnings, plus PVGO:

$$PV_t = \frac{earnings_{t+1}}{r} + PVGO$$

But what if PVGO = 0? At the horizon period H, then,

$$PV_H = \frac{earnings_{H+1}}{r}$$

In other words, when the competition catches up, the price–earnings ratio equals $1/r$, because PVGO disappears.

Suppose competition is expected to catch up by period 8. We can recalculate the value of the concatenator business as follows:[11]

$$PV(horizon\ value) = \frac{1}{(1+r)^8}\left(\frac{earnings\ in\ period\ 9}{r}\right)$$

$$= \frac{1}{(1.1)^8}\left(\frac{3.57}{.10}\right)$$

$$= \$16.7\ million$$

$$PV(business) = -2.0 + 16.7 = \$14.7\ million$$

We now have four estimates of what Establishment Industries ought to pay for the concatenator business. The estimates reflect four different methods of estimating horizon value. There is no best method, although in many cases we put most weight on the last method, which sets the horizon date at the point when management expects PVGO to disappear. The last method forces managers to remember that sooner or later competition catches up.

Our calculated values for the concatenator business range from $14.7 to $18.8 million, a difference of about $4 million. The width of the range may be disquieting, but it is not unusual. Discounted-cash-flow formulas only estimate market value, and the estimates change as forecasts and assumptions change. Managers cannot know market value for sure until an actual transaction takes place.

How Much Is the Concatenator Business Worth per Share?

Suppose the concatenator division is spun off from its parent as an independent company, Concatco, with one million outstanding shares. What would each share sell for?

We have already calculated the value of Concatco's free cash flow as $18.8 million, using the constant-growth DCF formula to calculate horizon value. If this value is right, and there are one million shares, each share should be worth $18.80. This amount should also be the present value of Concatco's *dividends* per share—although here we must slow down and be careful. Note from Table 4.7 that free cash flow is negative from years 1 to 6. Dividends can't be negative, so Concatco will have to raise outside financing. Suppose it issues additional shares. Then Concatco's one million *existing* shares will not receive all of Concatco's dividend payments when the company starts paying out cash in year 7.

---

[11]The PV of free cash flow before the horizon improves to −$2.0 million because inflows in years 7 and 8 are now included.

There are two approaches to valuing a company's existing shares when new shares will be issued. The first approach discounts the net cash flow to existing shareholders if they buy *all* the new shares issued. In this case the existing shareholders would pay out cash to Concatco in years 1 to 6, and then receive all subsequent dividends; they would pay for or receive all free cash flow from year 1 to year 8 and beyond. The value of a share therefore equals free cash flow for the company as a whole, taking account of negative as well as positive amounts, divided by the number of existing shares. We have already done this calculation: If the value of the company is $18.8 million, the value of each of the one million existing shares should be $18.80.

The second approach discounts the dividends that will be paid when free cash flow turns positive. But you must discount *only* the dividends paid on *existing* shares. The new shares issued to finance the negative free cash flows in years 1 to 6 will claim a portion of the dividends paid out later.

Let's check that the second method gives the same answer as the first. Note that the present value of Concatco's free cash flow from years 1 to 6 is −$3.6 million. Concatco decides to raise this amount now and put it in the bank to take care of the future cash outlays through year 6. To do this, the company has to issue 191,500 shares at a price of $18.80:

$$\text{Cash raised} = \text{price per share} \times \text{number of new shares}$$
$$= 18.80 \times 191,500 = \$3,600,000$$

If the existing stockholders buy none of the new issue, their ownership of the company shrinks to

$$\frac{\text{Existing shares}}{\text{Existing + new shares}} = \frac{1,000,000}{1,191,500} = .839, \text{ or } 83.9\%$$

The value of the existing shares should be 83.9 percent of the present value of each dividend paid after year 6. In other words, they are worth 83.9 percent of PV(horizon value), which we calculated as $22.4 million from the constant-growth DCF formula.

$$\text{PV to existing stockholders} = .839 \times \text{PV(horizon value)}$$
$$= .839 \times 22.4 = \$18.8 \text{ million}$$

Since there are one million existing shares, each is worth $18.80.

Finally, let's check whether the new stockholders are getting a fair deal. They end up with $100 − 83.9 = 16.1$ percent of the shares in exchange for an investment of $3.6 million. The NPV of this investment is

$$\text{NPV to new stockholders} = -3.6 + .161 \times \text{PV(horizon value)}$$
$$= -3.6 + .161 \times 22.4 = -3.6 + 3.6 = 0$$

On reflection, you will see that our two valuation methods must give the same answer. The first assumes that the existing shareholders provide all the cash whenever the firm needs cash. If so, they will also receive every dollar the firm pays out. The second method assumes that *new* investors put up the cash, relieving existing shareholders of this burden. But the new investors then receive a share of future payouts. If investment by new investors is a zero-NPV transaction, then it doesn't make existing stockholders any better or worse off than if they had invested themselves. The key assumption, of course, is that new shares are issued on fair terms, that is, at zero NPV.[12]

---

[12]The same two methods work when the company will use free cash flow to repurchase and retire outstanding shares. We discuss share repurchases in Chapter 16.

In this chapter we have used our newfound knowledge of present values to examine the market price of common stocks. The value of a stock is equal to the stream of cash payments discounted at the rate of return that investors expect to receive on other securities with equivalent risks.

Common stocks do not have a fixed maturity; their cash payments consist of an indefinite stream of dividends. Therefore, the present value of a common stock is

$$PV = \sum_{t=1}^{\infty} \frac{DIV_t}{(1 + r)^t}$$

However, we did not just *assume* that investors purchase common stocks solely for dividends. In fact, we began with the assumption that investors have relatively short horizons and invest for both dividends and capital gains. Our fundamental valuation formula is, therefore,

$$P_0 = \frac{DIV_1 + P_1}{1 + r}$$

This is a condition of market equilibrium. If it did not hold, the share would be overpriced or underpriced, and investors would rush to sell or buy it. The flood of sellers or buyers would force the price to adjust so that the fundamental valuation formula holds.

This formula will hold in each future period as well as the present. That allowed us to express next year's forecasted price in terms of the subsequent stream of dividends DIV_2, DIV_3, ...

We also made use of the formula for a growing perpetuity presented in Chapter 3. If dividends are expected to grow forever at a constant rate of g, then

$$P_0 = \frac{DIV_1}{r - g}$$

It is often helpful to twist this formula around and use it to estimate the market capitalization rate r, given P_0 and estimates of DIV_1 and g:

$$r = \frac{DIV_1}{P_0} + g$$

Remember, however, that this formula rests on a *very* strict assumption: constant dividend growth in perpetuity. This may be an acceptable assumption for mature, low-risk firms, but for many firms, near-term growth is unsustainably high. In that case, you may wish to use a *two-stage* DCF formula, where near-term dividends are forecasted and valued, and the constant-growth DCF formula is used to forecast the value of the shares at the start of the long run. The near-term dividends and the future share value are then discounted to present value.

The general DCF formula can be transformed into a statement about earnings and growth opportunities:

$$P_0 = \frac{EPS_1}{r} + PVGO$$

The ratio EPS_1/r is the capitalized value of the earnings per share that the firm would generate under a no-growth policy. PVGO is the net present value of the investments that the firm will make in order to grow. A growth stock is one for which PVGO is large relative to the capitalized value of EPS. Most growth stocks are stocks of rapidly expanding firms, but expansion alone does not create a high PVGO. What matters is the profitability of the new investments.

The same formulas that are used to value a single share can also be applied to value the total package of shares that a company has issued. In other words, we can use them to value an entire business. In this case we discount the free cash flow thrown off by the business. Here again a two-stage DCF model is deployed. Free cash flows are forecasted and discounted year by year out to a horizon, at which point a horizon value is estimated and discounted.

Valuing a business by discounted cash flow is easy in principle but messy in practice. We concluded this chapter with a detailed numerical example to show you what practice is really like. We extended this example to show how to value a company's existing shares when new shares will be issued to finance growth.

In earlier chapters you should have acquired—we hope painlessly—a knowledge of the basic principles of valuing assets and a facility with the mechanics of discounting. Now you know something of how common stocks are valued and market capitalization rates estimated. In Chapter 5 we can begin to apply all this knowledge in a more specific analysis of capital budgeting decisions.

FURTHER READING

There are a number of discussions of the valuation of common stocks in investment texts. We suggest:
Z. Bodie, A. Kane, and A. J. Marcus: *Investments*, 5th ed., Irwin/McGraw-Hill, 2002.

W. F. Sharpe, G. J. Alexander, and J. V. Bailey: *Investments*, 6th ed., Prentice-Hall, Inc., Englewood Cliffs, N.J., 1999.

J. B. Williams's original work remains very readable. See particularly Chapter V of:
J. B. Williams: *The Theory of Investment Value*, Harvard University Press, Cambridge, Mass., 1938.

The following articles provide important developments of Williams's early work. We suggest, however, that you leave the third article until you have read Chapter 16:
D. Durand: "Growth Stocks and the Petersburg Paradox," *Journal of Finance,* 12:348–363 (September 1957).

M. J. Gordon and E. Shapiro: "Capital Equipment Analysis: The Required Rate of Profit," *Management Science,* 3:102–110 (October 1956).

M. H. Miller and F. Modigliani: "Dividend Policy, Growth and the Valuation of Shares," *Journal of Business,* 34:411–433 (October 1961).

Leibowitz and Kogelman call PVGO the "franchise factor." They analyze it in detail in:
M. L. Leibowitz and S. Kogelman: "Inside the P/E Ratio: The Franchise Factor," *Financial Analysts Journal,* 46:17–35 (November–December 1990).

Myers and Borucki cover the practical problems encountered in estimating DCF costs of equity for regulated companies; Harris and Marston report DCF estimates of rates of return for the stock market as a whole:
S. C. Myers and L. S. Borucki: "Discounted Cash Flow Estimates of the Cost of Equity Capital—A Case Study," *Financial Markets, Institutions and Instruments,* 3:9–45 (August 1994).

R. S. Harris and F. C. Marston: "Estimating Shareholder Risk Premia Using Analysts' Growth Forecasts," *Financial Management*, 21:63–70 (Summer 1992).

The following book covers valuation of businesses in great detail:

T. Copeland, T. Koller, and J. Murrin: *Valuation: Measuring and Managing the Value of Companies*, John Wiley & Sons, Inc., New York, 1994.

QUIZ

1. True or false?
   a. All stocks in an equivalent-risk class are priced to offer the same expected rate of return.
   b. The value of a share equals the PV of future dividends per share.

2. Respond briefly to the following statement.

   "You say stock price equals the present value of future dividends? That's crazy! All the investors I know are looking for capital gains."

3. Company X is expected to pay an end-of-year dividend of $10 a share. After the dividend its stock is expected to sell at $110. If the market capitalization rate is 10 percent, what is the current stock price?

4. Company Y does not plow back any earnings and is expected to produce a level dividend stream of $5 a share. If the current stock price is $40, what is the market capitalization rate?

5. Company Z's earnings and dividends per share are expected to grow indefinitely by 5 percent a year. If next year's dividend is $10 and the market capitalization rate is 8 percent, what is the current stock price?

6. Company Z-prime is like Z in all respects save one: Its growth will stop after year 4. In year 5 and afterward, it will pay out all earnings as dividends. What is Z-prime's stock price? Assume next year's EPS is $15.

7. If company Z (see question 5) were to distribute all its earnings, it could maintain a level dividend stream of $15 a share. How much is the market actually paying per share for growth opportunities?

8. Consider three investors:
   a. Mr. Single invests for one year.
   b. Ms. Double invests for two years.
   c. Mrs. Triple invests for three years.

   Assume each invests in company Z (see question 5). Show that each expects to earn an expected rate of return of 8 percent per year.

9. True or false?
   a. The value of a share equals the discounted stream of future earnings per share.
   b. The value of a share equals the PV of earnings per share assuming the firm does not grow, plus the NPV of future growth opportunities.

10. Under what conditions does r, a stock's market capitalization rate, equal its earnings–price ratio EPS_1/P_0?

11. What do financial managers mean by "free cash flow"? How is free cash flow related to dividends paid out? Briefly explain.

12. What is meant by a two-stage DCF valuation model? Briefly describe two cases where such a model could be used.

13. What is meant by the *horizon value* of a business? How is it estimated?

14. Suppose the horizon date is set at a time when the firm will run out of positive-NPV investment opportunities. How would you calculate the horizon value?

PRACTICE QUESTIONS

1. Look in a recent issue of *The Wall Street Journal* at "NYSE-Composite Transactions."
   a. What is the latest price of IBM stock?
   b. What are the annual dividend payment and the dividend yield on IBM stock?
   c. What would the yield be if IBM changed its yearly dividend to $1.50?
   d. What is the P/E on IBM stock?
   e. Use the P/E to calculate IBM's earnings per share.
   f. Is IBM's P/E higher or lower than that of Exxon Mobil?
   g. What are the possible reasons for the difference in P/E?

2. The present value of investing in a stock should not depend on how long the investor plans to hold it. Explain why.

3. Define the market capitalization rate for a stock. Does it equal the opportunity cost of capital of investing in the stock?

4. Rework Table 4.1 under the assumption that the dividend on Fledgling Electronics is $10 next year and that it is expected to grow by 5 percent a year. The capitalization rate is 15 percent.

5. In March 2001, Fly Paper's stock sold for about $73. Security analysts were forecasting a long-term earnings growth rate of 8.5 percent. The company was paying dividends of $1.68 per share.

   a. Assume dividends are expected to grow along with earnings at $g = 8.5$ percent per year in perpetuity. What rate of return r were investors expecting?
   b. Fly Paper was expected to earn about 12 percent on book equity and to pay out about 50 percent of earnings as dividends. What do these forecasts imply for g? For r? Use the perpetual-growth DCF formula.

6. You believe that next year the Superannuation Company will pay a dividend of $2 on its common stock. Thereafter you expect dividends to grow at a rate of 4 percent a year in perpetuity. If you require a return of 12 percent on your investment, how much should you be prepared to pay for the stock?

7. Consider the following three stocks:
   a. Stock A is expected to provide a dividend of $10 a share forever.
   b. Stock B is expected to pay a dividend of $5 next year. Thereafter, dividend growth is expected to be 4 percent a year forever.
   c. Stock C is expected to pay a dividend of $5 next year. Thereafter, dividend growth is expected to be 20 percent a year for 5 years (i.e., until year 6) and zero thereafter.

   If the market capitalization rate for each stock is 10 percent, which stock is the most valuable? What if the capitalization rate is 7 percent?

8. Crecimiento S.A. currently plows back 40 percent of its earnings and earns a return of 20 percent on this investment. The dividend yield on the stock is 4 percent.
   a. Assuming that Crecimiento can continue to plow back this proportion of earnings and earn a 20 percent return on the investment, how rapidly will earnings and dividends grow? What is the expected return on Crecimiento stock?
   b. Suppose that management suddenly announces that future investment opportunities have dried up. Now Crecimiento intends to pay out all its earnings. How will the stock price change?
   c. Suppose that management simply announces that the expected return on new investment would in the future be the same as the market capitalization rate. Now what is Crecimiento's stock price?

9. Look up General Mills, Inc., and Kellogg Co. on the Standard & Poor's Market Insight website (**www.mhhe.com/edumarketinsight**). The companies' ticker symbols are GIS and K.
   a. What are the current dividend yield and price–earnings ratio (P/E) for each company? How do the yields and P/Es compare to the average for the food

STANDARD & POOR'S

industry and for the stock market as a whole? (The stock market is represented by the S & P 500 index.)

b. What are the growth rates of earnings per share (EPS) and dividends for each company over the last five years? Do these growth rates appear to reflect a steady trend that could be projected for the long-run future?

c. Would you be confident in applying the constant-growth DCF valuation model to these companies' stocks? Why or why not?

10. Look up the following companies on the Standard & Poor's Market Insight website (**www.mhhe.com/edumarketinsight**): Citigroup (C), Dell Computer (DELL), Dow Chemical (DOW), Harley Davidson (HDI), and Pfizer, Inc. (PFE). Look at "Financial Highlights" and "Company Profile" for each company. You will note wide differences in these companies' price–earnings ratios. What are the possible explanations for these differences? Which would you classify as growth (high-PVGO) stocks and which as income stocks?

> STANDARD
> &POOR'S

11. Vega Motor Corporation has pulled off a miraculous recovery. Four years ago, it was near bankruptcy. Now its charismatic leader, a corporate folk hero, may run for president.

Vega has just announced a $1 per share dividend, the first since the crisis hit. Analysts expect an increase to a "normal" $3 as the company completes its recovery over the next three years. After that, dividend growth is expected to settle down to a moderate long-term growth rate of 6 percent.

Vega stock is selling at $50 per share. What is the expected long-run rate of return from buying the stock at this price? Assume dividends of $1, $2, and $3 for years 1, 2, 3. A little trial and error will be necessary to find r.

12. P/E ratios reported in *The Wall Street Journal* use the latest closing prices and the last 12 months' reported earnings per share. Explain why the corresponding earnings–price ratios (the reciprocals of reported P/Es) are *not* accurate measures of the expected rates of return demanded by investors.

13. Each of the following formulas for determining shareholders' required rate of return can be right or wrong depending on the circumstances:

a. $r = \dfrac{DIV_1}{P_0} + g$

b. $r = \dfrac{EPS_1}{P_0}$

For each formula construct a *simple* numerical example showing that the formula can give wrong answers and explain why the error occurs. Then construct another simple numerical example for which the formula gives the right answer.

14. Alpha Corp's earnings and dividends are growing at 15 percent per year. Beta Corp's earnings and dividends are growing at 8 percent per year. The companies' assets, earnings, and dividends per share are now (at date 0) exactly the same. Yet PVGO accounts for a greater fraction of Beta Corp's stock price. How is this possible? *Hint:* There is more than one possible explanation.

15. Look again at the financial forecasts for Growth-Tech given in Table 4.3. This time assume you *know* that the opportunity cost of capital is $r = .12$ (discard the .099 figure calculated in the text). Assume you do *not* know Growth-Tech's stock value. Otherwise follow the assumptions given in the text.

a. Calculate the value of Growth-Tech stock.

b. What part of that value reflects the discounted value of P_3, the price forecasted for year 3?

c. What part of P_3 reflects the present value of growth opportunities (PVGO) after year 3?

d. Suppose that competition will catch up with Growth-Tech by year 4, so that it can earn only its cost of capital on any investments made in year 4 or subsequently. What is Growth-Tech stock worth now under this assumption? (Make additional assumptions if necessary.)

16. Look up Hawaiian Electric Co. (HI) on the Standard & Poor's Market Insight website (**www.mhhe.com/edumarketinsight**). Hawaiian Electric was one of the companies in Table 4.2. That table was constructed in 2001.
a. What is the company's dividend yield? How has it changed since 2001?
b. Table 4.2 projected growth of 2.6 percent. How fast have the company's dividends and EPS actually grown since 2001?
c. Calculate a sustainable growth rate for the company based on its five-year average return on equity (ROE) and plowback ratio.
d. Given this updated information, would you modify the cost-of-equity estimate given in Table 4.2? Explain.

17. Browse through the companies in the Standard & Poor's Market Insight website (**www.mhhe.com/edumarketinsight**). Find three or four companies for which the earnings-price ratio reported on the website drastically *under*states the market capitalization rate *r* for the company. (*Hint:* you don't have to estimate *r* to answer this question. You know that *r* must be higher than current interest rates on U.S. government notes and bonds.)

18. The Standard & Poor's Market Insight website (**www.mhhe.com/edumarketinsight**) contains information all of the companies in Table 4.6 except for Chubb and Weyerhaeuser. Update the calculations of PVGO as a percentage of stock price. For simplicity use the costs of equity given in Table 4.6. You will need to track down an updated forecast of EPS, for example from MSN money (**www.moneycentral.msn.com**) of Yahoo (**http://finance.yahoo.com**).

19. Compost Science, Inc. (CSI), is in the business of converting Boston's sewage sludge into fertilizer. The business is not in itself very profitable. However, to induce CSI to remain in business, the Metropolitan District Commission (MDC) has agreed to pay whatever amount is necessary to yield CSI a 10 percent book return on equity. At the end of the year CSI is expected to pay a $4 dividend. It has been reinvesting 40 percent of earnings and growing at 4 percent a year.
a. Suppose CSI continues on this growth trend. What is the expected long-run rate of return from purchasing the stock at $100? What part of the $100 price is attributable to the present value of growth opportunities?
b. Now the MDC announces a plan for CSI to treat Cambridge sewage. CSI's plant will, therefore, be expanded gradually over five years. This means that CSI will have to reinvest 80 percent of its earnings for five years. Starting in year 6, however, it will again be able to pay out 60 percent of earnings. What will be CSI's stock price once this announcement is made and its consequences for CSI are known?

20. List at least four different formulas for calculating PV(horizon value) in a two-stage DCF valuation of a business. For each formula, describe a situation where that formula would be the best choice.

21. Look again at Table 4.7.
a. How do free cash flow and present value change if asset growth rate is only 15 percent in years 1 to 5? If value declines, explain why.
b. Suppose the business is a publicly traded company with one million shares outstanding. Then the company issues new stock to cover the present value of negative free cash flow for years 1 to 6. How many shares will be issued and at what price?
c. Value the company's one million existing shares by the two methods described in Section 4.5.

22. Icarus Air has one million shares outstanding and expects to earn a constant $10 million per year on its existing assets. All earnings will be paid out as dividends. Suppose that next year Icarus plans to double in size by issuing an additional one million shares at $100 a share. Everything will be the same as before but twice as big. Thus from year 2 onward the company earns a constant $20 million, all of which is paid out as dividends on the 20 million shares. What is the value of the company? What is the value of each existing Icarus Air share?

23. Look one more time at Table 4.1, which applies the DCF stock valuation formula to Fledgling Electronics. The CEO, having just learned that stock value is the present value of future dividends, proposes that Fledgling pay a bumper dividend of $15 a share in period 1. The extra cash would have to be raised by an issue of new shares. Recalculate Table 4.1 assuming that profits and payout ratios in all subsequent years are unchanged. You should find that the total present value of dividends *per existing share* is unchanged at $100. Why?

CHALLENGE QUESTIONS

1. Look again at Tables 4.3 (Growth-Tech) and 4.7 (Concatenator Manufacturing). Note the discontinuous increases in dividends and free cash flow when asset growth slows down. Now look at your answer to Practice Question 11: Dividends are expected to grow smoothly, although at a lower rate after year 3. Is there an error or hidden inconsistency in Practice Question 11? Write down a general rule or procedure for deciding how to forecast dividends or free cash flow.

2. The constant-growth DCF formula

$$P_0 = \frac{DIV_1}{r - g}$$

is sometimes written as

$$P_0 = \frac{ROE(1 - b)BVPS}{r - bROE}$$

where BVPS is book equity value per share, b is the plowback ratio, and ROE is the ratio of earnings per share to BVPS. Use this equation to show how the price-to-book ratio varies as ROE changes. What is price-to-book when $ROE = r$?

3. Portfolio managers are frequently paid a proportion of the funds under management. Suppose you manage a $100 million equity portfolio offering a dividend yield (DIV_1/P_0) of 5 percent. Dividends and portfolio value are expected to grow at a constant rate. Your annual fee for managing this portfolio is .5 percent of portfolio value and is calculated at the end of each year. Assuming that you will continue to manage the portfolio from now to eternity, what is the present value of the management contract?

MINI-CASE

Reeby Sports

Ten years ago, in 1993, George Reeby founded a small mail-order company selling high-quality sports equipment. Reeby Sports has grown steadily and been consistently profitable (see Table 4.8). The company has no debt and the equity is valued in the company's books at nearly $41 million (Table 4.9). It is still wholly owned by George Reeby.

George is now proposing to take the company public by the sale of 90,000 of his existing shares. The issue would not raise any additional cash for the company, but it would allow

TABLE 4.8

Summary income data (figures in $ millions).

Note: Reeby Sports has never paid a dividend and all the earnings have been retained in the business.

	1999	2000	2001	2002	2003
Cash flow	5.84	6.40	7.41	8.74	9.39
Depreciation	1.45	1.60	1.75	1.97	2.22
Pretax profits	4.38	4.80	5.66	6.77	7.17
Tax	1.53	1.68	1.98	2.37	2.51
Aftertax profits	2.85	3.12	3.68	4.40	4.66

TABLE 4.9

Summary balance sheet for year ending December 31st (figures in $ millions).

Note: Reeby Sports has 200,000 common shares outstanding, wholly owned by George Reeby.

Assets			Liabilities and Equity		
	2002	2003		2002	2003
Cash & securities	3.12	3.61	Current liabilities	2.90	3.20
Other current assets	15.08	16.93			
Net fixed assets	20.75	23.38	Equity	36.05	40.71
Total	38.95	43.91	Total	38.95	43.91

George to cash in on part of his investment. It would also make it easier to raise the substantial capital sums that the firm would later need to finance expansion.

George's business has been mainly on the East Coast of the United States, but he plans to expand into the Midwest in 2005. This will require a substantial investment in new warehouse space and inventory. George is aware that it will take time to build up a new customer base, and in the meantime there is likely to be a temporary dip in profits. However, if the venture is successful, the company should be back to its current 12 percent return on book equity by 2010.

George settled down to estimate what his shares are worth. First he estimated the profits and investment through 2010 (Tables 4.10 and 4.11). The company's net working capital includes a growing proportion of cash and marketable securities which would help to meet the cost of the expansion into the Midwest. Nevertheless, it seemed likely that the company would need to raise about $4.3 million in 2005 by the sale of new shares. (George distrusted banks and was not prepared to borrow to finance the expansion.)

Until the new venture reached full profitability, dividend payments would have to be restricted to conserve cash, but from 2010 onward George expected the company to pay out about 40 percent of its net profits. As a first stab at valuing the company, George assumed that after 2010 it would earn 12 percent on book equity indefinitely and that the cost of capital for the firm was about 10 percent. But he also computed a more conservative valuation, which recognized that the mail-order sports business was likely to get intensely competitive by 2010. He also looked at the market valuation of a comparable business on the West Coast, Molly Sports. Molly's shares were currently priced at 50 percent above book value and were selling at a prospective price–earnings ratio of 12 and a dividend yield of 3 percent.

George realized that a second issue of shares in 2005 would dilute his holdings. He set about calculating the price at which these shares could be issued and the number of shares that would need to be sold. That allowed him to work out the dividends *per share* and to check his earlier valuation by calculating the present value of the stream of per-share dividends.

	2004	2005	2006	2007	2008	2009	2010
Cash flow	10.47	11.87	7.74	8.40	9.95	12.67	15.38
Depreciation	2.40	3.10	3.12	3.17	3.26	3.44	3.68
Pretax profits	8.08	8.77	4.62	5.23	6.69	9.23	11.69
Tax	2.83	3.07	1.62	1.83	2.34	3.23	4.09
Aftertax profits	5.25	5.70	3.00	3.40	4.35	6.00	7.60
Dividends	2.00	2.00	2.50	2.50	2.50	2.50	3.00
Retained profits	3.25	3.70	.50	.90	1.85	3.50	4.60

TABLE 4.10

Forecasted profits and dividends (figures in $ millions).

	2004	2005	2006	2007	2008	2009	2010
Gross investment in fixed assets	4.26	10.50	3.34	3.65	4.18	5.37	6.28
Investments in net working capital	1.39	.60	.28	.42	.93	1.57	2.00
Total	5.65	11.10	3.62	4.07	5.11	6.94	8.28

TABLE 4.11

Forecasted investment expenditures (figures in $ millions).

Questions

1. Use Tables 4.10 and 4.11 to forecast free cash flow for Reeby Sports from 2004 to 2010. What is the present value of these cash flows in 2003, including PV(horizon value) in 2010?

2. Use the information given for Molly Sports to check your forecast of horizon value. What would you recommend as a reasonable range for the present value of Reeby Sports?

3. What is the present value of a share of stock in the company? Give a reasonable range.

4. Reeby Sports will have to raise $4.3 million in 2005. Does this prospective share issue affect the per-share value of Reeby Sports in 2003? Explain.

CHAPTER FIVE

WHY NET PRESENT VALUE LEADS TO BETTER INVESTMENT DECISIONS THAN OTHER CRITERIA

IN THE FIRST four chapters we introduced, at times surreptitiously, most of the basic principles of the investment decision. In this chapter we begin by consolidating that knowledge. We then take a look at three other measures that companies sometimes use when making investment decisions. These are the project's payback period, its book rate of return, and its internal rate of return. The first two of these measures have little to do with whether the project will increase shareholders' wealth. The project's internal rate of return—if used correctly—should always identify projects that increase shareholder wealth. However, we shall see that the internal rate of return sets several traps for the unwary.

We conclude the chapter by showing how to cope with situations when the firm has only limited capital. This raises two problems. One is computational. In simple cases we just choose those projects that give the highest NPV per dollar of investment. But capital constraints and project interactions often create problems of such complexity that linear programming is needed to sort through the possible alternatives. The other problem is to decide whether capital rationing really exists and whether it invalidates net present value as a criterion for capital budgeting. Guess what? NPV, properly interpreted, wins out in the end.

 ## 5.1 A REVIEW OF THE BASICS

Vegetron's chief financial officer (CFO) is wondering how to analyze a proposed $1 million investment in a new venture called project X. He asks what you think.

Your response should be as follows: "First, forecast the cash flows generated by project X over its economic life. Second, determine the appropriate opportunity cost of capital. This should reflect both the time value of money and the risk involved in project X. Third, use this opportunity cost of capital to discount the future cash flows of project X. The sum of the discounted cash flows is called present value (PV). Fourth, calculate *net* present value (NPV) by subtracting the $1 million investment from PV. Invest in project X if its NPV is greater than zero."

However, Vegetron's CFO is unmoved by your sagacity. He asks why NPV is so important.

Your reply: "Let us look at what is best for Vegetron stockholders. They want you to make their Vegetron shares as valuable as possible."

"Right now Vegetron's total market value (price per share times the number of shares outstanding) is $10 million. That includes $1 million cash we can invest in project X. The value of Vegetron's other assets and opportunities must therefore be $9 million. We have to decide whether it is better to keep the $1 million cash and reject project X or to spend the cash and accept project X. Let us call the value of the new project PV. Then the choice is as follows:

| | Market Value ($ millions) | |
Asset	Reject Project X	Accept Project X
Cash	1	0
Other assets	9	9
Project X	0	PV
	10	9 + PV

FIGURE 5.1

The firm can either keep and reinvest cash or return it to investors. (Arrows represent possible cash flows or transfers.) If cash is reinvested, the opportunity cost is the expected rate of return that shareholders could have obtained by investing in financial assets.

"Clearly project X is worthwhile if its present value, PV, is greater than $1 million, that is, if net present value is positive."

CFO: "How do I know that the PV of project X will actually show up in Vegetron's market value?"

Your reply: "Suppose we set up a new, independent firm X, whose only asset is project X. What would be the market value of firm X?

"Investors would forecast the dividends firm X would pay and discount those dividends by the expected rate of return of securities having risks comparable to firm X. We know that stock prices are equal to the present value of forecasted dividends.

"Since project X is firm X's only asset, the dividend payments we would expect firm X to pay are exactly the cash flows we have forecasted for project X. Moreover, the rate investors would use to discount firm X's dividends is exactly the rate we should use to discount project X's cash flows.

"I agree that firm X is entirely hypothetical. But if project X is accepted, investors holding Vegetron stock will really hold a portfolio of project X and the firm's other assets. We know the other assets are worth $9 million considered as a separate venture. Since asset values add up, we can easily figure out the portfolio value once we calculate the value of project X as a separate venture.

"By calculating the present value of project X, we are replicating the process by which the common stock of firm X would be valued in capital markets."

CFO: "The one thing I don't understand is where the discount rate comes from."

Your reply: "I agree that the discount rate is difficult to measure precisely. But it is easy to see what we are *trying* to measure. The discount rate is the opportunity cost of investing in the project rather than in the capital market. In other words, instead of accepting a project, the firm can always give the cash to the shareholders and let them invest it in financial assets.

"You can see the trade-off (Figure 5.1). The opportunity cost of taking the project is the return shareholders could have earned had they invested the funds on their own. When we discount the project's cash flows by the expected rate of return on comparable financial assets, we are measuring how much investors would be prepared to pay for your project."

"But which financial assets?" Vegetron's CFO queries. "The fact that investors expect only 12 percent on IBM stock does not mean that we should purchase Fly-by-Night Electronics if it offers 13 percent."

Your reply: "The opportunity-cost concept makes sense only if assets of equivalent risk are compared. In general, you should identify financial assets with risks equivalent to the project under consideration, estimate the expected rate of return on these assets, and use this rate as the opportunity cost."

Net Present Value's Competitors

Let us hope that the CFO is by now convinced of the correctness of the net present value rule. But it is possible that the CFO has also heard of some alternative investment criteria and would like to know why you do not recommend any of them. Just so that you are prepared, we will now look at three of the alternatives. They are:

1. The book rate of return.
2. The payback period.
3. The internal rate of return.

Later in the chapter we shall come across one further investment criterion, the profitability index. There are circumstances in which this measure has some special advantages.

Three Points to Remember about NPV

As we look at these alternative criteria, it is worth keeping in mind the following key features of the net present value rule. First, the NPV rule recognizes that *a dollar today is worth more than a dollar tomorrow,* because the dollar today can be invested to start earning interest immediately. Any investment rule which does not recognize the *time value of money* cannot be sensible. Second, net present value depends solely on the *forecasted cash flows* from the project and the *opportunity cost of capital.* Any investment rule which is affected by the manager's tastes, the company's choice of accounting method, the profitability of the company's existing business, or the profitability of other independent projects will lead to inferior decisions. Third, *because present values are all measured in today's dollars, you can add them up.* Therefore, if you have two projects A and B, the net present value of the combined investment is

$$NPV(A + B) = NPV(A) + NPV(B)$$

This additivity property has important implications. Suppose project B has a negative NPV. If you tack it onto project A, the joint project (A + B) will have a lower NPV than A on its own. Therefore, you are unlikely to be misled into accepting a poor project (B) just because it is packaged with a good one (A). As we shall see, the alternative measures do not have this additivity property. If you are not careful, you may be tricked into deciding that a package of a good and a bad project is better than the good project on its own.

NPV Depends on Cash Flow, Not Accounting Income

Net present value depends only on the project's cash flows and the opportunity cost of capital. But when companies report to shareholders, they do not simply show the cash flows. They also report book—that is, accounting—income and book assets; book income gets most of the immediate attention.

Financial managers sometimes use these numbers to calculate a book rate of return on a proposed investment. In other words, they look at the prospective book income as a proportion of the book value of the assets that the firm is proposing to acquire:

$$\text{Book rate of return} = \frac{\text{book income}}{\text{book assets}}$$

Cash flows and book income are often very different. For example, the accountant labels some cash outflows as *capital investments* and others as *operating expenses.* The operating expenses are, of course, deducted immediately from each year's income. The capital expenditures are put on the firm's balance sheet and then depreciated according to an arbitrary schedule chosen by the accountant. The annual depreciation charge is deducted from each year's income. Thus the book rate of return depends on which items the accountant chooses to treat as capital investments and how rapidly they are depreciated.[1]

Now the merits of an investment project do not depend on how accountants classify the cash flows[2] and few companies these days make investment decisions just on the basis of the book rate of return. But managers know that the company's shareholders pay considerable attention to book measures of profitability and naturally, therefore, they think (and worry) about how major projects would affect the company's book return. Those projects that will reduce the company's book return may be scrutinized more carefully by senior management.

You can see the dangers here. The book rate of return may not be a good measure of true profitability. It is also an *average* across all of the firm's activities. The average profitability of past investments is not usually the right hurdle for new investments. Think of a firm that has been exceptionally lucky and successful. Say its average book return is 24 percent, double shareholders' 12 percent opportunity cost of capital. Should it demand that all *new* investments offer 24 percent or better? Clearly not: That would mean passing up many positive-NPV opportunities with rates of return between 12 and 24 percent.

We will come back to the book rate of return in Chapter 12, when we look more closely at accounting measures of financial performance.

 ## 5.2 PAYBACK

Some companies require that the initial outlay on any project should be recoverable within a specified period. The **payback** period of a project is found by counting the number of years it takes before the cumulative forecasted cash flow equals the initial investment.

---

[1]This chapter's mini-case contains simple illustrations of how book rates of return are calculated and of the difference between accounting income and project cash flow. Read the case if you wish to refresh your understanding of these topics. Better still, do the case calculations.

[2]Of course, the depreciation method used for tax purposes does have cash consequences which should be taken into account in calculating NPV. We cover depreciation and taxes in the next chapter.

Consider the following three projects:

	Cash Flows ($)				Payback	
Project	C_0	C_1	C_2	C_3	Period (years)	NPV at 10%
A	−2,000	500	500	5,000	3	+2,624
B	−2,000	500	1,800	0	2	−58
C	−2,000	1,800	500	0	2	+50

Project A involves an initial investment of $2,000 ($C_0 = -2,000$) followed by cash inflows during the next three years. Suppose the opportunity cost of capital is 10 percent. Then project A has an NPV of +$2,624:

$$NPV(A) = -2,000 + \frac{500}{1.10} + \frac{500}{1.10^2} + \frac{5,000}{1.10^3} = +\$2,624$$

Project B also requires an initial investment of $2,000 but produces a cash inflow of $500 in year 1 and $1,800 in year 2. At a 10 percent opportunity cost of capital project B has an NPV of −$58:

$$NPV(B) = -2,000 + \frac{500}{1.10} + \frac{1,800}{1.10^2} = -\$58$$

The third project, C, involves the same initial outlay as the other two projects but its first-period cash flow is larger. It has an NPV of +$50.

$$NPV(C) = -2,000 + \frac{1,800}{1.10} + \frac{500}{1.10^2} = +\$50$$

The net present value rule tells us to accept projects A and C but to reject project B.

The Payback Rule

Now look at how rapidly each project pays back its initial investment. With project A you take three years to recover the $2,000 investment; with projects B and C you take only two years. If the firm used the payback *rule* with a cutoff period of two years, it would accept only projects B and C; if it used the payback rule with a cutoff period of three or more years, it would accept all three projects. Therefore, regardless of the choice of cutoff period, the payback rule gives answers different from the net present value rule.

You can see why payback can give misleading answers:

1. *The payback rule ignores all cash flows after the cutoff date.* If the cutoff date is two years, the payback rule rejects project A regardless of the size of the cash inflow in year 3.
2. *The payback rule gives equal weight to all cash flows before the cutoff date.* The payback rule says that projects B and C are equally attractive, but, because C's cash inflows occur earlier, C has the higher net present value at any discount rate.

In order to use the payback rule, a firm has to decide on an appropriate cutoff date. If it uses the same cutoff regardless of project life, it will tend to accept many poor short-lived projects and reject many good long-lived ones.

Some companies discount the cash flows before they compute the payback period. The **discounted-payback rule** asks, How many periods does the project have to last in order to make sense in terms of net present value? This modification to the payback rule surmounts the objection that equal weight is given to all flows before the cutoff date. However, the discounted-payback rule still takes no account of any cash flows after the cutoff date.

5.3 INTERNAL (OR DISCOUNTED-CASH-FLOW) RATE OF RETURN

Whereas payback and return on book are ad hoc measures, internal rate of return has a much more respectable ancestry and is recommended in many finance texts. If, therefore, we dwell more on its deficiencies, it is not because they are more numerous but because they are less obvious.

In Chapter 2 we noted that net present value could also be expressed in terms of rate of return, which would lead to the following rule: "Accept investment opportunities offering rates of return in excess of their opportunity costs of capital." That statement, properly interpreted, is absolutely correct. However, interpretation is not always easy for long-lived investment projects.

There is no ambiguity in defining the true rate of return of an investment that generates a single payoff after one period:

$$\text{Rate of return} = \frac{\text{payoff}}{\text{investment}} - 1$$

Alternatively, we could write down the NPV of the investment and find that discount rate which makes NPV = 0.

$$\text{NPV} = C_0 + \frac{C_1}{1 + \text{discount rate}} = 0$$

implies

$$\text{Discount rate} = \frac{C_1}{-C_0} - 1$$

Of course C_1 is the payoff and $-C_0$ is the required investment, and so our two equations say exactly the same thing. *The discount rate that makes NPV = 0 is also the rate of return.*

Unfortunately, there is no wholly satisfactory way of defining the true rate of return of a long-lived asset. The best available concept is the so-called **discounted-cash-flow (DCF) rate of return** or **internal rate of return (IRR)**. The internal rate of return is used frequently in finance. It can be a handy measure, but, as we shall see, it can also be a misleading measure. You should, therefore, know how to calculate it and how to use it properly.

The internal rate of return is defined as the rate of discount which makes NPV = 0. This means that to find the IRR for an investment project lasting T years, we must solve for IRR in the following expression:

$$\text{NPV} = C_0 + \frac{C_1}{1 + \text{IRR}} + \frac{C_2}{(1 + \text{IRR})^2} + \cdots + \frac{C_T}{(1 + \text{IRR})^T} = 0$$

Actual calculation of IRR usually involves trial and error. For example, consider a project that produces the following flows:

Cash Flows ($)		
C_0	C_1	C_2
-4,000	+2,000	+4,000

The internal rate of return is IRR in the equation

$$NPV = -4,000 + \frac{2,000}{1 + IRR} + \frac{4,000}{(1 + IRR)^2} = 0$$

Let us arbitrarily try a zero discount rate. In this case NPV is not zero but +$2,000:

$$NPV = -4,000 + \frac{2,000}{1.0} + \frac{4,000}{(1.0)^2} = +\$2,000$$

The NPV is positive; therefore, the IRR must be greater than zero. The next step might be to try a discount rate of 50 percent. In this case net present value is -$889:

$$NPV = -4,000 + \frac{2,000}{1.50} + \frac{4,000}{(1.50)^2} = -\$889$$

The NPV is negative; therefore, the IRR must be less than 50 percent. In Figure 5.2 we have plotted the net present values implied by a range of discount rates. From this we can see that a discount rate of 28 percent gives the desired net present value of zero. Therefore IRR is 28 percent.

The easiest way to calculate IRR, if you have to do it by hand, is to plot three or four combinations of NPV and discount rate on a graph like Figure 5.2, connect the

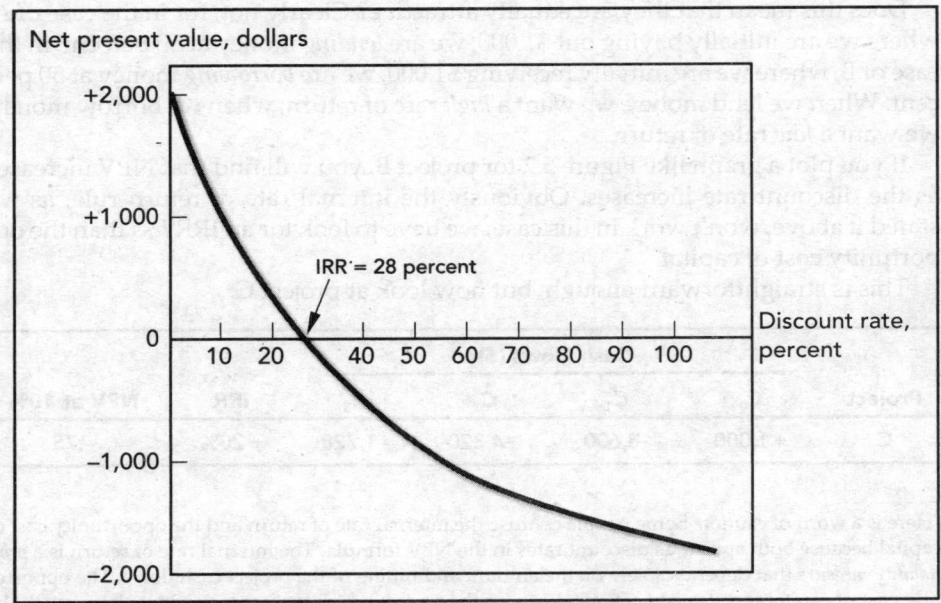

FIGURE 5.2

This project costs $4,000 and then produces cash inflows of $2,000 in year 1 and $4,000 in year 2. Its internal rate of return (IRR) is 28 percent, the rate of discount at which NPV is zero.

points with a smooth line, and read off the discount rate at which NPV = 0. It is of course quicker and more accurate to use a computer or a specially programmed calculator, and this is what most financial managers do.

Now, the *internal rate of return rule* is to accept an investment project if the opportunity cost of capital is less than the internal rate of return. You can see the reasoning behind this idea if you look again at Figure 5.2. If the opportunity cost of capital is less than the 28 percent IRR, then the project has a *positive* NPV when discounted at the opportunity cost of capital. If it is equal to the IRR, the project has a *zero* NPV. And if it is greater than the IRR, the project has a *negative* NPV. Therefore, when we compare the opportunity cost of capital with the IRR on our project, we are effectively asking whether our project has a positive NPV. This is true not only for our example. The rule will give the same answer as the net present value rule *whenever the NPV of a project is a smoothly declining function of the discount rate.*[3]

Many firms use internal rate of return as a criterion in preference to net present value. We think that this is a pity. Although, properly stated, the two criteria are formally equivalent, the internal rate of return rule contains several pitfalls.

Pitfall 1—Lending or Borrowing?

Not all cash-flow streams have NPVs that decline as the discount rate increases. Consider the following projects A and B:

Project	Cash Flows ($)		IRR	NPV at 10%
	C_0	C_1		
A	−1,000	+1,500	+50%	+364
B	+1,000	−1,500	+50%	−364

Each project has an IRR of 50 percent. (In other words, −1,000 + 1,500/1.50 = 0 *and* + 1,000 − 1,500/1.50 = 0.)

Does this mean that they are equally attractive? Clearly not, for in the case of A, where we are initially paying out $1,000, we are *lending* money at 50 percent; in the case of B, where we are initially receiving $1,000, we are *borrowing* money at 50 percent. When we lend money, we want a *high* rate of return; when we borrow money, we want a *low* rate of return.

If you plot a graph like Figure 5.2 for project B, you will find that NPV increases as the discount rate increases. Obviously the internal rate of return rule, as we stated it above, won't work in this case; we have to look for an IRR *less* than the opportunity cost of capital.

This is straightforward enough, but now look at project C:

Project	Cash Flows ($)				IRR	NPV at 10%
	C_0	C_1	C_2	C_3		
C	+1,000	−3,600	+4,320	−1,728	+20%	−.75

---

[3]Here is a word of caution: Some people confuse the internal rate of return and the opportunity cost of capital because both appear as discount rates in the NPV formula. The internal rate of return is a *profitability measure* that depends solely on the amount and timing of the project cash flows. The opportunity cost of capital is a *standard of profitability* for the project which we use to calculate how much the project is worth. The opportunity cost of capital is established in capital markets. It is the expected rate of return offered by other assets equivalent in risk to the project being evaluated.

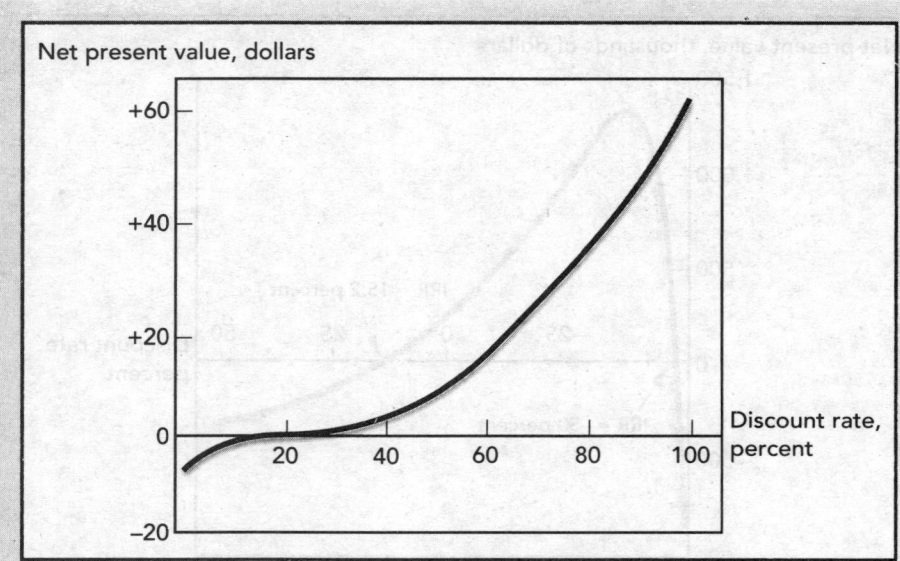

FIGURE 5.3

The NPV of project C increases as the discount rate increases.

It turns out that project C has zero NPV at a 20 percent discount rate. If the opportunity cost of capital is 10 percent, that means the project is a good one. Or does it? In part, project C is like borrowing money, because we receive money now and pay it out in the first period; it is also partly like lending money because we pay out money in period 1 and recover it in period 2. Should we accept or reject? The only way to find the answer is to look at the net present value. Figure 5.3 shows that the NPV of our project *increases* as the discount rate increases. If the opportunity cost of capital is 10 percent (i.e., less than the IRR), the project has a very small negative NPV and we should reject.

Pitfall 2—Multiple Rates of Return

In most countries there is usually a short delay between the time when a company receives income and the time it pays tax on the income. Consider the case of Albert Vore, who needs to assess a proposed advertising campaign by the vegetable canning company of which he is financial manager. The campaign involves an initial outlay of $1 million but is expected to increase pretax profits by $300,000 in each of the next five periods. The tax rate is 50 percent, and taxes are paid with a delay of one period. Thus the expected cash flows from the investment are as follows:

	Cash Flows ($ thousands)						
	Period						
	0	1	2	3	4	5	6
Pretax flow	−1,000	+300	+300	+300	+300	+300	
Tax		+500	−150	−150	−150	−150	−150
Net flow	−1,000	+800	+150	+150	+150	+150	−150

Note: The $1 million outlay in period 0 *reduces* the company's taxes in period 1 by $500,000; thus we enter +500 in year 1.

FIGURE 5.4

The advertising campaign has two internal rates of return. NPV = 0 when the discount rate is −50 percent and when it is +15.2 percent.

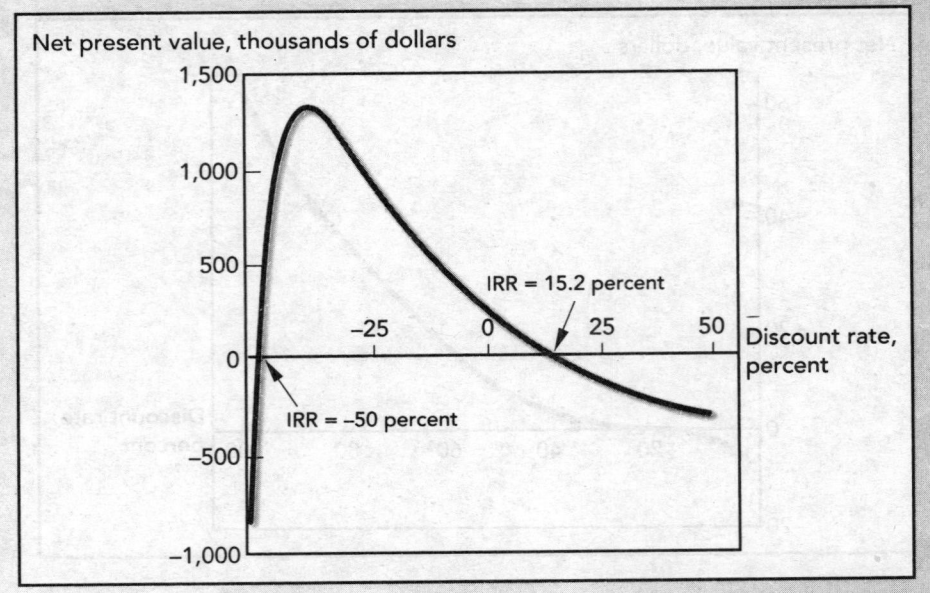

Mr. Vore calculates the project's IRR and its NPV as follows:

IRR (%)	NPV at 10%
−50 and 15.2	74.9 or $74,900

Note that there are *two* discount rates that make NPV = 0. That is, *each of the following statements holds:*

$$NPV = -1,000 + \frac{800}{.50} + \frac{150}{(.50)^2} + \frac{150}{(.50)^3} + \frac{150}{(.50)^4} + \frac{150}{(.50)^5} - \frac{150}{(.50)^6} = 0$$

and

$$NPV = -1,000 + \frac{800}{1.152} + \frac{150}{(1.152)^2} + \frac{150}{(1.152)^3} + \frac{150}{(1.152)^4} + \frac{150}{(1.152)^5}$$
$$- \frac{150}{(1.152)^6} = 0$$

In other words, the investment has an IRR of both −50 *and* 15.2 percent. Figure 5.4 shows how this comes about. As the discount rate increases, NPV initially rises and then declines. The reason for this is the double change in the sign of the cash-flow stream. There can be as many different internal rates of return for a project as there are changes in the sign of the cash flows.[4]

---

[4]By Descartes's "rule of signs" there can be as many different solutions to a polynomial as there are changes of sign. For a discussion of the problem of multiple rates of return, see J. H. Lorie and L. J. Savage, "Three Problems in Rationing Capital," *Journal of Business* 28 (October 1955), pp. 229–239; and E. Solomon, "The Arithmetic of Capital Budgeting," *Journal of Business* 29 (April 1956), pp. 124–129.

In our example the double change in sign was caused by a lag in tax payments, but this is not the only way that it can occur. For example, many projects involve substantial decommissioning costs. If you strip-mine coal, you may have to invest large sums to reclaim the land after the coal is mined. Thus a new mine creates an initial investment (negative cash flow up front), a series of positive cash flows, and an ending cash outflow for reclamation. The cash-flow stream changes sign twice, and mining companies typically see two IRRs.

As if this is not difficult enough, there are also cases in which *no* internal rate of return exists. For example, project D has a positive net present value at all discount rates:

Project	Cash Flows ($)			IRR (%)	NPV at 10%
	C_0	C_1	C_2		
D	+1,000	−3,000	+2,500	None	+339

A number of adaptations of the IRR rule have been devised for such cases. Not only are they inadequate, but they also are unnecessary, for the simple solution is to use net present value.[5]

Pitfall 3—Mutually Exclusive Projects

Firms often have to choose from among several alternative ways of doing the same job or using the same facility. In other words, they need to choose from among **mutually exclusive projects.** Here too the IRR rule can be misleading.

Consider projects E and F:

Project	Cash Flows ($)		IRR (%)	NPV at 10%
	C_0	C_1		
E	−10,000	+20,000	100	+ 8,182
F	−20,000	+35,000	75	+11,818

---

[5]Companies sometimes get around the problem of multiple rates of return by discounting the later cash flows back at the cost of capital until there remains only one change in the sign of the cash flows. A *modified internal rate of return* can then be calculated on this revised series. In our example, the modified IRR is calculated as follows:

1. Calculate the present value of the year 6 cash flow in year 5:

$$\text{PV in year } 5 = -150/1.10 = -136.36$$

2. Add to the year 5 cash flow the present value of subsequent cash flows:

$$C_5 + \text{PV(subsequent cash flows)} = 150 - 136.36 = 13.64$$

3. Since there is now only one change in the sign of the cash flows, the revised series has a unique rate of return, which is 15 percent:

$$\text{NPV} = -1,000 + \frac{800}{1.15} + \frac{150}{1.15^2} + \frac{150}{1.15^3} + \frac{150}{1.15^4} + \frac{13.64}{1.15^5} = 0$$

Since the modified IRR of 15 percent is greater than the cost of capital (and the initial cash flow is negative), the project has a positive NPV when valued at the cost of capital.

Of course, it would be much easier in such cases to abandon the IRR rule and just calculate project NPV.

Perhaps project E is a manually controlled machine tool and project F is the same tool with the addition of computer control. Both are good investments, but F has the higher NPV and is, therefore, better. However, the IRR rule seems to indicate that if you have to choose, you should go for E since it has the higher IRR. If you follow the IRR rule, you have the satisfaction of earning a 100 percent rate of return; if you follow the NPV rule, you are $11,818 richer.

You can salvage the IRR rule in these cases by looking at the internal rate of return on the incremental flows. Here is how to do it: First, consider the smaller project (E in our example). It has an IRR of 100 percent, which is well in excess of the 10 percent opportunity cost of capital. You know, therefore, that E is acceptable. You now ask yourself whether it is worth making the additional $10,000 investment in F. The incremental flows from undertaking F rather than E are as follows:

Project	Cash Flows ($)		IRR (%)	NPV at 10%
	C_0	C_1		
F–E	–10,000	+15,000	50	+3,636

The IRR on the incremental investment is 50 percent, which is also well in excess of the 10 percent opportunity cost of capital. So you should prefer project F to project E.[6]

Unless you look at the incremental expenditure, IRR is unreliable in ranking projects of different scale. It is also unreliable in ranking projects which offer different patterns of cash flow over time. For example, suppose the firm can take project G *or* project H but not both (ignore I for the moment):

Project	Cash Flows ($)							IRR (%)	NPV at 10%
	C_0	C_1	C_2	C_3	C_4	C_5	Etc.		
G	–9,000	+6,000	+5,000	+4,000	0	0	. . .	33	3,592
H	–9,000	+1,800	+1,800	+1,800	+1,800	+1,800	. . .	20	9,000
I		–6,000	+1,200	+1,200	±1,200	+1,200	. . .	20	6,000

Project G has a higher IRR, but project H has the higher NPV. Figure 5.5 shows why the two rules give different answers. The blue line gives the net present value of project G at different rates of discount. Since a discount rate of 33 percent produces a net present value of zero, this is the internal rate of return for project G. Similarly, the burgundy line shows the net present value of project H at different discount rates. The IRR of project H is 20 percent. (We assume project H's cash flows continue indefinitely.) Note that project H has a higher NPV so long as the opportunity cost of capital is less than 15.6 percent.

The reason that IRR is misleading is that the total cash inflow of project H is larger but tends to occur later. Therefore, when the discount rate is low, H has the higher NPV; when the discount rate is high, G has the higher NPV. (You can see from Figure 5.5 that the two projects have the *same* NPV when the discount rate is 15.6 percent.) The internal rates of return on the two projects tell us that at a discount rate of 20 percent H has a zero NPV (IRR = 20 percent) and G has a positive

---

[6]You may, however, find that you have jumped out of the frying pan into the fire. The series of incremental cash flows may involve several changes in sign. In this case there are likely to be multiple IRRs and you will be forced to use the NPV rule after all.

FIGURE 5.5

The IRR of project G exceeds that of project H, but the NPV of project G is higher *only* if the discount rate is greater than 15.6 percent.

NPV. Thus if the opportunity cost of capital were 20 percent, investors would place a higher value on the shorter-lived project G. But in our example the opportunity cost of capital is not 20 percent but 10 percent. Investors are prepared to pay relatively high prices for longer-lived securities, and so they will pay a relatively high price for the longer-lived project. At a 10 percent cost of capital, an investment in H has an NPV of $9,000 and an investment in G has an NPV of only $3,592.[7]

This is a favorite example of ours. We have gotten many businesspeople's reaction to it. When asked to choose between G and H, many choose G. The reason seems to be the rapid payback generated by project G. In other words, they believe that if they take G, they will also be able to take a later project like I (note that I can be financed using the cash flows from G), whereas if they take H, they won't have money enough for I. In other words they implicitly assume that it is a *shortage of capital* which forces the choice between G and H. When this implicit assumption is brought out, they usually admit that H is better if there is no capital shortage.

But the introduction of capital constraints raises two further questions. The first stems from the fact that most of the executives preferring G to H work for firms that would have no difficulty raising more capital. Why would a manager at IBM, say, choose G on the grounds of limited capital? IBM can raise plenty of capital and can take project I regardless of whether G or H is chosen; therefore I should not affect the choice between G and H. The answer seems to be that large firms usually impose capital budgets on divisions and subdivisions as a part of the firm's planning and control system. Since the system is complicated and cumbersome, the

---

[7]It is often suggested that the choice between the net present value rule and the internal rate of return rule should depend on the probable reinvestment rate. This is wrong. The prospective return on another *independent* investment should *never* be allowed to influence the investment decision. For a discussion of the reinvestment assumption see A. A. Alchian, "The Rate of Interest, Fisher's Rate of Return over Cost and Keynes' Internal Rate of Return," *American Economic Review* 45 (December 1955), pp. 938–942.

budgets are not easily altered, and so they are perceived as real constraints by middle management.

The second question is this. If there is a capital constraint, either real or self-imposed, should IRR be used to rank projects? The answer is no. The problem in this case is to find that package of investment projects which satisfies the capital constraint and has the largest net present value. The IRR rule will not identify this package. As we will show in the next section, the only practical and general way to do so is to use the technique of linear programming.

When we have to choose between projects G and H, it is easiest to compare the net present values. But if your heart is set on the IRR rule, you can use it as long as you look at the internal rate of return on the incremental flows. The procedure is exactly the same as we showed above. First, you check that project G has a satisfactory IRR. Then you look at the return on the additional investment in H.

	Cash Flows ($)							IRR	NPV
Project	C_0	C_1	C_2	C_3	C_4	C_5	Etc.	(%)	at 10%
H–G	0	–4,200	–3,200	–2,200	+1,800	+1,800	...	15.6	+5,408

The IRR on the incremental investment in H is 15.6 percent. Since this is greater than the opportunity cost of capital, you should undertake H rather than G.

Pitfall 4—What Happens When We Can't Finesse the Term Structure of Interest Rates?

We have simplified our discussion of capital budgeting by assuming that the opportunity cost of capital is the same for all the cash flows, C_1, C_2, C_3, etc. This is not the right place to discuss the term structure of interest rates, but we must point out certain problems with the IRR rule that crop up when short-term interest rates are different from long-term rates.

Remember our most general formula for calculating net present value:

$$NPV = C_0 + \frac{C_1}{1 + r_1} + \frac{C_2}{(1 + r_2)^2} + \frac{C_3}{(1 + r_3)^3} + \cdots$$

In other words, we discount C_1 at the opportunity cost of capital for one year, C_2 at the opportunity cost of capital for two years, and so on. The IRR rule tells us to accept a project if the IRR is greater than the opportunity cost of capital. But what do we do when we have several opportunity costs? Do we compare IRR with $r_1, r_2, r_3, \ldots$? Actually we would have to compute a complex weighted average of these rates to obtain a number comparable to IRR.

What does this mean for capital budgeting? It means trouble for the IRR rule whenever the term structure of interest rates becomes important.[8] In a situation where it is important, we have to compare the project IRR with the expected IRR (yield to maturity) offered by a traded security that (1) is equivalent in risk to the project and (2) offers the same time pattern of cash flows as the project. Such a comparison is easier said than done. It is much better to forget about IRR and just calculate NPV.

---

[8] The source of the difficulty is that the IRR is a derived figure without any simple economic interpretation. If we wish to define it, we can do no more than say that it is the discount rate which applied to all cash flows makes NPV = 0. The problem here is not that the IRR is a nuisance to calculate but that it is not a useful number to have.

Many firms use the IRR, thereby implicitly assuming that there is no difference between short-term and long-term rates of interest. They do this for the same reason that we have so far finessed the term structure: simplicity.[9]

The Verdict on IRR

We have given four examples of things that can go wrong with IRR. We spent much less space on payback or return on book. Does this mean that IRR is worse than the other two measures? Quite the contrary. There is little point in dwelling on the deficiencies of payback or return on book. They are clearly ad hoc measures which often lead to silly conclusions. The IRR rule has a much more respectable ancestry. It is a less easy rule to use than NPV, but, used properly, it gives the same answer.

Nowadays few large corporations use the payback period or return on book as their primary measure of project attractiveness. Most use discounted cash flow or "DCF," and for many companies DCF means IRR, not NPV. We find this puzzling, but it seems that IRR is easier to explain to nonfinancial managers, who think they know what it means to say that "Project G has a 33 percent return." But can these managers use IRR properly? We worry particularly about Pitfall 3. The financial manager never sees all possible projects. Most projects are proposed by operating managers. Will the operating managers' proposals have the highest NPVs or the highest IRRs?

A company that instructs nonfinancial managers to look first at projects' IRRs prompts a search for high-IRR projects. It also encourages the managers to *modify* projects so that their IRRs are higher. Where do you typically find the highest IRRs? In short-lived projects requiring relatively little up-front investment. Such projects may not add much to the value of the firm.

5.4 CHOOSING CAPITAL INVESTMENTS WHEN RESOURCES ARE LIMITED

Our entire discussion of methods of capital budgeting has rested on the proposition that the wealth of a firm's shareholders is highest if the firm accepts *every* project that has a positive net present value. Suppose, however, that there are limitations on the investment program that prevent the company from undertaking all such projects. Economists call this *capital rationing*. When capital is rationed, we need a method of selecting the package of projects that is within the company's resources yet gives the highest possible net present value.

An Easy Problem in Capital Rationing

Let us start with a simple example. The opportunity cost of capital is 10 percent, and our company has the following opportunities:

Project	Cash Flows ($ millions)			NPV at 10%
	C_0	C_1	C_2	
A	−10	+30	+5	21
B	−5	+5	+20	16
C	−5	+5	+15	12

[9]In Chapter 9 we will look at some other cases in which it would be misleading to use the same discount rate for both short-term and long-term cash flows.

All three projects are attractive, but suppose that the firm is limited to spending $10 million. In that case, it can invest *either* in project A *or* in projects B and C, but it cannot invest in all three. Although individually B and C have lower net present values than project A, when taken together they have the higher net present value. Here we cannot choose between projects solely on the basis of net present values. When funds are limited, we need to concentrate on getting the biggest bang for our buck. In other words, we must pick the projects that offer the highest net present value per dollar of initial outlay. This ratio is known as the **profitability index:**[10]

$$\text{Profitability index} = \frac{\text{net present value}}{\text{investment}}$$

For our three projects the profitability index is calculated as follows:[11]

Project	Investment ($ millions)	NPV ($ millions)	Profitability Index
A	10	21	2.1
B	5	16	3.2
C	5	12	2.4

Project B has the highest profitability index and C has the next highest. Therefore, if our budget limit is $10 million, we should accept these two projects.[12]

Unfortunately, there are some limitations to this simple ranking method. One of the most serious is that it breaks down whenever more than one resource is rationed. For example, suppose that the firm can raise only $10 million for investment in *each* of years 0 and 1 and that the menu of possible projects is expanded to include an investment next year in project D:

Project	Cash Flows ($ millions)			NPV at 10%	Profitability Index
	C_0	C_1	C_2		
A	−10	+30	+5	21	2.1
B	−5	+5	+20	16	3.2
C	−5	+5	+15	12	2.4
D	0	−40	+60	13	0.4

One strategy is to accept projects B and C; however, if we do this, we cannot also accept D, which costs more than our budget limit for period 1. An alternative is to

---

[10]If a project requires outlays in two or more periods, the denominator should be the present value of the outlays. (A few companies do not discount the benefits or costs before calculating the profitability index. The less said about these companies the better.)

[11]Sometimes the profitability index is defined as the ratio of the present value to initial outlay, that is, as PV/investment. This measure is also known as the *benefit–cost ratio*. To calculate the benefit–cost ratio, simply add 1.0 to each profitability index. Project rankings are unchanged.

[12]If a project has a positive profitability index, it must also have a positive NPV. Therefore, firms sometimes use the profitability index to select projects when capital is *not* limited. However, like the IRR, the profitability index can be misleading when used to choose between mutually exclusive projects. For example, suppose you were forced to choose between (1) investing $100 in a project whose payoffs have a present value of $200 or (2) investing $1 million in a project whose payoffs have a present value of $1.5 million. The first investment has the higher profitability index; the second makes you richer.

accept project A in period 0. Although this has a lower net present value than the combination of B and C, it provides a $30 million positive cash flow in period 1. When this is added to the $10 million budget, we can also afford to undertake D next year. A and D have *lower* profitability indexes than B and C, but they have a *higher* total net present value.

The reason that ranking on the profitability index fails in this example is that resources are constrained in each of two periods. In fact, this ranking method is inadequate whenever there is *any* other constraint on the choice of projects. This means that it cannot cope with cases in which two projects are mutually exclusive or in which one project is dependent on another.

Some More Elaborate Capital Rationing Models

The simplicity of the profitability-index method may sometimes outweigh its limitations. For example, it may not pay to worry about expenditures in subsequent years if you have only a hazy notion of future capital availability or investment opportunities. But there are also circumstances in which the limitations of the profitability-index method are intolerable. For such occasions we need a more general method for solving the capital rationing problem.

We begin by restating the problem just described. Suppose that we were to accept proportion x_A of project A in our example. Then the net present value of our investment in the project would be $21x_A$. Similarly, the net present value of our investment in project B can be expressed as $16x_B$, and so on. Our objective is to select the set of projects with the highest *total* net present value. In other words we wish to find the values of x that maximize

$$\text{NPV} = 21x_A + 16x_B + 12x_C + 13x_D$$

Our choice of projects is subject to several constraints. First, total cash outflow in period 0 must not be greater than $10 million. In other words,

$$10x_A + 5x_B + 5x_C + 0x_D \leq 10$$

Similarly, total outflow in period 1 must not be greater than $10 million:

$$-30x_A - 5x_B - 5x_C + 40x_D \leq 10$$

Finally, we cannot invest a negative amount in a project, and we cannot purchase more than one of each. Therefore we have

$$0 \leq x_A \leq 1, \quad 0 \leq x_B \leq 1, \ldots$$

Collecting all these conditions, we can summarize the problem as follows:

Maximize $21x_A + 16x_B + 12x_C + 13x_D$

Subject to

$$10x_A + 5x_B + 5x_C + 0x_D \leq 10$$
$$-30x_A - 5x_B - 5x_C + 40x_D \leq 10$$
$$0 \leq x_A \leq 1, \quad 0 \leq x_B \leq 1, \ldots$$

One way to tackle such a problem is to keep selecting different values for the x's, noting which combination both satisfies the constraints and gives the highest net present value. But it's smarter to recognize that the equations above constitute a linear programming (LP) problem. It can be handed to a computer equipped to solve LPs.

The answer given by the LP method is somewhat different from the one we obtained earlier. Instead of investing in one unit of project A and one of project D, we are told to take half of project A, all of project B, and three-quarters of D. The reason is simple. The computer is a dumb, but obedient, pet, and since we did not tell it that the x's had to be whole numbers, it saw no reason to make them so. By accepting "fractional" projects, it is possible to increase NPV by $2.25 million. For many purposes this is quite appropriate. If project A represents an investment in 1,000 square feet of warehouse space or in 1,000 tons of steel plate, it might be feasible to accept 500 square feet or 500 tons and quite reasonable to assume that cash flow would be reduced proportionately. If, however, project A is a single crane or oil well, such fractional investments make little sense.

When fractional projects are not feasible, we can use a form of linear programming known as *integer* (or *zero-one*) *programming*, which limits all the x's to integers.

Uses of Capital Rationing Models

Linear programming models seem tailor-made for solving capital budgeting problems when resources are limited. Why then are they not universally accepted either in theory or in practice? One reason is that these models can turn out to be very complex. Second, as with any sophisticated long-range planning tool, there is the general problem of getting good data. It is just not worth applying costly, sophisticated methods to poor data. Furthermore, these models are based on the assumption that all future investment opportunities are known. In reality, the discovery of investment ideas is an unfolding process.

Our most serious misgivings center on the basic assumption that capital is limited. When we come to discuss company financing, we shall see that most large corporations do not face capital rationing and can raise large sums of money on fair terms. Why then do many company presidents tell their subordinates that capital is limited? If they are right, the capital market is seriously imperfect. What then are they doing maximizing NPV?[13] We might be tempted to suppose that if capital is not rationed, they do not *need* to use linear programming and, if it is rationed, then surely they *ought* not to use it. But that would be too quick a judgment. Let us look at this problem more deliberately.

Soft Rationing Many firms' capital constraints are "soft." They reflect no imperfections in capital markets. Instead they are provisional limits adopted by management as an aid to financial control.

Some ambitious divisional managers habitually overstate their investment opportunities. Rather than trying to distinguish which projects really are worthwhile, headquarters may find it simpler to impose an upper limit on divisional expenditures and thereby force the divisions to set their own priorities. In such instances budget limits are a rough but effective way of dealing with biased cash-flow forecasts. In other cases management may believe that very rapid corporate growth could impose intolerable strains on management and the organization. Since it is difficult to quantify such constraints explicitly, the budget limit may be used as a proxy.

Because such budget limits have nothing to do with any inefficiency in the capital market, there is no contradiction in using an LP model in the division to maximize net present value subject to the budget constraint. On the other hand, there

---

[13]Don't forget that in Chapter 2 we had to assume perfect capital markets to derive the NPV rule.

is not much point in elaborate selection procedures if the cash-flow forecasts of the division are seriously biased.

Even if capital is not rationed, other resources may be. The availability of management time, skilled labor, or even other capital equipment often constitutes an important constraint on a company's growth.

Hard Rationing   Soft rationing should never cost the firm anything. If capital constraints become tight enough to hurt—in the sense that projects with significant positive NPVs are passed up—then the firm raises more money and loosens the constraint. But what if it *can't* raise more money—what if it faces *hard* rationing?

Hard rationing implies market imperfections, but that does not necessarily mean we have to throw away net present value as a criterion for capital budgeting. It depends on the nature of the imperfection.

Arizona Aquaculture, Inc. (AAI), borrows as much as the banks will lend it, yet it still has good investment opportunities. This is not hard rationing so long as AAI can issue stock. But perhaps it can't. Perhaps the founder and majority shareholder vetoes the idea from fear of losing control of the firm. Perhaps a stock issue would bring costly red tape or legal complications.[14]

This does not invalidate the NPV rule. AAI's *shareholders* can borrow or lend, sell their shares, or buy more. They have free access to security markets. The type of portfolio they hold is independent of AAI's financing or investment decisions. The only way AAI can help its shareholders is to make them richer. Thus AAI should invest its available cash in the package of projects having the largest aggregate net present value.

A barrier between the firm and capital markets does not undermine net present value so long as the barrier is the *only* market imperfection. The important thing is that the firm's *shareholders* have free access to well-functioning capital markets.

The net present value rule *is* undermined when imperfections restrict shareholders' portfolio choice. Suppose that Nevada Aquaculture, Inc. (NAI), is solely owned by its founder, Alexander Turbot. Mr. Turbot has no cash or credit remaining, but he is convinced that expansion of his operation is a high-NPV investment. He has tried to sell stock but has found that prospective investors, skeptical of prospects for fish farming in the desert, offer him much less than he thinks his firm is worth. For Mr. Turbot capital markets hardly exist. It makes little sense for him to discount prospective cash flows at a market opportunity cost of capital.

---

[14]A majority owner who is "locked in" and has much personal wealth tied up in AAI may be effectively cut off from capital markets. The NPV rule may not make sense to such an owner, though it will to the other shareholders.

SUMMARY

If you are going to persuade your company to use the net present value rule, you must be prepared to explain why other rules may *not* lead to correct decisions. That is why we have examined three alternative investment criteria in this chapter.

Some firms look at the book rate of return on the project. In this case the company decides which cash payments are capital expenditures and picks the appropriate rate to depreciate these expenditures. It then calculates the ratio of book income to the book value of the investment. Few companies nowadays base their investment decision simply on the book rate of return, but shareholders pay attention to book measures of firm profitability and some managers therefore look with a jaundiced eye on projects that would damage the company's book rate of return.

Some companies use the payback method to make investment decisions. In other words, they accept only those projects that recover their initial investment within some specified period. Payback is an ad hoc rule. It ignores the order in which cash flows come within the payback period, and it ignores subsequent cash flows entirely. It therefore takes no account of the opportunity cost of capital.

The simplicity of payback makes it an easy device for *describing* investment projects. Managers talk casually about quick-payback projects in the same way that investors talk about high-P/E common stocks. The fact that managers talk about the payback periods of projects does not mean that the payback rule governs their decisions. Some managers *do* use payback in judging capital investments. Why they rely on such a grossly oversimplified concept is a puzzle.

The internal rate of return (IRR) is defined as the rate of discount at which a project would have zero NPV. It is a handy measure and widely used in finance; you should therefore know how to calculate it. The IRR rule states that companies should accept any investment offering an IRR in excess of the opportunity cost of capital. The IRR rule is, like net present value, a technique based on discounted cash flows. It will, therefore, give the correct answer if properly used. The problem is that it is easily misapplied. There are four things to look out for:

1. *Lending or borrowing?* If a project offers positive cash flows followed by negative flows, NPV can *rise* as the discount rate is increased. You should accept such projects if their IRR is *less* than the opportunity cost of capital.

2. *Multiple rates of return.* If there is more than one change in the sign of the cash flows, the project may have several IRRs or no IRR at all.

3. *Mutually exclusive projects.* The IRR rule may give the wrong ranking of mutually exclusive projects that differ in economic life or in scale of required investment. If you insist on using IRR to rank mutually exclusive projects, you must examine the IRR on each incremental investment.

4. *Short-term interest rates may be different from long-term rates.* The IRR rule requires you to compare the project's IRR with the opportunity cost of capital. But sometimes there is an opportunity cost of capital for one-year cash flows, a different cost of capital for two-year cash flows, and so on. In these cases there is no simple yardstick for evaluating the IRR of a project.

If you are going to the expense of collecting cash-flow forecasts, you might as well use them properly. Ad hoc criteria should therefore have no role in the firm's decisions, and the net present value rule should be employed in preference to other techniques. Having said that, we must be careful not to exaggerate the payoff of proper technique. Technique is important, but it is by no means the only determinant of the success of a capital expenditure program. If the forecasts of cash flows are biased, even the most careful application of the net present value rule may fail.

In developing the NPV rule, we assumed that the company can maximize shareholder wealth by accepting every project that is worth more than it costs. But, if capital is strictly limited, then it may not be possible to take every project with a positive NPV. If capital is rationed in only one period, then the firm should follow a simple rule: Calculate each project's profitability index, which is the project's net present value per dollar of investment. Then pick the projects with the highest profitability indexes until you run out of capital. Unfortunately, this procedure fails when capital is rationed in more than one period or when there are other constraints on project choice. The only general solution is linear or integer programming.

Hard capital rationing always reflects a market imperfection—a barrier between the firm and capital markets. If that barrier also implies that the firm's shareholders lack free access to a well-functioning capital market, the very foundations of net present value crumble. Fortunately, hard rationing is rare for corporations in the United States. Many firms do use soft capital rationing, however. That is, they set up self-imposed limits as a means of financial planning and control.

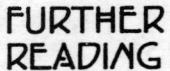

FURTHER READING

Classic articles on the internal rate of return rule include:

J. H. Lorie and L. J. Savage: "Three Problems in Rationing Capital," *Journal of Business,* 28:229–239 (October 1955).

E. Solomon: "The Arithmetic of Capital Budgeting Decisions," *Journal of Business,* 29:124–129 (April 1956).

A. A. Alchian: "The Rate of Interest, Fisher's Rate of Return over Cost and Keynes' Internal Rate of Return," *American Economic Review,* 45:938–942 (December 1955).

The classic treatment of linear programming applied to capital budgeting is:

H. M. Weingartner: *Mathematical Programming and the Analysis of Capital Budgeting Problems,* Prentice-Hall, Inc., Englewood Cliffs, N.J., 1963.

There is a long scholarly controversy on whether capital constraints invalidate the NPV rule. Weingartner has reviewed this literature:

H. M. Weingartner: "Capital Rationing: *n* Authors in Search of a Plot," *Journal of Finance,* 32:1403–1432 (December 1977).

QUIZ

1. What is the opportunity cost of capital supposed to represent? Give a concise definition.

2. **a.** What is the payback period on each of the following projects?

Cash Flows ($)

Project	C_0	C_1	C_2	C_3	C_4
A	−5,000	+1,000	+1,000	+3,000	0
B	−1,000	0	+1,000	+2,000	+3,000
C	−5,000	+1,000	+1,000	+3,000	+5,000

   b. *Given* that you wish to use the payback rule with a cutoff period of two years, which projects would you accept?

   c. If you use a cutoff period of three years, which projects would you accept?

   d. If the opportunity cost of capital is 10 percent, which projects have positive NPVs?

   e. "Payback gives too much weight to cash flows that occur after the cutoff date." True or false?

   f. "If a firm uses a single cutoff period for all projects, it is likely to accept too many short-lived projects." True or false?

   g. If the firm uses the discounted-payback rule, will it accept any negative-NPV projects? Will it turn down positive-NPV projects? Explain.

3. What is the book rate of return? Why is it *not* an accurate measure of the value of a capital investment project?

4. Write down the equation defining a project's internal rate of return (IRR). In practice how is IRR calculated?

5. a. Calculate the net present value of the following project for discount rates of 0, 50, and 100 percent:

Cash Flows ($)

C_0	C_1	C_2
−6,750	+4,500	+18,000

b. What is the IRR of the project?

6. You have the chance to participate in a project that produces the following cash flows:

Cash Flows ($)

C_0	C_1	C_2
+5,000	+4,000	−11,000

The internal rate of return is 13 percent. If the opportunity cost of capital is 10 percent, would you accept the offer?

7. Consider a project with the following cash flows:

C_0	C_1	C_2
−100	+200	−75

a. How many internal rates of return does this project have?
b. The opportunity cost of capital is 20 percent. Is this an attractive project? Briefly explain.

8. Consider projects Alpha and Beta:

Cash Flows ($)

Project	C_0	C_1	C_2	IRR (%)
Alpha	−400,000	+241,000	+293,000	21
Beta	−200,000	+131,000	+172,000	31

The opportunity cost of capital is 8 percent.
    Suppose you can undertake Alpha or Beta, but not both. Use the IRR rule to make the choice. *Hint:* What's the incremental investment in Alpha?

9. Suppose you have the following investment opportunities, but only $90,000 available for investment. Which projects should you take?

Project	NPV	Investment
1	5,000	10,000
2	5,000	5,000
3	10,000	90,000
4	15,000	60,000
5	15,000	75,000
6	3,000	15,000

10. What is the difference between hard and soft capital rationing? Does soft rationing mean the manager should stop trying to maximize NPV? How about hard rationing?

1. Consider the following projects:

Cash Flows ($)

Project	C_0	C_1	C_2	C_3	C_4	C_5
A	−1,000	+1,000	0	0	0	0
B	−2,000	+1,000	+1,000	+4,000	+1,000	+1,000
C	−3,000	+1.000	+1,000	0	+1,000	+1,000

a. If the opportunity cost of capital is 10 percent, which projects have a positive NPV?
b. Calculate the payback period for each project.
c. Which project(s) would a firm using the payback rule accept if the cutoff period were three years?

2. How is the discounted payback period calculated? Does discounted payback solve the deficiencies of the payback rule? Explain.

3. Does the following manifesto make sense? Explain briefly.

We're a darn successful company. Our book rate of return has exceeded 20 percent for five years running. We're determined that new capital investments won't drag down that average.

4. Respond to the following comments:
a. "I like the IRR rule. I can use it to rank projects without having to specify a discount rate."
b. "I like the payback rule. As long as the minimum payback period is short, the rule makes sure that the company takes no borderline projects. That reduces risk."

5. Unfortunately, your chief executive officer refuses to accept any investments in plant expansion that do not return their original investment in four years or less. That is, he insists on a *payback rule* with a *cutoff period* of four years. As a result, attractive long-lived projects are being turned down.

   The CEO is willing to switch to a *discounted payback* rule with the same four-year cutoff period. Would this be an improvement? Explain.

6. Calculate the IRR (or IRRs) for the following project:

C_0	C_1	C_2	C_3
−3,000	+3,500	+4,000	−4,000

For what range of discount rates does the project have positive-NPV?

7. Consider the following two mutually exclusive projects:

EXCEL

Cash Flows ($)

Project	C_0	C_1	C_2	C_3
A	−100	+60	+60	0
B	−100	0	0	+140

a. Calculate the NPV of each project for discount rates of 0, 10, and 20 percent. Plot these on a graph with NPV on the vertical axis and discount rate on the horizontal axis.
b. What is the approximate IRR for each project?

    c. In what circumstances should the company accept project A?

    d. Calculate the NPV of the incremental investment (B − A) for discount rates of 0, 10, and 20 percent. Plot these on your graph. Show that the circumstances in which you would accept A are also those in which the IRR on the incremental investment is less than the opportunity cost of capital.

8. Mr. Cyrus Clops, the president of Giant Enterprises, has to make a choice between two possible investments:

	Cash Flows ($ thousands)			
Project	C_0	C_1	C_2	IRR (%)
A	−400	+250	+300	23
B	−200	+140	+179	36

The opportunity cost of capital is 9 percent. Mr. Clops is tempted to take B, which has the higher IRR.

    a. Explain to Mr. Clops why this is not the correct procedure.

    b. Show him how to adapt the IRR rule to choose the best project.

    c. Show him that this project also has the higher NPV.

9. The Titanic Shipbuilding Company has a noncancelable contract to build a small cargo vessel. Construction involves a cash outlay of $250,000 at the end of each of the next two years. At the end of the third year the company will receive payment of $650,000. The company can speed up construction by working an extra shift. In this case there will be a cash outlay of $550,000 at the end of the first year followed by a cash payment of $650,000 at the end of the second year. Use the IRR rule to show the (approximate) range of opportunity costs of capital at which the company should work the extra shift.

10. "A company that ranks projects on IRR will encourage managers to propose projects with quick paybacks and low up-front investment." Is that statement correct? Explain.

11. Look again at projects E and F in Section 5.3. Assume that the projects are mutually exclusive and that the opportunity cost of capital is 10 percent.

    a. Calculate the profitability index for each project.

    b. Show how the profitability-index rule can be used to select the superior project.

12. In 1983 wealthy investors were offered a scheme that would allow them to postpone taxes. The scheme involved a debt-financed purchase of a fleet of beer delivery trucks, which were then leased to a local distributor. The cash flows were as follows:

Year	Cash Flow	
0	−21,750	
1	+7,861	
2	+8,317	
3	+7,188	Tax savings
4	+6,736	
5	+6,231	
6	−5,340	
7	−5,972	Additional taxes paid later
8	−6,678	
9	−7,468	
10	+12,578	Salvage value

Calculate the approximate IRRs. Is the project attractive at a 14 percent opportunity cost of capital?

13. Borghia Pharmaceuticals has $1 million allocated for capital expenditures. Which of the following projects should the company accept to stay within the $1 million budget? How much does the budget limit cost the company in terms of its market value? The opportunity cost of capital for each project is 11 percent.

Project	Investment ($ thousands)	NPV ($ thousands)	IRR (%)
1	300	66	17.2
2	200	-4	10.7
3	250	43	16.6
4	100	14	12.1
5	100	7	11.8
6	350	63	18.0
7	400	48	13.5

14. Consider the following capital rationing problem:

Project	C_0	C_1	C_2	NPV
W	-10,000	-10,000	0	+6,700
X	0	-20,000	+5,000	+9,000
Y	-10,000	+5,000	+5,000	+0
Z	-15,000	+5,000	+4,000	-1,500
Financing available	20,000	20,000	20,000	

Set up this problem as a linear program.

1. Some people believe firmly, even passionately, that ranking projects on IRR is OK if each project's cash flows can be reinvested at the project's IRR. They also say that the NPV rule "assumes that cash flows are reinvested at the opportunity cost of capital." Think carefully about these statements. Are they true? Are they helpful?

2. Look again at the project cash flows in Practice Question 6. Calculate the modified IRR as defined in footnote 5 in Section 5.3. Assume the cost of capital is 12 percent.
   Now try the following variation on the modified IRR concept. Figure out the fraction x such that x times C_1 and C_2 has the same present value as (minus) C_3.

$$xC_1 + \frac{xC_2}{1.12} = \frac{C_3}{1.12^2}$$

Define the modified project IRR as the solution of

$$C_0 + \frac{(1-x)C_1}{1+\text{IRR}} + \frac{(1-x)C_2}{(1+\text{IRR})^2} = 0$$

Now you have two modified IRRs. Which is more meaningful? If you can't decide, what do you conclude about the usefulness of modified IRRs?

3. Construct a series of cash flows with *no* IRR.

4. Solve the linear programming problem in Practice Question 14. You can allow partial investments, that is, $0 \le x \le 1$. Calculate and interpret the shadow prices[15] on the capital constraints.

---

[15] A shadow price is the marginal change in the objective for a marginal change in the constraint.

5. Look again at projects A, B, C, and D in Section 5.4. How would the linear programming setup change if:
   a. Cash not invested at date 0 could be invested at an interest rate r and used at date 1.
   b. Cash is not the only scarce resource. For example, there may not be enough people in the engineering department to complete necessary design work for all four projects.

MINI-CASE

Vegetron's CFO Calls Again

(The first episode of this story was presented in Section 5.1.)

Later that afternoon, Vegetron's CFO bursts into your office in a state of anxious confusion. The problem, he explains, is a last-minute proposal for a change in the design of the fermentation tanks that Vegetron will build to extract hydrated zirconium from a stockpile of powdered ore. The CFO has brought a printout (Table 5.1) of the forecasted revenues, costs, income, and book rates of return for the standard, low-temperature design. Vegetron's engineers have just proposed an alternative high-temperature design that will extract most of the hydrated zirconium over a shorter period, five instead of seven years. The forecasts for the high-temperature method are given in Table 5.2.[16]

TABLE 5.1

Income statement and book rates of return for high-temperature extraction of hydrated zirconium ($ thousands).

*Straight-line depreciation over five years is 400/5 = 80, or $80,000 per year.
†Capital investment is $400,000 in year 0.

	Year				
	1	2	3	4	5
1. Revenue	180	180	180	180	180
2. Operating costs	70	70	70	70	70
3. Depreciation*	80	80	80	80	80
4. Net income	30	30	30	30	30
5. Start-of-year book value†	400	320	240	160	80
6. Book rate of return (4 ÷ 5)	7.5%	9.4%	12.5%	18.75%	37.5%

TABLE 5.2

Income statement and book rates of return for low-temperature extraction of hydrated zirconium ($ thousands).

*Rounded. Straight-line depreciation over seven years is 400/7 = 57.14, or $57,140 per year.
†Capital investment is $400,000 in year 0.

	Year						
	1	2	3	4	5	6	7
1. Revenue	140	140	140	140	140	140	140
2. Operating costs	55	55	55	55	55	55	55
3. Depreciation*	57	57	57	57	57	57	57
4. Net income	28	28	28	28	28	28	28
5. Start-of-year book value†	400	343	286	229	171	114	57
6. Book rate of return (4 ÷ 5)	7%	8.2%	9.8%	12.2%	16.4%	24.6%	49.1%

[16]For simplicity we have ignored taxes. There will be plenty about taxes in Chapter 6.

CFO: Why do these engineers always have a bright idea at the last minute? But you've got to admit the high-temperature process looks good. We'll get a faster payback, and the rate of return beats Vegetron's 9 percent cost of capital in every year except the first. Let's see, income is $30,000 per year. Average investment is half the $400,000 capital outlay, or $200,000, so the average rate of return is 30,000/200,000, or 15 percent—a lot better than the 9 percent hurdle rate. The average rate of return for the low-temperature process is not that good, only 28,000/200,000, or 14 percent. Of course we might get a higher rate of return for the low-temperature proposal if we depreciated the investment faster—do you think we should try that?

You: Let's not fixate on book accounting numbers. Book income is not the same as cash flow to Vegetron or its investors. Book rates of return don't measure the true rate of return.

CFO: But people use accounting numbers all the time. We have to publish them in our annual report to investors.

You: Accounting numbers have many valid uses, but they're not a sound basis for capital investment decisions. Accounting changes can have big effects on book income or rate of return, even when cash flows are unchanged.

Here's an example. Suppose the accountant depreciates the capital investment for the low-temperature process over six years rather than seven. Then income for years 1 to 6 goes down, because depreciation is higher. Income for year 7 goes up because the depreciation for that year becomes zero. But there is no effect on year-to-year cash flows, because depreciation is not a cash outlay. It is simply the accountant's device for spreading out the "recovery" of the up-front capital outlay over the life of the project.

CFO: So how do we get cash flows?

You: In these cases it's easy. Depreciation is the only noncash entry in your spreadsheets (Tables 5.1 and 5.2), so we can just leave it out of the calculation. Cash flow equals revenue minus operating costs. For the high-temperature process, annual cash flow is:

$$\text{Cash flow} = \text{revenue} - \text{operating cost} = 180 - 70 = 110, \text{ or } \$110,000.$$

CFO: In effect you're adding back depreciation, because depreciation is a noncash accounting expense.

You: Right. You could also do it that way:

$$\text{Cash flow} = \text{net income} + \text{depreciation} = 30 + 80 = 110, \text{ or } \$110,000.$$

CFO: Of course. I remember all this now, but book returns seem important when someone shoves them in front of your nose.

You: It's not clear which project is better. The high-temperature process appears to be less efficient. It has higher operating costs and generates less total revenue over the life of the project, but of course it generates more cash flow in years 1 to 5.

CFO: Maybe the processes are equally good from a financial point of view. If so we'll stick with the low-temperature process rather than switching at the last minute.

You: We'll have to lay out the cash flows and calculate NPV for each process.

CFO: OK, do that. I'll be back in a half hour—and I also want to see each project's true, DCF rate of return.

Questions
1. Are the book rates of return reported in Table 5.1 useful inputs for the capital investment decision?
2. Calculate NPV and IRR for each process. What is your recommendation? Be ready to explain to the CFO.

CHAPTER SIX

MAKING INVESTMENT DECISIONS WITH THE NET PRESENT VALUE RULE

WE HOPE THAT by now you are convinced that wise investment decisions are based on the net present value rule. In this chapter we can think about how to apply the rule to practical capital investment decisions. Our task is threefold. First, what should be discounted? We know the answer in principle: discount cash flows. But useful forecasts of cash flows do not arrive on a silver platter. Often the financial manager has to make do with raw data supplied by specialists in product design, production, marketing, and so on.

This information has to be checked for completeness, consistency, and accuracy. The financial manager has to ferret out hidden cash flows and take care to reject accounting entries that look like cash flows but truly are not.

Second, how does the financial manager pull everything together into a forecast of overall, "bottom-line" cash flows? This requires careful tracking of taxes; changes in working capital; inflation; and the end-of-project "salvage values" of plant, property, and equipment. We will work through a realistic example.

Third, how should a financial manager apply the net present value rule when choosing between investments in plant or equipment with different economic lives? For example, suppose you must decide between machine Y, with a 5-year useful life, and machine Z, with a 10-year useful life. The present value of Y's lifetime investment and operating costs is naturally less than Z's, because Z will last twice as long. Does that necessarily make Y the better choice? Of course not.

We will show you how to transform the present value of an asset's investment and operating costs into an *equivalent annual cost,* that is, the total cost per year of buying and operating the asset. We will also show how to use equivalent annual costs to decide when to replace aging plant or equipment.

Choices between short- and long-lived production facilities, or between new and existing facilities, almost always involve *project interactions,* because a decision about one project cannot be separated from a decision about another, or from future decisions. We close this chapter with further examples of project interactions, for example, the choice between investing now and waiting to invest later.

 ## 6.1 WHAT TO DISCOUNT

Up to this point we have been concerned mainly with the mechanics of discounting and with the net present value rule for project appraisal. We have glossed over the problem of deciding *what* to discount. When you are faced with this problem, you should always stick to three general rules:

1. Only cash flow is relevant.
2. Always estimate cash flows on an incremental basis.
3. Be consistent in your treatment of inflation.

We will discuss each of these rules in turn.

Only Cash Flow Is Relevant

The first and most important point: Net present value depends on future cash flows. Cash flow is the simplest possible concept; it is just the difference between dollars received and dollars paid out. Many people nevertheless confuse cash flow with accounting profits.

Accountants *start* with "dollars in" and "dollars out," but to obtain accounting income they adjust these inputs in two important ways. First, they try to show profit as it is *earned* rather than when the company and the customer get around to paying their bills. Second, they sort cash outflows into two categories: current expenses and capital expenses. They deduct current expenses when calculating profit but do *not* deduct capital expenses. Instead they depreciate capital expenses over a number of years and deduct the annual depreciation charge from profits. As a result of these procedures, profits include some cash flows and exclude others, and they are reduced by depreciation charges, which are not cash flows at all.

It is not always easy to translate the customary accounting data back into actual dollars—dollars you can buy beer with. If you are in doubt about what is a cash flow, simply count the dollars coming in and take away the dollars going out. Don't assume without checking that you can find cash flow by routine manipulations of accounting data.

Always estimate cash flows on an after-tax basis. Some firms do not deduct tax payments. They try to offset this mistake by discounting the cash flows before taxes at a rate higher than the opportunity cost of capital. Unfortunately, there is no reliable formula for making such adjustments to the discount rate.

You should also make sure that cash flows are recorded *only when they occur* and not when work is undertaken or a liability is incurred. For example, taxes should be discounted from their actual payment date, not from the time when the tax liability is recorded in the firm's books.

Estimate Cash Flows on an Incremental Basis

The value of a project depends on *all* the additional cash flows that follow from project acceptance. Here are some things to watch for when you are deciding which cash flows should be included:

Do Not Confuse Average with Incremental Payoffs   Most managers naturally hesitate to throw good money after bad. For example, they are reluctant to invest more money in a losing division. But occasionally you will encounter turnaround opportunities in which the *incremental* NPV on investment in a loser is strongly positive.

Conversely, it does not always make sense to throw good money after good. A division with an outstanding past profitability record may have run out of good opportunities. You would not pay a large sum for a 20-year-old horse, sentiment aside, regardless of how many races that horse had won or how many champions it had sired.

Here is another example illustrating the difference between average and incremental returns: Suppose that a railroad bridge is in urgent need of repair. With the bridge the railroad can continue to operate; without the bridge it can't. In this case the payoff from the repair work consists of all the benefits of operating the railroad. The incremental NPV of such an investment may be enormous. Of course, these benefits should be net of all other costs and all subsequent repairs; otherwise the company may be misled into rebuilding an unprofitable railroad piece by piece.

Include All Incidental Effects   It is important to include all incidental effects on the remainder of the business. For example, a branch line for a railroad may have a negative NPV when considered in isolation, but still be a worthwhile investment when one allows for the additional traffic that it brings to the main line.

These incidental effects can extend into the far future. When GE, Pratt & Whitney, or Rolls Royce commits to the design and production of a new jet engine, cash inflows are not limited to revenues from engine sales. Once sold, an engine may be in service for 20 years or more, and during that time there is a steady demand for replacement parts. Some engine manufacturers also run profitable service and overhaul facilities. Finally, once an engine is proven in service, there are opportunities to offer modified or improved versions for other uses. All these "downstream" activities generate significant incremental cash inflows.

Do Not Forget Working Capital Requirements   Net working capital (often referred to simply as *working capital*) is the difference between a company's short-term assets and liabilities. The principal short-term assets are cash, accounts receivable (customers' unpaid bills), and inventories of raw materials and finished goods. The principal short-term liabilities are accounts payable (bills that *you* have not paid). Most projects entail an additional investment in working capital. This investment should, therefore, be recognized in your cash-flow forecasts. By the same token, when the project comes to an end, you can usually recover some of the investment. This is treated as a cash inflow.

Include Opportunity Costs   The cost of a resource may be relevant to the investment decision even when no cash changes hands. For example, suppose a new manufacturing operation uses land which could otherwise be sold for $100,000. This resource is not free: It has an opportunity cost, which is the cash it could generate for the company if the project were rejected and the resource were sold or put to some other productive use.

This example prompts us to warn you against judging projects on the basis of "before versus after." The proper comparison is "with or without." A manager comparing before versus after might not assign any value to the land because the firm owns it both before and after:

Before	Take Project	After	Cash Flow, Before versus After
Firm owns land	→	Firm still owns land	0

The proper comparison, with or without, is as follows:

With	Take Project	After	Cash Flow, with Project
Firm owns land	→	Firm still owns land	0

Without	Do Not Take Project	After	Cash Flow, without Project
	→	Firm sells land for $100,000	$100,000

Comparing the two possible "afters," we see that the firm gives up $100,000 by undertaking the project. This reasoning still holds if the land will not be sold but is worth $100,000 to the firm in some other use.

Sometimes opportunity costs may be very difficult to estimate; however, where the resource can be freely traded, its opportunity cost is simply equal to the market price. Why? It cannot be otherwise. If the value of a parcel of land to the firm is less than its market price, the firm will sell it. On the other hand, the opportunity cost of using land in a particular project cannot exceed the cost of buying an equivalent parcel to replace it.

Forget Sunk Costs   Sunk costs are like spilled milk: They are past and irreversible outflows. Because sunk costs are bygones, they cannot be affected by the decision to accept or reject the project, and so they should be ignored.

This fact is often forgotten. For example, in 1971 Lockheed sought a federal guarantee for a bank loan to continue development of the TriStar airplane. Lockheed and its supporters argued it would be foolish to abandon a project on which nearly $1 billion had already been spent. Some of Lockheed's critics countered that it would be equally foolish to continue with a project that offered no prospect of a satisfactory return on that $1 billion. Both groups were guilty of the *sunk-cost fallacy*; the $1 billion was irrecoverable and, therefore, irrelevant.[1]

Beware of Allocated Overhead Costs   We have already mentioned that the accountant's objective is not always the same as the investment analyst's. A case in point is the allocation of overhead costs. Overheads include such items as supervisory salaries, rent, heat, and light. These overheads may not be related to any particular project, but they have to be paid for somehow. Therefore, when the accountant assigns costs to the firm's projects, a charge for overhead is usually made. Now our principle of incremental cash flows says that in investment appraisal we should include only the *extra* expenses that would result from the project. A project may generate extra overhead expenses; then again, it may not. We should be cautious about assuming that the accountant's allocation of overheads represents the true extra expenses that would be incurred.

Treat Inflation Consistently

As we pointed out in Chapter 3, interest rates are usually quoted in *nominal* rather than *real* terms. For example, if you buy a one-year 8 percent Treasury bond, the government promises to pay you $1,080 at the end of the year, but it makes no promise what that $1,080 will buy. Investors take inflation into account when they decide what is a fair rate of interest.

Suppose that the yield on the Treasury bond is 8 percent and that next year's inflation is expected to be 6 percent. If you buy the bond, you get back $1,080 in year-1 dollars, which are worth 6 percent less than current dollars. The nominal payoff is $1,080, but the expected *real* value of your payoff is 1,080/1.06 = $1,019. Thus we could say, "The *nominal* rate of interest on the bond is 8 percent," *or* "The expected *real* rate of interest is 1.9 percent." Remember that the formula linking the nominal interest rate and the real rate is

$$1 + r_{nominal} = (1 + r_{real})(1 + \text{inflation rate})$$

If the discount rate is stated in nominal terms, then consistency requires that cash flows be estimated in nominal terms, taking account of trends in selling price, labor and materials cost, etc. This calls for more than simply applying a single assumed inflation rate to all components of cash flow. Labor cost per hour of work, for example, normally increases at a faster rate than the consumer price index because of improvements in productivity and increasing real wages throughout the economy. Tax savings from depreciation do not increase with inflation; they are

---

[1]See U. E. Reinhardt, "Break-Even Analysis for Lockheed's TriStar: An Application of Financial Theory," *Journal of Finance*, 28 (September 1973), pp. 821–838.

constant in nominal terms because tax law in the United States allows only the original cost of assets to be depreciated.

Of course, there is nothing wrong with discounting real cash flows at a real discount rate, although this is not commonly done. Here is a simple example showing the equivalence of the two methods.

Suppose your firm usually forecasts cash flows in nominal terms and discounts at a 15 percent nominal rate. In this particular case, however, you are given project cash flows estimated in real terms, that is, current dollars:

Real Cash Flows ($ thousands)			
C_0	C_1	C_2	C_3
-100	+35	+50	+30

It would be inconsistent to discount these real cash flows at 15 percent. You have two alternatives: Either restate the cash flows in nominal terms and discount at 15 percent, or restate the discount rate in real terms and use it to discount the real cash flows. We will now show you that both methods produce the same answer.

Assume that inflation is projected at 10 percent a year. Then the cash flow for year 1, which is $35,000 in current dollars, will be $35,000 \times 1.10 = \$38,500$ in year-1 dollars. Similarly the cash flow for year 2 will be $50,000 \times (1.10)^2 = \$60,500$ in year-2 dollars, and so on. If we discount these nominal cash flows at the 15 percent nominal discount rate, we have

$$NPV = -100 + \frac{38.5}{1.15} + \frac{60.5}{(1.15)^2} + \frac{39.9}{(1.15)^3} = 5.5, \text{ or } \$5,500$$

Instead of converting the cash-flow forecasts into nominal terms, we could convert the discount rate into real terms by using the following relationship:

$$\text{Real discount rate} = \frac{1 + \text{nominal discount rate}}{1 + \text{inflation rate}} - 1$$

In our example this gives

$$\text{Real discount rate} = \frac{1.15}{1.10} - 1 = .045, \text{ or } 4.5\%$$

If we now discount the real cash flows by the real discount rate, we have an NPV of $5,500, just as before:

$$NPV = -100 + \frac{35}{1.045} + \frac{50}{(1.045)^2} + \frac{30}{(1.045)^3} = 5.5, \text{ or } \$5,500$$

Note that the real discount rate is approximately equal to the *difference* between the nominal discount rate of 15 percent and the inflation rate of 10 percent. Discounting at $15 - 10 = 5$ percent would give NPV = $4,600—not exactly right, but close.

The message of all this is quite simple. Discount nominal cash flows at a nominal discount rate. Discount real cash flows at a real rate. Obvious as this rule is, it is sometimes violated. For example, in the 1970s there was a political storm in Ireland over the government's acquisition of a stake in Bula Mines. The price paid by the government reflected an assessment of £40 million as the value of Bula Mines; however, one group of consultants thought that the company's value was only £8 million and others thought that it was as high as £104 million. Although these valuations used different cash-flow projections, a significant part of the difference in views seemed to reflect confusion about real and nominal discount rates.[2]

6.2 EXAMPLE—IM&C'S FERTILIZER PROJECT

As the newly appointed financial manager of International Mulch and Compost Company (IM&C), you are about to analyze a proposal for marketing guano as a garden fertilizer. (IM&C's planned advertising campaign features a rustic gentleman who steps out of a vegetable patch singing, "All my troubles have guano way.")[3]

You are given the forecasts shown in Table 6.1. The project requires an investment of $10 million in plant and machinery (line 1). This machinery can be dismantled and sold for net proceeds estimated at $1.949 million in year 7 (line 1, column 7). This amount is your forecast of the plant's *salvage value*.

	Period							
	0	1	2	3	4	5	6	7
1. Capital investment	10,000							−1,949*
2. Accumulated depreciation		1,583	3,167	4,750	6,333	7,917	9,500	0
3. Year-end book value	10,000	8,417	6,833	5,250	3,667	2,083	500	0
4. Working capital		550	1,289	3,261	4,890	3,583	2,002	0
5. Total book value (3+4)	10,000	8,967	8,122	8,511	8,557	5,666	2,502	0
6. Sales		523	12,887	32,610	48,901	35,834	19,717	
7. Cost of goods sold[†]		837	7,729	19,552	29,345	21,492	11,830	
8. Other costs[‡]	4,000	2,200	1,210	1,331	1,464	1,611	1,772	
9. Depreciation		1,583	1,583	1,583	1,583	1,583	1,583	
10. Pretax profit (6 − 7 − 8 − 9)	−4,000	−4,097	2,365	10,144	16,509	11,148	4,532	1,449[§]
11. Tax at 35%	−1,400	−1,434	828	3,550	5,778	3,902	1,586	507
12. Profit after tax (10 − 11)	−2,600	−2,663	1,537	6,594	10,731	7,246	2,946	942

TABLE 6.1

IM&C's guano project—projections ($ thousands) reflecting inflation.

*Salvage value.

[†]We have departed from the usual income-statement format by *not* including depreciation in cost of goods sold. Instead, we break out depreciation separately (see line 9).

[‡]Start-up costs in years 0 and 1, and general and administrative costs in years 1 to 6.

[§]The difference between the salvage value and the ending book value of $500 is a taxable profit.

---

[2]In some cases it is unclear what procedure was used. At least one expert seems to have discounted nominal cash flows at a real rate. For a review of the Bula Mines controversy see E. Dimson and P. R. Marsh, *Cases in Corporate Finance* (London: Wiley International, 1987).

[3]Sorry.

	Period						
	0	**1**	**2**	**3**	**4**	**5**	**6**	**7**
1. Sales		523	12,887	32,610	48,901	35,834	19,717	
2. Cost of goods sold		837	7,729	19,552	29,345	21,492	11,830	
3. Other costs	4,000	2,200	1,210	1,331	1,464	1,611	1,772	
4. Tax on operations	−1,400	−1,434	828	3,550	5,778	3,902	1,586	
5. Cash flow from opera- tions (1 − 2 − 3 − 4)	−2,600	−1,080	3,120	8,177	12,314	8,829	4,529	
6. Change in working capital		−550	−739	−1,972	−1,629	1,307	1,581	2,002
7. Capital investment and disposal	−10,000							1,442*
8. Net cash flow (5 + 6 + 7)	−12,600	−1,630	2,381	6,205	10,685	10,136	6,110	3,444
9. Present value at 20%	−12,600	−1,358	1,654	3,591	5,153	4,074	2,046	961
Net present value = +3,519 (sum of 9)								

TABLE 6.2

IM&C's guano project—cash-flow analysis ($ thousands).

*Salvage value of $1,949 less tax of $507 on the difference between salvage value and ending book value.

Whoever prepared Table 6.1 depreciated the capital investment over six years to an arbitrary salvage value of $500,000, which is less than your forecast of salvage value. *Straight-line depreciation* was assumed. Under this method annual depreciation equals a constant proportion of the initial investment less salvage value ($9.5 million). If we call the depreciable life T, then the straight-line depreciation in year t is

Depreciation in year $t = 1/T \times$ depreciable amount $= 1/6 \times 9.5 = \$1.583$ million

Lines 6 through 12 in Table 6.1 show a simplified income statement for the guano project.[4] This will be our starting point for estimating cash flow. In preparing this table IM&C's managers recognized the effect of inflation on prices and costs. Not all cash flows are equally affected by inflation. For example, wages generally rise faster than the inflation rate. So labor costs per ton of guano will rise in real terms unless technological advances allow more efficient use of labor. On the other hand, inflation has no effect on the tax savings provided by the depreciation deduction, since the Internal Revenue Service allows you to depreciate only the original cost of the equipment, regardless of what happens to prices after the investment is made.

Table 6.2 derives cash-flow forecasts from the investment and income data given in Table 6.1. Cash flow from operations is defined as sales less cost of goods sold, other costs, and taxes. The remaining cash flows include the changes in working capital, the initial capital investment, and the recovery of your estimated salvage value. If, as you expect, the salvage value turns out higher than the depreciated value of the machinery, you will have to pay tax on the difference. So you must also include this figure in your cash-flow forecast.

---

[4]We have departed from the usual income-statement format by separating depreciation from costs of goods sold.

IM&C estimates the nominal opportunity cost of capital for projects of this type as 20 percent. When all cash flows are added up and discounted, the guano project is seen to offer a net present value of about $3.5 million:

$$NPV = -12,600 - \frac{1,630}{1.20} + \frac{2,381}{(1.20)^2} + \frac{6,205}{(1.20)^3} + \frac{10,685}{(1.20)^4} + \frac{10,136}{(1.20)^5}$$

$$+ \frac{6,110}{(1.20)^6} + \frac{3,444}{(1.20)^7} = +3,519, \text{ or } \$3,519,000$$

Separating Investment and Financing Decisions

Our analysis of the guano project takes no notice of how that project is financed. It may be that IM&C will decide to finance partly by debt, but if it does we will not subtract the debt proceeds from the required investment, nor will we recognize interest and principal payments as cash outflows. We analyze the project as if it were all equity-financed, treating all cash outflows as coming from stockholders and all cash inflows as going to them.

We approach the problem in this way so that we can separate the analysis of the investment decision from the financing decision. Then, when we have calculated NPV, we can undertake a separate analysis of financing. Financing decisions and their possible interactions with investment decisions are covered later in the book.

A Further Note on Estimating Cash Flow

Now here is an important point. You can see from line 6 of Table 6.2 that working capital increases in the early and middle years of the project. What is working capital? you may ask, and why does it increase?

Working capital summarizes the net investment in short-term assets associated with a firm, business, or project. Its most important components are *inventory, accounts receivable,* and *accounts payable.* The guano project's requirements for working capital in year 2 might be as follows:

Working capital = inventory + accounts receivable − accounts payable
$1,289   =   635   +   1,030   −   376

Why does working capital increase? There are several possibilities:

1. Sales recorded on the income statement overstate actual cash receipts from guano shipments because sales are increasing and customers are slow to pay their bills. Therefore, accounts receivable increase.
2. It takes several months for processed guano to age properly. Thus, as projected sales increase, larger inventories have to be held in the aging sheds.
3. An offsetting effect occurs if payments for materials and services used in guano production are delayed. In this case accounts payable will increase.

The additional investment in working capital from year 2 to 3 might be

Additional investment in working capital	=	increase in inventory	+	increase in accounts receivable	−	increase in accounts payable
$1,972	=	972	+	1,500	−	500

A more detailed cash-flow forecast for year 3 would look like Table 6.3.

		Data from Forecasted Income Statement		Working-Capital Changes
Cash inflow	=	Sales	−	Increase in accounts receivable
$31,110	=	32,610	−	1,500
Cash outflow	=	Cost of goods sold, other costs, and taxes	+	Increase in inventory net of increase in accounts payable
$24,905	=	(19,552 + 1,331 + 3,550)	+	(972 − 500)
		Net cash flow = cash inflow − cash outflow		
		$6,205 = 31,110 − 24,905		

TABLE 6.3

Details of cash-flow forecast for IM&C's guano project in year 3 ($ thousands).

Instead of worrying about changes in working capital, you could estimate cash flow directly by counting the dollars coming in and taking away the dollars going out. In other words,

1. If you replace each year's sales with that year's cash payments received from customers, you don't have to worry about accounts receivable.

2. If you replace cost of goods sold with cash payments for labor, materials, and other costs of production, you don't have to keep track of inventory or accounts payable.

However, you would still have to construct a projected income statement to estimate taxes.

We discuss the links between cash flow and working capital in much greater detail in Chapter 30.

A Further Note on Depreciation

Depreciation is a noncash expense; it is important only because it reduces taxable income. It provides an annual *tax shield* equal to the product of depreciation and the marginal tax rate:

$$\text{Tax shield} = \text{depreciation} \times \text{tax rate}$$
$$= 1{,}583 \times .35 = 554, \text{ or } \$554{,}000$$

The present value of the tax shields ($554,000 for six years) is $1,842,000 at a 20 percent discount rate.[5]

Now if IM&C could just get those tax shields sooner, they would be worth more, right? Fortunately tax law allows corporations to do just that: It allows *accelerated depreciation*.

The current rules for tax depreciation in the United States were set by the Tax Reform Act of 1986, which established a modified accelerated cost recovery system

---

[5]By discounting the depreciation tax shields at 20 percent, we assume that they are as risky as the other cash flows. Since they depend only on tax rates, depreciation method, and IM&C's ability to generate taxable income, they are probably less risky. In some contexts (the analysis of financial leases, for example) depreciation tax shields are treated as safe, nominal cash flows and are discounted at an after-tax borrowing or lending rate. See Chapter 26.

TABLE 6.4

Tax depreciation allowed under the modified accelerated cost recovery system (MACRS) (figures in percent of depreciable investment).

Notes:
1. Tax depreciation is lower in the first year because assets are assumed to be in service for only six months.
2. Real property is depreciated straight-line over 27.5 years for residential property and 31.5 years for nonresidential property.

	Tax Depreciation Schedules by Recovery-Period Class					
Year(s)	3-Year	5-Year	7-Year	10-Year	15-Year	20-Year
1	33.33	20.00	14.29	10.00	5.00	3.75
2	44.45	32.00	24.49	18.00	9.50	7.22
3	14.81	19.20	17.49	14.40	8.55	6.68
4	7.41	11.52	12.49	11.52	7.70	6.18
5		11.52	8.93	9.22	6.93	5.71
6		5.76	8.93	7.37	6.23	5.28
7			8.93	6.55	5.90	4.89
8			4.45	6.55	5.90	4.52
9				6.55	5.90	4.46
10				6.55	5.90	4.46
11				3.29	5.90	4.46
12					5.90	4.46
13					5.90	4.46
14					5.90	4.46
15					5.90	4.46
16					2.99	4.46
17–20						4.46
21						2.25

(MACRS). Table 6.4 summarizes the tax depreciation schedules. Note that there are six schedules, one for each recovery period class. Most industrial equipment falls into the five- and seven-year classes. To keep things simple, we will assume that all the guano project's investment goes into five-year assets. Thus, IM&C can write off 20 percent of its depreciable investment in year 1, as soon as the assets are placed in service, then 32 percent of depreciable investment in year 2, and so on. Here are the tax shields for the guano project:

	Year					
	1	2	3	4	5	6
Tax depreciation (MACRS percentage × depreciable investment)	2,000	3,200	1,920	1,152	1,152	576
Tax shield (tax depreciation × tax rate, $T = .35$)	700	1,120	672	403	403	202

The present value of these tax shields is $2,174,000, about $331,000 higher than under the straight-line method.

Table 6.5 recalculates the guano project's impact on IM&C's future tax bills, and Table 6.6 shows revised after-tax cash flows and present value. This time we have incorporated realistic assumptions about taxes as well as inflation. We of course arrive at a higher NPV than in Table 6.2, because that table ignored the additional present value of accelerated depreciation.

There is one possible additional problem lurking in the woodwork behind Table 6.5: It is the *alternative minimum tax*, which can limit or defer the tax shields of accelerated depreciation or other *tax preference* items. Because the alternative mini-

				Period				
	0	1	2	3	4	5	6	7
1. Sales*		523	12,887	32,610	48,901	35,834	19,717	
2. Cost of goods sold*		837	7,729	19,552	29,345	21,492	11,830	
3. Other costs*	4,000	2,200	1,210	1,331	1,464	1,611	1,772	
4. Tax depreciation		2,000	3,200	1,920	1,152	1,152	576	
5. Pretax profit (1 − 2 − 3 − 4)	−4,000	−4,514	748	9,807	16,940	11,579	5,539	1,949[†]
6. Taxes at 35%[‡]	−1,400	−1,580	262	3,432	5,929	4,053	1,939	682

TABLE 6.5

Tax payments on IM&C's guano project ($ thousands).

*From Table 6.1.
[†]Salvage value is zero, for tax purposes, after all tax depreciation has been taken. Thus, IM&C will have to pay tax on the full salvage value of $1,949.
[‡]A negative tax payment means a cash *inflow*, assuming IM&C can use the tax loss on its guano project to shield income from other projects.

				Period				
	0	1	2	3	4	5	6	7
1. Sales*		523	12,887	32,610	48,901	35,834	19,717	
2. Cost of goods sold*		837	7,729	19,552	29,345	21,492	11,830	
3. Other costs*	4,000	2,200	1,210	1,331	1,464	1,611	1,772	
4. Tax[†]	−1,400	−1,580	262	3,432	5,929	4,053	1,939	682
5. Cash flow from operations (1 − 2 − 3 − 4)	−2,600	−934	3,686	8,295	12,163	8,678	4,176	−682
6. Change in working capital		−550	−739	−1,972	−1,629	1,307	1,581	2,002
7. Capital investment and disposal	−10,000							1,949*
8. Net cash flow (5 + 6 + 7)	−12,600	−1,484	2,947	6,323	10,534	9,985	5,757	3,269
9. Present value at 20%	−12,600	−1,237	2,047	3,659	5,080	4,013	1,928	912

Net present value = +3,802 (sum of 9)

TABLE 6.6

IM&C's guano project—revised cash-flow analysis ($ thousands).

*From Table 6.1.
[†]From Table 6.5.

mum tax can be a motive for leasing, we discuss it in Chapter 26, rather than here. But make a mental note not to sign off on a capital budgeting analysis without checking whether your company is subject to the alternative minimum tax.

A Final Comment on Taxes

All large U.S. corporations keep two separate sets of books, one for stockholders and one for the Internal Revenue Service. It is common to use straight-line depreciation on the stockholder books and accelerated depreciation on the tax books. The IRS doesn't object to this, and it makes the firm's reported earnings higher than if accelerated depreciation were used everywhere. There are many other differences between tax books and shareholder books.[6]

The financial analyst must be careful to remember which set of books he or she is looking at. In capital budgeting only the tax books are relevant, but to an outside analyst only the shareholder books are available.

Project Analysis

Let's review. Several pages ago, you embarked on an analysis of IM&C's guano project. You started with a simplified statement of assets and income for the project that you used to develop a series of cash-flow forecasts. Then you remembered accelerated depreciation and had to recalculate cash flows and NPV.

You were lucky to get away with just two NPV calculations. In real situations, it often takes several tries to purge all inconsistencies and mistakes. Then there are "what if" questions. For example: What if inflation rages at 15 percent per year, rather than 10? What if technical problems delay start-up to year 2? What if gardeners prefer chemical fertilizers to your natural product?

You won't truly understand the guano project until all relevant what-if questions are answered. *Project analysis* is more than one or two NPV calculations, as we will see in Chapter 10.

Calculating NPV in Other Countries and Currencies

Before you become too deeply immersed in guano, we should take a quick look at another company that is facing a capital investment decision. This time it is the French firm, Flanel s.a., which is contemplating investment in a facility to produce a new range of fragrances. The basic principles are the same: Flanel needs to determine whether the present value of the future cash flows exceeds the initial investment. But there are a few differences that arise from the change in project location:

1. Flanel must produce a set of cash-flow forecasts like those that we developed for the guano project, but in this case the project cash flows are stated in euros, the European currency.

2. In developing these cash-flow forecasts, the company needs to recognize that prices and costs will be influenced by the French inflation rate.

3. When they calculate taxable income, French companies cannot use accelerated depreciation. (Remember that companies in the United States can use the MACRS depreciation rates which allow larger deductions in the early years of the project's life.)

4. Profits from Flanel's project are liable to the French rate of corporate tax. This is currently about 37 percent, a trifle higher than the rate in the United States.[7]

5. Just as IM&C calculated the net present value of its investment in the United States by discounting the expected *dollar* cash flows at the *dollar* cost

---

[6]This separation of tax accounts from shareholder accounts is not found worldwide. In Japan, for example, taxes reported to shareholders must equal taxes paid to the government; ditto for France and many other European countries.

[7]The French tax rate is made up of a basic corporate tax rate of 33.3 percent plus a surtax of 3.33 percent.

of capital, so Flanel can evaluate an investment in France by discounting the expected *euro* cash flows at the *euro* cost of capital. To calculate the opportunity cost of capital for the fragrances project, Flanel needs to ask what return its shareholders are giving up by investing their euros in the project rather than investing them in the capital market. If the project were risk-free, the opportunity cost of investing in the project would be the interest rate on safe euro investments, for example euro bonds issued by the French government.[8] As we write this, the 10-year euro interest rate is about 4.75 percent, compared with 4.5 percent on U.S. Treasury securities. But since the project is undoubtedly not risk-free, Flanel needs to ask how much risk it is asking its shareholders to bear and what extra return they demand for taking on this risk. A similar company in the United States might come up with a different answer to this question. We will discuss risk and the cost of capital in Chapters 7 through 9.

You can see from this example that the principles of valuation of capital investments are the same worldwide. A spreadsheet table for Flanel's project could have exactly the same format as Table 6.6.[9] But inputs and assumptions have to conform to local conditions.

6.3 EQUIVALENT ANNUAL COSTS

When you calculate NPV, you transform future, year-by-year cash flows into a lump-sum value expressed in today's dollars (or euros, or other relevant currency). But sometimes it's helpful to reverse the calculation, transforming a lump sum of investment today into an equivalent stream of future cash flows. Consider the following example.

Investing to Produce Reformulated Gasoline at California Refineries

In the early 1990s, the California Air Resources Board (CARB) started planning its "Phase 2" requirements for reformulated gasoline (RFG). RFG is gasoline blended to tight specifications designed to reduce pollution from motor vehicles. CARB consulted with refiners, environmentalists, and other interested parties to design these specifications.

As the outline for the Phase 2 requirements emerged, refiners realized that substantial capital investments would be required to upgrade California refineries. What might these investments mean for the retail price of gasoline? A refiner might ask: "Suppose my company invests $400 million to upgrade our refinery to meet Phase 2. How many cents per gallon extra would we have to charge to recover that cost?" Let's see if we can help the refiner out.

Assume $400 million of capital investment and a real (inflation-adjusted) cost of capital of 7 percent. The new equipment lasts for 25 years, and the refinery's total

---

[8]It is interesting to note that, while the United States Treasury can always print the money needed to repay its debts, national governments in Europe do not have the right to print euros. Thus there is always some possibility that the French government will not be able to raise sufficient taxes to repay its bonds, though most observers would regard the probability as negligible.

[9]You can tackle Flanel's project in Practice Question 13.

production of RFG will be 900 million gallons per year. Assume for simplicity that the new equipment does not change raw-material and operating costs.

How much additional revenue would the refinery have to receive each year, for 25 years, to cover the $400 million investment? The answer is simple: Just find the 25-year annuity with a present value equal to $400 million.

$$\text{PV of annuity} = \text{annuity payment} \times \text{25-year annuity factor}$$

At a 7 percent cost of capital, the 25-year annuity factor is 11.65.

$$\$400 \text{ million} = \text{annuity payment} \times 11.65$$
$$\text{Annuity payment} = \$34.3 \text{ million per year}^{10}$$

This amounts to 3.8 cents per gallon:

$$\frac{\$34.3 \text{ million}}{900 \text{ million gallons}} = \$.038 \text{ per gallon}$$

These annuities are called **equivalent annual costs.** Equivalent annual cost is the annual cash flow sufficient to recover a capital investment, including the cost of capital for that investment, over the investment's economic life.

Equivalent annual costs are handy—and sometimes essential—tools of finance. Here is a further example.

Choosing between Long- and Short-Lived Equipment

Suppose the firm is forced to choose between two machines, A and B. The two machines are designed differently but have identical capacity and do exactly the same job. Machine A costs $15,000 and will last three years. It costs $5,000 per year to run. Machine B is an economy model costing only $10,000, but it will last only two years and costs $6,000 per year to run. These are real cash flows: The costs are forecasted in dollars of constant purchasing power.

Because the two machines produce exactly the same product, the only way to choose between them is on the basis of cost. Suppose we compute the present value of cost:

| | Costs ($ thousands) | | | | |
Machine	C_0	C_1	C_2	C_3	PV at 6% ($ thousands)
A	+15	+5	+5	+5	28.37
B	+10	+6	+6		21.00

Should we take machine B, the one with the lower present value of costs? Not necessarily, because B will have to be replaced a year earlier than A. In other

---

[10]For simplicity we have ignored taxes. Taxes would enter this calculation in two ways. First, the $400 million investment would generate depreciation tax shields. The easiest way to handle these tax shields is to calculate their PV and subtract it from the initial outlay. For example, if the PV of depreciation tax shields is $83 million, equivalent annual cost would be calculated on an after-tax investment base of $400 − 83 = $317 million. Second, our cents-per-gallon calculation is after-tax. To actually earn 3.8 cents after tax, the refiner would have to charge the customer more. If the tax rate is 35 percent, the required extra pretax charge is:

$$\text{Pretax charge} \times (1 - .35) = \$.038$$
$$\text{Pretax charge} = \$.0585$$

words, the timing of a future investment decision is contingent on today's choice of A or B.

So, a machine with total PV(costs) of $21,000 spread over three years (0, 1, and 2) is not necessarily better than a competing machine with PV(costs) of $28,370 spread over four years (0 through 3). We have to convert total PV(costs) to a cost per year, that is, to an equivalent annual cost. For machine A, the annual cost turns out to be 10.61, or $10,610 per year:

Machine	Costs ($ thousands)				PV at 6% ($ thousands)
	C_0	C_1	C_2	C_3	
Machine A	+15	+5	+5	+5	28.37
Equivalent annual cost		+10.61	+10.61	+10.61	28.37

We calculated the equivalent annual cost by finding the three-year annuity with the same present value as A's lifetime costs.

PV of annuity = PV of A's costs = 28.37

= annuity payment × three-year annuity factor

The annuity factor is 2.673 for three years and a 6 percent real cost of capital, so

$$\text{Annuity payment} = \frac{28.37}{2.673} = 10.61$$

A similar calculation for machine B gives:

Machine	Costs ($ thousands)			PV at 6% ($ thousands)
	C_0	C_1	C_2	
Machine B	+10	+6	+6	21.00
Equivalent annual cost		+11.45	+11.45	21.00

Machine A is better, because its equivalent annual cost is less ($10,610 versus $11,450 for machine B).

You can think of the equivalent annual cost of machine A or B as an annual rental charge. Suppose the financial manager is asked to *rent* machine A to the plant manager actually in charge of production. There will be three equal rental payments starting in year 1. The three payments must recover both the original cost of machine A in year 0 and the cost of running it in years 1 to 3. Therefore the financial manager has to make sure that the rental payments are worth $28,370, the total PV(costs) of machine A. You can see that the financial manager would calculate a fair rental payment equal to machine A's equivalent annual cost.

Our rule for choosing between plant and equipment with different economic lines is, therefore, to select the asset with the lowest fair rental charge, that is, the lowest equivalent annual cost.

Equivalent Annual Cost and Inflation   The equivalent annual costs we just calculated are *real* annuities based on forecasted *real* costs and a 6 percent *real* discount rate. We could, of course, restate the annuities in nominal terms. Suppose the expected inflation rate is 5 percent; we multiply the first cash flow of the annuity by 1.05, the second by $(1.05)^2 = 1.105$, and so on.

		C_0	C_1	C_2	C_3
A	Real annuity		10.61	10.61	10.61
	Nominal cash flow		11.14	11.70	12.28
B	Real annuity			11.45	11.45
	Nominal cash flow			12.02	12.62

Note that B is still inferior to A. Of course the present values of the nominal and real cash flows are identical. Just remember to discount the real annuity at the real rate and the equivalent nominal cash flows at the consistent nominal rate.[11]

When you use equivalent annual costs simply for comparison of costs per period, as we did for machines A and B, we strongly recommend doing the calculations in real terms.[12] But if you actually rent out the machine to the plant manager, or anyone else, be careful to specify that the rental payments be "indexed" to inflation. If inflation runs on at 5 percent per year and rental payments do not increase proportionally, then the real value of the rental payments must decline and will not cover the full cost of buying and operating the machine.

Equivalent Annual Cost and Technological Change   So far we have the following simple rule: Two or more streams of cash outflows with different lengths or time patterns can be compared by converting their present values to equivalent annual costs. Just remember to do the calculations in real terms.

Now any rule this simple cannot be completely general. For example, when we evaluated machine A versus machine B, we implicitly assumed that their fair rental charges would *continue* at $10,610 versus $11,450. This will be so only if the *real* costs of buying and operating the machines stay the same.

Suppose that this is not the case. Suppose that thanks to technological improvements new machines each year cost 20 percent less in real terms to buy and operate. In this case future owners of brand-new, lower-cost machines will be able to cut their rental cost by 20 percent, and owners of old machines will be forced to match this reduction. Thus, we now need to ask: If the real level of rents declines by 20 percent a year, how much will it cost to rent each machine?

If the rent for year 1 is $rent_1$, rent for year 2 is $rent_2 = .8 \times rent_1$. $Rent_3$ is $.8 \times rent_2$, or $.64 \times rent_1$. The owner of each machine must set the rents sufficiently high to recover the present value of the costs. In the case of machine A,

$$\text{PV of renting machine A} = \frac{rent_1}{1.06} + \frac{rent_2}{(1.06)^2} + \frac{rent_3}{(1.06)^3} = 28.37$$

$$= \frac{rent_1}{1.06} + \frac{.8(rent_1)}{(1.06)^2} + \frac{.64(rent_1)}{(1.06)^3} = 28.37$$

$$rent_1 = 12.94, \text{ or } \$12,940$$

---

[11]The nominal discount rate is

$$r_{nominal} = (1 + r_{real})(1 + \text{inflation rate}) - 1$$
$$= (1.06)(1.05) - 1 = .113, \text{ or } 11.3\%$$

Discounting the nominal annuities at this rate gives the same present values as discounting the real annuities at 6 percent.

[12]Do *not* calculate equivalent annual costs as level *nominal* annuities. This procedure can give incorrect rankings of true equivalent annual costs at high inflation rates. See Challenge Question 2 at the end of this chapter for an example.

and for machine B,

$$\frac{\text{rent}_1}{1.06} + \frac{.8(\text{rent}_1)}{(1.06)^2} = 21.00$$

$$\text{rent}_1 = 12.69, \text{ or } \$12,690$$

The merits of the two machines are now reversed. Once we recognize that technology is expected to reduce the real costs of new machines, then it pays to buy the shorter-lived machine B rather than become locked into an aging technology with machine A in year 3.

You can imagine other complications. Perhaps machine C will arrive in year 1 with an even lower equivalent annual cost. You would then need to consider scrapping or selling machine B at year 1 (more on this decision below). The financial manager could not choose between machines A and B in year 0 without taking a detailed look at what each machine could be replaced with.

Our point is a general one: Comparing equivalent annual costs should never be a mechanical exercise; always think about the assumptions that are implicit in the comparison. Finally, remember why equivalent annual costs are necessary in the first place. The reason is that A and B will be replaced at different future dates. The choice between them therefore affects future investment decisions. If subsequent decisions are not affected by the initial choice (for example, because neither machine will be replaced) then we do *not need to take future decisions into account*.[13]

Equivalent Annual Cost and Taxes   We have not mentioned taxes. But you surely realized that machine A and B's lifetime costs should be calculated after-tax, recognizing that operating costs are tax-deductible and that capital investment generates depreciation tax shields.

Deciding When to Replace an Existing Machine

The previous example took the life of each machine as fixed. In practice the point at which equipment is replaced reflects economic considerations rather than total physical collapse. *We* must decide when to replace. The machine will rarely decide for us.

Here is a common problem. You are operating an elderly machine that is expected to produce a net cash *inflow* of $4,000 in the coming year and $4,000 next year. After that it will give up the ghost. You can replace it now with a new machine, which costs $15,000 but is much more efficient and will provide a cash inflow of $8,000 a year for three years. You want to know whether you should replace your equipment now or wait a year.

We can calculate the NPV of the new machine and also its *equivalent annual cash flow*, that is, the three-year annuity that has the same net present value:

	Cash Flows ($ thousands)			
	C_0	C_1	C_2	C_3	NPV at 6% ($ thousands)
New machine	−15	+8	+8	+8	6.38
Equivalent annual cash flow		+2.387	+2.387	+2.387	6.38

---

[13]However, if neither machine will be replaced, then we have to consider the extra revenue generated by machine A in its third year, when it will be operating but B will not.

In other words, the cash flows of the new machine are equivalent to an annuity of $2,387 per year. So we can equally well ask at what point we would want to replace our old machine with a new one producing $2,387 a year. When the question is put this way, the answer is obvious. As long as your old machine can generate a cash flow of $4,000 a year, who wants to put in its place a new one that generates only $2,387 a year?

It is a simple matter to incorporate salvage values into this calculation. Suppose that the current salvage value is $8,000 and next year's value is $7,000. Let's see where you come out next year if you wait and then sell. On one hand, you gain $7,000, but you lose today's salvage value *plus* a year's return on that money. That is, $8,000 \times 1.06 = \$8,480$. Your net loss is $8,480 - 7,000 = \$1,480$, which only partly offsets the operating gain. You should not replace yet.

Remember that the logic of such comparisons requires that the new machine be the best of the available alternatives and that it in turn be replaced at the optimal point.

Cost of Excess Capacity

Any firm with a centralized information system (computer servers, storage, software, and telecommunication links) encounters many proposals for using it. Recently installed systems tend to have excess capacity, and since the immediate marginal costs of using them seem to be negligible, management often encourages new uses. Sooner or later, however, the load on a system increases to the point at which management must either terminate the uses it originally encouraged or invest in another system several years earlier than it had planned. Such problems can be avoided if a proper charge is made for the use of spare capacity.

Suppose we have a new investment project that requires heavy use of an existing information system. The effect of adopting the project is to bring the purchase date of a new, more capable system forward from year 4 to year 3. This new system has a life of five years, and at a discount rate of 6 percent the present value of the cost of buying and operating it is $500,000.

We begin by converting the $500,000 present value of cost of the new system to an equivalent annual cost of $118,700 for each of five years.[14] Of course, when the new system in turn wears out, we will replace it with another. So we face the prospect of future information-system expenses of $118,700 a year. If we undertake the new project, the series of expenses begins in year 4; if we do not undertake it, the series begins in year 5. The new project, therefore, results in an *additional* cost of $118,700 in year 4. This has a present value of $118,700/(1.06)^4$, or about $94,000. This cost is properly charged against the new project. When we recognize it, the NPV of the project may prove to be negative. If so, we still need to check whether it is worthwhile undertaking the project now and abandoning it later, when the excess capacity of the present system disappears.

6.4 PROJECT INTERACTIONS

Almost all decisions about capital expenditure involve either–or choices. The firm can build either a 90,000-square-foot warehouse in northern South Dakota or a 100,000-square-foot warehouse in southern North Dakota. It can heat it either by

---

[14]The present value of $118,700 for five years discounted at 6 percent is $500,000.

oil or natural gas, and so on: These mutually exclusive options are simple examples of *project interactions*.

All of the examples in the last section involved project interactions. Think back to the first example, the choice between machine A, with a three-year life, and machine B, with a two-year life. A and B interact because they are mutually exclusive, and also because the choice of A or B ripples forward to affect future machine purchases.

Project interactions can arise in countless ways. The literature of operations research and industrial engineering sometimes addresses cases of extreme complexity and difficulty. We will be content with two more simple but important examples.

Case 1: Optimal Timing of Investment

The fact that a project has a positive NPV does not mean that it is best undertaken now. It might be even more valuable if undertaken in the future. Similarly, a project with a currently negative NPV might become a valuable opportunity if we wait a bit. Thus *any* project has two mutually exclusive alternatives: Do it now, or wait and invest later.

The question of optimal timing of investment is not difficult under conditions of certainty. We first examine alternative dates (t) for making the investment and calculate its net *future* value as of each date. Then, in order to find which of the alternatives would add most to the firm's *current* value, we must work out

$$\frac{\text{Net future value as of date } t}{(1 + r)^t}$$

For example, suppose you own a large tract of inaccessible timber. In order to harvest it, you have to invest a substantial amount in access roads and other facilities. The longer you wait, the higher the investment required. On the other hand, lumber prices will rise as you wait, and the trees will keep growing, although at a gradually decreasing rate.

Let us suppose that the net present value of the harvest at different *future* dates is as follows:

	Year of Harvest					
	0	**1**	**2**	**3**	**4**	**5**
Net *future* value ($ thousands)	50	64.4	77.5	89.4	100	109.4
Change in value from previous year (%)		+28.8	+20.3	+15.4	+11.9	+9.4

As you can see, the longer you defer cutting the timber, the more money you will make. However, your concern is with the date that maximizes the net *present* value of your investment, that is, its contribution to the value of your firm *today*. You therefore need to discount the net future value of the harvest back to the present. Suppose the appropriate discount rate is 10 percent. Then if you harvest the timber in year 1, it has a net *present* value of $58,500:

$$\text{NPV if harvested in year 1} = \frac{64.4}{1.10} = 58.5, \text{ or } \$58,500$$

The net present value (at $t = 0$) for other harvest dates is as follows:

	Year of Harvest					
	0	1	2	3	4	5
Net present value ($ thousands)	50	58.5	64.0	67.2	68.3	67.9

The optimal point to harvest the timber is year 4 because this is the point that maximizes NPV.

Notice that before year 4 the net future value of the timber increases by more than 10 percent a year: The gain in value is greater than the cost of the capital that is tied up in the project. After year 4 the gain in value is still positive but less than the cost of capital. You maximize the net present value of your investment if you harvest your timber as soon as the rate of increase in value drops below the cost of capital.[15]

The problem of optimal timing of investment under uncertainty is, of course, much more complicated. An opportunity not taken at $t = 0$ might be either more or less attractive at $t = 1$; there is rarely any way of knowing for sure. Perhaps it is better to strike while the iron is hot even if there is a chance it will become hotter. On the other hand, if you wait a bit you might obtain more information and avoid a bad mistake.[16]

Case 2: Fluctuating Load Factors

Although a $10 million warehouse may have a positive net present value, it should be built only if it has a higher NPV than a $9 million alternative. In other words, the NPV of the $1 million *marginal* investment required to buy the more expensive warehouse must be positive.

One case in which this is easily forgotten is when equipment is needed to meet fluctuating demand. Consider the following problem: A widget manufacturer operates two machines, each of which has a capacity of 1,000 units a year. They have an indefinite life and no salvage value, and so the only costs are the operating expenses of $2 per widget. Widget manufacture, as everyone knows, is a seasonal business, and widgets are perishable. During the fall and winter, when demand is high, each machine produces at capacity. During the spring and summer, each machine works at 50 percent of capacity. If the discount rate is 10 percent and the machines are kept indefinitely, the present value of the costs is $30,000:

---

[15]Our timber-cutting example conveys the right idea about investment timing, but it misses an important practical point: The sooner you cut the first crop of trees, the sooner the second crop can start growing. Thus, the value of the second crop depends on when you cut the first. This more complex and realistic problem might be solved in one of two ways:

1. Find the cutting dates that maximize the present value of a series of harvests, taking account of the different growth rates of young and old trees.
2. Repeat our calculations, counting the future market value of cut-over land as part of the payoff to the first harvest. The value of cut-over land includes the present value of all subsequent harvests.

The second solution is far simpler if you can figure out what cut-over land will be worth.

[16]We return to optimal investment timing under uncertainty in Chapters 10 and 22.

	Two Old Machines
Annual output per machine	750 units
Operating cost per machine	2 × 750 = $1,500
PV operating cost per machine	1,500/.10 = $15,000
PV operating cost of two machines	2 × 15,000 = $30,000

The company is considering whether to replace these machines with newer equipment. The new machines have a similar capacity, and so two would still be needed to meet peak demand. Each new machine costs $6,000 and lasts indefinitely. Operating expenses are only $1 per unit. On this basis the company calculates that the present value of the costs of two new machines would be $27,000:

	Two New Machines
Annual output per machine	750 units
Capital cost per machine	$6,000
Operating cost per machine	1 × 750 = $750
PV total cost per machine	6,000 + 750/.10 = $13,500
PV total cost of two machines	2 × 13,500 = $27,000

Therefore, it scraps both old machines and buys two new ones.

The company was quite right in thinking that two new machines are better than two old ones, but unfortunately it forgot to investigate a third alternative: to replace just one of the old machines. Since the new machine has low operating costs, it would pay to operate it at capacity all year. The remaining old machine could then be kept simply to meet peak demand. The present value of the costs under this strategy is $26,000:

	One Old Machine	One New Machine
Annual output per machine	500 units	1,000 units
Capital cost per machine	0	$6,000
Operating cost per machine	2 × 500 = $1,000	1 × 1,000 = $1,000
PV total cost per machine	1,000/.10 = $10,000	6,000 + 1,000/.10 = $16,000
PV total cost of both machines		$26,000

Replacing one machine saves $4,000; replacing two machines saves only $3,000. The net present value of the *marginal* investment in the second machine is −$1,000.

By now present value calculations should be a matter of routine. However, forecasting cash flows will never be routine. It will always be a skilled, hazardous occupation. Mistakes can be minimized by following three rules:

1. Concentrate on cash flows after taxes. Be wary of accounting data masquerading as cash-flow data.

2. Always judge investments on an incremental basis. Tirelessly track down all cash-flow consequences of your decision.

3. Treat inflation consistently. Discount nominal cash-flow forecasts at nominal rates and real forecasts at real rates.

SUMMARY

We worked through a detailed numerical example (IM&C's guano project), showing the basic steps in calculating project NPV. Remember to track changes in working capital, and stay alert for differences between tax depreciation and the depreciation used in reports to shareholders.

The principles of valuing capital investment projects are the same worldwide, but inputs and assumptions vary by country and currency. For example, cash flows from a project undertaken in France would be in euros, not dollars, and would be forecasted after French taxes.

We might add still another rule: Recognize project interactions. Decisions involving only a choice of accepting or rejecting a project rarely exist, since capital projects can rarely be isolated from other projects or alternatives. The simplest decision normally encountered is to accept or reject or delay. A project having a positive NPV if undertaken today may have a still higher NPV if undertaken tomorrow.

Projects also interact because they are mutually exclusive. You can install machine A or B, for example, but not both. When mutually exclusive choices involve different lengths or time patterns of cash outflows, comparison is difficult unless you convert present values to equivalent annual costs. Think of the equivalent annual cost as the period-by-period rental payment necessary to cover all the cash outflows. Choose A over B, other things equal, if A has the lower equivalent annual cost. Remember, though, to calculate equivalent annual costs in real terms and adjust for technological change if necessary.

This chapter is concerned with the mechanics of applying the net present value rule in practical situations. All our analysis boils down to two simple themes. First, be careful about the definition of alternative projects. Make sure you are comparing like with like. Second, make sure that your calculations include all incremental cash flows.

FURTHER READING

There are several good general texts on capital budgeting that cover project interactions. Two examples are:

E. L. Grant, W. G. Ireson, and R. S. Leavenworth: *Principles of Engineering Economy*, 8th ed., John Wiley & Sons, New York, 1990.

H. Bierman and S. Smidt: *The Capital Budgeting Decision*, 8th ed., Prentice-Hall, Inc., Englewood Cliffs, N.J., 1992.

Reinhardt provides an interesting case study of a capital investment decision in:

U. E. Reinhardt: "Break-Even Analysis for Lockheed's TriStar: An Application of Financial Theory," *Journal of Finance*, 32:821–838 (September 1973).

QUIZ

1. Which of the following should be treated as incremental cash flows when deciding whether to invest in a new manufacturing plant? The site is already owned by the company, but existing buildings would need to be demolished.
   a. The market value of the site and existing buildings.
   b. Demolition costs and site clearance.
   c. The cost of a new access road put in last year.
   d. Lost earnings on other products due to executive time spent on the new facility.
   e. A proportion of the cost of leasing the president's jet airplane.
   f. Future depreciation of the new plant.
   g. The reduction in the corporation's tax bill resulting from tax depreciation of the new plant.

h. The initial investment in inventories of raw materials.

i. Money already spent on engineering design of the new plant.

2. M. Loup Garou will be paid 100,000 euros one year hence. This is a nominal flow, which he discounts at an 8 percent nominal discount rate:

$$PV = \frac{100,000}{1.08} = €92,593$$

The inflation rate is 4 percent.

Calculate the PV of M. Garou's payment using the equivalent *real* cash flow and *real* discount rate. (You should get exactly the same answer as he did.)

3. True or false?

a. A project's depreciation tax shields depend on the actual future rate of inflation.

b. Project cash flows should take account of interest paid on any borrowing undertaken to finance the project.

c. In the U.S., income reported to the tax authorities must equal income reported to shareholders.

d. Accelerated depreciation reduces near-term project cash flows and therefore reduces project NPV.

4. How does the PV of depreciation tax shields vary across the recovery-period classes shown in Table 6.4? Give a general answer; then check it by calculating the PVs of depreciation tax shields in the five-year and seven-year classes. The tax rate is 35 percent. Use any reasonable discount rate.

5. The following table tracks the main components of working capital over the life of a four-year project.

	2000	2001	2002	2003	2004
Accounts receivable	0	150,000	225,000	190,000	0
Inventory	75,000	130,000	130,000	95,000	0
Accounts payable	25,000	50,000	50,000	35,000	0

Calculate net working capital and the cash inflows and outflows due to investment in working capital.

6. Suppose the guano project were undertaken in France by a French company. What inputs and assumptions would have to change? Make a checklist.

7. When appraising mutually exclusive investments in plant and equipment, many companies calculate the investments' equivalent annual costs and rank the investments on this basis. Why is this necessary? Why not just compare the investments' NPVs? Explain briefly.

8. Think back to the timber-cutting example in Section 6.4. State the rule for deciding *when* to undertake a project.

9. Air conditioning for a college dormitory will cost $1.5 million to install and $200,000 per year to operate. The system should last 25 years. The real cost of capital is 5 percent, and the college pays no taxes. What is the equivalent annual cost?

10. Machines A and B are mutually exclusive and are expected to produce the following cash flows:

Cash Flows ($ thousands)

Machine	C_0	C_1	C_2	C_3
A	−100	+110	+121	
B	−120	+110	+121	+133

The real opportunity cost of capital is 10 percent.

a. Calculate the NPV of each machine.
b. Calculate the equivalent annual cash flow from each machine.
c. Which machine should you buy?

11. Machine C was purchased five years ago for $200,000 and produces an annual cash flow of $80,000. It has no salvage value but is expected to last another five years. The company can replace machine C with machine B (see question 10 above) *either* now *or* at the end of five years. Which should it do?

PRACTICE QUESTIONS

1. Restate the net cash flows in Table 6.6 in real terms. Discount the restated cash flows at a real discount rate. Assume a 20 percent *nominal* rate and 10 percent expected inflation. NPV should be unchanged at +3,802, or $3,802,000.

2. In 1898 Simon North announced plans to construct a funeral home on land he owned and rented out as a storage area for railway carts. (A local newspaper commended Mr. North for not putting the cart before the hearse.) Rental income from the site barely covered real estate taxes, but the site was valued at $45,000. However, Mr. North had refused several offers for the land and planned to continue renting it out if for some reason the funeral home was not built. Therefore he did not include the value of the land as an outlay in his NPV analysis of the funeral home. Was this the correct procedure? Explain.

3. Discuss the following statement: "We don't want individual plant managers to get involved in the firm's tax position. So instead of telling them to discount after-tax cash flows at 10 percent, we just tell them to take the pretax cash flows and discount at 15 percent. With a 35 percent tax rate, 15 percent pretax generates approximately 10 percent after tax."

4. Consider the following statement: "We like to do all our capital budgeting calculations in real terms. It saves making any forecasts of the inflation rate." Discuss briefly.

5. Each of the following statements is true. Explain why they are consistent.
   a. When a company introduces a new product, or expands production of an existing product, investment in net working capital is usually an important cash outflow.
   b. Forecasting changes in net working capital is not necessary if the timing of *all* cash inflows and outflows is carefully specified.

6. Mrs. T. Potts, the treasurer of Ideal China, has a problem. The company has just ordered a new kiln for $400,000. Of this sum, $50,000 is described by the supplier as an installation cost. Mrs. Potts does not know whether the Internal Revenue Service (IRS) will permit the company to treat this cost as a tax-deductible current expense or as a capital investment. In the latter case, the company could depreciate the $50,000 using the five-year MACRS tax depreciation schedule. How will the IRS's decision affect the after-tax cost of the kiln? The tax rate is 35 percent and the opportunity cost of capital is 5 percent.

7. A project requires an initial investment of $100,000 and is expected to produce a cash inflow before tax of $26,000 per year for five years. Company A has substantial accumulated tax losses and is unlikely to pay taxes in the foreseeable future. Company B pays corporate taxes at a rate of 35 percent and can depreciate the investment for tax purposes using the five-year MACRS tax depreciation schedule.
   Suppose the opportunity cost of capital is 8 percent. Ignore inflation.
   a. Calculate project NPV for each company.
   b. What is the IRR of the after-tax cash flows for each company? What does comparison of the IRRs suggest is the effective corporate tax rate?

8. A widget manufacturer currently produces 200,000 units a year. It buys widget lids from an outside supplier at a price of $2 a lid. The plant manager believes that it

	2003	2004	2005	2006–2013
1. Capital expenditure	−10,400			
2. Research and development	−2,000			
3. Working capital	−4,000			
4. Revenue		8,000	16,000	40,000
5. Operating costs		−4,000	−8,000	−20,000
6. Overhead		−800	−1,600	−4,000
7. Depreciation		−1,040	−1,040	−1,040
8. Interest		−2,160	−2,160	−2,160
9. Income	−2,000	0	3,200	12,800
10. Tax	0	0	420	4,480
11. Net cash flow	−16,400	0	2,780	8,320
12. Net present value = +13,932				

TABLE 6.7

Cash flows and present value of Reliable Electric's proposed investment ($ thousands). See Practice Question 9.

Notes:
1. *Capital expenditure:* $8 million for new machinery and $2.4 million for a warehouse extension. The full cost of the extension has been charged to this project, although only about half of the space is currently needed. Since the new machinery will be housed in an existing factory building, no charge has been made for land and building.
2. *Research and development:* $1.82 million spent in 2002. This figure was corrected for 10 percent inflation from the time of expenditure to date. Thus 1.82 × 1.1 = $2 million.
3. *Working capital:* Initial investment in inventories.
4. *Revenue:* These figures assume sales of 2,000 motors in 2004, 4,000 in 2005, and 10,000 per year from 2006 through 2013. The initial unit price of $4,000 is forecasted to remain constant in real terms.
5. *Operating costs:* These include all direct and indirect costs. Indirect costs (heat, light, power, fringe benefits, etc.) are assumed to be 200 percent of direct labor costs. Operating costs per unit are forecasted to remain constant in real terms at $2,000.
6. *Overhead:* Marketing and administrative costs, assumed equal to 10 percent of revenue.
7. *Depreciation:* Straight-line for 10 years.
8. *Interest:* Charged on capital expenditure and working capital at Reliable's current borrowing rate of 15 percent.
9. *Income:* Revenue less the sum of research and development, operating costs, overhead, depreciation, and interest.
10. *Tax:* 35 percent of income. However, income is negative in 2003. This loss is carried forward and deducted from taxable income in 2005.
11. *Net cash flow:* Assumed equal to income less tax.
12. *Net present value:* NPV of net cash flow at a 15 percent discount rate.

would be cheaper to make these lids rather than buy them. Direct production costs are estimated to be only $1.50 a lid. The necessary machinery would cost $150,000. This investment could be written off for tax purposes using the seven-year tax depreciation schedule. The plant manager estimates that the operation would require additional working capital of $30,000 but argues that this sum can be ignored since it is recoverable at the end of the 10 years. If the company pays tax at a rate of 35 percent and the opportunity cost of capital is 15 percent, would you support the plant manager's proposal? State clearly any additional assumptions that you need to make.

9. Reliable Electric is considering a proposal to manufacture a new type of industrial electric motor which would replace most of its existing product line. A research breakthrough has given Reliable a two-year lead on its competitors. The project proposal is summarized in Table 6.7.
   a. Read the notes to the table carefully. Which entries make sense? Which do not? Why or why not?
   b. What additional information would you need to construct a version of Table 6.7 that makes sense?
   c. Construct such a table and recalculate NPV. Make additional assumptions as necessary.

10. Marsha Jones, whom you met in the Chapter 3 Mini-case, has bought a used Mercedes horse transporter for her Connecticut estate. It cost $35,000. The object is to save on horse transporter rentals.

    Marsha had been renting a transporter every other week for $200 per day plus $1.00 per mile. Most of the trips are 40 or 50 miles one-way. Marsha usually gives the driver a $40 tip. With the new transporter she will only have to pay for diesel fuel and mainte-nance, at about $.45 per mile. Insurance costs for Marsha's transporter are $1,200 per year.

    The transporter will probably be worth $15,000 (in real terms) after eight years, when Marsha's horse Nike will be ready to retire.

    Is the transporter a positive-NPV investment? Assume a nominal discount rate of 9 percent and a 3 percent forecasted inflation rate. Marsha's transporter is a personal out-lay, not a business or financial investment, so taxes can be ignored.

11. United Pigpen is considering a proposal to manufacture high-protein hog feed. The project would make use of an existing warehouse, which is currently rented out to a neighboring firm. The next year's rental charge on the warehouse is $100,000, and thereafter the rent is expected to grow in line with inflation at 4 percent a year. In addi-tion to using the warehouse, the proposal envisages an investment in plant and equip-ment of $1.2 million. This could be depreciated for tax purposes straight-line over 10 years. However, Pigpen expects to terminate the project at the end of eight years and to resell the plant and equipment in year 8 for $400,000. Finally, the project requires an ini-tial investment in working capital of $350,000. Thereafter, working capital is forecasted to be 10 percent of sales in each of years 1 through 7.

    Year 1 sales of hog feed are expected to be $4.2 million, and thereafter sales are fore-cast to grow by 5 percent a year, slightly faster than the inflation rate. Manufacturing costs are expected to be 90 percent of sales, and profits are subject to tax at 35 percent. The cost of capital is 12 percent.

    What is the NPV of Pigpen's project?

12. In the International Mulch and Compost example (Section 6.2), we assumed that losses on the project could be used to offset taxable profits elswhere in the corporation. Sup-pose that the losses had to be carried forward and offset against future taxable profits from the project. How would the project NPV change? What is the value of the com-pany's ability to use the tax deductions immediately?

13. Table 6.8 shows investment and projected income in euros for Flanel's new perfume factory. Forecast cash flows and calculate NPV. The nominal cost of capital in euros is 11 percent.

14. As a result of improvements in product engineering, United Automation is able to sell one of its two milling machines. Both machines perform the same function but differ in age. The newer machine could be sold today for $50,000. Its operating costs are $20,000 a year, but in five years the machine will require a $20,000 overhaul. Thereafter operat-ing costs will be $30,000 until the machine is finally sold in year 10 for $5,000.

    The older machine could be sold today for $25,000. If it is kept, it will need an im-mediate $20,000 overhaul. Thereafter operating costs will be $30,000 a year until the ma-chine is finally sold in year 5 for $5,000.

    Both machines are fully depreciated for tax purposes. The company pays tax at 35 per-cent. Cash flows have been forecasted in real terms. The real cost of capital is 12 percent.

    Which machine should United Automation sell? Explain the assumptions underly-ing your answer.

15. Hayden Inc. has a number of copiers that were bought four years ago for $20,000. Cur-rently maintenance costs $2,000 a year, but the maintenance agreement expires at the end of two years and thereafter the annual maintenance charge will rise to $8,000. The machines have a current resale value of $8,000, but at the end of year 2 their value will have fallen to $3,500. By the end of year 6 the machines will be valueless and would be scrapped.

	0	1	2	3	4	5	6	7	8
1. Capital investment	83.5								−12.0
2. Accumulated depreciation		11.9	23.9	35.8	47.7	59.6	71.6	83.5	
3. Year-end book value		71.6	59.6	47.7	35.8	23.9	11.9	0.0	
4. Working capital	2.3	4.4	7.6	6.9	5.3	3.2	2.5	0.0	
5. Total book value (3 + 4)	85.8	76.0	67.2	54.6	41.1	27.1	14.4	0.0	
6. Sales		27.0	51.3	89.1	81.0	62.1	37.8	29.7	
7. Cost of goods sold		9.2	17.4	30.3	27.5	21.1	12.9	10.1	
8. Other costs		15.5	15.5	5.2	5.2	5.2	5.2	5.2	
9. Depreciation		11.9	11.9	11.9	11.9	11.9	11.9	11.9	
10. Pretax profit (6 − 7 − 8 − 9)		−9.6	6.4	41.7	36.3	23.9	7.8	2.5	
11. Tax at 40%		−3.8	2.6	16.7	14.5	9.5	3.1	1.0	4.8
12. Profit after tax (10 − 11)		−5.8	3.9	25.0	21.8	14.3	4.7	1.5	7.2

TABLE 6.8

Projected investment and income for Flanel's new perfume factory. Figures in millions of euros.

Note: The format of this table matches Table 6.1. Cost of goods sold excludes depreciation.

Hayden is considering replacing the copiers with new machines that would do essentially the same job. These machines cost $25,000, and the company can take out an eight-year maintenance contract for $1,000 a year. The machines have no value by the end of the eight years and would be scrapped.

Both machines are depreciated by using seven-year MACRS, and the tax rate is 35 percent. Assume for simplicity that the inflation rate is zero. The real cost of capital is 7 percent.

When should Hayden replace its copiers?

16. Return to the start of Section 6.3, where we calculated the equivalent annual cost, in cents per gallon, of producing reformulated gasoline in California. Capital investment was $400 million. Suppose this amount can be depreciated for tax purposes on the 10-year MACRS schedule from Table 6.4. The marginal tax rate, including California taxes, is 39 percent, and the cost of capital is 7 percent. The refinery improvements have an economic life of 25 years.

a. Calculate the after-tax equivalent annual cost. *Hint:* It's easiest to use the PV of depreciation tax shields as an offset to the initial investment.

b. How much extra would retail gasoline customers have to pay to cover this equivalent annual cost? *Note:* Extra income from higher retail prices would be taxed.

17. You own 500 acres of timberland, with young timber worth $40,000 if logged now. This represents 1,000 cords of wood worth $40 per cord net of costs of cutting and hauling. A paper company has offered to purchase your tract for $140,000. Should you accept the offer? You have the following information:

Years	Yearly Growth Rate of Cords per Acre
1–4	16%
5–8	11
9–13	4
14 and subsequent years	1

- You expect price per cord to increase at 4 percent per year indefinitely.
- The cost of capital is 9 percent. Ignore taxes.

- The market value of your land would be $100 per acre if you cut and removed the timber this year. The value of cut-over land is also expected to grow at 4 percent per year indefinitely.

18. The Borstal Company has to choose between two machines that do the same job but have different lives. The two machines have the following costs:

Year	Machine A	Machine B
0	$40,000	$50,000
1	10,000	8,000
2	10,000	8,000
3	10,000 + replace	8,000
4		8,000 + replace

These costs are expressed in real terms.

a. Suppose you are Borstal's financial manager. If you had to buy one or the other machine and rent it to the production manager for that machine's economic life, what annual rental payment would you have to charge? Assume a 6 percent real discount rate and ignore taxes.

b. Which machine should Borstal buy?

c. Usually the rental payments you derived in part (a) are just hypothetical—a way of calculating and interpreting equivalent annual cost. Suppose you actually do buy one of the machines and rent it to the production manager. How much would you actually have to charge in each future year if there is steady 8 percent per year inflation? (*Note:* The rental payments calculated in part (a) are real cash flows. You would have to mark up those payments to cover inflation.)

19. Look again at your calculations for question 18 above. Suppose that technological change is expected to reduce costs by 10 percent per year. There will be new machines in year 1 that cost 10 percent less to buy and operate than A and B. In year 2 there will be a second crop of new machines incorporating a further 10 percent reduction, and so on. How does this change the equivalent annual costs of machines A and B?

20. The president's executive jet is not fully utilized. You judge that its use by other officers would increase direct operating costs by only $20,000 a year and would save $100,000 a year in airline bills. On the other hand, you believe that with the increased use the company will need to replace the jet at the end of three years rather than four. A new jet costs $1.1 million and (at its current low rate of use) has a life of six years. Assume that the company does not pay taxes. All cash flows are forecasted in real terms. The real opportunity cost of capital is 8 percent. Should you try to persuade the president to allow other officers to use the plane?

CHALLENGE QUESTIONS

1. One measure of the effective tax rate is the difference between the IRRs of pretax and after-tax cash flows, divided by the pretax IRR. Consider, for example, an investment I generating a perpetual stream of pretax cash flows C. The pretax IRR is C/I, and the after-tax IRR is $C(1 - T_c)/I$, where T_c is the statutory tax rate. The effective rate, call it T_E, is

$$T_E = \frac{C/I - C(1 - T_c)/I}{C/I} = T_c$$

In this case the effective rate equals the statutory rate.

a. Calculate T_E for the guano project in Section 6.2.

b. How does the effective rate depend on the tax depreciation schedule? On the inflation rate?

c. Consider a project where all of the up-front investment is treated as an expense for tax purposes. For example, R&D and marketing outlays are always expensed in the U.S. They create no tax depreciation. What is the effective tax rate for such a project?

2. We warned that equivalent annual costs should be calculated in real terms. We did not fully explain why. This problem will show you.

   Look back to the cash flows for machines A and B (in "Choosing between Long- and Short-Lived Equipment"). The present values of purchase and operating costs are 28.37 (over three years for A) and 21.00 (over two years for B). The real discount rate is 6 percent, and the inflation rate is 5 percent.

   a. Calculate the three- and two-year *level nominal* annuities which have present values of 28.37 and 21.00. Explain why these annuities are *not* realistic estimates of equivalent annual costs. (*Hint:* In real life machinery rentals increase with inflation.)

   b. Suppose the inflation rate increases to 25 percent. The real interest rate stays at 6 percent. Recalculate the level nominal annuities. Note that the *ranking* of machines A and B appears to change. Why?

3. Suppose that *after-tax* investment is defined as the investment outlay minus the present value of future depreciation tax shields. In the guano project, for example, after-tax investment would be $10,000,000 − 2,174,000 = $7,826,000. This figure would be entered as the investment outlay, then future cash flows would be calculated ignoring depreciation.

   a. Does this change in format affect bottom-line NPV? Does the format have any advantages or disadvantages?

   b. This format requires discounting depreciation tax shields separately. What should the discount rate be? Note that depreciation tax shields are safe if the company will be consistently profitable.

   c. If depreciation tax shields are not discounted at the ordinary cost of capital, should the discount rate for the other cash flows change? Why or why not?

MINI-CASE

New Economy Transport

The New Economy Transport Company (NETCO) was formed in 1952 to carry cargo and passengers between ports in the Pacific Northwest. By 2002 its fleet had grown to four vessels, one of which was a small dry-cargo vessel, the *Vital Spark*.

The *Vital Spark* is badly in need of an overhaul. Peter Handy, the finance director, has just been presented with a proposal, which would require the following expenditures:

Install new engine and associated equipment	$185,000
Replace radar and other electronic equipment	50,000
Repairs to hull and superstructure	130,000
Painting and other maintenance	35,000
	$400,000

NETCO's chief engineer, McPhail, estimates the postoverhaul operating costs as follows:[17]

Fuel	$ 450,000
Labor and benefits	480,000
Maintenance	141,000
Other	110,000
	$1,181,000

[17] All estimates of costs and revenues ignore inflation. Mr. Handy's bankers have suggested that inflation will average 3 percent a year.

The *Vital Spark* is carried on NETCO's books at a net value of only $30,000, but could probably be sold "as is," along with an extensive inventory of spare parts, for $100,000. The book value of the spare parts inventory is $40,000.

The chief engineer has also suggested installation of a more modern navigation and control system, which would cost an extra $200,000.[18] This additional equipment would not substantially affect the *Vital Spark's* performance, but it would result in the following reduced annual fuel, labor, and maintenance costs:

Fuel	$420,000
Labor and benefits	405,000
Maintenance	70,000
Other	90,000
	$985,000

There is no question that the *Vital Spark* needs a new engine and general overhaul soon. However, Mr. Handy feels it unwise to proceed without also considering the purchase of a new boat. Cohn and Doyle, Inc., a Wisconsin shipyard, has approached NETCO with a new design incorporating a Kort nozzle, extensively automated navigation and power control systems, and much more comfortable accommodations for the crew. Estimated annual operating costs of the new boat are

Fuel	$370,000
Labor and benefits	330,000
Maintenance	70,000
Other	74,000
	$844,000

The crew would require additional training to handle the new boat's more complex and sophisticated equipment and this would probably require an expenditure of $50,000 to $100,000.

The estimated operating costs for the new boat assume that it would be operated in the same way as the *Vital Spark*. However, the new boat should be able to handle a larger load on some routes, and this might generate additional revenues, net of additional out-of-pocket costs, of as much as $100,000 per year. Moreover, a new boat would have a useful service life of 20 years or more. The *Vital Spark*, even if rehabilitated, could not last that long—probably only 15 years. At that point it would be worth only its scrap value of about $40,000.

Cohn and Doyle offered the new boat for a fixed price of $2,000,000, payable half immediately and half on delivery in nine months. Of this amount $600,000 was for the engine and associated equipment and $510,000 was for navigation, control, and other electronic equipment.

NETCO was a private company, soundly financed and consistently profitable. Cash on hand was sufficient to rehabilitate or improve the *Vital Spark* but not to buy the new boat. However, Mr. Handy was confident that the new boat could be financed with medium-term debt, privately placed with an insurance company. NETCO had borrowed via a private placement once before when it negotiated a fixed rate of 12.5 percent on a seven-year loan. Preliminary discussions with NETCO's bankers led Mr. Handy to believe that the firm could arrange an 8 percent fixed-rate medium-term loan.

NETCO had traditionally estimated its opportunity cost of capital for major business investments by adding a risk premium of 10 percentage points to yields on newly issued

---

[18] All investments qualify for the seven-year MACRS class.

Treasury bonds.[19] Mr. Handy thought this was a reasonable rule of thumb for the dry-cargo business.

Questions

1. Calculate equivalent annual costs of the three alternatives—overhaul, overhaul with improved navigation and control, or a brand-new boat. To do the calculation, you will have to prepare a spreadsheet table showing all costs after taxes over each investment's economic life. Take special care with your assumptions about depreciation tax shields and inflation.

---

[19]In 2002 Treasury bonds were yielding 5 percent.

PART 1 RELATED WEBSITES

Chapter 1 described the role of the financial manager. More information on careers in finance can be found at:

www.careers-in-finance.com

The following websites, which are concerned largely with personal finance, provide discussions of the time value of money and calculators:

www.bankrate.com

www.financenter.com

www.financialplayerscenter.com

www.invest-faq.com

www.money.cnn.com

www.unb.ca/web/transpo/mynet/mtw21b.htm (how to use Excel for compound interest calculations)

One of the few sites with material on capital investment decisions is:

www.asbdc.ualr.edu/fod/1518.htm

Chapter 3 explained how bonds are valued. Helpful material and data on bond markets are available on:

www.bondsonline.com (good bond data)

http://bonds.yahoo.com

www.finpipe.com (good explanations of bond markets)

www.fintools.net (contains a bond calculator)

www.ganesha.org (explanation of bond markets and calculator)

www.hsh.com (good bond data)

www.investinginbonds.com (also contains links to related sites)

www.investorguide.com/university.html (good explanations of bond and equity markets)

http://money.cnn.com/markets/bondcenter

Chapter 4 was concerned with stock markets and equity valuation. Most major stock exchanges have good websites. See, for example:

www.nyse.com (New York Exchange)

www.nasdaq.com (NASDAQ)

www.londonstockexchange.com (London Exchange)

www.tse.or.jp (Tokyo Exchange)

www.123world.com/stockexchanges (links to exchanges)

www.fibv.com (The World Federation of Exchanges publishes useful comparative statistics)

Data on stock market indexes can be found on:

www.djindexes.com (Dow Jones index)

www.spglobal.com (Standard & Poor's indexes)

www.barra.com (market indices with information on dividend yields, P/Es etc.)

www.wilshire.com

There is a large number of sites with market commentary and data on individual firms and stocks. We find Finance.Yahoo particularly useful.

http://finance.yahoo.com

www.bloomberg.com

http://hoovers.com

www.cbs.marketwatch.com

www.finance.lycos.com

http://money.cnn.com

http://moneycentral.msn.com

www.wsrn.com

http://my.zacks.com (includes earnings forecasts)

The following sites provide useful software and data for calculating company values:

http://financialplayerscenter.com

www.valuepro.net

RI∫K

AMAZON.COM STOCK STARTED trading in May 1997 at a price of $1.73. By December 1999, the stock price had risen by over 6,000 percent. Within little more than a year it had slumped by 90 percent. These gyrations in Amazon's stock price were unusually large, but they remind us how risky investment in common stocks can be.

Most investors are not adrenaline junkies; they don't *enjoy* taking risks. Therefore they require a higher expected return from risky investments.

Companies recognize this in their capital budgeting decisions. An investment in a risky new project adds value only if the expected return is higher than investors could expect from an equally risky investment in the capital market.

But that raises two questions. How should risk be measured? And what is the relationship between risk and expected return? We tackle these two questions in Part Two.

CHAPTER SEVEN

INTRODUCTION TO RISK, RETURN, AND THE OPPORTUNITY COST OF CAPITAL

WE HAVE MANAGED to go through six chapters without directly addressing the problem of risk, but now the jig is up. We can no longer be satisfied with vague statements like "The opportunity cost of capital depends on the risk of the project." We need to know how risk is defined, what the links are between risk and the opportunity cost of capital, and how the financial manager can cope with risk in practical situations.

In this chapter we concentrate on the first of these issues and leave the other two to Chapters 8 and 9. We start by summarizing 75 years of evidence on rates of return in capital markets. Then we take a first look at investment risks and show how they can be reduced by portfolio diversification. We introduce you to beta, the standard risk measure for individual securities.

The themes of this chapter, then, are portfolio risk, security risk, and diversification. For the most part, we take the view of the individual investor. But at the end of the chapter we turn the problem around and ask whether diversification makes sense as a *corporate* objective.

7.1 SEVENTY-FIVE YEARS OF CAPITAL MARKET HISTORY IN ONE EASY LESSON

Financial analysts are blessed with an enormous quantity of data on security prices and returns. For example, the University of Chicago's Center for Research in Security Prices (CRSP) has developed a file of prices and dividends for each month since 1926 for every stock that has been listed on the New York Stock Exchange (NYSE). Other files give data for stocks that are traded on the American Stock Exchange and the over-the-counter market, data for bonds, for options, and so on. But this is supposed to be one easy lesson. We, therefore, concentrate on a study by Ibbotson Associates that measures the historical performance of five portfolios of securities:

1. A portfolio of Treasury bills, i.e., United States government debt securities maturing in less than one year.
2. A portfolio of long-term United States government bonds.
3. A portfolio of long-term corporate bonds.[1]
4. Standard and Poor's Composite Index (S&P 500), which represents a portfolio of common stocks of 500 large firms. (Although only a small proportion of the 7,000 or so publicly traded companies are included in the S&P 500, these companies account for over 70 percent of the *value* of stocks traded.)
5. A portfolio of the common stocks of small firms.

These investments offer different degrees of risk. Treasury bills are about as safe an investment as you can make. There is no risk of default, and their short maturity means that the prices of Treasury bills are relatively stable. In fact, an investor who wishes to lend money for, say, three months can achieve a perfectly certain payoff by purchasing a Treasury bill maturing in three months. However, the investor cannot lock in a *real* rate of return: There is still some uncertainty about inflation.

By switching to long-term government bonds, the investor acquires an asset whose price fluctuates as interest rates vary. (Bond prices fall when interest rates rise and rise when interest rates fall.) An investor who shifts from government to

---

[1]The two bond portfolios were revised each year to maintain a constant maturity.

FIGURE 7.1

How an investment of $1 at the start of 1926 would have grown, assuming reinvestment of all dividend and interest payments.

Source: Ibbotson Associates, Inc., *Stocks, Bonds, Bills, and Inflation, 2001 Yearbook*, Chicago, 2001; cited hereafter in this chapter as the *2001 Yearbook*. © 2001 Ibbotson Associates, Inc

corporate bonds accepts an additional *default* risk. An investor who shifts from corporate bonds to common stocks has a direct share in the risks of the enterprise.

Figure 7.1 shows how your money would have grown if you had invested $1 at the start of 1926 and reinvested all dividend or interest income in each of the five portfolios.[2] Figure 7.2 is identical except that it depicts the growth in the *real* value of the portfolio. We will focus here on nominal values.

Portfolio performance coincides with our intuitive risk ranking. A dollar invested in the safest investment, Treasury bills, would have grown to just over $16 by 2000, barely enough to keep up with inflation. An investment in long-term Treasury bonds would have produced $49, and corporate bonds a pinch more. Common stocks were in a class by themselves. An investor who placed a dollar in the stocks of large U.S. firms would have received $2,587. The jackpot, however, went to investors in stocks of small firms, who walked away with $6,402 for each dollar invested.

Ibbotson Associates also calculated the rate of return from these portfolios for each year from 1926 to 2000. This rate of return reflects both cash receipts—dividends or interest—and the capital gains or losses realized during the year. Averages of the 75 annual rates of return for each portfolio are shown in Table 7.1.

---

[2]Portfolio values are plotted on a log scale. If they were not, the ending values for the two common stock portfolios would run off the top of the page.

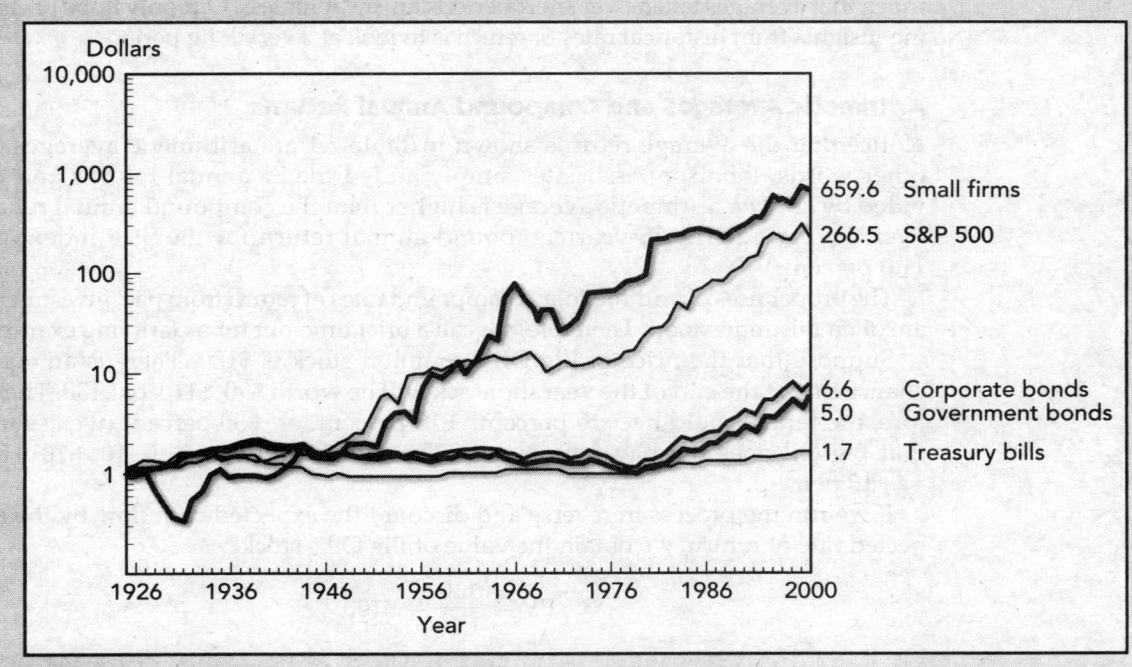

FIGURE 7.2

How an investment of $1 at the start of 1926 would have grown in real terms, assuming reinvestment of all dividend and interest payments. Compare this plot to Figure 7.1, and note how inflation has eroded the purchasing power of returns to investors.

Source: Ibbotson Associates, Inc., *2001 Yearbook.* © Ibbotson Associates, Inc.

TABLE 7.1

Average rates of return on Treasury bills, government bonds, corporate bonds, and common stocks, 1926–2000 (figures in percent per year).

Source: Ibbotson Associates, Inc., *2001 Yearbook.*

Portfolio	Average Annual Rate of Return		Average Risk Premium (Extra Return Versus Treasury Bills)
	Nominal	Real	
Treasury bills	3.9	.8	0
Government bonds	5.7	2.7	1.8
Corporate bonds	6.0	3.0	2.1
Common stocks (S&P 500)	13.0	9.7	9.1
Small-firm common stocks	17.3	13.8	13.4

Since 1926 Treasury bills have provided the lowest average return—3.9 percent per year in *nominal* terms and .8 percent in *real* terms. In other words, the average rate of inflation over this period was just over 3 percent per year. Common stocks were again the winners. Stocks of major corporations provided on average a *risk premium* of 9.1 percent a year over the return on Treasury bills. Stocks of small firms offered an even higher premium.

You may ask why we look back over such a long period to measure average rates of return. The reason is that annual rates of return for common stocks fluctuate so much that averages taken over short periods are meaningless. Our only hope of gaining insights from historical rates of return is to look at a very long period.[3]

Arithmetic Averages and Compound Annual Returns

Notice that the average returns shown in Table 7.1 are arithmetic averages. In other words, Ibbotson Associates simply added the 75 annual returns and divided by 75. The arithmetic average is higher than the compound annual return over the period. The 75-year compound annual return for the S&P index was 11.0 percent.[4]

The proper uses of arithmetic and compound rates of return from past investments are often misunderstood. Therefore, we call a brief time-out for a clarifying example.

Suppose that the price of Big Oil's common stock is $100. There is an equal chance that at the end of the year the stock will be worth $90, $110, or $130. Therefore, the return could be −10 percent, +10 percent, or +30 percent (we assume that Big Oil does not pay a dividend). The *expected* return is ⅓(−10 +10 +30) = +10 percent.

If we run the process in reverse and discount the expected cash flow by the expected rate of return, we obtain the value of Big Oil's stock:

$$PV = \frac{110}{1.10} = \$100$$

The expected return of 10 percent is therefore the correct rate at which to discount the expected cash flow from Big Oil's stock. It is also the opportunity cost of capital for investments that have the same degree of risk as Big Oil.

Now suppose that we observe the returns on Big Oil stock over a large number of years. If the odds are unchanged, the return will be −10 percent in a third of the years, +10 percent in a further third, and +30 percent in the remaining years. The arithmetic average of these yearly returns is

$$\frac{-10 + 10 + 30}{3} = +10\%$$

Thus the arithmetic average of the returns correctly measures the opportunity cost of capital for investments of similar risk to Big Oil stock.

The average compound annual return on Big Oil stock would be

$$(.9 \times 1.1 \times 1.3)^{1/3} - 1 = .088, \text{ or } 8.8\%,$$

---

[3]We cannot be sure that this period is truly representative and that the average is not distorted by a few unusually high or low returns. The reliability of an estimate of the average is usually measured by its *standard error*. For example, the standard error of our estimate of the average risk premium on common stocks is 2.3 percent. There is a 95 percent chance that the *true* average is within plus or minus 2 standard errors of the 9.1 percent estimate. In other words, if you said that the true average was between 4.5 and 13.7 percent, you would have a 95 percent chance of being right. (*Technical note*: The standard error of the average is equal to the standard deviation divided by the square root of the number of observations. In our case the standard deviation is 20.2 percent, and therefore the standard error is $20.2/\sqrt{75} = 2.3$.)

[4]This was calculated from $(1 + r)^{75} = 2,586.5$, which implies $r = .11$. *Technical note:* For lognormally distributed returns the annual compound return is equal to the arithmetic average return minus half the variance. For example, the annual standard deviation of returns on the U.S. market was about .20, or 20 percent. Variance was therefore $.20^2$, or .04. The compound annual return is $.04/2 = .02$, or 2 percentage points less than the arithmetic average.

less than the opportunity cost of capital. Investors would not be willing to invest in a project that offered an 8.8 percent expected return if they could get an expected return of 10 percent in the capital markets. The net present value of such a project would be

$$NPV = -100 + \frac{108.8}{1.1} = -1.1$$

Moral: If the cost of capital is estimated from historical returns or risk premiums, use arithmetic averages, not compound annual rates of return.

Using Historical Evidence to Evaluate Today's Cost of Capital

Suppose there is an investment project which you *know*—don't ask how—has the same risk as Standard and Poor's Composite Index. We will say that it has the same degree of risk as the *market portfolio*, although this is speaking somewhat loosely, because the index does not include all risky securities. What rate should you use to discount this project's forecasted cash flows?

Clearly you should use the currently expected rate of return on the market portfolio; that is the return investors would forgo by investing in the proposed project. Let us call this market return r_m. One way to estimate r_m is to assume that the future will be like the past and that today's investors expect to receive the same "normal" rates of return revealed by the averages shown in Table 7.1. In this case, you would set r_m at 13 percent, the average of past market returns.

Unfortunately, this is *not* the way to do it; r_m is not likely to be stable over time. Remember that it is the sum of the risk-free interest rate r_f and a premium for risk. We know that r_f varies. For example, in 1981 the interest rate on Treasury bills was about 15 percent. It is difficult to believe that investors in that year were content to hold common stocks offering an expected return of only 13 percent.

If you need to estimate the return that investors expect to receive, a more sensible procedure is to take the interest rate on Treasury bills and add 9.1 percent, the average *risk premium* shown in Table 7.1. For example, as we write this in mid-2001 the interest rate on Treasury bills is about 3.5 percent. Adding on the average risk premium, therefore, gives

$$r_m(2001) = r_f(2001) + \text{normal risk premium}$$
$$= .035 + .091 = .126, \text{ or about } 12.5\%$$

The crucial assumption here is that there is a normal, stable risk premium on the market portfolio, so that the expected *future* risk premium can be measured by the average past risk premium.

Even with 75 years of data, we can't estimate the market risk premium exactly; nor can we be sure that investors today are demanding the same reward for risk that they were 60 or 70 years ago. All this leaves plenty of room for argument about what the risk premium *really* is.[5]

Many financial managers and economists believe that long-run historical returns are the best measure available. Others have a gut instinct that investors

---

[5]Some of the disagreements simply reflect the fact that the risk premium is sometimes defined in different ways. Some measure the average difference between stock returns and the returns (or yields) on long-term bonds. Others measure the difference between the compound rate of growth on stocks and the interest rate. As we explained above, this is not an appropriate measure of the cost of capital.

don't need such a large risk premium to persuade them to hold common stocks.[6] In a recent survey of financial economists, more than a quarter of those polled believed that the expected risk premium was about 8 percent, but most of the remainder opted for a figure between 4 and 7 percent. The average estimate was just over 6 percent.[7]

If you believe that the expected market risk premium is a lot less than the historical averages, you probably also believe that history has been unexpectedly kind to investors in the United States and that their good luck is unlikely to be repeated. Here are three reasons why history *may* overstate the risk premium that investors demand today.

Reason 1   Over the past 75 years stock prices in the United States have outpaced dividend payments. In other words, there has been a long-term decline in the dividend yield. Between 1926 and 2000 this decline in yield added about 2 percent a year to the return on common stocks. Was this yield change anticipated? If not, it would be more reasonable to take the long-term growth in dividends as a measure of the capital appreciation that investors were expecting. This would point to a risk premium of about 7 percent.

Reason 2   Since 1926 the United States has been among the world's most prosperous countries. Other economies have languished or been wracked by war or civil unrest. By focusing on equity returns in the United States, we may obtain a biased view of what investors expected. Perhaps the historical averages miss the possibility that the United States could have turned out to be one of those less-fortunate countries.[8]

Figure 7.3 sheds some light on this issue. It is taken from a comprehensive study by Dimson, Marsh, and Staunton of market returns in 15 countries and shows the average risk premium in each country between 1900 and 2000.[9] Two points are worth making. Notice first that in the United States the risk premium over 101 years has averaged 7.5 percent, somewhat less than the figure that we cited earlier for the period 1926–2000. The period of the First World War and its aftermath was in many ways not typical, so it is hard to say whether we get a more or less representative picture of investor expectations by adding in the extra years. But the ef-

---

[6]There is some theory behind this instinct. The high risk premium earned in the market seems to imply that investors are extremely risk-averse. If that is true, investors ought to cut back their consumption when stock prices fall and wealth decreases. But the evidence suggests that when stock prices fall, investors spend at nearly the same rate. This is difficult to reconcile with high risk aversion and a high market risk premium. See R. Mehra and E. Prescott, "The Equity Premium: A Puzzle," *Journal of Monetary Economics* 15 (1985), pp. 145–161.

[7]I. Welch, "Views of Financial Economists on the Equity Premium and Other Issues," *Journal of Business* 73 (October 2000), pp. 501–537. In a later unpublished survey undertaken by Ivo Welch the average estimate for the equity risk premium was slightly lower at 5.5 percent. See I. Welch, "The Equity Premium Consensus Forecast Revisited," Yale School of Management, September 2001.

[8]This possibility was suggested in P. Jorion and W. N. Goetzmann, "Global Stock Markets in the Twentieth Century," *Journal of Finance* 54 (June 1999), pp. 953–980.

[9]See E. Dimson, P. R. Marsh, and M. Staunton, *Millenium Book II: 101 Years of Investment Returns*, APN-Amro and London Business School, London, 2001.

FIGURE 7.3

Average market risk premia, 1900–2000.

Source: E. Dimson, P. R. Marsh, and M. Staunton, *Millenium Book II: 101 Years of Investment Returns*, ABN-Amro and London Business School, London, 2001.

fect of doing so is an important reminder of how difficult it is to obtain an accurate measure of the risk premium.

Now compare the returns in the United States with those in the other countries. There is no evidence here that U.S. investors have been particularly fortunate; the USA was exactly average in terms of the risk premium. Danish common stocks came bottom of the league; the average risk premium in Denmark was only 4.3 percent. Top of the form was Italy with a premium of 11.1 percent. Some of these variations between countries may reflect differences in risk. For example, Italian stocks have been particularly variable and investors may have required a higher return to compensate. But remember how difficult it is to make precise estimates of what investors expected. You probably would not be too far out if you concluded that the *expected* risk premium was the same in each country.

Reason 3 During the second half of the 1990s U.S. equity prices experienced a remarkable boom, with the annual return averaging nearly 25 percent more than the return on Treasury bills. Some argued that this price rise reflected optimism that the new economy would lead to a golden age of prosperity and surging profits, but others attributed the rise to a reduction in the market risk premium.

To see how a rise in stock prices can stem from a fall in the risk premium, suppose that investors in common stocks initially look for a return of 13 percent, made up of a 3 percent dividend yield and 10 percent long-term growth in dividends. If they now decide that they are prepared to hold equities on a prospective return of 12 percent, then other things being equal the dividend yield must fall to 2 percent.

Thus a 1 percentage point fall in the risk premium would lead to a 50 percent rise in equity prices. If we include this price adjustment in our measures of past returns, we will be doubly wrong in our estimate of the risk premium. First, we will overestimate the return that investors required in the past. Second, we will not recognize that the return that investors require in the future is lower than in the past.

As stock prices began to slide back from their highs of March 2000, this belief in a falling market risk premium began to wane. It seems that if the risk premium truly did fall in the 1990s, then it also rose again as the new century dawned.[10]

Out of this debate only one firm conclusion emerges: Do not trust anyone who claims to *know* what returns investors expect. History contains some clues, but ultimately we have to judge whether investors on average have received what they expected. Brealey and Myers have no official position on the market risk premium, but we believe that a range of 6 to 8.5 percent is reasonable for the United States.[11]

7.2 MEASURING PORTFOLIO RISK

You now have a couple of benchmarks. You know the discount rate for safe projects, and you have an estimate of the rate for average-risk projects. But you *don't* know yet how to estimate discount rates for assets that do not fit these simple cases. To do that, you have to learn (1) how to measure risk and (2) the relationship between risks borne and risk premiums demanded.

Figure 7.4 shows the 75 annual rates of return calculated by Ibbotson Associates for Standard and Poor's Composite Index. The fluctuations in year-to-year returns are remarkably wide. The highest annual return was 54.0 percent in 1933—a partial rebound from the stock market crash of 1929–1932. However, there were losses exceeding 25 percent in four years, the worst being the −43.3 percent return in 1931.

Another way of presenting these data is by a histogram or frequency distribution. This is done in Figure 7.5, where the variability of year-to-year returns shows up in the wide "spread" of outcomes.

Variance and Standard Deviation

The standard statistical measures of spread are **variance** and **standard deviation**. The variance of the market return is the expected squared deviation from the expected return. In other words,

$$\text{Variance } (\tilde{r}_m) = \text{the expected value of } (\tilde{r}_m - r_m)^2$$

---

[10]The decline in the stock market in 2001 also reduces the long-term average risk premium. The average premium from 1926 to September 2001 is 8.7 percent, .4 percentage points lower than the figure quoted in Table 7.1.

[11]This range seems to be consistent with company practice. For example, Kaplan and Ruback, in an analysis of valuations in 51 takeovers between 1983 and 1998, found that acquiring companies appeared to base their discount rates on a market risk premium of about 7.5 percent over average returns on long-term Treasury bonds. The risk premium over Treasury bills would have been about a percentage point higher. See S. Kaplan and R. S. Ruback, "The Valuation of Cash Flow Forecasts: An Empirical Analysis," *Journal of Finance* 50 (September 1995), pp. 1059–1093.

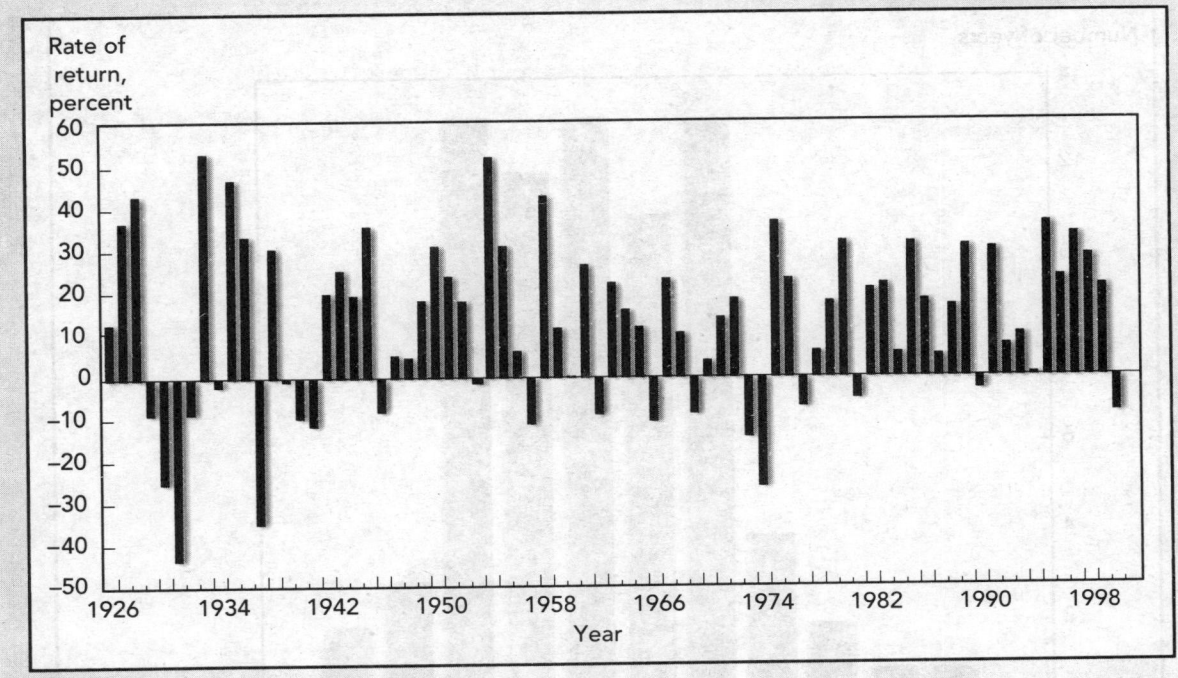

FIGURE 7.4

The stock market has been a profitable but extremely variable investment.

Source: Ibbotson Associates, Inc., *2001 Yearbook*, © 2001 Ibbotson Associates, Inc.

where $\tilde{r}_m$ is the actual return and r_m is the expected return.[12] The standard deviation is simply the square root of the variance:

$$\text{Standard deviation of } \tilde{r}_m = \sqrt{\text{variance } (\tilde{r}_m)}$$

Standard deviation is often denoted by σ and variance by σ^2.

Here is a very simple example showing how variance and standard deviation are calculated. Suppose that you are offered the chance to play the following game. You start by investing $100. Then two coins are flipped. For each head that comes up you get back your starting balance *plus* 20 percent, and for each tail that comes up you get back your starting balance *less* 10 percent. Clearly there are four equally likely outcomes:

- Head + head: You gain 40 percent.
- Head + tail: You gain 10 percent.

---

[12]One more technical point: When variance is estimated from a sample of *observed* returns, we add the squared deviations and divide by $N - 1$, where N is the number of observations. We divide by $N - 1$ rather than N to correct for what is called *the loss of a degree of freedom*. The formula is

$$\text{Variance } (\tilde{r}_m) = \frac{1}{N-1} \sum_{t=1}^{N} (\tilde{r}_{mt} - r_m)^2$$

where $\tilde{r}_{mt}$ is the market return in period t and r_m is the mean of the values of $\tilde{r}_{mt}$.

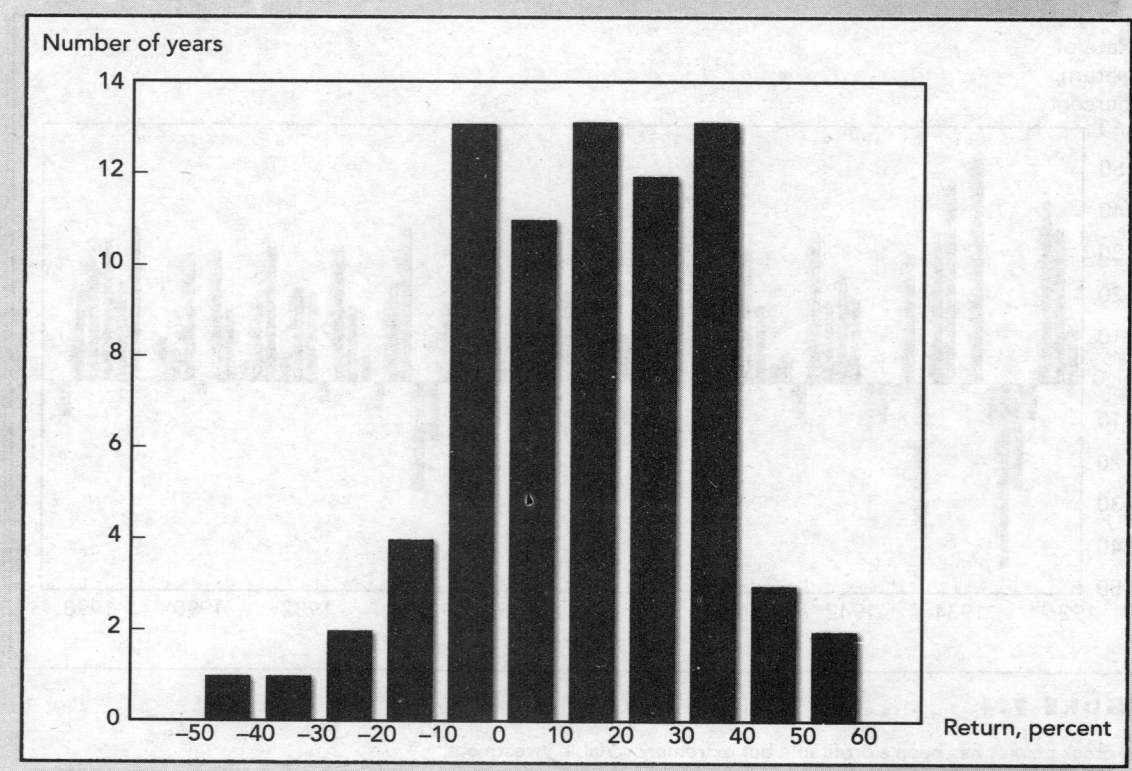

FIGURE 7.5

Histogram of the annual rates of return from the stock market in the United States, 1926–2000, showing the wide spread of returns from investment in common stocks.

Source: Ibbotson Associates, Inc., *2001 Yearbook.*

- Tail + head: You gain 10 percent.
- Tail + tail: You lose 20 percent.

There is a chance of 1 in 4, or .25, that you will make 40 percent; a chance of 2 in 4, or .5, that you will make 10 percent; and a chance of 1 in 4, or .25, that you will lose 20 percent. The game's expected return is, therefore, a weighted average of the possible outcomes:

$$\text{Expected return} = (.25 \times 40) + (.5 \times 10) + (.25 \times -20) = +10\%$$

Table 7.2 shows that the variance of the percentage returns is 450. Standard deviation is the square root of 450, or 21. This figure is in the same units as the rate of return, so we can say that the game's variability is 21 percent.

One way of defining uncertainty is to say that more things can happen than will happen. The risk of an asset can be completely expressed, as we did for the coin-tossing game, by writing all possible outcomes and the probability of each. In prac-

(1) Percent Rate of Return ($\tilde{r}$)	(2) Deviation from Expected Return ($\tilde{r} - r$)	(3) Squared Deviation ($\tilde{r} - r$)^2	(4) Probability	(5) Probability × Squared Deviation
+40	+30	900	.25	225
+10	0	0	.5	0
−20	−30	900	.25	225

Variance = expected value of $(\tilde{r} - r)^2$ = 450
Standard deviation = $\sqrt{\text{variance}}$ = $\sqrt{450}$ = 21

TABLE 7.2

The coin-tossing game: Calculating variance and standard deviation.

tice this is cumbersome and often impossible. Therefore we use variance or standard deviation to summarize the spread of possible outcomes.[13]

These measures are natural indexes of risk.[14] If the outcome of the coin-tossing game had been certain, the standard deviation would have been zero. The actual standard deviation is positive because we *don't* know what will happen.

Or think of a second game, the same as the first except that each head means a 35 percent gain and each tail means a 25 percent loss. Again, there are four equally likely outcomes:

- Head + head: You gain 70 percent.
- Head + tail: You gain 10 percent.
- Tail + head: You gain 10 percent.
- Tail + tail: You lose 50 percent.

For this game the expected return is 10 percent, the same as that of the first game. But its standard deviation is double that of the first game, 42 versus 21 percent. By this measure the second game is twice as risky as the first.

Measuring Variability

In principle, you could estimate the variability of any portfolio of stocks or bonds by the procedure just described. You would identify the possible outcomes, assign a probability to each outcome, and grind through the calculations. But where do the probabilities come from? You can't look them up in the newspaper; newspapers seem to go out of their way to avoid definite statements about prospects for securities. We once saw an article headlined "Bond Prices Possibly Set to Move Sharply Either Way." Stockbrokers are much the same. Yours may respond to your query about possible market outcomes with a statement like this:

The market currently appears to be undergoing a period of consolidation. For the intermediate term, we would take a constructive view, provided economic recovery

---

[13]Which of the two we use is solely a matter of convenience. Since standard deviation is in the same units as the rate of return, it is generally more convenient to use standard deviation. However, when we are talking about the *proportion* of risk that is due to some factor, it is usually less confusing to work in terms of the variance.

[14]As we explain in Chapter 8, standard deviation and variance are the correct measures of risk if the returns are normally distributed.

continues. The market could be up 20 percent a year from now, perhaps more if inflation continues low. On the other hand, . . .

The Delphic oracle gave advice, but no probabilities.

Most financial analysts start by observing past variability. Of course, there is no risk in hindsight, but it is reasonable to assume that portfolios with histories of high variability also have the least predictable future performance.

The annual standard deviations and variances observed for our five portfolios over the period 1926–2000 were:[15]

Portfolio	Standard Deviation (σ)	Variance (σ^2)
Treasury bills	3.2	10.1
Government bonds	9.4	88.7
Corporate bonds	8.7	75.5
Common stocks (S&P 500)	20.2	406.9
Small-firm common stocks	33.4	1118.4

As expected, Treasury bills were the least variable security, and small-firm stocks were the most variable. Government and corporate bonds hold the middle ground.[16]

You may find it interesting to compare the coin-tossing game and the stock market as alternative investments. The stock market generated an average annual return of 13.0 percent with a standard deviation of 20.2 percent. The game offers 10 and 21 percent, respectively—slightly lower return and about the same variability. Your gambling friends may have come up with a crude representation of the stock market.

Of course, there is no reason to believe that the market's variability should stay the same over more than 70 years. For example, it is clearly less now than in the Great Depression of the 1930s. Here are standard deviations of the returns on the S&P index for successive periods starting in 1926.[17]

---

[15]Ibbotson Associates, Inc., *2001 Yearbook.* In discussing the riskiness of *bonds,* be careful to specify the time period and whether you are speaking in real or nominal terms. The *nominal* return on a long-term government bond is absolutely certain to an investor who holds on until maturity; in other words, it is risk-free if you forget about inflation. After all, the government can always print money to pay off its debts. However, the real return on Treasury securities is uncertain because no one knows how much each future dollar will buy.

The bond returns reported by Ibbotson Associates were measured annually. The returns reflect year-to-year changes in bond prices as well as interest received. The *one-year* returns on long-term bonds are risky in *both* real and nominal terms.

[16]You may have noticed that corporate bonds come in just ahead of government bonds in terms of low variability. You shouldn't get excited about this. The problem is that it is difficult to get two sets of bonds that are alike in all other respects. For example, many corporate bonds are *callable* (i.e., the company has an option to repurchase them for their face value). Government bonds are not callable. Also interest payments are higher on corporate bonds. Therefore, investors in corporate bonds get their money sooner. As we will see in Chapter 24, this also reduces the bond's variability.

[17]These estimates are derived from *monthly* rates of return. Annual observations are insufficient for estimating variability decade by decade. The monthly variance is converted to an annual variance by multiplying by 12. That is, the variance of the monthly return is one-twelfth of the annual variance. The longer you hold a security or portfolio, the more risk you have to bear.

This conversion assumes that successive monthly returns are statistically independent. This is, in fact, a good assumption, as we will show in Chapter 13.

Because variance is approximately proportional to the length of time interval over which a security or portfolio return is measured, *standard deviation* is proportional to the square root of the interval.

Period	Market Standard Deviation (σ_m)
1926–1930	21.7
1931–1940	37.8
1941–1950	14.0
1951–1960	12.1
1961–1970	13.0
1971–1980	15.8
1981–1990	16.5
1991–2000	13.4

These figures do not support the widespread impression of especially volatile stock prices during the 1980s and 1990s. These years were below average on the volatility front.

However, there were brief episodes of extremely high volatility. On Black Monday, October 19, 1987, the market index fell by 23 percent *on a single day*. The standard deviation of the index for the week surrounding Black Monday was equivalent to 89 percent per year. Fortunately, volatility dropped back to normal levels within a few weeks after the crash.

How Diversification Reduces Risk

We can calculate our measures of variability equally well for individual securities and portfolios of securities. Of course, the level of variability over 75 years is less interesting for specific companies than for the market portfolio—it is a rare company that faces the same business risks today as it did in 1926.

Table 7.3 presents estimated standard deviations for 10 well-known common stocks for a recent five-year period.[18] Do these standard deviations look high to you? They should. Remember that the market portfolio's standard deviation was about 13 percent in the 1990s. Of our individual stocks only Exxon Mobil came close to this figure. Amazon.com was about eight times more variable than the market portfolio.

Take a look also at Table 7.4, which shows the standard deviations of some well-known stocks from different countries and of the markets in which they trade. Some of these stocks are much more variable than others, but you can see that once again the individual stocks are more variable than the market indexes.

This raises an important question: The market portfolio is made up of individual stocks, so why doesn't its variability reflect the average variability of its components? The answer is that *diversification reduces variability*.

Stock	Standard Deviation (σ)	Stock	Standard Deviation (σ)
Amazon.com*	110.6	General Electric	26.8
Boeing	30.9	General Motors	33.4
Coca-Cola	31.5	McDonald's	27.4
Dell Computer	62.7	Pfizer	29.3
Exxon Mobil	17.4	Reebok	58.5

TABLE 7.3

Standard deviations for selected U.S. common stocks, August 1996–July 2001 (figures in percent per year).

*June 1997–July 2001.

[18]These standard deviations are also calculated from monthly data.

Stock	Standard Deviation (σ)	Market	Standard Deviation (σ)	Stock	Standard Deviation (σ)	Market	Standard Deviation (σ)
Alcan	31.0	Canada	20.7	LVMH	41.9	France	21.5
BP Amoco	24.8	UK	14.5	Nestlé	19.7	Switzerland	19.0
Deutsche Bank	37.5	Germany	24.1	Nokia	57.6	Finland	43.2
Fiat	38.1	Italy	26.7	Sony	46.3	Japan	18.2
KLM	39.6	Netherlands	20.6	Telefonica de Argentina	45.4	Argentina	34.3

TABLE 7.4

Standard deviation for selected foreign stocks and market indexes, September 1996–August 2001 (figures in percent per year).

FIGURE 7.6

The risk (standard deviation) of randomly selected portfolios containing different numbers of New York Stock Exchange stocks. Notice that diversification reduces risk rapidly at first, then more slowly.

Source: M. Statman, "How Many Stocks Make a Diversified Portfolio?" *Journal of Financial and Quantitative Analysis* 22 (September 1987), pp. 353–363.

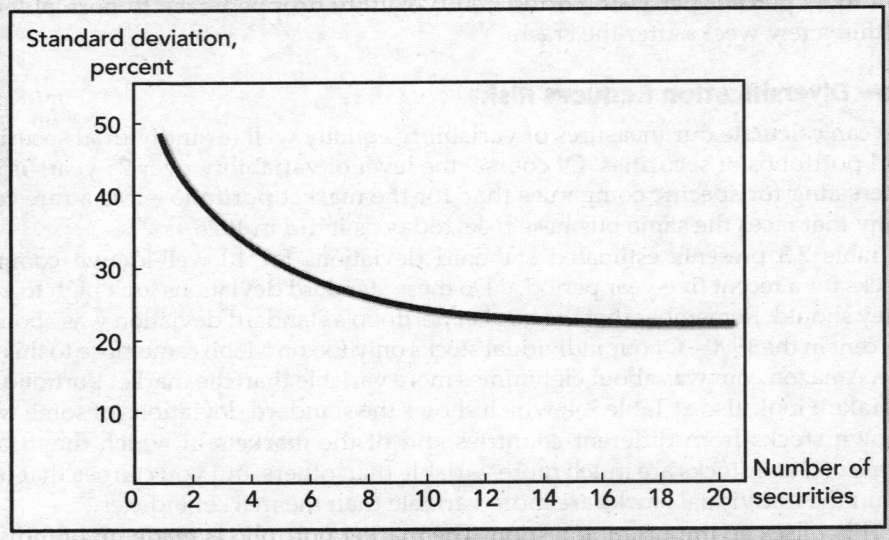

Even a little diversification can provide a substantial reduction in variability. Suppose you calculate and compare the standard deviations of randomly chosen one-stock portfolios, two-stock portfolios, five-stock portfolios, etc. A high proportion of the investments would be in the stocks of small companies and individually very risky. However, you can see from Figure 7.6 that diversification can cut the variability of returns about in half. Notice also that you can get most of this benefit with relatively few stocks: The improvement is slight when the number of securities is increased beyond, say, 20 or 30.

Diversification works because prices of different stocks do not move exactly together. Statisticians make the same point when they say that stock price changes are less than perfectly correlated. Look, for example, at Figure 7.7. The top panel shows returns for Dell Computer. We chose Dell because its stock has

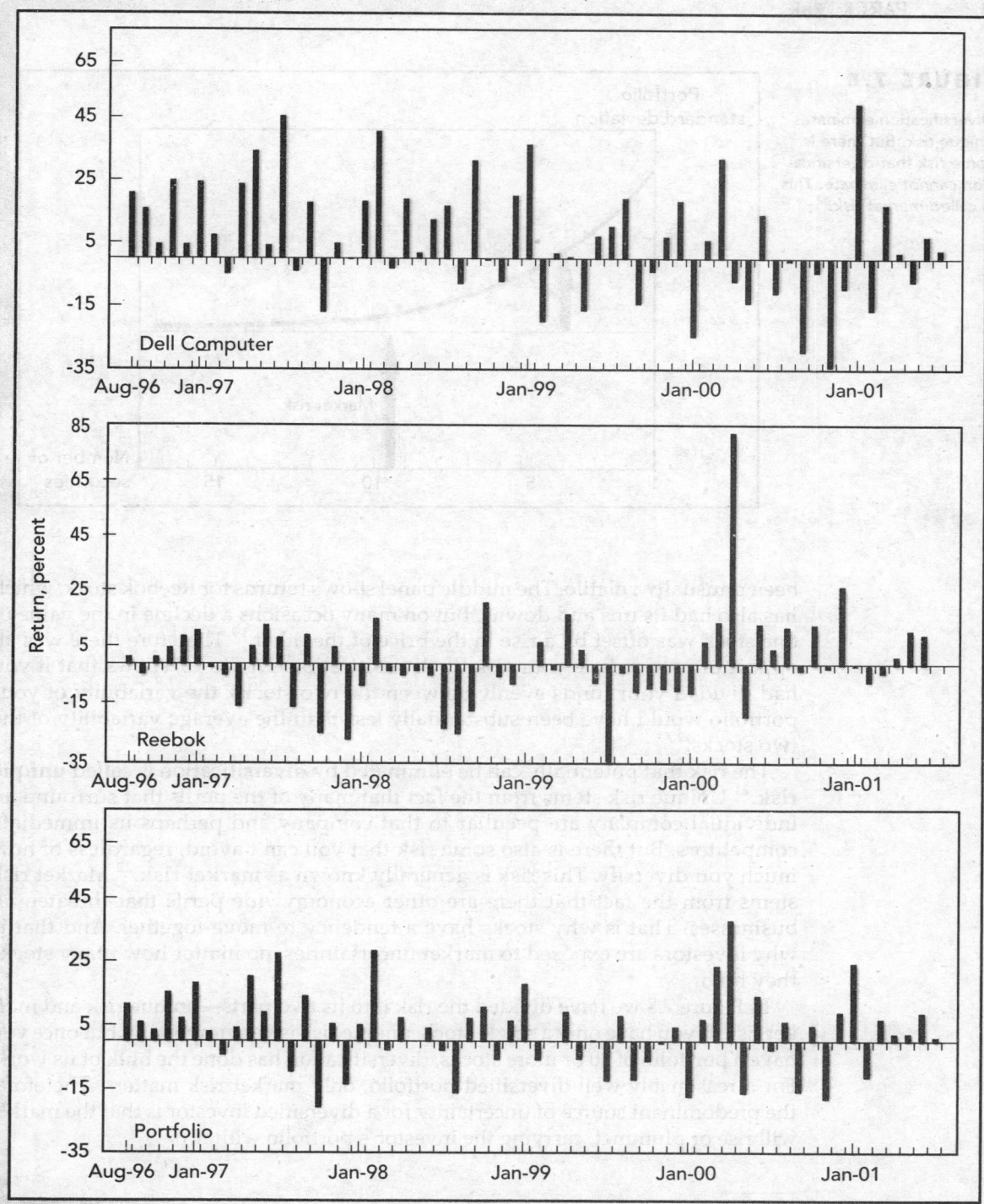

FIGURE 7.7

The variability of a portfolio with equal holdings in Dell Computer and Reebok would have been less than the average variability of the individual stocks. These returns run from August 1996 to July 2001.

FIGURE 7.8

Diversification eliminates
unique risk. But there is
some risk that diversification *cannot* eliminate. This
is called *market risk*.

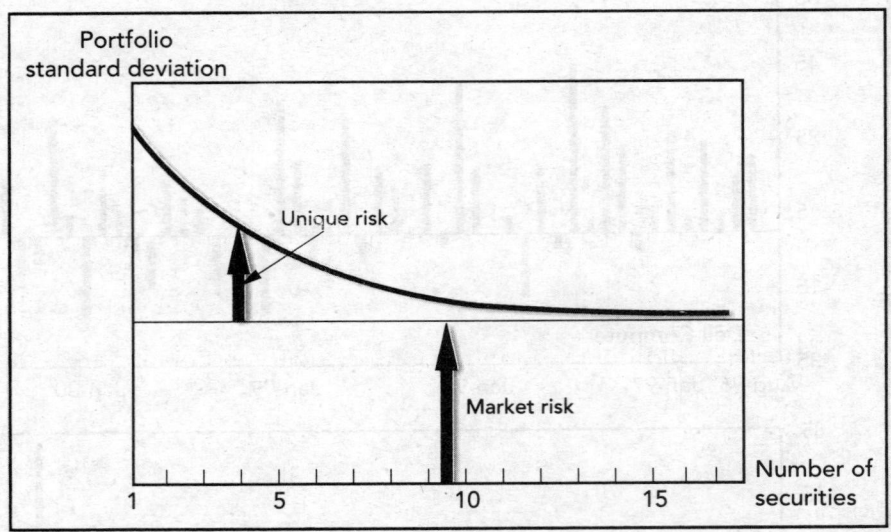

been unusually volatile. The middle panel shows returns for Reebok stock, which
has also had its ups and downs. But on many occasions a decline in the value of
one stock was offset by a rise in the price of the other.[19] Therefore there was an
opportunity to reduce your risk by diversification. Figure 7.7 shows that if you
had divided your funds evenly between the two stocks, the variability of your
portfolio would have been substantially less than the average variability of the
two stocks.[20]

The risk that potentially can be eliminated by diversification is called **unique
risk**.[21] Unique risk stems from the fact that many of the perils that surround an
individual company are peculiar to that company and perhaps its immediate
competitors. But there is also some risk that you can't avoid, regardless of how
much you diversify. This risk is generally known as **market risk**.[22] Market risk
stems from the fact that there are other economywide perils that threaten all
businesses. That is why stocks have a tendency to move together. And that is
why investors are exposed to market uncertainties, no matter how many stocks
they hold.

In Figure 7.8 we have divided the risk into its two parts—unique risk and market risk. If you have only a single stock, unique risk is very important; but once you
have a portfolio of 20 or more stocks, diversification has done the bulk of its work.
For a reasonably well-diversified portfolio, only market risk matters. Therefore,
the predominant source of uncertainty for a diversified investor is that the market
will rise or plummet, carrying the investor's portfolio with it.

---

[19]Over this period the correlation between the returns on the two stocks was approximately zero.

[20]The standard deviations of Dell Computer and Reebok were 62.7 and 58.5 percent, respectively. The
standard deviation of a portfolio with half invested in each was 43.3 percent.

[21]Unique risk may be called *unsystematic risk, residual risk, specific risk,* or *diversifiable risk.*

[22]Market risk may be called *systematic risk* or *undiversifiable risk.*

7.3 CALCULATING PORTFOLIO RISK

We have given you an intuitive idea of how diversification reduces risk, but to understand fully the effect of diversification, you need to know how the risk of a portfolio depends on the risk of the individual shares.

Suppose that 65 percent of your portfolio is invested in the shares of Coca-Cola and the remainder is invested in Reebok. You expect that over the coming year Coca-Cola will give a return of 10 percent and Reebok, 20 percent. The expected return on your portfolio is simply a weighted average of the expected returns on the individual stocks:[23]

$$\text{Expected portfolio return} = (0.65 \times 10) + (0.35 \times 20) = 13.5\%$$

Calculating the expected portfolio return is easy. The hard part is to work out the risk of your portfolio. In the past the standard deviation of returns was 31.5 percent for Coca-Cola and 58.5 percent for Reebok. You believe that these figures are a good forecast of the spread of possible *future* outcomes. At first you may be inclined to assume that the standard deviation of your portfolio is a weighted average of the standard deviations of the two stocks, that is $(.65 \times 31.5) + (.35 \times 58.5) = 41.0$ percent. That would be correct *only* if the prices of the two stocks moved in perfect lockstep. In any other case, diversification reduces the risk below this figure.

The exact procedure for calculating the risk of a two-stock portfolio is given in Figure 7.9. You need to fill in four boxes. To complete the top left box, you weight the variance of the returns on stock 1 (σ_1^2) by the *square* of the proportion invested in it (x_1^2). Similarly, to complete the bottom right box, you weight the variance of the returns on stock 2 (σ_2^2) by the *square* of the proportion invested in stock 2 (x_2^2).

The entries in these diagonal boxes depend on the variances of stocks 1 and 2; the entries in the other two boxes depend on their **covariance**. As you might guess, the covariance is a measure of the degree to which the two stocks "covary." The covariance can be expressed as the product of the correlation coefficient ρ_{12} and the two standard deviations:[24]

$$\text{Covariance between stocks 1 and 2} = \sigma_{12} = \rho_{12}\sigma_1\sigma_2$$

For the most part stocks tend to move together. In this case the correlation coefficient ρ_{12} is positive, and therefore the covariance σ_{12} is also positive. If the prospects of the stocks were wholly unrelated, both the correlation coefficient and the covariance would be zero; and if the stocks tended to move in opposite directions, the correlation coefficient and the covariance would be negative. Just as you

---

[23]Let's check this. Suppose you invest $65 in Coca-Cola and $35 in Reebok. The expected dollar return on your Coca-Cola holding is $.10 \times 65 = \$6.50$, and on Reebok it is $.20 \times 35 = \$7.00$. The expected dollar return on your portfolio is $6.50 + 7.00 = \$13.50$. The portfolio *rate* of return is $13.50/100 = 0.135$, or 13.5 percent.

[24]Another way to define the covariance is as follows:

$$\text{Covariance between stocks 1 and 2} = \sigma_{12} = \text{expected value of } (\tilde{r}_1 - r_1) \times (\tilde{r}_2 - r_2)$$

Note that any security's covariance with itself is just its variance:

$$\sigma_{11} = \text{expected value of } (\tilde{r}_1 - r_1) \times (\tilde{r}_1 - r_1)$$
$$= \text{expected value of } (\tilde{r}_1 - r_1)^2 = \text{variance of stock 1} = \sigma_1^2.$$

FIGURE 7.9

The variance of a two-stock portfolio is the sum of these four boxes. x_1, x_2 = proportions invested in stocks 1 and 2; σ_1, σ_2, = variances of stock returns; σ_{12} = covariance of returns ($\rho_{12}\,\sigma_1\,\sigma_2$); ρ_{12} = correlation between returns on stocks 1 and 2.

weighted the variances by the square of the proportion invested, so you must weight the covariance by the *product* of the two proportionate holdings x_1 and x_2.

Once you have completed these four boxes, you simply add the entries to obtain the portfolio variance:

$$\text{Portfolio variance} = x_1^2\sigma_1^2 + x_2^2\sigma_2^2 + 2(x_1 x_2 \rho_{12}\sigma_1\sigma_2)$$

The portfolio standard deviation is, of course, the square root of the variance.

Now you can try putting in some figures for Coca-Cola and Reebok. We said earlier that if the two stocks were perfectly correlated, the standard deviation of the portfolio would lie 45 percent of the way between the standard deviations of the two stocks. Let us check this out by filling in the boxes with $\rho_{12} = +1$.

	Coca-Cola	Reebok
Coca-Cola	$x_1^2\sigma_1^2 = (.65)^2 \times (31.5)^2$	$x_1 x_2 \rho_{12}\sigma_1\sigma_2$ $= (.65) \times (.35) \times 1 \times (31.5) \times (58.5)$
Reebok	$x_1 x_2 \rho_{12}\sigma_1\sigma_2$ $= .65 \times .35 \times 1 \times 31.5 \times 58.5$	$x_2^2\sigma_2^2 = (.35)^2 \times (58.5)^2$

The variance of your portfolio is the sum of these entries:

$$\text{Portfolio variance} = [(.65)^2 \times (31.5)^2] + [(.35)^2 \times (58.5)^2]$$
$$+ 2(.65 \times .35 \times 1 \times 31.5 \times 58.5) = 1,676.9$$

The standard deviation is $\sqrt{1,676.9} = 41.0$ percent or 35 percent of the way between 31.5 and 58.5.

Coca-Cola and Reebok do not move in perfect lockstep. If past experience is any guide, the correlation between the two stocks is about .2. If we go through the same exercise again with $\rho_{12} = +.2$, we find

$$\text{Portfolio variance} = [(.65)^2 \times (31.5)^2] + [(.35)^2 \times (58.5)^2]$$
$$+ 2(.65 \times .35 \times .2 \times 31.5 \times 58.5) = 1,006.1$$

The standard deviation is $\sqrt{1,006.1} = 31.7$ percent. The risk is now *less* than 35 percent of the way between 31.5 and 58.5; in fact, it is little more than the risk of investing in Coca-Cola alone.

The greatest payoff to diversification comes when the two stocks are negatively correlated. Unfortunately, this almost never occurs with real stocks, but just for illustration, let us assume it for Coca-Cola and Reebok. And as long as we are being unrealistic, we might as well go whole hog and assume perfect negative correlation ($\rho_{12} = -1$). In this case,

$$\text{Portfolio variance} = [(.65)^2 \times (31.5)^2] + [(.35)^2 \times (58.5)^2]$$
$$+ \, 2[.65 \times .35 \times (-1) \times 31.5 \times 58.5] = 0$$

When there is perfect negative correlation, there is always a portfolio strategy (represented by a particular set of portfolio weights) which will completely eliminate risk.[25] It's too bad perfect negative correlation doesn't really occur between common stocks.

General Formula for Computing Portfolio Risk

The method for calculating portfolio risk can easily be extended to portfolios of three or more securities. We just have to fill in a larger number of boxes. Each of those down the diagonal—the shaded boxes in Figure 7.10—contains the variance weighted by the square of the proportion invested. Each of the other boxes contains the covariance between that pair of securities, weighted by the product of the proportions invested.[26]

Limits to Diversification

Did you notice in Figure 7.10 how much more important the covariances become as we add more securities to the portfolio? When there are just two securities, there are equal numbers of variance boxes and of covariance boxes. When there are many securities, the number of covariances is much larger than the number of variances. Thus the variability of a well-diversified portfolio reflects mainly the covariances.

Suppose we are dealing with portfolios in which equal investments are made in each of N stocks. The proportion invested in each stock is, therefore, $1/N$. So in each variance box we have $(1/N)^2$ times the variance, and in each covariance box we have $(1/N)^2$ times the covariance. There are N variance boxes and $N^2 - N$ covariance boxes. Therefore,

$$\text{Portfolio variance} = N\left(\frac{1}{N}\right)^2 \times \text{average variance}$$
$$+ \, (N^2 - N)\left(\frac{1}{N}\right)^2 \times \text{average covariance}$$
$$= \frac{1}{N} \times \text{average variance} + \left(1 - \frac{1}{N}\right) \times \text{average covariance}$$

---

[25]Since the standard deviation of Reebok is 1.86 times that of Coca-Cola, you need to invest 1.86 times more in Coca-Cola to eliminate risk in this two-stock portfolio.

[26] The formal equivalent to "add up all the boxes" is

$$\text{Portfolio variance} = \sum_{i=1}^{N} \sum_{j=1}^{N} x_i x_j \sigma_{ij}$$

Notice that when $i = j$, σ_{ij} is just the variance of stock i.

FIGURE 7.10

To find the variance of an *N*-stock portfolio, we must add the entries in a matrix like this. The diagonal cells contain variance terms ($x_i^2\sigma_i^2$), and the off-diagonal cells contain covariance terms ($x_ix_j\sigma_{ij}$).

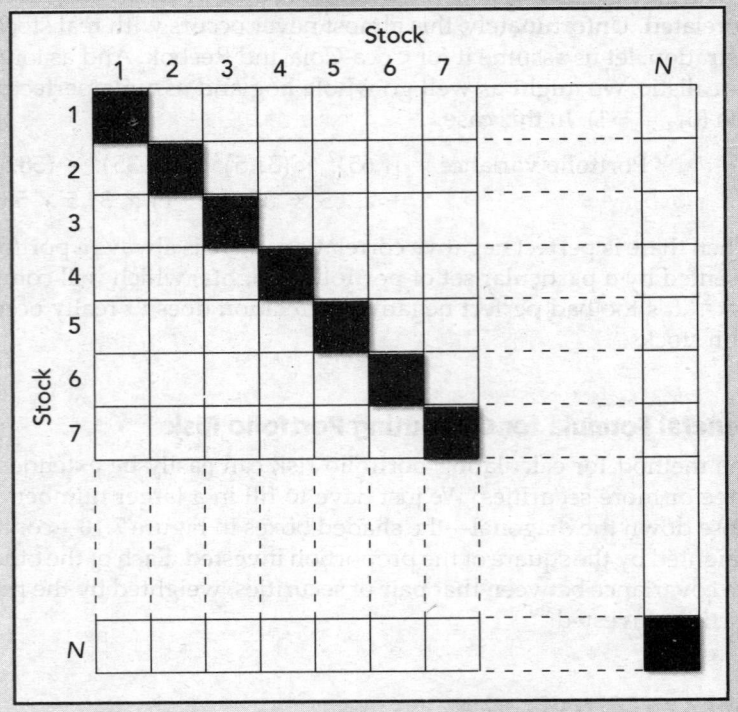

Notice that as *N* increases, the portfolio variance steadily approaches the average covariance. If the average covariance were zero, it would be possible to eliminate *all* risk by holding a sufficient number of securities. Unfortunately common stocks move together, not independently. Thus most of the stocks that the investor can actually buy are tied together in a web of positive covariances which set the limit to the benefits of diversification. Now we can understand the precise meaning of the market risk portrayed in Figure 7.8. It is the average covariance which constitutes the bedrock of risk remaining after diversification has done its work.

7.4 HOW INDIVIDUAL SECURITIES AFFECT PORTFOLIO RISK

We presented earlier some data on the variability of 10 individual U.S. securities. Amazon.com had the highest standard deviation and Exxon Mobil had the lowest. If you had held Amazon on its own, the spread of possible returns would have been six times greater than if you had held Exxon Mobil on its own. But that is not a very interesting fact. Wise investors don't put all their eggs into just one basket: They reduce their risk by diversification. They are therefore interested in the effect that each stock will have on the risk of their portfolio.

This brings us to one of the principal themes of this chapter. *The risk of a well-diversified portfolio depends on the market risk of the securities included in the portfolio.* Tattoo that statement on your forehead if you can't remember it any other way. It is one of the most important ideas in this book.

Stock	Beta (β)	Stock	Beta (β)
Amazon.com*	3.25	General Electric	1.18
Boeing	.56	General Motors	.91
Coca-Cola	.74	McDonald's	.68
Dell Computer	2.21	Pfizer	.71
Exxon Mobil	.40	Reebok	.69

TABLE 7.5

Betas for selected U.S. common stocks, August 1996–July 2001.

*June 1997–July 2001.

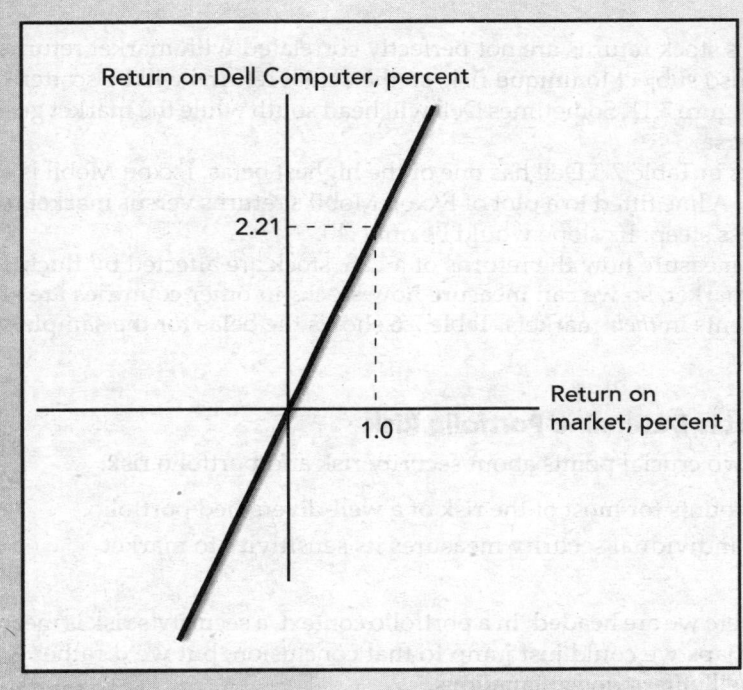

FIGURE 7.11

The return on Dell Computer stock changes on average by 2.21 percent for each additional 1 percent change in the market return. Beta is therefore 2.21.

Market Risk Is Measured by Beta

If you want to know the contribution of an individual security to the risk of a well-diversified portfolio, it is no good thinking about how risky that security is if held in isolation—you need to measure its *market* risk, and that boils down to measuring how sensitive it is to market movements. This sensitivity is called **beta** (β).

Stocks with betas greater than 1.0 tend to amplify the overall movements of the market. Stocks with betas between 0 and 1.0 tend to move in the same direction as the market, but not as far. Of course, the market is the portfolio of all stocks, so the "average" stock has a beta of 1.0. Table 7.5 reports betas for the 10 well-known common stocks we referred to earlier.

Over the five years from mid-1996 to mid-2001, Dell Computer had a beta of 2.21. If the future resembles the past, this means that *on average* when the market rises an extra 1 percent, Dell's stock price will rise by an extra 2.21 percent. When the market falls an extra 2 percent, Dell's stock prices will fall an extra 2 × 2.21 = 4.42 percent. Thus a line fitted to a plot of Dell's returns versus market returns has a slope of 2.21. See Figure 7.11.

TABLE 7.6

Betas for foreign stocks, September 1996–August 2001 (betas are measured relative to the stock's home market).

Stock	Beta	Stock	Beta
Alcan	.66	LVMH	1.42
BP Amoco	.82	Nestlé	.64
Deutsche Bank	1.18	Nokia	1.29
Fiat	1.03	Sony	1.38
KLM	.82	Telefonica de Argentina	1.06

Of course Dell's stock returns are not perfectly correlated with market returns. The company is also subject to unique risk, so the actual returns will be scattered about the line in Figure 7.11. Sometimes Dell will head south while the market goes north, and vice versa.

Of the 10 stocks in Table 7.5 Dell has one of the highest betas. Exxon Mobil is at the other extreme. A line fitted to a plot of Exxon Mobil's returns versus market returns would be less steep: Its slope would be only .40.

Just as we can measure how the returns of a U.S. stock are affected by fluctuations in the U.S. market, so we can measure how stocks in other countries are affected by movements in *their* markets. Table 7.6 shows the betas for the sample of foreign stocks.

Why Security Betas Determine Portfolio Risk

Let's review the two crucial points about security risk and portfolio risk:

- Market risk accounts for most of the risk of a well-diversified portfolio.
- The beta of an individual security measures its sensitivity to market movements.

It's easy to see where we are headed: In a portfolio context, a security's risk is measured by beta. Perhaps we could just jump to that conclusion, but we'd rather explain it. In fact, we'll offer two explanations.

Explanation 1: Where's Bedrock?   Look back to Figure 7.8, which shows how the standard deviation of portfolio return depends on the number of securities in the portfolio. With more securities, and therefore better diversification, portfolio risk declines until all unique risk is eliminated and only the bedrock of market risk remains.

Where's bedrock? It depends on the average beta of the securities selected.

Suppose we constructed a portfolio containing a large number of stocks—500, say—drawn randomly from the whole market. What would we get? The market itself, or a portfolio *very* close to it. The portfolio beta would be 1.0, and the correlation with the market would be 1.0. If the standard deviation of the market were 20 percent (roughly its average for 1926–2000), then the portfolio standard deviation would also be 20 percent.

But suppose we constructed the portfolio from a large group of stocks with an average beta of 1.5. Again we would end up with a 500-stock portfolio with virtually no unique risk—a portfolio that moves almost in lockstep with the market. However, *this* portfolio's standard deviation would be 30 percent, 1.5 times that of the market.[27] A well-diversified portfolio with a beta of 1.5 will amplify every market move by 50 percent and end up with 150 percent of the market's risk.

Of course, we could repeat the same experiment with stocks with a beta of .5 and end up with a well-diversified portfolio half as risky as the market. Figure 7.12 shows these three cases.

The general point is this: The risk of a well-diversified portfolio is proportional to the portfolio beta, which equals the average beta of the securities included in the portfolio. This shows you how portfolio risk is driven by security betas.

Explanation 2: Betas and Covariances. A statistician would define the beta of stock i as

$$\beta_i = \frac{\sigma_{im}}{\sigma_m^2}$$

where σ_{im} is the covariance between stock i's return and the market return, and σ_m^2 is the variance of the market return.

It turns out that this ratio of covariance to variance measures a stock's contribution to portfolio risk. You can see this by looking back at our calculations for the risk of the portfolio of Coca-Cola and Reebok.

Remember that the risk of this portfolio was the sum of the following cells:

	Coca-Cola	Reebok
Coca-Cola	$(.65)^2 \times (31.5)^2$	$.65 \times .35 \times .2 \times 31.5 \times 58.5$
Reebok	$.65 \times .35 \times .2 \times 31.5 \times 58.5$	$(.35)^2 \times (58.5)^2$

If we add each *row* of cells, we can see how much of the portfolio's risk comes from Coca-Cola and how much comes from Reebok:

Stock	Contribution to Risk		
Coca-Cola	$.65 \times \{[.65 \times (31.5)^2] + [.35 \times .2 \times 31.5 \times 58.5]\} = .65 \times$	774.0
Reebok	$.35 \times \{[.65 \times .2 \times 31.5 \times 58.5] + [.35 \times (58.5)^2]\} = .35 \times$	1,437.3
		Total portfolio	1,006.1

Coca-Cola's contribution to portfolio risk depends on its relative importance in the portfolio (.65) and its average covariance with the stocks in the portfolio (774.0). (Notice that the average covariance of Coca-Cola with the portfolio includes its covariance with itself, i.e., its variance.) The *proportion* of the risk that comes from the Coca-Cola holding is

$$\text{Relative market value} \times \frac{\text{average covariance}}{\text{portfolio variance}} = .65 \times \frac{774.0}{1,006.1} = .65 \times .77 = .5$$

Similarly, Reebok's contribution to portfolio risk depends on its relative importance in the portfolio (.35) and its average covariance with the stocks in the

---

[27] A 500-stock portfolio with $\beta = 1.5$ would still have some unique risk because it would be unduly concentrated in high-beta industries. Its actual standard deviation would be a bit higher than 30 percent. If that worries you, relax; we will show you in Chapter 8 how you can construct a fully diversified portfolio with a beta of 1.5 by borrowing and investing in the market portfolio.

FIGURE 7.12

(a) A randomly selected 500-stock portfolio ends up with β = 1 and a standard deviation equal to the market's—in this case 20 percent. (b) A 500-stock portfolio constructed with stocks with average β = 1.5 has a standard deviation of about 30 percent—150 percent of the market's. (c) A 500-stock portfolio constructed with stocks with average β = .5 has a standard deviation of about 10 percent—half the market's.

Standard deviation

Portfolio risk (σ_p) = 20 percent

Market risk (σ_m) = 20 percent

500

Number of securities

(a)

Standard deviation

Portfolio risk (σ_p) = 30 percent

Market risk (σ_m) = 20 percent

500

Number of securities

(b)

Standard deviation

Market risk (σ_m) = 20 percent

Portfolio risk (σ_p) = 10 percent

500

Number of securities

(c)

portfolio (1,437.3). The *proportion* of the risk that comes from the Reebok holding is also .5:

$$.35 \times \frac{1,437.3}{1,006.1} = .35 \times 1.43 = .5$$

In each case the proportion depends on two numbers: the relative size of the holding (.65 or .35) and a measure of the effect of that holding on portfolio risk (.77 or 1.43). The latter values are the betas of Coca-Cola and Reebok *relative to that portfolio.* On average, an extra 1 percent change in the value of the portfolio would be associated with an extra .77 percent change in the value of Coca-Cola and a 1.43 percent change in the value of Reebok.

To calculate Coca-Cola's beta relative to the portfolio, we simply take the covariance of Coca-Cola with the portfolio and divide by the portfolio variance. The idea is exactly the same if we wish to calculate the beta of Coca-Cola *relative to the market portfolio.* We just calculate its covariance with the market portfolio and divide by the variance of the market:

$$\text{Beta relative to market portfolio} \atop \text{(or, more simply, beta)} = \frac{\text{covariance with market}}{\text{variance of market}} = \frac{\sigma_{im}}{\sigma_m^2}$$

 ## 7.5 DIVERSIFICATION AND VALUE ADDITIVITY

We have seen that diversification reduces risk and, therefore, makes sense for investors. But does it also make sense for the firm? Is a diversified firm more attractive to investors than an undiversified one? If it is, we have an *extremely* disturbing result. If diversification is an appropriate corporate objective, each project has to be analyzed as a potential addition to the firm's portfolio of assets. The value of the diversified package would be greater than the sum of the parts. So present values would no longer add.

Diversification is undoubtedly a good thing, but that does not mean that firms should practice it. If investors were *not* able to hold a large number of securities, then they might want firms to diversify for them. But investors *can* diversify.[28] In many ways they can do so more easily than firms. Individuals can invest in the steel industry this week and pull out next week. A firm cannot do that. To be sure, the individual would have to pay brokerage fees on the purchase and sale of steel company shares, but think of the time and expense for a firm to acquire a steel company or to start up a new steel-making operation.

You can probably see where we are heading. If investors can diversify on their own account, they will not pay any *extra* for firms that diversify. And if they have a sufficiently wide choice of securities, they will not pay any *less* because they are unable to invest separately in each factory. Therefore, in countries like the United States, which have large and competitive capital markets, diversification does not add to a firm's value or subtract from it. The total value is the sum of its parts.

This conclusion is important for corporate finance, because it justifies adding present values. The concept of *value additivity* is so important that we will give a

---

[28]One of the simplest ways for an individual to diversify is to buy shares in a mutual fund that holds a diversified portfolio.

formal definition of it. If the capital market establishes a value PV(A) for asset A and PV(B) for B, the market value of a firm that holds only these two assets is

$$PV(AB) = PV(A) + PV(B)$$

A three-asset firm combining assets A, B, and C would be worth PV(ABC) = PV(A) + PV(B) + PV(C), and so on for any number of assets.

We have relied on intuitive arguments for value additivity. But the concept is a general one that can be proved formally by several different routes.[29] The concept of value additivity seems to be widely accepted, for thousands of managers add thousands of present values daily, usually without thinking about it.

---

[29]You may wish to refer to the Appendix to Chapter 33, which discusses diversification and value additivity in the context of mergers.

SUMMARY

Our review of capital market history showed that the returns to investors have varied according to the risks they have borne. At one extreme, very safe securities like U.S. Treasury bills have provided an average return over 75 years of only 3.9 percent a year. The riskiest securities that we looked at were common stocks. The stock market provided an average return of 13.0 percent, a premium of more than 9 percent over the safe rate of interest.

This gives us two benchmarks for the opportunity cost of capital. If we are evaluating a safe project, we discount at the current risk-free rate of interest. If we are evaluating a project of average risk, we discount at the expected return on the average common stock. Historical evidence suggests that this return is about 9 percent above the risk-free rate, but many financial managers and economists opt for a lower figure. That still leaves us with a lot of assets that don't fit these simple cases. Before we can deal with them, we need to learn how to measure risk.

Risk is best judged in a portfolio context. Most investors do not put all their eggs into one basket: They diversify. Thus the effective risk of any security cannot be judged by an examination of that security alone. Part of the uncertainty about the security's return is diversified away when the security is grouped with others in a portfolio.

Risk in investment means that future returns are unpredictable. This spread of possible outcomes is usually measured by standard deviation. The standard deviation of the *market portfolio*, generally represented by the Standard and Poor's Composite Index, is around 20 percent a year.

Most individual stocks have higher standard deviations than this, but much of their variability represents *unique* risk that can be eliminated by diversification. Diversification cannot eliminate *market* risk. Diversified portfolios are exposed to variation in the general level of the market.

A security's contribution to the risk of a well-diversified portfolio depends on how the security is liable to be affected by a general market decline. This sensitivity to market movements is known as *beta* (β). Beta measures the amount that investors expect the stock price to change for each additional 1 percent change in the market. The average beta of all stocks is 1.0. A stock with a beta greater than 1 is unusually sensitive to market movements; a stock with a beta below 1 is unusually insensitive to market movements. The standard deviation of a well-diversified portfolio is proportional to its beta. Thus a diversified portfolio invested in stocks with a beta of 2.0 will have twice the risk of a diversified portfolio with a beta of 1.0.

One theme of this chapter is that diversification is a good thing *for the investor.* This does not imply that *firms* should diversify. Corporate diversification is redundant if investors can diversify on their own account. Since diversification does not affect the firm value, present values add even when risk is explicitly considered. Thanks to *value additivity,* the net present value rule for capital budgeting works even under uncertainty.

FURTHER READING

A very valuable record of the performance of United States securities since 1926 is:
Ibbotson Associates, Inc.: *Stocks, Bonds, Bills, and Inflation, 2001 Yearbook,* Ibbotson Associates, Chicago, 2001.

Dimson, Marsh, and Staunton compare market returns in 15 countries over the years 1900–2000 in:
E. Dimson, P. R. Marsh, and M. Staunton: *Millenium Book II: 101 Years of Investment Returns,* ABN-Amro and London Business School, London, 2001.

Fama and French derive measures of expected dividend growth to argue that historical data on the market risk premium overstate the expected premium. See:
E. F. Fama and K. R. French: "The Equity Premium," *Journal of Finance,* forthcoming.

Merton discusses the problems encountered in measuring average returns from historical data:
R. C. Merton: "On Estimating the Expected Return on the Market: An Exploratory Investigation," *Journal of Financial Economics,* 8:323–361 (December 1980).

The classic analysis of the degree to which stocks move together is:
B. F. King: "Market and Industry Factors in Stock Price Behavior," *Journal of Business, Security Prices: A Supplement,* 39:179–190 (January 1966).

There have been several studies of the way that standard deviation is reduced by diversification, including:
M. Statman: "How Many Stocks Make a Diversified Portfolio?" *Journal of Financial and Quantitative Analysis,* 22:353–364 (September 1987).

Formal proofs of the value additivity principle can be found in:
S. C. Myers: "Procedures for Capital Budgeting under Uncertainty," *Industrial Management Review,* 9:1–20 (Spring 1968).

L. D. Schall: "Asset Valuation, Firm Investment and Firm Diversification," *Journal of Business,* 45:11–28 (January 1972).

QUIZ

1. a. What was the average annual return on United States common stocks from 1926 to 2000 (approximately)?
   b. What was the average difference between this return and the return on Treasury bills?
   c. What was the average return on Treasury bills in real terms?
   d. What was the standard deviation of returns on the market index?
   e. Was this standard deviation more or less than on most individual stocks?

2. A game of chance offers the following odds and payoffs. Each play of the game costs $100, so the net profit per play is the payoff less $100.

Probability	Payoff	Net Profit
.10	$500	$400
.50	100	0
.40	0	−100

What are the expected cash payoff and expected rate of return? Calculate the variance and standard deviation of this rate of return.

3. The following table shows the nominal returns on the Mexican stock market and the Mexican rate of inflation.
   a. What was the standard deviation of the market returns?
   b. Calculate the average real return.

Year	Nominal Return (%)	Inflation (%)
1995	16.5	52.0
1996	21.9	27.7
1997	53.4	15.7
1998	−20.8	18.6
1999	84.3	12.3

4. Fill in the missing words:

   Risk is usually measured by the variance of returns or the _____, which is simply the square root of the variance. As long as the stock price changes are not perfectly _____, the risk of a diversified portfolio is _____ than the average risk of the individual stocks. The risk that can be eliminated by diversification is known as _____ risk. But diversification cannot remove all risk; the risk that it cannot eliminate is known as _____ risk.

5. Lawrence Interchange, ace mutual fund manager, produced the following percentage rates of return from 1996 to 2000. Rates of return on the S&P 500 are given for comparison.

	1996	1997	1998	1999	2000
Mr. Interchange	+16.1	+28.4	+25.1	+14.3	−6.0
S&P 500	+23.1	+33.4	+28.6	+21.0	−9.1

Calculate the average return and standard deviation of Mr. Interchange's mutual fund. Did he do better or worse than the S&P by these measures?

6. True or false?
   a. Investors prefer diversified companies because they are less risky.
   b. If stocks were perfectly positively correlated, diversification would not reduce risk.
   c. The contribution of a stock to the risk of a well-diversified portfolio depends on its market risk.
   d. A well-diversified portfolio with a beta of 2.0 is twice as risky as the market portfolio.
   e. An undiversified portfolio with a beta of 2.0 is less than twice as risky as the market portfolio.

7. In which of the following situations would you get the largest reduction in risk by spreading your investment across two stocks?
   a. The two shares are perfectly correlated.
   b. There is no correlation.
   c. There is modest negative correlation.
   d. There is perfect negative correlation.

TABLE 7.7

See Quiz Question 11.

Stock	Expected Stock Return if Market Return Is:	
	−10%	+10%
A	0	+20
B	−20	+20
C	−30	0
D	+15	+15
E	+10	−10

8. To calculate the variance of a three-stock portfolio, you need to add nine boxes:

Use the same symbols that we used in this chapter; for example, x_1 = proportion invested in stock 1 and σ_{12} = covariance between stocks 1 and 2. Now complete the nine boxes.

9. Suppose the standard deviation of the market return is 20 percent.
   a. What is the standard deviation of returns on a well-diversified portfolio with a beta of 1.3?
   b. What is the standard deviation of returns on a well-diversified portfolio with a beta of 0?
   c. A well-diversified portfolio has a standard deviation of 15 percent. What is its beta?
   d. A poorly diversified portfolio has a standard deviation of 20 percent. What can you say about its beta?

10. A portfolio contains equal investments in 10 stocks. Five have a beta of 1.2; the remainder have a beta of 1.4. What is the portfolio beta?
   a. 1.3.
   b. Greater than 1.3 because the portfolio is not completely diversified.
   c. Less than 1.3 because diversification reduces beta.

11. What is the beta of each of the stocks shown in Table 7.7?

12. True or false? Why? "Diversification reduces risk. Therefore corporations ought to favor capital investments with low correlations with their existing lines of business."

1. Here are inflation rates and stock market and Treasury bill returns between 1996 and 2000:

PRACTICE QUESTIONS

Year	Inflation	S&P 500 Return	T-Bill Return
1996	3.3	23.1	5.2
1997	1.7	33.4	5.3
1998	1.6	28.6	4.9
1999	2.7	21.0	4.7
2000	3.4	−9.1	5.9

   a. What was the real return on the S&P 500 in each year?
   b. What was the average real return?

c. What was the risk premium in each year?

d. What was the average risk premium?

e. What was the standard deviation of the risk premium?

2. Most of the companies in Tables 7.3 are covered in the Standard & Poor's Market Insight website (**www.mhhe.com/edumarketinsight**). Pick at least three companies. For each company, download "Monthly Adjusted Prices" as an Excel spreadsheet. Calculate each company's variance and standard deviation from the monthly returns given on the spreadsheet. The Excel functions are VAR and STDEV. Convert the standard deviations from monthly to annual units by multiplying by the square root of 12. How has the stand-alone risk of these stocks changed, compared to the figures reported in Table 7.3?

3. Each of the following statements is dangerous or misleading. Explain why.

a. A long-term United States government bond is always absolutely safe.

b. All investors should prefer stocks to bonds because stocks offer higher long-run rates of return.

c. The best practical forecast of future rates of return on the stock market is a 5- or 10-year average of historical returns.

4. "There's upside risk and downside risk: Standard deviation doesn't distinguish between them." Do you think the speaker has a fair point?

5. Hippique s.a., which owns a stable of racehorses, has just invested in a mysterious black stallion with great form but disputed bloodlines. Some experts in horseflesh predict the horse will win the coveted Prix de Bidet; others argue that it should be put out to grass. Is this a risky investment for Hippique shareholders? Explain.

6. Lonesome Gulch Mines has a standard deviation of 42 percent per year and a beta of +.10. Amalgamated Copper has a standard deviation of 31 percent a year and a beta of +.66. Explain why Lonesome Gulch is the safer investment for a diversified investor.

7. Respond to the following comments:

a. "Risk is not variability. If I know a stock is going to fluctuate between $10 and $20, I can make myself a bundle."

b. "There are all sorts of risk in addition to beta risk. There's the risk that we'll have a downturn in demand, there's the risk that my best plant manager will drop dead, there's the risk of a hike in steel prices. You've got to take all these things into consideration."

c. "Risk to me is the probability of loss."

d. "Those guys who suggest beta is a measure of risk make the big assumption that betas don't change."

8. Lambeth Walk invests 60 percent of his funds in stock I and the balance in stock J. The standard deviation of returns on I is 10 percent, and on J it is 20 percent. Calculate the variance of portfolio returns, assuming

a. The correlation between the returns is 1.0.

b. The correlation is .5.

c. The correlation is 0.

9. a. How many variance terms and how many covariance terms do you need to calculate the risk of a 100-share portfolio?

b. Suppose all stocks had a standard deviation of 30 percent and a correlation with each other of .4. What is the standard deviation of the returns on a portfolio that has equal holdings in 50 stocks?

c. What is the standard deviation of a fully diversified portfolio of such stocks?

10. Suppose that the standard deviation of returns from a typical share is about .40 (or 40 percent) a year. The correlation between the returns of each pair of shares is about .3.

a. Calculate the variance and standard deviation of the returns on a portfolio that has equal investments in two shares, three shares, and so on, up to 10 shares.

| | | | Correlation Coefficients | | | | |
	Alcan	BP	Deutsche Bank	KLM	LVMH	Nestlé	Sony	Standard Deviation
Alcan	1.0	.48	.40	.32	.43	.26	.27	31.0%
BP		1.0	.05	.20	.08	.23	.15	24.8
Deutsche Bank			1.0	.45	.50	.37	.42	37.5
KLM				1.0	.31	.32	.01	39.6
LVMH					1.0	.16	.36	41.9
Nestlé						1.0	.14	19.7
Sony							1.0	46.3

TABLE 7.8

Standard deviations and correlation coefficients for a sample of seven stocks.

Note: Correlations and standard deviations are calculated using returns in each country's own currency; in other words, they assume that the investor is hedged against exchange risk.

b. Use your estimates to draw a graph like Figure 7.8. How large is the underlying market risk that cannot be diversified away?

c. Now repeat the problem, assuming that the correlation between each pair of stocks is zero.

11. Download the "Monthly Adjusted Prices" spreadsheets for Coca-Cola, Citigroup, and Pfizer from the Standard & Poor's Market Insight website (**www.mhhe.com/ edumarketinsight**).

a. Calculate the annual standard deviation for each company, using the most recent three years of monthly returns. Use the Excel function STDEV. Multiply by the square root of 12 to convert to annual units.

b. Use the Excel function CORREL to calculate the correlation coefficient between the monthly returns for each pair of stocks.

c. Calculate the standard deviation of a portfolio with equal investments in each of the three stocks.

12. Table 7.8 shows standard deviations and correlation coefficients for seven stocks from different countries. Calculate the variance of a portfolio 40 percent invested in BP, 40 percent invested in KLM, and 20 percent invested in Nestlé.

13. Most of the companies in Tables 7.5 are covered in the Standard & Poor's Market Insight website (**www.mhhe.com/edumarketinsight**). For those that are covered, you can easily calculate beta. Download the "Monthly Adjusted Prices" spreadsheet, and note the columns for returns on the stock and the S&P 500 index. Beta is calculated by the Excel function SLOPE, where the "y" range refers to the company's return (the dependent variable) and the "x" range refers to the market returns (the independent variable). Calculate the betas. How have they changed from the betas reported in Table 7.5?

14. Your eccentric Aunt Claudia has left you $50,000 in Alcan shares plus $50,000 cash. Unfortunately her will requires that the Alcan stock not be sold for one year and the $50,000 cash must be entirely invested in one of the stocks shown in Table 7.8. What is the safest attainable portfolio under these restrictions?

15. There are few, if any, real companies with negative betas. But suppose you found one with $\beta = -.25$.

a. How would you expect this stock's rate of return to change if the overall market rose by an extra 5 percent? What if the market fell by an extra 5 percent?

STANDARD &POOR'S

EXCEL

STANDARD &POOR'S

b. You have $1 million invested in a well-diversified portfolio of stocks. Now you receive an additional $20,000 bequest. Which of the following actions will yield the safest overall portfolio return?

    i. Invest $20,000 in Treasury bills (which have $\beta = 0$).

    ii. Invest $20,000 in stocks with $\beta = 1$.

    iii. Invest $20,000 in the stock with $\beta = -.25$.

    Explain your answer.

16. Download "Monthly Adjusted Prices" for General Motors (GM) and Harley David-son (HDI) from the Standard & Poor's Market Insight website (**www.mhhe.com/edumarketinsight**).

    a. Calculate each company's beta, following the procedure described in Practice Question 13.

    b. Calculate the annual standard deviation of the market from the monthly returns for the S&P 500. Use the Excel function STDEV, and multiply by the square root of 12 to convert to annual units. Also calculate the annual standard deviations for GM and HDI.

    c. Let's assume that your answers to (a) and (b) are good forecasts. What would be the standard deviation of a well-diversified portfolio of stocks with betas equal to Harley Davidson's beta? How about a well-diversified portfolio of stocks with GM's beta?

    d. How much of the total risk of GM was unique risk? How much of HDI's?

17. Diversification has enormous value to investors, yet opportunities for diversification should not sway capital investment decisions by corporations. How would you explain this apparent paradox?

CHALLENGE QUESTIONS

1. Here are some historical data on the risk characteristics of Dell and Microsoft:

	Dell	Microsoft
β (beta)	2.21	1.81
Yearly standard deviation of return (%)	62.7	50.7

Assume the standard deviation of the return on the market was 15 percent.

    a. The correlation coefficient of Dell's return versus Microsoft's is .66. What is the standard deviation of a portfolio invested half in Dell and half in Microsoft?

    b. What is the standard deviation of a portfolio invested one-third in Dell, one-third in Microsoft, and one-third in Treasury bills?

    c. What is the standard deviation if the portfolio is split evenly between Dell and Microsoft and is financed at 50 percent margin, i.e., the investor puts up only 50 percent of the total amount and borrows the balance from the broker?

    d. What is the *approximate* standard deviation of a portfolio composed of 100 stocks with betas of 2.21 like Dell? How about 100 stocks like Microsoft? *Hint:* Part (d) should not require anything but the simplest arithmetic to answer.

2. Suppose that Treasury bills offer a return of about 6 percent and the expected market risk premium is 8.5 percent. The standard deviation of Treasury-bill returns is zero and the standard deviation of market returns is 20 percent. Use the formula for portfolio risk to calculate the standard deviation of portfolios with different proportions in Treasury bills and the market. (Note that the covariance of two rates of return must be zero when the standard deviation of one return is zero.) Graph the expected returns and standard deviations.

3. It is often useful to know how well your portfolio is diversified. Two measures have been suggested:
   a. The variance of the returns on a fully diversified portfolio as a proportion of the variance of returns on *your* portfolio.
   b. The number of shares in a portfolio that (*i*) has the same risk as yours, (*ii*) is invested in "typical" shares, and (*iii*) has equal amounts invested in each share.
   Suppose that you hold eight stocks. All are fairly typical; they have a standard deviation of 40 percent a year and the correlation between each pair is .3. Of your fund, 20 percent is invested in one stock, 20 percent is invested in a second stock, and the remaining 60 percent is spread evenly over a further six stocks. Calculate each measure of portfolio diversification. What are the advantages and disadvantages of each?

4. Some stocks have high standard deviations and relatively low betas. Sometimes it is the other way around. Why do you think this is so? Illustrate your answer by calculating some standard deviations and betas using data for 60 recent months. (Monthly stock price and index data can be found on **finance.yahoo.com**.)

5. Select two bank stocks and two oil stocks and then calculate the returns for 60 recent months. (Monthly stock price and index data can be obtained from **finance.yahoo. com**.) Now
   a. Calculate the standard deviation of monthly returns for each of these stocks and the correlation between each pair of stocks.
   b. Use your results to find the standard deviation of a portfolio that is evenly divided between different pairs of stocks. Do you reduce risk more by diversifying across stocks in the same industry or those in different industries?

CHAPTER EIGHT

RISK AND RETURN

IN CHAPTER 7 we began to come to grips with the problem of measuring risk. Here is the story so far. The stock market is risky because there is a spread of possible outcomes. The usual measure of this spread is the standard deviation or variance. The risk of any stock can be broken down into two parts. There is the *unique risk* that is peculiar to that stock, and there is the *market risk* that is associated with marketwide variations. Investors can eliminate unique risk by holding a well-diversified portfolio, but they cannot eliminate market risk. *All* the risk of a fully diversified portfolio is market risk.

A stock's contribution to the risk of a fully diversified portfolio depends on its sensitivity to market changes. This sensitivity is generally known as *beta*. A security with a beta of 1.0 has average market risk—a well-diversified portfolio of such securities has the same standard deviation as the market index. A security with a beta of .5 has below-average market risk—a well-diversified portfolio of these securities tends to move half as far as the market moves and has half the market's standard deviation.

In this chapter we build on this newfound knowledge. We present leading theories linking risk and return in a competitive economy, and we show how these theories can be used to estimate the returns required by investors in different stock market investments. We start with the most widely used theory, the capital asset pricing model, which builds directly on the ideas developed in the last chapter. We will also look at another class of models, known as arbitrage pricing or factor models. Then in Chapter 9 we show how these ideas can help the financial manager cope with risk in practical capital budgeting situations.

 ## 8.1 HARRY MARKOWITZ AND THE BIRTH OF PORTFOLIO THEORY

Most of the ideas in Chapter 7 date back to an article written in 1952 by Harry Markowitz.[1] Markowitz drew attention to the common practice of portfolio diversification and showed exactly how an investor can reduce the standard deviation of portfolio returns by choosing stocks that do not move exactly together. But Markowitz did not stop there; he went on to work out the basic principles of portfolio construction. These principles are the foundation for much of what has been written about the relationship between risk and return.

We begin with Figure 8.1, which shows a histogram of the daily returns on Microsoft stock from 1990 to 2001. On this histogram we have superimposed a bell-shaped normal distribution. The result is typical: When measured over some fairly short interval, the past rates of return on any stock conform closely to a normal distribution.[2]

Normal distributions can be completely defined by two numbers. One is the average or expected return; the other is the variance or standard deviation. Now you can see why in Chapter 7 we discussed the calculation of expected return and standard deviation. They are not just arbitrary measures: If returns are normally distributed, they are the *only* two measures that an investor need consider.

[1]H. M. Markowitz, "Portfolio Selection," *Journal of Finance* 7 (March 1952), pp. 77–91.

[2]If you were to measure returns over *long* intervals, the distribution would be skewed. For example, you would encounter returns greater than 100 percent but none less than −100 percent. The distribution of returns over periods of, say, one year would be better approximated by a *lognormal* distribution. The lognormal distribution, like the normal, is completely specified by its mean and standard deviation.

FIGURE 8.1

Daily price changes for Microsoft are approximately normally distributed. This plot spans 1990 to 2001.

Figure 8.2 pictures the distribution of possible returns from two investments. Both offer an expected return of 10 percent, but A has much the wider spread of possible outcomes. Its standard deviation is 15 percent; the standard deviation of B is 7.5 percent. Most investors dislike uncertainty and would therefore prefer B to A.

Figure 8.3 pictures the distribution of returns from two other investments. This time both have the *same* standard deviation, but the expected return is 20 percent from stock C and only 10 percent from stock D. Most investors like high expected return and would therefore prefer C to D.

Combining Stocks into Portfolios

Suppose that you are wondering whether to invest in shares of Coca-Cola or Reebok. You decide that Reebok offers an expected return of 20 percent and Coca-Cola offers an expected return of 10 percent. After looking back at the past variability of the two stocks, you also decide that the standard deviation of returns is 31.5 percent for Coca-Cola and 58.5 percent for Reebok. Reebok offers the higher expected return, but it is considerably more risky.

Now there is no reason to restrict yourself to holding only one stock. For example, in Section 7.3 we analyzed what would happen if you invested 65 percent of your money in Coca-Cola and 35 percent in Reebok. The expected return on this portfolio is 13.5 percent, which is simply a weighted average of the expected returns on the two holdings. What about the risk of such a portfolio? We know that thanks to diversification the portfolio risk is less than the average of the risks of the

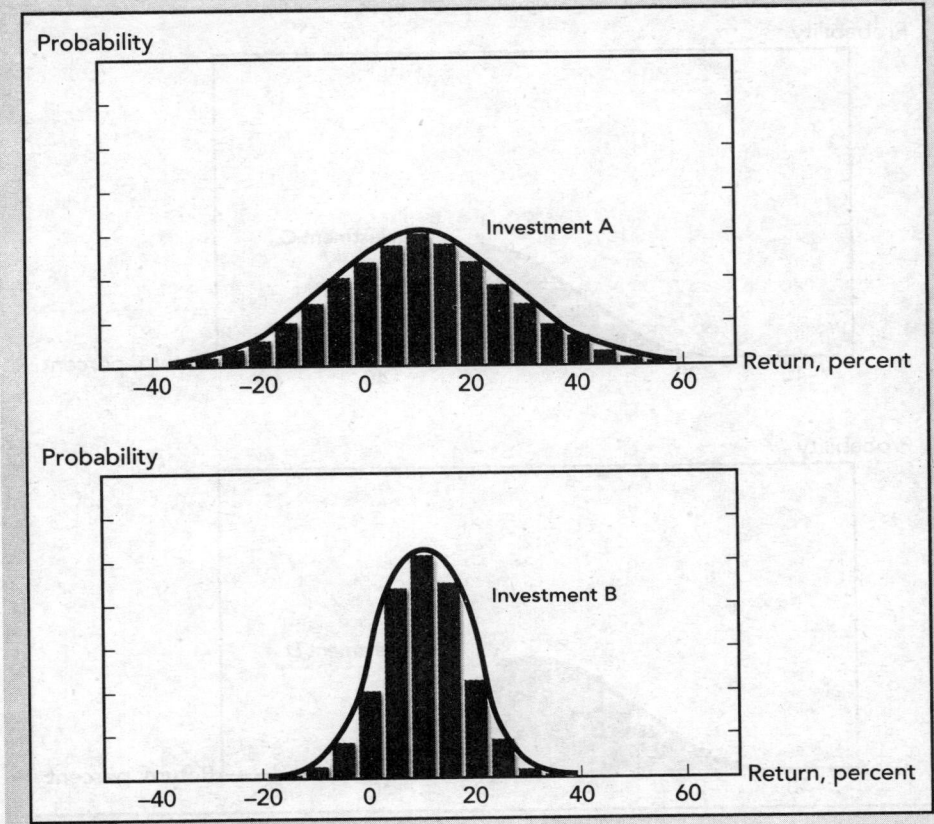

FIGURE 8.2

These two investments both have an *expected* return of 10 percent but because investment A has the greater spread of *possible* returns, it is more risky than B. We can measure this spread by the standard deviation. Investment A has a standard deviation of 15 percent; B, 7.5 percent. Most investors would prefer B to A.

separate stocks. In fact, on the basis of past experience the standard deviation of this portfolio is 31.7 percent.[3]

In Figure 8.4 we have plotted the expected return and risk that you could achieve by different combinations of the two stocks. Which of these combinations is best? That depends on your stomach. If you want to stake all on getting rich quickly, you will do best to put all your money in Reebok. If you want a more peaceful life, you should invest most of your money in Coca-Cola; to minimize risk you should keep a small investment in Reebok.[4]

In practice, you are not limited to investing in only two stocks. Our next task, therefore, is to find a way to identify the best portfolios of 10, 100, or 1,000 stocks.

---

[3]We pointed out in Section 7.3 that the correlation between the returns of Coca-Cola and Reebok has been about .2. The variance of a portfolio which is invested 65 percent in Coca-Cola and 35 percent in Reebok is

$$\text{Variance} = x_1^2\sigma_1^2 + x_2^2\sigma_2^2 + 2x_1x_2\rho_{12}\sigma_1\sigma_2$$
$$= [(.65)^2 \times (31.5)^2] + [(.35)^2 \times (58.5)^2] + 2(.65 \times .35 \times .2 \times 31.5 \times 58.5)$$
$$= 1006.1$$

The portfolio standard deviation is $\sqrt{1006.1} = 31.7$ percent.

[4]The portfolio with the minimum risk has 21.4 percent in Reebok. We assume in Figure 8.4 that you may not take negative positions in either stock, i.e., we rule out short sales.

FIGURE 8.3

The standard deviation
of possible returns is 15
percent for both these
investments, but the
expected return from C
is 20 percent compared
with an expected return
from D of only 10
percent. Most investors
would prefer C to D.

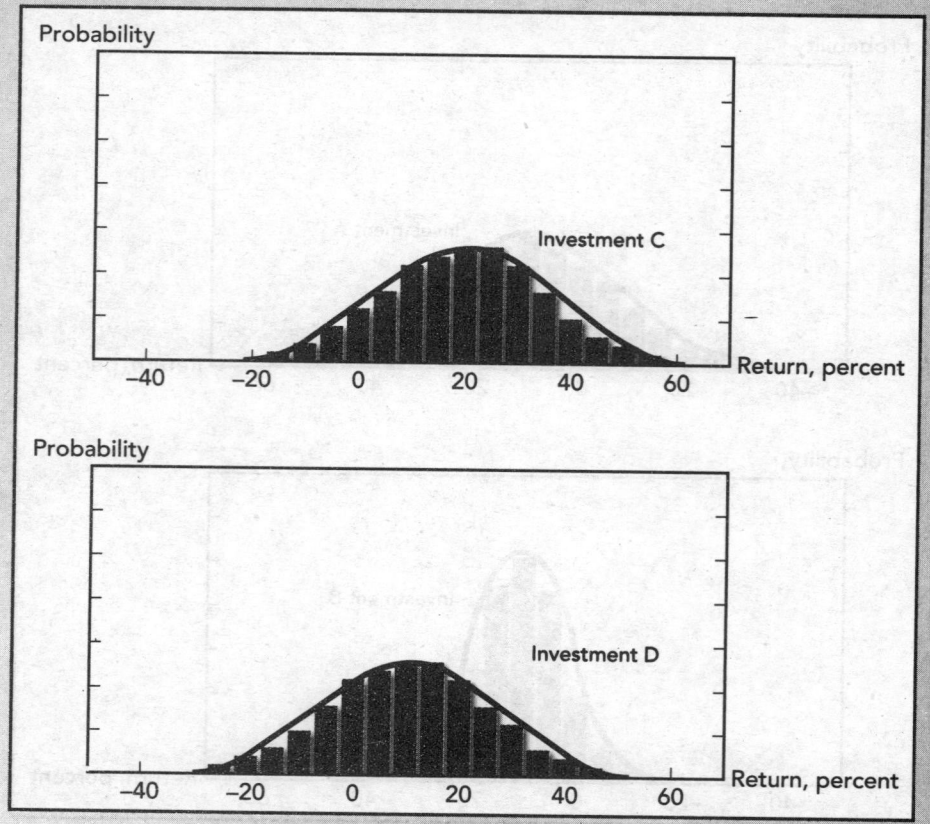

FIGURE 8.4

The curved line illustrates how
expected return and standard
deviation change as you hold
different combinations of two
stocks. For example, if you invest
35 percent of your money in
Reebok and the remainder in
Coca-Cola, your expected return
is 13.5 percent, which is 35
percent of the way between the
expected returns on the two
stocks. The standard deviation is
31.7 percent, which is *less* than
35 percent of the way between
the standard deviations on the
two stocks. This is because diversification reduces risk.

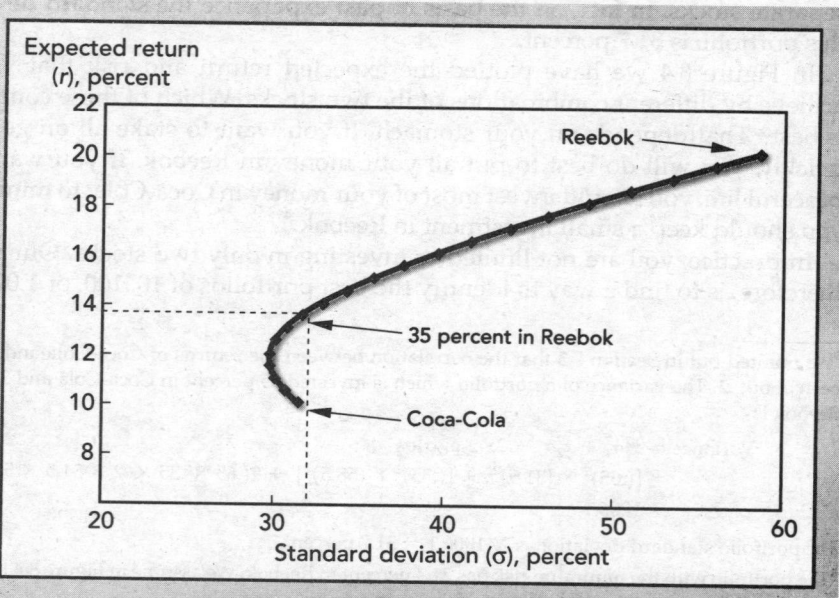

	Expected Return	Standard Deviation	Efficient Portfolios—Percentages Allocated to Each Stock			
			A	B	C	D
Amazon.com	34.6%	110.6%	100	9.3	4.5	
Boeing	13.0	30.9		2.1	9.6	0.6
Coca-Cola	10.0	31.5				0.4
Dell Computer	26.2	62.7		21.1	14.4	
Exxon Mobil	11.8	17.4			3.6	56.3
General Electric	18.0	26.8		46.8	39.7	10.2
General Motors	15.8	33.4				9
McDonald's	14.0	27.4			5.4	10
Pfizer	14.8	29.3			9.8	13.3
Reebok	20.0	58.5		20.7	13.0	
Expected portfolio return			34.6	21.6	19.0	13.4
Portfolio standard deviation			110.6	30.8	23.7	14.6

TABLE 8.1

Examples of efficient portfolios chosen from 10 stocks.

Note: Standard deviations and the correlations between stock returns were estimated from monthly stock returns, August 1996–July 2001. Efficient portfolios are calculated assuming that short sales are prohibited.

We'll start with 10. Suppose that you can choose a portfolio from any of the stocks listed in the first column of Table 8.1. After analyzing the prospects for each firm, you come up with the return forecasts shown in the second column of the table. You use data for the past five years to estimate the risk of each stock (column 3) and the correlation between the returns on each pair of stocks.[5]

Now turn to Figure 8.5. Each diamond marks the combination of risk and return offered by a different individual security. For example, Amazon.com has the highest standard deviation; it also offers the highest expected return. It is represented by the diamond at the upper right of Figure 8.5.

By mixing investment in individual securities, you can obtain an even wider selection of risk and return: in fact, *anywhere* in the shaded area in Figure 8.5. But where in the shaded area is best? Well, what is your goal? Which direction do you want to go? The answer should be obvious: You want to go up (to increase expected return) and to the left (to reduce risk). Go as far as you can, and you will end up with one of the portfolios that lies along the heavy solid line. Markowitz called them **efficient portfolios.** These portfolios are clearly better than any in the interior of the shaded area.

We will not calculate this set of efficient portfolios here, but you may be interested in how to do it. Think back to the capital rationing problem in Section 5.4. There we wanted to deploy a limited amount of capital investment in a mixture of projects to give the highest total NPV. Here we want to deploy an investor's funds to give the highest expected return for a given standard deviation. In principle, both problems can be solved by hunting and pecking—but only in principle. To solve the capital

---

[5]There are 90 correlation coefficients, so we have not listed them in Table 8.1.

FIGURE 8.5

Each diamond shows the expected return and standard deviation of one of the 10 stocks in Table 8.1. The shaded area shows the possible combinations of expected return and standard deviation from investing in a *mixture* of these stocks. If you like high expected returns and dislike high standard deviations, you will prefer portfolios along the heavy line. These are *efficient* portfolios. We have marked the four efficient portfolios described in Table 8.1 (A, B, C, and D).

rationing problem, we can employ linear programming; to solve the portfolio problem, we would turn to a variant of linear programming known as *quadratic programming*. Given the expected return and standard deviation for each stock, as well as the correlation between each pair of stocks, we could give a computer a standard quadratic program and tell it to calculate the set of efficient portfolios.

Four of these efficient portfolios are marked in Figure 8.5. Their compositions are summarized in Table 8.1. Portfolio A offers the highest expected return; A is invested entirely in one stock, Amazon.com. Portfolio D offers the minimum risk; you can see from Table 8.1 that it has a large holding in Exxon Mobil, which has had the lowest standard deviation. Notice that D has only a small holding in Boeing and Coca-Cola but a much larger one in stocks such as General Motors, even though Boeing and Coca-Cola are individually of similar risk. The reason? On past evidence the fortunes of Boeing and Coca-Cola are more highly correlated with those of the other stocks in the portfolio and therefore provide less diversification.

Table 8.1 also shows the compositions of two other efficient portfolios B and C with intermediate levels of risk and expected return.

We Introduce Borrowing and Lending

Of course, large investment funds can choose from thousands of stocks and thereby achieve a wider choice of risk and return. This choice is represented in Figure 8.6 by the shaded, broken-egg-shaped area. The set of efficient portfolios is again marked by the heavy curved line.

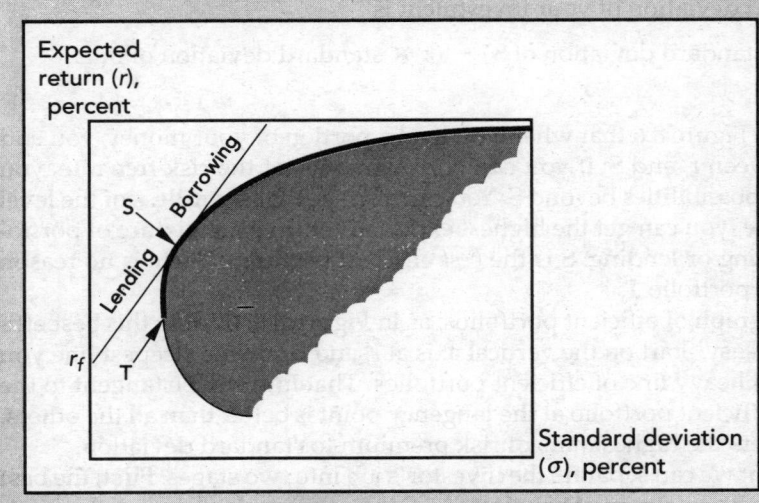

FIGURE 8.6

Lending and borrowing extend the range of investment possibilities. If you invest in portfolio S and lend or borrow at the risk-free interest rate, r_f, you can achieve any point along the straight line from r_f through S. This gives you a higher expected return for any level of risk than if you just invest in common stocks.

Now we introduce yet another possibility. Suppose that you can also lend and borrow money at some risk-free rate of interest r_f. If you invest some of your money in Treasury bills (i.e., lend money) and place the remainder in common stock portfolio S, you can obtain any combination of expected return and risk along the straight line joining r_f and S in Figure 8.6.[6] Since borrowing is merely negative lending, you can extend the range of possibilities to the right of S by borrowing funds at an interest rate of r_f and investing them as well as your own money in portfolio S.

Let us put some numbers on this. Suppose that portfolio S has an expected return of 15 percent and a standard deviation of 16 percent. Treasury bills offer an interest rate (r_f) of 5 percent and are risk-free (i.e., their standard deviation is zero). If you invest half your money in portfolio S and lend the remainder at 5 percent, the expected return on your investment is halfway between the expected return on S and the interest rate on Treasury bills:

$$r = (\tfrac{1}{2} \times \text{expected return on S}) + (\tfrac{1}{2} \times \text{interest rate})$$
$$= 10\%$$

And the standard deviation is halfway between the standard deviation of S and the standard deviation of Treasury bills:

$$\sigma = (\tfrac{1}{2} \times \text{standard deviation of S}) + (\tfrac{1}{2} \times \text{standard deviation of bills})$$
$$= 8\%$$

Or suppose that you decide to go for the big time: You borrow at the Treasury bill rate an amount equal to your initial wealth, and you invest everything in portfolio S. You have twice your own money invested in S, but you have to *pay* interest on the loan. Therefore your expected return is

$$r = (2 \times \text{expected return on S}) - (1 \times \text{interest rate})$$
$$= 25\%$$

---

[6]If you want to check this, write down the formula for the standard deviation of a two-stock portfolio:

$$\text{Standard deviation} = \sqrt{x_1^2 \sigma_1^2 + x_2^2 \sigma_2^2 + 2x_1 x_2 \rho_{12} \sigma_1 \sigma_2}$$

Now see what happens when security 2 is riskless, i.e., when $\sigma_2 = 0$.

And the standard deviation of your investment is

$$\sigma = (2 \times \text{standard deviation of S}) - (1 \times \text{standard deviation of bills})$$
$$= 32\%$$

You can see from Figure 8.6 that when you lend a portion of your money, you end up partway between r_f and S; if you can borrow money at the risk-free rate, you can extend your possibilities beyond S. You can also see that regardless of the level of risk you choose, you can get the highest expected return by a mixture of portfolio S and borrowing or lending. S is the *best* efficient portfolio. There is no reason ever to hold, say, portfolio T.

If you have a graph of efficient portfolios, as in Figure 8.6, finding this best efficient portfolio is easy. Start on the vertical axis at r_f and draw the steepest line you can to the curved heavy line of efficient portfolios. That line will be tangent to the heavy line. The efficient portfolio at the tangency point is better than all the others. Notice that it offers the highest *ratio* of risk premium to standard deviation.

This means that we can separate the investor's job into two stages. First, the best portfolio of common stocks must be selected—S in our example.[7] Second, this portfolio must be blended with borrowing or lending to obtain an exposure to risk that suits the particular investor's taste. Each investor, therefore, should put money into just two benchmark investments—a risky portfolio S and a risk-free loan (borrowing or lending).[8]

What does portfolio S look like? If you have better information than your rivals, you will want the portfolio to include relatively large investments in the stocks you think are undervalued. But in a competitive market you are unlikely to have a monopoly of good ideas. In that case there is no reason to hold a different portfolio of common stocks from anybody else. In other words, you might just as well hold the market portfolio. That is why many professional investors invest in a market-index portfolio and why most others hold well-diversified portfolios.

8.2 THE RELATIONSHIP BETWEEN RISK AND RETURN

In Chapter 7 we looked at the returns on selected investments. The least risky investment was U.S. Treasury bills. Since the return on Treasury bills is fixed, it is unaffected by what happens to the market. In other words, Treasury bills have a beta of 0. We also considered a much riskier investment, the market portfolio of common stocks. This has average market risk: Its beta is 1.0.

Wise investors don't take risks just for fun. They are playing with real money. Therefore, they require a higher return from the market portfolio than from Treasury bills. The difference between the return on the market and the interest rate is termed the *market risk premium.* Over a period of 75 years the market risk premium $(r_m - r_f)$ has averaged about 9 percent a year.

In Figure 8.7 we have plotted the risk and expected return from Treasury bills and the market portfolio. You can see that Treasury bills have a beta of 0 and a risk

---

[7]Portfolio S is the point of tangency to the set of efficient portfolios. It offers the highest expected risk premium $(r - r_f)$ per unit of standard deviation (σ).

[8]This *separation theorem* was first pointed out by J. Tobin in "Liquidity Preference as Behavior toward Risk," *Review of Economic Studies* 25 (February 1958), pp. 65–86.

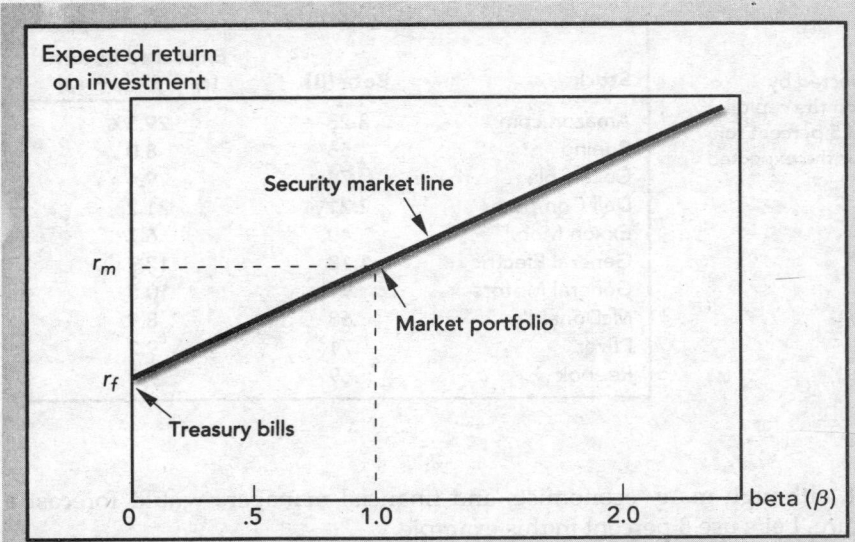

FIGURE 8.7

The capital asset pricing model states that the expected risk premium on each investment is proportional to its beta. This means that each investment should lie on the sloping security market line connecting Treasury bills and the market portfolio.

premium of 0.[9] The market portfolio has a beta of 1.0 and a risk premium of $r_m - r_f$. This gives us two benchmarks for the expected risk premium. But what is the expected risk premium when beta is not 0 or 1?

In the mid-1960s three economists—William Sharpe, John Lintner, and Jack Treynor—produced an answer to this question.[10] Their answer is known as the **capital asset pricing model,** or **CAPM.** The model's message is both startling and simple. In a competitive market, the expected risk premium varies in direct proportion to beta. This means that in Figure 8.7 all investments must plot along the sloping line, known as the **security market line.** The expected risk premium on an investment with a beta of .5 is, therefore, *half* the expected risk premium on the market; the expected risk premium on an investment with a beta of 2.0 is *twice* the expected risk premium on the market. We can write this relationship as

Expected risk premium on stock = beta × expected risk premium on market

$$r - r_f = \beta(r_m - r_f)$$

Some Estimates of Expected Returns

Before we tell you where the formula comes from, let us use it to figure out what returns investors are looking for from particular stocks. To do this, we need three numbers: β, r_f, and $r_m - r_f$. We gave you estimates of the betas of 10 stocks in Table 7.5. In July 2001 the interest rate on Treasury bills was about 3.5 percent.

How about the market risk premium? As we pointed out in the last chapter, we can't measure $r_m - r_f$ with precision. From past evidence it appears to be about

---

[9]Remember that the risk premium is the difference between the investment's expected return and the risk-free rate. For Treasury bills, the difference is zero.

[10]W. F. Sharpe, "Capital Asset Prices: A Theory of Market Equilibrium under Conditions of Risk," *Journal of Finance* 19 (September 1964), pp. 425–442 and J. Lintner, "The Valuation of Risk Assets and the Selection of Risky Investments in Stock Portfolios and Capital Budgets," *Review of Economics and Statistics* 47 (February 1965), pp. 13–37. Treynor's article has not been published.

TABLE 8.2

These estimates of the returns *expected* by investors in July 2001 were based on the capital asset pricing model. We assumed 3.5 percent for the interest rate r_f and 8 percent for the expected risk premium $r_m - r_f$.

Stock	Beta (β)	Expected Return $[r_f + \beta(r_m - r_f)]$
Amazon.com	3.25	29.5%
Boeing	.56	8.0
Coca-Cola	.74	9.4
Dell Computer	2.21	21.2
Exxon Mobil	.40	6.7
General Electric	1.18	12.9
General Motors	.91	10.8
McDonald's	.68	8.9
Pfizer	.71	9.2
Reebok	.69	9.0

9 percent, although many economists and financial managers would forecast a lower figure. Let's use 8 percent in this example.

Table 8.2 puts these numbers together to give an estimate of the expected return on each stock. The stock with the lowest beta in our sample is Exxon Mobil. Our estimate of the expected return from Exxon Mobil is 6.7 percent. The stock with the highest beta is Amazon.com. Our estimate of its expected return is 29.5 percent, 26 percent more than the interest rate on Treasury bills.

You can also use the capital asset pricing model to find the discount rate for a new capital investment. For example, suppose that you are analyzing a proposal by Pfizer to expand its capacity. At what rate should you discount the forecast cash flows? According to Table 8.2, investors are looking for a return of 9.2 percent from businesses with the risk of Pfizer. So the cost of capital for a further investment in the same business is 9.2 percent.[11]

In practice, choosing a discount rate is seldom so easy. (After all, you can't expect to be paid a fat salary just for plugging numbers into a formula.) For example, you must learn how to adjust for the extra risk caused by company borrowing and how to estimate the discount rate for projects that do not have the same risk as the company's existing business. There are also tax issues. But these refinements can wait until later.[12]

Review of the Capital Asset Pricing Model

Let's review the basic principles of portfolio selection:

1. Investors like high expected return and low standard deviation. Common stock portfolios that offer the highest expected return for a given standard deviation are known as *efficient portfolios.*

---

[11]Remember that instead of investing in plant and machinery, the firm could return the money to the shareholders. The opportunity cost of investing is the return that shareholders could expect to earn by buying financial assets. This expected return depends on the market risk of the assets.

[12]Tax issues arise because a corporation must pay tax on income from an investment in Treasury bills or other interest-paying securities. It turns out that the correct discount rate for risk-free investments is the *after-tax* Treasury bill rate. We come back to this point in Chapters 19 and 26.

Various other points on the practical use of betas and the capital asset pricing model are covered in Chapter 9.

2. If the investor can lend or borrow at the risk-free rate of interest, one efficient portfolio is better than all the others: the portfolio that offers the highest ratio of risk premium to standard deviation (that is, portfolio S in Figure 8.6). A risk-averse investor will put part of his money in this efficient portfolio and part in the risk-free asset. A risk-tolerant investor may put all her money in this portfolio or she may borrow and put in even more.

3. The composition of this best efficient portfolio depends on the investor's assessments of expected returns, standard deviations, and correlations. But suppose everybody has the same information and the same assessments. If there is no superior information, each investor should hold the same portfolio as everybody else; in other words, everyone should hold the market portfolio.

Now let's go back to the risk of individual stocks:

4. Don't look at the risk of a stock in isolation but at its contribution to portfolio risk. This contribution depends on the stock's sensitivity to changes in the value of the portfolio.

5. A stock's sensitivity to changes in the value of the *market* portfolio is known as *beta*. Beta, therefore, measures the marginal contribution of a stock to the risk of the market portfolio.

Now if everyone holds the market portfolio, and if beta measures each security's contribution to the market portfolio risk, then it's no surprise that the risk premium demanded by investors is proportional to beta. That's what the CAPM says.

What If a Stock Did Not Lie on the Security Market Line?

Imagine that you encounter stock A in Figure 8.8. Would you buy it? We hope not[13]—if you want an investment with a beta of .5, you could get a higher expected return by investing half your money in Treasury bills and half in the market portfolio. If everybody shares your view of the stock's prospects, the price of A will have to fall until the expected return matches what you could get elsewhere.

What about stock B in Figure 8.8? Would you be tempted by its high return? You wouldn't if you were smart. You could get a higher expected return for the same beta by borrowing 50 cents for every dollar of your own money and investing in the market portfolio. Again, if everybody agrees with your assessment, the price of stock B cannot hold. It will have to fall until the expected return on B is equal to the expected return on the combination of borrowing and investment in the market portfolio.

We have made our point. An investor can always obtain an expected risk premium of $\beta(r_m - r_f)$ by holding a mixture of the market portfolio and a risk-free loan. So in well-functioning markets nobody will hold a stock that offers an expected risk premium of *less* than $\beta(r_m - r_f)$. But what about the other possibility? Are there stocks that offer a higher expected risk premium? In other words, are there any that lie above the security market line in Figure 8.8? If we take all stocks together, we have the market portfolio. Therefore, we know that stocks *on average* lie on the line. Since none lies *below* the line, then there also can't be any that lie *above* the line. Thus

---

[13]Unless, of course, we were trying to sell it.

FIGURE 8.8

In equilibrium no stock can lie below the security market line. For example, instead of buying stock A, investors would prefer to lend part of their money and put the balance in the market portfolio. And instead of buying stock B, they would prefer to borrow and invest in the market portfolio.

each and every stock must lie on the security market line and offer an expected risk premium of

$$r - r_f = \beta(r_m - r_f)$$

8.3   VALIDITY AND ROLE OF THE CAPITAL ASSET PRICING MODEL

Any economic model is a simplified statement of reality. We need to simplify in order to interpret what is going on around us. But we also need to know how much faith we can place in our model.

Let us begin with some matters about which there is broad agreement. First, few people quarrel with the idea that investors require some extra return for taking on risk. That is why common stocks have given on average a higher return than U.S. Treasury bills. Who would want to invest in risky common stocks if they offered only the *same* expected return as bills? We wouldn't, and we suspect you wouldn't either.

Second, investors do appear to be concerned principally with those risks that they cannot eliminate by diversification. If this were not so, we should find that stock prices increase whenever two companies merge to spread their risks. And we should find that investment companies which invest in the shares of other firms are more highly valued than the shares they hold. But we don't observe either phenomenon. Mergers undertaken just to spread risk don't increase stock prices, and investment companies are no more highly valued than the stocks they hold.

The capital asset pricing model captures these ideas in a simple way. That is why many financial managers find it the most convenient tool for coming to grips with the slippery notion of risk. And it is why economists often use the capital asset pricing model to demonstrate important ideas in finance even when there are other ways to prove these ideas. But that doesn't mean that the capital asset pricing model is ultimate truth. We will see later that it has several unsatisfactory features, and we will look at some alternative theories. Nobody knows whether one of these alternative theories is eventually going to come out on top or whether there are other, better models of risk and return that have not yet seen the light of day.

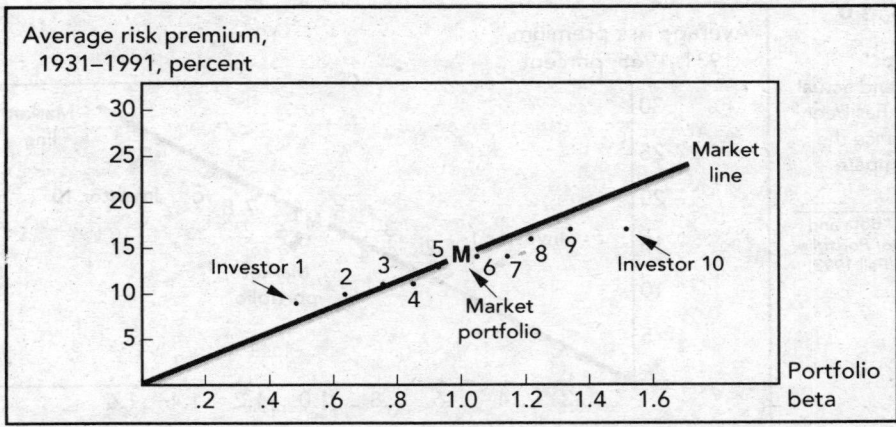

FIGURE 8.9

The capital asset pricing model states that the expected risk premium from any investment should lie on the market line. The dots show the actual average risk premiums from portfolios with different betas. The high-beta portfolios generated higher average returns, just as predicted by the CAPM. But the high-beta portfolios plotted below the market line, and four of the five low-beta portfolios plotted above. A line fitted to the 10 portfolio returns would be "flatter" than the market line.

Source: F. Black, "Beta and Return," *Journal of Portfolio Management* 20 (Fall 1993), pp. 8–18.

Tests of the Capital Asset Pricing Model

Imagine that in 1931 ten investors gathered together in a Wall Street bar to discuss their portfolios. Each agreed to follow a different investment strategy. Investor 1 opted to buy the 10 percent of New York Stock Exchange stocks with the lowest estimated betas; investor 2 chose the 10 percent with the next-lowest betas; and so on, up to investor 10, who agreed to buy the stocks with the highest betas. They also undertook that at the end of every year they would reestimate the betas of all NYSE stocks and reconstitute their portfolios.[14] Finally, they promised that they would return 60 years later to compare results, and so they parted with much cordiality and good wishes.

In 1991 the same 10 investors, now much older and wealthier, met again in the same bar. Figure 8.9 shows how they had fared. Investor 1's portfolio turned out to be much less risky than the market; its beta was only .49. However, investor 1 also realized the lowest return, 9 percent above the risk-free rate of interest. At the other extreme, the beta of investor 10's portfolio was 1.52, about three times that of investor 1's portfolio. But investor 10 was rewarded with the highest return, averaging 17 percent a year above the interest rate. So over this 60-year period returns did indeed increase with beta.

As you can see from Figure 8.9, the market portfolio over the same 60-year period provided an average return of 14 percent above the interest rate[15] and (of

---

[14]Betas were estimated using returns over the previous 60 months.

[15]In Figure 8.9 the stocks in the "market portfolio" are weighted equally. Since the stocks of small firms have provided higher average returns than those of large firms, the risk premium on an equally weighted index is higher than on a value-weighted index. This is one reason for the difference between the 14 percent market risk premium in Figure 8.9 and the 9.1 percent premium reported in Table 7.1.

FIGURE 8.10

The relationship between beta and actual average return has been much weaker since the mid-1960s. Compare Figure 8.9.

Source: F. Black, "Beta and Return," *Journal of Portfolio Management* 20 (Fall 1993), pp. 8–18.

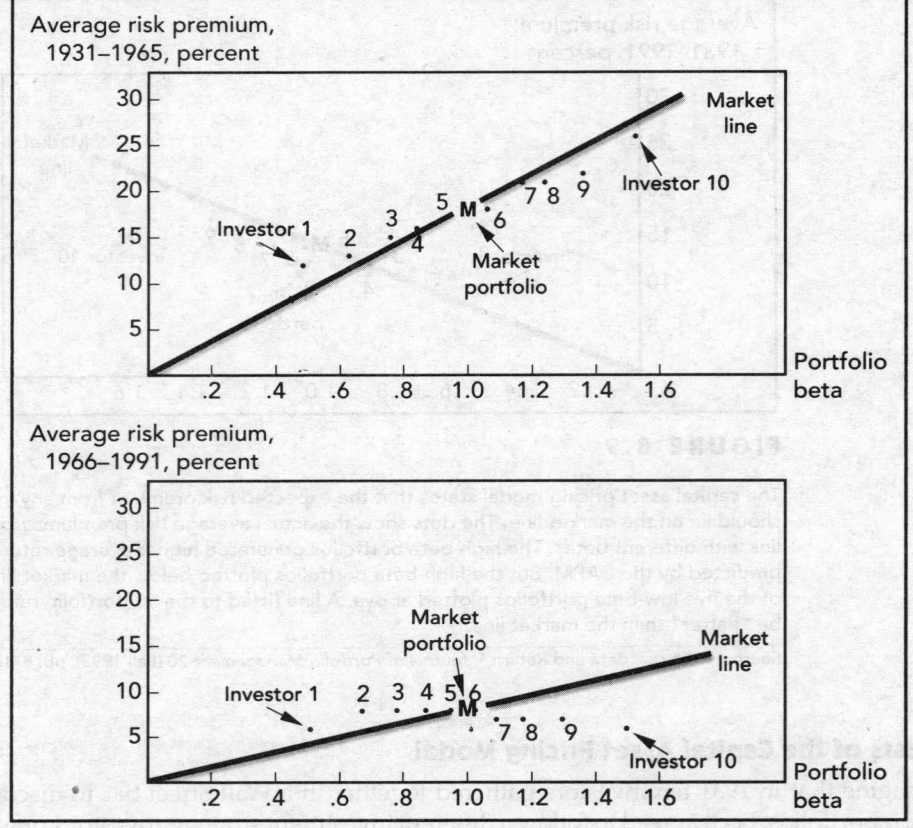

course) had a beta of 1.0. The CAPM predicts that the risk premium should increase in proportion to beta, so that the returns of each portfolio should lie on the upward-sloping security market line in Figure 8.9. Since the market provided a risk premium of 14 percent, investor 1's portfolio, with a beta of .49, should have provided a risk premium of a shade under 7 percent and investor 10's portfolio, with a beta of 1.52, should have given a premium of a shade over 21 percent. You can see that, while high-beta stocks performed better than low-beta stocks, the difference was not as great as the CAPM predicts.

Although Figure 8.9 provides broad support for the CAPM, critics have pointed out that the slope of the line has been particularly flat in recent years. For example, Figure 8.10 shows how our 10 investors fared between 1966 and 1991. Now it's less clear who is buying the drinks: The portfolios of investors 1 and 10 had very different betas but both earned the same average return over these 25 years. Of course, the line was correspondingly steeper before 1966. This is also shown in Figure 8.10

What's going on here? It is hard to say. Defenders of the capital asset pricing model emphasize that it is concerned with *expected* returns, whereas we can observe only *actual* returns. Actual stock returns reflect expectations, but they also embody lots of "noise"—the steady flow of surprises that conceal whether on av-

FIGURE 8.11

The burgundy line shows the cumulative difference between the returns on small-firm and large-firm stocks. The blue line shows the cumulative difference between the returns on high book-to-market-value stocks and low book-to-market-value stocks.

Source: **www.mba.tuck.dartmouth.edu/pages/faculty/ken.french/data_library.**

erage investors have received the returns they expected. This noise may make it impossible to judge whether the model holds better in one period than another.[16] Perhaps the best that we can do is to focus on the longest period for which there is reasonable data. This would take us back to Figure 8.9, which suggests that expected returns do indeed increase with beta, though less rapidly than the simple version of the CAPM predicts.[17]

The CAPM has also come under fire on a second front: Although return has not risen with beta in recent years, it has been related to other measures. For example, the burgundy line in Figure 8.11 shows the cumulative difference between the returns on small-firm stocks and large-firm stocks. If you had bought the shares with the smallest market capitalizations and sold those with the largest capitalizations, this is how your wealth would have changed. You can see that small-cap stocks did not always do well, but over the long haul their owners have made substantially

---

[16]A second problem with testing the model is that the market portfolio should contain all risky investments, including stocks, bonds, commodities, real estate—even human capital. Most market indexes contain only a sample of common stocks. See, for example, R. Roll, "A Critique of the Asset Pricing Theory's Tests; Part 1: On Past and Potential Testability of the Theory," *Journal of Financial Economics* 4 (March 1977), pp. 129–176.

[17]We say "simple version" because Fischer Black has shown that if there are borrowing restrictions, there should still exist a positive relationship between expected return and beta, but the security market line would be less steep as a result. See F. Black, "Capital Market Equilibrium with Restricted Borrowing," *Journal of Business* 45 (July 1972), pp. 444–455.

higher returns. Since 1928 the average annual difference between the returns on the two groups of stocks has been 3.1 percent.

Now look at the blue line in Figure 8.11 which shows the cumulative difference between the returns on value stocks and growth stocks. Value stocks here are defined as those with high ratios of book value to market value. Growth stocks are those with low ratios of book to market. Notice that value stocks have provided a higher long-run return than growth stocks.[18] Since 1928 the average annual difference between the returns on value and growth stocks has been 4.4 percent.

Figure 8.11 does not fit well with the CAPM, which predicts that beta is the *only* reason that expected returns differ. It seems that investors saw risks in "small-cap" stocks and value stocks that were not captured by beta.[19] Take value stocks, for example. Many of these stocks sold below book value because the firms were in serious trouble; if the economy slowed unexpectedly, the firms might have collapsed altogether. Therefore, investors, whose jobs could also be on the line in a recession, may have regarded these stocks as particularly risky and demanded compensation in the form of higher expected returns.[20] If that were the case, the simple version of the CAPM cannot be the whole truth.

Again, it is hard to judge how seriously the CAPM is damaged by this finding. The relationship among stock returns and firm size and book-to-market ratio has been well documented. However, if you look long and hard at past returns, you are bound to find some strategy that just by chance would have worked in the past. This practice is known as "data-mining" or "data snooping." Maybe the size and book-to-market effects are simply chance results that stem from data snooping. If so, they should have vanished once they were discovered. There is some evidence that this is the case. If you look again at Figure 8.11, you will see that in recent years small-firm stocks and value stocks have underperformed just about as often as they have overperformed.

There is no doubt that the evidence on the CAPM is less convincing than scholars once thought. But it will be hard to reject the CAPM beyond all reasonable doubt. Since data and statistics are unlikely to give final answers, the plausibility of the CAPM *theory* will have to be weighed along with the empirical "facts."

Assumptions behind the Capital Asset Pricing Model

The capital asset pricing model rests on several assumptions that we did not fully spell out. For example, we assumed that investment in U.S. Treasury bills is risk-free. It is true that there is little chance of default, but they don't guarantee a *real*

---

[18]The small-firm effect was first documented by Rolf Banz in 1981. See R. Banz, "The Relationship between Return and Market Values of Common Stock," *Journal of Financial Economics* 9 (March 1981), pp. 3–18. Fama and French calculated the returns on portfolios designed to take advantage of the size effect and the book-to-market effect. See E. F. Fama and K. R. French, "The Cross-Section of Expected Stock Returns," *Journal of Financial Economics* 47 (June 1992), pp. 427–465. When calculating the returns on these portfolios, Fama and French control for differences in firm size when comparing stocks with low and high book-to-market ratios. Similarly, they control for differences in the book-to-market ratio when comparing small- and large-firm stocks. For details of the methodology and updated returns on the size and book-to-market factors see Kenneth French's website (**www.mba.tuck.dartmouth.edu/pages/faculty/ken.french/data_library**).

[19]Small-firm stocks have higher betas, but the difference in betas is not sufficient to explain the difference in returns. There is no simple relationship between book-to-market ratios and beta.

[20]For a good review of the evidence on the CAPM, see J. H. Cochrane, "New Facts in Finance," *Journal of Economic Perspectives* 23 (1999), pp. 36–58.

return. There is still some uncertainty about inflation. Another assumption was that investors can *borrow* money at the same rate of interest at which they can lend. Generally borrowing rates are higher than lending rates.

It turns out that many of these assumptions are not crucial, and with a little pushing and pulling it is possible to modify the capital asset pricing model to handle them. The really important idea is that investors are content to invest their money in a limited number of benchmark portfolios. (In the basic CAPM these benchmarks are Treasury bills and the market portfolio.)

In these modified CAPMs expected return still depends on market risk, but the definition of market risk depends on the nature of the benchmark portfolios.[21] In practice, none of these alternative capital asset pricing models is as widely used as the standard version.

8.4 SOME ALTERNATIVE THEORIES

Consumption Betas versus Market Betas

The capital asset pricing model pictures investors as solely concerned with the level and uncertainty of their future wealth. But for most people wealth is not an end in itself. What good is wealth if you can't spend it? People invest now to provide future consumption for themselves or for their families and heirs. The most important risks are those that might force a cutback of future consumption.

Douglas Breeden has developed a model in which a security's risk is measured by its sensitivity to changes in investors' consumption. If he is right, a stock's expected return should move in line with its *consumption beta* rather than its market beta. Figure 8.12 summarizes the chief differences between the standard and consumption CAPMs. In the standard model investors are concerned exclusively with the amount and uncertainty of their future wealth. Each investor's wealth ends up perfectly correlated with the return on the market portfolio; the demand for stocks and other risky assets is thus determined by their market risk. The deeper motive for investing—to provide for consumption—is outside the model.

In the consumption CAPM, uncertainty about stock returns is connected directly to uncertainty about consumption. Of course, consumption depends on wealth (portfolio value), but wealth does not appear explicitly in the model.

The consumption CAPM has several appealing features. For example, you don't have to identify the market or any other benchmark portfolio. You don't have to worry that Standard and Poor's Composite Index doesn't track returns on bonds, commodities, and real estate.

However, you do have to be able to measure consumption. *Quick:* How much did you consume last month? It's easy to count the hamburgers and movie tickets, but what about the depreciation on your car or washing machine or the daily cost of your homeowner's insurance policy? We suspect that your estimate of total consumption will rest on rough or arbitrary allocations and assumptions. And if it's hard for you to put a dollar value on your total consumption, think of the

---

[21]For example, see M. C. Jensen (ed.), *Studies in the Theory of Capital Markets,* Frederick A. Praeger, Inc., New York, 1972. In the introduction Jensen provides a very useful summary of some of these variations on the capital asset pricing model.

FIGURE 8.12

(a) The standard CAPM concentrates on how stocks contribute to the level and uncertainty of investor's wealth. Consumption is outside the model. (b) The consumption CAPM defines risk as a stock's contribution to uncertainty about consumption. Wealth (the intermediate step between stock returns and consumption) drops out of the model.

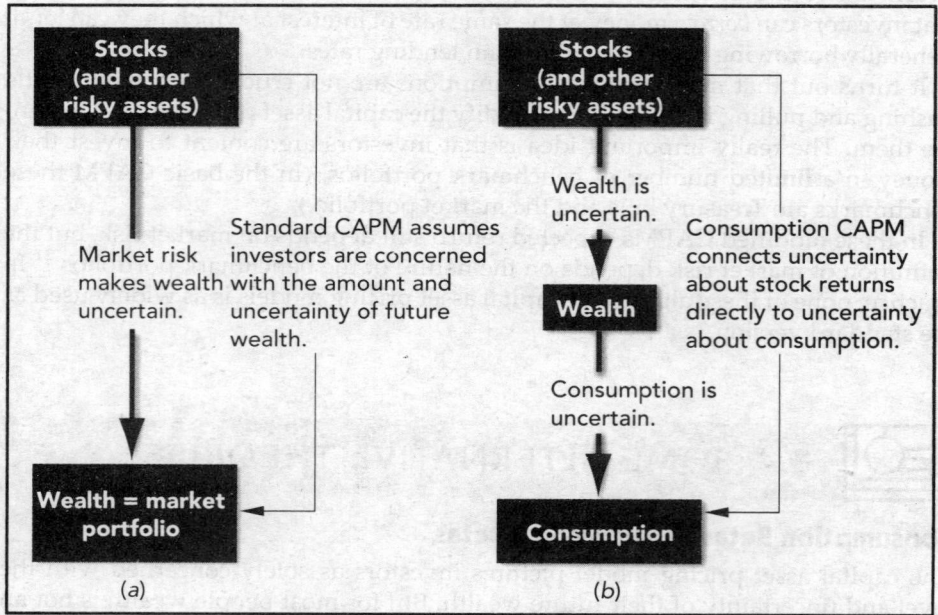

task facing a government statistician asked to estimate month-by-month consumption for all of us.

Compared to stock prices, estimated aggregate consumption changes smoothly and gradually over time. Changes in consumption often seem to be out of phase with the stock market. Individual stocks seem to have low or erratic consumption betas. Moreover, the volatility of consumption appears too low to explain the past average rates of return on common stocks unless one assumes unreasonably high investor risk aversion.[22] These problems may reflect our poor measures of consumption or perhaps poor models of how individuals distribute consumption over time. It seems too early for the consumption CAPM to see practical use.

Arbitrage Pricing Theory

The capital asset pricing theory begins with an analysis of how investors construct efficient portfolios. Stephen Ross's **arbitrage pricing theory,** or **APT,** comes from a different family entirely. It does not ask which portfolios are efficient. Instead, it starts by *assuming* that each stock's return depends partly on pervasive macroeconomic influences or "factors" and partly on "noise"—events that are unique to that company. Moreover, the return is assumed to obey the following simple relationship:

$$\text{Return} = a + b_1(r_{\text{factor }1}) + b_2(r_{\text{factor }2}) + b_3(r_{\text{factor }3}) + \cdots + \text{noise}$$

The theory doesn't say what the factors are: There could be an oil price factor, an interest-rate factor, and so on. The return on the market portfolio *might* serve as one factor, but then again it might not.

---

[22]See R. Mehra and E. C. Prescott, "The Equity Risk Premium: A Puzzle," *Journal of Monetary Economics* 15 (1985), pp. 145–161.

Some stocks will be more sensitive to a particular factor than other stocks. Exxon Mobil would be more sensitive to an oil factor than, say, Coca-Cola. If factor 1 picks up unexpected changes in oil prices, b_1 will be higher for Exxon Mobil.

For any individual stock there are two sources of risk. First is the risk that stems from the pervasive macroeconomic factors which cannot be eliminated by diversification. Second is the risk arising from possible events that are unique to the company. Diversification *does* eliminate unique risk, and diversified investors can therefore ignore it when deciding whether to buy or sell a stock. The expected risk premium on a stock is affected by factor or macroeconomic risk; it is *not* affected by unique risk.

Arbitrage pricing theory states that the expected risk premium on a stock should depend on the expected risk premium associated with each factor and the stock's sensitivity to each of the factors (b_1, b_2, b_3, etc.). Thus the formula is[23]

$$\text{Expected risk premium} = r - r_f$$
$$= b_1(r_{\text{factor 1}} - r_f) + b_2(r_{\text{factor 2}} - r_f) + \cdots$$

Notice that this formula makes two statements:

1. If you plug in a value of zero for each of the b's in the formula, the expected risk premium is zero. A diversified portfolio that is constructed to have zero sensitivity to each macroeconomic factor is essentially risk-free and therefore must be priced to offer the risk-free rate of interest. If the portfolio offered a higher return, investors could make a risk-free (or "arbitrage") profit by borrowing to buy the portfolio. If it offered a lower return, you could make an arbitrage profit by running the strategy in reverse; in other words, you would *sell* the diversified zero-sensitivity portfolio and *invest* the proceeds in U.S. Treasury bills.

2. A diversified portfolio that is constructed to have exposure to, say, factor 1, will offer a risk premium, which will vary in direct proportion to the portfolio's sensitivity to that factor. For example, imagine that you construct two portfolios, A and B, which are affected only by factor 1. If portfolio A is twice as sensitive to factor 1 as portfolio B, portfolio A must offer twice the risk premium. Therefore, if you divided your money equally between U.S. Treasury bills and portfolio A, your combined portfolio would have exactly the same sensitivity to factor 1 as portfolio B and would offer the same risk premium.

    Suppose that the arbitrage pricing formula did *not* hold. For example, suppose that the combination of Treasury bills and portfolio A offered a higher return. In that case investors could make an arbitrage profit by selling portfolio B and investing the proceeds in the mixture of bills and portfolio A.

The arbitrage that we have described applies to well-diversified portfolios, where the unique risk has been diversified away. But if the arbitrage pricing relationship holds for all diversified portfolios, it must generally hold for the individual stocks. Each stock must offer an expected return commensurate with its contribution to portfolio risk. In the APT, this contribution depends on the sensitivity of the stock's return to unexpected changes in the macroeconomic factors.

---

[23]There may be some macroeconomic factors that investors are simply not worried about. For example, some macroeconomists believe that money supply doesn't matter and therefore investors are not worried about inflation. Such factors would not command a risk premium. They would drop out of the APT formula for expected return.

A Comparison of the Capital Asset Pricing Model and Arbitrage Pricing Theory

Like the capital asset pricing model, arbitrage pricing theory stresses that expected return depends on the risk stemming from economywide influences and is not affected by unique risk. You can think of the factors in arbitrage pricing as representing special portfolios of stocks that tend to be subject to a common influence. If the expected risk premium on each of these portfolios is proportional to the portfolio's market beta, then the arbitrage pricing theory and the capital asset pricing model will give the same answer. In any other case they won't.

How do the two theories stack up? Arbitrage pricing has some attractive features. For example, the market portfolio that plays such a central role in the capital asset pricing model does not feature in arbitrage pricing theory.[24] So we don't have to worry about the problem of measuring the market portfolio, and in principle we can test the arbitrage pricing theory even if we have data on only a sample of risky assets.

Unfortunately you win some and lose some. Arbitrage pricing theory doesn't tell us what the underlying factors are—unlike the capital asset pricing model, which collapses *all* macroeconomic risks into a well-defined *single* factor, the return on the market portfolio.

APT Example

Arbitrage pricing theory will provide a good handle on expected returns only if we can (1) identify a reasonably short list of macroeconomic factors,[25] (2) measure the expected risk premium on each of these factors, and (3) measure the sensitivity of each stock to these factors. Let us look briefly at how Elton, Gruber, and Mei tackled each of these issues and estimated the cost of equity for a group of nine New York utilities.[26]

Step 1: Identify the Macroeconomic Factors   Although APT doesn't tell us what the underlying economic factors are, Elton, Gruber, and Mei identified five principal factors that could affect either the cash flows themselves or the rate at which they are discounted. These factors are

Factor	Measured by
Yield spread	Return on long government bond *less* return on 30-day Treasury bills
Interest rate	Change in Treasury bill return
Exchange rate	Change in value of dollar relative to basket of currencies
Real GNP	Change in forecasts of real GNP
Inflation	Change in forecasts of inflation

---

[24]Of course, the market portfolio *may* turn out to be one of the factors, but that is not a necessary implication of arbitrage pricing theory.

[25]Some researchers have argued that there are four or five principal pervasive influences on stock prices, but others are not so sure. They point out that the more stocks you look at, the more factors you need to take into account. See, for example, P. J. Dhrymes, I. Friend, and N. B. Gultekin, "A Critical Reexamination of the Empirical Evidence on the Arbitrage Pricing Theory," *Journal of Finance* 39 (June 1984), pp. 323–346.

[26]See E. J. Elton, M. J. Gruber, and J. Mei, "Cost of Capital Using Arbitrage Pricing Theory: A Case Study of Nine New York Utilities," *Financial Markets, Institutions, and Instruments* 3 (August 1994), pp. 46–73. The study was prepared for the New York State Public Utility Commission. We described a parallel study in Chapter 4 which used the discounted-cash-flow model to estimate the cost of equity capital.

Factor	Estimated Risk Premium * $(r_{factor} - r_f)$
Yield spread	5.10%
Interest rate	−.61
Exchange rate	−.59
Real GNP	.49
Inflation	−.83
Market	6.36

TABLE 8.3

Estimated risk premiums for taking on factor risks, 1978–1990.

*The risk premiums have been scaled to represent the annual premiums for the average industrial stock in the Elton–Gruber–Mei sample.

Source: E. J. Elton, M. J. Gruber, and J. Mei, "Cost of Capital Using Arbitrage Pricing Theory: A Case Study of Nine New York Utilities," *Financial Markets, Institutions, and Instruments* 3 (August 1994), pp. 46–73.

To capture any remaining pervasive influences, Elton, Gruber, and Mei also included a sixth factor, the portion of the market return that could not be explained by the first five.

Step 2: Estimate the Risk Premium for Each Factor   Some stocks are more exposed than others to a particular factor. So we can estimate the sensitivity of a sample of stocks to each factor and then measure how much extra return investors would have received in the past for taking on factor risk. The results are shown in Table 8.3.

For example, stocks with positive sensitivity to real GNP tended to have higher returns when real GNP increased. A stock with an average sensitivity gave investors an additional return of .49 percent a year compared with a stock that was completely unaffected by changes in real GNP. In other words, investors appeared to dislike "cyclical" stocks, whose returns were sensitive to economic activity, and demanded a higher return from these stocks.

By contrast, Table 8.3 shows that a stock with average exposure to *inflation* gave investors .83 percent a year *less* return than a stock with no exposure to inflation. Thus investors seemed to prefer stocks that protected them against inflation (stocks that did well when inflation accelerated), and they were willing to accept a lower expected return from such stocks.

Step 3: Estimate the Factor Sensitivities   The estimates of the premiums for taking on factor risk can now be used to estimate the cost of equity for the group of New York State utilities. Remember, APT states that the risk premium for any asset depends on its sensitivities to factor risks (*b*) and the expected risk premium for each factor ($r_{factor} - r_f$). In this case there are six factors, so

$$r - r_f = b_1(r_{factor\ 1} - r_f) + b_2(r_{factor\ 2} - r_f) + \cdots + b_6(r_{factor\ 6} - r_f)$$

The first column of Table 8.4 shows the factor risks for the portfolio of utilities, and the second column shows the required risk premium for each factor (taken from Table 8.3). The third column is simply the product of these two numbers. It shows how much return investors demanded for taking on each factor risk. To find the expected risk premium, just add the figures in the final column:

$$\text{Expected risk premium} = r - r_f = 8.53\%$$

TABLE 8.4

Using APT to estimate the expected risk premium for a portfolio of nine New York State utility stocks.

Source: E. J. Elton, M. J. Gruber, and J. Mei, "Cost of Capital Using Arbitrage Pricing Theory: A Case Study of Nine New York Utilities," *Financial Markets, Institutions, and Instruments* 3 (August 1994), tables 3 and 4.

Factor	Factor Risk (b)	Expected Risk Premium $(r_{factor} - r_f)$	Factor Risk Premium $b(r_{factor} - r_f)$
Yield spread	1.04	5.10%	5.30%
Interest rate	−2.25	−.61	1.37
Exchange rate	.70	−.59	−.41
GNP	.17	.49	.08
Inflation	−.18	−.83	.15
Market	.32	6.36	2.04
Total			8.53%

The one-year Treasury bill rate in December 1990, the end of the Elton–Gruber–Mei sample period, was about 7 percent, so the APT estimate of the expected return on New York State utility stocks was[27]

$$\text{Expected return} = \text{risk-free interest rate} + \text{expected risk premium}$$
$$= 7 + 8.53$$
$$= 15.53, \text{ or about } 15.5\%$$

The Three-Factor Model

We noted earlier the research by Fama and French showing that stocks of small firms and those with a high book-to-market ratio have provided above-average returns. This could simply be a coincidence. But there is also evidence that these factors are related to company profitability and therefore may be picking up risk factors that are left out of the simple CAPM.[28]

If investors do demand an extra return for taking on exposure to these factors, then we have a measure of the expected return that looks very much like arbitrage pricing theory:

$$r - r_f = b_{market}(r_{market\ factor}) + b_{size}(r_{size\ factor}) + b_{book\text{-}to\text{-}market}(r_{book\text{-}to\text{-}market\ factor})$$

This is commonly known as the Fama–French three-factor model. Using it to estimate expected returns is exactly the same as applying the arbitrage pricing theory. Here's an example.[29]

Step 1: Identify the Factors

Fama and French have already identified the three factors that appear to determine expected returns. The returns on each of these factors are

---

[27]This estimate rests on risk premiums actually earned from 1978 to 1990, an unusually rewarding period for common stock investors. Estimates based on long-run market risk premiums would be lower. See E. J. Elton, M. J. Gruber, and J. Mei, "Cost of Capital Using Arbitrage Pricing Theory: A Case Study of Nine New York Utilities," *Financial Markets, Institutions, and Instruments* 3 (August 1994), pp. 46–73.

[28]E. F. Fama and K. R. French, "Size and Book-to-Market Factors in Earnings and Returns," *Journal of Finance* 50 (1995), pp. 131–155.

[29]The example is taken from E. F. Fama and K. R. French, "Industry Costs of Equity," *Journal of Financial Economics* 43 (1997), pp. 153–193. Fama and French emphasize the imprecision involved in using either the CAPM or an APT-style model to estimate the returns that investors expect.

Factor	Measured by
Market factor	Return on market index *minus* risk-free interest rate
Size factor	Return on small-firm stocks *less* return on large-firm stocks
Book-to-market factor	Return on high book-to-market-ratio stocks *less* return on low book-to-market-ratio stocks

Step 2: Estimate the Risk Premium for Each Factor   Here we need to rely on history. Fama and French find that between 1963 and 1994 the return on the market factor averaged about 5.2 percent per year, the difference between the return on small and large capitalization stocks was about 3.2 percent a year, while the difference between the annual return on stocks with high and low book-to-market ratios averaged 5.4 percent.[30]

Step 3: Estimate the Factor Sensitivities   Some stocks are more sensitive than others to fluctuations in the returns on the three factors. Look, for example, at the first three columns of numbers in Table 8.5, which show some estimates by Fama and French of factor sensitivities for different industry groups. You can see, for example, that an increase of 1 percent in the return on the book-to-market factor *reduces* the return on computer stocks by .49 percent but *increases* the return on utility stocks by .38 percent.[31]

	Three-Factor Model				CAPM
	Factor Sensitivities			Expected Risk Premium*	Expected Risk Premium
	b_{market}	b_{size}	$b_{book-to-market}$		
Aircraft	1.15	.51	.00	7.54%	6.43%
Banks	1.13	.13	.35	8.08	5.55
Chemicals	1.13	−.03	.17	6.58	5.57
Computers	.90	.17	−.49	2.49	5.29
Construction	1.21	.21	−.09	6.42	6.52
Food	.88	−.07	−.03	4.09	4.44
Petroleum & gas	.96	−.35	.21	4.93	4.32
Pharmaceuticals	.84	−.25	−.63	.09	4.71
Tobacco	.86	−.04	.24	5.56	4.08
Utilities	.79	−.20	.38	5.41	3.39

TABLE 8.5

Estimates of industry risk premiums using the Fama–French three-factor model and the CAPM.

*The expected risk premium equals the factor sensitivities multiplied by the factor risk premiums, that is, (b_{market} × 5.2) + (b_{size} × 3.2) + ($b_{book-to-market}$ × 5.4).
Source: E. F. Fama and K. R. French, "Industry Costs of Equity," *Journal of Financial Economics* 43 (1997), pp. 153–193.

[30]We saw earlier that over the longer period 1928–2000 the average annual difference between the returns on small and large capitalization stocks was 3.1 percent. The difference between the returns on stocks with high and low book-to-market ratios was 4.4 percent.

[31]A 1 percent return on the book-to-market factor means that stocks with a high book-to-market ratio provide a 1 percent higher return than those with a low ratio.

Once you have an estimate of the factor sensitivities, it is a simple matter to multiply each of them by the expected factor return and add up the results. For example, the fourth column of numbers shows that the expected risk premium on computer stocks is $r - r_f = (.90 \times 5.2) + (.17 \times 3.2) - (.49 \times 5.4) = 2.49$ percent. Compare this figure with the risk premium estimated using the capital asset pricing model (the final column of Table 8.5). The three-factor model provides a substantially lower estimate of the risk premium for computer stocks than the CAPM. Why? Largely because computer stocks have a low exposure ($-.49$) to the book-to-market factor.

SUMMARY

The basic principles of portfolio selection boil down to a commonsense statement that investors try to increase the expected return on their portfolios and to reduce the standard deviation of that return. A portfolio that gives the highest expected return for a given standard deviation, or the lowest standard deviation for a given expected return, is known as an *efficient portfolio*. To work out which portfolios are efficient, an investor must be able to state the expected return and standard deviation of each stock and the degree of correlation between each pair of stocks.

Investors who are restricted to holding common stocks should choose efficient portfolios that suit their attitudes to risk. But investors who can also borrow and lend at the risk-free rate of interest should choose the *best* common stock portfolio *regardless* of their attitudes to risk. Having done that, they can then set the risk of their overall portfolio by deciding what proportion of their money they are willing to invest in stocks. The best efficient portfolio offers the highest ratio of forecasted risk premium to portfolio standard deviation.

For an investor who has only the same opportunities and information as everybody else, the best stock portfolio is the same as the best stock portfolio for other investors. In other words, he or she should invest in a mixture of the market portfolio and a risk-free loan (i.e., borrowing or lending).

A stock's marginal contribution to portfolio risk is measured by its sensitivity to changes in the value of the portfolio. The marginal contribution of a stock to the risk of the *market portfolio* is measured by *beta*. That is the fundamental idea behind the capital asset pricing model (CAPM), which concludes that each security's expected risk premium should increase in proportion to its beta:

$$\text{Expected risk premium} = \text{beta} \times \text{market risk premium}$$
$$r - r_f = \beta(r_m - r_f)$$

The capital asset pricing theory is the best-known model of risk and return. It is plausible and widely used but far from perfect. Actual returns are related to beta over the long run, but the relationship is not as strong as the CAPM predicts, and other factors seem to explain returns better since the mid-1960s. Stocks of small companies, and stocks with high book values relative to market prices, appear to have risks not captured by the CAPM.

The CAPM has also been criticized for its strong simplifying assumptions. A new theory called the *consumption* capital asset pricing model suggests that security risk reflects the sensitivity of returns to changes in investors' *consumption*.

This theory calls for a consumption beta rather than a beta relative to the market portfolio.

The arbitrage pricing theory offers an alternative theory of risk and return. It states that the expected risk premium on a stock should depend on the stock's exposure to several pervasive macroeconomic factors that affect stock returns:

$$\text{Expected risk premium} = b_1(r_{\text{factor 1}} - r_f) + b_2(r_{\text{factor 2}} - r_f) + \cdots$$

Here b's represent the individual security's sensitivities to the factors, and $r_{\text{factor}} - r_f$ is the risk premium demanded by investors who are exposed to this factor.

Arbitrage pricing theory does not say what these factors are. It asks for economists to hunt for unknown game with their statistical tool kits. The hunters have returned with several candidates, including unanticipated changes in

- The level of industrial activity.
- The rate of inflation.
- The spread between short- and long-term interest rates.

Fama and French have suggested three different factors:

- The return on the market portfolio less the risk-free rate of interest.
- The difference between the return on small- and large-firm stocks.
- The difference between the return on stocks with high book-to-market ratios and stocks with low book-to-market ratios.

In the Fama–French three-factor model, the expected return on each stock depends on its exposure to these three factors.

Each of these different models of risk and return has its fan club. However, all financial economists agree on two basic ideas: (1) Investors require extra expected return for taking on risk, and (2) they appear to be concerned predominantly with the risk that they cannot eliminate by diversification.

FURTHER READING

The pioneering article on portfolio selection is:
H. M. Markowitz: "Portfolio Selection," *Journal of Finance,* 7:77–91 (March 1952).

There are a number of textbooks on portfolio selection which explain both Markowitz's original theory and some ingenious simplified versions. See, for example:
E. J. Elton and M. J. Gruber: *Modern Portfolio Theory and Investment Analysis,* 5th ed., John Wiley & Sons, New York, 1995.

Of the three pioneering articles on the capital asset pricing model, Jack Treynor's has never been published. The other two articles are:
W. F. Sharpe: "Capital Asset Prices: A Theory of Market Equilibrium under Conditions of Risk," *Journal of Finance,* 19:425–442 (September 1964).

J. Lintner: "The Valuation of Risk Assets and the Selection of Risky Investments in Stock Portfolios and Capital Budgets," *Review of Economics and Statistics,* 47:13–37 (February 1965).

The subsequent literature on the capital asset pricing model is enormous. The following book provides a collection of some of the more important articles plus a very useful survey by Jensen:
M. C. Jensen (ed.): *Studies in the Theory of Capital Markets,* Frederick A. Praeger, Inc., New York, 1972.

The two most important early tests of the capital asset pricing model are:

E. F. Fama and J. D. MacBeth: "Risk, Return and Equilibrium: Empirical Tests," *Journal of Political Economy*, 81:607–636 (May 1973).

F. Black, M. C. Jensen, and M. Scholes: "The Capital Asset Pricing Model: Some Empirical Tests," in M. C. Jensen (ed.), *Studies in the Theory of Capital Markets*, Frederick A. Praeger, Inc., New York, 1972.

For a critique of empirical tests of the capital asset pricing model, see:

R. Roll: "A Critique of the Asset Pricing Theory's Tests; Part I: On Past and Potential Testability of the Theory," *Journal of Financial Economics*, 4:129–176 (March 1977).

Much of the recent controversy about the performance of the capital asset pricing model was prompted by Fama and French's paper. The paper by Black takes issue with Fama and French and updates the Black, Jensen, and Scholes test of the model:

E. F. Fama and K. R. French: "The Cross-Section of Expected Stock Returns," *Journal of Finance*, 47:427–465 (June 1992).

F. Black, "Beta and Return," *Journal of Portfolio Management*, 20:8–18 (Fall 1993).

Breeden's 1979 article describes the consumption asset pricing model, and the Breeden, Gibbons, and Litzenberger paper tests the model and compares it with the standard CAPM:

D. T. Breeden: "An Intertemporal Asset Pricing Model with Stochastic Consumption and Investment Opportunities," *Journal of Financial Economics*, 7:265–296 (September 1979).

D. T. Breeden, M. R. Gibbons, and R. H. Litzenberger: "Empirical Tests of the Consumption-Oriented CAPM," *Journal of Finance*, 44:231–262 (June 1989).

Arbitrage pricing theory is described in Ross's 1976 paper.

S. A. Ross: "The Arbitrage Theory of Capital Asset Pricing," *Journal of Economic Theory*, 13:341–360 (December 1976).

The most accessible recent implementation of APT is:

E. J. Elton, M. J. Gruber, and J. Mei, "Cost of Capital Using Arbitrage Pricing Theory: A Case Study of Nine New York Utilities," *Financial Markets, Institutions, and Instruments*, 3:46–73 (August 1994).

For an application of the Fama–French three-factor model, see:

E. F. Fama and K. R. French, "Industry Costs of Equity," *Journal of Financial Economics*, 43:153–193 (February 1997).

QUIZ

1. Here are returns and standard deviations for four investments.

	Return	Standard Deviation
Treasury bills	6%	0%
Stock P	10	14
Stock Q	14.5	28
Stock R	21.0	26

Calculate the standard deviations of the following portfolios.
a. 50 percent in Treasury bills, 50 percent in stock P.
b. 50 percent each in Q and R, assuming the shares have
   • perfect positive correlation
   • perfect negative correlation
   • no correlation

FIGURE 8.13

See Quiz Question 3.

c. Plot a figure like Figure 8.4 for Q and R, assuming a correlation coefficient of .5.

d. Stock Q has a lower return than R but a higher standard deviation. Does that mean that Q's price is too high or that R's price is too low?

2. For each of the following pairs of investments, state which would always be preferred by a rational investor (assuming that these are the *only* investments available to the investor):

a. Portfolio A	$r = 18$ percent	$\sigma = 20$ percent
Portfolio B	$r = 14$ percent	$\sigma = 20$ percent
b. Portfolio C	$r = 15$ percent	$\sigma = 18$ percent
Portfolio D	$r = 13$ percent	$\sigma = 8$ percent
c. Portfolio E	$r = 14$ percent	$\sigma = 16$ percent
Portfolio F	$r = 14$ percent	$\sigma = 10$ percent

3. Figures 8.13a and 8.13b purport to show the range of attainable combinations of expected return and standard deviation.

a. Which diagram is incorrectly drawn and why?

b. Which is the efficient set of portfolios?

c. If r_f is the rate of interest, mark with an X the optimal stock portfolio.

4. a. Plot the following risky portfolios on a graph:

				Portfolio				
	A	B	C	D	E	F	G	H
Expected return (r), %	10	12.5	15	16	17	18	18	20
Standard deviation (σ), %	23	21	25	29	29	32	35	45

b. Five of these portfolios are efficient, and three are not. Which are *in*efficient ones?

c. Suppose you can also borrow and lend at an interest rate of 12 percent. Which of the above portfolios is best?

d. Suppose you are prepared to tolerate a standard deviation of 25 percent. What is the maximum expected return that you can achieve if you cannot borrow or lend?

e. What is your optimal strategy if you can borrow or lend at 12 percent and are prepared to tolerate a standard deviation of 25 percent? What is the maximum expected return that you can achieve?

5. How could an investor identify the *best* of a set of efficient portfolios of common stocks? What does "best" mean? Assume the investor can borrow or lend at the risk-free interest rate.

6. Suppose that the Treasury bill rate is 4 percent and the expected return on the market is 10 percent. Use the betas in Table 8.2.
   a. Calculate the expected return from McDonald's.
   b. Find the highest expected return that is offered by one of these stocks.
   c. Find the lowest expected return that is offered by one of these stocks.
   d. Would Dell offer a higher or lower expected return if the interest rate was 6 rather than 4 percent? Assume that the expected market return stays at 10 percent.
   e. Would Exxon Mobil offer a higher or lower expected return if the interest rate was 6 percent?

7. True or false?
   a. The CAPM implies that if you could find an investment with a negative beta, its expected return would be less than the interest rate.
   b. The expected return on an investment with a beta of 2.0 is twice as high as the expected return on the market.
   c. If a stock lies below the security market line, it is undervalued.

8. The CAPM has great theoretical, intuitive, and practical appeal. Nevertheless, many financial managers believe "beta is dead." Why?

9. Write out the APT equation for the expected rate of return on a risky stock.

10. Consider a three-factor APT model. The factors and associated risk premiums are

Factor	Risk Premium
Change in GNP	5%
Change in energy prices	−1
Change in long-term interest rates	+2

Calculate expected rates of return on the following stocks. The risk-free interest rate is 7 percent.
   a. A stock whose return is uncorrelated with all three factors.
   b. A stock with average exposure to each factor (i.e., with $b = 1$ for each).
   c. A pure-play energy stock with high exposure to the energy factor ($b = 2$) but zero exposure to the other two factors.
   d. An aluminum company stock with average sensitivity to changes in interest rates and GNP, but negative exposure of $b = -1.5$ to the energy factor. (The aluminum company is energy-intensive and suffers when energy prices rise.)

11. Fama and French have proposed a three-factor model for expected returns. What are the three factors?

PRACTICE QUESTIONS

1. True or false? Explain or qualify as necessary.
   a. Investors demand higher expected rates of return on stocks with more variable rates of return.
   b. The CAPM predicts that a security with a beta of 0 will offer a zero expected return.
   c. An investor who puts $10,000 in Treasury bills and $20,000 in the market portfolio will have a beta of 2.0.

d. Investors demand higher expected rates of return from stocks with returns that are highly exposed to macroeconomic changes.

e. Investors demand higher expected rates of return from stocks with returns that are very sensitive to fluctuations in the stock market.

2. Look back at the calculation for Coca-Cola and Reebok in Section 8.1. Recalculate the expected portfolio return and standard deviation for different values of x_1 and x_2, assuming the correlation coefficient $\rho_{12} = 0$. Plot the range of possible combinations of expected return and standard deviation as in Figure 8.4. Repeat the problem for $\rho_{12} = +1$ and for $\rho_{12} = -1$.

3. Mark Harrywitz proposes to invest in two shares, X and Y. He expects a return of 12 percent from X and 8 percent from Y. The standard deviation of returns is 8 percent for X and 5 percent for Y. The correlation coefficient between the returns is .2.
   a. Compute the expected return and standard deviation of the following portfolios:

Portfolio	Percentage in X	Percentage in Y
1	50	50
2	25	75
3	75	25

   b. Sketch the set of portfolios composed of X and Y.
   c. Suppose that Mr. Harrywitz can also borrow or lend at an interest rate of 5 percent. Show on your sketch how this alters his opportunities. Given that he can borrow or lend, what proportions of the common stock portfolio should be invested in X and Y?

4. M. Grandet has invested 60 percent of his money in share A and the remainder in share B. He assesses their prospects as follows:

	A	B
Expected return (%)	15	20
Standard deviation (%)	20	22
Correlation between returns		.5

   a. What are the expected return and standard deviation of returns on his portfolio?
   b. How would your answer change if the correlation coefficient was 0 or $-.5$?
   c. Is M. Grandet's portfolio better or worse than one invested entirely in share A, or is it not possible to say?

5. Download "Monthly Adjusted Prices" for General Motors (GM) and Harley Davidson (HDI) from the Standard & Poor's Market Insight website (**www.mhhe.com/ edumarketinsight**). Use the Excel function SLOPE to calculate beta for each company. (See Practice Question 7.13 for details.)
   a. Suppose the S&P 500 index falls unexpectedly by 5 percent. By how much would you expect GM or HDI to fall?
   b. Which is the riskier company for the well-diversified investor? How much riskier?
   c. Suppose the Treasury bill rate is 4 percent and the expected return on the S&P 500 is 11 percent. Use the CAPM to forecast the expected rate of return on each stock.

EXCEL

STANDARD &POOR'S

6. Download the "Monthly Adjusted Prices" spreadsheets for Boeing and Pfizer from the Standard & Poor's Market Insight website (**www.mhhe.com/edumarketinsight**).
   a. Calculate the annual standard deviation for each company, using the most recent three years of monthly returns. Use the Excel function STDEV. Multiply by the square root of 12 to convert to annual units.
   b. Use the Excel function CORREL to calculate the correlation coefficient between the stocks' monthly returns.
   c. Use the CAPM to estimate expected rates of return. Calculate betas, or use the most recent beta reported under "Monthly Valuation Data" on the Market Insight website. Use the current Treasury bill rate and a reasonable estimate of the market risk premium.
   d. Construct a graph like Figure 8.5. What combination of Boeing and Pfizer has the lowest portfolio risk? What is the expected return for this minimum-risk portfolio?

7. The Treasury bill rate is 4 percent, and the expected return on the market portfolio is 12 percent. On the basis of the capital asset pricing model:
   a. Draw a graph similar to Figure 8.7 showing how the expected return varies with beta.
   b. What is the risk premium on the market?
   c. What is the required return on an investment with a beta of 1.5?
   d. If an investment with a beta of .8 offers an expected return of 9.8 percent, does it have a positive NPV?
   e. If the market expects a return of 11.2 percent from stock X, what is its beta?

8. Most of the companies in Table 8.2 are covered in the Standard & Poor's Market Insight website (**www.mhhe.com/edumarketinsight**). For those that are covered, use the Excel SLOPE function to recalculate betas from the monthly returns on the "Monthly Adjusted Prices" spreadsheets. Use as many monthly returns as available, up to a maximum of 60 months. Recalculate expected rates of return from the CAPM formula, using a current risk-free rate and a market risk premium of 8 percent. How have the expected returns changed from the figures reported in Table 8.2?

9. Go to the Standard & Poor's Market Insight website (**www.mhhe.com/edumarket insight**), and find a low-risk income stock—Exxon Mobil or Kellogg might be good candidates. Estimate the company's beta to confirm that it is well below 1.0. Use monthly rates of return for the most recent three years. For the same period, estimate the annual standard deviation for the stock, the standard deviation for the S&P 500, and the correlation coefficient between returns on the stock and the S&P 500. (The Excel functions are given in Practice Questions above.) Forecast the expected rate of return for the stock, assuming the CAPM holds, with a market return of 12 percent and a risk-free rate of 5 percent.
   a. Plot a graph like Figure 8.5 showing the combinations of risk and return from a portfolio invested in your low-risk stock and in the market. Vary the fraction invested in the stock from zero to 100 percent.
   b. Suppose you can borrow or lend at 5 percent. Would you invest in some combination of your low-risk stock and the market? Or would you simply invest in the market? Explain.
   c. Suppose you forecast a return on the stock that is 5 percentage points higher than the CAPM return used in part (a). Redo parts (a) and (b) with this higher forecasted return.
   d. Find a high-beta stock and redo parts (a), (b), and (c).

10. Percival Hygiene has $10 million invested in long-term corporate bonds. This bond portfolio's expected annual rate of return is 9 percent, and the annual standard deviation is 10 percent.
    Amanda Reckonwith, Percival's financial adviser, recommends that Percival consider investing in an index fund which closely tracks the Standard and Poor's 500 in-

dex. The index has an expected return of 14 percent, and its standard deviation is 16 percent.

   a. Suppose Percival puts all his money in a combination of the index fund and Treasury bills. Can he thereby improve his expected rate of return without changing the risk of his portfolio? The Treasury bill yield is 6 percent.

   b. Could Percival do even better by investing equal amounts in the corporate bond portfolio and the index fund? The correlation between the bond portfolio and the index fund is +.1.

11. "There may be some truth in these CAPM and APT theories, but last year some stocks did much better than these theories predicted, and other stocks did much worse." Is this a valid criticism?

12. True or false?

   a. Stocks of small companies have done better than predicted by the CAPM.

   b. Stocks with high ratios of book value to market price have done better than predicted by the CAPM.

   c. On average, stock returns have been positively related to beta.

13. Some true or false questions about the APT:

   a. The APT factors cannot reflect diversifiable risks.

   b. The market rate of return cannot be an APT factor.

   c. Each APT factor must have a positive risk premium associated with it; otherwise the model is inconsistent.

   d. There is no theory that specifically identifies the APT factors.

   e. The APT model could be true but not very useful, for example, if the relevant factors change unpredictably.

14. Consider the following simplified APT model (compare Tables 8.3 and 8.4):

Factor	Expected Risk Premium
Market	6.4%
Interest rate	−.6
Yield spread	5.1

Calculate the expected return for the following stocks. Assume $r_f = 5$ percent.

	Factor Risk Exposures		
	Market	**Interest Rate**	**Yield Spread**
Stock	(b_1)	(b_2)	(b_3)
P	1.0	−2.0	−.2
P^2	1.2	0	.3
P^3	.3	.5	1.0

15. Look again at Practice Question 14. Consider a portfolio with equal investments in stocks P, P^2, and P^3.

   a. What are the factor risk exposures for the portfolio?

   b. What is the portfolio's expected return?

16. The following table shows the sensitivity of four stocks to the three Fama–French factors in the five years to 2001. Estimate the expected return on each stock assuming that the interest rate is 3.5 percent, the expected risk premium on the market is 8.8 percent, the expected risk premium on the size factor is 3.1 percent, and the expected risk premium on the book-to-market factor is 4.4 percent. (These were the realized premia from 1928–2000.)

Factor	Factor Sensitivities			
	Coca-Cola	Exxon Mobil	Pfizer	Reebok
Market	.82	.50	.66	1.17
Size*	−.29	.04	−.56	.73
Book-to-market†	.24	.27	−.07	1.14

*Return on small-firm stocks less return on large-firm stocks.
†Return on high book-to-market-ratio stocks less return on low book-to-market-ratio stocks.

CHALLENGE QUESTIONS

1. In footnote 4 we noted that the minimum-risk portfolio contained an investment of 21.4 percent in Reebok and 78.6 in Coca-Cola. Prove it. *Hint:* You need a little calculus to do so.

2. Look again at the set of efficient portfolios that we calculated in Section 8.1.
   a. If the interest rate is 10 percent, which of the four efficient portfolios should you hold?
   b. What is the beta of each holding relative to that portfolio? *Hint:* Remember that if a portfolio is efficient, the expected risk premium on each holding must be proportional to the beta of the stock *relative to that portfolio.*
   c. How would your answers to (a) and (b) change if the interest rate was 5 percent?

3. "Suppose you could forecast the behavior of APT factors, such as industrial production, interest rates, etc. You could then identify stocks' sensitivities to these factors, pick the right stocks, and make lots of money." Is this a good argument favoring the APT? Explain why or why not.

4. The following question illustrates the APT. Imagine that there are only two pervasive macroeconomic factors. Investments X, Y, and Z have the following sensitivities to these two factors:

Investment	b_1	b_2
X	1.75	.25
Y	−1.00	2.00
Z	2.00	1.00

We assume that the expected risk premium is 4 percent on factor 1 and 8 percent on factor 2. Treasury bills obviously offer zero risk premium.
   a. According to the APT, what is the risk premium on each of the three stocks?
   b. Suppose you buy $200 of X and $50 of Y and sell $150 of Z. What is the sensitivity of your portfolio to each of the two factors? What is the expected risk premium?
   c. Suppose you buy $80 of X and $60 of Y and sell $40 of Z. What is the sensitivity of your portfolio to each of the two factors? What is the expected risk premium?

d. Finally, suppose you buy $160 of X and $20 of Y and sell $80 of Z. What is your portfolio's sensitivity now to each of the two factors? And what is the expected risk premium?

e. Suggest two possible ways that you could construct a fund that has a sensitivity of .5 to factor 1 only. Now compare the risk premiums on each of these two investments.

f. Suppose that the APT did *not* hold and that X offered a risk premium of 8 percent, Y offered a premium of 14 percent, and Z offered a premium of 16 percent. Devise an investment that has zero sensitivity to each factor and that has a positive risk premium.

CHAPTER NINE

CAPITAL BUDGETING AND RISK

LONG BEFORE THE development of modern theories linking risk and expected return, smart financial managers adjusted for risk in capital budgeting. They realized intuitively that, other things being equal, risky projects are less desirable than safe ones. Therefore, financial managers demanded a higher rate of return from risky projects, or they based their decisions on conservative estimates of the cash flows.

Various rules of thumb are often used to make these risk adjustments. For example, many companies estimate the rate of return required by investors in their securities and then use this **company cost of capital** to discount the cash flows on new projects. Our first task in this chapter is to explain when the company cost of capital can, and cannot, be used to discount a project's cash flows. We shall see that it is the right hurdle rate for those projects that have the same risk as the firm's existing business; however, if a project is more risky than the firm as a whole, the cost of capital needs to be adjusted upward and the project's cash flows discounted at this higher rate. Conversely, a lower discount rate is needed for projects that are safer than the firm as a whole.

The capital asset pricing model is widely used to estimate the return that investors require.[1] It states

$$\text{Expected return} = r = r_f + (\text{beta})\,(r_m - r_f)$$

We used this formula in the last chapter to figure out the return that investors expected from a sample of common stocks but we did not explain how to estimate beta. It turns out that we can gain some insight into beta by looking at how the stock price has responded in the past to market fluctuations. Beta is difficult to measure accurately for an individual firm: Greater accuracy can be achieved by looking at an average of similar companies. We will also look at what features make some investments riskier than others. If you know *why* Exxon Mobil has less risk than, say, Dell Computer, you will be in a better position to judge the relative risks of different capital investment opportunities.

Some companies are financed entirely by common stock. In these cases the company cost of capital and the expected return on the stock are the same thing. However, most firms finance themselves partly by debt and the return that they earn on their investments must be sufficient to satisfy both the stockholders and the debtholders. We will show you how to calculate the company cost of capital when the firm has more than one type of security outstanding.

There is still another complication: Project betas can shift over time. Some projects are safer in youth than in old age; others are riskier. In this case, what do we mean by the project beta? There may be a separate beta for each year of the project's life. To put it another way, can we jump from the capital asset pricing model, which looks one period into the future, to the discounted-cash-flow formula for valuing long-lived assets? Most of the time it is safe to do so, but you should be able to recognize and deal with the exceptions.

We will use the capital asset pricing model, or CAPM, throughout this chapter. But don't infer that it is therefore the last word on risk and return. The principles and procedures covered in this chapter work just as well with other models such as arbitrage pricing theory (APT).

---

[1]In a survey of financial practice, Graham and Harvey found that 74 percent of firms always, or almost always, used the capital asset pricing model to estimate the cost of capital. See J. Graham and C. Harvey, "The Theory and Practice of Corporate Finance: Evidence from the Field," *Journal of Financial Economics* 60 (May/June 2001), pp. 187–244.

9.1 COMPANY AND PROJECT COSTS OF CAPITAL

The **company cost of capital** is defined as the expected return on a portfolio of all the company's existing securities. It is used to discount the cash flows on projects that have similar risk to that of the firm as a whole. For example, in Table 8.2 we estimated that investors require a return of 9.2 percent from Pfizer common stock. If Pfizer is contemplating an expansion of the firm's existing business, it would make sense to discount the forecasted cash flows at 9.2 percent.[2]

The company cost of capital is *not* the correct discount rate if the new projects are more or less risky than the firm's existing business. Each project should in principle be evaluated at its *own* opportunity cost of capital. This is a clear implication of the value-additivity principle introduced in Chapter 7. For a firm composed of assets A and B, the firm value is

$$\text{Firm value} = PV(AB) = PV(A) + PV(B)$$
$$= \text{sum of separate asset values}$$

Here PV(A) and PV(B) are valued just as if they were mini-firms in which stockholders could invest directly. Investors would value A by discounting its forecasted cash flows at a rate reflecting the risk of A. They would value B by discounting at a rate reflecting the risk of B. The two discount rates will, in general, be different. If the present value of an asset depended on the identity of the company that bought it, present values would *not* add up. Remember, a good project is a good project is a good project.

If the firm considers investing in a third project C, it should also value C as if C were a mini-firm. That is, the firm should discount the cash flows of C at the expected rate of return that investors would demand to make a separate investment in C. *The true cost of capital depends on the use to which that capital is put.*

This means that Pfizer should accept any project that more than compensates for the *project's* beta. In other words, Pfizer should accept any project lying above the upward-sloping line that links expected return to risk in Figure 9.1. If the project has a high risk, Pfizer needs a higher prospective return than if the project has a low risk. Now contrast this with the company cost of capital rule, which is to accept any project *regardless of its risk* as long as it offers a higher return than the *company's* cost of capital. In terms of Figure 9.1, the rule tells Pfizer to accept any project above the horizontal cost of capital line, that is, any project offering a return of more than 9.2 percent.

It is clearly silly to suggest that Pfizer should demand the same rate of return from a very safe project as from a very risky one. If Pfizer used the company cost of capital rule, it would reject many good low-risk projects and accept many poor high-risk projects. It is also silly to suggest that just because another company has a low company cost of capital, it is justified in accepting projects that Pfizer would reject.

The notion that each company has some individual discount rate or cost of capital is widespread, but far from universal. Many firms require different returns

---

[2]Debt accounted for only about 0.3 percent of the total market value of Pfizer's securities. Thus, its cost of capital is effectively identical to the rate of return investors expect on its common stock. The complications caused by debt are discussed later in this chapter.

FIGURE 9.1

A comparison between the company cost of capital rule and the required return under the capital asset pricing model. Pfizer's company cost of capital is about 9.2 percent. This is the correct discount rate only if the project beta is .71. In general, the correct discount rate increases as project beta increases. Pfizer should accept projects with rates of return above the security market line relating required return to beta.

from different categories of investment. For example, discount rates might be set as follows:

Category	Discount Rate
Speculative ventures	30%
New products	20
Expansion of existing business	15 (company cost of capital)
Cost improvement, known technology	10

Perfect Pitch and the Cost of Capital

The true cost of capital depends on project risk, not on the company undertaking the project. So why is so much time spent estimating the company cost of capital?

There are two reasons. First, many (maybe, most) projects can be treated as average risk, that is, no more or less risky than the average of the company's other assets. For these projects the company cost of capital is the right discount rate. Second, the company cost of capital is a useful starting point for setting discount rates for unusually risky or safe projects. It is easier to add to, or subtract from, the company cost of capital than to estimate each project's cost of capital from scratch.

There is a good musical analogy here.[3] Most of us, lacking perfect pitch, need a well-defined reference point, like middle C, before we can sing on key. But anyone who can carry a tune gets *relative* pitches right. Businesspeople have good intuition about *relative* risks, at least in industries they are used to, but not about absolute risk or required rates of return. Therefore, they set a companywide cost of capital as a benchmark. This is not the right hurdle rate for everything the company does, but adjustments can be made for more or less risky ventures.

---

[3]The analogy is borrowed from S. C. Myers and L. S. Borucki, "Discounted Cash Flow Estimates of the Cost of Equity Capital—A Case Study," *Financial Markets, Institutions, and Investments* 3 (August 1994), p. 18.

9.2 MEASURING THE COST OF EQUITY

Suppose that you are considering an across-the-board expansion by your firm. Such an investment would have about the same degree of risk as the existing business. Therefore you should discount the projected flows at the company cost of capital.

Companies generally start by estimating the return that investors require from the company's common stock. In Chapter 8 we used the capital asset pricing model to do this. This states

$$\text{Expected stock return} = r_f + \beta(r_m - r_f)$$

An obvious way to measure the beta (β) of a stock is to look at how its price has responded in the past to market movements. For example, look at the three left-hand scatter diagrams in Figure 9.2. In the top-left diagram we have calculated monthly returns from Dell Computer stock in the period after it went public in 1988, and we have plotted these returns against the market returns for the same month. The second diagram on the left shows a similar plot for the returns on General Motors stock, and the third shows a plot for Exxon Mobil. In each case we have fitted a line through the points. The slope of this line is an estimate of beta.[4] It tells us how much on average the stock price changed for each additional 1 percent change in the market index.

The right-hand diagrams show similar plots for the same three stocks during the subsequent period, February 1995 to July 2001. Although the slopes varied from the first period to the second, there is little doubt that Exxon Mobil's beta is much less than Dell's or that GM's beta falls somewhere between the two. If you had used the past beta of each stock to predict its future beta, you wouldn't have been too far off.

Only a small portion of each stock's total risk comes from movements in the market. The rest is unique risk, which shows up in the scatter of points around the fitted lines in Figure 9.2. *R-squared* (R^2) measures the proportion of the total variance in the stock's returns that can be explained by market movements. For example, from 1995 to 2001, the R^2 for GM was .25. In other words, a quarter of GM's risk was market risk and three-quarters was unique risk. The variance of the returns on GM stock was 964.[5] So we could say that the variance in stock returns that was due to the market was .25 × 964 = 241, and the variance of unique returns was .75 × 964 = 723.

The estimates of beta shown in Figure 9.2 are just that. They are based on the stocks' returns in 78 particular months. The noise in the returns can obscure the true beta. Therefore, statisticians calculate the *standard error* of the estimated beta to show the extent of possible mismeasurement. Then they set up a *confidence interval* of the estimated value plus or minus two standard errors. For example, the standard error of GM's estimated beta in the most recent period is .20. Thus the confidence interval for GM's beta is 1.00 plus or minus 2 × .20. If you state that the *true* beta for GM is between .60 and 1.40, you have a 95 percent chance of being right. Notice that we can be more confident of our estimate of Exxon Mobil's beta and less confident of Dell's.

Usually you will have more information (and thus more confidence) than this simple calculation suggests. For example, you know that Exxon Mobil's estimated

---

[4]Notice that you must regress the *returns* on the stock on the market *returns*. You would get a very similar estimate if you simply used the percentage *changes* in the stock price and the market index. But sometimes analysts make the mistake of regressing the stock price *level* on the *level* of the index and obtain nonsense results.

[5]This is an annual figure; we annualized the monthly variance by multiplying by 12 (see footnote 17 in Chapter 7). The standard deviation was $\sqrt{964} = 31.0$ percent.

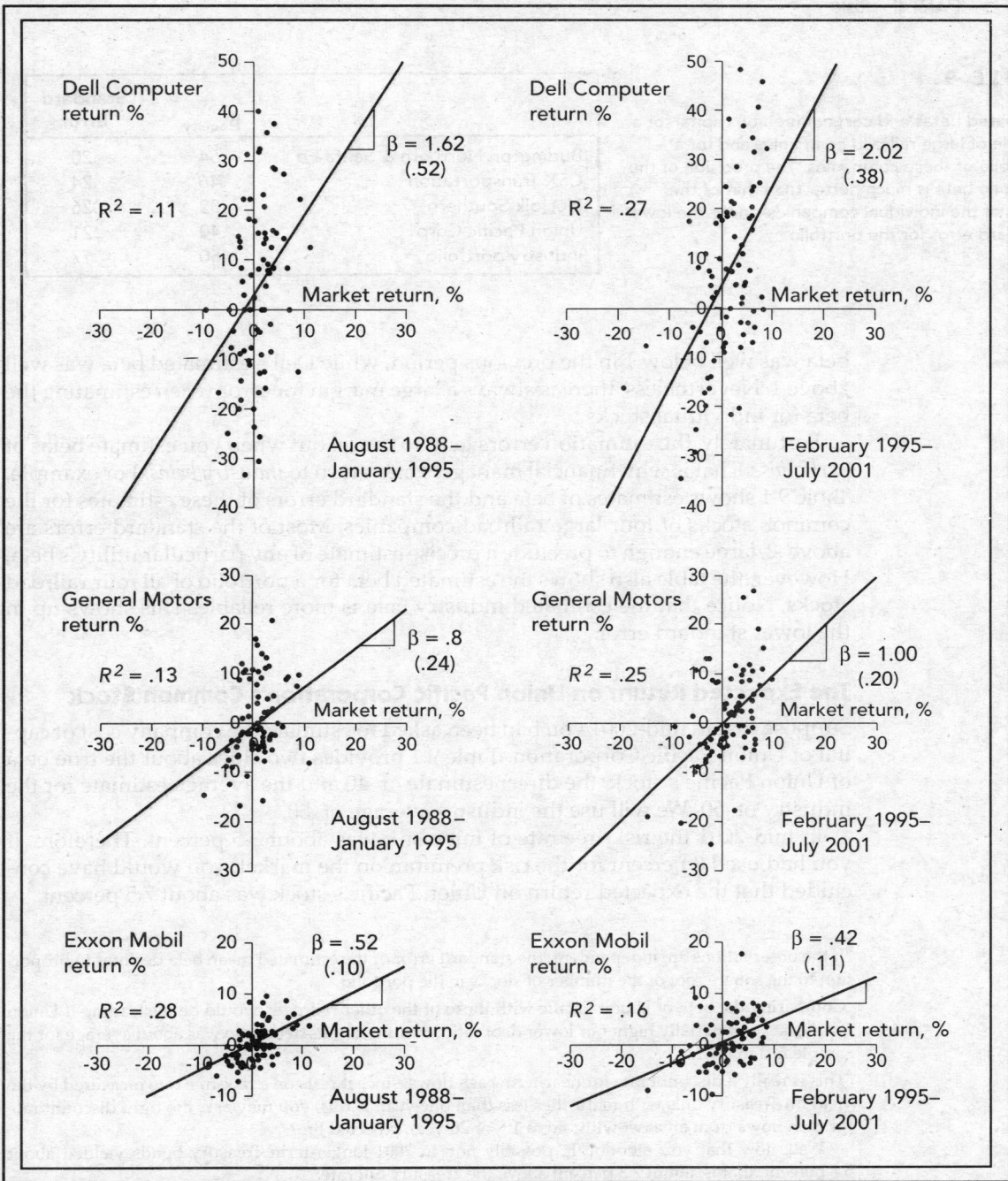

FIGURE 9.2

We have used past returns to estimate the betas of three stocks for the periods August 1988 to January 1995 (left-hand diagrams) and February 1995 to July 2001 (right-hand diagrams). Beta is the slope of the fitted line. Notice that in both periods Dell had the highest beta and Exxon Mobil the lowest. Standard errors are in parentheses below the betas. The standard error shows the range of possible error in the beta estimate. We also report the proportion of total risk that is due to market movements (R^2).

TABLE 9.1

Estimated betas and costs of (equity) capital for a sample of large railroad companies and for a portfolio of these companies. The precision of the portfolio beta is much better than that of the betas of the individual companies—note the lower standard error for the portfolio.

	β_{equity}	Standard Error
Burlington Northern & Santa Fe	.64	.20
CSX Transportation	.46	.24
Norfolk Southern	.52	.26
Union Pacific Corp.	.40	.21
Industry portfolio	.50	.17

beta was well below 1 in the previous period, while Dell's estimated beta was well above 1. Nevertheless, there is always a large margin for error when estimating the beta for individual stocks.

Fortunately, the estimation errors tend to cancel out when you estimate betas of *portfolios*.[6] That is why financial managers often turn to *industry betas.* For example, Table 9.1 shows estimates of beta and the standard errors of these estimates for the common stocks of four large railroad companies. Most of the standard errors are above .2, large enough to preclude a precise estimate of any particular utility's beta. However, the table also shows the estimated beta for a portfolio of all four railroad stocks. Notice that the estimated industry beta is more reliable. This shows up in the lower standard error.

The Expected Return on Union Pacific Corporation's Common Stock

Suppose that in mid-2001 you had been asked to estimate the company cost of capital of Union Pacific Corporation. Table 9.1 provides two clues about the true beta of Union Pacific's stock: the direct estimate of .40 and the average estimate for the industry of .50. We will use the industry average of .50.[7]

In mid-2001 the risk-free rate of interest r_f was about 3.5 percent. Therefore, if you had used 8 percent for the risk premium on the market, you would have concluded that the expected return on Union Pacific's stock was about 7.5 percent:[8]

---

[6]If the observations are independent, the standard error of the estimated mean beta declines in proportion to the square root of the number of stocks in the portfolio.

[7]Comparing the beta of Union Pacific with those of the other railroads would be misleading if Union Pacific had a materially higher or lower debt ratio. Fortunately, its debt ratio was about average for the sample in Table 9.1.

[8]This is really a discount rate for near-term cash flows, since it rests on a risk-free rate measured by the yield on Treasury bills with maturities less than one year. Is this, you may ask, the right discount rate for cash flows from an asset with, say, a 10- or 20-year expected life?

Well, now that you mention it, possibly not. In 2001 longer-term Treasury bonds yielded about 5.8 percent, that is, about 2.3 percent above the Treasury bill rate.

The risk-free rate could be defined as a long-term Treasury bond yield. If you do this, however, you should subtract the risk premium of Treasury bonds over bills, which we gave as 1.8 percent in Table 7.1. This gives a rough-and-ready estimate of the expected yield on short-term Treasury bills over the life of the bond:

$$\text{Expected average T-bill rate} = \text{T-bond yield} - \text{premium of bonds over bills}$$
$$= .058 - .019 = .039, \text{ or } 3.9\%$$

The expected average future Treasury bill rate should be used in the CAPM if a discount rate is needed for an extended stream of cash flows. In 2001 this "long-term r_f" was a bit higher than the Treasury bill rate.

$$\text{Expected stock return} = r_f + \beta(r_m - r_f)$$
$$= 3.5 + .5(8.0) = 7.5\%$$

We have focused on using the capital asset pricing model to estimate the expected returns on Union Pacific's common stock. But it would be useful to get a check on this figure. For example, in Chapter 4 we used the constant-growth DCF formula to estimate the expected rate of return for a sample of utility stocks.[9] You could also use DCF models with varying future growth rates, or perhaps arbitrage pricing theory (APT). We showed in Section 8.4 how APT can be used to estimate expected returns.

 ## 9.3 CAPITAL STRUCTURE AND THE COMPANY COST OF CAPITAL

In the last section, we used the capital asset pricing model to estimate the return that investors require from Union Pacific's common stock. Is this figure Union Pacific's company cost of capital? Not if Union Pacific has other securities outstanding. The company cost of capital also needs to reflect the returns demanded by the owners of these securities.

We will return shortly to the problem of Union Pacific's cost of capital, but first we need to look at the relationship between the cost of capital and the mix of debt and equity used to finance the company. Think again of what the *company* cost of capital is and what it is used for. We *define* it as the opportunity cost of capital for the firm's existing assets; we *use* it to value new assets that have the same risk as the old ones.

If you owned a portfolio of all the firm's securities—100 percent of the debt and 100 percent of the equity—you would own the firm's assets lock, stock, and barrel. You wouldn't share the cash flows with anyone; every dollar of cash the firm paid out would be paid to you. You can think of the company cost of capital as the expected return on this hypothetical portfolio. To calculate it, you just take a weighted average of the expected returns on the debt and the equity:

$$\text{Company cost of capital} = r_{\text{assets}} = r_{\text{portfolio}}$$
$$= \frac{\text{debt}}{\text{debt} + \text{equity}} r_{\text{debt}} + \frac{\text{equity}}{\text{debt} + \text{equity}} r_{\text{equity}}$$

For example, suppose that the firm's market-value balance sheet is as follows:

Asset value	100	Debt value (D)	30
		Equity value (E)	70
Asset value	100	Firm value (V)	100

Note that the values of debt and equity add up to the firm value ($D + E = V$) and that the firm value equals the asset value. (These figures are *market* values, not *book* values: The market value of the firm's equity is often substantially different from its book value.)

[9]The United States Surface Transportation Board uses the constant-growth model to estimate the cost of equity capital for railroad companies. We will review its findings in Chapter 19.

If investors expect a return of 7.5 percent on the debt and 15 percent on the equity, then the expected return on the assets is

$$r_{assets} = \frac{D}{V} r_{debt} + \frac{E}{V} r_{equity}$$

$$= \left(\frac{30}{100} \times 7.5 \right) + \left(\frac{70}{100} \times 15 \right) = 12.75\%$$

If the firm is contemplating investment in a project that has the same risk as the firm's existing business, the opportunity cost of capital for this project is the same as the firm's cost of capital; in other words, it is 12.75 percent.

What would happen if the firm issued an additional 10 of debt and used the cash to repurchase 10 of its equity? The revised market-value balance sheet is

Asset value	100	Debt value (D)	40
		Equity value (E)	60
Asset value	100	Firm value (V)	100

The change in financial structure does not affect the amount or risk of the cash flows on the total package of debt and equity. Therefore, if investors required a return of 12.75 percent on the total package before the refinancing, they must require a 12.75 percent return on the firm's assets afterward.

Although the required return on the *package* of debt and equity is unaffected, the change in financial structure does affect the required return on the individual securities. Since the company has more debt than before, the debtholders are likely to demand a higher interest rate. We will suppose that the expected return on the debt rises to 7.875 percent. Now you can write down the basic equation for the return on assets

$$r_{assets} = \frac{D}{V} r_{debt} + \frac{E}{V} r_{equity}$$

$$= \left(\frac{40}{100} \times 7.875 \right) + \left(\frac{60}{100} \times r_{equity} \right) = 12.75\%$$

and solve for the return on equity

$$r_{equity} = 16.0\%$$

Increasing the amount of debt increased debtholder risk and led to a rise in the return that debtholders required (r_{debt} rose from 7.5 to 7.875 percent). The higher leverage also made the equity riskier and increased the return that shareholders required (r_{equity} rose from 15 to 16 percent). The weighted average return on debt and equity remained at 12.75 percent:

$$r_{assets} = (.4 \times r_{debt}) + (.6 \times r_{equity})$$

$$= (.4 \times 7.875) + (.6 \times 16) = 12.75\%$$

Suppose that the company decided instead to repay all its debt and to replace it with equity. In that case all the cash flows would go to the equity holders. The company cost of capital, r_{assets}, would stay at 12.75 percent, and r_{equity} would also be 12.75 percent.

How Changing Capital Structure Affects Beta

We have looked at how changes in financial structure affect expected return. Let us now look at the effect on beta.

The stockholders and debtholders both receive a share of the firm's cash flows, and both bear part of the risk. For example, if the firm's assets turn out to be worthless, there will be no cash to pay stockholders or debtholders. But debtholders usually bear much less risk than stockholders. Debt betas of large blue-chip firms are typically in the range of .1 to .3.[10]

If you owned a portfolio of all the firm's securities, you wouldn't share the cash flows with anyone. You wouldn't share the risks with anyone either; you would bear them all. Thus the firm's asset beta is equal to the beta of a portfolio of all the firm's debt and its equity.

The beta of this hypothetical portfolio is just a weighted average of the debt and equity betas:

$$\beta_{assets} = \beta_{portfolio} = \frac{D}{V}\,\beta_{debt} + \frac{E}{V}\,\beta_{equity}$$

Think back to our example. If the debt before the refinancing has a beta of .1 and the equity has a beta of 1.1, then

$$\beta_{assets} = (.3 \times .1) + (.7 \times 1.1) = .8$$

What happens after the refinancing? The risk of the total package is unaffected, but both the debt and the equity are now more risky. Suppose that the debt beta increases to .2. We can work out the new equity beta:

$$\beta_{assets} = \beta_{portfolio} = \frac{D}{V}\,\beta_{dept} + \frac{E}{V}\,\beta_{equity}$$

$$.8 = (.4 \times .2) + (.6 \times \beta_{equity})$$

$$\beta_{equity} = 1.2$$

You can see why borrowing is said to create *financial leverage* or *gearing*. Financial leverage does not affect the risk or the expected return on the firm's assets, but it does push up the risk of the common stock. Shareholders demand a correspondingly higher return because of this *financial risk*.

Figure 9.3 shows the expected return and beta of the firm's assets. It also shows how expected return and risk are shared between the debtholders and equity holders before the refinancing. Figure 9.4 shows what happens after the refinancing. Both debt and equity are now more risky, and therefore investors demand a higher return. But equity accounts for a smaller proportion of firm value than before. As a result, the weighted average of both the expected return and beta on the two components is unchanged.

Now you can see how to *unlever* betas, that is, how to go from an observed β_{equity} to β_{assets}. You have the equity beta, say, 1.2. You also need the debt beta, say, .2, and the relative market values of debt (D/V) and equity (E/V). If debt accounts for 40 percent of overall value V,

$$\beta_{assets} = (.4 \times .2) + (.6 \times 1.2) = .8$$

---

[10]For example, in Table 7.1 we reported average returns on a portfolio of high-grade corporate bonds. In the 10 years ending December 2000 the estimated beta of this bond portfolio was .17.

FIGURE 9.3

Expected returns and betas before refinancing. The expected return and beta of the firm's assets are weighted averages of the expected return and betas of the debt and equity.

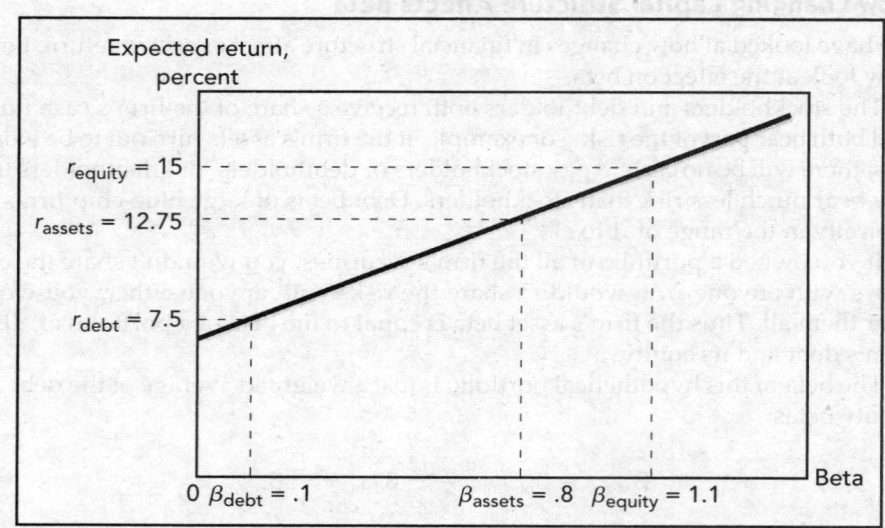

FIGURE 9.4

Expected returns and betas after refinancing.

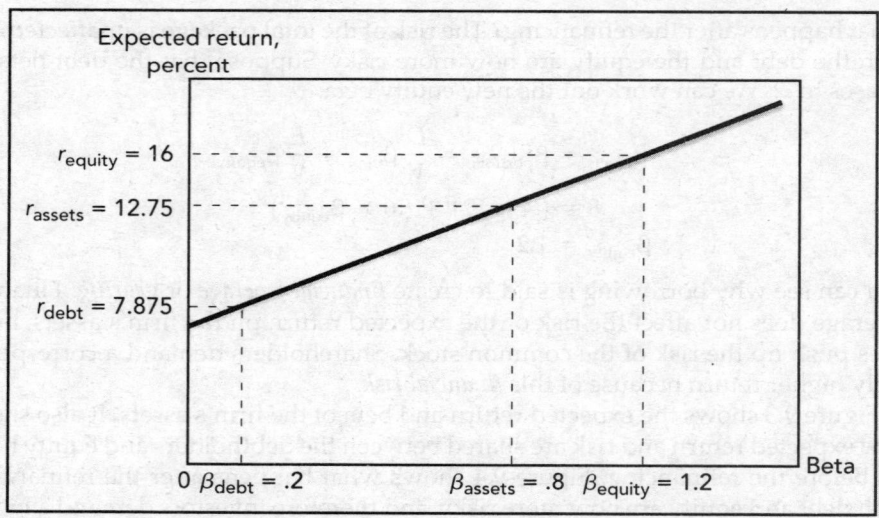

This runs the previous example in reverse. Just remember the basic relationship:

$$\beta_{assets} = \beta_{portfolio} = \frac{D}{V}\beta_{debt} + \frac{E}{V}\beta_{equity}$$

Capital Structure and Discount Rates

The company cost of capital is the opportunity cost of capital for the firm's assets. That's why we write it as r_{assets}. If a firm encounters a project that has the same beta as the firm's overall assets, then r_{assets} is the right discount rate for the project cash flows.

When the firm uses debt financing, the company cost of capital is not the same as r_{equity}, the expected rate of return on the firm's stock; r_{equity} is higher because of financial risk. However, the company cost of capital can be calculated as a weighted average of the returns expected by investors on the various debt and equity securities issued by the firm. You can also calculate the firm's asset beta as a weighted average of the betas of these securities.

When the firm changes its mix of debt and equity securities, the risk and expected returns of these securities change; however, the asset beta and the company cost of capital do not change.

Now, if you think all this is too neat and simple, you're right. The complications are spelled out in great detail in Chapters 17 through 19. But we must note one complication here: Interest paid on a firm's borrowing can be deducted from taxable income. Thus the after-tax cost of debt is $r_{debt}(1 - T_c)$, where T_c is the marginal corporate tax rate. When companies discount an average-risk project, they do not use the company cost of capital as we have computed it. They use the after-tax cost of debt to compute the after-tax weighted-average cost of capital or WACC:

$$\text{WACC} = r_{debt}(1 - T_c)\frac{D}{V} + r_{equity}\frac{E}{V}$$

More—lots more—on this in Chapter 19.

Back to Union Pacific's Cost of Capital

In the last section we estimated the return that investors required on Union Pacific's common stock. If Union Pacific were wholly equity-financed, the company cost of capital would be the same as the expected return on its stock. But in mid-2001 common stock accounted for only 60 percent of the market value of the company's securities. Debt accounted for the remaining 40 percent.[11] Union Pacific's company cost of capital is a weighted average of the expected returns on the different securities.

We estimated the expected return from Union Pacific's common stock at 7.5 percent. The yield on the company's debt in 2001 was about 5.5 percent.[12] Thus

$$\text{Company cost of capital} = r_{assets} = \frac{D}{V} r_{debt} + \frac{E}{V} r_{equity}$$

$$= \left(\frac{40}{100} \times 5.5\right) + \left(\frac{60}{100} \times 7.5\right) = 6.7\%$$

Union Pacific's WACC is calculated in the same fashion, but using the after-tax cost of debt.

[11]Union Pacific had also issued preferred stock. Preferred stock is discussed in Chapter 14. To keep matters simple here, we have lumped the preferred stock in with Union Pacific's debt.

[12]This is a *promised* yield; that is, it is the yield if Union Pacific makes all the promised payments. Since there is some risk of default, the *expected* return is always less than the promised yield. Union Pacific debt has an investment-grade rating and the difference is small. But for a company that is hovering on the brink of bankruptcy, it can be important.

9.4 DISCOUNT RATES FOR INTERNATIONAL PROJECTS

We have shown how the CAPM can help to estimate the cost of capital for domestic investments by U.S. companies. But can we extend the procedure to allow for investments in different countries? The answer is yes in principle, but naturally there are complications.

Foreign Investments Are Not Always Riskier

Pop quiz: Which is riskier for an investor in the United States—the Standard and Poor's Composite Index or the stock market in Egypt? If you answer Egypt, you're right, but *only* if risk is defined as *total* volatility or variance. But does investment in Egypt have a high *beta?* How much does it add to the risk of a diversified portfolio held in the United States?

Table 9.2 shows estimated betas for the Egyptian market and for markets in Poland, Thailand, and Venezuela. The standard deviations of returns in these markets were two or three times more than the U.S. market, but only Thailand had a beta greater than 1. The reason is low correlation. For example, the standard deviation of the Egyptian market was 3.1 times that of the Standard and Poor's index, but the correlation coefficient was only .18. The beta was $3.1 \times .18 = .55$.

Table 9.2 does not prove that investment abroad is always safer than at home. But it should remind you always to distinguish between diversifiable and market risk. The opportunity cost of capital should depend on market risk.

Foreign Investment in the United States

Now let's turn the problem around. Suppose that the Swiss pharmaceutical company, Roche, is considering an investment in a new plant near Basel in Switzerland. The financial manager forecasts the Swiss franc cash flows from the project and discounts these cash flows at a discount rate measured in francs. Since the project is risky, the company requires a higher return than the Swiss franc interest rate. However, the project is average-risk compared to Roche's other Swiss assets. To estimate the cost of capital, the Swiss manager proceeds in the same way as her counterpart in a U.S. pharmaceutical company. In other words, she first measures the risk of the investment by estimating Roche's beta and the beta of other Swiss pharmaceutical companies. However, she calculates these betas *relative to the Swiss market index.* Suppose that both measures point to a beta of 1.1 and that the expected

TABLE 9.2

Betas of four country indexes versus the U.S. market, calculated from monthly returns, August 1996–July 2001. Despite high volatility, three of the four betas are less than 1. The reason is the relatively low correlation with the U.S. market.

	Ratio of Standard Deviations*	Correlation Coefficient	Beta[†]
Egypt	3.11	.18	.56
Poland	1.93	.42	.81
Thailand	2.91	.48	1.40
Venezuela	2.58	.30	.77

*Ratio of standard deviations of country index to Standard & Poor's Composite Index.

[†]Beta is the ratio of covariance to variance. Covariance can be written as $\sigma_{IM} = \rho_{IM}\,\sigma_I\,\sigma_M$; $\beta = \rho_{IM}\,\sigma_I\,\sigma_M/\sigma_M^2 = \rho\,(\sigma_I/\sigma_M)$, where I indicates the country index and M indicates the U.S. market.

risk premium on the Swiss market index is 6 percent.[13] Then Roche needs to discount the Swiss franc cash flows from its project at $1.1 \times 6 = 6.6$ percent above the Swiss franc interest rate.

That's straightforward. But now suppose that Roche considers construction of a plant in the United States. Once again the financial manager measures the risk of this investment by its beta relative to the Swiss market index. But notice that the value of Roche's business in the United States is likely to be much less closely tied to fluctuations in the Swiss market. So the beta of the U.S. project relative to the *Swiss* market is likely to be less than 1.1. How much less? One useful guide is the U.S. pharmaceutical industry beta calculated *relative to the Swiss market index*. It turns out that this beta has been .36.[14] If the expected risk premium on the Swiss market index is 6 percent, Roche should be discounting the Swiss franc cash flows from its U.S. project at $.36 \times 6 = 2.2$ percent above the Swiss franc interest rate.

Why does Roche's manager measure the beta of its investments relative to the Swiss index, whereas her U.S. counterpart measures the beta relative to the U.S. index? The answer lies in Section 7.4, where we explained that risk cannot be considered in isolation; it depends on the other securities in the investor's portfolio. Beta measures risk *relative to the investor's portfolio*. If U.S. investors already hold the U.S. market, an additional dollar invested at home is just more of the same. But, if Swiss investors hold the *Swiss* market, an investment in the United States can reduce their risk. That explains why an investment in the United States is likely to have lower risk for Roche's shareholders than it has for shareholders in Merck or Pfizer. It also explains why Roche's shareholders are willing to accept a lower return from such an investment than would the shareholders in the U.S. companies.[15]

When Merck measures risk relative to the U.S. market and Roche measures risk relative to the Swiss market, their managers are implicitly assuming that the shareholders simply hold domestic stocks. That's not a bad approximation, particularly in the case of the United States.[16] Although investors in the United States can reduce their risk by holding an internationally diversified portfolio of shares, they generally invest only a small proportion of their money overseas. Why they are so shy is a puzzle.[17] It looks as if they are worried about the costs of investing overseas, but we don't understand what those costs include. Maybe it is more difficult to figure out which foreign shares to buy. Or perhaps investors are worried that a

---

[13]Figure 7.3 showed that this is the historical risk premium on the Swiss market. The fact that the realized premium has been lower in Switzerland than the United States may be just a coincidence and may not mean that Swiss investors *expected* the lower premium. On the other hand, if Swiss firms are generally less risky, then investors may have been content with a lower premium.

[14]This is the beta of the Standard and Poor's pharmaceutical index calculated relative to the Swiss market for the period August 1996 to July 2001.

[15]When investors hold efficient portfolios, the expected reward for risk on each stock in the portfolio is proportional to its beta *relative to the portfolio*. So, if the Swiss market index is an efficient portfolio for Swiss investors, then Swiss investors will want Roche to invest in a new plant if the expected reward for risk is proportional to its beta relative to the Swiss market index.

[16]But it can be a bad assumption elsewhere. For small countries with open financial borders—Luxembourg, for example—a beta calculated relative to the local market has little value. Few investors in Luxembourg hold only local stocks.

[17]For an explanation of the cost of capital for international investments when there are costs to international diversification, see I. A. Cooper and E. Kaplanis, "Home Bias in Equity Portfolios and the Cost of Capital for Multinational Firms," *Journal of Applied Corporate Finance* 8 (Fall 1995), pp. 95–102.

foreign government will expropriate their shares, restrict dividend payments, or catch them by a change in the tax law.

However, the world is getting smaller, and investors everywhere are increasing their holdings of foreign securities. Large American financial institutions have substantially increased their overseas investments, and literally dozens of funds have been set up for individuals who want to invest abroad. For example, you can now buy funds that specialize in investment in emerging capital markets such as Vietnam, Peru, or Hungary. As investors increase their holdings of overseas stocks, it becomes less appropriate to measure risk relative to the domestic market and more important to measure the risk of any investment relative to the portfolios that they actually hold.

Who knows? Perhaps in a few years investors will hold internationally diversified portfolios, and in later editions of this book we will recommend that firms calculate betas relative to the world market. If investors throughout the world held the world portfolio, then Roche and Merck would both demand the same return from an investment in the United States, in Switzerland, or in Egypt.

Do Some Countries Have a Lower Cost of Capital?

Some countries enjoy much lower rates of interest than others. For example, as we write this the interest rate in Japan is effectively zero; in the United States it is above 3 percent. People often conclude from this that Japanese companies enjoy a lower cost of capital.

This view is one part confusion and one part probable truth. The confusion arises because the interest rate in Japan is measured in yen and the rate in the United States is measured in dollars. You wouldn't say that a 10-inch-high rabbit was taller than a 9-foot elephant. You would be comparing their height in different units. In the same way it makes no sense to compare an interest rate in yen with a rate in dollars. The units are different.

But suppose that in each case you measure the interest rate in *real* terms. Then you are comparing like with like, and it does make sense to ask whether the costs of overseas investment can cause the *real* cost of capital to be lower in Japan. Japanese citizens have for a long time been big savers, but as they moved into a new century they were very worried about the future and were saving more than ever. That money could not be absorbed by Japanese industry and therefore had to be invested overseas. Japanese investors were not *compelled* to invest overseas: They needed to be enticed to do so. So the expected real returns on Japanese investments fell to the point that Japanese investors were willing to incur the costs of buying foreign securities, and when a Japanese company wanted to finance a new project, it could tap into a pool of relatively low-cost funds.

 ## 9.5 SETTING DISCOUNT RATES WHEN YOU CAN'T CALCULATE BETA

Stock or industry betas provide a rough guide to the risk encountered in various lines of business. But an asset beta for, say, the steel industry can take us only so far. Not all investments made in the steel industry are typical. What other kinds of evidence about business risk might a financial manager examine?

In some cases the asset is publicly traded. If so, we can simply estimate its beta from past price data. For example, suppose a firm wants to analyze the risks of holding a large inventory of copper. Because copper is a standardized, widely traded commodity, it is possible to calculate rates of return from holding copper and to calculate a beta for copper.

What should a manager do if the asset has no such convenient price record? What if the proposed investment is not close enough to business as usual to justify using a company cost of capital?

These cases clearly call for judgment. For managers making that kind of judgment, we offer two pieces of advice.

1. *Avoid fudge factors.* Don't give in to the temptation to add fudge factors to the discount rate to offset things that could go wrong with the proposed investment. Adjust cash-flow forecasts first.
2. *Think about the determinants of asset betas.* Often the characteristics of high- and low-beta assets can be observed when the beta itself cannot be.

Let us expand on these two points.

Avoid Fudge Factors in Discount Rates

We have defined risk, from the investor's viewpoint, as the standard deviation of portfolio return or the beta of a common stock or other security. But in everyday usage *risk* simply equals "bad outcome." People think of the risks of a project as a list of things that can go wrong. For example,

- A geologist looking for oil worries about the risk of a dry hole.
- A pharmaceutical manufacturer worries about the risk that a new drug which cures baldness may not be approved by the Food and Drug Administration.
- The owner of a hotel in a politically unstable part of the world worries about the political risk of expropriation.

Managers often add fudge factors to discount rates to offset worries such as these.

This sort of adjustment makes us nervous. First, the bad outcomes we cited appear to reflect unique (i.e., diversifiable) risks that would not affect the expected rate of return demanded by investors. Second, the need for a discount rate adjustment usually arises because managers fail to give bad outcomes their due weight in cash-flow forecasts. The managers then try to offset that mistake by adding a fudge factor to the discount rate.

Example   Project Z will produce just one cash flow, forecasted at $1 million at year 1. It is regarded as average risk, suitable for discounting at a 10 percent company cost of capital:

$$PV = \frac{C_1}{1 + r} = \frac{1,000,000}{1.1} = \$909,100$$

But now you discover that the company's engineers are behind schedule in developing the technology required for the project. They're confident it will work, but they admit to a small chance that it won't. You still see the *most likely* outcome as $1 million, but you also see some chance that project Z will generate *zero* cash flow next year.

Now the project's prospects are clouded by your new worry about technology. It must be worth less than the $909,100 you calculated before that worry arose. But how much less? There is *some* discount rate (10 percent plus a fudge factor) that will give the right value, but we don't know what that adjusted discount rate is.

We suggest you reconsider your original $1 million forecast for project Z's cash flow. Project cash flows are supposed to be *unbiased* forecasts, which give due weight to all possible outcomes, favorable and unfavorable. Managers making unbiased forecasts are correct on average. Sometimes their forecasts will turn out high, other times low, but their errors will average out over many projects.

If you forecast cash flow of $1 million for projects like Z, you will overestimate the average cash flow, because every now and then you will hit a zero. Those zeros should be "averaged in" to your forecasts.

For many projects, the most likely cash flow is also the unbiased forecast. If there are three possible outcomes with the probabilities shown below, the unbiased forecast is $1 million. (The unbiased forecast is the sum of the probability-weighted cash flows.)

Possible Cash Flow	Probability	Probability-Weighted Cash Flow	Unbiased Forecast
1.2	.25	.3	
1.0	.50	.5	1.0, or $1 million
.8	.25	.2	

This might describe the initial prospects of project Z. But if technological uncertainty introduces a 10 percent chance of a zero cash flow, the unbiased forecast could drop to $900,000:

Possible Cash Flow	Probability	Probability-Weighted Cash Flow	Unbiased Forecast
1.2	.225	.27	
1.0	.45	.45	.90, or $900,000
.8	.225	.18	
0	.10	.0	

The present value is

$$PV = \frac{.90}{1.1} = .818, \text{ or } \$818,000$$

Now, of course, you can figure out the right fudge factor to add to the discount rate to apply to the original $1 million forecast to get the correct answer. But you have to think through possible cash flows to get that fudge factor; and once you have thought through the cash flows, you don't *need* the fudge factor.

Managers often work out a range of possible outcomes for major projects, sometimes with explicit probabilities attached. We give more elaborate examples and further discussion in Chapter 10. But even when a range of outcomes and probabilities is not explicitly written down, the manager can still consider the good and bad outcomes as well as the most likely one. When the bad outcomes outweigh the good, the cash-flow forecast should be reduced until balance is regained.

Step 1, then, is to do your best to make unbiased forecasts of a project's cash flows. Step 2 is to consider whether *investors* would regard the project as more or less risky than typical for a company or division. Here our advice is to search for characteristics of the asset that are associated with high or low betas. We wish we had a more fundamental scientific understanding of what these characteristics are. We see business risks surfacing in capital markets, but as yet there is no satisfactory theory describing how these risks are generated. Nevertheless, some things are known.

What Determines Asset Betas?

Cyclicality   Many people intuitively associate risk with the variability of book, or accounting, earnings. But much of this variability reflects unique or diversifiable risk. Lone prospectors in search of gold look forward to extremely uncertain future earnings, but whether they strike it rich is not likely to depend on the performance of the market portfolio. Even if they do find gold, they do not bear much market risk. Therefore, an investment in gold has a high standard deviation but a relatively low beta.

What really counts is the strength of the relationship between the firm's earnings and the aggregate earnings on all real assets. We can measure this either by the *accounting beta* or by the *cash-flow beta*. These are just like a real beta except that changes in book earnings or cash flow are used in place of rates of return on securities. We would predict that firms with high accounting or cash-flow betas should also have high stock betas—and the prediction is correct.[18]

This means that cyclical firms—firms whose revenues and earnings are strongly dependent on the state of the business cycle—tend to be high-beta firms. Thus you should demand a higher rate of return from investments whose performance is strongly tied to the performance of the economy.

Operating Leverage   We have already seen that financial leverage (i.e., the commitment to fixed-debt charges) increases the beta of an investor's portfolio. In just the same way, *operating leverage* (i.e., the commitment to fixed *production* charges) must add to the beta of a capital project. Let's see how this works.

The cash flows generated by any productive asset can be broken down into revenue, fixed costs, and variable costs:

$$\text{Cash flow} = \text{revenue} - \text{fixed cost} - \text{variable cost}$$

Costs are variable if they depend on the rate of output. Examples are raw materials, sales commissions, and some labor and maintenance costs. Fixed costs are cash outflows that occur regardless of whether the asset is active or idle (e.g., property taxes or the wages of workers under contract).

We can break down the asset's present value in the same way:

$$PV(\text{asset}) = PV(\text{revenue}) - PV(\text{fixed cost}) - PV(\text{variable cost})$$

Or equivalently

$$PV(\text{revenue}) = PV(\text{fixed cost}) + PV(\text{variable cost}) + PV(\text{asset})$$

---

[18]For example, see W. H. Beaver and J. Manegold, "The Association between Market-Determined and Accounting-Determined Measures of Systematic Risk: Some Further Evidence," *Journal of Financial and Quantitative Analysis* 10 (June 1979), pp. 231–284.

Those who *receive* the fixed costs are like debtholders in the project; they simply get a fixed payment. Those who receive the net cash flows from the asset are like holders of common stock; they get whatever is left after payment of the fixed costs.

We can now figure out how the asset's beta is related to the betas of the values of revenue and costs. We just use our previous formula with the betas relabeled:

$$\beta_{\text{revenue}} = \beta_{\text{fixed cost}} \frac{PV(\text{fixed cost})}{PV(\text{revenue})}$$

$$+ \beta_{\text{variable cost}} \frac{PV(\text{variable cost})}{PV(\text{revenue})} + \beta_{\text{asset}} \frac{PV(\text{asset})}{PV(\text{revenue})}$$

In other words, the beta of the value of the revenues is simply a weighted average of the beta of its component parts. Now the fixed-cost beta is zero by definition: Whoever receives the fixed costs holds a safe asset. The betas of the revenues and variable costs should be approximately the same, because they respond to the same underlying variable, the rate of output. Therefore, we can substitute $\beta_{\text{variable cost}}$ and solve for the asset beta. Remember that $\beta_{\text{fixed cost}} = 0$.

$$\beta_{\text{assets}} = \beta_{\text{revenue}} \frac{PV(\text{revenue}) - PV(\text{variable cost})}{PV(\text{asset})}$$

$$= \beta_{\text{revenue}} \left[1 + \frac{PV(\text{fixed cost})}{PV(\text{asset})} \right]$$

Thus, given the cyclicality of revenues (reflected in β_{revenue}), the asset beta is proportional to the ratio of the present value of fixed costs to the present value of the project.

Now you have a rule of thumb for judging the relative risks of alternative designs or technologies for producing the same project. Other things being equal, the alternative with the higher ratio of fixed costs to project value will have the higher project beta. Empirical tests confirm that companies with high operating leverage actually do have high betas.[19]

Searching for Clues

Recent research suggests a variety of other factors that affect an asset's beta.[20] But going through a long list of these possible determinants would take us too far afield.

You cannot hope to estimate the relative risk of assets with any precision, but good managers examine any project from a variety of angles and look for clues as to its riskiness. They know that high market risk is a characteristic of cyclical ventures and of projects with high fixed costs. They think about the major uncertainties affecting the economy and consider how projects are affected by these uncertainties.[21]

---

[19]See B. Lev, "On the Association between Operating Leverage and Risk," *Journal of Financial and Quantitative Analysis* 9 (September 1974), pp. 627–642; and G. N. Mandelker and S. G. Rhee, "The Impact of the Degrees of Operating and Financial Leverage on Systematic Risk of Common Stock," *Journal of Financial and Quantitative Analysis* 19 (March 1984), pp. 45–57.

[20]This work is reviewed in G. Foster, *Financial Statement Analysis*, 2d ed., Prentice-Hall, Inc., Englewood Cliffs, N.J., 1986, chap. 10.

[21]Sharpe's article on a "multibeta" interpretation of market risk offers a useful way of thinking about these uncertainties and tracing their impact on a firm's or project's risk. See W. F. Sharpe, "The Capital Asset Pricing Model: A 'Multi-Beta' Interpretation," in H. Levy and M. Sarnat (eds.), *Financial Decision Making under Uncertainty*, Academic Press, New York, 1977.

9.6 ANOTHER LOOK AT RISK AND DISCOUNTED CASH FLOW

In practical capital budgeting, a single discount rate is usually applied to all future cash flows. For example, the financial manager might use the capital asset pricing model to estimate the cost of capital and then use this figure to discount each year's expected cash flow.

Among other things, the use of a constant discount rate assumes that project risk does not change.[22] We know that this can't be strictly true, for the risks to which companies are exposed are constantly shifting. We are venturing here onto somewhat difficult ground, but there is a way to think about risk that can suggest a route through. It involves converting the expected cash flows to **certainty equivalents.** We will first explain what certainty equivalents are. Then we will use this knowledge to examine when it is reasonable to assume constant risk. Finally we will value a project whose risk *does* change.

Think back to the simple real estate investment that we used in Chapter 2 to introduce the concept of present value. You are considering construction of an office building that you plan to sell after one year for $400,000. Since that cash flow is uncertain, you discount at a risk-adjusted discount rate of 12 percent rather than the 7 percent risk-free rate of interest. This gives a present value of 400,000/1.12 = $357,143.

Suppose a real estate company now approaches and offers to fix the price at which it will buy the building from you at the end of the year. This guarantee would remove any uncertainty about the payoff on your investment. So you would accept a lower figure than the uncertain payoff of $400,000. But how much less? If the building has a present value of $357,143 and the interest rate is 7 percent, then

$$PV = \frac{\text{Certain cash flow}}{1.07} = \$357,143$$

Certain cash flow = $382,143

In other words, a certain cash flow of $382,143 has exactly the same present value as an expected but uncertain cash flow of $400,000. The cash flow of $382,143 is therefore known as the *certainty-equivalent cash flow*. To compensate for both the delayed payoff and the uncertainty in real estate prices, you need a return of 400,000 − 357,143 = $42,857. To get rid of the risk, you would be prepared to take a cut in the return of 400,000 − 382,143 = $17,857.

Our example illustrates two ways to value a risky cash flow C_1:

Method 1: Discount the risky cash flow at a *risk-adjusted discount rate r* that is greater than r_f.[23] The risk-adjusted discount rate adjusts for both time and risk. This is illustrated by the clockwise route in Figure 9.5.

Method 2: Find the certainty-equivalent cash flow and discount at the risk-free interest rate r_f. When you use this method, you need to ask, What is the smallest *certain* payoff for which I would exchange the risky cash flow C_1?

---

[22]See E. F. Fama, "Risk-Adjusted Discount Rates and Capital Budgeting under Uncertainty," *Journal of Financial Economics* 5 (August 1977), pp. 3–24; or S. C. Myers and S. M. Turnbull, "Capital Budgeting and the Capital Asset Pricing Model: Good News and Bad News," *Journal of Finance* 32 (May 1977), pp. 321–332.

[23]The quantity r can be less than r_f for assets with negative betas. But the betas of the assets that corporations hold are almost always positive.

FIGURE 9.5

Two ways to calculate present value. "Haircut for risk" refers to the reduction of the cash flow from its fore-casted value to its certainty equivalent.

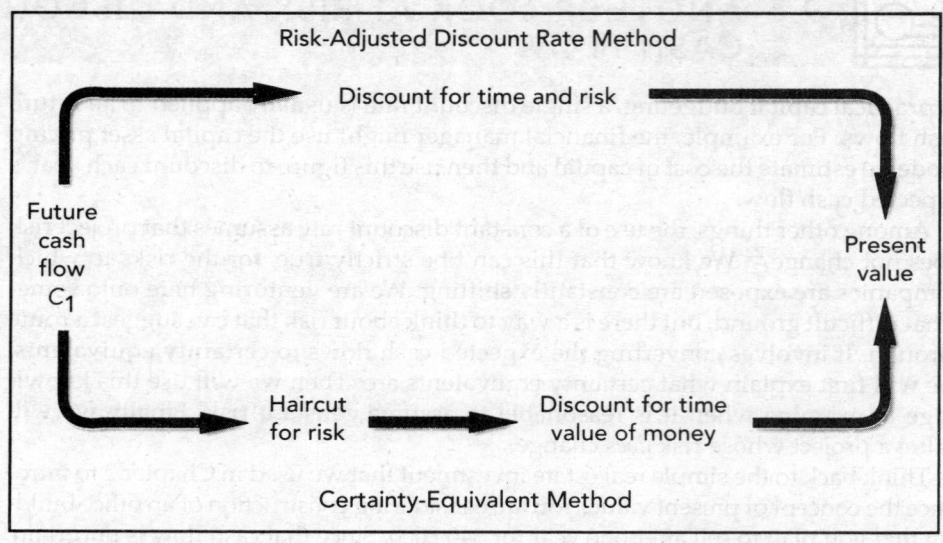

This is called the *certainty equivalent* of C_1 denoted by CEQ_1.[24] Since CEQ_1 is the value equivalent of a safe cash flow, it is discounted at the risk-free rate. The certainty-equivalent method makes *separate* adjustments for risk and time. This is illustrated by the counterclockwise route in Figure 9.5.

We now have two identical expressions for PV:

$$PV = \frac{C_1}{1 + r} = \frac{\text{CEQ}_1}{1 + r_f}$$

For cash flows two, three, or t years away,

$$PV = \frac{C_t}{(1 + r)^t} = \frac{\text{CEQ}_t}{(1 + r_f)^t}$$

When to Use a Single Risk-Adjusted Discount Rate for Long-Lived Assets

We are now in a position to examine what is implied when a constant risk-adjusted discount rate, r, is used to calculate a present value.

Consider two simple projects. Project A is expected to produce a cash flow of $100 million for each of three years. The risk-free interest rate is 6 percent, the market risk premium is 8 percent, and project A's beta is .75. You therefore calculate A's opportunity cost of capital as follows:

$$r = r_f + \beta(r_m - r_f)$$
$$= 6 + .75(8) = 12\%$$

Discounting at 12 percent gives the following present value for each cash flow:

---

[24]CEQ_1 can be calculated directly from the capital asset pricing model. The certainty-equivalent form of the CAPM states that the certainty-equivalent value of the cash flow, C_1, is $PV = C_1 - \lambda \, \text{cov}(\tilde{C}_1, \tilde{r}_m)$. Cov $(\tilde{C}_1, \tilde{r}_m)$ is the covariance between the uncertain cash flow, $\tilde{C}_1$, and the return on the market, r_m. Lambda, λ, is a measure of the market price of risk. It is defined as $(r_m - r_f)/\sigma_m^2$. For example, if $r_m - r_f = .08$ and the standard deviation of market returns is $\sigma_m = .20$, then lambda $= .08/.20^2 = 2$. We show on the Brealey-Myers website (**www.mhhe.com/bm7e**) how the CAPM formula can be twisted around into this certainty-equivalent form.

Project A		
Year	Cash Flow	PV at 12%
1	100	89.3
2	100	79.7
3	100	71.2
	Total PV	240.2

Now compare these figures with the cash flows of project B. Notice that B's cash flows are lower than A's; but B's flows are safe, and therefore they are discounted at the risk-free interest rate. The *present value* of each year's cash flow is identical for the two projects.

Project B		
Year	Cash Flow	PV at 6%
1	94.6	89.3
2	89.6	79.7
3	84.8	71.2
	Total PV	240.2

In year 1 project A has a risky cash flow of 100. This has the same PV as the safe cash flow of 94.6 from project B. Therefore 94.6 is the certainty equivalent of 100. Since the two cash flows have the same PV, investors must be willing to give up $100 - 94.6 = 5.4$ in expected year-1 income in order to get rid of the uncertainty.

In year 2 project A has a risky cash flow of 100, and B has a safe cash flow of 89.6. Again both flows have the same PV. Thus, to eliminate the uncertainty in year 2, investors are prepared to give up $100 - 89.6 = 10.4$ of future income. To eliminate uncertainty in year 3, they are willing to give up $100 - 84.8 = 15.2$ of future income.

To value project A, you discounted each cash flow at the same risk-adjusted discount rate of 12 percent. Now you can see what is implied when you did that. By using a constant rate, you effectively made a larger deduction for risk from the later cash flows:

Year	Forecasted Cash Flow for Project A	Certainty-Equivalent Cash Flow	Deduction for Risk
1	100	94.6	5.4
2	100	89.6	10.4
3	100	84.8	15.2

The second cash flow is riskier than the first because it is exposed to two years of market risk. The third cash flow is riskier still because it is exposed to three years of market risk. This increased risk is reflected in the steadily declining certainty equivalents:

Year	Forecasted Cash Flow for Project A (C_t)	Certainty-Equivalent Cash Flow (CEQ_t)	Ratio of CEQ_t to C_t
1	100	94.6	.946
2	100	89.6	$.896 = .946^2$
3	100	84.8	$.848 = .946^3$

Our example illustrates that if we are to use the same discount rate for every future cash flow, then the certainty equivalents must decline steadily as a fraction of the cash flow. There's no law of nature stating that certainty equivalents have to decrease in this smooth and regular way. It may be a fair assumption for most projects most of the time, but we'll sketch in a moment a real example in which that is not the case.

A Common Mistake

You sometimes hear people say that because distant cash flows are riskier, they should be discounted at a higher rate than earlier cash flows. That is quite wrong: We have just seen that using the same risk-adjusted discount rate for each year's cash flow implies a larger deduction for risk from the later cash flows. The reason is that the discount rate compensates for the risk borne *per period*. The more distant the cash flows, the greater the number of periods and the larger the *total* risk adjustment.

When You Cannot Use a Single Risk-Adjusted Discount Rate for Long-Lived Assets

Sometimes you will encounter problems where risk does change as time passes, and the use of a single risk-adjusted discount rate will then get you into trouble. For example, later in the book we will look at how options are valued. Because an option's risk is continually changing, the certainty-equivalent method needs to be used.

Here is a disguised, simplified, and somewhat exaggerated version of an actual project proposal that one of the authors was asked to analyze. The scientists at Vegetron have come up with an electric mop, and the firm is ready to go ahead with pilot production and test marketing. The preliminary phase will take one year and cost $125,000. Management feels that there is only a 50 percent chance that pilot production and market tests will be successful. If they are, then Vegetron will build a $1 million plant that would generate an expected annual cash flow in perpetuity of $250,000 a year after taxes. If they are not successful, the project will have to be dropped.

The expected cash flows (in thousands of dollars) are

$$C_0 = -125$$
$$C_1 = 50\% \text{ chance of } -1{,}000 \text{ and } 50\% \text{ chance of } 0$$
$$= .5(-1{,}000) + .5(0) = -500$$
$$C_t \text{ for } t = 2, 3, \cdots = 50\% \text{ chance of } 250 \text{ and } 50\% \text{ chance of } 0$$
$$= .5(250) + .5(0) = 125$$

Management has little experience with consumer products and considers this a project of extremely high risk.[25] Therefore management discounts the cash flows at 25 percent, rather than at Vegetron's normal 10 percent standard:

$$NPV = -125 - \frac{500}{1.25} + \sum_{t=2}^{\infty} \frac{125}{(1.25)^t} = -125, \text{ or } -\$125{,}000$$

This seems to show that the project is not worthwhile.

Management's analysis is open to criticism if the first year's experiment resolves a high proportion of the risk. If the test phase is a failure, then there's no risk at all—the project is *certain* to be worthless. If it is a success, there could well be only normal risk from then on. That means there is a 50 percent chance that in one year Vegetron will

---

[25]We will assume that they mean high *market* risk and that the difference between 25 and 10 percent is *not* a fudge factor introduced to offset optimistic cash-flow forecasts.

have the opportunity to invest in a project of *normal* risk, for which the *normal* discount rate of 10 percent would be appropriate. Thus the firm has a 50 percent chance to invest $1 million in a project with a net present value of $1.5 million:

$$\text{Success} \longrightarrow \text{NPV} = -1000 + \frac{250}{.10} = +1{,}500 \ (50\% \text{ chance})$$

Pilot production
and market tests

$$\text{Failure} \longrightarrow \text{NPV} = 0 \ (50\% \text{ chance})$$

Thus we could view the project as offering an expected payoff of $.5(1{,}500) + .5(0) = 750$, or $750,000, at $t = 1$ on a $125,000 investment at $t = 0$. Of course, the certainty equivalent of the payoff is less than $750,000, but the difference would have to be very large to justify rejecting the project. For example, if the certainty equivalent is half the forecasted cash flow and the risk-free rate is 7 percent, the project is worth $225,500:

$$\text{NPV} = C_0 + \frac{\text{CEQ}_1}{1 + r}$$

$$= -125 + \frac{.5(750)}{1.07} = 225.5, \text{ or } \$225{,}500$$

This is not bad for a $125,000 investment—and quite a change from the negative-NPV that management got by discounting all future cash flows at 25 percent.

In Chapter 8 we set out some basic principles for valuing risky assets. In this chapter we have shown you how to apply these principles to practical situations.

The problem is easiest when you believe that the project has the same market risk as the company's existing assets. In this case, the required return equals the required return on a portfolio of all the company's existing securities. This is called the *company cost of capital*.

Common sense tells us that the required return on any asset depends on its risk. In this chapter we have defined risk as beta and used the capital asset pricing model to calculate expected returns.

The most common way to estimate the beta of a stock is to figure out how the stock price has responded to market changes in the past. Of course, this will give you only an estimate of the stock's true beta. You may get a more reliable figure if you calculate an industry beta for a group of similar companies.

Suppose that you now have an estimate of the stock's beta. Can you plug that into the capital asset pricing model to find the company's cost of capital? No, the stock beta may reflect both business and financial risk. Whenever a company borrows money, it increases the beta (and the expected return) of its stock. Remember, the company cost of capital is the expected return on a portfolio of all the firm's securities, not just the common stock. You can calculate it by estimating the expected return on each of the securities and then taking a weighted average of these separate returns. Or you can calculate the beta of the portfolio of securities and then plug this *asset beta* into the capital asset pricing model.

The company cost of capital is the correct discount rate for projects that have the same risk as the company's existing business. Many firms, however, use the company cost of capital to discount the forecasted cash flows on all new projects. This

SUMMARY

is a dangerous procedure. In principle, each project should be evaluated at its own opportunity cost of capital; the true cost of capital depends on the use to which the capital is put. If we wish to estimate the cost of capital for a particular project, it is *project risk* that counts. Of course the company cost of capital is fine as a discount rate for average-risk projects. It is also a useful starting point for estimating discount rates for safer or riskier projects.

These basic principles apply internationally, but of course there are complications. The risk of a stock or real asset may depend on who's investing. For example, a Swiss investor would calculate a lower beta for Merck than an investor in the United States. Conversely, the U.S. investor would calculate a lower beta for a Swiss pharmaceutical company than a Swiss investor. Both investors see lower risk abroad because of the less-than-perfect correlation between the two countries' markets.

If all investors held the world market portfolio, none of this would matter. But there is a strong home-country bias. Perhaps some investors stay at home because they regard foreign investment as risky. We suspect they confuse total risk with market risk. For example, we showed examples of countries with extremely volatile stock markets. Most of these markets were nevertheless low-beta investments for an investor holding the U.S. market. Again, the reason was low correlation between markets.

Then we turned to the problem of assessing project risk. We provided several clues for managers seeking project betas. First, avoid adding fudge factors to discount rates to offset worries about bad project outcomes. Adjust cash-flow forecasts to give due weight to bad outcomes as well as good; *then* ask whether the chance of bad outcomes adds to the project's market risk. Second, you can often identify the characteristics of a high- or low-beta project even when the project beta cannot be calculated directly. For example, you can try to figure out how much the cash flows are affected by the overall performance of the economy: Cyclical investments are generally high-beta investments. You can also look at the project's operating leverage: Fixed production charges work like fixed debt charges; that is, they increase beta.

There is one more fence to jump. Most projects produce cash flows for several years. Firms generally use the same risk-adjusted rate to discount each of these cash flows. When they do this, they are implicitly assuming that cumulative risk increases at a constant rate as you look further into the future. That assumption is usually reasonable. It is precisely true when the project's future beta will be constant, that is, when risk *per period* is constant.

But exceptions sometimes prove the rule. Be on the alert for projects where risk clearly does not increase steadily. In these cases, you should break the project into segments within which the same discount rate can be reasonably used. Or you should use the certainty-equivalent version of the DCF model, which allows separate risk adjustments to each period's cash flow.

FURTHER READING

There is a good review article by Rubinstein on the application of the capital asset pricing model to capital investment decisions:

M. E. Rubinstein: "A Mean-Variance Synthesis of Corporate Financial Theory," *Journal of Finance,* 28:167–182 (March 1973).

There have been a number of studies of the relationship between accounting data and beta. Many of these are reviewed in:

G. Foster: *Financial Statement Analysis,* 2nd ed., Prentice-Hall, Inc., Englewood Cliffs, N.J., 1986.

For some ideas on how one might break down the problem of estimating beta, see:

W. F. Sharpe: "The Capital Asset Pricing Model: A 'Multi-Beta' Interpretation," in H. Levy and M. Sarnat (eds.), *Financial Decision Making under Uncertainty*, Academic Press, New York, 1977.

Fama and French present estimates of industry costs of equity capital from both the CAPM and APT models. The difficulties in obtaining precise estimates are discussed in:

E. F. Fama and K. R. French, "Industry Costs of Equity," *Journal of Financial Economics*, 43:153–193 (February 1997).

The assumptions required for use of risk-adjusted discount rates are discussed in:

E. F. Fama: "Risk-Adjusted Discount Rates and Capital Budgeting under Uncertainty," *Journal of Financial Economics*, 5:3–24 (August 1977).

S. C. Myers and S. M. Turnbull: "Capital Budgeting and the Capital Asset Pricing Model: Good News and Bad News," *Journal of Finance*, 32:321–332 (May 1977).

QUIZ

1. Suppose a firm uses its company cost of capital to evaluate all projects. Will it underestimate or overestimate the value of high-risk projects?

2. "A stock's beta can be estimated by plotting past prices against the level of the market index and drawing the line of best fit. Beta is the slope of this line." True or false? Explain.

3. Look back to the top-right panel of Figure 9.2. What proportion of Dell's return was explained by market movements? What proportion was unique or diversifiable risk? How does the unique risk show up in the plot? What is the range of possible error in the beta estimate?

4. A company is financed 40 percent by risk-free debt. The interest rate is 10 percent, the expected market return is 18 percent, and the stock's beta is .5. What is the company cost of capital?

5. The total market value of the common stock of the Okefenokee Real Estate Company is $6 million, and the total value of its debt is $4 million. The treasurer estimates that the beta of the stock is currently 1.5 and that the expected risk premium on the market is 9 percent. The Treasury bill rate is 8 percent. Assume for simplicity that Okefenokee debt is risk-free.
   a. What is the required return on Okefenokee stock?
   b. What is the beta of the company's existing portfolio of assets?
   c. Estimate the company cost of capital.
   d. Estimate the discount rate for an expansion of the company's present business.
   e. Suppose the company wants to diversify into the manufacture of rose-colored spectacles. The beta of unleveraged optical manufacturers is 1.2. Estimate the required return on Okefenokee's new venture.

6. Nero Violins has the following capital structure:

Security	Beta	Total Market Value, $ millions
Debt	0	100
Preferred stock	.20	40
Common stock	1.20	200

   a. What is the firm's asset beta (i.e., the beta of a portfolio of all the firm's securities)?
   b. How would the asset beta change if Nero issued an additional $140 million of common stock and used the cash to repurchase all the debt and preferred stock?
   c. Assume that the CAPM is correct. What discount rate should Nero set for investments that expand the scale of its operations without changing its asset beta? Assume a risk-free interest rate of 5 percent and a market risk premium of 6 percent.

7. True or false?
   a. Many foreign stock markets are much more volatile than the U.S. market.
   b. The betas of most foreign stock markets (calculated relative to the U.S. market) are usually greater than 1.0.
   c. Investors concentrate their holdings in their home countries. This means that companies domiciled in different countries may calculate different discount rates for the same project.

8. Which of these companies is likely to have the higher cost of capital?
   a. A's sales force is paid a fixed annual rate; B's is paid on a commission basis.
   b. C produces machine tools; D produces breakfast cereal.

9. Select the appropriate phrase from within each pair of brackets: "In calculating PV there are two ways to adjust for risk. One is to make a deduction from the expected cash flows. This is known as the [certainty-equivalent; risk-adjusted discount rate] method. It is usually written as PV = $[CEQ_t/(1 + r_f)^t; CEQ_t/(1 + r_m)^t]$. The certainty-equivalent cash flow, CEQ_t, is always [more than; less than] the forecasted risky cash flow. Another way to allow for risk is to discount the expected cash flows at a rate r. If we use the CAPM to calculate r, then r is $[r_f + \beta r_m; r_f + \beta(r_m - r_f); r_m + \beta(r_m - r_f)]$. This method is exact only if the ratio of the certainty-equivalent cash flow to the forecasted risky cash flow [is constant; declines at a constant rate; increases at a constant rate]. For the majority of projects, the use of a single discount rate, r, is probably a perfectly acceptable approximation."

10. A project has a forecasted cash flow of $110 in year 1 and $121 in year 2. The interest rate is 5 percent, the estimated risk premium on the market is 10 percent, and the project has a beta of .5. If you use a constant risk-adjusted discount rate, what is
    a. The PV of the project?
    b. The certainty-equivalent cash flow in year 1 and year 2?
    c. The ratio of the certainty-equivalent cash flows to the expected cash flows in years 1 and 2?

PRACTICE QUESTIONS

STANDARD & POOR'S

STANDARD & POOR'S

1. "The cost of capital always depends on the risk of the project being evaluated. Therefore the company cost of capital is useless." Do you agree?

2. Look again at the companies listed in Table 8.2. Monthly rates of return for most of these companies can be found on the Standard & Poor's Market Insight website (**www.mhhe.com/edumarketinsight**)—see the "Monthly Adjusted Prices" spreadsheet. This spreadsheet also shows monthly returns for the Standard & Poor's 500 market index. What percentage of the variance of each company's return is explained by the index? Use the Excel function RSQ, which calculates R^2.

3. Pick at least five of the companies identified in Practice Question 2. The "Monthly Adjusted Prices" spreadsheets should contain about four years of monthly rates of return for the companies' stocks and for the Standard & Poor's 500 index.
   a. Split the rates of return into two consecutive two-year periods. Calculate betas for each period using the Excel SLOPE function. How stable was each company's beta?
   b. Suppose you had used these betas to estimate expected rates of return from the CAPM. Would your estimates have changed significantly from period to period?
   c. You may find it interesting to repeat your analysis using weekly returns from the "Weekly Adjusted Prices" spreadsheets. This will give more than 100 weekly rates of return for each two-year period.

4. The following table shows estimates of the risk of two well-known British stocks during the five years ending July 2001:

	Standard Deviation	R^2	Beta	Standard Error of Beta
British Petroleum (BP)	25	.25	.90	.17
British Airways	38	.25	1.37	.22

a. What proportion of each stock's risk was market risk, and what proportion was unique risk?

b. What is the variance of BP? What is the unique variance?

c. What is the confidence level on British Airways beta?

d. If the CAPM is correct, what is the expected return on British Airways? Assume a risk-free interest rate of 5 percent and an expected market return of 12 percent.

e. Suppose that next year the market provides a zero return. What return would you expect from British Airways?

5. Identify a sample of food companies on the Standard & Poor's Market Insight website (**www.mhhe.com/edumarketinsight**). For example, you could try Campbell Soup (CPB), General Mills (GIS), Kellogg (K), Kraft Foods (KFT), and Sara Lee (SLE).

STANDARD &POOR'S

a. Estimate beta and R^2 for each company from the returns given on the "Monthly Adjusted Prices" spreadsheet. The Excel functions are SLOPE and RSQ.

b. Calculate an industry beta. Here is the best procedure: First calculate the monthly returns on an equally weighted portfolio of the stocks in your sample. Then calculate the industry beta using these portfolio returns. How does the R^2 of this portfolio compare to the average R^2 for the individual stocks?

c. Use the CAPM to calculate an average cost of equity (r_{equity}) for the food industry. Use current interest rates—take a look at footnote 8 in this chapter—and a reasonable estimate of the market risk premium.

6. Look again at the companies you chose for Practice Question 5.

a. Calculate the market-value debt ratio (D/V) for each company. Note that $V = D + E$, where equity value E is the product of price per share and number of shares outstanding. E is also called "market capitalization"—see the "Monthly Valuation Data" spreadsheet. To keep things simple, look only at long-term debt as reported on the most recent quarterly or annual balance sheet for each company.

b. Calculate the beta for each company's assets (β_{assets}), using the betas estimated in Practice Question 5(a). Assume that $\beta_{debt} = .15$.

c. Calculate the company cost of capital for each company. Use the debt beta of .15 to estimate the cost of debt.

d. Calculate an *industry* cost of capital using your answer to question 5(c). *Hint:* What is the average debt ratio for your sample of food companies?

e. How would you use this food industry cost of capital in practice? Would you recommend that an individual food company, Campbell Soup, say, should use this industry rate to value its capital investment projects? Explain.

7. You are given the following information for Lorelei Motorwerke. Note: €300,000 means 300,000 euros.

EXCEL

Long-term debt outstanding:	€300,000
Current yield to maturity (r_{debt}):	8%
Number of shares of common stock:	10,000
Price per share:	€50
Book value per share:	€25
Expected rate of return on stock (r_{equity}):	15%

a. Calculate Lorelei's company cost of capital. Ignore taxes.

b. How would r_{equity} and the cost of capital change if Lorelei's stock price fell to €25 due to declining profits? Business risk is unchanged.

8. Look again at Table 9.1. This time we will concentrate on Burlington Northern.

a. Calculate Burlington's cost of equity from the CAPM using its own beta estimate and the industry beta estimate. How different are your answers? Assume a risk-free rate of 3.5 percent and a market risk premium of 8 percent.

b. Can you be confident that Burlington's true beta is *not* the industry average?

c. Under what circumstances might you advise Burlington to calculate its cost of equity based on its own beta estimate?

d. Burlington's cost of debt was 6 percent and its debt-to-value ratio, D/V, was .40. What was Burlington's company cost of capital? Use the industry average beta.

9. Amalgamated Products has three operating divisions:

EXCEL

Division	Percentage of Firm Value
Food	50
Electronics	30
Chemicals	20

To estimate the cost of capital for each division, Amalgamated has identified the following three principal competitors:

	Estimated Equity Beta	Debt/(Debt + Equity)
United Foods	.8	.3
General Electronics	1.6	.2
Associated Chemicals	1.2	.4

Assume these betas are accurate estimates and that the CAPM is correct.

a. Assuming that the debt of these firms is risk-free, estimate the asset beta for each of Amalgamated's divisions.

b. Amalgamated's ratio of debt to debt plus equity is .4. If your estimates of divisional betas are right, what is Amalgamated's equity beta?

c. Assume that the risk-free interest rate is 7 percent and that the expected return on the market index is 15 percent. Estimate the cost of capital for each of Amalgamated's divisions.

d. How much would your estimates of each division's cost of capital change if you assumed that debt has a beta of .2?

10. Look at Table 9.2. What would the four countries' betas be if the correlation coefficient for each was 0.5? Do the calculation and explain.

11. "Investors' home country bias is diminishing rapidly. Sooner or later most investors will hold the world market portfolio, or a close approximation to it." Suppose that statement is correct. What are the implications for evaluating foreign capital investment projects?

12. Consider the beta estimates for the country indexes shown in Table 9.2. Could this information be helpful to a U.S. company considering capital investment projects in these countries? Would a German company find this information useful? Explain.

13. Mom and Pop Groceries has just dispatched a year's supply of groceries to the government of the Central Antarctic Republic. Payment of $250,000 will be made one year hence after the shipment arrives by snow train. Unfortunately there is a good chance of a coup d'état, in which case the new government will not pay. Mom and Pop's controller therefore decides to discount the payment at 40 percent, rather than at the company's 12 percent cost of capital.

a. What's wrong with using a 40 percent rate to offset political risk?

b. How much is the $250,000 payment really worth if the odds of a coup d'état are 25 percent?

14. An oil company is drilling a series of new wells on the perimeter of a producing oil field. About 20 percent of the new wells will be dry holes. Even if a new well strikes oil, there is still uncertainty about the amount of oil produced: 40 percent of new wells which strike oil produce only 1,000 barrels a day; 60 percent produce 5,000 barrels per day.

a. Forecast the annual cash revenues from a new perimeter well. Use a future oil price of $15 per barrel.

b. A geologist proposes to discount the cash flows of the new wells at 30 percent to offset the risk of dry holes. The oil company's normal cost of capital is 10 percent. Does this proposal make sense? Briefly explain why or why not.

15. Look back at project A in Section 9.6. Now assume that
    a. Expected cash flow is $150 per year for five years.
    b. The risk-free rate of interest is 5 percent.
    c. The market risk premium is 6 percent.
    d. The estimated beta is 1.2.

    Recalculate the certainty-equivalent cash flows, and show that the ratio of these certainty-equivalent cash flows to the risky cash flows declines by a constant proportion each year.

16. A project has the following forecasted cash flows:

Cash Flows, $ Thousands

C_0	C_1	C_2	C_3
−100	+40	+60	+50

The estimated project beta is 1.5. The market return r_m is 16 percent, and the risk-free rate r_f is 7 percent.
    a. Estimate the opportunity cost of capital and the project's PV (using the same rate to discount each cash flow).
    b. What are the certainty-equivalent cash flows in each year?
    c. What is the ratio of the certainty-equivalent cash flow to the expected cash flow in each year?
    d. Explain why this ratio declines.

17. The McGregor Whisky Company is proposing to market diet scotch. The product will first be test-marketed for two years in southern California at an initial cost of $500,000. This test launch is not expected to produce any profits but should reveal consumer preferences. There is a 60 percent chance that demand will be satisfactory. In this case McGregor will spend $5 million to launch the scotch nationwide and will receive an expected annual profit of $700,000 in perpetuity. If demand is not satisfactory, diet scotch will be withdrawn.

    Once consumer preferences are known, the product will be subject to an average degree of risk, and, therefore, McGregor requires a return of 12 percent on its investment. However, the initial test-market phase is viewed as much riskier, and McGregor demands a return of 40 percent on this initial expenditure.

    What is the NPV of the diet scotch project?

CHALLENGE QUESTIONS

1. Suppose you are valuing a future stream of high-risk (high-beta) cash *out*flows. High risk means a high discount rate. But the higher the discount rate, the less the present value. This seems to say that the higher the risk of cash outflows, the less you should worry about them! Can that be right? Should the sign of the cash flow affect the appropriate discount rate? Explain.

2. U.S. pharmaceutical companies have an average beta of about .8. These companies have very little debt financing, so the asset beta is also about .8. Yet a European investor would calculate a beta of much less than .8 relative to returns on European stock markets. (How do you explain this?) Now consider some possible implications.
    a. Should German pharmaceutical companies move their R&D and production facilities to the United States?
    b. Suppose the German company uses the CAPM to calculate a cost of capital of 9 percent for investments in the United States and 12 percent at home. As a result it plans to invest large amounts of its shareholders' money in the United States. But its shareholders have already demonstrated their home country bias. Should the German company respect its shareholders' preferences and also invest mostly at home?

    c. The German company can also buy shares of U.S. pharmaceutical companies. Suppose the expected rate of return in these shares is 13 percent, reflecting their beta of about 1.0 with respect to the U.S. market. Should the German company demand a 13 percent rate of return on investments in the United States?

3. An oil company executive is considering investing $10 million in one or both of two wells: Well 1 is expected to produce oil worth $3 million a year for 10 years; well 2 is expected to produce $2 million for 15 years. These are *real* (inflation-adjusted) cash flows.

    The beta for *producing wells* is .9. The market risk premium is 8 percent, the nominal risk-free interest rate is 6 percent, and expected inflation is 4 percent.

    The two wells are intended to develop a previously discovered oil field. Unfortunately there is still a 20 percent chance of a dry hole in each case. A dry hole means zero cash flows and a complete loss of the $10 million investment.

    Ignore taxes and make further assumptions as necessary.

    a. What is the correct real discount rate for cash flows from developed wells?

    b. The oil company executive proposes to add 20 percentage points to the real discount rate to offset the risk of a dry hole. Calculate the NPV of each well with this adjusted discount rate.

    c. What do *you* say the NPVs of the two wells are?

    d. Is there any *single* fudge factor that could be added to the discount rate for developed wells that would yield the correct NPV for both wells? Explain.

4. If you have access to "Data Analysis Tools" in Excel, use the "regression" functions to investigate the reliability of the betas estimated in Practice Questions 3 and 5 and the industry cost of capital calculated in question 6.

    a. What are the standard errors of the betas from questions 3(a) and 3(c)? Given the standard errors, do you regard the different beta estimates obtained for each company as signficantly different? (Perhaps the differences are just "noise.") What would you propose as the most reliable *forecast* of beta for each company?

    b. How reliable are the beta estimates from question 5(a)?

    c. Compare the standard error of the industry beta from question 5(b) to the standard errors for individual-company betas. Given these standard errors, would you change or amend your answer to question 6(e)?

MINI-CASE

Holiport Corporation

Holiport Corporation is a diversified company with three operating divisions:

- The construction division manages infrastructure projects such as roads and bridge construction.
- The food products division produces a range of confectionery and cookies.
- The pharmaceutical division develops and produces anti-infective drugs and animal healthcare products.

These divisions are largely autonomous. Holiport's small head-office financial staff is principally concerned with applying financial controls and allocating capital between the divisions. Table 9.3 summarizes each division's assets, revenues, and profits. Holiport has always been regarded as a conservative—some would say "stodgy"—company. Its bonds are highly rated and yield 7 percent, only 1.5 percent more than comparable government bonds.

Holiport's previous CFO, Sir Reginald Holiport-Bentley, retired last year after an autocratic 12-year reign. He insisted on a hurdle rate of 12 percent for all capital expenditures for all three divisions. This rate never changed, despite wide fluctuations in interest rates and inflation. However, the new CFO, Miss Florence Holiport-Bentley-Smythe (Sir Reginald's niece) had brought a breath of fresh air into the head office. She was determined to set dif-

	Construction	Food Products	Pharmaceuticals
Net working capital	47	373	168
Fixed assets	792	561	1083
Total net assets	839	934	1251
Revenues	1814	917	1271
Net profits	15	149	227

TABLE 9.3

Summary financial data for Holiport Corporation's three operating divisions (figures in £ millions).

	Holiport	Burchetts Green	Unifoods	Pharmichem
Cash and marketable securities	374	66	21	388
Other current assets	1596	408	377	1276
Fixed assets	2436	526	868	2077
Total assets	4406	1000	1266	3740
Short-term debt	340	66	81	21
Other current liabilities	1042	358	225	1273
Long-term debt	601	64	396	178
Equity	2423	512	564	2269
Total liabilities and equity	4406	1000	1266	3740
Number of shares, millions	1520	76	142	1299
Share price (£)	8.00	9.1	25.4	28.25
Dividend yield (%)	2.0	1.9	1.4	0.6
P/E ratio	31.1	14.5	27.6	46.6
Estimated β of stock	1.03	.80	1.15	.96

TABLE 9.4

Summary financial data for comparable companies (figures in £ millions, except as noted).

ferent costs of capital for each division. So when Henry Rodriguez returned from vacation, he was not surprised to find in his in-tray a memo from the new CFO. He was asked to determine how the company should establish divisional costs of capital and to provide estimates for the three divisions and for the company as a whole.

The new CFO's memo warned him not to confine himself to just one cookbook method, but to examine alternative estimates of the cost of capital. He also remembered a heated discussion between Florence and her uncle. Sir Reginald departed insisting that the only good forecast of the market risk premium was a long-run historical average; Florence argued strongly that alert, modern investors required much lower returns. Henry failed to see what "alert" and "modern" had to do with a market risk premium. Nevertheless, Henry decided that his report should address this question head on.

Henry started by identifying the three closest competitors to Holiport's divisions. Burchetts Green is a construction company, Unifoods produces candy, and Pharmichem is Holiport's main competitor in the animal healthcare business. Henry jotted down the summary data in Table 9.4 and poured himself a large cup of black coffee.

Questions

1. Help Henry Rogriguez by writing a memo to the CFO on Holiport's cost of capital. Your memo should (a) outline the merits of alternative methods for estimating the cost of capital, (b) explain your views on the market risk premium, and (c) provide an estimate of the cost of capital for each of Holiport's divisions.

PART TWO RELATED WEBSITES

Robert Shiller's home page includes long-term data on U.S. stock and bill returns:

www.aida.econ.yale.edu

Equity betas for individual stocks are found on Yahoo. (Or you can download the stock prices from Yahoo and calculate your own measures):

www.finance.yahoo.com

Aswath Damodoran's home page contains good long-term data on U.S. equities and average equity and asset betas for U.S. industries:

www.equity.stern.nyu.edu/~adamodar/
New_Home_Page

Another useful site is Campbell Harvey's home page. It contains data on past stock returns and risk, and software to calculate mean-variance efficient frontiers:

www.duke.edu/~charvey

Data on the Fama-French factors are published on Ken French's website:

www.mba.tuck.dartmouth.edu/pages/
faculty/ken.french

ValuePro provides software and data for estimating company cost of capital:

www.valuepro.net

For a collection of recent articles on the cost of capital see:

www.ibbotson.com

PRACTICAL PROBLEMS
IN CAPITAL BUDGETING

EUROTUNNEL'S CONSTRUCTION OF a tunnel between England and France cost a record $15 billion. Before proceeding, the company developed cash flow forecasts that indicated a 14 percent return. Unfortunately, meticulous DCF calculations do not guarantee success. The tunnel proved more costly and took longer to build than anticipated. Also revenues were disappointing, and for some time the company did not even generate enough profits to pay the debt interest.

Of course, life is full of unpleasant surprises, but Part Three shows how companies can take steps to minimize the chance that a project will turn out a loser. Chapter 10 describes how companies identify factors that could put a project below water. It also shows how firms build in the flex-ibility to expand if things go well, and cut back if disaster threatens.

Chapter 11 looks at how managers satisfy themselves that a project truly does have a positive NPV. They do not simply check the NPV calculations. They ask fundamental economic questions about the project. Does the firm have some special advantage or headstart over other firms? How will competitors react? Will their responses erode the project's profitability? For example, Eurotunnel's management would have thought hard about the response of existing operators of channel ferries.

Finally, Chapter 12 shows how firms organize the investment process and provide managers and employees with the proper incentives to maximize firm value.

CHAPTER TEN

A PROJECT IS NOT A BLACK BOX

A BLACK BOX is something that we accept and use but do not understand. For most of us a computer is a black box. We may know what it is supposed to do, but we do not understand how it works and, if something breaks, we cannot fix it.

We have been treating capital projects as black boxes. In other words, we have talked as if managers are handed unbiased cash-flow forecasts and their only task is to assess risk, choose the right discount rate, and crank out net present value. Actual financial managers won't rest until they understand what makes the project tick and what could go wrong with it. Remember Murphy's law, "If anything can go wrong, it will," and O'Reilly's corollary, "at the worst possible time."

Even if the project's risk is wholly diversifiable, you still need to understand why the venture could fail. Once you know that, you can decide whether it is worth trying to resolve the uncertainty. Maybe further expenditure on market research would clear up those doubts about acceptance by consumers, maybe another drill hole would give you a better idea of the size of the ore body, and maybe some further work on the test bed would confirm the durability of those welds. If the project really has a negative NPV, the sooner you can identify it, the better. And even if you decide that it is worth going ahead on the basis of present information, you do not want to be caught by surprise if things subsequently go wrong. You want to know the danger signals and the actions you might take.

We will show you how to use *sensitivity analysis,* *break-even analysis,* and *Monte Carlo simulation* to identify crucial assumptions and to explore what can go wrong. There is no magic in these techniques, just computer-assisted common sense. You don't need a license to use them.

Discounted-cash-flow analysis commonly assumes that companies hold assets passively, and it ignores the opportunities to expand the project if it is successful or to bail out if it is not. However, wise managers value these opportunities. They look for ways to capitalize on success and to reduce the costs of failure, and they are prepared to pay up for projects that give them this flexibility. Opportunities to modify projects as the future unfolds are known as *real options.* We describe several important real options, and we show how to use *decision trees* to set out these options' attributes and implications.

 ## 10.1 SENSITIVITY ANALYSIS

Uncertainty means that more things can happen than will happen. Whenever you are confronted with a cash-flow forecast, you should try to discover what else can happen.

Put yourself in the well-heeled shoes of the treasurer of the Otobai Company in Osaka, Japan. You are considering the introduction of an electrically powered motor scooter for city use. Your staff members have prepared the cash-flow forecasts shown in Table 10.1. Since NPV is positive at the 10 percent opportunity cost of capital, it appears to be worth going ahead.

$$NPV = -15 + \sum_{t=1}^{10} \frac{3}{(1.10)^t} = +¥3.43 \text{ billion}$$

Before you decide, you want to delve into these forecasts and identify the key variables that determine whether the project succeeds or fails. It turns out that the marketing department has estimated revenue as follows:

Unit sales = new product's share of market × size of scooter market
= .1 × 1 million = 100,000 scooters

TABLE 10.1

Preliminary cash-flow forecasts for Otobai's electric scooter project (figures in ¥ billions).

Assumptions:
1. Investment is depreciated over 10 years straight-line.
2. Income is taxed at a rate of 50 percent.

	Year 0	Years 1–10
Investment	15	
1. Revenue		37.5
2. Variable cost		30
3. Fixed cost		3
4. Depreciation		1.5
5. Pretax profit (1 − 2 − 3 − 4)		3
6. Tax		1.5
7. Net profit (5 − 6)		1.5
8. Operating cash flow (4 + 7)		3
Net cash flow	−15	+3

$$\text{Revenue} = \text{unit sales} \times \text{price per unit}$$
$$= 100{,}000 \times 375{,}000 = \text{¥}37.5 \text{ billion}$$

The production department has estimated variable costs per unit as ¥300,000. Since projected volume is 100,000 scooters per year, total variable cost is ¥30 billion. Fixed costs are ¥3 billion per year. The initial investment can be depreciated on a straight-line basis over the 10-year period, and profits are taxed at a rate of 50 percent.

These seem to be the important things you need to know, but look out for unidentified variables. Perhaps there are patent problems, or perhaps you will need to invest in service stations that will recharge the scooter batteries. The greatest dangers often lie in these *unknown* unknowns, or "unk-unks," as scientists call them.

Having found no unk-unks (no doubt you'll find them later), you conduct a **sensitivity analysis** with respect to market size, market share, and so on. To do this, the marketing and production staffs are asked to give optimistic and pessimistic estimates for the underlying variables. These are set out in the left-hand columns of Table 10.2. The right-hand side shows what happens to the project's net present value if the variables are set *one at a time* to their optimistic and pessimistic values. Your project appears to be by no means a sure thing. The most dangerous variables appear to be market share and unit variable cost. If market share is only .04 (and all other variables are as expected), then the project has an NPV of −¥10.4 billion. If unit variable cost is ¥360,000 (and all other variables are as expected), then the project has an NPV of −¥15 billion.

Value of Information

Now you can check whether an investment of time or money could resolve some of the uncertainty *before* your company parts with the ¥15 billion investment. Suppose that the pessimistic value for unit variable cost partly reflects the production department's worry that a particular machine will not work as designed and that the operation will have to be performed by other methods at an extra cost of ¥20,000 per unit. The chance that this will occur is only 1 in 10. But, if it does occur, the extra ¥20,000 unit cost will reduce after-tax cash flow by

$$\text{Unit sales} \times \text{additional unit cost} \times (1 - \text{tax rate})$$
$$= 100{,}000 \times 20{,}000 \times .50 = \text{¥}1 \text{ billion}$$

Variable	Range			NPV, ¥ Billions		
	Pessimistic	Expected	Optimistic	Pessimistic	Expected	Optimistic
Market size	.9 million	1 million	1.1 million	+1.1	+3.4	+5.7
Market share	.04	.1	.16	−10.4	+3.4	+17.3
Unit price	¥350,000	¥375,000	¥380,000	−4.2	+3.4	+5.0
Unit variable cost	¥360,000	¥300,000	¥275,000	−15.0	+3.4	+11.1
Fixed cost	¥4 billion	¥3 billion	¥2 billion	+.4	+3.4	+6.5

TABLE 10.2

To undertake a sensitivity analysis of the electric scooter project, we set each variable *in turn* at its most pessimistic or optimistic value and recalculate the NPV of the project.

It would reduce the NPV of your project by

$$\sum_{t=1}^{10} \frac{1}{(1.10)^t} = ¥6.14 \text{ billion,}$$

putting the NPV of the scooter project underwater at +3.43 − 6.14 = −¥2.71 billion.

Suppose further that a ¥10 million pretest of the machine will reveal whether it will work or not and allow you to clear up the problem. It clearly pays to invest ¥10 million to avoid a 10 percent probability of a ¥6.14 billion fall in NPV. You are ahead by −10 + .10 × 6,140 = +¥604 million.

On the other hand, the value of additional information about market size is small. Because the project is acceptable even under pessimistic assumptions about market size, you are unlikely to be in trouble if you have misestimated that variable.

Limits to Sensitivity Analysis

Sensitivity analysis boils down to expressing cash flows in terms of key project variables and then calculating the consequences of misestimating the variables. It forces the manager to identify the underlying variables, indicates where additional information would be most useful, and helps to expose confused or inappropriate forecasts.

One drawback to sensitivity analysis is that it always gives somewhat ambiguous results. For example, what exactly does *optimistic* or *pessimistic* mean? The marketing department may be interpreting the terms in a different way from the production department. Ten years from now, after hundreds of projects, hindsight may show that the marketing department's pessimistic limit was exceeded twice as often as the production department's; but what you may discover 10 years hence is no help now. One solution is to ask the two departments for a *complete* description of the various odds. However, it is far from easy to extract a forecaster's subjective notion of the complete probability distribution of possible outcomes.[1]

Another problem with sensitivity analysis is that the underlying variables are likely to be interrelated. What sense does it make to look at the effect in isolation of an increase in market size? If market size exceeds expectations, it is likely that

---

[1] If you doubt this, try some simple experiments. Ask the person who repairs your television to state a numerical probability that your set will work for at least one more year. Or construct your own subjective probability distribution of the number of telephone calls you will receive next week. That ought to be easy. Try it.

	Cash Flows, Years 1–10, ¥ Billions	
	Base Case	High Oil Prices and Recession Case
1. Revenue	37.5	44.9
2. Variable cost	30.0	35.9
3. Fixed cost	3.0	3.5
4. Depreciation	1.5	1.5
5. Pretax profit (1 − 2 − 3 − 4)	3.0	4.0
6. Tax	1.5	2.0
7. Net profit (5 − 6)	1.5	2.0
8. Net cash flow (4 + 7)	3.0	3.5
PV of cash flows	+18.4	+21.5
NPV	+3.4	+6.5
	Assumptions	
	Base Case	High Oil Prices and Recession Case
Market size	1 million	.8 million
Market share	.1	.13
Unit price	¥375,000	¥431,300
Unit variable cost	¥300,000	¥345,000
Fixed cost	¥3 billion	¥3.5 biilion

TABLE 10.3

How the NPV of the electric scooter project would be affected by higher oil prices and a world recession.

demand will be stronger than you anticipated and unit prices will be higher. And why look in isolation at the effect of an increase in price? If inflation pushes prices to the upper end of your range, it is quite probable that costs will also be inflated.

Sometimes the analyst can get around these problems by defining underlying variables so that they are roughly independent. But you cannot push *one-at-a-time* sensitivity analysis too far. It is impossible to obtain expected, optimistic, and pessimistic values for total *project* cash flows from the information in Table 10.2.

Scenario Analysis

If the variables are interrelated, it may help to consider some alternative plausible scenarios. For example, perhaps the company economist is worried about the possibility of another sharp rise in world oil prices. The direct effect of this would be to encourage the use of electrically powered transportation. The popularity of compact cars after the oil price increases in the 1970s leads you to estimate that an immediate 20 percent price rise in oil would enable you to capture an extra 3 percent of the scooter market. On the other hand, the economist also believes that higher oil prices would prompt a world recession and at the same time stimulate inflation. In that case, market size might be in the region of .8 million scooters and both prices and cost might be 15 percent higher than your initial estimates. Table 10.3 shows that this scenario of higher oil prices and recession would on balance help your new venture. Its NPV would increase to ¥6.5 billion.

Managers often find **scenario analysis** helpful. It allows them to look at different but *consistent* combinations of variables. Forecasters generally prefer to give an

| Inflows | | Outflows | | | | | | |
| | | Year 0 | Years 1–10 | | | | | |
Unit Sales, Thousands	Revenue, Years 1–10	Investment	Variable Costs	Fixed Costs	Taxes	PV Inflows	PV Outflows	NPV
0	0	15	0	3	−2.25	0	19.6	−19.6
100	37.5	15	30	3	1.5	230.4	227.0	3.4
200	75.0	15	60	3	5.25	460.8	434.4	26.4

TABLE 10.4

NPV of electric scooter project under different assumptions about unit sales (figures in ¥ billions except as noted).

estimate of revenues or costs under a particular scenario than to give some absolute optimistic or pessimistic value.

Break-Even Analysis

When we undertake a sensitivity analysis of a project or when we look at alternative scenarios, we are asking how serious it would be if sales or costs turned out to be worse than we forecasted. Managers sometimes prefer to rephrase this question and ask how bad sales can get before the project begins to lose money. This exercise is known as **break-even analysis.**

In the left-hand portion of Table 10.4 we set out the revenues and costs of the electric scooter project under different assumptions about annual sales.[2] In the right-hand portion of the table we discount these revenues and costs to give the *present value* of the inflows and the *present value* of the outflows. Net present value is of course the difference between these numbers.

You can see that NPV is strongly negative if the company does not produce a single scooter. It is just positive if (as expected) the company sells 100,000 scooters and is strongly positive if it sells 200,000. Clearly the *zero*-NPV point occurs at a little under 100,000 scooters.

In Figure 10.1 we have plotted the present value of the inflows and outflows under different assumptions about annual sales. The two lines cross when sales are 85,000 scooters. This is the point at which the project has zero NPV. As long as sales are greater than 85,000, the project has a positive NPV.[3]

Managers frequently calculate break-even points in terms of accounting profits rather than present values. Table 10.5 shows Otobai's after-tax profits at three levels of scooter sales. Figure 10.2 once again plots revenues and costs against sales. But the story this time is different. Figure 10.2, which is based on accounting profits, suggests a break-even of 60,000 scooters. Figure 10.1, which is based on present values, shows a break-even at 85,000 scooters. Why the difference?

When we work in terms of accounting profit, we deduct depreciation of ¥1.5 billion each year to cover the cost of the initial investment. If Otobai sells 60,000 scooters a year, revenues will be sufficient both to pay operating costs and to recover the

[2]Notice that if the project makes a loss, this loss can be used to reduce the tax bill on the rest of the company's business. In this case the project produces a tax saving—the tax outflow is negative.

[3]We could also calculate break-even sales by plotting equivalent annual costs and revenues. Of course, the break-even point would be identical at 85,000 scooters.

FIGURE 10.1

A break-even chart showing the present values of Otobai's cash inflows and outflows under different assumptions about unit sales. NPV is zero when sales are 85,000.

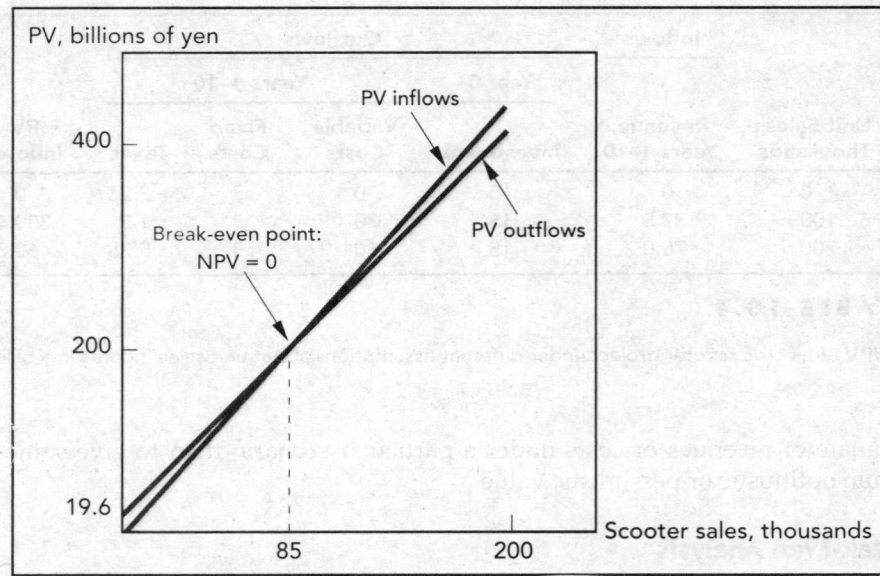

TABLE 10.5

The electric scooter project's accounting profit under different assumptions about unit sales (figures in ¥ billions except as noted).

Unit Sales, Thousands	Revenue	Variable Costs	Fixed Costs	Depreciation	Taxes	Total Costs	Profit after Tax
0	0	0	3	1.5	−2.25	2.25	−2.25
100	37.5	30	3	1.5	1.5	36.0	1.5
200	75.0	60	3	1.5	5.25	69.75	5.25

initial outlay of ¥15 billion. But they will *not* be sufficient to repay the *opportunity cost of capital* on that ¥15 billion. If we allow for the fact that the ¥15 billion could have been invested elsewhere to earn 10 percent, the equivalent annual cost of the investment is not ¥1.5 billion but ¥2.44 billion.[4]

---

[4]To calculate the equivalent annual cost of the initial ¥15 billion investment, we divide by the 10-year annuity factor for a 10 percent discount rate:

$$\text{Equivalent annual cost} = \frac{\text{investment}}{\text{10-year annuity factor}}$$

$$= \frac{15}{6.145} = ¥2.44 \text{ billion}$$

See Section 6.3.

The annual revenues at 85,000 scooters per year are about ¥31.9 billion. You can check that this is sufficient to cover variable costs, fixed costs, and taxes and still leave ¥2.44 billion per year to recover the ¥15 billion initial investment and a 10 percent return on that investment.

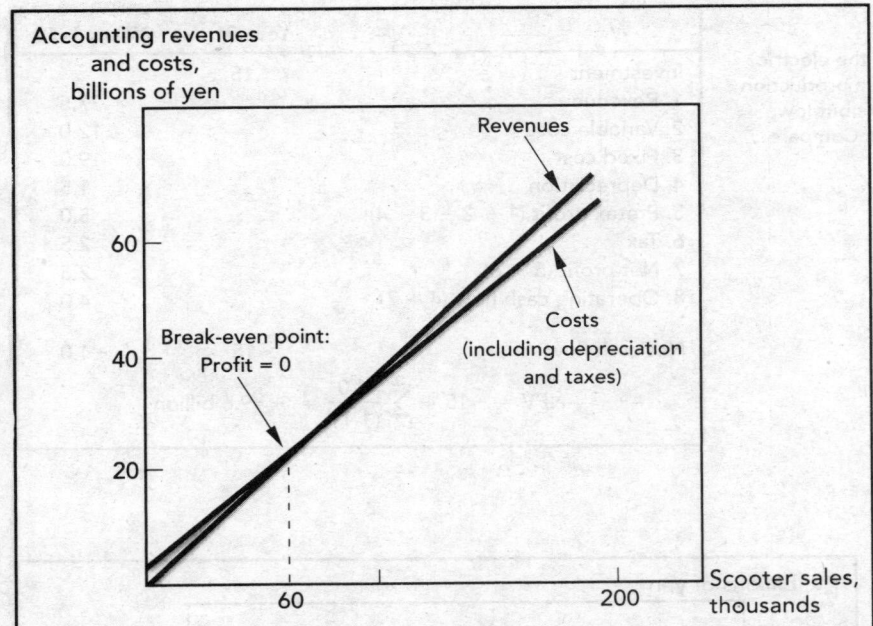

FIGURE 10.2

Sometimes break-even charts are constructed in terms of accounting numbers. After-tax profit is zero when sales are 60,000.

Companies that break even on an accounting basis are really making a loss—they are losing the opportunity cost of capital on their investment. Reinhardt has described a dramatic example of this mistake.[5] In 1971 Lockheed managers found themselves having to give evidence to Congress on the viability of the company's L-1011 TriStar program. They argued that the program appeared to be commercially attractive and that TriStar sales would eventually exceed the break-even point of about 200 aircraft. But in calculating this break-even point, Lockheed appears to have ignored the opportunity cost of the huge $1 billion capital investment on this project. Had it allowed for this cost, the break-even point would probably have been nearer to 500 aircraft.

Operating Leverage and Break-Even Points

Break-even charts like Figure 10.1 help managers appreciate *operating leverage,* that is, project exposure to fixed costs. Remember from Section 9.5 that high operating leverage means high risk, other things equal, of course.

The electric scooter project had low fixed costs, only ¥3 billion against projected revenues of ¥37.5 billion. But suppose Otobai now considers a different production technology with lower variable costs of only ¥120,000 per unit (versus ¥300,000 per unit) but higher fixed costs of ¥19 billion. Total forecasted production costs are lower (12 + 19 = ¥31 billion versus ¥33 billion), so profitability improves—compare Table 10.6 to Table 10.1. Project NPV increases to ¥9.6 billion.

Figure 10.3 is the new break-even chart. Break-even sales have *increased* to 88,000 (that's bad), even though total production costs have *fallen*. A new sensitivity analysis would show that project NPV is much more exposed to changes in market size,

---

[5]U. E. Reinhardt, "Break-Even Analysis for Lockheed's TriStar: An Application of Financial Theory," *Journal of Finance* 28 (September 1973), pp. 821–838.

TABLE 10.6

Cash-flow forecasts and PV for the electric scooter project, here assuming a production technology with high fixed costs but low total costs (figures in ¥ billions). Compare Table 10.1.

	Year 0	Years 1–10
Investment	15	
1. Revenue		37.5
2. Variable cost		12.0
3. Fixed cost		19.0
4. Depreciation		1.5
5. Pretax profit (1 − 2 − 3 − 4)		5.0
6. Tax		2.5
7. Net profit (5 − 6)		2.5
8. Operating cash flow (4 + 7)		4.0
Net cash flow	−15	+4.0

$$NPV = -15 + \sum_{t=1}^{10} \frac{4.0}{(1.1)^t} = +¥9.6 \text{ billion}$$

FIGURE 10.3

Break-even chart for an alternative production technology with higher fixed costs. Notice that break-even sales increase to 88,000. Compare Figure 10.1.

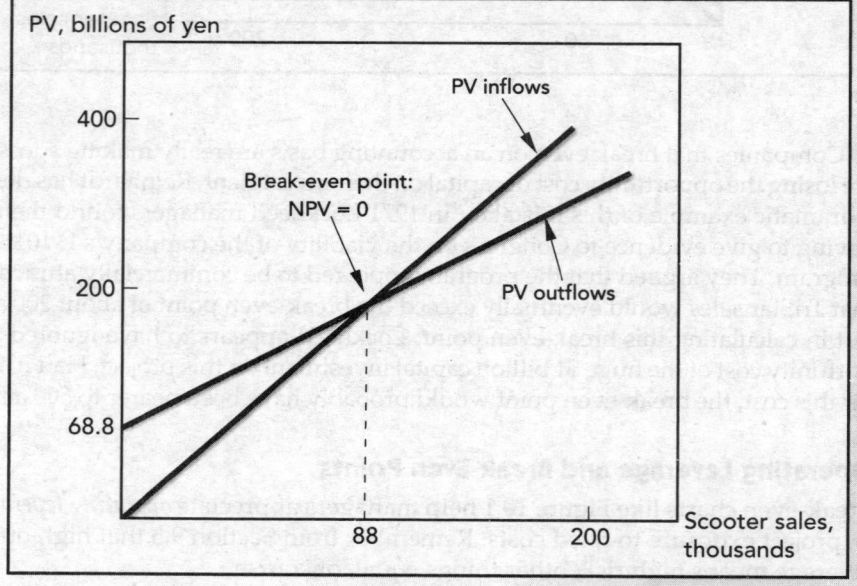

market share, or unit price. All of these differences can be traced to the higher fixed costs of the alternative production technology.

Is the alternative technology better than the original one? The financial manager would have to consider the alternative technology's higher business risk, and perhaps recompute NPV at a higher discount rate, before making a final decision.[6]

---

[6]He or she could use the procedures outlined in Section 9.5 to recalculate beta and come up with a new discount rate.

10.2 MONTE CARLO SIMULATION

Sensitivity analysis allows you to consider the effect of changing one variable at a time. By looking at the project under alternative scenarios, you can consider the effect of a *limited number* of plausible combinations of variables. **Monte Carlo simulation** is a tool for considering *all* possible combinations. It therefore enables you to inspect the entire distribution of project outcomes. The use of simulation in capital budgeting was first advocated by David Hertz[7] and McKinsey and Company, the management consultants.

Imagine that you are a gambler at Monte Carlo. You know nothing about the laws of probability (few casual gamblers do), but a friend has suggested to you a complicated strategy for playing roulette. Your friend has not actually tested the strategy but is confident that it will *on the average* give you a 2½ percent return for every 50 spins of the wheel. Your friend's optimistic estimate for any series of 50 spins is a profit of 55 percent; your friend's pessimistic estimate is a loss of 50 percent. How can you find out whether these really are the odds? An easy but possibly expensive way is to start playing and record the outcome at the end of each series of 50 spins. After, say, 100 series of 50 spins each, plot a frequency distribution of the outcomes and calculate the average and upper and lower limits. If things look good, you can then get down to some serious gambling.

An alternative is to tell a computer to simulate the roulette wheel and the strategy. In other words, you could instruct the computer to draw numbers out of its hat to determine the outcome of each spin of the wheel and then to calculate how much you would make or lose from the particular gambling strategy.

That would be an example of Monte Carlo simulation. In capital budgeting we replace the gambling strategy with a model of the project, and the roulette wheel with a model of the world in which the project operates. Let's see how this might work with our project for an electrically powered scooter.

Simulating the Electric Scooter Project

Step 1: Modeling the Project The first step in any simulation is to give the computer a precise model of the project. For example, the sensitivity analysis of the scooter project was based on the following implicit model of cash flow:

Cash flow = (revenues − costs − depreciation) × (1 − tax rate) + depreciation

Revenues = market size × market share × unit price

Costs = (market size × market share × variable unit cost) + fixed cost

This model of the project was all that you needed for the simpleminded sensitivity analysis that we described above. But if you wish to simulate the whole project, you need to think about how the variables are interrelated.

For example, consider the first variable—market size. The marketing department has estimated a market size of 1 million scooters in the first year of the project's life, but of course you do not know how things will work out. Actual market

---

[7]See D. B. Hertz, "Investment Policies that Pay Off," *Harvard Business Review* 46 (January–February 1968), pp. 96–108.

size will exceed or fall short of expectations by the amount of the department's forecast error:

$$\text{Market size, year 1} = \text{expected market size, year 1} \times \left(1 + \frac{\text{forecast error,}}{\text{year 1}}\right)$$

You *expect* the forecast error to be zero, but it could turn out to be positive or negative. Suppose, for example, that the actual market size turns out to be 1.1 million. That means a forecast error of 10 percent, or +.1:

$$\text{Market size, year 1} = 1 \times (1 + .1) = 1.1 \text{ million}$$

You can write the market size in the second year in exactly the same way:

$$\text{Market size, year 2} = \text{expected market size, year 2} \times \left(1 + \frac{\text{forecast error,}}{\text{year 2}}\right)$$

But at this point you must consider how the expected market size in year 2 is affected by what happens in year 1. If scooter sales are below expectations in year 1, it is likely that they will continue to be below in subsequent years. Suppose that a shortfall in sales in year 1 would lead you to revise down your forecast of sales in year 2 by a like amount. Then

$$\text{Expected market size, year 2} = \text{actual market size, year 1}$$

Now you can rewrite the market size in year 2 in terms of the actual market size in the previous year plus a forecast error:

$$\text{Market size, year 2} = \text{market size, year 1} \times \left(1 + \frac{\text{forecast error,}}{\text{year 2}}\right)$$

In the same way you can describe the expected market size in year 3 in terms of market size in year 2 and so on.

This set of equations illustrates how you can describe interdependence between different *periods*. But you also need to allow for interdependence between different *variables*. For example, the price of electrically powered scooters is likely to increase with market size. Suppose that this is the only uncertainty and that a 10 percent shortfall in market size would lead you to predict a 3 percent reduction in price. Then you could model the first year's price as follows:

$$\text{Price, year 1} = \text{expected price, year 1} \times \left(1 + \begin{array}{c}.3 \times \text{error in} \\ \text{market size} \\ \text{forecast,} \\ \text{year 1}\end{array}\right)$$

Then, if variations in market size exert a permanent effect on price, you can define the second year's price as

$$\text{Price, year 2} = \text{expected price, year 2} \times \left(1 + \begin{array}{c}.3 \times \text{error in} \\ \text{market size} \\ \text{forecast,} \\ \text{year 2}\end{array}\right)$$

$$= \text{actual price, year 1} \times \left(1 + \begin{array}{c}.3 \times \text{error in} \\ \text{market size} \\ \text{forecast,} \\ \text{year 2}\end{array}\right)$$

Notice how we have linked each period's selling price to the *actual* selling prices (including forecast error) in all previous periods. We used the same type of linkage for market size. These linkages mean that forecast errors accumulate; they do not cancel out over time. Thus, uncertainty *increases* with time: The farther out you look into the future, the more the actual price or market size may depart from your original forecast.

The complete model of your project would include a set of equations for each of the variables: market size, price, market share, unit variable cost, and fixed cost. Even if you allowed for only a few interdependencies between variables and across time, the result would be quite a complex list of equations.[8] Perhaps that is not a bad thing if it forces you to understand what the project is all about. Model building is like spinach: You may not like the taste, but it is good for you.

Step 2: Specifying Probabilities   Remember the procedure for simulating the gambling strategy? The first step was to specify the strategy, the second was to specify the numbers on the roulette wheel, and the third was to tell the computer to select these numbers at random and calculate the results of the strategy:

The steps are just the same for your scooter project:

Think about how you might go about specifying your possible errors in forecasting market size. You *expect* market size to be 1 million scooters. You obviously don't think that you are underestimating or overestimating, so the expected forecast error is zero. On the other hand, the marketing department has given you a range of possible estimates. Market size could be as low as .85 million scooters or as high as 1.15 million scooters. Thus the forecast error has an expected value of 0 and a range of plus or minus 15 percent. If the marketing department has in fact given you the lowest and highest possible outcomes, actual market size should fall somewhere within this range with near certainty.[9]

That takes care of market size; now you need to draw up similar estimates of the possible forecast errors for each of the other variables that are in your model.

---

[8] Specifying the interdependencies is the hardest and most important part of a simulation. If all components of project cash flows were unrelated, simulation would rarely be necessary.

[9] Suppose "near certainty" means "99 percent of the time." If forecast errors are normally distributed, this degree of certainty requires a range of plus or minus three standard deviations.

Other distributions could, of course, be used. For example, the marketing department may view any market size between .85 and 1.15 million scooters as *equally likely*. In that case the simulation would require a uniform (rectangular) distribution of forecast errors.

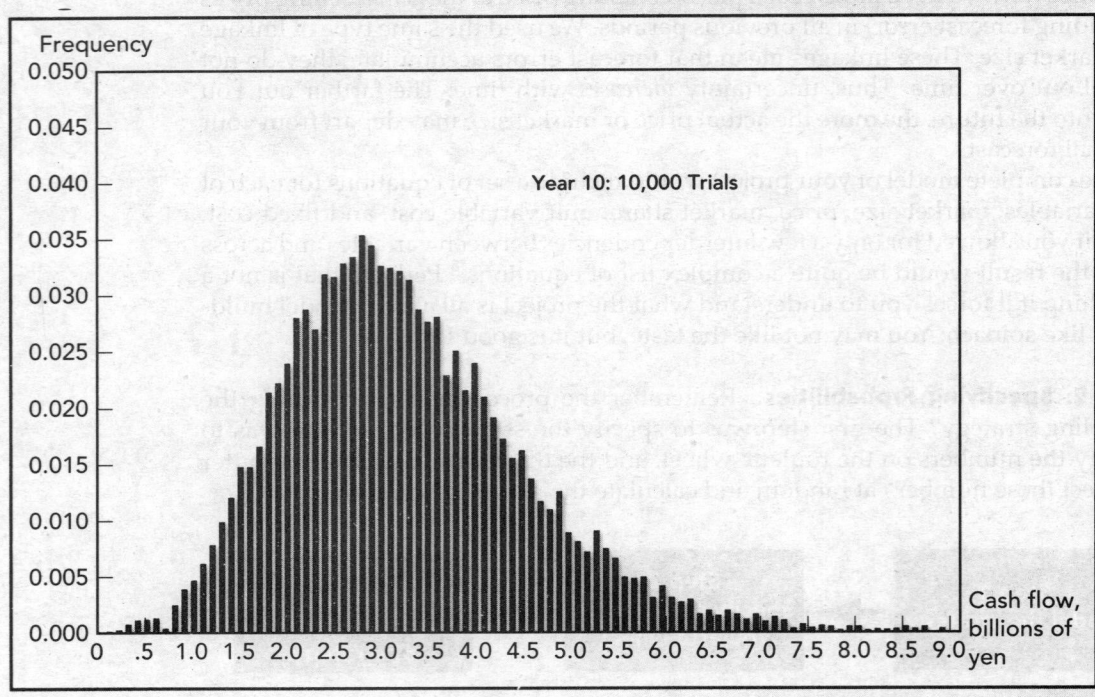

FIGURE 10.4

Simulation of cash flows for year 10 of the electric scooter project.

Step 3: Simulate the Cash Flows   The computer now *samples* from the distribution of the forecast errors, calculates the resulting cash flows for each period, and records them. After many iterations you begin to get accurate estimates of the probability distributions of the project cash flows—accurate, that is, only to the extent that your model and the probability distributions of the forecast errors are accurate. Remember the GIGO principle: "Garbage in, garbage out."

Figure 10.4 shows part of the output from an actual simulation of the electric scooter project.[10] Note the positive skewness of the outcomes—very large outcomes are more likely than very small ones. This is common and realistic when forecast errors accumulate over time. Because of the skewness the average cash flow is somewhat higher than the most likely outcome; in other words, a bit to the right of the peak of the distribution.[11]

Step 4: Calculate Present Value   The distributions of project cash flows should allow you to calculate the expected cash flows more accurately. In the final step you need to discount these expected cash flows to find present value.

---

[10]These are actual outputs from Crystal Ball™ software used with an EXCEL spreadsheet program. The simulation assumed annual forecast errors were normally distributed and ran through 10,000 trials. We thank Christopher Howe for running the simulation.

[11]When you are working with cash-flow forecasts, bear in mind the distinction between the expected value and the most likely (or modal) value. Present values are based on *expected* cash flows—that is, the probability-weighted average of the possible future cash flows. If the distribution of possible outcomes is skewed to the right as in Figure 10.4, the expected cash flow will be greater than the most likely cash flow.

FIGURE 10.5

Research and testing of a potential new drug from discovery to initial sales. This figure concentrates on the odds that the drug will pass all required clinical tests and be approved by the Food and Drug Administration (FDA). Only a small fraction of drug candidates identified in basic research prove safe and effective and achieve profitable production. The "Stop" signs indicate failure and abandonment.

Simulation of Pharmaceutical Research and Development

Simulation, though sometimes costly and complicated, has the obvious merit of compelling the forecaster to face up to uncertainty and to interdependencies. By constructing a detailed Monte Carlo simulation, you will gain a better understanding of how the project works and what could go wrong with it. You will have confirmed, or improved, your forecasts of future cash flows, and your calculations of project NPV will be more confident.

Several large pharmaceutical companies have used Monte Carlo simulation to analyze investments in research and development (R&D) of new drugs. Figure 10.5 sketches the progression of a new drug from its infancy, when it is identified as a promising chemical compound, all the way through the R&D required for approval for sale by the Food and Drug Administration (FDA). At each phase of R&D, the company must decide whether to press on to the next phase or halt. The R&D effort lasts 10 to 12 years from preclinical testing to FDA approval and can cost $300 million or more.[12]

The pharmaceutical companies face two kinds of uncertainty:

1. *Will the compound work?* Will it have harmful side effects? Will it ultimately gain FDA approval? (Most drugs do not: Of 10,000 promising compounds,

---

[12]Myers and Howe estimated the average cost of bringing one new drug to market as about $300 million after tax. The estimate was based on R&D costs and success rates from the 1970s and 1980s, but adjusted for inflation through 1994. See S. C. Myers and C. Howe, "A Life-Cycle Model of Pharmaceutical R&D," MIT Program on the Pharmaceutical Industry, April 1997.

only 1 or 2 may ever get to market. The 1 or 2 that are marketed have to generate enough cash flow to make up for the 9,999 or 9,998 that fail.)

2. *Market success.* FDA approval does not guarantee that a drug will sell. A competitor may be there first with a similar (or better) drug. The company may or may not be able to sell the drug worldwide. Selling prices and marketing costs are unknown.

Imagine that you are standing at the top left of Figure 10.5. A proposed research program will investigate a promising class of compounds. Could you write down the expected cash inflows and outflows of the program up to 25 or 30 years in the future? We suggest that no mortal could do so without a model to help; simulation may provide the answer.[13]

Simulation may sound like a panacea for the world's ills, but, as usual, you pay for what you get. Sometimes you pay for more than you get. It is not just a matter of the time and money spent in building the model. It is extremely difficult to estimate interrelationships between variables and the underlying probability distributions, even when you are trying to be honest.[14] But in capital budgeting, forecasters are seldom completely impartial and the probability distributions on which simulations are based can be highly biased.

In practice, a simulation that attempts to be realistic will also be complex. Therefore the decision maker may delegate the task of constructing the model to management scientists or consultants. The danger here is that, even if the builders understand their creation, the decision maker cannot and therefore does not rely on it. This is a common but ironic experience: The model that was intended to open up black boxes ends up creating another one.

10.3   REAL OPTIONS AND DECISION TREES

If financial managers treat projects as black boxes, they may be tempted to think only of the first accept–reject decision and to ignore the subsequent investment decisions that may be tied to it. But if subsequent investment decisions depend on those made today, then today's decision may depend on what you plan to do tomorrow.

When you use discounted cash flow (DCF) to value a project, you implicitly assume that the firm will hold the assets passively. But managers are not paid to be dummies. After they have invested in a new project, they do not simply sit back and watch the future unfold. If things go well, the project may be expanded; if they go badly, the project may be cut back or abandoned altogether. Projects that can easily be modified in these ways are more valuable than those that don't provide such flexibility. The more uncertain the outlook, the more valuable this flexibility becomes.

That sounds obvious, but notice that sensitivity analysis and Monte Carlo simulation do not recognize the opportunity to modify projects.[15] For example,

---

[13]N. A. Nichols, "Scientific Management at Merck: An Interview with CFO Judy Lewent," *Harvard Business Review* 72 (January–February 1994), p. 91.

[14]These difficulties are less severe for the pharmaceutical industry than for most other industries. Pharmaceutical companies have accumulated a great deal of information on the probabilities of scientific and clinical success and on the time and money required for clinical testing and FDA approval.

[15]Some simulation models *do* recognize the possibility of changing policy. For example, when a pharmaceutical company uses simulation to analyze its R&D decisions, it allows for the possibility that the company can abandon the development at each phase.

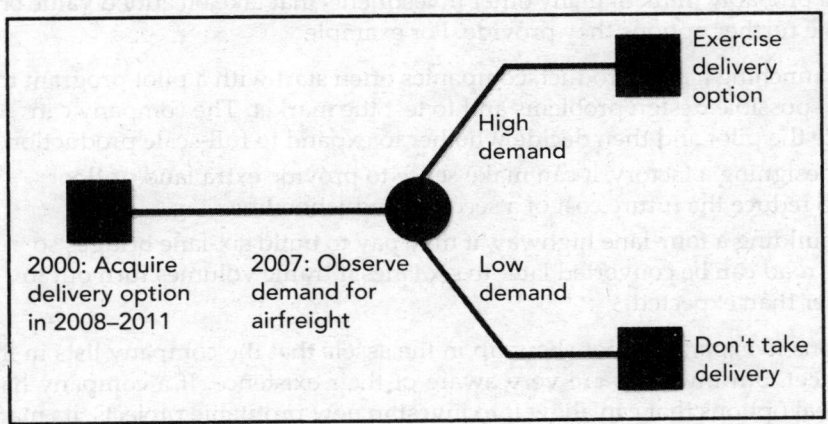

FIGURE 10.6

FedEx's expansion option expressed as a simple decision tree.

think back to the Otobai electric scooter project. In real life, if things go wrong with the project, Otobai would abandon to cut its losses. If so, the worst outcomes would not be as devastating as our sensitivity analysis and simulation suggested.

Options to modify projects are known as **real options.** Managers may not always use the term real option to describe these opportunities; for example, they may refer to "intangible advantages" of easy-to-modify projects. But when they review major investment proposals, these option intangibles are often the key to their decisions.

The Option to Expand

In 2000 FedEx placed an order for 10 Airbus A380 superjumbo transport planes for delivery in the years 2008–2011. Each flight of an A380 freighter will be capable of making a 200,000 pound dent in the massive volume of goods that FedEx carries each day, so the decision could have a huge impact on FedEx's worldwide business. If FedEx's long-haul airfreight business continues to expand and the superjumbo is efficient and reliable, the company will need more superjumbos. But it cannot be sure they will be needed.

Rather than placing further firm orders in 2000, FedEx has secured a place in the Airbus production line by acquiring *options* to buy a "substantial number" of additional aircraft at a predetermined price. These options do not commit the company to expand but give it the flexibility to do so.

Figure 10.6 displays FedEx's expansion option as a simple **decision tree.** You can think of it as a game between FedEx and fate. Each square represents an action or decision by the company. Each circle represents an outcome revealed by fate. In this case there is only one outcome in 2007,[16] when fate reveals the airfreight demand and FedEx's capacity needs. FedEx then decides whether to exercise its options and buy additional A380s. Here the future decision is easy: Buy the airplanes only if demand is high and the company can operate them profitably. If demand is low, FedEx walks away and leaves Airbus with the problem of selling the planes that were reserved for FedEx to some other customer.

---

[16]We assume that FedEx can wait until 2007 to decide whether to acquire the additional planes.

You can probably think of many other investments that take on added value because of the further options they provide. For example

- When launching a new product, companies often start with a pilot program to iron out possible design problems and to test the market. The company can evaluate the pilot and then decide whether to expand to full-scale production.
- When designing a factory, it can make sense to provide extra land or floor space to reduce the future cost of a second production line.
- When building a four-lane highway, it may pay to build six-lane bridges so that the road can be converted later to six lanes if traffic volumes turn out to be higher than expected.

Such options to expand do not show up in the assets that the company lists in its balance sheet, but investors are very aware of their existence. If a company has valuable real options that can allow it to invest in new profitable projects, its market value will be higher than the value of its physical assets now in place.

In Chapter 4 we showed how the present value of growth opportunities (PVGO) contributes to the value of a company's common stock. PVGO equals the forecasted total NPV of future investments. But it's better to think of PVGO as the value of the firm's *options* to invest and expand. The firm is not obliged to grow. It can invest more if the number of positive-NPV projects turns out high or slow down if that number turns out low. The flexibility to adapt investment to future opportunities is one of the factors that makes PVGO so valuable.

The Option to Abandon

If the option to expand has value, what about the decision to bail out? Projects don't just go on until assets expire of old age. The decision to terminate a project is usually taken by management, not by nature. Once the project is no longer profitable, the company will cut its losses and exercise its option to abandon the project.[17]

Some assets are easier to bail out of than others. Tangible assets are usually easier to sell than intangible ones. It helps to have active secondhand markets, which really exist only for standardized items. Real estate, airplanes, trucks, and certain machine tools are likely to be relatively easy to sell. On the other hand, the knowledge accumulated by a software company's research and development program is a specialized intangible asset and probably would not have significant abandonment value. (Some assets, such as old mattresses, even have *negative* abandonment value; you have to pay to get rid of them. It is costly to decommission nuclear power plants or to reclaim land that has been strip-mined.)

Example. Managers should recognize the option to abandon when they make the initial investment in a new project or venture. For example, suppose you must choose between two technologies for production of a Wankel-engine outboard motor.

1. Technology A uses computer-controlled machinery custom-designed to produce the complex shapes required for Wankel engines in high volumes and at low cost. But if the Wankel outboard doesn't sell, this equipment will be worthless.

---

[17]The abandonment option was first analyzed by A. A. Robichek and J. C. Van Horne, "Abandonment Value in Capital Budgeting," *Journal of Finance* 22 (December 1967), pp. 577–590.

2. Technology B uses standard machine tools. Labour costs are much higher, but the machinery can be sold for $10 million if the engine doesn't sell.

Technology A looks better in a DCF analysis of the new product because it was designed to have the lowest possible cost at the planned production volume. Yet you can sense the advantage of technology B's flexibility if you are unsure about whether the new outboard will sink or swim in the marketplace.

We can make the value of this flexibility concrete by expressing it as a real option. Just for simplicity, assume that the initial capital outlays for technologies A and B are the same. Technology A, with its low-cost customized machinery, will provide a payoff of $18.5 million if the outboard is popular with boat owners and $8.5 million if it is not. Think of these payoffs as the project's cash flow in its first year of production plus the present value of all subsequent cash flows. The corresponding payoffs to technology B are $18 million and $8 million.

	Payoffs from Producing Outboard ($ millions)	
	Technology A	Technology B
Buoyant demand	$18.5	$18
Sluggish demand	8.5	8

If you are obliged to continue in production regardless of how unprofitable the project turns out to be, then technology A is clearly the superior choice. But remember that at year-end you can bail out of technology B for $10 million. If the outboard is not a success in the market, you are better off selling the plant and equipment for $10 million than continuing with a project that has a present value of only $8 million.

Figure 10.7 summarizes this example as a decision tree. The abandonment option occurs at the right-hand boxes for Technology B. The decisions are obvious: continue if demand is buoyant, abandon otherwise. Thus the payoffs to Technology B are:

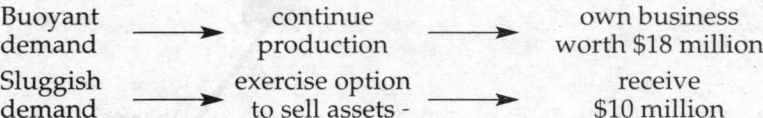

| Buoyant demand | → | continue production | → | own business worth $18 million |
| Sluggish demand | → | exercise option to sell assets - | → | receive $10 million |

Technology B provides an insurance policy: If the outboard's sales are disappointing, you can abandon the project and recover $10 million. You can think of this abandonment option as an option to sell the assets for $10 million. The total value of the project using technology B is its DCF value, assuming that the company does not abandon, *plus* the value of the abandonment option. When you value this option, you are placing a value on flexibility.

Two Other Real Options

These are not the only real options. For example, companies with positive-NPV projects are not obliged to undertake them right away. If the outlook is uncertain, you may be able to avoid a costly mistake by waiting a bit. Such options to postpone investment are called *timing options.*

FIGURE 10.7

Decision tree for the
Wankel outboard motor
project. Technology B
allows the firm to
abandon the project and
recover $10 million if
demand is sluggish.

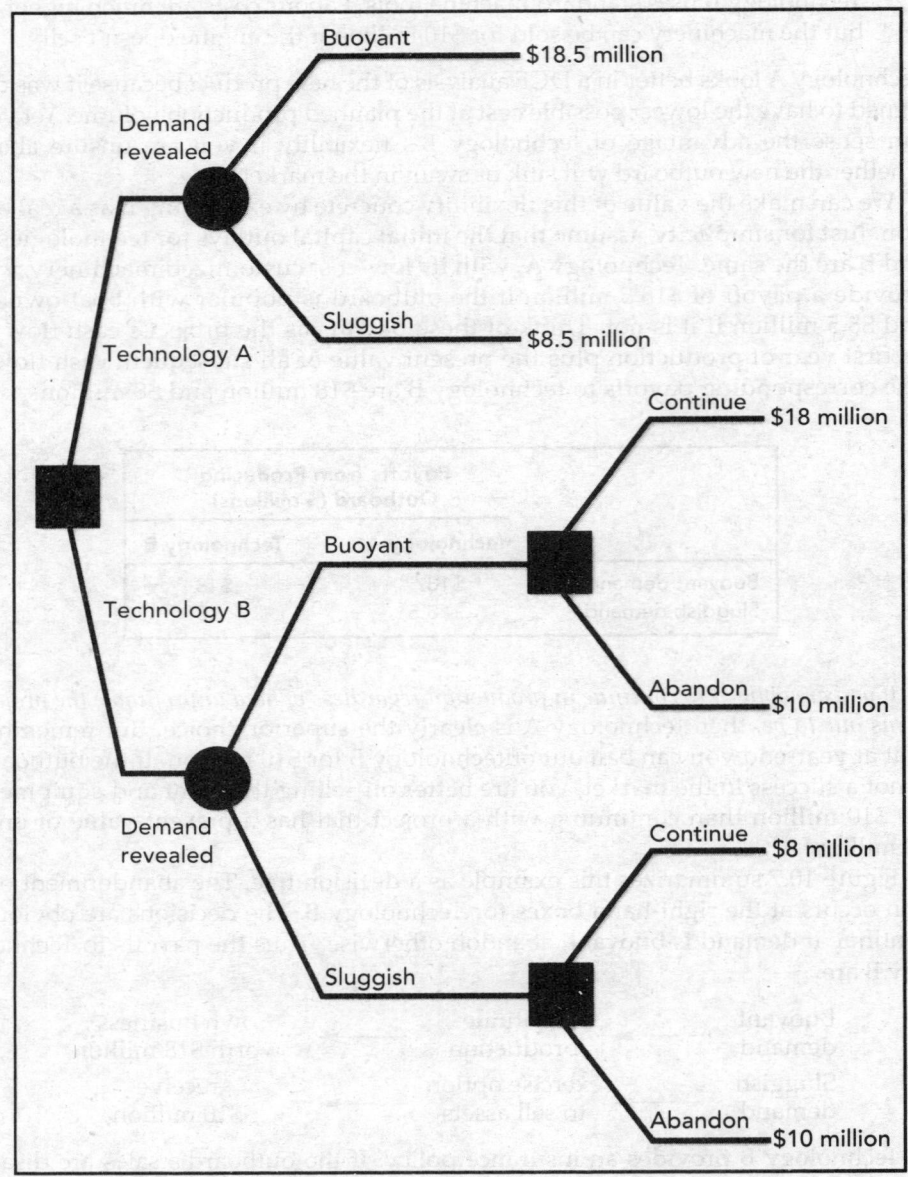

When companies undertake new investments, they generally think about the
possibility that at a later stage they may wish to modify the project. After all, today everybody may be demanding round pegs, but, who knows, tomorrow
square ones could be all the rage. In that case you need a plant that provides the
flexibility to produce a variety of peg shapes. In just the same way, it may be
worth paying up front for the flexibility to vary the inputs. For example, in Chapter 22 we will describe how electric utilities often build in the option to switch be-

tween burning oil to burning natural gas. We refer to these opportunities as *production options*.

More on Decision Trees

We will return to all these real options in Chapter 22, after we have covered the theory of option valuation in Chapters 20 and 21. But we will close this chapter with a closer look at decision trees.

Decision trees are commonly used to describe the real options imbedded in capital investment projects. But decision trees were used in the analysis of projects years before real options were first explicitly identified.[18] Decision trees can help to understand project risk and how future decisions will affect project cash flows. Even if you never learn or use option valuation theory, decision trees belong in your financial toolkit.

The best way to appreciate how decision trees can be used in project analysis is to work through a detailed example.

An Example: Magna Charter

Magna Charter is a new corporation formed by Agnes Magna to provide an executive flying service for the southeastern United States. The founder thinks there will be a ready demand from businesses that cannot justify a full-time company plane but nevertheless need one from time to time. However, the venture is not a sure thing. There is a 40 percent chance that demand in the first year will be low. If it is low, there is a 60 percent chance that it will remain low in subsequent years. On the other hand, if the initial demand is high, there is an 80 percent chance that it will stay high.

The immediate problem is to decide what kind of plane to buy. A turboprop costs $550,000. A piston-engine plane costs only $250,000 but has less capacity and customer appeal. Moreover, the piston-engine plane is an old design and likely to depreciate rapidly. Ms. Magna thinks that next year secondhand piston aircraft will be available for only $150,000.

That gives Ms. Magna an idea: Why not start out with one piston plane and buy another if demand is still high? It will cost only $150,000 to expand. If demand is low, Magna Charter can sit tight with one small, relatively inexpensive aircraft.

Figure 10.8 displays these choices. The square on the left marks the company's initial decision to purchase a turboprop for $550,000 or a piston aircraft for $250,000. After the company has made its decision, fate decides on the first year's demand. You can see in parentheses the probability that demand will be high or low, and you can see the expected cash flow for each combination of aircraft and demand level. At the end of the year the company has a second decision to make if it has a piston-engine aircraft: It can either expand or sit tight. This decision point is marked by the second square. Finally fate takes over again and selects the level of demand for year 2. Again you can see in parentheses the probability of high or low demand. Notice that the probabilities for the second year depend on the first-period outcomes. For example, if demand is high in the first period, then there is an 80 percent chance that it will also be high in the second. The chance of high

---

[18]The use of decision trees was first advocated by J. Magee in "How to Use Decision Trees in Capital Investment," *Harvard Business Review* 42(September–October 1964), pp. 79–96. Real options were first identified in S. C. Myers, "Determinants of Corporate Borrowing," *Journal of Financial Economics* 5 (November 1977), pp. 146–175.

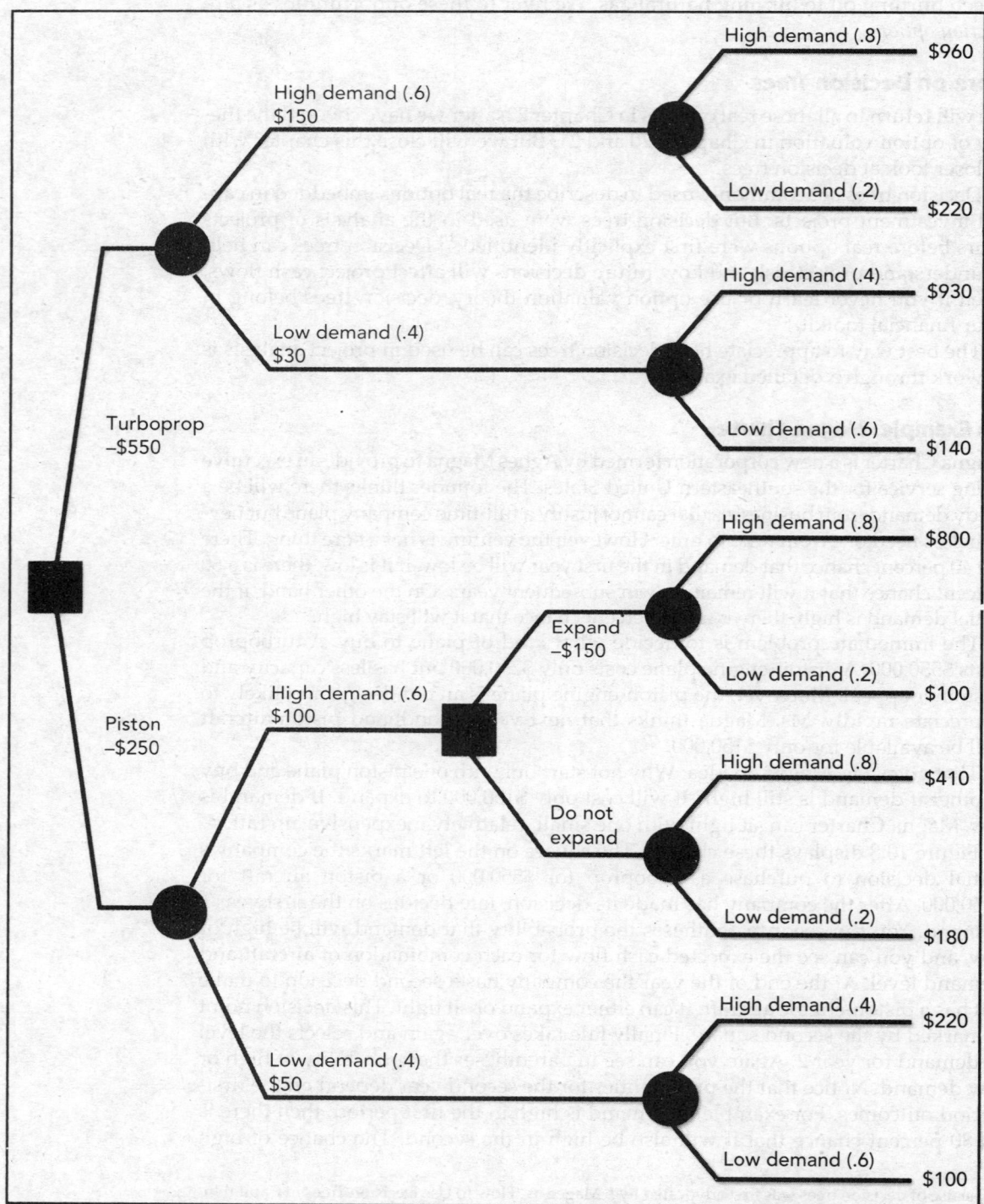

FIGURE 10.8

Decision tree for Magna Charter. Should it buy a turboprop or a smaller piston-engine plane? A second piston plane can be purchased in year 1 if demand turns out to be high. (All figures are in thousands. Probabilities are in parentheses.)

demand in *both* the first and second periods is .6 × .8 = .48. After the parentheses we again show the profitability of the project for each combination of aircraft and demand level. You can interpret each of these figures as the present value at the end of year 2 of the cash flows for that and all subsequent years.

The problem for Ms. Magna is to decide what to do today. We solve that problem by thinking first what she would do next year. This means that we start at the right side of the tree and work backward to the beginning on the left.

The only decision that Ms. Magna needs to make next year is whether to expand if purchase of a piston-engine plane is succeeded by high demand. If she expands, she invests $150,000 and receives a payoff of $800,000 if demand continues to be high and $100,000 if demand falls. So her *expected* payoff is

$$\text{(Probability high demand} \times \text{payoff with high demand)}$$
$$+ \text{(probability low demand} \times \text{payoff with}$$
$$\text{low demand)}$$
$$= (.8 \times 800) + (.2 \times 100) = +660, \text{ or } \$660,000$$

If the opportunity cost of capital for this venture is 10 percent,[19] then the net present value of expanding, computed as of year 1, is

$$\text{NPV} = -150 + \frac{660}{1.10} = +450, \text{ or } \$450,000$$

If Ms. Magna does *not* expand, the expected payoff is

$$\text{(Probability high demand} \times \text{payoff with high demand)}$$
$$+ \text{(probability low demand} \times \text{payoff with}$$
$$\text{low demand)}$$
$$= (.8 \times 410) + (.2 \times 180) = +364, \text{ or } \$364,000$$

The net present value of *not* expanding, computed as of year 1, is

$$\text{NPV} = 0 + \frac{364}{1.10} = +331, \text{ or } \$331,000$$

Expansion obviously pays if market demand is high.

Now that we know what Magna Charter ought to do if faced with the expansion decision, we can roll back to today's decision. If the first piston-engine plane is bought, Magna can expect to receive cash worth $550,000 in year 1 if demand is high and cash worth $185,000 if it is low:

____
[19]We are guilty here of assuming away one of the most difficult questions. Just as in the Vegetron mop case in Chapter 9, the most risky part of Ms. Magna's venture is likely to be the initial prototype project. Perhaps we should use a lower discount rate for the second piston-engine plane than for the first.

The net present value of the investment in the piston-engine plane is therefore $117,000:

$$\text{NPV} = -250 + \frac{.6(550) + .4(185)}{1.10} = +117, \text{ or } \$117,000$$

If Magna buys the turboprop, there are no future decisions to analyze, and so there is no need to roll back. We just calculate expected cash flows and discount:

$$\text{NPV} = -550 + \frac{.6(150) + .4(30)}{1.10}$$

$$+ \frac{.6[.8(960) + .2(220)] + .4[.4(930) + .6(140)]}{(1.10)^2}$$

$$= -550 + \frac{102}{1.10} + \frac{670}{(1.10)^2} = +96, \text{ or } \$96,000$$

Thus the investment in the piston-engine plane has an NPV of $117,000; the investment in the turboprop has an NPV of $96,000. The piston-engine plane is the better bet. Note, however, that the choice would be different if we forgot to take account of the option to expand. In that case the NPV of the piston-engine plane would drop from $117,000 to $52,000:

$$\text{NPV} = -250 + \frac{.6(100) + .4(50)}{1.10}$$

$$+ \frac{.6[.8(410) + .2(180)] + .4[.4(220) + .6(100)]}{(1.10)^2}$$

$$= +52, \text{ or } \$52,000$$

The value of the option to expand is, therefore,

$$117 - 52 = +65, \text{ or } \$65,000$$

The decision tree in Figure 10.8 recognizes that, if Ms. Magna buys one piston-engine plane, she is not stuck with that decision. She has the option to expand by buying an additional plane if demand turns out to be unexpectedly high. But Figure 10.8 also assumes that, if Ms. Magna goes for the big time by buying a turboprop, there is nothing that she can do if demand turns out to be unexpectedly *low*. That is unrealistic. If business in the first year is poor, it may pay for Ms. Magna to sell the turboprop and abandon the venture entirely. In Figure 10.8 we could represent this option to bail out by adding an extra decision point (a further square) if the company buys the turboprop and first-year demand is low. If that happens, Ms. Magna could decide either to sell the plane or to hold on and hope demand recovers. If the abandonment option is sufficiently valuable, it may make sense to take the turboprop and shoot for the big payoff.

Pro and Con Decision Trees

Any cash-flow forecast rests on some assumption about the firm's future investment and operating strategy. Often that assumption is implicit. Decision trees force the underlying strategy into the open. By displaying the links between today's and tomorrow's decisions, they help the financial manager to find the strategy with the highest net present value.

The trouble with decision trees is that they get so _____ complex so _____ quickly (insert your own expletives). What will Magna Charter do if demand is neither high nor low but just middling? In that event Ms. Magna might sell the turboprop and buy a piston-engine plane, or she might defer expansion and abandonment decisions until year 2. Perhaps middling demand requires a decision about a price cut or an intensified sales campaign.

We could draw a new decision tree covering this expanded set of events and decisions. Try it if you like: You'll see how fast the circles, squares, and branches accumulate.

Life is complex, and there is very little we can do about it. It is therefore unfair to criticize decision trees because they can become complex. Our criticism is reserved for analysts who let the complexity become overwhelming. The point of decision trees is to allow explicit analysis of possible future events and decisions. They should be judged not on their comprehensiveness but on whether they show the most important links between today's and tomorrow's decisions. Decision trees used in real life will be more complex than Figure 10.8, but they will nevertheless display only a small fraction of possible future events and decisions. Decision trees are like grapevines: They are productive only if they are vigorously pruned.

Decision trees can help identify the future choices available to the manager and can give a clearer view of the cash flows and risks of a project. However, our analysis of the Magna Charter project begged an important question. The option to expand enlarged the spread of possible outcomes and therefore increased the risk of investing in a piston aircraft. Conversely, the option to bail out would narrow the spread of possible outcomes, reducing the risk of investment. We should have used different discount rates to recognize these changes in risk, but decision trees do not tell us how to do this. But the situation is not hopeless. Modern techniques of option pricing can value these investment options. We will describe these techniques in Chapters 20 and 21, and turn again to real options in Chapter 22.

Decision Trees and Monte Carlo Simulation

We have said that any cash-flow forecast rests on assumptions about future investment and operating strategy. Think back to the Monte Carlo simulation model that we constructed for Otobai's electric scooter project. What strategy was that based on? We don't know. Inevitably Otobai will face decisions about pricing, production, expansion, and abandonment, but the model builder's assumptions about these decisions are buried in the model's equations. The model builder may have implicitly identified a future strategy for Otobai, but it is clearly not the optimal one. There will be some runs of the model when nearly everything goes wrong and when in real life Otobai would abandon to cut its losses. Yet the model goes on period after period, heedless of the drain on Otobai's cash resources. The most unfavorable outcomes reported by the simulation model would never be encountered in real life.

On the other hand, the simulation model probably understates the project's potential value if nearly everything goes right: There is no provision for expanding to take advantage of good luck.

Most simulation models incorporate a business-as-usual strategy, which is fine as long as there are no major surprises. The greater the divergence from expected levels of market growth, market share, cost, etc., the less realistic is the simulation. Therefore the extreme high and low simulated values—the "tails" of the simulated distributions—should be treated with extreme caution. Don't take the area under the tails as realistic probabilities of disaster or bonanza.

SUMMARY

There is more to capital budgeting than grinding out calculations of net present value. If you can identify the major uncertainties, you may find that it is worth undertaking some additional preliminary research that will *confirm* whether the project is worthwhile. And even if you decide that you have done all you can to resolve the uncertainties, you still want to be aware of the potential problems. You do not want to be caught by surprise if things go wrong: You want to be ready to take corrective action.

There are three ways in which companies try to identify the principal threats to a project's success. The simplest is *sensitivity analysis.* In this case the manager considers in turn each of the determinants of the project's success and recalculates NPV at very optimistic and very pessimistic levels of that variable. This establishes a range of possible values. The project is "sensitive to" the variable if the range is wide, especially on the pessimistic side.

Sensitivity analysis of this kind is easy, but it is not always helpful. Variables do not usually change one at a time. If costs are higher than you expect, it is a good bet that prices will be higher also. And if prices are higher, it is a good bet that sales volume will be lower. If you don't allow for the dependencies between the swings and the merry-go-rounds, you may get a false idea of the hazards of the fairground business. Many companies try to cope with this problem by examining the effect on the project of alternative plausible combinations of variables. In other words, they will estimate the net present value of the project under different *scenarios* and compare these estimates with the base case.

In a sensitivity analysis you change variables one at a time: When you analyze scenarios, you look at a limited number of alternative combinations of variables. If you want to go whole hog and look at *all* possible combinations of variables, then you will probably use *Monte Carlo simulation* to cope with the complexity. In that case you must construct a complete model of the project and specify the probability distribution of each of the determinants of cash flow. You can then ask the computer to select a random number for each of these determinants and work out the cash flows that would result. After the computer has repeated this process a few thousand times, you should have a fair idea of the expected cash flow in each year and the spread of possible cash flows.

Simulation can be a very useful tool. The discipline of building a model of the project can in itself lead you to a deeper understanding of the project. And once you have constructed your model, it is a simple matter to see how the outcomes would be affected by altering the scope of the project or the distribution of any of the variables.

Elementary treatises on capital budgeting sometimes create the impression that, once the manager has made an investment decision, there is nothing to do but sit back and watch the cash flows unfold. In practice, companies are constantly modifying their operations. If cash flows are better than anticipated, the project may be expanded; if they are worse, it may be contracted or abandoned altogether. Options to modify projects are known as *real options*. In this chapter we introduced the main categories of real options: *expansion* options, *abandonment* options, *timing* options, and options providing *flexibility in production*.

Good managers take account of real options when they value a project. One convenient way to summarize real options and their cash flow consequences is to create a *decision tree*. You identify the things that could happen to the project and the main counteractions that you might take. Then, working back from the future to the present, you can consider which action you *should* take in each case.

Decision trees can help the financial manager to identify real options and their impacts on project risks and cash flows. The options may increase or decrease project risk. Because risk changes, standard discounted-cash-flow techniques can only approximate the present value of real options. We will cover option-valuation methods in Chapter 21 and revisit real options in Chapter 22.

FURTHER READING

For an excellent case study of break-even analysis, see:

U. E. Reinhardt: "Break-Even Analysis for Lockheed's TriStar: An Application of Financial Theory," *Journal of Finance*, 28:821–838 (September 1973).

Hax and Wiig discuss how Monte Carlo simulation and decision trees were used in an actual capital budgeting decision:

A. C. Hax and K. M. Wiig: "The Use of Decision Analysis in Capital Investment Problems," *Sloan Management Review*, 17:19–48 (Winter 1976).

Merck's use of Monte Carlo simulation is discussed in:

N. A. Nichols: "Scientific Management at Merck: An Interview with Judy Lewent," *Harvard Business Review*, 72:89–99 (January–February 1994).

Three not-too-technical references on real options are listed below. Additional references follow Chapter 22.

M. Amram and N. Kulatilaka: *Real Options: Managing Strategic Investments in an Uncertain World*, Harvard Business School Press, Boston, 1999.

A. Dixit and R. Pindyck: "The Options Approach to Capital Investment," *Harvard Business Review*, 73:105–115 (May–June 1995).

W. C. Kester: "Today's Options for Tomorrow's Growth," *Harvard Business Review*, 62:153–160 (March–April 1984).

QUIZ

1. Define and briefly explain each of the following terms or procedures:
   a. Sensitivity analysis
   b. Scenario analysis
   c. Break-even analysis
   d. Monte Carlo simulation
   e. Decision tree
   f. Real option
   g. Abandonment value
   h. Expansion value

2. True or false?
   a. Sensitivity analysis is unnecessary for projects with asset betas that are equal to zero.

b. Sensitivity analysis can be used to identify the variables most crucial to a project's success.

c. If only one variable is uncertain, sensitivity analysis gives "optimistic" and "pessimistic" values for project cash flow and NPV.

d. The break-even sales level of a project is higher when *break even* is defined in terms of NPV rather than accounting income.

e. Monte Carlo simulation can be used to help forecast cash flows.

f. Monte Carlo simulation eliminates the need to estimate a project's opportunity cost of capital.

3. What are the advantages of scenario analysis compared to sensitivity analysis?

4. How should Monte Carlo simulation be used to help determine a project's NPV?

5. Suppose a manager has already estimated a project's cash flows, calculated its NPV, and done a sensitivity analysis like the one shown in Table 10.2. List the additional steps required to carry out a Monte Carlo simulation of project cash flows.

6. What are the four chief categories of real options?

7. True or false?
a. Decision trees can help identify and describe real options.
b. The option to expand increases NPV
c. High abandonment value decreases NPV.
d. If a project has positive NPV, the firm should always invest immediately.

8. Give an example of why flexible production facilities are valuable.

PRACTICE QUESTIONS

1. What is the NPV of the electric scooter project under the following scenario?

Market size	..1 million
Market share	.1
Unit price	¥400,000
Unit variable cost	¥360,000
Fixed cost	¥2 billion

2. Otobai's staff has come up with the following revised estimates for the electric scooter project:

	Pessimistic	Expected	Optimistic
Market size	.8 million	1.0 million	1.2 million
Market share	.04	.1	.16
Unit price	¥300,000	¥375,000	¥400,000
Unit variable cost	¥350,000	¥300,000	¥275,000
Fixed cost	¥5 billion	¥3 billion	¥1 billion

Conduct a sensitivity analysis. What are the principal uncertainties in the project?

3. Otobai is considering still another production method for its electric scooter. It would require an additional investment of ¥15 billion but would reduce variable costs by ¥40,000 per unit. Other assumptions follow Table 10.1.
a. What is the NPV of this alternative scheme?
b. Draw break-even charts for this alternative scheme along the lines of Figure 10.1.
c. Explain how you would interpret the break-even figure.

Now suppose Otobai's management would like to know the figure for variable cost per unit at which the electric scooter project in Section 10.1 would break even. Calculate the level of costs at which the project would earn zero profit and at which it would have zero NPV.

4. The Rustic Welt Company is proposing to replace its old welt-making machinery with more modern equipment. The new equipment costs $10 million and the company expects to sell its old equipment for $1 million. The attraction of the new machinery is that it is expected to cut manufacturing costs from their current level of $8 a welt to $4. However, as the following table shows, there is some uncertainty both about future sales and about the performance of the new machinery:

	Pessimistic	Expected	Optimistic
Sales, millions of welts	.4	.5	.7
Manufacturing cost with new machinery, dollars per welt	6	4	3
Economic life of new machinery, years	7	10	13

Conduct a sensitivity analysis of the replacement decision, assuming a discount rate of 12 percent. Rustic Welt does not pay taxes.

5. Rustic Welt could commission engineering tests to determine the actual improvement in manufacturing costs generated by the proposed new welt machines. (See problem 4 above.) The study would cost $450,000. Would you advise the company to go ahead with the study?

6. Summarize the problems that a manager would encounter in interpreting a standard sensitivity analysis, such as the one shown in Table 10.2. Which of these problems are alleviated by examining the project under alternative scenarios?

7. Operating leverage is often measured as the percentage increase in profits after depreciation for a 1 percent increase in sales.

   a. Calculate the operating leverage for the electric scooter project assuming unit sales are 100,000 (see Section 10.1).
   b. Now show that this figure is equal to 1 + (fixed costs/profits) including depreciation, divided by profits.
   c. Would operating leverage be higher or lower if sales were 200,000 scooters?

8. For what kinds of capital investment projects do you think Monte Carlo simulation would be most useful? For example, can you think of some industries in which this technique would be particularly attractive? Would it be more useful for large-scale investments than small ones? Discuss.

9. Look back at the Vegetron electric mop project in Section 9.6. Assume that if tests fail and Vegetron continues to go ahead with the project, the $1 million investment would generate only $75,000 a year. Display Vegetron's problem as a decision tree.

10. Describe the real option in each of the following cases:
   a. Deutsche Metall postpones a major plant expansion. The expansion has positive NPV on a discounted-cash-flow basis but top management wants to get a better fix on product demand before proceeding.
   b. Western Telecom commits to production of digital switching equipment specially designed for the European market. The project has a negative NPV, but it is justified on strategic grounds by the need for a strong market position in the rapidly growing, and potentially very profitable, market.
   c. Western Telecom vetoes a fully integrated, automated production line for the new digital switches. It relies on standard, less-expensive equipment. The automated

production line is more efficient overall, according to a discounted-cash-flow calculation.

d. Mount Fuji Airways buys a jumbo jet with special equipment that allows the plane to be switched quickly from freight to passenger use or vice versa.

e. The British–French treaty giving a concession to build a railroad link under the English Channel also required the concessionaire to propose by the year 2000 to build a "drive-through link" if "technical and economic conditions permit . . . and the decrease in traffic shall justify it without undermining the expected return on the first [rail] link." Other companies will not be permitted to build a link before the year 2020.

11. An auto plant that costs $100 million to build can produce a new line of cars that will generate cash flows with a present value of $140 million if the line is successful, but only $50 million if it is unsuccessful. You believe that the probability of success is only about 50 percent.

a. Would you build the plant?

b. Suppose that the plant can be sold for $90 million to another automaker if the line is not successful. Now would you build the plant?

c. Illustrate this option to abandon using a decision tree.

12. Agnes Magna has found some errors in her data (see Section 10.3). The corrected figures are as follows:

Price of turbo, year 0	$350,000
Price of piston, year 0	$180,000
Discount rate	8 percent

Redraw the decision tree with the changed data. Calculate the value of the option to expand. Which plane should Ms. Magna buy?

13. Ms. Magna has thought of another possibility. She could abandon the venture entirely by selling the plane at the end of the first year. Suppose that the piston-engine plane can be sold for $150,000 and the turboprop can be sold for $500,000.

a. In what circumstances would it pay for Ms. Magna to sell either plane?

b. Redraw the decision tree in Figure 10.8 to recognize that there will be circumstances in which Ms. Magna will choose to take the money and bail out.

c. Recalculate the value of the project recognizing the abandonment option.

d. How much does the option to abandon add to the value of the piston-engine project? How much does it add to the value of the turboprop project?

14. How can decision trees help the financial manager to "open up the black box" and understand a capital investment project better? Why are decision trees *not* complete solutions to the valuation of real options?

CHALLENGE
QUESTIONS

1. You own an unused gold mine that will cost $100,000 to reopen. If you open the mine, you expect to be able to extract 1,000 ounces of gold a year for each of three years. After that, the deposit will be exhausted. The gold price is currently $500 an ounce, and each year the price is equally likely to rise or fall by $50 from its level at the start of the year. The extraction cost is $460 an ounce and the discount rate is 10 percent.

a. Should you open the mine now or delay one year in the hope of a rise in the gold price?

b. What difference would it make to your decision if you could costlessly (but irreversibly) shut down the mine at any stage?

2. You are considering starting a company to provide a new Internet access service. There is a 60 percent chance the demand will be high in the first year. If it is high, there is an 80 percent chance that it will continue high indefinitely. If demand is low in the first year, there is a 60 percent chance that it will continue low indefinitely.

   If demand is high, forecasted revenue is $900,000 a year; if demand is low, forecasted revenue is $700,000 a year. You can cease to offer the service at any point, in which case, revenues are zero. Costs other than computing and telecommunications are forecasted at $500,000 a year regardless of demand. These costs also can be terminated at any point.

   You have a choice on computing and telecommunications. One possibility is to buy your own computers and software and to set up your own network and systems. This involves an initial outlay of $2,000,000 and no subsequent expenditure. The resulting system would have an economic life of 10 years and no salvage value. The alternative is to rent computer and telecommunications services as you need them from AT&T or one of the other major telecommunications companies. They propose to charge you 40 percent of your revenues.

   Assume that a decision to buy your own system cannot be reversed (i.e., if you buy a computer, you cannot resell it; if you do *not* buy it today, you cannot do so later). There are no taxes, and the opportunity cost of capital is 10 percent.

   Draw a decision tree showing your choices. Is it better to construct your own system or to rent it? State clearly any additional assumptions that you need to make.

3. Explain why real options are most valuable when forecasts of future cash flows are most uncertain.

MINI-CASE

Waldo County

Waldo County, the well-known real estate developer, worked long hours, and he expected his staff to do the same. So George Probit was not surprised to receive a call from the boss just as George was about to leave for a long summer's weekend.

Mr. County's success had been built on a remarkable instinct for a good site. He would exclaim "Location! Location! Location!" at some point in every planning meeting. Yet finance was not his strong suit. On this occasion he wanted George to go over the figures for a new $90 million outlet mall designed to intercept tourists heading downeast toward Maine. "First thing Monday will do just fine," he said as he handed George the file. "I'll be in my house in Bar Harbor if you need me."

George's first task was to draw up a summary of the projected revenues and costs. The results are shown in Table 10.7. Note that the mall's revenues would come from two sources: The company would charge retailers an annual rent for the space they occupied and in addition it would receive 5 percent of each store's gross sales.

Construction of the mall was likely to take three years. The construction costs could be depreciated straight-line over 15 years starting in year 3. As in the case of the company's other developments, the mall would be built to the highest specifications and would not need to be rebuilt until year 17. The land was expected to retain its value, but could not be depreciated for tax purposes.

Construction costs, revenues, operating and maintenance costs, and real estate taxes were all likely to rise in line with inflation, which was forecasted at 2 percent a year. The company's tax rate was 35 percent and the cost of capital was 9 percent in nominal terms.

	Year					
	0	1	2	3	4	5–17
Investment:						
Land	30					
Construction	20	30	10			
Operations:						
Rentals				12	12	12
Share of retail sales				24	24	24
Operating and maintenance costs	2	4	4	10	10	10
Real estate taxes	2	2	3	4	4	4

TABLE 10.7

Projected revenues and costs in real terms for the Downeast Tourist Mall (figures in $ millions).

George decided first to check that the project made financial sense. He then proposed to look at some of the things that might go wrong. His boss certainly had a nose for a good retail project, but he was not infallible. The Salome project had been a disaster because store sales had turned out to be 40 percent below forecast. What if that happened here? George wondered just how far sales could fall short of forecast before the project would be underwater.

Inflation was another source of uncertainty. Some people were talking about a zero long-term inflation rate, but George also wondered what would happen if inflation jumped to, say, 10 percent.

A third concern was possible construction cost overruns and delays due to required zoning changes and environmental approvals. George had seen cases of 25 percent construction cost overruns and delays up to 12 months between purchase of the land and the start of construction. He decided that he should examine the effect that this scenario would have on the project's profitability.

"Hey, this might be fun," George exclaimed to Mr. Waldo's secretary, Fifi, who was heading for Old Orchard Beach for the weekend. "I might even try Monte Carlo."

"Waldo went to Monte Carlo once," Fifi replied. "Lost a bundle at the roulette table. I wouldn't remind him. Just show him the bottom line. Will it make money or lose money? That's the bottom line."

"OK, no Monte Carlo," George agreed. But he realized that building a spreadsheet and running scenarios was not enough. He had to figure out how to summarize and present his results to Mr. County.

Questions

1. What is the project's NPV, given the projections in Table 10.7?
2. Conduct a sensitivity and a scenario analysis of the project. What do these analyses reveal about the project's risks and potential value?

CHAPTER ELEVEN

WHERE POSITIVE NET PRESENT VALUES COME FROM

WHY IS AN M.B.A. student who has learned about DCF like a baby with a hammer? Answer: Because to a baby with a hammer, everything looks like a nail.

Our point is that you should not focus on the arithmetic of DCF and thereby ignore the forecasts that are the basis of every investment decision. Senior managers are continuously bombarded with requests for funds for capital expenditures. All these requests are supported with detailed DCF analyses showing that the projects have positive NPVs.[1] How, then, can managers distinguish the NPVs that are truly positive from those that are merely the result of forecasting errors? We suggest that they should ask some probing questions about the possible sources of economic gain.

The first section in this chapter reviews certain common pitfalls in capital budgeting, notably the tendency to apply DCF when market values are already available and no DCF calculations are needed. The second section covers the *economic rents* that underlie all positive-NPV investments. The third section presents a case study describing how Marvin Enterprises, the gargle blaster company, analyzed the introduction of a radically new product.

11.1 LOOK FIRST TO MARKET VALUES

Let us suppose that you have persuaded all your project sponsors to give honest forecasts. Although those forecasts are unbiased, they are still likely to contain errors, some positive and others negative. The average error will be zero, but that is little consolation because you want to accept only projects with *truly* superior profitability.

Think, for example, of what would happen if you were to jot down your estimates of the cash flows from operating various lines of business. You would probably find that about half *appeared* to have positive NPVs. This may not be because you personally possess any superior skill in operating jumbo jets or running a chain of laundromats but because you have inadvertently introduced large errors into your estimates of the cash flows. The more projects you contemplate, the more likely you are to uncover projects that *appear* to be extremely worthwhile. Indeed, if you were to extend your activities to making cash-flow estimates for various companies, you would also find a number of *apparently* attractive takeover candidates. In some of these cases you might have genuine information and the proposed investment really might have a positive NPV. But in many other cases the investment would look good only because you made a forecasting error.

What can you do to prevent forecast errors from swamping genuine information? We suggest that you begin by looking at market values.

The Cadillac and the Movie Star

The following parable should help to illustrate what we mean. Your local Cadillac dealer is announcing a special offer. For $45,001 you get not only a brand new Cadillac but also the chance to shake hands with your favorite movie star. You wonder how much you are paying for that handshake.

There are two possible approaches to the problem. You could evaluate the worth of the Cadillac's power steering, disappearing windshield wipers, and other features and conclude that the Cadillac is worth $46,000. This would seem to suggest that the dealership is willing to pay $999 to have a movie star shake hands with

---

[1]Here is another riddle. Are projects proposed because they have positive NPVs, or do they have positive NPVs because they are proposed? No prizes for the correct answer.

you. Alternatively, you might note that the market price for Cadillacs is $45,000, so that you are paying $1 for the handshake. As long as there is a competitive market for Cadillacs, the latter approach is more appropriate.

Security analysts face a similar problem whenever they value a company's stock. They must consider the information that is already known to the market about a company, *and* they must evaluate the information that is known only to them. The information that is known to the market is the Cadillac; the private information is the handshake with the movie star. Investors have already evaluated the information that is generally known. Security analysts do not need to evaluate this information again. They can *start* with the market price of the stock and concentrate on valuing their private information.

While lesser mortals would instinctively accept the Cadillac's market value of $45,000, the financial manager is trained to enumerate and value all the costs and benefits from an investment and is therefore tempted to substitute his or her own opinion for the market's. Unfortunately this approach increases the chance of error. Many capital assets are traded in a competitive market, so it makes sense to *start* with the market price and then ask why these assets should earn more in your hands than in your rivals'.

Example: Investing in a New Department Store

We encountered a department store chain that estimated the present value of the expected cash flows from each proposed store, including the price at which it could eventually sell the store. Although the firm took considerable care with these estimates, it was disturbed to find that its conclusions were heavily influenced by the forecasted selling price of each store. Management disclaimed any particular real estate expertise, but it discovered that its investment decisions were unintentionally dominated by its assumptions about future real estate prices.

Once the financial managers realized this, they always checked the decision to open a new store by asking the following question: "Let us assume that the property is fairly priced. What is the evidence that it is best suited to one of our department stores rather than to some other use? In other words, *if an asset is worth more to others than it is to you, then beware of bidding for the asset against them.*

Let us take the department store problem a little further. Suppose that the new store costs $100 million.[2] You forecast that it will generate after-tax cash flow of $8 million a year for 10 years. Real estate prices are estimated to grow by 3 percent a year, so the expected value of the real estate at the end of 10 years is $100 \times (1.03)^{10}$ = $134 million. At a discount rate of 10 percent, your proposed department store has an NPV of $1 million:

$$\text{NPV} = -100 + \frac{8}{1.10} + \frac{8}{(1.10)^2} + \cdots + \frac{8 + 134}{(1.10)^{10}} = \$1 \text{ million}$$

Notice how sensitive this NPV is to the ending value of the real estate. For example, an ending value of $120 million implies an NPV of −$5 million.

It is helpful to imagine such a business as divided into two parts—a real estate subsidiary which buys the building and a retailing subsidiary which rents and operates it. Then figure out how much rent the real estate subsidiary would have to charge, and ask whether the retailing subsidiary could afford to pay the rent.

---

[2]For simplicity we assume the $100 million goes entirely to real estate. In real life there would also be substantial investments in fixtures, information systems, training, and start-up costs.

In some cases a fair market rental can be estimated from real estate transactions. For example, we might observe that similar retail space recently rented for $10 million a year. In that case we would conclude that our department store was an unattractive use for the site. Once the site had been acquired, it would be better to rent it out at $10 million than to use it for a store generating only $8 million.

Suppose, on the other hand, that the property could be rented for only $7 million per year. The department store could pay this amount to the real estate subsidiary and still earn a net operating cash flow of 8 − 7 = $1 million. It is therefore the best *current* use for the real estate.[3]

Will it also be the best *future* use? Maybe not, depending on whether retail profits keep pace with any rent increases. Suppose that real estate prices and rents are expected to increase by 3 percent per year. The real estate subsidiary must charge $7 \times 1.03 = \$7.21$ million in year 2, $7.21 \times 1.03 = \$7.43$ million in year 3, and so on.[4] Figure 11.1 shows that the store's income fails to cover the rental after year 5.

If these forecasts are right, the store has only a five-year economic life; from that point on the real estate is more valuable in some other use. If you stubbornly believe that the department store is the best long-term use for the site, you must be ignoring potential growth in income from the store.[5]

There is a general point here. Whenever you make a capital investment decision, think what bets you are placing. Our department store example involved at least two bets—one on real estate prices and another on the firm's ability to run a successful department store. But that suggests some alternative strategies. For instance, it would be foolish to make a lousy department store investment just because you are optimistic about real estate prices. You would do better to buy real estate and rent it out to the highest bidders. The converse is also true. You shouldn't be deterred from going ahead with a profitable department store because you are pessimistic about real estate prices. You would do better to sell the real estate and *rent* it back for the department store. We suggest that you separate the two bets by first asking, "Should we open a department store on this site, assuming that the real estate is fairly priced?" and then deciding whether you also want to go into the real estate business.

Another Example: Opening a Gold Mine

Here is another example of how market prices can help you make better decisions. Kingsley Solomon is considering a proposal to open a new gold mine. He estimates that the mine will cost $200 million to develop and that in each of the next 10 years it will produce .1 million ounces of gold at a cost, after mining and refining, of $200 an ounce. Although the extraction costs can be predicted with reasonable accuracy, Mr. Solomon is much less confident about future gold prices. His best guess is that

[3]The fair market rent equals the profit generated by the real estate's *second*-best use.

[4]This rental stream yields a 10 percent rate of return to the real estate subsidiary. Each year it gets a 7 percent "dividend" and 3 percent capital gain. Growth at 3 percent would bring the value of the property to $134 million by year 10.

The present value (at $r = .10$) of the growing stream of rents is

$$PV = \frac{7}{r - g} = \frac{7}{.10 - .03} = \$100 \text{ million}$$

This PV is the initial market value of the property.

[5]Another possibility is that real estate rents and values are expected to grow at less than 3 percent a year. But in that case the real estate subsidiary would have to charge more than $7 million rent in year 1 to justify its $100 million real estate investment (see footnote 4 above). That would make the department store even less attractive.

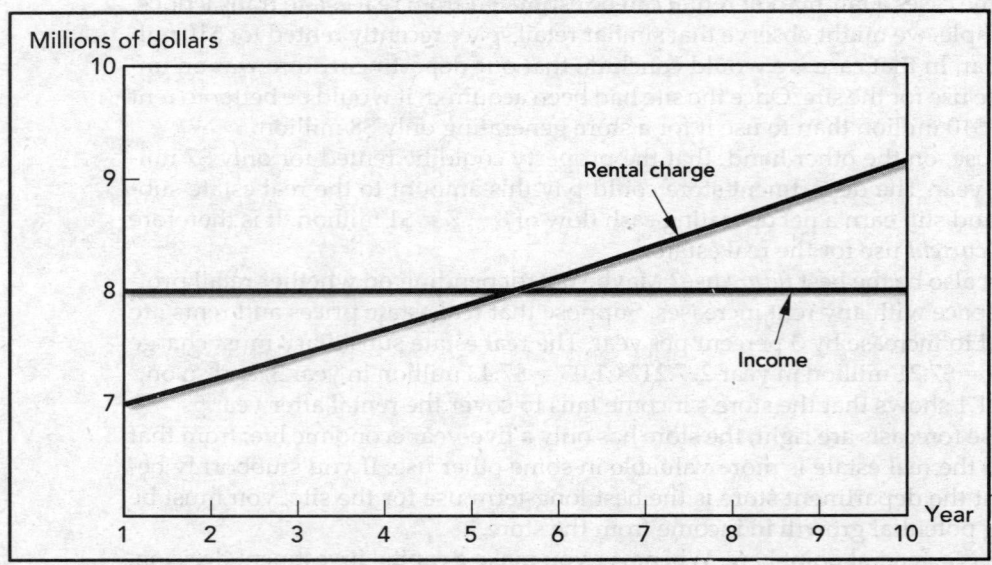

FIGURE 11.1

Beginning in year 6, the department store's income fails to cover the rental charge.

the price will rise by 5 percent per year from its current level of $400 an ounce. At a discount rate of 10 percent, this gives the mine an NPV of −$10 million:

$$\text{NPV} = -200 + \frac{.1(420 - 200)}{1.10} + \frac{.1(441 - 200)}{(1.10)^2} + \cdots + \frac{.1(652 - 200)}{(1.10)^{10}}$$

$$= -\$10 \text{ million}$$

Therefore the gold mine project is rejected.

Unfortunately, Mr. Solomon did not look at what the market was telling him. What is the PV of an ounce of gold? Clearly, if the gold market is functioning properly, it is the current price—$400 an ounce. Gold does not produce any income, so $400 is the discounted value of the expected future gold price.[6] Since the mine is

---

[6]Investing in an ounce of gold is like investing in a stock that pays no dividends: The investor's return comes entirely as capital gains. Look back at Section 4.2, where we showed that P_0, the price of the stock today, depends on DIV_1 and P_1, the expected dividend and price for next year, and the opportunity cost of capital r:

$$P_0 = \frac{\text{DIV}_1 + P_1}{1 + r}$$

But for gold $\text{DIV}_1 = 0$, so

$$P_0 = \frac{P_1}{1 + r}$$

In words, *today's price is the present value of next year's price.* Therefore, we don't have to know either P_1 or r to find the present value. Also since $\text{DIV}_2 = 0$,

$$P_1 = \frac{P_2}{1 + r}$$

expected to produce a total of 1 million ounces (.1 million ounces per year for 10 years), the present value of the revenue stream is $1 \times 400 = \$400$ million.[7] We assume that 10 percent is an appropriate discount rate for the relatively certain extraction costs. Thus

$$\text{NPV} = -\text{ initial investment} + \text{PV revenues} - \text{PV costs}$$
$$= -200 + 400 - \sum_{t=1}^{10} \frac{.1 \times 200}{(1.10)^t} = \$77 \text{ million}$$

It looks as if Kingsley Solomon's mine is not such a bad bet after all.[8]

Mr. Solomon's gold was just like anyone else's gold. So there was no point in trying to value it separately. By taking the PV of the gold sales as given, Mr. Solomon was able to focus on the crucial issue: Were the extraction costs sufficiently low to make the venture worthwhile? That brings us to another of those fundamental truths: If others are producing an article profitably and (like Mr. Solomon) you can make it more cheaply, then you don't need any NPV calculations to know that you are probably onto a good thing.

We confess that our example of Kingsley Solomon's mine is somewhat special. Unlike gold, most commodities are not kept solely for investment purposes, and therefore you cannot automatically assume that today's price is equal to the present value of the future price.[9]

---

and we can express P_0 as

$$P_0 = \frac{P_1}{1+r} = \frac{1}{1+r}\left(\frac{P_2}{1+r}\right) = \frac{P_2}{(1+r)^2}$$

In general,

$$P_0 = \frac{P_t}{(1+r)^t}$$

This holds for any asset which pays no dividends, is traded in a competitive market, and costs nothing to store. Storage costs for gold or common stocks are very small compared to asset value.

We also assume that guaranteed future delivery of gold is just as good as having gold in hand today. This is not quite right. As we will see in Chapter 27, gold in hand can generate a small "convenience yield."

[7]We assume that the extraction rate does not vary. If it can vary, Mr. Solomon has a valuable operating option to increase output when gold prices are high or to cut back when prices fall. Option pricing techniques are needed to value the mine when operating options are important. See Chapters 21 and 22.

[8]As in the case of our department store example, Mr. Solomon is placing two bets: one on his ability to mine gold at a low cost and the other on the price of gold. Suppose that he really does believe that gold is overvalued. That should not deter him from running a low-cost gold mine as long as he can place separate bets on gold prices. For example, he might be able to enter into a long-term contract to sell the mine's output or he could sell gold futures. (We explain *futures* in Chapter 27.)

[9]A more general guide to the relationship of current and future commodity prices was provided by Hotelling, who pointed out that if there are constant returns to scale in mining any mineral, the expected rise in the price of the mineral *less* extraction costs should equal the cost of capital. If the expected growth were faster, everyone would want to postpone extraction; if it were slower, everyone would want to exploit the resource today. In this case the value of a mine would be independent of when it was exploited, and you could value it by calculating the value of the mineral at today's price less the current cost of extraction. If (as is usually the case) there are declining returns to scale, then the expected price rise net of costs must be less than the cost of capital. For a review of Hotelling's Principle, see S. Devarajan and A. C. Fisher, "Hotelling's 'Economics of Exhaustible Resources': Fifty Years Later," *Journal of Economic Literature* 19 (March 1981), pp. 65–73. And for an application, see M. H. Miller and C. W. Upton, "A Test of the Hotelling Valuation Principle," *Journal of Political Economy* 93 (1985), pp. 1–25.

However, here's another way that you may be able to tackle the problem. Suppose that you are considering investment in a new copper mine and that someone offers to buy the mine's future output at a fixed price. If you accept the offer—and the buyer is completely creditworthy—the revenues from the mine are certain and can be discounted at the risk-free interest rate.[10] That takes us back to Chapter 9, where we explained that there are two ways to calculate PV:

- Estimate the expected cash flows and discount at a rate that reflects the risk of those flows.
- Estimate what sure-fire cash flows would have the same values as the risky cash flows. Then discount these *certainty-equivalent* cash flows at the risk-free interest rate.

When you discount the fixed-price revenues at the risk-free rate, you are using the certainty-equivalent method to value the mine's output. By doing so, you gain in two ways: You don't need to estimate future mineral prices, and you don't need to worry about the appropriate discount rate for risky cash flows.

But here's the question: What is the minimum fixed price at which you could agree today to sell your future output? In other words, what is the certainty-equivalent price? Fortunately, for many commodities there is an active market in which firms fix today the price at which they will buy or sell copper and other commodities in the future. This market is known as the *futures market,* which we will cover in Chapter 27. Futures prices are certainty equivalents, and you can look them up in the daily newspaper. So you don't need to make elaborate forecasts of copper prices to work out the PV of the mine's output. The market has already done the work for you; you simply calculate future revenues using the price in the newspaper of copper futures and discount these revenues at the risk-free interest rate.

Of course, things are never as easy as textbooks suggest. Trades in organized futures exchanges are largely confined to deliveries over the next year or so, and therefore your newspaper won't show the price at which you could sell output beyond this period. But financial economists have developed techniques for using the prices in the futures market to estimate the amount that buyers would agree to pay for more distant deliveries.[11]

Our two examples of gold and copper producers are illustrations of a universal principle of finance:

> When you have the market value of an asset, *use it,* at least as a starting point in your analysis.

11.2 FORECASTING ECONOMIC RENTS

We recommend that financial managers ask themselves whether an asset is more valuable in their hands than in another's. A bit of classical microeconomics can help to answer that question. When an industry settles into long-run competitive

---

[10]We assume that the volume of output is certain (or does not have any market risk).

[11]After reading Chapter 27, check out E. S. Schwartz, "The Stochastic Behavior of Commodity Prices: Implications for Valuation and Hedging," *Journal of Finance* 52 (July 1997), pp. 923–973; and A. J. Neuberger, "Hedging Long-Term Exposures with Multiple Short-Term Contracts," *Review of Financial Studies* 12 (1999), pp. 429–459.

equilibrium, all its assets are expected to earn their opportunity costs of capital—no more and no less. If the assets earned more, firms in the industry would expand or firms outside the industry would try to enter it.

Profits that *more* than cover the opportunity cost of capital are known as *economic rents*. These rents may be either temporary (in the case of an industry that is not in long-run equilibrium) or persistent (in the case of a firm with some degree of monopoly or market power). The NPV of an investment is simply the discounted value of the economic rents that it will produce. Therefore when you are presented with a project that appears to have a positive NPV, don't just accept the calculations at face value. They may reflect simple estimation errors in forecasting cash flows. Probe behind the cash-flow estimates, and *try to identify the source of economic rents*. A positive NPV for a new project is believable only if *you* believe that your company has some special advantage.

Such advantages can arise in several ways. You may be smart or lucky enough to be first to the market with a new, improved product for which customers are prepared to pay premium prices (until your competitors enter and squeeze out excess profits). You may have a patent, proprietary technology, or production cost advantage that competitors cannot match, at least for several years. You may have some valuable contractual advantage, for example, the distributorship for gargle blasters in France.

Thinking about competitive advantage can also help ferret out negative-NPV calculations that are negative by mistake. If you are the lowest-cost producer of a profitable product in a growing market, then you should invest to expand along with the market. If your calculations show a negative NPV for such an expansion, then you have probably made a mistake.

How One Company Avoided a $100 Million Mistake

A U.S. chemical producer was about to modify an existing plant to produce a specialty product, polyzone, which was in short supply on world markets.[12] At prevailing raw material and finished-product prices the expansion would have been strongly profitable. Table 11.1 shows a simplified version of management's analysis. Note the NPV of about $64 million at the company's 8 percent real cost of capital—not bad for a $100 million outlay.

Then doubt began to creep in. Notice the outlay for transportation costs. Some of the project's raw materials were commodity chemicals, largely imported from Europe, and much of the polyzone production was exported back to Europe. Moreover, the U.S. company had no long-run technological edge over potential European competitors. It had a head start perhaps, but was that really enough to generate a positive NPV?

Notice the importance of the price spread between raw materials and finished product. The analysis in Table 11.1 forecasted the spread at a constant $1.20 per pound of polyzone for 10 years. That had to be wrong: European producers, who did not face the U.S. company's transportation costs, would see an even larger NPV and expand capacity. Increased competition would almost surely squeeze the spread. The U.S. company decided to calculate the *competitive* spread—the spread at which a European competitor would see polyzone capacity as zero NPV. Table 11.2 shows management's analysis. The resulting spread of $.95 per

---

[12]This is a true story, but names and details have been changed to protect the innocent.

TABLE 11.1

NPV calculation for proposed investment in polyzone production by a U.S. chemical company (figures in $ millions except as noted).

Note: For simplicity, we assume no inflation and no taxes. Plant and equipment have no salvage value after 10 years.
*Production capacity is 80 million pounds per year.
†Production costs are $.375 per pound after start-up ($.75 per pound in year 2, when production is only 40 million pounds).
‡Transportation costs are $.10 per pound to European ports.

	Year 0	Year 1	Year 2	Years 3–10
Investment	100			
Production, millions of pounds per year*	0	0	40	80
Spread, dollars per pound	1.20	1.20	1.20	1.20
Net revenues	0	0	48	96
Production costs†	0	0	30	30
Transport‡	0	0	4	8
Other costs	0	20	20	20
Cash flow	−100	−20	−6	+38
NPV (at $r = 8\%$) = $63.6 million				

TABLE 11.2

What's the competitive spread to a European producer? About $.95 per pound of polyzone. Note that European producers face no transportation costs. Compare Table 11.1 (figures in $ millions except as noted).

	Year 0	Year 1	Year 2	Years 3–10
Investment	100			
Production, millions of pounds per year	0	0	40	80
Spread, dollars per pound	.95	.95	.95	.95
Net revenues	0	0	38	76
Production costs	0	0	30	30
Transport	0	0	0	0
Other costs	0	20	20	20
Cash flow	−100	−20	−12	+26
NPV (at $r = 8\%$) = 0				

pound was the best *long-run* forecast for the polyzone market, other things constant of course.

How much of a head start did the U.S. producer have? How long before competitors forced the spread down to $.95? Management's best guess was five years. It prepared Table 11.3, which is identical to Table 11.1 except for the forecasted spread, which would shrink to $.95 by the start of year 5. Now the NPV was negative.

The project might have been saved if production could have been started in year 1 rather than 2 or if local markets could have been expanded, thus reducing transportation costs. But these changes were not feasible, so management canceled the project, albeit with a sigh of relief that its analysis hadn't stopped at Table 11.1.

This is a perfect example of the importance of thinking through sources of economic rents. Positive NPVs are suspect without some long-run competitive advantage. When a company contemplates investing in a new product or expanding production of an existing product, it should specifically identify its advantages or disadvantages over its most dangerous competitors. It should calculate NPV from

	Year					
	0	1	2	3	4	5–10
Investment	100					
Production, millions of pounds per year	0	0	40	80	80	80
Spread, dollars per pound	1.20	1.20	1.20	1.20	1.10	.95
Net revenues	0	0	48	96	88	76
Production costs	0	0	30	30	30	30
Transport	0	0	4	8	8	8
Other costs	0	20	20	20	20	20
Cash flow	−100	−20	−6	+38	+30	+18
NPV (at $r = 8\%$) = −$10.3						

TABLE 11.3

Recalculation of NPV for polyzone investment by U.S. company (figures in $ millions except as noted). If expansion by European producers forces competitive spreads by year 5, the U.S. producer's NPV falls to −$10.3 million. Compare Table 11.1.

those competitors' points of view. If competitors' NPVs come out strongly positive, the company had better expect decreasing prices (or spreads) and evaluate the proposed investment accordingly.

11.3 EXAMPLE—MARVIN ENTERPRISES DECIDES TO EXPLOIT A NEW TECHNOLOGY

To illustrate some of the problems involved in predicting economic rents, let us leap forward several years and look at the decision by Marvin Enterprises to exploit a new technology.[13]

One of the most unexpected developments of these years was the remarkable growth of a completely new industry. By 2023, annual sales of gargle blasters totaled $1.68 billion, or 240 million units. Although it controlled only 10 percent of the market, Marvin Enterprises was among the most exciting growth companies of the decade. Marvin had come late into the business, but it had pioneered the use of integrated microcircuits to control the genetic engineering processes used to manufacture gargle blasters. This development had enabled producers to cut the price of gargle blasters from $9 to $7 and had thereby contributed to the dramatic growth in the size of the market. The estimated demand curve in Figure 11.2 shows just how responsive demand is to such price reductions.

---

[13]We thank Stewart Hodges for permission to adapt this example from a case prepared by him, and we thank the BBC for permission to use the term *gargle blasters*.

FIGURE 11.2

The demand "curve" for gargle blasters shows that for each $1 cut in price there is an increase in demand of 80 million units.

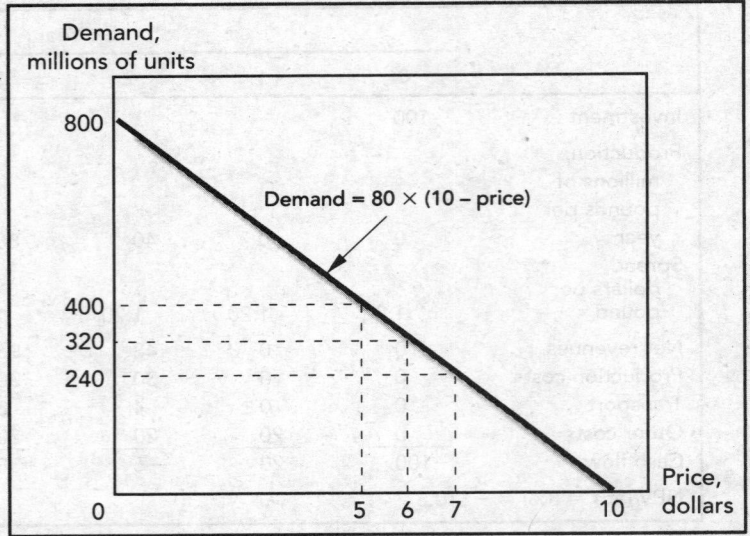

Table 11.4 summarizes the cost structure of the old and new technologies. While companies with the new technology were earning 20 percent on their initial investment, those with first-generation equipment had been hit by the successive price cuts. Since all Marvin's investment was in the 2019 technology, it had been particularly well placed during this period.

Rumors of new developments at Marvin had been circulating for some time, and the total market value of Marvin's stock had risen to $460 million by January 2024. At that point Marvin called a press conference to announce another technological breakthrough. Management claimed that its new third-generation process involving mutant neurons enabled the firm to reduce capital costs to $10 and manufacturing costs to $3 per unit. Marvin proposed to capitalize on this invention by embarking on a huge $1 billion expansion program that would add 100 million units to capacity. The company expected to be in full operation within 12 months.

Before deciding to go ahead with this development, Marvin had undertaken extensive calculations on the effect of the new investment. The basic assumptions were as follows:

1. The cost of capital was 20 percent.
2. The production facilities had an indefinite physical life.
3. The demand curve and the costs of each technology would not change.
4. There was no chance of a fourth-generation technology in the foreseeable future.
5. The corporate income tax, which had been abolished in 2014, was not likely to be reintroduced.

Marvin's competitors greeted the news with varying degrees of concern. There was general agreement that it would be five years before any of them would have access to the new technology. On the other hand, many consoled themselves with

| | Capacity, Millions of Units | | Capital Cost | Manufacturing | Salvage |
Technology	Industry	Marvin	per Unit ($)	Cost per Unit ($)	Value per Unit ($)
First generation (2011)	120	—	17.50	5.50	2.50
Second generation (2019)	120	24	17.50	3.50	2.50

TABLE 11.4

Size and cost structure of the gargle blaster industry before Marvin announced its expansion plans.

Note: Selling price is $7 per unit. One unit means one gargle blaster.

the reflection that Marvin's new plant could not compete with an existing plant that had been fully depreciated.

Suppose that you were Marvin's financial manager. Would you have agreed with the decision to expand? Do you think it would have been better to go for a larger or smaller expansion? How do you think Marvin's announcement is likely to affect the price of its stock?

You have a choice. You can go on *immediately* to read *our* solution to these questions. But you will learn much more if you stop and work out your own answer first. Try it.

Forecasting Prices of Gargle Blasters

Up to this point in any capital budgeting problem we have always given you the set of cash-flow forecasts. In the present case you have to *derive* those forecasts.

The first problem is to decide what is going to happen to the price of gargle blasters. Marvin's new venture will increase industry capacity to 340 million units. From the demand curve in Figure 11.2, you can see that the industry can sell this number of gargle blasters only if the price declines to $5.75:

$$\text{Demand} = 80 \times (10 - \text{price})$$
$$= 80 \times (10 - 5.75) = 340 \text{ million units}$$

If the price falls to $5.75, what will happen to companies with the 2011 technology? They also have to make an investment decision: Should they stay in business, or should they sell their equipment for its salvage value of $2.50 per unit? With a 20 percent opportunity cost of capital, the NPV of staying in business is

$$\text{NPV} = -\text{investment} + \text{PV(price} - \text{manufacturing cost)}$$
$$= -2.50 + \frac{5.75 - 5.50}{.20} = -\$1.25 \text{ per unit}$$

Smart companies with 2011 equipment will, therefore, see that it is better to sell off capacity. No matter what their equipment originally cost or how far it is depreciated, it is more profitable to sell the equipment for $2.50 per unit than to operate it and lose $1.25 per unit.

As capacity is sold off, the supply of gargle blasters will decline and the price will rise. An equilibrium is reached when the price gets to $6. At this point 2011 equipment has a zero NPV:

$$NPV = -2.50 + \frac{6.00 - 5.50}{.20} = \$0 \text{ per unit}$$

How much capacity will have to be sold off before the price reaches $6? You can check that by going back to the demand curve:

$$Demand = 80 \times (10 - price)$$
$$= 80 \times (10 - 6) = 320 \text{ million units}$$

Therefore Marvin's expansion will cause the price to settle down at $6 a unit and will induce first-generation producers to withdraw 20 million units of capacity.

But after five years Marvin's competitors will also be in a position to build third-generation plants. As long as these plants have positive NPVs, companies will increase their capacity and force prices down once again. A new equilibrium will be reached when the price reaches $5. At this point, the NPV of new third-generation plants is zero, and there is no incentive for companies to expand further:

$$NPV = -10 + \frac{5.00 - 3.00}{.20} = \$0 \text{ per unit}$$

Looking back once more at our demand curve, you can see that with a price of $5 the industry can sell a total of 400 million gargle blasters:

$$Demand = 80 \times (10 - price) = 80 \times (10 - 5) = 400 \text{ million units}$$

The effect of the third-generation technology is, therefore, to cause industry sales to expand from 240 million units in 2023 to 400 million five years later. But that rapid growth is no protection against failure. By the end of five years any company that has only first-generation equipment will no longer be able to cover its manufacturing costs and will be *forced* out of business.

The Value of Marvin's New Expansion

We have shown that the introduction of third-generation technology is likely to cause gargle blaster prices to decline to $6 for the next five years and to $5 thereafter. We can now set down the expected cash flows from Marvin's new plant:

	Year 0 (Investment)	Years 1–5 (Revenue − Manufacturing Cost)	Year 6, 7, 8, . . . (Revenue − Manufacturing Cost)
Cash flow per unit ($)	−10	6 − 3 = 3	5 − 3 = 2
Cash flow, 100 million units ($ millions)	−1,000	600 − 300 = 300	500 − 300 = 200

Discounting these cash flows at 20 percent gives us

$$NPV = -1,000 + \sum_{t=1}^{5} \frac{300}{(1.20)^t} + \frac{1}{(1.20)^5}\left(\frac{200}{.20}\right) = \$299 \text{ million}$$

It looks as if Marvin's decision to go ahead was correct. But there is something we have forgotten. When we evaluate an investment, we must consider *all* incremental cash flows. One effect of Marvin's decision to expand is to reduce the value of its existing 2019 plant. If Marvin decided not to go ahead with the new technology, the $7 price of gargle blasters would hold until Marvin's competitors started to cut prices in five years' time. Marvin's decision, therefore, leads to an immediate $1 cut in price. This reduces the present value of its 2019 equipment by

$$24 \text{ million} \times \sum_{t=1}^{5} \frac{1.00}{(1.20)^t} = \$72 \text{ million}$$

Considered in isolation, Marvin's decision has an NPV of $299 million. But it also reduces the value of existing plant by $72 million. The net present value of Marvin's venture is, therefore, $299 - 72 = \$227$ million.

Alternative Expansion Plans

Marvin's expansion has a positive NPV, but perhaps Marvin could do better to build a larger or smaller plant. You can check that by going through the same calculations as above. First you need to estimate how the additional capacity will affect gargle blaster prices. Then you can calculate the net present value of the new plant and the change in the present value of the existing plant. The total NPV of Marvin's expansion plan is

Total NPV = NPV of new plant + change in PV of existing plant

We have undertaken these calculations and plotted the results in Figure 11.3. You can see how total NPV would be affected by a smaller or larger expansion.

When the new technology becomes generally available in 2029, firms will construct a total of 280 million units of new capacity.[14] But Figure 11.3 shows that it would be foolish for Marvin to go that far. If Marvin added 280 million units of new capacity in 2024, the discounted value of the cash flows from the new plant would be zero *and* the company would have reduced the value of its old plant by $144 million. To maximize NPV, Marvin should construct 200 million units of new capacity and set the price just below $6 to drive out the 2011 manufacturers. Output is, therefore, less and price is higher than either would be under free competition.[15]

The Value of Marvin Stock

Let us think about the effect of Marvin's announcement on the value of its common stock. Marvin has 24 million units of second-generation capacity. In the absence of any

---

[14]Total industry capacity in 2029 will be 400 million units. Of this, 120 million units are second-generation capacity, and the remaining 280 million units are third-generation capacity.

[15]Notice that we are assuming that all customers have to pay the same price for their gargle blasters. If Marvin could charge each customer the maximum price which that customer would be willing to pay, output would be the same as under free competition. Such direct price discrimination is illegal and in any case difficult to enforce. But firms do search for indirect ways to differentiate between customers. For example, stores often offer free delivery which is equivalent to a price discount for customers who live at an inconvenient distance. Publishers differentiate their products by selling hardback copies to libraries and paperbacks to impecunious students. In the early years of electronic calculators, manufacturers put a high price on their product. Although buyers knew that the price would be reduced in a year or two, the convenience of having the machines for the extra time more than compensated for the additional outlay.

FIGURE 11.3

Effect on net present value of alternative expansion plans. Marvin's 100-million-unit expansion has a total NPV of $227 million (total NPV = NPV new plant + change in PV existing plant = 299 − 72 = 227). Total NPV is maximized if Marvin builds 200 million units of new capacity. If Marvin builds 280 million units of new capacity, total NPV is −$144 million.

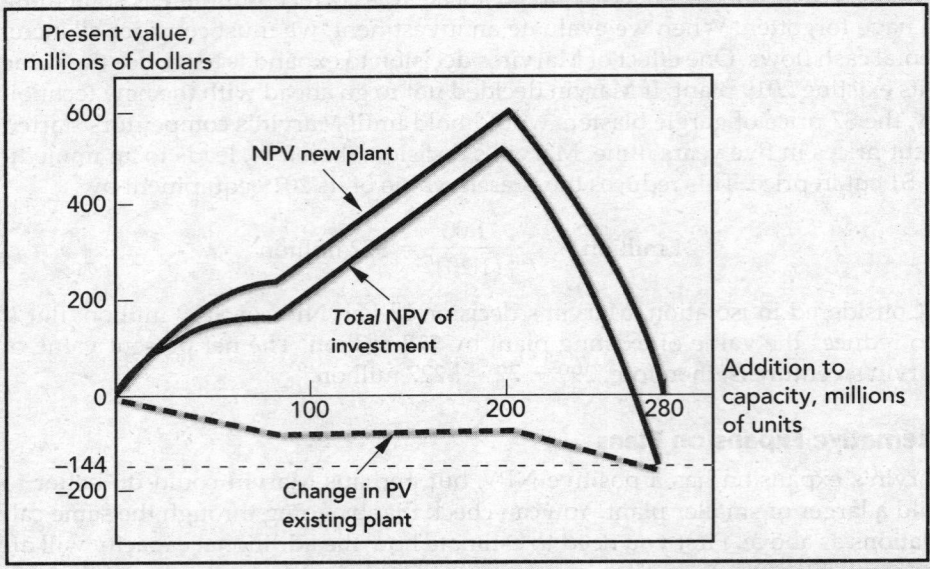

third-generation technology, gargle blaster prices would hold at $7 and Marvin's existing plant would be worth

$$PV = 24 \text{ million} \times \frac{7.00 - 3.50}{.20}$$
$$= \$420 \text{ million}$$

Marvin's new technology reduces the price of gargle blasters initially to $6 and after five years to $5. Therefore the value of existing plant declines to

$$PV = 24 \text{ million} \times \left[\sum_{t=1}^{5} \frac{6.00 - 3.50}{(1.20)^t} + \frac{5.00 - 3.50}{.20 \times (1.20)^5} \right]$$
$$= \$252 \text{ million}$$

But the *new* plant makes a net addition to shareholders' wealth of $299 million. So after Marvin's announcement its stock will be worth

$$252 + 299 = \$551 \text{ million}[16]$$

Now here is an illustration of something we talked about in Chapter 4: Before the announcement, Marvin's stock was valued in the market at $460 million. The difference between this figure and the value of the existing plant represented the present value of Marvin's growth opportunities (PVGO). The market valued Mar-

---

[16]In order to finance the expansion, Marvin is going to have to sell $1,000 million of new stock. Therefore the *total* value of Marvin's stock will rise to $1,551 million. But investors who put up the new money will receive shares worth $1,000 million. The value of Marvin's old shares after the announcement is therefore $551 million.

vin's ability to stay ahead of the game at $40 million even before the announcement. After the announcement PVGO rose to $299 million.[17]

The Lessons of Marvin Enterprises

Marvin Enterprises may be just a piece of science fiction, but the problems that it confronts are very real. Whenever Intel considers developing a new microprocessor or Biogen considers developing a new drug, these firms must face up to exactly the same issues as Marvin. We have tried to illustrate the *kind* of questions that you should be asking when presented with a set of cash-flow forecasts. Of course, no economic model is going to predict the future with accuracy. Perhaps Marvin can hold the price above $6. Perhaps competitors will not appreciate the rich pickings to be had in the year 2029. In that case, Marvin's expansion would be even more profitable. But would you want to bet $1 billion on such possibilities? We don't think so.

Investments often turn out to earn far more than the cost of capital because of a favorable surprise. This surprise may in turn create a temporary opportunity for further investments earning more than the cost of capital. But anticipated and more prolonged rents will naturally lead to the entry of rival producers. That is why you should be suspicious of any investment proposal that predicts a stream of economic rents into the indefinite future. Try to estimate *when* competition will drive the NPV down to zero, and think what that implies for the price of your product.

Many companies try to identify the major growth areas in the economy and then concentrate their investment in these areas. But the sad fate of first-generation gargle blaster manufacturers illustrates how rapidly existing plants can be made obsolete by changes in technology. It is fun being in a growth industry when you are at the forefront of the new technology, but a growth industry has no mercy on technological laggards.

You can expect to earn economic rents only if you have some superior resource such as management, sales force, design team, or production facilities. Therefore, rather than trying to move into growth areas, you would do better to identify your firm's comparative advantages and try to capitalize on them. These issues came to the fore during the boom in New Economy stocks in the late 1990s. The optimists argued that the information revolution was opening up opportunities for companies to grow at unprecedented rates. The pessimists pointed out that competition in e-commerce was likely to be intense and that competition would ensure that the benefits of the information revolution would go largely to consumers. The Finance in the News box, which contains an extract from an article by Warren Buffett, emphasizes the point that rapid growth is no guarantee of superior profits.

We do not wish to imply that good investment opportunities don't exist. For example, such opportunities frequently arise because the firm has invested money in the past which gives it the option to expand cheaply in the future. Perhaps the firm can increase its output just by adding an extra production line, whereas its rivals would need to construct an entirely new factory. In such cases, you must take into account not only *whether* it is profitable to exercise your option, but also *when* it is best to do so.

Marvin also reminded us of project interactions, which we first discussed in Chapter 6. When you estimate the incremental cash flows from a project, you must remember to include the project's impact on the rest of the business. By introducing the new

---

[17]Notice that the market value of Marvin stock will be greater than $551 million if investors expect the company to expand again within the five-year period. In other words, PVGO after the expansion may still be positive. Investors may expect Marvin to stay one step ahead of its competitors or to successfully apply its special technology in other areas.

WARREN BUFFETT ON GROWTH AND PROFITABILITY

I thought it would be instructive to go back and look at a couple of industries that transformed this country much earlier in this century: automobiles and aviation. Take automobiles first: I have here one page, out of 70 in total, of car and truck manufacturers that have operated in this country. At one time, there was a Berkshire car and an Omaha car. Naturally I noticed those. But there was also a telephone book of others.

All told, there appear to have been at least 2,000 car makes, in an industry that had an incredible impact on people's lives. If you had foreseen in the early days of cars how this industry would develop, you would have said, "Here is the road to riches." So what did we progress to by the 1990s? After corporate carnage that never let up, we came down to three U.S. car companies—themselves no lollapaloozas for investors. So here is an industry that had an enormous impact on America—and also an enormous impact, though not the anticipated one, on investors. Sometimes, incidentally, it's much easier in these transforming events to figure out the losers. You could have grasped the importance of the auto when it came along but still found it hard to pick companies that would make you money. But there was one obvious decision you could have made back then—it's better sometimes to turn these things upside down—and that was to short horses. Frankly, I'm disappointed that the Buffett family was not short horses through this entire period. And we really had no excuse: Living in Nebraska, we would have found it super-easy to borrow horses and avoid a "short squeeze."

U.S. Horse Population

1900: 21 million

1998: 5 million

The other truly transforming business invention of the first quarter of the century, besides the car, was the airplane—another industry whose plainly brilliant future would have caused investors to salivate. So I went back to check out aircraft manufacturers and found that in the 1919–39 period, there were about 300 companies, only a handful still breathing today. Among the planes made then—we must have been the Silicon Valley of that age—were both the Nebraska and the Omaha, two aircraft that even the most loyal Nebraskan no longer relies upon.

Move on to failures of airlines. Here's a list of 129 airlines that in the past 20 years filed for bankruptcy. Continental was smart enough to make that list twice. As of 1992, in fact—though the picture would have improved since then—the money that had been made since the dawn of aviation by all of this country's airline companies was zero. Absolutely zero.

Sizing all this up, I like to think that if I'd been at Kitty Hawk in 1903 when Orville Wright took off, I would have been farsighted enough, and public-spirited enough—I owed this to future capitalists—to shoot him down. I mean, Karl Marx couldn't have done as much damage to capitalists as Orville did.

I won't dwell on other glamorous businesses that dramatically changed our lives but concurrently failed to deliver rewards to U.S. investors: the manufacture of radios and televisions, for example. But I will draw a lesson from these businesses: The key to investing is not assessing how much an industry is going to affect society, or how much it will grow, but rather determining the competitive advantage of any given company and, above all, the durability of that advantage. The products or services that have wide, sustainable moats around them are the ones that deliver rewards to investors.

Source: C. Loomis, "Mr. Buffett on the Stock Market," *Fortune* (November 22, 1999), pp. 110–115.

technology immediately, Marvin reduced the value of its existing plant by $72 million. Sometimes the losses on existing plants may completely offset the gains from a new technology. That is why we sometimes see established, technologically advanced companies deliberately slowing down the rate at which they introduce new products.

Notice that Marvin's economic rents were equal to the difference between its costs and those of the marginal producer. The costs of the marginal 2011-generation plant consisted of the manufacturing costs plus the opportunity cost of not selling the equipment. Therefore, if the salvage value of the 2011 equipment were higher, Marvin's competitors would incur higher costs and Marvin could earn higher rents. We took the salvage value as given, but it in turn depends on the cost savings from substituting outdated gargle blaster equipment for some other asset. In a well-functioning economy, assets will be used so as to minimize the *total* cost of producing the chosen set of outputs. The economic rents earned by any asset are equal to the total extra costs that would be incurred if that asset were withdrawn.

Here's another point about salvage value which takes us back to our discussion of Magna Charter in the last chapter: A high salvage value gives the firm an option to abandon a project if things start to go wrong. However, if competitors *know* that you can bail out easily, they are more likely to enter your market. If it is clear that you have no alternative but to stay and fight, they will be more cautious about competing.

When Marvin announced its expansion plans, many owners of first-generation equipment took comfort in the belief that Marvin could not compete with their fully depreciated plant. Their comfort was misplaced. Regardless of past depreciation policy, it paid to scrap first-generation equipment rather than keep it in production. Do not expect that numbers in your balance sheet can protect you from harsh economic reality.

SUMMARY

It helps to use present value when you are making investment decisions, but that is not the whole story. Good investment decisions depend both on a sensible criterion and on sensible forecasts. In this chapter we have looked at the problem of forecasting.

Projects may look attractive for two reasons: (1) There may be some errors in the sponsor's forecasts, and (2) the company can genuinely expect to earn excess profit from the project. Good managers, therefore, try to ensure that the odds are stacked in their favor by expanding in areas in which the company has a comparative advantage. We like to put this another way by saying that good managers try to identify projects that will generate economic rents. Good managers carefully avoid expansion when competitive advantages are absent and economic rents are unlikely. They do not project favorable current product prices into the future without checking whether entry or expansion by competitors will drive future prices down.

Our story of Marvin Enterprises illustrates the origin of rents and how they determine a project's cash flows and net present value.

Any present value calculation, including our calculation for Marvin Enterprises, is subject to error. That's life: There's no other sensible way to value most capital investment projects. But some assets, such as gold, real estate, crude oil, ships, and airplanes, and financial assets, such as stocks and bonds, are traded in reasonably competitive markets. When you have the market value of such an asset, *use it*, at least as a starting point for your analysis.

FURTHER READING

For an interesting analysis of the likely effect of a new technology on the present value of existing assets, see:

S. P. Sobotka and C. Schnabei: "Linear Programming as a Device for Predicting Market Value: Prices of Used Commercial Aircraft, 1959–65," *Journal of Business*, 34:10–30 (January 1961).

QUIZ

1. You have inherited 250 acres of prime Iowa farmland. There is an active market in land of this type, and similar properties are selling for $1,000 per acre. Net cash returns per acre are $75 per year. These cash returns are expected to remain constant in real terms. How much is the land worth? A local banker has advised you to use a 12 percent discount rate.

2. True or false?
   a. A firm that earns the opportunity cost of capital is earning economic rents.
   b. A firm that invests in positive-NPV ventures expects to earn economic rents.
   c. Financial managers should try to identify areas where their firms can earn economic rents, because it's there that positive-NPV projects are likely to be found.
   d. Economic rent is the equivalent annual cost of operating capital equipment.

3. Demand for concave utility meters is expanding rapidly, but the industry is highly competitive. A utility meter plant costs $50 million to set up, and it has an annual capacity of 500,000 meters. The production cost is $5 per meter, and this cost is not expected to change. The machines have an indefinite physical life and the cost of capital is 10 percent. What is the competitive price of a utility meter?
   a. $5   b. $10   c. $15

4. Look back to the polyzone example at the end of Section 11.2. Explain why it was necessary to calculate the NPV of investment in polyzone capacity from the point of view of a potential European competitor.

5. Your brother-in-law wants you to join him in purchasing a building on the outskirts of town. You and he would then develop and run a Taco Palace restaurant. Both of you are extremely optimistic about future real estate prices in this area, and your brother-in-law has prepared a cash-flow forecast that implies a large positive NPV. This calculation assumes sale of the property after 10 years.
   What further calculations should you do before going ahead?

6. A new leaching process allows your company to recover some gold as a by-product of its aluminum mining operations. How would you calculate the PV of the future cash flows from gold sales?

7. On the London Metals Exchange the price for copper to be delivered in one year is $1,600 a ton. *Note:* Payment is made when the copper is delivered. The risk-free interest rate is 5 percent and the expected market return is 12 percent.
   a. Suppose that you expect to produce and sell 100,000 tons of copper next year. What is the PV of this output? Assume that the sale occurs at the end of the year.
   b. If copper has a beta of 1.2, what is the expected price of copper at the end of the year? What is the certainty-equivalent price?

8. New-model commercial airplanes are much more fuel-efficient than older models. How is it possible for airlines flying older models to make money when its competitors are flying newer planes? Explain briefly.

9. What are the lessons of Marvin Enterprises? Select from the following list. *Note:* Some of the following statements may be *partly* true, or true in some circumstances but not generally. Briefly explain your choices.
   a. Companies should try to concentrate their investments in high-tech, high-growth sectors of the economy.
   b. Think when your competition is likely to catch up, and what that will mean for product pricing and project cash flows.

c. Introduction of a new product may reduce the profits from an existing product but this project interaction should be ignored in calculating the new project's NPV.

d. In the long run, economic rents flow from some asset (usually intangible) or some advantage that your competitors do not have.

e. Do not attempt to enter a new market when your competitors can produce with fully depreciated plant.

1. Suppose that you are considering investing in an asset for which there is a reasonably good secondary market. Specifically, you're Delta Airlines, and the asset is a Boeing 757—a widely used airplane. How does the presence of a secondary market simplify your problem in principle? Do you think these simplifications could be realized in practice? Explain.

2. There is an active, competitive leasing (i.e., rental) market for most standard types of commercial jets. Many of the planes flown by the major domestic and international airlines are not owned by them but leased for periods ranging from a few months to several years.

   Gamma Airlines, however, owns two long-range DC-11s just withdrawn from Latin American service. Gamma is considering using these planes to develop the potentially lucrative new route from Akron to Yellowknife. A considerable investment in terminal facilities, training, and advertising will be required. Once committed, Gamma will have to operate the route for at least three years. One further complication: The manager of Gamma's international division is opposing commitment of the planes to the Akron–Yellowknife route because of anticipated future growth in traffic through Gamma's new hub in Ulan Bator.

   How would you evaluate the proposed Akron–Yellowknife project? Give a detailed list of the necessary steps in your analysis. Explain how the airplane leasing market would be taken into account. If the project is attractive, how would you respond to the manager of the international division?

3. Why is an M.B.A. student who has just learned about DCF like a baby with a hammer? What was the point of our answer?

4. Suppose the current price of gold is $280 per ounce. Hotshot Consultants advises you that gold prices will increase at an average rate of 12 percent for the next two years. After that the growth rate will fall to a long-run trend of 3 percent per year. What is the price of 1 million ounces of gold produced in eight years? Assume that gold prices have a beta of 0 and that the risk-free rate is 5.5 percent.

5. Thanks to acquisition of a key patent, your company now has exclusive production rights for barkelgassers (BGs) in North America. Production facilities for 200,000 BGs per year will require a $25 million immediate capital expenditure. Production costs are estimated at $65 per BG. The BG marketing manager is confident that all 200,000 units can be sold for $100 per unit (in real terms) until the patent runs out five years hence. After that the marketing manager hasn't a clue about what the selling price will be.

   What is the NPV of the BG project? Assume the real cost of capital is 9 percent. To keep things simple, also make the following assumptions:

   * The technology for making BGs will not change. Capital and production costs will stay the same in real terms.
   * Competitors know the technology and can enter as soon as the patent expires, that is, in year 6.
   * If your company invests immediately, full production begins after 12 months, that is, in year 1.
   * There are no taxes.
   * BG production facilities last 12 years. They have no salvage value at the end of their useful life.

6. How would your answer to question 5 change if:

   - Technological improvements reduce the cost of new BG production facilities by 3 percent per year?

   Thus a new plant built in year 1 would cost only 25 (1 − .03) = $24.25 million; a plant built in year 2 would cost $23.52 million; and so on. Assume that production costs per unit remain at $65.

7. Reevaluate the NPV of the proposed polyzone project under each of the following assumptions. Follow the format of Table 11.3. What's the right management decision in each case?

   a. Competitive entry does not begin until year 5, when the spread falls to $1.10 per pound, and is complete in year 6, when the spread is $.95 per pound.

   b. The U.S. chemical company can start up polyzone production at 40 million pounds in year 1 rather than year 2.

   c. The U.S. company makes a technological advance that reduces its annual production costs to $25 million. Competitors' production costs do not change.

8. Photographic laboratories recover and recycle the silver used in photographic film. Stikine River Photo is considering purchase of improved equipment for their laboratory at Telegraph Creek. Here is the information they have:

   - The equipment costs $100,000.
   - It will cost $80,000 per year to run.
   - It has an economic life of 10 years but can be depreciated over 5 years by the straight-line method (see Section 6.2).
   - It will recover an additional 5,000 ounces of silver per year.
   - Silver is selling for $20 per ounce. Over the past 10 years, the price of silver has appreciated by 4.5 percent per year in real terms. Silver is traded in an active, competitive market.
   - Stikine's marginal tax rate is 35 percent. Assume U.S. tax law.
   - Stikine's company cost of capital is 8 percent in real terms.

   What is the NPV of the new equipment? Make additional assumptions as necessary.

9. The Cambridge Opera Association has come up with a unique door prize for its December (2004) fund-raising ball: Twenty door prizes will be distributed, each one a ticket entitling the bearer to receive a cash award from the association on December 30, 2005. The cash award is to be determined by calculating the ratio of the level of the Standard and Poor's Composite Index of stock prices on December 30, 2005, to its level on June 30, 2005, and multiplying by $100. Thus, if the index turns out to be 1,000 on June 30, 2005, and 1,200 on December 30, 2005, the payoff will be 100 × (1,200/1,000) = $120.

   After the ball, a black market springs up in which the tickets are traded. What will the tickets sell for on January 1, 2005? On June 30, 2005? Assume the risk-free interest rate is 10 percent per year. Also assume the Cambridge Opera Association will be solvent at year-end 2005 and will, in fact, pay off on the tickets. Make other assumptions as necessary.

   Would ticket values be different if the tickets' payoffs depended on the Dow Jones Industrial index rather than the Standard and Poor's composite?

10. You are asked to value a large building in northern New Jersey. The valuation is needed for a bankruptcy settlement. Here are the facts:

    - The settlement *requires* that the building's value equal the PV value of the *net cash proceeds* the railroad would receive if it cleared the building and sold it for its highest and best nonrailroad use, which is as a warehouse.
    - The building has been appraised at $1 million. This figure is based on actual recent selling prices of a sample of similar New Jersey buildings used as, or available for use as, warehouses.

- If rented today as a warehouse, the building could generate $80,000 per year. This cash flow is calculated *after* out-of-pocket operating expenses and *after* real estate taxes of $50,000 per year:

Gross rents	$180,000
Operating expenses	50,000
Real estate taxes	50,000
Net	$80,000

Gross rents, operating expenses, and real estate taxes are uncertain but are expected to grow with inflation.

- However, it would take one year and $200,000 to clear out the railroad equipment and prepare the building for use as a warehouse. This expenditure would be spread evenly over the next year.
- The property will be put on the market when ready for use as a warehouse. Your real estate adviser says that properties of this type take, on average, 1 year to sell after they are put on the market. However, the railroad could rent the building as a warehouse while waiting for it to sell.
- The opportunity cost of capital for investment in real estate is 8 percent in *real* terms.
- Your real estate adviser notes that selling prices of comparable buildings in northern New Jersey have declined, in real terms, at an average rate of 2 percent per year over the last 10 years.
- A 5 percent sales commission would be paid by the railroad at the time of the sale.
- The railroad pays no income taxes. It would have to pay property taxes.

CHALLENGE
QUESTIONS

1. The manufacture of polysyllabic acid is a competitive industry. Most plants have an annual output of 100,000 tons. Operating costs are $.90 a ton, and the sales price is $1 a ton. A 100,000-ton plant costs $100,000 and has an indefinite life. Its current scrap value of $60,000 is expected to decline to $57,900 over the next two years.

Phlogiston, Inc., proposes to invest $100,000 in a plant that employs a new low-cost process to manufacture polysyllabic acid. The plant has the same capacity as existing units, but operating costs are $.85 a ton. Phlogiston estimates that it has two years' lead over each of its rivals in use of the process but is unable to build any more plants itself before year 2. Also it believes that demand over the next two years is likely to be sluggish and that its new plant will therefore cause temporary overcapacity.

You can assume that there are no taxes and that the cost of capital is 10 percent.

a. By the end of year 2, the prospective increase in acid demand will require the construction of several new plants using the Phlogiston process. What is the likely NPV of such plants?
b. What does that imply for the price of polysyllabic acid in year 3 and beyond?
c. Would you expect existing plant to be scrapped in year 2? How would your answer differ if scrap value were $40,000 or $80,000?
d. The acid plants of United Alchemists, Inc., have been fully depreciated. Can it operate them profitably after year 2?
e. Acidosis, Inc., purchased a new plant last year for $100,000 and is writing it down by $10,000 a year. Should it scrap this plant in year 2?
f. What would be the NPV of Phlogiston's venture?

2. The world airline system is composed of the routes X and Y, each of which requires 10 aircraft. These routes can be serviced by three types of aircraft—A, B, and C. There are 5 type A aircraft available, 10 type B, and 10 type C. These aircraft are identical except for their operating costs, which are as follows:

Aircraft Type	Annual Operating Cost ($ millions)	
	Route X	Route Y
A	1.5	1.5
B	2.5	2.0
C	4.5	3.5

The aircraft have a useful life of five years and a salvage value of $1 million.

The aircraft owners do not operate the aircraft themselves but rent them to the operators. Owners act competitively to maximize their rental income, and operators attempt to minimize their operating costs. Airfares are also competitively determined.

Assume the cost of capital is 10 percent.

a. Which aircraft would be used on which route, and how much would each aircraft be worth?
b. What would happen to usage and prices of each aircraft if the number of type A aircraft increased to 10?
c. What would happen if the number of type A aircraft increased to 15?
d. What would happen if the number of type A aircraft increased to 20?

State any additional assumptions you need to make.

3. Taxes are a cost, and, therefore, changes in tax rates can affect consumer prices, project lives, and the value of existing firms. The following problem illustrates this. It also illustrates that tax changes that appear to be "good for business" do not always increase the value of existing firms. Indeed, unless new investment incentives increase consumer demand, they can work only by rendering existing equipment obsolete.

The manufacture of bucolic acid is a competitive business. Demand is steadily expanding, and new plants are constantly being opened. Expected cash flows from an investment in a new plant are as follows:

	0	1	2	3
1. Initial investment	100			
2. Revenues		100	100	100
3. Cash operating costs		50	50	50
4. Tax depreciation		33.33	33.33	33.33
5. Income pretax		16.67	16.67	16.67
6. Tax at 40%		6.67	6.67	6.67
7. Net income		10	10	10
8. After-tax salvage				15
9. Cash flow (7 + 8 + 4 − 1)	−100	+43.33	+43.33	+58.33

NPV at 20% = 0

Assumptions:
1. Tax depreciation is straight-line over three years.
2. Pretax salvage value is 25 in year 3 and 50 if the asset is scrapped in year 2.
3. Tax on salvage value is 40 percent of the difference between salvage value and depreciated investment.
4. The cost of capital is 20 percent.

a. What is the value of a one-year-old plant? Of a two-year-old plant?
b. Suppose that the government now changes tax depreciation to allow a 100 percent writeoff in year 1. How does this affect the value of existing one- and two-year-old plants? Existing plants must continue using the original tax depreciation schedule.

c. Would it now make sense to scrap existing plants when they are two rather than three years old?

d. How would your answers change if the corporate income tax were abolished entirely?

MINI-CASE

Ecsy-Cola[18]

Libby Flannery, the regional manager of Ecsy-Cola, the international soft drinks empire, was reviewing her investment plans for Central Asia. She had contemplated launching Ecsy-Cola in the ex-Soviet republic of Inglistan in 2004. This would involve a capital outlay of $20 million in 2004 to build a bottling plant and set up a distribution system there. Fixed costs (for manufacturing, distribution, and marketing) would then be $3 million per year from 2003 onward. This would be sufficient to make and sell 200 million liters per year—enough for every man, woman, and child in Inglistan to drink four bottles per week! But there would be few savings from building a smaller plant, and import tariffs and transport costs in the region would keep all production within national borders.

The variable costs of production and distribution would be 12 cents per liter. Company policy requires a rate of return of 25 percent in nominal dollar terms, after local taxes but before deducting any costs of financing. The sales revenue is forecasted to be 35 cents per liter.

Bottling plants last almost forever, and all unit costs and revenues were expected to remain constant in nominal terms. Tax would be payable at a rate of 30 percent, and under the Inglistan corporate tax code, capital expenditures can be written off on a straight-line basis over four years.

All these inputs were reasonably clear. But Ms. Flannery racked her brain trying to forecast sales. Ecsy-Cola found that the "1-2-4" rule works in most new markets. Sales typically double in the second year, double again in the third year, and after that remain roughly constant. Libby's best guess was that, if she went ahead immediately, initial sales in Inglistan would be 12.5 million liters in 2005, ramping up to 50 million in 2007 and onward.

Ms. Flannery also worried whether it would be better to wait a year. The soft drink market was developing rapidly in neighboring countries, and in a year's time she should have a much better idea whether Ecsy-Cola would be likely to catch on in Inglistan. If it didn't catch on and sales stalled below 20 million liters, a large investment probably would not be justified.

Ms. Flannery had assumed that Ecsy-Cola's keen rival, Sparky-Cola, would not also enter the market. But last week she received a shock when in the lobby of the Kapitaliste Hotel she bumped into her opposite number at Sparky-Cola. Sparky-Cola would face costs similar to Ecsy-Cola. How would Sparky-Cola respond if Ecsy-Cola entered the market? Would it decide to enter also? If so, how would that affect the profitability of Ecsy-Cola's project?

Ms. Flannery thought again about postponing investment for a year. Suppose Sparky-Cola was interested in the Inglistan market. Would that favor delay or immediate action? Maybe Ecsy-Cola should announce its plans before Sparky-Cola had a chance to develop its own proposals. It seemed that the Inglistan project was becoming more complicated by the day.

Questions

1. Calculate the NPV of the proposed investment, using the inputs suggested in this case. How sensitive is this NPV to future sales volume?

2. What are the pros and cons of waiting for a year before deciding whether to invest? *Hint:* What happens if demand turns out high and Sparky-Cola also invests? What if Ecsy-Cola invests right away and gains a one-year head start on Sparky-Cola?

---

[18]We thank Anthony Neuberger for suggesting this topic.

CHAPTER TWELVE

MAKING SURE
MANAGERS
MAXIMIZE NPV

SO FAR WE'VE concentrated on criteria and procedures for identifying capital investments with positive NPVs. If a firm takes all (and only) positive-NPV projects, it maximizes the firm's value. But do the firm's managers *want* to maximize value?

Managers have no special gene or chromosome that automatically aligns their personal interests with outside investors' financial objectives. So how do shareholders ensure that top managers do not feather their own beds or grind their own axes? And how do top managers ensure that middle managers and employees try as hard as they can to find positive-NPV projects?

Here we circle back to the principal–agent problems first raised in Chapters 1 and 2. Shareholders are the ultimate principals; top managers are the stockholders' agents. But middle managers and employees are in turn agents of top management. Thus senior managers, including the chief financial officer, are simultaneously agents *vis-à-vis* shareholders and principals *vis-à-vis* the rest of the firm. The problem is to get everyone working together to maximize value.

This chapter summarizes how corporations grapple with that problem as they identify and commit to capital investment projects. We start with basic facts and tradeoffs and end with difficult problems in performance measurement. The main topics are as follows:

- **Process:** How companies develop plans and budgets for capital investments, how they authorize specific projects, and how they check whether projects perform as promised.
- **Information:** Getting accurate information and good forecasts to decision makers.
- **Incentives:** Making sure managers and employees are rewarded appropriately when they add value to the firm.
- **Performance Measurement:** You can't reward value added unless you can measure it. Since you get what you reward, and reward what you measure, you get what you measure. Make sure you are measuring the right thing.

In each case we will summarize standard practice and warn against common mistakes. The section on incentives probes more deeply into principal–agent relationships. The last two sections of the chapter describe performance measures, including residual income and economic value added. We also uncover the biases lurking in accounting rates of return. The pitfalls in measuring profitability are serious but are not as widely recognized as they should be.

12.1 THE CAPITAL INVESTMENT PROCESS

For most large firms, the investment process starts with preparation of an annual **capital budget,** which is a list of investment projects planned for the coming year. Since the capital budget does not give the final go-ahead to spend money, the description of each project is not as detailed at this stage as it is later.

Most firms let project proposals bubble up from plants, product lines, or regional operations for review by divisional management and then from divisions for review by senior management and their planning staff. Of course middle managers cannot identify all worthwhile projects. For example, the managers of plants A and B cannot be expected to see the potential economies of closing their plants and consolidating production at a new plant C. Divisional managers would propose plant C. Similarly, divisions 1 and 2 may not be eager to give up their own computers to a corporationwide information system. That proposal would come from senior management.

Preparation of the capital budget is not a rigid, bureaucratic exercise. There is plenty of give-and-take and back-and-forth. Divisional managers negotiate with plant managers and fine-tune the division's list of projects. There may be special analyses of major outlays or ventures into new areas.

The final capital budget must also reflect the corporation's strategic planning. Strategic planning takes a top-down view of the company. It attempts to identify businesses in which the company has a competitive advantage. It also attempts to identify businesses to sell or liquidate and declining businesses that should be allowed to run down.

In other words, a firm's capital investment choices should reflect both bottom-up and top-down processes—capital budgeting and strategic planning, respectively. The two processes should complement each other. Plant and division managers, who do most of the work in bottom-up capital budgeting, may not see the forest for the trees. Strategic planners may have a mistaken view of the forest because they do not look at the trees one by one.

Project Authorizations

Once the capital budget has been approved by top management and the board of directors, it is the official plan for the ensuing year. However, it is not the final sign-off for specific projects. Most companies require **appropriation requests** for each proposal. These requests include detailed forecasts, discounted-cash-flow analyses, and backup information.

Because investment decisions are so important to the value of the firm, final approval of appropriation requests tends to be reserved for top management. Companies set ceilings on the size of projects that divisional managers can authorize. Often these ceilings are surprisingly low. For example, a large company, investing $400 million per year, might require top management approval of all projects over $500,000.

Some Investments May Not Show Up in the Capital Budget

The boundaries of capital expenditure are often imprecise. Consider the investments in information technology, or IT (computers, software and systems, training, and telecommunications), made by large banks and securities firms. These investments soak up *hundreds* of millions of dollars annually, and some multiyear IT projects have costs well over $1 billion. Yet much of this expenditure goes to intangibles such as system design, testing, or training. Such outlays often bypass capital expenditure controls, particularly if the outlays are made piecemeal rather than as large, discrete commitments.

Investments in IT may not appear in the capital budget, but for financial institutions they are much more important than outlays for plant and equipment. An efficient information system is a valuable asset for any company, especially if it allows the company to offer a special product or service to its customers. Therefore outlays for IT deserve careful financial analysis.

Here are some further examples of important investments that rarely appear on the capital budget.

Research and Development   For many companies, the most important asset is technology. The technology is embodied in patents, licenses, unique products or services, or special production methods. The technology is generated by investment in research and development (R&D)

R&D budgets for major pharmaceutical companies routinely exceed $1 billion. Glaxo Smith Kline, one of the largest pharmaceutical companies, spent nearly $4 billion on R&D in 2000. The R&D cost of bringing *one* new prescription drug to market has been estimated at over $300 million.[1]

Marketing   In 1998 Gillette launched the Mach3 safety razor. It had invested $750 million in new, custom machinery and renovated production facilities. It planned to spend $300 million on the initial marketing program. Its goal was to make the Mach3 a long-lived, brand-name, cash-cow consumer product. This marketing outlay was clearly a capital investment, because it was cash spent to generate future cash inflows.

Training and Personnel Development   By launch of the Mach3, Gillette had hired 160 new workers and paid for 30,000 hours of training.

Small Decisions Add Up   Operating managers make investment decisions every day. They may carry extra inventories of raw materials or spare parts, just to be sure they won't be caught short. Managers at the confabulator plant in Quayle City, Arkansas, may decide they need one more forklift or a cappuccino machine for the cafeteria. They may hold on to an idle machine tool or an empty warehouse that could have been sold. These are not big investments ($5,000 here, $40,000 there) but they add up.

How can the financial manager assure that small investments are made for the right reasons? Financial staff can't second-guess every operating decision. They can't demand a discounted-cash-flow analysis of a cappuccino machine. Instead they have to make operating managers conscious of the cost of investment and alert for investments that add value. We return to this problem later in the chapter.

Our general point is this: The financial manager has to consider all investments, regardless of whether they appear in the formal capital budget. The financial manager has to decide which investments are most important to the success of the company and where financial analysis is most likely to pay off. The financial manager in a pharmaceutical company should be deeply involved in decisions about R&D. In a consumer goods company, the financial manager should play a key role in marketing decisions to develop and launch new products.

Postaudits

Most firms keep a check on the progress of large projects by conducting postaudits shortly after the projects have begun to operate. Postaudits identify problems that need fixing, check the accuracy of forecasts, and suggest questions that should have been asked before the project was undertaken. Postaudits pay off mainly by helping managers to do a better job when it comes to the next round of investments. After a postaudit the controller may say, "We should have anticipated the extra working capital needed to support the project." When the next proposal arrives, working capital will get the attention it deserves.

Postaudits may not be able to measure all cash flows generated by a project. It may be impossible to split the project away from the rest of the business. Suppose

---

[1]This figure is for drugs developed in the late 1980s and early 1990s. It is after-tax, stated in 1994 dollars. The comparable pretax figure is over $400 million. See S. C. Myers and C. D. Howe, *A Life-Cycle Model of Pharmaceutical R&D*, MIT Program on the Pharmaceutical Industry, 1997.

that you have just taken over a trucking firm that operates a merchandise delivery service for local stores. You decide to revitalize the business by cutting costs and improving service. This requires three investments:

1. Buying five new diesel trucks.
2. Constructing a dispatching center.
3. Buying a computer and special software to keep track of packages and schedule trucks.

A year later you try a postaudit of the computer. You verify that it is working properly and check actual costs of purchase, installation, and training against projections. But how do you identify the incremental cash inflows generated by the computer? No one has kept records of the extra diesel fuel that *would have been* used or the extra shipments that *would have been* lost had the computer not been installed. You may be able to verify that service is better, but how much of the improvement comes from the new trucks, how much comes from the dispatching center, and how much comes from the new computer? It is impossible to say. The only meaningful way to judge the success or failure of your revitalization program is to examine the delivery business as a whole.[2]

12.2 DECISION MAKERS NEED GOOD INFORMATION

Good investment decisions require good information. Decision makers get such information only if other managers are encouraged to supply it. Here are four information problems that financial managers need to think about.

Establishing Consistent Forecasts

Inconsistent assumptions often creep into investment proposals. Suppose the manager of your furniture division is bullish on housing starts but the manager of your appliance division is bearish. This inconsistency makes the furniture division's projects look better than the appliance division's. Senior management ought to negotiate a consensus estimate and make sure that all NPVs are recomputed using that joint estimate. Then projects can be evaluated consistently.

This is why many firms begin the capital budgeting process by establishing forecasts of economic indicators, such as inflation and growth in gross national product, as well as forecasts of particular items that are important to the firm's business, such as housing starts or the price of raw materials. These forecasts can then be used as the basis for all project analyses.

Reducing Forecast Bias

Anyone who is keen to get a project accepted is likely to look on the bright side when forecasting the project's cash flows. Such overoptimism seems to be a common feature in financial forecasts. Overoptimism afflicts governments too, probably more than private businesses. How often have you heard of a new dam, highway, or military aircraft that actually cost *less* than was originally forecasted?

---

[2]Even here you don't know the incremental cash flows unless you can establish what the business would have earned if you had not made the changes.

You will probably never be able to eliminate bias completely, but if you are aware of why bias occurs, you are at least part of the way there. Project sponsors are likely to overstate their case deliberately only if you, the manager, encourage them to do so. For example, if they believe that success depends on having the largest division rather than the most profitable one, they will propose large expansion projects that they do not truly believe have positive NPVs. Or if they believe that you won't listen to them unless they paint a rosy picture, you will be presented with rosy pictures. Or if you invite each division to compete for limited resources, you will find that each attempts to outbid the other for those resources. The fault in such cases is your own—if you hold up the hoop, others will try to jump through it.

Getting Senior Management the Information That It Needs

Valuing capital investment opportunities is hard enough when you can do the entire job yourself. In real life it is a cooperative effort. Although cooperation brings more knowledge to bear, it has its own problems. Some are unavoidable, just another cost of doing business. Others can be alleviated by adding checks and balances to the investment process.

Many of the problems stem from sponsors' eagerness to obtain approval for their favorite projects. As a proposal travels up the organization, alliances are formed. Preparation of the request inevitably involves compromises. But, once a division has agreed on its plants' proposals, the plants unite in competing against outsiders.

The competition among divisions can be put to good use if it forces division managers to develop a well-thought-out case for what they want to do. But the competition has its costs as well. Several thousand appropriation requests may reach the senior management level each year, all essentially sales documents presented by united fronts and designed to persuade. Alternative schemes have been filtered out at an earlier stage. The danger is that senior management cannot obtain (let alone absorb) the information to evaluate each project rationally.

The dangers are illustrated by the following practical question: Should we announce a definite opportunity cost of capital for computing the NPV of projects in our furniture division? The answer in theory is a clear yes, providing that the projects of the division are all in the same risk class. Remember that most project analysis is done at the plant or divisional level. Only a small proportion of project ideas analyzed survive for submission to top management. Plant and division managers cannot judge projects correctly unless they know the true opportunity cost of capital.

Suppose that senior management settles on 12 percent. That helps plant managers make rational decisions. But it also tells them exactly how optimistic they have to be to get their pet project accepted. Brealey and Myers's Second Law states: *The proportion of proposed projects having a positive NPV at the official corporate hurdle rate is independent of the hurdle rate.*[3]

This is not a facetious conjecture. The law was tested in a large oil company, whose capital budgeting staff kept careful statistics on forecasted profitability of proposed projects. One year top management announced a big push to conserve cash. It imposed discipline on capital expenditures by increasing the corporate hurdle rate by several percentage points. But staff statistics showed that the fraction of proposals

---

[3]There is no First Law; we thought that "Second Law" sounded better. There *is* a Third Law, but that is for another chapter.

with positive NPVs stayed rock-steady at about 85 percent of all proposals. Top management's tighter discipline was repaid with expanded optimism.

A firm that accepts poor information at the top faces two consequences. First, senior management cannot evaluate individual projects. In a study by Bower of a large multidivisional company, projects that had the approval of a division general manager were seldom turned down by his or her group of divisions, and those reaching top management were almost never rejected.[4] Second, since managers have limited control over project-by-project decisions, capital investment decisions are effectively decentralized regardless of what formal procedures specify.

Some senior managers try to impose discipline and offset optimism by setting rigid capital expenditure limits. This artificial capital rationing forces plant or division managers to set priorities. The firm ends up using capital rationing not because capital is truly unobtainable but as a way of decentralizing decisions.

Eliminating Conflicts of Interest

Plant and divisional managers are concerned about their own futures. Sometimes their interests conflict with stockholders' and that may lead to investment decisions that do not maximize shareholder wealth. For example, new plant managers naturally want to demonstrate good performance right away, in order to move up the corporate ladder, so they are tempted to propose quick-payback projects even if NPV is sacrificed. And if their performance is judged on book earnings, they will also be attracted by projects whose accounting results look good. That leads us to the next topic: how to motivate managers.

 ## 12.3 INCENTIVES

Managers will act in shareholders' interests only if they have the right incentives. Good capital investment decisions therefore depend on how managers' performance is measured and rewarded.

We start this section with an overview of agency problems encountered in capital investment, and then we look at how top management is actually compensated. Finally we consider how top management can set incentives for the middle managers and other employees who actually operate the business.

Overview: Agency Problems in Capital Budgeting

As you have surely guessed, there is no perfect system of incentives. But it's easy to see what *won't* work. Suppose shareholders decide to pay the financial managers a fixed salary—no bonuses, no stock options, just $X per month. The manager, as the stockholders' agent, is instructed to find and invest in all positive-NPV projects open to the firm. The manager may sincerely try to do so, but will face various tempting alternatives:

Reduced effort. Finding and implementing investment in truly valuable projects is a high-effort, high-pressure activity. The financial manager will be tempted to slack off.

---

[4]J. L. Bower, *Managing the Resource Allocation Process: A Study of Corporate Planning and Investment*, Division of Research, Graduate School of Business Administration, Harvard University, Boston, 1970.

Perks. Our hypothetical financial manager gets no bonuses. Only $X per month. But he or she may take a bonus anyway, not in cash, but in tickets to sporting events, lavish office accommodations, planning meetings scheduled at luxury resorts, and so on. Economists refer to these nonpecuniary rewards as *private benefits*. Ordinary people call them *perks* (short for perquisites.)

Empire building. Other things equal, managers prefer to run large businesses rather than small ones. Getting from small to large may not be a positive-NPV undertaking.

Entrenching investment. Suppose manager Q considers two expansion plans. One plan will require a manager with special skills that manager Q just happens to have. The other plan requires only a general-purpose manager. Guess which plan Q will favor. Projects designed to require or reward the skills of existing managers are called *entrenching investments*.[5]

Entrenching investments and empire building are typical symptoms of overinvestment, that is, investing beyond the point where NPV falls to zero. The temptation to overinvest is highest when the firm has plenty of cash but limited investment opportunities. Michael Jensen calls this a *free-cash-flow* problem: "The problem is how to motivate managers to disgorge the cash rather than investing it below the cost of capital or wasting it in organizational inefficiencies."[6]

Avoiding risk. If a financial manager receives only a fixed salary, and cannot share in the upside of risky projects, then safe projects are, from the manager's viewpoint, better than risky ones. But risky projects can have large, positive NPVs.

A manager on a fixed salary could hardly avoid all these temptations all of the time. The resulting loss in value is an agency cost.

Monitoring

Agency costs can be reduced in two ways: by *monitoring* the managers' effort and actions and by giving them the right *incentives* to maximize value.

Monitoring can prevent the more obvious agency costs, such as blatant perks or empire building. It can confirm that the manager is putting sufficient time on the job. But monitoring costs time, effort, and money. Some monitoring is almost always worthwhile, but a limit is soon reached at which an extra dollar spent on monitoring would not return an extra dollar of value from reduced agency costs. Like all investments, monitoring encounters diminishing returns.

Some agency costs can't be prevented even with spendthrift monitoring. Suppose a shareholder undertakes to monitor capital investment decisions. How could he or she ever know for sure whether a capital budget approved by top management includes (1) *all* the positive-NPV opportunities open to the firm and (2) *no* projects with negative NPVs due to empire-building or entrenching investments? The managers obviously know more about the firm's prospects than outsiders ever can. If the shareholder could list all projects and their NPVs, then the managers would hardly be needed!

[5]A. Shleifer and R. W. Vishny, "Management Entrenchment: The Case of Manager-Specific Investments," *Journal of Financial Economics* 25 (November 1989), pp. 123–140.

[6]M. C. Jensen, "Agency Costs of Free Cash Flow, Corporate Finance and Takeovers," *American Economic Review* 76 (May 1986), p. 323.

Who actually does the monitoring? Ultimately it is the shareholders' responsibility, but in large, public companies, monitoring is *delegated* to the board of directors, who are elected by shareholders and are supposed to represent their interests. The board meets regularly, both formally and informally, with top management. Attentive directors come to know a great deal about the firm's prospects and performance and the strengths and weaknesses of its top management.

The board also hires independent accountants to audit the firm's financial statements. If the audit uncovers no problems, the auditors issue an opinion that the financial statements fairly represent the company's financial condition and are consistent with generally accepted accounting principles (GAAP, for short).

If problems are found, the auditors will negotiate changes in assumptions or procedures. Managers almost always agree, because if acceptable changes are not made, the auditors will issue a *qualified opinion*, which is bad news for the company and its shareholders. A qualified opinion suggests that managers are covering something up and undermines investors' confidence that they can monitor effectively.

A qualified opinion may be bad news, but when investors learn of accounting problems that have escaped detection by auditors, there's hell to pay. On April 15, 1998, Cendant Corporation announced discovery of serious accounting irregularities. The next day Cendant shares fell by about 46 percent, wiping $14 billion off the market value of the company.[7]

Lenders also monitor. If a company takes out a large bank loan, the bank will track the company's assets, earnings, and cash flow. By monitoring to protect its loan, the bank protects shareholders' interests also.[8]

Delegated monitoring is especially important when ownership is widely dispersed. If there is a dominant shareholder, he or she will generally keep a close eye on top management. But when the number of stockholders is large, and each stockholding is small, individual investors cannot justify much time and expense for monitoring. Each is tempted to leave the task to others, taking a free ride on others' efforts. But if everybody prefers to let somebody else do it, then it won't get done; that is, monitoring by shareholders will not be strong or effective. Economists call this the *free-rider problem*.[9]

Compensation

Because monitoring is necessarily imperfect, compensation plans must be designed to give managers the right incentives.

---

[7]Cendant was formed in 1997 by the merger of HFS, Inc., and CUC International, Inc. It appears that about $500 million of CUC revenue from 1995 to 1997 was just made up and that about 60 percent of CUC's income in 1997 was fake. By August 1998, several CUC managers were fired or had resigned, including Cendant's chairman, the founder of CUC. Over 70 lawsuits had been filed on behalf of investors in the company. Investigations were continuing. See E. Nelson and J. S. Lubin. "Buy the Numbers? How Whistle-Blowers Set Off a Fraud Probe That Crushed Cendant," *The Wall Street Journal* (August 13, 1998), pp. A1, A8.

[8]Lenders' and shareholders' interests are not always aligned—see Chapter 18. But a company's ability to satisfy lenders is normally good news for stockholders, particularly when lenders are well placed to monitor. See C. James "Some Evidence on the Uniqueness of Bank Loans," *Journal of Financial Economics* 19 (December 1987), pp. 217–235.

[9]The free-rider problem might seem to drive out all monitoring by dispersed shareholders. But investors have another reason to investigate: They want to make money on their common stock portfolios by buying undervalued companies and selling overvalued ones. To do this they must investigate companies' performance.

Compensation can be based on input (for example, the manager's effort or demonstrated willingness to bear risk) or on output (actual return or value added as a result of the manager's decisions). But input is so difficult to measure; for example, how does an outside investor observe effort? Therefore incentives are almost always based on output. The trouble is that output depends not just on the manager's decisions but also on many other events outside his or her control.

The fortunes of a business never depend only on the efforts of a few key individuals. The state of the economy or the industry is usually at least as important for the firm's success. Unless you can separate out these influences, you face a dilemma. You want to provide managers with a high-powered incentive, so that they capture all the benefits of their contributions to the firm, but such an arrangement would load onto the managers all the risk of fluctuations in the firm's value. Think of what this would mean in the case of GE, where in a recession income can fall by more than $1 billion. No group of managers would have the wealth to stump up a significant fraction of $1 billion, and they would certainly be reluctant to take on the risk of huge personal losses in a recession. A recession is not their fault.

The result is a compromise. Firms do link managers' pay to performance, but fluctuations in firm value are shared by managers and shareholders. Managers bear some of the risks that are outside their control and shareholders bear some of the agency costs if managers shirk, empire build, or otherwise fail to maximize value. Thus, some agency costs are inevitable. For example, since managers split the gains from hard work with the stockholders but reap all the personal benefits of an idle or indulgent life, they will be tempted to put in less effort than if shareholders could reward their effort perfectly.

If the firm's fortunes are largely outside managers' control, it makes sense to offer the managers low-powered incentives. In such cases the managers' compensation should be largely in the form of a fixed salary. If success depends almost exclusively on individual skill and effort, then managers are given high-powered incentives and end up bearing substantial risks. For example, a large part of the compensation of traders and salespeople in securities firms is in the form of bonuses or stock options.

How do managers of large corporations share in the fortunes of their firms? Michael Jensen and Kevin Murphy found that the median holding of chief executive officers (CEOs) in their firms was only .14 percent of the outstanding shares. On average, for every $1,000 addition to shareholder wealth, the CEO received $3.25 in extra compensation. Jensen and Murphy conclude that "corporate America pays its most important leaders like bureaucrats," and ask "Is it any wonder then that so many CEOs act like bureaucrats rather than the value-maximizing entrepreneurs companies need to enhance their standing in world markets?"[10]

Jensen and Murphy may overstate their case. It is true that managers bear only a small portion of the gains and losses in firm value. However, the payoff to the manager of a large, successful firm can still be very large. For example, when

---

[10]M. C. Jensen and K. Murphy, "CEO Incentives—It's Not How Much You Pay, But How," *Harvard Business Review* 68 (May–June 1990), p. 138. The data for Jensen and Murphy's study ended in 1983. Hall and Liebman have updated the study and argue that the sensitivity of compensation to changes in firm value has increased significantly. See B. J. Hall and J. B. Liebman, "Are CEOs Really Paid Like Bureaucrats?" Harvard University working paper, August 1997.

Michael Eisner was hired as CEO by the Walt Disney Company, his compensation package had three main components: a base annual salary of $750,000; an annual bonus of 2 percent of Disney's net income above a threshold of normal profitability; and a 10-year option that allowed him to purchase 2 million shares of stock for $14 a share, which was about the price of Disney stock at the time. As it turned out, by the end of Eisner's six-year contract the value of Disney shares had increased by $12 billion, more than sixfold. While Eisner received only 1.6 percent of that gain in value as compensation, this still amounted to $190 million.[11]

Because most CEOs own stock and stock options in their firms, managers of poorly performing firms often actually lose money; they also often lose their jobs. For example, a study of the remuneration of the chief executives of large U.S. firms found that the heads of firms that were in the top 10 percent in terms of stock market performance received over $9 million more in compensation than their brethren at the bottom 10 percent of the spectrum.[12]

Chief executives in the United States are generally paid more than those in other countries and their pay is more closely tied to stock returns. For example, Kaplan found that top managers in the United States earn salary plus bonus five times that of their Japanese counterparts, although Japanese managers receive more noncash compensation. The United States managers' stakes in their companies averaged more than double the Japanese managers' stakes.[13]

In the ideal incentive scheme, management should bear all the consequences of their own actions, but should not be exposed to the fluctuations in firm value over which they have no control. That raises a question: Managers are not responsible for fluctuations in the general level of the stock market. So why don't companies tie top management's compensation to stock returns relative to the market or to the firm's close competitors? This would tie managers' compensation somewhat more closely to their own contributions.

Tying top management compensation to stock prices raises another difficult issue. The market value of a company's shares reflects investors' expectations. The stockholders' return depends on how well the company performs relative to expectations. For example, suppose a company announces the appointment of an outstanding new manager. The stock price leaps up in anticipation of improved performance. Thenceforth, if the new manager delivers exactly the good performance that investors expected, the stock will earn only a normal, average rate of return. In this case a compensation scheme linked to the stock return would fail to recognize the manager's special contribution.

---

[11]We don't know whether Michael Eisner's contribution to the firm over the six-year period was more or less than $190 million. However, one of the benefits of paying such a large sum to the CEO is that it provides a wonderful incentive for junior managers to compete for the prize. In effect the firm runs a *tournament*, in which there is a large prize for the winner and considerably smaller prizes for runners-up. The incentive effects of tournaments show up dramatically in PGA golf tournaments. Players who enter the final round within striking distance of big prize money perform much better than their past records would predict. Those who receive only a small increase in prize money by moving up the ranking are more inclined to relax and deliver only average performance. See R. G. Ehrenberg and M. L. Bognanno, "Do Tournaments Have Incentive Effects?" *Journal of Political Economy* 6 (December 1990), pp. 1307–1324.

[12]See B. J. Hall and J. B. Liebman, op. cit.

[13]S. Kaplan, "Top Executive Rewards and Firm Performance: A Comparison of Japan and the USA," *Journal of Political Economy* 102 (June 1994), pp. 510–546.

12.4 MEASURING AND REWARDING PERFORMANCE: RESIDUAL INCOME AND EVA

Almost all top executives of firms with publicly traded shares have compensation packages that depend in part on their firms' stock price performance. But their compensation also depends on increases in earnings or on other accounting measures of performance. For lower-level managers, compensation packages usually depend more on accounting measures and less on stock returns.

Accounting measures of performance have two advantages:

- They are based on absolute performance, rather than on performance relative to investors' expectations.
- They make it possible to measure the performance of junior managers whose responsibility extends to only a single division or plant.

Tying compensation to accounting profits also creates some obvious problems. First, accounting profits are partly within the control of management. For example, managers whose pay depends on near-term earnings may cut maintenance or staff training. This is not a recipe for adding value, but an ambitious manager hoping for a quick promotion will be tempted to pump up short-term profits, leaving longer-run problems to his or her successors.

Second, accounting earnings and rates of return can be severely biased measures of true profitability. We ignore this problem for now, but return to it in the next section.

Third, growth in earnings does not necessarily mean that shareholders are better off. Any investment with a positive rate of return (1 or 2 percent will do) will eventually increase earnings. Therefore, if managers are told to maximize growth in earnings, they will dutifully invest in projects offering 1 or 2 percent rates of return—projects that destroy value. But shareholders don't want growth in earnings for its own sake, and they are not content with 1 or 2 percent returns. They want positive-NPV investments, and *only* positive-NPV investments. They want the company to invest only if the expected rate of return exceeds the cost of capital.

In short, managers ought not to forget the cost of capital. In judging their performance, the focus should be on value added, that is, on returns over and above the cost of capital.

Look at Table 12.1, which contains a simplified income statement and balance sheet for your company's Quayle City confabulator plant. There are two methods for judging whether the plant has increased shareholder value.

Net Return on Investment   Does the return on investment exceed the cost of capital? The net return to investment method calculates the difference between them.

As you can see from Table 12.1, your corporation has invested $1,000 million ($1 billion) in the Quayle City plant.[14] The plant's net earnings are $130 million. Therefore the firm is earning a return on investment (ROI) of 130/1,000 = .13 or

---

[14]In practice, investment would be measured as the average of beginning- and end-of-year assets. See Chapter 29.

TABLE 12.1

Simplified statements of income and assets for the Quayle City confabulator plant (figures in $ millions).

*Includes depreciation expense.

†Current assets less current liabilities.

Income		Assets	
Sales	$550	Net working capital†	$80
Cost of goods sold*	275	Property, plant, and equipment investment	1,170
Selling, general, and administrative expenses	75	*Less* cumulative depreciation	360
	200	Net investment	810
Taxes at 35%	70	Other assets	110
Net income	$130	Total assets	$1,000

13 percent.[15] If the cost of capital is (say) 10 percent, then the firm's activities are adding to shareholder value. The *net* return is 13 − 10 = 3 percent. If the cost of capital is (say) 20 percent, then shareholders would have been better off investing $1 billion somewhere else. In this case the net return is negative, at 13 − 20 = −7 percent.

Residual Income or Economic Value Added (EVA ©)[16]   The second method calculates a net dollar return to shareholders. It asks, What are earnings after deducting a charge for the cost of capital?

When firms calculate income, they start with revenues and then deduct costs, such as wages, raw material costs, overhead, and taxes. But there is one cost that they do not commonly deduct: the cost of capital. True, they allow for depreciation of the assets financed by investors' capital, but investors also expect a positive return on their investment. As we pointed out in Chapter 10, a business that breaks even in terms of accounting profits is really making a loss; it is failing to cover the cost of capital.

To judge the net contribution to value, we need to deduct the cost of capital contributed to the plant by the parent company and its stockholders. For example, suppose that the cost of capital is 12 percent. Then the dollar cost of capital for the Quayle City plant is .12 × $1,000 = $120 million. The net gain is therefore 130 − 120 = $10 million. This is the addition to shareholder wealth due to management's hard work (or good luck).

Net income after deducting the dollar return required by investors is called *residual income, economic value added,* or *EVA.* The formula is

$$EVA = \text{residual income} = \text{income earned} - \text{income required}$$
$$= \text{income earned} - \text{cost of capital} \times \text{investment}$$

For our example, the calculation is

$$EVA = \text{residual income} = 130 - (.12 \times 1,000) = +\$10 \text{ million}$$

[15]Notice that earnings are calculated after tax but with no deductions for interest paid. The plant is evaluated as if it were all-equity financed. This is standard practice (see Chapter 6). It helps to separate investment and financing decisions. The tax advantages of debt financing supported by the plant are picked up not in the plant's earnings or cash flows but in the discount rate. The cost of capital is the after-tax weighted average cost of capital, or WACC. WACC is explained in Chapter 19.

[16]EVA is the term used by the consulting firm Stern–Stewart, which has done much to popularize and implement this measure of residual income. With Stern–Stewart's permission, we omit the copyright symbol in what follows.

But if the cost of capital were 20 percent, EVA would be negative by $70 million.

Net return on investment and EVA are focusing on the same question. When return on investment equals the cost of capital, net return and EVA are both zero. But the net return is a percentage and ignores the scale of the company. EVA recognizes the amount of capital employed and the number of dollars of additional wealth created.

A growing number of firms now calculate EVA and tie management compensation to it.[17] They believe that a focus on EVA can help managers concentrate on increasing shareholder wealth. One example is Quaker Oats:

> Until Quaker adopted [EVA] in 1991, its businesses had one overriding goal—increasing quarterly earnings. To do it, they guzzled capital. They offered sharp price discounts at the end of each quarter, so plants ran overtime turning out huge shipments of Gatorade, Rice-A-Roni, 100% Natural Cereal, and other products. Managers led the late rush, since their bonuses depended on raising profits each quarter.
>
> This is the pernicious practice known as trade loading (because it loads up the trade, or retailers, with product) and many consumer product companies are finally admitting it damages long-run returns. An important reason is that it demands so much capital. Pumping up sales requires many warehouses (capital) to hold vast temporary inventories (more capital). But who cared? Quaker's operating businesses paid no charge for capital in internal accounting, so they barely noticed. It took EVA to spot the problem.[18]

When Quaker Oats implemented EVA, most of the capital-guzzling stopped.

The term *EVA* has been popularized by the consulting firm Stern–Stewart. But the concept of residual income has been around for some time,[19] and many companies that are not Stern–Stewart clients use this concept to measure and reward managers' performance.

Other consulting firms have their own versions of residual income. McKinsey & Company uses *economic profit (EP)*, defined as capital invested multiplied by the spread between return on investment and the cost of capital. This is another expression of the concept of residual income. For the Quayle City plant, with a 12 percent cost of capital, economic profit is the same as EVA:

$$\text{Economic profit} = EP = (\text{ROI} - r) \times \text{capital invested}$$
$$= (.13 - .12) \times 1,000 = \$10 \text{ million}$$

Pros and Cons of EVA

Let's start with the pros. EVA, economic profit, and other residual income measures are clearly better than earnings or earnings growth for measuring performance. A plant or division that's generating lots of EVA should generate accolades

---

[17]It can be shown that compensation plans that are linked to economic value added can induce a manager to choose the efficient investment level. See W. P. Rogerson, "International Cost Allocation and Managerial Incentives: A Theory Explaining the Use of Economic Value Added as a Performance Measure," *Journal of Political Economy* 4 (August 1977), pp. 770–795.

[18]Shawn Tully, "The Real Key to Creating Shareholder Wealth," *Fortune* (September 20, 1993), p. 48.

[19]EVA is conceptually the same as the residual income measure long advocated by some accounting scholars. See, for example, R. Anthony, "Accounting for the Cost of Equity," *Harvard Business Review* 51 (1973), pp. 88–102 and "Equity Interest—Its Time Has Come," *Journal of Accountancy* 154 (1982), pp. 76–93.

for its managers as well as value for shareholders. EVA may also highlight parts of the business that are not performing up to scratch. If a division is failing to earn a positive EVA, its management is likely to face some pointed questions about whether the division's assets could be better employed elsewhere.

EVA sends a message to managers: Invest if and only if the increase in earnings is enough to cover the cost of capital. For managers who are used to tracking earnings or growth in earnings, this is a relatively easy message to grasp. Therefore EVA can be used down deep in the organization as an incentive compensation system. It is a substitute for explicit monitoring by top management. Instead of *telling* plant and divisional managers not to waste capital and then trying to figure out whether they are complying, EVA rewards them for careful and thoughtful investment decisions. Of course, if you tie junior managers' compensation to their economic value added, you must also give them power over those decisions that affect EVA. Thus the use of EVA implies delegated decision-making.

EVA makes the cost of capital *visible* to operating managers. A plant manager can improve EVA by (a) increasing earnings or (b) *reducing* capital employed. Therefore underutilized assets tend to be flushed out and disposed of. Working capital may be reduced, or at least not added to casually, as Quaker Oats did by trade loading in its pre-EVA era. The plant managers in Quayle City may decide to do without that cappuccino machine or extra forklift.

Introduction of residual income measures often leads to surprising reductions in assets employed—not from one or two big capital disinvestment decisions, but from many small ones. Ehrbar quotes a sewing machine operator at Herman Miller Corporation:

> [EVA] lets you realize that even assets have a cost. . . . we used to have these stacks of fabric sitting here on the tables until we needed them. . . . We were going to use the fabric anyway, so who cares that we're buying it and stacking it up there? Now no one has excess fabric. They only have the stuff we're working on today. And it's changed the way we connect with suppliers, and we're having [them] deliver fabric more often.[20]

Now we come to the first limitation to EVA. It does not involve forecasts of future cash flows and does not measure present value. Instead, EVA depends on the *current* level of earnings. It may, therefore, reward managers who take on projects with quick paybacks and penalize those who invest in projects with long gestation periods. Think of the difficulties in applying EVA to a pharmaceutical research program, where it typically takes 10 to 12 years to bring a new drug from discovery to final regulatory approval and the drug's first revenues. That means 10 to 12 years of guaranteed losses, even if the managers in charge do everything right. Similar problems occur in startup ventures, where there may be heavy capital outlays but low or negative earnings in the first years of operation. This does not imply negative NPV, so long as operating earnings and cash flows are sufficiently high later on. But EVA would be negative in the startup years, even if the project were on track to a strong positive NPV.

The problem in these cases lies not so much in EVA as in the measurement of income. The pharmaceutical R&D program may be showing accounting losses, be-

---

[20] A. Ehrbar, *EVA: The Real Key to Creating Wealth,* John Wiley & Sons, Inc., New York, 1998, pp. 130–131.

	Economic Value Added (EVA)	Capital Invested	Return on Capital	Cost of Capital
Philip Morris	$6,081	$57,220	17.4%	6.7%
General Electric	5,943	71,421	20.4	12.1
Microsoft	5,919	23,890	39.1	14.3
Exxon Mobil	5,357	·181,344	10.5	7.6
Citigroup	4,646	73,890	19.0	12.7
Coca-Cola	1,266	19,523	15.7	9.2
Boeing	94	40,651	8.0	7.8
General Motors	−1,065	110,111	5.7	6.7
Viacom	−4,370	52,045	2.0	10.4
AT&T Corp	−9,972	206,700	4.5	9.3

TABLE 12.2

EVA performance of selected U.S. companies, 2000 (dollar figures in millions).

Note: Economic value added is the rate of return on capital less the cost of capital times the amount of capital invested; e.g., for Coca-Cola EVA = (.157 − .092) × 19,523 = $1,266. Source: Data provided by Stern–Stewart.

cause generally accepted accounting principles require that outlays for R&D be written off as a current expense. But from an economic point of view, the outlays are an investment, not an expense. If a proposal for a new business forecasts accounting losses during a startup period, but the proposal nevertheless shows positive NPV, then the startup losses are really an investment—cash outlays made to generate larger cash inflows when the new business hits its stride.

In short, EVA and other measures of residual income depend on accurate measures of economic income and investment. Applying EVA effectively requires major changes in income statements and balance sheets.[21] We will pick up this point in the next section.

Applying EVA to Companies

EVA's most important use is in measuring and rewarding performance inside the firm. But it can also be applied to firms as a whole. Business periodicals regularly report EVAs for companies and industries. Table 12.2 shows the economic value added in 2000 for a sample of U.S. companies.[22] Notice that the firms with the highest return on capital did not necessarily add the most economic value. For example, Philip Morris was top of the class in terms of economic value added, but its return on capital was less than half that of Microsoft. This is partly because Philip Morris has more capital invested and partly because it is less risky than Microsoft and its cost of capital is correspondingly lower.

---

[21]For example, R&D should not be treated as an immediate expense but as an investment to be added to the balance sheet and written off over a reasonable period. Eli Lilly, a large pharmaceutical company, did this so that it could use EVA. As a result, the net value of its assets at the end of 1996 increased from $6 to $13 billion.

[22]Stern–Stewart makes some adjustments to income and assets before calculating these EVAs, but it is almost impossible to include the value of all assets. For example, did Microsoft really earn a 39 percent true, economic rate of return? We suspect that the value of its assets is understated. The value of its intellectual property—the fruits of its investment over the years in software and operating systems—is not shown on the balance sheet. If the denominator in a return on capital calculation is too low, the resulting profitability measure is too high.

12.5 BIASES IN ACCOUNTING MEASURES OF PERFORMANCE

Any method of performance measurement that depends on accounting profitability measures had better hope those numbers are accurate. Unfortunately they are often not accurate, but biased. We referred to this problem in the last section and return to it now.

Biases in Accounting Rates of Return

Business periodicals regularly report book (accounting) rates of return on investment (ROIs) for companies and industries. ROI is just the ratio of after-tax operating income to the net (depreciated) book value of assets. We rejected book ROI as a capital investment criterion in Chapter 5, and in fact few companies now use it for that purpose. But they do use it to evaluate profitability of existing businesses.

Consider the pharmaceutical and chemical industries. According to Table 12.3, pharmaceutical companies have done much better than chemical companies. Are the pharmaceutical companies *really* that profitable? If so, lots of companies should be rushing into the pharmaceutical business. Or is there something wrong with the ROI measure?

Pharmaceutical companies have done well, but they look more profitable than they really are. Book ROIs are biased upward for companies with intangible investments such as R&D, simply because accountants don't put these outlays on the balance sheet.

Table 12.4 shows cash inflows and outflows for two mature companies. Neither is growing. Each must plow back $400 million to maintain its existing business. The *only* difference is that the chemical company's plowback goes mostly to plant and

---

TABLE 12.3

After-tax accounting rates of return for pharmaceutical and chemical companies, 2000.

Source: Datastream.

Pharmaceutical		Chemical	
Abbot Laboratories	19.2%	Du Pont	7.3%
Bristol-Myers Squibb	24.0	Dow Chemical	7.5
Merck	19.7	Ethyl Corporation	8.5
Pfizer	14.9	Hercules Inc.	5.4

TABLE 12.4

Comparison of a pharmaceutical company and a chemical company, each in a no-growth steady state (figures in $ millions). Revenues, costs, total investment, and annual cash flow are identical. But the pharmaceutical company invests more in R&D.

*Operating costs do *not* include any charge for depreciation.

†Cash flow = revenues − operating costs − total investment.

	Pharmaceutical	Chemical
Revenues	1,000	1,000
Operating costs, out-of-pocket*	500	500
Net operating cash flow	500	500
Investment in:		
Plant and equipment	100	300
R&D	300	100
Total investment	400	400
Annual cash flow†	+100	+100

Age, Years	Pharmaceutical		Chemical	
	Original Cost of Investment	Net Book Value	Original Cost of Investment	Net Book Value
0 (new)	100	100	300	300
1	100	90	300	270
2	100	80	300	240
3	100	70	300	210
4	100	60	300	180
5	100	50	300	150
6	100	40	300	120
7	100	30	300	90
8	100	20	300	60
9	100	10	300	30
Total net book value		550		1,650

	Pharmaceutical	Chemical
Annual depreciation*	100	300
R&D expense	300	100
Total depreciation and R&D	400	400

TABLE 12.5

Book asset values and annual depreciation for the pharmaceutical and chemical companies described in Table 12.4 (figures in $ millions).

*The pharmaceutical company has 10 vintages of assets, each depreciated by $10 per year. Total depreciation per year is 10 × 10 = $100 million. The chemical company's depreciation is 10 × 30 = $300 million.

	Pharmaceutical	Chemical
Revenues	1,000	1,000
Operating costs, out-of-pocket	500	500
R&D expense	300	100
Depreciation*	100	300
Net income	100	100
Net book value*	550	1,650
Book ROI	18%	6%

TABLE 12.6

Book ROIs for the companies described in Table 12.4 (figures in $ millions). The chemical and pharmaceutical companies' cash flows and values are identical. But the pharmaceutical's accounting rate of return is triple the chemical's. This bias occurs because accountants do not show the value of investment in R&D on the balance sheet.

*Calculated in Table 12.5.

equipment; the pharmaceutical company invests mostly in R&D. The chemical company invests only one-third as much in R&D ($100 versus $300 million) but triples the pharmaceutical company's investment in fixed assets.

Table 12.5 calculates the annual depreciation charges. Notice that the sum of R&D and total annual depreciation is identical for the two companies.

The companies' cash flows, true profitability, and true present values are also identical, but as Table 12.6 shows, the pharmaceutical company's book ROI is 18 percent, *triple* the chemical company's. The accountants would get annual income right (in this case it is identical to cash flow) but understate the value of the pharmaceutical company's assets relative to the chemical company's. Lower asset value creates the upward-biased pharmaceutical ROI.

The first moral is this: Do not assume that businesses with high book ROIs are necessarily performing better. They may just have more hidden assets, that is, assets which accountants do not put on balance sheets.

Measuring the Profitability of the Nodhead Supermarket— Another Example

Supermarket chains invest heavily in building and equipping new stores. The regional manager of a chain is about to propose investing $1 million in a new store in Nodhead. Projected cash flows are

	Year						
	1	2	3	4	5	6	after 6
Cash flow ($ thousands)	100	200	250	298	298	298	0

Of course, real supermarkets last more than six years. But these numbers are realistic in one important sense: It may take two or three years for a new store to catch on—that is, to build up a substantial, habitual clientele. Thus cash flow is low for the first few years even in the best locations.

We will assume the opportunity cost of capital is 10 percent. The Nodhead store's NPV at 10 percent is zero. It is an acceptable project, but not an unusually good one:

$$\text{NPV} = -1,000 + \frac{100}{1.10} + \frac{200}{(1.10)^2} + \frac{250}{(1.10)^3} + \frac{298}{(1.10)^4} + \frac{298}{(1.10)^5} + \frac{298}{(1.10)^6} = 0$$

With NPV = 0, the true (internal) rate of return of this cash-flow stream is also 10 percent.

Table 12.7 shows the store's forecasted *book* profitability, assuming straight-line depreciation over its six-year life. The book ROI is lower than the true return for the first two years and higher afterward.[23] This is the typical outcome: Accounting profitability measures are too low when a project or business is young and are too high as it matures.

At this point the regional manager steps up on stage for the following soliloquy:

The Nodhead store's a decent investment. I really should propose it. But if we go ahead, I won't look very good at next year's performance review. And what if I also go ahead with the new stores in Russet, Gravenstein, and Sheepnose? Their cash-flow patterns are pretty much the same. I could actually appear to lose money next year. The stores I've got won't earn enough to cover the initial losses on four new ones.

Of course, everyone knows new supermarkets lose money at first. The loss would be in the budget. My boss will understand—I think. But what about her boss? What if the board of directors starts asking pointed questions about profitability in my region? I'm under a lot of pressure to generate better earnings. Pamela Quince, the upstate manager, got a bonus for generating a 40 percent increase in book ROI. She didn't spend much on expansion.

The regional manager is getting conflicting signals. On one hand, he is told to find and propose good investment projects. *Good* is defined by discounted cash flow. On the other hand, he is also urged to increase book earnings. But the two goals conflict because book earnings do not measure true earnings. The greater the

---

[23]The errors in book ROI always catch up with you in the end. If the firm chooses a depreciation schedule that overstates a project's return in some years, it must also understate the return in other years. In fact, you can think of a project's IRR as a kind of average of the book returns. It is not a simple average, however. The weights are the project's book values discounted at the IRR. See J. A. Kay, "Accountants, Too, Could Be Happy in a Golden Age: The Accountant's Rate of Profit and the Internal Rate of Return," *Oxford Economic Papers* 28 (1976), pp. 447–460.

	Year					
	1	**2**	**3**	**4**	**5**	**6**
Cash flow	100	200	250	298	298	298
Book value at *start* of year, straight-line depreciation	1,000	833	667	500	333	167
Book value at *end* of year, straight-line depreciation	833	667	500	333	167	0
Change in book value during year	−167	−167	−167	−167	−167	−167
Book income	−67	+33	+83	+131	+131	+131
Book ROI	−.067	+.04	+.124	+.262	+.393	+.784
Book depreciation	167	167	167	167	167	167

TABLE 12.7

Forecasted book income and ROI for the proposed Nodhead store. Book ROI is lower than the true rate of return for the first two years and higher thereafter.

pressure for immediate book profits, the more the regional manager is tempted to forgo good investments or to favor quick-payback projects over longer-lived projects, even if the latter have higher NPVs.

Would EVA solve this problem? No, EVA would be negative in the first two years of the Nodhead store. In year 2, for example,

$$\text{EVA} = 33 - (.10 \times 833) = -50, \text{ or } -\$50,000$$

This calculation risks reinforcing the regional manager's qualms about the new Nodhead store.

Again, the fault here is not in the principle of EVA but in the measurement of income. If the project performs as projected in Table 12.7, the negative EVA in year 2 is really an investment.

 ## 12.6 MEASURING ECONOMIC PROFITABILITY

Let us think for a moment about how profitability should be measured in principle. It is easy enough to compute the true, or economic, rate of return for a common stock that is continuously traded. We just record cash receipts (dividends) for the year, add the change in price over the year, and divide by the beginning price:

$$\text{Rate of return} = \frac{\text{cash receipts} + \text{change in price}}{\text{beginning price}}$$
$$= \frac{C_1 + (P_1 - P_0)}{P_0}$$

The numerator of the expression for rate of return (cash flow plus change in value) is called **economic income**:

$$\text{Economic income} = \text{cash flow} + \text{change in present value}$$

Any reduction in present value represents **economic depreciation;** any increase in present value represents *negative* economic depreciation. Therefore

$$\text{Economic depreciation} = \text{reduction in present value}$$

and

$$\text{Economic income} = \text{cash flow} - \text{economic depreciation}$$

The concept works for any asset. Rate of return equals cash flow plus change in value divided by starting value:

$$\text{Rate of return} = \frac{C_1 + (PV_1 - PV_0)}{PV_0}$$

where PV_0 and PV_1 indicate the present values of the business at the ends of years 0 and 1.

The only hard part in measuring economic income and return is calculating present value. You can observe market value if shares in the asset are actively traded, but few plants, divisions, or capital projects have shares traded in the stock market. You can observe the present market value of *all* the firm's assets but not of any one of them taken separately.

Accountants rarely even attempt to measure present value. Instead they give us net book value (BV), which is original cost less depreciation computed according to some arbitrary schedule. Companies use the book value to calculate the book return on investment:

$$\begin{aligned}\text{Book income} &= \text{cash flow} - \text{book depreciation}\\ &= C_1 + (BV_1 - BV_0)\end{aligned}$$

Therefore

$$\text{Book ROI} = \frac{C_1 + (BV_1 - BV_0)}{BV_0}$$

If book depreciation and economic depreciation are different (they are rarely the same), then the book profitability measures will be wrong; that is, they will not measure true profitability. (In fact, it is not clear that accountants should even *try* to measure true profitability. They could not do so without heavy reliance on subjective estimates of value. Perhaps they should stick to supplying objective information and leave the estimation of value to managers and investors.)

It is not hard to forecast economic income and rate of return. Table 12.8 shows the calculations. From the cash-flow forecasts we can forecast present value at the start of periods 1 to 6. Cash flow plus *change* in present value equals economic income. Rate of return equals economic income divided by start-of-period value.

Of course, these are forecasts. Actual future cash flows and values will be higher or lower. Table 12.8 shows that investors *expect* to earn 10 percent in each year of the store's six-year life. In other words, investors expect to earn the opportunity cost of capital each year from holding this asset.[24]

Notice that EVA calculated using present value and economic income is zero in each year of the Nodhead project's life. For year 2, for example,

$$\text{EVA} = 100 - (.10 \times 100) = 0$$

---

[24]This is a general result. Forecasted profitability always equals the discount rate used to calculate the estimated future present values.

	Year					
	1	2	3	4	5	6
Cash flow	100	200	250	298	298	298
PV, at *start* of year, 10 percent discount rate	1,000	1,000	901	741	517	271
PV at *end* of year, 10 percent discount rate	1,000	900	741	517	271	0
Change in value during year	0	−100	−160	−224	−246	−271
Economic income	100	100	90	74	52	27
Rate of return	.10	.10	.10	.10	.10	.10
Economic depreciation	0	100	160	224	246	271

TABLE 12.8

Forecasted economic income and rate of return for the proposed Nodhead store. Economic income equals cash flow plus change in present value. Rate of return equals economic income divided by value at start of year.

Note: There are minor rounding errors in some annual figures.

EVA *should* be zero, because the project's true rate of return is only equal to the cost of capital. EVA will always give the right signal if income equals economic income and asset values are measured accurately.

Do the Biases Wash Out in the Long Run?

Some people downplay the problem we have just described. Is a temporary dip in book profits a major problem? Don't the errors wash out in the long run, when the region settles down to a steady state with an even mix of old and new stores?

It turns out that the errors diminish but do *not* exactly offset. The simplest steady-state condition occurs when the firm does not grow, but reinvests just enough each year to maintain earnings and asset values. Table 12.9 shows steady-state book ROIs for a regional division which opens one store a year. For simplicity we assume that the division starts from scratch and that each store's cash flows are carbon copies of the Nodhead store. The true rate of return on each store is, therefore, 10 percent. But as Table 12.9 demonstrates, steady-state book ROI, at 12.6 percent, overstates the true rate of return. Therefore, you cannot assume that the errors in book ROI will wash out in the long run.

Thus we still have a problem even in the long run. The extent of the error depends on how fast the business grows. We have just considered one steady state with a zero growth rate. Think of another firm with a 5 percent steady-state growth rate. Such a firm would invest $1,000 the first year, $1,050 the second, $1,102.50 the third, and so on. Clearly the faster growth means more new projects relative to old ones. The greater weight given to young projects, which have low book ROIs, the lower the business' apparent profitability. Figure 12.1 shows how this works out for a business composed of projects like the Nodhead store. Book ROI will either overestimate or underestimate the true rate of return unless the amount that the firm invests each year grows at the same rate as the true rate of return.[25]

---

[25]This also is a general result. Biases in steady-state book ROIs disappear when the growth rate equals the true rate of return. This was discovered by E. Solomon and J. Laya, "Measurement of Company Profitability: Some Systematic Errors in Accounting Rate of Return," in A. A. Robichek (ed.), *Financial Research and Management Decisions*, John Wiley & Sons, Inc., New York, 1967, pp. 152–183.

TABLE 12.9

Book ROI for a group of stores like the Nodhead store. The steady-state book ROI overstates the 10 percent *economic* rate of return.

*Book income = cash flow + change in book value during year.

†Steady-state book ROI.

	Year					
	1	2	3	4	5	6
Book income for store*						
1	−67	+33	+83	+131	+131	+131
2		−67	+33	+83	+131	+131
3			−67	+33	+83	+131
4				−67	+33	+83
5					−67	+33
6						−67
Total book income	−67	−34	+49	+180	+311	+442
Book value for store						
1	1,000	833	667	500	333	167
2		1,000	833	667	500	333
3			1,000	833	667	500
4				1,000	833	667
5					1,000	833
6						1,000
Total book value	1,000	1,833	2,500	3,000	3,333	3,500
Book ROI for all stores = $\dfrac{\text{total book income}}{\text{total book value}}$	−.067	−.019	+.02	+.06	+.093	+.126†

FIGURE 12.1

The faster a firm grows, the lower its book rate of return is, providing true profitability is constant and cash flows are constant or increasing over project life. This graph is drawn for a firm composed of identical projects, all like the Nodhead store (Table 12.7), but growing at a constant compound rate.

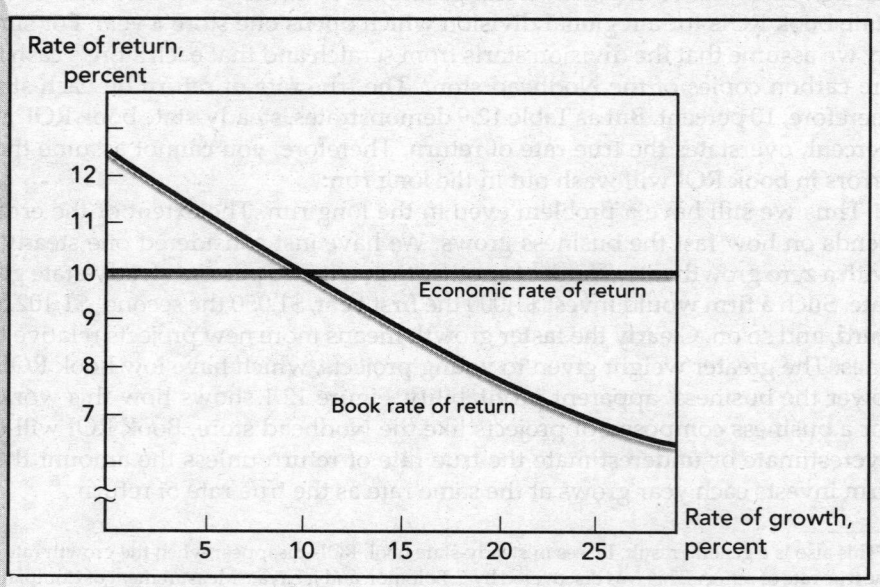

What Can We Do about Biases in Accounting Profitability Measures?

The dangers in judging profitability by accounting measures are clear from this chapter's discussion and examples. To be forewarned is to be forearmed. But we can say something beyond just "be careful."

It is natural for firms to set a standard of profitability for plants or divisions. Ideally that standard should be the opportunity cost of capital for investment in the plant or division. That's the whole point of EVA: to compare actual profits with the cost of capital. But if performance is measured by return on investment or EVA, then these measures need to recognize accounting biases. Ideally, the financial manager should identify and eliminate accounting biases before judging or rewarding performance.

This is easier said than done. Accounting biases are notoriously hard to get rid of. Thus, many firms end up asking not "Did the widget division earn more than its cost of capital last year?" but "Was the widget division's book ROI typical of a successful firm in the widget industry?" The underlying assumptions are that (1) similar accounting procedures are used by other widget manufacturers and (2) successful widget companies earn their cost of capital.

There are some simple accounting changes that could reduce biases in performance measures. Remember that the biases all stem from *not* using economic depreciation. Therefore why not switch to economic depreciation? The main reason is that each asset's present value would have to be reestimated every year. Imagine the confusion if this were attempted. You can understand why accountants set up a depreciation schedule when an investment is made and then stick to it apart from exceptional circumstances. But why restrict the choice of depreciation schedules to the old standbys, such as straight-line? Why not specify a depreciation pattern that at least matches *expected* economic depreciation? For example, the Nodhead store could be depreciated according to the expected economic depreciation schedule shown in Table 12.8.[26] This would avoid any systematic biases. It would break no law or accounting standard. This step seems so simple and effective that we are at a loss to explain why firms have not adopted it.[27]

One final comment: Suppose that you *do* conclude that a project has earned less than its cost of capital. This indicates that you made a mistake in taking on the project and, if you could have your time over again, you would not accept it. But does that mean you should bail out now? Not necessarily. That depends on how much the assets would be worth if you sold them or put them to an alternative use. A plant that produces low profits may still be worth operating if it has few alternative uses. Conversely, on some occasions it may pay to sell or redeploy a highly profitable plant.

Do Managers Worry Too Much about Book Profitability?

Book measures of profitability can be wrong or misleading because

1. Errors occur at different stages of project life. When true depreciation is decelerated, book measures are likely to understate true profitability for new projects and overstate it for old ones.

---

[26]Using expected economic depreciation will not generate book ROIs that are exactly right unless realized cash flows exactly match forecasted flows. But we expect forecasts to be right, on average.

[27]This procedure has been suggested by several authors, for example by Zvi Bodie in "Compound Interest Depreciation in Capital Investment," *Harvard Business Review* 60 (May–June 1982), pp. 58–60.

2. Errors also occur when firms or divisions have a balanced mix of old and new projects. Our steady-state analysis of Nodhead shows this.

3. Errors occur because of inflation, basically because inflation shows up in revenue faster than it shows up in costs. For example, a firm owning a plant built in 1980 will, under standard accounting procedures, calculate depreciation in terms of the plant's original cost in 1980 dollars. The plant's output is sold for current dollars. This is why the U.S. National Income and Product Accounts report corporate profits calculated under replacement cost accounting. This procedure bases depreciation not on the original cost of firms' assets, but on what it would cost to replace the assets at current prices.

4. Book measures are often confused by creative accounting. Some firms pick and choose among available accounting procedures, or even invent new ones, in order to make their income statements and balance sheets look good. This was done with particular imagination in the "go-go years" of the mid-1960s and the late 1990s.

Investors and financial managers have learned not to take accounting profitability at face value. Yet many people do not realize the depth of the problem. They think that if firms eschewed creative accounting, everything would be all right except perhaps for temporary problems with very old or very young projects. In other words, they worry about reason 4, and a little about reasons 1 and 3, but not at all about 2. We think reason 2 deserves more attention.

SUMMARY

We began this chapter by describing how capital budgeting is organized and ended by exposing serious biases in accounting measures of financial performance. Inevitably such discussions stress the mechanics of organization, control, accounting, and performance measurement. It is harder to talk about the informal procedures that reinforce the formal ones. But remember that it takes informal communication and personal initiative to make capital budgeting work. Also, the accounting biases are partly or wholly alleviated because managers and stockholders are smart enough to look behind book earnings.

Formal capital budgeting systems usually have four stages:

1. A *capital budget* for the firm is prepared. This is a plan for capital expenditure by plant, division, or other business unit.

2. *Project authorizations* are approved to give authority to go ahead with specific projects.

3. Procedures for *control of projects under construction* are established to warn if projects are behind schedule or are costing more than planned.

4. *Postaudits* are conducted to check on the progress of recent investments.

Capital budgeting is not entirely a bottom-up process. Strategic planners practice capital budgeting on a grand scale by attempting to identify those businesses in which the firm has a special advantage. Project proposals that support the firm's accepted overall strategy are much more likely to have clear sailing as they come up through the organization.

But don't assume that all important capital outlays appear as projects in the capital budgeting process. Many important investment decisions may never receive formal financial analysis. First, plant or division managers decide which projects to propose. Top management and financial staff may never see the alternatives. Second, investments in intangible assets, for example, marketing and R&D outlays, may bypass the capital budget. Third, there are countless routine investment decisions that must be made by middle management. These outlays are small if looked at one by one, but they add up.

Capital investment decisions must be decentralized to a large extent. Consequently agency problems are inevitable. Managers are tempted to slack off, to avoid risk, and to propose empire-building or entrenching investments. Empire building is a particular threat when plant and divisional managers' bonuses depend just on earnings or on growth in earnings.

Top management mitigates these agency problems by a combination of monitoring and incentives. Many large companies have implemented sophisticated incentive schemes based on residual income or economic value added (EVA). In these schemes, managers' bonuses depend on earnings minus a charge for capital employed. There is a strong incentive to dispose of unneeded assets and to acquire new ones only if additional earnings exceed the cost of capital. Of course EVA depends on accurate measures of earnings and capital employed.

Top management also create agency costs (e.g., empire building). In this case they are the agents and shareholders are the principals. Shareholders' interests are represented by the board of directors and are also protected by delegated monitors (e.g., the accountants who audit the company's books).

In most public corporations, top management's compensation is tied to the performance of the company's stock. This aligns their interests with shareholders'. But compensation tied to stock returns is not a complete solution. Stock returns respond to events outside management's control, and today's stock prices already reflect investors' expectations of managers' future performance.

Thus most firms also measure performance by accounting or book profitability. Unfortunately book income and return on investment (ROI) are often seriously biased measures of true profitability. For example, book ROIs are generally too low for new assets and too high for old ones. Businesses with important intangible assets generally have upward-biased ROIs because the intangibles don't appear on the balance sheet.

In principle, true or economic income is easy to calculate: You just subtract economic depreciation from the asset's cash flow. Economic depreciation is simply the decrease in the asset's present value during the period.

Unfortunately we can't ask accountants to recalculate each asset's present value every time income is calculated. But it does seem fair to ask why they don't try at least to match book depreciation schedules to typical patterns of economic depreciation.

The most extensive study of the capital budgeting process is:

J. L. Bower: *Managing the Resource Allocation Process*, Division of Research, Graduate School of Business Administration, Harvard University, Boston, 1970.

The article by Pohlman, Santiago, and Markel is a more up-to-date survey of current practice:

R. A. Pohlman, E. S. Santiago, and F. L. Markel: "Cash Flow Estimation Practices of Large Firms," *Financial Management*, 17:71–79 (Summer 1988).

FURTHER READING

For an easy-to-read description of EVA, with lots of success stories, see
A. Ehrbar: *EVA: The Real Key to Creating Wealth*, John Wiley & Sons, Inc., New York, 1998.

Biases in book ROI and procedures for reducing the biases are discussed by:
E. Solomon and J. Laya: "Measurement of Company Profitability: Some Systematic Errors in the Accounting Rate of Return," in A. A. Robichek (ed.), *Financial Research and Management Decisions*, John Wiley & Sons, Inc., New York, 1967, pp. 152–183.

F. M. Fisher and J. I. McGowan: "On the Misuse of Accounting Rates of Return to Infer Monopoly Profits," *American Economic Review*, 73:82–97 (March 1983).

J. A. Kay: "Accountants, Too, Could Be Happy in a Golden Age: The Accountant's Rate of Profit and the Internal Rate of Return," *Oxford Economic Papers*, 28:447–460 (1976).

Z. Bodie: "Compound Interest Depreciation in Capital Investment," *Harvard Business Review*, 60:58–60 (May–June 1982).

QUIZ

1. True or false?
   a. The approval of a capital budget allows managers to go ahead with any project included in the budget.
   b. Capital budgets and project authorizations are mostly developed "bottom up." Strategic planning is a "top-down" process.
   c. Project sponsors are likely to be overoptimistic.
   d. Investments in marketing (for new products) and R&D are not capital outlays.
   e. Many capital investments are not included in the company's capital budget. (If true, give some examples.)
   f. Postaudits are typically undertaken about five years after project completion.

2. Explain how each of the following actions or problems can distort or disrupt the capital budgeting process.
   a. Overoptimism by project sponsors.
   b. Inconsistent forecasts of industry and macroeconomic variables.
   c. Capital budgeting organized solely as a bottom-up process.
   d. A demand for quick results from operating managers, e.g., requiring new capital expenditures to meet a payback constraint.

3. What is the practical implication of Brealey and Myers's Second Law? The law reads, "The proportion of proposed projects having a positive NPV at the corporate hurdle rate is independent of the hurdle rate."

4. Define the following: **(a)** Agency costs in capital investment, **(b)** private benefits, **(c)** empire building, **(d)** free-rider problem, **(e)** entrenching investment, **(f)** delegated monitoring.

5. Monitoring alone can never completely eliminate agency costs in capital investment. Briefly explain why.

6. Here are several questions about economic value added or EVA.
   a. Is EVA expressed as a percentage or a dollar amount?
   b. Write down the formula for calculating EVA.
   c. What is the difference, if any, between EVA and residual income?
   d. What is the point of EVA? Why do firms use it?
   e. Does the effectiveness of EVA depend on accurate measures of accounting income and assets?

7. The Modern Language Division earned $1.6 million on net assets of $20 million. The cost of capital is 11.5 percent. Calculate the net percentage return on investment and EVA.

8. True or false? Briefly explain your answers.
   a. Accountants require companies to write off outlays for R&D as current expenses. This makes R&D-intensive companies look less profitable than they really are.

b. Companies with valuable intangible assets will show upward-biased accounting rates of return.

9. Fill in the blanks:

"A project's economic income for a given year equals the project's _____ less its _____ depreciation. Book income is typically _____ than economic income early in the project's life and _____ than economic income later in its life."

0. Consider the following project:

	Period			
	0	**1**	**2**	**3**
Net cash flow	−100	0	78.55	78.55

The internal rate of return is 20 percent. The NPV, assuming a 20 percent opportunity cost of capital, is exactly zero. Calculate the expected *economic* income and economic depreciation in each year.

PRACTICE QUESTIONS

1. Discuss the value of postaudits. Who should conduct them? When? Should they consider solely financial performance? Should they be confined to the larger projects?

2. Draw up an outline or flowchart tracing the capital budgeting process from the initial idea for a new investment project to the completion of the project and the start of operations. Assume the idea for a new obfuscator machine comes from a plant manager in the Deconstruction Division of the Modern Language Corporation.

   Here are some questions your outline or flowchart should consider: Who will prepare the original proposal? What information will the proposal contain? Who will evaluate it? What approvals will be needed, and who will give them? What happens if the machine costs 40 percent more to purchase and install than originally forecasted? What will happen when the machine is finally up and running?

3. Compare typical compensation and incentive arrangements for **(a)** top management, for example, the CEO or CFO, and **(b)** plant or division managers. What are the chief differences? Can you explain them?

4. Suppose all plant and division managers were paid only a fixed salary—no other incentives or bonuses.
   a. Describe the agency problems that would appear in capital investment decisions.
   b. How would tying the managers' compensation to EVA alleviate these problems?

5. Table 12.10 shows a condensed income statement and balance sheet for Androscoggin Copper's Rumford smelting plant.
   a. Calculate the plant's EVA. Assume the cost of capital is 9 percent.
   b. As Table 12.10 shows, the plant is carried on Androscoggin's books at $48.32 million. However, it is a modern design, and could be sold to another copper company for $95 million. How should this fact change your calculation of EVA?

6. Here are a few questions about compensation schemes that tie top management's compensation to the rate of return earned on the company's common stock.
   a. Today's stock price depends on investors' expectations of future performance. What problems does this create?
   b. Stock returns depend on factors outside the managers' control, for example, changes in interest rates or prices of raw materials. Could this be a serious problem? If so, can you suggest a partial solution?
   c. Compensation schemes that depend on stock returns do *not* depend on accounting income or ROI. Is that an advantage? Why or why not?

TABLE 12.10

Condensed financial statements for the Rumford smelting plant. See practice question 5 (figures in $ millions).

Income Statement for 2001		Assets, December 31, 2001	
Revenue	$56.66	Net working capital	$7.08
Raw materials cost	18.72		
Operating cost	21.09	Investment in plant and equipment	69.33
Depreciation	4.50	Less accumulated depreciation	21.01
Pretax income	12.35	Net plant and equipment	48.32
Tax at 35%	4.32		
Net income	$8.03	Total assets	$55.40

7. Herbal Resources is a small but profitable producer of dietary supplements for pets. This is not a high-tech business, but Herbal's earnings have averaged around $1.2 million after tax, largely on the strength of its patented enzyme for making cats nonallergenic. The patent has eight years to run, and Herbal has been offered $4 million for the patent rights.

   Herbal's assets include $2 million of working capital and $8 million of property, plant, and equipment. The patent is not shown on Herbal's books. Suppose Herbal's cost of capital is 15 percent. What is its EVA?

8. List and define the agency problems likely to be encountered in a firm's capital investment decisions.

9. Large brokerage and investment companies, such as Merrill Lynch and Morgan Stanley Dean Witter, employ squadrons of security analysts. Each analyst devotes full time to an industry—aerospace, for example, or insurance—and issues reports and buy, hold, or sell recommendations for companies in the industry. How do security analysts help overcome free-rider problems in monitoring management? How do they help avoid agency problems in capital investment?

10. What is meant by *delegated monitoring?* Who are these monitors and what roles do they play?

11. True or false? Explain briefly.
   a. Book profitability measures are biased measures of true profitability for individual assets. However, these biases "wash out" when firms hold a balanced mix of old and new assets.
   b. Systematic biases in book profitability would be avoided if companies used depreciation schedules that matched expected economic depreciation. However, few, if any, firms have done this.

12. Calculate the year-by-year book and economic profitability for investment in polyzone production, as described in Chapter 11. Use the cash flows and competitive spreads shown in Table 11.2.

   What is the steady-state book rate of return (ROI) for a mature company producing polyzone? Assume no growth and competitive spreads.

13. Suppose that the cash flows from Nodhead's new supermarket are as follows:

	Year					
	0	1	2	3	4	5	6
Cash flows ($ thousands)	−1,000	+298	+298	+298	+138	+138	+138

   a. Recalculate economic depreciation. Is it accelerated or decelerated?
   b. Rework Tables 12.7 and 12.8 to show the relationship between the "true" rate of return and book ROI in each year of the project's life.

STANDARD
&POOR'S

14. Use the Market Insight database (**www.mhhe.com/edumarketinsight**) to estimate the economic value added (EVA) for three firms. What problems did you encounter in doing this?

CHALLENGE QUESTIONS

1. Is there an *optimal* level of agency costs? How would you define it?

2. Suppose it were possible to measure and track economic income and the true economic value of a firm's assets. Would there be any remaining need for EVA? Discuss.

3. Reconstruct Table 12.9 assuming a steady-state growth rate of 10 percent per year. Your answer will illustrate a fascinating theorem, namely, that book rate of return equals the economic rate of return when the economic rate of return and the steady-state growth rate are the same.

4. Consider an asset with the following cash flows:

	Year			
	0	**1**	**2**	**3**
Cash flows ($ millions)	−12	+5.20	+4.80	+4.40

The firm uses straight-line depreciation. Thus, for this project, it writes off $4 million per year in years 1, 2, and 3. The discount rate is 10 percent.
a. Show that economic depreciation equals book depreciation.
b. Show that the book rate of return is the same in each year.
c. Show that the project's book profitability is its true profitability.

You've just illustrated another interesting theorem. If the book rate of return is the same in each year of a project's life, the book rate of return equals the IRR.

5. The following are extracts from two newsletters sent to a stockbroker's clients:

Investment Letter—March 2001

   Kipper Parlors was founded earlier this year by its president, Albert Herring. It plans to open a chain of kipper parlors where young people can get together over a kipper and a glass of wine in a pleasant, intimate atmosphere. In addition to the traditional grilled kipper, the parlors serve such delicacies as Kipper Schnitzel, Kipper Grandemere, and (for dessert) Kipper Sorbet.

   The economics of the business are simple. Each new parlor requires an initial investment in fixtures and fittings of $200,000 (the property itself is rented). These fixtures and fittings have an estimated life of 5 years and are depreciated straight-line over that period. Each new parlor involves significant start-up costs and is not expected to reach full profitability until its fifth year. Profits per parlor are estimated as follows:

	Year after Opening				
	1	**2**	**3**	**4**	**5**
Profit	0	40	80	120	170
Depreciation	40	40	40	40	40
Profit after depreciation	−40	0	40	80	130
Book value at start of year	200	160	120	80	40
Return on investment (%)	−20	0	33	100	325

   Kipper has just opened its first parlor and plans to open one new parlor each year. Despite the likely initial losses (which simply reflect start-up costs), our calculations show a dramatic profit growth and a long-term return on investment that is substantially higher than Kipper's 20 percent cost of capital.

The total market value of Kipper stock is currently only $250,000. In our opinion, this does not fully reflect the exciting growth prospects, and we strongly recommend clients to buy.

Investment Letter—April 2001

Albert Herring, president of Kipper Parlors, yesterday announced an ambitious new building plan. Kipper plans to open two new parlors next year, three the year after, and so on.

We have calculated the implications of this for Kipper's earnings per share and return on investment. The results are extremely disturbing, and under the new plan, there seems to be no prospect of Kipper's ever earning a satisfactory return on capital.

Since March, the value of Kipper's stock has fallen by 40 percent. Any investor who did not heed our earlier warnings should take the opportunity to sell the stock now.

Compare Kipper's accounting and economic income under the two expansion plans. How does the change in plan affect the company's return on investment? What is the PV of Kipper stock? Ignore taxes in your calculations.

6. In our Nodhead example, true depreciation was decelerated. That is not always the case. For instance, Figure 12.2 shows how on average the value of a Boeing 737 has varied with its age.[28] Table 12.11 shows the market value at different points in the plane's life and the cash flow needed in each year to provide a 10 percent return. (For example, if you bought a 737 for $19.69 million at the start of year 1 and sold it a year later, your total profit would be 17.99 + 3.67 − 19.69 = $1.97 million, 10 percent of the purchase cost.)

Many airlines write off their aircraft straight-line over 15 years to a salvage value equal to 20 percent of the original cost.

a. Calculate economic and book depreciation for each year of the plane's life.
b. Compare the true and book rates of return in each year.
c. Suppose an airline invested in a fixed number of Boeing 737s each year. Would steady-state book return overstate or understate true return?

FIGURE 12.2

Estimated value of Boeing 737 in January 1987 as a function of age.

_____

[28]We are grateful to Mike Staunton for providing us with these estimates.

Start of Year	Market Value	Cash Flow
1	19.69	
2	17.99	$3.67
3	16.79	3.00
4	15.78	2.69
5	14.89	2.47
6	14.09	2.29
7	13.36	2.14
8	12.68	2.02
9	12.05	1.90
10	11.46	1.80
11	10.91	1.70
12	10.39	1.61
13	9.91	1.52
14	9.44	1.46
15	9.01	1.37
16	8.59	1.32

TABLE 12.11

Estimated market values of a Boeing 737 in January 1987 as a function of age, plus the cash flows needed to provide a 10 percent true rate of return (figures in $ millions).

A discussion of capital budgeting procedures in the context of IT investments:

www.itpolicy.gsa.gov

Software for project analysis is available on:

www.decisioneering.com

www.kellogg.nwu.edu/faculty/myerson/
   ftp/addins.htm

The following sites provide articles and data on EVA:

www.sternstewart.com

www.financeadvisor.com

FINANCING DECISIONS AND MARKET EFFICIENCY

SO FAR OUR focus has been on the investment decision. Now we turn to the problem of paying for these investments. This can be a challenging task. For example, in the introduction to Part Three we described how construction of the tunnel between England and France cost $15 billion. The financial manager was responsible for finding this huge sum. It involved borrowing from more than 200 banks as well as public issues of stock and bonds.

Later chapters will describe in detail the principal sources of finance, but Part Four sets the scene. We begin in Chapter 13 with a fundamental question, Can managers be confident that investors will pay a fair price for the firm's securities? Many scholars believe that securities are competitively priced, but we will also encounter some conflicting evidence.

Chapter 14 takes a first look at the firm's securities and their relative importance. It shows how they differ in their rights to payment and in the control that their holders can exercise.

Part Four concludes by showing how infant companies finance themselves and how, after reaching adulthood, they sell their securities to the public.

CHAPTER THIRTEEN

CORPORATE FINANCING AND THE SIX LESSONS OF MARKET EFFICIENCY

UP TO THIS point we have concentrated almost exclusively on the left-hand side of the balance sheet—the firm's capital expenditure decision. Now we move to the right-hand side and to the problems involved in financing the capital expenditures. To put it crudely, you've learned how to spend money, now learn how to raise it.

Of course, we haven't totally ignored financing in our discussion of capital budgeting. But we made the simplest possible assumption: all-equity financing. That means we assumed the firm raises its money by selling stock and then invests the proceeds in real assets. Later, when those assets generate cash flows, the cash is returned to the stockholders. Stockholders supply all the firm's capital, bear all the business risks, and receive all the rewards.

Now we are turning the problem around. We take the firm's present portfolio of real assets and its future investment strategy as given, and then we determine the best financing strategy. For example,

- Should the firm reinvest most of its earnings in the business, or should it pay them out as dividends?
- If the firm needs more money, should it issue more stock or should it borrow?
- Should it borrow short-term or long-term?
- Should it borrow by issuing a normal long-term bond or a convertible bond (i.e., a bond which can be exchanged for stock by the bondholders)?

There are countless other financing trade-offs, as you will see.

The purpose of holding the firm's capital budgeting decision constant is to separate that decision from the financing decision. Strictly speaking, this assumes that capital budgeting and financing decisions are *independent*. In many circumstances this is a reasonable assumption. The firm is generally free to change its capital structure by repurchasing one security and issuing another. In that case there is no need to associate a particular investment project with a particular source of cash. The firm can think, first, about which projects to accept and, second, about how they should be financed.

Sometimes decisions about capital structure depend on project choice or vice versa, and in those cases the investment and financing decisions have to be considered jointly. However, we defer discussion of such interactions of financing and investment decisions until later in the book.

We start this chapter by contrasting investment and financing decisions. The objective in each case is the same—to maximize NPV. However, it may be harder to find positive-NPV financing opportunities. The reason it is difficult to add value by clever financing decisions is that capital markets are efficient. By this we mean that fierce competition between investors eliminates profit opportunities and causes debt and equity issues to be fairly priced. If you think that sounds like a sweeping statement, you are right. That is why we have devoted this chapter to explaining and evaluating the efficient-market hypothesis.

You may ask why we start our discussion of financing issues with this conceptual point, before you have even the most basic knowledge about securities and issue procedures. We do it this way because financing decisions seem overwhelmingly complex if you don't learn to ask the right questions. We are afraid you might flee from confusion to the myths that often dominate popular discussion of corporate financing. You need to understand the efficient-market hypothesis not because it is *universally* true but because it leads you to ask the right questions.

We define the efficient-market hypothesis more carefully in Section 13.2. The hypothesis comes in different strengths, depending on the information available to investors. Sections 13.2 and 13.3 review the evidence for and against efficient markets. The evidence "for" is massive, but over the years a number of puzzling anomalies have accumulated.

The chapter closes with *the six lessons of market efficiency*.

13.1 WE ALWAYS COME BACK TO NPV

Although it is helpful to separate investment and financing decisions, there are basic similarities in the criteria for making them. The decisions to purchase a machine tool and to sell a bond each involve valuation of a risky asset. The fact that one asset is real and the other is financial doesn't matter. In both cases we end up computing net present value.

The phrase *net present value of borrowing* may seem odd to you. But the following example should help to explain what we mean: As part of its policy of encouraging small business, the government offers to lend your firm $100,000 for 10 years at 3 percent. This means that the firm is liable for interest payments of $3,000 in each of the years 1 through 10 and that it is responsible for repaying the $100,000 in the final year. Should you accept this offer?

We can compute the NPV of the loan agreement in the usual way. The one difference is that the first cash flow is *positive* and the subsequent flows are *negative*:

$$NPV = \text{amount borrowed} - \text{present value of interest payments}$$
$$- \text{present value of loan repayment}$$
$$= +100,000 - \sum_{t=1}^{10} \frac{3,000}{(1 + r)^t} - \frac{100,000}{(1 + r)^{10}}$$

The only missing variable is r, the opportunity cost of capital. You need that to value the liability created by the loan. We reason this way: The government's loan to you is a financial asset: a piece of paper representing your promise to pay $3,000 per year plus the final repayment of $100,000. How much would that paper sell for if freely traded in the capital market? It would sell for the present value of those cash flows, discounted at r, the rate of return offered by other securities issued by your firm. All you have to do to determine r is to answer the question, What interest rate would my firm have to pay to borrow money directly from the capital markets rather than from the government?

Suppose that this rate is 10 percent. Then

$$NPV = +100,000 - \sum_{t=1}^{10} \frac{3,000}{(1.10)^t} - \frac{100,000}{(1.10)^{10}}$$
$$= +100,000 - 56,988 = +\$43,012$$

Of course, you don't need any arithmetic to tell you that borrowing at 3 percent is a good deal when the fair rate is 10 percent. But the NPV calculations tell you just how much that opportunity is worth ($43,012).[1] It also brings out the essential similarity of investment and financing decisions.

Differences between Investment and Financing Decisions

In some ways investment decisions are simpler than financing decisions. The number of different financing decisions (i.e., securities) is continually expanding. You will have to learn the major families, genera, and species. You will also need to become familiar with the vocabulary of financing. You will learn about such matters as caps, strips, swaps, and bookrunners; behind each of these terms lies an interesting story.

---

[1] We ignore here any tax consequences of borrowing. These are discussed in Chapter 18.

There are also ways in which financing decisions are much easier than investment decisions. First, financing decisions do not have the same degree of finality as investment decisions. They are easier to reverse. That is, their abandonment value is higher. Second, it's harder to make or lose money by smart or stupid financing strategies. That is, it is difficult to find financing schemes with NPVs significantly different from zero. This reflects the nature of the competition.

When the firm looks at capital investment decisions, it does *not* assume that it is facing perfect, competitive markets. It may have only a few competitors that specialize in the same line of business in the same geographical area. And it may own some unique assets that give it an edge over its competitors. Often these assets are intangible, such as patents, expertise, or reputation. All this opens up the opportunity to make superior profits and find projects with positive NPVs.

In financial markets your competition is all other corporations seeking funds, to say nothing of the state, local, and federal governments that go to New York, London, and other financial centers to raise money. The investors who supply financing are comparably numerous, and they are smart: Money attracts brains. The financial amateur often views capital markets as *segmented*, that is, broken down into distinct sectors. But money moves between those sectors, and it moves fast.

Remember that a good financing decision generates a positive NPV. It is one in which the amount of cash raised exceeds the value of the liability created. But turn that statement around. If selling a security generates a positive NPV for the seller, it must generate a negative NPV for the buyer. Thus, the loan we discussed was a good deal for your firm but a negative NPV from the government's point of view. By lending at 3 percent, it offered a $43,012 subsidy.

What are the chances that your firm could consistently trick or persuade investors into purchasing securities with negative NPVs to them? Pretty low. In general, firms should assume that the securities they issue are fairly priced. That takes us into the main topic of this chapter: efficient capital markets.

 13.2 WHAT IS AN EFFICIENT MARKET?

A Startling Discovery: Price Changes Are Random

As is so often the case with important ideas, the concept of efficient capital markets stemmed from a chance discovery. In 1953 Maurice Kendall, a British statistician, presented a controversial paper to the Royal Statistical Society on the behavior of stock and commodity prices.[2] Kendall had expected to find regular price cycles, but to his surprise they did not seem to exist. Each series appeared to be "a 'wandering' one, almost as if once a week the Demon of Chance drew a random number . . . and added it to the current price to determine the next week's price." In other words, the prices of stocks and commodities seemed to follow a *random walk*.

---

[2]See M. G. Kendall, "The Analysis of Economic Time Series, Part I. Prices," *Journal of the Royal Statistical Society* 96 (1953), pp. 11–25. Kendall's idea was not wholly new. It had been proposed in an almost forgotten thesis written 53 years earlier by a French doctoral student, Louis Bachelier. Bachelier's accompanying development of the mathematical theory of random processes anticipated by five years Einstein's famous work on the random Brownian motion of colliding gas molecules. See L. Bachelier, *Theorie de la Speculation*, Gauthiers-Villars, Paris, 1900. Reprinted in English (A. J. Boness, trans.) in P. H. Cootner (ed.), *The Random Character of Stock Market Prices*, M.I.T. Press, Cambridge, MA, 1964, pp. 17–78.

If you are not sure what we mean by "random walk," you might like to think of the following example: You are given $100 to play a game. At the end of each week a coin is tossed. If it comes up heads, you win 3 percent of your investment; if it is tails, you lose 2.5 percent. Therefore, your capital at the end of the first week is either $103.00 or $97.50. At the end of the second week the coin is tossed again. Now the possible outcomes are:

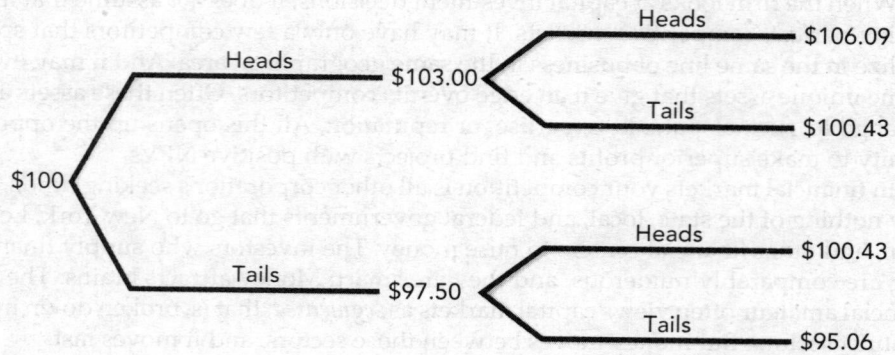

This process is a random walk with a positive drift of .25 percent per week.[3] It is a random walk because successive changes in value are independent. That is, the odds each week are the same, regardless of the value at the start of the week or of the pattern of heads and tails in the previous weeks.

If you find it difficult to believe that there are no patterns in share price changes, look at the two charts in Figure 13.1. One of these charts shows the outcome from playing our game for five years; the other shows the actual performance of the Standard and Poor's Index for a five-year period. Can you tell which one is which?[4]

When Maurice Kendall suggested that stock prices follow a random walk, he was implying that the price changes are independent of one another just as the gains and losses in our coin-tossing game were independent. Figure 13.2 illustrates this. Each dot shows the change in the price of Microsoft stock on successive days. The circled dot in the southeast quadrant refers to a pair of days in which a 1 percent increase was followed by a 1 percent decrease. If there was a systematic tendency for increases to be followed by decreases, there would be many dots in the southeast quadrant and few in the northeast quadrant. It is obvious from a glance that there is very little pattern in these price movements, but we can test this more precisely by calculating the coefficient of correlation between each day's price change and the next. If price movements persisted, the correlation would be positive; if there was no relationship, it would be 0. In our example, the correlation between successive price changes in Microsoft stock was +.022; there was a negligible tendency for price rises to be followed by further price rises.[5]

---

[3]The drift is equal to the expected outcome: $(1/2)(3) + (1/2)(-2.5) = .25\%$.

[4]The bottom chart in Figure 13.1 shows the real Standard and Poor's Index for the years 1980 through 1984; the top chart is a series of cumulated random numbers. Of course, 50 percent of you are likely to have guessed right, but we bet it was just a guess. A similar comparison between cumulated random numbers and actual price series was first suggested by H. V. Roberts, "Stock Market 'Patterns' and Financial Analysis: Methodological Suggestions," *Journal of Finance* 14 (March 1959), pp. 1–10.

[5]The correlation coefficient between successive observations is known as the *autocorrelation coefficient*. An autocorrelation of +.022 implies that, if Microsoft stock price rose by 1 percent more than average yesterday, your best forecast of today's price change would be a rise of .022 percent more than average.

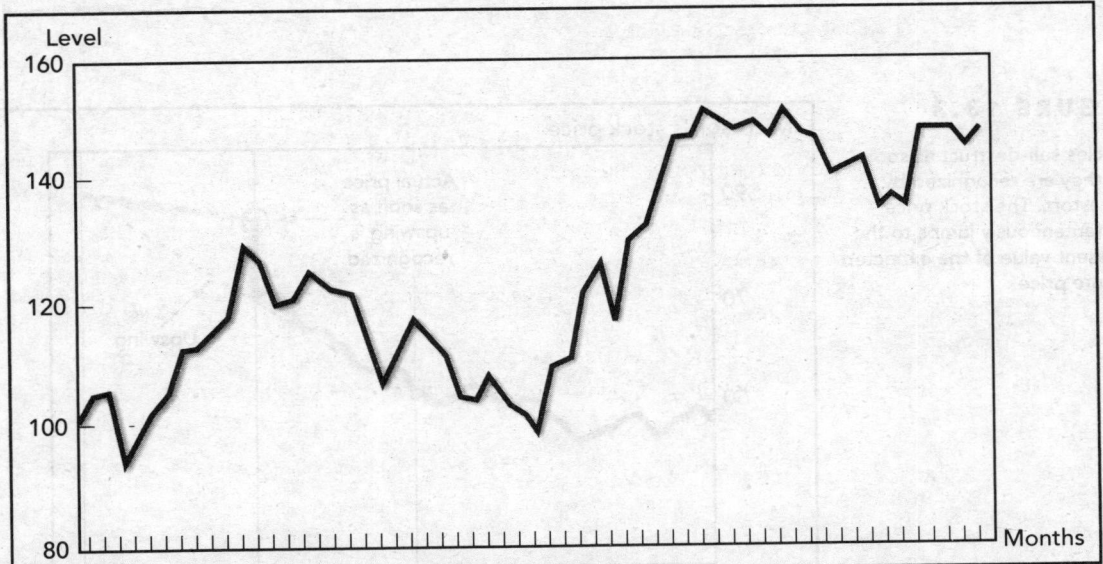

FIGURE 13.1

One of these charts shows the Standard and Poor's Index for a five-year period. The other shows the results of playing our coin-tossing game for five years. Can you tell which is which?

Figure 13.2 suggests that Microsoft's price changes were effectively uncorrelated. Today's price change gave investors almost no clue as to the likely change tomorrow. Does that surprise you? If so, imagine that it were not the case and that changes in Microsoft's stock price were expected to persist for several months. Figure 13.3 provides an example of such a predictable cycle. You can see that an

FIGURE 13.2

Each dot shows a pair of returns for Microsoft stock on two successive days between March 1990 and July 2001. The circled dot records a daily return of +1 percent and then −1 percent on the next day. The scatter diagram shows no significant relationship between returns on successive days.

FIGURE 13.3

Cycles self-destruct as soon as they are recognized by investors. The stock price instantaneously jumps to the present value of the expected future price.

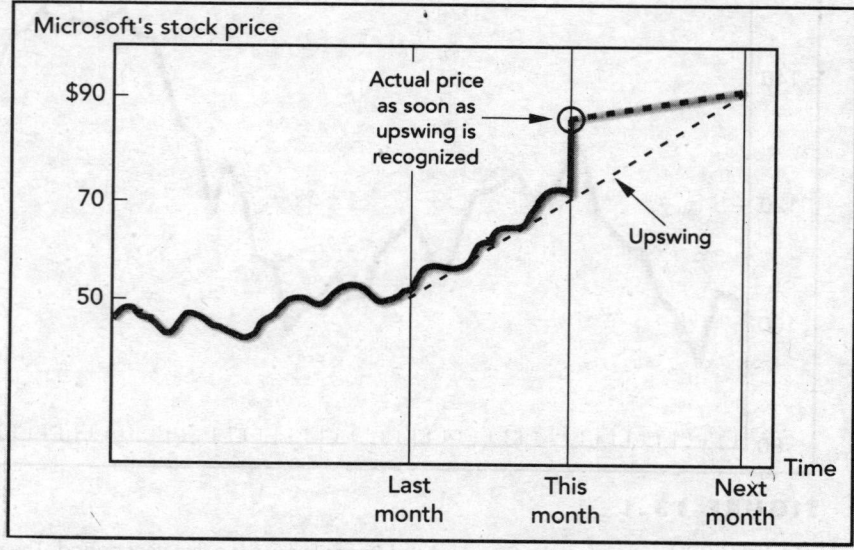

upswing in Microsoft's stock price started last month, when the price was $50, and it is expected to carry the price to $90 next month. What will happen when investors perceive this bonanza? It will self-destruct. Since Microsoft stock is a bargain at $70, investors will rush to buy. They will stop buying only when the stock offers a normal rate of return. Therefore, as soon as a cycle becomes apparent to investors, they immediately eliminate it by their trading.

Three Forms of Market Efficiency

You should see now why prices in competitive markets must follow a random walk. If past price changes could be used to predict future price changes, investors could make easy profits. But in competitive markets easy profits don't last. As investors try to take advantage of the information in past prices, prices adjust immediately until the superior profits from studying past price movements disappear. As a result, all the information in past prices will be reflected in *today's* stock price, not tomorrow's. Patterns in prices will no longer exist and price changes in one period will be independent of changes in the next. In other words, the share price will follow a random walk.

In competitive markets today's stock price must already reflect the information in past prices. But why stop there? If markets are competitive, shouldn't today's stock price reflect *all* the information that is available to investors? If so, securities will be fairly priced and security returns will be unpredictable, whatever information you consider.

Economists often define three levels of market efficiency, which are distinguished by the degree of information reflected in security prices. In the first level, prices reflect the information contained in the record of past prices. This is called the *weak* form of efficiency. If markets are efficient in the weak sense, then it is impossible to make consistently superior profits by studying past returns. Prices will follow a random walk.

The second level of efficiency requires that prices reflect not just past prices but all other published information, such as you might get from reading the financial press. This is known as the *semistrong* form of market efficiency. If markets are efficient in this sense, then prices will adjust immediately to public information such as the announcement of the last quarter's earnings, a new issue of stock, a proposal to merge two companies, and so on.

Finally, we might envisage a *strong* form of efficiency, in which prices reflect all the information that can be acquired by painstaking analysis of the company and the economy. In such a market we would observe lucky and unlucky investors, but we wouldn't find any superior investment managers who can consistently beat the market.

Efficient Markets: The Evidence

In the years that followed Maurice Kendall's discovery, financial journals were packed with tests of the efficient-market hypothesis. To test the weak form of the hypothesis, researchers measured the profitability of some of the trading rules used by those investors who claim to find patterns in security prices. They also employed statistical tests such as the one that we described when looking for patterns in the returns on Microsoft stock. For example, in Figure 13.4 we have used the same test to look for relationships between stock market returns in successive weeks. It appears that throughout the world there are few patterns in week-to-week returns.

To analyze the semistrong form of the efficient-market hypothesis, researchers have measured how rapidly security prices respond to different items of news, such as earnings or dividend announcements, news of a takeover, or macroeconomic information.

Before we describe what they found, we should explain how to isolate the effect of an announcement on the price of a stock. Suppose, for example, that you need

FIGURE 13.4

Each point in these scatter diagrams shows the return in successive weeks on four stock market indexes between September 1991 and July 2001. The wide scatter of points shows that there is almost no correlation between the return in one week and in the next. The four indexes are FTSE 100 (UK), the Nikkei 500 (Japan), DAX 30 (Germany), and Standard & Poor's Composite (USA).

to know how the stock price responds to news of a takeover. As a first stab, you could look at the returns on the stock in the months surrounding the announcement. But that would provide a very noisy measure, for the price would reflect among other things what was happening to the market as a whole. A second possibility would be to calculate a measure of relative performance.

Relative stock return = return on stock − return on market index

This is almost certainly better than simply looking at the returns on the stock. However, if you are concerned with performance over a period of several months or years, it would be preferable to recognize that fluctuations in the market have a larger effect on some stocks than others. For example, past experience might suggest that a change in the market index affected the value of a stock as follows:

Expected stock return = α + β × return on market index[6]

Alpha (α) states how much on average the stock price changed when the market index was unchanged. Beta (β) tells us how much *extra* the stock price moved for each 1 percent change in the market index.[7] Suppose that subsequently the stock price provides a return of $\tilde{r}$ in a month when the market return is $\tilde{r}_m$. In that case we would conclude that the abnormal return for that month is

Abnormal stock return = actual stock return − expected stock return

$$= \tilde{r} - (\alpha + \beta\tilde{r}_m)$$

This abnormal return abstracts from the fluctuations in the stock price that result from marketwide influences.[8]

Figure 13.5 illustrates how the release of news affects abnormal returns. The graph shows the price run-up of a sample of 194 firms that were targets of takeover attempts. In most takeovers, the acquiring firm is willing to pay a large premium over the current market price of the acquired firm; therefore when a firm becomes the target of a takeover attempt, its stock price increases in anticipation of the takeover premium. Figure 13.5 shows that on the day the public become aware of a takeover attempt (Day 0 in the graph), the stock price of the typical target takes a big upward jump. The adjustment in stock price is immediate: After the big price move on the public announcement day, the run-up is over, and there is no further drift in the stock price, either upward or downward.[9] Thus within the day, the new stock prices apparently reflect (at least on average) the magnitude of the takeover premium.

A study by Patell and Wolfson shows just how fast prices move when new information becomes available.[10] They found that, when a firm publishes its latest earnings or announces a dividend change, the major part of the adjustment in price occurs within 5 to 10 minutes of the announcement.

---

[6]This relationship is often referred to as the *market model.*

[7]It is important when estimating α and β that you choose a period in which you believe that the stock behaved normally. If its performance was abnormal, then estimates of α and β cannot be used to measure the returns that investors expected. As a precaution, ask yourself whether your estimates of expected returns look sensible. Methods for estimating abnormal returns are analyzed in S. J. Brown and J. B. Warner, "Measuring Security Performance," *Journal of Financial Economics* 8 (1980), pp. 205–258.

[8]The market is not the only common influence on stock prices. For example, in Section 8.4 we described the Fama–French three-factor model, which states that a stock's return is influenced by three common factors—the market factor, a size factor, and a book-to-market factor. In this case we would calculate the expected stock return as $a + b_{market}(\tilde{r}_{market\ factor}) + b_{size}(\tilde{r}_{size\ factor}) + b_{book-to-market}(\tilde{r}_{book-to-market\ factor})$.

[9]See A. Keown and J. Pinkerton, "Merger Announcements and Insider Trading Activity," *Journal of Finance* 36 (September 1981), pp. 855–869. Note that prices on the days *before* the public announcement do show evidence of a sustained upward drift. This is evidence of a gradual leakage of information about a possible takeover attempt. Some investors begin to purchase the target firm in anticipation of a public announcement. Consistent with efficient markets, however, once the information becomes public, it is reflected fully and immediately in stock prices.

[10]See J. M. Patell and M. A. Wolfson, "The Intraday Speed of Adjustment of Stock Prices to Earnings and Dividend Announcements," *Journal of Financial Economics* 13 (June 1984), pp. 223–252.

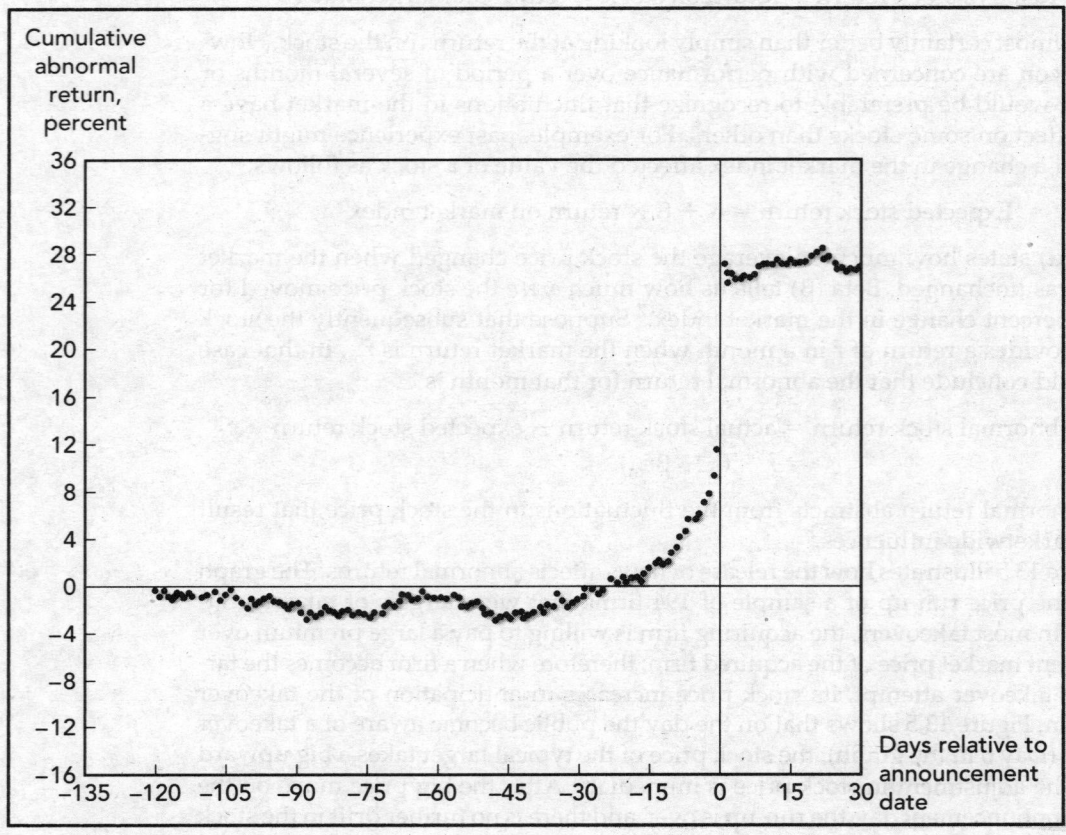

FIGURE 13.5

The performance of the stocks of target companies compared with that of the market. The prices of target stocks jump up on the announcement day, but from then on, there are no unusual price movements. The announcement of the takeover attempt seems to be fully reflected in the stock price on the announcement day.

Source: A. Keown and J. Pinkerton, "Merger Announcements and Insider Trading Activity," *Journal of Finance* 36 (September 1981), pp. 855–869.

Tests of the strong form of the hypothesis have examined the recommendations of professional security analysts and have looked for mutual funds or pension funds that could predictably outperform the market. Some researchers have found a slight persistent outperformance, but just as many have concluded that professionally managed funds fail to recoup the costs of management. Look, for example, at Figure 13.6, which is taken from a study by Mark Carhart of the average return on nearly 1,500 U.S. mutual funds. You can see that in some years the mutual funds beat the market, but as often as not it was the other way around. Figure 13.6 provides a fairly crude comparison, for mutual funds have tended to specialize in particular sectors of the market, such as low-beta stocks or large-firm stocks, that may have given below-average returns. To control for such differences, each fund needs to be compared with a benchmark portfolio of similar securities. The study by Mark Carhart did this, but the message was unchanged: The funds earned a lower return than the benchmark portfolios *after* expenses and roughly matched the benchmarks *before* expenses.

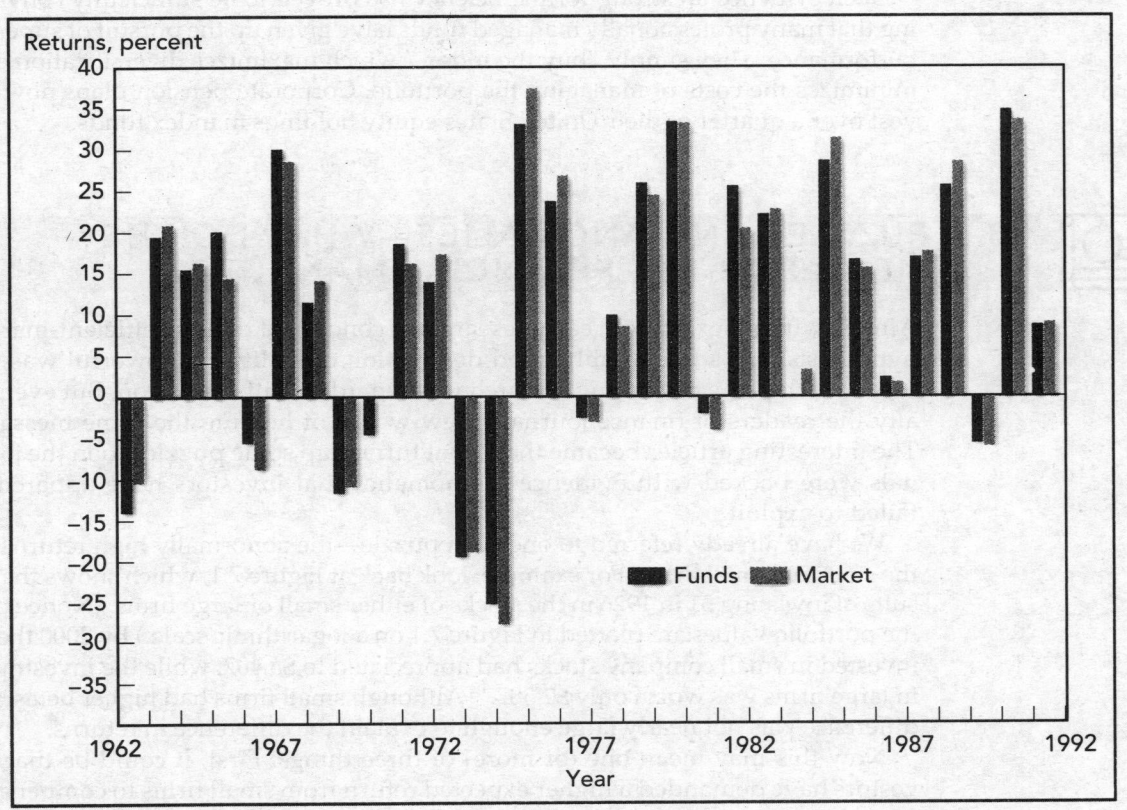

FIGURE 13.6

Average annual returns on 1,493 U.S. mutual funds and the market index, 1962–1992. Notice that mutual funds underperform the market in approximately half the years.

Source: M. M. Carhart, "On Persistence in Mutual Fund Performance," *Journal of Finance* 52 (March 1997), pp. 57–82.

It would be surprising if some managers were not smarter than others and could earn superior returns. But it seems difficult to spot the smart ones, and the top-performing managers one year have about an average chance of falling on their face the next year. For example, *Forbes Magazine*, a widely read investment periodical, has published annually since 1975 an "honor roll" of the most consistently successful mutual funds. Suppose that each year, when *Forbes* announced its honor roll, you had invested an equal sum in each of these exceptional funds. You would have outperformed the market in only 5 of the following 16 years, and your average annual return before paying any initial fees would have been more than 1 percent below the return on the market.[11]

---

[11]See B. G. Malkiel, "Returns from Investing in Equity Mutual Funds 1971 to 1991," *Journal of Finance* 50 (June 1995), pp. 549–572. It seems to be difficult to measure whether good performance does persist. Some contrary evidence is provided in E. J. Elton, M. J. Gruber, and C. R. Blake, "The Persistence of Risk-Adjusted Mutual Fund Performance," *Journal of Business* 69 (April 1996), pp. 133–157. There is, however, widespread agreement that the worst performing funds continue to underperform. That is not surprising, for they are shrinking and the costs of running them are proportionately higher.

Such evidence on strong-form efficiency has proved to be sufficiently convincing that many professionally managed funds have given up the pursuit of superior performance. They simply "buy the index," which maximizes diversification and minimizes the costs of managing the portfolio. Corporate pension plans now invest over a quarter of their United States equity holdings in index funds.

13.3 PUZZLES AND ANOMALIES—WHAT DO THEY MEAN FOR THE FINANCIAL MANAGER?

Almost without exception, early researchers concluded that the efficient-market hypothesis was a remarkably good description of reality. So powerful was the evidence that any dissenting research was regarded with suspicion. But eventually the readers of finance journals grew weary of hearing the same message. The interesting articles became those that turned up some puzzle. Soon the journals were packed with evidence of anomalies that investors have apparently failed to exploit.

We have already referred to one such puzzle—the abnormally high returns on the stocks of small firms. For example, look back at Figure 7.1, which shows the results of investing $1 in 1926 in the stocks of either small or large firms. (Notice that the portfolio values are plotted in Figure 7.1 on a logarithmic scale.) By 2000 the $1 invested in small company stocks had appreciated to $6,402, while the investment in large firms was worth only $2,587.[12] Although small firms had higher betas, the difference was not nearly large enough to explain the difference in returns.

Now this may mean one (or more) of three things. First, it could be that investors have demanded a higher expected return from small firms to compensate for some extra risk factor that is not captured in the simple capital asset pricing model. That is why we asked in Chapter 8 whether the small-firm effect is evidence against the CAPM.

Second, the superior performance of small firms could simply be a coincidence, a finding that stems from the efforts of many researchers to find interesting patterns in the data. There is evidence for and against the coincidence theory. Those who believe that the small-firm effect is a pervasive phenomenon can point to the fact that small-firm stocks have provided a higher return in many other countries. On the other hand, you can see from Figure 7.1 that the superior performance of small-firm stocks in the United States is limited to a relatively short period. Until the early 1960s small-firm and large-firm stocks were neck and neck. A wide gap then opened in the next two decades but it narrowed again in the 1980s when the small-firm effect first became known. If you looked simply at recent years, you might judge that there is a *large-firm* effect.

The third possibility is that we have here an important exception to the efficient-market theory, one that provided investors with an opportunity to make predictably superior profits over a period of two decades. If such anomalies offer easy pickings, you would expect to find a number of investors eager to take advantage of them. It turns out that, while many investors do try to exploit such anomalies, it is surprisingly difficult to get rich by doing so. For example, Professor Richard Roll, who probably knows as much as anyone about market anomalies, confesses

---

[12]In each case the portfolio values assume that dividends are reinvested.

Over the past decade, I have attempted to exploit many of the seemingly most promising "inefficiencies" by actually trading significant amounts of money according to a trading rule suggested by the "inefficiencies" . . . I have never yet found one that worked in practice, in the sense that it returned more after cost than a buy-and-hold strategy.[13]

Do Investors Respond Slowly to New Information?

We have dwelt on the small-firm effect, but there is no shortage of other puzzles and anomalies. Some of them relate to the short-term behavior of stock prices. For example, returns appear to be higher in January than in other months, they seem to be lower on a Monday than on other days of the week, and most of the daily return comes at the beginning and end of the day.

To have any chance of making money from such short-term patterns, you need to be a professional trader, with one eye on the computer screen and the other on your annual bonus. If you are a corporate financial manager, these short-term patterns in stock prices may be intriguing conundrums, but they are unlikely to change the major financial decisions about which projects to invest in and how they should be financed. The more troubling concern for the corporate financial manager is the possibility that it may be several years before investors fully appreciate the significance of new information. The studies of daily and hourly price movements that we referred to above may not pick up this long-term mispricing, but here are two examples of an apparent long-term delay in the reaction to news.

The Earnings Announcement Puzzle   The earnings announcement puzzle is summarized in Figure 13.7, which shows stock performance following the announcement of unexpectedly good or bad earnings during the years 1974 to 1986.[14] The 10 percent of the stocks of firms with the best earnings news outperform those with the worst news by more than 4 percent over the two months following the announcement. It seems that investors underreact to the earnings announcement and become aware of the full significance only as further information arrives.

The New-Issue Puzzle   When firms issue stock to the public, investors typically rush to buy. On average those lucky enough to receive stock receive an immediate capital gain. However, researchers have found that these early gains often turn into losses. For example, suppose that you bought stock immediately following each initial public offering and then held that stock for five years. Over the period 1970–1998 your average annual return would have been 33 percent less than the return on a portfolio of similar-sized stocks.

The jury is still out on these studies of longer-term anomalies. Take, for example, the new-issue puzzle. Most new issues during the past 30 years have involved growth stocks with high market values and limited book assets. When the long-run performance of new issues is compared with a portfolio that is matched in terms of both size and book-to-market, the difference in performance disappears.[15] So

---

[13]R. Roll, "What Every CFO Should Know about Scientific Progress in Financial Economics: What Is Known and What Remains to be Resolved," *Financial Management* 23 (Summer 1994), pp. 69–75.

[14]V. L. Bernard and J. K. Thomas, "Post-Earnings Announcement Drift: Delayed Price Response or Risk Premium?" *Journal of Accounting Research* 27 (Supplement 1989), pp. 1–36.

[15]The long-run underperformance of new issues was described in R. Loughran and J. R. Ritter, "The New Issues Puzzle," *Journal of Finance* 50 (1995), pp. 23–51. The figures are updated on Jay Ritter's website and the returns compared with those of a portfolio which is matched in terms of size and book-to-market. (See **http://bear.cba.ufl.edu/ritter.**)

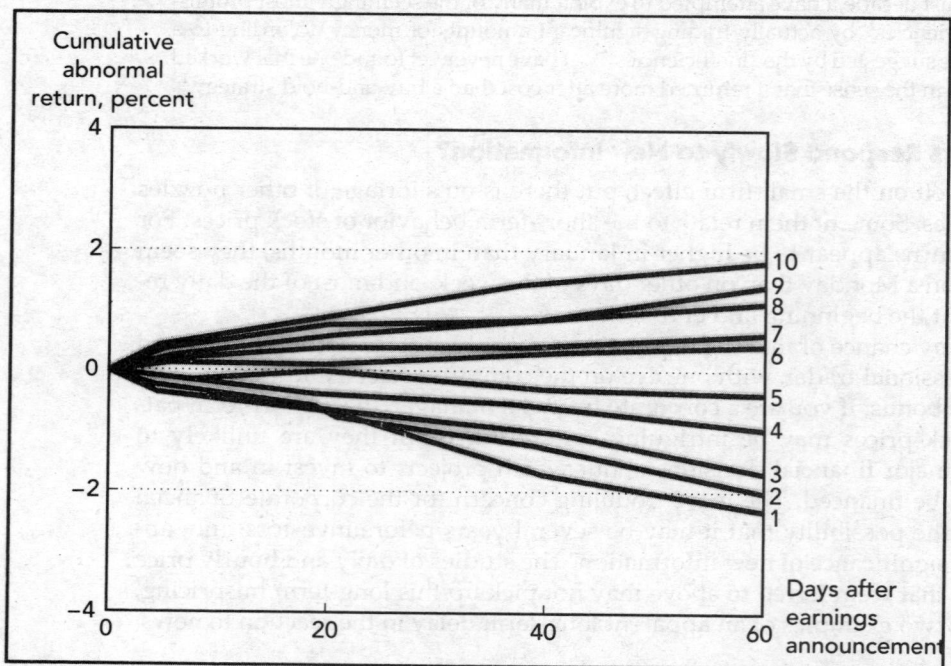

FIGURE 13.7

The cumulative abnormal returns of stocks of firms over the 60 days following an announcement of quarterly earnings. The 10 percent of the stocks with the best earnings news (Group 10) outperformed those with the worst news (Group 1) by more than 4 percent.

Source: V. L. Bernard and J. K. Thomas, "Post-Earnings-Announcement Drift: Delayed Price Response or Risk Premium?" *Journal of Accounting Research* 27 (Supplement 1989), pp. 1–36.

the new-issue puzzle could well turn out to be just the book-to-market puzzle in disguise.

Stock Market Anomalies and Behavioral Finance

In the meantime, some scholars are casting around for an alternative theory that might explain these apparent anomalies. Some argue that the answers lie in behavioral psychology. People are not 100 percent rational 100 percent of the time. This shows up in two broad areas—their attitudes to risk and the way that they assess probabilities.

1. *Attitudes toward risk* Psychologists have observed that, when making risky decisions, people are particularly loath to incur losses, even if those losses are small.[16] Losers tend to regret their actions and kick themselves for having been so foolish. To avoid this unpleasant possibility, individuals will tend to avoid those actions that may result in loss.

---

[16]This aversion to loss is modeled in D. Kahneman and A. Tversky, "Prospect Theory: An Analysis of Decision under Risk," *Econometrica* 47 (1979), pp. 263–291.

The pain of a loss seems to depend on whether it comes on the heels of earlier losses. Once investors have suffered a loss, they may be even more concerned not to risk a further loss and therefore they become particularly risk-averse. Conversely, just as gamblers are known to be more willing to make large bets when they are ahead, so investors may be more prepared to run the risk of a stock market dip after they have experienced a period of substantial gains.[17] If they do then suffer a small loss, they at least have the consolation of being up on the year.

When we discussed risk in Chapters 7 through 9, we pictured investors as concerned solely with the distribution of the possible returns, as summarized by the expected return and the variance. We did not allow for the possibility that investors may look back at the price at which they purchased stock and feel elated when their investment is in the black and depressed when it is in the red.

2. *Beliefs about probabilities* Most investors do not have a PhD in probability theory and may make systematic errors in assessing the probability of uncertain outcomes. Psychologists have found that, when judging the possible future outcomes, individuals commonly look back to what has happened in recent periods and then assume that this is representative of what may occur in the future. The temptation is to project recent experience into the future and to forget the lessons learned from the more distant past. Thus, an investor who places too much weight on recent events may judge that glamorous growth companies are very likely to continue to grow rapidly, even though very high rates of growth cannot persist indefinitely.

A second systematic bias is that of overconfidence. Most of us believe that we are better-than-average drivers, and most investors think that they are better-than-average stock pickers. Two speculators who trade with one another cannot both make money from the deal; for every winner there must be a loser. But presumably investors are prepared to continue trading because each is confident that it is the other one who is the patsy.

Now these behavioral tendencies have been well documented by psychologists, and there is plenty of evidence that investors are not immune to irrational behavior. For example, most individuals are reluctant to sell stocks that show a loss. They also seem to be overconfident in their views and to trade excessively.[18] What is less clear is how far such behavioral traits help to explain stock market anomalies. Take, for example, the tendency to place too much emphasis on recent events and therefore to overreact to news. This phenomenon fits with one of our possible long-term puzzles (the long-term underperformance of new issues). It looks as if investors observe the hot new issues, get carried away by the apparent profits to be made, and then spend the next few years regretting their enthusiasm. However, the tendency to overreact doesn't help to explain our other long-term puzzle (the *under-reaction* of investors to earnings announcements). Unless we have a theory of

---

[17]The effect is described in R. H. Thaler and E. J. Johnson, "Gambling with the House Money and Trying to Break Even: The Effects of Prior Outcomes on Risky Choice," *Management Science* 36 (1990), pp. 643–660. The implications for expected stock returns are explored in N. Barberis, M. Huang, and T. Santos, "Prospect Theory and Asset Prices," *Quarterly Journal of Economics* 116 (February 2001), pp. 1–53.

[18]See T. Odean, "Are Investors Reluctant to Realize their Losses?" *Journal of Finance* 53 (October 1998), pp. 1775–1798; and T. Odean, "Boys Will Be Boys: Gender, Overconfidence, and Common Stock Investment," *Quarterly Journal of Economics* 116 (February 2001), pp. 261–292.

human nature that can tell us when investors will overreact and when they will underreact, we are just as well off with the efficient-market theory which tells us that overreactions and underreactions are equally likely.[19]

There is another question that needs answering before we accept a behavioral bias as an explanation of an anomaly. It may well be true that many of us have a tendency to over- or underreact to recent events. However, hard-headed professional investors are constantly on the lookout for possible biases that may be a source of future profits.[20] So it is not enough to refer to irrationality on the part of individual investors; we also need to explain why professional investors have not competed away the apparent profit opportunities that such irrationality offers. The evidence on the performance of professionally managed portfolios suggests that many of these anomalies were not so easy to predict.

Professional Investors, Irrational Exuberance, and the Dot.com Bubble

Investors in technology stocks in the 1990s saw an extraordinary run-up in the value of their holdings. The Nasdaq Composite Index, which has a heavy weighting in high-tech stocks, rose 580 percent from the start of 1995 to its high in March 2000. Then even more rapidly than it began, the boom ended. By November 2001 the Nasdaq index had fallen 64 percent.

Some of the largest price gains and losses were experienced by the new "dot.com stocks." For example, Yahoo! shares, which began trading in April 1996, appreciated by 1,400 percent in just four years. At this point Yahoo! stock was valued at $124 billion, more than that of GM, Heinz, and Boeing combined. It was not, however, to last; just over a year later Yahoo!'s market capitalization was little more than $6 billion.

What caused the boom in high-tech stocks? Alan Greenspan, chairman of the Federal Reserve, attributed the run-up in prices to "irrational exuberance," a view that was shared by Professor Robert Shiller from Yale. In his book *Irrational Exuberance*[21] Shiller argued that, as the bull market developed, it generated optimism about the future and stimulated demand for shares.[22] Moreover, as investors racked up profits on their stocks, they became even more confident in their opinions.

But this brings us back to the $64,000 question. If Shiller was right and individual investors were carried away by irrational optimism, why didn't smart professional investors step in, sell high-tech stocks, and force their prices down to fair value? Were the pros also-carried away on the same wave of euphoria? Or were they rationally reluctant to undertake more than a limited amount of selling if they could not be sure where and when the boom would end?

---

[19]This point is made in E. F. Fama, "Market Efficiency, Long-Term Returns, and Behavioral Finance," *Journal of Financial Economics* 49 (September 1998), pp. 283–306. One paper that does seek to model why investors may both underreact and overreact is N. Barberis, A. Shleifer, and R. Vishny, "A Model of Investor Sentiment," *Journal of Financial Economics* 49 (September 1998), pp. 307–343.

[20]Many financial institutions employ behavioral finance specialists to advise them on these biases.

[21]See R. J. Shiller, *Irrational Exuberance*, Broadway Books, 2001. Shiller also discusses behavioral explanations for the boom in R. J. Shiller, "Bubbles, Human Judgment, and Expert Opinion," Cowles Foundation Discussion Paper No. 1303, Cowles Foundation for Research in Economics, Yale University, New Haven, CT, May 2001.

[22]Some economists believe that the market price is prone to "bubbles"—situations in which price grows faster than fundamental value, but investors don't sell because they expect prices to keep rising. Of course, all such bubbles pop eventually, but they can in theory be self-sustaining for a while. The *Journal of Economic Perspectives* 4 (Spring 1990) contains several nontechnical articles on bubbles.

The Crash of 1987 and Relative Efficiency

On Monday, October 19, 1987, the Dow Jones Industrial Average (the Dow) fell 23 percent in *one day*. Immediately after the crash, everybody started to ask two questions: Who were the guilty parties? and Do prices reflect fundamental values?

As in most murder mysteries, the immediate suspects are not the ones "who done it." The first group of suspects included *index arbitrageurs*, who trade back and forth between index futures[23] and the stocks comprising the market index, taking advantage of any price discrepancies. On Black Monday futures fell first and fastest because investors found it easier to bail out of the stock market by way of futures than by selling individual stocks. This pushed the futures price below the stock market index.[24] The arbitrageurs tried to make money by selling stocks and buying futures, but they found it difficult to get up-to-date quotes on the stocks they wished to trade. Thus the futures and stock markets were for a time disconnected. Arbitrageurs contributed to the trading volume that swamped the New York Stock Exchange, but they did not cause the crash; they were the messengers who tried to transmit the selling pressure in the futures market back to the exchange.

The second suspects were large institutional investors who were trying to implement *portfolio insurance* schemes. Portfolio insurance aims to put a floor on the value of an equity portfolio by progressively selling stocks and buying safe, short-term debt securities as stock prices fall. Thus the selling pressure that drove prices down on Black Monday led portfolio insurers to sell still more. One institutional investor on October 19 sold stocks and futures totalling $1.7 billion. The immediate cause of the price fall on Black Monday may have been a herd of elephants all trying to leave by the same exit.

Perhaps some large portfolio insurers can be convicted of disorderly conduct, but why did stocks fall *worldwide*,[25] when portfolio insurance was significant only in the United States? Moreover, if sales were triggered mainly by portfolio insurance or trading tactics, they should have conveyed little fundamental information, and prices should have bounced back after Black Monday's confusion had dissipated.

So why did prices fall so sharply? There was no obvious, new fundamental information to justify such a sharp and widespread decline in share values. For this reason, the idea that the market price is the best estimate of intrinsic value seems less compelling than before the crash. It appears that either prices were irrationally high before Black Monday or irrationally low afterward. Could the theory of efficient markets be another casualty of the crash?

The events of October 1987 remind us how exceptionally difficult it is to value common stocks. For example, imagine that in November 2001 you wanted to check whether common stocks were fairly valued. At least as a first stab you might use the constant-growth formula that we introduced in Chapter 4. The annual expected dividend on the Standard and Poor's Composite Index was about 18.7.

---

[23]An index future provides a way of trading in the stock market as a whole. It is a contract that pays investors the value of the stocks in the index at a specified future date. We discuss futures in Chapter 27.

[24]That is, sellers pushed the futures prices below their *proper relation* to the index (again, see Chapter 27). The proper relation is not exact equality.

[25]Some countries experienced even larger falls than the United States. For example, prices fell by 46 percent in Hong Kong, 42 percent in Australia, and 35 percent in Mexico. For a discussion of the worldwide nature of the crash, see R. Roll, "The International Crash of October 1987," in R. Kamphuis (ed.), *Black Monday and the Future of Financial Markets*, Richard D. Irwin, Inc., Homewood, IL, 1989.

Suppose this dividend was expected to grow at a steady rate of 10 percent a year and investors required an annual return of 11.7 percent from common stocks. The constant growth formula gives a value for the index of

$$PV(\text{index}) = \frac{DIV}{r - g} = \frac{18.7}{.117 - .10} = 1,100$$

which was roughly the actual level of the index in mid-November 2001. But how confident could you be about any of these figures? Perhaps the likely dividend growth was only 9.5 percent per year. This would produce a 23 percent downward revision in your estimate of the right level of the index, from 1,100 to 850!

$$PV(\text{index}) = \frac{DIV}{r - g} = \frac{18.7}{.117 - .095} = 850$$

In other words, a price drop like Black Monday's could have occurred if investors had become just 0.5 percentage point less optimistic about future dividend growth.

The extreme difficulty of valuing common stocks from scratch has two important consequences. First, investors almost always price a common stock relative to yesterday's price or relative to today's price of comparable securities. In other words, they generally take yesterday's price as correct, adjusting upward or downward on the basis of today's information. If information arrives smoothly, then as time passes, investors become more and more confident that today's price level is correct. However, when investors lose confidence in the benchmark of yesterday's price, there may be a period of confused trading and volatile prices before a new benchmark is established.

Second, the hypothesis that stock price *always* equals intrinsic value is nearly impossible to test, because it is so difficult to calculate intrinsic value without referring to prices. Thus the crash did not conclusively disprove the hypothesis, but many people find it less plausible.

However, the crash does not undermine the evidence for market efficiency with respect to *relative* prices. Take, for example, Hershey stock, which sold for $66 in November 2001. Could we prove that true intrinsic value is $66? No, but we could be more confident that the price of Hershey should be roughly double that of Smucker ($33) since Hershey's earnings per share and dividend were about twice those of Smucker and the two shares had similar growth prospects. Moreover, if either company announced unexpectedly higher earnings, we could be quite confident that its share price would respond instantly and without bias. In other words, the subsequent price would be set correctly relative to the prior price. The most important lessons of market efficiency for the corporate financial manager are concerned with relative efficiency.

Market Anomalies and the Financial Manager

The financial manager needs to be confident that, when the firm issues new securities, it can do so at a fair price. There are two reasons that this may not be the case. First, the strong form of the efficient-market hypothesis may not be 100 percent true, so that the financial manager may have information that other investors do not have. Alternatively, investors may have the *same* information as management, but be slow to react to it. For example, we described above some evidence that new issues of stock tend to be followed by a prolonged period of low stock returns.

You sometimes hear managers say something along the following lines:

Great! Our stock is clearly overpriced. This means we can raise capital cheaply and invest in Project X. Our high stock price gives us a big advantage over our competitors who could not possibly justify investing in Project X.

But that doesn't make sense. If your stock is truly overpriced, you can help your current shareholders by selling additional stock and using the cash to invest in other capital market securities. But you should *never* issue stock to invest in a project that offers a lower rate of return than you could earn elsewhere in the capital market. Such a project would have a negative NPV. You can always do better than investing in a negative-NPV project: Your company can go out and buy common stocks. In an efficient market, such purchases are always *zero* NPV.

What about the reverse? Suppose you know that your stock is *underpriced.* In that case, it certainly would not help your current shareholders to sell additional "cheap" stock to invest in other fairly priced stocks. If your stock is sufficiently underpriced, it may even pay to forego an opportunity to invest in a positive-NPV project rather than to allow new investors to buy into your firm at a low price. Financial managers who believe that their firm's stock is underpriced may be justifiably reluctant to issue more stock, but they may instead be able to finance their investment program by an issue of debt. In this case the market inefficiency would affect the firm's choice of financing but not its real investment decisions. In Chapter 15 we will have more to say about the financing choice when managers believe their stock is mispriced.

13.4 THE SIX LESSONS OF MARKET EFFICIENCY

Sorting out the puzzles will take time, but we believe that there is now widespread agreement that capital markets function sufficiently well that opportunities for easy profits are rare. So nowadays when economists come across instances where market prices apparently don't make sense, they don't throw the efficient-market hypothesis onto the economic garbage heap. Instead, they think carefully about whether there is some missing ingredient that their theories ignore.

We suggest therefore that financial managers should assume, at least as a starting point, that security prices are fair and that it is very difficult to outguess the market. This has some important implications for the financial manager.

Lesson 1: Markets Have No Memory

The weak form of the efficient-market hypothesis states that the sequence of past price changes contains no information about future changes. Economists express the same idea more concisely when they say that the market has no memory. Sometimes financial managers *seem* to act as if this were not the case. For example, studies by Taggart and others in the United States and by Marsh in the United Kingdom show that managers generally favor equity rather than debt financing after an abnormal price rise.[26] The idea is to catch the market while it is high. Similarly, they

---

[26]R. A. Taggart, "A Model of Corporate Financing Decisions," *Journal of Finance* 32 (December 1977), pp. 1467–1484; P. Asquith and D. W. Mullins, Jr., "Equity Issues and Offering Dilution," *Journal of Financial Economics* 15 (January–February 1986), pp. 16–89; P. R. Marsh, "The Choice between Debt and Equity: An Empirical Study," *Journal of Finance* 37 (March 1982), pp. 121–144.

are often reluctant to issue stock after a fall in price. They are inclined to wait for a rebound. But we know that the market has no memory and the cycles that financial managers seem to rely on do not exist.[27]

Sometimes a financial manager will have inside information indicating that the firm's stock is overpriced or underpriced. Suppose, for example, that there is some good news which the market does not know but you do. The stock price will rise sharply when the news is revealed. Therefore, if the company sold shares at the current price, it would be offering a bargain to new investors at the expense of present stockholders.

Naturally, managers are reluctant to sell new shares when they have favorable inside information. But such information has nothing to do with the history of the stock price. Your firm's stock could be selling at half its price of a year ago, and yet you could have special information suggesting that it is *still* grossly overvalued. Or it may be undervalued at twice last year's price.

Lesson 2: Trust Market Prices

In an efficient market you can trust prices, for they impound all available information about the value of each security. This means that in an efficient market, there is no way for most investors to achieve consistently superior rates of return. To do so, you not only need to know more than *anyone* else, but you also need to know more than *everyone* else. This message is important for the financial manager who is responsible for the firm's exchange-rate policy or for its purchases and sales of debt. If you operate on the basis that you are smarter than others at predicting currency changes or interest-rate moves, you will trade a consistent financial policy for an elusive will-o'-the-wisp.

The company's assets may also be directly affected by management's faith in its investment skills. For example, one company may purchase another simply because its management thinks that the stock is undervalued. On approximately half the occasions the stock of the acquired firm will with hindsight turn out to be undervalued. But on the other half it will be overvalued. On average the value will be correct, so the acquiring company is playing a fair game except for the costs of the acquisition.

Example—Orange County   In December 1994, Orange County, one of the wealthiest counties in the United States, announced that it had lost $1.7 billion on its investment portfolio. The losses arose because the county treasurer, Robert Citron, had raised large short-term loans which he then used to bet on a rise in long-term bond prices.[28] The bonds that the county bought were backed by government-guaranteed mortgage loans. However, some of them were of an unusual type known as *reverse*

---

[27]If high stock prices signal expanded investment opportunities and the need to finance these new investments, we would expect to see firms raise more money *in total* when stock prices are historically high. But this does not explain why firms prefer to raise the extra cash at these times by an issue of equity rather than debt.

[28]Orange County borrowed money in the following way. Suppose it bought bond A and then sold it to a bank with a promise to buy it back at a slightly higher price. The cash from this sale was then invested in bond B. If bond prices fell, the county lost twice over: Its investment in bond B was worth less than the purchase price, and it was obliged to repurchase bond A for more than the bond was now worth. The sale and repurchase of bond A is known as a reverse repurchase agreement, or reverse "repo." We describe repos in Chapter 31.

floaters, which means that as interest rates rise, the interest payment on each bond is reduced, and vice versa.

Reverse floaters are riskier than normal bonds. When interest rates rise, prices of all bonds fall, but prices of reverse floaters suffer a double whammy because the interest rate payments decline as the discount rate rises. Thus Robert Citron's policy of borrowing to invest in reverse floaters ensured that when, contrary to his forecast, interest rates subsequently rose, the fund suffered huge losses.

Like Robert Citron, financial managers sometimes take large bets because they believe that they can spot the direction of interest rates, stock prices, or exchange rates, and sometimes their employers may encourage them to speculate.[29] We do not mean to imply that such speculation always results in losses, as in Orange County's case, for in an efficient market speculators win as often as they lose.[30] But corporate and municipal treasurers would do better to trust market prices rather than incur large risks in the quest for trading profits.

Lesson 3: Read the Entrails

If the market is efficient, prices impound all available information. Therefore, if we can only learn to read the entrails, security prices can tell us a lot about the future. For example, in Chapter 29 we will show how information in a company's financial statements can help the financial manager to estimate the probability of bankruptcy. But the market's assessment of the company's securities can also provide important information about the firm's prospects. Thus, if the company's bonds are offering a much higher yield than the average, you can deduce that the firm is probably in trouble.

Here is another example: Suppose that investors are confident that interest rates are set to rise over the next year. In that case, they will prefer to wait before they make long-term loans, and any firm that wants to borrow long-term money today will have to offer the inducement of a higher rate of interest. In other words, the long-term rate of interest will have to be higher than the one-year rate. Differences between the long-term interest rate and the short-term rate tell you something about what investors expect to happen to short-term rates in the future.[31]

Example—Hewlett Packard Proposes to Merge with Compaq   On September 3, 2001, two computer companies, Hewlett Packard and Compaq, revealed plans to merge. Announcing the proposal, Carly Fiorina, the chief executive of Hewlett Packard, stated: "This combination vaults us into a leadership role" and creates "substantial shareowner value through significant cost structure improvements and access to new growth opportunities." But investors and analysts gave the proposal a big thumbs-down. Figure 13.8 shows that over the following two days the shares of Hewlett Packard underperformed the market by 21 percent, while Compaq shares underperformed by 16 percent. Investors, it seems, believed that the merger had a negative net present value of $13 billion. When on November 6 the Hewlett family announced that it would vote against the proposal, investors took

---

[29]We don't know why Robert Citron gambled with Orange County's money, but he was under pressure to make up for a shortfall in tax revenues.

[30]Watch out for the speculators who are making very large profits; they are almost certainly taking correspondingly large risks.

[31]We will discuss the relationship between short-term and long-term interest rates in Chapter 24. Notice, however, that in an efficient market the difference between the prices of *any* short-term and long-term contracts always says something about how participants expect prices to move.

FIGURE 13.8

Cumulative abnormal returns on Hewlett Packard and Compaq stocks during four-month period surrounding the announcement on September 3, 2001, of a proposed merger. Hewlett Packard stock recovered after the Hewlett family announced on November 6 that it would vote against the merger.

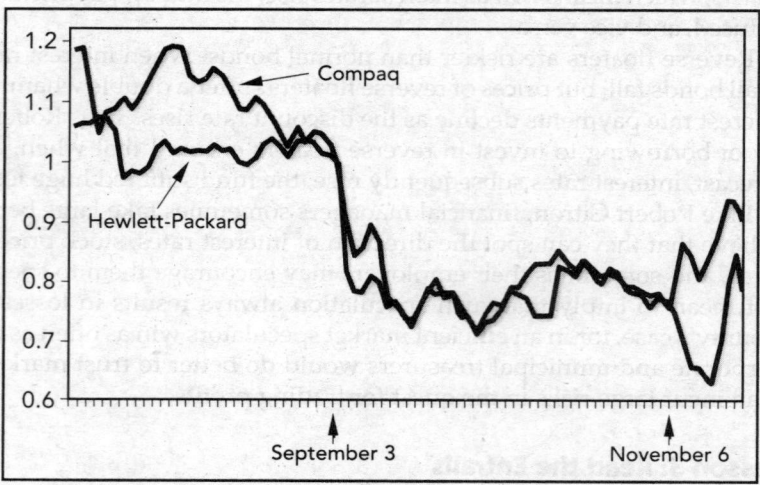

heart, and the next day Hewlett Packard shares gained 16 percent.[32] We do not wish to imply that investor concerns about the merger were justified, for management may have had important information that investors lacked. Our point is simply that the price reaction of the two stocks provided a potentially valuable summary of investor opinion about the effect of the merger on firm value.

Lesson 4: There Are No Financial Illusions

In an efficient market there are no financial illusions. Investors are unromantically concerned with the firm's cash flows and the portion of those cash flows to which they are entitled.

Example—Stock Dividends and Splits   We can illustrate our fourth lesson by looking at the effect of stock dividends and splits. Every year hundreds of companies increase the number of shares outstanding either by subdividing the existing shares or by distributing more shares as dividends. This does not affect the company's future cash flows or the proportion of these cash flows attributable to each shareholder. For example, suppose the stock of Chaste Manhattan is selling for $210 per share. A 3-for-1 stock split would replace each outstanding share with three new shares. Chaste would probably arrange this by printing two new shares for each original share and distributing the new shares to its stockholders as a "free gift." After the split we would expect each share to sell for 210/3 = $70. Dividends per share, earnings per share, and all other per-share variables would be one-third their previous levels.

Figure 13.9 summarizes the results of a classic study of stock splits during the years 1926 to 1960.[33] It shows the cumulative abnormal performance of stocks

---

[32]The stock of Compaq, which was thought to be less badly affected by the merger, fell on the news, before also rising.

[33]See E. F. Fama, L. Fisher, M. Jensen, and R. Roll, "The Adjustment of Stock Prices to New Information," *International Economic Review* 10 (February 1969), pp. 1–21. Later researchers have discovered that shareholders make abnormal gains both when the split or stock dividend is announced and when it takes place. Nobody has offered a convincing explanation for the latter phenomenon. See, for example, M. S. Grinblatt, R. W. Masulis, and S. Titman, "The Valuation Effects of Stock Splits and Stock Dividends," *Journal of Financial Economics* 13 (December 1984), pp. 461–490.

Change in stock price, percent

FIGURE 13.9

Cumulative abnormal returns at the time of a stock split. (Returns are adjusted for the increase in the number of shares.) Notice the rise before the split and the absence of abnormal changes after the split.

Source: E. Fama, L. Fisher, M. Jensen, and R. Roll, "The Adjustment of Stock Prices to New Information," *International Economic Review* 10 (February 1969), fig. 2b, p. 13.

around the time of the split after adjustment for the increase in the number of shares.[34] Notice the rise in price before the split. The announcement of the split would have occurred in the last month or two of this period. That means the decision to split is both the consequence of a rise in price and the cause of a further rise. It looks as if shareholders are not as hard-headed as we have been making out. They do seem to care about the form as well as the substance. However, during the subsequent year two-thirds of the splitting companies announced above-average increases in cash dividends. Normally such an announcement would cause an unusual rise in the stock price, but in the case of the splitting companies there was no such occurrence at any time after the split. The apparent explanation is that the split was accompanied by an explicit or implicit promise of a dividend increase and the rise in price at the time of the split had nothing to do with a predilection for splits as such but with the information that it was thought to convey.

This behavior does not imply that investors like the dividend increases for their own sake, for companies that split their stocks appear to be unusually successful in other ways. For example, Asquith, Healy, and Palepu found that stock splits are frequently preceded by sharp increases in earnings.[35] Such earnings increases are very often transitory, and investors rightly regard them with suspicion. However, the stock split appears to provide investors with an assurance that in this case the rise in earnings is indeed permanent.

Example—Accounting Changes   There are other occasions on which managers seem to assume that investors suffer from financial illusion. For example, some firms devote considerable ingenuity to the task of manipulating earnings reported to stockholders. This is done by "creative accounting," that is, by choosing accounting methods that stabilize and increase reported earnings. Presumably firms

[34]By this we mean that the study looked at the change in the shareholders' wealth. A decline in the price of Chaste Manhattan stock from $210 to $70 at the time of the split would not affect shareholders' wealth.

[35]See P. Asquith, P. Healy, and K. Palepu, "Earnings and Stock Splits," *Accounting Review* 64 (July 1989), pp. 387–403.

go to this trouble because management believes that stockholders take the figures at face value.[36]

One way that companies can affect their reported earnings is through the way that they cost the goods taken out of inventory. Companies can choose between two methods. Under the FIFO (first-in, first-out) method, the firm deducts the cost of the first goods to have been placed in inventory. Under the LIFO (last-in, first-out) method companies deduct the cost of the latest goods to arrive in the warehouse. When inflation is high, the cost of the goods that were bought first is likely to be lower than the cost of those that were bought last. So earnings calculated under FIFO appear higher than those calculated under LIFO.

Now, if it were just a matter of presentation, there would be no harm in switching from LIFO to FIFO. But the IRS insists that the same method that is used to report to shareholders also be used to calculate the firm's taxes. So the lower immediate tax payments from using the LIFO method also bring lower apparent earnings.

If markets are efficient, investors should welcome a change to LIFO accounting, even though it reduces earnings. Biddle and Lindahl, who studied the matter, concluded that this is exactly what happens, so that the move to LIFO is associated with an abnormal rise in the stock price.[37] It seems that shareholders look behind the figures and focus on the amount of the tax savings.

Lesson 5: The Do-It-Yourself Alternative

In an efficient market investors will not pay others for what they can do equally well themselves. As we shall see, many of the controversies in corporate financing center on how well individuals can replicate corporate financial decisions. For example, companies often justify mergers on the grounds that they produce a more diversified and hence more stable firm. But if investors can hold the stocks of both companies why should they thank the companies for diversifying? It is much easier and cheaper for them to diversify than it is for the firm.

The financial manager needs to ask the same question when considering whether it is better to issue debt or common stock. If the firm issues debt, it will create financial leverage. As a result, the stock will be more risky and it will offer a higher expected return. But stockholders can obtain financial leverage without the firm's issuing debt; they can borrow on their own accounts. The problem for the financial manager is, therefore, to decide whether the company can issue debt more cheaply than the individual shareholder.

Lesson 6: Seen One Stock, Seen Them All

The elasticity of demand for any article measures the percentage change in the quantity demanded for each percentage addition to the price. If the article has close substitutes, the elasticity will be strongly negative; if not, it will be near zero. For example, coffee, which is a staple commodity, has a demand elasticity of about $-.2$. This means that a 5 percent increase in the price of coffee changes sales by $-.2 \times .05 = -.01$; in other words, it reduces demand by only 1 percent. Consumers are likely to regard

---

[36]For a discussion of the evidence that investors are not fooled by earnings manipulation, see R. Watts, "Does It Pay to Manipulate EPS?" in J. M. Stern and D. H. Chew, Jr. (eds.), *The Revolution in Corporate Finance*, Oxford, Basil Blackwell, 1986.

[37]G. C. Biddle and F. W. Lindahl, "Stock Price Reactions to LIFO Adoptions: The Association between Excess Returns and LIFO Tax Savings," *Journal of Accounting Research* 20 (Autumn 1982, Part 2), pp. 551–588.

different *brands* of coffee as much closer substitutes for each other. Therefore, the demand elasticity for a particular brand could be in the region of, say, −2.0. A 5 percent increase in the price of Maxwell House relative to that of Folgers would in this case reduce demand by 10 percent.

Investors don't buy a stock for its unique qualities; they buy it because it offers the prospect of a fair return for its risk. This means that stocks should be like *very* similar brands of coffee, almost perfect substitutes. Therefore, the demand for a company's stock should be highly elastic. If its prospective return is too low relative to its risk, *nobody* will want to hold that stock. If the reverse is true, *everybody* will scramble to buy.

Suppose that you want to sell a large block of stock. Since demand is elastic, you naturally conclude that you need only to cut the offering price very slightly to sell your stock. Unfortunately, that doesn't necessarily follow. When you come to sell your stock, other investors may suspect that you want to get rid of it because you know something they don't. Therefore, they will revise their assessment of the stock's value downward. Demand is still elastic, but the whole demand curve moves down. Elastic demand does not imply that stock prices never change when a large sale or purchase occurs; it *does* imply that you can sell large blocks of stock at close to the market price *as long as you can convince other investors that you have no private information.*

Here is one case that supports this view: In June 1977 the Bank of England offered its holding of BP shares for sale at 845 pence each. The bank owned nearly 67 million shares of BP, so the total value of the holding was £564 million, or about $970 million. It was a huge sum to ask the public to find.

Anyone who wished to apply for BP stock had nearly two weeks within which to do so. Just before the Bank's announcement the price of BP stock was 912 pence. Over the next two weeks the price drifted down to 898 pence, largely in line with the British equity market. Therefore, by the final application date, the discount being offered by the Bank was only 6 percent. In return for this discount, any applicant had to raise the necessary cash, taking the risk that the price of BP would decline before the result of the application was known, and had to pass over to the Bank of England the next dividend on BP.

If Maxwell House coffee is offered at a discount of 6 percent, the demand is unlikely to be overwhelming. But the discount on BP stock was enough to bring in applications for $4.6 billion worth of stock, 4.7 times the amount on offer.

We admit that this case was unusual in some respects, but an important study by Myron Scholes of a large sample of secondary offerings confirmed the ability of the market to absorb blocks of stock. The average effect of the offerings was a slight reduction in the stock price, but the decline was almost independent of the amount offered. Scholes's estimate of the demand elasticity for a company's stock was −3,000. Of course, this figure was not meant to be precise, and some researchers have argued that demand is not as elastic as Scholes's study suggests.[38] However, there seems to be widespread agreement with the general point that you can sell large quantities of stock at close to the market price as long as other investors do not deduce that you have some private information.

---

[38]For example, see W. H. Mikkelson and M. M. Partch, "Stock Price Effects and Costs of Secondary Distributions," *Journal of Financial Economics* 14 (June 1985), pp. 165–194. Scholes's study is M. S. Scholes, "The Market for Securities: Substitution versus Price Pressure and the Effects of Information on Share Prices," *Journal of Business* 45 (April 1972), pp. 179–211.

Here again we encounter an apparent contradiction with practice. Many corporations seem to believe not only that the demand elasticity is low but also that it varies with the stock price, so that when the price is relatively low, new stock can be sold only at a substantial discount. State and federal regulatory commissions, which set the prices charged by local telephone companies, electric companies, and other utilities, have sometimes allowed significantly higher earnings to compensate the firm for price "pressure." This pressure is the decline in the firm's stock price that is supposed to occur when new shares are offered to investors. Yet Paul Asquith and David Mullins, who searched for evidence of pressure, found that new stock issues by utilities drove down their stock prices on average by only .9 percent.[39] We will come back to the subject of pressure when we discuss stock issues in Chapter 15.

---

[39]See P. Asquith and D. W. Mullins, "Equity Issues and Offering Dilution," *Journal of Financial Economics* 15 (January–February 1986), pp. 61–89.

SUMMARY

The patron saint of the Bolsa (stock exchange) in Barcelona, Spain, is Nuestra Senora de la Esperanza—Our Lady of Hope. She is the perfect patroness, for we all hope for superior returns when we invest. But competition between investors will tend to produce an efficient market. In such a market, prices will rapidly impound any new information, and it will be difficult to make consistently superior returns. We may indeed hope, but all we can rationally *expect* in an efficient market is a return just sufficient to compensate us for the time value of money and for the risks we bear.

The efficient-market hypothesis comes in three different flavors. The weak form of the hypothesis states that prices efficiently reflect all the information in the past series of stock prices. In this case it is impossible to earn superior returns simply by looking for patterns in stock prices; in other words, price changes are random. The semistrong form of the hypothesis states that prices reflect all published information. That means it is impossible to make consistently superior returns just by reading the newspaper, looking at the company's annual accounts, and so on. The strong form of the hypothesis states that stock prices effectively impound all available information. It tells us that superior information is hard to find because in pursuing it you are in competition with thousands, perhaps millions, of active, intelligent, and greedy investors. The best you can do in this case is to assume that securities are fairly priced and to hope that one day Nuestra Senora will reward your humility.

While there remain plenty of unsolved puzzles, there seems to be widespread agreement that consistently superior returns are hard to attain. Thirty years ago any suggestion that security investment is a fair game was generally regarded as bizarre. Today it is not only widely discussed in business schools but also permeates investment practice and government policy toward the securities markets.

For the corporate treasurer who is concerned with issuing or purchasing securities, the efficient-market theory has obvious implications. In one sense, however, it raises more questions than it answers. The existence of efficient markets does not mean that the financial manager can let financing take care of itself. It provides only a starting point for analysis. It is time to get down to details about securities and issue procedures. We start in Chapter 14.

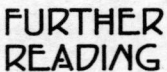

FURTHER READING

The classic review articles on market efficiency are:

E. F. Fama: "Efficient Capital Markets: A Review of Theory and Empirical Work," *Journal of Finance,* 25:383–417 (May 1970).

E. F. Fama: "Efficient Capital Markets: II," *Journal of Finance,* 46:1575–1617 (December 1991).

For evidence on possible exceptions to the efficient-market theory, we suggest:

G. Hawawini and D. B. Keim: "On the Predictability of Common Stock Returns: World-Wide Evidence," in R. A. Jarrow, V. Maksimovic, and W. T. Ziemba (eds.), *Finance,* North-Holland, Amsterdam, Netherlands, 1994.

Martin Gruber's Presidential Address to the American Finance Association is an interesting overview of the performance of mutual fund managers.

M. Gruber: "Another Puzzle: The Growth in Actively Managed Mutual Funds," *Journal of Finance,* 51:783–810 (July 1996).

Andre Shleifer's book and Robert Shiller's paper provide a good introduction to behavioral finance. A useful collection of papers on behavioral explanations for market anomalies is provided in Richard Thaler's book of readings, while Eugene Fama's paper offers a more skeptical view of these behavioral theories.

A. Shleifer: *Inefficient Markets: An Introduction to Behavioral Finance,* Oxford University Press, Oxford, 2000.

R. J. Shiller: "Human Behavior and the Efficiency of the Financial System," in J. B. Taylor and M. Woodford (eds.), *Handbook of Macroeconomics,* North-Holland, Amsterdam, 1999.

R. H. Thaler (ed.): *Advances in Behavioral Finance,* Russell Sage Foundation, New York, 1993.

E. F. Fama: "Market Efficiency, Long-Term Returns, and Behavioral Finance," *Journal of Financial Economics,* 49:283–306 (September 1998).

The following book contains an interesting collection of articles on the crash of 1987:

R. W. Kamphuis, Jr., et al. (eds.): *Black Monday and the Future of Financial Markets,* Dow-Jones Irwin, Inc., Homewood, IL, 1989.

QUIZ

1. Which (if any) of these statements are true? Stock prices appear to behave as though successive values **(a)** are random numbers, **(b)** follow regular cycles, **(c)** differ by a random number.

2. Supply the missing words:

   "There are three forms of the efficient-market hypothesis. Tests of randomness in stock returns provide evidence for the _____ form of the hypothesis. Tests of stock price reaction to well-publicized news provide evidence for the _____ form, and tests of the performance of professionally managed funds provide evidence for the _____ form. Market efficiency results from competition between investors. Many investors search for new information about the company's business that would help them to value the stock more accurately. Such research helps to ensure that prices reflect all available information; in other words, it helps to keep the market efficient in the _____ form. Other investors study past stock prices for recurrent patterns that would allow them to make superior profits. Such research helps to ensure that prices reflect all the information contained in past stock prices; in other words, it helps to keep the market efficient in the _____ form."

3. True or false? The efficient-market hypothesis assumes that
   a. There are no taxes.
   b. There is perfect foresight.
   c. Successive price changes are independent.
   d. Investors are irrational.

     e. There are no transaction costs.

     f. Forecasts are unbiased.

4. The stock of United Boot is priced at $400 and offers a dividend yield of 2 percent. The company has a 2-for-1 stock split.

     a. Other things equal, what would you expect to happen to the stock price?

     b. In practice would you expect the stock price to fall by more or less than this amount?

     c. Suppose that a few months later United Boot announces a rise in dividends that is exactly in line with that of other companies. Would you expect the announcement to lead to a slight abnormal rise in the stock price, a slight abnormal fall, or no change?

5. True or false?

     a. Financing decisions are less easily reversed than investment decisions.

     b. Financing decisions don't affect the total size of the cash flows; they just affect who receives the flows.

     c. Tests have shown that there is almost perfect negative correlation between successive price changes.

     d. The semistrong form of the efficient-market hypothesis states that prices reflect all publicly available information.

     e. In efficient markets the expected return on each stock is the same.

     f. Myron Scholes's study of the effect of secondary distributions provided evidence that the demand schedule for a single company's shares is highly elastic.

6. Analysis of 60 monthly rates of return on United Futon common stock indicates a beta of 1.45 and an alpha of $-.2$ percent per month. A month later, the market is up by 5 percent, and United Futon is up by 6 percent. What is Futon's abnormal rate of return?

7. True or false?

     a. Analysis by security analysts and investors helps keep markets efficient.

     b. Psychologists have found that, once people have suffered a loss, they are more relaxed about the possibility of incurring further losses.

     c. Psychologists have observed that people tend to regard recent events as representative of what might happen in the future.

     d. If the efficient-market hypothesis is correct, managers will not be able to increase stock prices by creative accounting that boosts reported earnings.

8. Geothermal Corporation has just received good news: its earnings increased by 20 percent from last year's value. Most investors are anticipating an increase of 25 percent. Will Geothermal's stock price increase or decrease when the announcement is made?

9. Here again are the six lessons of market efficiency. For each lesson give an example showing the lesson's relevance to financial managers.

     a. Markets have no memory.

     b. Trust market prices.

     c. Read the entrails.

     d. There are no financial illusions.

     e. The do-it-yourself alternative.

     f. Seen one stock, seen them all.

PRACTICE QUESTIONS

1. How would you respond to the following comments?

     a. "Efficient market, my eye! I know lots of investors who do crazy things."

     b. "Efficient market? Balderdash! I know at least a dozen people who have made a bundle in the stock market."

     c. "The trouble with the efficient-market theory is that it ignores investors' psychology."

d. "Despite all the limitations, the best guide to a company's value is its written-down book value. It is much more stable than market value, which depends on temporary fashions."

2. Respond to the following comments:
   a. "The random-walk theory, with its implication that investing in stocks is like playing roulette, is a powerful indictment of our capital markets."
   b. "If everyone believes you can make money by charting stock prices, then price changes won't be random."
   c. "The random-walk theory implies that events are random, but many events are not random. If it rains today, there's a fair bet that it will rain again tomorrow."

3. Which of the following observations *appear* to indicate market inefficiency? Explain whether the observation appears to contradict the weak, semistrong, or strong form of the efficient-market hypothesis.
   a. Tax-exempt municipal bonds offer lower pretax returns than taxable government bonds.
   b. Managers make superior returns on their purchases of their company's stock.
   c. There is a positive relationship between the return on the market in one quarter and the change in aggregate profits in the next quarter.
   d. There is disputed evidence that stocks which have appreciated unusually in the recent past continue to do so in the future.
   e. The stock of an acquired firm tends to appreciate in the period before the merger announcement.
   f. Stocks of companies with unexpectedly high earnings *appear* to offer high returns for several months after the earnings announcement.
   g. Very risky stocks on average give higher returns than safe stocks.

4. Look again at Figure 13.9.
   a. Is the steady rise in the stock price before the split evidence of market inefficiency?
   b. How do you think those stocks performed that did *not* increase their dividends by an above-average amount?

5. Stock splits are important because they convey information. Can you suggest some other financial decisions that do so?

6. Here are alphas and betas for Intel and Conagra for the 60 months ending October 2001. Alpha is expressed as a percent per month.

	Alpha	Beta
Intel	.77	1.61
Conagra	.17	.47

Explain how these estimates would be used to calculate an abnormal return.

7. It is sometimes suggested that stocks with low price–earnings ratios tend to be underpriced. Describe a possible test of this view. Be as precise as possible.

8. "If the efficient-market hypothesis is true, then it makes no difference what securities a company issues. All are fairly priced." Does this follow?

9. "If the efficient-market hypothesis is true, the pension fund manager might as well select a portfolio with a pin." Explain why this is not so.

10. The bottom graph in Figure 13.1 shows the actual performance of the Standard and Poor's 500 Index for a five-year period. Two financial managers, Alpha and Beta, are contemplating this chart. Each manager's company needs to issue new shares of common stock sometime in the next year.

Alpha: My company's going to issue right away. The stock market cycle has obviously topped out, and the next move is almost surely down. Better to issue now and get a decent price for the shares.

Beta: You're too nervous; we're waiting. It's true that the market's been going nowhere for the past year or so, but the figure clearly shows a basic upward trend. The market's on the way up to a new plateau.

What would you say to Alpha and Beta?

11. What does the efficient-market hypothesis have to say about these two statements?
    a. "I notice that short-term interest rates are about 1 percent below long-term rates. We should borrow short-term."
    b. "I notice that interest rates in Japan are lower than rates in the United States. We would do better to borrow Japanese yen rather than U.S. dollars."

12. We suggested that there are three possible interpretations of the small-firm effect: a required return for some unidentified risk factor, a coincidence, or market inefficiency. Write three brief memos, arguing each point of view.

13. "It may be true that in an efficient market there *should* be no patterns in stock prices, but, if everyone believes that they *do* exist, then this belief will be self-fulfilling." Discuss.

14. Column (a) in Table 13.1 shows the monthly return on the British FTSE 100 index from August 1999 through July 2001. Columns (b) and (c) show the returns on the stocks of two firms. Both announced dividend increases during this period—Executive Cheese

TABLE 13.1

See practice question 14. Rates of return in percent per month.

Month	(A) Market Return	(B) Executive Cheese Return	(C) Paddington Beer Return
1999:			
Aug.	.2	−1.9	−.5
Sept.	−3.5	−10.1	−6.1
Oct.	3.7	8.1	9.8
Nov.	5.5	7.5	16.5
Dec.	5.0	4.3	6.7
2000:			
Jan.	−9.5	−5.3	−11.1
Feb.	−.6	5.7	−7.3
Mar.	4.9	−9.7	4.5
Apr.	−3.3	−4.7	−14.8
May	.5	−10.0	−1.1
June	−.7	−2.7	−1.2
July	.8	.1	−2.6
Aug.	4.8	3.4	12.4
Sept.	−5.7	5.6	−7.9
Oct.	2.3	−2.2	11.5
Nov.	−4.6	−6.5	−14.4
Dec.	1.3	−.2	3.4
2001:			
Jan.	1.2	−3.7	4.1
Feb.	−6.0	−9.0	−14.1
Mar.	−4.8	7.3	−6.5
Apr.	5.9	4.7	12.6
May	−2.9	−7.1	−.7
June	−2.7	0.5	−14.5
July	−2.0	−0.5	−11.4

in September 2000 and Paddington Beer in January 2000. Calculate the average abnormal return of the two stocks during the month of the dividend announcement.

15. On May 15, 1997, the government of Kuwait offered to sell 170 million BP shares, worth about $2 billion. Goldman Sachs was contacted after the stock market closed in London and given one hour to decide whether to bid on the stock. They decided to offer 710.5 pence ($11.59) per share, and Kuwait accepted. Then Goldman Sachs went looking for buyers. They lined up 500 institutional and individual investors worldwide, and resold all the shares at 716 pence ($11.70). The resale was complete before the London Stock Exchange opened the next morning. Goldman Sachs made $15 million overnight.[40]

    What does this deal say about market efficiency? Discuss.

CHALLENGE QUESTIONS

1. Bond dealers buy and sell bonds at very low spreads. In other words, they are willing to sell at a price only slightly higher than the price at which they buy. Used-car dealers buy and sell cars at very wide spreads. What has this got to do with the strong form of the efficient-market hypothesis?

2. "An analysis of the behavior of exchange rates and bond prices around the time of international assistance for countries in balance of payments difficulties suggests that on average prices decline sharply for a number of months before the announcement of the assistance and are largely stable after the announcement. This suggests that the assistance is effective but comes too late." Does this follow?

3. Use either the Market Insight database (**www.mhhe.com/edumarketinsight**) or (**www.finance.yahoo.com**) to download daily prices for 5 U.S. stocks for a recent 12-month period. For each stock construct a scatter diagram of successive returns as in Figure 13.2. Then calculate the correlation between the returns on successive days. Do you find any consistent patterns?

---

[40]"Goldman Sachs Earns a Quick $15 Million Sale of BP Shares," *The Wall Street Journal*, May 16, 1997, p. A4.

CHAPTER FOURTEEN

AN OVERVIEW OF CORPORATE FINANCING

WE NOW BEGIN our analysis of long-term financing decisions—an undertaking we will not complete until Chapter 26. This chapter provides an introduction to corporate financing. It reviews with a broad brush several topics that will be explored more carefully later on.

We start the chapter by looking at aggregate data on the sources of financing for U.S. corporations. Much of the money for new investments comes from profits that companies retain and reinvest. The remainder comes from selling new debt or equity securities. These financing patterns raise several interesting questions. Do companies rely too heavily on internal financing rather than on new issues of debt or equity? Are debt ratios of U.S. corporations dangerously high? How do patterns of financing differ across the major industrialized countries?

Our second task in the chapter is to review some of the essential features of debt and equity. Lenders and stockholders have different *cash flow rights* and also different *control rights*. The lenders have first claim on cash flow, because they are promised definite cash payments for interest and principal. The stockholder receives whatever cash is left over after the lenders are paid. Stockholders, on the other hand, have complete control of the firm, providing that they keep their promises to lenders. As owners of the business, stockholders have the ultimate control over what assets the company buys, how the assets are financed, and how they are used. Of course, in large public corporations the stockholders delegate these decisions to the board of directors, who in turn appoint senior management. In these cases *effective* control often ends up with the company's management.

The simple division of sources of cash into debt and equity glosses over the many different types of debt that companies issue. Therefore, we close our discussion of debt and equity with a brief canter through the main categories of debt. We also pause to describe certain less common forms of equity, particularly preferred stock.

Financial institutions play an important role in supplying finance to companies. For example, banks provide short- and medium-term debt, help to arrange new public issues of securities, buy and sell foreign currencies, and so on. We introduce you to the major financial institutions and look at the roles that they play in corporate financing and in the economy at large.

 ## 14.1 PATTERNS OF CORPORATE FINANCING

Companies invest in long-term assets (mainly property, plant, and equipment) and net working capital. Table 14.1 shows where they get the cash to pay for these investments. You can see that by far the greater part of the money is generated internally. In other words, it comes from cash that the company has set aside as depreciation and from retained earnings (earnings not paid out as dividends).[1] Shareholders are happy for companies to plow back this money into the firm, so long as it goes to positive-NPV investments. Every positive-NPV investment generates a higher price for their shares.

In most years there is a gap between the cash that companies need and the cash that they generate internally. This gap is the financial deficit. To make up the deficit, companies must either sell new equity or borrow. So companies face two basic financing decisions: How much profit should be plowed back into the

---

[1] In Table 14.1, internally generated cash was calculated by adding depreciation to retained earnings. Depreciation is a noncash expense. Thus, retained earnings understate the cash flow available for reinvestment.

	1990	1991	1992	1993	1994	1995	1996	1997	1998	1999	2000
1. Capital expenditure	87.1%	104.5%	87.5%	87.3%	83.2%	77.6%	87.6%	81.0%	89.1%	80.4%	86.6%
2. Investment in net working capital and other uses	12.9%	−4.5%	12.5%	12.7%	16.8%	22.4%	12.4%	19.0%	10.9%	19.6%	13.4%
3. Total investment	100.0%	100.0%	100.0%	100.0%	100.0%	100.0%	100.0%	100.0%	100.0%	100.0%	100.0%
Total investment, billions	$ 498	$ 412	$ 517	$ 567	$ 754	$ 789	$ 755	$ 880	$ 872	$ 1,116	$ 1,162
4. Internally generated cash	86.8%	108.6%	90.0%	90.2%	87.7%	78.6%	89.5%	82.7%	85.7%	72.1%	76.7%
5. Financial deficit	13.2%	−8.6%	10.0%	9.8%	12.3%	21.4%	10.5%	17.3%	14.3%	27.9%	23.3%
Financial deficit covered by											
6. Net stock issues	−12.7%	4.4%	5.2%	3.8%	−6.9%	−7.4%	−9.2%	−13.0%	−30.6%	−12.9%	−14.3%
7. Net increase in debt	25.9%	−13.0%	4.8%	6.1%	19.3%	28.8%	19.7%	30.3%	45.0%	40.8%	37.6%

TABLE 14.1

Sources and uses of funds in nonfinancial corporations expressed as percentages of each year's total investment.

Source: Board of Governors of the Federal Reserve System, Division of Research and Statistics, Flow of Funds Accounts Table F.102 for Nonfarm, Nonfinancial Corporate Business, at www.federalreserve.gov/releases/z1/current/data.htm.

business rather than paid out as dividends? and What proportion of the deficit should be financed by borrowing rather than by an issue of equity? To answer the first question the firm requires a dividend policy (we discuss this in Chapter 16); and to answer the second it needs a debt policy (this is the topic of Chapters 17 and 18).

Notice that net stock issues were negative in most years. That means that the amount of new money raised by companies issuing equity was more than offset by the amount of money returned to shareholders by repurchase of previously outstanding shares. (Companies can buy back their own shares, or they may repurchase and retire other companies' shares in the course of mergers and acquisitions.) We discuss share repurchases in Chapter 16 and mergers and acquisitions in Chapter 33.

Net stock issues were positive in the early 1990s. Companies had entered the decade with uncomfortably high debt levels, so they paid down debt in 1991 and replenished equity in 1991, 1992, and 1993. But net stock issues turned negative in 1994 and stayed negative for the rest of the decade. Aggregate debt issues increased to cover both the financial deficit and the net retirements of equity.

Companies in the United States are not alone in their heavy reliance on internal funds. Internal funds make up more than two-thirds of corporate financing in Germany, Japan, and the United Kingdom.[2]

Do Firms Rely Too Much on Internal Funds?

We have seen that on average internal funds (retained earnings plus depreciation) cover most of the cash firms need for investment. It seems that internal financing is more convenient than external financing by stock and debt issues. But some observers worry that managers have an irrational or self-serving aversion to external finance. A manager seeking comfortable employment could be tempted to forego a risky but positive-NPV project if it involved launching a new stock issue and facing awkward questions from potential investors. Perhaps managers take the line of least resistance and dodge the "discipline of capital markets."

But there are also some good reasons for relying on internally generated funds. The cost of issuing new securities is avoided, for example. Moreover, the announcement of a new equity issue is usually bad news for investors, who worry that the decision signals lower future profits or higher risk.[3] If issues of shares are costly and send a bad-news signal to investors, companies may be justified in looking more carefully at those projects that would require a new stock issue.

Has Capital Structure Changed?

We commented that in recent years firms have, in the aggregate, issued much more debt than equity. But is there a long-run trend to heavier reliance on debt finance? This is a hard question to answer in general, because financing policy varies so

---

[2]See, for example, J. Corbett and T. Jenkinson, "How Is Investment Financed? A Study of Germany, Japan, the United Kingdom and the United States," *The Manchester School* 65 (Supplement 1997), pp. 69–93.

[3]Managers do have insiders' insights and naturally are tempted to issue stock when the price looks good to them, that is, when they are less optimistic than outside investors. The outside investors realize this and will buy a new issue only at a discount from the pre-announcement price. More on stock issues in Chapter 15.

Current assets[†]	$1,547	Current liabilities[†]	$1,234
Fixed assets	$2,361	Long-term debt	$1,038
Less depreciation	1,166	Other long-term liabilities[‡]	679
Net fixed assets	1,195	Total long-term liabilities	1,717
Other long-term assets	2,160	Stockholders' equity	1,951
Total assets[§]	$4,903	Total liabilities and stockholders' equity[§]	$4,903

TABLE 14.2

Aggregate balance sheet for manufacturing corporations in the United States, 1st quarter, 2001 (figures in $ billions)*.

*Excludes companies with less than $250,000 in assets.
[†]See Table 30.1 for a breakdown of current assets and liabilities.
[‡]Includes deferred taxes and several miscellaneous categories.
[§]Columns may not add up because of rounding.
Source: U.S. Census Bureau, *Quarterly Financial Report for Manufacturing, Mining and Trade Corporations*, 1st Quarter, 2001 (**www.census.gov/csd/qfr**).

much from industry to industry and from firm to firm. But a few statistics will do no harm as long as you keep these difficulties in mind.

Table 14.2 shows the aggregate balance sheet of all manufacturing corporations in the United States in 2001. If all manufacturing corporations were merged into one gigantic firm, Table 14.2 would be its balance sheet.

Assets and liabilities in Table 14.2 are entered at book, that is, accounting values. These do not generally equal market values. The numbers are nevertheless instructive. The table shows that manufacturing corporations had total book assets of $4,903 billion. On the right-hand-side of the balance sheet, we find total long-term liabilities of $1,717 billion and stockholders' equity of $1,951 billion.

So what was the book debt ratio of manufacturing corporations in 2001? It depends on what you mean by *debt*. If all liabilities are counted as debt, the debt ratio is .60:

$$\frac{\text{Debt}}{\text{Total assets}} = \frac{1,234 + 1,717}{4,903} = .60$$

This measure of debt includes both current liabilities and long-term obligations. Sometimes financial analysts focus on the proportions of debt and equity in *long-term* financing. The proportion of debt in long-term financing is

$$\frac{\text{Long-term liabilities}}{\text{Long-term liabilities + stockholders' equity}} = \frac{1,717}{1,717 + 1,951} = .47$$

The sum of long-term liabilities and stockholders' equity is called *total capitalization*. Figure 14.1 plots these two ratios from 1954 to 2001. There is a clear upward trend. But before we conclude that industry is becoming weighed down by a crippling debt burden, we need to put these changes in perspective.

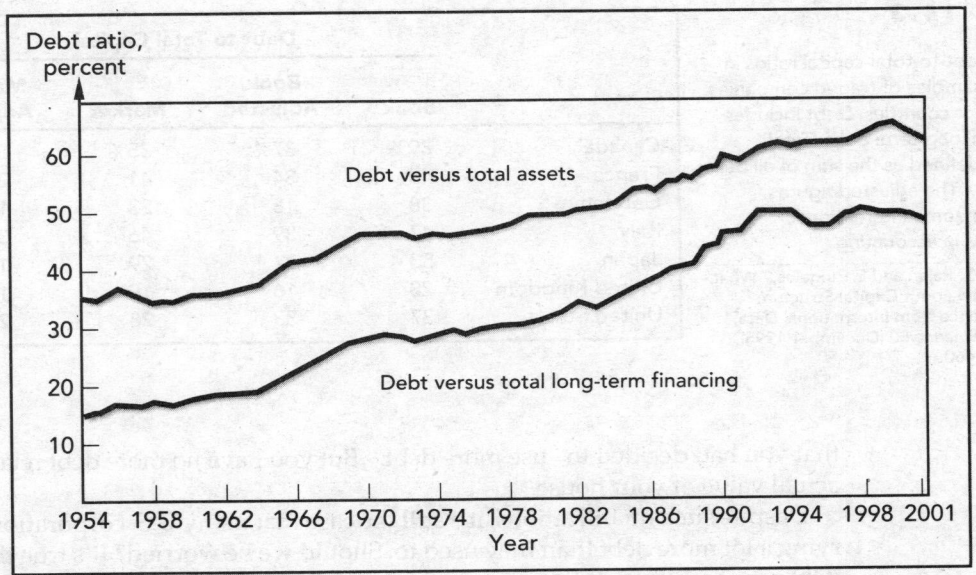

FIGURE 14.1

Average debt ratios for manufacturing corporations in the United States have increased in the postwar period. However, note that these ratios compare debt with the *book* value of total assets and total long-term financing. The actual value of corporate assets is higher as a result of inflation.

Source: U.S. Census Bureau, *Quarterly Financial Report for Manufacturing, Mining and Trade Corporations,* various issues.

1990 versus 1920   Debt ratios in the 1990s, though clearly higher than in the early postwar period, are no higher than in-the 1920s and 1930s. You could argue that Figure 14.1 starts from an abnormally low point.[4]

Inflation   Some of the upward movement in Figure 14.1 may have reflected inflation, which was especially rapid—by U.S. standards—throughout the 1970s and early 1980s. Rapid inflation means that the *book* value of corporate assets falls behind the actual value of those assets. If corporations were borrowing against *actual* value, it would not be surprising to observe rising ratios of debt-to-book asset values.

To illustrate, suppose that you bought a house 10 years ago for $60,000. You financed the purchase in part with a $30,000 mortgage, 50 percent of the purchase price. Today the house is worth $120,000. Suppose that you repay the remaining balance of your original mortgage and take out a new mortgage of $60,000, which is again 50 percent of current market value. Your *book* debt ratio would be 100 percent. The reason is that the book value of the house is its *original* cost of $60,000 (we assume no depreciation). An analyst having only book values to work with would observe that 10 years ago your book debt ratio was only 50 percent and might conclude

---

[4]See Figure 1.3 on p. 25 in R. A. Taggart, Jr., "Secular Patterns in the Financing of U.S. Corporations," in B. M. Friedman (ed.), *Corporate Capital Structures in the United States,* University of Chicago Press, 1985.

TABLE 14.3

Median debt-to-total-capital ratios in 1991 for samples of traded companies in the major countries. Debt includes short- and long-term debt. Total capital is defined as the sum of all debt and equity. The adjusted figures correct for some international differences in accounting.

Source: R. G. Rajan and L. Zingales, "What Do We Know about Capital Structure? Some Evidence from International Data," *Journal of Finance* 50 (December 1995), pp. 1421–1460.

| | Debt to Total Capital | | | |
	Book	Book, Adjusted	Market	Market, Adjusted
Canada	39%	37%	35%	32%
France	48	34	41	28
Germany	38	18	23	15
Italy	47	39	46	36
Japan	53	37	29	17
United Kingdom	28	16	19	11
United States	37	33	28	23

that you had decided to "use more debt." But you have no more debt relative to the actual value of your house.

Despite such qualifications, it's still the case that many U.S. corporations are carrying a lot more debt than they used to. Should we be worried? It's true that higher debt ratios mean that more companies will fall into financial distress if a serious recession hits the economy. But all companies live with this risk to some degree, and it does not follow that less risk is better. Finding the optimal debt ratio is like finding the optimal speed limit. We can agree that accidents at 30 miles per hour are generally less dangerous than accidents at 60 miles per hour, but we do not therefore set the speed limit on all roads at 30. Speed has benefits as well as risks. So does debt, as we will see in Chapter 18.

There is no God-given, correct debt ratio, and if there were, it would change. It may be that some of the new tools that allow firms to manage their risks have made higher debt ratios practicable.

International Comparisons   Corporations in the United States are generally viewed as having less debt than many of their foreign counterparts. That was surely true in the 1950s and 1960s. Now it is not so clear.

Rajan and Zingales examined the balance sheets of a large sample of publicly traded firms in the seven largest industrialized countries. They calculated debt ratios using both book and market values of shareholders' equity. (The book value of debt was assumed to approximate market value.) A taste of their results is given in Table 14.3. Notice that the debt ratios for the United States sample fall in the middle of the pack.

International comparisons of this sort are always muddied by differences in accounting methods. For example, German companies show pension liabilities as a debtlike obligation on their balance sheets, with no offsetting entry for pension assets.[5] They also report "reserves" separately from equity. These reserves do not cover any specific obligations but serve as equity for a rainy day. Reserves might be drawn down to offset a future drop in operating earnings, for example. (This would be unacceptably creative accounting in the United States.) When Rajan and Zingales crossed out the pension liabilities and added back reserves to equity, the *adjusted* debt ratios for German companies dropped to the low levels reported in Table 14.3.

---

[5]United States companies show a net liability only if the pension plan is underfunded.

14.2 COMMON STOCK

Corporations raise cash in two principal ways—by issuing equity or by issuing debt. The equity consists largely of common stock, but companies may also issue preferred stock. As we shall see, there is a much greater diversity of debt securities.

We start our brief tour of corporate securities by taking a closer look at common stock. Table 14.4 shows the common equity of H.J. Heinz Company. The maximum number of shares that can be issued is known as the *authorized share capital*; for Heinz it was 600 million shares. If management wishes to increase the number of authorized shares, it needs the agreement of shareholders to do so. By May 2000 Heinz had already issued 431 million shares, and so it could issue 169 million more without further shareholder approval.

Most of the issued shares were held by investors. These shares are said to be *issued and outstanding*. But Heinz has also bought back 84 million shares from investors. Repurchased shares are held in the company's treasury until they are either canceled or resold. Treasury shares are said to be *issued but not outstanding*.

The issued shares are entered into the company's books at their par value. Each Heinz share had a par value of $.25. Thus the total book value of the issued shares was $431 \times \$.25 = \$108$ million. Par value has little economic significance.[6] Some companies issue shares with no par value. In this case, the stock is listed in the accounts at an arbitrarily determined figure.

The price of new shares sold to the public almost always exceeds par value. The difference is entered in the company's accounts as additional paid-in capital or capital surplus. Thus, if Heinz had sold an additional 100,000 shares at $40 a share, the common stock account would have increased by $100,000 \times \$.25 = \$25,000$, and the capital surplus account would have increased by $100,000 \times \$39.75 = \$3,975,000$.

Heinz distributed about 50 percent of its earnings as dividends. The remainder was retained in the business and used to finance new investments. The cumulative amount of retained earnings was $4,757 million.

Common shares ($.25 par value per share)	$ 108
Additional paid-in capital	304
Retained earnings	4,757
Treasury shares	(2,920)
Other adjustments	(652)
Net common equity	$1,596
Note:	
Authorized shares	600
Issued shares, of which:	431
Outstanding shares	347
Treasury shares	84

TABLE 14.4

Book value of common stockholders' equity of H.J. Heinz Company, May 3, 2000 (figures in millions).

Sources: H.J. Heinz Company, *Annual Reports*.

---

[6]Because some states do not allow companies to sell shares below par value, par value is generally set at a low figure.

FIGURE 14.2

Holdings of corporate
equities, 2000.

Source: Board of Governors of
the Federal Reserve System,
Division of Research and Statistics, Flow of Funds Accounts
Table L.213 at **www.federal
reserve.gov/releases/z1/
current/data.htm**.

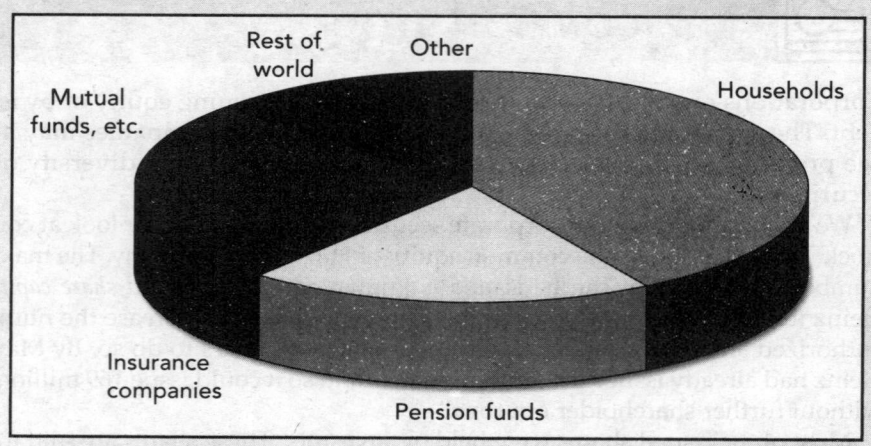

The next entry in the common stock account shows the amount that the company has spent on repurchasing its common stock. The repurchases have *reduced*
the stockholders' equity by $2,920 million. Finally, there is an entry for other ad-
justments, principally currency losses stemming from Heinz's foreign operations.
We would rather not get into these accounting adjustments here.

Heinz's net common equity had a book value in May 2000 of $1,596 million.
That works out at 1,596/347 = $4.60 per share. But in May 2000, Heinz's shares
were priced at about $35 each. So the *market value* of the common stock was 347 mil-
lion × $35 = $12.1 billion, over $10 billion higher than book.

Ownership of the Corporation

A corporation is owned by its common stockholders. Some of this common stock
is held directly by individual investors, but the greater proportion belongs to **financial institutions** such as banks, pension funds, and insurance companies. For
example, look at Figure 14.2. You can see that in the United States just over 60 percent of common stock is held by financial institutions, with pension funds and mutual funds each holding about 20 percent.

What do we mean when we say that these stockholders *own* the corporation?
The answer is obvious if the company has issued no other securities. Consider
the simplest possible case of a corporation financed solely by common stock, all
of which is owned by the firm's chief executive officer (CEO). This lucky
owner–manager receives all the cash flows and makes all investment and operating decisions. She has complete *cash-flow rights* and also complete *control rights*.

These rights are split up and reallocated as soon as the company borrows
money. If it takes out a bank loan, it enters into a contract with the bank promising
to pay interest and eventually repay the principal. The bank gets a privileged, but
limited, right to cash flows; the residual cash-flow rights are left to the stockholder.

The bank will typically protect its claim by imposing restrictions on what the
firm can or cannot do. For example, it may require the firm to limit future borrowing, and it may forbid the firm to sell off assets or to pay excessive dividends. The
stockholders' control rights are thereby limited. However, the contract with the

bank can never restrict or determine all the operating and investment decisions necessary to run the firm efficiently. (No team of lawyers, no matter how long they scribbled, could ever write a contract covering all possible contingencies.[7]) The owner of the common stock retains the rights of control over these decisions. For example, she may choose to increase the selling price of the firm's products, to hire temporary rather than permanent employees, or to construct a new plant in Miami Beach rather than Hollywood.[8]

Ownership of the firm can of course change. If the firm fails to make the promised payments to the bank, it may be forced into bankruptcy. Once the firm is under the "protection" of a bankruptcy court, shareholders' cash-flow and control rights are tightly restricted and may be extinguished altogether. Unless some rescue or reorganization plan can be implemented, the bank will become the new owner of the firm and will acquire the cash-flow and control rights of ownership. (We discuss bankruptcy in Chapter 25.)

There is no law of nature that says residual cash-flow rights and residual control rights have to go together. For example, one could imagine a situation where the debtholder gets to make all the decisions. But this would be inefficient. Since the benefits of good decisions are felt mainly by the common stockholders, it makes sense to give them control over how the firm's assets are used.

We have focused so far on a firm that is owned by a single stockholder. In many countries, such as Italy, Hong Kong, or Mexico, there is generally a dominant stockholder who controls 20 percent or more of the votes of even the largest corporations.[9] There are also a few major businesses in the United States that are controlled by one or two large stockholders. For example, at the beginning of 2001 Bill Gates owned 21 percent of the common stock of Microsoft as well as being chairman and chief executive. However, such concentration of control is the exception. Ownership of most major corporations in the United States is widely dispersed.

The common stockholders in widely held corporations still have the residual rights over the cash flows and have the ultimate right of control over the company's affairs. In practice, however, their control is limited to an entitlement to vote, either in person or by proxy, on appointments to the *board of directors*, and on other crucial matters such as the decision to merge. Many shareholders do not bother to vote. They reason that, since they own so few shares, their vote will have little impact on the outcome. The problem is that, if all shareholders think in the same way, they cede effective control and management gets a free hand to look after its own interests.

Voting Procedures and the Value of Votes

If the company's articles of incorporation specify a *majority voting* system, each director is voted upon separately and stockholders can cast one vote for each share that they own. If a company's articles permit *cumulative voting*, the directors are voted upon jointly and stockholders can, if they wish, allot all their votes to just

---

[7]Theoretical economists therefore stress the importance of *incomplete contracts*. Their point is that contracts pertaining to the management of the firm *must* be incomplete and that someone must exercise residual rights of control. See O. Hart, *Firms, Contracts, and Financial Structure*, Clarendon Press, Oxford, 1995.

[8]Of course, the bank manager may suggest that a particular decision is unwise, or even threaten to cut off future lending, but the bank does not have any *right* to make these decisions.

[9]See R. La Porta, F. Lopez-de-Silanes, and A. Shleifer, "Corporate Ownership around the World," *Journal of Finance* 54 (1999), pp 471–517.

one candidate.[10] Cumulative voting makes it easier for a minority group among the stockholders to elect directors who will represent the group's interests. That is why some shareholder groups campaign for cumulative voting.

On many issues a simple majority of votes cast is sufficient to carry the day, but the company charter may specify some decisions that require a *supermajority* of, say, 75 percent of those eligible to vote. For example, a supermajority vote is sometimes needed to approve a merger. Managers, who believe that their jobs may be threatened by a merger, are often anxious to persuade shareholders to agree that the charter should be amended to require a supermajority vote.[11]

The issues on which stockholders are asked to vote are rarely contested, particularly in the case of large, publicly traded firms. Occasionally, there are *proxy contests* in which the firm's existing management and directors compete with outsiders for effective control of the corporation. But the odds are stacked against the outsiders, for the insiders can get the firm to pay all the costs of presenting their case and obtaining votes.

Usually companies have one class of common stock and each share has one vote. Occasionally, however, a firm may have two classes of stock outstanding, which differ in their right to vote. Suppose that a firm needs fresh equity capital, but its present shareholders do not wish to relinquish their control of the firm. The existing shares could be labeled "class A," and then "class B" shares with limited voting privileges could be issued to outsiders.

Both classes of shareholders would have the same cash-flow rights but they would have different control rights. For example, each A share could have five votes, the B shares only one. However, the two classes would have identical claims to the corporation's assets, earnings, and dividends.

Holders of the A shares would have extra voting power to toss out bad management or to force management to adopt value-enhancing investment or operating policies. But both the A and B shares should benefit equally from such changes, since the two classes of shares have identical cash-flow rights. So here's the question: If everyone gains equally from better management, why would investors be prepared to pay more for one class of shares than for another? The only plausible reason is *private benefits* captured by the A shares. For example, a holder of a block of A shares might be able to obtain a seat on the board of directors or access to perquisites provided by the company. (How about a ride to Bermuda on the corporate jet?) The A shares might have extra bargaining power in an acquisition. The A shares might be held by another company, which could use its voting power and influence to secure a business advantage. These are some of the reasons why the A shares could sell for a higher price.

These private benefits of control seem to be much larger in some countries than others. For example, Luigi Zingales has looked at companies in the United States and Italy that have two classes of stock. In the United States investors were on average prepared to pay an extra 11 percent for the shares with the superior voting

[10]For example, suppose there are five directors to be elected and you own 100 shares. You therefore have a total of $5 \times 100 = 500$ votes. Under the majority voting system, you can cast a maximum of 100 votes for any one candidate. Under a cumulative voting system, you can cast all 500 votes for your favorite candidate.

[11]See, for example, R. M. Stulz, "Managerial Control of Voting Rights: Financing Policies and the Market for Corporate Control," *Journal of Financial Economics* 20 (January–March 1988), pp. 25–54.

A CONTEST OVER VOTING RIGHTS

"Not so long ago," wrote *The Economist* magazine, "shareholder friendly companies in Switzerland were as rare as Swiss admirals. Safe behind anti-takeover defences, most managers treated their shareholders with disdain." However, *The Economist* perceived one encouraging sign that these attitudes were changing. This was a proposal by the Union Bank of Switzerland (UBS) to change the rights of its equity holders.

UBS had two classes of shares—bearer shares, which are anonymous, and registered shares, which are not. In Switzerland, where anonymity is prized, bearer shares usually traded at a premium. UBS's bearer shares had sold at a premium for many years. However, there was another important distinction between the two share classes. The registered shares carried five times as many votes as an equivalent investment in the bearer shares. Presumably attracted by this feature, an investment company, BK Vision, began to accumulate a large position in the registered shares, and their price rose to a 38 percent premium over the bearer shares.

At this point UBS announced its plan to merge the two classes of share, so that the registered shares would become bearer shares and would lose their superior voting rights. Since all UBS's shares would then sell for the same price, UBS's announcement led to a rise in the price of the bearer shares and a fall in the price of the registered.

Martin Ebner, the president of BK Vision, objected to the change, complaining that it stripped the registered shareholders of some of their voting rights without providing compensation. The dispute highlighted the question of the value of superior voting stock. If the votes are used to secure benefits for *all* shareholders, then the stock should not sell at a premium. However, a premium would arise if holders of the superior voting stock expected to secure benefits for themselves alone.

To many observers UBS's proposal was a welcome attempt to prevent one group of shareholders from profiting at the expense of others and to unite all shareholders in the common aim of maximizing firm value. To others it represented an attempt to take away their rights. In any event, the debate over the proposal was never fully resolved, for UBS shortly afterward agreed to merge with SBC, another Swiss bank.

rights, but in Italy the average premium for a vote was 82 percent.[12] The Finance in the News box describes a major dispute in Switzerland over the value of superior voting rights.

Even when there is only one class of shares, minority stockholders may be at a disadvantage; the company's cash flow and potential value may be diverted to management or to one or a few dominant stockholders holding large blocks of shares. In the United States, the law protects minority stockholders from blatant or extreme exploitation. Minority stockholders in other countries do not always fare so well.[13]

---

[12]L. Zingales, "What Determines the Value of Corporate Votes?" *Quarterly Journal of Economics* 110 (1995), pp. 1047–1073; and L. Zingales, "The Value of the Voting Right: A Study of the Milan Stock Exchange," *Review of Financial Studies* 7 (1994), pp. 125–148. The data for the United States were for the period 1984–1990. This was the height of the leveraged buyout boom, when the value of control was likely to have been unusually large. An earlier study that looked at the period 1940–1978 found a premium of only 4 percent. See R. C. Lease, J. J. McConnell, and W. H. Mikkelson, "The Market Value of Control in Publicly-Traded Corporations," *Journal of Financial Economics* 11 (April 1983), pp. 439–471.

[13]International differences in the opportunities for dominant shareholders to exploit their position is discussed in S. Johnson et al., "Tunnelling," *American Economic Review* 90 (May 2000), pp. 22–27.

Example   Financial economists sometimes refer to the exploitation of minority shareholders as *tunneling;* the majority shareholder tunnels into the firm and acquires control of the assets for himself. Let us look at an example of tunneling Russian-style.

To grasp how the scam works, you first need to understand *reverse stock splits.* These are often used by companies with a large number of low-priced shares. The company making the reverse split simply combines its existing shares into a smaller (and, hopefully, more convenient) number of new shares. For example, the shareholders might be given 2 new shares in place of the 3 shares that they currently own. As long as all shareholdings are reduced by the same proportion, nobody gains or loses by such a move.

However, the majority shareholder of one Russian company realized that the reverse stock split could be used to loot the company's assets. He therefore proposed that existing shareholders receive 1 new share in place of every 136,000 shares they currently held.[14]

Why did the majority shareholder pick the number "136,000"? Answer: because the two minority shareholders owned less than 136,000 shares and therefore did not have the right to *any* shares. Instead they were simply paid off with the par value of their shares and the majority shareholder was left owning the entire company. The majority shareholders of several other companies were so impressed with this device that they also proposed similar reverse stock splits to squeeze out their minority shareholders.

Needless to say such blatant exploitation would not be permitted in the United States.

Equity in Disguise

Common stocks are issued by corporations. But a few equity securities are issued not by corporations but by partnerships or trusts. We will give some brief examples.

Partnerships   Newhall Land and Farming is a *master limited partnership* which owns large tracts of real estate, mostly in southern California. You can buy "units" in this partnership on the New York Stock Exchange, thus becoming a *limited* partner in Newhall. The most the limited partners can lose is their investment in the company.[15] In this and most other respects, the Newhall partnership units are just like the shares in an ordinary corporation. They share in the profits of the business and receive cash distributions (like dividends) from time to time.

Partnerships avoid corporate income tax; any profits or losses are passed straight through to the partners' tax returns. Offsetting this tax advantage are various limitations of partnerships. For example, the law regards a partnership merely as a voluntary association of individuals; like its partners, it is expected to have a limited life. A corporation, on the other hand, is an independent legal "person" that can, and often does, outlive all its original shareholders.

---

[14]Since a reverse stock split required only the approval of a simple majority of the shareholders, the proposal was voted through.

[15]A partnership can offer limited liability *only* to its limited partners. The partnership must also have one or more general partners, who have unlimited liability. However, general partners can be corporations. This puts the corporation's shield of limited liability between the partnership and the human beings who ultimately own the general partner.

Trusts and REITs   Would you like to own a part of the oil in the Prudhoe Bay field on the north slope of Alaska? Just call your broker and buy a few units of the Prudhoe Bay Royalty Trust. British Petroleum (BP) set up this trust and gave it a royalty interest in production from BP's share of the Prudhoe Bay revenues. As the oil is produced, each trust unit gets its share of the revenues.

This trust is the passive owner of a single asset: the right to a share of the revenues from BP's Prudhoe Bay production. Operating businesses, which cannot be passive, are rarely organized as trusts, though there are exceptions, notably *real estate investment trusts,* or *REITs* (pronounced "reets").

REITs were created to facilitate public investment in commercial real estate; there are shopping center REITs, office building REITs, apartment REITs, and REITs that specialize in lending to real estate developers. REIT "shares" are traded just like common stocks.[16] The REITs themselves are not taxed, so long as they pay out at least 95 percent of earnings to the REITs' owners, who must pay whatever taxes are due on the dividends. However, REITs are tightly restricted to real estate investment. You cannot set up a widget factory and avoid corporate taxes by calling it a REIT.

Preferred Stock

Usually when investors talk about equity or stock, they are referring to common stock. But Heinz has also issued $139,000 of **preferred stock,** and this too is part of the company's equity. Despite its name, preferred stock provides only a small part of most companies' cash needs and it will occupy less time in later chapters. However, it can be a useful method of financing in mergers and certain other special situations.

Like debt, preferred stock offers a series of fixed payments to the investor. The company can choose *not* to pay a preferred dividend, but in that case it may not pay a dividend to its common stockholders. Most issues of preferred are known as *cumulative preferred stock.* This means that the firm must pay *all* past preferred dividends before common stockholders get a cent. If the company does miss a preferred dividend, the preferred stockholders generally gain some voting rights, so that the common stockholders are obliged to share control of the company with the preferred holders. Directors are also aware that failure to pay the preferred dividend earns the company a black mark with investors, so they do not take such a decision lightly.

 14.3 DEBT

When companies borrow money, they promise to make regular interest payments and to repay the principal. However, this liability is limited. Stockholders have the right to default on the debt if they are willing to hand over the corporation's assets to the lenders. Clearly, they will choose to do this only if the value of the assets is less than the amount of the debt.[17]

---

[16]There are also some private REITs, whose shares are not publicly traded.

[17]In practice this handover of assets is far from straightforward. Sometimes there may be thousands of lenders with different claims on the firm. Administration of the handover is usually left to the bankruptcy court (see Chapter 25).

FIGURE 14.3

Holdings of corporate
and foreign bonds,
end 2000.

Source: Board of Governors
of the Federal Reserve
System, Division of Research
and Statistics, Flow of Funds
Accounts Table L.212 at
**www.federalreserve.gov/
releases/z1/current/data.
htm**.

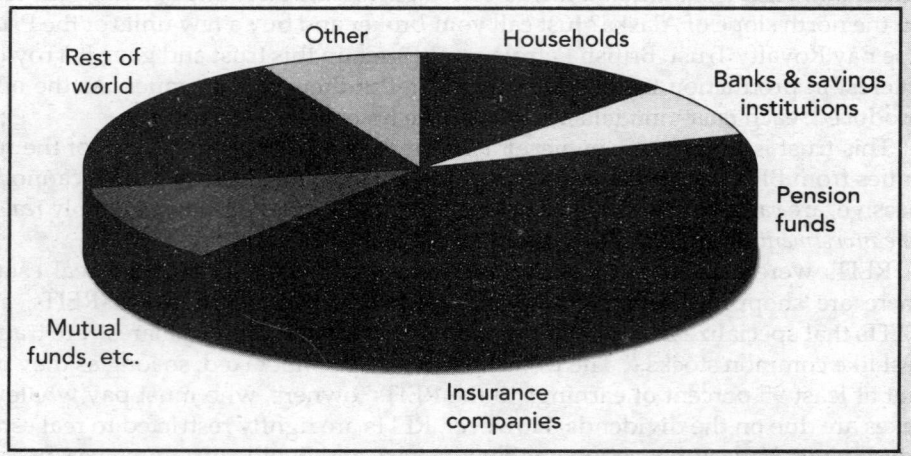

Because lenders are not regarded as owners of the firm, they do not normally have any voting power. The company's payments of interest are regarded as a cost and are deducted from taxable income. Thus interest is paid from *before-tax* income, whereas dividends on common and preferred stock are paid from *after-tax* income. Therefore the government provides a tax subsidy on the use of debt which it does not provide on equity. We will discuss debt and taxes in detail in Chapter 18.

We have seen that financial institutions own the majority of corporate equity. Figure 14.3 shows that this is also true of the company's bonds. In this case it is the insurance companies that own the largest stake.[18]

Debt Comes in Many Forms

The financial manager is faced with an almost bewildering choice of debt securities. For example, look at Table 14.5, which shows the many ways that H.J. Heinz has borrowed money. Heinz has also entered into a number of other arrangements that are not shown on the balance sheet. For example, it has arranged lines of credit that allow it to take out further short-term bank loans. Also it has entered into a swap that converts its fixed-rate sterling notes into floating-rate debt.

You are probably wondering what a swap or floating-rate debt is. Relax—later in the book we will spend several chapters explaining the various features of corporate debt. For the moment, simply notice that the mixture of loans that each company issues reflects the financial manager's response to a number of questions:

1. *Should the company borrow short-term or long-term?* If your company simply needs to finance a temporary increase in inventories ahead of the Christmas season, then it may make sense to take out a short-term bank loan. But suppose that the cash is needed to pay for expansion of an oil refinery. Refinery facilities can operate more or less continuously for

---

[18]Figure 14.3 does not include shorter-term debt such as bank loans. Almost all short-term debt issued by corporations is held by financial institutions.

US Dollar Debt	Foreign Currency Debt
Bank loans	Sterling notes
Commercial paper	Euro notes
Senior unsecured notes and debentures	Lire notes
Eurodollar notes	Australian dollar notes
Revenue bonds	

TABLE 14.5

Large firms issue many different securities. This table shows some of the debt securities on Heinz's balance sheet in May 2000.

15 or 20 years. In that case it would be more appropriate to issue a long-term bond.[19]

Some loans are repaid in a steady regular way; in other cases the entire loan is repaid at maturity. Occasionally either the borrower or the lender has the option to terminate the loan early and to demand that it be repaid immediately.

2. *Should the debt be fixed or floating rate?* The interest payment, or coupon, on long-term bonds is commonly fixed at the time of issue. If a $1,000 bond is issued when long-term interest rates are 10 percent, the firm continues to pay $100 per year regardless of how interest rates fluctuate.

Most bank loans and some bonds offer a variable, or *floating*, rate. For example, the interest rate in each period may be set at 1 percent above LIBOR (London Interbank Offered Rate), which is the interest rate at which major international banks lend dollars to each other. When LIBOR changes, the interest rate on your loan also changes.

3. *Should you borrow dollars or some other currency?* Many firms in the United States borrow abroad. Often they may borrow dollars abroad (foreign investors have large holdings of dollars), but firms with large overseas operations may decide to issue debt in a foreign currency. After all, if you need to spend foreign currency, it probably makes sense to borrow foreign currency.

Because these international bonds have usually been marketed by the London branches of international banks they have traditionally been known as **eurobonds** and the debt is called **eurocurrency** debt. A eurobond may be denominated in dollars, yen, or any other currency. Unfortunately, when the single European currency was established, it was called the *euro*. It is, therefore, easy to confuse a *eurobond* (a bond that is sold internationally) with a bond that is denominated in euros. (Notice that Heinz has issued both eurodollar debt and euro debt.)

4. *What promises should you make to the lender?* Lenders want to make sure that their debt is as safe as possible. Therefore, they may demand that their debt is senior to other debt. If default occurs, *senior* debt is first in line to be repaid. The *junior*, or *subordinated*, debtholders are paid only after all senior

---

[19]A company might choose to finance a long-term project with short-term debt if it wished to signal its confidence in the future. Investors would deduce that, if the company anticipated declining profits, it would not take the risk of being unable to take out a fresh loan when the first one matured. See D. Diamond, "Debt Maturity Structure and Liquidity Risk," *Quarterly Journal of Economics* 106 (1991), pp. 709–737.

debtholders are satisfied (though all debtholders rank ahead of the preferred and common stockholders).

The firm may also set aside some of its assets specifically for the protection of particular creditors. Such debt is said to be **secured** and the assets that are set aside are know as **collateral.** Thus a retailer might offer inventory or accounts receivable as collateral for a bank loan. If the retailer defaults on the loan, the bank can seize the collateral and use it to help pay off the debt.

Usually the firm also provides assurances to the lender that it will use the money well and not take unreasonable risks. For example, a firm that borrows in moderation is less likely to get into difficulties than one that is up to its gunwales in debt. So the borrower may agree to limit the amount of extra debt that it can issue. Lenders are also concerned that, if trouble occurs, others will push ahead of them in the queue. Therefore, the firm may agree not to create new debt that is senior to existing debtholders or to put aside assets for other lenders.

5. *Should you issue straight or convertible bonds?* Companies often issue securities that give the owner an option to convert them into other securities. These options may have a substantial effect on value. The most dramatic example is provided by a **warrant,** which is *nothing but* an option. The owner of a warrant can purchase a set number of the company's shares at a set price before a set date. Warrants and bonds are often sold together as a package.

A **convertible bond** gives its owner the option to exchange the bond for a predetermined number of shares. The convertible bondholder hopes that the issuing company's share price will zoom up so that the bond can be converted at a big profit. But if the shares zoom down, there is no obligation to convert; the bondholder remains a bondholder.[20]

Variety's the Very Spice of Life

We have indicated several dimensions along which corporate securities can be classified. That gives the financial manager plenty of choice in designing securities. As long as you can convince investors of its attractions, you can issue a convertible, subordinated, floating-rate bond denominated in Swedish kronor. Rather than combining features of existing securities, you may create an entirely new one. We can imagine a coal mining company issuing convertible bonds on which the payment fluctuates with coal prices. We know of no such security, but it is perfectly legal to issue it—and who knows?—it might generate considerable interest among investors.

14.4 FINANCIAL MARKETS AND INSTITUTIONS

That completes our tour of corporate securities. You may feel like the tourist who has just seen 12 cathedrals in five days. But there will be plenty of time in later chapters for reflection and analysis. It is now time to move on and to look briefly

---

[20]Companies may also issue convertible preferred stock. The Heinz preferred stock that we mentioned earlier is convertible.

at the markets in which the firm's securities are traded and at the financial institutions that hold them.

We have explained that corporations raise money by selling financial assets such as stocks and bonds. This increases the amount of cash held by the company and the amount of stocks and bonds held by the public. Such an issue of securities is known as a *primary issue* and it is sold in the **primary market.** But in addition to helping companies to raise cash, financial markets also allow investors to trade stocks or bonds between themselves. For example, Ms. Watanabe might decide to raise some cash by selling her Sony stock at the same time that Mr. Hashimoto invests his savings in Sony. So they make a trade. The result is simply a transfer of ownership from one person to another, which has no effect on the company's cash, assets, or operations. Such purchases and sales are known as *secondary transactions* and they take place in the **secondary market.**

Some financial assets have less active secondary markets than others. For example, when a company borrows money from the bank, the bank acquires a financial asset (the company's promise to repay the loan with interest). Banks do sometimes sell packages of loans to other banks, but usually they retain the loan until it is repaid by the borrower. Other financial assets are regularly traded and their prices are shown each day in the newspaper. Some, such as shares of stock, are traded on organized exchanges like the New York, London, or Tokyo stock exchanges. In other cases there is no organized exchange and the financial assets are traded by a network of dealers. For example, if General Motors needs to buy foreign currency for an overseas investment, it will do so from one of the major banks that deals regularly in currency. Markets where there is no organized exchange are known as *over-the-counter (OTC)* markets.

Financial Institutions

We have referred to the fact that a large proportion of the company's equity and debt is owned by financial institutions. Since we will be meeting some of these financial institutions in the following chapters, we should introduce them to you here and explain what functions they serve.

Financial institutions act as *financial intermediaries* that gather the savings of many individuals and reinvest them in the financial markets. For example, banks raise money by taking deposits and by selling debt and common stock to investors. They then lend the money to companies and individuals. Of course banks must charge sufficient interest to cover their costs and to compensate depositors and other investors.

Banks and their immediate relatives, such as savings and loan companies, are the most familiar intermediaries. But there are many others, such as insurance companies and mutual funds. In the United States insurance companies are more important than banks for the *long-term* financing of business. They are massive investors in corporate stocks and bonds, and they often make long-term loans directly to corporations. Most of the money for these loans comes from the sale of insurance policies. Say you buy a fire insurance policy on your home. You pay cash to the insurance company, which it invests in the financial markets. In exchange you get a financial asset (the insurance policy). You receive no interest on this asset, but if a fire does strike, the company is obliged to cover the damages up to the policy limit. This is the return on your investment. Of course, the company will issue not just one policy but thousands. Normally the incidence of fires averages out, leaving the company with a predictable obligation to its policy-holders as a group.

Why are financial intermediaries different from a manufacturing corporation? First, the financial intermediary may raise money in special ways, for example, by taking deposits or by selling insurance policies. Second, the financial intermediary invests in *financial assets,* such as stocks, bonds, or loans to businesses or individuals. By contrast, the manufacturing company's main investments are in *real* assets, such as plant and equipment. Thus the intermediary receives cash flows from its investment in one set of financial assets (stocks, bonds, etc.) and repackages those flows as a different set of financial assets (bank deposits, insurance policies, etc.). The intermediary hopes that investors will find the cash flows on this new package more attractive than those provided by the original security.

Financial intermediaries contribute in many ways to our individual well-being and the smooth functioning of the economy. Here are some examples.

The Payment Mechanism   Think how inconvenient life would be if all payments had to be made in cash. Fortunately, checking accounts, credit cards, and electronic transfers allow individuals and firms to send and receive payments quickly and safely over long distances. Banks are the obvious providers of payments services, but they are not alone. For example, if you buy shares in a money-market mutual fund, your money is pooled with that of other investors and is used to buy safe, short-term securities. You can then write checks on this mutual fund investment, just as if you had a bank deposit.

Borrowing and Lending   Almost all financial institutions are involved in channeling savings toward those who can best use them. Thus, if Ms. Jones has more money now than she needs and wishes to save for a rainy day, she can put the money in a bank savings deposit. If Mr. Smith wants to buy a car now and pay for it later, he can borrow money from the bank. Both the lender and borrower are happier than if they were forced to spend cash as it arrived. Of course, individuals are not alone in needing to raise cash. Companies with profitable investment opportunities may also wish to borrow from the bank, or they may raise the finance by selling new shares or bonds. Governments also often run at a deficit, which they fund by issuing large quantities of debt.

In principle, individuals or firms with cash surpluses could take out newspaper advertisements or surf the Net looking for those with cash shortages. But it can be cheaper and more convenient to use a financial intermediary, such as a bank, to link up the borrower and lender. For example, banks are equipped to check out the would-be borrower's creditworthiness and to monitor the use of cash lent out. Would you lend money to a stranger contacted over the Internet? You would be safer lending the money to the bank and letting the bank decide what to do with it.

Notice that banks promise their checking account customers instant access to their money and at the same time make long-term loans to companies and individuals. Since there is no marketplace in which bank loans are regularly bought and sold, most of the loans that banks make are illiquid. This mismatch between the liquidity of the bank's liabilities (the deposits) and most of its assets (the loans) is possible only because the number of depositors is sufficiently large so banks can be fairly sure that they won't all want to withdraw their money simultaneously.

Pooling Risk   Financial markets and institutions allow firms and individuals to pool their risks. For instance, insurance companies make it possible to share the risk of an automobile accident or a household fire. Here is another example. Suppose that you have only a small sum to invest. You could buy the stock of a single company, but then you would be wiped out if that company went belly-up. It's generally better to buy shares in a mutual fund that invests in a diversified portfolio of common stocks or other securities. In this case you are exposed only to the risk that security prices as a whole will fall.

The basic functions of financial markets are the same the world over. So it is not surprising that similar institutions have emerged to perform these functions. In almost every country you will find banks accepting deposits, making loans, and looking after the payments system. You will also encounter insurance companies offering life insurance and protection against accident. If the country is relatively prosperous, other institutions, such as pension funds and mutual funds, will also have been established to help manage people's savings.

Of course there are differences in institutional structure. Take banks, for example. In many countries where securities markets are relatively undeveloped, banks play a much more dominant role in financing industry. Often the banks undertake a wider range of activities than they do in the United States. For example, they may take large equity stakes in industrial companies; this would not generally be allowed in the United States.[21]

---

[21]U.S. banks are permitted to acquire temporary equity holdings as a result of company bankruptcy.

Financial managers are faced with two broad financing decisions:

1. What proportion of profits should the corporation reinvest in the business rather than distribute as dividends to its shareholders?

2. What proportion of the deficit should be financed by borrowing rather than by an issue of equity?

The answer to the first question reflects the firm's dividend policy and the answer to the second depends on its debt policy.

Table 14.1 summarized the ways that companies raise and spend money. Have another look at it and try to get a feel for the numbers. Notice that

1. Internally generated cash is the principal source of funds. Some people worry about this; they think that if management does not have to go to the trouble of raising the money, it won't think so hard when it comes to spending it.

2. The mix of financing changes from year to year. Sometimes companies prefer to issue equity and pay back part of their debt. At other times, they raise more debt than they need for investment and they use the balance to repurchase equity.

SUMMARY

Common stock is the simplest form of finance. The common stockholders own the corporation. They are therefore entitled to whatever earnings are left over after all the firm's debts are paid. Stockholders also have the ultimate control over how the firm's assets are used. They exercise this control by voting on important matters, such as membership of the board of directors.

The second source of finance is preferred stock. Preferred is like debt in that it promises a fixed dividend, but preferred dividends are within the discretion of the board of directors. The firm must pay any dividends on the preferred before it is allowed to pay a dividend on the common stock. Lawyers and tax experts treat preferred stock as part of the company's equity. This means that preferred dividends are not tax-deductible. That is one reason that preferred is less popular than debt.

The third important source of finance is debt. Debtholders are entitled to a regular payment of interest and the final repayment of principal. If the company cannot make these payments, it can file for bankruptcy. The usual result is that the debtholders then take over and either sell the company's assets or continue to operate them under new management.

Note that the tax authorities treat interest payments as a cost and therefore the company can deduct interest when calculating its taxable income. Interest is paid from pretax income, whereas dividends and retained earnings come from after-tax income.

Debt ratios in the United States have generally increased over the post–World War II period. However, they are not appreciably higher than the ratios in the other major industrialized countries.

The variety of debt instruments is almost endless. The instruments differ by maturity, interest rate (fixed or floating), currency, seniority, security, and whether the debt can be converted into equity.

The majority of the firm's debt and equity is owned by financial institutions—notably banks, insurance companies, pension funds, and mutual funds. These institutions provide a variety of services. They run the payment system, channel savings to those who can best use them, and help firms to manage their risk. These basic functions do not change but the ways that financial markets and institutions perform these functions is constantly changing.

FURTHER READING

A useful article for comparing financial structure in the United States and other major industrial countries is:

R. G. Rajan and L. Zingales: "What Do We Know about Capital Structure? Some Evidence from International Data," *Journal of Finance*, 50:1421–1460 (December 1995).

For a discussion of the allocation of control rights and cash-flow rights between stockholders and debtholders, see:

O. Hart: *Firms, Contracts, and Financial Structure*, Clarendon Press, Oxford, 1995.

Robert Merton gives an excellent overview of the functions of financial institutions in:

R. Merton: "A Functional Perspective of Financial Intermediation," *Financial Management*, 24: 23–41 (Summer 1995).

1. The figures in the following table are in the wrong order. Can you place them in their correct order?   **QUIZ**

	Percent of Total Sources, 2000
Internally generated cash	23
Financial deficit	−14
Net share issues	77
Debt issues	38

2. True or false?
   a. Net stock issues by U.S. nonfinancial corporations are in most years small but positive.
   b. Most capital investment by U.S. companies is funded by retained earnings and reinvested depreciation.
   c. Debt ratios in the U.S. have generally increased over the past 40 years.
   d. Debt ratios in the U.S. are lower than in other industrial countries.

3. The authorized share capital of the Alfred Cake Company is 100,000 shares. The equity is currently shown in the company's books as follows:

Common stock ($.50 par value)	$40,000
Additional paid-in capital	10,000
Retained earnings	30,000
Common equity	80,000
Treasury stock (2,000 shares)	5,000
Net common equity	$75,000

   a. How many shares are issued?
   b. How many are outstanding?
   c. Explain the difference between your answers to (a) and (b).
   d. How many more shares can be issued without the approval of shareholders?
   e. Suppose that Alfred Cake issues 10,000 shares at $2 a share. Which of the above figures would be changed?
   f. Suppose instead that the company bought back 5,000 shares at $5 a share. Which of the above figures would be changed?

4. There are 10 directors to be elected. A shareholder owns 80 shares. What is the maximum number of votes that he or she can cast for a favorite candidate under (a) majority voting? (b) cumulative voting?

5. In what ways is preferred stock like debt? In what ways is it like common stock?

6. Fill in the blanks, using the following terms: floating rate, common stock, convertible, subordinated, preferred stock, senior, warrant.
   a. If a lender ranks behind the firm's general creditors in the event of default, his or her loan is said to be _____.
   b. Interest on many bank loans is based on a _____ of interest.
   c. A(n) _____ bond can be exchanged for shares of the issuing corporation.
   d. A(n) _____ gives its owner the right to buy shares in the issuing company at a predetermined price.
   e. Dividends on _____ cannot be paid unless the firm has also paid any dividends on its _____.

7. True or false?
   a. In the United States, most common shares are owned by individual investors.
   b. An insurance company is a financial intermediary.
   c. Investments in partnerships cannot be publicly traded.

8. What is the traditional meaning of the term *eurobond?*

9. How do financial intermediaries contribute to the smooth functioning of the economy' Give three examples.

PRACTICE QUE∫TION∫

1. Use the Market Insight database (**www.mhhe.com/edumarketinsight**) to work out the financing proportions given in Table 14.1 for a particular industrial company for some recent year.

2. In Table 14.3 Rajan and Zingales use both book and market values of equity to measure debt ratios. Which measure results in the lower ratio? Why?

3. It is sometimes suggested that since retained earnings provide the bulk of industry's capital needs, the securities markets are largely redundant. Do you agree?

4. In 1999 Pfizer had 9,000 million shares of common stock authorized, 4,260 million in issue, and 3,847 million outstanding (figures rounded to the nearest million). Its equity account was as follows:

Common stock	$ 213
Additional paid-in capital	5,416
Retained earnings	10,109
Treasury shares	6,851

   Currency translation adjustment and contributions to an employee benefit trust have been deducted from retained earnings.
   a. What is the par value of each share?
   b. What was the average price at which shares were sold?
   c. How many shares have been repurchased?
   d. What was the average price at which the shares were repurchased?
   e. What is the value of the net common equity?

5. Inbox Software was founded in 1998. Its founder put up $2 million for 500,000 shares of common stock. Each share had a par value of $.10.
   a. Construct an equity account (like the one in Table 14.4) for Inbox on the day after its founding. Ignore any legal or administrative costs of setting up the company.
   b. After two years of operation, Inbox generated earnings of $120,000 and paid no dividends. What was the equity account at this point?
   c. After three years the company sold one million additional shares for $5 per share. It earned $250,000 during the year and paid no dividends. What was the equity account?

6. Look back at Table 14.4.
   a. Suppose that Heinz issued an additional 50 million shares at $30 a share. Rework Table 14.4 to show the company's equity after the issue.
   b. Suppose that Heinz *subsequently* repurchased 20 million shares at $35 a share. Rework Table 14.4 to show the effect of this further change.

7. Suppose that East Corporation has issued voting and nonvoting stock. Investors hope that holders of the voting stock will use their power to vote out the company's incompeten: management. Would you expect the voting stock to sell for a higher price? Explain.

8. In 2001 Beta Corporation earned gross profits of $760,000.
   a. Suppose that it is financed by a combination of common stock and $1 million of debt. The interest rate on the debt is 10 percent, and the corporate tax rate is 35 percent. How much profit is available for common stockholders after payment of interest and corporate taxes?
   b. Now suppose instead that Beta is financed by a combination of common stock and $1 million of preferred stock. The dividend yield on the preferred is 8 percent and the corporate tax rate is still 35 percent. How much profit is now available for common stockholders after payment of preferred dividends and corporate taxes?

9. Look up the financial statements for a U.S. corporation on the Internet and construct a table like Table 14.5 showing the types of debt that the company has issued. What arrangements has it made that would allow it to borrow more in the future? (You will need to look at the notes to the accounts to answer this.)

10. Which of the following features would increase the value of a corporate bond? Which would reduce its value?
    a. The borrower has the option to repay the loan before maturity.
    b. The bond is convertible into shares.
    c. The bond is secured by a mortgage on real estate.
    d. The bond is subordinated.

CHALLENGE QUESTIONS

1. The shareholders of the Pickwick Paper Company need to elect five directors. There are 200,000 shares outstanding. How many shares do you need to own to *ensure* that you can elect at least one director if (a) the company has majority voting? (b) it has cumulative voting?

2. Can you think of any new kinds of security that might appeal to investors? Why do you think they have not been issued?

CHAPTER FIFTEEN

HOW CORPORATIONS ISSUE SECURITIES

IN CHAPTER 11 we encountered Marvin Enterprises, one of the most remarkable growth companies of the twenty-first century. It was founded by George and Mildred Marvin, two high-school dropouts, together with their chum Charles P. (Chip) Norton. To get the company off the ground the three entrepreneurs relied on their own savings together with personal loans from a bank. However, the company's rapid growth meant that they had soon borrowed to the hilt and needed more equity capital. Equity investment in young private companies is generally known as **venture capital.** Such venture capital may be provided by investment institutions or by wealthy individuals who are prepared to back an untried company in return for a piece of the action. In the first part of this chapter we will explain how companies like Marvin go about raising venture capital.

Venture capital organizations aim to help growing firms over that awkward adolescent period before they are large enough to go public. For a successful firm such as Marvin, there is likely to come a time when it needs to tap a wider source of capital and therefore decides to make its first public issue of common stock. The next section of the chapter describes what is involved in such an issue. We will explain the process for registering the offering with the Securities and Exchange Commission and we will introduce you to the underwriters who buy the issue and resell it to the public. We will also see that new issues are generally sold below the price at which they subsequently trade. To understand *why* that is so, we will need to make a brief sortie into the field of auction procedures.

A company's first issue of stock is seldom its last. In Chapter 14 we saw that corporations face a persistent financial deficit which they meet by selling securities. We will therefore look at how established corporations go about raising more capital. In the process we will encounter another puzzle: When companies announce a new issue of stock, the stock price generally falls. We suggest that the explanation lies in the information that investors read into the announcement.

If a stock or bond is sold publicly, it can then be traded on the securities markets. But sometimes investors intend to hold onto their securities and are not concerned about whether they can sell them. In these cases there is little advantage to a public issue, and the firm may prefer to place the securities directly with one or two financial institutions. At the end of this chapter we will explain how companies arrange a private placement.

 ## 15.1 VENTURE CAPITAL

On April 1, 2013, George and Mildred Marvin met with Chip Norton in their research lab (which also doubled as a bicycle shed) to celebrate the incorporation of Marvin Enterprises. The three entrepreneurs had raised $100,000 from savings and personal bank loans and had purchased one million shares in the new company. At this *zero-stage* investment, the company's assets were $90,000 in the bank ($10,000 had been spent for legal and other expenses of setting up the company), plus the *idea* for a new product, the household gargle blaster. George Marvin was the first to see that the gargle blaster, up to that point an expensive curiosity, could be commercially produced using microgenetic refenestrators.

Marvin Enterprises' bank account steadily drained away as design and testing proceeded. Local banks did not see Marvin's idea as adequate collateral, so a transfusion of equity capital was clearly needed. Preparation of a *business plan* was a necessary first step. The plan was a confidential document describing the proposed product, its potential market, the underlying technology, and the resources (time, money, employees, plant, and equipment) needed for success.

Most entrepreneurs are able to spin a plausible yarn about their company. But it is as hard to convince a venture capitalist that your business plan is sound as to get a first novel published. Marvin's managers were able to point to the fact that they were prepared to put their money where their mouths were. Not only had they staked all their savings in the company but they were mortgaged to the hilt. This *signaled* their faith in the business.[1]

First Meriam Venture Partners was impressed with Marvin's presentation and agreed to buy one million new shares for $1 each. After this *first-stage* financing, the company's market-value balance sheet looked like this:

Marvin Enterprises First-Stage Balance Sheet (Market Values in $ Millions)

Cash from new equity	$1	$1	New equity from venture capital
Other assets, mostly intangible	1	1	Original equity held by entrepreneurs
Value	$2	$2	Value

By accepting a $2 million *after-the-money* valuation, First Meriam implicitly put a $1 million value on the entrepreneurs' idea and their commitment to the enterprise. It also handed the entrepreneurs a $900,000 paper gain over their original $100,000 investment. In exchange, the entrepreneurs gave up half their company and accepted First Meriam's representatives to the board of directors.[2]

The success of a new business depends critically on the effort put in by the managers. Therefore venture capital firms try to structure a deal so that management has a strong incentive to work hard. That takes us back to Chapters 1 and 12, where we showed how the shareholders of a firm (who are the principals) need to provide incentives for the managers (who are their agents) to work to maximize firm value.

If Marvin's management had demanded watertight employment contracts and fat salaries, they would not have found it easy to raise venture capital. Instead the Marvin team agreed to put up with modest salaries. They could cash in only from appreciation of their stock. If Marvin failed they would get nothing, because First Meriam actually bought *preferred* stock designed to convert automatically into common stock when and if Marvin Enterprises succeeded in an initial public offering or consistently generated more than a target level of earnings. But if Marvin Enterprises had failed, First Meriam would have been first in line to claim any salvageable assets. This raised even further the stakes for the company's management.[3]

---

[1] For a formal analysis of how management's investment in the business can provide a reliable signal of the company's value, see H. E. Leland and D. H. Pyle, "Informational Asymmetries, Financial Structure, and Financial Intermediation," *Journal of Finance* 32 (May 1977), pp. 371–387.

[2] Venture capital investors do not necessarily demand a majority on the board of directors. Whether they do depends, for example, on how mature the business is and on what fraction they own. A common compromise gives an equal number of seats to the founders and to outside investors; the two parties then agree to one or more additional directors to serve as tie-breakers in case a conflict arises. Regardless of whether they have a majority of directors, venture capital companies are seldom silent partners; their judgment and contacts can often prove useful to a relatively inexperienced management team.

[3] Notice the trade-off here. Marvin's management is being asked to put all its eggs into one basket. That creates pressure for managers to work hard, but it also means that they take on risk that could have been diversified away.

Venture capitalists rarely give a young company all the money it will need all at once. At each stage they give enough to reach the next major checkpoint. Thus in spring 2015, having designed and tested a prototype, Marvin Enterprises was back asking for more money for pilot production and test marketing. Its *second-stage* financing was $4 million, of which $1.5 million came from First Meriam, its original backers, and $2.5 million came from two other venture capital partnerships and wealthy individual investors. The balance sheet just after the second stage was as follows:

Marvin Enterprises Second-Stage Balance Sheet (Market Values in $ Millions)

Cash from new equity	$4	$4	New equity, second stage
Fixed assets	1	5	Equity from first stage
Other assets, mostly intangible	9	5	Original equity held by entrepreneurs
Value	$14	$14	Value

Now the after-the-money valuation was $14 million. First Meriam marked up its original investment to $5 million, and the founders noted an additional $4 million paper gain.

Does this begin to sound like a (paper) money machine? It was so only with hindsight. At stage 1 it wasn't clear whether Marvin would ever get to stage 2; if the prototype hadn't worked, First Meriam could have refused to put up more funds and effectively closed the business down.[4] Or it could have advanced stage 2 money in a smaller amount on less favorable terms. The board of directors could also have fired George, Mildred, and Chip and gotten someone else to try to develop the business.

In Chapter 14 we pointed out that stockholders and lenders differ in their cash-flow rights and control rights. The stockholders are entitled to whatever cash flows remain after paying off the other security holders. They also have control over how the company uses its money, and it is only if the company defaults that the lenders can step in and take control of the company. When a new business raises venture capital, these cash-flow rights and control rights are usually negotiated separately. The venture capital firm will want a say in how that business is run and will demand representation on the board and a significant number of votes. The venture capitalist may agree that it will relinquish some of these rights if the business subsequently performs well. However, if performance turns out to be poor, the venture capitalist may automatically get a greater say in how the business is run and whether the existing management should be replaced.

For Marvin, fortunately, everything went like clockwork. Third-stage *mezzanine financing* was arranged,[5] full-scale production began on schedule, and gargle blasters were acclaimed by music critics worldwide. Marvin Enterprises went public on February 3, 2019. Once its shares were traded, the paper gains earned by First Meriam

---

[4]If First Meriam had refused to invest at stage 2, it would have been an exceptionally hard sell convincing another investor to step in its place. The other outside investors knew they had less information about Marvin than First Meriam and would have read its refusal as a bad omen for Marvin's prospects.

[5]Mezzanine financing does not necessarily come in the third stage; there may be four or five stages. The point is that mezzanine investors come in late, in contrast to venture capitalists who get in on the ground floor.

FIGURE 15.1

U.S. venture capital disbursements by type of fund.

Source: Venture Economics/National Venture Capital Association.

and the company's founders turned into fungible wealth. Before we go on to this initial public offering, let us look briefly at the venture capital markets today.

The Venture Capital Market

Most new companies rely initially on family funds and bank loans. Some of them continue to grow with the aid of equity investment provided by wealthy individuals, known as *angel investors*. However, the bulk of the capital for adolescent companies comes from specialist venture-capital firms, which pool funds from a variety of investors, seek out fledgling companies to invest in, and then work with these companies as they try to grow. Figure 15.1 shows how the amount of venture capital investment has increased. During the heady days of 2000 venture capital funds invested nearly $140 billion in some 16,000 different companies.

Most venture capital funds are organized as limited private partnerships with a fixed life of about 10 years. The management company is the general partner, and the pension funds and other investors are limited partners. Some large industrial firms, such as Intel, General Electric, and Sun Microsystems also act as *corporate venturers* by providing equity capital to new innovative companies.[6] Finally, in the United States the government provides cheap loans to small-business investment companies (SBICs) that then relend the money to deserving entrepreneurs. SBICs occupy a small, specialized niche in the venture capital markets.

Venture capital firms are not passive investors. They provide ongoing advice to the firms that they invest in and often play a major role in recruiting the senior

---

[6]See, for example, H. Chesbrough, "Designing Corporate Ventures in the Shadow of Private Venture Capital," *California Management Review* 42 (Spring 2000), pp. 31–49.

management team. This advice can be valuable to businesses in their early years and helps them to bring their products more quickly to market.[7]

Venture capitalists may cash in on their investment in two ways. Sometimes, once the new business has established a track record, it may be sold out to a larger firm. However, many entrepreneurs do not fit easily into a corporate bureaucracy and would prefer instead to remain the boss. In this case, the company may decide, like Marvin, to go public and so provide the original backers with an opportunity to "cash out," selling their stock and leaving the original entrepreneurs in control. A thriving venture capital market therefore needs an active stock exchange, such as Nasdaq, that specializes in trading the shares of young, rapidly growing firms.[8]

In many countries, such as those of continental Europe, venture capital markets have been slower to develop. But this is changing and investment in high-tech ventures in Europe has begun to blossom. This has been helped by the formation of new European exchanges that model themselves on Nasdaq. These mini-Nasdaqs inlcude Aim in London, Neuer Markt in Frankfurt, and Nouveau Marché in Paris.

For every 10 first-stage venture capital investments, only two or three may survive as successful, self-sufficient businesses, and rarely will they pay off as big as Marvin Enterprises. From these statistics come two rules for success in venture capital investment. First, don't shy away from uncertainty; accept a low probability of success. But don't buy into a business unless you can see the *chance* of a big, public company in a profitable market. There's no sense taking a long shot unless it pays off handsomely if you win. Second, cut your losses; identify losers early, and if you can't fix the problem—by replacing management, for example—throw no good money after bad.

How successful is venture capital investment? Since you can't look up the value of new start-up businesses in *The Wall Street Journal*, it is difficult to say with confidence. However, *Venture Economics*, which tracks the performance of over 1,200 venture capital funds, calculated that from 1980 to 2000 investors in these funds would have earned an average annual return of nearly 20 percent after expenses.[9] That is about 3 percent a year more than they would have earned from investing in the stocks of large public corporations.

 ## 15.2 THE INITIAL PUBLIC OFFERING

Very few new businesses make it big, but venture capitalists keep sane by forgetting about the many failures and reminding themselves of the success stories—the investors who got in on the ground floor of firms like Federal Express, Genentech,

---

[7]For evidence on the role of venture capitalists in assisting new businesses, see T. Hellman and Manju Puri, "The Interaction between Product Market and Financial Strategy: The Role of Venture Capital," *Review of Financial Studies* 13 (2000), pp. 959–984; and S. N. Kaplan and P. Stromberg, "How Do Venture Capitalists Choose Investments," working paper, Graduate School of Business, University of Chicago, August 2000.

[8]This argument is developed in B. Black and R. Gilson, "Venture Capital and the Structure of Capital Markets: Banks versus Stock Markets," *Journal of Financial Economics* 47 (March 1998), pp. 243–277.

[9]See **www.ventureeconomics.com/news_ve.** Gompers and Lerner, who studied the period 1979–1997, found somewhat higher returns (see P. A. Gompers and J. Lerner, "Risk and Reward in Private Equity Investments: The Challenge of Performance Assessment," *Journal of Private Equity*, Winter 1997, pp. 5–12). In a study of a large sample of individual venture capital investments Cochrane tackles the problem of measuring returns on investments that remain unmarketable. The average *annually compounded* return on his sample is 57 percent, though the average *continuously compounded* return is much lower (see J. Cochrane, "The Risk and Return of Venture Capital," NBER Working Paper No. 8066, 2001).

Compaq, Intel, and Sun Microsystems. When First Meriam invested in Marvin Enterprises, it was not looking for cash dividends from its investment; instead it was hoping for rapid growth that would allow Marvin to go public and give First Meriam an opportunity to cash in on some of its gains.

By 2019 Marvin had grown to the point at which it needed still more capital to implement its second-generation production technology. At this point it decided to make an **initial public offering** of stock or **IPO**. This was to be partly a *primary* offering; that is, new shares were to be sold to raise additional cash for the company. It was also to be partly a *secondary* offering; that is, the venture capitalists and the company's founders were looking to sell some of their existing shares.

Often when companies go public, the issue is solely intended to raise new capital for the company. But there are also occasions when no new capital is raised and all the shares on offer are being sold as a secondary offering by existing shareholders. For example, in 1998 Du Pont sold off a large part of its holding in Conoco for $4.4 billion.[10]

Some of the biggest IPOs occur when governments sell off their shareholdings in companies. For example, the British government raised $9 billion from its sale of British Gas stock, while the secondary offering of Nippon Telegraph and Telephone by the Japanese government brought in nearly $13 billion.

For Marvin there were other benefits from going public. The market value of its stock would provide a readily available measure of the company's performance and would allow Marvin to reward its management team with stock options. Because information about the company would become more widely available, Marvin could diversify its sources of finance and reduce its costs of borrowing. These benefits outweighed the expense of the public issue and the continuing costs of administering a public company and communicating with its shareholders.

Instead of going public, many successful entrepreneurs may decide to sell out to a larger firm or they may continue to operate successfully as private, unlisted companies. Some very large companies in the United States are private. They include Bechtel, Cargill, and Levi Strauss. In other countries it is more common for large companies to remain privately owned. For example, since 1988 there have been only 70 listings of new, independent, nonfinancial companies on the Milan Stock Exchange.[11]

Arranging an Initial Public Offering[12]

Once Marvin had made the decision to go public, its first task was to select the *underwriters*. Underwriters act as financial midwives to a new issue. Usually they play a triple role: First they provide the company with procedural and financial advice, then they buy the issue, and finally they resell it to the public.

After some discussion Marvin settled on Klein Merrick as the managing underwriter and Goldman Stanley as the co-manager. Klein Merrick then formed a syndicate of underwriters who would buy the entire issue and reoffer it to the public.

---

[10]This is the largest U.S. IPO, but it is dwarfed by the Japanese telecom company NTT DoCoMo, which sold $18 billion of stock in 1998 and handed out $500 million in fees to the underwriters.

[11]The reasons for going public in Italy are analyzed in M. Pagano, F. Panetta, and L. Zingales, "Why Do Companies Go Public? An Empirical Analysis," *Journal of Finance* 53 (February 1998), pp. 27–64.

[12]For an excellent case study of how one company went public, see B. Uttal, "Inside the Deal That Made Bill Gates $350,000,000," *Fortune*, July 21, 1986.

Together with Klein Merrick and firms of lawyers and accountants, Marvin prepared a **registration statement** for the approval of the Securities and Exchange Commission (SEC).[13] This statement is a detailed and somewhat cumbersome document that presents information about the proposed financing and the firm's history, existing business, and plans for the future.

The most important sections of the registration statement are distributed to investors in the form of a **prospectus.** In Appendix B to this chapter we have reproduced the prospectus for Marvin's first public issue of stock.[14] Real prospectuses would go into much more detail on each topic, but this example should give you some feel for the mixture of valuable information and redundant qualification that characterizes these documents. The Marvin prospectus also illustrates how the SEC insists that investors' eyes are opened to the dangers of purchase (see "Certain Considerations" of the prospectus). Some investors have joked that if they read each prospectus carefully, they would not dare buy any new issue.

In addition to registering the issue with the SEC, Marvin needed to check that the issue complied with the so-called *blue-sky laws* of each state that regulate sales of securities within the state.[15] It also arranged for its newly issued shares to be traded on the Nasdaq exchange.

The Sale of Marvin Stock

While the registration statement was awaiting approval, Marvin and its underwriters began to firm up the issue price. First they looked at the price–earnings ratios of the shares of Marvin's principal competitors. Then they worked through a number of discounted-cash-flow calculations like the ones we described in Chapters 4 and 11. Most of the evidence pointed to a market value of $75 a share.

Marvin and Klein Merrick arranged a *road show* to talk to potential investors. Mostly these were institutional investors, such as managers of mutual funds and pension funds. The investors gave their reactions to the issue and indicated to the underwriters how much stock they wished to buy. Some stated the maximum price that they were prepared to pay, but others said that they just wanted to invest so many dollars in Marvin at whatever issue price was chosen. These discussions with fund managers allowed Klein Merrick to build up a book of potential orders.[16] Although the managers were not bound by their responses, they knew that, if they wanted to keep in the underwriters' good books, they should be careful not to go back on their expressions of interest. The underwriters also were not bound to treat all investors equally. Some investors who were keen to

---

[13]The rules governing the sale of securities derive principally from the Securities Act of 1933. The SEC is concerned solely with disclosure and it has no power to prevent an issue as long as there has been proper disclosure. Some public issues are exempt from registration. These include issues by small businesses and loans maturing within nine months.

[14]The company is allowed to circulate a preliminary version of the prospectus (known as a *red herring*) before the SEC has approved the registration statement.

[15]In 1980, when Apple Computer Inc. went public, the Massachusetts state government decided the offering was too risky and barred the sale of the shares to individual investors in the state. The state relented later after the issue was out and the price had risen. Needless to say, this action was not acclaimed by Massachusetts investors.

States do not usually reject security issues by honest firms through established underwriters. We cite the example to illustrate the potential power of state securities laws and to show why underwriters keep careful track of them.

[16]The managing underwriter is therefore often known as the *bookrunner*.

buy Marvin stock were disappointed in the allotment that they subsequently received.

Immediately after it received clearance from the SEC, Marvin and the underwriters met to fix the issue price. Investors had been enthusiastic about the story that the company had to tell and it was clear that they were prepared to pay more than $75 for the stock. Marvin's managers were tempted to go for the highest possible price, but the underwriters were more cautious. Not only would they be left with any unsold stock if they overestimated investor demand but they also argued that some degree of underpricing was needed to tempt investors to buy the stock. Marvin and the underwriters therefore compromised on an issue price of $80.

Although Marvin's underwriters were committed to buy only 900,000 shares from the company, they chose to sell 1,035,000 shares to investors. This left the underwriters short of 135,000 shares or 15 percent of the issue. If Marvin's stock had proved unpopular with investors and traded below the issue price, the underwriters could have bought back these shares in the marketplace. This would have helped to stabilize the price and would have given the underwriters a profit on these extra shares that they sold. As it turned out, investors fell over themselves to buy Marvin stock and by the end of the first day the stock was trading at $105. The underwriters would have incurred a heavy loss if they had been obliged to buy back the shares at $105. However, Marvin had provided underwriters with a *greenshoe* option which allowed them to buy an additional 135,000 shares from the company. This ensured that the underwriters were able to sell the extra shares to investors without fear of loss.

In choosing Klein Merrick to manage its IPO, Marvin was influenced by Merrick's proposals for making an active market in the stock in the weeks after the issue.[17] Merrick also planned to generate continuing investor interest in the stock by distributing a major research report on Marvin's prospects.[18]

The Underwriters

Companies get to make only one IPO, but underwriters are in the business all the time. Established underwriters are, therefore, careful of their reputation and will not handle a new issue unless they believe the facts have been presented fairly to investors. Thus, in addition to handling the sale of Marvin's issue, the underwriters in effect gave their seal of approval to it. This implied endorsement was worth quite a bit to a company like Marvin that was coming to the market for the first time.

Marvin's underwriters were prepared to enter into a firm commitment to buy the stock and then offer it to the public. Thus they took the risk that the issue might flop and they would be left with unwanted stock. Occasionally, where the sale of common stock is regarded as particularly risky, the underwriters may be

---

[17]On average the managing underwriter accounts for 40 to 60 percent of trading volume in the stock during the first 60 days after an IPO. See K. Ellis, R. Michaely, and M. O'Hara, "When the Underwriter is the Market Maker: An Examination of Trading in the IPO Aftermarket," *Journal of Finance* 55 (June 2000), pp. 1039–1074.

[18]The 25 days after the offer is designated as a *quiet period*. Merrick is obliged to wait until after this period before commenting on the valuation of the company. Survey evidence suggests that, in choosing an underwriter, firms place considerable importance on its ability to provide follow-up research reports. See L. Krigman, W. H. Shaw, and K. L. Womack, "Why Do Firms Switch Underwriters?" *Journal of Financial Economics* 60 (May–June 2001), pp. 245–284.

Underwriter	Value of Issues	Number of Issues
Merrill Lynch	$353	1,566
Citigroup/Salomon Smith Barney	334	1,039
Credit Suisse First Boston	252	996
JP Morgan	232	818
Morgan Stanley Dean Witter	211	656
Lehman Brothers	193	660
Goldman Sachs	189	598
UBS Warburg	172	690
Deutsche Bank	166	573
Banc of America Securities	125	571

TABLE 15.1

The top managing underwriters January 2001 to September 2001. Values include global debt and equity issues. Figures in billions.

Source: Thomson Financial Investment Banking/Capital Markets (**www.tfibcm.com**).

prepared to handle the sale only on a best-efforts basis. In this case the underwriters promise to sell as much of the issue as possible but do not guarantee to sell the entire amount.[19]

Successful underwriting requires financial muscle, considerable experience, and an established reputation. The names of Marvin's underwriters are of course fictitious, but Table 15.1 shows that underwriting in the United States is dominated by the major investment banks and large commercial banks. Foreign players are also heavily involved in underwriting securities that are sold internationally.

Underwriting is not always fun. On October 15, 1987, the British government finalized arrangements to sell its holding of BP shares at £3.30 a share.[20] This huge issue involved more than $12 billion and was underwritten by an international group of underwriters who marketed it in a number of countries. Four days after the underwriting was agreed, the October crash caused stock prices around the world to nose-dive. The underwriters unsuccessfully appealed to the British government to cancel the issue.[21] By the closing date of the offer, the price of BP stock had fallen to £2.96, and the underwriters had lost more than a billion dollars.

Underwriters face another danger. When a new issue goes wrong and the stock performs badly, they may be blamed for overhyping the issue. For example, in December 1999 the software company Va Linux went public at $30 a share. Next-day trading opened at $299 a share, but then the stock price began to sag. As we write this in November 2001, the stock is selling for less than $2. Disgruntled Va Linux investors sued the underwriters, complaining that the prospectus was "materially false." These underwriters had plenty of company; following the collapse of the "new economy" stocks in 2000, investors in almost one in three recent high-tech IPOs sued the underwriters.

---

[19]The alternative is to enter into an *all-or-none* arrangement. In this case, either the entire issue is sold at the offering price or the deal is called off and the issuing company receives nothing.

[20]The issue was partly a secondary issue (the sale of the British government's shares) and partly a primary issue (BP took the opportunity to raise additional capital by selling new shares).

[21]The government's only concession was to put a floor on the underwriters' losses by giving them the opportunity to resell their stock to the government at £2.80 a share.

Costs of a New Issue

We have described Marvin's underwriters as filling a triple role—providing advice, buying the new issue, and reselling it to the public. In return they received payment in the form of a *spread*; that is, they were allowed to buy the shares for less than the *offering price* at which the shares were sold to investors.[22] Klein Merrick as syndicate manager kept 20 percent of this spread. A further 25 percent of the spread was used to pay those underwriters who bought the issue. The remaining 55 percent went to the firms that provided the salesforce.

The underwriting spread on the Marvin issue amounted to 7 percent of the total sum raised from investors. Since many of the costs incurred by underwriters are fixed, you would expect that the percentage spread would decline with issue size. This in part is what we find. For example, a $5 million IPO might carry a spread of 10 percent, while the spread on a $300 million issue might be only 5 percent. However, Chen and Ritter found that with almost every IPO between $20 and $80 million the spread was exactly 7 percent.[23] Since it is difficult to believe that all these issues were equally costly to underwrite, this clustering at 7 percent is a puzzle.[24]

In addition to the underwriting fee, Marvin's new issue entailed substantial administrative costs. Preparation of the registration statement and prospectus involved management, legal counsel, and accountants, as well as the underwriters and their advisers. In addition, the firm had to pay fees for registering the new securities, printing and mailing costs, and so on. You can see from the first page of the Marvin prospectus (Appendix B) that these administrative costs totaled $820,000.

Underpricing of IPOs

Marvin's issue was costly in yet another way. Since the offering price was less than the true value of the issued securities, investors who bought the issue got a bargain at the expense of the firm's original shareholders.

These costs of *underpricing* are hidden but nevertheless real. For IPOs they generally exceed all other issue costs. Whenever any company goes public, it is very difficult for the underwriters to judge how much investors will be willing to pay for the stock. Sometimes they misjudge demand dramatically. For example, when the prospectus for the IPO of Netscape stock was first published, the underwriters indicated that the company would sell 3.5 million shares at a price between $12 and $14 each. However, the enthusiasm for Netscape's Internet browser system was such that the underwriters increased the shares available to 5 million and set an issue price of $28. The next morning the volume of orders was so large that trading was delayed by an hour and a half and, when trading did begin, the shares were quoted at $71, over five times the underwriters' initial estimates.

---

[22] In the more risky cases the underwriter usually receives some extra noncash compensation, such as warrants to buy additional common stock in the future.

[23] H. C. Chen and J. R. Ritter, "The Seven Percent Solution," *Journal of Finance* 55 (June 2000), pp. 1105–1132.

[24] Chen and Ritter argue that the fixed spread suggests the underwriting market is not competitive and the Justice Department was led to investigate whether the spread constituted evidence of price-fixing. Robert Hansen disagrees that the market is not competitive. See R. Hansen, "Do Investment Banks Compete in IPOs?: The Advent of the Seven Percent Plus Contract," *Journal of Financial Economics* 59 (2001) pp. 313–346.

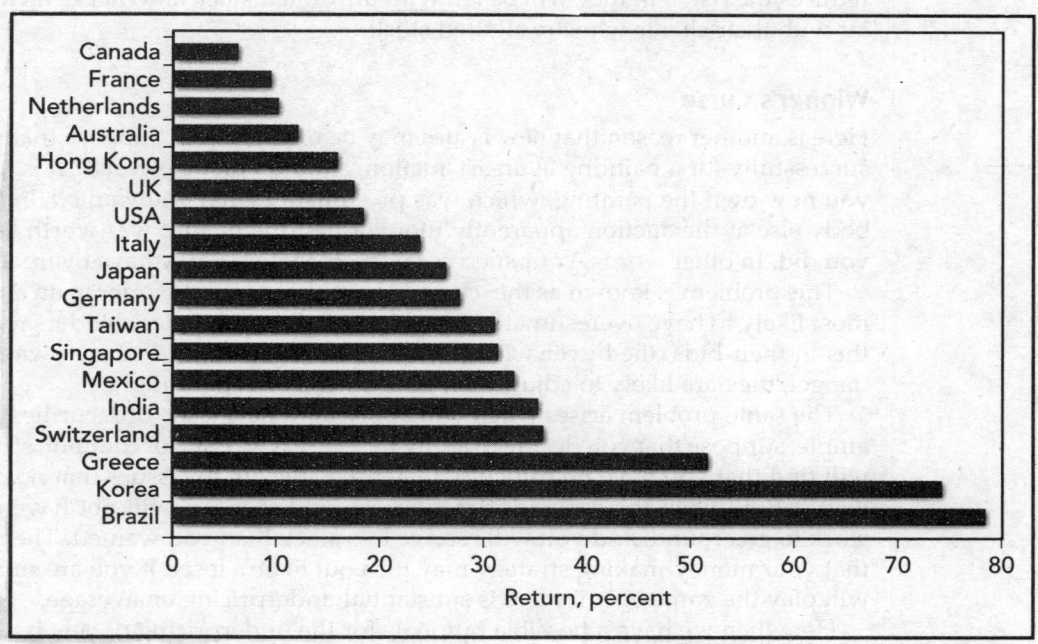

FIGURE 15.2

Average initial returns from investing in IPOs in different countries.

Source: T. Loughran, J. R. Ritter, and K. Rydqvist, "Initial Public Offerings: International Insights," *Pacific-Basin Finance Journal* 2 (1994), pp. 165–199, updated on **www.bear.cba.ufl.edu/ritter**.

We admit that the Netscape issue was unusual[25] but researchers have found that investors who buy at the issue price on average commonly realize very high returns over the following weeks. For example, a study by Ibbotson, Sindelar, and Ritter of nearly 15,000 U.S. new issues from 1960 to 2000 found average underpricing of 18.4 percent.[26] Figure 15.2 shows that the United States is not the only country in which IPOs are underpriced. In Brazil the gains from buying IPOs have averaged nearly 80 percent.[27]

You might think that shareholders would prefer not to sell their stock for less than its market price, but many investment bankers and institutional investors argue that underpricing is in the interests of the issuing firm. They say that a low offering price on the initial offer raises the price of the stock when it is subsequently traded in the market and enhances the firm's ability to raise further capital.[28] Skeptics respond that investment bankers push for a low offering price because it

[25]It does not, however, hold the record. That honor goes to Va Linux.

[26]R. G. Ibbotson, J. L. Sindelar, and J. R. Ritter, "The Market's Problems with the Pricing of Initial Public Offerings," *Journal of Applied Corporate Finance* 7 (Spring 1994), pp. 66–74, updated on **http://bear.cba.ufl.edu/ritter**. As we saw in Chapter 13, there is some evidence that these early gains are not maintained and in the five years following an IPO the shares underperform the market.

[27]There wasn't room on the chart to plot Chinese IPOs; their initial returns have averaged 257 percent.

[28]For an analysis of how a firm could rationally underprice to facilitate subsequent stock issues, see I. Welch, "Seasoned Offerings, Imitation Costs and the Underpricing of Initial Public Offerings," *Journal of Finance* 44 (June 1989), pp. 421–449.

reduces the risk that they will be left with unwanted stock and makes them popular with their clients who are allotted stock.

Winner's Curse

Here is another reason that new issues may be underpriced. Suppose that you bid successfully for a painting at an art auction. Should you be pleased? It is true that you now own the painting, which was presumably what you wanted, but everybody else at the auction apparently thought that the picture was worth less than you did. In other words, your success suggests that you may have overpaid.

This problem is known as the *winner's curse*. The highest bidder in an auction is most likely to have overestimated the object's value and, unless bidders recognize this in their bids, the buyer will on average overpay. If bidders are aware of the danger, they are likely to adjust their bids down correspondingly.

The same problem arises when you apply for a new issue of securities. For example, suppose that you decide to apply for every new issue of common stock. You will find that you have no difficulty in getting stock in the issues that no one else wants. But, when the issue is attractive, the underwriters will not have enough stock to go around, and you will receive less stock than you wanted. The result is that your money-making strategy may turn out to be a loser. If you are smart, you will play the game only if there is substantial underpricing on average.

Here then we have a possible rationale for the underpricing of new issues. Uninformed investors who cannot distinguish which issues are attractive are exposed to the winner's curse. Companies and their underwriters are aware of this and need to underprice on average to attract the uninformed investors.[29]

15.3 OTHER NEW-ISSUE PROCEDURES

Table 15.2 summarizes the main steps involved in making an initial public offering of stock in the United States. You can see that Marvin's new issue was a typical IPO in almost every respect. In particular most IPOs in the United States use the *bookbuilding* method in which the underwriter builds a book of likely orders and uses this information to set the issue price.

Although bookbuilding is rapidly gaining in popularity throughout the world,[30] firms and governments in different countries employ a variety of techniques for selling their securities. The main alternatives to bookbuilding are a fixed price offer or an auction. The fixed price offer is often used for IPOs in the UK. In this case the firm fixes the selling price and then advertises the number of shares on offer. If the price is set too high, investors will not apply for all the shares on offer and the underwriters will be obliged to buy the unsold shares. If the price is set too low, the applications will exceed the number of shares on offer and investors

---

[29]Notice that the winner's curse would disappear if only investors knew what the market price was going to be. One response is to allow trading in a security before it has been issued. This is known as a *gray market* and is most common for debt issues. Investors can observe the price in the gray market and can be more confident that they are not overbidding when the actual issue takes place.

[30]The growth in bookbuilding is discussed in A. E. Sherman, "Global Trends in IPO Methods: Book Building vs. Auctions," working paper, Department of Finance and Business Economics, University of Notre Dame, March 2001.

TABLE 15.2

The main steps involved in making an initial public offering of stock in the United States.

1. Company appoints managing underwriter (bookrunner) and co-manager(s). Underwriting syndicate formed.
2. Arrangement with underwriters includes agreement on spread (typically 7% for medium-sized IPOs) and on greenshoe option (typically allowing the underwriters to increase the number of shares bought by 15%).
3. Issue registered with SEC and preliminary prospectus (red herring) issued.
4. Roadshow arranged to market the issue to potential investors. Managing underwriter builds book of potential demand.
5. SEC approves registration. Company and underwriters agree on issue price.
6. Underwriters allot stock (typically with overallotment).
7. Trading starts. Underwriters cover short position by buying stock in the market or by exercising greenshoe option.
8. Managing underwriter makes liquid market in stock and provides research coverage.

will receive only a proportion of the shares that they applied for. Since the most underpriced offers are likely to be heavily oversubscribed, the fixed price offer leaves investors very exposed to the winner's curse.[31]

The alternative is to sell new securities by auction. In this case investors are invited to submit their bids, stating both how many securities they wish to buy and the price. The securities are then sold to the highest bidders. Most governments, including the U.S. Treasury, sell their bonds by auction. In recent years a few companies in the United States have made an IPO by auctioning stock on the Internet.

Notice that the bookbuilding method is in some ways like an auction, since potential buyers state how many shares they are prepared to buy at given prices. However, the bids are not binding and are used only as a guide to fix the price of the issue. Thus the issue price is commonly set below the price that is needed to sell the issue, and the underwriters are more likely to allot stock to their favorite clients and to those investors whose bids are most helpful in setting the issue price.[32]

Types of Auction

Suppose that a government wishes to auction four million bonds and three would-be buyers submit bids. Investor A bids $1,020 each for one million bonds, B bids $1,000 for three million bonds, and C bids $980 for two million bonds. The bids of the two highest bidders (A and B) absorb all the bonds on offer and C is left empty-handed. What price do the winning bidders, A and B, pay?

The answer depends on whether the sale is a *discriminatory auction* or a *uniform-price auction*. In a discriminatory auction every winner is required to pay the price that he or she bid. In this case A would pay $1,020 and B would pay $1,000. In a uniform-price auction both would pay $1,000, which is the price of the lowest winning bidder (investor B).

---

[31]Mario Levis found that, though IPOs in the UK offered an average first-day return of nearly 9 percent in the period 1985–1988, an investor who applied for an equal amount of each IPO would have done little better than break even. See M. Levis, "The Winner's Curse Problem, Interest Costs and the Underpricing of Initial Public Offerings," *Economics Journal* 100 (1990), pp. 76–89.

[32]F. Cornelli and D. Goldreich, "Bookbuilding and Strategic Allocation," *Journal of Finance* 56 (December 2001), pp. 2337–2369.

It might seem from our example that the proceeds from a uniform-price auction would be lower than from a discriminatory auction. But this ignores the fact that the uniform-price auction provides better protection against the winner's curse. Wise bidders know that there is little cost to overbidding in a uniform-price auction, but there is potentially a very high cost to doing so in a discriminatory auction.[33] Economists therefore often argue that the uniform-price auction should result in higher proceeds.[34]

Sales of bonds by the U.S. Treasury used to take the form of discriminatory auctions so that successful buyers paid their bid. However, governments do occasionally listen to economists, and the Treasury has now switched to a uniform-price auction. The Mexican government has also been sufficiently convinced to change from a discriminatory auction to a uniform-price auction.[35]

15.4   SECURITY SALES BY PUBLIC COMPANIES

For most companies their first public issue of stock is seldom their last. As they grow, they are likely to make further issues of debt and equity. Public companies can issue securities either by offering them to investors at large or by making a rights issue that is limited to existing stockholders. General cash offers are now used for virtually all debt and equity issues in the United States, but rights issues are widespread in other countries and you should understand how they work. Therefore in Appendix A to this chapter we describe rights issues.

General Cash Offers

When a corporation makes a general cash offer of debt or equity in the United States, it goes through much the same procedure as when it first went public. In other words, it registers the issue with the SEC and then sells the securities to an underwriter (or a syndicate of underwriters), who in turn offers the securities to the public. Before the price of the issue is fixed the underwriter will build up a book of likely demand for the securities just as in the case of Marvin's IPO.

The SEC allows large companies to file a single registration statement covering financing plans for up to two years into the future. The actual issues can then be done with scant additional paperwork, whenever the firm needs the cash or thinks it can issue securities at an attractive price. This is called *shelf registra-*

---

[33]In addition, the price in the uniform-price auction depends not only on the views of B but also on those of A (for example, if A had bid $990 rather than $1,020, then both A and B would have paid $990 for each bond). Since the uniform-price auction takes advantage of the views of both A and B, it reduces the winner's curse.

[34]Sometimes auctions reduce the winner's curse by allowing uninformed bidders to enter noncompetitive bids, whereby they submit a quantity but not a price. For example, in U.S. Treasury auctions investors may submit noncompetitive bids and receive their full allocation at the average price paid by competitive bidders.

[35]Experience in the United States and Mexico with uniform-price auctions suggests that they do indeed reduce the winner's curse problem and realize higher prices for the seller. See K. G. Nyborg and S. Sundaresan, "Discriminatory versus Uniform Treasury Auctions: Evidence from When-Issued Transactions," *Journal of Financial Economics* 42 (1996), pp. 63–105; and S. Umlauf, "An Empirical Study of the Mexican Treasury Bill Auction," *Journal of Financial Economics* 33 (1993), pp. 313–340.

tion—the registration statement is "put on the shelf," to be taken down and used as needed.

Think of how you as a financial manager might use shelf registration. Suppose your company is likely to need up to $200 million of new long-term debt over the next year or so. It can file a registration statement for that amount. It then has prior approval to issue up to $200 million of debt, but it isn't obligated to issue a penny. Nor is it required to work through any particular underwriters; the registration statement may name one or more underwriters the firm thinks it may work with, but others can be substituted later.

Now you can sit back and issue debt as needed, in bits and pieces if you like. Suppose Merrill Lynch comes across an insurance company with $10 million ready to invest in corporate bonds. Your phone rings. It's Merrill Lynch offering to buy $10 million of your bonds, priced to yield, say, 8½ percent. If you think that's a good price, you say OK and the deal is done, subject only to a little additional paperwork. Merrill then resells the bonds to the insurance company, it hopes at a higher price than it paid for them, thus earning an intermediary's profit.

Here is another possible deal: Suppose that you perceive a window of opportunity in which interest rates are temporarily low. You invite bids for $100 million of bonds. Some bids may come from large investment banks acting alone; others may come from ad hoc syndicates. But that's not your problem; if the price is right, you just take the best deal offered.

Not all companies eligible for shelf registration actually use it for all their public issues. Sometimes they believe they can get a better deal by making one large issue through traditional channels, especially when the security to be issued has some unusual feature or when the firm believes that it needs the investment banker's counsel or stamp of approval on the issue. Consequently, shelf registration is less often used for issues of common stock or convertible securities than for garden-variety corporate bonds.

International Security Issues

Well-established companies are not restricted to the capital market in the United States; they can also sell securities in the international capital markets. The procedures for such issues are broadly similar to those used in the United States. Here are two points to note:

1. As long as the issue is not publicly offered in the United States, it does not need to be registered with the SEC. However, the company must still provide a prospectus or offering circular.
2. Frequently an international sale of bonds takes the form of a *bought deal,* in which case one or a few underwriters buy the entire issue. Bought deals allow companies to issue bonds at very short notice.

Large debt issues are now often split, with part sold in the international debt market and part registered and sold in the United States. Likewise with equity issues. For example, in 1992 Wellcome Trust, a British charitable foundation, decided to sell part of its holdings in the Wellcome Group. To handle the sale, it paid about $140 million to a group of 120 underwriters from around the world. These underwriters collected bids from interested investors and forwarded them to Robert Fleming, a London merchant bank, which built up a book of the various bids. Particular classes of investors, such as existing shareholders or those who submitted

Type	Company	Issue Amount ($ millions)	Underwriter's Spread
Common Stock:			
IPO	Torch Offshore	$ 80	7.0 %
IPO	Alliance Imaging	122	7.0
IPO	United Surgical Partners	126	7.0
IPO	Tellium, Inc.	135	7.0
IPO	Agere Systems	3,600	3.9
Seasoned	National Golf Properties, Inc.	$ 29.6	5.126%
Seasoned	Lifepoint Hospitals	92.8	5.0
Seasoned	Valspar Corp.	168	4.25
Seasoned	Raytheon Co.	343.8	3.745
Seasoned	Pepsico, Inc.	534.6	2.0
Seasoned	Allegheny Energy, Inc.	598.3	3.005
Debt (coupon rate, type, maturity):			
8.3% Subordinated notes, 2011	Bank of the West	$ 50	.65 %
6.875% Medium-term notes, 2006	Maytag Corp.	185	.50
7.75% Notes, 2011	Shurgard Storage Centers	250	.65
8.5% Senior notes, 2011	Hilton Hotels	300	.875
5.875% Global bonds, 2004	American Home Products	500	.35
3.5% Convertible bonds, 2021	Cox Communications	685	2.25
7.45% Global bonds, 2031	Kellogg	1,100	.875
8.5% Senior notes, 2008	Calpine	1,500	1.00

TABLE 15.3

Gross underwriting spreads of selected issues, 2001. Spreads are percentages of gross proceeds.

their bids early, went to the front of the queue, while those who subsequently cut their bids or sold Wellcome stock were demoted.

By the end of the three-week issue period, Wellcome Trust was able to look at a demand curve showing how many shares investors were prepared to buy at each price. In the light of this information it decided to sell 270 million shares, with net proceeds of about $4 billion. Some 1,100 institutions and 30,000 individuals ended up buying the shares. About 40 percent of the issue was sold outside the United Kingdom, mainly in the United States, Japan, France, and Germany.

The shares of many companies are now listed and traded on major international exchanges. British Telecom trades on the New York Stock Exchange, as do Sony, Fiat, Telefonos de Mexico, and so on.[36] Several of these companies also trade on overseas exchanges. Citigroup, one of the largest banks in the United States, trades in New York, London, Amsterdam, Tokyo, Zurich, Toronto, and Frankfurt, as well as several smaller exchanges.

Some companies' stocks do not trade at all in their home country. For example, in 1998 Radcom Ltd., an Israeli manufacturer of network test equipment,

---

[36]Rather than issuing shares directly in the United States, foreign companies generally issue *American depository receipts (ADRs)*. These are simply claims to the shares of the foreign company that are held by a bank on behalf of the ADR owners.

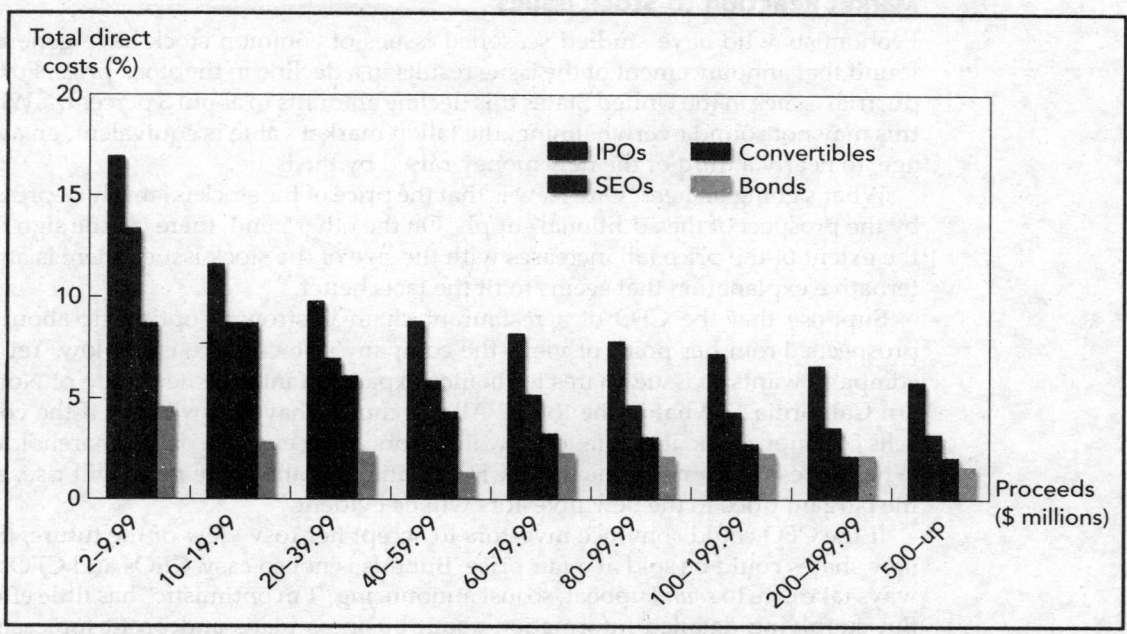

FIGURE 15.3

Total direct costs as a percentage of gross proceeds. The total direct costs for initial public offerings (IPOs), seasoned equity offerings (SEOs), convertible bonds, and straight bonds are composed of underwriter spreads and other direct expenses.

Source: I. Lee, S. Lochhead, J. R. Ritter, and Q. Zhao, "The Costs of Raising Capital," *Journal of Financial Research* 19 (Spring 1996), pp. 59–74.

raised $30 million by an IPO in the United States. Its stock was not traded in Israel. The company thought it could get a better price and more active follow-on trading in New York.[37]

The Costs of a General Cash Offer

Whenever a firm makes a cash offer of securities, it incurs substantial administrative costs. Also the firm needs to compensate the underwriters by selling them securities below the price that they expect to receive from investors. Table 15.3 lists underwriting spreads for a few issues in 2001. As the table shows, there are economies of scale in issuing securities: The underwriter's spread declines as the size of the issue increases. Spreads for debt securities are lower than for common stocks, less than 1 percent for many issues.

Figure 15.3 summarizes a study by Lee, Lochhead, Ritter, and Zhao of total issue costs (spreads plus administrative costs) for several thousand issues between 1990 and 1994.

[37]"High-tech firms are much better understood and valued in the U.S." "[The issuers] get a better price, a shareholder base that understands their business, and they can get publicity in a major market for their products." These are representative quotes from M. R. Sesit, "Foreign Firms Flock to U.S. for IPOs," *The Wall Street Journal*, June 23, 1995, p. C1.

Market Reaction to Stock Issues

Economists who have studied seasoned issues of common stock have generally found that announcement of the issue results in a decline in the stock price. For industrial issues in the United States this decline amounts to about 3 percent.[38] While this may not sound overwhelming, the fall in market value is equivalent, on average, to nearly a third of the new money raised by the issue.

What's going on here? One view is that the price of the stock is simply depressed by the prospect of the additional supply. On the other hand, there is little sign that the extent of the price fall increases with the size of the stock issue. There is an alternative explanation that seems to fit the facts better.

Suppose that the CFO of a restaurant chain is strongly optimistic about its prospects. From her point of view, the company's stock price is too low. Yet the company wants to issue shares to finance expansion into the new state of Northern California.[39] What is she to do? All the choices have drawbacks. If the chain sells common stock, it will favor new investors at the expense of old shareholders. When investors come to share the CFO's optimism, the share price will rise, and the bargain price to the new investors will be evident.

If the CFO could convince investors to accept her rosy view of the future, then new shares could be sold at a fair price. But this is not so easy. CEOs and CFOs always take care to *sound* upbeat, so just announcing "I'm optimistic" has little effect. But supplying detailed information about business plans and profit forecasts is costly and is also of great assistance to competitors.

The CFO could scale back or delay the expansion until the company's stock price recovers. That too is costly, but it may be rational if the stock price is severely undervalued and a stock issue is the only source of financing.

If a CFO knows that the company's stock is *over*valued, the position is reversed. If the firm sells new shares at the high price, it will help existing shareholders at the expense of the new ones. Managers might be prepared to issue stock even if the new cash was just put in the bank.

Of course, investors are not stupid. They can predict that managers are more likely to issue stock when they think it is overvalued and that optimistic managers may cancel or defer issues. Therefore, when an equity issue is announced, they mark down the price of the stock accordingly. Thus the decline in the price of the stock at the time of the new issue may have nothing to do with the increased supply but simply with the information that the issue provides.[40]

Cornett and Tehranian devised a natural experiment which pretty much proves this point.[41] They examined a sample of stock issues by commercial banks. Some of these issues were necessary to meet capital standards set by banking regulators. The rest were ordinary, voluntary stock issues designed to raise money for various corporate purposes. The necessary issues caused a much smaller drop in stock prices than the voluntary ones, which makes perfect sense. If the issue is outside

---

[38]See, for example, P. Asquith and D. W. Mullins, "Equity Issues and Offering Dilution," *Journal of Financial Economics* 15 (January–February 1986), pp. 61–90.

[39]Northern California seceded from California and became the fifty-second state in 2007.

[40]This explanation was developed in S. C. Myers and N. S. Majluf, "Corporate Financing and Investment Decisions When Firms Have Information That Investors Do Not Have," *Journal of Financial Economics* 35 (1994), pp. 99–122.

[41]M. M. Cornett and H. Tehranian, "An Examination of Voluntary versus Involuntary Issuances by Commercial Banks," *Journal of Financial Economics* 35 (1994), pp. 99–122.

the manager's discretion, announcement of the issue conveys no information about the manager's view of the company's prospects.[42]

Most financial economists now interpret the stock price drop on equity issue announcements as an information effect and not a result of the additional supply.[43] But what about an issue of preferred stock or debt? Are they equally likely to provide information to investors about company prospects? A pessimistic manager might be tempted to get a debt issue out before investors become aware of the bad news, but how much profit can you make for your shareholders by selling overpriced debt? Perhaps 1 or 2 percent. Investors know that a pessimistic manager has a much greater incentive to issue equity rather than preferred stock or debt. Therefore, when companies announce an issue of preferred or debt, there is a barely perceptible fall in the stock price.[44]

There is, however, at least one puzzle left. As we saw in Chapter 13, it appears that the long-run performance of companies that issue shares is substandard. Investors who bought these companies' shares *after* the stock issue earned lower returns than they would have if they had bought into similar companies. This result holds for both IPOs and seasoned issues.[45] It seems that investors failed to appreciate fully the issuing companies' information advantage. If so, we have an exception to the efficient-market theory.

 ## 15.5 PRIVATE PLACEMENTS AND PUBLIC ISSUES

Whenever a company makes a public offering, it is obliged to register the issue with the SEC. It could avoid this costly process by selling the securities privately. There are no hard-and-fast definitions of a private placement, but the SEC has insisted that the security should be sold to no more than a dozen or so knowledgeable investors.

One of the drawbacks of a private placement is that the investor cannot easily resell the security. However, institutions such as life insurance companies invest huge amounts in corporate debt for the long haul and are less concerned about its marketability. Consequently, an active private placement market has evolved for corporate debt. Often this debt is negotiated directly between the company and the lender, but, if the issue is too large to be absorbed by one institution, the company will generally employ an investment bank to draw up a prospectus and identify possible buyers.

---

[42]The "involuntary issuers" did make a choice: they could have foregone the stock issue and run the risk of failing to meet the regulatory capital standards. The banks that were more concerned with this risk were more likely to issue. Thus it's no surprise that Cornett and Tehranian found some drop in stock price even for the involuntary issues.

[43]There is another possible information effect. Just as an unexpected increase in the dividend suggests to investors that the company is generating more cash than they thought, the announcement of a new issue may have the reverse implication. However, this effect cannot explain why the announcement of an issue of debt does not result in a similar fall in the stock price.

[44]See L. Shyam-Sunder, "The Stock Price Effect of Risky vs. Safe Debt," *Journal of Financial and Quantitative Analysis* 26 (December 1991), pp. 549–558. Evidence on the price impact of issues of different types of security is summarized in C. Smith, "Investment Banking and the Capital Acquisition Process," *Journal of Financial Economics* 15 (January–February 1986), pp. 3–29.

[45]See, for example, T. Loughran and J. R. Ritter, "The New Issues Puzzle," *Journal of Finance* 50 (March 1995), pp. 23–51.

As you would expect, it costs less to arrange a private placement than to make a public issue. This is a particular advantage for companies making smaller issues.

In 1990 the SEC relaxed its restrictions on who can buy and trade unregistered securities. The new rule, Rule 144A, allows large financial institutions (known as *qualified institutional buyers*) to trade unregistered securities among themselves. Rule 144A was intended to increase liquidity and reduce interest rates and issue costs for private placements. It was aimed largely at foreign corporations deterred by registration requirements in the United States. The SEC argued that such firms would welcome the opportunity to issue unregistered stocks and bonds which could then be freely traded by large U.S. financial institutions.

Rule 144A issues have proved very popular, particularly with foreign issuers. There has also been an increasing volume of secondary trading in Rule 144A issues.

SUMMARY

In this chapter we have summarized the various procedures for issuing corporate securities. We first looked at how infant companies raise venture capital to carry them through to the point at which they can make their first public issue of stock. We then looked at how companies can make further public issues of securities by a general cash offer. Finally, we reviewed the procedures for a private placement.

It is always difficult to summarize a summary. Instead we will remind you of some of the most important implications for the financial manager who must decide how to issue capital.

Larger is cheaper   There are economies of scale in issuing securities. It is cheaper to go to the market once for $100 million than to make two trips for $50 million each. Consequently firms bunch security issues. That may often mean relying on short-term financing until a large issue is justified. Or it may mean issuing more than is needed at the moment in order to avoid another issue later.

Watch out for underpricing   Underpricing is a hidden cost to the existing shareholders. Fortunately, it is usually serious only for companies that are selling stock to the public for the first time.

The winner's curse may be a serious problem with IPOs   Would-be investors in an initial public offering (IPO) do not know how other investors will value the stock and they worry that they are likely to receive a larger allocation of the overpriced issues. Careful design of issue procedure may reduce the winner's curse.

New stock issues may depress the price   The extent of this price pressure varies, but for industrial issues in the United States the fall in the value of the existing stock may amount to a significant proportion of the money raised. This pressure is due to the information that the market reads into the company's decision to issue stock.

Shelf registration often makes sense for debt issues by blue-chip firms   Shelf registration reduces the time taken to arrange a new issue, it increases flexibility, and it may cut underwriting costs. It seems best suited for debt issues by large firms that are happy to switch between investment banks. It seems less suited for issues of unusually risky or complex securities or for issues by small companies that are likely to benefit from a close relationship with an investment bank.

The Privileged Subscription or Rights Issue

APPENDIX A

Instead of making an issue of stock to investors at large, companies sometimes give their existing shareholders the right of first refusal. Such issues are known as *privileged subscription,* or *rights, issues.* In some countries, such as the United States and Japan, rights issues have become a rarity and general cash offers are the norm. In Europe equity must generally be sold by rights, though companies have increasingly lobbied for the freedom to make general cash offers.

Here is an example of a rights issue. In January 2001 the French building-materials company, Lafarge, needed to raise €1.1 billion of new equity. It did so by offering its existing stockholders the right to buy one new share for every eight shares that they currently held. The new shares were priced at €80 each, nearly 20 percent below the preannouncement price of €99.65.

Imagine that you hold eight shares of Lafarge stock just prior to the rights issue. Your holding is therefore worth 8 × €99.65 = €797.20. Lafarge's offer gives you the opportunity to buy one additional share for €80. If you buy the new share, your holding increases to nine shares and the value of your holding increases by the extra €80 to 797.20 + 80 = €877.20. Therefore after the issue the value of each share is no longer €99.65, but slightly lower at 877.20/9 = €97.47.

How much is your right to buy one new share for €80 worth? The answer is €17.47. An investor, who could buy a share worth €97.47 for €80, would be willing to pay €17.47 for the right to do so.

It should be clear on reflection that Lafarge could have raised the same amount of money on a variety of terms. For example, instead of a 1-for-8 at €80, it could have made a 1-for-4 at €40. In this case it would have sold twice as many shares at half the price. If you held eight Lafarge shares before the issue, you could subscribe for two new shares at €40 each. This would give you 10 shares in total worth 797.20 + (2 × 40) = €877.20. After the issue the value of each share would be 877.20/10 = €87.72. This is less than in the case of the 1-for-8 issue but then you would have the compensation of owning 10 rather than 9 shares. Suppose you wanted to sell your right to buy a new share for €40? Investors would be prepared to pay you €47.72 for this right. They would then pay over €40 to Lafarge and receive a share with a market value of €87.72.

Our example illustrates that, as long as the company successfully sells the new shares, the issue price in a rights offering is irrelevant.[46] That is *not* the case in a general cash offer. If the company sells new stock for less than the market will bear, the buyer makes a profit at the expense of existing shareholders. Although this

---

[46]If the share price stayed at €97.47, Lafarge's shareholders would be very happy to buy new shares for €80. However, if the price fell below €80, shareholders would no longer exercise their option to buy new shares. To guard against this possibility, it is common to arrange standby agreements requiring the underwriters to buy any unwanted stock.

danger creates a natural presumption in favor of the rights issue, it can be argued that underpricing is a serious problem only in the case of an initial public offer, when a rights issue is not a feasible alternative.

APPENDIX B   Marvin's New-Issue Prospectus[47]

PROSPECTUS
900,000 Shares
Marvin Enterprises Inc.
Common Stock ($.10 par value)

Of the 900,000 shares of Common Stock offered hereby, 500,000 shares are being sold by the Company and 400,000 shares are being sold by the Selling Stockholders. See "Principal and Selling Stockholders." The Company will not receive any of the proceeds from the sale of shares by the Selling Stockholders.

Before this offering there has been no public market for the Common Stock. **These securities involve a high degree of risk. See "Certain Considerations."**

THESE SECURITIES HAVE NOT BEEN APPROVED OR DISAPPROVED BY THE SECURITIES AND EXCHANGE COMMISSION NOR HAS THE COMMISSION PASSED ON THE ACCURACY OR ADEQUACY OF THIS PROSPECTUS. ANY REPRESENTATION TO THE CONTRARY IS A CRIMINAL OFFENSE.

	Price to Public	Underwriting Discount	Proceeds to Company[1]	Proceeds to Selling Stockholders[1]
Per share	$80.00	$5.60	$74.40	$74.40
Total[2]	$72,000,000	$5,040,000	$37,200,000	$29,760,000

[1]Before deducting expenses payable by the Company estimated at $820,000, of which $455,555 will be paid by the Company and $364,445 will be paid by the Selling Stockholders.
[2]The Company has granted to the Underwriters an option to purchase up to an additional 135,000 shares at the initial public offering price, less the underwriting discount, solely to cover overallotment.

The Common Stock is offered subject to receipt and acceptance by the Underwriters, to prior sale, and to the Underwriters's right to reject any order in whole or in part and to withdraw, cancel, or modify the offer without notice.

Klein Merrick Inc.   **February 3, 2019**

No person has been authorized to give any information or to make any representations, other than as contained therein, in connection with the offer contained in this Prospectus, and, if given or made, such information or representations must not be relied upon. This Prospectus does not constitute an offer of any securities other than the registered securities to which it relates or an offer to any person in any jurisdiction where such an offer would be unlawful. The delivery of this Prospectus at any time does not imply that information herein is correct as of any time subsequent to its date.

---

[47]Most prospectuses have content similar to that of the Marvin prospectus but go into considerably more detail. Also we have omitted Marvin's financial statements.

IN CONNECTION WITH THIS OFFERING, THE UNDERWRITERS MAY OVER-ALLOT OR EFFECT TRANSACTIONS WHICH STABILIZE OR MAINTAIN THE MARKET PRICE OF THE COMMON STOCK OF THE COMPANY AT A LEVEL ABOVE THAT WHICH MIGHT OTHERWISE PREVAIL IN THE OPEN MARKET. SUCH STABILIZING, IF COMMENCED, MAY BE DISCONTINUED AT ANY TIME.

Prospectus Summary

The following summary information is qualified in its entirety by the detailed information and financial statements appearing elsewhere in this Prospectus.

The Offering

Common Stock offered by the Company ....500,000 shares
Common Stock offered by the Selling Stockholders ....400,000 shares
Common Stock to be outstanding after this offering ....4,100,000 shares

Use of Proceeds

For the construction of new manufacturing facilities and to provide working capital.

The Company

Marvin Enterprises Inc. designs, manufactures, and markets gargle blasters for domestic use. Its manufacturing facilities employ integrated microcircuits to control the genetic engineering processes used to manufacture gargle blasters.

The Company was organized in Delaware in 2013.

Use of Proceeds

The net proceeds of this offering are expected to be $36,744,445. Of the net proceeds, approximately $27.0 million will be used to finance expansion of the Company's principal manufacturing facilities. The balance will be used for working capital.

Certain Considerations

Investment in the Common Stock involves a high degree of risk. The following factors should be carefully considered in evaluating the Company:

Substantial Capital Needs The Company will require additional financing to continue its expansion policy. The Company believes that its relations with its lenders are good, but there can be no assurance that additional financing will be available in the future.

Licensing The expanded manufacturing facilities are to be used for the production of a new imploding gargle blaster. An advisory panel to the U.S. Food and Drug Administration (FDA) has recommended approval of this product for the U.S. market but no decision has yet been reached by the full FDA committee.

Dividend Policy

The company has not paid cash dividends on its Common Stock and does not anticipate that dividends will be paid on the Common Stock in the foreseeable future.

Management

The following table sets forth information regarding the Company's directors, executive officers, and key employees.

Name	Age	Position
George Marvin	32	President, Chief Executive Officer, & Director
Mildred Marvin	28	Treasurer & Director
Chip Norton	30	General Manager

George Marvin—George Marvin established the Company in 2013 and has been its Chief Executive Officer since that date. He is a past president of the Institute of

Gargle Blasters and has recently been inducted into the Confrèrie des gargarisateurs. *Mildred Marvin*—Mildred Marvin has been employed by the Company since 2013. *Chip Norton*—Mr. Norton has been General Manager of the Company since 2013. He is a former vice-president of Amalgamated Blasters, Inc.

Executive Compensation

The following table sets forth the cash compensation paid for services rendered for the year 2018 by the executive officers:

Name	Capacity	Cash Compensation
George Marvin	President and Chief Executive Officer	$300,000
Mildred Marvin	Treasurer	220,000
Chip Norton	General Manager	220,000

Certain Transactions

At various times between 2014 and 2017 First Meriam Venture Partners invested a total of $8.5 million in the Company. In connection with this investment, First Meriam Venture Partners was granted certain rights to registration under the Securities Act of 1933, including the right to have their shares of Common Stock registered at the Company's expense with the Securities and Exchange Commission.

Principal and Selling Stockholders

The following table sets forth certain information regarding the beneficial ownership of the Company's voting Common Stock as of the date of this prospectus by (i) each person known by the Company to be the beneficial owner of more than 5 percent of its voting Common Stock, and (ii) each director of the Company who beneficially owns voting Common Stock. Unless otherwise indicated, each owner has sole voting and dispositive power over his or her shares.

	Common Stock				
	Shares Beneficially Owned Prior to Offering			Shares Beneficially Owned After Offer[1]	
Name of Beneficial Owner	Number	Percent	Shares to Be Sold	Number	Percent
George Marvin	375,000	10.4	60,000	315,000	7.7
Mildred Marvin	375,000	10.4	60,000	315,000	7.7
Chip Norton	250,000	6.9	80,000	170,000	4.1
First Meriam Venture Partners	1,700,000	47.2	—	1,700,000	41.5
TFS Investors	260,000	7.2	—	260,000	6.3
Centri-Venture Partnership	260,000	7.2	—	260,000	6.3
Henry Pobble	180,000	5.0	—	180,000	4.4
Georgina Sloberg	200,000	5.6	200,000	—	—

[1]Assuming no exercise of the Underwriters' overallotment option.

Description of Capital Stock

The Company's authorized capital stock consists of 10,000,000 shares of voting Common Stock.

As of the date of this Prospectus, there are 10 holders of record of the Common Stock.

Under the terms of one of the Company's loan agreements, the Company may not pay cash dividends on Common Stock except from net profits without the written consent of the lender.

Underwriting

Subject to the terms and conditions set forth in the Underwriting Agreement, the Company has agreed to sell to each of the Underwriters named below, and each of the Underwriters, for whom Klein Merrick Inc. are acting as Representatives, has severally agreed to purchase from the Company, the number of shares set forth opposite its name below.

Underwriters	Number of Shares to Be Purchased
Klein Merrick, Inc.	300,000
Goldman Stanley, Inc.	300,000
Salomon, Buffett & Co.	100,000
Orange County Securities	100,000
Bank of New England	100,000

In the Underwriting Agreement, the several Underwriters have agreed, subject to the terms and conditions set forth therein, to purchase all shares offered hereby if any such shares are purchased. In the event of a default by any Underwriter, the Underwriting Agreement provides that, in certain circumstances, purchase commitments of the nondefaulting Underwriters may be increased or the Underwriting Agreement may be terminated.

There is no public market for the Common Stock. The price to the public for the Common Stock was determined by negotiation between the Company and the Underwriters and was based on, among other things, the Company's financial and operating history and condition, its prospects and the prospects for its industry in general, the management of the Company, and the market prices of securities for companies in businesses similar to that of the Company.

Legal Matters

The validity of the shares of Common Stock offered by the Prospectus is being passed on for the Company by Dodson and Fogg and for the Underwriters by Kenge and Carboy.

Experts

The consolidated financial statements of the Company have been so included in reliance on the reports of Hooper Firebrand, independent accountants, given on the authority of that firm as experts in auditing and accounting.

Financial Statements

[Text and tables omitted.]

FURTHER READING

The best sources on venture capital are the specialized journals. See, for example, recent issues of Venture Capital Journal. The paper by Gompers and Lerner provides a review of the venture capital industry. Sahlman's paper is a very readable analysis of how venture capital financing is structured to provide the right incentives and Kaplan and Stromberg's paper examines a sample of venture capital investments:

P. A. Gompers and J. Lerner: "The Venture Capital Revolution," *Journal of Economic Perspectives*, 15:145–168 (Spring 2001).

W. A. Sahlman: "Aspects of Financial Contracting in Venture Capital," *Journal of Applied Corporate Finance,* 1:23–26 (Summer 1988).

S. N. Kaplan and P. Stromberg, "Financial Contracting Theory Meets the Real World: An Empirical Analysis of Venture Capital Contracts," *Review of Financial Studies,* forthcoming.

There have been a number of studies of the market for initial public offerings of common stock. Good articles to start with are:

K. Ellis, R. Michaely, and M. O'Hara: "When the Underwriter Is the Market Maker: An Examination of Trading in the IPO Aftermarket," *Journal of Finance,* 55:1039–1074 (June 2000).

F. Cornelli and D. Goldreich: "Bookbuilding and Strategic Allocation," *Journal of Finance* 56 (December 2001), pp. 2337–2369.

R. G. Ibbotson, J. L. Sindelar, and J. R. Ritter: "The Market's Problems with the Pricing of Initial Public Offerings," *Journal of Applied Corporate Finance,* 7:66–74 (Spring 1994).

T. Loughran and J. R. Ritter: "The New Issues Puzzle," *Journal of Finance,* 50:23–51 (March 1995).

K. Rock: "Why New Issues Are Underpriced," *Journal of Financial Economics,* 15:187–212 (January–February 1986).

A useful introduction to the design of auction procedures is:
P. Milgrom, "Auctions and Bidding: A Primer," *Journal of Economic Perspectives,* 3:3–22 (1989).

The significant and permanent fall in price after a seasoned stock issue in the United States is documented in the Asquith and Mullins paper. Myers and Majluf relate this price fall to the information associated with security issues:

P. Asquith and D. W. Mullins: "Equity Issues and Offering Dilution," *Journal of Financial Economics,* 15:61–90 (January–February 1986).

S. C. Myers and N. S. Majluf: "Corporate Financing and Investment Decisions When Firms Have Information That Investors Do Not Have," *Journal of Financial Economics,* 13:187–222 (June 1984).

QUIZ

1. After each of the following issue methods we have listed two types of issue. Choose the one more likely to employ that method.
   a. Rights issue *(initial public offer/further sale of an already publicly traded stock)*
   b. Rule 144A issue *(international bond issue/U.S. bond issue by a foreign corporation)*
   c. Private placement *(issue of existing stock/bond issue by an industrial company)*
   d. Shelf registration *(initial public offer/bond issue by a large industrial company)*

2. Each of the following terms is associated with one of the events beneath. Can you match them up?
   a. Best efforts
   b. Bookbuilding
   c. Shelf registration
   d. Rule 144A
   Events:
   a. Investors indicate to the underwriter how many shares they would like to buy in a new issue and these indications are used to help set the price.
   b. The underwriter accepts responsibility only to *try* to sell the issue.
   c. Some issues are not registered but can be traded freely among qualified institutional buyers.
   d. Several tranches of the same security may be sold under the same registration. (A "tranche" is a batch, a fraction of a larger issue.)

3. Explain what each of the following terms or phrases means:
   a. Venture capital
   b. Primary offering

    c. Secondary offering

    d. Registration statement

    e. Winner's curse

    f. Bought deal

4. For each of the following pairs of issues, which is likely to involve the lower proportionate underwriting and administrative costs?

    a. A large issue/a small issue.

    b. A bond issue/a common stock issue.

    c. Initial public offering/subsequent issue of stock.

    d. A small private placement of bonds/a small general cash offer of bonds.

5. True or false?

    a. Venture capitalists typically provide first-stage financing sufficient to cover all development expenses. Second-stage financing is provided by stock issued in an IPO.

    b. Large companies' stocks may be listed and traded on several different international exchanges.

    c. Stock price generally falls when the company announces a new issue of shares. This is attributable to the information released by the decision to issue.

6. Look back at the prospectus for Marvin's IPO (Appendix B):

    a. If there is unexpectedly heavy demand for the issue, how many extra shares can the underwriter buy?

    b. How many shares are to be sold in the primary offering? How many will be sold in the secondary offering?

    c. One day post-IPO, Marvin shares traded at $105. What was the degree of underpricing? How does that compare with the average degree of underpricing for IPOs in the United States?

    d. There are three kinds of cost to Marvin's new issue—underwriting expense, administrative costs, and underpricing. What was the *total* dollar cost of the Marvin issue?

7. You need to choose between making a public offering and arranging a private placement. In each case the issue involves $10 million face value of 10-year debt. You have the following data for each:

    • *A public issue:* The interest rate on the debt would be 8.5 percent, and the debt would be issued at face value. The underwriting spread would be 1.5 percent, and other expenses would be $80,000.

    • *A private placement:* The interest rate on the private placement would be 9 percent, but the total issuing expenses would be only $30,000.

    a. What is the difference in the proceeds to the company net of expenses?

    b. Other things being equal, which is the better deal?

    c. What other factors beyond the interest rate and issue costs would you wish to consider before deciding between the two offers?

8. In what ways does the bookbuilding method of selling new issues differ from a formal auction?

9. Associated Breweries is planning to market unleaded beer. To finance the venture it proposes to make a rights issue at $10 of one new share for each two shares held. (The company currently has outstanding 100,000 shares priced at $40 a share.) Assuming that the new money is invested to earn a fair return, give values for the following:

    a. Number of new shares.

    b. Amount of new investment.

    c. Total value of company after issue.

    d. Total number of shares after issue.

    e. Stock price after the issue.

    f. Price of the right to buy one new share.

PRACTICE QUESTIONS

1. Here is a further vocabulary quiz. Briefly explain each of the following:
   a. Zero-stage vs. first- or second-stage financing.
   b. After-the-money valuation.
   c. Mezzanine financing.
   d. Road show.
   e. Best-efforts offer.
   f. Qualified institutional buyer.
   g. Blue-sky laws.

2. a. "A signal is credible only if it is costly." Explain why management's willingness to invest in Marvin's equity was a credible signal. Was its willingness to accept only part of the venture capital that would eventually be needed also a credible signal?
   b. "When managers take their reward in the form of increased leisure or executive jets, the cost is borne by the shareholders." Explain how First Meriam's financing package tackled this problem.

3. Describe the alternative procedures for IPOs of common stock. What are their advantages and disadvantages?

4. In the UK initial public offerings of common stock are usually sold by an *offer for sale*. Mr. Bean has observed that on average these stocks are underpriced by about 9 percent and for some years has followed a policy of applying for a constant proportion of each issue. He is therefore disappointed and puzzled to find that this policy has not resulted in a profit. Explain to him why this is so.

5. Get ahold of the prospectus for a recent IPO. How do the issue costs compare with (a) those of the Marvin issue and (b) those shown in Table 15.3? Can you suggest reasons for the differences?

6. Why are the costs of debt issues less than those of equity issues? List the possible reasons.

7. "For small issues of common stock, the issue costs to about 10 percent of the proceeds. This means that the opportunity cost of external equity capital is about 10 percentage points higher than that of retained earnings." Does the speaker have a point?

8. There are three reasons that a common stock issue might cause a fall in price: (a) the price fall is needed to absorb the extra supply, (b) the issue causes temporary price pressure until it has been digested, and (c) management has information that stockholders do not have. Explain these reasons more fully. Which do you find most plausible? Is there any way that you could seek to test whether you are right?

9. In what circumstances is a private placement preferable to a public issue? Explain.

10. Construct a simple example to show the following:
    a. Existing shareholders are made worse off when a company makes a cash offer of new stock below the market price.
    b. Existing shareholders are *not* made worse off when a company makes a rights issue of new stock below the market price even if the new stockholders do not wish to take up their rights.

11. In 1998 the Pandora Box Company made a rights issue at $5 a share of one new share for every four shares held. Before the issue there were 10 million shares outstanding and the share price was $6.
    a. What was the total amount of new money raised?
    b. What was the value of the right to buy one new share?
    d. What was the prospective stock price after the issue?
    e. How far could the total value of the company fall before shareholders would be unwilling to take up their rights?

12. Problem 11 contains details of a rights offering by Pandora Box. Suppose that the company had decided to issue new stock at $4. How many new shares would it have needed to sell to raise the same sum of money? Recalculate the answers to questions (b) to (d) in question 11. Show that the shareholders are just as well off if the company issues the shares at $4 rather than $5.

CHALLENGE QUESTIONS

1. a. Why do venture capital companies prefer to advance money in stages? If you were the management of Marvin Enterprises, would you have been happy with such an arrangement? With the benefit of hindsight did First Meriam gain or lose by advancing money in stages?
   b. The price at which First Meriam would invest more money in Marvin was not fixed in advance. But Marvin could have given First Meriam an *option* to buy more shares at a preset price. Would this have been better?
   c. At the second stage Marvin could have tried to raise money from another venture capital company in preference to First Meriam. To protect themselves against this, venture capital firms sometimes demand first refusal on new capital issues. Would you recommend this arrangement?

2. Explain the difference between a uniform-price auction and a discriminatory auction. Why might you prefer to sell securities by one method rather than another?

3. Here is recent financial data on Pisa Construction, Inc.

Stock price	$40	Market value of firm	$400,000
Number of shares	10,000	Earnings per share	$4
Book net worth	$500,000	Return on investment	8%

Pisa has not performed spectacularly to date. However, it wishes to issue new shares to obtain $80,000 to finance expansion into a promising market. Pisa's financial advisers think a stock issue is a poor choice because, among other reasons, "sale of stock at a price below book value per share can only depress the stock price and decrease shareholders' wealth." To prove the point they construct the following example: "Suppose 2,000 new shares are issued at $40 and the proceeds are invested. (Neglect issue costs.) Suppose return on investment doesn't change. Then

Book net worth = $580,000

Total earnings = .08(580,000) = $46,400

Earnings per share = $\frac{46,400}{12,000}$ = $3.87

Thus, EPS declines, book value per share declines, and share price will decline proportionately to $38.70."

Evaluate this argument with particular attention to the assumptions implicit in the numerical example.

4. Do you think that there could be a shortage of finance for new ventures? Should the government help to provide such finance and, if so, how?

PART FOUR RELATED WEBSITES

Useful sources of aggregate data on corporate financing for U.S. corporations include:

www.census.gov/csd/qfr (balance sheets and income statements)

www.federalreserve.gov/releases (sources and uses of funds data)

Material on the changing capital structure of corporations is provided on:

http://fisher.osu.edu/fin/resources education/credit

Sites on corporate governance and shareholder rights include:

www.corpgov.net

www.corpmon.com

www.thecorporatelibrary.com

For information on venture capital see:

www.ipo.com

www.nvca.org

www.redherring.com

www.tfibcm.com

www.thedeal.com

www.ventureeconomics.com

www.v1.com

www.vnpartners.com/primer (a useful primer on venture capital)

The following sites give information on recent IPOs:

www.hoovers.com/ipo

www.ipo.com

www.ipodata.com

www.redherring.com/ipo

www.thedeal.com

www.edgar-online.com/ipoexpress

Nasdaq provides a useful explanation of how to go public together with some data on new listings:

www.nasdaq.com/about/going_public.stm

Jay Ritter's home page is a mine of information on the behavior of IPOs:

http://bear.cba.ufl.edu/ritter

Underwriter league tables are published on:

www.tfibcm.com

This huge SEC database contains prospectuses and registration statements:

www.FreeEDGAR.com

PART FIVE

DIVIDEND POLICY
AND CAPITAL STRUCTURE

PHILIP MORRIS PRODUCES food, drink, and tobacco, including such well-known products as Marlboro cigarettes, Maxwell House coffee, and Miller's beer. In 2000 the company generated $11 billion in cash. From this it paid $4.5 billion as dividends and repurchased shares for $3.6 billion. The balance of $2.9 billion was reinvested in the business. This sum was far short of the cash needed to modernize production and to acquire new food businesses. To make up the shortfall, the company borrowed $10.9 billion and issued $100 million of common stock.

In considering how to finance its investments, Philip Morris's managers faced two basic decisions. One was the dividend decision. For example, the company could have paid a larger dividend. The cash for this would have had to come from buying back fewer shares or selling more stock. Chapter 16 discusses these choices.

The second decision was whether to raise cash by debt or equity. A company's mix of debt and equity is termed its *capital structure*. Chapters 17 through 19 examine the choice of capital structure and its implications for the cost of capital.

There are no simple answers to the dividend or capital structure decisions; for example, more debt can be good or bad, depending on the circumstances. But Part Five will supply the concepts and facts needed for assessing dividend policies or capital structure decisions in practice.

CHAPTER SIXTEEN

THE DIVIDEND CONTROVERSY

IN THIS CHAPTER we explain how companies set their dividend payments and we discuss the controversial question of how dividend policy affects the market value of the firm.

The first step toward understanding dividend policy is to recognize that the phrase means different things to different people. Therefore we must start by defining what *we* mean by it.

A firm's decisions about dividends are often mixed up with other financing and investment decisions. Some firms pay low dividends because management is optimistic about the firm's future and wishes to retain earnings for expansion. In this case the dividend is a by-product of the firm's capital budgeting decision. Suppose, however, that the future opportunities evaporate, that a dividend increase is announced, and that the stock price falls. How do we separate the impact of the dividend increase from the impact of investors' disappointment at the lost growth opportunities?

Another firm might finance capital expenditures largely by borrowing. This releases cash for dividends. In this case the firm's dividend is a by-product of the borrowing decision.

We must isolate dividend policy from other problems of financial management. The precise question we should ask is, What is the effect of a change in cash dividends paid, *given the firm's capital budgeting and borrowing decisions*? Of course the cash used to finance a dividend increase has to come from somewhere. If we fix the firm's investment outlays and borrowing, there is only one possible source—an issue of stock. Thus we define *dividend policy* as the trade-off between retaining earnings on the one hand and paying out cash and issuing new shares on the other.

This trade-off may seem artificial at first, for we do not observe firms scheduling a stock issue to offset every dividend payment. But there are many firms that pay dividends and also issue stock from time to time. They could avoid the stock issues by paying lower dividends. Many other firms restrict dividends so that they do *not* have to issue shares. They could issue stock occasionally and increase the dividend. Both groups of firms are facing the dividend policy trade-off.

Companies can hand back cash to their shareholders either by paying a dividend or by buying back their stock. So we start the chapter with some basic institutional material on dividends and stock repurchases. We then look at how companies decide on dividend payments and we show how both dividends and stock repurchases provide information to investors about company prospects. We then come to the central question, How does dividend policy affect firm value? You will see why we call this chapter "The Dividend Controversy."

 ## 16.1 HOW DIVIDENDS ARE PAID

The dividend is set by the firm's board of directors. The announcement of the dividend states that the payment will be made to all those stockholders who are registered on a particular *record date*. Then about two weeks later dividend checks are mailed to stockholders.

Shares are normally bought and sold *with dividend* or *cum dividend* until a few days before the record date, at which point they trade *ex dividend*. Investors who buy with dividend need not worry if their shares are not registered in time. The dividend must be paid over to them by the seller.

The company is not free to declare whatever dividend it chooses. Some restrictions may be imposed by lenders, who are concerned that excessive dividend payments would not leave enough in the kitty to pay the company's debts. State law also helps to protect the company's creditors against excessive dividend payments. For example, companies are not allowed to pay a dividend out of *legal capital,* which is generally defined as the par value of outstanding shares.[1]

Dividends Come in Different Forms

Most companies pay a *regular cash dividend* each quarter,[2] but occasionally this regular dividend is supplemented by a one-off *extra* or *special dividend.*[3]

Dividends are not always in the form of cash. Frequently companies also declare *stock dividends.* For example, Archer Daniels Midland has paid a yearly stock dividend of 5 percent for over 20 years. That means it sends each shareholder 5 extra shares for every 100 shares currently owned. You can see that a stock dividend is very much like a stock split. (For example, Archer Daniels Midland could have skipped one year's stock dividend and split each 100 shares into 105.) Both stock dividends and splits increase the number of shares, but the company's assets, profits, and total value are unaffected. So both reduce value *per share.* The distinction between the two is technical. A stock dividend is shown in the accounts as a transfer from retained earnings to equity capital, whereas a split is shown as a reduction in the par value of each share.

Many companies have automatic dividend reinvestment plans (DRIPs). Often the new shares are issued at a 5 percent discount from the market price; the firm offers this sweetener because it saves the underwriting costs of a regular share issue.[4] Sometimes 10 percent or more of total dividends will be reinvested under such plans.

Dividend Payers and Nonpayers

Fama and French, who have studied dividend payments in the United States, found that only about a fifth of public companies pay a dividend.[5] Some of the remainder paid dividends in the past but then fell on hard times and were forced to conserve cash. The other non-dividend-payers are mostly growth companies. They include such household names as Microsoft, Cisco, and Sun Microsystems, as well as many small, rapidly growing firms that have not yet reached full profitability. Of course, investors hope that these firms will eventually become profitable and that, when their rate of new investment slows down, they will be able to pay a dividend.

---

[1] Where there is no par value, legal capital is defined as part or all of the receipts from the issue of shares. Companies with wasting assets, such as mining companies, are sometimes permitted to pay out legal capital.

[2] In 1999 Disney changed to paying dividends once a year rather than quarterly. Disney has an unusually large number of investors with only a handful of shares. By making an annual payment, Disney reduced the substantial cost of mailing dividend checks to these investors.

[3] Special dividends are much less common than they used to be. The reasons are analyzed in H. DeAngelo, L. DeAngelo, and D. Skinner, "Special Dividends and the Evolution of Dividend Signaling," *Journal of Financial Economies* 57 (2000), pp. 309–354.

[4] Sometimes companies not only allow shareholders to reinvest dividends but also allow them to buy additional shares at a discount. In some cases substantial amounts of money have been invested. For example, AT&T has raised over $400 million a year through DRIPs. For an amusing and true rags-to-riches story, see M. S. Scholes and M. A. Wolfson, "Decentralized Investment Banking: The Case of Dividend-Reinvestment and Stock-Purchase Plans," *Journal of Financial Economics* 24 (September 1989), pp. 7–36.

[5] E. F. Fama and K. R. French, "Disappearing Dividends: Changing Firm Characteristics or Lower Propensity to Pay?" *Journal of Financial Economics* 60 (2001), pp. 3–43.

Fama and French also found that the proportion of dividend payers has declined sharply from a peak of 67 percent in 1978. One reason for this is that a large number of small growth companies have gone public in the last 20 years. Many of these newly listed companies were in high-tech industries, had no earnings, and did not pay dividends. But the influx of newly listed growth companies does not fully explain the declining popularity of dividends. It seems that even large and profitable firms are somewhat less likely to pay a dividend than was once the case.

Share Repurchase

When a firm wants to pay out cash to its shareholders, it usually declares a cash dividend. The alternative is to repurchase its own stock. The reacquired shares may be kept in the company's treasury and resold if the company needs money.

There is an important difference in the taxation of dividends and stock repurchases. Dividends are taxed as ordinary income, but stockholders who sell shares back to the firm pay tax only on capital gains realized in the sale. However, the Internal Revenue Service is on the lookout for companies that disguise dividends as repurchases, and it may decide that regular or proportional repurchases should be taxed as dividend payments.

There are three main ways to repurchase stock. The most common method is for the firm to announce that it plans to buy its stock in the open market, just like any other investor.[6] However, sometimes companies offer to buy back a stated number of shares at a fixed price, which is typically set at about 20 percent above the current market level. Shareholders can then choose whether to accept this offer. Finally, repurchase may take place by direct negotiation with a major shareholder. The most notorious instances are *greenmail* transactions, in which the target of a takeover attempt buys off the hostile bidder by repurchasing any shares that it has acquired. "Greenmail" means that these shares are repurchased by the target at a price which makes the bidder happy to leave the target alone. This price does not always make the target's shareholders happy, as we point out in Chapter 33.

Stock repurchase plans were big news in October 1987. On Monday, October 19, stock prices in the United States nose-dived more than 20 percent. The next day the board of Citicorp approved a plan to repurchase $250 million of the company's stock. Citicorp was soon joined by a number of other corporations whose managers were equally concerned about the market crash. Altogether, over a two-day period these firms announced plans to buy back $6.2 billion of stock. News of these huge buyback programs helped to stem the slide in stock prices.

Figure 16.1 shows that since the 1980s stock repurchases have mushroomed and are now larger in value than dividend payments. As we write this chapter at the end of October 2001, large new repurchase programs have just been announced in the last two weeks by IBM ($3.5 billion), McDonald's ($5 billion), and Citigroup ($5 billion). The biggest and most dramatic repurchases have been in the oil industry, where cash resources for a long time outran good capital investment opportunities. Exxon Mobil is in first place, having spent about $27 billion on repurchasing shares through year-end 2000.

---

[6]An alternative procedure is to employ a *Dutch auction*. In this case the firm states a series of prices at which it is prepared to repurchase stock. Shareholders submit offers declaring how many shares they wish to sell at each price and the company then calculates the lowest price at which it can buy the desired number of shares. This is another example of the uniform-price auction described in Section 15.3.

FIGURE 16.1

Stock repurchases and dividends in the United States, 1982–1999. (Figures in $ billions.)

Source: J. B. Carlson, "Why Is the Dividend Yield So Low?" *Federal Reserve Bank of Cleveland Economic Commentary*, April 1, 2001.

Repurchases are like bumper dividends; they cause large amounts of cash to be paid to investors. But they don't *substitute* for dividends. Most companies that repurchase stock are mature, profitable companies that also pay dividends. So the growth in stock repurchases cannot explain the declining proportion of dividend payers.

Suppose that a company has accumulated large amounts of unwanted cash or wishes to change its capital structure by replacing equity with debt. It will usually do so by repurchasing stock rather than by paying out large dividends. For example, consider the case of U.S. banks. In 1997 large bank holding companies paid out just under 40 percent of their earnings as dividends. There were few profitable investment opportunities for the remaining income, but the banks did not want to commit themselves in the long run to any larger dividend payments. They therefore returned the cash to shareholders not by upping the dividend rate, but by repurchasing $16 billion of stock.[7]

Given these differences in the way that dividends and repurchases are used, it is not surprising to find that repurchases are much more volatile than dividends. Repurchases mushroom during boom times as firms accumulate excess cash and wither in recessions.[8]

In recent years a number of countries, such as Japan and Sweden, have allowed repurchases for the first time. Some countries, however, continue to ban them entirely, while in many other countries repurchases are taxed as dividends, often at very high rates. In these countries firms that have amassed large mountains of cash may prefer to invest it on very low rates of return rather than to hand it back to shareholders, who could reinvest it in other firms that are short of cash.

---

[7]B. Hirtle, "Bank Holding Company Capital Ratios and Shareholder Payouts," *Federal Reserve Bank of New York: Current Issues in Economics and Finance* 4 (September 1998).

[8]These differences between dividends and repurchases are described in M. Jagannathan, C. Stephens, and M. S. Weisbach, "Financial Flexibility and the Choice between Dividends and Stock Repurchases," *Journal of Financial Economics* 57 (2000), pp. 355–384.

16.2 HOW DO COMPANIES DECIDE ON DIVIDEND PAYMENTS?

Lintner's Model

In the mid-1950s John Lintner conducted a classic series of interviews with corporate managers about their dividend policies.[9] His description of how dividends are determined can be summarized in four "stylized facts":[10]

1. Firms have long-run target dividend payout ratios. Mature companies with stable earnings generally pay out a high proportion of earnings; growth companies have low payouts (if they pay any dividends at all).

2. Managers focus more on dividend changes than on absolute levels. Thus, paying a $2.00 dividend is an important financial decision if last year's dividend was $1.00, but no big deal if last year's dividend was $2.00.

3. Dividend changes follow shifts in long-run, sustainable earnings. Managers "smooth" dividends. Transitory earnings changes are unlikely to affect dividend payouts.

4. Managers are reluctant to make dividend changes that might have to be reversed. They are particularly worried about having to rescind a dividend increase.

Lintner developed a simple model which is consistent with these facts and explains dividend payments well. Here it is: Suppose that a firm always stuck to its target payout ratio. Then the dividend payment in the coming year (DIV_1) would equal a constant proportion of earnings per share (EPS_1):

$$DIV_1 = \text{target dividend}$$
$$= \text{target ratio} \times EPS_1$$

The dividend *change* would equal

$$DIV_1 - DIV_0 = \text{target change}$$
$$= \text{target ratio} \times EPS_1 - DIV_0$$

A firm that always stuck to its target payout ratio would have to change its dividend whenever earnings changed. But the managers in Lintner's survey were reluctant to do this. They believed that shareholders prefer a steady progression in dividends. Therefore, even if circumstances appeared to warrant a large increase in their company's dividend, they would move only partway toward their target payment. Their dividend changes therefore seemed to conform to the following model:

$$DIV_1 - DIV_0 = \text{adjustment rate} \times \text{target change}$$
$$= \text{adjustment rate} \times (\text{target ratio} \times EPS_1 - DIV_0)$$

The more conservative the company, the more slowly it would move toward its target and, therefore, the *lower* would be its adjustment rate.

---

[9] J. Lintner, "Distribution of Incomes of Corporations among Dividends, Retained Earnings, and Taxes," *American Economic Review* 46 (May 1956), pp. 97–113.

[10] The stylized facts are given by Terry A. Marsh and Robert C. Merton, "Dividend Behavior for the Aggregate Stock Market," *Journal of Business* 60 (January 1987), pp. 1–40. See pp. 5–6. We have paraphrased and embellished.

Lintner's simple model suggests that the dividend depends in part on the firm's current earnings and in part on the dividend for the previous year, which in turn depends on that year's earnings and the dividend in the year before. Therefore, if Lintner is correct, we should be able to describe dividends in terms of a weighted average of current and past earnings.[11] The probability of an increase in the dividend rate should be greatest when *current* earnings have increased; it should be somewhat less when only the earnings from the previous year have increased; and so on. An extensive study by Fama and Babiak confirmed this hypothesis.[12] Their tests of Lintner's model suggest that it provides a fairly good explanation of how companies decide on the dividend rate, but it is not the whole story. We would expect managers to take future prospects as well as past achievements into account when setting the payment. As we shall see in the next section, that is indeed the case.

16.3 THE INFORMATION IN DIVIDENDS AND STOCK REPURCHASES

In some countries you cannot rely on the information that companies provide. Passion for secrecy and a tendency to construct multilayered corporate organizations produce asset and earnings figures that are next to meaningless. Some people say that, thanks to creative accounting, the situation is little better for some companies in the United States.

How does an investor in such a world separate marginally profitable firms from the real money makers? One clue is dividends. Investors can't read managers' minds, but they can learn from managers' actions. They know that a firm which reports good earnings and pays a generous dividend is putting its money where its mouth is. We can understand, therefore, why investors would value the information content of dividends and would refuse to believe a firm's reported earnings unless they were backed up by an appropriate dividend policy.

Of course, firms can cheat in the short run by overstating earnings and scraping up cash to pay a generous dividend. But it is hard to cheat in the long run, for a firm that is not making enough money will not have enough cash to pay out. If a firm chooses a high dividend payout without the cash flow to back it up, that firm will ultimately have to reduce its investment plans or turn to investors for additional debt or equity financing. All of these consequences are costly. Therefore, most managers don't increase dividends until they are confident that sufficient cash will flow in to pay them.

---

[11]This can be demonstrated as follows: Dividends per share in time t are

(1)
$$DIV_t = aT(EPS_t) + (1 - a)DIV_{t-1}$$

where a is the adjustment rate and T is the target payout ratio. But the same relationship holds in $t - 1$:

(2)
$$DIV_{t-1} = aT(EPS_{t-1}) + (1 - a)DIV_{t-2}$$

Substitute for DIV_{t-1} in (1):

$$DIV_t = aT(EPS_t) + aT(1 - a)(EPS_{t-1}) + (1 - a)^2 DIV_{t-2}$$

We can make similar substitutions for DIV_{t-2}, DIV_{t-3}, etc., thereby obtaining

$$DIV_t = aT(EPS_t) + aT(1 - a)(EPS_{t-1}) + aT(1 - a)^2(EPS_{t-2}) + \cdots + aT(1 - a)^n(EPS_{t-n})$$

[12]E. F. Fama and H. Babiak, "Dividend Policy: An Empirical Analysis," *Journal of the American Statistical Association* 63 (December 1968), pp. 1132–1161.

There is some evidence that managers do look to the future when they set the dividend payment. For example, Benartzi, Michaely, and Thaler found that dividend increases generally followed a couple of years of unusual earnings growth.[13] Although this rapid growth did not persist beyond the year in which the dividend was changed, for the most part the higher level of earnings was maintained and declines in earnings were relatively uncommon. More striking evidence that dividends are set with an eye to the future is provided by Healy and Palepu, who focus on companies that pay a dividend for the first time.[14] On average earnings jumped 43 percent in the year that the dividend was paid. If managers thought that this was a temporary windfall, they might have been cautious about committing themselves to paying out cash. But it looks as if they had good reason to be confident about prospects, for over the next four years earnings grew on average by a further 164 percent.

If dividends provide some reassurance that the new level of earnings is likely to be sustained, it is no surprise to find that announcements of dividend cuts are usually taken by investors as bad news (stock price falls) and that dividend increases are good news (stock price rises). For example, in the case of the dividend initiations studied by Healy and Palepu, the announcement of the dividend resulted in an abnormal rise of 4 percent in the stock price.[15]

Notice that investors do not get excited about the *level* of a company's dividend; they worry about the *change*, which they view as an important indicator of the sustainability of earnings. In Finance in the News we illustrate how an unexpected change in dividends can cause the stock price to bounce back and forth as investors struggle to interpret the significance of the change.

It seems that in some other countries investors are less preoccupied with dividend changes. For example, in Japan there is a much closer relationship between corporations and major stockholders, and therefore information may be more easily shared with investors. Consequently, Japanese corporations are more prone to cut their dividends when there is a drop in earnings, but investors do not mark the stocks down as sharply as in the United States.[16]

The Information Content of Share Repurchase

Share repurchases, like dividends, are a way to hand cash back to shareholders. But unlike dividends, share repurchases are frequently a one-off event. So a company that announces a repurchase program is not making a long-term commitment to earn and distribute more cash. The information in the announcement of a share repurchase program is therefore likely to be different from the information in a dividend payment.

Companies repurchase shares when they have accumulated more cash than they can invest profitably or when they wish to increase their debt levels. Neither

---

[13]See L. Benartzi, R. Michaely, and R. H. Thaler, "Do Changes in Dividends Signal the Future or the Past," *Journal of Finance* 52 (July 1997), pp. 1007–1034. Similar results are reported in H. DeAngelo, L. DeAngelo, and D. Skinner, "Reversal of Fortune: Dividend Signaling and the Disappearance of Sustained Earnings Growth," *Journal of Financial Economics* 40 (1996), pp. 341–372.

[14]See P. Healy and K. Palepu, "Earnings Information Conveyed by Dividend Initiations and Omissions," *Journal of Financial Economics* 21 (1988), pp. 149–175.

[15]Healy and Palepu also looked at companies that *stopped* paying a dividend. In this case the stock price on average declined by an abnormal 9.5 percent on the announcement and earnings fell over the next four quarters.

[16]The dividend policies of Japanese *keiretsus* are analyzed in K. L. Dewenter and V. A. Warther, "Dividends, Asymmetric Information, and Agency Conflicts: Evidence from a Comparison of the Dividend Policies of Japanese and U.S. Firms," *Journal of Finance* 53 (June 1998), pp. 879–904.

THE DIVIDEND CUT HEARD 'ROUND THE WORLD

On May 9, 1994, FPL Group, the parent company of Florida Power & Light Company, announced a 32 percent reduction in its quarterly dividend payout, from 62 cents per share to 42 cents. In its announcement, FPL did its best to spell out to investors why it had taken such an unusual step. It stressed that it had studied the situation carefully and that, given the prospect of increased competition in the electric utility industry, the company's high dividend payout ratio (which had averaged 90 percent in the past 4 years) was no longer in the shareholders' best interests. The new policy resulted in a payout of about 60 percent of the previous year's earnings. Management also announced that, starting in 1995, the dividend payout would be reviewed in February instead of May to reinforce the linkage between dividends and annual earnings. In doing so, the company wanted to minimize unintended "signaling effects" from any future changes in dividends.

At the same time that it announced this change in dividend policy, FPL Group's board authorized the repurchase of up to 10 million shares of common stock over the next 3 years. In adopting this strategy, the company noted that changes in the U.S. tax code since 1990 had made capital gains more attractive than dividends to shareholders.

Besides providing a more tax-efficient means of distributing excess cash to its stockholders, FPL's substitution of stock repurchases for dividends was also designed to increase the company's financial flexibility in preparation for a new era of heightened competition among utilities. Although much of the cash savings from the dividend cut would be returned to shareholders in the form of stock repurchases, the rest would be used to retire debt and so reduce the company's leverage ratio. This deleveraging was intended to prepare the company for the likely increase in business risk and to provide some slack that would allow the company to take advantage of future business opportunities.

All this sounded logical, but investors' first reaction was dismay. On the day of the announcement, the stock price fell nearly 14 percent. But, as analysis digested the news and considered the reasons for the reduction, they concluded that the action was not a signal of financial distress but a well-considered strategic decision. This view spread throughout the financial community, and FPL's stock price began to recover. By the middle of the following month at least 15 major brokerage houses had placed FPL's common stock on their "buy" lists and the price had largely recovered from its earlier fall.

Source: Modified from D. Soter, E. Brigham, and P. Evanson, "The Dividend Cut 'Heard 'Round the World': The Case of FPL," *Journal of Applied Corporate Finance* 9 (Spring 1996), pp. 4–15.

circumstance is good news in itself, but shareholders are frequently relieved to see companies paying out the excess cash rather than frittering it away on unprofitable investments. Shareholders also know that firms with large quantities of debt to service are less likely to squander cash. A study by Comment and Jarrell, who looked at the announcements of open-market repurchase programs, found that on average they resulted in an abnormal price rise of 2 percent.[17]

[17]See R. Comment and G. Jarrell, "The Relative Signalling Power of Dutch-Auction and Fixed Price Self-Tender Offers and Open-Market Share Repurchases," *Journal of Finance* 46 (September 1991), pp. 1243–1271. There is also evidence of continuing superior performance during the years following a repurchase announcement. See D. Ikenberry, J. Lakonishok, and T. Vermaelen, "Market Underreaction to Open Market Share Repurchases," *Journal of Financial Economics* 39 (1995), pp. 181–208.

Stock repurchases may also be used to signal a manager's confidence in the future. Suppose that you, the manager, believe that your stock is substantially undervalued. You announce that the company is prepared to buy back a fifth of its stock at a price that is 20 percent above the current market price. But (you say) you are certainly not going to sell any of your own stock at that price. Investors jump to the obvious conclusion—you must believe that the stock is good value even at 20 percent above the current price.

When companies offer to repurchase their stock at a premium, senior management and directors usually commit to hold onto their stock.[18] So it is not surprising that researchers have found that announcements of offers to buy back shares above the market price have prompted a larger rise in the stock price, averaging about 11 percent.[19]

 ## 16.4 THE DIVIDEND CONTROVERSY

We have seen that a dividend increase indicates management's optimism about earnings and thus affects the stock price. But the jump in stock price that accompanies an unexpected dividend increase would happen eventually anyway as information about future earnings comes out through other channels. We now ask whether the dividend decision *changes* the value of the stock, rather than simply providing a *signal* of stock value.

One endearing feature of economics is that it can always accommodate not just two but three opposing points of view. And so it is with the controversy about dividend policy. On the right there is a conservative group which believes that an increase in dividend payout increases firm value. On the left, there is a radical group which believes that an increase in payout reduces value. And in the center there is a middle-of-the-road party which claims that dividend policy makes no difference.

The middle-of-the-road party was founded in 1961 by Miller and Modigliani (always referred to as "MM" or "M and M"), when they published a theoretical paper showing the irrelevance of dividend policy in a world without taxes, transaction costs, or other market imperfections.[20] By the standards of 1961 MM were leftist radicals, because at that time most people believed that even under idealized assumptions increased dividends made shareholders better off.[21] But now MM's proof is generally accepted as correct, and the argument has shifted to whether taxes or other market imperfections alter the situation. In the process MM have been pushed toward the center by a new leftist party which argues for *low* dividends. The leftists' position is based on MM's argument modified to take account

---

[18]Not only do managers' hold onto their stock; on average they also add to their holdings *before* the announcement of a repurchase. See D. S. Lee, W. Mikkelson, and M. M. Partch, "Managers Trading around Stock Repurchases," *Journal of Finance* 47 (1992), pp. 1947–1961.

[19]See R. Comment and G. Jarrell, *op. cit.*

[20]M. H. Miller and F. Modigliani: "Dividend Policy, Growth and the Valuation of Shares," *Journal of Business* 34 (October 1961), pp. 411–433.

[21]Not *everybody* believed dividends make shareholders better off. MM's arguments were anticipated in 1938 in J. B. Williams, *The Theory of Investment Value*, Harvard University Press, Cambridge, MA, 1938. Also, a proof very similar to MM's was developed by J. Lintner in "Dividends, Earnings, Leverage, Stock Prices and the Supply of Capital to Corporations," *Review of Economics and Statistics* 44 (August 1962), pp. 243–269.

of taxes and costs of issuing securities. The conservatives are still with us, relying on essentially the same arguments as in 1961.

Why should you care about this debate? Of course, if you help to decide your company's dividend payment, you will want to know how it affects value. But there is a more general reason than that. We have up to this point assumed that the company's investment decision is independent of its financing policy. In that case a good project is a good project is a good project, no matter who undertakes it or how it is ultimately financed. If dividend policy does not affect value, that is still true. But perhaps it *does* affect value. In that case the attractiveness of a new project may depend on where the money is coming from. For example, if investors prefer companies with high payouts, companies might be reluctant to take on investments financed by retained earnings.

We begin our discussion of dividend policy with a presentation of MM's original argument. Then we will undertake a critical appraisal of the positions of the three parties. Perhaps we should warn you before we start that our own position is mostly middle of the road but sometimes marginally leftist. (As investors we prefer low dividends because we don't like paying taxes!)

Dividend Policy Is Irrelevant in Perfect Capital Markets

In their classic 1961 article MM argued as follows: Suppose your firm has settled on its investment program. You have worked out how much of this program can be financed from borrowing, and you plan to meet the remaining funds requirement from retained earnings. Any surplus money is to be paid out as dividends.

Now think what happens if you want to increase the dividend payment without changing the investment and borrowing policy. The extra money must come from somewhere. If the firm fixes its borrowing, the only way it can finance the extra dividend is to print some more shares and sell them. The new stockholders are going to part with their money only if you can offer them shares that are worth as much as they cost. But how can the firm do this when its assets, earnings, investment opportunities, and, therefore, market value are all unchanged? The answer is that there must be a *transfer of value* from the old to the new stockholders. The new ones get the newly printed shares, each one worth less than before the dividend change was announced, and the old ones suffer a capital loss on their shares. The capital loss borne by the old shareholders just offsets the extra cash dividend they receive.

Figure 16.2 shows how this transfer of value occurs. Our hypothetical company pays out a third of its total value as a dividend and it raises the money to do so by selling new shares. The capital loss suffered by the old stockholders is represented by the reduction in the size of the burgundy boxes. But that capital loss is exactly offset by the fact that the new money raised (the blue boxes) is paid over to them as dividends.

Does it make any difference to the old stockholders that they receive an extra dividend payment plus an offsetting capital loss? It might if that were the only way they could get their hands on cash. But as long as there are efficient capital markets, they can raise the cash by selling shares. Thus the old shareholders can cash in either by persuading the management to pay a higher dividend or by selling some of their shares. In either case there will be a transfer of value from old to new shareholders. The only difference is that in the former case this transfer is caused

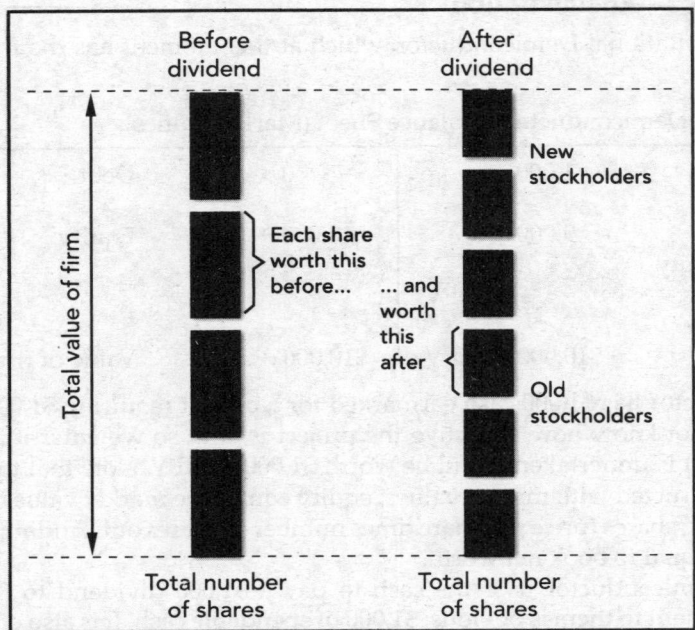

FIGURE 16.2

This firm pays out a third of its worth as a dividend and raises the money by selling new shares. The transfer of value to the new stockholders is equal to the dividend payment. The total value of the firm is unaffected.

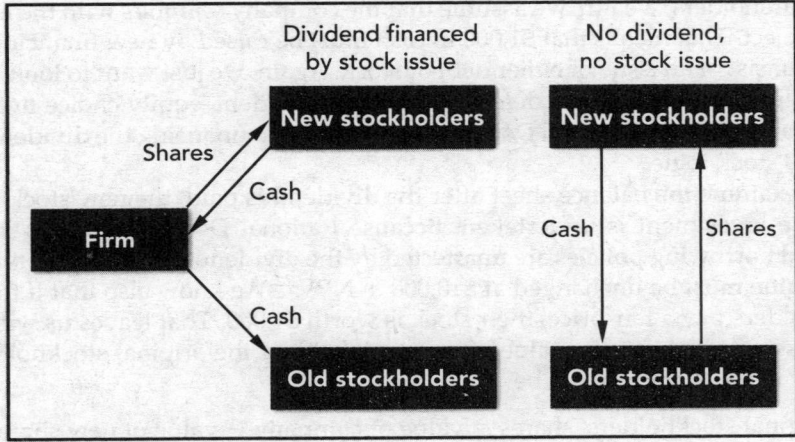

FIGURE 16.3

Two ways of raising cash for the firm's original shareholders. In each case the cash received is offset by a decline in the value of the old stockholders' claim on the firm. If the firm pays a dividend, each share is worth less because more shares have to be issued against the firm's assets. If the old stockholders sell some of their shares, each share is worth the same but the old stockholders have fewer shares.

by a dilution in the value of each of the firm's shares, and in the latter case it is caused by a reduction in the number of shares held by the old shareholders. The two alternatives are compared in Figure 16.3.

Because investors do not need dividends to get their hands on cash, they will not pay higher prices for the shares of firms with high payouts. Therefore firms ought not to worry about dividend policy. They should let dividends fluctuate as a by-product of their investment and financing decisions.

Dividend Irrelevance—An Illustration

Consider the case of Rational Demiconductor, which at this moment has the following balance sheet:

Rational Demiconductor's Balance Sheet (Market Values)

Cash ($1,000 held for investment)	1,000	0	Debt
Fixed assets	9,000	10,000 + NPV	Equity
Investment opportunity ($1,000 investment required)	NPV		
Total asset value	$10,000 + NPV	$10,000 + NPV	Value of firm

Rational Demiconductor has $1,000 cash earmarked for a project requiring $1,000 investment. We do not know how attractive the project is, and so we enter it at NPV; after the project is undertaken it will be worth $1,000 + NPV. Note that the balance sheet is constructed with market values; equity equals the market value of the firm's outstanding shares (price per share times number of shares outstanding). It is not necessarily equal to book net worth.

Now Rational Demiconductor uses the cash to pay a $1,000 dividend to its stockholders. The benefit to them is obvious: $1,000 of spendable cash. It is also obvious that there must be a cost. The cash is not free.

Where does the money for the dividend come from? Of course, the immediate source of funds is Rational Demiconductor's cash account. But this cash was earmarked for the investment project. Since we want to isolate the effects of dividend policy on shareholders' wealth, we assume that the company *continues* with the investment project. That means that $1,000 in cash must be raised by new financing. This could consist of an issue of either debt or stock. Again, we just want to look at dividend policy for now, and we defer discussion of the debt–equity choice until Chapters 17 and 18. Thus Rational Demiconductor ends up financing the dividend with a $1,000 stock issue.

Now we examine the balance sheet after the dividend is paid, the new stock is sold, and the investment is undertaken. Because Rational Demiconductor's investment and borrowing policies are unaffected by the dividend payment, its *overall* market value must be unchanged at $10,000 + NPV.[22] We know also that if the new stockholders pay a fair price, their stock is worth $1,000. That leaves us with only one missing number—the value of the stock held by the original stockholders. It is easy to see that this must be

$$\text{Value of original stockholders' shares} = \text{value of company} - \text{value of new shares}$$
$$= (10,000 + \text{NPV}) - 1,000$$
$$= \$9,000 + \text{NPV}$$

The old shareholders have received a $1,000 cash dividend and incurred a $1,000 capital loss. Dividend policy doesn't matter.

By paying out $1,000 with one hand and taking it back with the other, Rational Demiconductor is recycling cash. To suggest that this makes shareholders better off is like advising a cook to cool the kitchen by leaving the refrigerator door open.

---

[22]All other factors that might affect Rational Demiconductor's value are assumed constant. This is not a necessary assumption, but it simplifies the proof of MM's theory.

Of course, our proof ignores taxes, issue costs, and a variety of other complications. We will turn to those items in a moment. The really crucial assumption in our proof is that the new shares are sold at a fair price. The shares sold to raise $1,000 must actually be *worth* $1,000.[23] In other words, we have assumed efficient capital markets.

Calculating Share Price

We have assumed that Rational Demiconductor's new shares can be sold at a fair price, but what is that price and how many new shares are issued?

Suppose that before this dividend payout the company had 1,000 shares outstanding and that the project had an NPV of $2,000. Then the old stock was worth in total $10,000 + NPV = $12,000, which works out at $12,000/1,000 = $12 per share. After the company has paid the dividend and completed the financing, this old stock is worth $9,000 + NPV = $11,000. That works out at $11,000/1,000 = $11 per share. In other words, the price of the old stock falls by the amount of the $1 per share dividend payment.

Now let us look at the new stock. Clearly, after the issue this must sell at the same price as the rest of the stock. In other words, it must be valued at $11. If the new stockholders get fair value, the company must issue $1,000/$11 or 91 new shares in order to raise the $1,000 that it needs.

Share Repurchase

We have seen that any increased cash dividend payment must be offset by a stock issue if the firm's investment and borrowing policies are held constant. In effect the stockholders finance the extra dividend by selling off part of their ownership of the firm. Consequently, the stock price falls by just enough to offset the extra dividend.

This process can also be run backward. With investment and borrowing policy given, any *reduction* in dividends must be balanced by a reduction in the number of shares issued or by repurchase of previously outstanding stock. But if the process has no effect on stockholders' wealth when run forward, it must likewise have no effect when run in reverse. We will confirm this by another numerical example.

Suppose that a technical discovery reveals that Rational Demiconductor's new project is not a positive-NPV venture but a sure loser. Management announces that the project is to be discarded and that the $1,000 earmarked for it will be paid out as an extra dividend of $1 per share. After the dividend payout, the balance sheet is

Rational Demiconductor's Balance Sheet (Market Values)

Cash	$ 0	$ 0	Debt
Existing fixed assets	9,000	9,000	Equity
New project	0		
Total asset value	$ 9,000	$ 9,000	Total firm value

Since there are 1,000 shares outstanding, the stock price is $10,000/1,000 = $10 before the dividend payment and $9,000/1,000 = $9 *after* the payment.

---

[23]The "old" shareholders get all the benefit of the positive NPV project. The new shareholders require only a fair rate of return. They are making a zero-NPV investment.

What if Rational Demiconductor uses the $1,000 to repurchase stock instead? As long as the company pays a fair price for the stock, the $1,000 buys $1,000/$10 = 100 shares. That leaves 900 shares worth 900 × $10 = $9,000.

As expected, we find that switching from cash dividends to share repurchase has no effect on shareholders' wealth. They forgo a $1 cash dividend but end up holding shares worth $10 instead of $9.

Note that when shares are repurchased the transfer of value is in favor of those stockholders who do not sell. They forgo any cash dividend but end up owning a larger slice of the firm. In effect they are using their share of Rational Demiconductor's $1,000 distribution to buy out some of their fellow shareholders.

Stock Repurchase and Valuation

Valuing the equity of a firm that repurchases its own stock can be confusing. Let's work through a simple example.

Company X has 100 shares outstanding. It earns $1,000 a year, all of which is paid out as a dividend. The dividend per share is, therefore, $1,000/100 = $10. Suppose that investors expect the dividend to be maintained indefinitely and that they require a return of 10 percent. In this case the value of each share is $PV_{share} = $10/.10 = 100. Since there are 100 shares outstanding, the *total* market value of the equity is $PV_{equity} = 100 \times $100 = $10,000$. Note that we could reach the same conclusion by discounting the *total* dividend payments to shareholders ($PV_{equity} = $1,000/.10 = $10,000$).[24]

Now suppose the company announces that instead of paying a cash dividend in year 1, it will spend the same money repurchasing its shares in the open market. The total expected cash flows to shareholders (dividends and cash from stock repurchase) are unchanged at $1,000. So the total value of the equity also remains at $1,000/.10 = $10,000. This is made up of the value of the $1,000 received from the stock repurchase in year 1 ($PV_{repurchase} = $1,000/1.1 = 909.1) and the value of the $1,000-a-year dividend starting in year 2 [$PV_{dividends} = $1,000/(.10 \times 1.1) = $9,091$]. Each share continues to be worth $10,000/100 = $100 just as before.

Think now about those shareholders who plan to sell their stock back to the company. They will demand a 10 percent return on their investment. So the price at which the firm buys back shares must be 10 percent higher than today's price, or $110. The company spends $1,000 buying back its stock, which is sufficient to buy $1,000/$110 = 9.09 shares.

The company starts with 100 shares, it buys back 9.09, and therefore 90.91 shares remain outstanding. Each of these shares can look forward to a dividend stream of $1,000/90.91 = $11 per share. So after the repurchase shareholders have 10 percent fewer shares, but earnings and dividends per share are 10 percent higher. An investor who owns one share today that is not repurchased will receive no dividends in year 1 but can look forward to $11 a year thereafter. The value of each share is therefore $11/(.1 \times 1.1) = 100.

Our example illustrates several points. First, other things equal, company value is unaffected by the decision to repurchase stock rather than to pay a cash divi-

---

[24]When valuing the entire equity, remember that if the company is expected to issue additional shares in the future, we should include the dividend payments on these shares only if we also include the amount that investors pay for them. See Chapter 4.

dend. Second, when valuing the entire equity you need to include both the cash that is paid out as dividends and the cash that is used to repurchase stock. Third, when calculating the cash flow *per share*, it is double counting to include both the forecasted dividends per share *and* the cash received from repurchase (if you sell back your share, you don't get any subsequent dividends). Fourth, a firm that repurchases stock instead of paying dividends reduces the number of shares outstanding but produces an offsetting increase in earnings and dividends per share.

16.5 THE RIGHTISTS

Much of traditional finance literature has advocated high payout ratios. Here, for example, is a statement of the rightist position made by Graham and Dodd in 1951:

> The considered and continuous verdict of the stock market is overwhelmingly in favor of liberal dividends as against niggardly ones. The common stock investor must take this judgment into account in the valuation of stock for purchase. It is now becoming standard practice to evaluate common stock by applying one multiplier to that portion of the earnings paid out in dividends and a much smaller multiplier to the undistributed balance.[25]

This belief in the importance of dividend policy is common in the business and investment communities. Stockholders and investment advisers continually pressure corporate treasurers for increased dividends. When we had wage-price controls in the United States in 1974, it was deemed necessary to have dividend controls as well. As far as we know, no labor union objected that "dividend policy is irrelevant." After all, if wages are reduced, the employee is worse off. Dividends are the shareholders' wages, and so if the payout ratio is reduced the shareholder is worse off. Therefore fair play requires that wage controls be matched by dividend controls. Right?

Wrong! You should be able to see through that kind of argument by now. But there are more serious arguments for a high-payout policy that rely either on market imperfections or the effect of dividend policy on management incentives.

Market Imperfections

Those who favor large dividend payments point out that there is a natural clientele for high-payout stocks. For example, some financial institutions are legally restricted from holding stocks lacking established dividend records.[26] Trusts and endowment funds may prefer high-dividend stocks because dividends are regarded as spendable "income," whereas capital gains are "additions to principal." Some observers have argued that, although individuals are free to spend capital, they

---

[25]These authors later qualified this statement, recognizing the willingness of investors to pay high price–earnings multiples for growth stocks. But otherwise they stuck to their position. We quoted their 1951 statement because of its historical importance. Compare B. Graham and D. L. Dodd, *Security Analysis: Principles and Techniques*, 3rd ed., McGraw-Hill Book Company, New York, 1951, p. 432, with B. Graham, D. L. Dodd, and S. Cottle, *Security Analysis: Principles and Techniques*, 4th ed., McGraw-Hill Book Company, New York, 1962, p. 480.

[26]Most colleges and universities are legally free to spend capital gains from their endowments, but they usually restrict spending to a moderate percentage which can be covered by dividends and interest receipts.

may welcome the self-discipline that comes from spending only dividend in-come.[27] If so, they also may favor stocks that provide more spendable cash.

There is also a natural clientele of investors who look to their stock portfolios for a steady source of cash to live on. In principle this cash could be easily generated from stocks paying no dividends at all; the investor could just sell off a small frac-tion of his or her holdings from time to time. But it is simpler and cheaper for IBM to send a quarterly check than for its stockholders to sell, say, one share every three months. IBM's regular dividends relieve many of its shareholders of transaction costs and considerable inconvenience.[28]

Dividends, Investment Policy, and Management Incentives

If it is true that nobody gains or loses from shifts in dividend policy, why do share-holders often clamor for higher dividends? There is one good reason that applies particularly to mature companies with plenty of free cash flow but few profitable investment opportunities. Shareholders of such companies don't always trust managers to spend retained earnings wisely and they fear that the money will be plowed back into building a larger empire rather than a more profitable one. In such cases investors may clamor for generous dividends not because dividends are valuable in themselves, but because they signal a more careful, value-oriented in-vestment policy.[29]

 ## 16.6 TAXES AND THE RADICAL LEFT

The left-wing dividend creed is simple: Whenever dividends are taxed more heav-ily than capital gains, firms should pay the lowest cash dividend they can get away with. Available cash should be retained or used to repurchase shares.

By shifting their distribution policies in this way, corporations can transmute dividends into capital gains. If this financial alchemy results in lower taxes, it should be welcomed by any taxpaying investor. That is the basic point made by the leftist party when it argues for low-dividend payout.

If dividends are taxed more heavily than capital gains, investors should pay more for stocks with low dividend yields. In other words, they should accept a lower *pretax* rate of return from securities offering returns in the form of capital gains rather than dividends. Table 16.1 illustrates this. The stocks of firms A and B are equally risky. Investors expect A to be worth $112.50 per share next year. The

---

[27]See H. Shefrin and M. Statman, "Explaining Investor Preference for Cash Dividends," *Journal of Fi-nancial Economics* 13 (June 1984), pp. 253–282.

[28]Those advocating generous dividends might go on to argue that a regular cash dividend relieves stockholders of the risk of having to sell shares at "temporarily depressed" prices. Of course, the firm will have to issue shares eventually to finance the dividend, but (the argument goes) the firm can pick the *right time* to sell. If firms really try to do this and if they are successful—two big *ifs*—then stock-holders of high-payout firms might indeed get something for nothing.

[29]La Porta et al. argue that in countries such as the United States minority shareholders are able to pres-sure companies to disgorge cash and this prevents managers from using too high a proportion of earn-ings to benefit themselves. By contrast, companies pay out a smaller proportion of earnings in those countries where the law is more relaxed about overinvestment and empire building. See R. La Porta, F. Lopez-de-Silanes, A. Shleifer, and R. W. Vishny, "Agency Problems and Dividend Policies around the World," *Journal of Finance* 55 (February 2000), pp. 1–34.

	Firm A (No Dividend)	Firm B (High Dividend)
Next year's price	$112.50	$102.50
Dividend	$0	$10.00
Total pretax payoff	$112.50	$112.50
Today's stock price	$100	$97.78
Capital gain	$12.50	$4.72
Before-tax rate of return	$100 \times \left(\dfrac{12.5}{100}\right) = 12.5\%$	$100 \times \left(\dfrac{14.72}{97.78}\right) = 15.05\%$
Tax on dividend at 40%	$0	$.40 \times 10 = \$4.00$
Tax on capital gains at 20%	$.20 \times 12.50 = \$2.50$	$.20 \times 4.72 = \$.94$
Total after-tax income (dividends plus capital gains less taxes)	$(0 + 12.50) - 2.50 = \$10.00$	$(10.00 + 4.72) - (4.00 + .94)$ $= \$9.78$
After-tax rate of return	$100 \times \left(\dfrac{10}{100}\right) = 10.0\%$	$100 \times \left(\dfrac{9.78}{97.78}\right) = 10.0\%$

TABLE 16.1

Effects of a shift on dividend policy when dividends are taxed more heavily than capital gains. The high-payout stock (firm B) must sell at a lower price to provide the same after-tax return.

share price of B is expected to be only $102.50, but a $10 dividend is also forecasted, and so the total pretax payoff is the same, $112.50.

Yet we find B's stock selling for less than A's and therefore offering a higher pretax rate of return. The reason is obvious: Investors prefer A because its return comes in the form of capital gains. Table 16.1 shows that A and B are equally attractive to investors who pay a 40 percent tax on dividends and a 20 percent tax on capital gains. Each offers a 10 percent return after all taxes. The difference between the stock prices of A and B is exactly the present value of the extra taxes the investors face if they buy B.[30]

The management of B could save these extra taxes by eliminating the $10 dividend and using the released funds to repurchase stock instead. Its stock price should rise to $100 as soon as the new policy is announced.

Why Pay Any Dividends at All?

It is true that when companies make very large one-off distributions of cash to shareholders, they generally choose to do so by share repurchase than by a large temporary hike in dividends. But if dividends attract more tax than capital gains, why should any firm ever pay a cash dividend? If cash is to be distributed to stockholders, isn't share repurchase always the best channel for doing so? The leftist position seems to call not just for low payouts but for *zero* payouts whenever capital gains have a tax advantage.

---

[30]Michael Brennan has modeled what happens when you introduce taxes into an otherwise perfect market. He found that the capital asset pricing model continues to hold, but on an *after-tax* basis. Thus, if A and B have the same beta, they should offer the same after-tax rate of return. The spread between pretax and post-tax returns is determined by a weighted average of investors' tax rates. See M. J. Brennan, "Taxes, Market Valuation and Corporate Financial Policy," *National Tax Journal* 23 (December 1970), pp. 417–427.

Few leftists would go quite that far. A firm that eliminates dividends and starts repurchasing stock on a regular basis may find that the Internal Revenue Service recognizes the repurchase program for what it really is and taxes the payments accordingly. That is why financial managers do not usually announce that they are repurchasing shares to save stockholders taxes; they give some other reason.[31]

The low-payout party has nevertheless maintained that the market rewards firms that have low-payout policies. They have claimed that firms which paid dividends and as a result had to issue shares from time to time were making a serious mistake. Any such firm was essentially financing its dividends by issuing stock; it should have cut its dividends at least to the point at which stock issues were unnecessary. This would not only have saved taxes for shareholders but it would also have avoided the transaction costs of the stock issues.[32]

Empirical Evidence on Dividends and Taxes

It is hard to deny that taxes are important to investors. You can see that in the bond market. Interest on municipal bonds is not taxed, and so municipals sell at low pretax yields. Interest on federal government bonds is taxed, and so these bonds sell at higher pretax yields. It does not seem likely that investors in bonds just forget about taxes when they enter the stock market. Thus, we would expect to find a historical tendency for high-dividend stocks to sell at lower prices and therefore to offer higher returns, just as in Table 16.1.

Unfortunately, there are difficulties in measuring this effect. For example, suppose that stock A is priced at $100 and is expected to pay a $5 dividend. The *expected* yield is, therefore, $5/100 = .05$, or 5 percent. The company now announces bumper earnings and a $10 dividend. Thus with the benefit of hindsight, A's *actual* dividend yield is $10/100 = .10$, or 10 percent. If the unexpected increase in earnings causes a rise in A's stock price, we will observe that a high actual yield is accompanied by a high actual return. But that would not tell us anything about whether a high *expected* yield was accompanied by a high *expected* return. In order to measure the effect of dividend policy, we need to estimate the dividends that investors expected.

A second problem is that nobody is quite sure what is meant by high dividend yield. For example, utility stocks have generally offered high yields. But did they have a high yield all year, or only in months or on days that dividends were paid? Perhaps for most of the year, they had zero yields and were perfect holdings for the highly taxed individuals.[33] Of course, high-tax investors did not want to hold a stock on the days dividends were paid, but they could sell their stock temporarily to a security dealer. Dealers are taxed equally on dividends and capital gains and therefore should not have demanded any extra return for holding stocks over the dividend period.[34] If shareholders could pass stocks freely between each other at the time of the dividend payment, we should not observe any tax effects at all.

---

[31]They might say, "Our stock is a good investment," or, "We want to have the shares available to finance acquisitions of other companies." What do you think of these rationales?

[32]These costs can be substantial. Refer back to Chapter 15, especially Figure 15.3.

[33]Suppose there are 250 trading days in a year. Think of a stock paying quarterly dividends. We could say that the stock offers a high dividend yield on 4 days but a zero dividend yield on the remaining 246 days.

[34]The stock could also be sold to a corporation, which could "capture" the dividend and then resell the shares. Corporations are natural buyers of dividends, because they pay tax only on 30 percent of dividends received from other corporations. (We say more on the taxation of intercorporate dividends later in this section.)

A number of researchers have attempted to tackle these problems and to measure whether investors demand a higher return from high-yielding stocks. Their findings offer some limited comfort to the dividends-are-bad school, for most of the researchers have suggested that high-yielding stocks have provided higher returns. However, the estimated tax rates differ substantially from one study to another. For example, while Litzenberger and Ramaswamy concluded that investors have priced stocks as if dividend income attracted an extra 14 to 23 percent rate of tax, Miller and Scholes using a different methodology came up with a negligible 4 percent difference in the rate of tax.[35]

The Taxation of Dividends and Capital Gains

Many of these attempts to measure the effect of dividends are of more historical than current interest, for they look back at the years before 1986 when there was a dramatic difference between the taxation of dividends and capital gains.[36] Today, the tax rate on capital gains for most shareholders is 20 percent, while for taxable incomes above $65,550 the tax rate on dividends ranges from 30.5 to 39.1 percent.[37]

Tax law favors capital gains in another way. Taxes on dividends have to be paid immediately, but taxes on capital gains can be deferred until shares are sold and capital gains are realized. Stockholders can choose when to sell their shares and thus when to pay the capital gains tax. The longer they wait, the less the present value of the capital gains tax liability.[38]

---

[35]See R. H. Litzenberger and K. Ramaswamy, "The Effects of Dividends on Common Stock Prices: Tax Effects or Information Effects," *Journal of Finance* 37 (May 1982), pp. 429–443; and M. H. Miller and M. Scholes, "Dividends and Taxes: Some Empirical Evidence," *Journal of Political Economy* 90 (1982), pp. 1118–1141. Merton Miller provides a broad review of the empirical literature in "Behavioral Rationality in Finance: The Case of Dividends," *Journal of Business* 59 (October 1986), pp. S451–S468.

[36]The Tax Reform Act of 1986 equalized the tax rates on dividends and capital gains. A gap began to open up again in 1992.

[37]Here are two examples of 2001 marginal tax rates by income bracket:

	Income Bracket	
Marginal Tax Rate	Single	Married, Joint Return
15%	$0–$27,050	$0–$45,200
27.5	$27,051–$65,550	$45,201–$109,250
30.5	$65,551–$136,750	$109,251–$166,500
35.5	$136,751–$297,350	$166,501–$297,350
39.1	Over $297,350	Over $297,350

Source: http://taxes.yahoo.com/rates.html.

There are different schedules for married taxpayers filing separately and for single taxpayers who are heads of households.

[38]When securities are sold capital gains tax is paid on the difference between the selling price and the initial purchase price or *basis*. Thus, shares purchased in 1996 for $20 (the basis) and sold for $30 in 2001 would generate $10 per share in capital gains and a tax of $2.00 at a 20 percent marginal rate.

Suppose the investor now decides to defer sale for one year. Then, if the interest rate is 8 percent, the present value of the tax, viewed from 2001, falls to 2.00/1.08 = $1.85. That is, the *effective* capital gains rate is 18.5 percent. The longer sale is deferred, the lower the effective rate will be.

The effective rate falls to zero if the investor dies before selling, because the investor's heirs get to "step up" the basis without recognizing any taxable gain. Suppose the price is still $30 when the investor dies. The heirs could sell for $30 and pay no tax, because they could claim a $30 basis. The $10 capital gain would escape tax entirely.

The distinction between capital gains and dividends is less important for financial institutions, many of which operate free of all taxes and therefore have no tax reason to prefer capital gains to dividends or vice versa. For example, pension funds are untaxed. These funds hold more than $3 trillion in common stocks, so they have enormous clout in the U.S. stock market. Only corporations have a tax reason to *prefer* dividends. They pay corporate income tax on only 30 percent of any dividends received. Thus the effective tax rate on dividends received by large corporations is 30 percent of 35 percent (the marginal corporate tax rate), or 10.5 percent. But they have to pay a 35 percent tax on the full amount of any realized capital gain.

The implications of these tax rules for dividend policy are pretty simple. Capital gains have advantages to many investors, but they are far less advantageous than they were 20 or 30 years ago. Thus, the leftist case for minimizing cash dividends is weaker than it used to be. At the same time, the middle-of-the-road party has increased its share of the vote.

16.7 THE MIDDLE-OF-THE-ROADERS

The middle-of-the-road party, principally represented by Miller, Black, and Scholes, maintains that a company's value is not affected by its dividend policy.[39] We have already seen that this would be the case if there were no impediments such as transaction costs or taxes. The middle-of-the-roaders are aware of these phenomena but nevertheless raise the following disarming question: If companies could increase their share price by distributing more or less cash dividends, why have they not already done so? Perhaps dividends are where they are because no company believes that it could increase its stock price simply by changing its dividend policy.

This "supply effect" is not inconsistent with the existence of a clientele of investors who demand low-payout stocks. Firms recognized that clientele long ago. Enough firms may have switched to low-payout policies to satisfy fully the clientele's demand. If so, there is no incentive for *additional* firms to switch to low-payout policies.

Miller, Black, and Scholes similarly recognize possible high-payout clienteles but argue that they are satisfied also. If all clienteles are satisfied, their demands for high or low dividends have no effect on prices or returns. It doesn't matter which clientele a particular firm chooses to appeal to. If the middle-of-the-road party is right, we should not expect to observe any general association between dividend policy and market values, and the value of any individual company would be independent of its choice of dividend policy.

The middle-of-the-roaders stress that companies would not have generous payout policies unless they believed that this was what investors wanted. But this does not answer the question, Why *should* so many investors want high payouts?

---

[39]F. Black and M. S. Scholes, "The Effects of Dividend Yield and Dividend Policy on Common Stock Prices and Returns," *Journal of Financial Economics* 1 (May 1974), pp. 1–22; M. H. Miller and M. S. Scholes, "Dividends and Taxes," *Journal of Financial Economics* 6 (December 1978), pp. 333–364; and M. H. Miller, "Behavioral Rationality in Finance: The Case of Dividends," *Journal of Business* 59 (October 1986), pp. S451–S468.

Operating income	100	
Corporate tax at 35%	35	◄——— Corporate tax
After-tax income (paid out as dividends)	65	
Income tax paid by investor at 39.1%	25.4	◄——— Second tax paid by investor
Net income to shareholder	39.6	

TABLE 16.2

In the United States returns to shareholders are taxed twice. This example assumes that all income after corporate taxes is paid out as cash dividends to an investor in the top income tax bracket (figures in dollars per share).

This is the chink in the armor of the middle-of-the-roaders. If high dividends bring high taxes, it's difficult to believe that investors get what they want. The response of the middle-of-the-roaders has been to argue that there are plenty of wrinkles in the tax system which stockholders can use to avoid paying taxes on dividends. For example, instead of investing directly in common stocks, they can do so through a pension fund or insurance company, which receives more favorable tax treatment.

Here is another possible reason that U.S. companies may pay dividends even when these dividends result in higher tax bills. Companies that pay *low* dividends will be more attractive to highly taxed individuals; those that pay *high* dividends will have a greater proportion of pension funds or other tax-exempt institutions as their stockholders. These financial institutions are sophisticated investors; they monitor carefully the companies that they invest in and they bring pressure on poor managers to perform. Successful, well-managed companies are happy to have financial institutions as investors, but their poorly managed brethren would prefer unsophisticated and more docile stockholders.

You can probably see now where the argument is heading. Well-managed companies want to signal their worth. They can do so by having a high proportion of demanding institutions among their stockholders. How do they achieve this? By paying high dividends. Those shareholders who pay tax do not object to these high dividends as long as the effect is to encourage institutional investors who are prepared to put the time and effort into monitoring the management.[40]

Alternative Tax Systems

In the United States shareholders' returns are taxed twice. They are taxed at the corporate level (corporate tax) and in the hands of the shareholder (income tax or capital gains tax). These two tiers of tax are illustrated in Table 16.2, which shows the after-tax return to the shareholder if the company distributes all its income as dividends. We assume the company earns $100 a share before tax and therefore pays corporate tax of .35 × 100 = $35. This leaves $65 a share to be paid out as a dividend, which is then subject to a second layer of tax. For example, a shareholder who is taxed at the top marginal rate of 39.1 percent pays tax on this dividend of .391 × 65 = $25.4. Only a tax-exempt pension fund or charity would retain the full $65.

---

[40]This signaling argument is developed in F. Allen, A. E. Bernardo, and I. Welch, "A Theory of Dividends Based on Tax Clienteles," *Journal of Finance* 55 (December 2000), pp. 2499–2536.

TABLE 16.3

Under imputation tax systems, such as that in Australia, shareholders receive a tax credit for the corporate tax that the firm has paid (figures in Australian dollars per share).

	Rate of Income Tax		
	15%	**30%**	**47%**
Operating income	100	100	100
Corporate tax ($T_c = .30$)	30	30	30
After-tax income	70	70	70
Grossed-up dividend	100	100	100
Income tax	15	30	47
Tax credit for corporate payment	−30	−30	−30
Tax due from shareholder	−15	0	17
Available to shareholder	85	70	53

Of course, dividends are regularly paid by companies that operate under very different tax systems. In fact, the two-tier United States system is relatively rare. Some countries, such as Germany, tax investors at a higher rate on dividends than on capital gains, but they offset this by having a split-rate system of corporate taxes. Profits that are retained in the business attract a higher rate of corporate tax than profits that are distributed. Under this split-rate system, tax-exempt investors prefer that the company pay high dividends, whereas millionaires might vote to retain profits.

In some other countries, shareholders' returns are not taxed twice. For example, in Australia shareholders are taxed on dividends, but they may deduct from this tax bill their share of the corporate tax that the company has paid. This is known as an *imputation tax system*. Table 16.3 shows how the imputation system works. Suppose that an Australian company earns pretax profits of $A100 a share. After it pays corporate tax at 30 percent, the profit is $A70 a share. The company now declares a net dividend of $A70 and sends each shareholder a check for this amount. This dividend is accompanied by a tax credit saying that the company has already paid $A30 of tax on the shareholder's behalf. Thus shareholders are treated as if each received a total, or gross, dividend of 70 + 30 = $A100 and paid tax of $A30. If the shareholder's tax rate is 30 percent, there is no more tax to pay and the shareholder retains the net dividend of $A70. If the shareholder pays tax at the top personal rate of 47 percent, then he or she is required to pay an additional $17 of tax; if the tax rate is 15 percent (the rate at which Australian pension funds are taxed), then the shareholder receives a *refund* of 30 − 15 = $A15.[41]

Under an imputation tax system, millionaires have to cough up the extra personal tax on dividends. If this is more than the tax that they would pay on capital gains, then millionaires would prefer that the company does not distribute earnings. If it is the other way around, they would prefer dividends.[42] Investors with low tax rates have no doubts about the matter. If the company pays a dividend, these investors receive a check from the revenue service for the excess tax that the company has paid, and therefore they prefer high payout rates.

---

[41]In Australia, shareholders receive a credit for the full amount of corporate tax that has been paid on their behalf. In other countries the tax credit is less than the corporate tax rate. You can think of the tax system in these countries as lying between the Australian and United States systems.

[42]In the case of Australia the tax rate on capital gains is the same as the tax rate on dividends. However, for securities that are held for more than 12 months only half of the gain is taxed.

Look once again at Table 16.3 and think what would happen if the corporate tax rate was zero. The shareholder with a 15 percent tax rate would still end up with $A85, and the shareholder with the 47 percent rate would still receive $A53. Thus, under an imputation tax system, when a company pays out all its earnings, there is effectively only one layer of tax—the tax on the shareholder. The revenue service collects this tax through the company and then sends a demand to the shareholder for any excess tax or makes a refund for any overpayment.[43]

---

[43]This is only true for earnings that are paid out as dividends. Retained earnings are subject to corporate tax. Shareholders get the benefit of retained earnings in the form of capital gains.

SUMMARY

Dividends come in several forms. The most common is the regular cash dividend, but sometimes companies pay a dividend in the form of stock.

When managers decide on the dividend, their primary concern seems to be to give shareholders a "fair" level of dividends. Most managers have a conscious or subconscious long-term target payout rate. If firms simply applied the target payout rate to each year's earnings, dividends could fluctuate wildly. Managers therefore try to smooth dividend payments by moving only partway toward the target payout in each year. Also they don't just look at past earnings performance: They try to look into the future when they set the payment. Investors are aware of this and they know that a dividend increase is often a sign of optimism on the part of management.

As an alternative to dividend payments, the company can repurchase its own stock. Although this has the same effect of distributing cash to shareholders, the Internal Revenue Service taxes shareholders only on the capital gains that they may realize as a result of the repurchase.

In recent years many companies have bought back their stock in large quantities, but repurchases do not generally substitute for dividends. Instead, they are used to return unwanted cash to shareholders or to retire equity and replace it with debt. Investors usually interpret stock repurchases as an indication of managers' optimism.

If we hold the company's investment policy constant, then dividend policy is a trade-off between cash dividends and the issue or repurchase of common stock. Should firms retain whatever earnings are necessary to finance growth and pay out any residual as cash dividends? Or should they increase dividends and then (sooner or later) issue stock to make up the shortfall of equity capital? Or should they reduce dividends below the "residual" level and use the released cash to repurchase stock?

If we lived in an ideally simple and perfect world, there would be no problem, for the choice would have no effect on market value. The controversy centers on the effects of dividend policy in our flawed world. A common—though by no means universal—view in the investment community is that high payout enhances share price. Although there are natural clienteles for high-payout stocks, we find it difficult to explain a *general* preference for dividends. We suspect that investors often pressure companies to increase dividends when they do not trust management to spend free cash flow wisely. In this case a dividend increase may lead to a rise in the stock price not because investors like dividends as such but because they want management to run a tighter ship.

The most obvious and serious market imperfection has been the different tax treatment of dividends and capital gains. Currently in the United States the tax rate on dividend income can be almost 40 percent, whereas the rate of capital gains tax tops out at only 20 percent. Thus investors should have required a higher before-tax return on high-payout stocks to compensate for their tax disadvantage. High-income investors should have held mostly low-payout stocks.

This view has a respectable theoretical basis. It is supported by some evidence that gross returns have, on the average, reflected the tax differential. The weak link is the theory's silence on the question of why companies continue to distribute such large sums contrary to the preferences of investors.

The third view of dividend policy starts with the notion that the actions of companies *do* reflect investors' preferences; the fact that companies pay substantial dividends is the best evidence that investors want them. If the supply of dividends exactly meets the demand, no single company could improve its market value by changing its dividend policy. Although this explains corporate behavior, it is at a cost, for we cannot explain why dividends are what they are and not some other amount.

These theories are too incomplete and the evidence is too sensitive to minor changes in specification to warrant any dogmatism. Our sympathies, however, lie with the third, middle-of-the-road view. Our recommendations to companies would emphasize the following points: First, there is little doubt that sudden shifts in dividend policy can cause abrupt changes in stock price. The principal reason is the information that investors read into the company's actions. Given such problems, there is a clear case for smoothing dividends, for example, by defining the firm's target payout and making relatively slow adjustments toward it. If it is necessary to make a sharp dividend change, the company should provide as much forewarning as possible and take care to ensure that the action is not misinterpreted.

Subject to these strictures, we believe that, at the very least, a company should adopt a target payout that is sufficiently low as to minimize its reliance on external equity. Why pay out cash to stockholders if that requires issuing new shares to get the cash back? It's better to hold onto the cash in the first place.

If dividend policy doesn't affect firm value, then you don't need to worry about it when estimating the cost of capital. But if (say) you believe that tax effects are important, then in principle you should recognize that investors demand higher returns from high-payout stocks. Some financial managers do take dividend policy into account, but most become de facto middle-of-the-roaders when estimating the cost of capital. It seems that the effects of dividend policy are too uncertain to justify fine-tuning such estimates.

FURTHER READING

Lintner's classic analysis of how companies set their dividend payments is provided in:

J. Lintner: "Distribution of Incomes of Corporations among Dividends, Retained Earnings, and Taxes," *American Economic Review*, 46:97–113 (May 1956).

Marsh and Merton have reinterpreted Lintner's findings and used them to explain the aggregate dividends paid by U.S. corporations:

T. A. Marsh and R. C. Merton: "Dividend Behavior for the Aggregate Stock Market," *Journal of Business*, 60:1–40 (January 1987).

The pioneering article on dividend policy in the context of a perfect capital market is:

M. H. Miller and F. Modigliani: "Dividend Policy, Growth and the Valuation of Shares," *Journal of Business*, 34:411–433 (October 1961).

There are several interesting models explaining the information content of dividends. Two influential examples are:

S. Bhattacharya: "Imperfect Information, Dividend Policy and the Bird in the Hand Fallacy," *Bell Journal of Economics and Management Science*, 10:259–270 (Spring 1979).

M. H. Miller and K. Rock: "Dividend Policy under Asymmetric Information," *Journal of Finance*, 40:1031–1052 (September 1985).

Financial Management *published a special issue on dividend policy in Autumn 1998. It includes four articles on the information content of dividends.*

The effect of differential rates of tax on dividends and capital gains is analyzed rigorously in the context of the capital asset pricing model in:

M. J. Brennan: "Taxes, Market Valuation and Corporate Financial Policy," *National Tax Journal*, 23:417–427 (December 1970).

The argument that dividend policy is irrelevant even in the presence of taxes is presented in:

F. Black and M. S. Scholes: "The Effects of Dividend Yield and Dividend Policy on Common Stock Prices and Returns," *Journal of Financial Economics*, 1:1–22 (May 1974).

M. H. Miller and M. S. Scholes: "Dividends and Taxes," *Journal of Financial Economics*, 6:333–364 (December 1978).

A review of some of the empirical evidence is contained in:

R. Michaely and A. Kalay: "Dividends and Taxes: A Re-Examination," *Financial Management*, 29:55–75 (Summer 2000).

Merton Miller reviews research on the dividend controversy in:

M. H. Miller: "Behavioral Rationality in Finance: The Case of Dividends," *Journal of Business*, 59:S451–S468 (October 1986).

QUIZ

1. In the 1st quarter of 2001 Merck paid a regular quarterly dividend of $.34 a share.
   a. Match each of the following sets of dates:

(A1) 27 February 2001	(B1) Record date
(A2) 6 March 2001	(B2) Payment date
(A3) 7 March 2001	(B3) Ex-dividend date
(A4) 9 March 2001	(B4) Last with-dividend date
(A5) 2 April 2001	(B5) Declaration date

   b. On one of these dates the stock price is likely to fall by about the value of the dividend. Which date? Why?
   c. Merck's stock price at the end of February was $80.20. What was the dividend yield?
   d. If earnings per share for 2001 are $3.20, what is the percentage payout rate?
   e. Suppose that in 2001 the company paid a 10 percent stock dividend. What would be the expected fall in price?

2. Between 1986 and 2000 Textron dividend changes were described by the following equation:

$$\text{DIV}_t - \text{DIV}_{t-1} = .36(.26 \, \text{EPS}_t - \text{DIV}_{t-1})$$

What do you think were **(a)** Textron's target payout ratio? **(b)** the rate at which dividends adjusted toward the target?

3. True or false?
   a. Realized long-term gains are taxed at the marginal rate of income tax.
   b. The *effective* rate of tax on capital gains can be less than the tax rate on dividends.

4. Here are several "facts" about typical corporate dividend policies. Which are true and which false?
   a. Companies decide each year's dividend by looking at their capital expenditure requirements and then distributing whatever cash is left over.
   b. Most companies have some notion of a target payout ratio.
   c. They set each year's dividend equal to the target payout ratio times that year's earnings.
   d. Managers and investors seem more concerned with dividend changes than with dividend levels.
   e. Managers often increase dividends temporarily when earnings are unexpectedly high for a year or two.
   f. Companies undertaking substantial share repurchases usually finance them with an offsetting reduction in cash dividends.

5. a. Wotan owns 1,000 shares of a firm that has just announced an increase in its dividend from $2.00 to $2.50 a share. The share price is currently $150. If Wotan does not wish to spend the extra cash, what should he do to offset the dividend increase?
   b. Brunhilde owns 1,000 shares of a firm that has just announced a dividend cut from $8.00 a share to $5.00. The share price is currently $200. If Brunhilde wishes to maintain her consumption, what should she do to offset the dividend cut?

6. a. The London Match Company has 1 million shares outstanding, on which it currently pays an annual dividend of £5.00 a share. The chairman has proposed that the dividend should be increased to £7.00 a share. If investment policy and capital structure are not to be affected, what must the company do to offset the dividend increase?
   b. Patriot Games has 5 million shares outstanding. The president has proposed that, given the firm's large cash holdings, the annual dividend should be increased from $6.00 a share to $8.00. If you agree with the president's plans for investment and capital structure, what else must the company do as a consequence of the dividend increase?

7. House of Haddock has 5,000 shares outstanding and the stock price is $140. The company is expected to pay a dividend of $20 per share next year and thereafter the dividend is expected to grow indefinitely by 5 percent a year. The President, George Mullet, now makes a surprise announcement: He says that the company will henceforth distribute half the cash in the form of dividends and the remainder will be used to repurchase stock.
   a. What is the total value of the company before and after the announcement? What is the value of one share?
   b. What is the expected stream of dividends per share for an investor who plans to retain his shares rather than sell them back to the company? Check your estimate of share value by discounting this stream of dividends per share.

8. Here are key financial data for House of Herring, Inc.:

Earnings per share for 2009	$5.50
Number of shares outstanding	40 million
Target payout ratio	50%
Planned dividend per share	$2.75
Stock price, year-end 2009	$130

House of Herring plans to pay the entire dividend early in January 2010. All corporate and personal taxes were repealed in 2008.

a. Other things equal, what will be House of Herring's stock price after the planned dividend payout?

b. Suppose the company cancels the dividend and announces that it will use the money saved to repurchase shares. What happens to the stock price on the announcement date? Assume that investors learn nothing about the company's prospects from the announcement. How many shares will the company need to repurchase?

c. Suppose the company increases dividends to $5.50 per share and then issues new shares to recoup the extra cash paid out as dividends. What happens to the with- and ex-dividend share prices? How many shares will need to be issued? Again, assume investors learn nothing from the announcement about House of Herring's prospects.

9. Answer the following question twice, once assuming current tax law and once assuming the same rate of tax on dividends and capital gains.

Suppose all investments offered the same expected return *before* tax. Consider two equally risky shares, Hi and Lo. Hi shares pay a generous dividend and offer low expected capital gains. Lo shares pay low dividends and offer high expected capital gains. Which of the following investors would prefer the Lo shares? Which would prefer the Hi shares? Which shouldn't care? (Assume that any stock purchased will be sold after one year.)

a. A pension fund.

b. An individual.

c. A corporation.

d. A charitable endowment.

e. A security dealer.

PRACTICE
QUESTIONS

1. Look in a recent issue of *The Wall Street Journal* at "Dividend News" and choose a company reporting a regular dividend.

a. How frequently does the company pay a regular dividend?

b. What is the amount of the dividend?

c. By what date must your stock be registered for you to receive the dividend?

d. How many weeks later is the dividend paid?

e. Look up the stock price and calculate the annual yield on the stock.

2. "Risky companies tend to have lower target payout ratios and more gradual adjustment rates." Explain what is meant by this statement. Why do you think it is so?

3. Which types of companies would you expect to distribute a relatively high or low proportion of current earnings? Which would you expect to have a relatively high or low price–earnings ratio?

a. High-risk companies.

b. Companies that have experienced an unexpected decline in profits.

c. Companies that *expect* to experience a decline in profits.

d. Growth companies with valuable future investment opportunities.

4. Little Oil has outstanding 1 million shares with a total market value of $20 million. The firm is expected to pay $1 million of dividends next year, and thereafter the amount paid out is expected to grow by 5 percent a year in perpetuity. Thus the expected dividend is $1.05 million in year 2, $1.105 million in year 3, and so on. However, the company has heard that the value of a share depends on the flow of dividends, and therefore it announces that next year's dividend will be increased to $2 million and that the extra cash will be raised immediately by an issue of shares. After that, the total amount paid out each year will be as previously forecasted, that is, $1.05 million in year 2 and increasing by 5 percent in each subsequent year.

a. At what price will the new shares be issued in year 1?

b. How many shares will the firm need to issue?

c. What will be the expected dividend payments on these new shares, and what therefore will be paid out to the *old* shareholders after year 1?

d. Show that the present value of the cash flows to current shareholders remains $20 million.

5. We stated in Section 16.4 that MM's proof of dividend irrelevance assumes that new shares are sold at a fair price. Look back at question 4. Assume that new shares are issued in year 1 at $10 a share. Show who gains and who loses. Is dividend policy still irrelevant? Why or why not?

6. Respond to the following comment: "It's all very well saying that I can sell shares to cover cash needs, but that may mean selling at the bottom of the market. If the company pays a regular cash dividend, investors avoid that risk."

7. "Dividends are the shareholders' wages. Therefore, if a government adopts an incomes policy, restricting increases in wages, it should in all logic restrict increases in dividends." Does this make sense?

8. Refer to the first balance sheet prepared for Rational Demiconductor in Section 16.4. Again it uses cash to pay a $1,000 cash dividend, planning to issue stock to recover the cash required for investment. But this time catastrophe hits before the stock can be issued. A new pollution control regulation increases manufacturing costs to the extent that the value of Rational Demiconductor's existing business is cut in half, to $4,500. The NPV of the new investment opportunity is unaffected, however. Show that dividend policy is still irrelevant.

9. "Many companies use stock repurchases to increase earnings per share. For example, suppose that a company is in the following position:

Net profit	$10 million
Number of shares before repurchase	1 million
Earnings per share	$10
Price–earnings ratio	20
Share price	$200

The company now repurchases 200,000 shares at $200 a share. The number of shares declines to 800,000 shares and earnings per share increase to $12.50. Assuming the price–earnings ratio stays at 20, the share price must rise to $250." Discuss.

10. Hors d'Age Cheeseworks has been paying a regular cash dividend of $4 per share each year for over a decade. The company is paying out all its earnings as dividends and is not expected to grow. There are 100,000 shares outstanding selling for $80 per share. The company has sufficient cash on hand to pay the next annual dividend.

Suppose that Hors d'Age decides to cut its cash dividend to zero and announces that it will repurchase shares instead.

a. What is the immediate stock price reaction? Ignore taxes, and assume that the repurchase program conveys no information about operating profitability or business risk.

b. How many shares will Hors d'Age purchase?

c. Project and compare future stock prices for the old and new policies. Do this for at least years 1, 2, and 3.

11. An article on stock repurchase in the *Los Angeles Times* noted: "An increasing number of companies are finding that the best investment they can make these days is in themselves." Discuss this view. How is the desirability of repurchase affected by company prospects and the price of its stock?

12. It is well documented that stock prices tend to rise when firms announce increases in their dividend payouts. How, then, can it be said that dividend policy is irrelevant?

13. Comment briefly on each of the following statements:
    a. "Unlike American firms, which are always being pressured by their shareholders to increase dividends, Japanese companies pay out a much smaller proportion of earnings and so enjoy a lower cost of capital."
    b. "Unlike new capital, which needs a stream of new dividends to service it, retained earnings have zero cost."
    c. "If a company repurchases stock instead of paying a dividend, the number of shares falls and earnings per share rise. Thus stock repurchase must always be preferred to paying dividends."

14. Suppose the Miller–Modigliani (MM) theory of dividend policy is correct. How would a government-imposed dividend freeze affect (a) stock prices? (b) capital investment?

15. Formaggio Vecchio has just announced its regular quarterly cash dividend of $1 per share.
    a. When will the stock price fall to reflect this dividend payment—on the record date, the ex-dividend date, or the payment date?
    b. Assume that there are no taxes. By how much is the stock price likely to fall?
    c. Now assume that *all* investors pay tax of 30 percent on dividends and nothing on capital gains. What is the likely fall in the stock price?
    d. Suppose, finally, that everything is the same as in part (c), except that security dealers pay tax on *both* dividends and capital gains. How would you expect your answer to (c) to change? Explain.

16. Refer back to question 15. Assume no taxes and a stock price immediately after the dividend announcement of $100.
    a. If you own 100 shares, what is the value of your investment? How does the dividend payment affect your wealth?
    b. Now suppose that Formaggio Vecchio cancels the dividend payment and announces that it will repurchase 1 percent of its stock at $100. Do you rejoice or yawn? Explain.

17. The shares of A and B both sell for $100 and offer a pretax return of 10 percent. However, in the case of company A the return is entirely in the form of dividend yield (the company pays a regular annual dividend of $10 a share), while in the case of B the return comes entirely as capital gain (the shares appreciate by 10 percent a year). Suppose that dividends and capital gains are both taxed at 30 percent. What is the after-tax return on share A? What is the after-tax return on share B to an investor who sells after two years? What about an investor who sells after 10 years?

18. a. The Horner Pie Company pays a quarterly dividend of $1. Suppose that the stock price is expected to fall on the ex-dividend date by $.90. Would you prefer to buy on the with-dividend date or the ex-dividend date if you were (i) a tax-free investor, (ii) an investor with a marginal tax rate of 40 percent on income and 16 percent on capital gains?
    b. In a study of ex-dividend behavior, Elton and Gruber[44] estimate that the stock price fell on the average by 85 percent of the dividend. Assuming that the tax rate on capital gains was 40 percent of the rate on income tax, what did Elton and Gruber's result imply about investors' marginal rate of income tax?
    c. Elton and Gruber also observed that the ex-dividend price fall was different for high-payout stocks and for low-payout stocks. Which group would you expect to show the larger price fall as a proportion of the dividend?
    d. Would the fact that investors can trade stocks freely around the ex-dividend date alter your interpretation of Elton and Gruber's study?

E. J. Elton and M. J. Gruber, "Marginal Stockholders' Tax Rates and the Clientele Effect," *Review of Economics and Statistics* 52 (1970), pp. 68–74.

e. Suppose Elton and Gruber repeat their tests for the period after the 1986 Tax Reform Act, when the tax rate was the same on dividends and capital gains. How would you expect their results to change?

19. In the United States, where there is a two-tier tax system, which investors are indifferent to the dividend payout ratio? How about investors in Australia, where there is an imputation tax system? Describe how the Australian system works and what it could imply for dividend policy.

20. The middle-of-the-road party holds that dividend policy doesn't matter because the *supply* of high-, medium-, and low-payout stocks has already adjusted to satisfy investors' demands. Investors who like generous dividends hold stocks which give them all the dividends that they want. Investors who want capital gains see a surfeit of low-payout stocks to choose from. Thus, high-payout firms cannot gain by transforming to low-payout firms, or vice versa.

Suppose the government equalizes the tax rates on dividends and capital gains. Suppose that before this change the supply of dividends matched investor needs. How would you expect the tax change to affect the total cash dividends paid by U.S. corporations and the proportion of high- versus low-payout companies? Would dividend policy still be irrelevant after any dividend supply adjustments are completed? Explain.

CHALLENGE QUESTIONS

1. Table 16.4 lists the dividends and earnings per share (EPS) for Merck and International Paper. Estimate the target payout for each company and the rate at which the dividend is adjusted toward the target. Suppose that in 2001 Merck's earnings increase to $5 a share and International Paper's earnings increase to $3 per share. How would you predict their dividends to change?

2. Consider the following two statements: "Dividend policy is irrelevant," and "Stock price is the present value of expected future dividends." (See Chapter 4.) They *sound* contradictory. This question is designed to show that they are fully consistent.

TABLE 16.4

See Challenge Question 1.

Year	Merck EPS	Merck Dividend	International Paper EPS	International Paper Dividend
1983	.17	.08	1.16	.6
1984	.19	.09	.47	.6
1985	.21	.09	.54	.6
1986	.27	.11	1.45	.6
1987	.37	.14	1.84	.61
1988	.51	.22	3.28	.64
1989	.63	.28	3.86	.77
1990	.76	.32	2.60	.84
1991	.92	.39	1.80	.84
1992	1.56	.46	0.58	.84
1993	1.44	.52	1.17	.84
1994	1.19	.57	1.73	.84
1995	1.32	.62	4.50	.92
1996	1.56	.71	1.04	1.00
1997	1.87	.85	−.20	1.00
1998	2.15	.95	.60	1.00
1999	2.45	1.10	.48	1.00
2000	2.90	1.21	.32	1.00

The current price of the shares of Charles River Mining Corporation is $50. Next year's earnings and dividends per share are $4 and $2, respectively. Investors expect perpetual growth at 8 percent per year. The expected rate of return demanded by investors is $r = 12$ percent.

We can use the perpetual-growth model to calculate stock price.

$$P_0 = \frac{\text{DIV}}{r - g} = \frac{2}{.12 - .08} = 50$$

Suppose that Charles River Mining announces that it will switch to a 100 percent payout policy, issuing shares as necessary to finance growth. Use the perpetual-growth model to show that current stock price is unchanged.

3. Suppose management is expected to make a fixed-price tender offer to repurchase half of the stock at a 20 percent premium. How, if at all, would that affect today's market price of the company's shares?

4. Adherents of the "dividends-are-good" school sometimes point to the fact that stocks with high yields tend to have above-average price–earnings multiples. Is this evidence convincing? Discuss.

CHAPTER SEVENTEEN

DOES DEBT POLICY MATTER?

A FIRM'S BASIC resource is the stream of cash flows produced by its assets. When the firm is financed entirely by common stock, all those cash flows belong to the stockholders. When it issues both debt and equity securities, it undertakes to split up the cash flows into two streams, a relatively safe stream that goes to the debtholders and a more risky one that goes to the stockholders.

The firm's mix of different securities is known as its **capital structure.** The choice of capital structure is fundamentally a marketing problem. The firm can issue dozens of distinct securities in countless combinations, but it attempts to find the particular combination that maximizes its overall market value.

Are these attempts worthwhile? We must consider the possibility that *no* combination has any greater appeal than any other. Perhaps the really important decisions concern the company's assets, and decisions about capital structure are mere details—matters to be attended to but not worried about.

Modigliani and Miller (MM), who showed that dividend policy doesn't matter in perfect capital markets, also showed that financing decisions don't matter in perfect markets.[1] Their famous "proposition I" states that a firm cannot change the *total* value of its securities just by splitting its cash flows into different streams: The firm's value is determined by its real assets, not by the securities it issues. Thus capital structure is irrelevant as long as the firm's investment decisions are taken as given.

MM's proposition I allows complete separation of investment and financing decisions. It implies that any firm could use the capital budgeting procedures presented in Chapters 2 through 12 without worrying about where the money for capital expenditures comes from. In those chapters, we assumed all-equity financing without really thinking about it. If proposition I holds, that is exactly the right approach.

We believe that in practice capital structure *does* matter, but we nevertheless devote all of this chapter to MM's argument. If you don't fully understand the conditions under which MM's theory holds, you won't fully understand why one capital structure is better than another. The financial manager needs to know what kinds of market imperfection to look for.

In Chapter 18 we will undertake a detailed analysis of the imperfections that are most likely to make a difference, including taxes, the costs of bankruptcy, and the costs of writing and enforcing complicated debt contracts. We will also argue that it is naive to suppose that investment and financing decisions can be completely separated.

But in this chapter we isolate the decision about capital structure by holding the decision about investment fixed. We also assume that dividend policy is irrelevant.

17.1 THE EFFECT OF LEVERAGE IN A COMPETITIVE TAX-FREE ECONOMY

We have referred to the firm's choice of capital structure as a *marketing problem*. The financial manager's problem is to find the combination of securities that has the greatest overall appeal to investors—the combination that maximizes the market value of the firm. Before tackling this problem, we ought to make sure that a policy which maximizes firm value also maximizes the wealth of the shareholders.

---

[1]F. Modigliani and M. H. Miller, "The Cost of Capital, Corporation Finance and the Theory of Investment," *American Economic Review* 48 (June 1958), pp. 261–297. MM's basic argument was anticipated in 1938 by J. B. Williams and to some extent by David Durand. See J. B. Williams, *The Theory of Investment Value*, Harvard University Press, Cambridge, MA, 1938; and D. Durand, "Cost of Debt and Equity Funds for Business: Trends and Problems of Measurement," in *Conference on Research in Business Finance*, National Bureau of Economic Research, New York, 1952.

Let D and E denote the market values of the outstanding debt and equity of the Wapshot Mining Company. Wapshot's 1,000 shares sell for $50 apiece. Thus

$$E = 1{,}000 \times 50 = \$50{,}000$$

Wapshot has also borrowed $25,000, and so V, the aggregate market value of all Wapshot's outstanding securities, is

$$V = D + E = \$75{,}000$$

Wapshot's stock is known as *levered equity*. Its stockholders face the benefits and costs of **financial leverage,** or *gearing*. Suppose that Wapshot "levers up" still further by borrowing an additional $10,000 and paying the proceeds out to shareholders as a special dividend of $10 per share. This substitutes debt for equity capital with no impact on Wapshot's assets.

What will Wapshot's equity be worth after the special dividend is paid? We have two unknowns, E and V:

Old debt	$25,000	
New debt	$10,000	$35,000 = D
Equity		? = E
Firm value		? = V

If V is $75,000 as before, then E must be $V - D = 75{,}000 - 35{,}000 = \$40{,}000$. Stockholders have suffered a capital loss which exactly offsets the $10,000 special dividend. But if V *increases* to, say, $80,000 as a result of the change in capital structure, then $E = \$45{,}000$ and the stockholders are $5,000 ahead. In general, any increase or decrease in V caused by a shift in capital structure accrues to the firm's stockholders. We conclude that a policy which maximizes the market value of the firm is also best for the firm's stockholders.

This conclusion rests on two important assumptions: first, that Wapshot can ignore dividend policy and, second, that after the change in capital structure the old and new debt is *worth* $35,000.

Dividend policy may or may not be relevant, but there is no need to repeat the discussion of Chapter 16. We need only note that shifts in capital structure sometimes force important decisions about dividend policy. Perhaps Wapshot's cash dividend has costs or benefits which should be considered in addition to any benefits achieved by its increased financial leverage.

Our second assumption that old and new debt ends up worth $35,000 seems innocuous. But it could be wrong. Perhaps the new borrowing has increased the risk of the old bonds. If the holders of old bonds cannot demand a higher rate of interest to compensate for the increased risk, the value of their investment is reduced. In this case Wapshot's stockholders gain at the expense of the holders of old bonds even though the overall value of the debt and equity is unchanged.

But this anticipates issues better left to Chapter 18. In this chapter we will assume that any issue of debt has no effect on the market value of existing debt.[2]

---

[2]See E. F. Fama, "The Effects of a Firm's Investment and Financing Decisions," *American Economic Review* 68 (June 1978), pp. 272–284, for a rigorous analysis of the conditions under which a policy of maximizing the value of the firm is also best for the stockholders.

Enter Modigliani and Miller

Let us accept that the financial manager would like to find the combination of securities that maximizes the value of the firm. How is this done? MM's answer is that the financial manager should stop worrying: In a perfect market any combination of securities is as good as another. The value of the firm is unaffected by its choice of capital structure.

You can see this by imagining two firms that generate the same stream of operating income and differ only in their capital structure. Firm U is unlevered. Therefore the total value of its equity E_U is the same as the total value of the firm V_U. Firm, L, on the other hand, is levered. The value of its stock is, therefore, equal to the value of the firm less the value of the debt: $E_L = V_L - D_L$.

Now think which of these firms you would prefer to invest in. If you don't want to take much risk, you can buy common stock in the unlevered firm U. For example, if you buy 1 percent of firm U's shares, your investment is $.01V_U$ and you are entitled to 1 percent of the gross profits:

Dollar Investment	Dollar Return
$.01V_U$	.01 Profits

Now compare this with an alternative strategy. This is to purchase the same fraction of both the debt and the equity of firm L. Your investment and return would then be as follows:

	Dollar Investment	Dollar Return
Debt	$.01D_L$	.01 Interest
Equity	$.01E_L$	.01 (Profits − interest)
Total	$.01(D_L + E_L)$	.01 Profits
	$= .01V_L$	

Both strategies offer the same payoff: 1 percent of the firm's profits. In well-functioning markets two investments that offer the same payoff must have the same cost. Therefore, $.01V_U$ must equal $.01V_L$: The value of the unlevered firm must equal the value of the levered firm.

Suppose that you are willing to run a little more risk. You decide to buy 1 percent of the outstanding shares in the *levered* firm. Your investment and return are now as follows:

Dollar Investment	Dollar Return
$.01E_L$	.01 (Profits − interest)
$= .01(V_L - D_L)$	

But there is an alternative strategy. This is to borrow $.01D_L$ on your own account and purchase 1 percent of the stock of the *unlevered* firm. In this case, your borrowing gives you an immediate cash *inflow* of $.01D_L$, but you have to pay interest on your loan equal to 1 percent of the interest that is paid by firm L. Your total investment and return are, therefore, as follows:

	Dollar Investment	Dollar Return
Borrowing	$-.01D_L$	$-.01$ Interest
Equity	$.01V_U$	$.01$ Profits
Total	$.01(V_U - D_L)$	$.01$(Profits $-$ interest)

Again both strategies offer the same payoff: 1 percent of profits after interest. Therefore, both investments must have the same cost. The quantity $.01(V_U - D_L)$ must equal $.01(V_L - D_L)$ and V_U must equal V_L.

It does not matter whether the world is full of risk-averse chickens or venturesome lions. All would agree that the value of the unlevered firm U must be equal to the value of the levered firm L. As long as investors can borrow or lend on their own account on the same terms as the firm, they can "undo" the effect of any changes in the firm's capital structure. This is the basis for MM's famous proposition I: "The market value of any firm is independent of its capital structure."

The Law of the Conservation of Value

MM's argument that debt policy is irrelevant is an application of an astonishingly simple idea. If we have two streams of cash flow, A and B, then the present value of $A + B$ is equal to the present value of A plus the present value of B. We met this principle of *value additivity* in our discussion of capital budgeting, where we saw that in perfect capital markets the present value of two assets combined is equal to the sum of their present values considered separately.

In the present context we are not combining assets but splitting them up. But value additivity works just as well in reverse. We can slice a cash flow into as many parts as we like; the values of the parts will always sum back to the value of the unsliced stream. (Of course, we have to make sure that none of the stream is lost in the slicing. We cannot say, "The value of a pie is independent of how it is sliced," if the slicer is also a nibbler.)

This is really a *law of conservation of value*. The value of an asset is preserved regardless of the nature of the claims against it. Thus proposition I: Firm value is determined on the *left-hand* side of the balance sheet by real assets—not by the proportions of debt and equity securities issued by the firm.

The simplest ideas often have the widest application. For example, we could apply the law of conservation of value to the choice between issuing preferred stock, common stock, or some combination. The law implies that the choice is irrelevant, assuming perfect capital markets and providing that the choice does not affect the firm's investment, borrowing, and operating policies. If the total value of the equity "pie" (preferred and common combined) is fixed, the firm's owners (its common stockholders) do not care how this pie is sliced.

The law also applies to the *mix* of debt securities issued by the firm. The choices of long-term versus short-term, secured versus unsecured, senior versus subordinated, and convertible versus nonconvertible debt all should have no effect on the overall value of the firm.

Combining assets and splitting them up will not affect values as long as they do not affect an investor's choice. When we showed that capital structure does not af-

Data				
Number of shares	1,000			
Price per share	$10			
Market value of shares	$10,000			
			Outcomes	
Operating income ($)	500	1,000	**1,500**	2,000
Earnings per share ($)	.50	1.00	**1.50**	2.00
Return on shares (%)	5	10	**15**	20
			Expected outcome	

TABLE 17.1

Macbeth Spot Removers is entirely equity-financed. Although it *expects* to have an income of $1,500 a year in perpetuity, this income is not certain. This table shows the return to the stockholder under different assumptions about operating income. We assume no taxes.

fect choice, we implicitly assumed that both companies and individuals can borrow and lend at the same risk-free rate of interest. As long as this is so, individuals can undo the effect of any changes in the firm's capital structure.

In practice corporate debt is not risk-free and firms cannot escape with rates of interest appropriate to a government security. Some people's initial reaction is that this alone invalidates MM's proposition. It is a natural mistake, but capital structure can be irrelevant even when debt is risky.

If a company borrows money, it does not *guarantee* repayment: It repays the debt in full only if its assets are worth more than the debt obligation. The shareholders in the company, therefore, have limited liability.

Many individuals would like to borrow with limited liability. They might, therefore, be prepared to pay a small premium for levered shares *if the supply of levered shares were insufficient to meet their needs.*[3] But there are literally thousands of common stocks of companies that borrow. Therefore it is unlikely that an issue of debt would induce them to pay a premium for *your* shares.[4]

An Example of Proposition I

Macbeth Spot Removers is reviewing its capital structure. Table 17.1 shows its current position. The company has no leverage and all the operating income is paid as dividends to the common stockholders (we assume still that there are no taxes). The expected earnings and dividends per share are $1.50, but this figure is by no means certain—it could turn out to be more or less than $1.50. The price of each share is $10. Since the firm expects to produce a level stream of earnings in perpetuity, the expected return on the share is equal to the earnings–price ratio, $1.50/10.00 = .15$, or 15 percent.[5]

---

[3]Of course, individuals could *create* limited liability if they chose. In other words, the lender could agree that borrowers need repay their debt in full only if the assets of company X are worth more than a certain amount. Presumably individuals don't enter into such arrangements because they can obtain limited liability more simply by investing in the stocks of levered companies.

[4]Capital structure is also irrelevant if each investor holds a fully diversified portfolio. In that case he or she owns *all* the risky securities offered by a company (both debt and equity). But anybody who owns *all* the risky securities doesn't care about how the cash flows are divided between different securities.

[5]See Chapter 4, Section 4.

TABLE 17.2

Macbeth Spot Removers is wondering whether to issue $5,000 of debt at an interest rate of 10 percent and repurchase 500 shares. This table shows the return to the shareholder under different assumptions about operating income.

Data				
Number of shares	500			
Price per share	$10			
Market value of shares	$5,000			
Market value of debt	$5,000			
Interest at 10 percent	$500			
			Outcomes	
Operating income ($)	500	1,000	**1,500**	2,000
Interest ($)	500	500	**500**	500
Equity earnings ($)	0	500	**1,000**	1,500
Earnings per share ($)	0	1	**2**	3
Return on shares (%)	0	10	**20**	30
			Expected outcome	

Ms. Macbeth, the firm's president, has come to the conclusion that shareholders would be better off if the company had equal proportions of debt and equity. She therefore proposes to issue $5,000 of debt at an interest rate of 10 percent and use the proceeds to repurchase 500 shares. To support her proposal, Ms. Macbeth has analyzed the situation under different assumptions about operating income. The results of her calculations are shown in Table 17.2.

In order to see more clearly how leverage would affect earnings per share, Ms. Macbeth has also produced Figure 17.1. The burgundy line shows how earnings per share would vary with operating income under the firm's current all-equity financing. It is, therefore, simply a plot of the data in Table 17.1. The blue line shows how earnings per share would vary given equal proportions of debt and equity. It is, therefore, a plot of the data in Table 17.2.

Ms. Macbeth reasons as follows: "It is clear that the effect of leverage depends on the company's income. If income is greater than $1,000, the return to the equity holder is *increased* by leverage. If it is less than $1,000, the return is *reduced* by leverage. The return is unaffected when operating income is exactly $1,000. At this point the return on the market value of the assets is 10 percent, which is exactly equal to the interest rate on the debt. Our capital structure decision, therefore, boils down to what we think about income prospects. Since we expect operating income to be above the $1,000 break-even point, I believe we can best help our shareholders by going ahead with the $5,000 debt issue."

As financial manager of Macbeth Spot Removers, you reply as follows: "I agree that leverage will help the shareholder as long as our income is greater than $1,000. But your argument ignores the fact that Macbeth's shareholders have the alternative of borrowing on their own account. For example, suppose that an investor borrows $10 and then invests $20 in two unlevered Macbeth shares. This person has to put up only $10 of his or her own money. The payoff on the investment varies with Macbeth's operating income, as shown in Table 17.3. This is exactly the same set of payoffs as the investor would get by buying one share in the levered company. (Compare the last two lines of Tables 17.2 and 17.3.)

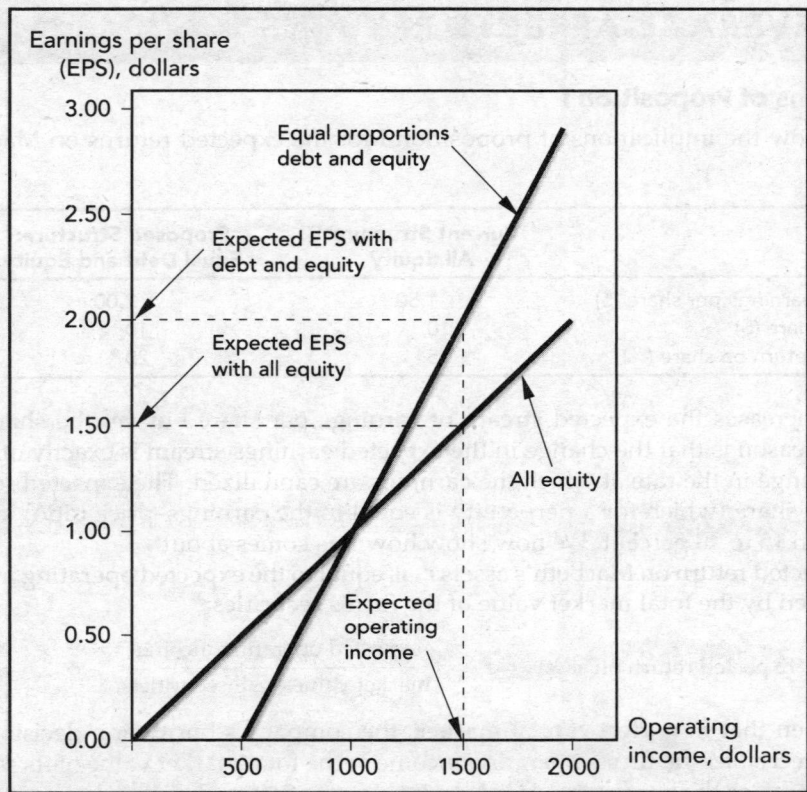

FIGURE 17.1

Borrowing increases Macbeth's EPS (earnings per share) when operating income is greater than $1,000 and reduces EPS when operating income is less than $1,000. Expected EPS rises from $1.50 to $2.

TABLE 17.3

Individual investors can replicate Macbeth's leverage.

	Operating Income ($)			
	500	**1,000**	**1,500**	**2,000**
Earnings on two shares ($)	1	2	3	4
Less interest at 10% ($)	1	1	1	1
Net earnings on investment ($)	0	1	2	3
Return on $10 investment (%)	0	10	20	30
			Expected outcome	

Therefore, a share in the levered company must also sell for $10. If Macbeth goes ahead and borrows, it will not allow investors to do anything that they could not do already, and so it will not increase value."

The argument that you are using is exactly the same as the one MM used to prove proposition I.

17.2 HOW LEVERAGE AFFECTS RETURNS

Implications of Proposition I

Consider now the implications of proposition I for the expected returns on Macbeth stock:

	Current Structure: All Equity	Proposed Structure: Equal Debt and Equity
Expected earnings per share ($)	1.50	2.00
Price per share ($)	10	10
Expected return on share (%)	15	20

Leverage increases the expected stream of earnings per share but *not* the share price. The reason is that the change in the expected earnings stream is exactly offset by a change in the rate at which the earnings are capitalized. The expected return on the share (which for a perpetuity is equal to the earnings–price ratio) increases from 15 to 20 percent. We now show how this comes about.

The expected return on Macbeth's assets r_A is equal to the expected operating income divided by the total market value of the firm's securities:

$$\text{Expected return on assets} = r_A = \frac{\text{expected operating income}}{\text{market value of all securities}}$$

We have seen that in perfect capital markets the company's borrowing decision does not affect *either* the firm's operating income *or* the total market value of its securities. Therefore the borrowing decision also does not affect the expected return on the firm's assets r_A.

Suppose that an investor holds all of a company's debt and all of its equity. This investor would be entitled to all the firm's operating income; therefore, the expected return on the portfolio would be equal to r_A.

The expected return on a portfolio is equal to a weighted average of the expected returns on the individual holdings. Therefore the expected return on a portfolio consisting of *all* the firm's securities is[6]

$$\text{Expected return} \atop \text{on assets} = \left({\text{proportion} \atop \text{in debt}} \times {\text{expected return} \atop \text{on debt}} \right)$$

$$+ \left({\text{proportion} \atop \text{in equity}} \times {\text{expected return} \atop \text{on equity}} \right)$$

$$r_A = \left(\frac{D}{D + E} \times r_D \right) + \left(\frac{E}{D + E} \times r_E \right)$$

We can rearrange this equation to obtain an expression for r_E, the expected return on the equity of a levered firm:

---

[6]This equation should look familiar. We introduced it in Chapter 9 when we showed that the company cost of capital is a weighted average of the expected returns on the debt and equity. (*Company cost of capital* is simply another term for the expected return on assets, r_A.) We also stated in Chapter 9 that changing the capital structure does not change the company cost of capital. In other words, we implicitly assumed MM's proposition I.

$$\underset{\text{on equity}}{\text{Expected return}} = \underset{\text{on assets}}{\text{expected return}} + \underset{\text{ratio}}{\text{debt–equity}} \times \left(\underset{\text{on assets}}{\text{expected return}} - \underset{\text{on debt}}{\text{expected return}} \right)$$

$$r_E = r_A + \frac{D}{E}(r_A - r_D)$$

Proposition II

This is MM's proposition II: The expected rate of return on the common stock of a levered firm increases in proportion to the debt–equity ratio (D/E), expressed in market values; the rate of increase depends on the spread between r_A, the expected rate of return on a portfolio of all the firm's securities, and r_D, the expected return on the debt. Note that $r_E = r_A$ if the firm has no debt.

We can check out this formula for Macbeth Spot Removers. Before the decision to borrow

$$r_E = r_A = \frac{\text{expected operating income}}{\text{market value of all securities}}$$

$$= \frac{1{,}500}{10{,}000} = .15, \text{ or } 15\%$$

If the firm goes ahead with its plan to borrow, the expected return on assets r_A is still 15 percent. The expected return on equity is

$$r_E = r_A + \frac{D}{E}(r_A - r_D)$$

$$= .15 + \frac{5{,}000}{5{,}000}(.15 - .10)$$

$$= .20, \text{ or } 20\%$$

The general implications of MM's proposition II are shown in Figure 17.2. The figure assumes that the firm's bonds are essentially risk-free at low debt levels. Thus r_D is independent of D/E, and r_E increases linearly as D/E increases. As the firm borrows more, the risk of default increases and the firm is required to pay higher rates of interest. Proposition II predicts that when this occurs the rate of increase in r_E slows down. This is also shown in Figure 17.2. The more debt the firm has, the less sensitive r_E is to further borrowing.

Why does the slope of the r_E line in Figure 17.2 taper off as D/E increases? Essentially because holders of risky debt bear some of the firm's business risk. As the firm borrows more, more of that risk is transferred from stockholders to bondholders.

The Risk–Return Trade-off

Proposition I says that financial leverage has no effect on shareholders' wealth. Proposition II says that the rate of return they can expect to receive on their shares increases as the firm's debt–equity ratio increases. How can shareholders be indifferent to increased leverage when it increases expected return? The answer is that any increase in expected return is exactly offset by an increase in risk and therefore in shareholders' *required* rate of return.

FIGURE 17.2

MM's proposition II. The expected return on equity r_E increases linearly with the debt–equity ratio so long as debt is risk-free. But if leverage increases the risk of the debt, debtholders demand a higher return on the debt. This causes the rate of increase in r_E to slow down.

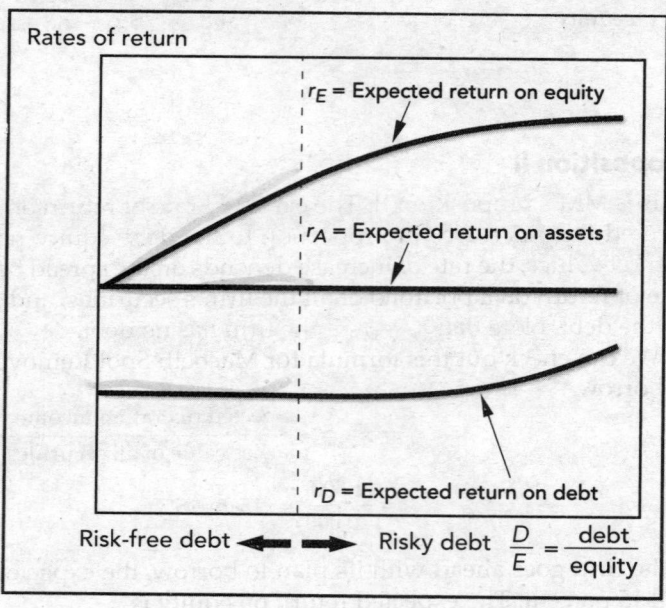

TABLE 17.4

Leverage increases the risk of Macbeth shares.

		Operating Income	
		$500	**$1,500**
All equity:	Earnings per share ($)	.50	1.50
	Return on shares (%)	5	15
50 percent debt:	Earnings per share ($)	0	2
	Return on shares (%)	0	20

Look at what happens to the risk of Macbeth shares if it moves to equal debt–equity proportions. Table 17.4 shows how a shortfall in operating income affects the payoff to the shareholders.

The debt–equity proportion does not affect the *dollar* risk borne by equity-holders. Suppose operating income drops from $1,500 to $500. Under all-equity financing, equity earnings drop by $1 per share. There are 1,000 outstanding shares, and so *total* equity earnings fall by $1 × 1,000 = $1,000. With 50 percent debt, the same drop in operating income reduces earnings per share by $2. But there are only 500 shares outstanding, and so total equity income drops by $2 × 500 = $1,000, just as in the all-equity case.

However, the debt–equity choice does amplify the spread of *percentage* returns. If the firm is all-equity-financed, a decline of $1,000 in the operating income reduces the return on the shares by 10 percent. If the firm issues risk-free debt with a fixed interest payment of $500 a year, then a decline of $1,000 in the operating income reduces the return on the shares by 20 percent. In other words,

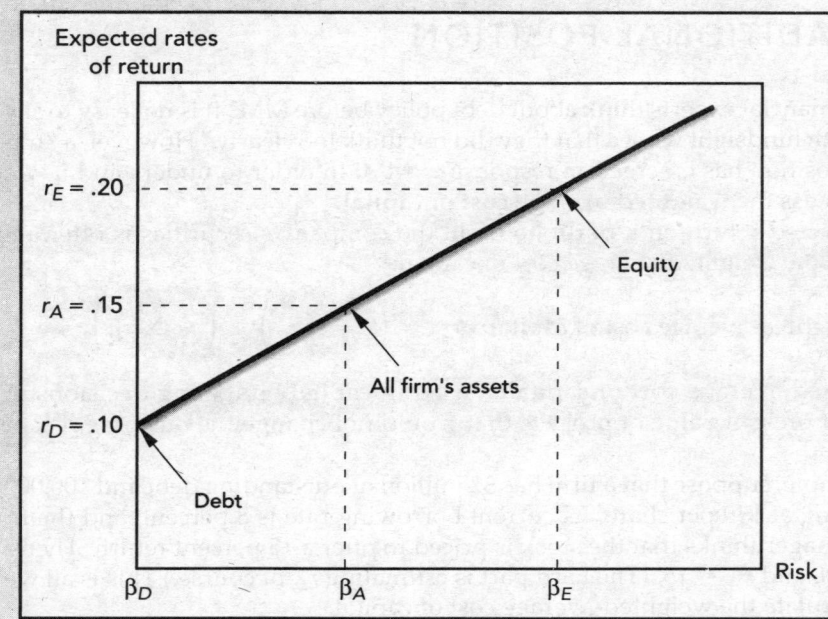

FIGURE 17.3

If Macbeth is unlevered, the expected return on its equity equals the expected return on its assets. Leverage increases both the expected return on equity (r_E) and the risk of equity (β_E).

the effect of leverage is to double the amplitude of the swings in Macbeth's shares. Whatever the beta of the firm's shares before the refinancing, it would be twice as high afterward.

Just as the expected return on the firm's assets is a weighted average of the expected return on the individual securities, so likewise is the beta of the firm's assets a weighted average of the betas of the individual securities:[7]

$$\text{Beta of assets} = \left(\begin{array}{c}\text{proportion}\\\text{of debt}\end{array} \times \begin{array}{c}\text{beta of}\\\text{debt}\end{array}\right) + \left(\begin{array}{c}\text{proportion}\\\text{of equity}\end{array} \times \begin{array}{c}\text{beta of}\\\text{equity}\end{array}\right)$$

$$\beta_A = \left(\frac{D}{D+E} \times \beta_D\right) + \left(\frac{E}{D+E} \times \beta_E\right)$$

We can rearrange this equation also to give an expression for β_E, the beta of the equity of a levered firm:

$$\text{Beta of equity} = \begin{array}{c}\text{beta of}\\\text{assets}\end{array} + \begin{array}{c}\text{debt-equity}\\\text{ratio}\end{array} \times \left(\begin{array}{c}\text{beta of}\\\text{assets}\end{array} - \begin{array}{c}\text{beta of}\\\text{debt}\end{array}\right)$$

$$\beta_E = \beta_A + \frac{D}{E}(\beta_A - \beta_D)$$

Now you can see why investors require higher returns on levered equity. The required return simply rises to match the increased risk.

In Figure 17.3, we have plotted the expected returns and the risk of Macbeth's securities, assuming that the interest on the debt is risk-free.[8]

---

[7]This equation should also look old-hat. We used it in Section 9.3 when we stated that changes in the capital structure change the beta of stock but not the asset beta.

[8]In this case $\beta_D = 0$ and $\beta_E = \beta_A + (D/E)\beta_A$.

17.3 THE TRADITIONAL POSITION

What did financial experts think about debt policy before MM? It is not easy to say because with hindsight we see that they did not think too clearly.[9] However, a "traditional" position has emerged in response to MM. In order to understand it, we have to discuss the **weighted-average cost of capital.**

The expected return on a portfolio of all the company's securities is often referred to as the weighted-average cost of capital:[10]

$$\text{Weighted-average cost of capital} = r_A = \left(\frac{D}{V} \times r_D \right) + \left(\frac{E}{V} \times r_E \right)$$

The weighted-average cost of capital is used in capital budgeting decisions to find the net present value of projects that would not change the business risk of the firm.

For example, suppose that a firm has $2 million of outstanding debt and 100,000 shares selling at $30 per share. Its current borrowing rate is 8 percent, and the financial manager thinks that the stock is priced to offer a 15 percent return. Therefore $r_D = .08$ and $r_E = .15$. (The hard part is estimating r_E, of course.) This is all we need to calculate the weighted-average cost of capital:

$$D = \$2 \text{ million}$$
$$E = 100{,}000 \text{ shares} \times \$30 \text{ per share} = \$3 \text{ million}$$
$$V = D + E = 2 + 3 = \$5 \text{ million}$$

$$\begin{aligned}
\text{Weighted-average cost of capital} &= \left(\frac{D}{V} \times r_D \right) + \left(\frac{E}{V} \times r_E \right) \\
&= \left(\frac{2}{5} \times .08 \right) + \left(\frac{3}{5} \times .15 \right) \\
&= .122, \text{ or } 12.2\%
\end{aligned}$$

Note that we are still assuming that proposition I holds. If it doesn't, we can't use this simple weighted average as the discount rate even for projects that do not change the firm's business "risk class." As we will see in Chapter 19, the weighted-average cost of capital is only a starting point for setting discount rates.

Two Warnings

Sometimes the objective in financing decisions is stated not as "maximize overall market value" but as "minimize the weighted-average cost of capital." If MM's proposition I holds, then these are equivalent objectives. If MM's proposition I does *not* hold, then the capital structure that maximizes the value of the firm also minimizes the weighted-average cost of capital, *provided* that operating income is independent of capital structure. Remember that the weighted-average cost of capital is the expected rate of return on the market value of all of the firm's securities.

---

[9]Financial economists in 20 years may remark on Brealey and Myers's blind spots and clumsy reasoning. On the other hand, they may not remember us at all.

[10]Remember that in this chapter we ignore taxes. In Chapter 19, we shall see that the weighted-average cost of capital formula needs to be amended when debt interest can be deducted from taxable profits.

Anything that increases the value of the firm reduces the weighted-average cost of capital if operating income is constant. But if operating income is varying too, all bets are off.

In Chapter 18 we will show that financial leverage can affect operating income in several ways. Therefore maximizing the value of the firm is *not* always equivalent to minimizing the weighted-average cost of capital.

Warning 1   Shareholders want management to increase the firm's value. They are more interested in being rich than in owning a firm with a low weighted-average cost of capital.

Warning 2   Trying to minimize the weighted-average cost of capital seems to encourage logical short circuits like the following. Suppose that someone says, "Shareholders demand—and deserve—higher expected rates of return than bondholders do. Therefore debt is the cheaper capital source. We can reduce the weighted-average cost of capital by borrowing more." But this doesn't follow if the extra borrowing leads stockholders to demand a still higher expected rate of return. According to MM's proposition II the cost of equity capital r_E increases by just enough to keep the weighted-average cost of capital constant.

This is not the only logical short circuit you are likely to encounter. We have cited two more in practice question 5 at the end of this chapter.

Rates of Return on Levered Equity—The Traditional Position

You may ask why we have even mentioned the aim of minimizing the weighted-average cost of capital if it is often wrong or confusing. We had to because the traditionalists accept this objective and argue their case in terms of it.

The logical short circuit we just described rested on the assumption that r_E, the expected rate of return demanded by stockholders, does not rise as the firm borrows more. Suppose, just for the sake of argument, that this is true. Then r_A, the weighted-average cost of capital, must decline as the debt–equity ratio rises.

Take Figure 17.4, for example, which is drawn on the assumption that shareholders demand 12 percent no matter how much debt the firm has and that bondholders always want 8 percent. The weighted-average cost of capital starts at 12 percent and ends up at 8. Suppose that this firm's operating income is a level, perpetual stream of $100,000 a year. Then firm value starts at

$$V = \frac{100,000}{.12} = \$833,333$$

and ends up at

$$V = \frac{100,000}{.08} = \$1,250,000$$

The gain of $416,667 falls into the stockholders' pockets.[11]

Of course this is absurd: A firm that reaches 100 percent debt *has to be bankrupt.* If there is *any* chance that the firm could remain solvent, then the equity retains

---

[11]Note that Figure 17.4 relates r_E and r_D to D/V, the ratio of debt to firm value, rather than to the debt–equity ratio D/E. In this figure we wanted to show what happens when the firm is 100 percent debt-financed. At that point $E = 0$ and D/E is infinite.

FIGURE 17.4

If the expected rate of return demanded by stockholders r_E is unaffected by financial leverage, then the weighted-average cost of capital r_A declines as the firm borrows more. At 100 percent debt r_A equals the borrowing rate r_D. Of course this is an absurd and totally unrealistic case.

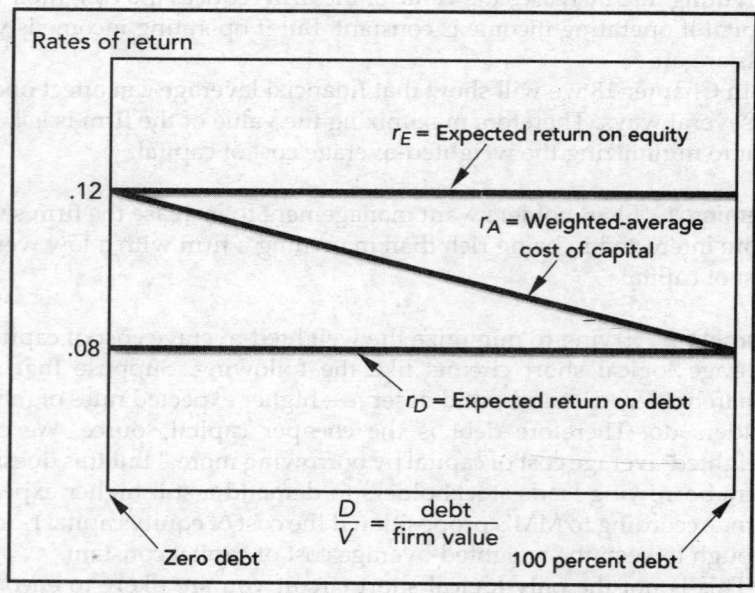

some value, and the firm cannot be 100 percent debt-financed. (Remember that we are working with the *market* values of debt and equity.)

But if the firm is bankrupt and its original shares are worthless pieces of paper, then its *lenders are its new shareholders.* The firm is back to all-equity financing! We assumed that the original stockholders demanded 12 percent—why should the new ones demand any less? They have to bear all of the firm's business risk.[12]

The situation described in Figure 17.4 is just impossible.[13] However, it is possible to stake out a position somewhere *between* Figures 17.3 and 17.4. That is exactly what the traditionalists have done. Their hypothesis is shown in Figure 17.5. They hold that a moderate degree of financial leverage may increase the expected equity return r_E, although not to the degree predicted by MM's proposition II. But irresponsible firms that borrow *excessively* find r_E shooting up faster than MM predict. Consequently, the weighted-average cost of capital r_A declines at first, then rises. Its minimum point is the point of optimal capital structure. Remember that minimizing r_A is equivalent to maximizing overall firm value if, as the traditionalists assume, operating income is unaffected by borrowing.

Two arguments might be advanced in support of the traditional position. First, it could be that investors don't notice or appreciate the financial risk created by "moderate" borrowing, although they wake up when debt is "excessive." If so, investors in moderately leveraged firms may accept a lower rate of return than they really should.

---

[12]We ignore the costs, delays, and other complications of bankruptcy. They are discussed in Chapter 18.

[13]This case is often termed the *net-income* (NI) approach because investors are assumed to capitalize income *after* interest at the same rate regardless of financial leverage. In contrast, MM's approach is a net-operating-income (NOI) approach because the value of the firm is fundamentally determined by operating income, the total dollar return to *both* bondholders and stockholders. This distinction was emphasized by D. Durand in his important, pre-MM paper, "Cost of Debt and Equity Funds for Business: Trends and Problems of Measurement," in *Conference on Research in Business Finance*, National Bureau of Economic Research, New York, 1952.

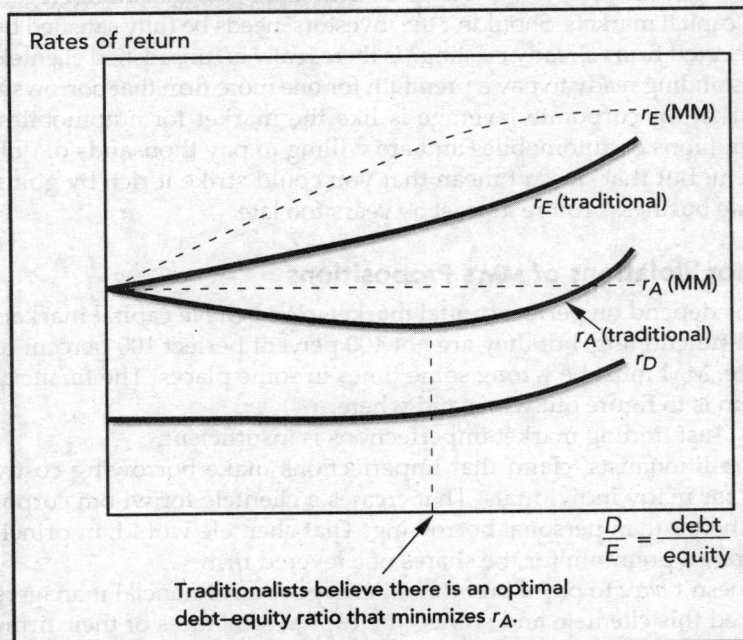

FIGURE 17.5

The dashed lines show MM's view of the effect of leverage on the expected return on equity r_E and the weighted-average cost of capital r_A. (See Figure 17.2.) The solid lines show the traditional view. Traditionalists say that borrowing at first increases r_E more slowly than MM predict but that r_E shoots up with excessive borrowing. If so, the weighted-average cost of capital can be minimized if you use just the right amount of debt.

In the figure, the vertical axis is labeled "Rates of return" and curves are labeled r_E (MM), r_E (traditional), r_A (MM), r_A (traditional), and r_D. The horizontal axis is labeled $\frac{D}{E} = \frac{debt}{equity}$. A note reads: "Traditionalists believe there is an optimal debt–equity ratio that minimizes r_A."

That seems naive.[14] The second argument is better. It accepts MM's reasoning as applied to perfect capital markets but holds that actual markets are imperfect. Imperfections may allow firms that borrow to provide a valuable service for investors. If so, levered shares might trade at premium prices compared to their theoretical values in perfect markets.

Suppose that corporations can borrow more cheaply than individuals. Then it would pay investors who want to borrow to do so indirectly by holding the stock of levered firms. They would be willing to live with expected rates of return that do not fully compensate them for the business and financial risk they bear.

Is corporate borrowing really cheaper? It's hard to say. Interest rates on home mortgages are not too different from rates on high-grade corporate bonds.[15] Rates on margin debt (borrowing from a stockbroker with the investor's shares tendered as security) are not too different from the rates firms pay banks for short-term loans.

There are some individuals who face relatively high interest rates, largely because of the costs lenders incur in making and servicing small loans. There are economies of scale in borrowing. A group of small investors could do better by borrowing via a corporation, in effect pooling their loans and saving transaction costs.[16]

---

[14]This first argument may reflect a confusion between financial risk and the risk of default. Default is not a serious threat when borrowing is moderate; stockholders worry about it only when the firm goes "too far." But stockholders bear financial risk—in the form of increased volatility of rate of return and higher beta—even when the chance of default is nil. We demonstrated this in Figure 17.3.

[15]One of the authors once obtained a home mortgage at a rate ½ percentage point *less* than the contemporaneous yield on long-term AAA bonds.

[16]Even here there are alternatives to borrowing on personal account. Investors can draw down their savings accounts or sell a portion of their investment in bonds. The impact of reductions in lending on the investor's balance sheet and risk position is exactly the same as increases in borrowing.

But suppose that this class of investors is large, both in number and in the aggregate wealth it brings to capital markets. Shouldn't the investors' needs be fully satisfied by the thousands of levered firms already existing? Is there really an unsatisfied clientele of small investors standing ready to pay a premium for one more firm that borrows?

Maybe the market for corporate leverage is like the market for automobiles. Americans need millions of automobiles and are willing to pay thousands of dollars apiece for them. But that doesn't mean that you could strike it rich by going into the automobile business. You're at least 50 years too late.

Where to Look for Violations of MM's Propositions

MM's propositions depend on perfect capital markets. We believe capital markets are generally well-functioning, but they are not 100 percent perfect 100 percent of the time. Therefore, MM must be wrong some times in some places. The financial manager's problem is to figure out when and where.

That is not easy. Just finding market imperfections is insufficient.

Consider the traditionalists' claim that imperfections make borrowing costly and inconvenient for many individuals. That creates a clientele for whom corporate borrowing is better than personal borrowing. That clientele would, in principle, be willing to pay a premium for the shares of a levered firm.

But maybe it doesn't *have* to pay a premium. Perhaps smart financial managers long ago recognized this clientele and shifted the capital structures of their firms to meet its needs. The shifts would not have been difficult or costly to make. But if the clientele is now satisfied, it is no longer willing to pay a premium for levered shares. Only the financial managers who *first* recognized the clientele extracted any advantage from it.

Today's Unsatisfied Clienteles Are Probably Interested in Exotic Securities

So far we have made little progress in identifying cases where firm value might plausibly depend on financing. But our examples illustrate what smart financial managers look for. They look for an *unsatisfied* clientele, investors who want a particular kind of financial instrument but because of market imperfections can't get it or can't get it cheaply.

MM's proposition I is violated when the firm, by imaginative design of its capital structure, can offer some *financial service* that meets the needs of such a clientele. Either the service must be new and unique or the firm must find a way to provide some old service more cheaply than other firms or financial intermediaries can.

Now, is there an unsatisfied clientele for garden-variety debt or levered equity? We doubt it. But perhaps you can invent an exotic security and uncover a latent demand for it.

In the next several chapters we will encounter a number of new securities that have been invented by companies and advisers. These securities take the company's basic cash flows and repackage them in ways that are thought to be more attractive to investors. However, while inventing these new securities is easy, it is more difficult to find investors who will rush to buy them.[17]

Imperfections and Opportunities

The most serious capital market imperfections are often those created by government. An imperfection which supports a violation of MM's proposition I *also* cre-

---

[17]We return to the topic of security innovation in Section 25.8.

ates a money-making opportunity. Firms and intermediaries will find some way to reach the clientele of investors frustrated by the imperfection.

For many years the United States government imposed a limit on the rate of interest that could be paid on savings accounts. It did so to protect savings institutions by limiting competition for their depositors' money. The fear was that depositors would run off in search of higher yields, causing a cash drain that savings institutions would not be able to meet. This would cut off the supply of funds from those institutions for new real estate mortgages and knock the housing market for a loop. The savings institutions could not have afforded to offer higher interest rates on deposits—even if the government had allowed them to—because most of their past deposits had been locked up in fixed-rate mortgages issued when interest rates were much lower.

These regulations created an opportunity for firms and financial institutions to design new savings schemes that were not subject to the interest-rate ceilings. One invention was the *floating-rate note,* first issued on a large scale and with terms designed to appeal to individual investors by Citicorp in July 1974. Floating-rate notes are medium-term debt securities whose interest payments "float" with short-term interest rates. On the Citicorp issue, for example, the coupon rate used to calculate each semiannual interest payment was set at 1 percentage point above the contemporaneous yield on Treasury bills. The holder of the Citicorp note was therefore protected against fluctuating interest rates, because Citicorp sent a larger semiannual check when interest rates rose (and, of course, a smaller check when rates fell).

Citicorp evidently found an untapped clientele of investors, for it was able to raise $650 million in the first offering. The success of the issue suggests that Citicorp was able to add value by changing its capital structure. However, other companies were quick to jump on Citicorp's bandwagon, and within five months an additional $650 million of floating-rate notes were issued by other companies. By the mid-1980s about $43 billion of floating-rate securities were outstanding, though by that time the interest-rate ceiling was no longer a motive.

Interest-rate regulation also provided financial institutions with an opportunity to create value by offering money-market funds. These are mutual funds invested in Treasury bills, commercial paper, and other high-grade, short-term debt instruments. Any saver with a few thousand dollars to invest can gain access to these instruments through a money-market fund and can withdraw money at any time by writing a check against his or her fund balance. Thus the fund resembles a checking or savings account which pays close to market interest rates.[18] These money-market funds have become enormously popular. By 2001, their assets had increased to $2 trillion.

As floating-rate notes, money-market funds, and other instruments became more easily available, the protection given by government restrictions on savings account rates became less and less helpful. Finally the restrictions were lifted, and savings institutions met their competition head-on.

Long before interest-rate ceilings were finally removed, most of the gains had gone out of issuing the new securities to individual investors. Once the clientele was finally satisfied, MM's proposition I was restored (until the government creates a new imperfection). The moral of the story is this: If you ever find an unsatisfied clientele, do something right away, or capital markets will evolve and steal it from you.

---

[18]Money-market funds offer rates slightly lower than those on the securities they invest in. This spread covers the fund's operating costs and profits.

SUMMARY

At the start of this chapter we characterized the firm's financing decision as a marketing problem. Think of the financial manager as taking all of the firm's real assets and selling them to investors as a package of securities. Some financial managers choose the simplest package possible: all-equity financing. Some end up issuing dozens of debt and equity securities. The problem is to find the particular combination that maximizes the market value of the firm.

Modigliani and Miller's (MM's) famous proposition I states that no combination is better than any other—that the firm's overall market value (the value of all its securities) is independent of capital structure. Firms that borrow do offer investors a more complex menu of securities, but investors yawn in response. The menu is redundant. Any shift in capital structure can be duplicated or "undone" by investors. Why should they pay extra for borrowing indirectly (by holding shares in a levered firm) when they can borrow just as easily and cheaply on their own accounts?

MM agree that borrowing increases the expected rate of return on shareholders' investments. But it also increases the risk of the firm's shares. MM show that the risk increase exactly offsets the increase in expected return, leaving stockholders no better or worse off.

Proposition I is an extremely general result. It applies not just to the debt–equity trade-off but to *any* choice of financing instruments. For example, MM would say that the choice between long-term and short-term debt has no effect on firm value.

The formal proofs of proposition I all depend on the assumption of perfect capital markets.[19] MM's opponents, the "traditionalists," argue that market imperfections make personal borrowing excessively costly, risky, and inconvenient for some investors. This creates a natural clientele willing to pay a premium for shares of levered firms. The traditionalists say that firms should borrow to realize the premium.

But this argument is incomplete. There may be a clientele for levered equity, but that is not enough; the clientele has to be *unsatisfied*. There are already thousands of levered firms available for investment. Is there still an unsatiated clientele for garden-variety debt and equity? We doubt it.

Proposition I is violated when financial managers find an untapped demand and satisfy it by issuing something new and different. The argument between MM and the traditionalists finally boils down to whether this is difficult or easy. We lean toward MM's view: Finding unsatisfied clienteles and designing exotic securities to meet their needs is a game that's fun to play but hard to win.

---

[19]Proposition I can be proved umpteen different ways. The references at the end of this chapter include several more abstract and general proofs. Our formal proofs have been limited to MM's own arguments.

FURTHER READING

The pioneering work on the theory of capital structure is:

F. Modigliani and M. H. Miller: "The Cost of Capital, Corporation Finance and the Theory of Investment," *American Economic Review*, 48:261–297 (June 1958).

However, Durand deserves credit for setting out the issues that MM later solved:

D. Durand: "Cost of Debt and Equity Funds for Business: Trends and Problems in Measurement," in *Conference on Research in Business Finance*, National Bureau of Economic Research, New York, 1952, pp. 215–247.

MM provided a shorter and clearer proof of capital structure irrelevance in:

F. Modigliani and M. H. Miller: "Reply to Heins and Sprenkle," *American Economic Review,* 59:592–595 (September 1969).

A somewhat difficult article which analyzes capital structure in the context of capital asset pricing theory is:

R. S. Hamada: "Portfolio Analysis, Market Equilibrium and Corporation Finance," *Journal of Finance,* 24:13–31 (March 1969).

More abstract and general theoretical treatments can be found in:

J. E. Stiglitz: "On the Irrelevance of Corporate Financial Policy," *American Economic Review,* 64:851–866 (December 1974).

E. F. Fama: "The Effects of a Firm's Investment and Financing Decisions," *American Economic Review,* 68:272–284 (June 1978).

The fall 1988 issue of the Journal of Economic Perspectives *contains an anniversary collection of articles, including one by Modigliani and Miller, which review and assess the MM propositions. The summer 1989 issue of* Financial Management *contains three more articles under the heading "Reflections on the MM Propositions 30 Years Later."*

QUIZ

1. Assume a perfectly competitive market with no corporate or personal taxes. Companies A and B each earn gross profits of P and differ only in their capital structure—A is wholly equity-financed and B has debt outstanding on which it pays a certain $100 of interest each year. Investor X purchases 10 percent of the equity of A.
   a. What profits does X obtain?
   b. What alternative strategy would provide the same result?
   c. Suppose investor Y purchases 10 percent of the equity of B. What profits does Y obtain?
   d. What alternative strategy would provide the same result?

2. Ms. Kraft owns 50,000 shares of the common stock of Copperhead Corporation with a market value of $2 per share, or $100,000 overall. The company is currently financed as follows:

	Book Value
Common stock (8 million shares)	$2 million
Short-term loans	$2 million

   Copperhead now announces that it is replacing $1 million of short-term debt with an issue of common stock. What action can Ms. Kraft take to ensure that she is entitled to exactly the same proportion of profits as before? (Ignore taxes.)

3. The common stock and debt of Northern Sludge are valued at $50 million and $30 million, respectively. Investors currently require a 16 percent return on the common stock and an 8 percent return on the debt. If Northern Sludge issues an additional $10 million of common stock and uses this money to retire debt, what happens to the expected return on the stock? Assume that the change in capital structure does not affect the risk of the debt and that there are no taxes. If the risk of the debt did increase, would your answer underestimate or overestimate the expected return on the stock?

4. Company C is financed entirely by common stock and has a β of 1.0. The stock has a price–earnings multiple of 10 and is priced to offer a 10 percent expected return. The company decides to repurchase half the common stock and substitute an equal value of debt. Assume that the debt yields a risk-free 5 percent.
   a. Give
      i. The beta of the common stock after the refinancing.
      ii. The beta of the debt.
      iii. The beta of the company (i.e., stock and debt combined).

    b. Give

        i. Investors' required return on the common stock before the refinancing.

        ii. The required return on the common stock after the refinancing.

        iii. The required return on the debt.

        iv. The required return on the company (i.e., stock and debt combined) after the refinancing.

    c. Assume that the operating profit of firm C is expected to remain constant. Give

        i. The percentage increase in earnings per share.

        ii. The new price–earnings multiple.

5. Suppose that Macbeth Spot Removers issues $2,500 of debt and uses the proceeds to repurchase 250 shares.

    a. Rework Table 17.2 to show how earnings per share and share return now vary with operating income.

    b. If the beta of Macbeth's assets is .8 and its debt is risk-free, what would be the beta of the equity after the increased borrowing?

6. True or false? Explain briefly.

    a. Stockholders always benefit from an increase in company value.

    b. MM's proposition I assumes that actions which maximize firm value also maximize shareholder wealth.

    c. The reason that borrowing increases equity risk is because it increases the probability of bankruptcy.

    d. If firms did not have limited liability, the risk of their assets would be increased.

    e. If firms did not have limited liability, the risk of their equity would be increased.

    f. Borrowing does not affect the return on equity if the return on the firm's assets is equal to the interest rate.

    g. As long as the firm is certain that the return on assets will be higher than the interest rate, an issue of debt makes the shareholders better off.

    h. MM's proposition I implies that an issue of debt increases expected earnings per share and leads to an offsetting fall in the price–earnings ratio.

    i. MM's proposition II assumes increased borrowing does not affect the interest rate on the firm's debt.

    j. Borrowing increases firm value if there is a clientele of investors with a reason to prefer debt.

7. Note the two blank graphs in Figure 17.6. On graph (*a*), assume MM are right, and plot the relationship between financial leverage and (i) the rates of return on debt and equity and (ii) the weighted-average cost of capital. Then fill in graph (*b*), assuming the traditionalists are right.

8. Look back to Section 17.1. Suppose that Ms. Macbeth's investment bankers have informed her that since the new issue of debt is risky, debtholders will demand a return of 12.5 percent, which is 2.5 percent above the risk-free interest rate.

    a. What are r_A and r_E?

    b. Suppose that the beta of the unlevered stock was .6. What will be β_A, β_E, and β_D after the change to the capital structure?

    c. Assuming that the capital asset pricing model is correct, what is the expected return on the market?

9. Capitale Netto s.a. is financed solely by common stock, which offers an expected return of 13 percent. Suppose now that the company issues debt and repurchases stock so that its debt ratio is .4. Investors note the extra risk and raise their required return on the stock to 15 percent.

    a. What is the interest rate on the debt?

    b. If the debt is risk-free and the beta of the equity after the refinancing is 1.5, what is the expected return on the market?

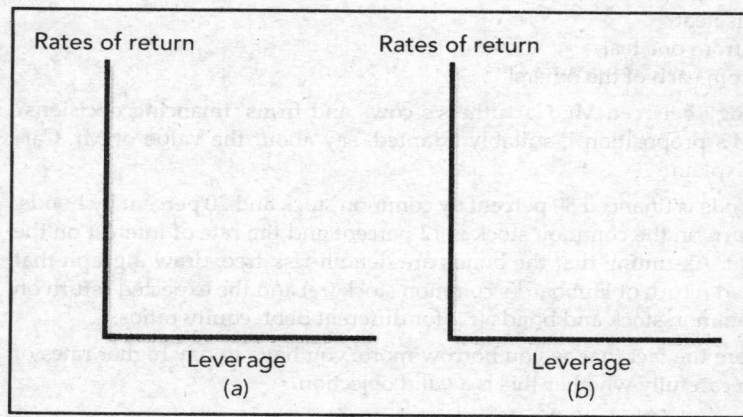

FIGURE 17.6

See quiz question 7.

10. Executive Chalk is financed solely by common stock and has outstanding 25 million shares with a market price of $10 a share. It now announces that it intends to issue $160 million of debt and to use the proceeds to buy back common stock.
    a. How is the market price of the stock affected by the announcement?
    b. How many shares can the company buy back with the $160 million of new debt that it issues?
    c. What is the market value of the firm (equity plus debt) after the change in capital structure?
    d. What is the debt ratio after the change in structure?
    e. Who (if anyone) gains or loses?

    Now try the next question.

11. Executive Cheese has issued debt with a market value of $100 million and has outstanding 15 million shares with a market price of $10 a share. It now announces that it intends to issue a further $60 million of debt and to use the proceeds to buy back common stock. Debtholders, seeing the extra risk, mark the value of the existing debt down to $70 million.
    a. How is the market price of the stock affected by the announcement?
    b. How many shares can the company buy back with the $60 million of new debt that it issues?
    c. What is the market value of the firm (equity plus debt) after the change in capital structure?
    d. What is the debt ratio after the change in structure?
    e. Who (if anyone) gains or loses?

PRACTICE QUESTIONS

1. Companies A and B differ only in their capital structure. A is financed 30 percent debt and 70 percent equity; B is financed 10 percent debt and 90 percent equity. The debt of both companies is risk-free.
   a. Rosencrantz owns 1 percent of the common stock of A. What other investment package would produce identical cash flows for Rosencrantz?
   b. Guildenstern owns 2 percent of the common stock of B. What other investment package would produce identical cash flows for Guildenstern?
   c. Show that neither Rosencrantz nor Guildenstern would invest in the common stock of B if the *total* value of company A were less than that of B.

2. Here is a limerick:

   There once was a man named Carruthers,
   Who kept cows with miraculous udders.

He said, "Isn't this neat?
They give cream from one teat,
And skim milk from each of the others!"

What is the analogy between Mr. Carruthers's cows and firms' financing decisions? What would MM's proposition I, suitably adapted, say about the value of Mr. Carruthers's cows? Explain.

3. Hubbard's Pet Foods is financed 80 percent by common stock and 20 percent by bonds. The expected return on the common stock is 12 percent and the rate of interest on the bonds is 6 percent. Assuming that the bonds are default-risk free, draw a graph that shows the expected return of Hubbard's common stock (r_E) and the expected return on the package of common stock and bonds (r_A) for different debt–equity ratios.

4. "MM totally ignore the fact that as you borrow more, you have to pay higher rates of interest." Explain carefully whether this is a valid objection.

5. Indicate what's wrong with the following arguments:
   a. "As the firm borrows more and debt becomes risky, both stockholders and bondholders demand higher rates of return. Thus by *reducing* the debt ratio we can reduce *both* the cost of debt and the cost of equity, making everybody better off."
   b. "Moderate borrowing doesn't significantly affect the probability of financial distress or bankruptcy. Consequently moderate borrowing won't increase the expected rate of return demanded by stockholders."

6. Each of the following statements is false or at least misleading. Explain why in each case.
   a. "A capital investment opportunity offering a 10 percent DCF rate of return is an attractive project if it can be 100 percent debt-financed at an 8 percent interest rate."
   b. "The more debt the firm issues, the higher the interest rate it must pay. That is one important reason why firms should operate at conservative debt levels."

7. Can you invent any new kinds of debt that might be attractive to investors? Why do you think they have not been issued?

8. It has been suggested that one disadvantage of common stock financing is that share prices tend to decline in recessions, thereby increasing the cost of capital and deterring investment. Discuss this view. Is it an argument for greater use of debt financing?

9. Figure 17.5 shows that r_D increases as the debt–equity ratio increases. In MM's world r_E also increases but at a declining rate. Explain why.
   Redraw Figure 17.5, showing how r_D and r_E change for increasingly high debt–equity ratios. Can r_D ever be higher than r_A? Can r_E decline beyond a certain debt–equity ratio?

10. Imagine a firm that is expected to produce a level stream of operating profits. As leverage is increased, what happens to
    a. The ratio of the market value of the equity to income after interest?
    b. The ratio of the market value of the *firm* to income before interest if (i) MM are right and (ii) the traditionalists are right?

11. Archimedes Levers is financed by a mixture of debt and equity. You have the following information about its cost of capital:

$$r_E = \underline{\quad} \qquad r_D = 12\% \qquad r_A = \underline{\quad}$$
$$\beta_E = 1.5 \qquad \beta_D = \underline{\quad} \qquad \beta_A = \underline{\quad}$$
$$r_f = 10\% \qquad r_m = 18\% \qquad D/V = .5$$

Can you fill in the blanks?

12. Look back at question 11. Suppose now that Archimedes repurchases debt and issues equity so that $D/V = .3$. The reduced borrowing causes r_D to fall to 11 percent. How do the other variables change?

13. Schuldenfrei a.g. pays no taxes and is financed entirely by common stock. The stock has a beta of .8, a price–earnings ratio of 12.5, and is priced to offer an 8 percent expected return. Schuldenfrei now decides to repurchase half the common stock and substitute an equal value of debt. If the debt yields a *risk-free* 5 percent, calculate
   a. The beta of the common stock after the refinancing.
   b. The required return and risk premium on the stock before the refinancing.
   c. The required return and risk premium on the stock after the refinancing.
   d. The required return on the debt.
   e. The required return on the company (i.e., stock and debt combined) after the refinancing.
   Assume that the operating profit of the firm is expected to remain constant in perpetuity. Give
   f. The percentage increase in expected earnings per share.
   g. The new price–earnings multiple.

14. Gamma Airlines is currently all-equity-financed, and its shares offer an expected return of 18 percent. The risk-free interest rate is 10 percent. Draw a graph with return on the vertical axis and debt–equity ratio (D/E) on the horizontal axis, and plot for different levels of leverage the expected return on assets (r_A), the expected return on equity (r_E), and the return on debt (r_D). Assume that the debt is risk-free. Now draw a similar graph with the debt ratio (D/V) on the horizontal axis.

15. Two firms, U and L, are identical except for their capital structure. Both will earn $150 in a boom and $50 in a slump. There is a 50 percent chance of each event. U is entirely equity-financed, and therefore shareholders receive the entire income. Its shares are valued at $500. L has issued $400 of risk-free debt at an interest rate of 10 percent, and therefore $40 of L's income is paid out as interest. There are no taxes or other market imperfections. Investors can borrow and lend at the risk-free rate of interest.
   a. What is the value of L's stock?
   b. Suppose that you invest $20 in U's stock. Is there an alternative investment in L that would give identical payoffs in boom and slump? What is the expected payoff from such a strategy?
   c. Now suppose that you invest $20 in L's stock. Design an alternative strategy with identical payoffs.
   d. Now show that MM's proposition II holds.

CHALLENGE
QUESTIONS

1. Consider the following three tickets: ticket A pays $10 if ____ is elected as president, ticket B pays $10 if ____ is elected, and ticket C pays $10 if neither is elected. (Fill in the blanks yourself.) Could the three tickets sell for less than the present value of $10? Could they sell for more? Try auctioning off the tickets. What are the implications for MM's proposition I?

2. People often convey the idea behind MM's proposition I by various supermarket analogies, for example, "The value of a pie should not depend on how it is sliced," or, "The cost of a whole chicken should equal the cost of assembling one by buying two drumsticks, two wings, two breasts, and so on."

   Actually proposition I doesn't work in the supermarket. You'll pay less for an uncut whole pie than for a pie assembled from pieces purchased separately. Supermarkets charge more for chickens after they are cut up. Why? What costs or imperfections cause proposition I to fail in the supermarket? Are these costs or imperfections likely to be important for corporations issuing securities on the U.S. or world capital markets? Explain.

CHAPTER EIGHTEEN

HOW MUCH SHOULD A FIRM BORROW?

IN CHAPTER 17 we found that debt policy rarely matters in well-functioning capital markets. Few financial managers would accept that conclusion as a practical guideline. If debt policy doesn't matter, then they shouldn't worry about it—financing decisions should be delegated to underlings. Yet financial managers do worry about debt policy. This chapter explains why.

If debt policy were *completely* irrelevant, then actual debt ratios should vary randomly from firm to firm and industry to industry. Yet almost all airlines, utilities, banks, and real estate development companies rely heavily on debt. And so do many firms in capital-intensive industries like steel, aluminum, chemicals, petroleum, and mining. On the other hand, it is rare to find a drug company or advertising agency that is not predominantly equity-financed. Glamorous growth companies rarely use much debt despite rapid expansion and often heavy requirements for capital.

The explanation of these patterns lies partly in the things we left out of the last chapter. We ignored taxes. We assumed bankruptcy was cheap, quick, and painless. It isn't, and there are costs associated with financial distress even if legal bankruptcy is ultimately avoided. We ignored potential conflicts of interest between the firm's security holders. For example, we did not consider what happens to the firm's "old" creditors when new debt is issued or when a shift in investment strategy takes the firm into a riskier business. We ignored the information problems that favor debt over equity when cash must be raised from new security issues. We ignored the incentive effects of financial leverage on management's investment and payout decisions.

Now we will put all these things back in: taxes first, then the costs of bankruptcy and financial distress. This will lead us to conflicts of interest and to information and incentive problems. In the end we will have to admit that debt policy *does* matter.

However, we will *not* throw away the MM theory we developed so carefully in Chapter 17. We're shooting for a theory combining MM's insights *plus* the effects of taxes, costs of bankruptcy and financial distress, and various other complications. We're not dropping back to the traditional view based on inefficiencies in the capital market. Instead, we want to see how well-functioning capital markets *respond* to taxes and the other things covered in this chapter.

 ## 18.1 CORPORATE TAXES

Debt financing has one important advantage under the corporate income tax system in the United States. The interest that the company pays is a tax-deductible expense. Dividends and retained earnings are not. Thus the return to bondholders escapes taxation at the corporate level.

Table 18.1 shows simple income statements for firm U, which has no debt, and firm L, which has borrowed $1,000 at 8 percent. The tax bill of L is $28 less than that of U. This is the *tax shield* provided by the debt of L. In effect the government pays 35 percent of the interest expense of L. The total income that L can pay out to its bondholders and stockholders increases by that amount.

Tax shields can be valuable assets. Suppose that the debt of L is fixed and permanent. (That is, the company commits to refinance its present debt obligations when they mature and to keep rolling over its debt obligations indefinitely.) It looks forward to a permanent stream of cash flows of $28 per year. The risk of these flows is likely to be less than the risk of the operating assets of L. The tax shields

TABLE 18.1

The tax deductibility of interest increases the total income that can be paid out to bondholders and stockholders.

	Income Statement of Firm U	Income Statement of Firm L
Earnings before interest and taxes	$1,000	$1,000
Interest paid to bondholders	0	80
Pretax income	1,000	920
Tax at 35%	350	322
Net income to stockholders	$ 650	$ 598
Total income to both bondholders and stockholders	$0 + 650 = $650	$80 + 598 = $678
Interest tax shield (.35 × interest)	$0	$28

depend only on the corporate tax rate[1] and on the ability of L to earn enough to cover interest payments. The corporate tax rate has been pretty stable. (It did fall from 46 to 34 percent after the Tax Reform Act of 1986, but that was the first material change since the 1950s.) And the ability of L to earn its interest payments must be reasonably sure; otherwise it could not have borrowed at 8 percent.[2] Therefore we should discount the interest tax shields at a relatively low rate.

But what rate? One common assumption is that the risk of the tax shields is the same as that of the interest payments generating them. Thus we discount at 8 percent, the expected rate of return demanded by investors who are holding the firm's debt:

$$PV(\text{tax shield}) = \frac{28}{.08} = \$350$$

In effect the government itself assumes 35 percent of the $1,000 debt obligation of L.

Under these assumptions, the present value of the tax shield is independent of the return on the debt r_D. It equals the corporate tax rate T_c times the amount borrowed D:

$$\text{Interest payment} = \text{return on debt} \times \text{amount borrowed}$$
$$= r_D \times D$$

$$PV(\text{tax shield}) = \frac{\text{corporate tax rate} \times \text{expected interest payment}}{\text{expected return on debt}}$$
$$= \frac{T_c(r_D D)}{r_D} = T_c D$$

Of course, PV(tax shield) is less if the firm does not plan to borrow permanently, or if it may not be able to use the tax shields in the future.

---

[1]Always use the marginal corporate tax rate, not the average rate. Average rates are often much lower than marginal rates because of accelerated depreciation and other tax adjustments. For large corporations, the marginal rate is usually taken as the statutory rate, which was 35 percent when this chapter was written (2001). However, effective marginal rates can be less than the statutory rate, especially for smaller, riskier companies which cannot be sure that they will earn taxable income in the future.

[2]If the income of L does not cover interest in some future year, the tax shield is not necessarily lost. L can carry back the loss and receive a tax refund up to the amount of taxes paid in the previous three years. If L has a string of losses, and thus no prior tax payments that can be refunded, then losses can be carried forward and used to shield income in subsequent years.

Normal Balance Sheet (Market Values)	
Asset value (present value of after-tax cash flows)	Debt
	Equity
Total assets	Total value
Expanded Balance Sheet (Market Values)	
Pretax asset value (present value of *pretax* cash flows)	Debt
	Government's claim (present value of future taxes)
	Equity
Total pretax assets	Total pretax value

TABLE 18.2

Normal and expanded market value balance sheets. In a normal balance sheet, assets are valued after tax. In the expanded balance sheet, assets are valued pretax, and the value of the government's tax claim is recognized on the right-hand side. Interest tax shields are valuable because they reduce the government's claim.

How Do Interest Tax Shields Contribute to the Value of Stockholders' Equity?

MM's proposition I amounts to saying that the value of a pie does not depend on how it is sliced. The pie is the firm's assets, and the slices are the debt and equity claims. If we hold the pie constant, then a dollar more of debt means a dollar less of equity value.

But there is really a third slice, the government's. Look at Table 18.2. It shows an *expanded* balance sheet with *pretax* asset value on the left and the value of the government's tax claim recognized as a liability on the right. MM would still say that the value of the pie—in this case *pretax* asset value—is not changed by slicing. But anything the firm can do to reduce the size of the government's slice obviously makes stockholders better off. One thing it can do is borrow money, which reduces its tax bill and, as we saw in Table 18.1, increases the cash flows to debt and equity investors. The *after-tax* value of the firm (the sum of its debt and equity values as shown in a normal market value balance sheet) goes up by PV(tax shield).

Recasting Pfizer's Capital Structure

Pfizer, Inc., is a large successful firm that uses essentially no long-term debt. Table 18.3(*a*) shows simplified book and market value balance sheets for Pfizer as of year-end 2000.

Suppose that you were Pfizer's financial manager in 2001 with complete responsibility for its capital structure. You decide to borrow $1 billion on a permanent basis and use the proceeds to repurchase shares.

Table 18.3(*b*) shows the new balance sheets. The book version simply has $1,000 million more long-term debt and $1,000 million less equity. But we know that Pfizer's assets must be worth more, for its tax bill has been reduced by 35 percent of the interest on the new debt. In other words, Pfizer has an increase in PV(tax shield), which is worth $T_cD = .35 \times \$1,000$ million = $350 million. If the MM theory holds *except* for taxes, firm value must increase by $350 million to $296,247 million. Pfizer's equity ends up worth $289,794 million.

TABLE 18.3(a)

Simplified balance sheets for Pfizer, Inc., December 31, 2000 (figures in millions).

Notes:
1. Market value is equal to book value for net working capital, long-term debt, and other long-term liabilities. Equity is entered at actual market value: number of shares times closing price on December 29, 2000. The difference between the market and book values of long-term assets is equal to the difference between the market and book values of equity.
2. The market value of the long-term assets includes the tax shield on the existing debt. This tax shield is worth $.35 \times 1{,}123 = \$393$ million.

Book Values			
Net working capital	$ 5,206	$ 1,123	Long-term debt
Long-term assets	16,323	4,330	Other long-term liabilities
		16,076	Equity
Total assets	$ 21,529	$ 21,529	Total value
Market Values			
Net working capital	$ 5,206	$ 1,123	Long-term debt
		4,330	Other long-term liabilities
Market value of long-term assets	290,691	290,444	Equity
Total assets	$295,897	$295,897	Total value

TABLE 18.3(b)

Balance sheets for Pfizer, Inc., with additional $1 billion of long-term debt substituted for stockholders' equity (figures in millions).

Notes:
1. The figures in Table 18.3(b) for net working capital, long-term assets, and other long-term liabilities are identical to those in Table 18.3(a).
2. Present value of tax shields assumed equal to corporate tax rate (35 percent) times additional long-term debt.

Book Values			
Net working capital	$ 5,206	$ 2,123	Long-term debt
Long-term assets	16,323	4,330	Other long-term liabilities
		15,076	Equity
Total assets	$ 21,529	$ 21,529	Total value
Market Values			
Net working capital	$ 5,206	$ 2,123	Long-term debt
		4,330	Other long-term liabilities
Market value of long-term assets	291,041	289,794	Equity
Total assets	$296,247	$296,247	Total value

Now you have repurchased $1,000 million worth of shares, but Pfizer's equity value has dropped by only $650 million. Therefore Pfizer's stockholders must be $350 million ahead. Not a bad day's work.[3]

MM and Taxes

We have just developed a version of MM's proposition I as corrected by them to reflect corporate income taxes.[4] The new proposition is

---

[3]Notice that as long as the bonds are sold at a fair price, all the benefits from the tax shield go to the shareholders.

[4]Interest tax shields are recognized in MM's original article, F. Modigliani and M. H. Miller, "The Cost of Capital, Corporation Finance and the Theory of Investment," *American Economic Review* 48 (June 1958), pp. 261–296. The valuation procedure used in Table 18.3(b) is presented in their 1963 article "Corporate Income Taxes and the Cost of Capital: A Correction," *American Economic Review* 53 (June 1963), pp. 433–443.

Value of firm = value if all-equity-financed + PV(tax shield)

In the special case of permanent debt,

Value of firm = value if all-equity-financed + $T_c D$

Our imaginary financial surgery on Pfizer provides the perfect illustration of the problems inherent in this "corrected" theory. That $350 million came too easily; it seems to violate the law that there is no such thing as a money machine. And if Pfizer's stockholders would be richer with $2,123 million of corporate debt, why not $3,123 or $17,199 million?[5] Our formula implies that firm value and stockholders' wealth continue to go up as D increases. The optimal debt policy appears to be embarrassingly extreme. All firms should be 100 percent debt-financed.

MM were not that fanatical about it. No one would expect the formula to apply at extreme debt ratios. There are several reasons why our calculations overstate the value of interest tax shields. First, it's wrong to think of debt as fixed and perpetual; a firm's ability to carry debt changes over time as profits and firm value fluctuate.[6] Second, many firms face marginal tax rates less than 35 percent. Third, you can't use interest tax shields unless there will be future profits to shield—and no firm can be absolutely sure of that.

But none of these qualifications explains why firms like Pfizer not only exist but also thrive with no debt at all. It is hard to believe that the management of Pfizer is simply missing the boat.

Therefore we have argued ourselves into a corner. There are just two ways out:

1. Perhaps a fuller examination of the U.S. system of corporate *and personal* taxation will uncover a tax disadvantage of corporate borrowing, offsetting the present value of the corporate tax shield.

2. Perhaps firms that borrow incur other costs—bankruptcy costs, for example—offsetting the present value of the tax shield.

We will now explore these two escape routes.

 18.2 CORPORATE AND PERSONAL TAXES

When personal taxes are introduced, the firm's objective is no longer to minimize the *corporate* tax bill; the firm should try to minimize the present value of *all* taxes paid on corporate income. "All taxes" include *personal* taxes paid by bondholders and stockholders.

Figure 18.1 illustrates how corporate and personal taxes are affected by leverage. Depending on the firm's capital structure, a dollar of operating income will

[5]The last figure would correspond to a 100 percent book debt ratio. But Pfizer's *market* value would be $301,524 million according to our formula for firm value. Pfizer's common shares would have an aggregate value of $279,995 million.

[6]The valuation of interest tax shields is discussed again in Section 19.4. Our calculation here adheres to Chapter 19's "Financing Rule 1," which assumes that debt is fixed regardless of future performance of the project or the firm.

FIGURE 18.1

The firm's capital structure determines whether operating income is paid out as interest or equity income. Interest is taxed only at the personal level. Equity income is taxed at both the corporate and the personal levels. However, T_{pE}, the personal tax rate on equity income, can be less than T_p, the personal tax rate on interest income.

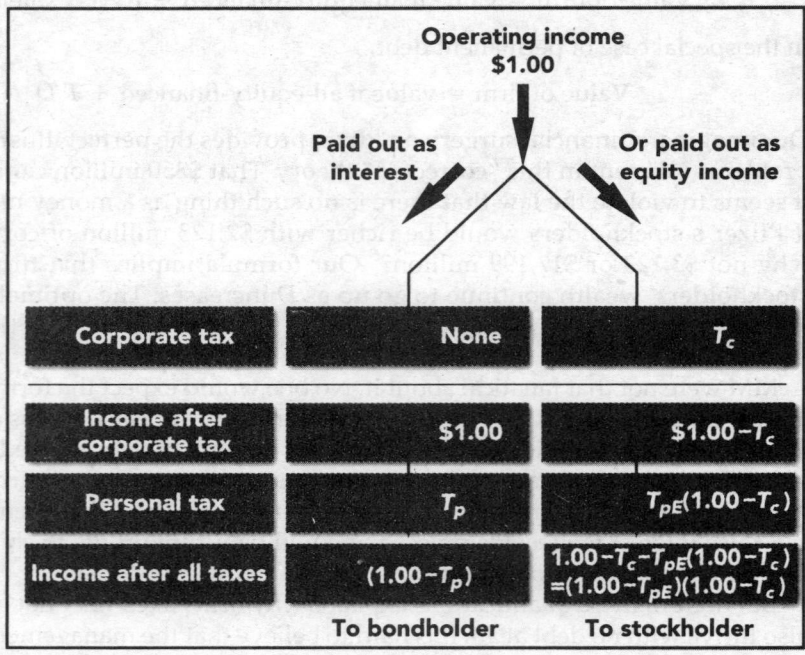

accrue to investors either as debt interest or equity income (dividends or capital gains). That is, the dollar can go down either branch of Figure 18.1.

Notice that Figure 18.1 distinguishes between T_p, the personal tax rate on interest, and T_{pE}, the effective personal rate on equity income. The two rates are equal if equity income comes entirely as dividends. But T_{pE} can be less than T_p if equity income comes as capital gains. In 2001 the top rate on ordinary income, including interest and dividends, was 39.1 percent. The rate on *realized* capital gains was 20 percent.[7] However, capital gains taxes can be deferred until shares are sold, so the top *effective* capital gains rate can be less than 20 percent.

The firm's objective should be to arrange its capital structure so as to maximize after-tax income. You can see from Figure 18.1 that corporate borrowing is better if $(1 - T_p)$ is more than $(1 - T_{pE}) \times (1 - T_c)$; otherwise it is worse. The *relative tax advantage of debt* over equity is

$$\text{Relative tax advantage of debt} = \frac{1 - T_p}{(1 - T_{pE})(1 - T_c)}$$

This suggests two special cases. First, suppose all equity income comes as dividends. Then debt and equity income are taxed at the same effective personal rate. But with $T_{pE} = T_p$, the relative advantage depends only on the *corporate rate*:

$$\text{Relative advantage} = \frac{1 - T_p}{(1 - T_{pE})(1 - T_c)} = \frac{1}{1 - T_c}$$

---

[7]See Section 16.6 for details. Note that we are simplifying by ignoring those corporate investors, such as banks, which pay top rates on capital gains of 35 percent.

In this case, we can forget about personal taxes. The tax advantage of corporate borrowing is exactly as MM calculated it.[8] They do not have to assume away personal taxes. Their theory of debt and taxes requires only that debt and equity be taxed at the same rate.

The second special case occurs when corporate and personal taxes cancel to make debt policy irrelevant. This requires

$$1 - T_p = (1 - T_{pE})(1 - T_c)$$

This case can happen only if T_c, the corporate rate, is less than the personal rate T_p *and* if T_{pE}, the effective rate on equity income, is small. Merton Miller explored this situation at a time when tax rates in the United States were very different from today, but we won't go into the details of his analysis here.[9]

In any event we seem to have a simple, practical decision rule. Arrange the firm's capital structure to shunt operating income down that branch of Figure 18.1 where the tax is least. Unfortunately that is not as simple as it sounds. What's T_{pE}, for example? The shareholder roster of any large corporation is likely to include tax-exempt investors (such as pension funds or university endowments) as well as millionaires. All possible tax brackets will be mixed together. And it's the same with T_p, the personal tax rate on interest. The large corporation's "typical" bondholder might be a tax-exempt pension fund, but many taxpaying investors also hold corporate debt.

Some investors may be much happier to buy your debt than others. For example, you should have no problems inducing pension funds to lend; they don't have to worry about personal tax. But taxpaying investors may be more reluctant to hold debt and will be prepared to do so only if they are compensated by a high rate of interest. Investors paying tax on interest at the top rate of 39.1 percent may be particularly unwilling to hold debt. They will prefer to hold common stock or municipal bonds whose interest is exempt from tax.

To determine the net tax advantage of debt, companies would need to know the tax rates faced by the marginal investor—that is, an investor who is equally happy to hold debt or equity. This makes it hard to put a precise figure on the tax benefit, but we can nevertheless provide a back-of-the-envelope calculation. One way to estimate the tax rate of the marginal debt investor is to see how much yield investors are prepared to give up when they invest in tax-exempt municipal bonds. As we write this in August 2001, short-term municipals yield 2.49 percent, while similar Treasury bonds yield 3.71 percent. An investor with a personal tax rate of 33 percent would receive exactly the same after-tax interest from the two securities and would be equally happy to hold them.[10]

---

[8]Of course, personal taxes reduce the dollar amount of corporate interest tax shields, but the appropriate discount rate for cash flows after personal tax is also lower. If investors are willing to lend at a prospective return *before* personal taxes of r_D, then they must also be willing to accept a return *after* personal taxes of $r_D(1 - T_p)$, where T_p is the marginal rate of personal tax. Thus we can compute the value after personal taxes of the tax shield on permanent debt:

$$PV(\text{tax shield}) = \frac{T_c \times (r_D D) \times (1 - T_p)}{r_D \times (1 - T_p)} = T_c D$$

This brings us back to our previous formula for firm value:

$$\text{Value of firm} = \text{value if all-equity-financed} + T_c D$$

[9]See M. H. Miller, "Debt and Taxes," *Journal of Finance* 32 (May 1977), pp. 261–276.

[10]That is, $(1 - .33) \times 3.71 = 2.49$ percent.

To work out how much tax such an investor would pay on equity income, we need to know the proportion of income that is in the form of capital gains and the tax that is paid on these gains. Companies currently (2001) pay out on average 28 percent of their earnings. So for each $1.00 of equity income, $.28 consists of dividends and the balance of $.72 comprises capital gains. We assume that by not realizing these capital gains immediately, investors can cut the effective tax to one-half the statutory rate on realized gains, that is, $20/2 = 10$ percent[11] Therefore, if our marginal investor invests in common stock, the tax on each $1.00 of equity income is $T_{pE} = (.28 \times .33) + (.72 \times .10) = .16$.

Now we can calculate the effect of shunting a dollar of income down each of the two branches in Figure 18.1:

	Interest	Equity Income
Income before tax	$1.00	$1.00
Less corporate tax at $T_c = .35$	0	.35
Income after corporate tax	1.00	.65
Personal tax at $T_p = .33$ and $T_{pE} = .16$	.33	.107
Income after all taxes	$ .67	$ .543
		Advantage to debt = $.127

The advantage to debt financing appears to be about $.13 on the dollar.

We should emphasize that our back-of-the-envelope calculation is just that. Economists have come up with differing figures for the tax rate of the marginal debtholder and the effective rate of capital gains tax. These estimates may give higher or lower figures for the tax advantage of debt. Also our calculation of the benefits of debt financing assumed that the firm could be confident that it would have sufficient income to shield. In practice few firms can be *sure* they will show a taxable profit in the future. If a firm shows a loss and cannot carry the loss back against past taxes, its interest tax shield must be carried forward with the hope of using it later. The firm loses the time value of money while it waits. If its difficulties are deep enough, the wait may be permanent and the interest tax shield may be lost forever.

Notice also that borrowing is not the only way to shield income against tax. Firms have accelerated write-offs for plant and equipment. Investment in many intangible assets can be expensed immediately. So can contributions to the firm's pension fund. The more that firms shield income in these ways, the lower is the expected shield from corporate borrowing.[12] Even if the firm is confident that it will earn a taxable profit with the current level of debt, it is unlikely to be so positive if the amount of debt is increased.[13]

---

[11]For an analysis of the effective rate of capital gains tax, see R. C. Green and B. Hollifield, "The Personal Tax Advantages of Equity," working paper, Graduate School of Industrial Administration, Carnegie Mellon University, January 2001.

[12]For a discussion of these and other tax shields on company borrowing, see H. DeAngelo and R. Masulis, "Optimal Capital Structure under Corporate and Personal Taxation," *Journal of Financial Economics* 8 (March 1980), pp. 5–29.

[13]For some evidence on the average marginal tax rate of U.S. firms, see J. R. Graham, "Debt and the Marginal Tax Rate," *Journal of Financial Economics* 41 (May 1996), pp. 41–73, and "Proxies for the Corporate Marginal Tax Rate," *Journal of Financial Economics* 42 (October 1996), pp. 187–221.

Thus corporate tax shields are worth more to some firms than to others. Firms with plenty of noninterest tax shields and uncertain future profits should borrow less than consistently profitable firms with lots of taxable profits to shield. Firms with large accumulated tax-loss carry-forwards shouldn't borrow at all. Why should such a firm pay a high rate of interest to induce taxpaying investors to hold its debt when it can't use interest tax shields? All this suggests that there is a moderate tax advantage to corporate borrowing, at least for companies that are reasonably sure they can use the corporate tax shields. For companies that do not expect corporate tax shields there is probably a moderate tax disadvantage.

Do companies make full use of interest tax shields? John Graham argues that they don't. His estimates suggest that for the typical firm unused tax shields are worth nearly 5 percent of company value.[14] Presumably, well-established companies like Pfizer, with effectively no long-term debt, are leaving even more money on the table. It seems either that managers of these firms are missing out or that there are some offsetting disadvantages to increased borrowing. We will now explore this second escape route.

 ## 18.3 COSTS OF FINANCIAL DISTRESS

Financial distress occurs when promises to creditors are broken or honored with difficulty. Sometimes financial distress leads to bankruptcy. Sometimes it only means skating on thin ice.

As we will see, financial distress is costly. Investors know that levered firms may fall into financial distress, and they worry about it. That worry is reflected in the current market value of the levered firm's securities. Thus, the value of the firm can be broken down into three parts:

$$\text{Value of firm} = \text{value if all-equity-financed} + \text{PV(tax shield)} - \text{PV(costs of financial distress)}$$

The costs of financial distress depend on the probability of distress and the magnitude of costs encountered if distress occurs.

Figure 18.2 shows how the trade-off between the tax benefits and the costs of distress determines optimal capital structure. PV(tax shield) initially increases as the firm borrows more. At moderate debt levels the probability of financial distress is trivial, and so PV(cost of financial distress) is small and tax advantages dominate. But at some point the probability of financial distress increases rapidly with additional borrowing; the costs of distress begin to take a substantial bite out of firm value. Also, if the firm can't be sure of profiting from the corporate tax shield, the tax advantage of additional debt is likely to dwindle and eventually disappear. The theoretical optimum is reached when the present value of tax savings due to further borrowing is just offset by increases in the present value of costs of distress. This is called the *trade-off theory* of capital structure.

Costs of financial distress cover several specific items. Now we identify these costs and try to understand what causes them.

---

[14]Graham's estimates for individual firms recognize both the uncertainty in future profits and the existence of noninterest tax shields. See J. R. Graham, "How Big Are the Tax Benefits of Debt?" *Journal of Finance* 55 (October 2000), pp. 1901–1941.

FIGURE 18.2

The value of the firm is equal to its value if all-equity-financed plus PV(tax shield) minus PV(costs of financial distress). According to the trade-off theory of capital structure, the manager should choose the debt ratio that maximizes firm value.

Bankruptcy Costs

You rarely hear anything nice said about corporate bankruptcy. But there is some good in almost everything. Corporate bankruptcies occur when stockholders exercise their *right to default*. That right is valuable; when a firm gets into trouble, limited liability allows stockholders simply to walk away from it, leaving all its troubles to its creditors. The former creditors become the new stockholders, and the old stockholders are left with nothing.

In our legal system all stockholders in corporations automatically enjoy limited liability. But suppose that this were not so. Suppose that there are two firms with identical assets and operations. Each firm has debt outstanding, and each has promised to repay $1,000 (principal and interest) next year. But only one of the firms, Ace Limited, enjoys limited liability. The other firm, Ace Unlimited, does not; its stockholders are personally liable for its debt.

Figure 18.3 compares next year's possible payoffs to the creditors and stockholders of these two firms. The only differences occur when next year's asset value turns out to be less than $1,000. Suppose that next year the assets of each company are worth only $500. In this case Ace Limited defaults. Its stockholders walk away; their payoff is zero. Bondholders get the assets worth $500. But Ace Unlimited's stockholders can't walk away. They have to cough up $500, the difference between asset value and the bondholders' claim. The debt is paid whatever happens.

Suppose that Ace Limited does go bankrupt. Of course, its stockholders are disappointed that their firm is worth so little, but that is an operating problem having nothing to do with financing. Given poor operating performance, the right to go bankrupt—the right to default—is a valuable privilege. As Figure 18.3 shows, Ace Limited's stockholders are in better shape than Unlimited's are.

The example illuminates a mistake people often make in thinking about the costs of bankruptcy. Bankruptcies are thought of as corporate funerals. The mourn-

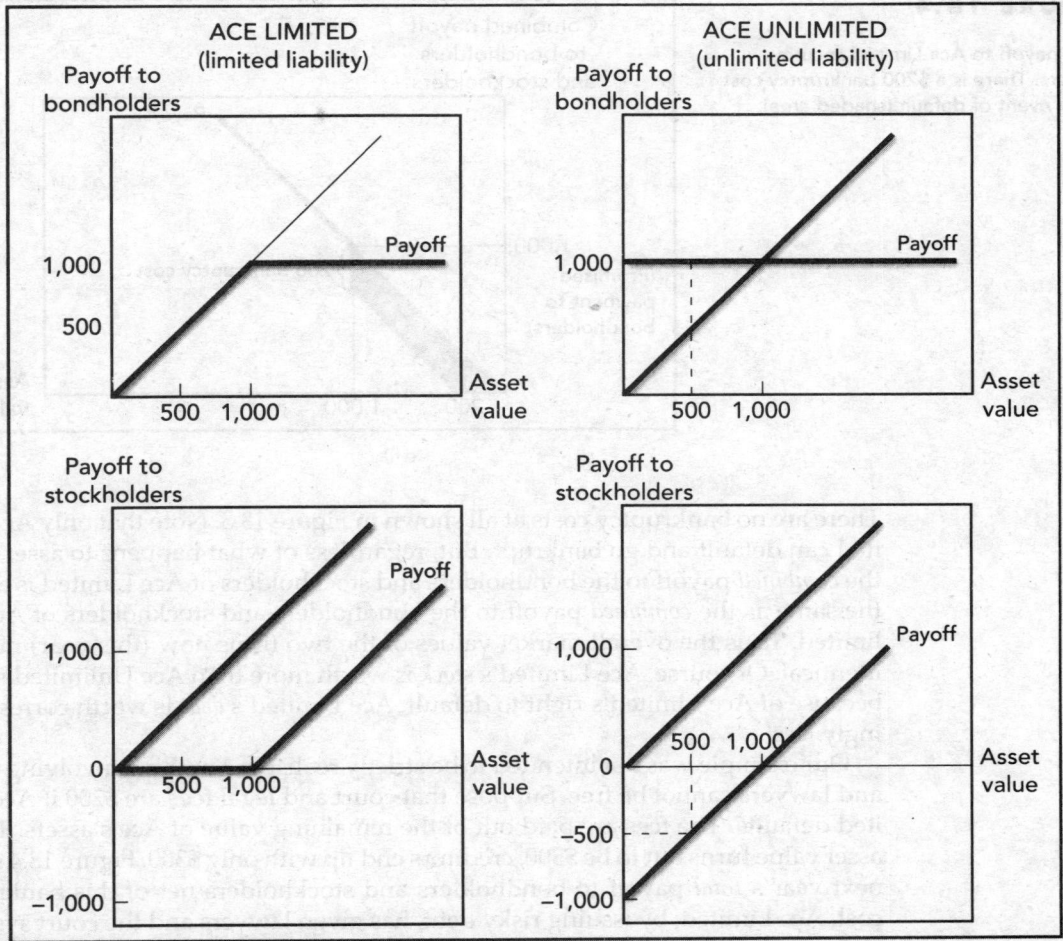

FIGURE 18.3

Comparison of limited and unlimited liability for two otherwise identical firms. If the two firms' asset values are less than $1,000, Ace Limited stockholders default and its bondholders take over the assets. Ace Unlimited stockholders keep the assets, but they must reach into their own pockets to pay off its bondholders. The total payoff to both stockholders and bondholders is the same for the two firms.

ers (creditors and especially shareholders) look at their firm's present sad state. They think of how valuable their securities used to be and how little is left. Moreover, they think of the lost value as a cost of bankruptcy. That is the mistake. The decline in the value of assets is what the mourning is really about. That has no necessary connection with financing. The bankruptcy is merely a legal mechanism for allowing creditors to take over when the decline in the value of assets triggers a default. Bankruptcy is not the *cause* of the decline in value. It is the result.

Be careful not to get cause and effect reversed. When a person dies, we do not cite the implementation of his or her will as the cause of death.

We said that bankruptcy is a legal mechanism allowing creditors to take over when a firm defaults. Bankruptcy costs are the costs of using this mechanism.

FIGURE 18.4

Total payoff to Ace Limited security holders. There is a $200 bankruptcy cost in the event of default (shaded area).

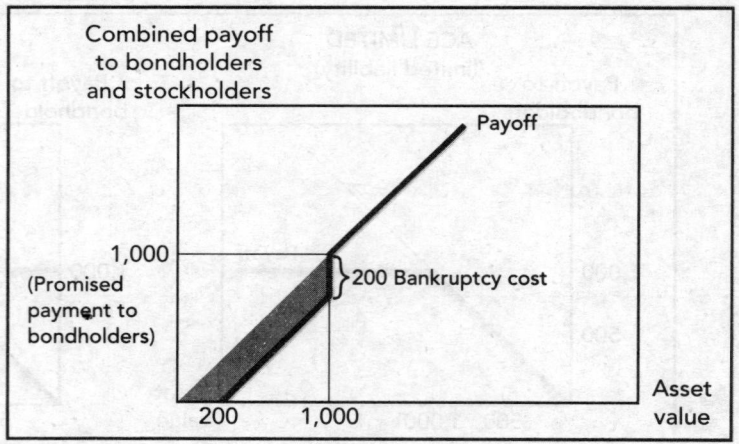

There are no bankruptcy costs at all shown in Figure 18.3. Note that only Ace Limited can default and go bankrupt. But, regardless of what happens to asset value, the *combined* payoff to the bondholders and stockholders of Ace Limited is always the same as the *combined* payoff to the bondholders and stockholders of Ace Unlimited. Thus the overall market values of the two firms now (this year) must be identical. Of course, Ace Limited's *stock* is worth more than Ace Unlimited's stock because of Ace Limited's right to default. Ace Limited's *debt* is worth correspondingly less.

Our example was not intended to be strictly realistic. Anything involving courts and lawyers cannot be free. Suppose that court and legal fees are $200 if Ace Limited defaults. The fees are paid out of the remaining value of Ace's assets. Thus if asset value turns out to be $500, creditors end up with only $300. Figure 18.4 shows next year's *total* payoff to bondholders and stockholders net of this bankruptcy cost. Ace Limited, by issuing risky debt, has given lawyers and the court system a claim on the firm if it defaults. The market value of the firm is reduced by the present value of this claim.

It is easy to see how increased leverage affects the present value of the costs of financial distress. If Ace Limited borrows more, it increases the probability of default and the value of the lawyers' claim. It increases PV (costs of financial distress) and reduces Ace's present market value.

The costs of bankruptcy come out of stockholders' pockets. Creditors foresee the costs and foresee that *they* will pay them if default occurs. For this they demand compensation in advance in the form of higher payoffs when the firm does *not* default; that is, they demand a higher promised interest rate. This reduces the possible payoffs to stockholders and reduces the present market value of their shares.

Evidence on Bankruptcy Costs

Bankruptcy costs can add up fast. Manville, which declared bankruptcy in 1982 because of expected liability for asbestos-related health claims, spent $200 million on fees before it emerged from bankruptcy in 1988.[15] While Eastern Airlines was in

---

[15]S. P. Sherman, "Bankruptcy's Spreading Blight," *Fortune*, June 3, 1991, pp. 123–132.

bankruptcy, it spent $114 million on professional fees.[16] Daunting as such numbers may seem, they are not a large fraction of the companies' asset values. For example, the fees incurred by Eastern amounted to only 3.5 percent of its assets when it entered bankruptcy, or about the equivalent of one jumbo jet.

Lawrence Weiss, who studied 31 firms that went bankrupt between 1980 and 1986, found average costs of about 3 percent of total book assets and 20 percent of the market value of equity in the year prior to bankruptcy. A study by Edward Altman found that costs were similar for retail companies but higher for industrial companies. Also, bankruptcy eats up a larger fraction of asset value for small companies than for large ones. There are significant economies of scale in going bankrupt.[17] Finally, a study by Andrade and Kaplan of a sample of troubled and highly leveraged firms estimated costs of financial distress amounting to 10 to 20 percent of predistress market value.[18] A breakdown of these costs of corporate bankruptcy is provided in the Finance in the News box.

Direct versus Indirect Costs of Bankruptcy

So far we have discussed the *direct* (that is, legal and administrative) costs of bankruptcy. There are indirect costs too, which are nearly impossible to measure. But we have circumstantial evidence indicating their importance.

Some of the indirect costs arise from the reluctance to do business with a firm that may not be around for long. Customers worry about the continuity of supplies and the difficulty of obtaining replacement parts if the firm ceases production. Suppliers are disinclined to put effort into servicing the firm's account and demand cash on the nail for their goods. Potential employees are unwilling to sign on and the existing staff keep slipping away from their desks for job interviews.

Managing a bankrupt firm is not easy. Consent of the bankruptcy court is required for many routine business decisions, such as the sale of assets or investment in new equipment. At best this involves time and effort; at worst the proposals are thwarted by the firm's creditors, who have little interest in the firm's long-term prosperity and would prefer the cash to be paid out to them.

Sometimes the problem is reversed: The bankruptcy court is so anxious to maintain the firm as a going concern that it allows the firm to engage in negative-NPV activities. When Eastern Airlines entered the "protection" of the bankruptcy court in 1989, it still had some valuable, profit-making routes and saleable assets such as planes and terminal facilities. The creditors would have been best served by a prompt liquidation, which probably would have generated enough cash to pay off all debt and preferred stockholders. But the bankruptcy judge was keen to keep Eastern's planes flying at all costs, so he allowed the company to sell many of its assets to fund

---

[16]L. Gibbs and A. Boardman, "A Billion Later, Eastern's Finally Gone," *American Lawyer Newspaper Groups*, February 6, 1995.

[17]The pioneering study of bankruptcy costs is J. B. Warner, "Bankruptcy Costs: Some Evidence," *Journal of Finance* 26 (May 1977), pp. 337–348. The Weiss and Altman papers are L. A. Weiss, "Bankruptcy Resolution: Direct Costs and Violation of Priority of Claims," *Journal of Financial Economics* 27 (October 1990), pp. 285–314, and E. I. Altman, "A Further Investigation of the Bankruptcy Cost Question," *Journal of Finance* 39 (September 1984), pp. 1067–1089.

[18]G. Andrade and S. N. Kaplan, "How Costly is Financial (not Economic) Distress? Evidence from Highly Leveraged Transactions that Became Distressed," *Journal of Finance* 53 (October 1998), pp. 1443–1493.

WHO CAN AFFORD TO GO BROKE?

The costs of going broke are spiralling. Consider what's happening to Pacific Gas & Electric Corp. Since seeking protection from creditors in April 2001, it has been billed more than $7 million in fees from lawyers, investment bankers, and accountants, according to court filings. The company's lead counsel has charged $2.6 million, its investment banker wants $350,000 a month and a $20 million success fee. PG&E will also have to pay the financial adviser

to its creditors, which has proposed $900,000 in fees for two months' work. Industry sources figure PG&E's final tab could total $98 million.

On average a bankrupt company with $1 billion in assets pays advisers as much as $60 million to help strike a deal with creditors (see table).

Source: "Who Can Afford to Go Broke," *Business Week*, September 10, 2001, p. 116.

The High Cost of Chapter 11		
Adviser	**Debtor**	**Creditor**
Lawyer	$500,000–$1 million per month	$300,000–$700,000 per month
Accountant	$200,000 per month	
Investment Banker	$200,000–$250,000 per month; $7 million–$10 million success fee	$175,000–$225,000 per month; $3 million–$8 million success fee
Total bill for $1 billion distressed company in 18 months	$23.2 million–$60.75 million	

hefty operating losses. When Eastern finally closed down after two years, it was not just bankrupt, but *administratively* insolvent: There was almost nothing for creditors, and the company was running out of cash to pay legal expenses.[19]

We do not know what the sum of direct and indirect costs of bankruptcy amounts to. We suspect it is a significant number, particularly for large firms for which proceedings would be lengthy and complex. Perhaps the best evidence is the reluctance of creditors to force bankruptcy. In principle, they would be better off to end the agony and seize the assets as soon as possible. Instead, creditors often overlook defaults in the hope of nursing the firm over a difficult period. They do this in part to avoid costs of bankruptcy.[20] There is an old financial saying, "Borrow $1,000 and you've got a banker. Borrow $10,000,000 and you've got a partner."

---

[19] The bankruptcy of Eastern Airlines is analyzed in L. A. Weiss and K. H. Wruck, "Information Problems, Conflicts of Interest, and Asset Stripping: Chapter 11's Failure in the Case of Eastern Airlines," *Journal of Financial Economics* 48 (1998), pp. 55–97.

[20] There is another reason. Creditors are not always given absolute priority in bankruptcy. *Absolute priority* means that creditors must be paid in full before stockholders receive a cent. Sometimes reorganizations are negotiated which provide something for everyone, even though creditors are *not* paid in full. Thus creditors can never be sure how they will fare in bankruptcy.

In all this discussion of bankruptcy costs we have said very little about bankruptcy *procedures*. These are described in the appendix at the end of Chapter 25.

Financial Distress without Bankruptcy

Not every firm that gets into trouble goes bankrupt. As long as the firm can scrape up enough cash to pay the interest on its debt, it may be able to postpone bankruptcy for many years. Eventually the firm may recover, pay off its debt, and escape bankruptcy altogether.

When a firm is in trouble, both bondholders and stockholders want it to recover, but in other respects their interests may be in conflict. In times of financial distress the security holders are like many political parties—united on generalities but threatened by squabbling on any specific issue.

Financial distress is costly when these conflicts of interest get in the way of proper operating, investment, and financing decisions. Stockholders are tempted to forsake the usual objective of maximizing the overall market value of the firm and to pursue narrower self-interest instead. They are tempted to play games at the expense of their creditors. We will now illustrate how such games can lead to costs of financial distress.

Here is the Circular File Company's book balance sheet:

Circular File Company (Book Values)

Net working capital	$ 20	$ 50	Bonds outstanding
Fixed assets	80	50	Common stock
Total assets	$100	$100	Total value

We will assume there is only one share and one bond outstanding. The stockholder is also the manager. The bondholder is somebody else.

Here is its balance sheet in market values—a clear case of financial distress, since the face value of Circular's debt ($50) exceeds the firm's total market value ($30):

Circular File Company (Market Values)

Net working capital	$20	$25	Bonds outstanding
Fixed assets	10	5	Common stock
Total assets	$30	$30	Total value

If the debt matured today, Circular's owner would default, leaving the firm bankrupt. But suppose that the bond actually matures one year hence, that there is enough cash for Circular to limp along for one year, and that the bondholder cannot "call the question" and force bankruptcy before then.

The one-year grace period explains why the Circular share still has value. Its owner is betting on a stroke of luck that will rescue the firm, allowing it to pay off the debt with something left over. The bet is a long shot—the owner wins only if firm value increases from $30 to more than $50.[21] But the owner has a secret weapon: He controls investment and operating strategy.

---

[21]We are not concerned here with how to work out whether $5 is a fair price for stockholders to pay for the bet. We will come to that in Chapter 20 when we discuss the valuation of options.

Risk Shifting: The First Game

Suppose that Circular has $10 cash. The following investment opportunity comes up:

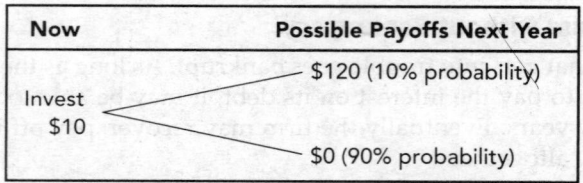

Now	Possible Payoffs Next Year
Invest $10	$120 (10% probability)
	$0 (90% probability)

This is a wild gamble and probably a lousy project. But you can see why the owner would be tempted to take it anyway. Why not go for broke? Circular will probably go under anyway, so the owner is essentially betting with the bondholder's money. But the owner gets most of the loot if the project pays off.

Suppose that the project's NPV is −$2 but that it is undertaken anyway, thus depressing firm value by $2. Circular's new balance sheet might look like this:

Circular File Company (Market Values)

Net working capital	$10	$20	Bonds outstanding
Fixed assets	18	8	Common stock
Total assets	$28	$28	Total value

Firm value falls by $2, but the owner is $3 ahead because the bond's value has fallen by $5.[22] The $10 cash that used to stand behind the bond has been replaced by a very risky asset worth only $8.

Thus a game has been played at the expense of Circular's bondholder. The game illustrates the following general point: Stockholders of levered firms gain when business risk increases. Financial managers who act strictly in their shareholders' interests (and *against* the interests of creditors) will favor risky projects over safe ones. They may even take risky projects with negative NPVs.

This warped strategy for capital budgeting clearly is costly to the firm and to the economy as a whole. Why do we associate the costs with financial distress? Because the temptation to play is strongest when the odds of default are high. A blue-chip company like Exxon Mobil would never invest in our negative-NPV gamble. Its creditors are not vulnerable to this type of game.

Refusing to Contribute Equity Capital: The Second Game

We have seen how stockholders, acting in their immediate, narrow self-interest, may take projects that reduce the overall market value of their firm. These are errors of commission. Conflicts of interest may also lead to errors of omission.

Assume that Circular cannot scrape up any cash, and therefore cannot take that wild gamble. Instead a *good* opportunity comes up: a relatively safe asset costing $10 with a present value of $15 and NPV = +$5.

This project will not in itself rescue Circular, but it is a step in the right direction. We might therefore expect Circular to issue $10 of new stock and to go ahead with the investment. Suppose that two new shares are issued to the original owner for $10 cash. The project is taken. The new balance sheet might look like this:

---

[22]We are not calculating this $5 drop. We are simply using it as a plausible assumption. The tools necessary for a calculation come in Chapter 21.

Circular File Company (Market Values)

Net working capital	$20	$33	Bonds outstanding
Fixed assets	25	12	Common stock
Total assets	$45	$45	Total value

The total value of the firm goes up by $15 ($10 of new capital and $5 NPV). Notice that the Circular bond is no longer worth $25, but $33. The bondholder receives a capital gain of $8 because the firm's assets include a new, safe asset worth $15. The probability of default is less, and the payoff to the bondholder if default occurs is larger.

The stockholder loses what the bondholder gains. Equity value goes up not by $15 but by $15 − $8 = $7. The owner puts in $10 of fresh equity capital but gains only $7 in market value. Going ahead is in the firm's interest but not the owner's.

Again, our example illustrates a general point. If we hold business risk constant, any increase in firm value is shared among bondholders and stockholders. The value of any investment opportunity to the firm's *stockholders* is reduced because project benefits must be shared with bondholders. Thus it may not be in the stockholders' self-interest to contribute fresh equity capital even if that means forgoing positive-NPV investment opportunities.

This problem theoretically affects all levered firms, but it is most serious when firms land in financial distress. The greater the probability of default, the more bondholders have to gain from investments that increase firm value.

And Three More Games, Briefly

As with other games, the temptation to play the next three games is particularly strong in financial distress.

Cash In and Run   Stockholders may be reluctant to put money into a firm in financial distress, but they are happy to take the money out—in the form of a cash dividend, for example. The market value of the firm's stock goes down by less than the amount of the dividend paid, because the decline in *firm* value is shared with creditors. This game is just "refusing to contribute equity capital" run in reverse.

Playing for Time   When the firm is in financial distress, creditors would like to salvage what they can by forcing the firm to settle up. Naturally, stockholders want to delay this as long as they can. There are various devious ways of doing this, for example, through accounting changes designed to conceal the true extent of trouble, by encouraging false hopes of spontaneous recovery, or by cutting corners on maintenance, research and development, and so on, in order to make this year's operating performance look better.

Bait and Switch   This game is not always played in financial distress, but it is a quick way to get *into* distress. You start with a conservative policy, issuing a limited amount of relatively safe debt. Then you suddenly switch and issue a lot more. That makes all your debt risky, imposing a capital loss on the "old" bondholders. Their capital loss is the stockholders' gain.

The most dramatic example of bait and switch occurred in October 1988, when the management of RJR Nabisco announced its intention to acquire the company in a *leveraged buy-out* (LBO). This put the company "in play" for a transaction in which existing shareholders would be bought out and the company would be "taken private." The cost of the buy-out would be almost entirely debt-financed. The new private company would start life with an extremely high debt ratio.

RJR Nabisco had debt outstanding with a market value of about $2.4 billion. The announcement of the coming LBO drove down this market value by $298 million.[23]

What the Games Cost

Why should anyone object to these games so long as they are played by consenting adults? Because playing them means poor decisions about investments and operations. These poor decisions are *agency costs* of borrowing.

The more the firm borrows, the greater is the temptation to play the games (assuming the financial manager acts in the stockholders' interest). The increased odds of poor decisions in the future prompt investors to mark down the present market value of the firm. The fall in value comes out of the shareholders' pockets. Therefore it is ultimately in their interest to avoid temptation. The easiest way to do this is to limit borrowing to levels at which the firm's debt is safe or close to it.

Banks and other corporate lenders are also not financial innocents. They realize that games may be played at their expense and so protect themselves by rationing the amount that they will lend or by imposing restrictions on the company's actions. For example, consider the case of Henrietta Ketchup, a budding entrepreneur with two possible investment projects that offer the following payoffs:

	Investment	Payoff	Probability of Payoff
Project 1	−12	+15	1.0
Project 2	−12	+24	.5
		0	.5

Project 1 is surefire and very profitable; project 2 is risky and a rotten project. Ms. Ketchup now approaches her bank and asks to borrow the present value of $10 (she will find the remaining money out of her own purse). The bank calculates that the payoff will be split as follows:

	Expected Payoff to Bank	Expected Payoff to Ms. Ketchup
Project 1	+10	+5
Project 2	(.5 × 10) + (.5 × 0) = +5	.5 × (24 − 10) = +7

If Ms. Ketchup accepts project 1, the bank's debt is certain to be paid in full; if she accepts project 2, there is only a 50 percent chance of payment and the expected payoff to the bank is only $5. Unfortunately, Ms. Ketchup will prefer to take project 2, for if things go well, she gets most of the profit, and if they go badly, the bank bears most of the loss. Unless Ms. Ketchup can convince the bank that she will not gamble with its money, the bank will limit the amount that it is prepared to lend.[24]

---

[23]We thank Paul Asquith for these figures. RJR Nabisco was finally taken private not by its management but by another LBO partnership. We discuss this LBO in Chapter 34.

[24]You might think that, if the bank suspects Ms. Ketchup will undertake project 2, it should just raise the interest rate on its loan. In this case Ms. Ketchup will not want to take on project 2 (they can't both be happy with a lousy project). But Ms. Ketchup also would not want to pay a high rate of interest if she is going to take on project 1 (she would do better to borrow less money at the risk-free rate). So simply raising the interest rate is not the answer.

How can Ms. Ketchup reassure the bank of her intentions? The obvious answer is to give it veto power over potentially dangerous decisions. There we have the ultimate economic rationale for all that fine print backing up corporate debt. Debt contracts frequently limit dividends or equivalent transfers of wealth to stockholders; the firm may not be allowed to pay out more than it earns, for example. Additional borrowing is almost always limited. For example, many companies are prevented by existing bond indentures from issuing any additional long-term debt unless their ratio of earnings to interest charges exceeds 2.0.[25]

Sometimes firms are restricted from selling assets or making major investment outlays except with the lenders' consent. The risks of playing for time are reduced by specifying accounting procedures and by giving lenders access to the firm's books and its financial forecasts.

Of course, fine print cannot be a complete solution for firms that insist on issuing risky debt. The fine print has its own costs; you have to spend money to save money. Obviously a complex debt contract costs more to negotiate than a simple one. Afterward it costs the lender more to monitor the firm's performance. Lenders anticipate monitoring costs and demand compensation in the form of higher interest rates; thus the monitoring costs—another agency cost of debt—are ultimately paid by stockholders.

Perhaps the most severe costs of the fine print stem from the constraints it places on operating and investment decisions. For example, an attempt to prevent the risk-shifting game may also prevent the firm from pursuing *good* investment opportunities. At the minimum there are delays in clearing major investments with lenders. In some cases lenders may veto high-risk investments even if net present value is positive. Lenders can lose from risk shifting even when the firm's overall market value increases. In fact, the lenders may try to play a game of their own, forcing the firm to stay in cash or low-risk assets even if good projects are forgone.

Thus, debt contracts cannot cover every possible manifestation of the games we have just discussed. Any attempt to do so would be hopelessly expensive and doomed to failure in any event. Human imagination is insufficient to conceive of all the possible things that could go wrong. We will always find surprises coming at us on dimensions we never thought to think about.

We hope we have not left the impression that managers and stockholders always succumb to temptation unless restrained. Usually they refrain voluntarily, not only from a sense of fair play but also on pragmatic grounds: A firm or individual that makes a killing today at the expense of a creditor will be coldly received when the time comes to borrow again. Aggressive game playing is done only by out-and-out crooks and by firms in extreme financial distress. Firms limit borrowing precisely because they don't wish to land in distress and be exposed to the temptation to play.

Costs of Distress Vary with Type of Asset

Suppose your firm's only asset is a large downtown hotel, mortgaged to the hilt. The recession hits, occupancy rates fall, and the mortgage payments cannot be met. The lender takes over and sells the hotel to a new owner and operator. You use your firm's stock certificates for wallpaper.

What is the cost of bankruptcy? In this example, probably very little. The value of the hotel is, of course, much less than you hoped, but that is due to the lack of

---

[25]We discuss covenants and the rest of the fine print in debt contracts in Section 25.6.

guests, not to the bankruptcy. Bankruptcy doesn't damage the hotel itself. The direct bankruptcy costs are restricted to items such as legal and court fees, real estate commissions, and the time the lender spends sorting things out.[26]

Suppose we repeat the story of Heartbreak Hotel for Fledgling Electronics. Everything is the same, except for the underlying real assets—not real estate but a high-tech going concern, a growth company whose most valuable assets are technology, investment opportunities, and its employees' human capital.

If Fledgling gets into trouble, the stockholders may be reluctant to put up money to cash in on its growth opportunities. Failure to invest is likely to be much more serious for Fledgling than for a company like Heartbreak Hotel.

If Fledgling finally defaults on its debt, the lender will find it much more difficult to cash in by selling off the assets. Many of them are intangibles which have value only as a part of a going concern.

Could Fledgling be kept as a going concern through default and reorganization? It may not be as hopeless as putting a wedding cake through a car wash, but there are a number of serious difficulties. First, the odds of defections by key employees are higher than they would be if the firm had never gotten into financial trouble. Special guarantees may have to be given to customers who have doubts about whether the firm will be around to service its products. Aggressive investment in new products and technology will be difficult; each class of creditors will have to be convinced that it is in its interest for the firm to invest new money in risky ventures.

Some assets, like good commercial real estate, can pass through bankruptcy and reorganization largely unscathed; the values of other assets are likely to be considerably diminished. The losses are greatest for the intangible assets that are linked to the health of the firm as a going concern—for example, technology, human capital, and brand image. That may be why debt ratios are low in the pharmaceutical industry, where value depends on continued success in research and development, and in many service industries where value depends on human capital. We can also understand why highly profitable growth companies, such as Microsoft or Pfizer, use mostly equity finance.[27]

The moral of these examples is this: *Do not think only about the probability that borrowing will bring trouble. Think also of the value that may be lost if trouble comes.*

The Trade-off Theory of Capital Structure

Financial managers often think of the firm's debt–equity decision as a trade-off between interest tax shields and the costs of financial distress. Of course, there is controversy about how valuable interest tax shields are and what kinds of financial

---

[26]In 1989 the Rockefeller family sold 80 percent of Rockefeller Center—several acres of extremely valuable Manhattan real estate—to Mitsubishi Estate Company for $1.4 billion. A REIT, Rockefeller Center Properties, held a $1.3 billion mortgage loan (the REIT's only asset) secured by this real estate. But rents and occupancy rates did not meet forecasts, and by 1995 Mitsubishi had incurred losses of about $600 million. Then Mitsubishi quit, and Rockefeller Center was bankrupt. That triggered a complicated series of maneuvers and negotiations. But did this damage the value of the Rockefeller Center properties? Was Radio City Music Hall, one of the properties, any less valuable because of the bankruptcy? We doubt it.

[27]Empirical research confirms that firms holding largely intangible assets borrow less. See, for example, M. Long and I. Malitz, "The Investment-Financing Nexus: Some Empirical Evidence," *Midland Corporate Finance Journal* 3 (Fall 1985), pp. 53–59.

trouble are most threatening, but these disagreements are only variations on a theme. Thus, Figure 18.2 illustrates the debt–equity trade-off.

This *trade-off theory* of capital structure recognizes that target debt ratios may vary from firm to firm. Companies with safe, tangible assets and plenty of taxable income to shield ought to have high target ratios. Unprofitable companies with risky, intangible assets ought to rely primarily on equity financing.

If there were no costs of adjusting capital structure, then each firm should always be at its target debt ratio. However, there are costs, and therefore delays, in adjusting to the optimum. Firms cannot immediately offset the random events that bump them away from their capital structure targets, so we should see random differences in actual debt ratios among firms having the same target debt ratio.

All in all, this trade-off theory of capital structure choice tells a comforting story. Unlike MM's theory, which seemed to say that firms should take on as much debt as possible, it avoids extreme predictions and rationalizes moderate debt ratios.

But what are the facts? Can the trade-off theory of capital structure explain how companies actually behave?

The answer is "yes and no." On the "yes" side, the trade-off theory successfully explains many industry differences in capital structure. High-tech growth companies, for example, whose assets are risky and mostly intangible, normally use relatively little debt. Airlines can and do borrow heavily because their assets are tangible and relatively safe.[28]

The trade-off theory also helps explain what kinds of companies "go private" in LBOs. LBOs are acquisitions of public companies by private investors who finance a large fraction of the purchase price with debt. The target companies for LBO takeovers are usually mature, cash-cow businesses with established markets for their products but little in the way of high-NPV growth opportunities. That makes sense by the trade-off theory, because these are exactly the kind of companies that *ought* to have high debt ratios.

The trade-off theory also says that companies saddled with extra heavy debt— too much to pay down with a couple of years' internally generated cash—should issue stock, constrain dividends, or sell off assets to raise cash to rebalance capital structure. Here again, we can find plenty of confirming examples. When Texaco bought Getty Petroleum in January 1984, it borrowed $8 billion from a consortium of banks to help finance the acquisition. (The loan was arranged and paid over to Texaco within two weeks!) By the end of 1984, it had raised about $1.8 billion to pay down this debt, mostly by selling assets and forgoing dividend increases. Chrysler, when it emerged from near-bankruptcy in 1983, sold $432 million of new common stock to help regain a conservative capital structure.[29] In 1991, after a second brush with bankruptcy, it again sold shares to replenish equity, this time for $350 million.[30]

---

[28]We are not suggesting that all airline companies are safe; many are not. But air*craft* can support debt where air*lines* cannot. If Fly-by-Night Airlines fails, its planes retain their value in another airline's operations. There's a good secondary market in used aircraft, so a loan secured by aircraft can be well protected even if made to an airline flying on thin ice (and in the dark).

[29]Note that Chrysler issued stock *after* it emerged from financial distress. It did not *prevent* financial distress by raising equity money when trouble loomed on its horizon. Why not? Refer back to "Refusing to Contribute Equity Capital: The Second Game" or forward to the analysis of asymmetric information in Section 18.4.

[30]Chrysler simultaneously contributed $300 million of newly issued shares to its underfunded pension plans.

On the "no" side, there are a few things the trade-off theory cannot explain. It cannot explain why some of the most successful companies thrive with little debt. Think of Pfizer, which as Table 18.3(a) shows, is basically all-equity-financed. Granted, Pfizer's most valuable assets are intangible, the fruits of its pharmaceutical research and development. We know that intangible assets and conservative capital structures go together. But Pfizer also has a very large corporate income tax bill (over $2 billion in 2000) and the highest possible credit rating. It could borrow enough to save tens of millions of dollars without raising a whisker of concern about possible financial distress.

Pfizer illustrates an odd fact about real-life capital structures: The most profitable companies commonly borrow the least.[31] Here the trade-off theory fails, for it predicts exactly the reverse. Under the trade-off theory, high profits should mean more debt-servicing capacity and more taxable income to shield and so should give a *higher* target debt ratio.[32]

In general it appears that public companies rarely make major shifts in capital structure just because of taxes,[33] and it is hard to detect the present value of interest tax shields in firms' market values.[34]

A final point on the "no" side for the trade-off theory: Debt ratios today are no higher than they were in the early 1900s, when income tax rates were low (or zero). Debt ratios in other industrialized countries are equal to or higher than those in the United States. Many of these countries have imputation tax systems, which should eliminate the value of the interest tax shields.[35]

None of this disproves the trade-off theory. As George Stigler emphasized, theories are not rejected by circumstantial evidence; it takes a theory to beat a theory. So we now turn to a completely different theory of financing.

---

[31]For example, in an international comparison Wald found that profitability was the single largest determinant of firm capital structure. See J. K. Wald, "How Firm Characteristics Affect Capital Structure: An International Comparison," *Journal of Financial Research* 22 (Summer 1999), pp. 161–187.

[32]Here we mean debt as a fraction of the book or replacement value of the company's assets. Profitable companies might not borrow a greater fraction of their market value. Higher profits imply higher market value as well as stronger incentives to borrow.

[33]Mackie-Mason found that tax-paying companies are more likely to issue debt (vs. equity) than non-taxpaying companies. This shows that taxes do affect financing choices. However, it is not necessarily evidence for the static trade-off theory. Look back to Section 18.2, and note the special case where corporate and personal taxes cancel to make debt policy irrelevant. In that case, taxpaying firms would see no net tax advantage to debt: corporate interest tax shields would be offset by the taxes paid by investors in the firm's debt. But the balance would tip in favor of equity for a firm that was losing money and reaping no benefits from interest tax shields. See J. Mackie-Mason, "Do Taxes Affect Corporate Financing Decisions?" *Journal of Finance* 45 (December 1990), pp. 1471–1493.

[34]A study by E. F. Fama and K. R. French, covering over 2,000 firms from 1965 to 1992, failed to find any evidence that interest tax shields contributed to firm value. See "Taxes, Financing Decisions and Firm Value," *Journal of Finance* 53 (June 1998), pp. 819–843.

[35]We described the Australian imputation tax system in Section 16.7. Look again at Table 16.3, supposing that an Australian corporation pays $A10 of interest. This reduces the corporate tax by $A3.00; it also reduces the tax credit taken by the shareholders by $A3.00. The final tax does not depend on whether the corporation or the shareholder borrows.

You can check this by redrawing Figure 18.1 for the Australian system. The corporate tax rate T_c will cancel out. Since income after all taxes depends only on investors' tax rates, there is no special advantage to corporate borrowing.

18.4 THE PECKING ORDER OF FINANCING CHOICES

The pecking-order theory starts with *asymmetric information*—a fancy term indicating that managers know more about their companies' prospects, risks, and values than do outside investors.

Managers obviously know more than investors. We can prove that by observing stock price changes caused by announcements by managers. When a company announces an increased regular dividend, stock price typically rises, because investors interpret the increase as a sign of management's confidence in future earnings. In other words, the dividend increase transfers information from managers to investors. This can happen only if managers know more in the first place.

Asymmetric information affects the choice between internal and external financing and between new issues of debt and equity securities. This leads to a *pecking order*, in which investment is financed first with internal funds, reinvested earnings primarily; then by new issues of debt; and finally with new issues of equity. New equity issues are a last resort when the company runs out of debt capacity, that is, when the threat of costs of financial distress brings regular insomnia to existing creditors and to the financial manager.

We will take a closer look at the pecking order in a moment. First, you must appreciate how asymmetric information can force the financial manager to issue debt rather than common stock.

Debt and Equity Issues with Asymmetric Information

To the outside world Smith & Company and Jones, Inc., our two example companies, are identical. Each runs a successful business with good growth opportunities. The two businesses are risky, however, and investors have learned from experience that current expectations are frequently bettered or disappointed. Current expectations price each company's stock at $100 per share, but the true values could be higher or lower:

	Smith & Co.	Jones, Inc.
True value could be higher, say	$120	$120
Best current estimate	100	100
True value could be lower, say	80	80

Now suppose that both companies need to raise new money from investors to fund capital investment. They can do this either by issuing bonds or by issuing new shares of common stock. How would the choice be made? One financial manager—we will not tell you which one—might reason as follows:

> Sell stock for $100 per share? Ridiculous! It's worth at least $120. A stock issue now would hand a free gift to new investors. I just wish those stupid, skeptical shareholders would appreciate the true value of this company. Our new factories will make us the world's lowest-cost producer. We've painted a rosy picture for the press and security analysts, but it just doesn't seem to be working. Oh well, the decision is obvious: we'll issue debt, not underpriced equity. A debt issue will save underwriting fees too.

The other financial manager is in a different mood:

> Beefalo burgers were a hit for a while, but it looks like the fad is fading. The fast-food division's gotta find some good new products or it's all downhill from here. Export markets are OK for now, but how are we going to compete with those new Siberian ranches? Fortunately the stock price has held up pretty well—we've had some good short-run news for the press and security analysts. Now's the time to issue stock. We have major investments underway, and why add increased debt service to my other worries?

Of course, outside investors can't read the financial managers' minds. If they could, one stock might trade at $120 and the other at $80.

Why doesn't the optimistic financial manager simply educate investors? Then the company could sell stock on fair terms, and there would be no reason to favor debt over equity or vice versa.

This is not so easy. (Note that both companies are issuing upbeat press releases.) Investors can't be told what to think; they have to be convinced. That takes a detailed layout of the company's plans and prospects, including the inside scoop on new technology, product design, marketing plans, and so on. Getting this across is expensive for the company and also valuable to its competitors. Why go to the trouble? Investors will learn soon enough, as revenues and earnings evolve. In the meantime the optimistic financial manager can finance growth by issuing debt.

Now suppose there are two press releases:

> Jones, Inc., will issue $120 million of five-year senior notes.

> Smith & Co. announced plans today to issue 1.2 million new shares of common stock. The company expects to raise $120 million.

As a rational investor, you immediately learn two things. First, Jones's financial manager is optimistic and Smith's is pessimistic. Second, Smith's financial manager is also stupid to think that investors would pay $100 per share. The *attempt* to sell stock shows that it must be worth less. Smith might sell stock at $80 per share, but certainly not at $100.[36]

Smart financial managers think this through ahead of time. The end result? Both Smith and Jones end up issuing debt. Jones, Inc., issues debt because its financial manager is optimistic and doesn't want to issue undervalued equity. A smart, but pessimistic, financial manager at Smith issues debt because an attempt to issue equity would force the stock price down and eliminate any advantage from doing so. (Issuing equity also reveals the manager's pessimism immediately. Most managers prefer to wait. A debt issue lets bad news come out later through other channels.)

The story of Smith and Jones illustrates how asymmetric information favors debt issues over equity issues. If managers are better informed than investors and both groups are rational, then any company that can borrow will do so rather than issuing fresh equity. In other words, debt issues will be higher in the pecking order.

Taken literally this reasoning seems to rule out any issue of equity. That's not right, because asymmetric information is not always important and there are other forces at work. For example, if Smith had already borrowed heavily, and would risk financial distress by borrowing more, then it would have a good reason to issue common stock. In this case announcement of a stock issue would not be en-

---

[36] A Smith stock issue might not succeed even at $80. Persistence in trying to sell at $80 could convince investors that the stock is worth even less!

tirely bad news. The announcement would still depress the stock price—it would highlight managers' concerns about financial distress—but the fall in price would not necessarily make the issue unwise or infeasible.

High-tech, high-growth companies can also be credible issuers of common stock. Such companies' assets are mostly intangible, and bankruptcy or financial distress would be especially costly. This calls for conservative financing. The only way to grow rapidly and keep a conservative debt ratio is to issue equity. If investors see equity issued for these reasons, problems of the sort encountered by Jones's financial manager become much less serious.

With such exceptions noted, asymmetric information can explain the dominance of debt financing over new equity issues in practice. Debt issues are frequent; equity issues, rare. The bulk of external financing comes from debt, even in the United States, where equity markets are highly information-efficient. Equity issues are even more difficult in countries with less well developed stock markets.

None of this says that firms ought to strive for high debt ratios—just that it's better to raise equity by plowing back earnings than issuing stock. In fact, a firm with ample internally generated funds doesn't have to sell any kind of security and thus avoids issue costs and information problems completely.[37]

Implications of the Pecking Order

The pecking-order theory of corporate financing goes like this.[38]

1. Firms prefer internal finance.
2. They adapt their target dividend payout ratios to their investment opportunities, while trying to avoid sudden changes in dividends.
3. Sticky dividend policies, plus unpredictable fluctuations in profitability and investment opportunities, mean that internally generated cash flow is sometimes more than capital expenditures and other times less. If it is more, the firm pays off debt or invests in marketable securities. If it is less, the firm first draws down its cash balance or sells its marketable securities.
4. If external finance is required, firms issue the safest security first. That is, they start with debt, then possibly hybrid securities such as convertible bonds, then perhaps equity as a last resort.

In this theory, there is no well-defined target debt–equity mix, because there are two kinds of equity, internal and external, one at the top of the pecking order and one at the bottom. Each firm's observed debt ratio reflects its cumulative requirements for external finance.

The pecking order explains why the most profitable firms generally borrow less—not because they have low target debt ratios but because they don't need outside money. Less profitable firms issue debt because they do not have internal funds sufficient for their capital investment programs and because debt financing is first on the pecking order of *external* financing.

---

[37] Even debt issues can create information problems if the odds of default are significant. A pessimistic manager may try to issue debt quickly, before bad news gets out. An optimistic manager will delay pending good news, perhaps arranging a short-term bank loan in the meantime. Rational investors will take this behavior into account in pricing the risky debt issue.

[38] The description is paraphrased from S. C. Myers, "The Capital Structure Puzzle," *Journal of Finance* 39 (July 1984), pp. 581–582. For the most part, this section follows Myers's arguments.

In the pecking-order theory, the attraction of interest tax shields is assumed to be a second-order effect. Debt ratios change when there is an imbalance of internal cash flow, net of dividends, and real investment opportunities. Highly profitable firms with limited investment opportunities work down to low debt ratios. Firms whose investment opportunities outrun internally generated funds are driven to borrow more and more.

This theory explains the inverse intraindustry relationship between profitability and financial leverage. Suppose firms generally invest to keep up with the growth of their industries. Then rates of investment will be similar within an industry. Given sticky dividend payouts, the least profitable firms will have less internal funds and will end up borrowing more.

The pecking order seems to predict changes in many mature firms' debt ratios to a T. These companies' debt ratios increase when the firms have financial deficits and decline when they have surpluses.[39] If asymmetric information makes major equity issues or retirements rare, this behavior is nearly inevitable.

The pecking order is less successful in explaining *inter*industry differences in debt ratios. For example, debt ratios tend to be low in high-tech, high-growth industries, even when the need for external capital is great. There are also mature, stable industries—electric utilities, for example—in which ample cash flow is *not* used to pay down debt. High dividend payout ratios give the cash flow back to investors instead.

Financial Slack

Other things equal, it's better to be at the top of the pecking order than at the bottom. Firms that have worked down the pecking order and need external equity may end up living with excessive debt or passing by good investments because shares can't be sold at what managers consider a fair price.

In other words, *financial slack* is valuable. Having financial slack means having cash, marketable securities, readily saleable real assets, and ready access to the debt markets or to bank financing. Ready access basically requires conservative financing so that potential lenders see the company's debt as a safe investment.

In the long run, a company's value rests more on its capital investment and operating decisions than on financing. Therefore, you want to make sure your firm has sufficient financial slack so that financing is quickly available for good investments. Financial slack is most valuable to firms with plenty of positive-NPV growth opportunities. That is another reason why growth companies usually aspire to conservative capital structures.

Free Cash Flow and the Dark Side of Financial Slack[40]

There is also a dark side to financial slack. Too much of it may encourage managers to take it easy, expand their perks, or empire-build with cash that should be paid back to stockholders. In other words, slack can make agency problems worse.

Michael Jensen has stressed the tendency of managers with ample free cash flow (or unnecessary financial slack) to plow too much cash into mature businesses or

---

[39]See L. Shyam Sunder and S. C. Myers, "Testing Static Tradeoff Against Pecking Order Models of Capital Structure," *Journal of Financial Economics* 51 (February 1999), pp. 219–244.

[40]Some of the following is drawn from S. C. Myers, "Still Searching for Optimal Capital Structure," *Journal of Applied Corporate Finance* 6 (Spring 1993), pp. 4–14.

ill-advised acquisitions. "The problem," Jensen says, "is how to motivate managers to disgorge the cash rather than investing it below the cost of capital or wasting it in organizational inefficiencies."[41]

If that's the problem, then maybe debt is an answer. Scheduled interest and principal payments are contractual obligations of the firm. Debt forces the firm to pay out cash. Perhaps the best debt level would leave just enough cash in the bank, after debt service, to finance all positive-NPV projects, with not a penny left over.

We do not recommend this degree of fine-tuning, but the idea is valid and important. Debt can discipline managers who are tempted to invest too much. It can also provide the pressure to force improvements in operating efficiency. We pick up this theme again in Chapters 33 and 34.

---

[41]M. C. Jensen, "Agency Costs of Free Cash Flow, Corporate Finance and Takeovers," *American Economic Review* 26 (May 1986), p. 323.

Our task in this chapter was to show why capital structure matters. We did not throw away MM's proposition I, that capital structure is irrelevant; we added to it. However, we did not arrive at any simple, satisfactory theory of optimal capital structure.

The traditional trade-off theory emphasizes taxes and financial distress. The value of the firm is broken down as

> Value if all-equity-financed + PV(tax shield) − PV(costs of financial distress)

According to this theory, the firm should increase debt until the value from PV(tax shield) is just offset, at the margin, by increases in PV(costs of financial distress).

The costs of financial distress can be broken down as follows:

1. Bankruptcy costs
   a. Direct costs such as court fees.
   b. Indirect costs reflecting the difficulty of managing a company undergoing liquidation or reorganization.
2. Costs of financial distress short of bankruptcy
   a. Conflicts of interest between bondholders and stockholders of firms in financial distress may lead to poor operating and investment decisions. Stockholders acting in their narrow self-interest can gain at the expense of creditors by playing "games" that reduce the overall value of the firm.
   b. The fine print in debt contracts is designed to prevent these games. But fine print increases the costs of writing, monitoring, and enforcing the debt contract.

The value of the tax shield is more controversial. It would be easy to compute if we had only corporate taxes to worry about. In that case the net tax saving from borrowing would be just the marginal corporate tax rate T_c times $r_D D$, the interest payment. This tax shield is usually valued by discounting at the borrowing rate r_D. In the special case of fixed, permanent debt

$$\text{PV(tax shield)} = \frac{T_c(r_D D)}{r_D} = T_c D$$

SUMMARY

However, corporate taxes are only part of the story. If investors are subject to higher taxes on interest income than on equity income (dividends and capital gains), they will be reluctant to hold corporate debt and will do so only if they are compensated by a sufficiently attractive rate of interest. Thus, ultimately firms end up paying for any additional personal taxes that are levied on debtholders. The personal tax disadvantage of debt is smaller today than it once was, but it probably still offsets to some degree the corporate tax advantage.

We suggest that borrowing may make sense for some firms but not for others. If a firm can be fairly sure of earning a profit, there is likely to be a net tax saving from borrowing. However, for firms that are unlikely to earn sufficient profits to benefit from the corporate tax shield, there is little, if any, net tax advantage to borrowing. For these firms the net tax saving could even be negative.

The trade-off theory balances the tax advantages of borrowing against the costs of financial distress. Corporations are supposed to pick a target capital structure that maximizes firm value. Firms with safe, tangible assets and plenty of taxable income to shield ought to have high targets. Unprofitable companies with risky, intangible assets ought to rely primarily on equity financing.

This theory of capital structure successfully explains many industry differences in capital structure, but it does not explain why the most profitable firms *within* an industry generally have the most conservative capital structures. Under the trade-off theory, high profitability should mean high debt capacity *and* a strong corporate tax incentive to use that capacity.

There is a competing, pecking-order theory, which states that firms use internal financing when available and choose debt over equity when external financing is required. This explains why the less profitable firms in an industry borrow more—not because they have higher target debt ratios but because they need more external financing and because debt is next on the pecking order when internal funds are exhausted.

The pecking order is a consequence of asymmetric information. Managers know more about their firms than outside investors do, and they are reluctant to issue stock when they believe the price is too low. They try to time issues when shares are fairly priced or overpriced. Investors understand this, and interpret a decision to issue shares as bad news. That explains why stock price usually falls when a stock issue is announced.

Debt is better than equity when these information problems are important. Optimistic managers will prefer debt to undervalued equity, and pessimistic managers will be pressed to follow suit. The pecking-order theory says that equity will be issued only when debt capacity is running out and financial distress threatens.

The pecking-order theory is clearly not 100 percent right. There are many examples of equity issued by companies that could easily have borrowed. But the theory does explain why most external financing comes from debt, and it explains why changes in debt ratios tend to follow requirements for external financing.

The pecking-order theory stresses the value of financial slack. Without sufficient slack, the firm may be caught at the bottom of the pecking order and be forced to choose between issuing undervalued shares, borrowing and risking financial distress, or passing up positive-NPV investment opportunities.

There is, however, a dark side to financial slack. Surplus cash or credit tempts managers to overinvest or to indulge an easy and glamorous corporate lifestyle. When temptation wins, or threatens to win, a high debt ratio can help: It forces the company to disgorge cash and prods managers and organizations to try harder to be more efficient.

Modigliani and Miller's analysis of the present value of interest tax shields at the corporate level is in:

F. Modigliani and M. H. Miller: "Corporate Income Taxes and the Cost of Capital: A Correction," *American Economic Review*, 53:433–443 (June 1963).

F. Modigliani and M. H. Miller: "Some Estimates of the Cost of Capital to the Electric Utility Industry, 1954–57," *American Economic Review*, 56:333–391 (June 1966).

Miller extends the MM model to personal as well as corporate taxes. DeAngelo and Masulis argue that firms with plenty of noninterest tax shields, for example, shields from depreciation, should borrow less. Graham's estimates of the tax benefits of debt recognize the possibility that firms will not earn taxable profits in the future:

M. H. Miller: "Debt and Taxes," *Journal of Finance*, 32:261–276 (May 1977).

H. DeAngelo and R. Masulis: "Optimal Capital Structure under Corporate Taxation," *Journal of Financial Economics*, 8:5–29 (March 1980).

J. R. Graham: "How Big Are the Tax Benefits of Debt?" *Journal of Finance*, 55:1901–1941 (October 2000).

The following articles analyze the conflicts of interest between bondholders and stockholders and their implications for financing policy (do not read the last article until you have read Chapter 20):

M. C. Jensen and W. H. Meckling: "Theory of the Firm: Managerial Behavior, Agency Costs and Ownership Structure," *Journal of Financial Economics*, 3:305–360 (October 1976).

S. C. Myers: "Determinants of Corporate Borrowing," *Journal of Financial Economics*, 5:146–175 (1977).

D. Galai and R. W. Masulis: "The Option Pricing Model and the Risk Factor of Stock," *Journal of Financial Economics*, 3:53–82 (January–March 1976).

Myers describes the pecking-order theory, which is in turn based on work by Myers and Majluf; Baskin and Shyam-Sunder and Myers survey some of the evidence for that theory:

S. C. Myers: "The Capital Structure Puzzle," *Journal of Finance*, 39:575–592 (July 1984).

S. C. Myers and N. S. Majluf: "Corporate Financing and Investment Decisions When Firms Have Information Investors Do Not Have," *Journal of Financial Economics*, 13:187–222 (June 1984).

J. Baskin: "An Empirical Investigation of the Pecking Order Hypothesis," *Financial Management*, 18:26–35 (Spring 1989).

L. Shyam-Sunder and S. C. Myers: "Testing Static Trade-Off Against Pecking-Order Models of Capital Structure," *Journal of Financial Economics*, 51:219–244 (February 1999).

Some useful reviews of theory and evidence on optimal capital structure are:

M. J. Barclay, C. W. Smith, and R. L. Watts: "The Determinants of Corporate Leverage and Dividend Policies," *Journal of Applied Corporate Finance*, 7:4–19 (Winter 1995).

M. Harris and A. Raviv: "The Theory of Optimal Capital Structure," *Journal of Finance*, 48:297–356 (March 1991).

S. C. Myers: "Capital Structure," *Journal of Economic Perspectives*, 15:81–102 (Spring 2000).

The Spring 1993 and Winter 1995 issues of the Journal of Applied Corporate Finance *contain several articles on the incentive effects of capital structure.*

The January–February 1986 issue of the Journal of Financial Economics *(vol. 15, no. 1/2) collects a series of empirical studies on the stock price impacts of debt and equity issues and capital structure changes.*

FURTHER READING

1. Compute the present value of interest tax shields generated by these three debt issues. Consider corporate taxes only. The marginal tax rate is $T_c = .35$.
   a. A $1,000, one-year loan at 8 percent.

QUIZ

b. A five-year loan of $1,000 at 8 percent. Assume no principal is repaid until maturity.

c. A $1,000 perpetuity at 7 percent.

2. Here are book and market value balance sheets of the United Frypan Company (UF):

Book				Market			
Net working capital	$ 20	Debt	$ 40	Net working capital	$ 20	Debt	$ 40
Long-term assets	80	Equity	60	Long-term assets	140	Equity	120
	$100		$100		$160		$160

Assume that MM's theory holds with taxes. There is no growth, and the $40 of debt is expected to be permanent. Assume a 40 percent corporate tax rate.

a. How much of the firm's value is accounted for by the debt-generated tax shield?

b. How much better off will UF's shareholders be if the firm borrows $20 more and uses it to repurchase stock?

c. Now suppose that subsequently Congress passes a law which eliminates the deductibility of interest for tax purposes after a grace period of five years. What will be the new value of the firm, other things equal? (Assume an 8 percent borrowing rate.)

3. What is the relative tax advantage of corporate debt if the corporate tax rate is $T_c = .35$, the personal tax rate is $T_p = .31$, but all equity income is received as capital gains and escapes tax entirely ($T_{pE} = 0$)? How does the relative tax advantage change if the company decides to pay out all equity income as cash dividends?

4. This question tests your understanding of financial distress.

a. What are the costs of going bankrupt? Define these costs carefully.

b. "A company can incur costs of financial distress without ever going bankrupt." Explain how this can happen.

c. Explain how conflicts of interest between bondholders and stockholders can lead to costs of financial distress.

5. On February 29, 2003, when PDQ Computers announced bankruptcy, its share price fell from $3.00 to $.50 per share. There were 10 million shares outstanding. Does that imply bankruptcy costs of 10 × (3.00 − .50) = $25 million? Explain.

6. "The firm can't use interest tax shields unless it has (taxable) income to shield." What does this statement imply for the debt policy? Explain briefly.

7. Let us go back to Circular File's market value balance sheet:

Net working capital	$20	$25	Bonds outstanding
Fixed assets	10	5	Common stock
Total assets	$30	$30	Total value

Who gains and who loses from the following maneuvers?

a. Circular scrapes up $5 in cash and pays a cash dividend.

b. Circular halts operations, sells its fixed assets, and converts net working capital into $20 cash. Unfortunately the fixed assets fetch only $6 on the secondhand market. The $26 cash is invested in Treasury bills.

c. Circular encounters an acceptable investment opportunity, NPV = 0, requiring an investment of $10. The firm borrows to finance the project. The new debt has the same security, seniority, etc., as the old.

d. Suppose that the new project has NPV = +$2 and is financed by an issue of preferred stock.

e. The lenders agree to extend the maturity of their loan from one year to two in order to give Circular a chance to recover.

8. What types of firms would be likely to incur heavy costs in the event of bankruptcy or financial distress? What types would incur relatively light costs? Give a few examples of each type.

9. The traditional theory of optimal capital structure states that firms trade off corporate interest tax shields against the possible costs of financial distress due to borrowing. What does this theory predict about the relationship between book profitability and target book debt ratios? Is the theory's prediction consistent with the facts?

10. What is meant by the pecking-order theory of capital structure? Could this theory explain the observed relationship between profitability and debt ratios? Explain briefly.

11. Why does asymmetric information push companies to raise external funds by borrowing rather than by issuing common stock?

12. For what kinds of companies is financial slack most valuable? Are there situations in which financial slack should be reduced by borrowing and paying out the proceeds to the stockholders? Explain.

PRACTICE QUESTIONS

1. Suppose that, in an effort to reduce the federal deficit, Congress increases the top personal tax rate on interest and dividends to 44 percent but retains a 20 percent tax rate on realized capital gains. The corporate tax rate stays at 35 percent. Compute the total corporate plus personal taxes paid on debt versus equity income if (a) all capital gains are realized immediately and (b) capital gains are deferred forever. Assume capital gains are half of equity income.

2. "The trouble with MM's argument is that it ignores the fact that individuals can deduct interest for personal income tax." Show why this is not an objection. What difference would it make if individuals were not allowed to deduct interest for personal tax?

3. Look back at the Pfizer example in Section 18.1. Suppose that Pfizer moves to a 40 percent book debt ratio by issuing debt and using the proceeds to repurchase shares. Consider only corporate taxes. Now reconstruct Table 18.3(b) to reflect the new capital structure.

4. Calculate the tax shield for an actual U.S. company assuming:
   a. Debt is permanent.
   b. Personal tax rates on debt and equity income are the same.

   How would the stock price change if the company announced tomorrow that it intended to replace all its debt with equity?

5. Tables 18.3(a) and 18.3(b), although pertaining to a real company, are really just a simplified numerical example. What factors would you expect to determine the value of interest tax shields in practice—not just for Pfizer, but for a range of companies with different profitability, risk, and types of business?

6. "The right of shareholders to default is a valuable privilege." Explain.

7. In Section 18.3, we briefly referred to three games: Playing for time, cash in and run, and bait and switch.

   For each game, construct a simple numerical example (like the example for the risk-shifting game) showing how shareholders can gain at the expense of creditors. Then explain how the temptation to play these games could lead to costs of financial distress.

8. Summarize the evidence pro and con the trade-off theory of capital structure.

9. Look at some real companies with different types of assets. What operating problems would each encounter in the event of financial distress? How well would the assets keep their value?

10. The Salad Oil Storage (SOS) Company has financed a large part of its facilities with long-term debt. There is a significant risk of default, but the company is not on the ropes yet. Explain:

    a. Why SOS stockholders could lose by investing in a positive-NPV project financed by an equity issue.

    b. Why SOS stockholders could gain by investing in a negative-NPV project financed by cash.

    c. Why SOS stockholders could gain from paying out a large cash dividend.

    How might the firm's adherence to a target debt ratio mitigate some or all of the problems noted above?

11. **a.** Who benefits from the fine print in bond contracts when the firm gets into financial trouble? Give a one-sentence answer.

    b. Who benefits from the fine print when the bonds are issued? Suppose the firm is offered the choice of issuing (i) a bond with standard restrictions on dividend payout, additional borrowing, etc., and (ii) a bond with minimal restrictions but a much higher interest rate? Suppose the interest rates on both (i) and (ii) are fair from the viewpoint of lenders. Which bond would you expect the firm to issue? Why?

12. Caldor, the retailing chain, filed for bankruptcy in September 1995. Shortly after the bankruptcy its stock traded at $5.25 per share, down from about $20 earlier in the year. How much of this drop should be attributed to bankruptcy costs—all, part, or none? Explain.

13. "I was amazed to find that the announcement of a stock issue drives down the value of the issuing firm by *30 percent*, on average, of the proceeds of the issue. That issue cost dwarfs the underwriter's spread and the administrative costs of the issue. It makes common stock issues prohibitively expensive."

    a. You are contemplating a $100 million stock issue. On past evidence, you anticipate that announcement of this issue will drive down stock price by 3 percent and that the market value of your firm will fall by 30 percent of the amount to be raised. On the other hand, additional equity funds are necessary to fund an investment project which you believe has a positive NPV of $40 million. Should you proceed with the issue?

    b. Is the fall in market value on announcement of a stock issue an *issue cost* in the same sense as an underwriter's spread? Respond to the quote that begins this question.

    Use your answer to (a) as a numerical example to explain your response to (b).

14. Ronald Masulis[42] has analyzed the stock price impact of *exchange offers* of debt for equity or vice versa. In an exchange offer, the firm offers to trade freshly issued securities for seasoned securities in the hands of investors. Thus, a firm that wanted to move to a higher debt ratio could offer to trade new debt for outstanding shares. A firm that wanted to move to a more conservative capital structure could offer to trade new shares for outstanding debt securities.

    Masulis found that debt for equity exchanges were good news (stock price increased on announcement) and equity for debt exchanges were bad news.

    a. Are these results consistent with the trade-off theory of capital structure?

    b. Are the results consistent with the evidence that investors regard announcements of (i) stock issues as bad news, (ii) stock repurchases as good news, and (iii) debt issues as no news, or at most trifling disappointments?

    c. How could Masulis's results be explained?

---

[42]R. W. Masulis, "The Effects of Capital Structure Change on Security Prices: A Study of Exchange Offers," *Journal of Financial Economics* 8 (June 1980), pp. 139–177, and "The Impact of Capital Structure Change on Firm Value," *Journal of Finance* 38 (March 1983), pp. 107–126.

15. Suppose the trade-off theory of capital structure is true. Can you predict how companies' debt ratios should change over time? How do these predictions differ from the pecking-order theory's?

16. Summarize the evidence pro and con the pecking-order theory of capital structure.

17. "Why are personal taxes on bond interest important? They are the bondholder's problem." Explain why they are also indirectly the shareholder's problem.

18. The possible payoffs from Ms. Ketchup's projects (see Section 18.3) have not changed but there is now a 40 percent chance that project 2 will pay off $24 and a 60 percent chance that it will pay off $0.
    a. Recalculate the expected payoffs to the bank and Ms. Ketchup if the bank lends the present value of $10. Which project would Ms. Ketchup undertake?
    b. What is the maximum amount the bank could lend that would induce Ms. Ketchup to take project 1?

19. Select a dozen companies from the Market Insight database (**www.mhhe.com/edumarketinsight**). Estimate how much more these companies could borrow before they would exhaust taxable profits.

1. Use the Market Insight database (**www.mhhe.com/edumarketinsight**) to see how well differences in company leverage seem to support the trade-off theory and the pecking-order theory.

CHALLENGE QUESTION

STANDARD &POOR'S

PART TWO RELATED WEBSITES

Robert Shiller's home page includes long-term data on U.S. stock and bill returns:

www.aida.econ.yale.edu

Equity betas for individual stocks are found on Yahoo. (Or you can download the stock prices from Yahoo and calculate your own measures):

www.finance.yahoo.com

Aswath Damodoran's home page contains good long-term data on U.S. equities and average equity and asset betas for U.S. industries:

www.equity.stern.nyu.edu/~adamodar/ New_Home_Page

Another useful site is Campbell Harvey's home page. It contains data on past stock returns and risk, and software to calculate mean-variance efficient frontiers:

www.duke.edu/~charvey

Data on the Fama-French factors are published on Ken French's website:

www.mba.tuck.dartmouth.edu/pages/ faculty/ken.french

ValuePro provides software and data for estimating company cost of capital:

www.valuepro.net

For a collection of recent articles on the cost of capital see:

www.ibbotson.com

CHAPTER NINETEEN

FINANCING AND VALUATION

WE FIRST ADDRESSED problems of capital budgeting in Chapter 2. At that point we said hardly a word about financing decisions; we proceeded under the simplest possible assumption about financing, namely, all-equity financing. We were really assuming an idealized Modigliani–Miller (MM) world in which all financing decisions are irrelevant. In a strict MM world, firms can analyze real investments as if they are to be all-equity-financed; the actual financing plan is a mere detail to be worked out later.

Under MM assumptions, decisions to spend money can be separated from decisions to raise money. In this chapter we reconsider the capital budgeting decision when investment and financing decisions *interact* and cannot be wholly separated.

In the early chapters you learned how to value a capital investment opportunity by a four-step procedure:

1. Forecast the project's incremental after-tax cash flow, assuming the project is entirely equity-financed.
2. Assess the project's risk.
3. Estimate the opportunity cost of capital, that is, the expected rate of return offered to investors by the equivalent-risk investments traded in capital markets.
4. Calculate NPV, using the discounted-cash-flow formula.

In effect, we were thinking of each project as a mini-firm, and asking, How much would that mini-firm be worth if we spun it off as a separate, all-equity-financed enterprise? How much would investors be willing to pay for shares in the project?

Of course, this procedure rests on the concept of *value additivity*. In well-functioning capital markets the market value of the firm is the sum of the present value of all the assets held by the firm[1]— the whole equals the sum of the parts.

In this chapter we stick with the value-additivity principle but extend it to include value contributed by financing decisions. There are two ways of doing this:

1. *Adjust the discount rate.* The adjustment is typically downward, to account for the value of interest tax shields. This is the most common approach. It is usually implemented via the after-tax weighted-average cost of capital or "WACC."
2. *Adjust the present value.* That is, start by estimating the project's "base-case" value as an all-equity-financed mini-firm, and then adjust this base-case NPV to account for the project's impact on the firm's capital structure. Thus

Adjusted NPV (APV for short) = base-case NPV

+NPV of financing decisions caused by project acceptance

Once you identify and value the side effects of financing a project, calculating its APV (adjusted net present value) is no more than addition or subtraction.

This is a how-to-do-it chapter. In the next section, we explain and derive the after-tax weighted-average cost of capital, reviewing required assumptions and the too-common mistakes people make using this formula. Section 19.2 then covers the tricks of the trade: helpful tips on how to estimate

continued

---

[1]*All assets* means intangible as well as tangible assets. For example, a going concern is usually worth more than a haphazard pile of tangible assets. Thus, the aggregate value of a firm's tangible assets often falls short of its market value. The difference is accounted for by going-concern value or by other intangible assets such as accumulated technical expertise, an experienced sales force, or valuable growth opportunities.

inputs and how the formula is used in practice. Section 19.3 shows how to recalculate the weighted-average cost of capital when capital structure or asset mix changes.

Section 19.4 turns to the Adjusted Present Value or APV method. This is simple enough in concept: Just value the project by discounting at the opportunity cost of capital––not the WACC––and then add the present values gained or lost due to financing side effects. But identifying and valuing the side effects is sometimes tricky, so we'll have to work through some numerical examples.

Section 19.5 reexamines a basic and apparently simple issue: What should the discount rate be for a risk-free project? Once we recognize the tax deductibility of debt interest, we will find that all risk-free, or *debt-equivalent*, cash flows can be evaluated by discounting at the *after-tax* interest rate. We show that this rule is consistent with both the weighted-average cost of capital and with APV.

We conclude the chapter with a question and answer section designed to clarify points that managers and students often find confusing. An Appendix providing more details and more formulas can be obtained from the Brealey–Myers website.[2]

 ## 19.1 THE AFTER-TAX WEIGHTED-AVERAGE COST OF CAPITAL

Think back to Chapter 17 and Modigliani and Miller's (MM's) proposition I. MM showed that, without taxes or financial market imperfections, the cost of capital does not depend on financing. In other words, the weighted average of the expected returns to debt and equity investors equals the opportunity cost of capital, regardless of the debt ratio:

$$\text{Weighted-average return to debt and equity} = r_D \frac{D}{V} + r_E \frac{E}{V}$$

$$= r, \text{a constant, independent of } D/V$$

Here r is the opportunity cost of capital, the expected rate of return investors would demand if the firm had no debt at all; r_D and r_E are the expected rates of return on debt and equity, the "cost of debt" and "cost of equity." The weights D/V and E/V are the fractions of debt and equity, based on market values; V, the total market value of the firm, is the sum of D and E.

But you can't look up r, the opportunity cost of capital, in *The Wall Street Journal* or find it on the Internet. So financial managers turn the problem around: They start with the estimates of r_D and r_E and then infer r. Under MM's assumptions,

$$r = r_D \frac{D}{V} + r_E \frac{E}{V}$$

This formula calculates r, the opportunity cost of capital, as the expected rate of return on a portfolio of all the firm's outstanding securities.

---

[2]www.mhhe.com/bm7e.

We have discussed this weighted-average cost of capital formula in Chapters 9 and 17. However, the formula misses a crucial difference between debt and equity: Interest payments are tax-deductible. Therefore we move on to the *after-tax* weighted-average cost of capital, nicknamed WACC:

$$\text{WACC} = r_D(1 - T_c)\frac{D}{V} + r_E\frac{E}{V}$$

Here T_c is the marginal corporate tax rate.

Notice that the after-tax WACC is less than the opportunity cost of capital (r), because the "cost of debt" is calculated after tax as $r_D(1 - T_c)$. Thus the tax advantages of debt financing are reflected in a lower discount rate. Notice too that all the variables in the weighted-average formula refer to the firm as a whole. As a result, the formula gives the right discount rate only for projects that are just like the firm undertaking them. The formula works for the "average" project. It is incorrect for projects that are safer or riskier than the average of the firm's existing assets. It is incorrect for projects whose acceptance would lead to an increase or decrease in the firm's debt ratio.

Example: Sangria Corporation

Let's calculate WACC for the Sangria Corporation. Its book and market value balance sheets are

Sangria Corporation (Book Values, millions)

Asset value	$100	$ 50	Debt
		50	Equity
	$100	$100	

Sangria Corporation (Market Values, millions)

Asset value	$125	$ 50	Debt (D)
		75	Equity (E)
	$125	$125	Firm Value (V)

We calculated the market value of equity on Sangria's balance sheet by multiplying its current stock price ($7.50) by 10 million, the number of its outstanding shares. The company has done well and future prospects are good, so the stock is trading above book value ($5.00 per share). However, the book and market values of Sangria's debt are in this case equal.

Sangria's cost of debt (the interest rate on its existing debt and on any new borrowing) is 8 percent. Its cost of equity (the expected rate of return demanded by investors in Sangria's stock) is 14.6 percent.

The market value balance sheet shows assets worth $125 million. Of course we can't observe this value directly, because the assets themselves are not traded. But we know what they are worth to debt and equity investors (50 + 75 = $125 million). This value is entered on the left of the market value balance sheet.

Why did we show the book balance sheet? Only so you could draw a big **X** through it. Do so now.

When estimating the weighted-average cost of capital, you are not interested in past investments but in current values and expectations for the future. Sangria's true debt ratio is not 50 percent, the book ratio, but 40 percent, because its assets are worth $125 million. The cost of equity, $r_E = .146$, is the expected rate of return from purchase of stock at $7.50 per share, the current market price. It is not the return on book value per share. You can't buy shares in Sangria for $5 anymore.

Sangria is consistently profitable and pays tax at the marginal rate of 35 percent. That is the final input for Sangria's WACC. The inputs are summarized here:

Cost of debt (r_D)	.08
Cost of equity (r_E)	.146
Marginal tax rate (T_c)	.35
Debt ratio (D/V)	50/125 = .4
Equity ratio (E/V)	75/125 = .6

The company's WACC is

$$WACC = .08(1 - .35)(.4) + .146(.6) = .1084, \text{ or } 10.84\%$$

That's how you calculate the weighted-average cost of capital.[3]

Now let's see how Sangria would use this formula. Sangria's enologists have proposed investing $12.5 million in construction of a perpetual crushing machine, which, conveniently for us, never depreciates and generates a perpetual stream of earnings and cash flow of $2.085 million per year pretax. The after-tax cash flow is

Pretax cash flow	$2.085
Tax at 35%	.730
After-tax cash flow	$1.355 million

Notice: This after-tax cash flow takes no account of interest tax shields on debt supported by the perpetual crusher project. As we explained in Chapter 6, standard capital budgeting practice calculates after-tax cash flows as if the project were all-equity-financed. However, the interest tax shields will not be ignored: We are about to discount the project cash flows by Sangria's WACC, in which the cost of debt is entered after tax. The value of interest tax shields is picked up not as higher after-tax cash flows, but in a lower discount rate.

The crusher generates a perpetual cash flow of C = $1.355 million, so NPV is

$$NPV = -12.5 + \frac{1.355}{.1084} = 0$$

NPV = 0 means a barely acceptable investment. The annual cash flow of $1.355 million per year amounts to a 10.84% rate of return on investment (1.355/12.5 = .1084), exactly equal to Sangria's WACC.

If project NPV = 0, the return to equity investors must exactly equal the cost of equity, 14.6%. Let's confirm that Sangria shareholders could actually forecast a 14.6% return on their investment in the perpetual crusher project.

---

[3]In practice it's pointless to calculate discount rates to four decimal places. We do so here to avoid confusion from rounding errors. Earnings and cash flows are carried to three decimal places for the same reason.

Suppose Sangria sets up this project as a mini-firm. Its market-value balance sheet looks like this:

Perpetual Crusher (Market Values, millions)

Project value	$12.5	$ 5.0	Debt (D)
		7.5	Equity (E)
	$12.5	$12.5	Project Value (V)

Calculate the expected dollar return to shareholders:

$$\text{After-tax interest} = r_D(1 - T_c)D = .08(1 - .35)(5) = .26$$
$$\text{Expected equity income} = C - (1 - T_c)r_D D = 1.355 - .26 = 1.095$$

The project's earnings are level and perpetual, so the expected rate of return on equity is equal to the expected equity income divided by the equity value:

$$\text{Expected equity return} = r_E = \frac{\text{expected equity income}}{\text{equity value}}$$
$$= \frac{1.095}{7.5} = .146, \text{ or } 14.6\%$$

The expected return on equity equals the cost of equity, so it makes sense that the project's NPV is zero.

Review of Assumptions

By discounting the perpetual crusher's cash flows at Sangria's WACC, we assume that

- The project's business risks are the same as Sangria's other assets.
- The project supports the same fraction of debt to value as in Sangria's overall capital structure.

You can see the importance of these two assumptions: If the perpetual crusher had greater business risk than Sangria's other assets, or if acceptance of the project would lead to a permanent, material[4] change in Sangria's debt ratio, then Sangria's shareholders would not be content with a 14.6 percent expected return on their equity investment in the project.

We have illustrated the WACC formula only for a project offering perpetual cash flows. But Miles and Ezzell have shown that the formula works for any cash-flow pattern if the firm adjusts its borrowing to maintain a constant debt ratio over time. When the firm departs from this borrowing policy, WACC is only approximately correct.[5]

---

[4]Users of WACC need not worry about small or temporary fluctuations in debt-to-value ratios. Suppose that Sangria management decided for convenience to borrow $12.5 million to allow immediate construction of the crusher. This does not necessarily change Sangria's long-term financing policy. If the crusher supports only $5.0 million of debt, Sangria would have to pay down debt to restore its overall debt ratio to 40 percent. For example, it could fund later projects with less debt and more equity.

[5]J. Miles and R. Ezzell, "The Weighted Average Cost of Capital, Perfect Capital Markets, and Project Life: A Clarification," *Journal of Financial and Quantitative Analysis* 15 (September 1980), pp. 719–730.

19.2 USING WACC—SOME TRICKS OF THE TRADE

Sangria had just one asset and two sources of financing. A real company's market value balance sheet has many more entries, for example:[6]

Current assets, including cash, inventory, and accounts receivable	Current liabilities, including accounts payable and short-term debt
Plant and equipment	Long-term debt (D)
	Preferred stock (P)
Growth opportunities	Equity (E)
	Firm value (V)

Several questions immediately arise:

1. *How does the formula change when there are more than two sources of financing?* Easy: There is one cost for each element. The weight for each element is proportional to its market value. For example, if the capital structure includes both preferred and common shares,

$$\text{WACC} = r_D(1 - T_c)\frac{D}{V} + r_P\frac{P}{V} + r_E\frac{E}{V}$$

where r_P is investors' expected rate of return on preferred stocks.

2. *What about short-term debt?* Many companies consider only long-term financing when calculating WACC. They leave out the cost of short-term debt. In principle this is incorrect. The lenders who hold short-term debt are investors who can claim their share of operating earnings. A company that ignores this claim will misstate the required return on capital investments.

    But "zeroing out" short-term debt is not a serious error if the debt is only temporary, seasonal, or incidental financing or if it is offset by holdings of cash and marketable securities.[7] Suppose, for example, that your company's Italian subsidiary takes out a six-month loan from an Italian bank to finance its inventory and accounts receivable. The dollar equivalent

---

[6]This balance sheet is for exposition and should not be confused with a real company's books. It includes the value of growth opportunities, which accountants do not recognize, though investors do. It excludes certain accounting entries, for example, deferred taxes.

Deferred taxes arise when a company uses faster depreciation for tax purposes than it uses in reports to investors. That means the company reports more taxes than it pays. The difference is accumulated as a liability for deferred taxes. In a sense there is a liability, because the Internal Revenue Service "catches up," collecting extra taxes, as assets age. But this is irrelevant in capital investment analysis, which focuses on actual after-tax cash flows and uses accelerated tax depreciation.

Deferred taxes should not be regarded as a source of financing or an element of the weighted-average cost of capital formula. The liability for deferred taxes is not a security held by investors. It is a balance sheet entry created to serve the needs of accounting.

Deferred taxes can be important in regulated industries, however. Regulators take deferred taxes into account in calculating allowed rates of return and the time patterns of revenues and consumer prices.

[7]Financial practitioners have rules of thumb for deciding whether short-term debt is worth including in the weighted-average cost of capital. Suppose, for example, that short-term debt is 10 percent of total liabilities and that net working capital is negative. Then short-term debt is almost surely being used to finance long-term assets and should be explicitly included in WACC.

of this loan will show up as a short-term debt on the parent's balance sheet. At the same time headquarters may be lending money by investing surplus dollars in short-term securities. If lending and borrowing offset, there is no point in including the cost of short-term debt in the weighted-average cost of capital, because the company is not a *net* short-term borrower.

3. *What about other current liabilities?* Current liabilities are usually "netted out" by subtracting them from current assets. The difference is entered as net working capital on the left-hand side of the balance sheet. The sum of long-term financing on the right is called *total capitalization*.

Net working capital = current assets − current liabilities	
Plant and equipment	Long-term debt (D)
Growth opportunities	Preferred stock (P)
	Equity (E)
	Total capitalization (V)

When net working capital is treated as an asset, forecasts of cash flows for capital investment projects must treat increases in net working capital as a cash outflow and decreases as an inflow. This is standard practice, which we followed in Section 6.2.

Since current liabilities include short-term debt, netting them out against current assets excludes the cost of short-term debt from the weighted-average cost of capital. We have just explained why this can be an acceptable approximation. But when short-term debt is an important, permanent source of financing—as is common for small firms and firms outside the United States—it should be shown explicitly on the right side of the balance sheet, not netted out against current assets. The interest cost of short-term debt is then one element of the weighted-average cost of capital.

4. *How are the costs of the financing elements calculated?* You can often use stock market data to get an estimate of r_E, the expected rate of return demanded by investors in the company's stock. With that estimate, WACC is not too hard to calculate, because the borrowing rate r_D and the debt and equity ratios D/V and E/V can be directly observed or estimated without too much trouble.[8] Estimating the value and required return for preferred shares is likewise usually not too complicated.

Estimating the required return on other security types can be troublesome. Convertible debt, where the investors' return comes partly from an option to exchange the debt for the company's stock, is one example. We will leave convertibles to Chapter 23.

Junk debt, where the risk of default is high, is likewise difficult. The higher the odds of default, the lower the market price of the debt and the higher the *promised* rate of interest. But the weighted-average cost of capital

---

[8]Most corporate debt is not actively traded, so its market value cannot be observed directly. But you can usually value a nontraded debt security by looking to securities that *are* traded and that have approximately the same default risk and maturity. See Chapter 24.

For healthy firms the market value of debt is usually not too far from book value, so many managers and analysts use book value for D in the weighted-average cost of capital formula. However, be sure to use *market*, not book, values for E.

is an *expected*, that is, average, rate of return, not a promised one. For example, in October 2001, Crown Cork bonds maturing in 2005 sold at only 76 percent of face value and offered an 18.6 percent promised yield, more than 14 percentage points above yields on the highest-quality debt issues maturing at the same time. The price and yield on the Crown Cork bond demonstrated investors' concern about the company's chronic financial ill-health. But the 18.6 percent yield was not an expected return, because it did not average in the losses to be incurred if Crown Cork defaults. Including 18.6 percent as a "cost of debt" in a calculation of WACC would therefore overstate Crown Cork's true cost of capital.

This is bad news: There is no easy or tractable way of estimating the expected rate of return on most junk debt issues.[9] The good news is that for most debt the odds of default are small. That means the promised and expected rates of return are close, and the promised rate can be used as an approximation in the weighted-average cost of capital.

Industry Costs of Capital

You can also calculate WACC for *industries*. Suppose that a pharmaceutical company has a subsidiary that produces specialty chemicals. What discount rate is better for the subsidiary's projects—the company WACC or a weighted-average cost of capital for a portfolio of "pure-play" specialty chemical companies? The latter rate is better in principle and also in practice if good data are available for firms with operations and markets similar to the subsidiary's.

An Application to the Railroad Industry Every year the United States Surface Transportation Board (STB) estimates a cost of capital for the railroad industry, defined as Class I (big) railroads. We will use the STB's data and estimates to calculate a railroad industry WACC for 1999.

The STB took care to estimate the market value of the railroads' common shares and all outstanding debt issues, including debt-equivalents such as equipment trust certificates and financial leases.[10] The aggregate industry capital structure was[11]

	Market Value (billions)	Financing Weights
Debt	$31,627.8	37.3%
Equity	53,210.0	62.7

The average cost of debt was 7.2 percent. To estimate the cost of equity, the STB used the constant-growth DCF model, which you will recall with pleasure from Section 4.3. If investors expect dividends to grow at a constant, perpetual rate, g, then the expected return is the sum of the dividend yield and the expected growth rate:

$$r_E = \frac{DIV_1}{P_0} + g$$

---

[9]When betas can be estimated for the junk issue or for a sample of similar issues, the expected return can be calculated from the capital asset pricing model. Otherwise, the yield should be adjusted for the probability of default. Evidence on historical default rates on junk bonds is described in Chapter 25.

[10]Equipment trust certificates are described in Section 25.3; financial leases are discussed in Chapter 26.

[11]There were three tiny preferred issues. For simplicity we have added them to debt.

An investor who bought a portfolio of the shares of Class I railroads in 1999 got a dividend yield of about 2.0 percent. A review of security analysts' forecasts gave an average expected growth rate for earnings and dividends of 10.9 percent. The cost of equity was thus estimated at $r_E = 2.0 + 10.9 = 12.9$ percent.

Using the statutory marginal tax rate of 35 percent,[12] the railroad industry WACC is

$$\text{WACC} = 0.072(1 - .35)(.373) + .129(.627) = .098, \text{ or about } 10\%$$

Valuing Companies: WACC vs. the Flow-to-Equity Method

WACC is normally used as a hurdle rate or discount rate to value proposed capital investments. But sometimes it is used as a discount rate for valuing whole companies. For example, the financial manager may need to value a target company to decide whether to go ahead with a merger.

Valuing companies raises no new conceptual problems. You just treat the company as if it were one big project. Forecast the company's cash flows (the hardest part of the exercise) and discount back to present value. The company's WACC is the right discount rate if the company's debt ratio is expected to remain reasonably close to constant. But remember:

- If you discount at WACC, cash flows have to be projected just as you would for a capital investment project. Do not deduct interest. Calculate taxes as if the company were all-equity-financed. The value of interest tax shields is picked up in the WACC formula.
- The company's cash flows will probably not be forecasted to infinity. Financial managers usually forecast to a medium-term horizon—10 years, say—and add a terminal value to the cash flows in the horizon year. The terminal value is the present value at the horizon of post-horizon flows. Estimating the terminal value requires careful attention because it often accounts for the majority of the value of the company. See Section 4.5.
- Discounting at WACC values the assets and operations of the company. If the object is to value the company's equity, that is, its common stock, don't forget to subtract the value of the company's outstanding debt.

If the task is to value equity, there's an obvious alternative to discounting company cash flows at its WACC. Discount the cash flows to *equity,* after interest and after taxes, at the cost of equity. This is called the *flow-to-equity* method. If the company's debt ratio is constant over time, the flow-to-equity method should give the same answer as discounting company cash flows at the WACC and subtracting debt.

The flow-to-equity method seems simple, and it is simple if the proportions of debt and equity financing stay reasonably close to constant for the life of the company. But the cost of equity depends on financial leverage; it depends on financial risk as well as business risk. If financial leverage will change significantly, discounting flows to equity at today's cost of equity will not give the right answer.

A one-shot change in financing can usually be accommodated. Think again of a proposed takeover. Suppose the financial manager decides that the target's 20 percent debt-to-value ratio is stodgy and too conservative. She decides the company

---

[12] The STB actually uses a pretax cost of debt. If the STB's reported WACC is used as a discount rate, interest tax shields have to be valued separately, as in the adjusted-present-value method described in Section 19.4.

could easily support 40 percent debt and asks you to value the target's shares on that assumption. Unfortunately you have estimated the cost of equity at the existing 20 percent ratio. No problem! Adjust the cost of equity (we will revisit the formula in the next section) and proceed as usual. Of course you must forecast and discount cash flows to equity at the new 40 percent debt ratio. You also have to assume that this debt ratio will be maintained after the takeover.

Mistakes People Make in Using the Weighted-Average Formula

The weighted-average formula is very useful but also dangerous. It tempts people to make logical errors. For example, manager Q, who is campaigning for a pet project, might look at the formula

$$\text{WACC} = r_D(1 - T_c)\frac{D}{V} + r_E\frac{E}{V}$$

and think, Aha! My firm has a good credit rating. It could borrow, say, 90 percent of the project's cost if it likes. That means $D/V = .9$ and $E/V = .1$. My firm's borrowing rate r_D is 8 percent, and the required return on equity, r_E, is 15 percent. Therefore

$$\text{WACC} = .08(1 - .35)(.9) + .15(.1) = .062$$

or 6.2 percent. When I discount at that rate, my project looks great.

Manager Q is wrong on several counts. First, the weighted-average formula works only for projects that are carbon copies of the firm. The firm isn't 90 percent debt-financed.

Second, the immediate source of funds for a project has no necessary connection with the hurdle rate for the project. What matters is the project's overall contribution to the firm's borrowing power. A dollar invested in Q's pet project will not increase the firm's debt capacity by $.90. If the firm borrows 90 percent of the project's cost, it is really borrowing in part against its *existing* assets. Any advantage from financing the new project with more debt than normal should be attributed to the old projects, not to the new one.

Third, even if the firm were willing and able to lever up to 90 percent debt, its cost of capital would not decline to 6.2 percent (as Q's naive calculation predicts). You cannot increase the debt ratio without creating financial risk for stockholders and thereby increasing r_E, the expected rate of return they demand from the firm's common stock. Going to 90 percent debt would certainly increase the borrowing rate, too.

19.3 ADJUSTING WACC WHEN DEBT RATIOS OR BUSINESS RISKS CHANGE

The WACC formula assumes that the project to be valued will be financed in the same proportions of debt and equity as the firm as a whole. What if that is not true? What if the perpetual crusher project supports debt equal to, say, 20 percent of project value, versus 40 percent debt financing for the firm as a whole?

Moving from 40 to 20 percent debt changes all the elements of the WACC formula except the tax rate.[13] Obviously the financing weights change. But the cost

---

[13]It could change the tax rate too. For example, the firm might have enough pretax income to cover interest payments at 20 percent debt but not at 40 percent. In this case the effective marginal tax rate would be higher at 20 percent debt.

Rates of return

Cost of equity (r_E)

Opportunity cost of capital (r)

WACC

Cost of debt (r_D)

r

Debt–equity ratio (D/E)

FIGURE 19.1

WACC plotted against the debt–equity ratio. WACC equals the opportunity cost of capital when there is no debt. WACC declines with financial leverage because of interest tax shields.

of equity r_E is less, because financial risk is reduced. The cost of debt may be lower too.

Figure 19.1 plots WACC and the costs of debt and equity as a function of the debt–equity ratio. The flat line is r, the opportunity cost of capital. Remember, this is the expected rate of return that investors would want from the project if it were all-equity-financed. The opportunity cost of capital depends only on business risk and is the natural reference point.

Suppose Sangria or the perpetual crusher project were all-equity-financed ($D/V = 0$). At that point WACC equals cost of equity, and both equal the opportunity cost of capital. Start from that point in Figure 19.1. As the debt ratio increases, the cost of equity increases, because of financial risk, but notice that WACC declines. The decline is *not* caused by use of "cheap" debt in place of "expensive" equity. It falls because of the tax shields on debt interest payments. If there were no corporate income taxes, the weighted-average cost of capital would be constant, and equal to the opportunity cost of capital, at all debt ratios. We showed this in Chapters 9 and 17.

Figure 19.1 shows the *shape* of the relationship between financing and WACC, but we have numbers only for Sangria's current 40 percent debt ratio. We want to recalculate WACC at a 20 percent ratio.

Here is the simplest way to do it. There are three steps.

Step 1   Calculate the opportunity cost of capital. In other words, calculate WACC and the cost of equity at zero debt. This step is called *unlevering* the WACC. The simplest unlevering formula is

$$\text{Opportunity cost of capital} = r = r_D D/V + r_E E/V$$

This formula comes directly from Modigliani and Miller's proposition I (see Section 17.1). If taxes are left out, the weighted-average cost of capital equals the opportunity cost of capital and is independent of leverage.

FIGURE 19.2

This plot shows WACC for the Sangria Corporation at debt-to-equity ratios of 25 and 67 percent. The corresponding debt-to-*value* ratios are 20 and 40 percent.

Step 2   Estimate the cost of debt, r_D, at the new debt ratio, and calculate the new cost of equity.

$$r_E = r + (r - r_D)D/E$$

This formula is Modigliani and Miller's proposition II (see Section 17.2). It calls for D/E, the ratio of debt to *equity*, not debt to value.

Step 3   Recalculate the weighted-average cost of capital at the new financing weights.

Let's do the numbers for the perpetual crusher project at $D/V = .20$ or 20 percent. *Step 1.* Sangria's current debt ratio is $D/V = .4$

$$r = .08(.4) + .146(.6) = .12 \text{ or } 12\%$$

Step 2. We will assume that the debt cost stays at 8 percent when the debt ratio is 20 percent. Then

$$r_E = .12 + (.12 - .08)(.25) = .13 \text{ or } 13\%$$

Note that the debt–*equity* ratio is $.2/.8 = .25$.
Step 3. Recalculate WACC.

$$\text{WACC} = .08(1 - .35)(.2) + .13(.8) = .114 \text{ or } 11.4\%$$

Figure 19.2 enters these numbers on the plot of WACC versus debt ratio. The 11.4 percent project discount rate at 20 percent debt to value is .56 percentage points higher than at 40 percent.

Another Example: WACC for U.S. Railroads at 45 percent Debt   Let's return to the WACC we calculated for large U.S. railroads. We assumed a debt-to-value ratio of 37.3 percent. How would the railroad industry WACC change at 45 percent debt?

Step 1. Calculate the unlevered opportunity cost of capital

$$r = .072(.373) + .129(.627) = .108$$

Step 2. Assume that the cost of debt increases to 8 percent at 45 percent debt. The cost of equity is

$$r_E = .108 + (.108 - .080)45/55 = .13$$

Step 3. Recalculate WACC. If the marginal tax rate stays at 35 percent,

$$WACC = .080(1 - .35).45 + .130(.55) = .095 \text{ or } 9.5\%$$

The cost of capital drops by more than one half percentage point. Is this a great deal? Not as good as it looks. In these simple calculations, the cost of capital drops as financial leverage increases, but only because of corporate interest tax shields. In Chapter 18 we reviewed all the reasons why just focusing on corporate interest tax shields overstates the advantages of debt. For example, costs of financial distress encountered at high debt levels appear nowhere in the WACC formula or in the standard formulas relating the cost of equity for leverage.[14]

Unlevering and Relevering Betas

Our three-step procedure (1) unlevers and then (2) relevers the cost of equity. Some financial managers find it convenient to (1) unlever and then (2) relever the equity beta. Given the beta of equity at the new debt ratio, the cost of equity is determined from the capital asset pricing model. Then WACC is recalculated.

The formula for unlevering beta was given in Section 9.2.

$$\beta_{asset} = \beta_{debt}(D/V) + \beta_{equity}(E/V)$$

This equation says that the beta of a firm's assets is revealed by the beta of a portfolio of all of the firm's outstanding debt and equity securities. An investor who bought such a portfolio would own the assets free and clear and absorb only business risks.

The formula for relevering beta closely resembles MM's proposition II, except that betas are substituted for rates of return:

$$\beta_{equity} = \beta_{asset} + (\beta_{asset} - \beta_{debt})D/E$$

The Importance of Rebalancing

The formulas for WACC and for unlevering and relevering expected returns are simple, but we must be careful to remember underlying assumptions. The most important point is *rebalancing*.

Calculating WACC for a company at its existing capital structure requires that the capital structure *not* change; in other words, the company must rebalance its capital structure to maintain the same market-value debt ratio for the relevant future. Take Sangria Corporation as an example. It starts with a debt-to-value ratio of 40 percent and a market value of $125 million. Suppose that Sangria's products do unexpectedly

---

[14]Some financial managers and analysts argue that the costs of debt and equity increase rapidly at high debt ratios because of costs of financial distress. This in turn would cause the WACC curve in Figure 19.1 to flatten out, and finally increase, as the debt ratio climbs. For practical purposes, this can be a sensible end result. However, formal modeling of the interactions between the cost of financial distress and the expected rates of return on the company's securities is not easy.

well in the marketplace and that market value increases to $150 million. Rebalancing means that it will then increase debt to $.4 \times 150 = \$60$ million,[15] thus regaining a 40 percent ratio. If market value instead falls, Sangria would have to pay down debt proportionally.

Of course real companies do not rebalance capital structure in such a mechanical and compulsive way. For practical purposes, it's sufficient to assume gradual but steady adjustment toward a long-run target. But if the firm plans significant changes in capital structure (for example, if it plans to pay off its debt), the WACC formula won't work. In such cases, you should turn to the APV method, which we describe in the next section.

Our three-step procedure for recalculating WACC makes a similar rebalancing assumption.[16] Whatever the starting debt ratio, the firm is assumed to rebalance to maintain that ratio in the future. The unlevering and relevering in steps 1 and 2 also ignore any impact of investors' personal income taxes on the costs of debt and equity.[17]

19.4 ADJUSTED PRESENT VALUE

We now take a different tack. Instead of messing around with the discount rate, we explicitly adjust cash flows and present values for costs or benefits of financing. This approach is called **adjusted present value,** or **APV.**

The adjusted-present-value rule is easiest to understand in the context of simple numerical examples. We start by analyzing a project under base-case assumptions and then consider possible financing side-effects of accepting the project.

The Base Case

The APV method begins by valuing the project as if it were a mini-firm financed solely by equity. Consider a project to produce solar water heaters. It requires a $10 million investment and offers a level after-tax cash flow of $1.8 million per year for 10 years. The opportunity cost of capital is 12 percent, which reflects the project's business risk. Investors would demand a 12 percent expected return to invest in the mini-firm's shares.

Thus the mini-firm's base-case NPV is

$$\text{NPV} = -10 + \sum_{t=1}^{10} \frac{1.8}{(1.12)^t} = +\$.17 \text{ million, or } \$170,000$$

Considering the project's size, this figure is not much greater than zero. In a pure MM world where no financing decision matters, the financial manager would lean toward taking the project but would not be heartbroken if it were discarded.

---

[15]The proceeds of the additional borrowing would be paid out to shareholders or used, along with additional equity investment, to finance Sangria's growth.

[16]Similar, but not identical. The basic WACC formula assumes that rebalancing occurs at the end of each period. The unlevering and relevering formulas used in steps 1 and 2 of our three-step procedure are exact only if rebalancing is continuous so that the debt ratio stays constant day-to-day and week-to-week. However, the errors introduced from annual rebalancing are very small and can be ignored for practical purposes.

[17]The response of the cost of equity to changes in financial leverage can be affected by personal taxes. This is not covered here and is rarely adjusted for in practice.

Issue Costs

But suppose that the firm actually has to finance the $10 million investment by issuing stock (it will not have to issue stock if it rejects the project) and that issue costs soak up 5 percent of the gross proceeds of the issue. That means the firm has to issue $10,526,000 in order to obtain $10,000,000 cash. The $526,000 difference goes to underwriters, lawyers, and others involved in the issue process.

The project's APV is calculated by subtracting the issue cost from base-case NPV:

$$APV = \text{base-case NPV} - \text{issue cost}$$
$$= +170,000 - 526,000 = -\$356,000$$

The firm would reject the project because APV is negative.

Additions to the Firm's Debt Capacity

Consider a different financing scenario. Suppose that the firm has a 50 percent target debt ratio. Its policy is to limit debt to 50 percent of its assets. Thus, if it invests more, it borrows more; in this sense investment adds to the firm's debt capacity.[18]

Is debt capacity worth anything? The most widely accepted answer is yes because of the tax shields generated by interest payments on corporate borrowing. (Look back to our discussion of debt and taxes in Chapter 18.) For example, MM's theory states that the value of the firm is independent of its capital structure *except* for the present value of interest tax shields:

$$\text{Firm value} = \text{value with all-equity financing} + \text{PV(tax shield)}$$

This theory tells us to compute the value of the firm in two steps: First compute its base-case value under all-equity financing, and then add the present value of taxes saved due to a departure from all-equity financing. This procedure is like an APV calculation for the firm as a whole.

We can repeat the calculation for a particular project. For example, suppose that the solar heater project increases the firm's assets by $10 million and therefore prompts it to borrow $5 million more. Suppose that this $5 million loan is repaid in equal installments, so that the amount borrowed declines with the depreciating book value of the solar heater project. We also assume that the loan carries an interest rate of 8 percent. Table 19.1 shows how the value of the interest tax shields is calculated. This is the value of the additional debt capacity contributed to the firm by the project. We obtain APV by adding this amount to the project's NPV:

$$APV = \text{base-case NPV} + \text{PV(tax shield)}$$
$$= +170,000 + 576,000 = \$746,000$$

With these numbers, the solar heater project looks like a "go." But notice the differences between this APV calculation and an NPV calculated with a WACC used as the discount rate. The APV calculation assumes debt equal to 50 percent of book value, paid down on a fixed schedule. NPV using WACC assumes debt is a constant fraction of market value in each year of the project's life. Since the project's value will inevitably turn out higher or lower than expected, using WACC also assumes that

---

[18]*Debt capacity* is potentially misleading because it seems to imply an absolute limit to the amount the firm is *able* to borrow. That is not what we mean. The firm limits borrowing to 50 percent of assets as a rule of thumb for optimal capital structure. It could borrow more if it wanted to run increased risks of costs of financial distress.

Year	Debt Outstanding at Start of Year	Interest	Interest Tax Shield	Present Value of Tax Shield
1	$5,000	$400	$140	$129.6
2	4,500	360	126	108.0
3	4,000	320	112	88.9
4	3,500	280	98	72.0
5	3,000	240	84	57.2
6	2,500	200	70	44.1
7	2,000	160	56	32.6
8	1,500	120	42	22.7
9	1,000	80	28	14.0
10	500	40	14	6.5
			Total	$576

TABLE 19.1

Calculating the present value of interest tax shields on debt supported by the solar heater project (dollar figures in thousands).

Assumptions:
1. Marginal tax rate = T_c = .35; tax shield = $T_c \times$ interest.
2. Debt principal is repaid at end of year in ten $500,000 installments.
3. Interest rate on debt is 8 percent.
4. Present value is calculated at the 8 percent borrowing rate. The assumption here is that the tax shields are just as risky as the interest payments generating them.

future debt levels will be increased or reduced as necessary to keep the future debt ratio constant.

APV can be used when debt supported by a project is tied to the project's book value or has to be repaid on a fixed schedule. For example, Kaplan and Ruback used APV to analyze the prices paid for a sample of leveraged buyouts (LBOs). LBOs are takeovers, typically of mature companies, financed almost entirely with debt. However, the new debt is not intended to be permanent. LBO business plans call for generating extra cash by selling assets, shaving costs, and improving profit margins. The extra cash is used to pay down the LBO debt. Therefore you can't use WACC as a discount rate to evaluate an LBO because its debt ratio will not be constant.

APV works fine for LBOs. The company is first evaluated as if it were all-equity-financed. That means that cash flows are projected after tax, but without any interest tax shields generated by the LBO's debt. The tax shields are then valued separately. The debt repayment schedule is set down in the same format as Table 19.1 and the present value of interest tax shields is calculated and added to the all-equity value. Any other financing side effects are added also. The result is an APV valuation for the company.[19] Kaplan and Ruback found that APV did a pretty good job explaining prices paid in these hotly contested takeovers, considering that not all the information available to bidders had percolated into the public domain. Kaplan and Ruback were restricted to publicly available data.

---

[19]Kaplan and Ruback actually used "compressed" APV, in which all cash flows, including interest tax shields, are discounted at the opportunity cost of capital. S. N. Kaplan and R. S. Ruback, "The Valuation of Cash Flow Forecasts: An Empirical Analysis," *Journal of Finance* 50 (September 1995), pp. 1059–1093.

The Value of Interest Tax Shields

In Table 19.1, we boldly assume that the firm can fully capture interest tax shields of $.35 on every dollar of interest. We also treat the interest tax shields as safe cash inflows and discount them at a low 8 percent rate.

The true present value of the tax shields is almost surely less than $576,000:

- You can't use tax shields unless you pay taxes, and you don't pay taxes unless you make money. Few firms can be sure that future profitability will be sufficient to use up the interest tax shields.
- The government takes two bites out of corporate income: the corporate tax and the tax on bondholders' and stockholders' personal income. The corporate tax favors debt; the personal tax favors equity.
- A project's debt capacity depends on how well it does. When profits exceed expectations, the firm can borrow more; if the project fails, it won't support any debt. If the future amount of debt is tied to future project value, then the interest tax shields given in Table 19.1 are estimates, not fixed amounts.

In Chapter 18, we argued that the effective tax shield on interest was probably not 35 percent ($T_c = .35$) but some lower figure, call it T^*. We were unable to pin down an exact figure for T^*.

Suppose, for example, that we believe $T^* = .25$. We can easily recalculate the APV of the solar heater project. Just multiply the present value of the interest tax shields by 25/35. The bottom line of Table 19.1 drops from $576,000 to $576,000(25/35) = $411,000. APV drops to

$$\text{APV} = \text{base-case NPV} + \text{PV(tax shield)}$$
$$= +170,000 + 411,000 = \$581,000$$

PV(tax shield) drops still further if the tax shields are treated as forecasts and discounted at a higher rate. Suppose the firm ties the amount of debt to actual future project cash flows. Then the interest tax shields become just as risky as the project and should be discounted at the 12 percent opportunity cost of capital. PV(tax shield) drops to $362,000 at $T^* = .25$.

Review of the Adjusted-Present-Value Approach

If the decision to invest in a capital project has important side effects on other financial decisions made by the firm, those side effects should be taken into account when the project is evaluated. They include interest tax shields on debt supported by the project (a plus), any issue costs of raising financing for the project (a minus), or perhaps other side effects such as the value of a government-subsidized loan tied to the project.

The idea behind APV is to divide and conquer. The approach does not attempt to capture all the side effects in a single calculation. A series of present value calculations is made instead. The first establishes a base-case value for the project: its value as a separate, all-equity-financed mini-firm. Then each side effect is traced out, and the present value of its cost or benefit to the firm is calculated. Finally, all the present values are added together to estimate the project's total contribution to the value of the firm. Thus, in general,

$$\text{Project APV} = \text{base-case NPV} + \frac{\text{sum of the present values of the side}}{\text{effects of accepting the project}}$$

The wise financial manager will want to see not only the adjusted present value but also where that value is coming from. For example, suppose that base-case NPV is positive but the benefits are outweighed by the costs of issuing stock to finance the project. That should prompt the manager to look around to see if the project can be rescued by an alternative financing plan.

APV for International Projects

APV is most useful when financing side effects are numerous and important. This is frequently the case for large international projects, which may have custom-tailored *project financing* and special contracts with suppliers, customers, and governments.[20] Here are a few examples of financing side effects encountered in the international arena.

We explain project finance in Chapter 25. It typically means very high debt ratios to start, with most or all of a project's early cash flows committed to debt service. Equity investors have to wait. Since the debt ratio will not be constant, you have to turn to APV.

Project financing may include debt available at favorable interest rates. Most governments subsidize exports by making special financing packages available, and manufacturers of industrial equipment may stand ready to lend money to help close a sale. Suppose, for example, that your project requires construction of an on-site electricity generating plant. You solicit bids from suppliers in various countries. Don't be surprised if the competing suppliers sweeten their bids with offers of low interest rate project loans or if they offer to lease the plant on favorable terms. You should then calculate the NPVs of these loans or leases and include them in your project analysis.

Sometimes international projects are supported by contracts with suppliers or customers. Suppose a manufacturer wants to line up a reliable supply of a crucial raw material—powdered magnoosium, say. The manufacturer could subsidize a new magnoosium smelter by agreeing to buy 75 percent of production and guaranteeing a minimum purchase price. The guarantee is clearly a valuable addition to project APV: If the world price of powdered magnoosium falls below the minimum, the project doesn't suffer. You would calculate the value of this guarantee (by the methods explained in Chapters 20 and 21) and add it to APV.

Sometimes local governments impose costs or restrictions on investment or disinvestment. For example, Chile, in an attempt to slow down a flood of short-term capital inflows in the 1990s, required investors to "park" part of their incoming money in non-interest-bearing accounts for a period of two years. An investor in Chile during this period would calculate the cost of this requirement and subtract it from APV.

APV for the Perpetual Crusher Project

Discounting at WACC and calculating APV may seem like totally disconnected approaches to valuation. But we can show that, with consistent assumptions, they give nearly identical answers. We demonstrate this for the perpetual crusher project introduced in Section 19.1.

In the following calculations, we ignore any issue costs and concentrate on the value of interest tax shields. To keep things simple, we assume throughout this sec-

---

[20]Use of APV for international projects was first advocated by D. L. Lessard, "Valuing Foreign Cash Flows: An Adjusted Present Value Approach," in D. L. Lessard, ed., *International Financial Management: Theory and Application,* Warren, Gorham and Lamont, Boston, MA, 1979.

tion that the only financing side effects are the interest tax shields on debt supported by the perpetual crusher project, and we consider corporate taxes only. (In other words, $T^* = T_c$.) As in Section 19.1, we assume that the perpetual crusher is an exact match, in business risk and financing, to its parent, the Sangria Corporation.

Base-case NPV is found by discounting after-tax project cash flows of $1.355 million at the opportunity cost of capital r of 12 percent and then subtracting the $12.5 million outlay. The cash flows are perpetual, so

$$\text{Base-case NPV} = -12.5 + \frac{1.355}{.12} = -\$1.21 \text{ million}$$

Thus the project would not be worthwhile with all-equity financing. But it actually supports debt of $5 million. At an 8 percent borrowing rate ($r_D = .08$) and a 35 percent tax rate ($T_c = .35$), annual interest tax shields are $.35 \times .08 \times 5 = .14$, or $140,000.

What are those tax shields worth? It depends on the *financing rule* the company follows. There are two common rules:

- Financing Rule 1: *Debt fixed*. Borrow a fraction of *initial* project value and make any debt repayments on a predetermined schedule. We followed this rule in Table 19.1.
- Financing Rule 2: *Debt rebalanced*. Adjust the debt in each future period to keep it at a constant fraction of future project value.

What do these rules mean for the perpetual crusher project? Under Financing Rule 1, debt stays at $5 million come hell or high water, and interest tax shields stay at $140,000 per year. The tax shields are tied to fixed interest payments, so the 8 percent cost of debt is a reasonable discount rate:

$$\text{PV(tax shields, debt fixed)} = \frac{140,000}{.08} = \$1,750,000, \text{ or } \$1.75 \text{ million}$$

$$\text{APV} = \text{base-case NPV} + \text{PV(tax shield)}$$
$$= -1.21 + 1.75 = +\$.54 \text{ million}$$

If the perpetual crusher were financed solely by equity, project value would be $11.29 million. With fixed debt of $5 million, value increases by PV(tax shield) to $11.29 + 1.75 = \$13.04$ million.

Under Financing Rule 2, debt is rebalanced to 40 percent of actual project value. That means future debt levels are not known at the start of the project. They shift up or down depending on the success or failure of the project. Interest tax shields therefore pick up the project's business risk.

If interest tax shields are just as risky as the project, they should be discounted at the project's opportunity cost of capital, in this case 12 percent.

$$\text{PV(tax shields, debt rebalanced)} = \frac{140,000}{.12} = 1,170,000, \text{ or } \$1.17 \text{ million}$$

$$\text{APV (debt rebalanced)} = -1.21 + 1.17 = -\$.04 \text{ million}$$

We have now valued the perpetual crusher project three different ways:

1. APV (debt fixed) = +$.54 million.
2. APV (debt rebalanced)= −$.04 million.
3. NPV (discounting at WACC)= $0 million.

The first APV is the highest, because it assumes that debt is fixed, not rebalanced, and that interest tax shields are as safe as the interest payments generating them.

A Technical Point on Financing Rule 2

But why don't APV calculations 2 and 3, which both follow Financing Rule 2, generate the same number? The answer is that our calculation of APV (debt rebalanced) gets the implications of Financing Rule 2 only approximately right.

Even when debt is rebalanced, *next year's* interest tax shields are fixed. Year 1's interest tax shield is fixed by the amount of debt at date 0, the start of the project. Therefore, year 1's interest tax shield should have been discounted at 8, not 12 percent.

Year 2's interest tax shield is not known at the start of the project, since debt is rebalanced at date 1, depending on the first year's performance. But once date 1's debt level is set, the interest tax shield is known. Therefore the forecasted interest tax shield at date 2 ($140,000) should be discounted for one year at 12 percent and one year at 8 percent.

The reasoning repeats. Every year, once debt is rebalanced, next year's interest tax shield is fixed. For example, year 15's interest tax shield is fixed once debt is rebalanced in year 14. Thus the present value of the year 15 tax shield is the date 0 forecast (again $140,000) discounted one year at 8 percent and 14 years at 12 percent.

So the procedure for calculating the exact value of tax shields under Financing Rule 2 is as follows:

1. Discount at the opportunity cost of capital, because future tax shields are tied to actual cash flows.
2. Multiply the resulting PV by $(1 + r)/(1 + r_D)$, because the tax shields are fixed one period before receipt.

For the perpetual crusher project, the forecasted interest tax shields are $140,000 or $.14 million. Their exact value is

$$\text{PV(approximate)} = \frac{.14}{.12} = \$1.17 \text{ million}$$

$$\text{PV(exact)} = 1.17 \times \left(\frac{1.12}{1.08}\right) = \$1.21 \text{ million}$$

The APV of the project, given these assumptions about future debt capacity, is

$$\text{APV} = \text{base-case NPV} + \text{PV(tax shield)}$$
$$= -1.21 + 1.21 = \$0 \text{ million}$$

This calculation exactly matches our first valuation of the perpetual crusher project based on WACC. Discounting at WACC implicitly recognizes that next year's interest tax shield is fixed by this year's debt level.[21]

---

[21]Miles and Ezzell (see footnote 5) have come up with a useful formula for modifying WACC:

$$\text{WACC} = r - Lr_D T^* \left(\frac{1 + r}{1 + r_D}\right)$$

where L is the debt-to-value ratio and T^* is the net tax saving per dollar of interest paid. In practice T^* is hard to pin down, so the marginal tax rate T_c is used instead.

The Miles–Ezzell formula assumes Financing Rule 2, that is, that debt is rebalanced at the end of every period (although next year's interest tax shield is fixed). You can check that it values the Sangria project exactly (NPV = $0 million).

In Section 19.3, we used a three-step procedure to calculate WACC at different debt ratios. It turns out that this procedure is not exactly the same as the changes in WACC calculated by the Miles–Ezzell formula. However, the numerical differences are in practice very small. In the Sangria example they are lost in rounding.

Which Financing Rule?

In practice it rarely pays to worry whether interest tax shields are valued approximately (giving APV = −$.04 million) or exactly ($0 million). Your worrying time will be much better spent in refining forecasts of operating cash flows and thinking through what-if scenarios.

But which financing rule is better—debt fixed or debt rebalanced?

Sometimes debt has to be paid down on a fixed schedule, as for the solar heater project in Table 19.1. This is the case for most LBOs. But as a general rule we vote for the assumption of rebalancing, that is, for Financing Rule 2. Any capital budgeting procedure that assumes debt levels are *always* fixed after a project is undertaken is grossly oversimplified. Should we assume that the perpetual crusher project contributes $5 million to the firm's debt capacity not just when the project is undertaken but from here to eternity? That amounts to saying that the future value of the project will not change—a strong assumption indeed.

Financing Rule 2 is better: not "Always borrow $5 million," but "Always borrow 40 percent of the perpetual crusher project value." Then if project value increases, the firm borrows more. If it decreases, the firm borrows less. Under this policy you can no longer discount future interest tax shields at the borrowing rate because the shields are no longer certain. Their size depends on the amount actually borrowed and, therefore, on the actual future value of the project.

APV and Hurdle Rates

APV tells you whether a project makes a net contribution to the value of the firm. It can also tell you a project's *break-even* cash flow or internal rate of return. Let's check this for the perpetual crusher project. We first calculate the income at which APV = 0. We will then determine the project's minimum acceptable internal rate of return (IRR).

$$\text{APV} = \frac{\text{annual income}}{r} - \text{investment} + \text{PV(tax shield)}$$

$$= \frac{\text{annual income}}{.12} - 12.5 + 1.21 = 0$$

$$\text{Annual income} = \$1.355 \text{ million}$$

or 10.84 percent of the $12.5 million outlay. In other words, the minimum acceptable IRR for the project is 10.84 percent. At this IRR project APV is zero.

Suppose that we encounter another project with perpetual cash flows. Its opportunity cost of capital is also $r = .12$, and it also expands the firm's borrowing power by 40 percent of project value. We know that if such a project offers an IRR greater than 10.84 percent, it will have a positive APV. Therefore, we could shorten the analysis by just discounting the project's cash inflows at 10.84 percent.[22] This discount rate is the *adjusted cost of capital*. It reflects both the project's business risk and its contribution to the firm's debt capacity.

We will call the adjusted cost of capital r^*. To calculate r^* we find the minimum acceptable internal rate of return—the IRR at which APV = 0. The rule is this: *Accept projects which have a positive NPV at the adjusted cost of capital r^*.*

---

[22]Remember that forecasted project cash flows do *not* reflect the tax shields generated by any debt the project may support. Project taxes are calculated assuming all-equity financing.

The 10.84 percent adjusted cost of capital for the perpetual crusher project is (no surprise) identical to Sangria Corporation's WACC, calculated in Section 19.1.

A General Definition of the Adjusted Cost of Capital

We recapitulate the two concepts of cost of capital:

- Concept 1: *The opportunity cost of capital (r).* This is the expected rate of return offered in capital markets by equivalent-risk assets. This depends on the risk of the project's cash flows. The opportunity cost of capital is the correct discount rate for the project if it is all-equity-financed.
- Concept 2: *The adjusted cost of capital (r*).* This is an adjusted opportunity cost or hurdle rate that reflects the financing side effects of an investment project.

Some people just say "cost of capital." Sometimes their meaning is clear in context. At other times, they don't know which concept they are referring to, and that can sow widespread confusion.

When financing side effects are important, you should accept projects with positive APVs. But if you know the adjusted discount rate, you don't have to calculate APV: You just calculate NPV at the adjusted rate. The weighted-average cost of capital formula is the most common way to calculate the adjusted cost of capital.

19.5 DISCOUNTING SAFE, NOMINAL CASH FLOWS

Suppose you're considering purchase of a $100,000 machine. The manufacturer sweetens the deal by offering to finance the purchase by lending you $100,000 for five years, with annual interest payments of 5 percent. You would have to pay 13 percent to borrow from a bank. Your marginal tax rate is 35 percent ($T_c = .35$).

How much is this loan worth? If you take it, the cash flows, in thousands of dollars, are

		Period				
	0	**1**	**2**	**3**	**4**	**5**
Cash flow	100	−5	−5	−5	−5	−105
Tax shield	-	+1.75	+1.75	+1.75	+1.75	+1.75
After-tax cash flow	100	−3.25	−3.25	−3.25	−3.25	−103.25

What is the right discount rate?

Here you are discounting *safe, nominal* cash flows—safe because your company must commit to pay if it takes the loan,[23] and nominal because the payments would be fixed regardless of future inflation. Now, the correct discount rate for safe, nominal cash flows is your company's *after-tax, unsubsidized* borrowing rate.[24] In this case $r^* = r_D(1 - T_c) = .13(1 - .35) = .0845$. Therefore

---

[23]In theory, *safe* means literally "risk-free," like the cash returns on a Treasury bond. In practice, it means that the risk of not paying or receiving a cash flow is small.

[24]In Section 13.1 we calculated the NPV of subsidized financing using the *pretax* borrowing rate. Now you can see that was a mistake. Using the pretax rate implicitly defines the loan in terms of its pretax cash flows, violating a rule promulgated way back in Section 6.1: *Always* estimate cash flows on an after-tax basis.

$$NPV = +100 - \frac{3.25}{1.0845} - \frac{3.25}{(1.0845)^2} - \frac{3.25}{(1.0845)^3} - \frac{3.25}{(1.0845)^4} - \frac{103.25}{(1.0845)^5}$$

$$= +20.52, \text{ or } \$20,520$$

The manufacturer has effectively cut the machine's purchase price from $100,000 to $100,000 − $20,520 = $79,480. You can now go back and recalculate the machine's NPV using this fire-sale price, or you can use the NPV of the subsidized loan as one element of the machine's adjusted present value.

A General Rule

Clearly, we owe an explanation of why $r_D(1 - T_c)$ is the right discount rate for safe, nominal cash flows. It's no surprise that the rate depends on r_D, the unsubsidized borrowing rate, for that is investors' opportunity cost of capital, the rate they would demand from your company's debt. But why should r_D be converted to an *after-tax* figure?

Let's simplify by taking a *one-year* subsidized loan of $100,000 at 5 percent. The cash flows, in thousands of dollars, are

	Period 0	Period 1
Cash flow	100	−105
Tax shield		+1.75
After-tax cash flow	100	−103.25

Now ask, What is the maximum amount X that could be borrowed for one year through regular channels if $103,250 is set aside to service the loan?

"Regular channels" means borrowing at 13 percent pretax and 8.45 percent after tax. Therefore you will need 108.45 percent of the amount borrowed to pay back principal plus after-tax interest charges. If $1.0845X = 103,250$, then $X = 95,205$. Now if you can borrow $100,000 by a subsidized loan, but only $95,205 through normal channels, the difference ($4,795) is money in the bank. Therefore, it must also be the NPV of this one-period subsidized loan.

When you discount a safe, nominal cash flow at an after-tax borrowing rate, you are implicitly calculating the *equivalent loan*, the amount you could borrow through normal channels, using the cash flow as debt service. Note that

$$\text{Equivalent loan} = PV\left(\begin{array}{c}\text{cash flow available}\\ \text{for debt service}\end{array}\right) = \frac{103,250}{1.0845} = 95,205$$

In some cases, it may be easier to think of taking the lender's side of the equivalent loan rather than the borrower's. For example, you could ask, How much would my company have to invest today in order to cover next year's debt service on the subsidized loan? The answer is $95,205: If you lend that amount at 13 percent, you will earn 8.45 percent after tax, and therefore have 95,205(1.0845) = $103,250. By this transaction, you can in effect cancel, or "zero out," the future obligation. If you can borrow $100,000 and then set aside only $95,205 to cover all the required debt service, you clearly have $4,795 to spend as you please. That amount is the NPV of the subsidized loan.

Therefore, regardless of whether it's easier to think of borrowing or lending, the correct discount rate for safe, nominal cash flows is an after-tax interest rate.[25]

In some ways, this is an obvious result once you think about it. Companies are free to borrow or lend money. If they *lend*, they receive the after-tax interest rate on their investment; if they *borrow* in the capital market, they pay the after-tax interest rate. Thus, the opportunity cost to companies of investing in debt-equivalent cash flows is the after-tax interest rate. This is the adjusted cost of capital for debt-equivalent cash flows.[26]

Some Further Examples

Here are some further examples of debt-equivalent cash flows.

Payout Fixed by Contract   Suppose you sign a maintenance contract with a truck leasing firm, which agrees to keep your leased trucks in good working order for the next two years in exchange for 24 fixed monthly payments. These payments are debt-equivalent flows.[27]

Depreciation Tax Shields   Capital projects are normally valued by discounting the total after-tax cash flows they are expected to generate. Depreciation tax shields contribute to project cash flow, but they are not valued separately; they are just folded into project cash flows along with dozens, or hundreds, of other specific inflows and outflows. The project's opportunity cost of capital reflects the average risk of the resulting aggregate.

However, suppose we ask what depreciation tax shields are worth *by themselves*. For a firm that's sure to pay taxes, depreciation tax shields are a safe, nominal flow. Therefore, they should be discounted at the firm's after-tax borrowing rate.[28]

Suppose we buy an asset with a depreciable basis of $200,000, which can be depreciated by the five-year tax depreciation schedule (see Table 6.4). The resulting tax shields are

---

[25]Borrowing and lending rates should not differ by much if the cash flows are truly safe, that is, if the chance of default is small. Usually your decision will not hinge on the rate used. If it does, ask which offsetting transaction—borrowing or lending—seems most natural and reasonable for the problem at hand. Then use the corresponding interest rate.

[26]All the examples in this section are forward-looking; they call for the value today of a stream of future debt-equivalent cash flows. But similar issues arise in legal and contractual disputes when a *past* cash flow has to be brought forward in time to a present value today. Suppose it's determined that company A should have paid B $1 million ten years ago. B clearly deserves more than $1 million today, because it has lost the time value of money. The time value of money should be expressed as an after-tax borrowing or lending rate, or if no risk enters, as the after-tax risk-free rate. The time value of money is *not* equal to B's overall cost of capital. Allowing B to "earn" its overall cost of capital on the payment allows it to earn a risk premium without bearing risk. For a broader discussion of these issues, see F. Fisher and C. Romaine, "Janis Joplin's Yearbook and Theory of Damages," *Journal of Accounting, Auditing & Finance* 5 (Winter/Spring 1990), pp. 145–157.

[27]We assume you are locked into the contract. If it can be canceled without penalty, you may have a valuable option.

[28]The depreciation tax shields are cash inflows, not outflows as for the contractual payout or the subsidized loan. For safe, nominal inflows, the relevant question is, How much could the firm borrow today if it uses the inflow for debt service? You could also ask, How much would the firm have to lend today to generate the same future inflow?

	Period					
	1	2	3	4	5	6
Percentage deductions	20	32	19.2	11.5	11.5	5.8
Dollar deductions (thousands)	$40	$64	$38.4	$23	$23	$11.6
Tax shields at $T_c = .35$ (thousands)	$14	$22.4	$13.4	$8.1	$8.1	$4.0

The after-tax discount rate is $r_D(1 - T_c) = .13(1 - .35) = .0845$. (We continue to assume a 13 percent pretax borrowing rate and a 35 percent marginal tax rate.) The present value of these shields is

$$PV = \frac{14}{1.0845} + \frac{22.4}{(1.0845)^2} + \frac{13.4}{(1.0845)^3} + \frac{8.1}{(1.0845)^4} + \frac{8.1}{(1.0845)^5} + \frac{4.0}{(1.0845)^6}$$
$$= +56.2, \text{ or } \$56,200$$

A Consistency Check

You may have wondered whether our procedure for valuing debt-equivalent cash flows is consistent with the WACC and APV approaches presented earlier in this chapter. Yes, it is consistent, as we will now illustrate.

Let's look at another very simple numerical example. You are asked to value a $1 million payment to be received from a blue-chip company one year hence. After taxes at 35 percent, the cash inflow is $650,000. The payment is fixed by contract.

Since the contract generates a debt-equivalent flow, the opportunity cost of capital is the rate investors would demand on a one-year note issued by the blue-chip company, which happens to be 8 percent. For simplicity, we'll assume this is your company's borrowing rate too. Our valuation rule for debt-equivalent flows is therefore to discount at $r^* = r_D(1 - T_c) = .08(1 - .35) = .052$:

$$PV = \frac{650,000}{1.052} = \$617,900$$

What is the *debt capacity* of this $650,000 payment? Exactly $617,900. Your company could borrow that amount and pay off the loan completely—principal and after-tax interest—with the $650,000 cash inflow. The debt capacity is 100 percent of the PV of the debt-equivalent cash flow.

If you think of it that way, our discount rate $r_D(1 - T_c)$ is just a special case of WACC with a 100 percent debt ratio ($D/V = 1$).

$$WACC = r_D(1 - T_c)D/V + r_E E/V$$
$$= r_D(1 - T_c) \text{ if } D/V = 1 \text{ and } E/V = 0$$

Now let's try an APV calculation. This is a two-part valuation. First, the $650,000 inflow is discounted at the opportunity cost of capital, 8 percent. Second, we add the present value of interest tax shields on debt supported by the project. Since the firm can borrow 100 percent of the cash flow's value, the tax shield is $r_D T_c$ APV, and APV is

$$APV = \frac{650,000}{1.08} + \frac{.08(.35)APV}{1.08}$$

Solving for APV, we get $617,900, the same answer we obtained by discounting at the after-tax borrowing rate. Thus our valuation rule for debt-equivalent flows is a special case of APV.

 ## 19.6 YOUR QUESTIONS ANSWERED

Question: All these cost of capital formulas—which ones do financial managers actually use?

Answer: The after-tax weighted-average cost of capital, most of the time. WACC is estimated for the company, or sometimes for an industry. We recommend industry WACCs when data are available for several closely comparable firms. The firms should have similar assets, operations, business risks, and growth opportunities.

Of course, conglomerate companies, with divisions operating in two or more unrelated industries, should not use a single company or industry WACC. Such firms should try to estimate a different industry WACC for each operating division.

Question: But WACC is the correct discount rate only for "average" projects. What if the project's financing differs from the company's or industry's?

Answer: Remember, investment projects are usually not separately financed. Even when they are, you should focus on the project's contribution to the firm's overall debt capacity, not on its immediate financing. (Suppose it's convenient to raise all the money for a particular project with a bank loan. That doesn't mean the project itself supports 100 percent debt financing. The company is borrowing against its existing assets as well as the project.)

But if the project's debt capacity is materially different from the company's existing assets, or if the company's overall debt policy changes, WACC should be adjusted. The adjustment can be done by the three-step procedure explained in Section 19.3.

Question: Could we do one more numerical example?

Answer: Sure. Suppose that WACC has been estimated as follows at a 30 percent debt ratio:

$$\text{WACC} = r_D(1 - T_c)\frac{D}{V} + r_E\frac{E}{V}$$
$$= .09(1 - .35)(.3) + .15(.7) = .1226, \text{ or } 12.26\%$$

What is the correct discount rate at a 50 percent debt ratio?

First, let's repeat the three-step procedure.

Step 1. Calculate the opportunity cost of capital.

$$r = r_D D/V + r_E E/V$$
$$= .09(.3) + .15(.7) = .132 \text{ or } 13.2\%$$

Step 2. Calculate the new costs of debt and equity. The cost of debt will be higher at 50 percent debt than 30 percent. Say it is $r_D = .095$. The new cost of equity is

$$r_E = r + (r - r_D)D/E$$
$$= .132 + (.132 - .095)50/50$$
$$= .169 \text{ or } 16.9\%$$

Step 3. Recalculate WACC.

$$\text{WACC} = r_D(1 - T_c)D/V + r_E E/V$$
$$= .095(1 - .35)(.5) + .169(.5) = .1154, \text{ or about } 11.5\%$$

Question: How do I use the capital asset pricing model to calculate the after-tax weighted-average cost of capital?

Answer: First plug the equity beta into the capital asset pricing formula to calculate r_E, the expected return to equity. Then use this figure, along with the after-tax cost of debt and the debt-to-value and equity-to-value ratios, in the WACC formula. We covered this in Chapter 9. The only change here is use of the after-tax cost of debt, $r_D(1 - T_c)$.

Of course the CAPM is not the only way to estimate the cost of equity. For example, you might be able to use arbitrage pricing theory (APT—see Section 8.4) or the dividend-discount model (see Section 4.3).

Question: But suppose I do use the CAPM? What if I have to recalculate the equity beta for a different debt ratio?

Answer: The formula for the equity beta is

$$\beta_E = \beta_A + (\beta_A - \beta_D)\frac{D}{E}$$

where β_E is the equity beta, β_A is the asset beta, and β_D is the beta of the company's debt.

Question: Can I use the capital asset pricing model to calculate the asset beta and the opportunity cost of capital?

Answer: Sure. We covered this in Chapter 9. The asset beta is a weighted average of the debt and equity betas:[29]

$$\beta_A = \beta_D\frac{D}{V} + \beta_E\frac{E}{V}$$

Suppose you needed the opportunity cost of capital r. You could calculate β_A and then r from the capital asset pricing model.

Question: I think I understand how to adjust for differences in debt capacity or debt policy. How about differences in business risk?

Answer: If business risk is different, then r, the opportunity cost of capital, is different.

Figuring out the right r for an unusually safe or risky project is never easy. Sometimes the financial manager can use estimates of risk and expected return for companies similar to the project. Suppose, for example, that a traditional pharmaceutical company is considering a major commitment to biotech research. The financial manager could pick a sample of biotech companies, estimate their

---

[29]This formula assumes Financing Rule 2. If debt is fixed, taxes complicate the formulas. For example, if debt is fixed and permanent, and only corporate taxes are considered, the formula for β_E changes to

$$\beta_E = \beta_A + (\beta_A - \beta_D)(1 - T_c)D/E$$

average beta and cost of capital, and use these estimates as benchmarks for the biotech investment.

But in many cases it's difficult to find a good sample of matching companies for an unusually safe or risky project. Then the financial manager has to adjust the opportunity cost of capital by judgment.[30] Section 9.5 may be helpful in such cases.

Question: Let's go back to the cost of capital formulas. The tax rates are confusing. When should I use T_c and when T^*?

Answer: Always use T_c, the marginal corporate tax rate, (1) when calculating WACC as a weighted average of the costs of debt and equity and (2) when discounting safe, nominal cash flows. In each case the discount rate is adjusted *only* for corporate taxes.[31]

APV in principle calls for T^*, the net tax saving per dollar of interest paid by the firm. This depends on the effective personal tax rates on debt and equity income. T^* is almost surely less than T_c, but it is very difficult to pin down the numerical difference. Therefore in practice T_c is almost always used as an approximation.

Question: When do I need adjusted present value (APV)?

Answer: The WACC formula picks up only one financing side effect: the value of interest tax shields on debt supported by a project. If there are other side effects—subsidized financing tied to a project, for example—you should use APV.

You can also use APV to show the value of interest tax shields:

$$\text{APV} = \text{base-case NPV} + \text{PV(tax shield)}$$

where base-case NPV assumes all-equity financing. But it's usually easier to do this calculation in one step, by discounting project cash flows at an adjusted cost of capital (usually WACC). Remember, though, that discounting by WACC usually assumes Financing Rule 2, that is, debt rebalanced to a constant fraction of future project value. If this financing rule is not right, you may need APV to calculate PV(tax shield), as we did for the solar heater project in Table 19.1.[32]

Suppose, for example, that you are analyzing a company just after a leveraged recapitalization. The company has a very high initial debt level but plans to pay down the debt as rapidly as possible. APV could be used to obtain an accurate valuation.

---

[30]The judgment may be implicit. That is, the manager may not explicitly announce that the discount rate for a high-risk project is, say, 2.5 percentage points above the standard rate. But the project will not be approved unless it offers a higher-than-standard rate of return.

[31]Any effects of personal income taxes are reflected in r_D and r_E, the rates of return demanded by debt and equity investors.

[32]Having read Section 19.5, you may be wondering why we did not discount at the *after-tax* borrowing rate in Table 19.1. The answer is that we wanted to simplify and take one thing at a time. If debt is fixed and the odds of financial distress are low, interest tax shields are safe, nominal flows, and there is a case for using the after-tax rate. Doing so assumes that the firm will, or can, take out an additional loan with debt service exactly covered by the interest tax shields.

Investment decisions always have side effects on financing: Every dollar spent has to be raised somehow. Sometimes the side effects are irrelevant or at least unimportant. In an ideal world with no taxes, transaction costs, or other market imperfections, only investment decisions would affect firm value. In such a world firms could analyze all investment opportunities as if they were all-equity-financed. Firms would decide which assets to buy and then worry about getting the money to pay for them. No one making investment decisions would worry about where the money might come from because debt policy, dividend policy, and all other financing choices would have no impact on stockholders' wealth.

Side effects cannot be ignored in practice. There are two ways to take them into account. You can calculate NPV by discounting at an adjusted discount rate, or you can discount at the opportunity cost of capital and then add or subtract the present value of financing side effects. The second approach is called adjusted present value, or APV.

The most commonly used adjusted discount rate is the after-tax weighted-average cost of capital, or WACC:

$$\text{WACC} = r_D(1 - T_c)\frac{D}{V} + r_E\frac{E}{V}$$

Here r_D and r_E are the expected rates of return demanded by investors in the firm's debt and equity securities, respectively; D and E are the current *market values* of debt and equity; and V is the total market value of the firm ($V = D + E$).

Strictly speaking, this formula works only for projects that are carbon copies of the existing firm—projects with the same business risk that will be financed to maintain the firm's current, market debt ratio. But firms can use WACC as a benchmark rate to be adjusted for differences in business risk or financing. We suggested a three-step procedure for adjusting a company's WACC for differences between project and company debt ratios.

Discounting project cash flows at the WACC assumes that debt is rebalanced every period to keep a constant debt-to-market-value ratio. The amount of debt supported by a project is supposed to rise or fall with the project's after-the-fact success or failure. We called this Financing Rule 2. The WACC formula also assumes that financing matters *only* because of interest tax shields. When this or other assumptions are violated, only APV will give an absolutely correct answer.

APV is, in concept at least, simple. First calculate the present value of the project as if there are no important side effects. Then adjust present value to calculate the project's total impact on firm value. The rule is to accept the project if APV is positive:

$$\text{Accept project if APV = base-case NPV} + \begin{array}{c}\text{present value}\\\text{of financing}\\\text{side effects}\end{array} > 0$$

The base-case NPV is the project's NPV computed assuming all-equity financing and perfect capital markets. Think of it as the project's value if it were set up as a separate mini-firm. You would compute the mini-firm's value by forecasting its cash flows and discounting at the opportunity cost of capital for the project. The cash flows should be net of the taxes that an all-equity-financed mini-firm would pay.

Financing side effects are evaluated one by one and their present values are added to or subtracted from base-case NPV. We looked at several cases:

1. *Issue costs.* If accepting the project forces the firm to issue securities, then the present value of issue costs should be subtracted from base-case NPV.
2. *Interest tax shields.* Debt interest is a tax-deductible expense. Most people believe that interest tax shields contribute to firm value. Thus a project that prompts the firm to borrow more generates additional value. The project's APV is increased by the present value of interest tax shields on debt the project supports.
3. *Special financing.* Sometimes special financing opportunities are tied to project acceptance. For example, the government might offer subsidized financing for socially desirable projects. You simply compute the present value of the financing opportunity and add it to base-case NPV.

Remember not to confuse *contribution to corporate debt capacity* with the immediate source of funds for investment. For example, a firm might, as a matter of convenience, borrow $1 million for a $1 million research program. But the research would be unlikely to contribute $1 million in debt capacity; a large part of the $1 million new debt would be supported by the firm's other assets.

Also remember that *debt capacity* is not meant to imply an absolute limit on how much the firm *can* borrow. The phrase refers to how much it *chooses* to borrow. Normally the firm's optimal debt level increases as its assets expand; that is why we say that a new project contributes to corporate debt capacity.

Calculating APV may require several steps: one step for base-case NPV and one for each financing side effect. Many firms try to calculate APV in a single calculation. They do so by the following procedure: After-tax cash flows are forecasted in the usual way—that is, as if the project is all-equity-financed. But the discount rate is adjusted to reflect the financing side effects. If the discount rate is adjusted correctly, the result is APV:

$$\begin{array}{c}\text{NPV at adjusted} \\ \text{discount rate}\end{array} = \text{APV} = \begin{array}{c}\text{NPV at opportunity} \\ \text{cost of capital}\end{array} + \begin{array}{c}\text{present value of} \\ \text{financing side effects}\end{array}$$

WACC is the leading example of an adjusted discount rate.

This chapter is almost 100 percent theory. The theory is difficult. If you think you understand all the formulas, assumptions, and relationships on the first reading, we suggest psychiatric assistance. We can, however, offer one simple, bullet-proof, easy-to-remember rule: Discount safe, nominal cash flows at the after-tax borrowing rate.

FURTHER READING

The adjusted-present-value rule was developed in:
S. C. Myers: "Interactions of Corporate Financing and Investment Decisions—Implications for Capital Budgeting," *Journal of Finance*, 29:1–25 (March 1974).

The Harvard Business Review *has published a popular account of APV:*
T. A. Luehrman, "Using APV: A Better Tool for Valuing Operations," *Harvard Business Review* 75:145–154 (May–June 1997).

There have been dozens of articles on the weighted-average cost of capital and other issues discussed in this chapter. Here are two:

J. Miles and R. Ezzell: "The Weighted Average Cost of Capital, Perfect Capital Markets, and Project Life: A Clarification," *Journal of Financial and Quantitative Analysis,* 15:719–730 (September 1980).

R. A. Taggart, Jr.: "Consistent Valuation and Cost of Capital Expressions with Corporate and Personal Taxes," *Financial Management,* 20:8–20 (Autumn 1991).

The valuation rule for safe, nominal cash flows is developed in:

R. S. Ruback: "Calculating the Market Value of Risk-Free Cash Flows," *Journal of Financial Economics,* 15:323–339 (March 1986).

1. Calculate the weighted-average cost of capital (WACC) for Federated Junkyards of America, using the following information:
   - Debt: $75,000,000 book value outstanding. The debt is trading at 90 percent of par. The yield to maturity is 9 percent.
   - Equity: 2,500,000 shares selling at $42 per share. Assume the expected rate of return on Federated's stock is 18 percent.
   - Taxes: Federated's marginal tax rate is $T_c = .35$.

   What are the key assumptions underlying your calculation? For what type of project would Federated's weighted-average cost of capital be the right discount rate?

2. Suppose Federated Junkyards decides to move to a more conservative debt policy. A year later its debt ratio is down to 15 percent $(D/V = .15)$. The interest rate has dropped to 8.6 percent. Recalculate Federated's WACC under these new assumptions. The company's business risk, opportunity cost of capital, and tax rate have not changed. Use the three-step procedure explained in Section 19.3.

3. True or false? Use of the WACC formula assumes
   a. A project supports a fixed amount of debt over the project's economic life.
   b. The *ratio* of the debt supported by a project to project value is constant over the project's economic life.
   c. The firm rebalances debt, each period, keeping the debt-to-value ratio constant.

4. What is meant by the flow-to-equity valuation method? What discount rate is used in this method? What assumptions are necessary for this method to give an accurate valuation?

5. True or false? The APV method
   a. Starts with a base-case value for the project.
   b. Calculates the base-case value by discounting project cash flows, forecasted assuming all-equity financing, at the WACC for the project.
   c. Is especially useful when debt is to be paid down on a fixed schedule.
   d. Can be used to calculate an adjusted discount rate for a company or a project.

6. Explain the difference between Financing Rules 1 (debt fixed) and 2 (debt rebalanced).

7. What is meant by financing "side effects" in an APV valuation? Give at least three examples of side effects encountered in practice.

8. A project costs $1 million and has a base-case NPV of exactly zero (NPV = 0). What is the project's APV in the following cases?
   a. If the firm invests, it has to raise $500,000 by stock issue. Issue costs are 15 percent of *net* proceeds.
   b. The firm has ample cash on hand. But if it invests, it will have access to $500,000 of debt financing at a subsidized interest rate. The present value of the subsidy is $175,000.

QUIZ

  c. If the firm invests, its debt capacity increases by $500,000. The present value of interest tax shields on this debt is $76,000.

 9. Whispering Pines, Inc., is all-equity-financed. The expected rate of return on the company's shares is 12 percent.

  a. What is the opportunity cost of capital for an average-risk Whispering Pines investment?

  b. Suppose the company issues debt, repurchases shares, and moves to a 30 percent debt-to-value ratio ($D/V = .30$). What will the company's weighted-average cost of capital be at the new capital structure? The borrowing rate is 7.5 percent and the tax rate is 35 percent.

 10. Consider the APV of the solar heater project, as calculated in Table 19.1. How would the APV change if the net tax shield per dollar of interest were not $T_c = .35$, but $T^* = .10$?

 11. Consider a project lasting one year only. The initial outlay is $1,000 and the expected inflow is $1,200. The opportunity cost of capital is $r = .20$. The borrowing rate is $r_D = .10$, and the net tax shield per dollar of interest is $T^* = T_c = .35$.

  a. What is the project's base-case NPV?

  b. What is its APV if the firm borrows 30 percent of the project's required investment?

 12. The WACC formula seems to imply that debt is "cheaper" than equity—that is, that a firm with more debt could use a lower discount rate. Does this make sense? Explain briefly.

 13. What discount rate should be used to value safe, nominal cash flows? Explain briefly.

 14. The U.S. government has settled a dispute with your company for $16 million. It is committed to pay this amount in exactly 12 months. However, your company will have to pay tax on the award at a marginal tax rate of 35 percent. What is the award worth? The one-year Treasury rate is 5.5 percent.

PRACTICE QUESTIONS

EXCEL

 1. Table 19.2 shows a *book* balance sheet for the Wishing Well Motel chain. The company's long-term debt is secured by its real estate assets, but it also uses short-term bank financing. It pays 10 percent interest on the bank debt and 9 percent interest on the secured debt. Wishing Well has 10 million shares of stock outstanding, trading at $90 per share. The expected return on Wishing Well's common stock is 18 percent.

  Calculate Wishing Well's WACC. Assume that the book and market values of Wishing Well's debt are the same. The marginal tax rate is 35 percent.

 2. Suppose Wishing Well is evaluating a new motel and resort on a romantic site in Madison County, Wisconsin. Explain how you would forecast the after-tax cash flows for this project. (*Hints:* How would you treat taxes? Interest expense? Changes in working capital?)

 3. To finance the Madison County project, Wishing Well will have to arrange an additional $80 million of long-term debt and make a $20 million equity issue. Underwriting fees,

TABLE 19.2

Balance sheet for Wishing Well, Inc. (figures in $ millions).

Cash, marketable securities	100	Accounts payable		120
Inventory	50	Bank loan		280
Accounts receivable	200	Current liabilities		400
Current assets	350			
Real estate	2,100	Long-term debt		1,800
Other assets	150	Equity		400
Total	2,600	Total		2,600

Cash and marketable			
securities	1,500	Short-term debt	75,600
Accounts receivable	120,000	Accounts payable	62,000
Inventories	125,000	Current liabilities	137,600
Current assets	246,500		
Property, plant,		Long-term debt	208,600
and equipment	302,000	Deferred taxes	45,000
Other assets	89,000	Shareholders' equity	246,300
Total	637,500	Total	637,500

TABLE 19.3

Simplified book balance sheet for Rensselaer Felt (figures in $ thousands).

spreads, and other costs of this financing will total $4 million. How would you take this into account in valuing the proposed investment?

4. Table 19.3 shows a simplified balance sheet for Rensselaer Felt. Calculate this company's weighted-average cost of capital. The debt has just been refinanced at an interest rate of 6 percent (short term) and 8 percent (long term). The expected rate of return on the company's shares is 15 percent. There are 7.46 million shares outstanding, and the shares are trading at $46. The tax rate is 35 percent.

EXCEL

5. How will Rensselaer Felt's WACC and cost of equity change if it issues $50 million in new equity and uses the proceeds to retire long-term debt? Assume the company's borrowing rates are unchanged. Use the three-step procedure from Section 19.3.

6. Look one more time at practice question 4. Renssalaer Felt's pretax operating income is $100.5 million. Assume for simplicity that this figure is expected to remain constant forever. Value the company by the flow-to-equity method.

7. Rapidly growing companies may have to issue shares to finance capital expenditures. In doing so, they incur underwriting and other issue costs. Some analysts have tried to adjust WACC to account for these costs. For example, if issue costs are 8 percent of equity issue proceeds, and equity issues account for all of equity financing, the cost of equity might be divided by $1 - .08 = .92$. This would increase a 15 percent cost of equity to $15/.92 = 16.3$ percent.

   Explain why this sort of adjustment is *not* a smart idea. What is the correct way to take issue costs into account in project valuation?

8. Digital Organics (DO) has the opportunity to invest $1 million now ($t = 0$) and expects after-tax returns of $600,000 in $t = 1$ and $700,000 in $t = 2$. The project will last for two years only. The appropriate cost of capital is 12 percent with all-equity financing, the borrowing rate is 8 percent, and DO will borrow $300,000 against the project. This debt must be repaid in two equal installments. Assume debt tax shields have a net value of $.30 per dollar of interest paid. Calculate the project's APV using the procedure followed in Table 19.1.

9. You are considering a five-year lease of office space for R&D personnel. Once signed, the lease cannot be canceled. It would commit your firm to six annual $100,000 payments, with the first payment due immediately. What is the present value of the lease if your company's borrowing rate is 9 percent and its tax rate is 35 percent? *Note:* The lease payments would be tax-deductible.

10. Consider another perpetual project like the crusher described in Section 19.1. Its initial investment is $1,000,000, and the expected cash inflow is $85,000 a year in perpetuity. The opportunity cost of capital with all-equity financing is 10 percent, and the project allows the firm to borrow at 7 percent. Assume the net tax advantage to borrowing is $.35 per dollar of interest paid ($T^* = T_c = .35$).

    Use APV to calculate this project's value.

a. Assume first that the project will be partly financed with $400,000 of debt and that the debt amount is to be fixed and perpetual.

b. Then assume that the initial borrowing will be increased or reduced in proportion to changes in the future market value of this project.

Explain the difference between your answers to **(a)** and **(b)**.

11. Suppose the project described in practice question 10 is to be undertaken by a university. Funds for the project will be withdrawn from the university's endowment, which is invested in a widely diversified portfolio of stocks and bonds. However, the university can also borrow at 7 percent. The university is tax exempt.

The university treasurer proposes to finance the project by issuing $400,000 of perpetual bonds at 7 percent and by selling $600,000 worth of common stocks from the endowment. The expected return on the common stocks is 10 percent. He therefore proposes to evaluate the project by discounting at a weighted-average cost of capital, calculated as

$$r = r_D \frac{D}{V} + r_E \frac{E}{V}$$

$$= .07\left(\frac{400,000}{1,000,000}\right) + .10\left(\frac{600,000}{1,000,000}\right)$$

$$= .088, \text{ or } 8.8\%$$

What's right or wrong with the treasurer's approach? Should the university invest? Should it borrow? Would the project's value to the university change if the treasurer financed the project entirely by selling common stocks from the endowment?

12. What is meant by an adjusted discount rate (r^* in our notation)? In what circumstances would an adjusted discount rate *not* equal WACC?

13. The Bunsen Chemical Company is currently at its target debt ratio of 40 percent. It is contemplating a $1 million expansion of its existing business. This expansion is expected to produce a cash inflow of $130,000 a year in perpetuity.

The company is uncertain whether to undertake this expansion and how to finance it. The two options are a $1 million issue of common stock or a $1 million issue of 20-year debt. The flotation costs of a stock issue would be around 5 percent of the amount raised, and the flotation costs of a debt issue would be around 1½ percent.

Bunsen's financial manager, Miss Polly Ethylene, estimates that the required return on the company's equity is 14 percent, but she argues that the flotation costs increase the cost of new equity to 19 percent. On this basis, the project does not appear viable.

On the other hand, she points out that the company can raise new debt on a 7 percent yield which would make the cost of new debt 8½ percent. She therefore recommends that Bunsen should go ahead with the project and finance it with an issue of long-term debt.

Is Miss Ethylene right? How would you evaluate the project?

14. Curtis Bog, chief financial officer of Sphagnum Paper Corporation, is reviewing a consultant's analysis of Sphagnum's weighted-average cost of capital. The consultant proposes

$$\text{WACC} = (1 - T_c)r_D \frac{D}{V} + r_E \frac{E}{V}$$

$$= (1 - .35)(.103)(.55) + .183(.45)$$

$$= .1192, \text{ or about } 12\%$$

Mr. Bog wants to check that this calculation is consistent with the capital asset pricing model. He has observed or estimated the following numbers:

Betas	$\beta_{debt} = .15, \beta_{equity} = 1.09$
Expected market risk premium ($r_m - r_f$)	.085
Risk-free rate of interest (r_f)	9 percent

Note: We suggest you simplify by ignoring personal income taxes and assuming that the promised and expected rates of returns on Sphagnum debt are equal.

15. Nevada Hydro is 40 percent debt-financed and has a weighted-average cost of capital of 9.7 percent:

$$\text{WACC} = (1 - T_c)r_D\frac{D}{V} + r_E\frac{E}{V}$$

$$= (1 - .35)(.085)(.40) + .125(.60) = .097$$

Banker's Tryst Company is advising Nevada Hydro to issue $75 million of preferred stock at a dividend yield of 9 percent. The proceeds would be used to repurchase and retire common stock. The preferred issue would account for 10 percent of the preissue market value of the firm.

Banker's Tryst argues that these transactions would reduce Nevada Hydro's WACC to 9.4 percent:

$$\text{WACC} = (1 - .35)(.085)(.40) + .09(.10) + .125(.50)$$
$$= .094, \text{ or } 9.4\%$$

Do you agree with this calculation? Explain.

16. Sometimes APV is particularly useful in international capital investment decisions. What kinds of tax or financing side effects are encountered in international projects?

17. Consider a different financing scenario for the solar water heater project discussed in Section 19.4. The project requires $10 million and has a base-case NPV of $170,000. Suppose the firm happens to have $5 million banked that could be used for the project.

The government, eager to encourage solar energy, offers to help finance the project by lending $5 million at a subsidized rate of 5 percent. The loan calls for the firm to pay the government $647,500 annually for 10 years (this amount includes both principal and interest).

a. What is the value of being able to borrow from the government at 5 percent? Assume the company's normal borrowing rate is 8 percent and the corporate tax rate is 35 percent.

b. Suppose the company's normal debt policy is to borrow 50 percent of the book value of its assets. It calculates the present value of interest tax shields by the procedure shown in Table 19.1 and includes this present value in APV. Should it do so here, given the government's offer of cheap financing?

18. Table 19.4 is a simplified book balance sheet for Phillips Petroleum in June 2001. Other information:

Number of outstanding shares (N)	256.2 million
Price per share (P)	$59
Beta based on 60 monthly returns, against the S&P Composite:	$\beta = .66$
Interest rates	
Treasury bills	3.5%
20-year Treasury bonds	5.8
New issue rate for Phillips assuming straight long-term debt	7.4
Marginal tax rate	35%

TABLE 19.4

Simplified book balance sheet for Phillips Petroleum, June 2001 (figures in $ millions).

Current assets	2,202	Current liabilities	2,780
Net property, plant, and equipment	15,124	Long-term debt	6,268
Investments and other assets	3,428	Deferred taxes	2,144
		Other liabilities	2,510
		Shareholders' equity	7,052
Total	20,754	Total	20,754

     a. Calculate Phillips's WACC. Use the capital asset pricing model and the data given above. Make additional assumptions and approximations as necessary.
     b. What would Phillips's WACC be if it moved to *and maintained* a debt—market value ratio (*D/V*) of 25 percent?

19. In question 18 you calculated a WACC for Phillips Petroleum. Phillips could also use an industry WACC. Under what conditions would the industry WACC be the better choice? Explain.

CHALLENGE QUESTIONS

1. In footnote 21 we referred to the Miles–Ezzell formula:

$$r^* = r - Lr_D T^* \left[\frac{1 + r}{1 + r_D} \right] = \text{WACC}$$

Derive this formula as the adjusted discount rate (r^*) for a one-period project. Then show that the formula correctly values projects of any life if the company follows Financing Rule 2.

2. In Section 19.3 we proposed a three-step procedure for calculating WACC at different debt ratios. The Miles–Ezzell formula can be used for the same purpose. Set up a numerical example and use these two approaches to calculate how WACC changes with financial leverage. Assume $T^* = T_c$. You will get slightly different numerical answers. Why?

3. Consider a project generating a level, perpetual stream of cash flows. The project is financed at an initial debt-to-value ratio L. The debt is likewise perpetual. But the company follows Financing Rule 1: The dollar amount of debt is kept constant. Derive a formula for the adjusted discount rate r^* to fit these assumptions.[33] What does this formula imply for **(a)** the difference between WACC and the opportunity cost of capital r and **(b)** the formulas for levering and relevering the cost of equity?

4. Financing Rule 2 ties the level of future interest tax shields to the future value of the project or company. That means the interest tax shields are risky and worth less than if the company followed Financing Rule 1. Does that mean that Financing Rule 1 is better for stockholders?

---

[33]Here you are following in MM's footsteps. See F. Modigliani and M. H. Miller, "Corporate Income Taxes and the Cost of Capital: A Correction," *American Economic Review* 53 (June 1963), pp. 433–443, and "Some Estimates of the Cost of Capital to the Electric Utility Industry," *American Economic Review* 56 (June 1966), pp. 333–391.

Some materials on cash and stock dividends is provided by:

www.e-analytics.com

www.dripcentral.com *(information on dividend reinvestment plans)*

John Graham's website contains material on capital structure:

www.duke.edu/~jgraham

ValuePro provides software and data for estimating WACCs:

www.valuepro.net

PART FIVE
RELATED
WEBSITES

OPTIONS

POP QUIZ: WHAT do the following events have in common?

- Flatiron offers its president a bonus if the company's stock price exceeds $120.
- BJ Services issues 4.8 million warrants as partial payment for an acquisition.
- Tyco issues a $3.5 billion convertible bond.
- Blitzen Computer dips a toe in the water and enters a new market.
- Malted Herring postpones investment in a positive-NPV plant.
- Hewlett-Packard exports partially assembled printers even though it would be cheaper to ship the finished product.
- An investment uses standard machinery rather than efficient custom-designed machinery.

Answers: (1) each of these events involves an *option*, and (2) each is analyzed in the next four chapters. But you must walk before you can run. Therefore we start by focusing on a simple option to buy the stock of AOL Time-Warner. Chapter 20 examines the payoffs from this option, and Chapter 21 shows how it is valued.

Chapter 22 looks at the *real options* that arise in capital budgeting decisions. We encountered these in Chapter 10, when we used decision trees to set out future opportunities to modify a project. Now we place a value on this flexibility.

Chapter 23 looks at two sources of finance involving an option—warrants and convertible bonds. Later chapters will encounter many other securities with a built-in option.

CHAPTER TWENTY

UNDERSTANDING OPTIONS

FIGURE 20.1(A) SHOWS your payoff if you buy AOL Time Warner (AOL) stock at $55. You gain dollar-for-dollar if the stock price goes up and you lose dollar-for-dollar if it falls. That's trite; it doesn't take a genius to draw a 45-degree line.

Look now at panel (*b*), which shows the payoffs from an investment strategy that retains the upside potential of AOL stock but gives complete downside protection. In this case your payoff stays at $55 even if the AOL stock price falls to $50, $40, or zero. Panel (*b*)'s payoffs are clearly better than panel (*a*)'s. If a financial alchemist could turn panel (*a*) into (*b*), you'd be willing to pay for the service.

Of course alchemy has its dark side. Panel (*c*) shows an investment strategy for masochists. You lose if the stock price falls, but you give up any chance of profiting from a rise in the stock price. If you *like* to lose, or if somebody pays you enough to take the strategy on, this is the strategy for you.

Now, as you have probably suspected, all this financial alchemy is for real. You really can do all the transmutations shown in Figure 20.1. You do them with options, and we will show you how.

But why should the financial manager of an industrial company be interested in options? There are several reasons. First, companies regularly use commodity, currency, and interest-rate options to reduce risk. For example, a meatpacking company that wishes to put a ceiling on the cost of beef might take out an option to buy live cattle. A company that wishes to limit its future borrowing costs might take out an option to sell long-term bonds. And so on. In Chapter 27 we will explain how firms employ options to limit their risk.

Second, many capital investments include an embedded option to expand in the future. For instance, the company may invest in a patent that allows it to exploit a new technology or it may purchase adjoining land that gives it the option in the future to increase capacity. In each case the company is paying money today for the opportunity to make a further investment. To put it another way, the company is acquiring *growth opportunities*.

Here is another disguised option to invest: You are considering the purchase of a tract of desert land that is known to contain gold deposits. Unfortunately, the cost of extraction is higher than the current price of gold. Does this mean the land is almost worthless? Not at all. You are not obliged to mine the gold, but ownership of the land gives you the option to do so. Of course, if you know that the gold price will remain below the extraction cost, then the option is worthless. But if there is uncertainty about future gold prices, you could be lucky and make a killing.[1]

If the option to expand has value, what about the option to bail out? Projects don't usually go on until the equipment disintegrates. The decision to terminate a project is usually taken by management, not by nature. Once the project is no longer profitable, the company will cut its losses and exercise its option to abandon the project. Some projects have higher abandonment value than others. Those that use standardized equipment may offer a valuable abandonment option. Others may actually cost money to discontinue. For example, it is very costly to decommission an offshore oil rig.

We took a peek at these investment options in Chapter 10, and we showed there how to use decision trees to analyze Magna Charter's options to expand its airline operation or abandon it. In Chapter 22 we will take a more thorough look at these *real* options.

The other important reason why financial managers need to understand options is that they are often tacked on to an issue of corporate securities and so provide the investor or the company with the flexibility to change the terms of the issue. For example, in Chapter 23 we will show how warrants and

continued

---

[1]In Chapter 11 we valued Kingsley Solomon's gold mine by calculating the value of the gold in the ground and then subtracting the value of the extraction costs. That is correct only if we *know* that the gold will be mined. Otherwise, the value of the mine is increased by the value of the option to leave the gold in the ground if its price is less than the extraction cost.

convertibles give their holders an option to buy common stock in exchange for cash or bonds. Then in Chapter 25 we will see how corporate bonds may give the issuer or the investor the option of early repayment.

In fact, we shall see that whenever a company borrows, it creates an option. The reason is that the borrower is not *compelled* to repay the debt at maturity. If the value of the company's assets is less than the amount of the debt, the company will choose to default on the payment and the bondholders will get to keep the company's assets. Thus, when the firm borrows, the lender effectively acquires the company and the shareholders obtain the option to buy it back by paying off the debt. This is an extremely important insight. It means that anything that we can learn about traded options applies equally to corporate liabilities.[2]

In this chapter we use traded stock options to explain how options work, but we hope that our brief survey has convinced you that the interest of financial managers in options goes far beyond traded stock options. That is why we are asking you to invest here to acquire several important ideas for use later.

If you are unfamiliar with the wonderful world of options, it may seem baffling on first encounter. We will therefore divide this chapter into three bite-sized pieces. Our first task is to introduce you to call and put options and to show you how the payoff on these options depends on the price of the underlying asset. We will then show how financial alchemists can combine options to produce the interesting strategies depicted in Figure 20.1 (*b*) and (*c*).

We conclude the chapter by identifying the variables that determine option values. Here you will encounter some surprising and counterintuitive effects. For example, investors are used to thinking that increased risk reduces present value. But for options it is the other way around.

20.1 CALLS, PUTS, AND SHARES

The Chicago Board Options Exchange (CBOE) was founded in 1973 to allow investors to buy and sell options on shares of common stock. The CBOE was an almost instant success and other exchanges have since copied its example. In addition to options on individual common stocks, investors can now trade options on stock indexes, bonds, commodities, and foreign exchange.

Table 20.1 reproduces quotes from the CBOE for June 22, 2001. It shows the prices for two types of options on AOL stock—calls and puts. We will explain each in turn.

Call Options and Position Diagrams

A **call option** gives its owner the right to buy stock at a specified *exercise* or *strike price* on or before a specified exercise date. If the option can be exercised only on one particular day, it is conventionally known as a *European call;* in other cases

[2]This relationship was first recognized by Fischer Black and Myron Scholes, in "The Pricing of Options and Corporate Liabilities," *Journal of Political Economy* 81 (May–June 1973), pp. 637–654.

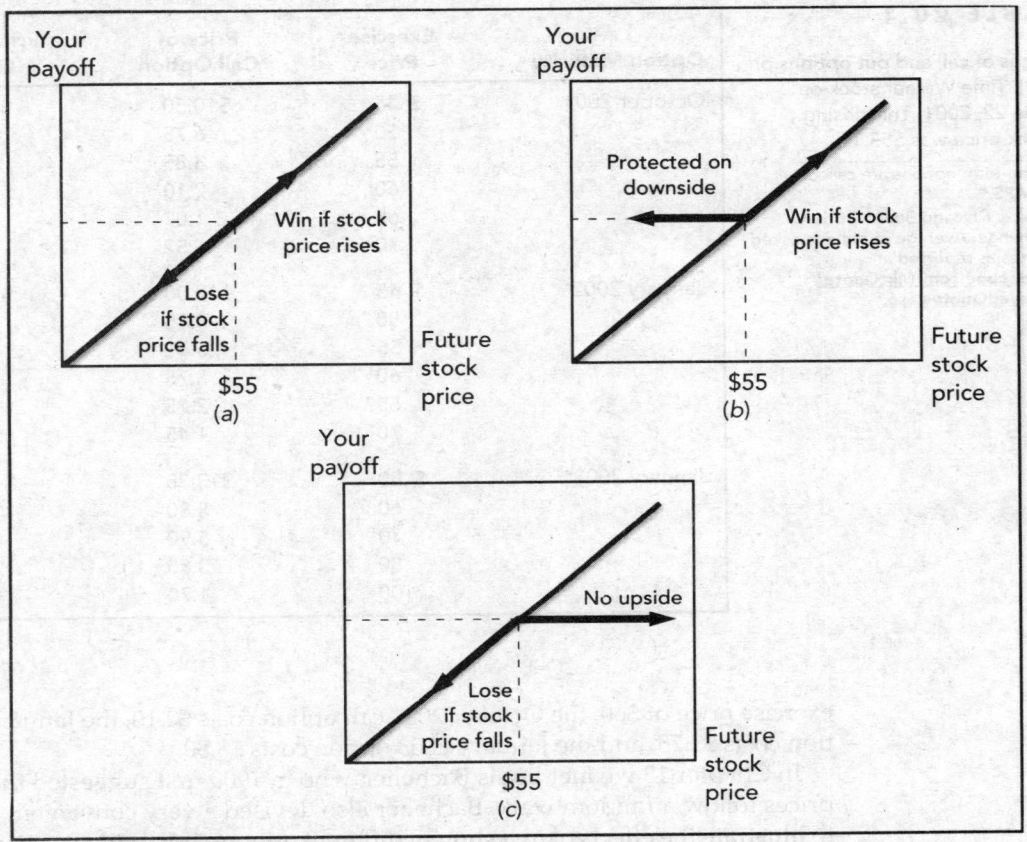

FIGURE 20.1

Payoffs to three investment strategies for AOL stock. (a) You buy one share for $55. (b) No downside. If stock price falls, your payoff stays at $55. (c) A strategy for masochists? You lose if stock price falls, but you don't gain if it rises.

(such as the AOL options shown in Table 20.1), the option can be exercised on or at any time before that day, and it is then known as an *American call.*

The third column of Table 20.1 sets out the prices of AOL Time Warner call options with different exercise prices and exercise dates. Look at the quotes for options maturing in October 2001. The first entry says that for $10.50 you could require an option to buy one share[3] of AOL stock for $45 on or before October 2001. Moving down to the next row, you can see that an option to buy for $5 more ($50 vs. $45) costs $3.75 less, that is $6.75. In general, the value of a call option goes down as the exercise price goes up.

Now look at the quotes for options maturing in January 2002 and 2003. Notice how the option price increases as option maturity is extended. For example, at an

---

[3]You can't actually buy an option on a single share. Trades are in multiples of 100. The minimum order would be for 100 options on 100 AOL shares.

TABLE 20.1

Prices of call and put options on AOL Time Warner stock on June 22, 2001. The closing stock price was $53.10.

---

*Long-term options are called "LEAPS."

Source: Chicago Board Options Exchange. Average of bid and asked quotes as reported at **www.cboe.com/MktQuote/ DelayedQuotes.asp.**

Option Maturity	Exercise Price	Price of Call Option	Price of Put Option
October 2001	$ 45	$10.50	$ 1.97
	50	6.75	3.15
	55	3.85	5.25
	60	2.10	8.50
	65	1.07	12.50
	70	.52	17.10
January 2002	$ 45	$12.00	$ 2.90
	50	8.45	4.35
	55	**5.75**	**6.55**
	60	3.75	9.55
	65	2.25	13.20
	70	1.45	17.50
January 2003*	$ 50	$13.30	$ 7.30
	60	8.80	12.40
	70	5.90	19.40
	80	3.85	27.80
	100	1.70	47.00

exercise price of $60, the October 2001 call option costs $2.10, the January 2002 option costs $3.75, and the January 2003 option costs $8.80.

In Chapter 13 we met Louis Bachelier, who in 1900 first suggested that security prices follow a random walk. Bachelier also devised a very convenient shorthand to illustrate the effects of investing in different options.[4] We will use this shorthand to compare three possible investments in AOL—a call option, a put option, and the stock itself.

The *position diagram* in Figure 20.2(*a*) shows the possible consequences of investing in AOL January 2002 call options with an exercise price of $55 (boldfaced in Table 20.1). The outcome from investing in AOL calls depends on what happens to the stock price. If the stock price at the end of this six-month period turns out to be less than the $55 exercise price, nobody will pay $55 to obtain the share via the call option. Your call will in that case be valueless, and you will throw it away. On the other hand, if the stock price turns out to be greater than $55, it will pay to exercise your option to buy the share. In this case the call will be worth the market price of the share minus the $55 that you must pay to acquire it. For example, suppose that the price of AOL stock rises to $100. Your call will then be worth $100 − $55 = $45. That is your payoff, but of course it is not all profit. Table 20.1 shows that you had to pay $5.75 to buy the call.

Put Options

Now let us look at the AOL **put options** in the right-hand column of Table 20.1. Whereas the call option gives you the right to *buy* a share for a specified exercise price, the comparable put gives you the right to *sell* the share. For example, the

---

[4]L. Bachelier, *Théorie de la Speculation*, Gauthier-Villars, Paris, 1900. Reprinted in English in P. H. Cootner (ed.), *The Random Character of Stock Market Prices*, M.I.T. Press, Cambridge, MA, 1964.

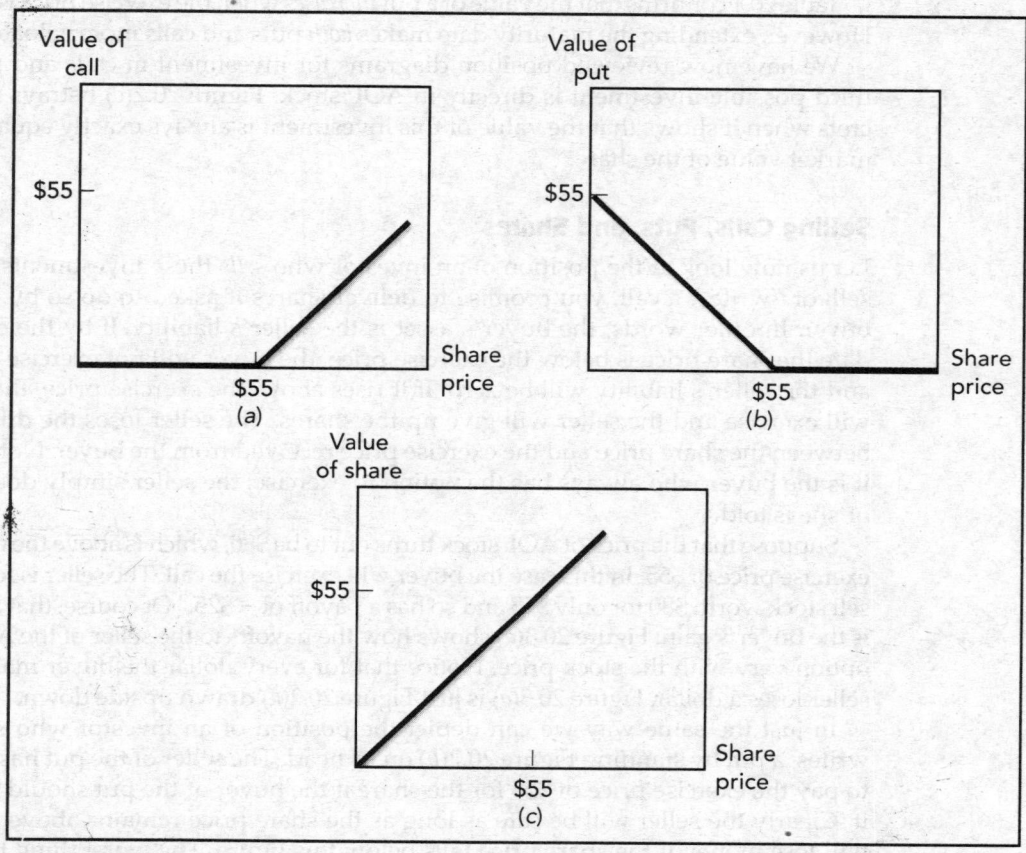

FIGURE 20.2

Position diagrams show how payoffs to owners of AOL calls, puts, and shares (shown by the colored lines) depend on the share price. (a) Result of buying AOL call exercisable at $55. (b) Result of buying AOL put exercisable at $55. (c) Result of buying AOL share.

boldfaced entry in the right-hand column of Table 20.1 shows that for $6.55 you could acquire an option to sell AOL stock for a price of $55 anytime before January 2002. The circumstances in which the put turns out to be profitable are just the opposite of those in which the call is profitable. You can see this from the position diagram in Figure 20.2(b). If AOL's share price immediately before expiration turns out to be *greater* than $55, you won't want to sell stock at that price. You would do better to sell the share in the market, and your put option will be worthless. Conversely, if the share price turns out to be *less* than $55, it will pay to buy stock at the low price and then take advantage of the option to sell it for $55. In this case, the value of the put option on the exercise date is the difference between the $55 proceeds of the sale and the market price of the share. For example, if the share is worth $35, the put is worth $20:

Value of put option at expiration = exercise price − market price of the share
= $55 − $35 = $20

Table 20.1 confirms that the value of a put *increases* when the exercise price is raised. However, extending the maturity date makes *both* puts and calls more valuable.

We have now reviewed position diagrams for investment in calls and puts. A third possible investment is directly in AOL stock. Figure 20.2(*c*) betrays few secrets when it shows that the value of this investment is always exactly equal to the market value of the share.

Selling Calls, Puts, and Shares

Let us now look at the position of an investor who *sells* these investments. If you sell, or "write," a call, you promise to deliver shares if asked to do so by the call buyer. In other words, the buyer's asset is the seller's liability. If by the exercise date the share price is below the exercise price, the buyer will not exercise the call and the seller's liability will be zero. If it rises above the exercise price, the buyer will exercise and the seller will give up the shares. The seller loses the difference between the share price and the exercise price received from the buyer. Notice that it is the buyer who always has the option to exercise; the seller simply does as he or she is told.

Suppose that the price of AOL stock turns out to be $80, which is above the option's exercise price of $55. In this case the buyer will exercise the call. The seller is forced to sell stock worth $80 for only $55 and so has a payoff of $-$25.[5] Of course, that $25 loss is the buyer's gain. Figure 20.3(*a*) shows how the payoffs to the seller of the AOL call option vary with the stock price. Notice that for every dollar the buyer makes, the seller loses a dollar. Figure 20.3(*a*) is just Figure 20.2(*a*) drawn upside down.

In just the same way we can depict the position of an investor who sells, or writes, a put by standing Figure 20.2(*b*) on its head. The seller of the put has agreed to pay the exercise price of $55 for the share if the buyer of the put should request it. Clearly the seller will be safe as long as the share price remains above $55 but will lose money if the share price falls below this figure. The worst thing that can happen is that the stock becomes worthless. The seller would then be obliged to pay $55 for a stock worth $0. The "value" of the option position would be $-$55.

Finally, Figure 20.3(*c*) shows the position of someone who sells AOL stock *short*. Short sellers sell stock which they do not yet own. As they say on Wall Street:

> He who sells what isn't his'n
> Buys it back or goes to prison.

Eventually, therefore, the short seller will have to buy the stock back. The short seller will make a profit if it has fallen in price and a loss if it has risen.[6] You can see that Figure 20.3(*c*) is simply an upside-down Figure 20.2(*c*).

Position Diagrams Are Not Profit Diagrams

Position diagrams show *only* the payoffs at option exercise; they do not account for the initial cost of buying the option or the initial proceeds from selling it.

This is a common point of confusion. For example, the position diagram in Figure 20.2(*a*) makes purchase of a call *look* like a sure thing—the payoff is at worst

---

[5]The seller has some consolation, for he or she was paid $5.75 in June for selling the call.

[6]Selling short is not as simple as we have described it. For example, a short seller usually has to put up margin, that is, deposit cash or securities with the broker. This assures the broker that the short seller will be able to repurchase the stock when the time comes to do so.

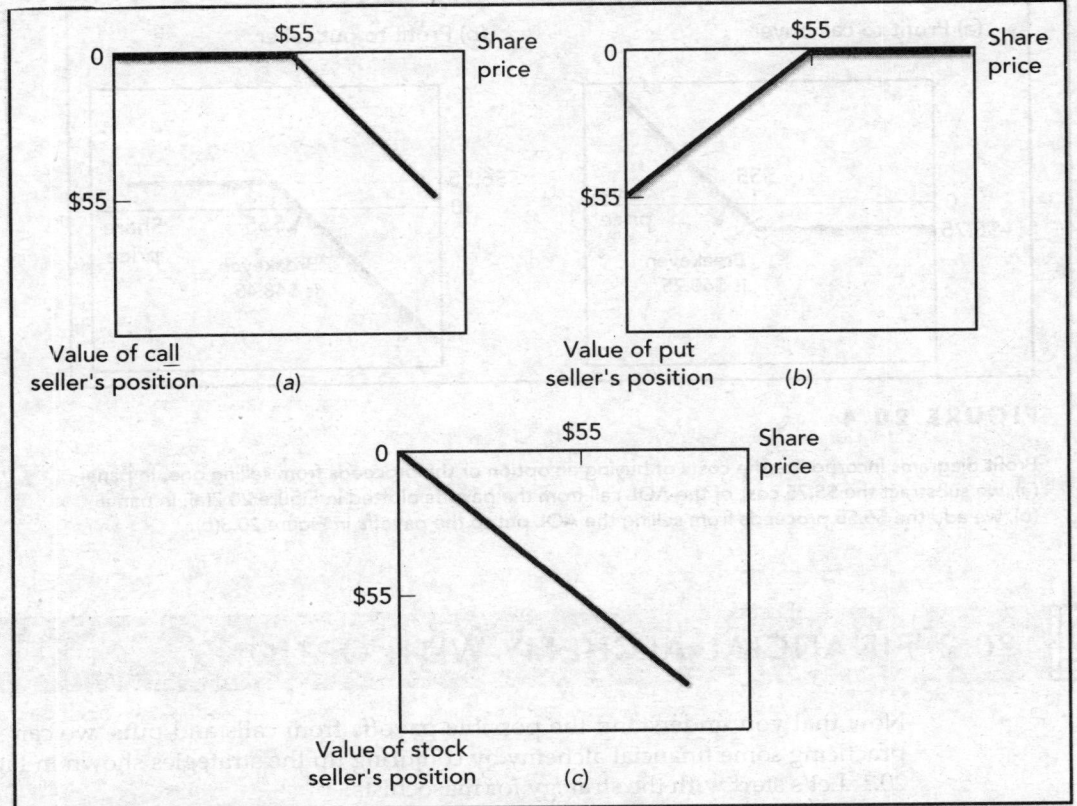

FIGURE 20.3

Payoffs to *sellers* of AOL calls, puts, and shares (shown by the colored lines) depend on the share price. (a) Result of selling AOL call exercisable at $55. (b) Result of selling AOL put exercisable at $55. (c) Result of selling AOL share short.

zero, with plenty of "upside" if AOL's stock price goes above $55 by January 2002. But compare the *profit diagram* in Figure 20.4(*a*), which subtracts the $5.75 *cost* of the call in June 2001 from the payoff at maturity. The call buyer loses money at all share prices less than $55 + 5.75 = $60.75. Take another example: The position diagram in Figure 20.3(*b*) makes selling a put *look* like a sure loss—the *best* payoff is zero. But the profit diagram in Figure 20.4(*b*), which recognizes the $6.55 received by the seller, shows that the seller gains at all prices above $55 − 6.55 = $48.45.[7]

Profit diagrams like those in Figure 20.4 may be helpful to the options beginner, but options experts rarely draw them. Now that you've graduated from the first options class we won't draw them either. We will stick to position diagrams, because you have to zero in on payoffs at exercise to understand options and to value them properly.

---

[7]Strictly speaking, the profit diagrams in Figure 20.4 should account for the time value of money, that is, the interest earned on the seller's initial proceeds and lost on the call buyer's outlay.

FIGURE 20.4

Profit diagrams incorporate the costs of buying an option or the proceeds from selling one. In panel (a), we substract the $5.75 cost of the AOL call from the payoffs plotted in Figure 20.2(a). In panel (b), we add the $6.55 proceeds from selling the AOL put to the payoffs in Figure 20.3(b).

 ## 20.2 FINANCIAL ALCHEMY WITH OPTIONS

Now that you understand the possible payoffs from calls and puts, we can start practicing some financial alchemy by conjuring up the strategies shown in Figure 20.1. Let's start with the strategy for masochists.

Look at row 1 of Figure 20.5. The first diagram shows the payoffs from buying a share of AOL stock, while the second shows the payoffs from *selling* a call option with a $55 exercise price. The third diagram shows what happens if you combine these two positions. The result is the no-win strategy that we depicted in panel (c) of Figure 20.1. You lose if the stock price declines below $55, but, if the stock price rises above $55, the owner of the call option will demand that you hand over your stock for the $55 exercise price. So you lose on the downside and give up any chance of a profit. That's the bad news. The good news is that you get paid for taking on this liability. In June 2001 you would have been paid $5.75, the price of a six-month call option.

Now, we'll create the downside protection shown in Figure 20.1(b). Look at row 2 of Figure 20.5. The first diagram again shows the payoff from buying a share of AOL stock, while the next diagram in row 2 shows the payoffs from buying an AOL put option with an exercise price of $55. The third diagram shows the effect of combining these two positions. You can see that, if AOL's stock price rises above $55, your put option is valueless, so you simply receive the gains from your investment in the share. However, if the stock price falls below $55, you can exercise your put option and sell your stock for $55. Thus, by adding a put option to your investment in the stock, you have protected yourself against loss.[8] This is the strategy that we depicted in panel (b) of Figure 20.1. Of course, there is no gain without pain. The *cost* of insuring yourself against loss is the amount that you pay for a put

---

[8]This combination of a stock and a put option is known as a *protective put*.

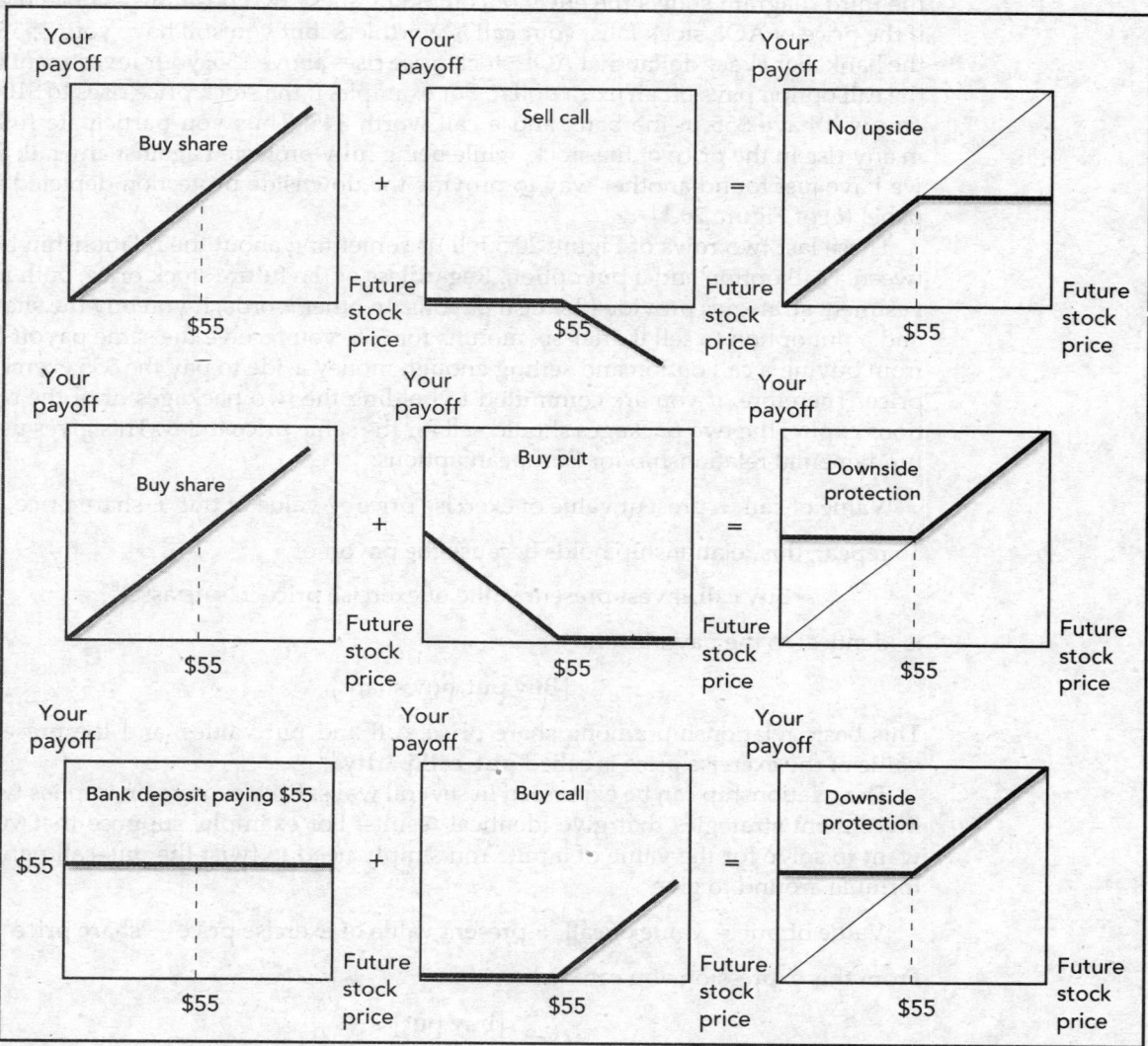

FIGURE 20.5

The first row shows how options can be used to create a strategy where you lose if the stock price falls but do not gain if it rises [strategy (c) in Figure 20.1]. The second and third rows show two ways to create the reverse strategy where you gain on the upside but are protected on the downside [strategy (b) in Figure 20.1].

option on AOL stock with an exercise price of $55. In June 2001 the price of this put was $6.55. This was the going rate for financial alchemists.

We have just seen how put options can be used to provide downside protection. We will now show you how call options can be used to get the same result. This is illustrated in row 3 of Figure 20.5. The first diagram shows the payoff from placing the present value of $55 in a bank deposit. Regardless of what happens to the price of AOL stock, your bank deposit will pay off $55. The second diagram in row 3 shows the payoff from a call option on AOL stock with an exercise price of $55, and the third diagram shows the effect of combining these two positions. Notice that, if the price of AOL stock falls, your call is worthless, but you still have your $55 in the bank. For every dollar that AOL stock price rises above $55, your investment in the call option pays off an extra dollar. For example, if the stock price rises to $100, you will have $55 in the bank and a call worth $45. Thus you participate fully in any rise in the price of the stock, while being fully protected against any fall. So we have just found another way to provide the downside protection depicted in panel (*b*) of Figure 20.1.

These last two rows of Figure 20.5 tell us something about the relationship between a call option and a put option. Regardless of the future stock price, both investment strategies provide identical payoffs. In other words, if you buy the share and a put option to sell it after six months for $55, you receive the same payoff as from buying a call option and setting enough money aside to pay the $55 exercise price. Therefore, if you are committed to holding the two packages until the options expire, the two packages should sell for the same price today. This gives us a fundamental relationship for European options:

Value of call + present value of exercise price = value of put + share price

To repeat, this relationship holds because the payoff of

[Buy call, invest present value of exercise price in safe asset[9]]

is identical to the payoff from

[Buy put, buy share]

This basic relationship among share price, call and put values, and the present value of the exercise price is called **put–call parity.**[10]

The relationship can be expressed in several ways. Each expression implies two investment strategies that give identical results. For example, suppose that you want to solve for the value of a put. You simply need to twist the put–call parity formula around to give

Value of put = value of call + present value of exercise price − share price

From this expression you can deduce that

[buy put]

is identical to

[Buy call, invest present value of exercise price in safe asset, sell share]

In other words, if puts are not available, you can create them by buying calls, putting cash in the bank, and selling shares.

---

[9]The present value is calculated at the *risk-free* rate of interest. It is the amount that you would have to invest today in a bank deposit or Treasury bills to realize the exercise price on the option's expiration date.

[10]Put–call parity holds only if you are committed to holding the options until the final exercise date. It therefore does not hold for American options, which you can exercise *before* the final date. We discuss possible reasons for early exercise in Chapter 21. Also if the stock makes a dividend payment before the final exercise date, you need to recognize that the investor who buys the call misses out on this dividend. In this case the relationship is

Value of call + present value of exercise price = value of put + share price − present value of dividend.

Default Puts and the Difference between Safe and Risky Bonds

In Chapter 18 we discussed the plight of Circular File Company, which borrowed $50 per share. Unfortunately the firm fell on hard times and the market value of its assets fell to $30. Circular's bond and stock prices fell to $25 and $5, respectively. Circular's *market* value balance sheet is now

Circular File Company (Market Values)

Asset value	$30	$25	Bonds
		5	Stock
	$30	$30	Firm value

If Circular's debt were due and payable now, the firm could not repay the $50 it originally borrowed. It would default, bondholders receiving assets worth $30 and shareholders receiving nothing. The reason Circular stock is worth $5 is that the debt is *not* due now but rather is due a year from now. A stroke of good fortune could increase firm value enough to pay off the bondholders in full, with something left over for the stockholders.

Let us go back to a statement that we made at the start of the chapter. Whenever a firm borrows, the lender effectively acquires the company and the shareholders obtain the option to buy it back by paying off the debt. The stockholders have in effect purchased a call option on the assets of the firm. The bondholders have sold them this call option. Thus the balance sheet of Circular File can be expressed as follows:

Circular File Company (Market Values)

Asset value	$30	$25	Bond value = asset value − value of call
		5	Stock value = value of call
	$30	$30	Firm value = asset value

If this still sounds like a strange idea to you, try drawing one of Bachelier's position diagrams for Circular File. It should look like Figure 20.6. If the future value of the assets is less than $50, Circular will default and the stock will be worthless. If the value of the assets exceeds $50, the stockholders will receive asset value *less* the $50 paid over to the bondholders. The payoffs in Figure 20.6 are identical to a call option on the firm's assets, with an exercise price of $50.

Now look again at the basic relationship between calls and puts:

Value of call + present value of exercise price = value of put + value of share

To apply this to Circular File, we have to interpret "value of share" as "asset value," because the common stock is a call option on the firm's assets. Also, "present value of exercise price" is the present value of receiving the promised payment of $50 to bondholders *for sure* next year. Thus

Value of call + present value of promised payment to bondholders
   = value of put + asset value

Now we can solve for the value of Circular's bonds. This is equal to the firm's asset value less the value of the shareholders' call option on these assets:

Bond value = asset value − value of call
      = present value of promised payment to bondholders − value of put

FIGURE 20.6

The value of Circular's common stock is the same as the value of a call option on the firm's assets with an exercise price of $50.

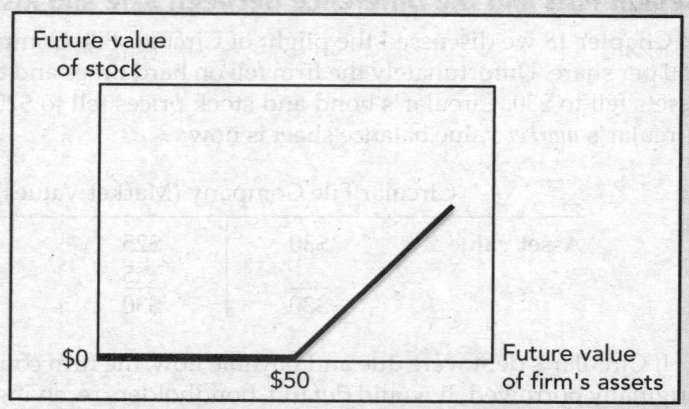

Circular's bondholders have in effect (1) bought a safe bond and (2) given the shareholders the option to sell them the firm's assets for the amount of the debt. You can think of the bondholders as receiving the $50 promised payment, but they have given the shareholders the option to take the $50 back in exchange for the assets of the company. If firm value turns out to be less than the $50 that is promised to bondholders, the shareholders will exercise their put option.

Circular's risky bond is equal to a safe bond less the value of the shareholders' option to default. To value this risky bond we need to value a safe bond and then subtract the value of the default option. The default option is equal to a put option on the firm's assets. Now you can see why bond traders, investors, and financial managers refer to *default puts*.

In the case of Circular File the option to default is extremely valuable because default is likely to occur. At the other extreme, the value of IBM's option to default is trivial compared to the value of IBM's assets. Default on IBM bonds is possible but extremely unlikely. Option traders would say that for Circular File the put option is "deep in the money" because today's asset value ($30) is well below the exercise price ($50). For IBM the put option is far "out of the money" because the value of IBM's assets substantially exceeds the value of IBM's debt.

We know that Circular's stock is equivalent to a call option on the firm's assets. It is also equal to (1) owning the firm's assets, (2) borrowing the present value of $50 with the obligation to repay regardless of what happens, but also (3) buying a put on the firm's assets with an exercise price of $50.

We can sum up by presenting Circular's balance sheet in terms of asset value, put value, and the present value of a sure $50 payment:

Circular File Company (Market Values)

Asset value	$30	$25	Bond value = present value of promised payment − value of default put
		5	Stock value = asset value − present value of promised payment + value of put
	$30	$30	Firm value = asset value

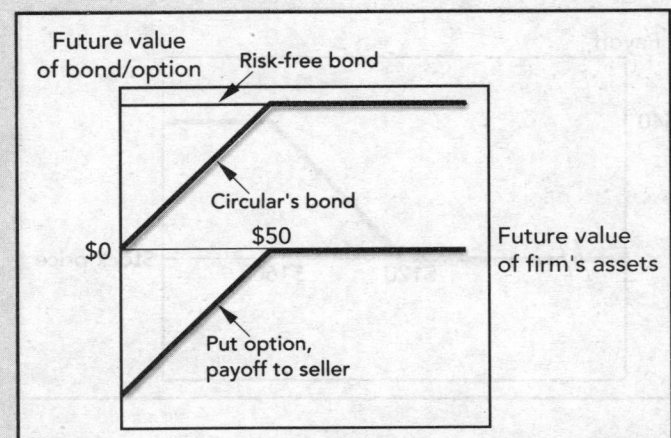

FIGURE 20.7

You can also think of Circular's bond (the colored line) as equivalent to a risk-free bond (the upper black line) *less* a put option on the firm's assets with an exercise price of $50 (the lower black line).

Again you can check this with a position diagram. The colored line in Figure 20.7 shows the payoffs to Circular's bondholders. If the firm's assets are worth more than $50, the bondholders are paid off in full; if the assets are worth less than $50, the firm defaults and the bondholders receive the value of the assets. You could get an identical payoff pattern by buying a safe bond (the upper black line) and selling a put option on the firm's assets (the lower black line).

Spotting the Option

Options rarely come with a large label attached. Often the trickiest part of the problem is to identify the option. For example, we suspect that until it was pointed out, you did not realize that every risky bond contains a hidden option. When you are not sure whether you are dealing with a put or a call or a complicated blend of the two, it is a good precaution to draw a position diagram. Here is an example.

The Flatiron and Mangle Corporation has offered its president, Ms. Higden, the following incentive scheme: At the end of the year Ms. Higden will be paid a bonus of $50,000 for every dollar that the price of Flatiron stock exceeds its current figure of $120. However, the maximum bonus that she can receive is set at $2 million.

You can think of Ms. Higden as owning 50,000 tickets, each of which pays nothing if the stock price fails to beat $120. The value of each ticket then rises by $1 for each dollar rise in the stock price up to the maximum of $2,000,000/50,000 = $40. Figure 20.8 shows the payoffs from just one of these tickets. The payoffs are not the same as those of the simple put and call options that we drew in Figure 20.2, but it is possible to find a combination of options that exactly replicates Figure 20.8. Before going on to read the answer, see if you can spot it yourself. (If you are someone who enjoys puzzles of the make-a-triangle-from-just-two-match-sticks type, this one should be a walkover.)

The answer is in Figure 20.9. The solid black line represents the purchase of a call option with an exercise price of $120, and the dotted line shows the sale of another call option with an exercise price of $160. The colored line shows the payoffs from a combination of the purchase and the sale—exactly the same as the payoffs from one of Ms. Higden's tickets.

FIGURE 20.8

The payoff from one of Ms. Higden's "tickets' depends on Flatiron's stock price.

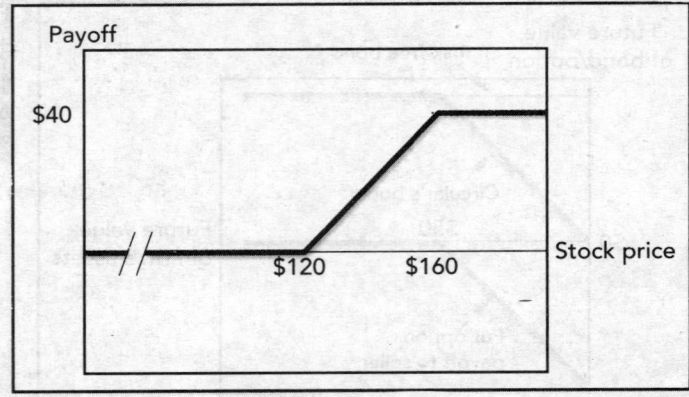

FIGURE 20.9

The solid black line shows the payoff from buying a call with an exercise price of $120. The dotted line shows the *sale* of a call with an exercise price of $160. The combined purchase and sale (shown by the colored line) is identical to one of Ms. Higden's "tickets."

Thus, if we wish to know how much the incentive scheme is costing the company, we need to calculate the difference between the value of 50,000 call options with an exercise price of $120 and the value of 50,000 calls with an exercise price of $160.

We could have made the incentive scheme depend in a much more complicated way on the stock price. For example, the bonus could peak at $2 million and then fall steadily back to zero as the stock price climbs above $160. (Don't ask why anyone would want to offer such an arrangement—perhaps there's some tax angle.) You could still have represented this scheme as a combination of options. In fact, we can state a general theorem:

Any set of contingent payoffs—that is, payoffs which depend on the value of some other asset—can be constructed with a mixture of simple options on that asset.

In other words, you can create any position diagram—with as many ups and downs or peaks and valleys as your imagination allows—by buying or selling the right combinations of puts and calls with different exercise prices.[11]

___

[11]In some cases you may also have to borrow or lend money to generate a position diagram with your desired pattern. Lending raises the payoff line in position diagrams, as in the bottom row of Figure 20.5. Borrowing lowers the payoff line.

20.3 WHAT DETERMINES OPTION VALUES?

So far we have said nothing about how the market value of an option is determined. We do know what an option is worth when it matures, however. Consider, for instance, our earlier example of an option to buy AOL stock at $55. If AOL's stock price is below $55 on the exercise date, the call will be worthless; if the stock price is above $55, the call will be worth $55 less than the value of the stock. In terms of Bachelier's position diagram, the relationship is depicted by the heavy, lower line in Figure 20.10.

Even before maturity the price of the option can never remain *below* the heavy, lower-bound line in Figure 20.10. For example, if our option were priced at $5 and the stock were priced at $70, it would pay any investor to sell the stock and then buy it back by purchasing the option and exercising it for an additional $55. That would give a money machine with a profit of $10. The demand for options from investors using the money machine would quickly force the option price up, at least to the heavy line in the figure. For options that still have some time to run, the heavy line is therefore a *lower-bound* limit on the market price of the option.

The diagonal line in Figure 20.10 is the *upper-bound* limit to the option price. Why? Because the stock gives a higher ultimate payoff than the option. If at the option's expiration the stock price ends up above the exercise price, the option is worth the stock price *less* the exercise price. If the stock price ends up below the exercise price, the option is worthless, but the stock's owner still has a valuable security. Let P be the stock price at the option's expiration date, and assume the option's exercise price is $55. Then the extra dollar returns realized by stockholders are

	Stock Payoff	Option Payoff	Extra Payoff from Holding Stock Instead of Option
Option exercised (P greater than $55)	P	$P - 55$	$55
Option expires unexercised (P less than or equal to $55)	P	0	P

FIGURE 20.10

Value of a call before its expiration date (dashed line). The value depends on the stock price. It is always worth more than its value if exercised now (heavy line). It is never worth more than the stock price itself.

If the stock and the option have the same price, everyone will rush to sell the option and buy the stock. Therefore, the option price must be somewhere in the shaded region of Figure 20.10. In fact, it will lie on a curved, upward-sloping line like the dashed curve shown in the figure. This line begins its travels where the upper and lower bounds meet (at zero). Then it rises, gradually becoming parallel to the upward-sloping part of the lower bound. This line tells us an important fact about option values: *The value of an option increases as stock price increases*, if the exercise price is held constant.

That should be no surprise. Owners of call options clearly hope for the stock price to rise and are happy when it does. But let us look more carefully at the shape and location of the dashed line. Three points, *A*, *B*, and *C*, are marked on the dashed line. As we explain each point you will see why the option price has to behave as the dashed line predicts.

Point A   *When the stock is worthless, the option is worthless:* A stock price of zero means that there is no possibility the stock will ever have any future value.[12] If so, the option is sure to expire unexercised and worthless, and it is worthless today.

Point B   *When the stock price becomes large, the option price approaches the stock price less the present value of the exercise price:* Notice that the dashed line representing the option price in Figure 20.10 eventually becomes parallel to the ascending heavy line representing the lower bound on the option price. The reason is as follows: The higher the stock price is, the higher is the probability that the option will eventually be exercised. If the stock price is high enough, exercise becomes a virtual certainty; the probability that the stock price will fall below the exercise price before the option expires becomes trivially small.

If you own an option that you *know* will be exchanged for a share of stock, you effectively own the stock now. The only difference is that you don't have to pay for the stock (by handing over the exercise price) until later, when formal exercise occurs. In these circumstances, buying the call is equivalent to buying the stock but financing part of the purchase by borrowing. The amount implicitly borrowed is the present value of the exercise price. The value of the call is therefore equal to the stock price less the present value of the exercise price.

This brings us to another important point about options. Investors who acquire stock by way of a call option are buying on credit. They pay the purchase price of the option today, but they do not pay the exercise price until they actually take up the option. The delay in payment is particularly valuable if interest rates are high and the option has a long maturity. *Thus, the value of an option increases with both the rate of interest and the time to maturity.*

Point C   *The option price always exceeds its minimum value* (except when stock price is zero): We have seen that the dashed and heavy lines in Figure 20.10 coincide when stock price is zero (point *A*), but elsewhere the lines diverge; that is, the option price must exceed the minimum value given by the heavy line. The reason for this can be understood by examining point *C*.

At point *C*, the stock price exactly equals the exercise price. The option is therefore worthless if exercised today. However, suppose that the option will not expire

---

[12]If a stock *can* be worth something in the future, then investors will pay *something* for it today, although possibly a very small amount.

until three months hence. Of course we do not know what the stock price will be at the expiration date. There is roughly a 50 percent chance that it will be higher than the exercise price and a 50 percent chance that it will be lower. The possible payoffs to the option are therefore

Outcome	Payoff
Stock price rises (50 percent probability)	Stock price less exercise price (option is exercised)
Stock price falls (50 percent probability)	Zero (option expires worthless)

If there is a positive probability of a positive payoff, and if the worst payoff is zero, then the option must be valuable. That means the option price at point C exceeds its lower bound, which at point C is zero. In general, the option prices will exceed their lower-bound values as long as there is time left before expiration.

One of the most important determinants of the *height* of the dashed curve (i.e., of the difference between actual and lower-bound value) is the likelihood of substantial movements in the stock price. An option on a stock whose price is unlikely to change by more than 1 or 2 percent is not worth much; an option on a stock whose price may halve or double is very valuable.

Panels (*a*) and (*b*) in Figure 20.11 illustrate this point. The panels compare the payoffs at expiration of two options with the same exercise price and the same stock price. The panels assume that stock price equals exercise price (like point C in Figure 20.10), although this is not a necessary assumption.[13] The only difference is that the price of stock Y at its option's expiration date is much harder to predict than the price of stock X at its option's expiration date. You can see this from the probability distributions superimposed on the figures.

In both cases there is roughly a 50 percent chance that the stock price will decline and make the options worthless, but if the prices of stocks X and Y rise, the odds are that Y will rise more than X. Thus there is a larger chance of a big payoff from the option on Y. Since the chance of a zero payoff is the same, the option on Y is worth more than the option on X. Figure 20.12 shows how the value of an option increases as stock price volatility increases. The upper curved line shows the values of the AOL call option assuming that the stock price is highly variable. The lower curved line assumes a lower (and more realistic) degree of volatility.[14]

The probability of large stock price changes during the remaining life of an option depends on two things: (1) the variance (i.e., volatility) of the stock price *per period* and (2) the number of periods until the option expires. If there are t remaining periods, and the variance per period is σ^2, the value of the option should depend on cumulative variability $\sigma^2 t$.[15] Other things equal, you would like to hold

---

[13]In drawing Figure 20.11 we have assumed that the distribution of possible stock prices is symmetric. This also is not a necessary assumption, and we will look more carefully at the distribution of price changes in the next chapter.

[14]The option values shown in Figure 20.12 were calculated by using the Black–Scholes option-valuation model. We explain this model in Chapter 21 and use it to value the AOL option.

[15]Here is an intuitive explanation: If the stock price follows a random walk (see Section 13.2), successive price changes are statistically independent. The cumulative price change before expiration is the sum of t random variables. The variance of a sum of independent random variables is the sum of the variances of those variables. Thus, if σ^2 is the variance of the daily price change, and there are t days until expiration, the variance of the cumulative price change is $\sigma^2 t$.

FIGURE 20.11

Call options are written against the shares of (a) firm X and (b) firm Y. In each case, the current share price equals the exercise price, so each option has a 50 percent chance of ending up worthless (if the share price falls) and a 50 percent chance of ending up "in the money" (if the share price rises). However, the chance of a *large* payoff is *greater* for the option on firm Y's share because Y's stock price is more volatile and therefore has more upside potential.

FIGURE 20.12

How the value of the AOL call option increases with the volatility of the stock price. Each of the curved lines shows the value of the option for different initial stock prices. The only difference is that the upper line assumes a much higher level of uncertainty about AOL's future stock price.

TABLE 20.2

1. If there is an *increase* in:	The change in the call option price is:
Stock price (P)	Positive
Exercise price (EX)	Negative
Interest rate (r_f)	Positive*
Time to expiration (t)	Positive
Volatility of stock price (σ)	Positive*

2. Other properties:
   a. *Upper bound.* The option price is always less than the stock price.
   b. *Lower bound.* The option price never falls below the payoff to immediate exercise (P − EX or zero, whichever is larger).
   c. If the stock is worthless, the option is worthless.
   d. As the stock price becomes very large, the option price approaches the stock price less the present value of the exercise price.

TABLE 20.2

What the price of a call option depends on.

*The *direct* effects of increases in r_f or σ on option price are positive. There may also be *indirect* effects. For example, an increase in r_f could reduce stock price P. This in turn could reduce option price.

an option on a volatile stock (high σ^2). Given volatility, you would like to hold an option with a long life ahead of it (large t). Thus the value of an option increases *with both the volatility of the share price and the time to maturity.*

It's a rare person who can keep all these properties straight at first reading. Therefore, we have summed them up in Table 20.2.

Risk and Option Values

In most financial settings, risk is a bad thing; you have to be paid to bear it. Investors in risky (high-beta) stocks demand higher expected rates of return. High-risk capital investment projects have correspondingly high costs of capital and have to beat higher hurdle rates to achieve positive NPV.

For options it's the other way around. As we have just seen, options written on volatile assets are worth *more* than options written on safe assets. If you can understand and remember that one fact about options, you've come a long way.

Example. Suppose you have to choose between two job offers, as CFO of either Establishment Industries or Digital Organics. Establishment Industries' compensation package includes a grant of the stock options described on the left side of Table 20.3. You demand a similar package from Digital Organics, and they comply. In fact they match the Establishment Industries options in every respect, as you can see on the right side of Table 20.3. (The two companies' current stock prices just happen to be the same.) The only difference is that Digital Organics' stock is half again as volatile as Establishment Industries' stock (36 percent annual standard deviation vs. 24 percent for Establishment Industries).

If your job choice hinges on the value of the executive stock options, you should take the Digital Organics offer. The Digital Organics options are written on the more volatile asset and therefore are worth more. We will value the two stock-option packages in the next chapter.

Asset Risk and Equity Values   In Section 18.3, we asserted that:

Financial managers who act strictly in their shareholders' interests (and against the interests of creditors) will favor risky projects over safe ones.

TABLE 20.3

Which package of executive stock options would you choose? The package offered by Digital Organics is more valuable, because the volatility of that company's stock is higher.

	Establishment Industries	Digital Organics
Number of options	100,000	100,000
Exercise price	$25	$25
Maturity	5 years	5 years
Current stock price	$22	$22
Stock price volatility (standard deviation of return)	24%	36%

Now you can see why this statement is generally true. Common stock is a call option written on the firm's assets, and like all call options, its value depends on the risk of the underlying asset. If the financial manager can swap a risky asset for a safe one—holding everything else, including the value of the firm's assets, constant—then the value of the firm's common stock increases and shareholders are better off.[16]

There is, of course, an offsetting decrease in the value of the firm's debt. The debtholders have given up a default put. The riskier the firm's assets, the more that put is worth. Since the put value is subtracted from the default-free value of the debt, increased risk makes the debtholders worse off.

Although the assertion from Chapter 18 is generally true, it is not important for established, blue-chip companies where the odds of default are miniscule. For example, the value of the default put on Exxon Mobil's debt is trivial. But there are always companies, even large companies, in financial distress. Financial distress means that the odds of default are *not* trivial, that the default put is valuable, and that increased asset risk benefits shareholders.

---

[16]In this context, risk means all sources of uncertainty, not just market risk. Option prices depend on the standard deviation or variance of returns, not just on beta. You'll see this more explicitly in the next chapter.

ƒUMMARY

If you have managed to reach this point, you are probably in need of a rest and a stiff gin and tonic. So we will summarize what we have learned so far and take up the subject of options again in the next chapter when you are rested (or drunk).

There are two types of option. An American call is an option to buy an asset at a specified exercise price on or before a specified exercise date. Similarly, an American put is an option to sell the asset at a specified price on or before a specified date. European calls and puts are exactly the same except that they cannot be exercised before the specified exercise date. Calls and puts are the basic building blocks that can be combined to give any pattern of payoffs.

What determines the value of a call option? Common sense tells us that it ought to depend on three things:

1. To exercise an option you have to pay the exercise price. Other things being equal, the less you are obliged to pay, the better. Therefore, the value of an option increases with the ratio of the asset price to the exercise price.

2. You do not have to pay the exercise price until you decide to exercise the option. Therefore, an option gives you a free loan. The higher the rate of interest and the longer the time to maturity, the more this free loan is worth. Therefore the value of an option increases with the interest rate and time to maturity.

3. If the price of the asset falls short of the exercise price, you won't exercise the option. You will, therefore, lose 100 percent of your investment in the option no matter how far the asset depreciates below the exercise price. On the other hand, the more the price rises *above* the exercise price, the more profit you will make. Therefore the option holder does not lose from increased volatility if things go wrong, but gains if they go right. The value of an option increases with the variance per period of the stock return multiplied by the number of periods to maturity.

Always remember that an option written on a risky (high-variance) asset is worth more than an option on a safe asset. It's easy to forget, because in most other financial contexts increases in risk reduce present value.

FURTHER READING

The classic articles on option valuation are:

F. Black and M. Scholes: "The Pricing of Options and Corporate Liabilities," *Journal of Political Economy*, 81:637–654 (May–June 1973).

R. C. Merton: "Theory of Rational Option Pricing," *Bell Journal of Economics and Management Science*, 4:141–183 (Spring 1973).

There are also a number of good texts on option valuation. They include:

J. Hull: *Options, Futures and Other Derivatives*, 5th ed., Prentice-Hall, Inc., Englewood Cliffs, NJ, 2003.

R. Jarrow and S. Turnbull: *Derivative Securities*, 2nd ed., South-Western College Publishing, Cincinnati, OH, 1999.

M. Rubinstein: *Derivatives: A PowerPlus Picture Book*, 1998.[17]

---

[17]This book is published by the author and is listed on **www.in-the-money.com**.

QUIZ

1. Complete the following passage:

   A ____ option gives its owner the opportunity to buy a stock at a specified price which is generally called the ____ price. A ____ option gives its owner the opportunity to sell stock at a specified price. Options that can be exercised only at maturity are called ____ options.

   The common stock of firms that borrow is a ____ option. Stockholders effectively sell the firm's ____ to ____ , but retain the option to buy the ____ back. The exercise price is the ____.

2. Note Figure 20.13. Match each diagram, (*a*) and (*b*), with one of the following positions:
   - Call buyer
   - Call seller
   - Put buyer
   - Put seller

FIGURE 20.13

See Quiz question 2.

(a)   (b)

3. Suppose that you hold a share of stock and a put option on that share. What is the pay-off when the option expires if **(a)** the stock price is below the exercise price? **(b)** the stock price is above the exercise price?

4. What is put–call parity and why does it hold? Could you apply the parity formula to a call and put with different exercise prices?

5. There is another strategy involving calls and borrowing and lending that gives the same payoffs as the strategy described in question 3. What is the alternative strategy?

6. Dr. Livingstone I. Presume holds £600,000 in East African gold stocks. Bullish as he is on gold mining, he requires absolute assurance that at least £500,000 will be available in six months to fund an expedition. Describe two ways for Dr. Presume to achieve this goal. There is an active market for puts and calls on East African gold stocks, and the rate of interest is 6 percent per year.

7. Suppose you buy a one-year European call option on Wombat stock with an exercise price of $100 and sell a one-year European put option with the same exercise price. The current stock price is $100, and the interest rate is 10 percent.
   a. Draw a position diagram showing the payoffs from your investments.
   b. How much will the combined position cost you? Explain.

8. Explain why the common stock of a firm that borrows is a call option. What is the underlying asset? What is the exercise price?

9. What does "default put" mean? When are default puts most important?

10. What is the lower bound to the price of a call option? If the price of a European call option were below the lower bound, how could you make a sure-fire profit? What is the upper bound to the price of a call option?

11. Look again at Figure 20.13. It appears that the call buyer in panel **(b)** can't lose and the call seller in panel **(a)** can't win. Is that correct? Explain. *Hint:* Draw a profit diagram for each panel.

12. What is a call option worth if **(a)** the stock price is zero? **(b)** the stock price is extremely high relative to the exercise price?

13. How does the price of a call option respond to the following changes, other things equal? Does the call price go up or down?
   a. Stock price increases.
   b. Exercise price is increased.
   c. Risk-free rate increases.
   d. Expiration date of the option is extended.

e. Volatility of the stock price falls.

f. Time passes, so the option's expiration date comes closer.

14. Respond to the following statements.
    a. "I'm a conservative investor. I'd much rather hold a call option on a safe stock like Exxon Mobil than a volatile stock like AOL Time Warner."
    b. "When a company lands in financial distress, stockholders are better off if the financial manager shifts to safer assets and operating strategies."

PRACTICE QUESTIONS

1. In everyday speech the term *option* often just means "choice," whereas in finance it refers specifically to the right to buy or sell an asset in the future on terms that are fixed today. Which of the following are the odd statements out? Are the options involved in the other statements puts or calls?
    a. "The preferred stockholders in Chrysalis Motors have the option to redeem their shares at par value after 2009."
    b. "What I like about Toit à Porcs is its large wine list. You have the option to choose from over 100 wines."
    c. "I don't have to buy IBM stock now. I have the option to wait and see if the stock price goes lower over the next month or two."
    d. "By constructing an assembly plant in Mexico, Chrysalis Motors gave itself the option to switch a substantial proportion of its production to that country if the dollar should appreciate in the future."

2. Discuss briefly the risks and payoffs of the following positions:
    a. Buy stock and a put option on the stock.
    b. Buy stock.
    c. Buy call.
    d. Buy stock and sell call option on the stock.
    e. Buy bond.
    f. Buy stock, buy put, and sell call.
    g. Sell put.

3. "The buyer of the call and the seller of the put both hope that the stock price will rise. Therefore the two positions are identical." Is the speaker correct? Illustrate with a position diagram.

4. Pintail's stock price is currently $200. A one-year *American* call option has an exercise price of $50 and is priced at $75. How would you take advantage of this great opportunity? Now suppose the option is a *European* call. What would you do?

5. It is possible to buy three-month call options and three-month puts on stock Q. Both options have an exercise price for $60 and both are worth $10. Is a six-month call with an exercise price of $60 more or less valuable than a similar six-month put? *Hint:* Use put–call parity.

6. In June 2001 a six-month call on Intel stock, with an exercise price of $22.50, sold for $2.30. The stock price was $27.27. The risk-free interest rate was 3.9 percent. How much would you be willing to pay for a put on Intel stock with the same maturity and exercise price?

7. Go to the Chicago Board Options Exchange website at **www.cboe.com.** Check out the delayed quotes for AOL Time Warner for different exercise prices and maturities.
    a. Confirm that higher exercise prices mean lower call prices and higher put prices.
    b. Confirm that longer maturity means higher prices for both puts and calls.
    c. Choose an AOL put and call with the same exercise price and maturity. Confirm that put–call parity holds (approximately). *Note:* You will have to use an up-to-date risk-free interest rate.

8. The Rank and File Company is considering a rights issue to raise $50 million (see Chapter 15 Appendix A). An underwriter offers to "stand by" (i.e., to guarantee the success of the issue by buying any unwanted stock at the issue price). The underwriter's fee is $2 million.
   a. What kind of option does Rank and File acquire if it accepts the underwriter's offer?
   b. What determines the value of the option?

9. FX Bank has succeeded in hiring ace foreign exchange trader, Lucinda Cable. Her remuneration package reportedly includes an annual bonus of 20 percent of the profits that she generates in excess of $100 million. Does Ms. Cable have an option? Does it provide her with the appropriate incentives?

10. Suppose that Mr. Colleoni borrows the present value of $100, buys a six-month put option on stock Y with an exercise price of $150, and sells a six-month put option on Y with an exercise price of $50.
    a. Draw a position diagram showing the payoffs when the options expire.
    b. Suggest two other combinations of loans, options, and the underlying stock that would give Mr. Colleoni the same payoffs.

11. Which *one* of the following statements is correct?
    a. Value of put + present value of exercise price = value of call + share price.
    b. Value of put + share price = value of call + present value of exercise price.
    c. Value of put − share price = present value of exercise price − value of call.
    d. Value of put + value of call = share price − present value of exercise price.

    The correct statement equates the value of two investment strategies. Plot the payoffs to each strategy as a function of the stock price. Show that the two strategies give identical payoffs.

12. Test the formula linking put and call prices by using it to explain the relative prices of traded puts and calls. (Note that the formula is exact only for European options. Most traded puts and calls are American.)

13. a. If you can't sell a share short, you can achieve exactly the same final payoff by a combination of options and borrowing or lending. What is this combination?
    b. Now work out the mixture of stock and options that gives the same final payoff as a risk-free loan.

14. The common stock of Triangular File Company is selling at $90. A 26-week call option written on Triangular File's stock is selling for $8. The call's exercise price is $100. The risk-free interest rate is 10 percent per year.
    a. Suppose that puts on Triangular stock are not traded, but you want to buy one. How would you do it?
    b. Suppose that puts *are* traded. What should a 26-week put with an exercise price of $100 sell for?

15. Digital Organics has 10 million outstanding shares trading at $25 per share. It also has a large amount of debt outstanding, all coming due in one year. The debt pays interest at 8 percent. It has a par (face) value of $350 million, but is trading at a market value of only $280 million. The one-year risk-free interest rate is 6 percent.
    a. Write out the put–call parity formula for Digital Organics' stock, debt, and assets.
    b. What is the value of the default put given up by Digital Organics' creditors?

16. Option traders often refer to "straddles" and "butterflies." Here is an example of each:
    • *Straddle:* Buy call with exercise price of $100 and simultaneously buy put with exercise price of $100.
    • *Butterfly:* Simultaneously buy one call with exercise price of $100, sell two calls with exercise price of $110, and buy one call with exercise price of $120.

Draw position diagrams for the straddle and butterfly, showing the payoffs from the investor's net position. Each strategy is a bet on variability. Explain briefly the nature of each bet.

17. Refer again to the Circular File balance sheet in Section 20.2. Suppose that the government suddenly offers to guarantee the $50 principal payment due bondholders next year and also to guarantee the interest payment. (In other words, if firm value falls short of the promised payments, the government will make up the difference.) This offer is a complete surprise to everyone. The government asks nothing in return, and so its offer is cheerfully accepted.
    a. Suppose that the promised interest rate on Circular's debt is 10 percent. The rate on one-year United States government notes is 8 percent. How will the guarantee affect bond value?
    b. The guarantee does *not* affect the value of Circular stock. Why? (*Note:* There could be some effect if the guarantee allows Circular to avoid costs of financial distress or bankruptcy. See Section 18.3.)
    c. How will the value of the firm (debt plus equity) change?

    Now suppose that the government offers the same guarantee for *new* debt issued by *Rectangular* File Company. Rectangular's assets are identical to Circular's, but Rectangular has no existing debt. Rectangular accepts the offer and uses the proceeds of a $50 debt issue to repurchase or retire stock.
    Will Rectangular stockholders gain from the opportunity to issue the guaranteed debt? By how much, approximately? (Ignore taxes.)

18. Look at actual trading prices of call options on stocks to check whether they behave as the theory presented in this chapter predicts. For example,
    a. Follow several options as they approach maturity. How would you expect their prices to behave? Do they actually behave that way?
    b. Compare two call options written on the same stock with the same maturity but different exercise prices.
    c. Compare two call options written on the same stock with the same exercise price but different maturities.

19. Is it more valuable to own an option to buy a portfolio of stocks or to own a portfolio of options to buy each of the individual stocks? Say briefly why.

20. Table 20.4 lists some prices of options on common stocks (prices are quoted to the nearest dollar). The interest rate is 10 percent a year. Can you spot any mispricing? What would you do to take advantage of it?

21. As manager of United Bedstead you own substantial executive stock options. These entitle you to buy the firm's shares during the next five years at a price of $100 a share. The plant manager has just outlined two alternative proposals to reequip the plant. Both proposals have the same net present value, but one is substantially riskier than the other. At first you are undecided about which to choose, but then you remember your stock options. How might these influence your choice?

TABLE 20.4

Prices of options on common stocks (in dollars). See Practice Question 20.

Stock	Time to Exercise (months)	Exercise Price	Stock Price	Put Price	Call Price
Drongo Corp.	6	50	80	20	52
Ragwort, Inc.	6	100	80	10	15
Wombat Corp.	3	40	50	7	18
	6	40	50	5	17
	6	50	50	8	10

22. You've just completed a month-long study of energy markets and conclude that energy prices will be *much* more volatile in the next year than historically. Assuming you're right, what types of option strategies should you undertake? *Note:* You can buy or sell options on oil-company stocks or on the price of future deliveries of crude oil, natural gas, fuel oil, etc.

CHALLENGE QUESTIONS

1. Figure 20.14 shows some complicated position diagrams. Work out the combination of stocks, bonds, and options that produces each of these positions.

2. In 1988 the Australian firm Bond Corporation sold a share in some land that it owned near Rome for $110 million and as a result boosted its 1988 earnings by $74 million. In 1989 a television program revealed that the buyer was given a put option to sell its share in the land back to Bond for $110 million and that Bond had paid $20 million for a call option to repurchase the share in the land for the same price.[18]
   a. What happens if the land is worth more than $110 million when the options expire? What if it is worth less than $110 million?
   b. Use position diagrams to show the net effect of the land sale and the option transactions.
   c. Assume a one-year maturity on the options. Can you deduce the interest rate?
   d. The television program argued that it was misleading to record a profit on the sale of land. What do you think?

3. Three six-month call options are traded on Hogswill stock:

Exercise Price	Call Option Price
$ 90	$ 5
100	11
110	15

FIGURE 20.14

Some complicated position diagrams. See Challenge Question 1.

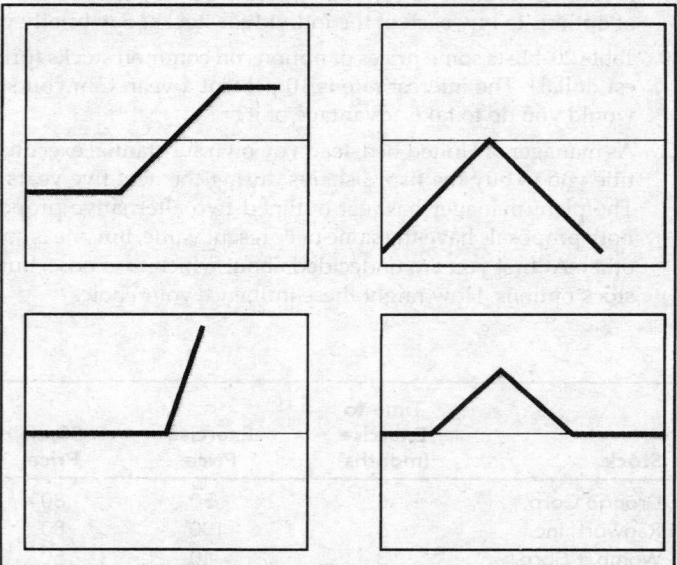

---

[18]See *Sydney Morning Herald*, March 14, 1989, p. 27. The options were subsequently renegotiated.

How would you make money by trading in Hogswill options? (*Hint:* Draw a graph with the option price on the vertical axis and the ratio of stock price to exercise price on the horizontal axis. Plot the three Hogswill options on your graph. Does this fit with what you know about how option prices should vary with the ratio of stock price to exercise price?) Now look in the newspaper at options with the same maturity but different exercise prices. Can you find any money-making opportunities?

4. Ms. Higden has been offered yet another incentive scheme (see Section 20.2). She will receive a bonus of $500,000 if the stock price at the end of the year is $120 or more; otherwise she will receive nothing.

   a. Draw a position diagram illustrating the payoffs from such a scheme.
   b. What combination of options would provide these payoffs? (*Hint:* You need to buy a large number of options with one exercise price and sell a similar number with a different exercise price.)

CHAPTER TWENTY-ONE

VALUING OPTIONS

IN THE LAST chapter we introduced you to call and put options. Call options give the owner the right to buy an asset at a specified exercise price; put options give the right to sell. We also took the first step toward understanding how options are valued. The value of a call option depends on five variables:

1. The higher the price of the asset, the more valuable an option to buy it.
2. The lower the price that you must pay to exercise the call, the more valuable the option.
3. You do not need to pay the exercise price until the option expires. This delay is most valuable when the interest rate is high.
4. If the stock price is *below* the exercise price at maturity, the call is valueless regardless of whether the price is $1 below or $100 below. However, for every dollar that the stock price rises *above* the exercise price, the option holder gains an additional dollar. Thus, the value of the call option increases with the volatility of the stock price.
5. Finally, a long-term option is more valuable than a short-term option. A distant maturity delays the point at which the holder needs to pay the exercise price and increases the chance of a large jump in the stock price before the option matures.

In this chapter we show how these variables can be combined into an exact option-valuation model—a formula we can plug numbers into to get a definite answer. We first describe a simple way to value options, known as the binomial model. We then introduce the Black–Scholes formula for valuing options. Finally, we provide a checklist showing how these two methods can be used to solve a number of practical option problems.

The only feasible way to value most options is to use a computer. But in this chapter we will work through some simple examples by hand. We do so because unless you understand the basic principles behind option valuation, you are likely to make mistakes in setting up an option problem and you won't know how to interpret the computer's answer and explain it to others.

In the last chapter we introduced you to the put and call options on AOL stock. In this chapter we will stick with that example and show you how to value the AOL options. But remember *why* you need to understand option valuation. It is not to make a quick buck trading on an options exchange. It is because many capital budgeting and financing decisions have options embedded in them. We will discuss a variety of these options in subsequent chapters.

 ## 21.1 A SIMPLE OPTION-VALUATION MODEL

Why Discounted Cash Flow Won't Work for Options

For many years economists searched for a practical formula to value options until Fisher Black and Myron Scholes finally hit upon the solution. Later we will show you what they found, but first we should explain why the search was so difficult.

Our standard procedure for valuing an asset is to (1) figure out expected cash flows and (2) discount them at the opportunity cost of capital. Unfortunately, this is not practical for options. The first step is messy but feasible, but finding *the* opportunity cost of capital is impossible, because the risk of an option changes every time the stock price moves,[1] and we know it *will* move along a random walk through the option's lifetime.

---

[1] It also changes over time even with the stock price constant.

When you buy a call, you are taking a position in the stock but putting up less of your own money than if you had bought the stock directly. Thus, an option is always riskier than the underlying stock. It has a higher beta and a higher standard deviation of return.

How much riskier the option is depends on the stock price relative to the exercise price. A call option that is in the money (stock price greater than exercise price) is safer than one that is out of the money (stock price less than exercise price). Thus a stock price increase raises the option's price *and* reduces its risk. When the stock price falls, the option's price falls *and* its risk increases. That is why the expected rate of return investors demand from an option changes day by day, or hour by hour, every time the stock price moves.

We repeat the general rule: The higher the stock price is relative to the exercise price, the safer is the call option, although the option is always riskier than the stock. The option's risk changes every time the stock price changes.

Constructing Option Equivalents from Common Stocks and Borrowing

If you've digested what we've said so far, you can appreciate why options are hard to value by standard discounted-cash-flow formulas and why a rigorous option-valuation technique eluded economists for many years. The breakthrough came when Black and Scholes exclaimed, "Eureka! We have found it![2] The trick is to set up an *option equivalent* by combining common stock investment and borrowing. The net cost of buying the option equivalent must equal the value of the option."

We'll show you how this works with a simple numerical example. We'll travel back to the end of June 2001 and consider a six-month call option on AOL Time Warner (AOL) stock with an exercise price of $55. We'll pick a day when AOL stock was also trading at $55, so that this option is *at the money*. The short-term, risk-free interest rate was a bit less than 4 percent per year, or about 2 percent for six months.

To keep the example as simple as possible, we assume that AOL stock can do only two things over the option's six-month life: either the price will fall by a quarter to $41.25 or rise by one-third to $73.33.

If AOL's stock price falls to $41.25, the call option will be worthless, but if the price rises to $73.33, the option will be worth $73.33 − 55 = $18.33. The possible payoffs to the option are therefore

	Stock Price = $41.25	Stock Price = $73.33
1 call option	$0	$18.33

Now compare these payoffs with what you would get if you bought .5714 AOL shares and borrowed $23.11 from the bank:[3]

	Stock Price = $41.25	Stock Price = $73.33
.5714 shares	$23.57	$41.90
Repayment of loan + interest	−23.57	−23.57
Total payoff	$ 0	$18.33

---

[2]We do not know whether Black and Scholes, like Archimedes, were sitting in bathtubs at the time.

[3]The amount that you need to borrow from the bank is simply the present value of the difference between the payoffs from the option and the payoffs from the .5714 shares. In our example, amount borrowed = $(55 − .5714 \times 55)/1.02 = \$23.11$.

Notice that the payoffs from the levered investment in the stock are identical to the payoffs from the call option. Therefore, both investments must have the same value:

$$\text{Value of call} = \text{value of .5714 shares} - \$23.11 \text{ bank loan}$$
$$= (55 \times .5714) - 23.11 = \$8.32$$

Presto! You've valued a call option.

To value the AOL option, we borrowed money and bought stock in such a way that we exactly replicated the payoff from a call option. This is called a **replicating portfolio.** The number of shares needed to replicate one call is called the **hedge ratio** or **option delta.** In our AOL example one call is replicated by a levered position in .5714 shares. The option delta is, therefore, .5714.

How did we know that AOL's call option was equivalent to a levered position in .5714 shares? We used a simple formula that says

$$\text{Option delta} = \frac{\text{spread of possible option prices}}{\text{spread of possible share prices}} = \frac{18.33 - 0}{73.33 - 41.25} = .5714$$

You have learned not only to value a simple option but also that you can replicate an investment in the option by a levered investment in the underlying asset. Thus, if you can't buy or sell an option on an asset, you can create a homemade option by a replicating strategy—that is, you buy or sell delta shares and borrow or lend the balance.

Risk-Neutral Valuation   Notice why the AOL call option should sell for $8.32. If the option price is higher than $8.32, you could make a certain profit by buying .5714 shares of stock, selling a call option, and borrowing $23.11. Similarly, if the option price is less than $8.32, you could make an equally certain profit by selling .5714 shares, buying a call, and lending the balance. In either case there would be a money machine.[4]

If there's a money machine, everyone scurries to take advantage of it. So when we said that the option price had to be $8.32 (or there would be a money machine), we did not have to know anything about investor attitudes to risk. The option price cannot depend on whether investors detest risk or do not care a jot.

This suggests an alternative way to value the option. We can *pretend* that all investors are *indifferent* about risk, work out the expected future value of the option in such a world, and discount it back at the risk-free interest rate to give the current value. Let us check that this method gives the same answer.

If investors are indifferent to risk, the expected return on the stock must be equal to the risk-free rate of interest:

$$\text{Expected return on AOL stock} = 2.0\% \text{ per six months}$$

We know that AOL stock can either rise by 33 percent to $73.33 or fall by 25 percent to $41.25. We can, therefore, calculate the probability of a price rise in our hypothetical risk-neutral world:

$$\text{Expected return} = [\text{probability of rise} \times 33]$$
$$+ [(1 - \text{probability of rise}) \times (-25)]$$
$$= 2.0 \text{ percent}$$

---

[4]Of course, you don't get seriously rich by dealing in .5714 shares. But if you multiply each of our transactions by a million, it begins to look like real money.

Therefore,[5]

$$\text{Probability of rise} = .463, \text{ or } 46.3\%$$

Notice that this is not the *true* probability that AOL stock will rise. Since investors dislike risk, they will almost surely require a higher expected return than the risk-free interest rate from AOL stock. Therefore the true probability is greater than .463.

We know that if the stock price rises, the call option will be worth $18.33; if it falls, the call will be worth nothing. Therefore, if investors are risk-neutral, the expected value of the call option is

$$[\text{Probability of rise} \times 18.33] + [(1 - \text{probability of rise}) \times 0]$$
$$= (.463 \times 18.33) + (.537 \times 0)$$
$$= \$8.49$$

And the current value of the call is

$$\frac{\text{Expected future value}}{1 + \text{interest rate}} = \frac{8.49}{1.02} = \$8.32$$

Exactly the same answer that we got earlier!

We now have two ways to calculate the value of an option:

1. Find the combination of stock and loan that replicates an investment in the option. Since the two strategies give identical payoffs in the future, they must sell for the same price today.
2. Pretend that investors do not care about risk, so that the expected return on the stock is equal to the interest rate. Calculate the expected future value of the option in this hypothetical *risk-neutral* world and discount it at the risk-free interest rate.[6]

Valuing the AOL Put Option

Valuing the AOL call option may well have seemed like pulling a rabbit out of a hat. To give you a second chance to watch how it is done, we will use the same method to value another option—this time, the six-month AOL put option with a $55 exercise price.[7] We continue to assume that the stock price will either rise to $73.33 or fall to $41.25.

---

[5]The general formula for calculating the risk-neutral probability of a rise in value is

$$p = \frac{\text{interest rate} - \text{downside change}}{\text{upside change} - \text{downside change}}$$

In the case of AOL stock

$$p = \frac{.02 - (-.25)}{.33 - (-.25)} = .463$$

[6]In Chapter 9 we showed how you can value an investment either by discounting the expected cash flows at a risk-adjusted discount rate or by adjusting the expected cash flows for risk and then discounting these *certainty-equivalent* flows at the risk-free interest rate. We have just used this second method to value the AOL option. The certainty-equivalent cash flows on the stock and option are the cash flows that would be expected in a risk-neutral world.

[7]When valuing *American* put options, you need to recognize the possibility that it will pay to exercise early. We discuss this complication later in the chapter, but it is not relevant for valuing the AOL put and we ignore it here.

If AOL's stock price rises to $73.33, the option to sell for $55 will be worthless. If the price falls to $41.25, the put option will be worth $55 − 41.25 = $13.75. Thus the payoffs to the put are

	Stock Price = $41.25	Stock Price = $73.33
1 put option	$13.75	$0

We start by calculating the option delta using the formula that we presented above:[8]

$$\text{Option delta} = \frac{\text{spread of possible option prices}}{\text{spread of possible stock prices}} = \frac{0 - 13.75}{73.33 - 41.25} = -.4286$$

Notice that the delta of a put option is always negative; that is, you need to *sell* delta shares of stock to replicate the put. In the case of the AOL put you can replicate the option payoffs by *selling* .4286 AOL shares and *lending* $30.81. Since you have sold the share short, you will need to lay out money at the end of six months to buy it back, but you will have money coming in from the loan. Your net payoffs are exactly the same as the payoffs you would get if you bought the put option:

	Stock Price = $41.25	Stock Price = $73.33
Sale of .4286 shares	−$17.68	−$31.43
Repayment of loan + interest	+31.43	+31.43
Total payoff	$13.75	$ 0

Since the two investments have the same payoffs, they must have the same value:

$$\text{Value of put} = -.4286 \text{ shares} + \$30.81 \text{ bank loan}$$
$$= -(.4286 \times 55) + 30.81 = \$7.24$$

Valuing the Put Option by the Risk-Neutral Method   Valuing the AOL put option with the risk-neutral method is a cinch. We already know that the probability of a rise in the stock price is .463. Therefore the expected value of the put option in a risk-neutral world is

$$[\text{Probability of rise} \times 0] + [(1 - \text{probability of rise}) \times 13.75]$$
$$= (.463 \times 0) + (.537 \times 13.75)$$
$$= \$7.38$$

And therefore the current value of the put is

$$\frac{\text{Expected future value}}{1 + \text{interest rate}} = \frac{7.38}{1.02} = \$7.24$$

The Relationship between Call and Put Prices   We pointed out earlier that for European options there is a simple relationship between the value of the call and that of the put:[9]

Value of put = value of call − share price + present value of exercise price

---

[8]The delta of a put option is always equal to the delta of a call option with the same exercise price minus one. In our example, delta of put = .5714 − 1 = −.4286.

[9]*Reminder:* This formula applies only when the two options have the same exercise price and exercise date.

Since we had already calculated the value of the AOL call, we could also have used this relationship to find the value of the put:

$$\text{Value of put} = 8.32 - 55 + \frac{55}{1.02} = \$7.24$$

Everything checks.

21.2 THE BINOMIAL METHOD FOR VALUING OPTIONS

The essential trick in pricing any option is to set up a package of investments in the stock and the loan that will exactly replicate the payoffs from the option. If we can price the stock and the loan, then we can also price the option. Equivalently, we can pretend that investors are risk-neutral, calculate the expected payoff on the option in this fictitious risk-neutral world, and discount by the rate of interest to find the option's present value.

These *concepts* are completely general, but there are several ways to find the replicating package of investments. The example in the last section used a simplified version of what is known as the **binomial method.** The method starts by reducing the possible changes in next period's stock price to two, an "up" move and a "down" move. This simplification is OK if the time period is very short, so that a large number of small moves is accumulated over the life of the option. But it was fanciful to assume just two possible prices for AOL stock at the end of six months.

We could make the AOL problem a trifle more realistic by assuming that there are two possible price changes in each three-month period. This would give a wider variety of six-month prices. And there is no reason to stop at three-month periods. We could go on to take shorter and shorter intervals, with each interval showing two possible changes in AOL's stock price and giving an even wider selection of six-month prices.

This is illustrated in Figure 21.1. The two left-hand diagrams show our starting assumption: just two possible prices at the end of six months. Moving to the right, you can see what happens when there are two possible price changes every three months. This gives three possible stock prices when the option matures. In Figure 21.1(c) we have gone on to divide the six-month period into 26 weekly periods, in each of which the price can make one of two small moves. The distribution of prices at the end of six months is now looking much more realistic.

We could continue in this way to chop the period into shorter and shorter intervals, until eventually we would reach a situation in which the stock price is changing continuously and there is a continuum of possible future stock prices.

Example: The Two-Stage Binomial Method

Dividing the period into shorter intervals doesn't alter the basic method for valuing a call option. We can still replicate the call by a levered investment in the stock, but we need to adjust the degree of leverage at each stage. We will demonstrate first with our simple two-stage case in Figure 21.1 (b). Then we will work up to the situation where the stock price is changing continuously.

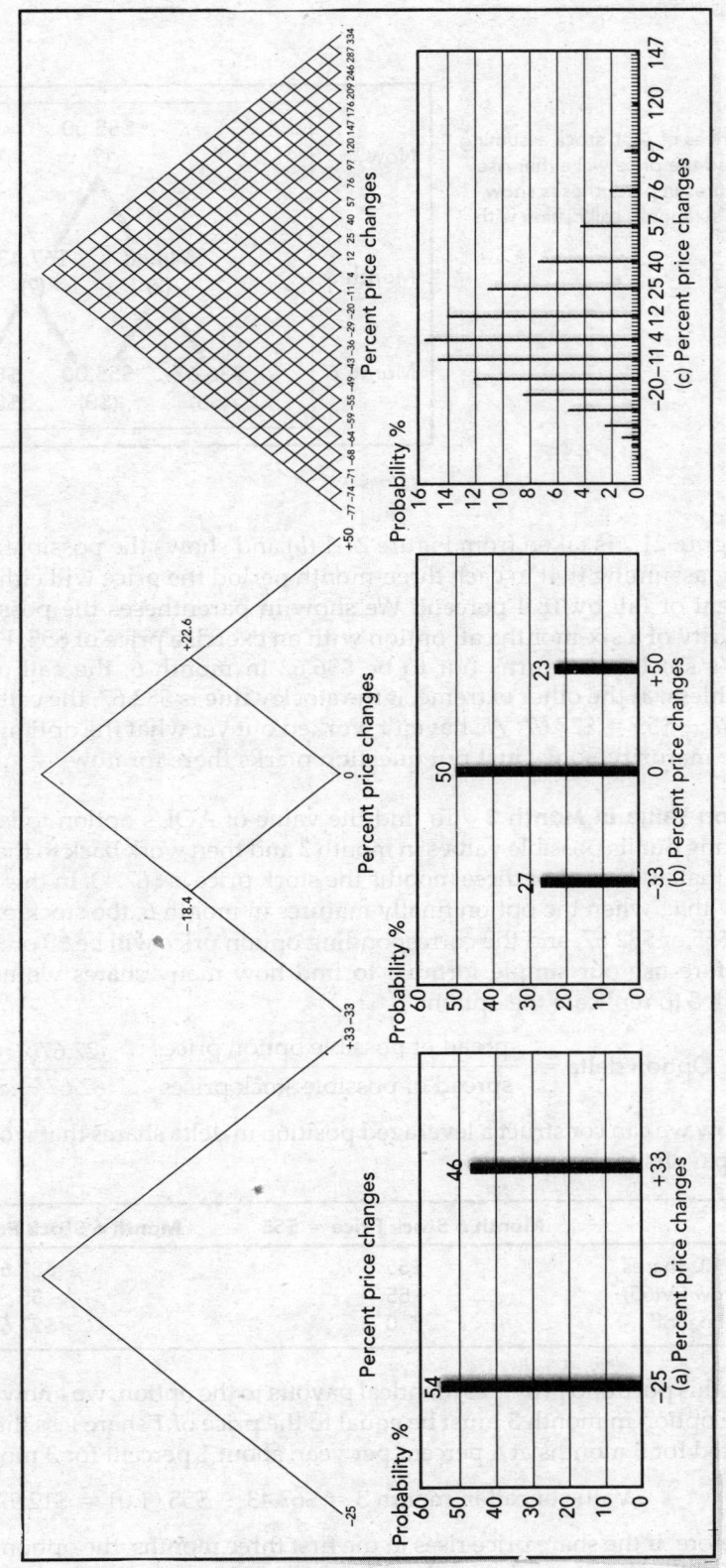

FIGURE 21.1

This figure shows the possible six-month price changes for AOL stock assuming that the stock makes a single up or down move each six months [Fig. 21.1(a)], each three months [Fig. 21.1(b)], or each week [Fig. 21.1(c)]. Beneath each tree we show a histogram of the possible six-month price changes, assuming investors are risk-neutral.

FIGURE 21.2

Present and possible future prices of AOL stock assuming that in each three-month period the price will either rise by 22.6% or fall by 18.4%. Figures in parentheses show the corresponding values of a six-month call option with an exercise price of $55.

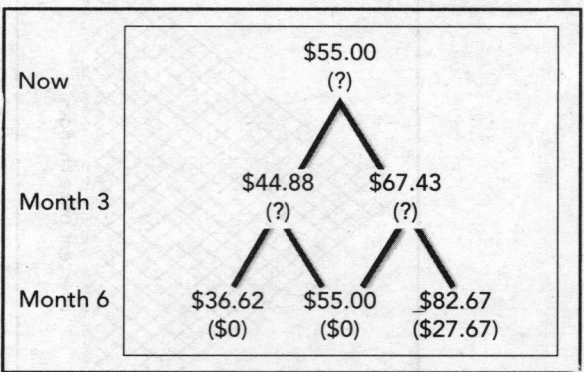

Figure 21.2 is taken from Figure 21.1 (*b*) and shows the possible prices of AOL stock, assuming that in each three-month period the price will either rise by 22.6 percent or fall by 18.4 percent. We show in parentheses the possible values at maturity of a six-month call option with an exercise price of $55. For example, if AOL's stock price turns out to be $36.62 in month 6, the call option will be worthless; at the other extreme, if the stock value is $82.67, the call will be worth $82.67 − $55 = $27.67. We haven't worked out yet what the option will be worth *before* maturity, so we just put question marks there for now.

Option Value in Month 3   To find the value of AOL's option today, we start by working out its possible values in month 3 and then work back to the present. Suppose that at the end of three months the stock price is $67.43. In this case investors know that, when the option finally matures in month 6, the stock price will be either $55 or $82.67, and the corresponding option price will be $0 or $27.67. We can therefore use our simple formula to find how many shares we need to buy in month 3 to replicate the option:

$$\text{Option delta} = \frac{\text{spread of possible option prices}}{\text{spread of possible stock prices}} = \frac{27.67 - 0}{82.67 - 55} = 1.0$$

Now we can construct a leveraged position in delta shares that would give identical payoffs to the option:

	Month 6 Stock Price = $55	Month 6 Stock Price = $82.67
Buy 1.0 shares	$55	$82.67
Borrow PV(55)	−55	−55
Total payoff	$ 0	$27.67

Since this portfolio provides identical payoffs to the option, we know that the value of the option in month 3 must be equal to the price of 1 share less the $55 loan discounted for 3 months at 4 percent per year, about 1 percent for 3 months:

$$\text{Value of call in month 3} = \$67.43 - \$55/1.01 = \$12.97$$

Therefore, if the share price rises in the first three months, the option will be worth $12.97. But what if the share price falls to $44.88? In that case the most that you can

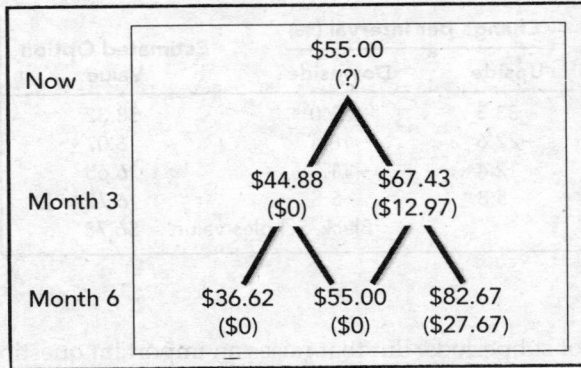

FIGURE 21.3

Present and possible future prices of AOL stock. Figures in parentheses show the corresponding values of a six-month call option with an exercise price of $55.

hope for is that the share price will recover to $55. Therefore the option is bound to be worthless when it matures and must be worthless at month 3.

Option Value Today   We can now get rid of two of the question marks in Figure 21.2. Figure 21.3 shows that if the stock price in month 3 is $67.43, the option value is $12.97 and, if the stock price is $44.88, the option value is zero. It only remains to work back to the option value today.

We again begin by calculating the option delta:

$$\text{Option delta} = \frac{\text{spread of possible option prices}}{\text{spread of possible stock prices}} = \frac{12.97 - 0}{67.43 - 44.88} = .575$$

We can now find the leveraged position in delta shares that would give identical payoffs to the option:

	Month 3 Stock Price = $44.88	Month 3 Stock Price = $67.43
Buy .575 shares	$25.81	$38.78
Borrow PV(25.81)	−25.81	−25.81
Total payoff	$ 0	$12.97

The value of the AOL option today is equal to the value of this leveraged position:

$$\text{PV option} = \text{PV}(.575 \text{ shares}) - \text{PV}(\$25.81)$$

$$= .575 \times \$55 - \frac{\$25.81}{1.01} = \$6.07$$

The General Binomial Method

Moving to two steps when valuing the AOL call probably added extra realism. But there is no reason to stop there. We could go on, as in Figure 21.1, to chop the period into smaller and smaller intervals. We could still use the binomial method to work back from the final date to the present. Of course, it would be tedious to do the calculations by hand, but simple to do so with a computer.

Since a stock can usually take on an almost limitless number of future values, the binomial method gives a more realistic and accurate measure of the option's value if

TABLE 21.1

As the number of intervals is increased, you must adjust the range of possible changes in the value of the asset to keep the same standard deviation. But you will get increasingly close to the Black–Scholes value of the AOL call option.

Note: The standard deviation is σ = .4069.

Intervals in a Year (1/h)	Change per Interval (%)		Estimated Option Value
	Upside	Downside	
2	+33.3	−25.0	$8.32
4	+22.6	−18.4	6.07
12	+12.4	−11.1	6.65
52	+5.8	−5.5	6.75
		Black–Scholes value =	$6.78

we work with a large number of subperiods. But that raises an important question. How do we pick sensible figures for the up and down changes in value? For example, why did we pick figures of +22.6 percent and −18.4 percent when we revalued AOL's option with two subperiods? Fortunately, there is a neat little formula that relates the up and down changes to the standard deviation of stock returns:

$$1 + \text{upside change} = u = e^{\sigma\sqrt{h}}$$
$$1 + \text{downside change} = d = 1/u$$

where

e = base for natural logarithms = 2.718

σ = standard deviation of (continuously compounded) stock returns

h = interval as fraction of a year

When we said that AOL's stock could either rise by 33.3 percent or fall by 25 percent over six months ($h = .5$), our figures were consistent with a figure of 40.69 percent for the standard deviation of annual returns:

$$1 + \text{upside change (6-month interval)} = u = e^{.4069\sqrt{.5}} = 1.333$$
$$1 + \text{downside change} = d = 1/u = 1/1.333 = .75$$

To work out the equivalent upside and downside changes when we divide the period into two three-month intervals ($h = .25$), we use the same formula:

$$1 + \text{upside change (3-month interval)} = u = e^{.4069\sqrt{.25}} = 1.226$$
$$1 + \text{downside change} = d = 1/u = 1/1.226 = .816$$

The center columns in Table 21.1 show the equivalent up and down moves in the value of the firm if we chop the period into monthly or weekly periods, and the final column shows the effect on the estimated option value. (We will explain the Black–Scholes value shortly.)

The Binomial Method and Decision Trees

Calculating option values by the binomial method is basically a process of solving decision trees. You start at some future date and work back through the tree to the present. Eventually the possible cash flows generated by future events and actions are folded back to a present value.

Is the binomial method *merely* another application of decision trees, a tool of analysis that you learned about in Chapter 10? The answer is no, for at least two reasons. First, option pricing theory is absolutely essential for discounting within decision trees. Standard discounting doesn't work within decision trees for the same reason that it doesn't work for puts and calls. As we pointed out in Section 21.1, there is no single, constant discount rate for options because the risk of the option changes as time and the price of the underlying asset change. There is no single discount rate inside a decision tree, because if the tree contains meaningful future decisions, it also contains options. The market value of the future cash flows described by the decision tree has to be calculated by option pricing methods.

Second, option theory gives a simple, powerful framework for describing complex decision trees. For example, suppose that you have the option to postpone an investment for many years. The complete decision tree would overflow the largest classroom chalkboard. But now that you know about options, the opportunity to postpone investment might be summarized as "an American call on a perpetuity with a constant dividend yield." Of course, not all real problems have such easy option analogues, but we can often approximate complex decision trees by some simple package of assets and options. A custom decision tree may get closer to reality, but the time and expense may not be worth it. Most men buy their suits off the rack even though a custom-made suit from Saville Row would fit better and look nicer.

21.3 THE BLACK–SCHOLES FORMULA

Look back at Figure 21.1, which showed what happens to the distribution of possible AOL stock price changes as we divide the option's life into a larger and larger number of increasingly small subperiods. You can see that the distribution of price changes becomes increasingly smooth.

If we continued to chop up the option's life in this way, we would eventually reach the situation shown in Figure 21.4, where there is a continuum of possible stock price changes at maturity. Figure 21.4 is an example of a lognormal distribution. The lognormal distribution is often used to summarize the probability of different stock price changes.[10] It has a number of good commonsense features. For example, it recognizes the fact that the stock price can never fall by more than 100 percent, but that there is some, perhaps small, chance that it could rise by much more than 100 percent.

Subdividing the option life into indefinitely small slices does not affect the principle of option valuation. We could still replicate the call option by a levered investment in the stock, but we would need to adjust the degree of leverage continuously as time went by. Calculating option value when there is an infinite number of subperiods may sound a hopeless task. Fortunately, Black and Scholes derived a formula that does the trick. It is an unpleasant-looking formula, but on

---

[10]When we first looked at the distribution of stock price changes in Chapter 8, we assumed that these changes were normally distributed. We pointed out at the time that this is an acceptable approximation for very short intervals, but the distribution of changes over longer intervals is better approximated by the lognormal.

FIGURE 21.4

As the option's life is divided into more and more sub-periods, the distribution of possible stock price changes approaches a lognormal distribution.

closer acquaintance you will find it exceptionally elegant and useful. The formula is

$$\text{Value of call option} = [\text{delta} \times \text{share price}] - [\text{bank loan}]$$

$$[N(d_1) \times P] - [N(d_2) \times \text{PV(EX)}]$$

where

$$d_1 = \frac{\log\left[P/\text{PV(EX)}\right]}{\sigma\sqrt{t}} + \frac{\sigma\sqrt{t}}{2}$$

$$d_2 = d_1 - \sigma\sqrt{t}$$

$N(d)$ = cumulative normal probability density function[11]

EX = exercise price of option; PV(EX) is calculated by discounting at the risk-free interest rate r_f

t = number of periods to exercise date

P = price of stock now

σ = standard deviation per period of (continuously compounded) rate of return on stock

Notice that the value of the call in the Black–Scholes formula has the same properties that we identified earlier. It increases with the level of the stock price P and decreases with the present value of the exercise price PV(EX), which in turn depends on the interest rate and time to maturity. It also increases with the time to maturity and the stock's variability ($\sigma\sqrt{t}$).

To derive their formula Black and Scholes assumed that there is a continuum of stock prices, and therefore to replicate an option investors must continuously adjust their holding in the stock. Of course this is not literally possible,

---

[11]That is, $N(d)$ is the probability that a normally distributed random variable $\tilde{x}$ will be less than or equal to d. $N(d_1)$ in the Black–Scholes formula is the option delta. Thus the formula tells us that the value of a call is equal to an investment of $N(d_1)$ in the common stock less borrowing of $N(d_2) \times \text{PV(EX)}$.

but even so the formula performs remarkably well in the real world, where stocks trade only intermittently and prices jump from one level to another. The Black–Scholes model has also proved very flexible; it can be adapted to value options on a variety of assets with special features, such as foreign currency, bonds, and commodities. It is not surprising therefore that it has been extremely influential and has become the standard model for valuing options. Every day dealers on the options exchanges use this formula to make huge trades. These dealers are not for the most part trained in the formula's mathematical derivation; they just use a computer or a specially programmed calculator to find the value of the option.

Using the Black–Scholes Formula

The Black–Scholes formula may look difficult, but it is very straightforward to apply. Let us practice using it to value the AOL call.

Here are the data that you need:

- Price of stock now $= P = 55$.
- Exercise price $= EX = 55$.
- Standard deviation of continuously compounded annual returns $= \sigma = .4069$.
- Years to maturity $= t = .5$.
- Interest rate per annum $= r_f = 4$ percent (equivalent to 1.98 percent for six months).[12]

Remember that the Black–Scholes formula for the value of a call is

$$[N(d_1) \times P] - [N(d_2) \times PV(EX)]$$

where

$$d_1 = \log [P/PV(EX)]/\sigma\sqrt{t} + \sigma\sqrt{t}/2$$
$$d_2 = d_1 - \sigma\sqrt{t}$$

$N(d)$ = cumulative normal probability function

There are three steps to using the formula to value the AOL call:

Step 1 Calculate d_1 and d_2. This is just a matter of plugging numbers into the formula (noting that "log" means *natural* log):

$$d_1 = \log [P/PV(EX)]/\sigma\sqrt{t} + \sigma\sqrt{t}/2$$
$$= \log [55/(55/1.0198)]/(.4069 \times \sqrt{.5}) + (.4069 \times \sqrt{.5})/2$$
$$= .2120$$
$$d_2 = d_1 - \sigma\sqrt{t} = .2120 - (.4069 \times \sqrt{.5}) = -.0757$$

---

[12]If the annually compounded rate of interest is 4 percent, the equivalent rate for six months is 1.98 percent. This will give PV(EX) $= 55/(1.04)^5 = \$53.93$. (In the earlier binomial examples, we used a 2 percent six-month rate.)

When valuing options, it is more common to use continuously compounded rates (see Section 3.3). If the annual rate is 4 percent, the equivalent continuously compounded rate is 3.92 percent. (The natural log of 1.04 is .0392, and $e^{.0392} = 1.04$.) Using continuous compounding, $55 \times e^{-.5 \times .0392} = \$53.93$.

There is only one trick here: If you are using a spreadsheet or computer program that calls for a continuously compounded interest rate, make sure that you *enter* a continuously compounded rate.

FIGURE 21.5

The curved line shows how the value of the AOL call option changs as the price of AOL stock changes.

Values of AOL call option

Share price

Exercise price = $55

Step 2   Find $N(d_1)$ and $N(d_2)$. $N(d_1)$ is the probability that a normally distributed variable will be less than d_1 standard deviations above the mean. If d_1 is large, $N(d_1)$ is close to 1.0 (i.e., you can be almost certain that the variable will be less than d_1 standard deviations above the mean). If d_1 is zero, $N(d_1)$ is .5 (i.e., there is a 50 percent chance that a normally distributed variable will be below the average).

The simplest way to find $N(d_1)$ is to use the Excel function NORMSDIST. For example, if you enter NORMSDIST(.2120) into an Excel spreadsheet, you will see that there is a .5840 probability that a normally distributed variable will be less than .2120 standard deviations above the mean. Alternatively, you can use a set of normal probability tables such as those in Appendix Table 6, in which case you need to interpolate between the cumulative probabilities for $d_1 = .21$ and $d_1 = .22$.

Again you can use the Excel function to find $N(d_2)$. If you enter NORMSDIST(−.0757) into an Excel spreadsheet, you should get the answer .4698. In other words, there is a probability of .4698 that a normally distributed variable will be less than .0757 standard deviations *below* the mean. Alternatively, if you use Appendix Table 6, you need to look up the value for +.0757 and subtract it from 1.0:

$$N(d_2) = N(-.0757) = 1 - N(+.0757)$$
$$= 1 - .5302 = .4698$$

Step 3   Plug these numbers into the Black–Scholes formula. You can now calculate the value of the AOL call:

$$[\text{Delta} \times \text{price}] - [\text{bank loan}]$$
$$= [N(d_1) \times P] - [N(d_2) \times PV(EX)]$$
$$= [.5840 \times 55] - [.4698 \times 55/(1.04)^5] = \$6.78$$

Some More Practice   Suppose you repeated the calculations for the AOL call for a wide range of stock prices. The result is shown in Figure 21.5. You can see that the option values lie along an upward-sloping curve that starts its travels in the bottom left-hand corner of the diagram. As the stock price increases, the option

	Establishment Industries	Digital Organics
Stock price (P)	$22	$22
Exercise price (EX)	$25	$25
Interest rate (r_f)	.04	.04
Maturity in years (t)	5	5
Standard deviation (σ)	.24	.36
$d_1 = \log[P/PV(EX)]/\sigma\sqrt{t} + \sigma\sqrt{t}/2$	.3955	.4873
$d_2 = d_1 - \sigma\sqrt{t}$	−.1411	−.3177
Value of call =		
$[N(d_1) \times P] - [N(d_2) \times PV(EX)]$	$5.26	$7.40
Value of 100,000 options	$526,000	$740,000

TABLE 21.2

Using the Black–Scholes formula to value the executive stock options for Establishment Industries and Digital Organics (see Table 20.3).

value rises and gradually becomes parallel to the lower bound for the option value. This is exactly the shape we deduced in Chapter 20 (see Figure 20.10).

The height of this curve of course depends on risk and time to maturity. For example, if the risk of AOL stock had suddenly decreased, the curve shown in Figure 21.5 would drop at every possible stock price.

Speaking of differences in risk, we can now use the Black–Scholes formula to value the executive stock option packages you were offered in Section 20.3 (see Table 20.3). Table 21.2 calculates the value of the package from safe-and-stodgy Establishment Industries at $526,000. The package from risky-and-glamorous Digital Organics is worth $740,000. Congratulations.

The Black–Scholes Formula and the Binomial Method

Look back at Table 21.1 where we used the binomial method to calculate the value of the AOL call. Notice that, as the number of intervals is increased, the values that you obtain from the binomial method begin to snuggle up to the Black–Scholes value of $6.78.

The Black–Scholes formula recognizes a continuum of possible outcomes. This is usually more realistic than the limited number of outcomes assumed in the binomial method. The formula is also more accurate and quicker to use than the binomial method. So why use the binomial method at all? The answer is that there are circumstances in which you cannot use the Black–Scholes formula but the binomial method will still give you a good measure of the option's value. We will look at several such cases in the next section.

Using the Black–Scholes Formula to Estimate Variability

So far we have used our option pricing model to calculate the value of an option *given* the standard deviation of the asset's returns. Sometimes it is useful to turn the problem around and ask what the option price is telling us about the asset's variability. For example, the Chicago Board Options Exchange trades options on several market indexes. As we write this, the Standard and Poor's 100-share index is 575, while a six-month at-the-money call option on the index is priced at 42. If the Black–Scholes formula is correct, then an option value of 42 makes sense

FIGURE 21.6

Standard deviations of market returns implied by prices of options on stock indexes.

Source: **www.cboe.com**.

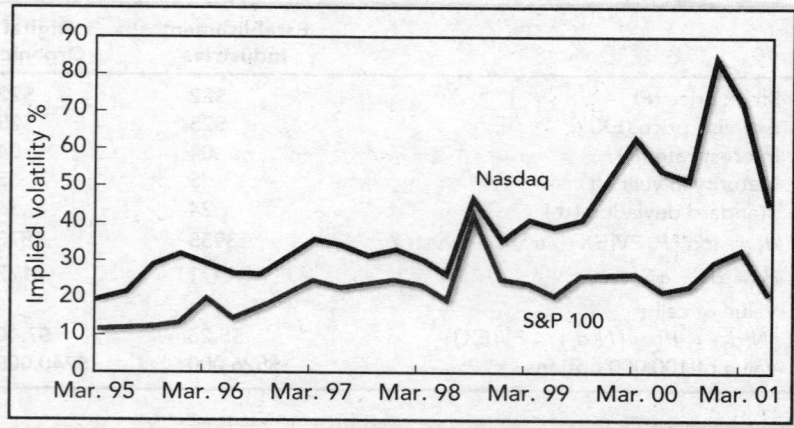

only if investors believe that the standard deviation of index returns is about 23 percent a year. You may be interested to compare this number with Figure 21.6, which shows the stock market volatility that was implied by the price of index options in earlier years. Notice the sharp increase in investor uncertainty about the value of Nasdaq stocks during the crash of the dot.com stocks in late 2000. This uncertainty showed up in the high price that investors were prepared to pay for options.

 ## 21.4 OPTION VALUES AT A GLANCE

So far our discussion of option values has assumed that investors hold the option until maturity. That is certainly the case with European options that *cannot* be exercised before maturity but may not be the case with American options that can be exercised at any time. Also, when we valued the AOL call, we could ignore dividends, because AOL did not pay any. Can the same valuation methods be extended to American options and to stocks that pay dividends? You may find it useful to have the following summary of how different combinations of features affect option value.

American Calls—No Dividends   Unlike European options, American options can be exercised anytime. However, we know that in the absence of dividends the value of a call option increases with time to maturity. So, if you exercised an American call option early, you would needlessly reduce its value. Since an American call should not be exercised before maturity, its value is the same as that of a European call, and the Black–Scholes model applies to both options.

European Puts—No Dividends   If we wish to value a European put, we can use the put–call parity formula from Chapter 20:

Value of put = value of call − value of stock + PV(exercise price)

American Puts—No Dividends   It can sometimes pay to exercise an American put before maturity to reinvest the exercise price. For example, suppose that immediately after you buy an American put, the stock price falls to zero. In this case there is no advantage to holding onto the option since it *cannot* become more valuable. It is better to exercise the put and invest the exercise money. Thus an American put is always more valuable than a European put. In our extreme example, the difference is equal to the present value of the interest that you could earn on the exercise price. In all other cases the difference is less.

Because the Black–Scholes formula does not allow for early exercise, it cannot be used to value an American put exactly. But you can use the step-by-step binomial method as long as you check at each point whether the option is worth more dead than alive and then use the higher of the two values.

European Calls on Dividend-Paying Stocks   Part of the share value comprises the present value of dividends. The option holder is not entitled to dividends. Therefore, when using the Black–Scholes model to value a European call on a dividend-paying stock, you should reduce the price of the stock by the present value of the dividends paid before the option's maturity.

Dividends don't always come with a big label attached, so look out for instances where the asset holder gets a benefit and the option holder does not. For example, when you buy foreign currency, you can invest it to earn interest; but if you own an option to buy foreign currency, you miss out on this income. Therefore, when valuing an option to buy foreign currency, you need to deduct the present value of this foreign interest from the current price of the currency.[13]

American Calls on Dividend-Paying Stocks   We have seen that when the stock does not pay dividends, an American call option is *always* worth more alive than dead. By holding onto the option, you not only keep your option open but also earn interest on the exercise money. Even when there are dividends, you should never exercise early if the dividend you gain is less than the interest you lose by having to pay the exercise price early. However, if the dividend is sufficiently large, you might want to capture it by exercising the option just before the ex-dividend date.

The only general method for valuing an American call on a dividend-paying stock is to use the step-by-step binomial method. In this case you must check at each stage to see whether the option is more valuable if exercised just before the ex-dividend date than if held for at least one more period.

Example. Here is a last chance to practice your option valuation skills by valuing an American call on a dividend-paying stock. Figure 21.7 summarizes the possible price movements in Consolidated Pork Bellies stock. The stock price is currently $100, but over the next year it could either fall by 20 percent to $80 or rise by 25 percent to $125. In either case the company will then pay its regular dividend of $20. Immediately after payment of this dividend the stock price will fall to 80 − 20 = $60, or 125 − 20 = $105. Over the second year the

---

[13]For example, suppose that it currently costs $2 to buy £1 and that this pound can be invested to earn interest of 5 percent. The option holder misses out on interest of .05 × $2 = $.10. So, before using the Black–Scholes formula to value an option to buy sterling, you must adjust the current price of sterling:

$$\text{Adjusted price of sterling} = \text{current price} - \text{PV(interest)}$$
$$= \$2 - .10/1.05 = \$1.905.$$

FIGURE 21.7

Possible values of Consolidated Pork Bellies stock.

price will again either fall by 20 percent from the ex-dividend price or rise by 25 percent.[14]

Suppose that you wish to value a two-year American call option on Consolidated stock. Figure 21.8 shows the possible option values at each point, assuming an exercise price of $70 and an interest rate of 12 percent. We won't go through all the calculations behind these figures, but we will focus on the option values at the end of year 1.

Suppose that the stock price has fallen in the first year. What is the option worth if you hold onto it for a further period? You should be used to this problem by now. First pretend that investors are risk-neutral and calculate the probability that the stock will rise in price. This probability turns out to be 71 percent.[15] Now calculate the expected payoff on the option and discount at 12 percent:

$$\text{Option value if not exercised in year 1} = \frac{(.71 \times 5) + (.29 \times 0)}{1.12} = \$3.18$$

Thus, if you hold onto the option, it is worth $3.18. However, if you exercise the option just before the ex-dividend date, you pay an exercise price of $70 for a stock worth $80. This $10 value from exercising is greater than the $3.18 from holding onto the option. Therefore in Figure 21.8 we put in an option value of $10 if the stock price falls in year 1.

You will also want to exercise if the stock price *rises* in year 1. The option is worth $42.45 if you hold onto it but $55 if you exercise. Therefore in Figure 21.8 we put in a value of $55 if the stock price rises.

The rest of the calculation is routine. Calculate the expected option payoff in year 1 and discount by 12 percent to give the option value today:

$$\text{Option value today} = \frac{(.71 \times 55) + (.29 \times 10)}{1.12} = \$37.50$$

---

[14]Notice that the payment of a fixed dividend in year 1 results in four possible stock prices at the end of year 2. In other words, 60×1.25 does not equal $105 \times .8$. Don't let that put you off. You still start from the end and work back one step at a time to find the possible option values at each date.

[15]Using the formula given in footnote 5,

$$p = \frac{\text{interest rate} - \text{downside change}}{\text{upside change} - \text{downside change}} = \frac{12 - (-20)}{25 - (-20)} = .71$$

FIGURE 21.8

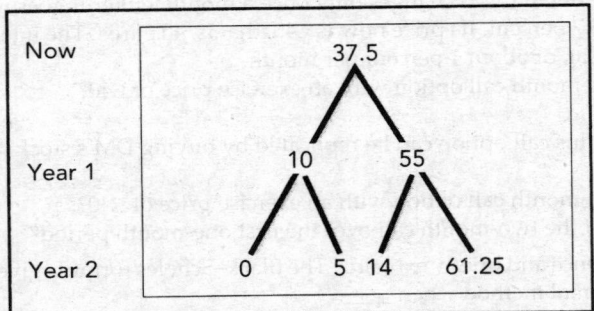

Now		37.5
Year 1	10	55
Year 2	0 5	14 61.25

Values of a two-year call option on Consolidated Pork Bellies stock. Exercise price is $70. Although we show option values for year 2, the option will not be alive then. It will be exercised in year 1.

SUMMARY

In this chapter we introduced the basic principles of option valuation by considering a call option on a stock that could take on one of two possible values at the option's maturity. We showed that it is possible to construct a package of the stock and a loan that would provide exactly the same payoff as the option *regardless* of whether the stock price rises or falls. Therefore the value of the option must be the same as the value of this replicating portfolio.

We arrived at the same answer by pretending that investors are risk-neutral, so that the expected return on every asset is equal to the interest rate. We calculated the expected future value of the option in this imaginary risk-neutral world and then discounted this figure at the interest rate to find the option's present value.

The general binomial method adds realism by dividing the option's life into a number of subperiods in each of which the stock price can make one of two possible moves. Chopping the period into these shorter intervals doesn't alter the basic method for valuing a call option. We can still replicate the call by a package of the stock and a loan, but the package changes at each stage.

Finally, we introduced the Black–Scholes formula. This calculates the option's value when the stock price is constantly changing and takes on a continuum of possible future values.

When valuing options in practical situations there are a number of features to look out for. For example, you may need to recognize that the option value is reduced by the fact that the holder is not entitled to any dividends.

FURTHER READING

The classic articles on option valuation are:

F. Black and M. Scholes: "The Pricing of Options and Corporate Liabilities," *Journal of Political Economy*, 81:637–654 (May–June 1973).

R. C. Merton: "Theory of Rational Option Pricing," *Bell Journal of Economics and Management Science*, 4:141–183 (Spring 1973).

The texts listed under "Further Reading" in Chapter 20 can be referred to for discussion of option-valuation models and the practical complications of applying them.

QUIZ

1. The stock price of Deutsche Metall (DM) changes only once a month: either it goes up by 20 percent or it falls by 16.7 percent. Its price now is €40, that is, 40 euros. The interest rate is 12.7 percent per year, or about 1 percent per month.
   a. What is the value of a one-month call option with an exercise price of €40?
   b. What is the option delta?
   c. Show how the payoffs of this call option can be replicated by buying DM's stock and borrowing.
   d. What is the value of a two-month call option with an exercise price of €40?
   e. What is the option delta of the two-month call over the first one-month period?

2. Complete the following sentence and briefly explain: "The Black–Scholes formula gives the same answer as the binomial method when ____."

3. a. Can the delta of a call option be greater than 1.0? Explain.
   b. Can it be less than zero?
   c. How does the delta of a call change if the stock price rises?
   d. How does it change if the risk of the stock increases?

4. Why can't you value options using a standard discounted-cash-flow formula?

5. Use either the replicating-portfolio method or the risk-neutral method to value the six-month call and put options on AOL stock with an exercise price of $60 (see Table 20.1). Assume AOL stock price = $55.

6. Imagine that AOL's stock price will either rise by 25 percent or fall by 20 percent over the next six months (see Section 21.1). Recalculate the value of the call option (exercise price = $55) using (a) the replicating portfolio method and (b) the risk-neutral method. Explain intuitively why the option value falls from the value computed in Section 21.1.

7. Over the coming year Ragwort's stock price will halve to $50 from its current level of $100 or it will rise to $200. The one-year interest rate is 10 percent.
   a. What is the delta of a one-year call option on Ragwort stock with an exercise price of $100?
   b. Use the replicating-portfolio method to value this call.
   c. In a risk-neutral world what is the probability that Ragwort stock will rise in price?
   d. Use the risk-neutral method to check your valuation of the Ragwort option.
   e. If someone told you that in reality there is a 60 percent chance that Ragwort's stock price will rise to $200, would you change your view about the value of the option? Explain.

8. Use the Black–Scholes formula with Appendix Table 6 to value the following options:
   a. A call option written on a stock selling for $60 per share with a $60 exercise price. The stock's standard deviation is 6 percent per month. The option matures in three months. The risk-free interest rate is 1 percent per month.
   b. A put option written on the same stock at the same time, with the same exercise price and expiration date.

   Now for each of these options find the combination of stock and risk-free asset that would replicate the option.

9. "An option is always riskier than the stock it is written on." True or false? How does the risk of an option change when the stock price changes?

10. For which of the following options *might* it be rational to exercise before maturity? Explain briefly why or why not.
    a. American put on a non-dividend-paying stock.
    b. American call—the dividend payment is 50 pesos per annum, the exercise price is 1,000 pesos, and the interest rate is 10 percent.

    c. American call—the interest rate is 10 percent, and the dividend payment is 5 percent of future stock price. *Hint:* The dividend depends on the stock price, which could either rise or fall.

1. Johnny Jones's high school derivatives homework asks for a binomial valuation of a 12-month call option on the common stock of the Overland Railroad. The stock is now selling for $45 per share and has a standard deviation of 24 percent. Johnny first constructs a binomial tree like Figure 21.2, in which stock price moves up or down every six months. Then he constructs a more realistic tree, assuming that the stock price moves up or down once every three months, or four times per year.
   a. Construct these two binomial trees.
   b. How would these trees change if Overland's standard deviation were 30 percent? *Hint:* Make sure to specify the right up and down percentage changes.

2. Suppose a stock price can go up by 15 percent or down by 13 percent over the next year. You own a one-year put on the stock. The interest rate is 10 percent, and the current stock price is $60.
   a. What exercise price leaves you indifferent between holding the put or exercising it now?
   b. How does this break-even exercise price change if the interest rate is increased?

3. Look back at Table 20.2. Now construct a similar table for put options. In each case construct a simple example to illustrate your point.

4. The price of Matterhorn Mining stock is 100 Swiss francs (SFr). During each of the next two six-month periods the price may either rise by 25 percent or fall by 20 percent (equivalent to a standard deviation of 31.5 percent a year). At month 6 the company will pay a dividend of SFr20. The interest rate is 10 percent per six-month period. What is the value of a one-year American call option with an exercise price of SFr80? Now recalculate the option value, assuming that the dividend is equal to 20 percent of the with-dividend stock price.

5. Buffelhead's stock price is $220 and could halve or double in each six-month period (equivalent to a standard deviation of 98 percent). A one-year call option on Buffelhead has an exercise price of $165. The interest rate is 21 percent a year.
   a. What is the value of the Buffelhead call?
   b. Now calculate the option delta for the second six months if (i) the stock price rises to $440 and (ii) the stock price falls to $110.
   c. How does the call option delta vary with the level of the stock price? Explain intuitively why.
   d. Suppose that in month 6 the Buffelhead stock price is $110. How at that point could you replicate an investment in the stock by a combination of call options and risk-free lending? Show that your strategy does indeed produce the same returns as those from an investment in the stock.

6. Suppose that you own an American put option on Buffelhead stock (see question 5) with an exercise price of $220.
   a. Would you ever want to exercise the put early?
   b. Calculate the value of the put.
   c. Now compare the value with that of an equivalent European put option.

7. Recalculate the value of the Buffelhead call option (see question 5), assuming that the option is American and that at the end of the first six months the company pays a dividend of $25. (Thus the price at the end of the year is either double or half the *ex*-dividend price in month 6.) How would your answer change if the option were European?

8. Suppose that you have an option which allows you to sell Buffelhead stock (see question 5) in month 6 for $165 *or* to buy it in month 12 for $165. What is the value of this unusual option?

9. The current price of the stock of Mont Tremblant Air is C$100. During each six-month period it will either rise by 11.1 percent or fall by 10 percent (equivalent to an annual standard deviation of 14.9 percent). The interest rate is 5 percent per six-month period.
   a. Calculate the value of a one-year European put option on Mont Tremblant's stock with an exercise price of C$102.
   b. Recalculate the value of the Mont Tremblant put option, assuming that it is an American option.

10. The current price of United Carbon (UC) stock is $200. The standard deviation is 22.3 percent a year, and the interest rate is 21 percent a year. A one-year call option on UC has an exercise price of $180.
   a. Use the Black–Scholes model to value the call option on UC.
   b. Use the formula given in Section 21.2 to calculate the up and down moves that you would use if you valued the UC option with the one-period binomial method. Now value the option by using that method.
   c. Recalculate the up and down moves and revalue the option by using the two-period binomial method.
   d. Use your answer to part (c) to calculate the option delta (i) today; (ii) next period if the stock price rises; and (iii) next period if the stock price falls. Show at each point how you would replicate a call option with a levered investment in the company's stock.

11. Suppose you construct an option hedge by buying a levered position in delta shares of stock and selling one call option. As the share price changes, the option delta changes, and you will need to adjust your hedge. You can minimize the cost of adjustments if changes in the stock price have only a small effect on the option delta. Construct an example to show whether the option delta is likely to vary more if you hedge with an in-the-money option, an at-the-money option, or an out-of-the-money option.

12. Other things equal, which of these American options are you most likely to want to exercise early?
   a. A put option on a stock with a large dividend or a call on the same stock.
   b. A put option on a stock that is selling below exercise price or a call on the same stock.
   c. A put option when the interest rate is high or the same put option when the interest rate is low.

   Illustrate your answer with examples.

13. Is it better to exercise a call option on the with-dividend date or on the ex-dividend date? How about a put option? Explain.

14. You can buy each of the following items of information about an American call option for $10 apiece: PV (exercise price); exercise price; standard deviation × square root of time to maturity; interest rate (per annum); time to maturity; value of European put; expected return on stock.

   How much would you need to spend to value the option? Explain.

15. Look back to the companies listed in Table 7.3. Most of these companies are covered in the Standard & Poor's Market Insight website (**www.mhhe.com/edumarketinsight**), and most will have traded options. Pick at least three companies. For each company, download "Monthly Adjusted Prices" as an Excel spreadsheet. Calculate each company's standard deviation from the monthly returns given on the spreadsheet. The Excel function is STDEV. Convert the standard deviations from monthly to annual units by multiplying by the square root of 12.
   a. Use the Black–Scholes formula to value 3, 6, and 9 month call options on each stock. Assume the exercise price equals the current stock price, and use a current, risk-free, annual interest rate.

b. For each stock, pick a traded option with an exercise price approximately equal to the current stock price. Use the Black–Scholes formula and your estimate of standard deviation to value the option. How close is your calculated value to the traded price of the option?

c. Your answer to part (b) will not exactly match the traded price. Experiment with different values for standard deviation until your calculations match the traded options prices as closely as possible. What are these this implied volatilites? What do the implied volatilities say about investors' forecasts of future volatility?

1. Use the formula that relates the value of the call and the put (see Section 21.1) and the one-period binomial model to show that the option delta for a put option is equal to the option delta for a call option minus 1.

2. Show how the option delta changes as the stock price rises relative to the exercise price. Explain intuitively why this is the case. (What happens to the option delta if the exercise price of an option is zero? What happens if the exercise price becomes indefinitely large?)

3. Write a spreadsheet program to value a call option using the Black–Scholes formula.

4. Your company has just awarded you a generous stock option scheme. You suspect that the board will either decide to increase the dividend or announce a stock repurchase program. Which do you secretly hope they will decide? Explain. (You may find it helpful to refer back to Chapter 16.)

5. In August 1986 Salomon Brothers issued four-year Standard and Poor's 500 Index Subordinated Notes (SPINS). The notes paid no interest, but at maturity investors received the face value plus a possible bonus. The bonus was equal to $1,000 times the proportionate appreciation in the market index.
   a. What would be the value of SPINS if issued today?
   b. If Salomon Brothers wished to hedge itself against a rise in the market index, how should it have done so?

6. Some corporations have issued *perpetual* warrants. Warrants are call options issued by a firm, allowing the warrant-holder to buy the firm's stock. We discuss warrants in Chapter 23. For now, just consider a perpetual call.
   a. What does the Black-Scholes formula predict for the value of an infinite-lived call option on a non-dividend paying stock? Explain the value you obtain. (*Hint:* what happens to the present value of the exercise price of a long-maturity option?)
   b. Do you think this prediction is realistic? If not, explain carefully why. (*Hint:* for one of several reasons: if a company's stock price followed the exact time-series process assumed by Black and Scholes, could the company ever be bankrupt, with a stock price of zero?)

CHALLENGE QUESTIONS

MINI-CASE

Bruce Honiball's Invention

It was another disappointing year for Bruce Honiball, the manager of retail services at the Gibb River Bank. Sure, the retail side of Gibb River was making money, but it didn't grow at all in 2000. Gibb River had plenty of loyal depositors, but few new ones. Bruce had to

Year	Interest Rate	Market Return	End-Year Dividend Yield	Year	Interest Rate	Market Return	End-Year Dividend Yield
1981	13.3%	−20.2%	4.5%	1991	10.0%	37.8%	3.8%
1982	14.6	−10.7	5.6	1992	6.3	−.5	3.8
1983	11.1	70.1	4.0	1993	5.0	38.7	3.2
1984	11.0	−4.8	5.1	1994	5.7	−6.8	4.1
1985	15.3	46.5	4.6	1995	7.6	17.3	3.9
1986	15.4	47.7	3.9	1996	7.0	10.4	3.6
1987	12.8	1.6	4.8	1997	5.3	10.3	3.6
1988	12.1	16.8	5.4	1998	4.8	14.5	3.8
1989	16.8	19.9	5.5	1999	4.7	13.8	3.5
1990	14.2	14.1	6.0	2000	5.9	−.9	3.2

TABLE 21.3

Australian interest rates and equity returns, 1981–2000.

figure out some new product or financial service—something that would generate some excitement and attention.

Bruce had been musing on one idea for some time. How about making it easy *and safe* for Gibb River's customers to put money in the stock market? How about giving them the upside of investing in equities—at least *some* of the upside—but none of the downside?

Bruce could see the advertisements now:

How would you like to invest in Australian stocks completely risk-free? You can with the new Gibb River Bank *Equity-Linked Deposit*. You share in the good years; we take care of the bad ones.

Here's how it works. Deposit $A100 with us for one year. At the end of that period you get back your $A100 *plus* $A5 for every 10 percent rise in the value of the Australian All Ordinaries stock index. But, if the market index falls during this period, the Bank will still refund your $A100 deposit in full.

There's no risk of loss. Gibbs River Bank is your safety net.

Bruce had floated the idea before and encountered immediate skepticism, even derision: "Heads they win, tails we lose—is that what you're proposing, Mr. Honiball?" Bruce had no ready answer. Could the bank really afford to make such an attractive offer? How should it invest the money that would come in from customers? The bank had no appetite for major new risks.

Bruce has puzzled over these questions for the past two weeks but has been unable to come up with a satisfactory answer. He believes that the Australian equity market is currently fully valued, but he realizes that some of his colleagues are more bullish than he is about equity prices.

Fortunately, the bank had just recruited a smart new MBA graduate, Sheila Cox. Sheila was sure that she could find the answers to Bruce Honiball's questions. First she collected data on the Australian market to get a preliminary idea of whether equity-linked deposits could work. These data are shown in Table 21.3. She was just about to undertake some quick calculations when she received the following further memo from Bruce:

Sheila, I've got another idea. A lot of our customers probably share my view that the market is overvalued. Why don't we also offer them a chance to make some money by offering a "bear market deposit"? If the market goes up, they would just get back their $A100 deposit. If it goes down, they get their $A100 back plus $5 for each 10 percent that the market falls. Can you figure out whether we could do something like this? Bruce.

Questions

1. What kinds of options is Bruce proposing? How much would the options be worth? Would the equity-linked and bear-market deposits generate positive NPV for Gibb River Bank?

CHAPTER TWENTY-TWO

REAL OPTIONS

WHEN YOU USE discounted cash flow (DCF) to value a project, you implicitly assume that your firm will hold the project passively. In other words, you are ignoring the *real options* attached to the project—options that sophisticated managers can take advantage of. You could say that DCF does not reflect the value of management. Managers who hold real options do not have to be passive; they can make decisions to capitalize on good fortune or to mitigate loss. The opportunity to make such decisions clearly adds value whenever project outcomes are uncertain.

Chapter 10 introduced the four main types of real options:

- The option to expand if the immediate investment project succeeds.
- The option to wait (and learn) before investing.
- The option to shrink or abandon a project.
- The option to vary the mix of output or the firm's production methods.

Chapter 10 gave several simple examples of real options. We also showed you how to use decision trees to set out possible future outcomes and decisions. But we did not show you how to value real options. That is our task in this chapter. We will apply the concepts and valuation principles you learned in Chapter 21.

For the most part we will work with simple numerical examples. The art and science of valuing real options are illustrated just as well with simple calculations as complex ones. But we will also show you results for several more complex examples, including:

- A strategic investment in the computer business.
- The valuation of an aircraft purchase option.
- The option to develop commercial real estate.
- The decision to operate or mothball an oil tanker.

These examples show how financial managers value real options in real life.

 ## 22.1 THE VALUE OF FOLLOW-ON INVESTMENT OPPORTUNITIES

It is 1982. You are assistant to the chief financial officer (CFO) of Blitzen Computers, an established computer manufacturer casting a profit-hungry eye on the rapidly developing personal computer market. You are helping the CFO evaluate the proposed introduction of the Blitzen Mark I Micro.

The Mark I's forecasted cash flows and NPV are shown in Table 22.1. Unfortunately the Mark I can't meet Blitzen's customary 20 percent hurdle rate and has a $46 million negative NPV, contrary to top management's strong gut feeling that Blitzen ought to be in the personal computer market.

The CFO has called you in to discuss the project:

"The Mark I just can't make it on financial grounds," the CFO says. "But we've got to do it for strategic reasons. I'm recommending we go ahead."

"But you're missing the all-important financial advantage, Chief," you reply.

"Don't call me 'Chief.' What financial advantage?"

"If we don't launch the Mark I, it will probably be too expensive to enter the micro market later, when Apple, IBM, and others are firmly established. If we go ahead, we have the opportunity to make follow-on investments which could be extremely profitable. The Mark I gives not only its own cash flows but also a call option to go on with a Mark II micro. That call option is the real source of strategic value."

TABLE 22.1

Summary of cash flows
and financial analysis
of the Mark I
microcomputer
($ millions).

*After-tax operating cash
flow is negative in 1982
because of R&D costs.

	Year					
	1982	**1983**	**1984**	**1985**	**1986**	**1987**
After-tax operating cash flow (1)*	−200	+110	+159	+295	+185	0
Capital investment (2)	250	0	0	0	0	0
Increase in working capital (3)	0	50	100	100	−125	−125
Net cash flow (1) − (2) − (3)	−450	+60	+59	+195	+310	+125
NPV at 20% = −$46.45, or about −$46 million						

"So it's strategic value by another name. That doesn't tell me what the Mark II investment's worth. The Mark II could be a great investment or a lousy one—we haven't got a clue."

"That's exactly when a call option is worth the most," you point out perceptively. "The call lets us invest in the Mark II if it's great and walk away from it if it's lousy."

"So what's it worth?"

"Hard to say precisely, but I've done a back-of-the-envelope calculation which suggests that the value of the option to invest in the Mark II could more than offset the Mark I's $46 million negative NPV. [The calculations are shown in Table 22.2.] If the option to invest is worth $55 million, the total value of the Mark I is its own NPV, −$46 million, plus the $55 million option attached to it, or +$9 million."

"You're just overestimating the Mark II," the CFO says gruffly. "It's easy to be optimistic when an investment is three years away."

"No, no," you reply patiently. "The Mark II is expected to be no more profitable than the Mark I—just twice as big and therefore twice as bad in terms of discounted cash flow. I'm forecasting it to have a negative NPV of about $100 million. But there's a chance the Mark II could be extremely valuable. The call option allows Blitzen to cash in on those upside outcomes. The chance to cash in could be worth $55 million."

"Of course, the $55 million is only a trial calculation, but it illustrates how valuable follow-on investment opportunities can be, especially when uncertainty is high and the product market is growing rapidly. Moreover, the Mark II will give us a call on the Mark III, the Mark III on the Mark IV, and so on. My calculations don't take subsequent calls into account."

"I think I'm beginning to understand a little bit of corporate strategy," mumbles the CFO.

Questions and Answers about Blitzen's Mark II

Question: I know how to use the Black–Scholes formula to value traded call options, but this case seems harder. What number do I use for the stock price? I don't see any traded shares.

Answer: With traded call options, you can see the value of the *underlying asset* that the call is written on. Here the option is to buy a nontraded real asset, the Mark II. We can't observe the Mark II's value; we have to compute it.

TABLE 22.2

Valuing the option to invest in the Mark II microcomputer.

Assumptions
1. The decision to invest in the Mark II must be made after 3 years, in 1985.
2. The Mark II investment is double the scale of the Mark I (note the expected rapid growth of the industry). Investment required is $900 million (the exercise price), which is taken as fixed.
3. Forecasted cash inflows of the Mark II are also double those of the Mark I, with present value of $807 million in 1985 and $807/(1.2)^3 = \$467$ million in 1982.
4. The future value of the Mark II cash flows is highly uncertain. This value evolves as a stock price does with a standard deviation of 35 percent per year. (Many high-technology stocks have standard deviations higher than 35 percent.)
5. The annual interest rate is 10 percent.

Interpretation
The opportunity to invest in the Mark II is a three-year call option on an asset worth $467 million with a $900 million exercise price.

Valuation

$$\text{PV(exercise price)} = \frac{900}{(1.1)^3} = 676$$

$$\text{Call value} = [N(d_1) \times P] - [N(d_2) \times \text{PV(EX)}]$$

$$d_1 = \log[P/\text{PV(EX)}]/\sigma\sqrt{t} + \sigma\sqrt{t}/2$$

$$= \log[.691]/.606 + .606/2 = -.3072$$

$$d_2 = d_1 - \sigma\sqrt{t} = -.3072 - .606 = -.9134$$

$$N(d_1) = .3793, N(d_2) = .1805$$

$$\text{Call value} = [.3793 \times 467] - [.1805 \times 676] = \$55.12 \text{ million}$$

The Mark II's forecasted cash flows are set out in Table 22.3. The project involves an initial outlay of $900 million in 1985. The cash inflows start in the following year and have a present value of $807 million in 1985, equivalent to $467 million in 1982 as shown in Table 22.3. So the real option to invest in the Mark II amounts to a three-year call on an underlying asset worth $467 million, with a $900 million exercise price.

Notice that real options analysis does *not* replace DCF. You typically need DCF to value the underlying asset.

Question: Table 22.2 uses a standard deviation of 35 percent per year. Where does that number come from?

Answer: We recommend you look for *comparables*, that is, traded stocks with business risks similar to the investment opportunity.[1] For the Mark II, the ideal comparables would be growth stocks in the personal computer business, or perhaps a broader sample of high-tech growth stocks. Use the average standard deviation of

---

[1]You could also use scenario analysis, which we described in Chapter 10. Work out "best" and "worst" scenarios to establish a range of possible future values. Then find the annual standard deviation that would generate this range over the life of the option. For the Mark II, a range from $300 million to $2 billion would cover about 90 percent of the possible outcomes. This range, shown in Figure 22.1, is consistent with an annual standard deviation of 35 percent.

		Year					
	1982	**1985**	**1986**	**1987**	**1988**	**1989**	**1990**
After-tax operating cash flow			+220	+318	+590	+370	0
Increase in working capital			100	200	200	−250	−250
Net cash flow			+120	+118	+390	+620	+250
Present value at 20%	+467	⟵ +807					
Investment, PV at 10%	676 (PV in 1982)	⟵ 900					
Forecasted NPV in 1985		−93					

TABLE 22.3

Cash flows of the Mark II microcomputer, as forecasted from 1982 ($ millions).

the comparable companies' returns as the benchmark for judging the risk of the investment opportunity.[2]

Question: Table 22.3 discounts the Mark II's cash flows at 20 percent. I understand the high discount rate, because the Mark II is risky. But why is the $900 million investment discounted at the risk-free interest rate of 10 percent? Table 22.3 shows the present value of the investment in 1982 of $676 million.

Answer: Black and Scholes assumed that the exercise price is a fixed, certain amount. We wanted to stick with their basic formula. If the exercise price is uncertain, you can switch to a slightly more complicated valuation formula.[3]

Question: Nevertheless, if I had to decide in 1982, once and for all, whether to invest in the Mark II, I wouldn't do it. Right?

Answer: Right. The NPV of a commitment to invest in the Mark II is negative:

$$NPV(1982) = PV(\text{cash inflows}) - PV(\text{investment}) = \$467 - 676$$
$$= -\$209 \text{ million}$$

The option to invest in the Mark II is "out of the money" because the Mark II's value is far less than the required investment. Nevertheless, the option is worth +$55 million. It is especially valuable because the Mark II is a risky project with lots of upside potential. Figure 22.1 shows the probability distribution of the

---

[2]Be sure to "unlever" the standard deviations, thereby eliminating volatility created by debt financing. Chapter 9 covered unlevering procedures for beta. The same principles apply for standard deviation: You want the standard deviation of a portfolio of all the debt and equity securities issued by the comparable firm.

[3]If the required investment is uncertain, you have, in effect, an option to exchange one risky asset (the future value of the exercise price) for another (the future value of the Mark II's cash inflows). See W. Margrabe, "The Value of an Option to Exchange One Asset for Another," *Journal of Finance* 33 (March 1978), pp. 177–186.

FIGURE 22.1

This distribution shows the range of possible present values for the Mark II project in 1985. The expected value is about $800 million, less than the required investment of $900 million. The *option* to invest pays off in the shaded area above $900 million.

possible present values of the Mark II in 1985. The expected (i.e., mean or average) outcome is our forecast of $807,[4] but the actual value could exceed $2 billion.

Question: Could it also be far below $807 million— $500 million or less?

Answer: The downside is irrelevant, because Blitzen won't invest unless the Mark II's actual value turns out higher than $900 million. The net option payoffs for all values less than $900 million are zero.

In a DCF analysis, you discount the expected outcome ($807 million), which averages the downside against the upside, the bad outcomes against the good. The value of a call option depends only on the upside. You can see the danger of trying to value a future investment option with DCF.

Question: What's the decision rule?

Answer: Adjusted present value. The Mark I project costs $46 million (NPV = −$46 million), but accepting it creates the expansion option for the Mark II. The expansion option is worth $55 million, so:

$$APV = -46 + 55 = +\$9 \text{ million}$$

---

[4]We have drawn the future values of the Mark II as a lognormal distribution, consistent with the assumptions of the Black–Scholes formula. Lognormal distributions are skewed to the right, so the average outcome is greater than the most likely outcome. (The most likely outcome is the highest point on the probability distribution.)

Of course we haven't counted other follow-on opportunities. If the Mark I and Mark II are successes, there will be an option to invest in the Mark III, possibly the Mark IV, and so on.

Other Expansion Options

You can probably think of many other cases where companies spend money today to create opportunities to expand in the future. A mining company may acquire rights to an ore body that is not worth developing today but could be very profitable if product prices increase. A real estate developer may invest in worn-out farmland that could be turned into a shopping mall if a new highway is built. A pharmaceutical company may acquire a patent that gives the right but not the obligation to market a new drug. In each case the company is acquiring a real option to expand.

22.2 THE TIMING OPTION

The fact that a project has a positive NPV does not mean that you should take it today. It may be better to wait and see how the market develops.

Suppose that you are contemplating a now-or-never opportunity to build a malted herring factory. In this case you have an about-to-expire call option on the present value of the factory's future cash flows. If the present value exceeds the cost of the factory, the call option's payoff is the project's NPV. But if NPV is negative, the call option's payoff is zero, because in that case the firm will not make the investment.

Now suppose that you can delay construction of the plant. You still have the call option, but you face a trade-off. If the outlook is highly uncertain, it is tempting to wait and see whether the malted herring market takes off or nose-dives. On the other hand, if the project is truly profitable, the sooner you can capture the project's cash flows, the better. If the cash flows are high enough, you will want to exercise your option right away.

The cash flows from an investment project play the same role as dividend payments on a stock. When a stock pays no dividends, an American call is always worth more alive than dead and should never be exercised early. But payment of a dividend before the option matures reduces the ex-dividend price and the possible payoffs to the call option price at maturity. Think of the extreme case: If a company pays out all its assets in one bumper dividend, the stock price must be zero and the call worthless. Therefore, any in-the-money call would be exercised just before this liquidating dividend.

Dividends do not always prompt early exercise, but if they are sufficiently large, call option holders capture them by exercising just before the ex-dividend date. We see managers acting in the same way: When a project's forecasted cash flows are sufficiently large, managers capture the cash flows by investing right away.[5] But when forecasted cash flows are small, managers are inclined to hold onto their call

[5]In this case the call's value equals its lower-bound value because it is exercised immediately.

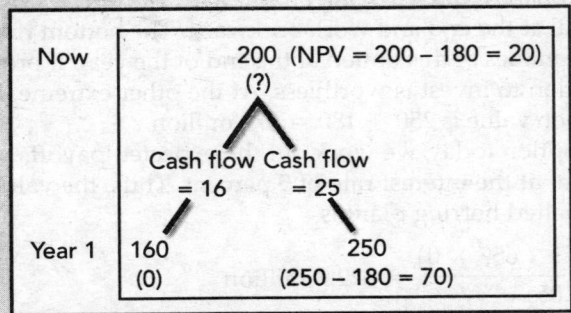

FIGURE 22.2

Possible cash flows and end-of-period values for the malted herring project are shown in blue. The project costs $180 million, either now or later. The burgundy figures in parentheses show payoffs from the option to wait and to invest later if the project is positive-NPV at year 1. Waiting means loss of the first year's cash flows. The problem is to figure out the current value of the option.

rather than to invest, even when project NPV is positive.[6] This explains why managers are sometimes reluctant to commit to positive-NPV projects. This caution is rational as long as the option to wait is open and sufficiently valuable.

Valuing the Malted Herring Option

Figure 22.2 shows the possible cash flows and end-of-year values for the malted herring project. If you commit and invest $180 million, you have a project worth $200 million. If demand turns out to be low in year 1, the cash flow is only $16 million and the value of the project falls to $160 million. But if demand is high in year 1, the cash flow is $25 million and value rises to $250 million. Although the project lasts indefinitely, we assume that investment cannot be postponed beyond the end of the first year, and therefore we show only the cash flows for the first year and the possible values at the end of the year. Notice that if you undertake the investment right away, you capture the first year's cash flow ($16 million or $25 million); if you delay, you miss out on this cash flow, but you will have more information on how the project is likely to work out.

We can use the binomial method to value this option. The first step is to pretend that investors are risk neutral and to calculate the probabilities of high and low demand in this risk-neutral world. If demand is high in the first year, the malted herring plant has a cash flow of $25 million and a year-end value of $250 million. The total return is $(25 + 250)/200 - 1 = .375$, or 37.5 percent. If demand is low, the plant has a cash flow of $16 million and a year-end value of $160 million. Total return is $(16 + 160)/200 - 1 = -.12$, or -12 percent. In a *risk-neutral* world, the expected return would be equal to the interest rate, which we assume is 5 percent:

$$\begin{array}{c}\text{Expected} \\ \text{return}\end{array} = \left(\begin{array}{c}\text{Probability of} \\ \text{high demand}\end{array}\right) \times 37.5 + \left(\begin{array}{c}1 - \text{probability of} \\ \text{high demand}\end{array}\right) \times (-12) = 5\%$$

Therefore the (pretend) probability of high demand is 34.3 percent.

---

[6]We have been a bit vague about forecasted project cash flows. If competitors can enter and take away cash that you could have earned, the meaning is clear. But what about the decision to, say, develop an oil well? Here delay doesn't waste barrels of oil in the ground; it simply postpones production and the associated cash flow. The cost of waiting is the decline in today's *present value* of revenues from production. Present value declines if the future rate of increase in oil prices is not sufficiently high, that is, if the discounted price of oil is less than the current price.

We want to value a call option on the malted herring project with an exercise price of $180 million. We begin as usual at the end and work backward. The bottom row of Figure 22.2 shows the possible values of this option at the end of the year. If project value is $160 million, the option to invest is worthless. At the other extreme, if project value is $250 million, option value is 250 − 180 = $70 million.

To calculate the value of the option today, we work out the expected payoffs in a risk-neutral world and discount at the interest rate of 5 percent. Thus, the value of your option to invest in the malted herring plant is

$$\frac{(.343 \times 70) + (.657 \times 0)}{1.05} = \$22.9 \text{ million}$$

But here is where we need to recognize the opportunity to exercise the option immediately. The option is worth $22.9 million if you keep it open, and it is worth the project's immediate NPV (200 − 180 = $20 million) if exercised now. Thus the fact that the malted herring project has a positive NPV is not sufficient reason for investing. There is a still better strategy: Wait and see.

Optimal Timing for Real Estate Development

Sometimes it pays to wait for a long time, even for projects with large positive NPVs. Suppose you own a plot of vacant land in the suburbs.[7] The land can be used for a hotel or an office building, but not for both. A hotel could be later converted to an office building, or an office building to a hotel, but only at significant cost. You are therefore reluctant to invest, even if both investments have positive NPVs.

In this case you have two options to invest, but only one can be exercised. You therefore learn two things by waiting. First, you learn about the general *level* of cash flows from development, for example, by observing changes in the value of developed properties near your land. Second, you can update your estimates of the *relative* size of the hotel's future cash flows versus the office building's.

Figure 22.3 shows the conditions in which you would finally commit to build either the hotel or the office building. The horizontal axis shows the current cash flows that a hotel would generate. The vertical axis shows current cash flows for an office building. For simplicity, we will assume that each investment would have NPV of exactly zero at current cash flow of 100. Thus, if you were forced to invest today, you would choose the building with the higher cash flow, assuming the cash flow is greater than 100. (What if you were forced to decide today and each building could generate the same cash flow, say, 150? You would flip a coin.)

If the two buildings' cash flows plot in the colored area at the lower right of Figure 22.3, you build the hotel. To fall in this area, the hotel's cash flows have to beat two hurdles. First, they must exceed a minimum level of about 240. Second, they must exceed the office building's cash flows by a sufficient amount. If the situation is reversed, with office building cash flows above the minimum level of 240, and also sufficiently above the hotel's, then you build the office building. In this case, the cash flows plot in the colored area at the top left of the figure.

Notice how the "Delay development" region extends upward along the 45-degree line in Figure 22.3. When the cash flows from the hotel and office building are nearly the same, you become *very* cautious before choosing one over the other.

---

[7]The following example is based on P. D. Childs, T. J. Riddiough, and A. J. Triantis, "Mixed Uses and the Redevelopment Option," *Real Estate Economics* 24 (Fall 1996), pp. 317–339.

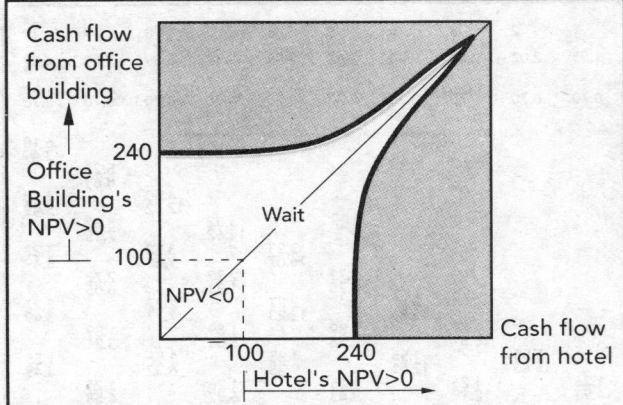

FIGURE 22.3

Development option for vacant land, assuming two mutually exclusive uses, either hotel or office building. The developer should "wait and see" unless the hotel's and office building's cash flows end up in one of the shaded areas.

Source: Adapted from Figure 1 in P. D. Childs, T. J. Riddiough, and A. J. Triantis, "Mixed Uses and the Redevelopment Option," *Real Estate Economics* 24 (Fall 1996), pp. 317–339.

You may be surprised at how high cash flows have to be in Figure 22.3 to justify investment. There are three reasons. First, building the office building means not building the hotel, and vice versa. Second, the calculations underlying Figure 22.3 assumed cash flows that were small, but growing; therefore, the costs of waiting to invest were small. Third, the calculations did not consider the threat that someone might build a competing hotel or office building right next door. In that case the "relax and wait" area of Figure 22.3 would shrink dramatically.

 ## 22.3 THE ABANDONMENT OPTION

Expansion value is important. When investments turn out well, the quicker and easier the business can be expanded, the better. But suppose bad news arrives, and cash flows are far below expectations. In that case it is useful to have the option to bail out and recover the value of the project's plant, equipment, or other assets. The option to abandon is equivalent to a put option. You exercise that abandonment option if the value recovered from the project's assets is greater than the present value of continuing the project for at least one more period.

The binomial method is tailor-made for most abandonment options. Here is an example.

The Zircon Subductor Project

Dawn East, the chief financial officer of Maine Subductor Corp., has to decide whether to start production of zircon subductors. The investment required is $12 million— $2 million for roads and site preparation and $10 million for equipment. The equipment costs $700,000 per year ($.7 million) to operate (a fixed cost). For simplicity, we will ignore other costs and taxes.

At today's prices, the project would generate revenues of $1.7 million per year. Annual output will be constant, so revenue is proportional to price. If the mine were operating today, cash flow would be $1.7 − .7 = $1.0 million.

FIGURE 22.4

Binomial tree for the Subductor project. Cash flow (top number) and end-of-period present value are shown for each node in millions of dollars. Abandonment occurs if cash flows drop to $.42 million (lighter shaded nodes) in years 3, 5, 7, or 9, and in year 10. Beginning present value is $13.84 million.

Year	0	1	2	3	4	5	6	7	8	9	10
Forecasted revenues / Present value	$17.00	1.85	2.02	2.20	2.40	2.62	2.85	3.11	3.39	3.69	4.02
Fixed costs / Present value	$5.15	0.70	0.70	0.70	0.70	0.70	0.70	0.70	0.70	0.70	0.70
NPV	−0.15										

Binomial tree (each node: cash flow / end-of-period present value), by year:

Level	0	1	2	3	4	5	6	7	8	9	10
											6.18 / 3.49
										5.28 / 8.61	
									4.50 / 12.22		4.50 / 3.49
								3.82 / 14.62		3.82 / 7.15	
							3.23 / 16.07		3.23 / 9.68		3.23 / 3.49
						2.72 / 16.75		2.72 / 11.31		2.72 / 6.05	
					2.27 / 16.86		2.27 / 12.23		2.27 / 7.77		2.27 / 3.49
				1.89 / 16.51		1.89 / 12.58		1.89 / 8.81		1.89 / 5.21	
			1.55 / 15.83		1.55 / 12.51		1.55 / 9.33		1.55 / 6.32		1.55 / 3.49
		1.26 / 14.91		1.26 / 12.10		1.26 / 9.43		1.26 / 6.92		1.26 / 4.58	
Cash flow / Present value	13.84		1.00 / 11.47		1.00 / 9.23		1.00 / 7.14		1.00 / 5.22		1.00 / 3.49
		0.78 / 10.73		0.78 / 8.83		0.78 / 7.09		0.78 / 5.50		0.78 / 4.11	
			0.59 / 8.49		0.59 / 6.95		0.59 / 5.60		0.59 / 4.43		0.59 / 3.49
				0.42 / 7.29		0.42 / 5.90		0.42 / 4.78		0.42 / 3.87	
					0.27 / 6.56		0.27 / 5.31		0.27 / 4.30		0.27 / 3.49
						0.15 / 5.90		0.15 / 4.78		0.15 / 3.87	
							0.03 / 5.31		0.03 / 4.30		0.03 / 3.49
								−0.06 / 4.78		−0.06 / 3.87	
									−0.14 / 4.30		−0.14 / 3.49
										−0.22 / 3.87	
											−0.28 / 3.49

Salvage value (years 1–10)		9.00	8.10	7.29	6.56	5.90	5.31	4.78	4.30	3.87	3.49

Calculate the Present Value of the Project   The first step in a real options analysis is to value the underlying asset, that is, the project if it had no options attached. Usually this is done by discounted cash flow (DCF). In this case the chief source of uncertainty is the future selling price of zircon subductors. Therefore Ms. East starts by calculating the present value of future revenues. She notes a strong upward trend in subductor prices, and ends up forecasting annual growth at 9 percent for the next 10 years. Fixed costs are constant at $.7 million. The top panel of Figure 22.4 shows these cash-flow forecasts and calculates present values: $17 million for revenues, after discounting at a risk-adjusted rate of 9 percent, and $5.15 million for fixed costs, after discounting at a risk-free rate of 6 percent.[8] The NPV of the project, assuming no salvage value or abandonment over its 10-year life, is

$$\text{NPV} = \text{PV(revenues)} - \text{PV(fixed costs)} - \text{investment required}$$
$$= \$17.00 - 5.15 - 12.00 = -\$.15 \text{ million}$$

This NPV is slightly negative, but Ms. East has so far made no provision for abandonment.

---

[8]Why calculate present values for revenues and fixed costs separately? Because it's easier to construct a binomial tree for revenues, which can be assumed to follow a random walk with constant standard deviation. We will subtract fixed costs after the binomial tree is constructed.

Build a Binomial Tree   Now Ms. East constructs a binomial tree for revenues and PV(revenues). She notes that subductor prices have followed a random walk with an annual standard deviation of about 14 percent. She constructs a binomial tree with one step per year. The "up" values for revenues are 115 percent of the prior year's revenues. The "down" values are 87 percent of prior revenues.[9] Thus, the up and down revenues for year 1 are $1.70 × 1.15 = $1.96 and $1.70 × .87 = $1.48 million, respectively.[10] After deduction of fixed costs, the up and down cash flows are $1.26 and $.78 million, respectively. The first two years of the resulting tree are shown below (figures in millions of dollars).

Figure 22.4 shows the whole tree, starting with cash flows in year 1. (Maine Subductor can't generate any revenues in year 0 because it hasn't started production yet.) The top number at each node is cash flow. The bottom number (in burgundy) is the *end*-of-year present value of *all* subsequent cash flows, including the value of the production equipment when the project ends or is abandoned. We will see in a moment how these present values are calculated.

Finally, Ms. East calculates the risk-neutral probabilities of up and down changes in revenues, p and $1 - p$, respectively. If the risk-free interest rate is 6 percent, $p = .6791$ and $1 - p = .3209$:

$$\text{Expected return} = .15p - .13(1 - p) = .06$$
$$\text{Probability of up change} = p = .6791$$
$$\text{Probability of down change} = 1 - p = .3209$$

Solve for Optimal Abandonment and Project Value   Ms. East has assumed a project life of 10 years. At that time the production equipment, which normally depreciates by about 10 percent per year, should be worth $3.49 million. This salvage value represents what the equipment could be sold for, or its value to Maine Subductor if shifted to another use. Forecasted salvage values are shown year-by-year at the bottom of Figure 22.4.

Now let's calculate this project's value in the binomial tree. We start at the far right of Figure 22.4 (year 10) and work back to the present. The company will

---

[9]The formula (given in Section 21.2) for the up percentage is $u = e^{\sigma \sqrt{h}}$ where σ is the standard deviation per year and h is the interval as a fraction of a year. In this case, $h = 1$ and $e^{\sigma} = e^{.14} = 1.15$. The down value is $d = 1/u = .87$.

[10]We do not build the 9 percent forecasted growth rate into the up and down steps of the tree. However, the "up" probabilities will be greater than the "down" probabilities, enough greater that the present value of next period's revenue will equal this year's revenue, using a risk-free discount rate of 6 percent. In other words, the tree will assume a 6 percent *risk-neutral* expected growth rate.

abandon for sure in year 10, when the ore body is exhausted. Thus we enter the ending salvage value ($3.49 million) as the end-of-year value in year 10. Then we step back to year 9.

Suppose that Maine Subductor ends up in the best possible place in that year, where cash flow is $5.28 million. The upside payoff if the company does not abandon is the "up" node in year 10: $6.18 + 3.49 = 9.67 million. The downside payoff is $4.50 + 3.49 = 7.99 million. The present value, using the risk-neutral probabilities, is

$$PV = \frac{(.6791 \times 9.67) + (.3209 \times 7.99)}{1.06} = \$8.61 \text{ million}$$

The company could abandon at the end of year 9, realizing salvage value of $3.87 million, but continuing is better. We therefore enter $8.61 million as the end-of-year value at the top node for year 9 in Figure 22.4.

We can fill in the end-of-period values for the other nodes in year 9 by the same procedure. But at some point, as we step down to lower and lower cash flows, there will come a node where it's better to bail out than continue. This occurs when cash flow is $.42 million. The present value of continuing is only

$$PV = \frac{.6791 \times (.59 + 3.49) + .3209 \times (.27 + 3.49)}{1.06} = \$3.75 \text{ million}$$

The payoff to abandonment is $3.87 million, so that payoff is entered as the value in year 9 at all nodes with cash flows equal to or less than $.42 million.

The cash flows and end-of-year values for year 9 are the payoffs to continuing from year 8. We then calculate values in year 8, checking at each node whether to abandon, for year 7, and so on back to year zero.[11] In this example, Maine Subductor should abandon the project in any year when cash flows fall to $.42 million. This means that it never encounters cash flows less than $.42 million.

The present value at year 0 is $13.84 million, so the project is worthwhile: NPV = $13.84 - 12.00 = +\$1.84$ million.

How much of this NPV is due to abandonment value?[12] The DCF valuation at the top of Figure 22.4 (which ignores salvage and abandonment) gives NPV of $-\$.15$ million, a drop of $1.99 million from the NPV with abandonment. Therefore, the value of the abandonment put is $1.99 million:

$$APV = NPV, \text{no abandonment} + \text{value of abandonment option}^{13}$$
$$= -.15 + 1.99 = \$1.84 \text{ million}$$

The project looks good, although Ms. East may wish to check out the timing option. She could decide to wait.

---

[11]We will spare you the calculations. You can check them, however. The spreadsheet for Figure 22.4 is on this book's website (**www.mhhe.com/bm7e**).

[12]You could also revalue the binomial tree with all salvage values set to zero. The present value in year 0 then falls to $11.85 million, implying NPV = $11.85 - 12.00 = -\$.15$ million. You can do this calculation in the spreadsheet program on the website. Just set "Salvage $t = 0$" equal to zero.

[13]It turns out, however, that the value of *early* abandonment in this example is relatively small. Suppose that Maine Subductor could recover salvage value of $3.49 million in year 10, but not before. The present value of this recovery in year 0, using a 6 percent discount rate, is $1.95 million. APV in this case is $-.15 + 1.95 = 1.8 million, only slightly less than the APV of $1.85 with early abandonment allowed.

Abandonment Value and Project Life

Ms. East assumed that the zircon subductor project had a definite 10 year life. But most projects' economic lives are not known at the start. Cash flows from a new product may last only a year or so if the product fails in the marketplace. But if it succeeds, that product, or variations or improvements of it, could be produced for decades.

A project's economic life can be just as hard to predict as the project's cash flows. Yet in standard DCF capital-budgeting analysis, that life is assumed to end at a fixed future date. Real options analysis allows us to relax that assumption. Here is the procedure.[14]

1. Forecast the range of possible cash flows well beyond your best guess of the project's economic life. Suppose, for example, that your guess is 10 years. You could prepare a binomial tree like Figure 22.4 stretching out 25 years into the future.

2. Then value the project, including its abandonment value. In the best upside scenarios, project life will be 25 years—it will never make sense to abandon before year 25. In the worst downside scenarios, project life will be much shorter, because the project will be more valuable dead than alive. If your original guess about project life is right, then in intermediate scenarios, where actual cash flows match expectations, abandonment will occur around year 10.

This procedure links project life to the performance of the project. It does not impose an arbitrary ending date, except in the far distant future.

Temporary Abandonment

Companies are often faced with complex options that allow them to abandon a project *temporarily*, that is, to mothball it until conditions improve. Suppose you own an oil tanker operating in the short-term spot market. (In other words, you charter the tanker voyage by voyage, at whatever short-term charter rates prevail at the start of the voyage.) The tanker costs $5 million a year to operate and at current tanker rates it produces charter revenues of $5.25 million per year. The tanker is therefore profitable but scarcely cause for celebration. Now tanker rates dip by about 10 percent, forcing revenues down to $4.7 million. Do you immediately lay off the crew and mothball the tanker until prices recover? The answer is clearly yes if the tanker business can be turned on and off like a faucet. But that is unrealistic. There is a fixed cost to mothballing the tanker. You don't want to incur this cost only to regret your decision next month if rates rebound to their earlier level. The higher the costs of mothballing and the more variable the level of charter rates, the greater the loss that you will be prepared to bear before you call it quits and lay up the boat.

Suppose that eventually you do decide to take the boat off the market. You lay up the tanker temporarily.[15] Two years later your faith is rewarded; charter rates rise, and the revenues from operating the tanker creep above the operating cost of

---

[14]See S. C. Myers and S. Majd, "Abandonment Value and Project Life," in F. J. Fabozzi (ed.), *Advances in Futures and Options Research*, JAI Press, 1990.

[15]We assume it makes sense to keep the tanker in mothballs. If rates fall sufficiently, it will pay to scrap the tanker.

FIGURE 22.5

An oil tanker should be mothballed when tanker rates fall to M, where the tanker's value if mothballed is enough above its value in operation to cover mothballing costs. The tanker is reactivated when rates recover to R.

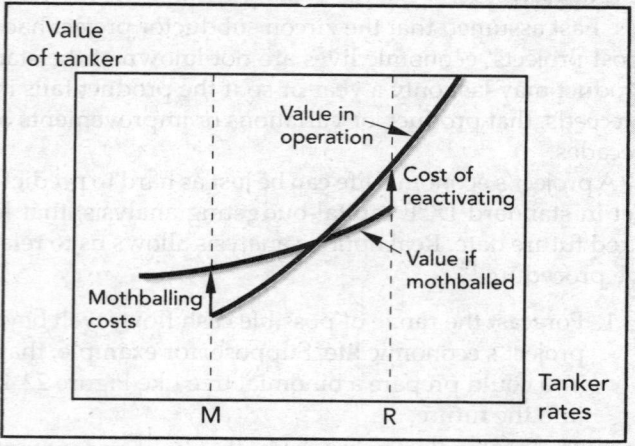

$5 million. Do you reactivate immediately? Not if there are costs to doing so. It makes more sense to wait until the project is well in the black and you can be fairly confident that you will not regret the cost of bringing the tanker back into operation.

These choices are illustrated in Figure 22.5. The colored line shows how the value of an operating tanker varies with the level of charter rates. The black line shows the value of the tanker when mothballed.[16] The level of rates at which it pays to mothball is given by M and the level at which it pays to reactivate is given by R. The higher the costs of mothballing and reactivating and the greater the variability in tanker rates, the further apart these points will be. You can see that it will pay for you to mothball as soon as the value of a mothballed tanker reaches the value of an operating tanker plus the costs of mothballing. It will pay to reactivate as soon as the value of a tanker that is operating in the spot market reaches the value of a mothballed tanker plus the costs of reactivating. If the level of rates falls below M, the value of the tanker is given by the black line; if the level is greater than R, value is given by the colored line. If rates lie between M and R, the tanker's value depends on whether it happens to be mothballed or operating.

22.4 FLEXIBLE PRODUCTION—AND ANOTHER LOOK AT AIRCRAFT PURCHASE OPTIONS

Companies often have an option to vary either the inputs in the production process or the outputs. For example, an electric utility plant may be designed to operate on either oil or natural gas. Or a manufacturer may invest in computer-integrated manufacturing (CIM) systems that allow it to vary the production mix.

In such cases the firm has the option to acquire one asset in exchange for another. Consider the electric utility's decision to build an oil-fired generating plant that can be converted to run on natural gas. You can think of the utility as having

---

[16]Dixit and Pindyck estimate these thresholds for a medium-sized tanker and show how they depend on costs and the volatility of freight rates. See A. K. Dixit and R. S. Pindyck, *Investment under Uncertainty*, Princeton University Press, Princeton, NJ, 1994, Chapter 7.

an option to "buy" a gas-fired plant in exchange for the oil-fired plant. If oil prices were certain, this would be a simple call option on a gas-fired plant with a fixed exercise price (the value of an oil-fired plant plus the cost of conversion). If the price of gas is sufficiently low, it pays to exercise the option and switch to gas.

In practice both oil and gas prices are likely to vary. This means that the exercise price of the utility's call option changes as the price of oil changes. Uncertainty about this exercise price could reduce or enhance the value of the option, depending on the correlation between the prices of the two fuels. If oil prices and gas prices moved together dollar for dollar, your option to switch fuels would be valueless. The benefit of a rise in the value of the underlying asset (the gas-fired plant) would be exactly offset by a rise in the option's exercise price (the value of the oil-fired plant). The best of all worlds would occur if the prices of the two fuels were negatively correlated. In this case whenever oil became expensive, the gas would become cheap. In these (unlikely) circumstances the option to switch between the two fuels would be particularly valuable.

In this example, the output is the same (electricity); option value comes from flexibility in raw materials (gas or oil). In other cases, option value comes from the flexibility to switch from product to product using the same production facilities. For example, textile firms have invested heavily in computer-controlled knitting machines, which allow production to shift from product to product, or from design to design, as demand and fashion dictate.

Flexibility in *procurement* can also have option value. For example, a computer manufacturer planning next year's production must also plan to buy components, such as disc drives and microprocessors, in large quantities. Should it strike a deal today with the component manufacturer? This locks in the quantity, price, and delivery dates. But it also gives up flexibility, for example, the ability to switch suppliers next year or buy at a "spot" price if next year's prices are lower.

The Finance in the News box features another example of the value of flexibility in production or procurement.

Another Look at Aircraft Purchase Options

For our final example, we return to the problem confronting airlines that order new airplanes for future use. In this industry "lead times" between an order and delivery can extend to several years. Long lead times mean that airlines which order planes today may end up not needing them. You can see why an airline might negotiate for an aircraft purchase *option*.

In Section 10.3, we used aircraft purchase options to illustrate the option to expand. That's true, but not the whole truth. Let's take another look. Suppose an airline forecasts a need for a new Airbus A320 four years hence.[17] It has at least three choices.

- *Commit now.* It can commit now to buy the plane, in exchange for Airbus's offer of locked-in price and delivery date.
- *Acquire option.* It can seek a purchase option from Airbus, allowing the airline to decide later whether to buy. A purchase option fixes the price and delivery date if the option is exercised.

---

[17]The following example is based on J. E. Stonier, "What is an Aircraft Purchase Option Worth? Quantifying Asset Flexibility Created through Manufacturer Lead-Time Reductions and Product Commonality," in G. F. Butler and M. R. Keller (eds.), *Handbook of Airline Finance*, Aviation Week Books, 1999.

VALUING FLEXIBILITY

With the help of faculty from Stanford University, Hewlett-Packard has experimented with real options since the beginning of the 1990s. Example: In the '80s, HP customized inkjet printers for foreign markets at the factory, then shipped them in finished form to warehouses. Customizing at the factory is cheaper than customizing in the field. But HP kept guessing wrong on demand and ending up with, say, too many printers configured for French customers but not enough for Germans.

Executives realized that it would be smarter to ship partially assembled printers and then customize them at the warehouse, once it had firm orders. True, local customization costs more. But even though production costs rose, HP saved $3 million a month by more effectively matching supply to demand, says Corey A. Billington, a former Stanford professor who directs HP's Strategic Planning & Modeling group.

Common sense? Sure. But you can also view it as a neat solution of a real-options problem. Increasing the cost of production—anathema to your average engineer—was in effect the price HP paid for the option to delay configuration choices until the optimal time.

Source: P. Coy, "Exploiting Uncertainty," *Business Week*, June 7, 1999.

- *Wait and decide later.* Airbus will be happy to sell another A320 at any time in the future if the airline wants to buy one. However, the airline may have to pay a higher price and wait longer for delivery, especially if the airline industry is flying high and many planes are on order.

The top half of Figure 22.6 shows the terms of a typical purchase option for an Airbus A320. The option must be exercised at year 3, when final assembly of the plane will begin. The option fixes the purchase price and the delivery date in year 4. The bottom half of the figure shows the consequences of "wait and decide later." We assume that the decision will come at year 3. If the decision is "buy," the airline pays the year-3 price and joins the queue for delivery in year 5 or later.

The payoffs from "wait and decide later" can never be better than the payoffs from an aircraft purchase option, since the airline can discard the option and negotiate afresh with Airbus if it wishes. In most cases the airline will be better off in the future with the option than without it; the airline is at least guaranteed a place in the production line, and it may have locked in a favorable purchase price. But how much are these advantages worth today, compared to the wait-and-see strategy?

Figure 22.7 illustrates Airbus's answers to this problem. It assumes a three-year purchase option with an exercise price equal to the current A320 price of $45 million. The present value of the purchase option depends on both the NPV of purchasing an A320 at that price and on the forecasted wait for delivery if the airline does *not* have a purchase option but nevertheless decides to place an order in year 3. The longer the wait in year 3, the more valuable it is to have the purchase option today. (Remember that the purchase option holds a place in the A320 production line and guarantees delivery in year 4.)

	Year 0	Year 3	Year 4	Year 5 or later
Buy option	Airline and manufacturer set price and delivery date	Exercise? (Yes or no)	Aircraft delivered if option exercised	
Wait	Wait	Buy now? If yes, negotiate price and wait for delivery.		Aircraft delivered if purchased at year 3.

FIGURE 22.6

This aircraft purchase option, if exercised at year 3, guarantees delivery at year 4 at a fixed price. Without the option, the airline can still order the plane at year 3, but the price is uncertain and the wait for delivery longer.

Source: Adapted from Figure 17-17 in J. Stonier, "What is an Aircraft Purchase Option Worth? Quantifying Asset Flexibility Created through Manufacturer Lead-Time Reductions and Product Commonality," in G. F. Butler and M. R. Keller (eds.), *Handbook of Airline Finance*, Aviation Week Books, 1999.

FIGURE 22.7

Value of aircraft purchase option—the *extra* value of the option versus waiting and possibly negotiating a purchase later. (See Figure 22.6.) The purchase option is worth most when NPV of purchase now is about zero and the forecasted wait for delivery is long.

Source: Adapted from Fig. 17-20 in J. Stonier, *op. cit.*

If the NPV of buying an A320 today is very high (the right-hand side of Figure 22.7), future NPV will probably be high as well, and the airline will want to buy regardless of whether it has a purchase option. In this case the value of the purchase option comes mostly from the value of guaranteed delivery in year 4.[18]

---

[18]The Airbus real-options model assumes that future A320 prices will be increased when demand is high, but only to an upper bound. Thus the airline that waits and decides later may still have a positive-NPV investment opportunity if future demand and NPV are high. Figure 22.7 plots the *difference* between the value of the purchase option and this wait-and-see opportunity. This difference can shrink when NPV is high, especially if forecasted waiting times are short.

If the NPV is very low, then the option has low value because the airline is unlikely to exercise it. (Low NPV today probably means low NPV in year 3.) The purchase option is worth the most, compared to the wait-and-decide-later strategy, when NPV is around zero. In this case the airline can exercise the option, getting a good price and early delivery, if future NPV is higher than expected, and walk away from the option if NPV disappoints. Of course, if it walks away, it may still wish to negotiate with Airbus for delivery at a price lower than the option's exercise price.

We have cruised by many of the technical details of Airbus's valuation model for purchase options. But the example does illustrate how real-options models are being built and used. By the way, Airbus offers more than just plain-vanilla purchase options. Airlines can negotiate "rolling options," which lock in price but do not guarantee a place on the production line. (Exercise of the rolling option means that the airline joins the end of the queue.) Airbus also offers a purchase option that includes the right to switch from delivery of an A320 to an A319, a somewhat smaller plane.

 ## 22.5 A CONCEPTUAL PROBLEM?

In this chapter we have suggested that option pricing models can help to value the real options embedded in capital investment decisions.

When we introduced option pricing models in Chapter 21, we suggested that the trick is to construct a package of the underlying asset and a loan that would give exactly the same payoffs as the option. If the two investments do not sell for the same price, then there are arbitrage possibilities. But many assets are not freely traded. This means that we can no longer rely on arbitrage arguments to justify the use of option models.

The risk-neutral method still makes practical sense, however. It's really just an application of the *certainty-equivalent* method introduced in Chapter 9.[19] The key assumption—implicit till now—is that the company's *shareholders* have access to assets with the same risk characteristics (e.g., the same beta) as the capital investments being evaluated by the firm.

Think of each real investment opportunity as having a "double," a security or portfolio with identical risk. Then the expected rate of return offered by the double is also the cost of capital for the real investment and the discount rate for a DCF valuation of the investment project. Now what would investors pay for a real *option* based on the project? The same as for an identical traded option written on the double. This traded option does not have to exist; it is enough to know how it would be valued by investors, who could employ either the arbitrage or the risk-neutral method. The two methods give the same answer, of course.

When we value a real option by the risk-neutral method, we are calculating the option's value if it could be traded. This exactly parallels standard capital budget-

---

[19]Use of risk-neutral probabilities converts future cash flows to certainty equivalents, which are then discounted to present value at a risk-free rate.

ing. If shareholders can buy traded securities or portfolios with the same risk characteristics as the real investments being evaluated by the firm, they would vote unanimous endorsement for any real investment whose market value if traded would exceed the investment required. This key assumption supports the use of both DCF and real-option-valuation methods.

In Chapter 21 you learned the basics of option valuation. In this chapter we described four important real options:

1. *The option to make follow-on investments.* Companies often cite "strategic" value when taking on negative-NPV projects. A close look at the projects' payoffs reveals call options on follow-on projects in addition to the immediate projects' cash flows. Today's investments can generate tomorrow's opportunities.

2. *The option to wait (and learn) before investing.* This is equivalent to owning a call option on the investment project. The call is exercised when the firm commits to the project. But often it's better to defer a positive-NPV project in order to keep the call alive. Deferral is most attractive when uncertainty is great and immediate project cash flows—which are lost or postponed by waiting—are small.

3. *The option to abandon.* The option to abandon a project provides partial insurance against failure. This is a put option; the put's exercise price is the value of the project's assets if sold or shifted to a more valuable use.

4. *The option to vary the firm's output or its production methods.* Firms often build flexibility into their production facilities so that they can use the cheapest raw materials or produce the most valuable set of outputs. In this case they effectively acquire the option to exchange one asset for another.

We should offer here a healthy warning: The real options encountered in practice are often complex. Each real option brings its own issues and trade-offs. Nevertheless the tools that you have learned in this and previous chapters can be used in practice. The Black–Scholes formula often suffices to value expansion options. Problems of investment timing and optimal abandonment can be tackled with binomial trees.

Binomial trees are cousins of decision trees. You work back through binomial trees from future payoffs to present value. Whenever a future decision needs to be made, you figure out the value-maximizing choice, using the principles of option pricing theory, and record the resulting value at the appropriate node of the tree.

Don't jump to the conclusion that real-option-valuation methods can replace discounted cash flow (DCF). First, DCF works fine for safe cash flows. It also works fine for "cash cow" assets—that is, for assets or businesses whose value depends primarily on forecasted cash flows, not on real options. Second, the starting point in most real-option analyses is the present value of an underlying asset. To value the underlying asset, you typically have to use DCF.

Real options are rarely traded assets. When we value a real option, we are estimating its value if it could be traded. This is the standard approach in corporate finance, the same approach taken in DCF valuations. The key assumption is that shareholders can buy traded securities or portfolios with the same risk character-istics as the real investments being evaluated by the firm. If so, they would vote unanimously for any real investment whose market value if traded would exceed the investment required. This key assumption supports the use of both DCF and real-option-valuation methods.

FURTHER READING

Further reading for Chapter 10 lists several introductory articles on real options. The Summer 2001 issue of the Journal of Applied Corporate Finance *contains several additional articles, includ-ing the following survey of how real options are used in practice:*

A. Triantis and A. Borison: "Real Options: State of the Practice," *Journal of Applied Corporate Finance,* 14:8–24 (Summer 2001).

The standard texts on real options include:

T. Copeland and V. Antikarov: *Real Options: A Practitioner's Guide,* Texere, New York, 2001.

A. K. Dixit and R. S. Pindyck: *Investment under Uncertainty,* Princeton University Press, Princeton, NJ, 1994.

M. Amran and N. Kulatilaka: *Real Options: Managing Strategic Investments in an Uncertain World,* Harvard Business School Press, Boston, 1999.

L. Trigeorgis: *Real Options,* MIT Press, Cambridge, MA, 1996.

The Autumn 1993 issue of Financial Management *includes six articles on real options, including a description of how to value an industrial facility that can be fueled with gas or oil:*

N. Kulatilaka: "The Value of Flexibility: The Case of a Dual-Fuel Industrial Steam Boiler," *Financial Management,* 22:271–280 (Autumn 1993).

Mason and Merton review a range of option applications to corporate finance:

S. P. Mason and R. C. Merton: "The Role of Contingent Claims Analysis in Corporate Fi-nance," in E. I. Altman and M. G. Subrahmanyan (eds.), *Recent Advances in Corporate Fi-nance,* Richard D. Irwin, Inc., Homewood, IL, 1985.

Brennan and Schwartz have worked out an interesting application to natural resource investments:

M. J. Brennan and E. S. Schwartz: "Evaluating Natural Resource Investments," *Journal of Business,* 58:135–157 (April 1985).

QUIZ

1. What are the four types of real options?
2. Look again at the valuation in Table 22.2 of the option to invest in the Mark II project. Consider a change in each of the following inputs. Would the change increase or de-crease the value of the expansion option?
   a. Increased uncertainty (higher standard deviation).
   b. More optimistic forecast (higher expected value) of the Mark II in 1985.
   c. Increase in the required investment in 1985.
3. Describe the real options in each of the following cases.
   a. United Airlines pays Boeing for the option to purchase ten 747 jets in 2005.
   b. United Airlines buys Boeing 767 passenger jets with reinforced floors, larger doors, and other features that would allow quick conversion to a cargo plane.

c. Exxon Mobil pays $75 million for oil drilling rights in Central Costaguana. The Costaguanan oil fields are too small and costly to develop now but development could be profitable if oil prices rise.

d. Forest Investors purchases a remote stand of Northern hardwoods. Harvest is positive-NPV now but the company nevertheless postpones logging.

e. Deutsche Motorwerke builds an automobile engine plant in China. The investment is negative-NPV. The company justifies the project as a strategic investment.

f. A biotech startup declines an opportunity to buy a building designed for biotech research. Instead it operates in a rented warehouse. It even rents its furniture and laboratory equipment.

g. A plot of land suitable for construction of an office building is left vacant, even though the present value of rents from a new office building would significantly exceed construction cost.

4. Respond to the following comments.
   a. "You don't need option pricing theories to value flexibility. Just use a decision tree. Discount the cash flows in the tree at the company cost of capital."
   b. "These option pricing methods are just plain nutty. They say that real options on risky assets are worth more than options on safe assets."
   c. "Real-options methods eliminate the need for DCF valuation of investment projects."

5. You own a parcel of vacant land. You can develop it now, or wait.
   a. What is the advantage of waiting?
   b. Why might you decide to develop the property immediately?

PRACTICE QUE/TION/

1. Describe each of the following situations in the language of options:
   a. Drilling rights to undeveloped heavy crude oil in Northern Alberta. Development and production of the oil is a negative-NPV endeavor. (The break-even oil price is C$32 per barrel, versus a spot price of C$20.) However, the decision to develop can be put off for up to five years. Development costs are expected to increase by 5 percent per year.
   b. A restaurant is producing net cash flows, after all out-of-pocket expenses, of $700,000 per year. There is no upward or downward trend in the cash flows, but they fluctuate, with an annual standard deviation of 15 percent. The real estate occupied by the restaurant is owned, not leased, and could be sold for $5 million. Ignore taxes.
   c. A variation on part (b): Assume the restaurant faces known fixed costs of $300,000 per year, incurred as long as the restaurant is operating. Thus

   Net cash flow = revenue less variable costs − fixed costs
       $700,000 = 1,000,000 − 300,000

   The annual standard deviation of the forecast error of revenue less variable costs is 10.5 percent. The interest rate is 10 percent. Ignore taxes.
   d. A paper mill can be shut down in periods of low demand and restarted if demand improves sufficiently. The costs of closing and reopening the mill are fixed.
   e. A real-estate developer uses a parcel of urban land as a parking lot, although construction of either a hotel or an apartment building on the land would be a positive-NPV investment.
   f. Air France negotiates a purchase option for the first 10 Sonic Cruisers produced by Boeing. Air France must confirm its order in 2005. Otherwise, Boeing will be free to sell the aircraft to other airlines.

2. After a good night's sleep, your boss, the CFO in Section 22.1, still doesn't understand. Try again. Explain why the Mark I microcomputer has a positive NPV even though DCF analyses of both the Mark I and the Mark II seem to show *negative* NPVs.

3. Look again at Table 22.2. How does the value in 1982 of the option to invest in the Mark II change if:
   a. The investment required for the Mark II is $800 million (vs. $900 million)?
   b. The present value of the Mark II in 1982 is $500 million (vs. $467 million)?
   c. The standard deviation of the Mark II's present value is only 20 percent (vs. 35 percent)?

4. You own a one-year call option on 1 acre of Los Angeles real estate. The exercise price is $2 million, and the current, appraised market value of the land is $1.7 million. The land is currently used as a parking lot, generating just enough money to cover real estate taxes. The annual standard deviation is 15 percent and the interest rate 12 percent. How much is your call worth? Use the Black–Scholes formula.

5. A variation on question 4: Suppose the land is occupied by a warehouse generating rents of $150,000 after real estate taxes and all other out-of-pocket costs. The value of the land plus warehouse is again $1.7 million. Other facts are as in question 4. You have a *European* call option. What is it worth?

6. In Section 22.4 we described the problem faced by a utility that was contemplating an investment in equipment that would allow it to burn either oil or gas. How would the value of the option to cofire be affected if **(a)** the prices of both oil and gas were very variable, but **(b)** the prices of oil and gas were highly correlated?

7. Look again at the malted herring example in Section 22.3. Suppose that by postponing the project for a year, you do not miss out on any cash flows. Instead all cash flows are simply delayed by one year. What is the value of the option to invest in the malted herring plant?

8. Suppose investment in the malted herring project (see Section 22.3) can be postponed to the end of year 2.
   a. Build a two-year binomial tree with cash flows proportional to end-of-year values. Under what circumstances would you want to delay construction for two years?
   b. How does this additional choice affect project NPV?
   c. Would NPV change if you could undertake the project *only* in years 0 or 2?

9. You have an option to purchase all of the assets of the Overland Railroad for $2.5 billion. The option expires in 9 months. You estimate Overland's current (month 0) present value (PV) as $2.7 billion. Overland generates after-tax free cash flow (FCF) of $50 million at the end of each quarter (i.e., at the end of each three-month period). If you exercise your option at the start of the quarter, that quarter's cash flow is paid out to you. If you do not exercise, the cash flow goes to Overland's current owners.

   In each quarter, Overland's PV either increases by 10 percent or decreases by 9.09 percent. This PV includes the quarterly FCF of $50 million. After the $50 million is paid out, PV drops by $50 million. Thus the binomial tree for the first quarter is (figures in millions):

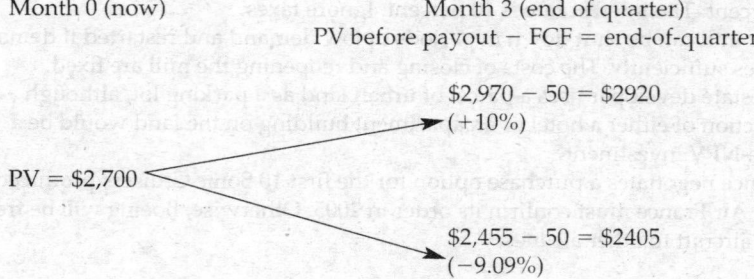

Month 0 (now)   Month 3 (end of quarter)
                          PV before payout − FCF = end-of-quarter PV

                                      $2,970 − 50 = $2920
                                      (+10%)
PV = $2,700
                                      $2,455 − 50 = $2405
                                      (−9.09%)

The risk-free interest rate is 2 percent per quarter.
   a. Build a binomial tree for Overland, with one up or down change for each 3-month period (three steps to cover your 9-month option).
   b. Suppose you can only exercise your option now, or after 9 months (not at month 3 or 6). Would you exercise now?
   c. Suppose you can exercise now, or at month 3, 6, or 9. What is your option worth today? Should you exercise today, or wait?

10. In Section 10.3 we considered two production technologies for a new Wankel-engined outboard motor. Technology A was the most efficient but had no salvage value if the new outboards failed to sell. Technology B was less efficient but offered a salvage value of $10 million.
    Figure 10.7 shows the present value of the project as either $18.5 or 8.5 million in year 1 if Technology A is used. Assume that the present value of these payoffs is $11.5 million at year 0.
    a. With Technology B, the payoffs at year 1 are $18 or 8 million. What is the present value in year 0 if Technology B is used? (*Hint:* The payoffs with Technology B vs. A differ by a constant $.5 million.) The risk-free rate is 7 percent.
    b. Technology B allows abandonment in year 1 for $10 million salvage value. Calculate abandonment value.

11. Look again at practice question 10. We will assume that Technology A has a salvage value of $7 million, rather than zero. The present value of the project with Technology A is $11.5 million at year 0, assuming no abandonment. The risk-free rate is 7 percent.
    a. Construct a one-year binomial tree for this project, with one up or down step every three months (four steps total). The up steps are +25 percent, the down steps are −16.7 percent.
    b. Suppose abandonment can only occur at year 1. In what circumstances would you abandon then? What is abandonment value at year 0?

12. How do the binomial trees used in this chapter differ from the decision trees discussed in Chapter 10?

13. Josh Kidding, who has only read part of Chapter 10, decides to value a real option by (1) setting out a decision tree, with cash flows and probabilities forecasted for each future outcome; (2) deciding what to do at each decision point in the tree; and (3) discounting the resulting expected cash flows at the company cost of capital. Will this procedure give the right answer? Why or why not?

14. Some argue that option pricing theory doesn't apply to real options, because the options are not traded in financial markets. Do you agree? Explain.

1. Suppose you expect to need a new plant that will be ready to produce turbo-encabulators in 36 months. If design A is chosen, construction must begin immediately. Design B is more expensive, but you can wait 12 months before breaking ground. Figure 22.8 shows the cumulative present value of construction costs for the two designs up to the 36-month deadline. Assume that the designs, once built, will be equally efficient and have equal production capacity.
   A standard discounted-cash-flow analysis ranks design A ahead of design B. But suppose the demand for turbo-encabulators falls and the new factory is not needed; then, as Figure 22.8 shows, the firm is better off with design B, provided the project is abandoned before month 24.

CHALLENGE QUESTIONS

FIGURE 22.8

Cumulative construction cost of the two plant designs. Plant A takes 36 months to build; plant B, only 24. But plant B costs more.

Describe this situation as the choice between two (complex) call options. Then describe the same situation in terms of (complex) abandonment options. The two descriptions should imply identical payoffs, given optimal exercise strategies.

2. Consumers appear to require returns of 25 percent or more before they are prepared to make energy-efficient investments, even though a more reasonable estimate of the cost of capital might be around 15 percent. Here is a highly simplified problem which illustrates that such behavior *could* be rational.[20]

   Suppose you have the opportunity to invest $1,000 in new space-heating equipment that would generate fuel savings of $250 a year forever given current fuel prices. What is the PV of this investment if the cost of capital is 15 percent? What is the NPV?

   Now recognize that fuel prices are uncertain and that the savings could well turn out to be $50 a year or $450 a year. If the risk-free interest rate is 10 percent, would you invest in the new equipment now or wait and see how fuel prices change? Explain.

3. In Chapter 4, we expressed the value of a share of stock as

$$P_0 = \frac{EPS_1}{r} + PVGO$$

---

[20]See, for example, A. H. Sanstad, C. Blumstein, and S. E. Stoft, "How High Are Option Values in Energy-Efficient Investments?" *Energy Policy* 9 (1995), pp. 739–743. However, the authors argue that the option to delay investment is not sufficiently valuable to explain consumer behavior.

where EPS$_1$ is earnings per share from existing assets, r is the expected rate of return required by investors, and PVGO is the present value of growth opportunities. PVGO really consists of a portfolio of expansion options.

a. What is the effect of an increase in PVGO on the standard deviation or beta of the stock's rate of return?

b. Suppose the CAPM is used to calculate the cost of capital for a growth (high-PVGO) firm. Assume all-equity financing. Will this cost of capital be the correct hurdle rate for investments to expand the firm's plant and equipment, or to introduce new products?

CHAPTER TWENTY-THREE

WARRANTS AND CONVERTIBLES

MANY DEBT ISSUES are either packages of bonds and warrants or convertibles. The warrant gives its owner the right to buy other company securities. A convertible bond gives its owner the right to exchange the bond for other securities.

There is also convertible preferred stock—it is often used to finance mergers, for example. Convertible preferred gives its owner the right to exchange the preferred share for other securities.

What are these strange hybrids, and how should you value them? Why are they issued? We will answer each of these questions in turn.

23.1 WHAT IS A WARRANT?

A significant proportion of private placement bonds and a smaller proportion of public issues are sold with warrants. In addition, warrants are sometimes sold with issues of common or preferred stock; they are also often given to investment bankers as compensation for underwriting services or used to compensate creditors in the case of bankruptcy.[1]

In April 1995 B.J. Services, a firm servicing the oil industry, issued 4.8 million warrants as partial payment for an acquisition. Each of these warrants allowed the holder to buy one share of B.J. Services for $30 at any time before April 2000. When the warrants were issued, the shares were priced at $19, so that the price needed to rise by more than 50 percent to make it worthwhile to exercise the warrants.

Warrant holders are not entitled to vote or to receive dividends. But the exercise price of a warrant is automatically adjusted for any stock dividends or stock splits. So, when in 1998 B.J. Services split its stock 2 for 1, each warrant holder was given the right to buy two shares and the exercise price was reduced to $30 \div 2 = \$15.00$ per share. By the time that the warrants finally expired in April 2000, the share price had reached $70 and so a warrant to buy two shares was worth $2 \times (\$70 - \$15) = \$110$.

Valuing Warrants

As a trained option spotter (having read Chapter 20), you have probably already classified the B.J. Services warrant as a five-year American call option exercisable at $15 (after adjustment for the 1998 stock split). You can depict the relationship between the value of the warrant and the value of the common stock with our standard option shorthand, as in Figure 23.1. The lower limit on the value of the warrant is the heavy line in the figure.[2] If the price of B.J. Services stock is less than $15, the lower limit on the warrant price is zero; if the price of the stock is greater than $15, the lower limit is equal to the stock price minus $15. Investors in warrants sometimes refer to this lower limit as the *theoretical* value of the warrant. It is a misleading term, because both theory and practice tell us that before the final exercise date the value of the warrant should lie *above* the lower limit, on a curve like the one shown in Figure 23.1.

---

[1] The term *warrant* usually refers to a long-term option issued by a company on its own stock or bonds, but investment banks and other financial institutions also issue "warrants" to buy the stock of another firm.

[2] Do you remember why this is a lower limit? What would happen if, by some accident, the warrant price was *less* than the stock price minus $15? (See Section 20.3.)

FIGURE 23.1

Relationship between the value of the
B.J. Services warrant and stock price.
The heavy line is the lower limit for
warrant value. Warrant value falls to
the lower limit just before the option
expires. Before expiration, warrant
value lies on a curve like the one
shown here.

The height of this curve depends on two things. As we explained in Section 20.3, it depends on the variance of the stock returns per period (σ^2) times the number of periods before the option expires ($\sigma^2 t$). It also depends on the rate of interest (r_f) times the number of option periods (t). Of course as time runs out on a warrant, its price snuggles closer and closer to the lower bound. On the final day of its life, its price hits the lower bound.

Two Complications: Dividends and Dilution

If the warrant has no unusual features and the stock pays no dividends, then the value of the option can be estimated from the Black–Scholes formula described in Section 21.3.

But there is a problem when warrants are issued against dividend-paying stocks. The warrant holder is not entitled to dividends. In fact the warrant holder loses every time a cash dividend is paid because the dividend reduces stock price and thus reduces the value of the warrant. It may pay to exercise the warrant before maturity in order to capture the extra income.[3]

Remember that the Black–Scholes option-valuation formula assumes that the stock pays no dividends. Thus it will not give the theoretically correct value for a warrant issued by a dividend-paying firm. However, we showed in Chapter 21 how you can use the one-step-at-a-time binomial method to value options on dividend-paying stocks.

Another complication is that exercise of the warrants increases the number of shares. Therefore, exercise means that the firm's assets and profits are spread over a larger number of shares. Firms with significant amounts of warrants or convertibles outstanding are required to report earnings on a "fully diluted" basis, which recognizes the potential increase in the number of shares.

---

[3] This cannot make sense unless the dividend payment is larger than the interest that could be earned on the exercise price. By *not* exercising, the warrant holder keeps the exercise price and can put this money to work.

TABLE 23.1

United Glue's market value balance sheet (in $ millions).

Before the Issue			
Existing assets	$16	$ 4	Existing loans
		12	Common stock
			(1 million shares
			at $12 a share)
Total	$16	$16	Total

After the Issue			
Existing assets	$16	$ 4	Existing loans
New assets financed		1.5	New loan without warrants
by debt and warrants	2	5.5	Total debt
		.5	Warrants
		12	Common stock
		12.5	Total equity
Total	$18	$18.0	Total

This problem of *dilution* never arises with call options. If you buy or sell an option on the Chicago Board Options Exchange, you have no effect on the number of shares outstanding.

Example: Valuing United Glue's Warrants

United Glue has just issued a $2 million package of debt and warrants. Here are some basic data that we can use to value the warrants:

- Number of shares outstanding (N):   1 million
- Current stock price (P): $12
- Number of warrants issued per share outstanding (q):   .10
- Total number of warrants issued (Nq):   100,000
- Exercise price of warrants (EX): $10
- Time to expiration of warrants (t):   4 years
- Annual standard deviation of stock price changes (σ):   .40
- Rate of interest (r):   10%
- United stock pays no dividends.

Suppose that without the warrants the debt is worth $1.5 million. Then investors must be paying $.5 million for the warrants:

Cost of warrants = total amount of financing − value of loan without warrants

500,000 =   2,000,000   −   1,500,000

$$\text{Each warrant costs investors } \frac{500,000}{100,000} = \$5$$

Table 23.1 shows the market value of United's assets and liabilities both before and after the issue.

Now let us take a stab at checking whether the warrants are really worth the $500,000 that investors are paying for them. Since the warrant is a call option to buy the United stock, we can use the Black–Scholes formula to value the warrant. It turns out that a four-year call to buy United stock at $10 is worth $6.15.[4] Thus the warrant issue looks like a good deal for investors and a bad deal for United. Investors are paying $5 a share for warrants that are worth $6.15.

How the Value of United Warrants Is Affected by Dilution

Unfortunately, our calculations for United warrants do not tell the whole story. Remember that when investors exercise a traded call or put option, there is no change in either the company's assets or the number of shares outstanding. But, if United's warrants are exercised, the number of shares outstanding will increase by $Nq = 100,000$. Also the assets will increase by the amount of the exercise money ($Nq \times EX = 100,000 \times \$10 = \$1$ million). In other words, there will be dilution. We need to allow for this dilution when we value the warrants.

Let us call the value of United's equity V:

$$\text{Value of equity} = V = \text{value of United's total assets} - \text{value of debt}$$

If the warrants are exercised, equity value will increase by the amount of the exercise money to $V + NqEX$. At the same time the number of shares will increase to $N + Nq$. So the share price after the warrants are exercised will be

$$\text{Share price after exercise} = \frac{V + NqEX}{N + Nq}$$

At maturity the warrant holder can choose to let the warrants lapse or to exercise them and receive the share price less the exercise price. Thus the value of the warrants will be the share price minus the exercise price or zero, whichever is the higher. Another way to write this is

$$\text{Warrant value at maturity} = \text{maximum (share price} - \text{exercise price, zero)}$$

$$= \text{maximum}\left(\frac{V + NqEX}{N + Nq} - EX, 0\right)$$

$$= \text{maximum}\left(\frac{V/N - EX}{1 + q}, 0\right)$$

$$= \frac{1}{1 + q}\text{maximum}\left(\frac{V}{N} - EX, 0\right)$$

This tells us the effect of dilution on the value of United's warrants. The warrant value is the value of $1/(1 + q)$ call options written on the stock of an alternative firm with the same total equity value V, *but with no outstanding warrants.* The alternative firm's stock price would be equal to V/N—that is, the total value of United's

---

[4]In Chapter 21 we saw that the Black–Scholes formula for the value of a call is

$$[N(d_1) \times P] - [N(d_2) \times PV(EX)]$$

where $d_1 = \log[P/PV(EX)]/\sigma\sqrt{t} + \sigma\sqrt{t}/2$
 $d_2 = d_1 - \sigma\sqrt{t}$
 $N(d_1)$ = cumulative normal probability function

Plugging the data for United into this formula gives

 $d_1 = \log[12/(10/1.1^4)]/(.40 \times \sqrt{4}) + .40 \times \sqrt{4}/2 = 1.104$ and $d_2 = 1.104 - .40 \times \sqrt{4} = .304$
Appendix Table 6 shows that $N(d_1) = .865$, and $N(d_2) = .620$. Therefore, estimated warrant value = $.865 \times 12 - .620 \times (10/1.1^4) = \$6.15$.

equity (V) divided by the number of shares outstanding (N).[5] The stock price of this alternative firm is more variable than United's stock price. So when we value the call option on the alternative firm, we must remember to use the standard deviation of the changes in V/N.

Now we can recalculate the value of United's warrants allowing for dilution. First we find the stock price of the alternative firm:

$$\text{Current equity value of alternative firm} = V = \text{value of United's total assets}$$
$$- \text{ value of loans}$$
$$= 18 - 5.5 = \$12.5 \text{ million}$$
$$\text{Current share price of alternative firm} = \frac{V}{N} = \frac{12.5 \text{ million}}{1 \text{ million}} = \$12.50$$

Also, suppose the standard deviation of the share price changes of this alternative firm is $\sigma^* = .41$.[6]

The Black–Scholes formula gives a value of $6.64 for a call option on a stock with a price of $12.50 and a standard deviation of .41. The value of United warrants is equal to the value of $1/(1 + q)$ call options on the stock of this alternative firm. Thus warrant value is

$$\frac{1}{1 + q} \times \text{value of call on alternative firm} = \frac{1}{1.1} \times 6.64 = \$6.04$$

This is a somewhat lower value than the one we computed when we ignored dilution but still a bad deal for United.

---

[5] The modifications to allow for dilution when valuing warrants were originally proposed in F. Black and M. Scholes, "The Pricing of Options and Corporate Liabilities," *Journal of Political Economy* 81 (May–June 1973), pp. 637–654. Our exposition follows a discussion in D. Galai and M. I. Schneller, "Pricing of Warrants and the Valuation of the Firm," *Journal of Finance* 33 (December 1978), pp. 1333–1342.

[6] How in practice could we compute σ^*? It would be easy if we could wait until the warrants had been trading for some time. In that case σ^* could be computed from the returns on a package of *all* the company's shares and warrants. In the present case we need to value the warrants *before* they start trading. We argue as follows: The standard deviation of the *assets* before the issue is equal to the standard deviation of a package of the common stock and the existing loans. For example, suppose that the company's debt is risk-free and that the standard deviation of stock returns *before* the bond–warrant issue is 38 percent. Then we calculate the standard deviation of the initial assets as follows:

$$\begin{array}{c}\text{Standard deviation} \\ \text{of initial assets}\end{array} = \begin{array}{c}\text{proportion in} \\ \text{common stock}\end{array} \times \begin{array}{c}\text{standard deviation} \\ \text{of common stock}\end{array}$$
$$= \frac{12}{16} \times 38 = 28.5\%$$

Now suppose that the assets after the issue are equally risky. Then

$$\begin{array}{c}\text{Standard deviation} \\ \text{of assets after issue}\end{array} = \begin{array}{c}\text{proportion of equity} \\ \text{after issue}\end{array} \times \begin{array}{c}\text{standard deviation} \\ \text{of equity } (\sigma^*)\end{array}$$
$$28.5 = \frac{12.5}{18} \times \text{standard deviation of equity } (\sigma^*)$$

$$\text{Standard deviation of equity } (\sigma^*) = 41\%$$

Notice that in our example the standard deviation of the stock returns *before* the warrant issue was slightly lower than the standard deviation of the package of stock and warrants. However, the warrant holders bear proportionately more of this risk than do the stockholders; so the bond–warrant package could either increase or reduce the risk of the stock.

It may sound from all this as if you need to know the value of United warrants to compute their value. This is not so. The formula does not call for warrant value but for V, the value of United's equity (that is, the shares *plus* warrants). Given equity value, the formula calculates how the overall value of equity should be split up between stock and warrants. Thus, suppose that United's underwriter advises that $500,000 extra can be raised by issuing a package of bonds and warrants rather than bonds alone. Is this a fair price? You can check using the Black–Scholes formula with the adjustment for dilution.

Finally, notice that these modifications are necessary to apply the Black–Scholes formula to value a warrant. They are not needed by the warrant holder, who must decide whether to exercise at maturity. If at maturity the price of the stock exceeds the exercise price of the warrant, the warrant holder will of course exercise.

23.2 WHAT IS A CONVERTIBLE BOND?

The convertible bond is a close relative of the bond–warrant package. Many companies choose to issue convertible preferred as an alternative to issuing packages of preferred stock and warrants. We will concentrate on convertible bonds, but almost all our comments apply to convertible preferred issues.

In 1999 Amazon.com issued $1.25 billion of 4 3/4 percent convertible bonds due in 2009.[7] These could be converted at any time to 6.41 shares of common stock. In other words, the owner had a 10-year option to return the bond to the company and receive 6.41 shares of stock in exchange. The number of shares into which each bond can be converted is called the bond's *conversion ratio.* The conversion ratio of the Amazon bond was 6.41.

To receive 6.41 shares of Amazon stock, the owner had to surrender bonds with a face value of $1,000. This means that to receive one share, the owner had to surrender a face amount of $1,000/6.41 = $156.01. This figure is called the *conversion price.* Anybody who bought the bond at $1,000 to convert it into 6.41 shares paid the equivalent of $156.01 per share.

At the time of issue the price of Amazon stock was about $120 so the conversion price was 30 percent higher than the stock price.

Convertibles are usually protected against stock splits or stock dividends. When Amazon subsequently split its stock 2 for 1, the conversion ratio was increased to 12.82 and the conversion price dropped to $1,000/12.82 = $78.00.

The Convertible Menagerie

Amazon's convertible issue is typical, but you may come across more complicated cases. For example, in November 2000 Tyco raised the record sum of $3.5 billion from a convertible issue. The Tyco issue was an example of a LYON (liquid yield option note). A LYON is a callable and puttable, zero-coupon convertible bond (and you can't get much more complicated than that).

---

[7]The Amazon issue consisted of convertible subordinated notes. The term *subordinated* indicates that the issue is a junior debt; its holders will be at the bottom of the heap of creditors in the event of default. Notes are simply unsecured bonds. Therefore there are no specific assets that have been reserved to pay off the holders in the event of default. There is more about these terms in Section 25.3.

The Tyco issue was a 20-year zero-coupon bond that was convertible at any time into 10.3 shares. The bonds were issued at a price of $741.65, which gave bond-holders a yield to maturity of 1.5 percent. When Tyco issued the convertible, corporate bonds were yielding roughly 8 percent. So an investor who converted immediately would be giving up a bond worth $1,000/1.08^{20} = $215. Investors who waited 20 years to convert would be relinquishing a bond worth $1,000 (as long as the firm is solvent). So the value of the bond that they give up increases each year.

The Tyco LYON contains two other options. Starting in 2007 the company has the right to call the bond for cash. The exercise price of this call option starts at 82.34 percent and increases by 1.5 percent each year until it reaches 100 percent in 2014. The bondholders also have an option, for there are five days between 2001 and 2014 on which they can demand repayment of their bonds. The repayment price starts at 75.28 percent and then is increased by 1.5 percent a year. These put options help to provide a more solid floor to the issue. Even if interest rates rise and prices of other bonds fall, LYON holders have a guaranteed price on these five days at which they can sell their bonds.[8] Obviously, investors who exercise the put give up the opportunity to convert their bonds into stock; it would be worth taking advantage of the guarantee only if the conversion price of the bonds was well below the exercise price of the put.[9]

Mandatory Convertibles

In recent years a number of companies have issued preferred stock or debt that is *automatically* converted into equity after several years. Investors in mandatory convertibles receive the benefit of a higher current income than common stockholders, but there is a limit on the value of the common stock that they ultimately receive. Thus they share in the appreciation of the common stock only up to this limit. As the stock price rises above this limit, the number of shares that the convertible holder receives is reduced proportionately.

Valuing Convertible Bonds

The owner of a convertible owns a bond and a call option on the firm's stock. So does the owner of a bond–warrant package. There are differences, of course, the most important being the requirement that a convertible owner give up the bond in order to exercise the call option. The owner of a bond–warrant package can (generally) exercise the warrant for cash and keep the bond. Nevertheless, understanding convertibles is easier if you analyze them first as bonds and then as call options.

Imagine that Eastman Kojak has issued convertible bonds with a total face value of $1 million and that these can be converted at any stage to one million shares of common stock. The price of Kojak's convertible bond depends on its *bond value* and its *conversion value*. The bond value is what each bond would sell for if it could not be converted. The conversion value is what the bond would sell for if it had to be converted immediately.

[8]Of course, this guarantee would not be worth much if the company was in financial distress and *couldn't* buy the bonds back.

[9]The reasons for issuing LYONs are discussed in J. J. McConnell and E. S. Schwartz, "The Origin of LYONs: A Case Study in Financial Innovation," *Journal of Applied Corporate Finance* 4 (Winter 1992), pp. 40–47. For a discussion of how to value an earlier LYON issue by Waste Management see J. McConnell and E. S. Schwartz, "Taming LYONs," *Journal of Finance* 41 (July 1986), pp. 561–576.

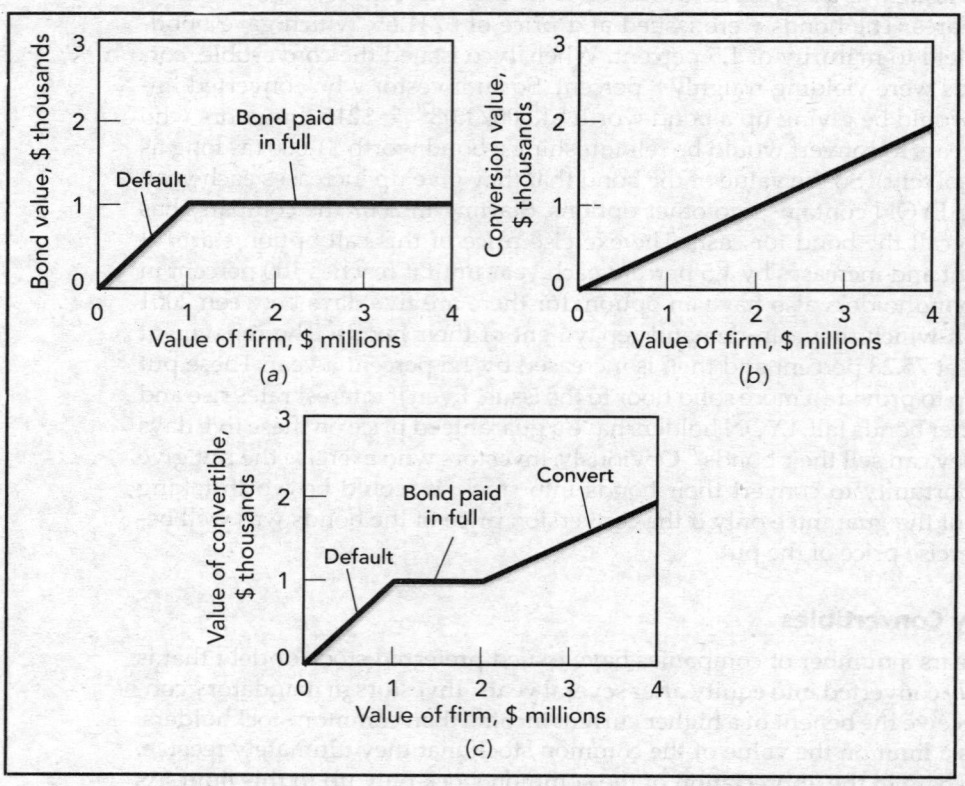

FIGURE 23.2

(a) The bond value when Eastman Kojak's convertible bond matures. If firm value is at least
$1 million, the bond is paid off at its face value of $1000; if it is less than $1 million, the bondholders
receive the value of the firm's assets. (b) The conversion value at maturity. If converted, the value of
the convertible bond rises in proportion to firm value. (c) At maturity the convertible bondholder can
choose to receive the principal repayment on the bond or convert to common stock. The value of the
convertible bond is therefore the higher of its bond value and its conversion value.

Value at Maturity   Figure 23.2(a) shows the possible *bond values* when the Kojak
convertible matures. As long as the value of the firm's assets does not fall below
$1 million, the bond will pay off in full. But if the firm value is *less* than $1 million,
there will not be enough to pay off the bondholders. In the extreme case that the
assets are worthless, the bondholders will receive nothing. Thus the horizontal line
in Figure 23.2(a) shows the payoff if the bond is repaid in full, and the sloping line
shows the payoffs if the firm defaults.[10]

You can think of the bond value as a lower bound, or "floor," to the price of
the convertible. But that floor has a nasty slope and, when the company falls on
hard times, the bonds may not be worth much. For example, we saw earlier how
Amazon.com issued a convertible bond in 1999. Over the following two years

---

[10]You may recognize this as the position diagram for a default-free bond *minus* a put option on the assets with an exercise price equal to the face value of the bonds. See Section 20.1.

investors became disenchanted with dot.com companies and Amazon's stock price fell by 75 percent to $15. This was well below the conversion price of $78.03. Convertible bondholders might have hoped that the bond value would provide a secure floor to the value of their investment. Unfortunately, by early 2001 Amazon's bonds no longer looked as safe as they once had, and Moody's placed its convertible in the junk bond category Caa. By the spring of that year the price of the convertible had fallen to about $400 and offered a promised yield to maturity of 20 percent.

Figure 23.2(*b*) shows the possible *conversion values* at maturity of Kojak's convertible. We assume that Kojak already has one million shares of common stock outstanding, so the convertible holders will be entitled to half the value of the firm. For example, if the firm is worth $2 million,[11] the one million shares obtained by conversion would be worth $1 each. Each convertible bond can be exchanged for 1,000 shares of stock and therefore would have a conversion value of $1,000 \times 1 = \$1,000$.

Kojak's convertible also cannot sell for less than its conversion value. If it did, smart investors would buy the convertible, exchange it rapidly for stock, and sell the stock. Their profit would be equal to the difference between the conversion value and the price of the convertible.

Therefore, there are *two* lower bounds to the price of the convertible: its bond value and its conversion value. Investors will not convert if bond value exceeds conversion value; they will do so if conversion value exceeds bond value. In other words, the price of the convertible at maturity is represented by the higher of the two lines in Figure 23.2(*a*) and (*b*). This is shown in Figure 23.2(*c*).

Value before Maturity   We can also draw a picture similar to Figure 23.2 when the convertible is *not* about to mature. Because even healthy companies may subsequently fall sick and default on their bonds, other things equal, the bond value will be lower when the bond has some time to run. Thus bond value before maturity is represented by the curved line in Figure 23.3(*a*).[12]

Figure 23.3(*b*) shows that the lower bound to the price of a convertible before maturity is again the higher of the bond value and conversion value. However, before maturity the convertible bondholders *do not have to make a now-or-never choice for or against conversion*. They can wait and then, with the benefit of hindsight, take whatever course turns out to give them the highest payoff. Thus before maturity a convertible is always worth more than its lower-bound value. Its actual selling price will behave as shown by the top line in Figure 23.3(*c*). The difference between the top line and the lower bound is the value of a call option on the firm. Remember, however, that this option can be exercised only by giving up the bond. In other words, the option to convert is a call option with an exercise price equal to the bond value.

Dilution and Dividends Revisited

If you want to value a convertible, it is easiest to break the problem down into two parts. First estimate bond value; then add the value of the conversion option.

When you value the conversion option, you need to look out for the same things that make warrants more tricky to value than traded options. For example,

---

[11]Firm value is equal to the value of Kojak's common stock *plus* the value of its convertible bonds.

[12]Remember, the value of a risky bond is the value of a safe bond *less* the value of a put option on the firm's assets. The value of this option increases with maturity.

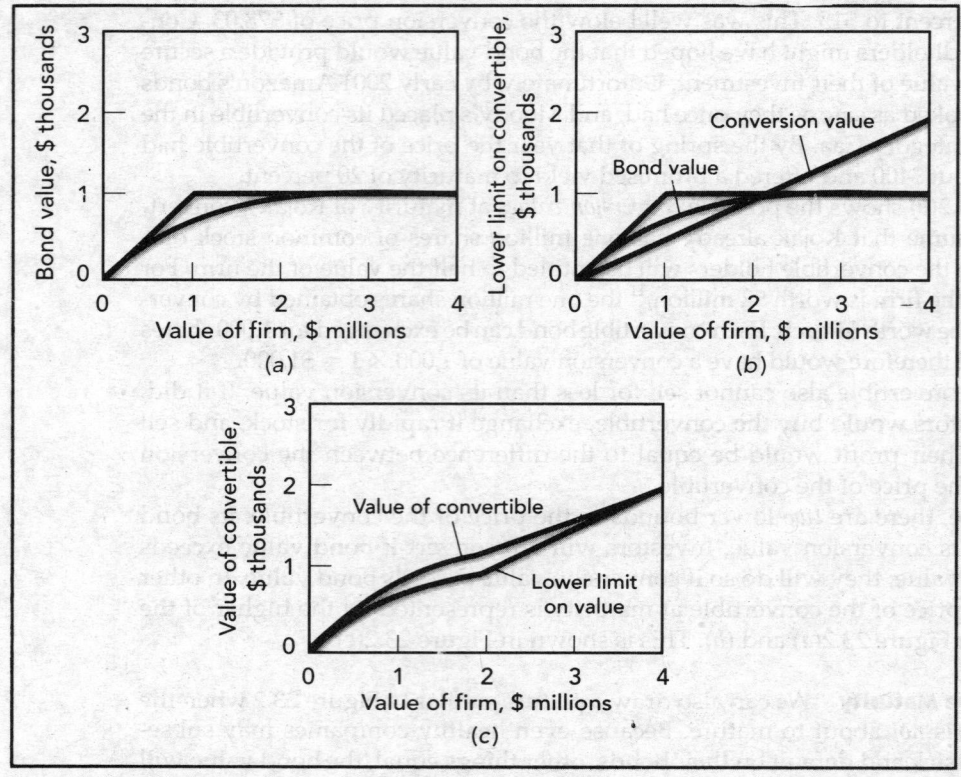

FIGURE 23.3

(a) Before maturity the bond value of Eastman Kojak's convertible bond is close to that of a similar default-free bond when firm value is high, but it falls sharply if firm value falls to a very low level. (b) If investors were obliged to make an immediate decision for or against conversion, the value of the convertible would be equal to the higher of bond value or conversion value. (c) Since convertible bondholders do not have to make a decision until maturity, (b) represents a lower limit. The value of the convertible bond is worth *more* than either bond value or conversion value.

dilution may be important. If the bonds are converted, the company saves on its interest payments and is relieved of having to eventually repay the loan; on the other hand, net profits have to be divided among a larger number of shares.[13] Companies are obliged to show in their financial statements how earnings would be affected by conversion.[14]

Also, you must remember that the convertible owner is missing out on the dividends on the common stock. If these dividends are higher than the interest on the

---

[13] In practice investors often ignore dilution and calculate conversion value as the share price times the number of shares into which the bonds can be converted. A convertible bond actually gives an option to acquire a fraction of the "new equity"—the equity *after* conversion. When we calculated the conversion value of Kojak's convertible, we recognized this by multiplying the proportion of common stock that the convertible bondholders would receive by the total value of the firm's assets (i.e., the value of the common stock plus the value of the convertible).

[14] These "diluted" earnings take into account the extra shares but not the savings in interest payments.

FIGURE 23.4

The decision to call a convertible. The financial manager should call at price C but wait at prices A and B. (*Note:* The conversion value is the straight upward-sloping line.)

bonds, it may pay to convert before the final exercise date in order to pick up the extra cash income.

Forcing Conversion

Companies usually retain an option to buy back or "call" the convertible bond at a preset price. If the company calls the bond, the owner has a brief period, usually about 30 days, within which to convert the bond or surrender it.[15] If a bond is surrendered, the investor receives the call price in cash. But if the share price is higher than the call price, the investor will convert the bond instead of surrendering it. Thus a call can *force conversion* if the stock price is high enough.

Most convertible bonds provide for two or more years of *call protection.* During this period the company is not permitted to call the bonds. However, many convertibles can be called early, before the end of the call protection, if the stock price has risen enough to provide a nice conversion profit. For example, a convertible with a call price of $40 might be callable early if the stock price trades above $65 for at least two weeks.

Calling the bond obviously does not affect the total size of the company pie, but it can affect the size of the individual slices. In other words, conversion has no effect on the total value of the firm's assets, but it does affect how asset value is *distributed* among the different classes of security holders. Therefore, if you want to maximize your shareholders' slice of the pie, you must minimize the convertible bondholders' slice. That means you must not call the bonds if they are worth *less* than the call price, for that would be giving the bondholders an unnecessary present. Similarly, you must not allow the bonds to remain uncalled if their value is *above* the call price, for that would not be minimizing the value of the bonds.

Let's apply this reasoning to specific cases. Refer to Figure 23.4, which matches Figure 23.3(*c*) but has the call price drawn in as a horizontal line. Consider the firm values corresponding to three stock prices, marked A, B, and C:

- At price A, the convertible is "out of the money." Calling the bond leads to redemption for cash and hands bondholders a free gift equal to the difference between the call price and the convertible value. Therefore the company should not call.

---

[15]Companies may also reserve the right to force conversion of warrants.

- Suppose call protection ends with price at level C. Then the financial manager should call immediately, forcing the convertible value down to the call price.[16]
- What if call protection ends with price at level B, barely above the call price? In this case the financial manager will probably wait. Remember, if a call is announced, bondholders have a 30-day period in which to decide whether to convert or redeem. The stock price could easily fall below the call price during this period, forcing the company to redeem for cash. Usually calls are not announced until the stock price is about 20 percent above the call price. This provides a safety margin to ensure conversion.[17]

Do companies follow these simple guidelines? On the surface they don't, for there are many instances of convertible bonds selling well above the call price. But the explanation seems to lie in the call-protection period, during which companies are not allowed to call their bonds. Paul Asquith found that most convertible bonds that are worth calling are called as soon as possible after this period ends.[18] The typical delay for bonds that can be called is slightly less than four months after the conversion value first exceeds the call price.

23.3 THE DIFFERENCE BETWEEN WARRANTS AND CONVERTIBLES

We have dwelt on the basic similarity between warrants and convertibles. Now let us look at some of the differences:

1. *Warrants are usually issued privately.* Packages of bonds with warrants or preferred stock with warrants tend to be more common in private placements. By contrast most convertible bonds are issued publicly.
2. *Warrants can be detached.* When you buy a convertible, the bond and the option are bundled up together. You cannot sell them separately. This may be inconvenient. If your tax position or attitude to risk inclines you to bonds, you may not want to hold options as well. Sometimes warrants are also "nondetachable," but usually you can keep the bond and sell the warrant.
3. *Warrants may be issued on their own.* Warrants do not have to be issued in conjunction with other securities. Often they are used to compensate investment bankers for underwriting services. Many companies also give their executives long-term options to buy stock. These executive stock options are not usually called warrants, but that is exactly what they are. Companies can also sell warrants on their own directly to investors, though they rarely do so.

---

[16] The financial manager might delay calling for a time at price C if interest payments on the convertible debt are less than the extra dividends that would be paid after conversion. This delay would reduce cash payments to bondholders. Nothing is lost if the financial manager always calls "on the way down" if stock price subsequently falls toward level B. Note that investors may convert voluntarily if dividends after conversion exceed interest on the convertible bond.

[17] See P. Asquith and D. Mullins, "Convertible Debt: Corporate Call Policy," *Journal of Finance* 46 (September 1991), pp. 1273–1290.

[18] See P. Asquith, "Convertible Bonds Are Not Called Late," *Journal of Finance* 50 (September 1995), pp. 1275–1289.

4. *Warrants are exercised for cash.* When you convert a bond, you simply exchange your bond for common stock. When you exercise warrants, you generally put up extra cash, though occasionally you have to surrender the bond or can choose to do so. This means that bond–warrant packages and convertible bonds usually have different effects on the company's cash flow and on its capital structure.

5. *A package of bonds and warrants may be taxed differently.* There are some tax differences between warrants and convertibles. Suppose that you are wondering whether to issue a convertible bond at 100. You can think of this convertible as a package of a straight bond worth, say, 90 and an option worth 10. If you issue the bond and option separately, the IRS will note that the bond is issued at a discount and that its price will rise by 10 points over its life. The IRS will allow you, the issuer, to spread this prospective price appreciation over the life of the bond and deduct it from your taxable profits. The IRS will also allocate the prospective price appreciation to the taxable income of the bondholder. Thus, by issuing a package of bonds and warrants rather than a convertible, you may reduce the tax paid by the issuing company and increase the tax paid by the investor.[19]

23.4 WHY DO COMPANIES ISSUE WARRANTS AND CONVERTIBLES?

You are approached by an investment banker who is anxious to persuade you that your company should issue warrants. She points out that the exercise price of the warrants could be set at 20 percent above the current stock price, so that you would effectively be selling stock at a hefty premium. And, if it turns out that the warrants are never exercised, the proceeds from their sale would become a clear profit to the company. Are you convinced?

You hear many similar arguments for issuing warrants and convertibles, but you should always be suspicious of any "Heads I win, tails you lose" argument. If the shareholder inevitably wins, the warrant holder must lose. But that doesn't make sense. Surely there must be some price at which it makes sense to buy warrants.[20]

Suppose that your company's stock is priced at $100 and that you are considering an issue of warrants exercisable at $120. You believe that you can sell these warrants at $10. If the stock price subsequently fails to reach $120, the warrants will not be exercised. You will have sold warrants for $10 each, which with the benefit of hindsight proved to be worthless to the buyer. If the stock price reaches $130, say, the warrants will be exercised. Your firm will have received the initial payment of $10 *plus* the exercise price of $120. On the other hand, it will have issued to the warrant holders stock worth $130 per share. The net result is a standoff. You have received a payment of $130 in exchange for a liability worth $130.

---

[19]See J. D. Finnerty, "The Case for Issuing Synthetic Convertible Bonds," *Midland Corporate Finance Journal* 4 (Fall 1986), pp. 73–82.

[20]Here is another "Heads I win, tails you lose" argument. You are an investor. Your broker calls you with an offer of ABC company warrants. ABC's share price is $10; the warrants expire in one year, have an exercise price of $10, and are selling at $1. Your broker points out that you are likely to make much larger percentage gains from buying the warrants rather than the shares. For example, if over the next year the share price rises by 20 percent to $12, the warrants will be worth $2, a gain of 100 percent. On the other hand, if the share price falls, the most that you can lose as a warrant holder is $1. How do you respond?

Think now what happens if the stock price rises above $130. Perhaps it goes to $200. In this case the warrant issue will end up producing a loss of $70. This is not a cash outflow but an opportunity loss. The firm receives $130, but in this case it could have sold stock for $200. On the other hand, the warrant holders gain $70: They invest $130 in cash to acquire stock that they can sell, if they like, for $200.

Our example is oversimplified—for instance, we have kept quiet about the time value of money and risk—but we hope it has made the basic point. When you sell warrants, you are selling options and getting cash in exchange. Options are valuable securities. If they are properly priced, this is a fair trade; in other words, it is a zero-NPV transaction.

Some managers look on convertibles as "cheap debt." Others regard them as a deferred sale of stock at an attractive price. These arguments also are misleading. We have seen that a convertible is like a package of a straight bond and an option. The difference between the market value of the convertible and that of the straight bond is therefore the price investors place on the call option. The convertible is "cheap" only if this price overvalues the option.

What then of the other managers—those who regard the issue as a deferred sale of common stock? A convertible bond gives you the right to buy stock by giving up a bond.[21] Bondholders may decide to do this, but then again they may not. Thus issue of a convertible bond *may* amount to a deferred stock issue. But if the firm *needs* equity capital, a convertible issue is an unreliable way of getting it.

Taken at their face value the motives of these managers are irrational. Convertibles are not just cheap debt, nor are they a deferred sale of stock. But we suspect that these simple phrases encapsulate some more complex and rational motives.

Notice that convertibles tend to be issued by the smaller and more speculative firms. They are almost invariably unsecured and generally subordinated. Now put yourself in the position of a potential investor. You are approached by a small firm with an untried product line that wants to issue some junior unsecured debt. You know that if things go well, you will get your money back, but if they do not, you could easily be left with nothing. Since the firm is in a new line of business, it is difficult to assess the chances of trouble. Therefore you don't know what the fair rate of interest is. Also, you may be worried that once you have made the loan, management will be tempted to run extra risks. It may take on additional senior debt, or it may decide to expand its operations and go for broke on your money. In fact, if you charge a very high rate of interest, you could be encouraging this to happen.

What can management do to protect you against a wrong estimate of the risk and to assure you that its intentions are honorable? In crude terms, it can give you a piece of the action. You don't mind the company running unanticipated risks as long as you share in the gains as well as the losses.[22]

---

[21]That is much the same as already having the stock together with the right to sell it for the convertible's bond value. In other words, instead of thinking of a convertible as a bond plus a call option, you could think of it as the stock plus a put option. Now you see why it is wrong to think of a convertible as equivalent to the sale of stock; it is equivalent to the sale of both stock *and* a put option. If there is any possibility that investors will want to hold onto their bond, the put option will have some value.

[22]See M. J. Brennan and E. S. Schwartz, "The Case for Convertibles," *Journal of Applied Corporate Finance* 1 (Summer 1988), pp. 55–64.

Convertible securities and warrants make sense whenever it is unusually costly to assess the risk of debt or whenever investors are worried that management may not act in the bondholders' interest.[23]

You can also think of a convertible issue as a *contingent* issue of equity. If a company's investment opportunities expand, its stock price is likely to increase, allowing the financial manager to call and force conversion of a convertible bond into equity. Thus the company gets fresh equity when it is most needed for expansion. Of course, it is also stuck with debt if the company does not prosper.[24]

The relatively low coupon rate on convertible bonds may also be a convenience for rapidly growing firms facing heavy capital expenditures. They may be willing to give up the conversion option to reduce immediate cash requirements for debt service. Without the conversion option, lenders might demand extremely high (promised) interest rates to compensate for the probability of default. This would not only force the firm to raise still more capital for debt service but also increase the risk of financial distress. Paradoxically, lenders' attempts to protect themselves against default may actually increase the probability of financial distress by increasing the burden of debt service on the firm.[25]

---

[23]Changes in risk ought to be more likely when the firm is small and its debt is low-grade. If so, we should find that the convertible bonds of such firms offer their owners a larger potential ownership share. This is indeed the case. See C. M. Lewis, R. J. Rogalski, and J. K. Seward, "Understanding the Design of Convertible Debt," *Journal of Applied Corporate Finance* 11 (Spring 1998), pp. 45–53.

[24]Jeremy Stein points out that an issue of a convertible sends a better signal to investors than a straight equity issue. As we explained in Chapter 15, announcement of a common stock issue prompts worries of overvaluation and usually depresses stock price. Convertibles are hybrids of debt and equity and send a less negative signal. If the company is likely to need equity, its willingness to issue a convertible, and to take the chance that stock price will rise enough to allow forced conversion, also signals management's confidence. See J. Stein, "Convertible Bonds as Backdoor Equity Financing," *Journal of Financial Economics* 32 (1992), pp. 3–21.

[25]This fact led to an extensive body of literature on "credit rationing." A lender rations credit if it is irrational to lend more to a firm regardless of the interest rate the firm is willing to *promise* to pay. Whether this can happen in efficient, competitive capital markets is controversial. We discussed credit rationing in Chapter 18. For a review of this literature, see E. Baltensperger, "Credit Rationing: Issues and Questions," *Journal of Money, Credit and Banking* 10 (May 1978), pp. 170–183.

SUMMARY

Instead of issuing straight bonds, companies may sell either packages of bonds and warrants or convertible bonds.

A warrant is just a long-term call option issued by the company. You already know a good deal about valuing call options. You know from Chapter 20 that call options must be worth at least as much as the stock price less the exercise price. You know that their value is greatest when they have a long time to expiration, when the underlying stock is risky, and when the interest rate is high.

Warrants are somewhat trickier to value than call options traded on the options exchanges. First, because they are long-term options, it is important to recognize that the warrant holder does not receive any dividends. Second, dilution must be allowed for.

A convertible bond gives its holder the right to swap the bond for common stock. The rate of exchange is usually measured by the *conversion ratio*—that is, the number of shares that the investor gets for each bond. Sometimes the rate of exchange is expressed in terms of the *conversion price*—that is, the face value of the bond that must be given up in order to receive one share.

Convertibles are like a package of a bond and a call option. When you evaluate the conversion option, you must again remember that the convertible holder does not receive dividends and that conversion results in dilution of the common stock. There are two other things to watch out for. One is the problem of default risk. If the company runs into trouble, you may have not only a worthless conversion option but also a worthless bond. Second, the company may be able to force conversion by calling the bond. It should do this when the market price of the convertible reaches the call price.

You hear a variety of arguments for issuing warrants or convertibles. Convertible bonds and bonds with warrants are almost always junior bonds and are frequently issued by risky companies. We think that this says something about the reasons for their issue. Suppose that you are lending to an untried company. You are worried that the company may turn out to be riskier than you thought or that it may issue additional senior bonds. You can try to protect yourself against such eventualities by imposing very restrictive conditions on the debt, but it is often simpler to allow some extra risk as long as you get a piece of the action. The convertible and bond–warrant package give you a chance to participate in the firm's successes as well as its failures. They diminish the possible conflicts of interest between bondholder and stockholder.

FURTHER READING

The items listed in Chapters 20 and 21 under "Further Reading" are also relevant to this chapter, in particular Black and Scholes's discussion of warrant valuation.

Ingersoll's work represents the "state of the art" in valuing convertibles:

J. E. Ingersoll: "A Contingent Claims Valuation of Convertible Securities," *Journal of Financial Economics*, 4:289–322 (May 1977).

Ingersoll also examines corporate call policies on convertible bonds in:

J. E. Ingersoll: "An Examination of Corporate Call Policies on Convertible Securities," *Journal of Finance*, 32:463–478 (May 1977).

Brennan and Schwartz's paper was written about the same time as Ingersoll's and reaches essentially the same conclusions; they also present a general procedure for valuing convertibles:

M. J. Brennan and E. S. Schwartz: "Convertible Bonds: Valuation and Optimal Strategies for Call and Conversion," *Journal of Finance*, 32:1699–1715 (December 1977).

Two useful articles on warrants are:

E. S. Schwartz: "The Valuation of Warrants: Implementing a New Approach," *Journal of Financial Economics*, 4:79–93 (January 1977).

D. Galai and M. A. Schneller: "Pricing of Warrants and the Value of the Firm," *Journal of Finance*, 33:1333–1342 (December 1978).

Asquith's analysis of the effect of call protection provides evidence that firms' decisions on calling convertibles are more rational than was previously believed:

P. Asquith: "Convertible Bonds Are Not Called Late," *Journal of Finance*, 50:1275–1289 (September 1995).

For nontechnical discussions of the pricing of convertibles and the reasons for their use, see:

M. J. Brennan and E. S. Schwartz: "The Case for Convertibles," *Journal of Applied Corporate Finance*, 1:55–64 (Summer 1988).

C. M. Lewis, R. J. Rogalski, and J. K. Seward, "Understanding the Design of Convertible Debt," *Journal of Applied Corporate Finance*, 11:45–53 (Spring 1998).

1. Associated Elk warrants entitle the owner to buy one share at $40.
    a. What is the "theoretical" value of the warrant if the stock price is: (i) $20? (ii) $30? (iii) $40? (iv) $50? (v) $60?
    b. Plot the theoretical value of the warrant against the stock price.
    c. Suppose the stock price is $60 and the warrant price is $5. What would you do?

2. In 1994 Viacom made a typical issue of warrants. Each warrant could be exercised before 1999 at a price of $70 per share. In September 1998 the stock price was $57 per share.
    a. Did the warrant holder have a vote?
    b. Did the warrant holder receive dividends?
    c. If the stock was split 3 for 1, how would the exercise price be adjusted?
    d. Suppose that instead of adjusting the exercise price after a 3-for-1 split, the company gives each warrant holder the right to buy *three* shares at $70 apiece. Would this have the same effect? Would it make the warrant holder better or worse off?
    e. What is the "theoretical" value of the warrant?
    f. Before maturity is the warrant worth more or less than the "theoretical" value?
    g. *Other things equal,* would the warrant be more or less valuable if:
        i. The company increased its rate of dividend payout?
        ii. The interest rate declined?
        iii. The stock became riskier?
        iv. The company extended the exercise period?
        v. The company reduced the exercise price?
    h. A few companies issue perpetual warrants that have no final exercise date. Suppose that Viacom warrants were perpetual. In what circumstances might it make sense for investors to exercise their warrants?
    i. If the stock price rises 5 percent, would you expect the price of a warrant to rise by more or less than 5 percent?

3. Company X has outstanding 1,000 shares and 200 warrants. Each warrant can be converted into one share at an exercise price of $20. What will be the *total* market value of X's shares after the warrants mature if the share price on that date is (a) $15, (b) $25?

4. Maple Aircraft has issued a 4 ¾ percent convertible subordinated debenture due 2008. The conversion price is $47.00 and the debenture is callable at $102.75 percent of face value. The market price of the convertible is 91 percent of face value, and the price of the common is $41.50. Assume that the value of the bond in the absence of a conversion feature is about 65 percent of face value.
    a. What is the conversion ratio of the debenture?
    b. If the conversion ratio were 50, what would be the conversion price?
    c. What is the conversion value?
    d. At what stock price is the conversion value equal to the bond value?
    e. Can the market price be less than the conversion value?
    f. How much is the convertible holder paying for the option to buy one share of common stock?
    g. By how much does the common have to rise by 2008 to justify conversion?
    h. When should Maple call the debenture?

5. a. Pi, Inc., has 30 million shares outstanding and has a net income of $210 million. Calculate Pi's earnings per share.
    b. Pi has also issued $50 million of 5 percent convertible bonds with a face value of $1,000 each and a conversion ratio of 3.142. How will earnings per share change if the bonds are converted?

6. True or false?
    a. Convertible bonds are usually senior claims on the firm.
    b. The higher the conversion ratio, the more valuable the convertible.

c. The higher the conversion price, the more valuable the convertible.

d. If a company splits its stock, the conversion price is increased.

e. Other things equal, if dividend payments rise, bondholders are more likely to convert before maturity.

f. Convertible bonds do not share fully in a rise in the price of the common stock, but they provide some protection against a decline.

PRACTICE QUESTIONS

1. Associated Elk warrants have an exercise price of $40. The share price is $50. The dividend on the stock is $3, and the interest rate is 10 percent.

   a. Would you exercise your warrants now or later? State why.

   b. If the dividend increased to $5, it could pay to exercise now if the stock price has low variability and it could be better to exercise later if the stock price has high variability. Explain why.

2. Moose Stores has outstanding one million shares of common stock with a total market value of $40 million. It now announces an issue of one million warrants at $5 each. Each warrant entitles the owner to buy one Moose share for a price of $30 any time within the next five years. Moose Stores has stated that it will not pay a dividend within this period.

   The standard deviation of the returns on Moose's equity is 20 percent a year, and the interest rate is 8 percent.

   a. What is the market value of each warrant?

   b. What is the market value of each share after the warrant issue? (*Hint:* The value of the shares is equal to the total value of the equity less the value of the warrants.)

3. Look again at question 2. Suppose that Moose now forecasts the following dividend payments:

End of Year	Dividend
1	$2
2	3
3	4
4	5
5	6

   Reestimate the market values of the warrant and stock.

4. Occasionally firms extend the life of warrants that would otherwise expire unexercised. What is the cost of doing this?

5. The Surplus Value Company had $10 million (face value) of convertible bonds outstanding in 2001. Each bond has the following features:

Par or face value	$1000
Conversion price	$25
Current call price	105 (percent of face value)
Current trading price	130 (percent of face value)
Maturity	2011
Current stock price	$30 (per share)
Interest rate	10 (coupon as percent of face value)

   a. What is the bond's conversion value?

   b. Can you explain why the bond is selling above conversion value?

   c. Should Surplus call? What will happen if it does so?

6. Piglet Pies has issued a zero-coupon 10-year bond that can be converted into 10 Piglet shares. Comparable straight bonds are yielding 8 percent. Piglet stock is priced at $50 a share.
   a. Suppose that you had to make a now-or-never decision on whether to convert or to stay with the bond. Which would you do?
   b. If the convertible bond is priced at $550, how much are investors paying for the option to buy Piglet shares?
   c. If after one year the value of the conversion option is unchanged, what is the value of the convertible bond?

7. Iota Microsystems' 10 percent convertible is about to mature. The conversion ratio is 27.
   a. What is the conversion price?
   b. The stock price is $47. What is the conversion value?
   c. Should you convert?

8. In each case, state which of the two securities is likely to provide the higher return:
   a. When the stock price rises (stock *or* convertible bond?).
   b. When interest rates fall (straight bond *or* convertible bond?).
   c. When the specific risk of the stock decreases (straight bond *or* convertible bond?).
   d. When the dividend on the stock increases (stock *or* convertible bond?).

9. In 1996 Marriott International made an issue of LYONS. The bond matured in 2011, had a zero coupon, and was issued at $532.15. It could be converted into 8.76 shares. Beginning in 1999 the bonds could be called by Marriott. The call price was $603.71 in 1999 and increased by 4.3 percent a year thereafter. Holders had an option to put the bond back to Marriott in 1999 at $603.71 and in 2006 at $810.36. At the time of issue the price of the common stock was about $50.50.
   a. What was the yield to maturity on the bond?
   b. Assuming that comparable nonconvertible bonds yielded 10 percent, how much were investors paying for the conversion option?
   c. What was the conversion value of the bonds at the time of issue?
   d. What was the initial conversion price of the bonds?
   e. What is the conversion price in 2005? Why does it change?
   f. If the price of the bond in 2006 is less than $810.36, would you put the bond back to Marriott?
   g. At what price can Marriott call the bonds in 2006? If the price of the bond in 2006 is more than this, should Marriott call them?

10. "The company's decision to issue warrants should depend on the management's forecast of likely returns on the stock." Do you agree?

11. If the riskiness of the firm's assets increases, does the value of its convertible rise or fall, or can't you say?

12. Financing with convertible debt is especially appropriate for small, rapidly growing, or risky companies. Explain why.

13. The Pork Barrel Company has issued three-year warrants to buy 12 percent perpetual debentures at a price of 120 percent. The current interest rate is 12 percent and the standard deviation of returns on the bond is 20 percent. Use the Black–Scholes model to obtain a rough estimate of the value of Pork Barrel warrants.

1. The B.J. Services warrant is described in Section 23.1. How would you use the Black–Scholes formula to compute the value of the warrant immediately after its issue, assuming a stock price of $19 and a warrant price of $5? Begin by ignoring the problem of dilution. Then go on to describe how dilution would affect your calculations.

CHALLENGE
QUESTIONS

2. Here is a question about dilution. The Electric Bassoon Company has outstanding 2,000 shares with a total market value of $20,000 *plus* 1,000 warrants with a total market value of $5,000. Each warrant gives its holder the option to buy one share at $20.

   a. To value the warrants, you first need to value a call option on an alternative share. How might you calculate its standard deviation?

   b. Suppose that the value of a call option on this alternative share was $6. Calculate whether the Electric Bassoon warrants were undervalued or overvalued.

3. This question illustrates that when there is scope for the firm to vary its risk, lenders may be more prepared to lend if they are offered a piece of the action through the issue of a convertible bond.

   Ms. Blavatsky is proposing to form a new start-up firm with initial assets of $10 million. She can invest this money in one of two projects. Each has the same expected payoff, but one has more risk than the other. The relatively safe project offers a 40 percent chance of a $12.5 million payoff and a 60 percent chance of an $8 million payoff. The risky project offers a 40 percent chance of a $20 million payoff and a 60 percent chance of a $5 million payoff.

   Ms. Blavatsky initially proposes to finance the firm by an issue of straight debt with a promised payoff of $7 million. Ms. Blavatsky will receive any remaining payoff. Show the possible payoffs to the lender and to Ms. Blavatsky if (a) she chooses the safe project and (b) she chooses the risky project. Which project is Ms. Blavatsky likely to choose? Which will the lender want her to choose?

   Suppose now that Ms. Blavatsky offers to make the debt convertible into 50 percent of the value of the firm. Show that in this case the lender receives the same expected payoff from the two projects.

4. Occasionally it is said that issuing convertible bonds is better than issuing stock when the firm's shares are undervalued. Suppose that the financial manager of the Butternut Furniture Company does have inside information indicating that the Butternut stock price is too low. Butternut's future earnings will in fact be higher than investors expect. Suppose further that the inside information cannot be released without giving away a valuable competitive secret. Clearly, selling shares at the present low price would harm Butternut's existing shareholders. Will they also lose if convertible bonds are issued? If they do lose in this case, is the loss more or less than it would be if common stock were issued?

   Now suppose that investors forecast earnings accurately, but still undervalue the stock because they overestimate Butternut's actual business risk. Does this change your answers to the questions posed in the preceding paragraph? Explain.

MINI-CASE

The Shocking Demise of Mr. Thorndike

It was one of Morse's most puzzling cases. That morning Rupert Thorndike, the autocratic CEO of Thorndike Oil, was found dead in a pool of blood on his bedroom floor. He had been shot through the head, but the door and windows were bolted on the inside and there was no sign of the murder weapon.

Morse looked in vain for clues in Thorndike's office. He had to take another tack. He decided to investigate the financial circumstances surrounding Thorndike's demise.

The company's capital structure was as follows:

- *Debt:* $200 million face value. The bonds had a coupon of 5 percent, matured in 10 years, and offered a yield of 12 percent (the risk-free interest rate was 6 percent).

- *Stock:* 36 million shares, which closed at $10 per share on the day before the murder. The company had just announced a regular quarterly dividend of $.10 per share, and the shares were due to go ex-dividend in two weeks.

- *Warrants:* Warrants to buy an additional four million shares at $10 per share, expiring in three months time on December 31, 2003. The recent volatility of the shares had been around 50 percent per annum.

Yesterday Thorndike had flatly rejected an offer by T. Spoone Dickens to buy all Thorndike's assets for $1 billion cash, effective January 1, 2004. With Thorndike out of the way, it appeared that Dickens's offer would be accepted, much to the profit of Thorndike Oil's other shareholders.[26]

Thorndike's two nieces, Doris and Patsy, and his nephew John all had substantial investments in Thorndike Oil and had bitterly disagreed with Thorndike's dismissal of Dickens's offer. Their stakes are shown in the table below.

All debt issued by Thorndike Oil would be paid off at face value if Dickens's offer went through.

Morse kept coming back to the problem of motive. Which niece or nephew, he wondered, stood to gain most by eliminating Thorndike and allowing Dickens's offer to succeed?

	Debt (Face Value)	Stock (Number of Shares, in Millions)	Warrants (Number, in Millions)
Doris	$6 million	1.0	0
John	0	.5	2
Patsy	0	1.5	1

Questions

Help Morse by answering the following questions:

1. Value the company's debt, stock, and warrants both before and after Mr. Thorndike's death.

2. Which of Thorndike's relatives stood to gain most from his death?

---

[26]Rupert Thorndike's shares would go to a charitable foundation formed to "advance the study of financial engineering and its crucial role in world peace and progress." The managers of the foundation's endowment were not expected to oppose the takeover.

PART SIX
RELATED
WEBSITES

The Chicago Board site contains explanations of options markets and lots of data:

www.cboe.com

There are a number of good options sites, many of which provide data and calculators for Black–Scholes values and implied standard deviations:

www.cfo.com

www.fintools.net/options/optcalc.html
  (very good calculators)

www.numa.com

www.optionscentral.com

www.pcquote.com/options

www.pmpublishing.com (includes historical implied volatilities)

www.schaffersresearch.com/stock/calculator.asp

Two sites devoted to real options are:

www.real-options.com

www.puc-rio.br/marco.ind

Examples of journals specializing in options and other derivatives include:

www.appliederivatives.com

www.erivativesreview.com

www.futuresmag.com

www.risk.com

PART SEVEN

DEBT FINANCING

FALLING STOCK PRICES and low interest rates made 2001 a boom year for company borrowing. The largest issue was a record-breaking $11.9 billion issue by WorldCom. This involved bonds with different maturities.[1] The 3-year bonds paid interest of 6.5 percent, 2.2 percent above the yield on comparable government bonds. The 10-year bonds paid 7.5 percent, 2.4 percent above the government-bond yield, while the 30-year bonds paid 8.25 percent or nearly 2.7 percent above goverment-bond yields.

Why did WorldCom issue 30-year bonds, when the interest rate was lower on 3-year debt? Were the 3-year bonds cheap and the 30-year bonds ex-

pensive? And why did the company pay more in interest than the U.S. government? Part Seven first explains how bonds are priced, why short-term interest rates differ from long-term rates, and why companies pay more to borrow than governments.

Companies have an enormous choice in how they borrow. For example, the WorldCom issue pays a fixed interest rate; others pay a variable rate. The WorldCom issue consists of senior unsecured notes; others may be junior or secured. Chapter 25 explains these and other differences.

Finally, Chapter 26 explains leases and shows how they are valued. Leases have many of the characteristics of bonds.

---

[1]The package also included euro and sterling bonds.

CHAPTER TWENTY-FOUR

VALUING DEBT

HOW DO YOU estimate the present value of a company's bonds? The answer is simple: You take the cash flows and discount them at the opportunity cost of capital. Therefore, if a bond produces cash flows of C dollars per year for N years and is then repaid at its face value ($1,000), the present value is

$$PV = \frac{C}{1 + r_1} + \frac{C}{(1 + r_2)^2} + \cdots + \frac{C}{(1 + r_N)^N} + \frac{\$1,000}{(1 + r_N)^N}$$

where $r_1, r_2, \ldots, r_N$ are the appropriate discount rates for the cash flows to be received by the bond owners in periods $1, 2, \ldots, N$.

That is correct as far as it goes but it does not tell us anything about what *determines* the discount rates. For example,

- In 1945 U.S. Treasury bills offered a return of .4 percent: At their 1981 peak they offered a return of over 17 percent. Why does the same security offer radically different yields at different times?
- In mid-2001 the U.S. Treasury could borrow for one year at an interest rate of 3.4 percent, but it had to pay nearly 6 percent for a 30-year loan. Why do bonds maturing at different dates offer different rates of interest? In other words, why is there a *term structure* of interest rates?
- In mid-2001 the United States government could issue long-term bonds at a rate of nearly 6 percent. But even the most blue-chip corporate issuers had to pay at least 50 basis points (.5 percent) more on their long-term borrowing. What explains the premium that firms have to pay?

These questions lead to deep issues that will keep economists simmering for years. But we can give general answers and at the same time present some fundamental ideas.

Why should the financial manager care about these ideas? Who needs to know how bonds are priced as long as the bond market is active and efficient? Efficient markets protect the ignorant trader. If it is necessary to know whether the price is right for a proposed bond issue, you can check the prices of similar bonds. There is no need to worry about the historical behavior of interest rates, about the term structure, or about the other issues discussed in this chapter.

We do not believe that ignorance is desirable even when it is harmless. At least you ought to be able to read the bond tables in *The Wall Street Journal* and talk to investment bankers about the prices of recently issued bonds. More important, you will encounter many problems of bond pricing where there are no similar instruments already traded. How do you evaluate a private placement with a custom-tailored repayment schedule? How about financial leases? In Chapter 26 we will see that they are essentially debt contracts, but often extremely complicated ones, for which traded bonds are not close substitutes. Many companies, notably banks and insurance firms, are exposed to the risk of interest rate fluctuations. To control their exposure, these companies need to understand how interest rates change.[1] You will find that the terms, concepts, and facts presented in this chapter are essential to the analysis of these and other practical problems.

We start the chapter with our first question: Why does the general level of interest rates change over time? Next we turn to the relationship between short- and long-term interest rates. We consider three issues:

- Each period's cash flow on a bond potentially needs to be discounted at a different interest rate, but bond investors often calculate the yield to maturity as a summary measure of the interest rate on the bond. We first explain how these measures are related.

continued

---

[1]We discuss in Chapter 27 how firms protect themselves against interest rate risk.

- Second, we show why a change in interest rates has a greater impact on the price of long-term loans than on short-term loans.
- Finally, we look at some theories that explain why short- and long-term interest rates differ.

To close the chapter we shift the focus to corporate bonds and examine the risk of default and its effect on bond prices.

24.1 REAL AND NOMINAL RATES OF INTEREST

Indexed Bonds and the Real Rate of Interest

In Chapter 3 we drew the distinction between the real and nominal rate of interest. Most bonds promise a fixed *nominal* rate of interest. The *real* interest rate that you receive depends on the inflation rate. For example, if a one-year bond promises you a return of 10 percent and the expected inflation rate is 4 percent, the expected real return on your bond is $1.10/1.04 - 1 = .058$, or 5.8 percent. Since future inflation rates are uncertain, the real return on a bond is also uncertain. For example, if inflation turns out to be higher than the expected 4 percent, the real return will be *lower* than 5.8 percent.

You *can* nail down a real return; you do so by buying an indexed bond whose payments are linked to inflation. Indexed bonds have been around in many countries for decades, but they were almost unknown in the United States until 1997 when the U.S. Treasury began to issue inflation-indexed bonds known as TIPs (Treasury Inflation-Protected Securities).[2]

The real cash flows on TIPs are fixed, but the nominal cash flows (interest and principal) are increased as the Consumer Price Index increases. For example, suppose that the U.S. Treasury issues 3 percent 20-year TIPs at a price of 100. If during the first year the Consumer Price Index rises by (say) 10 percent, then the coupon payment on the bond would be increased by 10 percent to $(1.1 \times 3) = 3.3$ percent. And the final payment of principal would also be increased in the same proportion to $(1.1 \times 100) = 110$ percent. Thus, an investor who buys the bond at the issue price and holds it to maturity can be assured of a real yield of 3 percent.

As we write this in the summer of 2001, long-term TIPs offer a yield of 3.46 percent. This yield is a *real* yield: It measures how much extra goods your investment would allow you to buy. The 3.46 percent yield on TIPs was about 2.3 percent less than on nominal Treasury bonds. If the annual inflation rate proves to be higher than 2.3 percent, you will earn a higher return by holding long-term TIPs; if the inflation rate is lower than 2.3 percent, the reverse will be true.

What determines the real interest rate that investors demand? The classical economist's answer to this question is summed up in the title of Irving Fisher's great book: *The Theory of Interest: As Determined by Impatience to Spend Income and Opportunity to Invest It.*[3] The real interest rate, according to Fisher, is the price which equates

---

[2]In 1988 Franklin Savings Association had issued a 20-year bond whose interest (but not principal) was tied to the rate of inflation. Since then a trickle of companies has also issued indexed bonds.

[3]August M. Kelley, New York, 1965; originally published in 1930.

FIGURE 24.1

The burgundy line shows the real yield on long-term indexed bonds issued by the UK government. The blue line shows the yield on UK government long-term nominal bonds. Notice that the real yield has been much more stable than the nominal yield

the supply and demand for capital. The supply depends on people's willingness to save.[4] The demand depends on the opportunities for productive investment.

For example, suppose that investment opportunities generally improve. Firms have more good projects, so they are willing to invest more than previously at any interest rate. Therefore, the rate has to rise to induce individuals to save the additional amount that firms want to invest.[5] Conversely, if investment opportunities deteriorate, there will be a fall in the real interest rate.

Fisher's theory emphasizes that the required real rate of interest depends on real phenomena. A high aggregate willingness to save may be associated with high aggregate wealth (because wealthy people usually save more), an uneven distribution of wealth (an even distribution would mean fewer rich people, who do most of the saving), and a high proportion of middle-aged people (the young don't need to save and the old don't want to—"You can't take it with you"). Correspondingly, a high propensity to invest may be associated with a high level of industrial activity or major technological advances.

Real interest rates do change but they do so gradually. We can see this by looking at the UK, where the government has issued indexed bonds since 1982. The colored line in Figure 24.1 shows that the (real) yield on these bonds has fluctuated within a relatively narrow range, while the yield on nominal government bonds has declined dramatically.

Inflation and Nominal Interest Rates

Now let us see what Irving Fisher had to say about inflation and interest rates. Suppose that consumers are equally happy with 100 apples today or 105 apples in a year's time. In this case the real or "apple" interest rate is 5 percent. Suppose also

---

[4]Some of this saving is done indirectly. For example, if you hold 100 shares of GM stock, and GM retains earnings of $1 per share, GM is saving $100 on your behalf.

[5]We assume that investors save more as interest rates rise. It doesn't have to be that way; here is an example of how a higher interest rate could mean *less* saving: Suppose that 20 years hence you will need $50,000 at current prices for your children's college expenses. How much will you have to set aside today to cover this obligation? The answer is the present value of a real expenditure of $50,000 after 20 years, or $50,000/(1 + real interest rate)^{20}$. The higher the real interest rate, the lower the present value and the less you have to set aside.

that I know the price of apples will increase over the year by 10 percent. Then I will part with $100 today if I am repaid $115 at the end of the year. That $115 is needed to buy me 5 percent more apples than I can get for my $100 today. In other words, the nominal, or "money," rate of interest must equal the required real, or "apple," rate plus the prospective rate of inflation.[6] A change of 1 percent in the expected inflation rate produces a change of 1 percent in the nominal interest rate. That is Fisher's theory: A change in the expected inflation rate will cause the same change in the *nominal* interest rate; it has no effect on the required real interest rate.[7]

Nominal interest rates cannot be negative; if they were, everyone would prefer to hold cash, which pays zero interest.[8] But what about *real* rates? For example, is it possible for the money rate of interest to be 5 percent and the expected rate of inflation to be 10 percent, thus giving a negative real interest rate? If this happens, you may be able to make money in the following way: You borrow $100 at an interest rate of 5 percent and you use the money to buy apples. You store the apples and sell them at the end of the year for $110, which leaves you enough to pay off your loan plus $5 for yourself.

Since easy ways to make money are rare, we can conclude that if it doesn't cost anything to store goods, the money rate of interest can't be less than the expected rise in prices. But many goods are even more expensive to store than apples, and others can't be stored at all (you can't store haircuts, for example). For these goods, the money interest rate can be less than the expected price rise.

How Well Does Fisher's Theory Explain Interest Rates?

Not all economists would agree with Fisher that the real rate of interest is unaffected by the inflation rate. For example, if changes in prices are associated with changes in the level of industrial activity, then in inflationary conditions I might want more or less than 105 apples in a year's time to compensate me for the loss of 100 today.

We wish we could show you the past behavior of interest rates and *expected* inflation. Instead we have done the next best thing and plotted in Figure 24.2 the return on U.S. Treasury bills against actual inflation. Notice that between 1926 and 1981 the return on Treasury bills was below the inflation rate about as often as it

---

[6]We oversimplify. If apples cost $1.00 apiece today and $1.10 next year, you need $1.10 \times 105 = \$115.50$ next year to buy 105 apples. The money rate of interest is 15.5 percent, not 15. Remember, the exact formula relating real and money rates is

$$1 + r_{money} = (1 + r_{real})(1 + i)$$

where i is the expected inflation rate. Thus

$$r_{money} = r_{real} + i + i(r_{real})$$

In our example, the money rate should be

$$r_{money} = .05 + .10 + .10(.05) = .155$$

When we said the money rate should be 15 percent, we ignored the cross-product term $i(r_{real})$. This is a common rule of thumb because the cross-product term is usually small. But there are countries where i is large (sometimes 100 percent or more). In such cases it pays to use the full formula.

[7]The apple example was taken from R. Roll, "Interest Rates on Monetary Assets and Commodity Price Index Changes," *Journal of Finance* 27 (May 1972), pp. 251–278.

[8]There seems to be an exception to almost every statement. In late 1998 concern about the solvency of some Japanese banks led to a large volume of yen deposits with Western banks. Some of these banks *charged* their customers interest on these deposits; the nominal interest rate was negative.

FIGURE 24.2

The return on U.S. Treasury bills and
the rate of inflation, 1926–2000.

Source: Ibbotson Associates, Inc.,
Chicago, 2001.

was above. The average real interest rate during this period was a mere 0.1 percent.
Since 1981 the return on bills has been significantly higher than the rate of inflation, so that investors have earned a positive real return on their savings.

  Fisher's theory states that changes in anticipated inflation produce corresponding changes in the rate of interest. But Figure 24.2 offers little evidence of this in
the 1930s and 1940s. During this period, the return on Treasury bills scarcely
changed even though the inflation rate fluctuated sharply. Either these changes in
inflation were unanticipated or Fisher's theory was wrong. Since the early 1950s,
there appears to have been a closer relationship between interest rates and inflation in the United States.[9] Thus, for today's financial managers Fisher's theory provides a useful rule of thumb. If the expected inflation rate changes, it is a good bet
that there will be a corresponding change in the interest rate.

 24.2 TERM STRUCTURE AND YIELDS TO MATURITY

We turn now to the relationship between short- and long-term rates of interest.
Suppose that we have a simple loan that pays $1 at time 1. The present value of this
loan is

$$PV = \frac{1}{1 + r_1}$$

Thus we discount the cash flow at r_1, the rate appropriate for a one-period loan.
This rate, which is fixed today, is often called today's one-period **spot rate.**

  If we have a loan that pays $1 at both time 1 and time 2, present value is

$$PV = \frac{1}{1 + r_1} + \frac{1}{(1 + r_2)^2}$$

---

[9]This probably reflects government policy, which before 1951 stabilized nominal interest rates. The 1951
"accord" between the Treasury and the Federal Reserve System permitted more flexible nominal interest rates after 1951.

Thus the first period's cash flow is discounted at today's one-period spot rate and the second period's flow is discounted at today's two-period spot rate. The series of spot rates r_1, r_2, etc., is one way of expressing the **term structure** of interest rates.

Yield to Maturity

Rather than discounting each of the payments at a different rate of interest, we could find a single rate of discount that would produce the same present value. Such a rate is known as the **yield to maturity,** though it is in fact no more than our old acquaintance, the internal rate of return (IRR), masquerading under another name. If we call the yield to maturity y, we can write the present value of the two-year loan as

$$PV = \frac{1}{1 + y} + \frac{1}{(1 + y)^2}$$

All you need to calculate y is the price of a bond, its annual payment, and its maturity. You can then rapidly work out the yield with the aid of a preprogrammed calculator.

The yield to maturity is unambiguous and easy to calculate. It is also the stock-in-trade of any bond dealer. By now, however, you should have learned to treat any internal rate of return with suspicion.[10] The more closely we examine the yield to maturity, the less informative it is seen to be. Here is an example.

Example. It is 2003. You are contemplating an investment in U.S. Treasury bonds and come across the following quotations for two bonds:[11]

Bond	Price	Yield to Maturity (IRR)
5s of '08	85.21%	8.78%
10s of '08	105.43	8.62

The phrase "5s of '08" refers to a bond maturing in 2008, paying annual interest of 5 percent of the bond's face value. The interest payment is called the *coupon* payment. In continental Europe coupons are usually paid annually; in the United States they are usually paid every six months, so the 5s of '08 would pay 2.5 percent of face value every six months. To simplify the arithmetic, we will pretend throughout this chapter that all coupon payments are annual. When the bonds mature in 2008, bondholders receive the bond's face value in addition to the final interest payment.

The price of each bond is quoted as a percent of face value. Therefore, if face value is $1,000, you would have to pay $852.11 to buy the bond and your yield would be 8.78 percent. Letting 2003 be $t = 0$, 2004 be $t = 1$, etc., we have the following discounted-cash-flow calculation:

Bond	Cash Flows						Yield
	C_0	C_1	C_2	C_3	C_4	C_5	
5s of '08	−852.11	+50	+50	+50	+50	+1,050	8.78%
10s of '08	−1,054.29	+100	+100	+100	+100	+1,100	8.62

---

[10]See Section 5.3.

[11]The quoted bond price is known as the *flat* (or *clean*) price. The price that the bond buyer pays (sometimes called the *dirty* price) is equal to the flat price *plus* the interest that the seller has already earned on the bond since the last interest payment date. You need to use the flat price to calculate yields to maturity.

TABLE 24.1

		Present Value Calculations			
		5s of '08		10s of '08	
Period	**Interest Rate**	**C_t**	**PV at r_t**	**C_t**	**PV at r_t**
$t = 1$	$r_1 = .05$	$ 50	$ 47.62	$ 100	$ 95.24
$t = 2$	$r_2 = .06$	50	44.50	100	89.00
$t = 3$	$r_3 = .07$	50	40.81	100	81.63
$t = 4$	$r_4 = .08$	50	36.75	100	73.50
$t = 5$	$r_5 = .09$	1,050	682.43	1,100	714.92
	Totals		$852.11		$1,054.29

Calculating present value of two bonds when long-term interest rates are higher than short-term rates.

Although the two bonds mature at the same date, they presumably were issued at different times—the 5s when interest rates were low and the 10s when interest rates were high.

Are the 5s of '08 a better buy? Is the market making a mistake by pricing these two issues at different yields? The only way you will know for sure is to calculate the bonds' present values by using spot rates of interest: r_1 for 2004, r_2 for 2005, etc. This is done in Table 24.1.

The important assumption in Table 24.1 is that long-term interest rates are higher than short-term interest rates. We have assumed that the one-year interest rate is $r_1 = .05$, the two-year rate is $r_2 = .06$, and so on. When each year's cash flow is discounted at the rate appropriate to that year, we see that each bond's present value is exactly equal to the quoted price. Thus each bond is fairly priced.

Why do the 5s have a higher yield? Because for each dollar that you invest in the 5s you receive relatively little cash inflow in the first four years and a relatively high cash inflow in the final year. Therefore, although the two bonds have identical maturity dates, the 5s provide a greater proportion of their cash flows in 2008. In this sense the 5s are a longer-term investment than the 10s. Their higher yield to maturity just reflects the fact that long-term interest rates are higher than short-term rates.

Notice why the yield to maturity can be misleading. When the yield is calculated, the *same* rate is used to discount *all* payments on the bond. But in our example bondholders actually demanded different rates of return (r_1, r_2, etc.) for cash flows that occurred at different times. Since the cash flows on the two bonds were not identical, the bonds had different yields to maturity. Therefore, the yield to maturity on the 5s of '08 offered only a rough guide to the appropriate yield on the 10s of '08.[12]

Measuring the Term Structure

Financial managers who just want a quick, summary measure of interest rates look in the financial press at the yields to maturity on government bonds. Thus managers will make broad generalizations such as "If we borrow money today, we will have to pay an interest rate of 8 percent." But if you wish to understand why different

---

[12]For a good analysis of the relationship between the yield to maturity and spot interest rates, see S. M. Schaefer, "The Problem with Redemption Yields," *Financial Analysts Journal* 33 (July–August 1977), pp. 59–67.

FIGURE 24.3

Spot rates on U.S. Treasury strips,
June 2001.

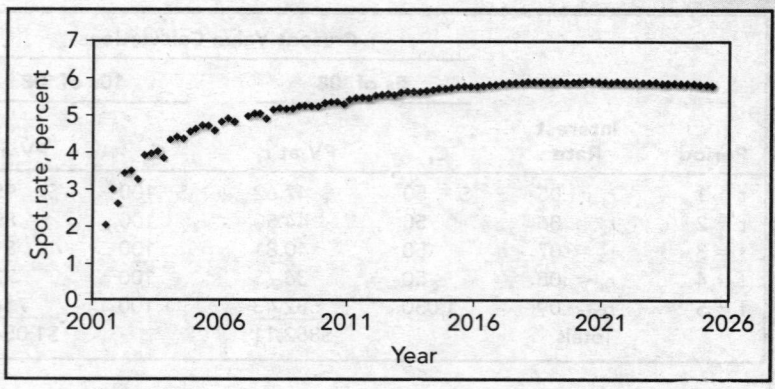

bonds sell at different prices, you must dig deeper and look at the separate interest rates for one-year cash flows, for two-year cash flows, and so on. In other words, you must look at the spot rates of interest.

To find the spot interest rate, you need the price of a bond that simply makes one future payment. Fortunately, such bonds do exist. They are known as *stripped bonds* or *strips*. Strips originated in 1982 when several investment bankers came up with a novel idea. They bought U.S. Treasury bonds and reissued their own separate mini-bonds, each of which made only one payment. The idea proved to be popular with investors, who welcomed the opportunity to buy the mini-bonds rather than the complete package. If you've got a smart idea, you can be sure that others will soon clamber onto your bandwagon. It was therefore not long before the Treasury issued its own mini-bonds.[13] The prices of these bonds are shown each day in the daily press. For example, in the summer of 2001, a strip maturing in May 2021 cost $316.55 and 20 years later will give the investors a single payment of $1,000. Thus the 20-year spot rate was $(1000/316.55)^{1/20} - 1 = .0592$, or 5.92 percent.[14]

In Figure 24.3 we have used the prices of strips with different maturities to plot the term structure of spot rates from 1 to 24 years. You can see that investors required an interest rate of 3.4 percent from a bond that made a payment only at the end of one year and a rate of 5.8 percent from a bond that paid off only in year 2025.

 24.3 HOW INTEREST RATE CHANGES AFFECT BOND PRICES

Duration and Bond Volatility

In Chapter 7 we reviewed the historical performance of different security classes. We showed that since 1926 long-term government bonds have provided a higher average return than short-term bills, but have also been more variable. The stan-

---

[13]The Treasury continued to auction coupon bonds in the normal way, but investors could exchange them at the Federal Reserve Bank for stripped bonds.

[14]This is an annually compounded rate. The yields quoted by investment dealers are semiannually compounded rates.

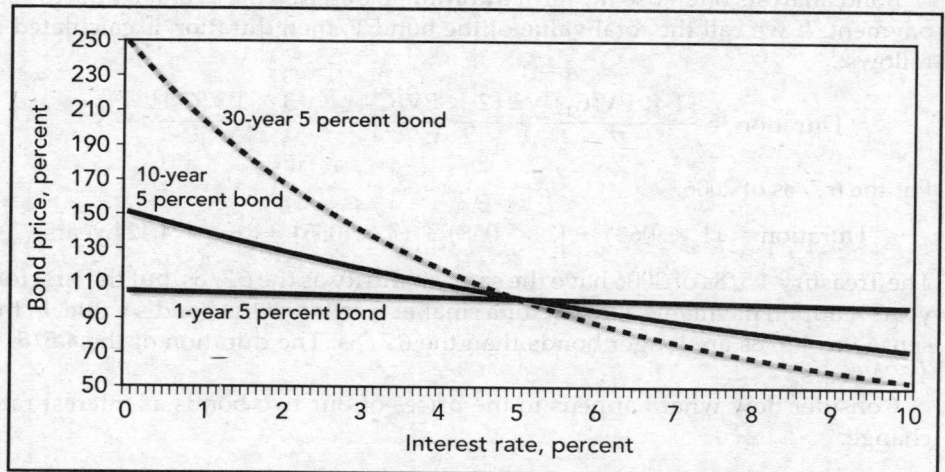

FIGURE 24.4

How bond prices change as interest rates change. Note that longer-term bonds are more sensitive to interest rate changes.

TABLE 24.2

The first four columns show that the cash flow in year 5 accounts for only 77.5 percent of the present value of the 6 7/8s of 2006. The final column shows how to calculate a weighted average of the time to each cash flow. This average is the bond's duration.

Year	C_t	PV(C_t) at 4.9%	Proportion of Total Value [PV(C_t)/V]	Proportion of Total Value × Time
1	68.75	65.54	0.060	0.060
2	68.75	62.48	0.058	0.115
3	68.75	59.56	0.055	0.165
4	68.75	56.78	0.052	0.209
5	1068.75	841.39	0.775	3.875
		V = 1085.74	1.000	Duration = 4.424 years

dard deviation of annual returns on a portfolio of long-term bonds was 9.4 percent compared with a standard deviation of 3.2 percent for bills.

Figure 24.4 illustrates why long-term bonds are more variable. Each line shows how the price of a 5-percent bond changes with the level of interest rates. You can see that the price of a longer-term bond is more sensitive to interest rate fluctuations than that of a shorter bond.

But what do we mean by long-term and short-term bonds? It is obvious in the case of strips that make payments in only one year. However, a coupon bond that matures in year 10 makes payments in *each* of years 1 through 10. Therefore, it is somewhat misleading to describe the bond as a 10-year bond; the average time to each cash flow is less than 10 years.

Consider the Treasury 6 7/8s of 2006. In mid-2001 these bonds had a present value of 108.57 percent of face value and yielded 4.9 percent. The third and fourth columns in Table 24.2 show where this present value comes from. Notice that the cash flow in year 5 accounts for only 77.5 percent of the bond's value. The remaining 22.5 percent of the value comes from the earlier cash flows.

Bond analysts often use the term **duration** to describe the average time to each payment. If we call the total value of the bond V, then duration is calculated as follows:[15]

$$\text{Duration} = \frac{[1 \times \text{PV}(C_1)]}{V} + \frac{[2 \times \text{PV}(C_2)]}{V} + \frac{[3 \times \text{PV}(C_3)]}{V} + \cdots$$

For the 6 7/8s of 2006,

$$\text{Duration} = (1 \times .060) + (2 \times .058) + (3 \times .055) + \cdots = 4.424 \text{ years}$$

The Treasury 4 5/8s of 2006 have the same maturity as the 6 7/8s, but the first four years' coupon payments account for a smaller fraction of the bond's value. In this sense the 4 5/8s are longer bonds than the 6 7/8s. The duration of the 4 5/8s is 4.574 years.

Consider now what happens to the prices of our two bonds as interest rates change:

	6 7/8s of 2006		4 5/8s of 2006	
	New Price	**Change**	**New Price**	**Change**
Yield falls .5%	1108.96	+2.14%	1009.91	+2.21%
Yield rises .5%	1063.16	−2.08%	966.81	−2.15%
Difference		4.22%		4.36%

Thus, a 1 percentage-point variation in yield causes the price of the 6 7/8s to change by 4.22 percent. We can say that the 6 7/8s have a **volatility** of 4.22 percent, while the 4 5/8s have a volatility of 4.36 percent.

Notice that the 4 5/8 percent bonds have the greater volatility and that they also have the longer duration. In fact, a bond's volatility is directly related to its duration:[16]

$$\text{Volatility (percent)} = \frac{\text{duration}}{1 + \text{yield}}$$

In the case of the 6 7/8s,

$$\text{Volatility (percent)} = \frac{4.424}{1.049} = 4.22$$

In Figure 24.4 we showed how bond prices vary with the level of interest rates. Each bond's volatility is simply the slope of the line relating the bond price to the interest rate. You can see this more clearly in Figure 24.5, where the convex curve shows the price of the 5 percent 30-year bond for different interest rates. The bond's volatility is measured by the slope of a tangent to this curve. For example, the dotted line in the figure shows that, if the interest rate is 5 percent, the curve has a slope of 15.4. At this point the change in bond price is 15.4 times a change in the interest rate. Notice that the bond's volatility changes as the interest rate changes. Volatility is higher at lower interest rates (the curve is steeper), and it is lower at higher rates (the curve is flatter).

---

[15]This measure is also known as *Macaulay duration* after its inventor. See F. Macaulay, *Some Theoretical Problems Suggested by the Movements of Interest Rates, Bond Yields, and Stock Prices in the United States since 1856*, National Bureau of Economic Research, New York, 1938.

[16]For this reason volatility is also called *modified duration*.

FIGURE 24.5

Volatility is the slope of the curve relating the bond price to the interest rate. For example, a 5 percent 30-year bond has a volatility of 15.4 when the interest rate is 5 percent. At this point the change in price is 15.4 times the change in the interest rate. Its volatility is higher at lower interest rates (the curve is steeper) and lower at higher rates (the curve is flatter).

Managing Interest Rate Risk

Volatility is a useful, summary measure of the likely effect of a change in interest rates on the value of a bond. The longer a bond's duration, the greater is its volatility. In Chapter 27 we will make use of this relationship between duration and volatility to describe how firms can protect themselves against interest rate changes. Here is an example that should give you a flavor of things to come.

Suppose your firm has promised to make pension payments to retired employees. The discounted value of these pension payments is $1 million; therefore, the firm puts aside $1 million in the pension fund and invests the money in government bonds. So the firm has a liability of $1 million and (through the pension fund) an offsetting asset of $1 million. But, as interest rates fluctuate, the value of the pension liability will change and so will the value of the bonds in the pension fund. How can the firm ensure that the value of the bonds in the fund is always sufficient to meet the liabilities? Answer: By making sure that the duration of the bonds is always the same as the duration of the pension liability.

A Cautionary Note

Bond volatility measures the effect on bond prices of a shift in interest rates. For example, we calculated that the 6 7/8s had a volatility of 4.22. This means a 1 percentage-point change in interest rates leads to a 4.22 percent change in bond price:

$$\text{Change in bond price} = 4.22 \times \text{change in interest rates}$$

This relationship is sometimes called a *one-factor model* of bond returns; it tells us how each bond's price changes in response to one factor—a change in the overall level of interest rates. One-factor models have proved very useful in helping firms to understand how they are affected by interest-rate changes and how they can protect themselves against these risks.

If the yields on all Treasury bonds moved in precise lockstep, then changes in the price of each bond would be exactly proportional to the bond's duration. For example, the price of a long-term bond with a duration of 20 years would always rise or fall twice as much as the price of a medium-term bond with a duration of 10 years. However, Figure 24.6 illustrates that short- and long-term interest rates do

FIGURE 24.6

Short-term and long-term interest rates do not always move in parallel. Between September 1992 and April 2000 short-term rates rose sharply while long-term rates declined.

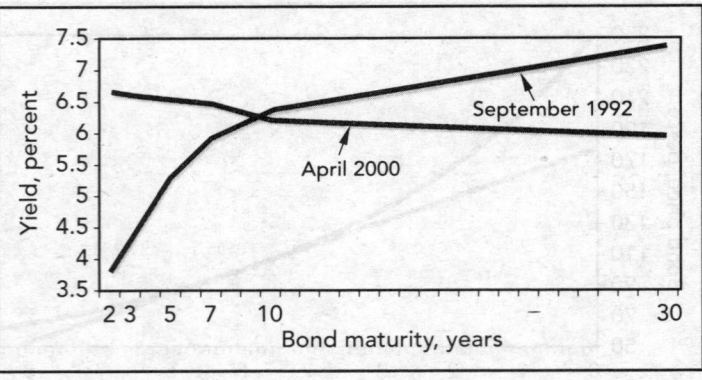

not always move in perfect unison. Between 1992 and 2000 short-term interest rates nearly doubled while long-term rates declined. As a result, the term structure, which initially sloped steeply upward, shifted to a downward slope. Because short- and long-term yields do not move in parallel, one-factor models cannot be the whole story, and managers need to worry not just about the risks of an overall change in interest rates but also about shifts in the term structure.

24.4 EXPLAINING THE TERM STRUCTURE

The term structure that we showed in Figure 24.3 was upward-sloping. In other words, long rates of interest are higher than short rates. This is the more common pattern but sometimes it is the other way around, with short rates higher than long rates. Why do we get these shifts in term structure?

Let us look at a simple example. Figure 24.3 showed that in the summer of 2001 the one-year spot rate (r_1) was about 3.5 percent. The two-year spot rate (r_2) was higher at 4 percent. Suppose that in 2001 you invest in a one-year U.S. Treasury strip. You would earn the one-year spot rate of interest and by the end of the year each dollar that you invested would have grown to $\$(1 + r_1) = \$1.035$. If instead you were prepared to invest for two years, you would earn the two-year spot rate of r_2 and by the end of the two years each dollar would have grown to $\$(1 + r_2)^2 = \$1.04^2 = \$1.0816$. By keeping your money invested for a further year, your savings grow from \$1.0350 to \$1.0816, an increase of 4.5 percent. This extra 4.5 percent that you earn by keeping your money invested for two years rather than one is termed the **forward interest rate** or f_2.

Notice how we calculated the forward rate. When you invest for one year, each dollar grows to $\$(1 + r_1)$. When you invest for two years, each dollar grows to $\$(1 + r_2)^2$. Therefore, the extra return that you earn for that second year is $f_2 = (1 + r_2)^2/(1 + r_1) - 1$. In our example,

$$f_2 = (1 + r_2)^2/(1 + r_1) - 1 = (1.04)^2/(1.035) - 1 = .045, \text{ or } 4.5\%$$

If you twist this equation around, you obtain an expression for the two-year spot rate, r_2, in terms of the one-year spot rate, r_1, and the forward rate, f_2:

$$(1 + r_2)^2 = (1 + r_1) \times (1 + f_2)$$

FIGURE 24.7

An investor can invest either in a two-year loan [a] or in two successive one-year loans [b]. The expectations theory says that in equilibrium the expected payoffs from these two strategies must be equal. In other words, the forward rate, f_2, must equal the expected spot rate, $_1r_2$.

(a) The future value of $1 invested in a two-year loan

Period 0 $\longrightarrow$ Period 2

$$(1 + r_2)^2 = (1 + r_1) \times (1 + f_2)$$

(b) The future value of $1 invested in two successive one-year loans

Period 0 $\longrightarrow$ Period 1 $\longrightarrow$ Period 2

$\quad(1 + r_1) \quad\quad \times \quad\quad (1 + {}_1r_2)$

In other words, you can think of the two-year investment as earning the one-year spot rate for the first year and the extra return, or forward rate, for the second year.

The Expectations Theory

Would you have been happy in the summer of 2001 to earn an extra 4.5 percent for investing for two years rather than one? The answer depends on how you expected interest rates to change over the coming year. Suppose, for example, that you were confident that interest rates would rise sharply, so that at the end of the year the one-year rate would be 5 percent. In that case rather than investing in a two-year bond and earning the extra 4.5 percent for the second year, you would do better to invest in a one-year bond and, when that matured, to reinvest the money for a further year at 5 percent. If other investors shared your view, no one would be prepared to hold the two-year bond and its price would fall. It would stop falling only when the extra return from holding the two-year bond equalled the expected future one-year rate. Let us call this expected rate $_1r_2$—that is, the spot rate of interest at year 1 on a loan maturing at the end of year 2.[17] Figure 24.7 shows that at that point investors would earn the same expected return from investing in a two-year loan as from investing in two successive one-year loans.

This is known as the **expectations theory** of term structure.[18] It states that in equilibrium the forward interest rate, f_2, must equal the expected one-year spot rate, $_1r_2$. The expectations theory implies that the *only* reason for an upward-sloping term structure, such as existed in the summer of 2001, is that investors expect short-term interest rates to rise; the *only* reason for a declining term structure is that investors expect short-term rates to fall.[19] The expectations theory also implies that investing in a succession of short-term bonds gives exactly the same expected return as investing in long-term bonds.

If short-term interest rates are significantly lower than long-term rates, it is often tempting to borrow short-term rather than long-term. The expectations theory

---

[17]Be careful to distinguish $_1r_2$ from r_2, the spot interest rate on a two-year bond held from time 0 to time 2. The quantity $_1r_2$ is a one-year spot rate established at time 1.

[18]The expectations theory is usually attributed to Lutz and Lutz. See F. A. Lutz and V. C. Lutz, *The Theory of Investment in the Firm*, Princeton University Press, Princeton, NJ, 1951.

[19]This follows from our example. If the two-year spot rate, r_2, exceeds the one-year rate, r_1, then the forward rate, f_2, also exceeds r_1. If the forward rate equals the expected spot rate, $_1r_2$ then $_1r_2$ must also exceed r_1. The converse is likewise true.

implies that such naïve strategies won't work. If short rates are lower than long rates, then investors must be expecting interest rates to rise. When the term structure is upward-sloping, you are likely to make money by borrowing short only if investors are *overestimating* future increases in interest rates.

Even on a casual glance the expectations theory does not seem to be the complete explanation of term structure. For example, if we look back over the period 1926–2000, we find that the return on long-term U.S. Treasury bonds was on average 1.9 percent higher than the return on short-term Treasury bills. Perhaps short-term interest rates did not go up as much as investors expected, but it seems more likely that investors wanted a higher expected return for holding long bonds and that on the average they got it. If so, the expectations theory is wrong.

The expectations theory has few strict adherents, but most economists believe that expectations about future interest rates have an important effect on term structure. For example, the expectations theory implies that if the forward rate of interest is 1 percent above the spot rate of interest, then your best estimate is that the spot rate of interest will rise by 1 percent. In a study of the U.S. Treasury bill market between 1959 and 1982, Eugene Fama found that a forward premium *does* on average precede a rise in the spot rate but the rise is less than the expectations theory would predict.[20]

The Liquidity-Preference Theory

What does the expectations theory leave out? The most obvious answer is "risk." If you are confident about the future level of interest rates, you will simply choose the strategy that offers the highest return. But, if you are not sure of your forecast, you may well opt for the less risky strategy even if it offers a lower expected return.

Remember that the prices of long-duration bonds are more volatile than those of short-term bonds. For some investors this extra volatility may not be a concern. For example, pension funds and life insurance companies with long-term liabilities may prefer to lock in future returns by investing in long-term bonds. However, the volatility of long-term bonds *does* create extra risk for investors who do not have such long-term fixed obligations.

Here we have the basis for the **liquidity-preference** theory of the term structure.[21] If investors incur extra risk from holding long-term bonds, they will demand the compensation of a higher expected return. In this case the forward rate must be higher than the expected spot rate. This difference between the forward rate and the expected spot rate is usually called the **liquidity premium.** If the liquidity-preference theory is right, the term structure should be upward-sloping more often than not. Of course, if future spot rates are expected to fall, the term structure could be downward-sloping and *still* reward investors for lending long. But the liquidity-preference theory would predict a less dramatic downward slope than the expectations theory.

---

[20]See E. F. Fama, "The Information in the Term Structure," *Journal of Financial Economics* 13 (December 1984), pp. 509–528. Evidence from the Treasury bond market that the forward premium has some power to predict changes in spot rates is provided in J. Y. Campbell, A. W. Lo, and A. C. MacKinlay, *The Econometrics of Financial Markets,* Princeton University Press, Princeton, NJ, 1997, pp. 421–422.

[21]The liquidity-preference hypothesis is usually attributed to Hicks. See J. R. Hicks, *Value and Capital: An Inquiry into Some Fundamental Principles of Economic Theory,* 2nd ed., Oxford University Press, Oxford, 1946. For a theoretical development, see R. Roll, *The Behavior of Interest Rates: An Application of the Efficient-Market Model to U.S. Treasury Bills,* Basic Books, Inc., New York, 1970.

Introducing Inflation

The money cash flows on a U.S. Treasury bond are certain, but the real cash flows are not. In other words, Treasury bonds are still subject to inflation risk. Let us look therefore at how uncertainty about inflation affects the risk of bonds with different maturities.[22]

Suppose that Irving Fisher is right and short rates of interest always incorporate fully the market's latest views about inflation. Suppose also that the market learns more as time passes about the likely inflation rate in a particular year. Perhaps today investors have only a very hazy idea about inflation in year 2, but in a year's time they expect to be able to make a much better prediction. Since investors expect to learn a good deal about the inflation rate in year 2 from experience in year 1, next year they will be in a much better position to judge the appropriate interest rate in year 2.

You are saving for your retirement. Which of the following strategies is the more risky? Invest in a succession of one-year Treasury bonds or invest in a 20-year bond?

If you buy the 20-year bond, you know what money you will have at the end of 20 years, but you will be making a long-term bet on inflation. Inflation may seem benign now, but who knows what it will be in 10 or 20 years? This uncertainty about inflation makes it more risky for you to fix today the rates at which you will lend in the distant future.

You can reduce this uncertainty by investing in successive short-term bonds. You do not know the interest rate at which you will be able to reinvest your money at the end of each year, but at least you know that it will incorporate the latest information about inflation in the coming year. So, if the prospects for inflation deteriorate, it is likely that you will be able to reinvest your money at a higher interest rate.

Inflation uncertainty may help to explain why long-term bonds provide a liquidity premium. If inflation creates additional risks for long-term lenders, borrowers must offer some incentive if they want investors to lend long. Therefore, the forward rate of interest f_2 must be greater than the expected spot rate $E(_1r_2)$ by an amount that compensates investors for the extra risk of inflation.

Relationships between Bond Returns

These term structure theories tell us how bond prices may be determined at a point in time. More recently, financial economists have proposed some important theories of how price *movements* are related. These theories take advantage of the fact that the returns on bonds with different maturities tend to move together. For example, if short-term interest rates are high, it is a good bet that long-term rates will also be high. If short-term rates fall, long-term rates usually keep them company. Such linkages between interest rate movements can tell us something about relationships between bond prices.

The models that bond traders use to exploit these relationships can be quite complex and we can't get deeply into the subject here. However, the following example will give you a flavor of how the models work.

Suppose that you can invest in three possible government loans: a three-month Treasury bill, a medium-term bond, and a long-term bond. The return on

---

[22]See R. A. Brealey and S. M. Schaefer, "Term Structure and Uncertain Inflation," *Journal of Finance* 32 (May 1977), pp. 277–290.

TABLE 24.3

Illustrative payoffs from three government securities. Note the wider range of outcomes from the longer-duration loans. We don't know what the medium-term bond sells for; we need to figure it out from how its value *changes* when interest rates rise or fall.

| | Beginning Price | Change in Value | | Ending Value |
		If Interest Rates Rise	If Interest Rates Fall	
Treasury bill	98	+2	+2	100
Medium-term bond	?	−6.5	+10	?
Long-term bond	105	−15	+18	90 or 123

the Treasury bill over the next three months is certain; we will assume it yields a 2 percent quarterly rate. The return on each of the other bonds depends on what happens to interest rates. Suppose that you foresee only two possible outcomes—a sharp rise in interest rates or a sharp fall. Table 24.3 summarizes how the prices of the three investments would be affected. Notice that the long-term bond has a longer duration and therefore a wider range of possible outcomes.

Here's the puzzle. You know the price of the Treasury bill and the long-term bond. But can you get rid of the two question marks in Table 24.3 and figure out what the medium-term bond should sell for?

Suppose that you start with $100. You invest half of this money in the Treasury bill and half in the long-term bond. In this case the change in the value of your portfolio will be $(.5 \times 2) + [.5 \times (-15)] = -\$6.5$ if interest rates rise and $(.5 \times 2) + (.5 \times 18) = +\$10$ if interest rates fall. Thus, regardless of whether interest rates rise or fall, your portfolio will provide exactly the same payoffs as an investment in the medium-term bond. Since the two investments provide identical payoffs, they must sell for the same price or there will be a money machine. So, the value of the medium-term bond must be halfway between the value of a three-month bill and that of the long-term bond, that is, $(98 + 105)/2 = 101.5$. Knowing this, you can calculate what the yield to maturity on the medium-term bond has to be. You can also calculate its value next year, either $101.5 - 6.5 = 95$ or $101.5 + 10 = 111.5$.

Everything now checks; regardless of whether interest rates rise or fall, the medium-term bond will provide the same payoff as the package of Treasury bill and long-term bond and therefore it must cost the same:

| | Initial Outlay | Ending Value | |
		If Interest Rates Rise	If Interest Rates Fall
Equal holdings of Treasury bill & long-term bond	$(.5 \times 98) + (.5 \times 105) = 101.5$	$(.5 \times 100) + (.5 \times 90) = 95$	$(.5 \times 100) + (.5 \times 123) = 111.5$
Medium-term bond	101.5	$101.5 - 6.5 = 95$	$101.5 + 10 = 111.5$

Our example is grossly oversimplified, but you have probably already noticed that the basic idea is the same that we used when valuing an option. To value an option on a share, we constructed a portfolio of a risk-free loan and the common stock that would exactly replicate the payoffs from the option. That allowed us to price the option *given* the price of the risk-free loan and the share. Here we value a bond by constructing a portfolio of two or more other bonds that will provide exactly the same payoffs.[23] That allows us to value one bond *given* the prices of the other bonds.

Our example carries three messages. First, bond traders focus on *changes* in bond prices and on how the changes for different bonds are linked. Second, changes in bond prices can be related to a small number of factors (in our example, the change in the overall level of interest rates completely defined the change in the price of each bond). Third, once the linkages between bond prices can be pinned down, then each bond can be priced relative to a package of other bonds.

24.5 ALLOWING FOR THE RISK OF DEFAULT

You should by now be familiar with some of the basic ideas about why interest rates change and why short rates may differ from long rates. It only remains to consider our third question: Why do some borrowers have to pay a higher rate of interest than others?

The answer is obvious: Bond prices go down, and interest rates go up, when the probability of default increases. But when we say "interest rates go up," we mean *promised* interest rates. If the borrower defaults, the *actual* interest rate paid to the lender is less than the promised rate. The *expected* interest rate may go up with increasing probability of default, but this is not a logical necessity.

These points can be illustrated by a simple numerical example. Suppose that the interest rate on one-year, *risk-free* bonds is 9 percent. Backwoods Chemical Company has issued 9 percent notes with face values of $1,000, maturing in one year. What will the Backwoods notes sell for?

The answer is easy—if the notes are risk-free, just discount principal ($1,000) and interest ($90) at 9 percent:

$$\text{PV of notes} = \frac{\$1,000 + 90}{1.09} = \$1,000$$

Suppose instead that there is a 20 percent chance that Backwoods will default and that, if default does occur, holders of its notes receive nothing. In this case, the possible payoffs to the noteholders are

	Payoff	Probability
Full payment	$1,090	.8
No payment	0	.2

The expected payment is .8($1,090) + .2($0) = $872.

We can value the Backwoods notes like any other risky asset, by discounting their expected payoff ($872) at the appropriate opportunity cost of capital. We might discount at the risk-free interest rate (9 percent) if Backwoods's possible default is

[23]Two early examples of models that use no-arbitrage conditions to model the term structure are O. Vasicek, "An Equilibrium Characterization of the Term Structure," *Journal of Financial Economics* 5 (November 1977), pp. 177–188; and J. C. Cox, J. E. Ingersoll, and S. A. Ross, "A Theory of the Term Structure of Interest Rates," *Econometrica* 53 (May 1985), pp. 385–407.

TABLE 24.4

Key to Moody's and Standard and Poor's bond ratings. The highest quality bonds are rated triple-A. Then come double-A bonds, and so on. Investment-grade bonds have to be Baa or higher. Bonds that don't make this cut are called junk bonds.

Moody's Ratings	Standard and Poor's Ratings
Investment-grade:	
Aaa	AAA
Aa	AA
A	A
Baa	BBB
Junk bonds:	
Ba	BB
B	B
Caa	CCC
Ca	CC
C	C

totally unrelated to other events in the economy. In this case the default risk is wholly diversifiable, and the beta of the notes is zero. The notes would sell for

$$\text{PV of notes} = \frac{\$872}{1.09} = \$800$$

An investor who purchased these notes for $800 would receive a *promised* yield of about 36 percent:

$$\text{Promised yield} = \frac{\$1,090}{\$800} - 1 = .363$$

That is, an investor who purchased the notes for $800 would earn a 36.3 percent rate of return if Backwoods does not default. Bond traders therefore might say that the Backwoods notes "yield 36 percent." But the smart investor would realize that the notes' *expected* yield is only 9 percent, the same as on risk-free bonds.

This of course assumes that risk of default with these notes is wholly diversifiable, so that they have no market risk. In general, risky bonds do have market risk (that is, positive betas) because default is more likely to occur in recessions when all businesses are doing poorly. Suppose that investors demand a 2 percent risk premium and an 11 percent expected rate of return. Then the Backwoods notes will sell for $872/1.11 = $785.59 and offer a promised yield of $(1,090/785.59) - 1 = .388$, or about 39 percent.

You rarely see traded bonds offering 39 percent yields, although we will soon encounter an example of one company's bonds that had a promised yield of 50 percent.

Bond Ratings

The relative quality of most traded bonds can be judged from bond ratings given by Moody's and Standard and Poor's. Table 24.4 summarizes these ratings. For example, the highest quality bonds are rated triple-A (Aaa) by Moody's, then come double-A (Aa) bonds, and so on. Bonds rated Baa or above are known as *investment-grade* bonds. Commercial banks, many pension funds, and other financial institutions are not allowed to invest in bonds unless they are investment-grade.[24]

---

[24]Investment-grade bonds can usually be entered at face value on the books of banks and life insurance companies.

Rating at Time of Issue	Percentage Defaulting within		
	1 Year after Issue	5 Years after Issue	10 Years after Issue
AAA	.0	.1	.1
AA	.0	.7	.7
A	.0	.2	.6
BBB	.0	1.6	2.8
BB	.4	8.3	16.4
B	1.5	22.0	33.0
CCC	2.3	35.4	47.5

TABLE 24.5

Default rates of corporate bonds 1971–1997 by Standard and Poor's rating at date of issue.

Source: R. A. Waldman, E. I. Altman, and A. R. Ginsberg, "Defaults and Returns on High Yield Bonds: Analysis through 1997," Salomon Smith Barney, New York, January 30, 1998.

Bond ratings are judgments about firms' financial and business prospects. There is no fixed formula by which ratings are calculated. Nevertheless, investment bankers, bond portfolio managers, and others who follow the bond market closely can get a fairly good idea of how a bond will be rated by looking at a few key numbers such as the firm's debt–equity ratio, the ratio of earnings to interest, and the return on assets.

Table 24.5 shows that bond ratings do reflect the probability of default. Since 1971 no bond that was initially rated triple-A by Standard and Poor's has defaulted in the year after issue and fewer than one in a thousand has defaulted within 10 years of issue. At the other extreme, over 2 percent of CCC bonds have defaulted in their first year and by year 10 almost half have done so. Of course, bonds rarely fall suddenly from grace. As time passes and the company becomes progressively more shaky, the agencies revise downward the bond's rating to reflect the increasing probability of default.

Since bond ratings reflect the probability of default, it is not surprising that there is also a close correspondence between a bond's rating and its promised yield. For example, in the postwar period the promised yield on Moody's Baa corporate bonds has been on average about .9 percent more than on Aaa's.

Firms and governments, having noticed the link between bond ratings and yields, worry that a reduction in rating will result in higher interest charges.[25] When the Asian currency crisis in 1998 led Moody's to downgrade the Malaysian government's risk rating, the government immediately canceled a much-needed $2 billion bond issue. Investors have a different concern; they worry that the rating agencies are slow to react when businesses are in trouble. When Enron went belly up in 2001, investors protested that only two months earlier the company's debt had an investment-grade rating.

Junk Bonds

Bonds rated below Baa are known as **junk bonds.** Most junk bonds used to be *fallen angels*, that is, bonds of companies that had fallen on hard times. But during the 1980s new issues of junk bonds multiplied tenfold as more and more companies issued large quantities of low-grade debt to finance takeovers or to defend themselves against being taken over.

[25]They almost certainly exaggerate the influence of the rating agencies, which are as much following investor opinion as leading it.

FIGURE 24.8

Cumulative value of investments in junk and Treasury bonds, 1978–2000. The plot assumes investment of $1 in 1977.

Source: E. I. Altman, "High Yield Bond and Default Study," Salomon Smith Barney, July 19, 2001.

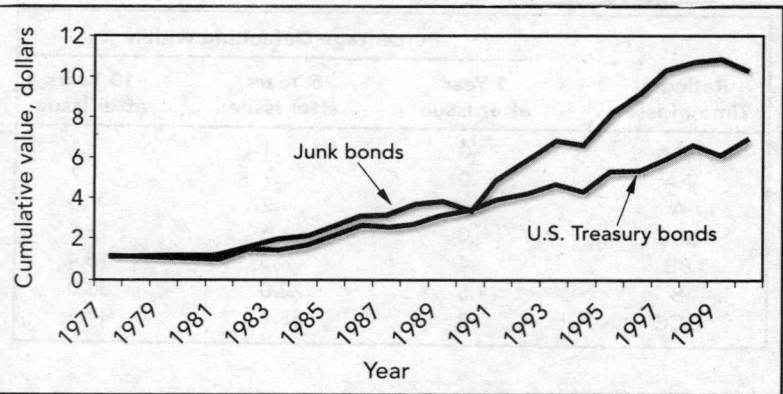

The development of this market for low-grade corporate bonds was largely the brainchild of the investment banking firm Drexel Burnham Lambert. The result was that for the first time corporate midgets were able to take control of corporate giants, because they could finance this activity by issues of debt. However, issuers of junk bonds often had debt ratios of 90 or 95 percent. Many worried that these high levels of leverage resulted in undue risk and pressed for legislation to ban junk bonds.

One of the largest issuers of junk bonds was Campeau Corporation. Between 1986 and 1988 Campeau amassed a huge retailing empire by acquiring major department store chains such as Federated Department Stores and Allied Stores. Unfortunately, it also amassed $10.9 billion in debt, which was supported by just $.9 billion of book equity. So when in September 1989 Campeau announced that it was having difficulties meeting the interest payments on its debt, the junk bond market took a nosedive and worries about the riskiness of junk bonds intensified. Campeau's own bonds fell to the point at which they offered a promised yield of nearly 50 percent. Campeau eventually filed for bankruptcy, and investors with holdings of junk bonds took large losses.

In 1990 and 1991 the default rate for junk bonds climbed to over 10 percent and the market for new issues of these bonds dried up. But later in the decade the market began to boom again and with increasing economic prosperity the annual default rate fell to below 2 percent before rising again in the new millenium.

Junk bonds promise a higher yield than U.S. Treasuries. When junk bonds were out of favor, their yields reached more than 9 percent above that of Treasuries, but the gap has since narrowed. Of course, companies can't always keep their promises. Many junk bonds have defaulted, while some of the more successful issuers have called their bonds, thus depriving their holders of the prospect of a continuing stream of high coupon payments. Figure 24.8 shows the performance since 1977 of a portfolio of junk bonds and 10-year Treasury bonds. On average, the *promised yield* on junk bonds was 4.8 percent higher than that on Treasuries, but the annual *realized return* was only 1.9 percent higher.

Option Pricing and Risky Debt

In Section 20.2 we showed that holding a corporate bond is equivalent to lending money with no chance of default *but* at the same time giving stockholders a put option on the firm's assets. When a firm defaults, its stockholders are in effect exercising their put. The put's value is the value of limited liability—the value of stockholders' right to walk away from their firm's debts in exchange for handing over the firm's assets to its creditors. Thus, valuing bonds should be a two-step process:

$$
\text{Bond value} = \begin{matrix} \text{bond value} \\ \text{assuming no chance} \\ \text{of default} \end{matrix} - \begin{matrix} \text{value} \\ \text{of put} \\ \text{option} \end{matrix}
$$

The first step is easy: Calculate the bond's value assuming no default risk. (Discount promised interest and principal payments at the rates offered by Treasury issues.) Second, calculate the value of a put written on the firm's assets, where the maturity of the put equals the maturity of the bond and the exercise price of the put equals the promised payments to bondholders.

Owning a corporate bond is also equivalent to owning the firm's assets *but* giving a call option on these assets to the firm's stockholders:

$$\text{Bond value} = \text{asset value} - \text{value of call option on assets}$$

Thus you can also calculate a bond's value, given the value of the firm's assets, by valuing a call option on these assets and subtracting the call value from the asset value. (The call value is just the value of the firm's common stock.) Therefore, if you can value puts and calls on a firm's assets, you can value its debt.[26]

Figure 24.9 shows a simple application of option theory to pricing corporate debt. It takes a company with average operating risk and shows how the promised interest rate on its debt should vary with its leverage and the maturity of the debt. For example, if the company has a 20 percent debt ratio and all its debt matures in 25 years, then it should pay about one-half percentage point above the government borrowing rate to compensate for default risk. Companies with more leverage ought to pay higher premiums. Notice that at relatively modest levels of leverage, promised yields increase with maturity. This makes sense, for the longer you have to wait for repayment, the greater is the chance that things will go wrong. However, if the company is already in distress and its assets are worth less than the face value of the debt, then promised yields are higher at low maturities. (In our example, they run off the top of the graph for maturities of less than four years.) This also makes sense, for in these cases the longer that you wait, the greater is the chance that the company will recover and avoid default.[27]

Notice that in constructing Figure 24.9 we made several artificial assumptions. One assumption is that the company does not pay dividends. If it does regularly pay out part of its assets to stockholders, there may be substantially fewer assets to protect the bondholder in the event of trouble. In this case, the market may be justified in requiring a higher yield on the company's bonds.

There are other complications that make the valuation of corporate debt and equity a good bit more difficult than it sounds. For example, in constructing Figure 24.9

---

[26]However, option-valuation procedures cannot value the *assets* of the firm. Puts and calls must be valued as a proportion of asset value. For example, note that the Black–Scholes formula (Section 21.3) requires stock price in order to compute the value of a call option.

[27]Sarig and Warga plot the difference between corporate bond yields and the yield on U.S. Treasuries. They confirm that the yield difference increases with maturity for high-grade bonds and declines for low-grade bonds. See O. Sarig and A. Warga, "Bond Price Data and Bond Market Liquidity," *Journal of Financial and Quantitative Analysis* 44 (1989), pp. 1351–1360. Incidentally, the shape of the curves in Figure 24.9 depends on how leverage is defined. If we had plotted curves for constant ratios of the *market* value of debt to debt plus equity, the curves would all have started at zero.

FIGURE 24.9

How the interest rate on risky corporate debt changes with leverage and maturity. These curves are calculated using option pricing theory under the following simplifying assumptions: (1) the risk-free interest rate is constant for all maturities; (2) the standard deviation of the returns on the company's assets is 25 percent per annum; (3) debt is in the form of zero-coupon bonds; and (4) leverage is the ratio $D/(D + E)$, where E is the market value of equity and D is the face value of the debt discounted at the risk-free interest rate.

we assumed that the company made only a single issue of zero-coupon debt. But suppose instead that it issues a 10-year bond which pays interest annually. We can still think of the company's stock as a call option that can be exercised by making the promised payments. But in this case there are 10 payments rather than just 1. To value the stock, we would have to value 10 sequential call options. The first option can be exercised by making the first interest payment when it comes due. By exercise the stockholders obtain a second call option, which can be exercised by making the second interest payment. The reward to exercising is that the stockholders get a third call option, and so on. Finally, in year 10 the stockholders can exercise the tenth option. By paying off both the principal and the last year's interest, the stockholders regain unencumbered ownership of the company's assets.

Of course, if the firm does not make any of these payments when due, bondholders take over and stockholders are left with nothing. In other words, by not exercising one call option, stockholders give up all subsequent call options.

Valuing the equity when the 10-year bond is issued is equivalent to valuing the first of the 10 call options. But you cannot value the first option without valuing the nine that follow.[28] Even this example understates the practical difficulties, because large firms may have dozens of outstanding debt issues with different interest rates and maturities, and before the current debt matures they may make further issues. But do not lose heart. Computers can solve these problems, more or less by brute force, even in the absence of simple, exact valuation formulas.

In practice, interest rate differentials tend to be greater than those shown in Figure 24.9. High-grade corporate bonds typically offer promised yields about 1 percentage point greater than U.S. Treasury bonds. It is very difficult to justify yield

---

[28]The other approach to valuing the company's debt (subtracting the value of a put option from risk-free bond value) is no easier. The analyst would be confronted by not one simple put but a package of 10 sequential puts.

differentials of this magnitude simply in terms of default risk.[29] So what is going on here? One possibility is that companies are paying too much for their debt, but it seems likely that the high yields on corporate bonds stem in part from some other drawback. One possibility is that investors demand additional yield to compensate for the illiquidity of corporate bonds. There is little doubt that investors prefer bonds that are easily bought and sold. We can even see small yield differences in the Treasury bond market, where the latest bonds to have been issued (known as "on-the-run" bonds) are traded much more heavily and typically yield a few basis points less than more seasoned issues.

Valuing Government Loan Guarantees

In the summer of 1971 Lockheed Corporation was in trouble. It was nearly out of cash after absorbing heavy cost overruns on military contracts and, at the same time, committing more than $800 million[30] to the development of the L1O11 Tri-Star airliner. After months of suspense and controversy, the U.S. government rescued Lockheed by agreeing to guarantee up to $250 million of new bank loans. If Lockheed had defaulted on these loans, the banks could have gotten their money back directly from the government.

From the banks' point of view, these loans were as safe as Treasury notes. Thus, Lockheed was assured of being able to borrow up to $250 million at a favorable rate.[31] This assurance in turn gave Lockheed's banks the confidence to advance the rest of the money the firm needed.

The loan guarantee was a helping hand—a subsidy—to bring Lockheed through a difficult period. What was it worth? What did it cost the government?

This loan guarantee did not turn out to cost the government anything, because Lockheed survived, recovered, and paid off the loans that the government had guaranteed. Does that mean that the value of the guarantee to Lockheed was also zero? Does it mean the government absorbed no risks when it gave the guarantee in 1971, when Lockheed's survival was still uncertain? Of course not. The government absorbed the risk of default. Obviously the banks' loans to Lockheed were worth more with the guarantee than they would have been without it.

The present value of a loan guarantee is the amount lenders would be willing to pay to relieve themselves of all risk of default on an otherwise equivalent unguaranteed loan. It is the difference between the present value of the loan with the guarantee and its present value without the guarantee. A guarantee can clearly have substantial value on a large loan when the chance of default by the firm is high.

It turns out that a loan guarantee can be valued as a put on the firm's assets, where the put's maturity equals the loan's maturity and its exercise price equals the interest and principal payments promised to lenders. We can easily show the equivalence by starting with the definition of the value of the guarantee.

$$\text{Value of guarantee} = \text{value of guaranteed loan} - \text{loan value without the guarantee}$$

[29]See, for example, J. Huang and M. Huang, "How Much of the Corporate-Treasury Yield is Due to Credit Risk? Results from a New Calibration Approach," working paper, Pennsylvania State University, August 2000.

[30]See U. Reinhardt, "Break-Even Analysis for Lockheed's TriStar: An Application of Financial Theory," *Journal of Finance* 28 (September 1973), pp. 821–838.

[31]Lockheed paid the current Treasury bill rate plus a fee of roughly 2 percent to the government.

FIGURE 24.10

Backwoods Chemical has issued five-year debt with a face value of $60. The shaded area shows that there is a 20 percent probability that the value of the company's assets in year 5 will be less than $60, in which case the company will choose to default.

Without a guarantee, the loan becomes an ordinary debt obligation of the firm. We know from Section 20.2 that

$$\begin{matrix} \text{Value of} \\ \text{ordinary} \\ \text{loan} \end{matrix} = \begin{matrix} \text{value assuming} \\ \text{no chance of} \\ \text{default} \end{matrix} - \text{value of put option}$$

The loan's value, assuming no chance of default, is exactly its guaranteed value; thus, the put value equals the difference between the values of a guaranteed and an ordinary loan. This is the value of the loan guarantee.

Thus, option pricing theory should lead to a way of calculating the actual cost of the government's many loan guarantee programs. This will be a healthy thing. The government's possible liability under existing guarantee programs has been enormous. In 1987, for example, $4 billion in loans to shipowners had been guaranteed under the so-called Title IX program to support shipyards in the United States.[32] This program was one of dozens. Yet the true cost of these programs is not widely recognized. Because loan guarantees involve no immediate outlay, they do not appear in the federal budget. Members of Congress sponsoring loan guarantee programs do not, as far as we know, present careful estimates of the value of the programs to business and the present value of the programs' cost to the public.

Calculating the Probability of Default

Banks and other financial institutions not only want to know the value of the loans that they have made but they also need to know the risk that they are incurring. Suppose that the assets of Backwoods Chemical have a current market value of $100 and its debt has a face value of $60 (i.e., 60 percent leverage), all of which is due to be repaid at the end of five years. Figure 24.10 shows the range

---

[32]The actual figure on March 31, 1987, was $4,497,365,297.98. Since 1987 these government guarantees to shipowners have been substantially reduced.

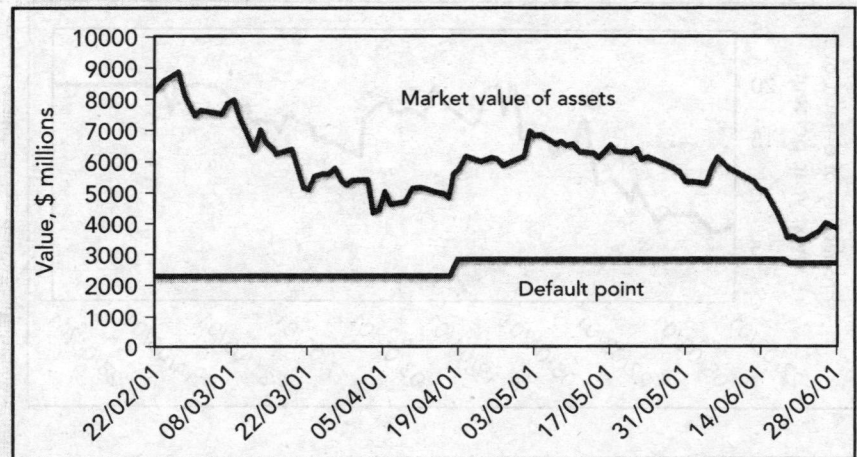

FIGURE 24.11

The market value of the assets of Metromedia Fiber Network crept closer to the point at which the firm would choose to default.

Source: KMV Credit Monitor.

of possible values of Backwoods's assets when the loan becomes due. The expected value of the assets is $120, but this value is by no means certain. There is a probability of 20 percent that the asset value could fall below $60, in which case the company will default on its debt. This probability is shown by the shaded area in Figure 24.10.

To calculate the probability that Backwoods will default, we need to know the expected growth in the market value of its assets, the face value and maturity of the debt, and the variability of future asset values. Real-world cases are likely to be more complex than our Backwoods example. For example, firms may have several classes of debt maturing on different dates. If so, shareholders have an option on an option. It may be worth their while to put up more money to pay off the short-term debt and thus keep alive the chance that the firm's fortunes will recover before the rest of the debt becomes due.

However, banks and consulting firms are now finding that they can use these ideas to measure the risk of actual loans.[33] For example, by mid-2001 the fiber-optics company, Metromedia Fiber Network, was a company in difficulties. Revenues had expanded rapidly, but so had losses. By 2000 the company was making operating losses of $329 million on revenues of $188 million. The stock price had fallen from a high of $50 to under $2, while the company's 8-year 10 percent notes were priced at 44 percent and offered a yield to maturity of 27 percent.

How close was Metromedia to default? Figure 24.11 provides an answer. The burgundy line shows the market value of Metromedia's assets, and the blue line shows the asset value at which the company would choose to default on its debts. You can see that during the first half of 2001 the value of the company's assets crept closer and closer to the default point.

---

[33]Banks are not just interested in the risk of individual loans; they would also like to know the risk of their entire portfolio. Therefore, specialists in credit risk also need to recognize the correlation between the outcomes. A portfolio of loans, all of which are to factory outlets in suburban Hicksville, is likely to be more risky than a portfolio with a wide variety of different borrowers.

FIGURE 24.12

Estimates by KMV Credit
Monitor of the probability that
Metromedia Fiber Network
would default on its debt
within a year.

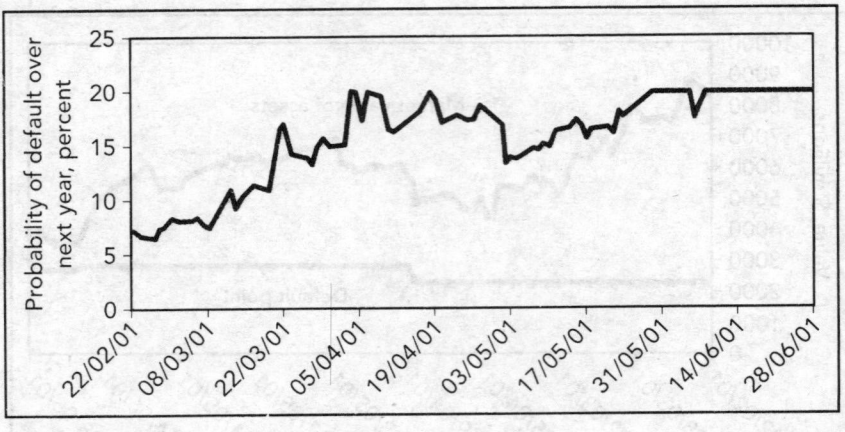

Of course, nobody had a crystal ball that could foresee what would happen to
Metromedia, but KMV, a consulting firm specializing in the assessment of credit
risk, estimated the *probability* at each point that the company would default in the
next year. Figure 24.12 shows how KMV progressively increased its assessment of
the probability of default.

SUMMARY

Efficient debt management presupposes that you understand how bonds are valued. That means you need to consider three problems:

1. What determines the general level of interest rates?
2. What determines the difference between long-term and short-term rates?
3. What determines the difference between the interest rates on company and government debt?

Here are some things to remember. The rate of interest depends on the demand
for savings and the supply. The *demand* comes from firms who wish to invest in
new plant and equipment. The supply of savings comes from individuals who are
willing to consume tomorrow rather than today. The equilibrium interest rate is the
rate that produces a *balance* between the demand and supply.

The best-known theory about the effect of inflation on interest rates was suggested by Irving Fisher. He argued that the nominal, or money, rate of interest is
equal to the expected real rate plus the expected inflation rate. If the expected inflation rate increases by 1 percent, so too will the money rate of interest. During the
past 50 years Fisher's simple theory has not done a bad job of explaining changes
in short-term interest rates in the United States.

The value of any bond is equal to the cash payments discounted at the spot
rates of interest. For example, the value of a 10-year bond with a 5 percent
coupon equals

$$PV(\text{percent of face value}) = \frac{5}{1 + r_1} + \frac{5}{(1 + r_2)^2} + \cdots + \frac{105}{(1 + r_{10})^{10}}$$

Bond dealers generally look at the yield to maturity on a bond. This is simply the internal rate of return y, the discount rate at which

$$\text{Bond price} = \frac{5}{1 + y} + \frac{5}{(1 + y)^2} + \cdots + \frac{105}{(1 + y)^{10}}$$

The yield to maturity y is a complex average of the spot interest rates r_1, r_2, etc. Like most averages it can be a useful summary measure, but it can also hide a lot of interesting information. We suggest you refer to yields on stripped bonds as measures of the spot rates of interest.

When you invest in a bond you usually receive a regular interest payment and then the final principal payment. Duration measures the *average* time to each payment. It is a useful summary measure of the length of a loan. It is also important because there is a direct relationship between the duration of a bond and its volatility. A change in interest rates has a greater effect on the price of a bond with a longer duration.

The one-period spot rate r_1 may be very different from the two-period spot rate r_2. In other words, investors often want a different annual rate of interest for lending for one year than for two years. Why is this? The *expectations theory* says that bonds are priced so that the expected rate of return from investing in bonds over any period is independent of the maturity of the bonds held by the investor. The expectations theory predicts that r_2 will exceed r_1 only if next year's one-period interest rate is expected to rise.

The expectations theory cannot be a complete explanation of the term structure if investors are worried about risk. Long bonds may be a safe haven for investors with long-term fixed liabilities. But other investors may not like the extra volatility of long-term bonds and may be concerned that a sudden burst in inflation could largely wipe out the real value of these bonds. Such investors will be prepared to hold long-term bonds only if they offer a liquidity premium—that is, a higher rate of interest.

Finally, we come to our third question: What determines the difference between interest rates on company and government debt? Company debt sells at a lower price than government debt. This discount represents the value of the company's option to default. We showed you how the value of this option varies with the degree of leverage and the time to maturity.

Ratings are widely used as a guide to the risk of loans. However, banks and consulting firms also recognize that the option to default is a put option and they have been developing models to estimate the probability that the borrower will exercise its option to default.

FURTHER READING

A good general text on debt markets is:

A. Sundaresan and S. Sundaresan: *Fixed Income Markets and Their Derivatives*, South-Western College Publishing, Cincinnati, Ohio, 2nd ed., 2001.

Nelson provides a useful review of some of the standard theories of the term structure literature:

C. R. Nelson: "The Term Structure of Interest Rates: Theories and Evidence," in J. L. Bicksler (ed.), *Handbook of Financial Economics*, North-Holland Publishing Company, Amsterdam, 1980.

Empirical tests of term structure theories are provided by Fama and Shiller, Campbell, and Schoenholtz:

E. F. Fama: "The Information in the Term Structure," *Journal of Financial Economics,* 13:509–528 (December 1984).

E. F. Fama: "Term Premiums in Bond Returns," *Journal of Financial Economics,* 13:529–546 (December 1984).

R. J. Shiller, J. Y. Campbell, and K. L. Schoenholtz: "Forward Rates and Future Policy: Interpreting the Term Structure of Interest Rates," *Brookings Papers on Economic Activity,* 1:173–217 (1983).

The following paper by Schaefer is a good review of duration and of how it is used to hedge fixed liabilities:

S. M. Schaefer: "Immunisation and Duration: A Review of Theory, Performance and Application," *Midland Corporate Finance Journal,* 3:41–58 (Autumn 1984).

We referred briefly to modern models of the term structure, which exploit the relationship between the price changes of bonds with different maturities. For more on this topic we suggest:

T. S. Y. Ho: "Evolution of Interest Rate Models: A Comparison," *Journal of Derivatives,* 2:9–20 (Summer 1995).

The classic paper on the valuation of the option to default on corporate debt is:

R. Merton: "On the Pricing of Corporate Debt: The Risk Structure of Interest Rates," *Journal of Finance,* 29:449–470 (May 1974).

QUIZ

1. The real interest rate is determined by the demand for, and supply of, capital. Draw a diagram showing how the demand by companies for capital and the supply of capital by investors vary with the interest rate. Use this diagram to show the following:
   a. What will happen to the amount of investment and saving if firms' investment prospects improve? How will the equilibrium interest rate change?
   b. What will happen to the amount of investment and saving if individuals' willingness to save increases at each possible interest rate? How will the equilibrium interest rate change? Assume firms' investment opportunities do not change.

2. In 2001 Treasury 13 7/8s of 2011 offered a semiannually compounded yield of 8.04 percent. Recognizing that coupons are paid semiannually, calculate the bond's price.

3. Here are the prices in 1998 of four Scandinavian government bonds with similar maturities:

Bond	Price (%)
Denmark 7s of 2007	116.58
Finland 6s of 2008	111.58
Norway 6 3/4s of 2007	108.15
Sweden 6 1/2s of 2008	113.19

   a. If coupons are paid annually, which bond offered the highest yield to maturity? Which had the lowest?
   b. Which bonds had the longest and shortest durations?

4. a. What is the formula for the value of a two-year, 5 percent bond in terms of spot rates?
   b. What is the formula for its value in terms of yield to maturity?
   c. If the two-year spot rate is higher than the one-year rate, is the yield to maturity greater or less than the two-year spot rate?

d. In each of the following sentences choose the correct term from within the parentheses:

"The (yield-to-maturity/spot-rate) formula discounts all cash flows from one bond at the same rate even though they occur at different points in time."
"The (yield-to-maturity/spot-rate) formula discounts all cash flows received at the same point in time at the same rate even though the cash flows may come from different bonds."

5. Construct some simple examples to illustrate your answers to the following:
   a. If interest rates rise, do bond prices rise or fall?
   b. If the bond yield is greater than the coupon, is the price of the bond greater or less than 100?
   c. If the price of a bond exceeds 100, is the yield greater or less than the coupon?
   d. Do high-coupon bonds sell at higher or lower prices than low-coupon bonds?
   e. If interest rates change, does the price of high-coupon bonds change proportionately more than that of low-coupon bonds?

6. The following table shows the prices of a sample of strips of UK gilts (government bonds) in December 1998. Each strip makes a single payment of £100 at maturity.

Maturity	Price (£)
December 2000	90.826
December 2005	73.565
December 2006	70.201
December 2007	67.787
December 2028	29.334

   a. Calculate the annually compounded, spot interest rate for each year.
   b. Is the term structure upward- or downward-sloping?
   c. Would you expect the yield on a *coupon* bond maturing in December 2028 to be higher or lower than the yield on the 2028 strip?
   d. Calculate the annually compounded, one-year forward rate of interest for December 2005. Now do the same for December 2006.

7. **a.** An 8 percent, five-year bond yields 6 percent. If the yield remains unchanged, what will be its price one year hence? Assume annual coupon payments.
   b. What is the total return to an investor who held the bond over this year?
   c. What can you deduce about the relationship between the bond return over a particular period and the yields to maturity at the start and end of that period?

8. True or false? Explain.
   a. Longer-maturity bonds necessarily have longer durations.
   b. The longer a bond's duration, the lower its volatility.
   c. Other things equal, the lower the bond coupon, the higher its volatility.
   d. If interest rates rise, bond durations rise also.

9. Calculate the durations and volatilities of securities A, B, and C. Their cash flows are shown below. The interest rate is 8 percent.

	Period 1	Period 2	Period 3
A	40	40	40
B	20	20	120
C	10	10	110

10. **a.** Suppose that the one-year spot rate of interest at time 0 is 1 percent and the two-year spot rate is 3 percent. What is the forward rate of interest for year 2?

b. What does the expectations theory of term structure say about the relationship between the forward rate and the one-year spot rate at time 1?

c. Over a very long period of time, the term structure in the United States has been on average upward-sloping. Is this evidence for or against the expectations theory?

d. What does the liquidity-preference theory say about the relationship between the forward rate and the one-year spot rate at time 1?

e. If the liquidity-preference theory is a good approximation and you have to meet long-term liabilities (college tuition for your children, for example), is it safer to invest in long- or short-term bonds? Assume inflation is predictable.

f. If inflation is very uncertain and you have to meet long-term real liabilities, is it safer to invest in long- or short-term bonds?

11. **a.** State the four Moody's ratings that are generally known as "investment-grade" ratings.

 b. Other things equal, would you expect the yield to maturity on a corporate bond to increase or decrease with
 i. The company's business risk?
 ii. The expected rate of inflation?
 iii. The risk-free rate of interest?
 iv. The degree of leverage?

12. The difference between the price of a government bond and a simple corporate bond is equal to the value of an option. What is this option and what is its exercise price?

13. How in principle would you calculate the value of a government loan guarantee?

PRACTICE QUESTIONS

1. Why might Fisher's theory about inflation and interest rates *not* be true?

2. Under what conditions can the expected real interest rate be negative?

3. A 6 percent six-year bond yields 12 percent and a 10 percent six-year bond yields 8 percent. Calculate the six-year spot rate. (Assume annual coupon payments.)

4. Is the yield on high-coupon bonds more likely to be higher than that on low-coupon bonds when the term structure is upward-sloping or when it is downward-sloping?

5. The one-year spot rate is $r_1 = 6$ percent, and the forward rate for a one-year loan maturing in year 2 is $f_2 = 6.4$ percent. Similarly, $f_3 = 7.1$ percent, $f_4 = 7.3$ percent, and $f_5 = 8.2$ percent. What are the spot rates $r_2, r_3, r_4,$ and r_5? If the expectations hypothesis holds, what can you say about expected future interest rates?

6. Suppose your company will receive $100 million at $t = 4$ but must make a $107 million payment at $t = 5$. Assume the spot and forward rates from question 5. Show how the company can lock in the interest rate at which it will invest at $t = 4$. Will the $100 million, invested at this locked-in rate, be sufficient to cover the $107 million liability?

7. Use the rates from question 5 one more time. Consider the following bonds, each with a five-year maturity. Calculate the yield to maturity for each. Which is the better investment (or are they equally attractive)? Each has $1,000 face value and pays coupons annually.

Coupon	Price
5	92.07%
7	100.31
12	120.92

8. You have estimated spot rates as follows:

Year	Spot Rate
1	$r_1 = 5.00\%$
2	$r_2 = 5.40$
3	$r_3 = 5.70$
4	$r_4 = 5.90$
5	$r_5 = 6.00$

    a. What are the discount factors for each date (that is, the present value of $1 paid in year t)?
    b. What are the forward rates for each period?
    c. Calculate the PV of the following Treasury notes:
       i. 5 percent, two-year note.
      ii. 5 percent, five-year note.
      iii. 10 percent, five-year note.
    d. Explain intuitively why the yield to maturity on the 10 percent bond is less than that on the 5 percent bond.
    e. What should be the yield to maturity on a five-year zero-coupon bond?
    f. Show that the correct yield to maturity on a five-year annuity is 5.75 percent.
    g. Explain intuitively why the yield on the five-year Treasury notes described in part (c) must lie between the yield on a five-year zero-coupon bond and a five-year annuity.

9. Look at the spot interest rates shown in question 8. Suppose that someone told you that the six-year spot interest rate was 4.80 percent. Why would you not believe him? How could you make money if he was right? What is the minimum sensible value for the six-year spot rate?

10. Look again at the spot interest rates shown in question 8. What can you deduce about the one-year spot interest rate in four years if
    a. The expectations theory of term structure is right?
    b. The liquidity-preference theory of term structure is right?
    c. The term structure contains an inflation uncertainty premium?

11. Look up prices of 10 U.S. Treasury bonds with different coupons and different maturities. Calculate how their prices would change if their yields to maturity increased by one percentage point. Are long- or short-term bonds most affected by the change in yields? Are high- or low-coupon bonds most affected?

12. Assume the term structure of interest rates is upward-sloping. How would you respond to the following comment? "The present term structure of interest rates makes short-term debt more attractive to corporate treasurers. Firms should avoid new long-term debt issues."

13. In Section 24.3 we stated that in 2001 the duration of the 4 5/8s of 2006 was 4.36 years. Construct a table like Table 24.2 to show that this is so.

14. The formula for the duration of a perpetual bond which makes an equal payment each year in perpetuity is $(1 + \text{yield})/\text{yield}$. If bonds yield 5 percent, which has the longer duration—a perpetual bond or a 15-year zero-coupon bond? What if the yield is 10 percent?

15. You have just been fired as CEO. As consolation the board of directors gives you a five-year consulting contract at $150,000 per year. What is the duration of this contract if your personal borrowing rate is 9 percent? Use duration to calculate the change in the contract's present value for a .5 percent increase in your borrowing rate.

16. Look at the example in Section 24.4 of the Treasury bill and the medium- and long-term bonds. Now assume that the price of the medium-term bond can either fall by $10.75 or

rise by $14.0. What can you say now about the relationship between the value of the three bonds?

17. Explain carefully what factors determine the yield on corporate bonds.

18. Companies sometimes issue floating-rate bonds. In this case the interest rate might be set at (say) 1 percent above the Treasury bill rate. Would you expect the price of a company's floating-rate bonds to vary? If so, why?

19. Company A has issued a single zero-coupon bond maturing in 10 years. Company B has issued a coupon bond maturing in 10 years. Explain why it is more complicated to value B's debt than A's.

20. Company X has borrowed $150 maturing this year and $50 maturing in 10 years. Company Y has borrowed $200 maturing in five years. In both cases asset value is $140. Why might X not default while Y does?

CHALLENGE QUESTIONS

1. It has been suggested that the Fisher theory is a tautology. If the real rate of interest is defined as the difference between the nominal rate and the expected inflation rate, then the nominal rate *must* equal the real rate plus the expected inflation rate. In what sense is Fisher's theory *not* a tautology?

2. Find the arbitrage opportunity (opportunities?). Assume for simplicity that coupons are paid annually. In each case the face value of the bond is $1,000.

Bond	Maturity (years)	Coupon ($)	Price ($)
A	3	zero	751.30
B	4	50	842.30
C	4	120	1,065.28
D	4	100	980.57
E	3	140	1,120.12
F	3	70	1,001.62
G	2	zero	834.00

3. The duration of a bond which makes an equal payment each year in perpetuity is $(1 + \text{yield})/\text{yield}$. Prove it.

4. What is the duration of a common stock whose dividends are expected to grow at a constant rate in perpetuity?

5. a. What spot and forward rates are embedded in the following Treasury bonds? The price of one-year (zero-coupon) Treasury bills is 93.46 percent. Assume for simplicity that bonds make only annual payments. *Hint:* Can you devise a mixture of long and short positions in these bonds that gives a cash payoff only in year 2? In year 3?

Coupon (%)	Maturity (years)	Price (%)
4	2	94.92
8	3	103.64

   b. A three-year bond with a 4 percent coupon is selling at 95.00 percent. Is there a profit opportunity here? If so, how would you take advantage of it?

6. Look back at our example in Section 24.4 of the short-, medium-, and long-term bonds. Remember that we said that the prices must stand in a particular relationship or there would be an arbitrage opportunity. This means that we can take advantage of the risk-

neutral trick that we used to value options. Pretend that investors are risk-neutral. Now answer the following questions:

a. Suppose that the price of the short bond is 98 and the price of the medium is 83. What is the price of the long bond?

b. What are the possible future prices of these three bonds at the end of three months if rates rise and if they fall?

c. What would be the expected return over the three months on each bond?

d. What is the probability of an interest rate rise?

e. Show that the expected return on each bond is equal.

7. Look up prices of 10 corporate bonds with different coupons and maturities. Be sure to include some low-rated bonds on your list. Now estimate what these bonds would sell for if the government had guaranteed them. Calculate the value of the guarantee for each bond. Can you explain the difference between the 10 guarantee values?

8. Bond rating services usually charge corporations for rating their bonds.

a. Why do they do this, rather than charge those investors who use the information?

b. Why will a company pay to have its bonds rated even when it knows the service is likely to assign a below-average rating?

c. A few companies are not willing to pay for their bonds to be rated. What can investors deduce about the quality of these bonds?

9. Look back to the first Backwoods Chemical example at the start of Section 24.5. Suppose that the firm's book balance sheet is

Backwoods Chemical Company (Book Values)

Net working capital	$ 400	$1,000	Debt
Net fixed assets	1,600	1,000	Equity (net worth)
Total assets	$2,000	$2,000	Total value

The debt has a one-year maturity and a promised interest rate of 9 percent. Thus, the promised payment to Backwoods's creditors is $1,090. The market value of the assets is $1,200, and the standard deviation of asset value is 45 percent per year. The risk-free interest rate is 9 percent. Calculate the value of Backwoods debt and equity.

10. Refer again to question 9. Suppose that the continuously compounded return on Backwoods's assets over the next year is normally distributed with a mean of 10 percent. What is the probability that Backwoods will default?

CHAPTER TWENTY-FIVE

THE MANY DIFFERENT KINDS OF DEBT

IN CHAPTERS 17 and 18 we discussed how much a company should borrow. But companies also need to think about what *type* of debt to issue. They must decide whether to issue short- or long-term debt, whether to issue straight bonds or convertible bonds, whether to issue in the United States or in the international debt market, and whether to sell the debt publicly or place it privately with a few large investors.

As a financial manager, you need to choose the type of debt that makes sense for your company. For example, foreign currency debt may be best suited for firms with a substantial overseas business. Short-term debt is generally used when the firm has only a temporary need for funds.[1] Sometimes competition between lenders opens a window of opportunity in a particular sector of the debt market. The effect may be only a few basis-points reduction in yield, but on a large issue that can translate into savings of several million dollars. Remember the saying, "A million dollars here and a million there—pretty soon it begins to add up to real money."[2]

Our focus in this chapter is on straight long-term debt.[3] We begin our discussion by looking at the different types of bonds. We examine the differences between senior and junior bonds and between secured and unsecured bonds. Then we describe how bonds may be repaid by means of a sinking fund and how the borrower or the lender may have an option for early repayment. We also look at some of the restrictive provisions that deter the company from taking actions that would damage the bonds' value. We not only describe the different features of corporate debt but also try to explain *why* sinking funds, repayment options, and the like exist. They are not simply matters of custom; there are generally good economic reasons for their use.

Debt may be sold to the public or placed privately with large financial institutions. Because privately placed bonds are broadly similar to public issues, we will not discuss them at length. However, we will discuss another form of private debt known as project finance. This is the glamorous part of the debt market. The words *project finance* conjure up images of multi-million-dollar loans to finance huge ventures in exotic parts of the world. You'll find there's something to the popular image, but it's not the whole story.

Finally, we look at a few unusual bonds and consider the reasons for innovation in the debt markets.

If a company cannot service its debt, it will need to come to some arrangement with its creditors or file for bankruptcy. In the appendix to this chapter we explain the procedures involved in such cases. We will also consider the efficiency of the bankruptcy rules in the United States and look at how some European countries handle the problem.

 ## 25.1 DOMESTIC BONDS AND INTERNATIONAL BONDS

A firm can issue a bond either in its home country or in another country. Of course, any firm that raises money abroad is subject to the rules of the country in which it does so. For example, any issue in the United States of publicly traded bonds needs to be registered with the SEC. Since the cost of registration can be particularly large for foreign firms, these firms often avoid registration by complying with the SEC's

---

[1]For example, Stohs and Mauer show that firms with a preponderance of short-term assets tend to issue short-term debt. See M. H. Stohs and D. C. Mauer, "The Determinants of Corporate Debt Maturity Structure," *Journal of Business* 69 (July 1996), pp. 279–312.

[2]The remark was made by the late Senator Everett Dirksen. However, he was talking billions.

[3]Short-term debt is discussed in Chapter 30.

Rule 144A for bond issues in the United States. Rule 144A bonds can be bought and sold only by large financial institutions.[4]

Bonds that are sold to local investors in another country's bond market are known as *foreign bonds.* The United States is by far the largest market for foreign bonds, but Japan and Switzerland are also important. These bonds have a variety of nicknames: A bond sold publicly by a foreign company in the United States is known as a *yankee bond;* a bond sold by a foreign firm in Japan is a *samurai.*

There is also a large international market for long-term bonds. These international bond issues are sold throughout the world by syndicates of underwriters, mainly located in London. They include the London branches of large U.S., European, and Japanese banks and security dealers. International issues are usually made in one of the major currencies. The U.S. dollar has been the most popular choice, but a high proportion of international bond issues are made in the euro, the currency of the European Monetary Union.

The international bond market arose during the 1960s because the U.S. government imposed an interest-equalization tax on the purchase of foreign securities and discouraged American corporations from exporting capital. Therefore both European and American multinationals were forced to tap an international market for capital.[5] This market came to be known as the *eurobond market,* but be careful not to confuse a eurobond (which may be in any currency) with a bond denominated in euros.

The interest-equalization tax was removed in 1974, and there are no longer any controls on capital exports from the United States. Since U.S. firms can now choose whether to borrow in New York or London, the interest rates in the two markets are usually similar. However, the international bond market is not directly subject to regulation by the U.S. authorities, and therefore the financial manager needs to be alert to small differences in the cost of borrowing in one market rather than another.

25.2   THE BOND CONTRACT

To give you some feel for the bond contract (and for some of the language in which it is couched), we have summarized in Table 25.1 the terms of an issue of 30-year bonds by Ralston Purina Company. We will look at each of the principal items in turn.

Indenture, or Trust Deed

The Ralston Purina offering was a public issue of bonds, which was registered with the SEC and listed on the New York Stock Exchange. In the case of a public issue, the bond agreement is in the form of an **indenture,** or **trust deed,** between the borrower and a trust company.[6] Continental Bank, which is the trust company for the Ralston

---

[4]We described Rule 144A in Section 15.5.

[5]Also, until 1984 the United States imposed a withholding tax on interest payments to foreign investors. Investors could avoid this tax by buying an international bond issued in London rather than a similar bond issued in New York.

[6]In the case of international bond issues, there is a *fiscal agent* who carries out somewhat similar functions to a bond trustee.

Listed	New York Stock Exchange
Trustee	Continental Bank, Chicago
Rights on default	The trustee or 25% of the debentures outstanding may declare interest due and payable.
Indenture modification	Indenture may not be modified except as provided with the consent of two-thirds of the debentures outstanding.
Registered	Fully registered
Denomination	$1,000
To be issued	$86.4 million
Issue date	June 4, 1986
Offered	Issued at a price of 97.60% plus accrued interest (proceeds to Company 96.725%) through First Boston Corporation, Goldman Sachs and Company, Shearson Lehman Brothers, Stifel Nicolaus and Company, and associates.
Interest	At a rate of 9½% per annum, payable June 1 and December 1 to holders registered on May 15 and November 15.
Security	Not secured. Company will not permit to have any lien on its property or assets without equally and ratably securing the debt securities.
Sale and lease-back	Company will not enter into any sale and lease-back transaction unless the Company within 120 days after the transfer of title to such principal property applies to the redemption of the debt securities at the then-applicable option redemption price an amount equal to the net proceeds received by the Company upon such sale.
Maturity	June 1, 2016
Sinking fund	Annually between June 2, 1996, and June 2, 2015, sufficient to redeem not less than $13.5 million principal amount, plus similar optional payments. Sinking fund is designed to redeem 90% of the debentures prior to maturity.
Callable	At whole or in part at any time at the option of the Company with at least 30, but not more than 60, days' notice on each May 31 as follows:

1989	106.390	1990	106.035	1991	105.680
1992	105.325	1993	104.970	1994	104.615
1995	104.260	1996	103.905	1997	103.550
1998	103.195	1999	102.840	2000	102.485
2001	102.130	2002	101.775	2003	101.420
2004	101.065	2005	100.710	2006	100.355

and thereafter at 100 plus accrued interest; provided, however, that prior to June 1, 1996, the Company may not redeem the bonds from, or in anticipation of, moneys borrowed having an effective interest cost of less than 9.748%.

TABLE 25.1

Summary of terms of 9½ percent sinking fund debenture 2016 issued by Ralston Purina Company.

Purina bond, represents the bondholders. It must see that the terms of the indenture are observed and look after the bondholders in the event of default. A copy of the bond indenture is included in the registration statement. It is a turgid legal document.[7] Its main provisions are summarized in the prospectus to the issue.

---

[7] For example, the indenture for one J.C. Penney bond stated: "In any case where several matters are required to be certified by, or covered by an opinion of, any specified Person, it is not necessary that all such matters be certified by, or covered by the opinion of, only one such Person, or that they be certified or covered by only one document, but one such Person may certify or give an opinion with respect to some matters and one or more such other Persons as to other matters, and any such Person may certify or give an opinion as to such matters in one or several documents." Try saying that three times fast.

Moving down Table 25.1, you will see that the Ralston Purina bonds are *registered*. This means that the company's registrar records the ownership of each bond and the company pays the interest and the final principal amount directly to each owner.[8]

Almost all bonds issued in the United States are issued in registered form, but in many countries bonds may be issued in *bearer* form. In this case, the certificate constitutes the primary evidence of ownership so the bondholder must send in coupons to claim interest and must send the certificate itself to claim the final repayment of principal. International bonds almost invariably allow the owner to hold them in bearer form. However, since the ownership of such bonds cannot be traced, the IRS has tried to deter U.S. residents from holding them.[9]

The Bond Terms

Like most dollar bonds, the Ralston Purina bonds have a face value of $1,000. Notice, however, that the bond price is shown as a percentage of face value. Also, the price is stated net of *accrued interest*. This means that the bond buyer must pay not only the quoted price but also the amount of any future interest that may have accrued. For example, an investor who bought bonds for delivery on (say) June 11, 1986, would be receiving them 10 days into the first interest period. Therefore, accrued interest would be $10/360 \times 9.5 = .26$ percent, and the investor would pay a price of 97.60 plus .26 percent of accrued interest.[10]

The Ralston Purina bonds were offered to the public at a price of 97.60 percent, but the company received only 96.725 percent. The difference represents the underwriters' spread. Of the $86.4 million raised, about $85.6 million went to the company and $.8 million went to the underwriters.

Since the bonds were issued at a price of 97.60 percent, investors who hold the bonds to maturity receive a capital gain over the 30 years of 2.40 percent.[11] However, the bulk of their return is provided by the regular interest payment. The annual interest or *coupon* payment on each bond is 9.50 percent of $1,000, or $95. This interest is payable semiannually, so every six months investors receive interest of $95/2 = \$47.50$. Most U.S. bonds pay interest semiannually, but a comparable international bond would generally pay interest annually.[12]

The regular interest payment on a bond is a hurdle that the company must keep jumping. If the company ever fails to pay the interest, lenders can demand their

---

[8]Often, investors do not physically hold the security; instead, their ownership is represented by a book entry. The "book" is in practice a computer.

[9]U.S. residents cannot generally deduct capital losses on bearer bonds. Also, payments on such bonds cannot be made to a bank account in the United States.

[10]In the U.S. corporate bond market accrued interest is calculated on the assumption that a year is composed of twelve 30-day months; in some other markets (such as the U.S. Treasury bond market) calculations recognize the actual number of days in each calendar month.

[11]This gain is not taxed as income as long as it amounts to less than .25 percent a year.

[12]If a bond pays interest semiannually, investors usually calculate a *semiannually* compounded yield to maturity on the bond. In other words, the yield is quoted as twice the six-month yield. Because international bonds pay interest annually, it is conventional to quote their yields to maturity on an *annually* compounded basis. Remember this when comparing yields.

money back instead of waiting until matters may have deteriorated further.[13] Thus, interest payments provide added protection for lenders.[14]

Sometimes bonds are sold with a lower interest payment but at a larger discount on their face value, so investors receive a significant part of their return in the form of capital appreciation.[15] The ultimate is the zero-coupon bond, which pays no interest at all; in this case the entire return consists of capital appreciation.[16]

The Ralston Purina interest payment is fixed for the life of the bond, but in some issues the payment varies with the general level of interest rates. For example, the payment may be tied to the U.S. Treasury bill rate or (more commonly) to the London interbank offered rate (LIBOR), which is the rate at which international banks lend to one another. Often these floating-rate notes specify a minimum (or floor) interest rate or they may specify a maximum (or cap) on the rate.[17] You may also come across "collars," which stipulate both a maximum and a minimum payment.

 ## 25.3 SECURITY AND SENIORITY

Almost all debt issues by industrial and financial companies are general unsecured obligations. Longer-term unsecured issues like the Ralston Purina bond are usually called **debentures;** shorter-term issues are usually called **notes.**

Utility company bonds are commonly secured. This means that if the company defaults on the debt, the trustee or lender may take possession of the relevant assets. If these are insufficient to satisfy the claim, the remaining debt will have a general claim, alongside any unsecured debt, against the other assets of the firm.

The majority of secured debt consists of **mortgage bonds.** These sometimes provide a claim against a specific building, but they are more often secured on all the firm's property.[18] Of course, the value of any mortgage depends on the extent of alternative uses of the property. A custom-built machine for producing buggy whips will not be worth much when the market for buggy whips dries up.

---

[13]There is one type of bond on which the borrower is obliged to pay interest only if it is covered by the year's earnings. These so-called *income bonds* are rare and have largely been issued as part of railroad reorganizations. For a discussion of the attraction of income bonds, see J. J. McConnell and G. G. Schlarbaum, "Returns, Risks, and Pricing of Income Bonds, 1956–1976 (Does Money Have an Odor?)," *Journal of Business* 54 (January 1981), pp. 33–64.

[14]See F. Black and J. C. Cox, "Valuing Corporate Securities: Some Effects of Bond Indenture Provisions," *Journal of Finance* 31 (May 1976), pp. 351–367. Black and Cox point out that the interest payment would be a trivial hurdle if the company could sell assets to make the payment. Such sales are, therefore, restricted.

[15]Any bond that is issued at a discount is known as an *original issue discount (OID)* bond. A zero coupon is often called a "pure discount bond."

[16]The ultimate of ultimates was an issue of a perpetual zero-coupon bond on behalf of a charity.

[17]Instead of issuing a capped floating-rate loan, a company will sometimes issue an uncapped loan and at the same time buy a cap from a bank. The bank pays the interest in excess of the specified level.

[18]If a mortgage is *closed*, no more bonds may be issued against the mortgage. However, usually there is no specific limit to the amount of bonds that may be secured (in which case the mortgage is said to be *open*). Many mortgage bonds are secured not only by existing property but also by "after-acquired" property. However, if the company buys only property that is already mortgaged, the bondholder would have only a junior claim on the new property. Therefore, mortgage bonds with after-acquired property clauses also limit the extent to which the company can purchase additional mortgaged property.

FIGURE 25.1

Average recovery rates per $100 face value on defaulting debt & preferred stock by seniority and security.

Source: "The Evolving Meaning of Moody's Bond Ratings," Moody's Investor Service, August 1999. See **www.moodys.com**.

Companies that own securities may use them as collateral for a loan. For example, holding companies are firms whose main assets consist of common stock in a number of subsidiaries. So, when holding companies wish to borrow, they generally use these investments as collateral. The problem for the lender is that this stock is junior to *all* other claims on the assets of the subsidiaries, and so these *collateral trust bonds* usually include detailed restrictions on the freedom of the subsidiaries to issue debt or preferred stock.

A third form of secured debt is the **equipment trust certificate.** This is most frequently used to finance new railroad rolling stock but may also be used to finance trucks, aircraft, and ships. Under this arrangement a trustee obtains formal ownership of the equipment. The company makes a down payment on the cost of the equipment, and the balance is provided by a package of equipment trust certificates with different maturities that might typically run from 1 to 15 years. Only when all these debts have finally been paid off does the company become the formal owner of the equipment. Bond rating agencies such as Moody's or Standard and Poor's usually rate equipment trust certificates one grade higher than the company's regular debt.

Bonds may be senior claims or they may be subordinated to the senior bonds or to *all* other creditors.[19] If the firm defaults, the senior bonds come first in the pecking order. The subordinated lender gets in line behind the firm's general creditors (but ahead of the preferred stockholder and the common stockholder).

As you can see from Figure 25.1, if default does occur, it pays to hold senior secured bonds. On average investors in these bonds can expect to recover over half of the amount of the loan. At the other extreme, recovery rates for junior unsecured bondholders are less than 20 percent of the face value of the debt.

---

[19]If a bond does not specifically state that it is junior, you can assume that it is senior.

25.4 ASSET-BACKED SECURITIES

Instead of borrowing money directly, companies sometimes bundle up a group of assets and then sell the cash flows from these assets. These securities are known as **asset-backed** securities.

Suppose your company has made a large number of mortgage loans to buyers of homes or commercial real estate. However, you don't want to wait until the loans are paid off; you would like to get your hands on the money now. Here is what you do.

You establish a separate company that buys a package of the mortgage loans. To finance this purchase, the company sells *mortgage pass-through certificates.*[20] The holders of these certificates simply receive a share of the mortgage payments. For example, if interest rates fall and the mortgages are repaid early, holders of the pass-through certificates are also repaid early. That's not generally popular with these holders, for they get their money back just when they don't want it—when interest rates are low.[21]

Real estate companies are not unique in wanting to turn future cash receipts into up-front cash. Automobile loans, student loans, and credit card receivables are also often bundled together and re-marketed as a bond. Indeed, investment bankers seem able to repackage any set of cash flows into a loan. In 1997 David Bowie, the British rock star, established a company that then purchased the royalties from his current albums. The company financed the purchase by selling $55 million of 10-year notes at an interest rate of 7.9 percent. The royalty receipts were used to make the interest and principal payments on the notes. When asked about the singer's reaction to the idea, his manager replied, "He kind of looked at me cross-eyed and said 'What?' "[22]

 25.5 REPAYMENT PROVISIONS

Sinking Funds

The maturity date of the Ralston Purina bond is June 1, 2016, but part of the issue is repaid on a regular basis before maturity. To do this, the company makes a regular repayment into a *sinking fund.* If the payment is in the form of cash, the trustee selects bonds by lottery and uses the cash to redeem them at their face value.[23]

---

[20]Mortgage-backed loans for commercial real estate are called (not surprisingly) *commercial mortgage backed securities* or *CMBS*.

[21]Sometimes, instead of issuing one class of pass-through certificates, the company will issue several different classes of security, known as *collateralized mortgage obligations* or *CMOs*. For example, any mortgage prepayments might be used first to pay off one class of security holders and only then will other classes start to be repaid.

[22]See J. Mathews, "David Bowie Reinvents Self, This Time as a Bond Issue," *Washington Post*, February 7, 1997.

[23]Every investor dreams of buying up the entire supply of a sinking-fund bond that is selling way below face value and then forcing the company to buy the bonds back at face value. Cornering the market in this way is fun to dream about but difficult to do. For a discussion, see K. B. Dunn and C. S. Spatt, "A Strategic Analysis of Sinking Fund Bonds," *Journal of Financial Economics* 13 (September 1984), pp. 399–424.

Instead of paying cash, the company can buy bonds in the marketplace and pay these into the fund.[24] This is a valuable option for the company. If the price of the bond is low, the firm will buy bonds in the market and hand them to the sinking fund; if the price is high, it will call the bonds by lottery.

Generally, there is a mandatory fund that *must* be satisfied and an optional fund which can be satisfied if the borrower chooses.[25] For example, Ralston Purina *must* contribute at least $13.5 million each year to the sinking fund but has the option to contribute a further $13.5 million.

As in the case of Ralston Purina, most "sinkers" begin to operate after about 10 years. For lower-quality issues the payments are usually sufficient to redeem the entire issue in equal installments over the life of the bond. In contrast, high-quality bonds often have light sinking fund requirements with large balloon payments at maturity.

We saw earlier that interest payments provide a regular test of the company's solvency. Sinking funds provide an additional hurdle that the firm must keep jumping. If it cannot pay the cash into the sinking fund, the lenders can demand their money back. That is why long-dated, low-quality issues usually involve larger sinking funds.

Unfortunately, a sinking fund is a weak test of solvency if the firm is allowed to repurchase bonds in the market. Since the *market* value of the debt must always be less than the value of the firm, financial distress reduces the cost of repurchasing debt in the market. The sinking fund, then, is a hurdle that gets progressively lower as the hurdler gets weaker.

Call Provisions

Corporate bonds sometimes include a call option that allows the company to pay back the debt early. Occasionally, you come across bonds that give the *investor* the repayment option. Retractable (or puttable) bonds give investors the option to demand early repayment, and extendible bonds give them the option to extend the bond's life.

For some companies callable bonds offer a natural form of insurance. For example, Fannie Mae and Freddie Mac are federal agencies that offer fixed- and floating-rate mortgages to home buyers. When interest rates fall, home owners are likely to repay their fixed-rate mortgage and take out a new mortgage at the lower interest rate. This can severely dent the income of the two agencies. Therefore, to protect themselves against the effect of falling interest rates, both agencies issue large quantities of long-term callable debt. When interest rates fall, the agencies can reduce their funding costs by calling their bonds and replacing them with new bonds at a lower rate. Ideally, the fall in bond interest payments should exactly offset the reduction in mortgage income.

These days, issues of straight bonds by industrial companies are much less likely to include a call provision.[26] However, Ralston Purina had the option to buy back the entire bond issue. The company was subject to two limitations on the use

---

[24]If the bonds are privately placed, the company cannot repurchase them in the marketplace; it *must* call them at their face value.

[25]A number of private placements (particularly those in extractive industries) require a payment only when net income exceeds some specified level.

[26]See, for example, L. Crabbe, "Callable Corporate Bonds: A Vanishing Breed," Board of Governors of the Federal Reserve System, Washington, D.C., 1991.

of this call option: Until 1989 the company was prohibited from calling the bond in any circumstances and from 1989 to 1996 it was not allowed to call the bond in order to replace it with new debt yielding less than the 9.748 percent yield on the original bond.

If interest rates fall and bond prices rise, the option to buy back the bond at a fixed price can be very attractive. The company can buy back the bond and issue another at a higher price and a lower interest rate. And so it proved with the Ralston Purina bond. By the time that the restrictions on calling the bonds were removed in 1996, interest rates had declined. The company was therefore able to repurchase the bond at the call price of 103.905, which was below the bond's potential value.

How does a company know when to call its bonds? The answer is simple: Other things equal, if it wishes to maximize the value of its stock, it must minimize the value of its bonds. Therefore, the company should never call the bond if its market value is less than the call price, for that would just be giving a present to the bondholders. Equally, a company *should* call the bond if it's worth *more* than the call price.

Of course, investors take the call option into account when they buy or sell the bond. They know that the company will call the bond as soon as it is worth more than the call price, so no investor will be willing to pay more than the call price for the bond. The market price of the bond may, therefore, reach the call price, but it will not rise above it. This gives the company the following rule for calling its bonds: *Call the bond when, and only when, the market price reaches the call price.*[27]

If we know how bond prices behave over time, we can modify the basic option-valuation model of Chapter 21 to find the value of the callable bond, *given* that investors know that the company will call the issue as soon as the market price reaches the call price. For example, look at Figure 25.2. It illustrates the relationship between the value of a straight 8 percent five-year bond and the value of a callable 8 percent five-year bond. Suppose that the value of the straight bond is very low. In this case there is little likelihood that the company will ever wish to call its bonds. (Remember that it will call the bonds only when their price equals the call price.) Therefore the value of the callable bond will be almost identical to the value of the straight bond. Now suppose that the straight bond is worth exactly 100. In this case there is a good chance that the company will wish at some time to call its bonds. Therefore the value of our callable bond will be slightly less than that of the straight bond. If interest rates decline further, the price of the straight bond will continue to rise, but nobody will ever pay more than the call price for the callable bond.

A call provision is not a free lunch. It provides the issuer with a valuable option, but that is recognized in a lower issue price. So why do companies bother with call provisions? One reason is that bond indentures often place a number of restrictions on what the company can do. Companies are happy to agree to these restrictions as long as they know they can escape from them if the restrictions prove too inhibiting. The call provision provides the escape route.

[27]See M. J. Brennan and E. S. Schwartz, "Savings Bonds, Retractable Bonds, and Callable Bonds," *Journal of Financial Economics* 5 (1997), pp. 67–88. Of course, this assumes that the bond is correctly priced, that investors are behaving rationally, and that investors expect the *firm* to behave rationally. Also, we ignore some complications. First, you may not wish to call a bond if you are prevented by a nonrefunding clause from issuing new debt. Second, the call premium is a tax-deductible expense for the company but is taxed as a capital gain to the bondholder. Third, there are other possible tax consequences to both the company and the investor from replacing a low-coupon bond with a higher-coupon bond. Fourth, there are costs to calling and reissuing debt.

FIGURE 25.2

Relationship between the value of a callable bond and that of a straight (noncallable) bond. Assumptions: (1) Both bonds have an 8 percent coupon and a five-year maturity; (2) the callable bond may be called at face value any time before maturity; (3) the short-term interest rate follows a random walk, and the expected returns on bonds of all maturities are equal.

Source: M. J. Brennan and E. S. Schwartz, "Savings Bonds, Retractable Bonds, and Callable Bonds," *Journal of Financial Economics* 5 (1977), pp. 67–88.

We mentioned earlier that some bonds also provide the investor with an option to demand early repayment. *Puttable* bonds exist largely because bond indentures cannot anticipate every action that the company may take which could harm the bondholder. If the value of the bonds is reduced, the put option allows bondholders to demand repayment.

Puttable loans can sometimes get their issuers into BIG trouble. During the 1990s many loans to Asian companies had given the lenders a repayment option. Consequently, when the Asian crisis struck in 1997, these companies were faced by a flood of lenders demanding their money back.

25.6 RESTRICTIVE COVENANTS

The difference between a corporate bond and a comparable Treasury bond is that the company has the option to default whereas the government supposedly doesn't. That is a valuable option. If you don't believe us, think about whether (other things equal) you would prefer to be a shareholder in a company with limited liability or in a company with unlimited liability. Of course you would prefer to have the option to walk away from your company's debts. Unfortunately, every silver lining has its cloud, and the drawback to having a default option is that corporate bondholders expect to be compensated for giving it to you. That is why corporate bonds sell at lower prices and therefore higher yields than government bonds.[28]

Investors know there is a risk of default when they buy a corporate bond. But they still want to make sure that the company plays fair. They don't want it to gam-

[28]In Chapters 20 and 24 we showed that this option to default is equivalent to a put option on the assets of the firm.

ble with their money or to take unreasonable risks. Therefore, the bond indenture may include a number of restrictive covenants to prevent the company from purposely increasing the value of its default option.[29]

After Ralston Purina had issued its bonds, the company had a total market value of $7.6 billion and total long-term debt of $2.1 billion. This meant that the company value would need to fall by over 70 percent before it would pay Ralston Purina to default. But suppose that after issuing the 9.5 percent bonds, Ralston Purina announced a bumper $3 billion bond issue. The company would have a market value of $10.6 billion and long-term debt of $5.1 billion. It would now pay the company to default if its value fell by little more than 50 percent $(1 - 5.1/10.6 = .52$, or 52 percent). The original bondholders would be worse off. If they had known about the new issue, they would not have been willing to pay such a high price for their bonds.

A new issue hurts the original bondholders because it increases the *ratio* of senior debt to company value. The bondholders would not object to an issue if the company kept the ratio the same by simultaneously issuing common stock. Therefore, the bond agreement often states that the company may issue more senior debt only if the ratio of senior debt to the value of net book assets is within a specified limit.

Why don't senior lenders demand limits on *subordinated* debt? The answer is that the subordinated lender does not get *any* money until the senior bondholders have been paid in full.[30] The senior bondholders, therefore, view subordinated bonds in much the same way that they view equity: They would be happy to see an issue of either. Of course, the converse is not true. Holders of subordinated debt *do* care both about the total amount of debt and the proportion that is senior to their claim. As a result, an issue of subordinated debt generally includes a restriction on both total debt and senior debt.

All bondholders worry that the company may issue more secured debt. An issue of mortgage bonds often imposes a limit on the amount of secured debt. This is not necessary when you are issuing unsecured debentures. As long as the debenture holders are given equal protection, they do not care how much you mortgage your assets. Therefore, the Ralston Purina debenture includes a so-called *negative pledge clause,* in which the debenture holders simply say, "Me, too."[31]

Instead of borrowing money to buy an asset, companies may enter into a long-term agreement to rent or lease it. For the debtholder this is very similar to secured borrowing. Therefore indentures also include limitations on leasing.

We have talked about how an unscrupulous borrower can try to increase the value of the default option by issuing more debt. But that is not the only way that such a company can exploit its existing bondholders. For example, we know that the value of an option is affected by dividend payments. If the company pays out large dividends to its shareholders and doesn't replace the cash by an issue of

---

[29]We described in Section 18.3 some of the games that managers can play at the expense of bondholders.

[30]In practice the courts do not always observe the strict rules of precedence (see the appendix to this chapter). Therefore the subordinated debtholder may receive *some* payment even when the senior debtholder is not fully paid off.

[31]"Me too" is not acceptable legal jargon. Instead the Ralston Purina bond agreement states that the company will not consent to any lien on its assets without securing the debentures "equally and ratably."

MARRIOTT PLAN ENRAGES HOLDERS OF ITS BONDS

Marriott Corp. has infuriated bond investors with a restructuring plan that may be a new way for companies to pull the rug out from under bondholders.

Prices of Marriott's existing bonds have plunged as much as 30% in the past two days in the wake of the hotel and food-services company's announcement that it plans to separate into two companies, one burdened with virtually all of Marriott's debt.

On Monday, Marriott said that it will divide its operations into two separate businesses. One, Marriott International Inc., is a healthy company that will manage Marriott's vast hotel chain; it will get most of the old company's revenue, a larger share of the cash flow and will be nearly debt-free.

The second business, called Host Marriott Corp., is a debt-laden company that will own Marriott hotels along with other real estate and retain essentially all of the old Marriott's $3 billion of debt.

The announcement stunned and infuriated bondholders, who watched nervously as the value of their Marriott bonds tumbled and as Moody's Investors Service Inc. downgraded the bonds to the junk-bond category from investment-grade.

PRICE PLUNGE

In trading, Marriott's 10% bonds that mature in 2012, which Marriott sold to investors just six months ago, were quoted yesterday at about 80 cents on the dollar, down from 110 Friday. The price decline translates into a stunning loss of $300 for a bond with a $1,000 face amount.

Marriott officials concede that the company's spinoff plan penalizes bondholders. However, the company notes that, like all public corporations, its fiduciary duty is to stockholders, not bondholders. Indeed, Marriott's stock jumped 12% Monday. (It fell a bit yesterday.)

Bond investors and analysts worry that if the Marriott spinoff goes through, other companies will soon follow suit by separating debt-laden units from the rest of the company. "Any company that fears it has underperforming divisions that are dragging down its stock price is a possible candidate [for such a restructuring]," says Dorothy K. Lee, an assistant vice president at Moody's.

If the trend heats up, investors said, the Marriott's structuring could be the worst news for corporate bondholders since RJR Nabisco Inc.'s managers shocked investors in 1987 by announcing they were taking the company private in a record $25 billion leveraged buyout. The move, which loaded RJR with debt and tanked the value of RJR bonds, triggered a deep slump of many investment-grade corporate bonds as investors backed away from the market.

STRONG COVENANTS MAY RE-EMERGE

Some analysts say the move by Marriott may trigger the re-emergence of strong covenants, or written protections in future corporate bond issues to protect bondholders against such restructurings as the one being engineered by Marriott. In the wake of the RJR buy-out, many investors demanded stronger covenants in new corporate bond issues.

Some investors blame themselves for not demanding stronger covenants. "It's our own fault," said Robert Hickey, a bond fund manager at Van Kampen Merritt. In their rush to buy bonds in an effort to lock in yields, many investors have allowed companies to sell bonds with covenants that have been "slim to none," Mr. Hickey said.

stock, there are fewer assets available to cover the debt. Therefore many bond issues restrict the amount of dividends that the company may pay.[32]

Changes in Covenant Protection

Before 1980 most bonds had covenants limiting further issues of debt and payments of dividends. But then institutions relaxed their requirements for lending to large public companies and accepted bonds with no such restrictions. This was the case with RJR Nabisco, the food and tobacco giant, which in 1988 had $5 billion of A-rated debt outstanding. In that year the company was taken over, and $19 billion of additional debt was substituted for equity. As soon as the first plans for the takeover were announced, the value of the existing debt fell by about 12 percent, and it was downrated to BB. For one of the bondholders, Metropolitan Life Insurance, this meant a $40 million loss. Metropolitan sued the company, arguing that the bonds contained an *implied* covenant preventing major financing changes that would undercut existing bondholders.[33] However, Metropolitan lost: The courts held that only the written covenants count.

Restrictions on debt issues and dividend payments quietly returned to fashion.[34] Bond analysts and lawyers started to look more closely at *event risks* like the debt-financed takeover that socked Metropolitan. Some companies agreed to *poison-put* clauses that oblige the borrower to repay the bonds if a large quantity of stock is bought by a single investor and the firm's bonds are downrated.

Unfortunately, there are always nasty surprises around the next corner. The Finance in the News box describes how one such surprise came in 1992 when the hotel chain, Marriott, antagonized its bondholders.

 ## 25.7 PRIVATE PLACEMENTS AND PROJECT FINANCE

The Ralston Purina debenture was registered with the SEC and sold to the public. However, debt is often placed privately with a small number of financial institutions. As we saw in Section 15.5, it costs less to arrange a private placement than to make a public debt issue. But there are three other ways in which the private placement bond may differ from its public counterpart.

First, if you place an issue privately with one or two financial institutions, it may be necessary to sign only a simple promissory note. This is just an IOU which lays down certain conditions that the borrower must observe. However, when you

---

[32]See A. Kalay, "Stockholder-Bondholder Conflict and Dividend Constraints," *Journal of Financial Economics* 10 (1982), pp. 211–233. A dividend restriction might typically prohibit the company from paying dividends if their cumulative amount would exceed the sum of (1) cumulative net income, (2) the proceeds from the sale of stock or conversion of debt, and (3) a dollar amount equal to one year's dividend.

[33]*Metropolitan Life Insurance Company* (plaintiff) *v. RJR Nabisco, Inc., and F. Ross Johnson* (defendants), Supreme Court of the State of New York, County of New York, Complaint, Nov. 16, 1988.

[34]A study by Paul Asquith and Thierry Wizman suggests that better covenants would have protected Metropolitan Life and other bondholders against loss. On average, the announcement of a leveraged buyout led to a fall of 5.2 percent in the value of the bond if there were no restrictions on further debt issues, dividend payments, or mergers. However, if the bond was protected by strong covenants, announcement of a leveraged buyout led to a *rise* in the bond price of 2.6 percent. See P. Asquith and T. A. Wizman, "Event Risk, Bond Covenants, and the Return to Existing Bondholders in Corporate Buyouts," *Journal of Financial Economics* 27 (September 1990), pp. 195–213.

make a public issue of debt, you must worry about who is to represent the bond-holders in any subsequent negotiations and what procedures are needed for paying interest and principal. Therefore the contractual arrangement has to be that much more complicated.

The second characteristic of publicly issued bonds is that they are highly standardized products. They *have* to be—investors are constantly buying and selling without checking the fine print in the agreement. This is not so necessary in private placements and so the debt contract can be custom-tailored for firms with special problems or opportunities. The relationship between borrower and lender is much more intimate. Imagine a $20 million debt issue privately placed with an insurance company, and compare it with an equivalent public issue held by 200 anonymous investors. The insurance company can justify a more thorough investigation of the company's prospects and therefore may be more willing to accept unusual terms or conditions.[35]

All bond agreements seek to protect the lender by imposing a number of conditions on the borrower. These conditions tend to be more severe in the case of privately placed debt. The borrowers are willing to agree to these conditions because they know that, if the debt is privately placed, the conditions can be modified later if it makes sense. However, in the case of a public issue it can be extremely cumbersome to get the permission of all the existing bondholders.

These features give private placements a particular niche in the corporate debt market, namely, loans to small and medium-sized firms. These are the firms that face the highest issue costs in public issues, that require the most detailed investigation, and that may require specialized, flexible loan arrangements. However, many large companies also use private placements.

Of course, the advantages of private placements are not free, for the lenders demand a higher rate of interest to compensate them for holding an illiquid asset. It is difficult to generalize about the differences in interest rates between private placements and public issues, but a typical differential is on the order of 50 basis points or .50 percentage points.

Project Finance

We are not going to dwell further on the topic of private placement bonds, because the greater part of what we have had to say about public issues is also true of private placements. However, we do need to discuss a different form of private loan, one that is tied as closely as possible to the fortunes of a particular project and that minimizes the exposure of the parent. Such a loan is usually referred to as **project finance** and is a specialty of large international banks.

Project finance means debt supported by the project, not by the project's sponsoring companies. Debt ratios are nevertheless very high. They can be high because the debt is supported not just by the project's assets but also by a variety of contracts and guarantees provided by customers, suppliers, and local governments, as well as by the project's owners.

Example   Here is how project finance was used to construct a large new oil-fired power plant in Pakistan. First, a separate firm, the Hub Power Company (Hubco), was established to own the power station. Hubco then engaged a consortium of

---

[35]Of course debt with the same terms could be offered publicly, but then 200 separate investigations would be required—a much more expensive proposition.

companies, headed by the Japanese company, Mitsui & Co., to build the power station, while the British company, National Power, became responsible for managing and running it. Hubco agreed to buy the fuel from the Pakistan State Oil Company and to sell the power station's output to another government body, the Water and Power Development Authority (WAPDA).

Hubco's lawyers drew up a complex series of contracts to make sure that each of these parties came up to scratch. For example, the contractors guaranteed to deliver the plant on time and to ensure that it would operate to specifications. National Power, the plant manager, agreed to maintain the plant and operate it efficiently. Pakistan State Oil Company entered into a long-term contract to supply oil to Hubco and WAPDA agreed to buy Hubco's output for the next 30 years.[36] Since WAPDA would pay for the electricity with rupees, Hubco was concerned about the possibility of a fall in the value of the rupee. The State Bank of Pakistan, therefore, arranged to provide Hubco with foreign exchange at guaranteed exchange rates.

The effect of these contracts was to ensure that each risk was borne by the party that was best able to measure and control it. For example, the contractors were best placed to ensure that the plant was completed on time, so it made sense to ask them to bear the risk of construction delays. Similarly, the plant operator was best placed to operate the plant efficiently and would be penalized if it failed to do so. The contractors and the plant manager were prepared to take on these risks because the project involved an established technology and there was relatively little chance of unpleasant surprises.

While these contracts sought to be as precise as possible about each party's responsibilities, they could not cover every eventuality; inevitably the contracts were incomplete. Therefore, to buttress the formal legal agreements, the contractors and the plant manager became major shareholders in Hubco. This meant that if they cut corners in building and running the plant, they would share in the losses.

The equity in Hubco was highly levered. Over 75 percent of the $1.8 billion investment in the project was financed by debt. Some of this was junior debt provided by a fund that was set up by the World Bank and western and Japanese government aid agencies. The bulk of the debt was senior debt provided by a group of major international banks.[37] The banks were encouraged to invest because they knew that the World Bank and several governments were in the frontline and would take a hit if the project were to fail. But they were still concerned that the government of Pakistan might prevent Hubco from paying out foreign currency or it might impose a special tax or prevent the company bringing in the specialist staff it needed. Therefore, to protect Hubco against these political risks, the government promised to pay compensation if it interfered in such ways with the operation of the project. Of course, the government could not be prevented from tearing up that agreement, but, if it did, Hubco was able to call on a $360 million guarantee by the

[36]WAPDA entered into a *take-or-pay* agreement with Hubco; if it did not take the electricity, it still had to pay for it. In the case of pipeline projects the contract with the customer is often in the form of a *throughput* agreement, whereby the customer agrees to make a minimum use of the pipeline. Another arrangement for transferring revenue risk to a customer is the tolling contract, whereby the customer agrees to deliver to the project company materials that it is to process and to return to the customer. One purpose of transferring revenue risk to customers is to encourage them to estimate their demand for the project's output thoroughly.

[37]Notice that the project was not financed by a public bond issue. The concentrated ownership of bank debt induces the lenders to evaluate the project carefully and to monitor its subsequent progress. It also facilitates the renegotiation of the debt if the project company runs into difficulties.

World Bank and the Export–Import Bank of Japan. This was supposed to keep the Pakistan government honest once the plant was built and operating. Governments can be surprisingly relaxed in the face of the wrath of a private corporation but are usually reluctant to break an agreement that lands the World Bank with a large bill.

The arrangements for the Hubco project were complex, costly, and time-consuming. Not everything was plain sailing. The project was suspended for over a year by the Gulf War and it looked at one time as if it would be spiked by a Pakistani court ruling that the interest on the loans contravened Islamic law. Ten years after the start of discussions the final agreement on financing the project was signed and within a short time Hubco was producing a fifth of all Pakistan's electricity.

However, that was not the end of the Hubco story. After the fall of Benazir Bhutto's government in Pakistan, the new government terminated the contract with Hubco and announced a 30 percent cut in electricity tariffs. This inevitably led to a dispute with the World Bank, which spelled out that, until the dispute could be resolved, nothing could move on new loans.[38]

Project Finance—Some Common Features

No two project financings are alike, but they have some common features:

- The project is established as a separate company.
- The contractors and the plant manager become major shareholders in the project and thus share in the risk of the project's failure.
- The project company enters into a complex series of contracts that distributes risk among the contractors, the plant manager, the suppliers, and the customers.
- The government may guarantee that it will provide the necessary permits, allow the purchase of foreign exchange, and so on.
- The detailed contractual arrangements and government guarantees allow a large part of the capital for the project to be provided in the form of bank debt or other privately placed borrowing.

The Role of Project Finance

Project finance is widely used in developing countries to fund power, telecommunication, and transportation projects, but it is also used in the major industrialized countries. In the United States project finance is most commonly used to fund power plants. For example, an electric utility company may get together with an industrial company to construct a cogeneration plant that provides electricity to the utility and waste heat to a nearby industrial plant. The utility stands behind the cogeneration project and guarantees its revenue stream. Banks are happy to lend as much as 90 percent of the cost of the project because they know that, once the project is up and running, the cash flow is insulated from most of the risks facing normal businesses.[39]

There are some interesting regulatory implications, however. When a utility builds a power plant, it is entitled to a fair return on its investment: Regulators are

---

[38]The confrontation between Hubco and the government of Pakistan is described in C. Hill, "Power Failure," *Institutional Investor* (November 1999), pp. 109–119.

[39]Such extremely high debt ratios must rest on the utility's creditworthiness. In a sense, the utility has borrowed money "off balance sheet."

TABLE 25.2

Some examples of
innovation in bond
design.

Liquid Yield Option Notes (LYONs)	Puttable, callable, convertible, zero-coupon debt
Asset-backed securities	Many small loans are packaged together and resold as a bond
Catastrophe (CAT) bonds	Payments are reduced in the event of a specified natural disaster
Reverse floaters (yield-curve notes)	Floating-rate bonds that pay a higher rate of interest when other interest rates fall and a lower rate when other rates rise
Equity-linked bonds	Payments are linked to the performance of a stock-market index
Pay-in-kind bonds (PIKs)	Issuer can choose to make interest payments either in cash or in more bonds with an equivalent face value
Rate-sensitive bonds	Coupon rate changes as company's credit rating changes
Ratchet bonds	Floating-rate bond whose coupon can only be reset downward

supposed to set customer charges that will allow the utility to earn its cost of capital. Unfortunately, the cost of capital is not easily measured and is a natural focus for argument in regulatory hearings. But when a utility buys electric power, the cost of capital is rolled into the contract price and treated as an operating cost. In this case the pass-through to customers may be less controversial.

 ## 25.8 INNOVATION IN THE BOND MARKET

Domestic and international bonds, fixed- and floating-rate bonds, coupon bonds and zeros, callable and puttable bonds, secured and unsecured bonds, senior and junior bonds, privately placed bonds and project finance—you might think that all this would give you as much choice as you need. Yet almost every day some new type of bond seems to be issued.

Table 25.2 lists some of the more interesting bonds that have been invented in recent years.[40] We have already encountered some of these exotic bonds. For example, you may remember from Chapter 23 the convertible zero-coupon LYONs, and in this chapter we cited the "Bowie bonds" as an example of asset-backed bonds. In Chapter 27 we will also discuss catastrophe bonds whose payoffs are linked to the occurrence of natural disasters.

Here are a couple more examples of unusual bonds. The first is an issue of a three-year Japanese yen bond that combined the features of two types of exotic bond—the reverse floater and the equity-linked bond. The issue by the Norwegian Christiania Bank came in two parts or *tranches*. Tranche A paid interest equal to the prime rate but subject to a maximum (or *cap*) of 12.8 percent. Tranche B paid interest of 12.8 percent *less* the prime rate. Thus, if the general level of interest rates rose, the interest payment on tranche B fell but it was not allowed to fall below zero. If

---

[40]For a more comprehensive list of innovations, see K. A. Carrow and J. J. McConnell, "A Survey of U.S. Corporate Financing Innovations: 1970–1997," *Journal of Applied Corporate Finance* 12 (Spring 1999), pp. 55–69.

you had invested an equal amount in each tranche, the average interest rate on your two holdings would have been 6.4 percent.

That was not the end of tranche B's complications, since the principal payment was not fixed at 100 percent. Instead it declined if the Japanese stock market fell. If the index fell by about 50 percent, the bondholder did not receive any principal payment at all. Thus, investing in tranche B was like buying an unusual floating-rate note and also selling a put option on the Japanese stock market. To compensate for the possible capital loss, the bonds offered a relatively high rate of interest.

For several years the majority of international issues of yen bonds involved similar options. Why? One reason is that life insurance companies in Japan cannot distribute capital gains to policyholders and therefore had a powerful appetite for high-yielding bonds even if such investments involved the risk of a capital loss. Christiania Bank paid a high rate of interest on the package, but it obtained a put option in exchange. If it did not want to hold onto this put option, it could easily sell it to foreign investors who were worried that the Japanese equity market was overpriced and wanted protection against a fall in that market.

Our second example is a *pay-in-kind* bond (or *PIK*) issued by RJR Nabisco. The bond carried an attractive coupon of 15 percent, but for the first few years of the bond's life, RJR could choose to pay interest either in the form of cash or of bonds with an equivalent face value. This gave the company a valuable option. If RJR fell on hard times and bond prices dropped, it could hand over low-priced bonds instead of hard cash. RJR also had the right to call the bonds. That provided another valuable option: If interest rates fell and bond prices rose, the company could buy back the bond for the call price.

It is often difficult to foresee which new securities will become popular and which will never get off the ground. Sometimes new financial instruments succeed because they widen investor choice. Economists refer to such securities as helping to "complete the market." For example, the unusual weather in 1997–1998 resulting from El Niño encouraged a number of firms to market financial contracts that would pay off in unfavorable weather conditions. These firms hoped that *weather derivatives* would prove popular with the newly deregulated energy companies, the agricultural community, and many other businesses that might wish to protect themselves against the vagaries of the weather.

Governments may unwittingly play a major role in stimulating financial innovation, for new types of security are often designed to circumvent government regulations. For instance, we have already seen how one unusual bond, the equity-linked yen bond, was a consequence of Japanese insurance regulation. Unforeseen changes in the bond market can also result from changes in the tax rules. One of the most striking examples was the U.S. government's imposition of a tax on purchases of foreign securities, which brought about the development of the eurobond market in the 1960s.

∫UMMARY

Now that you have read this chapter, you should have a fair idea of what you are letting yourself in for when you make a public issue of bonds. You can issue the bonds in the domestic U.S. market, in a foreign bond market, or in the international bond market. International bonds (also called eurobonds) are marketed simultaneously in a number of foreign countries, usually by the London branches of international banks and security dealers.

The detailed bond agreement is set out in the indenture between your company and a trustee, but the main provisions are summarized in the prospectus to the issue.

The indenture states whether the bonds are senior or subordinated and whether they are secured or unsecured. Most bonds are unsecured debentures or notes. This means that they are general claims on the corporation. The principal exceptions are utility mortgage bonds, collateral trust bonds, and equipment trust certificates. In the event of a default, the trustee to these issues can repossess the company's assets in order to pay off the debt.

Most long-term bond issues have a sinking fund. This means that the company must set aside enough money each year to retire a specified number of bonds. A sinking fund reduces the average life of the bond, and it provides a yearly test of the company's ability to service its debt. It therefore protects the bondholders against the risk of default.

Long-dated bonds may be callable before maturity. The company usually has to pay a call premium, which is initially equal to the coupon and which declines progressively to zero. The option to call the bond may be very valuable: If interest rates decline and bond values rise, you may be able to call a bond that would be worth substantially more than the call price. Of course, if investors know that you may call the bond, the call price will act as a ceiling on the market price. Your best strategy, therefore, is to call the bond as soon as the market price hits the call price. You are unlikely to do better than that.

The bond indenture also imposes certain conditions on the borrower. Here are some examples of covenants:

1. Issues of senior bonds prohibit the company from issuing further senior debt if the ratio of senior debt to net tangible assets is too high.

2. Issues of subordinated bonds may also prohibit the company from issuing further senior or junior debt if the ratio of *all* debt to net tangible assets is too high.

3. Unsecured bonds incorporate a negative pledge clause, which prohibits the company from securing additional debt without giving equal treatment to the existing unsecured bonds.

4. Many bonds place a limit on the company's dividend payments.

Private placements are less standardized than public issues, and they impose more stringent covenants. Otherwise, they are generally close counterparts of publicly issued bonds. Sometimes private debt takes the form of project finance. In this case the loan is tied to the fortunes of a particular project.

There is an enormous variety of bond issues, and new forms of bonds are spawned almost daily. By a principle of natural selection, some of these new instruments become popular and may even replace existing species. Others are ephemeral curiosities. Some innovations succeed because they widen investor choice and allow investors to manage their risks better. Others owe their origin to tax rules and government regulation.

Bankruptcy Procedures   APPENDIX

What do Pacific Gas and Electric, Global Crossing, Enron, Fruit of the Loom, and Kmart have in common? Answer: They have all filed for bankruptcy. In this appendix we will explain what this involves and we will look at some of the pros and cons of the U.S. bankruptcy laws.

Occasionally bankruptcy proceedings in the United States are initiated by the creditors, but usually it is the firm itself that decides to file. It can choose one of two procedures, which are set out in Chapters 7 and 11 of the 1978 Bankruptcy Reform Act. The purpose of Chapter 7 is to oversee the firm's death and dismemberment, while Chapter 11 seeks to nurse the firm back to health.

Most small firms make use of Chapter 7.[41] In this case the bankruptcy judge appoints a trustee, who then closes the firm down and auctions off the assets. The proceeds from the auction are used to pay off the creditors. There is a pecking order of unsecured creditors. The U.S. Treasury, court officers, and the trustee have first peck. Wages come next, followed by taxes and debts to some government agencies such as the Pension Benefit Guarantee Corporation. Frequently the trustee will need to prevent some creditors from trying to jump the gun and collect on their debts, and sometimes the trustee will retrieve property that a creditor has recently seized. Managers of small firms that are in trouble know that Chapter 7 bankruptcy means the end of the road and, therefore, will try to put off filing as long as possible. As a result, when the assets are eventually liquidated, the unsecured creditors usually receive only a few crumbs.[42]

Instead of agreeing to a liquidation, large public companies generally attempt to rehabilitate the business. This is in the shareholders' interests; they have nothing to lose if things deteriorate further and everything to gain if the firm recovers. The procedures for rehabilitation are set out in Chapter 11 of the 1978 act. Their purpose is to keep the firm alive and operating and to protect the value of its assets[43] while a plan of reorganization is worked out. During this period, other proceedings against the firm are halted, and the company usually continues to be run by its existing management.[44] The responsibility for developing the plan falls on the debtor firm but, if it cannot devise an acceptable plan, the court may invite anyone to do so—for example, a committee of creditors.

The plan goes into effect if it is accepted by the creditors and confirmed by the court. Acceptance requires approval by at least one-half of the creditors voting, and the creditors voting "aye" must represent two-thirds of the value of the creditors' aggregate claim against the firm. The plan also needs to be approved by two-thirds of the shareholders. Once the creditors and shareholders have accepted the plan, the court normally approves it, provided that *each class* of creditors is in favor and that the creditors will be no worse off under the plan than they would be if the firm's assets were liquidated and distributed. Under certain conditions the court may confirm a plan even if one or more classes of creditors votes against it,[45] but the rules for a "cram-down" are complicated and we will not attempt to cover them here.

The reorganization plan is basically a statement of who gets what; each class of creditors gives up its claim in exchange for new securities or a mixture of securities and cash. The problem is to design a new capital structure for the firm that will

---

[41]Sometimes small firms file under Chapter 11, but attempts to rehabilitate the firm are rarely successful and the assets eventually have to be liquidated.

[42]See M. J. White, "Survey Evidence on Business Bankruptcy," in J. S. Bhandari and L. A. Weiss (eds.), *Corporate Bankruptcy,* Cambridge University Press, Cambridge, 1996.

[43]To keep the firm alive, it may be necessary to continue to use assets that were offered as collateral, but this denies secured creditors access to their collateral. To resolve this problem, the Bankruptcy Reform Act makes it possible for firms operating under Chapter 11 to keep such assets as long as the creditors who have a claim on those assets are compensated for any decline in their value. Thus, the firm might make cash payments to the secured creditors to cover economic depreciation of the assets.

[44]Occasionally the court will appoint a trustee to manage the firm.

[45]But at least one class of creditors must vote for the plan; otherwise the court cannot approve it.

(1) satisfy the creditors and (2) allow the firm to solve the *business* problems that got the firm into trouble in the first place.[46] Sometimes satisfying these two conditions requires a plan of baroque complexity, involving the creation of a dozen or more new securities.

The Securities and Exchange Commission (SEC) plays a role in many reorganizations, particularly for large, public companies. Its interest is to ensure that all relevant and material information is disclosed to the creditors before they vote on a proposed plan of reorganization. The SEC may take part in a hearing before court approval of a plan, for example.

Chapter 11 proceedings are often successful, and the patient emerges fit and healthy. But in other cases rehabilitation proves impossible, and the assets are liquidated. Sometimes the firm may emerge from Chapter 11 for a brief period before it is once again submerged by disaster and back in the bankruptcy court. For example, TWA came out of Chapter 11 bankruptcy at the end of 1993, was back again less than two years later, and then for a third time in 1998, prompting jokes about "Chapter 22" and "Chapter 33."[47]

Is Chapter 11 Efficient?

Here is a simple view of the bankruptcy decision: Whenever a payment is due to creditors, management checks the value of the equity. If the value is positive, the firm pays the creditors (if necessary, raising the cash by an issue of shares). If the equity is valueless, the firm defaults on its debt and petitions for bankruptcy. If the assets of the bankrupt firm can be put to better use elsewhere, the firm is liquidated and the proceeds are used to pay off the creditors; otherwise the creditors simply become the new owners, and the firm continues to operate.[48]

In practice, matters are rarely so simple. For example, we observe that firms often petition for bankruptcy even when the equity has a positive value. And firms often continue to operate even when the assets could be used more efficiently elsewhere. The problems in Chapter 11 usually arise because the goal of paying off the creditors conflicts with the goal of maintaining the business as a going concern. We described in Chapter 18 how the assets of Eastern Airlines seeped away as the court attempted to keep the airline flying. When the company filed for bankruptcy, its assets were more than sufficient to repay in full its liabilities of $3.7 billion. But the bankruptcy judge was determined to keep Eastern flying. When it finally became clear that the airline was a terminal case, the assets were sold off and the creditors received less than $.9 billion. The creditors would clearly have been better off if Eastern had been liquidated immediately; the unsuccessful attempt at resuscitation cost the creditors $2.8 billion.[49]

---

[46] Although Chapter 11 is designed to keep the firm in business, the reorganization plan often involves the sale or closure of large parts of the business.

[47] One study found that after emerging from Chapter 11, about one in three firms reentered bankruptcy or privately restructured their debt. See E. S. Hotchkiss, "Postbankruptcy Reform and Management Turnover," *Journal of Finance* 50 (March 1995), pp. 3–21.

[48] If there are several classes of creditors, the junior creditors initially become the owners of the company and are responsible for paying off the senior debt. They now face exactly the same decision as the original owners. If their equity is valueless, they will also default and turn over ownership of the company to the next class of creditors.

[49] These estimates of creditor losses are taken from L. A. Weiss and K. H. Wruck, "Information Problems, Conflicts of Interest, and Asset Stripping: Chapter 11's Failure in the Case of Eastern Airlines," *Journal of Financial Economics* 48 (1998), pp. 55–97.

Here are some reasons that Chapter 11 proceedings do not always achieve an efficient solution:

1. Although the reorganized firm is legally a new entity, it is entitled to the tax-loss carryforwards belonging to the old firm. If the firm is liquidated rather than reorganized, the tax-loss carryforwards disappear. Thus there is a tax incentive to continue operating the firm even when its assets could be sold and put to better use elsewhere.

2. If the firm's assets are sold off, it is easy to determine what is available to pay the creditors. However, when the company is reorganized, it needs to conserve cash. Therefore, claimants are generally paid in a mixture of cash and securities. This makes it less easy to judge whether they receive a fair shake. For example, each bondholder may be offered $300 in cash and $700 in a new bond that pays no interest for the first two years and a low rate of interest thereafter. A bond of this kind in a company that is struggling to survive may not be worth much, but the bankruptcy court usually looks at the face value of the new bonds and may therefore regard the bondholders as paid off in full.

3. Senior creditors who know they are likely to get a raw deal in a reorganization are likely to press for a liquidation. Shareholders and junior creditors prefer a reorganization. They hope that the court will not interpret the pecking order too strictly and that they will receive some crumbs when the firm's remaining value is sliced up. In the majority of cases their hopes are realized; often they receive a substantial portion of the equity of the reorganized company even though the senior creditors receive less than they are owed.[50]

4. Although shareholders and junior creditors are at the bottom of the pecking order, they have a secret weapon—they can play for time. On average it takes two to three years before a plan is presented to the court and agreed to by each class of creditor. When they use delaying tactics, the junior claimants are betting on a stroke of luck that will rescue their investment. On the other hand, the senior claimants know that time is working against them, so they may be prepared to accept a smaller payoff as part of the price for getting a plan accepted. Also, prolonged bankruptcy cases are costly (the bankruptcy proceedings of Wickes Corporation involved about $250 million in legal and administrative costs).[51] Senior claimants may see their money seeping into lawyers' pockets and therefore decide to settle quickly.

5. While a reorganization plan is being drawn up, the company is likely to need additional working capital. It is therefore allowed to buy goods on credit and borrow money. The new creditors have priority over the old creditors, and their debt may even be secured by assets that are already mortgaged to existing debtholders. This also gives the old creditors an incentive to settle quickly, before their claims are diluted by the new debt.

6. While the firm is in Chapter 11, secured debt receives interest but unsecured debt does not. For unsecured debtholders that is another reason for a fast settlement.

---

[50]Franks and Torous found that stockholders received some payoff—usually securities—in two-thirds of Chapter 11 reorganizations. See J. R. Franks and W. N. Torous, "An Empirical Investigation of U.S. Firms in Reorganization," *Journal of Finance* 44 (July 1989), pp. 747–770. A similar study concluded that in a third of the cases shareholders received more than 25 percent of the equity in the new firm. See L. A. Weiss, "Bankruptcy Resolution: Direct Costs and Violation of Priority of Claims," *Journal of Financial Economics* 27 (October 1990), pp. 285–314.

[51]We reviewed these costs in Section 18.3.

7. Sometimes profitable companies have filed for Chapter 11 bankruptcy to protect themselves against burdensome suits.[52] For example, Continental Airlines, which was bedeviled by a costly labor contract, filed for Chapter 11 in 1982 and immediately cut pay by up to 50 percent.[53] In 1995 Dow Corning was threatened with costly litigation for damage allegedly caused by its silicone-gel breast implants. Dow filed for bankruptcy under Chapter 11, and the bankruptcy judge agreed to stay the damage suits. Needless to say, lawyers and legislators worry that these actions were contrary to the original intent of the bankruptcy acts.

Workouts

If Chapter 11 reorganizations are not efficient, why don't firms bypass the bankruptcy courts and get together with their creditors to work out a solution?

Many firms that are in distress *do* first seek a negotiated settlement. For example, they can seek to delay repayment of the debt or negotiate an interest rate holiday. However, shareholders and junior creditors know that senior creditors are anxious to avoid formal bankruptcy proceedings. So they are likely to be tough negotiators, and senior creditors generally need to make concessions to reach agreement.[54] The larger the firm, and the more complicated its capital structure, the less likely it is that everyone will agree to any proposal. For example, Wickes Corporation tried—and failed—to reach a negotiated settlement with its 250,000 creditors.

Sometimes the firm does agree to an informal workout with its creditors and then files under Chapter 11 to obtain the approval of the bankruptcy court.[55] Such *prepackaged bankruptcies* reduce the likelihood of subsequent litigation and allow the firm to gain the special tax advantages of Chapter 11.

Alternative Bankruptcy Procedures

The United States bankruptcy system is often described as a debtor-oriented system: Its principal focus is on rescuing firms in distress. But this comes at a cost, for there are many instances in which the firm's assets would be better redeployed in other uses. One critic of Chapter 11, Michael Jensen, has argued that "the U.S. bankruptcy system is fundamentally flawed. It is expensive, it exacerbates conflicts of interest among different classes of creditors, and it often takes years to resolve individual cases."[56] Jensen's proposed solution is to require that any bankrupt company be put immediately on the auction block and the proceeds distributed to claimants in accordance with the priority of their claims.[57]

---

[52]See, for example, A. Cifelli, "Management by Bankruptcy," *Fortune*, October 1983, pp. 69–73.

[53]The pay cut enabled Continental to reduce fares aggressively and improve its load factors, but it did not solve Continental's problems. Shortly after emerging from bankruptcy, it was back in the bankruptcy court.

[54]Franks and Torous show that creditors make even greater concessions to junior claimholders in informal workouts than in Chapter 11 reorganizations. See J. R. Franks and W. N. Torous, "How Shareholders and Creditors Fare in Workouts and Chapter 11 Reorganizations," *Journal of Financial Economics* 35 (May 1994), pp. 349–370.

[55]For example, when TWA reentered Chapter 11 in 1995, it had already agreed to a *prepack* with its creditors.

[56] M. C. Jensen, "Corporate Control and the Politics of Finance," *Journal of Applied Corporate Finance* 4 (Summer 1991), pp. 13–33.

[57]An ingenious alternative set of bankruptcy procedures is proposed in P. Aghion, O. Hart, and J. Moore, "The Economics of Bankruptcy Reform," *Journal of Law, Economics and Organization* 8 (1992), pp. 523–546.

In other countries the bankruptcy rules are often "creditor-oriented"; their object is to recover as much as possible for the lenders and to ensure that the senior claimants get first peck. For example, the bankruptcy procedures in Germany, Sweden, and the UK have much in common with Chapter 7 in the United States.[58] In other words, an outside official is appointed to take over the company and to sell the assets either piecemeal or as a going concern.[59] The proceeds are then distributed to creditors according to the priority of their claims.

Of course, the grass is always greener elsewhere. In the United States, critics of Chapter 11 complain about the costs of trying to save businesses that are no longer viable. By contrast, in Europe, bankruptcy laws are blamed for the demise of healthy businesses and governments there have looked for ways to encourage rehabilitation rather than liquidation.

---

[58]See, for example, M. J. White, "The Costs of Corporate Bankruptcy: A U.S.–European Comparison," in J. S. Bhandari and L. A. Weiss (eds.), *Corporate Bankruptcy*, Cambridge University Press, Cambridge, 1996; and P. Stromberg, "Conflicts of Interest and Market Illiquidity in Bankruptcy Auctions: Theory and Tests," *Journal of Finance* 55 (December 2000), pp. 2641–2692.

[59]Although the bankruptcy codes in these countries contain provisions to keep the firm operating, they are relatively rarely invoked.

FURTHER READING

A useful general work on debt securities is:

F. J. Fabozzi (ed.): *The Handbook of Fixed Income Securities*, Frank J. Fabozzi Associates, New Hope, PA, 2000.

The articles by Brennan and Schwartz and by Kraus are general discussions of call provisions:

M. J. Brennan and E. S. Schwartz: "Savings Bonds, Retractable Bonds and Callable Bonds," *Journal of Financial Economics*, 5:67–88 (1977).

A. Kraus: "An Analysis of Call Provisions and the Corporate Refunding Decision," *Midland Corporate Finance Journal*, 1:46–60 (Spring 1983).

Smith and Warner provide an extensive survey and analysis of covenants:

C. W. Smith and J. B. Warner: "On Financial Contracting: An Analysis of Bond Covenants," *Journal of Financial Economics*, 7:117–161 (June 1979).

Discussions of project finance include:

R. A. Brealey, I. A. Cooper, and M. Habib: "Using Project Finance to Fund Infrastructure Investments," *Journal of Applied Corporate Finance*, 9:25–38 (Fall 1996).

B. C. Esty: "Petrozuata: A Case Study on the Effective Use of Project Finance," *Journal of Applied Corporate Finance*, 12:26–42 (Fall 1999).

P. K. Nevitt and F. J. Fabozzi, *Project Financing*, American Educational Systems, London, 7th ed., 2000.

Altman's book is a general survey of the bankruptcy decision, while Bhandari and Weiss provide a useful collection of readings. Also listed below are several good studies of the conflicting interests of different security holders and the costs and consequences of reorganization:

E. A. Altman: *Corporate Financial Distress and Bankruptcy: A Complete Guide to Predicting and Avoiding Distress, and Profiting from Bankruptcy*, John Wiley & Sons, New York, 2nd ed., 1993.

J. S. Bhandari and L. A. Weiss (eds.), *Corporate Bankruptcy*, Cambridge University Press, Cambridge, 1996.

M. White: "The Corporate Bankruptcy Decision," *Journal of Economic Perspectives* 3:129–152 (Spring 1989).

J. R. Franks and W. N. Torous: "An Empirical Analysis of U.S. Firms in Reorganization," *Journal of Finance*, 44:747–770 (July 1989).

J. R. Franks and W. N. Torous: "How Shareholders and Creditors Fare in Workouts and Chapter 11 Reorganizations," *Journal of Financial Economics*, 35:349–370 (May 1994).

L. A. Weiss, "Bankruptcy Resolution: Direct Costs and Violation of Priority of Claims," *Journal of Financial Economics*, 27:285–314 (October 1990).

QUIZ

1. Select the most appropriate term from within the parentheses:
   a. (High-grade utility bonds/low-grade industrial bonds) generally have only light sinking-fund requirements.
   b. Collateral trust bonds are often issued by (utilities/industrial holding companies).
   c. (Utility bonds/industrial bonds) are usually unsecured.
   d. Equipment trust certificates are usually issued by (railroads/financial companies).
   e. Mortgage pass-through certificates are an example of (an asset-backed security/project finance).

2. *Vocabulary check.* Define the following terms: indenture or trust deed, debentures, mortgage bonds, call provision, sinking fund, foreign bond, negative pledge clause.

3. For each of the following sinking funds, state whether the fund increases or decreases the value of the bond at the time of issue (or whether it is impossible to say):
   a. An optional sinking fund operating by drawings at par.
   b. A mandatory sinking fund operating by drawings at par *or* by purchases in the market.
   c. A mandatory sinking fund operating by drawings at par.

4. a. As a senior bondholder, would you like the company to issue more junior debt, would you prefer it not to do so, or would you not care?
   b. You hold debt secured on the company's existing property. Would you like the company to issue more unsecured debt, would you prefer it not to do so, or would you not care?

5. Use Table 25.1 (but not the text) to answer the following questions:
   a. Who are the principal underwriters for the Ralston Purina bond issue?
   b. Who is the trustee for the issue?
   c. How many dollars does the company receive for each debenture after deduction of the underwriters' spread?
   d. Is the debenture "bearer" or "registered"?
   e. At what price was the issue callable in 1995?
   f. Could the company call the bond in 1990 and replace it with a debenture yielding 5 percent?

6. Look at Table 25.1:
   a. Suppose the debenture was issued on July 1, 1986, at 97.60 percent. How much would you have to pay to buy one bond delivered on July 1? Don't forget to include accrued interest.
   b. When is the first interest payment on the bond, and what is the amount of the payment?
   c. On what date do the bonds finally mature, and what is the principal amount of the bonds that is due to be repaid on that date?
   d. Suppose that the market price of the bonds rises to 102 and thereafter does not change. When should the company call the issue?

7. A security dealer in New York tells you that the yield to maturity on a 10 percent five-year corporate debenture is 7.80 percent. An international bond dealer in London tells you that the yield to maturity on an identical international bond (eurobond) is 7.90 percent. Which bond offers the higher return? Explain.

8. Explain the three principal ways in which the terms of private placement bonds commonly differ from those of public issues.

9. True or false? Briefly explain in each case.
   a. Lenders in project financings rarely have recourse against the project's owners if the project fails.
   b. Many new and exotic debt securities are triggered by government policies or regulations.
   c. Call provisions give a valuable option to debt investors.
   d. Restrictive covenants have been shown to protect debt investors when takeovers are financed with large amounts of debt.
   e. Privately placed debt issues often include stricter covenants than public debt. However, public debt covenants are more difficult and expensive to renegotiate.

10. What is the difference between Chapter 7 bankruptcy and Chapter 11 bankruptcy?

11. True or false?
   a. When a company becomes bankrupt, it is usually in the interests of the equityholders to seek a liquidation rather than a reorganization.
   b. A reorganization plan must be presented for approval by each class of creditor.
   c. The Internal Revenue Service has first claim on the company's assets in the event of bankruptcy.
   d. In a reorganization, creditors may be paid off with a mixture of cash and securities.
   e. When a company is liquidated, one of the most valuable assets to be sold is often the tax-loss carryforward.

12. Explain why equity can sometimes have a positive value even when companies petition for bankruptcy.

PRACTICE QUESTIONS

1. Suppose that the Ralston Purina bond was issued at face value and that investors continue to demand a yield of 9.5 percent. Sketch what you think would happen to the bond price as the first interest payment date approaches and then passes. What about the price of the bond plus accrued interest?

2. Find the terms and conditions of a recent bond issue and compare them with those of the Ralston Purina issue.

3. Bond prices can fall either because of a change in the general level of interest rates or because of an increased risk of default. To what extent do floating-rate bonds and puttable bonds protect the investor against each of these risks?

4. Proctor Power has fixed assets worth $200 million and net working capital worth $100 million. It is financed partly by equity and partly by three issues of debt. These consist of $250 million of First Mortgage Bonds secured only on the company's fixed assets, $100 million of senior debentures, and $120 million of subordinated debentures. If the debt were due today, how much would each debtholder be entitled to receive?

5. Elixir Corporation has just filed for bankruptcy. Elixir is a holding company whose assets consist of real estate worth $80 million and 100 percent of the equity of its two operating subsidiaries. It is financed partly by equity and partly by an issue of $400 million of senior collateral trust bonds that are just about to mature. Subsidiary A has issued directly $320 million of debentures and $15 million of preferred stock. Subsidiary B has issued $180 million of senior debentures and $60 million of subordinated debentures. A's assets have a market value of $500 million and B's have a value of $220 million. How much will each security holder receive if the assets are sold and distributed strictly according to precedence?

6. a. Residential mortgages may stipulate either a fixed rate or a variable rate. As a *borrower*, what considerations might cause you to prefer one rather than the other?
   b. Why might holders of mortgage pass-through certificates wish the mortgages to have a floating rate?

7. After a sharp change in interest rates, newly issued bonds generally sell at yields different from those of outstanding bonds of the same quality. One suggested explanation is that there is a difference in the value of the call provisions. Explain how this could arise.

8. Suppose that a company simultaneously issues a zero-coupon bond and a coupon bond with identical maturities. Both are callable at any time at their face values. Other things equal, which is likely to offer the higher yield? Why?

9. **a.** If interest rates rise, will callable or noncallable bonds fall more in price?
   b. Sometimes you encounter bonds that can be repaid after a fixed interval at the option of *either* the issuer or the bondholder. If the exercise price of each option is the same and both the issuer and bondholder act rationally, what will happen when the options can be exercised? (Ignore refinements such as transactions or issue costs.)

10. A puttable bond is a bond which may be repaid before maturity at the investor's option. Sketch a diagram similar to Figure 25.2 showing the relationship between the value of a straight bond and that of a puttable bond.

11. What restrictions are imposed on a company's freedom to issue further debt? Be as precise as possible. Explain carefully the reasons for such restrictions.

12. Does the issue of additional junior debt harm senior bondholders? Would your answer be the same if the junior debt matured *before* the senior debt? Explain.

13. Alpha Corp. is prohibited from issuing more senior debt unless net tangible assets exceed 200 percent of senior debt. Currently the company has outstanding $100 million of senior debt and has net tangible assets of $250 million. How much more senior debt can Alpha Corp. issue?

14. Explain carefully why bond indentures place limitations on the following actions:
   a. Sale of the company's assets.
   b. Payment of dividends to shareholders.
   c. Issue of additional senior debt.

15. Look up a recent issue of an unusual bond in, say, a recent issue of the periodical *Euromoney*. Why do you think this bond was issued? What investors do you think it would appeal to? How would you value the unusual features?

16. In Section 25.8 we referred to Christiania Bank's exotic bond. Explain how you would value tranche B. Assume that the principal repayment is fixed at 100 percent of par. *Hint:* Find a package of other securities that would produce identical cash flows.

17. Explain when it makes sense to use project finance rather than a direct debt issue by the parent company.

18. The appendix summarizes several problems with Chapter 11 bankruptcy. Which of these problems could be mitigated by negotiating a prepackaged bankruptcy?

CHALLENGE QUESTIONS

1. Dorlcote Milling has outstanding a $1 million 3 percent mortgage bond maturing in 10 years. The coupon on any new debt issued by the company is 10 percent. The finance director, Mr. Tulliver, cannot decide whether there is a tax benefit to repurchasing the existing bonds in the marketplace and replacing them with new 10 percent bonds. What do you think?

2. Refer back to the Hub Power project in Section 25.7. There were many other ways that the Hubco project could have been financed. For example, a government agency could have invested in the power plant and hired National Power to run it. Alternatively, National Power could have owned the power plant directly and funded its cost by a mixture of new borrowing and the sale of shares. What do you think were the advantages of setting up a separately financed company to undertake the project?

CHAPTER TWENTY-SIX

LEASING

MOST OF US occasionally rent a car, bicycle, or boat. Usually such personal rentals are short-lived; we may rent a car for a day or week. But in corporate finance longer-term rentals are common. A rental agreement that extends for a year or more and involves a series of fixed payments is called a **lease.**

Firms lease as an alternative to buying capital equipment. Computers are often leased; so are trucks, railroad cars, aircraft, and ships. Just about every kind of asset has been leased sometime by somebody, including electric power plants, nuclear fuel, handball courts, and zoo animals.

Every lease involves two parties. The *user* of the asset is called the *lessee*. The lessee makes periodic payments to the *owner* of the asset, who is called the *lessor*. For example, if you sign an agreement to rent an apartment for a year, you are the lessee and the owner is the lessor.

You often see references to the *leasing industry*. This refers to lessors. (Almost all firms are lessees to at least a minor extent.) Who are the lessors?

Some of the largest lessors are equipment manufacturers. For example, IBM is a large lessor of computers, and Deere is a large lessor of agricultural and construction equipment.

The other two major groups of lessors are banks and independent leasing companies. Leasing companies play an enormous role in the airline business. For example, in 2000 GE Capital Aviation Services, a subsidiary of GE Capital, owned and leased out 970 commercial aircraft. A large fraction of the world's airlines rely entirely on leasing to finance their fleets.

Leasing companies offer a variety of services. Some act as lease brokers (arranging lease deals) as well as lessors. Others specialize in leasing automobiles, trucks, and standardized industrial equipment; they succeed because they can buy equipment in quantity, service it efficiently, and if necessary resell it at a good price.

We begin this chapter by cataloging the different kinds of leases and some of the reasons for their use. Then we show how short-term, or cancelable, lease payments can be interpreted as equivalent annual costs. The remainder of the chapter analyzes long-term leases used as alternatives to debt financing.

 ## 26.1 WHAT IS A LEASE?

Leases come in many forms, but in all cases the lessee (user) promises to make a series of payments to the lessor (owner). The lease contract specifies the monthly or semiannual payments, with the first payment usually due as soon as the contract is signed. The payments are usually level, but their time pattern can be tailored to the user's needs. For example, suppose that a manufacturer leases a machine to produce a complex new product. There will be a year's "shakedown" period before volume production starts. In this case, it might be possible to arrange for lower payments during the first year of the lease.

When a lease is terminated, the leased equipment reverts to the lessor. However, the lease agreement often gives the user the option to purchase the equipment or take out a new lease.

Some leases are short-term or cancelable during the contract period at the option of the lessee. These are generally known as *operating leases*. Others extend over most of the estimated economic life of the asset and cannot be canceled or can be canceled only if the lessor is reimbursed for any losses. These are called *capital, financial,* or *full-payout leases.*[1]

Financial leases are a *source of financing.* Signing a financial lease contract is like borrowing money. There is an immediate cash inflow because the lessee is relieved of having to pay for the asset. But the lessee also assumes a binding obligation to make the payments specified in the lease contract. The user could have borrowed the full purchase price of the asset by accepting a binding obligation to make interest and principal payments to the lender. Thus the cash-flow consequences of leasing and borrowing are similar. In either case, the firm raises cash now and pays it back later. A large part of this chapter will be devoted to comparing leasing and borrowing as financing alternatives.

Leases also differ in the services provided by the lessor. Under a *full-service,* or *rental,* lease, the lessor promises to maintain and insure the equipment and to pay any property taxes due on it. In a *net* lease, the lessee agrees to maintain the asset, insure it, and pay any property taxes. Financial leases are usually net leases.

Most financial leases are arranged for brand new assets. The lessee identifies the equipment, arranges for the leasing company to buy it from the manufacturer, and signs a contract with the leasing company. This is called a *direct* lease. In other cases, the firm sells an asset it already owns and leases it back from the buyer. These *sale and lease-back* arrangements are common in real estate. For example, firm X may wish to raise cash by selling a factory but still retain use of the factory. It could do this by selling the factory for cash to a leasing company and simultaneously signing a long-term lease contract for the factory. Legal ownership of the factory passes to the leasing company, but the right to use it stays with firm X.

You may also encounter *leveraged* leases. These are financial leases in which the lessor borrows part of the purchase price of the leased asset, using the lease contract as security for the loan. This does not change the lessee's obligations, but it can complicate the lessor's analysis considerably.

26.2 WHY LEASE?

You hear many suggestions about why companies should lease equipment rather than buy it. Let us look at some sensible reasons and then at four more dubious ones.

Sensible Reasons for Leasing

Short-Term Leases Are Convenient   Suppose you want the use of a car for a week. You could buy one and sell it seven days later, but that would be silly. Quite apart from the fact that registering ownership is a nuisance, you would spend some time selecting a car, negotiating purchase, and arranging insurance. Then at the end of the week you would negotiate resale and cancel the registration and insurance. When you need a car only for a short time, it clearly makes sense to rent it. You save the trouble of registering ownership, and you know the effective cost. In the same way, it pays a company to lease equipment that it needs for only a year or two. Of course, this kind of lease is always an operating lease.

---

[1]In the shipping industry, a financial lease is called a *bareboat charter* or a *demise hire.*

Sometimes the cost of short-term rentals may seem prohibitively high, or you may find it difficult to rent at any price. This can happen for equipment that is easily damaged by careless use. The owner knows that short-term users are unlikely to take the same care they would with their own equipment. When the danger of abuse becomes too high, short-term rental markets do not survive. Thus, it is easy enough to buy a Lamborgini Diablo, provided your pockets are deep enough, but nearly impossible to rent one.

Cancellation Options Are Valuable   Some leases that *appear* expensive really are fairly priced once the option to cancel is recognized. We return to this point in the next section.

Maintenance Is Provided   Under a full-service lease, the user receives maintenance and other services. Many lessors are well equipped to provide efficient maintenance. However, bear in mind that these benefits will be reflected in higher lease payments.

Standardization Leads to Low Administrative and Transaction Costs   Suppose that you operate a leasing company that specializes in financial leases for trucks. You are effectively lending money to a large number of firms (the lessees) which may differ considerably in size and risk. But, because the underlying asset is in each case the same saleable item (a truck), you can safely "lend" the money (lease the truck) without conducting a detailed analysis of each firm's business. You can also use a simple, standard lease contract. This standardization makes it possible to "lend" small sums of money without incurring large investigative, administrative, or legal costs.

For these reasons leasing is often a relatively cheap source of cash for the small company. It offers financing on a flexible, piecemeal basis, with lower transaction costs than in a bond or stock issue.

Tax Shields Can Be Used   The lessor owns the leased asset and deducts its depreciation from taxable income. If the lessor can make better use of depreciation tax shields than an asset's user can, it may make sense for the leasing company to own the equipment and pass on some of the tax benefits to the lessee in the form of low lease payments.

Avoiding the Alternative Minimum Tax   Red-blooded financial managers want to earn lots of money for their shareholders but *report* low profits to the tax authorities. Tax law in the United States allows this. A firm may use straight-line depreciation in its annual report but choose accelerated depreciation (and the shortest possible asset life) for its tax books. By this and other perfectly legal and ethical devices, profitable companies have occasionally managed to escape tax entirely. Almost all companies pay less tax than their public income statements suggest.[2]

But there is a trap for companies that shield too much income: the alternative minimum tax (*AMT*). Corporations must pay the AMT whenever it is higher than their tax computed in the regular way.

---

[2]Year-by-year differences between reported tax expense and taxes actually paid are explained in footnotes to the financial statements. The cumulative difference is shown on the balance sheet as a deferred tax liability. (Note that accelerated depreciation *postpones* taxes; it does not eliminate taxes.)

Here is how the AMT works: It requires a second calculation of taxable income, in which part of the benefit of accelerated depreciation and other tax-reducing items[3] is added back. The AMT is 20 percent of the result.

Suppose Yuppytech Services would have $10 million in taxable income but for the AMT, which forces it to add back $9 million of tax privileges:

	Regular Tax	Alternative Minimum Tax
Income	$10	$10 + 9 = 19
Tax rate	.35	.20
Tax	$ 3.5	$3.8

Yuppytech must pay $3.8 million, not $3.5.[4]

How can this painful payment be avoided? How about leasing? Lease payments are *not* on the list of items added back in calculating the AMT. If you lease rather than buy, tax depreciation is less and the AMT is less. There is a net gain if the *lessor* is not subject to the AMT and can pass back depreciation tax shields in the form of lower lease payments.

Some Dubious Reasons for Leasing

Leasing Avoids Capital Expenditure Controls   In many companies lease proposals are scrutinized as carefully as capital expenditure proposals, but in others leasing may enable an operating manager to avoid the elaborate approval procedures needed to buy an asset. Although this is a dubious reason for leasing, it may be influential, particularly in the public sector. For example, city hospitals have sometimes found it politically more convenient to lease their medical equipment than to ask the city government to provide funds for purchase. Another example is provided by the United States Navy, which once leased a fleet of new tankers and supply ships instead of asking Congress for the money to buy them.

Leasing Preserves Capital   Leasing companies provide "100 percent financing"; they advance the full cost of the leased asset. Consequently, they often claim that leasing preserves capital, allowing the firm to save its cash for other things.

But the firm can also "preserve capital" by borrowing money. If Greymare Bus Lines leases a $100,000 bus rather than buying it, it does conserve $100,000 cash. It could also (1) buy the bus for cash and (2) borrow $100,000, using the bus as security. Its bank balance ends up the same whether it leases or buys and borrows. It has the bus in either case, and it incurs a $100,000 liability in either case. What's so special about leasing?

Leases May Be Off-Balance-Sheet Financing   In some countries, such as Germany, financial leases are off-balance-sheet financing; that is, a firm can acquire an asset,

---

[3]Other items include some interest receipts from tax-exempt municipal securities and taxes deferred by use of completed contract accounting. (The completed contract method allows a manufacturer to postpone reporting taxable profits until a production contract is completed. Since contracts may span several years, this deferral can have a substantial positive NPV.)

[4]But Yuppytech can carry forward the $.3 million difference. If later years' AMTs are *lower* than regular taxes, the difference can be used as a tax credit. Suppose the AMT next year is $4 million and the regular tax is $5 million. Then Yuppytech pays only 5 − .3 = $4.7 million.

finance it through a financial lease, and show neither the asset nor the lease contract on its balance sheet.

In the United States, the Financial Accounting Standards Board (FASB) requires that all *capital* (i.e., financial) leases be capitalized. This means that the present value of the lease payments must be calculated and shown alongside debt on the right-hand side of the balance sheet. The same amount must be shown as an asset on the left-hand side.[5]

The FASB defines capital leases as leases which meet *any one* of the following requirements:

1. The lease agreement transfers ownership to the lessee before the lease expires.
2. The lessee can purchase the asset for a bargain price when the lease expires.
3. The lease lasts for at least 75 percent of the asset's estimated economic life.
4. The present value of the lease payments is at least 90 percent of the asset's value.

All other leases are operating leases as far as the accountants are concerned.

Many financial managers have tried to take advantage of this arbitrary boundary between operating and financial leases. Suppose that you want to finance a computer-controlled machine tool costing $1 million. The machine tool's life is expected to be 12 years. You could sign a lease contract for 8 years, 11 months (just missing requirement 3) with lease payments having a present value of $899,000 (just missing requirement 4). You could also make sure the lease contract avoids requirements 1 and 2. Result? You have off-balance-sheet financing. This lease would not have to be capitalized, although it is clearly a long-term, fixed obligation.

Now we come to the $64,000 question: Why should anyone *care* whether financing is off balance sheet or on balance sheet? Shouldn't the financial manager worry about substance rather than appearance?

When a firm obtains off-balance-sheet financing, the conventional measures of financial leverage, such as the debt–equity ratio, understate the true degree of financial leverage. Some believe that financial analysts do not always notice off-balance-sheet lease obligations (which are still referred to in footnotes) or the greater volatility of earnings that results from the fixed lease payments. They may be right, but we would not expect such an imperfection to be widespread.

When a company borrows money, it must usually consent to certain restrictions on future borrowing. Early bond indentures did not include any restrictions on financial leases. Therefore leasing was seen as a way to circumvent restrictive covenants. Loopholes such as these are easily stopped, and most bond indentures now include limits on leasing.

Long-term lease obligations ought to be regarded as debt whether or not they appear on the balance sheet. Financial analysts may overlook moderate leasing activity, just as they overlook minor debts. But major lease obligations are generally recognized and taken into account.

Leasing Affects Book Income   Leasing can make the firm's balance sheet and income statement *look* better by increasing book income or decreasing book asset value, or both.

---

[5]This "asset" is then amortized over the life of the lease. The amortization is deducted from book income, just as depreciation is deducted for a purchased asset.

A lease which qualifies as off-balance-sheet financing affects book income in only one way: The lease payments are an expense. If the firm buys the asset instead and borrows to finance it, both depreciation and interest expense are deducted. Leases are usually set up so that payments in the early years are less than depreciation plus interest under the buy-and-borrow alternative. Consequently, leasing increases book income in the early years of an asset's life. The book rate of return can increase even more dramatically, because the book value of assets (the denominator in the book-rate-of-return calculation) is understated if the leased asset never appears on the firm's balance sheet.

Leasing's impact on book income should in itself have no effect on firm value. In efficient capital markets investors will look through the firm's accounting results to the true value of the asset and the liability incurred to finance it.

 ## 26.3 OPERATING LEASES

Remember our discussion of *equivalent annual costs* in Chapter 6? We defined the equivalent annual cost of, say, a machine as the annual rental payment sufficient to cover the present value of all the costs of owning and operating it.

In Chapter 6's examples, the rental payments were hypothetical—just a way of converting a present value to an annual cost. But in the leasing business the payments are real. Suppose you decide to lease a machine tool for one year. What will the rental payment be in a competitive leasing industry? The lessor's equivalent annual cost, of course.

Example of an Operating Lease

The boyfriend of the daughter of the CEO of Establishment Industries takes her to the senior prom in a pearly white stretch limo. The CEO is impressed. He decides Establishment Industries ought to have one for VIP transportation. Establishment's CFO prudently suggests a one-year operating lease instead and approaches Acme Limolease for a quote.

Table 26.1 shows Acme's analysis. Suppose it buys a new limo for $75,000 which it plans to lease out for seven years (years 0 through 6). The table gives Acme's forecasts of operating, maintenance, and administrative costs, the latter including the costs of negotiating the lease, keeping track of payments and paperwork, and finding a replacement lessee when Establishment's year is up. For simplicity we assume zero inflation and use a 7 percent real cost of capital. We also assume that the limo will have zero salvage value at the end of year 6. The present value of all costs, partially offset by the value of depreciation tax shields,[6] is $98,150. Now, how much does Acme have to charge to break even?

Acme can afford to buy and lease out the limo only if the rental payments forecasted over six years have a present value of at least $98,150. The problem, then, is

---

[6]The depreciation tax shields are safe cash flows if the tax rate does not change and Acme is sure to pay taxes. If 7 percent is the right discount rate for the other flows in Table 26.1, the depreciation tax shields deserve a lower rate. A more refined analysis would discount safe depreciation tax shields at an after-tax borrowing or lending rate. See Section 19.5 or the next section of this chapter.

				Year			
	0	1	2	3	4	5	6
Initial cost	−75						
Maintenance, insurance, selling, and administrative costs	−12	−12	−12	−12	−12	−12	−12
Tax shield on costs	+4.2	+4.2	+4.2	+4.2	+4.2	+4.2	+4.2
Depreciation tax shield*		+5.25	+8.40	+5.04	+3.02	+3.02	+1.51
Total	−82.80	−2.55	.60	−2.76	−4.78	−4.78	−6.29
PV at 7% = −$98.15[†]							
Break-even rent (level)	26.18	26.18	26.18	26.18	26.18	26.18	26.18
Tax	−9.16	−9.16	−9.16	−9.16	−9.16	−9.16	−9.16
Break-even rent after tax	17.02	17.02	17.02	17.02	17.02	17.02	17.02
PV at 7% = $98.15[†]							

TABLE 26.1

Calculating the zero-NPV rental rate (or equivalent annual cost) for Establishment Industries' pearly white stretch limo (figures in $ thousands).

Note: We assume no inflation and a 7 percent real cost of capital. The tax rate is 35 percent.
*Depreciation tax shields are calculated using the five-year schedule from Table 6.4.
†Note that the first payment of these annuities comes immediately. The standard annuity formula must be multiplied by $1 + r = 1.07$.

to calculate a six-year annuity with a present value of $98,150. We will follow common leasing practice and assume rental payments in advance.[7]

As Table 26.1 shows, the required annuity is $26,180, that is, about $26,000.[8] This annuity's present value (after taxes) exactly equals the present value of the after-tax costs of owning and operating the limo. The annuity provides Acme with a competitive expected rate of return (7 percent) on its investment. Acme could try to charge Establishment Industries more than $26,000, but if the CFO is smart enough to ask for bids from Acme's competitors, the winning lessor will end up receiving this amount.

Remember that Establishment Industries is not obligated to continue using the limo for more than one year. Acme may have to find several new lessees over the limo's economic life. Even if Establishment continues, it can renegotiate a new lease at whatever rates prevail in the future. Thus Acme does not know what it can charge in year 1 or afterward. If pearly white falls out of favor with teenagers and CEOs, Acme is probably out of luck.

In real life Acme would have several further things to worry about. For example, how long will the limo stand idle when it is returned at year 1? If idle time is likely before a new lessee is found, then lease rates have to be higher to compensate.[9]

---

[7]In Section 6.3 the hypothetical rentals were paid *in arrears*.

[8]This is a level annuity because we are assuming that (1) there is no inflation and (2) the services of a six-year-old limo are no different than a brand-new limo's. If users of aging limos see them as obsolete or unfashionable, or if new limos are cheaper, then lease rates for older limos would have to be cut. This would give a *declining* annuity: initial users would pay more than the amount shown in Table 26.1, later users, less.

[9]If, say, limos were off-lease and idle 20 percent of the time, lease rates would have to be 25 percent above those shown in Table 26.1.

In an operating lease, the *lessor* absorbs these risks, not the lessee. The discount rate used by the lessor must include a premium sufficient to compensate its shareholders for the risks of buying and holding the leased asset. In other words, Acme's 7 percent real discount rate must cover the risks of investing in stretch limos. (As we will see in the next section, risk bearing in *financial* leases is fundamentally different.)

Lease or Buy?

If you need a car or limo for only a day or a week you will surely rent it; if you need one for five years you will probably buy it. In between there is a gray region in which the choice of lease or buy is not obvious. The decision rule should be clear in concept, however: If you need an asset for your business, *buy it if the equivalent annual cost of ownership and operation is less than the best lease rate you can get from an outsider.* In other words, buy if you can "rent to yourself" cheaper than you can rent from others. (Again we stress that this rule applies to *operating* leases.)

If you plan to use the asset for an extended period, your equivalent annual cost of owning the asset will usually be less than the operating lease rate. The lessor has to mark up the lease rate to cover the costs of negotiating and administering the lease, the foregone revenues when the asset is off-lease and idle, and so on. These costs are avoided when the company buys and rents to itself.

There are two cases in which operating leases may make sense even when the company plans to use an asset for an extended period. First, the lessor may be able to buy and manage the asset at less expense than the lessee. For example, the major truck leasing companies buy thousands of new vehicles every year. That puts them in an excellent bargaining position with truck manufacturers. These companies also run very efficient service operations, and they know how to extract the most salvage value when trucks wear out and it is time to sell them. A small business, or a small division of a larger one, cannot achieve these economies and often finds it cheaper to lease trucks than to buy them.

Second, operating leases often contain useful options. Suppose Acme offers Establishment Industries the following two leases:

1. A one-year lease for $26,000.
2. A six-year lease for $28,000, *with the option to cancel the lease* at any time from year 1 on.[10]

The second lease has obvious attractions. Suppose Establishment's CEO becomes fond of the limo and wants to use it for a second year. If rates increase, lease 2 allows Establishment to continue at the old rate. If rates decrease, Establishment can cancel lease 2 and negotiate a lower rate with Acme or one of its competitors.

Of course, lease 2 is a more costly proposition for Acme: In effect it gives Establishment an insurance policy protecting it from increases in future lease rates. The difference between the costs of leases 1 and 2 is the annual insurance premium. But lessees may happily pay for insurance if they have no special knowledge of future asset values or lease rates. A leasing company acquires such knowledge in the course of its business and can generally sell such insurance at a profit.

---

[10]Acme might also offer a one-year lease for $28,000 but give the lessee an option to *extend* the lease on the same terms for up to five additional years. This is, of course, identical to lease 2. It doesn't matter whether the lessee has the (put) option to cancel or the (call) option to continue.

Airlines face fluctuating demand for their services and the mix of planes that they need is constantly changing. Most airlines, therefore, lease a proportion of their fleet on a short-term cancelable basis and are willing to pay a premium to lessors for bearing the cancelation risk. Specialist aircraft lessors are well-placed to bear this risk, for they will hope to find new customers for any aircraft that are returned to them.

Be sure to check out the options before you sign (or reject) an operating lease.[11]

26.4 VALUING FINANCIAL LEASES

For operating leases the decision centers on "lease versus buy." For *financial* leases the decision amounts to "lease versus borrow." Financial leases extend over most of the economic life of the leased equipment. They are *not* cancelable. The lease payments are fixed obligations equivalent to debt service.

Financial leases make sense when the company is prepared to take on the business risks of owning and operating the leased asset. If Establishment Industries signs a *financial* lease for the stretch limo, it is stuck with that asset. The financial lease is just another way of borrowing money to pay for the limo.

Financial leases do offer special advantages to some firms in some circumstances. However, there is no point in further discussion of these advantages until you know how to value financial lease contracts.

Example of a Financial Lease

Imagine yourself in the position of Thomas Pierce III, president of Greymare Bus Lines. Your firm was established by your grandfather, who was quick to capitalize on the growing demand for transportation between Widdicombe and nearby townships. The company has owned all its vehicles from the time the company was formed; you are now reconsidering that policy. Your operating manager wants to buy a new bus costing $100,000. The bus will last only eight years before going to the scrap yard. You are convinced that investment in the additional equipment is worthwhile. However, the representative of the bus manufacturer has pointed out that her firm would also be willing to lease the bus to you for eight annual payments of $16,900 each. Greymare would remain responsible for all maintenance, insurance, and operating expenses.

Table 26.2 shows the direct cash-flow consequences of signing the lease contract. (An important indirect effect is considered later.) The consequences are

1. Greymare does not have to pay for the bus. This is equivalent to a cash inflow of $100,000.

2. Greymare no longer owns the bus, and so it cannot depreciate it. Therefore it gives up a valuable depreciation tax shield. In Table 26.2, we have assumed depreciation would be calculated using five-year tax depreciation schedules. (See Table 6.4.)

3. Greymare must pay $16,900 per year for eight years to the lessor. The first payment is due immediately.

[11]McConnell and Schallheim calculate the value of options in operating leases under various assumptions about asset risk, depreciation rates, etc. See J. J. McConnell and J. S. Schallheim, "Valuation of Asset Leasing Contracts," *Journal of Financial Economics* 12 (August 1983), pp. 237–261.

	Year							
	0	1	2	3	4	5	6	7
Cost of new bus	+100							
Lost depreciation tax shield		−7.00	−11.20	−6.72	−4.03	−4.03	−2.02	0
Lease payment	−16.9	−16.9	−16.9	−16.9	−16.9	−16.9	−16.9	−16.9
Tax shield of lease payment	+5.92	+5.92	+5.92	+5.92	+5.92	+5.92	+5.92	+5.92
Cash flow of lease	+89.02	−17.99	−22.19	−17.71	−15.02	−15.02	−13.00	−10.98

TABLE 26.2

Cash-flow consequences of the lease contract offered to Greymare Bus Lines (figures in $ thousands; some columns do not add due to rounding).

4. However, these lease payments are fully tax-deductible. At a 35 percent marginal tax rate, the lease payments generate tax shields of $5,920 per year. You could say that the after-tax cost of the lease payment is $16,900 − $5,920 = $10,980.

We must emphasize that Table 26.2 assumes that Greymare will pay taxes at the full 35 percent marginal rate. If the firm were sure to lose money, and therefore pay no taxes, lines 2 and 4 would be left blank. The depreciation tax shields are worth nothing to a firm that pays no taxes, for example.

Table 26.2 also assumes the bus will be worthless when it goes to the scrap yard at the end of year 7. Otherwise there would be an entry for salvage value lost.

Who Really Owns the Leased Asset?

To a lawyer or a tax accountant, that would be a silly question: The lessor is clearly the *legal* owner of the leased asset. That is why the lessor is allowed to deduct depreciation from taxable income.

From an *economic* point of view, you might say that the *user* is the real owner, because in a *financial* lease, the user faces the risks and receives the rewards of ownership. Greymare cannot cancel a financial lease. If the new bus turns out to be hopelessly costly and unsuited for Greymare's routes, that is Greymare's problem, not the lessor's. If it turns out to be a great success, the profit goes to Greymare, not the lessor. The success or failure of the firm's business operations does not depend on whether the buses are financed by leasing or some other financial instrument.

In many respects, a financial lease is equivalent to a secured loan. The lessee must make a series of fixed payments; if the lessee fails to do so, the lessor can repossess the asset. Thus we can think of a balance sheet like this

Greymare Bus Lines (Figures in $ Thousands)

Bus	100	100	Loan secured by bus
All other assets	1,000	450	Other loans
		550	Equity
Total assets	1,100	1,100	Total liabilities

as being economically equivalent to a balance sheet like this

Greymare Bus Lines (Figures in $ Thousands)

Bus	100	100	Financial lease
All other assets	1,000	450	Other loans
		550	Equity
Total assets	1,100	1,100	Total liabilities

Having said this, we must immediately add two qualifications. First, legal ownership can make a big difference when a financial lease expires because the lessor gets the salvage value of the asset. Once a secured loan is paid off, the user owns the asset free and clear.

Second, lessors and secured creditors may be treated differently in bankruptcy. If a company defaults on a lease payment, you might think that the lessor could pick up the leased asset and take it home. But if the bankruptcy court decides the asset is "essential" to the lessee's business, it "affirms" the lease. Then the bankrupt firm can continue to use the asset, *but* it must also continue to make the lease payments. This can be *good* news for the lessor: It is paid cash while other creditors cool their heels. Even secured creditors are not paid until the bankruptcy process works itself out.

If the lease is not affirmed but "rejected," the lessor can of course recover the leased asset. If it is worth less than the future payments the lessee had promised, the lessor can try to recoup this loss. But in this case the lender must get in line with the unsecured creditors.

Of course, neither the lessor nor the secured lender can be sure it will come out whole. Our point is that lessors and secured creditors have different rights when the asset user gets into trouble.

Leasing and the Internal Revenue Service

We have already noted that the lessee loses the tax depreciation of the leased asset but can deduct the lease payment in full. The *lessor*, as legal owner, uses the depreciation tax shield but must report the lease payments as taxable rental income.

However, the Internal Revenue Service is suspicious by nature and will not allow the lessee to deduct the entire lease payment unless it is satisfied that the arrangement is a genuine lease and not a disguised installment purchase or secured loan agreement. Here are examples of lease provisions that will arouse its suspicion:

1. Designating any part of the lease payment as "interest."
2. Giving the lessee the option to acquire the asset for, say, $1 when the lease expires. Such a provision would effectively give the asset's salvage value to the lessee.
3. Adopting a schedule of payments such that the lessee pays a large proportion of the cost over a short period and thereafter is able to use the asset for a nominal charge.
4. Including a so-called hell-or-high-water clause that obliges the lessee to make payments regardless of what subsequently happens to the lessor or the equipment.
5. Limiting the lessee's right to issue debt or pay dividends while the lease is in force.

6. Leasing "limited use" property—for example, leasing a machine or production facility which is custom-designed for the lessee's operations and which therefore will have scant secondhand value.

Some leases are designed *not* to qualify as a true lease for tax purposes. Suppose a manufacturer finds it convenient to lease a new computer but wants to keep the depreciation tax shields. This is easily accomplished by giving the manufacturer the option to purchase the computer for $1 at the end of the lease. Then the Internal Revenue Service treats the lease as an installment sale, and the manufacturer can deduct depreciation and the interest component of the lease payment for tax purposes. But the lease is still a lease for all other purposes.

A First Pass at Valuing a Lease Contract

When we left Thomas Pierce III, president of Greymare Bus Lines, he had just set down in Table 26.2 the cash flows of the financial lease proposed by the bus manufacturer.

These cash flows are typically assumed to be about as safe as the interest and principal payments on a secured loan issued by the lessee. This assumption is reasonable for the lease payments because the lessor is effectively lending money to the lessee. But the various tax shields might carry enough risk to deserve a higher discount rate. For example, Greymare might be confident that it could make the lease payments but not confident that it could earn enough taxable income to use these tax shields. In that case the cash flows generated by the tax shields would probably deserve a higher discount rate than the borrowing rate used for the lease payments.

A lessee might, in principle, end up using a separate discount rate for each line of Table 26.2, each rate chosen to fit the risk of that line's cash flow. But established, profitable firms usually find it reasonable to simplify by discounting the types of flows shown in Table 26.2 at a single rate based on the rate of interest the firm would pay if it borrowed rather than leased. We will assume Greymare's borrowing rate is 10 percent.

At this point we must go back to our discussion in Chapter 19 of debt-equivalent flows. When a company lends money, it pays tax on the interest it receives. Its net return is the after-tax interest rate. When a company borrows money, it can *deduct* interest payments from its taxable income. The net cost of borrowing is the after-tax interest rate. Thus the after-tax interest rate is the effective rate at which a company can transfer debt-equivalent flows from one time period to another. Therefore, to value the incremental cash flows stemming from the lease, we need to discount them at the after-tax interest rate.

Since Greymare can borrow at 10 percent, we should discount the lease cash flows at $r_D(1 - T_c) = .10(1 - .35) = .065$, or 6.5 percent. This gives

$$\text{NPV lease} = +89.02 - \frac{17.99}{1.065} - \frac{22.19}{(1.065)^2} - \frac{17.71}{(1.065)^3} - \frac{15.02}{(1.065)^4}$$

$$- \frac{15.02}{(1.065)^5} - \frac{13.00}{(1.065)^6} - \frac{10.98}{(1.065)^7}$$

$$= -.70, \text{ or } -\$700$$

Since the lease has a negative NPV, Greymare is better off buying the bus.

A positive or negative NPV is not an abstract concept; in this case Greymare's shareholders really are $700 poorer if the company leases. Let us now check how this situation comes about.

Look once more at Table 26.2. The lease cash flows are

	Year							
	0	1	2	3	4	5	6	7
Lease cash flows, thousands	+89.02	−17.99	−22.19	−17.71	−15.02	−15.02	−13.00	−10.98

The lease payments are contractual obligations like the principal and interest payments on secured debt. Thus you can think of the incremental lease cash flows in years 1 through 7 as the "debt service" of the lease. Table 26.3 shows a loan with *exactly* the same debt service as the lease. The initial amount of the loan is 89.72 thousand dollars. If Greymare borrowed this sum, it would need to pay interest in the first year of $.10 \times 89.72 = 8.97$ and would *receive* a tax shield on this interest of $.35 \times 8.97 = 3.14$. Greymare could then repay 12.15 of the loan, leaving a net cash outflow of 17.99 (exactly the same as for the lease) in year 1 and an outstanding debt at the start of year 2 of 77.56.

As you walk through the calculations in Table 26.3, you see that it costs exactly the same to service a loan that brings an immediate inflow of 89.72 as it does to service the lease, which brings in only 89.02. That is why we say that the lease has a net present value of $89.02 − 89.72 = −.7$, or −$700. If Greymare leases the bus rather than raising an *equivalent loan*,[12] there will be $700 less in Greymare's bank account.

Our example illustrates two general points about leases and equivalent loans. First, if you can devise a borrowing plan that gives the same cash flow as the lease in every future period but a higher immediate cash flow, then you should not lease. If, however, the equivalent loan provides the same future cash outflows as the lease but a lower immediate inflow, then leasing is the better choice.

	Year							
	0	1	2	3	4	5	6	7
Amount borrowed at year-end	89.72	77.56	60.42	46.64	34.66	21.89	10.31	0
Interest paid at 10%		−8.97	−7.76	−6.04	−4.66	−3.47	−2.19	−1.03
Interest tax shield at 35%		+3.14	+2.71	+2.11	+1.63	+1.21	+.77	+.36
Interest paid after tax		−5.83	−5.04	−3.93	−3.03	−2.25	−1.42	−.67
Principal repaid		−12.15	−17.14	−13.78	−11.99	−12.76	−11.58	−10.31
Net cash flow of equivalent loan	89.72	−17.99	−22.19	−17.71	−15.02	−15.02	−13.00	−10.98

TABLE 26.3

Details of the equivalent loan to the lease offered to Greymare Bus Lines (figures in $ thousands; cash outflows shown with negative sign).

---

[12]When we compare the lease to its equivalent loan, we do not mean to imply that the bus alone could support all of that loan. Some part of the loan would be supported by Greymare's other assets. Some part of the lease would likewise be supported by the other assets.

Second, our example suggests two ways to value a lease:

1. *Hard way.* Construct a table like Table 26.3 showing the equivalent loan.
2. *Easy way.* Discount the lease cash flows at the *after-tax* interest rate that the firm would pay on an equivalent loan. Both methods give the same answer—in our case an NPV of −$700.

The Story So Far

We concluded that the lease contract offered to Greymare Bus Lines was *not* attractive because the lease provided $700 less financing than the equivalent loan. The underlying principle is as follows: A financial lease is superior to buying and borrowing if the financing provided by the lease exceeds the financing generated by the equivalent loan.

The principle implies this formula:

$$\frac{\text{Net value}}{\text{of lease}} = \frac{\text{initial financing}}{\text{provided}} - \sum_{t=1}^{N} \frac{\text{lease cash flow}}{[1 + r_D(1 - T_c)]^t}$$

where N is the length of the lease. Initial financing provided equals the cost of the leased asset minus any immediate lease payment or other cash outflow attributable to the lease.

Notice that the value of the lease is its incremental value relative to borrowing via an equivalent loan. A positive lease value means that *if* you acquire the asset, lease financing is advantageous. It does not prove you should acquire the asset.

However, sometimes favorable lease terms rescue a capital investment project. Suppose that Greymare had decided *against* buying a new bus because the NPV of the $100,000 investment was −$5,000 assuming normal financing. The bus manufacturer could rescue the deal by offering a lease with a value of, say, +$8,000. By offering such a lease, the manufacturer would in effect cut the price of the bus to $92,000, giving the bus-lease package a positive value to Greymare. We could express this more formally by treating the lease's NPV as a favorable financing side effect that adds to project adjusted present value (APV):[13]

$$\text{APV} = \text{NPV of project} + \text{NPV of lease}$$
$$= -5,000 + 8,000 = +\$3,000$$

Notice also that our formula applies to net financial leases. Any insurance, maintenance, and other operating costs picked up by the lessor have to be evaluated separately and added to the value of the lease. If the asset has salvage value at the end of the lease, that value should be taken into account also.

Suppose, for example, that the bus manufacturer offers to provide routine maintenance that would otherwise cost $2,000 per year after tax. However, Mr. Pierce reconsiders and decides that the bus will probably be worth $10,000 after eight years. (Previously he assumed the bus would be worthless at the end of the lease.) Then the value of the lease increases by the present value of the maintenance savings and decreases by the present value of the lost salvage value.

Maintenance and salvage value are harder to predict than the cash flows shown in Table 26.2, and normally deserve a higher discount rate. Suppose that Mr. Pierce uses 12 percent. Then the maintenance savings are worth

---

[13]See Chapter 19 for the general definition and discussion of APV.

$$\sum_{t=0}^{7} \frac{2000}{(1.12)^t} = \$11,100$$

The lost salvage value is worth $\$10,000/(1.12)^8 = \$4,000$.[14] Remember that we previously calculated the value of the lease as $-\$700$. The revised value is therefore $-700 + 11,100 - 4,000 = \$6,400$. Now the lease looks like a good deal.

 ## 26.5 WHEN DO FINANCIAL LEASES PAY?

We have examined the value of a lease from the viewpoint of the lessee. However, the lessor's criterion is simply the reverse. As long as lessor and lessee are in the same tax bracket, every cash outflow to the lessee is an inflow to the lessor, and vice versa. In our numerical example, the bus manufacturer would project cash flows in a table like Table 26.2, but with the signs reversed. The value of the lease to the bus manufacturer would be

$$\begin{aligned}
\text{Value of} \\
\text{lease to} &= -89.02 + \frac{17.99}{1.065} + \frac{22.19}{(1.065)^2} + \frac{17.71}{(1.065)^3} + \frac{15.02}{(1.065)^4} + \frac{15.02}{(1.065)^5} \\
\text{lessor} \\
&\quad + \frac{13.00}{(1.065)^6} + \frac{10.98}{(1.065)^7} \\
&= +.70, \text{ or } \$700
\end{aligned}$$

In this case, the values to lessee and lessor exactly offset ($-\$700 + \$700 = 0$). The lessor can win only at the lessee's expense.

But both lessee and lessor can win if their tax rates differ. Suppose that Greymare paid no tax ($T_c = 0$). Then the only cash flows of the bus lease would be

	Year							
	0	1	2	3	4	5	6	7
Cost of new bus	+100							
Lease payment	−16.9	−16.9	−16.9	−16.9	−16.9	−16.9	−16.9	−16.9

These flows would be discounted at 10 percent, because $r_D(1 - T_c) = r_D$ when $T_c = 0$. The value of the lease is

$$\text{Value of lease} = +100 - \sum_{t=0}^{7} \frac{16.9}{(1.10)^t}$$
$$= +100 - 99.18 = +.82, \text{ or } \$820$$

In this case there is a net gain of $\$700$ to the lessor (who has the 35 percent tax rate) *and* a net gain of $\$820$ to the lessee (who pays zero tax). This mutual gain is at the expense of the government. On one hand, the government gains from the lease contract because it can tax the lease payments. On the other hand, the contract allows the lessor to take advantage of depreciation and interest tax shields which are

---

[14]For simplicity, we have assumed that maintenance expenses are paid at the start of the year and that salvage value is measured at the *end* of year 8.

of no use to the lessee. However, because the depreciation is accelerated and the interest rate is positive, the government suffers a net loss in the present value of its tax receipts as a result of the lease.

Now you should begin to understand the circumstances in which the government incurs a loss on the lease and the other two parties gain. Other things being equal, the potential gains to lessor and lessee are highest when

- The lessor's tax rate is substantially higher than the lessee's.
- The depreciation tax shield is received early in the lease period.
- The lease period is long and the lease payments are concentrated toward the end of the period.
- The interest rate r_D is high—if it were zero, there would be no advantage in present value terms to postponing tax.

Lessors are constantly on the lookout for arrangements that increase the potential gains from leasing. Some of the most ingenious arrangements involve cross-border leases and take advantage of the fact that different tax authorities define "ownership" in different ways. For example, suppose that an asset is bought by a company in Switzerland, which then "leases" the asset to a firm in the United States. As the legal owner, the company can depreciate the asset for tax purposes in Switzerland. But the terms of the lease may be such that in the United States the user of the asset is regarded as the *effective* owner and therefore gets to depreciate it for tax purposes. Needless to say, the tax authorities are keen to prevent such "double-dipping," but, as soon as one opportunity is blocked off, another seems to arise.

∫UMMARY

A lease is just an extended rental agreement. The owner of the equipment (the *lessor*) allows the user (the *lessee*) to operate the equipment in exchange for regular lease payments.

There is a wide variety of possible arrangements. Short-term, cancelable leases are known as *operating leases*. In these leases the lessor bears the risks of ownership. Long-term, noncancelable leases are called *full-payout, financial*, or *capital* leases. In these leases the lessee bears the risks. Financial leases are *sources of financing* for assets the firm wishes to acquire and use for an extended period.

The key to understanding operating leases is equivalent annual cost. In a competitive leasing market, the annual operating lease payment will be forced down to the lessor's equivalent annual cost. Operating leases are attractive to equipment users if the lease payment is less than the *user's* equivalent annual cost of buying the equipment. Operating leases make sense when the user needs the equipment only for a short time, when the lessor is better able to bear the risks of obsolescence, or when the lessor can offer a good deal on maintenance. Remember too that operating leases often have valuable options attached.

A financial lease extends over most of the economic life of the leased asset and cannot be canceled by the lessee. Signing a financial lease is like signing a secured loan to finance purchase of the leased asset. With financial leases, the choice is not "lease versus buy" but "lease versus borrow."

Many companies have sound reasons for financing via leases. For example, companies that are not paying taxes can usually strike a favorable deal with a taxpaying lessor. Also, it may be less costly and time-consuming to sign a standardized lease contract than to negotiate a long-term secured loan.

When a firm borrows money, it pays the after-tax rate of interest on its debt. Therefore, the opportunity cost of lease financing is the after-tax rate of interest on the firm's bonds. To value a financial lease, we need to discount the incremental cash flows from leasing by the after-tax interest rate.

An equivalent loan is one that commits the firm to exactly the same future cash flows as a financial lease. When we calculate the net present value of the lease, we are measuring the difference between the amount of financing provided by the lease and the financing provided by the equivalent loan:

$$\begin{matrix} \text{Value} \\ \text{of lease} \end{matrix} = \begin{matrix} \text{financing provided} \\ \text{by lease} \end{matrix} - \begin{matrix} \text{value of} \\ \text{equivalent loan} \end{matrix}$$

We can also analyze leases from the lessor's side of the transaction, using the same approaches we developed for the lessee. If lessee and lessor are in the same tax bracket, they will receive exactly the same cash flows but with signs reversed. Thus, the lessee can gain only at the lessor's expense, and vice versa. However, if the lessee's tax rate is lower than the lessor's, then both can gain at the federal government's expense.

FURTHER READING

A useful general reference on leasing is:
J. S. Schallheim: *Lease or Buy? Principles for Sound Decisionmaking,* Harvard Business School Press, Boston, MA, 1994.

The approach to valuing financial leases presented in this chapter is based on:
S. C. Myers, D. A. Dill, and A. J. Bautista: "Valuation of Financial Lease Contracts," *Journal of Finance,* 31:799–819 (June 1976).

J. R. Franks and S. D. Hodges: "Valuation of Financial Lease Contracts: A Note," *Journal of Finance,* 33:647–669 (May 1978).

Other useful works include Nevitt and Fabozzi's book and the theoretical discussions of Miller and Upton and of Lewellen, Long, and McConnell:
P. K. Nevitt and F. J. Fabozzi: *Equipment Leasing,* 4th ed., Frank Fabozzi Associates, 2000.

M. H. Miller and C. W. Upton: "Leasing, Buying and the Cost of Capital Services," *Journal of Finance,* 31:761–786 (June 1976).

W. G. Lewellen, M. S. Long, and J. J. McConnell: "Asset Leasing in Competitive Capital Markets," *Journal of Finance,* 31:787–798 (June 1976).

Harold Bierman gives a detailed account of leasing and the AMT in:
H. Bierman: "Buy versus Lease with an Alternative Minimum Tax," *Financial Management,* 17:87–92 (Winter 1988).

The options embedded in many operating leases are discussed in:
T. E. Copeland and J. E. Weston: "A Note on the Evaluation of Cancelable Operating Leases," *Financial Management,* 11:68–72 (Summer 1982).

J. J. McConnell and J. S. Schallheim: "Valuation of Asset Leasing Contracts," *Journal of Financial Economics,* 12:237–261 (August 1983).

S. R. Grenadier, "Valuing Lease Contracts: A Real Options Approach," *Journal of Financial Economics,* 38:297–331 (July 1995).

QUIZ

1. The following terms are often used to describe leases:
   a. Direct
   b. Full-service
   c. Operating
   d. Financial
   e. Rental
   f. Net
   g. Leveraged
   h. Sale and lease-back
   i. Full-payout

   Match one or more of these terms with each of the following statements:

   A. The initial lease period is shorter than the economic life of the asset.
   B. The initial lease period is long enough for the lessor to recover the cost of the asset.
   C. The lessor provides maintenance and insurance.
   D. The lessee provides maintenance and insurance.
   E. The lessor buys the equipment from the manufacturer.
   F. The lessor buys the equipment from the prospective lessee.
   G. The lessor finances the lease contract by issuing debt and equity claims against it.

2. Some of the following reasons for leasing are rational. Others are irrational or assume imperfect or inefficient capital markets. Which of the following reasons are the rational ones?
   a. The lessee's need for the leased asset is only temporary.
   b. Specialized lessors are better able to bear the risk of obsolescence.
   c. Leasing provides 100 percent financing and thus preserves capital.
   d. Leasing allows firms with low marginal tax rates to "sell" depreciation tax shields.
   e. Leasing increases earnings per share.
   f. Leasing reduces the transaction cost of obtaining external financing.
   g. Leasing avoids restrictions on capital expenditures.
   h. Leasing can reduce the alternative minimum tax.

3. Explain why the following statements are true:
   a. In a competitive leasing market, the annual operating lease payment equals the lessor's equivalent annual cost.
   b. Operating leases are attractive to equipment users if the lease payment is less than the *user's* equivalent annual cost.

4. True or false?
   a. Lease payments are usually made at the start of each period. Thus the first payment is usually made as soon as the lease contract is signed.
   b. Financial leases can still provide off-balance-sheet financing.
   c. The cost of capital for a financial lease is the interest rate the company would pay on a bank loan.
   d. An equivalent loan's principal plus after-tax interest payments exactly match the after-tax cash flows of the lease.
   e. A financial lease should not be undertaken unless it provides more financing than the equivalent loan.
   f. It makes sense for firms that pay no taxes to lease from firms that do.
   g. Other things equal, the net tax advantage of leasing increases as nominal interest rates increase.

5. Acme has branched out to rentals of office furniture to start-up companies. Consider a $3,000 desk. Desks last for six years and can be depreciated on a five-year ACRS schedule (see Table 6.4). What is the break-even operating lease rate for a new desk? Assume that lease rates for old and new desks are the same and that Acme's pretax administrative costs are $400 per desk per year. The cost of capital is 9 percent and the tax rate is

35 percent. Lease payments are made in advance, that is, at the start of each year. The inflation rate is zero.

6. Refer again to quiz question 5. Suppose a blue-chip company requests a six-year *financial* lease for a $3,000 desk. The company has just issued five-year notes at an interest rate of 6 percent per year. What is the break-even rate in this case? Assume administrative costs drop to $200 per year. Explain why your answers to question 5 and this question differ.

7. Suppose that National Waferonics has before it a proposal for a four-year financial lease. The firm constructs a table like Table 26.2. The bottom line of its table shows the lease cash flows:

	Year 0	Year 1	Year 2	Year 3
Lease cash flow	+62,000	−26,800	−22,200	−17,600

These flows reflect the cost of the machine, depreciation tax shields, and the after-tax lease payments. Ignore salvage value. Assume the firm could borrow at 10 percent and faces a 35 percent marginal tax rate.
   a. What is the value of the equivalent loan?
   b. What is the value of the lease?
   c. Suppose the machine's NPV under normal financing is −$5,000. Should National Waferonics invest? Should it sign the lease?

PRACTICE QUESTIONS

1. A lessee does not have to pay to buy the leased asset. Thus it's said that "leases provide 100 percent financing." Explain why this is *not* a true advantage to the lessee.

2. In quiz question 5 we assumed identical lease rates for old and new desks.
   a. How does the initial break-even lease rate change if the expected inflation rate is 5 percent per year? Assume that the *real* cost of capital does not change. *Hint:* Look at the discussion of equivalent annual costs in Chapter 6.
   b. How does your answer to part (a) change if wear and tear force Acme to cut lease rates by 10 percent in real terms for every year of a desk's age?

3. Look at Table 26.1. How would the initial break-even operating lease rate change if rapid technological change in limo manufacturing reduces the costs of new limos by 5 percent per year? *Hint:* We discussed technological change and equivalent annual costs in Chapter 6.

4. Why do you think that leasing of trucks, airplanes, and computers is such big business? What efficiencies offset the costs of running these leasing operations?

5. Financial leases make sense when the lessee faces a lower marginal tax rate than the lessor. Does this tax advantage carry over to *operating* leases?

The following questions all apply to financial leases.

6. Look again at the bus lease described in Table 26.2.
   a. What is the value of the lease if Greymare's marginal tax rate is $T_c = .20$?
   b. What would the lease value be if Greymare had to use straight-line depreciation for tax purposes?

7. In Section 26.4 we showed that the lease offered to Greymare Bus Lines had a positive NPV of $820 if Greymare paid no tax *and* a +$700 NPV to a lessor paying 35 percent tax. What is the minimum lease payment the lessor could accept under these assumptions? What is the maximum amount that Greymare could pay?

8. In Section 26.5 we listed four circumstances in which there are potential gains from leasing. Check them out by conducting a sensitivity analysis on the Greymare Bus Lines lease, assuming that Greymare does not pay tax. Try, in turn, (a) a lessor tax rate of 50 percent (rather than 35 percent), (b) immediate 100 percent depreciation in year 0 (rather than five-year ACRS), (c) a three-year lease with four annual rentals (rather than an eight-year lease), and (d) an interest rate of 20 percent (rather than 10 percent). In each case, find the minimum rental that would satisfy the lessor and calculate the NPV to the lessee.

9. In Section 26.5 we stated that if the interest rate were zero, there would be no advantage in postponing tax and therefore no advantage in leasing. Value the Greymare Bus Lines lease with an interest rate of zero. Assume that Greymare does not pay tax. Can you devise any lease terms that would make both a lessee and a lessor happy? (If you can, we would like to hear from you.)

10. A lease with a varying rental schedule is known as a *structured lease*. Try structuring the Greymare Bus Lines lease to increase value to the lessee while preserving the value to the lessor. Assume that Greymare does not pay tax. (*Note:* In practice the tax authorities will allow some structuring of rental payments but might be unhappy with some of the schemes you devise.)

11. Nodhead College needs a new computer. It can either buy it for $250,000 or lease it from Compulease. The lease terms require Nodhead to make six annual payments (prepaid) of $62,000. Nodhead pays no tax. Compulease pays tax at 35 percent. Compulease can depreciate the computer for tax purposes over five years. The computer will have no residual value at the end of year 5. The interest rate is 8 percent.
   a. What is the NPV of the lease for Nodhead College?
   b. What is the NPV for Compulease?
   c. What is the overall gain from leasing?

12. The Safety Razor Company has a large tax-loss carryforward and does not expect to pay taxes for another 10 years. The company is therefore proposing to lease $100,000 of new machinery. The lease terms consist of eight equal lease payments prepaid annually. The lessor can write the machinery off over seven years using the tax depreciation schedules given in Table 6.4. There is no salvage value at the end of the machinery's economic life. The tax rate is 35 percent, and the rate of interest is 10 percent. Wilbur Occam, the president of Safety Razor, wants to know the maximum lease payment that his company should be willing to make and the minimum payment that the lessor is likely to accept. Can you help him? How would your answer differ if the lessor was obliged to use straight-line depreciation?

13. The overall gain from leasing is the sum of the lease's value to the lessee and its value to the lessor. Construct simple numerical examples showing how this gain is affected by
   a. The rate of interest.
   b. The choice of depreciation schedule.
   c. The difference between the tax rates of the lessor and lessee.
   d. The length of the lease.

14. Many companies calculate the internal rate of return of the incremental after-tax cash flows from financial leases. What problems do you think this may give rise to? To what rate should the IRR be compared?

15. Discuss the following two opposite statements. Which do you think makes more sense?
   a. "Leasing is tax avoidance and should be legislated against."
   b. "Leasing ensures that the government's investment incentives work. It does so by allowing companies in nontaxpaying positions to take advantage of depreciation allowances."

1. Magna Charter has been asked to operate a Beaver bush plane for a mining company exploring north and west of Fort Liard. Magna will have a firm one-year contract with the mining company and expects that the contract will be renewed for the five-year duration of the exploration program. If the mining company renews at year 1, it will commit to use the plane for four more years.

   Magna Charter has the following choices.

   • Buy the plane for $500,000.
   • Take a one-year operating lease for the plane. The lease rate is $118,000, paid in advance.
   • Arrange a five-year, noncancelable financial lease at a rate of $75,000 per year, paid in advance.

   These are net leases: all operating costs are absorbed by Magna Charter.

   How would you advise Agnes Magna, the charter company's CEO? For simplicity assume five-year, straight-line depreciation for tax purposes. The company's tax rate is 35 percent. The weighted-average cost of capital for the bush-plane business is 14 percent, but Magna can borrow at 9 percent. The expected inflation rate is 4 percent.

   Ms. Magna thinks the plane will be worth $300,000 after five years. But if the contract with the mining company is not renewed (there is a 20 percent probability of this outcome at year 1), the plane will have to be sold on short notice for $400,000.

   If Magna Charter takes the five-year financial lease and the mining company cancels at year 1, Magna can sublet the plane, that is, rent it out to another user.

   Make additional assumptions as necessary.

2. Here is a variation on challenge question 1. Suppose Magna Charter is offered a five-year *cancelable* lease at an annual rate of $125,000, paid in advance. How would you go about analyzing this lease? You do not have enough information to do a full option pricing analysis, but you can calculate costs and present values for different scenarios.

3. Recalculate the value of the lease to Greymare Bus Lines if the company pays no taxes until year 3. Calculate the lease cash flows by modifying Table 26.2. Remember that the after-tax borrowing rate for periods 1 and 2 differs from the rate for periods 3 through 7.

MINI-CASE

Halverton Corporation

Helen James, a newly recruited financial analyst at Halverton Corporation, had just been asked to analyze a proposal to acquire a new dredger.

She reviewed the capital appropriation request. The dredger would cost $3.5 million and was expected to generate cash flows of $470,000 a year for nine years. After that point, the dredger would almost surely be obsolete and have no significant salvage value. The company's weighted-average cost of capital was 16 percent.

Helen proposed a standard DCF analysis, but this suggestion was brushed off by Halverton's top management. They seemed to be convinced of the merits of the investment but were unsure of the best way to finance it. Halverton could raise the money by issuing a secured eight-year note at an interest rate of 12 percent. However, Halverton had large tax-loss carryforwards from a disastrous foray into foreign exchange options. As a result, the company was unlikely to be in a tax-paying position for many years. Halverton's CEO thought it might be better to lease the dredger than to buy it.

Helen's first step was to invite two leasing companies, Mount Zircon Finance and First Cookham Bank, to submit proposals. Both companies were in a tax-paying position and could write off their investment in the dredger using five-year MACRS tax depreciation.

Helen received the following letters, the first from Mount Zircon Finance:

February 29, 2006

Dear Helen,

We appreciated the opportunity to meet you the other day and to discuss the possibility of providing lease finance for your proposed new JLT4 dredger. As you know, Mount Zircon has extensive experience in this field and, because of our large volumes and low borrowing costs, we are able to offer very attractive terms.

We would envisage offering a 9-year lease with 10 annual payments of $544,300, with the initial lease payment due on entering into the lease contract. This is equivalent to a borrowing cost of 11.5 percent per annum (i.e., 10 payments of $544,300 paid at the beginning of each year discounted at 11.5 percent amounts to $3,500,000).

We hope that you agree with us that this is an attractive rate. It is well below your company's overall cost of capital. Our leasing proposal will cover the entire $3.5 million cost of the dredger, thereby preserving Halverton's capital for other uses. Leasing will also allow a very attractive return on equity from your company's acquisition of this new equipment.

This proposal is subject to a routine credit check and review of Halverton's financial statements. We expect no difficulties on that score, but you will understand the need for due diligence.

Thank you for contacting Mount Zircon Finance. We look forward to hearing your response.

Sincerely yours,

Henry Attinger

For and on behalf of Mount Zircon Finance

The next letter was from First Cookham.

February 29, 2006

Dear Helen,

It was an honor to meet you the other day and to discuss how First Cookham Bank can help your company to finance its new dredger. First Cookham has a small specialized leasing operation. This enables us to tailor our proposals to our clients' needs.

We recommend that Halverton consider leasing the dredger on a 7-year term. Subject to documentation and routine review of Halverton's financial statements, we could offer a 7-year lease on the basis of 8 payments of $619,400 due at the beginning of each year. This is equivalent to a loan at an interest rate of 11.41 percent.

We expect that this lease payment will be higher than quoted by the larger, mass-market leasing companies, but our financial analysts have determined that, by offering a shorter lease, we can quote a lower interest rate.

We are confident that this is a highly competitive offer, and we look forward to your response.

Yours sincerely,

George Bucknall,

First Cookham Bank

Both proposals appeared to be attractive. However, Helen realized the need to undertake careful calculations before deciding whether leasing made sense and which firm was offering the better deal. She also wondered whether the terms offered were really as attractive as the two lessors claimed. Perhaps she could persuade them to cut their prices.

Questions

1. Calculate the NPV to Halverton of the two lease proposals.

2. Does the dredger have a positive NPV with (a) ordinary financing, (b) lease financing?

3. Calculate the NPVs of the leases from the lessors' viewpoints. Is there a chance that they could offer more attractive terms?

4. Evaluate the arguments presented by each of the lessors.

Useful material and data on bond markets are available on:

www.bondmarkets.com *(website of the Bond Market Association. Includes useful statistics)*

www.bondsonline.com

www.bondresources.com/main.html

http://bonds.yahoo.com

www.duke.edu/~charvey/applets/Bond/test.html *(nice graphics illustrating effect of interest rate on bond prices)*

www.finpipe.com *(explanations of bond markets)*

www.hsh.com

www.investinginbonds.com *(also contains links to related sites)*

www.loanpricing.com *(useful statistics on corporate bond issuance)*

http://money.cnn.com/markets/bondcenter

http://ourworld.compuserve.com/homepages/martinhighmore *(bond calculator)*

The websites of the ratings services provide information and data on bond risk:

www.standardandpoors.com

www.moodys.com

For material on the estimation of default probabilities see:

www.kmv.com

www.riskmetrics.com

Here are some sites that focus on project finance:

www.hbs.edu/projfinportal

www.infrastructure.com

www.ipfa.org

For material on bankruptcies and bankruptcy procedures see:

www.abiworld.org

www.bankrupt.com

www.bankruptcydata.com

www.law.cornell.edu/uscode/11 *(a technical description of the bankruptcy code)*

The following sites contain material on leasing:

www.elaonline.com *(the site for the Equipment Leasing Association)*

www.gecapital.com

www.leasingcanada.com *(includes a lease calculator)*

RISK MANAGEMENT

TO ADD VALUE companies need to take risks. But they try to avoid those risks that carry no compensating gains. Consider, for example, Green Mountain Coffee, which buys and roasts each year about 11 million pounds of coffee. In the past four years the price of coffee has swung between about $.40 and $3.00 a pound. Green Mountain could be knocked badly off course by such fluctuations. It therefore fixes in advance the price for about 40 percent of its coffee needs and it uses coffee futures and options to reduce even further the risk of sudden price hikes.

No two companies are exposed to the same risks. Some financial managers lie awake worrying about the price of oil or copper; others may sweat about changes in interest rates or exchange rates. Part Eight explains how each can achieve peace of mind. We start in Chapter 27 with an overview of the objectives of risk management and with corporate purchases of insurance. The rest of the chapter focuses on the risk of changes in commodity prices and interest rates. You will discover there how commodity and financial futures markets work.

Chapter 28 turns to the special risks of doing business internationally. These largely follow from fluctuations in exchange rates, so we explain how exchange rates are related to international differences in interest rates and inflation.

CHAPTER TWENTY-SEVEN

MANAGING RISK

MOST OF THE time we take risk as God-given. An asset or business has its beta, and that's that. Its cash flow is exposed to unpredictable changes in raw material costs, tax rates, technology, and a long list of other variables. There's nothing the manager can do about it.

That's not wholly true. To some extent managers can choose the risks that the business takes. We have already come across one way that they can do so. In our discussion of real options in Chapter 22 we described how companies reduce risk by building flexibility into their operations. A company that uses standardized machine tools rather than specialized equipment lowers the cost of bailing out if things go wrong. A petrochemical plant that is designed to use either oil or natural gas as a feedstock reduces the impact of an unfavorable shift in relative fuel prices. And so on.

In this chapter we shall explain how companies also enter into financial contracts that insure against or hedge (i.e., offset) a variety of business hazards. But first we should give some reasons *why* they do so.

Insurance and hedging are seldom free: At best they are zero-NPV transactions.[1] Most businesses insure or hedge to reduce risk, not to make money. Why, then, bother to reduce risk in this way? For one thing, it makes financial planning easier and reduces the odds of an embarrassing cash shortfall. A shortfall might mean only an unexpected trip to the bank, but if financing is hard to obtain on short notice, the company might need to cut back its capital expenditure program. In extreme cases an un-hedged setback could trigger financial distress or even bankruptcy. Banks and bondholders are aware of this possibility, and, before lending to your firm, they will often insist that it is properly insured.

In some cases hedging also makes it easier to decide whether an operating manager deserves a stern lecture or a pat on the back. Suppose your confectionery division shows a 60 percent profit increase in a period when cocoa prices decline by 12 percent. How much of the increase is due to the change in cocoa prices and how much to good management? If cocoa prices were hedged, it's probably good management. If they were not, things have to be sorted out with hindsight by asking, What would profits have been *if* cocoa prices had been hedged?[2]

Finally, hedging extraneous events can help focus the operating manager's attention. It's naive to expect the manager of the confectionery division *not* to worry about cocoa prices if her bottom line and bonus depend on them. That worrying time would be better spent if the prices were hedged.[3]

Of course, managers are not paid to avoid all risks, but if they can reduce their exposure to risks for which there are no compensating rewards, they can afford to place larger bets when the odds are in their favor.

27.1 INSURANCE

Most businesses buy insurance against a variety of hazards—the risk that their plant will be damaged by fire; that their ships, planes, or vehicles will be involved in accidents; that the firm will be held liable for environmental damage; and so on.

---

[1]Hedging transactions are zero-NPV when trading is costless and markets are completely efficient. In practice the firm has to pay small trading costs at least.

[2]Many large firms insure or hedge away operating divisions' risk exposures by setting up internal, make-believe markets between each division and the treasurer's office. Trades in the internal markets are at real (external) market prices. The object is to relieve the operating managers of risks outside their control. The treasurer makes a separate decision on whether to offset the *firm's* exposure.

[3]A Texas oilman who lost hundreds of millions in ill-fated deals protested, "Why should I worry? Worry is for strong minds and weak characters." If there are any financial managers with weak minds and strong characters, we especially advise them to hedge whenever they can.

When a firm takes out insurance, it is simply transferring the risk to the insurance company. Insurance companies have some advantages in bearing risk. First, they may have considerable experience in insuring similar risks, so they are well placed to estimate the probability of loss and price the risk accurately. Second, they may be skilled at providing advice on measures that the firm can take to reduce the risk, and they may offer lower premiums to firms that take this advice. Third, an insurance company can *pool* risks by holding a large, diversified portfolio of policies. The claims on any individual policy can be highly uncertain, yet the claims on a portfolio of policies may be very stable. Of course, insurance companies cannot diversify away macroeconomic risks; firms use insurance policies to reduce their specific risk, and they find other ways to avoid macro risks.

Insurance companies also suffer some *disadvantages* in bearing risk, and these are reflected in the prices they charge. Suppose your firm owns a $1 billion offshore oil platform. A meteorologist has advised you that there is a 1-in-10,000 chance that in any year the platform will be destroyed as a result of a storm. Thus the *expected* loss from storm damage is $1 billion/10,000 = $100,000.

The risk of storm damage is almost certainly not a macroeconomic risk and can potentially be diversified away. So you might expect that an insurance company would be prepared to insure the platform against such destruction as long as the premium was sufficient to cover the expected loss. In other words, a fair premium for insuring the platform should be $100,000 a year.[4] Such a premium would make insurance a zero-NPV deal for your company. Unfortunately, no insurance company would offer a policy for only $100,000. Why not?

- *Reason 1: Administrative costs.* An insurance company, like any other business, incurs a variety of costs in arranging the insurance and handling any claims. For example, disputes about the liability for environmental damage can eat up millions of dollars in legal fees. Insurance companies need to recognize these costs when they set their premiums.

- *Reason 2: Adverse selection.* Suppose that an insurer offers life insurance policies with "no medical needed, no questions asked." There are no prizes for guessing who will be most tempted to buy this insurance. Our example is an extreme case of the problem of *adverse selection*. Unless the insurance company can distinguish between good and bad risks, the latter will always be most eager to take out insurance. Insurers increase premiums to compensate.

- *Reason 3: Moral hazard.* Two farmers met on the road to town. "George," said one, "I was sorry to hear about your barn burning down." "Shh," replied the other, "that's tomorrow night." The story is an example of another problem for insurers, known as *moral hazard*. Once a risk has been insured, the owner may be less careful to take proper precautions against damage. Insurance companies are aware of this and factor it into their pricing.

When these extra costs are small, insurance may be close to a zero-NPV transaction. When they are large, insurance may be a costly way to protect against risk.

Many insurance risks are *jump risks*; one day there is not a cloud on the horizon and the next day the hurricane hits. The risks can also be huge. For example, Hurricane Andrew, which devastated Florida, cost insurance companies $17 bil-

---

[4]This is imprecise. If the premium is paid at the beginning of the year and the claim is not settled until the end, then the zero-NPV premium equals the discounted value of the expected claim or $100,000/(1 + r)$.

lion; the attack on the World Trade Center is likely to involve payments of more than $35 billion.

Many in the industry worry that one day a major disaster will wipe out a large proportion of the capital of the U.S. insurance industry. Therefore, insurance companies have been looking for ways to share these risks with investors. One solution is for the insurance company to issue *catastrophe bonds* (or *Cat bonds*). The payment on a Cat bond depends on whether a catastrophe occurs and how much is lost.[5]

The first public issue of a Cat bond was made by the Swiss insurance giant, Winterthur. As a major provider of automobile insurance, Winterthur wanted to protect itself against the risk that storm damage could lead to an unusually large number of claims. Therefore, when it issued its bond, the company stated that it would not pay the annual interest if ever there was a hailstorm in Switzerland which damaged at least 6,000 cars that it had insured. In effect, owners of the Winterthur Cat bonds coinsured the company's risks.

How British Petroleum (BP) Changed Its Insurance Strategy[6]

Major public companies typically buy insurance against large potential losses and self-insure against routine ones. The idea is that large losses can trigger financial distress. On the other hand, routine losses for a corporation are predictable, so there is little point paying premiums to an insurance company and receiving back a fairly constant proportion as claims.

BP Amoco has challenged this conventional wisdom. Like all oil companies, BP is exposed to a variety of potential losses. Some arise from routine events such as vehicle accidents and industrial injuries. At the other extreme, they may result from catastrophes such as a major oil spill or the loss of an offshore oil rig. In the past BP purchased considerable external insurance.[7] During the 1980s it paid out an average of $115 million a year in insurance premiums and recovered $25 million a year in claims.

BP then took a hard look at its insurance strategy. It decided to allow local managers to insure against routine risks, for in those cases insurance companies have an advantage in assessing and pricing risk and compete vigorously against one another. However, it decided not to insure against most losses above $10 million. For these larger, more specialized risks BP felt that insurance companies had less ability to assess risk and were less well placed to advise on safety measures. As a result, BP concluded, insurance against large risks was not competitively priced.

How much extra risk did BP assume by its decision not to insure against major losses? BP estimated that large losses of above $500 million could be expected to occur once in 30 years. But BP is a huge company with equity worth about $180 billion. So even a $500 million loss, which could throw most companies into bankruptcy, would translate after tax into a fall of less than 1 percent in the value of

---

[5]For a discussion of Cat bonds and other techniques to spread insurance risk, see N. A. Doherty, "Financial Innovation in the Management of Catastrophe Risk," *Journal of Applied Corporate Finance* 10 (Fall 1997), pp. 84–95; and K. Froot, "The Market for Catastrophe Risk: A Clinical Examination," *Journal of Financial Economics* 60 (2001), pp. 529–571.

[6]Our description of BP's insurance strategy draws heavily on N. A. Doherty and C. W. Smith, Jr., "Corporate Insurance Strategy: The Case of British Petroleum," *Journal of Applied Corporate Finance* 6 (Fall 1993), pp. 4–15.

[7]However, with one or two exceptions insurance has not been available for the very largest losses of $500 million or more.

BP's equity. BP concluded that this was a risk worth taking. In other words, it concluded that for large, low-probability risks the stock market was a more efficient risk-absorber than the insurance industry.

BP Amoco is not the only company that has looked at the package of risks that it faces and the way that these risks should be managed. Here is how *The Economist* summarized risk management in Duke Energy:[8]

> Duke's risk managers are currently designing a model that examines different types of risk together: movements in exchange rates, changes in raw material prices, downtime caused by distribution failures, and so on. This is supposed to produce an "aggregate loss distribution," which estimates the likelihood that several events could happen at once and sink the company. With this better understanding of the company's aggregate risk, Duke's managers can make a more informed decision about how much of this potential loss should be absorbed by shareholders, how much hedged in the financial markets, and how much transferred to insurers.

 27.2 HEDGING WITH FUTURES

Hedging involves taking on one risk to offset another. We will explain shortly how to set up a hedge, but first we will give some examples and describe some tools that are specially designed for hedging. These are futures, forwards, and swaps. Together with options, they are known as *derivative instruments* or *derivatives* because their value depends on the value of another asset. You can think of them as side bets on the value of the underlying asset.[9]

We start with the oldest actively traded derivative instruments, **futures contracts.** Futures were originally developed for agricultural and other commodities. For example, suppose that a wheat farmer expects to have 100,000 bushels of wheat to sell next September. If he is worried that the price may decline in the interim, he can hedge by selling 100,000 bushels of September wheat futures. In this case he agrees to deliver 100,000 bushels of wheat in September at a price that is set today. Do not confuse this futures contract with an option, in which the holder has a choice whether to make delivery; the farmer's futures contract is a firm promise to deliver wheat.

A miller is in the opposite position. She needs to *buy* wheat after the harvest. If she would like to fix the price of this wheat ahead of time, she can do so by *buying* wheat futures. In other words, she agrees to take delivery of wheat in the future at a price that is fixed today. The miller also does not have an option; if she holds the contract to maturity, she is obliged to take delivery.

Both the farmer and the miller have less risk than before.[10] The farmer has hedged risk by *selling* wheat futures; this is termed a *short hedge*. The miller has hedged risk by *buying* wheat futures; this is known as a *long hedge*.

---

[8]"Meet the Riskmongers," *The Economist*, July 18, 1998, p. 93.

[9]"Side bet" conjures up an image of wicked speculators. Derivatives attract their share of speculators, some of whom may be wicked, but they are also used by sober and prudent businesspeople to reduce risk.

[10]We oversimplify. For example, the miller won't reduce risk if bread prices vary in proportion to the postharvest wheat price. In this case the miller is in the hazardous position of having fixed her cost but not her selling price. This point is discussed in A. C. Shapiro and S. Titman, "An Integrated Approach to Corporate Risk Management," *Midland Corporate Finance Journal* 3 (Summer 1985), pp. 41–56.

Future	Exchange	Future	Exchange
Barley	WPG	Orange juice	NYBOT
Corn	CBT, MCE	Sugar	LIFFE, NYBOT
Oats	CBT		
Wheat	CBT, KC, MCE, MPLS	Aluminum	LME
		Copper	COMEX, LME
		Gold	COMEX
Soybeans	CBT, MCE	Lead	LME
Soybean meal	CBT	Nickel	LME
Soybean oil	CBT	Silver	COMEX
		Tin	LME
Live cattle	CME	Zinc	LME
Lean hogs	CME		
		Crude oil	IPE, NYMEX
Cocoa	LIFFE, NYBOT	Gas oil	IPE
Coffee	LIFFE, NYBOT	Heating oil	NYMEX
Cotton	NYBOT	Natural gas	IPE, NYMEX
Lumber	CME	Unleaded gasoline	NYMEX

TABLE 27.1

Some commodity futures and the principal exchanges on which they are traded.

Key to abbreviations:

CBT	Chicago Board of Trade	LME	London Metal Exchange
CME	Chicago Mercantile Exchange	MCE	MidAmerica Commodity Exchange
COMEX	Commodity Exchange Division of NYMEX	MPLS	Minneapolis Grain Exchange
IPE	International Petroleum Exchange of London	NYBOT	New York Board of Trade
KC	Kansas City Board of Trade	NYMEX	New York Mercantile Exchange
LIFFE	London International Financial Futures and Options Exchange	WPG	Winnipeg Commodity Exchange

The price of wheat for immediate delivery is known as the *spot price*. When the farmer sells wheat futures, the price that he agrees to take for his wheat may be very different from the spot price. But as the date for delivery approaches, a futures contract becomes more and more like a spot contract and the price of the future snuggles up to the spot price.

The farmer may decide to wait until his futures contract matures and then deliver wheat to the buyer. In practice such delivery is very rare, for it is more convenient for the farmer to buy back the wheat futures just before maturity.[11] If he is properly hedged, any loss on his wheat crop will be exactly offset by the profit on his sale and subsequent repurchase of wheat futures.

Commodity and Financial Futures

Futures contracts are bought and sold on organized futures exchanges. Table 27.1 lists the principal commodity futures contracts and the exchanges on which they are traded. Notice that our farmer and miller are not the only businesses that can hedge

[11]In the case of some of the financial futures described below, you *cannot* deliver the asset. At maturity the buyer simply receives (or pays) the difference between the spot price and the price at which he or she agreed to purchase the asset.

Future	Exchange	Future	Exchange
U.S. Treasury bonds	CBT	Dow Jones Industrial Average	CBT
U.S. Treasury notes	CBT	S&P 500 Index	CME
U.S. agency notes	CBT	European equity index (Dow Jones	Eurex
German government bonds (bunds)	Eurex	Euro Stoxx)	
Japanese government bonds (JGBs)	Simex, TSE	French equity index (CAC)	MATIF
British government bonds (gilts)	LIFFE	German equity index (DAX)	Eurex
		Japanese equity index (Nikkei)	CME, OSE,
U.S. Treasury bills	CME		Simex
		UK equity index (FTSE)	LIFFE
LIBOR	CME	Individual stocks	LIFFE
Eurodollar deposits	CME	Euro	CME
Euroyen deposits	CME, Simex,		
	TIFFE	Japanese yen	CME

TABLE 27.2

Some financial futures and the principal exchanges on which they are traded.

Key to abbreviations:

CBT	Chicago Board of Trade
CME	Chicago Mercantile Exchange
LIFFE	London International Financial Futures and Options Exchange
MATIF	Marché à Terme d'Instruments Financiers
OSE	Osaka Securities Exchange
SIMEX	Singapore International Monetary Exchange
TIFFE	Tokyo International Financial Futures Exchange
TSE	Tokyo Stock Exchange

risk with commodity futures. The lumber company and the builder can hedge against changes in lumber prices, the copper producer and the cable manufacturer can hedge against changes in copper prices, the oil producer and the trucker can hedge against changes in gasoline prices, and so on.[12]

For many firms the wide fluctuations in interest rates and exchange rates have become at least as important a source of risk as changes in commodity prices. Financial futures are similar to commodity futures, but instead of placing an order to buy or sell a commodity at a future date, you place an order to buy or sell a financial asset at a future date. Table 27.2 lists some important financial futures. It is far from complete. You can trade futures on the Thailand stock market index, the South African rand, Finnish government bonds, and many other financial assets.

Financial futures have been a remarkably successful innovation. They were invented in 1972; within a few years, trading in financial futures significantly exceeded trading in commodity futures.

---

[12]By the time you read this, the list of futures contracts will almost certainly be out of date. Unsuccessful contracts are regularly dropped, and at any time the exchanges may be seeking approval for literally dozens of new contracts.

The Mechanics of Futures Trading

When you buy or sell a futures contract, the price is fixed today but payment is not made until later. You will, however, be asked to put up margin in the form of either cash or Treasury bills to demonstrate that you have the money to honor your side of the bargain. As long as you earn interest on the margined securities, there is no cost to you.

In addition, futures contracts are *marked to market*. This means that each day any profits or losses on the contract are calculated; you pay the exchange any losses and receive any profits. For example, suppose that our farmer agreed to deliver 100,000 bushels of wheat at $2.80 a bushel. The next day the price of wheat futures declines to $2.75 a bushel. The farmer now has a profit on his sale of $100,000 \times $.05 = $5,000$. The exchange's clearinghouse therefore pays this $5,000 to the farmer. You can think of the farmer as closing out his position every day and then opening up a new position. Thus after the first day the farmer has realized a profit of $5,000 on his trade and now has an obligation to deliver wheat for $2.75 a bushel. The $.05 that the farmer has already been paid *plus* the $2.75 that remains to be paid equals the $2.80 selling price at which the farmer originally agreed to deliver wheat.

Of course, our miller is in the opposite position. The fall in the futures price leaves her with a *loss* of $.05 a bushel. She must, therefore, pay over this loss to the exchange's clearinghouse. In effect the miller closes out her initial purchase at a $.05 loss and opens a new contract to take delivery at $2.75 a bushel.[13]

Spot and Futures Prices—Financial Futures

If you want to buy a security, you have a choice. You can buy it for immediate delivery at the spot price. Alternatively, you can place an order for later delivery; in this case you buy at the futures price. When you buy a financial future, you end up with exactly the same security that you would have if you bought in the spot market. However, there are two differences. First, you don't pay for the security up front, and so you can earn interest on its purchase price. Second, you miss out on any dividend or interest that is paid in the interim. This tells us something about the relationship between the spot and futures prices:[14]

$$\frac{\text{Futures price}}{(1 + r_f)^t} = \frac{\text{spot}}{\text{price}} - PV \left(\begin{array}{c} \text{dividends or} \\ \text{interest payments} \\ \text{forgone} \end{array} \right)$$

Here r_f is the t-period risk-free interest rate. An example will show how and why this formula works.

Example: Stock Index Futures   Suppose six-month stock index futures trade at 1,205 when the index is 1,190. The six-month interest rate is 4 percent, and the average dividend yield of stocks in the index is 1.6 percent per year. Are these numbers consistent?

---

[13]Notice that neither the farmer nor the miller need be concerned about whether the other party will honor his or her side of the bargain. The futures exchange guarantees the contract and protects itself by settling up profits and losses each day.

[14]This relationship is strictly true only if the contract is not marked to market. Otherwise the value of the future depends on the path of interest rates up to the delivery date. In practice this qualification is usually unimportant. See J. C. Cox, J. E. Ingersoll, and S. A. Ross, "The Relationship between Forward and Futures Prices," *Journal of Financial Economics* 9 (1981), pp. 321–346.

Suppose you buy the futures contract and set aside the money to exercise it. At a 4 percent annual rate, you'll earn about 2 percent interest over the next six months. Thus you invest

$$\frac{\text{Futures price}}{(1 + r_f)^t} = \frac{1,205}{1.02} = 1,181$$

What do you get in return? Everything you would have gotten by buying the index now at the spot price, except for the dividends paid over the next six months. If we assume, for simplicity, that a half-year's dividends are paid in month six (rather than evenly over six months), your payoff is

$$\text{Spot price} - \text{PV(dividends)} = 1,190 - \frac{1,190\,(.008)}{1.02} = 1,181$$

You get what you pay for.

Spot and Futures Prices—Commodities

The difference between buying *commodities* today and buying commodity futures is more complicated. First, because payment is again delayed, the buyer of the future earns interest on her money. Second, she does not need to store the commodities and, therefore, saves warehouse costs, wastage, and so on. On the other hand, the futures contract gives no *convenience yield*, which is the value of being able to get your hands on the real thing. The manager of a supermarket can't burn heating oil futures if there's a sudden cold snap, and he can't stock the shelves with orange juice futures if he runs out of inventory at 1 P.M. on a Saturday. All this means that for commodities,

$$\frac{\text{Futures price}}{(1 + r_f)^t} = \text{spot price} + \text{PV}\left(\begin{array}{c}\text{storage} \\ \text{costs}\end{array}\right) - \text{PV}\left(\begin{array}{c}\text{convenience} \\ \text{yield}\end{array}\right)$$

No one would be willing to hold the futures contract at a higher futures price or to hold the commodity at a lower futures price.[15]

It's interesting to compare the formulas for futures prices of commodities to the formulas for securities. PV(convenience yield) plays the same role as PV(dividends or interest payments forgone). But financial assets cost nothing to store, so PV(storage costs) does not appear in the formula for financial futures.

You can't observe PV(convenience yield) or PV(storage) separately, but you can infer the difference between them by comparing the spot price to the discounted futures price. This difference—that is, convenience yield less storage cost—is called *net convenience yield*.

Here is an example using quotes for August 2001. At that time the spot price of coffee was about 51 cents per pound. The futures price for March 2002 was 58.7 cents. Of course, if you bought and held the futures, you would not pay until March. The present value of this outlay is 57.4 cents, using a one-year interest rate of 4 percent. So PV(net convenience yield) is negative at 6.4 cents a pound:

$$\text{PV(net convenience yield)} = \text{spot price} - \frac{\text{futures price}}{1 + r_f}$$

$$= 51 - 57.4 = -6.4 \text{ cents}$$

---

[15]Our formula could overstate the futures price if no one is willing to hold the commodity, that is, if inventories fall to zero or some absolute minimum.

FIGURE 27.1

Weekly percentage net convenience yield (convenience yield *less* storage costs) for two commodities.

Source: R. S. Pindyck, "The Present Value Model of Rational Commodity Pricing," *Economic Journal* 103 (May 1993), pp. 511–530. We thank Professor Pindyck for updating the data.

Sometimes the net convenience yield is expressed as a percentage of the spot price, in this case as $-6.4/51 = -.125$, or -12.5 percent. Coffee in 2001 was in ample supply and evidently roasters had no worries that they would run short in the months ahead.

Figure 27.1 plots percentage net convenience yields for crude oil and gas oil (used for heating). Notice how much the spread between the spot and futures price for gas oil bounces around. When there are shortages or fears of an interruption of supply, traders may be prepared to pay 2 or more percent *per week* for the convenience of having oil in the tanks rather than the promise of future delivery.[16]

There is one further complication that we should note. There are some commodities that cannot be stored at all. You can't store electricity, for example. As a result, electricity supplied in, say, six-months' time is effectively a different commodity from electricity available now, and there is no simple link between today's price and that of a futures contract to buy or sell at the end of six months. Of course,

---

[16]For evidence that the net convenience yield is related to the level of inventories, see M. J. Brennan, "The Price of Convenience and the Valuation of Commodity Contingent Claims," in D. Lund and B. Øksendal (eds.), *Stochastic Models and Option Values*, North-Holland Publishing Company, Amsterdam, 1991.

generators and consumers will have their own views of what the spot price is likely to be when those six months have elapsed, and they may be more or less eager to fix today the price at which they buy or sell.

27.3 FORWARD CONTRACTS

Each day billions of dollars of futures contracts are bought and sold. This liquidity is possible only because futures contracts are standardized and mature on a limited number of dates each year.

Fortunately there is usually more than one way to skin a financial cat. If the terms of futures contracts do not suit your particular needs, you may be able to buy or sell a **forward contract.** Forward contracts are simply tailor-made futures contracts. The main forward market is in foreign currency. We will discuss forward exchange rates in the next chapter.

It is also possible to enter into a forward interest rate contract. For example, suppose that you know that at the end of six months you are going to need a three-month loan. You worry that interest rates will rise over the six-month period. You can lock in the interest rate on that loan by buying a *forward rate agreement (FRA)* from a bank.[17] For example, the bank might offer to sell you a six-month forward rate agreement on three-month LIBOR at 7 percent.[18] If at the end of six months the three-month LIBOR rate is greater than 7 percent, the bank will pay you the difference; if three-month LIBOR is less than 7 percent, you pay the bank the difference.[19]

Homemade Forward Contracts

Suppose that you borrow $90.91 for one year at 10 percent and lend $90.91 for two years at 12 percent. These interest rates are for loans made today; therefore, they are spot interest rates.

The cash flows on your transactions are as follows:

	Year 0	Year 1	Year 2
Borrow for 1 year at 10%	+90.91	−100	
Lend for 2 years at 12%	−90.91		+114.04
Net cash flow	0	−100	+114.04

Notice that you do not have any net cash outflow today but you have contracted to pay out money in year 1. The interest rate on this forward commitment is 14.04 percent. To calculate this forward interest rate, we simply worked out the extra return for lending for two years rather than one:

---

[17]Note that the party which profits from a rise in rates is described as the "buyer." In our example you would be said to "buy six against nine months" money, meaning that the forward rate agreement is for a three-month loan in six months' time.

[18]LIBOR (London interbank offered rate) is the interest rate at which major international banks in London lend each other dollars.

[19]Unlike futures contracts, forwards are not marked to market. Thus all profits or losses are settled when the contract matures.

$$\text{Forward interest rate} = \frac{(1 + 2\text{-year spot rate})^2}{1 + 1\text{-year spot rate}} - 1$$

$$= \frac{(1.12)^2}{1.10} - 1 = .1404, \text{ or } 14.04\%$$

In our example you manufactured a forward loan by borrowing short-term and lending long. But you can also run the process in reverse. If you wish to fix today the rate at which you borrow next year, you borrow long and lend the money until you need it next year.

27.4 SWAPS

Some company cash flows are fixed. Others vary with the level of interest rates, rates of exchange, prices of commodities, and so on. These characteristics may not always result in the desired risk profile. For example, a company that pays a fixed rate of interest on its debt might prefer to pay a floating rate, while another company that receives cash flows in euros might prefer to receive them in yen. Swaps allow them to change their risk in these ways.

The market for swaps is huge. In 2000 the total notional amount of swaps outstanding was estimated at over $50 trillion. The major part of this figure consisted of interest rate swaps, but it is also possible to swap different currencies, equity indexes, and commodities.[20] We will show first how interest rate swaps work, and then describe a currency swap. We conclude with a brief look at *default swaps*. The default swap is an example of a *credit derivative*, a relatively new box of tools for managing risk.

Interest Rate Swaps

Friendly Bancorp has made a five-year, $50 million loan to fund part of the construction cost of a large cogeneration project. The loan carries a fixed interest rate of 8 percent. Annual interest payments are therefore $4 million. Interest payments are made annually, and all the principal will be repaid at year 5.

Suppose that instead of receiving fixed interest payments of $4 million a year, the bank would prefer to receive floating-rate payments. It can do so by swapping the $4 million, five-year annuity (the fixed interest payments) into a five-year floating-rate annuity. We will show first how Friendly Bancorp can make its own homemade swap. Then we will describe a simpler procedure.

The bank can borrow at a 6 percent fixed rate for five years.[21] Therefore, the $4 million interest it receives can support a fixed-rate loan of $4/.06 = $66.67 million. The bank can now construct the homemade swap as follows: It borrows $66.67 million at a fixed interest rate of 6 percent for five years and simultaneously lends

---

[20]Data on swaps are provided by the Bank for International Settlements (see **www.bis.org/statistics**). Equity swaps typically involve one party receiving the dividends and capital gains on an equity index, while the other party receives a fixed or floating rate of interest. Similarly, in a commodity swap one party receives a payment linked to the commodity price and the other receives the interest rate.

[21]The spread between the bank's 6 percent borrowing rate and the 8 percent lending rate is the bank's profit on the project financing.

	Year					
	0	1	2	3	4	5
Homemade swap:						
1. Borrow $66.67 at 6% fixed rate	+66.67	−4	−4	−4	−4	−(4 + 66.67)
2. Lend $66.67 at LIBOR floating rate	−66.67	+.05 × 66.67	+LIBOR$_1$ × 66.67	+LIBOR$_2$ × 66.67	+LIBOR$_3$ × 66.67	+LIBOR$_4$ × 66.67 + 66.67
Net cash flow	0	−4+.05 × 66.67	−4 + LIBOR$_1$ × 66.67	−4 + LIBOR$_2$ × 66.67	−4 + LIBOR$_3$ × 66.67	−4 + LIBOR$_4$ × 66.67
Standard fixed-to-floating swap:						
Net cash flow	0	−4 + .05 × 66.67	−4 + LIBOR$_1$ × 66.67	−4 + LIBOR$_2$ × 66.67	−4 + LIBOR$_3$ × 66.67	−4 + LIBOR$_4$ × 66.67

TABLE 27.3

The top panel shows the cash flows to a homemade fixed-to-floating interest rate swap. The bottom panel shows the cash flows to a standard swap transaction.

the same amount at LIBOR. We assume that LIBOR is initially 5 percent.[22] LIBOR is a short-term interest rate, so future interest receipts will fluctuate as the bank's investment is rolled over.

The net cash flows to this strategy are shown in the top portion of Table 27.3. Notice that there is no net cash flow in year 0 and that in year 5 the principal amount of the short-term investment is used to pay off the $66.67 million loan. What's left? A cash flow equal to the *difference* between the interest earned (LIBOR × 66.67) and the $4 million outlay on the fixed loan. The bank also has $4 million per year coming in from the project financing, so it has transformed that fixed payment into a floating payment keyed to LIBOR.

Of course, there's an easier way to do this, shown in the bottom portion of Table 27.3. The bank can just enter into a five-year swap.[23] Naturally, Friendly Bancorp takes this easier route. Let's see what happens.

Friendly Bancorp calls a swap dealer, which is typically a large commercial or investment bank, and agrees to *swap* the payments on a $66.67 million fixed-rate loan for the payments on an equivalent floating-rate loan. The swap is known as a fixed-to-floating interest rate swap and the $66.67 million is termed the *notional principal* amount of the swap. Friendly Bancorp and the dealer are the *counterparties* to the swap.

The dealer is quoting a rate for five-year swaps of 6 percent against LIBOR.[24] This figure is sometimes quoted as a spread over the yield on U.S. Treasuries. For

---

[22]Maybe the short-term interest rate is below the five-year interest rate because investors expect interest rates to rise.

[23]Both strategies are equivalent to a series of forward contracts on LIBOR. The forward prices are $4 million each for LIBOR$_1$ × 66.67, LIBOR$_2$ × 66.67, and so on. Separately negotiated forward prices would not be $4 million for any one year, but the PVs of the "annuities" of forward prices would be identical.

[24]Notice that the swap rate always refers to the interest rate on the fixed leg of the swap. Rates are generally quoted against LIBOR, though dealers will also be prepared to quote rates against other short-term debt.

example, if the yield on five-year Treasury notes is 5.25 percent, the swap spread is .75 percent.[25]

The first payment on the swap occurs at the end of year 1 and is based on the starting LIBOR rate of 5 percent.[26] The dealer (who pays floating) owes the bank 5 percent of $66.67 million, while the bank (which pays fixed) owes the dealer $4 million (6 percent of $66.67 million). The bank therefore makes a net payment to the dealer of $4 - (.05 \times 66.67) = \$.67$ million:

Bank	←	.05 × $66.67 = $3.33	←	Counterparty
Bank	→	$4	→	Counterparty
Bank	→	Net = $.67	→	Counterparty

The second payment is based on LIBOR at year 1. Suppose it increases to 6 percent. Then the net payment is zero:

Bank	←	.06 × $66.67 = $4	←	Counterparty
Bank	→	$4	→	Counterparty
Bank	→	Net = 0	→	Counterparty

The third payment depends on LIBOR at year 2, and so on.

Notice that, when the two counterparties entered into the swap, the deal was fairly valued. In other words, the net cash flows had zero present value. What happens to the value of the swap as time passes? That depends on long-term interest rates. For example, suppose that after two years interest rates are unchanged, so a 6 percent note issued by the bank would continue to trade at its face value. In this case the swap still has zero value. (You can confirm this by checking that the NPV of a new three-year homemade swap is zero.) But if long rates increase over the two years to 7 percent (say), the value of a three-year note falls to

$$PV = \frac{4}{1.07} + \frac{4}{(1.07)^2} + \frac{4 + 66.67}{(1.07)^3} = \$64.92 \text{ million}$$

Now the fixed payments that the bank has agreed to make are less valuable and the swap is worth $66.67 - 64.92 = \$1.75$ million.

How do we know the swap is worth $1.75 million? Consider the following strategy:

1. The bank can enter a new three-year swap deal in which it agrees to *pay* LIBOR on the same notional principal of $66.67 million.

2. In return it receives fixed payments at the new 7 percent interest rate, that is, $.07 \times 66.67 = \$4.67$ per year.

The new swap cancels the cash flows of the old one, but it generates an extra $.67 million for three years. This extra cash flow is worth

$$PV = \sum_{t=1}^{3} \frac{.67}{(1.07)^t} = \$1.75 \text{ million}$$

---

[25]Swap spreads fluctuate. After Russia defaulted on its debt in 1998 and the U.S. hedge fund Long Term Capital Management (LTCM) came close to collapse, five-year swap spreads nearly doubled from 0.5 percent to 0.8 percent.

[26]More commonly, interest rate swaps are based on three-month LIBOR and involve quarterly cash payments.

Remember, ordinary interest rate swaps have no initial cost or value (NPV = 0), but their value drifts away from zero as time passes and long-term interest rates change. One counterparty wins as the other loses.

In our example, the swap dealer loses from the rise in interest rates. Dealers will try to hedge the risk of interest rate movements by engaging in a series of futures or forward contracts or by entering into an offsetting swap with a third party. As long as Friendly Bancorp and the other counterparty honor their promises, the dealer is fully protected against risk. The recurring nightmare for swap managers is that one party will default, leaving the dealer with a large unmatched position. This is called *counterparty risk*.

Currency Swaps

We now look briefly at an example of a currency swap.

Suppose that the Possum Company needs 11 million euros to help finance its European operations. We assume that the euro interest rate is about 5 percent, whereas the dollar rate is about 6 percent. Since Possum is better known in the United States, the financial manager decides not to borrow euros directly. Instead, the company issues $10 million of five-year 6 percent notes in the United States. Then it arranges with a counterparty to swap this dollar loan into euros. Under this arrangement the counterparty agrees to pay Possum sufficient dollars to service its dollar loan, and in exchange Possum agrees to make a series of annual payments in euros to the counterparty.

Here are Possum's cash flows (in millions):

	Year 0		Years 1–4		Year 5	
	Dollars	**Euros**	**Dollars**	**Euros**	**Dollars**	**Euros**
1. Issue dollar loan	+10		−.6		−10.6	
2. Swap dollars for euros	−10	+11	+.6	−.55	+10.6	−11.55
3. Net cash flow	0	+11	0	−.55	0	−11.55

Look first at the cash flows in year 0. Possum receives $10 million from its issue of dollar notes, which it then pays over to the swap counterparty. In return the counterparty sends Possum a check for €11 million. (We assume that at current rates of exchange $10 million is worth €11 million.)

Now move to years 1 through 4. Possum needs to pay interest of 6 percent on its debt issue, which works out at .06 × 10 = $.6 million. The swap counterparty agrees to provide Possum each year with sufficient cash to pay this interest and in return Possum makes an annual payment to the counterparty of 5 percent of €11 million, or €.55 million. Finally, in year 5 the swap counterparty pays Possum enough to make the final payment of interest and principal on its dollar notes ($10.6 million), while Possum pays the counterparty €11.55 million.

The combined effect of Possum's two steps (line 3) is to convert a 6 percent dollar loan into a 5 percent euro loan. You can think of the cash flows for the swap (line 2) as a series of contracts to buy euros in years 1 through 5. In each of years 1 through 4 Possum agrees to purchase $.6 million at a cost of .5 million euros; in year 5 it agrees to buy $10.6 million at a cost of 11.55 million euros.[27]

---

[27]Usually in a currency swap the two parties make an initial payment to each other (i.e., Possum pays the bank $10 million and receives €11 million). However, this is not necessary and Possum might prefer to buy the €11 million from another bank.

Credit Derivatives

In recent years there has been considerable growth in the use of *credit derivatives*, which protect lenders against the risk that a borrower will default. For example, bank A may be reluctant to refuse a loan to a major customer (customer X) but may be concerned about the total size of its exposure to that customer. Bank A can go ahead with the loan, but use credit derivatives to shuffle off the risk to bank B.

The most common credit derivative is known as a *default swap*. It works as follows. Bank A promises to pay a fixed sum each year to B as long as company X has not defaulted on its debts. If X defaults, B compensates A for the loss, but otherwise pays nothing. Thus you can think of B as providing A with long-term insurance against default in return for an annual insurance premium.[28]

Banks that have a portfolio of loans may be more concerned with the possibility of widespread defaults than with the risk of a single loan. In principle, they could negotiate a default swap on each individual loan. In practice, it is generally simpler to enter into a portfolio default swap that provides protection on the entire loan portfolio.

 27.5 HOW TO SET UP A HEDGE

To hedge risk the firm buys one asset and sells an equal amount of another asset. For example, our farmer owned 100,000 bushels of wheat and sold 100,000 bushels of wheat futures. As long as the wheat that the farmer owns is identical to the wheat that he has promised to deliver, this strategy minimizes risk.

In practice the wheat that the farmer owns and the wheat that he sells in the futures markets are unlikely to be identical. For example, if he sells wheat futures on the Kansas City exchange, he agrees to deliver hard, red winter wheat in Kansas City in September. But perhaps he is growing northern spring wheat many miles from Kansas City; in this case the prices of the two wheats will not move exactly together.

Figure 27.2 shows how changes in the prices of the two types of wheat may have been related in the past. Notice two things about this figure. First, the scatter of points suggests that the price changes are imperfectly related. If so, it is not possible to construct a hedge that eliminates all risk. Some residual, or *basis*, risk will remain. Second, the slope of the fitted line shows that a 1 percent change in the price of Kansas wheat was on average associated with an .8 percent change in the price of the farmer's wheat. Because the price of the farmer's wheat is relatively insensitive to changes in Kansas prices, he needs to sell $.8 \times 100,000$ bushels of wheat futures to minimize risk.

Let us generalize. Suppose that you already own an asset, A (e.g., wheat), and that you wish to hedge against changes in the value of A by making an offsetting sale of another asset, B (e.g., wheat futures). Suppose also that percentage changes in the value of A are related in the following way to percentage changes in the value of B:

$$\text{Expected change in value of A} = a + \delta \left(\text{change in value of B} \right)$$

---

[28] Another form of credit derivative is the credit option. In this case A would pay an up-front premium and B would assume the obligation to pay A in the event of X's default.

FIGURE 27.2

Hypothetical plot of past changes in the price of the farmer's wheat against changes in the price of Kansas City wheat futures. A 1 percent change in the futures price implies, on average, an .8 percent change in the price of the farmer's wheat.

Delta (δ) measures the sensitivity of A to changes in the value of B. It is also equal to the *hedge ratio*—that is, the number of units of B which should be sold to hedge the purchase of A. You minimize risk if you offset your position in A by the sale of delta units of B.[29]

The trick in setting up a hedge is to estimate the delta or hedge ratio. This often calls for a strong dose of judgment. For example, suppose that Antarctic Air would like to protect itself against a hike in oil prices. As the financial manager, you need to decide how much a rise in oil prices would affect firm value. Suppose the company spent $200 million on fuel last year. Other things equal, a 10 percent increase in the price of oil will cost the company an extra $.1 \times 200 = \$20$ million. But perhaps you can partially offset the higher costs by higher ticket prices, in which case earnings will fall by *less* than $20 million. Or perhaps an oil price rise will lead to a slowdown in business activity and therefore lower passenger numbers. In that case earnings will decline by *more* than $20 million. Working out the likely effect on firm *value* is even more tricky, because that depends on whether the rise is likely to be permanent. Perhaps the price rise will induce an increase in production or encourage consumers to economize on energy usage.

Sometimes in such cases some history may help. For example, you could look at how firm value changed in the past as oil prices changed. In other cases it may be possible to call on a little theory to set up the hedge.

Using Theory to Set Up the Hedge: An Example

Potterton Leasing has just purchased some equipment and arranged to rent it out for $2 million a year over eight years. At an interest rate of 12 percent, Potterton's rental income has a present value of $9.94 million:[30]

$$PV = \frac{2}{1.12} + \frac{2}{(1.12)^2} + \cdots + \frac{2}{(1.12)^8} = \$9.94 \text{ million}$$

---

[29]Notice that A, the item that you wish to hedge, is the dependent variable. Delta measures the sensitivity of A to changes in B.

[30]We ignore taxes in this example.

Potterton proposes to finance the deal by issuing a package of $1.91 million of one-year debt and $8.03 million of six-year debt, each with a 12 percent coupon. Think of its new asset (the stream of rental income) and the new liability (the issue of debt) as a package. Does Potterton stand to gain or lose on this package if interest rates change?

To answer this question, it is helpful to go back to the concept of duration that we introduced in Chapter 24. Duration, you may remember, is the weighted-average time to each cash flow. Duration is important because it is directly related to volatility. If two assets have the same duration, their prices will be equally affected by any change in interest rates. If we call the total value of Potterton's rental income V, then the duration of Potterton's rental income is calculated as follows:

$$\text{Duration} = \frac{1}{V} \left\{ [PV(C_1) \times 1] + [PV(C_2) \times 2] + [PV(C_3) \times 3] + \cdots \right\}$$

$$= \frac{1}{9.94} \left\{ \left[\frac{2}{1.12} \times 1 \right] + \left[\frac{2}{(1.12)^2} \times 2 \right] + \cdots + \left[\frac{2}{(1.12)^8} \times 8 \right] \right\}$$

$$= 3.9 \text{ years}$$

We can also calculate the duration of Potterton's new liabilities. The duration of the 1-year debt is 1 year, and the duration of the 6-year debt is 4.6 years. The duration of the package of 1- and 6-year debt is a weighted average of the durations of the individual issues:

$$\begin{aligned} \text{Duration of liability} &= (1.91/9.94) \times \text{duration of 1-year debt} \\ &\quad + (8.03/9.94) \times \text{duration of 6-year debt} \\ &= (.192 \times 1) + (.808 \times 4.6) = 3.9 \text{ years} \end{aligned}$$

Thus, both the asset (the lease) and the liability (the debt package) have a duration of 3.9 years. Therefore, both are affected equally by a change in interest rates. If rates rise, the present value of Potterton's rental income will decline, but the value of its debt obligation will also decline by the same amount. By equalizing the duration of the asset and that of the liability, Potterton has *immunized* itself against any change in interest rates. It looks as if Potterton's financial manager knows a thing or two about hedging.

When Potterton set up the hedge, it needed to find a package of loans that had a present value of $9.94 million and a duration of 3.9 years. Call the proportion of the proceeds raised by the six-year loan x and the proportion raised by the one-year loan $(1 - x)$. Then

$$\begin{aligned} \text{Duration of package} &= (x \times \text{duration of 6-year loan}) + [(1 - x) \\ &\quad \times \text{duration of 1-year loan}] \\ 3.9 \text{ years} &= (x \times 4.6 \text{ years}) + [(1 - x) \times 1 \text{ year}] \\ x &= .808 \end{aligned}$$

Since the package of loans must raise $9.94 million, Potterton needs to issue .808 × 9.94 = $8.03 million of the six-year loan.

An important feature of this hedge is that it is dynamic. As interest rates change and time passes, the duration of Potterton's asset may no longer be the same as that of its liability. Thus, to remain hedged against interest rate changes, Potterton must be prepared to keep adjusting the duration of its debt.

Cash Flows ($ millions)								
	Year							
	1	2	3	4	5	6	7	8
Balance at start of year	9.94	9.13	8.23	7.22	6.08	4.81	3.39	1.79
Interest at 12%	1.19	1.10	.99	.87	.73	.58	.40	.21
Sinking fund payment	.81	.90	1.01	1.13	1.27	1.42	1.60	1.79
Interest plus sinking fund payment	2.00	2.00	2.00	2.00	2.00	2.00	2.00	2.00

TABLE 27.4

Potterton can hedge by issuing this sinking fund bond that pays out $2 million each year.

If Potterton is not disposed to follow this dynamic hedging strategy, it has an alternative. It can devise a debt issue whose cash flows exactly match the rental income from the lease. For example, suppose that it issues an eight-year sinking fund bond; the amount of the sinking fund is $810,000 in year 1, and the payment increases by 12 percent annually. Table 27.4 shows that the bond payments (interest plus sinking fund) are $2 million in each year.

Since the cash flows on the asset exactly match those on the liability, Potterton's financial manager can now relax. Each year the manager simply collects the $2 million rental income and hands it to the bondholders. Whatever happens to interest rates, the firm is always perfectly hedged.

Why wouldn't Potterton's financial manager *always* prefer to construct matching assets and liabilities? One reason is that it may be relatively costly to devise a bond with a specially tailored pattern of cash flows. Another may be that Potterton is continually entering into new lease agreements and issuing new debt. In this case the manager can never relax; it may be simpler to keep the durations of the assets and liabilities equal than to maintain an exact match between the cash flows.

Options, Deltas, and Betas

Here's another case where some theory can help you set up a hedge. In Chapter 20 we came across options. These give you the right, but not the obligation, to buy or sell an asset. Options are derivatives; their value depends only on what happens to the price of the underlying asset.

The *option delta* summarizes the link between the option and the asset. For example, if you own an option to buy a share of Walt Disney stock, the change in the value of your investment will be the same as it would be if you held delta shares of Disney.

Since the option price is tied to the asset price, options can be used for hedging. Thus, if you own an option to buy a share of Disney and at the same time you sell delta shares of Disney, any change in the value of your position in the stock will be exactly offset by the change in the value of your option position.[31] In other words, you will be perfectly hedged—hedged, that is, for the next short period of time.

---

[31] We are assuming that you hold one option and hedge by selling δ shares. If you owned one share and wanted to hedge by selling options, you would need to sell 1/δ options.

Option deltas change as the stock price changes and time passes. Therefore, option-based hedges need to be adjusted frequently.

Options can be used to hedge commodities too. The miller could offset changes in the cost of future wheat purchases by buying call options on wheat (or on wheat futures). But this is not the simplest strategy if the miller is trying to lock in the future cost of wheat. She would have to check the option delta to determine how many options to buy, and she would have to keep track of changes in the option delta and reset the hedge as necessary.[32]

It's the same for financial assets. Suppose you hold a well-diversified portfolio of stocks with a beta of 1.0 and near-perfect correlation with the market return. You want to lock in the portfolio's value at year-end. You could accomplish this by selling call options on the index, but to maintain the hedge, the option position would have to be adjusted frequently. It's simpler just to sell index futures maturing at year-end.

Speaking of betas . . . what if your portfolio has a beta of .60, not 1.0? Then your hedge will require 40 percent fewer index futures contracts. And since your low-beta portfolio is probably not perfectly correlated with the market, there will be some basis risk as well. In this context our old friend beta (β) and the hedge ratio (δ) are one and the same. Remember, to hedge A with B, you need to know δ because

$$\text{Expected change in value of A} = a + \delta(\text{change in value of B})$$

When A is a stock or portfolio, and B is the market, we estimate beta from the same relationship:

$$\text{Expected change in stock or portfolio value} = a + \beta(\text{change in market index})$$

 ## 27.6 IS "DERIVATIVE" A FOUR-LETTER WORD?

Our earlier example of the farmer and miller showed how futures may be used to reduce business risk. However, if you were to copy the farmer and sell wheat futures without an offsetting holding of wheat, you would not be *reducing* risk: You would be *speculating*.

Speculators in search of large profits (and prepared to tolerate large losses) are attracted by the leverage that derivatives provide. By this we mean that it is not necessary to lay out much money up front and the profits or losses may be many times the initial outlay.[33] "Speculation" has an ugly ring, but a successful derivatives market needs speculators who are prepared to take on risk and provide more cautious people like our farmer and miller with the protection they need. For example, if an excess of farmers wish to sell wheat futures, the price of futures will be forced down until enough speculators are tempted to buy in the hope of a profit. If there is a surplus of millers wishing to buy wheat futures, the reverse will happen. The price of wheat futures will be forced *up* until speculators are drawn in to sell.

Speculation may be necessary to a thriving derivatives market, but it can get companies into serious trouble. Finance in the News describes how the German metals

---

[32]*Quiz:* What is the miller's position if she buys call options on wheat and simply holds them to maturity?

[33]For example, if you buy or sell forward, no money changes hands until the contract matures, though you may be required to put up margin to show that you can honor your commitment. This margin does not need to be cash; it can be in the form of safe securities.

THE DEBACLE AT METALLGESELLSCHAFT

In January 1994 the German industrial giant Metallgesellschaft shocked investors with news of huge losses in its U.S. oil subsidiary, MGRM. These losses, later estimated at over $1 billion, brought the firm to the brink of bankruptcy and it was saved only by a $1.9 billion rescue package from 120 banks.

The previous year MGRM had embarked on what looked like a sure-fire way to make money. It offered its customers forward contracts on deliveries of gasoline, heating oil, and diesel fuel for up to 10 years. These price guarantees proved extremely popular. By September 1993, MGRM had sold forward over 150 million barrels of oil at prices that were $3 to $5 a barrel over the prevailing spot prices.

As long as oil prices did not rise appreciably, MGRM stood to make a handsome profit from its forward sales, but if oil prices did return to their level of earlier years the result would be a calamitous loss. MGRM therefore sought to avoid such an outcome by buying energy futures. Unfortunately, the long-term futures contracts that were needed to offset MGRM's price guarantees did not exist. MGRM's solution was to enter into what is known as a "stack-and-roll" hedge. In other words, it bought a stack of short-dated futures contracts and, as these were about to expire, it rolled them over into a fresh stack of short-dated contracts.

MGRM was relaxed about the mismatch between the long-term maturity of its price guarantees and the much shorter maturity of its futures contracts. It could point to past history to justify its confidence, for in most years energy traders have placed a high value on owning the oil rather than having a promise of future delivery. In other words, the net convenience yield on oil has generally been positive (see Figure 27.1). As long as that continued to be the case, then each time that MGRM rolled over its futures contracts, it would be selling its maturing contracts at a higher price than it would need to pay for the stack of new contracts. However, if the net convenience yield were to become negative, the maturing futures contracts would sell for *less* than more distant ones. Unfortunately, this is what occurred in 1993. In that year there was a glut of oil, the storage tanks were full, and nobody was prepared to pay extra to get their hands on oil. The result was that MGRM was forced to pay a premium to roll over each stack of maturing contracts.

The fall in oil prices had another unfortunate consequence for MGRM. Futures contracts are marked to market. This means that the investor settles up the profits and losses on each contract as they arise. Therefore, as oil prices continued to fall in 1993, MGRM incurred losses on its purchases of oil futures. This resulted in huge margin calls.* The offsetting good news was that the fall in oil prices meant that its long-term forward contracts were looking increasingly profitable, but this profit was not money in the bank.

When Metallgesellschaft's board learned of these problems, it fired the chief executive and instructed the company to cease all hedging activities and to start negotiations with customers to cancel the long-term contracts. Almost immediately the fall in oil prices reversed. Within eight months the price had risen about 40 percent. If only MGRM had been able to hold on, it would have enjoyed a huge cash inflow.

Observers have continued to argue about the Metallgesellschaft debacle. Was the company's belief that the net convenience yield would remain positive a reasonable assumption or a gigantic speculation? How much did the company anticipate its cash needs and could it have financed them by borrowing on the strength of its long-term forward contracts? Did senior management mistake the margin calls for losses and just lose its nerve when it decided to liquidate the company's positions?

---

*In addition to buying futures contracts, MGRM also bought short-term over-the-counter forward contracts and commodity swaps. As these matured, MGRM had to make good the loss on them, even though it did not receive the gains on the price guarantees.

and oil trading company, Metallgesellschaft, took a $1 billion bath on its positions in oil futures. Metallgesellschaft had plenty of company. The Japanese company, Showa Shell, reported a loss of $1.5 billion on positions in foreign exchange futures. Another Japanese firm, Sumitomo Corporation, lost over $2 billion when a rogue trader tried to buy enough copper to control that market.[34] And in 1995 Baring Brothers, a blue-chip British merchant bank with a 200-year history, became insolvent. The reason: Nick Leeson, a trader in Baring's Singapore office, had placed very large bets on the Japanese stock market index resulting in losses of $1.4 billion.

These tales of woe have some cautionary messages for corporations. During the 1970s and 1980s many firms turned their treasury operations into profit centers and proudly announced their profits from trading in financial instruments. But it is not possible to make large profits in financial markets without also taking large risks, so these profits should have served as a warning rather than a matter for congratulation.

A Boeing 747 weighs 400 tons, flies at nearly 600 miles per hour, and is inherently very dangerous. But we don't ground 747s; we just take precautions to ensure that they are flown with care. Similarly, it is foolish to suggest that firms should ban the use of derivatives, but it makes obvious sense to take precautions against their misuse. Here are two bits of horse sense:

- *Precaution 1*. Don't be taken by surprise. By this we mean that senior management needs to monitor regularly the value of the firm's derivatives positions and to know what bets the firm has placed. At its simplest, this might involve asking what would happen if interest rates or exchange rates were to change by 1 percent. But large banks and consultants have also developed sophisticated models for measuring the risk of derivatives positions. J. P. Morgan, for example, offers corporate clients its *RiskMetrics* software to keep track of their risk.

- *Precaution 2*. Place bets only when you have some comparative advantage that ensures the odds are in your favor. If a bank were to announce that it was drilling for oil or launching a new soap powder, you would rightly be suspicious about whether it had what it takes to succeed. Conversely, when an industrial corporation places large bets on interest rates or exchange rates, it is competing against some highly paid pros in banks and other financial institutions. Unless it is better informed than they are about future interest rates or exchange rates, it should use derivatives for hedging, not for speculation.

Imprudent speculation in derivatives is undoubtedly an issue of concern for the company's shareholders, but is it a matter for more general concern? Some people believe so. They point to the huge volume of trading in derivatives and argue that speculative losses could lead to major defaults that might threaten the whole financial system. These worries have led to calls for increased regulation of derivatives markets.

Now, this is not the place for a discussion of regulation, but we should warn you about careless measures of the size of the derivatives markets and the possible losses. In December 2000 the notional value of outstanding derivative contracts was about $110 trillion.[35] This is a very large sum, but it tells you *nothing* about the

---

[34]The attempt failed, and the company later agreed to pay $150 million more in fines and restitution.

[35]Bank of International Settlements, *Derivatives Statistics* (**www.bis.org/statistics/derstats.htm**).

money that was being put at risk. For example, suppose that a bank enters into a $10 million interest rate swap and the other party goes bankrupt the next day. How much has the bank lost? Nothing. It hasn't paid anything up front; the two parties simply promised to pay sums to each other in the future. Now the deal is off.

Suppose that the other party does not go bankrupt until a year after the bank entered into the swap. In the meantime interest rates have moved in the bank's favor, so it should be receiving more money from the swap than it is paying out. When the other side defaults on the deal, the bank loses the difference between the interest that it is due to receive and the interest that it should pay. But it doesn't lose $10 million.[36]

The only meaningful measure of the potential loss from default is the amount that it would cost firms showing a profit to replace their swap positions. This figure is only a small fraction of the principal amount of swaps outstanding.[37]

---

[36]This does not mean that firms don't worry about the possibility of default, and there are a variety of ways that they try to protect themselves. In the case of swaps, firms are reluctant to deal with banks that do not have the highest credit rating.

[37]United States General Accounting Office, "Financial Derivatives: Actions Needed to Protect the Financial System," report to congressional requesters, May 1994. This does not mean that swaps have *increased* risk. If counterparties use swaps to hedge risk, they are *less likely* to default.

SUMMARY

As a manager, you are paid to take risks, but you are not paid to take *any* risks. Some are simply bad bets, and others could jeopardize the success of the firm. In these cases you should look for ways to insure or hedge.

Most businesses take out insurance against a variety of risks. Insurance companies have considerable expertise in assessing risk and may be able to pool risks by holding a diversified portfolio. Insurance works less well when the insurance policy attracts only the worst risks *(adverse selection)* or when the insured firm is tempted to skip on maintenance and safety procedures *(moral hazard)*.

Insurance is generally purchased from specialist insurance companies, but sometimes firms issue specialized securities instead. Cat (catastrophe) bonds are an example.

The idea behind hedging is straightforward. You find two closely related assets. You then buy one and sell the other in proportions that minimize the risk of your net position. If the assets are *perfectly* correlated, you can make the net position risk-free.

The trick is to find the hedge ratio or delta—that is, the number of units of one asset that is needed to offset changes in the value of the other asset. Sometimes the best solution is to look at how the prices of the two assets have moved together in the past. For example, suppose you observe that a 1 percent change in the value of B has been accompanied on average by a 2 percent change in the value of A. Then delta equals 2.0; to hedge each dollar invested in A, you need to sell two dollars of B.

On other occasions a little theory can help to set up the hedge. For example, the effect of a change in interest rates on an asset's value depends on the asset's duration. If two assets have the same duration, they will be equally affected by fluctuations in interest rates.

Many of the hedges described in this chapter are static. Once you have set up the hedge, you can take a long vacation, confident that the firm is well protected. However, some hedges, such as those that match durations, are dynamic. As time passes and prices change, you need to rebalance your position to maintain the hedge.

Firms use a number of tools to hedge:

1. Futures contracts are advance orders to buy or sell an asset. The price is fixed today, but the final payment does not occur until the delivery date. The futures markets allow firms to place advance orders for dozens of different commodities, securities, and currencies.

2. Futures contracts are highly standardized and are traded in huge volumes on the futures exchanges. Instead of buying or selling a standardized futures contract, you may be able to arrange a tailor-made contract with a bank. These tailor-made futures contracts are called forward contracts. Firms regularly protect themselves against exchange rate changes by buying or selling forward currency contracts. Forward rate agreements (FRAs) provide protection against interest rate changes.

3. It is also possible to construct homemade forward contracts. For example, if you borrow for two years and at the same time lend for one year, you have effectively taken out a forward loan.

4. In recent years firms have entered into a variety of swap arrangements. For example, a firm may arrange for the bank to make all the future payments on its fixed-rate debt in exchange for paying the bank the cost of servicing a floating-rate loan.

Instead of using derivatives for hedging, some companies have decided that speculation is more fun, and this has sometimes gotten them into serious trouble. We do not believe that such speculation makes sense for an industrial company, but we caution against the view that derivatives are a threat to the financial system.

FURTHER READING

Two general articles on corporate risk management are:
C. W. Smith and R. M. Stultz: "The Determinants of Firms' Hedging Policies," *Journal of Financial and Quantitative Analysis,* 20:391–405 (December 1985).

K. A. Froot, D. Scharfstein, and J. C. Stein: "A Framework for Risk Management," *Journal of Applied Corporate Finance,* 7:22–32 (Fall 1994).

Schaefer's paper is a useful review of how duration measures are used to immunize fixed liabilities:
S. M. Schaefer: "Immunisation and Duration: A Review of Theory, Performance and Applications," *Midland Corporate Finance Journal,* 3:41–58 (Autumn 1984).

The texts that we cited in the readings for Chapter 20 cover futures and swaps as well as options. There are also some useful texts that focus on futures and swaps. They include:
D. Duffie: *Futures Markets,* Prentice-Hall, Inc., Englewood Cliffs, NJ, 1989.

D. R. Siegel and D. F. Siegel: *Futures Markets,* Dryden Press, Chicago, 1990.

C. W. Smith, C. H. Smithson, and D. S. Wilford: *Managing Financial Risk,* 3rd ed., McGraw-Hill, Inc., New York, 1998.

The Metallgesellschaft debacle makes fascinating reading. The following three papers cover all sides of the debate:
C. Culp and M. H. Miller: "Metallgesellschaft and the Economics of Synthetic Storage," *Journal of Applied Corporate Finance,* 7:62–76 (Winter 1995).

F. Edwards: "The Collapse of Metallgesellschaft: Unhedgeable Risks, Poor Hedging Strategy, or Just Bad Luck?" *Journal of Futures Markets,* 15:211–264 (May 1995).

A. Mello and J. Parsons: "Maturity Structure of a Hedge Matters: Lessons from the Metallgesellschaft Debacle," *Journal of Applied Corporate Finance,* 7:106–120 (Spring 1995).

QUIZ

1. True or false?
   a. A perfect hedge of asset A requires an asset B that's perfectly correlated with A.
   b. Hedging transactions in an active futures market have zero or slightly negative NPVs.
   c. Longer maturity bonds necessarily have longer durations.
   d. The longer a bond's duration, the lower is its volatility.
   e. When you buy a futures contract, you pay now for delivery at a future date.
   f. The holder of a futures contract receives the convenience yield on the underlying commodity.
   g. The holder of a financial futures contract misses out on any dividend or interest payments made on the underlying security.

2. Yesterday you sold six-month futures on the German DAX stock market index at a price of 5,820. Today the DAX closed at 5,800 and DAX futures closed at 5,840. You get a call from your broker, who reminds you that your futures position is marked to market each day. Is she asking you to pay money, or is she about to offer to pay you?

3. Calculate the value of a six-month futures contract on a Treasury bond. You have the following information:
   - Six-month interest rate: 10 percent per year, or 4.9 percent for six months.
   - Spot price of bond: 95.
   - Coupon payments on the bond over the next six months: Present value of 4.

4. Calculate PV(convenience yield) for magnoosium scrap from the following information:
   - Spot price: $2,550 per ton.
   - Futures price: $2,408 for a one-year contract.
   - Interest rate: 12 percent.
   - PV(storage costs): $100 per year.

5. Residents of the northeastern United States suffered record-setting low temperatures throughout November and December 2015. Spot prices of heating oil rose 25 percent, to over $2 a gallon.
   a. What effect did this have on the net convenience yield and on the relationship between futures and spot prices?
   b. In late 2016 refiners and distributors were surprised by record-setting *high* temperatures. What was the effect on net convenience yield and spot and futures prices for heating oil?

6. After a record harvest, grain silos are full to the brim. Are storage costs likely to be high or low? What does this imply for the *net* convenience yield?

7. A year ago a British bank entered into a £50 million five-year interest rate swap. It agreed to pay company A each year a fixed rate of 6 percent and to receive in return LIBOR plus 1 percent. When the bank entered into this swap, LIBOR was 5 percent, but now interest rates have risen, so on a four-year interest rate swap the bank could expect to pay 6 1/2 percent and receive LIBOR plus 1 percent.
   a. Is the swap showing a profit or loss to the bank?
   b. Suppose that at this point company A approaches the bank and asks to terminate the swap. If there are four annual payments still remaining, how much should the bank charge A to terminate?

8. What is basis risk? In which of the following cases would you expect basis risk to be most serious?
   a. A broker owning a large block of Walt Disney common stock hedges by selling index futures.
   b. An Iowa corn farmer hedges the selling price of her crop by selling Chicago corn futures.
   c. An importer must pay 900 million euros in six months. He hedges by buying euros forward.

9. You own a $1 million portfolio of aerospace stocks with a beta of 1.2. You are very enthusiastic about aerospace but uncertain about the prospects for the overall stock market. Explain how you could hedge out your market exposure by selling the market short. How much would you sell? How in practice would you go about "selling the market"?

10. **a.** Marshall Arts has just invested one million euros in BTPs (long-term Italian government bonds). Marshall is concerned about increasing volatility in interest rates. He decides to hedge using bond futures contracts. Should he buy or sell such contracts?
    b. The treasurer of an Italian corporation plans to issue bonds in three months. She is also concerned about interest rate volatility and wants to lock in the price at which her company could sell 5 percent coupon bonds. How would she use bond futures contracts to hedge?

11. Securities A, B, and C have the following cash flows:

	Period 1	Period 2	Period 3
A	40	40	40
B	120	—	—
C	10	10	110

a. Calculate their durations if the interest rate is 8 percent.
b. Suppose that you have an investment of $10 million in A. What combination of B and C would immunize this investment against interest rate changes?
c. Now suppose that you have a $10 million investment in B. How would you immunize?

PRACTICE
QUESTIONS

1. Why might a large, multinational company choose to insure against common events, such as vehicle accidents, but not against rare events which could cause large losses? Explain briefly.

2. Large businesses spend millions of dollars annually on insurance. Why? Should they insure against all risks or does insurance make more sense for some risks than others?

3. What is meant by "moral hazard" and "adverse selection"? Explain why these effects tend to increase insurance premiums.

4. On some catastrophe bonds, payments are reduced if the claims against the issuer exceed a specified sum. In other cases payments are reduced only if claims against the entire industry exceed some sum. What are the advantages and disadvantages of the two structures? Which involves more basis risk? Which may create a problem of moral hazard?

5. "The farmer does not avoid risk by selling wheat futures. If wheat prices stay about $2.80 a bushel, then he will actually have lost by selling wheat futures at $2.50." Is this a fair comment?

6. Explain the chief differences between futures and forward contracts, e.g., for foreign exchange.

7. List some of the commodity futures contracts that are traded on exchanges. Who do you think could usefully reduce risk by buying each of these contracts? Who do you think might wish to sell each contract?

8. What is a currency swap? An interest rate swap? A default swap? Give an example of how each swap might be used.

9. In August 2001, six-month futures on the Brazilian Bovespa stock index traded at 15,330. Spot was 13,743. The interest rate was 19 percent and the dividend yield was about 4 percent. Were the futures fairly priced?

10. If you buy a nine-month T-bill future, you undertake to buy a three-month bill in nine months' time. Suppose that Treasury bills and notes currently offer the following yields:

Months to Maturity	Annual Yield
3	6%
6	6.5
9	7
12	8

What is the value of a nine-month bill future?

11. Table 27.5 contains spot and six-month futures prices for several commodities and financial instruments. There may be some money-making opportunities. See if you can find them, and explain how you would trade to take advantage of them. The interest rate is 14.5 percent, or 7 percent over the six-month life of the contracts.

12. The following table shows gold futures prices for varying contract lengths. Gold is predominantly an investment good, not an industrial commodity. Investors hold gold because it diversifies their portfolios and because they hope its price will rise. They do not hold it for its convenience yield.

Calculate the interest rate faced by traders in gold futures for each of the contract lengths shown below. The spot price is $295.2 per ounce.

	Contract Length (months)				
	1	3	9	15	21
Futures price	$296.49	$300.11	$312.32	$325.57	$339.65

13. In September 2001 swap dealers were quoting a rate for five-year euro interest-rate swaps of 4.5 percent against euribor (the short-term interest rate for euro loans). Euribor at the time was 4.1 percent. Suppose that A arranges with a dealer to swap a €10 million five-year fixed-rate loan for an equivalent floating-rate loan in euros.

Commodity	Spot Price	Futures Price	Comments
Magnoosium	$2,550 per ton	$2,728.50 per ton	PV(storage costs) = PV(convenience yield).
Frozen quiche	$.50 per pound	$.514 per pound	PV(storage costs) = $.10 per pound; PV(convenience yield) = $.05 per pound.
Nevada Hydro 8s of 2002	77	78.39	4% semiannual coupon payment is due just before futures contract expires.
Costaguanan pulgas (currency)	9,300 pulgas = $1	6,900 pulgas = $1	Costaguanan interest rate is 95% per year.
Establishment Industries common stock	$95	$97.54	Establishment pays dividends of $2 per quarter. Next dividend is paid 2 months from now.
Cheap white wine	$12,500 per 10,000-gal. tank	$14,200 per 10,000-gal. tank	PV(convenience yield) = $250 per tank. Your company unexpectedly has surplus storage and can store 50,000 gallons at no cost.

TABLE 27.5

Spot and six-month futures prices for selected commodities and securities. See problem 11.

a. What is the value of this swap at the time that it is entered into?

b. Suppose that immediately after A has entered into the swap, the long-term interest rate rises by 1 percent. Who gains and who loses?

c. What is now the value of the swap?

14. Firms A and B face the following borrowing rates for making a five-year fixed-rate debt issue in U.S. dollars or Swiss francs:

	U.S. Dollars	Swiss Francs
Firm A	10%	7%
Firm B	8	6

Suppose that A wishes to borrow U.S. dollars and B wishes to borrow Swiss francs. Show how a swap could be used to reduce the borrowing costs of each company. Assume a spot exchange rate of 2 Swiss francs per dollar.

15. What is meant by "delta" in the context of hedging? Give examples of how delta can be estimated or calculated.

16. A gold-mining firm is concerned about short-term volatility in its revenues. Gold currently sells for $300 an ounce, but the price is extremely volatile and could fall as low as $280 or rise as high as $320 in the next month. The company will bring 1,000 ounces to the market next month.

a. What will be total revenues if the firm remains unhedged for gold prices of $280, $300, and $320 an ounce?

b. The future price of gold for delivery one month ahead is $301. What will be the firm's total revenues at each gold price if the firm enters into a one-month futures contract to deliver 1,000 ounces of gold?

c. What will total revenues be if the firm buys a one-month put option to sell gold for $300 an ounce? The put option costs $2 per ounce.

17. Legs Diamond owns shares in Vanguard Index 500 mutual fund worth $1 million on July 15. (This is an index fund that tracks the Standard and Poor's 500 Index.) He wants to cash in now, but his accountant advises him to wait six months so as to defer a large capital gains tax. Explain to Legs how he can use stock index futures to hedge out his exposure to market movements over the next six months. Could Legs "cash in" without actually selling his shares?

18. Refer back to question 17. Suppose that the nearest index futures contract matures in seven months rather than in six. Show how Legs Diamond can still use index futures to hedge his position. How would the maturity date affect the hedge ratio?

19. Your investment bank has an investment of $100 million in the stock of the Swiss Roll Corporation and a short position in the stock of the Frankfurter Sausage Company. Here is the recent price history of the two stocks:

	Percentage Price Change	
Month	Frankfurter Sausage	Swiss Roll
January	−10	−10
February	−10	−5
March	−10	0
April	+10	0
May	+10	+5
June	+10	+10

On the evidence of these six months, how large would your short position in Frankfurter Sausage need to be to hedge you as far as possible against movements in the price of Swiss Roll?

20. Price changes on two gold-mining stocks have shown strong positive correlation. Their historical relationship is

$$\text{Average percentage change in A} = .001 + .75 \text{ (percentage change in B)}$$

Changes in B explain 60 percent of the variation of the changes in A ($R^2 = .6$).
   a. Suppose you own \$100,000 of A. How much of B should you sell to minimize the risk of your net position?
   b. What is the hedge ratio?
   c. Here is the historical relationship between stock A and gold prices:

$$\text{Average percentage change in A} = -.002 + 1.2 \text{ (percentage change in gold price)}$$

If $R^2 = .5$, can you lower the risk of your net position by hedging with gold (or gold futures) rather than with stock B? Explain.

21. In Section 27.5, we stated that the duration of Potterton's lease equals the duration of its debt.
   a. Show that this is so.
   b. Now suppose that the interest rate falls to 3 percent. Show how the value of the lease and the debt package are now affected by a .5 percent rise or fall in the interest rate. What would Potterton need to do to re-establish the interest rate hedge?

22. Line 1 of the following table shows cash payments that your company has just promised to make. Below that are the cash flows on a blue-chip corporate note. The interest rate is 10 percent. Your company can borrow at this rate if it wishes.

	Year 1	Year 2	Year 3	Year 4
Liability (millions)	0	0	−\$20	−\$20
Note's cash payments as percent of face value	12	12	12	112

   a. What is the present value of your liability?
   b. Calculate the durations of the liability and the note.
   c. Suppose you wish to hedge the liability by investing in a combination of the note and a short-term bank deposit with a duration of zero. How much must you invest in each?
   d. Would this hedge continue to protect your company if
      i. Interest rates dropped by 3 percent?
      ii. Short-term interest rates fluctuate while longer-term rates remain basically constant?
      iii. Interest rates remain the same but two years pass?
   e. Can you set up a hedge portfolio that relieves the financial manager of all the worries mentioned in (d)? Describe that portfolio.

23. Petrochemical Parfum (PP) is concerned about possible increases in the price of heavy fuel oil, which is one of its major inputs. Show how PP can use either options or futures contracts to protect itself against a rise in the price of crude oil. Show how the payoffs in each case would vary if the oil price were \$14, \$16, or \$18 a barrel. What are the advantages and disadvantages for PP of using futures rather than options to reduce risk?

24. Explain the difference between insurance and hedging. Give an example of how options can be used for each.

25. "Speculators want futures contracts to be incorrectly priced; hedgers want them to be correctly priced." Why?

CHALLENGE QUESTIONS

1. Phillip's Screwdriver Company has borrowed $20 million from a bank at a floating interest rate of 2 percentage points above three-month Treasury bills, which now yield 5 percent. Assume that interest payments are made quarterly and that the entire principal of the loan is repaid after five years.

Phillip's wants to convert the bank loan to fixed-rate debt. It could have issued a fixed-rate five-year note at a yield to maturity of 9 percent. Such a note would now trade at par. The five-year Treasury note's yield to maturity is 7 percent.

a. Is Phillip's stupid to want long-term debt at an interest rate of 9 percent? It is borrowing from the bank at 7 percent.

b. Explain how the conversion could be carried out by an interest rate swap. What will be the initial terms of the swap? (Ignore transaction costs and the swap dealer's profit.)

One year from now medium- and long-term Treasury yields *decrease* to 6 percent, so the term structure then is flat. (The changes actually occur in month 5.) Phillip's credit standing is unchanged; it can still borrow at 2 percentage points over Treasury rates.

c. What net swap payment will Phillip's make or receive?

d. Suppose that Phillip's now wants to cancel the swap. How much would it need to pay the swap dealer? Or would the dealer pay Phillip's? Explain.

2. Hoopoe Corporation wants to borrow 100 million Canadian dollars at a fixed rate with a maturity of five years. It calculates that it can make an international bond issue with the following terms:

* Interest: 10 5/8 percent payable annually.
* Maturity: 5 years.
* Issue expenses: .2 percent.

A bank has presented Hoopoe with a proposal for a Swiss franc issue combined with a currency swap into Canadian dollars. The proposed terms for the Swiss franc issue are

* Amount: 200 million Swiss francs.
* Interest: 5 3/8 percent annually.
* Maturity: 5 years.
* Issue expenses: .2 percent.

The counterparty of the swap would raise fixed dollars on the following terms:

* Amount: 100 million Canadian dollars (equivalent to 200 million Swiss francs).
* Interest: 10 5/8 percent annually.
* Maturity: 5 years.
* Issue expenses: .15 percent.

The counterparty would be happy with an all-in cost in Swiss francs of 6.45 percent.

a. Which alternative should Hoopoe take? (Ignore credit risk in your analysis.)

b. Suppose that you are the corporate treasurer of Hoopoe. Discuss the credit risk issues involved in the alternatives.

3. Consider the commodities and financial assets listed in Table 27.6. The risk-free interest rate is 6 percent a year, and the term structure is flat.

a. Calculate the six-month futures price for each case.

b. Explain how a magnoosium producer would use a futures market to lock in the selling price of a planned shipment of 1,000 tons of magnoosium six months from now.

c. Suppose the producer takes the actions recommended in your answer to (b), but after one month magnoosium prices have fallen to $2,200. What happens? Will the

TABLE 27.6

Spot prices for selected commodities and financial assets. See challenge question 3.

Asset	Spot Price	Comments
Magnoosium	$2,800 per ton	Net convenience yield = 4% per year
Oat bran	$.44 per bushel	Net convenience yield = .5% per month
Biotech stock index	140.2	Dividend = 0
Allen Wrench Co. common stock	$58.00	Cash dividend = $2.4 per year
5-year Treasury note	108.93	8% coupon
Westonian ruple	3.1 ruples = $1	12% interest rate in ruples

producer have to undertake additional futures market trades to restore its hedged position?

d. Does the biotech index futures price provide useful information about the expected future performance of biotech stocks?

e. Suppose Allen Wrench stock falls suddenly by $10 per share. Investors are confident that the cash dividend will not be reduced. What happens to the futures price?

f. Suppose interest rates suddenly fall. The spot rate for cash flows 6 months from now is 4 percent (per year); it is 4.5 percent for cash flows 12 months from now, 4.8 percent for cash flows 18 months from now, and 5 percent for all subsequent cash flows. What happens to the six-month futures price on the five-year Treasury note? What happens to a trader who shorted 100 notes at the futures price calculated in part (a)?

g. An importer must make a payment of one million ruples three months from now. Explain *two* strategies the importer could use to hedge against unfavorable shifts in the ruple–dollar exchange rate.

MANAGING INTERNATIONAL RISKS

IN THE LAST chapter we considered the risks that flow from changes in interest rates and commodity prices. But companies with substantial overseas interests encounter a variety of other hazards, including political risks and currency fluctuations. *Political risk* means the possibility that a hostile foreign government will expropriate your business without compensation or not allow profits to be taken out of the country.

To understand currency risk, you first need to understand how the foreign exchange market works and how prices for foreign currency are determined. We therefore start this chapter with some basic institutional detail about the foreign exchange market and we will look at some simple theories that link exchange rates, interest rates, and inflation. We will use these theories to show how firms assess and hedge their foreign currency exposure.

When we discussed investment decisions in Chapter 6, we showed that financial managers do not need to forecast exchange rates in order to evaluate overseas investment proposals. They can simply forecast the foreign currency cash flows and discount these flows at the foreign currency cost of capital. In this chapter we will explain *why* this rule makes sense. It turns out that it is the ability to hedge foreign exchange risk that allows companies to ignore future exchange rates when making investment decisions.

We conclude the chapter with a discussion of political risk. We show that, while companies cannot restrain a determined foreign government, they can structure their operations to reduce the risk of hostile actions.

28.1 THE FOREIGN EXCHANGE MARKET

An American company that imports goods from France may need to buy euros to pay for the purchase. An American company exporting to France may receive euros, which it sells in exchange for dollars. Both firms make use of the foreign exchange market.

The foreign exchange market has no central marketplace. Business is conducted electronically. The principal dealers are the larger commercial banks and investment banks. A corporation that wants to buy or sell currency usually does so through a commercial bank. Turnover in the foreign exchange market is huge. In London in April 2001 $504 billion of currency changed hands each day. That is equivalent to an annual turnover of $126 trillion ($126,000,000,000,000). New York and Tokyo together accounted for a further $400 billion of turnover per day.[1]

Table 28.1 is adapted from the table of exchange rates in the *Financial Times*. Exchange rates are generally expressed in terms of the number of units of the foreign currency needed to buy one U.S. dollar. This is termed an *indirect quote*. In the first column of Table 28.1, the indirect quote for the yen shows that you can buy 120.700 yen for $1. This is often written as ¥120.700/$.

A *direct* exchange rate quote states how many dollars you can buy for one unit of foreign currency. The euro and the British pound sterling are usually shown as direct quotes.[2] For example, Table 28.1 shows that £1 is equivalent to $1.4483 or, more concisely, $1.4483/£. If £1 buys $1.4483, then $1 must buy 1/1.4483 = £.6905. Thus the indirect quote for the pound is £.6905/$.[3]

---

[1]The results of the triennial survey of foreign exchange business are published on www.bis.org/publ.

[2]The euro is the common currency of the European Monetary Union. The 12 members of the Union are Austria, Belgium, Finland, France, Germany, Greece, Ireland, Italy, Luxembourg, Netherlands, Portugal, and Spain.

[3]Foreign exchange dealers usually refer to the exchange rate between pounds and dollars as *cable*. In Table 28.1 cable is 1.4483.

TABLE 28.1

Spot and forward exchange rates, August 28, 2001.

*Rates show the number of units of foreign currency per U.S. dollar, except for the euro and the UK pound, which show the number of U.S. dollars per unit of foreign currency.
Source: *Financial Times*, August 29, 2001.

	Spot Rate*	Forward Rate*		
		1 Month	3 Months	1 Year
Europe:				
EMU (euro)	.9094	.9088	.9076	.9057
Norway (krone)	8.8756	8.9006	8.9594	9.1889
Sweden (krona)	10.3159	10.3221	10.3389	10.4034
Switzerland (franc)	1.6680	1.6677	1.6667	1.6563
United Kingdom (pound)	1.4483	1.4468	1.4432	1.4289
Americas:				
Canada (dollar)	1.5397	1.5403	1.5415	1.545
Mexico (peso)	9.1390	9.1865	9.307	9.924
Pacific/Africa:				
Hong Kong (dollar)	7.7999	7.7987	7.7962	7.7954
Japan (yen)	120.700	120.36	119.66	116.535
Singapore (dollar)	1.7542	1.7525	1.7491	1.7322
South Africa (rand)	8.3693	8.4102	8.4963	8.8278
Thailand (baht)	44.3450	44.39	44.555	45.295

The exchange rates in the first column of Table 28.1 are the prices of currency for immediate delivery. These are known as **spot rates of exchange.** The spot rate for the yen is ¥120.700/$, and the spot rate for the pound is $1.4483/£.

In addition to the spot exchange market, there is a *forward market.* In the forward market you buy and sell currency for future delivery. If you know that you are going to pay out or receive foreign currency at some future date, you can insure yourself against loss by buying or selling forward. Thus, if you need one million yen in three months, you can enter into a three-month *forward contract.* The **forward rate** on this contract is the price you agree to pay in three months when the one million yen are delivered. If you look again at Table 28.1, you will see that the three-month forward rate for the yen is quoted at ¥119.66/$. If you buy yen for three months' delivery, you get fewer yen for your dollar than if you buy them spot. In this case the yen is said to trade at a forward *premium* relative to the dollar, because forward yen are more expensive than spot ones. Expressed as an annual rate, the forward premium is[4]

$$4 \times \left(\frac{120.700}{119.66} - 1 \right) = .035, \text{ or } 3.5\%$$

You could also say that the dollar was selling at a *forward discount.*

A forward purchase or sale is a made-to-measure transaction between you and the bank. It can be for any currency, any amount, and any delivery day. You could buy, say, 99,999 Vietnamese dong or Haitian gourdes for a year and a day forward as long as you can find a bank ready to deal. Most forward transactions are for six months or less, but banks are prepared to buy and sell the major currencies for several years forward.[5]

---

[4]Here is an occasional point of confusion. Since the quote for the yen is indirect, we calculate the premium by taking the ratio of the spot rate to the forward rate. If we use *direct* quotes, then we need to calculate the ratio of the forward rate to the spot rate. In the case of the yen, the forward premium with direct quotes is $4 \times [(1/119.66)/(1/120.7) - 1] = .035$, or 3.5 percent.

[5]Forward and spot trades are often undertaken together. For example, a company might need the use of Japanese yen for one month. In this case it would buy the yen spot and simultaneously sell them forward. This is known as a *swap* trade, but do not confuse it with the longer-term interest rate and currency swaps described in Chapter 27.

CHAPTER 28 Managing International Risks   789

There is also an organized market for currency for future delivery known as the currency *futures* market. Futures contracts are highly standardized; they exist only for the main currencies, and they are for specified amounts and for a limited choice of delivery dates.[6]

When you buy a forward or futures contract, you are committed to taking delivery of the currency. As an alternative, you can take out an *option* to buy or sell currency in the future at a price that is fixed today. Made-to-measure currency options can be bought from the major banks, and standardized options are traded on the options exchanges.

28.2 SOME BASIC RELATIONSHIPS

You can't develop a consistent international financial policy until you understand the reasons for the differences in exchange rates and interest rates. We will consider the following four problems:

- *Problem 1.* Why is the dollar rate of interest ($r_\$$) different from, say, the yen rate ($r_¥$)?
- *Problem 2.* Why is the forward rate of exchange ($f_{¥/\$}$) different from the spot rate ($s_{¥/\$}$)?
- *Problem 3.* What determines next year's expected spot rate of exchange between dollars and yen [$E(r_{¥/\$})$]?
- *Problem 4.* What is the relationship between the inflation rate in the United States ($i_\$$) and the inflation rate in Japan ($i_¥$)?

Suppose that individuals were not worried about risk and that there were no barriers or costs to international trade. In that case the spot exchange rates, forward exchange rates, interest rates, and inflation rates would stand in the following simple relationship to one another:

Why should this be so?

---

[6] See Chapter 27 for a further discussion of the difference between forward and futures contracts.

Interest Rates and Exchange Rates

It is August 2001 and you have $1 million to invest for one year. U.S. dollar deposits are offering an interest rate of about 3.65 percent; Japanese yen deposits are offering a meager .06 percent. Where should you put your money? Does the answer sound obvious? Let's check:

- *Dollar loan.* The rate of interest on one-year dollar deposits is 3.65 percent. Therefore at the end of the year you get $1,000,000 \times 1.0365 = \$1,036,500$.
- *Yen loan.* The current exchange rate is ¥120.700/$. For $1 million, you can buy $1,000,000 \times 120.700 = ¥120,700,000$. The rate of interest on a one-year yen deposit is .06 percent. Therefore at the end of the year you get $120,700,000 \times 1.0006 = ¥120,772,420$. Of course, you don't know what the exchange rate is going to be in one year's time. But that doesn't matter. You can fix today the price at which you sell your yen. The one-year forward rate is ¥116.535/$. Therefore, by selling forward, you can make sure that you will receive $120,772,420/116.535 = \$1,036,400$ at the end of the year.

Thus, the two investments offer almost exactly the same rate of return.[7] They have to—they are both risk-free. If the domestic interest rate were different from the *covered* foreign rate, you would have a money machine.

When you make the yen loan, you receive a lower interest rate. But you get an offsetting gain because you sell yen forward at a higher price than you pay for them today. The interest rate differential is

$$\frac{1 + r_¥}{1 + r_\$}$$

And the differential between the forward and spot exchange rates is

$$\frac{f_{¥/\$}}{s_{¥/\$}}$$

Interest rate parity theory says that the difference in interest rates must equal the difference between the forward and spot exchange rates:

| Difference in interest rates $\dfrac{1 + r_¥}{1 + r_\$}$ | equals | Difference between forward and spot rates $\dfrac{f_{¥/\$}}{s_{¥/\$}}$ |

In our example,

$$\frac{1.0006}{1.0365} = \frac{116.535}{120.700}$$

The Forward Premium and Changes in Spot Rates

Now let's consider how the forward premium is related to changes in spot rates of exchange. If people didn't care about risk, the forward rate of exchange would depend solely on what people expected the spot rate to be. For example, if the one-

---

[7]The minor difference in our calculated end-of-year payoffs was mostly due to rounding in the interest rates.

year forward rate on yen is ¥116.535/$, that could only be because traders expect the spot rate in one year's time to be ¥116.535/$. If they expected it to be, say, ¥125/$, nobody would be willing to buy yen forward. They could get more yen for their dollar by waiting and buying spot.

Therefore the *expectations theory* of exchange rates tells us that the percentage difference between the forward rate and today's spot rate is equal to the expected change in the spot rate:

$$\text{Difference between forward and spot rates } \frac{f_{¥/\$}}{s_{¥/\$}} \quad\text{equals}\quad \text{Expected change in spot rate } \frac{E(s_{¥/\$})}{s_{¥/\$}}$$

Of course, this assumes that traders don't care about risk. If they do care, the forward rate can be either higher or lower than the expected spot rate. For example, suppose that you have contracted to receive one million yen in three months. You can wait until you receive the money before you change it into dollars, but this leaves you open to the risk that the price of yen may fall over the next three months. Your alternative is to sell yen forward. In this case, you are fixing today the price at which you will sell your yen. Since you avoid risk by selling forward, you may be willing to do so even if the forward price of yen is a little *lower* than the expected spot price.

Other companies may be in the opposite position. They may have contracted to pay out yen in three months. They can wait until the end of the three months and then buy yen, but this leaves them open to the risk that the price of yen may rise. It is safer for these companies to fix the price today by *buying* yen forward. These companies may, therefore, be willing to buy forward even if the forward price of yen is a little *higher* than the expected spot price.

Thus some companies find it safer to sell yen forward, while others find it safer to buy yen forward. When the first group predominates, the forward price of yen is likely to be less than the expected spot price. When the second group predominates, the forward price is likely to be greater than the expected spot price. On average you would expect the forward price to underestimate the expected spot price just about as often as it overestimates it.

Changes in the Exchange Rate and Inflation Rates

Now we come to the third side of our quadrilateral—the relationship between changes in the spot exchange rate and inflation rates. Suppose that you notice that silver can be bought in the United States for $4.00 a troy ounce and sold in Japan for ¥675. You think you may be onto a good thing. You decide to buy silver for $4.00 and put it on the first plane to Tokyo, where you sell it for ¥675. Then you exchange your ¥675 for 675/120.700 = $5.59. You have made a gross profit of $1.59 an ounce. Of course, you have to pay transportation and insurance costs out of this, but there should still be something left over for you.

Money machines don't exist—not for long, anyway. As others notice the disparity between the price of silver in Japan and the price in the United States, the price will be forced down in Japan and up in the United States until the profit opportunity disappears. Arbitrage ensures that the dollar price of silver is about the same in the two countries. Of course, silver is a standard and easily transportable commodity, but the same forces should act to equalize the domestic and foreign prices of other goods. Those goods that can be bought more cheaply abroad will be imported, and that will force down the price of domestic products. Similarly, those goods that can be bought more cheaply in the United States will be exported, and that will force down the price of the foreign products.

This is often called *purchasing power parity.*[8] Just as the price of goods in Safeway must be roughly the same as the price of goods in A&P, so the price of goods in Japan when converted into dollars must be roughly the same as the price in the United States:

$$\text{Dollar price of goods in the USA} = \frac{\text{yen price of goods in Japan}}{\text{number of yen per dollar}}$$

Purchasing power parity implies that any differences in the rates of inflation will be offset by a change in the exchange rate. For example, if prices are rising by 2.6 percent in the United States while they are declining by −1.0 percent in Japan, the number of yen that you can buy for $1 must fall by .99/1.026 − 1, or about 3.5 percent. Therefore purchasing power parity says that to estimate changes in the spot rate of exchange, you need to estimate differences in inflation rates:[9]

Expected difference in inflation rates
$$\frac{E(1 + i_\yen)}{E(1 + i_\$)}$$

— equals —

Expected change in spot rate
$$\frac{E(s_{\yen/\$})}{s_{\yen/\$}}$$

In our example,

Current spot rate × expected difference in inflation rates = expected spot rate
120.700   ×   .99/1.026   =   116.5

Interest Rates and Inflation Rates

Now for the fourth leg! Just as water always flows downhill, so capital tends to flow where returns are greatest. But investors are not interested in *nominal* returns; they care about what their money will buy. So, if investors notice that real interest rates are higher in Japan than in the United States, they will shift their savings into Japan until the expected real returns are the same in the two countries. If the expected real interest rates are equal, then the difference in money rates must be equal to the difference in the expected inflation rates:[10]

---

[8]Economists use the term *purchasing power parity* to refer to the notion that the level of prices of goods in general must be the same in the two countries. They tend to use the phrase *law of one price* when they are talking about the price of a single good.

[9]In other words, the *expected* difference in inflation rates equals the *expected* change in the exchange rate. Strictly interpreted, purchasing power parity also implies that the *actual* difference in the inflation rates always equals the *actual* change in the exchange rate.

[10]In Section 24.1 we discussed Irving Fisher's theory that over time money interest rates change to reflect changes in anticipated inflation. Here we argue that international differences in money interest rates also reflect differences in anticipated inflation. This theory is sometimes known as the *international Fisher effect.*

In Japan the real one-year interest rate is just over 1 percent:

$$r_\yen(real) = \frac{1 + r_\yen}{E(1 + i_\yen)} - 1 = \frac{1.0006}{.99} - 1 = .0107$$

Ditto for the United States:

$$r_\$(real) = \frac{1 + r_\$}{E(1 + i_\$)} - 1 = \frac{1.0365}{1.026} - 1 = .0102$$

Is Life Really That Simple?

We have described above four theories that link interest rates, forward rates, spot exchange rates, and inflation rates. Of course, such simple economic theories are not going to provide an exact description of reality. We need to know how well they predict actual behavior. Let's check.

1. Interest Rate Parity Theory   Interest rate parity theory says that the yen rate of interest covered for exchange risk should be the same as the dollar rate. In the example that we gave you earlier we used the rates of interest on dollar and yen deposits in London. Since money can be moved easily between these deposits, interest rate parity almost always holds. In fact, dealers *set* the forward price of yen by looking at the difference between the interest rates on deposits of dollars and yen.[11]

The relationship does not hold so exactly for deposits made in different domestic money markets. In these cases taxes and government regulations sometimes prevent the citizens of one country from switching out of one country's bank deposits and covering their exchange risk in the forward market.

2. The Expectations Theory of Forward Rates   How well does the expectations theory explain the level of forward rates? Scholars who have studied exchange rates have found that forward rates typically exaggerate the likely change in the spot rate. When the forward rate appears to predict a sharp rise in the spot rate (a forward premium), the forward rate tends to overestimate the rise in the spot rate. Conversely, when the forward rate appears to predict a fall in the currency (a forward discount), it tends to overestimate this fall.[12]

This finding is *not* consistent with the expectations theory. Instead it looks as if sometimes companies are prepared to give up return to *buy* forward currency and other times they are prepared to give up return to *sell* forward currency. In

---

[11]The forward exchange rates shown in the *Financial Times* and reproduced in Table 28.1 are simply calculated from the differences in interest rates.

[12]Many researchers have even found that, when the forward rate predicts a rise, the spot rate is more likely to fall, and vice versa. For a readable discussion of this puzzling finding, see K. A. Froot and R. H. Thaler, "Anomalies: Foreign Exchange," *Journal of Political Economy* 4 (1990), pp. 179–192.

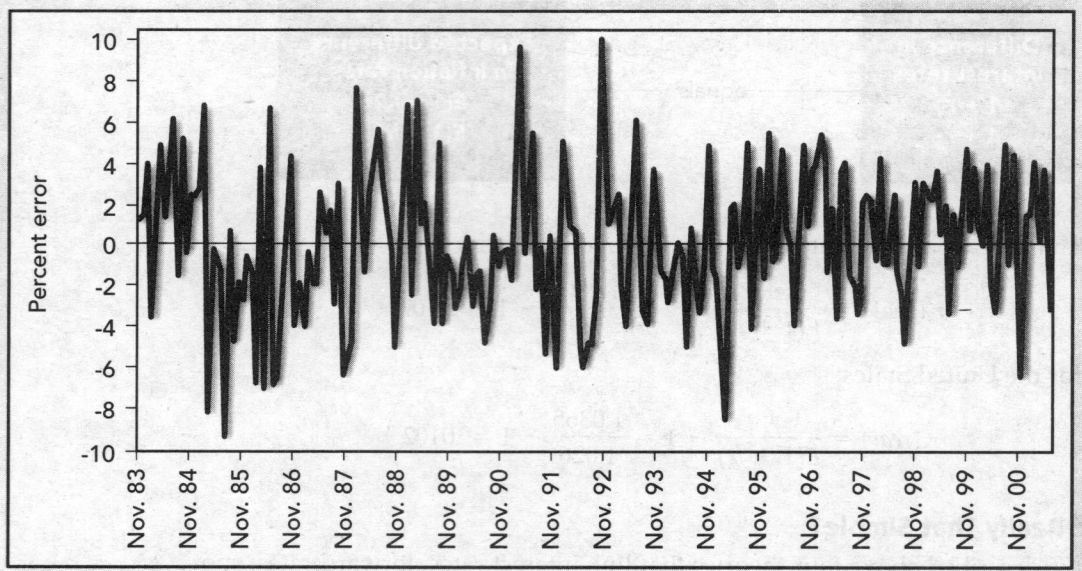

FIGURE 28.1

Percentage error from using the one-month forward rate for Swiss francs to forecast next month's spot rate. Note that the forward rate overestimates and underestimates the spot rate with about equal frequency.

other words, forward rates seem to contain a risk premium, but the sign of this premium swings backward and forward.[13] You can see this from Figure 28.1. Almost half the time the forward rate for the Swiss franc *overstates* the likely future spot rate and half the time it *understates* the likely spot rate. *On average* the forward rate and future spot rate are almost identical. This is important news for the financial manager; it means that a company which always uses the forward market to protect against exchange rate movements does not pay any extra for this insurance.

3. Purchasing Power Parity Theory   What about the third side of our quadrilateral—purchasing power parity theory? No one who has compared prices in foreign stores with prices at home really believes that prices are the same throughout the world. Look, for example, at Table 28.2, which shows the price of a Big Mac in different countries. Notice that at current rates of exchange a Big Mac costs $3.65 in Switzerland but only $2.54 in the United States. To equalize prices in Switzerland and the United States, the number of Swiss francs that you could buy for your dollar would need to increase by 3.65/2.54 − 1 = .44, or 44 percent.

This suggests a possible way to make a quick buck. Why don't you buy a hamburger-to-go in (say) the Philippines for the equivalent of $1.17 and take it for resale in Switzerland, where the price in dollars is $3.65? The answer, of course, is that the gain would not cover the costs. The same good can be sold for

---

[13]For evidence that forward exchange rates contain risk premia that are sometimes positive and sometimes negative, see, for example, E. F. Fama, "Forward and Spot Exchange Rates," *Journal of Monetary Economics* 14 (1984), pp. 319–338.

TABLE 28.2

Price of Big Mac hamburgers in different countries.

Source: "Big Mac Currencies," *The Economist*, April 21, 2001, p. 74.

Country	Local Price Converted to U.S. Dollars	Country	Local Price Converted to U.S. Dollars
Australia	1.52	Japan	2.38
Brazil	1.64	Mexico	2.36
Canada	2.14	Philippines	1.17
China	1.20	Russia	1.21
Denmark	2.93	Sweden	2.33
Germany	2.30	Switzerland	3.65
Hong Kong	1.37	United Kingdom	2.85
Hungary	1.32	United States	2.54

different prices in different countries because transportation is costly and inconvenient.[14]

On the other hand, there is clearly some relationship between inflation and changes in exchange rates. For example, between 1994 and 1999 prices in Turkey rose about 20 times. Or, to put it another way, you could say that the purchasing power of money in Turkey declined by about 95 percent. If exchange rates had not adjusted, Turkish exporters would have found it impossible to sell their goods. But, of course, exchange rates did adjust. In fact, the value of the Turkish currency declined by 92 percent relative to the U.S. dollar.

Turkey is an extreme case, but in Figure 28.2 we have plotted the relative change in purchasing power for a sample of countries against the change in the exchange rate. Turkey is tucked in the bottom left-hand corner; the United States is closer to the top right. You can see that although the relationship is far from exact, large differences in inflation rates are generally accompanied by an offsetting change in the exchange rate.

Strictly speaking, purchasing power parity theory implies that the differential inflation rate is always identical to the change in the spot rate. But we don't need to go as far as that. We should be content if the *expected* difference in the inflation rates equals the *expected* change in the spot rate. That's all we wrote on the third side of our quadrilateral. Look, for example, at Figure 28.3. The solid line shows that in 2000 £1 sterling bought almost 70 percent fewer dollars than it did at the beginning of the century. But this decline in the price of sterling was largely matched by the higher inflation rate in the United Kingdom. The thin line shows that the inflation-adjusted, or *real*, exchange rate ended the century at roughly the same level as it began.[15] Of course, the real exchange rate *does* change, sometimes dramatically. For example, the real value of sterling almost halved between 1980 and 1985 before recovering in the next five years. However, if you were a financial manager called on to make a long-term forecast of the exchange rate, you could not

---

[14]Of course, even within a currency area there may be considerable price variations. The price of a Big Mac, for example, differs substantially from one part of the United States to another. And even after the introduction of the euro, the price of Big Macs varied between $1.96 in Italy and $2.49 in France.

[15]The real exchange rate is equal to the nominal exchange rate multiplied by the inflation differential. For example, suppose that the value of sterling falls from $1.54 = £1 to $1.40 = £1 at the same time that the price of goods rises 10 percent faster in the United Kingdom than in the United States. The inflation-adjusted, or real, exchange rate is unchanged at

$$\text{Initial exchange rate} \times (1 + i_£)/(1 + i_\$) = 1.40 \times 1.1 = \$1.54/£$$

FIGURE 28.2

A decline in the exchange rate and a decline in a currency's purchasing power usually go hand in hand. In this diagram, each of the 138 points represents the experience of a different country between 1994 and 1999. The vertical axis shows the change in the value of the foreign currency relative to the average. The horizontal axis shows the change in purchasing power relative to the average. The × at the lower left is Turkey; the + at the upper right is the United States.

FIGURE 28.3

Since 1900 sterling has fallen sharply in value against the dollar. But this fall has largely offset the higher inflation rate in the UK. The *real* value of sterling has been roughly constant.

Source: N. Abuaf and P. Jorion, "Purchasing Power Parity in the Long Run," *Journal of Finance* 45 (March 1990), pp. 157–174. We are grateful to Li Jin for extending the data.

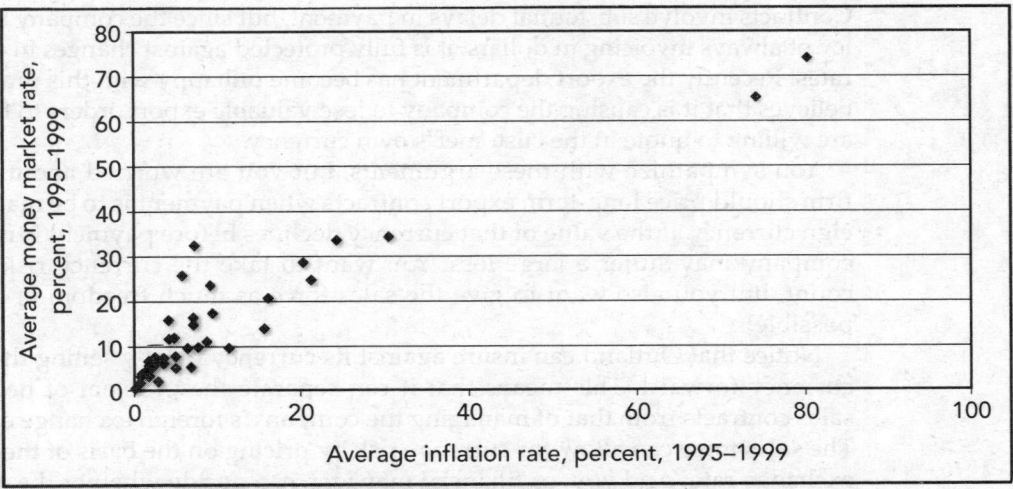

FIGURE 28.4

Countries with the highest interest rates generally have the highest inflation rates. In this diagram, each of the 51 points represents the experience of a different country.

have done much better than to assume that changes in the value of the currency would offset the difference in inflation rates.

4. Equal Real Interest Rates   Finally we come to the relationship between interest rates in different countries. Do we have a single world capital market with the same *real* rate of interest in all countries? Does the difference in money interest rates equal the difference in the expected inflation rates?

This is not an easy question to answer since we cannot observe *expected* inflation. However, in Figure 28.4 we have plotted the average interest rate in each of 51 countries against the inflation that subsequently occurred. Japan is tucked into the bottom-left corner of the chart, while Turkey is represented by the dot in the top-right corner. You can see that, in general, the countries with the highest interest rates also had the highest inflation rates. In other words, there were much smaller differences between the real rates of interest than between the nominal (or money) rates.[16]

 28.3 HEDGING CURRENCY RISK

Sharp exchange rate movements can make a large dent in corporate profits. To illustrate how companies cope with this problem, we will look at a typical company in the United States, Outland Steel, and walk through its foreign exchange operations.

---

[16]In Chapter 24 we saw that in some countries the government has issued indexed bonds promising a fixed real return. The annual interest payment and the amount repaid at maturity increase with the rate of inflation. In these cases, therefore, we can observe and compare the real rate of interest. As we write this, real interest rates in Australia, Canada, France, Sweden, and the United States cluster within the range of 3.3 to 3.7 percent. The exception is the UK, where the yield on indexed bonds is under 2.5 percent.

Example: Outland Steel　Outland Steel has a small but profitable export business. Contracts involve substantial delays in payment, but since the company has a policy of always invoicing in dollars, it is fully protected against changes in exchange rates. Recently the export department has become unhappy with this practice and believes that it is causing the company to lose valuable export orders to firms that are willing to quote in the customer's own currency.

You sympathize with these arguments, but you are worried about how the firm should price long-term export contracts when payment is to be made in foreign currency. If the value of that currency declines before payment is made, the company may suffer a large loss. You want to take the currency risk into account, but you also want to give the sales force as much freedom of action as possible.

Notice that Outland can insure against its currency risk by selling the foreign currency forward. This means that it can separate the problem of negotiating sales contracts from that of managing the company's foreign exchange exposure. The sales force can allow for currency risk by pricing on the basis of the forward exchange rate. And you, as financial manager, can decide whether the company *ought* to hedge.

What is the cost of hedging? You sometimes hear managers say that it is equal to the difference between the forward rate and *today's* spot rate. That is wrong. If Outland does not hedge, it will receive the spot rate at the time that the customer pays for the steel. Therefore, the cost of insurance is the difference between the forward rate and the expected spot rate when payment is received.

Insure or speculate? We generally vote for insurance. First, it makes life simpler for the firm and allows it to concentrate on its main business.[17] Second, it does not cost much. (In fact, the cost is zero on average if the forward rate equals the expected spot rate, as the expectations theory of forward rates implies.) Third, the foreign currency market seems reasonably efficient, at least for the major currencies. Speculation should be a zero-NPV game, unless financial managers have information that is not available to the pros who make the market.

Is there any other way that Outland can protect itself against exchange loss? Of course. It can borrow foreign currency against its foreign receivables, sell the currency spot, and invest the proceeds in the United States. Interest rate parity theory tells us that in free markets the difference between selling forward and selling spot should be equal to the difference between the interest that you have to pay overseas and the interest that you can earn at home. However, in countries where capital markets are highly regulated, it may be cheaper to arrange foreign borrowing rather than forward cover.[18]

Our discussion of Outland's export business illustrates four practical implications of our simple theories about forward exchange rates. First, you can use forward rates to adjust for exchange risk in contract pricing. Second, the expectations theory suggests that protection against exchange risk is usually worth having. Third, interest rate parity theory reminds us that you can hedge either by selling forward or by borrowing foreign currency and selling spot. Fourth, the cost of for-

---

[17]It also relieves shareholders of worrying about the foreign exchange exposure they may have acquired by purchase of the firm's shares.

[18]Sometimes governments also attempt to prevent currency speculation by limiting the amount that companies can sell forward.

ward cover is not the difference between the forward rate and *today's* spot rate; it is the difference between the forward rate and the expected spot rate when the forward contract matures.

Perhaps we should add a fifth implication. You don't make money simply by buying currencies that go up in value and selling those that go down. For example, suppose that you buy Narnian leos and sell them after a year for 2 percent more than you paid for them. Should you give yourself a pat on the back? That depends on the interest that you have earned on your leos. If the interest rate on leos is 2 percentage points less than the interest rate on dollars, the profit on the currency is exactly canceled out by the reduction in interest income. Thus you make money from currency speculation only if you can predict whether the exchange rate will change by more or less than the interest rate differential. In other words, you must be able to predict whether the exchange rate will change by more or less than the forward premium or discount.

Transaction Exposure and Economic Exposure

The exchange risk from Outland Steel's export business is due to delays in foreign currency payments and is therefore referred to as *transaction exposure*. Transaction exposure can be easily identified and hedged. Since a 1 percent fall in the value of the foreign currency results in a 1 percent fall in Outland's dollar receipts, for every euro or yen that Outland is owed by its customers, it needs to sell forward one euro or one yen.[19]

However, Outland may still be affected by currency fluctuations even if its customers do not owe it a cent. For example, Outland may be in competition with Swedish steel producers. If the value of the Swedish krona falls, Outland will need to cut its prices in order to compete.[20] Outland can protect itself against such an eventuality by selling the krona forward. In this case the loss on Outland's steel business will be offset by the profit on its forward sale.

Notice that Outland's exposure to the krona is not limited to specific transactions that have already been entered into. Financial managers often refer to this broader type of exposure as *economic exposure*.[21] Economic exposure is less easy to measure than transaction exposure. For example, it is clear that the value of Outland Steel is positively related to the value of the krona, so to hedge its position it needs to sell krona forward. But in practice it may be hard to say exactly how many krona Outland needs to sell.

Economic exposure is a major source of risk for many firms. When the deutschemark appreciated in value in 1991 and 1992, German luxury carmakers such as Porsche and Mercedes took a bath on their overseas sales. So did American dealers that had a franchise to sell these cars. Competitors such as Jaguar, however, benefited from their rivals' discomfiture. Thus the German and British car producers and their dealers were affected by exchange rate changes even

---

[19]To put it another way, the hedge ratio is 1.0.

[20]Of course, if purchasing power parity always held, the fall in the value of the krona would be matched by higher inflation in Sweden. The risk for Outland is that the *real* value of the krona may decline, so that when measured in dollars Swedish costs are lower than previously. Unfortunately, it is much easier to hedge against a change in the *nominal* exchange rate than against a change in the *real* rate.

[21]Financial managers also refer to *translation exposure*, which measures the effect of an exchange rate change on the company's financial statements.

though they may have had no fixed obligation to pay or receive dollars. They had economic exposure as well as possible transaction exposure.[22]

Most firms do not attempt to quantify economic exposure, but that does not mean that they ignore it. For example, when a company makes a major overseas investment, it often finances it by foreign currency borrowing. A subsequent fall in the value of the foreign currency may reduce the dollar value of the investment, but this is compensated by the fall in the dollar cost of servicing the foreign debt.

Currency Speculation

Outland Steel's currency exposure arose naturally from its business activity, but the risk was avoidable; it could have been hedged using either the forward markets or the loan markets. Sometimes, however, companies deliberately take on currency risk in the hope of gain. Now there is nothing wrong with that if you truly do have a forecasting edge, but we should warn you against the dangers of naive strategies.

Suppose, for example, that a company in the United States notices that the interest rate on the Swiss franc is lower than on the dollar. Does this mean that it is "cheaper" to borrow Swiss francs? Before jumping to that conclusion, you need to ask *why* the Swiss interest rate is so low. Unless the Swiss government is deliberately holding the rate down by restrictions on the export of capital, you should suspect that the real cost of capital is roughly the same in Switzerland as anywhere else. The nominal interest rate is low only because investors expect a low domestic rate of inflation and a strong currency. Therefore, the advantage of the low rate of interest is likely to be offset by the additional dollars required to buy the Swiss francs required to pay off the loan.

You cannot reliably make a profit simply by borrowing in countries with low nominal rates of interest and you may be taking on considerable currency exposure by doing so. If the currency subsequently appreciates *more* rapidly than investors expect, it could turn out to be very costly to buy the currency that you need to service the loan. In 1989 several Australian banks learned this lesson the hard way. They had induced their clients to borrow at the low Swiss interest rates. When the value of the Swiss franc rose sharply, the banks found themselves sued by irate clients for not having warned them of the risk of a rise in the price of Swiss francs.

 ## 28.4 EXCHANGE RISK AND INTERNATIONAL INVESTMENT DECISIONS

Suppose that the Swiss pharmaceutical company, Roche, is evaluating a proposal to build a new plant in the United States. To calculate the project's net present value, Roche forecasts the following dollar cash flows from the project:

Cash Flows ($ millions)					
C_0	C_1	C_2	C_3	C_4	C_5
−1,300	400	450	510	575	650

---

[22]The German car producers could have hedged their exposure by borrowing dollars. As the deutschemark appreciated, their dollar income fell but the cost of servicing dollar loans would also have fallen. However, while borrowing dollars would have reduced the risk for German car producers, it should not have affected their decisions about where to produce and sell cars.

These cash flows are stated in dollars. So to calculate their net present value Roche discounts them at the dollar cost of capital. (Remember dollars need to be discounted at a *dollar* rate, not the Swiss franc rate.) Suppose this cost of capital is 12 percent. Then

$$NPV = -1{,}300 + \frac{400}{1.12} + \frac{450}{1.12^2} + \frac{510}{1.12^3} + \frac{575}{1.12^4} + \frac{650}{1.12^5} = \$513 \text{ million}$$

To convert this net present value to Swiss francs, the manager can simply multiply the dollar NPV by the spot rate of exchange. For example, if the spot rate is 2 SFr/$, then the NPV in Swiss francs is

NPV in francs = NPV in dollars × SFr/$ = 513 × 2 = 1,026 million francs

Notice one very important feature of this calculation. Roche does not need to forecast whether the dollar is likely to strengthen or weaken against the Swiss franc. No currency forecast is needed, because the company can hedge its foreign exchange exposure. In that case, the decision to accept or reject the pharmaceutical project in the United States is totally separate from the decision to bet on the outlook for the dollar. For example, it would be foolish for Roche to accept a poor project in the United States just because management is optimistic about the outlook for the dollar; if Roche wishes to speculate in this way it can simply buy dollars forward. Equally, it would be foolish for Roche to reject a good project just because management is pessimistic about the dollar. The company would do much better to go ahead with the project and sell dollars forward. In that way, it would get the best of both worlds.[23]

When Roche ignores currency risk and discounts the dollar cash flows at a dollar cost of capital, it is implicitly assuming that the currency risk is hedged. Let us check this by calculating the number of Swiss francs that Roche would receive if it hedged the currency risk by selling forward each future dollar cash flow.

We need first to calculate the forward rate of exchange between dollars and francs. This depends on the interest rates in the United States and Switzerland. For example, suppose that the dollar interest rate is 6 percent and the Swiss franc interest rate is 4 percent. Then interest rate parity theory tells us that the one-year forward exchange rate is

$$s_{\text{SFr}/\$} \times (1 + r_{\text{SFr}})/(1 + r_\$) = \frac{2 \times 1.04}{1.06} = 1.962$$

Similarly, the two-year forward rate is

$$s_{\text{SFr}/\$} \times (1 + r_{\text{SFr}})^2/(1 + r_\$)^2 = \frac{2 \times 1.04^2}{1.06^2} = 1.925$$

So, if Roche hedges its cash flows against exchange rate risk, the number of Swiss francs it will receive in each year is equal to the dollar cash flow times the forward rate of exchange:

---

[23]There is a general point here that is not confined to currency hedging. Whenever you face an investment that appears to have a positive NPV, decide what it is that you are betting on and then think whether there is a more direct way to place the bet. For example, if a copper mine looks profitable only because you are unusually optimistic about the price of copper, then maybe you would do better to buy copper futures or the shares of other copper producers rather than opening a copper mine.

Cash Flows (millions of Swiss francs)					
C_0	C_1	C_2	C_3	C_4	C_5
$-1{,}300 \times 2$	400×1.962	450×1.925	510×1.889	575×1.853	650×1.818
$= -2{,}600$	$= 785$	$= 866$	$= 963$	$= 1{,}066$	$= 1{,}182$

These cash flows are in Swiss francs and therefore they need to be discounted at the risk-adjusted Swiss franc discount rate. Since the Swiss rate of interest is lower than the dollar rate, the risk-adjusted discount rate must also be correspondingly lower. The formula for converting from the required dollar return to the required Swiss franc return is[24]

$$(1 + \text{Swiss franc return}) = (1 + \text{dollar return}) \times \frac{(1 + \text{Swiss franc interest rate})}{(1 + \text{dollar interest rate})}$$

In our example

$$(1 + \text{Swiss franc return}) = 1.12 \times \frac{1.04}{1.06} = 1.099$$

Thus the risk-adjusted discount rate in dollars is 12 percent, but the discount rate in Swiss francs is only 9.9 percent.

All that remains is to discount the Swiss franc cash flows at the 9.9 percent risk-adjusted discount rate:

$$\text{NPV} = -2{,}600 + \frac{785}{1.099} + \frac{866}{1.099^2} + \frac{963}{1.099^3} + \frac{1{,}066}{1.099^4} + \frac{1{,}182}{1.099^5}$$

$$= 1{,}026 \text{ million francs}$$

Everything checks. We obtain exactly the same net present value by (a) ignoring currency risk and discounting Roche's dollar cash flows at the dollar cost of capital and (b) calculating the cash flows in francs on the assumption that Roche hedges the currency risk and then discounting these Swiss franc cash flows at the franc cost of capital.

To repeat: When deciding whether to invest overseas, separate out the investment decision from the decision to take on currency risk. This means that your views about future exchange rates should NOT enter into the investment decision. The simplest way to calculate the NPV of an overseas investment is to forecast the cash flows in the foreign currency and discount them at the foreign currency cost of capital. The alternative is to calculate the cash flows that you would receive if you hedged the foreign currency risk. In this case you need to translate the foreign currency cash flows into your own currency *using the forward exchange rate* and then discount these domestic currency cash flows at the domestic cost of capital. If the two methods don't give the same answer, you have made a mistake.

When Roche analyzes the proposal to build a plant in the United States, it is able to ignore the outlook for the dollar *only because it is free to hedge the currency risk.* Be-

---

[24]The following example should give you a feel for the idea behind this formula. Suppose the spot rate for Swiss francs is $2 \, \text{SFr} = \$1$. Interest rate parity tells us that the forward rate must be $2 \times 1.04/1.06 = 1.9623$ SFr/\$. Now suppose that a share costs \$100 and will pay an expected \$112 at the end of the year. The cost to Swiss investors of buying the share is $100 \times 2 = 200$ SFr. If the Swiss investors sell forward the expected payoff, they will receive an expected $112 \times 1.9623 = 219.8$ SFr. The expected return in Swiss francs is $219.8/200 - 1 = .099$ or 9.9 percent. More simply, the Swiss franc return is $1.12 \times 1.04/1.06 - 1 = .099$.

cause investment in a pharmaceutical plant does not come packaged with an investment in the dollar, the opportunity for firms to hedge allows for better investment decisions.

More about the Cost of Capital

In our discussion of Roche's investment decision we did not explain how Roche estimated the cost of capital for its investment in the United States. There is no simple agreed-upon procedure for doing this but we suggest that you first estimate the cost of capital in Swiss francs and then convert it to a dollar cost.

We discussed the problem of estimating the required return on Roche's overseas investment in Chapter 9. You need to decide how risky an investment in the U.S. pharmaceutical business would be to a Swiss investor. For example, a good starting point might be to look at the betas of a sample of U.S. pharmaceutical companies *relative to the Swiss market index*.[25]

Suppose that you decide that the investment's beta relative to the Swiss market is .7 and that the market risk premium in Switzerland is 8.4 percent. Then the required return on the project can be estimated as

$$\text{Required return} = \text{Swiss interest rate} + (\text{beta} \times \text{Swiss market risk premium})$$
$$= 4 + (.7 \times 8.4) = 9.9\%$$

This is the project's cost of capital measured in Swiss francs. We used it above to discount the expected *Swiss franc* cash flows if Roche hedged the project against currency risk. We cannot use it to discount the *dollar* cash flows from the project.

To discount the expected *dollar* cash flows, we need to convert the Swiss franc cost of capital to a dollar cost of capital. This means running our earlier calculation in reverse:

$$(1 + \text{dollar return}) = (1 + \text{Swiss franc return}) \times \frac{(1 + \text{dollar interest rate})}{(1 + \text{Swiss franc interest rate})}$$

In our example,

$$(1 + \text{dollar return}) = 1.099 \times \frac{1.06}{1.04} = 1.12$$

We used this 12 percent dollar cost of capital to discount the forecasted dollar cash flows from the project.

 ## 28.5 POLITICAL RISK

So far we have focused on the management of exchange rate risk, but managers also worry about political risk. By this they mean the threat that a government will change the rules of the game—that is, break a promise or understanding—*after* the

---

[25]We pointed out in Chapter 9 that when we use the beta relative to the U.S. index to estimate the returns required by U.S. investors, we are assuming that the U.S. market index is an efficient portfolio for these investors. Similarly, when we use the beta relative to the Swiss index to estimate the returns that Swiss investors require, we are assuming that the Swiss market index is an efficient portfolio for these investors. Investors do invest largely, but not exclusively, in their home markets.

	A	B	C	D	E	F	G	H	I	J	K	L	Total
Maximum score	12	12	12	12	12	6	6	6	6	6	6	4	100
Netherlands	9	10	10	12	12	6	6	6	6	6	6	4	93
USA	11	10	11	11	8	4	6	6	6	5	6	4	88
Germany	10	8	9	12	11	5	6	6	6	5	5	4	87
United Kingdom	11	10	11	9	9	5	6	6	6	4	6	4	87
France	10	7	9	10	11	3	5	6	5	5	5	4	80
Japan	10	6	6	12	10	2	6	5	6	5	5	4	78
Brazil	9	4	5	9	11	3	4	6	2	4	4	2	63
China	11	4	6	10	9	2	2	5	5	4	1	2	61
India	5	5	5	8	5	3	5	2	4	2	5	3	52
Russia	7	2	3	8	10	1	4	5	3	3	2	1	49
Indonesia	10	3	5	4	9	1	1	2	2	2	2	3	44
Iraq	8	3	4	3	4	1	0	5	2	2	0	0	32

TABLE 28.3

Political risk scores for a sample of countries, 1999.

Key:
A Government stability
B Socioeconomic conditions
C Investment profile
D Internal conflict
E External conflict
F Corruption

G Military in politics
H Religious tensions
I   Law and order
J   Ethnic tensions
K Democratic accountability
L Bureaucracy quality

Source: PRS Group (**www.prsgroup.com**).

investment is made. Of course political risks are not confined to overseas investments. Businesses in every country are exposed to the risk of unanticipated actions by governments or the courts. But in some parts of the world foreign companies are particularly vulnerable.

A number of consultancy services offer analyses of political and economic risks and draw up country rankings.[26] For example, Table 28.3 is an extract from the 1999 political risk rankings provided by the PRS Group. You can see that each country is scored on 12 separate dimensions. The Netherlands comes top of the class overall, while Iraq is near the bottom.

Some managers dismiss political risk as an act of God, like a hurricane or earthquake. But the most successful multinational companies structure their business to reduce political risk. Foreign governments are not likely to expropriate a local business if it cannot operate without the support of its parent. For example, the foreign subsidiaries of American computer manufacturers or pharmaceutical companies would have relatively little value if they were cut off from the know-how of their parents. Such operations are much less likely to be expropriated than, say, a mining operation that can be operated as a stand-alone venture.

We are not recommending that you turn your silver mine into a pharmaceutical company, but you may be able to plan your overseas manufacturing operations to

[26]For a discussion of these services see C. Erb, C. R. Harvey, and T. Viskanta, "Political Risk, Financial Risk, and Economic Risk," *Financial Analysts Journal* 52 (1996), pp. 28–46. Campbell Harvey's web page (**www.duke.edu/~charvey**) is also a useful source of information on political risk.

improve your bargaining position with foreign governments. For example, Ford has integrated its overseas operations so that the manufacture of components, sub-assemblies, and complete automobiles is spread across plants in a number of countries. None of these plants would have much value on its own, and Ford can switch production between plants if the political climate in one country deteriorates.

Multinational corporations have also devised financing arrangements to help keep foreign governments honest. For example, suppose your firm is contemplating an investment of $500 million to reopen the San Tomé silver mine in Costaguana with modern machinery, smelting equipment, and shipping facilities.[27] The Costaguanan government agrees to invest in roads and other infrastructure and to take 20 percent of the silver produced by the mine in lieu of taxes. The agreement is to run for 25 years.

The project's NPV on these assumptions is quite attractive. But what happens if a new government comes into power five years from now and imposes a 50 percent tax on "any precious metals exported from the Republic of Costaguana"? Or changes the government's share of output from 20 to 50 percent? Or simply takes over the mine "with fair compensation to be determined in due course by the Minister of Natural Resources of the Republic of Costaguana"?

No contract can absolutely restrain sovereign power. But you can arrange project financing to make these acts as painful as possible for the foreign government. For example, you might set up the mine as a subsidiary corporation, which then borrows a large fraction of the required investment from a consortium of major international banks. If your firm guarantees the loan, make sure the guarantee stands only if the Costaguanan government honors its contract. The government will be reluctant to break the contract if that causes a default on the loans and undercuts the country's credit standing with the international banking system.

If possible, you should arrange for the World Bank (or one of its affiliates) to finance part of the project or to guarantee your loans against political risk.[28] Few governments have the guts to take on the World Bank. Here is another variation on the same theme. Arrange to borrow, say, $450 million through the Costaguanan Development Agency. In other words, the development agency borrows in international capital markets and relends to the San Tomé mine. Your firm agrees to stand behind the loan as long as the government keeps its promises. If it does keep them, the loan is your liability. If not, the loan is *its* liability.

Political risk is not confined to the risk of expropriation. Multinational companies are always exposed to the criticism that they siphon funds out of countries in which they do business, and, therefore, governments are tempted to limit their freedom to repatriate profits. This is most likely to happen when there is considerable uncertainty about the rate of exchange, which is usually when you would most like to get your money out. Here again a little forethought can help. For example, there are often more onerous restrictions on the payment of dividends to the parent than on the payment of interest or principal on debt. Royalty payments and management fees are less sensitive than dividends, particularly if they are levied equally on all foreign operations. A company can also, within limits, alter the price of goods that are bought or sold within the group, and it can require more or less prompt payment for such goods.

---

[27]The early history of the San Tomé mine is described in Joseph Conrad's *Nostromo*.

[28]In Section 25.7 we described how the World Bank provided the Hubco power project with a guarantee against political risk.

SUMMARY

The international financial manager has to cope with different currencies, interest rates, and inflation rates. To produce order out of chaos, the manager needs some model of how they are related. We described four very simple but useful theories.

Interest rate parity theory states that the interest differential between two countries must be equal to the difference between the forward and spot exchange rates. In the international markets, arbitrage ensures that parity almost always holds. There are two ways to hedge against exchange risk: One is to take out forward cover; the other is to borrow or lend abroad. Interest rate parity tells us that the costs of the two methods should be the same.

The expectations theory of exchange rates tells us that the forward rate equals the expected spot rate. In practice forward rates seem to incorporate a risk premium, but this premium is about equally likely to be negative as positive.

In its strict form, purchasing power parity states that $1 must have the same purchasing power in every country. That doesn't square well with the facts, for differences in inflation rates are not perfectly related to changes in exchange rates. This means that there may be some genuine exchange risks in doing business overseas. On the other hand, the difference in inflation rates is just as likely to be above as below the change in the exchange rate.

Finally, we saw that in an integrated world capital market real rates of interest would have to be the same. In practice government regulation and taxes can cause differences in real interest rates. But do not simply borrow where interest rates are lowest. Those countries are also likely to have the lowest inflation rates and the strongest currencies.

With these precepts in mind we showed how you can use forward markets or the loan markets to hedge transactions exposure, which arises from delays in foreign currency payments and receipts. But the company's financing choices also need to reflect the impact of a change in the exchange rate on the value of the entire business. This is known as economic exposure.

Because companies can hedge their currency risk, the decision to invest overseas does not involve currency forecasts. There are two ways for a company to calculate the NPV of an overseas project. The first is to forecast the foreign currency cash flows and to discount them at the foreign currency cost of capital. The second is to translate the foreign currency cash flows into domestic currency assuming that they are hedged against exchange rate risk. These domestic currency flows can then be discounted at the domestic cost of capital. The answers should be identical.

In addition to currency risk, overseas operations may be exposed to extra political risk. However, firms may be able to structure the financing to reduce the chances that government will change the rules of the game.

FURTHER READING

There are a number of useful textbooks in international finance. Here is a small selection:

D. K. Eiteman and A. I. Stonehill: *Multinational Business Finance*, 8th ed., Addison-Wesley Publishing Company, Inc., Reading, MA, 1998.

J. O. Grabbe, *International Financial Markets*, 3rd ed., Prentice-Hall, Inc., Englewood Cliffs, NJ, 1995.

P. Sercu and R. Uppal: *International Financial Markets and the Firm*, South-Western College Publishing, Cincinnati, OH, 1995.

A. C. Shapiro: *Multinational Financial Management*, 6th ed., John Wiley & Sons, New York, 1999.

Here are some general discussions of international investment decisions and associated exchange risks:

G. W. Brown: "Managing Foreign Exchange Risk with Derivatives," *Journal of Financial Economics*, 60:401–448 (2001).

D. R. Lessard: "Global Competition and Corporate Finance in the 1990s," *Journal of Applied Corporate Finance*, 3:59–72 (Winter 1991).

M. D. Levi and P. Sercu: "Erroneous and Valid Reasons for Hedging Foreign Exchange Exposure," *Journal of Multinational Financial Management*, 1:25–37 (1991).

A. C. Shapiro: "International Capital Budgeting," *Midland Corporate Finance Journal*, 1:26–45 (Spring 1983).

Listed below are a few of the articles on the relationship between interest rates, exchange rates, and inflation:

Forward and spot exchange rates

M. D. D. Evans and K. K. Lewis: "Do Long-Term Swings in the Dollar Affect Estimates of the Risk Premia?" *Review of Financial Studies*, 8:709–742 (1995).

E. F. Fama: "Forward and Spot Exchange Rates," *Journal of Monetary Economics*, 14:319–338 (1984).

Interest-rate parity

K. Clinton: "Transaction Costs and Covered Interest Arbitrage: Theory and Evidence," *Journal of Political Economy*, 96:358–370 (April 1988).

J. A. Frenkel and R. M. Levich: "Covered Interest Arbitrage: Unexploited Profits?" *Journal of Political Economy*, 83:325–338 (April 1975).

Purchasing power parity

M. Adler and B. Lehmann: "Deviations from Purchasing Power Parity in the Long Run," *Journal of Finance*, 38:1471–1487 (December 1983).

K. Froot and K. Rogoff: "Perspectives on PPP and Long-run Real Exchange Rates," in G. Grossman and K. Rogoff (eds.), *Handbook of International Economics*, North-Holland Publishing Company, Amsterdam, 1995.

P. Jorion and R. Sweeney: "Mean Reversion in Real Exchange Rates: Evidence and Implications for Forecasting," *Journal of International Money and Finance*, 15:535–550 (1996).

K. Rogoff: "The Purchasing Power Parity Puzzle," *Review of Economic Literature*, 34:667–668 (June 1996).

QUIZ

1. Look at Table 28.1.
   a. How many Mexican pesos do you get for your dollar?
   b. What is the one-month forward rate for the peso?
   c. Is the dollar at a forward discount or premium on the peso?
   d. Use the one-year forward rate to calculate the annual percentage discount or premium on the peso.
   e. If the one-year interest rate on dollars is 3.7 percent annually compounded, what do you think is the one-year interest rate on pesos?
   f. According to the expectations theory, what is the expected spot rate for the peso in three months' time?
   g. According to the law of one price, what then is the expected difference in the rate of price inflation in the United States and Mexico?

2. Define each of the following theories in a sentence or simple equation:
   a. Interest rate parity theory.
   b. Expectations theory of forward rates.
   c. Purchasing power parity.
   d. International capital market equilibrium (relationship of real and nominal interest rates in different countries).

3. In March 1997 the exchange rate for the Indonesian rupiah was R2,419 = $1. Inflation in the year to March 1998 was about 30 percent in Indonesia and 2 percent in the United States.
   a. If purchasing power parity held, what should have been the nominal exchange rate in March 1998?
   b. The actual exchange rate in March 1998 (in the middle of the Asian currency crisis) was R8,325 = $1. What was the change in the *real* exchange rate?

4. The following table shows interest rates and exchange rates for the U.S. dollar and the Philippine peso. The spot exchange rate is 53.6 pesos = $1. Complete the missing entries:

	1 Month	3 Months	1 Year
Dollar interest rate (annually compounded)	3.60	3.50	?
Peso interest rate (annually compounded)	9.55	?	11.90
Forward pesos per dollar	?	?	57.844
Forward premium on peso (% per year)	?	−5.9	?

5. An importer in the United States is due to take delivery of clothing from Mexico in six months. The price is fixed in Mexican pesos. Which of the following transactions could eliminate the importer's exchange risk?
   a. Sell six-month call options on pesos.
   b. Buy pesos forward.
   c. Sell pesos forward.
   d. Sell pesos in the currency futures market.
   e. Borrow pesos; buy dollars at the spot exchange rate.
   f. Sell pesos at the spot exchange rate; lend dollars.

6. A U.S. company has committed to pay 10 million krona to a Swedish company in one year. What is the cost (in present value) of covering this liability by buying krona forward? The Swedish interest rate is 4.53 percent, and exchange rates are shown in Table 28.1. Briefly explain.

7. A firm in the United States is due to receive payment of €1 million in eight years' time. It would like to protect itself against a decline in the value of the euro, but finds it difficult to get forward cover for such a long period. Is there any other way in which it can protect itself?

8. In August 2001 short-term interest rates were about 3.65 percent in the United States and .06 percent in Japan. The spot exchange rate was ¥120.70/$. Suppose that one year later interest rates are 3 percent in both countries, while the value of the yen has appreciated to ¥115.00/$.
   a. Benjamin Pinkerton from New York invested in a U.S. two-year zero-coupon bond in August 2001 and sold it in August 2002. What was his return?
   b. Madame Butterfly from Osaka also invested in the two-year U.S. zero-coupon bond in August 2001 and sold it in August 2002. What was her return *in yen*?
   c. Suppose that Ms. Butterfly had correctly forecasted the price at which she sold her bond and that she hedged her investment against currency risk. How could she have done so? What would have been her return in yen?

9. It is the year 2006 and Pork Barrels Inc. is considering construction of a new barrel plant in Spain. The forecasted cash flows in millions of euros are as follows:

C_0	C_1	C_2	C_3	C_4	C_5
-80	$+10$	$+20$	$+23$	$+27$	$+25$

The spot exchange rate is $\$1.2 = \text{€}1$. The interest rate in the United States is 8 percent and the euro interest rate is 6 percent. You can assume that pork barrel production is effectively risk-free.

  a. Calculate the NPV of the euro cash flows from the project. What is the NPV in dollars?

  b. What are the dollar cash flows from the project if the company hedges against exchange rate changes?

  c. Suppose that the company expects the euro to depreciate by 5 percent a year. How does this affect the value of the project?

1. Look at the foreign exchange table in a recent issue of *The Wall Street Journal* or the London *Financial Times*.

  a. How many U.S. dollars are worth one Canadian dollar today?

  b. How many Canadian dollars are worth one U.S. dollar today?

  c. Suppose that you arrange today to buy Canadian dollars in 90 days. How many Canadian dollars could you buy for each U.S. dollar?

  d. If forward rates simply reflect market expectations, what is the likely spot exchange rate for the New Zealand dollar in 90 days' time?

  e. Look at the table of money rates in the same issue. What is the three-month interest rate on dollars?

  f. Can you deduce the likely three-month interest rate for the Swiss franc?

  g. You can also buy currency for future delivery in the financial futures market. Look at the table of futures prices. What is the rate of exchange for Canadian dollars to be delivered in approximately six months' time?

2. Table 28.1 shows the 90-day forward rate on the Thai baht.

  a. Is the dollar at a forward discount or premium on the baht?

  b. What is the annual *percentage* discount or premium?

  c. If you have no other information about the two currencies, what is your best guess about the spot rate on the baht three months hence?

  d. Suppose that you expect to receive 100,000 baht in three months. How many dollars is this likely to be worth?

3. Look at Table 28.1. If the three-month interest rate on dollars is 3.5 percent, what do you think is the three-month interest rate on South African rands? Explain what would happen if the rate were substantially above your figure.

4. Look in *The Wall Street Journal* or the *Financial Times.* How many Swiss francs can you buy for $1? How many Hong Kong dollars can you buy? What rate do you think a Swiss bank would quote for buying or selling Hong Kong dollars? Explain what would happen if it quoted a rate that was substantially above your figure.

5. What do our four basic relationships imply about the relationship between two countries' interest rates and the expected change in the exchange rate? Explain why you would or would not expect them to be related.

6. Ms. Rosetta Stone, the treasurer of International Reprints, Inc., has noticed that the interest rate in Japan is below the rates in most other countries. She is, therefore, sug-

PRACTICE QUESTIONS

gesting that the company should make an issue of Japanese yen bonds. Does this make sense?

7. What considerations should an American company take into account when deciding how to finance its overseas subsidiaries?

8. Suppose you are the treasurer of Lufthansa, the German international airline. How is company value likely to be affected by exchange rate changes? What policies would you adopt to reduce exchange rate risk?

9. Companies may be affected by changes in the nominal exchange rate or in the real exchange rate. Explain how this can occur. Which risks are easiest to hedge against?

10. A Ford dealer in the United States may be exposed to a devaluation of the yen if this leads to a cut in the price of Japanese cars. Suppose that the dealer estimates that a 1 percent decline in the value of the yen would result in a permanent decline of 5 percent in the dealer's profits. How should she hedge against this risk, and how should she calculate the size of the hedge position? You may find it helpful to refer back to Section 27.5.

11. You have bid for a possible export order that would provide a cash inflow of €1 million in six months. The spot exchange rate is $.9094 = €1 and the six-month forward rate is $.9070 = €1. There are two sources of uncertainty: (1) the euro could appreciate or depreciate and (2) you may or may not receive the export order. Illustrate in each case the profits or losses that you would make if (a) you sell one million euros forward, and (b) you buy a six-month option to sell euros with an exercise price of $.9070/€.

12. In August 2001, an American investor buys 1,000 shares in a Mexican company at a price of 500 pesos each. The share does not pay any dividend. A year later she sells the shares for 550 pesos each. The exchange rates when she buys the stock are shown in Table 28.1. Suppose that the exchange rate at the time of sale is pesos 9.50/$.
   a. How many dollars does she invest?
   b. What is her total return in pesos? In dollars?
   c. Do you think that she has made an exchange rate profit or loss? Explain.

13. Table 28.4 shows the foreign exchange rate for the Australian dollar and the Australian and U.S. inflation rates. Using these data, plot the nominal and real exchange rates. Which was more volatile, the nominal or the real exchange rate?

14. Look again at Table 28.4. George and Bruce each have an equal share in a trust fund that provides them with an income of US$100,000 a year. George lives in Seattle, but Bruce emigrated to Sydney in 1983. What has happened to George's *real* income since 1983? What was Bruce's income in 1983 in Australian dollars? What was it in 2000? What has happened to Bruce's *real* income?

15. In 1992 a liter of scotch cost $22.84 in New York, S$69 in Singapore, and 3,240 roubles in Moscow.
   a. If the law of one price held, what was the exchange rate between U.S. dollars and Singapore dollars? Between U.S. dollars and roubles?
   b. The actual exchange rates in 1992 were S$1.63 = US$1 and 250 roubles = US$1. Where would you prefer to buy your scotch?

16. Table 28.5 shows the annual interest rate (annually compounded) and exchange rates against the dollar for different currencies. Are there any arbitrage opportunities? If so, how would you secure a positive cash flow today, while zeroing out all future cash flows?

17. "Last year we had a substantial income in sterling, which we hedged by selling sterling forward. In the event sterling rose, and our decision to sell forward cost us a lot of money. I think that in the future we should either stop hedging our currency exposure or just hedge when we think sterling is overvalued." As financial manager, how would you respond to your chief executive's comment?

18. In 1985 a German corporation bought $250 million forward to cover a future purchase of goods from the United States. However, the dollar subsequently depreciated and the company found that, if it had waited and then bought the dollars spot, it would have

TABLE 28.4

Comparative data for Australia and the United States, 1983–2000.

	Foreign Exchange Rate, A$/US$	Consumer Price Index: 1983 = 100	
		Australia	United States
1983	1.108	100	100
1984	1.137	104	104
1985	1.427	111	108
1986	1.491	121	110
1987	1.427	131	114
1988	1.275	141	117
1989	1.262	151	121
1990	1.280	163	125
1991	1.284	168	129
1992	1.360	169	132
1993	1.470	172	134
1994	1.287	175	138
1995	1.342	184	142
1996	1.255	189	146
1997	1.532	189	149
1998	1.633	191	158
1999	1.524	193	158
2000	1.799	202	163

TABLE 28.5

Interest rates and exchange rates.

*Number of units of foreign currency that can be exchanged for $1.

	Interest Rate (%)	Spot Exchange Rate	1-Year Forward Exchange Rate*
United States (dollar)	3	—	—
Costaguana (pulga)	23	10,000	11,942
Westonia (ruple)	5	2.6	2.65
Gloccamorra (pint)	8	17.1	18.2
Anglosaxophonia (wasp)	4.1	2.3	2.28

paid 225 million deutschmarks (DM) less. One financial manager pointed out that the company could have waited to buy the dollars and meanwhile covered its exposure by using options. In that case it would have saved itself 225 million DM and would have lost only the cost of the option—around 20 million DM.[29] Evaluate the company's decision and the financial manager's criticism.

19. Carpet Baggers, Inc., is proposing to construct a new bagging plant in Europe. The two prime candidates are Germany and Switzerland. The forecasted cash flows from the proposed plants are as follows:

	C_0	C_1	C_2	C_3	C_4	C_5	C_6	IRR (%)
Germany (millions of euros)	−60	+10	+15	+15	+20	+20	+20	18.8
Switzerland (millions of Swiss francs)	−120	+20	+30	+30	+35	+35	+35	12.8

---

[29]Example cited in *Managing Risks and Costs through Financial Innovation*, Business International Corporation, New York, 1987.

The spot exchange rate for euros is $1.3/€, while the rate for Swiss francs is SFr1.5/$. The interest rate is 5 percent in the United States, 4 percent in Switzerland, and 6 percent in the euro countries. The financial manager has suggested that, if the cash flows were stated in dollars, a return in excess of 10 percent would be acceptable.

Should the company go ahead with either project? If it must choose between them, which should it take?

CHALLENGE QUESTIONS

1. If investors recognize the impact of inflation and exchange rate changes on a firm's cash flows, changes in exchange rates should be reflected in stock prices. How would the stock price of each of the following Swiss companies be affected by an unanticipated appreciation of the Swiss franc of 10 percent? Assume that only 2 percent of the appreciation can be attributed to increased inflation in the rest of the world (relative to the Swiss inflation rate).

   a. *A Swiss airline*: More than two-thirds of its employees are Swiss. Most revenues come from international fares set in U.S. dollars.

   b. *Nestlé*: Fewer than 5 percent of its employees are Swiss. Most revenues are derived from sales of consumer goods in a wide range of countries with competition from local producers.

   c. *Union Bank of Switzerland:* Most employees are Swiss. All non-Swiss franc monetary positions are fully hedged.

2. Alpha and Omega are U.S. corporations. Alpha has a plant in Hamburg that imports components from the United States, assembles them, and then sells the finished product in Germany. Omega is at the opposite extreme. It also has a plant in Hamburg, but it buys its raw material in Germany and exports its output back to the United States. How is each firm likely to be affected by a fall in the value of the euro? How could each firm hedge itself against exchange risk?

MINI-CASE

Exacta, s.a.

Exacta, s.a., is a major French producer, based in Lyons, of precision machine tools. About two-thirds of its output is exported. The majority of these sales is within the European Union. However, the company also has a thriving business in the United States, despite strong competition from several U.S. firms. Exacta usually receives payment for exported goods within two months of the invoice date, so that at any point in time only about one-sixth of annual exports to the United States is exposed to currency risk.

The company believes that its North American business is now large enough to justify a local manufacturing operation, and it has recently decided to establish a plant in South Carolina. Most of the output from this plant will be sold in the United States, but the company believes that there should also be opportunities for future sales in Canada and Mexico.

The South Carolina plant will involve a total investment of $380 million and is expected to be in operation by the year 2001. Annual revenues from the plant are expected to be about $420 million and the company forecasts net profits of $52 million a year. Once the plant is up and running, it should be able to operate for several years without substantial additional investment.

Although there is widespread enthusiasm for the project, several members of the management team have expressed anxiety about possible currency risk. M. Pangloss, the finance director, reassured them that the company was not a stranger to currency risk; after all, the company is already exporting about $320 million of machine tools each year to the United States and has managed to exchange its dollar revenue for French francs—and now for euros—without any major losses. But not everybody was convinced by this argument. For example, the CEO, M. B. Bardot, pointed out that the $380 million to be invested would substantially increase the amount of money at risk if the dollar fell relative to the euro. M. Bardot was notoriously risk-averse on financial matters and would push for complete hedging if practical.

M. Pangloss attempted to reassure the CEO. At the same time, he secretly shared some of the anxieties about exchange rate risk, particularly in the early years of the euro's existence. Nearly all the revenues from the South Carolina plant would be in U.S. dollars and the bulk of the $380 million investment would likewise be incurred in the United States. About two-thirds of the operating costs would be in dollars, but the remaining one-third would represent payment for components brought in from Lyons plus the charge by head office for management services and use of patents. The company has yet to decide whether to invoice its U.S. operation in dollars or euros for these purchases from the parent company.

M. Pangloss is optimistic that the company can hedge itself against currency risk. His favored solution is for Exacta to finance the plant by a $380 million issue of dollar bonds. That way the dollar investment would be offset by a matching dollar liability. An alternative is for the company to sell forward at the beginning of each year the expected revenues from the U.S. plant. But he realizes from experience that these simple solutions might carry hidden dangers. He decides to slow down and think more systematically about the additional exchange risk from the U.S. operation.

Questions

1. What would Exacta's true exposure be from its new U.S. operations, and how would it change from the company's current exposure?

2. Given that exposure, what would be the most effective and inexpensive approach to hedging?

PART EIGHT RELATED WEBSITES

The major futures exchanges have useful sites that provide data and explain how futures markets work:

www.cbot.com (Chicago Board of Trade)

www.cme.com (Chicago Mercantile Exchange)

www.eurexchange.com (Eurex)

www.liffe.com (London International Financial Futures Exchange)

The site for the Bank for International Settlements includes periodic surveys of derivative and currency markets:

www.bis.org

Commodity futures and options quotes and comment are available on:

www.cisco-futures.com

www.commoditytrader.net

www.io.com/~gibbonsb/wahoo (links to derivative sites)

Examples of journals specializing in derivatives include:

www.appliederivatives.com

www.erivativesreview.com

www.futuresmag.com

www.Risk.net

ISDA is the trade association for swap dealers:

www.isda.org

For data on companies in a number of countries and useful links to other finance-related sites for each country, see:

www.corporateinformation.com

A wonderful site for data and commentary on emerging markets is:

www.emgmkts.com

For sample rankings of countries by political risk see:

www.duke.edu/~charvey

www.prsgroup.com

FINANCIAL PLANNING AND
SHORT-TERM MANAGEMENT

W. T. GRANT WAS a large successful department store chain with 1,200 stores and $1.8 billion of sales. Yet in 1975 the company filed for bankruptcy, in what *Business Week* termed "the most significant bankruptcy in U.S. history."

The company's problems stemmed from the mid-1960s when it embarked on a rapid expansion policy. New stores take time to reach full profitability, so while profits initially increased, return on capital fell. Since the company chose to increase dividends, the money for the new investment had to be raised largely from the capital market. Instead of selling more shares, W. T. Grant preferred to raise the money by borrowing.

As the country slipped into recession, profits evaporated. Yet Grant insisted on maintaining its dividend. Effectively it was borrowing to pay the dividend. Within a year the company was bankrupt.

W. T. Grant failed because its goals for growth were unsustainable, and it had no plans for surviving a recession. Part Nine shows how firms can check that their growth strategy is consistent with their financing plans. Chapter 29 explains how managers monitor the company's financial health and develop long-term financial plans. Chapter 30 turns to short-term planning and examines how firms forecast and manage their short-term cash requirements. The remaining two chapters focus on two short-term issues— the collection and disbursement of cash and the management of credit.

CHAPTER TWENTY-NINE

FINANCIAL ANALYSIS AND PLANNING

A CAMEL LOOKS like an animal designed by a committee. If a firm made all its financial decisions piece-meal, it would end up with a financial camel. Therefore, smart financial managers consider the over-all effect of financing and investment decisions and ensure that they have the financial strategies in place to support the firm's plans for future growth.

Knowing where you stand today is a necessary prelude to contemplating where you might be in the future. Therefore we start the chapter with a brief review of a company's financial statements and we show how you can use these statements to assess the firm's overall performance and its current financial standing.

To produce order out of chaos, financial analysts calculate a few key financial ratios that summa-rize the company's financial strengths and weaknesses. These ratios are no substitute for a crystal ball, but they do help you to ask the right questions. For example, when the firm needs a loan from the bank, the financial manager can expect some searching questions about the firm's debt ratio and the proportion of profits that is absorbed by interest. Likewise, financial ratios may alert senior man-agement to potential problem areas. If a division is earning a low rate of return on its capital or its profit margins are under pressure, you can be sure that management will demand an explanation.

Growing firms need to invest in working capital, plant and equipment, product development, and so on. All this requires cash. We will, therefore, explain how firms use financial planning models to help them understand the financial implications of their business plans and to explore the conse-quences of alternative financial strategies.

Our focus in this chapter is on the long-term future. For example, firms may have a planning hori-zon of 5 or 10 years. In the next chapter we will look at how firms also develop more detailed strate-gies to ensure that they can get safely through the next few months.

29.1 FINANCIAL STATEMENTS

Public companies have a variety of stakeholders, such as shareholders, bondhold-ers, bankers, suppliers, employees, and management. All these stakeholders need to monitor the firm and to ensure that their interests are being served. They rely on the company's financial statements to provide the necessary information.

When reviewing a company's financial statements, it is important to remember that accountants still have a fair degree of leeway in reporting earnings and book val-ues. For example, accountants have discretion in the way they treat intangible assets, such as patents or franchises. Some believe that including these items on the balance sheet provides the best measure of the company's value as a going concern. Others take a more conservative approach and exclude intangible assets. They reason that, if the firm were liquidated, these assets would be largely valueless.

Although accountants around the world are working toward common prac-tices, there are considerable variations in the accounting rules of different coun-tries. In Anglo-Saxon countries such as the United States or the UK which have large and active equity markets, the rules have been designed with the shareholder very much in mind. By contrast, in Germany the focus of accounting standards is to verify that the creditors are properly protected.

Ray Ball has pointed out that differences between German and U.S. practice also arise because "German laws and institutional arrangements closely link German corporations' reported earnings to their dividend payments and to bonuses paid to managers and employees alike. The economic role of reported earnings is analogous to an annually-baked pie that is divided among the important stakeholders (government, employees, shareholders and managers alike), the size of the pie having first been determined with prudential regard for the financial stability of the corporation. . . . Reporting a loss would eliminate bonus, dividend and tax distributions, to the chagrin of all the stakeholders."[1]

Another difference is the way that taxes are shown in the income statement. For example, in Germany taxes are paid on the published profits and the depreciation method must therefore be approved by the revenue service. That is not so in Anglo-Saxon countries, where the numbers shown in the published accounts are generally *not* the basis for calculating the company's tax payments. For instance, the depreciation method used to calculate the published profits may differ from the depreciation method used by the tax authorities.

Sometimes the effect of these differences in accounting rules can be substantial. When the German car manufacturer, Daimler-Benz, decided to list its shares on the New York Stock Exchange in 1993, it was required to revise its accounting practices to conform to U.S. standards. While it reported a modest profit in the first half of 1993 using German accounting rules, it reported a loss of $592 million under U.S. rules, primarily because of differences in the treatment of reserves.

Countries also differ in the amount and accuracy of the information disclosed in a company's financial statements. For example, the Russian company, Lukoil, owns some of the largest oil reserves in the world and has 120,000 employees. Yet until recently its income statement reported just four numbers, with no accompanying notes. A study by LaPorta et al. rated a sample of countries on the quality of their accounting standards.[2] Table 29.1 provides an extract from their results. In general, they concluded that company accounts were more informative in those countries with a Scandinavian or English legal tradition and less so in those with a French or German tradition. However, there was a huge variation within each of these groups.

TABLE 29.1

Country ratings on quality of accounting standards (a high figure indicates high quality).

Source: LaPorta et al., "Law and Finance," *Journal of Political Economy* 106 (December 1998), 1113–1155.

Country	Legal Tradition	Rating
Sweden	Scandinavian	83
United Kingdom	English	78
United States	English	71
France	French	69
Hong Kong	English	69
Switzerland	German	68
Japan	German	65
Germany	German	62
South Korea	German	62
Mexico	French	60
India	English	57
Peru	French	38
Egypt	French	24

[1] See R. J. Ball, "Daimler-Benz (DaimlerChrysler) AG: Evolution of Corporate Governance from a Code-law 'Stakeholder' to a Common-law 'Shareholder Value' System," Graduate School of Business, University of Chicago.

[2] LaPorta et al., "Law and Finance," *Journal of Political Economy* 106 (December 1998), pp. 1113–1155.

29.2 EXECUTIVE PAPER'S FINANCIAL STATEMENTS

Your task is to assess the financial standing of the Executive Paper Corporation. Perhaps you are a financial analyst with Executive Paper and are helping to develop a five-year financial plan. Perhaps you are employed by a rival company that is contemplating a takeover bid for Executive Paper. Or perhaps you are a banker who needs to assess whether the bank should lend to the company. In each case your first step is to assess the company's *current* condition. You have before you the latest balance sheet, income statement, and sources and uses of funds.

The Balance Sheet

Executive Paper's balance sheet in Table 29.2 provides a snapshot of the company's assets and the sources of the money used to buy those assets.

The items in the balance sheet are listed in declining order of liquidity. For example, you can see that the accountant lists first those assets which are most likely to be turned into cash in the near future. They include cash itself, marketable securities and receivables (that is, bills to be paid by the firm's customers), and

Assets	Dec 1998	Dec 1999	Change
Current assets:			
Cash & securities	75	110	+35
Receivables	433.1	440	+6.9
Inventory	339.9	350	+10.1
Total current assets	848	900	+52
Fixed assets:			
Property, plant, and equipment	929.5	1,000	+70.5
Less accumulated depreciation	396.7	450	+53.3
Net fixed assets	532.8	550	+17.2
Total assets	1,380.8	1,450	+69.2
Liabilities and Shareholders' Equity	**Dec 1998**	**Dec 1999**	**Change**
Current liabilities:			
Debt due within 1 year	96.6	100	+3.4
Payables	349.9	360	+10.1
Total current liabilities	446.5	460	+13.5
Long-term debt	425	450	+25
Shareholders' equity	509.3	540	+30.7
Total liabilities & shareholders' equity	1,380.8	1,450	+69.2
Other financial information:			
Market value of equity	598	708	
Average number of shares (millions)	14.16	14.16	
Share price ($)	42.25	50.00	

TABLE 29.2

The balance sheet of Executive Paper Corporation (figures in $ millions).

inventories of raw materials, work in process, and finished goods. These assets are all known as *current assets.*

The remaining assets on the balance sheet consist of long-term, usually illiquid, assets such as pulp and paper mills, office buildings, and timberlands. The balance sheet does not show up-to-date market values of these long-term assets. Instead, the accountant records the amount that each asset originally cost and then, in the case of plant and equipment, deducts a fixed annual amount for depreciation. The balance sheet does not include all the company's assets. Some of the most valuable ones are intangible, such as patents, reputation, a skilled management, and a well-trained labor force. Accountants are generally reluctant to record these assets in the balance sheet unless they can be readily identified and valued.

Now look at the right-hand portion of Executive Paper's balance sheet, which shows where the money to buy the assets came from.[3] The accountant starts by looking at the liabilities, that is, the money owed by the company. First come those liabilities that need to be paid off in the near future. These *current liabilities* include debts that are due to be repaid within the next year and payables (that is, amounts owed by the company to its suppliers).

The difference between the current assets and current liabilities is known as the *net current assets* or *net working capital.* It roughly measures the company's potential reservoir of cash. For Executive Paper in 1999

$$\text{Net working capital} = \text{current assets} - \text{current liabilities}$$
$$= 900 - 460 = \$440 \text{ million}$$

The bottom portion of the balance sheet shows the sources of the cash that was used to acquire the net working capital and fixed assets. Some of the cash has come from the issue of bonds and leases that will not be repaid for many years. After all these long-term liabilities have been paid off, the remaining assets belong to the common stockholders. The company's equity is simply the total value of the net working capital and fixed assets less the long-term liabilities. Part of this equity has come from the sale of shares to investors and the remainder has come from earnings that the company has retained and invested on behalf of the shareholders.

Table 29.2 provides some other financial information about Executive Paper. For example, it shows the market value of the common stock. It is often helpful to compare the *book value* of the equity (shown in the company's accounts) with the *market value* established in the capital markets.

The Income Statement

If Executive Paper's balance sheet resembles a snapshot of the firm at a particular point in time, its income statement is like a video. It shows how profitable the firm has been over the past year.

Look at the summary income statement in Table 29.3. You can see that during 1999 Executive Paper sold goods worth $2,200 million and that the total costs of producing and selling these goods were $1,980 million. In addition to these out-of-pocket expenses, Executive Paper also made a deduction of $53.3 million for the value of the fixed assets used up in producing the goods. Thus Executive Paper's earnings before interest and taxes (EBIT) were

---

[3]The British and Americans can never agree whether to keep to the left or the right. British accountants list liabilities on the left and assets on the right.

	$ Millions
Revenues	2,200
Costs	1,980
Depreciation	53.3
EBIT	166.7
Interest	42.5
Tax	49.7
Net income	74.5
Dividends	43.8
Retained earnings	30.7
Earnings per share, dollars	5.26
Dividend per share, dollars	3.09

TABLE 29.3

The 1999 income statement of Executive Paper Corporation (figures in $ millions).

	$ Millions	Notes:
Sources:		
Net income	74.5	See Table 29.3
Depreciation	53.3	See Table 29.3
Operating cash flow	127.8	
Issues of long-term debt	25.0	See Table 29.2: 450 − 425
Issues of equity	0	See Tables 29.2 and 29.3:
		540 − 509.3 − (74.5 − 43.8)
Total sources	152.8	
Uses:		
Investment in net working capital	38.5	See Table 29.2: (900 − 460)
		− (848 − 446.5)
Investment in fixed assets	70.5	See Table 29.2: 1000 − 929.5
Dividends	43.8	See Table 29.3
Total uses	152.8	

TABLE 29.4

Sources and uses of funds for Executive Paper Corporation, 1999 (figures in $ millions).

$$EBIT = \text{Total revenues} - \text{costs} - \text{depreciation}$$
$$= 2,200 - 1,980 - 53.3 = \$166.7 \text{ million}$$

Of this sum $42.5 million went to pay the interest on the short- and long-term debt (remember debt interest is paid out of pretax income) and a further $49.7 million went to the government in the form of taxes. The $74.5 million that was left over belonged to the shareholders. Executive Paper paid out $43.8 million as dividends and reinvested the remaining $30.7 million in the business.

Sources and Uses of Funds

Table 29.4 shows where Executive Paper raised funds and how it spent them.[4] Beside each row in the table we have added a brief note on how the figure is calculated. We will explain each item in turn.

---

[4] Notice that in a *Sources and Uses of Funds* table the different components of net working capital are not separated out. When we discuss short-term planning in Chapter 30, we will show how to draw up a *Sources and Uses of Cash* table, which separates out different items of net working capital.

Look first at the uses of funds. The money that Executive Paper generates is either invested in net working capital and fixed assets or it is paid out to shareholders as dividends. Thus

$$\text{Total uses of funds} = \text{investment in net working capital} + \text{investment} \\ \text{in fixed assets} + \text{dividends paid to shareholders}$$

Table 29.2 shows that in 1999 Executive Paper started the year with net working capital of $848 - 446.5 = \$401.5$ million. By the end of the year it had grown to $900 - 460 = \$440$ million. So the company invested an additional $38.5 million in working capital. Over the same period fixed assets rose from $929.5 million to $1,000 million, an increase of $70.5 million. Finally, the income statement in Table 29.3 shows that Executive Paper distributed $43.8 million as dividends. Thus, in total, Executive Paper invested or paid out as dividends $38.5 + 70.5 + 43.8 = \$152.8$ million.

Where did the funds come from? There are two sources—the cash generated from operations and new money raised from investors:

$$\text{Total sources of funds} = \text{operating cash flow} + \text{new issues of long-term debt} \\ + \text{new issues of equity}$$

The income statement shows that in 1999 the company generated $127.8 million from operations. This included $53.3 million of depreciation (remember depreciation is not a cash outflow) and $74.5 million of net income. This left a deficiency of $152.8 - 127.8 = \$25$ million that Executive Paper needed to raise from the capital market. You can see from the balance sheet that Executive Paper raised this $25 million by an issue of long-term debt (debt increased from $425 million to $450 million). Executive Paper did not issue new equity capital in 1999. So why does the balance sheet show an increase in equity of $540 - 509.3 = \$30.7$ million? The answer is that this increase in equity came from income that the company retained and plowed back on behalf of its shareholders (retained earnings = net income dividends = $74.5 - 43.8 = \$30.7$ million).

29.3 MEASURING EXECUTIVE PAPER'S FINANCIAL CONDITION

Executive Paper's financial statements provide you with the basic information to assess its current financial standing. However, financial statements typically contain large amounts of data—far more than is contained in the simplified statements for Executive Paper. To condense these data into a convenient form, financial managers generally focus on a few key financial ratios.

Table 29.5 summarizes the key financial ratios for Executive Paper.[5] We will explain how to calculate these ratios and use them to shed light on five questions:

- How much has the company borrowed? Is the amount of debt likely to result in financial distress?
- How liquid is the company? Can it easily lay its hands on cash if needed?

---

[5]In addition to the ratios that we describe below, Table 29.5 includes a few other ratios that you may well encounter. Some are simply alternative ways to express the same result; others are variations on a theme.

		Executive Paper	Paper Industry[†]
Leverage Ratios:			
Debt ratio	(Long-term debt + leases)/(long-term debt + leases + equity)	.45	.53
Debt ratio (including short-term debt)*	(Long-term debt + short-term debt + leases)/(long-term debt + short-term debt + leases + equity)	.50	.56
Debt–equity ratio	(Long-term debt + leases)/equity	.83	1.12
Times-interest-earned	(EBIT + depreciation)/interest	5.2	2.9
Liquidity Ratios:			
Net-working-capital-to-total assets*	(Current assets − current liabilities)/total assets	.30	.06
Current ratio	Current assets/current liabilities	2.0	1.3
Quick ratio	(Cash + short-term securities + receivables)/current liabilities	1.2	.7
Cash ratio	(Cash + short-term securities)/current liabilities	.2	.1
Interval measure*	(Cash + short-term securities + receivables)/(costs from operations/365)	101.4	61.7
Efficiency Ratios:			
Sales-to-assets ratio	Sales/average total assets	1.55	.90
Sales-to-net-working-capital*	Sales/average net working capital	5.2	14.1
Days in inventory	Average inventory/(cost of goods sold/365)	63.6	59.1
Inventory turnover*	Cost of goods sold/average inventory	5.7	6.2
Average collection period (days)	Average receivables/(sales/365)	72.4	45.9
Receivables turnover*	Sales/average receivables	5.0	8.0
Profitability Ratios:			
Net profit margin	(EBIT − tax)/sales	5.3%	−0.5%
Return on assets (ROA)	(EBIT − tax)/average total assets	8.3%	−0.4%
Return on equity (ROE)	Earnings available for common stockholders/average equity	14.2%	−10.3%
Payout ratio	Dividend per share/earnings per share	.6	n.a.
Market-Value Ratios:			
Price–earnings ratio (P/E)	Stock price/earnings per share	9.5	n.a
Dividend yield	Dividend per share/stock price	6.2%	1.8%
Market-to-book ratio	Stock price/book value per share	1.3	3.6

TABLE 29.5

Financial ratios for Executive Paper and the paper industry, 1999.

*This ratio is an extra bonus not discussed in Section 29.2.
[†]1999 ratios for U.S. paper and allied products.
Source: Compustat.

- How productively is the company using its assets? Are there any signs that the assets are not being used efficiently?
- How profitable is the company?
- How highly is the firm valued by investors? Are investors' expectations reasonable?

When you calculate a company's financial ratios, you need some criteria to decide whether they are a cause for concern or a matter for congratulation. Unfortunately, there is no "right" set of financial ratios to which all companies should aspire. Take, for example, the company's capital structure. Debt has both advantages and disadvantages, and, even if there were an optimal level of debt for company A, it would not be appropriate for company B.

When managers review a company's financial position, they often start by comparing the current year's ratios with equivalent figures for earlier years. It is also helpful to look at how the company's financial position measures up to that of other firms in the same industry. Therefore, in Table 29.5 we have compared the financial ratios of Executive Paper with those for the U.S. paper industry.[6]

How Much Has Executive Paper Borrowed?

When Executive Paper borrows, it promises to make a series of fixed payments. Because its shareholders get only what is left over after the debtholders have been paid, the debt is said to create *financial leverage*. In extreme cases, if hard times come, a company may be unable to pay its debts.

The company's bankers and bondholders also want to make certain that Executive Paper does not borrow excessively. So, if Executive wishes to take out a new loan, the lenders will scrutinize several measures of whether the company is borrowing too much and will demand that it *keep* its debt within reasonable bounds. Such borrowing limits are stated in terms of financial ratios.

Debt Ratio   Financial leverage is usually measured by the ratio of long-term debt to total long-term capital. Since long-term lease agreements also commit the firm to a series of fixed payments, it makes sense to include the value of lease obligations with the long-term debt. For Executive Paper

$$\text{Debt ratio} = \frac{(\text{long-term debt} + \text{value of leases})}{(\text{long-term debt} + \text{value of leases} + \text{equity})}$$
$$= 450/(450 + 540) = .45$$

Another way to say the same thing is that Executive Paper has a debt-to-equity ratio of $450/540 = .83$:

$$\text{Debt–equity ratio} = \frac{(\text{long-term debt} + \text{value of leases})}{\text{equity}}$$
$$= 450/540 = .83$$

Notice that this measure makes use of book (i.e., accounting) values rather than market values.[7] The market value of the company finally determines whether the debtholders get their money back, so you might expect analysts to look at

---

[6]Financial ratios for different industries are published by the U.S. Department of Commerce, Dun and Bradstreet, The Risk Management Association, and others.

[7]In the case of leased assets accountants try to estimate the present value of the lease commitments. In the case of long-term debt they simply show the face value. This can sometimes be very different from present value. For example, the present value of low-coupon debt may be only a fraction of its face value. The difference between the book value of equity and its market value can be even more dramatic.

the face amount of the debt as a proportion of the total market value of debt and equity. On the other hand, the market value includes the value of intangible assets generated by research and development, advertising, staff training, and so on. These assets are not readily salable, and if the company falls on hard times, their value may disappear altogether. For some purposes, it may be just as good to follow the accountant and ignore these intangible assets. This is what lenders do when they insist that the borrower should not allow the book debt ratio to exceed a specified limit.

Debt ratios are sometimes defined in other ways. For example, analysts may include short-term debt or other obligations such as payables. There is a general point here. There are a variety of ways to define most financial ratios and there is no law stating how they *should* be defined. So be warned: Don't accept a ratio at face value without understanding how it has been calculated.

Times-Interest-Earned (or Interest Cover)   Another measure of financial leverage is the extent to which interest is covered by earnings before interest and taxes (EBIT) plus depreciation. For Executive Paper,[8]

$$\text{Times-interest-earned} = \frac{(\text{EBIT} + \text{depreciation})}{\text{interest}}$$

$$= \frac{(166.7 + 53.3)}{42.5} = 5.2$$

The regular interest payment is a hurdle that companies must keep jumping if they are to avoid default. The times-interest-earned ratio measures how much clear air there is between hurdle and hurdler.

Is Executive Paper's borrowing in the ballpark of standard practice or is it a matter for concern? Table 29.5 provides some clues. You can see that the debt ratio is slightly lower than that of the rest of the paper industry and the times-interest-earned is significantly higher than that of most companies.

How Liquid Is Executive Paper?

If Executive Paper is borrowing for a short period or has some large bills coming up for payment, you want to make sure that it can lay its hands on the cash when it is needed. The company's bankers and suppliers also need to keep an eye on Executive's liquidity. They know that illiquid firms are more likely to fail and default on their debts.

Another reason that analysts focus on liquid assets is that the figures are often more reliable. The book value of Executive's newsprint mill may be a poor guide to its true value, but at least you know what its cash in the bank is worth. Liquidity ratios also have some *less* desirable characteristics. Because short-term assets and liabilities are easily changed, measures of liquidity can rapidly become out-of-date. You may not know what that newsprint mill is worth, but you can be fairly sure that it won't disappear overnight.

---

[8]The numerator of times-interest-earned can be defined in several ways. Sometimes depreciation is excluded. Sometimes it is just earnings plus interest, that is, earnings before interest but *after* tax. This last definition seems nutty to us, because the point of interest earned is to assess the risk that the firm won't have enough money to pay interest. If EBIT falls below interest obligations, the firm won't have to worry about taxes. Interest is paid before the firm pays taxes.

Current Ratio   Executive Paper's current assets consist of cash and assets that can readily be turned into cash. Its current liabilities consist of payments that the company expects to make in the near future. Thus the ratio of the current assets to the current liabilities measures the margin of liquidity. It is known as the *current ratio:*

$$\text{Current ratio} = \frac{\text{current assets}}{\text{current liabilities}} = \frac{900}{460} = 1.96$$

Rapid decreases in the current ratio sometimes signify trouble. However, they can also be misleading. For example, suppose that a company borrows a large sum from the bank and invests it in short-term securities. If nothing else happens, net working capital is unaffected, but the current ratio changes. For this reason it might be preferable to net off the short-term investments and the short-term debt when calculating the current ratio.

Quick (or Acid-Test) Ratio   Some assets are closer to cash than others. If trouble comes, inventories may not sell at anything above fire-sale prices. (Trouble typically comes *because* customers are not buying and the firm's warehouse is stuffed with unwanted goods.) Thus, managers often focus only on cash, short-term securities, and bills that customers have not yet paid:

$$\text{Quick ratio} = \frac{(\text{cash } + \text{ short-term securities } + \text{ receivables})}{\text{current liabilities}}$$

$$= \frac{110 + 440}{460} = 1.20$$

Cash Ratio   A company's most liquid assets are its holdings of cash and marketable securities. That is why analysts also look at the cash ratio:

$$\text{Cash ratio} = \frac{(\text{cash } + \text{ short-term securities})}{\text{current liabilities}} = \frac{110}{460} = .24$$

Of course, these summary measures of liquidity are just that. They are no substitute for detailed plans to ensure that the company can pay its bills. In the next chapter we will describe how companies forecast their cash needs and draw up a short-term financial plan to deal with any cash shortage.

How Productively Is Executive Paper Using Its Assets?

Financial analysts employ another set of ratios to judge how efficiently the firm is using its investment in current and fixed assets. Later in the chapter we will look at the financial implications of Executive's ambitious plans to expand output, but understanding the investment in fixed assets and working capital that is needed to support Executive Paper's *current* output may help to uncover any inconsistencies in these plans for the future.

Sales-to-Assets (or Asset Turnover) Ratio   The sales-to-assets ratio shows how hard the firm's assets are being put to use:

$$\frac{\text{Sales}}{\text{average total assets}} = \frac{2,200}{(1,380.8 + 1,450)/2} = 1.55$$

Assets here are measured as the sum of current and fixed assets. Notice that since assets are likely to change over the course of a year, we use the *average* of the assets at the beginning and end of the year. Averages are commonly used whenever a *flow* figure (in this case, sales) is compared with a *stock* or snapshot figure (total assets).

Notice that for each dollar of investment Executive generates $1.55 of sales, a much higher figure than other paper companies. There are several possible explanations: (1) Executive uses its assets more efficiently; (2) Executive is working close to capacity, so that it may be difficult to increase sales without additional invested capital; or (3) compared with its rivals, Executive produces high volume, low margin products.[9] You need to dig deeper to know which explanation is correct. Remember our earlier comment—financial ratios help you to *ask* the right questions, not to *answer* them.

Instead of looking at the ratio of sales to *total assets*, managers sometimes look at how hard particular types of capital are being put to use. For example, it turns out that Executive's ratio of sales to *current assets* is less than that of other paper companies. It is the ratio of Executive's sales to its *fixed assets* that sets it apart from its rivals.

Days in Inventory The speed with which a company turns over its inventory is measured by the number of days that it takes for the goods to be produced and sold. First convert the cost of goods sold to a daily basis by dividing by 365. Then express inventories as a multiple of the daily cost of goods sold:

$$\text{Days in inventory} = \frac{\text{average inventory}}{\text{cost of goods sold} \div 365}$$

$$= \frac{(339.9 + 350)/2}{1,980/365} = 63.6 \text{ days}$$

Notice that Executive Paper appears to have a relatively low rate of inventory turnover. Perhaps there is scope for economizing on the company's investment in inventories.

Average Collection Period The average collection period measures how quickly customers pay their bills:

$$\text{Average collection period} = \frac{\text{average receivables}}{\text{sales} \div 365}$$

$$= \frac{(433.1 + 440)/2}{2,200/365} = 72.4 \text{ days}$$

The collection period for Executive Paper is somewhat longer than the industry average. The company may have a conscious policy of offering attractive credit terms to lure business, but it is worth looking at whether the credit manager is lax in chasing up the slow payers.

---

[9]We will see shortly that this last explanation does not hold up. The paper industry in 1999 earned a *negative* profit margin.

How Profitable Is Executive Paper?

Net Profit Margin   If you want to know the proportion of sales that finds its way into profits, you look at the profit margin. Thus[10]

$$\text{Net profit margin} = \frac{(\text{EBIT} - \text{tax})}{\text{sales}} = .053, \text{ or } 5.3\%$$

Return on Assets (ROA)   Managers often measure the performance of the firm by the ratio of income to total assets (income is usually defined as earnings before interest but after taxes). This is known as the firm's *return on assets* (ROA) or *return on investment* (ROI):[11]

$$\text{Return on assets} = \frac{(\text{EBIT} - \text{tax})}{(\text{average total assets})}$$

$$= \frac{(166.7 - 49.7)}{(1,380.8 + 1,450)/2} = .083, \text{ or } 8.3\%$$

Another measure focuses on the return on the firm's equity:

$$\text{Return on equity (ROE)} = \frac{(\text{earnings available for common stockholders})}{\text{average equity}}$$

$$= \frac{74.5}{(509.3 + 540)/2} = .142, \text{ or } 14.2\%$$

Executive Paper's return on assets and equity is in sharp contrast to the rest of the industry, which provided a negative return in 1999.

It is natural to compare the return earned by Executive Paper with the opportunity cost of capital. Of course, the assets in the financial statements are shown at *net book value*, that is, original cost less depreciation.[12] So a low ROA does not necessar-

---

[10]Net profit margin is sometimes measured as net income ÷ sales. This ignores the profits that are paid out to debtholders as interest and should therefore not be used to compare firms with different capital structures.

When making comparisons between firms, it makes sense to recognize that firms which pay more interest pay less tax. We suggest that you calculate the tax that the company would pay if it were all-equity-financed. To do this you need to adjust taxes by adding back interest tax shields (interest payments × marginal tax rate). Using an assumed tax rate of 40 percent,

$$\text{Net profit margin} = \frac{\text{EBIT} - (\text{tax} + \text{interest tax shields})}{\text{sales}}$$

$$= \frac{166.7 - [49.7 + (.4 \times 42.5)]}{2,200} = 0.45, \text{ or } 4.5\%$$

[11]When comparing the returns on total assets of firms with different capital structures, it makes sense to add back interest tax shields to tax payments (see footnote 10). This adjusted ratio then measures the returns that the company would have earned if it were all-equity-financed.

One other point about return on assets. Since profits are a flow figure and assets are a snapshot figure, analysts commonly divide profits by the average of assets at the start and end of the year. The reason that they do this is that the firm may raise large amounts of new capital during the year and then put it to work. Therefore part of the year's earnings is a return on this new capital.

However, this measure is potentially misleading and should not be compared closely with the cost of capital. After all, when we defined the return that shareholders require from investing in the capital market, we divided expected profit by the initial outlay, not by an average of starting and ending values.

[12]More careful comparisons between the return on assets and the cost of capital need to recognize the biases in accounting numbers. We discussed these biases in Chapter 12.

ily imply that those assets could be better employed elsewhere. Nor would a high ROA necessarily mean that you could buy similar assets today and get a high return. In a competitive industry, firms can expect to earn only their cost of capital. Therefore, managers whose businesses are earning more than the cost of capital are likely to earn a pat on the back, while those that are earning a low return may face some tough questions or worse. Although shareholders like to see their companies earn a high return on assets, consumers' groups or regulators often regard a high return as evidence that the firm is charging excessive prices. Naturally, such conclusions are seldom cut and dried. There is plenty of room for argument as to whether the return on assets is properly measured or whether it exceeds the cost of capital.

Payout Ratio   The payout ratio measures the proportion of earnings that is paid out as dividends. Thus

$$\text{Payout ratio} = \frac{\text{dividends}}{\text{earnings}} = \frac{43.8}{74.5} = .6$$

We saw in Section 16.2 that managers don't like to cut dividends if there is a shortfall in earnings. Therefore, if a company's earnings are particularly variable, management is likely to play it safe by setting a low average payout ratio. When earnings fall unexpectedly, the payout ratio will rise temporarily. Likewise, if earnings are expected to rise next year, management may feel that it can pay somewhat more generous dividends than it would otherwise have done.

How Highly Is Executive Paper Valued by Investors?

There is no law that prohibits you from introducing data that are not in the company accounts. For example, when you are assessing Executive Paper's efficiency, you might wish to look at the cost per ton of paper produced. Similarly, an airline might calculate revenues per passenger mile flown, and so on. If you want to gauge how highly Executive Paper is valued by investors, then you will need to calculate ratios that combine accounting and stock market data. Here are three examples.

Price–Earnings Ratio   The price–earnings, or P/E, ratio measures the price that investors are prepared to pay for each dollar of earnings. In the case of Executive Paper

$$\text{P/E ratio} = \frac{\text{stock price}}{\text{earnings per share}} = \frac{50}{5.26} = 9.5$$

In Section 4.4 we explained that a high P/E ratio may indicate that investors think the firm has good growth opportunities or that its earnings are relatively safe and therefore more valuable. Of course, it may also mean that earnings are temporarily depressed. If a company just breaks even with zero earnings, its P/E ratio is infinite.

Dividend Yield   Executive's dividend yield is simply its dividend as a proportion of the stock price. Thus

$$\text{Dividend yield} = \frac{\text{dividend per share}}{\text{stock price}} = \frac{3.09}{50} = .062, \text{ or } 6.2\%$$

Remember that the return to an investor comes in two forms—dividend yield and capital appreciation. Executive Paper's relatively high dividend yield may indicate that investors are demanding a relatively high rate of return or that they are not expecting rapid dividend growth with consequent capital gains.

Market-to-Book Ratio   The market-to-book ratio is the ratio of the stock price to book value per share. For Executive Paper

$$\text{Market-to-book ratio} = \frac{\text{stock price}}{\text{book value per share}} = \frac{50}{540/14.16} = 1.3$$

Book value per share is just stockholders' book equity divided by the number of shares outstanding. Book equity equals common stock plus retained earnings—the net amount that the firm has received from stockholders or reinvested on their behalf.[13] Thus Executive Paper's market-to-book ratio of 1.3 means that the firm is worth 30 percent more than past and present stockholders have put into it.

The Dupont System

Some of the profitability and efficiency ratios that we described above can be linked in useful ways. These relationships are often referred to as the **Dupont system,** in recognition of the chemical company that popularized them.

The first relationship links the return on assets (ROA) with the firm's sales-to-assets ratio and its profit margin:

$$\text{ROA} = \frac{\text{EBIT} - \text{tax}}{\text{assets}} = \underset{\substack{\uparrow \\ \text{sales-to-} \\ \text{assets ratio}}}{\frac{\text{sales}}{\text{assets}}} \times \underset{\substack{\uparrow \\ \text{profit} \\ \text{margin}}}{\frac{\text{EBIT} - \text{tax}}{\text{sales}}}$$

All firms would like to earn a higher return on assets but their ability to do so is limited by competition. If the expected return on assets is fixed by competition, firms face a trade-off between the sales-to-assets ratio and the profit margin. For example, fast-food chains, which turn over their capital frequently, also tend to operate on low profit margins. Classy hotels have relatively high margins, but this is offset by lower sales-to-assets ratios.

Firms often seek to increase their profit margins by becoming more vertically integrated; for example, they may acquire a supplier or one of their sales outlets. Unfortunately, unless they have some special skill in running these new businesses, they are likely to find that any gain in profit margin is offset by a decline in the sales-to-assets ratio.

The return on equity (ROE) can be broken down as follows:

$$\text{ROE} = \frac{\text{EBIT} - \text{tax} - \text{interest}}{\text{equity}}$$

$$= \underset{\substack{\uparrow \\ \text{leverage} \\ \text{ratio}}}{\frac{\text{assets}}{\text{equity}}} \times \underset{\substack{\uparrow \\ \text{sales-to-} \\ \text{assets} \\ \text{ratio}}}{\frac{\text{sales}}{\text{assets}}} \times \underset{\substack{\uparrow \\ \text{profit} \\ \text{margin}}}{\frac{\text{EBIT} - \text{tax}}{\text{sales}}} \times \underset{\substack{\uparrow \\ \text{"debt} \\ \text{burden"}}}{\frac{\text{EBIT} - \text{tax} - \text{interest}}{(\text{EBIT} - \text{tax})}}$$

---

[13]Retained earnings are measured net of depreciation. They represent stockholders' new investment in the business over and above the amount needed to maintain the firm's existing stock of assets.

Notice that the product of the two middle terms is the return on assets. This depends on the firm's production and marketing skills and is unaffected by the financing mix. However, the first and fourth terms do depend on the debt–equity mix.[14] The first term measures the ratio of gross assets to equity, while the last term measures the extent to which profits are reduced by interest. If the firm is leveraged, the first term is greater than 1.0 (assets are greater than equity) and the fourth term is less than 1.0 (part of the profits are absorbed by interest). Thus, leverage can either increase or reduce the return on equity. In the case of Executive Paper

$$\text{ROE} = \text{leverage ratio} \times \text{sales-to-assets ratio} \times \text{profit margin} \times \text{debt burden}$$
$$= 2.70 \times 1.55 \times .053 \times .637 = .14$$

So, for Executive Paper the leverage ratio (2.70) more than offsets the debt burden (.637). Executive's leverage increases its return on equity.

 ## 29.4 FINANCIAL PLANNING

Executive Paper's financial statements not only help you to understand the past, but they also provide the starting point for developing a financial plan for the future.

Financial plans begin with the firm's product development and sales objectives. For example, Executive Paper's corporate staff might ask each division to submit three alternative business plans covering the next five years:

1. A *best-case* or aggressive growth plan calling for heavy capital investment, new products, and an increased market share.

2. A *normal growth* plan in which the division grows with its markets but not at the expense of its competitors.

3. A plan of *retrenchment* designed to minimize capital outlays. This is planning for lean economic times.

Of course, the planners might also look at the opportunities for moving into a wholly new area where the company can exploit its existing strengths. Often they may recommend entering the market for strategic reasons, that is, not because the *immediate* investment is profitable but because it establishes the firm in the market and creates *options* for possibly valuable follow-on investments. In other words, there is a two-stage decision. At the second stage (the follow-on project) the financial manager faces a standard capital budgeting problem. But at the first stage projects may be valuable primarily for the options they bring with them.[15]

To see the financial consequences of the business plan, you need to develop forecasts of future cash flows. If the likely operating cash flow is insufficient to cover both the planned dividend payments and the investment in net working capital and fixed assets, then the firm needs to ensure that it can raise the balance by borrowing or by the sale of additional shares.

---

[14]There is a complication here because the amount of tax paid does depend on the financing mix. We suggested in footnote 10 that it would be better to add back any interest tax shields to the tax payment when calculating the firm's profit margin.

[15]The Blitzen Computers example in Section 22.1 illustrates how option theory can be used to quantify a project's strategic value.

Cash-flow forecasts should always be subjected to a reality check. For example, few companies can expect to continue to earn a high return on their investment without attracting competition. So firms are likely to find it difficult to maintain a high return on assets indefinitely. Conversely, those with a low return on assets may hope for some easing of competitive pressures and the arrival of more normal returns.[16]

When you prepare a financial plan, you shouldn't look just at the most likely financial consequences. You also need to plan for the unexpected. One way to do this is to work through the consequences of the plan under the most likely set of circumstances and then use *sensitivity analysis* to vary the assumptions one at a time. Another approach is to look at the implications of different plausible scenarios.[17] For example, one scenario might envisage high interest rates leading to a slowdown in world economic growth and lower commodity prices. The second scenario might involve a buoyant domestic economy, high inflation, and a weak currency.

29.5 FINANCIAL PLANNING MODELS

Suppose that management has asked you to assume a 20 percent annual growth in Executive Paper's sales and profits over the next five years. Can the company realistically expect to finance this out of retained earnings and borrowing, or should it plan for an issue of equity? Spreadsheet programs are tailor-made for such questions. Let's investigate.

The basic sources and uses relationship tells us that

> External capital required
> = operating cash flow
>   − investment in net working capital
>   − investment in fixed assets
>   − dividends

Thus there are four steps to finding how much extra cash Executive Paper will need and the implications for its debt ratio:

Step 1   Project next year's operating cash flow (depreciation provision plus net income) assuming the planned 20 percent increase in revenues. This gives the total sources of funds in the absence of any new issue of securities. Look, for example, at the second column of Table 29.6, which provides a forecast of operating cash flow in year 2000 for Executive Paper.

Step 2   Project what additional investment in net working capital and fixed assets will be needed to support this increased activity and how much of the net income will be paid out as dividends. The sum of these expenditures gives you the total

[16]For evidence that accounting returns tend to regress toward the mean, see Chapter 10 of K. G. Palepu, P. M. Healy, and V. L. Bernard, *Business Analysis and Valuation*, South-Western College Publishing, Cincinnati, OH, 2nd ed., 2000.

[17]For a description of the use of different planning scenarios in the Royal Dutch/Shell group, see P. Wack, "Scenarios: Uncharted Waters Ahead," *Harvard Business Review* 63 (September–October 1985) and "Scenarios: Shooting the Rapids," *Harvard Business Review* 64 (November–December 1985).

	1999	2000	2004
Revenues	2,200	2,640	5,474
Costs (90% of revenues)	1,980	2,376	4,927
Depreciation (10% of fixed assets at start of year)	53.3	55.0	114
EBIT	166.7	209.0	433.4
Interest (10% of long-term debt at start of year)	42.5	45	131.3
Tax (40% of pretax profit)	49.7	65.6	120.8
Net income	74.5	98.4	181.2
Operating cash flow	127.8	153.4	295.3

TABLE 29.6

Latest and pro forma income statements for Executive Paper (figures in $ millions).

	1999	2000	2004
Increase in net working capital (NWC) assuming NWC = 20% of revenues	38.5	88	182.5
Investment in fixed assets (FA) assuming FA = 25% of revenues	70.2	165	342.1
Dividend (60% of net income)	45.6	59.0	108.7
Total uses of funds	129.3	312.0	633.4
External capital required = total uses of funds − operating cash flow	25.0	158.6	338.1

TABLE 29.7

Latest and pro forma statements of sources and uses of funds for Executive Paper (figures in $ millions).

uses of funds. The second column of Table 29.7 provides a forecast of uses of funds for Executive Paper.

Step 3   Calculate the difference between the projected operating cash flow (from Step 1) and the projected uses (Step 2). This is the cash that will need to be raised from new sales of securities. For example, you can see from Table 29.7 that Executive Paper will need to issue $158.6 million of debt in 2000 if it is to expand at the planned rate and not sell more shares.

Step 4   Finally, construct a pro forma balance sheet that incorporates the additional assets and the increase in debt and equity. This is done in the second column of Table 29.8. Executive Paper's equity increases by the additional retained earnings (net income less dividends), while long-term debt is increased by the $158.6 million new issue.

Once you have set up the spreadsheet, it is easy to run out your projections for several years. The final columns in Tables 29.6–29.8 show the pro forma income statement, sources and uses of funds, and balance sheet for the year 2004, assuming Executive Paper continues to fund a 20 percent annual growth rate solely from retained earnings and new debt issues. Over the five-year period Executive Paper would need to borrow an additional $1.2 billion and by year 2004 its debt ratio would have increased to 67 percent. Most financial managers would regard this as sailing much too close to the wind, and the debt ratio would probably be above the limit set by the company's banks and bondholders.

TABLE 29.8

Latest and pro forma balance sheets for Executive Paper (figures in $ millions).

	1999	2000	2004
Net working capital (20% of revenues)	440	528	1,095
Net fixed assets (25% of revenues)	550	660	1,369
Total net assets	990	1,188	2,463
Long-term debt	450	608.6	1,651
Equity	540	579.4	812
Total long-term liabilities and equity	990	1,188	2,463

The obvious solution for Executive Paper is to issue a mix of debt and equity, but there are other possibilities that the financial manager may want to explore. One option may be to hold back dividends during this period of rapid growth, but it turns out that even a complete dividend freeze would still leave Executive Paper needing to raise just under $750 million of new funds. An alternative might be to investigate whether the company could cut back on net working capital. For example, we have seen that Executive Paper's customers take 72 days to pay their bills. Perhaps more careful control of credit collection could help to economize on capital.

We stated earlier that financial planning is not just about exploring how to cope with the most likely outcomes. It also needs to ensure that the firm is prepared for unlikely ones. For example, the paper industry is notoriously exposed to economic downturn. So you would certainly wish to check that Executive Paper could cope with a cyclical decline in sales and profit margins. Sensitivity analysis or scenario analysis can help you to do so.

Executive Paper's problem is not unique, for many companies find that rapid growth can bring burgeoning debt levels. Firms that fail to think through the financial consequences of their growth plans are liable to get into BIG trouble. Look, for example, at the Finance in the News box, which shows how British Telecom's attempt to become a global telecom company forced some hard thinking about how to finance this growth.

Pitfalls in Model Design

The Executive Paper model that we have developed is too simple for practical application. You probably have already thought of several ways to improve it—by keeping track of the outstanding shares, for example, and printing out earnings and dividends per share. Or you might want to distinguish between short-term lending and borrowing opportunities, now buried in working capital.

The model that we developed for Executive Paper is known as a *percentage of sales model*. Almost all the forecasts for the company are proportional to the forecasted level of sales. However, in reality many variables will *not* be proportional to sales. For example, important components of working capital such as inventory and cash balances will generally rise less rapidly than sales. In addition, fixed assets such as plant and equipment are typically not added in small increments as sales increase. Executive Paper's plant may well be operating at less than full capacity, so that the company can initially increase output without *any* additions to capacity. Eventually, however, if sales continue to increase, the firm may need to make a large new investment in plant and equipment.

INVESTORS QUESTION BRITISH TELECOM'S FINANCIAL PLANNING

As the country's principal telecom supplier, British Telecom (BT) was a safe, if somewhat uninspiring, investment. Including short-term loans, its debt ratio was a fairly conservative .38 and the volatility of its stock returns was well below the average for UK companies.

All that changed at the end of the 1990s when BT made a series of foreign acquisitions and paid several billion pounds for a license to offer third-generation mobile services in the UK. These expenditures were financed largely by new borrowing, including a record $10 billion bond issue in the United States. By December 2000 BT's debt had expanded to £30 billion and the debt ratio had climbed to .71. To reassure new bondholders BT had agreed that, if its debt rating were subsequently lowered, it would increase the interest payment on its bonds. Not long afterward the rating agencies announced that they were considering a downgrade, which would increase the cost of servicing BT's debt.

BT's aim was to reduce its debt by £10 billion, and it hoped to achieve this by selling off some recent acquisitions. Unfortunately, as the prices of high-tech stocks fell away in the spring of 2001, this plan began to look less and less attractive.

By March 2001 BT's share price had fallen 70 percent from its high, and anxious investors began to question whether the company had a coherent strategy to deal with its mountain of debt and to finance the heavy expenditures that would be needed to exploit its mobile licenses. Various questions were asked and debated. Should the company press ahead with its plans to sell off businesses? Could it live with its high debt ratio for the time being? Should it seek to build up equity by cutting its dividend or by issuing new equity? It was clear that for BT, financial planning had become central to the company's survival.

But beware of adding too much complexity: There is always the temptation to make a model bigger and more detailed. You may end up with an exhaustive model that is too cumbersome for routine use. The fascination of detail, if you give in to it, distracts attention from crucial decisions like stock issues and dividend policy.

There Is No Finance in Financial Planning Models

Why do we say there is no finance in these corporate financial models? The first reason is that they usually incorporate an accountant's view of the world. They are designed to forecast accounting statements. They do not emphasize the tools of financial analysis: incremental cash flow, present value, market risk, and so on.[18]

This may not matter as long as everyone recognizes the financial forecasts for what they are. However, you sometimes hear managers stating corporate goals in terms of accounting numbers. They may say, "Our objective is to achieve an

---

[18]Of course, there is no reason that the manager can't use the output to calculate the present value of the firm (given some assumption about growth beyond the planning period), and this is sometimes done.

annual sales growth of 20 percent," or "We want a 25 percent return on book equity and a profit margin of 10 percent." On the surface such objectives don't make sense. Shareholders want to be richer, not to have the satisfaction of a 10 percent profit margin. Also, a goal that is stated in terms of accounting ratios is not operational unless it is translated back into what the statement means for business decisions. For example, what does a 10 percent profit margin imply— higher prices, lower costs, increased vertical integration, or a move into new, high-margin products?

So why do managers define objectives in this way? In part such goals may be a mutual exhortation to try harder, like singing the company song before work. But we suspect that managers are often using a code to communicate real concerns. For example, the goal to increase sales rapidly may reflect managers' belief that increased market share is needed to achieve scale economies, or a target profit margin may be a way of saying that the firm has been pursuing sales growth at the expense of margins. The danger is that everyone may forget the code and the accounting targets may be seen as goals in themselves.

The second reason for saying that there is no finance in these planning models is that they produce no signposts pointing toward optimal decisions. They do not even tell us which alternatives are worth examining. For example, we saw that Executive Paper is planning for a rapid growth in sales and earnings per share. But is that good news for the shareholders? Well, not necessarily; it depends on the opportunity cost of the capital that Executive Paper needs to invest. If the new investment earns more than the cost of capital, it will have a positive NPV and add to shareholder wealth. However, the return that Executive Paper is forecasting to earn on its new investment is little more than the interest rate on its debt and almost certainly below Executive's cost of capital. In this case the company's planned investment will make shareholders worse off, even though the company expects steady growth in earnings per share.

The capital that Executive Paper needs to raise depends on its decision to pay out two-thirds of its earnings as a dividend. But the financial planning model does not tell us whether this dividend payment makes sense or what mixture of equity or debt the company should issue. In the end the management has to decide. We would like to tell you exactly how to make the choice, but we can't. There is no model that encompasses all the complexities encountered in financial planning.

As a matter of fact, there never will be one. This bold statement is based on Brealey and Myers's Third Law:[19]

- *Axiom:* The number of unsolved problems is infinite.
- *Axiom:* The number of unsolved problems that humans can hold in their minds is at any time limited to 10.
- *Law:* Therefore in any field there will always be 10 problems which can be addressed but which have no formal solution.

Brealey and Myers's Third Law implies that no model can find the best of all financial strategies.[20]

---

[19]The second law is presented in Section 12.2.

[20]It is possible to build linear programming models that help search for the best strategy subject to specified assumptions and constraints. These models can be more effective in screening alternative financial strategies.

29.6 GROWTH AND EXTERNAL FINANCING

We started this chapter by noting that financial plans force managers to be consistent in their goals for growth, investment, and financing. Before leaving the topic of financial planning, we should look at some general relationships between a firm's growth objectives and its financing needs.

Recall that Executive Paper ended 1999 with fixed assets and net working capital of $990 million. In 2000 it plans to plow back $39.4 million, so net assets will increase by 39.4/990 or 3.98 percent. Thus Executive Paper can grow by 3.98 percent without needing to raise additional capital. The growth rate that a company can achieve without external funds is known as the *internal growth rate.* For Executive Paper

$$\text{Internal growth rate} = \frac{\text{retained earnings}}{\text{net assets}} = 3.98\%$$

We can gain more insight into what determines this growth rate by multiplying the top and bottom of the expression for internal growth rate by *net income* and *equity* as follows:

$$\text{Internal growth rate} = \frac{\text{retained earnings}}{\text{net income}} \times \frac{\text{net income}}{\text{equity}} \times \frac{\text{equity}}{\text{net assets}}$$

$$= \text{plowback ratio} \times \text{return on equity} \times \frac{\text{equity}}{\text{net assets}}$$

In 2000 Executive Paper expects to plow back 40 percent of net income and to earn a return of 18.22 percent on the equity with which it began the year. At the start of the year equity finances 54.55 percent of Executive Paper's net assets. Therefore

$$\text{Internal growth rate} = .40 \times .1822 \times .5455 = .0398, \text{ or } 3.98\%$$

Notice that if Executive Paper wishes to grow faster than this without raising equity capital, it would need to (1) plow back a higher proportion of its earnings, (2) earn a higher return on equity (ROE), or (3) have a lower debt-to-equity ratio.[21]

Instead of focusing on how rapidly the company can grow without *any* external financing, Executive Paper's financial manager may be interested in the growth rate that can be sustained without additional *equity* issues. Of course, if the firm is able to raise enough debt, virtually any growth rate can be financed. It makes more sense to assume that the firm has settled on an optimal capital structure which it will maintain as equity is increased by the retained earnings. Thus the firm issues only enough debt to keep the debt–equity ratio constant. The *sustainable growth rate* is the highest growth rate the firm can maintain without increasing its financial leverage. It turns out that the sustainable growth rate depends only on the plowback rate and the return on equity:

$$\text{Sustainable growth rate} = \text{plowback ratio} \times \text{return on equity}$$

---

[21]Notice that the internal growth rate does not stay constant. As the firm plows back earnings, the debt-to-equity ratio declines and the internal growth rate increases.

For Executive Paper,

$$\text{Sustainable growth rate} = .40 \times .1822 = .0729, \text{ or } 7.29\%$$

We first encountered this formula in Chapter 4, where we used it to value the firm's equity.

These simple formulas remind us that financial plans need to be consistent. Firms may grow rapidly in the short term by relying on debt finance, but such growth cannot be maintained without incurring excessive debt levels.

SUMMARY

Managers use financial statements to monitor their own company's performance, to help understand the policies of a competitor, or to check on the health of a customer. But there is a danger of being overwhelmed by the sheer volume of data. That is why managers use a few salient ratios to summarize the firm's leverage, liquidity, efficiency, profitability, and market valuation. We have described some of the more popular financial ratios.

We offer the following general advice to users of these ratios:

1. Financial ratios seldom provide answers, but they do help you to ask the right questions.

2. There is no international standard for financial ratios. A little thought and common sense are worth far more than blind application of formulas.

3. You need a benchmark for assessing a company's financial position. Compare financial ratios with the company's ratios in earlier years and with the ratios of other firms in the same business.

Understanding the past is the first step to being prepared for the future. Most firms prepare a financial plan that describes the firm's strategy and projects its future consequences by means of pro forma balance sheets, income statements, and statements of sources and uses of funds. The plan establishes financial goals and is a benchmark for evaluating subsequent performance.

The plan is the end result, but the process that produces the plan is valuable in its own right. First, planning forces the financial manager to consider the combined effects of all the firm's investment and financing decisions. This is important because these decisions interact and should not be made independently. Second, planning requires the manager to consider events that could upset the firm's progress and to devise strategies to be held in reserve for counterattack when unhappy surprises occur.

There is no theory or model that leads straight to *the* optimal financial strategy. Consequently, financial planning proceeds by trial and error. Many different strategies may be projected under a range of assumptions about the future. The dozens of separate projections that may be made during this trial-and-error process generate a heavy load of arithmetic. Firms have responded by developing corporate financial planning models to forecast the financial consequences of different strategies. We showed how you can use a simple spreadsheet model to analyze Executive Paper's strategies. But remember there is no finance in these models. Their primary purpose is to produce accounting statements.

There are some good general texts on financial statement analysis. See, for example:

G. Foster: *Financial Statement Analysis*, 2nd ed., Prentice-Hall, Inc., Englewood Cliffs, NJ, 1986.

K. G. Palepu, V. L. Bernard, and P. M. Healy: *Business Analysis and Valuation*, South-Western College Publishing, Cincinnati, OH, 2nd ed., 2000.

Three classic articles on the application of financial ratios to specific problems are:

W. H. Beaver: "Financial Ratios as Predictors of Failure," *Empirical Research in Accounting: Selected Studies,* supplement to *Journal of Accounting Research,* 1966, pp. 77–111.

W. H. Beaver, P. Kettler, and M. Scholes: "The Association between Market-Determined and Accounting-Determined Risk Measures," *Accounting Review,* 45:654–682 (October 1970).

J. O. Horrigan: "The Determination of Long Term Credit Standing with Financial Ratios," *Empirical Research in Accounting: Selected Studies,* supplement to *Journal of Accounting Research,* 1966, pp. 44–62.

Corporate planning has an extensive literature of its own. Good books and articles include:

G. Donaldson: "Financial Goals and Strategic Consequences," *Harvard Business Review,* 63:57–66 (May–June 1985).

G. Donaldson: *Strategy for Financial Mobility,* Harvard Business School Press, Boston, 1986.

A. C. Hax and N. S. Majluf: *The Strategy Concept and Process—A Pragmatic Approach,* 2nd ed., Prentice-Hall, Inc., Englewood Cliffs, NJ, 1996.

The links between capital budgeting, strategy, and financial planning are discussed in:

S. C. Myers: "Finance Theory and Financial Strategy," *Interfaces,* 14:126–137 (January–February, 1984).

Here are three references on corporate planning models:

W. T. Carleton, C. L. Dick, Jr., and D. H. Downes: "Financial Policy Models: Theory and Practice," *Journal of Financial and Quantitative Analysis,* 8:691–709 (December 1973).

W. T. Carleton and J. M. McInnes: "Theory, Models and Implementation in Financial Management," *Management Science,* 28:957–978 (September 1982).

S. C. Myers and G. A. Pogue: "A Programming Approach to Corporate Financial Management," *Journal of Finance,* 29:579–599 (May 1974).

1. Table 29.9 gives abbreviated balance sheets and income statements for Weyerhaeuser Company. Calculate the following ratios:
   a. Debt ratio.
   b. Times-interest-earned ratio.
   c. Current ratio.
   d. Quick ratio.
   e. Net profit margin.
   f. Days in inventory.
   g. Return on equity.
   h. Payout ratio.

2. There are no universally accepted definitions of financial ratios, but five of the following ratios make no sense at all. Substitute the correct definitions.
   a. Debt–equity ratio = (long-term debt + value of leases)/(long-term debt + value of leases + equity)
   b. Return on equity = (EBIT − tax)/average equity

TABLE 29.9

Income statement
and balance sheet
for Weyerhaeuser
Company, 2000
(figures in millions).

Source: Weyerhaeuser
Company, 2000 annual
report.

Income Statement	
Net sales	$15,980
Cost of goods sold	12,035
Other expenses	1,412
Depreciation	859
Earnings before interest and tax (EBIT)	1,674
Net interest	351
Tax	483
Earnings	$ 840
Dividends	263

Balance Sheet		
	End of Year	Start of Year
Cash and short-term securities	115	1,640
Receivables	1,247	1,296
Inventories	1,499	1,329
Other current assets	427	278
Total current assets	3,288	4,543
Tangible fixed assets	10,427	9,582
Other long-term assets	4,480	4,214
Total assets	$18,195	$18,339
Short-term debt	733	909
Payables	921	961
Other current liabilities	1,050	1,083
Total current liabilities	2,704	2,953
Long-term debt and capital leases	5,114	5,100
Other long-term liabilities	3,544	3,113
Common shareholders' equity	6,832	7,173
Total liabilities	$18,195	$18,339

    c. Payout ratio = dividend/stock price
    d. Profit margin = (EBIT − tax)/sales
    e. Inventory turnover = sales/average inventory
    f. Current ratio = current liabilities/current assets
    g. Sales-to-net-working-capital = average sales/average net working capital
    h. Average collection period = sales/(average receivables ÷ 365)
    i. Quick ratio = (current assets − inventories)/current liabilities

3. True or false?
    a. A company's debt–equity ratio is always less than 1.
    b. The quick ratio is always less than the current ratio.
    c. The return on equity is always less than the return on assets.
    d. If a project is slow to reach full profitability, straight-line depreciation is likely to
       produce an overstatement of profits in the early years.
    e. A substantial new advertising campaign by a cosmetics company will tend to
       depress earnings and cause the stock to sell at a low price–earnings multiple.

4. In each of the following cases, explain briefly which of the two companies is likely to
   be characterized by the higher ratio:
    a. Debt–equity ratio: a shipping company or a computer software company.
    b. Payout ratio: United Foods Inc. or Computer Graphics Inc.

   c. Sales-to-assets ratio: an integrated pulp and paper manufacturer or a paper mill.

   d. Average collection period: a supermarket chain or a mail-order company.

   e. Price–earnings multiple: Basic Sludge Company or Fledgling Electronics.

5. A firm has $30,000 of inventory. If this represents 30 days' sales, what is the annual cost of goods sold? What is the inventory turnover ratio?

6. Keller Cosmetics maintains a profit margin of 4 percent and a sales-to-assets ratio of 3.

   a. What is its return on assets?

   b. If its debt–equity ratio is 1.0, its interest payments and taxes are each $10,000, and EBIT is $40,000, what is the return on equity?

7. A firm has a long-term debt–equity ratio of .4. Shareholders' equity is $1 million. Current assets are $200,000, and the current ratio is 2.0. Long-term assets total $1.5 million. What is the ratio of debt to total long-term capital?

8. Magic Flutes has total receivables of $3,000, which represent 20 days' sales. Average total assets are $75,000. The firm's profit margin is 5 percent. Find the firm's return on assets and sales-to-assets ratio.

9. Consider this simplified balance sheet for Geomorph Trading:

Current assets	100	60	Current liabilities
		280	Long-term debt
Long-term assets	500	70	Other liabilities
		190	Equity
	600	600	

   a. Calculate the ratio of debt to equity.

   b. What are Geomorph's net working capital and total long-term capital? Calculate the ratio of debt to total long-term capital.

10. Airlux Antarctica has current liabilities of $200 million and a crash—sorry—*cash* ratio of .05. How much cash and marketable securities does it hold?

11. On average, it takes Microlimp's customers 60 days to pay their bills. If Microlimp has annual sales of $500 million, what is the average value of unpaid bills?

12. Executive Paper's return on equity is higher than its return on assets. Is this always the case? Explain.

13. True or false?

   a. Financial planning should attempt to minimize risk.

   b. The primary aim of financial planning is to obtain better forecasts of future cash flows and earnings.

   c. Financial planning is necessary because financing and investment decisions interact and should not be made independently.

   d. Firms' planning horizons rarely exceed three years.

   e. Financial planning requires accurate forecasting.

   f. Financial planning models should include as much detail as possible.

14. Table 29.10 summarizes the 2002 income statement and end-year balance sheet of Drake's Bowling Alleys. Drake's financial manager forecasts a 10 percent increase in sales and costs in 2003. The ratio of sales to *average* assets is expected to remain at .40. Interest is forecasted at 5 percent of debt at start of year.

   a. What is the implied level of assets at the end of 2003?

   b. If the company pays out 50 percent of net income as dividends, how much cash will Drake need to raise in the capital markets in 2003?

   c. If Drake is unwilling to make an equity issue, what will be the debt ratio at the end of 2003?

TABLE 29.10

Financial statement for Drake's
Bowling Alleys, 2002 (figures in
thousands).

*Assets at end-2001 were
$2,400,000.
†Debt at end-2001 was $500,000.

Income Statement	
Sales	$1,000 (40% of *average* assets)*
Costs	750 (75% of sales)
Interest	25 (5% of debt at start of year)†
Pretax profit	225
Tax	90 (40% of pretax profit)
Net income	$ 135

Balance Sheet			
Assets	$2,600	Debt	$ 500
		Equity	2,100
Total	$2,600	Total	$2,600

TABLE 29.11

Financial statements for Archimedes
Levers, 2001.

Income Statement	
Sales	$4,000
Costs, including interest	3,500
Net income	$ 500

Balance Sheet, Year-end					
	2001	2000		2001	2000
Assets	$3,200	$2,700	Debt	$1,200	$1,033
			Equity	2,000	1,667
Total	$3,200	$2,700	Total	$3,200	$2,700

15. Abbreviated financial statements for Archimedes Levers are shown in Table 29.11. If sales increase by 10 percent in 2002 and all other items, including debt, increase correspondingly, what must be the balancing item? What will be its value?

16. What is the maximum possible growth rate for Archimedes (see question 15) if the payout ratio is set at 50 percent and **(a)** no external debt or equity is to be issued? **(b)** the firm maintains a fixed debt ratio but issues no equity?

PRACTICE QUESTIONS

1. Look up the latest financial statements for any company on the Market Insight database (**www.mhhe.com/edumarketinsight**) and calculate a sources and uses of funds table for the latest year. Don't be put off by the fact that actual financial statements are more complicated than the simplified ones we showed for Executive Paper.

2. Look up the latest financial statements for any company on the Market Insight database (**www.mhhe.com/edumarketinsight**) and calculate the following ratios for the latest year:
   a. Debt ratio.
   b. Times-interest-earned.
   c. Current ratio.
   d. Quick ratio.
   e. Net profit margin.
   f. Days in inventory.

g. Return on equity.

h. Payout ratio.

3. Select a sample of companies with financial statements on the Market Insight database (**www.mhhe.com/edumarketinsight**) and compare the days in inventory and the average collection period for receivables. Can you explain these differences?

4. This question reviews some of the difficulties encountered in interpreting accounting numbers.
   a. Give four examples of important assets, liabilities, or transactions which may not be shown on the company's books.
   b. How does investment in intangible assets, such as research and development, distort accounting ratios? Give at least two examples.
   c. Explain the three ways in which accelerating inflation affects earnings and profitability ratios based on historical-cost accounting.

5. Use financial ratio analysis to compare two companies chosen from the same industry.

6. Discuss alternative measures of financial leverage. Should the market value of equity be used or the book value? Is it better to use the market value of debt, the book value, or the book value discounted at the risk-free interest rate? How should you treat off-balance-sheet obligations such as pension liabilities? How would you treat preferred stock, deferred tax reserves, and minority interest?

7. Suppose that at year-end 1999 Executive Paper had unused lines of credit that would have allowed it to borrow a further $300 million. Suppose also that it used this line of credit to raise short-term loans of $300 million and invested the proceeds in marketable securities. Would the company have appeared to be (a) more or less liquid? (b) more or less highly levered? Calculate the appropriate ratios.

8. How would the following actions affect a firm's current ratio?
   a. Inventory is sold.
   b. The firm takes out a bank loan to pay its suppliers.
   c. A customer pays its overdue bills.
   d. The firm uses cash to purchase additional inventories.

9. Sara Togas sells all its output to Federal Stores. The following table shows selected financial data, in millions, for the two firms:

	Sales	Profits	Assets
Federal Stores	$100	$10	$50
Sara Togas	20	4	20

Calculate the sales-to-assets ratio, the profit margin, and the return on the two firms. Now assume that the two companies merge. If Federal continues to sell goods worth $100 million, how will the three financial ratios change?

10. United Ratio's common stock has a dividend yield of 4 percent. Its dividend per share is $2, and it has 10 million shares outstanding. If the market-to-book ratio is 1.5, what is the total book value of the equity?

11. As you can see, someone has spilled ink over some of the entries in the balance sheet and income statement of Transylvania Railroad (Table 29.12). Can you use the following information to work out the missing entries?
   • Financial leverage: .4.
   • Times-interest-earned: 8.
   • Current ratio: 1.4.
   • Quick ratio: 1.0.

TABLE 29.12

Balance sheet and income statement of Transylvania Railroad (figures in $ millions).

	December 2001	December 2000
Balance Sheet		
Cash	■■■	20
Accounts receivable	■■■	34
Inventory	■■■	26
Total current assets	■■■	80
Fixed assets, net	■■■■	25
Total	■■■	105
Notes payable	30	35
Accounts payable	25	20
Total current liabilities	■■■	55
Long-term debt	■■■	20
Equity	■■■	30
Total	115	105
Income Statement		
Sales	■■■	
Cost of goods sold	■■■	
Selling, general, and administrative expenses	10	
Depreciation	20	
EBIT	■■■	
Interest	■■■	
Earnings before tax	■■■	
Tax	■■■	
Earnings available for common stock	■■■	

- Cash ratio: .2.
- Return on total assets: .18.
- Return on equity: .41.
- Inventory turnover: 5.0.
- Receivables' collection period: 71.2 days.

12. Here are some data for five companies in the same industry:

	Company Code				
	A	B	C	D	E
Net income (millions)	$ 10	$ .5	$ 6.67	−$ 1	$ 6.67
Total book assets (millions)	$300	$30.0	$120.00	$50	$120.00
Shares outstanding (millions)	3	4	2	5	10
Share price	$100	$ 5	$ 50	$ 8	$ 10

You have been asked to calculate a measure of the industry price–earnings ratio. Discuss the possible ways that you might calculate such a measure. Does changing the method of calculation make a significant difference to the end result?

13. Describe some of the ways that the choice of accounting technique can temporarily depress or inflate earnings.

14. How would rapid inflation affect the accuracy and relevance of a manufacturing company's balance sheet and income statement? Does your answer depend on how much debt the company has issued?

15. In 1970 United Airlines bought four new jumbos for $21.8 million each. These planes were written down straight-line over 16 years to a residual value of $0.2 million each. However, they could have been sold in 1986 for about $20 million each.[22] How would the company's financial ratios have changed if it had used a depreciation schedule that more nearly reflected the actual decline in aircraft values?

16. The British food company Ranks Hovis McDougall (RHM) believed that some of its most valuable assets were its brand names. Yet these assets are not usually shown on the balance sheet. In 1988 RHM changed its accounting policy to include the value of brand names and thereby added £678 million (nearly $1.2 billion) to the balance sheet. Do you think that this change would facilitate comparisons between firms?

17. Suppose you wish to use financial ratios to estimate the risk of a company's stock. Which of those that we have described in this chapter are likely to be helpful? Can you think of other accounting measures of risk?

18. Look up some firms that have been in trouble. Plot the changes over the preceding years in the principal financial ratios. Are there any patterns?

19. List the major elements of a completed financial plan.

20. "There is no finance in financial planning models." Explain.

21. What are the dangers and disadvantages of using a financial model? Discuss.

22. Should a financial plan be considered an unbiased forecast of future cash flows, earnings, and other financial variables? Why or why not?

23. Our model of Executive Paper is an example of a top-down planning model. Some firms use a bottom-up financial planning model, which incorporates forecasts of revenues and costs for particular products, advertising plans, major investment projects, and so on. What sort of firms would you expect to use each type, and what would they use them for?

24. Corporate financial plans are often used as a basis for judging subsequent performance. What do you think can be learned from such comparisons? What problems are likely to arise, and how might you cope with these problems?

25. What problems are likely to be encountered in keeping the financial plan up-to-date?

26. The balancing item in the Executive Paper model is borrowing. What is meant by *balancing item?* How would the model change if dividends were made the balancing item instead? In that case how would you suggest that planned borrowing be determined?

27. Construct a new model for Executive Paper based on your answer to question 26. Does your model generate a feasible financial plan for 2000? (*Hint:* If it doesn't, you may have to allow the firm to issue stock.)

28. Executive Paper's financial manager believed that revenues in 2000 would rise by as much as 50 percent or by as little as 10 percent. Recalculate the pro forma financial statements under these two assumptions. How does the rate of growth in revenues affect the firm's borrowing requirement?

---

[22]See M. D. Staunton, *Pricing of Airline Assets and Their Valuation by Securities Markets,* unpublished PhD dissertation, London Business School, 1992.

TABLE 29.13

Financial statements for Executive Cheese
Company, 2001 (figures in thousands).

Income Statement	
Revenue	$1,785
Fixed costs	53
Variable costs (80% of revenue)	1,428
Depreciation	80
Interest (at 11.8%)	24
Taxes (at 40%)	80
Net income	$ 120

Sources and Uses of Funds	
Sources:	
Operating cash flow	$ 200
Borrowing	36
Stock issues	104
Total sources	$ 340
Uses:	
Increase in net working capital	$ 60
Investment	200
Dividends	80
Total uses	$ 340

Balance Sheet, Year-end		
	2001	2000
Assets:		
Net working capital	$ 400	$ 340
Fixed assets	800	680
Total assets	$1,200	$1,020
Liabilities:		
Debt	$ 240	$ 204
Book equity	960	816
Total liabilities	$1,200	$1,020

29. a. Use the Executive Paper model (Tables 29.6–29.8) to produce pro forma income statements, balance sheets, and sources and uses of funds statements for 2000 and 2001.
Assume business as usual except that sales and costs were planned to expand by
30 percent per year, as were fixed assets and net working capital. The interest rate
was forecasted to remain at 10 percent and stock issues were ruled out. Executive Paper also stuck to its 60 percent dividend payout ratio.
    b. What are the firm's debt ratio and interest coverage under this plan?
    c. Can the company continue to finance expansion by borrowing?

30. Table 29.13 shows the 2001 financial statements for the Executive Cheese Company. Annual depreciation is 10 percent of fixed assets at the beginning of the year, plus 10 percent of new investment. The company plans to invest a further $200 per year in fixed
assets for the next five years and forecasts that the ratio of revenues to total assets at the
start of each year will remain at 1.75. Fixed costs are expected to remain at $53, and vari-
able costs, at 80 percent of revenue. The company's policy is to pay out two-thirds of
net income as dividends and to maintain a book debt ratio of 20 percent.

Income Statement	
Revenue	$1,800
Fixed costs	56
Variable costs (80% of revenue)	1,440
Depreciation	80
Interest (8% of beginning-of-year debt)	24
Taxable income	200
Taxes (at 40%)	80
Net income	$ 120
Dividends	$80
Retained earnings	$40

Balance Sheet, Year-end		
	2002	2001
Assets:		
Net working capital	$ 400	$ 400
Fixed assets	800	800
Total assets	$1,200	$1,200
Liabilities and shareholders' equity:		
Debt	$ 300	$ 300
Equity	900	900
Total liabilities and shareholders' equity	$1,200	$1,200

TABLE 29.14

Financial statements for Dynastatics Corporation 2002 (figures in thousands).

Income Statement	
Sales	$950
Costs	250
EBIT	700
Taxes	200
Net income	$500

Balance Sheet, Year-end					
	2001	2002		2001	2002
Assets	$2,700	$3,000	Debt	$ 900	$1,000
			Equity	1,800	2,000
Total	$2,700	$3,000	Total	$2,700	$3,000

TABLE 29.15

Financial statements for Eagle Sport Supply, 2002.

a. Construct a model for Executive Cheese like the one in Tables 29.6–29.8.

b. Use your model to produce a set of financial statements for 2002.

31. Table 29.14 contains financial statements for Dynastatics Corporation. Although the company has not been growing, it now plans to expand and will increase net fixed assets (that is, assets net of depreciation) by $200 per year for the next five years. It forecasts that the ratio of revenues to total assets will remain fixed at 1.5. Annual

depreciation is 10 percent of fixed assets at the start of the year. Fixed costs are expected to remain at $56, and variable costs, at 80 percent of revenue. The company's policy is to pay out two-thirds of net income as dividends and to maintain a book debt ratio of 25 percent of total capital.

a. Produce a set of financial statements for 2007. Assume that net working capital will equal 50 percent of fixed assets.

b. Now assume that the balancing item is debt and that no equity is to be issued. Prepare a completed pro forma balance sheet for 2007. What is the projected debt ratio for 2003?

32. The financial statements of Eagle Sport Supply are shown in Table 29.15. For simplicity, "Costs" include interest. Assume that Eagle's assets are proportional to its sales.

a. Find Eagle's required external funds if it maintains a dividend payout ratio of 60 percent and plans a growth rate of 15 percent in 2003.

b. If Eagle chooses not to issue new shares of stock, what variable must be the balancing item? What will its value be?

c. Now suppose that the firm plans instead to increase long-term debt only to $1,100 and does not wish to issue any new shares of stock. Why must the dividend payment now be the balancing item? What will its value be?

33. a. What is the internal growth rate of Eagle Sports (see problem 32) if the dividend payout ratio is fixed at 60 percent and the equity-to-asset ratio is fixed at 2/3?

b. What is the sustainable growth rate?

34. Bio-Plasma Corp. is growing at 30 percent per year. It is all-equity-financed and has total assets of $1 million. Its return on equity is 20 percent. Its plowback ratio is 40 percent.

a. What is the internal growth rate?

b. What is the firm's need for external financing this year?

c. By how much would the firm increase its internal growth rate if it reduced its payout rate to zero?

d. By how much would such a move reduce the need for external financing? What do you conclude about the relationship between dividend policy and requirements for external financing?

CHALLENGE QUESTIONS

1. Take another look at Geomorph Trading's balance sheet in quiz question 9, and consider the following additional information:

Current Assets		Current Liabilities		Other Liabilities	
Cash	15	Payables	35	Deferred tax	32
Inventories	35	Taxes due	10	Unfunded pensions	22
Receivables	50	Bank loan	15	R&R reserve	16
	100		60		70

The "R&R reserve" covers the future costs of removal of an oil pipeline and environmental restoration of the pipeline route.

There are many ways to calculate a debt ratio for Geomorph. Suppose you are evaluating the safety of Geomorph's debt and want a debt ratio for comparison with the ratios of other companies in the same industry. Would you calculate the ratio in terms of total liabilities or total capitalization? What would you include in debt—the bank loan, the deferred tax account, the R&R reserve, the unfunded pension liability? Explain the pros and cons of these choices.

2. Take any firm whose financial statements are shown on the Market Insight database (**www.mhhe.com/edumarketinsight**) and make some plausible forecasts for future growth and the asset base needed to support that growth. Then use a spreadsheet program to develop a five-year financial plan. What financing is needed to support the planned growth? How vulnerable is the company to an error in your forecasts?

STANDARD
&POOR'S

CHAPTER THIRTY

SHORT-TERM FINANCIAL PLANNING

MOST OF THIS book is devoted to long-term financial decisions such as capital budgeting and the choice of capital structure. Such decisions are called *long-term* for two reasons. First, they usually involve long-lived assets or liabilities. Second, they are not easily reversed and therefore may commit the firm to a particular course of action for several years.

Short-term financial decisions generally involve short-lived assets and liabilities, and usually they are easily reversed. Compare, for example, a 60-day bank loan for $50 million with a $50 million issue of 20-year bonds. The bank loan is clearly a short-term decision. The firm can repay it two months later and be right back where it started. A firm might conceivably issue a 20-year bond in January and retire it in March, but it would be extremely inconvenient and expensive to do so. In practice, such a bond issue is a long-term decision, not only because of the bond's 20-year maturity but also because the decision to issue it cannot be reversed on short notice.

A financial manager responsible for short-term financial decisions does not have to look far into the future. The decision to take the 60-day bank loan could properly be based on cash-flow forecasts for the next few months only. The bond issue decision will normally reflect forecasted cash requirements 5, 10, or more years into the future.

Managers concerned with short-term financial decisions can avoid many of the difficult conceptual issues encountered elsewhere in this book. In a sense, short-term decisions are easier than long-term decisions, but they are not less important. A firm can identify extremely valuable capital investment opportunities, find the precise optimal debt ratio, follow the perfect dividend policy, and yet founder because no one bothers to raise the cash to pay this year's bills. Hence the need for short-term planning.

We start the chapter with an overview of the major classes of short-term assets and liabilities. We show how long-term financing decisions affect the firm's short-term financial planning problem. We describe how financial managers trace changes in cash and working capital, and we look at how they forecast month-by-month cash requirements or surpluses and develop short-term financing strategies. We conclude by examining more closely the principal sources of short-term finance.

 ## 30.1 THE COMPONENTS OF WORKING CAPITAL

Short-term, or *current*, assets and liabilities are collectively known as **working capital.** Table 30.1 gives a breakdown of current assets and liabilities for all manufacturing corporations in the United States in 2000. Note that current assets are larger than current liabilities. **Net working capital** (current assets less current liabilities) was positive.

Current Assets

One important current asset is *accounts receivable.* When one company sells goods to another company or a government agency, it does not usually expect to be paid immediately. These unpaid bills, or *trade credit,* make up the bulk of accounts receivable. Companies also sell goods on credit to the final consumer. This *consumer credit* makes up the remainder of accounts receivable. We will discuss the management of receivables in Chapter 32. You will learn how companies decide which customers are good or bad credit risks and when it makes sense to offer credit.

Another important current asset is *inventory.* Inventories may consist of raw materials, work in process, or finished goods awaiting sale and shipment. Firms

TABLE 30.1

Current assets and liabilities for U.S. manufacturing corporations, first quarter, 2001 (figures in $ billions).

Source: U.S. Census Bureau, *Quarterly Financial Report for Manufacturing, Mining and Trade Corporations, First Quarter, 2001* (**www.census. gov/prod/www/abs/qfr-mm**).

Current Assets		Current Liabilities	
Cash	156.3	Short-term loans	228.4
Marketable securities	104.4	Accounts payable	357.3
Accounts receivable	527.2	Accrued income taxes	55.5
Inventories	510.7	Current payments due on long-term debt	85.3
Other current assets	248.9	Other current liabilities	507.4
Total	1547.5	Total	1233.9

Net working capital (current assets − current liabilities) = $1,547.5 − 1,233.9 = $313.6 billion

invest in inventory. The cost of holding inventory includes not only storage cost and the risk of spoilage or obsolescence but also the opportunity cost of capital, that is, the rate of return offered by other, equivalent-risk investment opportunities.[1] The benefits of holding inventory are often indirect. For example, a large inventory of finished goods (large relative to expected sales) reduces the chance of a "stockout" if demand is unexpectedly high. A producer holding a small finished-goods inventory is more likely to be caught short, unable to fill orders promptly. Similarly, large inventories of raw materials reduce the chance that an unexpected shortage would force the firm to shut down production or use a more costly substitute material.

Bulk orders for raw materials lead to large average inventories but may be worthwhile if the firm can obtain lower prices from suppliers. (That is, bulk orders may yield quantity discounts.) Firms are often willing to hold large inventories of finished goods for similar reasons. A large inventory of finished goods allows longer, more economical production runs. In effect, the production manager gives the firm a quantity discount.

The task of inventory management is to assess these benefits and costs and to strike a sensible balance. In manufacturing companies the production manager is best placed to make this judgment. Since the financial manager is not usually directly involved in inventory management, we will not discuss the inventory problem in detail.

The remaining current assets are cash and marketable securities. The cash consists of currency, demand deposits (funds in checking accounts), and time deposits (funds in savings accounts). The principal marketable security is commercial paper (short-term, unsecured notes sold by other firms). Other securities include U.S. Treasury bills and state and local government securities.

In choosing between cash and marketable securities, the financial manager faces a task like that of the production manager. There are always advantages to holding large "inventories" of cash—they reduce the risk of running out of cash and having to raise more on short notice. On the other hand, there is a cost to holding idle

---

[1]How risky are inventories? It is hard to generalize. Many firms just assume inventories have the same risk as typical capital investments and therefore calculate the cost of holding inventories using the firm's average opportunity cost of capital. You can think of many exceptions to this rule of thumb however. For example, some electronics components are made with gold connections. Should an electronics firm apply its average cost of capital to its inventory of gold? (See Section 11.1.)

cash balances rather than putting the money to work in marketable securities. In Chapter 31 we will tell you how the financial manager collects and pays out cash and decides on an optimal cash balance.

Current Liabilities

We have seen that a company's principal current asset consists of unpaid bills from other companies. One firm's credit must be another's debit. Therefore, it is not surprising that a company's principal current liability often consists of *accounts payable*, that is, outstanding payments to other companies. A firm that delays paying its bills is in effect borrowing money from its suppliers. So companies that are strapped for cash sometimes solve the problem by *stretching payables*.

To finance its investment in current assets, a company may rely on a variety of short-term loans. Banks and finance companies are the largest source of such loans, but companies may also issue short-term debt, called *commercial paper*. We will describe the different kinds of short-term debt toward the end of the chapter.

30.2 LINKS BETWEEN LONG-TERM AND SHORT-TERM FINANCING DECISIONS

All businesses require capital, that is, money invested in plant, machinery, inventories, accounts receivable, and all the other assets it takes to run a business efficiently. Typically, these assets are not purchased all at once but obtained gradually over time. Let us call the total cost of these assets the firm's *cumulative capital requirement*.

Most firms' cumulative capital requirement grows irregularly, like the wavy line in Figure 30.1. This line shows a clear upward trend as the firm's business grows. But there is also seasonal variation around the trend: In the figure the capital requirements peak late in each year. Finally, there would be unpredictable week-to-week and month-to-month fluctuations, but we have not attempted to show these in Figure 30.1.

The cumulative capital requirement can be met from either long-term or short-term financing. When long-term financing does not cover the cumulative capital requirement, the firm must raise short-term capital to make up the difference. When long-term financing *more* than covers the cumulative capital requirement, the firm has surplus cash available for short-term investment. Thus the amount of long-term financing raised, given the cumulative capital requirement, determines whether the firm is a short-term borrower or lender.

Lines *A*, *B*, and *C* in Figure 30.1 illustrate this. Each depicts a different long-term financing strategy. Strategy *A* always implies a short-term cash surplus. Strategy *C* implies a permanent need for short-term borrowing. Under *B*, which is probably the most common strategy, the firm is a short-term lender during part of the year and a borrower during the rest.

What is the *best* level of long-term financing relative to the cumulative capital requirement? It is hard to say. There is no convincing theoretical analysis of this question. We can make practical observations, however. First, most financial managers attempt to "match maturities" of assets and liabilities. That is, they finance long-lived assets like plant and machinery with long-term borrowing and equity. Second, most firms make a permanent investment in net working capital (current assets less current liabilities). This investment is financed from long-term sources.

FIGURE 30.1

The firm's cumulative capital require-ment (colored line) is the cumulative investment in all the assets needed for the business. In this case the requirement grows year by year, but there is seasonal fluctuation within each year. The requirement for short-term financing is the differ-ence between long-term financing (lines A^+, A, B, and C) and the cumu-lative capital requirement. If long-term financing follows line C, the firm always needs short-term financing. At line B, the need is seasonal. At lines A and A^+, the firm never needs short-term financing. There is always extra cash to invest.

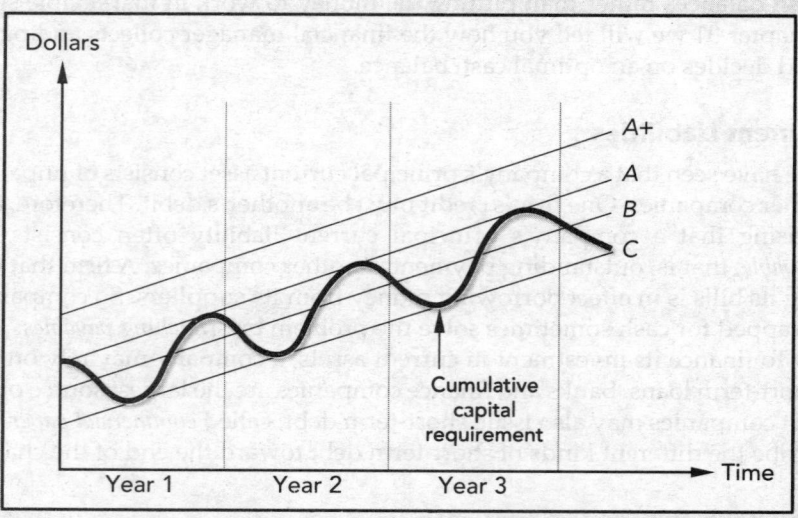

The Comforts of Surplus Cash

Many financial managers would feel more comfortable under strategy A than strat-egy C. Strategy A^+ (the highest line) would be still more relaxing. A firm with a sur-plus of long-term financing never has to worry about borrowing to pay next month's bills. But is the financial manager paid to be comfortable? Firms usually put surplus cash to work in Treasury bills or other marketable securities. This is at best a zero-NPV investment for a taxpaying firm.[2] Thus we think that firms with a *permanent* cash surplus ought to go on a diet, retiring long-term securities to reduce long-term financing to a level at or below the firm's cumulative capital requirement. That is, if the firm is on line A^+, it ought to move down to line A, or perhaps even lower.

30.3 TRACING CHANGES IN CASH AND WORKING CAPITAL

Table 30.2 compares 2000 and 2001 year-end balance sheets for Dynamic Mattress Company. Table 30.3 shows the firm's income statement for 2001. Note that Dynamic's cash balance increased by $1 million during 2001. What caused this increase? Did the extra cash come from Dynamic Mattress Company's additional long-term borrowing, from reinvested earnings, from cash released by reducing inventory, or from extra credit extended by Dynamic's suppliers? (Note the increase in accounts payable.)

The correct answer is "all the above." Financial analysts often summarize sources and uses of cash in a statement like the one shown in Table 30.4. The state-ment shows that Dynamic *generated* cash from the following sources:

1. It issued $7 million of long-term debt.
2. It reduced inventory, releasing $1 million.

---

[2]If there is a tax advantage to borrowing, as most people believe, there must be a corresponding tax *dis-*advantage to lending, and investment in Treasury bills has a negative NPV. See Section 18.1.

	2000	2001
Current assets:		
Cash	4	5
Marketable securities	0	5
Inventory	26	25
Accounts receivable	25	30
Total current assets	55	65
Fixed assets:		
Gross investment	56	70
Less depreciation	−16	−20
Net fixed assets	40	50
Total assets	95	115
Current liabilities:		
Bank loans	5	0
Accounts payable	20	27
Total current liabilities	25	27
Long-term debt	5	12
Net worth (equity and retained earnings)	65	76
Total liabilities and net worth	95	115

TABLE 30.2

Year-end balance sheets for 2000 and 2001 for Dynamic Mattress Company (figures in $ millions).

Sales	350
Operating costs	−321
	29
Depreciation	−4
	25
Interest	−1
Pretax income	24
Tax at 50%	−12
Net income	12

TABLE 30.3

Income statement for Dynamic Mattress Company, 2001 (figures in $ millions).

Note: Dividend = $1 million; retained earnings = $11 million.

3. It increased its accounts payable, in effect borrowing an additional $7 million from its suppliers.

4. By far the largest source of cash was Dynamic's operations, which generated $16 million. See Table 30.3, and note: Income ($12 million) understates cash flow because depreciation is deducted in calculating income. Depreciation is *not* a cash outlay. Thus, it must be added back in order to obtain operating cash flow.

Dynamic *used* cash for the following purposes:

1. It paid a $1 million dividend. (*Note:* The $11 million increase in Dynamic's equity is due to retained earnings: $12 million of equity income, less the $1 million dividend.)

TABLE 30.4

Sources and uses of cash for Dynamic Mattress Company, 2001 (figures in $ millions).

Sources:	
Issued long-term debt	7
Reduced inventories	1
Increased accounts payable	7
Cash from operations:	
Net income	12
Depreciation	4
Total sources	31
Uses:	
Repaid short-term bank loan	5
Invested in fixed assets	14
Purchased marketable securities	5
Increased accounts receivable	5
Dividend	1
Total uses	30
Increase in cash balance	1

2. It repaid a $5 million short-term bank loan.[3]
3. It invested $14 million. This shows up as the increase in gross fixed assets in Table 30.2.
4. It purchased $5 million of marketable securities.
5. It allowed accounts receivable to expand by $5 million. In effect, it lent this additional amount to its customers.

Tracing Changes in Net Working Capital

Financial analysts often find it useful to collapse all current assets and liabilities into a single figure for net working capital. Dynamic's net-working-capital balances were (in millions):

	Current Assets	Less	Current Liabilities	Equals	Net Working Capital
Year-end 2000	$55	−	$25	=	$30
Year-end 2001	$65	−	$27	=	$38

Table 30.5 gives balance sheets which report only net working capital, not individual current asset or liability items.

"Sources and uses" statements can likewise be simplified by defining *sources* as activities which contribute to net working capital and *uses* as activities which use up working capital. In this context working capital is usually referred to as *funds*, and a *sources and uses of funds statement* is presented.[4]

---

[3]This is principal repayment, not interest. Sometimes interest payments are explicitly recognized as a use of funds. If so, operating cash flow would be defined *before* interest, that is, as net income plus interest plus depreciation.

[4]We drew up a *sources and uses of funds* statement for Executive Paper in Section 29.1.

	2000	2001
Net working capital	30	38
Fixed assets:		
Gross investment	56	70
Less depreciation	−16	−20
Net fixed assets	40	50
Total net assets	70	88
Long-term debt	5	12
Net worth (equity and retained earnings)	65	76
Long-term liabilities and net worth*	70	88

TABLE 30.5

Condensed year-end balance sheets for 2000 and 2001 for Dynamic Mattress Company (figures in $ millions).

*When only *net working capital* appears on a firm's balance sheet, this figure (the sum of long-term liabilities and net worth) is often referred to as *total capitalization.*

Sources:	
Issued long-term debt	7
Cash from operations:	
Net income	12
Depreciation	4
	23
Uses:	
Invested in fixed assets	14
Dividend	1
	15
Increase in net working capital	8

TABLE 30.6

Sources and uses of funds (net working capital) for Dynamic Mattress Company, 2001 (figures in $ millions).

In 2000, Dynamic contributed to net working capital by

1. Issuing $7 million of long-term debt.
2. Generating $16 million from operations.

It used up net working capital by

1. Investing $14 million.
2. Paying a $1 million dividend.

The year's changes in net working capital are thus summarized by Dynamic Mattress Company's sources and uses of funds statement, given in Table 30.6.

Profits and Cash Flow

Now look back to Table 30.4, which shows sources and uses of *cash*. We want to register two warnings about the entry called *cash from operations*. It may not actually represent real dollars—dollars you can buy beer with.

First, depreciation may not be the only noncash expense deducted in calculating income. For example, most firms use different accounting procedures in their tax books than in their reports to shareholders. The point of special tax accounts is to minimize current taxable income. The effect is that the shareholder books overstate the firm's current cash tax liability,[5] and after-tax cash flow from operations is therefore understated.

Second, income statements record sales when made, not when the customer's payment is received. Think of what happens when Dynamic sells goods on credit. The company records a profit at the time of sale, but there is no cash inflow until the bills are paid. Since there is no cash inflow, there is no change in the company's cash balance, although there is an increase in working capital in the form of an increase in accounts receivable. No net addition to cash would be shown in a sources and uses statement like Table 30.4. The increase in cash from operations would be offset by an increase in accounts receivable.

Later, when the bills are paid, there is an increase in the cash balance. However, there is no further profit at this point and no increase in working capital. The increase in the cash balance is exactly matched by a decrease in accounts receivable.

That brings up an interesting characteristic of working capital. Imagine a company that conducts a very simple business. It buys raw materials for cash, processes them into finished goods, and then sells these goods on credit. The whole cycle of operations looks like this:

If you draw up a balance sheet at the beginning of the process, you see cash. If you delay a little, you find the cash replaced by inventories of raw materials and, still later, by inventories of finished goods. When the goods are sold, the inventories give way to accounts receivable, and finally, when the customers pay their bills, the firm draws out its profit and replenishes the cash balance.

There is only one constant in this process, namely, working capital. The components of working capital are constantly changing. That is one reason why (net) working capital is a useful summary measure of current assets and liabilities.

The strength of the working-capital measure is that it is unaffected by seasonal or other temporary movements between different current assets or liabilities. But the strength is also its weakness, for the working-capital figure hides a lot of interesting information. In our example cash was transformed into inventory, then into receivables, and back into cash again. But these assets have different degrees of risk and liquidity. You can't pay bills with inventory or with receivables, you must pay with cash.

---

[5]The difference between taxes reported and paid to the Internal Revenue Service shows up on the balance sheet as an increased deferred tax liability. The reason that a liability is recognized is that accelerated depreciation and other devices used to reduce current taxable income do not eliminate taxes; they only delay them. Of course, this reduces the present value of the firm's tax liability, but still the ultimate liability has to be recognized. In the sources and uses statements an increase in deferred taxes would be treated as a source of funds. In the Dynamic Mattress example we ignore deferred taxes.

FORD'S DISAPPEARING CASH MOUNTAIN

At the end of 1998 Ford had $23.8 billion in cash and marketable securities and only $9.8 billion in debt. But in the next three years Ford went on a shopping spree that resulted in the expenditure of more than $13 billion on acquisitions, such as Volvo Cars and Land Rover. In the same period Ford spent a total of $20 billion on new products and other capital projects. Within three years Ford's huge cash mountain had halved.

By most standards Ford remained relatively conservatively capitalized, but the outlook for the automobile industry was worsening rapidly. In the first nine months of 2001 Ford recorded a loss of nearly $5 billion, so that its operations became a cash drain rather than a source of cash. At the same time the company needed to set aside $3 billion to cover potential costs associated with alleged vehicle safety problems. As Ford faced a potential cash shortage, the company sought to conserve cash by halving its dividend payment and pruning its capital expenditure program.

Source: Ford Motor's cash drain is described in "Ford Motor's Cash Goes Subcompact," *The Wall Street Journal*, November 6, 2001.

30.4 CASH BUDGETING

The past is interesting only for what one can learn from it. The financial manager's problem is to forecast *future* sources and uses of cash. These forecasts serve two purposes. First, they provide a standard, or budget, against which subsequent performance can be judged. Second, they alert the manager to future cash-flow needs. Cash, as we all know, has a habit of disappearing fast. Look, for example, at Finance in the News, which describes how Ford's large cash surplus rapidly turned into a shortage. Ford's financial manager needed to *plan* for this deficiency.

Preparing the Cash Budget: Inflow

There are at least as many ways to produce a quarterly cash budget as there are to skin a cat. Many large firms have developed elaborate corporate models; others use a spreadsheet program to plan their cash needs. The procedures of smaller firms may be less formal. But there are common issues that all firms must face when they forecast. We will illustrate these issues by continuing the example of Dynamic Mattress.

Most of Dynamic's cash inflow comes from the sale of mattresses. We therefore start with a sales forecast by quarter[6] for 2002:

	First Quarter	Second Quarter	Third Quarter	Fourth Quarter
Sales ($ millions)	87.5	78.5	116	131

---

[6]Most firms would forecast by month instead of by quarter. Sometimes weekly or even daily forecasts are made. But presenting a monthly forecast would triple the number of entries in Table 30.7 and subsequent tables. We wanted to keep the examples as simple as possible.

TABLE 30.7

To forecast Dynamic Mattress's collections on accounts receivable, you have to forecast sales and collection rates (figures in $ millions).

*Sales in the fourth quarter of the previous year were $75 million.

	First Quarter	Second Quarter	Third Quarter	Fourth Quarter
1. Receivables at start of period	30	32.5	30.7	38.2
2. Sales	87.5	78.5	116	131
3. Collections:				
Sales in current period (80%)	70	62.8	92.8	104.8
Sales in last period (20%)	15*	17.5	15.7	23.2
Total collections	85	80.3	108.5	128.0
4. Receivables at end of period				
4 = 1 + 2 − 3	32.5	30.7	38.2	41.2

But sales become accounts receivable before they become cash. Cash flow comes from *collections* on accounts receivable.

Most firms keep track of the average time it takes customers to pay their bills. From this they can forecast what proportion of a quarter's sales is likely to be converted into cash in that quarter and what proportion is likely to be carried over to the next quarter as accounts receivable. Suppose that 80 percent of sales are "cashed in" in the immediate quarter and 20 percent are cashed in in the next. Table 30.7 shows forecasted collections under this assumption.

In the first quarter, for example, collections from current sales are 80 percent of $87.5, or $70 million. But the firm also collects 20 percent of the previous quarter's sales, or .2(75) = $15 million. Therefore total collections are $70 + $15 = $85 million.

Dynamic started the first quarter with $30 million of accounts receivable. The quarter's sales of $87.5 million were *added* to accounts receivable, but collections of $85 million were *subtracted*. Therefore, as Table 30.7 shows, Dynamic ended the quarter with accounts receivable of $30 + 87.5 − 85 = $32.5 million. The general formula is

$$\text{Ending accounts receivable} = \text{beginning accounts receivable} + \text{sales} - \text{collections}$$

The top section of Table 30.8 shows forecasted sources of cash for Dynamic Mattress. Collection of receivables is the main source, but it is not the only one. Perhaps the firm plans to dispose of some land or expects a tax refund or payment of an insurance claim. All such items are included as "other" sources. It is also possible that you may raise additional capital by borrowing or selling stock, but we don't want to prejudge that question. Therefore, for the moment we just assume that Dynamic will not raise further long-term finance.

Preparing the Cash Budget: Outflow

So much for the incoming cash. Now for the outgoing cash. There always seem to be many more uses for cash than there are sources. For simplicity, we have condensed the uses into four categories in Table 30.8.

1. *Payments on accounts payable.* You have to pay your bills for raw materials, parts, electricity, etc. The cash-flow forecast assumes all these bills are paid on time, although Dynamic could probably delay payment to some extent. Delayed payment is sometimes called *stretching your payables*. Stretching is one source of short-term financing, but for most firms it is an expensive

	First Quarter	Second Quarter	Third Quarter	Fourth Quarter
Sources of cash:				
Collections on accounts receivable	85	80.3	108.5	128
Other	0	0	12.5	0
Total sources	85	80.3	121	128
Uses of cash:				
Payments on accounts payable	65	60	55	50
Labor, administrative, and other expenses	30	30	30	30
Capital expenditures	32.5	1.3	5.5	8
Taxes, interest, and dividends	4	4	4.5	5
Total uses	131.5	95.3	95	93
Sources minus uses	−46.5	−15.0	+26	+35
Calculation of short-term financing requirement:				
1. Cash at start of period	5	−41.5	−56.5	−30.5
2. Change in cash balance (sources less uses)	−46.5	−15.0	+26	+35
3. Cash at end of period* 1 + 2 = 3	−41.5	−56.5	−30.5	+4.5
4. Minimum operating cash balance	5	5	5	5
5. Cumulative short-term financing required[†] 5 = 4 − 3	46.5	61.5	35.5	.5

TABLE 30.8

Dynamic Mattress's cash budget for 2002 (figures in $ millions).

*Of course, firms cannot literally hold a negative amount of cash. This is the amount the firm will have to raise to pay its bills.
[†]A negative sign would indicate a cash *surplus*. But in this example the firm must raise cash for all quarters.

source, because by stretching they lose discounts given to firms that pay promptly. This is discussed in more detail in Section 32.1.

2. *Labor, administrative, and other expenses.* This category includes all other regular business expenses.

3. *Capital expenditures.* Note that Dynamic Mattress plans a major capital outlay in the first quarter.

4. *Taxes, interest, and dividend payments.* This includes interest on presently outstanding long-term debt but does not include interest on any additional borrowing to meet cash requirements in 2002. At this stage in the analysis, Dynamic does not know how much it will have to borrow, or whether it will have to borrow at all.

The forecasted net inflow of cash (sources minus uses) is shown in the box in Table 30.8. Note the large negative figure for the first quarter: a $46.5 million forecasted *outflow*. There is a smaller forecasted outflow in the second quarter, and then substantial cash inflows in the second half of the year.

The bottom part of Table 30.8 (below the box) calculates how much financing Dynamic will have to raise if its cash-flow forecasts are right. It starts the year with $5 million in cash. There is a $46.5 million cash outflow in the first quarter, and so Dynamic will have to obtain at least $46.5 − 5 = $41.5 million of additional financing.

This would leave the firm with a forecasted cash balance of exactly zero at the start of the second quarter.

Most financial managers regard a planned cash balance of zero as driving too close to the edge of the cliff. They establish a *minimum operating cash balance* to absorb unexpected cash inflows and outflows. We will assume that Dynamic's minimum operating cash balance is $5 million. That means it will have to raise the full $46.5 million cash outflow in the first quarter and $15 million more in the second quarter. Thus its cumulative financing requirement is $61.5 million in the second quarter. This is the peak, fortunately: The cumulative requirement declines in the third quarter by $26 million to $35.5 million. In the final quarter Dynamic is almost out of the woods: Its cash balance is $4.5 million, just $.5 million shy of its minimum operating balance.

The next step is to develop a *short-term financing plan* that covers the forecasted requirements in the most economical way possible. We will move on to that topic after two general observations:

1. The large cash outflows in the first two quarters do not necessarily spell trouble for Dynamic Mattress. In part, they reflect the capital investment made in the first quarter: Dynamic is spending $32.5 million, but it should be acquiring an asset worth that much or more. In part, the cash outflows reflect low sales in the first half of the year; sales recover in the second half.[7] If this is a predictable seasonal pattern, the firm should have no trouble borrowing to tide it over the slow months.

2. Table 30.8 is only a best guess about future cash flows. It is a good idea to think about the *uncertainty* in your estimates. For example, you could undertake a sensitivity analysis, in which you inspect how Dynamic's cash requirements would be affected by a shortfall in sales or by a delay in collections. The trouble with such sensitivity analyses is that you are changing only one item at a time, whereas in practice a downturn in the economy might affect, say, sales levels *and* collection rates. An alternative but more complicated solution is to build a model of the cash budget and then to simulate to determine the probability of cash requirements significantly above or below the forecasts shown in Table 30.8.[8] If cash requirements are difficult to predict, you may wish to hold additional cash or marketable securities to cover a possible unexpected cash outflow.

30.5 THE SHORT-TERM FINANCING PLAN

Dynamic's cash budget defines its problem: Its financial manager must find short-term financing to cover the firm's forecasted cash requirements. There are dozens of sources of short-term financing, but for simplicity we assume that Dynamic has just two options.

Options for Short-Term Financing

1. *Bank loan:* Dynamic has an existing arrangement with its bank allowing it to borrow up to $38 million at an interest cost of 10 percent a year or 2.5

---

[7]Maybe people buy more mattresses late in the year when the nights are longer.

[8]In other words, you could use Monte Carlo simulation. See Section 10.2.

percent per quarter. The firm can borrow and repay whenever it wants to as long as it does not exceed its credit limit.

2. *Stretching payables:* Dynamic can also raise capital by putting off paying its bills. The financial manager believes that Dynamic can defer the following amounts in each quarter:

	First Quarter	Second Quarter	Third Quarter	Fourth Quarter
Amount deferrable ($ millions)	52	48	44	40

Thus, $52 million can be saved in the first quarter by *not* paying bills in that quarter. (Note that the cash-flow forecasts in Table 30.8 assumed that these bills *will* be paid in the first quarter.) If deferred, these payments *must* be made in the second quarter. Similarly, up to $48 million of the second quarter bills can be deferred to the third quarter, and so on.

Stretching payables is often costly, even if no ill will is incurred. The reason is that suppliers may offer discounts for prompt payment. Dynamic loses this discount if it pays late. In this example we assume the lost discount is 5 percent of the amount deferred. In other words, if a $100 payment is delayed, the firm must pay $105 in the next quarter.

Dynamic's Financing Plan

With these two options, the short-term financing strategy is obvious. Use the bank loan first, if necessary up to the $38 million limit. If there is still a shortage of cash, stretch payables.

Table 30.9 shows the resulting plan. In the first quarter the plan calls for borrowing the full amount available from the bank ($38 million) and stretching $3.5 million of payables (see lines 1 and 2 in the table). In addition the company sells the $5 million of marketable securities it held at the end of 1999 (line 8). Thus it raises 38 + 3.5 + 5 = $46.5 million of cash in the first quarter (line 10).

In the second quarter, the plan calls for Dynamic to continue to borrow $38 million from the bank and to stretch $19.7 million of payables. This raises a further $16.2 million after paying off the $3.5 million of bills deferred from the first quarter.

Why raise $16.2 million when Dynamic needs only an additional $15 million to finance its operations? The answer is that the company must pay interest on the borrowings that it undertook in the first quarter and it foregoes interest on the marketable securities that were sold.[9]

In the third and fourth quarters the plan calls for Dynamic to pay off its debt and to make a small purchase of marketable securities.

Evaluating the Plan

Does the plan shown in Table 30.9 solve Dynamic's short-term financing problem? No: The plan is feasible, but Dynamic can probably do better. The most glaring weakness is its reliance on stretching payables, an extremely expensive financing

[9]The bank loan calls for quarterly interest of .025 × 38 = $.95 million; the lost discount on the stretched payables amounts to .05 × 3.5 = $.175 million; and the interest lost on the marketable securities is .02 × 5 = $.1 million.

TABLE 30.9

Dynamic Mattress's financing plan (figures in $ millions).

Note: Column sums subject to rounding error.

*We assume that the first interest payment occurs one quarter after a loan is taken out.
†Dynamic sold $5 million of marketable securities in the first quarter. The yield is assumed to be 2 percent per quarter.
‡From Table 30.8.

	First Quarter	Second Quarter	Third Quarter	Fourth Quarter
New borrowing:				
1. Bank loan	38.0	0.0	0.0	0.0
2. Stretching payables	3.5	19.7	0.0	0.0
3. Total	41.5	19.7	0.0	0.0
Repayments:				
4. Bank loan	0.0	0.0	4.3	33.7
5. Stretching payables	0.0	3.5	19.7	0.0
6. Total	0.0	3.5	24.0	33.7
7. Net new borrowing	41.5	16.2	−24.0	−33.7
8. Plus securities sold	5.0	0.0	0.0	0.0
9. Less securities bought	0.0	0.0	0.0	0.4
10. Total cash raised	46.5	16.2	−24.0	−34.1
Interest payments*				
11. Bank loan	0.0	1.0	1.0	0.8
12. Stretching payables	0.0	0.2	1.0	0.0
13. Interest on securities sold†	0.0	0.1	0.1	0.1
14. Net interest paid	0.0	1.2	2.0	0.9
15. Cash required for operations‡	46.5	15.0	−26.0	−35.0
16. Total cash required	46.5	16.2	−24.0	−34.1

device. Remember that it costs Dynamic 5 percent *per quarter* to delay paying bills—20 percent per year at simple interest. The first plan would merely stimulate the financial manager to search for cheaper sources of short-term borrowing.

The financial manager would ask several other questions as well. For example:

1. Does the plan yield satisfactory current and quick ratios?[10] Its bankers may be worried if these ratios deteriorate.[11]

2. Are there intangible costs of stretching payables? Will suppliers begin to doubt Dynamic's creditworthiness?

3. Does the plan for 2002 leave Dynamic in good financial shape for 2003? (Here the answer is yes, since Dynamic will have paid off all short-term borrowing by the end of the year.)

4. Should Dynamic try to arrange long-term financing for the major capital expenditure in the first quarter? This seems sensible, following the rule of thumb that long-term assets deserve long-term financing. It would also reduce the need for short-term borrowing dramatically. A counterargument is that Dynamic is financing the capital investment *only temporarily* by short-term borrowing. By year-end, the investment is paid for by cash from operations. Thus Dynamic's initial decision not to seek immediate long-

[10]These ratios are discussed in Chapter 29.

[11]We have not worked out these ratios explicitly, but you can infer from Table 30.9 that they would be fine at the end of the year but relatively low in midyear, when Dynamic's borrowing is high.

term financing may reflect a preference for ultimately financing the investment with retained earnings.

5. Perhaps the firm's operating and investment plans can be adjusted to make the short-term financing problem easier. Is there any easy way of deferring the first quarter's large cash outflow? For example, suppose that the large capital investment in the first quarter is for new mattress-stuffing machines to be delivered and installed in the first half of the year. The new machines are not scheduled to be ready for full-scale use until August. Perhaps the machine manufacturer could be persuaded to accept 60 percent of the purchase price on delivery and 40 percent when the machines are installed and operating satisfactorily.

6. Dynamic may also be able to release cash by reducing the level of other current assets. For example, it could reduce receivables by getting tough with customers who are late paying their bills. (The cost is that in the future these customers may take their business elsewhere.) Or it may be able to get by with lower inventories of mattresses. (The cost is that it may lose business if there is a rush of orders that it cannot supply.)

Short-term financing plans are developed by trial and error. You lay out one plan, think about it, and then try again with different assumptions on financing and investment alternatives. You continue until you can think of no further improvements.

Trial and error is important because it helps you understand the real nature of the problem the firm faces. Here we can draw a useful analogy between the *process* of planning and Chapter 10, "A Project Is Not a Black Box." In Chapter 10 we described sensitivity analysis and other tools used by firms to find out what makes capital investment projects tick and what can go wrong with them. Dynamic's financial manager faces the same kind of task: not just to choose a plan but to understand what can go wrong with it and what will be done if conditions change unexpectedly.[12]

A Note on Short-Term Financial Planning Models

Working out a consistent short-term plan requires burdensome calculations.[13] Fortunately much of the arithmetic can be delegated to a computer. Many large firms have built *short-term financial planning models* to do this. Smaller companies like Dynamic Mattress do not face so much detail and complexity and find it easier to work with a spreadsheet program on a personal computer. In either case the financial manager specifies forecasted cash requirements or surpluses, interest rates, credit limits, etc., and the model grinds out a plan like the one shown in Table 30.9. The computer also produces balance sheets, income statements, and whatever special reports the financial manager may require.

Smaller firms that do not want custom-built models can rent general-purpose models offered by banks, accounting firms, management consultants, or specialized computer software firms.

---

[12]This point is even more important in *long-term* financial planning. See Chapter 29.

[13]If you doubt that, look again at Table 30.9. Notice that the cash requirements in each quarter depend on borrowing in the previous quarter, because borrowing creates an obligation to pay interest. Also, borrowing under a line of credit may require additional cash to meet compensating balance requirements; if so, that means still more borrowing and still higher interest charges in the next quarter. Moreover, the problem's complexity would have been tripled had we not simplified by forecasting per quarter rather than by month.

Most of these models are *simulation* programs.[14] They simply work out the consequences of the assumptions and policies specified by the financial manager. *Optimization* models for short-term financial planning are also available. These models are usually linear programming models. They search for the *best* plan from a range of alternative policies identified by the financial manager.

As a matter of fact, we used a linear programming model developed by Pogue and Bussard[15] to generate Dynamic Mattress's financial plans. Of course, in that simple example we hardly needed a linear programming model to identify the best strategy. It was obvious that Dynamic should always use the line of credit first, turning to the second-best alternative (stretching payables) only when the limit on the line of credit was reached. The Pogue–Bussard model nevertheless did the arithmetic quickly and easily.

Optimization helps when the firm faces complex problems with many interdependent alternatives and restrictions for which trial and error might never identify the *best* combination of alternatives.

Of course the best plan for one set of assumptions may prove disastrous if the assumptions are wrong. Thus the financial manager has to explore the implications of alternative assumptions about future cash flows, interest rates, and so on. Linear programming can help identify good strategies, but even with an optimization model the financial plan is still sought by trial and error.

 ## 30.6 SOURCES OF SHORT-TERM BORROWING

Dynamic solved the greater part of its cash shortage by borrowing from a bank. But banks are not the only source of short-term loans. Finance companies are also a major source of cash, particularly for financing receivables and inventories.[16] In addition to borrowing from an intermediary like a bank or finance company, firms also sell short-term commercial paper or medium-term notes directly to investors. It is time to look more closely at these sources of short-term funds.

Bank Loans

To finance its investment in current assets, a company may rely on a variety of short-term loans. Obviously, if you approach a bank for a loan, the bank's lending officer is likely to ask searching questions about your firm's financial position and its plans for the future. Also, the bank will want to monitor the firm's subsequent progress. There is, however, a good side to this. Other investors know that banks

---

[14]Like the simulation models described in Section 10.2, except that the short-term planning models rarely include uncertainty explicitly. The models referred to here are built and used in the same way as the long-term financial planning models described in Section 29.4.

[15]G. A. Pogue and R. N. Bussard, "A Linear Programming Model for Short-Term Financial Planning under Uncertainty," *Sloan Management Review*, 13 (Spring 1972), pp. 69–99.

[16]*Finance companies* are firms that specialize in lending to businesses or individuals. They include independent firms, such as Household Finance, as well as subsidiaries of nonfinancial corporations, such as General Motors Acceptance Corporation (GMAC). In their lending finance companies compete with banks. However, they raise funds not by attracting deposits, as banks do, but by issuing commercial paper and other longer-term securities.

are hard to convince, and, therefore, when a company announces that it has arranged a large bank facility, the share price tends to rise.[17]

Bank loans come in a variety of flavors.[18] Here are a few of the ways that they differ.

Commitment Companies sometimes wait until they need the money before they apply for a bank loan, but nearly three-quarters of commercial bank loans are made under commitment. In this case the company establishes a line of credit that allows it to borrow from the bank up to an established limit. This line of credit may be an *evergreen credit* with no fixed maturity, but more commonly it is a *revolving credit* (*revolver*) with a fixed maturity of up to three years.

Credit lines are relatively expensive, for in addition to paying interest on any borrowings the company must pay a commitment fee on the unused amount. In exchange for this extra cost, the firm receives a valuable option: It has guaranteed access to the bank's money at a fixed spread over the general level of interest rates. This amounts to a put option, because the firm can sell its debt to the bank on fixed terms even if its own creditworthiness deteriorates or the cost of credit rises. The growth in the use of credit lines is changing the role of banks. They are no longer simply lenders; they are also in the business of providing companies with liquidity insurance.

Many companies discovered the value of this insurance in 1998, when Russia defaulted on its borrowings and created turmoil in the world's debt markets. Companies in the United States suddenly found it much more expensive to issue their own debt to investors. Those who had arranged lines of credit with their banks rushed to take advantage of them. As a result, new debt issues languished, while bank lending boomed.[19]

Maturity Most bank loans are for only a few months. For example, a company may need a short-term *bridge loan* to finance the purchase of new equipment or the acquisition of another firm. In this case the loan serves as interim financing until the purchase is completed and long-term financing is arranged. Often a short-term loan may be needed to finance a temporary increase in inventory. Such a loan is described as *self-liquidating;* in other words, the sale of goods provides the cash to repay the loan.

Banks also provide longer-term loans, known as *term loans.* A term loan typically has a maturity of four to five years. Usually the loan is repaid in level amounts over this period, though there is sometimes a large final balloon payment or just a single bullet payment at maturity. Banks can accommodate the repayment pattern to the anticipated cash flows of the borrower. For example, the first repayment might be delayed a year until the new factory is completed. Term loans are often renegotiated before maturity. Banks are willing to do this if the

---

[17]See C. James, "Some Evidence on the Uniqueness of Bank Loans," *Journal of Financial Economics* 19 (1987), pp. 217–235.

[18]The results of a survey of the terms of business lending by banks in the United States are published quarterly in the *Federal Reserve Bulletin* (see **www.federalreserve.gov/releases/E2/**).

[19]The rush to draw on bank lines of credit is described in M. R. Saidenberg and P. E. Strahan, "Are Banks Still Important for Financing Large Businesses?" *Federal Reserve Bank of New York, Current Issues in Economics and Finance* 5 (August 1999), pp. 1–6.

borrower is an established customer, remains creditworthy, and has a sound business reason for making the change.[20]

Rate of Interest   Short-term bank loans are often made at a fixed rate of interest, which is often quoted as a discount. For example, if the interest rate on a one-year loan is stated as a discount of 5 percent, the borrower receives $100 - 5 = \$95$ and undertakes to pay $100 at the end of the year. The return on such a loan is not 5 percent, but $5/95 = .0526$, or 5.26 percent.

For longer-term bank loans the interest rate is usually linked to the general level of interest rates. The most common benchmarks are the London Interbank Offered Rate (LIBOR), the federal funds rate,[21] or the bank's prime rate. Thus, if the rate is set at "1 percent over LIBOR," the borrower may pay 5 percent in the first three months when LIBOR is 4 percent, 6 percent in the next three months when LIBOR is 5 percent, and so on.[22]

Syndicated Loans   Some bank loans are far too large for a single bank. In these cases the loan may be arranged by one or more lead banks and then parceled out among a syndicate of banks. For example, when Vodafone Airtouch needed to borrow $24 billion (€25 billion) to help finance its bid for the German telephone company, Mannesmann, it engaged 11 banks from around the world to arrange a large syndicate of banks that would lend the cash.

Loan Sales   Large banks often have more demand for loans than they can satisfy; for smaller banks it is the other way around. Banks with an excess demand for loans may solve the problem by selling a portion of their existing loans to other institutions. Loan sales have mushroomed in recent years. In 1991 they totalled only $8 million; by 2000 they had reached $129 billion.[23]

These loan sales generally take one of two forms: *assignments* or *participations*. In the former case a portion of the loan is transferred with the agreement of the borrower. In the second case the lead bank maintains its relationship with its borrowers but agrees to pay over to the buyer a portion of the cash flows that it receives.

Participations often involve a single loan, but sometimes they can be huge deals involving hundreds of loans. Because these deals change a collection of nonmarketable bank loans into marketable securities, they are known as *securitizations*. For example, in 1996 the British bank, Natwest, securitized about one-sixth of its loan book. Natwest first put together a $5 billion package of about 200 loans to major firms in 17 different countries. It then sold notes, each of which promised to pay a proportion of the cash that it received from the package of loans. Because the notes provided the chance to share in a diversified portfolio of high-quality loans, they proved very popular with investors from around the world.

Security   If a bank is concerned about a firm's credit risk, it will ask the firm to provide security for the loan. Since the bank is lending on a short-term basis, this

---

[20]Term loans typically allow the borrower to repay early, but in many cases the loan agreement specifies that the firm must pay a penalty for early repayment.

[21]The federal funds rate is the rate at which banks lend excess reserves to each other.

[22]In addition to paying interest, the borrower may be obliged to maintain a minimum interest-free deposit (*compensating balance*) with the bank. Compensating balances for bank loans are now relatively rare.

[23]Loan Pricing Corporation (**www.loanpricing.com**).

security usually consists of liquid assets such as receivables, inventories, or securities. Sometimes the bank will accept a *floating charge* against these assets.[24] This gives it a general claim if the firm defaults, but it does not specify the assets in detail, and it sets few restrictions on what the company can do with the assets.

More commonly, banks will require specific collateral. For example, suppose that there is a significant delay between the time that you ship your goods and when your customers pay you. If you need the money up front, you can borrow using these receivables as collateral. First, you must send the bank a copy of each invoice and provide it with a claim against the money that you receive from your customers. The bank will then lend up to 80 percent of the value of the receivables.

Each day, as you make more sales, your collateral increases and you can borrow more money. Each day also some customers pay their bills. This money is placed in a special collateral account under the bank's control and is periodically used to reduce the size of the loan. Therefore, as the firm's business fluctuates, so does the amount of the collateral and the size of the loan.[25]

You can also use inventories as security for a loan. For example, if your goods are stored in a warehouse, you need to arrange for an independent warehouse company to provide the bank with a receipt showing that the goods are held on the bank's behalf. When the loan is repaid, the bank returns the warehouse receipt and you are free to remove the goods.[26]

Banks are naturally choosy about the collateral that they will accept. They want to make sure that they can identify and sell the collateral if you default. For example, they may be happy to lend against a warehouse full of a standard nonperishable commodity, but they would turn up their nose at a warehouse of ripe Camemberts.

Banks also need to ensure that the collateral is kept safe and the borrower doesn't sell the assets and run off with the money. This is what happened in the great salad oil swindle. Fifty-one banks and companies made loans of nearly $200 million to the Allied Crude Vegetable Oil Refining Corporation. In return the company agreed to provide security in the form of storage tanks full of valuable salad oil. Unfortunately, the cursory inspections of the tanks failed to notice that they simply contained seawater and sludge. When the fraud was discovered, the president of Allied went to jail and the 51 lenders were left out in the cold, looking for their $200 million.[27] Lenders have been more careful since then, but Finance in the News shows that even old scams can still work.

Commercial Paper

Banks borrow money from one group of firms or individuals and relend the money to another group. They make their profit by charging the borrower a higher rate of interest than they offer the lender.

---

[24]Floating charges are common in other countries.

[25]In Chapter 32 we will describe how firms sometimes raise money by selling their receivables to a factor. The factor is responsible for collecting the debt and suffers any losses if the customers don't pay. When you pledge your receivables as collateral for a loan, *you* remain responsible for collecting the debt and *you* suffer if a customer is delinquent.

[26]It is not always practicable to keep inventory in a warehouse. For example, automobile dealers need to display their cars in a showroom. One solution is to enter into a floor-planning arrangement in which the finance company buys the cars and the dealer holds them in trust. When the cars are sold, the proceeds are used to redeem the cars from the finance company.

[27]See N.C. Miller, *The Great Salad Oil Swindle*, London, Gollancz, 1966.

THE HAZARDS OF SECURED BANK LENDING

The National Safety Council of Australia's Victoria Division had been a sleepy outfit until John Friedrich took over. Under its new management, NSC members trained like commandos and were prepared to go anywhere and do anything. They saved people from drowning, they fought fires, found lost bushwalkers and went down mines. Their lavish equipment included 22 helicopters, 8 aircraft and a mini-submarine. Soon the NSC began selling its services internationally.

Unfortunately the NSC's paramilitary outfit cost millions of dollars to run—far more than it earned in revenue. Friedrich bridged the gap by borrowing $A236 million of debt. The banks were happy to lend because the NSC's debt appeared well secured. At one point the company showed $A107 million of receivables (that is money owed by its customers), which it pledged as security for bank loans. Later checks revealed that many of these customers did not owe the NSC a cent. In other cases banks took comfort in the fact that their loans were secured by containers of valuable rescue gear. There were more than 100 containers stacked around the NSC's main base. Only a handful contained any equipment, but these were the ones that the bankers saw when they came to check that their loans were safe. Sometimes a suspicious banker would ask to inspect a particular container. Friedrich would then explain that it was away on exercise, fly the banker across the country in a light plane and point to a container well out in the bush. The container would of course be empty, but the banker had no way to know that.

Six years after Friedrich was appointed CEO, his massive fraud was uncovered. But a few days before a warrant could be issued, Friedrich disappeared. Although he was eventually caught and arrested, he shot himself before he could come to trial. Investigations revealed that Friedrich was operating under an assumed name, having fled from his native Germany, where he was wanted by the police. Many rumors continued to circulate about Friedrich. He was variously alleged to have been a plant of the CIA and the KGB and the NSC was said to have been behind an attempted counter-coup in Fiji. For the banks there was only one hard truth. Their loans to the NSC, which had appeared so well secured, would never be repaid.

Source: Adapted from Chapter 7 of T. Sykes, *The Bold Riders*, Allen & Unwin, St. Leonards, NSW, Australia, 1994.

Sometimes it is convenient to have a bank in the middle. It saves the lenders the trouble of looking for borrowers and assessing their creditworthiness, and it saves borrowers the trouble of looking for lenders. Depositors do not care whom the bank lends to: They need only satisfy themselves that the bank as a whole is safe.

There are also occasions on which it is *not* worth paying an intermediary to perform these functions. Large well-known companies can bypass the banking system by issuing their own short-term unsecured notes. These notes are known as **commercial paper (CP).** Financial institutions, such as bank holding companies and finance companies,[28] also issue commercial paper, sometimes in very large quantities. For example, GE Capital Corporation has nearly $70 billion of commercial paper in issue. The major issuers of commercial paper have set up their own marketing departments and sell their paper directly to investors, often

[28] *A bank holding company* is a firm that owns both a bank and nonbanking subsidiaries.

using the Web to do so. Smaller companies sell through dealers who receive a fee for marketing the issue.

Commercial paper in the United States has a maximum maturity of nine months, though most paper is for 60 days or less. Buyers of commercial paper generally hold it to maturity, but the company or dealer that sells the paper is usually prepared to repurchase it earlier.

The majority of commercial paper is issued by high-grade, nationally known companies.[29] Companies generally support their issue of commercial paper by arranging a backup line of credit with a bank, which guarantees that they can find the money to repay the paper.[30] The risk of default is, therefore, small.

Commercial paper is very popular with major companies. By cutting out the intermediary, they are able to borrow at rates that may be 1 to 1.5 percent below the prime rate charged by banks. Even after allowing for a dealer's commission and the cost of any backup line of credit, this is still a substantial savings. Banks have felt the competition from commercial paper and have been prepared to reduce their rates to blue-chip customers. As a result, "prime rate" doesn't mean what it used to. It once meant the rate banks charged their most creditworthy customers. Now the prime customers often pay less than the prime rate.

Medium-Term Notes

New issues of securities do not need to be registered with the SEC as long as they mature within 270 days. So by limiting the maturity of commercial paper issues, companies can avoid the delays and expense of registration. However, large blue-chip companies also make regular issues of unsecured **medium-term notes (MTNs).**

You can think of MTNs as a hybrid between corporate bonds and commercial paper. Like bonds, they are relatively long-term instruments; their maturity is never less than 270 days and may be as long as 30 years.[31] On the other hand, like commercial paper, MTNs are not underwritten but are sold on a regular basis either through dealers or, occasionally, direct to investors. Borrowers, such as finance companies, that are always needing cash, welcome the flexibility of MTNs. For example, a company may tell its dealer the amount of money that it needs to raise that week, the range of maturities that it can offer, and the maximum interest that it is prepared to pay. It is then up to the dealers to find the buyers.

---

[29]Moody's and Standard and Poor's publish quality ratings for commercial paper. For example, Moody's provides three ratings, from P-1 (denoting Prime 1, the highest-grade paper) to P-3. Most investors are reluctant to buy low-rated paper. For example, money-market funds are largely limited to holding P-1 paper.

[30]Banks often reserve the right to cancel this line of credit if there is a *material adverse change* in the company's condition. However, lower-rated companies may back their paper with an irrevocable line of credit.

[31]The Walt Disney Company has even used its MTN shelf registration to issue a 100-year bond.

Short-term financial planning is concerned with the management of the firm's short-term, or current, assets and liabilities. The most important current assets are cash, marketable securities, inventory, and accounts receivable. The most important current liabilities are short-term loans and accounts payable. The difference between current assets and current liabilities is called (net) working capital.

Current assets and liabilities are turned over much more rapidly than the other items on the balance sheet. Short-term financing and investment decisions are more quickly and easily reversed than long-term decisions. Consequently, the financial manager does not need to look so far into the future when making them.

The nature of the firm's short-term financial planning problem is determined by the amount of long-term capital it raises. A firm that issues large amounts of long-term debt or common stock, or which retains a large part of its earnings, may find that it has permanent excess cash. In such cases there is never any problem paying bills, and short-term financial planning consists of managing the firm's portfolio of marketable securities. We think that firms with permanent cash surpluses ought to return the excess cash to their stockholders.

Other firms raise relatively little long-term capital and end up as permanent short-term debtors. Most firms attempt to find a golden mean by financing all fixed assets and part of current assets with equity and long-term debt. Such firms may invest cash surpluses during part of the year and borrow during the rest of the year.

The starting point for short-term financial planning is an understanding of sources and uses of cash.[32] Firms forecast their net cash requirements by forecasting collections on accounts receivable, adding other cash inflows, and subtracting all cash outlays. If the forecasted cash balance is insufficient to cover day-to-day operations and to provide a buffer against contingencies, the company will need to find additional finance. The search for the best short-term financial plan inevitably proceeds by trial and error. The financial manager must explore the consequences of different assumptions about cash requirements, interest rates, sources of finance, and so on. Firms are increasingly using computerized financial models to help in this process. The models range from simple spreadsheet programs that merely help with the arithmetic to linear programming models that help to find the best financial plan.

If you foresee a large and permanent cash deficiency, the financial plan may involve raising long-term finance. If the shortage is temporary, you may be able to finance it by not paying your bills for a while or you can choose from a variety of short- and medium-term loans.

Often firms arrange a *revolving line of credit* with a bank that allows them to borrow up to an agreed amount whenever they need financing. This is usually intended to tide the firm over a temporary shortage of cash and is therefore repaid in only a few months. However, banks also make *term loans* that sometimes extend for five years or more. In addition to borrowing from their domestic banks, companies may borrow dollars (or any other currency) from overseas banks or the foreign branches of U.S. banks. These international bank loans often involve huge sums of money and in this case they may be *syndicated* among a group of major banks.

Many bank loans are unsecured, but less-creditworthy borrowers may be asked to provide security. Sometimes this consists of a floating charge on receivables and inventories, but usually you will be asked to pledge specific assets. When you borrow against receivables, the bank is informed of all sales of goods

---

[32]We pointed out in Section 30.3 that sources and uses of *funds* are often analyzed rather than sources and uses of cash. Anything that contributes to working capital is called a *source of funds*; anything that diminishes working capital is called a *use of funds*. Sources and uses of funds statements are relatively simple because many sources and uses of cash are buried in changes in working capital. However, in forecasting, the emphasis is on cash flow. You pay bills with cash, not working capital.

and the resulting receivables are pledged to the bank. As the customers pay their bills, the money is paid into a special collateral account under the bank's control. Similarly, when you borrow against stocks of raw materials, the bank may insist that the goods are under the control of an independent warehouse company. As long as the bank holds the warehouse receipt for these goods, they cannot be released without the bank's permission.

The interest rate on very short-term bank loans is generally fixed for the life of the loan, but in other cases the rate floats with the general level of short-term interest rates. For example, it might be set at 1 percent over LIBOR (the London Interbank Offered Rate).

Of course, the interest rate that the bank charges must be sufficient to cover not only the opportunity cost of capital for the loan but also the costs of running the loan department. As a result, large regular borrowers have found it cheaper to bypass the banking system and issue their own short-term unsecured debt. This is called *commercial paper*. Longer-term loans that are marketed on a regular basis are known as *medium-term notes*.

Here are some general textbooks on working-capital management:

G. W. Gallinger and P. B. Healey: *Liquidity Analysis and Management*, 2nd. ed., Addison-Wesley Publishing Company, Inc., Reading, MA, 1991.

N. C. Hill and W. L. Sartoris: *Short-Term Financial Management: Text and Cases*, 3rd. ed., Prentice-Hall, Inc., Englewood Cliffs, NJ, 1995.

K. V. Smith and G. W. Gallinger: *Readings on Short-Term Financial Management*, 3rd ed., West Publishing Company, New York, 1988.

J. H. Vander Weide and S. F. Maier: *Managing Corporate Liquidity: An Introduction to Working Capital Management*, John Wiley & Sons, Inc., New York, 1985.

F. C. Scherr: *Modern Working Capital Management: Text and Cases*, Prentice-Hall, Inc., Englewood Cliffs, NJ, 1989.

Pogue and Bussard present a linear programming model for short-term financial planning:

G. A. Pogue and R. N. Bussard: "A Linear Programming Model for Short-Term Financial Planning under Uncertainty," *Sloan Management Review*, 13:69–99 (Spring 1972).

FURTHER READING

QUIZ

1. Fill in the blanks in the following statements:
   a. A firm has a cash surplus when its _____ exceeds its _____. The surplus is normally invested in _____.
   b. In developing the short-term financial plan, the financial manager starts with a budget for the next year. This budget shows the _____ generated or absorbed by the firm's operations and also the minimum _____ needed to support these operations. The financial manager may also wish to invest in _____ as a reserve for unexpected cash requirements.
   c. Short-term financing plans are developed by _____ and _____, often aided by computerized _____.

2. Listed below are six transactions that Dynamic Mattress might make. Indicate how each transaction would affect (a) cash and (b) working capital.

The transactions are

i. Pay out $2 million cash dividend.
ii. Receive $2,500 from a customer who pays a bill resulting from a previous sale.
iii. Pay $5,000 previously owed to one of its suppliers.
iv. Borrow $1 million long term and invest the proceeds in inventory.
v. Borrow $1 million short term and invest the proceeds in inventory.
vi. Sell $5 million of marketable securities for cash.

3. State how each of the following events would affect the firm's balance sheet. State whether each change is a source or use of cash.
   a. An automobile manufacturer increases production in response to a forecasted increase in demand. Unfortunately, the demand does not increase.
   b. Competition forces the firm to give customers more time to pay for their purchases.
   c. Inflation increases the value of raw material inventories by 20 percent.
   d. The firm sells a parcel of land for $100,000. The land was purchased five years earlier for $200,000.
   e. The firm repurchases its own common stock.
   f. The firm doubles its quarterly dividend.
   g. The firm issues $1 million of long-term debt and uses the proceeds to repay a short-term bank loan.

4. Here is a forecast of sales by National Bromide for the first four months of 2003 (figures in $ thousands):

	Month 1	Month 2	Month 3	Month 4
Cash sales	15	24	18	14
Sales on credit	100	120	90	70

On the average 50 percent of credit sales are paid for in the current month, 30 percent are paid in the next month, and the remainder are paid in the month after that. What is the expected cash inflow from operations in months 3 and 4?

5. Dynamic Futon forecasts the following purchases from suppliers:

	Jan.	Feb.	Mar.	Apr.	May	Jun.
Value of goods ($ millions)	32	28	25	22	20	20

   a. Forty percent of goods are supplied cash on delivery. The remainder are paid with an average delay of one month. If Dynamic Futon starts the year with payables of $22 million, what is the forecasted level of payables for each month?
   b. Suppose that from the start of the year the company stretches payables by paying 40 percent after one month and 20 percent after two months. (The remainder continue to be paid cash on delivery.) Recalculate payables for each month assuming that there are no cash penalties for late payment.

6. Each of the following events affects one or more tables in the chapter. Show the effects of each event by adjusting the tables listed in parentheses:
   a. Dynamic repays only $2 million of short-term debt in 2001. (Tables 30.2, 30.4–30.6)
   b. Dynamic issues an additional $10 million of long-term debt in 2001 and invests $12 million in a new warehouse. (Tables 30.2, 30.4–30.6)
   c. In 2001 Dynamic reduces the quantity of stuffing in each mattress. Customers don't notice, but operating costs fall by 10 percent. (Tables 30.2–30.6)

d. Starting in the third quarter of 2002, Dynamic employs new staff members who will prove very effective in persuading customers to pay more promptly. As a result, 90 percent of sales are paid for immediately, and 10 percent are paid in the following quarter. (Tables 30.7 and 30.8)

e. Starting in the first quarter of 2002, Dynamic cuts wages by $4 million a quarter. (Table 30.8)

f. In the second quarter of 2002 a disused warehouse mysteriously catches fire. Dynamic receives a $10 million check from the insurance company. (Table 30.8)

g. Dynamic's treasurer decides he can scrape by on a $2 million operating cash balance. (Table 30.8)

7. True or false?
   a. Most commercial bank loans are made under commitment.
   b. A line of credit provides the lender with a put option.
   c. Bank term loans typically have a maturity of several years.
   d. If the interest rate on a one-year bank loan is stated as a discount of 10 percent, the actual yield on the loan is less than 10 percent.
   e. The interest rate on term loans is usually linked to LIBOR, the federal funds rate, or the bank's prime rate.

8. Complete the passage below by selecting the most appropriate terms from the following list: *floating charge, commercial paper, warehouse receipt, collateral, commitment fee, line of credit, medium-term notes.*

   Companies with fluctuating capital needs often arrange a _____ with their bank. This is relatively expensive because companies need to pay a _____ on any unused amount.

   Secured short-term loans are sometimes covered by a _____ on all receivables and inventory. Generally, however, the borrower pledges specific assets as _____. For example, if goods are stored in a warehouse, an independent warehouse company may issue a _____ to the lender. The goods can then only be released with the lender's consent.

   Banks are not the only source of short-term debt. Many large companies issue their own unsecured debt directly to investors, often on a regular basis. If the maturity is less than nine months, this debt is generally known as _____. Companies also make regular issues of longer term debt to investors. These are called _____.

1. Table 30.10 lists data from the budget of Ritewell Publishers. Half the company sales are for cash on the nail; the other half are paid for with a one-month delay. The company pays all its credit purchases with a one-month delay. Credit purchases in January were $30, and total sales in January were $180. Complete the cash budget in Table 30.11.

PRACTICE QUESTIONS

	February	March	April
Total sales	200	220	180
Purchases of materials			
For cash	70	80	60
For credit	40	30	40
Other expenses	30	30	30
Taxes, interest, and dividends	10	10	10
Capital investment	100	0	0

TABLE 30.10

Selected budget data for Ritewell Publishers.

TABLE 30.11

Cash budget for
Ritewell Publishers.

	February	March	April
Sources of cash:			
Collections on cash sales			
Collections on accounts receivable	—	—	—
Total sources of cash			
Uses of cash:			
Payments of accounts payable			
Cash purchases of materials			
Other expenses			
Capital expenditures			
Taxes, interest, and dividends			
Total uses of cash	—	—	—
Net cash inflow			
Cash at start of period	100		
+ Net cash inflow			
= Cash at end of period			
+ Minimum operating cash balance	100	100	100
= Cumulative short-term financing required			

TABLE 30.12

Year-end balance sheet for 1999
(figures in $ millions).

Current assets:		Current liabilities:	
Cash	4	Bank loans	4
Marketable securities	2	Accounts payable	15
Inventory	20	Total current liabilities	19
Accounts receivable	22		
Total current assets	48	Long-term debt	5
		Net worth (equity and retained earnings)	60
Fixed assets:			
Gross investment	50		
Less depreciation	−14		
Net fixed assets	36	Total liabilities	
Total assets	84	and net worth	84

2. If a firm pays its bills with a 30-day delay, what fraction of its purchases will be paid in the current quarter? In the following quarter? What if the delay is 60 days?

3. Which items in Table 30.9 would be affected by the following events?
   a. There is a rise in interest rates.
   b. Suppliers demand interest for late payment.
   c. Dynamic receives an unexpected bill in the third quarter from the Internal Revenue Service for underpayment of taxes in previous years.

4. Table 30.12 shows Dynamic Mattress's year-end 1999 balance sheet, and Table 30.13 shows its income statement for 2000. Work out statements of sources and uses of cash and sources and uses of funds for 2000.

Sales	300
Operating costs	−285
	15
Depreciation	−2
	13
Interest	−1
Pretax income	12
Tax at 50%	−6
Net income	6

TABLE 30.13

Income statement for 2000 (figures in $ millions).

Note: Dividend = $1 million; retained earnings = $5 million.

5. Work out a short-term financing plan for Dynamic Mattress Company, assuming the limit on the line of credit is raised from $38 to $50 million. Otherwise keep to the assumptions used in developing Table 30.9.

6. Dynamic Mattress decides to lease its new mattress-stuffing machines rather than buy them. As a result, capital expenditure in the first quarter is reduced by $30 million, but the company must make lease payments of $1.5 million for each of the four quarters. Assume that the lease has no effect on tax payments until after the fourth quarter. Construct two tables like Tables 30.8 and 30.9 showing Dynamic's cumulative financing requirement and a new financing plan.

7. You need to borrow $10 million for 90 days. You have the following alternatives:
   a. Issue high-grade commercial paper, with a back-up line of credit costing .3 percent a year.
   b. Borrow from First Cookham Bank at an interest rate of .25 percent over LIBOR.
   c. Borrow from the Test Bank at prime.

   Given the rates currently prevailing in the market (see, for example, *The Wall Street Journal*), which alternative would you choose?

8. Suppose that you are a banker responsible for approving corporate loans. Nine firms are seeking secured loans. They offer the following assets as collateral:
   a. Firm A, a heating oil distributor, offers a tanker load of fuel in transit from the Middle East.
   b. Firm B, a wine wholesaler, offers 1,000 cases of Beaujolais Nouveau, located in a warehouse.
   c. Firm C, a stationer, offers an account receivable for office supplies sold to the City of New York.
   d. Firm D, a bookstore, offers its entire inventory of 15,000 used books.
   e. Firm E, a wholesale grocer, offers a boxcar full of bananas.
   f. Firm F, an appliance dealer, offers its inventory of electric typewriters.
   g. Firm G, a jeweler, offers 100 ounces of gold.
   h. Firm H, a government securities dealer, offers its portfolio of Treasury bills.
   i. Firm I, a boat builder, offers a half-completed luxury yacht. The yacht will take four months more to complete.

   Which of these assets are most likely to be good collateral? Which are likely to be bad collateral? Explain.

9. Any of the assets mentioned in the preceding question *could* be acceptable collateral under certain circumstances if appropriate safeguards were taken. What circumstances? What safeguards? Explain.

10. Interest rates on bank loans exceed rates on commercial paper. Why don't all firms issue commercial paper rather than borrow from banks?

11. Do you think you could make money by setting up a firm which would **(a)** issue commercial paper and **(b)** relend money to businesses at a rate slightly higher than the commercial paper rate but still less than the rate charged by banks?

STANDARD
&POOR'S

12. Use the Market Insight database (**www.mhhe.com/edumarketinsight**) to find recent balance sheets and income statements for two companies. Draw up a sources and uses of cash statement and a sources and uses of funds statement as in Tables 30.4 and 30.6.

13. Use the Market Insight database (**www.mhhe.com/edumarketinsight**) to compare the investment in current assets of different companies. Which of these companies make a heavy investment in inventories or receivables? Can you explain why?

STANDARD
&POOR'S

14. The Federal Reserve Bulletin publishes the results of a quarterly survey of bank lending (see **www.federalreserve.gov/releases/E2/**). Use the latest survey to describe the pattern of bank lending by domestic banks. Examine, for example, whether most loans are secured and whether they are made under commitment. What are the different characteristics of small and large loans? Now compare the results of this survey with an earlier one. Have there been any important changes?

CHALLENGE QUESTIONS

1. In some countries the market for long-term corporate debt is limited, and firms turn to short-term bank loans to finance long-term investments in plant and machinery. When a short-term loan comes due, it is replaced by another one, so that the firm is always a short-term debtor. What are the advantages and disadvantages?

2. Axle Chemical Corporation's treasurer has forecasted a $1 million cash deficit for the next quarter. However, there is only a 50 percent chance this deficit will actually occur. The treasurer estimates that there is a 20 percent probability the company will have no deficit at all and a 30 percent probability that it will actually need $2 million in short-term financing. The company can either take out a 90-day unsecured loan for $2 million at 1 percent per month or establish a line of credit, costing 1 percent per month on the amount borrowed plus a commitment fee of $20,000. If excess cash can be reinvested at 9 percent, which source of financing gives the lower expected cost?

3. Term loans usually require firms to pay a fluctuating interest rate. For example, the interest rate may be set at "1 percent above prime." The prime rate sometimes varies by several percentage points within a single year. Suppose that your firm has decided to borrow $40 million for five years. It has three alternatives. It can (a) borrow from a bank at the prime rate, currently 10 percent. The proposed loan agreement requires no principal repayments until the loan matures in five years. It can (b) issue 26-week commercial paper, currently yielding 9 percent. Since funds are required for five years, the commercial paper will have to be rolled over semiannually. That is, financing the $40 million requirement for five years will require 10 successive commercial paper sales. Or, finally, it can (c) borrow from an insurance company at a fixed rate of 11 percent. As in the bank loan, no principal has to be repaid until the end of the five-year period. What factors would you consider in analyzing these alternatives? Under what circumstances would you choose (a)? Under what circumstances would you choose (b) or (c)? (*Hint:* Don't forget Chapter 24.)

CHAPTER THIRTY-ONE

CASH MANAGEMENT

CHAPTER 30 PROVIDED an overall idea of what is involved in short-term financial management. Now it is time to get down to detail. We begin in this chapter by looking at how companies manage their holdings of cash and marketable securities. Then in the next chapter we look at the terms on which firms sell their goods and how they ensure that their customers pay promptly.

Out first task is to explain how cash is collected and paid out. In the United States small routine payments are commonly made by check. You want to ensure that when customers pay by check, you can convert these payments into usable cash in the bank quickly and cheaply. The use of checks is on the decline and large payments are almost always made electronically. You therefore need to understand how electronic payment systems work.

Our second task is to consider how much cash the firm should hold. Companies have a choice between holding cash in the bank and investing it in short-term securities. There is a trade-off here. Cash gives you a store of liquidity, which can be used to pay employees and suppliers. However, cash has the disadvantage that it does not pay interest. As we explain in the second section of this chapter, the trick is to strike a sensible balance.

In the last chapter we explained how companies raise short-term loans to tide them over a temporary cash shortage. If you are in the opposite position and have surplus cash, you need to know where you can park it to earn interest. So in the final section of this chapter we look at the menu of short-term investments that are available to the financial manager.

31.1 CASH COLLECTION AND DISBURSEMENT

The majority of small face-to-face purchases are made with coins or dollar bills. The most popular alternative in the United States for retail purchases is to pay by check. Each year individuals and firms write about 70 billion checks.

Notice that the United States is unusual in this heavy use of checks. For example, Figure 31.1 compares retail payment methods in the United States and Holland. You can see that checks are almost unknown in Holland: Most payments there are made by debit cards, direct debit, or credit transfer.[1]

How Checks Create Float

How does the firm's cash balance change when it writes or deposits a check? Suppose that the United Carbon Company has $1 million on demand deposit with its bank. It now pays one of its suppliers by writing and mailing a check for $200,000. The company's ledgers are immediately adjusted to show a cash balance of $800,000. But the company's bank won't learn anything about this check until it has been received by the supplier, deposited at the supplier's bank, and finally presented to United Carbon's bank for payment.[2] During this time United Carbon's bank continues to show

---

[1]Debit cards allow the cardholder to transfer money directly to the receiver's bank account. With a credit transfer the payer initiates the transaction, for example by giving her bank a standing order to make a regular payment. With a direct debit the transaction is initiated by the payee and is usually processed electronically.

[2]Checks deposited with a bank are cleared through the Federal Reserve clearing system, through a correspondent bank, or through a clearinghouse of local banks.

FIGURE 31.1

Shares of noncash retail payments in the USA and Holland in 1997. Notice the heavy use of checks in the USA.

Source: "Retail Payments in Selected Countries: A Comparative Study," Bank for International Settlements, Basel, 1999.

in its ledger that the company has a balance of $1 million. The company obtains the benefit of an extra $200,000 in the bank while the check is clearing. This sum is often called *payment*, or *disbursement float*.

Float sounds like a marvelous invention, but unfortunately it can also work in reverse. Suppose that in addition to paying its supplier, United Carbon *receives* a check for $100,000 from a customer. It deposits the check, and both the company and the bank increase the ledger balance by $100,000:

But this money isn't available to the company immediately. The bank doesn't actually have the money in hand until it has sent the check to, and received payment from, the customer's bank. Since the bank has to wait, it makes United Carbon wait too—usually one or two business days. In the meantime, the bank will show that United Carbon has an *available balance* of $1 million and an *availability float* of $100,000:

Notice that the company gains as a result of the payment float and loses as a result of the availability float. The difference is often termed the *net float*. In our example, the net float is $100,000. The company's available balance is therefore $100,000 greater than the balance shown in its ledger.

As financial manager you are concerned with the available balance, not with the company's ledger balance. If you know that it is going to be a week or two before some of your checks are presented for payment, you may be able to get by on a smaller cash balance. This game is often called *playing the float*.

You can increase your available cash balance by increasing your net float. This means that you want to ensure that checks paid in by customers are cleared rapidly and those paid to suppliers are cleared slowly. Perhaps this may sound like rather small beer, but think what it can mean to a company like Ford. Ford's daily sales average about $450 million. Therefore if it can speed up the collection process by one day, it frees $450 million, which is available for investment or payment to Ford's stockholders.

Some financial managers have become overenthusiastic in managing the float. In 1985, the brokerage firm E. F. Hutton pleaded guilty to 2,000 separate counts of mail and wire fraud. Hutton admitted that it had created nearly $1 billion of float by shuffling funds between its branches, and through various accounts at different banks. These activities cost the company a $2 million fine and its agreement to repay the banks any losses they may have incurred.

Managing Float

Float is the child of delay. Actually there are several kinds of delay, and so people in the cash management business refer to several kinds of float. Figure 31.2 summarizes.

Of course the delays that help the payer hurt the recipient. Recipients try to speed up collections. Payers try to slow down disbursements.

Speeding Up Collections

Many companies use **concentration banking** to speed up collections. In this case customers in a particular area make payment to a local branch office rather than to company headquarters. The local branch office then deposits the checks into a

FIGURE 31.2

Delays create float. Each heavy arrow represents a source of delay. Recipients try to reduce delay to get available cash sooner. Payers prefer delay because they can use their cash longer.

Note: The delays causing availability float and presentation float are equal on average but can differ from case to case.

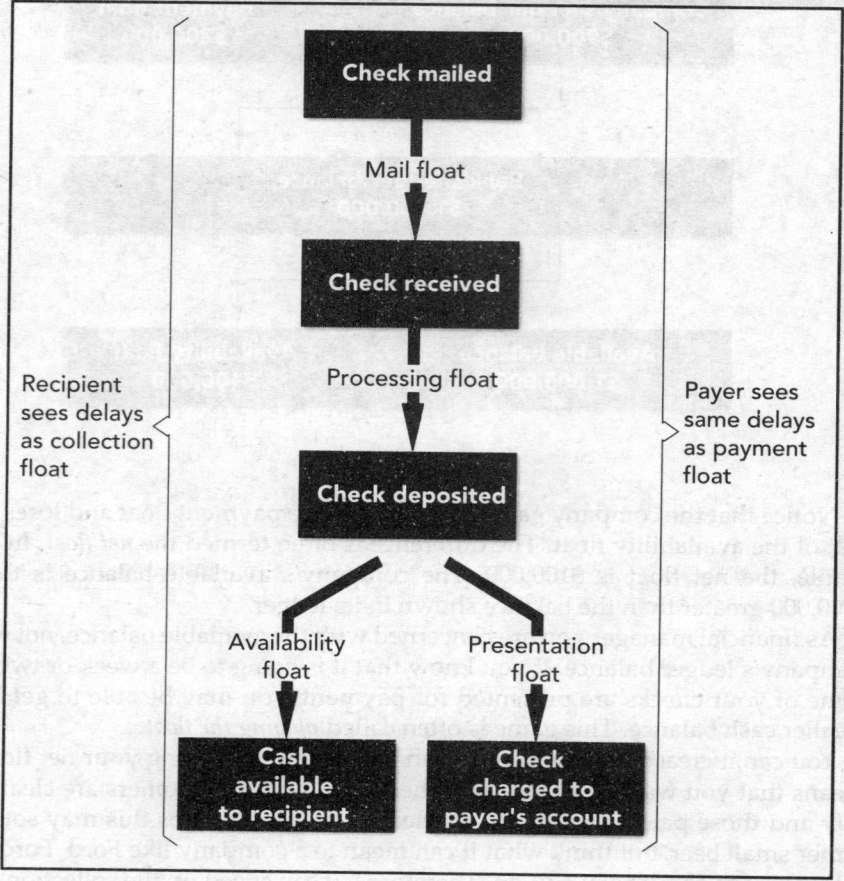

Recipient sees delays as collection float

Payer sees same delays as payment float

local bank account. Surplus funds are transferred to a *concentration account* at one of the company's principal banks.

Concentration banking reduces float in two ways. First, because the branch office is nearer to the customer, mailing time is reduced. Second, since the customer's check is likely to be drawn on a local bank, the time taken to clear the check is also reduced. Concentration banking brings many small balances together in one large, central balance, which can then be invested in interest-paying assets through a single transaction. For example, when Amoco streamlined its U.S. bank accounts in 1995, it was able to reduce its daily bank balances in non-interest-bearing accounts by almost 80 percent.[3]

Often concentration banking is combined with a **lock-box system.** In a lock-box system, you pay the local bank to take on the administrative chores. The system works as follows. The company rents a locked post office box in each principal region. All customers within a region are instructed to send their payments to the post office box. The local bank, as agent for the company, empties the box at regular intervals and deposits the checks in the company's local account. Surplus funds are transferred periodically to one of the company's principal banks.

---

[3]"Amoco Streamlines Treasury Operations," *The Citibank Globe,* November/December 1998.

How many collection points do you need if you use a lock-box system or concentration banking? The answer depends on where your customers are and on the speed of the U.S. mail. For example, suppose that you are thinking of opening a lock box. The local bank shows you a map of mail delivery times. From that and knowledge of your customers' locations, you come up with the following data:

- Average number of daily payments to lock box: 150
- Average size of payment: $1,200
- Rate of interest *per day:*   .02 percent
- Saving in mailing time: 1.2 days
- Saving in processing time: .8 day

On this basis, the lock box would increase your collected balance by

150 items per day × $1,200 per item × (1.2 + .8) days saved = $360,000

Invested at .02 percent per day, $360,000 gives a daily return of

.0002 × $360,000 = $72

The bank's charge for operating the lock-box system depends on the number of checks processed. Suppose that the bank charges $.26 per check. That works out to 150 × .26 = $39 per day. You are ahead by $72 − 39 = $33 per day, plus whatever your firm saves from not having to process the checks itself.

Our example assumes that the company has only two choices. It can do nothing, or it can operate the lock box. But maybe there is some other lock-box location, or some mixture of locations, that would be still more effective. Of course, you can always find this out by working through all possible combinations, but it may be simpler to solve the problem by linear programming. Many banks offer linear programming models to solve the problem of locating lock boxes.[4]

Controlling Disbursements

Speeding up collections is not the only way to increase the net float. You can also do so by slowing down disbursements. One tempting strategy is to increase mail time. For example, United Carbon could pay its New York suppliers with checks mailed from Nome, Alaska, and its Los Angeles suppliers with checks mailed from Vienna, Maine.

But on second thought you will realize that such post office tricks are unlikely to give more than a short-run payoff. Suppose you have promised to pay a New York supplier on February 29. Does it matter whether you mail the check from Alaska on the 26th or from New York on the 28th? Of course, you could use a remote mailing address as an excuse for paying late, but that's a trick easily seen through. If you have to pay late, you may as well mail late.[5]

There are effective ways of increasing presentation float, however. For example, suppose that United Carbon pays its suppliers with checks written on a New York City bank. From the time that the check has been deposited by the supplier, there

[4]See, for example, A. Kraus, C. Janssen, and A. McAdams, "The Lock-Box Location Problem," *Journal of Bank Research* 1 (Autumn 1970), pp. 50–58.

[5]Since the tax authorities look at the date of the postmark rather than the date of receipt, companies have been tempted to use a remote mailing address to pay their tax bills. But the tax authorities have reacted by demanding that large tax bills be paid by electronic transfer.

will be an average lapse of little more than a day before it is presented to United Carbon's bank for payment. The alternative is that United Carbon pays its suppliers with checks mailed to *arrive* on time but written on a bank in Helena, Montana; Midland, Texas; or Wilmington, Delaware. In these cases, it may take three or four days before each check is presented for payment. United Carbon, therefore, gains several days of additional float.[6]

Some firms even maintain disbursement accounts in different parts of the country. The computer looks up each supplier's zip code and automatically produces a check on the most distant bank.

The suppliers won't object to these machinations because the Federal Reserve guarantees a maximum clearing time of two days on all checks cleared through its system. The Federal Reserve, however, does object and has been trying to prevent remote disbursement.

A New York City bank receives several check deliveries each day from the Federal Reserve system as well as checks that come directly from other banks or through the local clearinghouse. Thus, if United Carbon uses a New York City bank for paying its suppliers, it will not know at the beginning of the day how many checks will be presented for payment. It must either keep a large cash balance to cover contingencies or be prepared to borrow. However, instead of having a disbursement account with a bank in New York, United Carbon could open a *zero-balance* account with a regional bank that receives almost all check deliveries in the form of a single, early-morning delivery from the Federal Reserve. Therefore, it can let the cash manager at United Carbon know early in the day exactly how much money will be paid out that day. The cash manager then arranges for this sum to be transferred from the company's concentration account to the disbursement account. Thus by the end of the day (and at the start of the next day), United Carbon has a zero balance in the disbursement account.

United Carbon's regional bank account has two advantages. First, by choosing a remote location, the company has gained several days of float. Second, because the bank can forecast early in the day how much money will be paid out, United Carbon does not need to keep extra cash in the account to cover contingencies.

The Finance in the News box describes how one Canadian company was able to reduce its cash needs by concentrating its cash holdings and using zero-balance accounts.

Electronic Funds Transfer

Throughout the world the use of checks is on the decline. For consumers they are being replaced by credit or debit cards. In the case of companies, payments are increasingly made electronically.[7] Electronic payments are relatively few in number but they account for the majority of transactions by value. Electronic payment systems may be of two kinds—a *gross* settlement system or a *net* settlement system. With gross settlement each payment is settled individually; with net settlement all payment instructions are accumulated and then at the end of the day any imbalances are settled.

---

[6]Remote disbursement accounts are described in I. Ross, "The Race Is to the Slow Payer," *Fortune*, April 18, 1983, pp. 75–80.

[7]Consumers also may receive and pay bills electronically via their personal computer. Currently Electronic Bill Presentment and Payment (EBPP) accounts for only a small proportion of payments but it is forecasted to grow rapidly.

HOW LAIDLAW RESTRUCTURED ITS CASH MANAGEMENT

The Canadian company, Laidlaw Inc., has more than 4,000 facilities throughout America, operating school bus services, ambulance services, and Greyhound coaches. During the 1990s the company expanded rapidly through acquisition, and its number of banking relationships multiplied until it had 1,000 separate bank accounts with more than 200 different banks. The head office had no way of knowing how much cash was stashed away in these accounts until the end of each quarter, when it was able to construct a consolidated balance sheet.

To economize on the use of cash, Laidlaw's financial manager sought to cut the company's average float from five days to two. At the same time management decided to consolidate cash management at five key banks. This enabled cash to be zero-balanced to a single account for each division and swept daily to Laidlaw's disbursement bank. Because the head office could obtain daily reports of the company's cash position, cash forecasting was improved and the company could reduce its cash needs still further.

Source: *Cash management at Laidlaw is described in G. Mann and S. Hutchison, "Driving Down Working Capital: Laidlaw's Story," Canadian Treasurer Magazine, August/September 1999.*

In the United States there are two systems for making large-value electronic payments—Fedwire (a gross system) and CHIPS (a net system). Fedwire is operated by the Federal Reserve system and connects over 10,000 financial institutions in the United States to the Fed and thereby to each other. Suppose Bank A instructs the Fed to transfer $1 million from its account with the Fed to the account of Bank B. Bank A's account is debited immediately and Bank B's account is credited at the same time. Fedwire is therefore an example of a *real-time gross settlement (RTGS)* system. Most developed countries now operate RTGS systems for large-value payments.

Real-time gross settlement suffers from a potential problem. If Bank A needs to pay Bank B, B needs to pay C, and C needs to pay A, there is a risk that the system could gridlock unless each bank kept a large reserve with the Fed. (A might not be able to pay B until it has been paid by C, C can't pay A until paid by B, and B in turn is awaiting payment by A.) To oil the wheels, therefore, the Fed takes on the credit risk by paying the receiving bank even if there are insufficient funds in the account of the payer. Since each payment is final and guaranteed by the Fed, each receiving bank can be sure that it has the money and can give its customer immediate access to the funds.

Cross-border high-value payments in dollars are handled by CHIPS, which is a privately owned system connecting 115 large domestic and foreign banks. CHIPS accumulates payment instructions throughout the day, and at the end of the day each bank settles up the net payment using Fedwire. This means that, if the bank receiving payments makes the funds available to its customers during the day, it would be at risk if the paying bank goes belly up during the day. Banks control this risk by imposing intraday credit limits on their exposure to each other.

Fedwire and CHIPS provide same-day settlement and are used to make high-value payments. Bulk payments such as wages, dividends, and payments to suppliers generally travel through the *Automated Clearinghouse (ACH)* system and take two to three days. In this case the company simply needs to provide a computer file of instructions to its bank, which then debits the corporation's account and forwards the payments to the ACH system. The ACH system is the largest payment system in the United States and in 1999 handled 6.2 billion payments with a value of $19 trillion.

For companies that are "wired" to their banks, customers, and suppliers, these electronic payment systems have at least three advantages:

- Record keeping and routine transactions are easy to automate when money moves electronically. Campbell Soup's Treasury Management Department discovered that it could handle cash management, short-term borrowing and lending, and bank relationships with a total staff of seven. The company's domestic cash flow was about $5 billion.[8]

- The marginal cost of transactions is very low. For example, it costs less than $10 to transfer huge sums of money using Fedwire and only a few cents to make an ACH transfer.

- Float is drastically reduced. Wire transfers generate no float at all. This can result in substantial savings. For example, cash managers at Occidental Petroleum found that one plant was paying out about $8 million per month three to five days early to avoid any risk of late fees if checks were delayed in the mail. The solution was obvious: The plant's managers switched to paying large bills electronically; that way they could ensure they arrived exactly on time.[9]

International Cash Management

Cash management in domestic firms is child's play compared with that in large multinational corporations operating in dozens of countries, each with its own currency, banking system, and legal structure.

A single, centralized cash management system is an unattainable ideal for these companies, although they are edging toward it. For example, suppose that you are the treasurer of a large multinational company with operations throughout Europe. You could allow the separate businesses to manage their own cash but that would be costly and would almost certainly result in each one accumulating little hoards of cash. The solution is to set up a regional system. In this case the company establishes a local concentration account with a bank in each country. Then any surplus cash is swept daily into central multicurrency accounts in London or another European banking center. This cash is then invested in marketable securities or used to finance any subsidiaries that have a cash shortage.

Payments also can be made out of the regional center. For example, to pay wages in each European country, the company just needs to send its principal bank a computer file with details of the payments to be made. The bank then finds the least costly way to transfer the cash from the company's central accounts and arranges for the funds to be credited on the correct day to the employees in each country.

---

[8]J. D. Moss, "Campbell Soup's Cutting-Edge Cash Management," *Financial Executive* 8 (September/October 1992), pp. 39–42.

[9]R. J. Pisapia, "The Cash Manager's Expanding Role: Working Capital," *Journal of Cash Management* 10 (November/December 1990), pp. 11–14.

Companies that maintain separate balances in each country are liable to find that they have a cash surplus in one country and a shortage in another. In this case the company could lend the surplus and borrow the deficit. However, that is likely to be costly, since banks need to charge a higher rate to borrowers than they pay to lenders. One alternative is to convert the surplus cash pool into the currency which is in short supply, but the simpler solution is to arrange for the bank to *pool* all your cash surpluses and shortages. In this case no money is transferred between accounts. Instead, the bank just adds together the credit and debit balances and pays you interest at its lending rate on the net surplus.

Most large multinationals have several banks in each country, but the more banks they use, the less control they have over their cash balances. So development of regional cash management systems favors banks that can offer a worldwide branch network. These banks also can afford to invest the several billion dollars that are needed to set up computer systems for handling cash payments and receipts in many different countries.

Paying for Bank Services

Much of the work of cash management—processing checks, transferring funds, running lock boxes, helping keep track of the company's accounts—is done by banks. And banks provide many other services not so directly linked to cash management, such as handling payments and receipts in foreign currency or acting as custodian for securities.[10]

All these services have to be paid for. Usually payment is in the form of a monthly fee, but banks may agree to waive the fee as long as the firm maintains a minimum average balance in an interest-free deposit. Banks are prepared to do this, because, after setting aside a portion of the money in a reserve account with the Fed, they can relend the money to earn interest. Demand deposits earmarked to pay for bank services are termed *compensating balances.* They used to be a very common way to pay for bank services, but there has been a steady trend away from using compensating balances and toward direct fees.

 ## 31.2 HOW MUCH CASH SHOULD THE FIRM HOLD?

Cash pays no interest. So why do individuals and corporations hold billions of dollars in cash and demand deposits? Why, for example, don't you take all your cash and invest it in interest-bearing securities? The answer of course is that cash gives you more *liquidity* than securities. You can use it to buy things. It is hard enough getting New York cab drivers to give you change for a $20 bill, but try asking them to split a Treasury bill.

In equilibrium all assets in the same risk class are priced to give the same expected marginal benefit. The benefit from holding Treasury bills is the interest that you receive; the benefit from holding cash is that it gives you a convenient store of liquidity. In equilibrium the marginal value of this liquidity is equal to the marginal value of the interest on Treasury bills. This is just another way of saying that Treasury bills are investments with zero net present value; they are fair value relative to cash.

---

[10]Of course, banks also lend money or give firms the *option* to borrow under a line of credit. See Section 30.6.

Does this mean that it does not matter how much cash you hold? Of course not. The marginal value of liquidity declines as you hold increasing amounts of cash. When you have only a small proportion of your assets in cash, a little extra can be extremely useful; when you have a substantial holding, any additional liquidity is not worth much. Therefore, as financial manager you want to hold cash balances up to the point where the marginal value of the liquidity is equal to the value of the interest forgone.

If that seems more easily said than done, you may be comforted to know that production managers must make a similar trade-off. Ask yourself why firms carry inventories of raw materials. They are not obliged to do so; they could simply buy materials day by day, as needed. But then they would pay higher prices for ordering in small lots, and they would risk production delays if the materials were not delivered on time. That is why they order more than the firm's immediate needs.[11]

But there is a cost to holding inventories. Interest is lost on the money that is tied up in inventories, storage must be paid for, and often there is spoilage and deterioration. Therefore production managers try to strike a sensible balance between the costs of holding too little inventory and those of holding too much.

It is exactly the same with cash. Cash is just another material that you require to carry on production. If you keep too small a proportion of your funds in the bank, you will need to make repeated sales of securities every time you want to pay your bills. On the other hand, if you keep excessive cash in the bank, you are losing interest.

The Inventory Decision

Let us look at what economists have had to say about managing inventories and then see whether some of these ideas may also help us to manage cash balances. Here is a simple inventory problem.

Everyman's Bookstore experiences a steady demand for *Principles of Corporate Finance* from customers who find that it makes a serviceable doorstop. There are two costs to holding an inventory of the book. First there is the *carrying cost*. This includes the cost of the capital that is tied up in the inventory, the cost of the shelf space, and so on. The second type of cost is the *order cost*. Each order involves a fixed handling expense and delivery charge.

These two costs are the kernel of the inventory problem. An increase in order size increases the average number of books in inventory, and therefore the carrying cost *rises*. However, as the store increases its order size, the number of orders falls, so that the order costs *decline*. The trick is to strike a sensible balance between these two costs. When carrying costs are high, you should hold a smaller inventory and replenish it more often. When order costs are high, you should hold a larger inventory and place orders less frequently.

Some numbers may help to illustrate. Suppose that the bookstore sells 100 copies of the book a year. Suppose also that the carrying cost of inventory works out at $4 per book and that each order placed with the publisher involves a fixed order cost of $2. The upward sloping line in Figure 31.3 shows that carrying costs increase in proportion to order size. The effect of order size on order costs is de-

---

[11]Not much more in many manufacturing operations. "Just-in-time" assembly systems provide for a continuous stream of parts deliveries, with no more than two or three hours' worth of parts inventory on hand. Financial managers likewise strive for just-in-time cash management systems, in which no cash lies idle anywhere in the company's business. This ideal is never quite reached because of the costs and delays discussed in this chapter. Large corporations get close, however.

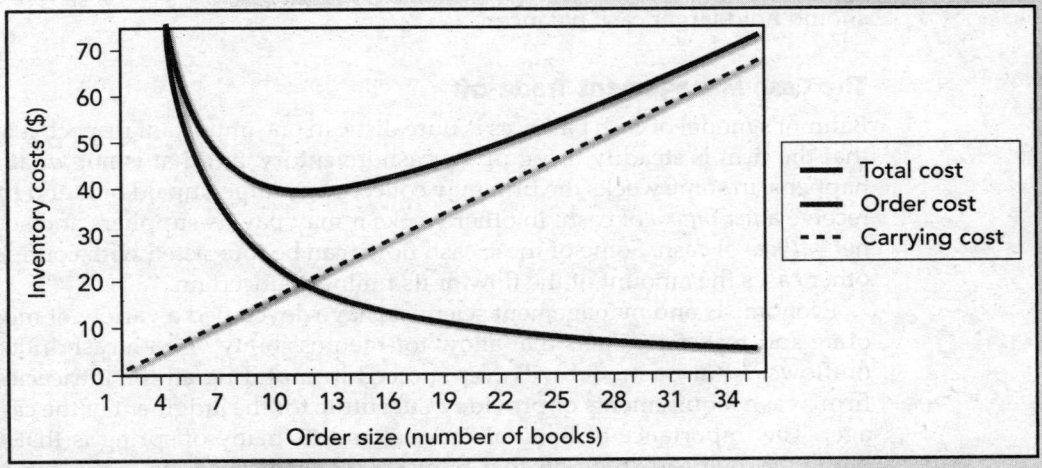

FIGURE 31.3

Optimal order size involves a trade-off between order costs and carrying costs.

picted by the downward sloping line. Order costs halve when the bookstore orders two books at a time rather than one, but thereafter the savings from increases in order size steadily diminish.

The upper curve in Figure 31.3 shows the sum of the carrying and order costs. You can see that total costs are minimized when the store orders 10 books at a time. Thus, 10 times a year the bookstore should place an order for 10 books and it should work off this inventory over the following five weeks.[12]

The Extension to Cash Balances

William Baumol was the first to point out that this simple inventory model can tell us something about the management of cash balances.[13] Suppose that you keep a reservoir of cash that is steadily drawn down to pay bills. When it runs out, you replenish the cash balance by selling Treasury bills. The order cost is the fixed administrative expense of each sale of Treasury bills. The main carrying cost of holding this cash is the interest that the firm is losing.

Deciding on the firm's cash holding is exactly analogous to the problem of optimum order size faced by Everyman's Bookstore. You just have to redefine the variables. For example, instead of referring to the number of books per order, order size becomes the amount of Treasury bills sold each time the cash balance is replenished. Order cost becomes cost per sale of Treasury bills, while carrying cost is just the interest lost from holding cash rather than bills.

If high interest rates increase the cost of carrying cash, you should hold a smaller inventory of cash and therefore make smaller and more frequent sales of Treasury

---

[12]See the *Principles of Corporate Finance* Web page (**www.mhhe.com/bm7e**) for an explanation of how to calculate the optimal order size.

[13]W. J. Baumol, "The Transactions Demand for Cash: An Inventory Theoretic Approach," *Quarterly Journal of Economics* 66 (November 1952), pp. 545–556.

bills. On the other hand, if the firm incurs high costs in selling securities, you should hold larger cash balances.

The Cash Management Trade-off

Baumol's model of cash balances is unrealistic in one important respect: It assumes that the firm is steadily using up its cash inventory. But that is not what usually happens. In some weeks the firm may collect some large unpaid bills and therefore receive a *net inflow* of cash. In other weeks it may pay its suppliers and so incur a net *outflow* of cash. Some of these cash flows can be forecasted with confidence; in other cases the amount of the flow or its timing is uncertain.

Economists and management scientists have developed a variety of more elaborate and realistic models that allow for the possibility of both cash inflows and outflows.[14] But no model will ever succeed in capturing all the intricacies of the firm's cash requirements or provide a substitute for the judgment of the cash manager. The importance of Baumol's model and its many offspring is that they all highlight the basic trade-off that the cash manager needs to make between the fixed costs of selling securities and the carrying costs of holding cash balances. Since there are economies of scale in buying or selling securities, the firm should wait and place a sufficiently large order rather than place a series of smaller orders.

Baumol's model helps us understand why small and medium-sized firms hold significant cash balances. But for very large firms, the transaction costs of buying and selling securities become trivial compared with the opportunity cost of holding idle cash balances.

Suppose that the interest rate is 8 percent per year, or roughly $8/365 = .022$ percent per day. Then the daily interest earned by $1 million is $.00022 \times 1,000,000 = 220. Even at a cost of $50 per transaction, which is generously high, it pays to buy Treasury bills today and sell them tomorrow rather than to leave $1 million idle overnight.

A corporation with $1 billion of annual sales has an average daily cash flow of $1,000,000,000/365$, about $2.7 million. Firms of this size end up buying or selling securities once a day, every day, unless by chance they have only a small positive cash balance at the end of the day.

Why do such firms hold any significant amounts of cash? There are basically two reasons. First, cash may be left in non-interest-bearing accounts to compensate banks for the services they provide. Second, large corporations may have literally hundreds of accounts with dozens of different banks. It is often better to leave idle cash in some of these accounts than to monitor each account daily and make daily transfers between them.

One major reason for the proliferation of bank accounts is decentralized management. You cannot give a subsidiary operating autonomy without giving its managers the right to spend and receive cash.

Good cash management nevertheless implies some degree of centralization. You cannot maintain your desired inventory of cash if all the subsidiaries in the group are responsible for their own private pools of cash. And you certainly want to avoid situations in which one subsidiary is investing its spare cash at 8 percent

---

[14]For example, the problem of cash management when inflows and outflows are unpredictable is analyzed in M. H. Miller and D. Orr, "A Model of the Demand for Money by Firms," *Quarterly Journal of Economics* 80 (August 1966), pp. 413–435. The Miller–Orr model is described in the *Principles of Corporate Finance* Web page.

while another is borrowing at 10 percent. It is not surprising, therefore, that even in highly decentralized companies there is generally central control over cash balances and bank relations.

 ## 31.3 INVESTING IDLE CASH

The Money Market

Temporary cash surpluses are generally invested in short-term securities. The market for these short-term investments is known as the **money market.** The money market has no physical marketplace. It consists of a loose agglomeration of banks and dealers linked together by telex, telephones, and computers. But a huge volume of securities is regularly traded on the money market, and competition is vigorous.

Most large corporations manage their own money-market investments, buying and selling through banks and dealers or over the Web. Small companies sometimes find it more convenient to hire a professional investment management firm or to put their cash into a money-market fund. This is a mutual fund that invests only in low-risk, short-term securities. We discussed money-market funds in Section 17.3.

Valuing Money-Market Investments

When we value long-term debt, it is important to take default risk into account. Almost anything may happen in 30 years, and even today's most respectable company may get into trouble eventually. This is the basic reason that corporate bonds offer higher yields than Treasury bonds.

Short-term debt is not risk-free either. When Penn Central failed, it had $82 million of short-term commercial paper outstanding.[15] After that shock, investors became much more discriminating in their purchases of commercial paper.

Such examples of failure are exceptions; in general, the danger of default is less for money-market securities issued by corporations than for corporate bonds. There are two reasons for this. First, the range of possible outcomes is smaller for short-term investments. Even though the distant future may be clouded, you can usually be confident that a particular company will survive for at least the next month. Second, for the most part only well-established companies can borrow in the money market. If you are going to lend money for only one day, you can't afford to spend too much time in evaluating the loan. Thus you will consider only blue-chip borrowers.

Despite the high quality of money-market investments, there are often significant differences in yield between corporate and U.S. government securities. Why is this? One answer is the risk of default. Another is that the investments have different degrees of liquidity or "moneyness." Investors like Treasury bills because they are easier to turn into cash on short notice. Securities that cannot be converted quickly and cheaply into cash need to offer relatively high yields.

During times of market turmoil investors often place a high value on having ready access to cash. On such occasions the yield on illiquid securities can increase dramatically. This happened in the fall of 1998 when a large hedge fund, Long

---

[15]Commercial paper is short-term debt issued by corporations. We described it in Section 30.6.

Term Capital Management (LTCM), came close to collapse.[16] Fearful that LTCM would be forced to liquidate its huge positions, investors shrank from securities that could not be converted easily into cash. The spread between the yield on commercial paper and Treasury bills rose to about 120 basis points (1.20 percent), almost four times its level at the beginning of the year.

Calculating the Yield on Money-Market Investments

Many money-market investments are pure discount securities. This means that they don't pay interest. The return consists of the difference between the amount you pay and the amount you receive at maturity. Unfortunately, it is no good trying to persuade the Internal Revenue Service that this difference represents capital gain. The IRS is wise to that one and will tax your return as ordinary income.

Interest rates on money-market investments are often quoted on a discount basis. For example, suppose that six-month bills are issued at a discount of 5 percent. This is rather a complicated way of saying that the price of a six-month bill is $100 - (6/12) \times 5 = \$97.50$. Therefore, for every $97.5 that you invest today, you receive $100 at the end of six months. The return over six months is $2.5/97.5 = .0256$, or 2.56 percent. This is equivalent to an annual yield of 5.12 percent simple interest or 5.19 percent if interest is compounded annually. Note that the return is always higher than the discount. When you read that an investment is selling at a discount of 5 percent, it is very easy to slip into the mistake of thinking that this is its return.[17]

The International Money Market

In Chapter 24 we pointed out that there are two main markets for dollar bonds. There is the domestic market in the United States and there is an international market. Similarly, in this chapter we shall see that in addition to the domestic money market, there is also an international market for short-term dollar investments. Since this market is based largely in Europe, it has traditionally been known as the *eurodollar* market. However, now that the European single currency has been called the euro, the term "eurodollar" is potentially confusing and we will just refer to "international dollars."

An international dollar is not some strange bank note; it is simply a dollar deposit in a bank outside the United States. For example, suppose that an American oil company buys crude oil from an Arab sheik and pays for it with a $1 million check drawn on Chase Manhattan Bank. The sheik then deposits the check into his account at Barclays Bank in London. As a result, Barclays has an asset in the form of a $1 million credit in its account with Chase Manhattan. It also has an offsetting liability in the form of a dollar deposit. That dollar deposit is placed in Europe; it is, therefore, an international dollar deposit.[18]

---

[16]Hedge funds specialize in making positive investments in securities that are believed to be undervalued, while selling short those that appear overvalued. The story of LTCM is told in R. Lowenstein, *When Genius Failed: The Rise and Fall of Long Term Capital Management*, Random House, New York, 2000; and N. Dunbar, *Inventing Money: The Story of Long Term Capital Management and the Legends behind It*, John Wiley, New York, 2000.

[17]To confuse things even more, dealers in the money market often quote rates as if there were only 360 days in a year. So a discount of 5 percent on a bill maturing in 182 days translates into a price of $100 - 5 \times (182/360) = 97.47$ percent.

[18]The sheik could equally well deposit the check with the London branch of a U.S. bank or a Japanese bank. He would still have made an international dollar deposit.

We will describe the principal domestic and international dollar investments shortly, but bear in mind that there is also an international market for investments in other currencies. For example, if a U.S. corporation wishes to make a short-term investment in yen, it can do so in the Tokyo money market or it can make an international yen deposit in London.

If we lived in a world without regulation and taxes, the interest rate on an international dollar loan would have to be the same as the rate on an equivalent domestic dollar loan, the rate on an international yen loan would have to be the same as that on a domestic yen loan, and so on. However, the international loan markets thrive because individual governments attempt to regulate domestic bank lending. For example, between 1963 and 1974 the U.S. government controlled the export of funds for corporate investment. Therefore, companies that wished to expand abroad were forced to borrow dollars outside the United States. This demand tended to push the interest rate on these loans above the domestic rate. At the same time the government limited the rate of interest that banks in the United States could pay on domestic deposits; this also tended to keep the rate of interest that you could earn on dollar deposits in Europe above the rate on domestic dollar deposits. By early 1974 the restrictions on the export of funds had been removed, and for large deposits the interest rate ceiling had also been abolished. In consequence, the difference between the interest rate on international dollar deposits and domestic deposits narrowed, but it did not disappear: Banks are not subject to Federal Reserve requirements on international dollar deposits and are not obliged to insure these deposits with the Federal Deposit Insurance Corporation. On the other hand, depositors are exposed to the (very low) risk that a foreign government could prohibit banks from repaying international dollar deposits. For these reasons international dollar investments continue to offer slightly higher rates of interest than domestic dollar deposits.

The U.S. government has become increasingly concerned that its regulations are driving banking business overseas to foreign banks and the overseas branches of American banks. To attract some of this business back to the States, the government in 1981 allowed U.S. and foreign banks to establish so-called *international banking facilities* (IBFs). An IBF is the financial equivalent of a free-trade zone; it is physically situated in the United States, but it is not required to maintain reserves with the Federal Reserve and depositors are not subject to any U.S. tax.[19] However, there are tight restrictions on what business an IBF can conduct. In particular, it cannot accept deposits from domestic United States corporations or make loans to them.

Banks in London lend dollars to one another at the *London interbank offered rate* (LIBOR). LIBOR is a benchmark for pricing many types of short-term loans in the United States and overseas. For example, a corporation in the United States may issue a floating-rate note with interest payments tied to LIBOR.

 ## 31.4 MONEY-MARKET INVESTMENTS

Table 31.1 summarizes the principal money-market investments. We will describe each in turn.

---

[19]For these reasons dollars held on deposit in an IBF are also classed as international dollars.

Investment	Borrower	Maturities When Issued	Marketability	Basis for Calculating Interest	Comments
Treasury bills	U.S. government	4 weeks, 3 months, or 6 months	Excellent secondary market	Discount	Auctioned weekly
Federal agency discount notes	FHLB, "Fannie Mae," "Sallie Mae," "Freddie Mac," etc.	Typically 3 to 6 months	Very good secondary market	Discount for securities of 6 months or less	Sold through dealers
Tax-exempt municipal notes	Municipalities, states, school districts, etc.	3 months to 1 year	Good secondary market	Usually interest-bearing; interest at maturity	Tax anticipation notes (TANs), revenue anticipation notes (RANs), bond anticipation notes (BANs), etc.
Tax-exempt variable-rate demand bonds (VRDBs)	Municipalities, states, state universities, etc.	20 to 40 years	Good secondary market	Variable interest rate	Long-term bonds but with put options to demand repayment
Non-negotiable time deposits and negotiable certificates of deposit (CDs)	Commercial banks, savings and loans	Usually 1 to 3 months; also longer-maturity variable-rate CDs	Poor secondary market for CDs	Interest-bearing with interest at maturity	Receipt for time deposit
Commercial paper (CP)	Industrial firms, finance companies, and bank holding companies; also municipalities	Maximum 270 days; usually 60 days or less	Dealers or issuer will repurchase paper	Usually discount	Unsecured promissory note; may be placed through dealer or directly with investor
Medium-term notes (MTNs)	Largely finance companies and banks; also industrial firms	Minimum 270 days; usually less than 10 years	Dealers will repurchase notes	Interest-bearing; usually fixed rate	Unsecured promissory note; placed through dealer
Bankers' acceptances (BAs)	Major commercial banks	1 to 6 months	Fair secondary market	Discount	Demands to pay that have been accepted by a bank
Repurchase agreements (repos)	Dealers in U.S. government securities	Overnight to about 3 months; also open repos (continuing contracts)	No secondary market	Repurchase price set higher than selling price; difference quoted as repo interest rate	Sales of government securities by dealer with simultaneous agreement to repurchase

TABLE 31.1

Money-market investments in the United States.

U.S. Treasury Bills

The first item in Table 31.1 is U.S. Treasury bills. These are usually issued weekly and mature in four weeks, three months, or six months.[20] Sales are by auction. You can enter a competitive bid and take your chance of receiving an allotment at your bid price. Alternatively, if you want to be sure of getting your bills, you can enter a noncompetitive bid. Noncompetitive bids are filled at the *average* price of the successful competitive bids. You don't have to participate in the auction to invest in Treasury bills. There is also an excellent secondary market in which billions of dollars of bills are bought and sold every day.

Federal Agency Securities

Agencies of the federal government such as the Federal Home Loan Bank (FHLB) and the Federal National Mortgage Association ("Fannie Mae") borrow both short and long term. The short-term debt consists of discount notes, which are similar to Treasury bills. They are very actively traded and are often held by corporations. Their yields are slightly above those on comparable Treasury securities. One reason for the slightly higher yields is that agency debt is not quite as marketable as Treasury issues.

Another is that most agency debt is backed not by the "full faith and credit" of the U.S. government but only by the agency itself.[21] Most investors do not believe that the U.S. government would allow one of its agencies to default, but in 2000 their faith and the price of agency debt both took a knock when a senior Treasury official reminded Congress that the government did *not* guarantee the debt. Soothing noises from the Treasury subsequently helped to reassure investors.

Short-Term Tax-Exempts

Short-term notes are also issued by municipalities, states, and agencies such as state universities and school districts.[22] These are slightly more risky than Treasury bills and not as easy to buy or sell.[23] Nevertheless they have one particular attraction—the interest is not subject to federal income tax.[24]

Pretax yields on tax-exempts are substantially lower than those on comparable taxed securities. But if your company pays tax at the standard 35 percent corporate rate, the lower gross yield of the municipals may be more than offset by the savings in tax.

Tax-exempt issues also include variable-rate demand bonds (VRDBs). These are long-term securities, whose interest payments are linked to the level of short-term interest rates. Whenever the interest rate is reset, investors have the right to sell the bonds back to the issuer for their face value. This ensures that on these reset dates the price of the bonds cannot be less than their face value. Therefore, although

---

[20]So-called three-month bills actually mature 91 days after issue, and six-month bills mature 182 days after issue.

[21]The exception is Ginnie Mae, whose debt is guaranteed by the U.S. government.

[22]Some of these notes are *general obligations* of the issuer; others are *revenue securities,* and in these cases payments are made from rent receipts or other user charges.

[23]Defaults on tax-exempts are rare but not unknown. For example, in 1983 the municipal utility Washington Public Power Supply System (unfortunately known as WPPSS) defaulted on $2.25 billion of bonds. The 1994 default of Orange County is described in Section 13.4.

[24]This advantage is partly offset by the fact that Treasury securities are free of state and local taxes.

VRDBs are long-term bonds, their prices are very stable and they compete with short-term tax-exempt notes as a home for spare cash.

Bank Time Deposits and Certificates of Deposit

If you make a time deposit with a bank, you are lending money to the bank for a fixed period. If you need the money before maturity, the bank will usually allow you to withdraw it but will exact a penalty in the form of a reduced rate of interest.

In the 1960s banks introduced the **negotiable certificate of deposit (CD)** for time deposits of $1 million or more. In this case, when the bank borrows, it issues a certificate of deposit, which is simply evidence of a time deposit with that bank. If a lender needs the money before maturity, it can sell the CD to another investor. When the loan matures, the new owner of the CD presents it to the bank and receives payment.

In recent years doubts about the creditworthiness of some banks have caused the secondary market in CDs to become less active, so that CDs are now much more like large non-negotiable time deposits.[25]

Instead of depositing dollars with a bank in the United States, a corporation can deposit them overseas with a foreign bank or the foreign branch of a U.S. bank. These deposits pay a fixed rate of interest, and either they are for a fixed term that may vary from one day to several years or they are for an undefined term but may be called at one or more days' notice. Since a time deposit is an illiquid investment, the London branches of the major banks also issue negotiable international dollar CDs.

Commercial Paper

We described commercial paper in the last chapter so we will not discuss it here beyond reminding you that it is short-term debt that is issued on a regular basis by both financial and nonfinancial companies. Commercial paper is popular with both industrial companies and money-market mutual funds as a parking place for short-term cash.

Bankers' Acceptances

In the next chapter we will explain how **bankers' acceptances (BAs)** may be used to finance exports or imports. An acceptance begins life as a written demand for the bank to pay a given sum at a future date. The bank then agrees to this demand by writing "accepted" on it. Once accepted, the draft becomes the bank's IOU and is a negotiable security that can be bought or sold through money-market dealers. Acceptances by the large U.S. banks generally mature in one to six months and involve very low credit risk.

Repurchase Agreements

Repurchase agreements, or *repos,* are effectively secured loans to a government security dealer. They work as follows: The investor buys part of the dealer's holding of Treasury securities and simultaneously arranges to sell them back again at a later date at a specified higher price. The borrower (the dealer) is said to have entered into a *repo;* the lender (who buys the securities) is said to have a *reverse repo.*

---

[25]Some CDs are not negotiable at all and are therefore *identical* to time deposits. For example, banks may sell low-value non-negotiable CDs to individuals.

Repos sometimes run for several months, but more frequently they are just overnight (24-hour) agreements. No other domestic money-market investment offers such liquidity. Corporations can treat overnight repos almost as if they were interest-bearing demand deposits.

Suppose that you decide to invest cash in repos for several days or weeks. You don't want to keep renegotiating agreements every day. One solution is to enter into an *open repo* with a security dealer. In this case there is no fixed maturity to the agreement; either side is free to withdraw at one day's notice. Alternatively, you may arrange with your bank to transfer any excess cash automatically into repos.

For many years repos appeared to be not only very liquid instruments but also very safe.[26] This reputation took a knock in 1982 when two money-market dealers went bankrupt. Each case involved heavy use of repos. One dealer, Drysdale Securities, had been in existence for only three months and had total capital of $20 million. However, it went bankrupt, owing Chase Bank $250 million. It's not easy to run up debts that fast, but Drysdale did it.

 ## 31.5 FLOATING-RATE PREFERRED STOCK—AN ALTERNATIVE TO MONEY-MARKET INVESTMENTS

There is no law preventing firms from making short-term investments in long-term securities. If a firm has $1 million set aside for an income tax payment, it could buy a long-term bond on January 1 and sell it on April 15, when the taxes must be paid. However, the danger in this strategy is obvious. What happens if bond prices fall by 10 percent between January and April? There you are, with a $1 million liability to the Internal Revenue Service, bonds worth only $900,000, and a very red face. Of course, bond prices could also go up, but why take the chance? Corporate treasurers entrusted with excess funds for short-term investment are naturally averse to the price volatility of long-term bonds.

We saw earlier how municipalities devised variable-rate demand bonds, which investors could periodically sell back to the issuer. The prices of these bonds are nearly immune to fluctuations in interest rates. In addition, the interest on municipal loans has the attraction of being tax-exempt. So a municipal variable-rate demand bond offers a safe, tax-free, short-term haven for your $1 million of cash.

Common stock and preferred stock also have an interesting tax advantage for corporations, since firms pay tax on only 30 percent of dividends received from other corporations. For each $1 of dividends received, the firm gets to keep $1 - .30 \times .35 = \$.895$. Thus the effective tax rate is only 10.5 percent. This is higher than the zero tax rate on the interest from municipal debt but much lower than the rate that the company pays on other debt interest.

Suppose you consider putting that $1 million in some other corporation's preferred shares.[27] The 10.5 percent tax rate is very tempting. On the other hand,

---

[26]To reduce the risk of repos, it is common to value the security at less than its market value. This difference is known as a *haircut*.

[27]Preferred shares are usually better short-term investments for a corporation than common shares. The preferred shares' expected return is virtually all dividends; most common shares are expected to generate capital gains, too. The corporate tax on capital gains is usually 35 percent. Corporations therefore have a strong incentive to like dividends and dislike capital gains.

since preferred dividends are fixed, the prices of preferred shares change when long-term interest rates change. A $1 million investment in preferred shares could be worth only $900,000 on April 15, when taxes are due. Wouldn't it be nice if someone invented a preferred share that was insulated from fluctuating interest rates?

Well, there are such securities, and you can probably guess how they work: Specify a dividend payment which goes up and down with the general level of interest rates.[28] The prices of these securities are less volatile than those of fixed-dividend preferreds.

Varying the dividend payment on preferred stock doesn't quite do the trick. For example, if investors become more concerned about the risk of preferred stock, they might demand a higher relative return and the price of the stock could fall. So companies sometimes add another wrinkle to floating-rate preferred. Instead of being tied rigidly to interest rates, the dividend can be reset periodically by means of an auction which is open to all investors. Existing shareholders can enter the auction by stating the minimum dividend they are prepared to accept; if this turns out to be higher than the rate that is needed to sell the issue, the shareholders sell the stock to the new investors at its face value. Alternatively, shareholders can simply enter a noncompetitive bid, keeping their shares and receiving whatever dividend is set by the other bidders. The result is similar to the variable-rate demand note: Because auction-rate preferred stock can be resold at regular intervals for its face value, its price cannot wander far in the interim.[29]

Why would any firm want to *issue* floating-rate preferreds? Dividends must be paid out of *after-tax* income, whereas interest comes out of before-tax income. Thus, if a taxpaying firm wants to issue a floating-rate security, it would normally choose to issue floating-rate debt to generate interest tax shields.

However, there are plenty of firms that are not paying taxes. These firms cannot make use of the interest tax shield. Moreover, they have been able to issue floating-rate preferreds at yields *lower* than what they would have to pay on a floating-rate debt issue. (The corporations buying the preferreds are happy with these lower yields because 70 percent of the dividends they receive escape tax.)

Floating-rate preferreds were invented in Canada in the mid-1970s, when several billion dollars' worth were issued before the Canadian tax authorities cooled off the market by limiting the dividend tax exclusion on some types of floating-rate issues. They were reinvented in the United States in May 1982, when Chemical New York Corporation, the holding company for Chemical Bank, raised $200 million. The securities proved so popular that over $4 billion of floating-rate preferreds were issued by the following spring. Then the novelty wore off, and the frequency of new issues slowed down. It was back to business as usual, with one important exception: There was one more item on the menu of investment opportunities open to corporate money managers.

---

[28]Usually there are limits on the maximum and minimum dividends that can be paid. Thus if interest rates leap to 100 percent, the preferred dividend would hit a ceiling of, say, 15 percent. If interest rates fall to 1 percent, the preferred dividend would hit a floor at say, 5 percent.

[29]See M. J. Alderson, K. C. Brown, and S. L. Lummer, "Dutch Auction Rate Preferred Stock," *Financial Management* 16 (Summer 1987), pp. 68–73.

In the United States a high proportion of small purchases are paid for by check. To make the best use of their cash, companies need to understand how a company's cash changes when it writes or deposits a check. The cash shown in the company's ledger is not the same as the available balance in your bank account. The difference is the net float. When you have written a large number of checks awaiting clearance, the available balance will be larger than the ledger balance. When you have just deposited a large number of checks that have not yet been cleared by the bank, the available balance will be smaller. If you can predict how long it will take checks to clear, you may be able to play the float and get by on a smaller cash balance.

You can also *manage* the float by speeding up collections and slowing down payments. One way to speed collections is to use concentration banking. Customers make payments to a regional office which then pays the checks into a local bank account. Surplus funds are transferred from the local account to a concentration bank. An alternative technique is lock-box banking. In this case customers send their payments to a local post office box. A local bank empties the box at regular intervals and clears the checks. Concentration banking and lock-box banking reduce mailing time and the time required to clear checks.

Large-value payments are almost always made electronically. In the United States there are two large-value systems—Fedwire (for dollar payments within the country) and CHIPS (for cross-border payments). Bulk payments, such as wages and dividends, are usually made by means of the Automated Clearinghouse (ACH) system.

Banks provide many services. They handle checks, manage lock boxes, provide advice, obtain references, and so on. Firms either pay cash for these services or pay by maintaining sufficient cash balances with the bank.

In many cases you will want to keep somewhat larger balances than are needed to pay for the tangible services. One reason is that the bank may be a valuable source of ideas and business connections. Another reason is that you may use the bank as a source of short-term funds. Leaving idle cash at your bank may be implicit compensation for the willingness of the bank to stand ready to advance credit when needed. A large cash balance may, therefore, be good insurance against a rainy day.

Cash provides liquidity, but it doesn't pay interest. Securities pay interest, but you can't use them to buy things. As financial manager you want to hold cash up to the point where the marginal value of liquidity is equal to the interest that you could earn on securities.

Cash is just one of the raw materials that you need to do business. It is expensive keeping your capital tied up in large inventories of raw materials when it could be earning interest. So why do you hold inventories at all? Why not order materials as and when you need them? The answer is that it is also expensive to keep placing many small orders. You need to strike a balance between holding too large an inventory of cash (and losing interest on the money) and making too many small adjustments to your stock of cash (and incurring additional administrative and transaction costs). If interest rates are high, you want to hold relatively small inventories of cash. If your cash needs are variable and your costs are high, you want to hold relatively large inventories.

If you have more cash than is currently needed, you can invest it in the money market. There is a wide choice of money-market investments, with different

FIGURE 31.4

Short-term assets held by U.S. nonfinancial corporations, 4th quarter, 2000.

Source: Federal Reserve System, Division of Research and Statistics, *Flow of Funds Accounts* (**www.federalreserve.gov/releases/Z1/current/data.htm**).

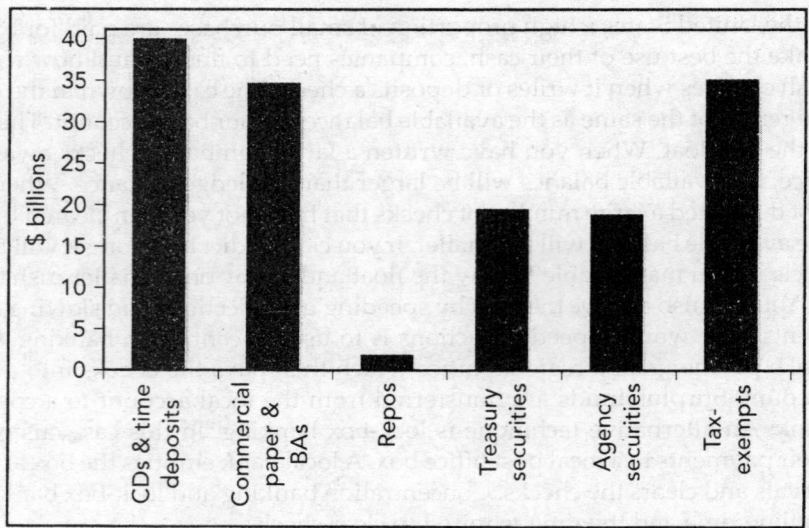

degrees of liquidity and risk. Remember that the interest rate on these investments is often quoted as a discount. The compound return is always higher than the rate of discount.

The principal money-market investments in the United States are

- U.S. Treasury bills
- Federal agency notes
- Short-term tax-exempts
- Time deposits and certificates of deposit
- Repurchase agreements
- Commercial paper
- Bankers' acceptances

Figure 31.4 should give you some feel for which of these investments are the most popular homes for surplus cash.

FURTHER READING

The next three articles analyze the design of lock-box and concentration banking systems:

A. Kraus, C. Janssen, and A. McAdams: "The Lock-Box Location Problem," *Journal of Bank Research*, 1:50–58 (Autumn 1970).

G. Cornuejols, M. L. Fisher, and G. L. Nemhauser: "Location of Bank Accounts to Optimize Float: An Analytic Study of Exact and Approximate Algorithms," *Management Science*, 23:789–810 (April 1977).

S. F. Maier and J. H. Vander Weide: "What Lock-Box and Disbursement Models Really Do," *Journal of Finance*, 37:361–371 (May 1983).

Baumol was the pioneer in applying inventory models to cash management. Miller and Orr extend the Baumol model to handling uncertain cash flows, and Mullins and Homonoff review tests of inventory models for cash management.

W. J. Baumol: "The Transactions Demand for Cash: An Inventory Theoretic Approach," *Quarterly Journal of Economics*, 66:545–556 (November 1952).

M. H. Miller and D. Orr: "A Model of the Demand for Money by Firms," *Quarterly Journal of Economics*, 80:413–435 (August 1966).

D. Mullins and R. Homonoff: "Applications of Inventory Cash Management Models," in S. C. Myers (ed.), *Modern Developments in Financial Management*, Frederick A. Praeger, Inc., New York, 1976.

The following article provides a useful description of electronic payments systems in the United States:

G. R. Junker, B. J. Summers, and F. M. Young: "A Primer on the Settlement of Payments in the United States," *Federal Reserve Bulletin*, 77:847–858 (November 1991).

Specialized "how-to" texts on cash management include:

J. E. Finnerty: *How to Manage Corporate Cash Effectively*, American Management Association, New York, 1991.

J. G. Kallberg and K. L. Parkinson: *Corporate Liquidity: Management and Measurement*, Richard D. Irwin, Homewood, IL, 1993.

C. R. Malburg: *The Cash Management Handbook*, Prentice-Hall, Englewood Cliffs, NJ, 1992.

For a detailed description of the money market and short-term lending opportunities, see:

L. Epstein: *Corporate Investing: A Treasurer's Reference*, John Wiley, New York, 2001.

F. J. Fabozzi, *The Handbook of Fixed Income Securities*, 6th ed., McGraw-Hill Companies, Inc., New York, 2000.

M. Stigum: *The Money Market*, 3rd ed., McGraw-Hill Professional Publishing, New York, 1990.

Chapter 4 of *U.S. Monetary Policy and Financial Markets*, which is available on the New York Federal Reserve website, **www.newyorkfed.org**.

QUIZ

1. A company has the following cash balances:

Company's ledger balance	$600,000
Bank's ledger balance	$625,000
Available balance	$550,000

   a. Calculate the payment float and availability float.
   b. Why does the company gain from the payment float?
   c. Suppose the company adopts a policy of writing checks on a remote bank. How is this likely to affect the three measures of cash balance?

2. Anne Teak, the financial manager of a furniture manufacturer, is considering operating a lock-box system. She forecasts that 300 payments a day will be made to lock boxes, with an average payment size of $1,500. The bank's charge for operating the lock boxes is *either* $.40 a check *or* compensating balances of $800,000.
   a. If the interest rate is 9 percent, which method of payment is cheaper?
   b. What reduction in the time to collect and process each check is needed to justify use of the lock-box system?

3. Complete the passage that follows by choosing the appropriate terms from the following list: *lock-box banking, Fedwire, CHIPS, payment float, concentration banking, availability float, net float.*

The firm's available balance is equal to its ledger balance plus the _____ and minus the _____. The difference between the available balance and the ledger balance is often called the _____. Firms can increase their cash resources by speeding up collections. One way to do this is to arrange for payments to be made to regional offices which pay the checks into local banks. This is known as _____. Surplus funds are then transferred from the local bank to one of the company's main banks. Transfers can be made electronically by the _____ or _____ systems. Another technique is to arrange for a local bank to collect the checks directly from a post office box. This is known as _____.

4. Everyman's Bookstore has experienced an increased demand for *Principles of Corporate Finance*. It now expects to sell 216 books a year. Unfortunately, inventory carrying costs have increased to $6 per book per year, whereas order costs have remained steady at $2 per order. How many orders should the store place per year and what is its average inventory? You can answer the question either by plotting store costs as in Figure 31.1 or using the formula shown on the *Principles of Corporate Finance* Web page (**www.mhhe.com/bm7e**)

5. Now assume that Everyman's Bookstore uses up cash at a steady rate of $20,000 a year. The interest rate is 2 percent, and each sale of securities costs $2. How many times a year should the store sell securities and what is its average cash balance? Either plot the costs as in Figure 31.1 or use the formula shown on the *Principles of Corporate Finance* Web page (**www.mhhe.com/bm7e**)

6. Suppose that you can hold cash that pays no interest or invest in securities that pay interest at 8 percent. The securities are not easily sold on short notice; therefore, you must make up any cash deficiency by drawing on a bank line of credit which charges interest at 10 percent. Should you invest more or less in securities under each of the following circumstances?
   a. You are unusually uncertain about future cash flows.
   b. The interest rate on bank loans rises to 11 percent.
   c. The interest rates on securities and on bank loans both rise by the same proportion.
   d. You revise downward your forecast of future cash needs.

7. In January 2002 six-month (182-day) Treasury bills were issued at a discount of 1.75 percent. What is the annual yield?

8. For each item below, choose the investment that best fits the accompanying description:
   a. Maturity often overnight (repurchase agreements/bankers' acceptances).
   b. Maturity never more than 270 days (tax-exempts/commercial paper).
   c. Often directly placed with investors (finance company commercial paper/industrial commercial paper).
   d. Registered with the SEC (commercial paper/medium-term notes).
   e. Issued by the U.S. Treasury (tax-exempts/3-month bills).
   f. Quoted on a discount basis (certificates of deposit/Treasury bills).
   g. Sold by auction (tax-exempts/Treasury bills).

9. Consider three securities:
   a. A floating-rate bond.
   b. A preferred share paying a fixed dividend.
   c. A floating-rate preferred.

   A financial manager responsible for short-term investment of excess cash would probably choose the floating-rate preferred over *either* of the other two securities. Why? Explain briefly.

1. Every day, Consolidated Blancmange writes checks worth $100,000. These checks take an average of five days to clear. The company also receives payments of $150,000 every day. These take three days to clear.

   a. Calculate payment float, availability float, and net float.

   b. What would be the company's annual savings if it could reduce availability float to one day? The interest rate is 6 percent a year. What would be the present value of these savings?

2. On January 25, Coot Company has $250,000 deposited with a local bank. On January 27, the company writes and mails checks of $20,000 and $60,000 to suppliers. At the end of the month, Coot's financial manager deposits a $45,000 check received from a customer in the morning mail and picks up the end-of-month account summary from the bank. The manager notes that only the $20,000 payment of the 27th has cleared the ·bank. What are the company's ledger balance and payment float? What is the company's net float?

3. Knob, Inc., is a nationwide distributor of furniture hardware. The company now uses a central billing system for credit sales of $180 million annually. First National, Knob's principal bank, offers to establish a new concentration banking system for a flat fee of $100,000 per year. The bank estimates that mailing and collection time can be reduced by three days. By how much will Knob's availability float be reduced under the new system? How much extra interest income will the new system generate if the extra funds are used to reduce borrowing under Knob's line of credit with First National? Assume that the borrowing rate is 12 percent. Finally, should Knob accept First National's offer if collection costs under the old system are $40,000 per year?

4. Explain why companies use zero-balance accounts to make disbursements.

5. A parent company settles the collection account balances of its subsidiaries once a week. (That is, each week it transfers any balances in the accounts to a central account.) The cost of a wire transfer is $10. A check costs $.80. Cash transferred by wire is available the same day, but the parent must wait three days for checks to clear. Cash can be invested at 12 percent per year. How much money must be in a collection account before it pays to use a wire transfer?

6. The financial manager of JAC Cosmetics is considering opening a lock box in Pittsburgh. Checks cleared through the lock box will amount to $300,000 per month. The lock box will make cash available to the company three days earlier than is currently the case.

   a. Suppose that the bank offers to run the lock box for a $20,000 compensating balance. Is the lock box worthwhile?

   b. Suppose that the bank offers to run the lock box for a fee of $.10 per check cleared instead of a compensating balance. What must the average check size be for the fee alternative to be less costly? Assume an interest rate of 6 percent per year.

   c. Why did you need to know the interest rate to answer (b) but not to answer (a)?

7. Some years ago, Merrill Lynch increased its float by mailing checks drawn on west coast banks to customers in the east and checks drawn on east coast banks to customers in the west. A subsequent class action suit against Merrill Lynch revealed that in 28 months, from September 1976, Merrill Lynch disbursed $1.25 billion in 365,000 checks to New York State customers alone. The plaintiffs' lawyer calculated that by using a remote bank Merrill Lynch had increased its average float by 1.5 days.

   a. How much did Merrill Lynch disburse per day to New York State customers?

   b. What was the total gain to Merrill Lynch over the 28 months, assuming an interest rate of 8 percent?

   c. What was the present value of the increase in float if the benefits were expected to be permanent?

d. Suppose that the use of remote banks had involved Merrill Lynch in extra expenses. What was the maximum extra cost per check that Merrill Lynch would have been prepared to pay?

8. The processing cost of making a payment through the ACH system is roughly half the cost of making the same payment by check. Why, therefore, do firms often rationally choose to make payments by check?

9. How would you expect a firm's cash balance to respond to the following changes?
   a. Interest rates increase.
   b. The volatility of daily cash flow decreases.
   c. The transaction cost of buying or selling marketable securities goes up.

10. A firm maintains a separate account for cash disbursements. Total disbursements are $100,000 per month, spread evenly over the month. Administrative and transaction costs of transferring cash to the disbursement account are $10 per transfer. Marketable securities yield 1 percent per month. Determine the size and number of transfers that will minimize the cost of maintaining the special account.

11. Suppose that the rate of inflation accelerates from 5 to 10 percent per year. Would firms' cash balances go up or down relative to sales? Explain.

12. Suppose that interest rates double.
   a. What, according to the Baumol model, would happen to the firm's average cash balances?
   b. Recalculate the gain from operating the lock-box system described in Section 31.1 given the new level of interest rates.

13. A three-month Treasury bill and a six-month bill both sell at a discount of 10 percent. Which offers the higher annual yield?

14. In Section 31.3 we described a six-month bill that was issued on an annually compounded yield of 5.19 percent. Suppose that one month has passed and the investment still offers the same annually compounded return. What is the percentage discount? What was your return over the month?

15. Look again at question 14. Suppose another month has passed, so the bill has only one month left to run. It is now selling at a discount of 5 percent. What is the yield calculated on a simple interest basis? What was your realized return over the two months?

16. Look up current interest rates offered by short-term investment alternatives. Suppose that your firm has $1 million excess cash to invest for the next two months. How would you invest this cash? How would your answer change if the excess cash were $5,000, $20,000, $100,000, or $100 million?

17. In February 2002 high-grade corporate bonds sold at a yield of 5.89 percent, while tax-exempts of comparable maturity offered 3.99 percent annually. If an investor receives the same *after-tax* return from corporates and tax-exempts, what is that investor's marginal rate of tax? What other factors might affect an investor's choice between the two types of securities?

18. The IRS prohibits companies from borrowing money to buy tax-exempts and also deducting the interest payments on the borrowing from taxable income. Should the IRS prohibit such activity? If it didn't, would you advise the company to borrow to buy tax-exempts?

19. Suppose you are a wealthy individual paying 39.1 percent tax on income. What is the expected after-tax yield on each of the following investments?
   a. A municipal note yielding 6.5 percent pretax.
   b. A Treasury bill yielding 10 percent pretax.
   c. A floating-rate preferred stock yielding 7.5 percent pretax.

How would your answer change if the investor is a corporation paying tax at 35 percent? What other factors would you need to take into account when deciding where to invest the corporation's spare cash?

20. Most floating-rate preferreds have both a floor and a ceiling on their dividend rate. (See Section 31.5, footnote 28.) How do these limits affect the behavior of the *prices* of these securities as interest rates change? Why do you think the companies included the limits in the first place?

1. The first floating-rate preferreds were successfully issued at initial yields *below* yields on Treasury bills. How was this possible? The preferreds were clearly riskier than the bills. What would you predict for the *long-run* relationship between yields on bills and on floating-rate preferreds? (We say "long-run" to give time for all firms that will want to issue floating-rate preferreds to get around to doing so.)

CHALLENGE QUESTION

CHAPTER THIRTY-TWO

CREDIT MANAGEMENT

WHEN COMPANIES SELL their products, they sometimes demand cash on or before delivery, but in most cases they allow some delay in payment. If you turn back to the balance sheet in Table 30.1, you can see that for the average manufacturing company, *accounts receivable* constitute about one-third of its current assets. Receivables include both trade credit and consumer credit. The former is by far the larger and will, therefore, be the main focus of this chapter.

Companies that do not pay for their purchases immediately are effectively borrowing money from their suppliers. Such "debts" show up as *accounts payable* in the purchasing companies' balance sheets. Table 30.1 shows that payables are the most important source of short-term finance, much larger than short-term loans from banks and other institutions.

Management of trade credit requires answers to five sets of questions:

1. On what terms do you propose to sell your goods or services? How long are you going to give customers to pay their bills? Are you prepared to offer a cash discount for prompt payment?
2. What evidence do you need of indebtedness? Do you just ask the buyer to sign a receipt, or do you insist on some more formal commitment?
3. Which customers are likely to pay their bills? To find out, do you consult a credit agency or ask for a bank reference? Or do you analyze the customer's financial statements?
4. How much credit are you prepared to extend to each customer? Do you play it safe by turning down any doubtful prospects? Or do you accept the risk of a few bad debts as part of the cost of building up a large regular clientele?
5. How do you collect the money when it becomes due? How do you keep track of payments? What do you do about reluctant payers or deadbeats?

We will discuss each set of questions in turn.

 ## 32.1 TERMS OF SALE

Not all sales involve credit. For example, if you are producing goods to the customer's specification or incurring substantial delivery costs, then it may be sensible to ask for cash before delivery (CBD). If you are supplying goods to a wide variety of irregular customers, you may prefer cash on delivery (COD).[1] If your product is expensive and custom-designed, you may require **progress payments** as work is carried out. For example, a large, extended consulting contract might call for 30 percent payment after completion of field research, 30 percent more on submission of a draft report, and the remaining 40 percent when the project is finally completed.

When we look at transactions that do involve credit, we find that each industry seems to have its own particular usage with regard to payment terms.[2] These norms have a rough logic. For example, firms selling consumer durables may allow the buyer a month to pay, while those selling perishable goods, such as cheese or fresh fruit, typically demand payment in a week. Similarly, a seller will generally allow more extended payment if its customers are in low-risk businesses, if

---

[1] Some goods *can't* be sold on credit—a glass of beer, for example.

[2] Standard credit terms in different industries are reported in O. K. Ng, J. K. Smith, and R. L. Smith, "Evidence on the Determinants of Credit Terms Used in Interfirm Trade," *Journal of Finance* 54 (June 1999), pp. 1109–1129.

their accounts are large, if the customers need time to ascertain the quality of the goods, and if the goods are not quickly resold.

To induce customers to pay before the final date, it is common to offer a cash discount for prompt settlement. For example, pharmaceutical manufacturers commonly require payment within 30 days but may offer a 2 percent discount to customers who pay within 10 days. These terms are referred to as "2/10, net 30."

Cash discounts are often very large. For example, a customer who buys on terms of 2/10, net 30 may decide to forgo the cash discount and pay on the thirtieth day. This means that the customer obtains an extra 20 days' credit but pays about 2 percent more for the goods. This is equivalent to borrowing money at a rate of 44.6 percent per annum.[3] Of course, any firm that delays payment beyond the due date gains a cheaper loan but damages its reputation for creditworthiness.

You can think of the terms of sale as fixing both the price for the cash buyer and the rate of interest charged for credit. For example, suppose that a firm reduces the cash discount from 2 to 1 percent. That would represent an *increase* in the price for the cash buyer of 1 percent but a *reduction* in the implicit rate of interest charged the credit buyer from just over 2 percent per 20 days to just over 1 percent per 20 days.

For many items that are bought on a recurrent basis, it is inconvenient to require separate payment for each delivery. A common solution is to pretend that all sales during the month in fact occur at the end of the month (EOM). Thus goods may be sold on terms of 8/10, EOM, net 60. This arrangement allows the customer a cash discount of 8 percent if the bill is paid within 10 days of the end of the month; otherwise, the full payment is due within 60 days of the invoice date.[4] When purchases are subject to seasonal fluctuations, manufacturers often encourage customers to take early delivery by allowing them to delay payment until the usual order season. This practice is known as "season dating."

 ## 32.2 COMMERCIAL CREDIT INSTRUMENTS

The terms of sale define when payment is due but not the nature of the contract. Repetitive sales to domestic customers are almost always made on *open account* and involve only an implicit contract. There is simply a record in the seller's books and a receipt signed by the buyer.

If you want a clear commitment from the buyer, before you deliver the goods, you can arrange a **commercial draft**.[5] This works as follows: You draw a draft ordering payment by the customer and send this draft to the customer's bank together with the shipping documents. If immediate payment is required, the draft is termed a *sight draft*; otherwise, it is known as a *time draft*. Depending on whether it is a sight or a time

---

[3]The cash discount allows you to pay $98 rather than $100. If you do not take the discount, you get a 20-day loan, but you pay $2/98 = 2.04$ percent more for your goods. The number of 20-day periods in a year is $365/20 = 18.25$. A dollar invested for 18.25 periods at 2.04 percent per period grows to $(1.0204)^{18.25} = \$1.446$, a 44.6 percent return on the original investment. If a customer is happy to borrow at this rate, it's a good bet that he or she is desperate for cash (or can't work out compound interest). For a discussion of this issue, see J. K. Smith, "Trade Credit and Information Asymmetry," *Journal of Finance* 42 (September 1987), pp. 863–872.

[4]Terms of 8/10, prox., net 60 would entitle the customer to a discount if the bill is paid within 10 days of the end of the following (or "proximo") month.

[5]Commercial drafts are sometimes known by the more general term *bills of exchange*.

draft, the customer either pays up or acknowledges the debt by adding the word *accepted* and his or her signature. The bank then hands the shipping documents to the customer and forwards the money or the **trade acceptance** to you, the seller.[6] You may hold the trade acceptance to maturity or use it as security for a loan.

If your customer's credit is for any reason suspect, you may ask the customer to arrange for his or her bank to *accept* the time draft. In this case, the bank guarantees the customer's debt. These **bankers' acceptances** are often used in overseas trade; they have a higher standing and greater negotiability than trade acceptances.

If you are selling goods overseas, you may ask the customer to arrange for an *irrevocable letter of credit*. In this case the customer's bank sends you a letter stating that it has established a credit in your favor at a bank in the United States. You then draw a draft on the customer's bank and present it to your bank in the United States together with the letter of credit and the shipping documents. The bank in the United States arranges for this draft to be accepted or paid and forwards the documents to the customer's bank.

If you sell goods to a customer who proves unable to pay, you cannot get your goods back. You simply become a general creditor of the company, in common with other unfortunates. You can avoid this situation by making a *conditional sale*, whereby title to the goods remains with the seller until full payment is made. The conditional sale is common practice in Europe. In the United States it is used only for goods that are bought on an installment basis. In this case, if the customer fails to make the agreed number of payments, then the goods can be immediately repossessed by the seller.

 ## 32.3 CREDIT ANALYSIS

Firms are not allowed to discriminate between customers by charging them different prices. Neither may they discriminate by offering the same prices but different credit terms.[7] You *can* offer different terms of sale to different *classes* of buyers. You can offer volume discounts, for example, or discounts to customers willing to accept long-term purchase contracts. But as a rule, if you have a customer of doubtful standing, you should keep to your regular terms of sale and protect yourself by restricting the volume of goods that the customer may buy on credit.

There are a number of ways to find out whether customers are likely to pay their debts. For example, you are likely to have more confidence in those existing customers that have paid promptly in the past. For new customers there are three broad sources of information about their creditworthiness. You can seek the views of a specialist credit analyst, you can look at the information embedded in the firm's security prices, or you can use the firm's financial statements to make your own assessment.

Specialist Credit Analysts   The simplest way to assess a customer's credit standing is to seek the views of a specialist in credit assessment. For example, in Chapter 24 we described how bond rating agencies, such as Moody's and Standard and Poor's, provide a useful guide to the riskiness of the firm's bonds.

---

[6]You often see the terms of sale defined as "SD-BL." This means that the bank will hand over the bill of lading in return for payment on a sight draft.

[7]Price discrimination, and by implication credit discrimination, is prohibited by the Robinson-Patman Act.

Bond ratings are usually available only for relatively large firms. However, you can obtain information on many smaller companies from a credit agency. Dun and Bradstreet is by far the largest of these agencies and its database contains reports on more than 10 million companies.

Credit agencies usually report the experience that other firms have had with your customer. Alternatively, you may be able to get this information by checking with a credit bureau or by contacting the firms directly. You can also ask your bank to undertake a credit check. It will contact the customer's bank and ask for information on the customer's average balance, access to bank credit, and general reputation.

Security Prices In addition to checking with a credit agency or your bank, it may make sense to check what everybody else in the financial community thinks about your customer's credit standing. Does that sound expensive? It isn't if your customer is a public company. For example, you can learn what other investors think by comparing the yield on the firm's bonds with the yields on those of other firms. (Of course, the comparison should be between bonds of similar maturity, coupon, etc.) You can also look at how the customer's stock price has been behaving. A sharp fall in stock price doesn't mean that the company is in trouble, but it does suggest that prospects are less bright than they were formerly.

In Chapter 24 we saw how information on security prices can be used to put a figure on the chances of default. Companies have an incentive to exercise their option to default when the value of their assets is less than the amount of their debt. So, if you know how much the value of the firm's assets may fluctuate, you can estimate the probability that the asset value will fall below the default point. In Chapter 24 we looked at an example of how one consulting firm, KMV, uses this market-based approach to estimate default probabilities.

Financial Statements Security price data may not be available for many customers, and in these cases you will need to rely on the customers' financial statements to make your own assessment of their credit standing. In Chapter 29 we saw how managers calculate a few key financial ratios to measure the firm's financial strength. Firms that are highly leveraged, illiquid, and unprofitable generally don't make dependable customers.

If you have a large number of customers, it may be useful to combine different financial indicators into a single measure of which companies or individuals are most likely to default. For example, if you apply for a credit card or a bank loan, you will be asked various questions about your financial position. The information that you provide is then used to calculate an overall credit score. One widely used system, designed by the consultancy firm Fair Isaacs, takes account of five factors: (1) How promptly the applicant has paid in the past (35 percent of score); (2) how much debt of each type is outstanding (30 percent of score); (3) the length of the applicant's credit history (15 percent of score); (4) the number of credit cards and recently opened credit accounts that the applicant has (10 percent of score); and (5) the mix of regular credit cards, store cards, and margin accounts (10 percent of score). Applicants who fail to make the grade on the score are likely to be refused credit or subjected to more detailed analysis.

Suppose you want to devise a scoring system that will help you to decide whether to extend credit to small businesses. You suspect that there is an above-average probability that firms with a low return on assets and a low current ratio

FIGURE 32.1

The black x's represent a hypothetical group of firms that subsequently repaid their loans; the burgundy +'s represent those that defaulted. The sloping line discriminates between the two groups on the basis of return on assets and current ratio. The line represents the equation

Z = return on assets
    +10(current ratio)
  = 15

Firms that plot above the line have Z scores greater than 15.

will default on their debts.[8] To test this, you take a sample of past loans and construct a scatter diagram showing for each borrower the return on assets and the current ratio (see Figure 32.1). Those businesses that repaid their loans are shown by a blue x; the ones that defaulted are shown in burgundy. Now try to draw a straight dividing line between the two groups. You can't completely separate them, but the line in our diagram keeps the two groups as far apart as possible. (Note that there are only three blue x's below the line and three burgundy +'s above it.) This line tells us that if you wish to *discriminate* between the good and the bad risks, you should give 10 times as much weight to the current ratio as you give to return on assets. The index of creditworthiness is

Index of creditworthiness = Z = return on assets, percent + 10 (current ratio)

You minimize the degree of misclassification if you predict that applicants with Z scores over 15 will pay their debts and that those with Z scores below 15 will not pay.[9]

In practice you do not need to consider only two variables, nor do you need to estimate the equation by eye. *Multiple-discriminant analysis* (MDA) is a straightforward statistical technique for calculating how much weight to put on each variable to separate the creditworthy sheep from the impecunious goats.[10]

---

[8] The current ratio is the ratio of current assets to current liabilities. It is commonly used as a measure of the company's ability to lay its hands on cash. See Chapter 29.

[9] The quantity 15 is an arbitrary constant. We could just as well have used 150, in which case the Z score is

$$Z = 10(\text{return on assets, percent}) + 100(\text{current ratio})$$

[10] MDA is not the only statistical technique that you can use for this purpose. Probit and logit are two other potentially useful techniques. These estimate the probability of some event (e.g., default) as a function of observable attributes.

Edward Altman has used discriminant analysis to come up with the following index of creditworthiness:[11]

$$Z = .72 \frac{\text{(net working capital)}}{\text{total assets}} + .85 \frac{\text{(retained earnings)}}{\text{total assets}} + 3.1 \frac{\text{(EBIT)}}{\text{total assets}}$$

$$+ .42 \frac{\text{(shareholders' equity)}}{\text{total liabilities}} + 1.0 \frac{\text{sales}}{\text{total assets}}$$

Those companies with a Z-score of less than 1.20 were predicted to go bankrupt. Companies with Z-scores between 1.20 and 2.90 were hovering in the grey area between decline and recovery.

Updated and refined versions of Altman's Z-score model are regularly used by banks and industrial companies. We wish we could show you one of these recent versions, but they are all top secret. A company with a superior method for identifying good and bad borrowers has a significant leg up on the competition.[12]

Credit scoring systems should carry a health warning. When you construct a risk index, it is tempting to experiment with many different combinations of variables until you find the equation that would have worked best in the past. Unfortunately, if you "mine" the data in this way, you are likely to find that the system works less well in the future than it did previously. If you are misled by the past successes into placing too much faith in your model, you may refuse credit to a number of potentially good customers. The profits that you lose by turning away these customers could more than offset the gains that you make from avoiding a few bad eggs. As a result, you could be worse off than if you had pretended that you could not tell one customer from another and extended credit to all of them.

Does this mean that you should not use credit scoring systems? Not a bit. It simply implies that it is not sufficient to have a good credit scoring system; you also need to know how much to rely on it. That is the topic of the next section.

32.4 THE CREDIT DECISION

Let us suppose that you have taken the first three steps toward an effective credit operation. In other words, you have fixed your terms of sale; you have decided on the contract that customers must sign, and you have established a procedure for estimating the probability that they will pay up. Your next step is to work out which of your customers should be offered credit.

If there is no possibility of repeat orders, the decision is relatively simple. Figure 32.2 summarizes your choice. On one hand, you can refuse credit. In this case you make neither a profit nor a loss. The alternative is to offer credit. Suppose that the probability that the customer will pay up is p. If the customer does pay, you receive additional revenues (REV) and you incur additional costs; your

---

[11]EBIT is earnings before interest and taxes. Z-score models for predicting bankruptcy were originally developed in E. I. Altman, "Financial Ratios, Discriminant Analysis and the Prediction of Corporate Bankruptcy," *Journal of Finance* 23 (September 1968), pp. 589–609. The equation cited here comes from E. I. Altman, *Corporate Financial Distress*, John Wiley, New York, 1983.

[12]When a British bank laid off a number of employees, one unhappy staff member decided that the best way to retaliate was to leak details of the bank's credit scoring system to the press. See V. Orvice, "Would You Get a Loan?" *Daily Mail*, March 16, 1994, p. 29.

FIGURE 32.2

If you refuse credit, you make neither profit nor loss. If you offer credit, there is a probability p that the customer will pay and you will make REV − COST; there is a probability $(1 − p)$ that the customer will default and you will lose COST.

net gain is the present value of REV − COST. Unfortunately, you can't be certain that the customer will pay; there is a probability $(1 − p)$ of default. Default means you receive nothing and incur the additional costs. The *expected* profit from each course of action is therefore as follows:

	Expected Profit
Refuse credit	0
Grant credit	pPV(REV − COST) − (1 − p)PV(COST)

You should grant credit if the expected profit from doing so is greater than the expected profit from refusing.

Consider, for example, the case of the Cast Iron Company. On each nondelinquent sale Cast Iron receives revenues with a present value of $1,200 and incurs costs with a value of $1,000. Therefore the company's expected profit if it offers credit is

$$p\text{PV(REV} - \text{COST)} - (1 - p)\text{PV(COST)} = p \times 200 - (1 - p) \times 1,000$$

If the probability of collection is 5/6, Cast Iron can expect to break even:

$$\text{Expected profit} = \frac{5}{6} \times 200 - \left(1 - \frac{5}{6}\right) \times 1,000 = 0$$

Therefore Cast Iron's policy should be to grant credit whenever the chances of collection are better than 5 out of 6.

When to Stop Looking for Clues

We told you earlier where to *start* looking for clues about a customer's creditworthiness, but we never said anything about when to *stop*. Now we can work out how your profits would be affected by more detailed credit analysis.

Suppose that Cast Iron Company's credit department undertakes a study to determine which customers are most likely to default. It appears that 95 percent of its customers have been prompt payers and 5 percent have been slow payers. However, customers with a record of slow payment are much more likely to default on the next order than those with a record of prompt payment. On the average 20 percent of the slow payers subsequently default, but only 2 percent of the prompt payers do so.

Suppose Cast Iron reviews a sample of 1,000 customers, none of whom has defaulted yet. Of these, 950 have a record of prompt payment, and 50 have a record of slow payment. On the basis of past experience Cast Iron should expect 19 of the prompt payers to default in the future and 10 of the slow payers to do so:

Category	Number of Customers	Probability of Default	Expected Number of Defaults
Prompt payers	950	.02	19
Slow payers	50	.20	10
All customers	1,000	.029	29

Now the credit manager must make a decision: Should the company refuse to give any more credit to customers that have been slow payers in the past?

If you are aware that a customer has been a slow payer, the answer is clearly yes. Every sale to a slow payer has only an 80 percent chance of payment ($p = .8$). Selling to a *slow* payer, therefore, gives an expected *loss* of $40:

$$\text{Expected profit} = p\text{PV(REV} - \text{COST)} - (1 - p)\text{PV(COST)}$$
$$= .8(200) - .2(1,000) = -\$40$$

But suppose that it costs $10 to search through Cast Iron's records to determine whether a customer has been a prompt or slow payer. Is it worth doing so? The expected payoff to such a check is

$$\begin{aligned}\text{Expected payoff} \atop \text{to credit check} = &\text{(probability of identifying a slow payer} \\ &\times \text{gain from not extending credit)} - \text{cost of credit check}\end{aligned}$$
$$= (.05 \times 40) - 10 = -\$8$$

In this case checking isn't worth it. You are paying $10 to avoid a $40 loss 5 percent of the time. But suppose that a customer orders 10 units at once. Then checking is worthwhile because you are paying $10 to avoid a *$400* loss 5 percent of the time:

$$\text{Expected payoff to credit check} = (.05 \times 400) - 10 = \$10$$

The credit manager therefore decides to check customers' past payment records only on orders of more than five units. You can verify that a credit check on a five-unit order just pays for itself.

Our illustration is simplistic, but you have probably grasped the message: You don't want to subject each order to the same credit analysis. You want to concentrate your efforts on the large and doubtful orders.

Credit Decisions with Repeat Orders

So far we have ignored the possibility of repeat orders. But one of the reasons for offering credit today is that you may get yourself a good, regular customer by doing so.

Figure 32.3 illustrates the problem.[13] Cast Iron has been asked to extend credit to a new customer. You can find little information on the firm, and you believe that

---

[13]Our example is adapted from H. Bierman, Jr., and W. H. Hausman, "The Credit Granting Decision," *Management Science* 16 (April 1970), pp. B519–B532.

FIGURE 32.3

In this example there is only a .8 probability that your customer will pay in period 1; but if payment is made, there will be another order in period 2. The probability that the customer will pay for the second order is .95. The possibility of this good repeat order more than compensates for the expected loss in period 1.

the probability of payment is no better than .8. If you grant credit, the expected profit on this customer's order is

$$\text{Expected profit on initial order} = p_1 \times \text{PV(REV} - \text{COST)}$$
$$- (1 - p_1) \times \text{PV(COST)}$$
$$= (.8 \times 200) - (.2 \times 1,000) = -\$40$$

You decide to refuse credit.

This is the correct decision if there is no chance of a repeat order. But look again at the decision tree in Figure 32.3. If the customer does pay up, there will be a re-order next year. Because the customer has paid once, you can be 95 percent sure that he or she will pay again. For this reason any repeat order is very profitable.

$$\text{Next year's expected profit on repeat order} = p_2\text{PV(REV}_2 - \text{COST}_2) - (1 - p_2)$$
$$\text{PV(COST}_2)$$
$$= (.95 \times 200) - (.05 \times 1,000) = \$140$$

Now you can reexamine today's credit decision. If you grant credit today, you receive the expected profit on the initial order *plus* the possible opportunity to extend credit next year:

$$\text{Total expected profit} = \text{expected profit on initial order}$$
$$+ \text{probability of payment and repeat order}$$
$$\times \text{PV(next year's expected profit on repeat order)}$$
$$= -40 + .80 \times \text{PV}(140)$$

At any reasonable discount rate, you ought to extend credit. For example, if the discount rate is 20 percent,

$$\text{Total expected profit (present value)} = -40 + \frac{.8(140)}{1.2} = \$53.33$$

In this example you should grant credit even though you expect to take a loss on the order. The expected loss is more than outweighed by the possibility that you will secure a reliable and regular customer.

Some General Principles

Sometimes the credit manager faces clear-cut choices. In such circumstances it may be possible to estimate fairly precisely the consequences of a more liberal or a more stringent credit policy. But real-life situations are generally far more complex than our simple examples. Customers are not all good or all bad. Many of them pay consistently late; you get your money, but it costs more to collect and you lose a few months' interest. Then there is the question of risk: You may be able to measure the revenues and costs, but at what rate do you discount them?

Like almost all financial decisions, credit allocation involves a strong dose of judgment. Our examples are intended as reminders of the issues involved rather than as cookbook formulas. Here are the basic things to remember.

1. *Maximize profit.* As credit manager, you should not focus on minimizing the number of bad accounts; your job is to maximize expected profit. You must face up to the following facts: The best that can happen is that the customer pays promptly; the worst is default. In the best case, the firm receives the full additional revenues from the sale less the additional costs; in the worst, it receives nothing and loses the costs. You must weigh the chances of these alternative outcomes. If the margin of profit is high, you are justified in a liberal credit policy; if it is low, you cannot afford many bad debts.

2. *Concentrate on the dangerous accounts.* You should not expend the same effort on analyzing all credit applications. If an application is small or clear-cut, your decision should be largely routine; if it is large or doubtful, you may do better to move straight to a detailed credit appraisal. Most credit managers don't make credit decisions on an order-by-order basis. Instead, they set a credit limit for each customer. The sales representative is required to refer the order for approval only if the customer exceeds this limit.

3. *Look beyond the immediate order.* The credit decision is a dynamic problem. You cannot look only at the present. Sometimes it may be worth accepting a relatively poor risk as long as there is a likelihood that the customer will become a regular and reliable buyer. New businesses must, therefore, be prepared to incur more bad debts than established businesses. This is part of the cost of building up a good customer list.

32.5 COLLECTION POLICY

It would be nice if all customers paid their bills by the due date. But they don't—and since you may also occasionally "stretch" your payables, you can't altogether blame them.

The credit manager keeps a record of payment experiences with each customer. Thus the manager knows that company Alpha always takes the discount and that Omega generally takes 90 days to pay. When a customer is in arrears, the usual procedure is to send a statement of account and to follow this at intervals with increasingly insistent letters or telephone calls. If none of these has any effect, most companies turn the debt over to a collection agency or an attorney. The fee for such services is usually between 15 and 40 percent of the amount collected.

There is always a potential conflict of interest between the collection department and the sales department. Sales representatives commonly complain that they no sooner win new customers than the collection department frightens them off with threatening letters. The collection manager, on the other hand, bemoans the fact that the sales force is concerned only with winning orders and does not care whether the goods are subsequently paid for.

There are also many instances of cooperation between sales managers and the financial managers who worry about collections. For example, the specialty chemicals division of a major pharmaceutical company actually made a business loan to an important customer that had been suddenly cut off by its bank. The pharmaceutical company bet that it knew its customer better than the customer's bank did. The bet paid off. The customer arranged alternative bank financing, paid back the pharmaceutical company, and became an even more loyal customer. It was a nice example of financial management supporting sales.

It is not common for suppliers to make business loans to customers in this way, but they lend money indirectly whenever they allow a delay in payment. Trade credit can be an important source of short-term funds for indigent customers that cannot obtain a bank loan. But that raises an important question: If the bank is unwilling to lend, does it make sense for you, the supplier, to continue to extend trade credit? Here are two possible reasons why it may make sense: First, as in the case of our pharmaceutical company, you may have more information than the bank does about the customer's business. Second, you need to look beyond the immediate transaction and recognize that your firm may stand to lose some profitable future sales if the customer goes out of business.[14]

Factoring and Credit Insurance

A large firm has some advantages in managing its accounts receivable. There are potential economies of scale in record keeping, billing, and so on. Also debt collection is a specialized business that calls for experience and judgment. The small firm may not be able to hire or train a specialized credit manager. However, it may be able to obtain some of these economies by farming out part of the job to a **factor**.

Factoring works as follows: The factor and the client agree on credit limits for each customer and on the average collection period. The client then notifies each customer that the factor has purchased the debt. Thereafter, for any sale, the client sends a copy of the invoice to the factor, the customer makes payment directly to the factor, and the factor pays the client on the basis of the agreed average collection period regardless of whether the customer has paid. There are, of course, costs

---

[14]Of course, banks also need to recognize future opportunities to make profitable loans to the firm. The question therefore is whether suppliers have a *greater* stake in the continued prosperity of the firm. For some evidence on the determinants of the supply and demand for trade credit, see M. A. Petersen and R. G. Rajan, "Trade Credit: Theories and Evidence," *Review of Financial Studies* 10 (1997), pp. 661–692.

to such an operation, and the factor typically charges a fee of 1 to 2 percent of the value of the invoice.[15]

This factoring arrangement, known as *maturity factoring*, provides assistance with collection and insurance against bad debts. Generally, the factor is also willing to advance 70 to 80 percent of the value of the accounts at an interest cost of 2 or 3 percent above the prime rate. Factoring that provides collection, insurance, and finance is generally termed *old-line factoring*.[16]

Factoring is most common in industries such as clothing and toys. These industries are characterized by many small producers and retailers that do not have long-established relationships with each other. Because a factor may be employed by a number of manufacturers, it sees a larger proportion of the transactions than any single firm and therefore is better placed to judge the creditworthiness of each customer.[17]

If you don't want help with collection but do want protection against bad debts, you can obtain credit insurance. The credit insurance company obviously wants to be certain that you do not throw caution to the winds by extending boundless credit to the most speculative accounts. It therefore generally imposes a maximum amount that it will cover for accounts with a particular credit rating. Thus it may agree to insure up to a total of $100,000 of sales to customers with the highest Dun and Bradstreet rating, up to $50,000 to those with the next-highest rating, and so on. You may claim not only if the customer actually becomes insolvent but also if an account is overdue. Such a delinquent account is then turned over to the insurance company, which makes vigorous efforts to collect.

Most governments have established agencies to insure export credits. In the United States this insurance is provided by the *Export–Import Bank* (*Ex–Im Bank*) in association with a group of insurance companies known as the *Foreign Credit Insurance Association* (*FCIA*). Banks are much more willing to lend against export credits that have been insured.

---

[15] Many factors are subsidiaries of commercial banks. Their typical client is a relatively small manufacturing company selling on a repetitive basis to a large number of industrial or retail customers.

[16] Under an arrangement known as *with-recourse factoring*, the company is liable for any delinquent accounts. In this case the factor provides collection, but not insurance.

[17] This point is made in S. L. Mian and C. W. Smith, Jr., "Accounts Receivable Management Policy: Theory and Evidence," *Journal of Finance* 47 (March 1992), pp. 169–200.

SUMMARY

Credit management involves five steps. The first is to establish normal terms of sale. This means that you must decide the length of the payment period and the size of any cash discounts. In most industries these conditions are standardized.

The second step is to decide the form of the contract with your customer. Most domestic sales are made on open account. In this case the only evidence that the customer owes you money is the entry in your ledger and a receipt signed by the customer. Particularly if the customer is located in a foreign country, you may require a more formal contract. We looked at two such devices—the trade acceptance and the letter of credit.

The third step is to assess each customer's creditworthiness. There are a variety of sources of information—your own experience with the customer, the experience of other creditors, the assessment of a credit agency, a check with the customer's bank, the market value of the customer's securities, and an analysis of the customer's financial statements. Firms that handle a large volume of credit information often use a formal system for combining the data from various sources into an overall credit score. Such numerical scoring systems help separate the borderline cases from the obvious sheep or goats. We showed how you can use statistical techniques such as multiple-discriminant analysis to give an efficient measure of default risk.

When you have made an assessment of the customer's credit standing, you can move to the fourth step in credit management, which is to establish sensible credit limits. The job of the credit manager is not to minimize the number of bad debts; it is to maximize profits. This means that you should increase the customer's credit limit as long as the probability of payment times the expected profit is greater than the probability of default times the cost of the goods. Remember not to be too shortsighted in reckoning the expected profit. It is often worth accepting the marginal applicant if there is a chance that the applicant may become a regular and reliable customer.

The fifth, and final, step is to *collect*. Doing so requires tact and judgment. You want to be firm with the truly delinquent customer, but you don't want to offend the good one by writing demanding letters just because a check has been delayed in the mail. You will find it easier to spot troublesome accounts if you keep a careful record of the aging of receivables.

These five steps are interrelated. For example, you can afford more liberal terms of sale if you are very careful about whom you grant credit to. You can accept higher-risk customers if you are very active in pursuing any late payers. A good credit policy is one that adds up to a sensible whole.

FURTHER READING

A standard text on the practice and institutional background of credit management is:
R. H. Cole and L. Mishler: *Consumer and Business Credit Management*, 11th ed., McGraw-Hill, New York, 1998.

For a more analytical discussion of credit policy, see:
S. Mian and C. W. Smith: "Extending Trade Credit and Financing," *Journal of Applied Corporate Finance*, 7:75–84 (Spring 1994).

M. A. Peterson and R. G. Rajan: "Trade Credit: Theories and Evidence," *Review of Financial Studies*, 10:661–692 (1997).

Altman's paper is the classic on numerical credit scoring:
E. I. Altman: "Financial Ratios, Discriminant Analysis and the Prediction of Corporate Bankruptcy," *Journal of Finance*, 23:589–609 (September 1968).

Altman also provides a review of credit scoring models in:
E. I. Altman: *Corporate Financial Distress and Bankruptcy*, 2nd ed., John Wiley, New York, 1993.

QUIZ

1. Company X sells on a 1/30, net 60 basis. Customer Y buys goods invoiced at $1,000.
   a. How much can Y deduct from the bill if Y pays on day 30?
   b. What is the effective annual rate of interest if Y pays on the due date rather than on day 30?
   c. How would you expect payment terms to change if
      i. The goods are perishable.
      ii. The goods are not rapidly resold.
      iii. The goods are sold to high-risk firms.
2. The lag between the purchase date and the date on which payment is due is known as the *terms lag*. The lag between the due date and the date on which the buyer actually

pays is the *due lag*, and the lag between the purchase and actual payment dates is the *pay lag*. Thus,

$$\text{Pay lag} = \text{terms lag} + \text{due lag}$$

State how you would expect the following events to affect each type of lag:

a. The company imposes a service charge on late payers.
b. A recession causes customers to be short of cash.
c. The company changes its terms from net 10 to net 20.

3. Complete the passage below by selecting the appropriate terms for each blank from the following list (some terms may be used more than once): *acceptance, open, commercial, trade, the United States, his or her own, draft, account, bank, the customer's, letter of credit, shipping documents.*

   Most goods are sold on _____ _____. In this case the only evidence of the debt is a record in the seller's books and a signed receipt. If you wish to ensure that its buyer will pay, you can arrange a(n) _____ _____, ordering payment by the customer. In order to obtain the _____ _____, the customer must acknowledge this order and sign the document. The signed acknowledgment is known as a(n) _____ _____. Sometimes the seller may ask _____ _____ bank to sign the document. In this case it is known as a(n) _____ _____. The fourth form of contract is used principally in overseas trade. The customer's bank sends the exporter a(n) _____ _____ _____ stating that it has established a credit in his or her favor at a bank in the United States. The exporter then draws a draft on _____ bank and presents it to _____ _____ bank together with the _____ _____ and _____ _____. The bank then arranges for this draft to be accepted and forwards the _____ _____ to the customer's bank.

4. The Branding Iron Company sells its irons for $50 apiece wholesale. Production cost is $40 per iron. There is a 25 percent chance that wholesaler Q will go bankrupt within the next year. Q orders 1,000 irons and asks for six months' credit. Should you accept the order? Assume that the discount rate is 10 percent per year, there is no chance of a repeat order, and Q will pay either in full or not at all.

5. Look back at Section 32.4. Cast Iron's costs have increased from $1,000 to $1,050. Assuming there is no possibility of repeat orders, answer the following:

   a. When should Cast Iron grant or refuse credit?
   b. If it costs $12 to determine whether a customer has been a prompt or slow payer in the past, when should Cast Iron undertake such a check?

6. Look back at the discussion in Section 32.4 of credit decisions with repeat orders. If $p_1 = .8$, what is the minimum level of p_2 at which Cast Iron is justified in extending credit?

7. True or False?

   a. Exporters who require greater certainty of payment arrange for the customers to sign a bill of lading in exchange for a sight draft.
   b. Multiple-discriminant analysis is often used to construct an index of creditworthiness. This index is generally called a Z score.
   c. It makes sense to monitor the credit manager's performance by looking at the proportion of bad debts.
   d. If a customer refuses to pay despite repeated reminders, the company will usually turn the debt over to a factor or an attorney.
   e. The Foreign Credit Insurance Association insures export credits.

PRACTICE QUESTIONS

1. Listed below are some common terms of sale. Can you explain what each means?

   a. 2/30, net 60.
   b. net 10.
   c. 2/5, EOM, net 30.

2. Some of the items in question 1 involve a cash discount. For each of these, calculate the rate of interest paid by customers who pay on the due date instead of taking the cash discount.

3. Phoenix Lambert currently sells its goods cash on delivery. However, the financial manager believes that by offering credit terms of 2/10 net 30 the company can increase sales by 4 percent, without significant additional costs. If the interest rate is 6 percent and the profit margin is 5 percent, would you recommend offering credit? Assume first that all customers take the cash discount. Then assume that they all pay on day 30.

4. As treasurer of the Universal Bed Corporation, Aristotle Procrustes is worried about his bad debt ratio, which is currently running at 6 percent. He believes that imposing a more stringent credit policy might reduce sales by 5 percent and reduce the bad debt ratio to 4 percent. If the cost of goods sold is 80 percent of the selling price, should Mr. Procrustes adopt the more stringent policy?

5. Jim Khana, the credit manager of Velcro Saddles, is reappraising the company's credit policy. Velcro sells on terms of net 30. Cost of goods sold is 85 percent of sales, and fixed costs are a further 5 percent of sales. Velcro classifies customers on a scale of 1 to 4. During the past five years, the collection experience was as follows:

EXCEL

Classification	Defaults as Percent of Sales	Average Collection Period in Days for Nondefaulting Accounts
1	.0	45
2	2.0	42
3	10.0	40
4	20.0	80

The average interest rate was 15 percent.

What conclusions (if any) can you draw about Velcro's credit policy? What other factors should be taken into account before changing this policy?

6. Look again at question 5. Suppose (a) that it costs $95 to classify each new credit applicant and (b) that an almost equal proportion of new applicants falls into each of the four categories. In what circumstances should Mr. Khana not bother to undertake a credit check?

7. Until recently, Augean Cleaning Products sold its products on terms of net 60, with an average collection period of 75 days. In an attempt to induce customers to pay more promptly, it has changed its terms to 2/10, EOM, net 60. The initial effect of the changed terms is as follows:

EXCEL

	Average Collection Periods, Days	
Percent of Sales with Cash Discount	Cash Discount	Net
60	30*	80

*Some customers deduct the cash discount even though they pay after the specified date.

Calculate the effect of the changed terms. Assume
• Sales volume is unchanged.
• The interest rate is 12 percent.
• There are no defaults.
• Cost of goods sold is 80 percent of sales.

8. Look back at question 7. Assume that the change in credit terms results in a 2 percent increase in sales. Recalculate the effect of the changed credit terms.

9. Financial ratios were described in Chapter 29. If you were a credit manager, to which financial ratios would you pay most attention? Which do you think would be the least informative?

10. Discuss the problems with developing a numerical credit scoring system for evaluating personal loans. You can only test your system using data for applicants who have in the past been granted credit. Is this a potential problem?

11. Discuss ways in which real-life decisions are more complex than the decision illustrated in Figure 32.3. How do you think these differences ought to affect the credit decision?

12. How should your willingness to grant credit be affected by differences in (a) the profit margin, (b) the interest rate, (c) the probability of repeat orders? In each case illustrate your answer with a simple example.

13. Select two companies from the Market Insight database (**www.mhhe.com/ edumarketinsight**). Use their latest financial statements to calculate some financial ratios that throw light on their relative creditworthiness. Calculate a Z-score for each, using the formula shown in Section 32.3. Now look at other indicators of creditworthiness, such as the company's bond rating or the return on its stock. Are the different indicators providing consistent messages?

14. Use the Market Insight database (**www.mhhe.com/edumarketinsight**) to compare the average collection periods (see Section 29.3) for different companies. Can you explain why some companies grant more credit than others?

CHALLENGE QUESTIONS

1. Why do firms grant "free" credit? Would it be more efficient if all sales were for cash and late payers were charged interest?

2. Sometimes a firm sells its receivables at a discount to a wholly owned captive finance company. This captive finance company is partly financed by the parent, but it also issues substantial amounts of debt. What are the possible advantages of such an arrangement?

3. Reliant Umbrellas has been approached by Plumpton Variety Stores of Nevada. Plumpton has expressed interest in an initial purchase of 5,000 umbrellas at $10 each on Reliant's standard terms of 2/30, net 60. Plumpton estimates that if the umbrellas prove popular with customers, its purchases could be in the region of 30,000 umbrellas a year. After deductions for variable costs, this account would add $47,000 per year to Reliant's profits.

   Reliant has been anxious for some time to break into the lucrative Nevada market, but its credit manager has some doubts about Plumpton. In the past five years, Plumpton had embarked on an aggressive program of store openings. In 2001, however, it went into reverse. The recession, combined with aggressive price competition, caused a cash shortage. Plumpton laid off employees, closed one store, and deferred store openings. The company's Dun and Bradstreet rating is only fair, and a check with Plumpton's other suppliers reveals that, although Plumpton traditionally took cash discounts, it has recently been paying 30 days slow. A check through Reliant's bank indicates that Plumpton has unused credit lines of $350,000 but has entered into discussions with the banks for a renewal of a $1,500,000 term loan due at the end of the year. Table 32.1 summarizes Plumpton's latest financial statements.

   As credit manager of Reliant, how do you feel about extending credit to Plumpton?

4. Galenic, Inc., is a wholesaler for a range of pharmaceutical products. Before deducting any losses from bad debts, Galenic operates on a profit margin of 5 percent. For a long time the firm has employed a numerical credit scoring system based on a small number of key ratios. This has resulted in a bad debt ratio of 1 percent.

   Galenic has recently commissioned a detailed statistical study of the payment record of its customers over the past eight years and, after considerable experimentation, has identified five variables that could form the basis of a new credit scoring system. On the evidence of the past eight years, Galenic calculates that for every 10,000 accounts it would have experienced the following default rates:

Credit Score under	Number of Accounts		
Proposed System	Defaulting	Paying	Total
Greater than 80	60	9,100	9,160
Less than 80	40	800	840
Total	100	9,900	10,000

By refusing credit to firms with a low credit score (less than 80), Galenic calculates that it would reduce its bad debt ratio to 60/9,160, or just under .7 percent. While this may not seem like a big deal, Galenic's credit manager reasons that this is equivalent to a decrease of one-third in the bad debt ratio and would result in a significant improvement in the profit margin.

a. What is Galenic's current profit margin, allowing for bad debts?
b. Assuming that the firm's estimates of default rates are right, how would the new credit scoring system affect profits?
c. Why might you suspect that Galenic's estimates of default rates will not be realized in practice? What are the likely consequences of overestimating the accuracy of such a credit scoring scheme?
d. Suppose that one of the variables in the proposed scoring system is whether the customer has an existing account with Galenic (new customers are more likely to default). How would this affect your assessment of the proposal?

	2001	2000		2001	2000
Cash	$ 1.0	$ 1.2	Payables	$ 2.3	$ 2.5
Receivables	1.5	1.6	Short-term loans	3.9	1.9
Inventory	10.9	11.6	Long-term debt	1.8	2.6
Fixed assets	5.1	4.3	Equity	10.5	11.7
Total assets	$18.5	$18.7	Total liabilities	$18.5	$18.7
				2001	2000
Sales				$55.0	$59.0
Cost of goods sold				32.6	35.9
Selling, general, and administrative expenses				20.8	20.2
Interest				.5	.3
Tax				.5	1.3
Net income				$ .6	$ 1.3

TABLE 32.1

Plumpton Variety Stores: summary financial statements (figures in millions).

PART NINE RELATED WEBSITES

For an introductory guide to understanding financial statements see:

www.ibm.com/investor/financialguide

For easy access to annual reports see:

www.reportgallery.com

www.prars.com

Downloadable software for short- and long-term financial planning is available on:

www.decisioneering.com

Journals with articles on short-term financial management include:

www.americanbanker.com

www.intltreasurer.com

www.treasuryandrisk.com

The Federal Reserve Bank sites are good general sources of reference for short-term interest rates and material on payment systems. See, for example:

www.federalreserve.gov

www.ny.frb.org

www.stls.frb.org

Sites on short-term debt markets include:

www.afponline.org (money market and interest rate data)

www.gecfosolutions.com (GE Capital's website contains information on sources and costs of short-term finance)

www.ny.frb.org/pihome/addpub/credit.pdf (a guide to sources of credit)

The websites of most major banks provide material on cash management services. See, for example:

www.bankone.com

www.bankofamerica.com

Other sites dealing with cash management include:

www.nacha.org (material on electronic payment)

www.phoenixhecht.com (a comprehensive website on cash management with useful links)

Some sites that are concerned with credit management:

www.creditworthy.com (credit management)

www.dnb.com (examples of Dun and Bradstreet credit reports, articles on credit management, and an introductory guide to understanding financial statements)

www.ftc.gov/bcp/conline/pubs/credit/scoring.htm (a guide to credit scoring)

www.nacm.org (contains links to sites on credit-related issues)

PART TEN

MERGERS, CORPORATE CONTROL, AND GOVERNANCE

THE JOURNAL *Mergers and Acquisitions* listed over 5,000 mergers involving U.S. corporations in 2000, and the total value of the companies acquired was $1.7 trillion. The year included the announcement of the U.S.'s largest merger, as AOL and Time Warner agreed to form a company valued at $350 billion.

What are the likely gains from mergers? How can managers calculate their benefits and costs? How can target companies defend themselves against unwelcome bidders? Who gains and who loses in mergers? Chapter 33 considers these questions.

Mergers are partly about economies from combining two businesses, but they are also about who gets to run the company. Chapter 34 circles back and considers other ways that companies may change their ownership and control. For example, we look at cases where a company spins off part of its business or where the firm is bought out by a group of investors who then take the business private. Chapter 34 also considers differences in the financial organization of corporations. For example, we contrast diversified conglomerates with more focused corporations and ask why conglomerates are more common outside the United States. Finally, we note some international differences in the financing and control of corporations.

CHAPTER THIRTY-THREE

MERGERS

THE SCALE AND pace of merger activity in the United States have been remarkable. In 2000, the peak of the merger boom, U.S. companies were involved in deals totaling more than $1.7 trillion. Table 33.1 lists just a few of the more important recent mergers, including several that involved overseas companies.

During these periods of intense merger activity, management spends significant amounts of time either searching for firms to acquire or worrying about whether some other firm will acquire their company.

A merger adds value only if the two companies are worth more together than apart. This chapter covers why two companies could be worth more together and how to get the merger deal done if they are. We proceed as follows.

- *Motives.* Sources of value added.
- *Dubious motives.* Don't be tempted.
- *Benefits and costs.* It's important to estimate them consistently.
- *Mechanics.* Legal, tax, and accounting issues.
- *Takeover battles and tactics.* We look back to several famous takeover battles. This history illustrates merger tactics and shows some of the economic forces driving merger activity.
- *Mergers and the economy.* How can we explain merger waves? Who gains and who loses as a result of mergers?

This chapter concentrates on ordinary mergers, that is, combinations of two established firms. We keep asking, What makes two firms worth more together than apart? We assume mergers are undertaken to cut costs, add revenues, or create growth opportunities.

But mergers also change *control* and *ownership.* Pick a merger, and you'll almost always find that one firm is the protagonist and the other is the target. The top management of the target firm usually departs after the merger.

Financial economists now view mergers as part of a broader *market for corporate control.* The activity in this market goes far beyond ordinary mergers. It includes spin-offs and divestitures, where a company splits off part of its assets and operations into an independent corporation. It includes restructurings, where a company reshapes its capital structure to change incentives for managers. It includes buyouts of public companies by groups of private investors.

When corporate control changes, the first questions to ask are: Who owns the business now? Who is running it? How closely do the owners control the managers? What incentives do the managers now have?

Such questions take us well beyond the analysis of ordinary mergers. In this chapter we concentrate on mergers. In the next, we move on to the market for corporate control.

TABLE 33.1

Some important mergers in 2000 and 2001.

Source: *Mergers and Acquisitions,* various issues.

Acquiring Company	Selling Company	Payment ($ billions)
Vodafone Air Touch (UK)	Mannesmann (Ger)	202.8
America Online	Time Warner	106.0
Pfizer	Warner-Lambert	89.2
Glaxo Wellcome (UK)	SmithKline Beecham (UK/US)	76.0
Bell Atlantic	GTE	53.4
Total Fina (Fr)	Elf Aquitaine (Fr)	50.1
AT&T	MediaOne	49.3
France Telecom (Fr)	Orange (UK)	46.0
Viacom	CBS	39.4
Chase Manhattan	J.P. Morgan	33.6
Citigroup	Associates First Capital	31.0
BP Amoco (UK)	Atlantic Richfield	27.2

33.1 SENSIBLE MOTIVES FOR MERGERS

Mergers that take place between two firms in the same line of business are known as *horizontal mergers*. Recent examples include bank mergers, such as Chemical Bank's merger with Chase and Nationsbank's purchase of BankAmerica. Other headline-grabbing horizontal mergers include those between oil giants Exxon and Mobil, and between British Petroleum (BP) and Amoco.

A *vertical merger* involves companies at different stages of production. The buyer expands back toward the source of raw materials or forward in the direction of the ultimate consumer. An example is Walt Disney's acquisition of the ABC television network. Disney planned to use the ABC network to show *The Lion King* and other recent movies to huge audiences.

A *conglomerate merger* involves companies in unrelated lines of businesses. The majority of mergers in the 1960s and 1970s were conglomerate. They became less popular in the 1980s. In fact, much of the action since the 1980s has come from breaking up the conglomerates that had been formed 10 to 20 years earlier.

With these distinctions in mind, we are about to consider motives for mergers, that is, reasons why two firms may be worth more together than apart. We proceed with some trepidation. The motives, though they often lead the way to real benefits, are sometimes just mirages that tempt unwary or overconfident managers into takeover disasters. This was the case for AT&T, which spent $7.5 billion to buy NCR. The aim was to shore up AT&T's computer business and to "link people, organizations and their information into a seamless, global computer network."[1] It didn't work. Even more embarrassing (on a smaller scale) was the acquisition of Apex One, a sporting apparel company, by Converse Inc. The purchase was made on May 18, 1995. Apex One was closed down on August 11, after Converse failed to produce new designs quickly enough to satisfy retailers. Converse lost an investment of over $40 million in 85 days.[2]

Many mergers that seem to make economic sense fail because managers cannot handle the complex task of integrating two firms with different production processes, accounting methods, and corporate cultures. This was one of the problems in the AT&T–NCR merger. It also beddeviled Novell's acquisition of Wordperfect. That merger at first seemed a perfect fit between Novell's strengths in networks for personal computers and Wordperfect's applications software. But Wordperfect's postacquisition sales were horrible, partly because of competition from other word processing systems but also because of a series of battles over turf and strategy:

> Wordperfect executives came to view Novell executives as rude invaders of the corporate equivalent of Camelot. They repeatedly fought with . . . Novell's staff over everything from expenses and management assignments to Christmas bonuses. [This led to] a strategic mistake: dismantling a Wordperfect sales team . . . needed to push a long-awaited set of office software products.[3]

The value of most businesses depends on *human assets*—managers, skilled workers, scientists, and engineers. If these people are not happy in their new roles

---

[1]Robert E. Allen, AT&T chairman, quoted in J. J. Keller, "Disconnected Line: Why AT&T Takeover of NCR Hasn't Been a Real Bell Ringer," *The Wall Street Journal*, September 9, 1995, p. A1.

[2]Mark Maremount, "How Converse Got Its Laces All Tangled," *Business Week*, September 4, 1995, p. 37.

[3]D. Clark, "Software Firm Fights to Remake Business after Ill-Fated Merger," *The Wall Street Journal*, January 12, 1996, p. A1.

in the acquiring firm, the best of them will leave. One Portuguese bank (BCP) learned this lesson the hard way when it bought an investment management firm against the wishes of the firm's employees. The entire workforce immediately quit and set up a rival investment management firm with a similar name. Beware of paying too much for assets that go down in the elevator and out to the parking lot at the close of each business day. They may drive into the sunset and never return.

There are also occasions when the merger does achieve gains but the buyer nevertheless loses because it pays too much. For example, the buyer may overestimate the value of stale inventory or underestimate the costs of renovating old plant and equipment, or it may overlook the warranties on a defective product. Buyers need to be particularly careful about environmental liabilities. If there is pollution from the seller's operations or toxic waste on its property, the costs of cleaning up will probably fall on the buyer.

Economies of Scale

Just as most of us believe that we would be happier if only we were a little richer, so every manager seems to believe that his or her firm would be more competitive if only it were just a little bigger. Achieving *economies of scale* is the natural goal of horizontal mergers. But such economies have been claimed in conglomerate mergers, too. The architects of these mergers have pointed to the economies that come from sharing central services such as office management and accounting, financial control, executive development, and top-level management.[4]

The most prominent recent examples of mergers in pursuit of economies of scale come from the banking industry. The United States entered the 1990s with far too many banks, largely as a result of outdated regulations on interstate banking. As these regulations eroded and communications and technology improved, hundreds of small banks were bought out and merged into regional or "supra-regional" firms. When Chase and Chemical, two of the largest money-center banks, merged, they forecasted that the merger would reduce costs by 16 percent a year, or $1.5 billion. The savings would come from consolidating operations and eliminating redundant costs.[5]

Optimistic financial managers can see potential economies of scale in almost any industry. But it is easier to buy another business than to integrate it with yours afterward. Some companies that have gotten together in pursuit of scale economies still function as a collection of separate and sometimes competing operations with different production facilities, research efforts, and marketing forces.

Economies of Vertical Integration

Vertical mergers seek economies in vertical integration. Some companies try to gain control over the production process by expanding back toward the output of the raw material and forward to the ultimate consumer. One way to achieve this is to merge with a supplier or a customer.

---

[4]Economies of scale are enjoyed when the average unit cost of production goes down as production increases. One way to achieve economies of scale is to spread fixed costs over a larger volume of production.

[5]Houston et al. examine 41 large bank mergers in which the companies provided forecasts of cost savings. On average the estimated present value of these savings was about 12 percent of the market value of the combined companies. See J. F. Houston, C. M. James, and M. D. Ryngaert, "Where Do Merger Gains Come from? Bank Mergers from the Perspective of Insiders and Outsiders," *Journal of Financial Economics* 60 (2001), pp. 285–331.

Vertical integration facilitates coordination and administration. We illustrate via an extreme example. Think of an airline that does not own any planes. If it schedules a flight from Boston to San Francisco, it sells tickets and then rents a plane for that flight from a separate company. This strategy might work on a small scale, but it would be an administrative nightmare for a major carrier, which would have to coordinate hundreds of rental agreements daily. In view of these difficulties, it is not surprising that all major airlines have integrated backward, away from the consumer, by buying and flying airplanes rather than patronizing rent-a-plane companies.

Do not assume that more vertical integration is better than less. Carried to extremes, it is absurdly inefficient, as in the case of LOT, the Polish state airline, which in the late 1980s found itself raising pigs to make sure that its employees had fresh meat on their tables. (Of course, in a centrally managed economy it may be necessary to raise your own cattle or pigs, since you can't be sure you'll be able to buy meat.)

Nowadays the tide of vertical integration seems to be flowing out. Companies are finding it more efficient to *outsource* the provision of many services and various types of production. For example, back in the 1950s and 1960s, General Motors was deemed to have a cost advantage over its main competitors, Ford and Chrysler, because a greater fraction of the parts used in GM's automobiles were produced in-house. By the 1990s, Ford and Chrysler had the advantage: They could buy the parts cheaper from outside suppliers. This was partly because the outside suppliers tended to use nonunion labor at lower wages. But it also appears that manufacturers have more bargaining power versus independent suppliers than versus a production facility that's part of the corporate family. In 1998 GM decided to spin off Delphi, its automotive parts division, as a separate company.[6] After the spin-off, GM can continue to buy parts from Delphi in large volumes, but it negotiates the purchases at arm's length.[7]

Complementary Resources

Many small firms are acquired by large ones that can provide the missing ingredients necessary for the small firms' success. The small firm may have a unique product but lack the engineering and sales organization required to produce and market it on a large scale. The firm could develop engineering and sales talent from scratch, but it may be quicker and cheaper to merge with a firm that already has ample talent. The two firms have *complementary resources*—each has what the other needs—and so it may make sense for them to merge. The two firms are worth more together than apart because each acquires something it does not have and gets it cheaper than it would by acting on its own. Also, the merger may open up opportunities that neither firm would pursue otherwise.

Of course, two large firms may also merge because they have complementary resources. Consider the 1989 merger between two electric utilities, Utah Power & Light and PacifiCorp, which served customers in California. Utah Power's peak demand came in the summer, for air conditioning. PacifiCorp's peak came in the winter, for heating. The savings from combining the two firms' generating systems were estimated at $45 million annually.

---

[6]We cover spin-offs in the next chapter.

[7]In 2000 Ford followed GM by announcing plans to spin off its auto-parts business, Visteon Corporation.

Surplus Funds

Here's another argument for mergers: Suppose that your firm is in a mature industry. It is generating a substantial amount of cash, but it has few profitable investment opportunities. Ideally such a firm should distribute the surplus cash to shareholders by increasing its dividend payment or repurchasing stock. Unfortunately, energetic managers are often reluctant to adopt a policy of shrinking their firm in this way. If the firm is not willing to purchase its own shares, it can instead purchase another company's shares. Firms with a surplus of cash and a shortage of good investment opportunities often turn to mergers *financed by cash* as a way of redeploying their capital.

Some firms have excess cash and do not pay it out to stockholders or redeploy it by wise acquisitions. Such firms often find themselves targeted for takeover by other firms that propose to redeploy the cash for them.[8] During the oil price slump of the early 1980s, many cash-rich oil companies found themselves threatened by takeover. This was not because their cash was a unique asset. The acquirers wanted to capture the companies' cash flow to make sure it was not frittered away on negative-NPV oil exploration projects. We return to this *free-cash-flow* motive for takeovers later in this chapter.

Eliminating Inefficiencies

Cash is not the only asset that can be wasted by poor management. There are always firms with unexploited opportunities to cut costs and increase sales and earnings. Such firms are natural candidates for acquisition by other firms with better management. In some instances "better management" may simply mean the determination to force painful cuts or realign the company's operations. Notice that the motive for such acquisitions has nothing to do with benefits from combining two firms. Acquisition is simply the mechanism by which a new management team replaces the old one.

A merger is not the only way to improve management, but sometimes it is the only simple and practical way. Managers are naturally reluctant to fire or demote themselves, and stockholders of large public firms do not usually have much *direct* influence on how the firm is run or who runs it.[9]

If this motive for merger is important, one would expect to observe that acquisitions often precede a change in the management of the target firm. This seems to be the case. For example, Martin and McConnell found that the chief executive is four times more likely to be replaced in the year after a takeover than during earlier years.[10] The firms they studied had generally been poor performers; in the four years before acquisition their stock prices had lagged behind those of other firms in the same industry by 15 percent. Apparently many of these firms fell on bad times and were rescued, or reformed, by merger.

Of course, it is easy to criticize another firm's management but not so easy to improve it. Some of the self-appointed scourges of poor management turn out to be

---

[8]Takeovers in this case often take the form of leveraged buy-outs. See Chapter 34.

[9]It is difficult to assemble a large-enough block of stockholders to effectively challenge management and the incumbent board of directors. Stockholders can have enormous indirect influence, however. Their displeasure shows up in the firm's stock price. A low stock price may encourage a takeover bid by another firm.

[10]K. J. Martin and J. J. McConnell, "Corporate Performance, Corporate Takeovers, and Management Turnover," *Journal of Finance* 46 (June 1991), pp. 671–687.

less competent than those they replace. Here is how Warren Buffet, the chairman of Berkshire Hathaway, summarizes the matter:[11]

> Many managers were apparently over-exposed in impressionable childhood years to the story in which the imprisoned, handsome prince is released from the toad's body by a kiss from the beautiful princess. Consequently, they are certain that the managerial kiss will do wonders for the profitability of the target company. Such optimism is essential. Absent that rosy view, why else should the shareholders of company A want to own an interest in B at a takeover cost that is two times the market price they'd pay if they made direct purchases on their own? In other words investors can always buy toads at the going price for toads. If investors instead bankroll princesses who wish to pay double for the right to kiss the toad, those kisses better pack some real dynamite. We've observed many kisses, but very few miracles. Nevertheless, many managerial princesses remain serenely confident about the future potency of their kisses, even after their corporate backyards are knee-deep in unresponsive toads.

33.2 SOME DUBIOUS REASONS FOR MERGERS

The benefits that we have described so far all make economic sense. Other arguments sometimes given for mergers are dubious. Here are a few of the dubious ones.

To Diversify

We have suggested that the managers of a cash-rich company may prefer to see it use that cash for acquisitions rather than distribute it as extra dividends. That is why we often see cash-rich firms in stagnant industries merging their way into fresh woods and pastures new.

What about diversification as an end in itself? It is obvious that diversification reduces risk. Isn't that a gain from merging?

The trouble with this argument is that diversification is easier and cheaper for the stockholder than for the corporation. No one has shown that investors pay a premium for diversified firms; in fact, discounts are common. For example, Kaiser Industries was dissolved as a holding company because its diversification apparently *subtracted* from its value. Kaiser Industries' main assets were shares of Kaiser Steel, Kaiser Aluminum, and Kaiser Cement. These were independent companies, and the stock of each was publicly traded. Thus you could value Kaiser Industries by looking at the stock prices of Kaiser Steel, Kaiser Aluminum, and Kaiser Cement. But Kaiser Industries' stock was selling at a price reflecting a significant *discount* from the value of its investment in these companies. The discount vanished when Kaiser Industries revealed its plan to sell its holdings and distribute the proceeds to its stockholders.

Why the discount existed in the first place is a puzzle. But the example at least shows that diversification does not *increase* value. The appendix to this chapter provides a simple proof that corporate diversification does not affect value in perfect markets as long as investors' diversification opportunities are unrestricted. This is the *value-additivity* principle introduced in Chapter 7.

---

[11]Berkshire Hathaway 1981 Annual Report, cited in G. Foster. "Comments on M&A Analysis and the Role of Investment Bankers," *Midland Corporate Finance Journal* 1 (Winter 1983), pp. 36–38.

	World Enterprises before Merger	Muck and Slurry	World Enterprises after Merger
1. Earnings per share	$2.00	$2.00	$2.67
2. Price per share	$40	$20	$40
3. Price–earnings ratio	20	10	15
4. Number of shares	100,000	100,000	150,000
5. Total earnings	$200,000	$200,000	$400,000
6. Total market value	$4,000,000	$2,000,000	$6,000,000
7. Current earnings per dollar invested in stock (line 1 ÷ line 2)	$.05	$.10	$.067

TABLE 33.2

Impact of merger on market value and earnings per share of World Enterprises.

Note: When World Enterprises purchases Muck and Slurry, there are no gains. Therefore, total earnings and total market value should be unaffected by the merger. But earnings *per share* increase. World Enterprises issues only 50,000 of its shares (priced at $40) to acquire the 100,000 Muck and Slurry shares (priced at $20).

Increasing Earnings per Share: The Bootstrap Game

During the 1960s some conglomerate companies made acquisitions that offered no evident economic gains. Nevertheless the conglomerates' aggressive strategy produced several years of rising earnings per share. To see how this can happen, let us look at the acquisition of Muck and Slurry by the well-known conglomerate World Enterprises.[12]

The position before the merger is set out in the first two columns of Table 33.2. Notice that because Muck and Slurry has relatively poor growth prospects, its stock sells at a lower price–earnings ratio than does World Enterprises' stock (line 3). The merger, we assume, produces no economic benefits, and so the firms should be worth exactly the same together as they are apart. The market value of World Enterprises after the merger should be equal to the sum of the separate values of the two firms (line 6).

Since World Enterprises' stock is selling for double the price of Muck and Slurry stock (line 2), World Enterprises can acquire the 100,000 Muck and Slurry shares for 50,000 of its own shares. Thus World will have 150,000 shares outstanding after the merger.

Total earnings double as a result of the merger (line 5), but the number of shares increases by only 50 percent. Earnings *per share* rise from $2.00 to $2.67. We call this the *bootstrap effect* because there is no real gain created by the merger and no increase in the two firms' combined value. Since the stock price is unchanged, the price–earnings ratio falls (line 3).

Figure 33.1 illustrates what is going on here. Before the merger $1 invested in World Enterprises bought 5 cents of current earnings and rapid growth prospects. On the other hand, $1 invested in Muck and Slurry bought 10 cents of current earnings but slower growth prospects. If the *total* market value is not altered by the merger, then $1 invested in the merged firm gives 6.7 cents of immediate earnings but slower growth than World Enterprises offered alone. Muck and Slurry shareholders get lower immediate earnings but faster growth. Neither side gains or loses provided everybody understands the deal.

Financial manipulators sometimes try to ensure that the market does *not* understand the deal. Suppose that investors are fooled by the exuberance of the president

[12]The discussion of the bootstrap game follows S. C. Myers, "A Framework for Evaluating Mergers," in S. C. Myers (ed.), *Modern Developments in Financial Management*, Frederick A. Praeger, Inc., New York, 1976.

FIGURE 33.1

Effects of merger on earnings growth. By merging with Muck and Slurry, World Enterprises increases current earnings but accepts a slower rate of future growth. Its stockholders should be no better or worse off unless investors are fooled by the bootstrap effect.

Source: S. C. Myers, "A Framework for Evaluating Mergers," in S. C. Myers, ed., *Modern Developments in Financial Management*, Frederick A. Praeger, Inc., New York, 1976, Figure 1, p. 639.

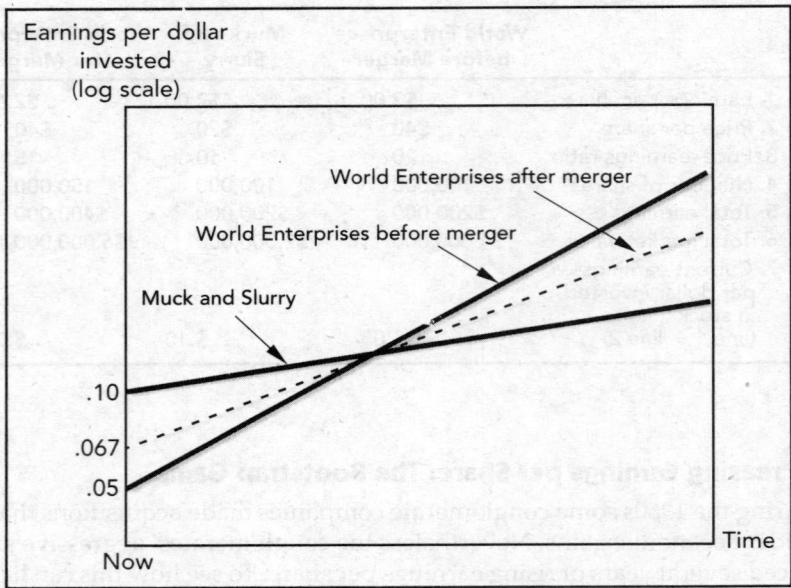

of World Enterprises and by plans to introduce modern management techniques into its new Earth Sciences Division (formerly known as Muck and Slurry). They could easily mistake the 33 percent postmerger increase in earnings per share for real growth. If they do, the price of World Enterprises stock rises and the shareholders of both companies receive something for nothing.

You should now see how to play the bootstrap, or "chain letter," game. Suppose that you manage a company enjoying a high price–earnings ratio. The reason why it is high is that investors anticipate rapid growth in future earnings. You achieve this growth not by capital investment, product improvement, or increased operating efficiency but by the purchase of slow-growing firms with low price–earnings ratios. The long-run result will be slower growth and a depressed price–earnings ratio, but in the short run earnings per share can increase dramatically. If this fools investors, you may be able to achieve higher earnings per share without suffering a decline in your price–earnings ratio. But to *keep* fooling investors, you must continue to expand by merger *at the same compound rate*. Obviously you cannot do this forever; one day expansion must slow down or stop. Then earnings growth will cease, and your house of cards will fall.

This kind of game is not played so often now. But there is still a widespread belief that a firm should not acquire companies with higher price–earnings ratios than its own. Of course you know better than to believe that low-P/E stocks are cheap and high-P/E stocks are dear. If life were as simple as that, we should all be wealthy by now. Beware of false prophets who suggest that you can appraise mergers just on the basis of their immediate impact on earnings per share.

Lower Financing Costs

You often hear it said that a merged firm is able to borrow more cheaply than its separate units could. In part this is true. We have already seen (in Section 15.4) that there are significant economies of scale in making new issues. Therefore, if firms can make fewer, larger security issues by merging, there are genuine savings.

But when people say that borrowing costs are lower for the merged firm, they usually mean something more than lower issue costs. They mean that when two firms merge, the combined company can borrow at lower interest rates than either firm could separately. This, of course, is exactly what we should expect in a well-functioning bond market. While the two firms are separate, they do not guarantee each other's debt; if one fails, the bondholder cannot ask the other for money. But after the merger each enterprise effectively does guarantee the other's debt; if one part of the business fails, the bondholders can still take their money out of the other part. Because these mutual guarantees make the debt less risky, lenders demand a lower interest rate.

Does the lower interest rate mean a net gain to the merger? Not necessarily. Compare the following two situations:

- *Separate issues.* Firm A and firm B each make a $50 million bond issue.
- *Single issue.* Firms A and B merge, and the new firm AB makes a single $100 million issue.

Of course AB would pay a lower interest rate, other things being equal. But it does not make sense for A and B to merge just to get that lower rate. Although AB's shareholders do gain from the lower rate, they lose by having to guarantee each other's debt. In other words, they get the lower interest rate only by giving bond-holders better protection. There is no *net* gain.

In Sections 20.2 and 24.5 we showed that

$$\text{Bond value} = \begin{matrix} \text{bond value} \\ \text{assuming no} \\ \text{chance of default} \end{matrix} - \begin{matrix} \text{value of} \\ \text{shareholders' (put)} \\ \text{option to default} \end{matrix}$$

Merger increases bond value (or reduces the interest payments necessary to support a *given* bond value) only by reducing the value of stockholders' options to default. In other words, the value of the default option for AB's $100 million issue is less than the combined value of the two default options on A's and B's separate $50 million issues.

Now suppose that A and B each borrow $50 million and *then* merge. If the merger is a surprise, it is likely to be a happy one for the bondholders. The bonds they thought were guaranteed by one of the two firms end up guaranteed by both. The stockholders lose in this case because they have given bondholders better protection but have received nothing for it.

There is one situation in which mergers can create value by making debt safer. In Section 18.3 we described the choice of an optimal debt ratio as a trade-off of the value of tax shields on interest payments made by the firm against the present value of possible costs of financial distress due to borrowing too much. Merging decreases the probability of financial distress, other things being equal. If it allows increased borrowing, and increased value from the interest tax shields, there will be a net gain to the merger.[13]

---

[13]This merger rationale was first suggested by W. G. Lewellen, "A Pure Financial Rationale for the Conglomerate Merger," *Journal of Finance* 26 (May 1971), pp. 521–537. If you want to see some of the controversy and discussion that this idea led to, look at R. C. Higgins and L. D. Schall, "Corporate Bankruptcy and Conglomerate Merger," *Journal of Finance* 30 (March 1975), pp. 93–114; and D. Galai and R. W. Masulis, "The Option Pricing Model and the Risk Factor of Stock," *Journal of Financial Economics* 3 (January–March 1976), especially pp. 66–69.

33.3 ESTIMATING MERGER GAINS AND COSTS

Suppose that you are the financial manager of firm A and you want to analyze the possible purchase of firm B.[14] The first thing to think about is whether there is an *economic gain* from the merger. There is an economic gain *only if the two firms are worth more together than apart*. For example, if you think that the combined firm would be worth PV_{AB} and that the separate firms are worth PV_A and PV_B, then

$$\text{Gain} = PV_{AB} - (PV_A + PV_B) = \Delta PV_{AB}$$

If this gain is positive, there is an economic justification for merger. But you also have to think about the *cost* of acquiring firm B. Take the easy case in which payment is made in cash. Then the cost of acquiring B is equal to the cash payment minus B's value as a separate entity. Thus

$$\text{Cost} = \text{cash paid} - PV_B$$

The net present value to A of a merger with B is measured by the difference between the gain and the cost. Therefore, you should go ahead with the merger if its net present value, defined as

$$
\begin{aligned}
NPV &= \text{gain} - \text{cost} \\
&= \Delta PV_{AB} - (\text{cash} - PV_B)
\end{aligned}
$$

is positive.

We like to write the merger criterion in this way because it focuses attention on two distinct questions. When you estimate the benefit, you concentrate on whether there are any gains to be made from the merger. When you estimate cost, you are concerned with the division of these gains between the two companies.

An example may help make this clear. Firm A has a value of $200 million, and B has a value of $50 million. Merging the two would allow cost savings with a present value of $25 million. This is the gain from the merger. Thus,

$$
\begin{aligned}
PV_A &= \$200 \\
PV_B &= \$50 \\
\text{Gain} = \Delta PV_{AB} &= +\$25 \\
PV_{AB} &= \$275 \text{ million}
\end{aligned}
$$

Suppose that B is bought for cash, say, for $65 million. The cost of the merger is

$$
\begin{aligned}
\text{Cost} &= \text{cash paid} - PV_B \\
&= 65 - 50 = \$15 \text{ million}
\end{aligned}
$$

Note that the stockholders of firm B—the people on the other side of the transaction—are ahead by $15 million. *Their* gain is *your* cost. They have captured $15 million of the $25 million merger gain. Thus when we write down the NPV of the merger from A's viewpoint, we are really calculating that part of the gain which A's stockholders get

---

[14]This chapter's definitions and interpretations of the gains and costs of merger follow those set out in S. C. Myers, "A Framework for Evaluating Mergers," op. cit.

to keep. The NPV to A's stockholders equals the overall gain from the merger less that part of the gain captured by B's stockholders:

$$NPV = 25 - 15 = +\$10 \text{ million}$$

Just as a check, let's confirm that A's stockholders really come out $10 million ahead. They start with a firm worth $PV_A = \$200$ million. They end up with a firm worth $275 million and then have to pay out $65 million to B's stockholders.[15] Thus their net gain is

$$NPV = \text{wealth with merger} - \text{wealth without merger}$$
$$= (PV_{AB} - \text{cash}) - PV_A$$
$$= (\$275 - \$65) - \$200 = +\$10 \text{ million}$$

Suppose investors do not anticipate the merger between A and B. The announcement will cause the value of B's stock to rise from $50 million to $65 million, a 30 percent increase. If investors share management's assessment of the merger gains, the market value of A's stock will increase by $10 million, only a 5 percent increase.

It makes sense to keep an eye on what investors think the gains from merging are. If A's stock price falls when the deal is announced, then investors are sending the message that the merger benefits are doubtful or that A is paying too much for them.[16]

Right and Wrong Ways to Estimate the Benefits of Mergers

Some companies begin their merger analyses with a forecast of the target firm's future cash flows. Any revenue increases or cost reductions attributable to the merger are included in the forecasts, which are then discounted back to the present and compared with the purchase price:

$$\begin{matrix} \text{Estimated} \\ \text{net gain} \end{matrix} = \begin{matrix} \text{DCF valuation} \\ \text{of target, including} \\ \text{merger benefits} \end{matrix} - \begin{matrix} \text{cash required} \\ \text{for acquisition} \end{matrix}$$

This is a dangerous procedure. Even the brightest and best-trained analyst can make large errors in valuing a business. The estimated net gain may come up positive not because the merger makes sense but simply because the analyst's cash-flow forecasts are too optimistic. On the other hand, a good merger may not be pursued if the analyst fails to recognize the target's potential as a stand-alone business.

Our procedure *starts* with the target's stand-alone market value (PV_B) and concentrates on the *changes* in cash flow that would result from the merger. *Ask yourself why the two firms should be worth more together than apart.*

The same advice holds when you are contemplating the *sale* of part of your business. There is no point in saying to yourself, This is an unprofitable business and should be sold. Unless the buyer can run the business better than you can, the price you receive will reflect the poor prospects.

---

[15]We are assuming that PV_A includes enough cash to finance the deal, or that the cash can be borrowed at a market interest rate. Notice that the value to A's stockholders after the deal is done and paid for is $275 - 65 = $210 million—a gain of $10 million.

[16]Think back to Section 13.4, where we saw how Hewlett Packard's stock price fell when it announced its plans to merge with Compaq.

Sometimes you may come across managers who believe that there are simple rules for identifying good acquisitions. They may say, for example, that they always try to buy into growth industries or that they have a policy of acquiring companies that are selling below book value. But our comments in Chapter 11 about the characteristics of a good investment decision also hold true when you are buying a whole company. *You add value only if you can generate additional economic rents*—some competitive edge that other firms can't match and the target firm's managers can't achieve on their own.

One final piece of horse sense: Often two companies bid against each other to acquire the same target firm. In effect, the target firm puts itself up for auction. In such cases, ask yourself whether the target is worth more to you than to the other bidder. If the answer is no, you should be cautious about getting into a bidding contest. Winning such a contest may be more expensive than losing it. If you lose, you have simply wasted your time; if you win, you have probably paid too much.

More on Estimating Costs—What If the Target's Stock Price Anticipates the Merger?

The cost of a merger is the premium that the buyer pays over the seller's stand-alone value. How can that value be determined? If the target is a public company, you can start with its market value; just observe price per share and multiply by the number of shares outstanding. But bear in mind that if investors *expect* A to acquire B, or if they expect *somebody* to acquire B, the market value of B may overstate its stand-alone value.

This is one of the few places in this book where we draw an important distinction between market value (MV) and the true, or "intrinsic," value (PV) of the firm as a separate entity. The problem here is not that the market value of B is wrong but that it may not be the value of firm B as a separate entity. Potential investors in B's stock will see two possible outcomes and two possible values:

Outcome	Market Value of B's Stock
1. No merger	PV_B: Value of B as a separate firm
2. Merger occurs	PV_B *plus* some part of the benefits of the merger

If the second outcome is possible, MV_B, the stock market value we observe for B, will overstate PV_B. This is exactly what *should* happen in a competitive capital market. Unfortunately, it complicates the task of a financial manager who is evaluating a merger.

Here is an example: Suppose that just before A and B's merger announcement we observe the following:

	Firm A	Firm B
Market price per share	$200	$100
Number of shares	1,000,000	500,000
Market value of firm	$200 million	$50 million

Firm A intends to pay $65 million cash for B. If B's market price reflects only its value as a separate entity, then

$$\text{Cost} = (\text{cash paid} - PV_B)$$
$$= (65 - 50) = \$15 \text{ million}$$

However, suppose that B's share price has already risen $12 because of rumors that B might get a favorable merger offer. That means that its intrinsic value is over-stated by $12 \times 500{,}000 = \$6$ million. Its true value, PV_B, is only $44 million. Then

$$\text{Cost} = (65 - 44) = \$21 \text{ million}$$

Since the merger gain is $25 million, this deal still makes A's stockholders better off, but B's stockholders are now capturing the lion's share of the gain.

Notice that if the market made a mistake, and the market value of B was *less* than B's true value as a separate entity, the cost could be negative. In other words, B would be a *bargain* and the merger would be worthwhile from A's point of view, even if the two firms were worth no more together than apart. Of course, A's stock-holders' gain would be B's stockholders' loss, because B would be sold for less than its true value.

Firms have made acquisitions just because their managers believed they had spotted a company whose intrinsic value was not fully appreciated by the stock market. However, we know from the evidence on market efficiency that "cheap" stocks often turn out to be expensive. It is not easy for outsiders, whether investors or managers, to find firms that are truly undervalued by the market. Moreover, if the shares are bargain-priced, A doesn't need a merger to profit by its special knowledge. It can just buy up B's shares on the open market and hold them pas-sively, waiting for other investors to wake up to B's true value.

If firm A is wise, it will not go ahead with a merger if the cost exceeds the gain. Conversely, firm B will not consent to a merger if it thinks the cost to A is negative, for a negative cost to A means a negative gain to B. This gives us a range of possi-ble cash payments that would allow the merger to take place. Whether the pay-ment is at the top or the bottom of this range depends on the relative bargaining power of the two participants.

Estimating Cost When the Merger Is Financed by Stock

In recent years about 70 percent of mergers have involved payment wholly or partly in the form of the acquirer's stock. When a merger is financed by stock, cost depends on the value of the shares in the new company received by the shareholders of the selling company. If the sellers receive N shares, each worth P_{AB}, the cost is

$$\text{Cost} = N \times P_{AB} - PV_B$$

Just be sure to use the price per share *after the merger is announced* and its benefits are appreciated by investors.

Suppose that A offers 325,000 (.325 million) shares instead of $65 million in cash. A's share price before the deal is announced is $200. If B is worth $50 million stand-alone,[17] the cost of the merger *appears* to be

$$\text{Apparent cost} = .325 \times 200 - 50 = \$15 \text{ million}$$

However, the apparent cost may not be the true cost. A's stock price is $200 before the merger announcement. At the announcement it ought to go up.

Given the gain and the terms of the deal, we can calculate share prices and mar-ket values after the deal. The new firm will have 1.325 million shares outstanding

---

[17]In this case we assume that B's stock price has *not* risen on merger rumors and accurately reflects B's stand-alone value.

and will be worth $275 million.[18] The new share price is $275/1.325 = \$207.55$. The true cost is

$$\text{Cost} = .325 \times 207.55 - 50 = \$17.45 \text{ million}$$

This cost can also be calculated by figuring out the gain to B's shareholders. They end up with .325 million shares, or 24.5 percent of the new firm AB. Their gain is

$$.245(275) - 50 = \$17.45 \text{ million}$$

In general, if B's shareholders are given the fraction x of the combined firms,

$$\text{Cost} = x\text{PV}_{AB} - \text{PV}_B$$

We can now understand the first key distinction between cash and stock as financing instruments. If cash is offered, the cost of the merger is unaffected by the merger gains. If stock is offered, the cost depends on the gains because the gains show up in the postmerger share price.

Stock financing also mitigates the effect of overvaluation or undervaluation of either firm. Suppose, for example, that A overestimates B's value as a separate entity, perhaps because it has overlooked some hidden liability. Thus A makes too generous an offer. Other things being equal, A's stockholders are better off if it is a stock offer rather than a cash offer. With a stock offer, the inevitable bad news about B's value will fall partly on the shoulders of B's stockholders.

Asymmetric Information

There is a second key difference between cash and stock financing for mergers. A's managers will usually have access to information about A's prospects that is not available to outsiders. Economists call this *asymmetric information*.

Suppose A's managers are more optimistic than outside investors. They may think that A's shares will really be worth $215 after the merger, $7.45 higher than the $207.55 market price we just calculated. If they are right, the true cost of a stock-financed merger with B is

$$\text{Cost} = .325 \times 215 - 50 = \$19.88$$

B's shareholders would get a "free gift" of $7.45 for every A share they receive—an extra gain of $7.45 \times .325 = 2.42$, that is, $2.42 million.

Of course, if A's managers were really this optimistic, they would strongly prefer to finance the merger with cash. Financing with stock would be favored by *pessimistic* managers who think their company's shares are *over*valued.

Does this sound like "win-win" for A—just issue shares when overvalued, cash otherwise? No, it's not that easy, because B's shareholders, and outside investors generally, understand what's going on. Suppose you are negotiating on behalf of B. You find that A's managers keep suggesting stock rather than cash financing. You quickly infer A's managers' pessimism, mark down your own opinion of what the shares are worth, and drive a harder bargain.

---

[18]In this case no cash is leaving the firm to finance the merger. In our example of a cash offer, $65 million would be paid out to B's stockholders, leaving the final value of the firm at $275 - 65 = \$210$ million. There would only be one million shares outstanding, so share price would be $210. The cash deal is better for A's shareholders.

This asymmetric-information story explains why buying-firms' share prices generally fall when stock-financed mergers are announced.[19] Andrade, Mitchell, and Stafford found an average market-adjusted fall of 1.5 percent on the announcement of stock-financed mergers between 1973 and 1998. There was a small *gain* (.4 percent) for a sample of cash-financed deals.[20]

33.4 THE MECHANICS OF A MERGER

Buying a company is a much more complicated affair than buying a piece of machinery. Thus we should look at some of the problems encountered in arranging mergers. In practice, these problems are often *extremely* complex, and specialists must be consulted. We are not trying to replace those specialists; we simply want to alert you to the kinds of legal, tax, and accounting issues they deal with.

Mergers and Antitrust Law

Mergers can get bogged down in the federal antitrust laws. The most important statute here is the Clayton Act of 1914, which forbids an acquisition whenever "in any line of commerce or in any section of the country" the effect "*may be* substantially to lessen competition, or to *tend* to create a monopoly."

Antitrust law can be enforced by the federal government in either of two ways: by a civil suit brought by the Justice Department or by a proceeding initiated by the Federal Trade Commission (FTC).[21] The Hart–Scott–Rodino Antitrust Act of 1976 requires that these agencies be informed of all acquisitions of stock amounting to $15 million or 15 percent of the target's stock, whichever is less. Thus, almost all large mergers are reviewed at an early stage.[22] Both the Justice Department and the FTC then have the right to seek injunctions delaying a merger. Often this injunction is enough to scupper the companies' plans.

Both the FTC and the Justice Department have been flexing their muscles in recent years. Here is an example. After the end of the Cold War, sharp declines in defense budgets triggered consolidation in the U.S. aerospace industry. By 1998 there remained just three giant companies—Boeing, Lockheed Martin, and Raytheon—plus several smaller ones, including Northrup Grumman. Thus, when Lockheed Martin and Northrup Grumman announced plans to get together, the Departments of Justice and Defense decided that this was a merger too far. In the face of this opposition, the two companies broke off their engagement.

---

[19]The same reasoning applies to stock issues. See Sections 15.4 and 18.4.

[20]See G. Andrade, M. Mitchell, and E. Stafford, "New Evidence and Perspectives on Mergers," *Journal of Economic Perspectives* 15 (Spring 2001), pp. 103–120. This result confirms earlier work by Travlos and by Franks, Harris, and Titman. See N. Travlos, "Corporate Takeover Bids, Methods of Payment, and Bidding Firms' Stock Returns," *Journal of Finance* 42 (September 1987), pp. 943–963; and J. R. Franks, R. S. Harris, and S. Titman, "The Postmerger Share-Price Performance of Acquiring Firms," *Journal of Financial Economics* 29 (March 1991), pp. 81–96.

[21]Competitors or third parties who think they will be injured by the merger can also bring antitrust suits.

[22]The target has to be notified also, and it in turn informs investors. Thus the Hart–Scott–Rodino Act effectively forces an acquiring company to "go public" with its bid.

The merger boom of the late 1990s has kept antitrust regulators busy. Other industries in which large mergers have been blocked on antitrust grounds include aluminum (Reynolds and Alcoa), telecoms (WorldCom and Sprint), supermarkets (Kroger and WinnDixie), video rentals (Hollywood Entertainment and Blockbuster), and office equipment (Office Depot and Staples).

Companies that do business outside the USA also have to worry about foreign antitrust laws. For example, GE's $46 billion takeover bid for Honeywell was blocked by the European Commission, which argued that the combined company would have too much power in the aircraft industry.

Sometimes trustbusters will object to a merger, but then relent if the companies agree to divest certain assets and operations. For example, the Justice Department has insisted that any joint venture between American Airlines and British Airways would be permitted to go ahead only if the airlines relinquished some of their take-off and landing slots at London's Heathrow airport.

The Form of Acquisition

Suppose you are confident that the purchase of company B will not be challenged on antitrust grounds. Next you will want to consider the form of the acquisition.

One possibility is literally to *merge* the two companies, in which case one company automatically assumes *all* the assets and *all* the liabilities of the other. Such a merger must have the approval of at least 50 percent of the stockholders of each firm.[23]

An alternative is simply to buy the seller's stock in exchange for cash, shares, or other securities. In this case the buyer can deal individually with the shareholders of the selling company. The seller's managers may not be involved at all. Their approval and cooperation are generally sought, but if they resist, the buyer will attempt to acquire an effective majority of the outstanding shares. If successful, the buyer has control and can complete the merger and, if necessary, toss out the incumbent management.

The third approach is to buy some or all of the seller's assets. In this case ownership of the assets needs to be transferred, and payment is made to the selling firm rather than directly to its stockholders.

Merger Accounting

When one company buys another, its management worries about how the purchase will show up in its financial statements. Before 2001 the company had a choice of accounting method, but in that year the Financial Accounting Standards Board (FASB) introduced new rules that required the buyer to use the *purchase method* of merger accounting. This is illustrated in Table 33.3, which shows what happens when A Corporation buys B Corporation, leading to the new AB Corporation. The two firms' initial balance sheets are shown at the top of the table. Below this we show what happens to the balance sheet when the two firms merge. We assume that B Corporation has been purchased for $1.8 million, 180 percent of book value.

Why did A Corporation pay an $800,000 premium over B's book value? There are two possible reasons. First, the true values of B's *tangible* assets—its working capital, plant, and equipment—may be greater than $1 million. We will assume that this is *not* the reason; that is, we assume that the assets listed on its balance

---

[23]Corporate charters and state laws sometimes specify a higher percentage.

TABLE 33.3

Accounting for the merger of A Corporation and B Corporation assuming that A Corporation pays $1.8 million for B Corporation (figures in $ millions).

Key: NWC = net working capital; FA = net book value of fixed assets; D = debt; E = book value of equity.

Initial Balance Sheets

A Corporation				B Corporation			
NWC	2.0	3.0	D	NWC	.1	0	D
FA	8.0	7.0	E	FA	.9	1.0	E
	10.0	10.0			1.0	1.0	

Balance Sheet of AB Corporation

NWC	2.1	3.0	D
FA	8.9	8.8	E
Goodwill	.8		
	11.8	11.8	

sheet are valued there correctly.[24] Second, A Corporation may be paying for an *intangible* asset that is not listed on B Corporation's balance sheet. For example, the intangible asset may be a promising product or technology. Or it may be no more than B Corporation's share of the expected economic gains from the merger.

A Corporation is buying an asset worth $1.8 million. The problem is to show that asset on the left-hand side of AB Corporation's balance sheet. B Corporation's tangible assets are worth only $1 million. This leaves $.8 million. Under the purchase method, the accountant takes care of this by creating a new asset category called *goodwill* and assigning $.8 million to it.[25] As long as the goodwill continues to be worth at least $.8 million, it stays on the balance sheet and the company's earnings are unaffected. However, the company is obliged each year to estimate the fair value of the goodwill. If the estimated value ever falls below $.8 million, the amount shown on the balance sheet must be adjusted downward and the write-off deducted from that year's earnings. Some companies have found that this can make a nasty dent in profits. For example, when the new accounting rules were introduced, AOL announced that it would need to write down its assets by as much as $60 billion.

Some Tax Considerations

An acquisition may be either taxable or tax-free. If payment is in the form of cash, the acquisition is regarded as taxable. In this case the selling stockholders are treated as having *sold* their shares, and they must pay tax on any capital gains. If payment is largely in the form of shares, the acquisition is tax-free and the shareholders are viewed as *exchanging* their old shares for similar new ones; no capital gains or losses are recognized.

The tax status of the acquisition also affects the taxes paid by the merged firm afterward. After a tax-free acquisition, the merged firm is taxed as if the two firms had always been together. In a taxable acquisition, the assets of the selling firm are

[24]If B's tangible assets are worth more than their previous book values, they would be reappraised and their current values entered on AB Corporation's balance sheet.

[25]If part of the $.8 million consisted of payment for identifiable intangible assets such as patents, the accountant would place these under a separate category of assets. Identifiable intangible assets that have a finite life need to be written off over their life.

	Taxable Merger	Tax-free Merger
Impact on Captain B	Captain B must recognize a $30,000 capital gain.	Capital gain can be deferred until Captain B sells the Baycorp shares.
Impact on Baycorp	Boat is revalued at $280,000. Baycorp must pay tax on the $130,000 write-up, but tax depreciation increases to $280,000/10 = $28,000 per year (assuming 10 years of remaining life).	Boat's value remains at $150,000, and tax depreciation continues at $15,000 per year.

TABLE 33.4

Possible tax consequences when Baycorp buys Seacorp for $330,000. Captain B's original investment in Seacorp was $300,000. Just before the merger Seacorp's assets were $50,000 of marketable securities and one boat with a book value of $150,000 but a market value of $280,000.

revalued, the resulting write-up or write-down is treated as a taxable gain or loss, and tax depreciation is recalculated on the basis of the restated asset values.

A very simple example will illustrate these distinctions. In 1990 Captain B forms Seacorp, which purchases a fishing boat for $300,000. Assume, for simplicity, that the boat is depreciated for tax purposes over 20 years on a straight-line basis (no salvage value). Thus annual depreciation is $300,000/20 = $15,000, and in 2000 the boat has a net book value of $150,000. But in 2000, Captain B finds that, owing to careful maintenance, inflation, and good times in the local fishing industry, the boat is really worth $280,000. In addition, Seacorp holds $50,000 of marketable securities.

Now suppose that Captain B sells the firm to Baycorp for $330,000. The possible tax consequences of the acquisition are shown in Table 33.4. In this case, Captain B is better off with a tax-free deal because capital gains taxes can be deferred. Baycorp will probably go along; it covets the $13,000-per-year extra depreciation tax shield that a taxable merger would generate, but the increased annual tax shields do not justify forcing Captain B to pay taxes on a $130,000 write-up.

33.5 TAKEOVER BATTLES AND TACTICS

Many mergers are negotiated by the two firms' top managements and boards of directors. When the companies are similar in size, these friendly mergers are often presented as "a merger between equals." However, in practice one of the management teams usually comes out on top. Consider, for example, the merger between Daimler-Benz and Chrysler. As Chrysler's profits slumped, the plans to integrate the two management teams with co-chairmen in Stuttgart and Dearborn rapidly fell apart; many of Chrysler's senior executives left and Daimler's management took control.[26]

If a negotiated merger appears impossible the acquirer can instead go over the heads of the target firm's management and appeal directly to its stockholders. There

---

[26]The story of the Daimler/Chrysler merger is told in B. Vlasic and B. A. Stertz, *Taken for a Ride: How Daimler-Benz Drove Off with Chrysler*, William Morrow & Co., 2000.

are two ways of doing this. First, the acquirer can seek the support of the target firm's stockholders at the next annual meeting. This is called a *proxy fight* because the right to vote someone else's share is called a *proxy.*[27]

Proxy fights are expensive and difficult to win. The alternative for the would-be acquirer is to make a *tender offer* directly to the shareholders. The management of the target firm may advise its shareholders to accept the tender, or it may attempt to fight the bid.

Tender battles resemble a complex game of poker. The rules are set mostly by the Williams Act of 1968, by state law, and by the courts. The problem in setting the rules is that it is unclear who requires protection. Should the management of the target firm be given more weapons to defend itself against unwelcome predators? Or should it simply be encouraged to sit the game out? Or should it be obliged to conduct an auction to obtain the highest price for its shareholders? And what about would-be acquirers? Should they be forced to reveal their intentions at an early stage, or would that allow other firms to piggy-back on their good ideas and enter competing bids?[28]

Keep these questions in mind as we review one of the more interesting chapters in merger history.

Boone Pickens Tries to Take Over Cities Service, Gulf Oil, and Phillips Petroleum

The 1980s saw a series of pitched takeover battles in the oil industry. The most interesting and visible player in these battles was Boone Pickens, chairman of Mesa Petroleum and a self-styled advocate for shareholders everywhere. Pickens and Mesa didn't win many battles, but they made a lot of money losing them, and they helped force major changes in oil companies' investment and financing policies.

Mesa's attack on Cities Service[29] illustrates Pickens's *modus operandi.* The battle began in May 1982, when Mesa bought Cities shares in preparation for a takeover bid. Cities counterattacked. It issued more shares to dilute Mesa's holdings, and it made a retaliatory offer for Mesa. (This is called a *pacman defense*—try to take over the attacker before it takes over you!) Over the following month Mesa upped its bid for Cities, and Cities twice increased its bid for Mesa. But in the end Cities won: Mesa agreed to call off its bid and not to make another one for Cities for at least five years. In exchange, Cities agreed to repurchase Mesa's holdings at an $80 million profit to Mesa. This is called a *greenmail* payment.

Though Cities escaped Mesa, it was still in play. It looked for a *white knight*, that is, a friendly acquirer, and found one in Gulf Oil. But the Federal Trade Commission raised various objections to that deal, and Gulf backed out.

In the end, Cities was bought by Occidental Petroleum. Occidental made a tender offer of $55 per share in cash for 45 percent of Cities, followed by a package of fixed income securities for the remaining stock. This is called a *two-tier offer.* In effect, Occidental was saying, "Last one through the door does the washing up."

---

[27]Peter Dodd and Jerrold Warner have written a detailed description and analysis of proxy fights. See "On Corporate Governance: A Study of Proxy Contests," *Journal of Financial Economics* 2 (April 1985), pp. 401–438.

[28]The Williams Act obliges firms who own 5 percent or more of another company's shares to tip their hand by reporting their holding in a Schedule 13(d) filing with the SEC.

[29]See R. S. Ruback, "The Cities Service Takeover: A Case Study," *Journal of Finance* 38 (May 1983), pp. 319–330.

TABLE 33.5

Phillips's balance sheet was dramatically changed by its leveraged repurchase (figures in billions).

	1985	1984		1985	1984
Current assets	$ 3.1	$ 4.6	Current liabilities	$ 3.1	$ 5.3
Fixed assets	10.3	11.2	Long-term debt	6.5	2.8
Other	.6	1.2	Other long-term liabilities	2.8	2.3
			Equity	1.6	6.6
Total assets	$14.0	$17.0	Total liabilities	$14.0	$17.0

Almost all Cities stockholders rushed to take advantage of the cash offer, and Occidental gained control.

One year after its brief engagement with Cities, Gulf itself became a takeover target. Pickens and Mesa were again on the warpath. At this point Chevron came to the rescue and acquired Gulf for $13.2 billion, more than double its value six months earlier. Chevron's bid gave Mesa a profit of $760 million on the Gulf shares it had bought. Asked for his views, Pickens commented, "Shucks, I guess we lost another one."

But why was Gulf worth that much more to Chevron than to investors just a few months earlier? Where was the added value? The answer will emerge as we look at Pickens's next foray, against Phillips Petroleum.

By 1984 Mesa had accumulated 6 percent of Phillips at an average price of $38 per share and made a bid for a further 15 percent at $60 per share. Phillips's first response was predictable: It bought out Mesa's shareholding. This greenmail payment gave Mesa a profit of $89 million.[30]

The other two responses reveal why Phillips was such an attractive target. It raised its dividend by 25 percent, reduced capital spending, and announced a program to sell $2 billion of assets. It also agreed to repurchase about 50 percent of its stock and to issue instead $4.5 billion of debt. Table 33.5 shows how this *leveraged repurchase* changed Phillips's balance sheet. The new debt ratio was about 80 percent, and book equity shrank by $5 billion to $1.6 billion.

This massive debt burden put Phillips on a strict cash diet. It was forced to sell assets and pinch pennies wherever possible. Capital expenditures were cut back from $1,065 million in 1985 to $646 million in 1986. In the same years, the number of employees fell from 25,300 to 21,800. Austerity continued through the late 1980s.

How did this *restructuring* shield Phillips from takeover? Certainly not by making purchase of the company more expensive. On the contrary, restructuring drastically reduced the total market value of Phillips's outstanding stock and therefore reduced the likely cost of buying out its remaining shareholders.

But restructuring removed the chief *motive* for takeover, which was to force Phillips to generate and pay out more cash to investors. Before the restructuring, investors sensed that Phillips was not running a tight ship and worried that it would plow back its ample operating cash flow into mediocre capital investments or ill-advised expansion. They wanted Phillips to pay out its free cash flow rather than let it be soaked up by a too-comfortable organization or plowed into negative-

---

[30]Giving in to greenmail can be dangerous, as Phillips soon discovered. Just six weeks later another corporate raider, Carl Icahn, acquired nearly 5 percent of Phillips stock and made an offer for the remainder. Phillips responded with a second greenmail payment, buying out Icahn and his pals for a profit (to them) of about $35 million.

NPV investments. Consequently, Phillips's share price did not reflect the potential value of its assets and operations. *That* created the opportunity for a takeover. One can almost hear the potential raider thinking:

> So what if I have to pay a 30 or 40 percent premium to take over Phillips? I can borrow most of the purchase price and then pay off the loan by selling surplus assets, cutting out all but the best capital investments, and wringing out slack in the organization. It'll be a rough few years, but if surgery's necessary, I might as well be the doctor and get paid for doing it.

Phillips's managers did not agree that the company was slack or prone to overinvestment. Nevertheless, they bowed to pressure from the stock market and undertook the surgery themselves. They paid out billions to repurchase stock and to service the $6.5 billion in long-term debt. They sold assets, cut back capital investment, and put their organization on the diet investors were calling for.

There are two lessons here. First, when the merger motive is to eliminate inefficiency or to distribute excess cash, the target's best defense is to do what the bidder would do, and thus avoid the cost, confusion, and random casualties of a takeover battle. Second, you can see why a company with ample free cash flow can be a tempting target for takeover.

The oil industry entered the 1980s with more-than-ample free cash flow. Rising oil prices had greatly increased revenues and operating profits. Investment opportunities had not expanded proportionally. Many companies overinvested. Investors foresaw massive, negative-NPV outlays and marked down the companies' stock prices accordingly. This created the opportunity for takeovers. Pickens and other acquirers could afford to offer a premium over the prebid stock price, knowing that if they did gain control they could increase value by putting the target company on a diet.

Pickens never succeeded in taking over a major oil company, but he and other "raiders" helped force the industry to cut back investment, reduce operating costs, and return cash to investors. Much of the cash was returned by stock repurchases.

Takeover Defenses

The Cities Service case illustrates several tactics managers use to fight takeover bids. Frequently they don't wait for a bid before taking defensive action. Instead, they deter potential bidders by devising *poison pills* that make their companies unappetizing or they persuade shareholders to agree to *shark-repellent* changes to the company charter.[31] Table 33.6 summarizes the principal first and second levels of defense.

Why do managers contest takeover bids? One reason is to extract a higher price from the bidder. Another possible reason is that managers believe their jobs may be at risk in the merged company. These managers are not trying to obtain a better price; they want to stop the bid altogether.

Some companies reduce these conflicts of interest by offering their managers *golden parachutes*, that is, generous payoffs if the managers lose their jobs as the result of a takeover. It may seem odd to reward managers for being taken over. However, if a soft landing overcomes their opposition to takeover bids, a few million dollars may be a small price to pay.

---

[31]Since shareholders expect to gain if their company is taken over, it is no surprise that they do not welcome these impediments. See, for example, G. Jarrell and A. Poulsen, "Shark Repellents and Stock Prices: The Effects of Antitakeover Amendments since 1980," *Journal of Financial Economics* 19 (1987), pp. 127–168.

Type of Defense	Description
Preoffer Defenses	
Shark-repellent charter amendments:	
Staggered board	The board is classified into three equal groups. Only one group is elected each year. Therefore the bidder cannot gain control of the target immediately.
Supermajority	A high percentage of shares is needed to approve a merger, typically 80%.
Fair price	Mergers are restricted unless a fair price (determined by formula or appraisal) is paid.
Restricted voting rights	Shareholders who own more than a specified proportion of the target have no voting rights unless approved by the target's board.
Waiting period	Unwelcome acquirers must wait for a specified number of years before they can complete the merger.
Other:	
Poison pill	Existing shareholders are issued rights which, if there is a significant purchase of shares by a bidder, can be used to purchase additional stock in the company at a bargain price.
Poison put	Existing bondholders can demand repayment if there is a change of control as a result of a hostile takeover.
Postoffer Defenses	
Litigation	File suit against bidder for violating antitrust or securities laws.
Asset restructuring	Buy assets that bidder does not want or that will create an antitrust problem.
Liability restructuring	Issue shares to a friendly third party or increase the number of share-holders. Repurchase shares from existing shareholders at a premium.

TABLE 33.6

A summary of takeover defenses.

Source: This table is loosely adapted from R. S. Ruback, "An Overview of Takeover Defenses," working paper no. 1836–86, Sloan School of Management, MIT, Cambridge, MA, September 1986, tables 1 and 2. See also L. Herzel and R. W. Shepro, *Bidders and Targets: Mergers and Acquisitions in the U.S.*, Basil Blackwell, Inc., Cambridge, MA, 1990, chap. 8.

Any management team that tries to develop improved weapons of defense must expect challenge in the courts. In the early 1980s the courts tended to give managers the benefit of the doubt and respect their business judgment about whether a takeover should be resisted. But the courts' attitudes to takeover battles have changed. For example, in 1993 a court blocked Viacom's agreed takeover of Paramount on the grounds that Paramount's directors did not do their homework before turning down a higher offer from QVC. Paramount was forced to give up its poison-pill defense and the stock options that it had offered to Viacom. Because of such decisions, managers have become much more careful in opposing bids, and they do not throw themselves blindly into the arms of any white knight.[32]

At the same time, state governments have provided some new defensive weapons. In 1987 the Supreme Court upheld state laws that allow companies to deprive an investor of voting rights as soon as the investor's share in the company ex-

---

[32]In 1985 a shiver ran through many boardrooms when the directors of Trans Union Corporation were held personally liable for being too hasty in accepting a takeover bid. Changes in judicial attitudes to takeover defenses are reviewed in L. Herzel and R. W. Shepro, *Bidders and Targets: Mergers and Acquisitions in the U.S.*, Basil Blackwell, Inc., Cambridge, MA, 1990.

ceeds a certain level. Since then state antitakeover laws have proliferated. Many allow boards of directors to block mergers with hostile bidders for several years and to consider the interests of employees, customers, suppliers, and their communities in deciding whether to try to block a hostile bid.

AlliedSignal vs. AMP

The hostile attacks of the 1980s were rarely repeated in the 1990s, when most mergers were friendly.[33] But now and then a battle flared up. The following example illustrates takeover tactics and defenses near the end of the millennium.

In the first week of August 1998, AlliedSignal, Inc., announced that it would bid $44.50 per share, or $9.8 billion, for AMP, Inc. AMP's stock price immediately jumped by nearly 50 percent to about $43 per share.

AMP was the world's largest producer of cables and connectors for computers and other electronic equipment. It had just announced a fall of nearly 50 percent in quarterly profits from the previous year. The immediate cause for this bad news was economic troubles in Southeast Asia, one of AMP's most important export markets. But longer-run performance had also disappointed investors, and the company was widely viewed as ripe for change in operations and management. AlliedSignal was betting that it could make these changes faster and better than the incumbent management.

AMP at first seemed impregnable. It was chartered in Pennsylvania, which had passed tough antitakeover laws. Pennsylvania corporations could "just say no" to takeovers that might adversely affect employees and local communities. The company also had a strong poison pill.[34]

AlliedSignal held out an olive branch, hinting that price was flexible if AMP was ready to talk turkey. But the offer was rebuffed. A tender offer went out to AMP shareholders, and 72 percent accepted. However, the terms of the offer did not require AlliedSignal to buy any shares until the poison pill was removed. In order to do that, AlliedSignal would have to appeal again to AMP's shareholders, asking them to approve a *solicitation of consent* blocking AMP's directors from enforcing the pill.

AMP fought back vigorously and imaginatively. It announced a plan to borrow $3 billion to repurchase its shares at $55 per share—its management's view of the true value of AMP stock. It convinced a federal court to delay AlliedSignal's solicitation of consent. At the same time it asked the Pennsylvania legislature to pass a law which would effectively bar the merger. The governor announced his support. Both companies sent teams of lobbyists to the state capitol. In October the bill was approved in the Pennsylvania House of Representatives and sent to the Senate for consideration.

Yet AlliedSignal discovered it had powerful allies. About 80 percent of AMP's shares were owned by mutual funds, pension funds, and other institutional investors. Many of these institutions bluntly and publicly disagreed with AMP's intransigence. The College Retirement Equities Fund (CREF), one of the largest U.S. pension funds, called AMP's defensive tactics "entirely inimical to the principles of shareholder democracy and good corporate governance." CREF then took an extraordinary step: It filed a legal brief supporting AlliedSignal's case in the federal court.[35] Then the Hixon family, descendants of AMP's co-founder, made public a

---

[33]By contrast, a number of hostile takeovers took place in continental European countries where such activity had been almost unknown.

[34]It was a *dead-hand* poison pill: Even if AlliedSignal gained a majority of AMP's board of directors, only the *previous* directors were empowered to vote to remove the pill.

[35]G. Faircloth, "AMP's Tactics Against AlliedSignal Bid Are Criticized by Big Pension Fund," *The Wall Street Journal*, September 28, 1998, p. A17.

letter to AMP's management and directors expressing "dismay," and asking, "Who do management and the board work for? The central issue is that AMP's management will not permit shareholders to voice their will."[36]

AMP had complained all along that AlliedSignal's bid was too low. Robert Ripp, AMP's chairman, reiterated this point in his reply to the Hixons and also said, "As a board, we have an overarching responsibility to AMP, all of its shareholders, and its other constituencies—which we believe we are serving on a basis consistent with your interests."[37]

But as the weeks passed, AMP's defenses, while still intact, did not look quite so strong. By mid-October it became clear that AMP would not receive timely help from the Pennsylvania legislature. In November, the federal court finally gave AlliedSignal the go-ahead for its solicitation of consent to remove the poison pill. Remember, 72 percent of its stockholders had already accepted AlliedSignal's tender offer.

Then, suddenly, AMP gave up: It agreed to be acquired by a white knight, Tyco International, for $55 per AMP share, paid for in Tyco stock. AlliedSignal dropped out of the bidding; it didn't think AMP was worth that much.

What are the lessons? First is the strength of poison pills and other takeover defenses, especially in a state like Pennsylvania where the law leans in favor of local targets. AlliedSignal's offensive gained ground, but with great expense and effort and at a very slow pace.

The second lesson is the potential power of institutional investors. We believe AMP gave in not because its legal and procedural defenses failed but largely because of economic pressure from its major shareholders.

Did AMP's management and board act in shareholders' interests? In the end, yes. They said that AMP was worth more than AlliedSignal's offer, and they found another buyer to prove them right. However, they would not have searched for a white knight absent AlliedSignal's bid.

Who Gains Most in Mergers?

As our brief history illustrates, in mergers sellers generally do better than buyers. Andrade, Mitchell, and Stafford found that following the announcement of the bid, selling shareholders received a healthy gain averaging 16 percent.[38] On the other hand, it appears that investors expected acquiring companies to just about break even. The prices of their shares fell by .7 percent.[39] The value of the *total* package—buyer plus seller—increased by 1.8 percent. Of course, these are averages; selling shareholders sometimes obtain much higher returns. When IBM took over Lotus Corporation, it paid a premium of 100 percent, or about $1.7 billion, for Lotus stock.

Why do sellers earn higher returns? There are two reasons. First, buying firms are typically larger than selling firms. In many mergers the buyer is so much larger that even substantial net benefits would not show up clearly in the buyer's share price. Suppose, for example, that company A buys company B, which is only one-tenth A's size. Suppose the dollar value of the net gain from the merger is split

---

[36]S. Lipin and G. Faircloth, "AMP's Antitakeover Tactics Rile Holder," *The Wall Street Journal,* October 5, 1998, p. A18.

[37]Ibid.

[38]See G. Andrade, M. Mitchell, and E. Stafford, "New Evidence and Perspectives on Mergers," *Journal of Economic Perspectives* 15 (Spring 2001), pp. 103–120.

[39]The small loss to the shareholders of acquiring firms is not statistically significant. Other studies using different samples have observed a small positive return.

equally between A and B.[40] Each company's shareholders receive the same *dollar* profit, but B's receive 10 times A's *percentage* return.

The second, and more important, reason is the competition among potential bidders. Once the first bidder puts the target company "in play," one or more additional suitors often jump in, sometimes as white knights at the invitation of the target firm's management. Every time one suitor tops another's bid, more of the merger gain slides toward the target. At the same time, the target firm's management may mount various legal and financial counterattacks, ensuring that capitulation, if and when it comes, is at the highest attainable price.

Of course, bidders and targets are not the only possible winners. Unsuccessful bidders often win, too, by selling off their holdings in target companies at substantial profits.

Other winners include investment bankers, lawyers, accountants, and in some cases arbitrageurs, or "arbs," who speculate on the likely success of takeover bids.[41] "Speculate" has a negative ring, but it can be a useful social service. A tender offer may present shareholders with a difficult decision. Should they accept, should they wait to see if someone else produces a better offer, or should they sell their stock in the market? This dilemma presents an opportunity for the arbitrageurs, who specialize in answering such questions. In other words, they buy from the target's shareholders and take on the risk that the deal will not go through.

As Ivan Boesky demonstrated, arbitrageurs can make even more money if they learn about the offer *before* it is publicly announced. Because arbitrageurs may accumulate large amounts of stock, they can have an important effect on whether a deal goes through, and the bidding company or its investment bankers may be tempted to take the arbitrageurs into their confidence. This is the point at which a legitimate and useful activity becomes an illegal and harmful one.

 ## 33.6 MERGERS AND THE ECONOMY

Merger Waves

Mergers come in waves. The first episode of intense merger activity occurred at the turn of the 20th century and the second occurred in the 1920s. There was a further boom from 1967 to 1969 and then again in the 1980s and 1990s (1999 and 2000 were record years). Each episode coincided with a period of buoyant stock prices, though there were substantial differences in the types of companies that merged and the ways they went about it.

We don't really understand why merger activity is so volatile. If mergers are prompted by economic motives, at least one of these motives must be "here today and gone tomorrow," and it must somehow be associated with high stock prices. But none of the economic motives that we review in this chapter has anything to do with the general level of the stock market. None burst on the scene in 1967, departed in 1970, and reappeared for most of the 1980s and again in the mid-1990s.

---

[40]In other words, the *cost* of the merger to A is one-half the gain ΔPV_{AB}.

[41]Strictly speaking, an arbitrageur is an investor who takes a fully hedged, that is, riskless, position. But arbitrageurs in merger battles often take very large risks indeed. Their activities are oxymoronically known as "risk arbitrage."

Some mergers may result from mistakes in valuation on the part of the stock market. In other words, the buyer may believe that investors have underestimated the value of the seller or may hope that they *will* overestimate the value of the combined firm. But we see (with hindsight) that mistakes are made in bear markets as well as bull markets. Why don't we see just as many firms hunting for bargain acquisitions when the stock market is low? It is possible that "suckers are born every minute," but it is difficult to believe that they can be harvested only in bull markets.

Merger activity tends to be concentrated in a relatively small number of industries and is often prompted by deregulation and by changes in technology or the pattern of demand. Take the merger wave of the 1990s, for example. Deregulation of telecoms and banking earlier in the decade led to a spate of mergers in both industries. Elsewhere, the decline in military spending brought about a number of mergers between defense companies until the Department of Justice decided to call a halt. And in the entertainment industry the prospective advantages from controlling both content and distribution led to mergers between such giants as AOL and Time Warner.

Do Mergers Generate Net Benefits?

There are undoubtedly good acquisitions and bad acquisitions, but economists find it hard to agree on whether acquisitions are beneficial *on balance.* Indeed, since there seem to be transient fashions in mergers, it would be surprising if economists could come up with simple generalizations.

We do know that mergers generate substantial gains to acquired firms' stockholders. Since buyers roughly break even and sellers make substantial gains, it seems that there are positive overall benefits from mergers.[42] But not everybody is convinced. Some believe that investors analyzing mergers pay too much attention to short-term earnings gains and don't notice that these gains are at the expense of long-term prospects.[43]

Since we can't observe how companies would have fared in the absence of a merger, it is difficult to measure the effects on profitability. Ravenscroft and Scherer, who looked at mergers during the 1960s and early 1970s, argued that productivity declined in the years following a merger.[44] But studies of subsequent merger activity suggest that mergers *do* seem to improve real productivity. For example, Paul Healy, Krishna Palepu, and Richard Ruback examined 50 large mergers between 1979 and 1983 and found an average increase of 2.4 percentage points in the companies' pretax

---

[42]M. C. Jensen and R. S. Ruback, "The Market for Corporate Control: The Scientific Evidence," *Journal of Financial Economics* 11 (April 1983), pp. 5–50, after an extensive review of empirical work, conclude that "corporate takeovers generate positive gains" (p. 47). Richard Roll reviewed the same evidence and argues that "takeover gains may have been overestimated if they exist at all." See "The Hubris Hypothesis of Corporate Takeovers," *Journal of Business* 59 (April 1986), pp. 198–216.

[43]There have been a number of attempts to test whether investors are myopic. For example, McConnell and Muscarella examined the reaction of stock prices to announcements of capital expenditure plans. If investors were interested in short-term earnings, which are generally depressed by major capital expenditure programs, then these announcements should depress stock price. But they found that increases in capital spending were associated with *increases* in stock prices and reductions were associated with *falls.* Similarly, Jarrell, Lehn, and Marr found that announcements of expanded R&D spending prompted a *rise* in stock price. See J. McConnell and C. Muscarella, "Corporate Capital Expenditure Decisions and the Market Value of the Firm," *Journal of Financial Economics* 14 (July 1985), pp. 399–422; and G. Jarrell, K. Lehn, and W. Marr, "Institutional Ownership, Tender Offers, and Long-Term Investments," Office of the Chief Economist, Securities and Exchange Commission (April 1985).

[44]See D. J. Ravenscroft and F. M. Scherer, "Mergers and Managerial Performance," in J. C. Coffee, Jr., L. Lowenstein, and S. Rose-Ackerman (eds.), *Knights, Raiders, and Targets: The Impact of the Hostile Takeover,* Oxford University Press, New York, 1988.

returns.[45] They argue that this gain came from generating a higher level of sales from the same assets. There was no evidence indicating that the companies were mortgaging their long-term future by cutting back on long-term investments; expenditures on capital equipment and research and development tracked industry averages.[46]

Perhaps the most important effect of acquisitions is felt by the managers of companies that are *not* taken over. Perhaps the threat of takeover spurs the whole of corporate America to try harder. Unfortunately, we don't know whether, on balance, the threat of merger makes for active days or sleepless nights.

The threat of takeover may be a spur to inefficient management, but it is also costly. It can soak up large amounts of management time and effort. When a company is planning a takeover, it can be difficult to pay as much attention as one should to the firm's existing business.[47] In addition, the company needs to pay for the services provided by the investment bankers, lawyers, and accountants. In the year 2000 merging companies paid in total more than $2 billion for professional assistance.

---

[45]See P. Healy, K. Palepu, and R. Ruback, "Does Corporate Performance Improve after Mergers?" *Journal of Financial Economics* 31 (April 1992), pp. 135–175. The study examined the pretax returns of the merged companies relative to industry averages. A study by Lichtenberg and Siegel came to similar conclusions. Before merger, acquired companies had lower levels of productivity than did other firms in their industries, but by seven years after the control change, two-thirds of the productivity gap had been eliminated. See F. Lichtenberg and D. Siegel, "The Effect of Control Changes on the Productivity of U.S. Manufacturing Plants," *Journal of Applied Corporate Finance* 2 (Summer 1989), pp. 60–67.

[46]Maintained levels of capital spending and R&D are also observed by Lichtenberg and Siegel, op. cit.; and B. H. Hall, "The Effect of Takeover Activity on Corporate Research and Development," in A. J. Auerbach (ed.), *Corporate Takeover: Causes and Consequences*, University of Chicago Press, Chicago, 1988.

[47]There is some evidence that, while acquisitions lead to improvements in the productivity of the new plant, productivity in the firm's existing plant languishes. See R. McGuckin and S. Nguyen, "On Productivity and Plant Ownership Change: New Evidence from the Longitudinal Research Database," *Rand Journal of Economics* 26 (1995), pp. 257–276.

SUMMARY

A merger generates an economic gain if the two firms are worth more together than apart. Suppose that firms A and B merge to form a new entity, AB. Then the gain from the merger is

$$\text{Gain} = PV_{AB} - (PV_A + PV_B) = \Delta PV_{AB}$$

Gains from mergers may reflect economies of scale, economies of vertical integration, improved efficiency, the combination of complementary resources, or redeployment of surplus funds. In other cases there may be no advantage in combining two businesses, but the object of the acquisition is to install a more efficient management team. There are also dubious reasons for mergers. There is no value added by merging just to diversify risks, to reduce borrowing costs, or to pump up earnings per share.

In many cases the object of merging is to replace management or to force changes in investment or financing policies. Many of the takeovers in the 1980s were diet deals, in which companies were forced to sell assets, cut costs, or reduce capital expenditures. The changes added value when the target company had ample free cash flow but was overinvesting or not trying hard enough to reduce costs or dispose of underutilized assets.

You should go ahead with the acquisition if the gain exceeds the cost. Cost is the premium that the buyer pays for the selling firm over its value as a separate entity. It is easy to estimate when the merger is financed by cash. In that case,

$$\text{Cost} = \text{cash paid} - PV_B$$

When payment is in the form of shares, the cost naturally depends on what those shares are worth after the merger is complete. If the merger is a success, B's stockholders will share the merger gains.

The mechanics of buying a firm are much more complex than those of buying a machine. First, you have to make sure that the purchase does not fall afoul of the antitrust laws. Second, you have a choice of procedures: You can merge all the assets and liabilities of the seller into those of your own company; you can buy the stock of the seller rather than the company itself; or you can buy the individual assets of the seller. Third, you have to worry about the tax status of the merger. In a tax-free merger the tax position of the corporation and the stockholders is not changed. In a taxable merger the buyer can depreciate the full cost of the tangible assets acquired, but tax must be paid on any write-up of the assets' taxable value, and the stockholders in the selling corporation are taxed on any capital gains.

Mergers are often amicably negotiated between the management and directors of the two companies; but if the seller is reluctant, the would-be buyer can decide to make a tender offer or engage in a proxy fight. We sketched some of the offensive and defensive tactics used in takeover battles. We also observed that when the target firm loses, its shareholders typically win: Selling shareholders earn large abnormal returns, while the bidding firm's shareholders roughly break even. The typical merger appears to generate positive net benefits for investors, but competition among bidders, plus active defense by target management, pushes most of the gains toward the selling shareholders.

APPENDIX   Conglomerate Mergers and Value Additivity

A pure conglomerate merger is one that has no effect on the operations or profitability of either firm. If corporate diversification is in stockholders' interests, a conglomerate merger would give a clear demonstration of its benefits. But if present values add up, the conglomerate merger would not make stockholders better or worse off.

In this appendix we examine more carefully our assertion that present values add. It turns out that values *do* add as long as capital markets are perfect and investors' diversification opportunities are unrestricted.

Call the merging firms A and B. Value additivity implies

$$PV_{AB} = PV_A + PV_B$$

where

PV_{AB} = market value of combined firms just after merger;
PV_A, PV_B = separate market values of A and B just before merger.

For example, we might have

PV_A = $100 million ($200 per share × 500,000 shares outstanding)

and

PV_B = $200 million ($200 per share × 1,000,000 shares outstanding)

Suppose A and B are merged into a new firm, AB, with one share in AB exchanged for each share of A or B. Thus there are 1,500,000 AB shares issued. *If* value additivity holds, then PV_{AB} must equal the sum of the separate values of A and B just before the merger, that is, $300 million. That would imply a price of $200 per share of AB stock.

But note that the AB shares represent a portfolio of the assets of A and B. Before the merger investors could have bought one share of A and two of B for $600. Afterward they can obtain a claim on *exactly* the same real assets by buying three shares of AB.

Suppose that the opening price of AB shares just after the merger is $200, so that $PV_{AB} = PV_A + PV_B$. Our problem is to determine if this is an equilibrium price, that is, whether we can rule out excess demand or supply at this price.

For there to be excess demand, there must be some investors who are willing to increase their holdings of A and B as a consequence of the merger. Who could they be? The only thing new created by the merger is diversification, but those investors who want to hold assets of A *and* B will have purchased A's and B's stock before the merger. The diversification is redundant and consequently won't attract new investment demand.

Is there a possibility of excess supply? The answer is yes. For example, there will be some shareholders in A who did not invest in B. After the merger they cannot invest solely in A, but only in a fixed combination of A and B. Their AB shares will be less attractive to them than the pure A shares, so they will sell part of or all their AB stock. In fact, the only AB shareholders who will *not* wish to sell are those who happened to hold A and B in exactly a 1:2 ratio in their premerger portfolios!

Since there is no possibility of excess demand but a definite possibility of excess supply, we seem to have

$$PV_{AB} \leq PV_A + PV_B$$

That is, corporate diversification can't help, but it may hurt investors by restricting the types of portfolios they can hold. This is not the whole story, however, since investment demand for AB shares might be attracted from other sources if PV_{AB} drops below $PV_A + PV_B$. To illustrate, suppose there are two other firms, A* and B*, which are judged by investors to have the same risk characteristics as A and B, respectively. Then before the merger,

$$r_A = r_{A^*} \quad \text{and} \quad r_B = r_{B^*}$$

where r is the rate of return expected by investors. We'll assume $r_A = r_{A^*} = .08$ and $r_B = r_{B^*} = .20$.

Consider a portfolio invested one-third in A* and two-thirds in B*. This portfolio offers an expected return of 16 percent:

$$r = x_{A^*} r_{A^*} + x_{B^*} r_{B^*}$$
$$= \tfrac{1}{3}(.08) + \tfrac{2}{3}(.20) = .16$$

A similar portfolio of A and B before their merger also offered a 16 percent return.

As we have noted, a new firm AB is really a portfolio of firms A and B, with portfolio weights of $\tfrac{1}{3}$ and $\tfrac{2}{3}$. Thus it is equivalent in risk to the portfolio of A* and B*. Thus the price of AB shares must adjust so that it likewise offers a 16 percent return.

What if AB shares drop below $200, so that PV_{AB} is less than $PV_A + PV_B$? Since the assets and earnings of firms A and B are the same, the price drop means that the expected rate of return on AB shares has risen above the return offered by the A*B* portfolio. That is, if r_{AB} exceeds $\tfrac{1}{3} r_A + \tfrac{2}{3} r_B$, then r_{AB} must also exceed $\tfrac{1}{3} r_{A^*} + \tfrac{2}{3} r_{B^*}$. But this is untenable: Investors A* and B* could sell part of their holdings (in a 1:2 ratio), buy AB, and obtain a higher expected rate of return with no increase in risk.

On the other hand, if PV_{AB} rises above $PV_A + PV_B$, the AB shares will offer an expected return less than that offered by the A*B* portfolio. Investors will unload the AB shares, forcing their price down.

A stable result occurs only if AB shares stick at $200. Thus, value additivity will hold exactly in a perfect-market equilibrium if there are ample substitutes for the A and B assets. If A and B have unique risk characteristics, however, then PV_{AB} can fall below $PV_A + PV_B$. The reason is that the merger curtails investors' opportunity to custom-tailor their portfolios to their own needs and preferences. This makes investors worse off, reducing the attractiveness of holding the shares of firm AB.

In general, the condition for value additivity is that investors' opportunity set—that is, the range of risk characteristics attainable by investors through their portfolio choices—is independent of the particular portfolio of real assets held by the firm. Diversification per se can never expand the opportunity set given perfect security markets. Corporate diversification may reduce the investors' opportunity set, but only if the real assets the corporations hold lack substitutes among traded securities or portfolios.

In a few cases the firm may be able to expand the opportunity set. It can do so if it finds an investment opportunity that is unique—a real asset with risk characteristics shared by few or no other financial assets. In this lucky event the firm should not diversify, however. It should set up the unique asset as a separate firm so as to expand investors' opportunity set to the maximum extent. If Gallo by chance discovered that a small portion of its vineyards produced wine comparable to Chateau Margaux, it would not throw that wine into the Hearty Burgundy vat.

FURTHER READING

Here are two useful books on takeovers:

L. Herzel and R. Shepro: *Bidders and Targets: Mergers and Acquisitions in the U.S.*, Basil Blackwell, Inc., Cambridge, MA, 1990.

J. F. Weston, K. S. Chung, and J. A. Siu: *Takeovers, Restructuring and Corporate Finance*, 3rd ed., Prentice-Hall, Upper Saddle River, NJ, 2000.

A good review of the mechanics of acquisitions is provided in:

S. M. Litwin: "The Merger and Acquisition Process: A Primer on Getting the Deal Done," *The Financier: ACMT*, 2:6–17 (November 1995).

Recent merger waves are reviewed in:

G. Andrade, M. Mitchell, and E. Stafford: "New Evidence and Perspectives on Mergers," *Journal of Economic Perspectives*, 15:103–120 (Spring 2001).

Jensen and Ruback review the early empirical work on mergers. The April 1983 issue of the Journal of Financial Economics *also contains a collection of some of the more important empirical studies.*

M. C. Jensen and R. S. Ruback: "The Market for Corporate Control: The Scientific Evidence," *Journal of Financial Economics*, 11:5–50 (April 1983).

Finally, here are some informative case studies:

G. P. Baker: "Beatrice: A Study in the Creation and Destruction of Value," *Journal of Finance*, 47:1081–1119 (July 1992).

R. Bruner: "An Analysis of Value Destruction and Recovery in the Alliance and Proposed Merger of Volvo and Renault," *Journal of Financial Economics*, 51:125–166 (1999).

R. S. Ruback: "The Cities Service Takeover: A Case Study," *Journal of Finance*, 38:319–330 (May 1983).

B. Burrough and J. Helyar: *Barbarians at the Gate: The Fall of RJR Nabisco*, Harper & Row, New York, 1990.

1. Are the following hypothetical mergers horizontal, vertical, or conglomerate?
   a. IBM acquires Dell Computer.
   b. Dell Computer acquires Kroger.
   c. Kroger acquires H. J. Heinz.
   d. H. J. Heinz acquires IBM.

2. Which of the following motives for mergers make economic sense?
   a. Merging to achieve economies of scale.
   b. Merging to reduce risk by diversification.
   c. Merging to redeploy cash generated by a firm with ample profits but limited growth opportunities.
   d. Merging to combine complementary resources.
   e. Merging just to increase earnings per share.

3. Velcro Saddles is contemplating the acquisition of Pogo Ski Sticks, Inc. The values of the two companies as separate entities are $20 million and $10 million, respectively. Velcro Saddles estimates that by combining the two companies, it will reduce marketing and administrative costs by $500,000 per year in perpetuity. Velcro Saddles can either pay $14 million cash for Pogo or offer Pogo a 50 percent holding in Velcro Saddles. The opportunity cost of capital is 10 percent.
   a. What is the gain from merger?
   b. What is the cost of the cash offer?
   c. What is the cost of the stock alternative?
   d. What is the NPV of the acquisition under the cash offer?
   e. What is its NPV under the stock offer?

4. Which of the following transactions are *not* likely to be classed as tax-free?
   a. An acquisition of assets.
   b. A merger in which payment is entirely in the form of voting stock.

5. True or false?
   a. Sellers almost always gain in mergers.
   b. Buyers usually gain more than sellers.
   c. Firms that do unusually well tend to be acquisition targets.
   d. Merger activity in the United States varies dramatically from year to year.
   e. On the average, mergers produce large economic gains.
   f. Tender offers require the approval of the selling firm's management.
   g. The cost of a merger to the buyer equals the gain realized by the seller.

6. Mature companies with ample free cash flow are often targets for takeovers. Briefly explain why.

7. Briefly define the following terms:
   a. Purchase accounting
   b. Tender offer
   c. Poison pill
   d. Greenmail
   e. White knight

1. Examine several recent mergers and suggest the principal motives for merging in each case.

2. Examine a recent merger in which at least part of the payment made to the seller was in the form of stock. Use stock market prices to obtain an estimate of the gain from the merger and the cost of the merger.

3. Respond to the following comments.
   a. "Our cost of debt is too darn high, but our banks won't reduce interest rates as long as we're stuck in this volatile widget-trading business. We've got to acquire other companies with safer income streams."

b. "Merge with Fledgling Electronics? No way! Their P/E's too high. That deal would knock 20 percent off our earnings per share."

c. "Our stock's at an all-time high. It's time to make our offer for Digital Organics. Sure, we'll have to offer a hefty premium to Digital stockholders, but we don't have to pay in cash. We'll give them new shares of our stock."

4. Explain how you would estimate the gain and cost of a merger financed by stock. What stock price should be used to calculate the cost?

5. Sometimes the stock price of a possible target company rises in anticipation of a merger bid. Explain how this complicates the bidder's evaluation of the target company.

6. Suppose you obtain special information—information unavailable to investors— indicating that Backwoods Chemical's stock price is 40 percent undervalued. Is that a reason to launch a takeover bid for Backwoods? Explain carefully.

7. As treasurer of Leisure Products, Inc., you are investigating the possible acquisition of Plastitoys. You have the following basic data:

	Leisure Products	Plastitoys
Earnings per share	$ 5.00	$ 1.50
Dividend per share	$ 3.00	$ .80
Number of shares	1,000,000	600,000
Stock price	$90	$20

You estimate that investors currently expect a steady growth of about 6 percent in Plastitoys' earnings and dividends. Under new management this growth rate would be increased to 8 percent per year, without any additional capital investment required.

a. What is the gain from the acquisition?

b. What is the cost of the acquisition if Leisure Products pays $25 in cash for each share of Plastitoys?

c. What is the cost of the acquisition if Leisure Products offers one share of Leisure Products for every three shares of Plastitoys?

d. How would the cost of the cash offer and the share offer alter if the expected growth rate of Plastitoys were not changed by the merger?

8. The Muck and Slurry merger has fallen through (see Section 33.2). But World Enterprises is determined to report earnings per share of $2.67. It therefore acquires the Wheelrim and Axle Company. You are given the following facts:

	World Enterprises	Wheelrim and Axle	Merged Firm
Earnings per share	$2.00	$2.50	$2.67
Price per share	$40	$25	?
Price–earnings ratio	20	10	?
Number of shares	100,000	200,000	?
Total earnings	$200,000	$500,000	?
Total market value	$4,000,000	$5,000,000	?

Once again there are no gains from merging. In exchange for Wheelrim and Axle shares, World Enterprises issues just enough of its own shares to ensure its $2.67 earnings per share objective.

a. Complete the above table for the merged firm.

b. How many shares of World Enterprises are exchanged for each share of Wheelrim and Axle?

c. What is the cost of the merger to World Enterprises?

d. What is the change in the total market value of the World Enterprises shares that were outstanding before the merger?

9. Explain the distinction between a tax-free and a taxable merger. Are there circumstances in which you would expect buyer and seller to agree to a taxable merger?

10. Look again at Table 33.3. Suppose that B Corporation's fixed assets are reexamined and found to be worth $1.2 million instead of $.9 million. How would this affect the AB Corporation's balance sheet under purchase accounting? How would the value of AB Corporation change? Would your answer depend on whether the merger is taxable?

11. What was the common theme in Boone Pickens's attempts to take over Cities Service, Gulf Oil, and Phillips Petroleum? Did his efforts create value for these companies' shareholders? How? Was economic efficiency enhanced?

12. In July 1994 the top managers of Sovereign Bancorp were at loggerheads:[48]

- Jay Sidhu, president and chief executive officer of the $5 billion bank, wants to be an acquirer. Only by buying up other banks, he argues, will Sovereign gain the financial clout it needs to survive in the increasingly competitive industry.

- But Fred Jaindl, the bank's chairman and largest stockholder, wants it to *be* acquired. A buy-out, he figures, would deliver big profits to stockholders, including $50 million on his own stock.

a. Are shareholders generally better off as sellers, rather than buyers, in mergers and acquisitions? Why?

b. Under what conditions would the active acquisition strategy advocated by Sidhu make sense for Sovereign *and* its shareholders?

13. In December 1995 NatWest, one of the largest British banks, sold its U.S. retail banking operations to Fleet Financial for about $3.5 billion. This price was much less than industry observers had expected, but NatWest's stock price nevertheless sharply increased. "The central explanation [for the stock price rise] was found in the strong hints in NatWest's announcement that it would not rush out immediately and spend the sale money on some ill-judged and overpriced acquisition."[49] NatWest also announced that it was considering repurchasing shares.

How would you interpret this episode?

1. Examine a hostile acquisition and discuss the tactics employed by both the predator and the target companies. Do you think that the management of the target firm was trying to defeat the bid or to secure the highest price for its stockholders? How did each announcement by the protagonists affect their stock prices?

2. How do you think mergers should be regulated? For example, what defenses should target companies be allowed to employ? Should managers of target firms be compelled to seek out the highest bids? Should they simply be passive and watch from the sidelines?

3. In Italy the first firm to bid for a target is allowed to revise its offer, but subsequent bidders may enter only one bid and they are not allowed to revise it. What do you think is the reason for this rule? Do you think that it should be introduced in the United States?

4. Do you have any rational explanation for the great fluctuations in aggregate merger activity and the apparent relationship between merger activity and stock prices?

CHALLENGE QUESTIONS

---

[48]G. Bruce Knecht, "Nationwide Banking Is around the Corner, but Obstacles Remain," *The Wall Street Journal*, July 26, 1994, p. A1.

[49]George Graham, "NatWest Bids Farewell to an Albatross," *Financial Times*, December 23–24, 1995, p. 2.

CHAPTER THIRTY-FOUR

CONTROL, GOVERNANCE, AND FINANCIAL ARCHITECTURE

FIRST, SOME DEFINITIONS. *Corporate control* means the power to make investment and financing decisions. A hostile takeover bid is an attempt to force a change in corporate control. In popular usage, *corporate governance* refers to the role of the board of directors, shareholder voting, proxy fights, and to other actions taken by shareholders to influence corporate decisions. In the last chapter we saw a striking example: Pressure from institutional shareholders helped force AMP Corporation to abandon its legal defenses and accept a takeover.

Economists use the term governance more generally to cover all the mechanisms by which managers are led to act in the interests of the corporation's owners. A perfect system of corporate governance would give managers all the right incentives to make value-maximizing investment and financing decisions. It would assure that cash is paid out to investors when the company runs out of positive-NPV investment opportunities. It would give managers and employees fair compensation but prevent excessive perks and other private benefits.

This chapter considers control and governance in the United States and other industrialized countries. It picks up where the last chapter left off—mergers and acquisitions are, after all, changes in corporate control. We will cover other mechanisms for changing or exercising control, including leveraged buyouts (LBOs), spin-offs and carve-outs, and conglomerates versus private equity partnerships.

The first section starts with yet another famous takeover battle, the leveraged buyout of RJR Nabisco. Then we move to a general evaluation of LBOs, leveraged restructurings, privatizations, and spin-offs. The main point of these transactions is not just to change control, although existing management is often booted out, but also to change incentives for managers and improve financial performance.

Section 34.3 looks at conglomerates. "Conglomerate" usually means a large, public company with operations in several unrelated businesses or markets. We ask why conglomerates in the United States are a declining species, while in some other countries, for example Korea and India, they seem to be the dominant corporate form. Even in the United States, there are many successful *temporary* conglomerates, although they are not public companies.[1]

Section 34.4 shows how ownership and control vary internationally. We use Germany and Japan as the main examples.

There is a common theme to these three sections. You can't think about control and governance without thinking still more broadly about *financial architecture*, that is, about the financial organization of the business. Financial architecture is partly corporate control (who runs the business?) and partly governance (making sure managers act in shareholders' interests). But it also includes the legal form of organization (e.g., corporation vs. partnership), sources of financing (e.g., public vs. private equity), and relationships with financial institutions. The financial architectures of LBOs and most public corporations are fundamentally different. The financial architecture of a Korean conglomerate (a *chaebol*) is fundamentally different from a conglomerate in the United States. Where financial architecture differs, governance and control are different too.

Much of corporate finance (and much of this book) assumes a particular financial architecture—that of a public corporation with actively traded shares, dispersed ownership, and relatively easy access to financial markets. But there are other ways to organize and finance a business. Arrangements for ownership and control vary greatly country by country. Even in the United States many successful businesses are not corporations, many corporations are not public, and many public corporations have concentrated, not dispersed, ownership.

---

[1]What's a temporary conglomerate? Sorry, you'll have to wait for the punch line.

34.1 LEVERAGED BUYOUTS, SPIN-OFFS, AND RESTRUCTURINGS

Leveraged buyouts differ from ordinary acquisitions in two immediately obvious ways. First, a large fraction of the purchase price is debt-financed. Some, often all, of this debt is junk, that is, below investment-grade. Second, the LBO goes private, and its shares no longer trade on the open market.[2] The LBO's stock is held by a partnership of (usually institutional) investors. When this group is led by the company's management, the acquisition is called a **management buyout (MBO).**

In the 1970s and 1980s many management buyouts were arranged for unwanted divisions of large, diversified companies. Smaller divisions outside the companies' main lines of business sometimes lacked top management's interest and commitment, and divisional management chafed under corporate bureaucracy. Many such divisions flowered when spun off as MBOs. Their managers, pushed by the need to generate cash for debt service and encouraged by a substantial personal stake in the business, found ways to cut costs and compete more effectively.

In the 1980s MBO/LBO activity shifted to buyouts of entire businesses, including large, mature public corporations. Table 34.1 lists the largest LBOs of the 1980s plus examples of transactions from 1997 to 2001. More recent LBOs are generally smaller and not leveraged as aggressively as the deals of the 1980s. But LBO activity is still impressive in aggregate: Buyout firms raised over $60 billion in new capital in 2000.[3]

Acquirer	Target	Industry	Year	Price
KKR	RJR Nabisco	Food, tobacco	1989	$24,720
KKR	Beatrice	Food	1986	6,250
KKR	Safeway	Supermarkets	1986	4,240
Thompson Co.	Southland (7-11)	Convenience stores	1987	4,000
Wings Holdings	NWA, Inc.	Airlines	1989	3,690
KKR	Owens-Illinois	Glass	1987	3,690
TF Investments	Hospital Corp of America	Hospitals	1989	3,690
Macy Acquisitions Corp.	R. H. Macy & Co.	Department stores	1986	3,500
Bain Capital	Sealy Corp.	Mattresses	1997	811
Cyprus Group, with management*	WESCO Distribution, Inc.	Data communications	1998	1,100
Clayton, Dubilier, & Rice	North American Van Lines	Trucking	1998	200
Berkshire Partners	William Carter Co.	Children's clothing	2001	450
Heartland Industrial Partners	Springs Industries	Household textiles	2001	846

TABLE 34.1

The 10 largest LBOs of the 1980s, plus examples of more recent deals. Price in $ millions.

*Management participated in the buyout—a partial MBO.
Source: A. Kaufman and E. J. Englander, "Kohlberg Kravis Roberts & Co. and the Restructuring of American Capitalism," *Business History Review* 67 (Spring 1993), p. 78; *Mergers and Acquisitions* 33 (November/December 1998), p. 43, and various later issues.

---

[2]Sometimes a small *stub* of stock is not acquired and continues to trade.

[3]LBO Signposts, *Mergers & Acquisitions,* March 2001, p. 24.

Table 34.1 starts with the largest, most dramatic, and best-documented LBO of all time: the $25 billion takeover of RJR Nabisco by Kohlberg, Kravis, Roberts (KKR). The players, tactics, and controversies of LBOs are writ large in this case.

RJR Nabisco

On October 28, 1988, the board of directors of RJR Nabisco revealed that Ross Johnson, the company's chief executive officer, had formed a group of investors that was prepared to buy all RJR's stock for $75 per share in cash and take the company private. Johnson's group was backed up and advised by Shearson Lehman Hutton, the investment banking subsidiary of American Express. RJR's share price immediately moved to about $75, handing shareholders a 36 percent gain over the previous day's price of $56. At the same time RJR's bonds fell, since it was clear that existing bondholders would soon have a lot more company.[4]

Johnson's offer lifted RJR onto the auction block. Once the company was in play, its board of directors was obliged to consider other offers, which were not long in coming. Four days later KKR bid $90 per share, $79 in cash plus PIK preferred valued at $11. (PIK means "pay in kind." The preferred dividends would be paid not in cash but in more preferred shares.)[5]

The resulting bidding contest had as many turns and surprises as a Dickens novel. In the end it was Johnson's group against KKR. KKR offered $109 per share, after adding $1 per share (roughly $230 million) in the last hour.[6] The KKR bid was $81 in cash, convertible subordinated debentures valued at about $10, and PIK preferred shares valued at about $18. Johnson's group bid $112 in cash and securities.

But the RJR board chose KKR. Although Johnson's group had offered $3 per share more, its security valuations were viewed as "softer" and perhaps overstated. The Johnson group's proposal also contained a management compensation package that seemed extremely generous and had generated an avalanche of bad press.

But where did the merger benefits come from? What could justify offering $109 per share, about $25 billion in all, for a company that only 33 days previously was selling for $56 per share? KKR and the other bidders were betting on two things. First, they expected to generate billions in additional cash from interest tax shields, reduced capital expenditures, and sales of assets not strictly necessary to RJR's core businesses. Asset sales alone were projected to generate $5 billion. Second, they expected to make the core businesses significantly more profitable, mainly by cutting back on expenses and bureaucracy. Apparently there was plenty to cut, including the RJR "Air Force," which at one point included 10 corporate jets.

In the year after KKR took over, new management was installed that sold assets and cut back operating expenses and capital spending. There were also layoffs. As expected, high interest charges meant a net loss of $976 million for 1989, but pretax operating income actually increased, despite extensive asset sales, including the sale of RJR's European food operations.

Inside the firm, things were going well. But outside there was confusion, and prices in the junk bond market were rapidly declining, implying much higher future

---

[4]N. Mohan and C. R. Chen track the abnormal returns of RJR securities in "A Review of the RJR Nabisco Buyout," *Journal of Applied Corporate Finance* 3 (Summer 1990), pp. 102–108.

[5]See Section 25.8.

[6]The whole story is reconstructed by B. Burrough and J. Helyar in *Barbarians at the Gate: The Fall of RJR Nabisco*, Harper & Row, New York, 1990—see especially Ch. 18—and in a movie with the same title.

interest charges for RJR and stricter terms on any refinancing. In mid-1990 KKR made an additional equity investment, and in December 1990 it announced an offer of cash and new shares in exchange for $753 million of junk bonds. RJR's chief financial officer described the exchange offer as "one further step in the deleveraging of the company."[7] For RJR, the world's largest LBO, it seemed that high debt was a temporary, not permanent, virtue.

RJR, like many other firms that were taken private through LBOs, enjoyed only a short period as a private company. In 1991 RJR went public again with the sale of $1.1 billion of stock.[8] KKR progressively sold off its investment, and its remaining stake in the company was sold in 1995 at roughly the original purchase price.

Barbarians at the Gate?

The RJR Nabisco LBO crystallized views on LBOs, the junk bond market, and the takeover business. For many it exemplified all that was wrong with finance in the 1980s, especially the willingness of "raiders" to carve up established companies, leaving them with enormous debt burdens, basically in order to get rich quick.

There was plenty of confusion, stupidity, and greed in the LBO business. Not all the people involved were nice. On the other hand, LBOs generated enormous increases in market value, and most of the gains went to the selling stockholders, not to the raiders. For example, the biggest winners in the RJR Nabisco LBO were the company's stockholders.

The most important sources of added value came from making RJR Nabisco leaner and meaner. The company's new management was obliged to pay out massive amounts of cash to service the LBO debt. It also had an equity stake in the business and therefore had strong incentives to sell off nonessential assets, cut costs, and improve operating profits.

LBOs are almost by definition *diet deals*. But there were other motives. Here are some of them.

The Junk Bond Markets   LBOs and debt-financed takeovers may have been driven by artificially cheap funding from the junk bond markets. With hindsight, it seems that investors in junk bonds underestimated the risks of default in junk bonds. Default rates climbed painfully from 1988 through 1991, when 10 percent of outstanding junk bonds with a face value of $18.9 billion defaulted.[9] The junk bond market also became much less liquid after the demise in 1990 of Drexel Burnham, the chief market maker, although the market recovered in the mid-1990s.

Leverage and Taxes   Borrowing money saves taxes, as we explained in Chapter 18. But taxes were not the main driving force behind LBOs. The value of interest tax shields was just not big enough to explain the observed gains in market value.[10]

---

[7]G. Andress, "RJR Swallows Hard, Offers $5-a-Share Stock," *The Wall Street Journal*, December 18, 1990, pp. C1–C2.

[8]Northwest Airlines, Safeway Stores, Kaiser Aluminum, and Burlington Industries are other examples of LBOs that reverted to being public companies.

[9]See R. A. Waldman, E. I. Altman, and A. R. Ginsberg, "Defaults and Returns on High Yield Bonds: Analysis through 1997," Salomon Smith Barney, New York, January 30, 1998. See also Section 24.5.

[10]Moreover, there are some tax costs to LBOs. For example, selling shareholders realize capital gains and pay taxes that otherwise could be deferred. See L. Stiglin, S. N. Kaplan, and M. C. Jensen, "Effects of LBOs on Tax Revenues of the U.S. Treasury," *Tax Notes* 42 (February 6, 1989), pp. 727–733.

For example, Richard Ruback estimated the present value of additional interest tax shields generated by the RJR LBO at $1.8 billion.[11] But the gain in market value to RJR stockholders was about $8 billion.

Of course, if interest tax shields were the main motive for LBOs' high debt, then LBO managers would not be so concerned to pay off debt. We saw that this was one of the first tasks facing RJR Nabisco's new management.

Other Stakeholders   We should look at the total gain to *all* investors in an LBO, not just to the selling stockholders. It's possible that the latter's gain is just someone else's loss and that no value is generated overall.

Bondholders are the obvious losers. The debt they thought was well secured may turn into junk when the borrower goes through an LBO. We noted how market prices of RJR Nabisco debt fell sharply when Ross Johnson's first LBO offer was announced. But again, the value losses suffered by bondholders in LBOs are not nearly large enough to explain stockholder gains. For example, Mohan and Chen's estimate[12] of losses to RJR bondholders was at most $575 million—painful to the bondholders, but far below the stockholders' gain.

Leverage and Incentives   Managers and employees of LBOs work harder and often smarter. They have to generate cash for debt service. Moreover, managers' personal fortunes are riding on the LBO's success. They become owners rather than organization men and women.

It's hard to measure the payoff from better incentives, but there is some preliminary evidence of improved operating efficiency in LBOs. Kaplan, who studied 48 MBOs between 1980 and 1986, found average increases in operating income of 24 percent three years after the LBO. Ratios of operating income and net cash flow to assets and sales increased dramatically. He observed cutbacks in capital expenditures but not in employment. Kaplan suggests that these "operating changes are due to improved incentives rather than layoffs or managerial exploitation of shareholders through inside information."[13]

We have reviewed several motives for LBOs. We do not say that all LBOs are good. On the contrary, there have been many mistakes, and even soundly motivated LBOs are dangerous, at least for the buyers, as the bankruptcies of Campeau, Revco, National Gypsum, and other highly leveraged transactions (*HLTs*) proved. Yet, we do quarrel with those who portray LBOs solely as undertaken by Wall Street barbarians breaking up the traditional strengths of corporate America.

Leveraged Restructurings

The essence of a leveraged buyout is of course leverage. Why not take on the leverage and dispense with the buyout?

We reviewed one prominent example in the last chapter. Phillips Petroleum was attacked by Boone Pickens and Mesa Petroleum. Phillips dodged the takeover with a *leveraged restructuring*. It borrowed $4.5 billion and repurchased one-half of its outstanding shares. To service this debt, it sold assets for $2 billion and cut back

---

[11]R. S. Ruback, "RJR Nabisco," case study, Harvard Business School, Cambridge, MA, 1989.

[12]Mohan and Chen, op. cit.

[13]S. Kaplan, "The Effects of Management Buyouts on Operating Performance and Value," *Journal of Financial Economics* 24 (October 1989), pp. 217–254.

capital expenditure and operating costs. It put itself on a cash diet. The demands of servicing $4.5 billion of extra debt made sure it stayed on the diet.

Let's look at another *diet deal*.

Sealed Air's Leveraged Restructuring[14]   In 1989 Sealed Air Corporation undertook a *leveraged restructuring*. It borrowed the money to pay a $328 million special cash dividend. In one stroke the company's debt increased 10 times. Its book equity (accounting net worth) went from $162 million to *minus* $161 million. Debt went from 13 percent of total book assets to 136 percent.

Sealed Air was a profitable company. The problem was that its profits were coming too easily because its main products were protected by patents. When the patents expired, strong competition was inevitable, and the company was not ready for it. In the meantime, there was too much financial slack:

> We didn't need to manufacture efficiently; we didn't need to worry about cash. At Sealed Air, capital tended to have limited value attached to it—cash was perceived as being free and abundant.

So the leveraged recap was used to "disrupt the status quo, promote internal change," and simulate "the pressures of Sealed Air's more competitive future." This shakeup was reinforced by new performance measures and incentives, including increases in stock ownership by employees.

It worked. Sales and operating profits increased steadily without major new capital investments, and net working capital *fell* by half, releasing cash to help service the company's debt. The company's stock price quadrupled in the five years after the restructuring.

Sealed Air's restructuring was not typical. It is an exemplar chosen with hindsight. It was also undertaken by a successful firm under no outside pressure. But it clearly shows the motive for most leveraged restructurings. They are designed to force mature, successful, but overweight companies to disgorge cash, reduce operating costs, and use assets more efficiently.

Financial Architecture of LBOs and Leveraged Restructurings

The financial structures of LBOs and leveraged restructurings are similar. The three main characteristics of LBOs are

1. *High debt.* The debt is not intended to be permanent. It is designed to be paid down. The requirement to generate cash for debt service is designed to curb wasteful investment and force improvements in operating efficiency.
2. *Incentives.* Managers are given a greater stake in the business via stock options or direct ownership of shares.
3. *Private ownership.* The LBO *goes private*. It is owned by a partnership of private investors who monitor performance and can act right away if something goes awry. But private ownership is not intended to be permanent. The most successful LBOs go public again as soon as debt has been paid down sufficiently and improvements in operating performance have been demonstrated.

Leveraged restructurings share the first two characteristics but continue as public companies.

---

[14]See K. H. Wruck, "Financial Policy as a Catalyst for Organizational Change: Sealed Air's Leveraged Special Dividend," *Journal of Applied Corporate Finance* 7 (Winter 1995), pp. 20–37.

34.2 FUSION AND FISSION IN CORPORATE FINANCE

Figure 34.1 shows some of AT&T's acquisitions and divestitures. Prior to 1984, AT&T controlled most of the local, and virtually all of the long-distance telephone service in the United States. (Customers used to speak of the ubiquitous "Ma [Mother] Bell.") In 1984 the company accepted an antitrust settlement requiring local telephone service to be spun off to seven new, independent companies.[15] AT&T was left with its long-distance business plus Bell Laboratories, Western Electric (telecommunications manufacturing), and various other assets. As the communications industry became increasingly competitive, AT&T acquired several other businesses, notably in computers, cellular telephone service, and cable television. Some of these acquisitions are shown as the burgundy incoming arrows in Figure 34.1.

AT&T was an unusually active acquirer. It was a giant company trying to respond to rapidly changing technologies and markets. But AT&T was simultaneously *divesting* dozens of other businesses. For example, its credit card operations (the AT&T Universal Card) were sold to Citicorp. In 1996, AT&T created two new companies by spinning off Lucent (incorporating Bell Laboratories and Western Electric) and its computer business (NCR). AT&T had paid $7.5 billion to acquire NCR in 1990. These and several other important divestitures are shown as the burgundy outgoing arrows in Figure 34.1.

In the market for corporate control, fusion—mergers and acquisitions—gets the most publicity. But fission—the separation of assets and operations from the whole—can be just as important. We will now see how these separations are carried out by spin-offs, carve-outs, asset sales, and privatizations.

Spin-offs

A **spin-off** is a new, independent company created by detaching part of a parent company's assets and operations. Shares in the new company are distributed to the parent company's stockholders. Here are some recent examples.

- Sears Roebuck spun off Allstate, its insurance subsidiary, in 1995.
- In 1998 the Brazilian government completed privatization of Telebras, the Brazilian national telecommunications company. Before the final auction, the company was split into 12 separate pieces—one long-distance, three local, and eight wireless communications companies. In other words, 12 companies were spun out of the one original.
- In 2001 Thermo Electron spun off its healthcare and paper machinery and systems divisions as two new companies, Viasys and Kadant, respectively.
- In 2001 Canadian Pacific Ltd. spun off its oil and gas, shipping, coal mining, and hotel businesses as four new companies traded on the Toronto stock exchange.

Spin-offs are not taxed so long as shareholders in the parent are given at least 80 percent of the shares in the new company.[16]

---

[15]Subsequent mergers reduced these seven companies to four: Bell South, SBC Communications, Qwest, and Verizon.

[16]If less than 80 percent of the shares are distributed, the value of the distribution is taxed as a dividend to the investor.

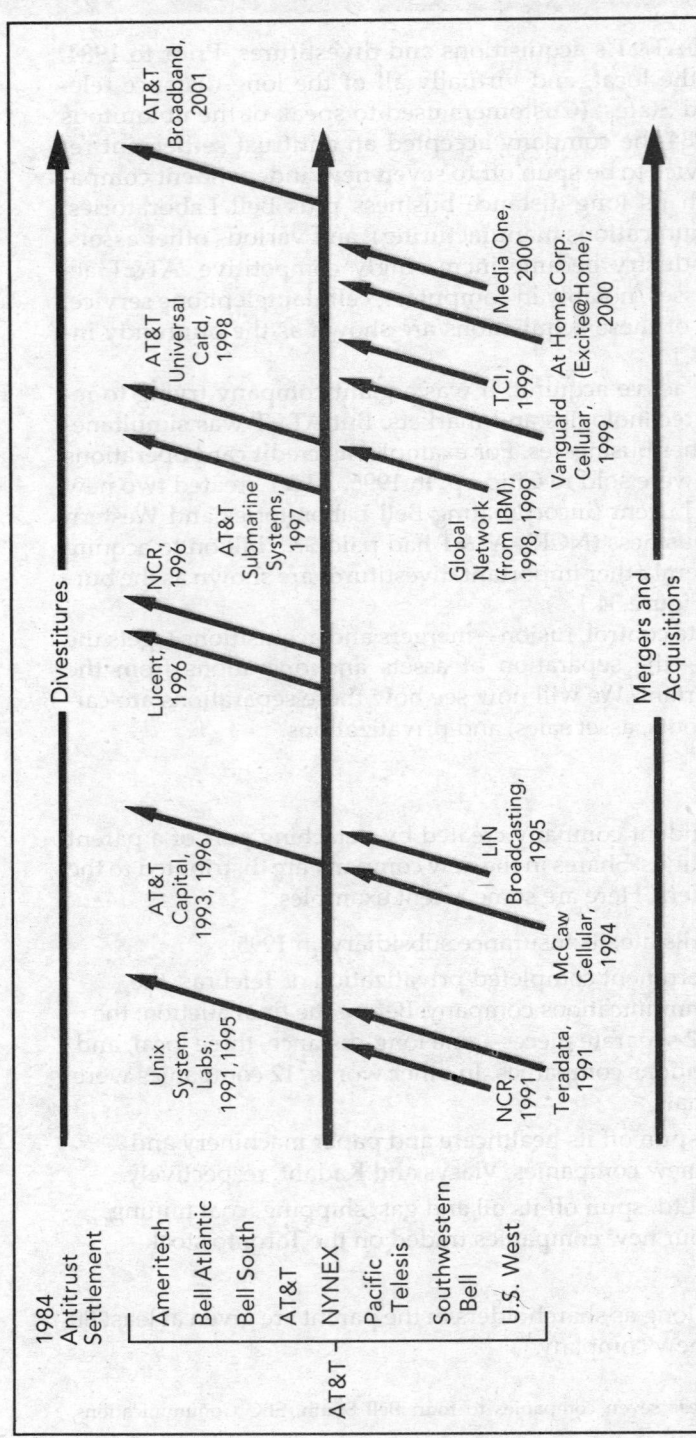

FIGURE 34.1

The effects of AT&T's antitrust settlement in 1984, and a few of AT&T's acquisitions and divestitures from 1991 to 2001. Divestitures are shown by the outgoing burgundy arrows. When two years are given, the transaction was completed in two steps.

Spin-offs widen investors' choice by allowing them to invest in just one part of the business. More important, spin-offs can improve incentives for managers. Companies sometimes refer to divisions or lines of business as "poor fits." By spinning these businesses off, management of the parent company can concentrate on its main activity.[17] If the businesses are independent, it is easier to see the value and performance of each and reward managers accordingly. Managers can be given stock or stock options in the spun-off company. Also, spin-offs relieve investors of the worry that funds will be siphoned from one business to support unprofitable capital investments in another.

Announcement of a spin-off is generally greeted as good news by investors.[18] Investors in U.S. companies seem to reward focus and penalize diversification. Consider the dissolution of John D. Rockefeller's Standard Oil trust in 1911. The company he founded, Standard Oil of New Jersey, was split up into seven separate corporations. Within a year of the breakup, the combined value of the successor companies' shares had more than doubled, increasing Rockefeller's personal fortune to about $900 million (about $15 billion in 2002 dollars). Theodore Roosevelt, who as president had led the trustbusters, ran again for president in 1912:[19]

> "The price of stock has gone up over 100 percent, so that Mr. Rockefeller and his associates have actually seen their fortunes doubled," he thundered during the campaign. "No wonder that Wall Street's prayer now is: 'Oh Merciful Providence, give us another dissolution.'"

Why is the value of the parts so often greater than the value of the whole? The best place to look for an answer to that question is in the financial architecture of conglomerates. But first, we take a brief look at carve-outs, asset sales, and privatizations.

Carve-outs

Carve-outs are similar to spin-offs, except that shares in the new company are not given to existing shareholders but are sold in a public offering. Recent carve-outs include Pharmacia's sale of part of its Monsanto subsidiary, and Philip Morris's sale of part of its Kraft Foods subsidiary. The latter sale raised $8.7 billion.

Most carve-outs leave the parent with majority control of the subsidiary, usually about 80 percent ownership.[20] This may not reassure investors who worry about

---

[17]The other way of getting rid of "poor fits" is to sell them to another company. One study found that over 30 percent of assets acquired in a sample of hostile takeovers from 1984 to 1986 were subsequently sold. See S. Bhagat, A. Shleifer, and R. Vishny, "Hostile Takeovers in the 1980s: The Return to Corporate Specialization," *Brookings Papers on Economic Activity: Microeconomics* (1990), pp. 1–12.

[18]Research on spin-offs includes K. Schipper and A. Smith, "Effects of Recontracting on Shareholder Wealth: The Case of Voluntary Spin-offs," *Journal of Financial Economics* 12 (December 1983), pp. 409–436; G. Hite and J. Owers, "Security Price Reactions around Corporate Spin-off Announcements," *Journal of Financial Economics* 12 (December 1983), pp. 437–467; and J. Miles and J. Rosenfeld, "An Empirical Analysis of the Effects of Spin-off Announcements on Shareholder Wealth," *Journal of Finance* 38 (December 1983), pp. 1597–1615. P. Cusatis, J. Miles, and J. R. Woolridge report improvements of operating performance in spun-off companies. See "Some New Evidence that Spin-offs Create Value," *Journal of Applied Corporate Finance* 7 (Summer 1994), pp. 100–107.

[19]D. Yergin: *The Prize*, Simon & Schuster, New York, 1991, p. 113.

[20]The parent must retain an 80 percent interest to consolidate the subsidiary with the parent's tax accounts. Otherwise the subsidiary is taxed as a freestanding corporation.

lack of focus or a poor fit, but it does allow the parent to set managers' compensation based on the performance of the subsidiary's stock price.

Some companies carve out a minority interest in a subsidiary and later sell or spin off the remaining shares. For example, Sara Lee, the food company, carved out a 19.5 percent stake in the luxury leather goods retailer Coach in 2000. The remaining 80.5 percent of the Coach shares were sold to Sara Lee stockholders in 2001.[21]

Perhaps the most enthusiastic carver-outer of the 1980s and 1990s was Thermo Electron, with operations in healthcare, power generation equipment, instrumentation, environmental monitoring and cleanup, and various other areas. At year-end 1997, it had seven publicly traded subsidiaries, which in turn had carved out 15 further public companies. The 15 were grandchildren of the ultimate parent, Thermo Electron.[22]

Some companies have distributed *tracking stock* tied to the performance of particular divisions. This does not require a spin-off or carve-out, only the creation of a new class of common stock. For example, in 1997 Georgia Pacific distributed a special class of shares tied to the performance of its Timber Group. The company noted that having two classes of shares "provides the opportunity to structure incentives for employees of each Group that are tied directly to the share price performance of that Group."[23]

Asset Sales

The simplest way to divest an asset is to sell it. **Asset sale** refers to the acquisition of *part* of one firm by another. The record asset sale is Comcast's acquisition of AT&T Broadband, AT&T's cable television division, for $42 billion in 2001.

We have mentioned the sale of AT&T's credit card division to Citibank. Asset sales are common in the credit card business. The largest credit card issuers, including Citibank, MBNA, and First USA, grew during the 1980s and 1990s by acquiring the credit card operations of hundreds of smaller banks.

Asset sales are also common in manufacturing. Maksimovic and Phillips examined a sample of about 50,000 U.S. manufacturing plants each year from 1974 to 1992. About 35,000 plants in the sample changed hands during that period. About one-half of the ownership changes were the result of mergers or acquisitions of entire firms. The other half of the ownership changes came about by asset sales, that is, sale of part or all of a division. On average, about 4 percent of the plants in the sample changed hands each year, about 2 percent by merger or acquisition, and about 2 percent by asset sales.[24]

---

[21]Sara Lee stockholders were allowed to exchange Sara Lee shares for Coach shares. The terms of the exchange gave Sara Lee's stockholders the opportunity to get Coach shares at a discount, so all of the Coach shares were issued in short order.

[22]In 1998 Thermo Electron announced a plan to consolidate several of its children and grandchildren in order to move to a less complicated structure. In 2001, it began to spin off some of its peripheral operations as separate companies.

[23]Georgia Pacific Corporation, Proxy Statement and Prospectus, November 11, 1997, p. 35. The Timber Group was sold to Plum Creek Timber Company in 2001. Timber Group tracking stock was exchanged for Plum Creek shares.

[24]V. Maksimovic and G. Phillips, "The Market for Corporate Assets: Who Engages in Mergers and Asset Sales and Are There Efficiency Gains?" *Journal of Finance* 56 (December 2001), Table I, p. 2030.

Announcements of asset sales are good news for investors in the selling firm, and productivity of the assets sold increases, on average, after the sale.[25] It appears that asset sales transfer business units to the companies that can manage them most effectively.

Privatization

A **privatization** is a sale of a government-owned company to private investors. For example, the government of Germany originally owned Volkswagen but sold it in 1961. Britain sold British Telecom in 1984. The United States sold Conrail in 1987.

Most privatizations are more like carve-outs than spin-offs, because shares are sold for cash, not distributed to the ultimate "shareholders," that is, to the people of the selling country. But several former Communist countries, including Russia, Poland, and the Czech Republic, privatized by means of vouchers distributed to citizens. The vouchers could be used to bid for shares in newly privatized companies. Thus the companies were not sold for cash, but for vouchers.[26]

Privatizations raised enormous sums for selling governments. France raised $17.6 billion in two share issues for France Telecom in 1997 and 1998. Japan raised over $80 billion in the privatization of NTT (Nippon Telephone and Telegraph) in 1987 and 1988. Privatizations have also been common in airlines (e.g., Japan Airlines and Air New Zealand) and banking (e.g., the French bank Paribas).

The motives for privatization seem to boil down to the following three points:

1. *Increased efficiency.* Through privatization, the enterprise is exposed to the discipline of competition and insulated from political influence on investment and operating decisions. Managers and employees can be given stronger incentives to cut costs and add economic value.
2. *Share ownership.* Privatizations encourage share ownership. Many privatizations give special terms or allotments to employees or small investors.
3. *Revenue for the government.* Last but not least!

There were fears that privatizations would lead to massive layoffs and unemployment, but that does not appear to be the case. While it is true that privatized companies operate more efficiently and thus reduce employment, they also grow faster as privatized companies, which increases employment. In many cases the net effect on employment is positive.

On other dimensions, the impact of privatization is almost always positive. A review of research on privatization concludes that privatized firms "almost always become more efficient, more profitable, . . . financially healthier and increase their capital investment spending."[27] It seems clear that changing from state to private ownership is in general a valuable change in financial architecture.

---

[25]See Maksimovic and Phillips, op. cit.

[26]There is extensive research on voucher privatizations. See, for example, M. Boyco, A. Shleifer, and R. Vishny, "Voucher Privatizations," *Journal of Financial Economics* 35 (April 1994), pp. 249–266; and R. Aggarwal and J. T. Harper, "Equity Valuation in the Czech Voucher Privatization Auctions," *Financial Management* 29 (Winter 2000), pp. 77–100.

[27]W. L. Megginson and J. M. Netter, "From State to Market: A Survey of Empirical Studies on Privatization," *Journal of Economic Literature* 39 (June 2001), p. 381.

34.3 CONGLOMERATES

We now examine a different form of financial architecture, the conglomerate. Conglomerates are firms investing in several unrelated industries. Large public conglomerates are now rare in the United States, though common elsewhere. We will try to figure out why. We will also examine the financial architecture of the private conglomerates that invest in venture capital and LBOs.

Pros and (Mostly) Cons of U.S. Conglomerates

Conglomerates were the corporate celebrities of the 1960s. They grew by leaps and bounds through aggressive programs of acquisitions in unrelated industries. By the 1970s, the largest conglomerates had achieved amazing scopes and spans. Table 34.2 shows that by 1979 ITT was operating in 38 different industries and ranked eighth in total sales among U.S. corporations.

In 1995 ITT, which had already sold or spun off several lines of business, split its remaining operations into three separate firms. One acquired ITT's interests in hotels and gambling; a second took over ITT's automotive parts, defense, and electronics businesses; and a third specialized in insurance and financial services (ITT Hartford). Most of the conglomerates created in the 1960s were broken up in the 1980s and early 1990s; however, a few successful new conglomerates have sprung up. Tyco International, AMP's white knight, is one of these.[28]

What advantages were claimed for conglomerates? First, diversification across industries was supposed to stabilize earnings and reduce risk. That's hardly compelling, because shareholders can diversify much more efficiently and flexibly on their own.[29] Second, and more important, was the idea that good managers were fungible; in other words, that modern management would work as well in the manufacture of auto parts as in running a hotel chain. Neil Jacoby, writing in 1969, argued that computers and new methods of quantitative, scientific management had "created opportunities for profits through mergers that remove assets from the

TABLE 34.2

The largest U.S. conglomerates in 1979, ranked by sales compared to all U.S. industrial corporations. Most of these companies have been broken up.

Source: A. Chandler and R. S. Tetlow, eds., *The Coming of Managerial Capitalism*, Richard D. Irwin, Inc., Homewood, IL, 1985, p. 772; see also J. Baskin and P. J. Miranti, Jr., *A History of Corporate Finance*, Cambridge University Press, Cambridge, UK: 1997, chap. 7.

Sales Rank	Company	Number of Industries
8	International Telephone & Telegraph (ITT)	38
15	Tenneco	28
42	Gulf & Western Industries	41
51	Litton Industries	19
66	LTV	18
73	Illinois Central Industries	26
103	Textron	16
104	Greyhound	19
128	Martin Marietta	14

---

[28]See Section 33.5.

[29]See the Appendix to Chapter 33.

inefficient control of old-fashioned managers and place them under men schooled in the new management science."[30]

There was some truth in this. The most successful early conglomerates did force dramatic improvements in some mature and slackly managed businesses. The problem is, of course, that a company doesn't need to be diversified to take over and improve a lagging business.

Third, conglomerates' wide diversification meant that their top managements could operate an *internal capital market*. Free cash flow generated by divisions in mature industries could be funneled within the company to other divisions with profitable growth opportunities. There was no need for fast-growing divisions to raise financing from outside investors.

There are some good arguments for internal capital markets. The company's own managers probably know more about its investment opportunities than do outside investors, and transaction costs of issuing securities are avoided. Nevertheless, it appears that attempts by conglomerates to allocate capital investment across many unrelated industries are more likely to subtract value than add it. Trouble is, internal capital markets are not really markets but combinations of central planning (by the conglomerates' top management and financial staff) and intracompany bargaining. Divisional capital budgets depend on politics as well as pure economics. Large, profitable divisions with plenty of free cash flow may have more bargaining power than growth opportunities; they may get generous capital budgets while smaller divisions with good prospects but less bargaining power are reined in.

Berger and Ofek estimate the average conglomerate discount at 12 to 15 percent.[31] *Conglomerate discount* means that the market value of the whole conglomerate is less than the sum of the values of its parts. The chief cause of this discount, at least in Berger and Ofek's sample, seemed to be overinvestment and misallocation of investment. In other words, investors were marking down the value of the conglomerates' shares from worry that their managements would make negative-NPV investments in mature divisions and forego positive-NPV opportunities elsewhere.

Conglomerates face further problems. Their divisions' market values can't be observed independently, and it is difficult to set incentives for division managers. This is particularly serious when managers are asked to commit to risky ventures. For example, how would a biotech startup fare as a division of a traditional conglomerate? Would the conglomerate be as patient and risk-tolerant as investors in the stock market? How are the scientists and clinicians doing the biotech R&D rewarded if they succeed? We don't mean to say that high-tech innovation and risk-taking is impossible in public conglomerates, but the difficulties are evident.

Internal Capital Markets in the Oil Business Misallocations in internal capital markets are not restricted to pure conglomerates. For example, Lamont found that, when oil prices fell by half in 1986, diversified oil companies cut back capital investment in their *non-oil* divisions.[32] The non-oil divisions were forced to "share

---

[30]Quoted in A. Chandler and R. S. Tetlow, eds., *The Coming of Managerial Capitalism*, Richard D. Irwin, Inc., Homewood, IL: 1985, p. 746.

[31]P. Berger and E. Ofek, "Diversification's Effect on Firm Value," *Journal of Financial Economics* 37 (January 1995), pp. 39–65.

[32]O. Lamont, "Cash Flow and Investment: Evidence from Internal Capital Markets," *Journal of Finance* 52 (March 1997), pp. 83–109.

the pain," even though the drop in oil prices did not diminish their investment opportunities. *The Wall Street Journal* reported one example:[33]

> Chevron Corp. cut its planned 1986 capital and exploratory budget by about 30 percent because of the plunge in oil prices . . . A Chevron spokesman said that spending cuts would be across the board and that no particular operations will bear the brunt.
>
> About 65 percent of the $3.5 billion budget will be spent on oil and gas exploration and production—about the same proportion as before the budget revision.
>
> Chevron also will cut spending for refining and marketing, oil and natural gas pipelines, minerals, chemicals, and shipping operations.

Why cut back on capital outlays for minerals, say, or chemicals? Low oil prices are generally good news, not bad, for chemical manufacturing, because oil distillates are an important raw material.

By the way, most of the oil companies in Lamont's sample were large, blue-chip companies. They could have raised additional capital from investors to maintain spending in their non-oil divisions. They chose not to. We do not understand why.

All large companies must allocate capital among divisions or lines of business. Therefore they all have internal capital markets and must worry about mistakes and misallocations. But this danger probably increases as a company moves from a focus on one, or a few related industries, to unrelated conglomerate diversification. Look again at Table 34.2: How could the top management of ITT keep accurate track of investment opportunities in 38 different industries?

Fifteen Years after Reading this Chapter

You have just seized control of Establishment Industries, the blue-chip conglomerate, after a high-stakes, high-profile takeover battle. You are a financial celebrity, hounded by business reporters every time you step out of your stretch limo. You're contemplating a Ferrari and a trophy spouse. Fundraisers from your college or university are suddenly very attentive. But first you've got to deliver on promises to add shareholder value to your renamed New Establishment Corporation.

Fortunately you remember *Principles of Corporate Finance.* First you identify New Establishment's neglected divisions—the poor fits that have not received their share of capital or top management attention. These you spin off; no more internal capital market. As independent companies, these divisions can set their own capital budgets, but to obtain financing, they have to convince outside investors that their growth opportunities are truly positive-NPV. The managers of these spun-off companies can buy stock or be given stock options as part of their compensation packages. Therefore incentives to maximize value are stronger. Investors understand this, so New Establishment's stock price jumps as soon as the spin-offs are announced.

Establishment Industries also has some large, mature, cash-cow businesses. You add still more value by selling some of these divisions to LBO partnerships. You bargain hard and get a good price, so the stock price jumps again.

The remaining divisions will be the core of New Establishment. You consider pushing through a leveraged restructuring of these core activities to make sure that free cash flow is paid out to investors rather than invested in negative-NPV ventures. But you decide instead to implement a performance measurement and compensation system based on residual income.[34] You also make sure managers and key employees have significant equity stakes. You take over as CEO, and New Establishment survives and prospers. Your celebrity status fades away, except that once a year you are listed in *Forbes* magazine's annual compilation of the 400 wealthiest executives and investors. It could happen.

Financial Architecture of Traditional U.S. Conglomerates

This fanciful tale sums up the argument for *focus* and against conglomerate diversification. We must be careful not to push the argument too far, however. GE, an exceptionally successful company, operates in a wide range of unrelated industries, including jet engines, equipment leasing, broadcasting, home appliances, and medical equipment.

But we can confidently identify the challenges set by the financial architecture of conglomerates.

To add value in the long run, the conglomerate structure sets two tasks for top management: (1) Make sure divisional management and operating performance are better than could be achieved if the divisions were independent and (2) operate an internal capital market that beats the external capital market. In other words, conglomerate management has to make better capital investment decisions than could be achieved by independent companies responsible for their own financing.

Task (1) is difficult because divisions' market values can't be observed separately, and it is difficult to set incentives for divisional managers. Task (2) is difficult because the conglomerate's central planners have to fully understand investment opportunities in many different industries and because internal capital markets are prone to allocations by bargaining and politics.

Now we turn to a class of conglomerates that does seem to add value. We will find, however, that they have a different financial architecture.

Temporary Conglomerates

Table 34.3 lists the businesses in which a Kohlberg, Kravis, Roberts (KKR) LBO fund operated in 1998. Looks like a conglomerate, right? But this fund is not a public company. It is a private partnership.

Books, cards, other publishing (2 companies)
Communications
Consumer services (Kindercare Learning Centers)
Fiber optics (coupling and connections)
General food products
Golf and healthcare products (1 company)
Hospital and institutional management
Insurance (in Canada)
Other consumer products (1 company)
Printing and binding
Transportation equipment and parts

TABLE 34.3

KKR formed an LBO partnership in 1993. By 1998 this fund held companies in the following industries. The partnership was a (temporary) conglomerate.

---

[34]That is, on EVA. See Section 12.4.

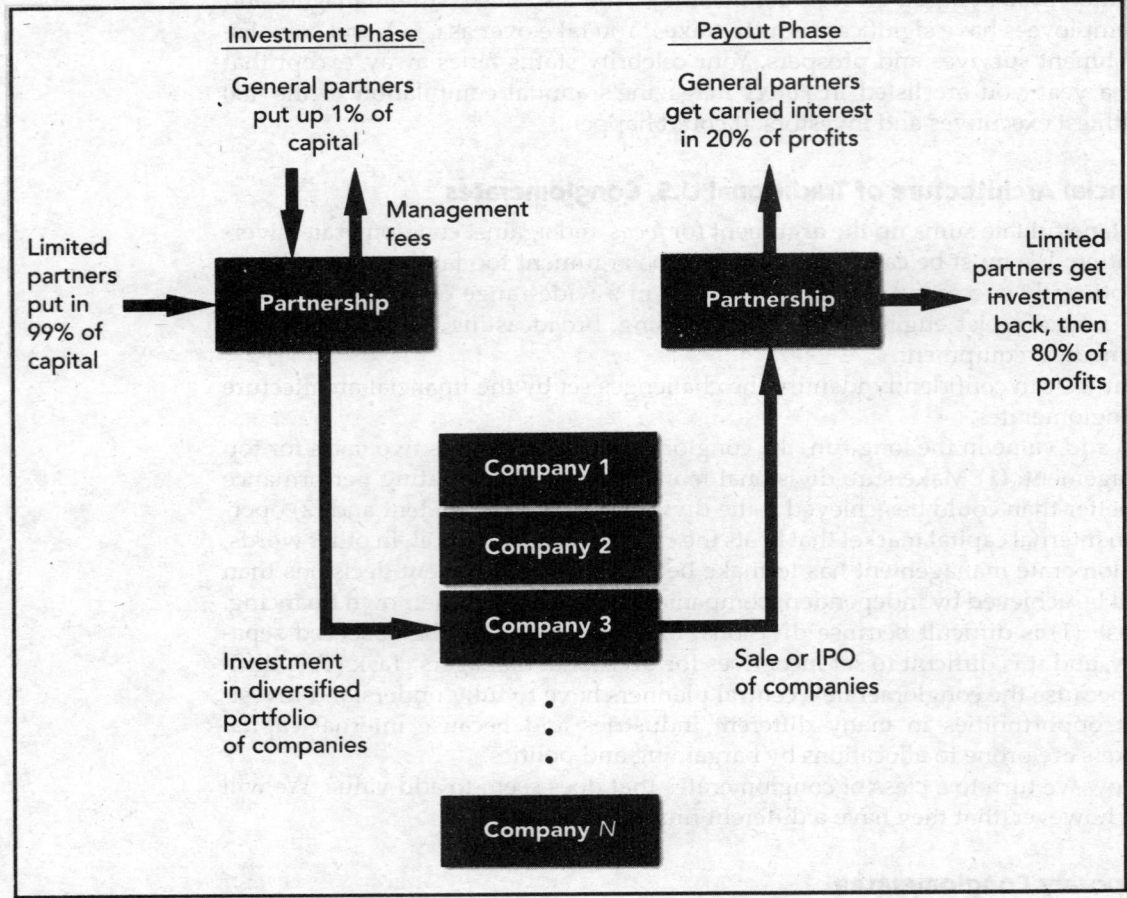

FIGURE 34.2

Organization of a typical private equity partnership. The limited partners, having put up almost all of the money, get first crack at the proceeds from sale or IPO of the portfolio companies. Once their investment is returned, they get 80 percent of any profits. The general partners, who organize and manage the partnership, get a 20 percent carried interest in profits.

This KKR fund is a private investment partnership and a *temporary conglomerate*. It buys up companies, generally in unrelated industries, but it does not buy and hold. It tries to buy, fix, and sell. It buys to restructure, to dispose of incidental assets, and to improve operations and management. If the program of improvement is a success, it sells out, either by taking the company public again or by selling it to another firm.

KKR is famous for LBOs. But its financial structure is shared by venture capital partnerships formed to invest in startup companies and by partnerships formed to buy up private companies without LBO financing. These are all *private equity partnerships*. Figure 34.2 shows how such a partnership is organized. The *general partners* organize and manage the venture. The *limited partners*[35] put up most of the

---

[35]Limited partners enjoy limited liability. See Section 14.2.

money. Limited partners are generally institutional investors, such as pension funds, endowments, and insurance companies. Wealthy individuals or families may also participate.

Once the partnership is formed, the general partners seek out companies to invest in. Venture capital partnerships look for high-tech startups, LBO partnerships for mature businesses with ample free cash flow and a need for new or reinvigorated management. Some partnerships specialize in particular industries, for example biotechnology or real estate. But most end up with a portfolio of companies in different industries.

The partnership agreement has a limited term, 10 years or less. The portfolio companies must be sold and the proceeds must be distributed. The general partners *cannot reinvest* the limited partners' money. Of course, once a fund is proved successful, the general partners can usually go back to the limited partners, or to other institutional investors, and form another one.

The general partners get a management fee, typically 1 or 2 percent of capital committed, plus a *carried interest*, usually 20 percent of the fund's profits. In other words the limited partners get paid off first, but then get only 80 percent of any further returns. (The general partners have a call option on 20 percent of the partnership's value, with an exercise price equal to the limited partners' investment.)

Table 34.4 summarizes a comparison by Baker and Montgomery of the financial structures of an LBO fund and a typical public conglomerate. Both are diversified, but the fund's limited partners do not have to worry that free cash flow will be plowed back into unprofitable investments. The fund has no internal capital market. Monitoring and compensation of management also differ. In the LBO fund, each company is run as a separate business. The managers report directly to the owners, the fund's partners. Each company's managers own shares or stock options in that company, not in the fund. Their compensation depends on their company's market value in a sale or IPO.

In a public conglomerate, these businesses would be divisions, not freestanding companies. Ownership of the conglomerate would be dispersed, not concentrated. The divisions would not be valued by investors in the stock market, but by the conglomerate's corporate staff, the very people who run the internal capital market.

LBO Partnerships	Public Conglomerates
Widely diversified, investment in unrelated industries	Widely diversified, investment in unrelated industries
Limited-life partnership forces sale of portfolio companies.	Public corporations designed to operate divisions for the long run
No financial links or transfers between portfolio companies	Internal capital market
General partners "do the deal," then monitor; lenders also monitor.	Hierarchy of corporate staff evaluates divisions' plans and performance.
Managers' compensation depends on exit value of company.	Divisional managers' compensation depends mostly on earnings—"smaller upside, softer downside."

TABLE 34.4

LBO funds vs. public conglomerates. Both diversify, investing in a portfolio of unrelated businesses, but their financial structures are otherwise fundamentally different.

Source: Adapted from G. Baker and C. Montgomery, "Conglomerates and LBO Associations: A Comparison of Organizational Forms," working paper, Harvard Business School, Cambridge, MA, July 1996.

Managers' compensation wouldn't depend on divisions' market values because no shares in the divisions would be traded and plans for sale or spin-off would not be part of the conglomerate's financial architecture.

The advantages of LBO partnerships are obvious: strong incentives to managers, concentrated ownership (no separation of ownership and control), and limited life, which reassures limited partners that cash flow will not be reinvested wastefully.

These advantages carry over to other types of private equity partnerships, including venture capital funds. We do not say that this financial structure is appropriate for most businesses. It is designed for change, not for the long run. But traditional conglomerates don't seem to work well for the long run, either.

Conglomerates around the World

Nevertheless, conglomerates are common outside the United States. In some emerging economies, they are the dominant financial structure. In Korea, for example, the 10 largest conglomerates control roughly two-thirds of the corporate economy. These *chaebols* are also strong exporters so that names like Samsung and Hyundai are recognized worldwide.

Conglomerates are common in Latin America. One of the more successful, the holding company[36] Quinenco, is in a dizzying variety of businesses, including hotels and brewing in Chile, pasta making in Peru, and the manufacture of copper and fiber optic cable in Brazil.

Why are conglomerates so common in such countries? There are several possible reasons.

Size   You can't be big *and* focused in a small, closed economy: The scale of one-industry companies is limited by the local market. Scale may require diversification. There are various reasons why size can be an advantage. For example, larger companies have easier access to international financial markets. This is important if local financial markets are inefficient.

Size means political power; this is especially important in managed economies or in countries where the government economic policy is unpredictable. In Korea, for example, the government has controlled access to bank loans. Bank lending has been directed to government-approved uses. The Korean conglomerate chaebols have usually been first in line.

Undeveloped Financial Markets   If a country's financial markets are substandard, an internal capital market may not be so bad after all.

"Substandard" does not just mean lack of scale or trading activity. It may mean government regulations limiting access to bank financing or requiring government approval before bonds or shares are issued.[37] It may mean information inefficiency: If accounting standards are loose and companies are secretive, monitoring by outside investors becomes especially costly and difficult, and agency costs proliferate.

---

[36]A holding company owns controlling blocks of shares in two or more subsidiary companies. The holding company and its subsidiaries operate as a group under common top management.

[37]In the United States, the SEC does *not* have the power to deny share issues. Its mandate is only to assure that investors are given adequate information.

In many countries, including some advanced economies, minority investors are not well protected by law and securities regulation. Sometimes there are blatant transfers of wealth from outside shareholders to insiders' pockets. It's no surprise that financial markets in such countries are relatively small.

Recent research by Rafael LaPorta and his colleagues finds a strong association between legal systems and the development of financial markets and the volume of external finance.[38] Minority shareholders seem to be best protected in common-law systems such as those in the United States, Great Britain, and other English-speaking countries. Civil-law systems, such as those in France and Spanish-speaking countries, offer less effective protection; consequently, financial markets are less important in such countries. The volume of external financing is low. Financing tends to flow instead through banks, within large, diversified companies, or among members of groups of associated companies. Many of these companies or groups are controlled by families.

The Bottom Line on Conglomerates

Are conglomerates good or bad? Does corporate diversification make sense? It depends on the task at hand and on the business, financial, and legal environments.

If the task is fundamental change, then the required management skills and knowledge may not be industry-specific. For example, the general partners in LBO funds are not industry experts. They specialize in identifying potential diet deals, negotiating financing, buying and selling assets, setting incentives, and choosing and monitoring management. It's no surprise that LBO funds end up with diversified portfolios; they invest wherever opportunities crop up. But these same skills are not best for long-run operation and growth. Thus LBO funds and other private equity partnerships are designed to force the managers of change to hand over the reins once change is accomplished.

If the task is managing for the long run, and the company has access to well-functioning financial markets, then focus usually beats diversification. Conglomerates have a hard time setting the right incentives for divisional managers and avoiding cross-subsidies and overinvestment in the internal capital market.

In less developed countries, conglomerates can be effective. Local history and practice have led to diversified companies or groups of companies. Also, diversification means scale, and size counts when local financial markets are small or undeveloped, when the company needs to attract the best professional managers, and when assistance or protection from the government is required.

 ## 34.4 GOVERNANCE AND CONTROL IN THE UNITED STATES, GERMANY, AND JAPAN

For public corporations in the United States, the agency problems created by the separation of ownership and control are offset by

- Incentives for management, particularly compensation tied to changes in earnings and stock price.

[38]R. LaPorta, F. Lopez-de-Silanes, A. Shleifer, and R. Vishny, "Law and Finance," *Journal of Political Economy* 106 (December 1998), pp. 1113–1155 and "Legal Determinants of External Finance," *Journal of Finance* 52 (July 1997), pp. 1131–1150.

- The legal duty of managers and directors to act in shareholders' interest, backed up by monitoring by auditors, lenders, security analysts, and large institutional investors.

- The threat of a takeover, either by another public company or a private investment partnership.

But don't assume that ownership and control are always separated. A large block of shares may give effective control even when there is no majority owner.[39] For example, Bill Gates owns over 20 percent of Microsoft. Barring some extreme catastrophe, that block means that he can run the company as he wants to and as long as he wants to. Henry Ford's descendants still hold a class of Ford Motor Company shares with extra voting rights and thereby retain great power should they decide to exercise it.[40]

Nevertheless, the concentration of ownership of public U.S. corporations is much less than in some other industrialized countries. The differences are not so apparent in Canada, Britain, Australia, and other English-speaking countries, but there are dramatic differences in Japan and continental Europe. We start with Germany.

Ownership and Control in Germany

Figure 34.3 summarizes the ownership in 1990 of Daimler-Benz, one of the largest German companies. The immediate owners were Deutsche Bank, the largest German bank, with 28 percent; Mercedes Automobil Holding, with 25 percent; and the Kuwait government, with 14 percent. The remaining 32 percent of the shares were widely held by about 300,000 individual and institutional investors.

But this was only the top layer. Mercedes Automobil Holding was half owned by two holding companies, "Stella" and "Stern" for short. The rest of its shares were widely held. Stella's shares were in turn split four ways: between two banks; Robert Bosch, an industrial company; and another holding company, "Komet." Stern's ownership was split four ways too, but we ran out of space.[41]

The differences between German and U.S. ownership patterns leap out from Figure 34.3. Note the concentration of ownership of Daimler-Benz shares in large blocks and the several layers of owners. A similar figure for General Motors would just say, "General Motors, 100 percent widely held."

In Germany these blocks are often held by other companies—a *cross-holding* of shares—or by holding companies for families. Franks and Mayer, who examined the ownership of 171 large German companies in 1990, found 47 with blocks of

---

[39] A surprising number of public U.S. corporations do have majority owners. A study by Clifford Holderness and Dennis Sheehan identified over 650. See "The Role of Majority Shareholders in Publicly Held Corporations: An Exploratory Analysis," *Journal of Financial Economics* 20 (January/March 1988), pp. 317–346.

[40] You would predict that companies with concentrated ownership would show better financial performance simply because the blockholders face less of a free-rider problem when they represent shareholders' interests. This prediction appears to be true. However, investors who accumulate very large stakes and gain effective control of the firm may act in their own interests and against the interests of the remaining minority shareholders. See R. Morck, A. Shleifer, and R. Vishny, "Management Ownership and Market Valuation: An Empirical Analysis," *Journal of Financial Economics* 20 (January/March 1988), pp. 293–315.

[41] A five-layer ownership tree for Daimler-Benz is given in S. Prowse, "Corporate Governance in an International Perspective: A Survey of Corporate Control Mechanisms among Large Firms in the U.S., U.K., Japan and Germany," *Financial Markets, Institutions, and Instruments* 4 (February 1995), Table 16.

FIGURE 34.3

Ownership of
Daimler-Benz, 1990.

Source: J. Franks and C.
Mayer, "The Ownership
and Control of German
Corporations," *Review
of Financial Studies* 14
(Winter 2001), Figure 1,
p. 949.

shares held by other companies and 35 with blocks owned by families. Only 26 of the companies did *not* have a substantial block of stock held by some company or institution.[42]

Note also the bank ownership of Daimler-Benz. This would be impossible in the United States, where federal law prohibits equity investments by banks in nonfinancial corporations. Germany's *universal banking* system allows such investments. Moreover, German banks customarily hold shares for safekeeping on behalf of individual and institutional investors and often acquire proxies to vote these shares on the investors' behalf. For example, Deutsche Bank held 28 percent of Daimler-Benz for its own account and had proxies for 14 percent more. Therefore it *voted* 42 percent, which approaches a majority.

The ownership structures illustrated in Figure 34.3 are common for large German corporations. Control rests mainly with banks and blockholders, not with ordinary stockholders. Corporate control is achieved by buying or assembling blocks of shares. When control changes, selling blockholders receive premiums of 9 to 16 percent over the trading price of the shares. That price increases by 2 or 3 percent

---

[42]See J. Franks and C. Mayer, "The Ownership and Control of German Corporations," *Review of Financial Studies* 14 (Winter 2001), Table 1, p. 947. A block was defined as at least 25 percent ownership. In Germany, a block of this size can veto certain corporate actions, including share issues and changes in corporate charters.

only, so the gains to ordinary stockholders from changes in control are small.[43] In the United States, by contrast, the big winners in acquisitions are usually the selling firm's ordinary stockholders.

Blockholders in Germany do not have unchecked power, however. Large German companies have *two* boards of directors: the supervisory board (*Aufsichtsrat*) and management board (*Vorstand*). Half of the supervisory board's members are elected by employees, including management and staff as well as labor unions. The other half represents stockholders, often including bank executives. (There is also a chairman who can cast tie-breaking votes if necessary.) The supervisory board oversees strategy and elects and monitors the management board which operates the company. Thus control of shares does not mean control of the company—100 percent ownership controls only half of the supervisory board.

This two-tier governance structure reflects a belief, widespread in Europe, that the firm should act in the interests of all its stakeholders, including its employees and the public at large, and not just seek to maximize shareholder value. This structure does not mean poor financial performance or an easy life for management— poor performance leads to management turnover, just as in the United States,[44] and the German economy has, in general, thrived over the last 50 years. One may ask, however, whether German companies which undertake extensive international operations, and seek financing in international capital markets, are best served by a financial architecture that skimps on protection for outside minority investors and discourages attempts to maximize the market value of the firm.

Daimler-Benz, now DaimlerChrysler, is an interesting case study. In the mid-1990s it reversed an unsuccessful diversification strategy that had led it into several other industries, including aerospace and defense. In 1998 it took over Chrysler. It listed its shares on the New York Stock Exchange and issued financial statements conforming to U.S. accounting standards. It turned to international capital markets for financing, including a share issue in the U.S. At the same time Deutsche Bank was reducing its stake in the company. DaimlerChrysler has formally announced a commitment to increasing shareholder value.

. . . And in Japan

Japan's system of corporate governance is in some ways in between the systems of Germany and the United States and in other ways different from both.

The most notable feature of Japanese corporate finance is the **keiretsu.** A keiretsu is a network of companies, usually organized around a major bank. There are long-standing business relationships between the group companies; a manufacturing company might buy a substantial part of its raw materials from group suppliers and in turn sell much of its output to other group companies.

The bank and other financial institutions at the keiretsu's center own shares in most of the group companies (though a commercial bank in Japan is limited to 5 percent ownership of each company). Those companies may in turn hold the bank's shares or each others' shares. Here are the cross-holdings at the end of 1991 between Sumitomo Bank; the Sumitomo Corporation, a trading company; and Sumitomo Trust, which concentrates on investment management:

---

[43]Franks and Mayer, op. cit., Table 9, p. 969.

[44]See Franks and Mayer, op. cit.; and S. Kaplan, "Top Executives, Turnover and Firm Performance in Germany," *Journal of Law and Economics* 10 (1994), pp. 142–159.

Thus the bank owns 4.8 percent of Sumitomo Corporation, which owns 1.8 percent of the bank. Both own shares in Sumitomo Trust . . . and so on. Table 34.5 illustrates the myriad of cross-holdings in a keiretsu. Because of the cross-holdings, the supply of shares available for purchase by outside investors is much less than the total number outstanding.

The keiretsu is tied together in other ways. Most debt financing comes from the keiretsu's banks or from elsewhere in the group. (Until the mid-1980s, all but a handful of Japanese companies were forbidden access to public debt markets. The fraction of debt provided by banks is still much greater than that in the United States.) Managers may sit on the boards of directors of other group companies, and a "presidents' council" of the CEOs of the most important group companies meets regularly.

Think of the keiretsu as a system of corporate governance, where power is split between the main bank, the largest companies, and the group as a whole. This confers certain financial advantages. First, firms have access to additional "internal" financing—internal to the group, that is. Thus a company with capital budgets exceeding

Shareholder	Percentage of Shares Held in:					
	Sumitomo Bank	Sumitomo Metal Industries	Sumitomo Chemical	Sumitomo Trust	Sumitomo Corporation	NEC
S. Bank	—	4.1	4.6	3.4	4.8	5.0
S. Metal Industries	*	—	*	2.5	2.8	*
S. Chemical	*	*	—	*	*	*
S. Trust	2.4	5.9	4.4	—	5.9	5.8
S. Corporation	1.8	1.6	*	3.4	—	2.2
NEC	*	*	*	2.9	3.7	—
Other[†]	9.7	4.8	9.8	10.4	9.5	11.6
Total[†]	13.9	16.4	18.8	22.6	26.7	24.6

TABLE 34.5

Cross-holdings of common stock between six companies in the Sumitomo group in 1991. Read *down* the columns to see holdings of each of the companies by the five others. Thus 4.6 percent of Sumitomo Chemical was owned by Sumitomo Bank, 4.4 percent by Sumitomo Trust, and 9.8 percent by other Sumitomo companies. These figures were compiled by examining the 10 largest shareholders of each company. Smaller cross-holdings are not reflected.

[*]Cross-holding does not appear in the 10 largest shareholdings.
[†]Based on the 10 largest shareholdings in 1991.
Source: Compiled from Dodwell Marketing Consultants, *Industrial Groupings in Japan*, 10th ed., Tokyo, 1992.

operating cash flows can turn to the main bank or other keiretsu companies for financing. This avoids the cost or possible bad-news signal of a public sale of securities. Second, when a keiretsu firm falls into financial distress, with insufficient cash to pay bills or fund necessary capital investments, a "workout" can usually be arranged. New management can be brought in from elsewhere in the group, and financing can be obtained, again "internally."

Hoshi, Kashyap, and Scharfstein tracked capital expenditure programs of a large sample of Japanese firms—many, but not all, members of keiretsus. The keiretsu companies' investments were more stable and less exposed to the ups and downs of operating cash flows or to episodes of financial distress.[45] It seems that the financial support of the keiretsus enabled their members to invest for the long run.

The Japanese system of corporate control has its disadvantages too, notably for outside investors, who have very little influence. Japanese managers' compensation is rarely tied to shareholder returns. Takeovers are unthinkable. Japanese companies have been particularly stingy with cash dividends; this was hardly a concern when growth was rapid and stock prices were stratospheric but is a serious issue for the future.

Corporate Ownership around the World

The theory of modern finance is most readily applied to public corporations with shares traded in active and efficient capital markets. The theory assumes that stockholders' interests are protected, so that ownership can be dispersed across thousands of minority stockholders. The protection comes from managers' incentives, particularly compensation tied to stock price; from supervision by the board of directors; and by the threat of hostile takeover of poorly performing companies.

This is a reasonable description of the corporate sector in the U.S., UK, and other "Anglo-Saxon" countries such as Canada and Australia. But as Germany and Japan illustrate, it is not an accurate description elsewhere. Corporate ownership in Germany is typical of continental Europe. The ownership diagram for a large French company would resemble Figure 34.3.[46]

The financial architecture of public companies in "Anglo-Saxon" economies may be the exception, not the rule. La Porta, Lopez-de-Silanes, and Shleifer surveyed the ownership of the largest companies in 27 developed countries. They found that "except in economies with very good shareholder protection, relatively few of these firms are widely held. Rather these firms are typically controlled by families or the State," or in some cases by financial institutions.[47]

This finding has various possible interpretations. The first is obvious: Protection for outside minority stockholders is a prerequisite for dispersed ownership and a broad and active stock market. Second, in countries that lack effective legal protection for minority stockholders, concentrated ownership may be the only feasible financial architecture.

---

[45]T. Hoshi, A. Kashyap, and D. Scharfstein, "Corporate Structure, Liquidity and Investment: Evidence from Japanese Industrial Groups," *Quarterly Journal of Economics* 106 (February 1991), pp. 33–60, and "The Role of Banks in Reducing the Costs of Financial Distress in Japan," *Journal of Financial Economics* 27 (September 1990), pp. 67–88.

[46]See J. Franks and C. Mayer, "Corporate Ownership and Control in the U. K., Germany and France," *Journal of Applied Corporate Finance* 9 (Winter 1997), pp. 30–45.

[47]R. La Porta, F. Lopez-de-Silanes, and A. Shleifer, "Corporate Ownership around the World," *Journal of Finance* 59 (April 1999), pp. 471–517.

We started with LBOs. An LBO is a takeover or buyout financed mostly with debt. The LBO is owned privately, usually by an investment partnership. Debt financing is not the objective of most LBOs; it is a means to an end. Most LBOs are diet deals. The cash requirements for debt service force managers to shed unneeded assets, improve operating efficiency, and forego wasteful capital expenditure. The managers and key employees are given a significant equity stake in the business, so they have strong incentives to make these improvements.

Leveraged restructurings are in many ways similar to LBOs. Large amounts of debt are added and the proceeds are paid out. The company is forced to generate cash to cover debt service, but there is no change in control and the company stays public.

Most investments in LBOs are made by private equity partnerships. We called these temporary conglomerates. They are conglomerates because they assemble a portfolio of companies in several unrelated industries. They are temporary because the partnership has limited life, usually about 10 years. At the end of this period, the partnership's investments must be sold or taken public again in IPOs. Private equity funds do not buy and hold; they buy, fix, and sell. Investors in the partnership therefore do not have to worry about wasteful reinvestment of free cash flow. LBO managers know that they will be able to cash out their equity stakes if their company succeeds in improving efficiency and paying down debt.

The private equity partnership (or fund) is also common in venture capital and other areas of private investment. The limited partners, who put up almost all of the money, are mostly institutional investors such as pension funds, endowments, and insurance companies. The limited partners are first in line when the partnership's investments are sold. The general partners, who organize and manage the fund, get a carried interest in the fund's profits.

The private equity market has been growing steadily. In contrast to these temporary conglomerates, public conglomerates have been declining in the United States. In public companies, unrelated diversification seems to destroy value—the whole is worth less than the sum of its parts. There are two possible reasons for this conglomerate discount. First, the value of the parts can't be observed separately and it is difficult to set incentives for divisional managers. Second, conglomerates' internal capital markets are inefficient. It is difficult for management to appreciate investment opportunities in many different industries, and internal capital markets are prone to overinvestment and cross-subsidies. The difficulties of running internal capital markets are not restricted to pure conglomerates, but they are most acute there.

Of course corporations shed assets as well as acquire them. Divisions are divested by asset sales, carve-outs, or spin-offs. These divestitures are generally good news to investors; it appears that the divisions are moving to better homes, where they can be better managed and more profitable. The same improvements in efficiency and profitability are observed in privatizations, which are spin-offs or carve-outs of businesses owned by governments.

Although conglomerates are a declining species in the United States, they are common elsewhere, particularly in emerging economies. An internal capital market can make sense when a country's financial markets are not well developed. Diversification also brings scale, which may make it easier to attract professional management, to gain access to international financial markets, or to gain political power in countries where the government tries to manage the economy or where laws and regulations are erratically enforced.

We wonder, though, whether some of these emerging-market conglomerates will be temporary rather than permanent. In a rapidly growing and modernizing economy, opportunities to buy and fix are spread across many industries. If these investments are successful, the next logical step may be to sell and focus on one or a few core businesses.

Our discussion of LBOs, private equity partnerships, and conglomerates illustrates how much financial architecture varies and how it depends on the financial and business environment and on the task at hand. The conglomerate financial architecture thrives in much of the world but not in the United States. LBOs are designed to force change in mature businesses. Private equity partnerships eliminate the separation of ownership and control and make sure that the general partners have strong incentives to achieve high exit values for the partnership's investments.

We also sketched typical arrangements for ownership and control in Germany and Japan. We did so especially for readers in the United States, who may regard their system as natural. In some circumstances the German or Japanese system can work better. Here are two key differences.

First, corporate finance in the United States, Britain, and the other English-speaking countries relies more on financial markets and less on banks or other financial intermediaries than is the case in most other countries. United States corporations routinely issue publicly traded debt in situations where Japanese or European companies borrow from banks.

Second, U.S.-style corporate finance puts fewer buffers between managers and the stock market. The block holdings and layered ownership structure of German companies are rare in the United States, and of course there is nothing remotely like a Japanese keiretsu. So CEOs and CFOs in the United States usually find their paychecks tied to stockholder returns. Negative returns may bring insomnia or bad dreams about takeovers.

These international comparisons illustrate different approaches to the problem of corporate governance—the problem of ensuring that managers act in shareholders' interest.

FURTHER READING

Some of the ideas in this chapter were drawn from:

S. C. Myers: "Financial Architecture," European Financial Management, 5:133–142 (July 1999).

The papers by Kaplan and by Kaplan and Stein provide evidence on the evolution and performance of LBOs; Jensen, the chief proponent of the free-cash-flow theory of takeovers, gives a spirited and controversial defense of LBOs:

S. N. Kaplan: "The Effects of Management Buyouts on Operating Performance and Value," Journal of Financial Economics, 24:217–254 (October 1989).

S. N. Kaplan and J. C. Stein: "The Evolution of Buyout Pricing and Financial Structure (Or, What Went Wrong) in the 1980s," Journal of Applied Corporate Finance, 6:72–88 (Spring 1993).

M. C. Jensen: "The Eclipse of the Public Corporation," Harvard Business Review, 67:61–74 (September/October 1989).

Privatization is reviewed in:

W. L. Megginson and J. M. Nutter: "From State to Market: A Survey of Empirical Studies on Privatization," Journal of Economic Literature, 39:321–389 (June 2001).

The Winter 1997 issue of the Journal of Applied Corporate Finance contains several articles on governance and control in different countries. See also the following survey article:

A. Shleifer and R. Vishny: "A Survey of Corporate Governance," *Journal of Finance*, 52:737–783 (June 1997).

Here are five useful articles on corporate finance in Germany and Japan:

S. Prowse: "Corporate Governance in an International Perspective: A Survey of Corporate Control Mechanisms among Large Firms in the U.S., U.K., Japan and Germany," *Financial Markets, Institutions, and Investments*, 4:1–63 (1995).

J. Franks and C. Mayer: "Ownership and Control of German Corporations," *Review of Financial Studies*, 14:943–977 (Winter 2001).

T. Jenkinson and A. Ljungqvist: "The Role of Hostile Stakes in German Corporate Performance," *Journal of Corporate Finance*, 7:397–446 (December 2001).

D. E. Logue and J. K. Seward: "Anatomy of a Governance Transformation: The Case of Daimler-Benz," *Law and Contemporary Problems*, 62:87–111 (Summer 1999).

E. Berglof and E. Perotti: "The Governance Structure of the Japanese Keiretsu," *Journal of Financial Economics*, 36:259–284 (October 1994).

Here are some interesting case studies pertinent to this chapter.

J. Allen: "Reinventing the Corporation: The Satellite Structure of Thermo Electron," *Journal of Applied Corporate Finance*, 11:38–47 (Summer 1998).

R. Parrino: "Spinoffs and Wealth Transfers: the Marriott Case," *Journal of Financial Economics*, 43:241–274 (February 1997).

C. Eckel, D. Eckel, and V. Singal: "Privatization and Efficiency: Industry Effects of the Sale of British Airways," *Journal of Financial Economics*, 43:275–298 (February 1997).

B. Burrough and J. Helyar: *Barbarians at the Gate: The Fall of RJR Nabisco*, Harper & Row, New York, 1990.

G. P. Baker: "Beatrice: A Study in the Creation and Destruction of Value," *Journal of Finance*, 47:1081–1120 (July 1992).

D. J. Denis: "Organizational Form and the Consequences of Highly Leveraged Transactions," *Journal of Financial Economics*, 36:193–224 (October 1994).

QUIZ

1. Define the following terms: (a) LBO, (b) MBO, (c) spin-off, (d) carve-out, (e) asset sale, (f) privatization, and (g) leveraged restructuring.

2. True or false?
   a. One of the first tasks of an LBO's financial manager is to pay down debt.
   b. Once an LBO or MBO goes private it almost always stays private.
   c. Privatizations are generally followed by massive layoffs.
   d. On average, privatization seems to improve efficiency and add value.
   e. Targets for LBOs in the 1980s tended to be profitable companies in mature industries.
   f. "Carried interest" refers to the deferral of interest payments on LBO debt.
   g. By the late 1990s, new LBO transactions were extremely rare.

3. What are the government's motives in a privatization?

4. a. List the *disadvantages* of a traditional conglomerate in the United States.
   b. What advantages might a conglomerate have in other countries, particularly less-developed economies? List some examples.

5. What are the chief differences in the role of banks in corporate governance in the United States, Germany, and Japan?

6. What is meant by a "temporary conglomerate"? Give an example.

PRACTICE QUESTIONS

1. True, false, or "It depends on . . ."?
   a. Most large corporations are controlled by families, governments, or financial institutions.
   b. Top managers in Germany are much more secure in their jobs than managers in the U.S. because German shareholders have less power than U.S. shareholders.
   c. Carve-out or spin-off of a division improves incentives for the division's managers.
   d. Private-equity partnerships have limited lives. The main purpose is to force the general partners to seek out quick-payout investments.
   e. Managers of private-equity partnerships have an incentive to make risky investments.

2. For what kinds of companies would an LBO or MBO transaction *not* be productive?

3. What was the common theme in both the Phillips Petroleum restructuring and the RJR Nabisco LBO? Why was financial leverage a necessary part of both deals?

4. Outline the similarities and differences between the RJR Nabisco LBO and the Sealed Air leveraged restructuring. Were the economic motives the same? Were the results the same? Do you think it was an advantage for Sealed Air to remain a public company?

5. Examine some recent examples of divestitures and spin-offs. What do you think were the underlying reasons for them? How did investors react to the news?

6. Read *Barbarians at the Gate* (Further Reading). What agency costs can you identify? *Hint:* See Chapter 12. Do you think the LBO was well designed to reduce these costs?

7. Explain the financial architecture of a private-equity partnership. Pay particular attention to incentives and compensation. What types of investments were such partnerships designed to make?

8. Traditional conglomerates are now rare in the United States, but in many other countries, conglomerates are the dominant firms. Explain why.

9. What is meant by an internal capital market? When would you expect such a market to add value? When and why would it be expected to misallocate capital?

CHALLENGE QUESTION

1. We devoted considerable space in this chapter to the problems encountered in the financial management of conglomerates. Could these problems be cured by basing performance measurement and compensation on residual income or EVA? See Chapter 12.

The sites that provide market commentary (see list at end of Part One) contain material on recent mergers. Other sites concerned with mergers include:

www.thedeal.com

www.mergernetwork.com *(information on businesses for sale)*

www.mergerstat.com *(articles and some data on merger activity)*

PART ELEVEN

CONCLUSION

The end is nigh!

CHAPTER THIRTY-FIVE

CONCLUSION: WHAT WE DO AND DO NOT KNOW ABOUT FINANCE

35.1 WHAT WE DO KNOW: THE SEVEN MOST IMPORTANT IDEAS IN FINANCE

What would you say if you were asked to name the seven most important ideas in finance? Here is our list.

1. Net Present Value

When you wish to know the value of a used car, you look at prices in the second-hand car market. Similarly, when you wish to know the value of a future cash flow, you look at prices quoted in the capital markets, where claims to future cash flows are traded (remember, those highly paid investment bankers are just secondhand cash-flow dealers). If you can buy cash flows for your shareholders at a cheaper price than they would have to pay in the capital market, you have increased the value of their investment.

This is the simple idea behind *net present value* (NPV). When we calculate a project's NPV, we are asking whether the project is worth more than it costs. We are estimating its value by calculating what its cash flows would be worth if a claim on them were offered separately to investors and traded in the capital markets.

That is why we calculate NPV by discounting future cash flows at the opportunity cost of capital—that is, at the expected rate of return offered by securities having the same degree of risk as the project. In well-functioning capital markets, all equivalent-risk assets are priced to offer the same expected return. By discounting at the opportunity cost of capital, we calculate the price at which investors in the project could expect to earn that rate of return.

Like most good ideas, the net present value rule is "obvious when you think about it." But notice what an important idea it is. The NPV rule allows thousands of shareholders, who may have vastly different levels of wealth and attitudes toward risk, to participate in the same enterprise and to delegate its operation to a professional manager. They give the manager one simple instruction: "Maximize present value."

2. The Capital Asset Pricing Model

Some people say that modern finance is all about the capital asset pricing model. That's nonsense. If the capital asset pricing model had never been invented, our advice to financial managers would be essentially the same. The attraction of the model is that it gives us a manageable way of thinking about the required return on a risky investment.

Again, it is an attractively simple idea. There are two kinds of risk: risks that you can diversify away and those that you can't. You can measure the *nondiversifiable*, or *market*, risk of an investment by the extent to which the value of the investment is affected by a change in the *aggregate* value of all the assets in the economy. This is called the *beta* of the investment. The only risks that people care about are the ones that they can't get rid of—the nondiversifiable ones. This is why the required return on an asset increases in line with its beta.

Many people are worried by some of the rather strong assumptions behind the capital asset pricing model, or they are concerned about the difficulties of estimating a project's beta. They are right to be worried about these things. In 10 or 20 years' time we will probably have much better theories than we do now. But we will be extremely surprised if those future theories do not still insist on the crucial distinction between diversifiable and nondiversifiable risks—and that, after all, is the main idea underlying the capital asset pricing model.

3. Efficient Capital Markets

The third fundamental idea is that security prices accurately reflect available information and respond rapidly to new information as soon as it becomes available. This *efficient-market theory* comes in three flavors, corresponding to different definitions of "available information." The weak form (or random-walk theory) says that prices reflect all the information in past prices. The semistrong form says that prices reflect all publicly available information, and the strong form holds that prices reflect all acquirable information.

Don't misunderstand the efficient-market idea. It doesn't say that there are no taxes or costs; it doesn't say that there aren't some clever people and some stupid ones. It merely implies that competition in capital markets is very tough— there are no money machines, and security prices reflect the true underlying values of assets.

Extensive empirical testing of the efficient-market hypothesis began around 1970. By 2001, after 30 years of work, the tests have uncovered dozens of statistically significant anomalies. Sorry, but this work does *not* translate into dozens of ways to make easy money. Superior returns are elusive. For example, only a few mutual fund managers can generate superior returns for a few years in a row, and then only in small amounts.[1] Statisticians can beat the market, but real investors have a much harder time of it.

4. Value Additivity and the Law of Conservation of Value

The principle of *value additivity* states that the value of the whole is equal to the sum of the values of the parts. It is sometimes called the *law of the conservation of value*.

When we appraise a project that produces a succession of cash flows, we always assume that values add up. In other words, we assume

$$\text{PV(project)} = \text{PV}(C_1) + \text{PV}(C_2) + \cdots + \text{PV}(C_t) + \cdots$$

$$= \frac{C_1}{1 + r} + \frac{C_2}{(1 + r)^2} + \cdots + \frac{C_t}{(1 + r)^t} + \cdots$$

We similarly assume that the sum of the present values of projects A and B equals the present value of a composite project AB.[2] But value additivity also means that you can't increase value by putting two whole companies together unless you thereby increase the total cash flow. In other words, there are no benefits to mergers solely for diversification.

---

[1] See, for example, M. J. Gruber, "Another Puzzle: The Growth in Actively Managed Mutual Funds," *Journal of Finance* 51 (July 1996), pp. 783–810.

[2] That is, if

$$\text{PV(A)} = \text{PV}[C_1(A)] + \text{PV}[C_2(A)] + \cdots + \text{PV}[C_t(A)] + \cdots$$
$$\text{PV(B)} = \text{PV}[C_1(B)] + \text{PV}[C_2(B)] + \cdots + \text{PV}[C_t(B)] + \cdots$$

and if for each period t, $C_t(AB) = C_t(A) + C_t(B)$, then

$$\text{PV(AB)} = \text{PV(A)} + \text{PV(B)}$$

5. Capital Structure Theory

If the law of the conservation of value works when you add up cash flows, it must also work when you subtract them.[3] Therefore, financing decisions that simply divide up operating cash flows don't increase overall firm value. This is the basic idea behind Modigliani and Miller's famous proposition I: In perfect markets changes in capital structure do not affect value. As long as the *total* cash flow generated by the firm's assets is unchanged by capital structure, value is independent of capital structure. The value of the whole pie does not depend on how it is sliced.

Of course, MM's proposition is not The Answer, but it does tell us where to look for reasons why capital structure decisions may matter. Taxes are one possibility. Debt provides a corporate interest tax shield, and this tax shield may more than compensate for any extra personal tax that the investor has to pay on debt interest. Also, high debt levels may spur managers to work harder and to run a tighter ship. But debt has its drawbacks if it leads to costly financial distress.

6. Option Theory

In everyday conversation we often use the word *option* as synonymous with *choice* or *alternative*; thus we speak of someone as "having a number of options." In finance *option* refers specifically to the opportunity to trade in the future on terms that are fixed today. Smart managers know that it is often worth paying today for the option to buy or sell an asset tomorrow.

Since options are so important, the financial manager needs to know how to value them. Finance experts always knew the relevant variables—the exercise price and the exercise date of the option, the risk of the underlying asset, and the rate of interest. But it was Black and Scholes who first showed how these can be put together in a usable formula.

The Black–Scholes formula was developed for simple call options and does not directly apply to the more complicated options often encountered in corporate finance. But Black and Scholes's most basic ideas—for example, the risk-neutral valuation method implied by their formula—work even where the formula doesn't. Valuing the real options described in Chapter 22 may require extra number crunching but no extra concepts.

7. Agency Theory

A modern corporation is a team effort involving a number of players, such as managers, employees, shareholders, and bondholders. For a long time economists used to assume without question that all these players acted for the common good, but in the last 30 years they have had a lot more to say about the possible conflicts of interest and how companies attempt to overcome such conflicts. These ideas are known collectively as *agency theory*.

Consider, for example, the relationship between the shareholders and the managers. The shareholders (the *principals*) want managers (their *agents*) to maximize firm value. In the United States the ownership of major corporations is widely dispersed and no single shareholder can check on the managers or reprimand those who are slacking. So, to encourage managers to pull their weight, firms seek to tie the managers' compensation to the value that they have added. For those managers

---

[3]If you *start* with the cash flow $C_t(AB)$ and split it into two pieces, $C_t(A)$ and $C_t(B)$, then total value is unchanged. That is, $PV[C_t(A)] + PV[C_t(B)] = PV[C_t(AB)]$. See footnote 2.

who persistently neglect shareholders' interests, there is the threat that their firm will be taken over and they will be turfed out.

In some other countries corporations are more likely to be owned by a few major shareholders and therefore there is less distance between ownership and control. For example, the families, companies, and banks which hold large stakes in many German companies can review top management's plans and decisions as insiders. In most cases they have the power to force changes as necessary. However, hostile takeovers in Germany are very rare.

We discussed the problems of management incentives and corporate control in Chapters 12, 14, and 34, but they were not the only places in the book where agency issues arose. For example, in Chapters 18 and 25 we looked at some of the conflicts that arise between shareholders and bondholders, and we described how loan agreements try to anticipate and minimize these conflicts.

Are these seven ideas exciting theories or plain common sense? Call them what you will, they are basic to the financial manager's job. If by reading this book you really understand these ideas and know how to apply them, you have learned a great deal.

35.2 WHAT WE DO NOT KNOW: 10 UNSOLVED PROBLEMS IN FINANCE

Since the unknown is never exhausted, the list of what we do not know about finance could go on forever. But, following Brealey and Myers's Third Law (see Section 29.4), we will list and briefly discuss 10 unsolved problems that seem ripe for productive research.

1. What Determines Project Risk and Present Value?

A good capital investment is one that has a positive NPV. We have talked at some length about how to calculate NPV, but we have given you very little guidance about how to find positive-NPV projects, except to say in Section 11.2 that projects have positive NPVs when the firm can earn economic rents. But why do some companies earn economic rents while others in the same industry do not? Are the rents merely windfall gains, or can they be anticipated and planned for? What is their source, and how long do they persist before competition destroys them? Very little is known about any of these important questions.

Here is a related question: Why are some real assets risky and others relatively safe? In Section 9.5 we suggested a few reasons for differences in project betas—differences in operating leverage, for example, or in the extent to which a project's cash flows respond to the performance of the national economy. These are useful clues, but we have as yet no general procedure for estimating project betas. Assessing project risk is therefore still largely a seat-of-the-pants matter.

2. Risk and Return—What Have We Missed?

In 1848 John Stuart Mill wrote, "Happily there is nothing in the laws of value which remains for the present or any future writer to clear up; the theory is complete." Economists today are not so sure about that. For example, the capital asset pricing model is an enormous step toward understanding the effect of risk on the value of an asset, but there are many puzzles left, some statistical and some theoretical.

The statistical problems arise because the capital asset pricing model is hard to prove or disprove conclusively. It appears that average returns from low-beta stocks are too high (that is, higher than the capital asset pricing model predicts) and that those from high-beta stocks are too low; but this could be a problem with the way that the tests are conducted and not with the model itself.[4] We also described the puzzling discovery by Fama and French that expected returns appear to be related to the firm's size and to the ratio of the book value of the stock to its market value. Nobody understands why this should be so; perhaps these variables are related to variable x, that mysterious second risk variable that investors may rationally take into account in pricing shares.[5]

Meanwhile scholars toil on the theoretical front. We discussed some of their work in Section 8.4. But just for fun, here is another example: Suppose that you love fine wine. It may make sense for you to buy shares in a grand cru chateau, even if doing so soaks up a large fraction of your personal wealth and leaves you with a relatively undiversified portfolio. However, you are *hedged* against a rise in the price of fine wine: Your hobby will cost you more in a bull market for wine, but your stake in the chateau will make you correspondingly richer. Thus you are holding a relatively undiversified portfolio for a good reason. We would not expect you to demand a premium for bearing that portfolio's undiversifiable risk.

In general, if two people have different tastes, it may make sense for them to hold different portfolios. You may hedge your consumption needs with an investment in wine making, whereas somebody else may do better to invest in Baskin-Robbins. The capital asset pricing model isn't rich enough to deal with such a world. It assumes that all investors have similar tastes: The "hedging motive" does not enter, and therefore they hold the same portfolio of risky assets.

Merton has extended the capital asset pricing model to accommodate the hedging motive.[6] If enough investors are attempting to hedge against the same thing, the model implies a more complicated risk–return relationship. However, it is not yet clear who is hedging against what, and so the model remains difficult to test.

So the capital asset pricing model survives not from a lack of competition but from a surfeit. There are too many plausible alternative risk measures, and so far no consensus exists on the right course to plot if we abandon beta.

In the meantime we must recognize the capital asset pricing model for what it is: an incomplete but extremely useful way of linking risk and return. Recognize too that the model's most basic message, that diversifiable risk doesn't matter, is accepted by nearly everyone.

---

[4]See R. Roll, "A Critique of the Asset Pricing Theory's Tests: Part 1: On Past and Potential Testability of the Theory," *Journal of Financial Economics* 4 (March 1977), pp. 129–176; and, for a critique of the critique, see D. Mayers and E. M. Rice, "Measuring Portfolio Performance and the Empirical Content of Asset Pricing Models," *Journal of Financial Economics* 7 (March 1979), pp. 3–28.

[5]Fama and French point out that small firms, and firms with high book-to-market ratios, are also low-profitability firms. Such firms may suffer more in downturns in the economy. Thus size and book-to-market measures may be proxies for exposure to business-cycle risk. See E. F. Fama and K. R. French, "Size and Book-to-Market Factors in Earnings and Returns," *Journal of Finance* 50 (March 1995), pp. 131–155.

[6]See R. Merton, "An Intertemporal Capital Asset Pricing Model," *Econometrica* 41 (1973), pp. 867–887.

3. How Important Are the Exceptions to the Efficient-Market Theory?

The efficient-market theory is strong, but no theory is perfect; there must be exceptions.

Now some of the apparent exceptions could simply be coincidences, for the more that researchers study stock performance, the more strange coincidences they are likely to find. For example, there is evidence that daily returns around new moons have been roughly double those around full moons.[7] It seems difficult to believe that this is anything other than a chance relationship—fun to read about but not a concern for serious investors or financial managers. But not all exceptions can be dismissed so easily. We saw that the stocks of firms which announce unexpectedly good earnings continue to perform well for a couple of months after the announcement date. Some scholars believe that this may mean that the stock market is inefficient and investors have consistently been slow to react to earnings announcements. Of course, we can't expect investors never to make mistakes. If they have been slow to react in the past, it will be interesting to see whether they learn from their mistake and price the stocks more efficiently in the future.

If stocks are fairly priced, there are no easy ways to make superior profits. Unfortunately, the converse does *not* hold: Stock prices could deviate substantially from fair value, and yet it could be difficult to make superior profits. For example, suppose that the price of IBM stock is always one-half of its fair value. As long as IBM is *consistently* underpriced, the percentage capital gain is the same as it would be if the stock always sold at a fair price. Of course, if IBM stock is underpriced, you get correspondingly more future dividends for your money, but for low-yield stocks that does not make much difference to your total returns. So, while the bulk of the evidence shows that it is difficult to earn high returns, we should be cautious about assuming that stocks are necessarily fairly priced.

Some researchers believe that the efficient-market hypothesis ignores important aspects of human behavior. For example, psychologists find that people tend to place too much emphasis on recent events when they are predicting the future. If so, we may find that investors are liable to overreact to new information. It will be interesting to see how far such behavioral observations can help us to understand apparent anomalies.

4. Is Management an Off-Balance-Sheet Liability?

Closed-end funds are firms whose only asset is a portfolio of common stocks. One might think that if you knew the value of these common stocks, you would also know the value of the firm. However, this is not the case. The stock of the closed-end fund often sells for substantially less than the value of the fund's portfolio.[8]

All this might not matter much except that it could be just the tip of the iceberg. For example, real estate stocks appear to sell for less than the market values of the firms' net assets. In the late 1970s and early 1980s the market values of many large oil companies were less than the market values of their oil reserves. Analysts joked that you could buy oil cheaper on Wall Street than in west Texas.

All these are special cases in which it was possible to compare the market value of the whole firm with the values of its separate assets. But perhaps if we could ob-

---

[7] K. Yuan, L. Zheng, and Q. Zhu, "Are Investors Moonstruck? Lunar Phases and Stock Returns," working paper, University of Michigan, September 2001.

[8] There are relatively few closed-end funds. Most mutual funds are *open-end*. This means that they stand ready to buy or sell additional shares at a price equal to the fund's net asset value per share. Therefore the share price of an open-end fund always equals net asset value.

serve the values of other firms' separate parts, we might find that the value of the whole was often less than the sum of the values of the parts.

Whenever firms calculate the net present value of a project, they implicitly assume that the value of the whole project is simply the sum of the values of all the years' cash flows. We referred to this earlier as the law of the conservation of value. If we cannot rely on that law, the tip of the iceberg could turn out to be a hot potato.

We don't understand why closed-end investment companies or any of the other firms sell at a discount on the market values of their assets. One explanation is that the value added by the firm's management is less than the cost of the management. That is why we suggest that management may be an off-balance-sheet liability. For example, the discount of oil company shares from oil-in-the-ground value can be explained if investors expected the profits from oil production to be frittered away in negative-NPV investments and bureaucratic excess. The present value of growth opportunities (PVGO) was negative!

We do not mean to portray managers as leeches soaking up cash flows meant for investors. Managers commit their human capital to the firm and rightfully expect a reasonable cash return on these personal investments. If investors extract too great a share of the firm's cash flow, the personal investments are discouraged, and the long-run health and growth of the firm can be damaged.

In most firms, managers and employees coinvest with stockholders and creditors—human capital from the insiders and financial capital from outside investors. So far we know very little about how this coinvestment works.

5. How Can We Explain the Success of New Securities and New Markets?

In the last 20 years companies and the securities exchanges have created an enormous number of new securities: options, futures, options on futures; zero-coupon bonds, floating-rate bonds; bonds with collars and caps, asset-backed bonds; catastrophe bonds, . . . the list is endless. In some cases, it is easy to explain the success of new markets or securities; perhaps they allow investors to insure themselves against new risks or they result from a change in tax or in regulation. Sometimes a market develops because of a change in the costs of issuing or trading different securities. But there are many successful innovations that cannot be explained so easily. Why do investment bankers continue to invent, and successfully sell, complex new securities that outstrip our ability to value them? The truth is we don't understand why some innovations in markets succeed and others never get off the ground.

6. How Can We Resolve the Dividend Controversy?

We spent all of Chapter 16 on dividend policy without being able to resolve the dividend controversy. Many people believe dividends are good; others believe they are bad; and still others believe they are irrelevant. If pressed, we stand somewhere in the middle, but we can't be dogmatic about it.

We don't mean to disparage existing research; rather, we say that more is in order. Whether future research will change anybody's mind is another matter. The problem is to disentangle several possible reasons that dividend policy *may* matter. For example, a firm that pays dividends rather than repurchases stock is likely to land its shareholders with heavier tax bills. On the other hand, a commitment to pay regular dividends may also provide a signal of the company's prosperity; in effect, a company that pays dividends is putting its money where its mouth is.

The way that companies distribute cash has been changing. An increasing number of companies do not pay any dividends, while the volume of stock repurchases has mushroomed. However, these repurchases are not substitutes for dividends; companies that repurchase stock do not at the same time reduce their dividend payments. Thus we need to understand better both how companies determine their payout policy and how that policy affects firm value.

7. What Risks Should a Firm Take?

Financial managers end up managing risk. For example,

- When a firm expands production, managers often reduce the cost of failure by building in the option to alter the product mix or to bail out of the project altogether.
- By reducing the firm's borrowing, managers can spread operating risks over a larger equity base.
- Most businesses take out insurance against a variety of specific hazards.
- Managers often use futures or other derivatives to protect against adverse movements in commodity prices, interest rates, and exchange rates.

All these actions reduce risk. But less risk can't always be better. The point of risk management is not to reduce risk but to add value. We wish we could give general guidance on what bets the firm should place and what the *appropriate* level of risk is.

In practice, risk management decisions interact in complicated ways. For example, firms that are hedged against commodity price fluctuations may be able to afford more debt than those that are not hedged. Hedging can make sense if it allows the firm to take greater advantage of interest tax shields, provided the costs of hedging are sufficiently low.

How can a company set a risk management strategy that adds up to a sensible whole?

8. What Is the Value of Liquidity?

Unlike Treasury bills, cash pays no interest. On the other hand, cash provides more liquidity than Treasury bills. People who hold cash must believe that this additional liquidity offsets the loss of interest. In equilibrium, the marginal value of the additional liquidity must equal the interest rate on bills.

Now what can we say about corporate holdings of cash? It is wrong to ignore the liquidity gain and to say that the cost of holding cash is the lost interest. This would imply that cash always has a *negative* NPV. It is equally foolish to say that, because the marginal value of liquidity is equal to the loss of interest, it doesn't matter how much cash the firm holds. This would imply that cash always has a *zero* NPV. We know that the marginal value of cash to a holder declines with the size of the cash holding, but we don't really understand how to value the liquidity service of cash and therefore we can't say how much cash is enough or how readily the firm should be able to raise it. To complicate matters further, we note that cash can be raised on short notice by borrowing, or by issuing other new securities, as well as by selling assets. The financial manager with a $1 million unused line of credit may sleep just as soundly as one whose firm holds $1 million in marketable securities. In our chapters on working-capital management we largely finessed these questions by presenting models that are really too simple or by speaking vaguely of the need to ensure an "adequate" liquidity reserve.

A better knowledge of liquidity would also help us to understand better how corporate bonds are priced. We already know part of the reason that corporate bonds sell for lower prices than Treasury bonds—companies have the option to walk away from their debts. However, the differences between the prices of corporate bonds and Treasury bonds are too large to be explained just by the company's default option. It seems likely that the price difference is partly due to the fact that corporate bonds are less liquid than Treasury bonds. But, until we know how to price differences in liquidity, we can't really say much more than this.

Investors seem to value liquidity much more highly at some times than at others. When liquidity suddenly dries up, asset prices can become very volatile. This happened in 1998 when Long-Term Capital Management, a large hedge fund, collapsed.[9] Since its formation four years earlier LTCM had generated high returns by holding large positions in "cheap" illiquid assets, which it hedged by selling liquid assets. LTCM, therefore, served as a supplier of liquidity to other investors. When Russia defaulted on its debt in 1998, there was a rush by investors to get out of illiquid assets. As the value of LTCM's holdings declined, its banks demanded additional collateral for their loans and LTCM was forced to liquidate its positions in a market that was already short of liquidity. Eventually, the New York Fed encouraged a group of institutions to take over LTCM, but not before there had been very sharp swings in asset prices.

9. How Can We Explain Merger Waves?

In 1968 at the first peak of the postwar merger movement, Joel Segall noted: "There is no single hypothesis which is both plausible and general and which shows promise of explaining the current merger movement. If so, it is correct to say that there is nothing known about mergers; there are no useful generalizations."[10] Of course there are many plausible motives for merging. If you single out a *particular* merger, it is usually possible to think up a reason why that merger could make sense. But that leaves us with a special hypothesis for each merger. What we need is a general hypothesis to explain merger waves. For example, in the late 1990s everybody seemed to be merging, while at the beginning of the twenty-first century mergers were out of fashion.

There are other instances of apparent financial fashions. For example, from time to time there are hot new-issue periods when there seems to be an insatiable supply of speculative new issues and an equally insatiable demand for them. We don't understand why hard-headed businessmen sometimes seem to behave like a flock of sheep, but the following story may contain the seeds of an explanation.

It is early evening and George is trying to decide between two restaurants, the Hungry Horse and the Golden Trough. Both are empty and, since there seems to be little reason to prefer one to the other, George tosses a coin and opts for the Hungry Horse. Shortly afterward Georgina pauses outside the two restaurants. She somewhat prefers the Golden Trough, but observing George inside the Hungry Horse while the other restaurant is empty, she decides that George may know something that she doesn't and therefore the rational decision is to copy George. Fred is the third person to arrive. He sees that George and Georgina have both chosen the Hungry Horse, and, putting aside his own judgment, decides to go with the flow. And so it is with subsequent diners, who simply look at the packed tables in the one restaurant and the empty tables elsewhere and draw the obvious conclusions. Each diner

---

[9]Hedge funds attempt to buy underpriced securities and to sell short overpriced ones. They are typically organized as partnerships and owned by a small number of institutions or wealthy individuals.

[10]J. Segall, "Merging for Fun and Profit," *Industrial Management Review* 9 (Winter 1968), pp. 17–30.

behaves fully rationally in balancing his or her own views with the revealed prefer-ences of the other diners. Yet the popularity of the Hungry Horse owed much to the toss of George's coin. If Georgina had been the first to arrive or if all diners could have pooled their information before coming to a decision, the Hungry Horse might not have scooped the jackpot.

Economists refer to this imitative behavior as a cascade.[11] It remains to be seen how far cascades or some alternative theory can help to explain financial fashions.

10. How Can We Explain International Differences in Financial Architecture?

In Chapter 34 we showed how financial architecture varies internationally. By this we mean that there are important international differences in the legal form of the business, its ownership, governance, and sources of financing. In the United States and most other English-speaking countries large firms are commonly organized as public corporations with actively traded shares, dispersed ownership, and rela-tively easy access to financial markets. In other countries businesses are often more closely held, and the owners have more say in how the business is run. Banks of-ten play a much larger role in financing businesses and keeping an eye on their progress. Also, in many countries businesses are combined together into diversi-fied conglomerates which can allocate capital from the parts that have a capital sur-plus to those that are short of capital.

We don't fully understand why these differences in organizational structure ex-ist, though we suggested that part of the answer may lie in differences in legal and accounting systems. We also made some qualitative statements about the advan-tages and disadvantages of different structures, but commentators continue to de-bate which arrangements are most efficient. Some worry that the preoccupation of managers in the United States with enhancing shareholder value leads to a focus on short-term profits; others assert that too cozy a relationship between a company and its sources of capital can lead to a lack of discipline in managers.

 ## 35.3 A FINAL WORD

That concludes our list of unsolved problems. We have given you the 10 upper-most in our minds. If there are others that you find more interesting and challeng-ing, by all means construct your own list and start thinking about it.

It will take years for our 10 problems to be finally solved and replaced with a fresh list. In the meantime, we invite you to go on to further study what we *already* know about finance. We also invite you to apply what you have learned from read-ing this book.

Now that the book is done, we sympathize with Huckleberry Finn. At the end of his book he says:

> So there ain't nothing more to write, and I am rotten glad of it, because if I'd a'knowed what a trouble it was to make a book I wouldn't a' tackled it, and I ain't a'going to no more.

---

[11]For an introduction to cascades, see S. Bikhchandani, D. Hirschleifer, and I. Welch, "Learning from the Behavior of Others: Conformity, Fads, and Informational Cascades," *Journal of Economic Perspectives* 12 (Summer 1998), pp. 151–170.

PRESENT VALUE TABLES

APPENDIX TABLE 1

Discount factors: Present value of $1 to be received after t years $= 1/(1 + r)^t$.

Number of Years	Interest Rate per Year														
	1%	2%	3%	4%	5%	6%	7%	8%	9%	10%	11%	12%	13%	14%	15%
1	.990	.980	.971	.962	.952	.943	.935	.926	.917	.909	.901	.893	.885	.877	.870
2	.980	.961	.943	.925	.907	.890	.873	.857	.842	.826	.812	.797	.783	.769	.756
3	.971	.942	.915	.889	.864	.840	.816	.794	.772	.751	.731	.712	.693	.675	.658
4	.961	.924	.888	.855	.823	.792	.763	.735	.708	.683	.659	.636	.613	.592	.572
5	.951	.906	.863	.822	.784	.747	.713	.681	.650	.621	.593	.567	.543	.519	.497
6	.942	.888	.837	.790	.746	.705	.666	.630	.596	.564	.535	.507	.480	.456	.432
7	.933	.871	.813	.760	.711	.665	.623	.583	.547	.513	.482	.452	.425	.400	.376
8	.923	.853	.789	.731	.677	.627	.582	.540	.502	.467	.434	.404	.376	.351	.327
9	.914	.837	.766	.703	.645	.592	.544	.500	.460	.424	.391	.361	.333	.308	.284
10	.905	.820	.744	.676	.614	.558	.508	.463	.422	.386	.352	.322	.295	.270	.247
11	.896	.804	.722	.650	.585	.527	.475	.429	.388	.350	.317	.287	.261	.237	.215
12	.887	.788	.701	.625	.557	.497	.444	.397	.356	.319	.286	.257	.231	.208	.187
13	.879	.773	.681	.601	.530	.469	.415	.368	.326	.290	.258	.229	.204	.182	.163
14	.870	.758	.661	.577	.505	.442	.388	.340	.299	.263	.232	.205	.181	.160	.141
15	.861	.743	.642	.555	.481	.417	.362	.315	.275	.239	.209	.183	.160	.140	.123
16	.853	.728	.623	.534	.458	.394	.339	.292	.252	.218	.188	.163	.141	.123	.107
17	.844	.714	.605	.513	.436	.371	.317	.270	.231	.198	.170	.146	.125	.108	.093
18	.836	.700	.587	.494	.416	.350	.296	.250	.212	.180	.153	.130	.111	.095	.081
19	.828	.686	.570	.475	.396	.331	.277	.232	.194	.164	.138	.116	.098	.083	.070
20	.820	.673	.554	.456	.377	.312	.258	.215	.178	.149	.124	.104	.087	.073	.061
25	.780	.610	.478	.375	.295	.233	.184	.146	.116	.092	.074	.059	.047	.038	.030
30	.742	.552	.412	.308	.231	.174	.131	.099	.075	.057	.044	.033	.026	.020	.015

Note: For example, if the interest rate is 10 percent per year, the present value of $1 received at year 5 is $.621.

Number of Years	Interest Rate per Year														
	16%	17%	18%	19%	20%	21%	22%	23%	24%	25%	26%	27%	28%	29%	30%
1	.862	.855	.847	.840	.833	.826	.820	.813	.806	.800	.794	.787	.781	.775	.769
2	.743	.731	.718	.706	.694	.683	.672	.661	.650	.640	.630	.620	.610	.601	.592
3	.641	.624	.609	.593	.579	.564	.551	.537	.524	.512	.500	.488	.477	.466	.455
4	.552	.534	.516	.499	.482	.467	.451	.437	.423	.410	.397	.384	.373	.361	.350
5	.476	.456	.437	.419	.402	.386	.370	.355	.341	.328	.315	.303	.291	.280	.269
6	.410	.390	.370	.352	.335	.319	.303	.289	.275	.262	.250	.238	.227	.217	.207
7	.354	.333	.314	.296	.279	.263	.249	.235	.222	.210	.198	.188	.178	.168	.159
8	.305	.285	.266	.249	.233	.218	.204	.191	.179	.168	.157	.148	.139	.130	.123
9	.263	.243	.225	.209	.194	.180	.167	.155	.144	.134	.125	.116	.108	.101	.094
10	.227	.208	.191	.176	.162	.149	.137	.126	.116	.107	.099	.092	.085	.078	.073
11	.195	.178	.162	.148	.135	.123	.112	.103	.094	.086	.079	.072	.066	.061	.056
12	.168	.152	.137	.124	.112	.102	.092	.083	.076	.069	.062	.057	.052	.047	.043
13	.145	.130	.116	.104	.093	.084	.075	.068	.061	.055	.050	.045	.040	.037	.033
14	.125	.111	.099	.088	.078	.069	.062	.055	.049	.044	.039	.035	.032	.028	.025
15	.108	.095	.084	.074	.065	.057	.051	.045	.040	.035	.031	.028	.025	.022	.020
16	.093	.081	.071	.062	.054	.047	.042	.036	.032	.028	.025	.022	.019	.017	.015
17	.080	.069	.060	.052	.045	.039	.034	.030	.026	.023	.020	.017	.015	.013	.012
18	.069	.059	.051	.044	.038	.032	.028	.024	.021	.018	.016	.014	.012	.010	.009
19	.060	.051	.043	.037	.031	.027	.023	.020	.017	.014	.012	.011	.009	.008	.007
20	.051	.043	.037	.031	.026	.022	.019	.016	.014	.012	.010	.008	.007	.006	.005
25	.024	.020	.016	.013	.010	.009	.007	.006	.005	.004	.003	.003	.002	.002	.001
30	.012	.009	.007	.005	.004	.003	.003	.002	.002	.001	.001	.001	.001	.000	.000

APPENDIX TABLE 2

Future value of $1 after t years $= (1 + r)^t$.

Number of Years	\multicolumn{15}{c}{Interest Rate per Year}
	1%	2%	3%	4%	5%	6%	7%	8%	9%	10%	11%	12%	13%	14%	15%
1	1.010	1.020	1.030	1.040	1.050	1.060	1.070	1.080	1.090	1.100	1.110	1.120	1.130	1.140	1.150
2	1.020	1.040	1.061	1.082	1.102	1.124	1.145	1.166	1.188	1.210	1.232	1.254	1.277	1.300	1.323
3	1.030	1.061	1.093	1.125	1.158	1.191	1.225	1.260	1.295	1.331	1.368	1.405	1.443	1.482	1.521
4	1.041	1.082	1.126	1.170	1.216	1.262	1.311	1.360	1.412	1.464	1.518	1.574	1.630	1.689	1.749
5	1.051	1.104	1.159	1.217	1.276	1.338	1.403	1.469	1.539	1.611	1.685	1.762	1.842	1.925	2.011
6	1.062	1.126	1.194	1.265	1.340	1.419	1.501	1.587	1.677	1.772	1.870	1.974	2.082	2.195	2.313
7	1.072	1.149	1.230	1.316	1.407	1.504	1.606	1.714	1.828	1.949	2.076	2.211	2.353	2.502	2.660
8	1.083	1.172	1.267	1.369	1.477	1.594	1.718	1.851	1.993	2.144	2.305	2.476	2.658	2.853	3.059
9	1.094	1.195	1.305	1.423	1.551	1.689	1.838	1.999	2.172	2.358	2.558	2.773	3.004	3.252	3.518
10	1.105	1.219	1.344	1.480	1.629	1.791	1.967	2.159	2.367	2.594	2.839	3.106	3.395	3.707	4.046
11	1.116	1.243	1.384	1.539	1.710	1.898	2.105	2.332	2.580	2.853	3.152	3.479	3.836	4.226	4.652
12	1.127	1.268	1.426	1.601	1.796	2.012	2.252	2.518	2.813	3.138	3.498	3.896	4.335	4.818	5.350
13	1.138	1.294	1.469	1.665	1.886	2.133	2.410	2.720	3.066	3.452	3.883	4.363	4.898	5.492	6.153
14	1.149	1.319	1.513	1.732	1.980	2.261	2.579	2.937	3.342	3.797	4.310	4.887	5.535	6.261	7.076
15	1.161	1.346	1.558	1.801	2.079	2.397	2.759	3.172	3.642	4.177	4.785	5.474	6.254	7.138	8.137
16	1.173	1.373	1.605	1.873	2.183	2.540	2.952	3.426	3.970	4.595	5.311	6.130	7.067	8.137	9.358
17	1.184	1.400	1.653	1.948	2.292	2.693	3.159	3.700	4.328	5.054	5.895	6.866	7.986	9.276	10.76
18	1.196	1.428	1.702	2.026	2.407	2.854	3.380	3.996	4.717	5.560	6.544	7.690	9.024	10.58	12.38
19	1.208	1.457	1.754	2.107	2.527	3.026	3.617	4.316	5.142	6.116	7.263	8.613	10.20	12.06	14.23
20	1.220	1.486	1.806	2.191	2.653	3.207	3.870	4.661	5.604	6.727	8.062	9.646	11.52	13.74	16.37
25	1.282	1.641	2.094	2.666	3.386	4.292	5.427	6.848	8.623	10.83	13.59	17.00	21.23	26.46	32.92
30	1.348	1.811	2.427	3.243	4.322	5.743	7.612	10.06	13.27	17.45	22.89	29.96	39.12	50.95	66.21

Note: For example, if the interest rate is 10 percent per year, the investment of $1 today will be worth $1.611 at year 5.

Number of Years	16%	17%	18%	19%	20%	21%	22%	23%	24%	25%	26%	27%	28%	29%	30%
1	1.160	1.170	1.180	1.190	1.200	1.210	1.220	1.230	1.240	1.250	1.260	1.270	1.280	1.290	1.300
2	1.346	1.369	1.392	1.416	1.440	1.464	1.488	1.513	1.538	1.563	1.588	1.613	1.638	1.664	1.690
3	1.561	1.602	1.643	1.685	1.728	1.772	1.816	1.861	1.907	1.953	2.000	2.048	2.097	2.147	2.197
4	1.811	1.874	1.939	2.005	2.074	2.144	2.215	2.289	2.364	2.441	2.520	2.601	2.684	2.769	2.856
5	2.100	2.192	2.288	2.386	2.488	2.594	2.703	2.815	2.932	3.052	3.176	3.304	3.436	3.572	3.713
6	2.436	2.565	2.700	2.840	2.986	3.138	3.297	3.463	3.635	3.815	4.002	4.196	4.398	4.608	4.827
7	2.826	3.001	3.185	3.379	3.583	3.797	4.023	4.259	4.508	4.768	5.042	5.329	5.629	5.945	6.275
8	3.278	3.511	3.759	4.021	4.300	4.595	4.908	5.239	5.590	5.960	6.353	6.768	7.206	7.669	8.157
9	3.803	4.108	4.435	4.785	5.160	5.560	5.987	6.444	6.931	7.451	8.005	8.595	9.223	9.893	10.60
10	4.411	4.807	5.234	5.695	6.192	6.728	7.305	7.926	8.594	9.313	10.09	10.92	11.81	12.76	13.79
11	5.117	5.624	6.176	6.777	7.430	8.140	8.912	9.749	10.66	11.64	12.71	13.86	15.11	16.46	17.92
12	5.936	6.580	7.288	8.064	8.916	9.850	10.87	11.99	13.21	14.55	16.01	17.61	19.34	21.24	23.30
13	6.886	7.699	8.599	9.596	10.70	11.92	13.26	14.75	16.39	18.19	20.18	22.36	24.76	27.39	30.29
14	7.988	9.007	10.15	11.42	12.84	14.42	16.18	18.14	20.32	22.74	25.42	28.40	31.69	35.34	39.37
15	9.266	10.54	11.97	13.59	15.41	17.45	19.74	22.31	25.20	28.42	32.03	36.06	40.56	45.59	51.19
16	10.75	12.33	14.13	16.17	18.49	21.11	24.09	27.45	31.24	35.53	40.36	45.80	51.92	58.81	66.54
17	12.47	14.43	16.67	19.24	22.19	25.55	29.38	33.76	38.74	44.41	50.85	58.17	66.46	75.86	86.50
18	14.46	16.88	19.67	22.90	26.62	30.91	35.85	41.52	48.04	55.51	64.07	73.87	85.07	97.86	112.5
19	16.78	19.75	23.21	27.25	31.95	37.40	43.74	51.07	59.57	69.39	80.73	93.81	108.9	126.2	146.2
20	19.46	23.11	27.39	32.43	38.34	45.26	53.36	62.82	73.86	86.74	101.7	119.1	139.4	162.9	190.0
25	40.87	50.66	62.67	77.39	95.40	117.4	144.2	176.9	216.5	264.7	323.0	393.6	478.9	581.8	705.6
30	85.85	111.1	143.4	184.7	237.4	304.5	389.8	497.9	634.8	807.8	1026	1301	1646	2078	2620

Interest Rate per Year

APPENDIX TABLE 3

Annuity table: Present value of $1 *per year* for each of *t* years $= 1/r - 1/[r(1 + r)^t]$.

Number of Years	Interest Rate per Year														
	1%	2%	3%	4%	5%	6%	7%	8%	9%	10%	11%	12%	13%	14%	15%
1	.990	.980	.971	.962	.952	.943	.935	.926	.917	.909	.901	.893	.885	.877	.870
2	1.970	1.942	1.913	1.886	1.859	1.833	1.808	1.783	1.759	1.736	1.713	1.690	1.668	1.647	1.626
3	2.941	2.884	2.829	2.775	2.723	2.673	2.624	2.577	2.531	2.487	2.444	2.402	2.361	2.322	2.283
4	3.902	3.808	3.717	3.630	3.546	3.465	3.387	3.312	3.240	3.170	3.102	3.037	2.974	2.914	2.855
5	4.853	4.713	4.580	4.452	4.329	4.212	4.100	3.993	3.890	3.791	3.696	3.605	3.517	3.433	3.352
6	5.795	5.601	5.417	5.242	5.076	4.917	4.767	4.623	4.486	4.355	4.231	4.111	3.998	3.889	3.784
7	6.728	6.472	6.230	6.002	5.786	5.582	5.389	5.206	5.033	4.868	4.712	4.564	4.423	4.288	4.160
8	7.652	7.325	7.020	6.733	6.463	6.210	5.971	5.747	5.535	5.335	5.146	4.968	4.799	4.639	4.487
9	8.566	8.162	7.786	7.435	7.108	6.802	6.515	6.247	5.995	5.759	5.537	5.328	5.132	4.946	4.772
10	9.471	8.983	8.530	8.111	7.722	7.360	7.024	6.710	6.418	6.145	5.889	5.650	5.426	5.216	5.019
11	10.37	9.787	9.253	8.760	8.306	7.887	7.499	7.139	6.805	6.495	6.207	5.938	5.687	5.453	5.234
12	11.26	10.58	9.954	9.385	8.863	8.384	7.943	7.536	7.161	6.814	6.492	6.194	5.918	5.660	5.421
13	12.13	11.35	10.63	9.986	9.394	8.853	8.358	7.904	7.487	7.103	6.750	6.424	6.122	5.842	5.583
14	13.00	12.11	11.30	10.56	9.899	9.295	8.745	8.244	7.786	7.367	6.982	6.628	6.302	6.002	5.724
15	13.87	12.85	11.94	11.12	10.38	9.712	9.108	8.559	8.061	7.606	7.191	6.811	6.462	6.142	5.847
16	14.72	13.58	12.56	11.65	10.84	10.11	9.447	8.851	8.313	7.824	7.379	6.974	6.604	6.265	5.954
17	15.56	14.29	13.17	12.17	11.27	10.48	9.763	9.122	8.544	8.022	7.549	7.120	6.729	6.373	6.047
18	16.40	14.99	13.75	12.66	11.69	10.83	10.06	9.372	8.756	8.201	7.702	7.250	6.840	6.467	6.128
19	17.23	15.68	14.32	13.13	12.09	11.16	10.34	9.604	8.950	8.365	7.839	7.366	6.938	6.550	6.198
20	18.05	16.35	14.88	13.59	12.46	11.47	10.59	9.818	9.129	8.514	7.963	7.469	7.025	6.623	6.259
25	22.02	19.52	17.41	15.62	14.09	12.78	11.65	10.67	9.823	9.077	8.422	7.843	7.330	6.873	6.464
30	25.81	22.40	19.60	17.29	15.37	13.76	12.41	11.26	10.27	9.427	8.694	8.055	7.496	7.003	6.566

Note: For example, if the interest rate is 10 percent per year, the present value of $1 received in each of the next 5 years is $3.791.

Number of Years	16%	17%	18%	19%	20%	21%	22%	23%	24%	25%	26%	27%	28%	29%	30%
							Interest Rate per Year								
1	.862	.855	.847	.840	.833	.826	.820	.813	.806	.800	.794	.787	.781	.775	.769
2	1.605	1.585	1.566	1.547	1.528	1.509	1.492	1.474	1.457	1.440	1.424	1.407	1.392	1.376	1.361
3	2.246	2.210	2.174	2.140	2.106	2.074	2.042	2.011	1.981	1.952	1.923	1.896	1.868	1.842	1.816
4	2.798	2.743	2.690	2.639	2.589	2.540	2.494	2.448	2.404	2.362	2.320	2.280	2.241	2.203	2.166
5	3.274	3.199	3.127	3.058	2.991	2.926	2.864	2.803	2.745	2.689	2.635	2.583	2.532	2.483	2.436
6	3.685	3.589	3.498	3.410	3.326	3.245	3.167	3.092	3.020	2.951	2.885	2.821	2.759	2.700	2.643
7	4.039	3.922	3.812	3.706	3.605	3.508	3.416	3.327	3.242	3.161	3.083	3.009	2.937	2.868	2.802
8	4.344	4.207	4.078	3.954	3.837	3.726	3.619	3.518	3.421	3.329	3.241	3.156	3.076	2.999	2.925
9	4.607	4.451	4.303	4.163	4.031	3.905	3.786	3.673	3.566	3.463	3.366	3.273	3.184	3.100	3.019
10	4.833	4.659	4.494	4.339	4.192	4.054	3.923	3.799	3.682	3.571	3.465	3.364	3.269	3.178	3.092
11	5.029	4.836	4.656	4.486	4.327	4.177	4.035	3.902	3.776	3.656	3.543	3.437	3.335	3.239	3.147
12	5.197	4.988	4.793	4.611	4.439	4.278	4.127	3.985	3.851	3.725	3.606	3.493	3.387	3.286	3.190
13	5.342	5.118	4.910	4.715	4.533	4.362	4.203	4.053	3.912	3.780	3.656	3.538	3.427	3.322	3.223
14	5.468	5.229	5.008	4.802	4.611	4.432	4.265	4.108	3.962	3.824	3.695	3.573	3.459	3.351	3.249
15	5.575	5.324	5.092	4.876	4.675	4.489	4.315	4.153	4.001	3.859	3.726	3.601	3.483	3.373	3.268
16	5.668	5.405	5.162	4.938	4.730	4.536	4.357	4.189	4.033	3.887	3.751	3.623	3.503	3.390	3.283
17	5.749	5.475	5.222	4.990	4.775	4.576	4.391	4.219	4.059	3.910	3.771	3.640	3.518	3.403	3.295
18	5.818	5.534	5.273	5.033	4.812	4.608	4.419	4.243	4.080	3.928	3.786	3.654	3.529	3.413	3.304
19	5.877	5.584	5.316	5.070	4.843	4.635	4.442	4.263	4.097	3.942	3.799	3.664	3.539	3.421	3.311
20	5.929	5.628	5.353	5.101	4.870	4.657	4.460	4.279	4.110	3.954	3.808	3.673	3.546	3.427	3.316
25	6.097	5.766	5.467	5.195	4.948	4.721	4.514	4.323	4.147	3.985	3.834	3.694	3.564	3.442	3.329
30	6.177	5.829	5.517	5.235	4.979	4.746	4.534	4.339	4.160	3.995	3.842	3.701	3.569	3.447	3.332

APPENDIX TABLE 4

Values of e^{rt}. Future value of $1 invested at a *continuously compounded* rate r for t years.

rt	.00	.01	.02	.03	.04	.05	.06	.07	.08	.09
.00	1.000	1.010	1.020	1.030	1.041	1.051	1.062	1.073	1.083	1.094
.10	1.105	1.116	1.127	1.139	1.150	1.162	1.174	1.185	1.197	1.209
.20	1.221	1.234	1.246	1.259	1.271	1.284	1.297	1.310	1.323	1.336
.30	1.350	1.363	1.377	1.391	1.405	1.419	1.433	1.448	1.462	1.477
.40	1.492	1.507	1.522	1.537	1.553	1.568	1.584	1.600	1.616	1.632
.50	1.649	1.665	1.682	1.699	1.716	1.733	1.751	1.768	1.786	1.804
.60	1.822	1.840	1.859	1.878	1.896	1.916	1.935	1.954	1.974	1.994
.70	2.014	2.034	2.054	2.075	2.096	2.117	2.138	2.160	2.181	2.203
.80	2.226	2.248	2.271	2.293	2.316	2.340	2.363	2.387	2.411	2.435
.90	2.460	2.484	2.509	2.535	2.560	2.586	2.612	2.638	2.664	2.691
1.00	2.718	2.746	2.773	2.801	2.829	2.858	2.886	2.915	2.945	2.974
1.10	3.004	3.034	3.065	3.096	3.127	3.158	3.190	3.222	3.254	3.287
1.20	3.320	3.353	3.387	3.421	3.456	3.490	3.525	3.561	3.597	3.633
1.30	3.669	3.706	3.743	3.781	3.819	3.857	3.896	3.935	3.975	4.015
1.40	4.055	4.096	4.137	4.179	4.221	4.263	4.306	4.349	4.393	4.437
1.50	4.482	4.527	4.572	4.618	4.665	4.711	4.759	4.807	4.855	4.904
1.60	4.953	5.003	5.053	5.104	5.155	5.207	5.259	5.312	5.366	5.419
1.70	5.474	5.529	5.585	5.641	5.697	5.755	5.812	5.871	5.930	5.989
1.80	6.050	6.110	6.172	6.234	6.297	6.360	6.424	6.488	6.553	6.619
1.90	6.686	6.753	6.821	6.890	6.959	7.029	7.099	7.171	7.243	7.316

Note: For example, if the continuously compounded interest rate is 10 percent per year, the investment of $1 today will be worth $1.105 at year 1 and $1.221 at year 2.

rt	.00	.01	.02	.03	.04	.05	.06	.07	.08	.09
2.00	7.389	7.463	7.538	7.614	7.691	7.768	7.846	7.925	8.004	8.085
2.10	8.166	8.248	8.331	8.415	8.499	8.585	8.671	8.758	8.846	8.935
2.20	9.025	9.116	9.207	9.300	9.393	9.488	9.583	9.679	9.777	9.875
2.30	9.974	10.07	10.18	10.28	10.38	10.49	10.59	10.70	10.80	10.91
2.40	11.02	11.13	11.25	11.36	11.47	11.59	11.70	11.82	11.94	12.06
2.50	12.18	12.30	12.43	12.55	12.68	12.81	12.94	13.07	13.20	13.33
2.60	13.46	13.60	13.74	13.87	14.01	14.15	14.30	14.44	14.59	14.73
2.70	14.88	15.03	15.18	15.33	15.49	15.64	15.80	15.96	16.12	16.28
2.80	16.44	16.61	16.78	16.95	17.12	17.29	17.46	17.64	17.81	17.99
2.90	18.17	18.36	18.54	18.73	18.92	19.11	19.30	19.49	19.69	19.89
3.00	20.09	20.29	20.49	20.70	20.91	21.12	21.33	21.54	21.76	21.98
3.10	22.20	22.42	22.65	22.87	23.10	23.34	23.57	23.81	24.05	24.29
3.20	24.53	24.78	25.03	25.28	25.53	25.79	26.05	26.31	26.58	26.84
3.30	27.11	27.39	27.66	27.94	28.22	28.50	28.79	29.08	29.37	29.67
3.40	29.96	30.27	30.57	30.88	31.19	31.50	31.82	32.14	32.46	32.79
3.50	33.12	33.45	33.78	34.12	34.47	34.81	35.16	35.52	35.87	36.23
3.60	36.60	36.97	37.34	37.71	38.09	38.47	38.86	39.25	39.65	40.04
3.70	40.45	40.85	41.26	41.68	42.10	42.52	42.95	43.38	43.82	44.26
3.80	44.70	45.15	45.60	46.06	46.53	46.99	47.47	47.94	48.42	48.91
3.90	49.40	49.90	50.40	50.91	51.42	51.94	52.46	52.98	53.52	54.05

APPENDIX TABLE 5

Present value of $1 per year received in a continuous stream for each of t years (discounted at an *annually compounded* rate r) = $\{1 - 1/(1 + r)^t\}/\{\ln(1 + r)\}$.

Number of Years	Interest Rate per Year														
	1%	2%	3%	4%	5%	6%	7%	8%	9%	10%	11%	12%	13%	14%	15%
1	.995	.990	.985	.981	.976	.971	.967	.962	.958	.954	.950	.945	.941	.937	.933
2	1.980	1.961	1.942	1.924	1.906	1.888	1.871	1.854	1.837	1.821	1.805	1.790	1.774	1.759	1.745
3	2.956	2.913	2.871	2.830	2.791	2.752	2.715	2.679	2.644	2.609	2.576	2.543	2.512	2.481	2.450
4	3.922	3.846	3.773	3.702	3.634	3.568	3.504	3.443	3.383	3.326	3.270	3.216	3.164	3.113	3.064
5	4.878	4.760	4.648	4.540	4.437	4.337	4.242	4.150	4.062	3.977	3.896	3.817	3.741	3.668	3.598
6	5.825	5.657	5.498	5.346	5.202	5.063	4.931	4.805	4.685	4.570	4.459	4.353	4.252	4.155	4.062
7	6.762	6.536	6.323	6.121	5.930	5.748	5.576	5.412	5.256	5.108	4.967	4.832	4.704	4.582	4.465
8	7.690	7.398	7.124	6.867	6.623	6.394	6.178	5.974	5.780	5.597	5.424	5.260	5.104	4.956	4.816
9	8.609	8.243	7.902	7.583	7.284	7.004	6.741	6.494	6.261	6.042	5.836	5.642	5.458	5.285	5.121
10	9.519	9.072	8.657	8.272	7.913	7.579	7.267	6.975	6.702	6.447	6.208	5.983	5.772	5.573	5.386
11	10.42	9.884	9.391	8.935	8.512	8.121	7.758	7.421	7.107	6.815	6.542	6.287	6.049	5.826	5.617
12	11.31	10.68	10.10	9.572	9.083	8.633	8.218	7.834	7.478	7.149	6.843	6.559	6.294	6.048	5.818
13	12.19	11.46	10.79	10.18	9.627	9.116	8.647	8.216	7.819	7.453	7.115	6.802	6.512	6.242	5.992
14	13.07	12.23	11.46	10.77	10.14	9.571	9.048	8.570	8.131	7.729	7.359	7.018	6.704	6.413	6.144
15	13.93	12.98	12.12	11.34	10.64	10.00	9.423	8.897	8.418	7.980	7.579	7.212	6.874	6.563	6.276
16	14.79	13.71	12.75	11.88	11.11	10.41	9.774	9.201	8.681	8.209	7.778	7.385	7.024	6.694	6.390
17	15.64	14.43	13.36	12.41	11.55	10.79	10.10	9.482	8.923	8.416	7.957	7.539	7.158	6.809	6.490
18	16.48	15.14	13.96	12.91	11.98	11.15	10.41	9.742	9.144	8.605	8.118	7.676	7.275	6.910	6.577
19	17.31	15.83	14.54	13.39	12.39	11.49	10.69	9.983	9.347	8.777	8.263	7.799	7.380	6.999	6.652
20	18.14	16.51	15.10	13.86	12.77	11.81	10.96	10.21	9.533	8.932	8.394	7.909	7.472	7.077	6.718
25	22.13	19.72	17.67	15.93	14.44	13.16	12.06	11.10	10.26	9.524	8.877	8.305	7.797	7.344	6.938
30	25.94	22.62	19.89	17.64	15.75	14.17	12.84	11.70	10.73	9.891	9.164	8.529	7.973	7.482	7.047

Note: For example, if the interest rate is 10 percent per year, a continuous cash flow of $1 a year for each of 5 years is worth $3.977. A continuous flow of $1 in year 5 only is worth $3.977 − $3.326 = $.651.

Number of Years	Interest Rate per Year														
	16%	17%	18%	19%	20%	21%	22%	23%	24%	25%	26%	27%	28%	29%	30%
1	.929	.925	.922	.918	.914	.910	.907	.903	.900	.896	.893	.889	.886	.883	.880
2	1.730	1.716	1.703	1.689	1.676	1.663	1.650	1.638	1.625	1.613	1.601	1.590	1.578	1.567	1.556
3	2.421	2.392	2.365	2.337	2.311	2.285	2.259	2.235	2.211	2.187	2.164	2.141	2.119	2.098	2.077
4	3.016	2.970	2.925	2.882	2.840	2.799	2.759	2.720	2.682	2.646	2.610	2.576	2.542	2.509	2.477
5	3.530	3.464	3.401	3.340	3.281	3.223	3.168	3.115	3.063	3.013	2.964	2.917	2.872	2.828	2.785
6	3.972	3.886	3.804	3.724	3.648	3.574	3.504	3.436	3.370	3.307	3.246	3.187	3.130	3.075	3.022
7	4.354	4.247	4.145	4.048	3.954	3.865	3.779	3.696	3.617	3.542	3.469	3.399	3.331	3.266	3.204
8	4.682	4.555	4.434	4.319	4.209	4.104	4.004	3.909	3.817	3.730	3.646	3.566	3.489	3.415	3.344
9	4.966	4.819	4.680	4.547	4.422	4.302	4.189	4.081	3.978	3.880	3.786	3.697	3.612	3.530	3.452
10	5.210	5.044	4.887	4.739	4.599	4.466	4.340	4.221	4.108	4.000	3.898	3.801	3.708	3.619	3.535
11	5.421	5.237	5.063	4.900	4.747	4.602	4.465	4.335	4.213	4.096	3.986	3.882	3.783	3.689	3.599
12	5.603	5.401	5.213	5.036	4.870	4.713	4.566	4.428	4.297	4.173	4.057	3.946	3.841	3.742	3.648
13	5.759	5.542	5.339	5.150	4.972	4.806	4.650	4.503	4.365	4.235	4.112	3.997	3.887	3.784	3.686
14	5.894	5.662	5.446	5.245	5.058	4.882	4.718	4.564	4.420	4.284	4.157	4.036	3.923	3.816	3.715
15	6.010	5.765	5.537	5.326	5.129	4.945	4.774	4.614	4.464	4.324	4.192	4.068	3.951	3.841	3.737
16	6.111	5.853	5.614	5.393	5.188	4.998	4.820	4.655	4.500	4.355	4.220	4.092	3.973	3.860	3.754
17	6.197	5.928	5.679	5.450	5.238	5.041	4.858	4.687	4.529	4.381	4.242	4.112	3.990	3.875	3.767
18	6.272	5.992	5.735	5.498	5.279	5.076	4.889	4.714	4.552	4.401	4.259	4.127	4.003	3.887	3.778
19	6.336	6.047	5.781	5.538	5.313	5.106	4.914	4.736	4.571	4.417	4.273	4.139	4.014	3.896	3.785
20	6.391	6.094	5.821	5.571	5.342	5.130	4.935	4.754	4.586	4.430	4.284	4.149	4.022	3.903	3.791
25	6.573	6.244	5.945	5.674	5.427	5.201	4.994	4.803	4.627	4.464	4.314	4.173	4.042	3.920	3.806
30	6.659	6.312	6.000	5.718	5.462	5.229	5.016	4.821	4.641	4.476	4.323	4.181	4.048	3.925	3.810

APPENDIX TABLE 6

Cumulative probability [N(d)] that a normally distributed variable will be less than d standard deviations above the mean.

d	0	0.01	0.02	0.03	0.04	0.05	0.06	0.07	0.08	0.09
0	.5000	.5040	.5080	.5120	.5160	.5199	.5239	.5279	.5319	.5359
0.1	.5398	.5438	.5478	.5517	.5557	.5596	.5636	.5675	.5714	.5753
0.2	.5793	.5832	.5871	.5910	.5948	.5987	.6026	.6064	.6103	.6141
0.3	.6179	.6217	.6255	.6293	.6331	.6368	.6406	.6443	.6480	.6517
0.4	.6554	.6591	.6628	.6664	.6700	.6736	.6772	.6808	.6844	.6879
0.5	.6915	.6950	.6985	.7019	.7054	.7088	.7123	.7157	.7190	.7224
0.6	.7257	.7291	.7324	.7357	.7389	.7422	.7454	.7486	.7517	.7549
0.7	.7580	.7611	.7642	.7673	.7704	.7734	.7764	.7794	.7823	.7852
0.8	.7881	.7910	.7939	.7967	.7995	.8023	.8051	.8078	.8106	.8133
0.9	.8159	.8186	.8212	.8238	.8264	.8289	.8315	.8340	.8365	.8389
1	.8413	.8438	.8461	.8485	.8508	.8531	.8554	.8577	.8599	.8621
1.1	.8643	.8665	.8686	.8708	.8729	.8749	.8770	.8790	.8810	.8830
1.2	.8849	.8869	.8888	.8907	.8925	.8944	.8962	.8980	.8997	.9015
1.3	.9032	.9049	.9066	.9082	.9099	.9115	.9131	.9147	.9162	.9177
1.4	.9192	.9207	.9222	.9236	.9251	.9265	.9279	.9292	.9306	.9319
1.5	.9332	.9345	.9357	.9370	.9382	.9394	.9406	.9418	.9429	.9441
1.6	.9452	.9463	.9474	.9484	.9495	.9505	.9515	.9525	.9535	.9545
1.7	.9554	.9564	.9573	.9582	.9591	.9599	.9608	.9616	.9625	.9633
1.8	.9641	.9649	.9656	.9664	.9671	.9678	.9686	.9693	.9699	.9706
1.9	.9713	.9719	.9726	.9732	.9738	.9744	.9750	.9756	.9761	.9767
2	.9772	.9778	.9783	.9788	.9793	.9798	.9803	.9808	.9812	.9817
2.1	.9821	.9826	.9830	.9834	.9838	.9842	.9846	.9850	.9854	.9857
2.2	.9861	.9864	.9868	.9871	.9875	.9878	.9881	.9884	.9887	.9890
2.3	.9893	.9896	.9898	.9901	.9904	.9906	.9909	.9911	.9913	.9916
2.4	.9918	.9920	.9922	.9925	.9927	.9929	.9931	.9932	.9934	.9936
2.5	.9938	.9940	.9941	.9943	.9945	.9946	.9948	.9949	.9951	.9952

Note: For example, if d = .22, N(d) = .5871 (i.e., there is a .5871 probability that a normally distributed variable will be less than .22 standard deviations above the mean).

Chapter 1

1. **(a)** Real; **(b)** executive airplanes; **(c)** brand names; **(d)** financial; **(e)** bonds; **(f)** investment; **(g)** capital budgeting; **(h)** financing.

2. **a.** Financial assets, such as stocks or bank loans, are claims held by investors. Corporations sell financial assets to raise the cash to invest in real assets such as plant and equipment. Some real assets are intangible.

   b. Capital budgeting means investment in real assets. Financing means raising the cash for this investment.

   c. The shares of public corporations are traded on stock exchanges and can be purchased by a wide range of investors. The shares of closely held corporations are not traded and are not generally available to investors.

   d. Unlimited liability: investors are responsible for all the firm's debts. A sole proprietor has unlimited liability. Investors in corporations have limited liability. They can lose their investment, but no more.

   e. A corporation is a separate legal "person" with unlimited life. Its owners hold shares in the business. A partnership is a limited-life agreement to establish and run a business.

3. *c, d, e,* and *g* are real assets. Others are financial.

4. Double taxation and agency costs due to separation of ownership and control. Public organizations also face the higher costs of complying with legal requirements and communicating with dispersed shareholders.

5. *a, c, d.*

6. *c, d.*

7. Principal–agent issues, often amplified by asymmetric information.

8. Conflicts of interest or differences in incentives create principal–agent problems. Agency costs are incurred if value-maximizing decisions are not made and if principals incur costs of monitoring or control.

Chapter 2

1. **(a)** Negative; **(b)** $PV = C_1/(1 + r)$; **(c)** $NPV = C_0 + (C_1/(1 + r))$; **(d)** r is the return foregone by investing in the project rather than the capital market; **(e)** the return offered by default-free U.S. Treasury securities.

2. $DF_1 = .867$; discount rate $= .154$, or 15.4%.

3. **(a)** .909; **(b)** .833; **(c)** .769.

4. **(a)** Return $=$ profit/investment $= (132 - 100)/100 = .32$, or 32%; **(b)** Negative (if the rate of interest r equals 32%, NPV $= 0$); **(c)** $PV = 132/1.10 = 120$, or \$120,000; **(d)** $NPV = -100 + 120 = 20$, or \$20,000.

5. Net present value rule: Invest if NPV is positive. Rate of return rule: Invest if the rate of return exceeds the opportunity cost of capital. They give the same answer.

6. The return foregone by investing in a project rather than in securities. The opportunity cost of capital for a risk-free investment is the interest rate on government bonds. For risky investments firms need to estimate the return expected by investors from securities of similar risk.

7. A would lend and consume \$120 next year. G would consume now. Neither would invest at 14%.

8. They will vote for *a* only. The other tasks can be carried out just as efficiently by stockholders.

9. To protect and enhance their reputations; because compensation is tied to earnings and stock price; supervision by the board of directors; the threat of takeover.

10. Investors were concerned that Salomon's damaged reputation would drive away its customers.

Chapter 3

1. $1.00.

2. $125/139 = .899$.

3. $596 \times .285 = \$170$.

4. $374/(1.09)^9 = \$172$.

5. $PV = 432/1.15 + 137/(1.15)^2 + 797/(1.15)^3$
$= 376 + 104 + 524 = 1,004$.

6. $100 \times (1.15)^8 = \$305.90$.

7. $NPV = -1548 + 138/.09 = -\$14.67$.

8. $PV = 4/(.14 - .04) = \$40$.

9. $1,006,512.

10. (a) $PV = 1/.10 = \$10$; (b) $PV = (1/.10)/(1.10)^7 = 10/2 = \$5$ (approximately); (c) $PV = 10 - 5 = \$5$ (approximately); (d) $PV = C/(r - g) = 10,000/(.10 - .05) = \$200,000$.

11. a. From Appendix Table 1, $1/(1.05)^5 = .784$. You therefore need to set aside $10,000 \times .784 = \$7,840$.
    b. From Appendix Table 3, the present value of $1 a year for 6 years at 8% is $4.623. Therefore you need to set aside $12,000 \times 4.623 = \$55,476$.
    c. From Appendix Table 2, $1.08^6 = 1.587$. Therefore, at the end of 6 years you would have $1.587 \times (60,476 - 55,476) = \$7,935$.

12. $(1.25)/(1.21) - 1 = .033$, or 3.3%.

13. (a) $1,000e^{.12 \times 5} = 1,000e^{.6} = \$1,822$; (b) $PV = 5e^{-.12 \times 8} = 5e^{-.96} = \$1.915$ million; (c) $PV = C/r(1 - e^{-rt}) = 2,000/.12(1 - e^{-.12 \times 15}) = \$13,912$.

14. (a) $12.625 million; (b) $12.705 million; (c) $12.712 million.

15. $1,133.55. This calculation assumes annual coupon payments and compounding.

16. The yield to maturity is the (single) discount rate that gives a present value equal to a bond's price. It is calculated by trial and error, by computer or calculator, or from bond tables.

Chapter 4

1. (a) True; (b) true.

2. Investors who buy stocks may get their return from capital gains as well as dividends. But the future stock price always depends on subsequent dividends. There is no inconsistency.

3. $P_0 = (10 + 110)/1.10 = \$109.09$.

4. $r = 5/40 = .125$.

5. $P_0 = 10/(.08 - .05) = \$333.33$.

6. By year 4, earnings will grow to $18.23 per share. Forecasted price per share at year 4 is $18.23/.08 = \$227.91$.

$$P_0 = \frac{10}{1.08} + \frac{10.50}{(1.08)^2} + \frac{11.03}{(1.08)^3} + \frac{11.58}{(1.08)^4}$$
$$+ \frac{227.91}{(1.08)^4} = 203.05.$$

7. $15/.08 + PVGO = 333.33$; therefore $PVGO = \$145.83$.

8. Z's forecasted dividends and prices grow as follows:

	Year 1	Year 2	Year 3
Dividend	10	10.50	11.03
Price	350	367.50	385.88

Calculate the expected rates of return:

From year 0 to 1: $\dfrac{10 + (350 - 333.33)}{333.33} = .08$.

From year 1 to 2: $\dfrac{10.50 + (367.50 - 350)}{350} = .08$.

From year 2 to 3: $\dfrac{11.03 + (385.88 - 367.50)}{367.50} = .08$

Double expects 8% in *each* of the first 2 years. Triple expects 8% in *each* of the first 3 years.

9. (a) False; (b) true.

10. $PVGO = 0$, and EPS_1 equals the average future earnings the firm could generate under no-growth policy.

11. Free cash flow equals the net cash flow available to shareholders after paying for all future investments. Free cash flow can be negative if investments are large. Dividends are the cash paid out to stockholders. A company could have negative free cash flow but sell new shares and still pay a dividend.

12. Dividends or free cash flow are forecasted to a horizon, and a horizon value is added. Two-stage models are used when near-term cash flows grow at irregular or unsustainable rates. For example, the company may be recovering from a period of low profits, or profitability and growth may be high for a limited period.

13. The value at the end of a forecast period. It can be estimated by the constant-growth DCF formula or by using price–earnings or market–book ratios for similar companies. If $PVGO = 0$ at the horizon date H, horizon value equals earnings forecasted at date $H + 1$ divided by r.

14. Earnings forecasted for date $H + 1$ divided by r.

Chapter 5

1. The opportunity cost of capital is the expected rate of return investors could earn in financial markets at the same level of risk as the asset to be valued.

2. (a) A = 3 years, B = 2 years, C = 3 years; (b) B; (c) A, B, and C; (d) B and C (NPV$_B$ = $3,378; NPV$_C$ = $2,405); (e) false; (f) true; (g) It will accept no negative-NPV projects but will turn down some with positive NPVs. A project can have positive NPV if all future cash flows are considered but still not meet the stated cutoff period.

3. The ratio of book (accounting) income to book assets. This ratio depends on accounting procedures. It is not calculated from project cash flows. The time value of money is ignored.

4. Given the cash flows $C_0, C_1, \ldots, C_T$, IRR is defined by

$$NPV = C_0 + \frac{C_1}{1 + IRR} + \frac{C_2}{(1 + IRR)^2}$$
$$+ \cdots + \frac{C_T}{(1 + IRR)^T} = 0.$$

It is calculated by trial and error, by financial calculators, or by spreadsheet programs.

5. (a) $15,750; $4,250; $0; (b) 100%.

6. No (you are effectively "borrowing" at a rate of interest higher than the opportunity cost of capital).

7. (a) Two, −50% and +50%; (b) yes, NPV = +14.6.

8. The incremental flows from investing in Alpha rather than Beta are −200,000; +110,000; and 121,000. The IRR on the incremental cash flow is 10 percent (i.e., −200 + 110/1.10 + 121/1.10^2 = 0). The IRR on Beta exceeds the cost of capital and so does the IRR on the incremental investment in Alpha. Choose Alpha.

9. 1, 2, 4, and 6.

10. Soft rationing means provisional capital constraints imposed by management as an aid to financial control. This doesn't rule out raising more money if necessary. Firms facing hard rationing can't raise money from capital markets. NPV is not ruled out as long as shareholders have access to capital markets.

Chapter 6

1. a, b, d, g, h.

2. Real cash flow = 100,000/1.04 = 96,154; real discount rate = 1.08/1.04 − 1 = .0385.

$$PV = \frac{96,154}{1.0385} = 92,589, \text{ four euros short}$$

because of rounding error.

3. (a) False; (b) false; (c) false; (d) false.

4. The longer the recovery period, the less the present value of depreciation tax shields. This is true regardless of the discount rate. If, say, r = .10, then 35% of the 5-year schedule's PV is .271. The same calculation for the 7-year schedule yields .253.

5.

	2000	2001	2002	2003	2004
Working capital	50,000	230,000	305,000	250,000	0
Cash flows	+50,000	+180,000	+75,000	−55,000	−250,000

6. The checklist would include: forecasting cash flows in euros (taking account of French inflation); recognizing French corporate tax rules and rates; and discounting at a euro cost of capital.

7. Comparing present values can be misleading when projects have different economic lives and the projects are part of an ongoing business. For example, a machine that costs $100,000 per year to buy and lasts 5 years is not necessarily more expensive than a machine that costs $75,000 per year to buy but lasts only 3 years. Calculating the machines' equivalent annual costs allows an unbiased comparison.

8. Plan to undertake the project at the future date which yields the highest NPV *today*. (This assumes certainty. We consider timing under uncertainty in Chapter 22.)

9. PV cost = 1.5 + .2 × 14.09 = $4.319 million. Equivalent annual cost = 4.319/14.09 = .306, or $306,000.

10. a. NPV$_A$ = $100,000; NPV$_B$ = $180,000.
    b. Equivalent cash flow of   A = 100,000/1.736 = $57,604; equivalent cash flow of B = 180,000/2.487 = $72,376.
    c. Machine B.

11. Replace at end of 5 years ($80,000 > $72,376).

Chapter 7

1. **(a)** About 13%; **(b)** about 9%; **(c)** about 1%; **(d)** about 20% (less in recent years); **(e)** less (diversification reduces risk).

2. Expected payoff is $100 and expected return is zero. Variance is 20,000 (percent squared) and standard deviation is 141%.

3. **(a)** 35.5%; **(b)** 7.1%.

4. Standard deviation of returns, correlated, less, unique, market.

5. Mr. Interchange had a lower average return than the S&P (15.6% versus 19.4%) but also a lower standard deviation (12.0% versus 14.9%).

6. **(a)** False; **(b)** true; **(c)** true; **(d)** true; **(e)** false.

7. *d*

8.

$x_1^2\sigma_1^2$	$x_1x_2\sigma_{12}$	$x_1x_3\sigma_{13}$
$x_1x_2\sigma_{12}$	$x_2^2\sigma_2^2$	$x_2x_3\sigma_{23}$
$x_1x_3\sigma_{13}$	$x_2x_3\sigma_{23}$	$x_3^2\sigma_3^2$

9. **(a)** 26%; **(b)** zero; **(c)** .75; **(d)** less than 1.0 (the portfolio's risk is the same as the market, but some of this risk is unique risk).

10. 1.3 (Diversification does not affect market risk.)

11. A, 1.0; B, 2.0; C, 1.5; D, 0; E, −1.0.

12. False. Corporations can reduce risk by diversifying but so can investors. Therefore they will not be prepared to pay extra for the stocks of diversified companies.

Chapter 8

1. **(a)** 7%; **(b)** 27% with perfect positive correlation; 1% with perfect negative correlation; 19.1% with no correlation; **(c)** See Figure 1; **(d)** No, measure risk by beta, not by standard deviation.

2. **(a)** Portfolio A (higher expected return, same risk); **(b)** Cannot say (depends on investor's attitude toward risk); **(c)** Portfolio F (lower risk, same expected return).

3. **a.** Figure 8.13b: Diversification reduces risk (e.g., a mixture of portfolios A and B would have less risk than the average of A and B).
   b. Those along line *AB* in Figure 8.13a.
   c. See Figure 2.

4. **(a)** See Figure 3; **(b)** A, D, G; **(c)** F; **(d)** 15% in C. **(e)** Put 25/32 of your money in F and lend 7/32 at 12%: Expected return = 7/32 × 12 + 25/32 × 18 = 16.7%; standard deviation = 7/32 × 0 + (25/32) × 32 = 25%. If you could borrow without limit, you would achieve as high an expected return as you'd like, with correspondingly high risk, of course.

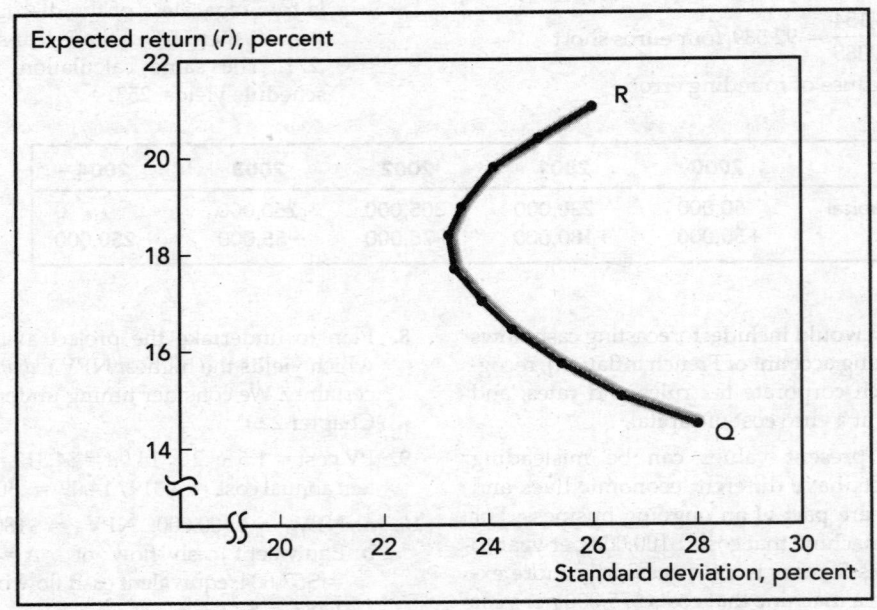

FIGURE 1

Chapter 8, Quiz question 1(c).

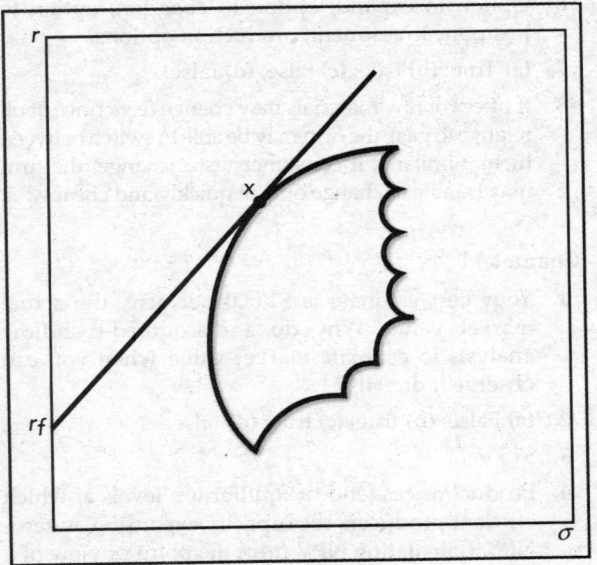

FIGURE 2

Chapter 8, Quiz question 3(c).

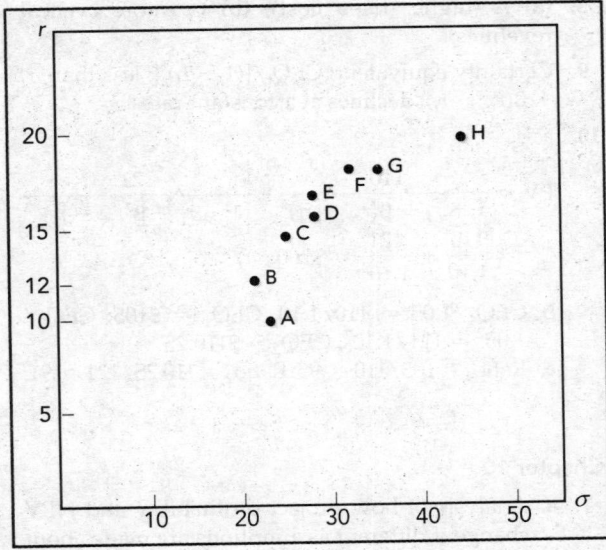

FIGURE 3

Chapter 8, Quiz question 4(a).

5. The best portfolio will be a combination of lending or borrowing, plus investment in the stock portfolio with the highest *ratio* of expected risk premium to standard deviation. See Figure 8.6.

6. **(a)** $r = 4 + .68(10 - 4) = 8.08\%$; **(b)** Amazon.com at 23.5%; **(c)** Exxon Mobil at 6.4%; **(d)** lower; **(e)** higher.

7. **(a)** True; **(b)** false (it offers twice the market *risk premium*); **(c)** false.

8. Because beta does not seem to explain average returns. The relationship between beta and average return has been too "flat"—see Figure 8.9. Other factors, such as the book-to-market ratio, seem to explain differences in average returns.

9. $r - r_f = b_1(r_{factor\,1} - r_f) + b_2(r_{factor\,2} - r_f) + \cdots$,

   r = expected return on stock,

   r_f = risk-free interest rate,

   $r_{factor\,j}$ = expected return on portfolio of stocks that is exposed only to the jth economic factor,

   b_j = sensitivity of stock to returns on jth factor.

10. **(a)** 7%; **(b)** $7 + 1(5) + 1(-1) + 1(2) = 13\%$; **(c)** $7 + 0(5) + 2(-1) + 0(2) = 5\%$; **(d)** $7 + 1(5) + (-1.5)(-1) + 1(2) = 15.5\%$.

11. Market factor (risk premium), size factor (return on small-firm stocks less return on large-firm stocks), book-to-market factor (return on high book-to-market stocks less return on low book-to-market stocks).

Chapter 9

1. Overestimate.

2. False. Beta depends on returns, not on the levels of stock price or the market index.

3. 27% was explained by market movements, 73% by unique risk. Unique risk shows up as the scatter of points around the fitted line. The standard error is .38, so plus or minus two standard errors gives a range of 1.26 to 2.78.

4. $\beta_{assets} = 0 \times .40 + .5 \times .60 = .30$,
   $r = 10 + .30(18 - 10) = 12.4\%$.

5. **a.** $r_f + \beta(r_m - r_f) = 8 + 1.5 \times 9 = 21.5\%$.

   b. $\beta_{assets} = \beta_{debt}\left(\dfrac{debt}{debt + equity}\right)$
   $\qquad + \beta_{equity}\left(\dfrac{equity}{debt + equity}\right)$
   $\qquad = 0 \times \dfrac{4}{4 + 6} + 1.5 \times \dfrac{6}{4 + 6}$
   $\qquad = .9.$

   c. $r_f + \beta_{assets}(r_m - r_f) = 8 + .9 \times 9 = 16.1\%$;
   d. $r = 16.1\%$; **(e)** $r_f + \beta(r_m - r_f) = 8 + 1.2 \times 9 = 18.8\%$.

6. **(a)** .73; **(b)** It would not change at all; **(c)** $r = 5 + .73(6) = 9.4\%$.

7. **(a)** True; **(b)** false; **(c)** true.

8. (a) A (higher fixed cost); (b) C (more cyclical revenues).

9. Certainty equivalent; $CEQ_t/[(1 + r_f)^t]$; less than; $r_f + \beta(r_m - r_f)$; declines at a constant rate.

10. a.

$$PV = \frac{110}{1 + r_f + \beta(r_m - r_f)} + \frac{121}{[1 + r_f + \beta(r_m - r_f)]^2}$$

$$= \frac{110}{1.10} + \frac{121}{1.10^2} = \$200.$$

b. $CEQ_1/1.05 = 110/1.10$, $CEQ_1 = \$105$; $CEQ_2/1.05^2 = 121/1.10^2$, $CEQ_2 = \$110.25$.

c. $Ratio_1 = 105/110 = .95$; $Ratio_2 = 110.25/121 = .91$.

Chapter 10

1. a. Analysis of how project profitability and NPV change if different assumptions are made about sales, cost, and other key variables.
   b. Project NPV is recalculated by changing several inputs to new, but consistent values.
   c. Determines the level of future sales at which project profitability or NPV equals zero.
   d. An extension of sensitivity analysis which explores all possible outcomes and weights each by its probability.
   e. A graphical technique for displaying possible future events and decisions taken in response to those events.
   f. Option to modify a project at a future date.
   g. The additional present value created by the option to bail out of a project, and recover part of the initial investment, if the project performs poorly.
   h. The additional present value created by the option to invest more and expand output, if a project performs well.

2. (a) False; (b) true; (c) true; (d) true; (e) true; (f) false.

3. It shows how the project would fare under consistent combinations of input assumptions. Sensitivity analysis changes only one input at a time.

4. Monte Carlo helps reveal what can go wrong (or right) with a project. It helps the manager to obtain an accurate forecast of expected cash flows. It also helps in assessing project risk and determining the appropriate discount rate.

5. a. Describe how project cash flow depends on the underlying variables.
   b. Specify probability distributions for forecast errors for these cash flows.
   c. Draw from the probability distributions to simulate the cash flows.

6. Option to expand; option to abandon; option to postpone investment; production options.

7. (a) True; (b) true; (c) false; (d) false.

8. If prices of raw materials may change (e.g., price of oil relative to gas), the firm may be able to switch between them. Similarly, if consumer tastes change, the firm may be able to change output quickly and cheaply.

Chapter 11

1. Your best estimate is $1,000 per acre, the actual market value. Why do a discounted-cash-flow analysis to estimate market value when you can observe it directly?

2. (a) False; (b) true; (c) true; (d) false.

3. $15

4. Product prices tend to equilibrium levels at which efficient producers see capacity expansion as zero-NPV. Calculating NPV from the point of view of a European competitor allowed estimation of this equilibrium price.

5. First consider whether *renting* the building and opening the Taco Palace is positive NPV. Then consider whether to buy (instead of renting) based on your optimistic view of local real estate.

6. The present value of the future price of gold is equal to today's price. Just multiply production volume by today's gold price.

7. (a) $160/1.05 = \$152.4$ million; (b) The expected rate of return is $r_f + \beta(r_m - r_f) = .05 + 1.2(.12 - .05) = .134$, or 13.4%. The expected price is $1,524 \times 1.134 = 1,728$. The certainty equivalent price is 1,600.

8. The second-hand market value of older planes falls by enough to make up for their higher fuel consumption. Also, the older planes are used on routes where fuel efficiency is relatively less important.

9. *b* and *d* are clear lessons. *c* can be true: reduction in profits from an existing project is a valid concern. But if competitor's new products would harm existing projects in any case, there is no reason to hold back on *your* new product. *a* is wrong: growth or high-tech products do not necessarily mean positive NPV. *e* is wrong: the book value of a plant does not show the opportunity cost of using it.

Chapter 12

1. (a) False; (b) true; (c) true; (d) false; (e) true (e.g., marketing programs and training); (f) false.

2. a. Can lead to investment in negative-NPV projects.
   b. Confuses the relative NPVs of projects proposed by different business units.

c. Project interactions may be ignored. Some opportunities, such as the closing or sale of a division, will not be considered. Strategic investments may be missed.

d. Creates a bias in favor of quick payback projects and against long-lived projects that may have large NPVs.

3. A change in the hurdle rate is offset by more or less optimistic forecasts by project sponsors. There's no way out: the financial manager can't avoid careful assessment of cash-flow forecasts.

4. *Agency costs:* value lost when managers do not act to maximize value. This includes costs of monitoring and control.

Private benefits: perks or other advantages enjoyed by managers.

Empire building: investing for size, not NPV.

Free-rider problem: when one shareholder, or group of shareholders, acts to monitor and control management, all shareholders benefit.

Entrenching investment: managers choose or design investment projects which increase the managers' value to the firm.

10.

	Year 1	Year 2	Year 3
Cash flow	0	78.55	78.55
PV at start of year	100.00	120.00	65.45
PV at end of year	120.00	65.45	0
Change in value during year	+20.00	−54.55	−65.45
Expected economic income	+20.00	+24.00	+13.10

Delegated monitoring: monitoring on behalf of principals. For example, the board of directors monitors management performance on behalf of stockholders.

5. Monitoring is costly and encounters diminishing returns. Also, completely effective monitoring would require perfect information.

6. **(a)** Dollar amount; **(b)** EVA = Income earned − (cost of capital × investment); **(c)** They are essentially the same; **(d)** EVA makes the cost of capital visible to managers. Compensation based on EVA encourages them to dispose of unnecessary assets and to forego investment unless it earns more than the cost of capital; **(e)** Yes.

7. Return on investment = 1.6/20 = .08 or 8%. EVA = 1.6 − (.115 × 20) = −$.7 million. EVA is negative.

8. **(a)** False: profits may be depressed temporarily, but in a steady state, writing off R&D can increase the book rate of return; **(b)** true—because asset value is understated, the ratio of income to assets is biased upward.

9. Cash flow, economic, less, greater.

Chapter 13

1. *c*

2. Weak, semistrong, strong, strong, weak.

3. **(a)** False; **(b)** false; **(c)** true; **(d)** false; **(e)** false; **(f)** true.

4. **(a)** Decline to $200; **(b)** less; **(c)** A slight abnormal fall (the split is likely to have led investors to expect an above-average rise in dividends).

5. **(a)** False; **(b)** true; **(c)** false; **(d)** true; **(e)** false; **(f)** true (a small change in price *in the absence of new information* causes a large increase in demand).

6. 6 − (−.2 + 1.45 × 5) = −1.05%.

7. **(a)** True; **(b)** false; **(c)** true; **(d)** true.

8. Decrease. The stock price already reflects an expected 25% increase. The 20% increase conveys bad news relative to expectations.

9. **a.** An investor should not buy or sell shares based on apparent trends or cycles in returns.

b. A CFO should not speculate on changes in interest rates or foreign exchange rates. There is no reason to think that the CFO has superior information.

c. A financial manager evaluating the creditworthiness of a large customer could check the customer's stock price and the yield on its debt. A falling stock price or a high yield could indicate trouble ahead.

d. Don't assume that accounting choices which increase or decrease earnings will have any effect on stock price.

e. The company should not seek diversification just to reduce risk. Investors can diversify on their own.

f. Stock issues do not depress price if investors believe the issuer has no private information.

Chapter 14

1.

Internally generated cash	77
Financial deficit	23
Net share issues	−14
Debt issues	38

2. **(a)** False; **(b)** true; **(c)** true; **(d)** false.

3. **(a)** 40,000/.50 = 80,000 shares; **(b)** 78,000 shares; **(c)** 2,000 shares are held as Treasury stock; **(d)** 20,000 shares.

	(e)	**(f)**
Common stock	$ 45,000	$40,000
Additional paid-in capital	25,000	10,000
Retained earnings	30,000	30,000
Common equity	100,000	80,000
Treasury stock	5,000	30,000
Net common equity	$ 95,000	$50,000

4. **(a)** 80 votes; **(b)** 10 × 80 = 800 votes.

5. *Similarities with debt:* **(a)** Fixed income; **(b)** preferred stockholders have limited voting rights.
   Similarities with equity: **(a)** Dividend is within discretion of directors; **(b)** no final repayment date; **(c)** dividend is not an allowable deduction from taxable profits.

6. **(a)** subordinated; **(b)** floating rate; **(c)** convertible; **(d)** warrant; **(e)** common stock; preferred stock.

7. **(a)** False; **(b)** true; **(c)** false.

8. A debt issue sold in international markets.

9. Support of the payment mechanism, facilitating borrowing and lending, pooling risk.

Chapter 15

1. **(a)** Further sale of an already publicly traded stock; **(b)** U.S. bond issue by foreign corporation; **(c)** Bond issue by industrial company; **(d)** Bond issue by large industrial company.

2. **(a)** B; **(b)** A; **(c)** D; **(d)** C.

3. **a.** Financing of startup companies.
   b. First sale of a security to public investors.
   c. Trading of a security after it is issued.
   d. Description of a security offering filed with the SEC.
   e. Winning bidders for a new issue tend to overpay.
   f. One or a few underwriters buy an entire issue.

4. **(a)** A large issue; **(b)** a bond issue; **(c)** subsequent issue of stock; **(d)** a small private placement of bonds.

5. **(a)** False; **(b)** true; **(c)** true.

6. **(a)** 135,000 shares; **(b)** primary: 500,000 shares; secondary: 400,000 shares; **(c)** $25 or 31%, which is higher than the average underpricing.

(d)

	Millions
Underwriting cost	$ 5.04
Administrative cost	.82
Underpricing	22.5
Total	$28.36

Note: Calculation ignores cost of shares sold under greenshoe option.

7. **a.** Net proceeds of public issue = 10,000,000 − 150,000 − 80,000 = $9,770,000; net proceeds of private placement = $9,970,000.
   b. PV of extra interest on private placement =
   $$\sum_{t=1}^{10} \frac{.005 \times 10,000,000}{1.085^t} = \$328,000,$$
   i.e., extra cost of higher interest on private placement more than outweighs saving in issue costs. N.b. We ignore taxes.
   c. Private placement debt can be custom-tailored and the terms more easily renegotiated.

8. An underwriter building a book solicits bids from investors, but the bids are not binding and are used only as a guide to set the issue price.

9. **(a)** Number of new shares, 50,000; **(b)** Amount of new investment, $500,000; **(c)** Total value of company after issue, $4,500,000; **(d)** Total number of shares after issue, 150,000; **(e)** Stock price after issue, $4,500,000/150,000 = $30; **(f)** The opportunity to buy one share is worth $20.

Chapter 16

1. **(a)** A1, B5; A2, B4; A3, B3; A4, B1; A5, B2. **(b)** March 7 = ex-dividend date; **(c)** (.34 × 4)/80.20 = .017, or 1.7%; **(d)** (.34 × 4)/3.20 = .43 or 43%; **(e)** The price would fall to 80.20/1.1 = $72.91.

2. **(a)** .26; **(b)** .36.

3. **(a)** False; **(b)** true.

4. **a.** False. The dividend depends on past dividends and current and forecasted earnings.
   b. True. This target does reflect growth opportunities and capital expenditure requirements.
   c. False. Dividends are adjusted gradually to a target. The target is based on current or forecasted earnings multiplied by the target payout ratio.
   d. True. Dividend changes convey information to investors.
   e. False. Dividends are "smoothed." Managers rarely increase regular dividends temporarily. They may pay a special dividend, however.
   f. False. Dividends are rarely cut when repurchases are being made.

5. a. Reinvest $1,000 \times \$.50 = \$500$ in the stock. If the ex-dividend price is $\$150 - \$2.50$, this should involve the purchase of $500/147.50$, or about 3.4 shares.

b. Sell shares worth $1,000 \times \$3 = \$3,000$. If the ex-dividend price is $\$200 - \$5$, this should involve the sale of $3,000/195$, or about 15 shares.

6. (a) Raise an additional £2 million by an issue of shares; (b) Reduce cash by $10 million or issue new shares for $10 million.

7. a. Company value is unchanged at $5,000 \times 140 = \$700,000$. Share price stays at $140.

b. The discount rate $r = (DIV_1/P_0) + g = (20/140) + .05 = .193$. The price at which shares are repurchased in year 1 is $140 \times (1 + r) = 140 \times 1.193 = \$167$. Therefore the firm repurchases $50,000/167 = 299$ shares. Total dividend payments in year 1 fall to $5,000 \times 10 = \$50,000$, which is equivalent to $50,000/(5000 - 299) =$

$10.64 a share. Similarly, in year 2 the firm repurchases 281 shares at $186.52 and the dividend per share increases by 11.7% to $11.88. In each subsequent year total dividends increase by 5%, the number of shares declines by 6% and therefore dividends per share increase by 11.7%. The constant growth model gives PV share $= 10.64/(.193 - .117) = \$140$.

8. a. $127.25.

b. Nothing; the stock price will stay at $130. 846,154 shares will be repurchased.

c. The with-dividend price stays at $130. Ex-dividend it drops to $124.50; 883,534 shares will be issued.

9. *Current tax law:* (a) shouldn't care; (b) prefers Lo; (c) prefers Hi; (d) shouldn't care; (e) shouldn't care. *Same rate of tax:* An individual now shouldn't care. Otherwise preferences do not change.

Chapter 17

1. (a) $.10P$; (b) Buy 10% of B's debt + 10% of B's equity; (c) $.10(P - 100)$; (d) Borrow an amount equal to 10% of B's debt and buy 10% of A's equity.

2. Note the market value of Copperhead is far in excess of its book value:

	Market Value
Common stock (8 million shares at $2)	$16,000,000
Short-term loans	$ 2,000,000

Ms. Kraft owns .625% of the firm, which proposes to increase common stock to $17 million and cut short-term debt. Ms. Kraft can offset this by (a) borrowing $.00625 \times 1,000,000 = \$6,250$, and (b) buying that much more Copperhead stock.

3. Expected return on assets is $r_A = .08 \times 30/80 + .16 \times 50/80 = .13$. The new return on equity will be r_E

$= .13 + 20/60(.13 - .08) = .147$. If stockholders pass on more of the firm's risk to debtholders, expected return on equity will be *less* than 14.7%.

4. a. (i) $\beta_A = \left(\dfrac{D}{D + E} \times \beta_D\right) + \left(\dfrac{E}{D + E} \times \beta_E\right)$

$1.0 = (.5 \times 0) + (.5 \times \beta_E)$

$\beta_E = 2.0$.

(ii) $\beta_D = 0$; (iii) $\beta_A = 1.0$.

b. (i) .10.

(ii) $r_A = \left(\dfrac{D}{D + E} \times r_D\right) + \left(\dfrac{E}{D + E} \times r_E\right)$

$.10 = (.5 \times .05) + (.5 \times r_E)$

$r_E = .15$.

(iii) $r_D = .05$; (iv) $r_A = .10$.

c. (i) 50%; (ii) 6.7 (i.e., the P/E ratio falls to offset the increase in EPS).

5. a.

Operating income ($)	500	1,000	1,500	2,000
Interest ($)	250	250	250	250
Equity earnings ($)	250	750	1,250	1,750
Earnings per share	.33	1.00	1.67	2.33
Return on shares (%)	3.3	10	16.7	23.3

b. $\beta_A = \left(\dfrac{D}{D + E} \times \beta_D\right) + \left(\dfrac{E}{D + E} \times \beta_E\right)$

$.8 = (.25 \times 0) + (.75 \times \beta_E)$

$\beta_E = 1.07$

6. a. True, so long as the market value of "old" debt does not change.

b. False. MM's Proposition I says only that overall firm value $(V = D + E)$ does not depend on capital structure.

c. False. Borrowing increases equity risk even if debt is default-risk-free.

d. False. Limited liability affects the relative values of debt and equity, not their sum.

e. True. Limited liability protects shareholders if the firm defaults.

f. True—but the required rate of return on equity and the firm's assets are the same only if the firm holds risk-free assets. In this case $r_A, r_D,$ and r_E all equal the risk-free rate of interest.

g. False. The shareholders could make the same debt issue on their own account.

h. True. To put it more precisely, it assumes that the expected rate of return to equity goes up, but stockholders' required rate of return goes up proportionately. Therefore, stock price is unchanged.

i. False. The formula $r_E = r_A + (D/E)(r_A - r_D)$ does not require r_D = a constant.

j. False. The clientele has to be willing to pay extra for the debt, which it will not do if plenty of corporate debt issues are already available.

7. See Figure 17.5.

8. **(a)** $r_A = .15, r_E = .175;$ **(b)** $\beta_A = .6$ (unchanged), $\beta_D = .3, \beta_E = .9;$ **(c)** 18.3%.

9. **(a)** 10%; **(b)** 13.3%.

10. **(a)** Not affected; **(b)** 16 million; **(c)** $250 million; **(d)** $D/V = 160/250 = .64;$ **(e)** No one.

11. **(a)** It rises by $2 per share or $30 million; **(b)** 5 million; **(c)** $250 million (unchanged); **(d)** $130/250 = .52$ (using market values); **(e)** Shareholders gain, investors in old debt lose.

Chapter 18

1. a. PV tax shield $= \dfrac{T_C(r_D D)}{1 + r_D} = \dfrac{.35(.08 \times 1000)}{1.08}$
$= 25.93.$

b. PV tax shield $= \displaystyle\sum_{t=1}^{5} \dfrac{.35(.08 \times 1000)}{(1.08)^t} = \$111.80.$

c. PV tax shield $= T_C D = \$350.$

2. a. PV tax shield $= T_C D = \$16.$

b. $T_C \times 20 = \$8.$

c. New PV tax shield $= \displaystyle\sum_{t=1}^{5} \dfrac{.40(.08 \times 60)}{(1.08)^t} = \$7.67.$

Therefore, company value $= 168 - 24 + 7.67 = \$151.67.$

3. a. Relative advantage of debt $= \dfrac{1 - T_p}{(1 - T_{pE})(1 - T_C)}$
$= \dfrac{.69}{(1)(.65)} = 1.06.$

b. Relative advantage $= .69/(.69)(.65) = 1.54.$

4. a. Direct costs of financial distress are the legal and administrative costs of bankruptcy. Indirect costs include possible delays in liquidation (Eastern Airlines) or poor investment or operating decisions while bankruptcy is being resolved. Also the *threat* of bankruptcy can lead to costs.

b. If financial distress increases odds of default, managers' and shareholders' incentives change. This can lead to poor investment or financing decisions.

c. See the answer to 4(*b*). Examples are the "games" described in Section 18.3.

5. Not necessarily. Announcement of bankruptcy can send a message of poor profits and prospects. Part of the share price drop can be attributed to anticipated bankruptcy costs, however.

6. A firm with no taxable income saves no taxes by borrowing and paying interest. The interest payments would simply add to its tax-loss carry-forwards. Such a firm would have little tax incentive to borrow.

7. a. Stockholders win. Bond value falls, since the value of assets securing the bond has fallen.

b. Bondholder wins if we assume the cash is left invested in Treasury bills. The bondholder is sure to get $26 plus interest. Stock value is zero, because there is no chance that firm value can rise above $50.

c. The bondholders lose. The firm adds assets worth $10 and debt worth $10. This would increase Circular's debt ratio, leaving the old bondholders more exposed. The old bondholders' loss is the stockholders' gain.

d. Both bondholders and stockholders win. They share the (net) increase in firm value. The bondholders' position is not eroded by the issue of a junior security. (We assume that the preferred does not lead to still more game playing and that the new investment does not make the firm's *assets* safer or riskier.)

e. Bondholders lose because they are at risk for longer. Stockholders win.

8. Specialized, intangible assets such as growth opportunities are most likely to lose value in financial distress. Safe, tangible assets with good second-hand markets are least likely to lose value. Costs of financial distress are thus likely to be less for, say, real estate firms or trucking companies than for advertising firms or high-tech growth companies.

9. More profitable firms have more taxable income to shield and are less likely to incur the costs of distress. Therefore the trade-off theory predicts high (book) debt ratios. In practice the more profitable companies borrow least.

10. Firms have a pecking order for new financing. Internal finance is preferred, followed by debt and then by external equity. Each firm's observed debt ratio reflects its cumulative requirements for external finance. The more profitable companies borrow least because they have sufficient internal finance.

11. When a company issues securities, outside investors worry that management may have unfavorable information. If so the securities can be overpriced. This worry is much less with debt than equity. Debt securities are safer than equity, and their price is less affected if unfavorable news comes out later.

 A company that can borrow (without incurring substantial costs of financial distress) usually does so. An issue of equity would be read as "bad news" by investors, and the new stock could be sold only at a discount to the previous market price.

12. Financial slack is most valuable to growth companies with good but uncertain investment opportunities. Slack means that financing can be raised quickly for positive-NPV investments. But too much financial slack can tempt mature companies to overinvest. Increased borrowing can force such firms to pay out cash to investors.

Chapter 19

1. Market values of debt and equity are $D = .9 \times 75 = \$67.5$ million and $E = 42 \times 2.5 = \$105$ million. $D/V = .39$.

$$WACC = .09(1 - .35).39 + .18(.61) = .1325, \text{ or } 13.25\%.$$

 The key assumptions: stable capital structure (D/V constant); Federated will pay taxes at 35% marginal rate in all relevant future years; use WACC as discount rate for projects with same risk as average of firm's assets.

2. Step 1: $r = .09(.39) + .18(.61) = .145$.

 Step 2: $r_D = .086$, $r_E = .145 + (.145 - .086)(15/85) = .155$.

 Step 3: WACC $= .086(1 - .35).15 + .155(.85) = .14$.

3. (a) False; (b) true; (c) true.

4. The method values the equity of a company by discounting cash flows to stockholders at the cost of equity. See Section 4.5 for more details. The method assumes that the debt-to-equity ratio will remain constant.

5. (a) True; (b) false, if interest tax shields are valued separately; (c) true; (d) true.

6. Rule 1 assumes that debt supported by a project is paid off on a fixed schedule regardless of project performance. Rule 2 assumes that debt is rebalanced to keep the ratio of debt to project value constant.

7. Acceptance of a project triggers financing costs or benefits. Examples: interest tax shields, issue costs, subsidized financing tied to the project. Other side effects are encountered in international investment.

8. APV = base-case NPV ± PV financing side effects

 (a) APV $= 0 - .15(500,000) = -75,000$; (b) APV $= 0 + 175,000 = +175,000$; (c) APV $= 0 + 76,000 = +76,000$

9. a. 12%, of course.
 b. $r_E = .12 + (.12 - .075)(30/70) = .139$,

 WACC $= .075(1 - .35)(.30) + .139(.70) = .112$, or 11.2%.

10. PV tax shield $= (.10/.35)576,000 = \$164,600$; APV $= 170,000 + 164,600 = \$334,600$.

11. a. Base-case NPV $= -1,000 + 1200/1.20 = 0$.
 b. PV tax shield $= (.35 \times .1 \times .3(1000))/1.1 = 9.55$. APV $= 0 + 9.55 = \$9.55$.

12. No. The more debt you use, the higher rate of return equity investors will require. (Lenders may demand more also.) Thus there is a hidden cost of the "cheap" debt: It makes equity more expensive.

13. The after-tax borrowing or lending rate. This assumes that the company can lend or borrow at a safe after-tax rate.

14. PV $= 16(1 - .35)/(1 + .055(1 - .35)) = \$10.04$ million.

Chapter 20

1. Call; exercise; put; European; call; assets; bondholders (lenders); assets; promised payment to bondholders.

2. Figure 20.13a represents a call seller; Figure 20.13b represents a call buyer.

3. a. The exercise price of the put option (i.e., you'd sell stock for the exercise price);
 b. The value of the stock (i.e., you would throw away the put and keep the stock).

4. Value of call + PV(exercise price) = value of put + value of asset (e.g., share).
 See table below.

At Maturity:	Share Price Exceeds Exercise Price		Share Price Below Exercise Price	
	Action	Value	Action	Value
Call + PV(EX) - Put + share	Exercise call	Stock price	Don't exercise call	Exercise price
	Don't exercise put	Stock price	Exercise put	Exercise price

- Relationship holds only for European options with same exercise price.

5. Buy a call and lend the present value of the exercise price.

6. **a.** Keep gold stocks and buy 6-month puts with an exercise price equal to 83.3% of the current price.

b. Sell gold stocks, invest £485,000 for 6 months at 6%. The remaining £115,000 can be used to buy calls on the gold stocks with the same exercise price.

7. **(a)** See Figure 4; **(b)** stock price − PV(EX) = 100 − 100/1.1 = $9.09.

8.

At Maturity:	Asset Value Exceeds Loan		Asset Value Below Loan	
	Action	Value	Action	Value
Call on assets with exercise price = amount of loan	Exercise call	Assets − amount of loan	Don't exercise call	Zero
Common stock	Repay loan	Assets − amount of loan	Default	Zero

9. Stockholders have the option to walk away from their debts, in which case lender takes over assets. Default put is important for firms in distress (i.e., asset value low relative to amount of loan).

10. The lower bound is the option's value if it expired immediately: either zero or the stock price less the exercise price, whichever is larger. If an (American) call option's price were less than the lower bound, you could exercise immediately and make a sure profit. The upper bound is the stock price.

11. Figure 20.13(b) doesn't show the cost of purchasing the call. The profit from call purchase would be negative for all stock prices less than exercise price plus cost of call. Figure 20.13(a) doesn't record the proceeds from selling the call.

12. **(a)** Zero; **(b)** Stock price less the present value of the exercise price.

13. The call price **(a)** increases; **(b)** decreases; **(c)** increases; **(d)** increases; **(e)** decreases; **(f)** decreases.

14. **a.** All investors, however risk-averse, should value more highly an option on a volatile stock. For both Exxon Mobil and AOL the option is valueless if stock price is below the exercise price, but the option on AOL has more upside potential.

b. Other things equal, stockholders lose and debtholders gain if the company shifts to safer assets. When the assets are risky, the default put is more valuable. Debtholders bear much of the losses if asset value declines, but shareholders get the gains if asset value increases.

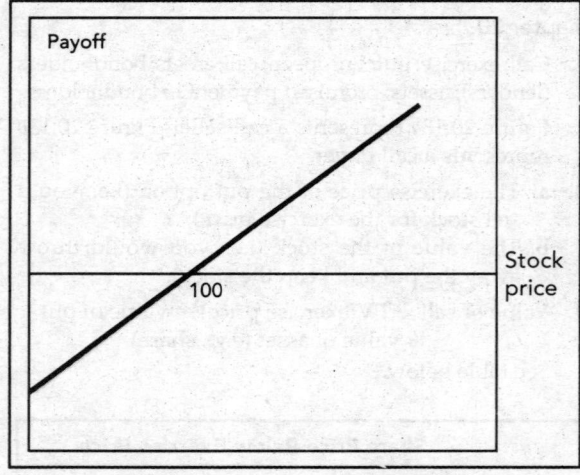

FIGURE 4

Chapter 20, Quiz question 7.

Chapter 21

1. **a.** Using risk-neutral method, $(p \times 20) + (1 - p)(-16.7) = 1$, $p = .48$.

$$\text{Value of call} = \frac{(.48 \times 8) + (.52 \times 0)}{1.01} = 3.8.$$

b. $\text{Delta} = \dfrac{\text{spread of option prices}}{\text{spread of stock prices}}$

$$= \frac{8}{14.7} = .544.$$

c.

	Current Cash Flow	Possible Future Cash Flows	
Buy call	−3.8	0	+8.0
equals			
Buy .544 shares	−21.8	−18.2	+26.2
Borrow 18.0	+18.0	−18.2	−18.2
	−3.8	0	+8.0

d. Possible stock prices with call option prices in parentheses:

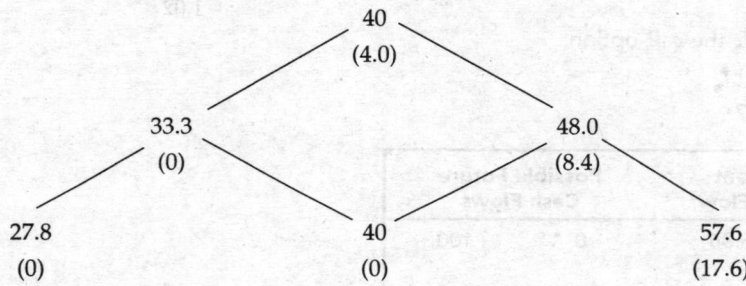

Option prices were calculated as follows:

Month 1: (i) $\dfrac{(.48 \times 0) + (.52 \times 0)}{1.01} = 0,$

(ii) $\dfrac{(.48 \times 17.6) + (.52 \times 0)}{1.01} = 8.4.$

Month 0: $\dfrac{(.48 \times 8.4) + (.52 \times 0)}{1.01} = 4.0.$

e. Delta $= \dfrac{\text{spread of option prices}}{\text{spread of stock prices}} = \dfrac{8.4}{14.7} = .57.$

2. The period to expiration is subdivided into an indefinitely large number of subperiods (and when there is no incentive to early exercise).

3. **(a)** No. The maximum delta is 1.0 when the ratio of stock price to exercise price is very high. **(b)** No. **(c)** Delta increases. **(d)** Delta increases.

4. Because option risk changes as time passes and the stock price changes.

5. Using the replicating portfolio method, delta = 13.33/(73.33 − 41.25) = .416.

	Current Cash Flow	Possible Future Cash Flows	
Buy call	−6.05	0	+13.33
equals			
Buy .416 shares	−22.86	+17.14	+30.48
Borrow 16.81	+16.81	−17.14	−17.14
	−6.05	0	+13.33

Using the risk-neutral method, $(p \times 33.3) + (1 - p)$
$(-25) = 2, p = .463.$

The put price is 9.87.

Value of call $= \dfrac{(.463 \times 13.33) + (.537 \times 0)}{1.02} = 6.05.$

6. Using the replicating portfolio method, delta = 13.75/(68.75 − 44) = .556.

	Current Cash Flow	Possible Future Cash Flows	
Buy call	−6.59	0	+13.75
equals			
Buy .556 shares	−30.56	+24.44	+38.19
Borrow 23.97	+23.97	−24.44	−24.44
	−6.59	0	+13.75

Using the risk-neutral method, $(p \times 25) + (1 - p)(-20) = 2, p = .489$.

$$\text{Value of call} = \frac{(.489 \times 13.75) + (.511 \times 0)}{1.02} = 6.59.$$

Lower risk means less upside for the call option. Thus option value falls.

7. **a.** Delta $= 100/(200 - 50) = .667$.

   b.

	Current Cash Flow	Possible Future Cash Flows	
Buy call	−36.36	0	+100
equals			
Buy .667 shares	−66.67	+33.33	+133.33
Borrow 30.30	+30.30	−33.33	−33.33
	−36.36	0	+100

   c. $(p \times 100) + (1 - p)(-50) = 10, p = .4$.

   d. Value of call $= \dfrac{(.4 \times 100) + (.6 \times 0)}{1.10} = 36.36$.

   e. No. The true probability of a price rise is almost certainly higher than the risk-neutral probability, but it does not help to value the option.

8. **a.** Call value = $3.44.

   b. Put value = call value + PV(exercise price) − stock price = $1.67.

9. True; as the stock price rises, the risk of the option falls.

10. **a.** You would exercise early if the stock price was sufficiently low. There may be little opportunity for further gains in the option value and it would be better to invest the exercise price to earn interest.

   b. Don't exercise early. The interest savings from delaying payment of the exercise price is larger than the dividend foregone.

   c. If the stock price and dividend are sufficiently high, it may pay to exercise early to capture the dividend.

Chapter 22

1. Expansion option; abandonment option; timing option (i.e., option to postpone investment); flexi-

ble production (i.e., option to exchange one asset for another).

2. **a.** Increase value (unless the cash flows from the Mark II needed to be discounted at a higher rate).

   b. Increase value.

   c. Reduce value.

3. **a.** Call (i.e., expansion option); **(b)** option to exchange one asset for another; **(c)** call on oil price; **(d)** timing option (Forest has an in-the-money call); **(e)** call (option to make subsequent investment in China); **(f)** put (i.e., abandonment option); **(g)** timing option (owner has an in-the-money call).

4. **a.** You can't use *any* single discount rate for option payoffs. The risk of an option changes as asset price changes and time passes.

   b. The risky *asset* may be worth less as a result, but option owner can capitalize from up moves while not losing from down moves.

   c. Option value depends on value of underlying asset. DCF is needed to get this value.

5. **a.** You learn more about land prices and best use of the land.

   b. By developing immediately, you capture rents immediately.

Chapter 23

1. **a.** (i) 0; (ii) 0; (iii) 0; (iv) \$10; (v) \$20.
   b.

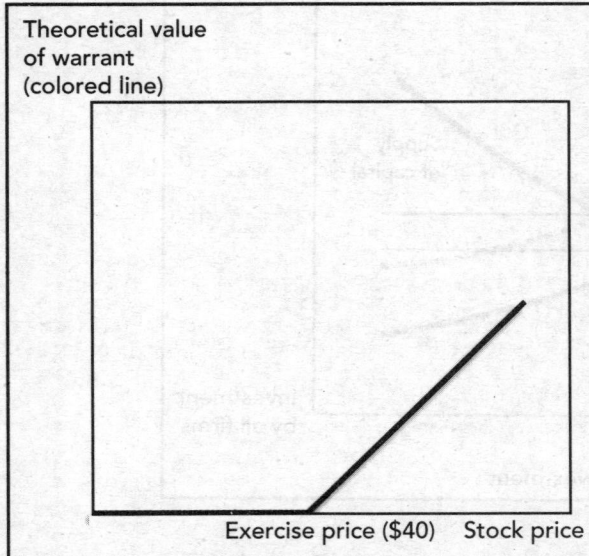

Theoretical value
of warrant
(colored line)

Exercise price (\$40)   Stock price

   c. Buy the warrant and exercise, then sell the stock.

   Net gain = −5 − 40 + 60 = +\$15.

2. **(a)** No; **(b)** no; **(c)** 1/3 × 70 = \$23.33; **(d)** no, worse off; **(e)** zero; **(f)** more; **(g)** (i) less, (ii) less, (iii) more, (iv) more, (v) more; **(h)** when the dividends on the stock outweigh the interest on the exercise price; **(i)** more.

3. **(a)** \$15,000; **(b)** \$29,000.

4. **(a)** 1,000/47 = 21.28; **(b)** 1,000/50 = \$20.00; **(c)** 21.28 × 41.50 = \$883.12, or 88.31%; **(d)** 650/21.28 = \$30.55; **(e)** no (not if the investor is free to convert immediately); **(f)** \$12.22, i.e., (910 − 650)/21.28; **(g)** (47/41.50) − 1 = .13, or 13%; **(h)** when the price reaches 102.75% of par.

5. **(a)** \$7.00; **(b)** \$7.05.

6. **(a)** False; **(b)** true; **(c)** false; **(d)** false; **(e)** true; **(f)** true.

Chapter 24

1 **a.** Figure 5 shows that an increase in the demand for capital increases investment and savings. The rate of interest also rises.
   b. Figure 6 shows that an increase in the supply of capital also increases investment and savings. The rate of interest falls.

2. There are 20 coupon payments of 6.9375 plus a principal payment of 100. With a discount rate of 8.04/2 = 4.02%, PV is

$$\frac{6.9375}{1.0402} + \frac{6.9375}{1.0402^2} + \cdots + \frac{106.9375}{1.0402^{20}} = 139.57$$

3. **a** The Norwegian bond has the highest yield (5.6%) and the Finnish bond has the lowest (4.5%).
   b. The Finnish bond has the longest duration (7.9 years) and the Norwegian has the shortest (7.1 years).

4. **a.** $PV = \dfrac{50}{1 + r_1} + \dfrac{1,050}{(1 + r_2)^2}$

   b. $PV = \dfrac{50}{1 + y} + \dfrac{1,050}{(1 + y)^2}$

   c. Less (it is between the 1-year and 2-year spot rates).
   d. Yield to maturity; spot rate.

5. **a.** Fall (e.g., 1-year 10% bond is worth 110/1.1 = 100 if r = 10% and is worth 110/1.15 = 95.65 if r = 15%).
   b. Less (e.g., see 5(a)).
   c. Less (e.g., with r = 5%, 1-year 10% bond is worth 110/1.05 = 104.76).
   d. Higher (e.g., if r = 10%, 1-year 10% bond is worth 110/1.1 = 100, while 1-year 8% bond is worth 108/1.1 = 98.18).
   e. No, low-coupon bonds have longer durations (unless there is only one period to maturity) and are therefore more volatile (e.g., if r falls from 10% to 5%, the value of a 2-year 10% bond rises from 100 to 109.3 (a rise of 9.3%). The value of a 2-year 5% bond rises from 91.3 to 100 (a rise of 9.5%).

6. **a.** $(100/90.826)^{(1/2)} - 1 = .0493$, or 4.93%;
   $(100/73.565)^{(1/7)} - 1 = .0448$, or 4.48%;
   $(100/70.201)^{(1/8)} - 1 = .0452$, or 4.52%;
   $(100/67.787)^{(1/9)} - 1 = .0441$, or 4.41%;
   $(100/29.334)^{(1/30)} - 1 = .0417$, or 4.17%.
   b. Downward.
   c. Higher (the yield is a complicated average of the different spot rates).
   d. 73.565/70.201 − 1 = .0479, or 4.79%; 70.201/ 67.787 − 1 = .0356, or 3.56%.

7. **a.** Price today is 108.425; price after 1 year is 106.930.
   b. Return = (106.930 + 8)/108.425 − 1 = .06, or 6%.
   c. If a bond's yield to maturity is unchanged, the return to the bondholder is equal to the yield.

8. **a.** False. Duration depends on the coupon as well as the maturity.
   b. False. Given the yield to maturity, volatility is proportional to duration.
   c. True. A lower coupon rate means longer duration and therefore higher volatility.
   d. False. A higher interest rate reduces the relative present value of (distant) principal repayments.

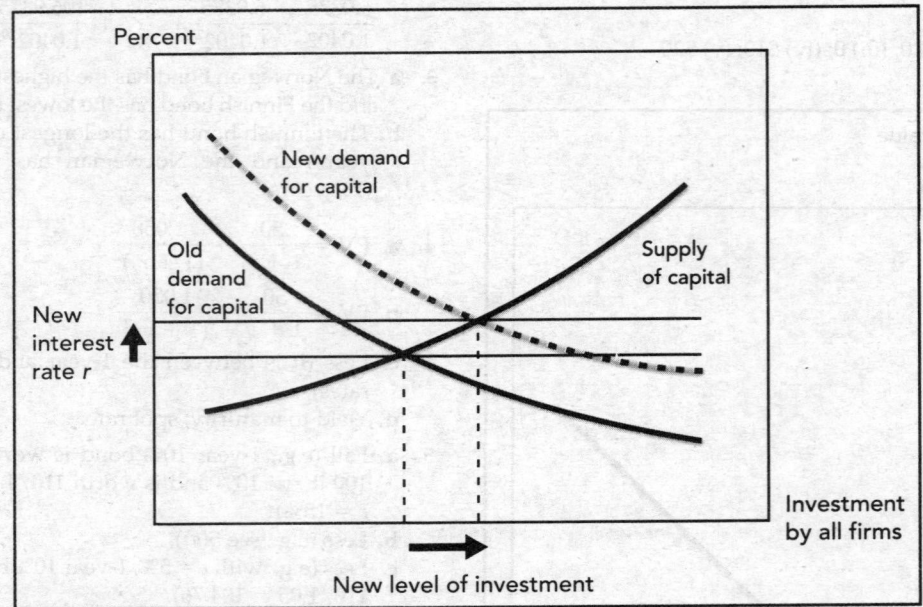

FIGURE 5

Chapter 24, Quiz question 1(a).

FIGURE 6

Chapter 24, Quiz question 1(b).

9.

	Year	C_t	PV(C_t)	Proportion of Total Value	Proportion × Time
Security A	1	40	37.04	.359	.359
	2	40	34.29	.333	.666
	3	40	31.75	.308	.924
	V =		103.08	1.0	Duration = 1.949 years
Security B	1	20	18.52	.141	.141
	2	20	17.15	.131	.262
	3	120	95.26	.728	2.184
	V =		130.93	1.0	Duration = 2.587 years
Security C	1	10	9.26	.088	.088
	2	10	8.57	.082	.164
	3	110	87.32	.830	2.490
	V =		105.15	1.0	Duration = 2.742 years

Volatilities: A, 1.80; B, 2.40; C, 2.49.

10. **a.** $(1 + r_2)^2 = (1 + r_1)(1 + f_2)$
$1.03^2 = 1.01 \times (1 + f_2)$
$f_2 = .05$, or 5%.
b. The expected 1-year spot rate at time 1 equals the forward rate f_2.
c. Against (unless one believes that investors have generally expected interest rates to rise).
d. The forward rate equals the expected spot rate *plus* a liquidity premium.
e. Long-term bonds.
f. Short-term bonds.

11. **a.** Aaa, Aa, A, and Baa
b. (i) Increase; (ii) increase; (iii) increase; (iv) increase.

12. Option to put (i.e., sell) company assets to the bondholders for the face value of the debt.

13. Value an option to put (i.e., sell) the company's assets to the government for the amount of the loan.

Chapter 25

1. **(a)** High-grade utility bonds; **(b)** industrial holding companies; **(c)** industrial bonds; **(d)** railroads; **(e)** asset-backed security.

2. • Indenture or trust deeds—agreement between the borrower and a trust company representing bondholders.
• Debentures—long-term unsecured bonds.
• Mortgage bonds—debt secured by property.
• Call provision—company has right to call and pay off debt.
• Sinking fund—provision for repayment of part or most of principal prior to maturity.
• Foreign bond—bond sold in another country's market.

• Negative pledge clause—if secured debt is issued, existing debt will also become secured.

3. **(a)** Decreases; **(b)** impossible to say; **(c)** impossible to say. For example, if the bond has a high coupon and is sold at a premium at issue, the prospect of drawings at par could decrease value. For an original-issue discount bond, the effect could be reversed.

4. **a.** You would like an issue of junior debt.
b. You prefer it not to do so (unless it is also junior debt). The existing property may not be sufficient to pay off your debt.

5. **(a)** First Boston, Goldman Sachs, Shearson Lehman, Stifel Nicholaus; **(b)** Continental Bank; **(c)** $967.25; **(d)** registered; **(e)** 104.26 (percent of par); **(f)** no.

6. **a.** Issue price + approximately 1 month's interest = 976.00 + 95/12 = $983.92.
b. December 1, 1986; $47.50.
c. 2016. The sinking fund was designed to pay off all but $8.64 million of principal by that date. The company must pay off the remaining $8.64 million.
d. 2002.

7. The 7.8 percent rate is actually 3.9 percent semiannually. The effective annual rate is $1.039^2 - 1 = .0795$, slightly higher than the London quote. International bonds pay interest annually.

8. Private placements: typically have simpler loan agreements—which may nevertheless contain "custom" features; have more stringent covenants; are more easily renegotiated.

9. **a.** False. Lenders usually retain some recourse; e.g., they may demand a completion guarantee.
b. True, but some new securities (e.g., zero-coupon bonds) survive even when the original motive for issuing them disappears.

c. False. The borrower has the option.

d. True. But debt issues with weak covenants suffered in such takeovers.

e. True. The costs of renegotiation are less for private placements.

10. Chapter 7 usually leads to liquidation. Chapter 11 "protects" the firm from its creditors while a reorganization plan is developed.

11. (a) False; (b) true; (c) true, except for costs incurred by the bankruptcy court or trustee; (d) true; (e) false. Tax-loss carry-forwards do not survive liquidation.

12. There is always a chance that the company can recover, allowing creditors to be paid off and leaving something for shareholders. Also, shareholders may retain some claims on the firm after reorganization in Chapter 11.

Chapter 26

1. A, c; B, d or i; C, b or e; D, f; E, a; F, h; G, g.

2. a, b, d, f, and h (though there may be other ways to reduce AMT).

3. a. The lessor must charge enough to cover the present value of the costs of owning and operating the asset over its expected economic life. In a competitive leasing market the present value of rentals cannot exceed the present value of costs. The competitive rental payment ends up equal to the lessor's equivalent annual cost.

   b. The user's equivalent annual cost is the annual cost to the user of owning and operating the asset. If the operating lease rate is less than this cost, it pays to lease.

4. (a) True; (b) true; (c) true, but compare after-tax rates; (d) true; (e) true; (f) true; (g) true.

5. The present value of depreciation tax shields on the $3,000 desk, using the 5-year schedule from Table 6.4, is

$$PV \text{ (at 9 percent)} = .35 \times PV \text{ (5-year schedule)} \times 3,000$$
$$= \$832.$$

After-tax administrative costs are $400(1 - .35) = \$260$ per year for 6 years. If the first costs are incurred immediately, their present value is $1,271. Thus the present value of all costs is $3,000 - 832 + 1,271 = \$3,439$. The break-even lease rate is about $703 after tax. In other words, the present value of six payments of $703, with the first payment due immediately, is about $3,439. The breakeven rate pretax is $703/.65 = \$1,082$.

6. Administrative costs drop to $200 per year. Moreover, the lease payments are a fixed commitment of the blue-chip company. The six lease payments are discounted at the after-tax rate at which Acme would lend money; that is, $6(1 - .35) = 3.9\%$. The break-even lease rate falls to about $514 after tax. The pretax break-even rate is $791.

7. a. $59,307; the present value of the lease cash flows from $t = 1$ to $t = 3$, discounted at $r(1 - T_c) = .10(1 - .35) = .065$.

   b. $62,000 - 59,307 = 2,693$.

   c. It should not invest. The lease's value of +2,693 does not offset the machine's negative NPV. It would be happy to sign the same lease on a more attractive asset.

Chapter 27

1. (a) True; (b) true; (c) false (depends on coupon); (d) false; (e) false; (f) false; (g) true.

2. Since the futures price has risen, your sale is now showing a loss. Your broker will ask you for money.

3. $\dfrac{\text{Value of future}}{1.049} = 95 - 4$.

   Value of future $= 95.46$.

4. $\dfrac{2,408}{1.12} = 2,550 + 100 - PV \text{ (convenience yield)}$.

   PV (convenience yield) $= \$500$.

5. a. A shortage of heating oil increases net convenience yield and reduces the futures price relative to spot price.

   b. Spot and futures prices decrease. The futures price rises relative to spot because convenience yield falls and storage costs rise.

6. Storage costs are likely to be high. Other things equal, firms will prefer to hold the future rather than the spot commodity, and net convenience yield will be low.

7. (a) Profit; (b) If the bank took out a new 4-year swap, it would need to pay an extra $.25 million a year. At the new interest rate of 6.5%, the extra payment has a present value of $856,000. This is the amount that the bank should charge to terminate.

8. Basis risk means that the hedging instrument is imperfectly correlated with the risk to be hedged. It is highest in a, because Disney stock has considerable nonmarket risk. In b basis risk is likely to be small, and in c it should disappear.

9. Sell short $1.2 million of the market portfolio. In practice rather than "sell the market" you would sell futures on $1.2 million of the market index.

10. (a) Sell; (b) sell 3-month futures on Italian government bonds.

11. **a.** The calculations for A and C are given for Quiz question 9, Chapter 24. For B, the calculations change to

Year	C_T	PV(C_T)	Proportion	Proportion × Time
1	120	111.11	1.0	1.0
2	0	0	0	0
3	0	0	0	0
		V = 111.11	1.0	Duration = 1.0 years

b. A has a duration of 1.949 years. So does a portfolio with 45.5% invested in B and 54.5% invested in C. To hedge A sell $4.55 million of B and $5.45 million of C.

c. Sell $5.13 million of A, borrow 10 − 5.13 = $4.87 million short-term. Alternatively, sell $3.65 million of C and borrow $6.35 million.

Chapter 28

1. **a.** 9.139.
   b. 9.1865 pesos = $1.
   c. premium.
   d. Using the 1-year forward rate, (9.924 − 9.139)/9.924 = .0791, or 7.91%.
   e. By interest rate parity $1 + r_{peso} = 1.05 \times 12.36/9.84$; $r_{peso} = .126$, or 12.6%.
   f. 9.307 pesos = $1.
   g. If real exchange rate is constant, expected inflation in Mexico over 3 months must be 9.307/9.139 − 1 = .018, or 1.8%, greater in Mexico than in the USA (equivalent to $1.018^4 - 1 = .076$, or 7.6%, a year).

2. **a.** The interest rate differential equals the forward premium or discount, i.e.,
$$\frac{1 + r_x}{1 + r_\$} = \frac{f_{x/\$}}{s_{x/\$}}.$$

   b. The expected change in the spot rate equals the forward premium or discount, i.e.,

$$\frac{f_{x/\$}}{s_{x/\$}} = \frac{E(s_{x/\$})}{s_{x/\$}}$$

   c. Prices of goods in different countries are equal when measured in terms of the same currency. It follows that the expected change in the spot rate equals the expected inflation differential; i.e.,

$$\frac{E(1 + i_x)}{E(1 + i_\$)} = \frac{E(s_{x/\$})}{s_{x/\$}}.$$

   d. Expected real interest rates in different countries are equal; i.e.,

$$\frac{1 + r_x}{1 + r_\$} = \frac{E(1 + i_x)}{E(1 + i_\$)}$$

3. **a.** $2,419 \times 1.3/1.02 = R3,083 = \$1$.
   b. Real value of rupiah fell by 3,083/8,325 − 1 = .63, or 63%.

4.

	1 Month	3 Months	1 Year
Dollar interest rate, %	3.60	3.70	3.70
Peso interest rate, %	9.55	9.99	11.90
Forward pesos per dollar	53.85	54.40	57.844
Forward premium on peso (% per year)	5.6	−5.7	−6.0

5. *b.*

6. Zero, of course. You don't need to do any calculations.

7. It can borrow the present value of €1 million, sell the euros in the spot market, and invest the proceeds in an 8-year dollar loan.

8. **(a)** $(100/1.03)/(100/1.0365^2) - 1 = .043$, or 4.3%;
   (b) $1.043 \times 115/120.7 - 1 = -.006$, or −.6%;
   (c) $1.043 \times 116.52/120.7 - 1 = .007$ or .7%.

9. **a.** NPV = $6.61 \times 1.2 = \$7.94$ million.

b.

Year	0	1	2	3	4	5
Forward rate	1.2	1.223	1.246	1.269	1.293	1.318
$ million	−96	12.23	24.91	29.19	34.92	32.94

c. It doesn't. The company can always hedge against a fall in the euro.

Chapter 29

1. **(a)** 5,114/(5114 + 6,832) = .43; **(b)** (1,674 + 859)/351 = 7.2; **(c)** 3,288/2,704 = 1.2; **(d)** (115 + 1,247)/2,704 = .5; **(e)** (1,674 − 483)/15,980 = .07; **(f)** ((1,499 + 1,329) ÷ 2)/(12,035 ÷ 365) = 42.9; **(g)** 840/((6,832 + 7,173) ÷ 2) = .120; **(h)** 263/840 = .31.

2. The illogical ratios are *a, b, c, f,* and *i.* The correct definitions are

$$\text{Debt–equity ratio} = \frac{\text{long-term debt + value of leases}}{\text{equity}}$$

$$\text{Return on equity} = \frac{\text{earnings available for common}}{\text{average equity}}$$

$$\text{Payout ratio} = \frac{\text{dividend}}{\text{earnings per share}}$$

$$\text{Current ratio} = \frac{\text{current assets}}{\text{current liabilities}}$$

$$\text{Average collection period} = \frac{\text{average receivables}}{\text{sales} \div 365}$$

3. **(a)** False; **(b)** true; **(c)** false; **(d)** false; **(e)** false—it will tend to increase the price–earnings multiple.

4. **(a)** Shipping company; **(b)** United Foods; **(c)** paper mill; **(d)** mail order company; **(e)** Fledgling Electronics.

5. $365,000; 12.2.

6. **(a)** 12%; **(b)** 16%.

7. .25.

8. 3.65%; .73.

9. **(a)** 1.47; **(b)** Net working capital = 40. Total capitalization = 540. Debt to total capitalization = .52.

10. $10 million.

11. $82 million.

12. The return on equity is higher when the return on assets exceeds the debt interest rate.

13. **a.** False (it is a process of deciding which risks to take).
   b. False (financial planning is concerned with possible surprises as well as expected outcomes).
   c. True (financial planning considers both the investment and financing decisions).
   d. False (a typical horizon for long-term planning is 5 years).
   e. True (perfect accuracy is unlikely to be obtainable, but the firm needs to produce the best possible consistent forecasts).
   f. False (excessive detail distracts attention from the crucial decisions).

14. **(a)** $2,900,000; **(b)** $225,000; **(c)** .25.

15. Archimedes will earn $550 and invest $320 to expand assets. Additional borrowing is $120, so retained earnings is $320 − 120 = $200. The residual dividend is $550 − 200 = $350.

16. **(a)** 8.6%; **(b)** 13.75%.

Chapter 30

1. **a.** Long-term financing, cumulative capital requirements, marketable securities
   b. Cash, cash, cash balance, marketable securities
   c. Trial, error, financial models

2.

Cash	Working Capital
1. $2 million decline	$2 million decline
2. $2,500 increase	Unchanged
3. $5,000 decline	Unchanged
4. Unchanged	$1 million increase
5. Unchanged	Unchanged
6. $5 million increase	Unchanged

3. **(a)** Inventories go up (use). **(b)** Accounts receivable go up (use). **(c)** No change shown on the firm's books. **(d)** Increase in cash (source) and reduction in assets. A loss of $100,000 is deducted from retained earnings. **(e)** Cash declines (use) and equity declines. **(f)** Cash unchanged, although net working capital increases (the debt issue is a source of *funds*).

4. Month 3: 18 + (.5 × 90) + (.3 × 120) + (.2 × 100) − $119,000.

   Month 4: 14 + (.5 × 70) + (.3 × 90) + (.2 × 120) = $100,000.

5. **(a)** 19.2, 16.8, 15, 13.2, 12, 12; **(b)** 19.2, 23.2, 20.6, 18.2, 16.4, 16.

6. a. Table 30.2: Bank loans = 3, Cash = 8, Current assets = 68, Current liabilities = 30, Total assets = Total liabilities and net worth = 118. Table 30.4: Repaid short-term bank loan = 2, Increase in cash balance = 4. Tables 30.5 and 30.6 unchanged.

b. Table 30.2: Long-term debt = 22, Gross investment = 82, Net fixed assets = 62, Cash = 3, Total assets = Total liabilities and net worth = 125. Table 30.4: Issued long-term debt = 17, Total sources = 41, Invested in fixed assets = 26, Total uses = 42, Increases in cash balance = −1. Table 30.5: Fixed and Total assets change as in Table 30.2, as do Long term debt and Total liabilities and net worth. Table 30.6: same changes as in Table 30.4, except Increase in net working capital = 6.

c. Table 30.3: Operating costs = 289, Pretax income = 56, Net income = 28, Retained earnings = 27. Table 30.2: Net worth = 92, Total liabilities and net worth = Total assets = 131; Inventory = 22.5, Cash = 23.5. Table 30.5: Net worth = 92, Long-term liabilities and net worth = Total assets = 104, Net working capital = 54. Table 30.6: Net income = 28, increase in Net working capital = 24.

d. Table 30.7: Third quarter, Total collections = 120.1, Ending receivables = 26.6. Fourth quarter, Total collections = 129.5, Ending receivables = 28.1. Table 30.8, Third quarter: Sources minus uses and Cash at end of period increase by 11.6, Cumulative financing required decreases by 11.6. Fourth quarter: Sources minus uses increase by 1.5, Cumulative financing required decreases by 13.1 to −12.6.

e. Table 30.8: Labor, etc. = 26, Sources minus uses decrease by 4 in each quarter. Cumulative financing required decreases by 4 in first quarter, 8 in second, etc.

f. Table 30.8: Other sources of cash increase by 10 in the second quarter, increasing Sources minus uses and decreasing Cumulative financing required.

g. Table 30.8: Minimum operating cash balance = 2, Cumulative financing required decreases by 2 in all quarters.

7. (a) True; **(b)** false (borrower has a call); **(c)** true; **(d)** false ($100/90 − 1 = .111$, or 11.1%); **(e)** true.

8. (a) Line of credit; **(b)** commitment fee; **(c)** floating charge; **(d)** collateral; **(e)** warehouse receipt; **(f)** commercial paper; **(g)** medium-term notes.

Chapter 31

1. a. Payment float = $25,000. Availability float = $75,000.

b. It can earn interest on these funds.

c. Payment float increases. The bank's gross ledger balance and available balance increase by the same amount.

2. a. The $.40 per check fee is cheaper at $300 \times .40 = \$120$ per day. The cost of putting up $800,000 of compensating balances is $.09 \times 800,000 = \$72,000$ per year, or $72,000/365 = \$197$ per day.

b. The lock-box system costs $120 per day, or $43,800 per year. You would need $486,700 additional cash to generate this much interest. Thus, the lock-box system must generate at least this much cash. The cash flow is $300 \times 1,500 = \$450,000$ per day. Thus the lock box must speed up average collection time by $486,700/450,000 = 1.08$ days.

3. Payment float; availability float; net float; concentration banking; FEDWIRE; CHIPS; lock-box banking.

4. The formula for optimal order size is

$$Q = \sqrt{(2 \times \text{sales} \times \text{cost per order})/\text{carrying cost}}$$
$$= \sqrt{(2 \times 216 \times 2)/6} = \sqrt{144} = 12 \text{ books.}$$

Everyman should place $216/12 = 18$ orders a year and its average inventory should be $12/2 = 6$ books.

5. The formula gives

$$Q = \sqrt{\frac{(2 \times \text{annual cash disbursements} \times \text{cost per sale of securities})}{\text{interest rate}}}$$
$$= \sqrt{(2 \times 20,000 \times 2)/.02} = \sqrt{4,000,000}$$
$$= \$2,000.$$

Everyman should sell securities $20,000/2,000 = 10$ times a year and its average cash balance should be $2,000/2 = \$1,000$.

6. (a) Less; **(b)** less; **(c)** invest the same amount; **(d)** more.

7. Price = $100 − (182/360)1.75 = 99.115$. Compound annual return $= (100/99.115)^2 − 1 = .0179$, or 1.79%.

8. (a) Repurchase agreements; **(b)** commercial paper; **(c)** finance company commercial paper; **(d)** medium-term notes; **(e)** 3-month bills; **(f)** Treasury bills; **(g)** Treasury bills.

9. Only 30% of the floating-rate preferred dividend is taxed versus 100% of bond interest. The fixed-dividend preferred also has this advantage but its price fluctuates more than the floating-rate preferred's.

Chapter 32

1. a. 1% of $1,000 = $10.

b. 1% for 30 days = 12.2% per annum simple interest or 12.9% compound interest.

c. (i) Shorter; (ii) longer; (iii) shorter.

2. a. Due lag decreases, therefore pay lag decreases;

b. Due lag increases, therefore pay lag increases;

c. Terms lag increases, therefore pay lag increases.

3. Open account, commercial draft, shipping documents, trade acceptance, the customer's banker's acceptance, letter of credit, the customer's, his or her own, letter of credit, shipping documents, shipping documents.

4. Reject because PV of Q's order = $(.75 \times 50)/1.10^{1/2}$ − 40 = −$4.25 per iron, or −$4,250 in total.

5. **a.** Expected profit = $p(1,200 - 1,050) - 1,050$ $(1 - p) = 0$

$$p = .875$$

Therefore, grant credit if probability of payment exceeds 87.5%.

   b. Expected profit from selling to slow payer:

   $.8(150) - .2(1050) = -90$. Break-even point for credit check: $(.05 \times 90 \times \text{units}) - 12 = 0$. Units = 2.67.

6. Total expected profit on initial order = $-40 + .8[(p_2 \times 200) - 1,000(1 - p_2)]/1.2 = 0$

$$p_2 = .88, \text{ or } 88\%$$

7. **(a)** False; **(b)** true; **(c)** false; **(d)** false—should be collection agency or attorney; **(e)** true.

Chapter 33

1. **(a)** Horizontal; **(b)** conglomerate; **(c)** vertical; **(d)** conglomerate.

2. *a* and *d*; *c* can also make sense, although merging is not the only way to redeploy excess cash.

3. **(a)** $5 million (We assume that the $500,000 saving is an after-tax figure.); **(b)** $4 million; **(c)** $7.5 million; **(d)** +$1 million; **(e)** −$2.5 million.

4. a, b.

5. **(a)** True; **(b)** false; **(c)** false; **(d)** true; **(e)** false (They may produce gains, but "large" is stretching it.); **(f)** false; **(g)** true.

6. Such companies are tempted to undertake negative-NPV investments. If they do, a bidder may try to take over and force a cutback of investment.

7. **a.** Any premium paid by the bidder over the book value of the target's equity is reflected in the bidder's balance sheet, e.g., it is shown as "goodwill."
   b. The bidder offers to buy the target's stock directly from its shareholders.
   c. The target's stockholders can purchase additional shares at a bargain price.
   d. The target purchases shares held by the bidder; the bidder agrees to go away.

   e. The target frustrates a hostile bidder by agreeing to merge with a friendlier and more compatible suitor.

Chapter 34

1. **a.** Purchase of a business using mostly debt financing. The company goes private. Management is given a substantial equity stake.
   b. An LBO undertaken by management.
   c. A parent company creates a new company with part of its assets and operations. Shares in the new business are distributed to the parent's stockholders.
   d. Like a spin-off, but shares in the new business are sold to investors.
   e. Sale of specific assets rather than entire firm. A company borrows to repurchase a large fraction of its shares. Like an LBO, except that the company remains public.
   f. A government-owned business is sold to private investors.
   g. A company moves to a much higher debt ratio. Proceeds of additional borrowing are paid out to stockholders.

2. **(a)** True; **(b)** false; **(c)** false; **(d)** true; **(e)** true; **(f)** false; **(g)** false.

3. Increased efficiency, broader share ownership, and revenue for the government.

4. **a.** Internal capital markets often misallocate capital. The market values of the conglomerate's divisions can't be observed separately, so it's hard to set incentives and to reward risk-taking.
   b. In a smaller, developing economy, size may give easier access to capital markets and make it easier to attract professional management. It may also give political power. An internal capital market may be helpful when external markets are undeveloped or inefficient.

5. In Germany, banks own large, often controlling stakes in nonfinancial corporations. In the U.S. this is not allowed. In Japan, banks play central roles in keiretsus, groups of companies linked by cross-ownership.

6. Temporary conglomerates, such as LBO funds, purchase businesses in different industries but not to invest and manage for the long run. The objective is to buy, fix, and sell.

GLOSSARY*

A

Abnormal return   Part of return that is not due to systematic influences, e.g., marketwide price movements.

Absolute priority   Rule in bankruptcy proceedings whereby senior creditors are required to be paid in full before junior creditors receive any payment.

Accelerated depreciation   Any *depreciation* method that produces larger deductions for depreciation in the early years of a project's life.

Accounts payable (payables, trade debt)   Money owed to suppliers.

Accounts receivable (receivables, trade credit)   Money owed by customers.

Accrued interest   Interest that has been earned but not yet paid.

ACH   *Automated Clearing House.*

Acid-test ratio   *Quick ratio.*

Adjusted present value (APV)   *Net present value* of an asset if financed solely by equity plus the *present value* of any financing side effects.

ADR   *American depository receipt.*

Adverse selection   A situation in which a pricing policy causes only the less desirable customers to do business, e.g., a rise in insurance prices that leads only the worst risks to buy insurance.

Agency theory   Theory of the relationship between a principal, e.g., a shareholder, and an agent of the principal, e.g., the company's manager.

Aging schedule   Record of the length of time that *accounts receivable* have been outstanding.

All-or-none underwriting   An arrangement whereby a security issue is canceled if the *underwriter* is unable to resell the entire issue.

American depository receipt (ADR)   A security issued in the United States to represent shares of a foreign company.

American option   *Option* that can be exercised any time before the final exercise date (cf. *European option*).

Amex   American Stock Exchange.

Amortization   (1) Repayment of a loan by installments; (2) allowance for *depreciation*.

Annual percentage rate (APR)   Annual interest rate calculated using *simple interest.*

Annuity   Investment that produces a level stream of cash flows for a limited number of periods.

Annuity due   *Annuity* whose payments occur at the start of each period.

Annuity factor   *Present value* of $1 paid for each of t periods.

*Italicized words are listed elsewhere in the glossary.

Anticipation   Arrangements whereby customers who pay before the final date may be entitled to deduct a normal rate of interest.

Appraisal rights   A right of shareholders in a *merger* to demand the payment of a fair price for their shares, as determined independently.

Appropriation request   Formal request for funds for a capital investment project.

APR   *Annual percentage rate.*

APT   Arbitrage pricing theory.

APV   *Adjusted present value.*

Arbitrage   Purchase of one security and simultaneous sale of another to give a risk-free profit.

"Arbitrage" or "risk arbitrage"   Often used loosely to describe the taking of offsetting positions in related securities, e.g., at the time of a takeover bid.

Articles of incorporation   Legal document establishing a corporation and its structure and purpose.

Asian currency units   Dollar deposits held in Singapore or other Asian centers.

Asian option   *Option* based on the average price of the asset during the life of the option.

Ask price (offer price)   Price at which a dealer is willing to sell (cf. *bid price*).

Asset-backed securities   Securities issued by a special purpose company that holds a package of low-risk assets whose cash flows are sufficient to service the *bonds.*

Auction-rate preferred   A variant of *floating-rate preferred* stock where the dividend is reset every 49 days by auction.

Authorized share capital   Maximum number of shares that a company can issue, as specified in the firm's *articles of incorporation.*

Automated Clearing House (ACH)   Private electronic system run by banks for high-volume, low-value payments.

Availability float   Checks deposited by a company that have not yet been cleared.

Aval   Bank guarantee for debt purchased by *forfaiter.*

B

BA   *Banker's acceptance.*

Backwardation   Condition in which *spot price* of commodity exceeds price of *future* (cf. *contango*).

Balloon payment   Large final payment (e.g., when a loan is repaid in installments).

Banker's acceptance (BA)   Written demand that has been accepted by a bank to pay a given sum at a future date (cf. *trade acceptance*).

Barrier option   *Option* whose existence depends on asset price hitting some specified barrier (cf. *down-and-out option, down-and-in option*).

Basis point (bp)   0.01 percent.

Basis risk   Residual risk that results when the two sides of a hedge do not move exactly together.

Bearer security   Security for which primary evidence of ownership is possession of the certificate (cf. *registered security*).

Bear market   Widespread decline in security prices (cf. *bull market*).

Benchmark maturity   Maturity of a newly issued Treasury bond.

Benefit–cost ratio   One plus *profitability index*.

Best-efforts underwriting   An arrangement whereby *underwriters* do not commit themselves to selling a security issue but promise only to use best efforts.

Beta   Measure of *market risk*.

Bid price   Price at which a dealer is willing to buy (cf. *ask price*).

Bill of exchange   General term for a document demanding payment.

Bill of lading   Document establishing ownership of goods in transit.

Blue-chip company   Large and creditworthy company.

Blue-sky laws   State laws covering the issue and trading of securities.

Boilerplate   Standard terms and conditions, e.g., in a debt contract.

Bond   Long-term debt.

Bookbuilding   The procedure whereby *underwriters* gather nonbinding indications of demand for a new issue.

Book entry   System whereby only one global certificate is issued for *bond* and evidence of ownership is receipt showing interest in this certificate.

Book runner   The managing *underwriter* for a new issue. The book runner maintains the book of securities sold.

Bought deal   Security issue where one or two *underwriters* buy the entire issue.

bp   *Basis point.*

Bracket   A term signifying the extent of an *underwriter's* commitment in a new issue, e.g., major bracket, minor bracket.

Break-even analysis   Analysis of the level of sales at which a project would just break even.

Bridging loan   Short-term loan to provide temporary financing until more permanent financing is arranged.

Bull–bear bond   *Bond* whose *principal* repayment is linked to the price of another security. The bonds are issued in two *tranches*: In the first the repayment increases with the price of the other security; in the second the repayment decreases with the price of the other security.

Bulldog bond   *Foreign bond* issue made in London.

Bullet payment   Single final payment, e.g., of a loan (in contrast to payment in installments).

Bull market   Widespread rise in security prices (cf. *bear market*).

Buy-back   *Repurchase agreement.*

C

Cable   The exchange rate between U.S. dollars and sterling.

Call option   Option to buy an asset at a specified *exercise price* on or before a specified exercise date (cf. *put option*).

Call premium   (1) Difference between the price at which a company can call its *bonds* and their *face value;* (2) price of an *option.*

Call provision   Provision that allows an issuer to buy back the *bond* issue at a stated price.

Cap   An upper limit on the interest rate on a *floating-rate note.*

Capital budget   List of planned investment projects, usually prepared annually.

Capitalization   Long-term debt plus *preferred stock* plus *net worth.*

Capital lease   *Financial lease.*

Capital market   Financial market (particularly the market for long-term securities).

Capital rationing   Shortage of funds that forces a company to choose between worthwhile projects.

Capital structure   Mix of different securities issued by a firm.

CAPM   Capital asset pricing model.

CAR   Cumulative *abnormal return.*

CARDs (Certificates for Amortizing Revolving Debt)   *Pass-through securities* backed by credit card *receivables.*

CARs (Certificates of Automobile Receivables)   *Pass-through securities* backed by automobile *receivables.*

Carve-out   Public offering of shares in a subsidiary.

Cascade   Rational herding in which each individual deduces that previous decisions by others may have been based on extra information.

Cash and carry   Purchase of a security and simultaneous sale of a *future,* with the balance being financed with a loan or *repo.*

Cash budget   Forecast of sources and uses of cash.

Cash-deficiency arrangement   Arrangement whereby a project's shareholders agree to provide the operating company with sufficient *net working capital.*

CAT bond   *Catastrophe bond.*

Catastrophe bond (CAT bond)   *Bond* whose payoffs are linked to a measure of catastrophe losses such as insurance claims.

CD   *Certificate of deposit.*

Certainty equivalent   A certain cash flow that has the same present value as a specified risky cash flow.

Certificate of deposit (CD) A certificate providing evidence of a bank time deposit.

CFTC Commodity Futures Trading Commission.

CFO Chief financial officer.

Chaebol A Korean conglomerate.

CHIPS *Clearing House Interbank Payments System.*

Clean price (flat price) *Bond* price excluding *accrued interest* (cf. *dirty price*).

Clearing House Interbank Payments System (CHIPS) An international wire transfer system operated by a group of major banks for high-value dollar payments.

Closed-end mortgage Mortgage against which no additional debt may be issued (cf. *open-end mortgage*).

CMOs *Collateralized mortgage obligations.*

Collar An upper and lower limit on the interest rate on a *floating-rate note.*

Collateral Assets that are given as security for a loan.

Collateralized mortgage obligations (CMOs) A variation on the mortgage *pass-through security,* in which the cash flows from a pool of mortgages are repackaged into several *tranches* of *bonds* with different maturities.

Collateral trust bonds *Bonds* secured by *common stocks* or other securities that are owned by the borrower.

Collection float Customer-written checks that have not been received, deposited, and added to the company's available balance (cf. *payment float*).

Commercial draft (bill of exchange) Demand for payment.

Commercial paper Unsecured *notes* issued by companies and maturing within nine months.

Commitment fee Fee charged by bank on an unused *line of credit.*

Common stock Security representing ownership of a corporation.

Compensating balance Non-interest-bearing demand deposits to compensate banks for bank loans or services.

Competitive bidding Means by which public utility *holding companies* are required to choose their *underwriter* (cf. *negotiated underwriting*).

Completion bonding Insurance that a construction contract will be successfully completed.

Compound interest Reinvestment of each interest payment on money invested to earn more interest (cf. *simple interest*).

Compound option Option on an *option.*

Concentration banking System whereby customers make payments to a regional collection center. The collection center pays the funds into a regional bank account and surplus money is transferred to the company's principal bank.

Conditional sale Sale in which ownership does not pass to the buyer until payment is completed.

Conglomerate merger *Merger* between two companies in unrelated businesses (cf. *horizontal merger, vertical merger*).

Consol Name of a perpetual *bond* issued by the British government. Sometimes used as a general term for *perpetuity.*

Contango Condition in which *spot price* of a commodity is below that of the *future* (cf. *backwardation*).

Contingent claim Claim whose value depends on the value of another asset.

Contingent project Project that cannot be undertaken unless another project is also undertaken.

Continuous compounding Interest compounded continuously rather than at fixed intervals.

Controller Officer responsible for budgeting, accounting, and auditing in a firm (cf. *treasurer*).

Convenience yield The extra advantage that firms derive from holding the commodity rather than the *future.*

Conversion price *Par value* of a *convertible bond* divided by the number of shares into which it may be exchanged.

Conversion ratio Number of shares for which a *convertible bond* may be exchanged.

Convertible bond *Bond* that may be converted into another security at the holder's option. Similarly convertible *preferred stock.*

Convexity Term often used to describe the fact that the effect of an interest rate change on *bond* prices declines as the interest rate rises.

Correlation coefficient Measure of the closeness of the relationship between two variables.

Cost company arrangement Arrangement whereby the shareholders of a project receive output free of charge but agree to pay all operating and financing charges of the project.

Cost of capital *Opportunity cost of capital.*

Coupon (1) Specifically, an attachment to the certificate of a *bearer security* that must be surrendered to collect interest payment; (2) more generally, interest payment on debt.

Covariance Measure of the comovement between two variables.

Covenant Clause in a loan agreement.

Credit derivative Contract for *hedging* against loan default or changes in credit risk (see *default swap, credit option*).

Credit option Similar to a long-term insurance policy against loan default.

Credit scoring A procedure for assigning scores to borrowers on the basis of the risk of default.

Cross-default clause Clause in a loan agreement stating that the company is in default if it fails to meet its obligation on any other debt issue.

Cum dividend *With dividend.*

Cum rights *With rights.*

Cumulative preferred stock Stock that takes priority over *common stock* in regard to dividend payments. Dividends may not be paid on the common stock until all past *dividends* on the *preferred stock* have been paid.

Cumulative voting   Voting system under which a stockholder may cast all of his or her votes for one candidate for the board of directors (cf. *majority voting*).

Current asset   Asset that will normally be turned into cash within a year.

Current liability   Liability that will normally be repaid within a year.

Current ratio   *Current assets* divided by *current liabilities*—a measure of liquidity.

D

DCF   *Discounted cash flow.*

Debenture   Unsecured *bond.*

Decision tree   Method of representing alternative sequential decisions and the possible outcomes from these decisions.

Default swap   *Credit derivative* in which one party makes fixed payments while the payments by the other party depend on the occurrence of a loan default.

Defeasance   Practice whereby the borrower sets aside cash or *bonds* sufficient to service the borrower's debt. Both the borrower's debt and the offsetting cash or bonds are removed from the balance sheet.

Delta   *Hedge ratio.*

Depository transfer check (DTC)   Check made out directly by a local bank to a particular company.

Depreciation   (1) Reduction in the book or market value of an asset; (2) portion of an investment that can be deducted from taxable income.

Derivative   Asset whose value derives from that of some other asset (e.g., a *future* or an *option*).

Diff   *Differential swap.*

Differential swap (diff, quanto swap)   Swap between two *LIBOR* rates of interest, e.g., yen LIBOR for dollar LIBOR. Payments are in one currency.

Dilution   Diminution in the proportion of income to which each share is entitled.

Direct lease   *Lease* in which the *lessor* purchases new equipment from the manufacturer and leases it to the *lessee* (cf. *sale and lease-back*).

Direct quote   For foreign exchange, the number of U.S. dollars needed to buy one unit of a foreign currency (cf. *indirect quote*).

Dirty price   *Bond* price including *accrued interest*, i.e., the price paid by the bond buyer (cf. *clean price*).

Discount bond   Debt sold for less than its *principal* value. If a discount bond pays no interest, it is called a "pure" discount, or *zero-coupon*, bond.

Discounted cash flow (DCF)   Future cash flows multiplied by *discount factors* to obtain *present value.*

Discount factor   *Present value* of $1 received at a stated future date.

Discount rate   Rate used to calculate the *present value* of future cash flows.

Discriminatory price auction   Auction in which successful bidders pay the price that they bid (cf. *uniform price auction*).

Disintermediation   Withdrawal of funds from a financial institution in order to invest them directly (cf. *intermediation*).

Dividend   Payment by a company to its stockholders.

Dividend reinvestment plan (DRIP)   Plan that allows shareholders to reinvest dividends automatically.

Dividend yield   Annual *dividend* divided by share price.

Double-declining-balance depreciation   Method of *accelerated depreciation.*

Double-tax agreement   Agreement between two countries that taxes paid abroad can be offset against domestic taxes levied on foreign *dividends.*

Down-and-in option   *Barrier option* that comes into existence if asset price hits a barrier.

Down-and-out option   *Barrier option* that expires if asset price hits a barrier.

DRIP   *Dividend reinvestment plan.*

Drop lock   An arrangement whereby the interest rate on a *floating-rate note* or *preferred stock* becomes fixed if it falls to a specified level.

DTC   *Depository transfer check.*

Dual-currency bond   *Bond* with interest paid in one currency and *principal* paid in another.

Duration   The average number of years to an asset's *discounted cash flows.*

E

EBIT   Earnings before interest and taxes.

Economic exposure   Risk that arises from changes in real exchange rates (cf. *transaction exposure, translation exposure*).

Economic income   Cash flow plus change in *present value.*

Economic rents   Profits in excess of the competitive level.

Economic Value Added (EVA)   A measure of *residual income* implemented by the consulting firm Stern Stewart.

Efficient market   Market in which security prices reflect information instantaneously.

Efficient portfolio   Portfolio that offers the lowest risk (*standard deviation*) for its *expected return* and the highest expected return for its level of risk.

Employee stock ownership plan (ESOP)   A company contributes to a trust fund that buys stock on behalf of employees.

EPS   Earnings per share.

Equipment trust certificate Form of *secured debt* generally used to finance railroad equipment. The trustee retains ownership of the equipment until the debt is repaid.

Equity (1) *Common stock* and *preferred stock*. Often used to refer to common stock only. (2) *Net worth*.

Equivalent annual cash flow *Annuity* with the same *net present value* as the company's proposed investment.

ESOP *Employee stock ownership plan*.

Euribor *Euro Interbank Offered Rate*.

Euro Interbank Offered Rate (Euribor) The interest rate at which major international banks in Europe lend euros to each other.

Eurobond *Bond* that is marketed internationally.

Eurodollar deposit Dollar deposit with a bank outside the United States.

European option *Option* that can be exercised only on final exercise date (cf. *American option*).

EVA *Economic Value Added*.

Evergreen credit *Revolving credit* without maturity.

Exchange of assets Acquisition of another company by purchase of its assets in exchange for cash or shares.

Exchange of stock Acquisition of another company by purchase of its stock in exchange for cash or shares.

Ex dividend Purchase of shares in which the buyer is not entitled to the forthcoming *dividend* (cf. *with dividend, cum dividend*).

Exercise price (striking price) Price at which a *call option* or *put option* may be exercised.

Expectations hypothesis Theory that *forward interest rate* (*forward exchange rate*) equals expected *spot rate*.

Expected return Average of possible returns weighted by their probabilities.

Ex rights Purchase of shares in which the buyer is not entitled to the rights to buy shares in the company's *rights issue* (cf. *with rights, cum rights, rights on*).

Extendable bond *Bond* whose maturity can be extended at the option of the lender (or issuer).

External finance Finance that is not generated by the firm: new borrowing or an issue of stock (cf. *internal finance*).

Extra dividend *Dividend* that may or may not be repeated (cf. *regular dividend*).

F

Face value *Par value*.

Factoring Arrangement whereby a financial institution buys a company's *accounts receivable* and collects the debt.

Fair price provision *Appraisal* rights.

FASB Financial Accounting Standards Board.

FCIA Foreign Credit Insurance Association.

FDIC Federal Deposit Insurance Corporation.

Federal funds Non-interest-bearing deposits by banks at the Federal Reserve. Excess reserves are lent by banks to each other.

Fedwire A wire transfer system for high-value payments operated by the Federal Reserve System (cf. *CHIPS*).

Field warehouse Warehouse rented by a warehouse company on another firm's premises (cf. *public warehouse*).

Financial assets Claims on *real assets*.

Financial engineering Combining or dividing existing instruments to create new financial products.

Financial lease (capital lease, full-payout lease) Long-term, noncancelable *lease* (cf. *operating lease*).

Financial leverage (gearing) Use of debt to increase the *expected return* on *equity*. Financial leverage is measured by the ratio of debt to debt plus equity (cf. *operating leverage*).

Fiscal agency agreement An alternative to a bond *trust deed*. Unlike the trustee, the fiscal agent acts as an agent of the borrower.

Flat price *Clean price*.

Float See *availability float, payment float*.

Floating lien General *lien* against a company's assets or against a particular class of assets.

Floating-rate note (FRN) *Note* whose interest payment varies with the short-term interest rate.

Floating-rate preferred *Preferred stock* paying dividends that vary with short-term interest rates.

Floor planning Arrangement used to finance inventory. A finance company buys the inventory, which is then held in trust by the user.

Foreign bond A *bond* issued on the domestic *capital market* of another country.

Forex Foreign exchange.

Forfaiter Purchaser of promises to pay (e.g., *bills of exchange* or *promissory notes*) issued by importers.

Forward cover Purchase or sale of forward foreign currency in order to offset a known future cash flow.

Forward exchange rate Exchange rate fixed today for exchanging currency at some future date (cf. *spot exchange rate*).

Forward interest rate Interest rate fixed today on a loan to be made at some future date (cf. *spot interest rate*).

Forward rate agreement (FRA) Agreement to borrow or lend at a specified future date at an interest rate that is fixed today.

FRA *Forward rate agreement*.

Free cash flow Cash not required for operations or for reinvestment.

FRN *Floating-rate note*.

Full-payout lease *Financial lease*.

Full-service lease (rental lease)   *Lease* in which the *lessor* promises to maintain and insure the equipment (cf. *net lease*).

Fundamental analysis   Security analysis that seeks to detect misvalued securities by an analysis of the firm's business prospects (cf. *technical analysis*).

Funded debt   Debt maturing after more than one year (cf. *unfunded debt*).

Future   A contract to buy a commodity or security on a future date at a price that is fixed today. Unlike forward contracts, futures are generally traded on organized exchanges and are *marked to market* daily.

G

GAAP   Generally accepted accounting principles.

Gearing   *Financial leverage.*

General cash offer   Issue of securities offered to all investors (cf. *rights issue*).

Golden parachute   A large termination payment due to a company's management if they lose their jobs as a result of a merger.

Goodwill   The difference between the amount paid for a firm in a *merger* and its book value.

Gray market   Purchases and sales of *eurobonds* that occur before the issue price is made.

Greenmail   Situation in which a large block of stock is held by an unfriendly company, forcing the target company to repurchase the stock at a substantial premium to prevent a takeover.

Greenshoe option   *Option* that allows the *underwriter* for a new issue to buy and resell additional shares.

Growth stock   *Common stock* of a company that has an opportunity to invest money to earn more than the *opportunity cost of capital* (cf. *income stock*).

H

Haircut   An additional margin of *collateral* for a loan.

Hedge ratio (delta, option delta)   The number of shares to buy for each *option* sold in order to create a safe position; more generally, the number of units of an asset that should be bought to hedge one unit of a liability.

Hedging   Buying one security and selling another in order to reduce risk. A perfect hedge produces a riskless portfolio.

Hell-or-high-water clause   Clause in a *lease* agreement that obligates the *lessee* to make payments regardless of what happens to the *lessor* or the equipment.

Highly leveraged transaction (HLT)   Bank loan to a highly leveraged firm (formerly needed to be separately reported to the Federal Reserve Board).

HLT   *Highly leveraged transaction.*

Holding company   Company whose sole function is to hold stock in other companies or subsidiaries.

Horizontal merger   Merger between two companies that manufacture similar products (cf. *vertical merger, conglomerate merger*).

Horizontal spread   The simultaneous purchase and sale of two *options* that differ only in their exercise date (cf. *vertical spread*).

Hurdle rate   Minimum acceptable rate of return on a project.

I

IBF   *International Banking Facility.*

IMM   *International Monetary Market.*

Immunization   The construction of an asset and a liability that are subject to offsetting changes in value.

Imputation tax system   Arrangement by which investors who receive a *dividend* also receive a tax credit for corporate taxes that the firm has paid.

Income bond   *Bond* on which interest is payable only if earned.

Income stock   *Common stock* with high *dividend yield* and few profitable investment opportunities (cf. *growth stock*).

Indenture   Formal agreement, e.g., establishing the terms of a *bond* issue.

Indexed bond   *Bond* whose payments are linked to an index, e.g., a consumer price index (see *TIPs*).

Index fund   Investment fund designed to match the returns on a stockmarket index.

Indirect quote   For foreign exchange, the number of units of a foreign currency needed to buy one U.S. dollar (cf. *direct quote*).

Industrial revenue bond (IRB)   Bond issued by local government agencies on behalf of corporations.

Initial public offering (IPO)   A company's first public issue of *common stock*.

In-substance defeasance   *Defeasance* whereby debt is removed from the balance sheet but not canceled (cf. *novation*).

Intangible asset   Nonmaterial asset, such as technical expertise, a trademark, or a patent (cf. *tangible asset*).

Integer programming   Variant of *linear programming* whereby the solution values must be integers.

Interest cover   *Times interest earned.*

Interest equalization tax   Tax on foreign investment by residents of the United States (abolished 1974).

Interest-rate parity   Theory that the differential between the *forward exchange rate* and the *spot exchange rate* is equal to the differential between the foreign and domestic interest rates.

Intermediation   Investment through a financial institution (cf. *disintermediation*).

Internal finance   Finance generated within a firm by *retained earnings* and *depreciation* (cf. *external finance*).

Internal growth rate   The maximum rate of firm growth without *external finance* (cf. *sustainable growth rate*).

Internal rate of return (IRR)   *Discount rate* at which investment has zero *net present value.*

International Banking Facility (IBF)   A branch that an American bank establishes in the United States to do eurocurrency business.

International Monetary Market (IMM)   The financial futures market within the Chicago Mercantile Exchange.

Interval measure   The number of days that a firm can finance operations without additional cash income.

In-the-money option   An *option* that would be worth exercising if it expired immediately (cf. *out-of-the-money option*).

Inverse FRN   *Floating-rate note* whose payments rise as the general level of interest rates falls and vice versa.

Investment-grade bond   *Bond* rated at least Baa by Moody's or BBB by Standard and Poor's.

Investment tax credit   Proportion of new capital investment that can be used to reduce a company's tax bill (abolished 1986).

IPO   *Initial public offering.*

IRB   *Industrial revenue bond.*

IRR   *Internal rate of return.*

IRS   Internal Revenue Service.

ISDA   International Swap and Derivatives Association.

ISMA   International Securities Market Association.

Issued share capital   Total amount of shares that are in issue (cf. *outstanding share capital*).

J

Junior debt   *Subordinated debt.*

Junk bond   Debt that is rated below an *investment-grade bond.*

K

Keiretsu   A network of Japanese companies organized around a major bank.

L

LBO   *Leveraged buyout.*

Lease   Long-term rental agreement.

Legal capital   Value at which a company's shares are recorded in its books.

Legal defeasance - *Novation.*

Lessee   User of a leased asset (cf. *lessor*).

Lessor   Owner of a leased asset (cf. *lessee*).

Letter of credit   Letter from a bank stating that it has established a credit in the company's favor.

Letter stock   Privately placed *common stock,* so-called because the *SEC* requires a letter from the purchaser that the stock is not intended for resale.

Leverage   See *financial leverage, operating leverage.*

Leveraged buyout (LBO)   Acquisition in which (1) a large part of the purchase price is debt-financed and (2) the remaining *equity* is privately held by a small group of investors.

Leveraged lease   *Lease* in which the *lessor* finances part of the cost of the asset by an issue of debt secured by the asset and the lease payments.

Liabilities, total liabilities   Total value of financial claims on a firm's assets. Equals (1) total assets or (2) total assets minus *net worth.*

LIBOR   *London interbank offered rate.*

Lien   Lender's claims on specified assets.

Limited liability   Limitation of a shareholder's losses to the amount invested.

Limited partnership   *Partnership* in which some partners have *limited liability* and general partners have unlimited liability.

Linear programming (LP)   Technique for finding the maximum value of some equation subject to stated linear constraints.

Line of credit   Agreement by a bank that a company may borrow at any time up to an established limit.

Liquid asset   Asset that is easily and cheaply turned into cash—notably cash itself and short-term securities.

Liquidating dividend   *Dividend* that represents a return of capital.

Liquidator   Person appointed by unsecured creditors in the United Kingdom to oversee the sale of an insolvent firm's assets and the repayment of debts.

Liquidity premium   (1) Additional return for investing in a security that cannot easily be turned into cash; (2) difference between the *forward* interest rate and the expected *spot interest rate.*

Liquid yield option note (LYON)   *Zero-coupon,* callable, puttable, *convertible bond.*

Load-to-load   Arrangement whereby the customer pays for the last delivery when the next one is received.

Lock-box system   Form of *concentration banking.* Customers send payments to a post office box. A local bank collects and processes the checks and transfers surplus funds to the company's principal bank.

London interbank offered rate (LIBOR)   The interest rate at which major international banks in London lend to each other. (LIBID is London interbank bid rate; LIMEAN is mean of bid and offered rate.)

Long hedge   Purchase of a *hedging* instrument (e.g., a *future*) to hedge a short position in the underlying asset (cf. *short hedge*).

Lookback option   *Option* whose payoff depends on the highest asset price recorded over the life of the option.

LP   *Linear programming.*

LYON   *Liquid yield option note.*

M

MACRS   *Modified accelerated cost recovery system.*

Maintenance margin   Minimum margin that must be maintained on a *futures* contract.

Majority voting   Voting system under which each director is voted upon separately (cf. *cumulative voting*).

Management buyout (MBO)   *Leveraged buyout* whereby the acquiring group is led by the firm's management.

Margin   Cash or securities set aside by an investor as evidence that he or she can honor a commitment.

Marked-to-market   An arrangement whereby the profits or losses on a *futures* contract are settled up each day.

Market capitalization rate   *Expected return* on a security.

Market risk (systematic risk)   Risk that cannot be diversified away.

Maturity factoring   *Factoring* arrangement that provides collection and insurance of *accounts receivable*.

MBO   *Management buyout.*

MDA   *Multiple-discriminant analysis.*

Medium-term note (MTN)   Debt with a typical maturity of 1 to 10 years offered regularly by a company using the same procedure as *commercial paper.*

Merger   (1) Acquisition in which all assets and liabilities are absorbed by the buyer (cf. *exchange of assets, exchange of stock*); (2) more generally, any combination of two companies.

MIP (Monthly income preferred security)   *Preferred stock* issued by a subsidiary located in a tax haven. The subsidiary relends the money to the parent.

Mismatch bond   *Floating-rate note* whose interest rate is reset at more frequent intervals than the rollover period (e.g., a note whose payments are set quarterly on the basis of the one-year interest rate).

Modified accelerated cost recovery system (MACRS)   Schedule of *depreciation* deductions allowed for tax purposes.

Money center bank   A major U.S. bank that undertakes a wide range of banking activities.

Money market   Market for short-term safe investments.

Money-market fund   *Mutual fund* that invests solely in short-term safe securities.

Monte Carlo simulation   Method for calculating the probability distribution of possible outcomes, e.g., from a project.

Moral hazard   The risk that the existence of a contract will change the behavior of one or both parties to the contract; e.g., an insured firm may take fewer fire precautions.

Mortgage bond   *Bond* secured against plant and equipment.

MTN   *Medium-term note.*

Multiple-discriminant analysis (MDA)   Statistical technique for distinguishing between two groups on the basis of their observed characteristics.

Mutual fund   Managed investment fund whose shares are sold to investors.

Mutually exclusive projects   Two projects that cannot both be undertaken.

N

Naked option   *Option* held on its own, i.e., not used for *hedging* a holding in the asset or other options.

NASD   National Association of Security Dealers.

Negative pledge clause   Clause under which the borrower agrees not to permit an exclusive *lien* on any of its assets.

Negotiated underwriting   Method of choosing an *underwriter*. Most firms may choose their *underwriter* by negotiation (cf. *competitive bidding*).

Net lease   *Lease* in which the *lessee* promises to maintain and insure the equipment (cf. *full-service lease*).

Net present value (NPV)   A project's net contribution to wealth—*present value* minus initial investment.

Net working capital   *Current assets* minus *current liabilities.*

Net worth   Book value of a company's *common stock*, surplus, and *retained earnings.*

Nominal interest rate   Interest rate expressed in money terms (cf. *real interest rate*).

Nonrefundable debt   Debt that may not be called in order to replace it with another issue at a lower interest cost.

Normal distribution   Symmetric bell-shaped distribution that can be completely defined by its mean and *standard deviation.*

Note   Unsecured debt with a maturity of up to 10 years.

Novation (legal defeasance)   *Defeasance* whereby the firm's debt is canceled (cf. *in-substance defeasance*).

NPV   *Net present value.*

NYSE   New York Stock Exchange.

O

Odd lot   A trade of less than 100 shares (cf. *round lot*).

Off-balance-sheet financing   Financing that is not shown as a liability in a company's balance sheet.

Offer price   *Ask price.*

OID debt   *Original issue discount debt.*

Old-line factoring *Factoring* arrangement that provides collection, insurance, and finance for *accounts receivable.*

On the run The most recently issued (and, therefore, typically the most liquid) government *bond* in a particular maturity range.

Open account Arrangement whereby sales are made with no formal debt contract. The buyer signs a receipt, and the seller records the sale in the sales ledger.

Open-end mortgage Mortgage against which additional debt may be issued (cf. *closed-end mortgage*).

Open interest The number of currently outstanding *futures* contracts.

Operating lease Short-term, cancelable *lease* (cf. *financial lease*).

Operating leverage Fixed operating costs, so-called because they accentuate variations in profits (cf. *financial leverage*).

Opportunity cost of capital (hurdle rate, cost of capital) *Expected return* that is forgone by investing in a project rather than in comparable financial securities.

Option See *call option, put option.*

Option delta *Hedge ratio.*

Original issue discount debt (OID debt) Debt that is initially offered at a price below *face value.*

OTC *Over-the-counter.*

Out-of-the-money option An *option* that would not be worth exercising if it matured immediately (cf. *in-the-money option*).

Outstanding share capital *Issued share capital* less the *par value* of shares that are held in the company's treasury.

Oversubscription privilege In a *rights issue,* arrangement by which shareholders are given the right to apply for any shares that are not taken up.

Over-the-counter (OTC) Informal market that does not involve a securities exchange. Specifically used to refer to the NASDAQ dealer market for *common stocks.*

P

Partnership Joint ownership of business whereby general partners have unlimited liability.

Par value (face value) Value of a security shown on the certificate.

Pass-through securities *Notes* or *bonds* backed by a package of assets (e.g., mortgage pass-throughs, *CARs, CARDs*).

Path-dependent option *Option* whose value depends on the sequence of prices of the underlying asset rather than just the final price of the asset.

Payables *Accounts payable.*

Payback period Time taken for a project to recover its initial investment.

Pay-in-kind bond (PIK) *Bond* that allows the issuer to choose to make interest payments in the form of additional bonds.

Payment float Company-written checks that have not yet cleared (cf. *availability float*).

Payout ratio *Dividend* as a proportion of earnings per share.

PBGC Pension Benefit Guarantee Corporation.

P/E ratio Share price divided by earnings per share.

PERC (Preferred equity redemption cumulative stock) *Preferred stock* that converts automatically into equity at a stated date. A limit is placed on the value of the shares that the investor receives.

Perpetuity Investment offering a level stream of cash flows in perpetuity (cf. *consol*).

PIK *Pay-in-kind bond.*

PN *Project note.*

Poison pill An issue of securities that is convertible, in the event of a *merger,* into the shares of the acquiring firm or must be repurchased by the acquiring firm.

Poison put A *covenant* allowing the *bond*holder to demand repayment in the event of a hostile *merger.*

Pooling of interest Method of accounting for *mergers* (no longer available in the USA). The consolidated balance sheet of the merged firm is obtained by combining the balance sheets of the separate firms (cf. *purchase accounting*).

Position diagram Diagram showing the possible payoffs from a *derivative* investment.

Postaudit Evaluation of an investment project after it has been undertaken.

Preemptive right Common stockholder's right to anything of value distributed by the company.

Preferred stock Stock that takes priority over common stock in regard to *dividends.* Dividends may not be paid on *common stock* unless the dividend is paid on all preferred stock (cf. *cumulative preferred stock*). The dividend rate on preferred is usually fixed at time of issue.

Prepack *Prepackaged bankruptcy.*

Prepackaged bankruptcy (prepack) Bankruptcy proceedings intended to confirm a reorganization plan that has already been agreed to informally.

Present value Discounted value of future cash flows.

Present value of growth opportunities (PVGO) *Net present value* of investments the firm is expected to make in the future.

PRIDE Similar to a *PERC* except that as the equity price rises beyond a specified point, the investor shares in the stock appreciation.

Primary issue Issue of new securities by a firm (cf. *secondary issue*).

Prime rate Benchmark lending rate set by U.S. banks.

Principal Amount of debt that must be repaid.

Principal–agent problem Problem faced by a principal (e.g., shareholder) in ensuring that an agent (e.g., manager) acts on his or her behalf.

Privileged subscription issue *Rights issue.*

Production payment Loan in the form of advance payment for future delivery of a product.

Profitability index Ratio of a project's *NPV* to the initial investment.

Pro forma Projected.

Project finance Debt that is largely a claim against the cash flows from a particular project rather than against the firm as a whole.

Project note (PN) *Note* issued by public housing or urban renewal agencies.

Promissory note Promise to pay.

Prospectus Summary of the *registration* statement providing information on an issue of securities.

Proxy vote Vote cast by one person on behalf of another.

Public warehouse (terminal warehouse) Warehouse operated by an independent warehouse company on its own premises (cf. *field warehouse*).

Purchase accounting Method of accounting for *mergers.* The assets of the acquired firm are shown at market value on the balance sheet of the acquiror (cf. *pooling of interest*).

Purchase fund Resembles a *sinking fund* except that money is used only to purchase bonds if they are selling below their *par value*.

Put option *Option* to sell an asset at a specified *exercise price* on or before a specified exercise date (cf. *call option*).

PVGO *Present value of growth opportunities.*

Q

q Ratio of the market value of an asset to its replacement cost.

QIBs *Qualified Institutional Buyers.*

Quadratic programming Variant of *linear programming* whereby the equations are quadratic rather than linear.

Qualified Institutional Buyers (QIBs) Institutions that are allowed to trade unregistered stock among themselves.

Quanto swap *Differential swap.*

Quick ratio (acid-test ratio) Measure of liquidity: (*current assets* – inventory) divided by *current liabilities*.

R

Range forward A *forward exchange rate* contract that places upper and lower bounds on the cost of foreign exchange.

Real assets *Tangible assets* and *intangible assets* used to carry on business (cf. *financial assets*).

Real estate investment trust (REIT) Trust company formed to invest in real estate.

Real interest rate Interest rate expressed in terms of real goods, i.e., *nominal interest rate* adjusted for inflation.

Receivables *Accounts receivable.*

Receiver A bankruptcy practitioner appointed by secured creditors in the United Kingdom to oversee the repayment of debts.

Record date Date set by directors when making dividend payment. *Dividends* are sent to stockholders who are registered on the record date.

Recourse Term describing a type of loan. If a loan is with recourse, the lender has a general claim against the parent company if the *collateral* is insufficient to repay the debt.

Red herring Preliminary *prospectus.*

Refunding Replacement of existing debt with a new issue of debt.

Registered security Security whose ownership is recorded by the company's *registrar* (cf. *bearer security*).

Registrar Financial institution appointed to record issue and ownership of company securities.

Registration Process of obtaining *SEC* approval for a public issue of securities.

Regression analysis In statistics, a technique for finding the line of best fit.

Regular dividend *Dividend* that the company expects to maintain in the future.

Regulation A issue Small security issues that are partially exempt from *SEC registration* requirements.

REIT *Real estate investment trust.*

Rental lease *Full-service lease.*

Repo *Repurchase agreement.*

Repurchase agreement (RP, repo, buy-back) Purchase of Treasury securities from a securities dealer with an agreement that the dealer will repurchase them at a specified price.

Residual income After-tax profit less the *opportunity cost of capital* employed by the business (see also *Economic Value Added*).

Residual risk *Unique risk.*

Retained earnings Earnings not paid out as *dividends*.

Return on equity Usually, equity earnings as a proportion of the book value of equity.

Return on investment (ROI) Generally, book income as a proportion of net book value.

Revolving credit Legally assured *line of credit* with a bank.

Rights issue (privileged subscription issue) Issue of securities offered to current stockholders (cf. *general cash offer*).

Rights on *With rights.*

Risk premium Expected additional return for making a risky investment rather than a safe one.

ROI *Return on investment.*

Roll-over CD A package of successive *certificates of deposit.*

Round lot A trade of 100 shares (cf. *odd lot*).

RP   *Repurchase agreement*.

R squared (R²)   Square of the *correlation coefficient*—the proportion of the variability in one series that can be explained by the variability of one or more other series.

Rule 144a   *SEC* rule allowing *qualified institutional buyers* to buy and trade unregistered securities.

S

Sale and lease-back   Sale of an existing asset to a financial institution that then *leases* it back to the user (cf. *direct lease*).

Salvage value   Scrap value of plant and equipment.

Samurai bond   A yen *bond* issued in Tokyo by a non-Japanese borrower (cf. *bulldog bond, Yankee bond*).

SBIC   Small Business Investment Company.

Seasoned issue   Issue of a security for which there is an existing market (cf. *unseasoned issue*).

Season datings   Extended credit for customers who order goods out of the peak season.

SEC   Securities and Exchange Commission.

Secondary issue   (1) Procedure for selling blocks of *seasoned issues* of stock; (2) more generally, sale of already issued stock.

Secondary market   Market in which one can buy or sell *seasoned issues* of securities.

Secured debt   Debt that, in the event of default, has first claim on specified assets.

Securitization   Substitution of tradable securities for privately negotiated instruments.

Security market line   Line representing the relationship between *expected return* and *market risk*.

Self-liquidating loan   Loan to finance *current assets*. The sale of the current assets provides the cash to repay the loan.

Self-selection   Consequence of a contract that induces only one group (e.g., low-risk individuals) to participate.

Semistrong-form efficient market   Market in which security prices reflect all publicly available information (cf. *weak-form efficient market* and *strong-form efficient market*).

Senior debt   Debt that, in the event of bankruptcy, must be repaid before *subordinated debt* receives any payment.

Sensitivity analysis   Analysis of the effect on project profitability of possible changes in sales, costs, and so on.

Serial bonds   Package of *bonds* that mature in successive years.

Series bond   *Bond* that may be issued in several series under the same *indenture*.

Shark repellant   Amendment to company charter intended to protect against takeover.

Shelf registration   A procedure that allows firms to file one *registration* statement covering several issues of the same security.

Shogun bond   Dollar *bond* issued in Japan by a nonresident.

Short hedge   Sale of a *hedging* instrument (e.g., a *future*) to *hedge* a long position in the underlying asset (cf. *long hedge*).

Short sale   Sale of a security the investor does not own.

Sight draft   Demand for immediate payment (cf. *time draft*).

Signal   Action that demonstrates an individual's unobservable characteristics (because it would be unduly costly for someone without those characteristics to take the action).

Simple interest   Interest calculated only on the initial investment (cf. *compound interest*).

Simulation   *Monte Carlo simulation*.

Sinker   *Sinking fund*.

Sinking fund (sinker)   Fund established by a company to retire debt before maturity.

Skewed distribution   Probability distribution in which an unequal number of observations lie below and above the mean.

Special dividend (extra dividend)   *Dividend* that is unlikely to be repeated.

Specific risk   *Unique risk*.

Spin-off   Distribution of shares in a subsidiary to the company's shareholders so that they hold shares separately in the two firms.

Spot exchange rate   Exchange rate on currency for immediate delivery (cf. *forward exchange rate*)

Spot interest rate   Interest rate fixed today on a loan that is made today (cf. *forward interest rate*).

Spot price   Price of asset for immediate delivery (in contrast to forward or futures price).

Spread   Difference between the price at which an *underwriter* buys an issue from a firm and the price at which the underwriter sells it to the public.

Standard deviation   Square root of the *variance*—a measure of variability.

Standard error   In statistics, a measure of the possible error in an estimate.

Standby agreement   In a *rights issue*, agreement that the *underwriter* will purchase any stock not purchased by investors.

Step-up bond   *Bond* whose *coupon* is stepped up over time (also step-down bond).

Stock dividend   *Dividend* in the form of stock rather than cash.

Stock split   "Free" issue of shares to existing shareholders.

Straddle   The combination of a *put option* and a *call option* with the same *exercise price*.

Straight-line depreciation   An equal dollar amount of *depreciation* in each period.

Striking price   *Exercise price* of an *option*.

Stripped bond   *Bond* that can be subdivided into a series of *zero-coupon bonds*.

Strong-form efficient market   Market in which security prices reflect instantaneously *all* information available to investors (cf. *weak-form efficient market* and *semistrong-form efficient market*).

Structured debt   Debt that has been customized for the buyer, often by incorporating unusual *options*.

Subordinated debt (junior debt)   Debt over which *senior debt* takes priority. In the event of bankruptcy, subordinated debtholders receive payment only after senior debt is paid off in full.

Sum-of-the-years'-digits depreciation   Method of *accelerated depreciation*.

Sunk costs   Costs that have been incurred and cannot be reversed.

Supermajority   Provision in a company's charter requiring a majority of, say, 80 percent of shareholders to approve certain changes, such as a *merger*.

Sushi bond   A *eurobond* issued by a Japanese corporation.

Sustainable growth rate   Maximum rate of firm growth without increasing financial leverage (cf. *internal growth rate*).

Swap   An arrangement whereby two companies lend to each other on different terms, e.g., in different currencies, or one at a fixed rate and the other at a floating rate.

Swaption   *Option* on a *swap*.

Swingline facility   Bank borrowing facility to provide finance while the firm replaces U.S. *commercial paper* with eurocommercial paper.

Systematic risk   *Market risk*.

T

Take-up fee   Fee paid to *underwriters* of a *rights issue* on any stock they are obliged to purchase.

Tangible asset   Physical asset, such as plant, machinery, and offices (cf. *intangible assets*).

Tax-anticipation bill   Short-term bill issued by the U.S. Treasury that can be surrendered at *face value* in payment of taxes.

T-bill   *Treasury bill*.

Technical analysis   Security analysis that seeks to detect and interpret patterns in past security prices (cf. *fundamental analysis*).

TED spread   Difference between *LIBOR* and U.S. *Treasury bill* rate.

Tender offer   General offer made directly to a firm's shareholders to buy their stock.

Tenor   Maturity of a loan.

Terminal warehouse   *Public warehouse*.

Term loan   Medium-term, privately placed loan, usually made by a bank.

Term structure of interest rates   Relationship between interest rates on loans of different maturities (cf. *yield curve*).

Throughput arrangement   Arrangement by which shareholders of a pipeline company agree to make sufficient use of pipeline to enable the pipeline company to service its debt.

Tick   Minimum amount the price of a security may change.

Time draft   Demand for payment at a stated future date (cf. *sight draft*).

Times interest earned (interest cover)   Earnings before interest and tax, divided by interest payments.

TIPS (Treasury Inflation Protected Securities)   U.S. Treasury *bonds* whose *coupon* and *principal* payments are linked to the Consumer Price Index.

Tombstone   Advertisement listing the *underwriters* to a security issue.

Trade acceptance   Written demand that has been accepted by an industrial company to pay a given sum at a future date (cf. *banker's acceptance*).

Trade credit   *Accounts receivable*.

Trade debt   *Accounts payable*.

Tranche   Portion of a new issue sold at a point in time different from the remainder or that has different terms.

Transaction exposure   Risk to a firm with known future cash flows in a foreign currency that arises from possible changes in the exchange rate (cf. *economic exposure, translation exposure*).

Transfer agent   Individual or institution appointed by a company to look after the transfer of securities.

Translation exposure   Risk of adverse effects on a firm's financial statements that may arise from changes in exchange rates (cf. *economic exposure, transaction exposure*).

Treasurer   Principal financial manager (cf. *controller*).

Treasury bill (T-bill)   Short-term discount debt maturing in less than one year, issued regularly by the government.

Treasury stock   *Common stock* that has been repurchased by the company and held in the company's treasury.

Trust deed   Agreement between trustee and borrower setting out terms of *bond*.

Trust receipt   Receipt for goods that are to be held in trust for the lender.

U

Underpricing   Issue of securities below their market value.

Underwriter   Firm that buys an issue of securities from a company and resells it to investors.

Unfunded debt Debt maturing within one year (cf. *funded debt*).

Uniform price auction Auction in which all successful bidders pay the same price (cf. *discriminatory price auction*).

Unique risk (residual risk, specific risk, unsystematic risk) Risk that can be eliminated by diversification.

Unseasoned issue Issue of a security for which there is no existing market (cf. *seasoned issue*).

Unsystematic risk *Unique risk.*

V

Value additivity Rule that the value of the whole must equal the sum of the values of the parts.

Value-at-risk model (VAR model) Procedure for estimating the probability of portfolio losses exceeding some specified proportion.

Vanilla issue Issue without unusual features.

Variable-rate demand bond (VRDB) Floating-rate *bond* that can be sold back periodically to the issuer.

Variance Mean squared deviation from the expected value—a measure of variability.

Variation margin The daily gains or losses on a *futures* contract credited to the investor's margin account.

VAR model *Value-at-risk model.*

Venture capital Capital to finance a new firm.

Vertical merger *Merger* between a supplier and its customer (cf. *horizontal merger, conglomerate merger*).

Vertical spread Simultaneous purchase and sale of two options that differ only in their *exercise price* (cf. *horizontal spread*).

VRDB *Variable rate demand bond.*

W

WACC *Weighted-average cost of capital.*

Warehouse receipt Evidence that a firm owns goods stored in a warehouse.

Warrant Long-term *call option* issued by a company.

Weak-form efficient market Market in which security prices instantaneously reflect the information in the history of security prices. In such a market security prices follow a random walk (cf. *semistrong-form efficient market* and *strong-form efficient market*).

Weighted-average cost of capital (WACC) *Expected return* on a portfolio of all the firm's securities. Used as *hurdle rate* for capital investment.

White knight A friendly potential acquirer sought out by a target company threatened by a less welcome suitor.

Wi. When issued.

Winner's curse Problem faced by uninformed bidders. For example, in an *initial public offering* uninformed participants are likely to receive larger allotments of issues that informed participants know are overpriced.

With dividend (cum dividend) Purchase of shares in which the buyer is entitled to the forthcoming *dividend* (cf. *ex dividend*).

Withholding tax Tax levied on *dividends* paid abroad.

With rights (cum rights, rights on) Purchase of shares in which the buyer is entitled to the rights to buy shares in the company's *rights issue* (cf. *ex rights*).

Working capital *Current assets* and *current liabilities.* The term is commonly used as synonymous with *net working capital.*

Workout Informal arrangement between a borrower and creditors.

Writer *Option* seller.

Y

Yankee bond A dollar *bond* issued in the United States by a non-U.S. borrower (cf. *bulldog bond, Samurai bond*).

Yield curve *Term structure of interest rates.*

Yield to maturity *Internal rate of return* on a bond.

Z

Zero-coupon bond *Discount bond* making no *coupon* payments.

Z score Measure of the likelihood of bankruptcy.

GLOBAL INDEX

INDEX

$\int$OME COMMON$\int$Y U$\int$ED $\int$YMBOL$\int$

APV	Adjusted present value
BV	Book value
C_t	Cash flow at time t
$\mathbf{CEQ}_t$	Certainty-equivalent cash flow at time t
$\mathbf{DIV}_t$	Dividend payment at time t
D	Market value of firm's debt
$\mathbf{DEP}_t$	Depreciation in year t
$\mathbf{DF}_t$	Discount factor for cash flow in period t
e	2.718 (base for natural logarithms)
E	Market value of firm's equity
$\mathbf{EPS}_t$	Earnings per share in year t
EX	Exercise price of option
f_t	Expected return on a one-period forward loan maturing at time t
$f_{\$/£}$	Forward rate of exchange between dollars and pounds
g	Growth rate
i_t	Expected inflation in year t
IRR	Internal rate of return
$\mathbf{LCF}_t$	Lease's cash outflow in year t
NPV	Net present value
P_t	Price at time t
PV	Present value
PVGO	Present value of growth opportunities
r_t	Expected rate of return (or cost of capital) in period t. We omit the subscript where the expected return is identical in each period. Sometimes we use a *second* subscript to define the date at which the investment is made. Thus, $_{t-1}r_t$ is the (spot) rate of return on an investment made at $t-1$ and paying off at time t.

$\tilde{r}_t$	Uncertain actual rate of return in period t
r_D	Expected rate of return on firm's debt
r_E	Expected rate of return on firm's equity
r_f	Risk-free interest rate
r_m	Expected rate of return on the market portfolio
$r_\$$	Dollar rate of interest
$s_{\text{SFr}/\$}$	Spot rate of exchange between Swiss francs and dollars
t	Time
$\mathbf{T}_c$	Rate of corporate income tax
$\mathbf{T}_p$	Rate of personal income tax
V	Market value of firm: $V = D + E$
y	Yield to maturity
β	Beta: A measure of market risk
δ	Delta: Hedge ratio
ρ_{12}	Rho: Correlation coefficient between investments 1 and 2
σ	Sigma: Standard deviation
σ_{12}	Covariance of investment 1 with investment 2
σ^2	Sigma squared: Variance
Σ	Capital sigma: "The sum of"

SOME USEFUL FORMULAS

(The section number indicates the principal reference in the text.)

Perpetuity (3-2)

The value of a perpetuity of $1 per year is:

$$PV = \frac{1}{r}$$

Annuity (3-2)

The value of an annuity of $1 per period for t years (t-year annuity factor) is:

$$PV = \frac{1}{r} - \frac{1}{r(1 + r)^t}$$

A Growing Perpetuity
(the "Gordon" model) (3-2)

If the first period's cash flow is $1 at year 1 and if cash flows thereafter grow at a constant rate of g in perpetuity,

$$PV = \frac{1}{r - g}$$

Continuous Compounding (3-3)

If r is the continuously compounded rate of interest, the present value of $1 received in year t is:

$$PV = \frac{1}{e^{rt}}$$

Equivalent Annual Cost (6-3)

If an asset has a life of t years, the equivalent annual cost is:

$$\frac{PV\ (costs)}{t\text{-year annuity factor}}$$

Measures of Risk (7-2 to 7-4)

Variance of returns = σ^2

$\qquad$ = expected value of $(\tilde{r} - r)^2$

Standard deviation of returns = $\sqrt{\text{variance}} = \sigma$
Covariance between returns of stocks 1 and 2
= σ_{12} = expected value of $[(\tilde{r}_1 - r_1)(\tilde{r}_2 - r_2)]$

Correlation between returns of stocks 1 and 2:

$$\rho_{12} = \frac{\sigma_{12}}{\sigma_1 \sigma_2}$$

Beta of stock $i = \beta_i = \dfrac{\sigma_{im}}{\sigma_m^2}$

The variance of returns on a portfolio with proportion x_i invested in stock i is:

$$\sum_{i=1}^{N} \sum_{j=1}^{N} x_i x_j \sigma_{ij}$$

Capital Asset Pricing Model (8-2)

The expected risk premium on a risky investment is:

$$r - r_f = \beta(r_m - r_f)$$

Unlevering Betas (9-3 and 19-1)

$$\beta_{assets} = \beta_{debt}\left(\frac{D}{V}\right) + \beta_{equity}\left(\frac{E}{V}\right)$$

where
D and E = the market values of debt and equity ($V = D + E$)

Weighted Average Cost of Capital (9-3 and 19-1)

$$WACC = r_D(1 - T_c)D/V + r_E E/V$$

where
r_D and r_E = the expected returns on debt and equity
T_c = the marginal rate of corporate tax
D and E = the market values of debt and equity
($V = D + E$)

MM's Proposition II (17-2 and 19-3)

The required return on equity (r_E) increases in line with the debt–equity ratio calculated using market values (D/E):

$$r_E = r + (r - r_D)D/E$$

where r is the opportunity cost of capital.

Relationship between the Value of a Call and a Put (20-2)

The relationship between the value of a European call and a European put is:

Value of call + present value of exercise price
$$= \text{value of put} + \text{share price}$$

Black–Scholes Formula for Value of a Call (21-3)

Value of a call $= [N(d_1) \times P] - [N(d_2) \times PV(EX)]$

where

$$d_1 = \log[P/PV(EX)]/\sigma\sqrt{t} + \sigma\sqrt{t}/2$$
$$d_2 = d_1 - \sigma\sqrt{t}$$

$N(d)$ = cumulative normal probability function
$PV(EX)$ = present value of exercise price
t = number of periods to exercise date
P = current price of stock
σ = standard deviation per period
    of continuously compounded rate
    of return on stock
$\log$ = natural logarithm

Inputs to Binomial Option Valuation Model (21-1 and 21-2)

$$\begin{array}{l}\text{Probability of upside change} \\ \text{in risk-neutral world}\end{array} = p = \frac{r_f - d}{u - d}$$

$$1 + \text{Upside change} = u = e^{\sigma\sqrt{h}}$$

$$1 + \text{Downside change} = d = 1/u$$

where σ = standard deviation of price changes
    per year
  h = interval as fraction of a year

$$\text{Option delta} = \frac{\text{spread of possible option prices}}{\text{spread of possible stock prices}}$$

Bond Duration and Volatility (24.3)

$$\text{Duration of T-period bond} = \frac{\sum_{t=1}^{T} t \times C_t/(1 + y)^t}{\sum_{t=1}^{T} C_t/(1 + y)^t}$$

$$\text{Volatility (modified duration)} = \text{Duration}/(1 + y)$$

Value of Lease (26-4)

If LCF_t is the lease's cash outflow in period t, the value of an N-period lease of an asset costing INV is:

$$\text{INV} - \sum_{t=0}^{N} \frac{LCF_t}{[1 + r(1 - T_c)]^t}$$

Value of a Future (27-2)

$$\frac{\text{Futures price}}{(1 + r_f)^t} = \frac{\text{spot}}{\text{price}} + PV\left(\begin{array}{c}\text{storage}\\\text{costs}\end{array}\right)$$
$$- PV\left(\begin{array}{c}\text{convenience}\\\text{yield}\end{array}\right)$$

Interest Rate Parity (28-2)

$$\frac{1 + r_\yen}{1 + r_\$} = \frac{f_{\yen/\$}}{s_{\yen/\$}}$$

Growth Rates (29-5)

Sustainable growth rate (no increase in leverage)
= plowback ratio $\times$ return on equity

Internal growth rate (no external finance)
= retained earnings/net assets
= plowback ratio $\times$ return on equity $\times$ equity/net assets

TIME
ALMANAC
2001
with INFORMATION PLEASE

BORGNA BRUNNER
EDITOR IN CHIEF

Information Please
www.infoplease.com
Part of LEARNING NETWORK

Information Please
www.infoplease.com
Part of **LEARNING** NETWORK

Editor in Chief Borgna Brunner

Editor Ann-Marie Imbornoni

Senior Contributing Editors
Elissa Haney, Otto T. Johnson,
Beth Rowen

Contributing Editors Susanna Brougham
(Religion), Christine Frantz (Sports),
David P. Johnson, Jr. (Countries),
Arthur Reed (Current Events)

Contributors Holly Hartman,
Michael Rozett, Ricco Villanueva Siasoco

Senior Vice President
Elizabeth Buckley Kubik

Production Director
Susan Hyde

Production Editor Christine Frantz

Proofreading and Fact-checking
Amy Smith Bell, Katie Blatt, Laura Lutz K

Editorial Assistants Andrew Nyberg,
Kate Pritchard, Jarrett Tolman, Kate Wrig

Graphics Sean Dessureau,
Barbara Pennucci

Technical Support Karl DeBisschop

Time Inc.
HOME ENTERTAINMENT

Contributing Editor Kelly Knauer

Design Anthony Kosner

Pictures Patricia Cadley

President Rob Gursha

Executive Director David Arfine

Associate Director Kenneth Maehlum

Product Manager Ann Marie Ross

Associate Product Manager
Jennifer Dowell

Director, Retail & Special Sales
Thomas Mifsud

Editorial Operations Manager
John Calvano

Assistant Editorial Operations Manag
Emily Rabin

Book Production Manager
Jessica McGrath

Associate Book Production Managers
Jonathan Polsky, Suzanne DeBenedetto

The *TIME Almanac* welcomes comments and suggestions from readers. Although the editors c
fully consider each suggestion, because of the volume of correspondence we receive we ca
respond personally to each writer. The *TIME Almanac* does not rule on bets or wagers.

Editorial Office
Information Please
20 Park Plaza, Suite 1420
Boston, MA 02116
Email: ipa@infoplease.com

Customer Service
Attention: TIME Almanac
PO Box 11016
Des Moines, IA 50336-1016

ISBN: 1-929049-11-0 Paperback
ISBN: 1-929049-12-9 Hardcover
ISSN: 0073-7860

If you would like to order copies of the hardcover almanac, please call us at 1-800-327-6388 (I
day through Friday, 7:00 a.m.–8:00 p.m. or Saturday, 7:00 a.m.–6:00 p.m. Central Time), or visi
website at www.TimeBookstore.com.

Printed in the United States of America.
WP Pa BP Hbd 10 9 8 7 6 5 4 3 2 1

Keyword Index

Section Index

NOTE ON THE 2001 EDITION: Some would claim this to be the official millennium edition. Although Jan. 1, 2000 celebrated throughout the world as the start of the new millennium, that honor should technically have been reserv Jan. 1, 2001. Because there is no year zero in our calendar—the sequence of years passes directly from 1 B.C. to A. the first millennium actually began in A.D. 1. Adding a thousand years to the year 1 equals the year 1001 (the start second millennium); adding another thousand brings us to 2001 (the dawn of the third). Opinion seems to be divided whether the insistence on 2001 as the true millennium is overbearingly pedantic or simply sticking to the facts.

Page numbers followed by "n" indicate information in footnotes.

The News of 2000: Nation

(Through Oct. 31; for U.S. election results, *see* pp. 42–48.)

The presidential election of 2000 between Vice President Al Gore (D) and Texas governor George W. Bush (R) was expected to be the tightest election in four decades. The neck-and-neck race, however, was also perceived to be one of the least dynamic on issues.

Election Ennui

The longest period of uninterrupted economic growth in American history continued in 2000 with the third federal budget surplus in a row, low inflation, and an unemployment rate less than 4%. The conventional wisdom that peace and prosperity in an election year leads to voter ennui was never more evident: the party conventions and presidential debates drew smaller audiences than in previous elections, and voter participation was not expected to exceed the 1996 turnout (49%), the lowest since 1924.

While the candidates were divided sharply along ideological lines on issues such as gun control, abortion, taxes, and the role of government, Gore and Bush both avoided emphasizing hot-button issues, hovering cautiously on either side of the political center. Beyond their core positions—Bush advocated smaller government and a $1.3 trillion across-the-board tax cut (two-thirds of the budget surplus); Gore supported governmental activism and a much smaller tax cut ($500 billion) targeted at middle- and lower-income Americans—the candidates' differences were often lost in a welter of detail about prescription drug benefits and school vouchers. These specific domestic policies were meant to appeal to various important voting blocs, but the strategy failed to generate any real passion among mainstream voters. The Center for the Study of the American Electorate has observed that "there's a broad mass of the American people who are not involved in most of the issues at stake. The candidates are not talking to a lot of people." Campaign finance reform galvanized a broad swath of voters for a short time, but soon went the way of its bipartisan champions, Bill Bradley (D) and John McCain (R), whose campaigns folded after Super Tuesday.

The Contenders

George W. Bush, son of former president George Bush and governor of Texas since 1995, characterized himself as a "compassionate conservative," an all-purpose mantra meant to convey a kinder, gentler Republican. His running mate, former Secretary of Defense Dick Cheney, added a seasoned Washington résumé to a ticket sometimes faulted for its lack of political experience and gravitas. Al Gore, vice president under Bill Clinton and a former congressman and senator (D-Tenn.), chose Sen. Joe Lieberman (D-Conn.) as his running mate in an effort to rid himself of the Clinton albatross (Lieberman was perhaps the most outspoken Democrat critic of the Lewinsky affair). Gore, perceived as strong on character but weak on inspirational leadership, struggled throughout the campaign with his relationship to his tarnished yet charismatic mentor, whose job approval ratings remained high (60%) up to the election. Significant third-party candidates included Patrick Buchanan (Reform) and Ralph Nader (Green)—the latter's undiluted liberal message threatened to siphon off votes from Gore.

In Senate races, 34 seats were at stake (19 Republican and 15 Democrat). In the House, all seats were up (223 Republican, 211 Democrat, and one Independent). Eleven governorships were also up for grabs.

Questions of Execution

While public support for capital punishment has dropped from a high of 80% in 1994, a Gallup Poll in Feb. 2000 found that the majority of Americans (66%) continue to support it. Almost half of those polled, however, expressed reservations about how the death penalty is carried out. Since 1976, 82 death-row prisoners have been found innocent. In Jan. 2000, Gov. George Ryan (Ill.-R), a death penalty supporter, announced that he had "grave concerns about our state's shameful record of convicting innocent people," and called for a moratorium. In June, a Columbia University study indicated that two-thirds of all capital punishment cases contained flaws serious enough to warrant retrial, and in September a Justice Dept. report condemned the federal death penalty system for glaring geographical and racial disparities. Bills have been introduced in both the Senate and the House to provide for post-conviction DNA testing in death penalty cases and to ensure that defendants receive competent defense.

Elián and the Cold War

Elián González, a young Cuban boy found clinging to an inner tube off the Florida coast in Nov. 1999, became the subject of an international dispute between the U.S. and Cuba. The boy's American relatives and the U.S. Cuban community demanded that the six-year-old refugee remain in Miami rather than be returned to his father in Cuba, arguing that American democracy would benefit the boy more than life in Castro's Cuba. A dramatic raid by armed federal agents on April 22 ended the standoff, and the boy was reunited with his father. The influential Cuban-American community lost a good deal of public sympathy by pitting political ideology against familial bonds. For Castro it was a publicity bonanza, emphasizing the intransigence of the official U.S. policy toward Cuba, which has imposed a 38-year-old trade embargo and other cold war–era sanctions.

Gathering China into the Fold

On Oct. 10, 2000, China was granted permanent normal trade relations (PNTR), a 14-year effort that generated enormous controversy in Congress but ultimately received bipartisan support. The agreement drastically reduces Chinese tariffs on many farm and industrial goods and gives some U.S. industries access to Chinese markets. Expected to be President Clinton's final major policy success, the agreement reflects the administration's philosophy that easing up trade restrictions will integrate China into the world market and lead to a better human rights record and weapons treaties. Unions and other groups vociferously opposed the agreement, anticipating the loss of American jobs.

The News of 2000: World

Electoral Revolution: Yugoslavia and Mexico

In Sept. 2000, federal elections in Yugoslavia formally ended the autocratic rule of Slobodan Milosevic, who had entangled his country in almost continuous war, first with the breakaway republics of Croatia and Bosnia (1991–1995) and then in the Serbian province of Kosovo in 1998, which ended with the NATO bombing of 1999. Despite dragging Yugoslavia into economic collapse and relegating it to pariah status throughout much of the world, Milosevic had managed to hold fast to the presidency after the Kosovo debacle—opposition parties remained disorganized and mired in internecine squabbles, and public dissent was sporadic.

In the Sept. 24 elections, Vojislav Kostunica, a constitutional law professor and political outsider, won the presidency in spite of widespread reports of fraud and voter intimidation. When Milosevic refused to honor the results and demanded a runoff election, the country erupted in massive public demonstrations, ultimately forcing Milosevic to step down on Oct. 5. Milosevic's Socialist Party, with its monopoly on political clout, thereafter agreed to share power with the two opposition parties. New parliamentary elections were scheduled for Dec. 2000.

The U.S. and the European Union quickly lifted some economic sanctions against Yugoslavia, and the new government was recognized by Russia and China, both of whom had been strong allies of Milosevic's Socialist Party government. But Kostunica was quick to assert himself as a true-believing Serb nationalist with no plans for becoming the darling of the West. He faced a daunting task in revitalizing the nation's shattered economy and in rebuilding the infrastructure destroyed during the NATO bombing.

Mexico also launched a promising electoral revolution, on July 2, 2000, by electing reformer and businessman Vicente Fox Quesada of the center-right National Action Party (PAN) as president, thereby ending 71 years of one-party rule by the Institutional Revolutionary Party (PRI). Like his counterpart in Yugoslavia, Fox faced an overwhelming task in rectifying the sins of the former government, which in Mexico's case involved colossal corruption, economic incompetence, and a multi-party democracy in name only.

Iran: "Islamic Democracy" Evolves

Signaling a seismic change in Iran's political environment, reform candidates won the overwhelming majority of seats in Feb. 2000 parliamentary elections, thereby wresting control from hard-liners, who had dominated the parliament since the 1979 Islamic revolution. The parliament's reformist transformation greatly buttressed the efforts of moderate president Mohammad Khatami in constructing what he intends to become a nation of "lasting pluralism and Islamic democracy." Khatami has walked a jittery tightrope between student groups and other liberals pressuring him to introduce bolder freedoms, and Iran's military and conservative clerical elite (including Iran's supreme leader, Ayatollah Khamenei), who have expressed growing impatience with the president's liberalizing measures. By Oct. 2000, however, the deeply conservative judiciary dampened the reformist impulse by systematically closing down every remaining pro-democracy publication. The new parliament soon countered by introducing legislation that would limit the judiciary's authority to crack down on the press.

Korea: Meeting of North and South

The half-century of antagonism between North and South Korea, who officially remain in a state of war, eased dramatically in June 2000 when South Korea's Kim Dae Jung met with Kim Jong Il in North Korea's capital, Pyongyang. The summit marked the first-ever meeting of the leaders of the two countries, whose simmering animosity erupted into open aggression as recently as 1999. Although largely symbolic at this stage, the officials signed a hopeful, yet vague, agreement that outlined plans for unification and peace, reunions of families separated since the war, and open communication between the leaders. In Sept. 2000 defense ministers from the two nations met to discuss a range of military issues, including the restoration of rail links between the north and south, which would require the clearance of thousands of landmines. Solidifying this unexpected shift in relations was the awarding of the Nobel Peace Prize to Kim Dae Jung in Oct. 2000. His North Korean counterpart Kim Jong Il also made news in October by playing lavish host to U.S. Secretary of State Madeleine Albright on Oct. 23–24, cracking the diplomatic door even further on what is considered the world's most reclusive nation.

Peace on Hold—Again: Northern Ireland and the Middle East

Another recent Nobel Peace Prize winner, David Trimble, leader of the Ulster Unionists and first minister of the coalition government of Northern Ireland, found himself on shaky political ground in the fall of 2000, with both the Irish peace accord and his own political future uncertain. Trimble, who received the peace prize in 1998 for his role in the Good Friday Agreement, faced increasing disaffection from fellow Protestant politicians regarding his handling of the IRA's disarmament.

The first "devolved" government formed on Dec. 2, 1999, when the British government formally transferred governing powers to the Northern Irish parliament. Trimble became first minister, and two leaders of Sinn Fein, Gerry Adams and Martin McGuinness, received seats in the four-party, twelve-member parliament. But this milestone in Irish self-government quickly crumbled. Protestant politicians had taken a difficult leap of faith in agreeing to allow the IRA to begin giving up its illegal weapons after the government formed. Sinn Fein, however, failed to live up to its promise of home rule first, disarmament later. As a result, the British government suspended parliament on Feb. 12, 2000, and once again imposed direct rule. On May 30, 2000, Sinn Fein again pledged to put the IRA's weapons "beyond use," and Britain restored parliamentary powers. While the IRA did allow for the inspection of some of its arms dumps, the months limped by without real progress, and Sinn Fein's commitment to disarmament once again appeared strikingly disingenuous. Trimble, caught in the middle, appeared to many of his Protestant compatriots as a pawn of the Republicans, and was nearly ousted by his own party on Oct. 28. Had he been forced to step down, there is little doubt that the Good Friday Agreement would have toppled with him. But Trimble survived, pledging to get tough by imposing sanctions on Sinn Fein.

Under Prime Minister Ehud Barak of the Labour Party, who took office in July 1999, Israel made promising forays into peace on three fronts—with Syria, Lebanon, and the Palestinian Authority—but only its withdrawal from Lebanon proved an enduring, positive change. After 22 years of occupation, on May 24, 2000, the remaining Israeli troops pulled out of the Lebanese security zone Israel had set up to safeguard its borders. Public pressure in Israel had been mounting for years to end the war of attrition between Hezbollah guerrillas in Lebanon, backed by Syria, and Israeli troops and their allies, the South Lebanon Army militia.

In Dec. 1999, Israeli-Syrian talks resumed after an almost four-year hiatus, fostered on the Syrian side by President Hafez al-Assad's wish to shore up his legacy (the ailing leader died in June). From Syria's point of view, normalization of relations between the two countries largely depended on Isra-

el's withdrawal from the Golan Heights, which was territory that Israel had captured from Syria during the Middle East war of 1967. From Israel's point of view, relinquishing the Golan Heights, which serves as a buffer zone between the two nations, could not occur without a guarantee of Israel's security from Syria. By Jan. 2000, however, talks ended when Syria rejected an Israeli offer to withdraw from most but not all of the Golan Heights.

Despite President Clinton's strongest efforts, July 2000 peace talks at Camp David between Barak and the Palestinian Authority's president Yasir Arafat ended unsuccessfully—although the negotiations made some progress, the status of Jerusalem remained the primary sticking point. Clinton lauded Barak's flexibility and called Arafat intransigent, but Palestinian supporters and much of the Arab world praised Arafat's strong stand. Barak, on the other hand, returned to a volatile political situation, with conservatives angered by his concessions and threatening to abandon his fragile parliamentary coalition.

At the end of September, however, the stalemate disintegrated into the worst violence between Israelis and Palestinians in years, provoked by right-wing Likud leader Ariel Sharon's incendiary visit on Sept. 28 to a Jerusalem religious complex sacred to both Jews and Muslims—the fiercely contested holy site is known as the Temple Mount to Jews and as Haram al Sharif to Muslims. Clashes between Palestinians and the Israeli police followed, giving rise to what has been called the Al Aksa intifada (named after the Al Aksa mosque where the fighting originated). The violence continued unabated through October, with no foreseeable end in sight, and with the political futures of Arafat and Barak in flux.

What Happened in 2000: Month by Month

January 2000

WORLD

Acting President Takes Charge of Kremlin (Jan. 3): In one of his first actions, Vladimir V. Putin dismisses Tatyana Dyachenko, daughter of former president Boris N. Yeltsin, and other staff members who had been loyal to Yeltsin. **(Jan. 10):** Putin distances himself from allegedly corrupt Yeltsin regime by demoting two high-ranking officials.

Pro-Western Bloc Elected in Croatia (Jan. 3): Center-left opposition, composed of Social Democrats and Social Liberals, emerges victorious in parliamentary balloting, overthrowing the nationalist Croatian Democratic Union. Former Communist Party leader Ivica Racan will become prime minister.

Pinochet Ruled Medically Unfit for Trial (Jan. 11): British Home Secretary Jack Straw, reviewing medical reports, says the ailing 84-year-old Chilean dictator Augusto Pinochet, who had spent 15 months under house arrest in London, is unfit to stand trial in Spain on charges of war crimes stemming from his 17-year rule in Chile.

War Crimes Tribunal Sentences Five (Jan. 14): Hague court convicts Bosnian Croat militiamen for part in 1993 massacre of 116 Muslims in the central Bosnian village of Ahmici.

Socialist President Elected in Chile (Jan. 16): Ricardo Lagos wins by narrow margin to become first Socialist executive in 27 years.

Israel and Syria Postpone Talks (Jan. 17): Scheduled conference in W. Va. hits snag over Syrian demand that Golan Heights issue be settled.

Helmut Kohl Quits German Party Post (Jan. 18): Former chancellor resigns as honorary chairman of opposition Christian Democrats amid controversy over his refusal to identify donors of more than $1 million in secret payments during his tenure as party leader.

Jesse Helms Rebukes UN on Policies (Jan. 20): Chairman of the Senate Foreign Relations Committee warns Security Council that Congress has no right to determine conditions on which U.S. will pay off its debt to the organization.

Protesters March in Madrid (Jan. 23): One million people rally against Basque separatist group, E.T.A.

China Issues Controls on Internet (Jan. 26): Bans posting and dissemination of "state secrets," a vague term the government applies to any information it has not approved.

NATION

Federal Reserve Head Nominated Again (Jan. 4): Alan Greenspan chosen by President Clinton to serve fourth four-year term as chairman.

Drug Companies Drop Medicare Opposition (Jan. 13): Executives say they want to work with President Clinton and Congress to set plan for Medicare coverage of prescription drugs. Industry would accept such legislation as step toward comprehensive changes in Medicare program.

Antimissile Test Called Flawed (Jan. 13): Pentagon concedes that Oct. test was not as successful as first claimed. Technical mistakes caused the interceptor to lock in on decoy balloon before changing course at last minute to hit target mock warhead.

Union Membership Gains (Jan. 19): Bureau of Labor Statistics reports 265,000 new members in 1999, bringing total to 16.5 million. Largest increase in two decades.

Bush and Gore Take Iowa Caucuses (Jan. 22): Texas governor is clear G.O.P. winner. On the Democratic front, Vice President Al Gore soundly defeats former senator Bill Bradley.

President Clinton Delivers Final Message to Congress (Jan. 27): In State of the Union speech, president hails nation's record prosperity. Proposes modest tax relief for lower and middle classes, especially for married couples.

BUSINESS/SCIENCE/SOCIETY

World Enters New Century Smoothly (Jan. 1): Computer experts surprised by smooth transition after widespread fears that computers might not adapt to year 2000.

New Cervical Cancer Test Acclaimed (Jan. 5): *Journal of the American Medical Association* reports that newer laboratory test is more accurate and more accessible than Pap tests.

Internet Thief Steals Credit Card Data (Jan. 9): Releases some customer information after Internet music retailer CD Universe refuses to meet $100,000 extortion demand.

Biggest Merger in History (Jan. 10): America Online agrees to buy Time Warner, largest traditional media company, for $165 billion.

Ice Storm Wreaks Havoc in Southeast (Jan. 23): Fallen pines close hundreds of roads from Georgia to North Carolina. Storm causes more than 500,000 homes to lose power. Meteorologist calls ice storm worst in 18 years.

International Safety Rules for Biotech Food Established (Jan. 29): More than 130 nations establish first global treaty regulating trade in genetically modified products. Allows countries to refuse to import certain items that may threaten environment.

Jet Carrying 88 Crashes in Pacific (Jan. 31): Alaska Airlines flight from Mexico to San Francisco goes down northwest of Malibu. Pilot had reported problem with plane's stabilizer trim. All on board are killed.

February 2000

WORLD

Albright Meets New Russian Leader (Feb. 2): Secretary of State praises Vladimir V. Putin as "well-informed" and eager for a "normal position with the West." War in Chechnya remains a point of dispute.

Israeli-Palestinian Summit Fails (Feb. 3): Leaders end Gaza Strip session without resolving disagreement on interim issues or setting new deadline for final accord.

Austria at Center of European Dispute (Feb. 3): After conservative People's Party forms coalition with the far-right Freedom Party, headed by Jörg Haider. A nationalist against immigration, Haider had made several controversial remarks praising some Nazi policies, which he has since recanted. The European Union condemns new coalition, freezes diplomatic contacts, and imposes sanctions, accusing Haider of being a racist and xenophobe. **(Feb. 28):** Under international pressure, Haider resigns as leader of Freedom Party.

Hijackers Seize Afghan Plane (Feb. 6): Boeing 727 with 186 passengers makes erratic flight through Russia and Central Asia. Hijackers demand release of jailed opposition leader Ismail Khan. **(Feb. 12):** After negotiating with government, hijackers release hostages and land plane in Stansted, England. About half onboard plane, including hijackers, request asylum in Britain.

Yugoslav Defense Minister Slain (Feb. 7): Gunmen kill Pavle Bulatovic, 51, a member of Montenegro's Socialist People's Party, and a close ally of President Slobodan Milosevic. **(Feb. 15):** Milosevic appoints Serbian Gen. Dragoljub Ojdanic, 58, as new defense minister.

Ojdanic and Milosevic were indicted in 1999 by the United Nations for suspected war crimes.

Kurdish Rebels End War on Turkey (Feb. 9): Announce plan to seek self-rule by nonviolent means. First step made by Kurdistan Workers Party in heeding captured leader Abdullah Ocalan's plea to lay down arms.

Britain Ends Self-Rule in Northern Ireland (Feb. 12): Britain suspends self-government in Belfast after Irish Republican Army misses disarmament deadline. I.R.A. takes action as a result, offering plan to disarm.

Russia Cuts Off Chechnya Capital (Feb. 14): Military orders surviving residents of Grozny to evacuate. City to be off-limits for two weeks while officials check for bombs and weapons.

German Conservative Party Leader Resigns (Feb. 16): Wolfgang Schäuble steps down, deepening crisis for Christian Democratic Union. The party of former chancellor Helmut Kohl has been shaken by recent evidence of embezzlement and illicit payments.

NATO Chief Seeks More Kosovo Troops (Feb. 23): Gen. Wesley K. Clark calls for immediate dispatch of additional 1,800 to maintain order in Yugoslav province. Fighting between ethnic Albanians and Serbian nationalists has continued since June 1999 accord.

U.S. Critical of China and Russia (Feb. 25): Charges leveled in State Department's annual report on human rights. Report especially harsh in criticizing China for what it calls marked deterioration in rights.

Reformists Win Control in Iran (Feb. 26): Gain firm control of parliament, with near sweep of Tehran district in final tally from Feb. elections. Hard-liners ousted from control for first time since 1979 Islamic revolution.

U.S. Expels Cuban Diplomat (Feb. 26): Accused spy José Imperatori gives up immunity and challenges officials to arrest him so that he can prove his innocence.

Taiwan Asks U.S. for Advanced Arms (Feb. 29): In bold move, seeks to buy defensive weapons to counter China's growing military power.

NATION

McCain and Gore Win in N.H. (Feb. 1): Sen. John McCain defeats Texas governor George W. Bush by unexpectedly large margin in first major Republican primary. Vice President Al Gore narrowly defeats former senator Bill Bradley in Democratic contest.

First Lady Enters N.Y. Senate Race (Feb. 6): Hillary Rodham Clinton officially declares candidacy.

Clinton Submits Year's Budget (Feb. 7): Outlines $1.84 trillion federal budget proposal. President calls for using much of projected surplus to bolster Medicare system over coming decade.

Mixed Results in Primaries (Feb. 19): In S.C., Gov. George W. Bush reclaims front-runner status in G.O.P. balloting. **(Feb. 22):** In Mich., Sen. John McCain rebounds to defeat Bush on wave of independent voters and Democrats. McCain also wins primary in home state of Ariz.

BUSINESS/SCIENCE/SOCIETY

Federal Reserve Raises Two Key Rates (Feb. 2): Increases interest rates quarter of percentage point. Warns of further advances to keep strong economy from generating inflation.

Hackers Attack Several Web Sites (Feb. 7 et seq.): Internet's vulnerability demonstrated as several major commercial sites are crippled, including Yahoo, Amazon, and eBay.

U.S. Productivity Continues to Grow (Feb. 8): Labor Dept. reports rate advanced 5% in last half of 1999.

Spacecraft First to Orbit an Asteroid (Feb. 14): The NEAR links up with Eros to become first artificial satellite to circle an asteroid.

Tornadoes Kill Many in Georgia (Feb. 14): Eighteen die in overnight twister that caught area off-guard. More than 100 injured.

Cats Closing after 18 Years on Broadway (Feb. 19): Musical, which is Broadway's longest-running production, will shut down on June 25.

Wary Investors Bring Stock Plunge (Feb. 25): Dow Jones Industrial Average falls below 10,000 level for first time in ten months. Investors dump shares in reaction to fears of higher interest rates.

First-Grader Accused of Killing Classmate (Feb. 29): Six-year-old boy shoots Kayla Rolland, also 6, at an elementary school in Mount Morris Township, Mich.

March 2000

WORLD

Britain Frees Gen. Augusto Pinochet (March 2): Drops extradition charges because of general's poor health. (March 3): Pinochet greeted as hero by military high command on return to Chile. Thousands of detractors and supporters stage competing demonstrations in Santiago.

Croatian General Sentenced for War Crimes (March 3): UN war crimes tribunal metes 45-year prison term to Gen. Tihomir Blaskic for directing attacks on Bosnian Muslim villagers between 1992 and 1994.

Pope Apologizes for Church Errors (March 12): John Paul II delivers unprecedented, broad papal apology for church errors over last 2,000 years.

Iranian Capital Scene of New Attack (March 13): Mortar shells fired into residential area next to military base in Tehran. Radical leftist group, Mujahedeen Khala, claims responsibility.

U.S. Accepts New I.M.F. Head (March 13): Clinton reluctantly endorses Horst Köhler as next managing director of International Monetary Fund.

Agreement Reached on West Bank Control (March 15): Israelis and Palestinians resolve dispute on next area to be transferred to Palestinians. Israeli security cabinet approves the move.

U.S. Relaxes Sanctions on Iran (March 17): Secretary of State Madeleine K. Albright lifts some economic penalties and vows to work toward normalized relations.

Taiwan Ends Nationalist Rule (March 18): Opposition leader Chen Shui-bian, who has supported independence from China, elected president. Some fear results may spark armed conflict with China.

Mass Murder Suspected in Uganda (March 18): More than 235 members of a doomsday cult, Movement for the Restoration of the Ten Commandments, reported to have died in what first appeared to be mass suicide.

President Visits South Asia (March 19): Clinton welcomed in India on state visit. (March 26): In Geneva at end of tour, Clinton fails to persuade Syrian leader, Hafez al-Assad, to resume talks with Israel.

Vladimir V. Putin Elected in Russia (March 25): Acting president formally chosen for post.

OPEC Nations Plan Oil Output Increase (March 29): Rise less than U.S. had expected. Iran, second-largest producer, dissents. Later, Iran reverses action.

NATION

Curb on Social Security Ends (March 1): House, 422–0, votes to remove earnings limit on recipients while maintaining benefits. (March 22): Senate, 100–0, votes for measure. Clinton says he'll sign bill.

Gore and Bush Win in Primaries (March 7): Vice president trounces Bill Bradley in Democratic balloting. Texas governor prevails over Sen. John McCain in Republican voting. (March 9): McCain and Bradley concede.

White House Cleared in Files Inquiry (March 16): Independent Counsel Robert W. Ray announces that no criminal wrongdoing had been involved in acquisition of several hundred confidential F.B.I. papers, many of which concerned prominent Republicans.

F.D.A. Withdraws Diabetes Drug (March 21): Removes Rezulin from market because of link to liver failure.

Record Settlement for Sex Discrimination (March 22): U.S. to pay $508 million in action brought by 1,100 women who charged they were denied jobs and promotions at U.S. Information Agency from 1974 to 1984.

Female General Charges Sexual Harassment (March 30): Lieut. Gen. Claudia J. Kennedy, the army's highest-ranking woman, files complaint charging a general, whose name was withheld, groped her in 1996.

BUSINESS/SCIENCE/SOCIETY

Admission by Philip Morris (March 2): A top official of nation's largest cigarette maker alludes to nicotine as a "drug" and says company would be open to F.D.A.'s limited regulation of nicotine.

Coal Mine Blast Kills 80 in Ukraine (March 11): Methane gas explosion 530 miles east of Kiev kills more than 80 people; worst accident since independence.

Two Big Newspaper Companies Merge (March 13): Tribune Company and Times Mirror Company announce merger, ending 119 years of ownership of *L.A. Times* by Otis and Chandler families.

Court Blocks Florida's School Vouchers (March 14): Judge rules state constitution prohibits the use of taxpayers' money to send students to private schools.

Gay Rights Bill Voted in Vermont (March 16): House approves "civil unions" that give gay and lesbian couples nearly all benefits of marriage. When enacted, legislation will give state the nation's most sweeping rights for same-sex couples.

Gun Maker Accepts Restrictions (March 17): Smith & Wesson agrees to widen limits on how it makes, sells, and distributes hundreds of thousands of handguns annually. It acted in exchange for the end of some prohibitively expensive lawsuits.

Tornadoes Sweep through Texas Cities (March 29): At least three reported dead and 100 injured after storms ravage Fort Worth and Arlington.

April 2000

WORLD

Beijing Court Frees Researcher (April 3): In reversal, quashes conviction of Chinese-born Stanford University scientist, Hua Di, who had been jailed for more than two years for "revealing state secrets."

Japanese Premier Suffers Stroke (April 3): Prime Minister Keizo Obuchi, 62, in intensive care. Senior cabinet minister, Mikio Aoki, appointed acting chief. (April 5): Ruling party names Yoshiro Mori to succeed Keizo Obuchi, who fell into coma after stroke.

Ousted Pakistani Leader Convicted (April 6): Nawaz Sharif, deposed as prime minister in Oct. military coup, found guilty of hijacking and sentenced to life imprisonment. Six codefendants acquitted.

Peru President Suffers Setback (April 9): Alberto K. Fujimori fails to secure first-round victory in contest with Alejandro Toledo, a business school professor. President had been regarded as shoo-in, but Toledo rallied amid accusations that Fujimori tried to steal the vote.

Greek Prime Minister Reelected (April 10): By narrow margin, voters retain Socialist Costas Simitis.

Russia Ratifies Arms Reduction Treaty (April 14): Lower house of parliament approves long-delayed nuclear Start II pact. (April 19): Upper house approves treaty. Passage indicates Putin wants a productive relationship with West.

World Trade Leaders Convene (April 16): Finance ministers and other leaders meet in Washington as thousands protest. (April 17): Conferees agree that World Bank should step up fight against AIDS and assist those adversely affected by globalization.

UN Rights Group Defies U.S. (April 18): Votes in Geneva not to act on U.S. resolution critical of China's human rights record. Embarrassing defeat for Clinton.

Iran's Reformers under Attack (April 27): Hard-line Islamic clerics bolster crackdown and close several reform newspapers.

NATION

Microsoft Loses in Antitrust Suit (April 3): U.S. judge Thomas Penfield Jackson rules software giant displayed anticompetitive behavior and sides with government on most important points. Options range from imposing restrictions on company's conduct to a breakup.

Plane Crash Kills 19 Marines (April 8): Controversial *Osprey*, a hybrid craft, destroyed in Arizona.

Congress Limits Assets Seizures (April 11): Completes legislation that protects a citizen's personal property from government seizure before trials begin.

Capitol Agreement on Patients' Rights (April 14): Senate and House reach preliminary agreement on appeals process for patients refused care by health maintenance organizations.

Cuban Boy Reunited with Father After Raid (April 22): Armed immigration agents storm Miami home where boy had been living with great-uncle's family. Child reunited with father outside Washington.

Albright Acts after Security Lapse (April 24): Orders shakeup in State Department's Bureau of Intelligence and Research as F.B.I. investigates disappearance of laptop computer that contained highly sensitive files.

U.S. Seeks Breakup of Microsoft (April 26): Joins 17 states in asking for ruling by federal judge. Calls for restraints on software company while split is implemented.

Gay Rights Parade in Washington (April 30): Hundreds of thousands celebrate progress of gay rights movement and press for legislation against hate crimes.

BUSINESS/SCIENCE/SOCIETY

Estrogen Tied to Heart Disorders (April 4): Researchers tell 25,000 women in federal study that instead of protecting the heart, as had been assumed, estrogen may have resulted in a slightly higher risk of heart attack and stroke.

Most Nations Fail to Supply Safe Blood (April 6): World Health Organization reports blood supplies in two-thirds of the world may contribute to spread of AIDS virus, some forms of hepatitis, and other diseases.

Holocaust Denier Loses Libel Suit (April 11): British court drops libel suit brought by David Irving against U.S. professor and author Deborah Lipstadt. Judge calls Irving "an active Holocaust denier."

Stock Market Recovers after Sharp Drop (April 14): Rampant selling closes one of worst weeks in history of U.S. markets. Dow Jones average down 5.55%; Nasdaq index off nearly 10%. **(April 17):** Stock prices level off, then rocket. Recovery calms fears of market collapse.

Fiber Studies Find No Benefit to Colon (April 19): Two tests involving thousands of persons contradict wide belief that low-fat, high-fiber foods can reduce risk of colon and rectal cancer.

Gun Makers Sue to Block Controls (April 26): Seven large manufacturers seek to keep New York, Connecticut, and 16 local governments from favoring purchases from companies that agree to stringent rules.

First Success of Gene Therapy Reported (April 27): French doctors use treatment to save several infants who might have died from severe immune disorder.

Mozambique Assesses Flood Losses (April 29): Thousands homeless as floods sweep away schools and clinics, crops, and cattle. Durban government says country needs about $427 million for reconstruction.

May 2000

WORLD

Rebels Seize Peacekeepers in Sierra Leone (May 4): UN intervention erupts into violence as Revolutionary United Front rebels kill seven and capture at least 500 of UN force. **(May 17):** Rebel leader Foday Sankoh captured and arrested outside his Freetown home. **(May 29):** UN reports rebels have released all 500 seized personnel.

British Prime Minister Rebuffed (May 5): Despite appeals from Tony Blair, London voters elect left-wing populist Ken Livingstone as city's first elected mayor.

New Russian President Sworn In (May 6): Vladimir V. Putin takes oath in nation's first free transfer of power. **(May 10):** Putin appoints Mikhail M. Kasyanov as prime minister.

Serbian Government Seizes TV Station (May 17): Charges main opposition outlet with encouraging an uprising. Thousands jam Belgrade streets to protest action.

New President of Taiwan Sworn In (May 20): Chen Shuibian, member of the Democratic Progressive Party, inaugurated, ending 50 years of rule by the Nationalist Party that fled China under Chiang Kai-shek.

Israeli Troops Leave Southern Lebanon (May 23): Shiite Muslims seize Israeli-occupied zone in south, accelerating withdrawal of Israeli troops. **(May 24):** Israeli troops pull out of Lebanon after 22 years of occupation.

Chile Ends Pinochet's Immunity (May 24): Chilean court clears way for trial on charges of kidnapping, murder, and torture of thousands during 17 years as dictator.

Reform Parliament Convenes in Iran (May 27): First since Islamic revolution to include majority of members eager to challenge conservative clergy's dominance.

Ulster Unionists Back Joint Rule (May 27): Largest Protestant party votes to rejoin power-sharing administration with Roman Catholic rivals in Sinn Fein, the political arm of the Irish Republican Army. **(May 30):** Britain restores Northern Ireland's government. Self-rule returns to Belfast from London.

Fujimori Wins in Peru's Runoff (May 28): President's victory tarnished as opposition candidate Alejandro Toledo withdrew, alleging vote fraud and campaign irregularities. **(May 29):** U.S. and allies warn that Fujimori reelection jeopardizes Peru's position in international community.

Suharto under House Arrest (May 29): Former Indonesian president, 78, faces charges of corruption and abuse of power.

NATION

McCain Endorses Former Rival (May 9): G.O.P. united as senator pledges to help Texas governor George W. Bush in campaign for presidency.

Moms March for Gun Control (May 14): Hundreds of thousands rally in Washington and several other cities to demand stricter gun laws.

South Carolina Removes Confederate Flag (May 18): Both houses of General Assembly vote to take it from Capitol dome. Smaller flag will be flown in front of building.

Panel Requests Clinton Be Disbarred (May 22): Arkansas court disciplinary committee recommends penalty because of "serious misconduct" in Paula Jones sexual harassment case.

Army Cancels General's Appointment (May 22): Holds up naming of Maj. Gen. Larry G. Smith as deputy inspector general in wake of sexual harassment charges brought by Lieut. Gen. Claudia J. Kennedy.

House Votes to Lift Trade Curbs on China (May 24): In victory for President Clinton, House votes, 237–197, to give Beijing permanent normal trading privileges.

BUSINESS/SCIENCE/SOCIETY

Cable Blackout Affects Millions (May 1): Time Warner contract dispute with Disney, parent company of ABC, results in blackout of network in 3.5 million homes.

Virus Disrupts Worldwide Computers (May 4): Invasive software program with "I love you" message crashes e-mail systems and destroys data on hundreds of thousands of computers worldwide.

Jobless Rate Lowest since 1970 (May 5): Unemployment level falls below 4%. In continuing boom, employers hire hundreds of thousands of workers.

Thousands Flee New Mexico Fire (May 8 et seq.): Control blaze set by National Park Service blown out of control in densely wooded area by 50-mile-an-hour winds. Blaze forces evacuation of as many as 25,000 and destroys hundreds of homes in Los Alamos.

Two Winners Share Record Lottery Jackpot (May 10): Total in Big Game seven-state drawing is $366 million, biggest lottery jackpot in U.S. history.

Federal Reserve Acts against Inflation (May 16): Raises short-term interest rates half a percentage point.

Two Charged in 1963 Church Bombing (May 17): Thomas E. Blanton and Bobby Frank Cherry held in Birmingham, Ala., as murder suspects in deaths of four black girls at Baptist church.

U.S. Takes Blame for Los Alamos Fire (May 18): Interior Secretary Bruce Babbitt admits errors and vows to compensate victims.

Thalidomide Proves Useful in Treating Disease (May 21): Specialists report promising role treating AIDS, leprosy, and some cancers. Drug banned worldwide in the 1960s for harming thousands of children.

Giant Airline Merger Planned (May 23): United, world's largest, agrees to acquire biggest carrier in Northeast, US Airways, for $4.3 billion.

June 2000

WORLD

Clinton and Putin Unable to Agree (June 4): End cordial two-day Moscow conference without compromise on U.S. plans for national missile defense system. Presidents, however, do pledge to destroy 34 metric tons of plutonium.

Suicide Bomber Kills 21 in Sri Lanka (June 7): Cabinet Minister C. V. Goonertne among victims at fund-raising event on nation's first War Heroes Day.

Putin Asserts Rule over Chechnya (June 8): Places civil administration in Chechnya directly under his control. **(June 12):** Putin appoints Muslim cleric, Mufti Akhmed Kadyrov, a Chechen, to govern breakaway republic.

President of Syria Dies at 69 (June 10): Sudden death of Hafez al-Assad dims prospects for peace talks in Middle East.

Italy Pardons Turk Who Shot Pope (June 13): Clears way for Mehmet Ali Agca to face murder charges in Turkey. Agca, 42, tried to kill Pope John Paul II in 1981.

Media Magnate Arrested in Russia (June 13): Vladimir A. Gusinsky, 47, jailed after weeks of government pressure on his Media-Most news group, which has been critical of the Kremlin.

Korean Leaders Move toward Peace (June 15): Presidents of North and South sign broad accord for peace and unity at summit meeting in North's capital, Pyongyang. Major points agreed on include need for reconciliation and unification.

Ethiopia and Eritrea End War (June 18): Two nations sign a preliminary cease-fire and agree to seek a final settlement, ending one of Africa's most enduring wars.

British Find 58 Bodies on Dutch Truck (June 19): Remains of Asian men and women discovered in airless space with cargo of tomatoes. **(June 20):** Police seize Perry Wacker, a Dutch truck driver, on suspicion of manslaughter. **(June 22):** Two more arrested in connection with suffocation of illegal immigrants.

Candidate for President Named in Syria (June 20): Baath Party nominates Bashar al-Assad, 34, an ophthalmologist, to succeed his late father, Hafez al-Assad.

Russia Unveils Economic Program (June 28): Bold plan designed to overhaul faltering economy. Upper house of Parliament rejects President Putin's plan to disband it in favor of an elected senate.

Iraq Resumes Missile Program (June 30): Government report reveals testing of short-range ballistic missile. Tests said to involve liquid-fueled ballistic missile able to carry conventional explosives or chemical and biological weapons.

NATION

Slowdown in Economy Signaled (June 2): Nation's private employers cut 116,000 jobs in May, the first decline since economy began rise in 1990s.

Court Orders Breakup of Microsoft (June 7): Federal judge Thomas Penfield Jackson says corporation seems not to have accepted his ruling that it had broadly violated antitrust law. Order would divide Microsoft into two companies, one for its Windows operating system, and one for its Internet businesses.

Senate Votes Campaign Finance Check (June 8): Seeks to require tax-exempt groups to disclose contributions and spending on political activities.

Microsoft Wins Delay on Penalties (June 20): U.S. judge in antitrust case defers his sweeping restrictions on company's conduct pending higher court action. Judge sends case to Supreme Court for direct review.

No Charges against First Lady (June 22): Independent Counsel Robert W. Ray plans no action against Hillary Rodham Clinton in 1993 dismissal of seven employees from White House travel office.

Cuban Boy Returns Home with Father (June 23): U.S. appeals court rejects plea by Miami relatives to keep custody of Elián González, 6. **(June 28):** Supreme Court declines to hear arguments in case. Boy and father fly home to Cuba.

Navy Resumes Puerto Rico Shelling (June 25): Training exercise on Vieques Island is first since fatal accident caused yearlong protest occupation of the range.

BUSINESS/SCIENCE/SOCIETY

Stroke Rehabilitation Reported (June 5): Scientists find that new course of therapy can coax brain into reorganizing circuitry so that nearly full use of paralyzed limbs can be obtained.

Nuclear Secrets Reported Missing (June 12): Computer hard drives containing sensitive data reported to have disappeared at Los Alamos National Laboratory. **(June 16):** Hard drives discovered behind copying machine. Officials call incident suspicious.

Signs of Water Detected on Mars (June 21): Orbiting spacecraft reports grooved surfaces suggesting relatively recent water flow on planet.

Two Food Company Giants to Merge (June 25): Philip Morris, parent of Kraft Foods, plans to buy Nabisco Holdings, maker of Oreo cookies, Ritz crackers, and other classics, for $14.9 billion.

Human Genome Deciphered (June 26): Two rival groups of scientists, led by J. Craig Venter and Francis S. Collins, announce major achievement in solving secrets of hereditary scripts that define the human organism. Understanding the human genome is expected to revolutionize the practice of medicine.

July 2000

WORLD

Mexico Elects Reform President (July 1): Leader of center-right party, Vicente Fox Quesada, soundly defeats governing party's candidate, Francisco Labastida Ochoa. Election ends 71 years of rule by Institutional Revolutionary Party (PRI).

Ten Jews Convicted by Iranian Court (July 1): Found guilty of spying and aiding Israel, Iran enemy. Western leaders criticize verdict.

Israeli Government Collapses (July 9): Prime Minister Ehud Barak's fragile coalition crumbles as rightist parties desert on eve of Camp David conference in protest of anticipated concessions to Palestinians.

President of Israel Resigns (July 10): Ezer Weizman, 75, quits amid accusations of financial misdealings.

Syrian Voters Confirm President (July 10): Referendum approves Bashar al-Assad to succeed late father, Hafez al-Assad, who ruled autocratically for 30 years.

Israel Ends Arms Deal with China (July 12): Cancels plan to sell Beijing elaborate $250 million airborne radar system. Israeli prime minister Ehud Barak makes announcement at Camp David summit.

Germany Agrees to Compensate Forced Laborers (July 17): Approves $5 billion package to settle claims stemming from atrocities of Nazi regime.

U.S. Commits to Help Africa Fight AIDS (July 18): Pledges $1 billion year in loans to fund purchase of American AIDS drugs and medical services.

Aid to Poor Countries Promised (July 23): Group of eight major powers ends Japan economic conference with promise to end extreme poverty and the spread of infectious diseases, such as AIDS and malaria.

Mideast Peace Talks Fail (July 25): President Clinton ends summit after two weeks of negotiations between Israeli and Palestinian leaders at Camp David. Leaders could not reach compromise on Jerusalem.

NATION

Vermont Legalizes Civil Unions (July 1): Becomes first state recognizing same-sex unions.

Crucial Pentagon Missile Test Fails (July 8): High-speed interceptor intended to destroy dummy warhead fails to separate from booster rocket. Malfunction hinders Pentagon's chance to prove effectiveness of $60 billion defense system and President Clinton's plan to move ahead with system.

U.S. and Vietnam Agree on Trade (July 13): Accord would permit nearly unrestrained commerce between the countries.

Congress Votes to Repeal Estate Tax (July 14): Senate, 59–39, disregards veto threat by president. House had previously passed measure.

Senate Passes Married Couples Tax Cut (July 18): Approves measure, 61–38, to reduce income levies for most couples by $248 billion over next ten years.

U.S. Officials Cleared in Waco Deaths (July 21): Special counsel John Danforth exonerates Attorney General Janet Reno and the government of any wrongdoing in 1993 tear-gas assault on Branch Davidian cult compound. Counsel blames religious sect members, notably the group's leader, David Koresh, for deaths.

Bush Chooses Running Mate (July 25): Names Richard B. Cheney, 59, former defense secretary and longtime family friend. As a Congress member, Cheney was considered extremely conservative.

BUSINESS / SCIENCE / SOCIETY

Wildfire Rages in Far West (July 2 et seq.): Destroys nearly 500,000 acres in California, Arizona, Colorado, Idaho, and Montana. Damage in millions. **(July 31):** Hundreds of firefighters and fleet of helicopters and tankers battle 63,270-acre blaze in Sierra Nevada.

Blast Kills Hundreds in South Nigeria (July 10): School-children among victims as damaged gasoline pipeline explodes. Fuel-scavenging villagers among dead.

Black Church Names Woman as Bishop (July 11): African Methodist Episcopal Church elects Rev. Vashti Murphy McKenzie as its first female leader.

Death Toll Past 100 in Philippine Catastrophe (July 12): Mountain of rubbish collapses and crushes hundreds of huts in squatters' colony called Promised Land.

Record Damages in Tobacco Lawsuit (July 14): Florida jury orders industry to pay $144.8 billion in punitive damages to some 500,000 Florida smokers. Award is largest in United States history.

Concorde Crash Kills 113 near Paris (July 25): Air France craft carrying mainly German passengers bound for New York. All 109 crew members and passengers are killed, as well as at least four on ground. First Concorde crash since this first supersonic passenger plane began commercial operation in 1976. Craft had been delayed by repairs to engine that caught fire. **(July 28):** Officials say evidence suggests burst tire caused fire that engulfed Concorde.

August 2000

WORLD

Queen Mother Turns 100 (Aug. 4): Elizabeth celebrates with three generations of royal family.

Free Press Bill Killed in Iran (Aug. 6): Ayatollah Ali Khamenei sides with conservatives and blocks legislation vaunted by President Khatami.

Anwar Ibrahim Convicted of Sodomy (Aug. 8): Former deputy prime minister sentenced to nine years in jail; currently serving six years for suspect corruption charge. International condemnation swift.

Pinochet Stripped of Immunity (Aug. 8): Chilean Supreme Court lifts senatorial privileges, removing major legal barrier to trial of former dictator.

Iran Closes Last Reformist Newspaper (Aug. 8): Hard-line judiciary shutters popular daily, *Bahar.*

Russian Submarine Sinks, 118 Dead (Aug. 12 et seq.): Entire crew aboard nuclear-powered *Kursk* perish on floor of Barents Sea. Russian seamen fail to dock rescue capsule.

Nicholas II and Family Canonized (Aug. 14): Russian Orthodox Church honors last czar and kin, imprisoned and executed by Bolsheviks in 1908.

Budget Cuts Blamed in *Kursk* Disaster (Aug. 21): Russian defense minister blames reduction in military funds for failure to rescue crew of doomed submarine. **(Aug. 22):** President Putin pledges families of victims will receive payment equal to 10 years of an officer's salary.

British Arrest Protestant Leader (Aug. 22): Arrest of infamous Ulster militant Johnny Adair follows recent surge of Protestant paramilitary violence.

NATION

U.S. Offers New Tactic on Global Warming (Aug. 1): Proposes that countries get credit for using forests and farmers' fields to absorb carbon dioxide. Proposal an alternative to curbing the burning of coal and oil.

Republicans Pick Candidates (Aug. 2 et seq.): Philadelphia convention nominates Texas governor George W. Bush as presidential candidate for 2000 election. Delegates chose Dick Cheney, a former congressman and secretary of defense, as Bush's running mate.

Clinton Vetoes Marriage Tax Relief (Aug. 5): Terms proposal too costly. Measure had been centerpiece of Republican efforts for tax reduction.

Dangerous Tires Recalled (Aug. 9): Bridgestone/Firestone admits the treads on millions of tires it produced since 1991 are prone to shredding. Ford Explorer especially vulnerable. Death toll set at 46.

Democrats Nominate Gore for Presidency (Aug. 14 et seq.): Los Angeles convention picks vice president to head ticket. Delegates select Sen. Joseph I. Lieberman of Conn. as vice presidential candidate; Gore gains slight edge over Gov. George W. Bush in post-convention bounce.

Clinton Vetoes Estate Tax Repeal (Aug. 31): President rejects Republican measure, saying it "fails the test of fairness and fiscal responsibility."

BUSINESS / SCIENCE / SOCIETY

Evolution Foes Defeated in Kansas Primaries (Aug. 2): Voters oust state school-board candidates who supported removing evolution from state curriculum.

North Pole Icecap Melting (Aug. 18): Arctic visitors report about a mile-wide swath of ice-free ocean. Global warming link suggested.

Senator McCain Undergoes Cancer Surgery (Aug. 19): Operation successfully removes two malignant melanomas. No evidence that cancer has spread.

Accord Reached in Phone Walkout (Aug. 20): Strike ends as unions reach contract agreement at Verizon Communications, nation's largest telecommunications employer, after 15-day tie-up.

Mitsubishi Admits to Defect Cover-up (Aug. 22): Japanese auto company says it concealed thousands of customer complaints about defective cars. Recall affects more than 600,000 vehicles.

Jet Crash Kills 143 off Bahrain (Aug. 23): All aboard Gulf Air Airbus perish in Persian Gulf.

Fire in Russian Broadcast Tower (Aug. 28): Firemen extinguish blaze in 1,772-foot Ostankino tower, Moscow's communications center and Europe's tallest structure. Several deaths reported.

Wildfires Rage across West (Aug. 30): Cost of fighting them expected to exceed $1 billion, federal officials estimate. Fires have devastated vast areas from Montana to New Mexico. Daily cost set at $18 million.

September 2000

WORLD

Burmese Opposition Leader under House Arrest (Sept. 4): Government and police shut down activities of National League for Democracy, led by Nobel Peace Prize winner Aung San Suu Kyi. Move follows nine-day roadside standoff between Suu Kyi and military.

OPEC Agrees on Production Increase (Sept. 10): Under world pressure, members will output crude oil output by 800,000 barrels daily.

Palestinian Statehood Postponed (Sept. 10): Leadership assembly in Gaza City calls off Sept. 13 announcement of Palestinian statehood.

High Fuel Prices Spark Protest in Europe (Sept. 11): Truck drivers, farm workers, and taxi drivers blockade oil refineries and cut off deliveries to thousands of gasoline stations.

EU Ends Sanctions against Austria (Sept. 12): Lifts restrictions imposed after far-right Freedom Party joined government. Vows to closely monitor party activities.

U.S. Moves to Revive Mideast Peace Talks (Sept. 14): Seeks action at informal New York meeting, but Secretary of State Albright is doubtful of progress.

Debt Relief Planned for Poor Nations (Sept. 16): Financial leaders of wealthy countries promise campaign to double number of poor countries given debt relief.

Blast Damages British Spy Headquarters (Sept. 20): Explosion goes off in London's M.I.6 intelligence building. No casualties reported.

Iran Court Cuts Sentences for Jews (Sept. 21): Appeals bench reduces terms of 10 who had been convicted of cooperating with Israel.

Central Banks Act to Save Euro (Sept. 22): European, American, and Japanese institutions seek to bolster Europe's unified currency to combat what they regard as a threat to world economy.

Separation of Twins Approved (Sept. 22): British Court of Appeal rules that doctors can operate on pair joined at birth. Procedure would sacrifice one to save the other.

Yugoslav Opposition Claims Victory (Sept. 25): Supporters of Vojislav Kostunica say he leads President Slobodan Milosevic in presidential election. **(Sept. 28):** Milosevic government calls for runoff election.

Danish Voters Reject Euro (Sept. 26): Block move to join Europe's common currency in first popular test. Vote threatens already fragile monetary experiment and rejects rapid European political integration.

Charges against Netanyahu Dropped (Sept. 27): Israeli attorney general says no grounds to prosecute former prime minister on corruption charges.

Palestinians and Israelis Clash (Sept. 30): At least 12 Palestinians killed and hundreds wounded on the third day of fighting set off by visit of right-wing Israeli leader Ariel Sharon to mosque in Jerusalem's Old City.

NATION

House Upholds Marriage Penalty Bill Veto (Sept. 13): Republicans fail to override president's rejection.

Los Alamos Scientist Released (Sept. 13): Wen Ho Lee, accused of stealing sensitive nuclear weapons data, freed after serving nine months in prison, mostly in solitary confinement. Pleads guilty to one count of mishandling classified nuclear information. **(Sept. 14):** President Clinton criticizes Justice Department and F.B.I. for handling of case against Wen Ho Lee.

Senate Approves China Trade Bill (Sept. 19): Votes, 83–15, in favor of broadening trade with China, giving President Clinton historic foreign policy victory. Measure, approved by House in May, ends annual congressional review of China's trade status.

Whitewater Inquiry Ends (Sept. 20): Special Prosecutor Robert W. Ray reports no evidence in six-year investigation that either President or Mrs. Clinton had committed crimes.

Release of Some Reserve Oil Approved (Sept. 22): Clinton orders 30 million barrels to offset rise in fuel costs.

Senate Approves Aid for Everglades (Sept. 25): Overwhelmingly passes $7.8 billion plan to restore ecosystem in Florida.

Abortion Pill Wins U.S. Approval (Sept. 28): Food and Drug Administration announces acceptance of marketing of drug, mifepristone, or RU-486, a prescription drug that is first alternative to surgical abortion approved in U.S.

BUSINESS / SCIENCE / SOCIETY

Indiana U. Coach Dismissed (Sept. 10): Bob Knight fired for repeated abuse of student players and staff of basketball teams.

Ford Was Aware of Engine Defect (Sept. 11): Company documents show knowledge of safety hazard despite dismissal of thousands of car owners' complaints.

Violent Entertainment Targeted at Youth (Sept. 11): F.T.C. report condemns "pervasive and aggressive marketing" of best-selling restricted movies, music, and video games to children as young as 12.

Selma Chooses Black for Mayor (Sept. 12): In historic election, Joseph J. Smitherman, former segregationist, loses after 35 years as mayor of Alabama city during turbulent era of South. Electorate supports James Perkins Jr., former computer consultant.

Olympic Games Open in Australia (Sept. 15): Air of reconciliation marks 27th summer games in Sydney. Host nation reaches out to native people, who were long a target of discrimination.

40 States Forfeit Health Care Funds (Sept. 23): Will lose hundreds of millions in federal money supposed to provide insurance for children in poor families.

Drug Fights Multiple Sclerosis (Sept. 25): Scientists find disease can be delayed in patients at risk and severity reduced by injections of Avonex, also called interferon.

October 2000

WORLD

Milosevic Dispatches Police to End Strike (Oct. 4): Kolubara coal miners, committed to halting electricity production in protest of President Slobodan Milosevic's refusal to concede recent election to Vojislav Kostunica, defy orders to end action and are joined by 20,000 supporters.

Yugoslav Court Annuls Parts of Election (Oct. 4): Government's Federal Election Commission alleges fraud in Sept. balloting, suggesting new vote necessary.

Palestinian and Israeli Leaders Fail to End Hostilities (Oct. 4): Palestinian leader Yasir Arafat and Israeli Prime Minister Ehud Barak leave Paris negotiations without accord to end violence in West Bank and Gaza Strip. **(Oct. 5):** Both leaders order commanders to stem rioting, but fighting persists.

Nationwide Uprising Ends Milosevic Era (Oct. 5): President Slobodan Milosevic overthrown after several hundred thousand protesters swarm Belgrade and take over Parliament and state-run television station. Police back down, and some join in revolt against Milosevic. **(Oct. 7):** Vojislav Kostunica sworn in as president. Vows to restore Yugoslavia's "integrity, sovereignty, and independence."

Lebanese Guerrillas Abduct Israeli Soldiers (Oct. 7): Hezbollah militants cross border into Israel and take three hostage. Barak gives Arafat 48 hours to quell protests or else he'll instruct Israeli military to "use all available means to stop the violence."

Palestinians Destroy Israeli Shrine (Oct. 7): Rioters and police demolish Joseph's Tomb at Nablus after Israeli troops evacuate holy site.

Clinton Meets with North Korean Military Leader (Oct. 10): First president to host North Korean official. Discuss further reducing tensions between North and South Korea.

Seats on UN Security Council Awarded (Oct. 10): Mauritius, Colombia, Ireland, Norway, and Singapore win two-year terms.

Israeli Soldiers Slain by Palestinian Mob (Oct. 12): Vigilantes stab and trample two soldiers who were in custody in a Palestinian police station. Israel retaliates by bombing Ramallah and Gaza City. Government offices among targets.

U.S. Sailors Die in Yemen Explosion (Oct. 12): Seventeen Americans die when a raft carrying powerful explosives collides with Navy destroyer *Cole,* which was refueling in Yemen. Terrorism suspected.

U.S. Adviser Meets with Kostunica (Oct. 12): James O'Brien, special adviser to President Clinton on the Balkans, visits newly elected president of Yugoslavia. Leaders vow to reestablish diplomatic ties. **(Oct. 12):** Clinton lifts some sanctions on Yugoslavia. Ends oil embargo and ban on American flights.

China Vows to Honor Trade Pact (Oct. 12): Prime Minister Zhu Rongji assures U.S. trade official Charlene Barshefsky that China will fulfill market-opening commitments made to gain permanent normal trading relations with U.S.

Barak and Arafat Call Cease-fire (Oct. 16): Leaders convene in Sharm el-Sheikh, Egypt, with President Clinton, and agree to end violence that has claimed about 100 lives and put Middle East on brink of war. **(Oct. 21 et seq.):** Continued violence threatens cease-fire and any prospect for peace. Death toll passes 150.

Violent Demonstrations Rock Ivory Coast (Oct. 26): Clashes intensify between supporters of socialist politician Laurent Gbagbo, who assumed presidency a day after military leader Gen. Robert Guei ousted in a coup, and opposition leader Alassane Dramane Ouattara, who was excluded from the Oct. 22 election. Gbagbo is popular in the Christian South, while Ouattara is favored in the Islamic North.

Euro Plunges to New Low (Oct. 26): The European currency hits new lows against the dollar and the Japanese yen. European Central Bank and the Bank of Japan plan intervention to stop slide.

New Lebanese Government Chosen (Oct. 27): Prime Minister Rafik Hariri, who was elected in September, announces new cabinet.

NATION

Gore and Bush Meet in First Debate (Oct. 3): Boston meeting contentious, with issues ranging from foreign policy to tax cuts to Medicare. Green Party candidate Ralph Nader, who was banned from participating in debate, is denied entrance to the event.

Vice Presidential Candidates Square Off (Oct. 5): Dick Cheney and Sen. Joseph Lieberman meet in first and only vice-presidential debate. Cordial meeting covers taxes, education, and national defense.

Clinton Signs China Trade Bill (Oct. 10): Law gives China permanent normal trading relations. Sends warning to China, however, not to back down on concessions it made for bill's passage and entry into World Trade Organization.

Bush and Gore Face Off in Second Debate (Oct. 11): Accord on many foreign and domestic issues prompt Gov. George W. Bush to call meeting a "lovefest."

Bush and Gore Meet in Final Debate (Oct. 17): Candidates square off in town-meeting-style forum in St. Louis a day after Missouri governor Mel Carnahan died in a plane crash.

Government Announces Record Surplus (Oct. 24): Administration posts $237 billion surplus, third in a row, for the fiscal year that ended in September.

BUSINESS/SCIENCE/SOCIETY

Library of Congress Announces Record Gift (Oct. 4): Receives $60 million from entertainment and telecommunications magnate John W. Kluge.

Former Sotheby's Chief Admits to Colluding with Rival (Oct. 5): Diana Brooks pleads guilty to conspiring to violate antitrust laws by engaging in price-fixing scheme with Christie's. Could face prison sentence and heavy fines.

Miss Hawaii Named Miss America (Oct. 14): Elementary school gym teacher Angela Perez Baraquio wins crown at Atlantic City ceremony.

Chevron to Buy Texaco (Oct. 16): Oil giant agrees to pay $36 billion in stock for Texaco. Combined entity will be world's fourth-largest oil company.

2000 Nobel Prize Winners

Peace: Kim Dae Jung, president of South Korea, was cited "for his work for democracy and human rights in South Korea and in East Asia in general, and for peace and reconciliation with North Korea in particular."

Literature: Gao Xingjian (China) "for an oeuvre of universal validity, bitter insights, and linguistic ingenuity, which has opened new paths for the Chinese novel and drama." His first novel, *Soul Mountain*, recounts impressions from journeys in remote districts in China, and his second, *One Man's Bible*, draws on his experiences as a political activist during China's Cultural Revolution.

Physics: One-half jointly to Zhores I. Alferov (Russia) and Herbert Kroemer (U.S.) "for developing semiconductor heterostructures used in high-speed- and optoelectronics," and one-half to Jack S. Kilby (U.S.) "for his part in the invention of the integrated circuit." Alferov and Kroemer's inventions led to the development of fast transistors, which are used in radio link satellites and mobile telephone base stations. Kilby contributed to the development of the microchip, the basis of all modern technology.

Chemistry: Alan J. Heeger, Alan G. MacDiarmid (both U.S.), and Hideki Shirakawa (Japan) "for the discovery and development of conductive polymers." Conductive polymers are plastics that can conduct electric current. They are used in antistatic substances for photographic film and in shields for computer screens against electromagnetic radiation.

Medicine: Arvid Carlsson (Sweden), Paul Greengard, and Eric Kandel (both U.S.) "for their discoveries concerning signal transduction in the nervous system." Their findings have led to the development of new drugs to treat neurological and psychiatric diseases.

Economics: James J. Heckman and Daniel L. McFadden (U.S.). "To James Heckman for his development of theory and methods for analyzing selective samples and to Daniel McFadden for his development of theory and methods for analyzing discrete choice." The laureates have developed methods that are widely used in the statistical analysis of individual and household behavior within the social sciences.

ELECTION 2000: A CLIFFHANGER

PRESIDENTIAL ELECTION

	Popular votes	Electoral votes
Gore (Dem.)	48.5%	255
Bush (Rep.)	48.3%	246
Nader (Green)	2.6%	
Undecided		37

Electoral votes

Map electoral votes by state:

ORE. 7
WASH. 11
CALIF. 54
NEV. 4
IDAHO 4
MONT. 3
WYO. 3
UTAH 5
ARIZ. 8
COLO. 8
N. DAK. 3
S. DAK. 3
NEB. 5
KANS. 6
OKLA. 8
TEXAS 32
N. MEX. 5
HAWAII 4
ALASKA 3
MINN. 10
IOWA 7
MO. 11
ARK. 6
LA. 9
WIS. 11
ILL. 22
MISS. 7
ALA. 9
MICH. 18
IND. 12
KY. 8
TENN. 11
GA. 13
OHIO 21
W.VA. 5
VA. 13
N.C. 14
S.C. 8
PA. 23
N.Y. 33
VT. 3
N.H. 4
ME. 4
MASS. 12
R.I. 4
CONN. 8
N.J. 15
DEL. 3
MD. 10
D.C. 3
FLA. 25

HOUSE OF REPRESENTATIVES
All 435 seats up for re-election

	Democrats	Republicans	Independent
107th Congress	211	220	2
Undecided	2		
106th Congress	210	223	2

UNITED STATES SENATE
34 seats up for re-election

	Democrats	Republicans	Undecided
107th Congress	49	50	1
106th Congress	46	54	

PRELIMINARY RESULTS: As of noon, Nov. 9, 2000, the presidential election was still undecided. Results in Florida, Oregon and New Mexico were too close to call.

Presidential Election of 2000, Preliminary Electoral and Popular Vote Summary[1]

Principal Candidates for President and Vice President:
Democratic—Albert A. Gore, Jr.; Joseph I. Lieberman
Republican—George W. Bush; Richard B. Cheney
Green—Ralph Nader; Winona LaDuke

	Albert A. Gore, Jr.		George W. Bush		Ralph Nader		Electoral votes			
	Popular vote	%	Popular vote	%	Popular vote	%	D	R	G	Undecided
Alabama	699,815	42%	944,155	56%	17,983	1%		9		
Alaska	63,437	28	134,829	59	22,601	10		3		
Arizona	609,937	46	673,657	50	40,301	3		8		
Arkansas	417,949	45	469,918	51	13,205	2		6		
California	5,254,500	54	4,054,756	42	372,543	4	54			
Colorado	725,950	42	870,303	51	90,723	5		8		
Connecticut	789,532	56	544,704	39	59,950	4	8			
Delaware	180,638	55	137,081	42	8,288	3	3			
D.C.	162,004	86	17,020	9	9,925	5	3			
Florida[1]										25
Georgia	1,101,101	43	1,404,058	55	—	—		13		
Hawaii	205,209	56	137,785	38	21,609	6	4			
Idaho	138,354	28	336,299	69				4		
Illinois	2,566,489	55	2,012,154	43	103,028	2	22			
Indiana	888,201	41	1,231,713	57	—	—		12		
Iowa	633,969	49	628,716	48	27,898	2	7			
Kansas	391,026	37	614,419	58	35,583	3		6		
Kentucky	637,518	41	869,946	57	23,125	2		8		
Louisiana	789,837	45	924,670	53	20,817	1		9		
Maine	315,466	49	283,988	44	37,757	6	4			
Maryland	1,093,344	57	770,911	40	51,078	3	10			
Massachusetts	1,610,175	60	876,106	33	173,758	6	12			
Michigan	2,140,755	51	1,936,288	47	81,089	2	18			
Minnesota	1,168,091	48	1,110,192	46	126,579	5	10			
Mississippi	399,306	42	548,634	57	7,890	1		7		
Missouri	1,110,826	47	1,189,521	51	38,488	2		11		
Montana	137,264	34	239,755	58	24,487	6		3		
Nebraska	215,616	33	408,719	63	22,975	3		5		
Nevada	279,949	46	301,539	49	15,004	2		4		
New Hampshire	265,853	47	273,135	48	22,156	4		4		
New Jersey	1,729,021	56	1,247,791	41	92,333	3	15			
New Mexico[1]										5
New York	3,742,101	60	2,218,620	35	222,075	4	33			
North Carolina	1,236,721	43	1,607,238	56	—	—		14		
North Dakota	95,723	33	175,547	61	9,524	3		3		
Ohio	2,117,555	46	2,294,049	50	114,474	3		21		
Oklahoma	474,326	38	744,335	60	—	—		8		
Oregon[1]										7
Pennsylvania	2,465,412	51	2,264,309	47	102,453	2	23			
Rhode Island	252,844	61	132,212	32	24,115	6	4			
South Carolina	578,143	41	804,826	57	21,008	2		8		
South Dakota	118,750	38	190,515	60	—	—		3		
Tennessee	977,789	48	1,056,480	51	19,694	1		11		
Texas	2,427,785	38	3,796,249	59	137,706	2		32		
Utah	201,732	26	512,161	67	35,661	5		5		
Vermont	148,166	51	119,273	41	19,810	7	3			
Virginia	1,216,925	45	1,426,951	52	58,864	2		13		
Washington	883,794	50	794,567	45	69,578	4	11			
West Virginia	291,088	46	329,708	52	10,440	2		5		
Wisconsin	1,242,115	48	1,235,991	48	92,925	4	11			
Wyoming	60,421	28	147,674	69	—	—		3		
Total[1]	45,252,522	48%	45,043,467	48%	2,499,600	3%	255	246		37

NOTE: Total electoral votes = 538. Total electoral votes needed to win = 270. Dash (—) indicates not on ballot. 1. The states of Florida, Oregon, and New Mexico were undecided as of noon, Nov. 9, 2000. *Source:* Voter News Service.

The One Hundred Seventh Congress
Composition of the 106th and 107th Congresses

107th Congress	Rep.	Dem.	Ind.	Undecided[1]	106th Congress	Rep.	Dem.	Ind.	Male	Female
Senate	50	49	0	1	Senate	54	46	0	91	9
House	220	211	2	2	House	223	210	2	377	58

1. As of noon, Nov. 9, 2000.

The Senate

In the following list, the senior senator is listed first. Dates in left column indicate term in office; birthdates are given in parentheses after name and party affiliation. All terms are for six years and expire in January. Senators listed in italics were elected or reelected in 2000.

Alabama
1987–2005 Richard Shelby (R) (1934)
1997–2003 Jeff Sessions (R) (1946)
Alaska
1969–2003 Ted Stevens (R) (1923)
1981–2005 Frank H. Murkowski (R) (1933)
Arizona
1987–2005 John McCain (R) (1936)
1995–2007 Jon Kyl (R) (1942)
Arkansas
1997–2003 Tim Hutchinson (R) (1949)
1999–2005 Blanche Lincoln (D) (1960)
California
1993–2007 Dianne Feinstein (D) (1933)
1993–2005 Barbara Boxer (D) (1940)
Colorado
1993–2005 Ben Nighthorse Campbell (R) (1933)
1997–2003 Wayne Allard (R) (1943)
Connecticut
1981–2005 Christopher J. Dodd (D) (1944)
1989–2007 Joseph I. Lieberman (D) (1942)
Delaware
1973–2003 Joseph R. Biden, Jr. (D) (1942)
2001–2007 Thomas R. Carper (D) (1947)
Florida
1987–2005 Bob Graham (D) (1936)
2001–2007 Bill Nelson (D) (1942)
Georgia
1997–2003 Max Cleland (D) (1942)
2000–2005[1] Zell Miller (D) (1932)
Hawaii
1963–2005 Daniel K. Inouye (D) (1924)
1990–2007 Daniel K. Akaka (D) (1924)
Idaho
1991–2003 Larry E. Craig (R) (1945)
1999–2005 Mike Crapo (R) (1951)
Illinois
1997–2003 Richard J. Durbin (D) (1944)
1999–2005 Peter G. Fitzgerald (R) (1960)
Indiana
1977–2007 Richard G. Lugar (R) (1932)
1999–2005 Evan Bayh (D) (1955)
Iowa
1981–2005 Chuck Grassley (R) (1933)
1985–2003 Tom Harkin (D) (1939)
Kansas
1997–2005 Sam Brownback (R) (1956)
1997–2003 Pat Roberts (R) (1936)
Kentucky
1985–2003 Mitch McConnell (R) (1942)
1999–2005 Jim Bunning (R) (1931)
Louisiana
1987–2005 John B. Breaux (D) (1944)
1997–2003 Mary L. Landrieu (D) (1955)
Maine
1995–2007 Olympia J. Snowe (R) (1947)
1997–2003 Susan M. Collins (R) (1952)

Maryland
1977–2007 Paul S. Sarbanes (D) (1933)
1987–2005 Barbara A. Mikulski (D) (1936)
Massachusetts
1963–2007 Edward M. Kennedy (D) (1932)
1985–2003 John F. Kerry (D) (1943)
Michigan
1979–2003 Carl Levin (D) (1934)
2001–2007 Debbie A. Stabenow (D) (1950)
Minnesota
1991–2003 Paul Wellstone (D) (1944)
2001–2007 Mark Dayton (D) (1947)
Mississippi
1979–2003 Thad Cochran (R) (1937)
1989–2007 Trent Lott (R) (1941)
Missouri
1987–2005 Christopher S. "Kit" Bond (R) (1939)
2001–2007 Jean Carnahan (D) (1933)
Montana
1978–2003 Max Baucus (D) (1941)
1989–2007 Conrad Burns (R) (1935)
Nebraska
1997–2003 Charles Hagel (R) (1946)
2001–2007 Ben Nelson (D) (1941)
Nevada
1987–2005 Harry Reid (D) (1939)
2001–2007 John Ensign (R) (1958)
New Hampshire
1991–2003 Bob Smith (R) (1941)
1993–2005 Judd Gregg (R) (1947)
New Jersey
1997–2003 Robert Torricelli (D) (1951)
2001–2007 Jon Corzine (D) (1947)
New Mexico
1973–2003 Pete V. Domenici (R) (1932)
1983–2007 Jeff Bingaman (D) (1943)
New York
1999–2005 Charles E. Schumer (D) (1950)
2001–2007 Hillary Rodham Clinton (D) (1947)
North Carolina
1973–2003 Jesse Helms (R) (1921)
1999–2005 John Edwards (D) (1953)
North Dakota
1987–2007 Kent Conrad (D) (1948)
1993–2005 Byron L. Dorgan (D) (1942)
Ohio
1995–2007 Mike DeWine (R) (1947)
1999–2005 George Voinovich (R) (1936)
Oklahoma
1989–2005 Don Nickles (R) (1948)
1994–2003 James M. Inhofe (R) (1934)
Oregon
1996–2005 Ron Wyden (D) (1949)
1997–2003 Gordon Smith (R) (1952)
Pennsylvania
1981–2005 Arlen Specter (R) (1930)
1995–2007 Rick Santorum (R) (1958)

Rhode Island
1997–2003 Jack Reed (D) (1949)
1999–2007 Lincoln Chafee (R) (1953)
South Carolina
1957–2003 Strom Thurmond (R) (1902)
1966–2005 Ernest Hollings (D) (1922)
South Dakota
1987–2005 Thomas A. Daschle (D) (1947)
1997–2003 Tim Johnson (D) (1946)
Tennessee
1995–2003 Fred Thompson (R) (1942)
1995–2007 William Frist (R) (1952)
Texas
1985–2003 Phil Gramm (R) (1942)
1995–2007 Kay Bailey Hutchison (R) (1943)
Utah
1977–2007 Orrin G. Hatch (R) (1934)
1993–2005 Robert F. Bennett (R) (1933)

Vermont
1975–2005 Patrick Leahy (D) (1940)
1989–2007 James M. Jeffords (R) (1934)
Virginia
1979–2003 John Warner (R) (1927)
2001–2007 George Allen (R) (1952)
Washington
1993–2005 Patty Murray (D) (1950)
UNDECIDED[2]
West Virginia
1959–2007 Robert C. Byrd (D) (1917)
1985–2003 John D. "Jay" Rockefeller IV (D) (1937)
Wisconsin
1989–2007 Herbert Kohl (D) (1935)
1993–2005 Russ Feingold (D) (1953)
Wyoming
1995–2007 Craig Thomas (R) (1933)
1997–2003 Michael B. Enzi (R) (1944)

1. Zell Miller was appointed and then elected to serve out the remaining term of Paul Coverdell, who died in July 2000. 2. Race undecided between incumbent Slade Gorton (R) and Maria Cantwell (D), as of noon, Nov. 9, 2000.

The House of Representatives

In the following lists, the numeral indicates the Congressional District represented; AL is for representatives At Large. All terms run from Jan. 2001 to Jan. 2003.

Alabama
1. Sonny Callahan (R)
2. Terry Everett (R)
3. Bob Riley (R)
4. Robert B. Aderholt (R)
5. Robert E. "Bud" Cramer, Jr. (D)
6. Spencer Bachus (R)
7. Earl F. Hilliard (D)

Alaska
AL Don Young (R)

Arizona
1. Jeff Flake (R)
2. Ed Pastor (D)
3. Bob Stump (R)
4. John B. Shadegg (R)
5. Jim Kolbe (R)
6. J. D. Hayworth (R)

Arkansas
1. Marion Berry (D)
2. Vic Snyder (D)
3. Asa Hutchinson (R)
4. Mike Ross (D)

California
1. Mike Thompson (D)
2. Wally Herger (R)
3. Doug Ose (R)
4. John T. Doolittle (R)
5. Robert T. Matsui (D)
6. Lynn C. Woolsey (D)
7. George Miller (D)
8. Nancy Pelosi (D)
9. Barbara Lee (D)
10. Ellen O. Tauscher (D)
11. Richard W. Pombo (R)
12. Tom Lantos (D)
13. Fortney Pete Stark (D)
14. Anna G. Eshoo (D)
15. Mike Honda (D)
16. Zoe Lofgren (D)
17. Sam Farr (D)
18. Gary A. Condit (D)
19. George P. Radanovich (R)
20. Calvin M. Dooley (D)
21. William M. Thomas (R)
22. Lois Capps (D)
23. Elton Gallegly (R)
24. Brad Sherman (D)
25. Howard P. "Buck" McKeon (R)

26. Howard L. Berman (D)
27. Adam Schiff (D)
28. David Dreier (R)
29. Henry A. Waxman (D)
30. Xavier Becerra (D)
31. Hilda L. Solis (D)
32. Julian C. Dixon (D)
33. Lucille Roybal-Allard (D)
34. Grace F. Napolitano (D)
35. Maxine Waters (D)
36. Jane Harman (D)
37. Juanita Millender-McDonald (D)
38. Steve Horn (R)
39. Edward R. Royce (R)
40. Jerry Lewis (R)
41. Gary G. Miller (R)
42. Joe Baca (D)
43. Ken Calvert (R)
44. Mary Bono (R)
45. Dana Rohrabacher (R)
46. Loretta Sanchez (D)
47. Christopher Cox (R)
48. Darrell Issa (R)
49. Susan A. Davis (D)
50. Bob Filner (D)
51. Randy "Duke" Cunningham (R)
52. Duncan Hunter (R)

Colorado
1. Diana DeGette (D)
2. Mark Udall (D)
3. Scott McInnis (R)
4. Bob Schaffer (R)
5. Joel Hefley (R)
6. Thomas G. Tancredo (R)

Connecticut
1. John B. Larson (D)
2. Rob Simmons (R)
3. Rosa L. DeLauro (D)
4. Christopher Shays (R)
5. James H. Maloney (D)
6. Nancy L. Johnson (R)

Delaware
AL Michael N. Castle (R)

Florida
1. Joe Scarborough (R)
2. Allen Boyd (D)
3. Corrine Brown (D)
4. Ander Crenshaw (R)

5. Karen L. Thurman (D)
6. Cliff Stearns (R)
7. John L. Mica (R)
8. Richard "Ric" Keller (R)
9. Michael Bilirakis (R)
10. C. W. Bill Young (R)
11. Jim Davis (D)
12. Adam Putnam (R)
13. Dan Miller (R)
14. Porter J. Goss (R)
15. Dave Weldon (R)
16. Mark Foley (R)
17. Carrie P. Meek (D)
18. Ileana Ros-Lehtinen (R)
19. Robert Wexler (D)
20. Peter Deutsch (D)
21. Lincoln Diaz-Balart (R)
22. UNDECIDED[1]
23. Alcee L. Hastings (D)

Georgia
1. Jack Kingston (R)
2. Sanford D. Bishop, Jr. (D)
3. Mac Collins (R)
4. Cynthia A. McKinney (D)
5. John Lewis (D)
6. Johnny Isakson (R)
7. Bob Barr (R)
8. Saxby Chambliss (R)
9. Nathan Deal (R)
10. Charlie Norwood (R)
11. John Linder (R)

Hawaii
1. Neil Abercrombie (D)
2. Patsy T. Mink (D)

Idaho
1. C. L. "Butch" Otter (R)
2. Michael K. Simpson (R)

Illinois
1. Bobby L. Rush (D)
2. Jesse L. Jackson, Jr. (D)
3. William O. Lipinski (D)
4. Luis V. Gutierrez (D)
5. Rod R. Blagojevich (D)
6. Henry J. Hyde (R)
7. Danny K. Davis (D)
8. Philip M. Crane (R)
9. Janice D. Schakowsky (D)
10. Mark Steven Kirk (R)

11. Jerry Weller (R)
12. Jerry F. Costello (D)
13. Judy Biggert (R)
14. J. Dennis Hastert (R)
15. Timothy V. Johnson (R)
16. Donald A. Manzullo (R)
17. Lane Evans (D)
18. Ray LaHood (R)
19. David D. Phelps (D)
20. John Shimkus (R)

Indiana
1. Peter J. Visclosky (D)
2. Mike Pence (R)
3. Tim Roemer (D)
4. Mark E. Souder (R)
5. Steve Buyer (R)
6. Dan Burton (R)
7. Brian D. Kerns (R)
8. John N. Hostettler (R)
9. Baron P. Hill (D)
10. Julia Carson (D)

Iowa
1. James A. Leach (R)
2. Jim Nussle (R)
3. Leonard L. Boswell (D)
4. Greg Ganske (R)
5. Tom Latham (R)

Kansas
1. Jerry Moran (R)
2. Jim Ryun (R)
3. Dennis Moore (D)
4. Todd Tiahrt (R)

Kentucky
1. Edward Whitfield (R)
2. Ron Lewis (R)
3. Anne M. Northup (R)
4. Ken Lucas (D)
5. Harold Rogers (R)
6. Ernie Fletcher (R)

Louisiana
1. David Vitter (R)
2. William J. Jefferson (D)
3. W. J. "Billy" Tauzin (R)
4. Jim McCrery (R)
5. John Cooksey (R)
6. Richard H. Baker (R)
7. Christopher John (D)

Maine
1. Thomas H. Allen (D)
2. John E. Baldacci (D)

Maryland
1. Wayne T. Gilchrest (R)
2. Robert L. Ehrlich, Jr. (R)
3. Benjamin L. Cardin (D)
4. Albert Russell Wynn (D)
5. Steny H. Hoyer (D)
6. Roscoe G. Bartlett (R)
7. Elijah E. Cummings (D)
8. Constance A. Morella (R)

Massachusetts
1. John W. Olver (D)
2. Richard E. Neal (D)
3. James P. McGovern (D)
4. Barney Frank (D)
5. Martin T. Meehan (D)
6. John F. Tierney (D)
7. Edward J. Markey (D)
8. Michael E. Capuano (D)
9. John Joseph Moakley (D)
10. William D. Delahunt (D)

Michigan
1. Bart Stupak (D)
2. Peter Hoekstra (R)

3. Vernon J. Ehlers (R)
4. Dave Camp (R)
5. James A. Barcia (D)
6. Fred Upton (R)
7. Nick Smith (R)
8. Mike Rogers (R)
9. Dale E. Kildee (D)
10. David E. Bonior (D)
11. Joe Knollenberg (R)
12. Sander M. Levin (D)
13. Lynn N. Rivers (D)
14. John Conyers, Jr. (D)
15. Carolyn C. Kilpatrick (D)
16. John D. Dingell (D)

Minnesota
1. Gil Gutknecht (R)
2. Mark Kennedy (R)
3. Jim Ramstad (R)
4. Betty McCollum (D)
5. Martin Olav Sabo (D)
6. Bill Luther (D)
7. Collin C. Peterson (D)
8. James L. Oberstar (D)

Mississippi
1. Roger F. Wicker (R)
2. Bennie G. Thompson (D)
3. Charles W. "Chip" Pickering (R)
4. Ronnie Shows (D)
5. Gene Taylor (D)

Missouri
1. William Lacy Clay, Jr. (D)
2. Todd Akin (R)
3. Richard A. Gephardt (D)
4. Ike Skelton (D)
5. Karen McCarthy (D)
6. Samuel Graves (R)
7. Roy Blunt (R)
8. Jo Ann Emerson (R)
9. Kenny C. Hulshof (R)

Montana
AL Dennis Rehberg (R)

Nebraska
1. Doug Bereuter (R)
2. Lee Terry (R)
3. Tom Osborne (R)

Nevada
1. Shelley Berkley (D)
2. Jim Gibbons (R)

New Hampshire
1. John E. Sununu (R)
2. Charles F. Bass (R)

New Jersey
1. Robert E. Andrews (D)
2. Frank A. LoBiondo (R)
3. Jim Saxton (R)
4. Christopher H. Smith (R)
5. Marge Roukema (R)
6. Frank Pallone, Jr. (D)
7. Mike Ferguson (R)
8. Bill Pascrell, Jr. (D)
9. Steven R. Rothman (D)
10. Donald M. Payne (D)
11. Rodney P. Frelinghuysen (R)
12. UNDECIDED[2]
13. Robert Menendez (D)

New Mexico
1. Heather Wilson (R)
2. Joe Skeen (R)
3. Tom Udall (D)

New York
1. Felix J. Grucci, Jr. (R)
2. Steven J. Israel (D)
3. Peter T. King (R)

4. Carolyn McCarthy (D)
5. Gary L. Ackerman (D)
6. Gregory W. Meeks (D)
7. Joseph Crowley (D)
8. Jerrold Nadler (D)
9. Anthony D. Weiner (D)
10. Edolphus Towns (D)
11. Major R. Owens (D)
12. Nydia M. Velázquez (D)
13. Vito Fossella (R)
14. Carolyn B. Maloney (D)
15. Charles B. Rangel (D)
16. José E. Serrano (D)
17. Eliot L. Engel (D)
18. Nita M. Lowey (D)
19. Sue W. Kelly (R)
20. Benjamin A. Gilman (R)
21. Michael R. McNulty (D)
22. John E. Sweeney (R)
23. Sherwood L. Boehlert (R)
24. John M. McHugh (R)
25. James T. Walsh (R)
26. Maurice D. Hinchey (D)
27. Thomas M. Reynolds (R)
28. Louise McIntosh Slaughter (D)
29. John J. LaFalce (D)
30. Jack Quinn (R)
31. Amo Houghton (R)

North Carolina
1. Eva M. Clayton (D)
2. Bob Etheridge (D)
3. Walter B. Jones (R)
4. David E. Price (D)
5. Richard Burr (R)
6. Howard Coble (R)
7. Mike McIntyre (D)
8. Robin Hayes (R)
9. Sue Wilkins Myrick (R)
10. Cass Ballenger (R)
11. Charles H. Taylor (R)
12. Melvin L. Watt (D)

North Dakota
AL Earl Pomeroy (D)

Ohio
1. Steve Chabot (R)
2. Rob Portman (R)
3. Tony P. Hall (D)
4. Michael G. Oxley (R)
5. Paul E. Gillmor (R)
6. Ted Strickland (D)
7. David L. Hobson (R)
8. John A. Boehner (R)
9. Marcy Kaptur (D)
10. Dennis J. Kucinich (D)
11. Stephanie Tubbs Jones (D)
12. Pat Tiberi (R)
13. Sherrod Brown (D)
14. Tom Sawyer (D)
15. Deborah Pryce (R)
16. Ralph Regula (R)
17. James A. Traficant, Jr. (D)
18. Robert W. Ney (R)
19. Steven C. LaTourette (R)

Oklahoma
1. Steve Largent (R)
2. Brad Carson (D)
3. Wes Watkins (R)
4. J. C. Watts, Jr. (R)
5. Ernest J. Istook, Jr. (R)
6. Frank D. Lucas (R)

Oregon
1. David Wu (D)
2. Greg Walden (R)
3. Earl Blumenauer (D)
4. Peter A. DeFazio (D)
5. Darlene Hooley (D)

Pennsylvania
1. Robert A. Brady (D)
2. Chaka Fattah (D)
3. Robert A. Borski (D)
4. Melissa Hart (R)
5. John E. Peterson (R)
6. Tim Holden (D)
7. Curt Weldon (R)
8. James C. Greenwood (R)
9. Bud Shuster (R)
10. Don Sherwood (R)
11. Paul E. Kanjorski (D)
12. John P. Murtha (D)
13. Joseph M. Hoeffel (D)
14. William J. Coyne (D)
15. Patrick J. Toomey (R)
16. Joseph R. Pitts (R)
17. George W. Gekas (R)
18. Michael F. Doyle (D)
19. Todd Platts (R)
20. Frank Mascara (D)
21. Phil English (R)

Rhode Island
1. Patrick J. Kennedy (D)
2. James R. Langevin (D)

South Carolina
1. Henry Brown (R)
2. Floyd Spence (R)
3. Lindsey O. Graham (R)
4. Jim DeMint (R)
5. John M. Spratt, Jr. (D)
6. James E. Clyburn (D)

South Dakota
AL John R. Thune (R)

Tennessee
1. William L. Jenkins (R)
2. John J. Duncan, Jr. (R)
3. Zach Wamp (R)
4. Van Hilleary (R)
5. Bob Clement (D)
6. Bart Gordon (D)
7. Ed Bryant (R)
8. John S. Tanner (D)
9. Harold E. Ford, Jr. (D)

Texas
1. Max Sandlin (D)
2. Jim Turner (D)
3. Sam Johnson (R)
4. Ralph M. Hall (D)
5. Pete Sessions (R)
6. Joe Barton (R)
7. John Culberson (R)
8. Kevin Brady (R)
9. Nick Lampson (D)
10. Lloyd Doggett (D)
11. Chet Edwards (D)
12. Kay Granger (R)
13. William "Mac" Thornberry (R)
14. Ron Paul (R)
15. Rubén Hinojosa (D)
16. Silvestre Reyes (D)
17. Charles W. Stenholm (D)
18. Sheila Jackson-Lee (D)
19. Larry Combest (R)
20. Charles A. Gonzalez (D)
21. Lamar S. Smith (R)
22. Tom DeLay (R)
23. Henry Bonilla (R)
24. Martin Frost (D)
25. Ken Bentsen (D)
26. Richard K. Armey (R)
27. Solomon P. Ortiz (D)
28. Ciro D. Rodriguez (D)
29. Gene Green (D)
30. Eddie Bernice Johnson (D)

Utah
1. James V. Hansen (R)
2. Jim Matheson (D)
3. Christopher B. Cannon (R)

Vermont
AL Bernard Sanders (I)

Virginia
1. Jo Ann S. Davis (R)
2. Edward L. Schrock (R)
3. Robert C. Scott (D)
4. Norman Sisisky (D)
5. Virgil H. Goode, Jr. (I)
6. Robert W. Goodlatte (R)
7. Eric I. Cantor (R)
8. James P. Moran (D)
9. Rick Boucher (D)
10. Frank R. Wolf (R)
11. Thomas M. Davis (R)

Washington
1. Jay Inslee (D)
2. Rick Larsen (D)
3. Brian Baird (D)
4. Richard "Doc" Hastings (R)
5. George R. Nethercutt, Jr. (R)
6. Norman D. Dicks (D)
7. Jim McDermott (D)
8. Jennifer Dunn (R)
9. Adam Smith (D)

West Virginia
1. Alan B. Mollohan (D)
2. Shelley Moore Capito (R)
3. Nick J. Rahall II (D)

Wisconsin
1. Paul D. Ryan (R)
2. Tammy Baldwin (D)
3. Ron Kind (D)
4. Gerald D. Kleczka (D)
5. Thomas M. Barrett (D)
6. Thomas E. Petri (R)
7. David R. Obey (D)
8. Mark Green (R)
9. F. James Sensenbrenner, Jr. (R)

Wyoming
AL Barbara Cubin (R)

1. Race undecided between incumbent E. Clay Shaw, Jr. (R) and Elaine Bloom (D), as of noon, Nov. 9, 2000. 2. Race undecided between incumbent Rush Holt (D) and Dick Zimmer (R), as of noon, Nov. 9, 2000.

The Governors of the Fifty States

State	Governor	Current term[1]	State	Governor	Current term[1]
Ala.	Don Siegelman (D)	1999–2003	Mont.	Judy Martz (R)	2001–2005
Alaska	Tony Knowles (D)	1998–2002[2]	Nebr.	Mike Johanns (R)	1999–2003
Ariz.	Jane Dee Hull (R)	1999–2003	Nev.	Kenny Guinn (R)	1999–2003
Ark.	Mike Huckabee (R)	1999–2003	N.H.	Jeanne Shaheen (D)	2001–2005
Calif.	Gray Davis (D)	1999–2003	N.J.	Christine Todd Whitman (R)	1998–2002
Colo.	Bill Owens (R)	1999–2003	N.M.	Gary E. Johnson (R)	1999–2003
Conn.	John G. Rowland (R)	1999–2003	N.Y.	George E. Pataki (R)	1999–2003
Del.	Ruth Ann Minner (D)	2001–2005	N.C.	Mike Easley (D)	2001–2005
Fla.	Jeb Bush (R)	1999–2003	N.D.	John Hoeven (R)	2001–2005
Ga.	Roy E. Barnes (D)	1999–2003	Ohio	Bob Taft (R)	1999–2003
Hawaii	Benjamin J. Cayetano (D)	1998–2002[2]	Okla.	Frank Keating (R)	1999–2003
Idaho	Dirk Kempthorne (R)	1999–2003	Ore.	John Kitzhaber (D)	1999–2003
Ill.	George H. Ryan (R)	1999–2003	Pa.	Tom Ridge (R)	1999–2003
Ind.	Frank O'Bannon (D)	2001–2005	R.I.	Lincoln C. Almond (R)	1999–2003
Iowa	Tom Vilsack (D)	1999–2003	S.C.	Jim Hodges (D)	1999–2003
Kans.	Bill Graves (R)	1999–2003	S.D.	William J. Janklow (R)	1999–2003
Ky.	Paul E. Patton (D)	1999–2003[2]	Tenn.	Don Sundquist (R)	1999–2003
La.	Mike Foster (R)	2000–2004	Tex.	George W. Bush (R)	1999–2003
Maine	Angus S. King, Jr. (I)	1999–2003	Utah	Michael O. Leavitt (R)	2001–2005
Md.	Parris N. Glendening (D)	1999–2003	Vt.	Howard Dean (D)	2001–2005
Mass.	Argeo Paul Cellucci (R)	1999–2003	Va.	James S. Gilmore (R)	1998–2002
Mich.	John Engler (R)	1999–2003	Wash.	Gary Locke (D)	2001–2005
Minn.	Jesse Ventura (IP)[3]	1999–2003	W. Va.	Bob Wise (D)	2001–2005
Miss.	Ronnie Musgrove (D)	2000–2004	Wis.	Tommy G. Thompson (R)	1999–2003
Mo.	Bob Holden (D)	2001–2005	Wyo.	Jim Geringer (R)	1999–2003

NOTE: Governors listed in italics were elected or reelected in 2000. 1. Except where indicated, all terms begin and end in January. 2. Term begins and ends in December. 3. Independence Party.

How a President Is Nominated and Elected

The Conventions

The National Conventions of both major parties are held during the summer of a presidential-election year. Earlier, each party selects delegates by primaries, conventions, committees, etc.

At each convention, a temporary chairman is chosen. After a credentials committee seats the delegates, a permanent chairman is elected. The convention then votes on a platform, drawn up by the platform committee.

By the third or fourth day, presidential nominations begin. The chairman calls the roll of states alphabetically. A state may place a candidate in nomination or yield to another state.

Voting, again alphabetically by roll call of states, begins after all nominations have been made and seconded. A simple majority is required in each party, although this may require many ballots.

Finally, the vice-presidential candidate is selected. Although there is no law saying that the candidates *must* come from different states, it is, practically, necessary for this to be the case. Otherwise, according to the Constitution (*see* the 12th Amendment), electors from that state could vote for only one of the candidates and would have to cast their other vote for some person of another state. This could result in a presidential candidate's receiving a majority electoral vote and his or her running mate's failing to do so.

The Electoral College

The next step in the process is the nomination of electors in each state, according to its laws. These electors must not be Federal office holders. In the November election, the voters cast their votes for electors, not for president. In some states, the ballots include only the names of the presidential and vice-presidential candidates; in others, they include only names of the electors. Nowadays, it is rare for electors to be split between parties. The last such occurrence was in North Carolina in 1968[1]; the last before that, in Tennessee in 1948. On three occasions (1824, 1876, and 1888), the presidential candidate with the largest popular vote failed to obtain an electoral-vote majority.

Each state has as many electors as it has Senators and Representatives. For the 1992 election, the total electors were 538, based on 100 Senators and 435 Representatives, plus 3 electoral votes from the District of Columbia as a result of the 23rd Amendment to the Constitution.

On the first Monday after the second Wednesday in December, the electors cast their votes in their respective state capitols. Constitutionally they may vote for someone other than the party candidate but usually they do not since they are pledged to one party and its candidate on the ballot. Should the presidential or vice-presidential candidate die between the November election and the December meetings, the electors pledged to vote for him or her could vote for whomever they pleased. However, it seems certain that the national committee would attempt to get an agreement among the state party leaders for a replacement candidate.

The votes of the electors, certified by the states, are sent to Congress, where the president of the Senate opens the certificates and has them counted in the presence of both houses on January 6. The new president is inaugurated at noon on January 20.

Should no candidate receive a majority of the electoral vote for president, the House of Representatives chooses a president from among the three highest candidates, voting, not as individuals, but as states, with a majority (now 26) needed to elect. Should no vice-presidential candidate obtain the majority, the Senate, voting as individuals, chooses from the highest two.

1. In 1956, one of Alabama's 11 electoral votes was cast for Walter B. Jones. In 1960, six of Alabama's 11 electoral votes and one of Oklahoma's eight electoral votes were cast for Harry Flood Byrd. (Byrd also received all eight of Mississippi's electoral votes.)

Electoral College Votes by State, 1996 and 2000 Presidential Elections

(total electoral votes: 538; majority needed to elect: 270)

State	Votes	State	Votes	State	Votes
Alabama	9	Kentucky	8	North Dakota	3
Alaska	3	Louisiana	9	Ohio	21
Arizona	8	Maine	4	Oklahoma	8
Arkansas	6	Maryland	10	Oregon	7
California	54	Massachusetts	12	Pennsylvania	23
Colorado	8	Michigan	18	Rhode Island	4
Connecticut	8	Minnesota	10	South Carolina	8
Delaware	3	Mississippi	7	South Dakota	3
District of Columbia	3	Missouri	11	Tennessee	11
Florida	25	Montana	3	Texas	32
Georgia	13	Nebraska	5	Utah	5
Hawaii	4	Nevada	4	Vermont	3
Idaho	4	New Hampshire	4	Virginia	13
Illinois	22	New Jersey	15	Washington	11
Indiana	12	New Mexico	5	West Virginia	5
Iowa	7	New York	33	Wisconsin	11
Kansas	6	North Carolina	14	Wyoming	3

National Political Conventions Since 1856

Opening date	Party	Where held	Opening date	Party	Where held
June 17, 1856	Republican	Philadelphia	June 14, 1932	Republican	Chicago
June 2, 1856	Democratic	Cincinnati	June 27, 1932	Democratic	Chicago
May 16, 1860	Republican	Chicago	June 9, 1936	Republican	Cleveland
April 23, 1860	Democratic	Charleston and Baltimore	June 23, 1936	Democratic	Philadelphia
June 7, 1864	Republican[1]	Baltimore	June 24, 1940	Republican	Philadelphia
Aug. 29, 1864	Democratic	Chicago	July 15, 1940	Democratic	Chicago
May 20, 1868	Republican	Chicago	June 26, 1944	Republican	Chicago
July 4, 1868	Democratic	New York City	July 19, 1944	Democratic	Chicago
June 5, 1872	Republican	Philadelphia	June 21, 1948	Republican	Philadelphia
June 9, 1872	Democratic	Baltimore	July 12, 1948	Democratic	Philadelphia
June 14, 1876	Republican	Cincinnati	July 17, 1948	(3)	Birmingham
June 28, 1876	Democratic	St. Louis	July 22, 1948	Progressive	Philadelphia
June 2, 1880	Republican	Chicago	July 7, 1952	Republican	Chicago
June 23, 1880	Democratic	Cincinnati	July 21, 1952	Democratic	Chicago
June 3, 1884	Republican	Chicago	Aug. 20, 1956	Republican	San Francisco
July 11, 1884	Democratic	Chicago	Aug. 13, 1956	Democratic	Chicago
June 19, 1888	Republican	Chicago	July 25, 1960	Republican	Chicago
June 6, 1888	Democratic	St. Louis	July 11, 1960	Democratic	Los Angeles
June 7, 1892	Republican	Minneapolis	July 13, 1964	Republican	San Francisco
June 21, 1892	Democratic	Chicago	Aug. 24, 1964	Democratic	Atlantic City
June 16, 1896	Republican	St. Louis	Aug. 5, 1968	Republican	Miami Beach
July 7, 1896	Democratic	Chicago	Aug. 26, 1968	Democratic	Chicago
June 19, 1900	Republican	Philadelphia	July 10, 1972	Democratic	Miami Beach
July 4, 1900	Democratic	Kansas City	Aug. 21, 1972	Republican	Miami Beach
June 21, 1904	Republican	Chicago	July 12, 1976	Democratic	New York City
July 6, 1904	Democratic	St. Louis	Aug. 16, 1976	Republican	Kansas City, Mo.
June 16, 1908	Republican	Chicago	Aug. 11, 1980	Democratic	New York City
July 7, 1908	Democratic	Denver	July 14, 1980	Republican	Detroit
June 18, 1912	Republican	Chicago	Aug. 20, 1984	Republican	Dallas
June 25, 1912	Democratic	Baltimore	July 16, 1984	Democratic	San Francisco
June 7, 1916	Republican	Chicago	July 18, 1988	Democratic	Atlanta
June 14, 1916	Democratic	St. Louis	Aug. 15, 1988	Republican	New Orleans
June 8, 1920	Republican	Chicago	July 13, 1992	Democratic	New York City
June 28, 1920	Democratic	San Francisco	Aug. 17, 1992	Republican	Houston
June 10, 1924	Republican	Cleveland	Aug. 10, 1996	Republican	San Diego
June 24, 1924[2]	Democratic	New York City	Aug. 26, 1996	Democratic	Chicago
June 12, 1928	Republican	Kansas City	July 29, 2000	Republican	Philadelphia
June 26, 1928	Democratic	Houston	Aug. 14, 2000	Democratic	Los Angeles

1. The Convention adopted name Union party to attract War Democrats and others favoring prosecution of war. 2. In session until July 10, 1924. 3. States' Rights delegates from 13 southern states.

National Committee Chairs Since 1944

Chairman and (state)	Term	Chairman and (state)	Term
Republican		**Democratic**	
Herbert Brownell, Jr. (N.Y.)	1944–1946	Robert E. Hannegan (Mo.)	1944–1947
Carroll Reece (Tenn.)	1946–1948	J. Howard McGrath (R.I.)	1947–1949
Hugh D. Scott, Jr. (Pa.)	1948–1949	William M. Boyle, Jr. (Mo.)	1949–1951
Guy G. Gabrielson (N.J.)	1949–1952	Frank E. McKinney (Ind.)	1951–1952
Arthur E. Summerfield (Mich.)	1952–1953	Stephen A. Mitchell (Ill.)	1952–1954
Wesley Roberts (Kan.)	1953	Paul M. Butler (Ind.)	1955–1960
Leonard W. Hall (N.Y.)	1953–1957	Henry M. Jackson (Wash.)	1960–1961
Meade Alcorn (Conn.)	1957–1959	John M. Bailey (Conn.)	1961–1968
Thruston B. Morton (Ky.)	1959–1961	Lawrence F. O'Brien (Mass.)	1968–1969
William E. Miller (N.Y.)	1961–1964	Fred R. Harris (Okla.)	1969–1970
Dean Burch (Ariz.)	1964–1965	Lawrence F. O'Brien (Mass.)	1970–1972
Ray C. Bliss (Ohio)	1965–1969	Jean Westwood (Utah)	1972
Rogers C. B. Morton (Md.)	1969–1971	Robert S. Strauss (Tex.)	1972–1977
Robert Dole (Kan.)	1971–1973	Kenneth M. Curtis (Me.)	1977
George H. Bush (Tex.)	1973–1974	John C. White (Tex.)	1977–1981
Mary Louise Smith (Iowa)	1974–1977	Charles T. Manatt (Calif.)	1981–1985
William E. Brock III (Tenn.)	1977–1981	Paul G. Kirk, Jr. (Mass.)	1985–1989
Richard Richards (Utah)	1981–1983	Ronald H. Brown (D.C.)	1989–1993
Frank J. Fahrenkopf, Jr. (Nevada)	1983–1989	David Wilhelm (Ill.)	1993–1994
Lee Atwater (S.C.)	1989–1991	Christopher J. Dodd (Conn.)	1995–1996
Clayton K. Yeutter (Neb.)	1991–1992	Steven Grossman (Mass.)	1996–1999
Richard Bond (N.Y.)	1992–1993	Joe Andrew (Ind.)	1999–
Haley Barbour (Miss.)	1993–1997		
Jim Nicholson (Colo.)	1997–		

Republican National Committee: 310 First St., S.E., Washington, D. C. 20003. *Democratic National Committee:* 430 South Capitol St., S.E., Washington, D.C. 20003.

Presidential Elections, 1789–1996

For the original method of electing the president and the vice president (elections of 1789, 1792, 1796, and 1800), *see* Article II, Section 1, of the Constitution. The election of 1804 was the first one in which the electors voted for president and vice president on separate ballots. (See Amendment XII to the Constitution.)

Year	Presidential candidate	Party	Electoral votes	Year	Presidential candidate	Party	Electoral votes
1789[1]	George Washington	(no party)	69	1796	John Adams	Federalist	71
	John Adams	(no party)	34		Thomas Jefferson	Dem.-Rep.	68
	Scattering	(no party)	35		Thomas Pinckney	Federalist	59
	Votes not cast		8		Aaron Burr	Dem.-Rep.	30
1792	George Washington	Federalist	132		Scattering		48
	John Adams	Federalist	77	1800[2]	Thomas Jefferson	Dem.-Rep.	73
	George Clinton	Anti-Federalist	50		Aaron Burr	Dem.-Rep.	73
	Thomas Jefferson	Anti-Federalist	4		John Adams	Federalist	65
	Aaron Burr	Anti-Federalist	1		Charles C. Pinckney	Federalist	64
	Votes not cast		6		John Jay	Federalist	1

Year	Presidential candidate	Party	Electoral votes	Vice-presidential candidate	Party	Electoral votes
1804	Thomas Jefferson	Dem.-Rep.	162	George Clinton	Dem.-Rep.	162
	Charles C. Pinckney	Federalist	14	Rufus King	Federalist	14
1808	James Madison	Dem.-Rep.	122	George Clinton	Dem.-Rep.	113
	Charles C. Pinckney	Federalist	47	Rufus King	Federalist	47
	George Clinton	Dem.-Rep.	6	John Langdon	Ind. (no party)	9
	Votes not cast		1	James Madison	Dem.-Rep.	3
				James Monroe	Dem.-Rep.	3
				Votes not cast		1
1812	James Madison	Dem.-Rep.	128	Elbridge Gerry	Dem.-Rep.	131
	De Witt Clinton	Federalist	89	Jared Ingersoll	Federalist	86
	Votes not cast		1	Votes not cast		1
1816	James Monroe	Dem.-Rep.	183	Daniel D. Tompkins	Dem.-Rep.	183
	Rufus King	Federalist	34	John E. Howard	Federalist	22
	Votes not cast		4	James Ross	Ind. (no party)	5
				John Marshall	Federalist	4
				Robert G. Harper	Ind. (no party)	3
				Votes not cast		4
1820	James Monroe	Dem-Rep	231	Daniel D. Tompkins	Dem.-Rep.	218
	John Quincy Adams	Ind. (no party)	1	Richard Stockton	Ind. (no party)	8
	Votes not cast		3	Daniel Rodney	Ind. (no party)	4
				Richard Rush	Ind. (no party)	1
				Robert G. Harper	Ind. (no party)	1
				Votes not cast		3
1824[3]	John Quincy Adams	(no party)	84	John C. Calhoun	(no party)	182
	Andrew Jackson	(no party)	99	Nathan Sanford	(no party)	30
	William H. Crawford	(no party)	41	Nathaniel Macon	(no party)	24
	Henry Clay	(no party)	37	Andrew Jackson	(no party)	13
				Martin Van Buren	(no party)	9
				Henry Clay	(no party)	2
				Votes not cast		1
1828	Andrew Jackson	Democratic	178	John C. Calhoun	Democratic	171
	John Quincy Adams	Natl. Rep.	83	Richard Rush	Natl. Rep.	83
				William Smith	Democratic	7
1832	Andrew Jackson	Democratic	219	Martin Van Buren	Democratic	189
	Henry Clay	Natl. Rep.	49	John Sergeant	Natl. Rep.	49
	John Floyd	Ind. (no party)	11	Henry Lee	Ind. (no party)	11
	William Wirt	Antimasonic[4]	7	Amos Ellmaker	Antimasonic	7
	Votes not cast		2	William Wilkins	Ind. (no party)	30
				Votes not cast		2
1836	Martin Van Buren	Democratic	170	Richard M. Johnson[5]	Democratic	147
	William H. Harrison	Whig	73	Francis Granger	Whig	77
	Hugh L. White	Whig	26	John Tyler	Whig	47
	Daniel Webster	Whig	14	William Smith	Ind. (no party)	23
	W. P. Mangum	Ind. (no party)	11			

Year	Presidential candidate	Party	Electoral votes	Vice-presidential candidate	Party	Electoral votes
1840	William H. Harrison[6]	Whig	234	John Tyler	Whig	234
	Martin Van Buren	Democratic	60	Richard M. Johnson	Democratic	48
				L. W. Tazewell	Ind. (no party)	11
				James K. Polk	Democratic	1
1844	James K. Polk	Democratic	170	George M. Dallas	Democratic	170
	Henry Clay	Whig	105	Theo. Frelinghuysen	Whig	105
1848	Zachary Taylor[7]	Whig	163	Millard Fillmore	Whig	163
	Lewis Cass	Democratic	127	William O. Butler	Democratic	127
1852	Franklin Pierce	Democratic	254	William R. King	Democratic	254
	Winfield Scott	Whig	42	William A. Graham	Whig	42
1856	James Buchanan	Democratic	174	John C. Breckinridge	Democratic	174
	John C. Fremont	Republican	114	William L. Dayton	Republican	114
	Millard Fillmore	American[8]	8	A. J. Donelson	American[8]	8
1860	Abraham Lincoln	Republican	180	Hannibal Hamlin	Republican	180
	John C. Breckinridge	Democratic	72	Joseph Lane	Democratic	72
	John Bell	Const. Union	39	Edward Everett	Const. Union	39
	Stephen A. Douglas	Democratic	12	H. V. Johnson	Democratic	12
1864	Abraham Lincoln[9]	Union[10]	212	Andrew Johnson	Union[15]	212
	George B. McClellan	Democratic	21	G. H. Pendleton	Democratic	21
1868	Ulysses S. Grant	Republican	214	Schuyler Colfax	Republican	214
	Horatio Seymour	Democratic	80	Francis P. Blair, Jr.	Democratic	80
	Votes not counted[11]		23	Votes not counted[11]		23

NOTE: Due to the communications constrictions of the time and the lack of formal political party organizations, the framers of the Constitution specified that the president and vice president be chosen based upon the votes cast by members of an electoral college rather than by a direct popular vote. Eventually, states began to change the method by which electors cast their votes. Today, all but two states, Maine and Nebraska, have a winner-take-all system in which a popular vote decides which candidates will be given all of a given state's electoral votes. The number of popular votes won by each presidential candidate are listed here for elections beginning in 1872.

Year	Presidential candidate	Party	Electoral votes	Popular votes	Vice-presidential candidate and party
1872	Ulysses S. Grant	Republican	286	3,597,132	Henry Wilson—R
	Horace Greeley	Dem., Liberal Rep.	(12)	2,834,125	B. Gratz Brown—D, LR—(47)
	Thomas A. Hendricks	Democratic	42		Scattering—(19)
	B. Gratz Brown	Dem., Liberal Rep.	18		Votes not counted—(14)
	Charles J. Jenkins	Democratic	2		
	David Davis	Democratic	1		
	Votes not counted		17		
1876[13]	Rutherford B. Hayes	Republican	185	4,033,768	William A. Wheeler—R
	Samuel J. Tilden	Democratic	184	4,285,992	Thomas A. Hendricks—D
	Peter Cooper	Greenback	0	81,737	Samuel F. Cary—G
1880	James A. Garfield[14]	Republican	214	4,449,053	Chester A. Arthur—R
	Winfield S. Hancock	Democratic	155	4,442,035	William H. English—D
	James B. Weaver	Greenback	0	308,578	B. J. Chambers—G
1884	Grover Cleveland	Democratic	219	4,911,017	Thomas A. Hendricks—D
	James G. Blaine	Republican	182	4,848,334	John A. Logan—R
	Benjamin F. Butler	Greenback	0	175,370	A. M. West—G
	John P. St. John	Prohibition	0	150,369	William Daniel—P
1888	Benjamin Harrison	Republican	233	5,440,216	Levi P. Morton—R
	Grover Cleveland	Democratic	168	5,538,233	A. G. Thurman—D
	Clinton B. Fisk	Prohibition	0	249,506	John A. Brooks—P
	Alson J. Streeter	Union Labor	0	146,935	Charles E. Cunningham—UL
1892	Grover Cleveland	Democratic	277	5,556,918	Adlai E. Stevenson—D
	Benjamin Harrison	Republican	145	5,176,108	Whitelaw Reid—R
	James B. Weaver	People's[15]	22	1,041,028	James G. Field—Peo
	John Bidwell	Prohibition	0	264,133	James B. Cranfill—P
1896	William McKinley	Republican	271	7,035,638	Garret A. Hobart—R
	William J. Bryan	Dem., People's[15]	176	6,467,946	Arthur Sewall—D—(149)
					Thomas E. Watson—Peo—(27)
	John M. Palmer	Natl. Dem.	0	133,148	Simon B. Buckner—ND
	Joshua Levering	Prohibition	0	132,007	Hale Johnson—P

Year	Presidential candidate	Party	Electoral votes	Popular votes	Vice-presidential candidate and party
1900	William McKinley[16]	Republican	292	7,219,530	Theodore Roosevelt—R
	William J. Bryan	Dem., People's[15]	155	6,358,071	Adlai E. Stevenson—D, Peo
	Eugene V. Debs	Social Democratic	0	94,768	Job Harriman—SD
1904	Theodore Roosevelt	Republican	336	7,628,834	Charles W. Fairbanks—R
	Alton B. Parker	Democratic	140	5,084,491	Henry G. Davis—D
	Eugene V. Debs	Socialist	0	402,400	Benjamin Hanford—S
1908	William H. Taft	Republican	321	7,679,006	James S. Sherman—R
	William J. Bryan	Democratic	162	6,409,106	John W. Kern—D
	Eugene V. Debs	Socialist	0	402,820	Benjamin Hanford—S
1912	Woodrow Wilson	Democratic	435	6,286,214	Thomas R. Marshall—D
	Theodore Roosevelt	Progressive	88	4,126,020	Hiram Johnson—Prog
	William H. Taft	Republican	8	3,483,922	Nicholas M. Butler—R[17]
	Eugene V. Debs	Socialist	0	897,011	Emil Seidel—S
1916	Woodrow Wilson	Democratic	277	9,129,606	Thomas R. Marshall—D
	Charles E. Hughes	Republican	254	8,538,221	Charles W. Fairbanks—R
	A. L. Benson	Socialist	0	585,113	G. R. Kirkpatrick—S
1920	Warren G. Harding[18]	Republican	404	16,152,200	Calvin Coolidge—R
	James M. Cox	Democratic	127	9,147,353	Franklin D. Roosevelt—D
	Eugene V. Debs	Socialist	0	917,799	Seymour Stedman—S
1924	Calvin Coolidge	Republican	382	15,725,016	Charles G. Dawes—R
	John W. Davis	Democratic	136	8,385,586	Charles W. Bryan—D
	Robert M. LaFollette	Progressive, Socialist	13	4,822,856	Burton K. Wheeler—Prog, S
1928	Herbert Hoover	Republican	444	21,392,190	Charles Curtis—R
	Alfred E. Smith	Democratic	87	15,016,443	Joseph T. Robinson—D
	Norman Thomas	Socialist	0	267,420	James H. Maurer—S
1932	Franklin D. Roosevelt	Democratic	472	22,821,857	John N. Garner—D
	Herbert Hoover	Republican	59	15,761,841	Charles Curtis—R
	Norman Thomas	Socialist	0	884,781	James H. Maurer—S
1936	Franklin D. Roosevelt	Democratic	523	27,751,597	John N. Garner—D
	Alfred M. Landon	Republican	8	16,679,583	Frank Knox—R
	Norman Thomas	Socialist	0	187,720	George Nelson—S
1940	Franklin D. Roosevelt	Democratic	449	27,244,160	Henry A. Wallace—D
	Wendell L. Willkie	Republican	82	22,305,198	Charles L. McNary—R
	Norman Thomas	Socialist	0	99,557	Maynard C. Krueger—S
1944	Franklin D. Roosevelt[19]	Democratic	432	25,602,504	Harry S. Truman—D
	Thomas E. Dewey	Republican	99	22,006,285	John W. Bricker—R
	Norman Thomas	Socialist	0	80,518	Darlington Hoopes—S
1948	Harry S. Truman	Democratic	303	24,179,345	Alben W. Barkley—D
	Thomas E. Dewey	Republican	189	21,991,291	Earl Warren—R
	J. Strom Thurmond	States' Rights Dem.	39	1,176,125	Fielding L. Wright—SR
	Henry A. Wallace	Progressive	0	1,157,326	Glen Taylor—Prog
	Norman Thomas	Socialist	0	139,572	Tucker P. Smith—S
1952	Dwight D. Eisenhower	Republican	442	33,936,234	Richard M. Nixon—R
	Adlai E. Stevenson	Democratic	89	27,314,992	John J. Sparkman—D
1956	Dwight D. Eisenhower	Republican	457	35,590,472	Richard M. Nixon—R
	Adlai E. Stevenson	Democratic	73[20]	26,022,752	Estes Kefauver—D
1960	John F. Kennedy[21]	Democratic	303	34,226,731	Lyndon B. Johnson—D
	Richard M. Nixon	Republican	219[22]	34,108,157	Henry Cabot Lodge—R
1964	Lyndon B. Johnson	Democratic	486	43,129,484	Hubert H. Humphrey—D
	Barry M. Goldwater	Republican	52	27,178,188	William E. Miller—R
1968	Richard M. Nixon	Republican	301	31,785,480	Spiro T. Agnew—R
	Hubert H. Humphrey	Democratic	191	31,275,166	Edmund S. Muskie—D
	George C. Wallace	American Independent	46	9,906,473	Curtis F. LeMay—AI
1972	Richard M. Nixon[23]	Republican	520[24]	47,169,911	Spiro T. Agnew—R
	George McGovern	Democratic	17	29,170,383	Sargent Shriver—D
	John G. Schmitz	American	0	1,099,482	Thomas J. Anderson—A
1976	Jimmy Carter	Democratic	297	40,830,763	Walter F. Mondale—D
	Gerald R. Ford	Republican	240[25]	39,147,973	Robert J. Dole—R
	Eugene J. McCarthy	Independent	0	756,631	None

Year	Presidential candidate	Party	Electoral votes	Popular votes	Vice-presidential candidate and party
1980	Ronald Reagan	Republican	489	43,899,248	George Bush—R
	Jimmy Carter	Democratic	49	36,481,435	Walter F. Mondale—D
	John B. Anderson	Independent	0	5,719,437	Patrick J. Lucey—I
1984	Ronald Reagan	Republican	525	54,455,075	George Bush—R
	Walter F. Mondale	Democratic	13	37,577,185	Geraldine A. Ferraro—D
1988	George H. Bush	Republican	426	48,886,097	J. Danforth Quayle—R
	Michael S. Dukakis	Democratic	111[26]	41,809,074	Lloyd Bentsen—D
1992	William J. Clinton	Democratic	370	44,909,889	Albert A. Gore, Jr.—D
	George H. Bush	Republican	168	39,104,545	J. Danforth Quayle—R
	H. Ross Perot	Independent	0	19,742,267	James B. Stockdale—I
1996	William J. Clinton	Democratic	379	47,402,357	Albert A. Gore, Jr.—D
	Robert J. Dole	Republican	159	39,198,755	Jack F. Kemp—R
	H. Ross Perot	Reform Party[27]	0	8,085,402	Pat Choate—RP[27]

1. Only 10 states participated in the election. The New York legislature chose no electors, and North Carolina and Rhode Island had not yet ratified the Constitution. 2. As Jefferson and Burr were tied, the House of Representatives chose the president. In a vote by states, 10 votes were cast for Jefferson, 4 for Burr; 2 votes were not cast. 3. As no candidate had an electoral-vote majority, the House of Representatives chose the president from the first three. In a vote by states, 13 votes were cast for Adams, 7 for Jackson, and 4 for Crawford. 4. The Antimasonic Party on Sept. 26, 1831, was the first party to hold a nominating convention to choose candidates for president and vice president. 5. As Johnson did not have an electoral-vote majority, the Senate chose him 33–14 over Granger, the others being legally out of the race. 6. Harrison died April 4, 1841, and Tyler succeeded him. 7. Taylor died July 9, 1850, and Fillmore succeeded him July 10. 8. Also known as the Know-Nothing Party. 9. Lincoln died April 15, 1865, and Johnson succeeded him the same day. 10. Name adopted by the Republican National Convention of 1864. Johnson was a War Democrat. 11. 23 Southern electoral votes were excluded. 12. See Election of 1872 in Unusual Voting Results. 13. See Election of 1876 in Unusual Voting Results. 14. Garfield died Sept. 19, 1881, and Arthur succeeded him Sept. 20. 15. Members of People's Party were called Populists. 16. McKinley died Sept. 14, 1901, and Roosevelt succeeded him the same day. 17. James S. Sherman, Republican candidate for vice president, died Oct. 30, 1912, and the Republican electoral votes were cast for Butler. 18. Harding died Aug. 2, 1923, and Coolidge succeeded him Aug. 3. 19. Roosevelt died April 12, 1945, and Truman succeeded him the same day. 20. One electoral vote from Alabama was cast for Walter B. Jones. 21. Kennedy died Nov. 22, 1963, and Johnson succeeded him the same day. 22. Sen. Harry F. Byrd received 15 electoral votes. 23. Nixon resigned Aug. 9, 1974, and Gerald R. Ford succeeded him the same day. 24. One electoral vote from Virginia was cast for John Hospers, Libertarian Party. 25. One electoral vote from Washington was cast for Ronald Reagan. 26. One electoral vote from West Virginia was cast for Lloyd Bentsen. 27. Perot helped establish the Reform Party following his defeat in the 1992 election.

Participation in Elections for President and U.S. Representatives, 1930–1996

(in thousands)

Year	Population of voting age	Percent of voting-age population that voted for President	Percent of voting-age population that voted for U.S. Representative	Year	Population of voting age	Percent of voting-age population that voted for President	Percent of voting-age population that voted for U.S. Representative
1930	73,623	n.a.	33.7	1964	114,090	61.9	57.8
1932	75,768	52.5	49.7	1966	116,638	n.a.	45.4
1934	77,997	n.a.	41.4	1968	120,285	60.9	55.1
1936	80,174	56.9	53.5	1970	124,498	n.a.	43.5
1938	82,354	n.a.	44.0	1972	140,777	55.2	50.7
1940	84,728	58.9	55.4	1974	146,338	n.a.	35.9
1942	86,465	n.a.	32.5	1976	152,308	53.5	48.9
1944	85,654	56.0	52.7	1978	158,369	n.a.	34.9
1946	82,659	n.a.	37.1	1980	163,945	52.9	47.6
1948	95,573	51.1	48.1	1982	169,643	n.a.	38.0
1950	98,134	n.a.	41.1	1984	173,995	53.3	47.8
1952	99,929	61.6	57.6	1986	177,922	n.a.	33.5
1954	102,075	n.a.	41.7	1988	181,956	50.3	44.9
1956	104,515	59.3	55.9	1990	185,888	n.a.	33.1
1958	106,447	n.a.	43.0	1992	189,687	55.1	50.7
1960	109,672	62.8	58.5	1994	193,163	n.a.	36.6
1962	112,952	n.a.	45.4	1996	196,928	48.9	45.6

n.a. = not applicable *Notes:* Prior to 1960, excludes Alaska and Hawaii. Population 18 years and over beginning 1972; prior to 1972, population 21 years and over except population 18 years and over in Georgia since 1944, 18 years and over in Kentucky since 1956, 19 years and over in Alaska since 1959, and 20 years and over in Hawaii since 1959. Beginning in 1972, includes votes cast for the delegate in the District of Columbia. *Source:* U.S. Bureau of the Census, Current Population Reports, April 1998.

National Voter Turnout in Federal Elections: 1960–1998

Year	Voting-age population	Voter registration	Voter turnout	Turnout of voting-age population (percent)
1998	200,929,000	141,850,558	73,117,022	36.4%
1996	**196,511,000**	**146,211,960**	**96,456,345**	**49.1**
1994	193,650,000	130,292,822	75,105,860	38.8
1992	**189,529,000**	**133,821,178**	**104,405,155**	**55.1**
1990	185,812,000	121,105,630	67,859,189	36.5
1988	**182,778,000**	**126,379,628**	**91,594,693**	**50.1**
1986	178,566,000	118,399,984	64,991,128	36.4
1984	**174,466,000**	**124,150,614**	**92,652,680**	**53.1**
1982	169,938,000	110,671,225	67,615,576	39.8
1980	**164,597,000**	**113,043,734**	**86,515,221**	**52.6**
1978	158,373,000	103,291,265	58,917,938	37.2
1976	**152,309,190**	**105,037,986**	**81,555,789**	**53.6**
1974	146,336,000	96,199,020[1]	55,943,834	38.2
1972	**140,776,000**	**97,328,541**	**77,718,554**	**55.2**
1970	124,498,000	82,496,747[2]	58,014,338	46.6
1968	**120,328,186**	**81,658,180**	**73,211,875**	**60.8**
1966	116,132,000	76,288,283[3]	56,188,046	48.4
1964	**114,090,000**	**73,715,818**	**70,644,592**	**61.9**
1962	112,423,000	65,393,751[4]	53,141,227	47.3
1960	**109,159,000**	**64,833,096[5]**	**68,838,204**	**63.1**

NOTE: Presidential election years are in boldface. 1. Registrations from Iowa not included. 2. Registrations from Iowa and Mo. not included. 3. Registrations from Iowa, Kans., Miss., Mo., Nebr., and Wyo. not included. D.C. did not have independent status. 4. Registrations from Ala., Alaska, D.C., Iowa, Kans., Ky., Miss., Mo., Nebr., N.C., N.D., Okla., S.D., Wis., and Wyo. not included. 5. Registrations from Ala., Alaska, D.C., Iowa, Kans., Ky., Miss., Mo., Nebr., N.M., N.C., N.D., Okla., S.D., Wis., and Wyo. not included. *Source:* Federal Election Commission. Data drawn from Congressional Research Service reports, Election Data Services Inc., and State Election Offices.

Plurality and Majority

In order to win a plurality, a candidate must receive a greater number of votes than anyone running against him. If he receives 50 votes, for example, and two other candidates receive 49 and 2, he will have a plurality of one vote over his closest opponent.

However, a candidate does not have a majority unless he receives more than 50% of the total votes cast. In the example above, the candidate does not have a majority, because his 50 votes are less than 50% of the 101 votes cast.

Presidents Elected Without a Majority

Fourteen candidates (three of them twice) have become president of the United States with a popular vote less than 50% of the total cast. It should be noted, however, that in elections before 1872, presidential electors were not chosen by popular vote in all states. Adams's election in 1824 was by the House of Representatives, which chose him over Jackson, who had a plurality of both electoral and popular votes, but not a majority in the electoral college.

The "minority" presidents are listed below.

Year	President	Electoral percent	Popular percent
1824	John Q. Adams	31.8%	29.8%
1844	James K. Polk (D)	61.8	49.3
1848	Zachary Taylor (W)	56.2	47.3
1856	James Buchanan (D)	58.7	45.3
1860	Abraham Lincoln (R)	59.4	39.9
1876	Rutherford B. Hayes (R)	50.1	47.9
1880	James A. Garfield (R)	57.9	48.3
1884	Grover Cleveland (D)	54.6	48.8
1888	Benjamin Harrison (R)	58.1	47.8

Year	President	Electoral percent	Popular percent
1892	Grover Cleveland (D)	62.4%	46.0%
1912	Woodrow Wilson (D)	81.9	41.8
1916	Woodrow Wilson (D)	52.1	49.3
1948	Harry S. Truman (D)	57.1	49.5
1960	John F. Kennedy (D)	56.4	49.7
1968	Richard M. Nixon (R)	56.1	43.4
1992	William J. Clinton (D)	68.8	43.0
1996	William J. Clinton (D)	70.4	49.0

Facts About Elections

Candidate with highest popular vote: Reagan (1984), 54,455,075.
Candidate with highest electoral vote: Reagan (1984), 525.
Candidate carrying most states: Nixon (1972) and Reagan (1984), 49.

Candidate running most times: Norman Thomas, six (1928, 1932, 1936, 1940, 1944, 1948).
Candidate elected, defeated, then reelected: Cleveland (1884, 1888, 1892).

Presidential Election of 1996, Electoral and Popular Vote Summary

Principal Candidates for President and Vice President:
Democratic—William J. Clinton; Albert A. Gore, Jr.
Republican—Robert J. Dole; Jack F. Kemp
Reform Party—H. Ross Perot; Pat Choate

| | William J. Clinton | | Robert J. Dole | | H. Ross Perot | | Electoral votes | | |
	Popular vote	%	Popular vote	%	Popular vote	%	D	R	RP
Alabama	662,165	43%	769,044	50%	92,149	6%	0	9	0
Alaska	80,380	33	122,746	51	26,333	11	0	3	0
Arizona	653,288	46	622,073	44	112,072	8	8	0	0
Arkansas	475,171	54	325,416	37	69,884	8	6	0	0
California	5,119,835	51	3,828,380	38	697,847	7	54	0	0
Colorado	671,152	44	691,848	46	99,629	7	0	8	0
Connecticut	735,740	52	483,109	35	139,523	10	8	0	0
Delaware	140,355	52	99,062	37	28,719	11	3	0	0
D.C.	158,220	85	17,339	9	3,611	2	3	0	0
Florida	2,546,870	48	2,244,536	42	483,870	9	25	0	0
Georgia	1,053,849	46	1,080,843	47	146,337	6	0	13	0
Hawaii	205,012	57	113,943	32	27,358	7	4	0	0
Idaho	165,443	34	256,595	52	62,518	13	0	4	0
Illinois	2,341,744	54	1,587,021	37	346,408	8	22	0	0
Indiana	887,424	42	1,006,693	47	224,299	10	0	12	0
Iowa	620,258	50	492,644	40	105,159	8	7	0	0
Kansas	387,659	36	583,245	54	92,639	9	0	6	0
Kentucky	636,614	46	623,283	45	120,396	9	8	0	0
Louisiana	927,837	52	712,586	40	123,293	7	9	0	0
Maine	312,788	52	186,378	31	85,970	14	4	0	0
Maryland	966,207	54	681,530	38	115,812	6	10	0	0
Massachusetts	1,571,763	61	718,107	28	227,217	9	12	0	0
Michigan	1,989,653	52	1,481,212	38	336,670	9	18	0	0
Minnesota	1,120,438	51	766,476	35	257,704	12	10	0	0
Mississippi	394,022	44	439,838	49	52,222	6	0	7	0
Missouri	1,025,935	47	890,016	41	217,188	10	11	0	0
Montana	167,922	41	179,652	44	55,229	13	0	3	0
Nebraska	236,761	35	363,467	54	71,278	10	0	5	0
Nevada	203,974	44	199,244	43	43,986	9	4	0	0
New Hampshire	246,214	49	196,532	39	48,390	10	4	0	0
New Jersey	1,652,329	54	1,103,078	36	262,134	8	15	0	0
New Mexico	273,495	49	232,751	42	32,257	6	5	0	0
New York	3,756,177	59	1,933,492	31	503,458	8	33	0	0
North Carolina	1,107,849	44	1,225,938	49	168,059	7	0	14	0
North Dakota	106,905	40	125,050	47	32,515	12	0	3	0
Ohio	2,148,222	47	1,859,883	40	483,207	11	21	0	0
Oklahoma	488,105	40	582,315	48	130,788	11	0	8	0
Oregon	649,641	47	538,152	39	121,221	9	7	0	0
Pennsylvania	2,215,819	49	1,801,169	40	430,984	10	23	0	0
Rhode Island	233,050	60	104,683	27	43,723	11	4	0	0
South Carolina	506,283	44	573,458	50	64,386	5	0	8	0
South Dakota	139,333	43	150,543	46	31,250	10	0	3	0
Tennessee	909,146	48	863,530	46	105,918	5	11	0	0
Texas	2,459,683	44	2,736,167	49	378,537	7	0	32	0
Utah	221,633	33	361,911	54	66,461	10	0	5	0
Vermont	137,894	53	80,352	31	31,024	12	3	0	0
Virginia	1,091,060	45	1,138,350	47	159,861	7	0	13	0
Washington	1,123,323	50	840,712	37	201,003	9	11	0	0
West Virginia	327,812	51	233,946	37	71,639	11	5	0	0
Wisconsin	1,071,971	49	845,029	39	227,339	10	11	0	0
Wyoming	77,934	37	105,388	50	25,928	12	0	3	0
Total	**47,402,357**	**49%**	**39,198,755**	**41%**	**8,085,402**	**8%**	**379**	**159**	**0**

NOTE: Total electoral votes = 538. Total electoral votes needed to win = 270. *Source:* Federal Election Commission.

Residency Requirements for Voting

The Supreme Court decision of March 21, 1972, declared lengthy requirements for voting in state and local elections unconstitutional and suggested that 30 days was an ample period. Most of the states have changed or eliminated their durational residency requirements to comply with the ruling, as shown.

State	Residency requirement
Alabama	No durational residency requirement. 10-day registration requirement. In-person registration by 5 p.m., eleven days before election date.
Alaska	30-day residency requirement. If otherwise qualified but has not been a resident of the election district for at least 30 days preceding the date of a presidential election, is entitled to register and vote for presidential and vice-presidential candidates.
Arizona	30-day residency requirement. Residency in the state 29 days preceding the election.
Arkansas	No durational residency requirement.
California	Must be a registered voter 29 days before an election; 20-day residency requirement.
Colorado	Residency requirement of 25 days immediately preceding the election.
Connecticut	No durational residency requirement. Registration deadline 14th day before election; registration and party enrollment deadline by 12 noon the day before primary.
Delaware	No durational residency requirement. Must reside in Delaware and register by the last day that the books are open for registration.
District of Columbia	No durational residency requirement. Registration stops 30 days before any election. Voters must inform Board of Elections of change of address within 30 days of moving.
Florida	No durational residency requirement. 29-day registration requirement before national election; 29-day registration requirement before first and second state primary.
Georgia	No durational residency requirement. 30-day registration requirement.
Hawaii	No durational residency requirement. 30-day registration requirement.
Idaho	30-day residency requirement. May register 25 days prior to any election with County Clerk. If eligible to vote, an individual may register in person at the polling place on election day at the resident precinct and complete a registration card, make an oath, and provide proof of residence.
Illinois	30-day residency requirement.
Indiana	30-day residency requirement.
Iowa	No durational residency requirement. 10-day registration requirement. In-person registration by 5 p.m., eleven days before election date.
Kansas	14-day residency requirement.
Kentucky	28-day residency requirement.
Louisiana	No durational residency requirement. Register 24 days prior to any election.
Maine	No durational residency requirement.
Maryland	No durational residency requirement.
Massachusetts	No durational residency requirement. No residency required to register to vote.
Michigan	30-day residency requirement.
Minnesota	Permits registration and voting on election day with approved ID; 20-day residency requirement.
Mississippi	30-day residency requirement. 30 days registration required; 60 days if registration is by mail.
Missouri	No durational residency requirement. Must be registered by the fourth Wednesday prior to election.
Montana	30-day residency requirement.
Nebraska	No durational residency requirement. Registration deadline is second Friday prior to election.
Nevada	30-day residency requirement.
New Hampshire	No durational residency requirement. Registration deadline is 10 days prior to election. Same-day registrations for federal and state elections.
New Jersey	30-day residency requirement.
New Mexico	No durational residency requirement. Must register 28 days before election.
New York	30-day residency requirement.
North Carolina	30-day residency requirement.
North Dakota	30-day residency requirement.
Ohio	30-day residency requirement.
Oklahoma	No durational residency requirement.
Oregon	Must register by close of business day of registering agencies (which varies), 21st day before the election.
Pennsylvania	30-day residency requirement. 30-day registration requirement.
Rhode Island	30-day residency requirement.
South Carolina	No durational residency requirement. Registration certificate not valid for 30 days, but if you move within the state you can vote in old precinct during the 30 days.
South Dakota	No durational residency requirement. 15-day registration requirement.
Tennessee	30-day residency requirement. 30-day registration requirement.
Texas	No durational residency requirement. 30-day registration requirement.
Utah	30-day residency requirement.
Vermont	10–12 day residency requirement. Administrative cut-off date for processing applications is second Saturday before the election, by 12 noon.
Virginia	No durational residency requirement.
Washington	30-day residency requirement. 30-day registration requirement.
West Virginia	No durational residency requirement. 30-day registration requirement.
Wisconsin	10-day residency requirement.
Wyoming	No durational residency requirement. 30-day registration requirement.

Source: Questionnaires to the states.

Presidents

	Name and (party)[1]	Term	State of birth	Born	Died	Religion	Age at inaug.	Age at death
1.	Washington (F)[2]	1789–1797	Va.	2/22/1732	12/14/1799	Episcopalian	57	67
2.	J. Adams (F)	1797–1801	Mass.	10/30/1735	7/4/1826	Unitarian	61	90
3.	Jefferson (DR)	1801–1809	Va.	4/13/1743	7/4/1826	Deist	57	83
4.	Madison (DR)	1809–1817	Va.	3/16/1751	6/28/1836	Episcopalian	57	85
5.	Monroe (DR)	1817–1825	Va.	4/28/1758	7/4/1831	Episcopalian	58	73
6.	J. Q. Adams (DR)	1825–1829	Mass.	7/11/1767	2/23/1848	Unitarian	57	80
7.	Jackson (D)	1829–1837	S.C.	3/15/1767	6/8/1845	Presbyterian	61	78
8.	Van Buren (D)	1837–1841	N.Y.	12/5/1782	7/24/1862	Reformed Dutch	54	79
9.	W. H. Harrison (W)[3]	1841	Va.	2/9/1773	4/4/1841	Episcopalian	68	68
10.	Tyler (W)	1841–1845	Va.	3/29/1790	1/18/1862	Episcopalian	51	71
11.	Polk (D)	1845–1849	N.C.	11/2/1795	6/15/1849	Methodist	49	53
12.	Taylor (W)[3]	1849–1850	Va.	11/24/1784	7/9/1850	Episcopalian	64	65
13.	Fillmore (W)	1850–1853	N.Y.	1/7/1800	3/8/1874	Unitarian	50	74
14.	Pierce (D)	1853–1857	N.H.	11/23/1804	10/8/1869	Episcopalian	48	64
15.	Buchanan (D)	1857–1861	Pa.	4/23/1791	6/1/1868	Presbyterian	65	77
16.	Lincoln (R)[4]	1861–1865	Ky.	2/12/1809	4/15/1865	Liberal	52	56
17.	A. Johnson (U)[5]	1865–1869	N.C.	12/29/1808	7/31/1875	(6)	56	66
18.	Grant (R)	1869–1877	Ohio	4/27/1822	7/23/1885	Methodist	46	63
19.	Hayes (R)	1877–1881	Ohio	10/4/1822	1/17/1893	Methodist	54	70
20.	Garfield (R)[4]	1881	Ohio	11/19/1831	9/19/1881	Disciples of Christ	49	49
21.	Arthur (R)	1881–1885	Vt.	10/5/1830	11/18/1886	Episcopalian	50	56
22.	Cleveland (D)	1885–1889	N.J.	3/18/1837	6/24/1908	Presbyterian	47	71
23.	B. Harrison (R)	1889–1893	Ohio	8/20/1833	3/13/1901	Presbyterian	55	67
24.	Cleveland (D)[7]	1893–1897	—	—	—	—	55	—
25.	McKinley (R)[4]	1897–1901	Ohio	1/29/1843	9/14/1901	Methodist	54	58
26.	T. Roosevelt (R)	1901–1909	N.Y.	10/27/1858	1/6/1919	Reformed Dutch	42	60
27.	Taft (R)	1909–1913	Ohio	9/15/1857	3/8/1930	Unitarian	51	72
28.	Wilson (D)	1913–1921	Va.	12/28/1856	2/3/1924	Presbyterian	56	67
29.	Harding (R)[3]	1921–1923	Ohio	11/2/1865	8/2/1923	Baptist	55	57
30.	Coolidge (R)	1923–1929	Vt.	7/4/1872	1/5/1933	Congregationalist	51	60
31.	Hoover (R)	1929–1933	Iowa	8/10/1874	10/20/1964	Quaker	54	90
32.	F. D. Roosevelt (D)[3]	1933–1945	N.Y.	1/30/1882	4/12/1945	Episcopalian	51	63
33.	Truman (D)	1945–1953	Mo.	5/8/1884	12/26/1972	Baptist	60	88
34.	Eisenhower (R)	1953–1961	Tex.	10/14/1890	3/28/1969	Presbyterian	62	78
35.	Kennedy (D)[4]	1961–1963	Mass.	5/29/1917	11/22/1963	Roman Catholic	43	46
36.	L. B. Johnson (D)	1963–1969	Tex.	8/27/1908	1/22/1973	Disciples of Christ	55	64
37.	Nixon (R)[8]	1969–1974	Calif.	1/9/1913	4/22/1994	Quaker	56	81
38.	Ford (R)	1974–1977	Neb.	7/14/1913	—	Episcopalian	61	—
39.	Carter (D)	1977–1981	Ga.	10/1/1924	—	Southern Baptist	52	—
40.	Reagan (R)	1981–1989	Ill.	2/6/1911	—	Disciples of Christ	69	—
41.	Bush (R)	1989–1993	Mass.	6/12/1924	—	Episcopalian	64	—
42.	Clinton (D)	1993– 2001	Ark.	8/19/1946	—	Baptist	46	—

1. F—Federalist; DR—Democratic-Republican; D—Democratic; W—Whig; R—Republican; U—Union. 2. No party for first election. The party system in the U.S. made its appearance during Washington's first term. 3. Died in office. 4. Assassinated in office. 5. The Republican National Convention of 1864 adopted the name Union Party. It renominated Lincoln for president; for vice president it nominated Johnson, a War Democrat. Although frequently listed as a Republican vice president and president, Johnson undoubtedly considered himself strictly a member of the Union Party. When that party broke apart after 1868, he returned to the Democratic Party. 6. Johnson was not a professed church member; however, he admired the Baptist principles of church government. 7. Second nonconsecutive term. 8. Resigned Aug. 9, 1974.

Vice Presidents

	Name and (party)[1]	Term	State of birth	Birth and death dates	President served under
1.	John Adams (F)[2]	1789–1797	Massachusetts	1735–1826	Washington
2.	Thomas Jefferson (DR)	1797–1801	Virginia	1743–1826	J. Adams
3.	Aaron Burr (DR)	1801–1805	New Jersey	1756–1836	Jefferson
4.	George Clinton (DR)[3]	1805–1812	New York	1739–1812	Jefferson and Madison
5.	Elbridge Gerry (DR)[3]	1813–1814	Massachusetts	1744–1814	Madison
6.	Daniel D. Tompkins (DR)	1817–1825	New York	1774–1825	Monroe
7.	John C. Calhoun[4]	1825–1832	South Carolina	1782–1850	J. Q. Adams and Jackson
8.	Martin Van Buren (D)	1833–1837	New York	1782–1862	Jackson
9.	Richard M. Johnson (D)	1837–1841	Kentucky	1780–1850	Van Buren
10.	John Tyler (W)[5]	1841	Virginia	1790–1862	W. H. Harrison
11.	George M. Dallas (D)	1845–1849	Pennsylvania	1792–1864	Polk
12.	Millard Fillmore (W)[5]	1849–1850	New York	1800–1874	Taylor
13.	William R. King (D)[3]	1853	North Carolina	1786–1853	Pierce
14.	John C. Breckinridge (D)	1857–1861	Kentucky	1821–1875	Buchanan

	Name and (party)[1]	Term	State of birth	Birth and death dates	President served under
15.	Hannibal Hamlin (R)	1861–1865	Maine	1809–1891	Lincoln
16.	Andrew Johnson (U)[5]	1865	North Carolina	1808–1875	Lincoln
17.	Schuyler Colfax (R)	1869–1873	New York	1823–1885	Grant
18.	Henry Wilson (R)[3]	1873–1875	New Hampshire	1812–1875	Grant
19.	William A. Wheeler (R)	1877–1881	New York	1819–1887	Hayes
20.	Chester A. Arthur (R)[5]	1881	Vermont	1830–1886	Garfield
21.	Thomas A. Hendricks (D)[3]	1885	Ohio	1819–1885	Cleveland
22.	Levi P. Morton (R)	1889–1893	Vermont	1824–1920	B. Harrison
23.	Adlai E. Stevenson (D)	1893–1897	Kentucky	1835–1914	Cleveland
24.	Garrett A. Hobart (R)[3]	1897–1899	New Jersey	1844–1899	McKinley
25.	Theodore Roosevelt (R)[5]	1901	New York	1858–1919	McKinley
26.	Charles W. Fairbanks (R)	1905–1909	Ohio	1852–1918	T. Roosevelt
27.	James S. Sherman (R)[3]	1909–1912	New York	1855–1912	Taft
28.	Thomas R. Marshall (D)	1913–1921	Indiana	1854–1925	Wilson
29.	Calvin Coolidge (R)[5]	1921–1923	Vermont	1872–1933	Harding
30.	Charles G. Dawes (R)	1925–1929	Ohio	1865–1951	Coolidge
31.	Charles Curtis (R)	1929–1933	Kansas	1860–1936	Hoover
32.	John N. Garner (D)	1933–1941	Texas	1868–1967	F. D. Roosevelt
33.	Henry A. Wallace (D)	1941–1945	Iowa	1888–1965	F. D. Roosevelt
34.	Harry S. Truman (D)[5]	1945	Missouri	1884–1972	F. D. Roosevelt
35.	Alben W. Barkley (D)	1949–1953	Kentucky	1877–1956	Truman
36.	Richard M. Nixon (R)	1953-1961	California	1913–1994	Eisenhower
37.	Lyndon B. Johnson (D)[5]	1961–1963	Texas	1908–1973	Kennedy
38.	Hubert H. Humphrey (D)	1965–1969	South Dakota	1911–1978	L. B. Johnson
39.	Spiro T. Agnew (R)[6]	1969–1973	Maryland	1918–1996	Nixon
40.	Gerald R. Ford (R)[7]	1973–1974	Nebraska	1913–	Nixon
41.	Nelson A. Rockefeller (R)[8]	1974–1977	Maine	1908–1979	Ford
42.	Walter F. Mondale (D)	1977–1981	Minnesota	1928–	Carter
43.	George Bush (R)	1981–1989	Massachusetts	1924–	Reagan
44.	J. Danforth Quayle (R)	1989–1993	Indiana	1947–	Bush
45.	Albert A. Gore, Jr. (D)	1993–2001	Washington, D.C.	1948–	Clinton

1. F—Federalist; DR—Democratic-Republican; D—Democratic; W—Whig; R—Republican; U—Union. 2. No party for first election. The party system in the U.S. made its appearance during Washington's first term as president. 3. Died in office. 4. Democratic-Republican with J. Q. Adams; Democratic with Jackson. Calhoun resigned in 1832 to become a U.S. Senator. 5. Succeeded to presidency on death of president. 6. Resigned Oct. 10, 1973, after pleading no contest to Federal income tax evasion charges. 7. Nominated by Nixon on Oct. 12, 1973, under provisions of 25th Amendment. Confirmed by Congress on Dec. 6, 1973, and was sworn in same day. He became president Aug. 9, 1974, upon Nixon's resignation. 8. Nominated by Ford Aug. 20, 1974; confirmed by Congress on Dec. 19, 1974, and was sworn in same day.

Presidential Libraries

The presidential library system is made up of ten presidential libraries and one presidential project. These are not traditional libraries, but rather repositories for preserving and making available the papers, records, and other historical materials of the presidents since Herbert Hoover. The presidential library system formally began in 1939, when President Franklin Roosevelt donated his personal and presidential papers to the federal government. Roosevelt believed that presidential papers are an important part of the national heritage and should be accessible to the public.

Hoover Library
210 Parkside Drive
P.O. Box 488
West Branch, IA 52358-0488
http://hoover.nara.gov

Roosevelt Library
4079 Albany Post Road
Hyde Park, NY 12538-1999
http://www.fdrlibrary.mariest.edu/

Truman Library
500 West U.S. Highway 24
Independence, MO 64050-1798
http://www.trumanlibrary.org

Eisenhower Library
200 SE 4th Street
Abilene, KS 67410-2900
http://www.eisenhower.utexas.edu

Kennedy Library
Columbia Point
Boston, MA 02125-3398
http://www.jfklibrary.org

Johnson Library
2313 Red River Street
Austin, TX 78705-5702
http://www.lbjlib.utexas.edu

The Nixon Project[1]
National Archives at College Park
8601 Adelphi Road
College Park, MD 20740-6001
http://www.nara.gov/nixon/

Ford Library
1000 Beal Avenue
Ann Arbor, MI 48109-2114
http://www.ford.utexas.edu

Carter Library
441 Freedom Parkway
Atlanta, GA 30307-1498
http://carterlibrary.galileo.peachnet.edu

Reagan Library
40 Presidential Drive
Simi Valley, CA 93065-0666
http://www.reagan.utexas.edu

Bush Library
1000 George Bush Drive West
College Station, TX 77845
http://bushlibrary.tamu.edu/

1. The Nixon Project is not affiliated with the Richard Nixon Library and Birthplace in Yorba Linda, Calif., a private institution that was established by Nixon in 1990. *Source:* National Archives and Records Administration; Web: www.nara.gov/nara/president.

Wives and Children of the Presidents

President	Wife's name	Year and place of wife's birth	Married	Wife died	Children[1] Sons	Children[1] Daughters
Washington	Martha Dandridge Custis	1732, Va.	1759	1802	—	—
John Adams	Abigail Smith	1744, Mass.	1764	1818	3	2
Jefferson [2]	Martha Wayles Skelton	1748, Va.	1772	1782	1	5
Madison	Dorothy "Dolley" Payne Todd	1768, N.C.	1794	1849	—	—
Monroe	Elizabeth "Eliza" Kortright	1768, N.Y.	1786	1830	—	2
J. Q. Adams	Louisa Catherine Johnson	1775, England	1797	1852	3	1
Jackson	Rachel Donelson Robards	1767, Va.	1791	1828	—	—
Van Buren	Hannah Hoes	1788, N.Y.	1807	1819	4	—
W. H. Harrison	Anna Symmes	1775, N.J.	1795	1864	6	4
Tyler	Letitia Christian	1790, Va.	1813	1842	3	4
	Julia Gardiner	1820, N.Y.	1844	1889	5	2
Polk	Sarah Childress	1803, Tenn.	1824	1891	—	—
Taylor	Margaret Smith	1788, Md.	1810	1852	1	5
Fillmore	Abigail Powers	1798, N.Y.	1826	1853	1	1
	Caroline Carmichael McIntosh	1813, N.J.	1858	1881	—	—
Pierce	Jane Means Appleton	1806, N.H.	1834	1863	3	—
Buchanan	(Unmarried)	—	—	—	—	—
Lincoln	Mary Todd	1818, Ky.	1842	1882	4	—
A. Johnson	Eliza McCardle	1810, Tenn.	1827	1876	3	2
Grant	Julia Dent	1826, Mo.	1848	1902	3	1
Hayes	Lucy Ware Webb	1831, Ohio	1852	1889	7	1
Garfield	Lucretia Rudolph	1832, Ohio	1858	1918	5	2
Arthur	Ellen Lewis Herndon	1837, Va.	1859	1880	2	1
Cleveland	Frances Folsom	1864, N.Y.	1886	1947	2	3
B. Harrison	Caroline Lavinia Scott	1832, Ohio	1853	1892	1	1
	Mary Scott Lord Dimmick	1858, Pa.	1896	1948	—	1
McKinley	Ida Saxton	1847, Ohio	1871	1907	—	2
T. Roosevelt	Alice Hathaway Lee	1861, Mass.	1880	1884	—	1
	Edith Kermit Carow	1861, Conn.	1886	1948	4	1
Taft	Helen Herron	1861, Ohio	1886	1943	2	1
Wilson	Ellen Louise Axson	1860, Ga.	1885	1914	—	3
	Edith Bolling Galt	1872, Va.	1915	1961	—	—
Harding	Florence Kling DeWolfe	1860, Ohio	1891	1924	—	—
Coolidge	Grace Anna Goodhue	1879, Vt.	1905	1957	2	—
Hoover	Lou Henry	1875, Iowa	1899	1944	2	—
F. D. Roosevelt	(Anna) Eleanor Roosevelt	1884, N.Y.	1905	1962	5	1
Truman	Bess Wallace	1885, Mo.	1919	1982	—	1
Eisenhower	Mamie Geneva Doud	1896, Iowa	1916	1979	2	—
Kennedy	Jacqueline Lee Bouvier	1929, N.Y.	1953	1994	2	1
L. B. Johnson	Claudia Alta "Lady Bird" Taylor	1912, Tex.	1934	—	—	2
Nixon	Thelma Catherine "Pat" Ryan	1912, Nev.	1940	1993	—	2
Ford	Elizabeth "Betty" Bloomer Warren	1918, Ill.	1948	—	3	1
Carter	Rosalynn Smith	1928, Ga.	1946	—	3	1
Reagan	Jane Wyman	1914, Mo.	1940[3]	—	1[4]	1
	Nancy Davis	1921 (?)[5], N.Y.	1952	—	1	1
Bush	Barbara Pierce	1925, N.Y.	1945	—	4	2
Clinton	Hillary Rodham	1947, Ill.	1975	—	—	1

1. Includes children who died in infancy. 2. Number of children listed here reflects only children Jefferson had with Martha Wayles Skelton. Scientists and historians agree, based on DNA evidence, that Jefferson probably fathered at least one child with slave Sally Hemings. 3. Divorced in 1948. 4. Adopted. 5. Birthday officially given as 1923 but her high school and college records show 1921 for year of birth.

Biographies of the Presidents

GEORGE WASHINGTON was born on Feb. 22, 1732 (Feb. 11, 1731/2, old style) in Westmoreland County, Va. While in his teens, he trained as a surveyor, and at the age of 20 he was appointed adjutant in the Va. militia. For the next three years, he fought in the wars against the French and Indians, serving as Gen. Edward Braddock's aide in the disastrous campaign against Ft. Duquesne. In 1759, he resigned from the militia, married Martha Dandridge Custis, a widow with children, and settled down as a gentleman farmer at Mount Vernon, Va.

As a militiaman, Washington had been exposed to the arrogance of the British officers, and his experience as a planter with British commercial restrictions increased his anti-British sentiment. He opposed the Stamp Act of 1765 and after 1770 became increasingly prominent in organizing resistance. A delegate to the Continental Congress, Washington was selected as commander in chief of the Continental Army and took command at Cambridge, Mass., on July 3, 1775.

Inadequately supported and sometimes covertly sabotaged by the Congress, in charge of troops who were inexperienced, badly equipped, and impatient of discipline, Washington conducted the war on the policy of avoiding major engagements with the British and wearing them down by harassing tactics. His able generalship, along with the French alliance and the growing weariness within Britain, brought the war to a conclusion with the surrender of Cornwallis at Yorktown, Va., on Oct. 19, 1781.

The chaotic years under the Articles of Confederation led Washington to return to public life in the hope of promoting the formation of a strong central government. He presided over the Constitutional Convention and yielded to the universal demand that he serve as first president. He was inaugurated on April 30, 1789, in New York, the first national capital. In office, he sought to unite the nation and establish the authority of the new government at home and abroad. Greatly distressed by the emergence of the Hamilton-Jefferson rivalry, Washington worked to maintain neutrality but actually sympathized more with Hamilton. Following his unanimous re-election in 1792, his second term was dominated by the Federalists. His Farewell Address on Sept. 17, 1796 (published but never delivered) rebuked party spirit and warned against "permanent alliances" with foreign powers.

He died at Mount Vernon on Dec. 14, 1799.

JOHN ADAMS born on Oct. 30 (Oct. 19, old style), 1735, at Braintree (now Quincy), Mass. A Harvard graduate, he considered teaching and the ministry but finally turned to law and was admitted to the bar in 1758. Six years later, he married Abigail Smith. He opposed the Stamp Act, served as lawyer for patriots indicted by the British, and by the time of the Continental Congresses, was in the vanguard of the movement for independence. In 1778, he went to France as commissioner. Subsequently he helped negotiate the peace treaty with Britain, and in 1785 became envoy to London. Resigning in 1788, he was elected vice president under Washington and was re-elected in 1792.

Though a Federalist, Adams did not get along with Hamilton, who sought to prevent his election to the presidency in 1796 and thereafter intrigued against his administration. In 1798, Adams's independent policy averted a war with France but completed the break with Hamilton and the right-wing Federalists; at the same time, the enactment of the Alien and Sedition Acts, directed against foreigners and against critics of the government, exasperated the Jeffersonian opposition. The split between Adams and Hamilton resulted in Jefferson's becoming the next president. Adams retired to his home in Quincy. He and Jefferson died on the same day, July 4, 1826, the 50th anniversary of the adoption of the Declaration of Independence.

His *Defence of the Constitutions of Government of the United States* (1787) contains original and striking, if conservative, political ideas.

THOMAS JEFFERSON was born on April 13 (April 2, old style), 1743, at Shadwell in Goochland (now Albemarle) County, Va. A William and Mary graduate, he studied law, but from the start showed an interest in science and philosophy. His literary skill and political clarity brought him to the fore-front of the revolutionary movement in Virginia. As delegate to the Continental Congress, he drafted the Declaration of Independence. In 1776, he entered the Virginia House of Delegates and initiated a comprehensive reform program for the abolition of feudal survivals in land tenure and the separation of church and state.

In 1779, he became governor, but constitutional limitations on his power, combined with his own lack of executive energy, caused an unsatisfactory administration, culminating in Jefferson's virtual abdication when the British invaded Virginia in 1781. He retired to his beautiful home at Monticello, Va., to his family. His wife, Martha Wayles Skelton, whom he married in 1772, died in 1782.

Jefferson's *Notes on Virginia* (1784–85) illustrate his many-faceted interests, his limitless intellectual curiosity, his deep faith in agrarian democracy. Sent to Congress in 1783, he helped lay down the decimal system and drafted basic reports on the organization of the western lands. In 1785 he was appointed minister to France, where the Anglo-Saxon liberalism he had drawn from John Locke, the British philosopher, was stimulated by contact with the thought that would soon ferment in the French Revolution. In 1789, Washington appointed him Secretary of State. While favoring the Constitution and a strengthened central government, Jefferson came to believe that Hamilton contemplated the establishment of a monarchy. Growing differences resulted in Jefferson's resignation on Dec. 31, 1793.

Elected vice president in 1796, Jefferson continued to serve as spiritual leader of the opposition to Federalism, particularly to the repressive Alien and Sedition Acts. He was elected president in 1801 by the House of Representatives as a result of Hamilton's decision to throw the Federalist votes to him rather than to Aaron Burr, who had tied him in electoral votes. He was the first president to be inaugurated in Washington, which he had helped to design.

The purchase of Louisiana from France in 1803, though in violation of Jefferson's earlier constitutional scruples, was the most notable act of his administration. Re-elected in 1804, with the Federalist Charles C. Pinckney opposing him, Jefferson tried desperately to keep the United States out of the Napoleonic Wars in Europe, employing to this end the unpopular embargo policy.

After his retirement to Monticello in 1809, he developed his interest in education, founding the University of Virginia and watching its development with never-flagging interest. He died at Monticello on July 4, 1826. Jefferson had an enormous variety of interests and skills, ranging from education and science to architecture and music.

JAMES MADISON was born in Port Conway, Va., on March 16, 1751 (March 5, 1750/1, old style). A Princeton graduate, he joined the struggle for independence on his return to Virginia in 1771. In the 1770s and 1780s he was active in state politics, where he championed the Jefferson reform program, and in the Continental Congress. Madison was influential in the Constitutional Convention as leader of the group favoring a strong central government and as recorder of the debates; and he subsequently wrote, in collaboration with Alexander Hamilton and John Jay, the *Federalist* papers to aid the campaign for the adoption of the Constitution.

Serving in the new Congress, Madison soon emerged as the leader in the House of the men who opposed Hamilton's financial program and his pro-British leanings in foreign policy. Retiring from Congress in 1797, he continued to be active in Virginia and drafted the Virginia Resolution protesting the Alien and Sedition Acts. His intimacy with Jefferson made him the natural choice for Secretary of State in 1801.

In 1809, Madison succeeded Jefferson as president, defeating Charles C. Pinckney. His wife, Dolley Payne Todd, whom he married in 1794, brought a new social sparkle to the executive mansion. In the meantime, increasing tension with Britain culminated in the War of 1812—a war for which the United States was unprepared and for which Madison lacked the executive talent to clear out incompetence and mobilize the nation's energies. Madison was re-elected in 1812, running against the Federalist De Witt Clinton. In 1814, the British actually captured Washington and forced Madison to flee to Virginia.

Madison's domestic program capitulated to the Hamiltonian policies that he had resisted 20 years before and he now signed bills to establish a United States Bank and a higher tariff.

After his presidency, he remained in retirement in Virginia until his death on June 28, 1836.

JAMES MONROE was born on April 28, 1758, in Westmoreland County, Va. A William and Mary graduate, he served in the army during the first years of the Revolution and was wounded at Trenton. He then entered Virginia politics and later national politics under the sponsorship of Jefferson. In 1786, he married Elizabeth (Eliza) Kortright.

Fearing centralization, Monroe opposed the adoption of the Constitution and, as senator from Virginia, was highly critical of the Hamiltonian program. In 1794, he was appointed minister to France, where his ardent sympathies with the Revolution exceeded the wishes of the State Department. His troubled diplomatic career ended with his recall in 1796. From 1799 to 1802, he was governor of Virginia. In 1803, Jefferson sent him to France to help negotiate the Louisiana Purchase and for the next few years he was active in various negotiations on the Continent.

In 1808, Monroe flirted with the radical wing of the Republican Party, which opposed Madison's candidacy; but the presidential boom came to naught and, after a brief term as governor of Virginia in 1811, Monroe accepted Madison's offer to become Secretary of State. During the War of 1812, he vainly sought a field command and instead served as Secretary of War from September 1814 to March 1815.

Elected president in 1816 over the Federalist Rufus King, and re-elected without opposition in 1820, Monroe, the last of the Virginia dynasty, pursued the course of systematic tranquilization that won for his administrations the name "the era of good feeling." He continued Madison's surrender to the Hamiltonian domestic program, signed the Missouri Compromise, acquired Florida, and with the able assistance of his Secretary of State, John Quincy Adams, promulgated the Monroe Doctrine in 1823, declaring against foreign colonization or intervention in the Americas. He died in New York City on July 4, 1831, the third president to die on the anniversary of Independence.

JOHN QUINCY ADAMS was born on July 11, 1767, at Braintree (now Quincy), Mass., the son of John Adams, the second president. He spent his early years in Europe with his father, graduated from Harvard, and entered law practice. His anti-Paine newspaper articles won him political attention. In 1794, he became minister to the Netherlands, the first of several diplomatic posts that occupied him until his return to Boston in 1801. In 1797, he married Louisa Catherine Johnson.

In 1803, Adams was elected to the Senate, nominally as a Federalist, but his repeated displays of independence on such issues as the Louisiana Purchase and the embargo caused his party to demand his resignation and ostracize him socially. In 1809, Madison rewarded him for his support of Jefferson by appointing him minister to St. Petersburg. He helped negotiate the Treaty of Ghent in 1814, and in 1815 became minister to London. In 1817 Monroe appointed him Secretary of State where he served with great distinction, gaining Florida from Spain without hostilities and playing an equal part with Monroe in formulating the Monroe Doctrine.

When no presidential candidate received a majority of electoral votes in 1824, Adams, with the support of Henry Clay, was elected by the House in 1825 over Andrew Jackson, who had the original plurality. Adams had ambitious plans of government activity to foster internal improvements and promote the arts and sciences, but congressional obstructionism, combined with his own unwillingness or inability to play the role of a politician, resulted in little being accomplished. After being defeated for re-election by Jackson in 1828, he successfully ran for the House of Representatives in 1830. There, though nominally a Whig, he pursued as ever an independent course. He led the fight to force Congress to receive antislavery petitions and fathered the Smithsonian Institution.

Adams had a stroke while on the floor of the House, and died two days later on Feb. 23, 1848. His long and detailed *Diary* gives a unique picture of the personalities and politics of the times.

ANDREW JACKSON was born on March 15, 1767, in what is now generally agreed to be Waxhaw, S.C. After a turbulent boyhood as an orphan and a British prisoner, he moved west to Tennessee, where he soon qualified for law practice but found time for such frontier pleasures as horse racing, cockfighting, and dueling. His marriage to Rachel Donelson Robards in 1791 was complicated by subsequent legal uncertainties about the status of her divorce. During the 1790s, Jackson served in the Tennessee Constitutional Convention, the United States House of Representatives and Senate, and on the Tennessee Supreme Court.

After some years as a country gentleman, living at the Hermitage near Nashville, Jackson in 1812 was given command of Tennessee troops sent against the Creeks. He defeated the Indians at Horseshoe Bend in 1814; subsequently he became a major general and won the Battle of New Orleans over veteran British troops, though after the treaty of peace had been signed at Ghent. In 1818, Jackson invaded Florida, captured Pensacola, and hanged two

Englishmen named Arbuthnot and Ambrister, creating an international incident. A presidential boom began for him in 1821, and to foster it, he returned to the Senate (1823–25). Though he won a plurality of electoral votes in 1824, he lost in the House when Clay threw his strength to Adams. Four years later, he easily defeated Adams.

As president, Jackson greatly expanded the power and prestige of the presidential office and carried through an unprecedented program of domestic reform, vetoing the bill to extend the United States Bank, moving toward a hard-money currency policy, and checking the program of federal internal improvements. He also vindicated federal authority against South Carolina with its doctrine of nullification and against France on the question of debts. The support given his policies by the workingmen of the East as well as by the farmers of the East, West, and South resulted in his triumphant re-election in 1832 over Clay.

After watching the inauguration of his handpicked successor, Martin Van Buren, Jackson retired to the Hermitage, where he maintained a lively interest in national affairs until his death on June 8, 1845.

MARTIN VAN BUREN was born on Dec. 5, 1782, at Kinderhook, N.Y. After graduating from the village school, he became a law clerk, entered practice in 1803, and soon became active in state politics as state senator and attorney general. In 1820, he was elected to the United States Senate. He threw the support of his efficient political organization, known as the Albany Regency, to William H. Crawford in 1824 and to Jackson in 1828. After leading the opposition to Adams's administration in the Senate, he served briefly as governor of New York (1828–1829) and resigned to become Jackson's Secretary of State. He was soon on close personal terms with Jackson and played an important part in the Jacksonian program.

In 1832, Van Buren became vice president; in 1836, president. The Panic of 1837 overshadowed his term. He attributed it to the overexpansion of the credit and favored the establishment of an independent treasury as repository for the federal funds. In 1840, he established a 10-hour day on public works. Defeated by Harrison in 1840, he was the leading contender for the Democratic nomination in 1844 until he publicly opposed immediate annexation of Texas, and was subsequently beaten by the Southern delegations at the Baltimore convention. This incident increased his growing misgivings about the slave power.

After working behind the scenes among the antislavery Democrats, Van Buren joined in the movement that led to the Free-Soil Party and became its candidate for president in 1848. He subsequently returned to the Democratic Party while continuing to object to its pro-Southern policy. He died in Kinderhook on July 24, 1862. His *Autobiography* throws valuable sidelights on the political history of the times.

His wife, Hannah Hoes, whom he married in 1807, died in 1819.

WILLIAM HENRY HARRISON was born in Charles City County, Va., on Feb. 9, 1773. Joining the army in 1791, he was active in Indian fighting in the Northwest, became secretary of the Northwest

Territory in 1798 and governor of Indiana in 1800. He married Anna Symmes in 1795. Growing discontent over white encroachments on Indian lands led to the formation of an Indian alliance under Tecumseh to resist further aggressions. In 1811, Harrison won a nominal victory over the Indians at Tippecanoe and in 1813 a more decisive one at the Battle of the Thames, where Tecumseh was killed.

After resigning from the army in 1814, Harrison had an obscure career in politics and diplomacy, ending up 20 years later as a county recorder in Ohio. Nominated for president in 1835 as a military hero whom the conservative politicians hoped to be able to control, he ran surprisingly well against Van Buren in 1836. Four years later, he defeated Van Buren but caught pneumonia and died in Washington on April 4, 1841, a month after his inauguration. Harrison was the first president to die in office.

JOHN TYLER was born in Charles City County, Va., on March 29, 1790. A William and Mary graduate, he entered law practice and politics, serving in the House of Representatives (1817–21), as governor of Virginia (1825–27), and as senator (1827–36). A strict constructionist, he supported Crawford in 1824 and Jackson in 1828, but broke with Jackson over his United States Bank policy and became a member of the Southern state-rights group that cooperated with the Whigs. In 1836, he resigned from the Senate rather than follow instructions from the Virginia legislature to vote for a resolution expunging censure of Jackson from the Senate record.

Elected vice president on the Whig ticket in 1840, Tyler succeeded to the presidency on Harrison's death. His strict-constructionist views soon caused a split with the Henry Clay wing of the Whig party and a stalemate on domestic questions. Tyler's more considerable achievements were his support of the Webster-Ashburton Treaty with Britain and his success in bringing about the annexation of Texas.

After his presidency he lived in retirement in Virginia until the outbreak of the Civil War, when he emerged briefly as chairman of a peace convention and then as delegate to the provisional Congress of the Confederacy. He died on Jan. 18, 1862. He married Letitia Christian in 1813 and, two years after her death in 1842, Julia Gardiner.

JAMES KNOX POLK was born in Mecklenburg County, N.C., on Nov. 2, 1795. A graduate of the University of North Carolina, he moved west to Tennessee, was admitted to the bar, and soon became prominent in state politics. In 1825, he was elected to the House of Representatives, where he opposed Adams and, after 1829, became Jackson's floor leader in the fight against the Bank. In 1835, he became Speaker of the House. Four years later, he was elected governor of Tennessee, but was beaten in tries for re-election in 1841 and 1843.

The supporters of Van Buren for the Democratic nomination in 1844 counted on Polk as his running mate, but when Van Buren's stand on Texas alienated Southern support, the convention swung to Polk on the ninth ballot. He was elected over Henry Clay, the Whig candidate. Rapidly disillusioning those who thought that he would not run his own administration, Polk proceeded steadily and precisely to achieve four major objectives—the acquisition of California, the settlement of the Oregon question, the reduction of the tariff, and the establishment of the independent treasury. He also enlarged the Monroe Doctrine to exclude all non-American intervention in American affairs, whether forcible or not, and he forced Mexico into a war that he waged to a successful conclusion.

His wife, Sarah Childress, whom he married in 1824, was a woman of charm and ability. Polk died in Nashville, Tenn., on June 15, 1849.

ZACHARY TAYLOR was born at Montebello, Orange County, Va., on Nov. 24, 1784. Embarking on a military career in 1808, Taylor fought in the War of 1812, the Black Hawk War, and the Seminole War, meanwhile holding garrison jobs on the frontier or desk jobs in Washington. A brigadier general as a result of his victory over the Seminoles at Lake Okeechobee (1837), Taylor held a succession of Southwestern commands and in 1846 established a base on the Rio Grande, where his forces engaged in hostilities that precipitated the war with Mexico. He captured Monterrey in September 1846 and, disregarding Polk's orders to stay on the defensive, defeated Santa Anna at Buena Vista in February 1847, ending the war in the northern provinces.

Though Taylor had never cast a vote for president, his party affiliations were Whiggish and his availability was increased by his difficulties with Polk. He was elected president over the Democrat Lewis Cass. During the revival of the slavery controversy, which was to result in the Compromise of 1850, Taylor began to take an increasingly firm stand against appeasing the South; but he died in Washington on July 9, 1850, during the fight over the Compromise. He married Margaret Mackall Smith in 1810. His bluff and simple soldierly qualities won him the name Old Rough and Ready.

MILLARD FILLMORE was born at Locke, Cayuga County, N.Y., on Jan. 7, 1800. A lawyer, he entered politics with the Anti-Masonic Party under the sponsorship of Thurlow Weed, editor and party boss, and subsequently followed Weed into the Whig Party. He served in the House of Representatives (1833–35 and 1837–43) and played a leading role in writing the tariff of 1842. Defeated for governor of New York in 1844, he became State comptroller in 1848, was put on the Whig ticket with Taylor as a concession to the Clay wing of the party, and became president upon Taylor's death in 1850.

As president, Fillmore broke with Weed and William H. Seward and associated himself with the pro-Southern Whigs, supporting the Compromise of 1850. Defeated for the Whig nomination in 1852, he ran for president in 1856 as candidate of the American, or Know-Nothing, Party, which sought to unite the country against foreigners in the alleged hope of diverting it from the explosive slavery issue. Fillmore opposed Lincoln during the Civil War. He died in Buffalo on March 8, 1874.

He was married in 1826 to Abigail Powers, who died in 1853, and in 1858 to Caroline Carmichael McIntosh.

FRANKLIN PIERCE was born at Hillsboro, N.H., on Nov. 23, 1804. A Bowdoin graduate, lawyer, and Jacksonian Democrat, he won rapid political advancement in the party, in part because of the prestige of his father, Gov. Benjamin Pierce. By 1831 he was Speaker of the New Hampshire House of Representatives; from 1833 to 1837, he served in the federal House and from 1837 to 1842 in the Senate. His wife, Jane Means Appleton, whom he married in 1834, disliked Washington and the somewhat dissipated life led by Pierce; in 1842 Pierce resigned from the Senate and began a successful law practice in Concord, N.H. During the Mexican War, he was a brigadier general.

Thereafter Pierce continued to oppose antislavery tendencies within the Democratic Party. As a result, he was the Southern choice to break the deadlock at the Democratic convention of 1852 and was nominated on the 49th ballot. In the election, Pierce overwhelmed Gen. Winfield Scott, the Whig candidate.

As president, Pierce followed a course of appeasing the South at home and of playing with schemes of territorial expansion abroad. The failure of his foreign and domestic policies prevented his renomination. He died in Concord on Oct. 8, 1869, in relative obscurity.

JAMES BUCHANAN was born near Mercersburg, Pa., on April 23, 1791. A Dickinson graduate and a lawyer, he entered Pennsylvania politics as a Federalist. With the disappearance of the Federalist Party, he became a Jacksonian Democrat. He served with ability in the House (1821–31), as minister to St. Petersburg (1832–33), and in the Senate (1834–45), and in 1845 became Polk's Secretary of State. In 1853, Pierce appointed Buchanan minister to Britain, where he participated with other American diplomats in Europe in drafting the expansionist Ostend Manifesto.

He was elected president in 1856, defeating John C. Frémont, the Republican candidate, and former President Millard Fillmore of the American Party. The growing crisis over slavery presented Buchanan with problems he lacked the will to tackle. His appeasement of the South alienated the Stephen Douglas wing of the Democratic Party without reducing Southern militancy on slavery issues. While denying the right of secession, Buchanan also denied that the federal government could do anything about it. He supported the administration during the Civil War and died in Lancaster, Pa., on June 1, 1868.

The only president to remain a bachelor throughout his term, Buchanan used his charming niece, Harriet Lane, as White House hostess.

ABRAHAM LINCOLN was born in Hardin (now Larue) County, Ky., on Feb. 12, 1809. His family moved to Indiana and then to Illinois, and Lincoln gained what education he could along the way. While reading law, he worked in a store, managed a mill, surveyed, and split rails. In 1834, he went to the Illinois legislature as a Whig and became the party's floor leader. For the next 20 years he practiced law in Springfield, except for a single term (1847–49) in Congress, where he denounced the Mexican War. In 1855, he was a candidate for senator and the next year he joined the new Republican Party.

A leading but unsuccessful candidate for the vice-presidential nomination with Frémont, Lincoln gained national attention in 1858 when, as Republican candidate for senator from Illinois, he engaged in a series of debates with Stephen A. Douglas, the

Democratic candidate. He lost the election, but continued to prepare the way for the 1860 Republican convention and was rewarded with the presidential nomination on the third ballot. He won the election over three opponents.

From the start, Lincoln made clear that, unlike Buchanan, he believed the national government had the power to crush the rebellion. Not an abolitionist, he held the slavery issue subordinate to that of preserving the Union, but soon perceived that the war could not be brought to a successful conclusion without freeing the slaves. His administration was hampered by the incompetence of many Union generals, the inexperience of the troops, and the harassing political tactics both of the Republican Radicals, who favored a hard policy toward the South, and the Democratic Copperheads, who desired a negotiated peace. The Gettysburg Address of Nov. 19, 1863, marks the high point in the record of American eloquence. Lincoln's long search for a winning combination finally brought Generals Ulysses S. Grant and William T. Sherman to the top; and their series of victories in 1864 dispelled the mutterings from both Radicals and Peace Democrats that at one time seemed to threaten Lincoln's re-election. He was re-elected in 1864, defeating Gen. George B. McClellan, the Democratic candidate. His inaugural address urged leniency toward the South: "With malice toward none, with charity for all . . . let us strive on to finish the work we are in; to bind up the nation's wounds . . ." This policy aroused growing opposition on the part of the Republican Radicals, but before the matter could be put to the test, Lincoln was shot by the actor John Wilkes Booth at Ford's Theater, Washington, on April 14, 1865. He died the next morning.

Lincoln's marriage to Mary Todd in 1842 was often unhappy and turbulent, in part because of his wife's pronounced instability.

ANDREW JOHNSON was born at Raleigh, N.C., on Dec. 29, 1808. Self-educated, he became a tailor in Greeneville, Tenn., but soon went into politics, where he rose steadily. He served in the House of Representatives (1843–54), as governor of Tennessee (1853–57), and as a senator (1857–62). Politically he was a Jacksonian Democrat and his specialty was the fight for a more equitable land policy. Alone among the Southern Senators, he stood by the Union during the Civil War. In 1862, he became war governor of Tennessee and carried out a thankless and difficult job with great courage. Johnson became Lincoln's running mate in 1864 as a result of an attempt to give the ticket a nonpartisan and nonsectional character. Succeeding to the presidency on Lincoln's death, Johnson sought to carry out Lincoln's policy, but without his political skill. The result was a hopeless conflict with the Radical Republicans who dominated Congress, passed measures over Johnson's vetoes, and attempted to limit the power of the executive concerning appointments and removals. The conflict culminated with Johnson's impeachment for attempting to remove his disloyal Secretary of War in defiance of the Tenure of Office Act which required senatorial concurrence for such dismissals. The opposition failed by one vote to get the two thirds necessary for conviction.

After his presidency, Johnson maintained an interest in politics and in 1875 was again elected to the Senate. He died near Carter Station, Tenn., on July 31, 1875. He married Eliza McCardle in 1827.

ULYSSES SIMPSON GRANT was born (as Hiram Ulysses Grant) at Point Pleasant, Ohio, on April 27, 1822. He graduated from West Point in 1843 and served without particular distinction in the Mexican War. In 1848 he married Julia Dent. He resigned from the army in 1854, after warnings from his commanding officer about his drinking habits, and for the next six years held a wide variety of jobs in the Middle West. With the outbreak of the Civil War, he sought a command and soon, to his surprise, was made a brigadier general. His continuing successes in the western theaters, culminating in the capture of Vicksburg, Miss., in 1863, brought him national fame and soon the command of all the Union armies. Grant's dogged, implacable policy of concentrating on dividing and destroying the Confederate armies brought the war to an end in 1865. The next year, he was made full general.

In 1868, as Republican candidate for president, Grant was elected over the Democrat, Horatio Seymour. From the start, Grant showed his unfitness for the office. His Cabinet was weak, his domestic policy was confused, and many of his intimate associates were corrupt. The notable achievement in foreign affairs was the settlement of controversies with Great Britain in the Treaty of London (1871), negotiated by his able Secretary of State, Hamilton Fish.

Running for re-election in 1872, he defeated Horace Greeley, the Democratic and Liberal Republican candidate. The Panic of 1873 graft scandals close to the presidency created difficulties for his second term.

After retiring from office, Grant toured Europe for two years and returned in time to accede to a third-term boom, but was beaten in the convention of 1880. Illness and bad business judgment darkened his last years, but he worked steadily at the *Personal Memoirs,* which were to be successful when published after his death at Mount McGregor, near Saratoga, N.Y., on July 23, 1885.

RUTHERFORD BIRCHARD HAYES was born in Delaware, Ohio, on Oct. 4, 1822. A graduate of Kenyon College and the Harvard Law School, he practiced law in Lower Sandusky (now Fremont) and then in Cincinnati. In 1852 he married Lucy Webb. A Whig, he joined the Republican party in 1855. During the Civil War he rose to major general. He served in the House of Representatives from 1865 to 1867 and then confirmed a reputation for honesty and efficiency in two terms as Governor of Ohio (1868–72). His election to a third term in 1875 made him the logical candidate for those Republicans who wished to stop James G. Blaine in 1876, and he was nominated.

The result of the election was in doubt for some time and hinged upon disputed returns from South Carolina, Louisiana, Florida, and Oregon. Samuel J. Tilden, the Democrat, had the larger popular vote but was adjudged by the strictly partisan decisions of the Electoral Commission to have one fewer electoral vote, 185 to 184. The national acceptance of this result was due in part to the general understanding that Hayes would pursue a conciliatory policy toward the South. He withdrew the troops from the South, took a conservative position on financial and labor issues, and urged civil service reform.

Hayes served only one term by his own wish and spent the rest of his life in various humanitarian endeavors. He died in Fremont on Jan. 17, 1893.

JAMES ABRAM GARFIELD, the last president to be born in a log cabin, was born in Cuyahoga County, Ohio, on Nov. 19, 1831. A Williams graduate, he taught school for a time and entered Republican politics in Ohio. In 1858, he married Lucretia Rudolph. During the Civil War, he had a promising career, rising to major general of volunteers; but he resigned in 1863, having been elected to the House of Representatives, where he served until 1880. His oratorical and parliamentary abilities soon made him the leading Republican in the House, though his record was marred by his unorthodox acceptance of a fee in the DeGolyer paving contract case and by suspicions of his complicity in the Crédit Mobilier scandal.

In 1880, Garfield was elected to the Senate, but instead became the presidential candidate on the 36th ballot as a result of a deadlock in the Republican convention. In the election, he defeated Gen. Winfield Scott Hancock, the Democratic candidate. Garfield's administration was barely under way when he was shot by Charles J. Guiteau, a disappointed office seeker, in Washington on July 2, 1881. He died in Elberton, N.J., on Sept. 19.

CHESTER ALAN ARTHUR was born at Fairfield, Vt., on Oct. 5, 1830. A graduate of Union College, he became a successful New York lawyer. In 1859, he married Ellen Herndon. During the Civil War, he held administrative jobs in the Republican state administration and in 1871 was appointed collector of the Port of New York by Grant. This post gave him control over considerable patronage. Though not personally corrupt, Arthur managed his power in the interests of the New York machine so openly that President Hayes in 1877 called for an investigation and the next year Arthur was suspended.

In 1880 Arthur was nominated for vice president in the hope of conciliating the followers of Grant and the powerful New York machine. As president upon Garfield's death, Arthur, stepping out of his familiar role as spoilsman, backed civil service reform, reorganized the Cabinet, and prosecuted political associates accused of post office graft. Losing machine support and failing to gain the reformers, he was not nominated for a full term in 1884. He died in New York City on Nov. 18, 1886.

(STEPHEN) GROVER CLEVELAND was born at Caldwell, N.J., on March 18, 1837. He was admitted to the bar in Buffalo, N.Y., in 1859 and lived there as a lawyer, with occasional incursions into Democratic politics, for more than 20 years. He did not participate in the Civil War. As mayor of Buffalo in 1881, he carried through a reform program so ably that the Democrats ran him successfully for governor in 1882. In 1884 he won the Democratic nomination for president. The campaign contrasted Cleveland's spotless public career with the uncertain record of James G. Blaine, the Republican candidate, and Cleveland received enough Mugwump (independent Republican) support to win.

As president, Cleveland pushed civil service reform, opposed the pension grab and attacked the high tariff rates. While in the White House, he married Frances Folsom in 1886. Renominated in 1888, Cleveland was defeated by Benjamin Harrison, polling more popular but fewer electoral votes. In 1892, he was elected over Harrison. When the Panic of 1893 burst upon the country, Cleveland's attempts to solve it by sound-money measures alienated the free-silver wing of the party, while his tariff policy alienated the protectionists. In 1894, he sent troops to break the Pullman strike. In foreign affairs, his firmness caused Great Britain to back down in the Venezuela border dispute.

In his last years Cleveland was an active and much-respected public figure. He died in Princeton, N.J., on June 24, 1908.

BENJAMIN HARRISON was born in North Bend, Ohio, on Aug. 20, 1833, the grandson of William Henry Harrison, the ninth president. A graduate of Miami University in Ohio, he took up the law in Indiana and became active in Republican politics. In 1853, he married Caroline Lavinia Scott. During the Civil War, he rose to brigadier general. A sound-money Republican, he was elected senator from Indiana in 1880. In 1888, he received the Republican nomination for president on the eighth ballot. Though behind on the popular vote, he won over Grover Cleveland in the electoral college by 233 to 168.

As president, Harrison failed to please either the bosses or the reform element in the party. In foreign affairs he backed Secretary of State Blaine, whose policy foreshadowed later American imperialism. Harrison was renominated in 1892 but lost to Cleveland. His wife died in the White House in 1892 and Harrison married her niece, Mary Scott (Lord) Dimmick, in 1896. After his presidency, he resumed law practice. He died in Indianapolis on March 13, 1901.

WILLIAM McKINLEY was born in Niles, Ohio, on Jan. 29, 1843. He taught school, then served in the Civil War, rising from the ranks to become a major. Subsequently he opened a law office in Canton, Ohio, and in 1871 married Ida Saxton. Elected to Congress in 1876, he served there until 1891, except for 1883–85. His faithful advocacy of business interests culminated in the passage of the highly protective McKinley Tariff of 1890. With the support of Mark Hanna, a shrewd Cleveland businessman interested in safeguarding tariff protection, McKinley became governor of Ohio in 1892 and Republican presidential candidate in 1896. The business community, alarmed by the progressivism of William Jennings Bryan, the Democratic candidate, spent considerable money to assure McKinley's victory.

The chief event of McKinley's administration was the war with Spain, which resulted in the United States' acquisition of the Philippines and other islands. With imperialism an issue, McKinley defeated Bryan again in 1900. On Sept. 6, 1901, he was shot at Buffalo, N.Y., by Leon F. Czolgosz, an anarchist, and he died there eight days later.

THEODORE ROOSEVELT was born in New York City on Oct. 27, 1858. A Harvard graduate, he was early interested in ranching, in politics, and in writing picturesque historical narratives. He was a Republican member of the New York Assembly in 1882–84, an unsuccessful candidate for mayor of

New York in 1886, a U.S. Civil Service Commissioner under Benjamin Harrison, Police Commissioner of New York City in 1895, and Assistant Secretary of the Navy under McKinley in 1897. He resigned in 1898 to help organize a volunteer regiment, the Rough Riders, and take a more direct part in the war with Spain. He was elected governor of New York in 1898 and vice president in 1900, in spite of lack of enthusiasm on the part of the bosses.

Assuming the presidency of the assassinated McKinley in 1901, Roosevelt embarked on a wide-ranging program of government reform and conservation of natural resources. He ordered antitrust suits against several large corporations, threatened to intervene in the anthracite coal strike of 1902, which prompted the operators to accept arbitration, and, in general, championed the rights of the "little man" and fought the "malefactors of great wealth." He was also responsible for such progressive legislation as the Elkins Act of 1901, which outlawed freight rebates by railroads; the bill establishing the Department of Commerce and Labor; the Hepburn Act, which gave the I.C.C. greater control over the railroads; the Meat Inspection Act; and the Pure Food and Drug Act.

In foreign affairs, Roosevelt pursued a strong policy, permitting the instigation of a revolt in Panama to dispose of Colombian objections to the Panama Canal and helping to maintain the balance of power in the East by bringing the Russo-Japanese War to an end, for which he won the Nobel Peace Prize, the first American to achieve a Nobel prize in any category. In 1904, he decisively defeated Alton B. Parker, his conservative Democratic opponent.

Roosevelt's increasing coldness toward his successor, William Howard Taft, led him to overlook his earlier disclaimer of third-term ambitions and to re-enter politics. Defeated by the machine in the Republican convention of 1912, he organized the Progressive Party (Bull Moose) and polled more votes than Taft, though the split brought about the election of Woodrow Wilson. From 1915 on, Roosevelt strongly favored intervention in the European war. He became deeply embittered at Wilson's refusal to allow him to raise a volunteer division. He died in Oyster Bay, N.Y., on Jan. 6, 1919. He was married twice: in 1880 to Alice Hathaway Lee, who died in 1884, and in 1886 to Edith Kermit Carow.

WILLIAM HOWARD TAFT was born in Cincinnati on Sept. 15, 1857. A Yale graduate, he entered Ohio Republican politics in the 1880s. In 1886 he married Helen Herron. From 1887 to 1890, he served on the Ohio Superior Court; 1890–92, as solicitor general of the United States; 1892–1900, on the federal circuit court. In 1900 McKinley appointed him president of the Philippine Commission and in 1901 governor general. Taft had great success in pacifying the Filipinos, solving the problem of the church lands, improving economic conditions, and establishing limited self-government. His period as Secretary of War (1904–08) further demonstrated his capacity as administrator and conciliator, and he was Roosevelt's hand-picked successor in 1908. In the election, he polled 321 electoral votes to 162 for William Jennings Bryan, who was running for the presidency for the third time.

Though he carried on many of Roosevelt's policies, Taft got into increasing trouble with the progressive wing of the party and displayed mounting irritability and indecision. After his defeat in 1912, he became professor of constitutional law at Yale. In 1921 he was appointed Chief Justice of the United States Supreme Court. He died in Washington, D.C., on March 8, 1930.

(THOMAS) WOODROW WILSON was born in Staunton, Va., on Dec. 28, 1856. A Princeton graduate, he turned from law practice to post-graduate work in political science at Johns Hopkins University, receiving his Ph.D. in 1886. He taught at Bryn Mawr, Wesleyan, and Princeton, and in 1902 was made president of Princeton. After an unsuccessful attempt to democratize the social life of the university, he welcomed an invitation in 1910 to be the Democratic gubernatorial candidate in New Jersey, and was elected. His success in fighting the machine and putting through a reform program attracted national attention.

In 1912, at the Democratic convention in Baltimore, Wilson won the nomination on the 46th ballot and went on to defeat Roosevelt and Taft in the election. Wilson proceeded under the standard of the New Freedom to enact a program of domestic reform, including the Federal Reserve Act, the Clayton Antitrust Act, the establishment of the Federal Trade Commission, and other measures designed to restore competition in the face of the great monopolies. In foreign affairs, while privately sympathetic with the Allies, he strove to maintain neutrality in the European war and warned both sides against encroachments on American interests.

Re-elected in 1916 as a peace candidate, he tried to mediate between the warring nations; but when the Germans resumed unrestricted submarine warfare in 1917, Wilson brought the United States into what he now believed was a war to make the world safe for democracy. He supplied the classic formulations of Allied war aims and the armistice of Nov. 11, 1918 was negotiated on the basis of Wilson's Fourteen Points. In 1919 he strove at Versailles to lay the foundations for enduring peace. He accepted the imperfections of the Versailles Treaty in the expectation that they could be remedied by action within the League of Nations. He probably could have secured ratification of the treaty by the Senate if he had adopted a more conciliatory attitude toward the mild reservationists; but his insistence on all or nothing eventually caused the diehard isolationists and diehard Wilsonites to unite in rejecting a compromise.

In September 1919 Wilson suffered a paralytic stroke that limited his activity. After leaving the presidency he lived on in retirement in Washington, dying on Feb. 3, 1924. He was married twice—in 1885 to Ellen Louise Axson, who died in 1914, and in 1915 to Edith Bolling Galt.

WARREN GAMALIEL HARDING was born in Morrow County, Ohio, on Nov. 2, 1865. After attending Ohio Central College, Harding became interested in journalism and in 1884 bought the *Marion* (Ohio) *Star.* In 1891 he married a wealthy widow, Florence Kling De Wolfe. As his paper prospered, he entered Republican politics, serving as state senator (1899–1903) and as lieutenant governor (1904–06). In 1910, he was defeated for governor, but in 1914 was elected to the Senate. His reputation as an orator made him the keynoter at the 1916 Republican convention.

When the 1920 convention was deadlocked between Leonard Wood and Frank O. Lowden, Harding became the dark-horse nominee on his solemn affirmation that there was no reason in his past that he should not be. Straddling the League question, Harding was easily elected over James M. Cox, his Democratic opponent. His Cabinet contained some able men, but also some manifestly unfit for public office. Harding's own intimates were mediocre when they were not corrupt. The impending disclosure of the Teapot Dome scandal in the Interior Department and illegal practices in the Justice Department and Veterans' Bureau, as well as political setbacks, profoundly worried him. On his return from Alaska in 1923, he died unexpectedly in San Francisco on Aug. 2.

(JOHN) CALVIN COOLIDGE was born in Plymouth, Vt., on July 4, 1872. An Amherst graduate, he went into law practice at Northampton, Mass., in 1897. He married Grace Anna Goodhue in 1905. He entered Republican state politics, becoming successively mayor of Northampton, state senator, lieutenant governor and, in 1919, governor. His use of the state militia to end the Boston police strike in 1919 won him a somewhat undeserved reputation for decisive action and brought him the Republican vice-presidential nomination in 1920. After Harding's death Coolidge handled the Washington scandals with care and finally managed to save the Republican Party from public blame for the widespread corruption.

In 1924, Coolidge was elected without difficulty, defeating the Democrat, John W. Davis, and Robert M. La Follette running on the Progressive ticket. His second term, like his first, was characterized by a general satisfaction with the existing economic order. He stated that he did not choose to run in 1928.

After his presidency, Coolidge lived quietly in Northampton, writing an unilluminating autobiography and conducting a syndicated column. He died there on Jan. 5, 1933.

HERBERT CLARK HOOVER was born at West Branch, Iowa, on Aug. 10, 1874, the first president to be born west of the Mississippi. A Stanford graduate, he worked from 1895 to 1913 as a mining engineer and consultant throughout the world. In 1899, he married Lou Henry. During World War I, he served with distinction as chairman of the American Relief Committee in London, as chairman of the Commission for Relief in Belgium, and as U.S. Food Administrator. His political affiliations were still too indeterminate for him to be mentioned as a possibility for either the Republican or Democratic nomination in 1920, but after the election he served Harding and Coolidge as Secretary of Commerce.

In the election of 1928, Hoover overwhelmed Gov. Alfred E. Smith of New York, the Democratic candidate and the first Roman Catholic to run for the presidency. He soon faced the worst depression in the nation's history, but his attacks upon it were hampered by his devotion to the theory that the forces that brought the crisis would soon bring the revival and then by his belief that there were too many areas in which the federal government had no power to act. In a succession of vetoes, he struck down measures proposing a national employment system or national relief, he reduced income tax rates, and only at the end of his term did he yield to popular pressure and set up agencies such as the Reconstruction Finance Corporation to make emergency loans to assist business.

After his 1932 defeat, Hoover returned to private business. In 1946, President Truman charged him with various world food missions; and from 1947 to 1949 and 1953 to 1955, he was head of the Commission on Organization of the Executive Branch of the Government. He died in New York City on Oct. 20, 1964.

FRANKLIN DELANO ROOSEVELT was born in Hyde Park, N.Y., on Jan. 30, 1882. A Harvard graduate, he attended Columbia Law School and was admitted to the New York bar. In 1910, he was elected to the New York State Senate as a Democrat. Reelected in 1912, he was appointed Assistant Secretary of the Navy by Woodrow Wilson the next year. In 1920, his radiant personality and his war service resulted in his nomination for vice president as James M. Cox's running mate. After his defeat, he returned to law practice in New York. In August 1921, Roosevelt was stricken with infantile paralysis while on vacation at Campobello, New Brunswick. After a long and gallant fight, he recovered partial use of his legs. In 1924 and 1928, he led the fight at the Democratic national conventions for the nomination of Gov. Alfred E. Smith of New York, and in 1928 Roosevelt was himself induced to run for governor of New York. He was elected, and was reelected in 1930.

In 1932, Roosevelt received the Democratic nomination for president and immediately launched a campaign that brought new spirit to a weary and discouraged nation. He defeated Hoover by a wide margin. His first term was characterized by an unfolding of the New Deal program, with greater benefits for labor, the farmers, and the unemployed, and the progressive estrangement of most of the business community.

At an early stage, Roosevelt became aware of the menace to world peace posed by totalitarian fascism, and from 1937 on he tried to focus public attention on the trend of events in Europe and Asia. As a result, he was widely denounced as a warmonger. He was re-elected in 1936 over Gov. Alfred M. Landon of Kansas by the overwhelming electoral margin of 523 to 8, and the gathering international crisis prompted him to run for an unprecedented third term in 1940. He defeated Wendell L. Willkie.

Roosevelt's program to bring maximum aid to Britain and, after June 1941, to Russia was opposed, until the Japanese attack on Pearl Harbor restored national unity. During the war, Roosevelt shelved the New Deal in the interests of conciliating the business community, both in order to get full production during the war and to prepare the way for a united acceptance of the peace settlements after the war. A series of conferences with Winston Churchill and Joseph Stalin laid down the bases for the postwar world. In 1944 he was elected to a fourth term, running against Gov. Thomas E. Dewey of New York.

On April 12, 1945, Roosevelt died of a cerebral hemorrhage at Warm Springs, Ga., shortly after his return from the Yalta Conference. His wife, (Anna) Eleanor Roosevelt, whom he married in 1905, was a woman of great ability who made significant contributions to her husband's policies.

HARRY S. TRUMAN was born on a farm near Lamar, Mo., on May 8, 1884. During World War I, he served in France as a captain with the 129th Field Artillery. He married Bess Wallace in 1919. After engaging briefly and unsuccessfully in the haberdashery business in Kansas City, Mo., Truman entered local politics. Under the sponsorship of Thomas Pendergast, Democratic boss of Missouri, he held a number of local offices, preserving his personal honesty in the midst of a notoriously corrupt political machine. In 1934, he was elected to the Senate and was re-elected in 1940. During his first term he was a loyal but quiet supporter of the New Deal, but in his second term, an appointment as head of a Senate committee to investigate war production brought out his special qualities of honesty, common sense, and hard work, and he won widespread respect.

Elected vice president in 1944, Truman became president upon Roosevelt's sudden death in April 1945 and was immediately faced with the problems of winding down the war against the Axis and preparing the nation for postwar adjustment.

The years 1947–48 were distinguished by civil-rights proposals, the Truman Doctrine to contain the spread of Communism, and the Marshall Plan to aid in the economic reconstruction of war-ravaged nations. Truman's general record, highlighted by a vigorous Fair Deal campaign, brought about his unexpected election in 1948 over the heavily favored Thomas E. Dewey.

Truman's second term was primarily concerned with the Cold War with the Soviet Union, the implementing of the North Atlantic Pact, the United Nations police action in Korea, and the vast rearmament program with its accompanying problems of economic stabilization.

On March 29, 1952, Truman announced that he would not run again for the presidency. After leaving the White House, he returned to his home in Independence, Mo., to write his memoirs. He further busied himself with the Harry S. Truman Library there. He died in Kansas City, Mo., on Dec. 26, 1972.

DWIGHT DAVID EISENHOWER was born in Denison, Tex., on Oct. 14, 1890. His ancestors lived in Germany and emigrated to America, settling in Pennsylvania, early in the 18th century. His father, David, had a general store in Hope, Kans., which failed. After a brief time in Texas, the family moved to Abilene, Kan.

After graduating from Abilene High School in 1909, Eisenhower did odd jobs for almost two years. He won an appointment to the Naval Academy at Annapolis, but was too old for admittance. Then he received an appointment in 1910 to West Point, from which he graduated as a second lieutenant in 1915.

He did not see service in World War I, having been stationed at Fort Sam Houston, Tex. There he met Mamie Geneva Doud, whom he married in Denver on July 1, 1916, and by whom he had two sons: Doud Dwight (died in infancy) and John Sheldon Doud.

Eisenhower served in the Philippines from 1935 to 1939 with Gen. Douglas MacArthur. Afterward, Gen. George C. Marshall, the Army Chief of Staff, brought him into the War Department's General Staff and in 1942 placed him in command of the invasion of North Africa. In 1944, he was made Supreme Allied Commander for the invasion of Europe.

After the war, Eisenhower served as Army Chief of Staff from November 1945 until February 1948, when he was appointed president of Columbia University.

In December 1950, President Truman recalled Eisenhower to active duty to command the North Atlantic Treaty Organization forces in Europe. He held his post until the end of May 1952.

At the Republican convention of 1952 in Chicago, Eisenhower won the presidential nomination on the first ballot in a close race with Senator Robert A. Taft of Ohio. In the election, he defeated Gov. Adlai E. Stevenson of Illinois.

Through two terms, Eisenhower hewed to moderate domestic policies. He sought peace through Free World strength in an era of new nationalisms, nuclear missiles, and space exploration. He fostered alliances pledging the United States to resist "Red" aggression in Europe, Asia, and Latin America. The Eisenhower Doctrine of 1957 extended commitments to the Middle East.

At home, the popular president lacked Republican Congressional majorities after 1954, but he was re-elected in 1956 by 457 electoral votes to 73 for Stevenson.

While retaining most Fair Deal programs, he stressed "fiscal responsibility" in domestic affairs. A moderate in civil rights, he sent troops to Little Rock, Ark., to enforce court-ordered school integration.

With his wartime rank restored by Congress, Eisenhower returned to private life and the role of elder statesman, with his vigor hardly impaired by a heart attack, an ileitis operation, and a mild stroke suffered while in office. He died in Washington, D.C., on March 28, 1969.

JOHN FITZGERALD KENNEDY was born in Brookline, Mass., on May 29, 1917. His father, Joseph P. Kennedy, was Ambassador to Great Britain from 1937 to 1940.

Kennedy was graduated from Harvard University in 1940 and joined the Navy the next year. He became skipper of a PT boat that was sunk in the Pacific by a Japanese destroyer. Although given up for lost, he swam to a safe island, towing an injured enlisted man.

After recovering from a war-aggravated spinal injury, Kennedy entered politics in 1946 and was elected to Congress. In 1952, he ran against Senator Henry Cabot Lodge, Jr., of Massachusetts, and won.

Kennedy was married on Sept. 12, 1953, to Jacqueline Lee Bouvier, by whom he had three children: Caroline, John Fitzgerald, Jr. (died in a 1999 plane crash), and Patrick Bouvier (died in infancy). In 1957 Kennedy won the Pulitzer Prize for a book he had written earlier, *Profiles in Courage*.

After strenuous primary battles, Kennedy won the Democratic presidential nomination on the first ballot at the 1960 Los Angeles convention. With a plurality of only 118,574 votes, he carried the election over Vice President Richard M. Nixon and became the first Roman Catholic president.

Kennedy brought to the White House the dynamic idea of a "New Frontier" approach in dealing with problems at home, abroad, and in the dimensions of space. Out of his leadership in his first few months in office came the 10-year Alliance for Progress to aid Latin America, the Peace Corps, and accelerated programs that brought the first Americans into orbit in the race in space.

Failure of the U.S.-supported Cuban invasion in April 1961 led to the entrenchment of the Communist-backed Castro regime, only 90 miles from United States soil. When it became known that Soviet offensive missiles were being installed in Cuba in 1962, Kennedy ordered a naval "quarantine" of the island and moved troops into position to eliminate this threat to U.S. security. The world seemed on the brink of a nuclear war until Soviet Premier Khrushchev ordered the removal of the missiles.

A sudden "thaw," or the appearance of one, in the cold war came with the agreement with the Soviet Union on a limited test-ban treaty signed in Moscow on Aug. 6, 1963.

In his domestic policies, Kennedy's proposals for medical care for the aged and aid to education were defeated, but on minimum wage, trade legislation, and other measures he won important victories.

Widespread racial disorders and demonstrations led to Kennedy's proposing sweeping civil rights legislation. As his third year in office drew to a close, he also recommended an $11-billion tax cut to bolster the economy. Both measures were pending in Congress when Kennedy, looking forward to a second term, journeyed to Texas for a series of speeches.

While riding in an automobile procession in Dallas on Nov. 22, 1963, he was shot to death by an assassin firing from an upper floor of a building. The alleged assassin, Lee Harvey Oswald, was killed two days later in the Dallas city jail by Jack Ruby, owner of a strip-tease place.

At 46 years of age, Kennedy became the fourth president to be assassinated and the eighth to die in office.

LYNDON BAINES JOHNSON was born in Stonewall, Tex., on Aug. 27, 1908. On both sides of his family he had a political heritage mingled with a Baptist background of preachers and teachers. Both his father and his paternal grandfather served in the Texas House of Representatives.

After his graduation from Southwest Texas State Teachers College, Johnson taught school for two years. He went to Washington in 1932 as secretary to Rep. Richard M. Kleberg. During this time, he married Claudia Alta Taylor, known as "Lady Bird." They had two children: Lynda Bird and Luci Baines.

In 1935, Johnson became Texas administrator for the National Youth Administration. Two years later, he was elected to Congress as an all-out supporter of Franklin D. Roosevelt, and served until 1949. He was the first member of Congress to enlist in the armed forces after the attack on Pearl Harbor. He served in the Navy in the Pacific and won a Silver Star.

Johnson was elected to the Senate in 1948 after he had captured the Democratic nomination by only 87 votes. He was 40 years old. He became the Senate Democratic leader in 1953. A heart attack in 1955 threatened to end his political career, but he recovered fully and resumed his duties.

At the height of his power as Senate leader, Johnson sought the Democratic nomination for president in 1960. When he lost to John F. Kennedy, he surprised even some of his closest associates by accepting second place on the ticket.

Johnson was riding in another car in the motorcade when Kennedy was assassinated in Dallas on Nov. 22, 1963. He took the oath of office in the presidential jet on the Dallas airfield.

With Johnson's insistent backing, Congress finally adopted a far-reaching civil-rights bill, a voting-rights bill, a Medicare program for the aged, and measures to improve education and conservation. Congress also began what Johnson described as "an all-out war" on poverty.

Amassing a record-breaking majority of nearly 16 million votes, Johnson was elected president in his own right in 1964, defeating Senator Barry Goldwater of Arizona.

The double tragedy of a war in Southeast Asia and urban riots at home marked Johnson's last two years in office. Faced with disunity in the nation and challenges within his own party, Johnson surprised the country on March 31, 1968, with the announcement that he would not be a candidate for re-election. He died of a heart attack suffered at his LBJ Ranch on Jan. 22, 1973.

RICHARD MILHOUS NIXON was born in Yorba Linda, Calif., on Jan. 9, 1913, to Midwestern-bred parents, Francis A. and Hannah Milhous Nixon, who raised their five sons as Quakers.

Nixon was a high school debater and was undergraduate president at Whittier College in California, where he was graduated in 1934. As a scholarship student at Duke University Law School in North Carolina, he graduated third in his class in 1937.

After five years as a lawyer, Nixon joined the Navy in August 1942. He was an air transport officer in the South Pacific and a legal officer stateside before his discharge in 1946 as a lieutenant commander.

Running for Congress in California as a Republican in 1946, Nixon defeated Rep. Jerry Voorhis. As a member of the House Un-American Activities Committee, he made a name as an investigator of Alger Hiss, a former high State Department official, who was later jailed for perjury. In 1950, Nixon defeated Rep. Helen Gahagan Douglas, a Democrat, for the Senate. He was criticized for portraying her as a Communist dupe.

Nixon's anti-Communism ideals, his Western roots, and his youth figured into his selection in 1952 to run for vice president on the ticket headed by Dwight D. Eisenhower. Demands for Nixon's withdrawal followed disclosure that California businessmen had paid some of his Senate office expenses. His televised rebuttal, known as "the Checkers speech" (named for a cocker spaniel given to the Nixons), brought him support from the public and from Eisenhower. The ticket won easily in 1952 and again in 1956.

Eisenhower gave Nixon substantive assignments, including missions to 56 countries. In Moscow in 1959, Nixon won acclaim for his defense of U.S. interests in an impromptu "kitchen debate" with Soviet Premier Nikita S. Khrushchev.

Nixon lost the 1960 race for the presidency to John F. Kennedy.

In 1962, Nixon failed in a bid for California's governorship and seemed to be finished as a national candidate. He became a Wall Street lawyer, but kept his old party ties and developed new ones through constant travels to speak for Republicans.

Nixon won the 1968 Republican presidential nomination after a shrewd primary campaign, then made Gov. Spiro T. Agnew of Maryland his surprise choice for vice president. In the election, they edged out the Democratic ticket headed by Vice President Hubert H. Humphrey by 510,314 votes out of 73,212,065 cast.

Committed to winding down the U.S. role in the Vietnamese War, Nixon pursued "Vietnamization"—training and equipping South Vietnamese to do their own fighting. American ground combat forces in Vietnam fell steadily from 540,000 when Nixon took office to none in 1973 when the military draft was ended. But there was heavy continuing use of U.S. air power.

Nixon improved relations with Moscow and reopened the long-closed door to mainland China with a good-will trip there in February 1972. In May of that year, he visited Moscow and signed agreements on arms limitation and trade expansion and approved plans for a joint U.S.–Soviet space mission in 1975.

Inflation was a campaign issue for Nixon, but he failed to master it as president. On Aug. 15, 1971, with unemployment edging up, Nixon abruptly announced a new economic policy: a 90-day wage-price freeze, stimulative tax cuts, a temporary 10% tariff, and spending cuts. A second phase, imposing guidelines on wage, price, and rent boosts, was announced October 7.

The economy responded in time for the 1972 campaign, in which Nixon played up his foreign-policy achievements. Played down was the burglary on June 17, 1972, of Democratic national headquarters in the Watergate apartment complex in Washington. The Nixon–Agnew re-election campaign cost a record $60 million and swamped the Democratic ticket headed by Senator George McGovern of South Dakota with a plurality of 17,999,528 out of 77,718,554 votes. Only Massachusetts, with 14 electoral votes, and the District of Columbia, with 3, went for McGovern.

In January 1973, hints of a cover-up emerged at the trial of six men found guilty of the Watergate burglary. With a Senate investigation under way, Nixon announced on April 30 the resignations of his top aides, H. R. Haldeman and John D. Ehrlichman, and the dismissal of White House counsel John Dean III. Dean was the star witness at televised Senate hearings that exposed both a White House cover-up of Watergate and massive illegalities in Republican fund-raising in 1972.

The hearings also disclosed that Nixon had routinely tape-recorded his office meetings and telephone conversations.

On Oct. 10, 1973, Agnew resigned as vice president, then pleaded no-contest to a negotiated federal charge of evading income taxes on alleged bribes. Two days later, Nixon nominated the House minority leader, Rep. Gerald R. Ford of Michigan, as the new vice president. Congress confirmed Ford on Dec. 6, 1973.

In June 1974, Nixon visited Israel and four Arab nations. Then he met in Moscow with Soviet leader Leonid I. Brezhnev and reached preliminary nuclear arms limitation agreements.

But, in the month after his return, Watergate ended the Nixon regime. On July 24 the Supreme Court ordered Nixon to surrender subpoenaed tapes. On July 30 the Judiciary Committee referred three impeachment articles to the full membership. On August 5, Nixon bowed to the Supreme Court and released tapes showing he halted an FBI probe of the Watergate burglary six days after it occurred. It was in effect an admission of obstruction of justice, and impeachment appeared inevitable.

Nixon resigned on Aug. 9, 1974, the first president ever to do so. A month later, President Ford issued an unconditional pardon for any offenses Nixon might have committed as president, thus forestalling possible prosecution.

In 1940, Nixon married Thelma Catherine (Pat) Ryan. They had two daughters, Patricia (Tricia) and Julie, who married Dwight David Eisenhower II, grandson of the former president.

He died on April 22, 1994, in New York City of a massive stroke.

GERALD RUDOLPH FORD was born Leslie King Jr. in Omaha, Neb., on July 14, 1913, the only child of Leslie and Dorothy Gardner King. His parents were divorced in 1915. His mother moved to Grand Rapids, Mich., and married Gerald R. Ford. The boy was renamed for his stepfather.

Ford captained his high school football team in Grand Rapids, and a football scholarship took him to the University of Michigan, where he starred as varsity center before his graduation in 1935. A job as assistant football coach at Yale gave him an opportunity to attend Yale Law School, from which he graduated in the top third of his class in 1941.

He returned to Grand Rapids to practice law, but entered the Navy in April 1942. He saw wartime service in the Pacific on the light aircraft carrier *Monterey* and was a lieutenant commander when he returned to Grand Rapids early in 1946 to resume law practice and dabble in politics.

Ford was elected to Congress in 1948 for the first of his 13 terms in the House. He was soon assigned to the influential Appropriations Committee and rose to become the ranking Republican on the subcommittee on Defense Department appropriations.

As a legislator, Ford described himself as "a moderate on domestic issues, a conservative in fiscal affairs, and a dyed-in-the-wool internationalist." He carried the ball for Pentagon appropriations, was a hawk on the war in Vietnam, and kept a low profile on civil-rights issues.

Ford was also dependable and hard-working and popular with his colleagues. In 1963, he was elected chairman of the House Republican Conference. He served in 1963-1964 as a member of the Warren Commission, which investigated the assassination of John F. Kennedy. A revolt by dissatisfied younger Republicans in 1965 made him minority leader.

Ford shelved his hopes for the speakership on Oct. 12, 1973, when Nixon nominated him to fill the vice presidency left vacant by Agnew's resignation under it. It was the first use of the procedures for filling vacancies in the vice presidency laid down in the 25th Amendment to the Constitution, which Ford had helped enact.

Congress confirmed Ford as vice president on Dec. 6, 1973. Once in office, he said he did not believe Nixon had been involved in the Watergate scandals, but criticized his stubborn court battle against releasing tape recordings of Watergate-related conversations for use as evidence.

The scandals led to Nixon's unprecedented resignation on Aug. 9, 1974, and Ford was sworn in immediately as the 38th president, the first to enter the White House without winning a national election.

Ford assured the nation when he took office that "our long national nightmare is over" and pledged "openness and candor" in all his actions. He won a warm response from the Democratic 93rd Congress when he said he wanted "a good marriage" rather than a honeymoon with his former colleagues. In December 1974 Congressional majorities backed his choice of former New York Gov. Nelson A. Rockefeller as his successor in the again-vacant vice presidency.

The cordiality was chilled by Ford's announcement on Sept. 8, 1974, that he had granted an unconditional pardon to Nixon for any crimes he might have committed as president. Although no formal charges were pending, Ford said he feared "ugly passions" would be aroused if Nixon were brought to trial. The pardon was widely criticized.

To fight inflation, the new president first proposed fiscal restraints and spending curbs and a 5% tax surcharge that got nowhere in the Senate and House. Congress again rebuffed Ford in the spring of 1975 when he appealed for emergency military aid to help the governments of South Vietnam and Cambodia resist massive Communist offensives.

In November 1974, Ford visited Japan, South Korea, and the Soviet Union, where he and Soviet leader Leonid I. Brezhnev conferred in Vladivostok and reached a tentative agreement to limit the number of strategic offensive nuclear weapons. It was Ford's first meeting as president with Brezhnev, who planned a return visit to Washington in the fall of 1975.

Politically, Ford's fortunes improved steadily in the first half of 1975. Badly divided Democrats in Congress were unable to muster votes to override his vetoes of spending bills that exceeded his budget. He faced some right-wing opposition in his own party, but moved to pre-empt it with an early announcement—on July 8, 1975—of his intention to be a candidate in 1976.

Early state primaries in 1976 suggested an easy victory for Ford despite Ronald Reagan's bitter attacks on administration foreign policy and defense programs. But later Reagan primary successes threatened the President's lead. At the Kansas City convention, Ford was nominated by the narrow margin of 1,187 to 1,070. But Reagan had moved the party to the right, and Ford himself was regarded as a caretaker president lacking in strength and vision. He was defeated in November by Jimmy Carter.

In 1948, Ford married Elizabeth Anne (Betty) Bloomer. They had four children, Michael Gerald, John Gardner, Steven Meigs, and Susan Elizabeth.

JAMES EARL CARTER, JR., was born in the tiny village of Plains, Ga., Oct. 1, 1924, and grew up on the family farm at nearby Archery. Both parents were fifth-generation Georgians. His father, James Earl Carter, was known as a segregationist, but treated his black and white workers equally. Carter's mother, Lillian Gordy, was a matriarchal presence in home and community and opposed the then-prevailing code of racial inequality. The future president was baptized in 1935 in the conservative Southern Baptist Church and spoke often of being a "born again" Christian, although committed to the separation of church and state.

Carter married Rosalynn Smith, a neighbor, in 1946. Their first child, John William, was born a year later in Portsmouth, Va. Their other children are James Earl III, born in Honolulu in 1950; Donnel Jeffrey, born in New London, Conn., in 1952; and Amy Lynn, born in Plains in 1967.

In 1946 Carter was graduated from the U.S. Naval Academy at Annapolis and served in the nuclear-submarine program under Adm. Hyman G. Rickover. In 1954, after his father's death, he resigned from the Navy to take over the family's flourishing warehouse and cotton gin, with several thousand acres for growing seed peanuts.

Carter was elected to the Georgia Senate in 1962. In 1966 he lost the race for Governor, but was elected in 1970. His term brought a state government reorganization, sharply reduced agencies, increased economy and efficiency, and new social programs, all with no general tax increase. In 1972 the peanut farmer–politician set his sights on the presidency and in 1973 built a base for himself as he criss-crossed the country as chairman of the Democratic Campaign Committee, appealing for revival and reform. In 1975 his image as a typical Southern white was erased when he won support of most of the old Southern civil-rights coalition after endorsement by Rep. Andrew Young, black Democrat from Atlanta, who had been the closest aide to the Rev. Martin Luther King, Jr. At Carter's 1971 inauguration as Governor he had called for an end to all forms of racial discrimination.

In the 1976 spring primaries, he won 19 out of 31 with a broad appeal to conservatives and liberals, black and white, poor and well-to-do. Throughout his campaigning Carter set forth his policies in his soft Southern voice, and with his electric-blue stare faced down skeptics who joked about "Jimmy Who?" He defeated Gerald R. Ford in Nov. 1976. Likewise, in 1980 he was renominated on the first ballot after vanquishing Senator Edward M. Kennedy of Massachusetts in the primaries. In the election campaign, Carter attacked his rivals, Ronald Reagan and John B. Anderson, independent, with the warning that a Reagan Republican victory would heighten the risk of war and impede civil rights and economic opportunity. In November Carter lost to Reagan, who won 489 Electoral College votes and 51% of the popular tally, to 49 electoral votes and 41% for Carter.

In his one term, Carter fought hard for his programs against resistance from an independent-minded Democratic Congress that frustrated many pet projects although it overrode only two vetoes. Observers generally viewed public dissatisfaction with the "stagflation" economy as a principal factor in his defeat. Others included his jittery performance in the debate Oct. 28 with Reagan, staff problems, friction with Congress, long gasoline lines, and the months-long Iranian crisis, including the abortive sally in April 1980 to free the hostages. Yet, assessments of his record noted many positive elements. There was, for one thing, peace throughout his term, with no American combat deaths and with a brake on the advocates of force. Regarded as perhaps his greatest personal achievements were the Camp David accords between Israel and Egypt and the resulting treaty—the first between Israel and an Arab neighbor. The treaty with China and the Panama Canal treaties were also major achievements. Carter worked for nuclear-arms control. His concern for international human rights was credited with saving lives and reducing torture, and he supported the British policy that ended internecine warfare in Rhodesia, now Zimbabwe. Domestically, his environmental record was a major accomplishment. His judicial appointments won acclaim; the Southerner who had forsworn racism made 265 choices for the Federal bench that included minority members and women. He also ended the U.S. practice of holding petroleum prices far below world levels with price decontrols.

RONALD WILSON REAGAN rode to the presidency in 1980 on a tide of resurgent right-wing sentiment among an electorate battered by winds of unwanted change, longing for a distant, simpler era.

He left office in Jan. 1989 with two-thirds of the American people approving his performance during his two terms. It was the highest rating for any retiring president since World War II.

His place in history will rest, perhaps, on the short- and intermediate-range missile treaty consummated on a cordial visit to the Soviet Union that he had once reviled as an "evil empire." Its provisions, including a ground-breaking agreement on verification inspection, were formulated in four days of summit talks in. Moscow in May 1988 with the Soviet leader, Mikhail S. Gorbachev.

Reagan can point to numerous domestic achievements as well: sharp cuts in income tax rates, sweeping tax reform, creating economic growth without inflation, and reducing the unemployment rate, among others. He failed, however, to win the "Reagan Revolution" on such issues as abortion and school prayer, and he seemed aloof from "sleazy" conduct by some top officials.

In his final months Reagan campaigned aggressively to win election as president for his two-term vice president, George Bush.

Reagan's popularity with the public dipped sharply in 1986 when the Iran-Contra scandal broke, shortly after the Democrats gained control of the Senate. Observers agreed that Reagan's presidency had been weakened, if temporarily, by the two unrelated events. Then the weeks-long Congressional hearings in the summer of 1987 heard an array of Administration officials, present and former, tell their tales of a White House riven by deceit and undercover maneuvering. Yet no breath of illegality touched the President's personal reputation; on Aug. 12, 1987, he told the nation that he had not known of questionable activities but agreed that he was "ultimately accountable."

Ronald Reagan, actor turned politician, New Dealer turned conservative, came to films and politics from a thoroughly Middle-American background—middle class, Middle West, and small town. He was born in Tampico, Ill., Feb. 6, 1911, the second son of John Edward Reagan and Nelle Wilson Reagan, and the family later moved to Dixon, Ill. The father, of Irish descent, was a shop clerk and merchant with Democratic sympathies. It was an impoverished family; young Ronald sold homemade popcorn at high school games and worked as a lifeguard to earn money for his college tuition. When the father got a New Deal WPA job, the future president became an ardent Roosevelt Democrat.

Reagan won a B.A. degree in 1932 from Eureka (Ill.) College, where a photographic memory aided in his studies and in debating and college theatricals. In a Depression year, he was making $100 a week as a sports announcer for radio station WHO in Des Moines, Iowa, from 1932 to 1937. His career as a film and TV actor stretched from 1937 to 1966, and his salary climbed to $3,500 a week. As a World War II captain in Army film studios, Reagan recoiled from what he saw as the laziness of Civil Service workers, and moved to the Right. As president of the Screen Actors Guild, he resisted what he considered a Communist plot to subvert the film industry. With advancing age, Reagan left leading-man roles and became a television spokesman for the General Electric Company.

With oratorical skill his trademark, Reagan became an active Republican. At the behest of a small group of conservative Southern California businessmen, he ran for governor with a pledge to cut spending, and was elected by almost a million votes over the political veteran, Democratic Gov. Edmund G. Brown, father of later governor Jerry Brown.

In the 1980 election battle against Jimmy Carter, Reagan broadened his appeal by espousing moderate policies, gaining much of his support from disaffected Democrats and blue-collar workers. The incoming Administration immediately set out to "turn the government around" with a new economic program. Over strenuous Congressional opposition, Reagan triumphed on his "supply side" theory to stimulate production and control inflation through tax cuts and sharp reductions in government spending.

The president won high acclaim for his nomination of Sandra Day O'Connor as the first woman on the Supreme Court. His later nominations met increasing opposition but did much to tilt the Court's orientation to the Right.

In 1982, the President's popularity had slipped as the economy declined into the worst recession in 40 years, with persistent high unemployment and interest rates. Initial support for "supply side" economics faded but the President won crucial battles in Congress.

Internationally, Reagan confronted numerous critical problems in his first term. The successful invasion of Grenada accomplished much diplomatically. But the intervention in Lebanon and the withdrawal of Marines after a disastrous terrorist attack were regarded as military failures.

The popular president won reelection in the 1984 landslide, with the economy improving and inflation under control. Domestically, a tax reform bill that Reagan backed became law. But the constantly growing budget deficit remained a constant irritant, with the President and Congress persistently at odds over priorities in spending for defense and domestic programs. His foreign policy met stiffening opposition, with Congress increasingly reluctant to increase spending for the Nicaraguan "Contras" and the Pentagon and to expand the development of the MX missile. But even severe critics praised Reagan's restrained but decisive handling of the crisis following the hijacking of an American plane in Beirut by Muslim extremists. The attack on Libya in April 1986 galvanized the nation, although it drew scathing disapproval from the NATO alliance.

Barely three months into his first term, Reagan was the target of an assassin's bullet; his courageous comeback won public admiration.

Reagan is devoted to his wife, Nancy, whom he married after his divorce from the screen actress Jane Wyman. The children from his first marriage are Maureen, his daughter by Wyman, and Michael, an adopted son. He had two children by Nancy: Patricia and Ron. Reagan continues to struggle with Alzheimer's disease, which he developed in the years following his presidency.

GEORGE HERBERT WALKER BUSH was born June 12, 1924, in Milton, Mass., to Prescott and Dorothy Bush. The family later moved to Connecticut. The youth studied at the elite Phillips Academy in Andover, Mass.

The future president joined the Navy after war broke out and at 18 became the Navy's youngest commissioned pilot, serving from 1942 to 1945. The man later derided by some as a "wimp" fought the Japanese on 58 missions and was shot down once. He won the Distinguished Flying Cross.

After the war, Bush earned an economics degree and a Phi Beta Kappa key in two and a half years at Yale University. While there he captained the baseball team and was initiated into "Skull and Bones," the prestigious Yale secret society.

In 1945 Bush married Barbara Pierce of Rye, N.Y., daughter of a magazine publisher. With his bride, Bush moved to Texas instead of entering his father's investment banking business. There he founded his oil company and by 1980 reported an estimated wealth of $1.4 million.

Throughout his whole career, Bush had the backing of an established family, headed by his father, Prescott Bush, who was elected to the Senate from Connecticut in 1952. The family helped the young patrician become established in his early business ventures, a rich uncle raising most of the capital required for founding the oil company.

In the 1960s, Bush won two contests for a Texas Republican seat in the House of Representatives, but lost two bids for a Senate seat and one for the presidency. After Bush's second race for the Senate, President Nixon appointed him U.S. delegate to the United Nations with the rank of Ambassador and he later became Republican National Chairman. He headed the United States liaison office in Beijing before becoming Director of Central Intelligence.

In 1980 Bush became Reagan's running mate despite earlier criticism of Reagan "voodoo economics" and by the 1984 election had won acclaim for devotion to Reagan's conservative agenda despite his own reputation as somewhat more liberally inclined. Nevertheless, die-hard right-wingers could find satisfaction in Bush's war record and his government service, particularly with the C.I.A. Throughout he remained influential in White House decisions, particularly in foreign affairs.

In the 1988 campaign, Bush's choice of Senator Dan Quayle of Indiana for vice president surprised his friends and provoked criticism and ridicule that continued even after the Administration was established in office. Nonetheless Bush strongly defended his choice.

George Herbert Walker Bush became president on Jan. 20, 1989, with his theme harmony and conciliation after the often-turbulent Reagan years. With his calm and unassuming manner, he emerged from his subordinate vice-presidential role with an air of quiet authority. His Inaugural address emphasized "A new breeze is blowing, and the old bipartisanship must be made new again."

In his first months, the president, the nation's 41st, established himself as his own man and all but erased memories of what many had regarded as his fiercely abrasive presidential election campaign of 1988 and questionable tactics against his Democratic opponent. People liked his easy style and readiness to compromise even as he remained a staunch conservative, although that readiness had disconcerted some conservatives.

Bush's early Cabinet choices reflected a pragmatic desire for an efficient, nonideological government. And with his usual cautious instinct, in 1990 he nominated to the Supreme Court the scholarly David H. Souter, with broadly conservative views. Souter was confirmed without a bruising battle.

In his first year, Bush, a World War II hero, had won plaudits at home and abroad for his confident, competent conduct at the NATO 40th anniversary summit meeting in Brussels, the Paris economic conference, on his tour of Eastern Europe, and at the Malta conference with Gorbachev. Grave challenges in that year were the Lebanese hostage crisis and the ongoing war against drug trafficking.

Domestically, Bush had to cope with such issues as the *Exxon Valdez* oil spill in Alaska and the dispute over flag-burning restrictions, which was resolved, if only for a time, in mid-1990.

But in his second year, 1990, the president confronted a mounting array of problems, chief among them the staggering budget deficit and the savings and loan crisis. The president's popularity dipped sharply from its near-record public approval following the invasion of Panama in late 1989. This plunge followed Bush's recantation of his campaign "no new taxes" pledge as he sat down with Congressional leaders to tame the budget deficit and deal with a faltering economy.

In 1991, the 67-year-old president emerged as the leader of an international coalition of Western democracies, Japan, and even some Arab states that freed invaded Kuwait and vanquished, at least for a time, Iraq's President Saddam Hussein and his armies.

A nation grateful at feeling the end of the "Vietnam syndrome" gave the president an overall rating of 89 percent in a Gallup poll in March after the end of the war. The approval rate fell as the year went on, but a solid majority continued to approve the president's performance, although with growing concern about the faltering economy and other domestic problems. And there were nagging doubts about the Persian Gulf war, its motives and conduct, and about the ensuing refugee crisis.

A major Bush accomplishment in 1991 was the Strategic Arms Reduction Treaty (START), signed in July with Soviet president Mikhail S. Gorbachev at their fourth summit conference, marking the end of the long weapons buildup. Succeeding events in the Soviet Union and the disintegration of the Communist empire could only enhance his status.

The year also saw the president undergoing treatment for Graves' disease, a thyroid disorder, from which he suffered serious side effects.

In the 1992 presidential election, Bush was defeated by Gov. Bill Clinton of Arkansas.

The Bushes have lived in 17 cities and more than a score of homes and have traveled in as many countries. In her husband's frequent absences during the early years, Mrs. Bush was matriarch of a family of four boys (George, Jeb, Neil, and Marvin) and a girl (Dorothy).

After the Clinton inauguration in January, the Bushes returned to Houston, Texas.

WILLIAM JEFFERSON CLINTON was born William Jefferson Blythe III in Hope, Ark., on Aug. 19, 1946. He was named for his father, who was killed in an automobile accident before Clinton's birth. Virginia Kelley, his mother, eventually married Roger Clinton, a car dealer, whose surname the future president later adopted.

In high school in Hot Springs, Ark., Clinton considered becoming a doctor, but politics beckoned after a meeting with President John F. Kennedy in Washington, D.C., on a Boys' Nation trip. He earned a B.S. in international affairs in 1968 at Georgetown University, having spent his junior year working for Arkansas Senator J. William Fulbright. He was a Rhodes scholar at Oxford between 1968 and 1970. He then attended Yale Law School, where he met his future wife, Hillary Rodham, a Wellesley graduate. The couple has one child, Chelsea.

Clinton taught at the University of Arkansas (1974–1976), was elected state attorney general (1976), and in 1979 became the nation's youngest governor. But he was defeated for reelection in 1980 by voters irate at a rise in the state's automobile license fees. In 1982 he was elected again. This time he reined in liberal tendencies to accommodate the conservative bent of the voters.

Clinton became the 42nd U.S. president following a turbulent political campaign. He overcame vigorous personal attacks on his character and on his actions during the Vietnam War, which he actively opposed. The "character issue" stemmed from allegations of infidelity, which Clinton refuted in a television interview in which he and Hillary avowed their relationship was solid. Throughout his term in office, Clinton was dogged by allegations relating to the Whitewater real estate deal in which he and Hillary were involved prior to the 1992 election. Though the Clintons were never accused of any wrongdoing, partners in the venture were convicted of fraud and conspiracy in a trial in 1996.

The problems faced by the new president were as daunting as they were varied. In January 1993 he became embroiled with the military leadership over his campaign pledge to allow homosexuals to serve openly in the armed services. He ultimately agreed to a compromise, dubbed the "don't ask, don't tell" policy. Clinton's first year also saw him wrangling with Congress over the Federal budget and economic policy.

In his second year, Clinton faced persistent troubles on the domestic front, with acrimonious battles raging over health care, welfare reform, and crime prevention. A health care reform package crafted by his wife failed to gain sufficient support. Clinton had to reduce his objective from massive overhaul to incremental reform.

Clinton won major victories with the passage of the North American Free Trade Agreement (NAFTA), which took effect Jan. 1, 1994, and the Global Agreement on Tariffs and Trade (GATT), which led to the establishment in 1995 of the World Trade Organization (WTO). Congress also approved a deficit reduction bill, rules allowing abortion counseling in federally funded clinics, a waiting period for handgun purchases (the Brady Bill), and a national service program.

Foreign affairs, once a weak point for a man elected on a domestic economic agenda, became a proving ground for Clinton. He improved his international image when the Israel–Jordan peace agreement was signed at the White House in the summer of 1994 by Israeli prime minister Yitzhak Rabin and Jordan's King Hussein. In the fall of that year, the administration succeeded in restoring Haiti's ousted president, Jean-Bertrand Aristide, to power. Clinton scored again by bolstering Russian president Boris Yeltsin's popularity with promises of economic aid.

The problems in Eastern Europe were Clinton's next big challenge. Though he wanted desperately to end the brutal ethnic cleansing in Bosnia, he did not want to commit American ground troops to do so. A peace accord involving American peacekeeping troops was ultimately signed in Dayton, Ohio, in November 1995.

The 1994 elections resulted in a Republican-controlled Congress, and 1995 was largely a tug-of-war between the White House and Capitol Hill over budget-balancing and other key points of the G.O.P.'s "Contract with America," crafted by Speaker of the House Newt Gingrich.

In 1996, aided by a booming economy, Clinton won reelection to a second term, becoming the first Democratic president since Franklin D. Roosevelt to do so. The country's general prosperity also made it possible in 1997 for Clinton and the Republicans to reach an agreement to balance the federal budget in three decades.

However, the character issues that had followed Clinton for years soon began to emerge once again. A series of investigations was begun to determine whether Clinton and Vice President Gore had participated in questionable fund-raising practices in their 1996 campaign.

As his tenure wore on, Clinton came under increasing pressure from Kenneth Starr, the independent counsel who in 1994 took over the investigation of the Clintons' involvement in the Whitewater land deal. Over time, Starr's brief was expanded to include other matters, such as the death of White House lawyer Vincent Foster, the handling of firings in the White House travel office, and shocking allegations of sexual misconduct by Clinton.

In Jan. 1998, Clinton was called to testify in a long-pending sexual harassment suit brought against him by Paula Corbin Jones, a former Arkansas state employee. In his testimony, Clinton denied that he had had a sexual relationship with a young White House intern, Monica Lewinsky, and that he had attempted to cover it up. Although a federal judge in Arkansas threw out the Jones sexual harassment suit in April 1998, by this time the Lewinsky affair had become the focus of Kenneth Starr's investigation as well as a national obsession.

Finally, on Aug. 17, 1998, after relentless media attention, leaks, and news of Lewinsky's upcoming testimony, Clinton made history by becoming the first U.S. president to testify in front of a grand jury in an investigation of his own possibly criminal conduct. In an address to the nation that evening, he admitted to having had an "inappropriate relationship" with Lewinsky, but reaffirmed that he did not ask anyone to lie about or cover up the affair.

Paradoxically, however, in spite of the scandalous outcome of events, Clinton's overall popularity among Americans remained high. The country seemed willing to ignore his weaknesses in character, much as they did in the 1992 elections, as long as the economy was good, his policies were popular, and the United States remained strong abroad.

On Sept. 9, Starr—a conservative Republican whose investigation was seen by Clinton supporters as a politically inspired vendetta—delivered his report to the House of Representatives. While the report outlined 11 possible grounds for impeachment, none stemmed from the initial subjects of the investigation, including the Whitewater real estate deal. The real focus of the accusations seemed to be Clinton's moral conduct, and the "Starr Report" graphically detailed his sexual affair.

Despite the American population's general disapproval of a trial (which was reflected in poll after poll), Congress moved forward in its highly partisan impeachment proceedings and on Dec. 19, Clinton became the second president in American history to be impeached. Two of the four articles of impeachment passed (Article I, grand jury perjury, and Article III, obstruction of justice), the votes drawn along party lines. After a Senate trial in Jan.–Feb. 1999, Clinton was acquitted on both counts.

While the impeachment trial overshadowed all other activity in Washington for a good portion of 1998, Clinton was forced to respond to continued problems with Iraq at the end of the year. In December, Saddam Hussein blocked a weapons inspection by the United Nations. The U.N. responded with airstrikes that would continue on a nearly daily basis for the next three months, and then off and on through the spring and summer, as Iraq taunted the U.S. and its allies further by shooting at jets patrolling the no-fly zones set up after the Persian Gulf war.

In the spring of 1999, reports of continued ethnic cleansing in the Serbian province of Kosovo were growing. Clinton and his British counterpart, Tony Blair, led the push for NATO intervention, which resulted in a 78-day bombing campaign against Serbia that began in March. Although Clinton received some sharp criticism for holding back on the deployment of NATO ground troops, he was ultimately justified, as Serbian president Slobodan Milosevic finally agreed to a peace treaty, signed June 9.

In his final year of office, the president maintained a relatively low profile but took several major trips overseas, to South Asia, Europe, and Africa. He also prepared for the 2000 elections, lending his support not only to presidential hopeful Al Gore, but also to his wife, Hillary Clinton, who ran for U.S. senator from New York.

Burial Places of the Presidents

President	Burial place	President	Burial place
Washington	Mt. Vernon, Va.	Hayes	Fremont, Ohio
J. Adams	Quincy, Mass.	Garfield	Cleveland, Ohio
Jefferson	Charlottesville, Va.	Arthur	Albany, N.Y.
Madison	Montpelier Station, Va.	Cleveland	Princeton, N.J.
Monroe	Richmond, Va.	B. Harrison	Indianapolis, Ind.
J. Q. Adams	Quincy, Mass.	McKinley	Canton, Ohio
Jackson	The Hermitage, nr. Nashville, Tenn.	T. Roosevelt	Oyster Bay, N.Y.
Van Buren	Kinderhook, N.Y.	Taft	Arlington National Cemetery
W. H. Harrison	North Bend, Ohio	Wilson	Washington National Cathedral
Tyler	Richmond, Va.	Harding	Marion, Ohio
Polk	Nashville, Tenn.	Coolidge	Plymouth, Vt.
Taylor	Louisville, Ky.	Hoover	West Branch, Iowa
Fillmore	Buffalo, N.Y.	F. D. Roosevelt	Hyde Park, N.Y.
Pierce	Concord, N.H.	Truman	Independence, Mo.
Buchanan	Lancaster, Pa.	Eisenhower	Abilene, Kan.
Lincoln	Springfield, Ill.	Kennedy	Arlington National Cemetery
A. Johnson	Greeneville, Tenn.	L. B. Johnson	Stonewall, Tex.
Grant	New York City	Nixon	Yorba Linda, Calif.

Senate and House Standing Committees, 106th Congress

Committees of the Senate

Aging (20 members)
Chairman: Charles E. Grassley (Iowa)
Ranking Dem.: John B. Breaux (La.)

Agriculture, Nutrition, and Forestry (17 members)
Chairman: Richard G. Lugar (Ind.)
Ranking Dem.: Tom Harkin (Iowa)

Appropriations (28 members)
Chairman: Ted Stevens (Alaska)
Ranking Dem.: Robert C. Byrd (W.Va.)

Armed Services (20 members)
Chairman: John Warner (Va.)
Ranking Dem.: Carl Levin (Mich.)

Banking, Housing, and Urban Affairs (20 members)
Chairman: Phil Gramm (Tex.)
Ranking Dem.: Paul S. Sarbanes (Md.)

Budget (22 members)
Chairman: Pete V. Domenici (N.M.)
Ranking Dem.: Frank R. Lautenberg (N.J.)

Commerce, Science, and Transportation (20 members)
Chairman: John McCain (Ariz.)
Ranking Dem.: Ernest F. Hollings (S.C.)

Energy and Natural Resources (20 members)
Chairman: Frank H. Murkowski (Alaska)
Ranking Dem.: Jeff Bingaman (N.M.)

Environment and Public Works (18 members)
Chairman: Robert C. Smith (N.H.)
Ranking Dem.: Max Baucus (Mont.)

Ethics (6 members)
Chairman: Pat Roberts (Kans.)
Ranking Dem.: Harry Reid (Nev.)

Finance (19 members)
Chairman: William V. Roth, Jr. (Del.)
Ranking Dem.: Daniel Patrick Moynihan (N.Y.)

Foreign Relations (18 members)
Chairman: Jesse Helms (N.C.)
Ranking Dem.: Joseph R. Biden Jr. (Del.)

Governmental Affairs (16 members)
Chairman: Fred Thompson (Tenn.)
Ranking Dem.: Joseph Lieberman (Conn.)

Health, Education, Labor, and Pensions (18 members)
Chairman: James M. Jeffords (Vt.)
Ranking Dem.: Edward M. Kennedy (Mass.)

Indian Affairs (14 members)
Chairman: Ben Nighthorse Campbell (Colo.)
Ranking Dem.: Daniel K. Inouye (Hawaii)

Intelligence (16 members)
Chairman: Richard C. Shelby (Ala.)
Ranking Dem.: Richard Bryan (Nev.)

Judiciary (18 members)
Chairman: Orrin G. Hatch (Utah)
Ranking Dem.: Patrick J. Leahy (Vt.)

Rules and Administration (16 members)
Chairman: Mitch McConnell (Ky.)
Ranking Dem.: Christopher Dodd (Conn.)

Small Business (17 members)
Chairman: Christopher S. Bond (Mo.)
Ranking Dem.: John Kerry (Mass.)

Veterans' Affairs (12 members)
Chairman: Arlen Specter (Pa.)
Ranking Dem: John D. Rockefeller IV (W.Va.)

Year 2000 Technology Problem (7 members)[1]
Chairman: Robert F. Bennett (Utah)
Ranking Dem: Christopher J. Dodd (Conn.)

Committees of the House

Agriculture (51 members)
Chairman: Larry Combest (Tex.)
Ranking Dem.: Charles W. Stenholm (Tex.)

Appropriations (61 members)
Chairman: C. W. Bill Young (Fla.)
Ranking Dem.: David R. Obey (Wis.)

Armed Services (60 members)
Chairman: Floyd D. Spence (S.C.)
Ranking Dem.: Ike Skelton (Mo.)

Banking and Financial Services (60 members)
Chairman: James A. Leach (Iowa)
Ranking Dem.: John J. LaFalce (N.Y.)

Budget (43 members)
Chairman: John R. Kasich (Ohio)
Ranking Dem.: John M. Spratt Jr. (S.C.)

Commerce (53 members)
Chairman: Thomas J. Bliley, Jr. (Va.)
Ranking Dem.: John D. Dingell (Mich.)

Education and the Workforce (49 members)
Chairman: William F. Goodling (Pa.)
Ranking Dem.: William L. Clay (Mo.)

Government Reform (44 members)
Chairman: Dan Burton (Ind.)
Ranking Dem.: Henry A. Waxman (Calif.)

House Administration (9 members)
Chairman: William M. Thomas (Calif.)
Ranking Dem.: Steny H. Hoyer (Md.)

International Relations (49 members)
Chairman: Benjamin A. Gilman (N.Y.)
Ranking Dem.: Sam Gejdenson (Conn.)

Judiciary (37 members)
Chairman: Henry J. Hyde (Ill.)
Ranking Dem.: John Conyers, Jr. (Mich.)

Resources (52 members)
Chairman: Don Young (Alaska)
Ranking Dem.: George Miller (Calif.)

Rules (13 members)
Chairman: David Dreier (Calif.)
Ranking Dem.: J. Joseph Moakley (Mass.)

Science (47 members)
Chairman: F. James Sensenbrenner, Jr. (Wis.)
Ranking Dem.: Ralph M. Hall (Tex.)

Small Business (36 members)
Chairman: James M. Talent (Mo.)
Ranking Dem.: Nydia M. Velázquez (N.Y.)

Standards of Official Conduct (10 members)
Chairman: Lamar S. Smith (Tex.)
Ranking Dem.: Howard L. Berman (Calif.)

Transportation and Infrastructure (75 members)
Chairman: Bud Shuster (Pa.)
Ranking Dem.: James L. Oberstar (Minn.)

Veterans' Affairs (31 members)
Chairman: Bob Stump (Ariz.)
Ranking Dem.: Lane Evans (Ill.)

Ways and Means (39 members)
Chairman: Bill Archer (Texas)
Ranking Dem.: Charles B. Rangel (N.Y.)

1. Committee disbanded as of Feb. 29, 2000.

Speakers of the House of Representatives

Dates served	Congress	Name and state	Dates served	Congress	Name and state
1789–1791	1	Frederick A. C. Muhlenberg (Pa.)	1869–1875	41–43	James G. Blaine (Maine)
1791–1793	2	Jonathan Trumbull (Conn.)	1875–1876	44	Michael C. Kerr (Ind.)[6]
1793–1795	3	Frederick A. C. Muhlenberg (Pa.)	1876–1881	44–46	Samuel J. Randall (Pa.)
1795–1799	4–5	Jonathan Dayton (N.J.)[1]	1881–1883	47	J. Warren Keifer (Ohio)
1799–1801	6	Theodore Sedgwick (Mass.)	1883–1889	48–50	John G. Carlisle (Ky.)
1801–1807	7–9	Nathaniel Macon (N.C.)	1889–1891	51	Thomas B. Reed (Maine)
1807–1811	10–11	Joseph B. Varnum (Mass.)	1891–1895	52–53	Charles F. Crisp (Ga.)
1811–1814	12–13	Henry Clay (Ky.)[2]	1895–1899	54–55	Thomas B. Reed (Maine)
1814–1815	13	Langdon Cheves (S.C.)	1899–1903	56–57	David B. Henderson (Iowa)
1815–1820	14–16	Henry Clay (Ky.)[3]	1903–1911	58–61	Joseph G. Cannon (Ill.)
1820–1821	16	John W. Taylor (N.Y.)	1911–1919	62–65	Champ Clark (Mo.)
1821–1823	17	Philip P. Barbour (Va.)	1919–1925	66–68	Frederick H. Gillett (Mass.)
1823–1825	18	Henry Clay (Ky.)	1925–1931	69–71	Nicholas Longworth (Ohio)
1825–1827	19	John W. Taylor (N.Y.)	1931–1933	72	John N. Garner (Tex.)
1827–1834	20–23	Andrew Stevenson (Va.)[4]	1933–1934	73	Henry T. Rainey (Ill.)[7]
1834–1835	23	John Bell (Tenn.)	1935–1936	74	Joseph W. Byrns (Tenn.)[8]
1835–1839	24–25	James K. Polk (Tenn.)	1936–1940	74–76	William B. Bankhead (Ala.)[9]
1839–1841	26	Robert M. T. Hunter (Va.)	1940–1947	76–79	Sam Rayburn (Tex.)
1841–1843	27	John White (Ky.)	1947–1949	80	Joseph W. Martin, Jr. (Mass.)
1843–1845	28	John W. Jones (Va.)	1949–1953	81–82	Sam Rayburn (Tex.)
1845–1847	29	John W. Davis (Ind.)	1953–1955	83	Joseph W. Martin, Jr. (Mass.)
1847–1849	30	Robert C. Winthrop (Mass.)	1955–1961	84–87	Sam Rayburn (Tex.)[10]
1849–1851	31	Howell Cobb (Ga.)	1963–1971	87–91	John W. McCormack (Mass.)[11]
1851–1855	32–33	Linn Boyd (Ky.)	1971–1977	92–94	Carl Albert (Okla.)[12]
1855–1857	34	Nathaniel P. Banks (Mass.)	1977–1987	95–99	Thomas P. O'Neill, Jr. (Mass.)[13]
1857–1859	35	James L. Orr (S.C.)	1987–1989	100–101	James C. Wright, Jr. (Tex.)[14]
1859–1861	36	Wm. Pennington (N.J.)	1989–1995	101–103	Thomas S. Foley (Wash.)
1861–1863	37	Galusha A. Grow (Pa.)	1995–1999	104–105	Newt Gingrich (Ga.)[15]
1863–1869	38–40	Schuyler Colfax (Ind.)	1999–	106–	Dennis Hastert (Ill.)
1869–1869	40	Theodore M. Pomeroy (N.Y.)[5]			

1. George Dent (Md.) was elected Speaker pro tempore for April 20 and May 28, 1798. 2. Resigned during second session of 13th Congress. 3. Resigned between first and second sessions of 16th Congress. 4. Resigned during first session of 23rd Congress. 5. Elected Speaker and served the day of adjournment. 6. Died between first and second sessions of 44th Congress. During first session, there were two Speakers pro tempore: Samuel S. Cox (N.Y.), appointed for Feb. 17, May 12, and June 19, 1876, and Milton Sayler (Ohio), appointed for June 4, 1876. 7. Died in 1934 after adjournment of second session of 73rd Congress. 8. Died during second session of 74th Congress. 9. Died during third session of 76th Congress. 10. Died between first and second sessions of 87th Congress. 11. Not a candidate in 1970 election. 12. Not a candidate in 1976 election. 13. Not a candidate in 1986 election. 14. Resigned during first session of 101st Congress. 15. Resigned Jan. 3, 1999, three days before the first session of the 106th Congress. *Source: Congressional Directory.*

Floor Leaders of the Senate

Democratic	Republican
Gilbert M. Hitchcock, Neb. (Min. 1919–20)	Charles Curtis, Kan. (Maj. 1925–29)
Oscar W. Underwood, Ala. (Min. 1920–23)	James E. Watson, Ind. (Maj. 1929–33)
Joseph T. Robinson, Ark. (Min. 1923–33, Maj. 1933–37)	Charles L. McNary, Ore. (Min. 1933–44)
Alben W. Barkley, Ky. (Maj. 1937–46, Min. 1947–48)	Wallace H. White, Jr., Maine (Min. 1944–47, Maj. 1947–48)
Scott W. Lucas, Ill. (Maj. 1949–50)	Kenneth S. Wherry, Neb. (Min. 1949–51)
Ernest W. McFarland, Ariz. (Maj. 1951–52)	Styles Bridges, N.H. (Min. 1951–52)
Lyndon B. Johnson, Tex. (Min. 1953–54, Maj. 1955–60)	Robert A. Taft, Ohio (Maj. 1953)
Mike Mansfield, Mont. (Maj. 1961–77)	William F. Knowland, Calif. (Maj. 1953–54, Min. 1955–58)
Robert C. Byrd, W. Va. (Maj. 1977–81, Min. 1981–86, Maj. 1987–88)	Everett M. Dirksen, Ill. (Min. 1959–69)
George John Mitchell, Maine (Maj. 1989–1994)	Hugh Scott, Pa. (Min. 1969–1977)
Thomas A. Daschle, S.D. (Min. 1995–)	Howard H. Baker, Jr., Tenn. (Min. 1977–81, Maj. 1981–84)
	Robert J. Dole, Kan. (Maj. 1985–86, Min. 1987–94, Maj. 1995–96)
	Trent Lott, Miss. (Maj. 1996–)

NOTE: Min. = Minority Leader; Maj. = Majority Leader. *Source:* United States Senate, Secretary for the Majority.

Composition of Congress, by Political Party, 1855–2001

Congress	Years	Senate					House				
		Total	Dems	Reps	Others	Vacant	Total	Dems	Reps	Others	Vacant
34th	1855–1857	62	42	15	5	—	234	83	108	43	—
35th	1857–1859	64	39	20	5	—	237	131	92	14	—
36th	1859–1861	66	38	26	2	—	237	101	113	23	—
37th	1861–1863	50	11	31	7	1	178	42	106	28	2
38th	1863–1865	51	12	39	—	—	183	80	103	—	—
39th	1865–1867	52	10	42	—	—	191	46	145	—	—
40th	1867–1869	53	11	42	—	—	193	49	143	—	1
41st	1869–1871	74	11	61	—	2	243	73	170	—	—
42nd	1871–1873	74	17	57	—	—	243	104	139	—	—
43rd	1873–1875	74	19	54	—	1	293	88	203	—	2
44th	1875–1877	76	29	46	—	1	293	181	107	3	2
45th	1877–1879	76	36	39	1	—	293	156	137	—	—
46th	1879–1881	76	43	33	—	—	293	150	128	14	1
47th	1881–1883	76	37	37	2	—	293	130	152	11	—
48th	1883–1885	76	36	40	—	—	325	200	119	6	—
49th	1885–1887	76	34	41	—	1	325	182	140	2	1
50th	1887–1889	76	37	39	—	—	325	170	151	4	—
51st	1889–1891	84	37	47	—	—	330	156	173	1	—
52nd	1891–1893	88	39	47	2	—	333	231	88	14	—
53rd	1893–1895	88	44	38	3	3	356	220	126	10	—
54th	1895–1897	88	39	44	5	—	357	104	246	7	—
55th	1897–1899	90	34	46	10	—	357	134	206	16	1
56th	1899–1901	90	26	53	11	—	357	163	185	9	—
57th	1901–1903	90	29	56	3	2	357	153	198	5	1
58th	1903–1905	90	32	58	—	—	386	178	207	—	1
59th	1905–1907	90	32	58	—	—	386	136	250	—	—
60th	1907–1909	92	29	61	—	2	386	164	222	—	—
61st	1909–1911	92	32	59	—	1	391	172	219	—	—
62nd	1911–1913	92	42	49	—	1	391	228	162	1	—
63rd	1913–1915	96	51	44	1	—	435	290	127	18	—
64th	1915–1917	96	56	39	1	—	435	231	193	8	3
65th	1917–1919	96	53	42	1	—	435	210[1]	216	9	—
66th	1919–1921	96	47	48	1	—	435	191	237	7	—
67th	1921–1923	96	37	59	—	—	435	132	300	1	2
68th	1923–1925	96	43	51	2	—	435	207	225	3	—
69th	1925–1927	96	40	54	1	1	435	183	247	5	—
70th	1927–1929	96	47	48	1	—	435	195	237	3	—
71st	1929–1931	96	39	56	1	—	435	163	267	1	4
72nd	1931–1933	96	47	48	1	—	435	216[2]	218	1	—
73rd	1933–1935	96	59	36	1	—	435	313	117	5	—
74th	1935–1937	96	69	25	2	—	435	322	103	10	—
75th	1937–1939	96	75	17	4	—	435	333	89	13	—
76th	1939–1941	96	69	23	4	—	435	262	169	4	—
77th	1941–1943	96	66	28	2	—	435	267	162	6	—
78th	1943–1945	96	57	38	1	—	435	222	209	4	—
79th	1945–1947	96	57	38	1	—	435	243	190	2	—
80th	1947–1949	96	45	51	—	—	435	188	246	1	—
81st	1949–1951	96	54	42	—	—	435	263	171	1	—
82nd	1951–1953	96	48	47	1	—	435	234	199	2	—
83rd	1953–1955	96	46	48	2	—	435	213	221	1	—
84th	1955–1957	96	48	47	1	—	435	232	203	—	—
85th	1957–1959	96	49	47	—	—	435	234	201	—	—
86th	1959–1961	98	64	34	—	—	436[3]	283	153	—	—
87th	1961–1963	100	64	36	—	—	437[4]	262	175	—	—
88th	1963–1965	100	67	33	—	—	435	258	176	—	1
89th	1965–1967	100	68	32	—	—	435	295	140	—	—
90th	1967–1969	100	64	36	—	—	435	248	187	—	—
91st	1969–1971	100	58	42	—	—	435	243	192	—	—
92nd	1971–1973	100	54	44	2	—	435	255	180	—	—
93rd	1973–1975	100	56	42	2	—	435	242	192	1	—
94th	1975–1977	100	61	37	2	—	435	291	144	—	—
95th	1977–1979	100	61	38	1	—	435	292	143	—	—
96th	1979–1981	100	58	41	1	—	435	277	158	—	—
97th	1981–1983	100	46	53	1	—	435	242	192	1	—
98th	1983–1985	100	46	54	—	—	435	269	166	—	—
99th	1985–1987	100	47	53	—	—	435	253	182	—	—

Congress	Years	Senate					House				
		Total	Dems	Reps	Others	Vacant	Total	Dems	Reps	Others	Vacant
100th	1987–1989	100	55	45	—	—	435	258	177	—	—
101st	1989–1991	100	55	45	—	—	435	260	175	—	—
102nd	1991–1993	100	56	44	—	—	435	267	167	1	—
103rd	1993–1995	100	57	43	—	—	435	258	176	1	—
104th	1995–1997	100	48	52	—	—	435	204	230	1	—
105th	1997–1999	100	45	55	—	—	435	207	227	1	—
106th	1999–2001	100	45	55	—	—	435	211	222	1	1

1. Democrats organized House with help of other parties. 2. Democrats organized House due to Republican deaths. 3. Proclamation declaring Alaska a state issued Jan 3., 1959. 4. Proclamation declaring Hawaii a state issued Aug. 21, 1959. *Source:* Office of the Clerk of the House of Representatives. Web: http://clerkweb.house.gov/histrecs/history/history.htm.

Salaries of the President, Vice President, and Other U.S. Officials, 2000

(per year)

Position	Salary	Position	Salary
President	$200,000	Vice President	$181,000
1789	25,000	Representative	141,300
1873	50,000	President Pro Tempore	157,000
1909	75,000	Majority and Minority Leaders	157,000
1949	100,000	Speaker of the House	181,400
1969	200,000	Chief Justice, U.S. Supreme Court	181,400
2001	400,000[1]	Assoc. Justice, U.S. Supreme Court	173,600

1. Plus $50,000 expense allowance to assist in defraying expenses relating to or resulting from the discharge of his official duties. *Source:* Office of Personnel Management. Web: www.opm.gov/.

Senate Salaries since 1789

(per year unless noted)

Year	Salary	Year	Salary	Year	Salary
1789–1815	$6.00 per day	1935–1947	$10,000	1987 (Jan. 1–Feb. 3)	$77,400
1815–1817	$1,500	1947–1955	$12,500	1987–1990	$89,500
1817–1855	$8.00 per day	1955–1965	$22,500	1990 (as of Feb. 1)	$98,400
1855–1865	$3,000	1965–1969	$30,000	1991	$101,900
1865–1871	$5,000	1969–1975	$42,500	1991 (as of Aug. 15)	$125,100
1871–1873	$7,500	1975–1977	$44,600	1992	$129,500
1873–1907	$5,000	1977–1978	$57,500	1993–1997	$133,600
1907–1925	$7,500	1979–1983	$60,662.50	1998	$136,700
1925–1932	$10,000	1983	$69,800	1999	$136,700
1932–1933	$9,000	1984	$72,600	2000	$141,300
1933–1935	$8,500	1985–1986	$75,100		

NOTE: Since the early 1980s, Senate leaders—majority and minority leaders, and the president *pro tempore*—have received slightly higher salaries than other members. *Source:* United States Senate. Web: www.senate.gov/learning.

How a Bill Becomes a Law

When a senator or a representative introduces a bill, he sends it to the clerk of his house, who gives it a number and title. This is the *first reading,* and the bill is referred to the proper committee.

The committee may decide the bill is unwise or unnecessary and *table* it, thus killing it at once. Or it may decide the bill is worthwhile and hold hearings to listen to facts and opinions presented by experts and other interested persons. After members of the committee have debated the bill and perhaps offered amendments, a vote is taken; and if the vote is favorable, the bill is sent back to the floor of the house.

The clerk reads the bill sentence by sentence to the house, and this is known as the *second reading.* Members may then debate the bill and offer amendments. In the House of Representatives, the time for debate is limited by a *cloture rule,* but there is no such restriction in the Senate for cloture, where 60

votes are required. This makes possible a *filibuster,* in which one or more opponents hold the floor to defeat the bill.

The *third reading* is by title only, and the bill is put to a vote, which may be by voice or roll call, depending on the circumstances and parliamentary rules. Members who must be absent at the time but who wish to record their vote may be paired if each negative vote has a balancing affirmative one.

The bill then goes to the other house of Congress, where it may be defeated, or passed with or without amendments. If the bill is defeated, it dies. If it is passed with amendments, a joint Congressional committee must be appointed by both houses to iron out the differences.

After its final passage by both houses, the bill is sent to the president. If he approves, he signs it, and the bill becomes a law. However, if he disapproves, he *vetoes* the bill by refusing to sign it and sending it back to the house of origin with his reasons for the veto. The objections are read and debated, and a roll-call vote is taken. If the bill receives less than a two-thirds vote, it is defeated and goes no further. But if it receives a two-thirds vote or greater, it is sent to the other house for a vote. If that house also passes it by a two-thirds vote, the president's veto is *overridden,* and the bill becomes a law.

Should the president desire neither to sign nor to veto the bill, he may retain it for ten days, Sundays excepted, after which time it automatically becomes a law without signature. However, if Congress has adjourned within those ten days, the bill is automatically killed, that process of indirect rejection being known as a *pocket veto.*

Presidential Vetoes, 1789–1999

President	Coincident Congresses	Regular vetoes	Pocket vetoes	Total vetoes	Vetoes overridden
Washington	1st–4th	2	—	2	—
Adams	5th–6th	—	—	—	—
Jefferson	7th–10th	—	—	—	—
Madison	11th–14th	5	2	7	—
Monroe	15th–18th	1	—	1	—
J. Q. Adams	19th–20th	—	—	—	—
Jackson	21st–24th	5	7	12	—
Van Buren	25th–26th	—	1	1	—
W. H. Harrison	27th	—	—	—	—
Tyler	27th–28th	6	4	10	1
Polk	29th–30th	2	1	3	—
Taylor	31st	—	—	—	—
Fillmore	31st–32nd	—	—	—	—
Pierce	33rd–34th	9	—	9	5
Buchanan	35th–36th	4	3	7	—
Lincoln	37th–39th	2	5	7	—
A. Johnson	39th–40th	21	8	29	15
Grant	41st–44th	45	48	93	4
Hayes	45th–46th	12	1	13	1
Garfield	47th	—	—	—	—
Arthur	47th–48th	4	8	12	1
Cleveland	49th–50th	304	110	414	2
B. Harrison	51st–52nd	19	25	44	1
Cleveland	53rd–54th	42	128	170	5
McKinley	55th–57th	6	36	42	—
T. Roosevelt	57th–60th	42	40	82	1
Taft	61st–62nd	30	9	39	1
Wilson	63rd–66th	33	11	44	6
Harding	67th	5	1	6	—
Coolidge	68th–70th	20	30	50	4
Hoover	71st–72nd	21	16	37	3
F. D. Roosevelt	73rd–79th	372	263	635	9
Truman	79th–82nd	180	70	250	12
Eisenhower	83rd–86th	73	108	181	2
Kennedy	87th–88th	12	9	21	—
L. B. Johnson	88th–90th	16	14	30	—
Nixon	91st–93rd	26	17	43	7
Ford	93rd–94th	48	18	66	12
Carter	95th–96th	13	18	31	2
Reagan	97th–100th	39	39	78	9
Bush[1]	101st–102nd	29	15	44	1
Clinton	103rd–106th	30	0	30	2
Total		**1,478**	**1,065**	**2,543**	**106**

1. President Bush attempted to pocket veto two bills during intrasession recess periods. Congress considered the two bills enacted into law because of the president's failure to return the legislation. The bills are not counted as pocket vetoes in this table. *Source: Presidential Vetoes, 1789–Present: A Summary Overview, 98–148 GOV. Nov. 12, 1999.*

Order of Presidential Succession

1. The Vice President
2. Speaker of the House
3. President pro tempore of the Senate
4. Secretary of State
5. Secretary of the Treasury
6. Secretary of Defense
7. Attorney General
8. Secretary of the Interior
9. Secretary of Agriculture
10. Secretary of Commerce
11. Secretary of Labor
12. Secretary of Health and Human Services
13. Secretary of Housing and Urban Development
14. Secretary of Transportation
15. Secretary of Energy
16. Secretary of Education
17. Secretary of Veterans Affairs

NOTE: An official cannot succeed to the Presidency unless that person meets the Constitutional requirements.

Executive Departments and Agencies

Source: United States Government Manual, 1998–1999.

Unless otherwise indicated, addresses shown are in Washington, D.C.

White House Offices and Agencies

Office of Administration
Old Executive Office Bldg., 725 17th St., N.W. (20503)
  Established: Dec. 12, 1977
  Director: Michael J. Lyle
Office of National Drug Control Policy
Executive Office of the President (20503)
  Established: Jan. 29, 1989
  Director: Barry R. McCaffrey
Council of Economic Advisers (CEA)
Room 314, Old Executive Office Bldg. (20501)
  Members: 3
  Established: Feb. 20, 1946
  Chair: Martin N. Baily
Council on Environmental Quality
Room 360, Old Executive Office Bldg. (20501)
  Established: 1969
  Chair: George T. Frampton (acting)
Office of Management and Budget
Executive Office Bldg. (20503)
  Established: July 1, 1939
  Director: Jacob J. Lew
Office of Science and Technology Policy
Old Executive Office Building (20502)
  Established: May 11, 1976
  Director: Neal F. Lane
National Security Council (NSC)
Old Executive Office Bldg. (20506)
  Members: 4
  Established: July 26, 1947
  Chair: The President
  National Security Adviser: Samuel R. Berger
  Other members: Vice President; Secretary of State; Secretary of Defense
Office of the United States Trade Representative
600 17th St., N.W. (20508)
  Established: Jan. 15, 1963
  Trade Representative: Charlene Barshefsky

Executive Departments

Department of Agriculture
14th & Independence Ave., S.W. (20250).
  Established: May 15, 1862. Administered by Commissioner of Agriculture until 1889, when it was made executive department.
  Secretary: Dan Glickman
  Deputy Secretary: Richard Rominger
Department of Commerce
14th St. between Constitution Ave. & Pennsylvania Ave., N.W. (20230)
  Established: Department of Commerce and Labor was created Feb. 14, 1903. On March 4, 1913, all labor activities were transferred out of Department of Commerce and Labor and it was renamed Department of Commerce.
  Secretary: Norman Y. Mineta
Department of Defense
Office of the Secretary, The Pentagon (20301-1155)
  Established: July 26, 1947, as National Military Establishment; name changed to Department of Defense on Aug. 10, 1949. Subordinate to Secretary of Defense are Secretaries of Army, Navy, Air Force.
  Secretary: William S. Cohen
  Deputy Secretary: Rudy de Leon
  Secretary of Army: Louis Caldera
  Secretary of Navy: Richard Danzig
  Secretary of Air Force: F. Whitten Peters

Commandant of Marine Corps: Gen. James L. Jones
Joint Chiefs of Staff: Gen. Harry Shelton, Chairman; Gen. Richard B. Myers, Vice Chairman; Gen. Eric K. Shinseki, Army; Adm. Jay L. Johnson, Navy; Gen. Michael E. Ryan, Air Force; Gen. James L. Jones, Marine Corps.
Department of Education
600 Independence Ave., S.W. (20202)
  Established: Oct. 17, 1979
  Secretary: Richard Riley
  Deputy Secretary: Frank S. Holleman, III
Department of Energy
1000 Independence Ave., S.W. (20585)
  Established: Oct. 1, 1977
  Secretary: Bill Richardson
  Deputy Secretary: T. J. Glauthier
Department of Health and Human Services
200 Independence Ave., S.W. (20201)
  Established: Department of Health, Education, and Welfare was created April 11, 1953, replacing Federal Security Agency created in 1939. On Oct. 17, 1979, the Department of Education became a separate department.
  Secretary: Donna Shalala
  Surgeon General: David Satcher
Department of Housing and Urban Development
451 7th St., S.W. (20410)
  Established: Nov. 9, 1965, replacing Housing and Home Finance Agency created in 1947
  Secretary: Andrew M. Cuomo
  Deputy Secretary: Saul Ramirez, Jr.
Department of the Interior
1849 C St., N.W. (20240)
  Established: March 3, 1849
  Secretary: Bruce Babbitt
  Deputy Secretary: Ken Smith
Department of Justice
10th St. and Constitution Ave., N.W. (20530)
  Established: Office of Attorney General was created Sept. 24, 1789. Although one of the original Cabinet members, the Attorney General was not an executive department head until June 22, 1870, when the Department of Justice was established.
  Attorney General: Janet Reno
  Deputy Attorney General: Eric H. Holder, Jr.
  Solicitor General: Seth P. Waxman
  Director of FBI: Louis J. Freeh
Department of Labor
200 Constitution Ave., N.W. (20210)
  Established: Bureau of Labor was created in 1884 under Department of the Interior; later became independent department without executive rank. Returned to bureau status in Department of Commerce and Labor, but on March 4, 1913, became independent executive department under its present name.
  Secretary: Alexis M. Herman
  Deputy Secretary: Edward Montgomery
Department of State
2201 C St., N.W. (20520)
  Established: 1781 as Department of Foreign Affairs; reconstituted, 1789, following adoption of Constitution; name changed to Department of State Sept. 15, 1789.
  Secretary: Madeleine Albright
  U.N. Ambassador: Richard Holbrooke
Department of Transportation
400 7th St., S.W. (20590)
  Established: Oct. 15, 1966, as result of Department of Transportation Act, which became effective April 1, 1967.
  Secretary: Rodney E. Slater
  Deputy Secretary: Mortimer L. Downey
Department of the Treasury

1500 Pennsylvania Ave., N.W. (20220)
Established: Sept. 2, 1789
Secretary: Lawrence H. Summers
Deputy Secretary: Stuart E. Eizenstat
Treasurer of the U.S.: Mary Ellen Withrow
Department of Veterans' Affairs
810 Vermont Ave., N.W. (20420)
Established: March 15, 1989, replacing Veterans Administration created in 1930
Secretary: Hershel W. Gober (acting)
Deputy Secretary: Edward A. Powell, Jr. (acting)

Major Independent Agencies

U.S. Arms Control and Disarmament Agency
320 21st St., N.W. (20451)
Established: Sept. 26, 1961
Director: John Holum
Central Intelligence Agency (CIA)
Washington, D.C. (20505)
Established: 1947
Director of Central Intelligence: George J. Tenet
U.S. Commission on Civil Rights
624 9th St., N.W. (20425)
Established: 1957
Chair: Mary Frances Berry
Consumer Product Safety Commission
East West Towers, 4330 East West Highway, Bethesda, Md. 20814
Established: Oct. 27, 1972
Chair: Ann Brown
Corporation for National Service
1201 New York Ave., N.W. (20525)
Established: Sept. 1993
CEO: Harris Wofford
Environmental Protection Agency (EPA)
401 M St., S.W. (20460)
Established: Dec. 2, 1970
Administrator: Carol M. Browner
Equal Employment Opportunity Commission (EEOC)
1801 L St., N.W. (20507)
Members: 5
Established: July 2, 1965
Chair: Ida L. Castro
Farm Credit Administration (FCA)
1501 Farm Credit Dr., McLean, Va. 22102-5090
Members: 13
Established: March 27, 1933
Chair: Michael M. Reyna
Federal Deposit Insurance Corporation (FDIC)
550 17th St., N.W. (20429)
Established: June 16, 1933
Chair: Donna Tanoue
Federal Election Commission (FEC)
999 E St., N.W. (20463)
Members: 6
Established: 1975
Chair: Darryl R. Wold
Federal Maritime Commission
800 North Capitol St., N.W. (20573-0001)
Members: 5
Established: Aug. 12, 1961
Chair: Harold J. Creel, Jr.
Federal Mediation and Conciliation Service (FMCS)
2100 K St., N.W. (20427)
Established: 1947
Director: C. Richard Barnes
Federal Reserve System (FRS), Board of Governors of
20th St. & Constitution Ave., N.W. (20551)
Members: 7
Established: Dec. 23, 1913
Chair: Alan Greenspan
Federal Trade Commission (FTC)
Pennsylvania Ave. at 6th St., N.W. (20580)
Members: 5

Established: Sept. 26, 1914
Chair: Robert Pitofsky
General Services Administration (GSA)
General Services Building, 18th and F Sts., N.W. (20405)
Established: July 1, 1949
Administrator: David J. Barram
U.S. Information Agency
301 Fourth St., S.W. (20547)
Established: Aug. 1, 1953. Reorganized April 1, 1978.
Director: Theodore C. Streibert
U.S. International Trade Commission
500 E St., S.W. (20436)
Members: 6
Established: Sept. 8, 1916
Chair: Stephen Koplan
National Aeronautics and Space Administration (NASA)
300 E St., S.W. (20546)
Established: 1958
Administrator: Daniel S. Goldin
National Foundation on the Arts and the Humanities
1100 Pennsylvania Ave., N.W. (20506-0001)
Established: 1965
Chairs: National Endowment for the Arts, Chair, William Ivey; National Endowment for the Humanities, Chair, William R. Ferris
National Labor Relations Board (NLRB)
1099 14th St., N.W. (20570)
Members: 5
Established: July 5, 1935
Chair: John C. Truesdale
National Mediation Board
Suite 250 East, 1301 K St., N.W. (20572)
Established: June 21, 1934
Chair: Ernest W. DuBester
National Science Foundation (NSF)
4201 Wilson Blvd., Arlington, Va. 22230
Established: 1950
Director: Rita R. Colwell
National Transportation Safety Board
490 L'Enfant Plaza, S.W. (20594)
Members: 5
Established: April 1, 1967, as an independent agency supported by the Dept. of Transportation. Ties with Dept. of Transportation officially ended in 1975.
Chair: James Hall
Nuclear Regulatory Commission (NRC)
One White Flint North, 11555 Rockville Pike, Rockville, Md. 20852-2738
Members: 5
Established: Jan. 19, 1975
Chair: Richard A. Meserve
Office of Personnel Management (OPM)
1900 E St., N.W. (20415-0001)
Established: Jan. 1, 1979
Director: Janice R. Lachance
U.S. Postal Service
475 L'Enfant Plaza West, S.W. (20260-0010)
Established: In 1775 with the appointment of Benjamin Franklin as the first Postmaster General under the Continental Congress. In 1970 became independent agency headed by 11-member board of governors.
Postmaster General: William J. Henderson
Deputy Postmaster General: John Nolan
Securities and Exchange Commission (SEC)
450 5th St., N.W. (20549)
Members: 5
Established: July 2, 1934
Chair: Arthur Levitt
Selective Service System (SSS)
1515 Wilson Blvd., Arlington, Va., 22209-2425
Established: Sept. 16, 1940
Director: Gil Coronado
Small Business Administration (SBA)
409 3rd St., S.W. (20416)

Established: July 30, 1953
Administrator: Aida Alvarez
Tennessee Valley Authority (TVA)
400 West Summit Hill Drive, Knoxville, Tenn. 37902. Washington office: One Massachusetts Ave., N.W. (20444-0001).
Members of Board of Directors: 3
Established: May 18, 1933
Chairman: Craven H. Crowell, Jr.

Other Independent Agencies

Administrative Conference of the United States—2120 L St., N.W., Ste. 500 (20037)
American Battle Monuments Commission—Pulaski Bldg., 20 Massachusetts Ave., N.W., Room 5127 (20314)
Appalachian Regional Commission—1666 Connecticut Ave., N.W., Room 601 (20235)
Commission of Fine Arts—441 F St., N.W., Ste. 312 (20001)
Commodity Futures Trading Commission—1155 21st St., N.W. (20581)
Export-Import Bank of the United States—811 Vermont Ave., N.W. (20571)
Federal Emergency Management Agency—500 C St., S.W. (20472)
Federal Housing Finance Board—1777 F St., N.W. (20006)
Federal Labor Relations Authority—607 14th St., N.W. (20424-0001)
Inter-American Foundation—901 N. Stuart St., Arlington, Va. 22203
National Commission on Libraries and Information Science—1110 Vermont Ave., N.W., Ste. 820 (20005-3552)
National Credit Union Administration—1775 Duke St., Alexandria, Va. 22314-3428
Occupational Safety and Health Review Commission—1120 20th St., N.W. (20036-3419)

Panama Canal Commission—1825 I St., N.W., Ste. 1050 (20006-5402)
U.S. Parole Commission—Dept. of Justice, 5550 Friendship Blvd., Ste. 420, Chevy Chase, Md. 20815
Peace Corps—1111 20th St., N.W. (20526)
Pension Benefit Guaranty Corporation—1200 K St., N.W. (20005-4026)
Postal Rate Commission—1333 H St., N.W. (20268-0001)
President's Committee on Employment of People With Disabilities—1331 F St., N.W., Ste. 300 (20004)
President's Council on Physical Fitness and Sports—701 Pennsylvania Ave., N.W., Ste. 250 (20004)
Railroad Retirement Board (RRB)—844 N. Rush St., Ninth Floor, Chicago, Ill. 60611-2092; Office of Legislative Affairs: 1310 G St., N.W, Ste. 500 (20005-3004).

Legislative Department

Architect of the Capitol—U.S. Capitol Building (20515)
General Accounting Office (GAO)—441 G St., N.W. (20548)
Government Printing Office (GPO)—732 North Capitol St., N.W. (20401)
Library of Congress—101 Independence Ave., S.E. (20540)
United States Botanic Garden—Office of Executive Director, 245 1st St., S.W. (20024)

Quasi-Official Agencies

American National Red Cross—430 17th St., N.W. (20006)
Legal Services Corporation—750 1st St., N.E. (20002-4250)
National Academy of Sciences, National Academy of Engineering, National Research Council, Institute of Medicine—2101 Constitution Ave., N.W. (20418)
National Railroad Passenger Corporation (Amtrak)—60 Massachusetts Ave., N.E. (20002)
Smithsonian Institution—1000 Jefferson Dr., S.W. (20560)

Government Officials

Cabinet Members With Dates of Appointment

Although the Constitution made no provision for a president's advisory group, the heads of the three executive departments (State, Treasury, and War) and the Attorney General were organized by Washington into such a group; and by about 1793, the name "Cabinet" was applied to it. With the exception of the Attorney General up to 1870 and the Postmaster General from 1829 to 1872, Cabinet members have been heads of executive departments.

Cabinet members are appointed by the president, subject to the confirmation of the Senate; and as their terms are not fixed, they may be replaced at any time by the president. At a change in Administration, it is customary for Cabinet members to resign, but they remain in office until successors are appointed.

The table of Cabinet members lists only those members who actually served after being duly commissioned. The dates shown are those of appointment. "Cont." indicates that the term continued from the previous Administration for a substantial amount of time.

Washington

Secretary of State	Thomas Jefferson, 1789
	Edmund Randolph, 1794
	Timothy Pickering, 1795
Secretary of the Treasury	Alexander Hamilton, 1789
	Oliver Wolcott, Jr., 1795
Secretary of War	Henry Knox, 1789
	Timothy Pickering, 1795
	James McHenry, 1796
Attorney General	Edmund Randolph, 1789
	William Bradford, 1794
	Charles Lee, 1795

J. Adams

Secretary of State	Timothy Pickering (Cont.)
	John Marshall, 1800
Secretary of the Treasury	Oliver Wolcott, Jr. (Cont.)
	Samuel Dexter, 1801
Secretary of War	James McHenry (Cont.)
	Samuel Dexter, 1800
Attorney General	Charles Lee (Cont.)
Secretary of the Navy	Benjamin Stoddert, 1798

Jefferson

Secretary of State	James Madison, 1801
Secretary of the Treasury	Samuel Dexter (Cont.)
	Albert Gallatin, 1801
Secretary of War	Henry Dearborn, 1801
Attorney General	Levi Lincoln, 1801
	Robert Smith, 1805
	John Breckinridge, 1805
	Caesar A. Rodney, 1807
Secretary of the Navy	Benjamin Stoddert (Cont.)
	Robert Smith, 1801

Madison

Secretary of State	Robert Smith, 1809
	James Monroe, 1811
Secretary of the Treasury	Albert Gallatin (Cont.)
	George W. Campbell, 1814
	Alexander J. Dallas, 1814
	William H. Crawford, 1816
Secretary of War	William Eustis, 1809
	John Armstrong, 1813
	James Monroe, 1814
	William H. Crawford, 1815
Attorney General	Caesar A. Rodney (Cont.)
	William Pinckney, 1811
	Richard Rush, 1814
Secretary of the Navy	Paul Hamilton, 1809
	William Jones, 1813
	B. W. Crowninshield, 1814

Monroe

Secretary of State	John Quincy Adams, 1817
Secretary of the Treasury	William H. Crawford (Cont.)
Secretary of War	John C. Calhoun, 1817
Attorney General	Richard Rush (Cont.)
	William Wirt, 1817
Secretary of the Navy	B. W. Crowninshield (Cont.)
	Smith Thompson, 1818
	Samuel L. Southard, 1823

J. Q. Adams

Secretary of State	Henry Clay, 1825
Secretary of the Treasury	Richard Rush, 1825
Secretary of War	James Barbour, 1825
	Peter B. Porter, 1828
Attorney General	William Wirt (Cont.)
Secretary of the Navy	Samuel L. Southard (Cont.)

Jackson

Secretary of State	Martin Van Buren, 1829
	Edward Livingston, 1831
	Louis McLane, 1833
	John Forsyth, 1834
Secretary of the Treasury	Samuel D. Ingham, 1829
	Louis McLane, 1831
	William J. Duane, 1833
	Roger B. Taney[1], 1833
	Levi Woodbury, 1834
Secretary of War	John H. Eaton, 1829
	Lewis Cass, 1831
Attorney General	John M. Berrien, 1829
	Roger B. Taney, 1831
	Benjamin F. Butler, 1833
Postmaster General[2]	William T. Barry, 1829
	Amos Kendall, 1835
Secretary of the Navy	John Branch, 1829
	Levi Woodbury, 1831
	Mahlon Dickerson, 1834

1. Not confirmed by the Senate. 2. The Postmaster General did not become a Cabinet member until 1829. Earlier Postmasters General were: Samuel Osgood (1789), Timothy Pickering (1791), Joseph Habersham (1795), Gideon Granger (1801), Return J. Meigs, Jr. (1814), and John McLean (1823).

Van Buren

Secretary of State	John Forsyth (Cont.)
Secretary of the Treasury	Levi Woodbury (Cont.)
Secretary of War	Joel R. Poinsett, 1837
Attorney General	Benjamin F. Butler (Cont.)
	Felix Grundy, 1838
	Henry D. Gilpin, 1840
Postmaster General	Amos Kendall (Cont.)
	John M. Niles, 1840
Secretary of the Navy	Mahlon Dickerson (Cont.)
	James K. Paulding, 1838

W. H. Harrison

Secretary of State	Daniel Webster, 1841
Secretary of the Treasury	Thomas Ewing, 1841
Secretary of War	John Bell, 1841
Attorney General	John J. Crittenden, 1841
Postmaster General	Francis Granger, 1841
Secretary of the Navy	George E. Badger, 1841

Tyler

Secretary of State	Daniel Webster (Cont.)
	Abel P. Upshur, 1843
	John C. Calhoun, 1844
Secretary of the Treasury	Thomas Ewing (Cont.)
	Walter Forward, 1841
	John C. Spencer[1], 1843
	George M. Bibb, 1844
Secretary of War	John Bell (Cont.)
	John C. Spencer, 1841
	James M. Porter[1], 1843
	William Wilkins, 1844
Attorney General	John J. Crittenden (Cont.)
	Hugh S. Legaré, 1841
	John Nelson, 1843
Postmaster General	Francis Granger (Cont.)
	Charles A. Wickliffe, 1841
Secretary of the Navy	George E. Badger (Cont.)
	Abel P. Upshur, 1841
	David Henshaw[1], 1843
	Thomas W. Gilmer, 1844
	John Y. Mason, 1844

1. Not confirmed by the Senate.

Polk

Secretary of State	James Buchanan, 1845
Secretary of the Treasury	Robert J. Walker, 1845
Secretary of War	William L. Marcy, 1845
Attorney General	John Y. Mason, 1845
	Nathan Clifford, 1846
	Isaac Toucey, 1848
Postmaster General	Cave Johnson, 1845
Secretary of the Navy	George Bancroft, 1845
	John Y. Mason, 1846

Taylor

Secretary of State	John M. Clayton, 1849
Secretary of the Treasury	William M. Meredith, 1849
Secretary of War	George W. Crawford, 1849
Attorney General	Reverdy Johnson, 1849
Postmaster General	Jacob Collamer, 1849
Secretary of the Navy	William B. Preston, 1849
Secretary of the Interior	Thomas Ewing, 1849

Fillmore

Secretary of State	Daniel Webster, 1850
	Edward Everett, 1852
Secretary of the Treasury	Thomas Corwin, 1850
Secretary of War	Charles M. Conrad, 1850
Attorney General	John J. Crittenden, 1850
Postmaster General	Nathan K. Hall, 1850
	Samuel D. Hubbard, 1852
Secretary of the Navy	William A. Graham, 1850
	John P. Kennedy, 1852
Secretary of the Interior	Thos. M. T. McKennan, 1850
	Alex. H. H. Stuart, 1850

Pierce

Secretary of State	William L. Marcy, 1853
Secretary of the Treasury	James Guthrie, 1853
Secretary of War	Jefferson Davis, 1853
Attorney General	Caleb Cushing, 1853
Postmaster General	James Campbell, 1853
Secretary of the Navy	James C. Dobbin, 1853
Secretary of the Interior	Robert McClelland, 1853

Buchanan

Secretary of State	Lewis Cass, 1857
	Jeremiah S. Black, 1860
Secretary of the Treasury	Howell Cobb, 1857
	Philip F. Thomas, 1860
	John A. Dix, 1861
Secretary of War	John B. Floyd, 1857
	Joseph Holt, 1861
Attorney General	Jeremiah S. Black, 1857
	Edwin M. Stanton, 1860
Postmaster General	Aaron V. Brown, 1857
	Joseph Holt, 1859
	Horatio King, 1861
Secretary of the Navy	Isaac Toucey, 1857
Secretary of the Interior	Jacob Thompson, 1857

Lincoln

Secretary of State	William H. Seward, 1861
Secretary of the Treasury	Salmon P. Chase, 1861
	William P. Fessenden, 1864
	Hugh McCulloch, 1865
Secretary of War	Simon Cameron, 1861
	Edwin M. Stanton, 1862
Attorney General	Edward Bates, 1861
	James Speed, 1864
Postmaster General	Montgomery Blair, 1861
	William Dennison, 1864
Secretary of the Navy	Gideon Welles, 1861
Secretary of the Interior	Caleb B. Smith, 1861
	John P. Usher, 1863

A. Johnson

Secretary of State	William H. Seward (Cont.)
Secretary of the Treasury	Hugh McCulloch (Cont.)
Secretary of War	Edwin M. Stanton (Cont.)
	John M. Schofield, 1868
Attorney General	James Speed (Cont.)
	Henry Stanbery, 1866
	William M. Evarts, 1868
Postmaster General	William Dennison (Cont.)
	Alexander W. Randall, 1866
Secretary of the Navy	Gideon Welles (Cont.)
Secretary of the Interior	John P. Usher (Cont.)
	James Harlan, 1865
	Orville H. Browning, 1866

Grant

Secretary of State	Elihu B. Washburne, 1869
	Hamilton Fish, 1869
	George S. Boutwell, 1869
	William A. Richardson, 1873
	Benjamin H. Bristow, 1874
	Lot M. Morrill, 1876
Secretary of War	John A. Rawlins, 1869
	William W. Belknap, 1869
	Alphonso Taft, 1876
	James D. Cameron, 1876
Attorney General	Ebenezer R. Hoar, 1869
	Amos T. Akerman, 1870
	George H. Williams, 1871
	Edwards Pierrepont, 1875
	Alphonso Taft, 1876
Postmaster General	John A. J. Creswell, 1869
	Marshall Jewell, 1874
	James N. Tyner, 1876
Secretary of the Navy	Adolph E. Borie, 1869
	George M. Robeson, 1869
Secretary of the Interior	Jacob D. Cox, 1869
	Columbus Delano, 1870
	Zachariah Chandler, 1875

Hayes

Secretary of State	William M. Evarts, 1877
Secretary of the Treasury	John Sherman, 1877
Secretary of War	George W. McCrary, 1877
	Alexander Ramsey, 1879
Attorney General	Charles Devens, 1877
Postmaster General	David M. Key, 1877
	Horace Maynard, 1880
	Richard W. Thompson, 1877
	Nathan Goff, Jr., 1881
Secretary of the Interior	Carl Schurz, 1877

Garfield

Secretary of State	James G. Blaine, 1881
Secretary of the Treasury	William Windom, 1881
Secretary of War	Robert T. Lincoln, 1881
Attorney General	Wayne MacVeagh, 1881
Postmaster General	Thomas L. James, 1881
Secretary of the Navy	William H. Hunt, 1881
Secretary of the Interior	Samuel J. Kirkwood, 1881

Arthur

Secretary of State	James G. Blaine (Cont.)
	F. T. Frelinghuysen, 1881
Secretary of the Treasury	William Windom (Cont.)
	Charles J. Folger, 1881
	Walter Q. Gresham, 1884
	Hugh McCulloch, 1884
Secretary of War	Robert T. Lincoln (Cont.)
Attorney General	Wayne MacVeagh (Cont.)
	Benjamin H. Brewster, 1881
Postmaster General	Thomas L. James (Cont.)
	Timothy O. Howe, 1881
	Walter Q. Gresham, 1883
	Frank Hatton, 1884
Secretary of the Navy	William H. Hunt (Cont.)
	William E. Chandler, 1882
Secretary of the Interior	Samuel J. Kirkwood (Cont.)
	Henry M. Teller, 1882

Cleveland

Secretary of State	Thomas F. Bayard, 1885
Secretary of the Treasury	Daniel Manning, 1885
	Charles S. Fairchild, 1887
Secretary of War	William C. Endicott, 1885
Attorney General	Augustus H. Garland, 1885
Postmaster General	William F. Vilas, 1885
	Don M. Dickinson, 1888
Secretary of the Navy	William C. Whitney, 1885
Secretary of the Interior	Lucius Q. C. Lamar, 1885
	William F. Vilas, 1888
Secretary of Agriculture	Norman J. Colman, 1889

B. Harrison

Secretary of State	James G. Blaine, 1889
	John W. Foster, 1892
Secretary of the Treasury	William Windom, 1889
	Charles Foster, 1891
Secretary of War	Redfield Proctor, 1889
	Stephen B. Elkins, 1891
Attorney General	William H. H. Miller, 1889
Postmaster General	John Wanamaker, 1889
Secretary of the Navy	Benjamin F. Tracy, 1889
Secretary of the Interior	John W. Noble, 1889
Secretary of Agriculture	Jeremiah M. Rusk, 1889

Cleveland

Secretary of State	Walter Q. Gresham, 1893
	Richard Olney, 1895
Secretary of the Treasury	John G. Carlisle, 1893
Secretary of War	Daniel S. Lamont, 1893
Attorney General	Richard Olney, 1893
	Judson Harmon, 1895
Postmaster General	Wilson S. Bissell, 1893
	William L. Wilson, 1895
Secretary of the Navy	Hilary A. Herbert, 1893
Secretary of the Interior	Hoke Smith, 1893
	David R. Francis, 1896
Secretary of Agriculture	Julius Sterling Morton, 1893

McKinley

Secretary of State	John Sherman, 1897
	William R. Day, 1898
	John Hay, 1898
Secretary of the Treasury	Lyman J. Gage, 1897
Secretary of War	Russell A. Alger, 1897
	Elihu Root, 1899
Attorney General	Joseph McKenna, 1897
	John W. Griggs, 1898
	Philander C. Knox, 1901
Postmaster General	James A. Gary, 1897
	Charles E. Smith, 1898
Secretary of the Navy	John D. Long, 1897
Secretary of the Interior	Cornelius N. Bliss, 1897
	Ethan A. Hitchcock, 1898
Secretary of Agriculture	James Wilson, 1897

T. Roosevelt

Secretary of State	John Hay (Cont.)
	Elihu Root, 1905
	Robert Bacon, 1909
Secretary of the Treasury	Lyman J. Gage (Cont.)
	Leslie M. Shaw, 1902
	George B. Cortelyou, 1907
Secretary of War	Elihu Root (Cont.)
	William H. Taft, 1904
	Luke E. Wright, 1908
Attorney General	Philander C. Knox (Cont.)
	William H. Moody, 1904
	Charles J. Bonaparte, 1906
Postmaster General	Charles E. Smith (Cont.)
	Henry C. Payne, 1902
	Robert J. Wynne, 1904
	George B. Cortelyou, 1905
	George von L. Meyer, 1907
Secretary of the Navy	John D. Long (Cont.)
	William H. Moody, 1902
	Paul Morton, 1904
	Charles J. Bonaparte, 1905
	Victor H. Metcalf, 1906
	Truman H. Newberry, 1908
Secretary of the Interior	Ethan A. Hitchcock (Cont.)
	James R. Garfield, 1907
Secretary of Agriculture	James Wilson (Cont.)
Secretary of Commerce and Labor	George B. Cortelyou, 1903
	Victor H. Metcalf, 1904
	Oscar S. Straus, 1906

Taft

Secretary of State	Philander C. Knox, 1909
Secretary of the Treasury	Franklin MacVeagh, 1909
Secretary of War	Jacob M. Dickinson, 1909
	Henry L. Stimson, 1911
Attorney General	George W. Wickersham, 1909
Postmaster General	Frank H. Hitchcock, 1909
Secretary of the Navy	George von L. Meyer, 1909
Secretary of the Interior	Richard A. Ballinger, 1909
	Walter L. Fisher, 1911
Secretary of Agriculture	James Wilson (Cont.)
Secretary of Commerce and Labor	Charles Nagel, 1909

Wilson

Secretary of State	William J. Bryan, 1913
	Robert Lansing, 1915
	Bainbridge Colby, 1920
Secretary of the Treasury	William G. McAdoo, 1913
	Carter Glass, 1918
	David F. Houston, 1920
Secretary of War	Lindley M. Garrison, 1913
	Newton D. Baker, 1916
Attorney General	James C. McReynolds, 1913
	Thomas W. Gregory, 1914
	A. Mitchell Palmer, 1919
Postmaster General	Albert S. Burleson, 1913

Secretary of the Navy	Josephus Daniels, 1913
Secretary of the Interior	Franklin K. Lane, 1913
	John B. Payne, 1920
Secretary of Agriculture	David F. Houston, 1913
	Edwin T. Meredith, 1920
Secretary of Commerce	William C. Redfield, 1913
	Joshua W. Alexander, 1919
Secretary of Labor	William B. Wilson, 1913

Harding

Secretary of State	Charles E. Hughes, 1921
Secretary of the Treasury	Andrew W. Mellon, 1921
Secretary of War	John W. Weeks, 1921
Attorney General	Harry M. Daugherty, 1921
Postmaster General	Will H. Hays, 1921
	Hubert Work, 1922
	Harry S. New, 1923
Secretary of the Navy	Edwin Denby, 1921
Secretary of the Interior	Albert B. Fall, 1921
	Hubert Work, 1923
Secretary of Agriculture	Henry C. Wallace, 1921
Secretary of Commerce	Herbert Hoover, 1921
Secretary of Labor	James J. Davis, 1921

Coolidge

Secretary of State	Charles E. Hughes (Cont.)
	Frank B. Kellogg, 1925
Secretary of the Treasury	Andrew W. Mellon (Cont.)
Secretary of War	John W. Weeks (Cont.)
	Dwight F. Davis, 1925
Attorney General	Harry M. Daugherty (Cont.)
	Harlan F. Stone, 1924
	John G. Sargent, 1925
Postmaster General	Harry S. New (Cont.)
Secretary of the Navy	Edwin Denby (Cont.)
	Curtis D. Wilbur, 1924
Secretary of the Interior	Hubert Work (Cont.)
	Roy O. West, 1928
Secretary of Agriculture	Henry C. Wallace (Cont.)
	Howard M. Gore, 1924
	William M. Jardine, 1925
Secretary of Commerce	Herbert Hoover (Cont.)
	William F. Whiting, 1928
Secretary of Labor	James J. Davis (Cont.)

Hoover

Secretary of State	Frank B. Kellogg (Cont.)
	Henry L. Stimson, 1929
Secretary of the Treasury	Andrew W. Mellon (Cont.)
	Ogden L. Mills, 1932
Secretary of War	James W. Good, 1929
	Patrick J. Hurley, 1929
Attorney General	William D. Mitchell, 1929
Postmaster General	Walter F. Brown, 1929
Secretary of the Navy	Charles F. Adams, 1929
Secretary of the Interior	Ray Lyman Wilbur, 1929
Secretary of Agriculture	Arthur M. Hyde, 1929
Secretary of Commerce	Robert P. Lamont, 1929
	Roy D. Chapin, 1932
Secretary of Labor	James J. Davis (Cont.)
	William N. Doak, 1930

F. D. Roosevelt

Secretary of State	Cordell Hull, 1933
	E. R. Stettinius, Jr., 1944
Secretary of the Treasury	William H. Woodin, 1933
	Henry Morgenthau, Jr., 1934
Secretary of War	George H. Dern, 1933
	Harry H. Woodring, 1936
	Henry L. Stimson, 1940
Attorney General	Homer S. Cummings, 1933
	Frank Murphy, 1939
	Robert H. Jackson, 1940
	Francis Biddle, 1941

Postmaster General	James A. Farley, 1933
	Frank C. Walker, 1940
Secretary of the Navy	Claude A. Swanson, 1933
	Charles Edison, 1940
	Frank Knox, 1940
	James Forrestal, 1944
Secretary of the Interior	Harold L. Ickes, 1933
Secretary of Agriculture	Henry A. Wallace, 1933
	Claude R. Wickard, 1940
Secretary of Commerce	Daniel C. Roper, 1933
	Harry L. Hopkins, 1938
	Jesse H. Jones, 1940
	Henry A. Wallace, 1945
Secretary of Labor	Frances Perkins, 1933

Truman

Secretary of State	E. R. Stettinius, Jr. (Cont.)
	James F. Byrnes, 1945
	George C. Marshall, 1947
	Dean Acheson, 1949
Secretary of the Treasury	Henry Morgenthau, Jr. (Cont.)
	Frederick M. Vinson, 1945
	John W. Snyder, 1946
Secretary of Defense	James Forrestal, 1947
	Louis A. Johnson, 1949
	George C. Marshall, 1950
	Robert A. Lovett, 1951
Attorney General	Francis Biddle (Cont.)
	Tom C. Clark, 1945
	J. Howard McGrath, 1949
	James P. McGranery, 1952
Postmaster General	Frank C. Walker (Cont.)
	Robert E. Hannegan, 1945
	Jesse M. Donaldson, 1947
Secretary of the Interior	Harold L. Ickes (Cont.)
	Julius A. Krug, 1946
	Oscar L. Chapman, 1949
Secretary of Agriculture	Claude R. Wickard (Cont.)
	Clinton P. Anderson, 1945
	Charles F. Brannan, 1948
Secretary of Commerce	Henry A. Wallace (Cont.)
	W. Averell Harriman, 1946
	Charles Sawyer, 1948
Secretary of Labor	Frances Perkins (Cont.)
	Lewis B. Schwellenbach, 1945
	Maurice J. Tobin, 1948
Secretary of War[1]	Henry L. Stimson (Cont.)
	Robert P. Patterson, 1945
	Kenneth C. Royall, 1947
Secretary of the Navy[1]	James Forrestal (Cont.)

1. On July 26, 1947, the Departments of War and of the Navy were incorporated into the Department of Defense.

Eisenhower

Secretary of State	John Foster Dulles, 1953
	Christian A. Herter, 1959
Secretary of the Treasury	George M. Humphrey, 1953
	Robert B. Anderson, 1957
Secretary of Defense	Charles E. Wilson, 1953
	Neil H. McElroy, 1957
	Thomas S. Gates, Jr., 1959
Attorney General	Herbert Brownell, Jr., 1953
	William P. Rogers, 1958
Postmaster General	Arthur E. Summerfield, 1953
Secretary of the Interior	Douglas McKay, 1953
	Frederick A. Seaton, 1956
Secretary of Agriculture	Ezra Taft Benson, 1953
Secretary of Commerce	Sinclair Weeks, 1953
	Lewis L. Strauss[1], 1958
	Frederick H. Mueller, 1959
Secretary of Health, Edu-	Oveta Culp Hobby, 1953
cation, and Welfare	Marion B. Folsom, 1955
	Arthur S. Flemming, 1958

1. Not confirmed by the Senate.

Secretary of Labor	Martin P. Durkin, 1953
	James P. Mitchell, 1953

Kennedy

Secretary of State	Dean Rusk, 1961
Secretary of the Treasury	C. Douglas Dillon, 1961
Secretary of Defense	Robert S. McNamara, 1961
Attorney General	Robert F. Kennedy, 1961
Postmaster General	J. Edward Day, 1961
	John A. Gronouski, 1963
Secretary of the Interior	Stewart L. Udall, 1961
Secretary of Agriculture	Orville L. Freeman, 1961
Secretary of Commerce	Luther H. Hodges, 1961
Secretary of Labor	Arthur J. Goldberg, 1961
	W. Willard Wirtz, 1962
Secretary of Health, Edu-	Abraham A. Ribicoff, 1961
cation, and Welfare	Anthony J. Celebrezze, 1962

L. B. Johnson

Secretary of State	Dean Rusk (Cont.)
Secretary of the Treasury	C. Douglas Dillon (Cont.)
	Henry H. Fowler, 1965
	Joseph W. Barr[1], 1968
Secretary of Defense	Robert S. McNamara (Cont.)
	Clark M. Clifford, 1968
Attorney General	Robert F. Kennedy (Cont.)
	N. de B. Katzenbach, 1965
	Ramsey Clark, 1967
Postmaster General	John A. Gronouski (Cont.)
	Lawrence F. O'Brien, 1965
	W. Marvin Watson, 1968
Secretary of the Interior	Stewart L. Udall (Cont.)
Secretary of Agriculture	Orville L. Freeman (Cont.)
Secretary of Commerce	Luther H. Hodges (Cont.)
	John T. Connor, 1964
	A. B. Trowbridge, 1967
	C. R. Smith, 1968
Secretary of Labor	W. Willard Wirtz (Cont.)
Secretary of Health, Edu-	Anthony J. Celebrezze (Cont.)
cation, and Welfare	John W. Gardner, 1965
	Wilbur J. Cohen, 1968
Secretary of Housing and	Robert C. Weaver, 1966
Urban Development	Robert C. Wood[1], 1969
Secretary of Transportation	Alan S. Boyd, 1966

1. Recess appointment.

Nixon

Secretary of State	William P. Rogers, 1969
	Henry A. Kissinger, 1973
Secretary of the Treasury	David M. Kennedy, 1969
	John B. Connally, 1971
	George P. Shultz, 1972
	William E. Simon, 1974
Secretary of Defense	Melvin R. Laird, 1969
	Elliot L. Richardson, 1973
	James R. Schlesinger, 1973
Attorney General	John N. Mitchell, 1969
	Richard G. Kleindienst, 1972
	Elliot L. Richardson, 1973
	William B. Saxbe, 1974
Postmaster General[1]	William M. Blount, 1969
Secretary of the Interior	Walter J. Hickel, 1969
	Rogers C. B. Morton, 1971
Secretary of Agriculture	Clifford M. Hardin, 1969
	Earl L. Butz, 1971
Secretary of Commerce	Maurice H. Stans, 1969
	Peter G. Peterson, 1972
	Frederick B. Dent, 1973
Secretary of Labor	George P. Shultz, 1969
	James D. Hodgson, 1970
	Peter J. Brennan, 1973
Secretary of Health, Edu-	Robert H. Finch, 1969
cation, and Welfare	Elliot L. Richardson, 1970
	Caspar W. Weinberger, 1973

Secretary of Housing and Urban Development	George Romney, 1969
	James T. Lynn, 1973
Secretary of Transportation	John A. Volpe, 1969
	Claude S. Brinegar, 1973

1. The Postmaster General is no longer a Cabinet member.

Ford

Secretary of State	Henry A. Kissinger (Cont.)
Secretary of the Treasury	William E. Simon (Cont.)
Secretary of Defense	James R. Schlesinger (Cont.)
	Donald H. Rumsfeld, 1975
Attorney General	William B. Saxbe (Cont.)
	Edward H. Levi, 1975
Secretary of the Interior	Rogers C. B. Morton (Cont.)
	Stanley K. Hathaway, 1975
	Thomas S. Kleppe, 1975
Secretary of Agriculture	Earl L. Butz (Cont.)
	John Knebel, 1976
Secretary of Commerce	Frederick B. Dent (Cont.)
	Rogers C. B. Morton, 1975
	Elliot L. Richardson, 1976
Secretary of Labor	Peter J. Brennan (Cont.)
	John T. Dunlop, 1975
	William J. Usery, Jr., 1976
Secretary of Health, Education, and Welfare	Caspar W. Weinberger (Cont.)
	F. David Mathews, 1975
Secretary of Housing and Urban Development	James T. Lynn (Cont.)
	Carla A. Hills, 1975
Secretary of Transportation	Claude S. Brinegar (Cont.)
	William T. Coleman, Jr., 1975

Carter

Secretary of State	Cyrus R. Vance, 1977
	Edmund S. Muskie, 1980
Secretary of the Treasury	W. Michael Blumenthal, 1977
	G. William Miller, 1979
Secretary of Defense	Harold Brown, 1977
Attorney General	Griffin B. Bell, 1977
	Benjamin R. Civiletti, 1979
Secretary of the Interior	Cecil D. Andrus, 1977
Secretary of Agriculture	Bob S. Bergland, 1977
Secretary of Commerce	Juanita M. Kreps, 1977
	Philip M. Klutznick, 1979
Secretary of Labor	F. Ray Marshall, 1977
Secretary of Health and Human Services[1]	Joseph A. Califano, Jr., 1977
	Patricia Roberts Harris, 1979
Secretary of Housing and Urban Development	Patricia Roberts Harris, 1977
	Moon Landrieu, 1979
Secretary of Transportation	Brock Adams, 1977
	Neil E. Goldschmidt, 1979
Secretary of Energy	James R. Schlesinger, 1977
	Charles W. Duncan, Jr., 1979
Secretary of Education	Shirley Mount Hufstedler, 1979

1. Known as Department of Health, Education, and Welfare until May 1980.

Reagan

Secretary of State	Alexander M. Haig, Jr., 1981
	George P. Shultz, 1982
Secretary of the Treasury	Donald T. Regan, 1981
	James A. Baker 3rd, 1985
	Nicholas F. Brady, 1988
Secretary of Defense	Caspar W. Weinberger, 1981
	Frank C. Carlucci, 1987
Attorney General	William French Smith, 1981
	Edwin Meese 3rd, 1985
	Richard L. Thornburgh, 1988
Secretary of the Interior	James G. Watt, 1981
	William P. Clark, 1983
	Donald P. Hodel, 1985
Secretary of Agriculture	John R. Block, 1981
	Richard E. Lyng, 1986
Secretary of Commerce	Malcolm Baldrige, 1981
	C. William Verity, Jr., 1987

Secretary of Labor	Raymond J. Donovan, 1981
	William E. Brock, 1985
	Ann Dore McLaughlin, 1987
Secretary of Health and Human Services	Richard S. Schweiker, 1981
	Margaret M. Heckler, 1983
	Otis R. Bowen, 1985
Secretary of Housing and Urban Development	Samuel R. Pierce, Jr., 1981
Secretary of Transportation	Andrew L. Lewis, Jr., 1981
	Elizabeth H. Dole, 1983
	James H. Burnley 4th, 1987
Secretary of Energy	James B. Edwards, 1981
	Donald P. Hodel, 1983
	John S. Herrington, 1985
Secretary of Education	T. H. Bell, 1981
	William J. Bennett, 1985
	Lauro F. Cavazos, 1988

Bush

Secretary of State	James A. Baker 3d, 1989
	Lawrence S. Eagleburger, 1992
Secretary of the Treasury	Nicholas F. Brady (Cont.)
Secretary of Defense	Richard Cheney, 1989
Attorney General	Richard L. Thornburgh (Cont.)
	William P. Barr, 1992
Secretary of the Interior	Manuel Lujan Jr., 1989
Secretary of Agriculture	Clayton K. Yeutter, 1989
	Edward Madigan, 1991
Secretary of Commerce	Robert A. Mosbacher Sr., 1989
	Barbara H. Franklin, 1992
Secretary of Labor	Elizabeth H. Dole, 1989
	Lynn Martin, 1991
Secretary of Health and Human Services	Louis W. Sullivan, 1989
Secretary of Housing and Urban Development	Jack F. Kemp, 1989
Secretary of Transportation	Samuel K. Skinner, 1989
	Andrew Card, 1992
Secretary of Energy	James D. Watkins, 1989
Secretary of Education	Lauro F. Cavazos (Cont.)
	Lamar Alexander, 1991
Secretary of Veterans' Affairs	Edward J. Derwinski, 1989

Clinton

Secretary of State	Warren M. Christopher, 1993
	Madeleine Albright, 1996
Secretary of the Treasury	Lloyd Bentsen, 1993
	Robert E. Rubin, 1995–1999
	Lawrence H. Summers, 1999
Secretary of Defense	Les Aspin, 1993
	William J. Perry, 1994
	William S. Cohen, 1997
Attorney General	Janet Reno, 1993
Secretary of the Interior	Bruce Babbitt, 1993
Secretary of Agriculture	Mike Espy, 1993
	Dan Glickman, 1995
Secretary of Commerce	Ronald H. Brown, 1993
	Mickey Kantor, 1996
	William M. Daley, 1997
	Norman Y. Mineta, 2000
Secretary of Labor	Robert B. Reich, 1993
	Alexis Herman, 1997
Secretary of Health and Human Services	Donna E. Shalala, 1993
Secretary of Housing and Urban Development	Henry G. Cisneros, 1993
	Andrew M. Cuomo, 1997
Secretary of Transportation	Federico F. Pena, 1993
	Rodney Slater, 1997
Secretary of Energy	Hazel R. O'Leary, 1993
	Frederico F. Pena, 1997
	Bill Richardson, 1998
Secretary of Education	Richard W. Riley, 1993
Secretary of Veterans' Affairs	Jesse Brown, 1993
	Togo D. West, Jr., 1998

"High Crimes and Misdemeanors:" A Short History of Impeachment

The right to impeach public officials is secured by the U.S. Constitution in Article I, Sections 2 and 3, which discuss the procedure, and in Article II, Section 4, which indicates the grounds for impeachment: "the President, Vice President, and all civil officers of the United States shall be removed from office on impeachment for, and conviction of, treason, bribery, or other high crimes and misdemeanors."

Removing an official from office requires two steps: (1) a formal accusation, or impeachment, by the House of Representatives, and (2) a trial and conviction by the Senate. Impeachment requires a majority vote of the House; conviction is more difficult, requiring a two-thirds vote by the Senate. The vice president presides over the Senate proceedings in the case of all officials except the president, whose trial is presided over by the Chief Justice of the Supreme Court. This is because the vice president can hardly be considered a disinterested party—if his or her boss is forced out of office he or she is next in line for the top job!

What are "High Crimes and Misdemeanors"?

Bribery and treason are among the least ambiguous reasons meriting impeachment, but the ocean of wrongdoing encompassed by the Constitution's stipulation of "high crimes and misdemeanors" is vast. Abuse of power and serious misconduct in office fit this category, but one act that is definitely not grounds for impeachment is partisan discord. Several impeachment cases have confused political animosity with genuine crimes. Since Congress, the vortex of partisanship, is responsible for indicting, trying, and convicting public officials, it is necessary for the legislative branch to temporarily cast aside its factional nature and adopt a judicial role.

The Infamous Sixteen

Since 1797 the House of Representatives has impeached sixteen federal officials. These include two presidents, a cabinet member, a senator, a justice of the Supreme Court, and eleven federal judges. Of those, the Senate has convicted and removed seven, all of them judges. Not included in this list are the office holders who have resigned rather than face impeachment, most notably, President Richard M. Nixon.

The One That Got Away

Of thirty-five attempts at impeachment, only nine have come to trial. Because it cripples Congress with a lengthy trial, impeachment is infrequent. Many officials, seeing the writing on the wall, resign rather than face the ignominy of a public trial.

The most famous of these cases is of course that of President Richard Nixon, a Republican. After five men hired by Nixon's reelection committee were caught burglarizing Democratic party headquarters at the Watergate Complex on June 17, 1972, President Nixon's subsequent behavior—his cover-up of the burglary and refusal to turn over evidence—led the House Judiciary Committee to issue three articles of impeachment on July 30, 1974. The document also indicted Nixon for illegal wiretapping, misuse of the CIA, perjury, bribery, obstruction of justice, and other abuses of executive power. "In all of this," the Articles of Impeachment summarize, "Richard M. Nixon has acted in a manner contrary to his trust as president and subversive of constitutional government, to the great prejudice of the cause of law and justice, and to the manifest injury of the people of the United States." Impeachment appeared inevitable, and Nixon resigned on Aug. 9, 1974.

Impeachments of Federal Officials

Source: Congressional Directory.

The procedure for the impeachment of federal officials is detailed in Article I, Section 3, of the Constitution. The Senate has sat as a court of impeachment in the following cases:

William Blount, Senator from Tennessee; charges dismissed for want of jurisdiction, Jan. 14, 1799.

John Pickering, Judge of the U.S. District Court for New Hampshire; removed from office March 12, 1804.

Samuel Chase, Associate Justice of the Supreme Court; acquitted March 1, 1805.

James H. Peck, Judge of the U.S. District Court for Missouri; acquitted Jan. 31, 1831.

West H. Humphreys, Judge of the U.S. District Court for the middle, eastern, and western districts of Tennessee; removed from office June 26, 1862.

Andrew Johnson, President of the United States; acquitted May 26, 1868.

William W. Belknap, Secretary of War; acquitted Aug. 1, 1876.

Charles Swayne, Judge of the U.S. District Court for the northern district of Florida; acquitted Feb. 27, 1905.

Robert W. Archbald, Associate Judge, U.S. Commerce Court; removed Jan. 13, 1913.

George W. English, Judge of the U.S. District Court for eastern district of Illinois; resigned Nov. 4, 1926; proceedings dismissed.

Harold Louderback, Judge of the U.S. District Court for the northern district of California; acquitted May 24, 1933.

Halsted L. Ritter, Judge of the U.S. District Court for the southern district of Florida; removed from office April 17, 1936.

Harry E. Claiborne, Judge of the U.S. District Court for the district of Nevada; removed from office Oct. 9, 1986.

Alcee L. Hastings, Judge of the U.S. District Court for the southern district of Florida; removed from office Oct. 20, 1988.

Walter L. Nixon, Judge of the U.S. District Court for Mississippi; removed from office Nov. 3, 1989.

William J. Clinton, President of the United States; acquitted Feb. 12, 1999.

Members of the Supreme Court of the United States

Mailing address for the Supreme Court: U.S. Supreme Court Building, 1 First Street NE, Washington, D.C. 20543.

Name, state	Service Term	Yrs	Birth Place	Date	Died	Religion
Chief Justices						
John Jay, N.Y.	1789–1795	5	N.Y.	1745	1829	Episcopal
John Rutledge, S.C.	1795	0	S.C.	1739	1800	Church of England
Oliver Ellsworth, Conn.	1796–1800	4	Conn.	1745	1807	Congregational
John Marshall, Va.	1801–1835	34	Va.	1755	1835	Episcopal
Roger B. Taney, Md.	1836–1864	28	Md.	1777	1864	Roman Catholic
Salmon P. Chase, Ohio	1864–1873	8	N.H.	1808	1873	Episcopal
Morrison R. Waite, Ohio	1874–1888	14	Conn.	1816	1888	Episcopal
Melville W. Fuller, Ill.	1888–1910	21	Maine	1833	1910	Episcopal
Edward D. White, La.	1910–1921	10	La.	1845	1921	Roman Catholic
William H. Taft, Conn.	1921–1930	8	Ohio	1857	1930	Unitarian
Charles E. Hughes, N.Y.	1930–1941	11	N.Y.	1862	1948	Baptist
Harlan F. Stone, N.Y.	1941–1946	4	N.H.	1872	1946	Episcopal
Frederick M. Vinson, Ky.	1946–1953	7	Ky.	1890	1953	Methodist
Earl Warren, Calif.	1953–1969	15	Calif.	1891	1974	Protestant
Warren E. Burger, Va.	1969–1986	17	Minn.	1907	1995	Presbyterian
William H. Rehnquist, Ariz.	1986–	—	Wis.	1924	—	Lutheran
Associate Justices						
James Wilson, Pa.	1789–1798	8	Scotland	1742	1798	Episcopal
John Rutledge, S.C.	1790–1791	1	S.C.	1739	1800	Church of England
William Cushing, Mass.	1790–1810	20	Mass.	1732	1810	Unitarian
John Blair, Va.	1790–1796	5	Va.	1732	1800	Presbyterian
James Iredell, N.C.	1790–1799	9	England	1751	1799	Episcopal
Thomas Johnson, Md.	1792–1793	0	Md.	1732	1819	Episcopal
William Paterson, N.J.	1793–1806	13	Ireland	1745	1806	Protestant
Samuel Chase, Md.	1796–1811	15	Md.	1741	1811	Episcopal
Bushrod Washington, Va.	1799–1829	30	Va.	1762	1829	Episcopal
Alfred Moore, N.C.	1800–1804	3	N.C.	1755	1810	Episcopal
William Johnson, S.C.	1804–1834	30	S.C.	1771	1834	Presbyterian
Brockholst Livingston, N.Y.	1807–1823	16	N.Y.	1757	1823	Presbyterian
Thomas Todd, Ky.	1807–1826	18	Va.	1765	1826	Presbyterian
Gabriel Duval, Md.	1811–1835	23	Md.	1752	1844	French Protestant
Joseph Story, Mass.	1812–1845	33	Mass.	1779	1845	Unitarian
Smith Thompson, N.Y.	1823–1843	20	N.Y.	1768	1843	Presbyterian
Robert Trimble, Ky.	1826–1828	2	Va.	1777	1828	Protestant
John McLean, Ohio	1830–1861	31	N.J.	1785	1861	Methodist-Epis.
Henry Baldwin, Pa.	1830–1844	14	Conn.	1780	1844	Trinity Church
James M. Wayne, Ga.	1835–1867	32	Ga.	1790	1867	Protestant
Philip P. Barbour, Va.	1836–1841	4	Va.	1783	1841	Episcopal
John Catron, Tenn.	1837–1865	28	Pa.	1786	1865	Presbyterian
John McKinley, Ala.	1837–1852	14	Va.	1780	1852	Protestant
Peter V. Daniel, Va.	1841–1860	18	Va.	1784	1860	Episcopal
Samuel Nelson, N.Y.	1845–1872	27	N.Y.	1792	1873	Protestant
Levi Woodbury, N.H.	1845–1851	5	N.H.	1789	1851	Protestant
Robert C. Grier, Pa.	1846–1870	23	Pa.	1794	1870	Presbyterian
Benjamin R. Curtis, Mass.	1851–1857	5	Mass.	1809	1874	(2)
John A. Campbell, Ala.	1853–1861	8	Ga.	1811	1889	Episcopal
Nathan Clifford, Maine	1858–1881	23	N.H.	1803	1881	(1)
Noah H. Swayne, Ohio	1862–1881	18	Va.	1804	1884	Quaker
Samuel F. Miller, Iowa	1862–1890	28	Ky.	1816	1890	Unitarian
David Davis, Ill.	1862–1877	14	Md.	1815	1886	(4)
Stephen J. Field, Calif.	1863–1897	34	Conn.	1816	1899	Episcopal
William Strong, Pa.	1870–1880	10	Conn.	1808	1895	Presbyterian
Joseph P. Bradley, N.J.	1870–1892	21	N.Y.	1813	1892	Presbyterian
Ward Hunt, N.Y.	1872–1882	9	N.Y.	1810	1886	Episcopal
John M. Harlan, Ky.	1877–1911	33	Ky.	1833	1911	Presbyterian
William B. Woods, Ga.	1880–1887	6	Ohio	1824	1887	Protestant
Stanley Matthews, Ohio	1881–1889	7	Ohio	1824	1889	Presbyterian
Horace Gray, Mass.	1882–1902	20	Mass.	1828	1902	(3)
Samuel Blatchford, N.Y.	1882–1893	11	N.Y.	1820	1893	Presbyterian
Lucius Q. C. Lamar, Miss.	1888–1893	5	Ga.	1825	1893	Methodist
David J. Brewer, Kan.	1889–1910	20	Asia Minor	1837	1910	Protestant
Henry B. Brown, Mich.	1890–1906	15	Mass.	1836	1913	Protestant

| Name, state | Service | | Birth | | Died | Religion |
	Term	Yrs	Place	Date		
George Shiras, Jr., Pa.	1892–1903	10	Pa.	1832	1924	Presbyterian
Howell E. Jackson, Tenn.	1893–1895	2	Tenn.	1832	1895	Baptist
Edward D. White, La.*	1894–1910	16	La.	1845	1921	Roman Catholic
Rufus W. Peckham, N.Y.	1895–1909	13	N.Y.	1838	1909	Episcopal
Joseph McKenna, Calif.	1898–1925	26	Pa.	1843	1926	Roman Catholic
Oliver W. Holmes, Mass.	1902–1932	29	Mass.	1841	1935	Unitarian
William R. Day, Ohio	1903–1922	19	Ohio	1849	1923	Protestant
William H. Moody, Mass.	1906–1910	3	Mass.	1853	1917	Episcopal
Horace H. Lurton, Tenn.	1909–1914	4	Ky.	1844	1914	Episcopal
Charles E. Hughes, N.Y.*	1910–1916	5	N.Y.	1862	1948	Baptist
Willis Van Devanter, Wyo.	1910–1937	26	Ind.	1859	1941	Episcopal
Joseph R. Lamar, Ga.	1910–1916	4	Ga.	1857	1916	Ch. of Disciples
Mahlon Pitney, N.J.	1912–1922	10	N.J.	1858	1924	Presbyterian
James C. McReynolds, Tenn.	1914–1941	26	Ky.	1862	1946	Disciples of Christ
Louis D. Brandeis, Mass.	1916–1939	22	Ky.	1856	1941	Jewish
John H. Clarke, Ohio	1916–1922	5	Ohio	1857	1945	Protestant
George Sutherland, Utah	1922–1938	15	England	1862	1942	Episcopal
Pierce Butler, Minn.	1923–1939	16	Minn.	1866	1939	Roman Catholic
Edward T. Sanford, Tenn.	1923–1930	7	Tenn.	1865	1930	Episcopal
Harlan F. Stone, N.Y.*	1925–1941	16	N.H.	1872	1946	Episcopal
Owen J. Roberts, Pa.	1930–1945	15	Pa.	1875	1955	Episcopal
Benjamin N. Cardozo, N.Y.	1932–1938	6	N.Y.	1870	1938	Jewish
Hugo L. Black, Ala.	1937–1971	34	Ala.	1886	1971	Baptist
Stanley F. Reed, Ky.	1938–1957	19	Ky.	1884	1980	Protestant
Felix Frankfurter, Mass.	1939–1962	23	Austria	1882	1965	Jewish
William O. Douglas, Conn.	1939–1975	36	Minn.	1898	1980	Presbyterian
Frank Murphy, Mich.	1940–1949	9	Mich.	1890	1949	Roman Catholic
James F. Byrnes, S.C.	1941–1942	1	S.C.	1879	1972	Episcopal
Robert H. Jackson, Pa.	1941–1954	13	N.Y.	1892	1954	Episcopal
Wiley B. Rutledge, Iowa	1943–1949	6	Ky.	1894	1949	Unitarian
Harold H. Burton, Ohio	1945–1958	13	Mass.	1888	1964	Unitarian
Tom C. Clark, Tex.	1949–1967	17	Tex.	1899	1977	Presbyterian
Sherman Minton, Ind.	1949–1956	7	Ind.	1890	1965	Roman Catholic
John M. Harlan, N.Y.	1955–1971	16	Ill.	1899	1971	Presbyterian
William J. Brennan, Jr., N.J.	1956–1990	33	N.J.	1906	1997	Roman Catholic
Charles E. Whittaker, Mo.	1957–1962	5	Kan.	1901	1973	Methodist
Potter Stewart, Ohio	1958–1981	23	Mich.	1915	1985	Episcopal
Byron R. White, Colo.	1962–1993	31	Colo.	1917	—	Episcopal
Arthur J. Goldberg, Ill.	1962–1965	2	Ill.	1908	1990	Jewish
Abe Fortas, Tenn.	1965–1969	3	Tenn.	1910	1982	Jewish
Thurgood Marshall, N.Y.	1967–1991	24	Md.	1908	1993	Episcopal
Harry A. Blackmun, Minn.	1970–1994	24	Ill.	1908	—	Methodist
Lewis F. Powell, Jr., Va.	1972–1987	15	Va.	1907	1998	Presbyterian
William H. Rehnquist, Ariz.*	1972–1986	14	Wis.	1924	—	Lutheran
John Paul Stevens, Ill.	1975–	—	Ill.	1920	—	Protestant
Sandra Day O'Connor, Ariz.	1981–	—	Tex.	1930	—	Episcopal
Antonin Scalia, D.C.	1986–	—	N.J.	1936	—	Roman Catholic
Anthony M. Kennedy, Calif.	1988–	—	Calif.	1936	—	Roman Catholic
David H. Souter, N.H.	1990–	—	Mass.	1939	—	Episcopal
Clarence Thomas, D.C.	1991–	—	Ga.	1948	—	Roman Catholic
Ruth Bader Ginsburg, D.C.	1993–	—	N.Y.	1933	—	Jewish
Stephen G. Breyer, Mass.	1994–	—	Calif.	1938	—	n.a.

NOTE: n.a. = not available. *Served as both Chief Justice and Associate Justice. 1. Congregational; later Unitarian. 2. Unitarian; then Episcopal. 3. Unitarian or Congregational. 4. Not a member of any church.

Supreme Court Facts

Youngest justice appointed: Joseph Story (age 32)

Oldest justice appointed: Horace Lurton (age 65)

Oldest justice to serve: Oliver Wendell Holmes (retired at age 90)

Shortest term: John Rutledge (1 year associate justice; 4 months chief justice)

Longest term: William O. Douglas (36 years, 209 days)

First Catholic justice: Roger B. Taney

First Jewish justice: Louis Brandeis

First African-American justice: Thurgood Marshall

First woman justice: Sandra Day O'Connor

President to appoint the most justices: George Washington (11)

President to appoint the most justices in the 20th century: Franklin Roosevelt (9)

Milestone Cases in Supreme Court History

1803 *Marbury v. Madison* was the first instance in which a law passed by Congress was declared unconstitutional. The decision greatly expanded the power of the Court by establishing its right to overturn acts of Congress, a power not explicitly granted by the Constitution.

1819 *McCulloch v. Maryland* upheld the right of Congress to create a Bank of the United States, ruling that it was a power implied but not enumerated by the Constitution. The case is significant because it advanced the doctrine of implied powers, or a loose construction of the Constitution. The Court, Chief Justice John Marshall wrote, would sanction laws reflecting "the letter and spirit" of the Constitution.

1857 *Dred Scott v. Sanford* was a highly controversial case that intensified the national debate over slavery. The case involved Dred Scott, a slave, who was taken from a slave state to a free territory. Scott filed a lawsuit claiming that because he had lived on free soil he was entitled to his freedom. Chief Justice Roger B. Taney disagreed, ruling that blacks were not citizens and therefore could not sue in Federal Court. Taney further inflamed anti-slavery forces by declaring that Congress had no right to ban slavery from U.S. territories.

1896 *Plessy v. Ferguson* was the infamous case that asserted that "equal but separate accommodations" for blacks on railroad cars did not violate the "equal protection under the laws" clause of the 14th Amendment. By defending the constitutionality of racial segregation, the Court paved the way for the repressive Jim Crow laws of the south. The lone dissenter on the Court, Justice John Marshall Harlan, protested, "The thin disguise of 'equal' accommodations . . . will not mislead anyone."

1954 *Brown v. Board of Education of Topeka* invalidated racial segregation in schools, and led to the unraveling of de jure segregation in all areas of public life. In the unanimous decision spearheaded by Chief Justice Earl Warren, the Court invalidated the Plessy ruling, declaring "in the field of public education, the doctrine of 'separate but equal' has no place," and contending that "separate educational facilities are inherently unequal." Future Supreme Court Justice Thurgood Marshall was one of the NAACP lawyers who successfully argued the case.

1973 *Roe v. Wade* legalized abortion and is at the center of the current controversy between "Pro-Life" and "Pro-Choice" advocates. The Court ruled that a woman has the right to an abortion without interference from the government in the first trimester of pregnancy, contending that it is part of her "right to privacy." The Court maintained that right to privacy is not absolute, however, and granted states the right to intervene in the second and third trimesters of pregnancy.

Notable Decisions of the U.S. Supreme Court, 1999–2000 Term

Ban on Opening Police Records Upheld (Dec. 7, 1999): Justices, 7–2, approve California law barring commercial information services from access to data routinely made available to journalists and others.

States Protected from Lawsuits on Age Bias (Jan. 11, 2000): In 5–4 ruling, Court decides Congress has no authority to make state governments subject to federal law that prohibits discrimination against older workers.

Flight Upheld as Cause for Police Search (Jan. 12, 2000): Justices all agree that police can be justified in detaining person who bolts at sight of officers. Court splits, 5–4, however, on acceptable level of suspicion.

Ban on State Data Sales Upheld (Jan. 12, 2000): Unanimous decision approves federal law preventing states from selling databases of personal information.

Ruling on Defendants' Rights (Jan. 13, 2000): Justices decide, 9–0, that criminal defendants do not have right to represent themselves while appealing their case.

Important Voting Rights Case Resolved (Jan. 24, 2000): Court rules, 5–4, that Justice Dept. must approve districting changes, even those with discriminatory intent, if minority voters will not be negatively impacted.

State Codes on Oil Tankers Limited (March 6, 2000): Court rules unanimously that states cannot set safety and environmental standards that conflict with or supplement federal regulations.

F.D.A. Power on Tobacco Denied (March 21, 2000): Justices rule unanimously that Congress had never given Food and Drug Administration authority to regulate industry's products.

Police Limited on Gun Searches (March 28, 2000): Court rules unanimously that an anonymous tip does not justify a stop-and-frisk action against a person.

Bans on Nude Dancing Upheld (March 29, 2000): Ruling, 6–3, says cities and states may restrict it as a step to combat crime and other negative secondary effects associated with such entertainment.

Women's Rights Law Overturned (May 15, 2000): In 5–4 decision, Court invalidates six-year-old provision of federal law that permits victims of rape, domestic violence, and other crimes to sue attackers in federal court. Justices declare "Constitution requires a distinction between what is truly national and what is truly local."

Curb on Cable Sex Shows Overruled (May 22, 2000): Justices, 5–4, declare for first time that cable TV programming is entitled to highest level of First Amendment protection. Court struck down federal law requiring many systems to limit sexually explicitly channels to the late-night hours.

Grandparents Denied Visiting Rights (June 5, 2000): In 6–3 decision, Court overrules Washington State law permitting a judge to order rights for grandparents over a mother's objection. Justices declare parents have "fundamental right to make decisions concerning the care, custody, and control" of their children.

H.M.O.s Upheld in Lawsuits (June 12, 2000): Justices rule unanimously that financial incentives given doctors to hold down costs do not make health care organizations liable in federal court for violating a duty to put their patients first.

Ruling in Job Discrimination Case (June 12, 2000): Court holds unanimously that a plaintiff can prevail, even without direct evidence, by showing that an employer's innocent-sounding explanation of actions was a lie.

Public Student Prayers Forbidden (June 19, 2000): Court rules, 6–3, that prayers led by students at high school football games are no exception to earlier decisions against officially sponsored prayer in public schools. All prayers at school and games are declared unconstitutional.

Miranda Decision Reaffirmed (June 26, 2000): By 7–2 vote, justices rebuff move to overthrow requirement for warning to suspected criminals before police interrogation.

Boy Scouts Backed in Ban on Gays (June 28, 2000): Justices rule, 5–4, that Boy Scouts have a constitutional right because of organization's opposition to homosexuality as part of its "expressive message."

Bar on Abortion Procedure Rejected (June 28, 2000): Court rules, 5–4, that government cannot prohibit "partial birth" operation when doctors believe it is most medically approved way to terminate some pregnancies.

Aid to Parochial Schools Upheld (June 28, 2000): By 6–3 vote, Court rules that federal program providing computers and other "instructional equipment" does not violate constitutional separation of church and state.

The Supreme Court Building

Source: U.S. Supreme Court. Web: www.supremecourtus.gov.

Despite its role as a coequal branch of government, the Supreme Court was not provided with a building of its own until 1935, the 146th year of its existence. Initially, the Court met in the Merchants Exchange Building in New York City. When the national capital moved to Philadelphia in 1790, the Court moved with it, establishing Chambers first in Independence Hall and later in the City Hall.

When the Federal Government moved, in 1800, to the permanent capital in Washington, D.C., Congress lent the Court space in the new Capitol Building. The Court was to change its meeting place a half dozen times within the Capitol. Additionally, the Court convened for a short period in a private house after the British set fire to the Capitol during the War of 1812. Following this episode, the Court returned to the Capitol and met from 1819 to 1860 in a chamber now restored as the "Old Supreme

Court Chamber." Then from 1860 until 1935, the Court sat in what is now known as the "Old Senate Chamber."

Finally in 1929, Chief Justice William Howard Taft, who had been president of the United States from 1909 to 1913, persuaded Congress to end this arrangement and authorize the construction of a permanent home for the Court. Architect Cass Gilbert was charged by Chief Justice Taft to design "a building of dignity and importance suitable for its use as the permanent home of the Supreme Court of the United States."

Neither Taft nor Gilbert survived to see the Supreme Court Building completed. The construction, begun in 1932, was completed in 1935, when the Court was finally able to occupy its own building.

Assassinations and Attempts in U.S. Since 1865

Lincoln, Abraham (President of U.S.): Shot April 14, 1865, in Washington, D.C., by John Wilkes Booth; died April 15.

Seward, William H. (Secretary of State): Escaped assassination (though injured) April 14, 1865, in Washington, D.C., by Lewis Powell (or Paine), accomplice of John Wilkes Booth.

Garfield, James A. (President of U.S.): Shot July 2, 1881, in Washington, D.C., by Charles J. Guiteau; died Sept. 19.

McKinley, William (President of U.S.): Shot Sept. 6, 1901, in Buffalo by Leon Czolgosz; died Sept. 14.

Roosevelt, Theodore (ex-President of U.S.): Escaped assassination (though shot) Oct. 14, 1912, in Milwaukee while campaigning for President.

Cermak, Anton J. (Mayor of Chicago): Shot Feb. 15, 1933, in Miami by Giuseppe Zangara, who attempted to assassinate Franklin D. Roosevelt; Cermak died March 6.

Roosevelt, Franklin D. (President-elect of U.S.): Escaped assassination unhurt Feb. 15, 1933, in Miami.

Long, Huey P. (U.S. Senator from Louisiana): Shot Sept. 8, 1935, in Baton Rouge by Dr. Carl A. Weiss; died Sept. 10.

Truman, Harry S. (President of U.S.): Escaped assassination unhurt Nov. 1, 1950, in Washington, D.C., as 2 Puerto Rican nationalists attempted to shoot their way into Blair House.

Kennedy, John F. (President of U.S.): Shot Nov. 22, 1963, in Dallas, Tex., allegedly by Lee Harvey Oswald; died same day. Injured was Gov. John B. Connally of Texas. Oswald was shot and killed two days later by Jack Ruby.

Malcolm X, also known as El-Hajj Malik El-Shabazz (black activist): Shot and killed in a New York City auditorium, Feb. 21, 1965; his killer(s) were never positively identified.

King, Martin Luther, Jr. (civil rights leader): Shot April 4, 1968, in Memphis by James Earl Ray; died same day.

Kennedy, Robert F. (U.S. Senator from New York): Shot June 5, 1968, in Los Angeles by Sirhan Bishara Sirhan; died June 6.

Wallace, George C. (Governor of Alabama): Shot and critically wounded in assassination attempt May 15, 1972, at Laurel, Md., by Arthur Herman Bremer. Wallace paralyzed from waist down.

Ford, Gerald R. (President of U.S.): Escaped assassination attempt Sept. 5, 1975, in Sacramento, Calif., by Lynette Alice (Squeaky) Fromme, who pointed but did not fire .45-caliber pistol. Escaped assassination attempt in San Francisco, Calif., Sept. 22, 1975, by Sara Jane Moore, who fired one shot from a .38-caliber pistol that was deflected.

Jordan, Vernon E., Jr. (civil rights leader): Shot and critically wounded in assassination attempt May 29, 1980, in Fort Wayne, Ind.

Reagan, Ronald (President of U.S.): Shot in left lung in Washington by John W. Hinckley, Jr., on March 30, 1981; three others also wounded.

The Early Congresses

At the urging of Massachusetts and Virginia, the First Continental Congress met in Philadelphia on Sept. 5, 1774, and was attended by representatives of all the colonies except Georgia. Patrick Henry of Virginia declared: "The distinctions between Pennsylvanians, New Yorkers, and New Englanders are no more. I am not a Virginian but an American." This Congress, which adjourned Oct. 26, 1774, passed intercolonial resolutions calling for extensive boycott by the colonies against British trade.

The following year, most of the delegates from the colonies were chosen by popular election to attend the Second Continental Congress, which assembled in Philadelphia on May 10. As war had already begun between the colonies and England, the chief problems before the Congress were the procuring of military supplies, the establishment of an army and proper defenses, the issuing of continental bills of credit, etc. On June 15, 1775, George Washington was elected to command the Continental army. Congress adjourned Dec. 12, 1776.

Other Continental Congresses were held in Baltimore (1776–1777), Philadelphia (1777), Lancaster, Pa. (1777), York, Pa. (1777–1778), and Philadelphia (1778–1781).

In 1781, the Articles of Confederation, although establishing a league of the thirteen states rather than a strong central government, provided for the continuance of Congress. Known thereafter as the Congress of the Confederation, it held sessions in Philadelphia (1781–1783), Princeton, N.J. (1783), Annapolis, Md. (1783–1784), and Trenton, N.J. (1784). Five sessions were held in New York City between the years 1785 and 1789.

The Congress of the United States, established by the ratification of the Constitution, held its first meeting on March 4, 1789, in New York City. Several sessions of Congress were held in Philadelphia, and the first meeting in Washington, D.C., was on Nov. 17, 1800.

Presidents of the Continental Congresses

Name	Elected	Birth and death dates	Name	Elected	Birth and death dates
Peyton Randolph, Va.	9/5/1774	c.1721–1775	John Hanson, Md.	11/5/1781	1715–1783
Henry Middleton, S.C.	10/22/1774	1717–1784	Elias Boudinot, N.J.	11/4/1782	1740–1821
Peyton Randolph, Va.	5/10/1775	c.1721–1775	Thomas Mifflin, Pa.	11/3/1783	1744–1800
John Hancock, Mass.	5/24/1775	1737–1793	Richard Henry Lee, Va.	11/30/1784	1732–1794
Henry Laurens, S.C.	11/1/1777	1724–1792	John Hancock, Mass.[1]	11/23/1785	1737–1793
John Jay, N.Y.	12/10/1778	1745–1829	Nathaniel Gorham, Mass.	6/6/1786	1738–1796
Samuel Huntington, Conn.	9/28/1779	1731–1796	Arthur St. Clair, Pa.	2/2/1787	1734–1818
Thomas McKean, Del.	7/10/1781	1734–1817	Cyrus Griffin, Va.	1/22/1788	1748–1810

1. Resigned May 29, 1786, never having served, because of continued illness.

States by Order of Entry into Union

State	Entered Union	Year settled	Representatives in Congress[1]	State	Entered Union	Year settled	Representatives in Congress[1]
1. Delaware	Dec. 7, 1787	1638	1	26. Michigan	Jan. 26, 1837	1668	16
2. Pennsylvania	Dec. 12, 1787	1682	21	27. Florida	Mar. 3, 1845	1565	23
3. New Jersey	Dec. 18, 1787	1660	13	28. Texas	Dec. 29, 1845	1682	30
4. Georgia	Jan. 2, 1788	1733	11	29. Iowa	Dec. 28, 1846	1788	5
5. Connecticut	Jan. 9, 1788	1634	6	30. Wisconsin	May 29, 1848	1766	9
6. Massachusetts	Feb. 6, 1788	1620	10	31. California	Sept. 9, 1850	1769	52
7. Maryland	Apr. 28, 1788	1634	8	32. Minnesota	May 11, 1858	1805	8
8. South Carolina	May 23, 1788	1670	6	33. Oregon	Feb. 14, 1859	1811	5
9. New Hampshire	June 21, 1788	1623	2	34. Kansas	Jan. 29, 1861	1727	4
10. Virginia	June 25, 1788	1607	11	35. West Virginia	June 20, 1863	1727	3
11. New York	July 26, 1788	1614	31	36. Nevada	Oct. 31, 1864	1849	2
12. North Carolina	Nov. 21, 1789	1660	12	37. Nebraska	Mar. 1, 1867	1823	3
13. Rhode Island	May 29, 1790	1636	2	38. Colorado	Aug. 1, 1876	1858	6
14. Vermont	Mar. 4, 1791	1724	1	39. North Dakota	Nov. 2, 1889	1812	1
15. Kentucky	June 1, 1792	1774	6	40. South Dakota	Nov. 2, 1889	1859	1
16. Tennessee	June 1, 1796	1769	9	41. Montana	Nov. 8, 1889	1809	1
17. Ohio	Mar. 1, 1803	1788	19	42. Washington	Nov. 11, 1889	1811	9
18. Louisiana	Apr. 30, 1812	1699	7	43. Idaho	July 3, 1890	1842	2
19. Indiana	Dec. 11, 1816	1733	10	44. Wyoming	July 10, 1890	1834	1
20. Mississippi	Dec. 10, 1817	1699	5	45. Utah	Jan. 4, 1896	1847	3
21. Illinois	Dec. 3, 1818	1720	20	46. Oklahoma	Nov. 16, 1907	1889	6
22. Alabama	Dec. 14, 1819	1702	7	47. New Mexico	Jan. 6, 1912	1610	3
23. Maine	Mar. 15, 1820	1624	2	48. Arizona	Feb. 14, 1912	1776	6
24. Missouri	Aug. 10, 1821	1735	9	49. Alaska	Jan. 3, 1959	1784	1
25. Arkansas	June 15, 1836	1686	4	50. Hawaii	Aug. 21, 1959	1820	2

1. Does not include Senators. *Source:* Compiled from various sources by the editors.

The Confederate States of America

State	Seceded from Union	Readmitted to Union[1]	State	Seceded from Union	Readmitted to Union[1]
1. South Carolina	Dec. 20, 1860	July 9, 1868	7. Texas	March 2, 1861	March 30, 1870
2. Mississippi	Jan. 9, 1861	Feb. 23, 1870	8. Virginia	April 17, 1861	Jan. 26, 1870
3. Florida	Jan. 10, 1861	June 25, 1868	9. Arkansas	May 6, 1861	June 22, 1868
4. Alabama	Jan. 11, 1861	July 13, 1868	10. North Carolina	May 20, 1861	July 4, 1868
5. Georgia	Jan. 19, 1861	July 15, 1870[2]	11. Tennessee	June 8, 1861	July 24, 1866
6. Louisiana	Jan. 26, 1861	July 9, 1868			

NOTE: Four other slave states—Delaware, Maryland, Kentucky, and Missouri—remained in the Union. The latter two were actually represented on the Confederate flag, which, like the Stars and Stripes, featured a star for every state. 1. Date of readmission to representation in U.S. House of Representatives. 2. Second readmission date. First date was July 21, 1868, but the representatives were unseated March 5, 1869.

Territorial Expansion

Accession	Date	Area[1]	Accession	Date	Area[1]
United States	—	3,536,278	Other territory	—	4,664
Territory in 1790	—	891,364	Philippines	1898	115,600[2]
Louisiana Purchase	1803	831,321	Puerto Rico	1899	3,426
Florida	1819	69,866	Guam	1899	209
Texas	1845	384,958	American Samoa	1900	77
Oregon	1846	283,439	Canal Zone[3]	1904	553
Mexican Cession	1848	530,706	Virgin Islands of U.S.	1917	134
Gadsden Purchase	1853	29,640	Trust Territory of Pacific Islands	1947	177[4]
Alaska	1867	591,004	All other	—	14
Hawaii	1898	6,471	**Total, 1990**	—	**3,787,319**

1. Total land and water area in square miles. 2. Became independent in 1946. 3. Reverted to Panama in 1979. 4. Land area only. Palau, the last remaining Trust Territory, became a soverign state in 1994. *Source:* U.S. Bureau of the Census, Web: www.census.gov.

The Monroe Doctrine

The Monroe Doctrine was announced in President James Monroe's message to Congress, during his second term on Dec. 2, 1823, in part as follows:

"In the discussions to which this interest has given rise, and in the arrangements by which they may terminate, the occasion has been deemed proper for asserting as a principle in which rights and interests of the United States are involved, that the American continents, by the free and independent condition which they have assumed and maintain, are henceforth not to be considered as subjects for future colonization by any European power. . . . We owe it, therefore, to candor and to the amicable relations existing between the United States and those powers to declare that we should consider any attempt on their part to extend their system to any portion of this hemisphere as dangerous to our peace and safety. With the existing colonies and dependencies of any European power we have not interfered and shall not interfere. But with the governments who have declared their independence and maintain it, and whose independence we have, on great consideration and on just principles, acknowledged, we could not view any interposition for the purpose of oppressing them or controlling in any other manner their destiny by any European power in any other light than as the manifestation of an unfriendly disposition toward the United States."

Figures and Legends in American Folklore

Appleseed, Johnny (John Chapman, 1774–1847): Massachusetts-born nurseryman; reputed to have spread seeds and seedlings out of which grew the apple orchards of the Midwest.

Billy the Kid (William H. Bonney, 1859–1881): Desperado who killed his first man before he reached his teens; after short life of crime in Wild West was gunned down by Sheriff Pat Garrett; symbol of lawless West.

Boone, Daniel (1734–1820): Frontiersman and Indian fighter, about whom legends of early America have been built; figured in Byron's *Don Juan.*

Buffalo Bill (William F. Cody, 1846–1917): Buffalo hunter and Indian scout; many of the legends about him stem from his own Wild West show, which he operated in late 19th century.

Bunyan, Paul: Mythical lumberjack; subject of tall tales throughout timber country (that he dug Grand Canyon, for example).

Crockett, Davy (1786–1836): Frontiersman, Congressman, and defender of the Alamo, his backwoods humor and larger-than-life adventures made him synonymous with the Wild West.

Jones, Casey (John Luther Jones, 1863–1900): Example of heroic locomotive engineer given to feats of prowess; died in wreck when his Illinois Central "Cannonball" express hit a freight train at Vaughan, Miss.

Uncle Sam: Personification of U.S. and its people; origin uncertain; may be based on inspector of government supplies in Revolutionary War and War of 1812.

The EXPANSION of the UNITED STATES

Just Where Was Columbus?

Pinpointing the explorer's whereabouts on October 12, 1492.

Christopher Columbus, of course, thought he had arrived in the "Indies," the medieval name for Asia. Using Marco Polo's *Travels* among other sources, Columbus calculated that his voyage would lead him to Cathay (China), Cipango (Japan), the Spice Islands (the Mollucas), and India.

A Slow Boat to China

After landing on a small island on Oct. 12, 1492, in what he believed were the Indies, Columbus sailed along the coast of Cuba, certain that he had finally reached the continent of Cathay. He searched in vain for the magnificent cities Marco Polo had described, hoping to deliver a letter from the Spanish monarchs to "the great Khan," the Chinese emperor. "Afterwards," Columbus wrote on Oct. 21, "I shall set sail for another very large island which I believe to be Cipango, according to the indications I receive from the Indians on board." Columbus's Japan proved to be the island of Hispaniola.

Refusing to Ask for Directions

Three voyages later, Columbus still resolutely maintained that he had reached Asia despite growing contrary evidence. Amerigo Vespucci's 1501 voyage along the coast of South America convinced most explorers and their patrons that a huge unexplored continent existed across the Atlantic—what Vespucci called *Mundus Novus,* the New World. Columbus, however, died in 1506 still insisting that he had found a new route to Asia.

Where in the New World is San Salvador?

But confusion over where Columbus landed in the New World has not been restricted to the explorer himself. For centuries scholars have hotly debated where Columbus first set foot in the Western Hemisphere—the so-called landfall controversy. All have agreed that Columbus arrived on an island in the Bahamas that he named San Salvador (Holy Savior), and that the island's Arawak inhabitants called Guanahani. But dozens of different islands have been bandied about by numerous historians as the genuine San Salvador. The three most popular contestants have been Watling's Island (called San Salvador today), Cat Island, and Grand Turk (which today is no longer part of the Bahamas).

More than 500 years later, there still is no definitive answer to the landfall question, but the general consensus is that Columbus landed on what was known until 1926 as Watlings Island. The island was named for a local pirate famous for his piety—marauding and pillaging were strictly forbidden on Sundays. The residents of Watlings renamed their island San Salvador in 1926, figuring the right name was key to their claim as Columbus's island.

The 400th Centennial

Among the early historians involved in the landfall controversy was Washington Irving, whose volume, *Life and Voyages of Christopher Columbus* (1828), suggested that the explorer first landed on Cat Island, to the northeast of Watlings. As the 400th anniversary of Columbus's arrival in the New World drew near, a special investigation of various Bahamian islands was commissioned, meant to clear up the controversy once and for all. The report, however, just emphasized how muddled the controversy had become:

> " . . . No two investigators agree as to the first landfall without disagreeing as to the second; and if they happen to coincide on the first, it is only to fall out over the fourth." —Frederick A. Ober, *In the Wake of Columbus* (1893)

Not Just Another Pretty Island

The difficulty in pinpointing Columbus's first landing is in part the result of the sketchy information provided in his captain's log. The island is described as large, level, and with a lagoon, and like all the other islands he encounters, "these lands are the most fertile, temperate, level, and beautiful countries in the world." With so little to go on, it is easy to make an argument for nearly any beautiful lagoon in the Bahamas.

Another difficulty is the lack of archeological evidence. Columbus landed only briefly on the island—he was far more interested in moving on to richer and more promising parts of the Indies. No definitive trace of his presence has been uncovered. And although a number of early maps show the island of Guanahani, the island is found in various locations depending on the vagaries of the cartographer.

More Centennial Squabbling

In 1986, the landfall controversy again grew tempestuous. As the 500th Columbus centennial approached, *National Geographic* presented a sophisticated argument claiming that Samana Cay was the true island of Columbus's landing. This stirred up the waters, but most historians, including such luminaries as Samuel Eliot Morison, maintained that Watlings/San Salvador was the true landfall.

This is a perfectly agreeable conclusion according to San Salvador's 539 inhabitants, who depend on Columbus-inspired tourism for their livelihood. The present-day San Salvadorans are the descendents of freed slaves-the original inhabitants, the Arawaks, have long since vanished.

The Voyages

First voyage, 1492–1493: San Salvador, The Bahamas, Cuba, Hispaniola

Second voyage, 1493–1494: Dominica, Hispaniola, Guadeloupe, Antiqua, Puerto Rico, Cuba, Jamaica

Third voyage, 1498–1500: St. Vincent, Grenada, Trinidad, Margarita, Venezuela

Fourth voyage, 1502–1504: St. Lucia, Martinique, Honduras, Nicaragua, Costa Rica, Panama

Firsts in America

This selection is based on our editorial judgment. Other sources may list different firsts.

Admiral in U.S. Navy: David Glasgow Farragut, 1866.

Airmail route, first transcontinental: Between New York City and San Francisco, 1920.

Assembly, representative: House of Burgesses, founded in Virginia, 1619.

Bank established: Bank of North America, Philadelphia, 1781.

Birth in America to English parents: Virginia Dare, born Roanoke Island, N.C., 1587.

Black newspaper: *Freedom's Journal,* 1827, edited by John B. Russworm.

Black U.S. diplomat: Ebenezer D. Bassett, 1869, minister-resident to Haiti.

Black elected governor of a state: L. Douglas Wilder, Virginia, 1990.

Black elected to U.S. Senate: Hiram Revels, 1870, Mississippi.

Black elected to U.S. House of Representatives: Jefferson Long, Georgia, 1870.

Black associate justice of U.S. Supreme Court: Thurgood Marshall, Oct. 2, 1967.

Black U.S. cabinet minister: Robert C. Weaver, 1966, Secretary of the Department of Housing and Urban Development.

Botanic garden: Established by John Bartram in Philadelphia, 1728, and is still in existence in its original location.

Cartoon, colored: "The Yellow Kid," by Richard Outcault, in *New York World,* 1895.

College: Harvard, founded 1636.

College to establish coeducation: Oberlin College (Ohio), 1833.

Electrocution of a criminal: William Kemmler in Auburn Prison, Auburn, N.Y., Aug. 6, 1890.

Five and Dime Store: Founded by Frank Woolworth, Utica, N.Y., 1879 (moved to Lancaster, Pa., same year).

Fraternity, Greek-letter: Phi Beta Kappa; founded Dec. 5, 1776, at College of William and Mary.

Gay and lesbian civil rights advocacy organization: National Gay and Lesbian Task Force, founded in New York City, 1973.

Homosexual, acknowledged, elected to high local office: Harvey Milk, 1977, San Francisco Board of Supervisors.

Law to be declared unconstitutional by U.S. Supreme Court: Judiciary Act of 1789. Case: *Marbury* v. *Madison,* 1803.

Library, circulating: Philadelphia, 1731.

Newspaper, illustrated daily: *New York Daily Graphic,* 1873.

Newspaper published daily: *Pennsylvania Packet and General Advertiser,* Philadelphia, Sept. 1784.

Newspaper published over a continuous period: *The Boston News-Letter,* April 1704.

Oil well, commercial: Titusville, Pa., 1859.

Panel quiz show on radio: *Information Please,* May 17, 1938.

Postage stamps issued: 1847.

Public School: Boston Latin School, Boston, 1635.

Radio station licensed: KDKA, Pittsburgh, Pa., Oct. 27, 1920.

Railroad, transcontinental: Central Pacific and Union Pacific railroads, joined at Promontory, Utah, May 10, 1869.

Savings bank: The Provident Institute for Savings, Boston, 1816.

Science museum: Founded by Charleston (S.C.) Library Society, 1773.

Skyscraper: Home Insurance Co., Chicago, 1885 (10 floors, 2 added later).

Slaves brought into America: At Jamestown, Va., 1619, from a Dutch ship.

Sorority: Alpha Delta Pi, at Wesleyan Female College, 1851.

State to abolish capital punishment: Michigan, 1847.

State to enter Union after original 13: Vermont, 1791.

Steam-heated building: Eastern Hotel, Boston, 1845.

Steam railroad (carried passengers and freight): Baltimore & Ohio, 1830.

Strike on record by union: Journeymen Printers, New York City, 1776.

Subway: Opened in Boston, 1897.

"Tabloid" picture newspaper: *The Illustrated Daily News* (now *The Daily News*), New York City, 1919.

Vaudeville theater: Gaiety Museum, Boston, 1883.

Woman astronaut appointed shuttle commander: Lt. Col. Eileen Collins, *Columbia,* launched July 1999.

Woman astronaut to ride in space: Dr. Sally K. Ride, 1983.

Woman cabinet member: Frances Perkins, Secretary of Labor, 1933.

Woman candidate for President: Victoria Claflin Woodhull, nominated by National Woman's Suffrage Assn. on ticket of Nation Radical Reformers, 1872.

Woman candidate for Vice President: Geraldine A. Ferraro, nominated on a major party ticket, Democratic Party, 1984.

Woman doctor of medicine: Elizabeth Blackwell; M.D. from Geneva Medical College of Western New York, 1849.

Woman elected governor of a state: Nellie Tayloe Ross, Wyoming, 1925.

Woman elected to U.S. Senate: Hattie Caraway, Arkansas; elected Nov. 1932.

Woman member of U.S. House of Representatives: Jeannette Rankin (Mont.); elected Nov. 1916.

Woman member of U.S. Senate: Rebecca Latimer Felton (Ga.); appointed Oct. 3, 1922.

Woman member of U.S. Supreme Court: Sandra Day O'Connor; appointed July 1981.

Woman Secretary of State: Madeleine Albright, appointed Dec. 1996.

Woman suffrage granted: Wyoming Territory, 1869.

Written constitution: *Fundamental Orders of Connecticut,* 1639.

The Great Seal of the U.S.

On July 4, 1776, the Continental Congress appointed a committee consisting of Benjamin Franklin, John Adams, and Thomas Jefferson "to bring in a device for a seal of the United States of America." After many delays, a verbal description of a design by William Barton was finally approved by Congress on June 20, 1782. The seal shows an American bald eagle with a ribbon in its mouth bearing the device *E pluribus unum* (One out of many). In its talons are the arrows of war and an olive branch of peace. On the reverse side it shows an unfinished pyramid with an eye (the eye of Providence) above it. Although this description was adopted in 1782, the first drawing was not made until four years later, and no die has ever been cut.

The Star-Spangled Banner

Francis Scott Key, 1814

O say, can you see, by the dawn's early light,
What so proudly we hail'd at the twilight's last gleaming?
Whose broad stripes and bright stars, thro' the perilous fight,
O'er the ramparts we watch'd, were so gallantly streaming?
And the rockets' red glare, the bombs bursting in air,
Gave proof thro' the night that our flag was still there.
O say, does that star-spangled banner yet wave
O'er the land of the free and the home of the brave?

On the shore dimly seen thro' the mists of the deep,
Where the foe's haughty host in dread silence reposes,
What is that which the breeze, o'er the towering steep,
As it fitfully blows, half conceals, half discloses?
Now it catches the gleam of the morning's first beam,
In full glory reflected, now shines on the stream:
'Tis the star-spangled banner: O, long may it wave
O'er the land of the free and the home of the brave!

And where is that band who so vauntingly swore
That the havoc of war and the battle's confusion,
A home and a country should leave us no more?
Their blood has wash'd out their foul footsteps' pollution.
No refuge could save the hireling and slave
From the terror of flight or the gloom of the grave:
And the star-spangled banner in triumph doth wave
O'er the land of the free and the home of the brave.

O thus be it ever when free-men shall stand
Between their lov'd home and the war's desolation;
Blest with vict'ry and peace, may the heav'n-rescued land
Praise the Pow'r that hath made and preserv'd us a nation!
Then conquer we must, when our cause it is just,
And this be our motto: "In God is our trust!"
And the star-spangled banner in triumph shall wave
O'er the land of the free and the home of the brave!

On Sept. 13, 1814, Francis Scott Key visited the British fleet in Chesapeake Bay to secure the release of Dr. William Beanes, who had been captured after the burning of Washington, D.C. The release was secured, but Key was detained on ship overnight during the shelling of Fort McHenry, one of the forts defending Baltimore. In the morning, he was so delighted to see the American flag still flying over the fort that he began a poem to commemorate the occasion. First published under the title "Defense of Fort M'Henry," the poem soon attained wide popularity as sung to the tune "To Anacreon in Heaven." The origin of this tune is obscure, but it may have been written by John Stafford Smith, a British composer born in 1750. "The Star-Spangled Banner" was officially made the National Anthem by Congress in 1931, although it already had been adopted as such by the Army and the Navy.

History of the American Flag

According to popular legend, the first American flag was made by Betsy Ross, a Philadelphia seamstress who was acquainted with George Washington, leader of the Continental Army, and other influential Philadelphians. In May 1776, so the story goes, General Washington and two representatives from the Continental Congress visited Ross at her upholstery shop and showed her a rough design of the flag. Although Washington initially favored using a star with six points, Ross advocated for a five-pointed star, which could be cut with just one quick snip of the scissors, and the gentlemen were won over.

Unfortunately, historians have never been able to verify this charming version of events, although it is known that Ross made flags for the navy of Pennsylvania. The story of Washington's visit to the flagmaker became popular about the time of the country's first centennial, after William Canby, a grandson of Ross, told about her role in shaping U.S. history in a speech given at the Philadelphia Historical Society in March 1870.

What is known, is that the first unofficial national flag, called the Grand Union Flag or the Continental Colours, was raised at the behest of General Washington near his headquarters outside Boston, Mass., on Jan. 1, 1776. The flag had 13 alternating red and white horizontal stripes and the British Union Flag (a predecessor of the Union Jack) in the canton. Another early flag had a rattlesnake on a background of 13 red and white stripes with the motto "Don't Tread on Me."

The first official national flag, also known as the Stars and Stripes or Old Glory, was approved by the Continental Congress on June 14, 1777. The blue canton contained 13 stars, representing the original 13 colonies, but the layout varied. After Vermont and Kentucky were admitted to the Union in 1791 and 1792, respectively, two more stars and two more stripes were added in 1795. In 1818, after five more states had gained admittance, Congress passed legislation fixing the number of stripes at 13 and requiring that the number of stars equal the number of states. The last new star, bringing the total to 50, was added on July 4, 1960, after Hawaii became a state.

Confederate Flag Controversy

In 1962 the Confederate battle flag was placed on top of the South Carolina statehouse by vote of the all-white legislature. While other Southern states eventually removed the flag from their statehouses, South Carolina refused to follow suit. This prompted the NAACP to organize a national economic boycott against South Carolina's $14 billion-a-year tourism industry, and since the summer of 1999, more than 100 conventions and business organizations have participated in the boycott.

On April 12, 2000, the South Carolina state senate finally passed a bill to remove the flag by a majority of 36–7. The bill specified that a more traditional version of the battle flag (square shaped as opposed to the rectangular flag then flying above the statehouse) would be flown in front of the Capitol next to a monument honoring fallen Confederate soldiers. The bill then went to the House, where it encountered some difficulty. But on May 18, 2000, after the bill was modified to ensure that the flag's new pole would be 30 feet high, it was passed by a majority of 66–43, and Governor Jim Hodges signed the bill five days later. On July 1, the flag was removed from the South Carolina statehouse.

A Controversial Symbol

The Confederate battle flag, also known as the Southern Cross, has been described variously as a proud emblem of Southern heritage and as a shameful reminder of slavery and segregation. Today two states (Mississippi and Georgia) incorporate the Confederate battle flag in their official state flag, and the flags of two other states (Arkansas and Alabama) use elements of the Southern Cross. The Confederate battle flag has also been appropriated by the Ku Klux Klan and other racist hate groups. According to the Southern Poverty Law Center, more than 500 extremist groups use the Southern Cross as one of their symbols.

Common Misperceptions

There is a common misperception that the Confederate battle flag (the Southern Cross) was the national flag of the Confederacy. In reality, the flag we usually associate with the Confederacy was strictly a battle flag—and not the only battle flag used. The Confederacy actually changed its national flag three times during the course of the war.

Another misperception is that in some Southern states the Confederate flag was flown without interruption since the 1860s. For the most part, the Southern states that raised the Confederate flag did so during the 1950s and 1960s, in a defiant stand against integration.

The Pledge of Allegiance to the Flag[1]

I pledge allegiance to the Flag of the United States of America, and to the Republic for which it stands, one Nation under God,[2] indivisible, with liberty and justice for all.

1. The original pledge was published in the Sept. 8, 1892, issue of *The Youth's Companion* in Boston. For years, the authorship was in dispute between James B. Upham and Francis Bellamy of the magazine's staff. In 1939, after a study of the controversy, the United States Flag Association decided that authorship be credited to Bellamy.
2. The phrase "under God" was added to the pledge on June 14, 1954.

The White House

Source: Department of the Interior, U.S. National Park Service.

The White House, the official residence of the president, is at 1600 Pennsylvania Avenue in Washington, D.C. 20500. The site, covering about 18 acres, was selected by President Washington and Pierre Charles L'Enfant, and the architect was James Hoban. The design appears to have been influenced by Leinster House, Dublin, and James Gibb's *Book of Architecture.* The cornerstone was laid Oct. 13, 1792, and the first residents were President John Adams and First Lady Abigail Adams in November 1800. The building was burned by the British in 1814 during the War of 1812.

From Dec. 1948 to March 1952, the interior of the White House was rebuilt, and the outer walls were strengthened.

The rooms for public functions are on the first floor; the second and third floors are used as the residence of the president and first family. The most celebrated public room is the East Room, where formal receptions take place. Other public rooms are the Red Room, the Green Room, and the Blue Room. The State Dining Room is used for formal dinners. There are 132 rooms.

U.S. Capitol

When the French architect and engineer Maj. Pierre L'Enfant first began to lay out the plans for a new federal city (now Washington, D.C.), he noted that Jenkins' Hill, overlooking the area, seemed to be "a pedestal waiting for a monument." It was here that the U.S. Capitol would be built. The basic structure as we know it today evolved over a period of more than 150 years. In 1792 a competition was held for the design of a capitol building. Dr. William Thornton, a physician and amateur architect, submitted the winning plan, a simple, low-lying structure of classical proportions with a shallow dome. Later, internal modifications were made by Benjamin Henry Latrobe. After the building was burned by the British in 1814, Latrobe and architect Charles Bulfinch were responsible for its reconstruction. Finally, under Thomas Walter, who was Architect of the Capitol from 1851 to 1865, the House and Senate wings and the imposing cast iron dome topped with the Statue of Freedom were added, and the Capitol assumed the form we see today. In Statuary Hall, which used to be the old House chamber, a small disk on the floor marks the spot where John Quincy Adams was fatally stricken after more than

50 years of service to his country. A whisper from one side of this room can be heard across the vast space of the hall. Visitors can see the original Supreme Court chamber a floor below the Rotunda.

The Capitol Building is also a vast artistic treasure house. The works of such famous artists as Gilbert Stuart, Rembrandt Peale, and John Trumbull are displayed on the walls. The Great Rotunda, with its 180-foot- (54.9-m-) high dome, is decorated with a fresco by Constantino Brumidi, which extends some 300 feet (90 m) in circumference. Throughout the building are many paintings of events in U.S. history and sculptures of outstanding Americans. The 68-acre (27.5-ha) park that the Capitol is situated on was designed by the 19th-century landscape architect Frederick Law Olmsted.

There are free guided tours of the Capitol, which include admission to the House and Senate galleries. Those who wish to visit the visitors' gallery in either wing without taking the tour may obtain passes from their Senators or Representatives. Visitors may ride on the monorail subway that joins the House and Senate wings of the Capitol with the Congressional office buildings.

The Liberty Bell

The Liberty Bell was cast in England in 1752 for the Pennsylvania Statehouse (now named Independence Hall) in Philadelphia. It was recast in Philadelphia in 1753. It is inscribed with the words, "Proclaim liberty throughout all the land unto all the inhabitants thereof" (Lev. 25:10). The bell was rung on July 8, 1776, for the first public reading of the

Declaration of Independence. Hidden in Allentown during the British occupation of Philadelphia, it was replaced in Independence Hall in 1778. The bell cracked on July 8, 1835, while tolling the death of Chief Justice John Marshall. In 1976 the Liberty Bell was moved to a special exhibition building near Independence Hall.

Washington Monument

Construction of this magnificent Washington, D.C., monument, which draws some two million visitors a year, took nearly a century of planning, building, and controversy. Provision for a large equestrian statue of George Washington was made in the original city plan, but the project was soon dropped. After Washington's death it was taken up again, and a number of false starts and changes of design were made. Finally, in 1848, work was begun on the monument that stands today. The design, by architect Robert Mills, then featured an ornate base. In 1854, however, political squabbling and a lack of

money brought construction to a halt. Work was resumed in 1880, and the monument was completed in 1884 and opened to the public in 1888. The tapered shaft, faced with white marble and rising from walls 15 feet thick (4.6 m) at the base was modeled after the obelisks of ancient Egypt. The monument, one of the tallest masonry constructions in the world, stands just over 555 feet (169 m). Memorial stones from the 50 States, foreign countries, and organizations line the interior walls. The top, reached only by elevator, commands a panoramic view of the city.

Arlington National Cemetery

Arlington National Cemetery occupies 612 acres in Virginia on the Potomac River, directly opposite Washington. This land was part of the estate of John Parke Custis, Martha Washington's son. His son, George Washington Parke Custis, built the mansion which later became the home of Robert E. Lee. In 1864, Arlington became a military cemetery. More than 240,000 service members and their dependents are buried there. Expansion of the cemetery began in 1966, using a 180-acre tract of land directly east of the present site.

In 1921, an Unknown American Soldier of World War I was buried in the cemetery; the monument at the Tomb of the Unknown Soldier was opened to the public without ceremony in 1932. Two additional Unknowns, one from World War II and one from the Korean War, were buried May 30, 1958.

The Unknown Serviceman of Vietnam was buried on May 28, 1984. In June 1998 his body was disinterred and recent DNA-testing technology was used to identify him as First Lt. Michael Blassie, an Air Force pilot from St. Louis. It is possible that technology will prevent there from ever being another "unknown" buried in the tomb.

The inscription carved on the Tomb of the Unknowns reads:

HERE RESTS IN
HONORED GLORY
AN AMERICAN
SOLDIER
KNOWN BUT TO GOD

The Statue of Liberty

The Statue of Liberty ("Liberty Enlightening the World") is a 225-ton, steel-reinforced copper female figure, 152 ft. in height, facing the ocean from Liberty Island[1] in New York Harbor. The right hand holds aloft a torch, and the left hand carries a tablet upon which is inscribed: "July IV MDCCLXXVI."

The statue was designed by Frédéric Auguste Bartholdi of Alsace as a gift to the United States from the people of France to memorialize the alliance of the two countries in the American Revolution and their abiding friendship. The French people contributed the $250,000 cost.

The 150-foot pedestal was designed by Richard M. Hunt and built by Gen. Charles P. Stone, both Americans. It contains steel underpinnings designed by Alexander Eiffel of France to support the statue. The $270,000 cost was borne by popular subscription in this country. President Grover Cleveland accepted the statue for the United States on Oct. 28, 1886.

On Sept. 26, 1972, President Richard M. Nixon dedicated the American Museum of Immigration, housed in structural additions to the base of the statue. In 1984 scaffolding went up for a major res-

toration and the torch was extinguished on July 4. It was relit with much ceremony July 4, 1986 to mark its centennial.

On a tablet inside the pedestal is engraved the following sonnet, written by Emma Lazarus (1849–1887):

The New Colossus
Not like the brazen giant of Greek fame.
With conquering limbs astride from land to land;
Here at our sea-washed, sunset gates shall stand
A mighty woman with a torch, whose flame
Is the imprisoned lightning, and her name
Mother of Exiles. From her beacon-hand
Glows world-wide welcome; her mild eyes command
The air-bridged harbor that twin cities frame.
"Keep, ancient lands, your storied pomp!" cries she
With silent lips. "Give me your tired, your poor,
Your huddled masses yearning to breathe free,
The wretched refuse of your teeming shore.
Send these, the homeless, tempest-tost to me,
I lift my lamp beside the golden door!"

1. Called Bedloe's Island prior to 1956.

The Mayflower Compact

On Sept. 6, 1620, the *Mayflower*, a sailing vessel of about 180 tons, started her memorable voyage from Plymouth, England, with about 100[1] pilgrims aboard, bound for Virginia to establish a private permanent colony in North America.

Arriving at what is now Provincetown, Mass., on Nov. 11 (Nov. 21, new-style calendar), 41 of the passengers signed the famous "Mayflower Compact" as the boat lay at anchor in that Cape Cod harbor. A small detail of the pilgrims, led by William Bradford, assigned to select a place for permanent settlement, landed at what is now Plymouth, Mass., on Dec. 21 (n.s.).

The text of the compact follows:

In the name of God, Amen. We, whose names are underwritten, the Loyal Subjects of our dread Sovereign Lord, King *James,* by the Grace of God, of *Great Britain, France* and *Ireland,* King, *Defender of the Faith,* &c.

Having undertaken for the Glory of God, and Advancement of the Christian Faith, and the Honour of our King and Country, a voyage to plant the first colony in the northern Parts of Virginia; do by these Presents, solemnly and mutually in the Presence of God and one of another, covenant and combine ourselves together into a civil Body Politick, for our better Ordering and Preservation, and Furtherance of the Ends aforesaid; And by Virtue hereof to enact, constitute, and frame, such just and equal Laws, Ordinances, Acts, Constitutions and Offices, from time to time, as shall be thought most meet and convenient for the General good of the Colony; unto which we promise all due Submission and Obedience.

In Witness whereof we have hereunto subscribed our names at *Cape Cod* the eleventh of *November,* in the Reign of our Sovereign Lord, King *James* of *England, France* and *Ireland,* the eighteenth, and of *Scotland* the fifty-fourth. *Anno Domini,* 1620

John Carver	William Mullins	John Billington	Peter Brown
Digery Priest	Thomas English	Thomas Tinker	John Turner
William Brewster	John Howland	Samuel Fuller	Edward Tilly
Edmund Margesson	Stephen Hopkins	Richard Clark	John Craxton
John Alden	Edward Winslow	John Allerton	Thomas Rogers
George Soule	Gilbert Winslow	Richard Warren	John Goodman
James Chilton	Miles Standish	Edward Liester	Edward Fuller
Francis Cooke	Richard Bitteridge	William Bradford	Richard Gardiner
Moses Fletcher	Francis Eaton	Thomas Williams	William White
John Ridgate	John Tilly	Isaac Allerton	Edward Doten
Christopher Martin			

1. Historians differ as to whether 100, 101, or 102 passengers were aboard.

The Declaration of Independence

On April 12, 1776, the legislature of North Carolina authorized its delegates to the Continental Congress to join with others in a declaration of separation from Great Britain; the first colony to instruct its delegates to take the actual initiative was Virginia on May 15. On June 7, 1776, Richard Henry Lee of Virginia offered a resolution to the Congress to the effect "that these United Colonies are, and of right ought to be, free and independent States. . . ." A committee consisting of Thomas Jefferson, John Adams, Benjamin Franklin, Robert R. Livingston, and Roger Sherman was organized to "prepare a declaration to the effect of the said first resolution." The Declaration of Independence was adopted on July 4, 1776. Most delegates signed the Declaration August 2, but George Wythe (Va.) signed August 27; Richard Henry Lee (Va.), Elbridge Gerry (Mass.), and Oliver Wolcott (Conn.) in September; Matthew Thornton (N.H.), not a delegate until September, in November; and Thomas McKean (Del.), although present on July 4, not until 1781 by special permission, having served in the army in the interim.

In Congress, July 4, 1776
The unanimous Declaration of the thirteen United States of America

When in the Course of human events it becomes necessary for one people to dissolve the political bands which have connected them with another, and to assume among the powers of the earth, the separate and equal station to which the Laws of Nature and of Nature's God entitle them, a decent respect to the opinions of mankind requires that they should declare the causes which impel them to the separation.

We hold these truths to be self-evident, that all men are created equal, that they are endowed by their Creator with certain unalienable Rights, that among these are Life, Liberty and the pursuit of Happiness.—That to secure these rights, Governments are instituted among Men, deriving their just powers from the consent of the governed.—That whenever any Form of Government becomes destructive of these ends, it is the Right of the People to alter or to abolish it, and to institute new Government, laying its foundation on such principles and organizing its powers in such form, as to them shall seem most likely to effect their Safety and Happiness. Prudence, indeed, will dictate that Governments long established should not be changed for light and transient causes; and accordingly all experience hath shewn that mankind are more disposed to suffer, while evils are sufferable, than to right themselves by abolishing the forms to which they are accustomed. But when a long train of abuses and usurpations, pursuing invariably the same Object evinces a design to reduce them under absolute Despotism, it is their right, it is their duty, to throw off such Government, and to provide new Guards for their future security.—Such has been the patient sufferance of these Colonies; and such is now the necessity which constrains them to alter their former Systems of Government. The history of the present King of Great Britain is a history of repeated injuries and usurpations, all having in direct object the establishment of an absolute Tyranny over these States. To prove this, let Facts be submitted to a candid world.

He has refused his Assent to Laws, the most wholesome and necessary for the public good.

He has forbidden his Governors to pass Laws of immediate and pressing importance, unless suspended in their operation till his Assent should be obtained; and when so suspended, he has utterly neglected to attend to them.

He has refused to pass other Laws for the accommodation of large districts of people, unless those people would relinquish the right of Representation in the Legislature, a right inestimable to them and formidable to tyrants only.

He has called together legislative bodies at places unusual, uncomfortable, and distant from the depository of their Public Records, for the sole purpose of fatiguing them into compliance with his measures.

He has dissolved Representative Houses repeatedly, for opposing with manly firmness his invasions on the rights of the people.

He has refused for a long time, after such dissolutions, to cause others to be elected; whereby the Legislative Powers, incapable of Annihilation, have returned to the People at large for their exercise; the State remaining in the mean time exposed to all the dangers of invasion from without, and convulsions within.

He has endeavoured to prevent the population of these States; for that purpose obstructing the Laws for Naturalization of Foreigners; refusing to pass others to encourage their migrations hither, and raising the conditions of new Appropriations of Lands.

He has obstructed the Administration of Justice, by refusing his Assent to Laws for establishing Judiciary Powers.

He has made Judges dependent on his Will alone, for the tenure of their offices, and the amount and payment of their salaries.

He has erected a multitude of New Offices, and sent hither swarms of Officers to harass our people, and eat out their substance.

He has kept among us, in times of peace, Standing Armies without the Consent of our legislatures.

He has affected to render the Military independent of and superior to the Civil Power.

He has combined with others to subject us to a jurisdiction foreign to our constitution, and unacknowledged by our laws; giving his Assent to their Acts of pretended Legislation:

For quartering large bodies of armed troops among us:

For protecting them, by a mock Trial, from punishment for any Murders which they should commit on the Inhabitants of these States:

For cutting off our Trade with all parts of the world:

For imposing Taxes on us without our Consent:

For depriving us in many cases, of the benefits of Trial by Jury:

For transporting us beyond Seas to be tried for pretended offences:

For abolishing the free System of English Laws in a neighbouring Province, establishing therein an Arbitrary government, and enlarging its Boundaries so as to render it at once an example and fit instrument for introducing the same absolute rule into these Colonies:

For taking away our Charters, abolishing our most valuable Laws and altering fundamentally the Forms of our Governments:

For suspending our own Legislatures, and declaring themselves invested with power to legislate for us in all cases whatsoever.

He has abdicated Government here, by declaring us out of his Protection and waging War against us.

He has plundered our seas, ravaged our Coasts, burnt our towns, and destroyed the lives of our people.

He is at this time transporting large Armies of foreign Mercenaries to compleat the works of death, desolation, and tyranny, already begun with circumstances of Cruelty & Perfidy scarcely paralleled in the most barbarous ages, and totally unworthy the Head of a civilized nation.

He has constrained our fellow Citizens taken Captive on the high Seas to bear Arms against their Country, to become the executioners of their friends and Brethren, or to fall themselves by their Hands.

He has excited domestic insurrections amongst us, and has endeavoured to bring on the inhabitants of our frontiers, the merciless Indian Savages, whose known rule of warfare, is an undistinguished destruction of all ages, sexes and conditions.

In every stage of these Oppressions We have Petitioned for Redress in the most humble terms: Our repeated Petitions have been answered only by repeated injury. A Prince, whose character is thus marked by every act which may define a Tyrant, is unfit to be the ruler of a free people.

Nor have We been wanting in attentions to our British brethren. We have warned them from time to time of attempts by their legislature to extend an unwarrantable jurisdiction over us. We have reminded them of the circumstances of our emigration and settlement here. We have appealed to their native justice and magnanimity, and we have conjured them by the ties of our common kindred to disavow these usurpations, which would inevitably interrupt our connections and correspondence. They too have been deaf to the voice of justice and of consanguinity. We must, therefore, acquiesce in the necessity, which denounces our Separation, and hold them, as we hold the rest of mankind, Enemies in War, in Peace Friends.

We, therefore, the Representatives of the United States of America, in General Congress, Assembled, appealing to the Supreme Judge of the world for the rectitude of our intentions, do, in the Name, and by Authority of the good People of these Colonies, solemnly publish and declare, That these United Colonies are, and of Right ought to be Free and Independent States; that they are Absolved from all Allegiance to the British Crown, and that all political connection between them and the State of Great Britain, is and ought to be totally dissolved; and that as Free and Independent States, they have full Power to levy War, conclude Peace, contract Alliances, establish Commerce, and to do all other Acts and Things which Independent States may of right do.—And for the support of this Declaration, with a firm reliance on the protection of Divine Providence, we mutually pledge to each other our Lives, our Fortunes and our sacred Honor.

—John Hancock

New Hampshire
Josiah Bartlett
Wm. Whipple
Matthew Thornton

Rhode Island
Step. Hopkins
William Ellery

Connecticut
Roger Sherman
Sam'el Huntington
Wm. Williams
Oliver Wolcott

New York
Wm. Floyd
Phil. Livingston
Frans. Lewis
Lewis Morris

New Jersey
Richd. Stockton
Jno. Witherspoon
Fras. Hopkinson
John Hart
Abra. Clark

Pennsylvania
Robt. Morris
Benjamin Rush
Benj. Franklin
John Morton
Geo. Clymer
Jas. Smith
Geo. Taylor
James Wilson
Geo. Ross

Massachusetts-Bay
Saml. Adams

John Adams
Robt. Treat Paine
Elbridge Gerry

Delaware
Caesar Rodney
Geo. Read
Tho. M'Kean

Maryland
Samuel Chase
Wm. Paca
Thos. Stone
Charles Carroll of
  Carrollton

Virginia
George Wythe
Richard Henry Lee
Th. Jefferson

Benj. Harrison
Ths. Nelson, Jr.
Francis Lightfoot Lee
Carter Braxton

North Carolina
Wm. Hooper
Joseph Hewes
John Penn

South Carolina
Edward Rutledge
Thos. Heyward, Junr.
Thomas Lynch, Junr.
Arthur Middleton

Georgia
Button Gwinnett
Lyman Hall
Geo. Walton

Constitution of the United States of America

(Historical text has been edited to conform to contemporary American usage. The bracketed words are designations for your convenience; they are not part of the Constitution.)

The oldest federal constitution in existence was framed by a convention of delegates from twelve of the thirteen original states in Philadelphia in May, 1787, Rhode Island failing to send a delegate. George Washington presided over the session, which lasted until September 17, 1787. The draft (originally a preamble and seven Articles) was submitted to all thirteen states and was to become effective when ratified by nine states. It went into effect on the first Wednesday in March, 1789, having been ratified by New Hampshire, the ninth state to approve, on June 21, 1788. The states ratified the Constitution in the following order:

Delaware	December 7, 1787	South Carolina	May 23, 1788
Pennsylvania	December 12, 1787	New Hampshire	June 21, 1788
New Jersey	December 18, 1787	Virginia	June 25, 1788
Georgia	January 2, 1788	New York	July 26, 1788
Connecticut	January 9, 1788	North Carolina	November 21, 1789
Massachusetts	February 6, 1788	Rhode Island	May 29, 1790
Maryland	April 28, 1788		

[Preamble]

We the people of the United States, in order to form a more perfect Union, establish justice, insure domestic tranquility, provide for the common defence, promote the general welfare, and secure the blessings of liberty to ourselves and our posterity, do ordain and establish this Constitution for the United States of America.

Article I

Section 1

[Legislative powers vested in Congress.] All legislative powers herein granted shall be vested in a Congress of the United States, which shall consist of a Senate and House of Representatives.

Section 2

[Composition of the House of Representatives.—1.] The House of Representatives shall be composed of members chosen every second year by the people of the several States, and the electors in each State shall have the qualifications requisite for electors of the most numerous branch of the State Legislature.

[Qualifications of Representatives.—2.] No Person shall be a Representative who shall not have attained to the age of twenty-five years, and been seven years a citizen of the United States, and who shall not, when elected, be an inhabitant of that State in which he shall be chosen.

[Apportionment of Representatives and direct taxes—census.[1]—3.] (Representatives and direct taxes shall be apportioned among the several States which may be included within this Union, according to their respective numbers, which shall be determined by adding to the whole number of free persons, including those bound to service for a term of years, and excluding Indians not taxed, three fifths of all other persons.) The actual enumeration shall be made within three years after the first meeting of the Congress of the United States, and within every subsequent term of ten years, in such manner as they shall by law direct. The number of Representatives shall not exceed one for every thirty thousand, but each State shall have at least one Representa-

tive; and until such enumeration shall be made, the State of New Hampshire shall be entitled to choose three, Massachusetts eight, Rhode-Island and Providence Plantations one, Connecticut five, New York six, New Jersey four, Pennsylvania eight, Delaware one, Maryland six, Virginia ten, North Carolina five, South Carolina five, and Georgia three.

[Filling of vacancies in representation.—4.] When vacancies happen in the representation from any State, the Executive Authority thereof shall issue writs of election to fill such vacancies.

[Selection of officers; power of impeachment.—5.] The House of Representatives shall choose their Speaker and other officers; and shall have the sole power of impeachment.

Section 3[2]

[The Senate.—1.] The Senate of the United States shall be composed of two Senators from each State, chosen by the Legislature thereof, for six years; and each Senator shall have one vote.

[Classification of Senators; filling of vacancies.—2.] Immediately after they shall be assembled in consequence of the first election, they shall be divided as equally as may be into three classes. The seats of the Senators of the first class shall be vacated at the expiration of the second year, of the second class at the expiration of the fourth year, and of the third class at the expiration of the sixth year, so that one-third may be chosen every second year; and if vacancies happen by resignation, or otherwise, during the recess of the Legislature of any State, the Executive thereof may make temporary appointments (until the next meeting of the Legislature, which shall then fill such vacancies).

[Qualification of Senators.—3.] No person shall be a Senator who shall not have attained to the age of thirty years, and been nine years a citizen of the United States, and who shall not, when elected, be an inhabitant of that State for which he shall be chosen.

[Vice President to be President of Senate.—4.] The Vice President of the United States shall be President of the Senate, but shall have no vote, unless they be equally divided.

[Selection of Senate officers; President pro tempore.—5.] The Senate shall choose their other

---

1. The clause included in parentheses is amended by the 14th Amendment, Section 2. 2. The first paragraph of this section and the part of the second paragraph included in parentheses are amended by the 17th Amendment.

officers, and also a President pro tempore, in the absence of the Vice President, or when he shall exercise the office of President of the United States.

[Senate to try impeachments.—6.] The Senate shall have the sole power to try all impeachments. When sitting for that purpose, they shall be on oath or affirmation. When the President of the United States is tried, the Chief Justice shall preside: and no person shall be convicted without the concurrence of two thirds of the members present.

[Judgment in cases of Impeachment.—7.] Judgment in cases of impeachment shall not extend further than to removal from office, and disqualification to hold and enjoy any office of honor, trust, or profit under the United States: but the party convicted shall nevertheless be liable and subject to indictment, trial, judgment and punishment, according to Law.

Section 4

[Control of congressional elections.—1.] The times, places, and manner of holding elections for Senators and Representatives, shall be prescribed in each State by the Legislature thereof; but the Congress may at any time by law make or alter such regulations, except as to the places of choosing Senators.

[Time for assembling of Congress[3]—2.] The Congress shall assemble at least once in every year, and such meeting shall be on the first Monday in December, unless they shall by law appoint a different day.

Section 5

[Each house to be the judge of the election and qualifications of its members; regulations as to quorum.—1.] Each House shall be the judge of the elections, returns, and qualifications of its own members, and a majority of each shall constitute a quorum to do business; but a smaller number may adjourn from day to day, and may be authorized to compel the attendance of absent members, in such manner, and under such penalties as each House may provide.

[Each house to determine its own rules.—2.] Each House may determine the rules of its proceedings, punish its members for disorderly behavior, and, with the concurrence of two thirds, expel a member.

[Journals and yeas and nays.—3.] Each House shall keep a journal of its proceedings, and from time to time publish the same, excepting such parts as may in their judgment require secrecy; and the yeas and nays of the members of either House on any question shall, at the desire of one fifth of those present, be entered on the journal.

[Adjournment.—4.] Neither House, during the session of Congress, shall, without the consent of the other, adjourn for more than three days, nor to any other place than that in which the two Houses shall be sitting.

Section 6

[Compensation and privileges of members of Congress.—1.] The Senators and Representatives shall receive a compensation for their services, to be ascertained by law, and paid out of the Treasury of the United States. They shall in all cases, except

treason, felony, and breach of the peace, be privileged from arrest during their attendance at the session of their respective Houses, and in going to and returning from the same; and for any speech or debate in either House, they shall not be questioned in any other place.

[Incompatible offices; exclusions.—2.] No Senator or Representative shall, during the time for which he was elected, be appointed to any civil office under the authority of the United States, which shall have been created, or the emoluments whereof shall have been increased during such time; and no person holding any office under the United States shall be a member of either House during his continuance in office.

Section 7

[Revenue bills to originate in House.—1.] All bills for raising revenue shall originate in the House of Representatives; but the Senate may propose or concur with amendments as on other bills.

[Manner of passing bills; veto power of President.—2.] Every bill which shall have passed the House of Representatives and the Senate, shall, before it becomes a law, be presented to the President of the United States; if he approve he shall sign it, but if not he shall return it, with his objections to that House in which it shall have originated, who shall enter the objections at large on their journal, and proceed to reconsider it. If after such reconsideration two thirds of that House shall agree to pass the bill, it shall be sent, together with the objections, to the other House, by which it shall likewise be reconsidered, and if approved by two thirds of that House, it shall become a law. But in all such cases the votes of both Houses shall be determined by yeas and nays, and the names of the persons voting for and against the bill shall be entered on the journal of each house, respectively. If any bill shall not be returned by the President within ten days (Sundays excepted) after it shall have been presented to him, the same shall be a law, in like manner as if he had signed it, unless the Congress by their adjournment prevent its return, in which case it shall not be a law.

[Concurrent orders or resolutions, to be passed by President.—3.] Every order, resolution, or vote to which the concurrence of the Senate and House of Representatives may be necessary (except on a question of adjournment) shall be presented to the President of the United States; and before the same shall take effect, shall be approved by him, or being disapproved by him, shall be repassed by two thirds of the Senate and House of Representatives, according to the rules and limitations prescribed in the case of a bill.

Section 8

[General powers of Congress.[4]]
[Taxes, duties, imposts, and excises.—1.] The Congress shall have power to lay and collect taxes, duties, imposts and excises, to pay the debts and provide for the common defense and general welfare of the United States; but all duties, imposts and excises shall be uniform throughout the United States;

---

3. Amended by the 20th Amendment, Section 2. 4. By the 16th Amendment, Congress is given the power to lay and collect taxes on income.

[**Borrowing of money.—2.**] To borrow money on the credit of the United States;

[**Regulation of commerce.—3.**] To regulate commerce with foreign nations, and among the several States, and with the Indian tribes;

[**Naturalization and bankruptcy.—4.**] To establish a uniform rule of naturalization, and uniform laws on the subject of bankruptcies throughout the United States;

[**Money, weights and measures.—5.**] To coin money, regulate the value thereof, and of foreign coin, and fix the standard of weights and measures;

[**Counterfeiting.—6.**] To provide for the punishment of counterfeiting the securities and current coin of the United States;

[**Post offices.—7.**] To establish post offices and post roads;

[**Patents and copyrights.—8.**] To promote the progress of science and useful arts, by securing for limited times to authors and inventors the exclusive right to their respective writings and discoveries;

[**Inferior courts.—9.**] To constitute tribunals inferior to the Supreme Court;

[**Piracies and felonies.—10.**] To define and punish piracies and felonies committed on the high seas, and offences against the law of nations;

[**War; marque and reprisal.—11.**] To declare war, grant letters of marque and reprisal, and make rules concerning captures on land and water;

[**Armies.—12.**] To raise and support armies, but no appropriation of money to that use shall be for a longer term than two years;

[**Navy.—13.**] To provide and maintain a navy;

[**Land and naval forces.—14.**] To make rules for the government and regulation of the land and naval forces;

[**Calling out militia.—15.**] To provide for calling forth the militia to execute the laws of the Union, suppress insurrections, and repel invasions;

[**Organizing, arming, and disciplining militia. —16.**] To provide for organizing, arming, and disciplining, the militia, and for governing such part of them as may be employed in the service of the United States, reserving to the States, respectively, the appointment of the officers, and the authority of training the militia according to the discipline prescribed by Congress;

[**Exclusive legislation over District of Columbia.—17.**] To exercise exclusive legislation in all cases whatsoever, over such district (not exceeding ten miles square) as may, by cession of particular States, and the acceptance of Congress, become the seat of the Government of the United States, and to exercise like authority over all places purchased by the consent of the Legislature of the State in which the same shall be, for the erection of forts, magazines, arsenals, dock-yards, and other needful buildings;—And

[**To enact laws necessary to enforce Constitution.—18.**] To make all laws which shall be necessary and proper for carrying into execution the foregoing powers, and all other powers vested by this Constitution in the Government of the United States, or in any department or officer thereof.

Section 9

[**Migration or importation of certain persons not to be prohibited before 1808.—1.**] The migration or importation of such persons as any of the States now existing shall think proper to admit, shall not be prohibited by the Congress prior to the year one thousand eight hundred and eight, but a tax or duty may be imposed on such importation, not exceeding ten dollars for each person.

[**Writ of habeas corpus not to be suspended; exception.—2.**] The privilege of the writ of habeas corpus shall not be suspended, unless when in cases of rebellion or invasion the public safety may require it.

[**Bills of attainder and ex post facto laws prohibited.—3.**] No bill of attainder or ex post facto law shall be passed.

[**Capitation and other direct taxes.—4.**] No capitation, or other direct, tax shall be laid, unless in proportion to the census or enumeration herein before directed to be taken.[5]

[**Exports not to be taxed.—5.**] No tax or duty shall be laid on articles exported from any State.

[**No preference to be given to ports of any States; interstate shipping.—6.**] No preference shall be given by any regulation of commerce or revenue to the ports of one State over those of another: nor shall vessels bound to, or from, one State, be obliged to enter, clear, or pay duties in another.

[**Money, how drawn from treasury; financial statements to be published.—7.**] No money shall be drawn from the Treasury, but in consequence of appropriations made by law; and a regular statement and account of the receipts and expenditures of all public money shall be published from time to time.

[**Titles of nobility not to be granted; acceptance by government officers of favors from foreign powers.—8.**] No title of nobility shall be granted by the United States: and no person holding any office of profit or trust under them, shall, without the consent of the Congress, accept of any present, emolument, office, or title, of any kind whatever, from any king, prince, or foreign state.

Section 10

[**Limitations of the powers of the several States.—1.**] No State shall enter into any treaty, alliance, or confederation; grant letters of marque and reprisal; coin money; emit bills of credit; make any thing but gold and silver coin a tender in payment of debts; pass any bill of attainder, ex post facto law, or law impairing the obligation of contracts, or grant any title of nobility.

[**State imposts and duties.—2.**] No State shall, without the consent of the Congress, lay any imposts or duties on imports or exports, except what may be absolutely necessary for executing its inspection laws; and the net produce of all duties and imposts, laid by any State on imports or exports, shall be for the use of the Treasury of the United States; and all such laws shall be subject to the revision and control of the Congress.

[**Further restrictions on powers of States.—3.**] No State shall, without the consent of Congress, lay any duty of tonnage, keep troops, or ships of war in time of peace, enter into any agreement or compact

5. *See* the 16th Amendment.

with another state, or with a foreign power, or engage in war, unless actually invaded, or in such imminent danger as will not admit of delay.

Article II

Section 1

[**The President; the executive power.—1.**] The executive power shall be vested in a President of the United States of America. He shall hold his office during the term of four years, and, together with the Vice President, chosen for the same term, be elected, as follows

[**Appointment and qualifications of presidential electors.—2.**] Each State shall appoint, in such manner as the Legislature thereof may direct, a number of electors, equal to the whole number of Senators and Representatives to which the State may be entitled in the Congress: but no Senator or Representative, or person holding an office of trust or profit under the United States, shall be appointed an elector.

[**Original method of electing the President and Vice President.**[6]] (The electors shall meet in their respective States, and vote by ballot for two persons, of whom one at least shall not be an inhabitant of the same State with themselves. And they shall make a list of all the persons voted for, and of the number of votes for each; which list they shall sign and certify, and transmit sealed to the seat of the Government of the United States, directed to the President of the Senate. The President of the Senate shall, in the presence of the Senate and House of Representatives, open all the certificates, and the votes shall then be counted. The person having the greatest number of votes shall be the President, if such number be a majority of the whole number of electors appointed; and if there be more than one who have such majority, and have an equal number of votes, then the House of Representatives shall immediately choose by ballot one of them for President; and if no person have a majority, then from the five highest on the list the said House shall in like manner choose the President. But in choosing the President, the votes shall be taken by States, the representation from each State having one vote; A quorum for this purpose shall consist of a member or members from two thirds of the States, and a majority of all the states shall be necessary to a choice. In every case, after the choice of the President, the person having the greatest number of votes of the electors shall be the Vice President. But if there should remain two or more who have equal votes, the Senate shall choose from them by ballot the Vice President.)

[**Congress may determine time of choosing electors and day for casting their votes.—3.**] The Congress may determine the time of choosing the electors, and the day on which they shall give their votes; which day shall be the same throughout the United States.

[**Qualifications for the office of President.**[7]**—4.**] No person except a natural born citizen, or a citizen of the United States, at the time of the adoption of this Constitution, shall be eligible to the office of President; neither shall any person be eligible to that office who shall not have attained to the age of thirty-five years, and been fourteen years a resident within the United States.

[**Filling vacancy in the office of President.**[8]**—5.**] In case of the removal of the President from office, or of his death, resignation, or inability to discharge the powers and duties of the said office, the same shall devolve on the Vice President, and the Congress may by law provide for the case of removal, death, resignation or inability, both of the President and Vice President, declaring what officer shall then act as President, and such officer shall act accordingly, until the disability be removed, or a President shall be elected.

[**Compensation of the President.—6.**] The President shall, at stated times, receive for his services, a compensation, which shall neither be increased nor diminished during the period for which he shall have been elected, and he shall not receive within that period any other emolument from the United States, or any of them.

[**Oath to be taken by the President.—7.**] Before he enter on the execution of his office, he shall take the following oath or affirmation:—"I do solemnly swear (or affirm) that I will faithfully execute the office of President of the United States, and will to the best of my ability, preserve, protect, and defend the Constitution of the United States."

Section 2

[**The President to be commander in chief of army and navy and head of executive departments; may grant reprieves and pardons.—1.**] The President shall be Commander in Chief of the Army and Navy of the United States, and of the militia of the several States, when called into the actual service of the United States; he may require the opinion, in writing, of the principal officer in each of the executive departments, upon any subject relating to the duties of their respective offices, and he shall have power to grant reprieves and pardons for offences against the United States, except in cases of impeachment.

[**President may, with concurrence of Senate, make treaties, appoint ambassadors, etc.; appointment of inferior officers, authority of Congress over.—2.**] He shall have power, by and with the advice and consent of the Senate, to make treaties, provided two thirds of the Senators present concur; and he shall nominate, and by and with the advice and consent of the Senate, shall appoint ambassadors, other public ministers and consuls, judges of the Supreme Court, and all other officers of the United States, whose appointments are not herein otherwise provided for, and which shall be established by law: but the Congress may by law vest the appointment of such inferior officers, as they think proper, in the President alone, in the courts of law, or in the heads of departments.

[**President may fill vacancies in office during recess of Senate.—3.**] The President shall have power to fill up all vacancies that may happen during the recess of the Senate, by granting commissions which shall expire at the end of their session.

---

6. This clause has been superseded by the 12th Amendment. 7. For qualifications of the Vice President, *see* the 12th Amendment. 8. Amended by the 20th Amendment, Sections 3 and 4.

Section 3

[President to give advice to Congress; may convene or adjourn it on certain occasions; to receive ambassadors, etc.; have laws executed and commission all officers.] He shall from time to time give to the Congress information of the state of the Union, and recommend to their consideration such measures as he shall judge necessary and expedient; he may, on extraordinary occasions, convene both Houses, or either of them, and in case of disagreement between them, with respect to the time of adjournment, he may adjourn them to such time as he shall think proper; he shall receive ambassadors and other public ministers: he shall take care that the laws be faithfully executed, and shall commission all the officers of the United States.

Section 4

[All civil officers removable by impeachment.] The President, Vice President, and all civil officers of the United States shall be removed from office on impeachment for, and conviction of, treason, bribery, or other high crimes and misdemeanors.

Article III

Section 1

[Judicial powers; how vested; term of office and compensation of judges.] The judicial Power of the United States, shall be vested in one Supreme Court, and in such inferior courts as the Congress may from time to time ordain and establish. The judges, both of the supreme and inferior courts, shall hold their offices during good behavior, and shall, at stated times, receive for their services, a compensation, which shall not be diminished during their continuance in office.

Section 2

[Jurisdiction of Federal courts[9]—1.] The judicial power shall extend to all cases, in law and equity, arising under this Constitution, the laws of the United States, and treaties made, or which shall be made, under their authority; to all cases affecting ambassadors, other public ministers and consuls; to all cases of admiralty and maritime jurisdiction; to controversies to which the United States, shall be a party; to controversies between two or more States; between a State and citizens of another State; between citizens of different States; between citizens of the same State claiming lands under grants of different states, and between a State, or the citizens thereof, and foreign states, citizens, or subjects.

[Original and appellate jurisdiction of Supreme Court.—2.] In all cases affecting ambassadors, other public ministers and consuls, and those in which a State shall be party, the Supreme Court shall have original jurisdiction. In all the other cases before mentioned, the Supreme Court shall have appellate jurisdiction, both as to law and fact, with such exceptions, and under such regulations, as the Congress shall make.

[Trial of all crimes, except impeachment, to be by jury.—3.] The trial of all crimes, except in cases of impeachment, shall be by jury; and such trial shall be held in the State where the said crimes shall have been committed; but when not committed within any State, the trial shall be at such place or places as the Congress may by law have directed.

Section 3

[Treason defined; conviction of.—1.] Treason against the United States, shall consist only in levying war against them, or, in adhering to their enemies, giving them aid and comfort. No person shall be convicted of treason unless on the testimony of two witnesses to the same overt act, or on confession in open court.

[Congress to declare punishment for treason; proviso.—2.] The Congress shall have power to declare the punishment of treason, but no attainder of treason shall work corruption of blood, or forfeiture except during the life of the person attained.

Article IV

Section 1

[Each State to give full faith and credit to the public acts and records of other States.] Full faith and credit shall be given in each State to the public acts, records, and judicial proceedings of every other State. And the Congress may by general laws prescribe the manner in which such acts, records, and proceedings shall be proved, and the effect thereof.

Section 2

[Privileges of citizens.—1.] The citizens of each State shall be entitled to all privileges and immunities of citizens in the several States.

[Extradition between the several States.—2.] A person charged in any State with treason, felony, or other crime, who shall flee from justice, and be found in another State, shall on demand of the Executive authority of the State from which he fled, be delivered up, to be removed to the State having jurisdiction of the crime.

[Persons held to labor or service in one State, fleeing to another, to be returned.—3.] No person held to service or labor in one State, under the laws thereof, escaping into another, shall, in consequence of any law or regulation therein, be discharged from such service or labor, but shall be delivered up on claim of the party to whom such service or labor may be due.

Section 3

[New States.—1.] New States may be admitted by the Congress into this Union; but no new State shall be formed or erected within the jurisdiction of any other State; nor any State be formed by the junction of two or more States, or parts of States, without the consent of the Legislatures of the States concerned as well as of the Congress.

[Regulations concerning territory.—2.] The Congress shall have power to dispose of and make all needful rules and regulations respecting the territory or other property belonging to the United States; and nothing in this Constitution shall be so construed as to prejudice any claims of the United States, or of any particular State.

Section 4

[Republican form of government and protection guaranteed the several States.] The United States shall guarantee to every State in this Union a Republican form of government, and shall protect each of them against invasion; and on application of the Legislature, or of the Executive (when the Legislature cannot be convened) against domestic violence.

9. This section is abridged by the 11th Amendment.

Article V

[Ways in which the Constitution can be amended.] The Congress, whenever two thirds of both Houses shall deem it necessary, shall propose amendments to this Constitution, or, on the application of the Legislatures of two thirds of the several States shall call a convention for proposing amendments, which, in either case, shall be valid to all intents and purposes, as part of this Constitution, when ratified by the Legislatures of three fourths of the several States, or by conventions in three fourths thereof, as the one or the other mode of ratification may be proposed by the Congress; provided that no amendment which may be made prior to the year one thousand eight hundred and eight shall in any manner affect the first and fourth clauses in the ninth Section of the first Article; and that no State, without its consent, shall be deprived of its equal suffrage in the Senate.

Article VI

[Debts contracted under the confederation secured.—1.] All debts contracted and engagements entered into, before the adoption of this Constitution, shall be as valid against the United States under this Constitution, as under the Confederation. [Constitution, laws, and treaties of the United States to be supreme.—2.] This Constitution, and the laws of the United States which shall be made in pursuance thereof; and all treaties made, or which shall be made, under the authority of the United States, shall be the supreme law of the land; and the judges in every State shall be bound thereby, any thing in the Constitution or laws of any State to the contrary notwithstanding.

[Who shall take constitutional oath; no religious test as to official qualification.—3.] The Senators and Representatives before mentioned, and the members of the several State Legislatures, and all executive and judicial officers, both of the United States and of the several States, shall be bound by oath or affirmation, to support this Constitution; but no religious test shall ever be required as a qualification to any office or public trust under the United States.

Article VII

[Constitution to be considered adopted when ratified by nine States.] The ratification of the conventions of nine States shall be sufficient for the establishment of this Constitution between the States so ratifying the same.

Done in convention by the unanimous consent of the States present the seventeenth day of September in the year of our Lord one thousand seven hundred and eighty seven and of the independence of the United States of America the Twelfth. In witness whereof we have hereunto subscribed our names.

George Washington
President and Deputy from Virginia

New Hampshire
John Langdon
Nicholas Gilman

Massachusetts
Nathaniel Gorham
Rufus King

Connecticut
Wm. Saml. Johnson
Roger Sherman

New York
Alexander Hamilton

New Jersey
Wil. Livingston
Wm. Paterson

David Brearley
Jona. Dayton

Pennsylvania
B. Franklin
Thomas Mifflin
Robt. Morris
Geo. Clymer
Thos. FitzSimons
Jared Ingersoll
James Wilson
Gouv. Morris

Delaware
Geo. Read
Gunning Bedford Jun.

John Dickinson
Richard Bassett
Jaco. Broom

Maryland
James McHenry
Dan. of St. Thos. Jenifer
Danl. Carroll

Virginia
John Blair
James Madison, Jr.

North Carolina
Wm. Blount
Richd Dobbs Spaight
Hu. Williamson

South Carolina
J. Rutledge
Charles Cotesworth
  Pinckney
Charles Pinckney
Pierce Butler

Georgia
William Few
Abr. Baldwin
Attest: William Jackson,
  Secretary

Amendments to the Constitution of the United States

(Amendments I to X inclusive, popularly known as the Bill of Rights, were proposed and sent to the states by the first session of the First Congress. They were ratified Dec. 15, 1791.)

Amendment I

[Freedom of religion, speech, of the press, and right of petition.] Congress shall make no law respecting an establishment of religion, or prohibiting the free exercise thereof; or abridging the freedom of speech, or of the press; or the right of the people peaceably to assemble, and to petition the Government for a redress of grievances.

Amendment II

[Right of people to bear arms not to be infringed.] A well regulated militia, being necessary to the security of a free State, the right of the people to keep and bear arms, shall not be infringed.

Amendment III

[Quartering of troops.] No soldier shall, in time of peace be quartered in any house, without the consent of the owner, nor in time of war, but in a manner to be prescribed by law.

Amendment IV

[Persons and houses to be secure from unreasonable searches and seizures.] The right of the people to be secure in their persons, houses, papers, and effects, against unreasonable searches and seizures, shall not be violated, and no warrants shall issue, but upon probable cause, supported by oath or affirmation, and particularly describing the place to be searched, and the persons or things to be seized.

Amendment V

[Trials for crimes; just compensation for private property taken for public use.] No person shall be held to answer for a capital, or otherwise infamous crime, unless on a presentment or indictment of a Grand Jury, except in cases arising in the land or naval forces, or in the militia, when in actual service in time of war or public danger; nor shall any person be subject for the same offence to be twice put in jeopardy of life or limb; nor shall be compelled in any criminal case to be a witness, against himself, nor be deprived of life, liberty, or property, without due process of law; nor shall private property be taken for public use, without just compensation.

Amendment VI

[Civil rights in trials for crimes enumerated.] In all criminal prosecutions, the accused shall enjoy the right to a speedy and public trial, by an impartial jury of the State and district wherein the crime shall have been committed, which district shall have been previously ascertained by law, and to be informed of the nature and cause of the accusation; to be confronted with the witnesses against him; to have compulsory process for obtaining witnesses in his favor, and to have the assistance of counsel for his defense.

Amendment VII

[Civil rights in civil suits.] In suits at common law, where the value in controversy shall exceed twenty dollars, the right of trial by jury shall be preserved, and no fact tried by a jury, shall be otherwise re-examined in any court of the United States, than according to the rules of the common law.

Amendment VIII

[Excessive bail, fines, and punishments prohibited.] Excessive bail shall not be required, nor excessive fines imposed, nor cruel and unusual punishments inflicted.

Amendment IX

[Reserved rights of people.] The enumeration in the Constitution, of certain rights, shall not be construed to deny or disparage others retained by the people.

Amendment X

[Powers not delegated, reserved to states and people respectively.] The powers not delegated to the United States by the Constitution, nor prohibited by it to the States, are reserved to the States, respectively, or to the people.

Amendment XI

(The proposed amendment was sent to the states Mar. 5, 1794, by the Third Congress. It was ratified Feb. 7, 1795.)

[Judicial power of United States not to extend to suits against a State.] The judicial power of the United States shall not be construed to extend to any suit in law or equity, commenced or prosecuted against one of the United States by citizens of another State, or by citizens or subjects of any foreign state.

Amendment XII

(The proposed amendment was sent to the states Dec. 12, 1803, by the Eighth Congress. It was ratified July 27, 1804.)

[Present mode of electing President and Vice-President by electors.[1]]

The electors shall meet in their respective states, and vote by ballot for President and Vice President, one of whom, at least, shall not be an inhabitant of the same state with themselves; they shall name in their ballots the person voted for as President, and in distinct ballots the person voted for as Vice President, and they shall make distinct lists of all persons voted for as President, and of all persons voted for as Vice President, and of the number of votes for each, which lists they shall sign and certify, and transmit sealed to the seat of the government of the United States, directed to the President of the Senate; the President of the Senate shall, in the presence of the Senate and House of Representatives, open all the certificates and the votes shall then be counted; the person having the greatest number of votes for President, shall be the President, if such number be a majority of the whole number of electors appointed; and if no person have such majority, then from the persons having the highest numbers not exceeding three on the list of those voted for as President, the House of Representatives shall choose immediately, by ballot, the President. But in choosing the President, the votes shall be taken by states, the representation from each State having one vote; a quorum for this purpose shall consist of a member or members from two thirds of the states, and a majority of all the states shall be necessary to a choice. And if the House of Representatives shall not choose a President whenever the right of choice shall devolve upon them, before the fourth day of March next following, then the Vice President shall act as President, as in the case of the death or other constitutional disability of the President. The person having the greatest number of votes as Vice President, shall be the Vice President, if such number be a majority of the whole number of electors appointed, and if no person have a majority, then from the two highest numbers on the list, the Senate shall choose the Vice President; a quorum for the purpose shall consist of two thirds of the whole

---

1. Amended by the 20th Amendment, Sections 3 and 4.

number of Senators, and a majority of the whole number shall be necessary to a choice. But no person constitutionally ineligible to the office of President shall be eligible to that of Vice President of the United States.

Amendment XIII

(The proposed amendment was sent to the states Feb. 1, 1865, by the Thirty-eighth Congress. It was ratified Dec. 6, 1865.)

Section 1

[Slavery prohibited.] Neither slavery nor involuntary servitude, except as a punishment for crime whereof the party shall have been duly convicted, shall exist within the United States, or any place subject to their jurisdiction.

Section 2

[Congress given power to enforce this article.] Congress shall have power to enforce this article by appropriate legislation.

Amendment XIV

(The proposed amendment was sent to the states June 16, 1866, by the Thirty-ninth Congress. It was ratified July 9, 1868.)

Section 1

[Citizenship defined; privileges of citizens.] All persons born or naturalized in the United States, and subject to the jurisdiction thereof, are citizens of the United States and of the State wherein they reside. No State shall make or enforce any law which shall abridge the privileges or immunities of citizens of the United States; nor shall any State deprive any person of life, liberty, or property, without due process of law; nor deny to any person within its jurisdiction the equal protection of the laws.

Section 2

[Apportionment of Representatives.] Representatives shall be apportioned among the several States according to their respective numbers, counting the whole number of persons in each State, excluding Indians not taxed. But when the right to vote at any election for the choice of electors for President and Vice President of the United States, Representatives in Congress, the executive and judicial officers of a State, or the members of the Legislature thereof, is denied to any of the male inhabitants of such State, being twenty-one years of age, and citizens of the United States, or in any way abridged, except for participation in rebellion, or other crime, the basis of representation therein shall be reduced in the proportion which the number of such male citizens shall bear to the whole number of male citizens twenty-one years of age in such State.

Section 3

[Disqualification for office; removal of disability.] No person shall be a Senator or Representative in Congress, or elector of President and Vice President, or hold any office, civil or military, under the United States, or under any State, who, having previously taken an oath, as a member of Congress, or as an officer of the United States, or as a member of any State Legislature, or as an executive or judicial officer of any State, to support the Constitution of the United States, shall have engaged in insurrection or rebellion against the same, or given aid or comfort to the enemies thereof. But Congress may, by a vote of two thirds of each House, remove such disability.

Section 4

[Public debt not to be questioned; payment of debts and claims incurred in aid of rebellion forbidden.] The validity of the public debt of the United States, authorized by law, including debts incurred for payment of pensions and bounties for services in suppressing insurrection or rebellion, shall not be questioned. But neither the United States nor any State shall assume or pay any debt or obligation incurred in aid of insurrection or rebellion against the United States, or any claim for the loss or emancipation of any slave; but all such debts, obligations, and claims shall be held illegal and void.

Section 5

[Congress given power to enforce this article.] The Congress shall have power to enforce, by appropriate legislation, the provisions of this article.

Amendment XV

(The proposed amendment was sent to the states Feb. 27, 1869, by the Fortieth Congress. It was ratified Feb. 3, 1870.)

Section 1

[Right of certain citizens to vote established.] The right of citizens of the United States to vote shall not be denied or abridged by the United States or by any State on account of race, color, or previous condition of servitude.

Section 2

[Congress given power to enforce this article.] The Congress shall have power to enforce this article by appropriate legislation.

Amendment XVI

(The proposed amendment was sent to the states July 12, 1909, by the Sixty-first Congress. It was ratified Feb. 3, 1913.)

[Taxes on income; Congress given power to lay and collect.] The Congress shall have power to lay and collect taxes on incomes, from whatever source derived, without apportionment among the several States, and without regard to any census or enumeration.

Amendment XVII

(The proposed amendment was sent to the states May 16, 1912, by the Sixty-second Congress. It was ratified April 8, 1913.)

[Election of United States Senators; filling of vacancies; qualifications of electors.] The Senate of the United States shall be composed of two Senators from each State, elected by the people thereof, for six years; and each Senator shall have one vote. The electors in each State shall have the qualifications requisite for electors of the most numerous branch of the State Legislatures.

When vacancies happen in the representation of any State in the Senate, the executive authority of such State shall issue writs of election to fill such vacancies: Provided, that the legislature of any State may empower the executive thereof to make temporary appointment until the people fill the vacancies by election as the legislature may direct.

This amendment shall not be so construed as to affect the election or term of any Senator chosen before it becomes valid as part of the Constitution.

Amendment XVIII[2]

(The proposed amendment was sent to the states Dec. 18, 1917, by the Sixty-fifth Congress. It was ratified by three quarters of the states by Jan. 16, 1919, and became effective Jan. 16, 1920.)

Section 1

[Manufacture, sale, or transportation of intoxicating liquors, for beverage purposes, prohibited.] After one year from the ratification of this article the manufacture, sale, or transportation of intoxicating liquors within, the importation thereof into, or the exportation thereof from the United States and all territory subject to the jurisdiction thereof for beverage purposes is hereby prohibited.

Section 2

[Congress and the several States given concurrent power to pass appropriate legislation to enforce this article.] The Congress and the several States shall have concurrent power to enforce this article by appropriate legislation.

Section 3

[Provisions of article to become operative, when adopted by three fourths of the States.] This article shall be inoperative unless it shall have been ratified as an amendment to the Constitution by the legislatures of the several States, as provided in the Constitution, within seven years from the date of the submission hereof to the States by Congress.

Amendment XIX

(The proposed amendment was sent to the states June 4, 1919, by the Sixty-sixth Congress. It was ratified Aug. 18, 1920.)

[The right of citizens to vote shall not be denied because of sex.] The right of citizens of the United States to vote shall not be denied or abridged by the United States or by any State on account of sex.

[Congress given power to enforce this article.] Congress shall have power to enforce this article by appropriate legislation.

Amendment XX

(The proposed amendment, sometimes called the "Lame Duck Amendment," was sent to the states Mar. 3, 1932, by the Seventy-second Congress. It was ratified Jan. 23, 1933; but, in accordance with Section 5, Sections 1 and 2 did not go into effect until Oct. 15, 1933.)

Section 1

[Terms of President, Vice President, Senators, and Representatives.] The terms of the President and Vice President shall end at noon on the twentieth day of January, and the terms of Senators and Representatives at noon on the third day of January, of the years in which such terms would have ended if this article had not been ratified; and the terms of their successors shall then begin.

Section 2

[Time of assembling Congress.] The Congress shall assemble at least once in every year, and such meeting shall begin at noon on the third day of January, unless they shall by law appoint a different day.

Section 3

[Filling vacancy in office of President.] If, at the time fixed for the beginning of the term of the President, the President-elect shall have died, the Vice President-elect shall become President. If a President shall not have been chosen before the time fixed for the beginning of his term, or if the President-elect shall have failed to qualify, then the Vice President shall have qualified; and the Congress may by law provide for the case wherein neither a President-elect nor a Vice President-elect shall have qualified, declaring who shall then act as President, or the manner in which one who is to act shall be selected, and such person shall act accordingly until a President or Vice President shall have qualified.

Section 4

[Power of Congress in Presidential succession.] The Congress may by law provide for the case of the death of any of the persons from whom the House of Representatives may choose a President whenever the right of choice shall have devolved upon them, and for the case of the death of any of the persons from whom the Senate may choose a Vice President whenever the right of choice shall have devolved upon them.

Section 5

[Time of taking effect.] Sections 1 and 2 shall take effect on the 15th day of October following the ratification of this article.

Section 6

[Ratification.] This article shall be inoperative unless it shall have been ratified as an amendment to the Constitution by the legislatures of three fourths of the several States within seven years from the date of its submission.

Amendment XXI

(The proposed amendment was sent to the states Feb. 20, 1933, by the Seventy-second Congress. It was ratified Dec. 5, 1933.)

Section 1

[Repeal of Prohibition Amendment.] The eighteenth article of amendment to the Constitution of the United States is hereby repealed.

Section 2

[Transportation of intoxicating liquors.] The transportation or importation into any State, territory, or possession of the United States for delivery or use therein of intoxicating liquors, in violation of the laws thereof, is hereby prohibited.

Section 3

[Ratification.] This article shall be inoperative unless it shall have been ratified as an amendment to the Constitution by convention in the several States, as provided in the Constitution, within seven years from the date of the submission thereof to the States by the Congress.

Amendment XXII

(The proposed amendment was sent to the states Mar. 21, 1947, by the Eightieth Congress. It was ratified Feb. 27, 1951.)

---

2. Repealed by the 21st Amendment.

Section 1

[Limit to number of terms a President may serve.] No person shall be elected to the office of the President more than twice, and no person who has held the office of President, or acted as President, for more than two years of a term to which some other person was elected President shall be elected to the office of the President more than once. But this article shall not apply to any person holding the office of President when this article was proposed by the Congress, and shall not prevent any person who may be holding the office of President, or acting as President, during the term within which this article becomes operative from holding the office of President or acting as President during the remainder of such term.

Section 2

[Ratification.] This article shall be inoperative unless it shall have been ratified as an amendment to the Constitution by the legislatures of three fourths of the several States within seven years from the date of its submission to the States by the Congress.

Amendment XXIII

(The proposed amendment was sent to the states June 16, 1960, by the Eighty-sixth Congress. It was ratified March 29, 1961.)

Section 1

[Electors for the District of Columbia.] The District constituting the seat of Government of the United States shall appoint in such manner as the Congress may direct: A number of electors of President and Vice President equal to the whole number of Senators and Representatives in Congress to which the District would be entitled if it were a State, but in no event more than the least populous State; they shall be in addition to those appointed by the States, but they shall be considered, for the purposes of the election of President and Vice President, to be electors appointed by a State; and they shall meet in the District and perform such duties as provided by the twelfth article of amendment.

Section 2

[Congress given power to enforce this article.] The Congress shall have the power to enforce this article by appropriate legislation.

Amendment XXIV

(The proposed amendment was sent to the states Aug. 27, 1962, by the Eighty-seventh Congress. It was ratified Jan. 23, 1964.)

Section 1

[Payment of poll tax or other taxes not to be prerequisite for voting in federal elections.] The right of citizens of the United States to vote in any primary or other election for President or Vice President, for electors for President or Vice President, or for Senator or Representative in Congress, shall not be denied or abridged by the United States or any State by reasons of failure to pay any poll tax or other tax.

Section 2

[Congress given power to enforce this article.] The Congress shall have the power to enforce this article by appropriate legislation.

Amendment XXV

(The proposed amendment was sent to the states July 6, 1965, by the Eighty-ninth Congress. It was ratified Feb. 10, 1967.)

Section 1

[Succession of Vice President to Presidency.] In case of the removal of the President from office or of his death or resignation, the Vice President shall become President.

Section 2

[Vacancy in office of Vice President.] Whenever there is a vacancy in the office of the Vice President, the President shall nominate a Vice President who shall take office upon confirmation by a majority vote of both Houses of Congress.

Section 3

[Vice President as Acting President.] Whenever the President transmits to the President pro tempore of the Senate and the Speaker of the House of Representatives his written declaration that he is unable to discharge the powers and duties of his office, and until he transmits to them a written declaration to the contrary, such powers and duties shall be discharged by the Vice President as Acting President.

Section 4

[Vice President as Acting President.] Whenever the Vice President and a majority of either the principal officers of the executive departments or of such other body as Congress may by law provide, transmit to the President pro tempore of the Senate and the Speaker of the House of Representatives their written declaration that the President is unable to discharge the powers and duties of his office, the Vice President shall immediately assume the powers and duties of the office as Acting President.

Thereafter, when the President transmits to the President pro tempore of the Senate and the Speaker of the House of Representatives his written declaration that no inability exists, he shall resume the powers and duties of his office unless the Vice President and a majority of either the principal officers of the executive department or of such other body as Congress may by law provide, transmit within four days to the President pro tempore of the Senate and the Speaker of the House of Representatives their written declaration that the President is unable to discharge the powers and duties of his office. Thereupon Congress shall decide the issue, assembling within forty-eight hours for that purpose if not in session. If the Congress, within twenty-one days after receipt of the latter written declaration, or, if Congress is not in session, within twenty-one days after Congress is required to assemble, determines by two thirds vote of both Houses that the President is unable to discharge the powers and duties of his office, the Vice President shall continue to discharge the same as Acting President; otherwise, the President shall resume the powers and duties of his office.

Amendment XXVI

(The proposed amendment was sent to the states Mar. 23, 1971, by the Ninety-second Congress. It was ratified July 1, 1971.)

Section 1

[Voting for 18-year-olds.] The right of citizens of the United States, who are 18 years of age or older, to vote shall not be denied or abridged by the United States or by any state on account of age.

Section 2
[Congress given power to enforce this article.] The Congress shall have power to enforce this article by appropriate legislation.

Amendment XXVII
(Ratified May 7, 1992.)
[Congressional raises.] No law, varying the compensation for the services of the Senators and Representatives, shall take effect, until an election of Representatives shall have intervened.

"In God We Trust"

"In God We Trust" first appeared on U.S. coins after April 22, 1864, when Congress passed an act authorizing the coinage of a 2-cent piece bearing this motto. Thereafter, Congress extended its use to other coins. On July 30, 1956, it became the national motto.

The Emancipation Proclamation
January 1, 1863

By the president of the United States of America: A Proclamation.

Whereas on the 22d day of September, A.D. 1862, a proclamation was issued by the president of the United States, containing, among other things, the following, to wit:

"That on the 1st day of January, A.D. 1863, all persons held as slaves within any State or designated part of a State the people whereof shall then be in rebellion against the United States shall be then, thenceforward, and forever free; and the executive government of the United States, including the military and naval authority thereof, will recognize and maintain the freedom of such persons and will do not act or acts to repress such persons, or any of them, in any efforts they may make for their actual freedom."

"That the executive will on the 1st day of January aforesaid, by proclamation, designate the States and parts of States, if any, in which the people thereof, respectively, shall then be in rebellion against the United States; and the fact that any State or the people thereof shall on that day be in good faith represented in the Congress of the United States by members chosen thereto at elections wherein a majority of the qualified voters of such States shall have participated shall, in the absence of strong countervailing testimony, be deemed conclusive evidence that such State and the people thereof are not then in rebellion against the United States."

Now, therefore, I, Abraham Lincoln, president of the United States, by virtue of the power in me vested as Commander-in-Chief of the Army and Navy of the United States in time of actual armed rebellion against the authority and government of the United States, and as a fit and necessary war measure for suppressing said rebellion, do, on this 1st day of January, A.D. 1863, and in accordance with my purpose so to do, publicly proclaimed for the full period of one hundred days from the first day above mentioned, order and designate as the States and parts of States wherein the people thereof, respectively, are this day in rebellion against the United States the following, to wit:

Arkansas, Texas, Louisiana (except the parishes of St. Bernard, Plaquemines, Jefferson, St. John, St. Charles, St. James, Ascension, Assumption, Terrebonne, Lafourche, St. Mary, St. Martin, and Orleans, including the city of New Orleans), Mississippi, Alabama, Florida, Georgia, South Carolina, North Carolina, and Virginia (except the forty-eight counties designated as West Virginia, and also the counties of Berkeley, Accomac, Northhampton, Elizabeth City, York, Princess Anne, and Norfolk, including the cities of Norfolk and Portsmouth), and which excepted parts are for the present left precisely as if this proclamation were not issued.

And by virtue of the power and for the purpose aforesaid, I do order and declare that all persons held as slaves within said designated States and parts of States are, and henceforward shall be, free; and that the Executive Government of the United States, including the military and naval authorities thereof, will recognize and maintain the freedom of said persons.

And I hereby enjoin upon the people so declared to be free to abstain from all violence, unless in necessary self-defense; and I recommend to them that, in all cases when allowed, they labor faithfully for reasonable wages.

And I further declare and make known that such persons of suitable condition will be received into the armed service of the United States to garrison forts, positions, stations, and other places, and to man vessels of all sorts in said service.

And upon this act, sincerely believed to be an act of justice, warranted by the Constitution upon military necessity, I invoke the considerate judgment of mankind and the gracious favor of Almighty God.

Lincoln's Gettysburg Address

The Battle of Gettysburg, one of the most noted battles of the Civil War, was fought on July 1–3, 1863. On Nov. 19, 1863, the field was dedicated as a national cemetery by President Lincoln in a two-minute speech that was to become immortal. At the time of its delivery the speech was relegated to the inside pages of the papers, while a two-hour address by Edward Everett, the leading orator of the time, caught the headlines.

The following is the text of the address revised by President Lincoln from his own notes:

Fourscore and seven years ago our fathers brought forth on this continent a new nation conceived in liberty and dedicated to the proposition that all men are created equal. Now we are engaged in a great civil war testing whether that nation, or any nation so conceived and so dedicated, can long endure. We are met on a great battlefield of that war. We have come to dedicate a portion of that field as a final resting-place for those who here gave their lives that that nation might live. It is altogether fitting and proper that we should do this. But, in a larger sense, we cannot dedicate, we cannot consecrate, we cannot hallow this ground. The brave men, living and dead, who struggled here have consecrated it far above our poor power to add or detract. The world will little note nor long remember what we say here, but it can never forget what they did here. It is for us the living rather to be dedicated here to the unfinished work which they who fought here have thus far so nobly advanced. It is rather for us to be here dedicated to the great task remaining before us—that from these honored dead we take increased devotion to that cause for which they gave the last full measure of devotion—that we here highly resolve that these dead shall not have died in vain, that this nation under God shall have a new birth of freedom, and that government of the people, by the people, for the people shall not perish from the earth.

The Declaration of Sentiments

Seneca Falls, New York, 1848
Source: U.S. Dept. of State

The Declaration of Sentiments and Resolutions was drafted by Elizabeth Cady Stanton for the women's rights convention at Seneca Falls, New York in 1848. Based on the American Declaration of Independence, the Sentiments demanded equality with men before the law, in education and employment. Here, too, was the first pronouncement demanding that women be given the right to vote.

Sentiments

When, in the course of human events, it becomes necessary for one portion of the family of man to assume among the people of the earth a position different from that which they have hitherto occupied, but one to which the laws of nature and of nature's God entitle them, a decent respect to the opinions of mankind requires that they should declare the causes that impel them to such a course.

We hold these truths to be self-evident: that all men and women are created equal; that they are endowed by their Creator with certain inalienable rights; that among these are life, liberty, and the pursuit of happiness; that to secure these rights governments are instituted, deriving their just powers from the consent of the governed. Whenever any form of government becomes destructive of these ends, it is the right of those who suffer from it to refuse allegiance to it, and to insist upon the institution of a new government, laying its foundation on such principles, and organizing its powers in such form, as to them shall seem most likely to effect their safety and happiness.

Prudence, indeed, will dictate that governments long established should not be changed for light and transient causes; and, accordingly, all experience has shown that mankind are more disposed to suffer, while evils are sufferable, than to right themselves by abolishing the forms to which they were accustomed. But when a long train of abuses and usurpations, pursuing invariably the same object, evinces a design to reduce them under absolute despotism, it is their duty to throw off such government and to provide new guards for their future security. Such has been the patient sufferance of the women under this government, and such is now the necessity which constrains them to demand the equal station to which they are entitled.

The history of mankind is a history of repeated injuries and usurpations on the part of man toward woman, having in direct object the establishment of an absolute tyranny over her. To prove this, let facts be submitted to a candid world.

He has never permitted her to exercise her inalienable right to the elective franchise.

He has compelled her to submit to law in the formation of which she had no voice.

He has withheld from her rights which are given to the most ignorant and degraded men, both natives and foreigners.

Having deprived her of this first right as a citizen, the elective franchise, thereby leaving her without representation in the halls of legislation, he has oppressed her on all sides.

He has made her, if married, in the eye of the law, civilly dead. He has taken from her all right in property, even to the wages she earns.

He has made her morally, an irresponsible being, as she can commit many crimes with impunity, provided they be done in the presence of her husband. In the covenant of marriage, she is compelled to promise obedience to her husband, he becoming, to all intents and purposes, her master-the law giving him power to deprive her of her liberty and to administer chastisement.

He has so framed the laws of divorce, as to what shall be the proper causes and, in case of separation, to whom the guardianship of the children shall be given, as to be wholly regardless of the happiness of the women-the law, in all cases, going upon a false supposition of the supremacy of man and giving all power into his hands.

After depriving her of all rights as a married woman, if single and the owner of property, he has taxed her to support a government which recognizes her only when her property can be made profitable to it.

He has monopolized nearly all the profitable employments, and from those she is permitted to follow, she receives but a scanty remuneration. He closes against her all the avenues to wealth and distinction which he considers most honorable to himself. As a teacher of theology, medicine, or law, she is not known.

He has denied her the facilities for obtaining a thorough education, all colleges being closed against her.

He allows her in church, as well as state, but a subordinate position, claiming apostolic authority for her exclusion from the ministry, and, with some exceptions, from any public participation in the affairs of the church.

He has created a false public sentiment by giving to the world a different code of morals for men and women, by which moral delinquencies which exclude women from society are not only tolerated but deemed of little account in man.

He has usurped the prerogative of Jehovah himself, claiming it as his right to assign for her a sphere of action, when that belongs to her conscience and to her God.

He has endeavored, in every way that he could, to destroy her confidence in her own powers, to lessen her self-respect, and to make her willing to lead a dependent and abject life.

Now, in view of this entire disfranchisement of one-half the people of this country, their social and religious degradation, in view of the unjust laws above mentioned, and because women do feel themselves aggrieved, oppressed, and fraudulently deprived of their most sacred rights, we insist that they have immediate admission to all the rights and privileges which belong to them as citizens of the United States.

In entering upon the great work before us, we anticipate no small amount of misconception, misrepresentation, and ridicule; but we shall use every instrumentality within our power to effect our object. We shall employ agents, circulate tracts, petition the state and national legislatures, and endeavor to enlist the pulpit and the press in our behalf. We hope this Convention will be followed by a series of conventions embracing every part of the country.

Resolutions

Whereas, the great precept of nature is conceded to be that "man shall pursue his own true and substantial happiness." Blackstone in his Commentaries remarks that this law of nature, being coeval with mankind and dictated by God himself, is, of course, superior in obligation to any other. It is binding over all the globe, in all countries and at all times; no human laws are of any validity if contrary to this, and such of them as are valid derive all their force, and all their validity, and all their authority, mediately and immediately, from this original; therefore,

Resolved, That such laws as conflict, in any way, with the true and substantial happiness of woman, are contrary to the great precept of nature and of no validity, for this is superior in obligation to any other.

Resolved, that all laws which prevent woman from occupying such a station in society as her conscience shall dictate, or which place her in a position inferior to that of man, are contrary to the great precept of nature and therefore of no force or authority.

Resolved, that woman is man's equal, was intended to be so by the Creator, and the highest good of the race demands that she should be recognized as such.

Resolved, that the women of this country ought to be enlightened in regard to the laws under which they live, that they may no longer publish their degradation by declaring themselves satisfied with their present position, nor their ignorance, by asserting that they have all the rights they want.

Resolved, that inasmuch as man, while claiming for himself intellectual superiority, does accord to woman moral superiority, it is preeminently his duty to encourage her to speak and teach, as she has an opportunity, in all religious assemblies.

Resolved, that the same amount of virtue, delicacy, and refinement of behavior that is required of woman in the social state also be required of man, and the same transgressions should be visited with equal severity on both man and woman.

Resolved, that the objection of indelicacy and impropriety, which is so often brought against woman when she addresses a public audience, comes with a very ill grace from those who encourage, by their attendance, her appearance on the stage, in the concert, or in feats of the circus.

Resolved, that woman has too long rested satisfied in the circumscribed limits which corrupt customs and a perverted application of the Scriptures have marked out for her, and that it is time she should move in the enlarged sphere which her great Creator has assigned her.

Resolved, that it is the duty of the women of this country to secure to themselves their sacred right to the elective franchise.

Resolved, that the equality of human rights results necessarily from the fact of the identity of the race in capabilities and responsibilities.

Resolved, that the speedy success of our cause depends upon the zealous and untiring efforts of both men and women for the overthrow of the monopoly of the pulpit, and for the securing to woman an equal participation with men in the various trades, professions, and commerce.

Resolved, therefore, that, being invested by the Creator with the same capabilities and same consciousness of responsibility for their exercise, it is demonstrably the right and duty of woman, equally with man, to promote every righteous cause by every righteous means; and especially in regard to the great subjects of morals and religion, it is self-evidently her right to participate with her brother in teaching them, both in private and in public, by writing and by speaking, by any instrumentalities proper to be used, and in any assemblies proper to be held; and this being a self-evident truth growing out of the divinely implanted principles of human nature, any custom or authority adverse to it, whether modern or wearing the hoary sanction of antiquity, is to be regarded as a self-evident falsehood, and at war with mankind.

Profile of the United States

This profile was created by the editors of the almanac from many data sources. Most figures are approximate. For additional details about the U.S., please refer to the appropriate sections of the almanac.

Geography

Number of states: 50
Land area (1990): 3,536,338 sq. mi. Share of world land area (1990): 6.2%
Population density (1990): 70.3 people per sq. mi.
Northernmost point: Point Barrow, Alaska
Easternmost point: West Quoddy Head, Maine
Southernmost point: Ka Lae (South Cape), Hawaii
Westernmost point: Cape Wrangell, Alaska[1]
Geographic center (50 states): in Butte County, S.D. (44′ 58′ N. lat., 103′ 46′ W. long)
Highest point: Mt. McKinley, Alaska (20,320 ft.)
Lowest point: Death Valley, Calif. (282 ft. below sea level)

1. The extreme points are measured from the geographic center of the United States (incl. Alaska and Hawaii), west of Castle Rock, S.D., 44° 58′ N. lat., 103° 46′ W. long. If measured from the prime meridian in Greenwich, England, Cape Wrangell, Alaska would be the easternmost point.

Population

Total Resident Pop.[1] (July 1999): 272,878,000
Mean center of population (1990): 10 miles southeast of Steelville in Crawford County, Mo.
Males (July 1999): 133,352,000
Females (July 1999): 139,526,000
White (July 1999): 224,692,000 (82.3% of pop.)
Black (July 1999): 34,903,000 (12.8% of pop.)
Asian and Pacific Islander (July 1999): 10,887,000 (4.0% of pop.)
American Indian, Eskimo, and Aleut (July 1999): 2,396,000 (0.9% of pop.)
Hispanic origin (can be of any race) (July 1999): 31,365,000 (11.5% of pop.)
Median age (July 1999): 35.5
Baby boomers (1992): 77,000,000
Rural population (1990): 66,964,000
Metropolitan population (1990): 192,725,741
Families (1998): 70,880,000
Average family size (1998): 3.18
Home ownership (1995): 64.7% of pop.
Married (March 1998): 117,965,000
Never married (March 1998): 58,303,000
Divorced (March 1998): 19,424,000
Unmarried couples (1995): 3,661,000
Single parents (1995): female, 12,514,000; male, 3,513,000
Widowed (March 1998): 13,599,000
1. Excludes the United States Armed Forces overseas.

Vital Statistics

Births (1998): 3,941,553 (14.6 per 1,000)
Deaths (1998): 2,337,256 (8.6 per 1,000)
Marriages (1998): 2,244,000 (8.3 per 1,000)
Divorces (1998): 1,135,000 (4.2 per 1,000)
Infant mortality rate (1998): 7.2 per 1,000
Legal abortions (1995): 1,210,883
Life expectancy (1998): Total U.S., both sexes, 76.7; total men, 73.8; total women, 79.5; white men, 74.5; white women, 80.0; black men, 67.6; black women, 74.8

Civilian Labor Force

All (1998): 137,673,000 (4.5% unemployed)
Males (1998): 73,959,000 (4.4% unemployed)
Females (1998): 63,714,000 (4.6% unemployed)
Work at home (telecommuters, est. 1997): 21.5 million
Farms (1998): 2,191,510; total acres (1998): 953,765,000
Avg. hourly earnings of workers (1999): $13.24
Avg. weekly hours of workers (1999): 34.5

Income and Credit

Gross Domestic Product (1999): $9,248.4 billion
Federal budget (est. 2000): total receipts, $1,956,252 million; total outlays, $1,789,562 million
Personal income per capita (1999): $28,518
Median four-person family income (1998): $56,061
Families with stockholdings (1998): 48.8%
Number below poverty level (1998): total, 34,476,000; white, 23,454,000; black, 9,091,000; Hispanic, 8,070,000

Education

Elementary school pupils, grades K–8 (2000)[1]: 38,543,000
Secondary school pupils, grades 9–12 (2000)[1]: 14,902,000
High school dropout rate, ages 16–24 (1998): 11.8%
College enrollment (2000)[1]: 14,889,000
Number of college students age 25 and older (1997): 2,408,000 (male), 3,652,000 (female)
Money spent on public elementary and secondary education (1996–97): $313,131,180,000
Public school teachers (1998): 2,705,000; elementary, 1,608,000; secondary, 1,097,000
Private elementary and secondary school teachers (1998)[1]: 391,000
Average salary for public school teachers (1998): $39,385
1. Projected.

Conveniences

Radio stations (Sept. 1999): AM, 4,783; FM, 5,766
Television stations (Sept. 1999): 1,616
Registered automobiles (1997): 129,749,000
Newspaper circulation (1995): 58,193,391
Cable TV households (1998): 74,550,000
Total TV households (Jan. 1999): 99,400,000
Percent of TV households with two or more sets (Jan. 1999): 74
TV Homes with VCRs (est. 1997): 74%
Internet users per 1,000 people (1998): 283

Crime

Total arrests (1998): 10,295,129
State and federal prison inmates (1996): 419,219
Prisoners under sentence of death (1996): 3,335
Law enforcement officers killed (1997): 132
Total murder victims (1998): 14,088
Violent crimes per 100,000 people (1998): 566.4
Property crimes per 100,000 people (1998): 4,049.1
Homicides per 100,000 people (1998): 6.3
Persons executed under civil authority (1998): 500
Hate crime victims (1998): 7,755

From Horseback to the Internet, Census 1790–2000

With its use of the Internet, sophisticated computers, and advanced statistical analysis, the census has indeed come a long way from 1790, when a group of federal marshals rode on horseback through the original 13 states counting the U.S. population, which was then just shy of four million.

That first census was the product of political compromise. Article I, Section 2, of the U.S. Constitution requires a census every ten years to determine how many members of Congress can be allocated to each state. However, the Founding Fathers suspected that each state would try to augment its population to increase its representation. So, the first census was also used to allocate the cost of the Revolutionary War, with more populous states paying more. Since no state would want to pay more than its fair share, it was thought that each would seek a truly accurate count.

In those days, there was no form to fill out; marshals asked the questions and recorded the results in notebooks or on whatever bits of paper were handy. It took 18 months to count 3.9 million inhabitants. The marshals recorded the number of free white males 16 and older, free white males under 16, free white females, all other free persons by sex and color, and slaves. Slaves were counted as three-fifths of a person, while Indians were excluded.

With each new decade, the form and purpose of the census evolved somewhat. Between 1790 and 1840 the number of census questions ballooned from six to over 70. In 1850 Congress revised the process, including questions on national birth and occupation and establishing a Census Office. Following the Civil War, the Thirteenth Amendment abolished the three-fifths compromise. The census of 1890 was the first to be tabulated by machine.

Changes continued to be made in the 20th century. The 1920 census indicated that for the first time more Americans lived in cities than rural areas. During the Great Depression of the 1930s, the census department began measuring unemployment and income. The first nondefense computer was developed to tabulate the 1950 census. Mail-in forms took precedence over door-to-door enumerators in 1970.

In Jan. 1999 the Supreme Court ruled that statistical sampling—which allows for the estimation of certain populations, such as the homeless or minorities, based on other data—could not be used to redistribute congressional seats. The Court did say,

however, that statistical sampling could be used to draw legislative districts, and to determine population for federal spending.

The Census Bureau was heavily criticized following the 1990 census, which missed an estimated 8.4 million people and counted some 4.4 million people twice. An additional 13 million people were counted in the wrong place, made up, or included by mistake. Part of the problem has been the declining levels of census participation. Some 30 million households did not respond, partly because their members may not have been able to read English.

Census 2000

Employing some 860,000 temporary workers and costing $6 billion, Census 2000 is the largest peacetime mobilization of resources and personnel. Officials reported that 80 million households, or 67% of the 120 million families in the U.S., did return their forms by the April 17 deadline. By early July, census workers had either counted or declared vacant the 42 million housing units that did not return a questionnaire in the mail. Later in the summer, 12 million households were revisited in an effort to verify the data collected. A separate sampling of 314,000 households nationwide was also undertaken to measure the accuracy of the count.

In an effort to reach everyone, Census 2000 used forms printed in English, Spanish, Korean, Chinese, Vietnamese, and Tagalog (spoken in the Philippines).

The Census Bureau expects the state population count to be completed by Dec. 31, 2000. (Information from the 2000 census was not available as the almanac went to print; therefore earlier figures are used.) The population of a given state or municipality is the basis for the distribution of an estimated $185 billion in federal funds, for everything from schools, highway and mass transit, aid to the elderly, and hospitals, to name a few.

The federal government also relies on race and ethnicity data collected by the census to determine whether states and municipalities are in compliance with the Voting Rights Act of 1964. The Census Bureau expects to make racial information available by April 1, 2001. All other information, including housing and economic statistics, will be released periodically between June 2001 and Sept. 2003 in both printed reports and on-line (www.census.gov).

National Censuses[1]

Year	Resident population[2]	Land area, sq mi.	Pop. per sq mi.	Year	Resident population[2]	Land area, sq mi.	Pop. per sq mi.
1790	3,929,214	864,746	4.5	1900	75,994,575	2,969,834	25.6
1800	5,308,483	864,746	6.1	1910	91,972,266	2,969,565	31.0
1810	7,239,881	1,681,828	4.3	1920	105,710,620	2,969,451	35.6
1820	9,638,453	1,749,462	5.5	1930	122,775,046	2,977,128	41.2
1830	12,866,020	1,749,462	7.4	1940	131,669,275	2,977,128	44.2
1840	17,069,453	1,749,462	9.8	1950	150,697,361	2,974,726	50.7
1850	23,191,876	2,940,042	7.9	1960	179,323,175	3,540,911	50.6
1860	31,443,321	2,969,640	10.6	1970	203,302,031	3,540,023	57.4
1870	39,818,449	2,969,640	13.4	1980	226,545,805	3,539,289	64.0
1880	50,155,783	2,969,640	16.9	1990	248,709,873	3,536,278	70.3
1890	62,947,714	2,969,640	21.2				

1. Beginning with 1960, figures include Alaska and Hawaii. 2. Excludes armed forces overseas. *Source:* U.S. Bureau of the Census; Web: www.census.gov.

Population

Colonial Population Estimates

(in round numbers)

Year	Population	Year	Population
1610	350	1700	250,900
1620	2,300	1710	331,700
1630	4,600	1720	466,200
1640	26,600	1730	629,400
1650	50,400	1740	905,600
1660	75,100	1750	1,170,800
1670	111,900	1760	1,593,600
1680	151,500	1770	2,148,100
1690	210,400	1780	2,780,400

Covers years before the establishment of the U.S. Census in 1790. *See* following page for National Census figures, 1790 to 1990.

Total Population

Area	1990	1980	1970
50 states of U.S.	248,709,873	226,545,805	203,302,031
48 conterminous	247,051,601	225,179,263	202,229,535
Alaska	550,043	401,851	302,583
Hawaii	1,108,229	964,691	769,913
American Samoa	46,773	32,297	27,159
Canal Zone	(1)	(1)	44,198
Corn Islands	—	—	(2)
Guam	133,152	105,979	84,996
Johnston Atoll	n.a.	327	1,007
Midway	(3)	453	2,220
Puerto Rico	3,522,037	3,196,520	2,712,033
Swan Islands	n.a.	n.a.	22
Trust Ter. of Pac. Is.	15,122[5]	132,929[4]	90,940
Virgin Is. of U.S.	101,809	96,569	62,468
Wake Island	(3)	302	1,647
Population abroad	922,819	995,546	1,737,836
Armed forces	910,611	515,408	1,057,776
Total	**253,451,585**	**231,106,727**	**208,066,557**

1. Reverted to Panama. 2. Returned to Nicaragua April 25, 1971. 3. No indigenous population. 4. Includes Northern Mariana Islands. 5. Palau only Trust Territory remaining. NOTE: n.a. = not available. *Source:* U.S. Bureau of the Census; Web: www.census.gov.

Population Distribution by Age, Race, Nativity, and Sex Ratio

Year	Total	Age Under 5	5–19	20–44	45–64	65 and over	White[1] Total	Native born	Foreign born	Black	Other races[1]
Percent Distribution											
1860[2]	100.0%	15.4%	35.8%	35.7%	10.4%	2.7%	85.6%	72.6%	13.0%	14.1%	0.3%
1870[2]	100.0	14.3	35.4	35.4	11.9	3.0	87.1	72.9	14.2	12.7	0.2
1880[2]	100.0	13.8	34.3	35.9	12.6	3.4	86.5	73.4	13.1	13.1	0.3
1890[3]	100.0	12.2	33.9	36.9	13.1	3.9	87.5	73.0	14.5	11.9	0.3
1900	100.0	12.1	32.3	37.7	13.7	4.1	87.9	74.5	13.4	11.6	0.5
1910	100.0	11.6	30.4	39.0	14.6	4.3	88.9	74.4	14.5	10.7	0.4
1920	100.0	10.9	29.8	38.4	16.1	4.7	89.7	76.7	13.0	9.9	0.4
1930	100.0	9.3	29.5	38.3	17.4	5.4	89.8	78.4	11.4	9.7	0.5
1940	100.0	8.0	26.4	38.9	19.8	6.8	89.8	81.1	8.7	9.8	0.4
1950	100.0	10.7	23.2	37.6	20.3	8.1	89.5	82.8	6.7	10.0	0.5
1960	100.0	11.3	27.1	32.2	20.1	9.2	88.6	83.4	5.2	10.5	0.9
1970[2]	100.0	8.4	29.5	31.7	20.6	9.8	87.6	83.4	4.3	11.1	1.4
1980	100.0	7.2	24.8	37.1	19.6	11.3	83.1	—	—	11.7	5.2
1990	100.0	7.6	21.3	40.1	18.6	12.5	83.9	—	—	12.3	3.8
Males per 100 Females											
1860[2]	104.7	102.4	101.2	107.9	111.5	98.3	105.3	103.7	115.1	99.6	260.8
1870[2]	102.2	102.9	101.2	99.2	114.5	100.5	102.8	100.6	115.3	96.2	400.7
1880[2]	103.6	103.0	101.3	104.0	110.2	101.4	104.0	102.1	115.9	97.8	362.2
1890[3]	105.0	103.6	101.4	107.3	108.3	104.2	105.4	102.9	118.7	99.5	165.2
1900	104.4	102.1	100.9	105.8	110.7	102.0	104.9	102.8	117.4	98.6	185.2
1910	106.0	102.5	101.3	108.1	114.4	101.1	106.6	102.7	129.2	98.9	185.6
1920	104.0	102.5	100.8	102.8	115.2	101.3	104.4	101.7	121.7	99.2	156.6
1930	102.5	103.0	101.4	100.5	109.1	100.5	102.9	101.1	115.8	97.0	150.6
1940	100.7	103.2	102.0	98.1	105.2	95.5	101.2	100.1	111.1	95.0	140.5
1950	98.6	103.9	102.5	96.2	100.1	89.6	99.0	98.8	102.0	93.7	129.7
1960	97.1	103.4	102.7	95.6	95.7	82.8	97.4	97.6	94.2	93.3	109.7
1970[2]	94.8	104.0	103.3	95.1	91.6	72.1	95.3	95.9	83.8	90.8	100.2
1980	94.5	104.7	104.0	98.1	90.7	67.6	94.8	—	—	89.6	100.3
1990	95.1	104.8	105.0	99.8	92.5	67.2	95.9	—	—	89.8	96.5

NOTES: Data exclude armed forces overseas. Beginning in 1960, includes Alaska and Hawaii. (—) Data not available. 1. The 1980 and 1990 census data for white and other race categories are not directly comparable to those shown for the preceding years because of changes in the way some persons reported their race, as well as changes in procedures relating to racial classification. 2. Excludes persons for whom age is not available. 3. Excludes persons enumerated in the Indian Territory and on Indian reservations. *Source:* U.S. Bureau of the Census; Web: www.census.gov.

Resident Population—Selected Characteristics, 1790–1999

(in thousands)

Date	Male	Female	White	Black	Total other	Other — American Indian, Eskimo, Aleut	Other — Asian and Pacific Islanders	Hispanic origin[1]
1790 (Aug. 2)[2]	n.a.	n.a.	3,172	757	n.a.	n.a.	n.a.	n.a.
1800 (Aug. 4)[2]	n.a.	n.a.	4,306	1,002	n.a.	n.a.	n.a.	n.a.
1850 (June 1)[2]	11,838	11,354	19,553	3,639	n.a.	n.a.	n.a.	n.a.
1900 (June 1)[2]	38,816	37,178	66,809	8,834	351	n.a.	n.a.	n.a.
1910 (Apr. 15)[2]	47,332	44,640	81,732	9,828	413	n.a.	n.a.	n.a.
1920 (Jan. 1)[2]	53,900	51,810	94,821	10,463	427	n.a.	n.a.	n.a.
1930 (Apr. 1)[2]	62,137	60,638	110,287	11,891	597	n.a.	n.a.	n.a.
1940 (Apr. 1)[2]	66,062	65,608	118,215	12,866	589	n.a.	n.a.	n.a.
1950 (Apr. 1)[2]	74,833	75,864	134,942	15,042	713	n.a.	n.a.	n.a.
1950 (Apr. 1)	75,187	76,139	135,150	15,045	1,131	n.a.	n.a.	n.a.
1960 (Apr. 1)	88,331	90,992	158,832	18,872	1,620	n.a.	n.a.	n.a.
1970 (Apr. 1)[3]	98,926	104,309	178,098	22,581	2,557	n.a.	n.a.	n.a.
1980 (Apr. 1)[4, 5]	110,053	116,493	194,713	26,683	5,150	1,420	3,729	14,609
1990 (Apr. 1)[4, 6]	121,271	127,494	208,727	30,511	9,527	2,065	7,462	22,372
1991 (July 1)[7]	122,943	129,184	210,961	31,131	10,035	2,110	7,925	23,384
1992 (July 1)[7]	124,404	130,590	212,860	31,667	10,467	2,148	8,319	24,275
1993 (July 1)[7]	125,767	131,979	214,677	32,179	10,890	2,185	8,705	25,214
1994 (July 1)[7]	127,028	133,261	216,365	32,654	11,271	2,221	9,050	26,152
1995 (July 1)[7]	128,272	134,493	218,010	33,098	11,657	2,254	9,403	27,099
1996 (July 1)[7]	129,483	135,707	219,623	33,518	12,050	2,289	9,761	28,092
1997 (July 1)[7]	130,760	136,984	221,317	33,973	12,454	2,324	10,130	29,160
1998 (July 1)[7]	132,046	138,252	223,001	34,431	12,867	2,360	10,507	30,250
1999 (July 1)[7]	133,352	139,526	224,692	34,903	13,283	2,396	10,887	31,365

NOTES: n.a. = not available. 1. Persons of Hispanic origin may be of any race. 2. Excludes Alaska and Hawaii. 3. The revised 1970 resident population count is 203,302,031, which incorporates changes due to errors found after tabulations were completed. The race and sex data shown here reflect the official 1970 census count. 4. The race data shown have been modified to be consistent with the guidelines in Federal Statistical Directive No. 15 issued by the Office of Management and Budget. Figures are not comparable to the 1990 census race categories. 5. Total population count has been revised since the 1980 census publications. Numbers by age, race, Hispanic origin, and sex have not been corrected. 6. The April 1, 1990, census count (248,765,170) includes count resolution corrections processed through Aug. 1997, and does not include adjustments for census coverage errors except for adjustments estimated for the 1995 Census Test in Oakland, Calif.; Paterson, N.J.; and six Louisiana parishes. These adjustments amounted to a total of 55,297 persons. 7. Estimated. *Source: Statistical Abstract of the United States 1999.*

Population Trends by Region

	July 1990	July 1995	July 1996	July 1997	July 1998	July 1999
United States	249,439,545	262,760,639	265,179,411	267,636,061	270,298,524	272,690,813
Northeast[1]	50,873,469	51,428,139	51,502,371	51,588,281	51,721,625	51,829,962
New England	13,219,210	13,280,586	13,326,211	13,378,545	13,429,862	13,495,933
Middle Atlantic	37,654,259	38,147,553	38,176,160	38,209,736	38,291,763	38,334,029
Midwest[2]	59,763,595	61,837,876	62,181,664	62,460,453	62,889,382	63,242,284
East North Central	42,075,499	43,483,513	43,713,327	43,889,857	44,194,756	44,442,146
West North Central	17,688,096	18,354,363	18,468,337	18,570,596	18,694,626	18,800,138
South[3]	85,731,322	91,824,747	93,009,528	94,187,161	95,429,486	96,468,455
South Atlantic	43,756,608	46,962,293	47,588,515	48,230,168	48,944,678	49,560,021
East South Central	15,208,424	16,044,096	16,187,380	16,325,977	16,471,211	16,582,841
West South Central	26,766,290	28,818,358	29,233,633	29,631,016	30,013,597	30,325,593
West[4]	53,071,159	57,669,877	58,485,848	59,400,166	60,258,031	61,150,112
Mountain	13,716,651	15,752,130	16,124,450	16,482,103	16,813,233	17,127,479
Pacific	39,354,508	41,917,747	42,361,398	42,918,063	43,444,798	44,022,633

NOTES: These population estimates incorporate revisions of estimates from previous years and the results of special censuses and test censuses conducted by the Bureau of the Census. Data released to public in Dec. 1998. 1. The Northeast region includes the New England division: Conn., Maine, Mass., N.H., R.I., and Vt.; and the Middle Atlantic division: N.J., N.Y., and Pa. 2. The Midwest region includes the East North Central division: Ill., Ind., Mich., Ohio, and Wis.; and the West North Central division: Iowa, Kans., Minn., Mo., Nebr., N.D., and S.D. 3. The South region includes the South Atlantic division: Del., D.C., Fla., Ga., Md., N.C., S. C., Va., and W.Va.; the East South Central division: Ala., Ky., Miss., Tenn.; and the West South Central division: Ark., La., Okla., and Tex. 4. The West region includes the Mountain division: Ariz., Colo., Idaho, Mont., Nev., N.M., Utah, Wyo.; and the Pacific division: Alaska, Calif., Hawaii, Ore., and Wash. *Source: Population Estimates Program, Population Division, U.S. Bureau of the Census; Web: www.census.gov/population.*

Population by State

State	1990	Percent change, 1980–1990	Pop. per sq mi., 1990	Pop. rank, 1990	1980	1950	1900	1790
Alabama	4,040,587	3.8%	79.6	22	3,893,888	3,061,743	1,828,697	—
Alaska	550,403	36.8	1.0	49	401,851	128,643	63,592	—
Arizona	3,665,228	34.9	32.3	24	2,718,215	749,587	122,931	—
Arkansas	2,350,725	2.8	45.1	33	2,286,435	1,909,511	1,311,564	—
California	29,786,021	25.8	191.4	1	23,667,902	10,586,223	1,485,053	—
Colorado	3,294,394	14.0	31.8	26	2,889,964	1,325,089	539,700	—
Connecticut	3,287,116	5.8	678.5	27	3,107,576	2,007,280	908,420	237,946
Delaware	666,168	12.1	340.8	46	594,338	318,085	184,735	59,096
D.C.	606,900	−4.9	884.4	—	638,333	802,178	278,718	—
Florida	12,937,926	32.8	239.9	4	9,746,324	2,771,305	528,542	—
Georgia	6,478,216	18.6	111.8	11	5,463,105	3,444,578	2,216,331	82,548
Hawaii	1,108,229	14.8	172.5	41	964,691	499,794	154,001	—
Idaho	1,006,749	6.6	12.2	42	943,935	588,637	161,772	—
Illinois	11,430,602	0.0	205.6	6	11,426,518	8,712,176	4,821,550	—
Indiana	5,544,159	1.0	154.6	14	5,490,224	3,934,224	2,516,462	—
Iowa	2,776,755	−4.7	49.7	30	2,913,808	2,621,073	2,231,853	—
Kansas	2,477,574	4.8	30.3	32	2,363,679	1,905,299	1,470,495	—
Kentucky	3,687,000	0.7	92.8	23	3,660,777	2,944,806	2,147,174	73,677
Louisiana	4,222,000	0.4	96.9	21	4,205,900	2,683,516	1,381,625	—
Maine	1,227,928	9.1	39.8	38	1,124,660	913,774	694,466	96,540
Maryland	4,781,468	13.4	489.1	19	4,216,975	2,343,001	1,188,044	319,728
Massachusetts	6,016,425	4.9	767.6	13	5,737,037	4,690,514	2,805,346	378,787
Michigan	9,295,297	0.4	163.6	8	9,262,078	6,371,766	2,420,982	—
Minnesota	4,375,099	7.4	55.0	20	4,075,970	2,982,483	1,751,394	—
Mississippi	2,575,000	2.2	54.9	31	2,520,638	2,178,914	1,551,270	—
Missouri	5,117,073	4.1	74.3	15	4,916,686	3,954,653	3,106,665	—
Montana	799,065	1.5	5.5	44	786,690	591,024	243,329	—
Nebraska	1,578,385	0.5	20.6	36	1,569,825	1,325,510	1,066,300	—
Nevada	1,201,833	50.2	10.9	39	800,493	160,083	42,335	—
New Hampshire	1,109,252	20.4	123.7	40	920,610	533,242	411,588	141,885
New Jersey	7,748,000	5.2	1,044.3	9	7,364,823	4,835,329	1,883,669	184,139
New Mexico	1,515,069	16.3	12.5	37	1,302,894	681,187	195,310	—
New York	17,990,455	2.5	384.1	2	17,558,072	14,830,192	7,268,894	340,120
North Carolina	6,632,000	12.8	136.1	10	5,881,766	4,061,929	1,893,810	393,751
North Dakota	638,800	−2.2	9.3	47	652,717	619,636	319,146	—
Ohio	10,847,115	0.5	264.9	7	10,797,630	7,946,627	4,157,545	—
Oklahoma	3,145,585	4.0	45.8	28	3,025,290	2,233,351	790,391[1]	—
Oregon	2,842,321	8.0	29.6	29	2,633,105	1,521,341	413,536	—
Pennsylvania	11,883,000	0.2	265.1	5	11,863,895	10,498,012	6,302,115	434,373
Rhode Island	1,003,464	6.0	960.3	43	947,154	791,896	428,556	68,825
South Carolina	3,486,703	11.7	115.4	25	3,121,820	2,117,027	1,340,316	249,073
South Dakota	696,004	0.7	9.2	45	690,768	652,740	401,570	—
Tennessee	4,877,185	6.2	118.3	17	4,591,120	3,291,718	2,020,616	35,691
Texas	16,986,510	19.4	64.9	3	14,229,191	7,711,194	3,048,710	—
Utah	1,722,850	17.9	21.0	35	1,461,037	688,862	276,749	—
Vermont	562,758	10.1	60.8	48	511,456	377,747	343,641	85,425
Virginia	6,189,000	15.8	156.3	12	5,346,818	3,318,680	1,854,184	747,610[2]
Washington	4,866,692	17.8	73.1	18	4,132,156	2,378,963	518,103	—
West Virginia	1,793,477	−8.0	74.5	34	1,949,644	2,005,552	958,800	—
Wisconsin	4,891,769	3.9	90.1	16	4,705,767	3,434,575	2,069,042	—
Wyoming	453,588	−3.5	4.7	50	469,557	290,529	92,531	—
Total U.S.	248,709,873	9.8	—	—	226,545,805	151,325,798	76,212,168	3,929,214

1. Includes population of Indian Territory, 1900: 392,960. 2. Until 1863, Virginia included what is now West Virginia. *Source:* U.S. Bureau of the Census; Web: www.census.gov.

Resident Population of the United States:
Estimates, by Sex, Race, and Hispanic Origin, with Median Age, 1999
(in thousands)

	Total population	% of population	Median age	Male population	Female population
All races	272,878	100.0%	35.5	133,352	139,526
White	224,692	82.3	36.6	110,372	114,320
Black	34,903	12.8	30.1	16,573	18,329
American Indian, Eskimo, and Aleut	2,396	0.9	27.6	1,186	1,211
Asian and Pacific Islander	10,887	4.0	31.7	5,221	5,667
Hispanic origin (of any race)	31,365	11.5	26.5	15,774	15,591

NOTES: As of July 1, 1999. Percentages add up to more than 100% because Hispanics may be of any race and are therefore counted under more than one category. *Source:* U.S. Bureau of the Census; Web: www.census.gov.

Resident Population Estimates by Age and Sex, 1999

	Both sexes	Male	Female
Population, all ages	272,878,000	133,352,000	139,526,000
Median age	35.5	34.3	36.6
Five-year age groups			
Under 5 years	18,918,000	9,668,000	9,250,000
5 to 9 years	19,957,000	10,213,000	9,744,000
10 to 14 years	19,554,000	10,015,000	9,540,000
15 to 19 years	19,762,000	10,159,000	9,603,000
20 to 24 years	18,061,000	9,197,000	8,864,000
25 to 29 years	18,240,000	9,067,000	9,174,000
30 to 34 years	19,750,000	9,780,000	9,970,000
35 to 39 years	22,556,000	11,221,000	11,335,000
40 to 44 years	22,278,000	11,045,000	11,233,000
45 to 49 years	19,363,000	9,505,000	9,858,000
50 to 54 years	16,452,000	8,001,000	8,451,000
55 to 59 years	12,883,000	6,186,000	6,697,000
60 to 64 years	10,526,000	4,973,000	5,553,000
65 to 69 years	9,455,000	4,339,000	5,116,000
70 to 74 years	8,779,000	3,866,000	4,914,000
75 to 79 years	7,337,000	3,060,000	4,277,000
80 to 84 years	4,823,000	1,816,000	3,007,000
85 to 89 years	2,629,000	848,000	1,781,000
90 to 94 years	1,151,000	308,000	843,000
95 to 99 years	344,000	76,000	269,000
100 years and over	60,000	11,000	49,000
Special age categories			
18 years and over	202,682,000	97,395,000	105,287,000
65 years and over	34,578,000	14,323,000	20,255,000

NOTE: As of July 1, 1999. *Source:* U.S. Bureau of the Census. Web: www.census.gov.

Ratio of Males to Females, by Age Group, 1950–2025

(number of males per 100 females, total resident population)

							Projections	
Age	1950	1960	1970	1980	1990[1]	1998	2000	2025
All ages	**98.6**	**97.1**	**94.8**	**94.5**	**95.1**	**95.5**	**95.5**	**96.0**
Under 14 years	103.7	103.4	103.9	104.6	104.9	104.8	104.8	105.1
14 to 24 years	98.2	98.7	98.7	101.9	104.6	104.8	104.1	104.2
25 to 44 years	96.4	95.7	95.5	97.4	98.9	98.6	98.9	97.7
45 to 64 years	100.1	95.7	91.6	90.7	92.5	93.7	93.8	93.5
65 years and over	89.6	82.8	72.1	67.6	67.2	70.3	70.4	82.9

NOTES: As of April 1 for 1950–1990. As of July 1 for 1998–2025. 1. The April 1, 1990, census count (248,765,170) includes count resolution corrections processed through August 1997, and does not include adjustments for census coverage errors except for adjustments estimated for the 1995 Census Test in Oakland, Calif.; Paterson, N.J.; and six Louisiana parishes. These adjustments amounted to a total of 55,297 persons. *Source:* U.S. Census Bureau, *Current Population Reports*, P25-1095 and P25-1130; and unpublished data. From *Statistical Abstract of the United States 1999*.

Population Explosion among Older Americans

The United States has seen a rapid growth in its elderly population during the 20th century. The number of Americans aged 65 and older climbed above 34.6 million in 1999, compared with 3.1 million in 1900. For the same years, the ratio of elderly Americans to the total population jumped from one in 25 to one in eight. The trend is guaranteed to continue in the coming century as the baby-boom generation grows older. Between 1990 and 2020, the population aged 65 to 74 is projected to grow 74 percent.

The elderly population explosion is a result of impressive increases in life expectancy. When the nation was founded, the average American could expect to live to the age of 35. Life expectancy at birth had increased to 47.3 by 1900 and in 1997 stood at 76.5.

Along with the growth of the general elderly population has come a remarkable increase in the number of Americans reaching age 100. The 1990 census found that there were 37,306 centenarians in the U.S. Current projections estimate that the number will reach 131,000 in the year 2010 and as many as 834,000 by 2050.

Source: Based on U.S. Census Bureau data.

Population Aged 100 and Over, 1990

	Total	White	Black	American Indian, Eskimo, and Aleut	Asian and Pacific Islander	Other	Hispanic[1]	Non-Hispanic White	Non-Hispanic All other races
Both sexes	37,306	30,105	5,874	264	492	571	1,642	29,130	6,534
100 to 104 years	30,947	25,881	4,208	180	357	321	1,051	25,186	4,710
105 years and over	6,359	4,224	1,666	84	135	250	591	3,944	1,824
Males	7,901	5,799	1,587	99	175	241	581	5,490	1,830
100 to 104 years	5,944	4,616	1,025	68	122	113	317	4,421	1,206
105 years and over	1,957	1,183	562	31	53	128	264	1,069	624
Females	29,405	24,306	4,287	165	317	330	1,061	23,640	4,704
100 to 104 years	25,003	21,265	3,183	112	235	208	734	20,765	3,504
105 years and over	4,402	3,041	1,104	53	82	122	327	2,875	1,200

1. Persons of Hispanic origin may be of any race. Source: U.S. Bureau of the Census, 1990 Census of Population—General Population Characteristics, United States.

Persons 65 Years Old and Over—Characteristics by Sex, 1980–1998

Characteristic	Total 1980	Total 1990	Total 1998	Male 1980	Male 1990	Male 1998	Female 1980	Female 1990	Female 1998
Total[1] (million)	24.2	29.6	32.1	9.9	12.3	13.5	14.2	17.2	18.6
White (million)	21.9	26.5	n.a.	9.0	11.0	n.a.	12.9	15.4	n.a.
Black (million)	2.0	2.5	n.a.	0.8	1.0	n.a.	1.2	1.5	n.a.
Percent below poverty level[2]	15.2%	11.4%	10.5%	11.1%	7.8%	7.0%	17.9%	13.9%	13.1%
Percent distribution									
Marital status:									
Single	5.5%	4.6%	4.3%	4.9%	4.2%	3.8%	5.9%	4.9%	4.7%
Married	55.4	56.1	56.6	78.0	76.5	75.1	39.5	41.4	42.9
Spouse present	53.6	54.1	54.2	76.1	74.2	72.6	37.9	39.7	40.7
Spouse absent	1.8	2.0	2.4	1.9	2.3	2.5	1.7	1.7	2.2
Widowed	35.7	34.2	32.5	13.5	14.2	14.9	51.2	48.6	45.2
Divorced	3.5	5.0	6.7	3.6	5.0	6.1	3.4	5.1	7.1
Family status:									
In families[3]	67.6%	66.7%	66.8%	83.0%	81.9%	79.6%	56.8%	55.8%	57.5%
Nonfamily householders	31.2	31.9	31.9	15.7	16.6	18.4	42.0	42.8	41.7
Secondary individuals	1.2	1.4	1.3	1.3	1.5	2.0	1.1	1.4	0.7
Living arrangements:									
Living in household	99.8%	99.7%	100.0%	99.9%	99.9%	100.0%	99.7%	99.5%	100.0%
Living alone	30.3	31.0	30.9	14.9	15.7	17.3	41.0	42.0	40.8
Spouse present	53.6	54.1	54.2	76.1	74.3	72.6	37.9	39.7	40.7
Living with someone else	15.9	14.6	14.9	8.9	9.9	10.0	20.8	17.8	18.4
Not in household[4]	0.2	0.3	—	0.1	0.1	—	0.3	0.5	—
Years of school completed:									
8 years or fewer	43.1%	28.5%	18.1%	45.3%	30.0%	18.3%	41.6%	27.5%	17.9%
1 to 3 years of high school	16.2	16.1	14.9[5]	15.5	15.7	14.1[5]	16.7	16.4	15.4[5]
4 years of high school	24.0	32.9	35.0[6]	21.4	29.0	30.2[6]	25.8	35.6	38.4[6]
1 to 3 years of college	8.2	10.9	17.2[7]	7.5	10.8	17.6[7]	8.6	11.0	17.0[7]
4 years or more of college	8.6	11.6	14.8[8]	10.3	14.5	19.8[8]	7.4	9.5	11.2[8]
Labor force participation[9]:									
Employed	12.2%	11.5%	11.6%	18.4%	15.9%	15.9%	7.8%	8.4%	8.3%
Unemployed	0.4	0.4	0.4	0.6	0.5	0.5	0.3	0.3	0.3
Not in labor force	87.5	88.1	88.1	81.0	83.6	83.5	91.9	91.3	91.4

NOTES: n.a. = not available. (—) Represents zero. 1. Includes other races, not shown separately. 2. Poverty status based on income in preceding year. 3. Excludes those living in unrelated subfamilies. 4. In group quarters other than institutions. 5. Represents those who completed 9th to 12th grade, but have no high school diploma. 6. High school graduate. 7. Some college or associate degree. 8. Bachelor's or advanced degree. 9. Annual averages of monthly figures (from U.S. Bureau of Labor Statistics, Employment and Earnings, January issues. Data beginning 1994 not directly comparable with earlier years). Source: Except as noted, U.S. Bureau of the Census, Current Population Reports. From Statistical Abstract of the United States 1999.

Marital Status and Household Characteristics

Marriages and Divorces, 1900–1998

Year	Marriage Number	Marriage Rate[2]	Divorce[1] Number	Divorce[1] Rate[2]	Year	Marriage Number	Marriage Rate[2]	Divorce[1] Number	Divorce[1] Rate[2]
1900	709,000	9.3	55,751	0.7	1985	2,425,000	10.2	1,187,000	5.0
1910	948,166	10.3	83,045	0.9	1986	2,400,000	10.0	1,159,000	4.8
1920	1,274,476	12.0	170,505	1.6	1987	2,421,000	9.9	1,157,000	4.8
1930	1,126,856	9.2	195,961	1.6	1988	2,389,000	9.7	1,183,000	4.8
1940	1,595,879	12.1	264,000	2.0	1989	2,404,000	9.7	1,163,000	4.7
1950	1,667,231	11.1	385,144	2.6	1990	2,448,000	9.8	1,175,000	4.7
1960	1,523,000	8.5	393,000	2.2	1991	2,371,000	9.4	1,187,000	4.7
1965	1,800,000	9.3	479,000	2.5	1992	2,362,000	9.2	1,215,000	4.8
1970	2,158,802	10.6	708,000	3.5	1993	2,334,000	9.0	1,187,000	4.6
1975	2,152,662	10.1	1,036,000	4.9	1994	2,362,000	9.1	1,191,000	4.6
1980	2,406,708	10.6	1,182,000	5.2	1995	2,336,000	8.9	1,169,000	4.4
1982	2,495,000	10.8	1,180,000	5.1	1996	2,344,000	8.8	1,150,000	4.3
1983	2,444,000	10.5	1,179,000	5.0	1997	2,384,000	8.9	1,163,000	4.3
1984	2,487,000	10.5	1,155,000	4.9	1998	2,256,000	8.4	955,000	3.5

1. Includes annulments. 2. Per 1,000 population. Divorce rates for 1941–1946 are based on population including armed forces overseas. Marriage rates are based on population excluding armed forces overseas. NOTE: Marriage and divorce figures for most years include some estimated data. Alaska is included beginning 1959, Hawaii beginning 1960. *Source:* Department of Health and Human Services, National Center for Health Statistics; Web: www.dhhs.gov.

Median Age at First Marriage

Year	Males	Females	Year	Males	Females	Year	Males	Females
1890	26.1	22.0	1950	22.8	20.3	1994	26.7	24.5
1900	25.9	21.9	1960	22.8	20.3	1995	26.9	24.5
1910	25.1	21.6	1970	23.2	20.8	1996	27.1	24.8
1920	24.6	21.2	1980	24.7	22.0	1997	26.8	25.0
1930	24.3	21.3	1990	26.1	23.9	1998	26.7	25.0
1940	24.3	21.5	1993	26.5	24.5			

Source: U.S. Bureau of the Census; Web: www.census.gov.

Singles in the United States

The ratio of unmarried men per 100 unmarried women in U.S. Metro Areas, 1990

Highest Ratio Men to Women

Rank	Metro Area	Ratio
1	Jacksonville, N.C. MSA	223.64
2	Killeen–Temple, Tex. MSA	122.75
3	Fayetteville, N.C. MSA	117.66
4	Brazoria, Tex. PMSA	116.71
5	Lawton, Okla. MSA	115.63
6	State College, Pa. MSA	112.98
7	Clarksville–Hopkinsville, Tenn.–Ky. MSA	112.71
8	Anchorage, Alaska MSA	112.45
9	Salinas–Seaside–Monterey, Calif. MSA	112.01
10	Bryan–College Station, Tex. MSA	111.40
11	Bremerton, Wash. MSA	108.30
12	San Diego, Calif. MSA	105.33
13	Honolulu, Hawaii MSA	105.22
14	Las Vegas, Nev. MSA	104.65
15	Yuma, Ariz. MSA	104.64
16	Grand Forks, N.D. MSA	104.19
17	San Jose, Calif. PMSA	103.63
18	Reno, Nev. MSA	103.52
19	Lafayette–West Lafayette, Ind. MSA	102.01
20	Fort Walton Beach, Fla. MSA	101.70
21	Vallejo–Fairfield–Napa, Calif. PMSA	101.68
22	Lake County, Ill. PMSA	101.56
23	Champaign–Urbana–Rantoul, Ill. MSA	101.33
24	Jackson, Miss. MSA	101.24
25	Colorado Springs, Colo. MSA	99.42

Lowest Ratio Men to Women

Rank	Metro Area	Ratio
1	Sarasota, Fla. MSA	65.57
2	Bradenton, Fla. MSA	68.41
3	Altoona, Pa. MSA	69.42
4	Springfield, Ill. MSA	69.63
5	Jacksonville, Tenn. MSA	69.72
6	Gadsden, Ala. MSA	69.86
7	Wheeling, W.Va.–Ohio MSA	70.48
8	Charleston, W.Va. MSA	70.65
9	St. Joseph, Mo. MSA	70.93
10	Lynchburg, Va. MSA	71.04
11	Roanoke, Va. MSA	71.09
12	Asheville, N.C. MSA	71.14
13	Shreveport, La. MSA	71.54
14	Birmingham, Ala. MSA	71.63
15	Danville, Va. MSA	71.72
16	Pittsburgh, Pa. PMSA	72.04
17	Monroe, La. MSA	72.06
18	Owensboro, Ky. MSA	72.14
19	Pittsburgh–Beaver Valley, Pa. (CMSA)	72.16
20	Florence, Ala. MSA	72.20
21	Sherman–Denison, Tex. MSA	72.27
22	Florence, S.C. MSA	72.32
23	Huntington–Ashland, W.Va.–Ky.–Ohio MSA	72.67
24	Cumberland, Md.–W.Va. MSA	72.73
25	Steubenville–Weirton, Ohio–W.Va. MSA	72.87

NOTE: Unmarried includes never-married, widowed, and divorced persons, 15 years or older. Metro Areas as defined June 30, 1990. The presence of a military base, college or university, etc. in a metropolitan area may have a significant impact on the size of the ratio. MSA—Metropolitan Statistical Area. CMSA—Consolidated Metropolitan Statistical Area. PMSA—Primary Metropolitan Statistical Area. *Source:* U.S. Bureau of the Census; Web: www.census.gov.

Percent Never Married, 1970 and 1998

Age	1970	1998	Age	1970	1998
Male:			Female:		
20 to 24 years	35.8%	83.4%	20 to 24 years	54.7%	70.3%
25 to 29 years	10.5	51.0	25 to 29 years	19.1	38.6
30 to 34 years	6.2	29.2	30 to 34 years	9.4	21.6
35 to 39 years	5.4	21.6	35 to 39 years	7.2	14.3
40 to 44 years	4.9	15.6	40 to 44 years	6.3	9.9

NOTE: Data applies to the U.S. *Source:* U.S. Bureau of the Census, *Current Population Reports.* From *Statistical Abstract of the United States 1999.*

Persons Living Alone, by Sex and Age

(in thousands)

Sex and Age	1998 Number	1998 Percent	1995 Number	1995 Percent	1990 Number	1990 Percent	1980 Number	1980 Percent
Both sexes								
15 to 24 years	1,251	5%	1,196	5%	1,210	5%	1,726	9%
25 to 34 years	3,679	14	3,653	15	3,972	17	4,729[1]	26[1]
35 to 44 years	4,054	15	3,663	15	3,138	14	(1)	(1)
45 to 64 years	7,421	28	6,377	26	5,502	24	4,514	25
65 to 74 years	4,098	16	4,374	18	4,350	19	3,851	21
75 years and over	5,825	22	5,470	22	4,825	21	3,477	19
Total, 15 years and over	**26,327**	**100**	**24,732**	**100**	**22,999**	**100**	**18,296**	**100**
Male								
15 to 24 years	722	3	623	3	674	3	947	5
25 to 34 years	2,222	8	2,213	9	2,395	10	2,920[1]	16[1]
35 to 44 years	2,555	10	2,263	9	1,836	8	(1)	(1)
45 to 64 years	3,164	12	2,787	11	2,203	10	1,613	9
65 to 74 years	1,111	4	1,134	5	1,042	5	775	4
75 years and over	1,234	5	1,120	5	901	4	711	4
Total, 15 years and over	**11,010**	**42**	**10,140**	**41**	**9,049**	**39**	**6,966**	**38**
Female								
15 to 24 years	528	2	572	2	536	2	779	4
25 to 34 years	1,456	6	1,440	6	1,578	7	1,809[1]	10[1]
35 to 44 years	1,499	6	1,399	6	1,303	6	(1)	(1)
45 to 64 years	4,257	16	3,589	15	3,300	14	2,901	16
65 to 74 years	2,987	11	3,240	13	3,309	14	3,076	17
75 years and over	4,590	17	4,351	18	3,924	17	2,766	15
Total, 15 years and over	**15,317**	**58**	**14,592**	**59**	**13,950**	**61**	**11,330**	**62**

NOTE: As of March. 1. Data for persons 35 to 44 years old included with persons 25 to 34 years old. *Source:* U.S. Bureau of the Census; Web: www.census.gov.

Marital Status of the Population, 1980–1998

(numbers are in millions)

Marital status	Total 1998	Total 1995	Total 1990	Total 1980	Male 1998	Male 1995	Male 1990	Male 1980	Female 1998	Female 1995	Female 1990	Female 1980
Total	197.4	191.6	181.8	159.5	95.0	92.0	86.9	75.7	102.4	99.6	95.0	83.8
Never married	46.6	43.9	40.4	32.3	25.5	24.6	22.4	18.0	21.0	19.3	17.9	14.3
Married	117.9	116.7	112.6	104.6	58.6	57.7	55.8	51.8	59.3	58.9	56.7	52.8
Widowed	13.6	13.4	13.8	12.7	2.6	2.3	2.3	2.0	11.0	11.1	11.5	10.8
Divorced	19.4	17.6	15.1	9.9	8.3	7.4	6.3	3.9	11.1	10.3	8.8	6.0
Percent of total	100.0%	100.0%	100.0%	100.0%	100.0%	100.0%	100.0%	100.0%	100.0%	100.0%	100.0%	100.0%
Never married	23.6	22.9	22.2	20.3	26.9	26.8	25.8	23.8	20.5	19.4	18.9	17.1
Married	59.7	60.9	61.9	65.5	61.7	62.7	64.3	68.4	57.9	59.2	59.7	63.0
Widowed	6.9	7.0	7.6	8.0	2.7	2.5	2.7	2.6	10.8	11.1	12.1	12.8
Divorced	9.8	9.2	8.3	6.2	8.8	8.0	7.2	5.2	10.8	10.3	9.3	7.1

Source: U.S. Bureau of the Census, *Current Population Reports*, Series P20–514 and earlier reports; and unpublished data. From *Statistical Abstract of the United States 1999.*

Births

Births, Birth Rates, and Fertility Rates by State, 1998

State	Number of births	Birth rate[1]	Fertility rate[2]	State	Number of births	Birth rate[1]	Fertility rate[2]
United States[3]	3,941,553	14.6	65.6	Nebraska	23,534	14,2	65.2
Alabama	62,074	14.3	63.2	Nevada	28,699	16.4	77.9
Alaska	9,926	16.2	73.1	New Hampshire	14,429	12.2	52.3
Arizona	78,243	16.8	78.2	New Jersey	114,550	14.1	64.3
Arkansas	36,865	14.5	67.5	New Mexico	27,318	15.7	72.2
California	521,661	16.0	70.7	New York	258,207	14.2	63.9
Colorado	59,577	15.0	67.2	North Carolina	111,688	14.8	66.6
Connecticut	43,820	13.4	61.3	North Dakota	7,932	12.4	58.3
Delaware	10,578	14.2	61.2	Ohio	152,794	13.6	61.2
D.C.	7,686	14.7	60.8	Oklahoma	49,461	14.8	69.0
Florida	195,637	13.1	65.1	Oregon	45,273	13.8	64.7
Georgia	122,368	16.0	67.2	Pennsylvania	145,899	12.2	56.9
Hawaii	17,583	14.7	69.6	Rhode Island	12,599	12.7	57.5
Idaho	19,391	15.8	72.3	South Carolina	53,877	14.0	61.3
Illinois	182,588	15.2	68.3	South Dakota	10,288	13.9	65.1
Indiana	85,122	14.4	64.3	Tennessee	77,396	14.3	63.1
Iowa	37,282	13.0	61.4	Texas	342,283	17.3	76.2
Kansas	38,422	14.6	67.1	Utah	45,165	21.5	91.4
Kentucky	54,329	13.8	61.6	Vermont	6,582	11.1	49.1
Louisiana	66,888	15.3	66.7	Virginia	94,351	13.9	59.1
Maine	13,733	11.0	49.7	Washington	79,663	14.0	62.3
Maryland	71,972	14.0	60.1	West Virginia	20,747	11.5	53.7
Massachusetts	81,411	13.2	58.5	Wisconsin	67,450	12.9	58.5
Michigan	133,666	13.6	60.4	Wyoming	6,252	13.0	60.9
Minnesota	65,202	13.8	61.8	Puerto Rico	60,412	15.7	66.8
Mississippi	42,939	15.6	68.3	Virgin Islands	1,800	15.2	69.6
Missouri	75,358	13.9	62.9	Guam	4,318	29.0	139.0
Montana	10,795	12.3	59.0				

NOTE: Data by place of residence. 1. Total births per 1,000 total population. 2. Total births per 1,000 women aged 15–44. 3. Excludes data for Puerto Rico, Virgin Islands, and Guam. Source: National Center for Health Statistics, National Vital Statistics Reports, vol. 48, no. 3, March 28, 2000. Web: www.cdc.gov/nchs.

Live Births by Age and Race of Mother, 1940–1998

Year[1]/race	Total	Age of Mother							
		Under 15	15–19	20–24	25–29	30–34	35–39	40–44	45–49[2]
1940	2,558,647	3,865	332,667	799,537	693,268	431,468	222,015	68,269	7,558
1945	2,858,449	4,028	298,868	832,746	785,299	554,906	296,852	78,853	6,897
1950	3,631,512	5,413	432,911	1,155,167	1,041,360	610,816	302,780	77,743	5,322
1955	4,014,112	6,181	493,770	1,290,939	1,133,155	732,540	352,320	89,777	5,430
1960	4,257,850	6,780	586,966	1,426,912	1,092,816	687,722	359,908	91,564	5,182
1965	3,760,358	7,768	590,894	1,337,350	925,732	529,376	282,908	81,716	4,614
1970	3,731,386	11,752	644,708	1,418,874	994,904	427,806	180,244	49,952	3,146
1975	3,144,198	12,642	582,238	1,093,676	936,786	375,500	115,409	26,319	1,628
1980	3,612,258	10,169	552,161	1,226,200	1,108,291	550,354	140,793	23,090	1,200
1985	3,760,561	10,220	467,485	1,141,320	1,201,350	696,354	214,336	28,334	1,162
1990	4,158,212	11,657	521,826	1,093,730	1,277,108	886,063	317,583	48,607	1,638
1995	3,899,589	12,242	499,873	965,547	1,063,539	904,666	383,745	67,250	2,727
1996	3,914,953	11,242	494,272	951,247	1,078,411	904,329	400,810	71,663	2,980
1997	3,880,894	10,121	483,220	942,048	1,069,436	886,798	409,710	76,084	3,333
1998	3,941,553	9,462	484,895	965,122	1,083,010	889,365	424,890	81,027	3,782[2]
White	3,118,727	4,801	340,694	736,664	880,688	737,532	349,799	65,485	3,064[2]
Black	609,902	4,289	126,937	189,088	139,302	93,785	46,657	9,496	348[2]
American Indian[3]	40,272	197	8,201	13,046	9,529	5,930	2,795	555	19[2]
Asian or Pacific Islander	172,652	175	9,063	26,324	53,491	52,118	25,639	5,491	351[2]
Hispanic origin[4]	734,661	2,716	121,388	223,113	196,012	125,702	54,195	11,056	479[2]

NOTE: Data refer only to births occurring within the U.S. 1. Data for 1940–55 are adjusted for under-registration. Beginning 1960, only registered births are shown. Data for 1960–70 based on a 50% sample of births. For 1972–84, based on 100% of births in selected states and on 50% sample in all other states. Beginning 1989, births are tabulated by race of mother; previously based on race of child. 2. Beginning 1998, ages 45–54. 3. Includes births to Aleuts and Eskimos. 4. Persons of Hispanic origin may be any race. Source: National Center for Health Statistics, National Vital Statistics Reports, vol. 48, no. 3, March 28, 2000. Web: www.cdc.gov/nchs.

Live Births by Sex and Sex Ratio

	Total[1,2]			White			Black		
Year	Male	Female	Males per 1,000 females	Male	Female	Males per 1,000 females	Male	Female	Males per 1,000 females
1985	1,927,983	1,832,578	1,052	1,536,646	1,454,727	1,056	308,575	299,618	1,030
1986	1,924,868	1,831,679	1,051	1,523,914	1,446,525	1,053	315,788	305,433	1,034
1987	1,951,153	1,858,241	1,050	1,535,517	1,456,971	1,054	325,259	316,308	1,028
1988	2,002,424	1,907,086	1,050	1,562,675	1,483,487	1,053	341,441	330,535	1,033
1989	2,069,490	1,971,468	1,050	1,606,757	1,525,234	1,053	360,131	349,264	1,031
1990	2,129,495	2,028,717	1,050	1,654,928	1,570,415	1,054	367,455	357,121	1,029
1991	2,101,518	2,009,389	1,046	1,659,077	1,582,196	1,049	346,455	336,147	1,031
1992	2,082,097	1,982,917	1,050	1,641,811	1,559,867	1,053	342,726	330,907	1,036
1993	2,048,861	1,951,379	1,050	1,616,332	1,533,501	1,054	333,984	324,891	1,028
1994	2,022,589	1,930,178	1,048	1,599,803	1,521,401	1,051	322,554	313,837	1,028
1995	1,996,355	1,930,234	1,049	1,588,427	1,510,458	1,052	308,115	297,024	1,031
1996	1,990,480	1,901,014	1,047	—	—	1,050	—	—	1,028
1997	1,985,596	1,895,298	1,048	—	—	1,052	—	—	1,031
1998	2,016,205	1,925,348	1,047	—	—	1,052	—	—	1,034

NOTE: (—) Data not available. 1. Excludes births to nonresidents of U.S. 2. Includes races other than white and black. *Source:* National Center for Health Statistics, *National Vital Statistics Reports*, vol. 48, no. 3, March 28, 2000. Web: www.cdc.gov/nchs.

Selected Characteristics of Births by Race of Mother, 1998

Characteristic	All races	White	Black	American Indian[1]	Asian or Pacific Islander	Hispanic origin[2]
Percentage of mothers who:						
Had prenatal care beginning in the first trimester	82.8	84.8	73.3	68.8	83.1	74.3
Had late or no prenatal care	3.9	3.3	7.0	8.5	3.6	6.3
Were tobacco users[3]	12.9	14.0	9.5	20.2	3.1	4.0
Were alcohol users[4]	1.1	1.0	1.4	3.2	0.4	0.6
Gained less than 16 lbs[5]	11.3	10.2	16.7	15.3	9.6	13.4
Median weight gain[5]	30.5	30.7	29.9	30.2	30.1	30.0
Had cesarean births	21.2	21.0	22.4	18.6	19.4	20.6
Percentage of infants who:						
Were born prior to 37 full weeks	11.6	10.5	17.5	12.2	10.4	11.4
Weighed less than 1,500 grams (3 lb 4 oz.)	1.4	1.1	3.1	1.2	1.1	1.1
Weighed less than 2,500 grams (5 lb 8 oz.)	7.6	6.5	13.0	6.8	7.4	6.4
Weighed 4,000 grams (8 lb 14 oz.) or more	10.1	11.2	5.4	12.4	5.9	9.0
Had five-minute Apgar scores of less than 7[6]	1.4	1.2	2.4	1.4	1.1	1.2

1. Includes births to Aleuts and Eskimos. 2. Hispanic origin may be of any race. 3. Excludes data for Calif., Ind., N.Y. (but includes N.Y.C.), and S.D., which did not report tobacco use on birth certificate. 4. Excludes data for Calif. and S.D., which did not report alcohol use on birth certificate. 5. Excludes data for Calif., which did not report weight gain on birth certificate. Median weight gain was 30.5 pounds in 1998. 6. Excludes data for Calif. and Tex., which did not report Apgar scores on birth certificate. Apgar scores are derived from evaluations of five major signs at one minute and five minutes after birth. Each sign is given a score of 0–2 for a total of ten possible points; scores of 7–10 are considered normal, 4–7 may require resuscitative measures, and 0–3 require immediate resuscitation. The signs and scores (0-1-2) are as follows: Activity or muscle tone (absent—arms and legs flexed—active movement); Pulse (absent—below 100 bpm—above 100 bpm); Grimace or reflex irritability (no response—grimace—sneeze, cough, pulls away); Appearance or skin color (blue-gray, pale all over—normal, except for extremities—normal over entire body); Respiration (absent—slow, irregular—good, crying). *Source:* National Center for Health Statistics, *National Vital Statistics Reports*, vol. 48, no. 3, March 28, 2000. Web: www.cdc.gov/nchs.

Teen Birth Rates Continue to Decline

Source: Centers for Disease Control and Prevention, National Center for Health Statistics

The birth rate for U.S. teenagers in 1998 was 51.1 live births per 1,000 women aged 15–19 years, 2 percent lower than in 1997 and 18 percent lower than in 1991, when it reached its recent peak. The 1998 rate is close to the 1986 record low of 50.2.

Several factors likely account for the falling teenage birth (and pregnancy) rates. One is changing attitudes toward premarital sex, possibly reflecting the influence of widespread public and private efforts focusing teenagers' attention on the importance of pregnancy prevention through abstinence and responsible behavior. Teenage sexual activity has leveled off according to several national surveys. Also important are increases in condom use and the adoption of the effective injectable and implant contraceptives. Another factor is the long economic expansion in the 1990s, increasing economic opportunity for teenagers (as well as older women). Economic opportunity may have given teenagers a reason to value education and work more highly and to postpone early pregnancy and parenthood. □

Teen Birth Rates in the U.S., Selected Years
(rates per 1,000 females in specified group)

Age	1980	1985	1990	1991	1993	1995	1997	1998
All races								
10–14 years	1.1	1.2	1.4	1.4	1.4	1.3	1.1	1.0
15–19 years	53.0	51.0	59.9	62.1	59.6	56.8	52.3	51.1
White, total								
10–14 years	—	—	0.7	0.8	0.8	0.8	0.7	0.6
15–19 years	—	—	50.8	52.8	51.1	50.1	46.3	45.4
White, non-Hispanic								
10–14 years	0.4	—	0.5	0.5	0.5	0.4	0.4	0.3
15–19 years	41.2	—	42.5	43.4	40.7	39.3	36.0	35.2
Black								
10–14 years	4.3	4.5	4.9	4.8	4.6	4.2	3.3	2.9
15–19 years	97.8	95.4	112.8	115.5	108.6	96.1	88.2	85.4
American Indian[1]								
10–14 years	1.9	1.7	1.6	1.6	1.4	1.8	1.7	1.6
15–19 years	82.2	79.2	81.1	85.0	83.1	78.0	71.8	72.1
Asian/Pacific Islander								
10–14 years	0.3	0.4	0.7	0.8	0.6	0.7	0.5	0.4
15–19 years	26.2	23.8	26.4	27.4	27.0	26.1	23.7	23.1
Hispanic[2]								
10–14 years	1.7	—	2.4	2.4	2.7	2.7	2.3	2.1
15–19 years	82.2	—	100.3	106.7	106.8	106.7	97.4	93.6

1. Includes births to Aleuts and Eskimos. 2. Persons of Hispanic origin may be of any race. *Source:* Centers for Disease Control and Prevention, National Center for Health Statistics. *National Vital Statistics Reports,* Vol. 48, No. 6. April 24, 2000.

Contraceptive Use by Women, 15 to 44 Years Old, 1995

		Age			Marital status		
Contraceptive status and method	All women	15–24 years	25–34 years	35–44 years	Never married	Currently married	Formerly married
All women (in thousands)	60,201	18,002	20,758	21,440	22,679	29,673	7,849
Percent distribution							
Sterile[1]	29.7%	2.6%	25.0%	57.0%	6.9%	43.2%	45.1%
Surgically sterile	27.9	1.8	23.6	54.0	5.7	41.1	42.5
Nonsurgically sterile[2]	1.7	0.7	1.3	2.8	1.1	2.0	2.2
Pill	17.3	23.1	23.7	6.3	20.4	15.6	14.6
IUD	0.5	0.1	0.6	0.8	0.3	0.7	0.4
Diaphragm	1.2	0.2	1.2	2.0	0.5	1.8	0.9
Condom	13.1	13.9	15.0	10.7	13.9	13.3	10.1
Periodic abstinence	1.5	0.5	1.8	2.0	0.6	2.3	0.7
Withdrawal	2.0	1.6	2.3	1.9	1.5	2.3	1.8
Other methods[3]	3.9	5.6	4.2	2.1	4.6	3.3	3.9

1. Total sterile includes male sterile for unknown reasons. 2. Persons sterile from illness, accident, or congenital conditions. 3. Includes implants, injectables, morning-after-pill, suppository, Today(TM) sponge, and less frequently used methods. *Source:* U.S. National Center for Health Statistics. From *Statistical Abstract of the United States 1999.*

Abortion Statistics, 1972–1997

	1972	1980	1985	1990	1995	1997[1]
Reported no. legal abortions	586,760	1,297,606	1,328,570	1,429,577	1,210,883	1,184,758
Abortion ratio[2]	180	359	354	345	311	305
Abortion rate[3]	13	25	24	24	20	20
			Percentage distribution			
Age group (yrs)						
≤19	32.6%	29.2%	26.3%	22.4%	20.1%	20.1%
20–24	32.5	35.5	34.7	33.2	32.5	31.7
≥25	34.9	35.3	39.0	44.4	47.4	48.2
Marital status						
Married	29.7	23.1	19.3	21.7	19.7	19.0
Unmarried	70.3	76.9	80.7	78.3	80.3	81.0

1. Preliminary data. The number of areas reporting a given characteristic varied. 2. Number of legal induced abortions per 1,000 live births. 3. Number of legal induced abortions per 1,000 women aged 15–44 years. *Source:* U.S. Centers for Disease Control and Prevention. *Abortion Surveillance: Preliminary Analysis—United States, 1997.* Jan. 7, 2000.

Abortions and Abortion Rates

State	Number of abortions			Abortion occurrence rate[1]		
	1996	1992	1988	1996	1992	1988
Alabama	13,826	17,450	18,220	14	18.2	18.7
Alaska	2,139	2,370	2,390	15	16.5	18.2
Arizona	11,016	20,600	23,070	11	24.1	28.8
Arkansas	5,882	7,130	6,250	11	13.5	11.6
California	280,180[2]	304,230	311,720	39	42.1	45.9
Colorado	9,710	19,880	18,740	11	23.6	22.4
Connecticut	14,094	19,720	23,630	20	26.2	31.2
Delaware	4,482	5,730	5,710	26	35.2	35.7
District of Columbia	13,674	21,320	26,120	(3)	138.4	163.3
Florida	80,040	84,680	82,850	27	30.0	31.5
Georgia	35,790	39,680	36,720	20	24.0	23.5
Hawaii	4,916	12,190	11,170	19	46.0	43.0
Idaho	1,022	1,710	1,920	4	7.2	8.2
Illinois	53,613	68,420	72,570	20	25.4	26.4
Indiana	13,341	15,840	15,760	10	12.0	11.9
Iowa	7,602[4]	6,970	9,420	12	11.4	14.6
Kansas	10,685	12,570	11,440	19	22.4	20.1
Kentucky	7,000	10,000	11,520	8	11.4	13.0
Louisiana	11,865	13,600	17,340	12	13.4	16.3
Maine	2,615	4,200	4,620	9	14.7	16.2
Maryland	12,363	31,260	32,670	10	26.4	28.6
Massachusetts	29,293	40,660	43,720	21	28.4	30.2
Michigan	30,208	55,580	63,410	14	25.2	28.5
Minnesota	14,193	16,180	18,580	13	15.6	18.2
Mississippi	4,206	7,550	5,120	7	12.4	8.4
Missouri	11,629	13,510	19,490	10	11.6	16.4
Montana	2,763	3,330	3,050	15	18.2	16.5
Nebraska	5,214	5,580	6,490	14	15.7	17.7
Nevada	6,965	13,300	10,190	20	44.2	40.3
New Hampshire	2,300[4]	3,890	4,710	8	14.6	17.5
New Jersey	31,860	55,320	63,900	18	31.0	35.1
New Mexico	5,033	6,410	6,810	13	17.7	19.1
New York	152,991	195,390	183,980	37	46.2	43.3
North Carolina	33,554	36,180	39,720	20	22.4	25.4
North Dakota	1,291	1,490	2,230	9	10.7	14.9
Ohio	36,530	49,520	53,040	15	19.5	21.0
Oklahoma	6,769[4]	8,940	12,120	10	12.5	16.2
Oregon	13,767	16,060	15,960	20	23.9	23.9
Pennsylvania	38,004	49,740	51,830	15	18.6	18.9
Rhode Island	5,437	6,990	7,190	24	30.0	30.6
South Carolina	9,326	12,190	14,160	11	14.2	16.7
South Dakota	901	1,040	900	6	6.8	5.7
Tennessee	17,989	19,060	22,090	15	16.2	18.9
Texas	91,470	97,400	100,690	21	23.1	24.8
Utah	3,639	3,940	5,030	8	9.3	12.8
Vermont	2,139	2,900	3,580	16	21.2	25.8
Virginia	25,770	35,020	35,420	16	22.7	23.7
Washington	26,138	33,190	31,220	21	27.7	27.6
West Virginia	2,470	3,140	3,270	6	7.7	7.5
Wisconsin	13,673	15,450	18,040	12	13.6	16.0
Wyoming	208	460	600	2	4.3	5.1
Total	**1,221,585**	**1,528,930**	**1,590,750**	**20**	**25.9**	**27.3**

NOTE: Abortion data reported by central health agencies unless otherwise specified. 1. Rate per 1,000 women aged 15-44. 2. CDC estimate. 3. 100 abortions per 1,000 women aged 15–44 years. 4. Reported by hospitals and/or other medical facilities in state. Source: U.S. Centers for Disease Control and Prevention. *Abortion Surveillance—United States, 1996.* July 30, 1999.

Abortion Rates Decline

Source: Centers for Disease Control

From 1990 (the year in which the number of abortions was highest) to 1995, the annual number of legal induced abortions in the United States declined by 15%. However, from 1995 to 1996, the number increased slightly. This change in the number of abortions reported to the Centers for Disease Control may indicate that the number of legal abortions in the U.S. is leveling off. In 1996, one-half of the states reported fewer abortions than in 1995.

Since 1990, factors contributing to the continued decrease in the proportion of pregnancies that ended in abortion might include a decrease in the number of unintended pregnancies, changes in contraceptive practices (including an increased use of condoms among young women), reduced access to abortion services, and possible changes in attitudes concerning abortion.

Mortality

10 Leading Causes of Death in the U.S., 1998

Leading causes of death differ somewhat by age, sex, and race. In 1998 accidents were the leading cause of death for those under 44 years. (In 1995 HIV infection was the leading cause of death for the age group 25–44, but in 1997 and 1998 it dropped to fifth rank.) In older age groups, cancer and heart disease were the leading causes. Seven of the ten leading causes of death were the same for males and females, although there were differences in ranking. Accidents were the third leading cause for males but seventh for females. Suicide, chronic liver disease, and homicide were among the leading causes of deaths for males but not for females. Likewise, seven of the leading causes were the same for the white and black populations. However, suicide, chronic liver disease, and kidney disease were among the ten leading causes for whites but not for blacks. Homicide, HIV infection, and perinatal conditions were among the ten leading causes for blacks but not for whites.

Rank[1]	Causes of death	Number	Deaths per 100,000 pop.
	All causes	2,337,256	864.7
1	Diseases of heart	724,859	268.2
2	Malignant neoplasms, including neoplasms of lymphatic and hematopoietic tissues	541,532	200.3
3	Cerebrovascular diseases	158,448	58.6
4	Chronic obstructive pulmonary diseases and allied conditions	112,584	41.7
5	Accidents and adverse effects	97,835	36.2
	Motor vehicle accidents	43,501	16.1
	All other accidents and adverse effects	54,334	20.1
6	Pneumonia and influenza	91,871	34.0
7	Diabetes mellitus	64,751	24.0
8	Suicide	30,575	11.3
9	Nephritis, nephrotic syndrome, and nephrosis	26,182	9.7
10	Chronic liver disease and cirrhosis	25,192	9.3
	All other causes	463,427	171.5

1. Rank based on number of deaths. *Source:* U.S. National Center for Health Statistics, *National Vital Statistics Reports,* vol. 48, no. 11, July 24, 2000. Web: www.cdc.gov/nchs.

Life Expectancy at Birth by Race and Sex, 1940–1998

	All races			White			Black		
Year	Both sexes	Male	Female	Both sexes	Male	Female	Both sexes	Male	Female
1998	76.7	73.8	79.5	77.3	74.5	80.0	71.3	67.6	74.8
1997	76.5	73.6	79.4	77.1	74.3	79.9	71.1	67.2	74.7
1996	76.1	73.1	79.1	76.8	73.9	79.7	70.2	66.1	74.2
1995	75.8	72.5	78.9	76.5	73.4	79.6	69.6	65.2	73.9
1994	75.7	72.4	79.0	76.5	73.3	79.6	69.5	64.9	73.9
1993	75.5	72.2	78.8	76.3	73.1	79.5	69.2	64.6	73.7
1992	75.8	72.3	79.1	76.5	73.2	79.8	69.6	65.0	73.9
1991	75.5	72.0	78.9	76.3	72.9	79.6	69.3	64.6	73.8
1990	75.4	71.8	78.8	76.1	72.7	79.4	69.1	64.5	73.6
1989	75.1	71.7	78.5	75.9	72.5	79.2	68.8	64.3	73.3
1988	74.9	71.4	78.3	75.6	72.2	78.9	68.9	64.4	73.2
1987	74.9	71.4	78.3	75.6	72.1	78.9	69.1	64.7	73.4
1986	74.7	71.2	78.2	75.4	71.9	78.8	69.1	64.8	73.4
1985	74.7	71.1	78.2	75.3	71.8	78.7	69.3	65.0	73.4
1984	74.7	71.1	78.2	75.3	71.8	78.7	69.5	65.3	73.6
1983	74.6	71.0	78.1	75.2	71.6	78.7	69.4	65.2	73.5
1982	74.5	70.8	78.1	75.1	71.5	78.7	69.4	65.1	73.6
1981	74.1	70.4	77.8	74.8	71.1	78.4	68.9	64.5	73.2
1980	73.7	70.0	77.4	74.4	70.7	78.1	68.1	63.8	72.5
1979	73.9	70.0	77.8	74.6	70.8	78.4	68.5	64.0	72.9
1978	73.5	69.6	77.3	74.1	70.4	78.0	68.1	63.7	72.4
1977	73.3	69.5	77.2	74.0	70.2	77.9	67.7	63.4	72.0
1976	72.9	69.1	76.8	73.6	69.9	77.5	67.2	62.9	71.6
1975	72.6	68.8	76.6	73.4	69.5	77.3	66.8	62.4	71.3
1974	72.0	68.2	75.9	72.8	69.0	76.7	66.0	61.7	70.3
1973	71.4	67.6	75.3	72.2	68.5	76.1	65.0	60.9	69.3
1972[1]	71.2	67.4	75.1	72.0	68.3	75.9	64.7	60.4	69.1
1971	71.1	67.4	75.0	72.0	68.3	75.8	64.6	60.5	68.9
1970	70.8	67.1	74.7	71.7	68.0	75.6	64.1	60.0	68.3
1960	69.7	66.6	73.1	70.6	67.4	74.1	—	—	—
1950	68.2	65.6	71.1	69.1	66.5	72.2	—	—	—
1940	62.9	60.8	65.2	64.2	62.1	66.6	—	—	—

(—) Data not available. 1. Deaths based on a 50-percent sample. *Source:* U.S. National Center for Health Statistics, *National Vital Statistics Reports,* vol. 47, no. 25, Oct. 5, 1999 and vol. 48, no. 11, July 24, 2000. Web: www.cdc.gov/nchs.

Life Expectancy by Age, 1850–1998

The expectation of life at a specified age is the average number of years that members of a hypothetical group of people of the same age would continue to live if they were subject throughout the remainder of their lives to the mortality rates for specified age groups observed in a given time period.

Calendar period	Age								
	0	10	20	30	40	50	60	70	80
White males									
1850[1]	38.3	48.0	40.1	34.0	27.9	21.6	15.6	10.2	5.9
1890[1]	42.50	48.45	40.66	34.05	27.37	20.72	14.73	9.35	5.40
1900–1902[2]	48.23	50.59	42.19	34.88	27.74	20.76	14.35	9.03	5.10
1909–1911[2]	50.23	51.32	42.71	34.87	27.43	20.39	13.98	8.83	5.09
1919–1921[3]	56.34	54.15	45.60	37.65	29.86	22.22	15.25	9.51	5.47
1929–1931	59.12	54.96	46.02	37.54	29.22	21.51	14.72	9.20	5.26
1939–1941	62.81	57.03	47.76	38.80	30.03	21.96	15.05	9.42	5.38
1949–1951	66.31	58.98	49.52	40.29	31.17	22.83	15.76	10.07	5.88
1959–1961[5]	67.55	59.78	50.25	40.98	31.73	23.22	16.01	10.29	5.89
1969–1971[6]	67.94	59.69	50.22	41.07	31.87	23.34	16.07	10.38	6.18
1979–1981	70.82	61.98	52.45	43.31	34.04	25.26	17.56	11.35	6.76
1990	72.7	63.5	54.0	44.7	35.6	26.7	18.7	12.1	7.1
1998	74.5	65.2	55.5	46.1	36.8	27.9	19.7	12.8	7.5
White females									
1850[1]	40.5	47.2	40.2	35.4	29.8	23.5	17.0	11.3	6.4
1890[1]	44.46	49.62	42.03	35.36	28.76	22.09	15.70	10.15	5.75
1900–1902[2]	51.08	52.15	43.77	36.42	29.17	21.89	15.23	9.59	5.50
1909–1911[2]	53.62	53.57	44.88	36.96	29.26	21.74	14.92	9.38	5.35
1919–1921[3]	58.53	55.17	46.46	38.72	30.94	23.12	15.93	9.94	5.70
1929–1931	62.67	57.65	48.52	39.99	31.52	23.41	16.05	9.98	5.63
1939–1941	67.29	60.85	51.38	42.21	33.25	24.72	17.00	10.50	5.88
1949–1951	72.03	64.26	54.56	45.00	35.64	26.76	18.64	11.68	6.59
1959–1961[5]	74.19	66.05	56.29	46.63	37.13	28.08	19.69	12.38	6.67
1969–1971[6]	75.49	66.97	57.24	47.60	38.12	29.11	20.79	13.37	7.59
1979–1981	78.22	69.21	59.44	49.76	40.16	30.96	22.45	14.89	8.65
1990	79.4	70.1	60.3	50.6	41.0	31.6	23.0	15.4	9.0
1998	80.0	70.6	60.8	51.0	41.4	32.0	23.3	15.6	9.1
All other males[4]									
1900–1902[2]	32.54	41.90	35.11	29.25	23.12	17.34	12.62	8.33	5.12
1909–1911[2]	34.05	40.65	33.46	27.33	21.57	16.21	11.67	8.00	5.53
1919–1921[3]	47.14	45.99	38.36	32.51	26.53	20.47	14.74	9.58	5.83
1929–1931	47.55	44.27	35.95	29.45	23.36	17.92	13.15	8.78	5.42
1939–1941	52.33	48.54	39.74	32.25	25.23	19.18	14.38	10.06	6.46
1949–1951	58.91	52.96	43.73	35.31	27.29	20.25	14.91	10.74	7.07
1959–1961[5]	61.48	55.19	45.78	37.05	28.72	21.28	15.29	10.81	6.87
1969–1971[6]	60.98	53.67	44.37	36.20	28.29	21.24	15.35	10.68	7.57
1979–1981	65.63	57.40	47.87	39.13	30.64	22.92	16.54	11.36	7.22
1990	67.0	58.5	49.0	40.3	31.9	23.9	17.0	11.4	7.0
1998	67.6	59.0	49.5	40.6	31.9	23.9	17.1	11.5	7.1
All other females[4]									
1900–1902[2]	35.04	43.02	36.89	30.70	24.37	18.67	13.60	9.62	6.48
1909–1911[2]	37.67	42.84	36.14	29.61	23.34	17.65	12.78	9.22	6.05
1919–1921[3]	46.92	44.54	37.15	31.48	25.60	19.76	14.69	10.25	6.58
1929–1931	49.51	45.33	37.22	30.67	24.30	18.60	14.22	10.38	6.90
1939–1941	55.51	50.83	42.14	34.52	27.31	21.04	16.14	11.81	8.00
1949–1951	62.70	56.17	46.77	38.02	29.82	22.67	16.95	12.29	8.15
1959–1961[5]	66.47	59.72	50.07	40.83	32.16	24.31	17.83	12.46	7.66
1969–1971[6]	69.05	61.49	51.85	42.61	33.87	25.97	19.02	13.30	9.01
1979–1981	74.00	65.64	55.88	46.39	37.16	28.59	20.49	14.44	9.17
1990	75.2	66.6	56.8	47.3	38.1	29.2	21.3	14.5	8.8
1998	74.8	66.0	56.2	46.7	37.5	28.8	21.0	14.1	8.7

1. Massachusetts only; white and nonwhite combined, the latter being about 1% of the total. *Source:* Historical Statistics of the United States. 2. Original Death Registration States. 3. Death Registration States of 1920. 4. Data for periods 1900–1902 to 1929–1931 and 1998 relate to blacks only. 5. Alaska and Hawaii included beginning in 1959. 6. Deaths of nonresidents of the United States excluded starting in 1970. *Sources:* Department of Health and Human Services, National Center for Health Statistics; Web: www.dhhs.gov.

U.S. Annual Death Rates per 1,000 Population

Year	Rate	Year	Rate	Year	Rate	Year	Rate	Year	Rate	Year	Rate	Year	Rate
1900	17.2	1935	10.9	1946	10.0	1957	9.6	1969	9.5	1980	8.7	1991	8.5
1905	15.9	1936	11.6	1947	10.1	1958	9.5	1970[1]	9.5	1981	8.6	1992	8.5
1910	14.7	1937	11.3	1948	9.9	1959	9.4	1971	9.3	1982	8.5	1993	8.8
1915	13.2	1938	10.6	1949	9.7	1960	9.5	1972	9.4	1983	8.6	1994	8.8
1920	13.0	1939	10.6	1950	9.6	1962	9.5	1973	9.3	1984	8.6	1995	8.8
1925	11.7	1940	10.8	1951	9.7	1963	9.6	1974	9.1	1985	8.7	1996	8.8
1930	11.3	1941	10.5	1952	9.6	1964	9.4	1975	8.8	1986	8.7	1997	8.6
1931	11.1	1942	10.3	1953	9.6	1965	9.4	1976	8.8	1987	8.7	1998	8.6
1932	10.9	1943	10.9	1954	9.2	1966	9.5	1977	8.6	1988	8.8		
1933	10.7	1944	10.6	1955	9.3	1967	9.4	1978	8.7	1989	8.7		
1934	11.1	1945	10.6	1956	9.4	1968	9.7	1979	8.5	1990	8.6		

NOTES: Includes only deaths occurring within the registration states. Beginning with 1933, area includes entire U.S.; with 1959 includes Alaska, and with 1960 includes Hawaii. Excludes fetal deaths. Rates as of April 1 for 1940, 1950, 1960, 1970, and 1980, and estimated as of July 1 for all other years. 1. First year for which deaths of nonresidents are excluded. *Sources:* Department of Health and Human Services, National Center for Health Statistics. Web: www.dhhs.gov.

Infant Mortality Rates, 1950–1998

		Deaths per 1,000 live births				
		Neonatal			Fetal mortality rate[1]	Late fetal mortality rate[2]
Year	Infant	Under 28 days	Under 7 days	Postneonatal		
1950[3]	29.2	20.5	17.8	8.7	18.4	14.9
1960[3]	26.0	18.7	16.7	7.3	15.8	12.1
1970	20.0	15.1	13.6	4.9	14.0	9.5
1980	12.6	8.5	7.1	4.1	9.1	6.2
1985	10.6	7.0	5.8	3.7	7.8	4.9
1988	10.0	6.3	5.2	3.6	7.5	4.5
1989	9.8	6.2	5.1	3.6	7.5	4.5
1990	9.2	5.8	4.8	3.4	7.5	4.3
1991	8.9	5.6	4.6	3.4	7.3	4.1
1992	8.5	5.4	4.4	3.1	7.4	4.1
1993	8.4	5.3	4.3	3.1	7.1	3.8
1994	8.0	5.1	4.2	2.9	7.0	3.7
1995	7.6	4.9	4.0	2.7	7.0	3.6
1996	7.3	4.8	3.8	2.5	6.9	3.6
1997	7.2	4.8	3.8	2.5	6.8	3.5
1998	7.2	4.8	3.8	2.4	—	—

NOTES: "Infant" is defined as under 1 year of age; "neonatal" is under 28 days; "postneonatal" is 28–365 days. (—) Data not available. 1. Number of fetal deaths of 20 weeks or more gestation per 1,000 live births plus fetal deaths. 2. Number of fetal deaths of 28 weeks or more gestation per 1,000 live births plus late fetal deaths. 3. Includes birth and deaths of persons who were not residents of the 50 states and the District of Columbia. *Sources:* Centers for Disease Control and Prevention, National Center for Health Statistics. From *Health, United States, 2000.*

Deaths and Death Rates from Accidents, by Type: 1980–1996

	Deaths (number)					Rate per 100,000 population				
Type of accident	1980	1990	1994	1995	1996	1980	1990	1994	1995	1996
Motor vehicle accidents	53,172	46,814	42,524	43,363	43,649	23.5	18.8	16.3	16.5	16.5
Traffic	51,930	45,827	41,507	42,331	42,522	22.9	18.4	15.9	16.1	16.0
Nontraffic	1,242	987	1,017	1,032	1,127	0.5	0.4	0.4	0.4	0.4
Water-transport accidents	1,429	923	723	762	675	0.6	0.4	0.3	0.3	0.3
Air and space transport accidents	1,494	941	1,075	851	1,061	0.7	0.4	0.4	0.3	0.4
Railway accidents	632	663	635	569	565	0.3	0.3	0.2	0.2	0.2
Accidental falls	13,294	12,313	13,450	13,986	14,986	5.9	5.0	5.2	5.3	5.6
Accidental drowning	6,043	3,979	3,404	3,790	3,488	2.7	1.6	1.3	1.4	1.3
Accidents caused by—										
Fires and flames	5,822	4,175	3,986	3,761	3,741	2.6	1.7	1.5	1.4	1.4
Firearms, unspecified and other	1,667	1,175	1,123	992	947	0.7	0.5	0.4	0.4	0.4
Handguns	288	241	233	233	187	0.1	0.1	0.1	0.1	0.1
Electric current	1,095	670	561	559	482	0.5	0.3	0.2	0.2	0.2
Accidental poisoning by—										
Drugs and medicines	2,492	4,506	7,828	8,000	8,431	1.1	1.8	3.0	3.0	3.2
Other solid and liquid substances	597	549	481	461	441	0.3	0.2	0.2	0.2	0.2
Gases and vapors	1,242	748	685	611	638	0.5	0.3	0.3	0.2	0.2
Complications due to medical procedures	2,282	2,669	2,616	2,712	2,919	1.0	1.1	1.0	1.0	1.0
Inhalation and ingestion of objects	3,249	3,303	3,065	3,185	3,206	1.4	1.3	1.2	1.2	1.2

NOTE: Excludes deaths of nonresidents of the United States. *Source: Statistical Abstract of the United States 1999.*

Deaths by Firearms, 1979–1998

(per 100,000 population in specified group)

Year	All races		White		Black	
	Number of deaths	Death rate[1]	Number of deaths	Death rate[1]	Number of deaths	Death rate[1]
1979	33,019	14.7	24,234	12.5	8,304	31.6
1980	33,780	14.9	24,849	12.8	8,505	31.9
1981	34,050	14.8	25,237	12.8	8,324	30.7
1982	32,957	14.2	25,071	12.7	7,415	27.0
1983	31,099	13.3	24,038	12.1	6,589	23.6
1984	31,331	13.3	24,419	12.2	6,449	22.9
1985	31,566	13.3	24,507	12.1	6,565	23.0
1986	33,373	13.9	25,339	12.5	7,494	25.9
1987	32,895	13.6	24,789	12.1	7,586	25.9
1988	33,989	13.9	24,892	12.1	8,475	28.5
1989	34,776	14.1	25,023	12.1	9,077	30.1
1990	37,155	14.9	26,299	12.6	10,175	33.4
1991	38,317	15.2	26,455	12.5	11,025	35.4
1992	37,776	14.8	26,120	12.3	10,906	34.5
1993	39,595	15.4	26,948	12.5	11,763	36.6
1994	38,505	14.8	26,403	12.2	11,223	34.4
1995	35,957	13.7	25,438	11.7	9,643	29.1
1996	34,040	12.8	24,114	11.0	9,175	27.4
1997	32,436	12.1	23,270	10.5	8,389	24.7
1998	30,708	11.4	22,480	10.1	7,503	21.8

1. On an annual basis, per 100,000 population in specified group. *Source:* Centers for Disease Control and Prevention, *National Vital Statistics Reports,* vol. 48, no. 11, July 24, 2000.

Death Rates for Suicide, 1950–1998

(deaths per 100,000 resident population)

Characteristic	1950[1]	1960[1]	1970	1980	1990	1996	1997	1998
All ages[2]	**11.0**	**10.6**	**11.8**	**11.4**	**11.5**	**10.8**	**10.6**	**10.4**
5 to 14 years	0.2	0.3	0.3	0.4	0.8	0.8	0.8	0.8
15 to 24 years	4.5	5.2	8.8	12.3	13.2	12.0	11.4	11.1
25 to 34 years	9.1	10.0	14.1	16.0	15.2	14.5	14.3	13.8
35 to 44 years	14.3	14.2	16.9	15.4	15.3	15.5	15.3	15.4
45 to 54 years	20.9	20.7	20.0	15.9	14.8	14.9	14.7	14.8
55 to 64 years	27.0	23.7	21.4	15.9	16.0	13.7	13.5	13.1
65 to 74 years	29.3	23.0	20.8	16.9	17.9	15.0	14.4	14.1
75 to 84 years	31.1	27.9	21.2	19.1	24.9	20.0	19.3	19.7
85 years and over	28.8	26.0	19.0	19.2	22.2	20.2	20.8	21.0
Male, all ages[2]	**17.3**	**16.6**	**17.3**	**18.0**	**19.0**	**18.0**	**17.4**	**17.2**
Female, all ages[2]	**4.9**	**5.0**	**6.8**	**5.4**	**4.5**	**4.0**	**4.1**	**4.0**

1. Includes deaths of persons who were not residents of the 50 states and the District of Columbia. 2. Data are age-adjusted. *Sources:* Centers for Disease Control and Prevention, National Center for Health Statistics. From *Health, United States, 2000.*

Miscellaneous

Most Common Last Names in the U.S.

Rank	Name	Frequency[1]	Rank	Name	Frequency[1]	Rank	Name	Frequency[1]
Last names			11.	Anderson	0.31	22.	Rodriguez	0.23
1.	Smith	1.01%	12.	Thomas	0.31	23.	Lewis	0.23
2.	Johnson	0.81	13.	Jackson	0.31	24.	Lee	0.22
3.	Williams	0.70	14.	White	0.28	25.	Walker	0.22
4.	Jones	0.62	15.	Harris	0.28	26.	Hall	0.20
5.	Brown	0.62	16.	Martin	0.27	27.	Allen	0.20
6.	Davis	0.48	17.	Thompson	0.27	28.	Young	0.19
7.	Miller	0.42	18.	Garcia	0.25	29.	Hernandez	0.19
8.	Wilson	0.34	19.	Martinez	0.23	30.	King	0.19
9.	Moore	0.31	20.	Robinson	0.23			
10.	Taylor	0.31	21.	Clark	0.23			

NOTE: Based on 1990 Census data. Numbers are rounded. 1. Percent of U.S. population sample. *Source:* U.S. Census Bureau. Web: www.census.gov/genealogy/names/dist.all.last.

Most Popular Given Names, 1880–1999

Boys

1880: John, William, Charles, George, James, Joseph, Frank, Henry, Thomas, Harry

1890: John, William, James, George, Charles, Joseph, Frank, Harry, Henry, Edward

1900: John, William, James, George, Charles, Joseph, Frank, Henry, Robert, Harry

1910: John, William, James, Robert, Joseph, Charles/George (tie), Edward, Frank, Henry

1920: John, William, James, Robert, Joseph, Charles, George, Edward, Thomas, Frank

1930: Robert, James, John, William, Richard, Charles, Donald, George, Joseph, Edward

1940: James, Robert, John, William, Richard, Charles, David, Thomas, Donald, Ronald

1950: John, James, Robert, William, Michael, David, Richard, Thomas, Charles, Gary

1960: David, Michael, John, James, Robert, Mark, William, Richard, Thomas, Steven

1970: Michael, David, John, James, Robert, Christopher, William, Mark, Richard, Brian

1980: Michael, Jason, Christopher, David, James, Matthew, John, Joshua, Robert, Daniel

1990: Michael, Christopher, Joshua, Matthew, David, Daniel, Andrew, Joseph, Justin, James

1999: Jacob, Michael, Matthew, Joshua, Christopher, Nicholas, Andrew, Joseph, Daniel, Tyler

Girls

1880: Mary, Anna, Elizabeth, Margaret, Minnie, Emma, Martha, Alice, Marie, Annie/Sarah (tie)

1890: Mary, Anna, Elizabeth, Emma, Margaret, Rose, Ethel, Florence, Ida, Bertha/Helen (tie)

1900: Mary, Helen, Anna, Margaret, Ruth, Elizabeth, Marie, Rose, Florence, Bertha

1910: Mary, Helen, Margaret, Dorothy, Ruth, Anna, Mildred, Elizabeth, Alice, Ethel

1920: Mary, Dorothy, Helen, Margaret, Ruth, Virginia, Elizabeth, Anna, Mildred, Betty

1930: Mary, Betty, Dorothy, Helen, Barbara, Margaret, Maria, Patricia, Doris, Joan/Ruth (tie)

1940: Mary, Barbara, Patricia, Carol, Judith, Betty, Nancy, Maria, Margaret, Linda

1950: Linda, Mary, Patricia, Barbara, Susan, Maria, Sandra, Nancy, Deborah, Kathleen

1960: Mary, Susan, Maria, Karen, Lisa, Linda, Donna, Patricia, Debra, Deborah

1970: Jennifer, Lisa, Kimberly, Michelle, Angela, Maria, Amy, Melissa, Mary, Tracy

1980: Jennifer, Jessica, Amanda, Melissa, Sarah, Nicole, Heather, Amy, Michelle, Elizabeth

1990: Jessica, Ashley, Brittany, Amanda, Stephanie, Jennifer, Samantha, Sarah, Megan, Lauren

1999: Emily, Hannah, Alexis, Samantha, Sarah, Ashley, Madison, Taylor, Jessica, Elizabeth

NOTE: Represents the most frequently used given names for births, based on a sampling of Social Security Number card applications. *Source:* Social Security Administration. Web: www.ssa.gov/OACT/NOTES/note139/note139.html.

Participation in Various Leisure Activities, 1997

	Adult population (mil.)	Attendance at			Participation in				
		Movies	Sports events	Amusement park	Exercise program	Playing sports	Charity work	Home improvement/ repair	Computer hobbies
Total	195.6	66%	41%	57%	76%	45%	43%	66%	40%
Sex:									
Male	94.2	66	49	58	75	56	40	71	44
Female	101.4	65	34	57	77	35	46	61	37
Race or ethnicity:									
Hispanic[1]	19.1	59	35	66	69	35	31	61	25
White	146.1	68	44	56	78	48	45	70	43
Black	22.1	60	35	55	74	34	44	51	37
American Indian	3.0	65	34	59	83	49	34	58	37
Asian	5.3	76	29	58	70	48	41	58	62
Age:									
18 to 24 years	23.7	88	51	76	85	67	35	57	68
25 to 34 years	40.1	79	51	70	82	63	41	63	51
35 to 44 years	45.3	73	46	68	79	52	50	76	47
45 to 54 years	33.7	65	42	53	77	40	46	75	40
55 to 64 years	20.9	46	33	40	69	19	44	71	23
65 to 74 years	19.6	38	21	29	65	23	40	55	11
75 years and over	12.3	28	16	18	56	13	40	44	7

NOTE: Covers activities engaged in at least once in the prior 12 months. 1. People of Hispanic origin may be of any race. *Source:* U.S. National Endowment for the Arts, *1997 Survey of Public Participation in the Arts.* From *Statistical Abstract of the United States 1999.*

Most Popular Pet Names

The American Society for the Prevention of Cruelty to Animals (ASPCA) has conducted a veterinarian survey to find out which pet names are most popular in the United States today. Here are the top 25:

1. Max
2. Sam
3. Lady
4. Bear
5. Smokey
6. Shadow
7. Kitty
8. Molly
9. Buddy
10. Brandy
11. Ginger
12. Baby
13. Misty
14. Missy
15. Pepper
16. Jake
17. Bandit
18. Tiger
19. Samantha
20. Lucky
21. Muffin
22. Princess
23. Maggie
24. Charlie
25. Sheba

Household Pet Ownership, 1996

Item	Dog	Cat	Pet bird	Horse
Households owning companion pets[1] (millions)	31.20	27.00	4.60	1.50
Percent of all households	31.60%	27.30%	4.60%	1.50%
Average number owned	1.70	2.20	2.70	2.70
Total companion pet population[1] (millions)	52.90	59.10	12.60	4.00
Households obtaining veterinary care[2]	88.70%	72.90%	15.80%	66.30%
Average visits per household per year	2.60	1.90	0.20	2.30
Average annual costs per household	$ 186.80	$ 112.24	$10.95	$226.26
Total expenditures (millions)	$5,828.00	$3,030.00	$50.00	$339.00
Percent distribution of households owning pets				
Annual household income: Under $12,500	12.70%	13.90%	17.30%	9.50%
$12,500 to $24,999	19.10	19.70	20.90	20.30
$25,000 to $39,999	21.60	21.50	22.00	21.80
$40,000 to $59,999	21.50	21.20	17.50	23.10
$60,000 and over	25.20	23.70	22.30	25.40
Family size:[1] One person	13.20%	16.80%	12.70%	12.10%
Two persons	31.00	32.60	27.90	29.10
Three persons	21.40	20.60	20.40	22.00
Four or more persons	34.50	29.90	38.90	36.70

NOTE: Based on a sample survey of 80,000 households in 1996. 1. As of December. 2. During 1996. Source: American Veterinary Medical Association, Schaumburg, Ill., *U.S. Pet Ownership and Demographics Sourcebook, 1997.* Reprinted with permission.

Hunger Still a Problem in U.S.

Source: Economic Research Service, U.S. Dept. of Agriculture, *Household Food Security in the United States, 1999.*

According to a report released by the U.S. Department of Agriculture, 10.1% of U.S. households, 31 million Americans, were food insecure during the 12 months ending April 1999. "Food insecure" means that at some time during the previous year they were uncertain of having or unable to acquire adequate food sufficient to meet basic needs. Of these, about 3 million households were food insecure to the extent that one or more household members were hungry due to inadequate resources at least some time during the year.

The prevalence of food insecurity and hunger varied considerably among household types, and some groups, including 29.7% of households with children headed by a single woman, 21.2% of black households, and 20.8% of Hispanic households, experienced rates of food insecurity greater than the national average. Overall, households with children experienced food insecurity at double the rate for households without children (14.8% versus 7.4%).

Food Insecurity and Hunger, 1999
(numbers in thousands)

Category	Total number[1]	Food secure		Food insecure					
				Total		Without hunger		With hunger	
		Number	Percent	Number	Percent	Number	Percent	Number	Percent
All households	104,684	94,154	89.9%	10,529	10.1%	7,420	7.1%	3,109	3.0%
All persons in households	270,318	239,304	88.5	31,015	11.5	23,237	8.6	7,779	2.9
Adults in households	198,900	179,960	90.5	18,941	9.5	13,869	7.0	5,072	2.5
Children in households	71,418	59,344	83.1	12,074	16.9	9,368	13.1	2,707	3.8
Household composition:									
With children < 18	37,884	32,290	85.2	5,594	14.8	4,340	11.5	1,254	3.3
Married couple families	26,303	23,771	90.4	2,532	9.6	2,105	8.0	428	1.6
Female head, no spouse	8,744	6,146	70.3	2,598	29.7	1,890	21.6	709	8.1
Male head, no spouse	2,187	1,817	83.1	370	16.9	280	12.8	89	4.1
Other household with child[2]	650	556	85.6	94	14.4	66	10.1	28	4.3
With no children < 18	66,800	61,865	92.6	4,935	7.4	3,080	4.6	1,855	2.8
More than one adult	39,568	37,380	94.5	2,188	5.5	1,470	3.7	718	1.8
Women living alone	16,046	14,473	90.2	1,573	9.8	908	5.7	665	4.1
Men living alone	11,187	10,013	89.5	1,174	10.5	701	6.3	473	4.2
Households with elderly	24,704	23,265	94.2	1,439	5.8	1,055	4.3	385	1.6
Elderly living alone	10,049	9,413	93.7	636	6.3	423	4.2	214	2.1
Race/ethnicity of households:									
White non-Hispanic	78,998	73,451	93.0	5,546	7.0	3,873	4.9	1,673	2.1
Black non-Hispanic	12,616	9,936	78.8	2,680	21.2	1,866	14.8	814	6.4
Hispanic[3]	9,192	7,285	79.2	1,907	20.8	1,406	15.3	502	5.5
Other non-Hispanic	3,878	3,482	89.8	396	10.2	275	7.1	121	3.1

1. Total households in each category exclude households whose food security status is unknown. 2. Households with children in complex living arrangements, e.g., children of other relatives or unrelated roommate or boarder. 3. Hispanics may be of any race. Source: Economic Research Service, U.S. Dept. of Agriculture, *Household Food Security in the United States, 1999.* Fall, 2000. Web: www.ers.usda.gov/briefing/foodsecurity/.

U.S. Charities Receiving Highest Donations in 1998

1998 Rank	Charity	Private support	Year Ending	1997 rank
1.	Salvation Army[1]	$1,234,953,000	9/30/1998	1
2.	YMCA of the USA[1, 2]	629,330,000	12/31/1998	2
3.	Fidelity Investments Charitable Gift Fund	571,914,529	6/30/1998	5
4.	American Cancer Society[1]	556,195,000	8/31/1998	4
5.	American Red Cross[1]	543,254,564	6/30/1998	3
6.	Harvard University	462,762,925	6/30/1998	6
7.	Catholic Charities USA[1]	446,266,726	12/31/1998	7
8.	Boys & Girls Clubs of America[1]	430,736,157	12/31/1998	9
9.	Emory University	423,039,313	8/31/1998	70
10.	America's Second Harvest	392,434,067	6/30/1998	8
11.	American Heart Association[1]	325,907,000	6/30/1998	11
12.	Stanford University	312,590,717	8/31/1998	10
13.	World Vision[1]	297,205,000	9/30/1998	14
14.	Nature Conservancy[3]	289,774,421	6/30/1998	17
15.	Gifts in Kind International	288,460,191	12/31/1998	13
16.	Partners HealthCare System[1]	277,744,781	9/30/1998	143
17.	Boy Scouts of America[1]	269,570,000	12/31/1998	15
18.	Columbia University	267,013,191	6/30/1998	24
19.	Campus Crusade for Christ International	264,656,000	8/31/1998	16
20.	Duke University	254,837,289	6/30/1998	21
21.	Cornell University	253,193,696	6/30/1998	20
22.	Shriners Hospitals for Children	249,001,000	12/31/1998	19
23.	Habitat for Humanity International[4]	233,335,000	12/31/1997	18
24.	University of Wisconsin at Madison	230,356,973	6/30/1998	22
25.	Public Broadcasting Service	224,980,779	6/30/1998	31

1. Includes affiliates. 2. Affiliates have different fiscal years. 3. Another $92,864,000 was spent to purchase land, which is no[t] included in program services. An additional $189,291,000 was put into an endowment to be used for future land acquisitions and land management. 4. Changed fiscal year; figures are not available for 1998. *Source: The Chronicle of Philanthropy* Nov. 4, 1999. Reprinted with permission.

Percent of Adult Population Doing Volunteer Work, 1995

Age, sex, race, and Hispanic origin	Percent of population volunteering	Average hours volunteered per week	Educational attainment and household income	Percent of population volunteering	Average hours volunteered per week
Total	48.8%	4.2	Elementary school	18.7%	(B)
			Some high school	26.1	3.3
18–24 years	38.4	2.8	High-school graduate	43.1	4.0
25–34 years	50.8	4.3	Technical, trade, or	51.2	4.4
35–44 years	55.0	4.3	business school		
45–54 years	55.3	4.5	Some college	56.3	3.9
55–64 years	47.9	4.8	College graduate	70.7	4.8
65–74 years	44.7	4.1			
75 years and over	33.7	4.4	Under $10,000	34.7	3.6
			10,000–19,999	34.3	3.2
Male	45.1	4.2	20,000–29,999	45.2	3.7
Female	52.2	4.2	30,000–39,999	46.0	3.7
			40,000–49,999	52.7	5.8
White	51.9	4.2	50,000–59,999	64.1	5.1
Black	35.3	4.5	60,000–74,999	56.4	4.4
Hispanic[1]	40.4	4.3	75,000–99,999	64.8	4.0
			100,000 or more	69.4	4.4

Type of activity	Percent of population involved in activity	Type of activity	Percent of population involved in activity
Arts, culture, humanities	6.2%	Political organizations	3.8%
Education	17.5	Private, community foundations	2.7
Environment	7.1	Public and societal benefit	6.7
Health	13.2	Recreation—adults	7.3
Human services	12.7	Religion	25.8
Informal	20.3	Work-related organizations	7.9
International, foreign	1.6	Youth development	15.4

(B) = Base figure too small to meet statistical standards for reliability. 1. Hispanic persons may be of any race. NOTE: Cov[]ers persons 18 years and over. Volunteers are persons who worked in some way to help others for no monetary pay dur[]ing the previous year. Based on a sample survey conducted during the spring of the following year and subject to samplin[g] variability. *Source: Statistical Abstract of the United States 1999.*

Homeownership Rates by Select Characteristics, 1950–1990

Characteristic	1950	1960	1970	1980	1990
U.S. total	**55.0%**	**61.9%**	**62.9%**	**64.4%**	**64.2%**
Mobile homeowners	79.4	88.3	84.5	79.8	79.8
One-person households	42.1	40.8	42.4	43.5	48.7
Recent movers	n.a.	34.0	31.4	33.5	28.8
Age of householder					
Under 35	n.a.	n.a.	41.2	43.8	39.6
65 and over	67.9	68.8	67.5	70.1	75.2
Black householder	34.5	n.a.	41.6	44.4	43.4
Hispanic householder[1]	n.a.	n.a.	43.7	43.4	42.4

NOTES: n.a. = not available. 1. Persons of Hispanic origin may be of any race. *Source:* U.S. Census Bureau. Web: www.census.gov/hhes/www/housing/census/historic/ownrate.html.

Homeownership by State, 1990

State	Homeownership rate (%)	State	Homeownership rate (%)	State	Homeownership rate (%)
U.S. total	**64.2%**	Louisiana	65.9%	Oklahoma	68.1%
Alabama	70.5	Maine	70.5	Oregon	63.1
Alaska	56.1	Maryland	65.0	Pennsylvania	70.6
Arizona	64.2	Massachusetts	59.3	Rhode Island	59.5
Arkansas	69.6	Michigan	71.0	South Carolina	69.8
California	55.6	Minnesota	71.8	South Dakota	66.1
Colorado	62.2	Mississippi	71.5	Tennessee	68.0
Connecticut	65.6	Missouri	68.8	Texas	60.9
Delaware	70.2	Montana	67.3	Utah	68.1
Florida	67.2	Nebraska	66.5	Vermont	69.0
Georgia	64.9	Nevada	54.8	Virginia	66.3
Hawaii	53.9	New Hampshire	68.2	Washington	62.6
Idaho	70.1	New Jersey	64.9	Washington, D.C.	38.9
Illinois	64.2	New Mexico	67.4	West Virginia	74.1
Indiana	70.2	New York	52.2	Wisconsin	66.7
Iowa	70.0	North Carolina	68.0	Wyoming	67.8
Kansas	67.9	North Dakota	65.6		
Kentucky	69.6	Ohio	67.5		

Source: U.S. Census Bureau. Web:www.census.gov/hhes/www/housing/census/historic/ownrate.html.

Characteristics of the Homeless, 1996

Characteristic	U.S. adult population (1996)	All homeless persons	Persons in homeless families	Single homeless persons
Sex:				
Male	48%	68%	16%	77%
Female	52	32	84	23
Race/ethnicity:				
White non-Hispanic	75	41	38	41
Black non-Hispanic	11	40	43	40
Hispanic	10	11	15	10
Native American	1	8	3	8
Age:				
Under 25	13	12	26	10
25 to 54 yrs.	59	80	75	81
55 or more yrs.	28	8	(1)	9
Marital status:				
Never married	23	48	41	50
Married	60	9	23	7
Separated	(2)	15	23	14
Divorced	10	24	13	26
Widowed	7	3	0	4
Educational attainment:				
Less than high school	25	38	53	37
High school graduate/G.E.D.	30	34	21	36
More than high school	45	28	27	28
Veteran	13	23	5	26

NOTE: Numbers do not add up to 100% due to rounding. 1. Denotes percentage less than 0.5 percent but greater than 0. 2. Included in "married." *Source:* U.S. Bureau of the Census. From Interagency Council on the Homeless, *Homelessness: Programs and the People They Serve,* 1999.

States

Data for state populations are the latest available from the U.S. Census Bureau. NOTE: Persons of Hispanic origin can be of any race. "American Indian" includes American Indians, Eskimos, and Aleuts. "Asian" includes Asians and Pacific Islanders. Largest cities include incorporated places only, as defined by the U.S. Census Bureau. They do not include adjacent or suburban areas. Population data for U.S. cities are also the latest available from the U.S. Census Bureau.

For secession and readmission dates of the former Confederate states, *see* U.S. Government & History: The Confederate States of America. Governors and senators listed here are as of Sept. 2000. For a list of governors, and lists of senators and representatives elected to terms beginning in 2001, *see* U.S. Government & History: The Governors of the Fifty States, The Senate, and The House of Representatives. For U.S. Territories, *see* Countries of the World: United States.

Alabama

Capital: Montgomery
Governor: Don Siegelman, D (to Jan. 2003)
Lieut. Governor: Steve Windom, R (to Jan. 2003)
Senators: Jeff Sessions, R (to Jan. 2003); Richard C. Shelby, R (to Jan. 2005)
Secy. of State: Jim Bennett, R (to Jan. 2003)
Treasurer: Lucy Baxley, D (to Jan. 2003)
Atty. General: William Pryor, R (to Jan. 2003)
Auditor: Susan D. Parker, D (to Jan. 2003)
Organized as territory: March 3, 1817
Entered Union (rank): Dec. 14, 1819 (22)
Present constitution adopted: 1901
Motto: *Audemus jura nostra defendere* (We dare defend our rights)
State Symbols: flower, camellia (1959); **bird,** yellowhammer (1927); **song,** "Alabama" (1931); **tree,** Southern longleaf pine (1949, 1997); **salt water fish,** fighting tarpon (1955); **fresh water fish,** largemouth bass (1975); **horse,** racking horse (1975); **mineral,** hematite (1967); **rock,** marble (1969); **game bird,** wild turkey (1980); **dance,** square dance (1981); **nut,** pecan (1982); **fossil,** species *Basilosaurus Cetoides* (1984); **official mascot and butterfly,** eastern tiger swallowtail (1989); **insect,** monarch butterfly (1989); **reptile,** Alabama red-bellied turtle (1990); **gemstone,** star blue quartz (1990); **shell,** *scaphella junonia johnstoneae* (1990);
Nickname: Yellowhammer State
Origin of name: May come from Choctaw meaning "thicket-clearers" or "vegetation-gatherers"
10 largest cities (1998 est.): Birmingham, 252,997; Mobile, 202,181; Montgomery, 197,014; Huntsville, 175,979; Tuscaloosa, 83,376; Hoover, 59,551; Dothan, 57,069; Decatur, 54,694; Gadsden, 42,158; Auburn, 40,425
Land area: 50,750 sq mi. (131,443 sq km)
Geographic center: In Chilton Co., 12 mi. SW of Clanton
Number of counties: 67
Largest county by population and area: Jefferson, 657,422 (1999 est.); Baldwin, 1,596 sq mi.
State forests: 21 (48,000 ac.)
State parks: 22 (45,614 ac.)
Residents: Alabamian, Alabaman
1999 resident population est.: 4,369,862
1990 resident census population (rank): 4,040,587 (22). **Male:** 1,936,162; **Female:** 2,104,425. **White:** 2,975,797 (73.6%); **Black:** 1,020,705 (25.3%); **American Indian:** 16,506 (0.4%); **Asian:** 21,797 (0.5%); **Other race:** 5,782 (0.1%); **Hispanic:** 24,629 (0.6%). **1990 percent population under 18:** 26.2; **65 and over:** 12.9; **median age:** 32.9.

Spanish explorers are believed to have arrived at Mobile Bay in 1519, and the territory was visited in 1540 by the explorer Hernando de Soto. The first permanent European settlement in Alabama was founded by the French at Fort Louis de la Mobile in 1702. The British gained control of the area in 1763 by the Treaty of Paris, but had to cede almost all the Alabama region to the U.S. and Spain after the American Revolution. The Confederacy was founded at Montgomery in February 1861 and, for a time, the city was the Confederate capital.

During the last part of the 19th century, the economy of the state slowly improved. At Tuskegee Institute, founded in 1881 by Booker T. Washington, Dr. George Washington Carver carried out his famous agricultural research.

In the 1950s and '60s, Alabama was the site of such landmark civil-rights actions as the bus boycott in Montgomery (1955–56) and the "Freedom March" from Selma to Montgomery (1965).

Today paper, chemicals, rubber and plastics, apparel and textiles, primary metals, and automobile manufacturing constitute the leading industries of Alabama. Continuing as a major manufacturer of coal, iron, and steel, Birmingham is also noted for its world-renowned medical center. The state ranks high in the production of poultry, soybeans, milk, vegetables, livestock, wheat, cattle, cotton, peanuts, fruits, hogs, and corn.

Points of interest include the Helen Keller birthplace at Tuscumbia, the Space and Rocket Center at Huntsville, the White House of the Confederacy, the restored state Capitol, the Civil Rights Memorial, the Shakespeare Festival Theater Complex in Montgomery, the Civil Rights Institute, the McWane Center in Birmingham, the Russell Cave near Bridgeport, the Bellingrath Gardens at Theodore, the USS *Alabama* at Mobile, Mound State Monument near Tuscaloosa, and the Gulf Coast area.

Famous natives and residents: Hank Aaron, baseball player; Ralph Abernathy, civil rights activist; Tallulah Bankhead, actress; Hugo L. Black, jurist; George Washington Carver, educator, agricultural chemist; Nat "King" Cole, entertainer; Marva Collins, educator; Kenneth Gibson, first black mayor of major eastern city (Newark); Lionel Hampton, jazz musician; W. C. Handy, composer; Kate Jackson, actress; Helen Keller, author and educator; Coretta Scott King, civil rights leader; Harper Lee, writer; Joe Louis, boxer; Willie Mays, baseball player; Jim Nabors, actor; Jesse Owens, athlete; Rosa Parks, civil rights activist; Wayne Rogers, actor; Tascaluza, Choctaw chief; George Wallace, former governor; William Weatherford (Red Eagle), Creek leader; Heather Whitestone, Miss America (1995).

Alaska

Capital: Juneau
Governor: Tony Knowles, D (to Dec. 2002)
Lieut. Governor: Fran Ulmer, D (to Dec. 2002)
Senators: Frank H. Murkowski, R (to Jan. 2005); Ted Stevens, R (to Jan. 2003)
Commissioner of Administration: Bob Poe
Atty. General: Bruce M. Bothelho, D
Organized as territory: 1912
Entered Union (rank): Jan. 3, 1959 (49)
Constitution ratified: April 24, 1956
Motto: North to the Future
State Symbols: flower, forget-me-not (1949); **tree,** sitka spruce (1962); **bird,** willow ptarmigan (1955); **fish,** king salmon (1962); **song,** "Alaska's Flag" (1955); **gem,** jade (1968); **marine mammal,** bowhead whale (1983); **fossil,** woolly mammoth (1986); **mineral,** gold (1968); **sport,** dog mushing (1972);
Nickname: The state is commonly called "The Last Frontier" or "Land of the Midnight Sun"
Origin of name: Corruption of Aleut word meaning "great land" or "that which the sea breaks against"
10 largest cities (1998 est.): Anchorage, 254,982; Fairbanks, 33,295; Juneau, 30,191; Sitka, 8,338; Kenai, 7,943; Kodiak, 7,720; Ketchikan, 7,543; Bethel, 6,342; Wasilla, 5,791; Homer, 4,794
Land area: 570,374 sq mi. (1,477,267 sq km)
Geographic center: 60 mi. NW of Mt. McKinley
Number of boroughs: 16
Largest borough by population and area: Anchorage, 257,808 (1999 est.); Yukon-Koyukuk, 157,121 sq mi.
State parks: more than 100 (3.5 million acres)
Residents: Alaskan
1999 resident population est.: 619,500
1990 resident census population (rank): 550,043 (49). **Male:** 289,867; **Female:** 260,176. **White:** 415,492 (75.5%); **Black:** 22,451 (4.1%); **American Indian:** 85,698 (15.6%); **Asian:** 19,728 (3.6%); **Other race:** 6,675 (1.2%); **Hispanic:** 17,803 (3.2%). **1990 percent population under 18:** 31.3; **65 and over:** 4.1; **median age:** 29.3.

Vitus Bering, a Dane working for the Russians, and Alexei Chirikov discovered the Alaskan mainland and the Aleutian Islands in 1741. The tremendous land mass of Alaska—equal to one-fifth of the continental U.S.—was unexplored in 1867 when Secretary of State William Seward arranged for its purchase from the Russians for $7,200,000. The transfer of the territory took place on Oct. 18, 1867. Despite a price of about two cents an acre, the purchase was widely ridiculed as "Seward's Folly." The first official census (1880) reported a total of 33,426 Alaskans, all but 430 being of aboriginal stock. The Gold Rush of 1898 resulted in a mass influx of more than 30,000 people. Since then, Alaska has contributed billions of dollars' worth of products to the U.S. economy.

In 1968, a large oil and gas reservoir near Prudhoe Bay on the Arctic Coast was found. The Prudhoe Bay reservoir, with an estimated recoverable 10 billion barrels of oil and 27 trillion cubic feet of gas, is twice as large as any other oil field in North America. The Trans-Alaska pipeline was completed in 1977 at a cost of $7.7 billion. On June 20, oil started flowing through the 800-mile-long pipeline from Prudhoe Bay to the port of Valdez.

Other important industries are fisheries, wood and wood products, furs, and tourism.

Denali National Park and Mendenhall Glacier in North Tongass National Forest are of interest, as is the large totem pole collection at Sitka National Historical Park. The Katmai National Park includes the "Valley of Ten Thousand Smokes," an area of active volcanoes.

The Alaska Native population, the indigenous peoples of Alaska, include Eskimos, Indians, and Aleuts. More than half of all Alaska Natives are Eskimos. (*Eskimo* is used for Alaska Natives; *Inuit* is used for Eskimos living in Canada.) The two main Eskimo groups, Inupiat and Yupik, are distinguished by their language and geography. The former live in the north and northwest parts of Alaska and speak Inupiaq, while the latter live in the south and southwest and speak Yupik.

About 36% of Alaska Natives are American Indians. The major tribes are the Alaskan Athabaskan (11,696) in the central part of the state, and the Tlingit (9,448), Tsimshian (1,653), and Haida (1,083) in the southeast.

The Aleuts, native to the Aleutian Islands, Kodiak Island, the lower Alaska and Kenai Peninsulas, and Prince William Sound, are physically and culturally related to the Eskimos. About 12% of Alaska Natives are Aleuts, and in 1990, they made up 10,052 of the indigenous population.

Famous natives and residents: Clarence L. Andrews, author; Aleksandr Baranov, first governor of Russian America; Margaret Elizabeth Bell, author; Benny Benson, designed state flag at age 13; Vitus Bering, explorer; Charles E. Bunnell, educator; Susan Butcher, sled-dog racer; William A. Egan, first state governor; Carl Ben Eielson, pioneer pilot; Henry E. Gruennig, political leader; B. Frank Heintzleman, territorial governor; Walter J. Hickel, former governor; Sheldon Jackson, educator and missionary; Joe Juneau, prospector; Austin Lathrop, industrialist; Sydney Lawrence, painter; Ray Mala, actor; Virgil F. Partch, cartoonist; Joe Redington, Sr., sled-dog musher and promoter; Peter Trinble Rowe, first Episcopal bishop; Ivan Popov-Veniaminov (St. Innocent), Russian Orthodox missionary; Ferdinand Wrangel, educator; Samuel Hall Young, founder of first American church.

Arizona

Capital: Phoenix
Governor: Jane Dee Hull, R (to Jan. 2003)
Senators: Jon Kyl, R (to Jan. 2001); John McCain, R (to Jan. 2005)
Secy. of State: Betsey Bayless, R (to Jan. 2003)
Atty. General: Janet Napolitano, D (to Jan. 2003)
Treasurer: Carol Springer, R (to Jan. 2003))
Organized as territory: Feb. 24, 1863
Entered Union (rank): Feb. 14, 1912 (48)
Present constitution adopted: 1911
Motto: *Ditat Deus* (God enriches)
State Symbols: flower, flower of saguaro cactus (1931); **bird,** cactus wren (1931); **colors,** blue and old gold (1915); **song,** "Arizona" (1919); **tree,** palo verde (1954); **neckwear,** bola tie (1971); **fossil,** petrified wood (1988); **gemstone,** turquoise (1974); **mammal,** ringtail (1986); **reptile,** Arizona ridgenose rattlesnake (1986); **fish,** Arizona trout (1986); **amphibian,** Arizona tree frog (1986);
Nickname: Grand Canyon State
Origin of name: From the Indian "Arizonac," meaning "little spring" or "young spring"
10 largest cities (1998 est.): Phoenix, 1,198,064; Tucson, 460,466; Mesa, 360,076; Scottsdale, 195,394; Glendale, 193,482; Tempe, 167,622; Chandler, 160,329; Gilbert, 88,840; Peoria, 87,048; Yuma, 62,433
Land area: 113,642 sq mi. (296,400 sq km)
Geographic center: In Yavapai Co., 55 mi. ESE of Prescott
Number of counties: 15

Largest county by population and area: Maricopa, 2,861,395 (1999 est.); Coconino, 18,619 sq mi.
State parks: 28
Residents: Arizonan, Arizonian
1999 resident population est.: 4,778,332
1990 resident census population (rank): 3,665,228 (24). **Male:** 1,810,691; **Female:** 1,854,537. **White:** 2,963,186 (80.8%); **Black:** 110,524 (3.0%); **American Indian:** 203,527 (5.6%); **Asian:** 55,206 (1.5%) **Other race:** 332,785 (9.1%); **Hispanic:** 688,338 (18.8%). **1990 percent population under 18:** 26.8; **65 and over:** 13.1; median age: 32.0.

Marcos de Niza, a Spanish Franciscan friar, was the first European to explore Arizona. He entered the area in 1539 in search of the mythical Seven Cities of Gold. Although he was followed a year later by another gold seeker, Francisco Vásquez de Coronado, most of the early settlement was for missionary purposes. In 1775 the Spanish established Fort Tucson. In 1848, after the Mexican War, most of the Arizona territory became part of the U.S., and the southern portion of the territory was added by the Gadsden Purchase in 1853.

Arizona history is rich in legends of America's Old West. It was here that the great Indian chiefs Geronimo and Cochise led their people against the frontiersmen. Tombstone, Ariz., was the site of the West's most famous shoot-out—the gunfight at the O.K. Corral. Today, Arizona has one of the largest U.S. Indian populations; more than 14 tribes are represented on 20 reservations.

Manufacturing has become Arizona's most important industry. Principal products include electrical, communications, and aeronautical items. The state produces over half of the country's copper. Agriculture is also important to the state's economy. In 1973 one of the world's most massive dams, the New Cornelia Tailings, was completed near Ajo.

State attractions include the Grand Canyon, the Petrified Forest, the Painted Desert, Hoover Dam, Lake Mead, Fort Apache, and the reconstructed London Bridge at Lake Havasu City.

Famous natives and residents: Apache Kid, Indian outlaw; Erma Bombeck, humorist and writer; Glen Campbell, singer; Lynda Carter, actress; Cesar Chavez, labor leader; Cochise, Apache chief; Alice Cooper, singer and songwriter; Wyatt Earp, marshall; Max Ernst, painter; Geronimo (Goyathlay), Apache chief; Barry Goldwater, politician; Zane Grey, novelist; Carl Trumbull Hayden, politician; George W. P. Hunt, first state governor; Bill Keane, cartoonist; Eusebio Kino, missionary; Percival Lowell, astronomer; Frank Luke, Jr., WWI fighter ace; Charles Mingus, jazz musician and composer; Carlos Montezuma, doctor and Indian spokesman; Stevie Nicks, singer; Sandra Day O'Connor, jurist; William O'Neill, frontier sheriff; Alexander M. Patch, general; William H. Pickering, astronomer; Linda Ronstadt, singer; Paolo Soleri, architect; Clyde W. Tombaugh, astronomer; Tanya Tucker, singer; Stewart Udall, former Secretary of the Interior; Pauline Weaver, frontier person; Frank Lloyd Wright, architect.

Arkansas

Capital: Little Rock
Governor: Mike Huckabee, R (to Jan. 2003)
Lieut. Governor: Winthrop Rockefeller, R (to 2002)
Senators: Tim Hutchinson, R (to Jan. 2003); Blanche Lambert Lincoln, D (to Jan. 2005)
Secy. of State: Sharon Priest, D (to Jan. 2003)
Atty. General: Mark Pryor, D (to Jan. 2003)
Auditor of State: Gus Wingfield, D (to Jan. 2003)
Treasurer of State: Jimmie Lou Fisher, D (to Jan. 2003)

Land Commissioner: Charles Daniels, D (to Jan. 2003)
Organized as territory: March 2, 1819
Entered Union (rank): June 15, 1836 (25)
Present constitution adopted: 1874
Motto: *Regnat populus* (The people rule)
State Symbols: flower, apple blossom (1901); **tree,** pine (1939); **bird,** mockingbird (1929); **insect,** honeybee (1973); **song,** "Arkansas" (1963).
Nickname: The Natural State
Origin of name: From the Quapaw Indians
10 largest cities (1998 est.): Little Rock, 175,303; Fort Smith, 75,637; North Little Rock, 1,217,649. White: Fayetteville, 53,300; Pine Bluff, 52,968; Jonesboro, 52,250; Springdale, 40,287; Conway, 39,164; Hot Springs, 37,961; Rogers, 37,073
Land area: 52,075 sq mi. (134,874 sq km)
Geographic center: In Pulaski Co., 12 mi. NW of Little Rock
Number of counties: 75
Largest county by population and area: Pulaski, 349,232 (1999 est.); Union, 1,039 sq mi.
State parks: 50
Residents: Arkansan
1999 resident population est.: 2,551,373
1990 resident census population(rank): 2,350,725 (33). **Male:** 1,133,076; **Female:** 1,217,649. **White:** 1,944,744 (82.7%); **Black:** 373,912 (15.9%); **American Indian:** 12,773 (0.5%); **Asian:** 12,530 (0.5%); **Other race:** 6,766 (0.3%); **Hispanic:** 19,876 (0.8%). **1990 percent population under 18:** 26.4; **65 and over:** 14.9; **median age:** 33.7.

Spaniard Hernando de Soto, in 1541, was among the early European explorers to visit the territory, but it was a Frenchman, Henri de Tonti, who in 1686 founded the first permanent white settlement—the Arkansas Post. In 1803 the area was acquired by the U.S. as part of the Louisiana Purchase.

Part of the Territory of Missouri from 1812, the area became a separate entity in 1819 after the first large wave of settlers arrived. The next several decades were marked by the development of the cotton industry and the spread of the Southern plantation system west into Arkansas. Arkansas joined the Confederacy in 1861, but from 1863 the northern part of the state was occupied by Union troops.

Food products are the state's largest employing sector, with lumber and wood products a close second. Arkansas is also a leader in the production of cotton, rice, and soybeans. It also has the country's only active diamond mine; located near Murfreesboro, it is operated as a tourist attraction.

Hot Springs National Park, and Buffalo National River in the Ozarks are major state attractions.

Blanchard Springs Caverns, the Arkansas Territorial Restoration at Little Rock, and the Arkansas Folk Center in Mountain View are of interest.

Famous natives and residents: G. M. "Broncho Billy" Anderson, actor; Maya Angelou, author and poet; Katharine Susan Anthony, author; Helen Gurley Brown, editor; Glen Campbell, singer; Hattie Caraway, first elected woman senator; Johnny Cash, singer; Eldridge Cleaver, black activist; William Jefferson Clinton, 42nd President; Dizzy Dean, baseball player; Orval Faubus, former governor; John Gould Fletcher, writer; James W. Fulbright, former senator; John H. Johnson, publisher; Alan Ladd, actor; Douglas MacArthur, 5-star general; John Paul McConnell, U.S. Air Force officer; Ben Murphy, actor; Frank Pace, Jr., public official; Ben Piazza, actor; Albert Pike, pioneer teacher and lawyer; Dick Powell, actor; Opie P. Read, writer; Jenny D. Rice-Meyrowitz, painter; Brehon Burke Somervell, World Wars I and II U.S. Army officer; Mary Steenburgen, actress; Edward Durell Stone, architect; William C. Warfield, concert singer and actor.

California

Capital: Sacramento
Governor: Gray Davis, D (to Jan. 2003)
Lieut. Governor: Cruz M. Bustamante, D (to Jan. 2003)
Senators: Barbara Boxer, D (to Jan. 2005);
 Dianne Feinstein, D (to Jan. 2001)
Secy. of State: Bill Jones, R (to Jan. 2003)
Controller: Kathleen Connell, D (to Jan. 2003)
Atty. General: Bill Lockyer, D (to Jan. 2003)
Treasurer: Phil Angelides, D (to Jan. 2003)
Supt. of Public Instruction: Delaine Eastin
Entered Union (rank): Sept. 9, 1850 (31)
Present constitution adopted: 1879
Motto: *Eureka* (I have found it)
State Symbols: flower, golden poppy (1903); **tree,**
 California redwoods (*Sequoia sempervirens & Sequoia gigantec*) (1937, 1953); **bird,** California valley quail
 (1931); **animal,** California grizzly bear (1953); **fish,**
 California golden trout (1947); **colors,** blue and gold
 (1951); **song,** "I Love You, California" (1951);
Nickname: Golden State
Origin of name: From a book, *Las Sergas de Esplandián,* by Garcia Ordóñez de Montalvo, c. 1500
10 largest cities (1998 est.): Los Angeles, 3,597,556;
 San Diego, 1,220,666; San Jose, 861,284; San
 Francisco, 745,774; Long Beach, 430,905;
 Sacramento, 404,168; Fresno, 398,133; Oakland,
 365,874; Santa Ana, 305,955; Anaheim, 295,153
Land area: 155,973 sq mi. (403,970 sq km)
Geographic center: In Madera Co., 35 mi. NE of
 Madera
Number of counties: 58
Largest county by population and area: Los Angeles,
 9,329,989 (1999 est.); San Bernardino, 20,062 sq mi.
National forests: 18
State parks and beaches: 264
Residents: Californian
1999 resident population est.: 33,145,121
1990 resident census population(rank): 29,760,021
 (1). **Male:** 14,897,627; **Female:** 14,862,394. **White:**
 20,524,327 (69.9%); **Black:** 2,208,801 (7.4%); **American Indian:** 242,164 (0.8%); **Asian:** 2,845,659 (9.6%);
 Other race: 3,939,070 (13.2%); **Hispanic:** 7,687,938
 (25.8%). **1990 percent population under 18:** 26.0; **65
 and over:** 10.5; **median age:** 31.3.

Although California was sighted by Spanish navigator Juan Rodríguez Cabrillo in 1542, its first Spanish mission (at San Diego) was not established until 1769. California became a U.S. territory in 1847 when Mexico surrendered it to John C. Frémont. On Jan. 24, 1848, James W. Marshall discovered gold at Sutter's Mill, starting the California Gold Rush and bringing settlers to the state in large numbers. In 1964, the U.S. Census Bureau estimated that California had become the most populous state, surpassing New York. One reason for this may be that more immigrants settle in California than any other state—more than one-third of the nation's total in 1994. Asians and Pacific Islanders led the influx.

Leading industries include agriculture, manufacturing (transportation equipment, machinery, and electronic equipment), biotechnology, aerospace-defense, and tourism. Principal natural resources include timber, petroleum, cement, and natural gas.

Death Valley, in the southeast, is 282 feet below sea level, the lowest point in the nation. Mt. Whitney (14,491 ft.) is the highest point in the contiguous 48 states. Lassen Peak is one of two active U.S. volcanoes outside of Alaska and Hawaii; its last eruptions were recorded in 1917.

Other points of interest include Yosemite National Park, Disneyland, Hollywood, the Golden Gate Bridge, Sequoia National Park, San Simeon State Park, and Point Reyes National Seashore.

Famous natives and residents: Gertrude Atherton, author; David Belasco, playwright and producer; Shirley Temple Black, actress, ambassador; Dave Brubeck, musician; Luther Burbank, horticulturalist; Julia Child, chef; Joe DiMaggio, baseball player; James H. Doolittle, air force general; Isadora Duncan, dancer; John Frémont, explorer; Robert Frost, poet; Henry George, economist; Richard "Pancho" Gonzales, tennis player; George E. Hale, astronomer; Bret Harte, writer; William Randolph Hearst, publisher; Sidney Howard, playwright; Collis Potter Huntington, financier; Helen Hunt Jackson, writer; Robinson Jeffers, poet; Anthony M. Kennedy, jurist; Jack London, author; James W. Marshall, first discovered gold; Aimee Semple McPherson, evangelist; Marilyn Monroe, actress; John Muir, naturalist; Richard M. Nixon, President; Isamu Noguchi, sculptor; Frank Norris, novelist; Kathleen Norris, novelist; George S. Patton, Jr., general; Robert Redford, actor; Sally K. Ride, astronaut; William Saroyan, author; Junípero Serra, missionary; Upton Sinclair, novelist; Leland Stanford, railroad magnate; Lincoln Steffens, journalist, author; John Steinbeck, author; Adlai Stevenson, statesman; Johann Sutter, pioneer; Michael Tilson Thomas, conductor; Earl Warren, jurist.

Colorado

Capital: Denver
Governor: Bill Owens, R (to Jan. 2003)
Lieut. Governor: Joe Rogers, D (to Jan. 2003)
Senators: Wayne A. Allard, R (to Jan. 2003);
 Ben Nighthorse Campbell, R (to Jan. 2005)
Secy. of State: Vikki Buckley, R (to Jan 2003)
Treasurer: Mike Coffman, R (to Jan. 2003)
Controller: Arthur Barnhart
Atty. General: Ken Salazar, D (to Jan. 2003)
Organized as territory: Feb. 28, 1861
Entered Union (rank): Aug. 1, 1876 (38)
Present constitution adopted: 1876
Motto: *Nil sine Numine* (Nothing without Providence)
State Symbols: flower, Rocky Mountain columbine
 (1899); **tree,** Colorado blue spruce (1939); **bird,** lark
 bunting (1931); **animal,** Rocky Mountain bighorn
 sheep (1961); **gemstone,** aquamarine (1971); **colors,**
 blue and white (1911); **song,** "Where the Columbines
 Grow" (1915); **fossil,** stegosaurus (1991);
Nickname: Centennial State
Origin of name: From the Spanish, "ruddy" or "red"
10 largest cities (1998 est.): Denver, 499,055; Colorado
 Springs, 344,987; Aurora, 250,604; Lakewood,
 136,883; Fort Collins, 108,905; Pueblo, 107,301;
 Arvada, 97,610; Westminster, 95,691; Boulder, 90,543;
 Thornton, 74,139
Land area: 103,730 sq mi. (268,660 sq km)
Geographic center: In Park Co., 30 mi. NW of
 Pikes Peak
Number of counties: 63
Largest county by population and area: Jefferson,
 509,222 (1999 est.); Las Animas, 4,773 sq mi.
State forests: 1 (71,000 ac.)
State parks: 44 (160,000 ac.)
Residents: Coloradan, Coloradoan
1999 resident population est.: 4,056,133
1990 resident census population (rank): 3,294,394
 (26). **Male:** 1,631,295; **Female:** 1,663,099. **White:**
 2,095,474 (88.2%); **Black:** 133,146 (4.0%); **American
 Indian:** 27,776 (0.8%); **Asian:** 59,862 (1.8%); **Other
 race:** 186,136 (5.1%); **Hispanic:** 424,302 (12.9%).
 1990 percent population under 18: 26.1; **65 and
 over:** 10.0; **median age:** 32.4.

First visited by Spanish explorers in the 1500s, the territory was claimed for Spain by Juan de Ulibarri in 1706. The U.S. obtained eastern Colorado as part of the Louisiana Purchase in 1803, the central portion in 1845 with the admission of Texas as a state, and the western part in 1848 as a result of the Mexican War.

Colorado has the highest mean elevation of any state, with more than 1,000 Rocky Mountain peaks over 10,000 feet high and 54 towering above 14,000 feet. Pikes Peak, the most famous of these mountains, was discovered by U.S. Army Lieut. Zebulon M. Pike in 1806.

Once primarily a mining and agricultural state, Colorado's economy is now driven by the service industries, including medical providers and other business and professional services. Colorado's economy also has a strong manufacturing base. The primary manufactures are food products, printing and publishing, machinery, and electrical instruments. The state is also a communications and transportation hub for the Rocky Mountain region.

Breathtaking scenery and world-class skiing make Colorado a prime tourist destination. The main tourist attractions in the state include Rocky Mountain National Park, Curecanti National Recreation Area, Mesa Verde National Park, the Great Sand Dunes and Dinosaur National Monuments, Colorado National Monument, and the Black Canyon of the Gunnison National Monument.

The farm industry, which is primarily concentrated in livestock, is also an important element of the state's economy. The primary crops in Colorado are corn, hay, and wheat.

Famous natives and residents: Tim Allen, actor and comedian; William E. Barrett, writer; William Bent, fur trader and pioneer; Charles F. Brannan, lawyer and public official; M. Scott Carpenter, astronaut; Lon Chaney, actor; Mary Coyle Chase, playwright; Jack Dempsey, boxer; Ralph Edwards, entertainer; John Evans, physician, educator; Douglas Fairbanks, actor; John Thomas Fante, writer; Eugene Fodor, violinist; Gene Fowler, writer; Erick Hawkins, choreographer; Homer Lea, soldier, writer; Ted Mack, TV host; Jaye P. Morgan, singer; Peg Murray, actress; Ouray, Ute Indian chief; Anne Parrish, writer; Barbara Rush, actress; Horace A. Tabor, silver king and lieut. governor; Lowell Thomas, commentator and author; Dalton Trumbo, screenwriter, novelist; Byron R. White, jurist; Paul Whiteman, conductor; Don Wilson, announcer.

Connecticut

Capital: Hartford
Governor: John G. Rowland, R (to Jan. 2003)
Lieut. Governor: M. Jodi Rell, R (to Jan. 2003)
Senators: Christopher J. Dodd, D (to Jan. 2005); Joseph I. Lieberman, D (to Jan. 2001)
Secy. of the State: Susan Bysiewicz, D (to Jan. 2003)
Comptroller: Nancy Wyman, D (to Jan. 2003)
Treasurer: Denise Nappier, D (to Jan. 2003)
Atty. General: Richard Blumenthal, D (to Jan. 2003)
Entered Union (rank): Jan. 9, 1788 (5)
Present constitution adopted: Dec. 30, 1965
Motto: *Qui transtulit sustinet* (He who transplanted still sustains)
State Symbols: flower, mountain laurel (1907); **tree,** white oak (1947); **animal,** sperm whale (1975); **bird,** American robin (1943); **hero,** Nathan Hale (1985); **heroine,** Prudence Crandall (1995); **insect,** praying mantis (1977); **mineral,** garnet (1977); **song,** "Yankee Doodle" (1978); **ship,** USS *Nautilus* (1983); **shellfish,** eastern oyster (1989); **fossil,** *Eubrontes Giganteus* (1991); **composer,** Charles Edward Ives (1991).
Official designation: *Constitution State* (1959)
Nickname: Nutmeg State
Origin of name: From an Indian word (Quinnehtukqut)

meaning "beside the long tidal river"
10 largest cities (1998 est.): Bridgeport, 137,425; Hartford, 131,523; New Haven, 123,189; Stamford, 110,689; Waterbury, 105,346; Norwalk, 78,064; New Britain, 70,492; Danbury, 65,829; Bristol, 59,158; Meriden, 56,667
Land area: 4,845 sq mi. (12,550 sq km)
Geographic center: In Hartford Co., at East Berlin
Number of counties: 8
Largest county by population and area: Fairfield, 841,334 (1999 est.); Litchfield, 920 sq mi.
State forests: 30 (145,529 ac.)
State parks: 91 (31,884 ac.)
Residents: Nutmegger
1999 resident population est.: 3,282,031
1990 resident census population(rank): 3,287,116 (27). **Male:** 1,592,873; **Female:** 1,694,243. **White:** 2,859,353 (87.0%); **Black:** 274,269 (8.3%); **American Indian:** 6,654 (0.2%); **Asian:** 50,698 (1.5%); **Other race:** 96,142 (2.9%); **Hispanic:** 213,116 (6.5%). **1990 percent population under 18:** 22.8; **65 and over:** 13.6; **median age:** 34.3.

The Dutch navigator, Adriaen Block, was the first European of record to explore the area, sailing up the Connecticut River in 1614. In 1633, Dutch colonists built a fort and trading post near present-day Hartford, but soon lost control to English Puritans migrating south from the Massachusetts Bay Colony.

English settlements, established in the 1630s at Windsor, Wethersfield, and Hartford, united in 1639 to form the Connecticut Colony and adopted the *Fundamental Orders*.

Connecticut played a prominent role in the Revolutionary War, serving as the Continental Army's major supplier. Sometimes called the "Arsenal of the Nation," the state became one of the most industrialized in the nation.

Today, Connecticut factories produce weapons, sewing machines, jet engines, helicopters, motors, hardware and tools, cutlery, clocks, locks, silverware, and submarines. Hartford has the oldest U.S. newspaper still being published—the *Hartford Courant*, established 1764—and is the insurance capital of the nation.

Poultry, fruit, and dairy products account for the largest portion of farm income, and Connecticut's shade-grown tobacco is acknowledged to be the state's most valuable crop per acre.

Connecticut is a popular resort area with its 250-mile Long Island Sound shoreline and many inland lakes. Among the major points of interest are Yale University's Gallery of Fine Arts and Peabody Museum. Other famous museums include the P. T. Barnum, Winchester Gun, and American Clock and Watch. The town of Mystic features a recreated 19th-century New England seaport and the Mystic Marinelife Aquarium.

Famous natives and residents: Dean Acheson, statesman; Ethan Allan, American Revolutionary soldier; Benedict Arnold, American Revolutionary general; P. T. Barnum, showman; Henry Ward Beecher, clergyman; John Brown, abolitionist; Oliver Ellsworth, jurist; Eileen Farrell, soprano; Charles Goodyear, inventor; Nathan Hale, American Revolutionary officer; Dorothy Hamill, ice skater; Katharine Hepburn, actress; Charles Ives, composer; Edwin H. Land, inventor; John Pierpont Morgan, financier; Frederick Law Olmsted, landscape designer; Rosa Ponselle, soprano; Adam Clayton Powell, Jr., congressman; Benjamin Spock, pediatrician; Harriet Beecher Stowe, author; Mark Twain, author; Morris R. Waite, jurist; Noah Webster, lexicographer.

Delaware

Capital: Dover
Governor: Thomas R. Carper, D (to Jan. 2001)
Lieut. Governor: Ruth Ann Minner, D (to Jan. 2001)
Senators: Joseph R. Biden, Jr., D (to Jan. 2003);
    William V. Roth, Jr., R (to Jan. 2001)
Secy. of State: Edward J. Freel, D (Pleasure
    of Governor)
State Treasurer: Jack Markell, D. (to Jan. 2002)
Atty. General: M. Jane Brady, R (to Jan. 2002)
Entered Union (rank): Dec. 7, 1787 (1)
Present constitution adopted: 1897
Motto: Liberty and independence
State Symbols: colors, colonial blue and buff; **flower,**
    peach blossom (1895); **tree,** American holly (1939);
    bird, blue hen chicken (1939); **insect,** ladybug (1974);
    fish, weakfish, *cynoscion regalis* (1981); **song,** "Our
    Delaware";
Nicknames: Diamond State; First State; Small Wonder
Origin of name: From Delaware River and Bay; named
    in turn for Sir Thomas West, Baron De La Warr
10 largest cities (1998 est.): Wilmington, 71,678;
    Dover, 30,369; Newark, 28,000; Milford, 6,665;
    Seaford, 6,600; Elsmere, 5,764; Smyrna, 5,652; New
    Castle 4,888; Middletown, 4,434; Georgetown, 4,185
Land area: 1,955 sq mi. (5,153 sq km)
Geographic center: In Kent Co., 11 mi. S of Dover
Number of counties: 3
Largest county by population and area: New Castle,
    487,182 (1999 est.); Sussex, 938 sq mi.
State forests: 3 (9,353 ac.)
State parks: 13
Residents: Delawarean
1999 resident population est.: 753,538
1990 resident census population (rank): 666,168 (46).
    Male: 322,968; **Female:** 343,200. **White:** 535,094
    (80.3%); **Black:** 112,460 (16.9%); **American Indian:**
    2,019 (0.3%); **Asian:** 9,057 (1.4%); **Other race:** 7,538
    (1.1%); **Hispanic:** 15,820 (2.4%). **1990 percent popu-
    lation under 18:** 24.5; **65 and over:** 12.1; **median
    age:** 32.7.

Henry Hudson, sailing under the Dutch flag, is
credited with Delaware's discovery in 1609. The
following year, Capt. Samuel Argall of Virginia
named Delaware for his colony's governor, Thomas
West, Baron De La Warr. An attempted Dutch settlement failed in 1631. Swedish colonization began at
Fort Christina (now Wilmington) in 1638, but New
Sweden fell to Dutch forces led by New Netherlands' Gov. Peter Stuyvesant in 1655.

England took over the area in 1664 and it was
transferred to William Penn as the southern Three
Counties in 1682. Semiautonomous after 1704,
Delaware fought as a separate state in the American
Revolution and became the first state to ratify the
Constitution in 1787.

During the Civil War, although a slave state,
Delaware did not secede from the Union.

In 1802, Éleuthère Irénée du Pont established a
gunpowder mill near Wilmington that laid the foundation for Delaware's huge chemical industry. Delaware's manufactured products now also include vul-
canized fiber, textiles, paper, medical supplies, metal
products, machinery, machine tools, and automobiles.

Delaware also grows a great variety of fruits and
vegetables and is a U.S. pioneer in the food-canning
industry. Corn, soybeans, potatoes, and hay are
important crops. Delaware's broiler-chicken farms
supply the big Eastern markets, and fishing and
dairy products are other important industries.

Points of interest include the Fort Christina
Monument, Hagley Museum, Holy Trinity Church
(erected in 1698, the oldest Protestant church in the
United States still in use), and Winterthur Museum,
in and near Wilmington; central New Castle, an
almost unchanged late 18th-century capital; and the
Delaware Museum of Natural History.

Popular recreation areas include Cape Henlopen,
Delaware Seashore, Trapp Pond State Park, and
Rehoboth Beach.

Famous natives and residents: Richard Allen, founder of
the African Methodist Episcopal Church; Valerie Bertinelli,
actress; Robert Montgomery Bird, writer and artist; Henry
S. Canby, editor and author; Annie Jump Cannon,
astronomer; Elizabeth Margaret Chandler, author; Felix
Darley, artist; John Dickinson, statesman; E. I. du Pont,
industrialist; Oliver Evans, inventor; Thomas Garrett,
abolitionist; Henry Heimlich, surgeon, inventor; William
Julius "Judy" Johnson, baseball player; J. P. Marquand,
novelist; Howard Pyle, artist and author; George Read,
jurist, signer of Declaration of Independence; Jay
Saunders Redding, educator and author; Caesar Rodney,
patriot, signer of Declaration of Independence; Frank
Stephens, sculptor; Estelle Taylor, actress; George Alfred
Townsend, journalist and author.

District of Columbia

See Washington, D.C., listing in U.S. Cities.

Florida

Capital: Tallahassee
Governor: Jeb Bush, R (to Jan. 2003)
Lieut. Governor: Frank Brogan, R (to Jan. 2003)
Senators: Bob Graham, D (to Jan. 2005); Connie Mack
    III, R (to Jan. 2001)
Secy. of State: Katherine Harris, R (to Jan. 2003)
Comptroller: Bob Milligan, R (to Jan. 2003)
Commissioner of Agriculture: Bob Crawford, D
    (to Jan. 2003)
Atty. General: Bob Butterworth, D (to Jan. 2003)
Organized as territory: March 30, 1821
Entered Union (rank): March 3, 1845 (27)
Present constitution adopted: 1969
Motto: In God we trust (1868)
State Symbols: flower, orange blossom (1909); **bird,**
    mockingbird (1927); **song,** "Suwannee River" (1935);
Nickname: Sunshine State (1970)
Origin of name: From the Spanish, meaning "feast of
    flowers" (Easter)
10 largest cities (1998 est.): Jacksonville (CC[1]), 693,630;
    Miami, 368,624; Tampa, 289,156; St. Petersburg,
    236,029; Hialeah, 211,392; Orlando, 181,175; Fort
    Lauderdale, 153,728; Tallahassee, 136,628; Hollywood,
    130,026; Pembroke Pines, 115,361
Land area: 54,153 sq mi. (140,256 sq km)
Geographic center: In Hernando Co., 12 mi. NNW of
    Brooksville
Number of counties: 67
Largest county by population and area: Miami-Dade,
    2,175,634 (1999 est.); Palm Beach, 2,034 sq mi.
State forests: 35 (550,000 ac.)
State parks: 151 (523,920 ac.)
Residents: Floridian, Floridan
1999 resident population est.: 15,111,244
1990 resident census population (rank): 12,937,926
    (4). **Male:** 6,261,719; **Female:** 6,676,207. **White:**
    10,749,285 (83.1%); **Black:** 1,759,534 (13.6%);
    American Indian: 36,335 (0.3%); **Asian:** 154,302
    (1.2%); **Other race:** 238,470 (1.8%); **Hispanic:**
    1,574,143 (12.2%). **1990 percent population under
    18:** 22.2; **65 and over:** 18.3; **median age:** 36.2.

1. Consolidated City (Coextensive with Duval County).
In 1513, Ponce De Leon, seeking the mythical
"Fountain of Youth," discovered and named Florida,

claiming it for Spain. Later, Florida would be held at different times by Spain and England until Spain finally sold it to the United States in 1819. (Incidentally, France established a colony named Fort Caroline in 1564 in the state that was to become Florida.)

Florida's early-19th-century history as a U.S. territory was marked by wars with the Seminole Indians that did not end until 1842, although a treaty was actually never signed.

Florida's economy rests on a solid base of tourism, manufacturing, agriculture, and international trade.

In recent years, oranges, grapefruit, and other citrus fruits led Florida's agricultural-product list, followed by potatoes, melons, strawberries, sugar cane, peanuts, dairy products, and cattle.

Major tourist attractions are Miami Beach, Palm Beach, St. Augustine (founded in 1565, thus the oldest permanent city in the U.S.), Daytona Beach, and Fort Lauderdale on the East Coast. Other resorts include Sarasota, Tampa, and St. Petersburg on the West Coast and Key West off the southern tip of Florida. The Orlando area, where Disney World is located on a 27,000-acre site, is Florida's most popular tourist destination. Also drawing many visitors are the NASA Kennedy Space Center's Spaceport USA, Everglades National Park, and the Epcot Center.

Famous natives and residents: Julian "Cannonball" Adderley, jazz saxophonist; Pat Boone, singer; Fernando Bujones, ballet dancer; Steve Carlton, baseball player; Faye Dunaway, actress; Stepin Fetchit (Lincoln Theodore Perry), comedian; Lue Gim Gong, horticulturist; Dwight Gooden, baseball player; Zora Neale Hurston, writer; Daniel James, four-star general; James Weldon Johnson, author and educator; Frances Langford, singer; Little Richard, singer; Butterfly McQueen, actress; Jim Morrison, singer; Osceola, Seminole Indian leader; Sidney Poitier, actor; A. Philip Randolph, labor leader; Marjorie Kinnan Rawlings, author; Burt Reynolds, actor; Charles and John Ringling, circus entrepreneurs; Joseph W. Stilwell, army general; Norman E. Thargard, astronaut; Clarence Thomas, jurist; Ben Vereen, actor.

Georgia

Capital: Atlanta
Governor: Roy E. Barnes, D (to Jan. 2003)
Lieut. Governor: Mark Taylor, D (to Jan. 2003)
Senators: Max Cleland, D (to Jan. 2003);
Zell Miller, D (to Jan. 2001)
Secy. of State: Cathy Cox, D (to Jan. 2003)
Insurance Commissioner: John Oxendine, R
(to Jan. 2003)
Atty. General: Thurbert Baker, D (to Jan. 2003)
Entered Union (rank): Jan. 2, 1788 (4)
Present constitution adopted: 1977
Motto: Wisdom, justice, and moderation
State Symbols: flower, Cherokee rose (1916); **tree,** live oak (1937); **bird,** brown thrasher (1935); **song,** "Georgia on My Mind" (1922).
Nicknames: Peach State, Empire State of the South
Origin of name: In honor of George II of England
10 largest cities (1998 est.): Atlanta, 403,819; Columbus[1], 182,219; Savannah, 131,674; Macon, 114,336; Athens-Clarke County, 89,361; Albany, 77,545; Roswell, 57,102; Marietta, 51,362; Warner Robins, 46,698; Valdosta, 41,390
Land area: 57,919 sq mi. (150,010 sq km)
Geographic center: In Twiggs Co., 18 mi. SE of Macon
Number of counties: 159
Largest county by population and area: Fulton, 744,827 (1999 est.); Ware, 903 sq mi.

State forests: 25,258,000 ac. (67% of total state area)
State parks: 53 (42,600 ac.)
Residents: Georgian
1999 resident population est.: 7,788,240
1990 resident census population (rank): 6,478,216 (11). **Male:** 3,144,503; **Female:** 3,333,713. **White:** 4,600,148 (71.0%); **Black:** 1,746,565 (27.0%); **American Indian:** 13,348 (0.2%); **Asian:** 75,781 (1.2%); **Other race:** 42,374 (0.7%); **Hispanic:** 108,922 (1.7%). **1990 percent population under 18:** 26.7; **65 and over:** 10.1; **median age:** 31.4.

1. Consolidated City (Coextensive with Muscogee County).

Hernando de Soto, the Spanish explorer, first traveled parts of Georgia in 1540. British claims later conflicted with those of Spain. After obtaining a royal charter, Gen. James Oglethorpe established the first permanent settlement in Georgia in 1733 as a refuge for English debtors. In 1742, Oglethorpe defeated Spanish invaders in the Battle of Bloody Marsh.

A Confederate stronghold, Georgia was the scene of extensive military action during the Civil War. Union General William T. Sherman burned Atlanta and destroyed a 60-mile-wide path to the coast, where he captured Savannah in 1864.

The largest state east of the Mississippi, Georgia is typical of the changing South with an ever-increasing industrial development. Atlanta, largest city in the state, is the communications and transportation center for the Southeast and the area's chief distributor of goods.

Georgia leads the nation in the production of paper and board, tufted textile products, and processed chicken. Other major manufactured products are transportation equipment, food products, apparel, and chemicals.

Important agricultural products are corn, cotton, tobacco, soybeans, eggs, and peaches. Georgia produces twice as many peanuts as the next leading state. From its vast stands of pine come more than half of the world's resins and turpentine and 74.4 percent of the U.S. supply. Georgia is a leader in the production of marble, kaolin, barite, and bauxite.

Principal tourist attractions in Georgia include the Okefenokee National Wildlife Refuge, Andersonville Prison Park and National Cemetery, Chickamauga and Chattanooga National Military Park, the Little White House at Warm Springs where Pres. Franklin D. Roosevelt died in 1945, Sea Island, the enormous Confederate Memorial at Stone Mountain, Kennesaw Mountain National Battlefield Park, and Cumberland Island National Seashore.

Famous natives and residents: Conrad Aiken, poet; James Bowie, soldier; James Brown, singer; Jim Brown, actor and athlete; Erskine Caldwell, writer; James E. Carter, former president; Ray Charles, singer; Lucius D. Clay, banker and former general; Ty Cobb, baseball player; Ossie Davis, actor and writer; James Dickey, poet; Melvyn Douglas, actor; Rebecca Latimer Felton, first appointed woman U.S. senator; Roosevelt Grier, entertainer and former athlete; Oliver Hardy, comedian; Joel Chandler Harris, journalist and author; Larry Holmes, boxer; Miriam Hopkins, actress; Harry James, trumpeter; Jasper Johns, painter and sculptor; Bobby Jones, golfer; Stacy Keach, actor; DeForest Kelley, actor; Martin Luther King, Jr., civil rights leader; Gladys Knight, singer; Joseph R. Lamar, jurist; Juliette Gordon Low, U.S. Girl Scouts founder; Carson McCullers, novelist; Johnny Mercer, songwriter; Margaret Mitchell, novelist; Elijah Muhammad, religious leader; Jessye Norman, soprano; Otis Redding, singer; Burt Reynolds, actor; Jackie Robinson, baseball player; Dean Rusk, former secretary of state; Nipsey Russell, comedian; Alice Walker, author; Joanne Woodward, actress.

Hawaii

Capital: Honolulu (on Oahu)
Governor: Benjamin Cayetano, D (to Dec. 2002)
Lieut. Governor: Mazie Hirono, D
Senators: Daniel K. Akaka, D (to Jan. 2001); Daniel K. Inouye, D (to Jan. 2005)
Comptroller: Raymond Sato (to Dec. 2002)
Atty. General: Earl Anzai (to Dec. 2002)
Organized as territory: 1900
Entered Union (rank): Aug. 21, 1959 (50)
Motto: *Ua Mau Ke Ea O Ka Aina I Ka Pono* (The life of the land is perpetuated in righteousness)
State Symbols: flower, hibiscus (yellow) (1988); **song,** "Hawaii Ponoi" (1967); **bird,** nene (hawaiian goose) (1957); **tree,** kukui (candlenut) (1959);
Nickname: Aloha State (1959)
Origin of name: Uncertain. The islands may have been named by Hawaii Loa, their traditional discoverer. Or they may have been named after Hawaii or Hawaiki, the traditional home of the Polynesians.
10 largest cities[1] (1996 est.): Honolulu, 377,059; Hilo, 37,808; Kailua, 36,818; Kaneohe, 35,448; Waipahu, 31,435; Pearl City, 30,993; Waimalu, 29,967; Mililani Town, 29,359; Schofield Barracks, 19,597; Wahiawa, 17,386
Land area: 6,423 sq mi. (16,637 sq km)
Geographic center: Between islands of Hawaii and Maui
Number of counties: Four plus one non-functioning county (Kalawao)
Largest county by population and area: Honolulu, 864,571 (1999 est.); Hawaii, 4,028 sq mi.
State parks and historic sites: 67
Residents: Hawaiian
1999 resident population est.: 1,185,497
1990 resident census population (rank): 1,108,229 (41). **Male:** 563,891; **Female:** 544,338. **White:** 369,616 (33.4%); **Black:** 27,195 (2.5%); **American Indian:** 5,099 (0.5%); **Asian and Pacific Islander:** 685,236 (61.8%); **Other race:** 21,083 (1.9%); **Hispanic:** 81,390 (7.3%). **1990 percent population under 18:** 25.3; **65 and over:** 11.3; **median age:** 32.5.

1. Census Designated Place. There are no political boundaries to Honolulu or any other place, but statistical boundaries are assigned under state law.

First settled by Polynesians sailing from other Pacific islands between A.D. 300 and 600, Hawaii was visited in 1778 by British Captain James Cook, who called the group the Sandwich Islands.

Hawaii was a native kingdom throughout most of the 19th century, when the expansion of the vital sugar industry (pineapple came after 1898) meant increasing U.S. business and political involvement. In 1893, Queen Liliuokalani was deposed and a year later the Republic of Hawaii was established with Sanford B. Dole as president. Then, following its annexation in 1898, Hawaii became a U.S. territory in 1900.

The Japanese attack on the naval base at Pearl Harbor on Dec. 7, 1941, was directly responsible for U.S. entry into World War II.

Hawaii, 2,397 miles west-southwest of San Francisco, is a 1,523-mile chain of islets and eight main islands—Hawaii, Kahoolawe, Maui, Lanai, Molokai, Oahu, Kauai, and Niihau. The Northwestern Hawaiian Islands, other than Midway, are administratively part of Hawaii.

The temperature is mild and Hawaii's soil is fertile for tropical fruits and vegetables. Cane sugar, pineapple, and flowers and nursery products are the chief products. Hawaii also grows coffee beans, bananas, and macadamia nuts. The tourist business is Hawaii's largest source of outside income.

Hawaii's highest peak is Mauna Kea (13,796 ft.). Mauna Loa (13,679 ft.) is the largest volcanic mountain in the world by volume.

Among the major points of interest are Hawaii Volcanoes National Park (Hawaii), Haleakala National Park (Maui), Puuhonua o Honaunau National Historical Park (Hawaii), Polynesian Cultural Center (Oahu), the USS *Arizona* and USS *Missouri* Memorial at Pearl Harbor, The National Memorial Cemetery of the Pacific (Oahu), and Iolani Palace (the only royal palace in the U.S.), Bishop Museum, and Waikiki Beach (all in Honolulu).

Famous natives and residents: Salevaa Atisanoe (Konishiki), sumo wrestler; George Ariyoshi, first Japanese-American elected governor; Hiram Bingham, missionary; Charles R. Bishop, banker and philanthropist; Tia Carrere, singer, actress; Samuel N. Castle, missionary, founder of Castle & Cooke Ltd. with Amos S. Cooke, missionary and educator; Father Damien, priest; Sanford B. Dole, territorial governor; Jean Erdman, dancer, choreographer; Hiram L. Fong, first Chinese-American senator; Don Ho, entertainer; Gerrit P. Judd, advisor to the Hawaiian king; Kaahumanu, Hawaiian queen; Duke Paoa Kahanamoku, Olympic swimming champion; Kamehameha I, first Hawaiian king; Kamehameha V, last of the dynasty; George Parsons Lathrop, journalist and poet; Liliuokalani, queen, last Hawaiian monarch; Bette Midler, singer; Ellison Onizuka, astronaut; Kawaipuna Prejean, Hawaiian activist, proponent of Hawaiian sovereignty; Chad Rowan (Akebono), sumo wrestler; Harold Sakata, actor; Carolyn Suzanne Sapp, Miss America (1991); James Shigeta, actor; Claus Spreckels, developer of Hawaiian sugar industry; Don Stroud, actor; John Waihee, first Hawaiian elected Governor.

Idaho

Capital: Boise
Governor: Dirk Kempthorne, R (to Jan. 2003)
Lieut. Governor: C. L. "Butch" Otter, R (to Jan. 2003)
Senators: Larry E. Craig, R (to Jan. 2003); Mike Crapo, R (to Jan. 2005)
Secy. of State: Pete T. Cenarrusa, R (to Jan. 2003)
State Controller: J. D. Williams, D (to Jan. 2003)
Atty. General: Alan G. Lance, R (to Jan. 2003)
Treasurer: Ron G. Crane, R (to Jan. 2003)
Organized as territory: March 3, 1863
Entered Union (rank): July 3, 1890 (43)
Present constitution adopted: 1890
Motto: *Esto perpetua* (It is forever)
State Symbols: flower, syringa (1931); **tree,** white pine (1935); **bird,** mountain bluebird (1931); **horse,** Appaloosa (1975); **gem,** star garnet (1967); **song,** "Here We Have Idaho"; **folk dance,** square dance; **fish,** cutthroat trout (1990); **fossil,** Hagerman horse fossil (1988);
Nickname: Gem State
Origin of name: Unknown. Though popularly believed to be an Indian word, it is an invented name whose meaning is unknown.
10 largest cities (1998 est.): Boise, 157,452; Pocatello, 53,074; Idaho Falls, 48,122; Nampa, 41,951; Twin Falls, 33,296; Coeur d'Alene, 32,565; Lewiston, 30,363; Meridian, 25,377; Caldwell, 22,340; Moscow, 19,312
Land area: 82,751 sq mi. (214,325 sq km)
Geographic center: In Custer Co., at Custer, SW of Challis
Number of counties: 44, plus small part of Yellowstone National Park
Largest county by population and area: Ada, 283,402 (1999 est.); Idaho, 8,485 sq mi.
State forests: 881,000 ac.
State parks: 23
Residents: Idahoan

1999 resident population est.: 1,251,700
1990 resident census population (rank): 1,006,749
(42). **Male:** 500,956; **Female:** 505,793. **White:**
950,451 (94.4%); **Black:** 3,370 (0.3%); **American
Indian:** 13,780 (1.4%); **Asian:** 9,365 (0.9%); **Other
race:** 29,783 (3.0%); **Hispanic:** 52,927 (5.3%). **1990
percent population under 18:** 30.6; **65 and over:**
12.0; **median age:** 31.5.

After its acquisition by the U.S. as part of the
Louisiana Purchase in 1803, the region was
explored by Meriwether Lewis and William Clark in
1805–06. Northwest boundary disputes with Great
Britain were settled by the Oregon Treaty in 1846
and the first permanent U.S. settlement in Idaho was
established by the Mormons at Franklin in 1860.

After gold was discovered on Orofino Creek in
1860, prospectors swarmed into the territory, but left
little more than a number of ghost towns.

In the 1870s, growing white occupation of Indian
lands led to a series of battles between U.S. forces
and the Nez Percé, Bannock, and Sheepeater tribes.

Mining, lumbering, and irrigation farming have
been important for years. Idaho produces more than
one fifth of all the silver mined in the U.S. It also
ranks high among the states in antimony, lead,
cobalt, garnet, phosphate rock, vanadium, zinc, and
mercury.

Idaho's most impressive growth began when
World War II military needs made processing agricultural products a big industry, particularly the
dehydrating and freezing of potatoes. The state produces about one fourth of the nation's potato crop,
as well as wheat, apples, corn, barley, sugar beets,
and hops.

With the growth of winter sports, tourism now
outranks mining in dollar revenue. Idaho's many
streams and lakes provide fishing, camping, and
boating sites. The nation's largest elk herds draw
hunters from all over the world and the famed Sun
Valley resort attracts thousands of visitors to its
swimming and skiing facilities.

Other points of interest are the Craters of the Moon
National Monument; Nez Percé National Historic
Park, which includes many sites visited by Lewis and
Clark; and the State Historical Museum in Boise.

Famous natives and residents: Joe Albertson, grocery
chain founder; Cecil Andrus, former governor; T. H. Bell,
educator; Ezra Taft Benson, Eisenhower's Secretary of
Agriculture, pres. LDS church, marketing specialist; William
E. Borah, former senator; Gutzon Borglum, Mt. Rushmore
sculptor; Carol R. Brink, author; Frank F. Church, former
senator; Fred Dubois, senator; Vardis Fisher, novelist;
Lawrence H. Gipson, historian; Ernest Hemingway, author;
Mariel Hemingway, actress; Chief Joseph, Nez Percé
chief; Harmon Killebrew, baseball player; Jerry Kramer,
football player, author; Ezra Pound, poet; Sacagawea,
Shoshonean guide; J. R. Simplot, industrialist; Robert E.
Smylie, political leader; Henry Spalding, missionary; Frank
Steunenberg, former governor; Picabo Street, skier; David
Tompson, founded first trading post; Lana Turner, actress.

Illinois

Capital: Springfield
Governor: George H. Ryan, R (to Jan. 2003)
Lieut. Governor: Corinne G. Wood, R (to Jan. 2003)
Senators: Richard J. Durbin, D (to Jan. 2003); Peter G.
Fitzgerald, R (to Jan. 2005)
Atty. General: Jim Ryan, R (to Jan. 2003)
Secy. of State: Jesse White, D (to Jan. 2003)
Comptroller: Daniel W. Hynes, D (to Jan. 2003)
Treasurer: Judith Barr Topinka, R (to Jan. 2003)
Organized as territory: Feb. 3, 1809

Entered Union (rank): Dec. 3, 1818 (21)
Present constitution adopted: 1970
Motto: State sovereignty, national union
State Symbols: flower, violet (1908); **tree,** white oak
(1973); **bird,** cardinal (1929); **animal,** white-tailed deer
(1982); **fish,** bluegill (1987); **insect,** monarch butterfly
(1975); **song,** "Illinois" (1925); **mineral,** fluorite (1965);
Nickname: Prairie State
Origin of name: Algonquin for "tribe of superior men"
10 largest cities (1998 est.): Chicago, 2,802,079;
Rockford, 143,656; Aurora, 124,736; Springfield,
117,098; Naperville, 117,091; Peoria, 111,148; Joliet,
92,285; Elgin, 87,507; Decatur, 79,972; Arlington
Heights, 76,522
Land area: 55,593 sq mi. (143,987 sq km)
Geographic center: Chestnut, on Illinois route 54
between Mt. Pulaski and Clinton.
Number of counties: 102
Largest county by population and area: Cook,
5,192,326 (1999 est.); McLean, 1,184 sq mi.
Public use areas: 187 (275,000 ac.), incl. state parks,
memorials, forests and conservation areas
Residents: Illinoisan
1999 resident population est.: 12,128,370
1990 resident census population (rank): 11,430,602
(6). **Male:** 5,552,233; **Female:** 5,878,369. **White:**
8,952,978 (78.3%); **Black:** 1,694,273 (14.8%); **American Indian:** 21,836 (0.2%); **Asian:** 285,311 (2.5%);
Other race: 476,204 (4.2%); **Hispanic:** 904,446
(7.9%). **1990 percent population under 18:** 25.8; **65
and over:** 12.6; **median age:** 32.7.

French explorers Jacques Marquette and Louis
Joliet, in 1673, were the first Europeans of record to
visit the region. In 1699 French settlers established
the first permanent settlement at Cahokia, near
present-day East St. Louis.

Great Britain obtained the region at the end of the
French and Indian Wars in 1763. The area figured
prominently in frontier struggles during the Revolutionary War and in Indian wars during the early 19th
century.

Significant episodes in the state's early history
include the growing migration of Eastern settlers
following the opening of the Erie Canal in 1825; the
Black Hawk War, which virtually ended the Indian
troubles in the area; and the rise of Abraham Lincoln from farm laborer to president.

Today, Illinois stands high in manufacturing, coal
mining, agriculture, and oil production. The sprawling Chicago district (including a slice of Indiana) is
a great iron and steel producer, meat packer, grain
exchange, and railroad center. Chicago is also
famous as a Great Lakes port.

The state manufactures a great variety of industrial and consumer products: railroad cars, clothing,
furniture, tractors, liquor, watches, and farm implements are just some of the items made in its factories and plants.

Illinois ranks third in the nation in the sale of
agricultural products, second in corn and soybeans,
and fourth in hog production.

Central Illinois is noted for shrines and memorials
associated with the life of Abraham Lincoln. In
Springfield are the Lincoln Home, the Lincoln Tomb,
and the restored Old State Capitol. Other points of
interest are the home of Mormon leader Joseph Smith
in Nauvoo and, in Chicago: the Art Institute, Field
Museum, Museum of Science and Industry, Shedd
Aquarium, Adler Planetarium, Merchandise Mart, and
Chicago Portage National Historic Site.

Famous natives and residents: Franklin Pierce Adams, author; Jane Addams, social worker; Mary Astor, actress; Jack Benny, comedian; Black Hawk, Sauk Indian chief; Harry A. Blackmun, jurist; Ray Bradbury, author; William Jennings Bryan, orator and politician; Edgar Rice Burroughs, novelist; Gower Champion, choreographer; John Chancellor, TV commentator; Raymond Chandler, writer; Jimmy Connors, tennis champion; James Gould Cozzens, novelist; Richard J. Daley, former mayor of Chicago; Miles Davis, musician; Peter DeVries, novelist; Walt Disney, film animator and producer; John Dos Passos, author; James T. Farrell, novelist; Betty Friedan, feminist; Benny Goodman, musician; John Gunther, author; Ernest Hemingway, author; Charlton Heston, actor; Wild Bill Hickok, scout; William Holden, actor; Rock Hudson, actor; Burl Ives, singer; James Jones, novelist; John Jones, civil rights leader; Quincy Jones, composer; Keokuk (Watchful Fox), chief of the Sac and Fox Indians; Walter Kerr, drama critic; Shelley Long, actress; Archibald MacLeish, poet; David Mamet, playwright; Robert A. Millikan, physicist; Sherrill Milnes, baritone; Bill Murray, actor; Bob Newhart, actor and comedian; William S. Paley, broadcasting executive; Drew Pearson, columnist; Richard Pryor, comedian and actor; Ronald Reagan, former President and actor; Carl Sandburg, poet; Sam Shepard, playwright; William L. Shirer, author and historian; John Paul Stevens, jurist; McLean Stevenson, actor; Preston Sturges, director; Gloria Swanson, actress; Carl Van Doren, writer and educator; Melvin Van Peebles, playwright; Irving Wallace, novelist; Alfred Wallenstein, conductor; Raquel Welch, actress; Oprah Winfrey, television talk show host and actress; Florenz Ziegfeld, theatrical producer.

Indiana

Capital: Indianapolis
Governor: Frank O'Bannon, D (to Jan. 2001)
Lieut. Governor: Joseph E. Kernan, D (to Jan. 2001)
Senators: Evan Bayh, D (to Jan. 2005); Richard G. Lugar, R (to Jan. 2001)
Secy. of State: Sue Anne Gilroy, R (to Dec. 2002)
Treasurer: Tim Berry, R (to Feb. 2003)
Atty. General: Karen Freeman-Wilson, D (to Jan. 2001)
Auditor: Connie Kay Nass, R (to Dec. 2002)
Organized as territory: May 7, 1800
Entered Union (rank): Dec. 11, 1816 (19)
Present constitution adopted: 1851
Motto: The Crossroads of America
State Symbols: flower, peony (1957); **tree,** tulip tree (1931); **bird,** cardinal (1933); **song,** "On the Banks of the Wabash, Far Away" (1913); **river,** Wabash; **stone,** limestone;
Official language: English
Nickname: Hoosier State
Origin of name: Meaning "land of Indians"
10 largest cities (1998 est.): Indianapolis, 741,304; Fort Wayne, 185,716; Evansville, 122,779; Gary, 108,469; South Bend, 99,417; Hammond, 78,212; Muncie, 67,476; Bloomington, 65,065; Anderson, 58,528; Terre Haute, 53,355
Land area: 35,870 sq mi. (92,904 sq km)
Geographic center: In Boone Co., 14 mi. NNW of Indianapolis
Number of Counties: 92
Largest county by population and area: Marion, 810,946 (1999 est.); Allen, 657 sq mi.
State parks: 23 (56,409 ac.)
State historic sites: 17 (2,007 ac.)
Residents: Indianan, Indianian
1999 resident population est.: 5,942,901
1990 resident census population(rank): 5,544,159 (14). **Male:** 2,688,281; **Female:** 2,855,878. **White:** 5,020,700 (90.6%); **Black:** 432,092 (7.8%); **American Indian:** 12,720 (0.2%); **Asian:** 37,617 (0.7%); **Other race:** 41,030 (0.7%); **Hispanic:** 98,788 (1.8%). **1990 percent population under 18:** 26.3; **65 and over:** 12.6; **median age:** 32.7.

First explored for France by sieur de la Salle in 1679–1680, the region figured importantly in the Franco-British struggle for North America that culminated with British victory in 1763.

George Rogers Clark led American forces against the British in the area during the Revolutionary War and, prior to becoming a state, Indiana was the scene of frequent Indian uprisings until the victory of Gen. William Henry Harrison at Tippecanoe in 1811.

Indiana's 41-mile Lake Michigan waterfront—one of the world's great industrial centers—turns out iron, steel, and oil products. Products include automobile parts and accessories, mobile homes and recreational vehicles, truck and bus bodies, aircraft engines, farm machinery, and fabricated structural steel. Wood office furniture and pharmaceuticals are also manufactured.

The state is a leader in agriculture with corn the principal crop. Hogs, soybeans, wheat, oats, rye, tomatoes, onions, and poultry also contribute heavily to Indiana's agricultural output. Much of the building limestone used in the U.S. is quarried in Indiana, which is also a large producer of coal.

Wyandotte Cave, one of the largest in the U.S., is located in Crawford County in southern Indiana, and West Baden and French Lick are well known for their mineral springs. Other attractions include Indiana Dunes National Lakeshore, Indianapolis Motor Speedway, Lincoln Boyhood National Memorial, and the George Rogers Clark National Historical Park.

Famous natives and residents: George Ade, humorist; Leon Ames, actor; Anne Baxter, actress; Albert J. Beveridge, political leader; Larry Bird, basketball player; Bill Blass, fashion designer; Frank Borman, astronaut; Hoagy Carmichael, songwriter; James Dean, actor; Eugene V. Debs, Socialist leader; Lloyd C. Douglas, author; Theodore Dreiser, writer; Bernard F. Gimbel, merchant; Virgil Grissom, astronaut; Phil Harris, actor and band leader; John Milton Hay, statesman; James R. Hoffa, labor leader; Michael Jackson, singer; Buck Jones, actor; Alfred C. Kinsey, zoologist; David Letterman, TV host and comedian; Eli Lilly, pharmaceuticals manufacturer; Carole Lombard, actress; Shelley Long, actress; Marjorie Main, actress; James McCracken, tenor; Joaquin Miller, poet; Paul Osborn, playwright; Cole Porter, songwriter; Gene Stratton Porter, naturalist and author; Ernest Taylor Pyle, journalist; J. Danforth Quayle, former vice president; James Whitcomb Riley, poet; Knute Rockne, football coach; Ned Rorem, composer; Red Skelton, comedian; Rex Stout, mystery writer; Booth Tarkington, author; Twyla Tharp, dancer and choreographer; Forrest Tucker, actor; Harold C. Urey, physicist; Kurt Vonnegut, Jr., author; Dan Wakefield, author; Robert Wise, director; Jessamyn West, novelist; Wendell Willkie, lawyer; Wilbur Wright, inventor.

Iowa

Capital: Des Moines
Governor: Tom Vilsack, D (to Jan. 2003)
Lieut. Governor: Sally Pederson, D (to Jan. 2003)
Senators: Chuck Grassley, R (to Jan. 2005); Tom Harkin, D (to Jan. 2003)
Secy. of State: Chet Culver, D (to Jan. 2003)
Treasurer: Michael L. Fitzgerald, D (to Jan. 2003)
Atty. General: Tom Miller, D (to Jan. 2003)
Organized as territory: June 12, 1838
Entered Union (rank): Dec. 28, 1846 (29)
Present constitution adopted: 1857
Motto: Our liberties we prize and our rights we will maintain
State Symbols: flower, wild rose (1897); **bird,** eastern goldfinch (1933); **colors,** red, white, and blue (in state flag); **song,** "Song of Iowa";
Nickname: Hawkeye State
Origin of name: Probably from an Indian word meaning "this is the place" or "the Beautiful Land"

10 largest cities (1998 est.): Des Moines, 191,293;
Cedar Rapids, 114,563; Davenport, 96,842; Sioux City,
82,697; Waterloo, 63,703; Iowa City, 60,897; Dubuque,
56,467; Council Bluffs, 56,312; Ames, 48,415; West
Des Moines, 42,333
Land area: 55,875 sq mi. (144,716 sq km)
Geographic center: In Story Co., 5 mi. NE of Ames
Number of counties: 99
Largest county by population and area: Polk, 364,672
(1999 est.); Kossuth, 973 sq mi.
State forests: 4 (39,500 ac.)
State parks: 83 (53,000 ac.)
Residents: Iowan
1999 resident population est.: 2,869,413
1990 resident census population (rank): 2,776,755 (30).
Male: 1,344,802; **Female:** 1,431,953. **White:** 2,683,090
(96.6%); **Black:** 48,090 (1.7%); **American Indian:**
7,349 (0.3%); **Asian:** 25,476 (0.9%); **Other race:**
12,750 (0.5%); **Hispanic:** 32,647 (1.2%). **1990 percent
population under 18:** 25.9; **65 and over:** 15.3;
median age: 34.0.

The first Europeans to visit the area were the
French explorers Father Jacques Marquette and
Louis Joliet in 1673. The U.S. obtained control of
the area in 1803 as part of the Louisiana Purchase.

During the first half of the 19th century, there was
heavy fighting between white settlers and Indians.
Lands were taken from the Indians after the Black
Hawk War in 1832 and again in 1836 and 1837.

When Iowa became a state in 1846, its capital was
Iowa City; the more centrally located Des Moines
became the new capital in 1857. At that time, the
state's present boundaries were also drawn.

Although Iowa produces a tenth of the nation's
food supply, the value of Iowa's manufactured products is twice that of its agriculture. Major industries
are food and associated products, non-electrical
machinery, electrical equipment, printing and publishing, and fabricated products.

Iowa stands in a class by itself as an agricultural
state. Its farms sell over $10 billion worth of crops
and livestock annually. Iowa leads the nation in all
corn, soybean, and hog marketings, and comes in
third in total livestock sales. Iowa's forests produce
hardwood lumber, particularly walnut, and its mineral products include cement, limestone, sand,
gravel, gypsum, and coal.

Tourist attractions include the Herbert Hoover
birthplace and library near West Branch; the Amana
Colonies; Fort Dodge Historical Museum, Fort, and
Stockade; the Iowa State Fair at Des Moines in
August; and the Effigy Mounds National Monument,
a prehistoric Indian burial site at Marquette.
Famous natives and residents: Bix Beiderbecke, jazz
musician; Norman Borlang, plant pathologist, geneticist, and
Nobel Peace Prize winner; William "Buffalo Bill" F. Cody,
scout; Johnny Carson, TV entertainer; Gardner Cowles, Jr.,
publisher; Simon Estes, bass-baritone; William Frawley,
actor; George H. Gallup, poll taker; Susan Glaspell, writer;
Herbert Hoover, former president; MacKinlay Kantor,
novelist; Charles A. Kettering, inventor; Ann Landers,
columnist; Cloris Leachman, actress; John L. Lewis, labor
leader; Glenn L. Martin, aviator and manufacturer; Elsa
Maxwell, writer; Frederick L. Maytag, inventor and
manufacturer; Glenn Miller, bandleader; Kate Mulgrew,
actress; Harriet Nelson, actress; Nathan M. Pusey, educator;
David Rabe, playwright; Harry Reasoner, TV commentator;
Donna Reed, actress; Lillian Russell, soprano; Robert
Schiller, evangelist; Wallace Stegner, novelist and critic; Billy
Sunday, evangelist; James A. Van Allen, space physicist;
Abigail Van Buren, columnist; Henry A. Wallace, statesman
and vice president; John Wayne, actor; Andy Williams,
singer; Meredith Willson, composer; Grant Wood, painter.

Kansas

Capital: Topeka
Governor: Bill Graves, R (to Jan. 2003)
Lieut. Governor: Gary Sherrer, R (to Jan. 2003)
Senators: Sam Brownback, R (to Jan. 2005);
Pat Roberts, R (to Jan. 2003)
Secy. of State: Ron Thornburgh, R (to Jan. 2003)
Treasurer: Tim Shallenburger, R (to Jan. 2003)
Atty. General: Carla Stovall, R (to Jan. 2003)
Commission of Insurance: Kathleen Sebelius, D
(to Jan. 2003)
Organized as territory: May 30, 1854
Entered Union (rank): Jan. 29, 1861 (34)
Present constitution adopted: 1859
Motto: *Ad astra per aspera* (To the stars through
difficulties)
State Symbols: flower, sunflower (1903); **tree,**
cottonwood (1937); **bird,** western meadowlark (1937);
animal, buffalo (1955); **song,** "Home on the Range"
(1947);
Nicknames: Sunflower State; Jayhawk State
Origin of name: From a Sioux word meaning "people of
the south wind"
10 largest cities (1998 est.): Wichita, 329,211; Kansas
City, 141,297; Overland Park, 139,685; Topeka,
118,977; Olathe, 85,035; Lawrence, 74,244; Shawnee,
45,250; Salina, 44,022; Manhattan, 41,318;
Leavenworth, 39,227
Land area: 81,823 sq mi. (211,922 sq km)
Geographic center: In Barton Co., 15 mi. NE of
Great Bend
Number of counties: 105
Largest county by population and area: Sedgwick,
451,684 (1999 est.); Butler, 1,428 sq mi.
State parks: 22 (14,394 ac.)
Residents: Kansan
1999 resident population est.: 2,654,052
1990 resident census population (rank): 2,477,574
(32). **Male:** 1,214,645; **Female:** 1,262,929. **White:**
2,231,986 (90.1%); **Black:** 143,076 (5.8%); **American
Indian:** 21,965 (0.9%); **Asian:** 31,750 (1.3%); **Other
race:** 48,797 (2.0%); **Hispanic:** 93,670 (3.8%). **1990
percent population under 18:** 26.7; **65 and over:**
13.8; **median age:** 32.8.

Spanish explorer Francisco de Coronado, in 1541,
is considered the first European to have traveled this
region. Sieur de la Salle's extensive land claims for
France (1682) included present-day Kansas. Ceded
to Spain by France in 1763, the territory reverted to
France in 1800 and was sold to the U.S. as part of
the Louisiana Purchase in 1803.

Lewis and Clark, Zebulon Pike, and Stephen H.
Long explored the region between 1803 and 1819.
The first permanent settlements in Kansas were
outposts—Fort Leavenworth (1827), Fort Scott
(1842), and Fort Riley (1853)—established to protect travelers along the Santa Fe and Oregon Trails.

Just before the Civil War, the conflict between the
pro- and anti-slavery forces earned the region the
grim title of Bleeding Kansas.

Today, wheat fields, oil-well derricks, herds of
cattle, and grain-storage elevators are chief features
of the Kansas landscape. A leading wheat-growing
state, Kansas also raises corn, sorghum, oats, barley,
soybeans, and potatoes. Kansas stands high in petroleum production and mines zinc, coal, salt, and lead.
It is also the nation's leading producer of helium.

Wichita is one of the nation's leading aircraft-
manufacturing centers, ranking first in production of
private aircraft. Kansas City is an important transportation, milling, and meat-packing center.

Points of interest include the Kansas History Center at Topeka, the Eisenhower boyhood home and the new Eisenhower Memorial Museum and Presidential Library at Abilene, John Brown's cabin at Osawatomie, recreated Front Street in Dodge City, Fort Larned (once the most important military post on the Santa Fe Trail), and Fort Leavenworth and Fort Riley.

Famous natives and residents: Roscoe "Fatty" Arbuckle, actor; Clarence D. Batchelor, political cartoonist; Gwendolyn Brooks, poet; Walter P. Chrysler, auto manufacturer; Clark M. Clifford, former secretary of defense; John Steuart Curry, painter; Amelia Earhart, aviator; Milton S. Eisenhower, educator; Gary Hart, politician; William Inge, playwright; Walter Johnson, baseball pitcher; Osa L. Johnson, documentary film producer; Buster Keaton, comedian; Emmett Kelly, clown; Stan Kenton, jazz musician; James Lehrer, broadcast journalist; Edgar Lee Masters, poet; Mary McCarthy, actress; Hattie McDaniel, actress; Karl Menninger, psychiatrist; Gordon Parks, film director; Zasu Pitts, actress; Samuel Ramey, opera singer; Charles Robinson, statesman and first governor; Charles (Buddy) Rogers, actor; Damon Runyon, journalist; Eugene W. Smith, photojournalist; Milburn Stone, actor; John Cameron Swayze, news commentator; William Allen White, journalist; Charles E. Whittaker, jurist; Jess Willard, boxer.

Kentucky

Capital: Frankfort
Governor: Paul E. Patton, D (to Dec. 2003)
Lieut. Governor: Stephen L. Henry, D (to Dec. 2003)
Senators: Jim Bunning, R (to Jan. 2005);
    Mitch McConnell, R (to Jan. 2003)
Secy. of State: John Y. Brown III, D (to Dec. 2003)
Treasurer: Jonathan Miller
    (to Dec. 2003)
Auditor: Ed Hatchett, D (to Dec. 2003)
Atty. General: A. B. "Ben" Chandler, D (to Dec. 2003)
Entered Union (rank): June 1, 1792 (15)
Present constitution adopted: 1891
Motto: United we stand, divided we fall
State Symbols: tree, tulip poplar (1994); **flower,** goldenrod; **bird,** Kentucky cardinal; **song,** "My Old Kentucky Home";
Nickname: Bluegrass State
Origin of name: From an Iroquoian word "Ken-tah-ten" meaning "land of tomorrow"
10 largest cities (1998 est.): Louisville, 255,045; Lexington-Fayette, 241,749; Owensboro, 54,041; Bowling Green, 44,822; Covington, 40,389; Hopkinsville, 32,045; Richmond, 27,644; Henderson, 26,457; Frankfort, 26,418; Paducah, 25,883
Land area: 39,732 sq mi. (102,907 sq km)
Geographic center: In Marion Co., 3 mi. NNW of Lebanon
Number of counties: 120
Largest county by population and area: Jefferson, 672,900 (1999 est.); Pike, 788 sq mi.
State forests: 9 (44,173 ac.)
State parks: 49
Residents: Kentuckian
1999 resident population est.: 3,960,825
1990 resident census population (rank): 3,685,296 (23). **Male:** 1,785,235; **Female:** 1,900,061. **White:** 3,391,832 (92.0%); **Black:** 262,907 (7.1%); **American Indian:** 5,769 (0.2%); **Asian:** 17,812 (0.5%); **Other race:** 6,976 (0.2%); **Hispanic:** 21,984 (0.6%). **1990 percent population below age 18:** 25.9; **65 and over:** 12.7; **median age:** 32.9.

Kentucky was the first region west of the Allegheny Mountains to be settled by American pioneers. James Harrod established the first permanent settlement at Harrodsburg in 1774; the following year

Daniel Boone, who had explored the area in 1767, blazed the Wilderness Trail and founded Boonesboro.

Politically, the Kentucky region was originally part of Virginia, but early statehood was gained in 1792. During the Civil War, as a slaveholding state with a considerable abolitionist population, Kentucky was caught in the middle of the conflict, supplying both Union and Confederate forces with thousands of troops.

In recent years, manufacturing has shown important gains, particularly in automotive assembly and parts manufacturing. Kentucky also prides itself on producing some of the nation's best tobacco, horses, and whiskey. Corn, soybeans, wheat, fruit, hogs, cattle, and dairy products are among the agricultural items produced.

Among the manufactured items produced in the state are motor vehicles, furniture, aluminum ware, brooms, apparel, lumber products, machinery, textiles, and iron and steel products. Kentucky also produces significant amounts of petroleum, natural gas, fluorspar, clay, and stone. However, coal accounts for 90% of the total mineral income.

Louisville, the largest city, famed for the Kentucky Derby at Churchill Downs, is also the location of a large state university, whiskey distilleries, and cigarette factories. The Bluegrass country around Lexington is the home of some of the world's finest race horses. Other attractions are Mammoth Cave, the George S. Patton, Jr., Military Museum at Fort Knox, and Old Fort Harrod State Park.

Famous natives and residents: John Adair, pioneer and political leader; Muhammad Ali, boxer; Alben W. Barkley, former vice president; Louis D. Brandeis, jurist; John Mason Brown, critic; Kit Carson, scout; Champ Clark, politician; Rosemary Clooney, singer; Irvin S. Cobb, humorist; Jefferson Davis, president of the Confederacy; Irene Dunne, actress; Crystal Gayle, singer; David W. Griffith, film producer; John M. Harlan, jurist; Elizabeth Hardwick, writer; Casey Jones, celebrated locomotive engineer; Abraham Lincoln, former president; Loretta Lynn, singer; Carry Amelia Nation, temperance leader; Patricia Neal, actress; George Reeves, actor; Wiley B. Rutledge, jurist; Diane Sawyer, broadcast journalist; Phil Simms, football player; Adlai Stevenson, former vice president; Allen Tate, poet and critic; Hunter Thompson, writer; Frederick M. Vinson, jurist; Robert Penn Warren, novelist.

Louisiana

Capital: Baton Rouge
Governor: Murphy J. "Mike" Foster, R (to Jan. 2004)
Lieut. Governor: Kathleen Blanco, D (to Jan. 2004)
Senators: John B. Breaux, D (to Jan. 2005);
    Mary Landrieu, D (to Jan. 2003)
Secy. of State: W. Fox McKeithen, R (to Jan. 2004)
Treasurer: John Neely Kennedy, D (to Jan. 2004)
Atty. General: Richard P. Ieyoub, D (to Jan. 2004)
Organized as territory: March 26, 1804
Entered Union (rank): April 30, 1812 (18)
Present constitution adopted: 1974
Motto: Union, justice, and confidence
State Symbols: flower, magnolia (1900); **tree,** bald cypress (1963); **bird,** eastern brown pelican (1958); **songs,** "Give Me Louisiana" and "You Are My Sunshine";
Nickname: Pelican State
Origin of name: In honor of Louis XIV of France
10 largest cities (1998 est.): New Orleans, 465,538; Baton Rouge, 211,551; Shreveport, 188,319; Lafayette, 113,615; Kenner, 71,641; Lake Charles, 70,766; Bossier City, 56,637; Monroe, 53,612; Alexandria, 45,800; New Iberia, 32,664
Land area: 43,566 sq mi. (112,836 sq km)

Geographic center: In Avoyelles Parish, 3 mi. SE of Marksville
Number of parishes (counties): 64
Largest parish by population and area: Orleans, 460,913 (1999 est.); Vernon, 1,328 sq mi.
State forests: 1 (8,000 ac.)
State parks: 30 (13,932 ac.)
Residents: Louisianan, Louisianian
1999 resident population est.: 4,372,035
1990 resident census population (rank): 4,219,973 (21). **Male:** 2,031,386; **Female:** 2,188,587. **White:** 2,839,138 (67.3%); **Black:** 1,299,281 (30.8%); **American Indian:** 18,541 (0.4%); **Asian:** 41,099 (1.0%); **Other race:** 21,914 (0.5%); **Hispanic:** 93,044 (2.2%). **1990 percent population under 18:** 29.1; **65 and over:** 11.1; **median age:** 30.9.

Louisiana has a rich, colorful historical background. Early Spanish explorers were Alvárez Piñeda, 1519; Álvar Núñez Cabeza de Vaca, 1528; and Hernando De Soto in 1541. Sieur de la Salle reached the mouth of the Mississippi and claimed all the land drained by it and its tributaries for Louis XIV of France in 1682.

Louisiana became a French crown colony in 1731, was ceded to Spain in 1763, returned to France in 1800, and was sold by Napoleon to the U.S. as part of the Louisiana Purchase (with large territories to the north and northwest) in 1803.

In 1815, Gen. Andrew Jackson's troops defeated a larger British army in the Battle of New Orleans, neither side aware that the treaty ending the War of 1812 had been signed.

Louisiana is a leader in natural gas, salt, petroleum, and sulfur production. Much of the oil and sulfur comes from offshore deposits. The state also produces large crops of sweet potatoes, rice, sugar cane, pecans, soybeans, corn, and cotton.

Leading manufactured items include chemicals, processed food, petroleum and coal products, paper, lumber and wood products, transportation equipment, and apparel.

Louisiana marshes supply most of the nation's muskrat fur as well as that of opossum, raccoon, mink, and otter, and large numbers of game birds.

Major points of interest include New Orleans with its French Quarter and Superdome, plantation homes near Natchitoches and New Iberia, Cajun country in the Mississippi Delta region, Chalmette National Historical Park, and the state capital at Baton Rouge.

Famous natives and residents: Louis Armstrong, musician; Geoffrey Beene, fashion designer; Truman Capote, writer; Kitty Carlisle, singer and actress; Van Cliburn, concert pianist; Michael De Bakey, heart surgeon; Fats Domino, musician; Donna Douglas, actress; Louis Moreau Gottschalk, pianist and composer; Jean Laffite, privateer; Lillian Hellman, playwright; Al Hirt, trumpeter; Mahalia Jackson, gospel singer; Jean Laffite, privateer; Dorothy Lamour, actress; John A. Lejeune, Marine Corps general; Elmore Leonard, author; Jerry Lee Lewis, singer; Huey P. Long, politician; Wynton Marsalis, musician; Jelly Roll Morton, jazz musician and composer; Huey Newton, black activist; Marguerite Piazza, soprano; Paul Prudhomme, chef; Howard K. Smith, TV commentator; Ben Turpin, comedian; Ray Walston, actor; Edward Douglas White, jurist.

Maine

Capital: Augusta
Governor: Angus S. King, Jr., I (to Jan. 2003)
Senators: Susan Collins, R (to Jan. 2003); Olympia J. Snowe, R (to Jan. 2001)
Secy. of State: Dan A. Gwadosky, D (to Jan. 1999)

Controller: Carol Whitney, R (to Jan. 1999)
Atty. General: Andrew Ketterer, D (to Jan. 1999)
Entered Union (rank): March 15, 1820 (23)
Present constitution adopted: 1820
Motto: *Dirigo* (I lead)
State Symbols: flower, white pine cone and tassel (1895); **tree,** white pine tree (1945); **bird,** chickadee (1927); **fish,** landlocked salmon (1969); **mineral,** tourmaline (1971); **song,** "State of Maine Song" (1937); **animal,** moose (1979); **cat,** Maine coon cat (1985); **fossil,** *pertica quadrifaria* (1985); **insect,** honeybee (1975);
Nickname: Pine Tree State
Origin of name: First used to distinguish the mainland from the offshore islands. It has been considered a compliment to Henrietta Maria, queen of Charles I of England. She was said to have owned the province of Mayne in France.
10 largest cities (1998 est.): Portland, 62,786; Lewiston, 36,186; Bangor, 30,508; South Portland, 22,810; Auburn, 22,617; Biddeford, 20,851; Augusta, 19,978; Westbrook, 16,679; Waterville, 16,263; Saco, 16,068
Largest town (1990 census): Brunswick, 20,906
Land area: 30,865 sq mi. (79,939 sq km)
Geographic center: In Piscataquis Co., 18 mi. N of Dover-Foxcroft
Number of counties: 16
Largest county by population and area: Cumberland, 256,437 (1999 est.); Aroostook, 6,672 sq mi.
State forests: 1 (21,000 ac.)
State parks: 26 (247,627 ac.)
State historic sites: 18 (403 ac.)
Residents: Mainer
1999 resident population est.: 1,253,040
1990 resident census population (rank): 1,227,928 (38). **Male:** 597,850; **Female:** 630,078. **White:** 1,208,360 (98.4%); **Black:** 5,138 (0.4%); **American Indian:** 5,998 (0.5%); **Asian:** 6,683 (0.5%); **Other race:** 1,749 (0.1%); **Hispanic:** 6,829 (0.6%).; **median age:** 33.8

John Cabot and his son, Sebastian, are believed to have visited the Maine coast in 1498. However, the first permanent English settlements were not established until more than a century later, in 1623.

The first naval action of the Revolutionary War occurred in 1775 when colonials captured the British sloop *Margaretta* off Machias on the Maine coast. In that same year, the British burned Falmouth (now Portland).

Long governed by Massachusetts, Maine became the 23rd state as part of the Missouri Compromise in 1820.

Maine produces 98% of the nation's low-bush blueberries. Farm income is also derived from apples, potatoes, dairy products, and vegetables, with poultry and eggs the largest selling items.

The state is one of the world's largest pulp-paper producers. With almost 89% of its area forested, Maine turns out wood products from boats to toothpicks.

Maine leads the world in the production of the familiar flat tins of sardines, producing more than 75 million of them annually. Lobstermen normally catch 50% of the nation's total of lobsters. The 1996 catch was 16,435 metric tons, the second-largest lobster catch in history.

A scenic seacoast, beaches, lakes, mountains, and resorts make Maine a popular vacationland. There are more than 2,500 lakes and 5,000 streams, plus 26 state parks to attract hunters, fishermen, skiers, and campers.

Major points of interest are Bar Harbor, Acadia National Park, Allagash National Wilderness Waterway, the Wadsworth-Longfellow House in Portland, Roosevelt Campobello International Park, and the St. Croix Island National Monument.

Famous natives and residents: F. Lee Bailey, defense attorney; Charles F. Browne (Artemus Ward), humorist; Cyrus Curtis, publisher; Dorothea Dix, civil rights reformer; John Ford, film director; Melville Fuller, jurist; Marsden Hartley, painter; Henry Wadsworth Longfellow, poet; Sarah Orne Jewett, author; Stephen King, writer; Linda Lavin, actress; Edna St. Vincent Millay, poet; Marston Morse, mathematician; Frank Munsey, publisher; Walter Piston, composer; George Putnam, publisher; Kenneth Roberts, historical novelist; Edwin Arlington Robinson, poet; Margaret Chase Smith, politician; Samantha Smith, peacemaker and actress; John Hay Whitney, publisher.

Maryland

Capital: Annapolis
Governor: Parris N. Glendening, D (to Jan. 2003)
Lieut. Gov.: Kathleen Kennedy Townsend, D (to Jan. 2003)
Senators: Barbara A. Mikulski, D (to Jan. 2005); Paul S. Sarbanes, D (to Jan. 2001)
Secy. of State: John T. Willis, D (to Jan. 2003)
Comptroller of the Treasury: William Donald Schaefer, D (to Jan. 2003)
Treasurer: Richard N. Dixon, D (to Jan. 2003)
Atty. General: J. Joseph Curran, Jr., D (to Jan. 2003)
Entered Union (rank): April 28, 1788 (7)
Present constitution adopted: 1867
Motto: *Fatti maschii, parole femine* (Manly deeds, womanly words)
State Symbols: bird, Baltimore oriole (1947); **boat,** skipjack (1985); **crustacean,** Maryland blue crab (1989); **dinosaur,** Astrodon johnstoni (1998); **dog,** Chesapeake Bay retriever (1964); **beverage,** milk (1998); **flower,** black-eyed susan (1918); **fish,** rockfish (1965); **folk dance,** square dance (1994); **fossil shell,** *ecphora gardnerae gardnerae* (Wilson) (1994); **insect,** Baltimore checkerspot butterfly (1973); **reptile,** Diamondback terrapin (1994); **song,** "Maryland! My Maryland!" (1939); **sport,** jousting (1962); **tree,** white oak (1941);
Nicknames: Free State; Old Line State
Origin of name: In honor of Henrietta Maria (queen of Charles I of England)
10 largest cities (1998 est.): Baltimore, 645,593; Frederick, 47,468; Gaithersburg, 46,980; Rockville, 46,788; Bowie, 40,704; Hagerstown, 34,105; Annapolis, 33,585; College Park, 25,855; Greenbelt, 22,076; Cumberland, 21,521
Land area: 9,775 sq mi. (25,316 sq km)
Geographic center: In Prince Georges Co., 4½ mi. NW of Davidsonville
Number of counties: 23, and 1 independent city
Largest county by population and area: Montgomery, 852,174 (1999 est.); Frederick, 663 sq mi.
State forests: 13 (132,944 ac.)
State parks: 47 (87,670 ac.)
Residents: Marylander
1999 resident population est.: 5,171,634
1990 resident census population (rank): 4,781,468 (19). **Male:** 2,318,671; **Female:** 2,462,997. **White:** 3,393,964 (71.0%); **Black:** 1,189,899 (24.9%); **American Indian:** 12,972 (0.3%); **Asian:** 139,719 (2.9%); **Other race:** 44,914 (0.9%); **Hispanic:** 125,102 (2.6%). **1990 percent population under 18:** 24.3; **65 and over:** 10.8; **median age:** 32.9.

Maryland was inhabited by Indians as early as circa 10,000 B.C. Permanent Indian villages were established by circa A.D. 1000.

In 1608, Capt. John Smith explored Chesapeake Bay. Charles I granted a royal charter for Maryland to Cecil Calvert, Lord Baltimore, in 1632, and English settlers, many of whom were Roman Catholic, landed on St. Clement's (now Blakistone) Island in 1634. Religious freedom, granted all Christians in the Toleration Act passed by the Maryland assembly in 1649, was ended by a Puritan revolt, 1654–58.

From 1763 to 1767, Charles Mason and Jeremiah Dixon surveyed Maryland's northern boundary line with Pennsylvania. In 1791, Maryland ceded land to form the District of Columbia.

In 1814, when the British attempted to capture Baltimore, the bombardment of Fort McHenry inspired Francis Scott Key to write the words to "The Star-Spangled Banner." During the Civil War, Maryland was a slave state but remained in the Union. Consequently, Marylanders fought on both sides and many families were split.

Maryland's Eastern Shore and Western Shore embrace the Chesapeake Bay, and the many estuaries and rivers create one of the longest waterfronts of any state. The Bay produces more seafood—oysters, crabs, clams, fin fish—than any comparable body of water. Important agricultural products are greenhouse and nursery products, chickens, dairy products, soybeans, corn, eggs, vegetables, melons, and wheat. Maryland is a leader in vegetable canning. Stone, coal, sand, gravel, cement, and clay are the chief mineral products.

Manufacturing industries produce food and kindred products, instruments, chemicals, printing and publishing, transportation equipment, and primary metals. Baltimore, home of the Johns Hopkins University and Hospital, ranks as the nation's second port in foreign tonnage. Annapolis, site of the U.S. Naval Academy, has one of the earliest state houses (1772–79) still in regular use by a state government.

Among the popular attractions in Maryland are the Fort McHenry National Monument; Harpers Ferry and Chesapeake and Ohio Canal National Historic Parks; Antietam National Battlefield; National Aquarium, USS *Constellation*, and Maryland Science Center at Baltimore's Inner Harbor; Historic St. Mary's City; Jefferson Patterson Historical Park and Museum at St. Leonard; U.S. Naval Academy in Annapolis; Goddard Space Flight Center at Greenbelt; Assateague Island National Park Seashore; Ocean City beach resort; and Catoctin Mountain, Fort Frederick, and Piscataway parks.

Famous natives and residents: Benjamin Banneker, almanacker and mathematician-astronomer; John Barth, writer; Eubie Blake, musician; John Wilkes Booth, actor and Lincoln assassin; Francis X. Bushman, actor; James M. Cain, writer; Samuel Chase, jurist; Frederick Douglass, abolitionist; John Hurst Fletcher, Methodist bishop and educator; Christopher Gist, frontiersman; Philip Glass, composer; Matthew Henson, reached North Pole with Peary; Billie Holiday, jazz-blues singer; Johns Hopkins, financier; Reverdy Johnson, lawyer and statesman; Thomas Johnson, political leader; Francis Scott Key, laywer and author of the words to the national anthem; Thurgood Marshall, jurist; H. L. Mencken, writer; Hezekiah Niles, journalist; Charles Wilson Peale, painter; Frank Perdue, farmer, businessman; James R. Randall, journalist and writer of the state song; Babe Ruth, baseball player; Upton Sinclair, novelist; Roger B. Taney, jurist; George Alfred Townsend (Gath), journalist; Harriet Tubman, abolitionist; Leon Uris, novelist; Frank Zappa, singer.

Massachusetts

Capital: Boston
Governor: Argeo Paul Cellucci, R (to Jan. 2003)
Lieut. Governor: Jane Swift, R (to Jan. 2003)
Senators: Edward M. Kennedy, D (to Jan. 2001);
John F. Kerry, D (to Jan. 2003)
Secy. of the Commonwealth: William F. Galvin, D
(to Jan. 2003)
Treasurer & Receiver-General: Shannon P. O'Brien, D
(to Jan. 2003)
Auditor of the Commonwealth: A. Joseph DeNucci, D
(to Jan. 2003)
Atty. General: Thomas F. Reilly, D (to Jan. 2003)
Present constitution drafted: 1780 (oldest U.S. state
constitution in effect today)
Entered Union (rank): Feb. 6, 1788 (6)
Motto: *Ense petit placidam sub libertate quietem*
(By the sword we seek peace, but peace only
under liberty)
State Symbols: flower, mayflower (1918); **tree,**
American elm (1941); **bird,** chickadee (1941); **song,**
"All Hail to Massachusetts" (1966); **beverage,**
cranberry juice (1970); **insect,** ladybug (1974);
cookie, chocolate chip (1997); **muffin,** corn muffin
(1986); **dessert,** Boston cream pie (1996);
Nicknames: Bay State; Old Colony State
Origin of name: From Massachusett tribe of Native
Americans, meaning "at or about the great hill"
10 largest cities (1998 est.): Boston, 555,447;
Worcester, 166,535; Springfield, 148,144; Lowell,
101,075; New Bedford, 96,353; Cambridge, 96,352;
Brockton, 93,173; Fall River, 90,654; Quincy, 85,752;
Lynn, 81,075
Land area: 7,838 sq mi. (20,300 sq km)
Geographic center: In Worcester Co., in S part of city
of Worcester
Number of counties: 14
Largest county by population and area: Middlesex,
1,426,606 (1999 est.); Worcester, 1,513 sq mi.
State forests and parks: 129 (242,000 ac.)[1]
Residents: Bay Stater
1999 resident population est.: 6,175,169
1990 resident census population (rank): 6,016,425
(13). **Male:** 2,888,745; **Female:** 3,127,680. **White:**
5,405,374 (89.8%); **Black:** 300,130 (5.0%); **American
Indian:** 12,241 (0.2%); **Asian:** 143,392 (2.4%); **Other
race:** 155,288 (2.6%); **Hispanic:** 287,549 (4.8%).
1990 percent population under 18: 22.5; **65 and
over:** 13.6; **median age:** 33.4.

1. The Metropolitan District Commission, an agency of
the Commonwealth serving municipalities in the Boston
area, has about 14,000 acres of parkways and reservations under its jurisdiction.

Massachusetts has played a significant role in
American history since the Pilgrims, seeking religious freedom, founded Plymouth Colony in 1620.
As one of the most important of the 13 colonies,
Massachusetts became a leader in resisting British
oppression. In 1773, the Boston Tea Party protested
unjust taxation. The Minute Men started the American Revolution by battling British troops at Lexington and Concord on April 19, 1775.

During the 19th century, Massachusetts was
famous for the vigorous intellectual activity of its
renowned writers and educators and for its expanding commercial fishing, shipping, and manufacturing interests.

Massachusetts pioneered the manufacture of textiles and shoes. Today, these industries have been
replaced in importance by activity in the electronics
and communications equipment fields.

The state's cranberry crop is the nation's largest.
Also important are dairy and poultry products, nursery and greenhouse produce, vegetables, and fruit.

Tourism has become an important factor in the
economy of the state because of its numerous recreational areas and historical landmarks. Cape Cod
has summer theaters, water sports, and an artists'
colony at Provincetown. Tanglewood, in the Berk-
shires, features the summer concerts of the Boston
Symphony.

Among the many other points of interest are Old
Sturbridge Village in Sturbridge in central Massa-
chusetts, Minute Man National Historical Park
between Lexington and Concord, and Plimoth
Plantation in Plymouth. In Boston there are many
places of historical interest, including Old North
Church, Old State House, Faneuil Hall, the USS
Constitution, and the John F. Kennedy Library and
Museum.

Famous natives and residents: John Adams, former
president; John Quincy Adams, former president; Samuel
Adams, patriot; Horatio Alger, novelist; Susan B. Anthony,
woman suffragist; Clara Barton, American Red Cross
founder; Leonard Bernstein, conductor; George Bush,
former president; William Cullen Bryan, poet and editor;
Luther Burbank, horticulturalist; John Cheever, novelist;
John Singleton Copley, painter; e.e. cummings, poet;
Jacques d'Amboise, ballet dancer; Bette Davis, actress;
Cecil B. DeMille, film director; Emily Dickinson, poet; Ralph
Waldo Emerson, philosopher and poet; Geraldine Farrar,
soprano, actress; Benjamin Franklin, statesman and
scientist; Buckminster Fuller, architect and educator;
Robert Goddard, father of modern rocketry; John Hancock,
statesman; Nathaniel Hawthorne, novelist; Oliver Wendell
Holmes, jurist; Winslow Homer, painter; Elias Howe,
inventor; John F. Kennedy, former president; Amy Lowell,
poet; James Russell Lowell, poet; Robert Lowell, poet;
Horace Mann, educator; Cotton Mather, clergyman;
Samuel F. B. Morse, painter and inventor; Edgar Allan
Poe, writer; Paul Revere, silversmith and Revolutionary
War figure; Dr. Seuss (Theodore Geisel), author and
illustrator; David Souter, jurist; Lucy Stone, woman
suffragist; Louis Henry Sullivan, architect; Henry David
Thoreau, author; Barbara Walters, TV commentator;
James McNeill Whistler, painter; Eli Whitney, inventor;
John Greenleaf Whittier, poet.

Michigan

Capital: Lansing
Governor: John Engler, R (to Jan. 2003)
Lieut. Governor: Dick Posthumus, R (to Jan. 2003)
Senators: Spencer Abraham, R (to Jan. 2001);
Carl Levin, D (to Jan. 2003)
Secy. of State: Candace S. Miller, R (to Jan. 2003)
Atty. General: Jennifer Granholm, D (to Jan. 2003)
Organized as territory: Jan. 11, 1805
Entered Union (rank): Jan. 26, 1837 (26)
Present constitution adopted: April 1, 1963, (effective
Jan. 1, 1964)
Motto: *Si quaeris peninsulam amoenam circumspice*
(If you seek a pleasant peninsula, look around you)
State Symbols: flower, apple blossom (1897); **bird,**
robin (1931); **mammal,** white-tailed deer (1997);
fishes, trout (1965), brook trout (1988); **gem,** isle
royal greenstone (chlorastrolite) (1972); **stone,**
petoskey stone (1965); **tree,** white pine (1955); **soil,**
kalkaska soil series (1990); **reptile,** painted turtle
(1996); **flag,** "Blue charged with the arms of the state"
(1911); **wildflower,** Dwarf Lake iris (1998).
Nickname: Wolverine State
Origin of name: From Indian word "Michigana" meaning
"great or large lake"
10 largest cities (1998 est.): Detroit, 970,196; Grand
Rapids, 185,437; Warren, 142,455; Flint, 131,668;
Lansing, 127,825; Sterling Heights, 124,339; Ann

Arbor, 109,967; Livonia, 101,358; Dearborn, 91,691; Westland, 86,227

Land area: 56,809 sq mi.

Geographic center: In Wexford Co., 5 mi. NNW of Cadillac

Number of counties: 83

Largest county by population and area: Wayne, 2,106,495 (1999 est.); Marquette, 1,821 sq mi.

State parks and recreation areas: 96 (265,000 ac.)

Residents: Michigander, Michiganite

1999 resident population est.: 9,863,775

1990 resident census population (rank): 9,295,297 (8). **Male:** 4,512,781; **Female:** 4,787,516. **White:** 7,756,086 (83.4%); **Black:** 1,291,706 (13.9%); **American Indian:** 55,638 (0.6%); **Asian:** 104,983 (1.1%); **Other race:** 86,884 (0.9%); **Hispanic:** 201,596 (2.2%). **1990 percent population under 18:** 26.5; **65 and over:** 11.9; **median age:** 32.5.

Indian tribes were living in the Michigan region when the first European, Étienne Brulé of France, arrived in 1618. Other French explorers, including Jacques Marquette, Louis Joliet, and sieur de la Salle, followed, and the first permanent settlement was established in 1668 at Sault Ste. Marie. France was ousted from the territory by Great Britain in 1763, following the French and Indian Wars.

After the Revolutionary War, the U.S. acquired most of the region, which remained the scene of constant conflict between the British and U.S. forces and their respective Indian allies through the War of 1812.

Bordering on four of the five Great Lakes, Michigan is divided into Upper and Lower peninsulas by the Straits of Mackinac, which link lakes Michigan and Huron. The two parts of the state are connected by the Mackinac Bridge, one of the world's longest suspension bridges. To the north, connecting lakes Superior and Huron, are the busy Sault Ste. Marie Canals.

While Michigan ranks first among the states in production of motor vehicles and parts, it is also a leader in many other manufacturing and processing lines, including prepared cereals, machine tools, airplane parts, refrigerators, hardware, steel springs, and furniture.

The state produces important amounts of iron, copper, iodine, gypsum, bromine, salt, lime, gravel, and cement. Michigan's farms grow apples, cherries, beans, pears, grapes, potatoes, and sugar beets. Michigan's forests contribute significantly to the state's economy, supporting thousands of jobs in the wood-product, tourism, and recreation industries. With 10,083 inland lakes and 3,288 miles of Great Lakes shoreline, Michigan is a prime area for both commercial and sport fishing.

Points of interest are the automobile plants in Dearborn, Detroit, Flint, Lansing, and Pontiac; Mackinac Island; Pictured Rocks and Sleeping Bear Dunes National Lakeshores; Greenfield Village in Dearborn; and the many summer resorts along both the inland lakes and Great Lakes.

Famous natives and residents: Nelson Algren, novelist; Tim Allen, actor and comedian; Ralph J. Bunche, statesman; Ellen Burstyn, actress; Bruce Catton, historian; Roger Chaffee, astronaut; Francis Ford Coppola, film director; Thomas E. Dewey, politician; Edna Ferber, novelist; Gerald Ford, former president; Henry Ford, industrialist; Ali Haji-Sheikh, football player; Julie Harris, actress; Earvin "Magic" Johnson, basketball player; Ring Lardner, writer; Charles A. Lindbergh, aviator; Madonna, singer; Dick Martin, comedian; Terry McMillan, author; John N. Mitchell, former attorney general; Ted Nugent, singer; Gilda Radner, comedienne; Della Reese, singer; Jason Robards, Sr., actor; Diana Ross, singer; Steven Seagal, actor; Bob Seger, singer; Tom Selleck, actor; Thomas Schippers, conductor; Potter Stewart, jurist; Lily Tomlin, actress; Danny Thomas, entertainer; Margaret Whiting, singer; Robin Williams, comedian and actor; Stevie Wonder, singer.

Minnesota

Capital: St. Paul

Governor: Jesse Ventura, IP[1] (to Jan. 2003)

Lieut. Governor: Mae Schunk, IP[1] (to Jan. 2003)

Senators: Rod Grams, R (to Jan. 2001); Paul Wellstone, D (to Jan. 2003)

Secy. of State: Mary Kiffmeyer, R (to Jan. 2003)

State Auditor: Judi Dutcher, D (to Jan. 2003)

Atty. General: Mike Hatch, D (to Jan. 2003)

State Treasurer: Carol Johnson, D (to Jan. 2003)

Organized as territory: March 3, 1849

Entered Union (rank): May 11, 1858 (32)

Present constitution adopted: 1858

Motto: L'Étoile du Nord (The North Star)

State Symbols: flower, lady slipper (1902); **tree,** red (or Norway) pine (1953); **bird,** common loon (also called great northern diver) (1961); **song,** "Hail Minnesota" (1945); **fish,** walleye (1965); **mushroom,** morel (1984);

Nicknames: North Star State; Gopher State; Land of 10,000 Lakes

Origin of name: From a Dakota Indian word meaning "sky-tinted water"

10 largest cities (1998 est.): Minneapolis, 351,731; St. Paul, 257,284; Bloomington, 86,186; Duluth, 81,228; Rochester, 78,173; Coon Rapids, 63,674; Brooklyn Park, 63,115; Plymouth, 61,509; Eagan, 60,042; Burnsville, 59,334

Land area: 79,617 sq mi. (206,207 sq km)

Geographic center: In Crow Wing Co., 10 mi. SW of Brainerd

Number of counties: 87

Largest county by population and area: Hennepin, 1,064,419 (1999 est.); St. Louis, 6,226 sq mi.

State forests: 55

State parks: 66 (226,000 ac.)

Residents: Minnesotan

1999 resident population est.: 4,775,508

1990 resident census population (rank): 4,375,099 (20). **Male:** 2,145,183; **Female:** 2,229,916. **White:** 4,130,395 (94.4%); **Black:** 94,944 (2.2%); **American Indian:** 49,909 (1.1%); **Asian:** 77,886 (1.8%); **Other race:** 21,965 (0.5%); **Hispanic:** 53,884 (1.2%). **1990 percent population under 18:** 26.7; **65 and over:** 12.5; **median age:** 32.4.

1. Independence Party.

Following the visits of several French explorers, fur traders, and missionaries, including Jacques Marquette, Louis Joliet, and sieur de la Salle, the region was claimed for Louis XIV by Daniel Greysolon, sieur Duluth, in 1679.

The U.S. acquired eastern Minnesota from Great Britain after the Revolutionary War and 20 years later bought the western part from France in the Louisiana Purchase of 1803. Much of the region was explored by U.S. Army Lt. Zebulon M. Pike before the northern strip of Minnesota bordering Canada was ceded by Britain in 1818.

The state is rich in natural resources. A few square miles of land in the north in the Mesabi, Cuyuna, and Vermillion ranges produce more than 75% of the nation's iron ore. The state's farms rank high in yields of corn, wheat, rye, alfalfa, and sugar beets. Other leading farm products include butter, eggs, milk, potatoes, green peas, barley, soybeans, oats, and livestock.

Minnesota's factory production includes nonelectrical machinery, fabricated metals, flour-mill products, plastics, electronic computers, scientific instruments, and processed foods. It is also one of the nation's leaders in the printing and paper-products industries.

Minneapolis is the trade center of the Midwest, and the headquarters of the world's largest supercomputer and grain distributor. St. Paul is the nation's biggest publisher of calendars and law books. These "twin cities" are the nation's third-largest trucking center. Duluth has the nation's largest inland harbor and now handles a significant amount of foreign trade. Rochester is the home of the Mayo Clinic, an internationally famous medical center.

Today, tourism is a major revenue producer in Minnesota, with arts, fishing, hunting, water sports, and winter sports bringing in millions of visitors each year.

Among the most popular attractions are the St. Paul Winter Carnival; the Tyrone Guthrie Theatre, the Institute of Arts, Walker Art Center, and Minnehaha Park, in Minneapolis; Boundary Waters Canoe Area; Voyageurs National Park; North Shore Drive; the Minnesota Zoological Gardens; and the state's more than 10,000 lakes.

Famous natives and residents: LaVerne, Maxene, and Patti Andrews, singers; Warren E. Burger, jurist; William E. Colby, former director of the CIA; William Demarest, actor; William O. Douglas, jurist; Bob Dylan, singer and composer; F. Scott Fitzgerald, novelist; Judy Garland, singer and actress; J. Paul Getty, oil executive; Cass Gilbert, architect; Duane Hanson, sculptor; Hubert H. Humphrey, senator and vice president; Jessica Lange, actress; Sinclair Lewis, novelist; Cornell MacNeil, baritone; Roger Maris, baseball player; E. G. Marshall, actor; Charles H. Mayo, surgeon; William J. Mayo, surgeon; Eugene J. McCarthy, former senator; Kate Millett, feminist; Walter F. Mondale, former U.S. vice president; Gen. Lauris Norstad, former commander of NATO forces; Westbrook Pegler, columnist; John Sargent Pillsbury, businessman; Marion Ross, actress; Jane Russell, actress; Harrison E. Salisbury, journalist; Charles M. Schulz, cartoonist; Max Shulman, novelist; Maurice H. Stans, former secretary of commerce; Harold E. Stassen, former government official; Michael Todd, producer; Frederick Weyerhaeuser, businessman; Gig Young, actor.

Mississippi

Capital: Jackson
Governor: Ronnie Musgrove, D (to Jan. 2004)
Lieut. Governor: Amy Tuck, D (to Jan. 2004)
Senators: Thad Cochran, R (to Jan. 2003);
Trent Lott, R (to Jan. 2001)
Secy. of State: Eric Clark, D (to Jan. 2004)
Treasurer: Marshall Bennett, D (to Jan. 2004)
Auditor: Phil Bryant, R (to Jan. 2004)
Atty. General: Mike Moore, D (to Jan. 2004)
Agriculture and Commerce Commissioner:
Lester Spell, Jr., D (to Jan. 2004)
Insurance Commissioner: George Dale, D (to Jan. 2004)
Organized as territory: April 7, 1798
Entered Union (rank): Dec. 10, 1817 (20)
Present constitution adopted: 1890
Motto: *Virtute et armis* (By valor and arms)
State Symbols: flower, flower or bloom of the magnolia or evergreen magnolia (1952); **wildflower,** coreopsis (1991); **tree,** magnolia (1938); **bird,** mockingbird (1944); **song,** "Go, Mississippi" (1962); **stone,** petrified wood (1976); **fish,** largemouth or black bass (1974); **insect,**

honeybee (1980); **shell,** oyster shell (1974); **water mammal,** bottlenosed dolphin or porpoise (1974); **fossil,** prehistoric whale (1981); **land mammal,** white-tailed deer (1974), red fox (1997); **waterfowl,** wood duck (1974); **beverage,** milk (1984); **butterfly,** spicebush swallowtail (1991); **dance,** square dance (1995);
Nickname: Magnolia State
Origin of name: From an Indian word meaning "Father of Waters"
10 largest cities (1998 est.): Jackson, 188,419; Gulfport, 64,762; Hattiesburg, 48,806; Biloxi, 47,316; Greenville, 42,042; Meridian, 40,255; Tupelo, 35,589; Vicksburg, 27,221; Pascagoula, 27,163; Southaven, 23,434
Land area: 46,914 sq mi. (121,506 sq km)
Geographic center: In Leake Co., 9 mi. WNW of Carthage
Number of counties: 82
Largest county by population and area: Hinds, 245,737 (1999 est.); Yazoo, 920 sq mi.
State forests: 1 (1,760 ac.)
State parks: 29 (24,521 ac.)
Residents: Mississippian
1999 resident population est.: 2,768,619
1990 resident census population (rank): 2,573,216 (31). **Male:** 1,230,617; **Female:** 1,342,599. **White:** 1,633,461 (63.5%); **Black:** 915,057 (35.6%); **American Indian,** 8,525 (0.3%); **Asian:** 13,016 (0.5%); **Other race:** 3,157 (0.1%); **Hispanic:** 15,931 (0.6%). **1990 percent population under 18:** 29.0; **65 and over:** 12.5; **median age:** 31.1.

First explored for Spain by Hernando De Soto, who discovered the Mississippi River in 1540, the region was later claimed by France. In 1699, a French group under Sieur d'Iberville established the first permanent settlement near present-day Ocean Springs.

Great Britain took over the area in 1763 after the French and Indian Wars, ceding it to the U.S. in 1783 after the Revolution. Spain did not relinquish its claims until 1798, and in 1810 the U.S. annexed West Florida from Spain, including what is now southern Mississippi.

For a little more than one hundred years, from shortly after the state's founding through the Great Depression, cotton was the undisputed king of Mississippi's largely agrarian economy. Over the last half-century, however, Mississippi has diversified its economy by balancing agricultural output with increased industrial activity.

Today, agriculture continues as a major segment of the state's economy. While the most acreage is devoted to soybeans, cotton is the largest cash crop—Mississippi remains fourth in the nation in cotton production. The state's farmlands yield important harvests of corn, peanuts, pecans, rice, sugar cane, sweet potatoes, soybeans, and food grains as well as poultry, eggs, meat animals, dairy products, feed crops, and horticultural crops. Mississippi remains the world's leading producer of pond-raised catfish.

The state abounds in historical landmarks and is the home of the Vicksburg National Military Park. Other National Park Service areas are Brices Cross Roads National Battlefield Site, Tupelo National Battlefield, and part of Natchez Trace National Parkway. Pre-Civil War mansions are the special pride of Natchez, Oxford, Columbus, Vicksburg, and Jackson.

Famous natives and residents: Red Barber, sportscaster; Jimmy Buffett, singer and songwriter; Craig Claiborne, columnist and restaurant critic; Bo Diddley, guitarist;

Charles Evers, civil rights leader; Medgar Evers, civil rights leader; William Faulkner, novelist; Shelby Foote, historian; Richard Ford, novelist; John Grisham, novelist; Barry Hannah, novelist; Beth Henley, playwright and actress; Jim Henson, puppeteer; James Earl Jones, actor; B. B. King, guitarist; Mary Ann Mobley, actress; Willie Morris, writer; Elvis Presley, singer and actor; Leontyne Price, soprano; William Raspberry, columnist; Jerry Rice, football player; Jimmie Rodgers, singer; Sela Ward, actress; Muddy Waters, singer and guitarist; Eudora Welty, novelist; Tennessee Williams, playwright; Oprah Winfrey, talk-show host and actress; Richard Wright, novelist; Tammy Wynette, country music star; Zig Ziglar, speaker and author.

Missouri

Capital: Jefferson City
Governor: Mel Carnahan, D (to Jan. 2001)
Lieut. Governor: Roger Wilson, D (to Jan. 2001)
Senators: John Ashcroft, R (to Jan. 2001); Christopher S. Bond, R (to Jan. 2005)
Secy. of State: Rebecca ("Bekki") McDowell Cook, D (to Jan. 2001)
Auditor: Claire C. McCaskill, D (to Jan. 2003)
Treasurer: Bob Holden, D (to Jan. 2001)
Atty. General: Jeremiah "Jay" W. Nixon, D (to Jan. 2001)
Organized as territory: June 4, 1812
Entered Union (rank): Aug. 10, 1821 (24)
Present constitution adopted: 1945
Motto: *Salus populi suprema lex esto* (The welfare of the people shall be the supreme law)
State Symbols: flower, hawthorn (1923); **bird,** bluebird (1927); **fish,** paddlefish (1997), channel catfish (1997); **song,** "Missouri Waltz" (1949); **fossil,** crinoid (1989); **musical instrument,** fiddle (1987); **rock,** mozarkite (1967); **mineral,** galena (1967); **insect,** honeybee (1985); **tree,** flowering dogwood (1955); **tree nut,** eastern black walnut (1990); **animal,** mule (1995); **dance,** square dance (1995); **Missouri Day,** third Wednesday in October (1915);
Nickname: Show-me State
Origin of name: Named after the Missouri Indian tribe. "Missouri" means "town of the large canoes."
10 largest cities (1998 est.): Kansas City, 441,574; St. Louis, 339,316; Springfield, 142,898; Independence, 116,832; Columbia, 78,915; St. Joseph, 69,622; Lee's Summit, 66,623; St. Charles, 58,166; St. Peter's, 50,297; Florissant, 47,069
Land area: 68,898 sq mi. (178,446 sq km)
Geographic center: In Miller Co., 20 mi. SW of Jefferson City
Number of counties: 114, plus 1 independent city
Largest county by population and area: St. Louis, 996,181 (1999 est.); Texas, 1,179 sq mi.
Conservation areas[1]: leased, 287 (194,381 ac.); owned, 785 (761,842 ac.)
Conservation accesses: leased, 72; owned, 251
State parks and historic sites: 80
Residents: Missourian
1999 resident population est.: 5,468,338
1990 resident census population (rank): 5,117,073 (15). **Male:** 2,464,315; **Female:** 2,652,758. **White:** 4,486,228 (87.7%); **Black:** 548,208 (10.7%); **American Indian:** 19,835 (0.4%); **Asian:** 41,277 (0.8%); **Other race:** 21,525 (0.4%); **Hispanic:** 61,702 (1.2%). **1990 percent population under 18:** 25.7; **65 and over:** 14.0; **median age:** 33.4.

1. Includes wildlife areas, natural history areas, state forests, and tower sites.

Hernando De Soto visited the Missouri area in 1541. France's claim to the entire region was based on sieur de la Salle's travels in 1682. French fur traders established Ste. Genevieve in 1735 and St. Louis was first settled in 1764.

The U.S. gained Missouri from France as part of the Louisiana Purchase in 1803, and the territory was admitted as a state following the Missouri Compromise of 1820. Throughout the pre–Civil War period and during the war, Missourians were sharply divided in their opinions about slavery and in their allegiances, supplying both Union and Confederate forces with troops. However, the state itself remained in the Union.

Historically, Missouri played a leading role as a gateway to the West, St. Joseph being the eastern starting point of the Pony Express, while the much-traveled Santa Fe and Oregon trails began in Independence.

Missouri's economy relies on a diversified industrial base. Service industries provide more income and jobs than any other segment, and include a growing tourism and travel sector. Wholesale and retail trade, manufacturing, and agriculture also play significant roles in the state's economy. Missouri is a leading producer of transportation equipment (including automobile manufacturing and auto parts), beer and beverages, and defense and aerospace technology. Food processing is the state's fastest-growing industry, well suited to the state's blend of agricultural, natural, energy, and transportation resources. Missouri mines produce 90% of the nation's principal (non-recycled) lead supply.

The state's top agricultural products include grain, sorghum, hay, corn, soybeans, wheat, oats, barley, tobacco, and rice. A well-established grape and wine program brings together aspects of agriculture, manufacturing, and tourism to support a vibrant vintner industry.

Tourism draws hundreds of thousands of visitors to a number of Missouri points of interest: the country-music shows of Branson; Bass Pro Shops national headquarters (Springfield); the Gateway Arch at the Jefferson National Expansion (St. Louis); Mark Twain's boyhood home (Hannibal); the Harry S Truman home and library (Independence); the scenic beauty of the Ozark National Scenic Riverways; and the Pony Express and Jesse James museums (St. Joseph). The state's different lake regions also attract fishermen and sun-seekers from throughout the Midwest.

Famous natives and residents: Robert Altman, film director; Burt Bacharach, songwriter; Josephine Baker, singer and dancer; Wallace Beery, actor; Robert Russell Bennett, composer; Yogi Berra, baseball player; Thomas Hart Benton, painter; Bill Bradley, basketball player and former N.J. senator; Omar N. Bradley, five-star general; Grace Bumbry, soprano; William Burroughs, writer; Sarah Caldwell, opera director and conductor; Martha Jane Canary (Calamity Jane), frontierswoman; George Washington Carver, scientist; Walter Cronkite, TV newscaster; Robert Cummings, actor; Jane Darwell, actress; Walt Disney, artist; T. S. Eliot, poet; Redd Foxx, actor and comedian; Betty Grable, actress; Dick Gregory, comic and activist; Jean Harlow, actress; George Hearn, actor; Edwin Hubble, astronomer; Langston Hughes, poet; John Huston, film director; Jesse James, outlaw; Scott Joplin, composer; Marianne Moore, poet; Geraldine Page, actress; James C. Penney, merchant; John Joseph Pershing, general; Vincent Price, actor; Joseph Pulitzer, journalist; Ginger Rogers, dancer and actress; Sacajawea, Indian guide for Lewis and Clark; Casey Stengel, baseball player; Gladys Swarthout, soprano; Sara Teasdale, poet; Virgil Thomson, composer; Harry S Truman, former president; Mark Twain, author; Dick Van Dyke, actor; Ruth Warrick, actress; Dennis Weaver, actor; Mary Wickes, actress; Laura Ingalls Wilder, author; Roy Wilkins, civil rights leader.

Montana

Capital: Helena
Governor: Marc Racicot, R (to Jan. 2001)
Lieut. Governor: Judy Martz, R (to Jan. 2001)
Senators: Max Baucus, D (to Jan. 2003);
Conrad R. Burns, R (to Jan. 2001)
Secy. of State: Mike Cooney, D (to Jan. 2001)
Auditor: Mark O'Keefe, D (to Jan. 2001)
Atty. General: Joe Mazurek, D (to Jan. 2001)
Organized as territory: May 26, 1864
Entered Union (rank): Nov. 8, 1889 (41)
Present constitution adopted: 1972
Motto: *Oro y plata* (Gold and silver)
State Symbols: flower, bitterroot (1895); **tree,**
ponderosa pine (1949); **stones,** sapphire and agate
(1969); **bird,** Western meadowlark (1981); **song,**
"Montana" (1945);
Nickname: Treasure State
Origin of name: Chosen from Latin dictionary by J. M.
Ashley. It is a Latinized Spanish word meaning
"mountainous."
10 largest cities (1998 est.): Billings, 91,750; Great
Falls, 56,395; Missoula, 52,239; Butte-Silver Bow[1],
33,994; Bozeman, 29,936; Helena, 28,306; Kalispell,
16,089; Havre, 10,015; Anaconda–Deer Lodge County,
9,999; Miles City, 8,685
Land area: 145,556 sq mi. (376,991 sq km)
Geographic center: In Fergus Co., 12 mi. W
of Lewistown
Number of counties: 56, plus small part of Yellowstone
National Park
Largest county by population and area: Yellowstone,
127,258 (1999 est.); Beaverhead, 5,543 sq mi.
State forests: 7 (214,000 ac.)
State parks and recreation areas: 110 (18,273 ac.)
Residents: Montanan
1999 resident population est.: 882,779
1990 resident census population (rank): 799,065 (44).
Male: 395,769; **Female:** 403,296. **White:** 741,111
(92.7%); **Black:** 2,381 (0.3%); **American Indian:**
47,679 (6.0%); **Asian:** 4,259 (0.5%); **Other race:**
3,635 (0.5%); **Hispanic:** 12,174 (1.5%). **1990 percent
population under 18:** 27.8; **65 and over:** 13.3;
median age: 33.8.

1. Consolidated City.

First explored for France by François and Louis-
Joseph Verendrye in the early 1740s, much of the
region was acquired by the U.S. from France as part
of the Louisiana Purchase in 1803. Before western
Montana was obtained from Great Britain in the
Oregon Treaty of 1846, American trading posts and
forts had been established in the territory.

The major Indian Wars (1867–1877) included the
famous 1876 Battle of the Little Big Horn, better
known as "Custer's Last Stand," in which Cheyenne
and Sioux defeated George A. Custer and more than
200 of his men in southeastern Montana.

Much of Montana's early history was concerned
with mining, with copper, lead, zinc, silver, coal,
and oil as principal products. Butte is the center of
the area that once supplied half of the U.S. copper.

Fields of grain cover much of Montana's plains. It
ranks high among the states in wheat and barley,
with rye, oats, flaxseed, sugar beets, and potatoes as
other important crops. Sheep and cattle raising make
significant contributions to the economy.

Tourist attractions include hunting, fishing, skiing,
and dude ranching. Glacier National Park, on the
Continental Divide, is a scenic and vacation wonderland with 60 glaciers, 200 lakes, and many
streams with good trout fishing.

Other major points of interest include the Little
Bighorn Battlefield National Monument, Virginia
City, Yellowstone National Park, Museum of the
Plains Indians at Browning, and the Fort Union
Trading Post and Grant-Kohr's Ranch National His-
toric Sites.

Famous natives and residents: Dorothy Baker, author; Dirk
Benedict, actor; W. A. (Tony) Boyle, labor union official;
Gary Cooper, actor; John Cowan, prospector and founder
of Last Chance Gulch (now Helena); Alfred Bertram
Guthrie, Pulitzer Prize–winning author; Chet Huntley, TV
newscaster; Will James, writer and artist; Dorothy
Johnson, author; Evel Knievel, daredevil motorcyclist;
Myrna Loy, actress; David Lynch, filmmaker; Mike
Mansfield, former senator; George Montgomery, actor;
Jeannette Rankin, first woman elected to Congress;
Martha Raye, actress; Charles M. Russell, Old West
painter; Michael Smuin, choreographer; Lester C. Thurow,
economist and educator.

Nebraska

Capital: Lincoln
Governor: Mike Johanns, R (to Jan. 2003)
Lieut. Governor: Dave Maurstad, R (to Jan. 2003)
Senators: Chuck Hagel, R (to Jan. 2003);
J. Robert Kerrey, D (to Jan. 2001)
Secy. of State: Scott Moore, R (to Jan. 2003)
Atty. General: Don Stenberg, R (to Jan. 2003)
Auditor: Kate Witek, R (to Jan. 2003)
Treasurer: David Heineman, R (to Jan. 2003)
Organized as territory: May 30, 1854
Entered Union (rank): March 1, 1867 (37)
Present constitution adopted: Oct. 12, 1875 (exten-
sively amended 1919–20)
Motto: Equality before the law
State Symbols: flower, goldenrod (1895); **fish,** channel
catfish (1997); **American folk dance,** square dance
(1997); **ballad,** "A Place Like Nebraska" (1997); **tree,**
cottonwood (1972); **bird,** Western meadowlark (1929);
insect, honeybee (1975); **gemstone,** blue agate
(1967); **rock,** prairie agate (1967); **fossil,** mammoth
(1967); **song,** "Beautiful Nebraska" (1967); **soil,** typic
argiustolls, holdreges series (1979); **mammal,** whitetail
deer (1981); **grass,** little bluestem (1969); **beverage,**
milk (1998);
Nicknames: Cornhusker State (1945); Beef State
Origin of name: From an Oto Indian word meaning
"flat water"
10 largest cities (1998 est.): Omaha, 371,291; Lincoln,
213,088; Bellevue, 44,047; Grand Island, 41,392;
Kearney, 27,968; Fremont, 24,429; Norfolk, 23,476;
North Platte, 23,307; Hastings, 21,356; Columbus,
20,898
Land area: 76,878 sq mi. (199,113 sq km)
Geographic center: In Custer Co., 10 mi. NW of
Broken Bow
Number of counties: 93
Largest county by population and area: Douglas,
446,277 (1999 est.); Cherry, 5,961 sq mi.
State parks: 85 areas, historical and recreational;
8 major areas
Residents: Nebraskan
1999 resident population est.: 1,666,028
1990 resident census population (rank): 1,578,417
(36). **Male:** 769,439; **Female:** 808,946. **White:**
1,480,558 (93.8%); **Black:** 57,404 (3.6%); **American
Indian:** 12,410 (0.8%); **Asian:** 12,422 (0.8%); **Other
race:** 15,591 (1.0%); **Hispanic:** 36,969 (2.3%). **1990
percent population under 18:** 27.2; **65 and over:**
14.1; **median age:** 32.9.

French fur traders first visited Nebraska in the late
1600s. Part of the Louisiana Purchase in 1803, eastern Nebraska was explored by Lewis and Clark in
1804–1806.

Robert Stuart pioneered the Oregon Trail across Nebraska in 1812–1813 and the first permanent white settlement was established at Bellevue in 1823. Western Nebraska was acquired by treaty following the Mexican War in 1848. The Union Pacific began its transcontinental railroad at Omaha in 1865. In 1937, Nebraska became the only state in the Union to have a unicameral (one-house) legislature. Members are elected to it without party designation.

Nebraska is a leading grain-producer with bumper crops of grain, sorghum, corn, and wheat. More varieties of grass, valuable for forage, grow in this state than in any other in the nation. The state's sizable cattle and hog industries make Dakota City and Lexington among the nation's largest meat-packing centers.

Manufacturing has become diversified in Nebraska, strengthening the state's economic base. Firms making electronic components, auto accessories, pharmaceuticals, and mobile homes have joined such older industries as clothing, farm machinery, chemicals, and transportation equipment. Oil was discovered in 1939 and natural gas in 1949.

Among the principal attractions are Agate Fossil Beds, Homestead, and Scotts Bluff National Monuments; Chimney Rock National Historic Site; a recreated pioneer village at Minden; SAC Museum near Ashland; the Stuhr Museum of the Prairie Pioneer with 57 original 19th-century buildings near Grand Island; Boys Town; the Sheldon Memorial Art Gallery and the Lied Center for the Performing Arts located on the University of Nebraska campus in Lincoln; the State Capitol in Lincoln; the Joslyn Art Museum in Omaha; the Henry Doorly Zoo in Omaha; Museum of Nebraska Art in Kearney; Museum of Nebraska History in Lincoln; and the University of Nebraska State Museum in Lincoln.

Famous natives and residents: Grace Abbott, social worker; Bess Streeter Aldrich, author; Grover Cleveland Alexander, Hall of Fame pitcher; Fred Astaire, dancer and actor; Max Baer, boxer; Bil Baird, puppeteer; George Beadle, geneticist; Marlon Brando, actor; William Jennings Bryan, three-time U.S. presidential candidate; Warren Buffett, investor; Johnny Carson, TV host; Willa Cather, author; Dick Cavett, TV entertainer; Richard B. Cheney, former secretary of Defense; Montgomery Clift, actor; James Coburn, actor; William "Buffalo Bill" Cody, showman of the Old West; Sandy Dennis, actress; Mignon Eberhart, author; Harold "Doc" Edgerton, inventor; Ruth Etting, singer and actress; Fr. Edward J. Flanagan, founder of Boys Town; Henry Fonda, actor; Gerald Ford, former president; Bob Gibson, baseball player; Howard Hanson, conductor; Leland Hayward, producer; Robert Henri, painter; David Janssen, actor; Francis La Flesche, ethnologist; Melvin Laird, politician and former secretary of defense; Frank W. Leahy, football coach; Harold Lloyd, actor; Malcolm X, civil rights advocate; Dorothy McGuire, actress; Julius Sterling Morton, politician and journalist; John G. Neihardt, epic poet; Nick Nolte, actor; George W. Norris, U.S. Senator; John J. Pershing, Army leader and founder of Pershing Rifles; Nathan Roscoe Pound, dean of Harvard Law School and botanist; Red Cloud, Indian rights advocate; Mari Sandoz, author; Standing Bear, Indian rights advocate; Robert Taylor, actor; Susette La Flesche Tibbles, Omaha Indian activist; Paul Williams, singer, composer, and actor; Julie Wilson, singer and actress; Darryl F. Zanuck, film producer.

Nevada

Capital: Carson City
Governor: Kenny Guinn, R (to Jan. 2003)
Lieut. Governor: Lorraine Hunt, R (to Jan. 2003)
Senators: Richard Bryan, D (to Jan. 2001); Harry Reid, D (to Jan. 2005)

Secy. of State: Dean Heller, R (to Jan. 2003)
Treasurer: Brian Krolicki, R (to Jan. 2003)
Controller: Kathy Augustine, R (to Jan. 2003)
Atty. General: Frankie Sue Del Papa, D (to Jan. 2003)
Organized as territory: March 2, 1861
Entered Union (rank): Oct. 31, 1864 (36)
Present constitution adopted: 1864
Motto: All for Our Country
State Symbols: flower, sagebrush (1959); **trees,** single-leaf pinon (1953) and bristlecone pine (1987); **bird,** mountain bluebird (1967); **animal,** desert bighorn sheep (1973); **colors,** silver and blue (1983); **song,** "Home Means Nevada" (1933); **rock,** sandstone (1987); **precious gemstone,** virgin valley black fire opal (1987); **semiprecious gemstone,** Nevada turquoise (1987); **grass,** Indian ricegrass (1977); **metal,** silver (1977); **fossil,** ichthyosaur (1977); **fish,** lahontan cutthroat trout (1981); **reptile,** desert tortoise (1989); **state artifact,** tule duck decoy (1995);
Nicknames: Sagebrush State; Silver State; Battle Born State
Origin of name: Spanish: "snowcapped"
10 largest cities (1998 est.): Las Vegas, 404,288; Reno, 163,334; Henderson, 152,717; North Las Vegas, 94,218; Sparks, 62,432; Carson, 49,301; Elko, 19,204; Boulder City, 14,166; Mesquite, 10,125; Winnemucca, 9,404
Land area: 109,806 sq mi. (284,397 sq km)
Geographic center: In Lander Co., 26 mi. SE of Austin
Number of counties: 16, plus 1 independent city
Largest county by population and area: Clark, 1,217,155 (1999 est.); Nye, 18,147 sq mi.
State parks: 20 (150,000 ac., including leased lands)
Residents: Nevadan, Nevadian
1999 resident population est.: 1,809,253
1990 resident census population (rank): 1,201,833 (39). **Male:** 611,880; **Female:** 589,953. **White:** 1,012,695 (84.3%); **Black:** 78,771 (6.6%); **American Indian:** 19,637 (1.6%); **Asian:** 38,127 (3.2%); **Other race:** 52,603 (4.4%); **Hispanic:** 124,419 (10.4%). **1990 percent population under 18:** 24.7; **65 and over:** 10.6; **median age:** 33.2.

Trappers and traders, including Jedediah Smith and Peter Skene Ogden, entered the Nevada area in the 1820s. In 1843–1845, John C. Frémont and Kit Carson explored the Great Basin and Sierra Nevada.

In 1848 following the Mexican War, the U.S. obtained the region and the first permanent settlement was a Mormon trading post near present-day Genoa.

The driest state in the nation, with an average annual rainfall of only about 7 inches, much of Nevada is uninhabited, sagebrush-covered desert. The wettest part of the state receives about 40 inches of precipitation per year, while the driest spot has less than four inches per year.

Nevada was made famous by the discovery of the fabulous Comstock Lode in 1859 and its mines have produced large quantities of gold, silver, copper, lead, zinc, mercury, barite, and tungsten. Oil was discovered in 1954. Gold now far exceeds all other minerals in value of production.

In 1931, the state created two industries, divorce and gambling. For many years, Reno and Las Vegas were the "divorce capitals of the nation." More liberal divorce laws in many states have ended this distinction, but Nevada is still the gambling capital of the U.S. and a leading entertainment center. State gambling taxes account for 35.2% of general fund tax revenues. Although Nevada leads the nation in per capita gambling revenue, it ranks only tenth in total gambling revenue.

The state's leading agricultural industry is cattle and calves. Agricultural crops consist mainly of hay, alfalfa seed, barley, wheat, and potatoes.

Nevada manufactures gaming equipment; lawn and garden irrigation devices; titanium products; seismic and machinery monitoring devices; and specialty printing.

Major resort areas flourish in Lake Tahoe, Reno, and Las Vegas. Recreation areas include those at Pyramid Lake, Lake Tahoe, and Lake Mead and Lake Mohave, both in Lake Mead National Recreation Area. Among the other attractions are Hoover Dam, Virginia City, and Great Basin National Park (includes Lehman Caves).

Famous natives and residents: Eva Adams, former director of U.S. Mint; Andre Agassi, tennis player; Raymond T. Baker, former director of U.S. Mint; Helen Delich Bentley, government official and newspaperwoman; Robert Caples, painter; Walter Van Tilburg Clark, writer; Henry Comstock, prospector of "Comstock Lode" fame; Abby Dalton, actress; Michele Greene, actress; Sarah Winnemucca Hopkins, author and Paiute interpreter and peacemaker; Jack Kramer, tennis player; Paul Laxalt, politician; William Lear, aviation inventor; Robert C. Lynch, surgeon; John W. Mackay, benefactor, one of Big Four of Comstock Lode; Emma Nevada, opera singer; Thelma "Pat" Nixon, former First Lady; James W. Nye, territory governor and former senator; Lute Pease, cartoonist and Pulitzer Prize winner; Edna Purviance, actress; Patty Sheehan, golfer; Jack Wilson, Paiute Indian prophet; George Wingfield, mining millionaire.

New Hampshire

Capital: Concord
Governor: Jeanne Shaheen, D (to Jan. 2001)
Senators: Judd Gregg, R (to Jan. 2005); Bob Smith, R (to Jan. 2003)
Treasurer: Georgie A. Thomas, R (to Dec. 1998)
Secy. of State: William M. Gardner, D (to Dec. 1998)
Atty. General: Philip T. McLaughlin (to March 2001)
Entered Union (rank): June 21, 1788 (9)
Present constitution adopted: 1784
Motto: Live free or die
State Symbols: flower, purple lilac (1919); **tree,** white birch (1947); **animal,** white-tailed deer (1983); **insect,** ladybug (1977); **saltwater fish,** striped bass (1994); **freshwater fish,** brook trout (1995); **amphibian,** spotted newt (1985); **butterfly,** karner blue (1992); **bird,** purple finch (1957); **songs,** "Old New Hampshire" (1949) and "New Hampshire, My New Hampshire" (1963)
Nickname: Granite State
Origin of name: From the English county of Hampshire
10 largest cities (1998 est.): Manchester, 102,524; Nashua, 82,169; Concord, 37,444; Rochester, 27,869; Dover, 25,953; Portsmouth, 25,388; Keene, 22,313; Laconia, 16,435; Claremont, 13,868; Lebanon, 12,461
Land area: 8,969 sq mi. (23,231 sq km)
Geographic center: In Belknap Co., 3 mi. E of Ashland
Number of counties: 10
Largest county by population and area: Hillsborough, 367,233 (1999 est.); Coos, 1,801 sq mi.
State parks: 42 (50,000+ ac.)
Residents: New Hampshirite
1999 resident population est.: 1,201,134
1990 resident census population (rank): 1,109,252 (41). **Male:** 543,544; **Female:** 565,708. **White:** 1,087,433 (98.0%); **Black:** 7,198 (0.6%); **American Indian:** 2,134 (0.2%); **Asian:** 9,343 (0.8%); **Other race:** 3,144 (0.3%); **Hispanic:** 11,333 (1.0%). **1990 percent population under 18:** 25.1; **65 and over:** 11.3; **median age:** 32.7.

Under an English land grant, Capt. John Smith sent settlers to establish a fishing colony at the mouth of the Piscataqua River, near present-day Rye and Dover, in 1623. Capt. John Mason, who participated in the founding of Portsmouth in 1630, gave New Hampshire its name.

After a 38-year period of union with Massachusetts, New Hampshire was made a separate royal colony in 1679. As leaders in the revolutionary cause, New Hampshire delegates received the honor of being the first to vote for the Declaration of Independence on July 4, 1776. New Hampshire gained a measure of international attention in 1905 when Portsmouth Naval Base played host to the signing of the treaty ending the Russo-Japanese War, known as the Treaty of Portsmouth.

Abundant water power early turned New Hampshire into an industrial state, and manufacturing is the principal source of income in the state. The most important industrial products are electrical and other machinery, textiles, pulp and paper products, and stone and clay products.

Dairy and poultry farming and growing fruit, truck vegetables, corn, potatoes, and hay are the major agricultural pursuits.

Tourism, because of New Hampshire's scenic and recreational resources, now brings over $3.5 billion into the state annually.

Vacation attractions include Lake Winnipesaukee, largest of 1,300 lakes and ponds; the 724,000-acre White Mountain National Forest; Daniel Webster's birthplace near Franklin; Strawbery Banke, restored buildings of the original settlement at Portsmouth; and the famous "Old Man of the Mountain" granite head profile, the state's official emblem, at Franconia.

Famous natives and residents: Sherman Adams, former governor and presidential advisor; Salmon P. Chase, jurist; Charles Anderson Dana, editor; Mary Baker Eddy, founder of the Christian Science Church; Dustin Farnum, actor; Thomas Green Fessenden, journalist and satirical poet; Daniel Chester French, sculptor; Horace Greeley, journalist and politician; Sarah J. Hale, editor; John Irving, writer; Benjamin F. Keith, theater entrepreneur; Jackson Hall Kelly, promoter of Oregon settlement; John Langdon, political leader; Sharon Christa McAuliffe, teacher and astronaut; Franklin Pierce, former president; Augustus Saint-Gaudens, sculptor; Alan Shepard, astronaut; Harlan F. Stone, jurist; Daniel Webster, statesman; Henry Wilson, politician and former vice president; Noah Worcester, clergyman and pacifist.

New Jersey

Capital: Trenton
Governor: Christine Todd Whitman, R (to Jan. 2002)
Senators: Robert Torricelli, D (to Jan. 2003); Frank R. Lautenberg, D (to Jan. 2001)
Secy. of State: DeForest B. Soaries, Jr., R (to Jan. 2002)
Treasurer: Roland Machold (to Jan. 2002)
Atty. General: John Farmer, Jr., R (to Jan. 2002)
Chief Justice: Deborah T. Poritz, R
Entered Union (rank): Dec. 18, 1787 (3)
Present constitution adopted: 1947
Motto: Liberty and prosperity
State Symbols: flower, purple violet (1913); **bird,** eastern goldfinch (1935); **insect,** honeybee (1974); **tree,** red oak (1950); **animal,** horse (1977); **colors,** buff and blue (1965); **folk dance,** square dance; **dinosaur,** hadrosaurus foulkii; **fish,** brook trout; **shell,** knobbed whelk;
Nickname: Garden State
Origin of name: From the Channel Isle of Jersey

10 largest cities (1998 est.)[1]: Newark, 267,823; Jersey City, 232,429; Paterson, 148,212; Elizabeth, 110,661; Trenton, 84,494; Camden, 83,546; Clifton, 76,180; East Orange, 69,598; Bayonne, 61,051; Passaic, 60,817
Land area: 7,419 sq mi. (19,215 sq km)
Geographic center: In Mercer Co., 5 mi. SE of Trenton
Number of counties: 21
Largest county by population and area: Bergen, 857,052 (1999 est.); Burlington, 805 sq mi.
State forests: 11
State parks: 35 (67,111 ac.)
Residents: New Jerseyite, New Jerseyan
1999 resident population est.: 8,143,412
1990 resident census population (rank): 7,730,188 (9). **Male:** 3,735,685; **Female:** 3,994,503. **White:** 6,130,465 (79.3%); **Black:** 1,036,825 (13.4%); **American Indian:** 14,970 (0.2%); **Asian:** 272,521 (3.5%); **Other race:** 275,407 (3.6%); **Hispanic:** 739,861 (9.6%). **1990 percent population under 18:** 23.3; **65 and over:** 13.4; **median age:** 34.3.

New Jersey's early colonial history was involved with that of New York (New Netherlands), of which it was a part. One year after the Dutch surrender to England in 1664, New Jersey was organized as an English colony under Gov. Philip Carteret.

In 1676 the colony was divided between Carteret and a company of English Quakers who had obtained the rights belonging to John, Lord Berkeley. New Jersey became a united, crown colony in 1702, administered by the royal governor of New York. Finally, in 1738, New Jersey was separated from New York under its own royal governor, Lewis Morris. Because of its key location between New York City and Philadelphia, New Jersey saw much fighting during the American Revolution.

Today, New Jersey, an area of wide industrial diversification, is known as the Crossroads of the East. Products from over 15,000 factories can be delivered overnight to almost 60 million people, representing 12 states and the District of Columbia. The greatest single industry is chemicals; New Jersey is one of the foremost research centers in the world. Many large oil refineries are located in northern New Jersey. Other important manufactured items are pharmaceuticals, instruments, electrical goods, and apparel.

Of the total land area, 36% is forested (1992). In 1995 there were about 9,000 farms, with over 850,000 acres under harvest. The state ranks high in the production of almost all garden vegetables. Tomatoes, asparagus, corn, and blueberries are important crops, and poultry and dairy farming make significant contributions to the state's economy.

Tourism is the second-largest industry in New Jersey. The state has numerous resort areas on 127 miles of Atlantic coastline. In 1977, New Jersey voters approved legislation allowing legalized casino gambling in Atlantic City. Points of interest include the Delaware Water Gap, the Edison National Historic Site in West Orange, Princeton University, Liberty State Park, Jersey City, and the N.J. State Aquarium in Camden (opened 1992).

Famous natives and residents: Bud Abbott, comedian; Charles Addams, cartoonist; Edwin Aldrin, astronaut; Count Basie, band leader; Joan Bennett, actress; Jon Bon Jovi, musician; William J. Brennan, jurist; Aaron Burr, political leader; James Fenimore Cooper, novelist; Lou Costello, comedian; Stephen Crane, writer; Helen Gahagan Douglas, former representative; Allen Ginsberg, poet; William Frederick Halsey, Jr., admiral; Alfred Joyce Kilmer, poet; Ernie Kovacs, comedian; Jerry Lewis, comedian and film director; Anne Morrow Lindbergh, author; Norman Mailer, novelist; Patricia McBride, ballerina; Richard Nixon, former president; Dorothy Parker, author; Joe Piscopo, comedian and actor; Paul Robeson, singer and actor; Philip Roth, novelist; Ruth St. Denis, dancer and choreographer; Antonin Scalia, jurist; H. Norman Schwarzkopf, general; Frank Sinatra, singer and actor; Bruce Springsteen, musician; Alfred Stieglitz, photographer; Albert Payson Terhune, journalist and novelist; Sarah Vaughan, singer; William Carlos Williams, physician and poet; Edmund Wilson, literary critic and author.

New Mexico

Capital: Santa Fe
Governor: Gary E. Johnson, R (to Jan. 2003)
Lieut. Governor: Walter Bradley, R (to Jan. 2003)
Senators: Jeff Bingaman, D (to Jan. 2001); Pete V. Domenici, R (to Jan. 2003)
Secy. of State: Rebecca Vigil-Giron, D (to Jan. 2003)
Atty. General: Patricia A. Madrid, D (to Jan. 2003)
State Auditor: Domingo P. Martinez, D (to Jan. 2003)
State Treasurer: Michael A. Montoya, D (to Jan. 2003)
Commissioner of Public Lands: Ray Powell, D (to Jan. 2003)
Organized as territory: Sept. 9, 1850
Entered Union (rank): Jan. 6, 1912 (47)
Present constitution adopted: 1911
Motto: *Crescit eundo* (It grows as it goes)
State Symbols: flower, yucca (1927); **tree,** pinon (1949); **animal,** black bear (1963); **bird,** roadrunner (1949); **fish,** cutthroat trout (1955); **vegetables,** chili and frijol (1965); **gem,** turquoise (1967); **song,** "O Fair New Mexico" (1917); **Spanish-language song,** "Asi Es Nuevo Méjico" (1971); **poem,** A Nuevo México (1991); **grass,** blue gramma (1973); **fossil,** coelophysis (1981); **cookie,** bizcochito (1989); **insect,** tarantula hawk wasp (1989); **ballad,** "Land of Enchantment" (1989); **bilingual song,** "New Mexico— Mi Lindo Nuevo Mexico", (1995); **question,** "Red or Green?" (1999);
Nickname: Land of Enchantment (1999)
Origin of name: From the country of Mexico
10 largest cities (1998 est.): Albuquerque, 419,311; Las Cruces, 76,102; Santa Fe, 67,879; Rio Rancho, 50,041; Roswell, 47,624; Farmington, 39,028; Clovis, 32,394; Alamogordo, 28,312; Hobbs, 27,156; Carlsbad, 26,315
Land area: 121,365 sq mi. (314,334 sq km)
Geographic center: In Torrance Co., 12 mi. SSW of Willard
Number of counties: 33
Largest county by population and area: Bernalillo, 523,472 (1999 est.); Catron, 6,928 sq mi.
State-owned forested land: 933,000 ac.
State parks: 31 (267,302 ac.)
Residents: New Mexican
1999 resident population est.: 1,739,844
1990 resident census population (rank): 1,515,069 (37). **Male:** 745,253; **Female:** 769,816. **White:** 1,146,028 (75.6%); **Black:** 30,210 (2.0%); **American Indian:** 134,355 (8.9%); **Asian:** 14,124 (0.9%); **Other race:** 190,352 (12.6%); **Hispanic:** 579,224 (38.2%). **1990 percent population under 18:** 29.5; **65 and over:** 10.8; **median age:** 31.1.

Francisco Vásquez de Coronado, a Spanish explorer searching for gold, traveled the region that became New Mexico in 1540–42. In 1598 the first Spanish settlement was established on the Rio Grande River by Juan de Onate; in 1610 Santa Fe was founded and made the capital of New Mexico.

The U.S. acquired most of New Mexico in 1848, as a result of the Mexican War, and the remainder in the 1853 Gadsden Purchase. Union troops captured the territory from the Confederates during the Civil War. With the surrender of Geronimo in 1886, the Apache Wars and most of the Indian conflicts in the area were ended.

Since 1945, New Mexico has been a leader in energy research and development with extensive experiments conducted at Los Alamos Scientific Laboratory and Sandia Laboratories in the nuclear, solar, and geothermal areas.

Minerals are the state's richest natural resource and New Mexico is one of the U.S. leaders in output of uranium and potassium salts. Petroleum, natural gas, copper, gold, silver, zinc, lead, and molybdenum also contribute heavily to the state's income.

The principal manufacturing industries include food products, chemicals, transportation equipment, lumber, electrical machinery, and stone-clay-glass products. More than two-thirds of New Mexico's farm income comes from livestock products, especially sheep. Cotton, pecans, and sorghum are the most important field crops. Corn, peanuts, beans, onions, chilies, and lettuce are also grown.

Tourist attractions in New Mexico include the Carlsbad Caverns National Park, Inscription Rock at El Morro National Monument, the ruins at Fort Union, Billy the Kid mementos at Lincoln, the White Sands and Gila Cliff Dwellings National Monuments, and the Chaco Culture National Historical Park.

Famous natives and residents: Kathy Baker, actress; Judy Blume, author; Ernest L. Blumenschein, artist; William "Billy the Kid" Bonney, outlaw; Richard Bradford, author; Ralph Bunche, Nobel Peace Prize winner; Bruce Cabot, actor; Glen Campbell, singer; Kit Carson, army scout and trapper; Dennis Chavez, former senator; John Chisum, cattle king; Mangus Coloradas, Apache leader; Edward Condon, physicist; Bill Daily, actor; John Denver, singer; Bo Diddley, blues guitarist; Patrick Garrett, lawman; Greer Garson, actress; Sid Gutierrez, astronaut; William Hanna, animator; Neil Patrick Harris, actor; Carl Hatch, former senator; Tony Hillerman, author; Conrad Hilton, hotel executive; Dennis Hopper, actor; Peter Hurd, artist; Preston Jones, playwright and actor; Ralph Kiner, baseball player and sportscaster; Nancy Lopez, golfer; Maria Martínez, San Ildefonso Pueblo potter; Demi Moore, actress; Jim Morrison, singer and songwriter; Bill Mauldin, political cartoonist; Popé, San Juan Pueblo medicine man and leader; Georgia O'Keeffe, painter; Harrison Schmitt, astronaut and U.S. representative; Kim Stanley, actress; Slim Summerville, actor; Clyde Tombaugh, astronomer; Al Unser, Bobby Unser, auto racers; Victorio, Apache chief; Linda Wertheimer, NPR correspondent; Kathy Whitworth, golfer.

New York

Capital: Albany
Governor: George E. Pataki, R (to Jan. 2003)
Lieut. Governor: Mary Donohue, R (to Jan. 2003)
Senators: Charles E. Schumer, D (to Jan. 2005); Daniel P. Moynihan, D (to Jan. 2001)
Secy. of State: Alexander Treadwell, R (to Jan. 1999)
Comptroller: Carl McCall, D (to Jan. 2003)
Atty. General: Eliot Spitzer, D (to Jan. 2003)
Entered Union (rank): July 26, 1788 (11)
Present constitution adopted: 1777 (last revised 1938)
Motto: *Excelsior* (Ever upward)
State Symbols: animal, beaver (1975); **fish,** brook trout (1975); **gem,** garnet (1969); **flower,** rose (1955); **tree,** sugar maple (1956); **bird,** bluebird (1970); **insect,** ladybug (1989); **song,** "I Love New York" (1980);
Nickname: Empire State
Origin of name: In honor of the Duke of York

10 largest cities (1998 est.): New York, 7,420,166; Buffalo, 300,717; Rochester, 216,887; Yonkers, 190,153; Syracuse, 152,215; Albany, 94,305; New Rochelle, 67,225; Mount Vernon, 66,824; Schenectady, 61,698; Utica, 59,334
Land area: 47,224 sq mi. (122,310 sq km)
Geographic center: In Madison Co., 12 mi. S of Oneida and 26 mi. SW of Utica
Number of counties: 62
Largest county by population and area: Kings, 2,268,297 (1999 est.); St. Lawrence, 2,686 sq mi.
State forest preserves: Adirondacks, 2,500,000 ac.; Catskills, 250,000 ac.
State parks: 152
Residents: New Yorker
1999 resident population est.: 18,196,601
1990 resident census population (rank): 17,990,455 (2). **Male:** 8,625,673; **Female:** 9,364,782. **White:** 13,385,255 (74.4%); **Black:** 2,859,055 (15.9%); **American Indian:** 62,651 (0.3%); **Asian:** 693,760 (3.9%); **Other race:** 989,734 (5.5%); **Hispanic:** 2,214,026 (12.3%). **1990 percent population under 18:** 23.7; **65 and over:** 13.1; **median age:** 33.7.

Giovanni da Verrazano, an Italian-born navigator sailing for France, discovered New York Bay in 1524. Henry Hudson, an Englishman employed by the Dutch, reached the bay and sailed up the river now bearing his name in 1609, the same year that northern New York was explored and claimed for France by Samuel de Champlain.

In 1624 the first permanent Dutch settlement was established at Fort Orange (now Albany); one year later Peter Minuit is said to have purchased Manhattan Island from the Indians for trinkets worth about $24 and founded the Dutch colony of New Amsterdam (now New York City), which was surrendered to the English in 1664.

For a short time, New York City was the U.S. capital and George Washington was inaugurated there as the first president on April 30, 1789.

New York's extremely rapid commercial growth may be partly attributed to Governor De Witt Clinton, who pushed through the construction of the Erie Canal (Buffalo to Albany), which was opened in 1825. Today, the 559-mile Governor Thomas E. Dewey Thruway connects New York City with Buffalo and with Connecticut, Massachusetts, and Pennsylvania express highways. Two toll-free superhighways, the Adirondack Northway (linking Albany with the Canadian border) and the North-South Expressway (crossing central New York from the Pennsylvania border to the Thousand Islands), have been opened.

The great metropolis of New York City is the nerve center of the nation. It is a leader in manufacturing, foreign trade, commerce and banking, book and magazine publishing, and theatrical production. A leading seaport, its John F. Kennedy International Airport is one of the busiest airports in the world. New York is also home to the New York Stock Exchange, the largest in the world. The printing and publishing industry is the city's largest manufacturing employer, with the apparel industry second.

Nearly all the rest of the state's manufacturing is done on Long Island, along the Hudson River north to Albany, and through the Mohawk Valley, Central New York, and Southern Tier regions to Buffalo. The St. Lawrence seaway and power projects have opened the North Country to industrial expansion and have given the state a second seacoast.

The state ranks seventh in the nation in manufacturing, with 893,000 employees in 1999. The principal industries are printing and publishing, industrial machinery and equipment, electronic equipment, and instruments. The convention and tourist business is also an important source of income.

New York farms produce cattle and calves, corn and poultry, and vegetables and fruits. The state is a leading wine producer.

Among the major points of interest are Castle Clinton, Fort Stanwix, and Statue of Liberty National Monuments; Niagara Falls; U.S. Military Academy at West Point; National Historic Sites that include homes of Franklin D. Roosevelt at Hyde Park and Theodore Roosevelt in Oyster Bay and New York City; the Women's Rights National Historical Park in Seneca Falls; National Memorials, including Grant's Tomb and Federal Hall in New York City; Fort Ticonderoga; the Baseball Hall of Fame in Cooperstown; and the United Nations, skyscrapers, museums, theaters, and parks in New York City.

Famous natives and residents: Kareem Abdul-Jabbar, basketball player; Lucille Ball, actress; Humphrey Bogart, actor; James Cagney, actor; Maria Callas, soprano; Benjamin N. Cardozo, jurist; Paddy Chayefsky, playwright; Peter Cooper, industrialist and philanthropist; Aaron Copland, composer; Sammy Davis, Jr., actor and singer; Agnes de Mille, choreographer; Eamon De Valera, former president of Ireland; George Eastman, inventor; Millard Fillmore, former president; Lou Gehrig, baseball player; George Gershwin, composer; Learned Hand, jurist; Edward Hopper, painter; Julia Ward Howe, poet and reformer; Charles Evans Hughes, jurist; Washington Irving, author; Henry James, novelist; John Jay, jurist; Michael Jordan, basketball player; Jerome Kern, composer; Rockwell Kent, painter; Vince Lombardi, football coach; Chico, Groucho, Harpo, and Zeppo Marx, comedians; Herman Melville, author; Ethel Merman, singer and actress; Ogden Nash, poet; Eugene O'Neill, playwright; Red Jacket, Seneca chief; John D. Rockefeller, industrialist; Norman Rockwell, painter and illustrator; Mickey Rooney, actor; Anna Eleanor Roosevelt, reformer and humanitarian; Franklin D. Roosevelt, former president; Theodore Roosevelt, former president; Jonas Salk, polio researcher; Margaret Sanger, birth control leader; Barbara Stanwyck, actress; Risë Stevens, mezzo-soprano; Richard Tucker, tenor; Martin Van Buren, former president; Mae West, actress; Walt Whitman, poet; Edith Wharton, novelist.

North Carolina

Capital: Raleigh
Governor: James B. Hunt, Jr., D (to Jan. 2001)
Lieut. Governor: Dennis A. Wicker, D (to Jan. 2001)
Senators: John Edwards, D (to Jan. 2005);
 Jesse Helms, R (to Jan. 2003)
Secy. of State: Elaine F. Marshall, D (to Jan. 2001)
Treasurer: Harlan E. Boyles, D (to Jan. 2001)
Auditor: Ralph Campbell, D (to Jan. 2001)
Atty. General: Michael Easley, D (to Jan. 2001)
Entered Union (rank): Nov. 21, 1789 (12)
Present constitution adopted: 1971
Motto: *Esse quam videri* (To be rather than to seem)
State Symbols: flower, dogwood (1941); **tree,** pine (1963); **bird,** cardinal (1943); **mammal,** gray squirrel (1969); **insect,** honeybee (1973); **reptile,** eastern box turtle (1979); **gemstone,** emerald (1973); **shell,** scotch bonnet (1965); **historic boat,** shad boat (1987); **beverage,** milk (1987); **rock,** granite (1979); **dog,** plott hound (1989); **song,** "The Old North State" (1927); **colors,** red and blue (1945);
Nickname: Tar Heel State
Origin of name: In honor of Charles I of England
10 largest cities (1998 est.): Charlotte, 504,637;

Raleigh, 259,423; Greensboro, 197,910; Winston-Salem, 164,316; Durham, 153,513; Cary, 82,071; Fayetteville, 77,295; High Point, 76,117; Jacksonville, 68,380; Wilmington, 68,062
Land area: 48,718 sq mi. (126,180 sq km)
Geographic center: In Chatham Co., 10 mi. NW of Sanford
Number of counties: 100
Largest county by population and area: Mecklenburg, 648,400 (1999 est.); Robeson, 949 sq mi.
State forests: 1
State parks: 30 (125,000 ac.)
Residents: North Carolinian
1999 resident population est.: 7,650,789
1990 resident census population (rank): 6,628,637 (10). **Male:** 3,214,290; **Female:** 3,414,347. **White:** 5,008,491 (75.6%); **Black:** 1,456,323 (22.0%); **American Indian:** 80,155 (1.2%); **Asian:** 52,166 (0.8%); **Other race:** 31,502 (0.5%); **Hispanic:** 76,726 (1.2%). **1990 percent population under 18:** 24.2; **65 and over:** 12.1; **median age:** 33.0.

English colonists, sent by Sir Walter Raleigh, unsuccessfully attempted to settle Roanoke Island in 1585 and 1587. Virginia Dare, born there in 1587, was the first child of English parentage born in America.

In 1653 the first permanent settlements were established by English colonists from Virginia near the Roanoke and Chowan rivers. The region was established as an English proprietary colony in 1663–65 and in its early history was the scene of Culpepper's Rebellion (1677), the Quaker-led Cary Rebellion of 1708, the Tuscarora Indian War in 1711–13, and many pirate raids.

During the American Revolution, there was relatively little fighting within the state, but many North Carolinians saw action elsewhere. Despite considerable pro-Union, anti-slavery sentiment, North Carolina joined the Confederacy during the Civil War.

North Carolina is the nation's largest furniture, tobacco, brick, and textile producer. It holds second place in the Southeast in population and first place in the value of its industrial and agricultural production. This production is highly diversified, with metalworking, chemicals, and paper constituting enormous industries. Tobacco, corn, cotton, hay, peanuts, and vegetable crops are of major importance. It is the country's leading producer of mica and lithium.

Tourism is also important, with travelers and vacationers spending more than $1 billion annually in North Carolina. Sports include year-round golfing, skiing at mountain resorts, both fresh- and saltwater fishing, and hunting.

Among the major attractions are the Great Smoky Mountains, the Blue Ridge National Parkway, the Cape Hatteras and Cape Lookout National Seashores, the Wright Brothers National Memorial at Kitty Hawk, Guilford Courthouse and Moores Creek National Military Parks, Carl Sandburg's home near Hendersonville, and the Old Salem Restoration in Winston-Salem.

Famous natives and residents: David Brinkley, TV newscaster; Howard Cosell, sportscaster; Virginia Dare, first person born in America to English parents; James B. Duke, industrialist; Roberta Flack, singer; Ava Gardner, actress; Richard Gatling, inventor; Billy Graham, evangelist; Kathryn Grayson, singer and actress; Jesse Helms, politician; O. Henry, writer; Barbara Howar, broadcaster and writer; Andrew Johnson, former president; Charles Kuralt, TV journalist; Sugar Ray Leonard, boxer; Dolley Madison, former first lady; Ronni Milsap, country music singer; Thelonious Monk, pianist; Alfred Moore, jurist; Edward R.

Murrow, commentator and government official; Walter Hines Page, journalist and ambassador; Floyd Patterson, boxer; Richard Petty, auto racer; James K. Polk, former president; Soupy Sales, comedian; Earl Scruggs, bluegrass musician; Randy Travis, musician; John Scott Trotter, orchestra leader; Thomas Wolfe, novelist.

North Dakota

Capital: Bismarck
Governor: Edward T. Schafer, R (to Dec. 15, 2000)
Lieut. Governor: Rosemarie Myrdal, R (to Dec. 15, 2000)
Senators: Kent Conrad, D (to Jan. 2001);
    Byron L. Dorgan, D (to Jan. 2005)
Secy. of State: Alvin A. Jaeger, R (to Dec. 31, 2000)
Auditor: Robert R. Peterson, R (to Dec. 31, 2000)
Treasurer: Kathi Gilmore, D (to Dec. 31, 2000)
Atty. General: Heidi Heitkamp, D (to Dec. 31, 2000)
Organized as territory: March 2, 1861
Entered Union (rank): Nov. 2, 1889 (39)
Present constitution adopted: 1889
Motto: Liberty and union, now and forever: one and inseparable
State Symbols: tree, American elm (1947); **bird,** western meadowlark (1947); **song,** "North Dakota Hymn" (1947); **fish,** northern pike (1969); **grass,** western wheatgrass (1977); **fossil,** teredo petrified wood (1967); **beverage,** milk (1983); **state march,** Spirit of the Land (1975); **flower,** wild prairie rose (1907); **equine,** Nokota horse (1993); **dance,** square dance (1995);
Nickname: Sioux State; Flickertail State; Peace Garden State; Rough Rider State
Origin of name: From the Sioux tribe, meaning "allies"
10 largest cities (1998 est.): Fargo, 86,718; Bismarck, 54,040; Grand Forks, 47,327; Minot, 35,286; Dickinson, 16,221; Mandan, 15,860; Jamestown, 14,713; West Fargo, 14,091; Williston, 12,446; Wahpeton, 9,322
Land area: 70,704 sq mi. (183,123 sq km)
Geographic center: In Sheridan Co., 5 mi. SW of McClusky
Number of counties: 53
Largest county by population and area: Cass, 118,405 (1999 est.); McKenzie, 2,742 sq mi.
State parks: 20 (14,822 ac.)
Residents: North Dakotan
1999 resident population est.: 633,666
1990 resident census population (rank): 638,800 (47). **Male:** 318,201; **Female:** 320,599. **White:** 604,142 (94.6%); **Black:** 3,524 (0.6%); **American Indian:** 25,917 (4.1%); **Asian:** 3,462 (0.5%); **Other race:** 1,755 (0.3%); **Hispanic:** 4,665 (0.7%). **1990 percent population under 18:** 27.5; **65 and over:** 14.3; **median age:** 32.3.

North Dakota was explored in 1738–40 by French Canadians led by sieur de la Verendrye. In 1803, the U.S. acquired most of North Dakota from France in the Louisiana Purchase. Lewis and Clark explored the region in 1804–06 and the first settlements were made at Pembina in 1812 by Scottish and Irish families while this area was still in dispute between the U.S. and Great Britain.

In 1818, the U.S. obtained the northeastern part of North Dakota by treaty with Great Britain and took possession of Pembina in 1823.

North Dakota is the most rural of all the states, with farms covering more than 90% of the land. North Dakota ranks first in the nation's production of spring and durum wheat, and the state's coal and oil reserves are plentiful.

Other agricultural products include barley, rye, sunflowers, dry edible beans, honey, oats, flaxseed, sugar beets, hay, beef cattle, sheep, and hogs.

Recently, manufacturing industries have grown, especially food processing and farm equipment. The state also produces natural gas, lignite, salt, clay, sand, and gravel.

The Garrison Dam on the Missouri River provides extensive irrigation and produces 400,000 kilowatts of electricity for the Missouri Basin areas.

Known for its waterfowl, grouse, and deer hunting and bass, trout, and pike fishing, North Dakota has 20 state parks and recreation areas. Points of interest include the International Peace Garden near Dunseith, Fort Union Trading Post National Historic Site near Williston, Knife River Indian Villages National Historic Site in Stanton, the State Capitol at Bismarck, the Badlands, Theodore Roosevelt National Park, and Fort Abraham Lincoln State Park.

Famous natives and residents: Lynn Anderson, singer; Maxwell Anderson, playwright; Dr. Robert H. Bahmer, U.S. archivist; Elizabeth Bodine, humanitarian; Dr. Anne Carlsen, educator; Warren Christopher, former U.S. Secretary of State; Ronald N. Davies, jurist; Angie Dickinson, actress; Ivan Dmitre, artist; Carl Ben Eielson, aviator; Phyllis Frelich, actress; Bertin C. Gamble, founder of Gamble-Skogmo; William H. Gass, writer and philosopher; Rev. Richard C. Halverson, U.S. Senate chaplain; Brynhild Haugland, state legislator; Phil D. Jackson, basketball player and coach; Dr. Leon O. Jacobson, researcher and educator; Harold K. Johnson, former army general and U.S. Army Chief of Staff; David C. Jones, former Chairman, Joint Chiefs of Staff; Louis L'Amour, author; Peggy Lee, singer; William Lemke, former representative; Roger Maris, baseball player; Marquis de Mores, cattleman who established Medora; Gerald P. Nye, former senator; Casper Oimoen, skier; William A. Owens, former Vice Chairman, Joint Chiefs of Staff; Arthur Peterson, radio and TV actor; Cliff (Fido) Purpur, hockey player and coach; James Rosenquist, painter; Harold Schafer, founder of Gold Seal Co.; Eric Sevareid, TV commentator; Ann Sothern, actress; Dorothy Stickney, actress; Edward K. Thompson, *Life* magazine editor; Era Bell Thompson, *Ebony* magazine editor; Tommy Tucker, band leader; Bobby Vee, entertainer; Lawrence Welk, band leader; Larry Woiwode, writer.

Ohio

Capital: Columbus
Governor: Bob Taft, R (to Jan. 2003)
Lieut. Governor: Maureen O'Connor, R (to Jan. 2003)
Senators: Mike DeWine, R (to Jan. 2001);
    George V. Voinovich, R (to Jan. 2005)
Secy. of State: J. Kenneth Blackwell, R (to Jan. 2003)
Auditor: Jim Petro, R (to Jan. 2003)
Treasurer: Joseph T. Deters, R (to Jan. 2003)
Atty. General: Betty D. Montgomery, R (to Jan. 2003)
Entered Union (rank): March 1, 1803 (17)
Present constitution adopted: 1851
Motto: (none)
State Symbols: flower, scarlet carnation (1904); **tree,** buckeye (1953); **bird,** cardinal (1933); **insect,** ladybug (1975); **gemstone,** flint (1965); **song,** "Beautiful Ohio" (1969); **beverage,** tomato juice (1965);
Nickname: Buckeye State
Origin of name: From an Iroquoian word meaning "great river"
10 largest cities (1998 est.): Columbus, 670,234; Cleveland, 495,817; Cincinnati, 336,400; Toledo, 312,174; Akron, 215,712; Dayton, 167,475; Youngstown, 84,650; Parma, 83,347; Canton, 79,259; Lorain, 68,857
Land area: 40,953 sq mi. (106,067 sq km)
Geographic center: In Delaware Co., 25 mi. NNE of Columbus
Number of counties: 88
Largest county by population and area: Cuyahoga, 1,371,717 (1999 est.); Ross, 688 sq mi.

State forests: 19 (172,744 ac.)
State parks: 71 (198,027 ac.)
Residents: Ohioan
1999 resident population est.: 11,256,654
1990 resident census population (rank): 10,847,115
(7). Male: 5,226,340; Female: 5,620,775. White:
9,521,756 (87.8%); Black: 1,154,826 (10.6%); American Indian: 20,358 (0.2%); Asian: 91,179 (0.8%);
Other race: 58,996 (0.5%); Hispanic: 139,696
(1.3%). 1990 percent population under 18: 25.8; 65
and over: 13.0; median age: 33.3.

First explored for France by sieur de la Salle in 1669, the Ohio region became British property after the French and Indian Wars. Ohio was acquired by the U.S. after the Revolutionary War in 1783. In 1788, the first permanent settlement was established at Marietta, capital of the Northwest Territory.

The 1790s saw severe fighting with the Indians in Ohio; a major battle was won by Maj. Gen. Anthony Wayne at Fallen Timbers in 1794. In the War of 1812, Commodore Oliver H. Perry defeated the British in the Battle of Lake Erie on Sept. 10, 1813.

Ohio is one of the nation's industrial leaders, ranking third in the value of manufactured products. Important manufacturing centers are located in or near Ohio's major cities. Akron is known for rubber; Canton for roller bearings; Cincinnati for jet engines and machine tools; Cleveland for auto assembly and parts, refining, and steel; Dayton for office machines, refrigeration, and heating and auto equipment; Youngstown and Steubenville for steel; and Toledo for glass and auto parts.

The state's fertile soil produces soybeans, corn, oats, grapes, and clover. More than half of Ohio's farm receipts come from dairy farming and sheep and hog raising. Ohio is the top state in lime production and among the leaders in coal, clay, salt, sand, and gravel. Petroleum, gypsum, cement, and natural gas are also important.

Tourism is a valuable revenue producer, bringing in $9.9 billion in 1996, and ranking 7th among the 50 states. Attractions include the Rock and Roll Hall of Fame, Indian burial grounds at Mound City Group National Monument, Perry's Victory International Peace Memorial, the Pro Football Hall of Fame at Canton, and the homes of presidents Grant, Taft, Hayes, Harding, and Garfield.

Famous natives and residents: Neil Armstrong, astronaut; Kathleen Battle, soprano; George Bellows, painter and lithographer; Ambrose Bierce, journalist; Erma Bombeck, columnist; Bill Boyd (Hopalong Cassidy), actor; Milton Caniff, cartoonist; Hart Crane, poet; George Armstrong Custer, army officer; Dorothy Dandridge, actress; Doris Day, singer and actress; Clarence Darrow, lawyer; Ruby Dee, actress; Rita Dove, former U.S. poet laureate; Hugh Downs, TV broadcaster; Thomas A. Edison, inventor; Clark Gable, actor; James A. Garfield, former president; Lillian Gish, actress; John Glenn, astronaut and senator; Ulysses S. Grant, former president; Warren G. Harding, former president; Rutherford Hayes, former president; Benjamin Harrison, former president; William Dean Howells, novelist and critic; Zane Grey, author; Robert Henri, painter; Kenisaw Mountain Landis, first baseball commissioner; Dean Martin, singer and actor; William McKinley, former president; Paul Newman, actor; Jack Nicklaus, golfer; Annie Oakley, markswoman; Norman Vincent Peale, clergyman; Tyrone Power, actor; Judith Resnik, astronaut; Eddie Rickenbacker, aviator; Arthur M. Schlesinger, Jr., historian; William Tecumseh Sherman, army general; Gloria Steinem, feminist; William H. Taft, former president; Tecumseh, Shawnee Indian chief; Lowell Thomas, explorer and commentator; James Thurber, author and cartoonist; Orville Wright, inventor; Cy Young, baseball player.

Oklahoma

Capital: Oklahoma City
Governor: Frank Keating, R (to Jan. 2003)
Lieut. Governor: Mary Fallin, R (to Jan. 2003)
Senators: James M. Inhofe, R (to Jan. 2003);
Don Nickles, R (to Jan. 2005)
Secy. of State: Mike Hunter, R (to Jan. 2003)
Treasurer: Robert Butkin, D (to Jan. 2003)
Atty. General: Drew Edmondson, D (to Jan. 2003)
Organized as territory: May 2, 1890
Entered Union (rank): Nov. 16, 1907 (46)
Present constitution adopted: 1907
Motto: *Labor omnia vincit* (Labor conquers all things)
State Symbols: flower, mistletoe (1893); tree, redbud
(1937); bird, scissor-tailed flycatcher (1951); animal,
bison (1972); reptile, mountain boomer lizard (1969);
stone, rose rock (barite rose) (1968); colors, green
and white (1915); song, "Oklahoma" (1953);
beverage, milk; butterfly, black swallowtail; fish,
white or sand bass; folk dance, square dance;
furbearer, raccoon; game animal, white-tailed deer;
grass, Indiangrass; insect, honeybee; musical
instrument, fiddle; poem, "Howdy Folks," David
Randolph Milsten; waltz, "Oklahoma Wind";
wildflower, Indian blanket;
Nickname: Sooner State
Origin of name: From two Choctaw Indian words meaning "red people"
10 largest cities (1998 est.): Oklahoma City, 472,221;
Tulsa, 381,393; Norman, 93,019; Lawton, 81,107;
Broken Arrow, 72,564; Edmond, 64,962; Midwest City,
54,037; Moore, 45,318; Enid, 45,234;
Stillwater, 38,765
Land area: 68,679 sq mi. (177,877 sq km)
Geographic center: In Oklahoma Co., 8 mi. N of Okla-
homa City
Number of counties: 77
Largest county by population and area: Oklahoma,
636,539 (1999 est.); Osage, 2,251 sq mi.
State parks: 51 (72,000 ac.)
Residents: Oklahoman
1999 resident population est.: 3,358,044
1990 resident census population (rank): 3,145,585
(28). Male: 1,530,819; Female: 1,614,766. White:
2,583,512 (82.1%); Black: 233,801 (7.4%); American
Indian: 252,420 (8.0%); Asian: 33,563 (1.1%); Other
race: 42,289 (1.3%); Hispanic: 86,160 (2.7%). 1990
percent population under 18: 26.6; 65 and over:
13.5; median age: 33.1.

Francisco Vásquez de Coronado first explored the region for Spain in 1541. The U.S. acquired most of Oklahoma in 1803 in the Louisiana Purchase from France; the Western Panhandle region became U.S. territory with the annexation of Texas in 1845.

Set aside as Indian Territory in 1834, the region was divided into Indian Territory and Oklahoma Territory on May 2, 1890. The two were combined to make a new state, Oklahoma, on Nov. 16, 1907.

On April 22, 1889, the first day homesteading was permitted, 50,000 people swarmed into the area. Those who tried to beat the noon starting gun were called "Sooners," hence the state's nickname.

Oil made Oklahoma a rich state, but natural-gas production has now surpassed it. Oil refining, meat packing, food processing, and machinery manufacturing (especially construction and oil equipment) are important industries.

Other minerals produced in Oklahoma include helium, gypsum, zinc, cement, coal, copper, and silver. Oklahoma's rich plains produce bumper yields of wheat, as well as large crops of sorghum, hay, cotton, and peanuts. More than half of Oklahoma's annual farm receipts are contributed by livestock products, including cattle, dairy products, swine, and broilers.

Tourist attractions include the National Cowboy Hall of Fame in Oklahoma City, the Will Rogers Memorial in Claremore, the Cherokee Cultural Center with a restored Cherokee village, the restored Fort Gibson Stockade near Muskogee, the Lake Texoma recreation area, Pari-Mutual horse racing at Remington Park in Oklahoma City, and Blue Ribbon Downs in Sallisaw.

Famous natives and residents: Johnny Bench, baseball player; John Berryman, poet; Garth Brooks, singer; Iron Eyes Cody, Cherokee actor; L. Gordon Cooper, astronaut; Ralph Ellison, writer; James Garner, actor; Owen K. Garriott, astronaut; Vince Gill, singer; Chester Gould, cartoonist; Woody Guthrie, singer and composer; Roy Harris, composer; Paul Harvey, broadcaster; Van Heflin, actor; Ron Howard, actor and director; Ben Johnson, actor; Jennifer Jones, actress; Jeane Kirkpatrick, educator and public-affairs spokesperson; Shannon Lucid, astronaut; Wilma P. Mankiller, principal chief of the Cherokee Nation of Oklahoma; Mickey Mantle, baseball player; Reba McEntire, singer; Shannon Miller, Olympic gymnast; Bill Moyers, journalist; Daniel Patrick Moynihan, N.Y. senator; Patti Page, singer; Mary Kay Place, actress and writer; Tony Randall, actor; Oral Roberts, evangelist; Dale Robertson, actor; Will Rogers, humorist; Dan Rowan, comedian; Thomas P. Stafford, astronaut; Maria Tallchief, ballerina; Jim Thorpe, athlete; Alfre Woodard, actress.

Oregon

Capital: Salem
Governor: John A. Kitzhaber, D (to Jan. 2003)
Senators: Gordon Smith, R (to Jan. 2003); Ron Wyden, D (to Jan. 2005)
Secy. of State: Bill Bradbury, D (to Jan. 2001)
Treasurer: James A. Hill, D (to Jan. 2001)
Atty. General: Hardy Myers, D (to Jan. 2001)
Organized as territory: Aug. 14, 1848
Entered Union (rank): Feb. 14, 1859 (33)
Present constitution adopted: 1859
Motto: *Alis volat Propriis* (She flies with her own wings) (1987)
State Symbols: flower, Oregon grape (1899); **tree,** douglas fir (1939); **animal,** beaver (1969); **bird,** western meadowlark (1927); **fish,** chinook salmon (1961); **rock,** thunderegg (1965); **colors,** navy blue and gold (1959); **song,** "Oregon, My Oregon" (1927); **insect,** swallowtail butterfly (1979); **dance,** square dance (1997); **nut,** hazelnut (1989); **gemstone,** sunstone (1987);
Nickname: Beaver State
Origin of name: Unknown. However, it is generally accepted that the name, first used by Jonathan Carver in 1778, was taken from the writings of Maj. Robert Rogers, an English army officer.
10 largest cities (1998 est.): Portland, 503,891; Eugene, 128,240; Salem, 126,702; Gresham, 85,021; Beaverton, 82,111; Hillsboro, 61,111; Medford, 57,156; Springfield, 50,682; Corvallis, 50,202; Albany, 38,832
Land area: 96,003 sq mi. (248,647 sq km)
Geographic center: In Crook Co., 25 mi. SSE of Prineville
Number of counties: 36
Largest county by population and area: Multnomah, 633,224 (1999 est.); Harney, 10,135 sq mi.
State forests: 820,000 ac.
State parks: 240 (93,330 ac.)
Residents: Oregonian
1999 resident population est.: 3,316,154
1990 resident census population (rank): 2,842,321 (29). **Male:** 1,397,073; **Female:** 1,445,248. **White:** 2,636,787 (92.8%); **Black:** 46,178 (1.6%); **American Indian:** 38,496 (1.4%); **Asian:** 69,269 (2.4%); **Other**

race: 51,591 (1.8%); **Hispanic:** 112,707 (4.0%). **1990 percent population under 18:** 25.5; **65 and over:** 13.8; **median age:** 34.5.

Spanish and English sailors are believed to have sighted the Oregon coast in the 1500s and 1600s. Capt. James Cook, seeking the Northwest Passage, charted some of the coastline in 1778. In 1792, Capt. Robert Gray, in the *Columbia,* discovered the river named after his ship and claimed the area for the U.S.

In 1805 the Lewis and Clark expedition explored the area. John Jacob Astor's fur depot, Astoria, was founded in 1811. Disputes for control of Oregon between American settlers and the Hudson Bay Company were finally resolved in the 1846 Oregon Treaty in which Great Britain gave up claims to the region.

Oregon has a $3.3 billion lumber and wood products industry, and an $859 million paper and allied manufacturing industry. Its salmon-fishing industry is one of the world's largest.

In agriculture, the state leads in growing peppermint, cover seed crops, blackberries, boysenberries, loganberries, black raspberries, and hazelnuts. It is second in raising hops, raspberries, sweet cherries, prunes, snap beans, and onions. Oregon has the only nickel smelter in the United States.

With the low-cost electric power provided by dams, Oregon has developed steadily as a manufacturing state. Leading manufactured items are lumber and plywood, metalwork, machinery, aluminum, chemicals, paper, food packing, and electronic equipment.

Crater Lake National Park, Mount Hood, and Bonneville Dam on the Columbia are major tourist attractions. Oregon Dunes National Recreation Area has been established near Florence. Other points of interest include the Oregon Caves National Monument, Cape Perpetua in Siuslaw National Forest, Columbia River Gorge between The Dalles and Troutdale, Hells Canyon, Newberry Volcanic National Monument, and John Day Fossil Beds National Monument.

Famous natives and residents: James Beard, food expert; Raymond Carver, writer and poet; Homer C. Davenport, political cartoonist; David Douglas, botanist; Abigail Scott Duniway, women's suffrage advocate; John E. Frohnmeyer, former chairman of the National Endowment for the Arts; Robert Gray, sea captain and discoverer of Columbia River; Matt Groening, cartoonist; Mark Hatfield, senator; Donald P. Hodel, former secretary of the Interior; Chief Joseph, Nez Percé chief; Dave Kingman, baseball player; Ursula LeGuin, writer; Edwin Markham, poet; Phyllis McGinley, author; Linus Pauling, chemist; Jane Powell, actress and singer; John Reed, poet and author; Harvey W. Scott, editor; Doc Severinsen, band leader; Norton Simon, business executive; Paul M. Simon, Illinois senator; William E. Stafford, poet; Sally Struthers, actress.

Pennsylvania

Capital: Harrisburg
Governor: Tom Ridge, R (to Jan. 2003)
Lieut. Governor: Mark Schweiker, R (to Jan. 2003)
Senators: Rick Santorum, R (to Jan. 2001); Arlen Specter, R (to Jan. 2005)
Acting Secy. of the Commonwealth: Kim Pizzingrilli, R (at the pleasure of the governor)
Auditor General: Robert P. Casey, Jr., D (to Jan. 2001)
Atty. General: Mike Fisher, R (to Jan. 2001)
Entered Union (rank): Dec. 12, 1787 (2)
Present constitution adopted: 1968

Motto: Virtue, liberty, and independence
State Symbols: flower, mountain laurel (1933); **tree,** hemlock (1931); **bird,** ruffed grouse (1931); **dog,** Great Dane (1965); **colors,** blue and gold (1907); **song,** "Pennsylvania" (1990);
Nickname: Keystone State
Origin of name: In honor of Adm. Sir William Penn, father of William Penn. It means "Penn's Woodland."
10 largest cities (1998 est.): Philadelphia, 1,436,287; Pittsburgh, 340,520; Erie, 102,640; Allentown, 100,757; Reading, 74,762; Scranton, 74,683; Bethlehem, 69,383; Lancaster, 52,951; Harrisburg, 49,502; Altoona, 49,226
Land area: 44,820 sq mi. (116,083 sq km)
Geographic center: In Centre Co., 2½ mi. SW of Bellefonte
Number of counties: 67
Largest county by population and area: Philadelphia, 1,417,601 (1999 est.); Lycoming, 1,235 sq mi.
State forests: over 2 mil. ac.
State parks: 116
Residents: Pennsylvanian
1999 resident population est.: 11,994,016
1990 resident census population (rank): 11,881,643 (5). **Male:** 5,694,265; **Female:** 6,187,378. **White:** 10,520,201 (88.5%); **Black:** 1,089,795 (9.2%); **American Indian:** 14,733 (0.1%); **Asian:** 137,438 (1.2%); **Other race:** 119,476 (1.0%); **Hispanic:** 232,262 (2.0%). **1990 percent population under 18:** 23.5; **65 and over:** 15.4; **median age:** 34.9.

Rich in historic lore, Pennsylvania territory was disputed in the early 1600s among the Dutch, the Swedes, and the English. England acquired the region in 1664 with the capture of New York and in 1681 Pennsylvania was granted to William Penn, a Quaker, by King Charles II.

Philadelphia was the seat of the federal government almost continuously from 1776 to 1800; there the Declaration of Independence was signed in 1776 and the U.S. Constitution drawn up in 1787. Valley Forge, of Revolutionary War fame, and Gettysburg, site of the pivotal battle of the Civil War, are both in Pennsylvania. The Liberty Bell is located in a glass pavilion across from Independence Hall in Philadelphia.

With the decline of the coal, steel, and railroad industries, Pennsylvania's industry has diversified, although the state still leads the country in the production of specialty steel. Pennsylvania is a leader in the production of chemicals, food, and electrical machinery and produces 10% of the nation's cement. Also important are brick and tiles, glass, limestone, and slate. Data processing is also increasingly important.

Pennsylvania's 8 million-plus agricultural acres (over 4 million acres for crops, 4 million acres in farm woodlands and pasture) produce a wide variety of crops, and its 51,000 farms are the backbone of the state's economy. Leading products are milk, poultry, eggs, a variety of fruits, sweet corn, potatoes, mushrooms, cheese, beans, hay, maple syrup, and Christmas trees.

Pennsylvania has the largest rural population in the nation. The state's farmers sell more than $3.6 billion in crops and livestock annually, and agribusiness and food-related industries account for another $39 billion in economic activity annually.

Tourists now spend approximately $6 billion in Pennsylvania annually. Among the chief attractions are the Gettysburg National Military Park, Valley Forge National Historical Park, Independence National Historical Park in Philadelphia, the Pennsylvania Dutch region, the Eisenhower farm near Gettysburg, and the Delaware Water Gap National Recreation Area.

Famous natives and residents: Louisa May Alcott, novelist; Marian Anderson, contralto; Maxwell Anderson, dramatist; Samuel Barber, composer; John Barrymore, actor; Donald Barthelme, author; Stephen Vincent Benet, poet and story writer; Daniel Boone, frontiersman; Ed Bradley, TV anchorman; James Buchanan, former president; Alexander Calder, sculptor; Rachel Carson, biologist and author; Mary Cassatt, painter; Henry Steele Commager, historian; Bill Cosby, actor; Stuart Davis, painter; Jimmy and Tommy Dorsey, band leaders; W. C. Fields, comedian; Stephen Foster, composer; Robert Fulton, inventor; Grace, Princess of Monaco; Martha Graham, choreographer; Alexander Haig, former secretary of state; Marilyn Horne, mezzo-soprano; Lee Iacocca, auto executive; Reggie Jackson, baseball player; Gene Kelly, dancer and actor; Gelsey Kirkland, ballerina; S. S. Kresge, merchant; Mario Lanza, actor and singer; George C. Marshall, five-star general; George McClellan, former general; Margaret Mead, anthropologist; Andrew Mellon, financier; Tom Mix, actor; Arnold Palmer, golfer; Robert E. Peary, explorer; Man Ray, painter; Mary Roberts Rinehart, novelist; Betsy Ross, flagmaker; B. F. Skinner, psychologist; John Sloan, painter; Gertrude Stein, author; James Stewart, actor; John Updike, novelist; Honus Wagner, baseball player; Fred Waring, band leader; Ethel Waters, singer and actress; Anthony Wayne, military officer; August Wilson, poet, writer, and playwright; Wallis Warfield, Duchess of Windsor; Andrew Wyeth, painter.

Rhode Island

Capital: Providence
Governor: Lincoln C. Almond, R (to Jan. 2003)
Lieut. Governor: Charles J. Fogarty, D (to Jan. 2003)
Senators: Jack Reed, D (to Jan. 2003); Lincoln Chafee, R (to Jan. 2001)
Secy. of State: Jim Langevin, D (to Jan. 2003)
Atty. General: Sheldon Whitehouse, D (to Jan. 2003)
General Treasurer: Paul J. Tavares, D (to Jan. 2003)
Entered Union (rank): May 29, 1790 (13)
Present constitution adopted: 1843
Motto: Hope
State Symbols: flower, violet (unofficial) (1968); **tree,** red maple (official) (1964); **bird,** Rhode Island red hen (official) (1954); **shell,** quahog (official); **mineral,** bowenite (1966); **stone,** cumberlandite (1966); **colors,** blue, white, and gold (in state flag); **song,** "Rhode Island" (1946);
Nickname: The Ocean State
Origin of name: From the Greek Island of Rhodes
Largest cities (1998 est.): Providence, 150,890; Warwick, 84,094; Cranston, 74,521; Pawtucket, 68,169; East Providence, 47,882; Woonsocket, 41,034; Newport, 24,279; Central Falls, 16,364
Land area: 1,045 sq mi. (2,706 sq km)
Geographic center: In Kent Co., 1 mi. SSW of Compton
Number of counties: 5
Largest county by population and area: Providence, 574,108 (1999 est.); Providence, 413 sq mi.
State forests: 11 (20,900 ac.)
State parks: 14
Residents: Rhode Islander
1999 resident population est.: 990,819
1990 resident census population (rank): 1,003,464 (43). **Male:** 481,496; **Female:** 521,968. **White:** 917,375 (91.4%); **Black:** 38,861 (3.9%); **American Indian:** 4,071 (0.4%); **Asian:** 18,325 (1.8%); **Other race:** 24,832 (2.5%); **Hispanic:** 45,752 (4.6%). **1990 percent population under 18:** 22.5; **65 and over:** 15.0; **median age:** 33.8.

From its beginnings, Rhode Island has been distinguished by its support for freedom of conscience and action, started by Roger Williams, who was exiled by the Massachusetts Bay Colony Puritans in 1636, and was the founder of the present state capital, Providence. Williams was followed by other religious exiles who founded Pocasset, now Portsmouth, in 1638 and Newport in 1639.

Rhode Island's rebellious, authority-defying nature was further demonstrated by the burnings of the British revenue cutters *Liberty* and *Gaspee* prior to the Revolution, by its early declaration of independence from Great Britain in May 1776, its refusal to participate actively in the War of 1812, and by Dorr's Rebellion of 1842, which protested property requirements for voting.

Rhode Island, smallest of the fifty states, is densely populated and highly industrialized. It is a major center for jewelry manufacturing. Electronics, metal, plastic products, and boat and ship construction are other important industries. Non-manufacturing employment includes research in health, medicine, and the ocean environment. Providence is a wholesale distribution center for New England.

Fishing ports are at Galilee and Newport. Rural areas of the state support small-scale farming, including grapes for local wineries, turf grass, and nursery stock. Tourism generates over a billion dollars a year in revenue.

Newport became famous as the summer capital of high society in the mid-19th century. Touro Synagogue (1763) is the oldest in the U.S. Other points of interest include the Roger Williams National Memorial in Providence, Samuel Slater's Mill in Pawtucket, the General Nathanael Greene Homestead in Coventry, and Block Island.

Famous natives and residents: Harry Anderson, actor; George M. Cohan, actor and dramatist; Eddie Dowling, actor and stage producer; Nelson Eddy, baritone and actor; Ann Smith Franklin, printer and almanac publisher; Charles Gorham, silversmith; Spalding Gray, writer, performance artist; Bobby Hackett, trumpeter; David Hartman, TV newscaster; Ruth Hussey, actress; Anne Hutchinson, religious leader; Thomas H. Ince, film producer; Wilbur John, Quaker leader; Van Johnson, actor; Clarence King, first director of the U.S. Geological Survey; Galway Kinnell, poet; Oliver LaFarge, writer; Irving R. Levine, news correspondent; H. P. Lovecraft, author; Ida Lewis, lighthouse keeper; John McLaughlin, political commentator, broadcaster; Dana C. Munro, educator and historian; Matthew C. Perry, naval officer; Oliver Hazard Perry, naval officer; King Philip (Metacomet), Indian leader; Anthony Quinn, actor; Gilbert Stuart, painter; Sarah Helen (Power) Whitman, poet; Jemima Wilkinson, religious leader; Roger Williams, clergyman and founder of Rhode Island; Leonard Woodcock, labor union official; James Woods, actor.

South Carolina

Capital: Columbia
Governor: Jim Hodges, D (to Jan. 2003)
Lieut. Governor: Robert L. Peeler, R (to Jan. 2003)
Senators: Ernest Hollings, D (to Jan. 2005); Strom Thurmond, R (to Jan. 2003)
Secy. of State: Jim Miles, R (to Jan. 2003)
Comptroller General: Jim Lander, D (to Jan. 2003)
Atty. General: Charles M. Condon, R (to Jan. 2003)
Entered Union (rank): May 23, 1788 (8)
Present constitution adopted: 1895
Mottoes: *Animis opibusque parati* (Prepared in mind and resources) and *Dum spiro spero* (While I breathe, I hope)

State Symbols: flower, Carolina yellow jessamine (1924); **tree,** palmetto tree (1939); **bird,** Carolina wren (1948); **song,** "Carolina" (1911);
Nickname: Palmetto State
Origin of name: In honor of Charles I of England
10 largest cities (1998 est.): Columbia, 110,840; Charleston, 87,044; North Charleston, 68,072; Greenville, 56,436; Rock Hill, 46,218; Mount Pleasant, 41,330; Spartanburg, 40,954; Sumter, 40,518; Hilton Head Island, 30,377; Florence, 29,511
Land area: 30,111 sq mi. (77,988 sq km)
Geographic center: In Richland Co., 13 mi. SE of Columbia
Number of counties: 46
Largest county by population and area: Greenville, 358,936 (1999 est.); Horry, 1,134 sq mi.
State forests: 4 (124,052 ac.)
State parks: 50 (61,726 ac.)
Residents: South Carolinian
1999 resident population est.: 3,885,736
1990 resident census population (rank): 3,486,703 (25). **Male:** 1,688,510; **Female:** 1,798,193. **White:** 2,406,974 (69.0%); **Black:** 1,039,884 (29.8%); **American Indian:** 8,246 (0.2%); **Asian:** 22,382 (0.6%); **Other race:** 9,217 (0.3%); **Hispanic:** 30,551 (0.9%)
1990 percent population under 18: 26.4; **65 and over:** 11.4; **median age:** 31.9.

Following exploration of the coast in 1521 by Francisco de Gordillo, the Spanish tried unsuccessfully to establish a colony near present-day Georgetown in 1526 and the French also failed to colonize Parris Island near Fort Royal in 1562.

The first English settlement was made in 1670 at Albemarle Point on the Ashley River, but poor conditions drove the settlers to the site of Charleston (originally called Charles Town). South Carolina, officially separated from North Carolina in 1729, was the scene of extensive military action during the Revolution and again during the Civil War. The Civil War began in 1861 as South Carolina troops fired on federal Fort Sumter in Charleston Harbor and the state was the first to secede from the Union.

Once primarily agricultural, South Carolina today has many large textile and other mills that produce eight times the output of its farms in cash value. Charleston makes asbestos, wood, pulp, steel products, chemicals, machinery, and apparel.

Farms have become fewer but larger in recent years. South Carolina grows more peaches than any other state except California; it ranks fifth in overall tobacco production. Other farm products include cotton, peanuts, sweet potatoes, soybeans, corn, and oats. Poultry and dairy products are also important.

Points of interest include Fort Sumter National Monument, Fort Moultrie, Fort Johnson, and aircraft carrier USS *Yorktown* in Charleston Harbor; the Middleton, Magnolia, and Cypress Gardens in Charleston; Cowpens National Battlefield; the Hilton Head resorts; and the Riverbanks 200 and Botanical Garden in Columbia.

Famous natives and residents: Bernard Baruch, statesman; Mary McLeod Bethune, educator; James F. Byrnes, senator, jurist and secretary of state; John C. Calhoun, statesman; Mark Clark, general; Joe Frazier, prize fighter; Althea Gibson, tennis champion; Dizzy Gillespie, jazz trumpeter; DuBose Heyward, poet, playwright, and novelist; Andrew Jackson, former president; Jesse Jackson, civil rights leader; Eartha Kitt, singer; Francis Marion ("Swamp Fox"), Revolutionary general; Ronald McNair, astronaut; John Rutledge, jurist; Strom Thurmond, politician; Charles Townes, physicist; William Westmoreland, former army chief of staff; Vanna White, TV personality.

South Dakota

Capital: Pierre
Governor: William J. Janklow, R (to Jan. 2003)
Lieut. Governor: Carole Hillard, R (to Jan. 3003)
Senators: Thomas A. Daschle, D (to Jan. 2005);
   Tim Johnson, D (to Jan. 2003)
Atty. General: Mark Barnett, R (to Jan. 2003)
Secy. of State: Joyce Hazeltine, R (to Jan. 2003)
Auditor: Vern Larson, R (to Jan. 2003)
Treasurer: Richard Butler, D (to Jan. 2003)
Organized as territory: March 2, 1861
Entered Union (rank): Nov. 2, 1889 (40)
Present constitution adopted: 1889
Motto: Under God the people rule
State Symbols: flower, American pasqueflower (1903);
   grass, Western wheat grass (1970); **soil,** houdek
   (1990); **tree,** black hills spruce (1947); **bird,**
   ring-necked pheasant (1943); **insect,** honeybee
   (1978); **animal,** coyote (1949); **mineral stone,** rose
   quartz (1966); **gemstone,** fairburn agate (1966);
   colors, blue and gold (in state flag); **song,** "Hail!
   South Dakota" (1943); **fish,** walleye (1982); **musical
   instrument,** fiddle (1989); **dessert,** kuchen (2000);
Nicknames: Mount Rushmore State; Coyote State
Origin of name: From the Sioux tribe, meaning "allies"
10 largest cities (1998 est.): Sioux Falls, 116,762;
   Rapid City, 57,513; Aberdeen, 24,865; Watertown,
   19,909; Brookings, 17,138; Mitchell, 14,386;
   Yankton, 14,325; Pierre, 13,267; Vermillion, 11,967;
   Huron, 11,778
Land area: 75,898 sq mi. (196,575 sq km)
Geographic center: In Hughes Co., 8 mi. NE of Pierre
Number of counties: 67 (64 county governments)
Largest county by population and area: Minnehaha,
   142,821 (1999 est.); Meade, 3,471 sq mi.
State forests: None[1]
State parks: 13 plus 39 recreational areas (87,269 ac.)[2]
Residents: South Dakotan
1999 resident population est.: 733,133
1990 resident census population (rank): 696,004 (45).
   Male: 342,498; **Female:** 353,506. **White:** 637,515
   (91.6%); **Black:** 3,258 (0.5%); **American Indian:**
   50,575 (7.3%); **Asian:** 3,123 (0.4%); **Other race:**
   1,533 (0.2%); **Hispanic:** 5,252 (0.8%). **1990 percent
   population under 18:** 28.5; **65 and over:** 14.7;
   median age: 32.4.

1. No designated state forests; about 13,000 ac. of
state land is forestland. 2. Acreage includes 39 recreation areas and 80 roadside parks, in addition to 12
state parks.

Exploration of this area began in 1743 when
Louis-Joseph and François Verendrye came from
France in search of a route to the Pacific.

The U.S. acquired the region as part of the Louisiana Purchase in 1803 and it was explored by
Lewis and Clark in 1804–06. Fort Pierre, the first
permanent settlement, was established in 1817.

Settlement of South Dakota did not begin in earnest until the arrival of the railroad in 1873 and the
discovery of gold in the Black Hills the following
year.

Agriculture is a cultural and economic mainstay,
but it no longer leads the state in employment or
share of gross state product. Durable-goods manufacturing and private services have evolved as the
drivers of the economy. Tourism is also a booming
industry in the state, generating approximately $1.25
billion worth of economic activity each year.

South Dakota is the second largest producer of
flaxseed and sunflower seed in the nation. It is the
third largest producer of hay and rye.

South Dakota is the nation's second leading
producer of gold and the Homestake Mine is the
richest in the U.S. Other minerals produced
include berylium, bentonite, granite, silver, and
uranium.

The Black Hills are the highest mountains east of
the Rockies. Mt. Rushmore, in this group, is famous
for the likenesses of Washington, Jefferson, Lincoln,
and Theodore Roosevelt, which were carved in
granite by Gutzon Borglum. A memorial to Crazy
Horse is also being carved in granite near Custer.

Other tourist attractions include the Badlands; the
World's Only Corn Palace, in Mitchell; and the city
of Deadwood, where Wild Bill Hickok was killed in
1876 and where gambling was recently legalized.

Famous natives and residents: Sparky Anderson, baseball
manager; Gertrude Bonnin (Zitkala-Sa), Sioux writer and
pan-Indian activist; Tom Brokaw, TV newscaster; Robert
Casey, writer; Myron Floren, accordionist; Joseph J. Foss,
WW II Marine fighter ace; Mary Hart, TV host; Crazy
Horse, Oglala chief; Oscar Howe, Sioux artist; Hubert H.
Humphrey, former vice president; Cheryl Ladd, actress;
Ernest Orlando Lawrence, physicist; Russell Means,
American Indian activist; George McGovern, politician;
Arthur C. Mellette, first governor; Dorothy Provine, actress;
Rain-in-the-Face, Hunkpapa Sioux chief; Red Cloud, chief
of the Oglala Sioux; Ben Reifel, Brulé Sioux congressman;
Ole Edvart Rölvaag, writer; Sitting Bull, chief of
Hunkpappa Sioux; Norm Van Brocklin, football player;
Mamie Van Doren, actress.

Tennessee

Capital: Nashville
Governor: Don Sundquist, R (to Jan. 2003)
Lieut. Governor: John S. Wilder, D (to Jan. 2000)
Senators: William Frist, R (to Jan. 2001);
   Fred Thompson, R (to Jan. 2003)
Secy. of State: Riley C. Darnell, D (to Jan. 2001)
Atty. General: Paul G. Summers, D (to Aug. 2005)
Treasurer: Steve Adams, D (to Jan. 2001)
Comptroller: John G. Morgan (to Jan. 2001)
Entered Union (rank): June 1, 1796 (16)
Present constitution adopted: 1870; amended 1953,
   1960, 1966, 1972, 1978
Motto: Agriculture and Commerce (1987)
Slogan: Tennessee—America at its best! (1965)
State Symbols: flower, iris (1933); **tree,** tulip poplar
   (1947); **bird,** mockingbird (1933); **horse,** Tennessee
   walking horse; **animal,** raccoon (1971); **wild flower,**
   passion flower (1973); **songs,** "Tennessee Waltz"
   (1965); "My Homeland, Tennessee" (1925); "When It's
   Iris Time in Tennessee" (1935); "My Tennessee"
   (1955); "Rocky Top" (1982); "Tennessee" (1992);
Nickname: Volunteer State
Origin of name: Of Cherokee origin; the exact meaning
   is unknown
10 largest cities (1998 est.): Memphis, 603,507;
   Nashville-Davidson (CC[1]), 510,274; Knoxville,
   165,540; Chattanooga, 147,790; Clarksville, 97,978;
   Murfreesboro, 58,430; Johnson City, 57,079; Jackson,
   51,115; Kingsport, 41,139; Hendersonville, 38,625
Land area: 41,220 sq mi. (106,759 sq km)
Geographic center: In Rutherford Co., 5 mi. NE
   of Murfreesboro
Number of counties: 95
Largest county by population and area: Shelby,
   873,000 (1999 est.); Shelby, 755 sq mi.
State forests: 13 (155,000 ac.)
State parks: 50 (133,000 ac.)
Residents: Tennessean, Tennesseean

1999 resident population est.: 5,483,535
1990 resident census population (rank): 4,877,185
(17). **Male:** 2,348,928; **Female:** 2,528,257. **White:**
4,048,068 (83.0%); **Black:** 778,035 (16.0%); **American Indian:** 10,039 (0.2%); **Asian:** 31,839 (0.7%);
Other race: 9,204 (0.2%); **Hispanic:** 32,741 (0.7%).
1990 percent population under 18: 24.9; **65 and
over:** 12.7; **median age:** 33.5.

1. Consolidated City.

First visited by the Spanish explorer Hernando de
Soto in 1540, the Tennessee area would later be
claimed by both France and England as a result of
the 1670s and 1680s explorations of Jacques Marquette and Louis Joliet, sieur de la Salle, and James
Needham and Gabriel Arthur. Great Britain obtained
the region following the French and Indian Wars in
1763.

During 1784–87, the settlers formed the "state" of
Franklin, which was disbanded when the region was
allowed to send representatives to the North Carolina legislature. In 1790 Congress organized the territory south of the Ohio River, and Tennessee joined
the Union in 1796.

Although Tennessee joined the Confederacy during the Civil War, there was much pro-Union sentiment in the state, which was the scene of extensive
military action.

The state is now predominantly industrial; the
majority of its population lives in urban areas.
Among the most important products are chemicals,
textiles, apparel, electrical machinery, furniture, and
leather goods. Other lines include food processing,
lumber, primary metals, and metal products. The
state is known as the U.S. hardwood-flooring center
and ranks first in the production of marble, zinc,
pyrite, and ball clay.

Tennessee is one of the leading tobacco-
producing states in the nation. Its farming income is
derived from livestock and dairy products, as well
as corn, cotton, and soybeans.

With six other states, Tennessee shares the extensive federal reservoir developments on the Tennessee and Cumberland River systems. The Tennessee
Valley Authority operates a number of dams and
reservoirs in the state.

Among the major points of interest are the
Andrew Johnson National Historic Site at Greenville, the American Museum of Atomic Energy at
Oak Ridge, Great Smoky Mountains National Park,
the Hermitage (home of Andrew Jackson near Nashville), Rock City Gardens near Chattanooga, and
three National Military Parks.

Famous natives and residents: James Agee, writer; Eddy
Arnold, singer; Chet Atkins, guitarist; Julian Bond, Georgia
legislator; Davy Crockett, frontiersman; David G. Farragut,
first American admiral; Lester Flatt, bluegrass musician;
Tennessee Ernie Ford, singer; Abe Fortas, jurist; Aretha
Franklin, singer; Nikki Giovanni, poet; Al Gore, Jr., vice
president; Red Grooms, artist; Isaac Hayes, composer;
Benjamin L. Hooks, civil rights activist; Cordell Hull, former
secretary of state; Andrew Jackson, former president;
Andrew Johnson, former president; Estes Kefauver,
legislator; Anita Kerr, singer; Grace Moore, soprano; Dolly
Parton, singer; Minnie Pearl, singer and comedienne;
James K. Polk, president; Grantland Rice, sportswriter;
Carl Rowan, journalist; Wilma Rudolph, sprinter; Sequoia,
Cherokee scholar and educator; Cybil Shepherd, actress;
Dinah Shore, actress and singer; Tina Turner, singer; Alvin
York, World War I hero.

Texas

Capital: Austin
Governor: George W. Bush, R (to Jan. 2003)
Lieut. Governor: Rick Perry, R (to Jan. 2003)
Senators: Phil Gramm, R (to Jan. 2003);
    Kay Bailey Hutchison, R (to Jan. 2001)
Secy. of State: Alberto Gonzales (apptd. by gov.)
Comptroller: Carole Keeton Rylander, R (to Jan. 2003)
Atty. General: John Cornyn, R (to Jan. 2003)
Entered Union (rank): Dec. 29, 1845 (28)
Present constitution adopted: 1876
Motto: Friendship
State Symbols: flower, bluebonnet (1901); **tree,** pecan
    (1919); **bird,** mockingbird (1927); **song,** "Texas, Our
    Texas" (1929); **fish,** guadalupe bass (1989); **seashell,**
    lightning whelk (1987); **dish,** chili (1977); **folk dance,**
    square dance (1991); **fruit,** Texas red grapefruit
    (1993); **gem,** Texas blue topaz (1969); **gemstone cut,**
    Lone Star cut (1977); **grass,** sideoats grass (1971);
    reptile, horned lizard (1993); **stone,** petrified
    palmwood (1969); **plant,** prickly pear cactus; **insect,**
    monarch butterfly; **pepper,** jalapeño pepper; **mammal,**
    longhorn; **small mammal,** armadillo; **flying mammal,**
    Mexican free-tailed bat;
Nickname: Lone Star State
Origin of name: From an Indian word meaning "friends"
10 largest cities (1998 est.): Houston, 1,786,691; San
    Antonio, 1,114,130; Dallas, 1,075,894; El Paso,
    615,032; Austin, 552,434; Fort Worth, 491,801;
    Arlington, 306,497; Corpus Christi, 281,453; Plano,
    219,486; Garland, 193,408
Land area: 261,914 sq mi. (678,358 sq km)
Geographic center: In McCulloch Co., 15 mi. NE of Brady
Number of counties: 254
Largest county by population and area: Harris,
    3,250,404 (1999 est.); Brewster, 6,193 sq mi.
State forests: 5 (7,609 ac.)
State parks: 123
Residents: Texan
1999 resident population est.: 20,044,141
1990 resident census population (rank): 16,986,510
    (3). **Male:** 8,365,963; **Female:** 8,620,547. **White:**
    12,774,762 (75.2%); **Black:** 2,021,632 (11.9%);
    American Indian: 65,877 (0.4%); **Asian:** 319,459
    (1.9%); **Other race:** 1,804,780 (10.6%); **Hispanic:**
    4,339,905 (25.5%). **1990 percent population under
    18:** 28.5; **65 and over:** 10.1; **median age:** 30.6.

Spanish explorers, including Álvar Núñez Cabeza
de Vaca and Francisco Vásquez de Coronado, were
the first to visit the region in the 16th and 17th centuries, settling at Ysleta near El Paso in 1682. In
1685, sieur de la Salle established a short-lived
French colony at Matagorda Bay.

Americans, led by Stephen F. Austin, began to
settle along the Brazos River in 1821 when Texas
was controlled by Mexico, recently independent
from Spain. In 1836, following a brief war between
the American settlers in Texas and the Mexican government, the Independent Republic of Texas was
proclaimed with Sam Houston as president. This
war was famous for the battles of the Alamo and
San Jacinto. After Texas became the 28th U.S. state
in 1845, border disputes led to the Mexican War of
1846–48.

Possessing enormous natural resources, Texas is a
major agricultural state and an industrial giant. Second only to Alaska in land area, it leads all other
states in such categories as oil, cattle, sheep, and
cotton. Texas ranches and farms also produce poultry, rice, pecans, peanuts, sorghum, and an extensive
variety of fruits and vegetables.

Sulfur, salt, helium, asphalt, graphite, bromine, natural gas, cement, and clays are among the state's valuable resources. Chemicals, oil refining, food processing, machinery, and transportation equipment are among the major Texas manufacturing industries.

Millions of tourists spend well over $20.6 billion annually visiting 123 state parks, recreation areas, and points of interest such as the Gulf Coast resort area, the Lyndon B. Johnson Space Center in Houston, the Alamo in San Antonio, the state capital in Austin, and the Big Bend and Guadalupe Mountains National Park.

Famous natives and residents: Alvin Ailey, choreographer; Mary Kay Ash, cosmetics entrepreneur; Steven Fuller Austin, founding father of Texas; Gene Autry, singer and actor; Carol Burnett, comedienne; Cyd Charisse, actress and dancer; Denton A. Cooley, heart surgeon; Joan Crawford, actress; Dwight David Eisenhower, former president and general; A. J. Foyt, auto racer; Ben Hogan, golfer; Sam Houston, general and statesman; Howard Hughes, industrialist and film producer; Jack Johnson, boxer; Lyndon B. Johnson, former president; George Jones, singer; Tommy Lee Jones, actor; Scott Joplin, composer; Trini Lopez, singer; Mary Martin, singer and actress; Spanky McFarland, actor; Audie Murphy, actor and war hero; Chester Nimitz, admiral; Sandra Day O'Connor, jurist; Buck Owens, singer; Selena Pérez, singer; Lou Diamond Phillips, actor; Katherine Anne Porter, novelist; Wiley Post, aviator; Dan Rather, TV newscaster; Robert Rauschenberg, painter; Tex Ritter, singer; Rip Torn, actor and director; Tommy Tune, dancer and choreographer; Lupe Velez, actress; Dooley Wilson, actor and musician; Babe Didrikson Zaharias, athlete and golfer.

Utah

Capital: Salt Lake City
Governor: Michael O. Leavitt, R (to Jan. 2001)
Lieut. Governor: Olene Walker, R (to Jan. 2001)
Senators: Robert F. Bennett, R (to Jan. 2005);
    Orrin G. Hatch, R (to Jan. 2001)
Atty. General: Jan Graham, D (to Jan. 2001)
Organized as territory: Sept. 9, 1850
Entered Union (rank): Jan. 4, 1896 (45)
Present constitution adopted: 1896
Motto: Industry
State Symbols: flower, sego lily (1911); **tree,** blue spruce (1933); **bird,** California gull (1955); **emblem,** beehive (1959); **song,** "Utah, We Love Thee" (1953); **gem,** topaz; **animal,** Rocky Mountain elk (1971); **insect,** honeybee (1983); **grass,** Indian rice grass (1990); **fossil,** allosaurus (1988); **cooking pot,** dutch oven (1997); **fish,** Bonneville cutthroat trout (1997); **fruit,** cherry (1997); **mineral,** copper; **rock,** coal (1991);
Nickname: Beehive State
Origin of name: From the Ute tribe, meaning "people of the mountains"
10 largest cities (1998 est.): Salt Lake City, 174,348; Provo, 110,419; West Valley City, 99,372; Sandy, 99,186; Orem, 78,937; Ogden, 66,507; West Jordan, 60,804; Taylorsville, 56,753; Layton, 55,112; St. George, 46,186
Land area: 82,168 sq mi. (212,816 sq km)
Geographic center: In Sanpete Co., 3 mi. N. of Manti
Number of counties: 29
Largest county by population and area: Salt Lake, 850,243 (1999 est.); San Juan, 7,821 sq mi.
National parks: 5
National monuments: 7
State parks/forests: 45 (64,097 ac.)
Residents: Utahan, Utahn
1999 resident population est.: 2,129,836
1990 resident census population (rank): 1,722,850 (35). **Male:** 855,759; **Female:** 867,091. **White:** 1,615,845 (93.8%); **Black:** 11,576 (0.7%); **American**

Indian: 24,283 (1.4%); **Asian:** 33,371 (1.9%); **Other race:** 37,775 (2.2%); **Hispanic:** 84,597 (4.9%). **1990 percent population under 18:** 36.4; **65 and over:** 8.7; **median age:** 26.2.

The region was first explored for Spain by Franciscan friars Escalante and Dominguez in 1776. In 1824 the famous American frontiersman Jim Bridger discovered the Great Salt Lake.

Fleeing religious persecution in the East and Midwest, the Mormons arrived in 1847 and began to build Salt Lake City. The U.S. acquired the Utah region in the treaty ending the Mexican War in 1848, and the first transcontinental railroad was completed with the driving of a golden spike at Promontory Summit in 1869.

Mormon difficulties with the federal government about polygamy did not end until the Mormon Church renounced the practice in 1890, six years before Utah became a state.

Rich in natural resources, Utah has long been a leading producer of copper, gold, silver, lead, zinc, and molybdenum. Oil has also become a major product. Utah shares rich oil shale deposits with Colorado and Wyoming. Utah also has large deposits of low sulphur coal.

Ranked fifth among the states in number of sheep in 1998, Utah also produces large crops of alfalfa, winter wheat, and beans.

Utah's traditional industries of agriculture and mining are complemented by increased tourism and growing aerospace, biomedical, and computer-related businesses.

Utah is a great vacationland with 11,000 miles of fishing streams and 147,000 acres of lakes and reservoirs. Among the many tourist attractions are Arches, Bryce Canyon, Canyonlands, Capitol Reef, and Zion National Parks; Cedar Breaks, Dinosaur, Hovenweep, Natural Bridges, Rainbow Bridge, Timpanogos Cave, and Grand Staircase (Escalante) National Monuments; the Mormon Tabernacle in Salt Lake City; and Monument Valley. Salt Lake City will be the site of the 2002 Winter Olympics.

Famous natives and residents: Maude Adams, actress; Roseanne, actress; Frank Borzage, film director and producer; John M. Browning, inventor; Butch Cassidy, outlaw; Laraine Day, actress; Bernard De Voto, writer; Avard Fairbanks, sculptor; Philo Farnsworth, television pioneer; Jake Garn, senator; John Gilbert, actor; J. Willard Marriott, restaurant and hotel chain founder; Peter Skene Ogden, fur trader and trapper; Merlin Olsen, football player; Donny Osmond, Marie Osmond, singers; Ivy Baker Priest, former U.S. treasurer; Lee Greene Richards, painter; Leroy Robertson, composer; Brent Scowcroft, business executive and consultant; Reed Smoot, first Mormon elected to U.S. Senate; Mack Swain, actor; Everett Thorpe, painter; Robert Walker, actor; James Woods, actor; Brigham Young, territory governor and religious leader; Loretta Young, actress.

Vermont

Capital: Montpelier
Governor: Howard Dean, D (to Jan. 2001)
Lieut. Governor: Douglas A. Racine, D (to Jan. 2001)
Senators: James M. Jeffords, R (to Jan. 2001);
    Patrick Leahy, D (to Jan. 2005)
Secy. of State: Deb Markowitz, D (to Jan. 2001)
Treasurer: James H. Douglas, R (to Jan. 2001)
Auditor of Accounts: Edward S. Flanagan, D (to Jan. 2001)
Atty. General: William Sorrell, D (to Jan. 2001)
Entered Union (rank): March 4, 1791 (14)
Present constitution adopted: 1793

Motto: Vermont, Freedom and Unity
State Symbols: flower, red clover (1894); **tree,** sugar maple (1949); **bird,** hermit thrush (1941); **animal,** Morgan horse (1961); **insect,** honeybee (1978); **song,** "Hail, Vermont!" (1938);
Nickname: Green Mountain State
Origin of name: From the French "vert mont," meaning "green mountain"
10 largest cities (1998): Burlington, 38,453; Rutland, 17,348; South Burlington, 14,037; Barre, 9,066; Essex Junction, 8,705; Montpelier, 7,734; St. Albans, 7,308; Winooski, 6,619; Newport, 4,537; Bellows Falls, 3,231
Land area: 9,249 sq mi. (23,956 sq km)
Geographic center: In Washington Co., 3 mi. E of Roxbury
Number of counties: 14
Largest county by population and area: Chittenden, 143,947 (1999 est.); Windsor, 971 sq mi.
State forests: 34 (113,953 ac.)
State parks: 45 (31,325 ac.)
Residents: Vermonter
1999 resident population est.: 593,740
1990 resident census population (rank): 562,758 (48). **Male:** 275,492; **Female:** 287,266. **White:** 555,088 (98.6%); **Black:** 1,951 (0.3%); **American Indian:** 1,696 (0.3%); **Asian:** 3,215 (0.6%); **Other race:** 808 (0.1%); **Hispanic:** 3,661 (0.7%). **1990 percent population under 18:** 25.4; **65 and over:** 11.8; **median age:** 32.9.

The Vermont region was explored and claimed for France by Samuel de Champlain in 1609 and the first French settlement was established at Fort Ste. Anne in 1666. The first English settlers moved into the area in 1724 and built Fort Dummer on the site of present-day Brattleboro. England gained control of the area in 1763 after the French and Indian Wars.

First organized to drive settlers from New York out of Vermont, the Green Mountain Boys, led by Ethan Allen, won fame by capturing Fort Ticonderoga from the British on May 10, 1775, in the early days of the Revolutionary War. In 1777 Vermont adopted its first constitution abolishing slavery and providing for universal male suffrage without property qualifications.

Vermont leads the nation in the production of monument granite, marble, and maple syrup. It is also a leader in the production of talc. Vermont's rugged, rocky terrain discourages extensive agricultural farming, but is well suited to raising fruit trees, and to dairy farming.

Principal industrial products include electrical equipment, fabricated metal products, printing and publishing, and paper and allied products.

Tourism is a major industry in Vermont. Vermont's many famous ski areas include Stowe, Killington, Mt. Snow, Bromley, Jay Peak, and Sugarbush. Hunting and fishing also attract many visitors to Vermont each year. Among the many points of interest are the Green Mountain National Forest, Bennington Battle Monument, the Calvin Coolidge Homestead at Plymouth, and the Marble Exhibit in Proctor.

Famous natives and residents: Chester A. Arthur, former president; Orson Bean, actor; Calvin Coolidge, former president; George Dewey, admiral; John Dewey, philosopher and educator; Stephen A. Douglas, politician; James Fisk, financial speculator; Wilbur Fisk, clergyman and educator; Richard Morris Hunt, architect; William Morris Hunt, painter; Elisha Otis, inventor; Moses Pendleton, choreographer; Joseph Smith, religious leader; Ernest Thompson, actor and writer; Rudy Vallee, singer and band leader; Henry Wells, pioneer entrepreneur (Wells Fargo & Co.); Brigham Young, religious leader.

Virginia

Capital: Richmond
Governor: James S. Gilmore, R (to Jan. 2002)
Lieut. Governor: John H. Hager, R (to Jan. 2002)
Senators: Charles Robb, D (to Jan. 2001); John Warner, R (to Jan. 2003)
Secy. of the Commonwealth: Anne P. Petera (apptd. by governor)
Comptroller: William E. Landsidle (apptd. by governor)
Atty. General: Mark L. Earley
Entered Union (rank): June 25, 1788 (10)
Present constitution adopted: 1970
Motto: *Sic semper tyrannis* (Thus always to tyrants)
State Symbols: flower, American dogwood (1918); **bird,** cardinal (1950); **dog,** American foxhound (1966); **shell,** oyster shell (1974); **tree,** dogwood (1956);
Nicknames: The Old Dominion; Mother of Presidents
Origin of name: In honor of Elizabeth "Virgin Queen" of England
10 largest cities (1998 est.): Virginia Beach, 432,380; Norfolk, 215,215; Chesapeake, 199,564; Richmond, 194,173; Newport News, 178,615; Arlington CDP, 177,275; Hampton, 136,968; Alexandria, 118,300; Portsmouth, 98,936; Roanoke, 93,749
Land area: 39,598 sq mi. (102,558 sq km)
Geographic center: In Buckingham Co., 5 mi. SW of Buckingham
Number of counties: 95, plus 40 independent cities
Largest county by population and area: Fairfax, 945,717 (1999 est.); Augusta, 972 sq mi.
State forests: 11 (50,636 ac.)
State parks and recreational parks: 43
Residents: Virginian
1999 resident population est.: 6,872,912
1990 resident census population (rank): 6,187,358 (12). **Male:** 3,033,974; **Female:** 3,153,384. **White:** 4,791,739 (77.4%); **Black:** 1,162,994 (18.8%); **American Indian:** 15,282 (0.2%); **Asian:** 159,053 (2.6%); **Other race:** 58,290 (0.9%); **Hispanic:** 160,288 (2.6%). **1990 percent population under 18:** 24.3; **65 and over:** 10.7; **median age:** 32.5.

The history of America is closely tied to that of Virginia, particularly during the Colonial period. Jamestown, founded in 1607, was the first permanent English settlement in North America and slavery was introduced there in 1619. The surrenders ending both the American Revolution (Yorktown) and the Civil War (Appomattox) occurred in Virginia. The state is called the "Mother of Presidents" because eight U.S. Presidents were born there.

Today, Virginia has a large number of diversified manufacturing industries, including transportation equipment, textiles, food processing, and printing. Other important lines are electronic and other electrical equipment, chemicals, apparel, lumber and wood products, furniture, and industrial machinery and equipment.

Agriculture remains an important sector in the Virginia economy and the state ranks among the top 10 in the U.S. in tomatoes, tobacco, peanuts, summer potatoes, turkeys, apples, broilers, and sweet potatoes. Other crops include corn, vegetables, and barley. Famous for Smithfield hams, Virginia also has a large dairy industry.

Coal mining accounts for roughly 75% of Virginia's mineral output, and lime, kyanite, and stone are also mined.

Points of interest include Mt. Vernon and other places associated with George Washington; Monticello, home of Thomas Jefferson; Stratford, home of the Lees; Richmond, capital of the Confederacy and of Virginia; and Williamsburg, the restored Colonial capital.

Other attractions are the Shenandoah National Park, Colonial National Historical Park, Fredericksburg and Spotsylvania National Military Park, the Booker T. Washington birthplace near Roanoke, Arlington House (the Robert E. Lee Memorial), the Skyline Drive, and the Blue Ridge National Parkway.

Famous natives and residents: Richard Arlen, actor; Arthur Ashe, tennis player; Pearl Bailey, singer; Russell Baker, columnist; Warren Beatty, actor; George Bingham, painter; Richard E. Byrd, polar explorer; Willa Cather, novelist; Roy Clark, country music artist; William Clark, explorer; Henry Clay, statesman; Joseph Cotten, actor; Ella Fitzgerald, singer; William H. Harrison, former president; Patrick Henry, statesman; Sam Houston, political leader; Thomas Jefferson, former president; Robert E. Lee, Confederate general; Meriwether Lewis, explorer; Shirley MacLaine, actress; James Madison, former president; John Marshall, jurist; Cyrus McCormick, inventor; James Monroe, former president; Opechancanough, Powhatan leader; John Payne, actor; Walter Reed, army surgeon; Matthew Ridgway, former Army Chief of Staff; Bill "Bojangles" Robinson, dancer; George C. Scott, actor; Sam Snead, golfer; James "Jeb" Stuart, Confederate army officer; Zachary Taylor, former president; Nat Turner, leader of slave uprising; John Tyler, former president; Booker T. Washington, educator; George Washington, first president; Woodrow Wilson, former president; Tom Wolfe, journalist.

Washington

Capital: Olympia
Governor: Gary Locke, D (to Jan. 2001)
Lieut. Governor: Brad Owen, D (to Jan. 2001)
Senators: Slade Gorton, R (to Jan. 2001);
Patty Murray, D (to Jan. 2005)
Secy. of State: Ralph Munro, R (to 2001)
State Treasurer: Michael J. Murphy (to 2001)
Atty. General: Christine Gregoire, D (to 2001)
Organized as territory: March 2, 1853
Entered Union (rank): Nov. 11, 1889 (42)
Present constitution adopted: 1889
Motto: Al-Ki (Indian word meaning "by and by")
State Symbols: flower, coast rhododendron (1949); **tree,** western hemlock (1947); **bird,** willow goldfinch (1951); **fish,** steelhead trout (1969); **gem,** petrified wood (1975); **colors,** green and gold (1925); **song,** "Washington, My Home" (1959); **folk song,** "Roll On Columbia, Roll On" (1987); **dance,** square dance (1979); **grass,** bluebunch wheatgrass (1989); **insect,** blue darner dragonfly (1997); **fossil,** Columbian mammoth (1998).
Nicknames: Evergreen State
Origin of name: In honor of George Washington
10 largest cities (1998 est.): Seattle, 536,978; Spokane, 184,058; Tacoma, 179,814; Bellevue, 104,052; Everett, 88,625; Federal Way, 74,254; Vancouver, 73,526; Lakewood, 65,933; Yakima, 64,967; Bellingham, 61,894
Land area: 66,582 sq mi. (172,447 sq km)
Geographic center: In Chelan Co., 10 mi. WSW of Wenatchee
Number of counties: 39
Largest county by population and area: King, 1,664,846 (1999 est.); Okanogan, 5,268 sq mi.
State forest lands: 2.1 million ac.
State parks: 215 (260,000 ac.)[1]
Residents: Washingtonian
1999 resident population est.: 5,756,361
1990 resident census population (rank): 4,866,692 (18). **Male:** 2,413,747; **Female:** 2,452,945. **White:** 4,308,937 (88.5%); **Black:** 149,801 (3.1%); **American Indian:** 81,483 (1.7%); **Other race:** 115,513 (2.4%); **Hispanic:** 214,570 (4.4%). **1990 percent population under 18:** 25.9; **65 and over:** 11.8; **median age:** 33.0.

1. Parks and undeveloped areas administered by State Parks and Recreation Commission. Dept. of Wildlife administers wildlife and recreation areas totaling 428,989.5 acres.

As part of the vast Oregon Country, Washington territory was visited by Spanish, American, and British explorers—Bruno Heceta for Spain in 1775, the American Capt. Robert Gray in 1792, and Capt. George Vancouver for Britain in 1792–1794. Lewis and Clark explored the Columbia River region and coastal areas for the U.S. in 1805–1806.

Rival American and British settlers and conflicting territorial claims threatened war in the early 1840s. However, in 1846 the Oregon Treaty set the boundary at the 49th parallel and war was averted.

Washington is a leading lumber producer. Its rugged surface is rich in stands of Douglas fir, hemlock, ponderosa and white pine, spruce, larch, and cedar. The state holds first place in apples, lentils, dry edible peas, hops, pears, red raspberries, spearmint oil, and sweet cherries, and ranks high in apricots, asparagus, grapes, peppermint oil, and potatoes. Livestock and livestock products make important contributions to total farm revenue and the commercial fishing catch of salmon, halibut, and bottomfish makes a significant contribution to the state's economy.

Manufacturing industries in Washington include aircraft and missiles, shipbuilding and other transportation equipment, lumber, food processing, metals and metal products, chemicals, and machinery.

Washington has over 1,000 dams, including the Grand Coulee, built for a variety of purposes including irrigation, power, flood control, and water storage. Its abundance of electrical power makes Washington one of the nation's major producers of refined aluminum.

Among the major points of interest: Mt. Rainier, Olympic, and North Cascades National Parks. Mount St. Helens, a peak in the Cascade Range, erupted in May 1980. Also of interest are Whitman Mission and Fort Vancouver National Historic Sites; and the Pacific Science Center and the Space Needle, in Seattle.

Famous natives and residents: Earl Anthony, professional bowler; Mildred Bailey, singer; Bob Barker, TV host; Dyan Cannon, actress; Raymond Carver, writer; Carol Channing, actress; Ray Charles, singer and musician; Kurt Cobain, rock musician; Judy Collins, singer; Chris Cornell, rock musician; Fred Couples, professional golfer; Bing Crosby, singer and actor; Bob Crosby, musician; Merce Cunningham, choreographer; Howard Duff, actor; Frances Farmer, actress; Kenny G., saxophonist; Bill Gates, software executive; Jimi Hendrix, guitarist; Frank Herbert, writer; Robert Joffrey, choreographer; Chuck Jones, animator; Quincy Jones, music producer; Hank Ketcham, cartoonist; Gary Larson, cartoonist; Gypsy Rose Lee, entertainer; Kenny Loggins, rock musician; Mary McCarthy, novelist; Guthrie McClintic, theatrical producer and director; John McIntire, actor; Steve Miller, rock musician; Robert Motherwell, artist; Patrice Munsel, soprano; Craig T. Nelson, actor; Ella Raines, actress; Ahmad Rashad, football player; Ann Reinking, dancer and actress; Tom Robbins, novelist; Ann Rule, writer; Francis Scobee, astronaut; Seattle, Dwamish, Suquamish chief; Smohalla, Indian prophet and chief; Hillary Swank, actress; Julia Sweeney, actress; Adam West, actor; Audrey Wurdemann, poet.

West Virginia

Capital: Charleston
Governor: Cecil H. Underwood, R (to Jan. 2001)
Senators: Robert C. Byrd, D (to Jan. 2001);
John D. "Jay" Rockefeller IV, D (to Jan. 2003)
Secy. of State: Ken Heckler, D

State Auditor: Glen Gainer
Atty. General: Darrell McGraw, D
Entered Union (rank): June 20, 1863 (35)
Present constitution adopted: 1872
Motto: *Montani semper liberi* (Mountaineers are always free)
State Symbols: flower, rhododendron (1903); **tree,** sugar maple (1949); **bird,** cardinal (1949); **animal,** black bear (1973); **colors,** blue and gold (official) (1863); **songs,** "West Virginia, My Home Sweet Home," "The West Virginia Hills," and "This Is My West Virginia" (adopted by Legislature in 1947, 1961, and 1963 as official state songs);
Nickname: Mountain State
Origin of name: In honor of Elizabeth, "Virgin Queen" of England
10 largest cities (1998 est.): Charleston, 55,056; Huntington, 52,571; Wheeling, 32,541; Parkersburg, 31,715; Morgantown, 26,751; Weirton, 21,206; Fairmont, 19,088; Beckley, 18,187; Clarksburg, 17,011; Martinsburg, 15,049
Land area: 24,087 sq mi. (62,384 sq km)
Geographic center: In Braxton Co., 4 mi. E of Sutton
Number of counties: 55
Largest county by population and area: Kanawha, 199,263 (1999 est.); Randolph, 1,040 sq mi.
State forests: 9 (79,502 ac.)
State parks: 35 (74,508 ac.)
Residents: West Virginian
1999 resident population est.: 1,806,928
1990 resident census population (rank): 1,793,477 (34). **Male:** 861,536; **Female:** 931,941. **White:** 1,725,523 (96.2%); **Black:** 56,295 (3.1%); **American Indian:** 2,458 (0.1%); **Asian:** 7,459 (0.4%); **Other race:** 1,742 (0.1%); **Hispanic:** 8,489 (0.5%). **1990 percent population under 18:** 24.7; **65 and over:** 15.0; **median age:** 35.3.

West Virginia's early history from 1609 until 1863 is largely shared with Virginia, of which it was a part until Virginia seceded from the Union in 1861. Then the delegates of 40 western counties formed their own government, which was granted statehood in 1863.

First permanent settlement dates from 1731 when Morgan Morgan founded Mill Creek. In 1742 coal was discovered on the Coal River, an event that would be of great significance in determining West Virginia's future.

The state usually ranks third in total coal production with about 15% of the U.S. total. It also is a leader in steel, glass, aluminum, and chemical manufactures; natural gas; oil; quarry products; and hardwood lumber.

Major cash farm products are poultry and eggs, dairy products, apples, and feed crops. Nearly 75% of West Virginia is covered with forests.

Tourism is increasingly popular in mountainous West Virginia and visitors spent $2.475 billion in 1990. More than a million acres have been set aside in 35 state parks and recreation areas and in 9 state forests and national forests.

Major points of interest include Harpers Ferry and New River Gorge National River, The Greenbrier and Berkeley Springs resorts, the scenic railroad at Cass, and the historic homes in the Eastern Panhandle.

Famous natives and residents: George Brett, baseball player; Pearl S. Buck, author; Phyllis Curtin, soprano; Martin R. Delany, first Black Army major; Billy Dixon, frontiersman and scout; Joanne Dru, actress; Thomas "Stonewall" Jackson, Confederate general; John S. Knight, publisher; Don Knotts, actor; Peter Marshall, TV host; Kathy Mattea, country music superstar; Whitney D. Morrow, banker and diplomat; Mary Lou Retton, gymnast; Walter Reuther, labor leader; Eleanor Steber, soprano; Lewis L. Strauss, naval officer and scientist; Cyrus Vance, government official; William Lyne Wilson, legislator and university president; Chuck Yeager, test pilot and Air Force general.

Wisconsin

Capital: Madison
Governor: Tommy G. Thompson, R (to Jan. 2003)
Lieut. Governor: Scott McCallum, R (to Jan. 2003)
Senators: Russell D. Feingold, D (to Jan. 2005); Herb Kohl, D (to Jan. 2001)
Secy. of State: Douglas J. La Follette, D (to Jan. 2003)
State Treasurer: Jack C. Voight, R (to Jan. 2003)
Atty. General: James E. Doyle, D (to Jan. 2003)
Superintendent of Public Instruction: John Benson, Nonpartisan (to July 2001)
Organized as territory: July 4, 1836
Entered Union (rank): May 29, 1848 (30)
Present constitution adopted: 1848
Motto: Forward
State Symbols: flower, wood violet (1949); **tree,** sugar maple (1949); **grain,** corn (1990); **bird,** robin (1949); **animal,** badger; **wild life animal,** white-tailed deer (1957); **domestic animal,** dairy cow (1971); **insect,** honeybee (1977); **fish,** musky (muskellunge) (1955); **song,** "On Wisconsin"; **mineral,** galena (1971); **rock,** red granite (1971); **symbol of peace,** mourning dove (1971); **soil,** antigo silt loam (1983); **fossil,** trilobite (1985); **dog,** American Water Spaniel (1986); **beverage,** milk (1988); **dance,** polka (1994);
Nickname: Badger State
Origin of name: French corruption of an Indian word whose meaning is disputed
10 largest cities (1998 est.): Milwaukee, 578,364; Madison, 209,306; Green Bay, 97,789; Kenosha, 87,849; Racine, 81,095; Appleton, 65,514; Waukesha, 61,989; West Allis, 59,974; Eau Claire, 59,200; Janesville, 59,149
Land area: 54,314 sq mi. (140,673 sq km)
Geographic center: In Wood Co., 9 mi. SE of Marshfield
Number of counties: 72
Largest county by population and area: Milwaukee, 906,248 (1999 est.); Marathon, 1,545 sq mi.
State forests: 9 (476,004 ac.)
State parks & scenic trails: 45 parks, 14 trails (66,185 ac.)
Residents: Wisconsinite
1999 resident population est.: 5,250,446
1990 resident census population (rank): 4,891,769 (16). **Male:** 2,392,935; **Female:** 2,498,834. **White:** 4,512,523 (92.2%); **Black:** 244,539 (5.0%); **American Indian:** 39,387 (0.8%); **Asian:** 53,583 (1.1%); **Other race:** 41,737 (0.9%); **Hispanic:** 93,194 (1.9%). **1980 percent population under 18:** 26.4; **65 and over:** 13.3; **median age:** 32.8.

The Wisconsin region was first explored for France by Jean Nicolet, who landed at Green Bay in 1634. In 1660 a French trading post and Roman Catholic mission were established near present-day Ashland.

Great Britain obtained the region in settlement of the French and Indian Wars in 1763; the U.S. acquired it in 1783 after the Revolutionary War. However, Great Britain retained actual control until after the War of 1812. The region was successively governed as part of the territories of Indiana, Illinois, and Michigan between 1800 and 1836, when it became a separate territory.

Wisconsin is a leading state in milk and cheese production. In 1998 the state ranked second in the number of milk cows (1,370,000) and produced 29% of the nation's total output of cheese. Other important farm products are peas, beans, beets, corn, potatoes, oats, hay, and cranberries.

The chief industrial products of the state are automobiles, machinery, furniture, paper, beer, and processed foods. Wisconsin ranks second among the 47 paper-producing states.

Wisconsin is a pioneer in social legislation, providing pensions for the blind (1907), aid to dependent children (1913), and old-age assistance (1925). In labor legislation, the state was the first to enact an unemployment compensation law (1932) and the first in which a workman's compensation law actually took effect. In 1984, Wisconsin became the first state to adopt the Uniform Marital Property Act.

The state has over 14,000 lakes, of which Winnebago is the largest. Water sports, ice-boating, and fishing are popular, as are skiing and hunting. Public parks and forests take up one-seventh of the land, with 45 state parks, 9 state forests, 14 state trails, 3 recreational areas, and 2 national forests.

Among the many points of interest are the Apostle Islands National Lakeshore; Ice Age National Scientific Reserve; the Circus World Museum at Baraboo; the Wolf, St. Croix, and Lower St. Croix national scenic riverways; and the Wisconsin Dells.

Famous natives and residents: Don Ameche, actor; Ray Chapman Andrews, naturalist and explorer; Walter Annenberg, media tycoon and philanthropist; Carrie Catt, woman suffragist; John R. Commons, economist; Tyne Daly, actress; August Derleth, author; Jeanne Dixon, seer; Zona Gale, novelist; Eric Heiden, skater; Woody Herman, band leader; Hildegarde, singer; Harry Houdini, magician; Hans V. Kaltenborne, journalist; Pee Wee King, singer; George F. Kennan, diplomat; Robert La Follette, politician; William D. Leahy, Fleet Admiral; Liberace, pianist; Charles Litel, actor; Allen Ludden, TV host; Alfred Lunt, actor; Frederic March, actor; Jackie Mason, comedian; John Ringling North, circus director; Pat O'Brien, actor; Georgia O'Keeffe, painter; Charlotte Rae, actress; William H. Rehnquist, jurist; Gena Rowlands, actress; Tom Snyder, newscaster; Spencer Tracy, actor; Thorstein Veblen, economist; Orson Welles, actor and producer; Thornton Wilder, author; Charles Winninger, actor; Frank Lloyd Wright, architect.

Wyoming

Capital: Cheyenne
Governor: Jim Geringer, R (to Jan. 2003)
Senators: Michael B. Enzi, R (to Jan. 2003); Craig Thomas, R (to Jan. 2001)
Secy. of State: Joe Meyer, R (to Jan. 2003)
Auditor: Max Maxfield, R (to Jan. 2003)
Supt. of Public Instruction: Judy Catchpole, R (to Jan. 2003)
Treasurer: Cynthia M. Lummis, R (to Jan. 2003)
Atty. General: Gay Woodhouse, R
Organized as territory: May 19, 1869
Entered Union (rank): July 10, 1890 (44)
Present constitution adopted: 1890
Motto: Equal rights (1955)
State Symbols: flower, Indian paintbrush (1917); **tree,** cottonwood (1947); **bird,** meadowlark (1927); **gemstone,** jade (1967); **insignia,** bucking horse (unofficial); **song,** "Wyoming" (1955);
Nickname: Equality State
Origin of name: From the Delaware Indian word, meaning "mountains and valleys alternating"; the same as the Wyoming Valley in Pennsylvania
10 largest cities (1998 est.): Cheyenne, 53,640; Casper, 48,283; Laramie, 25,035; Gillette, 19,463; Rock Springs, 19,408; Sheridan, 14,591; Green River,

13,059; Evanston, 11,475; Riverton, 10,126; Cody, 8,807
Land area: 97,105 sq mi. (251,501 sq km)
Geographic center: In Fremont Co., 58 mi. ENE of Lander
Number of counties: 23, plus Yellowstone National Park
Largest county by population and area: Laramie, 78,877 (1999 est.); Sweetwater, 10,426 sq mi.
State parks and historic sites: 23 (58,498 ac.)
Residents: Wyomingite
1999 resident population est.: 479,602
1990 resident census population (rank): 453,588 (50). **Male:** 227,007; **Female:** 226,581. **White:** 427,061 (94.2%); **Black:** 3,606 (0.8%); **American Indian:** 9,479 (2.1%); **Asian:** 2.806 (0.6%); **Other race:** 10,636 (2.3%); **Hispanic:** 25,751 (5.7%). **1990 percent population under 18:** 29.9; **65 and over:** 10.4; **median age:** 32.0.

The U.S. acquired the land comprising Wyoming from France as part of the Louisiana Purchase in 1803. John Colter, a fur-trapper, is the first white man known to have entered present Wyoming. In 1807 he explored the Yellowstone area and brought back news of its geysers and hot springs.

Robert Stuart pioneered the Oregon Trail across Wyoming in 1812–13 and, in 1834, Fort Laramie, the first permanent trading post in Wyoming, was built. Western Wyoming was obtained by the U.S. in the 1846 Oregon Treaty with Great Britain and as a result of the treaty ending the Mexican War in 1848.

When the Wyoming Territory was organized in 1869, Wyoming women became the first in the nation to obtain the right to vote. In 1925 Mrs. Nellie Tayloe Ross was elected first woman governor in the United States.

Wyoming's towering mountains and vast plains provide spectacular scenery, grazing lands for sheep and cattle, and rich mineral deposits.

Mining, particularly oil and natural gas, is the most important industry. Wyoming has the world's largest sodium carbonate (natrona) deposits and has the nation's second largest uranium deposits.

Wyoming ranks second among the states in wool production. In January 1998, it ranked third in sheep and lambs, exceeded only by Texas and California; it also had 1,660,000 cattle. Principal crops include wheat, oats, sugar beets, corn, barley, and alfalfa.

Second in mean elevation to Colorado, Wyoming has many attractions for the tourist trade, notably Yellowstone National Park. Cheyenne is famous for its annual "Frontier Days" celebration. Flaming Gorge, the Fort Laramie National Historic Site, and Devils Tower and Fossil Butte National Monuments are other points of interest.

Famous natives and residents: James Bridger, trapper, guide and storyteller; Dick Cheney, former Secretary of Defense; Buffalo Bill Cody, scout; John Colter, trader and first white man to enter Wyoming; June E. Downey, educator; Thomas Fitzpatrick, mountain man and guide; Curt Gowdy, sportscaster; Tom Horn, detective; Isabel Jewell, actress; Velma Linford, writer; Esther Morris, first woman judge; Ted Olson, writer; John "Portugee" Phillips, frontiersman; Jackson Pollock, painter; Nellie Tayloe Ross, first woman elected governor of a state; Alan K. Simpson, senator; Jedediah S. Smith, mountain man and first American to reach California from the East; Alan Swallow, publisher and author; Willis Van Devanter, Supreme Court justice; Francis E. Warren, first state governor; Chief Washakie, chief of the Shoshone; James G. Watt, former secretary of the Interior.

Tabulated Data on State Governments

State	Governor Term, years	Governor Annual salary	Legislature[1] Membership U[3]	L[4]	Term, years U[3]	L[4]	Salaries of members[5]		Highest Court[2] Members	Term, years	Annual salary
Alabama	4[6]	$ 94,655	35	105	4	4	$ 10	per diem	9	6	$126,117[7]
Alaska	4	81,648	20	40	4	2	24,012[8]	per annum	5	3[9]	99,996[7]
Arizona	4	95,000	30	60	2	2	24,000	per annum	5	6	120,000[7]
Arkansas	4	60,000	35	100	4	2	12,500	per annum	7	8	95,216[7]
California	4	114,000	40	80	4	2	72,500	per annum	7	12	127,276[7]
Colorado	4	90,000	35	65	4	2	30,000	per annum	7	10	95,090[7]
Connecticut	4	78,000	36	151	2	2	21,788[8]	per annum	7	8	119,962[7]
Delaware	4[10]	107,000	21	41	4	2	28,300	per annum	5	12	121,200[7]
Florida	4[6]	110,962	40	120	4[6]	2[11]	26,388	per annum	7	6	137,314
Georgia	4[6]	119,416	56	180	2	2	11,348	per annum	7	6	143,601
Hawaii	4	94,780	25	51	4	2	32,000[8]	per annum	5	10	93,780[7]
Idaho	4	95,500	35	70	2	2	14,760[8]	per annum	5	6	94,423[7]
Illinois	4	140,132	59	118	4-2	2	53,581	per annum	7	10	147,024
Indiana	4[6]	77,200	50	100	4	2	11,600	per annum	5	2[9]	81,000
Iowa	4	104,352	50	100	4	2	20,758	per annum	9	8	109,900[7]
Kansas	4	80,355	40	125	4	2	138	per diem[12]	7	6	82,005[7]
Kentucky	4	99,657	38	100	4	2	154	per diem[13]	7	8	114,373[7]
Louisiana	4	95,000	39	105	4	4	16,800	per annum	7	10	85,000
Maine	4	70,000	35	151	2	2	18,000	per biennium	7	7	80,392
Maryland	4[6]	120,000	47	141	4	4	29,700	per annum	7	10	107,300[7]
Massachusetts	4	100,000	40	160	2	2	46,410	per annum	7	(15)	95,880[7]
Michigan	4	151,245	38	110	4	2	56,981	per annum	7	8	140,816
Minnesota	4	114,000	67	134	4[15]	2	27,979	per annum	7	6	83,494
Mississippi	4	83,160	52	122	4	4	10,000	per session	9	8	90,800[7]
Missouri	4[10]	112,755	34	163	4[16]	2	29,080	per annum	7	12	114,348[7]
Montana	4	83,672	50	100	4	2	55	per diem	7	8	83,550
Nebraska	4[6]	85,000	49[17]	—	4[17]	—	12,000	per annum	7	6	111,003
Nevada	4[6]	117,000	21	42	4	2	7,800	per biennium	7	6	107,600
New Hampshire	2	93,263	24	(18)	2	2	200	per biennium	5	(14)	103,416[7]
New Jersey	4[6]	130,000[19]	40	80	4[16]	2	35,000	per annum	7	7[20]	128,800[7]
New Mexico	4[6]	90,000	42	70	4	2	136	per diem	5	8	90,407[7]
New York	4	179,000	61	150	2	2	79,500	per annum	7	14	151,200[7]
North Carolina	4[6]	107,132	50	120	2	2	13,951	per annum	7	8	110,687[7]
North Dakota	4	83,013	49	98	4	4	111	per diem[21]	5	10	83,107[7]
Ohio	4	115,752	33	99	4	2	42,427	per annum	7	6	101,150[7]
Oklahoma	4	101,140	48	101	4	2	38,400	per annum	(22)	6	97,807[7]
Oregon	4[6]	80,000	30	60	4	2	1,092	per month	7	6	83,700
Pennsylvania	4[6]	125,000	50	203	4	2	47,000	per annum	7	10	119,750[7]
Rhode Island	4	69,900	50	100	2	2	10,000	per annum	5	(23)	104,403
South Carolina	4	106,078	46	124	4	2	10,400	per annum	5	10	106,061[7]
South Dakota	4[6]	89,868	35	70	2	2	6,000	per annum	5	3[24]	92,123[7]
Tennessee	4	85,000	33	99	4	2	16,500	per annum	5	8	101,820
Texas	4	99,122	31	150	4	2	7,200	per annum	9	6	94,686[7]
Utah	4	96,700	29	75	4	2	120[8]	per diem	5	3	109,650[7]
Vermont	2	96,661	30	150	2	2	536[25]	per week	5	6	90,584[7]
Virginia	4	124,855	40	100	4	2	17,640[26]	per annum	7	12	128,352[7]
Washington	4[27]	135,960	49	98	4[11]	2	32,064	per annum	9	6	123,600
West Virginia	4[6]	72,000	34	100	4	2	15,000	per annum	5	12	72,000
Wisconsin	4	102,882	33	99	4	2	44,233	per annum	7	10	118,824[7]
Wyoming	4	95,000	30	60	4	2	125	per diem	5	10	93,000

NOTE: Salaries are rounded to nearest dollar. 1. Known as *General Assembly* in Ark., Colo., Conn., Del., Ga., Ill., Iowa, Ind., Ky., Md., Mo., N.C., Ohio, Pa., R.I., S.C., Tenn., Vt., Va.; *Legislative Assembly* in N.D., Ore.; *General Court* in Mass., N.H.; *Legislature* in other states. Meets biennially in Ark., Mont., Nev., N.D., Ore., Texas. Wyoming Legislature has regular general session on odd-numbered years and a budget session on even-numbered years. Arkansas General Assembly meets every other year for 60 days in odd numbered years. Ohio General Assembly meets when deemed necessary. Legislative bodies meet annually in other states. 2. Known as *Court of Appeals* in Md., N.Y.; *Supreme Court of Virginia* in Va.; *Supreme Judicial Court* in Maine, Mass.; *Supreme Court* in other states. 3. Upper house: *Senate* in all states except Neb., which has a single-house legislative body, "the Legislature." 4. Lower house: *Assembly* in Calif., Nev., N.Y., Wis.; *House of Delegates* in Md., Va., W.Va.; *General Assembly* in N.J.; *House of Representatives* in other states. 5. Base salary. Does not include additional payments for expenses, mileage, special sessions, etc., or additional per diem payments. 6. May not serve third consecutive term. 7. Chief justice receives a higher salary. 8. Leaders receive a higher salary. 9. Initial term; thereafter elected popularly for 10-year term. 10. May serve only two terms, consecutive or otherwise. 11. Have term limitations. 12. When in session, plus $600/mo. when not in session. 13. $1,459 per month when not in session. 14. Until 70 years old. 15. Every 10 years (the year after census) term is only for 2 years. 16. Legislators may serve only 8 years in each house, 16 combined. 17. Unicameral legislature. 18. Constitutional number: 375-400. 19. Legislated salary; salary received is $85,000. 20. Second term receive tenure, mandatory retirement at 70. 21. When in session, plus $250 per month when not in session. 22. Nine members in Supreme Court, highest in civil cases; five in Court of Criminal Appeals. 23. Term of good behavior. 24. Subsequent terms, eight years. 25. To limit of $13,000 per biennium; $105 per diem for Special Session. 26. Upper house receives higher salary. 27. No person is eligible who would have served during 8 of the previous 14 years. *Source:* questionnaires to the states.

Land and Water Area of States, 1990
(in square miles)

State	Rank (total area)	Land[1] area	Water[2] area	Total area	State	Rank (total area)	Land[1] area	Water[2] area	Total area
Alabama	30	50,750.23	1,672.71	52,422.94	Montana	4	145,556.34	1,489.82	147,046.16
Alaska	1	570,373.55	86,050.59	656,424.14	Nebraska	16	76,877.73	480.67	77,358.40
Arizona	6	113,642.26	364.00	114,006.26	Nevada	7	109,805.89	761.02	110,566.91
Arkansas	29	52,075.29	1,107.07	53,182.36	New Hampshire	46	8,969.36	381.57	9,350.93
California	3	155,973.09	7,734.06	163,707.15	New Jersey	47	7,418.84	1,303.11	8,721.95
Colorado	8	103,729.54	370.78	104,100.32	New Mexico	5	121,364.54	233.69	123,598.23
Connecticut	48	4,845.39	698.26	5,543.65	New York	27	47,223.85	7,250.71	54,474.56
Delaware	49	1,954.62	534.76	2,489.38	North Carolina	28	48,718.08	5,103.27	53,821.35
Dist. of Columbia	—	61.41	6.95	68.36	North Dakota	19	68,994.24	1,709.59	70,703.83
Florida	22	53,997.08	11,761.00	65,758.08	Ohio	34	40,952.59	3,874.94	44,827.53
Georgia	24	57,918.73	1,522.49	59,441.22	Oklahoma	20	68,678.57	1,224.33	69,902.90
Hawaii	43	6,423.34	4,508.24	10,931.58	Oregon	9	96,002.58	2,383.17	98,385.75
Idaho	14	82,750.93	822.84	83,573.77	Pennsylvania	33	44,819.61	1,238.63	46,058.24
Illinois	25	55,593.29	2,324.55	57,917.84	Rhode Island	50	1,044.98	500.12	1,545.10
Indiana	38	35,870.18	549.91	36,420.09	South Carolina	40	30,111.12	1,895.99	32,007.11
Iowa	26	55,874.90	400.64	56,275.54	South Dakota	17	75,897.74	1,223.72	77,121.46
Kansas	15	81,823.02	458.98	82,282.00	Tennessee	36	41,219.52	926.49	42,146.01
Kentucky	37	39,732.31	678.93	40,411.24	Texas	2	261,914.26	6,686.70	268,600.96
Louisiana	31	43,566.03	8,277.44	51,843.47	Utah	13	82,168.15	2,735.97	84,904.12
Maine	39	30,864.55	4,522.78	35,387.33	Vermont	45	9,249.33	365.67	9,615.00
Maryland	42	9,774.65	2,632.80	12,407.45	Virginia	35	39,597.79	3,171.09	42,768.88
Massachusetts	44	7,837.98	2,716.81	10,554.79	Washington	18	66,581.95	4,720.70	71,302.65
Michigan	11	56,809.18	40,001.04	96,810.22	West Virginia	41	24,086.55	144.89	24,231.44
Minnesota	12	79,616.66	7,326.05	86,942.71	Wisconsin	23	54,313.71	11,189.50	65,503.21
Mississippi	32	46,913.64	1,519.95	48,433.59	Wyoming	10	97,104.55	713.56	97,818.11
Missouri	21	68,898.01	810.80	69,708.81	**U.S. Total**		**3,536,341.73**	**251,083.35**	**3,787,425.08**

1. Dry land and land temporarily or partially covered by water, such as marshland, swamps, etc.; streams and canals under one-eighth statute mile wide; and lakes, reservoirs, and ponds under 40 acres. 2. Permanent inland water surface, such as lakes, reservoirs, and ponds having an area of 40 acres or more; streams, sloughs, estuaries, and canals one-eighth statute mile or more in width; deeply indented embayments and sounds, and other coastal waters behind or sheltered by headlands or islands separated by less than 1 nautical mile of water, and islands under 40 acres in area. Excludes areas of oceans, bays, sounds, etc. lying within U.S. jurisdiction but not defined as inland water. Source: Department of Commerce, Bureau of the Census.

State Capitals and Largest Cities

State	Capital	Largest city	State	Capital	Largest city
Alabama	Montgomery	Birmingham	Montana	Helena	Billings
Alaska	Juneau	Anchorage	Nebraska	Lincoln	Omaha
Arizona	Phoenix	Phoenix	Nevada	Carson City	Las Vegas
Arkansas	Little Rock	Little Rock	New Hampshire	Concord	Manchester
California	Sacramento	Los Angeles	New Jersey	Trenton	Newark
Colorado	Denver	Denver	New Mexico	Santa Fe	Albuquerque
Connecticut	Hartford	Bridgeport	New York	Albany	New York City
Delaware	Dover	Wilmington	North Carolina	Raleigh	Charlotte
Florida	Tallahassee	Jacksonville	North Dakota	Bismarck	Fargo
Georgia	Atlanta	Atlanta	Ohio	Columbus	Columbus
Hawaii	Honolulu	Honolulu	Oklahoma	Oklahoma City	Oklahoma City
Idaho	Boise	Boise	Oregon	Salem	Portland
Illinois	Springfield	Chicago	Pennsylvania	Harrisburg	Philadelphia
Indiana	Indianapolis	Indianapolis	Rhode Island	Providence	Providence
Iowa	Des Moines	Des Moines	South Carolina	Columbia	Columbia
Kansas	Topeka	Wichita	South Dakota	Pierre	Sioux Falls
Kentucky	Frankfort	Louisville	Tennessee	Nashville	Memphis
Louisiana	Baton Rouge	New Orleans	Texas	Austin	Houston
Maine	Augusta	Portland	Utah	Salt Lake City	Salt Lake City
Maryland	Annapolis	Baltimore	Vermont	Montpelier	Burlington
Massachusetts	Boston	Boston	Virginia	Richmond	Virginia Beach
Michigan	Lansing	Detroit	Washington	Olympia	Seattle
Minnesota	St. Paul	Minneapolis	West Virginia	Charleston	Charleston
Mississippi	Jackson	Jackson	Wisconsin	Madison	Milwaukee
Missouri	Jefferson City	Kansas City	Wyoming	Cheyenne	Cheyenne

Source: U.S. Bureau of the Census, 1990 figures.

50 Largest Cities of the United States

(According to 1998 Census Bureau data)

Data supplied by Bureau of the Census and by the cities in response to questionnaires. Ranking of 50 largest cities based on June 30, 1998, census estimates. (Census data for 1999 was released after the almanac went to press.) Per capita personal income data is given for the Metropolitan Statistical Area (MSA), the Primary Metropolitan Statistical Area (PMSA), the New England County Metropolitan Area (NECMA), or the Consolidated Metropolitan Statistical Area (CMSA), as noted. Average daily temperature data is from *County and City Data Book*. Population breakdown figures available only for original 1990 census data. For the revised 1990 census total population figures, see "Top 50 Cities in the U.S. by Estimated 1998 Population and Rank," p. 201. NOTE: Persons of Hispanic origin may be of any race.

Albuquerque, N.M.

Mayor: Jim Baca (to Dec. 2001)
1998 est. population (rank): 419,311 (36)
1990 census population (rank): 384,736 (38); **% change,** 8.9; **Male,** 186,584; **Female,** 198,152; **White,** 301,010 (78.3%); **Black,** 11,484 (3.0%); **American Indian, Eskimo, or Aleut,** 11,708 (3.0%); **Asian or Pacific Islander,** 6,660 (1.7%); **Other race,** 53,874; **Hispanic origin,** 132,706 (34.5%). **1990 population under 18:** 25.0%; **65 and over:** 11.1%; **median age:** 32.5.
Land area: 163 sq mi. (422 sq km); **Alt.:** 4,958 ft.
Avg. daily temp. (1998): Jan., 34.8° F; July, 78.8° F
Churches: 211; **City-owned parks:** 189; **Radio stations:** 43 (AM, 17; FM, 26); **Television stations:** 11
Civilian Labor Force: 224,003; **Unemployed:** 10,305, **Percent:** 4.6; **Per capita personal income (MSA) 1992:** $17,758
Chamber of Commerce: Greater Albuquerque Chamber of Commerce, 401 2nd St. N.W., Albuquerque, N.M. 87125. Albuquerque Hispanic Chamber of Commerce, 202 Central Ave. S.E., Albuquerque, N.M. 87102

Albuquerque is the largest city in New Mexico and the seat of Bernalillo County. It is situated in west central New Mexico on the upper Rio Grande River. Early Spanish settlers arrived there in the mid-1600s. The old town was founded in 1706 by Don Francisco Cuervo y Valdés, the governor of New Mexico, and named after the Duke of Albuquerque, the viceroy of New Spain. During the Civil War, Confederate forces briefly occupied the city in 1862. The new town section was founded in 1880. In 1883, Albuquerque became the county seat and was incorporated as a city in 1891.

The city is noted as a center for health and medical services in the region, and government agencies, nuclear research, banking, and tourism are important to the economy. There is a growing high-tech center in Albuquerque and Intel Corp.'s largest manufacturing facility is located there.

Famous natives: Erna Fergusson, author; Annabeth Gish, actress; Fred Haney, baseball player, executive; Ernie Pyle, World War II war correspondent; Slim Summerville, actor; Al and Bobby Unser, auto racers.

Atlanta, Ga.[1]

Mayor: Bill Campbell (to Jan. 2002)
1998 est. population (rank): 403,819 (39)[2]
1990 census population (rank): 394,017 (36), **% change,** 2.5; **Male,** 187,877; **Female,** 206,140; **White,** 122,327 (31.1%); **Black,** 264,262 (67.1%); **American Indian, Eskimo, or Aleut,** 563 (0.1%); **Asian or Pacific Islander,** 3,498 (0.9%); **Other race,** 3,367; **Hispanic origin,** 7,525 (1.9%).

1990 population under 18: 24.1%; **65 and over:** 11.3%; **median age:** 31.5.
City land area: 136 sq mi. (352.2 sq km); **Alt.:** Highest, 1,050 ft.; lowest, 940 ft.
Avg. daily temp.: Jan., 41.9° F; July, 78.6° F
Churches: 1,500; **City-owned parks:** 277 (3,178 ac.); **Radio stations:** AM, 7; FM, 20; **Television stations:** 8 commercial; 2 PBS
Civilian Labor Force (1999): 2,149,100; **Unemployed:** 66,622, **Percent:** 3.1; **Per capita personal income (MSA) 1999:** $31,229
Chamber of Commerce: Metro Atlanta Chamber of Commerce, 235 International Blvd., Atlanta, Ga. 30303

1. Information is gathered on the 20-county MSA.
2. 1999 est. population: 3,857,097 (metro area).

Atlanta, the largest city and capital of Georgia, is the seat of Fulton County. It is situated in the northwest part of the state at the base of the Blue Ridge Mountains near the Chattahoochee River. The first European settler was Hardy Ivy, who built a cabin there in 1833.

Founded as Terminus in 1837, the town served as the end of the Georgia railroad line (Western and Atlantic Railroad) and later became incorporated as Marthasville in 1843 in honor of ex-governor Lumpkin's daughter Martha. It was renamed Atlanta in 1845 and incorporated as a city in 1847. The name was suggested by the railroad's chief engineer, J. Edgar Thomson, and was derived from its location at the end of the Georgia and Atlantic railroad line. The city became the capital of Georgia in 1868.

During the Civil War, the city was burned and almost completely destroyed while occupied by Gen. W. T. Sherman's troops in Nov. 1864. It was quickly rebuilt after the war and it grew rapidly due to the expansion of the railroads in the southwest. Atlanta's diverse economy is led by the service, communications, retail trade, manufacturing, finance, and insurance industries. The convention business is also important, and in 1996 the Summer Olympic Games were held there.

Famous natives: Hank Aaron, baseball player; Arrested Development, recording artists; Jimmy Carter, former president; Ray Charles, singer; James Dickey, poet; Mattivilda Dobbs, soprano; Evander Holyfield, boxer; Allan Jackson, singer; Bobby Jones, golfer; DeForest Kelley, actor; Martin Luther King, Jr., civil rights leader and Nobel Peace Prize winner; Gladys Knight, singer; Kriss Kross, recording artists; Margaret Mitchell, novelist; Bert Parks, entertainer; Eric Roberts, actor; Julia Roberts, actress; Doug Stone, singer; Gwen Torrence, Olympic athlete; Lee Tracy, actor; Travis Tritt, singer; Ted Turner, TBS and CNN founder; Jane Withers, actress; Joanne Woodward, actress; Andrew Young, civil rights activist.

Austin, Tex.

Mayor: Kirk Watson (to June 2003)
1998 est. population (rank): 552,434 (21)[1]
1990 census population (rank): 465,622
(27); **% change,** 17.0; **Male,** 232,473; **Female,**
233,149; **White,** 328,542 (70.6%); **Black,** 57,868
(12.4%); **American Indian, Eskimo, or Aleut:,** 1,756
(0.4%); **Asian or Pacific Islander,** 14,141 (3.0%);
Other race, 63,315; **Hispanic origin,** 106,868
(23.0%). **1990 population under 18:** 23.1%; **65 and over:** 7.4%; **median age:** 28.9
Land area: 252.3 sq mi. (653 sq km); **Alt.:** From 425 ft. to over 1000 ft.
Avg. daily temp.: Jan., 49.1° F; July, 84.7° F
Churches: 353 churches, representing 45 denominations; **City-owned parks and playgrounds:** 169
(11,800 ac.); **Radio stations:** AM, 12; FM, 27;
Television stations: 7 commercial; 1 PBS;
1 independent
Civilian Labor Force (1998): 681,732; **Unemployed:**
17,899, **Percent:** 2.6; **Per capita personal income (MSA) 1992:** $26,700, Austin–San Marcos
Chamber of Commerce: Greater Austin Chamber of Commerce, P.O. Box 1967, Austin, Tex. 78767

1. 1997 est. population 561,045.

Austin, the state capital of Texas and seat of Travis County, is the fifth-largest city in Texas. It is situated in the south central part of the state on the Colorado River. The site was called Waterloo in 1838, and in 1839 it was incorporated as a city and chosen as the capital of the independent Republic of Texas. Waterloo was renamed Austin in honor of Stephen F. Austin, the founder of the Texas Republic. It became the permanent capital of the state of Texas in 1870.

Austin's growth was spurred by several developments after the Civil War—the railroads reached the city in the 1870s; it was crossed by the important Chisholm cattle trail; and it became the seat of the state university in 1883.

Austin has a growing commercial and diversified manufacturing sector. Civilian government employment is 20% of the labor force and is important to the economy. As home to the University of Texas, Austin is a major center for research and development, and is nationally recognized as a high-technology center. The city has a new convention center downtown.

Famous natives: Don Baylor, baseball player and manager; Earl Campbell, football player; Liz Carpenter, author; Dabney Coleman, actor; Ben Crenshaw, golfer; Michael Dell, founder Dell Computer Corp.; Tobe Hooper, film director; Lady Bird Johnson, former First Lady; Tom Kite, golfer; James Michener, author; Willie Nelson, musician; Amado Pena, artist; Darrell Royal, football coach; Zachary Scott, actor; Jerry Jeff Walker, musician; Dalhart Windberg, artist.

Baltimore, Md.

Mayor: Martin O'Malley (to Dec. 2003)
1998 est. population (rank): 645,593 (16)
1990 census population (rank): 736,014
(13); **% change,** –12.3; **Male,** 343,513; **Female:**
392,501; **White,** 287,753 (39.1%); **Black,** 435,768
(59.2%); **American Indian, Eskimo, or Aleut:** 2,555
(0.3%); **Asian or Pacific Islander:** 7,942 (1.1%);
Other race: 1,996; **Hispanic origin:** 7,602 (1.0%).
1990 population under 18: 24.4%; **65 and over:**
13.7%; **Median age:** 32.6.
Land area: 80.3 sq mi. (208 sq km); **Alt.:** Highest,
490 ft.; lowest, sea level

Avg. daily temp.: Jan., 35.5° F; July, 79.9° F
Churches: Roman Catholic, 72; Jewish, 50; Protestant and others, 344; **City-owned parks:** 347 park areas and tracts (6,314 ac.); **Radio stations:** AM, 10; FM, 11; **Television stations:** 7 (including Home Shopping Network)
Civilian Labor Force: 333,043; **Unemployed:** 35,531, **Percent:** 10.7; **Per capita personal income (PMSA) 1992:** $22,412
Chamber of Commerce: Greater Baltimore Committee, 111 S. Calvert St., Ste. 1500, Baltimore, Md. 21202

Baltimore, the largest city in Maryland, is situated in the northern part of the state on the Patapsco River estuary, an arm of Chesapeake Bay. The city is independent and does not fall within any county.

The site was settled in the early 17th century and founded as a town in 1729. The town was named after Lord Baltimore, the founder of Maryland, and was incorporated as a city in 1797. It has an excellent harbor and has been a principal port since the 18th century. Baltimore was a pioneer ship-building center and the Baltimore clipper, one of the best sailing ships of its day, was used extensively in world trade.

Baltimore's economy is focused on manufacturing, in steel and heavy and light industries; ship construction; and scientific research and development.

Famous natives: Larry Adler, musician; John Astin, actor; Eubie Blake, pianist; Francis X. Bushman, actor; Charlie Chase, actor; Hans Conried, actor; Mildred Dunnock, actress; "Mama" Cass Elliot, singer; Barry Farber, broadcaster; Paul Ford, actor; Philip Glass, composer; Billie Holiday, singer; Barry Levinson, director; H. L. Mencken, writer; Babe Ruth, baseball player; Upton Sinclair, novelist; Leon Uris, novelist; Frank Zappa, musician.

Boston, Mass.

Mayor: Thomas Menino (to Dec. 2001)
1998 est. population (rank): 555,447 (20)
1990 census population (rank): 574,283
(20); **% change,** –3.3; **Male,** 275,972; **Female,**
298,311; **White,** 360,875 (62.8%); **Black,** 146,945
(25.6%); **American Indian, Eskimo, or Aleut,** 1,884
(0.3%); **Asian or Pacific Islander,** 30,388 (5.3%);
Other race, 34,191; **Hispanic origin,** 61,955 (10.8%).
1990 population under 18: 19.1%; **65 and over:**
11.5%; **median age:** 30.3.
Land area: 47.2 sq mi. (122 sq km); **Alt.:** Highest, 330 ft.; lowest, sea level
Avg. daily temp.: Jan., 29.6° F; July, 73.5° F
Churches: Protestant, 187; Roman Catholic, 71; Jewish, 13; others, 100; **City-owned parks, playgrounds, etc.:** 2,276.36 ac.; **Radio stations:** AM, 7; FM, 17; **Television stations:** 8
Civilian Labor Force (Jan. 1999): 295,689;
Unemployed: 9,951, **Percent:** 3.4; **Per capita personal income (1996):** $32,150[1]
Chamber of Commerce: Boston Chamber of Commerce, 600 Atlantic Ave., Boston, Mass. 02210

1. Suffolk County.

Boston is the state capital and seat of Suffolk County, and the largest city in Massachusetts. It is located in the eastern part of the state at the head of Boston Bay. It was incorporated as a city in 1822. No city in the U.S. is richer in historical associations than Boston, and no city has retained more of its original buildings as memorials to America's past.

Puritans from England settled at Boston in 1630, only ten years after the Pilgrims had landed at Plymouth in 1620. They named their new town Boston, after the former home of many of the Pilgrims in

Lincolnshire, England. Fourteen years later, the pioneer Bostonians set aside the first public park in the U.S.—the Boston Common. The following year, 1635, they opened the first free public school in America. Today, the Boston metropolitan area is home to 68 colleges and universities.

Boston is a major industrial, financial, and educational hub and has one of the finest ports in the world. The port of Boston handled more than 16.8 million tons of cargo in 1999.

The city's banking and financial services, insurance, and real estate sectors continue to drive Boston's economy. Boston is also a leading city in health care, with 25 inpatient hospitals and numerous community health centers. The city's unique cultural and historic heritage makes it a center of tourism, and its hotel industry ranks first in the nation in occupancy. Boston's other businesses are in high technology, biotechnology, software, and electronics.

Famous natives: Samuel Adams, patriot; Louisa May Alcott, author; John Singleton Copley, painter; Ralph Waldo Emerson, philosopher and poet; Arthur Fiedler, conductor; Benjamin Franklin, statesman and scientist; Edward Everett Hale, clergyman and author; Oliver Wendell Holmes, Supreme Court justice; Winslow Homer, painter; Joseph P. Kennedy, financier; Jack Lemmon, actor; Robert Lowell, poet; Edgar Allan Poe, writer; Paul Revere, patriot and silversmith; John L. Sullivan, boxer; Barbara Walters, TV journalist.

Charlotte, N.C.

Mayor: Pat McCrory (to Nov. 2001)
1998 est. population: 504,637 (25)[1]
1990 census population (rank): 395,934 (35);
  % change, 20.3; **Male,** 188,088; **Female,** 207,846;
  White, 259,760 (65.6%); **Black,** 125,827 (31.8%);
  American Indian, Eskimo, or Aleut: 1,425 (0.4%);
  Asian or Pacific Islander: 7,211 (1.8%); **Other race,**
  1,711; **Hispanic origin,** 5,571 (1.4%). **1990 population under 18:** 24.2%; **65 and over:** 9.8%;
  median age: 32.1.
Land area: 234 sq mi. (606.2 sq km); **Alt.:** 765 ft.
Avg. daily temp.: Jan., 40.5° F; July, 78.5° F
Churches: Protestant, over 400; Roman Catholic, 8;
  Jewish, 3; Greek Orthodox, 1; **City-owned parks and parkways:** 130; **Radio stations:** AM, 10; FM, 19;
  Television stations: 6 commercial; 1 PBS
Civilian Labor Force (1999): 362,040; **Unemployed:**
  7,280, **Percent:** 2.0; **Per capita personal income (MSA) 1999:** $17,779[2]
Chamber of Commerce: Charlotte Chamber, P.O. Box 32785, Charlotte, N.C., 28232

1. 1997 est. population: 470,553. 2. Charlotte–Gastonia Rock Hill, N.C.–S.C.

Charlotte, North Carolina's largest city and the seat of Mecklenburg County, is located in the southern part of the state near the South Carolina border. It was named for King George III of England's wife, Charlotte Sophia of Mecklenburg-Strelitz.

Settled about 1750, Charlotte was incorporated as a city in 1768 and made the county seat in 1774. From 1800 to 1848, Charlotte was the center of U.S. gold production. A branch of the U.S. mint operated there from 1837 to 1913. Charlotte was a leading Confederate city during the Civil War and was the last meeting place of the full Confederate cabinet.

The city has a highly diversified economy and is a major center for distribution, retailing, technology, and manufacturing. It is the second-largest banking center in the U.S. It is the seat of the University of North Carolina at Charlotte.

Famous natives: Romare Bearden, artist; Richard G. Darman, government official; Billy Graham, evangelist; Charles Gwathmey, architect; Hamilton Jordan, government official; Donald Schollander, swimmer; Randolph Scott, actor.

Chicago, Ill.

Mayor: Richard M. Daley (to April 2003)
1998 est. population (rank): 2,802,079 (3)
1990 census population (rank): 2,783,726 (3);
  % change, 0.7; **Male,** 1,334,705; **Female,** 1,449,021;
  White, 1,263,524 (45.4%); **Black,** 1,087,711 (39.1%);
  American Indian, Eskimo, or Aleut, 7,064 (0.3%);
  Asian or Pacific Islander, 104,118 (3.7%); **Other race,** 321,309; **Hispanic origin,** 545,852 (19.6%).
  1990 population under 18: 26.0%; **65 and over:** 11.9%; **median age:** 31.3.
Land area: 228.443 sq mi. (592 sq km); **Alt.:** Highest, 672 ft.; lowest, 578.5 ft.
Avg. daily temp. (1998): Jan., 29.6° F; July, 74.5° F
Churches: Protestant, 850; Roman Catholic, 252; Jewish, 51; **City-owned parks:** 551; **Radio stations (1999):** AM, 16; FM, 28; **Television stations:** 14
Civilian Labor Force (PMSA 1996): 4,120,400;
  Unemployed: 194,400, **Percent:** 4.7; **Per capita personal income (PMSA) 1997:** $30,717
Chamber of Commerce: Chicagoland Chamber of Commerce, 330 N. Wabash, One IBM Plaza, Suite 2800, Chicago, Ill. 60611

Chicago is the largest city in Illinois and the seat of Cook County. Built directly on the lake front, it stretches for 22 miles along the southwestern shore of Lake Michigan.

The first white men known to have visited Chicago were Louis Joliet and Jacques Marquette in 1673. The first permanent white settler in the area was John Kinzie, who is sometimes called the Father of Chicago. He took over a trading post in 1796 that had been established in 1791 by Jean-Baptiste Point du Sable, a black fur trapper. Fort Dearborn, a blockhouse and stockade, was built in 1804 but was evacuated in 1812, with more than half of its garrison massacred at what is now the foot of 18th Street. Not until 1830 was the town laid out. The name Chicago is thought to come from the Algonquian word "Chicagou" meaning strong or powerful. Some early Frenchmen believed that the name was derived from the Algonquian word for "onion place" because wild onions grew there.

Chicago was incorporated as a village in 1833 and as a city in 1837. Thirty-four years later, it was destroyed in the great Chicago fire of 1871.

Chicago is a major Great Lakes port and the commercial, financial, industrial, and cultural center of the Midwest. The manufacturing industries dominate the wholesale and retail trade, and trade in agricultural commodities is important to the economy. The Chicago Board of Trade is the largest agricultural futures market in the world.

Famous natives: Jack Benny, comedian; Edgar Rice Burroughs, author; Raymond Chandler, author; Hillary Rodham Clinton, lawyer and First Lady; Michael Crichton, author; Walt Disney, filmmaker; John Dos Passos, author; Bobby Fischer, chess player; Bob Fosse, choreographer and director; Benny Goodman, clarinetist; Dorothy Hamill, figure skater; Quincy Jones, composer; Gene Krupa, drummer; David Mamet, playwright; Bob Newhart, comedian; Kim Novak, actress; Donald O'Connor, actor; William L. Shirer, journalist and historian; Gloria Swanson, actress; Melvin Van Peebles, playwright; Alfred Wallenstein, conductor; Robin Williams, comedian and actor; Robert Young, actor.

Cleveland, Ohio

Mayor: Michael R. White (to Dec. 2001)
1998 est. population (rank): 495,817 (28)
1990 census population (rank): 505,616 (24);
   % change, –1.9; **Male,** 237,211; **Female,** 268,405;
   White, 250,234 (49.5%); **Black,** 235,405 (46.6%);
   American Indian, Eskimo, or Aleut, 1,562 (0.3%);
   Asian or Pacific Islander, 5,115 (1.0%); **Other race,**
   13,300; **Hispanic origin,** 23,197 (4.6%). **1990 population under 18:** 26.9%; **65 and over:** 14.0%; **median age:** 31.9.
Land area: 79 sq mi. (205 sq km); **Alt.:** Highest, 1048 ft.; lowest, 573 ft.
Avg. daily temp.: Jan., 25.5° F; July, 71.6° F
Churches[1]: Protestant, 980; Roman Catholic, 187; Jewish, 31; Eastern Orthodox, 22; **City-owned parks:** 41 (1,930 ac.); **Radio stations:** AM, 15; FM, 17; **Television stations:** 7
Civilian Labor Force: 209,700; **Unemployed:** 19,900, **Percent:** 9.7; **Per capita personal income (PMSA) 1992:** $21,533[1]
Chamber of Commerce: Greater Cleveland Growth Association, 200 Tower City Center, Cleveland, Ohio 44113

1. Cleveland–Lorain–Elyria.

Cleveland is the second-largest city in Ohio and the seat of Cuyahoga County. It is located in the northeastern part of the state on Lake Erie. In the colonial era, the Cleveland area was known as the Connecticut Western Reserve, part of a land grant made to Connecticut by King Charles II in 1662. The city was founded in 1796 by Gen. Moses Cleaveland, who was the head surveyor of the Connecticut Land Company. This company had bought three million acres in what is now northern Ohio. A permanent settlement was founded in 1799, named after the general, and the spelling was shortened to Cleveland. The city was incorporated in 1836.

Cleveland's industrial growth was stimulated by the opening of the Ohio and Erie canals in 1832 and, later, by the advent of the Civil War, with the increasing demand for machinery, railroad equipment, ships, and other items.

The port of Cleveland is the largest overseas general cargo port on Lake Erie. Greater Cleveland has long been famous as a diversified durable goods manufacturing area. Following the national trend, Cleveland has been shifting to a more services-based economy. Greater Cleveland is a world corporate center for leading national and multinational companies in industries ranging from transportation, insurance, retailing, and utilities, to commercial banking and finance.

Famous natives: Jim Backus, actor; Drew Carey, actor and comedian; Dorothy Dandridge, actress; Ruby Dee, actress; Phil Donahue, talk-show host; Joel Grey, actor; Arsenio Hall, talk-show host; Margaret Hamilton, actress; Philip Johnson, architect; Henry Mancini, composer; Burgess Meredith, actor; Paul Newman, actor; Carl Stokes, jurist.

Colorado Springs, Colo.

Mayor: Mary Lou Makepeace (to April 2001)
1998 est. population (rank): 344,987 (48)
1990 census population (rank): 281,140
   (54); **% change,** 23.0; **Male,** 137,611; **Female,**
   143,529; **White,** 241,513 (85.9%); **Black,** 19,746
   (7.0%); **American Indian, Eskimo, or Aleut,** 2,335
   (0.8%); **Asian or Pacific Islander,** 6,845 (2.4%);
   Other race, 10,701; **Hispanic origin,** 25,662 (9.1%).
   1990 population under 18: 26.7%; **65 and over:**
   9.2%; **median age:** 31.1.

Land area: 183.2 sq mi. (474.49 sq km); **Alt.:** 6,035 ft.
Avg. daily temp.: Jan., 28.8° F; July, 71.2° F
Churches: Protestant, 400+; Roman Catholic, 20; Jewish, 3; others, **City parks and playgrounds:** 156 (10,762 ac.); **Radio stations:** AM, 7; FM, 17; **Television stations:** 7
Civilian Labor Force: 138,239; **Unemployed:** 10,084, **Percent:** 6.68; **Per capita personal income (1989):** $14,243
Chamber of Commerce: Colorado Springs Chamber of Commerce, 2 N. Cascade Ave., Suite 110, Colorado Springs, Colo. 80903

Colorado Springs is the second-largest city in Colorado, after Denver. It is the seat of El Paso County, making up about three-quarters of the county's population. It is located on the edge of the Rocky Mountains, with Pikes Peak (14,110 feet) towering beside it to the west. To the east begin the Great Plains.

The city was founded in 1871. Gen. William Jackson Palmer, a Pennsylvania-born Civil War veteran, came across the scenic spot in his railroad travels and was inspired to begin a new resort community there. The subsequent development of Colorado Springs was influenced in part by an influx of English tourists later in the 1870s and by the discovery of gold in nearby Cripple Creek in the 1890s. Millionaire businessmen and philanthropists, such as Spencer Penrose, Charles Tutt, and Winfield Scott Stratton, helped to establish the city's infrastructure and shape its popularity as a tourist destination.

During World War II, Colorado Springs sold a large amount of land just south of the city to the military. The U.S. Army established Fort Carson as a training facility. The military presence in Colorado Springs would continue to grow, with the establishment of the United States Air Force Academy there in the 1950s, and later, the construction of Peterson Air Force Base, Falcon Air Force Base, and Cheyenne Mountain Air Force Base. The bases are all home to space command centers (with Cheyenne Mountain housing the headquarters for the North American Aerospace Defense Command [NORAD]) and have collectively earned Colorado Springs its national reputation as the leading center for military space operations.

The city's economy is still based heavily on tourism. In more recent years, Colorado Springs has gained a strong foothold in the electronics, high-technology, and manufacturing industries. The city is also a large center for amateur sports, as it is home to the headquarters of the U.S. Olympic Committee and Olympic Training Center facility.

Famous natives: Bert Andrews, journalist; Kelly Bishop, actress; Spring Byington, actress; Lon Chaney, actor; Marjorie Daw, actress; Marceline Day, actress; Rich "Goose" Gossage, baseball player; Helen Hunt Jackson, writer and poet; Chase Masterson, actress; Sherry Stringfield, actress.

Columbus, Ohio

Mayor: Michael B. Coleman (to Nov. 2003)
1998 est. population (rank): 670,234 (15)
1990 census population (rank): 632,910 (16);
   % change, 5.9; **Male,** 305,574; **Female,** 327,336;
   White, 471,025 (74.4%); **Black,** 142,748 (22.6%);
   American Indian, Eskimo, or Aleut, 1,469 (0.2%);
   Asian or Pacific Islander, 14,993 (2.4%); **Other race,**
   2,675; **Hispanic origin,** 6,741 (1.1%). **1990 population under 18:** 23.7%; **65 and over:** 9.2%; **median age:** 29.4.

Land area: 211 sq mi. (546.4 sq km); **Alt.:** Highest, 902 ft.; lowest, 702 ft.
Avg. daily temp.: Jan., 27.1° F; July, 73.8° F
Churches: Protestant, 436; Roman Catholic, 62; Jewish, 5; Other, 8; **City-owned parks:** 203 (12,891 ac.);
Radio stations: AM, 10; FM, 16; **Television stations:** 9 commercial, 3 PBS
Civilian Labor Force (2000): 393,500; **Unemployed:** 11,500, **Percent:** 2.9; **Per capita personal income (1998):** $18,584
Chamber of Commerce: Columbus Area Chamber of Commerce, P.O. Box 1527, Columbus, Ohio 43216

Columbus, the largest city in Ohio, is the state capital and the seat of Franklin County. It is located in central Ohio on the Scioto River.

The first structures near the site of downtown Columbus were earthen mounds constructed by Indian tribes known as Mound Builders. Native Americans lived undisturbed in Central Ohio until the 1700s, when the first explorers entered the Midwest. The first permanent settlement in the area was founded by a surveyor from Kentucky, Lucas Sullivant, in 1797 and was named Franklinton. The state capital was laid out nearby in 1812 and named after Christopher Columbus. It became the capital in 1816. Columbus was chartered as a city in 1834 and annexed Franklinton in 1870. The city's growth was stimulated by the development of transportation facilities—a feeder to the Ohio Canal completed in 1832, the National Road in 1833, and the arrival of the railroad in 1850.

Columbus is a port of entry and a major industrial, commercial, manufacturing, and cultural center. It is the seat of Ohio State University. The city has enjoyed steady growth over the years due to its economic diversity—no single activity dominates the economy.

Famous natives: Warner Baxter, actor; George Bellows, painter; Michael Feinstein, singer and pianist; Eileen Heckart, actress; Jack Nicklaus, golfer; Tom Poston, actor; Eddie Rickenbacker, aviator; Arthur M. Schlesinger, historian; James Thurber, writer; Nancy Wilson, singer.

Dallas, Tex.

Mayor: Ron Kirk (to May 2001)
City Manager: Teodoro J. Benavides
1998 est. population (rank): 1,075,894 (9)
1990 census population (rank): 1,006,877 (8);
% change, 6.8; **Male,** 495,141; **Female,** 511,736; **White,** 556,760 (55.3%); **Black,** 296,994 (29.5%); **American Indian, Eskimo, or Aleut,** 4,792 (0.5%); **Asian or Pacific Islander,** 21,952 (2.2%); **Other race,** 126,379; **Hispanic origin,** 210,240 (20.9%). **1990 population under 18:** 25.0%; **65 and over:** 9.7%; **median age:** 30.6.
Land area: 378 sq mi. (979 sq km); **Alt.:** Highest, 750 ft.; lowest, 375 ft.
Avg. daily temp.: Jan., 45.0° F; July, 86.3° F
Churches: 1,974 (in Dallas Co.); **City-owned parks:** 296 (47,025 ac.); **Radio stations:** AM, 19; FM, 30; **Television stations:** 10 commercial, 1 PBS
Civilian Labor Force: 570,661; **Unemployed:** 50,526, **Percent:** 8.9; **Per capita personal income (PMSA)** 1992: $22,424
Chamber of Commerce: Dallas Chamber of Commerce, 1201 Elm, Dallas, Tex. 75270

Dallas is the second-largest city in Texas and is the seat of Dallas County. It is situated 185 miles northeast of Austin on the Trinity River near the junction of its three forks. It was first settled by Tennessee lawyer John Neely Bryan as a trading post on the Trinity River in 1841. Many historians believe that Bryan named the city after George Mifflin Dallas, vice president under James K. Polk, but there is no official agreement on this. It was incorporated as a town in 1856 and as a city in 1871. Located in the chief cotton-producing region of Texas, the city developed as a cotton market in the 1870s.

The economy is highly diversified, and the city is the leading commercial, marketing, and industrial center of the southwest. The insurance business is important, and the service sector has experienced rapid growth. Dallas is also a popular tourist and convention city.

Famous natives: Tex Avery, animator and director; Robby Benson, actor; Ernie Banks, baseball player; Bebe Daniels, actress; Linda Darnell, actress; Lee Elder, golfer; Morgan Fairchild, actress; Trini Lopez, singer; Aaron Spelling, producer; Stephen Stills, singer; Sharon Tate, actress; Lee Trevino, golfer.

Denver, Colo.

Mayor: Wellington Webb (to June 30, 2003)
1998 est. population (rank): 499,055 (27)
1990 census population (rank): 467,610 (26);
% change, 6.7; **Male,** 227,517; **Female,** 240,093; **White,** 337,198 (72.1%); **Black,** 60,046 (12.8%); **American Indian, Eskimo, or Aleut,** 5,381 (1.2%); **Asian or Pacific Islander,** 11,005 (2.4%); **Other race,** 53,980; **Hispanic origin,** 107,382 (23.0%); **1990 population under 18:** 22.0%; **65 and over:** 13.9%; **median age:** 33.9.
Land area: 154.63 sq mi. (400.5 sq km); **Alt.:** Highest, 5,494 ft.; lowest, 5,140 ft.
Avg. daily temp.: Jan., 29.5° F; July, 73.3° F
Churches:[1] Protestant, 859; Roman Catholic, 60; Jewish, 13; **City-owned parks:** 205 (4,166 ac.); **City-owned mountain parks:** 40 (13,600 ac.); **Radio stations:** AM, 23; FM, 20[1]; **Television stations:** 17[1]
Civilian Labor Force: 245,495[2]; **Unemployed:** 17,527[2]; **Percent:** 7.1[2]; **Per capita personal income (PMSA)** 1992: $22,930
Chamber of Commerce: Greater Denver Chamber of Commerce, 1445 Market Street, Denver, Colo. 80202

1. Metropolitan area. 2. Denver City/County.

Denver is the largest city in Colorado. It is the state capital and the seat of Denver County. It lies at the foot of the Rocky Mountains and is situated at the junction of the South Platte River and Cherry Creek. The city was born in 1858, when gold was discovered in the sands of Cherry Creek, at first just a tough village of cabins, shacks, and tents. It was incorporated as a city in 1861 and became the territorial capital in 1867. The city is named for James W. Denver, governor of the Kansas Territory, which included part of Colorado. The city prospered from the famous gold and silver mines of the 1870s and 1880s.

Denver International Airport, the first major new airport constructed in the U.S. in 21 years, opened to passenger traffic on Feb. 28, 1995, at a cost of $4.9 billion. At 53 square miles, it is the largest airport in North America.

Denver is an important cultural, industrial, transportation, tourist, and marketing center. It is also a regional center for many federal government agencies and a leader in the development of western energy resources.

Denver's fastest-growing industries include contract construction, real estate, retail trade, and government.

Famous natives: Tim Allen, comedian and actor; Ward Bond, actor; Douglas Fairbanks, Sr., actor; John Hart, newsman; Pat Hingle, actor; Ted Mack, TV host; Barbara Rush, actress; Alan K. Simpson, senator; Paul Whiteman, bandleader; Don Wilson, announcer.

Detroit, Mich.

Mayor: Dennis W. Archer (to Nov. 2002)
1998 est. population (rank): 970,196 (10)
1990 census population (rank): 1,027,974 (7);
  % change, –5.6; **Male,** 476,814; **Female,** 551,160;
  White, 222,316 (21.6%); **Black,** 777,916 (75.7%);
  American Indian, Eskimo, or Aleut, 3,655 (0.4%);
  Asian or Pacific Islander, 8,461 (0.8%); **Other race,**
  15,626; **Hispanic origin,** 28,473 (2.8%). **1990 population under 18:** 29.4%; **65 and over:** 12.2%; **median age:** 30.8.
Land area: 143 sq mi. (370 sq km), **Alt.:** Highest, 685 ft.; lowest, 574 ft.
Avg. daily temp.: Jan., 23.4° F; July, 71.9° F
Churches[1]: Protestant, 1,165; Roman Catholic, 89; Jewish, 2; **City-owned parks:** 56 parks (3,843 ac.); 393 sites (5,838 ac.); **Radio stations:** AM, 27; FM, 30 (includes 3 in Windsor, Ont.); **Television stations:** 8[2] (includes 1 in Windsor, Ont.)
Civilian Labor Force (1997): 394,050; **Unemployed:** 31,100; **Percent:** 7.9; **Per capita personal income (1992):** $21,000
Chamber of Commerce: Detroit Regional Chamber of Commerce, One Woodward Avenue, P.O. Box 33840, Detroit MI 48232-0840

1. Six-county metropolitan area. 2. Within four counties of Metro Detroit.

Detroit, the largest city in Michigan, is situated in the southeastern part of the state on the Detroit River. It is the seat of Wayne County. Detroit was incorporated as a city in 1815 and reincorporated in 1824.

Detroit is the oldest city of any size west of the seaboard colonies, having been founded by Antoine de la Mothe Cadillac on July 24, 1701, more than a century before Chicago was founded. The French were the first settlers, and they gave the city its name from their word meaning "strait," referring to the 27-mile-long Detroit River, which connects Lake Erie and Lake St. Clair. The river forms part of the international boundary, and marks the only point where Canada lies directly south of U.S. territory.

Because of its strategic location, Detroit was fought over by the French, the British, and the Indians. It was the headquarters for the British forces in the Northwest Territory during the American Revolutionary War.

The first steam vessel, the *Walk-in-the-Water*, made its appearance on the Great Lakes in 1818, and Detroit was the western terminus for most of its voyages from Buffalo. Its link to all the important cities on the Great Lakes made it a major exporting center.

Detroit is one of the largest manufacturing cities in the U.S. and is the center of the automobile manufacturing industry, which has experienced a decline due to foreign competition in the past decade. The health and medical care sector is important to the economy, and employment in the finance, insurance, and real-estate industries has inched up in the Detroit metropolitan area since 1991.

Famous natives: Ralph Bunche, statesman; Francis Ford Coppola, director; Charles Lindbergh, aviator; Madonna, singer and actress; John Mitchell, former U.S. Attorney General; George Peppard, actor; Gilda Radner, comedian; Della Reese, singer; Sugar Ray Robinson, boxer; Diana Ross, singer; Tom Selleck, actor; Margaret Whiting, singer.

El Paso, Tex.

Mayor: Carlos Ramirez (to May 2001)
1998 est. population (rank): 615,032 (17)[1]
1990 census population (rank): 515,342 (22);
  % change, 19.3; **Male,** 247,163; **Female,** 268,179;
  White, 396,122 (76.9%); **Black,** 17,708 (3.4%);
  American Indian, Eskimo, or Aleut, 2,239 (0.4%);
  Asian or Pacific Islander, 5,956 (1.2%); **Other race,**
  93,317; **Hispanic origin,** 355,669 (69.0%). **1990 population under 18:** 31.9%; **65 and over:** 8.7%; **median age:** 28.7
Land area: 250.9 sq mi. (649.8 sq km), **Alt.:** 4,000 ft.
Avg. daily temp.: Jan., 44.2° F; July, 82.5° F
Churches: Protestant, 320; Roman Catholic, 39; Jewish, 3; others, 20; **City-owned parks:** 116[2] (1,180 ac.); **Radio Stations:** AM, 18; FM, 17; **Television stations:** 6
Civilian Labor Force (1999): 291,300; **Unemployed:** 23,300, **Percent:** 8.0; **Per capita personal income (1997):** $15,216
Chamber of Commerce: El Paso Chamber of Commerce, Hispanic Chamber of Commerce, Black Chamber of Commerce, and Korean Chamber of Commerce, 10 Civic Center Plaza, El Paso, Tex. 79944

1. 1997 est. population: 596,804. 2. Includes 109 developed and 7 undeveloped parks.

El Paso, the fourth-largest city in Texas and the seat of El Paso County, is located in the far western part of the state on the north bank of the Rio Grande River, opposite the Mexican city of Ciudad Juárez on the south bank.

In 1581, Spanish explorers came through the Pass of the North to test the missionary and mining possibilities of New Mexico. The area had been inhabited for centuries by various Indian groups. On April 30, 1598, Juan de Onate took formal possession of the area for King Philip II of Spain and subsequently crossed the Rio Grande River near a site west of the present downtown El Paso that he called "El Paso del Rio del Norte," meaning the crossing of the river—the first use of the name "El Paso." In 1659, the mission of Nuestra Senora de Guadalupe was founded on a site that is present-day downtown Ciudad Juárez; the mission is still in use today. In 1682, Spanish colonists from Mexico founded the settlement of Ysleta on the site of the present-day city. However, it wasn't until 1827 that the first permanent settlement at El Paso was established by Juan María Ponce de León. The city's real growth started with the arrival of the Southern Pacific Railroad in 1881. El Paso was incorporated as a city in 1873.

In 1888, Mexico changed the name of Paso del Norte to Ciudad Juárez in honor of Benito Juárez. Later, in 1967, the U.S. agreed to cede a long-disputed part of El Paso to Mexico due to changes in the course of the Rio Grande, which forms the international boundary between the two countries. El Paso and its sister city of Ciudad Juárez across the U.S./Mexico border are inexorably joined by culture and economy. El Paso and Juárez make up the largest international metroplex in the world.

El Paso is an important port of entry to the U.S. from Mexico. The high technology, medical device manufacturing, plastics, refining, automotive, food processing, and defense-related industries are important to the economy. El Paso's service sector has experienced healthy growth since 1983. El Paso is also a major tourist resort.

Famous natives: Manuel Acosta, artist; Don Bluth, animation director; Vicki Carr, singer; Jose Cisneros, artist;

Sam Donaldson, newsman; Judith Ivey, actress; Guy Kibbee, actor; Sandra Day O'Connor, Supreme Court justice; Debbie Reynolds, actress; Irene Ryan, actress.

Fort Worth, Tex.

Mayor: Kenneth Barr (to May 2001)
City Manager: Bob Terrell
1998 est. population (rank): 491,801 (29)[1]
1990 census population (rank): 447,619 (28);
  % change, 9.9; **Male,** 220,268; **Female:** 227,351;
  White, 285,549 (63.8%); **Black,** 98,532 (22.0%);
  American Indian, Eskimo, or Aleut, 1,914 (0.4%);
  Asian or Pacific Islander, 8,910 (2.0%); **Other race,** 52,714; **Hispanic origin,** 87,345 (19.5%). **1990 population under 18:** 26.6%; **65 and over:** 11.2%; **median age:** 30.3.
Land area: 303 sq mi. (784.7 sq km); **Alt.:** Highest, 780 ft.; lowest, 520 ft.
Avg. daily temp.: Jan., 44.2° F; July, 82.5° F
Churches: 941, representing 72 denominations; **City-owned parks:** 200 (9,906.7 ac.); **Radio stations:** AM, 12; FM, 18; **Television stations:** 13
Civilian Labor Force (1999): 276,108; **Unemployed:** 11,261, **Percent:** 4.1; **Per capita personal income (MSA) 1997:** $25,818 [2]
Chamber of Commerce: Fort Worth Chamber of Commerce, 777 Taylor Street, Suite 900, Fort Worth, Tex. 76102

1. 1997 est. population: 484,500. 2. Tarrant County.

Fort Worth, seat of Tarrant County, is situated in the north central part of Texas on the Trinity River.

The city was founded by Maj. Ripley Arnold in 1849 as a military outpost on the Trinity River to protect settlers moving westward from frequent Indian attacks. It was named after Gen. William J. Worth, the commander of the Texas army. Fort Worth was incorporated in 1873. Its growth was stimulated in the 1870s by its proximity to the Chisholm cattle trail. It prospered as a meat-packing and shipping center when the Texas and Pacific Railway arrived in 1876 and later experienced a new boom when oil was discovered nearby in 1917. The establishment of military installations in the area during both world wars also spurred the economy.

Fort Worth has traditionally been a diverse center of manufacturing and is not dependent on the oil or financial sectors. The city's industries range from clothing and food products to jet fighters, helicopters, computers, pharmaceuticals, and plastics. Fort Worth is a national leader in aviation products, electronic equipment, and refrigeration equipment. It is home to a multitude of major corporate headquarters, offices, and distribution centers.

Famous natives: Robert Bass, financier; Mark Brooks, golfer; Betty Buckley, singer and actress; Kate Capshaw, actress; Ornette Coleman, composer; Sandra Haynie, golfer; Patricia Highsmith, writer; Spanky McFarland, actor; R. Bruce Merrifield, Nobelist in chemistry; Roger Miller, singer; Fess Parker, actor; Bill Paxton, actor; Rex Reed, critic; Johnny Rutherford, auto racer; Liz Smith, columnist.

Fresno, Calif.

Mayor: Jim Patterson (to Jan. 2001)
City Manager: Jeffrey M. Reid
1998 est. population (rank): 398,133 (40)
1990 census population (rank): 354,202 (47);
  % change, 12.4; **Male,** 172,241; **Female,** 181,961;
  White, 209,604 (59.2%); **Black,** 29,409 (8.3%);
  American Indian, Eskimo, or Aleut, 3,729 (1.1%);
  Asian or Pacific Islander, 44,358 (12.5%); **Other race,** 67,102; **Hispanic origin,** 105,787 (29.9%). **1990 population under 18:** 31.7%; **65 and over:** 10.1%; **median age:** 28.4.
Land area: 99.38 sq mi. (257.39 sq km); **Alt.:** 328 ft.
Avg. daily temp.: Jan., 45.5° F; July, 81.0° F
Churches: 450 (approximate); **City-owned parks:** 38 (690 ac.); **Radio stations:** AM 11[1]; FM 13[1]; Bilingual 1; **Television stations:** 8[1]
Civilian Labor Force: 174,496; **Unemployed:** 22,708, **Percent:** 13.0; **Per capita personal income (MSA) 1992:** $16,376
Chamber of Commerce: Fresno County and City Chamber of Commerce, P.O. Box 1469, 2331 Fresno St., Fresno, Calif. 93716

1. Metropolitan area.

Fresno is located in central California, 184 miles southeast of San Francisco and 222 miles northwest of Los Angeles. It is the seat of Fresno County. Fresno was incorporated as a city in 1885.

Fresno began as a station for the Central Pacific Railroad in 1872 and was made the seat of Fresno County in 1874. The city's name is Spanish for the ash trees that the early explorers found in the area.

Fresno is a leading agribusiness hub, with 250 different crops produced by 7,500 farmers on 1.9 million irrigated acres, worth $3 billion a year. Fresno county's top five agricultural products are grapes, cotton, tomatoes, cattle and calves, and turkeys. The city is also a trade, financial, media, and commercial center. Its diverse industries include agricultural chemicals, farm equipment, canned fruit and vegetables, clothing, computer software, electric wire, pumps, glass, and plastic products.

Famous natives: Mike Connors, actor; Maynard Dixon, painter; Bruce Furniss, swimmer; Jon Hall, actor; Daryle Lamonica, football player; Sam Peckinpah, director; William Saroyan, novelist; Tom Seaver, baseball player.

Honolulu, Hawaii

Mayor: Jeremy Harris (to Jan. 2001)
1998 est. population (rank): 395,789 (41)
1990 census population (rank): 377,059 (39)[1];
  % change, 5.0; **Male,** 186,371; **Female,** 190,688;
  White, 104,038 (27.6%); **Black,** 7,371 (1.95%);
  American Indian, Eskimo, or Aleut, 1,197 (0.3%);
  Asian or Pacific Islander, 259,629 (68.9%); **Other race,** 4,824 (1.3%); **Hispanic origin,** 18,017 (4.8%).
  1990 population under 18: 19.8%; **65 and over:** 15.5%; **median age:** n.a.
Land area: 85.7 sq mi. (221.9 sq km)[1]; **Alt.:** Highest, 2,013 ft.[1]; lowest, sea level
Avg. daily temp.: Jan., 72.6° F; July, 81° F
Churches: Roman Catholic, 39; Buddhist, 51; Jewish, 2; Protestant and others, 402; **City-owned parks:** 2,056 ac.[1]; **Radio stations:** AM, 17[1]; FM, 11[1]; **Television stations:** 12[1]
Civilian Labor Force (1998): 429,050[2]; **Unemployed:** 22,950[2], **Percent:** 5.4[2]; **Per capita personal income (1997):** $27,259
Chamber of Commerce: Chamber of Commerce of Hawaii, 1132 Bishop St., Suite 200, Honolulu, Hawaii 96813

1. Census Designated Place, approximately Salt Lake to Hawaii Kai. The 1990 census population and rank for the entire city and county of Honolulu would be 836,231 (12). 2. City and county.

Honolulu is the capital and largest city of Hawaii, on the southeastern coast of Oahu. The city is legally coextensive with the county of Honolulu, which includes the entire island of Oahu and most of the northwestern Hawaiian Islands, from Nihoa to

Kure Atoll, except Midway. The population of Oahu makes up 73% of the state's total population. It is situated in the central Pacific Ocean 2,397 miles west-southwest of San Francisco. Honolulu's name means "sheltered harbor" and derives from the native words *hono,* meaning "a bay," and *lulu,* meaning "sheltered."

Honolulu's early history was one of turbulence and conflict. One of the last areas on the globe to be explored and exploited by Europeans (it was first visited by British captain James Cook in 1778), Hawaii was subject to strong pressures from many forces, including American missionaries, who arrived in 1820, and opportunistic whalers. These whalers were among those who built Honolulu originally, bringing trade, commerce, and prosperity that led to expansion into the sugar and pineapple industries.

As early as 1814, Russia tried to move in, and Russian soldiers built a bastion at the harbor's edge. The British flag was raised in 1843 and French forces occupied Honolulu in 1849. Each time control was returned to the independent native kingdom without bloodshed. In 1898, a group of Americans completed a project attempted at intervals during the previous 65 years—annexation to the United States. Honolulu was incorporated as a city in 1907.

The Honolulu area was bombed by Japan in a surprise attack on the unprepared U.S. naval base at Pearl Harbor on Dec. 7, 1941. This action forced the United States to enter World War II. "Remember Pearl Harbor" became a famous American wartime slogan.

Hawaiian statehood in 1959 and the viability of commercial air travel to the island brought boom times to Honolulu. Tourism is the city's principal industry, followed by federal defense expenditures and agricultural exports (chiefly pineapples).

Famous natives: Hiram Bingham, explorer; Jean Erdman, dancer and choreographer; Hiram Fong, senator; Daniel Inouye, senator; Duke Kahanamoku, surfer and Olympian swimmer; Bette Midler, actress and singer; Kelly Preston, actress; Louise Morgan Sill, author; Don Stroud, actor; Merlin D. Tuttle, biologist and wildlife photographer.

Houston, Tex.

Mayor: Lee P. Brown (to Dec. 2001)
1998 est. population (rank): 1,786,691 (4)
1990 census population (rank): 1,630,553 (4);
  % change, 8.0; **Male,** 809,048; **Female,** 821,505;
  White, 859,069 (52.7%); **Black,** 457,990 (28.1%);
  American Indian, Eskimo, or Aleut, 4,126 (0.3%);
  Asian or Pacific Islander, 67,113 (4.1%); **Other race,**
  242,255; **Hispanic origin,** 450,483 (27.6%). **1990
  population under 18:** 26.7%; **65 and over:** 8.3%;
  median age: 30.4.
Land area: 617.48 sq mi. (1,521 sq km); **Alt.:** Highest,
  120 ft.; lowest, sea level
Avg. daily temp.: Jan., 50.4° F; July, 82.6° F
Churches: 1,750[1]; **City-owned parks:** 311 (32,655 ac.);
  Radio stations: AM, 22; FM, 32[1]; **Television stations:** 15 commercial, 1 PBS
Civilian Labor Force (1999): 2,147,700[2]; **Unemployed:**
  96,700[2], **Percent:** 4.5[2]; **Per capita personal income
  1997:** $28,977[2]
Chamber of Commerce: Greater Houston Partnership,
  1200 Smith, Suite 700, Houston, Tex. 77002

1. Harris County. 2. Primary Metropolitan Statistical Area.

Houston, the largest city in Texas and seat of Harris County, is located in the southeastern part of the state near the Gulf of Mexico.

Sam Houston was the commander-in-chief of the Texas troops who fought a successful war of rebellion against domination by Mexico, which had been in possession of Texas. On April 21, 1836, Houston's men won a decisive victory in which the Mexican dictator, Gen. Santa Anna, was taken prisoner and forced to sign the treaty that launched the Republic of Texas. In September, a constitution was ratified, and Houston was elected president. The Texas Republic was recognized by the U.S. and by the major European powers. The present city of Houston was incorporated in 1837 and named after Sam Houston; it was the Republic's first capital.

The port of Houston ranks first among U.S. ports in foreign tonnage handled. The city is a major business, financial, science, and technology center. Houston is outstanding in oil and natural-gas production and is the energy capital of the world. It is the home of one of the largest medical facilities in the world—the Texas Medical Center—and the focus of the aerospace industry. The Lyndon B. Johnson Space Center is the nation's headquarters for staffed spaceflight.

Famous natives: Debbie Allen, choreographer; Lance Alworth, football player; Denton Cooley, heart surgeon; Jim Demaret, golfer; Allen Drury, novelist; Shelly Duvall, actress; A. J. Foyt, auto racer; Howard Hughes, industrialist and film producer; Barbara C. Jordan, educator, lawyer, and politician; Barbara Mandrell, singer; Annette O'Toole, actress; Dennis and Randy Quaid, actors; Kenny Rogers, singer; Patrick Swayze, actor and dancer.

Indianapolis, Ind.

Mayor: Bart Peterson (to Dec. 31, 2003)
1998 est. population (rank): 741,304 (13)
1990 census population (rank)[1]: 741,952 (12);
  % change, 1.4; **Male,** 352,309; **Female,** 389,643;
  White, 564,447 (77.2%); **Black,** 166,031 (22.4%);
  American Indian, Eskimo, or Aleut, 1,580 (0.2%);
  Asian or Pacific Islander, 6,943 (0.9%); **Other race,**
  2,951; **Hispanic origin,** 7,790 (1.0%). **1990 population under 18:** 25.6%; **65 and over:** 11.5%; **median
  age:** 31.8.
Land area: 352 sq mi. (912 sq km); **Alt.:** Highest, 840
  ft.; lowest, 700 ft.
Avg. daily temp.: Jan., 25.5 F; July, 75.4° F
Churches: 1,191[2]; **City-owned parks:** 211 (9,866 ac.);
  Radio stations: AM, 8[3]; FM, 17[3]; **Television
  stations:** 7[2]
Civilian Labor Force (1999): 453,890[2] **Unemployed:**
  13,160[2], **Per capita personal income (MSA) 1997:**
  $26,577
Chamber of Commerce: Indianapolis Chamber of Com-
  merce, 320 N. Meridian St., Indianapolis, Ind. 46204

1. Consolidated city. 2. Marion County. 3. Metropolitan area.

Indianapolis, the largest city in Indiana and seat of Marion County, is located in the central part of the state on the West Fork of the White River. Its name derives from combining "Indiana" with "polis," the Greek word for city.

Indianapolis was settled in 1820, and five years later it was chosen as the state capital. It was incorporated as a city in 1832 and reincorporated in 1838. The city's growth began when the railroad reached it in 1847. Toward the end of the 19th century, the discovery of nearby natural gas and the start of the automobile industry hastened its industrial expansion. On Jan. 1, 1970, Indianapolis merged with surrounding Marion County.

Indianapolis is at the center of a rich agricultural region and is a major grain and livestock market. It is also a focal point of commerce, transportation, and manufacturing for the region. Some leading industries are electronics, pharmaceuticals, and food processing. The financial sector and service and insurance industries are growing rapidly.

Indianapolis is the site of the world-famous 500-mile automobile race and the Indiana State Fair.

Famous natives: Monte Blue, actor; David Letterman, TV host; Steve McQueen, actor; Jane Pauley, TV newscaster; Booth Tarkington, author; Kurt Vonnegut, Jr., author; Harry Von Zell, announcer; Clifton Webb, actor.

Jacksonville, Fla.

Mayor: John Delaney (to June 30, 2003)
1998 est. population (rank): 693,630 (14)
1990 census population (rank)[1]: 672,971 (15); **% change,** 9.2; **Male,** 328,737; **Female,** 344,234; **White,** 489,604 (77.1%); **Black,** 163,902 (24.4%); **American Indian, Eskimo, or Aleut,** 1,904 (0.3%); **Asian or Pacific Islander,** 12,940 (1.9%); **Other race,** 4,621; **Hispanic origin,** 17,333 (2.6%). **1990 population under 18:** 25.9%; **65 and over:** 10.7%; **median age:** 31.5.
Land area: 759.6 sq mi. (1,967 sq km); **Alt.:** Highest, 71 ft.; lowest, sea level
Avg. daily temp.: Jan., 53.2° F; July, 81.3° F
Churches: Protestant, 794; Roman Catholic, 21; Jewish, 5; others, 22; **City-owned parks and playgrounds:** 19 (7,404 ac.); **Radio stations:** AM, 14; FM, 16; **Television stations:** 6 commercial, 1 PBS, 1 religious
Civilian Labor Force: 328,211; **Unemployed:** 24,051, **Percent:** 7.3; **Per capita personal income (MSA) 1992:** $19,146
Chamber of Commerce: Jacksonville Area Chamber of Commerce, Jacksonville, Fla. 32202

1. Consolidated city.

Jacksonville, Florida's largest city, is located in Duval County in the northeast corner of Florida, on the banks of the St. Johns River and adjacent to the Atlantic Ocean. It is the largest metropolitan area in northeast Florida and southeast Georgia.

Starting in the 16th century, French, Spanish, and English explorers and colonists were attracted to the region by the St. Johns River. The site was settled by Lewis Hogans in 1816. Jacksonville was laid out in 1822 and was named after Gen. Andrew Jackson, the first military governor of Florida. It was incorporated as a city in 1832.

During the Civil War, much of the city was destroyed by Union forces, who occupied Jacksonville four times. The city was rebuilt and, following the development of its harbor and the railroads, quickly became the transportation hub and leading industrial city in Florida by the 1880s. In 1968, the city and county governments consolidated.

Jacksonville is the leading transportation and distribution hub in the state. However, the strength of the city's economy lies in its broad diversification. The area's economy is balanced among distribution, financial services, biomedical, consumer goods, information services, manufacturing, and other industries. Jacksonville has the largest deepwater port in the South Atlantic and is the leading port in the U.S. for automobile imports.

Famous natives: Mae Axton, songwriter; Pat Boone, singer; Judy Canova, comedian; Harold Carmichael, football player; Merion C. Cooper, producer and director; Billy Daniels, vocalist; Storm Davis, athlete; Bob Hayes,

athlete; Wanda Hendrix, actress; James Weldon Johnson, author and educator; John Rosamond Johnson, musician and composer; Mark McCumber, pro golfer; Ray Mercer, boxer; Charles "Hoss" Singleton, songwriter; Bill Terry, member of Baseball Hall of Fame; Donnie Van Zant, rock musician; Ronnie Van Zant, rock musician; Leeroy Yarbrough, auto racer.

Kansas City, Mo.

Mayor: Kay Barnes (to April 2003)
City Manager: Robert L. Collins (apptd. July 1997)
1998 est. population (rank): 441,574 (33)
1990 census population (rank): 435,146 (31); **% change:** 1.6; **Male,** 206,965; **Female,** 228,181; **White,** 290,572 (66.8%); **Black,** 128,768 (29.6%); **American Indian, Eskimo, or Aleut,** 2,144 (0.5%); **Asian or Pacific Islander,** 5,239 (1.2%); **Other race,** 8,423; **Hispanic origin,** 17,017 (3.9%). **1990 population under 18:** 24.8%; **65 and over:** 12.9%; **median age:** 32.8.
Land area: 317 sq mi. (821 sq km); **Alt.:** Highest, 1,014 ft.; lowest, 722 ft.
Avg. daily temp.: Jan., 28.4° F; July, 80.9 F
Churches: 1,100 churches of all denominations[1]; **City-owned parks and playgrounds:** 189 (10,647 ac.); **Radio stations:** AM, 14; FM, 19[1]; **Television stations:** 7[1]
Civilian Labor Force: 239,600; **Unemployed:** 15,400, **Percent:** 6.4; **Per capita personal income (MSA) 1992:** $24,576[2]
Chamber of Commerce: Chamber of Commerce of Greater Kansas City, 911 Main St., Kansas City, Mo. 64105

1. Metropolitan area. 2. Kansas City, Mo.–Kan.

Kansas City is the largest city in Missouri. It is located in the western part of the state, at the junction of the Missouri and Kansas rivers. Kansas City is located in Jackson, Clay, Platte, and Cass counties.

In 1821, the year Missouri entered the Union, French trader François Chouteau came from St. Louis to establish a trading post on the site of the present city to take advantage of the growing fur trade with the Kansa, Osage, Wyandotte, and other tribes. In 1833, a settlement, called the town of Westport Landing, was laid out by John Calvin McCoy and developed. The community became the Town of Kansas and was incorporated as a city in 1850 and renamed Kansas City in 1889. The city's name reflects its Native American heritage—its site was within the territory of the Kansa or Kaw Indians.

The city grew rapidly in the mid-1880s as the starting point for gold prospectors and settlers heading westward. The coming of the Missouri-Pacific Railroad in 1865 and the spanning of the Missouri River by the Hannibal Bridge in 1869 also contributed to the city's growth. It also prospered as a center for the nation's cattle business.

The Kansas City metropolitan area, once known primarily for agriculture and manufacturing, has expanded its economic base to include strong growth in areas of telecommunications, banking and finance, and the service industry. A transportation hub since the 1800s, the area enjoys a national and regional prominence as a distribution and manufacturing center. Kansas City ranks nationally as first in greeting-card publishing, frozen food storage and distribution, and hard winter-wheat marketing; second in wheat flour production; and third in auto and truck assembly. The area is one of ten federal regional centers and employs over 25,000 in local, state, and federal government. The city is also a regional center for health care, employing over 55,000 in this industry.

Famous natives: Robert Altman, director; Edward Asner, actor; Burt Bacharach, composer; Noah and Wallace Beery, actors; Robert Russell Bennett, composer; Jeanne Eagels, actress; Jean Harlow, actress; Ted Shawn, dancer and choreographer; Casey Stengel, baseball player; Virgil Thompson, composer; Tom Watson, golfer.

Las Vegas, Nev.

Mayor: Oscar Goodman (to May 2003)
1998 est. population (rank): 404,288 (37)
1990 census population (rank): 258,295 (63);
   % change: 56.2; **Male,** 130,981; **Female,** 127,314;
   White, 202,549 (78.4%); **Black,** 29,529 (11.4%);
   American Indian, Eskimo, or Aleut, 2,282 (0.9%);
   Asian or Pacific Islander, 9,325 (3.6%); **Other race,**
   14,610; **Hispanic origin,** 32,369 (12.5%); **1990 popu-**
   lation under 18: 25.0%; **65 and over:** 10.3%; **median**
   age: 32.5.
Land area: 83.3 sq mi. (1,215.7 sq km); **Alt.:** 2,174 ft.
Avg. daily temp.: Jan., 45.5° F; July, 91° F
Churches: over 500 churches and synagogues; **Radio**
   stations: AM 8; FM 18; **Television stations:** 7
Civilian Labor Force: (1990 census): 131,001;
   Unemployed: 19,043, **Percent:** 4.9; **Per capita per-**
   sonal income (MSA) 1992: $19,994
Chamber of Commerce: 3720 Howard Hughes Park-
   way, Las Vegas, NV 89109

Las Vegas, seat of Clark County in southeastern Nevada, is the largest city in the state and one of the fastest-growing cities in the United States. Between April 1990 and July 1998, the Las Vegas metropolitan area population increased by 55%, growing from 852,646 to 1,321,546.

The area was discovered by Spanish explorers in 1829. The site of Las Vegas ("The Meadows" in Spanish) was originally a watering place for travelers on their way to southern California. It was first settled by Mormons in 1855, who were attracted by its artesian springs. They abandoned their settlement two years later in 1857, and the U.S. Army established Fort Baker there in 1864. In 1867, Las Vegas was detached from the Arizona Territory and joined with Nevada.

The town was established in 1905 and started to grow with the arrival of the San Pedro, Los Angeles, and Salt Lake Railroad in 1905. However, its growth did not really begin until shortly after 1931, when the Nevada legislature legalized gambling in an effort to lift the state from the Great Depression. The construction of nearby Hoover Dam economically aided the area as well.

The Las Vegas that we know today basically began after World War II, when the idea of large hotels along the brand new "strip" was developed. Las Vegas is the "marriage capital" of America; there are 50 wedding chapels in the city. Tourism and the convention industry are the city's major sources of income. In addition, manufacturing, government, warehousing, and trucking are major sources of employment. Many high-technology companies are also located in Las Vegas, in close proximity to sophisticated military technology centers like Nellis Air Force Base, the top-secret Nuclear Testing Grounds, and the College of Engineering at the University of Nevada, Las Vegas.

Las Vegas has a favorable business climate: taxes are relatively low, and there are neither city nor state income taxes. This is because gambling and sales taxes, paid by tourists, have allowed the city and state governments to avoid personal and corporate income taxes.

Popular nearby tourist attractions are Hoover Dam and Lake Mead (the largest man-made lake in the U.S.), Lake Mojave, the Mt. Charleston Recreation Area, Red Rock Canyon, and the Death Valley National Monument.

Famous natives: Andre Agassi, tennis player; Clara Bow, actress; Jack Kramer, tennis player; Phyllis McGuire, singer; Benjamin Siegel, hotel-casino promoter; Orson Welles, actor and producer; Joe Williams, jazz singer.

Long Beach, Calif.

Mayor: Beverly O'Neill (to April 2002)
City Manager: Henry Taboada
1998 est. population (rank): 430,905 (35)
1990 census population (rank): 429,433 (32);
   % change, 0.4; **Male,** 216,685; **Female,** 212,748;
   1996 est. population breakdown: **White,** 168,074
   (39.1%); **Black,** 63,376 (14.8%); **American Indian,**
   Eskimo, or Aleut, 2,322 (0.5%); **Asian or Pacific**
   Islander, 66,767 (15.6%); **Hispanic origin,** 125,269
   (29.3%). **1990 population under 18:** 25.5%; **65 and**
   over: 10.8%; **median age:** 30.0.
Land area: 49.8 sq mi. (129 sq km); **Alt.:** Highest,
   170 ft.; lowest, sea level
Avg. daily temp.: Jan., 55.2° F; July, 72.8° F
Churches: 236; **City-owned parks:** 58 (plus 5 golf
   courses); **Radio stations:** AM, 2; FM, 2; **Television**
   stations: 8 (metro area)
Civilian Labor Force: 212,700; **Unemployed:** 11,800,
   Percent: 5.6; **Per capita personal income (MSA)**
   1992: $21,434[1]
Chamber of Commerce: Long Beach Area Chamber of
   Commerce, One World Trade Center, Suite 350, Long
   Beach, Calif. 90831-0350

1. Los Angeles–Long Beach MSA.

Long Beach is the fifth-largest city in California and is situated on San Pedro Bay, south of Los Angeles, in Los Angeles County.

The town was laid out and settled in 1881 by developer W. E. Willmore, who sold lots in the site as a seaside resort community called Willmore City. It was renamed Long Beach for its 8½-mi. beach in 1884. The city was incorporated in 1888 and reincorporated in 1897.

Long Beach is a major industrial port. The services and manufacturing industries together account for over 50% of the local economy. Retail trade and government are the next largest sectors, accounting for an additional 30% of employment. Tourism is also important to the economy. The Aquarium of the Pacific opened on June 20, 1998. Minor industries include transportation, communication and utilities, wholesale trade, finance, insurance, and real estate. Long Beach's economy has been adversely affected by cutbacks in the defense and aircraft production industries.

Famous natives: Jack Anderson, journalist; Jennifer Bartlett, artist; Barbara Britton, actress; Nicholas Cage, actor; Spike Jones, orchestra leader; Sally Kellerman, actress; Billie Jean King, tennis player; Martha Rae Watson, track star; Heather Watts, dancer.

Los Angeles, Calif.

Mayor: Richard Riordan (to June 2001)
1998 est. population (rank): 3,597,556 (2)
1990 census population (rank): 3,485,398 (2);
  % change, 3.2; **Male,** 1,750,055; **Female,** 1,735,343;
  White, 1,841,182 (52.8%); **Black,** 487,674 (14.0%);
  American Indian, Eskimo, or Aleut, 16,379 (0.5%);
  Asian or Pacific Islander, 341,807 (9.8%); **Other
  race,** 798,356; **Hispanic origin,** 1,391,411 (39.9%).
  1990 population under 18: 24.8%; **65 and over:**
  10.0%; **median age:** 30.7.
Land area: 467.4 sq mi. (1,210.57 sq km); **Alt.:** Highest,
  5,081 ft.; lowest, sea level
Avg. daily temp.: Jan., 57.2° F; July, 74.1° F
Churches: 2,000 of all denominations; **City-owned
  parks:** 355 (15,357 ac.); **Radio stations:** AM, 35; FM,
  53; **Television stations:** 19
Civilian Labor Force: 1,827,505; **Unemployed:**
  198,626, **Percent:** 10.9; **Per capita personal income
  (PMSA) 1992:** $21,434[1]
Chamber of Commerce: Los Angeles Chamber of
  Commerce, 404 S. Bixel St., Los Angeles, Calif. 90017

1. Los Angeles–Long Beach.

Los Angeles is the largest city in California and
the second-largest urban area in the nation. It is
located in the southern part of the state on the
Pacific Ocean. It is the seat of Los Angeles County.
Geographically, it extends more than 40 miles from
the mountains to the sea.

The Spanish explorer Gaspar de Portolá visited the
site in 1769. On Sept. 4, 1781, the Mexican provincial
governor, Filipe de Neve, founded "El Pueblo de
Nuestra Señora la Reina de Los Angeles," meaning
"The Village of Our Lady, the Queen of the Angels."
The pueblo became the capital of the Mexican province, Alta California, and it was the last place to surrender to the U.S. at the time of the American occupation in 1847. By the Treaty of Guadalupe Hidalgo in
1848, Mexico ceded California to the United States,
and Los Angeles was incorporated as a city in 1850.

The city's phenomenal growth was brought about
by its equable climate, which attracted people and
industry from all parts of the nation; the development of its citrus-fruit industry; the discovery of oil
in the area during the early 1890s; the development
of its man-made harbor—its port is one of the busiest in the U.S.; and the growth of the motion picture
industry in the early 20th century. Today, Hollywood is a suburb of Los Angeles.

Los Angeles is a major hub of shipping, manufacturing, industry, and finance, and is world-renowned
in the entertainment and communications fields. It is
a favorite vacation destination and attracts millions of
tourists to the area each year from all over the world.

Los Angeles County is the nation's largest manufacturing center, surpassing Chicago, New York, and
Detroit. The ports of Los Angeles and Long Beach
are second only to New York as the largest customs
district in the United States.

Major employers in the Los Angeles Five-County
area are in the business and management sector.
Growth in the key wholesale industries—apparel and
textiles, furniture, jewelry, and toys—and the boom
in industrial trade were the trend for the region in the
1990s. Other important sectors are health services
and international trade and investment. The aerospace and technology industries have declined due to
defense cutbacks but are projected to remain a viable
part of the region's economy.

Famous natives: Busby Berkeley, choreographer and
director; Marge Champion, dancer and choreographer;
Jackie Coogan, actor; Jackie Cooper, actor; Linda
Fratianne, figure skater; Jodie Foster, actress and director;
John Gavin, actor and diplomat; Pancho Gonzalez, tennis
player; Cynthia Gregory, ballerina; Jerome Hines, basso;
Dustin Hoffman, actor; Theodore Harold Maiman, laser
inventor; Marilyn Monroe, actress; Isamu Noguchi,
sculptor; Leonard Slotkin, conductor; Duke Snider,
baseball player; Adlai E. Stevenson, statesman; Madeleine
Stowe, actress; Darryl Strawberry, baseball player.

Memphis, Tenn.

Mayor: W. W. Herenton (to Dec. 2003)
1998 est. population (rank): 603,507 (18)
1990 census population (rank): 610,337 (18);
  % change, –2.4; **Male,** 285,010; **Female,** 325,327;
  White, 268,600 (43.4%); **Black,** 334,737 (54.8%);
  American Indian, Eskimo, or Aleut, 960 (0.2%);
  Asian or Pacific Islander, 4,805 (0.8%); **Other race,**
  1,235; **Hispanic origin,** 4,455 (0.7%). **1990 popula-
  tion under 18:** 26.9%; **65 and over:** 12.2%; **median
  age:** 31.5.
Land area: 277 sq mi. (702 sq km); **Alt.:** Highest, 417 ft.
Avg. daily temp.: Jan., 39.6° F; July, 82.1° F
Churches: 2000+; **Parks and playgrounds:** 230
  (13,291 ac.); **Radio stations:** AM, 14; FM, 15;
  Television stations: 6
Civilian Labor Force: 292,819; **Unemployed:** 25,640,
  Percent: 8.8; **Per capita personal income (MSA)
  1992:** $19,517
Chamber of Commerce: Memphis Area Chamber of
  Commerce, P.O. Box 224, Memphis, Tenn. 38103

Memphis, the largest city in Tennessee and the
seat of Shelby County, is located in the southwestern corner of the state, on the Mississippi River.

The first settlers of Memphis were the Chickasaw
Indians, who had a village named Chisca there on
the bluffs overlooking the Mississippi River. Hernando de Soto, in 1541, is said to have had his first
glimpse of the Mississippi from the site of Memphis; in the next century, Louis Joliet and Jacques
Marquette stopped there to trade with the Indians.
The French explorer Sieur de La Salle tried to claim
the region for France in 1682 and built Fort Prudhomme there. The area was ceded to the United
States by the Chickasaw Indians in 1818. Memphis
was officially established in 1819 by three enterpris-
ing businessmen from Nashville, James Winchester,
John Overton, and future president Andrew Jackson.
Jackson named it after the ancient Egyptian city
because of its site on the Nile-like Mississippi River.
Memphis was incorporated as a city in 1826 and
became an important Mississippi River port.

During the Civil War, Memphis was a Confederate military center. In 1862, Federal forces won a
gunboat battle on the river at Memphis, and General
Sherman was able to take the city.

Memphis's population was devastated by several
yellow-fever epidemics during the 1870s. The city
did not recover its prosperity until the end of the
19th century.

Memphis is one of the country's largest inland
ports and is known as "America's Distribution Center," serving the northeast, southeast, and southwest
regions of the country. Memphis is a leader in agribusiness, soybean cultivation, rice, grain sorghum,
winter wheat, and corn, and raising livestock. The
city is the world's largest trading center for spot
cotton, handling over 40% of the nation's crops
annually. It is the largest hardwood lumber trading

and processing center in the world and is estimated to be the nation's third-largest total food processor.

Health care and related activities such as medical education and biomedical research are Memphis's largest industries, bringing over $2.5 billion a year to the local economy. Also important are high-technology communications.

Famous natives: Kathy Bates, actress; Dixie Carter, actress; Rosalind Cash, singer; Aretha Franklin, singer; Morgan Freeman, actor; Al Green, singer; George Hamilton, actor; Anfernee "Penny" Hardaway, basketball player; Isaac Hayes, singer; Hal Holbrook, actor; Benjamin Hooks, organization official; Hal Needham, director; Charlie Rich, singer; Cybill Shepherd, actress; Robert Siodmak, director; Fred Smith, business executive; Rufus Thomas, singer; Kemmons Wilson, business executive.

Mesa, Arizona

Mayor: Keno Hawker (to June 2004)
City Manager: Mike Hutchinson
1998 est. population (rank): 360,076 (46)
1990 census population (rank): 288,091 (53);
  % change, 25; **Male,** 141,470; **Female,** 146,621;
  White, 259,472 (90.1%); **Black,** 5,342 (19.0%);
  American Indian, Eskimo, or Aleut, 3,018 (1.0%);
  Asian or Pacific Islander, 4,355 (1.5%); **Other race,**
  15,904 (5.5%); **Hispanic origin,** 31,357 (10.9%). **1990 population under 18:** 28.5%; **65 and over:** 12.4%;
  median age: 32.
Land area: 124.62 sq mi. (319 sq km); **Alt.:** 1,241 ft.
Avg. daily temp.: Jan., 52.9° F; July, 84.9° F
 City-owned parks: 52; **Radio stations:** AM, 20;
  FM, 17; **Television stations:** 7
Civilian Labor Force: 194,569; **Unemployed:** 4,401,
  Percent: 2.3; **Per capita personal income (1989):**
  $13,506
Chamber of Commerce: 120 N. Center St., P.O. Box
  5820, Mesa, AZ 85211–5820

Mesa is the third-largest city in Arizona and is located in the south central portion of the state in Maricopa County. Sitting atop a plateau overlooking the Valley of the Sun, the city gets its name from the Spanish word for "tabletop."

Prior to the arrival of Europeans, the area had been inhabited for centuries by native peoples, including the Hohokam and later, the Pima. The Hohokam culture developed an extensive system of irrigation canals, some of which are still used today.

Controlled by Spain and then by Mexico, the area was ceded to the U.S. following the Mexican War (1846–1848). Mormon settlers arrived on the site in 1878, and the city was incorporated five years later, in 1883.

The population of the area grew rapidly after World War II, as a result, in part, of the increased use of air conditioning; and the manufacturing, tourism, and retail trades became increasingly important. With 313 days of sunshine a year, Mesa was an ideal choice for several major-league baseball spring training camps. It is also the winter home of the Chicago Cubs.

Currently, Mesa is one of the fastest-growing cities in the U.S. due to its excellent climate and strong local economy, which boasts some of the country's top manufacturers. Electronics, automotive testing, propulsion equipment, aerospace, and heavy machinery firms are among the most significant in the region.

Famous natives: Danielle Fishel, actress; Liz Reney, actress; John J. Rhodes, politician; Keri Russell, actress.

Miami, Fla.

Mayor: Joe Carollo (to Nov. 2001)
City Manager: Carlos Gimenez (apptd. May 2000)
1998 est. population (rank): 368,624 (44)
1990 census population (rank): 358,548 (46);
  % change, 2.8; **Male,** 173,223; **Female,** 185,325;
  White, 235,358 (65.6%); **Black,** 98,207 (27.4%);
  American Indian, Eskimo, or Aleut, 545 (0.2%);
  Asian or Pacific Islander, 2,272 (0.6%); **Other race,**
  22,166; **Hispanic origin,** 223,964 (62.5%). **1990 population under 18:** 23.0%; **65 and over,** 16.6%;
  median age: 36.0.
Land area: 34.3 sq mi. (89 sq km); **Water area:** 19.5 sq
  mi.; **Alt.:** Average, 12 ft.
Avg. daily temp.: Jan., 67.1° F; July, 82.4° F
Churches (Dade County): Protestant, 850; Roman
  Catholic, 61; Jewish, 64; **City-owned parks (Miami):**
  109; **Radio stations (Dade County):** 29; **Television
  stations (Dade County):** 9 TV, 1 Cable
Civilian Labor Force: 181,684; **Unemployed:** 21,348,
  Percent: 11.8; **Per capita personal income (PMSA)**
  1992: $17,124
Chamber of Commerce: Greater Miami Chamber of
  Commerce, 1601 Biscayne Blvd., Miami, Fla. 33132

Miami, the second-largest city in Florida and seat of Dade County, is located in the southeastern part of the state, on Biscayne Bay.

The area was once the home of the Tequesta Indians until they were nearly wiped out by European diseases and warfare brought on by two centuries of Spanish control of Florida. Miami was founded in 1870 near the site of Ft. Dallas, built in 1835 during the Seminole Indian wars. The city's name is probably derived from "Mayaimi," an Indian word for "big water."

Miami is the only U.S. city to have been planned by a woman. Julia Tuttle, a Clevelander, arrived there in 1891 and bought several hundred acres on the bank of the Miami River. She convinced New York financier Henry M. Flagler of the area's vast potential and persuaded him to extend his Florida East Coast Railroad to Miami in 1896, the year the city was incorporated. Flagler dredged Miami Harbor, built the renowned Royal Palm Hotel, which opened Jan. 1, 1897, and promoted the area as a winter playground. Tourists flocked there, and by 1910 the city was a thriving recreational area. Miami survived the collapse of a land speculation boom in the 1920s and severe hurricanes in 1926 and 1935, and it continued to grow in the aftermath of these disasters.

Miami experienced one of its most monumental population boosts during the 1960s, when about 260,000 Cuban refugees arrived on its shore seeking freedom. They made a great impact on Miami, now a bilingual metropolis, and spurred economic growth.

Miami is an international banking and finance center, and the city has the greatest concentration of international and Edge Act banks[1] in North America; these constitute a major employment base. Greater Miami[2] has a highly diversified economy with over 170 multinational Miami-based companies, a bevy of Fortune 500 companies, and rapidly growing manufacturing and distribution industries. Miami ranks number one in Florida for total manufacturing income, employment, and number of manufacturing establishments. Greater Miami is the nation's leader in biomedical technology, and the health care sector is a major industry. It is also part of an area known as the Computer Coast of Florida, and its growing technologies include computers, electrical engineering, and plastics manufacturing.

Miami is one of the world's leading year-round resort centers with tourism contributing over 60% of the area's economy. The city is a major transportation hub, and the port of Miami is the world's largest cruise port and a major seaport for cargo. The famous island resort of Miami Beach, incorporated in 1915, is part of Greater Miami and is connected to Miami by four causeways.

1. Edge Act banks may make only foreign loans and accept foreign deposits. 2. Greater Miami is made up of 27 municipalities of which the city of Miami is the largest.

Famous natives: Fernando Bujones, dancer; Steve Carlton, baseball player; Debbie Harry, singer; Dick Howser, baseball player and manager; Sidney Poitier, actor; Janet Reno, attorney general of the U.S.; Ben Vereen, actor; Ellen Zwilich, composer.

Milwaukee, Wis.

Mayor: John O. Norquist (to April 2004)
1998 est. population (rank): 578,364 (19)
1990 census population (rank): 628,088 (17);
% change, −7.9; **Male,** 296,837; **Female,** 331,251; **White,** 398,033 (63.4%); **Black,** 191,255 (30.5%); **American Indian, Eskimo, or Aleut,** 5,858 (0.9%); **Asian or Pacific Islander,** 11,817 (1.9%); **Other race,** 21,125; **Hispanic origin,** 39,409 (6.3%). **1990 population under 18:** 27.4%; **65 and over:** 12.4%; **median age:** 30.3.
Land area: 95.8 sq mi. (248 sq km); **Alt.:** 580.60 ft.
Avg. daily temp.: Jan., 26.9° F; July, 72.4° F
Churches: 411; **County-owned parks:** 14,785 ac.; **Radio stations:** AM, 10; FM, 20; **Television stations:** 11
Civilian Labor Force (1999): 297,707; **Unemployed:** 15,859; **Percent:** 5.3; **Per capita personal income (PMSA) 1995:** $23,822
Chamber of Commerce: Metropolitan Milwaukee Association of Commerce, 756 N. Milwaukee St., Milwaukee, Wis. 53202; Milwaukee Minority Chamber of Commerce, 509 W. Wisconsin Ave. #606, Milwaukee, Wis. 53203; Hispanic Chamber of Commerce, 816 W. National Ave., Milwaukee, Wis. 53204

Milwaukee, the largest city in Wisconsin and seat of Milwaukee County, is located in the southeastern part of the state on Lake Michigan.

French missionaries visited the site of Milwaukee in the seventeenth century, but it was not until 1795 that Jacques Vieau established a fur-trading post there. The first permanent white settler, Vieau's son-in-law, Solomon Juneau, an agent of the American Fur Company, made his home there in 1818. The settlement merged with several neighboring villages in 1838 to form Milwaukee, and the city was incorporated in 1846. The origins of the word "Milwaukee" are disputed; it may come from the Potawatomi "Mahn-ah-wauk," meaning council grounds of the Potawatomi; "Mah-an-wauk-seepe," meaning gathering place of rivers; or the Algonquian "Milo-aki," meaning beautiful land. A large wave of German immigrants arrived after 1848 and contributed greatly to the city's political, economic, and cultural development.

Milwaukee is one of the great industrial centers in the country and one of the largest Great Lakes ports. Currently, port commerce runs almost 3 million tons per year.

Its economy was forged by heavy industries but is now diversified. Manufacturing remains strong, and

Milwaukee manufacturers are national leaders in lithographic commercial printing and the production of medical diagnostic instruments, small gasoline engines, malt beverages, iron and steel forgings, mining and construction machinery, robotics, speed changers and drives, and electronic controls. Milwaukee's high-tech manufacturing community is the ninth-largest among the nation's 31 major metropolitan areas. Though Milwaukee was once known as a "beer town," less than 1% of its workforce is now involved in beer production. However, beer still plays an important role, and almost 11% of the nation's malt beverage is produced there.

Tourism is important to the economy. About 5 million people visit Milwaukee every year.

Famous natives: Donald Gramm, bass-baritone; Woody Herman, band leader; Al Jarreau, singer; Kristen Johnston, actress; George F. Kennan, diplomat; Alfred Lunt, actor; Douglas MacArthur, army general; Pat O'Brien, actor; Tom Snyder, TV personality; Speech, member of the rap group "Arrested Development;" Spencer Tracy, actor; Gene Wilder, actor; Jerry and David Zucker, film producers.

Minneapolis, Minn.

Mayor: Sharon Sayles Belton (to Jan. 2002)
1998 est. population (rank): 351,731 (47)
1990 census population (rank): 368,383 (42);
% change, −4.5; **Male,** 178,671; **Female,** 189,712; **White,** 288,967 (78.4%); **Black,** 47,948 (13.0%); **American Indian, Eskimo, or Aleut,** 12,335 (3.3%); **Asian or Pacific Islander,** 15,723 (4.3%); **Other race,** 3,410; **Hispanic origin,** 7,900 (2.1%). **1990 population under 18:** 20.6%; **65 and over:** 13.0%; **median age:** 31.7
Land area: 58.7 sq mi. (143 sq km); **Alt.:** Highest, 945 ft.; lowest, 695 ft.
Avg. daily temp.: Jan., 11.2° F; July, 73.1° F
Churches: 419; **City-owned parks:** 153; **Radio stations:** AM, 17; FM, 15 (metro area); **Television stations:** 6 (metro area)
Civilian Labor Force: 204,477; **Unemployed:** 9,905, **Percent:** 4.8; **Per capita personal income (MSA) 1992:** $23,284[1]
Chamber of Commerce: Greater Minneapolis Chamber of Commerce, Young Quinlan Building, 81 S. Ninth Street, Suite 200, Minneapolis, Minn. 55402-3223

1. Minneapolis–St. Paul Minn.–Wis.

Minneapolis, the largest city in Minnesota and the seat of Hennepin County, is located in the southeast central part of the state on the Mississippi River. It is adjacent to its "twin city" of St. Paul. The Minneapolis–St. Paul Standard Metropolitan Statistical Area is the 15th-largest in the United States.

In 1680, Father Louis Hennepin visited the future site of Minneapolis and gave the Falls of St. Anthony their name. Lt. Zebulon Pike made a treaty with the Sioux Indians in 1805–1806, by which they ceded to the whites much land, including the Falls of St. Anthony and the site of Minneapolis. Fort Snelling was built in 1819–1820, and in 1823 the government built a lumber and flour mill. Flour milling became the major industry of early Minneapolis and made the city the milling capital of the world. The town of St. Anthony was established on the east bank of the Mississippi in 1848, and the town of Minneapolis grew up on the opposite bank of the river. The name Minneapolis is a combination of the Dakota Sioux word "minna," for water, and the Greek word "polis," for city. Minneapolis was incorporated as a city in 1867, and in 1872 the city of St. Anthony (chartered in 1860) was annexed to it. After the spread of the railroads in the 1870s, Minneapolis became the gateway to the Northern Great Plains.

Minneapolis is a center of industry and commerce serving a large agricultural region. During the 20th century, manufacturing, food processing, milling, computers, health services, and graphic arts developed as Minneapolis's major industries. Thirteen Fortune 500 companies are headquartered in the Minneapolis-St. Paul metropolitan area. The city is the home of the world's largest cash grain market and is the headquarters of the Ninth Federal Reserve Bank.

Famous natives: La Verne, Maxene, and Patti Andrews, singers; James Arness, actor; Lew Ayres, actor; Patty Berg, golfer; Virginia Bruce, actress; J. Paul Getty, oil executive; Peter Graves, actor; George Roy Hill, director; Cornell MacNeil, baritone; Ralph Meeker, actor; Westbrook Pegler, columnist; Prince, singer; Harrison Salisbury, journalist; Charles Schulz, cartoonist; Anne Tyler, writer; Bud Wilkinson, football coach; David Winfield, baseball player.

Nashville-Davidson, Tenn.

Mayor: Bill Purcell (to Oct. 2003)
1998 est. population (rank): 510,274 (24)[1]
1990 census population (rank)[2]: 510,784 (23);
  % change, 4.5; **Male,** 242,492; **Female,** 268,292;
  White, 381,740 (78.2%); **Black,** 119,273 (23.4%);
  American Indian, Eskimo, or Aleut, 1,162 (0.2%);
  Asian or Pacific Islander, 7,081 (1.4%); **Other race,**
  1,528; **Hispanic origin,** 4,775 (0.9%). **1990 population under 18:** 22.8%; **65 and over:** 11.6%; **median age:** 32.6.
Land area: 533 sq mi. (1,380 sq km); **Altitude:** Highest, 1,100 ft.; lowest, approx. 400 ft.
Avg. daily temp.: Jan., 36.7° F; July, 76.6° F
Churches: Protestant, 781; Roman Catholic, 18; Jewish, 3; **City-owned parks:** 76 (6,650 ac.); **Radio stations:** AM, 15; FM, 19; **Television stations:** 11
Civilian Labor Force: 315,480; **Unemployed:** 7,490, **Percent:** 2.4; **Per capita personal income (1995):** $23,655
Chamber of Commerce: Nashville Area Chamber of Commerce, 211 Commerce Street, Suite 100, Nashville, Tenn. 37201

1. 1997 est. population: 536,650. 2. Consolidated city.
The consolidated city of Nashville-Davidson is the capital of and second-largest city in Tennessee and is located in the north central part of the state on the Cumberland River. It is the seat of Davidson County.

During the winter of 1779–1780, James Robertson and John Donelson founded a settlement at Big Salt Lick by the Cumberland River at the present site of the city. They built forts on both sides of the river, naming one of them Fort Nashborough in honor of Francis Nash, a Revolutionary War general. In 1784, the town was named Nashville, and it was incorporated as a city in 1806.

Nashville became the capital of Tennessee in 1843 and was the seat of Davidson County until 1963, when it merged with the county to become Nashville-Davidson.

Nashville's best-known industries are the recording, publishing, and distribution of music, especially country music. The city is a port of entry and an important industrial and commercial center serving the Upper South. Its diverse economy includes automobiles, apparel, publishing, insurance, and banking. Health care services are the largest industry. Nashville is the home of several religious organizations and is a major tourist attraction and convention center.

Famous natives: Roy Acuff, singer; Gregg Allman, singer; Pat Boone, singer; Rita Coolidge, singer; Jeff Gordon, race car driver; Al Gore, vice president; Red Grooms, artist; Alex Haley, author; Barbara Howar, hostess and writer; Brenda Lee, singer; Minnie Pearl, comedienne; Annie Potts, actress; Paula Robeson, flutist; Wilma Rudolph, athlete; Dinah Shore, actress and singer; Tina Turner, singer; Oprah Winfrey, entertainer.

New Orleans, La.

Mayor: Marc H. Morial (to Feb. 2002)
1998 est. population (rank): 465,538 (31)
1990 census population (rank): 496,938 (25);
  % change, –6.3; **Male,** 230,883; **Female,** 266,055;
  White, 173,554 (34.9%); **Black,** 307,728 (61.9%);
  American Indian, Eskimo, or Aleut, 759 (0.2%);
  Asian or Pacific Islander, 9,678 (1.9%); **Other race,**
  5,219; **Hispanic origin,** 17,238 (3.5%). **1990 population under 18:** 27.5%; **65 and over,** 13.0%; **median age:** 31.6.
Land area: 199.4 sq mi. (516 sq km); **Alt.:** Highest, 15 ft.; lowest, –4 ft.
Avg. daily temp.: Jan., 52.4° F; July, 77° F
Churches: 712; **City-owned parks:** 165 (299 ac.); **Radio stations:** AM, 12; FM, 14; **Television stations:** 7
Civilian Labor Force: 205,610[1]; **Unemployed:** 15,055[1], **Percent:** 7.3[1]; **Per capita personal income (MSA) 1992:** $18,087
Chamber of Commerce: The Chamber/New Orleans and the River Region, 301 Camp Street, New Orleans, La. 70130

1. New Orleans City/Orleans Parish.
New Orleans, the largest city in Louisiana and seat of Orleans Parish, is located in the southeastern part of the state, between the Mississippi River and Lake Ponchartrain.

One of the few cities of the nation that has been under three flags, New Orleans has belonged to Spain, France, and the U.S. The French founded it in 1718 and named it in honor of the Duke of Orleans. In 1762, France ceded the city and the territory to Spain. In 1800, the territory was returned to France, but government authorities did not take over until 1803, only 20 days before the region became part of the U.S. in the Louisiana Purchase.

New Orleans is famous for its French Quarter. The Mardi Gras—a week of carnival held in New Orleans before the beginning of Lent—is the most spectacular festival in the U.S. and is a popular tourist attraction. Tourism has grown rapidly in recent years, and New Orleans hosts more than seven million visitors annually.

New Orleans has one of the world's greatest international ports, one of the largest in the nation, and it is a major focus of the city's economy. New Orleans is home to the corporate offices of oil companies with major offshore operations in the Gulf of Mexico, as well as the distribution and service centers of offshore equipment suppliers and fabricators.

The manufacturing industry is a significant part of the economy, with petroleum, petrochemical, shipbuilding, and aerospace industries all playing a role. The New Orleans region also functions as a mining, processing, and transportation center for other minerals, principally sulfur. Service industries are playing a larger role, with health care and telecommunications leading the way. The information services sector is one of the fastest-growing, and the New Orleans region is widely regarded as a leading center of medicine and health care in the South.

Famous natives: Louis Armstrong, musician; Truman Capote, author; Fats Domino, musician; Louis Gottschalk, pianist and composer; Bryant Gumbel, TV personality; Lillian Hellman, playwright and author; Al Hirt, musician; Mahalia Jackson, singer; Dorothy Lamour, actress; Wynton Marsalis, musician; Huey Newton, activist; Marguerite Piazza, soprano; Rusty Staub, baseball player; Ben Turpin, comedian; Shirley Verrett, mezzo-soprano; Carl Weathers, actor; Del Williams, football player.

New York, N.Y.

Mayor: Rudolph W. Giuliani (to Dec. 2001)
Borough Presidents: Bronx, Fernando Ferrer; Brooklyn, Howard Golden; Manhattan, C. Virginia Fields; Queens, Claire Shulman; Staten Island, Guy V. Molinari
1998 est. population (rank): 7,420,166 (1)
1990 census population (rank): 7,322,564 (1)[1];
% change, 1.3; **Male,** 3,437,687; **Female,** 3,884,877; **White,** 3,827,088 (52.2%); **Black,** 2,102,512 (28.7%); **American Indian, Eskimo, or Aleut,** 27,531 (0.4%); **Asian or Pacific Islander,** 512,719 (7.0%); **Other race,** 852,714; **Hispanic origin,** 1,783,511 (24.4%).[1] **1990 population under 18:** 23.0%; **65 and over:** 13.0%; **median age:** 33.7.
Land area: 321.8 sq mi. (826.68 sq km) (Queens, 112.1; Brooklyn, 81.8; Staten Island, 60.2; Bronx, 44.0; Manhattan, 23.7); **Alt.:** Highest, 426 ft.; lowest, sea level
Avg. daily temp.: Jan., 31.8° F; July, 76.7° F
Churches: Protestant, 1,766; Jewish, 1,256; Roman Catholic, 437; Orthodox, 66; **City-owned parks:** 1,701 (28,131.54 ac.); **Radio stations:** AM, 13; FM, 18; **Television stations:** 6 commercial, 1 public
Civilian Labor Force: 3,311,000; **Unemployed:** 359,000, **Percent:** 10.8; **Per capita personal income (PMSA) 1992:** $27,039
Chamber of Commerce: New York Chamber of Commerce and Industry, One Battery Park Plaza, New York, N.Y. 10004

1. Race breakdown figures according to N.Y.C. Dept. of City Planning: White, non-Hispanic, 3,163,125; Black, non-Hispanic, 1,847,049; American Indian, non-Hispanic, 17,871; Asian, non-Hispanic, 489,157; Hispanic, 1,783,511.

New York City is the largest city in the United States. It is located in the southern part of New York State, at the mouth of the Hudson River (also known as North River as it passes Manhattan Island).

In 1609, Henry Hudson, who worked for the Dutch East India Company, sailed up the river that now bears his name and went as far as Albany. Five years later, a permanent settlement was established at what is now New York, but it was originally called New Amsterdam by the Dutch governors. One of them, Peter Minuit, was said to have bought Manhattan Island from the Indians for $24 worth of beads, buttons, and trinkets. In 1664, Great Britain's Duke of York sent a fleet that quietly seized the settlement from the Dutch without bloodshed and rechristened the colony in honor of the duke.

Control of New York passed to the young U.S. at the end of the Revolutionary War, and George Washington was inaugurated president in New York's old City Hall. Congress met in New York from 1785 to 1790.

In 1898, when Greater New York was chartered, the city expanded to include the following five boroughs, which are also counties in New York State: Manhattan (New York County); Brooklyn (Kings County); Bronx (Bronx County); Queens (Queens County); and Staten Island (Richmond County).

There are recurrent efforts among Staten Island residents to separate from Greater New York and become the independent city of Staten Island.

"The Big Apple" is the most populous city in the United States, a major world capital, and a world leader in finance, the arts, and communications. The city is also the center of advertising, fashion, publishing, and radio broadcasting in the United States. New York has many museums, art galleries, and educational institutions. The port of New York is one of the finest in the world. The city is the home of the United Nations and is headquarters for some of the world's largest corporations.

Famous natives: Kareem Abdul-Jabbar, basketball player; Woody Allen, actor and director; Martina Arroyo, soprano; Lauren Bacall, actress; James Baldwin, novelist; Harry Belafonte, singer and actor; Humphrey Bogart, actor; James Cagney, actor; Maria Callas, soprano; Aaron Copland, composer; Sammy Davis, Jr., singer and actor; Agnes de Mille, choreographer; Robert De Niro, actor; Eamon De Valera, former president of Ireland; Gertrude Elion, Nobel Prize winner in medicine; Lou Gehrig, baseball player; George Gershwin, composer; Ira Gershwin, lyricist; Jackie Gleason, actor; Rita Hayworth, actress; Lena Horne, singer; Julia Ward Howe, poet and reformer; Washington Irving, author; Henry James, novelist; Michael Jordan, basketball player; Sandy Koufax, baseball player; Roy Lichtenstein, painter; Vince Lombardi, football player and coach; Chico, Groucho, Harpo, and Zeppo Marx, comedians; Herman Melville, novelist; Yehudi Menuhin, violinist; James Michener, novelist; Arthur Miller, playwright; Eugene O'Neill, playwright; J. Robert Oppenheimer, nuclear physicist; Al Pacino, actor; Jerome Robbins, choreographer; Eleanor Roosevelt, reformer and humanitarian; Theodore Roosevelt, former president; Jonas Salk, polio researcher; Beverly Sills, soprano; Neil Simon, playwright; Barbra Streisand, singer and actress; Ed Sullivan, TV personality; Mae West, actress; Edith Wharton, novelist; Rosalyn Yalow, Nobel Prize winner in medicine.

Oakland, Calif.

Mayor: Jerry Brown (to 2003)
City Manager: Robert C. Bobb
1998 est. population (rank): 365,874 (45)[1]
1990 census population (rank): 372,242 (39); **% change,** −1.7; **Male,** 178,824; **Female,** 193,418; **White,** 120,845 (32.5%); **Black,** 163,335 (43.9%); **American Indian, Eskimo, or Aleut,** 2,371 (0.6%); **Asian or Pacific Islander,** 54,931 (14.8%); **Other race,** 30,756; **Hispanic origin,** 51,711 (13.9%). **1990 population under 18,** 24.9%; **65 and over,** 12.0%; **median age:** 32.7.
Land area: 53.9 sq mi. (140 sq km); **Alt.:** Highest, 1,700 ft.; lowest, sea level
Avg. daily temp.: Jan., 49.0° F; July, 63.7° F
Churches: 374, representing over 78 denominations in the City; over 500 churches in Alameda County; **City-owned parks:** 2,196 ac.; **Radio stations:** AM, 1; **Television stations:** 1 commercial
Civilian Labor Force: 180,624; **Unemployed:** 18,148, **Percent:** 10.0; **Per capita personal income (PMSA) 1992:** $24,359
Chamber of Commerce: Oakland Chamber of Commerce, 475 Fourteenth St., Oakland, Calif. 94612-1903

1. 1997 est. population: 386,100

Oakland is located in the west central part of California on the east side of San Francisco Bay. It is the seat of Alameda County.

Don Luis Peralta first settled the site of Oakland in 1820 when he established the Rancho San Antonio. The gold rush of 1849 attracted more people to the area and the city's population continued to grow after a ferry service to San Francisco was started in

1851. Oakland was incorporated as a town in 1852 and as a city in 1854. It was named after the numerous oak trees found in the area. Oakland became the western terminus of the Central Pacific Railroad in 1869 and the seat of Alameda County in 1873.

In the latter part of the 19th century and also in 1910, additional territory was annexed to Oakland and the city assumed its present size. In 1906, thousands of people fled to Oakland in the aftermath of the San Francisco earthquake and settled there permanently, furthering the city's growth. Oakland's economic development continued to rise with the opening of the San Francisco–Oakland Bay Bridge in 1936.

Oakland is a major center of culture and commerce. It is an important container shipping port and the terminus of three transcontinental railroads. Oakland's industries include shipbuilding, food processing, chemicals, pharmaceuticals, electrical and high technology manufacturing. Oakland is also a leading importer of foreign cars. The city is the headquarters of many national and international corporations.

Famous natives: Buster Crabbe, actor; Frederick Cottrell, inventor; Dennis Eckersley, athlete; Hammer, singer, dancer, and songwriter; Rod McKuen, singer and composer; Russ Meyer, producer and director; Eddie (Anderson) Rochester, actor; George Stevens, director; Amy Tan, writer; Jo Van Fleet, actress.

Oklahoma City, Okla.

Mayor: Kirk Humphreys (to April 2002)
City Manager: Glen E. Deck
1998 est. population (rank): 472,221 (30)
1990 census population (rank): 444,719 (29);
% change, 6.2; **Male,** 214,466; **Female,** 230,253;
White, 332,539 (74.8%); **Black,** 71,064 (16.0%);
American Indian, Eskimo, or Aleut, 18,794 (4.2%);
Asian or Pacific Islander, 10,491 (2.4%); **Other race,** 11,831; **Hispanic origin,** 22,033 (5.0%). **1990 population under 18:** 26.0%; **65 and over:** 11.9%; **median age:** 32.4.
Land area: 608.2 sq mi. (1,575 sq km); **Alt.:** Highest, 1,320 ft.; lowest, 1,140 ft.
Avg. daily temp.: Jan., 35.9° F; July, 82.1° F
Churches: Roman Catholic, 25; Jewish, 4; Protestant and others, 741; **City-owned parks:** 144 (5,225 ac.); **Television stations:** 8; **Radio stations:** AM, 10; FM, 14
Civilian Labor Force (1999): 549,730; **Unemployed:** 14,079; **Percent:** 2.6; **Per capita personal income (MSA) 1998:** $23,337
Chamber of Commerce: Greater Oklahoma City Chamber of Commerce, 123 Park Ave., Oklahoma City, Okla. 73102

Oklahoma City, the state capital and seat of Oklahoma County, is the largest city in Oklahoma. It is located in the central part of the state on the North Canadian River.

Oklahoma City sprang into being almost overnight. On April 22, 1889, the U.S. government threw open the territory for settlement, and there was a rush across the line to stake claims. A sprawling tent city sprang up near the Santa Fe railroad tracks, and within a short time Oklahoma City was a bustling town of 10,000. The city was incorporated in 1890 and replaced Guthrie as the state capital in 1910. Oil was discovered in the city in 1928, and petroleum production became a mainstay of the city's economy.

Oklahoma City is the wholesale and distributing center for the state, and the city's stockyards are the largest stocker and feeder cattle market in the world.

Following the decline of the energy sector, Oklahoma City is fostering a private entrepreneurial environment and a more diversified economy. Within the service sector, health services are projected to grow, followed by retail trade and business services. Aerospace, distribution, and telecommunications have been targeted for business attraction. Nearby Tinker Air Force Base, one of the world's largest air depots, is a major city employer.

Famous natives: Johnny Bench, baseball; Lon Chaney, Jr., actor; Ralph Ellison, writer; Kay Francis, actress; Dale Robertson, actor; Ted Shackleford, actor; Pamela Tiffin, actress; Vince Gill, country singer.

Omaha, Neb.

Mayor: Hal Daub (to 2001)
1998 est. population (rank): 371,291 (43)
1990 census population (rank): 335,795 (48);
% change, 7.8; **Male,** 160,392; **Female,** 175,403;
White, 281,603 (83.9%); **Black,** 43,989 (13.1%);
American Indian, Eskimo, or Aleut, 2,274 (0.7%);
Asian or Pacific Islander, 3,412 (1.0%); **Other race,** 4,517; **Hispanic origin,** 10,288 (3.1%). **1990 population under 18:** 25.4%; **65 and over:** 12.9%; **median age:** 32.2.
Land area: 117 sq mi. (303 sq km); **Alt.:** Highest, 1,270 ft.
Avg. daily temp.: Jan., 20.2° F; July, 77.7° F
Churches: Protestant, 192; Roman Catholic, 44; Jewish, 4; **City-owned parks:** 192 (over 8,000 ac.); **Radio stations:** AM, 7; FM, 13; **Television stations:** 4
Civilian Labor Force: 177,387; **Unemployed:** 8,298, **Percent:** 4.7; **Per capita personal income (MSA) 1992:** $20,242[1]
Chamber of Commerce: Omaha Chamber of Commerce, 1301 Harney St., Omaha, Neb. 68102

1. Omaha, Neb.–Iowa.

Omaha, the largest city in Nebraska and the seat of Douglas County, is located in the eastern part of the state on the west bank of the Missouri River, opposite Council Bluffs, Iowa.

The Lewis and Clark expedition visited the area in 1804, and the U.S. Army built Ft. Atkinson nearby in 1819. Pierre Cabanne established a fur-trading post at the site in 1825. The first Mormon migrants wintered there in 1846–1847 on their way to Utah. The city grew rapidly as the most northerly supply point for overland wagons to the Far West.

The city was officially founded in 1854 after the Nebraska Territory was opened for settlement. It was named for the Omaha Indians living nearby, whose tribal name means "those who go upstream or against the current." Omaha was incorporated as a city in 1857 and was the capital of the Nebraska Territory from 1855 to 1867. The city continued to thrive as a point of entry and a major transportation center when the Union Pacific transcontinental railroad arrived in 1869.

Omaha is a major market for food processing, telecommunications, and insurance. Other important industries include electrical equipment and finance as well as printing and publishing.

Famous natives: Fred Astaire, dancer and actor; Max Baer, boxer; Ronald Boone, former NBA professional; Robert Boozer, former NBA professional; Marlon Brando, actor; Montgomery Clift, actor; Gerald Ford, former president; Bob Gibson, baseball player; Swoosie Kurtz, actress; Melvin Laird, former secretary of defense; Dorothy McGuire, actress; Nick Nolte, actor; Gale Sayers, football player; Malcolm X, political activist; Paul Williams, singer and composer.

Philadelphia, Pa.

Mayor: John F. Street (to Jan. 2004)
1998 est. population (rank): 1,436,287 (5)
1990 census population (rank): 1,585,577 (5);
 % change, −9.4; **Male,** 737,763; **Female,** 847,814;
 White, 848,586 (53.5%); **Black,** 631,936 (39.9%);
 American Indian, Eskimo, or Aleut, 3,454 (0.2%);
 Asian or Pacific Islander, 43,522 (2.7%); **Other race,**
 58,079; **Hispanic origin,** 89,193 (5.6%). **1990 popu-**
 lation under 18: 23.9%; **65 and over:** 15.2%; **median**
 age: 33.2.
Land area: 136 sq mi. (352 sq km); **Alt.:** Highest, 440
 ft.; lowest, sea level
Avg. daily temp.: Jan., 31.2° F; July, 76.5° F
Churches: Roman Catholic, 133; Jewish, 55; Protestant
 and others, 830; **City-owned parks:** 630 (10,252 ac.);
 Radio stations: AM, 40[1]; FM, 43[1]; **Television**
 stations: 14[1]
Civilian Labor Force (1997 est.): 652,126[1];
 Unemployed: 41,085[1], **Percent:** 8.8[2]; **Per capita per-**
 sonal income (PMSA) 1994: $25,220[1]
Chamber of Commerce: Philadelphia Chamber of Com-
 merce, 1234 Market Street, Suite 1800, Philadelphia,
 Pa. 19107

1. Philadelphia City/County.

Philadelphia, the largest city in Pennsylvania and
seat of Philadelphia County (coterminous), is
located in the southeastern part of the state at the
junction of the Schuylkill and Delaware Rivers.

Philadelphia, the City of Brotherly Love, was
settled in 1681 by Capt. William Markham, who, with
a small band of colonists, was sent out by his cousin,
William Penn. Penn arrived the following year.

In the period before the American Revolution, the
city outstripped all others in the colonies in education, arts, science, industry, and commerce. In 1774–
1776, the First and Second Continental Congresses
met in Philadelphia; and, from 1781–1783, the city
was the capital of the U.S. under the Articles of
Confederation. In 1790, it became the nation's capital under the Constitution and remained so until the
seat of the federal government moved to Washington in 1800.

Within a half-century of the founding of the
nation at Independence Hall, Philadelphia had
emerged as the "world's greatest workshop." The
steam locomotives and hat factories of the 19th century have been replaced by diverse manufacturing
specialties such as chemicals (including pharmaceuticals), medical devices, transportation equipment,
and printing and publishing. In the services sector,
Philadelphia is a major net "exporter" in subsectors
such as health services, insurance carriers, legal services, and architecture and engineering services.

The city abounds in landmarks of early American history, including Independence Hall and the
Liberty Bell.

Famous natives: Marian Anderson, contralto; Frankie
Avalon, singer and actor; John, Lionel, and Ethel
Barrymore, actors; Kevin Bacon, actor; Boyz II Men, R&B
group; Mary Cassatt, artist; Wilt Chamberlain, basketball
player; Chubby Checker, singer; Bill Cosby, actor; Stuart
Davis, painter; Thomas Eakins, painter and sculptor; W. C.
Fields, comedian; Benjamin Franklin, inventor and
statesman; Grace (Kelly), actress and Princess of Monaco;
Walt Kelly, cartoonist; Patti LaBelle, singer; Mario Lanza,
singer and actor; George McClellan, general; Margaret
Mead, anthropologist; Edgar Allen Poe, author; Anna
Quindlen, writer and Pulitzer Prize winner; Man Ray,
painter; Betsy Ross, flagmaker; Will Smith, actor;
Jacqueline Susann, novelist; Robert Venturi, architect.

Phoenix, Ariz.

Mayor: Skip Rimsza (to Oct. 2003)
City Manager: Frank Fairbanks (apptd. May 1990)
1998 est. population (rank): 1,198,064 (7)[1]
1990 census population (rank): 983,403 (9);
 % change, 21.3; **Male,** 487,589; **Female,** 495,814;
 White, 803,332 (81.6%); **Black,** 51,053 (5.2%);
 American Indian, Eskimo, or Aleut, 18,225 (1.9%);
 Asian or Pacific Islander, 16,303 (1.7%); **Other race,**
 94,490; **Hispanic origin,** 197,103 (20.0%). **1990**
 population under 18: 27.2%; **65 and over,** 9.7%;
 median age: 31.1.
Land area: 476.7 sq mi. (1,216.8 sq km); **Alt.:** Highest,
 2,740 ft..; lowest, 1,017 ft.
Avg. daily temp.: Jan., 53.6° F; July, 93.5° F
City-owned parks: 170 (25,235 ac.); **Radio stations:**
 AM, 20; FM, 20; **Television stations:** 9 commercial;
 1 PBS
Civilian Labor Force: 1,482,000; **Unemployed:** 51,200,
 Percent: 3.3; **Per capita personal income (MSA)**
 1992: $19,018
Chamber of Commerce: Phoenix Chamber of Com-
 merce, 201 N. Central, Phoenix, Ariz. 85073

1. 1997 est. population: 1,187,944.

Phoenix, the capital of Arizona and seat of Maricopa County, is the largest city in the state. It is
located in the center of Arizona, on the Salt River.

The prehistoric Hohokam Indians first settled the
area about 300 B.C. and dug a system of extensive
irrigation canals for farming. The Indian culture
mysteriously broke up in the 1400s. The site was
permanently resettled again by Jack Swilling and
"Lord Darrell" Duppa about 1867. Because the city
was founded on the ruins of the ancient civilization,
it was named Phoenix after the legendary Phoenix
bird that could regenerate itself. The irrigation
canals were restored for farming, and ranching and
prospecting began in the surrounding area. The city
quickly grew as an important trading center.

Phoenix was incorporated as a city in 1881 and
was made the territorial capital in 1889. It became
the state capital when Arizona was admitted to the
Union in 1912.

Phoenix is a center of agriculture and commerce.
Major industries include government, agricultural
products, aerospace technology, electronics, air-
conditioning, leather goods, and Indian arts and
crafts. The city of Phoenix is renowned as a leader
in local government management and received the
1993 Bertelsmann Foundation award for the best-
managed city in the world.

Famous natives: Lynda Carter, actress; Joan Ganz
Cooney, TV executive; Alice Cooper, musician; Arthur A.
Fletcher, government official; Barry Goldwater, politician;
Stevie Nicks, musician; Charles S. Robb, politician; Mare
Winningham, actress.

Pittsburgh, Pa.

Mayor: Tom Murphy (to Jan. 2002)
1998 est. population (rank): 340,520 (49)
1990 census population (rank): 369,879 (40);
 % change, −7.9; **Male,** 171,722; **Female,** 198,157;
 White, 266,791 (72.1%); **Black,** 95,362 (25.8%);
 American Indian, Eskimo, or Aleut, 671 (0.2%);
 Asian or Pacific Islander, 5,937 (1.6%); **Other race,**
 1,118; **Hispanic origin,** 3,468 (0.9%). **1990 popula-**
 tion under 18: 19.8%; **65 and over,** 17.9%; **median**
 age: 34.6.
Land area: 55.5 sq mi. (144 sq km); **Alt.:** Highest, 1,240
 ft.; lowest, 715 ft.
Avg. daily temp.: Jan., 26.7° F; July, 72.0° F

Churches: Protestant, 348; Roman Catholic, 86; Jewish, 28; Orthodox, 26; **City-owned parks and playgrounds:** 270 (2,572 ac.); **Radio stations:** AM, 12; FM, 20; **Television stations:** 11
Civilian Labor Force: 157,500; **Unemployed:** 5,355, **Percent:** 3.4; **Per capita personal income (MSA) 1996 :** $24,957
Chamber of Commerce: The Chamber of Commerce of Greater Pittsburgh, 425 Sixth Ave., Pittsburgh, Pa. 15219

Pittsburgh, the second-largest city in Pennsylvania and seat of Allegheny County, is located in the southwestern part of the state at the junction where the Allegheny and Monongahela rivers join to form the Ohio River.

Some of the first inhabitants of the area were the Shawnee, Seneca, Delaware, and Iroquois Indians, who had left the area by 1754. That year a detachment of troops from Virginia put a fort on the site of present Pittsburgh (Ft. Prince George), considering it a strategic spot. Following the original Virginia settlers, the French seized the spot and named it Ft. Duquesne; in 1758, the British took it away from the French. The British built a new fort and named it after the British prime minister, William Pitt. A town developed around the fort and was incorporated as the City of Pittsburgh in 1816.

By the late 1800s, Pittsburgh had become a world leader in iron and steelmaking, and it remained so for nearly a century. In the early 1980s, the country's domestic steel industry collapsed, causing major upheavals in Pittsburgh's manufacturing sector.

The Pittsburgh region underwent a successful diversified economic transition, shifting from heavy industries to light manufacturing, advanced technologies such as industrial automation, advanced materials, software engineering, and biomedical technology, medicine, education, finance, and corporate services. Pittsburgh is a national leader in health care services and is the world's leading center for organ transplantation.

Pittsburgh is also a major U.S. transportation center and is one of the nation's largest inland ports in terms of tonnage.

Famous natives: Rachel Carson, ecologist and writer; Henry Steele Commager, historian; Bill Cullen, radio and TV entertainer; John Davidson, singer and actor; Billy Eckstine, singer; Erroll Garner, jazz pianist; Scott Glenn, actor; Martha Graham, dancer and choreographer; George S. Kaufman, playwright; Michael Keaton, actor; Gene Kelly, actor and dancer; Oscar Levant, pianist; Andrew Mellon, financier; Adolphe Menjou, actor; William Powell, actor; Mary Roberts Rinehart, novelist; Peter Sellars, theater director; David O. Selznick, producer; Joseph Wambaugh, novelist; Andy Warhol, artist; August Wilson, playwright.

Portland, Ore.

Mayor: Vera Katz (to Jan. 2001)
1998 est. population (rank): 503,891 (26)
1990 census population (rank): 437,319 (30); **% change,** 3.7; **Male,** 211,914; **Female,** 225,405; **White,** 370,135 (84.4%); **Black,** 33,530 (7.7%); **American Indian, Eskimo, or Aleut,** 5,399 (1.2%); **Asian or Pacific Islander,** 23,185 (5.3%); **Other race,** 5,070; **Hispanic origin,** 13,874 (3.2%). **1990 population under 18:** 21.9%; **65 and over,** 14.6%; **median age:** 34.5.
Land area: 137.8 sq mi. (357 sq km), **Alt.:** Highest, 1073 ft.; lowest, sea level
Avg. daily temp.: Jan., 38.9° F; July, 67.7° F
Churches: Protestant, 450; Roman Catholic, 48; Jewish, 9; Buddhist, 6; other, 190; **City-owned parks:** 200 (over 9,400 ac.);

Radio stations: AM: 14, FM: 14; **Television stations:** 5 commercial, 1 public
Civilian Labor Force: 248,724; **Unemployed:** 18,372, **Percent:** 7.4; **Per capita personal income (PMSA) 1992:** $20,681
Chamber of Commerce: Portland Chamber of Commerce, 221 NW 2nd Ave., Portland, Ore. 97209

Portland, the largest city in Oregon and seat of Multnomah County, is located in the northwestern part of the state on the Willamette River.

Lewis and Clark camped at the site of Portland in 1805 on their expedition across the continent. Portland was founded in 1845 and was almost called Boston after the city in Massachusetts. Founders Amos Lovejoy from Massachusetts and Francis Pettygrove from Maine flipped a coin to decide the name of the new town. Pettygrove won the toss and named the place Portland after his hometown. Portland was incorporated as a city in 1851.

In the 1850s Portland served as a supply base for the California gold rush, and it grew with the development of its salmon and lumber industries and the arrival of the railroad in 1883. The city continued to grow during 1879 to 1900 as a supply point for the Alaska gold rush and as the site of the Lewis and Clark Centennial Exposition in 1905.

The port of Portland leads the west in grain exports and is among the top five auto-import centers in the United States. The port ranks third in overall volume behind Los Angeles and Long Beach.

Portland has a diverse economy with a broad base of manufacturing, distribution, wholesale and retail trade, regional government, and business services. Major manufacturing industries include machinery, electronics, metals, transportation equipment, and lumber and wood products. Technology is a thriving part of Portland's economy, with over 500 high-tech companies located in the metropolitan area. Tourism is also important to Portland's economy.

Famous natives: James Beard, food expert; Pietro Belluschi, architect; Richard Fosbury, high jumper; Matt Groening, cartoonist; Margaux Hemingway, actress; Phil Knight, founder of Nike; Terrance Knox, actor; Jeff Lorber, jazz musician; Linus Pauling, chemist; Jane Powell, singer and actress; Ahmad Rashad, football player and sportscaster; Susan Ruttan, actress; Doc Severinson, band leader; Norton Simon, business executive; Sally Ann Struthers, actress; Gus Van Sant, film director; Lindsay Wagner, actress; Mitch Williams, baseball pitcher.

Sacramento, Calif.

Mayor: Jimmy Yee (to Nov. 2000)
1998 est. population (rank): 404,168 (38)
1990 census population (rank): 369,365 (42); **% change,** 9.4; **Male,** 178,737; **Female,** 190,628; **White,** 221,963 (60.1%); **Black,** 56,521 (15.3%); **American Indian, Eskimo, or Aleut,** 4,561 (1.2%); **Asian or Pacific Islander,** 55,426 (15.0%); **Other race,** 30,894; **Hispanic origin,** 60,007 (16.2%). **1990 population under 18:** 26.2%; **65 and over,** 12.1%; **median age:** 31.8.
Land area: 123 sq mi. (318.7 sq km)
Avg. daily temp.: Jan., 53.5° F; July, 88.4° F
City park & recreational facilities: 134+ (1,427+ ac.); **Television stations:** 7
Civilian Labor Force: 188,670; **Unemployed:** 13,070, **Percent:** 6.9; **Per capita personal income (PMSA) 1992:** $23,038
Chamber of Commerce: Sacramento Chamber of Commerce, 917 7th St., Sacramento, Calif. 95814; West Sacramento Chamber of Commerce, 834-C Jefferson Blvd., Sacramento, Calif. 95691

Sacramento is the capital of and seventh-largest city in California and is the seat of Sacramento County. It is located in the north central part of the state at the confluence of the Sacramento and American rivers.

In 1839, German-born Swiss citizen John Augustus Sutter obtained a grant from the Mexican governor to establish a colony for fellow Swiss emigrants on a large tract of land in the vicinity that he named New Helvetia (New Switzerland), and established Fort Sutter there as a trading post.

After gold was discovered on Sutter's property in 1848, the settlement rapidly expanded as the prominent supply point for gold prospectors coming from the East. Sacramento was laid out in 1848 and named after California's principal river, which ran beside it. The river's name in Spanish honors the Holy Sacrament. It became incorporated as a city in 1849 and was made the state capital in 1854. Sacramento was the terminus of the first railroad in 1856 and the western terminus of the Pony Express in 1860.

The city has always been a hub of river transportation and is a major deep-water port connected to the Pacific Ocean. Sacramento's economy is highly diversified and, along with state government and military installations, its industries include aerospace, high technology, furniture, chemicals, pharmaceuticals, meat packing, and food processing of crops from the Central Valley.

The defense sector of the economy declined and Mather Air Force Base and the Army Depot were closed in 1995.

Famous natives: Joan Didion, author; Mark Goodson, TV producer; Tom Hanks, actor; Henry Hathaway, director; Anthony M. Kennedy, Supreme Court justice; Molly Ringwald, actress.

St. Louis, Mo.

Mayor: Clarence Harmon, Jr. (to April 2001)
1998 est. population (rank): 339,316 (50)
1990 census population (rank): 396,685 (34); **% change,** −14.5; **Male,** 180,680; **Female,** 216,005; **White,** 202,085 (50.9%); **Black,** 188,408 (47.5%); **American Indian, Eskimo, or Aleut,** 950 (0.2%); **Asian or Pacific Islander,** 3,733 (0.9%); **Other race,** 1,509; **Hispanic origin,** 5,124 (1.3%). **1990 population under 18:** 25.2%; **65 and over:** 16.6%; **median age:** 32.8.
Land area: 61.4 sq mi. (159 sq km); **Alt.:** Highest, 616 ft.; lowest, 413 ft.
Avg. daily temp.: Jan., 28.8° F; July, 78.9° F
Churches: 900[1]; **City-owned parks:** 106 (3,136 ac.); **Radio stations:** AM, 21; FM 27[1]; **Television stations:** 6 commercial; 1 PBS
Civilian Labor Force: 179,278; **Unemployed:** 14,379, **Percent:** 8.0; **Per capita personal income (MSA) 1992:** $22,002[2]
Chamber of Commerce: St. Louis Regional Chamber and Growth Association, One Metropolian Square, Suite 1300, St. Louis, Mo. 63102

1. Metropolitan area. 2. St. Louis, Mo.–Ill.

St. Louis, the second-largest city in Missouri, is located in the east central part of the state on the Mississippi River. The city is independent and is not part of any county.

St. Louis was founded by the French in 1764 when Auguste Chouteau established a fur-trading post and Pierre Laclède Liguest, a New Orleans merchant, founded a town at the present site. They named it after King Louis XV of France and his patron saint,

Louis IX. From 1770 to 1803, St. Louis was a Spanish possession, but it was ceded back to France in 1803 in accordance with the Treaty of San Ildefonso (1800), only to be acquired by the U.S. as part of the Louisiana purchase that year.

The town was incorporated in 1809. From 1812 to 1821, St. Louis was the capital of the Missouri Territory and was incorporated as a city in 1822.

John Jacob Astor opened the Western branch of the American Fur Company in 1819, and the city prospered during the early part of the 19th century as a commercial center for the fur trade. St. Louis continued to grow as a major transportation hub with the development of steamboat traffic and the later expansion of the railroads in the 1850s. The world-famous Louisiana Purchase Exposition was held here in 1904.

Manufacturing is important to the city's economy, and its highly developed industries include automobiles, aircraft and space technology, metal fabrication, beer, steelmaking, chemicals, food processing, and storage and distribution.

The giant stainless steel Gateway Arch, 630 feet high, standing on the banks of the Mississippi, symbolizes St. Louis as the Gateway to the West.

Famous natives: Josephine Baker, singer; Yogi Berra, baseball player; Grace Bumbry, mezzo-soprano; Morris Carnovsky, actor; T. S. Eliot, poet; Eugene Field, poet; Redd Foxx, comedian; Joe Garagiola, baseball player; John Goodman, actor; Betty Grable, actress; Dick Gregory, comedian; Al Hirschfeld, cartoonist; Kevin Kline, actor; David Merrick, producer; Vincent Price, actor; Judy Rankin, golfer; Leon Spinks, boxer; Herbert Bayard Swope, journalist; Sara Teasdale, poet; Helen Traubel, soprano; Roy Wilkins, civil rights leader.

San Antonio, Tex.

Mayor: Howard Peak (to June 2001)
City Manager: Alexander E. Briseno (apptd. April 27, 1990)
1998 est. population (rank): 1,114,130 (8)[1]
1990 census population (rank): 935,933 (10); **% change,** 14.1; **Male,** 450,695; **Female,** 485,238; **White,** 676,082 (72.3%); **Black,** 65,884 (7.0%); **American Indian, Eskimo, or Aleut,** 3,303 (0.4%); **Asian or Pacific Islander,** 10,703 (1.1%); **Other race,** 179,961; **Hispanic origin,** 520,282 (55.6%). **1990 population under 18:** 29.0%; **65 and over:** 10.5%; **median age:** 29.8.
Land area: 417.13 sq mi. (1080.3 sq km); **Alt.:** 700 ft.
Avg. daily temp.: Jan., 51.2° F; July, 86.1° F
City-owned parks: 6,717 ac.; **Radio stations:** AM, 20; FM, 22; **Television stations:** 9
Civilian Labor Force: 695,110; **Unemployed:** 32,177, **Percent:** 4.6; **Per capita personal income (MSA) 1992:** $17,282
Chamber of Commerce: Greater San Antonio Chamber of Commerce, P.O. Box 1628, 602 E. Commerce, San Antonio, Tex. 78296

1. 1997 est. population: 1,115,600.

San Antonio, the third-largest city in Texas and the seat of Bexar County, is located in the south central part of the state, on the San Antonio River.

The site of San Antonio was first visited in 1691 by a Franciscan friar on the feast day of St. Anthony and was named San Antonio de Padua in his honor. San Antonio was permanently settled on May 1, 1718, when the Spanish governor of Coahuila and Texas, Martin de Alarcón, founded the presidio (a fort) of San Antonio de Bejar (Bexar) and the mission of San Antonio de Valero (later called the

Alamo[1]) on the site of a Coahuiltecan Indian village. San Antonio remained almost continuously under Spanish rule until 1812, when Mexico won its independence from Spain.

During the outbreak of the Texas revolution (1835) against the tyranny of Mexican dictator General Santa Anna, San Antonio was captured by a small band of rebels who occupied the fortified mission of the Alamo in Dec. 1835. The historic battle of the Alamo was fought there (Feb. 24 to March 6, 1836) and its 183 besieged defenders were massacred by Santa Anna's troops. Their heroism aroused the anger and fighting spirit of Texans and led them to shout their famous battle cry "Remember the Alamo!" and defeat the Mexicans six weeks later (April 21, 1836) at the battle of San Jacinto. Texas became an independent republic in 1836 and San Antonio was incorporated as a city on Jan. 5, 1837.

After the Civil War, with the arrival of the railroad in 1877, San Antonio prospered as a major shipping point for cattle. The city has been an important military center since World War II and is the home to five of the largest military installations in the nation, including Fort Sam Houston, constructed in 1876. San Antonio is a leading livestock center and one of the largest produce exchange markets. The city's industries are highly diversified, and tourism is also important to the economy.

1. Spanish for the cottonwood tree.

Famous natives: Carol Burnett, comedienne; Cody Carlson, football player; Henry G. Cisneros, secretary of HUD; Joan Crawford, actress; Cito Gaston, baseball manager; Ann Harding, actress; Jesse James Leija, boxer; Emilio Navaira, Tejano music singer; Oliver North, military officer and government official; Suzy Parker, model and actress; Paula Prentiss, actress; Kyle Rote, football player; David R. Scott, astronaut; John Silber, university president; Patsy Torres, Tejano music singer; Edward H. White, astronaut.

San Diego, Calif.

Mayor: Susan Golding (to Dec. 2000)
City Manager: Michael Uberuaga (apptd. Nov. 1997)
1998 est. population (rank): 1,220,666 (6)
1990 census population (rank): 1,110,549 (6);
  % change, 9.9; **Male,** 566,464; **Female,** 544,085;
  White, 745,406 (67.1%); **Black,** 104,261 (9.4%);
  American Indian, Eskimo, or Aleut, 6,800 (0.6%);
  Asian or Pacific Islander, 130,945 (11.8%); **Other race,** 123,137; **Hispanic origin,** 229,519 (20.7%).
  1990 population under 18: 23.1%; **65 and over:** 10.2%; **median age:** 30.5.
Land area: 330.7 sq miles (857 sq km); **Alt.:** Highest, 1,591 ft.; lowest, sea level
Avg. daily temp.: Jan., 56.8° F; July, 70.3° F
Churches: Roman Catholic, 39; Jewish, 9; Protestant, 334; Eastern Orthodox, 8; other, 18; **City park and recreation facilities:** 164 (17,207 ac.); **Radio stations:** AM, 8; FM, 18; **Television stations:** 9
Civilian Labor Force: 548,687; **Unemployed:** 41,301, **Percent:** 7.5; **Per capita personal income (MSA) 1992:** $20,384
Chamber of Commerce: San Diego Chamber of Commerce, 402 West Broadway, Suite 1000, San Diego, Calif. 92101

San Diego is the second-largest city in California. It is located in the southwestern part of the state, on San Diego Bay.

Portuguese navigator Juan Rodríguez Cabrillo claimed the bay in 1542 for Spain. The site was named San Miguel by Cabrillo. On Nov. 12, 1602, Don Sebastian de Viscaíno came ashore with his party on the day of St. Didacus (San Diego in Spanish) and celebrated a mass in the saint's honor. By coincidence, Viscaíno's flagship was named *San Diego.* He renamed the place San Diego after the 15th-century saint.

In 1769, Franciscan father Junípero Serra established the first California mission there—San Diego del Alcala. In 1822, Mexico won control of the town after it declared its independence from Spain. In 1846, during the Mexican War, San Diego was seized by the United States and incorporated into a city in 1850, just after California joined the Union that same year.

Today, San Diego's excellent natural harbor is a busy commercial port and a hub of U.S. naval operations. However, the naval training center at San Diego has closed due to defense cutbacks. Other leading industries are electronics, aerospace and missiles, medical and scientific research, oceanography, and agriculture. Its magnificent climate and proximity to Mexico have made tourism a significant part of the city's economy.

Famous natives: Billy Casper, golfer; Florence Chadwick, swimmer; Dennis Conner, yacht racer; Ted Danson, actor; Robert Duvall, actor; Nanette Fabray, actress; Robert Lansing, actor; Margaret O'Brien, actress; Carol Vaness, soprano; Ted Williams, baseball player; Mickey Wright, golfer.

San Francisco, Calif.

Mayor: Willie L. Brown, Jr. (to Jan. 2004)
1998 est. population (rank): 745,774 (12)
1990 census population (rank): 723,959 (14);
  % change, 3.0; **Male,** 362,497; **Female,** 361,462;
  White, 387,783 (53.6%); **Black,** 79,039 (10.9%);
  American Indian, Eskimo, or Aleut, 3,456 (0.5%);
  Asian or Pacific Islander, 210,876 (29.1%); **Other race,** 42,805; **Hispanic origin,** 100,717 (13.9%). **1990 population under 18:** 16.1%; **65 and over:** 14.6%; **median age:** 35.8.
Land area: 46.1 sq mi. (120 sq km); **Alt.:** Highest, 925 ft.; lowest, sea level
Avg. daily temp.: Jan., 48.5° F; July, 62.2° F
Churches: 540 of all denominations; **City-owned parks and squares:** 225; **Radio stations:** 29; **Television stations:** 10
Civilian Labor Force (1995): 398,000[1]; **Unemployed (S.F. residents):** 26,000[1], **Percent:** 6.4[1]; **Per capita personal income (PMSA) 1992:** $31,262
Chamber of Commerce: Greater San Francisco Chamber of Commerce, 465 California St., San Francisco, Calif. 94104

1. San Francisco City/County.

San Francisco, the fourth-largest city in California, is coextensive with San Francisco County. It is located in the northern part of the state between the Pacific Ocean and San Francisco Bay. A narrow arm of land embraces San Francisco Bay, the largest land-locked harbor in the world, and shelters it from the Pacific Ocean. On this arm of land is San Francisco, a city on hills, almost surrounded by water.

A Franciscan father who was sailing with Sebastián Rodríguez Cermeño named the bay San Francisco on Nov. 7, 1595. In 1776, the Spaniards established a presidio, or military post, and a Franciscan mission on the end of the beautiful peninsula. In the following year, a little town was founded around the mission. It was called Yerba Buena, Spanish for "Good Herb," because mint grew in abundance there.

In 1846, during the Mexican War, Yerba Buena was taken over by the United States. It was renamed San Francisco in 1847 and became incorporated as a city in 1850.

When gold was discovered in California in 1848, the city's population jumped to 10,000, and it experienced turbulent years until order was established by Vigilance Committees, first in 1851, and again in 1856. Then followed a period of more orderly growth, and the foundations of the great commerce and industry of today were laid.

In 1906, San Francisco experienced the nation's most destructive earthquake, which, together with the fire that followed, practically destroyed the city. The city was quickly rebuilt and grew rapidly as a leading transportation, industrial, and cultural center. In the 19th century, the American explorer and soldier John C. Frémont, known as The Pathfinder, named the entrance to the bay the Golden Gate, and the famous bright orange Golden Gate Bridge was dedicated in May 1937.

A vital part of the economic and cultural fabric of northern California, the port of San Francisco covers 7½ miles of waterfront. The port is home to a broad range of commercial, maritime, and public activities. Its major shipping terminals serve shipping lines from around the world. Fisherman's Wharf, Alcatraz, Hyde St. Pier, and Pier 39 all make the port of San Francisco one of the world's leading visitor destinations.

Small businesses have a very important place in the economy. More than 80% of the city's 33,800 businesses have fewer than 15 employees. The high-technology industries of electronics and biotechnology are well represented throughout the Bay Area. With nearly 30% of the worldwide biotechnology labor force, and 360 biotech firms, the Bay Area has been appropriately called "Bionic Bay." Tourism is one of San Francisco's largest industries and the largest employer of city residents. Nearly 13.4 million persons visit San Francisco each year, and annual visitor spending is $231 million, providing 66,400 jobs.

The military has played an important role in San Francisco and the Bay Area's economies, but its impact will decline due to defense cutbacks. San Francisco is also the banking and financial center of the West and is home to a Federal Reserve Bank and a United States Mint. More than 60 foreign banks maintain offices there.

Famous natives: Gracie Allen, comedienne; Luis Walter Alvarez, Nobel Prize winner in physics; David Belasco, dramatist and producer; Mel Blanc, actor and voice specialist; Rosemary Casals, tennis player; Isadora Duncan, dancer; Clint Eastwood, actor; Robert Frost, poet; Rube Goldberg, cartoonist; William Randolph Hearst, publisher; Bruce Lee, actor; Mervyn LeRoy, director; Jack London, novelist; Johnny Mathis, singer; Lloyd Nolan, actor; O. J. Simpson, football player; Robert G. Sproul, educator; Irving Stone, novelist; Natalie Wood, actress.

San Jose, Calif.

Mayor: Ron Gonzales (to Dec. 31, 2002)
Acting City Manager: Debra Figone
1998 population (est): 861,284 (11)[1]
1990 census population (rank): 782,248 (11);
  % change, 10.1; **Male,** 397,709; **Female,** 384,539;
  White, 491,280 (62.8%); **Black,** 36,790 (4.7%);
  American Indian, Eskimo, or Aleut, 5,416 (0.7%);
  Asian or Pacific Islander, 152,815 (19.5%); **Other

race,** 95,947; **Hispanic origin,** 208,388 (26.6%). **1990 population under 18:** 26.7%; **65 and over:** 7.2%; **median age:** 30.4.
Land area: 180.8 sq mi. (468.27 sq km); **Alt.:** Highest, 4,372 ft.; lowest, sea level
Avg. daily temp.: Jan., 49.5° F; July, 68.8° F
Churches: 403; **City-owned parks and playgrounds:** 152 (3,136 ac.); **Radio stations:** 14; **Television stations:** 4
Civilian Labor Force: 420,686; **Unemployed:** 33,484, **Percent:** 8.0; **Per capita personal income (PMSA) 1992:** $25,924[1]
Chamber of Commerce: San Jose Chamber of Commerce, One Paseo de San Antonio, San Jose, Calif. 95113

1. 1999 est. population: 909,100

San Jose, the third-largest city in California and seat of Santa Clara County, is located in the northern part of the state in the Santa Clara Valley near San Francisco Bay, 50 miles south of downtown San Francisco.

San Jose was founded on Nov. 29, 1777, by Spanish colonizers who named the settlement Pueblo de San José de Guadalupe in honor of Saint Joseph and after the Guadalupe River on which the pueblo (town) was situated. San Jose was the first city to be established in California.

After California became a U.S. territory in 1847, San Jose was the state capital from 1849 to 1852 and was incorporated as a city in 1850. It developed commercially as a supply base for gold prospectors and, when the railroad connected it with San Francisco in 1864, it became the distribution point for agricultural products from the Santa Clara Valley.

Today, the city continues to be the distribution and food-processing center for the surrounding rich agricultural region, which produces seasonal fruits and grapes. More than 50 wineries grace the valley.

San Jose is the capital of Silicon Valley (Santa Clara), the nation's center of high technology, where more than 3,000 high-tech companies are located. Silicon Valley is also one of the world's leading centers for medical treatment and research. Heart transplants, gene splicing, and transportable baby incubators were developed there.

San Jose has healthy retail, transportation, and tourism industries and is the primary center for real estate and industrial development in the area.

Famous natives: "Fatty" Arbuckle, actor; Chuck Berry, singer and guitarist; Cesar Chavez, labor leader; Peggy Fleming, figure skater; Farley Granger, actor; Edmund Lowe, actor; Jim Plunkett, football player.

Seattle, Wash.

Mayor: Paul Schell (to Dec. 31, 2001)
1998 est. population (rank): 536,978 (22)
1990 census population (rank): 516,259 (21);
  % change, 4.0; **Male,** 252,042; **Female,** 264,217;
  White, 388,858 (75.3%); **Black,** 51,948 (10.1%);
  American Indian, Eskimo, or Aleut, 7,326 (1.4%);
  Asian or Pacific Islander, 60,819 (11.8%); **Other race,** 7,308 (1.4%); **Hispanic origin,** 18,349 (3.6%).
  1990 population under 18: 16.5%; **65 and over:** 15.2%; **median age:** 34.9.
Land area: 144.6 sq mi. (375 sq km); **Alt.:** Highest, 521 ft.; lowest, sea level
Avg. daily temp.: Jan., 42.2° F; July, 67.6° F
Churches: Roman Catholic, 35; Jewish, 12; Protestant, 447; others, 42; **City-owned parks, playgrounds, etc.:** 397 (6,000+ ac.); **Radio stations:** AM, 15; FM, 22; **Television stations:** 6

Civilian Labor Force (1999): (3 counties) 1,206,089; **Unemployed:** 37,389, **Percent:** 3.1; **Per capita personal income:** $35,019
Chamber of Commerce: Greater Seattle Chamber of Commerce, 1301 5th Ave., Suite 2400, Seattle, Wash. 98101-2603

Seattle is the largest city in Washington and the seat of King County. A city of steep hills, Seattle lies in western Washington between two bodies of water—Puget Sound on the west and Lake Washington on the east. Its fine landlocked harbor has made Seattle one of the major ports in the United States.

Seattle was first settled by five pioneer families from Illinois at Alki Point at the south end of Elliott Bay in 1851. They moved in 1852 to the eastern shore of the bay and laid out a town in 1853. It was named Seattle after a friendly Suquamish Indian chief (Seattle is only an approximation of his name).

Seattle successfully withstood an Indian attack in 1856 and was incorporated as a city in 1869. A disastrous fire almost destroyed the entire business district in 1889. When the Great Northern Railway arrived in 1893, the city became a major rail terminus and it grew rapidly. It was a boom town during the Alaska gold rush of 1897 and continued to prosper as a major Pacific port of entry with the opening of the Panama Canal in 1914.

Seattle is the region's commercial and transportation hub and the center of manufacturing, trade, and finance. Its important diversified industries include aircraft, lumber and forest products, fishing, high technology, food processing, boat building, machinery, fabricated metals, chemicals, pharmaceuticals, and apparel.

Famous natives: Chester Carlson, Xerox inventor; Carol Channing, actress; Judy Collins, singer; Fred Couples, golfer; Gail Devers, athlete; Frances Farmer, actress; William Gates, Microsoft founder; June Havoc, actress; Jimi Hendrix, guitarist; Robert Joffrey, choreographer; Gypsy Rose Lee, entertainer; Mary Livingstone, comedienne; Kevin McCarthy, actor; Mary McCarthy, novelist; Jeff Smith, food expert; Martha Wright, singer.

Tucson, Ariz.

Mayor: Bob Walkup (to Dec. 2003)
1998 est. population (rank): 460,466 (32)[1]
1990 census population (rank): 405,390 (33); **% change,** 10.8; **Male,** 197,319; **Female,** 208,071; **White,** 305,055 (74.6%); **Black,** 17,366 (4.3%); **American Indian, Eskimo, or Aleut,** 6,464 (1.6%); **Asian or Pacific Islander,** 8,901 (2.2%); **Other race,** 67,604; **Hispanic origin,** 118,595 (29.3%). **1990 population under 18:** 24.5%; **65 and over:** 12.6%; **median age:** 30.6.
Land area: 162 sq mi. (419 sq km); **Alt.:** 2,400 ft.
Avg. daily temp.: Jan., 51.1° F; July, 86.2° F
Churches: Protestant, 340; Roman Catholic, 42; other, 150; **City-owned parks and parkways:** (25,349 ac.); **Radio stations:** AM, 15; FM, 17; **Television stations:** 3 commercial; 1 educational; 3 other
Civilian Labor Force (1997): 364,700; **Unemployed:** 10,300, **Percent:** 2.8; **Per capita personal income (1997):** $22,307
Chamber of Commerce: Tucson Metropolitan Chamber of Commerce, P.O. Box 991, Tucson, Ariz. 85702

1. 1997 est. population: 452,298.

Tucson is the second-largest city in Arizona and the seat of Pima County. It is located in the southeastern part of the state on the Santa Cruz River.

The site was originally settled by the prehistoric Hohokam Indians (300 B.C.–A.D.1400s). The first

Europeans to visit the area were Spanish missionaries in the 17th century. In 1700, the Jesuit missionary explorer Father Eusebio Francisco Kino founded the mission of San Xavier del Bac close to the Papago Indian village of Stjukshon (later called Tucson). Stjukshon is an Indian word meaning "village of the dark spring at the foot of the mountain." The Papago Indians are descendants of the ancient Hohokam peoples.

In 1776, Spanish colonists from Mexico constructed a presidio (fort) at Tucson as protection against the hostile Apache Indians and also established the mission of San Jose de Tucson nearby. Tucson remained a military outpost under Spanish rule and later Mexican control until the area was sold to the United States as part of the Gadsden Purchase in 1853. Tucson was the capital of the Arizona Territory from 1867 to 1877. It was incorporated as a city in 1877. The town grew rapidly when the Southern Pacific Railroad arrived in 1880 and silver and copper deposits were discovered nearby.

Tucson is a popular vacation and health resort due to its sunny, mild, and dry climate and unique desert location. Tourism is important to the city's economy. Major industries include aerospace and missile production, high technology, optics, biotechnology, environmental technology, software, and electronics. Tucson is also the commercial center for the surrounding area's agriculture and mining industries. The city is the home of the University of Arizona.

Famous natives: Rose E. Bird, jurist; Dennis De Concini, senator; Barbara Eden, actress; Linda Ronstadt, singer.

Tulsa, Okla.

Mayor: M. Susan Savage (to May 2002)
1998 est. population (rank): 381,393 (42)
1990 census population (rank): 367,302 (43); **% change,** 3.8; **Male,** 175,538; **Female,** 191,764; **White,** 291,444 (79.3%); **Black,** 49,825 (13.6%); **American Indian, Eskimo, or Aleut,** 17,091 (4.7%); **Asian or Pacific Islander,** 5,133 (1.4%); **Other race,** 3,809; **Hispanic origin,** 9,564 (2.6%). **1990 population under 18:** 24.4%; **65 and over:** 12.7%; **median age:** 33.1.
Land area: 186.9 sq mi. (484 sq km); **Alt.:** 674 ft.
Avg. daily temp.: Jan., 35.2° F; July, 83.2° F
Churches: Protestant, 290; Roman Catholic, 40; Jewish, 3; others, 4; **City parks and playgrounds:** 131 (6,000 ac.); **Radio stations:** AM, 10; FM, 16; **Television stations:** 7 commercial; 1 PBS; 123 cable
Civilian Labor Force (1999): 387,500; **Unemployed:** 14,100, **Percent:** 3.4; **Per capita personal income (1999):** $26,687
Chamber of Commerce: Metropolitan Tulsa Chamber of Commerce, 616 S. Boston, Tulsa, Okla. 74119

Tulsa, the second-largest city in Oklahoma and seat of Tulsa County, is located in the northeastern part of the state on the Arkansas River.

Tulsa was settled in the 1830s by Creek Indians from Alabama who were forcibly sent to the area (then part of Indian Territory) under the Indian Removal Act of 1830. Creek medicine men planted ashes from their old home at the new site, and the Creeks named their new village "Tulsy," meaning old town, in memory of their former home in Tallassee, Ala. In time, the village became the town of Tulsa.

The coming of the first railroad in 1882 attracted white settlers to Tulsa and the town developed into a cattle-shipping center. When enormous oil deposits were discovered at nearby Red Fork in 1901 and at Glenn Pool in 1905, the city experienced rapid growth as a center of a booming petroleum industry. Tulsa was incorporated as a city in 1898 and chartered in 1908.

Tulsa is the center of the state's petroleum industry and has a diversified economy. Important industries include aerospace, chemicals, computer parts, automobile glass, fabricated metals, and industrial machinery. The city became a major inland port when the Tulsa port of Catoosa opened in 1971.

Famous natives: Garth Brooks, singer; Blake Edwards, director; Paul Harvey, commentator; Jennifer Jones, actress; Henry R. Kravis, investment banker; Daniel Patrick Moynihan, senator; Tony Randall, actor; Alfre Woodard, actress; Judy Woodruff, journalist.

Virginia Beach, Va.

Mayor: Meyera E. Obendorf (to June 2004)
1998 est. population (rank): 432,380 (34)
1990 census population (rank): 393,069 (37);
  % change, 10.0; **Male,** 199,571; **Female,** 193,498;
  White, 316,408 (80.5%); **Black,** 54,671 (13.9%);
  American Indian, Eskimo, or Aleut, 1,384 (0.4%);
  Asian or Pacific Islander, 17,025 (4.3%); **Other race,** 3,581; **Hispanic origin,** 12,137 (3.1%); **1990 population under 18:** 28.0%; **65 and over:** 5.9%; **median age:** 28.9.
Land area: 258.7 sq mi. (670 sq km); **Alt.:** 12 ft.
Avg. daily temp.: Jan., 39.9° F; July, 78.4° F
Churches: Protestant, 235; Catholic, 13; Jewish, 5;
  City-owned parks: 182 (1,748 ac.); **Radio stations:** AM 18, FM 26; **Television stations:** 4 commercial, 1 PBS, 1 cable
Civilian Labor Force: 216,590; **Unemployed:** 5,055, **Percent:** 2.3; **Per capita personal income (MSA) 1992:** $18,077[1]
Chamber of Commerce: Hampton Roads Chamber of Commerce, 4512 Virginia Beach Blvd., Virginia Beach, Va., 23463

1. Norfolk–Virginia Beach–Newport News.
Virginia Beach, the largest city in Virginia, is located in the southeasternmost portion of the state on the Atlantic coastline. It is independent and is not part of any county.

The first English settlers to set foot in America landed at Cape Henry at the tip of Virginia Beach on April 29, 1607. They were led by John Smith on his way to establishing Jamestown. The first permanent settlement within the city limits was made at Lynnhaven Bay in 1621. Cape Henry became an important port for British merchant ships calling on America, and it was here that the French Fleet led by Admiral Comte de Grasse blockaded the British Fleet during the American Revolution.

Virginia Beach gained its reputation as a famous vacation resort in the 19th century, following the building of a railroad connecting its oceanfront with Norfolk and the construction of its first hotel in 1883. Virginia Beach was incorporated as a town in 1906 and as a city in 1952. In 1963, Princess Anne County and Virginia Beach merged, giving the present city an area of 310 square miles of oceanfront.

Tourism is the mainstay of the economy, and 2.5 million people visit Virginia Beach overnight each year. Virginia Beach's economy is supported by four nearby military bases and diverse industries, including agriculture (165 farms), computer software, engineering, and technical services.

Famous natives and residents: V. C. Andrews, novelist; Raymond Brian Buckland, occult writer; Ann Woodruff Compton, news correspondent; D. J. Dozier, football and baseball player; George Eastman, inventor; Juice Newton, singer; Kenneth S. Reightler, Jr., astronaut; Pat Robertson, evangelist; Henry Walke, naval officer in Mexican and Civil wars; Pernell "Sweet Pea" Whitaker, boxer; Skip Wilkins, wheelchair athlete.

Washington, D.C.

Created municipal corporation: Feb. 21, 1871
Mayor: Anthony Williams (to Jan. 2003)
Motto: *Justitia omnibus* (Justice to all)
Flower: American beauty rose; **Tree:** Scarlet oak
1998 est. population: 523,124 (23)
1990 census population (rank): 606,900 (19);
  % change, –13.8; **Male,** 282,970; **Female,** 323,930;
  White, 179,667 (29.6%); **Black,** 399,604 (65.8%);
  American Indian, Eskimo, or Aleut, 1,466 (0.2%);
  Asian or Pacific Islander, 11,214 (1.8%); **Other race,** 14,949; **Hispanic origin,** 32,710 (5.4%)
Land area: 68.25 sq mi. (177 sq km); **Alt.:** Highest, 420 ft.; lowest, sea level
Avg. daily temp.: Jan., 35.2° F; July, 78.9° F
Churches: Protestant, 610; Roman Catholic, 132; Jewish, 9; **City parks:** 753 (7,725 ac.); **Radio stations:** AM, 9; FM, 38; **Television stations:** 19
Civilian Labor Force: 276,000; **Unemployed:** 23,000, **Percent:** 8.4; **Per capita personal income (PMSA) 1992:** $26,817[1]
Board of Trade: Greater Washington Board of Trade, 1129 20th Street, N.W., Washington, D.C. 20036
Chamber of Commerce: D.C. Chamber of Commerce, 1319 F St., NW, Washington, D.C. 20004

1. Washington, D.C.–Md.–Va.–W.Va.
The District of Columbia—identical with the City of Washington—is the capital of the United States. It is located between Virginia and Maryland on the Potomac River. The district is named after Columbus.

D.C. history began in 1790 when Congress directed selection of a new capital site, 100 square miles, along the Potomac. When the site was determined, it included 30.75 square miles on the Virginia side of the river. In 1846, however, Congress returned that area to Virginia, leaving the 68.25 square miles ceded by Maryland in 1788. The seat of government was transferred from Philadelphia to Washington on Dec. 1, 1800, and President John Adams became the first resident in the White House.

The city was planned and partly laid out by Maj. Pierre Charles L'Enfant, a French engineer. This work was perfected and completed by Maj. Andrew Ellicott and Benjamin Banneker, a freeborn black man, who was an astronomer and mathematician. In 1814, during the War of 1812, a British force burned the capital including the White House.

Until Nov. 3, 1967, the District of Columbia was administered by three commissioners appointed by the president. On that day, a government consisting of a mayor-commissioner and a 9-member council, all appointed by the president with the approval of the Senate, took office. On May 7, 1974, the citizens of the District of Columbia approved a Home Rule Charter, giving them an elected mayor and 13-member council—their first elected municipal government in more than a century. The district also has one non-voting member in the House of Representatives and an elected Board of Education.

On Aug. 22, 1978, Congress passed a proposed constitutional amendment to give Washington, D.C., voting representation in the Congress. The amendment had to be ratified by at least 28 state legislatures within seven years to become effective. It died in 1985.

A petition asking for the district's admission to the Union as the 51st state was filed in Congress on Sept. 9, 1983. The district is continuing this drive for statehood.

The federal government and tourism are the mainstays of the city's economy, and many unions, business, professional, and nonprofit organizations are headquartered there.

Famous natives: Edward Albee, playwright; Billie Burke, comedienne; Ina Claire, actress; John Foster Dulles, statesman; Duke Ellington, musician; Jane Greer, actress; Goldie Hawn, actress; Helen Hayes, actress; J. Edgar Hoover, former director of the F.B.I.; William Hurt, actor; Noor al-Hussein, queen of Jordan; Michael Learned, actress; Roger Mudd, newscaster; Eleanor Holmes Norton, government official; Chita Rivera, dancer and actress; Leonard Rose, cellist; John Philip Sousa, composer; Frances Sternhagen, actress.

Top 50 Cities in the U.S. by Estimated 1998 Population and Rank

	7/1/98 population estimate	4/1/90 population census	Numeric population change 1990–1998	Percent population change 1990–1998	Size rank 1990	Size rank 1998
New York, N.Y.	7,420,166	7,322,564	97,602	1.3%	1	1
Los Angeles, Calif.	3,597,556	3,485,557	111,999	3.2	2	2
Chicago, Ill.	2,802,079	2,783,726	18,353	0.7	3	3
Houston, Tex.	1,786,691	1,654,348	132,343	8.0	4	4
Philadelphia, Pa.	1,436,287	1,585,577	−149,290	−9.4	5	5
San Diego, Calif.	1,220,666	1,110,623	110,043	9.9	6	6
Phoenix, Ariz.	1,198,064	988,015	210,049	21.3	9	7
San Antonio, Tex.	1,114,130	976,514	137,616	14.1	10	8
Dallas, Tex.	1,075,894	1,007,618	68,276	6.8	8	9
Detroit, Mich.	970,196	1,027,974	−57,778	−5.6	7	10
San Jose, Calif.	861,284	782,224	79,060	10.1	11	11
San Francisco, Calif.	745,774	723,959	21,815	3.0	14	12
Indianapolis (remainder),[1] Ind.	741,304	731,278	10,026	1.4	13	13
Jacksonville (remainder),[1] Fla.	693,630	635,230	58,400	9.2	15	14
Columbus, Ohio	670,234	632,945	37,289	5.9	16	15
Baltimore, Md.	645,593	736,014	−90,421	−12.3	12	16
El Paso, Tex.	615,032	515,342	99,690	19.3	22	17
Memphis, Tenn.	603,507	618,652	−15,145	−2.4	18	18
Milwaukee, Wis.	578,364	628,088	−49,724	−7.9	17	19
Boston, Mass.	555,447	574,283	−18,836	−3.3	20	20
Austin, Tex.	552,434	472,020	80,414	17.0	27	21
Seattle, Wash.	536,978	516,259	20,719	4.0	21	22
Washington, D.C.	523,124	606,900	−83,776	−13.8	19	23
Nashville-Davidson (remainder),[1] Tenn.	510,274	488,366	21,908	4.5	25	24
Charlotte, N.C.	504,637	419,558	85,079	20.3	33	25
Portland, Ore.	503,891	485,975	17,916	3.7	26	26
Denver, Colo.	499,055	467,610	31,445	6.7	28	27
Cleveland, Ohio	495,817	505,616	−9,799	−1.9	23	28
Fort Worth, Tex.	491,801	447,619	44,182	9.9	29	29
Oklahoma City, Okla.	472,221	444,724	27,497	6.2	30	30
New Orleans, La.	465,538	496,938	−31,400	−6.3	24	31
Tucson, Ariz.	460,466	415,444	45,022	10.8	34	32
Kansas City, Mo.	441,574	434,829	6,745	1.6	31	33
Virginia Beach, Va.	432,380	393,089	39,291	10.0	37	34
Long Beach, Calif.	430,905	429,321	1,584	0.4	32	35
Albuquerque, N.M.	419,311	384,915	34,396	8.9	38	36
Las Vegas, Nev.	404,288	258,877	145,411	56.2	63	37
Sacramento, Calif.	404,168	369,365	34,803	9.4	42	38
Atlanta, Ga.	403,819	393,929	9,890	2.5	36	39
Fresno, Calif.	398,133	354,091	44,042	12.4	47	40
Honolulu CDP,[2] Hawaii	395,789	377,059	18,730	5.0	39	41
Tulsa, Okla.	381,393	367,302	14,091	3.8	44	42
Omaha, Neb.	371,291	344,463	26,828	7.8	48	43
Miami, Fla.	368,624	358,648	9,976	2.8	46	44
Oakland, Calif.	365,874	372,242	−6,368	−1.7	40	45
Mesa, Ariz.	360,076	289,199	70,877	24.5	53	46
Minneapolis, Minn.	351,731	368,383	−16,652	−4.5	43	47
Colorado Springs, Colo.	344,987	280,430	64,557	23.0	54	48
Pittsburgh, Pa.	340,520	369,879	−29,359	−7.9	41	49
St. Louis, Mo.	339,316	396,685	−57,369	−14.5	35	50

1. "Remainder" indicates that the city is part of a consolidated city-county government and that the populations of other incorporated places in the county have been excluded from the totals shown here. 2. Honolulu CDP (census designated place) is not incorporated as a city but is recognized for census purposes as a large urban place. Honolulu CDP is coextensive with Honolulu Judicial District within the city and county of Honolulu. NOTE: 1990 population figures in this table reflect most recent revisions by the Census Bureau. They are not the same as those used in the individual city profiles. *Source:* U.S. Census Bureau.

Tabulated Data on City Governments

City	Mayor		City manager's salary[1,2]	Council or Commission			
	Term, years	Salary[1]		Name	Members	Term, years	Salary[1,3]
Albuquerque, N.M.	4	$ 83,491	$109,096	Council	9	4	$ 7,028
Atlanta, Ga.	4	100,000	—	Council	18	4	22,000
Austin, Tex.	3	35,006	$171,018	Council	7	3	45,011
Baltimore, Md.	4	125,000	—	Council	19	4	48,000
Boston, Mass.	4	125,000	—	Council	13	2	62,500
Charlotte, N.C.	2	30,635	144,387	Council	11	2	21,425
Chicago, Ill.	4	192,100	—	Council	50	4	85,000
Cleveland, Ohio	4	101,286	—	Council	21	4	47,751
Colorado Springs, Colo.	4	6,250	137,000	Council	9	4	6,200
Columbus, Ohio	4	98,000	—	Council	7	4	25,000
Dallas, Tex.	2	50[4]	179,001	Council	15	2	50[4]
Denver, Colo.	4	109,992	—	Council	13	4	55,800
Detroit, Mich.	4	143,000	—	Council	9	4	66,000
El Paso, Tex.	2	25,000	—	Council	9[5]	2	15,000
Fort Worth, Tex.	2	75[4]	170,112	Council	9[5]	2	75[4]
Fresno, Calif.	4	99,369	120,000	Council	8[5]	4	33,120
Honolulu, Hawaii	4	110,000	105,000[6]	Council	9	4	42,500
Houston, Tex.	2	166,500	—	Council	14	2	44,400
Indianapolis, Ind.	4	95,000	—	Council	29	4	11,400
Jacksonville, Fla.	2	110,000	105,000[7]	Council	19	4	24,000
Kansas City, Mo.	4	83,208	126,000	Council	13[5]	4	41,592
Las Vegas, Nev.	4	75,800	112,499	Council	4	4	33,480
Long Beach, Calif.	4	93,238	181,500	Council	9	4	23,310
Los Angeles, Calif.	4[8]	139,607	193,224[6]	Council	15	4	107,390
Memphis, Tenn.	4	110,000	98,000[6]	Council	13	4	20,100
Mesa, Ariz.	4	33,600	144,860	Council	6	4	16,800
Miami, Fla.	4	97,000	100,000	Commission	5	4	5,000
Milwaukee, Wis.	4	120,548	—	Council	17	4	60,074
Minneapolis, Minn.	4	83,775	114,228	Council	13	4	63,722
Nashville, Tenn.	4	75,000	8,900[9]	Council	40	4	6,900
New Orleans, La.	4	90,000	57,900	Council	7	4	42,500
New York, N.Y.	4	195,000	156,000[9]	Council	51	4	90,000
Oakland, Calif.	4	97,740	207,505[10]	Council	9[5]	4	60,000[8,11]
Oklahoma City, Okla.	4	2,000	100,000	Council	8	4	20[12]
Omaha, Neb.	4	90,618	—	Council	7	4	26,423
Philadelphia, Pa.	4	110,000	95,000[7]	Council	17	4	65,000
Phoenix, Ariz.	4	56,000	183,810	Council	9[5]	4	35,999
Pittsburgh, Pa.	4	85,751	—	Council	9	4	48,894
Portland, Ore.	4	83,416	—	Council	4	4	70,261
Sacramento, Calif,	4	1,652[13]	124,963	Council	9	4	1,251[13]
St. Louis, Mo.	4	97,422	—	Board of Alderman	29	4	28,745
San Antonio, Tex.	2	3,000[14]	160,422	Council	11[5]	2	20[4]
San Diego, Calif.	4	80,913	172,692	Council	8	4	56,479
San Francisco, Calif.	4	155,688	155,052	Bd. of Supvrs.	11	4	37,584
San Jose, Calif.	4	87,550	158,000	Council	10	4	58,240
Seattle, Wash.	4	122,691	—	Council	9	4	75,505
Tucson, Ariz.	4	42,000	127,000	Council	7[5]	4	24,000
Tulsa, Okla.	4	70,000	—	Council	9	2	12,000
Virginia Beach, Va.	4	20,000	143,116	Council	11	4	18,000
Washington, D.C.	4	90,705	115,700	Council	13	4	71,885

1. Annual salary unless otherwise indicated; does not include additional payments for expenses, special sessions, etc. 2. City manager's term is indefinite and at will of council (or mayor). 3. In some cities, leaders receive a higher salary. 4. Per council meeting, with an annual cap. 5. Including mayor. 6. Appointed by mayor, approved by council. 7. Appointed by mayor; not subject to council confirmation. 8. At mayor's request; limited to 2 terms. 9. No city manager; salary is for deputy or vice mayor. 10. Denotes average based on range. 11. Council also serves as the Redevelopment Agency for which there is additional compensation. 12. Per council meeting; not to exceed 5 meetings a month. 13. Per month. 14. Plus council pay. *Source:* Questionnaires to the cities.

U.S. Cities with Population Over 50,000

ZIP codes provided below indicate the primary ZIP code for each city; please consult a ZIP code directory to find the appropriate ZIP code for a particular address.

City	ZIP code	1998 pop. est.	1998 rank	City	ZIP code	1998 pop. est.	1998 rank
Alabama				Huntington Beach	92647	195,316	87
Birmingham	35203	252,997	66	Huntington Park	90255	58,209	466
Decatur	35601	54,694	508	Inglewood	90311	111,618	189
Dothan	36302	57,069	480	Irvine	92713	136,446	147
Hoover	35216	59,551	448	Laguna Niguel	92607	53,615	522
Huntsville	35813	175,979	109	La Habra	90631	54,294	512
Mobile	36601	202,181	82	La Mesa	90241	55,986	498
Montgomery	36119	197,014	85	Lake Forest	92630	79,923	303
Tuscaloosa	35401	83,376	286	Lakewood	90714	76,222	323
Alaska				Lancaster	93534	118,518	172
Anchorage	99501	254,982	65	Livermore	94550	72,284	351
Arizona				Lodi	95240	56,173	497
Chandler	85225	160,329	121	Long Beach	90809	430,905	35
Flagstaff	86004	56,657	489	Los Angeles	90052	3,597,556	2
Gilbert	85234	88,840	261	Lynwood	90262	63,360	412
Glendale	85301	193,482	89	Merced	95340	59,380	449
Mesa	85201	360,076	46	Milpitas	95035	60,738	437
Peoria	85345	87,048	268	Mission Viejo	92690	95,440	237
Phoenix	85026	1,198,064	7	Modesto	95350	182,016	103
Scottsdale	85251	195,394	86	Montebello	90640	60,530	440
Tempe	85282	167,622	114	Monterey Park	91754	62,531	418
Tucson	85726	460,466	32	Moreno Valley	92388	144,613	135
Yuma	85364	62,433	419	Mountain View	94041	72,192	352
Arkansas				Napa	94558	66,548	386
Fayetteville	72701	53,300	529	National City	92050	54,994	507
Fort Smith	72917	75,637	329	Newport Beach	92658	72,416	350
Jonesboro	72401	52,250	541	Norwalk	90650	97,518	231
Little Rock	72231	175,303	111	Oakland	94615	365,874	45
North Little Rock	72114	59,184	454	Oceanside	92054	152,367	127
Pine Bluff	71601	52,968	532	Ontario	91761	147,188	134
California				Orange	92613	123,820	164
Alameda	94501	78,695	311	Oxnard	93030	154,622	123
Alhambra	91715	84,124	280	Palmdale	93550	100,157	218
Anaheim	92803	295,153	57	Palo Alto	94303	59,098	457
Antioch	94509	81,428	292	Paramount	90723	51,131	551
Apple Valley	92307	56,440	492	Pasadena	91109	134,587	149
Arcadia	91006	50,157	570	Petaluma	94952	50,913	557
Bakersfield	93380	210,284	79	Pico Rivera	90660	60,683	439
Baldwin Park	91706	71,953	353	Pittsburg	94565	52,796	536
Bellflower	90706	63,609	410	Pleasanton	94566	64,039	406
Berkeley	94704	108,101	204	Pomona	91768	135,659	148
Buena Park	90622	73,373	346	Rancho Cucamonga	91739	120,047	170
Burbank	91505	97,430	232	Redding	96049	77,944	315
Camarillo	93010	59,348	450	Redlands	92373	67,309	382
Carlsbad	92008	74,732	333	Redondo Beach	92077	63,075	414
Carson	90745	87,647	266	Redwood City	94063	73,438	344
Cerritos	90703	53,883	518	Rialto	92376	83,933	283
Chino	91710	65,766	392	Richmond	94802	93,470	243
Chula Vista	92010	160,553	120	Riverside	92517	262,140	61
Clovis	93612	63,962	407	Rosemead	91770	53,186	530
Compton	90221	92,269	249	Roseville	95678	71,609	358
Concord	94520	117,708	174	Sacramento	95813	404,168	38
Corona	91720	112,815	186	Salinas	93907	121,458	168
Costa Mesa	92628	102,348	211	San Bernardino	92403	186,402	97
Daly City	94015	99,231	224	San Buenaventura (Ventura)	93001	98,366	227
Davis	95616	54,405	511	San Diego	92199	1,220,666	6
Diamond Bar	91765	54,470	510	San Francisco	94188	745,774	12
Downey	90241	93,653	242	San Jose	95101	861,284	11
El Cajon	92020	94,259	239	San Leandro	94577	74,387	337
El Monte	91731	111,653	188	San Mateo	94402	91,282	253
Encinitas	92024	59,943	444	San Rafael	94901	51,057	553
Escondido	92025	120,578	169	Santa Ana	92799	305,955	55
Fairfield	94533	89,854	257	Santa Barbara	93102	86,645	271
Fontana	92335	109,777	199	Santa Clara	95050	100,370	217
Fountain Valley	92708	56,679	487	Santa Clarita	91380	127,001	159
Fremont	94537	204,298	81	Santa Cruz	95060	52,853	535
Fresno	93706	398,133	40	Santa Maria	93454	68,121	375
Fullerton	92634	121,954	167	Santa Monica	90406	89,522	258
Garden Grove	92642	151,264	129	Santa Rosa	95402	126,891	160
Gardena	90247	53,642	519	Santee	92071	57,740	471
Glendale	92109	185,086	100	Simi Valley	93065	110,463	195
Hawthorne	90250	73,413	345	South Gate	90280	88,384	263
Hayward	94544	128,872	155	South San Francisco	94080	58,829	459
Hemet	92543	52,781	537	Stockton	95213	240,143	69
Hesperia	92345	62,309	422	Sunnyvale	94086	127,444	158

City	ZIP code	1998 pop. est.	1998 rank	City	ZIP code	1998 pop. est.	1998 rank
Thousand Oaks	91359	117,199	175	Tallahassee	32301	136,628	146
Torrance	90510	137,533	142	Tamarac	33309	52,929	534
Turlock	95380	50,266	568	Tampa	33630	289,156	58
Tustin	92681	64,370	401	West Palm Beach	33406	76,308	321
Union City	94587	64,085	405	**Georgia**			
Upland	91786	67,826	379	Albany	31706	77,545	316
Vacaville	95687	83,362	287	Athens–Clarke County (remainder)	30601	89,361	259
Vallejo	94590	111,539	190	Atlanta	30304	403,819	39
Victorville	92392	68,914	369	Augusta-Richmond County (remainder)	30901	187,689	96
Visalia	93277	89,308	260				
Vista	92083	80,909	298	Columbus (remainder)	31908	182,219	102
Walnut Creek	94596	64,306	402	Macon	31201	114,336	183
West Covina	91790	99,455	220	Marietta	30060	51,362	548
Westminster	92684	84,042	282	Roswell	30075	57,102	478
Whittier	90605	79,135	308	Savannah	31402	131,674	151
Yorba Linda	92686	60,156	441	**Hawaii**			
Colorado				Honolulu CDP	96820	395,789	41
Arvada	80001	97,610	230	**Idaho**			
Aurora	80010	250,604	67	Boise City	83708	157,452	122
Boulder	80302	90,543	256	Pocatello	83201	53,074	531
Colorado Springs	80910	344,987	48	**Illinois**			
Denver	80201	499,055	27	Arlington Heights	60005	76,522	320
Fort Collins	80521	108,905	200	Aurora	60505	124,736	162
Greeley	80631	70,434	362	Bloomington	61701	58,841	458
Lakewood	80215	136,883	145	Bolingbrook	60440	54,288	513
Longmont	80501	62,078	424	Champaign	61820	64,280	404
Pueblo	81003	107,301	205	Chicago	60607	2,802,079	3
Thornton	80229	74,139	341	Cicero	60650	71,289	359
Westminster	80030	95,691	236	Decatur	62523	79,972	302
Connecticut				Des Plaines	60018	55,272	504
Bridgeport	06602	137,425	143	Downers Grove	60515	51,716	545
Bristol	06010	59,158	455	Elgin	60120	87,507	267
Danbury	06810	65,829	391	Evanston	60201	71,928	354
Hartford	06101	131,523	153	Joliet	60436	92,285	248
Meriden	06450	56,667	488	Mount Prospect	60056	53,581	525
New Britain	06050	70,492	361	Naperville	60540	117,091	177
New Haven	06511	123,189	165	Oak Lawn	60455	57,730	472
Norwalk	06856	78,064	314	Oak Park	60301	50,646	563
Stamford	06910	110,689	193	Peoria	61601	111,148	191
Waterbury	06701	105,346	207	Rockford	61125	143,656	136
West Haven	06616	51,639	546	Schaumburg	60194	74,481	336
Delaware				Skokie	60077	58,628	461
Wilmington	19850	71,678	356	Springfield	62703	117,098	176
District of Columbia				Waukegan	60085	75,999	327
Washington	20066	523,124	23	Wheaton	60187	55,308	503
Florida				**Indiana**			
Boca Raton	33431	71,761	355	Anderson	46011	58,528	463
Boynton Beach	33436	53,607	524	Bloomington	47408	65,065	397
Cape Coral	33990	91,180	254	Evansville	47708	122,779	166
Clearwater	34618	101,474	212	Fort Wayne	46802	185,716	98
Coral Springs	33075	111,744	187	Gary	46401	108,469	201
Davie	33329	62,061	425	Hammond	46320	78,212	312
Daytona Beach	32114	65,136	396	Indianapolis (remainder)	46206	741,304	13
Deerfield Beach	33441	50,921	556	Muncie	47302	67,476	380
Delray Beach	33444	53,618	521	South Bend	46624	99,417	221
Deltona	32725	58,168	468	Terre Haute	47808	53,355	528
Fort Lauderdale	33310	153,728	124	**Iowa**			
Gainesville	32602	92,648	247	Cedar Rapids	52401	114,563	182
Hialeah	33010	211,392	78	Council Bluffs	51501	56,312	495
Hollywood	33022	130,026	154	Davenport	52802	96,842	234
Jacksonville (remainder)	32203	693,630	14	Des Moines	50318	191,293	91
Lakeland	33805	74,204	340	Dubuque	52001	56,467	491
Largo	34640	66,264	388	Iowa City	52240	60,897	434
Lauderhill	33152	50,814	559	Sioux City	51101	82,697	289
Margate	33063	51,268	550	Waterloo	50703	63,703	408
Melbourne	32901	69,057	367	**Kansas**			
Miami	33152	368,624	44	Kansas City	66106	141,297	139
Miami Beach	33119	97,053	233	Lawrence	66044	74,244	339
Miramar	33023	57,215	475	Olathe	66061	85,035	276
North Miami	33261	50,772	560	Overland Park	66204	139,685	140
Orlando	32862	181,175	104	Topeka	66603	118,977	171
Palm Bay	32901	77,486	317	Wichita	67276	329,211	52
Pembroke Pines	33084	115,361	180	**Kentucky**			
Pensacola	32501	58,193	467	Lexington-Fayette	40511	241,749	68
Plantation	33318	81,424	293	Louisville	40231	255,045	64
Pompano Beach	33060	75,982	328	Owensboro	42301	54,041	515
Port St. Lucie	34985	79,351	305	**Louisiana**			
Sarasota	34230	51,035	554	Baton Rouge	70821	211,551	77
St. Petersburg	33730	236,029	70	Bossier City	71111	56,637	490
Sunrise	33322	80,338	301	Kenner	70062	71,641	357

City	ZIP code	1998 pop. est.	1998 rank
Lafayette	70501	113,615	184
Lake Charles	70601	70,766	360
Monroe	71203	53,612	523
New Orleans	70113	465,538	31
Shreveport	71102	188,319	95
Maine			
Portland	04101	62,786	416
Maryland			
Baltimore	21233	645,593	16
Massachusetts			
Boston	02205	555,447	20
Brockton	02402	93,173	245
Cambridge	02139	93,352	244
Chicopee	01020	54,049	514
Fall River	02720	90,654	255
Haverhill	01830	55,321	502
Lawrence	01842	69,420	365
Lowell	01853	101,075	214
Lynn	01901	81,075	297
Malden	02148	52,644	538
Medford	02155	55,981	499
New Bedford	02740	96,353	235
Newton	02164	80,345	300
Quincy	02369	85,752	275
Somerville	02143	74,100	342
Springfield	01101	148,144	132
Taunton	02780	52,553	540
Waltham	02154	58,540	462
Worcester	01613	166,535	116
Michigan			
Ann Arbor	48103	109,967	197
Battle Creek	49016	53,496	527
Dearborn	48120	91,691	251
Dearborn Heights	48127	59,805	445
Detroit	48283	970,196	10
Farmington Hills	48333	79,784	304
Flint	48502	131,668	152
Grand Rapids	49501	185,437	99
Kalamazoo	49001	76,241	322
Lansing	48924	127,825	157
Livonia	48150	101,358	213
Pontiac	48343	68,916	368
Rochester Hills	48309	67,413	381
Roseville	48066	51,390	547
Royal Oak	48068	64,290	403
Saginaw	48605	63,464	411
Southfield	48037	75,104	331
St. Clair Shores	48080	66,056	389
Sterling Heights	48311	124,339	163
Taylor	48180	72,551	348
Troy	48099	79,303	306
Warren	48090	142,455	138
Westland	48185	86,227	272
Wyoming	49509	68,671	371
Minnesota			
Bloomington	55431	86,186	273
Brooklyn Park	55429	63,115	413
Burnsville	55337	59,334	452
Coon Rapids	55433	63,674	409
Duluth	55806	81,228	294
Eagan	55121	60,042	442
Eden Prairie	55343	50,279	567
Minneapolis	55401	351,731	47
Minnetonka	55345	50,952	555
Plymouth	55441	61,509	431
Rochester	55901	78,173	313
St. Cloud	56301	50,745	561
St. Paul	55101	257,284	63
Mississippi			
Gulfport	39500	64,762	400
Jackson	39205	188,419	94
Missouri			
Columbia	65201	78,915	310
Independence	64050	116,832	178
Kansas City	64108	441,574	33
Lee's Summit	64063	66,623	385
Springfield	65801	142,898	137
St. Charles	63301	58,166	469
St. Joseph	64501	69,622	363
St. Louis	63155	339,316	50

City	ZIP code	1998 pop. est.	1998 rank
St. Peters	63303	50,297	566
Montana			
Billings	59101	91,750	250
Great Falls	59401	56,395	494
Missoula	59801	52,239	542
Nebraska			
Lincoln	68501	213,088	76
Omaha	68108	371,291	43
Nevada			
Henderson	89015	152,717	126
Las Vegas	89199	404,288	37
North Las Vegas	89030	94,218	240
Reno	89510	163,334	119
Sparks	89431	62,432	420
New Hampshire			
Manchester	03103	102,524	210
Nashua	03060	82,169	290
New Jersey			
Bayonne	07002	61,051	433
Camden	08101	83,546	285
Clifton	07015	76,180	324
East Orange	07019	69,598	364
Elizabeth	07207	110,661	194
Jersey City	07303	232,429	71
Newark	07101	267,823	60
Passaic	07055	60,817	435
Paterson	07510	148,212	131
Trenton	08650	84,494	279
Union City	07087	57,621	473
Vineland	08360	55,484	501
New Mexico			
Albuquerque	87101	419,311	36
Las Cruces	88001	76,102	326
Rio Rancho	87124	50,041	572
Santa Fe	87501	67,879	378
New York			
Albany	12288	94,305	238
Buffalo	14240	300,717	56
Mount Vernon	10551	66,824	384
New Rochelle	10802	67,225	383
New York	10199	7,420,166	1
Niagara Falls	14302	56,768	485
Rochester	14692	216,887	73
Schenectady	12305	61,698	430
Syracuse	13220	152,215	128
Troy	12180	51,320	549
Utica	13504	59,334	452
Yonkers	10702	190,153	93
North Carolina			
Asheville	28801	63,031	415
Cary	27511	82,071	291
Charlotte	28228	504,637	25
Durham	27701	153,513	125
Fayetteville	28302	77,295	318
Gastonia	28052	56,977	482
Greensboro	27420	197,910	84
Greenville	27833	57,005	481
High Point	27260	76,117	325
Jacksonville	28540	68,380	373
Raleigh	27611	259,423	62
Rocky Mount	27801	56,901	483
Wilmington	28402	68,062	377
Winston-Salem	27102	164,316	118
North Dakota			
Bismarck	58501	54,040	516
Fargo	58102	86,718	270
Ohio			
Akron	44309	215,712	74
Canton	44711	79,259	307
Cincinnati	45234	336,400	51
Cleveland	44101	495,817	28
Cleveland Heights	44118	53,533	526
Columbus	43216	670,234	15
Dayton	45401	167,475	115
Elyria	44035	56,278	496
Euclid	44117	50,644	564
Hamilton	45011	61,808	429
Kettering	45429	57,205	476
Lakewood	44107	55,682	500
Lorain	44052	68,857	370

City	ZIP code	1998 pop. est.	1998 rank
Parma	44129	83,347	288
Springfield	45501	65,568	393
Toledo	43601	312,174	53
Youngstown	44501	84,650	278
Oklahoma			
Broken Arrow	74012	72,564	347
Edmond	73034	64,962	399
Lawton	73501	81,107	295
Midwest City	73125	54,037	517
Norman	73069	93,019	246
Oklahoma City	73125	472,221	30
Tulsa	74103	381,393	42
Oregon			
Beaverton	97005	62,111	423
Corvallis	97330	50,202	569
Eugene	97401	128,240	156
Gresham	97030	85,021	277
Hillsboro	97123	61,111	432
Medford	97501	57,156	477
Portland	97208	503,891	26
Salem	97301	126,702	161
Springfield	97477	50,682	562
Pennsylvania			
Allentown	18101	100,757	215
Bethlehem	18016	69,383	366
Erie	16515	102,640	209
Lancaster	17604	52,951	533
Philadelphia	19104	1,436,287	5
Pittsburgh	15290	340,520	49
Reading	19612	74,762	332
Scranton	18505	74,683	334
Rhode Island			
Cranston	02920	74,521	335
Pawtucket	02860	68,169	374
Providence	02904	150,890	130
Warwick	02886	84,094	281
South Carolina			
Charleston	29423	87,044	269
Columbia	29292	110,840	192
Greenville	29602	56,436	493
North Charleston	29406	68,072	376
South Dakota			
Rapid City	57701	57,513	474
Sioux Falls	57101	116,762	179
Tennessee			
Chattanooga	37421	147,790	133
Clarksville	37040	97,978	228
Jackson	38301	51,115	552
Johnson City	37601	57,079	479
Knoxville	37950	165,540	117
Memphis	38101	603,507	18
Murfreesboro	37130	58,430	464
Nashville-Davidson (remainder)	37229	510,274	24
Texas			
Abilene	79604	108,257	203
Amarillo	79120	171,207	113
Arlington	76010	306,497	54
Austin	78710	552,434	21
Baytown	77520	68,588	372
Bedford	76021	50,148	571
Beaumont	77707	109,841	198
Brownsville	78520	137,883	141
Bryan	77801	58,763	460
Carrollton	75006	100,463	216
College Station	77840	59,742	446
Corpus Christi	78469	281,453	59
Dallas	75260	1,075,894	9
Denton	76201	76,933	319
El Paso	79910	615,032	17
Fort Worth	76161	491,801	29
Galveston	77550	59,567	447
Garland	75040	193,408	90
Grand Prairie	75051	113,329	185
Harlingen	78550	58,210	465
Houston	77201	1,786,691	4
Irving	75015	178,253	107
Killeen	76541	80,720	299
Laredo	78041	175,783	110
Lewisville	75067	72,466	349
Longview	75602	75,576	330
Lubbock	79402	190,974	92
McAllen	78501	106,822	206
Mesquite	75149	114,632	181
Midland	79711	99,621	219
Missouri City	77459	62,371	421
North Richland Hills	76182	54,622	509
Odessa	79761	91,572	252
Pasadena	77501	133,964	150
Plano	75075	219,486	72
Port Arthur	77640	56,827	484
Richardson	75080	86,020	274
Round Rock	78664	60,686	438
San Angelo	76902	88,233	264
San Antonio	78284	1,114,130	8
Sugar Land	77478	51,725	544
Tyler	75712	83,908	284
Victoria	77901	61,882	428
Waco	76702	108,272	202
Wichita Falls	76307	99,236	223
Utah			
Layton	84040	55,112	505
Ogden	84441	66,507	387
Orem	84057	78,937	309
Provo	84601	110,419	196
Salt Lake City	84199	174,348	112
Sandy	84070	99,186	225
Taylorsville	84118	56,753	486
West Jordan	84084	60,804	436
West Valley City	84199	99,372	222
Virginia			
Alexandria	22313	118,300	173
Arlington CDP	22210	177,275	108
Chesapeake	23320	199,564	83
Danville	24541	50,868	558
Hampton	23670	136,968	144
Lynchburg	24506	65,473	395
Newport News	23607	178,615	106
Norfolk	23501	215,215	75
Portsmouth	23707	98,936	226
Richmond	23232	194,173	88
Roanoke	24022	93,749	241
Suffolk	23434	62,703	417
Virginia Beach	23450	432,380	34
Washington			
Bellevue	98009	104,052	208
Bellingham	98225	61,894	427
Everett	98201	88,625	262
Federal Way	98063	74,254	338
Kennewick	99336	50,316	565
Lakewood	98439	65,933	390
Seattle	98109	536,978	22
Shoreline	98133	52,116	543
Spokane	99210	184,058	101
Tacoma	98413	179,814	105
Vancouver	98661	73,526	343
Yakima	98903	64,967	398
West Virginia			
Charleston	25301	55,056	506
Huntington	25704	52,571	539
Wisconsin			
Appleton	54911	65,514	394
Eau Claire	54703	59,200	453
Green Bay	54303	97,789	229
Janesville	53545	59,149	456
Kenosha	53140	87,849	265
Madison	53714	209,306	80
Milwaukee	53203	578,364	19
Oshkosh	54901	57,955	470
Racine	53403	81,095	296
Waukesha	53186	61,989	426
West Allis	53214	59,974	443
Wyoming			
Cheyenne	82001	53,640	520

U.S. Telephone Area Codes and Time Zones

NOTES: Data as of July 2000. "Overlay" area codes span across geographical areas that may already include one or more other area codes. *Source:* Bell Atlantic Yellow Pages Company, with additional information from the North American Numbering Plan Administration.

Twelve Terrific Train Trips

Traveling by rail is regaining popularity

By TIME correspondents around the world

Airplanes are faster, automobiles more adaptable. Yet more and more Americans are choosing to take their vacations on the railroad. While some trains are not yet up to European standards of luxury and convenience, rail tours in Canada and the Americas offer reasonable comfort, good food, and some spectacular scenery. Here are some of the options:

VIA Rail Across Canada

Train buffs consider this 2,750-mile, three-day, five-province journey one of the best in the world because of the train's refurbished Art Deco–style cars and first-rate service and the stunning scenery. Owen Hardy, president of the Society of International Railway Travelers, praises the *Canadian* as "a classic example of the elegant modern trains rolled out by the private railroads in their last-ditch battle against the automobile and interstate highways." **www.viarail.ca** (888-VIARail)

Rocky Mountaineer Railtours

On any of 30 different trips and tours offered by Rocky Mountaineer Railtours, you travel in daylight hours so that you don't miss any of the heart-stopping scenery. Choose the GoldLeaf Service because you'll be assigned a seat in the dome car, which offers a 360° view of the most dramatic sights in the world, and you'll eat in a first-class dining room with picture windows. You can stand on an open-air observation platform at the rear of the train, the wind on your face and moose, bear, eagles, bighorn sheep, and mountain goats in your view. **www.rockymountaineer.com** (800-665-7245)

American Orient Express

The elegant paneled dining car, its tables covered with crisp linen and set with silver, china, and glassware, comes from another, golden era of train travel, but it is alive and well aboard the *American Orient Express*, the only private luxury train in North America. From March through November this year, you can choose from five regional itineraries or select a transcontinental rail journey, either from Washington to Los Angeles or across Canada between Vancouver and Montreal. **www.americanorientexpress.com** (888-759-3944)

In the Path of Lewis & Clark

For their corps of discovery, Meriwether Lewis and William Clark selected men with grit and guts. Both qualities were put to the test: the group battled rattlesnakes and grizzlies, suffered boils and dysentery, portaged canoes up hills and through rocky ravines, and were reduced to eating dogs and horses in the course of their 28-month, 8,000-mile trek to chart the western wilderness.

Two hundred years later, you can re-live that historic exploration—without the danger or the dogmeat—by taking the seven-day rail-and-road tour "In the Path of Lewis and Clark." Traveling part of the way by motor coach and the remainder aboard the *American Spirit*—a daylight train with refurbished passenger cars and vista domes from the late '40s and '50s—you set out from Billings, Mont., and end up near Astoria, Ore., journeying through large swaths of Lewis and Clark territory in between.

You will cross the rugged Bitterroot Mountains—where the corps nearly starved; navigate the Clearwater River in canoes like those used by the expedition; stop at the Nez Perce National Historical Park to learn about the Native Americans who befriended the explorers; and visit a replica of Fort Clatsop, which sheltered the bedraggled group during the cold, wet winter of 1805–06. **www.americanspiritrail.com** (888-533-7245)

Mexico's Copper Canyon

Refurbished World War II–era Pullman cars twist and turn from the sea-level Sonoran Desert to 8,000 ft. along the rim of Copper Canyon, crossing 39 bridges and plunging through 86 tunnels. Those who know this route from Los Mochis to Chihuahua, Mexico, rate it as one of the last great American wilderness areas south of the Arctic Circle. With stops at Divisadero and Creel, the *Sierra Madre Express* allows you to visit the Tarahumara Indians, distant relatives of the Aztecs.

A fleet of five railcars make up the *Sierra Madre Express*. From the train's dome car, called the *Tucson*, and the *Divisadero* car, an open observation deck, you can gaze upon rivers with rushing waterfalls as well as lush bird life and wildflowers. **www.sierramadreexpress.com** (800-666-0346)

BC Rail's Royal Hudson

King George VI and his wife, Queen Elizabeth, were so pleased with the Hudson locomotive on the train that carried them across Canada on their 1939 royal tour that they granted the title Royal to a group of Hudson locomotives. One of these, Locomotive 2860, traveled proudly through British Columbia for 16 years before it was forced off the tracks by diesel engines. Rescued from the Winnipeg scrap yards by the government of British Columbia, the *Royal Hudson* was refurbished in 1974 and is now the only steam engine in regular mainline service in North America. During the spring and summer months, the *Royal Hudson* pulls a string of vintage passenger cars along tracks that hug the top of a cliff 100 ft. above Howe Sound, north of Vancouver. The 80-mile round trip, much of it poised over the water below, offers views of pretty islands, the Strait of Georgia, lush forests, a span of glaciers, coastal mountains that sweep into the sea and waterfalls so close you can almost touch them. **www.bcrail.com/bcrpass** (800-663-8238)

The Cascades

This sleek new European-built train may be the best—and cheapest—way to see the Pacific Northwest. Subsidized by the states of Oregon and Washington, the nine-hour trip costs only $44 for coach.

The *Cascades*, built for ultrahigh speeds, can do only 79 m.p.h. on existing tracks, but its pendular suspension means it doesn't have to slow down going around curves—of which this route has many. For much of the way, you skirt the shores of the lovely Willamette, Columbia, and Toutle rivers. The view gets even more spectacular as you follow the coastline of the vast and misty Puget Sound. So close to the water do you ride that you often feel you're not on a train at all but on a boat, with blue water and skies as far as you can see. If the day is clear, you can catch glimpses of Mount Hood and Mount Rainier, and you'll pass forests of fir and cedar. **www.amtrakcascades.com** (800-USA-RAIL)

The Overland Trail

If there is a time machine that allows you to relive the days when going by rail meant going in style, when women dressed up and wore gloves and men sported fedoras and suits with wide lapels, it is the *Overland Trail*, a 1949 club lounge car that was once a part of the Southern Pacific streamliner that ran from Oakland, Calif., to Chicago.

In 2000, the Overland Trail traveled from Oakland to either Santa Barbara or Los Angeles. Going along for the ride on every trip is Earl Nickles, a train buff and local barber who'll give you an on-train trim for a $5 donation. Most of the streamliners of yesteryear had barbershops, Nickles explains. "It was all part of the time when train travel was gracious." **www.overlandtrail.com** (800-KEY-RAIL)

Cumbres & Toltec Scenic Railroad

In the opening scene of *Indiana Jones and the Last Crusade,* young Indy gallops toward a smoke-billowing circus train and leaps aboard. That engine and those tracks are part of the Cumbres & Toltec Scenic Railroad, a Hollywood favorite and the highest and longest narrow-gauge railroad in the U.S. But seeing it onscreen doesn't compare with riding it firsthand, as 70,000 tourists and train buffs do each year.

The C&TS, built in the 1880s as part of a rail empire connecting commercial outposts and mining camps, cuts a meandering 64-mile-long swath through frontier history along the mountainous border between Colorado and New Mexico. Fired by tons of hand-stoked coal, steam-driven locomotives

maneuver around bends and across streambeds and pant up grades as steep as 4% on a track measuring just 36 in. between the rails. **www.cumbrestoltec.com** (888-CUMBRES)

Slow Train from Cuzco

The main streets of Cuzco, the majestic Inca capital of Peru, are still slumbering in the half-light between dawn and day as minibuses and taxis take tourists to the small San Pedro rail station. There, behind the chaotic stalls of the city market, crowds jostle in the entrance waiting for the three services that run from Cuzco to the famed Inca citadel of Machu Picchu. The most comfortable is the one-stop, 3¼-hour Inca service that leaves Cuzco at 6:15 a.m. daily for Machu Picchu. For railroad buffs, this 70-mile Cuzco-to-Machu Picchu line—another of the few remaining narrow-gauge passenger services still operating in the world—is one of the great rail experiences. (011-51-84-238722, or fax 011-51-84-222114)

Napa Valley Wine Train

The French proverb "a day without wine is like a day without sunshine" fits the Napa Valley to a T. Even on the rare cloudy days, there's plenty of sunshine aboard the *Napa Valley Wine Train*, a 10-year-old cruise ship on land that offers white-linen dining—and plenty of the local agricultural product—on a three-hour rail voyage through the heart of California's famed wine country.

The multisensory experience begins even before the train pulls out of the Napa depot, with an art show and a complimentary wine-tasting seminar. Then you climb onboard for the feast. As the train rolls at a peaceful pace past 27 wineries and manicured vineyards, passengers can sip local Chardonnays, Cabernet Sauvignons, Pinot Noirs, or other premium varietals as they dine in luxuriously refurbished Pullman cars, vintage 1915–70. **www.winetrain.com** (800-427-4124)

The Old Patagonian Express

Ever since the Old Patagonian Express rose to fame from the pages of Paul Theroux's 1979 best seller, this narrow-gauge line in southern Argentina has been a Mecca for steam-train lovers. "We're still running the same original engines from the year 1922," says El Maiten stationmaster Marcelo Ballerini. "Tourists arrive from all over the world to ride it." Threatened with extinction at various times, this fully steam-operated line running across the dry Patagonian steppes has been kept alive by Theroux's readers and a few locals who still board it along the way.

Known in Argentina as *La Trochita* (from trocha angosta, or "narrow gauge"), the old carriages run through the foothills of the majestic Andes mountain range. As much fun as the scenery is the train itself. Visitors can stand alongside the engineer as he operates the brakes and the burner on the steep grades along the way. (El Maiten train station: 011-54-2945-49-5190)   □

For more information on trains and railroads, *see* pp. 218–219.

Current Travel Warnings

(for U.S. citizens; as of Sept. 20, 2000)

Travel Warnings are issued when the State Department recommends that Americans avoid a certain country. The countries listed below are currently on that list. In addition to this list, the State Department issues Consular Information Sheets for every country of the world with information on such matters as the health conditions, crime, unusual currency or entry requirements, any areas of instability, and the location of the nearest U.S. embassy or consulate in the subject country.

Country	Most recent warning issued	Country	Most recent warning issued
Afghanistan	7/8/99	Iran	9/14/99
Albania	4/14/99	Iraq	9/10/99
Algeria	3/31/00	Lebanon	8/28/00
Angola	9/8/00	Liberia	8/25/00
Bosnia and Herzegovina	7/30/99	Libya	8/4/99
Burundi	1/20/00	Nigeria	4/7/00
Central African Republic	6/7/99	Pakistan	8/10/99
Colombia	1/28/00	Serbia and Montenegro	8/14/00
Republic of Congo (Brazzaville)	5/3/00	Sierra Leone	9/16/99
Dem. Rep. of the Congo (formerly Zaire)	5/2/00	Solomon Islands	6/30/00
Eritrea	6/15/99	Somalia	12/21/99
Ethiopia	5/12/00	Sudan	6/19/00
Guinea-Bissau	6/14/98	Tajikistan	8/31/00
Fiji	6/2/00	Yemen	2/23/00

Source: U.S. Department of State. Web: http://travel.state.gov.

U.S. Passport Information

Source: Department of State, Bureau of Consular Affairs. Web: http://travel.state.gov.

With a few exceptions, a passport is required for all U.S. citizens to depart and enter the United States and to enter most foreign countries. Persons who travel to a country where a U.S. passport is not required should be in possession of documentary evidence of their U.S. citizenship and identity to facilitate reentry into the United States. Travelers should check passport and visa requirements with consular officials of the countries to be visited well in advance of their departure date.

Application for a passport may be made at a passport agency, many federal and state courts, probate courts, some county and municipal offices, and some post offices. The thirteen major cities with U.S. passport agencies are Boston, Chicago, Honolulu, Houston, Los Angeles, Miami, New Orleans, New York, Philadelphia, San Francisco, Seattle, Stamford, Conn., and Washington, D.C.

All persons are required to obtain individual passports in their own names. Neither spouses nor children may be included in each other's passports. Applicants age 13 years and older must appear in person before the clerk or agent executing the application if it is their first time applying. For children under the age of 13, a parent or legal guardian may execute an application for them.

First-time passport applicants must apply in person. Applicants must present the following items at a passport facility:

• Completed Form DSP-11, Application for Passport (available at passport agencies, many travel agencies, or on the Web). This form may be completed in advance; however, it must be signed by you in person before a passport agent.

• Proof of U.S. citizenship. You may use one of the following: previous U.S. passport; certified birth certificate issued by the city, county, or state; Consular Report of Birth Abroad; Naturalization Certificate; or Certificate of Citizenship.

• Proof of identity. Acceptable proof includes: previous U.S. passport; Naturalization Certificate; Certificate of Citizenship; current, valid driver's license; government ID (city, state, or federal); military ID (military and dependents); work ID (must be currently employed by the company); student ID (must be currently enrolled); Merchant Marines card (also known as a "Seamen's" or "Z" card); pilot or flight attendant ID. *Note:* Social Security cards are NOT acceptable as identification.

Travel Web Sites

Adventurous Traveler Bookstore:
www.adventuroustraveler.com
Amtrak: www.amtrak.com
Bureau of Consular Affairs: travel.state.gov
CIA World Factbook:
www.odci.gov/cia/publications/factbook
Exchange Rates: www.x-rates.com
Expedia Travel (Microsoft): www.expedia.com
Fodor's Travel Online: www.fodors.com
Frommer's: www.frommers.com
Greyhound: www.greyhound.com
Hostelling International: www.iyhf.org
Lonely Planet: www.lonelyplanet.com
National Park Service ParkNet: www.nps.gov
Preview Travel: www.previewtravel.com
Priceline: www.priceline.com
Rail Connection (Europe): www.railconnection.com
Travelocity: www.travelocity.com
Zagat (restaurants): www.zagat.com

• Two passport photographs. Photographs must be 2×2 inches in size. The image size from the bottom of the chin to the top of the head should be between 1 inch and 1⅜ inches. They may be in color or black and white. They must be full face, front view with a plain white or off-white background. Photographs should be taken in normal street attire, without a hat or headgear that obscures the hair or hairline.

• The applicable fee. A fee of $45 plus a $15 execution fee is charged for adults 16 years and older for a passport valid for ten years from the date of issue. The fee for children under 16 years of age is $25 for a five-year passport plus $15 for the execution of the application. Persons of all ages born outside the U.S. are required to pay an additional $100 complex case fee. The fee for passport renewals by mail is $40 (there is no execution fee added).

• DSP-64 Lost or Stolen Passport Form (if necessary). In addition to the items listed above, if your passport was lost or stolen, you will need to complete and submit this form (available at passport facilities and on the Web).

Passport renewals can be handled through the mail in some instances. You may apply by mail if: (1) you can submit your most recent passport and it is not mutilated, altered, or damaged; (2) you were at least 16 years old when your most recent passport was issued; (3) you were issued your most recent passport less than 12 years ago; and (4) you use the same name as on your most recent passport, OR, you have had your name changed by marriage or court order and can submit proper documentation to reflect your name changes.

In order to apply for a renewal by mail, you must fill out and submit Form DSP-82, which can be obtained at a passport facility or downloaded from the Web site. Attach to it the following: (1) your most recent passport; (2) two identical passport photographs; and (3) the $40 fee. If your name changed, enclose a certified copy of the Court Order, Adoption Decree, Marriage Certificate, or Divorce Decree specifying another name for you to use. Mail the above items to: National Passport Center; P.O. Box 371971, Pittsburgh, PA 15250-7971.

Normal processing time for a passport application is 25 working days. However, it is recommended that you apply for your passport several months in advance of your planned departure. If you will need visas from foreign embassies, allow more time. If you need to leave in a hurry, you may expedite the process for an additional fee of $35 per passport. When requesting expedited service, two-way overnight mail for each application is strongly suggested. If you are applying by mail and wish to have your processing EXPEDITED, clearly mark the envelope EXPEDITED. You should receive your passport in 7–10 business days if using expedited service and two-way overnight delivery, depending upon the reliability of your overnight service.

If your passport is lost or stolen, report the loss on Form DSP-64 when you apply, in person, for your new passport. If you are abroad, report the loss immediately to local police authorities and the nearest U.S. embassy or consulate. Remember to write your current address in the space provided in your passport, so that, if it is found, it can be returned to you.

The State Dept. suggests you make two copies of the identification page—one to leave with a friend or relative at home in case of an emergency, and one to keep with you in the event that your passport is lost or stolen while abroad. This will make it easier to get a new passport, should it be necessary. It is also a good idea to carry two extra passport-size photos with you.

If you have questions or would like more information about obtaining or renewing a passport, visit the State Dept. Web site (http://travel.state.gov) or call the National Passport Information Center, 1-888-362-8668.

State Tourism Offices

The following is a selected list of state tourism office Web addresses and phone numbers. Where a toll-free 800 or 888 number is available, it is given. However, the numbers are subject to change.

Alabama
1-800-ALABAMA
www.touralabama.org

Alaska
907-465-2010
www.travelalaska.com

Arizona
1-800-842-8257
www.arizonaguide.com

Arkansas
1-800-NATURAL
www.arkansas.com

California
1-800-GOCALIF
www.gocalif.ca.gov

Colorado
1-800-COLORADO
www.colorado.com

Connecticut
1-800-CT-BOUND
www.ctbound.org

Delaware
1-800-441-8846
www.state.de.us/tourism

**District of Columbia
(Washington, D.C.)**
202-789-7000
www.washington.org

Florida
888-7FLA-USA
www.flausa.com

Georgia
1-800-VISIT-GA
www.georgia.com

Hawaii
1-800-GO-HAWAII
www.gohawaii.com

Idaho
1-800-635-7820
www.visitid.org

Illinois
1-800-2-CONNECT
www.enjoyillinois.com

Indiana
1-800-ENJOY-IN
www.enjoyindiana.com

Iowa
1-888-472-6035
www.traveliowa.com/

Kansas
1-800-2-KANSAS
www.kansascommerce.com/
0400travel.html

Kentucky
1-800-225-TRIP
www.tourky.com

Louisiana
1-800-677-4082
www.louisianatravel.com

Maine
1-888-MAINE-45
www.visitmaine.com

Average Daily Temperatures (°F) in Tourist Cities

(For U.S. cities, *see* Climate of Selected U.S. Cities)

Location	January High	January Low	April High	April Low	July High	July Low	October High	October Low
Acapulco (Mexico)	87	72	87	73	89	77	89	77
Amsterdam (Netherlands)	41	34	53	40	69	55	57	46
Athens (Greece)	54	42	67	52	90	72	74	60
Auckland (New Zealand)	73	60	67	56	56	46	63	52
Bangkok (Thailand)	89	69	94	78	91	77	89	76
Beijing (China)	35	15	68	44	87	71	67	44
Belgrade (Yugoslavia)	38	28	62	43	81	60	64	46
Berlin (Germany)	35	26	55	38	74	55	55	41
Bombay (India)	83	67	89	76	85	77	89	76
Cairo (Egypt)	65	47	83	57	96	70	86	65
Calcutta (India)	80	55	97	75	89	79	89	74
Cape Town (South Africa)	69	56	66	54	60	50	65	53
Caracas (Venezuela)	75	56	81	60	78	61	79	61
Copenhagen (Denmark)	36	29	50	37	72	55	53	42
Dublin (Ireland)	47	35	54	38	67	51	57	43
Glasgow (Scotland)	43	34	53	38	66	52	54	43
Hamilton (Bermuda)	68	58	71	59	85	73	79	69
Helsinki (Finland)	27	17	43	31	71	57	45	37
Hong Kong (China)	67	51	79	67	90	78	84	70
Istanbul (Turkey)	48	36	59	45	78	64	66	53
Jerusalem (Israel)	55	41	73	50	87	63	81	59
Kingston (Jamaica)	86	67	87	70	90	73	88	73
Lagos (Nigeria)	88	74	89	77	82	74	85	74
Lisbon (Portugal)	56	46	64	52	79	63	69	57
London (United Kingdom)	44	35	56	40	73	55	58	44
Madrid (Spain)	50	34	63	43	89	61	67	48
Mexico City (Mexico)	66	42	77	51	73	53	70	50
Montreal (Canada)	22	6	51	33	79	60	56	39
Moscow (Russia)	21	9	47	31	76	55	46	34
Nairobi (Kenya)	77	53	75	57	69	51	77	54
Nassau (Bahamas)	77	65	81	69	88	75	85	73
Oslo (Norway)	30	20	50	34	73	56	49	37
Paris (France)	42	32	60	41	76	55	59	44
Prague (Czech Republic)	34	25	55	40	74	58	54	44
Quebec (Canada)	19	3	45	30	77	58	51	37
Rio de Janeiro (Brazil)	84	73	80	69	75	63	77	66
Rome (Italy)	54	39	68	46	88	64	73	53
San José (Costa Rica)	75	58	79	62	77	62	77	60
San Juan (Puerto Rico)	81	70	83	72	86	76	86	75
Seoul (Korea)	33	17	62	42	84	70	67	47
Singapore	86	73	89	75	87	75	88	74
Stockholm (Sweden)	31	23	45	32	70	55	48	39
Sydney (Australia)	79	65	73	57	62	44	72	55
Taipei (Taiwan)	66	54	77	63	92	76	81	67
Tokyo (Japan)	48	31	64	48	84	71	70	56
Toronto (Canada)	30	17	51	35	79	60	57	42
Vancouver (Canada)	42	32	55	41	71	55	57	44
Vienna (Austria)	34	26	57	41	75	59	55	44
Zurich (Switzerland)	36	26	60	41	77	56	57	43

Maryland
1-800-MDISFUN
www.mdisfun.org

Massachusetts
1-800-227-MASS
www.massvacation.com

Michigan
1-888-78-GREAT
www.michigan.org

Minnesota
1-800-657-3700
www.exploreminnesota.com

Mississippi
1-800-WARMEST
www.visitmississippi.org

Missouri
1-800-877-1234
www.missouritourism.org

Montana
1-800-VISIT-MT
www.visitmt.com

Nebraska
1-800-228-4307, ext. 926
www.visitnebraska.org

Nevada
1-800-NEVADA-8
www.travelnevada.com

New Hampshire
1-800-FUN-IN-NH
www.visitnh.gov

New Jersey
1-800-VISIT-NJ
www.state.nj.us/travel

New Mexico
1-800-SEE-NEWMEX
www.newmexico.org

New York
1-800-CALL-NYS
www.iloveny.state.ny.us

North Carolina
1-800-VISIT-NC
www.visitnc.com

North Dakota
1-800-HELLO-ND
www.ndtourism.com

Ohio
1-800-BUCKEYE
www.ohiotourism.com

Oklahoma
1-800-654-8240
www.touroklahoma.com

Oregon
1-800-547-7842
www.traveloregon.com

Pennsylvania
1-800-VISIT-PA
www.experiencepa.com

Rhode Island
1-800-556-2484
www.visitrhodeisland.com

South Carolina
803-734-1700
www.travelsc.com

South Dakota
1-800-S-DAKOTA
www.travelsd.com

Tennessee
1-800-836-6200
www.tourism.state.tn.us/

Texas
1-800-452-9292
www.state.tx.us/Travel

Utah
1-800-200-1160
www.state.ut.us/visiting/
travel.html

Vermont
1-800-VERMONT
www.1-800-vermont.com

Virginia
1-800-932-5827
www.virginia.org

Washington
360-586-2088
www.tourism.wa.gov

Washington, D.C.
See District of Columbia

West Virginia
1-800-CALL-WVA
www.state.wv.us/tourism

Wisconsin
1-800-432-TRIP
www.travelwisconsin.com

Wyoming
1-800-225-5996
www.wyomingtourism.org

The World's Top Tourism Destinations[1]
International tourist arrivals

1999 rank	Country	Arrivals (million) 1998	Arrivals (million) 1999	% change 1999/1998	1999 market share	1999 rank	Country	Arrivals (million) 1998	Arrivals (million) 1999	% change 1999/1998	1999 market share
1.	France	70.0	71.4	2.0%	10.7	9.	Poland	18.8	17.9	−4.5%	2.9
2.	Spain	47.7	52.0	8.8	7.3	10.	Austria	17.4	17.6	1.6	2.6
3.	United States	46.4	47.0	1.3	7.1	11.	Germany	16.5	17.1	3.5	2.5
4.	Italy	34.8	35.8	2.9	5.3	12.	Russian Fed.	15.8	16.4	3.9	2.4
5.	China	25.1	27.0	7.9	3.8	13.	Czech Rep.	16.3	16.0	−1.8	2.5
6.	United Kingdom	25.7	25.7	0.0	3.9	14.	Hungary	15.0	12.9	−13.8	2.3
7.	Mexico	19.8	20.2	2.0	3.0	15.	Portugal	11.3	11.6	2.7	1.7
8.	Canada	18.8	19.6	3.8	2.9						

1. Preliminary data as of Jan. 2000. *Source:* World Tourism Organization (WTO). Web: www.world-tourism.org.

Top International Destinations of American Tourists
(numbers in thousands)

1998 rank	Country	1998 travelers	1998 rank	Country	1998 travelers	1998 rank	Country	1998 travelers
1.	Mexico	18,338	10.	Spain	946	18.	Australia	531
2.	Canada	14,880	11.	Switzerland	830	19.	People's Republic of China	508
3.	United Kingdom	3,645	12.	Hong Kong	738	20.	Belgium	484
4.	France	2,399	13.	South Korea	692	20.	India	484
5.	Germany	1,892	14.	Bahamas	623	22.	Austria	461
5.	Italy	1,892	15.	Brazil	577	22.	Ireland	461
7.	Jamaica	1,546	15.	Republic of China (Taiwan)	577	24.	Philippines	415
8.	Japan	1,061	17.	Greece	554	24.	Singapore	415
9.	Netherlands	1,015						

Source: U.S. Dept. of Commerce, International Trade Administration. Web: www.tinet.ita.doc.gov/research/reports.

Top Nationalities of Travelers to the U.S.

1999 rank	Country of residence	1999 total	% of total travelers to U.S.	1999 rank	Country of residence	1999 total	% of total travelers to U.S.
1.	Japan	4,826,000	20%	9.	Argentina	502,000	2%
2.	United Kingdom	4,252,000	17	10.	South Korea	499,000	2
3.	Germany	1,985,000	8	11.	Australia	483,000	2
4.	France	1,059,000	4	12.	Taiwan	453,000	2
5.	Brazil	665,000	3	13.	Colombia	416,000	2
6.	Italy	626,000	3	14.	Switzerland	406,000	2
7.	Venezuela	552,000	2	15.	People's Republic of China/ Hong Kong	384,000	2
8.	Netherlands	527,000	2				

Source: U.S. Dept. of Commerce, International Trade Administration. Web: www.tinet.ita.doc.gov/research/reports.

Transportation

Consumer Complaints Against Top U.S. Airlines by Airline[1]

Rank	Airline	Complaints	Systemwide enplanements	Complaints per 100,000 enplanements
1.	Southwest	259	65,483,849	0.40
2.	Alaska	223	13,620,053	1.64
3.	Delta	1,916	105,455,960	1.82
4.	Continental	1,153	44,012,311	2.62
5.	United	2,317	87,156,921	2.66
6.	Northwest	1,646	56,206,471	2.93
7.	U.S. Airways	1,759	55,892,604	3.15
8.	TWA	891	25,845,788	3.45
9.	American	2,848	81,452,089	3.50
10.	America West	697	18,703,607	3.73
	Total	**13,709**	**553,829,653**	**2.48**

NOTE: Data for Jan. 1999–Dec. 1999. 1. Includes U.S. airlines with at least 1% of total domestic scheduled-service passenger revenues. *Source:* Office of Aviation Enforcement and Proceedings, U.S. Dept. of Transportation, *Air Travel Consumer Report.*

Consumer Complaints Against Top U.S. Airlines by Category

Complaint category	1990	1991	1992	1993	1994	1995	1996	1997	1998	1999
TOTAL	7,703	6,106	5,639	4,438	5,179	4,629	5,782	6,394	7,994	17,381
Flight problems[1]	3,034	1,877	1,624	1,211	1,586	1,133	1,628	1,699	2,277	6,469
Customer service[2]	758	714	695	599	805	667	999	1,418	1,715	3,664
Baggage	1,329	883	752	627	761	628	882	826	1,108	2,353
Reservations/ticketing/boarding[3]	624	659	680	577	598	666	857	904	1,137	1,328
Refunds	701	783	721	482	393	576	521	531	602	940
Oversales[4]	399	301	265	257	301	263	353	414	388	673
Fares[5]	312	388	573	398	267	185	180	195	277	584
Disability[3]	n.a.	n.a.	n.a.	n.a.	n.a.	n.a.	n.a.	n.a.	n.a.	526
Advertising	96	96	54	51	94	66	61	57	40	57
Tours	29	23	12	16	127	18	16	13	23	28
Smoking[6]	74	30	25	30	20	15	13	5	4	n.a.
Credit[6]	5	10	10	4	2	4	3	1	1	n.a.
Other[6]	342	342	228	186	225	408	269	331	422	759

NOTE: Data for Jan. 1999–Dec. 1999. 1. Cancellations, delays, and other deviations from schedule. 2. Rude or unhelpful employees, inadequate meals or cabin service, treatment of delayed passengers. 3. Effective with the Sept. 1999 report, "disability" complaints are listed as a separate category. Previously, disability complaints were included in the "Reservations/ticketing/boarding" category. 4. All bumping problems, whether or not airline complied with DOT regulations. 5. Incorrect or incomplete information about fares, discount fare conditions and availability, overcharges, fare increases, and level of fares in general. 6. Complaints about "smoking" and "credit," which were formerly separate categories, are now included in the "other" category. *Source:* Office of Aviation Enforcement and Proceedings, U.S. Dept. of Transportation, *Air Travel Consumer Report.*

Passengers Denied Boarding by Top U.S. Airlines,[1] 1999

Rank Airline	Denied boardings (DBs)		Enplaned passengers	Involuntary DBs per 10,000 passengers
	Voluntary	Involuntary		
1. Northwest	68,573	772	38,374,040	0.20
2. Continental	46,975	839	29,496,569	0.28
3. American	192,119	2,278	54,433,093	0.42
4. U.S. Airways	60,149	2,302	40,517,315	0.57
5. United	102,185	4,170	60,254,240	0.69
6. TWA	52,952	1,652	18,717,037	0.88
7. Alaska	17,928	1,018	10,312,660	0.99
8. America West	41,091	1,949	14,160,423	1.38
9. Southwest	59,775	6,816	48,558,809	1.40
10. Delta	143,707	15,230	76,926,030	1.98
Total	**785,454**	**37,026**	**391,750,216**	**0.95**

NOTE: Data for Jan. 1999–Sept. 1999. 1. Includes U.S. airlines with at least 1% of total domestic scheduled-service passenger revenues. *Source:* Office of Aviation Enforcement and Proceedings, U.S. Dept. of Transportation, *Air Travel Consumer Report.*

World's 25 Busiest Airports by Passengers and Cargo, 1999

Airport	Total passengers[1]	1998–1999 percent change	Airport	Total cargo[1]	1998–1999 percent change
1. Atlanta, Hartsfield (ATL)	77,939,536	6.1%	Memphis (MEM)	2,412,905	1.9%
2. Chicago, O'Hare (ORD)	72,568,076	0.1	Hong Kong (HKG)	1,988,838	20.2
3. Los Angeles (LAX)	63,876,561	4.3	Los Angeles (LAX)	1,951,942	4.9
4. London, Heathrow (LHR)	62,263,710	2.6	Tokyo, Narita (NRT)	1,841,572	12.5
5. Dallas/Ft. Worth (DFW)	60,000,125	n.a.	New York (JFK)	1,737,000	8.9
6. Tokyo, Haneda (HND)	54,338,212	6.0	Anchorage (ANC)[2]	1,676,503	20.2
7. Frankfurt-Main (FRA)	45,858,315	7.3	Seoul (SEL)	1,655,344	16.2
8. Paris, Charles de Gaulle (CDG)	43,596,943	12.9	Miami (MIA)	1,651,062	−7.9
9. San Francisco (SFO)	40,387,422	0.7	Frankfurt-Main (FRA)	1,539,048	5.0
10. Denver (DEN)	38,034,231	3.3	Chicago, O'Hare (ORD)	1,531,809	6.2
11. Amsterdam, Schiphol (AMS)	36,781,015	6.9	Singapore (SIN)	1,522,984	16.7
12. Minneapolis/St. Paul (MSP)	34,216,331	12.7	Louisville (SDF)	1,486,205	6.5
13. Detroit (DTW)	34,038,381	7.9	London, Heathrow (LHR)	1,355,419	4.2
14. Miami (MIA)	33,899,246	−0.1	Paris, Charles de Gaulle (CDG)	1,226,924	22.1
15. Newark (EWR)	33,814,000	4.1	Amsterdam, Schiphol (AMS)	1,225,284	0.5
16. Las Vegas (LAS)	33,669,185	11.4	Indianapolis (IND)	1,107,985	36.1
17. Phoenix, Sky Harbor (PHX)	33,533,353	5.6	Newark (EWR)	1,078,000	−1.4
18. Seoul (SEL)	33,371,074	13.4	Taipei (TPE)	1,055,370	15.4
19. Houston (IAH)	33,089,333	6.3	Dayton (DAY)	894,389	0.8
20. New York (JFK)	32,003,000	2.9	Atlanta, Hartsfield (ATL)	883,149	−2.6
21. London, Gatwick (LGW)	30,559,461	4.8	Osaka (KIX)	864,318	12.7
22. St. Louis (STL)	30,188,973	5.4	San Francisco (SFO)	844,556	9.4
23. Hong Kong (HKG)	29,733,470	6.7	Dallas/Ft. Worth (DFW)	844,075	5.3
24. Orlando (MCO)	29,173,491	5.2	Bangkok (BKK)	809,302	12.5
25. Toronto (YYZ)	27,771,473	3.9	Tokyo, Haneda (HND)	724,318	4.5

NOTES: Total passengers enplaned and deplaned, passengers in transit counted once. Cargo loaded and unloaded freight and mail (in metric tons). 1. Results are preliminary. 2. Includes transit freight. *Source:* Airports Council International World Headquarters, Geneva, Switzerland. Web: www.airports.org.

Getting to Work in the City
Commuting characteristics for the 15 largest U.S. cities by population, 1990

1990 rank	City of residence	Total workers 16 years and over	Means of transportation (%)				Average travel time to work (min.)
			Drove alone	Carpool	Public transit	Other means[1]	
1.	New York, N.Y.	3,183,088	24.0%	8.5%	53.4%	14.0%	36.5
2.	Los Angeles, Calif.	1,629,096	65.2	15.4	10.5	8.9	26.5
3.	Chicago, Ill.	1,181,677	46.3	14.8	29.7	9.2	31.5
4.	Houston, Tex.	772,957	71.7	15.5	6.5	6.3	24.7
5.	Philadelphia, Pa.	640,577	44.7	13.2	28.7	13.5	27.4
6.	San Diego, Calif.	560,913	70.7	12.8	4.2	12.2	20.4
7.	Detroit, Mich.	325,054	67.8	16.1	10.7	5.3	24.7
8.	Dallas, Tex.	500,566	72.5	15.2	6.7	5.7	24.0
9.	Phoenix, Ariz.	473,966	73.7	15.1	3.3	7.9	23.0
10.	San Antonio, Tex.	395,551	73.4	15.5	4.9	6.2	21.7
11.	San Jose, Calif.	400,932	76.9	14.6	3.5	5.1	25.5
12.	Indianapolis, Ind.	362,777	78.0	13.4	3.3	5.2	20.8
13.	Baltimore, Md.	307,679	50.9	16.8	22.0	10.2	26.0
14.	San Francisco, Calif.	382,309	38.5	11.5	33.5	16.5	26.9
15.	Jacksonville, Fla.	312,958	75.5	14.2	2.7	7.6	21.6
	Total for U.S.	**115,070,274**	**73.2%**	**13.4%**	**5.3%**	**0.7%**	**n.a.**

NOTES: n.a. = not available. Percentages may not add up to 100%, due to rounding. 1. Includes commuting by motorcycle, bicycle, walking, and all other means. Also includes those who worked at home. *Source:* U.S. Bureau of the Census; Web: www.census.gov/population/socdemo/journey/city.txt.

World's Largest Subway Systems
(by 1997 usage)

City	Date system completed	Number of riders in 1997 (in millions)	Length (km)	City	Date system completed	Number of riders in 1997 (in millions)	Length (km)
Moscow	1935	3,160	200+	Paris	1900	1,120	200.9
Tokyo	1927	2,740	169.3	Osaka	1933	1,000	99.1
Mexico City	n.a.	1,420	178.0	Hong Kong	n.a.	779	28.2
Seoul	n.a.	1,390	n.a.	London	1863	770	391.0
New York City	1904	1,130	320.0	São Paulo	n.a.	701	n.a.

NOTE: n.a. = not available.

Driving Laws, 2000

Currently all states have child safety seat laws and enforce a drinking age of 21. Mandatory belt-use laws are in effect in 49 states plus D.C. Laws regulating breath-alcohol ignition interlock devices are currently in effect in 35 states. A national speed limit of 55 mph was imposed in 1974, and in 1987 it was modified to allow 65-mile-per-hour speeds on some rural freeways. The federal law was entirely repealed in 1995, giving states the right to set their own limits. In 2000, the maximum daylight speed limit on interstates is 65 mph or greater in 49 states—Hawaii is the exception. Montana, which had been the only state with no speed limit, imposed a 75-mile-an-hour limit in 1999.

State	Age for driver's license[1]	License revocation for alcohol offenses since	Blood alcohol concentration limit[2]	Alcohol ignition interlock device[3]	Mandatory belt-use law seating positions	Motorcycle helmet law[4]	Maximum allowable speed limit 1995[5]	1999
Alabama	16	1996	0.08	no	front	yes	65	70
Alaska	16	1983	0.10	yes	all	18[6]	—	65
Arizona	16	1992	0.10	no	front	18	55	75
Arkansas	16	1995	0.10	yes	front	21	65	70
California	17	1989	0.08	yes	all	yes	55	70
Colorado	16	1983	0.10	yes	front	no	65	75
Connecticut	16 + 4 mo.	1990	0.10	no	front[7]	18	55	65
Delaware	16 + 10 mo.	yes	0.10	yes	front	19[8]	—	65
D.C.	16	yes	0.08	no	all	yes	—	—
Florida	18	1990	0.08	yes	front	yes	65	70
Georgia	18	1995	0.10	yes	front[7]	yes	55	70
Hawaii	15 + 3 mo.	1990	0.08	no	front	18	—	55
Idaho	16	1994	0.08	yes	front	18	65	75
Illinois	17	1986	0.08	yes	front	no	65	65
Indiana	18	yes	0.10	yes	front	18	65	65
Iowa	17	1963	0.10	yes	front	no	55	65
Kansas	16	1988	0.08	yes	front	18	65	70
Kentucky	16 + 6 mo.	no	0.10	no	all	21[9, 10, 11]	65	65
Louisiana	17	1984	0.10	yes	front[7]	18[9]	65	70
Maine	16	1984	0.08	yes	all	15	65	65
Maryland	17 + 7 mo.	1989	0.10	yes	front[7]	yes	55	65
Massachusetts	18	1994	0.08	no	all	yes	55	65
Michigan	17	no	0.10	yes	front[7]	yes	55	70
Minnesota	17	1976	0.10	no	front[7]	18	65	70
Mississippi	16	1983	0.10	no	front	yes	65	70
Missouri	16	1987	0.10	yes	front[7]	yes	70	70
Montana	15	no	0.10	yes	all	18	65	75
Nebraska	17	1993	0.10	yes	front	yes	65	75
Nevada	16	1983	0.10	yes	all	yes	55	75
New Hampshire	18	1994	0.08	no	—	18	65	65
New Jersey	18	no	0.10	no	front	yes	—	65
New Mexico	15	1984	0.08	yes	front	18	65	75
New York	17	1994	0.10	yes	front[7]	yes	55	65
North Carolina	16 + 6 mo.	1983	0.08	yes	front	yes	55	70
North Dakota	16	1983	0.10	yes	front	18	65	70
Ohio	17	1993	0.10	yes	front	18[11]	65	65
Oklahoma	16	1983	0.10	yes	front	18	65	75
Oregon	16	1983	0.08	yes	all	yes	65	65
Pennsylvania	17	no	0.10	no	front	yes	55	65
Rhode Island	17 + 6 mo.	no	0.10	yes	all	21[6, 11]	55	65
South Carolina	16 + 3 mo.	1998	0.10	no	front[7]	21	65	65
South Dakota	16	no	0.10	no	front	18	65	75
Tennessee	16	no	0.10	yes	front	yes	65	70
Texas	16	1995	0.10	yes	front	21[9]	65	70
Utah	16	1983	0.08	yes	front	18	65	75
Vermont	16	1969	0.08	no	all	yes	65	65
Virginia	18	1995	0.08	yes	front	yes	65	65
Washington	16	1994	0.08	yes	all	yes	65	70
West Virginia	16	1981	0.10	yes	front	yes	65	70
Wisconsin	16	1988	0.10[12]	yes	front[7]	18[10]	65	65
Wyoming	16	1973	0.10	no	front	18	65	75

NOTES: A driver's license is required in every state. 1. Refers to minimum age for unrestricted driver's license. 2. Blood alcohol concentration that constitutes the threshold of legal intoxication. 3. Legislation for instruments designed to prevent drivers from starting their cars when breath alcohol content is at or above a set point. 4. Presence of law, or age below which riders are required to wear helmet. 5. In 1995, Congress repealed the national 55-miles-per-hour speed limit. 6. All passengers required to wear helmet. 7. Required for certain ages at all seating positions. 8. Helmet must also be carried on the motorcycle, whether or not it is worn, for persons 19 and older. 9. Helmet optional for those over listed age if they have proper insurance. 10. Helmets must be worn by cyclists holding learners' permits. 11. First-year novices required to wear helmet. 12. 0.08 after second DUI conviction. *Sources:* National Safety Council, National Motorists Organization.

Traffic Congestion in U.S. Cities, 1997

Urban area	Travel Rate Index[1]		Annual delay per eligible driver		Annual congestion cost			
	TRI	Rank	Hours	Rank	Total	Rank	Per eligible driver	Rank
Los Angeles, Calif.	1.51	1	82	1	$12,405	1	$1,370	1
Seattle-Everett, Wash.	1.43	2	69	3	1,805	11	1,165	3
San Francisco-Oakland, Calif.	1.42	3	58	7	3,065	6	995	7
Washington, D.C.-Md.-Va.	1.41	4	76	2	3,560	4	1,260	2
Chicago, Ill.-Northwestern Ind.	1.37	5	44	20	4,400	3	720	20
Atlanta, Ga.	1.34	6	68	4	2,270	8	1,125	4
Miami-Hialeah, Fla.	1.34	6	57	10	1,515	13	930	10
Boston, Mass.	1.32	8	66	5	2,635	7	1,095	5
Detroit, Mich.	1.31	9	62	6	3,145	5	1,010	6
Las Vegas, Nev.	1.31	9	34	32	505	29	575	32
San Diego, Calif.	1.31	9	36	29	1,265	16	635	29
Houston, Tex.	1.30	12	58	7	2,210	9	960	9
New York, N.Y.-Northeastern N.J.	1.30	12	38	26	8,885	2	640	27
Portland-Vancouver, Ore.-Wash.	1.30	12	52	12	930	21	885	11
San Jose, Calif.	1.29	15	45	18	955	20	765	17
Denver, Colo.	1.28	16	45	18	1,050	17	760	19
Phoenix, Ariz.	1.28	16	35	30	1,050	17	580	30
San Bernardino-Riverside, Calif.	1.28	16	47	15	790	22	815	15
Minneapolis-St. Paul, Minn.	1.26	19	34	32	1,030	19	570	33
Tacoma, Wash.	1.26	19	29	39	225	50	500	40

NOTE: Study conducted in 68 urbanized areas. 1. The Travel Rate Index is defined as the travel rate (in minutes per mile) during the peak period divided by the rate in the off-peak. A TRI of 1.30 indicates that the average peak trip takes 30% longer than in uncongested conditions—a 20-minute trip becomes a 26-minute trip. *Source:* Texas Transportation Institute, the Texas A&M University System. *The 1999 Annual Mobility Report,* David Schrank and Tim Lomax. Web: http://mobility.tamu.edu.

Improper Driving as a Factor in Accidents

Kind of improper driving	Fatal accidents		Injury accidents		All accidents	
	1998	1995	1998	1995	1998	1995
Improper driving	60.0%	68.1%	62.3%	73.5%	61.5%	75.5%
Speed too fast or unsafe	16.8	19.8	12.8	13.9	13.3	14.0
Right of way	16.0	15.2	21.9	25.5	18.4	22.9
Failed to yield	11.1	10.2	15.9	18.1	13.8	17.0
Passed stop sign	2.6	2.2	4.2	2.4	3.1	1.9
Disregarded signal	2.3	3.0	1.8	5.0	1.5	4.0
Drove left of center	7.3	9.1	1.7	2.4	1.6	2.2
Improper overtaking	1.2	1.5	0.6	1.3	1.0	1.5
Made improper turn	4.1	2.3	4.0	2.8	5.0	4.2
Followed too closely	0.5	0.5	4.3	7.0	5.4	7.2
Other improper driving	14.1	19.7	17.0	20.7	16.8	23.6
No improper driving stated	40.0	31.9	37.7	26.5	38.5	24.5
Total	100.0%	100.0%	100.0%	100.0%	100.0%	100.0%

NOTE: Based on reports from 12 state traffic authorities. *Source:* National Safety Council. *Injury Facts, 1999 Edition.* Web: www.nsc.org.

Alcohol-Related Traffic Fatalities on Holidays, 1998

Holiday 1998	Total traffic fatalities	Total fatalities alcohol-related	Percent fatalities alcohol-related	Time period monitored
New Year's Eve	122	62	51.0%	12/31/97
New Year's Day	142	97	68.4	1/1/98
St. Patrick's Day	86	36	41.3	6 p.m. 3/17/98–5:59 a.m. 3/18/98
Memorial Day weekend	393	204	51.9	6 p.m. 5/22/98–5:59 a.m. 5/26/98
Fourth of July weekend	443	220	49.7	6 p.m. 7/3/98–5:59 a.m. 7/6/98
Labor Day weekend	381	201	52.8	6 p.m. 9/4/98–5:59 a.m. 9/7/98
Halloween	200	113	56.6	6 p.m. 10/31/98–5:59 a.m. 11/1/98
Thanksgiving weekend	550	260	47.3	6 p.m. 11/26/98–5:59 a.m. 11/30/98
Thanksgiving—New Year's	4,356	1,644	37.7	6 a.m. 11/26/98–12/31/98
Christmas weekend	364	173	47.6	6 p.m. 12/24/98–5:59 a.m. 12/28/98

Source: Mothers Against Drunk Driving (MADD).

Fatalities by Transportation Mode, 1970–1998

Mode	1970	1980	1990	1995	1998[1]	Mode	1970	1980	1990	1995	1998[1]
Large air carrier	146	1	39	168	1	Waterborne					
Commuter air	n.a.	37	7	9	0	Vessel casualties	178	206	85	46	31
On-demand air taxi	n.a.	105	50	52	45	Nonvessel	420	281	101	137	76
General aviation	1,310	1,239	765	734	621	casualties					
Highway[2]	52,627	51,091	44,599	41,817	41,171	Recreational boating	1,418	1,360	865	829	813
Railroad[3]	785	584	599	567	577	Gas and hazardous	30	19	9	21	18
Transit[4]	n.a.	n.a.	339	274	n.a.	liquid pipeline					

NOTES: n.a. = not available. 1. Preliminary data. 2 Includes occupants, nonoccupants, and motor vehicle fatalities at railroad crossings. 3. Includes fatalities from nontrain incidents, as well as train incidents and accidents. Also includes train occupants and nonoccupants, except motor vehicle occupants at grade crossings. 4. Fatalities resulting from all reportable incidents, not just accidents. Includes commuter rail, heavy rail, light rail, motor bus, demand responsive, van pool, and automated guideway. *Source:* U.S. Dept. of Transportation, Bureau of Transportation Statistics, *Transportation Statistics Annual Report, 1999.*

Most Popular Car Colors, 1998–1999

(percentage of vehicles manufactured during 1999 model year in North America)

Luxury	1999	1998	Sport compact	1999	1998
1. White Met.	15.8%	12.3%	1. Silver	16.2%	10.4%
2. Silver	14.8	9.2	2. Black	14.7	15.0
3. Lt. Brown	12.9	17.7	3. White	14.0	14.7
4. White	10.3	11.3	4. Med./Dk. Green	12.4	15.9
5. Black	9.4	12.3	5. Med./Dk. Blue	8.5	5.3
6. Med. Gray	8.3	5.3	6. Lt. Brown	8.5	7.0
7. Gold	7.0	4.8	7. Bright Red	7.5	9.5
8. Med. Red	6.0	7.5	8. Med. Red	7.0	6.4
9. Med./Dk. Green	6.1	10.0	9. Dk. Red	4.5	n.a.
10. Med./Dk. Blue	4.9	4.8	10. Lt. Green	1.7	n.a.

Full/Intermediate	1999	1998	SUV/Truck/Van	1999	1998
1. White	15.4%	15.6%	1. White	26.2%	22.5%
2. Silver	14.1	11.0	2. Black	11.2	15.5
3. Lt. Brown	14.0	14.1	3. Med./Dk. Green	11.0	7.2
4. Med./Dk. Green	13.9	16.4	4. Med./Dk. Blue	8.4	4.7
5. Black	11.7	8.9	5. Silver	7.7	6.2
6. Med./Dk. Blue	6.4	6.0	6. Med. Red	7.4	7.2
7. Med. Red	5.7	6.5	7. Lt. Brown	6.2	6.1
8. Bright Red	4.9	n.a.	8. Bright Red	6.1	7.1
9. Med. Gray	4.3	n.a.	9. Med./Dk. Gray	4.5	n.a.
10. Gold	1.8	n.a.	10. Dk. Red	3.1	4.5

Source: DuPont Herberts Automotive Systems, Troy, Mich. 1999 DuPont Automotive Color Popularity Survey Results. Web: www.dupont.com.

Two Centuries of Railroading

Source: Association of American Railroads. Web: www.aar.org.

1797   The steam locomotive is invented in England.

1823   The first public railway in the world opens in England.

1827   The first railroad in North America—the Baltimore & Ohio—is chartered by Baltimore merchants.

1830   The first regularly scheduled steam-powered rail passenger service in the U.S. begins operation in South Carolina, utilizing the U.S.-built locomotive *The Best Friend of Charleston.*

1833   Andrew Jackson travels from Baltimore to Ellicott's Mills, becoming the first sitting U.S. president to ride the rails.

1838   Five of the six New England states have rail service, as do such frontier states as Kentucky and Indiana.

1840   More than 2,800 miles of track are in operation.

1850   More than 9,000 miles of track are in operation in the U.S., as much as in the rest of the world combined.

1860   More than 30,000 miles of track are in operation in the U.S.

1862   President Abraham Lincoln signs the Pacific Railroad Act for the construction of the transcontinental railroad that will ultimately link California with the rest of the nation.

1865   The "golden age" of railroads begins. For nearly half a century, no other mode of transportation challenges railroads. During these years, the rail network grows from 35,000 to a peak of 254,000 miles in 1916.

1869   On May 10, at Promontory, in the Utah Territory, the "Golden Spike" joins the Union Pacific and Central Pacific railroads, marking completion of the first transcontinental railroad.

1917   The federal government seizes control of the railroads for the duration of World War I.

1900–1940   By the eve of World War II, automobiles, large buses, trucks, planes, and pipelines—supported by government subsidies and less burdened by regulation than railroads—have become full-fledged competitors to railroads.

1945–1970   Railroads enter the post-war era with a new sense of optimism that leads them to invest billions of dollars in new locomotives, freight equipment, and passenger trains. That investment would see retirement of the last steam locomotive by the late 1950s in favor of diesel engines. In spite of this modernization, the decline in rail market share that began before the war resumes.

1970–1975 Burdened by regulation and faced with subsidized competition, nine Class I railroads, representing almost one-quarter of the industry's trackage, file for bankruptcy protection.

1970 The Rail Passenger Service Act creates Amtrak to take over intercity rail passenger service.

1971 Amtrak officially begins service on May 1.

1980 The Staggers Rail Act reduces the Interstate Commerce Commission's regulatory jurisdiction over railroads and sparks competition that stimulates advances in technology and a restructuring of the industry.

1987 Conrail is privatized in what—at that time—was the largest share offering in U.S. history as investors pay $1.9 billion to buy shares in the railroad.

1998 U.S. freight railroads move 1.38 trillion ton-miles of freight, more than ever before, setting new safety records in the process.

Railroad Ridership, 1988–1999

(millions)

	1988	1989	1990	1991	1992	1993	1994	1995	1996	1997	1998	1999
Amtrak system	21.5	21.4	22.2	22.0	21.3	22.1	21.2	20.7	19.7	20.2	21.1	21.5
Northeast Corridor	11.2	11.1	11.2	10.9	10.1	10.3	11.7	11.6	11.0	11.1	11.9	12.3
Intercity + West	10.3	10.3	11.0	11.1	11.2	11.8	9.4	9.1	8.7	9.1	9.2	9.2
Commuter trains[1]	15.4	17.4	18.0	18.1	20.3	32.9	39.5	42.2	45.9	48.5	54.0	58.3
Total	36.9	38.8	40.2	40.1	41.6	55.0	60.7	62.9	65.6	68.7	75.1	79.8

1. Includes only commuter trains run by Amtrak under contract. *Source:* National Assoc. of Railroad Passengers. Based on Amtrak annual reports. Web: www.narprail.org.

Ten Famous Trains

Trans-Siberian Express

Traveling between Moscow and Vladivostok, the *Trans-Siberian Express* makes the longest regular train trip in the world, covering 5,778 miles and making 91 stops over the course of nine days. During the Cold War, Westerners could travel only in compartments, where they were subject to Stalinist propaganda played on loudspeakers.

Blue Train

The *Blue Train* has run between Cape Town and Pretoria, South Africa, since 1939 and derives its name from its blue locomotives, railroad cars, and leather seats. It is still considered one of the most luxurious trains running, having been upgraded in 1997 to include televisions and phones in all of its suites.

Indian Pacific

Connecting the east and west coasts of Australia, the *Indian Pacific* runs from Sydney to Perth in three days, over a distance of 2,461 miles. This route has the world's longest stretch of straight track, which lasts for 297 miles.

Super Chief

Originally operated by the Santa Fe Railroad beginning in 1936, the *Super Chief* ran from Chicago to Los Angeles. It was considered one of the best long-distance trains in the U.S. and was renowned for its gourmet food and Hollywood clientele. Amtrak currently operates a version of this train.

TGV

The French *TGV* (train à grande vitesse or high speed train) is an electric train that runs between Paris and Lyons, regularly traveling at speeds of more than 130 miles per hour. A modified *TGV* set a world speed record in 1990 when it hit 320 miles per hour in trial runs.

Orient Express

In 1883 the *Orient Express* began service from Paris to Istanbul, crossing six countries. The train was famous for its five-course French meals and for its passengers, who were often diplomats, royalty, or government couriers.

20th Century Limited

The *20th Century Limited* debuted in 1902 as the New York Central's luxury train, operating between New York and Chicago. It traveled the smooth "water level route" alongside the Hudson River and the shores of Lake Erie. The railroad would roll out a crimson carpet to welcome passengers to the train, giving rise to the phrase the "red carpet treatment."

The Flying Scotsman

Running between King's Cross station in London and Edinburgh, Scotland, the *Flying Scotsman* was a luxury express train full of amenities. It featured a hairdressing salon, a Louis the XVI–style restaurant and bar, and, for a short time, a cinema coach.

Peruvian Central Railway

The highest railway in the world, the Peruvian Central Railway is an engineering marvel, climbing 13,000 feet on its trip from Juliaca to Cuzco, Peru. The railroad, which features 66 tunnels and 59 bridges, zigzags across valleys in order to minimize the steepness of its climb. There is an onboard doctor who administers oxygen to passengers who get altitude sickness.

Bullet Train

The Japanese *Shinkansen,* or *Bullet Train,* runs at speeds of more than 100 miles per hour over special tracks with minimal curves. In 1997, a newer version of the *Bullet Train* became the fastest scheduled train in the world, regularly reaching speeds of up to 186 miles per hour.

Many public figures not listed here may be found elsewhere in the almanac.

U.S. Presidents	British Prime Ministers
U.S. Vice Presidents	Rulers of England
Families of U.S. Presidents	Rulers of France
U.S. Governors	Rulers of Judah and Israel
U.S. Congress	Rulers of Prussia
U.S. Supreme Court Justices	Rulers of Russia
U.S. Government Officials	Sports Personalities

Names in parentheses indicate a person's original name or nickname. Locations in parentheses are the present-day name of the birthplace. Dates of birth appear as month/day/year. **Boldface** years in parentheses are dates of **(birth–death).**

Information has been gathered from many sources, including the individuals themselves. However, the almanac cannot guarantee the accuracy of every item.

A

Aalto, Alvar (architect); Kuortane, Finland **(1898–1976)**
Abbado, Claudio (orchestra conductor); Milan, Italy, 6/26/33
Abbott, Bud (William Abbott) (comedian); Asbury Park, N.J. **(1898–1974)**
Abbott, George (stage producer); Forestville, N.Y. **(1887–1995)**
Abelard, Peter (theologian); nr. Nantes, France **(1079–1142)**
Abernathy, Ralph (civil rights leader); Linden, Ala. **(1926–1990)**
Abraham, F(ahrid) Murray (actor); Pittsburgh, 10/24/39
Achebe, Chinua (writer); Ogidi, Nigeria, 11/16/30
Acheson, Dean (statesman); Middletown, Conn. **(1893–1971)**
Acuff, Roy Claxton (musician); nr. Maynardsville, Tenn. **(1903–1992)**
Adams, Abigail (First Lady, writer); Weymouth, Mass. **(1744–1818)**
Adams, Bryan (singer, songwriter); Kingston, Ont., Canada, 11/5/59
Adams, Charles Francis (diplomat); Boston **(1807–1886)**
Adams, Don (actor); New York City, 4/19/26
Adams, Edie (Edie Enke) (actress); Kingston, Pa., 4/16/29
Adams, Franklin Pierce (columnist, author); Chicago **(1881–1960)**
Adams, Gerry (political leader); West Belfast, Northern Ireland, 10/6/48
Adams, Henry Brooks (historian); Boston **(1838–1918)**
Adams, Joey (comedian); New York City, 1/6/11
Adams, John (2nd U.S. president); Braintree (Quincy), Mass. **(1735–1826)**
Adams, John Quincy (6th U.S. president); Braintree (Quincy), Mass. **(1767–1848)**
Adams, Maude (Maude Kiskadden) (actress); Salt Lake City **(1872–1953)**
Adams, Samuel (American Revolutionary patriot); Boston **(1722–1803)**
Adams, Scott (cartoonist); Catskill, N.Y., 6/8/57
Adamson, Joy (naturalist, writer); Troppau, Silesia **(1910–1980)**
Addams, Charles (cartoonist); Westfield, N.J. **(1912–1988)**
Addams, Jane (social worker, Nobel laureate); Cedarville, Ill. **(1860–1935)**
Adderley, Julian "Cannonball" (jazz saxophonist); Tampa, Fla. **(1928–1975)**
Ade, George (humorist); Kentland, Ind. **(1866–1944)**
Adenauer, Konrad (statesman); Cologne, Germany **(1876–1967)**
Adler, Alfred (psychoanalyst); Vienna **(1870–1937)**
Adler, Larry (musician); Baltimore, 2/10/14
Adler, Richard (songwriter); New York City, 8/3/21
Aeschylus (dramatist); Eleusis, Greece **(525–456 B.C.)**
Aesop (fabulist); Samos?, Greece, fl. c. 500 B.C.
Agnew, Spiro (political figure); Baltimore **(1905–1996)**
Aiello, Danny (actor); New York City, 6/20/33
Aiken, Conrad (poet); Savannah, Ga. **(1889–1973)**
Ailey, Alvin (choreographer); Rogers, Tex. **(1931–1989)**
Akhmatova, Anna (poet); Odessa, Ukraine **(1889–1966)**
Akihito, Tsugunomiya (Emperor of Japan); Tokyo, 12/23/33
Albanese, Licia (operatic soprano); Bari, Italy, 7/22/13
Albee, Edward (playwright); Washington, D.C., 3/12/28
Albers, Josef (painter); Bottrop, Germany **(1888–1976)**
Albert, Eddie (Edward Albert Heimberger) (actor); Rock Island, Ill., 4/22/08
Albert, Edward (actor); Los Angeles, 2/20/51
Albertson, Jack (actor); Malden, Mass. **(1907–1981)**
Albright, Madeleine (diplomat, U.S. Secretary of State); Prague, Czechoslovakia, 5/15/37

Alcott, Louisa May (novelist); Germantown, Pa. **(1832–1888)**
Alda, Alan (actor); New York City, 1/28/36
Alden, John (American Pilgrim); England **(c. 1599–1687)**
Alexander, Jane (Quigley) (actress); Boston, 10/28/39
Alexander, Jason (Jay Scott Greenspan) (actor); Newark, N.J., 9/23/59
Alexander the Great (monarch, conqueror); Pella, Macedonia, Greece **(356–323 B.C.)**
Alger, Horatio (author); Revere, Mass. **(1834–1899)**
Algren, Nelson (novelist); Detroit **(1909–1981)**
Allen, Debbie (dancer-choreographer, actress); Houston, 1/16/50
Allen, Ethan (American Revolutionary soldier); Litchfield, Conn. **(1738–1789)**
Allen, Fred (John Florence Sullivan) (comedian); Cambridge, Mass. **(1894–1956)**
Allen, Gracie (Grace Ethel Cecile Rosalie Allen) (comedienne); San Francisco **(1906–1964)**
Allen, Joan (actress); Rochelle, Ill., 8/20/56
Allen, Mel (Melvin Israel) (sportscaster); Birmingham, Ala. **(1913–1996)**
Allen, Peter (actor, songwriter); Tenterfield, Australia **(1944–1992)**
Allen, Steve (TV entertainer); New York City, 12/26/21
Allen, Woody (Allen Stewart Konigsberg) (actor, writer, director); Brooklyn, N.Y., 12/1/35
Allende, Isabel (novelist); Lima, Peru, 8/2/42
Alley, Kirstie (actress); Wichita, Kans., 1/12/55
Allison, Fran (actress); LaPorte City, Iowa **(1908?–1989)**
Allman, Gregg (singer); Nashville, Tenn., 12/8/47
Allyson, June (Ella Geisman) (actress); New York City, 10/7/17
Alonso, Alicia (ballet dancer); Havana, 12/21/21?
Alpert, Herb (band leader); Los Angeles, 3/31/35?
Alsop, Joseph W., Jr. (journalist); Avon, Conn. **(1910–1989)**
Alsop, Stewart (journalist); Avon, Conn. **(1914–1974)**
Alt, Carol (model); Flushing, New York, 12/1/60
Altman, Robert (director); Kansas City, Mo., 2/20/25
Amanpour, Christiane (broadcast journalist); London, 1958
Amati, Nicola (violin maker); Cremona, Italy **(1596–1684)**
Ambler, Eric (suspense writer); London **(1909–1998)**
Ameche, Don (Dominic Amici) (actor); Kenosha, Wis. **(1908–1993)**
Amis, Kingsley (novelist); London **(1922–1995)**
Amis, Martin (novelist); Oxford, England, 8/25/49
Amory, Cleveland (writer, conservationist); Nahant, Mass. **(1917–1998)**
Amos (Freeman F. Gosden) (radio comedian); Richmond, Va. **(1899–1982)**
Amos, John (actor); Newark, N.J., 12/27/41
Amos, Tori (singer); Newton, N.C., 8/22/63
Amsterdam, Morey (actor); Chicago **(1914–1996)**
Andersen, Hans Christian (author of fairy tales); Odense, Denmark **(1805–1875)**
Anderson, Eddie (Rochester) (actor); Oakland, Calif. **(1905–1977)**
Anderson, Gillian (actress); Chicago, 8/9/68
Anderson, Harry (actor); Newport, R.I., 10/14/52
Anderson, Ib (ballet dancer); Copenhagen, 12/14/54
Anderson, Jack (journalist); Long Beach, Calif., 10/19/22
Anderson, Dame Judith (actress); Adelaide, Australia **(1898–1992)**
Anderson, Lindsay (Gordon) (director); Bangalore, India **(1923–1994)**
Anderson, Loni (actress); St. Paul, Minn., 8/5/45

Anderson, Lynn (singer); Grand Forks, N.D., 9/26/47
Anderson, Marian (contralto); Philadelphia **(1897–1993)**
Anderson, Maxwell (dramatist); Atlantic, Pa. **(1888–1959)**
Anderson Lee, Pamela (Pamela Anderson) (model, actress); Ladysmith, B.C., Canada, 7/1/67
Anderson, Richard Dean (actor); Minneapolis, Minn., 1/23/50
Anderson, Robert (playwright); New York City, 4/28/17
Anderson, Sherwood (novelist); Camden, Ohio **(1876–1941)**
Andress, Ursula (actress); Bern, Switzerland, 3/19/38
Andrews, Julie (Julia Wells) (actress, singer); Walton-on-Thames, England, 10/1/35
Andrews, La Verne (singer); Minneapolis **(1916–1967)**
Andrews, Maxene (singer); Minneapolis **(1918–1995)**
Andrews, Patti (singer); Minneapolis, 2/16/20
Andy (Charles J. Correll) (radio comedian); Peoria, Ill. **(1890–1972)**
Angelico, Fra (Guido di Pietro; Giovanni de Fiesole) (painter); nr. Florence **(c. 1400–1455)**
Angelou, Maya (Marguerite Johnson) (poet, novelist); St. Louis, 4/4/28
Aniston, Jennifer (Jennifer Anistonapoulos) (actress); Sherman Oaks, Calif., 2/11/69
Anka, Paul (singer, composer); Ottawa, Ont., Canada, 7/30/41
Annan, Kofi (diplomat, U.N. secretary general); Kumasi, Ghana, 4/8/38
Ann-Margret (Ann-Margaret Olsson) (actress); Valsjobyn, Sweden, 4/28/41
Anouilh, Jean (playwright); Bordeaux, France **(1910–1987)**
Anthony, Susan Brownell (woman suffragist); Adams, Mass. **(1820–1906)**
Antonioni, Michelangelo (director); Ferrara, Italy, 9/29/12
Antony, Mark (Marcus Antonius) (statesman); Rome **(c. 83– 30 B.C.)**
Anuszkiewicz, Richard (painter); Erie, Pa., 5/23/30
Apple, Fiona (singer); New York City, 4/8/68
Applegate, Christina (actress); Los Angeles, Calif., 11/25/71
Aquinas, St. Thomas (philosopher); nr. Aquino, Italy **(1225–1274)**
Arafat, Yasir (Mohammed Abdel-Raouf Arafat al Qudwa al Husseini) (chairman of the Palestine Liberation Organization); Cairo, Egypt, 8/24/29
Arbuckle, Roscoe "Fatty" (actor, director); Smith Center, Kans. **(1887–1933)**
Archimedes (physicist, mathematician); Syracuse, Sicily **(287–212 B.C.)**
Archipenko, Alexandre (sculptor); Kiev, Ukraine **(1887–1964)**
Arden, Elizabeth (Florence Nightingale Graham) (cosmetics executive); Woodbridge, Canada **(1891–1966)**
Arden, Eve (Eunice Quedens) (actress); Mill Valley, Calif. **(1912– 1990)**
Arendt, Hannah (historian); Hanover, Germany **(1906–1975)**
Aristophanes (dramatist); Athens **(c. 448–c. 385 B.C.)**
Aristotle (philosopher); Stagirus, Macedonia **(384–322 B.C.)**
Arkin, Adam (actor); New York City, 8/19/57
Arkin, Alan (actor, director); New York City, 3/26/34
Arledge, Roone (TV executive); Forest Hills, N.Y., 7/8/31
Arlen, Harold (Hyman Arluck) (composer); Buffalo, N.Y. **(1905– 1986)**
Armani, Georgio (fashion designer); Piacenza, Italy, 7/11/34
Armstrong, Louis ("Satchmo") (musician); New Orleans **(1900– 1971)**
Arnaz, Desi (Desiderio Alberto Araz y de Acha III) (actor, producer); Santiago, Cuba **(1917–1986)**
Arness, James (James Aurness) (actor); Minneapolis, 5/26/23
Arno, Peter (cartoonist); New York City **(1904–1968)**
Arnold, Benedict (American Revolutionary War general, charged with treason); Norwich, Conn. **(1741–1801)**
Arnold, Matthew (poet, critic); Laleham, England **(1822–1888)**
Arp, Jean (sculptor, painter); Strasbourg, France **(1887–1966)**
Arquette, Cliff (actor); Toledo, Ohio **(1905–1974)**
Arquette, Patricia (actress); Chicago, 4/8/68
Arquette, Rosanna (actress); New York City, 8/10/59
Arrau, Claudio (pianist); Chillán, Chile **(1903–1991)**
Arroyo, Martina (soprano); New York City, 2/2/40
Arthur, Bea (Bernice Frankel) (actress); New York City, 5/13/23
Arthur, Chester Alan (21st U.S. president); Fairfield, Vt. **(1830– 1886)**
Ashcroft, Dame Peggy (actress); Croydon, England **(1907–1991)**
Ashkenazy, Vladimir (concert pianist); Gorki, U.S.S.R., 7/6/37
Ashley, Elizabeth (actress); Ocala, Fla., 8/30/39
Ashton, Sir Frederick William Mallandaine (choreographer); Guayaquil, Ecuador **(1904–1988)**
Asimov, Isaac (author); Petrovichi, Russia **(1920–1992)**
Asner, Edward (actor); Kansas City, Mo., 11/15/29
Assante, Armand (actor); New York City, 10/4/49

Astaire, Fred (Frederick Austerlitz) (dancer, actor); Omaha, Neb. **(1899–1987)**
Astin, John (actor, director); Baltimore, 3/30/30
Astor, Brooke (socialite, philanthropist); Portsmouth, N.H., 3/16/05
Astor, John Jacob (financier); Waldorf, Germany **(1763–1848)**
Astor, Mary (Lucile Langhanke) (actress); Quincy, Ill. **(1906–1987)**
Ataturk, Kemal (Mustafa Kemal) (Turkish soldier, statesman); Salonika, Greece **(1881–1938)**
Atkins, Chet (guitarist); nr. Luttrell, Tenn., 6/20/24
Atkinson, Rowan (actor); Newcastle-Upon-Tyne, England, 1/6/55
Attenborough, Richard (actor, director); Cambridge, England, 8/29/23
Attila (King of Huns); **(406?–453)**
Attucks, Crispus (American Revolutionary Patriot); Boston **(c. 1723–1770)**
Auberjonois, Rene (actor); New York City, 6/1/40
Auchincloss, Louis (author); Lawrence, N.Y., 9/27/17
Auden, W(ystan) H(ugh) (poet); York, England **(1907–1973)**
Audubon, John James (naturalist, painter); Haiti **(1785–1851)**
Auer, Leopold (violinist, teacher); Veszprém, Hungary **(1845–1930)**
Augustine, Saint (Aurelius Augustinus) (theologian); Tagaste, Numidia, Algeria **(354–430)**
Augustus (Gaius Octavius) (Roman emperor); Rome **(63 B.C.– A.D. 14)**
Aung San Suu Kyi (human rights activist); Rangoon, Burma, 6/19/45
Austen, Jane (novelist); Steventon, England **(1775–1817)**
Autry, Gene (singer, actor); Tioga, Tex. **(1907–1998)**
Avalon, Frankie (singer); Philadelphia, 9/18/39
Avedon, Richard (photographer); New York City, 5/15/23
Avery, Milton (painter); Altmar, N.Y. **(1893–1965)**
Ax, Emanuel (pianist); Lvov, Ukraine, 6/8/49
Axelrod, George (playwright); New York City, 6/9/22
Ayckbourn, Alan (playwright); London, 4/12/39
Aykroyd, Dan (actor); Ottawa, Ont., Canada, 7/1/52
Ayres, Lew (actor); Minneapolis **(1908–1996)**

B

Bacall, Lauren (Betty Joan Perske) (actress); New York City, 9/16/24
Bach, Carl Phillipp Emanuel (composer); Weimar, Germany **(1714– 1788)**
Bach, Johann Sebastian (composer); Eisenach, Germany **(1685– 1750)**
Bacharach, Burt (songwriter); Kansas City, Mo., 5/12/29
Backus, Jim (actor); Cleveland **(1913–1989)**
Bacon, Francis (philosopher, essayist); London **(1561–1626)**
Bacon, Francis (painter); Dublin **(1910–1992)**
Bacon, Kevin (actor); Philadelphia, 7/8/58
Bacon, Roger (philosopher, scientist); Ilchester, England **(c. 1214– 1294?)**
Badu, Erykah (Erykah Wright) (singer); Dallas, 1971
Baez, Joan (folk singer); Staten Island, N.Y., 1/9/41
Bailey, F. Lee (lawyer); Waltham, Mass., 6/10/33
Bailey, Pearl (singer); Newport News, Va. **(1918–1990)**
Bain, Conrad (actor); Lethbridge, Alba., Canada, 2/4/23
Baio, Scott (actor); Brooklyn, N.Y., 9/22/61
Baird, Bil (William B. Baird) (puppeteer); Grand Island, Neb. **(1904– 1987)**
Baker, Anita (singer); Toledo, Ohio, 1958
Baker, Carroll (actress); Johnstown, Pa., 5/28/31
Baker, Josephine (singer, dancer); St. Louis **(1906–1975)**
Baker, Russell (columnist); Loudoun County, Va., 8/14/25
Balanchine, George (choreographer); St. Petersburg, Russia **(1904–1983)**
Balboa, Vasco Nuñez de (explorer); Jerez de los Caballeros, Spain **(1475–1517)**
Baldwin, Alec (actor); Massapequa, N.Y., 4/3/58
Baldwin, James (novelist); New York City **(1924–1987)**
Bale, Christian (actor); Pembrokeshire, Wales, 1/30/74
Balenciaga, Cristóbal (fashion designer); Guetaria, Spain **(1895– 1972)**
Ball, Lucille (Lucille Désirée Ball) (actress, producer); Celoron (nr. Jamestown), N.Y. **(1911–1989)**
Balsam, Martin (actor); Bronx, New York **(1919–1996)**
Balzac, Honoré de (novelist); Tours, France **(1799–1850)**
Bancroft, Anne (Annemarie Italiano) (actress); New York City, 9/17/31
Banderas, Antonio (José Antonio Dominguez Banderas) (actor, model); Málaga, Spain, 8/10/60
Bankhead, Tallulah (actress); Huntsville, Ala. **(1903–1968)**
Banks, Tyra (model); Los Angeles, 12/4/73

Banting, Fredrick Grant (physiologist); Alliston, Ont., Canada (1891–1941)
Bara, Theda (Theodosia Goodman) (actress); Cincinnati (1890–1955)
Barak, Ehud (Israeli prime minister); Kibbutz Mishmar Hasharon, Israel, 2/12/42
Barbera, Joseph (animator, producer); New York City, 1911
Baraka, Imamu Amiri (LeRoi Jones) (playwright); Newark, N.J., 10/7/34
Baranski, Christine (actress); Buffalo, N.Y., 5/2/52
Barber, Red (Walter Lanier) (sportscaster); Columbus, Miss. (1908–1992)
Barber, Samuel (composer); West Chester, Pa. (1910–1981)
Barbie, Klaus (Nazi, "The Butcher of Lyon"); Bad Godesberg, Germany (1913–1991)
Bardot, Brigitte (Camille Javal) (actress); Paris, 9/28/34
Barenboim, Daniel (concert pianist, conductor); Buenos Aires, 11/15/42
Barker, Bob (game-show host); Darrington, Wash., 12/12/23
Barkin, Ellen (actress); Bronx, N.Y., 4/16/54
Barnard, Christiaan N. (heart surgeon); Beauford West, South Africa, 10/8/22
Barnum, Phineas Taylor (showman); Bethel, Conn. (1810–1891)
Barrie, Sir James Matthew (author); Kirriemuir, Scotland (1860–1937)
Barry, John (naval officer); County Wexford, Ireland (1745–1803)
Barrymore, Diana (actress); New York City (1921–1960)
Barrymore, Drew (actress); Los Angeles, 2/22/75
Barrymore, Ethel (Ethel Blythe) (actress); Philadelphia (1879–1959)
Barrymore, Georgiana Drew (actress); Philadelphia (1856–1893)
Barrymore, John (John Blythe) (actor); Philadelphia (1882–1942)
Barrymore, Lionel (Lionel Blythe) (actor); Philadelphia (1878–1954)
Barrymore, Maurice (Herbert Blythe) (actor, playwright); Agra, India (1847–1905)
Barth, John (novelist); Cambridge, Md., 5/27/30
Barthelme, Donald (novelist); Philadelphia (1931 –1989)
Bartók, Béla (composer); Nagyszentmiklo, Hungary (1881–1945)
Barton, Clara (founder of American Red Cross); Oxford, Mass. (1821–1912)
Baruch, Bernard Mannes (statesman); Camden, S.C. (1870–1965)
Baryshnikov, Mikhail Nikolayevich (ballet dancer, artistic director); Riga, Latvia, 1/27/48
Basie, Count (William Basie) (band leader); Red Bank, N.J. (1904–1984)
Basinger, Kim (actress); Athens, Ga., 12/8/53
Bassett, Angela (actress); New York City, 8/16/58
Bassey, Shirley (singer); Cardiff, Wales, 1/8/37
Batchelor, Clarence Daniel (political cartoonist); Osage City, Kans. (1888–1977)
Bateman, Jason (actor); Rye, N.Y., 1/14/69
Bateman, Justine (actress); Rye, N.Y., 2/19/66
Bates, Alan (actor); Allestree, England, 2/17/34
Bates, Kathy (Kathleen Doyle Bates) (actress); Memphis, Tenn., 6/28/48
Battle, Kathleen (soprano); Portsmouth, Ohio, 8/13/48
Baudelaire, Charles Pierre (poet); Paris (1821–1867)
Baxter, Anne (actress); Michigan City, Ind. (1923–1985)
Baxter, Meredith (actress); Los Angeles, 6/21/47
Beardsley, Aubrey Vincent (illustrator); Brighton, England (1872–1898)
Beaton, Cecil (photographer, designer); London (1904–1980)
Beatty, Clyde (animal trainer); Bainbridge, Ohio (1903–1965)
Beatty, Warren (Henry Warren Beaty) (actor, producer); Richmond, Va., 3/30/37
Beaumont, Francis (dramatist); Grace-Dieu, England (1584–1616)
Becket, Thomas à (archbishop of Canterbury); London (1118?–1170)
Beckett, Samuel (playwright); Dublin (1906–1989)
Beckmann, Max (painter); Leipzig, Germany (1884–1950)
Bede, Saint ("The Venerable Bede") (scholar); Monkwearmouth, England (673–735)
Beecham, Sir Thomas (conductor); St. Helens, England (1879–1961)
Beecher, Henry Ward (clergyman); Litchfield, Conn. (1813–1887)
Beerbohm, Sir Max (author); London (1872–1956)
Beery, Noah (actor); Kansas City, Mo. (1884–1946)
Beery, Noah, Jr. (actor); New York City (1913–1994)
Beery, Wallace (actor); Kansas City, Mo. (1886–1949)
Beethoven, Ludwig van (composer); Bonn, Germany (1770–1827)
Begin, Menachem (Israeli prime minister); Brest-Litovsk, Belarus (1913–1992)
Begley, Ed (actor); Hartford, Conn. (1901–1970)

Beiderbecke, Bix (jazz musician); Davenport, Iowa (1903–1931)
Beineix, Jean-Jacques (director, producer, screenwriter) 1946
Belafonte, Harry (singer, actor); New York City, 3/1/27
Belafonte-Harper, Shari (actress); New York City, 9/22/54
Belasco, David (dramatist, producer); San Francisco (1854–1931)
Bel Geddes, Barbara (actress); New York City, 10/31/22
Bell, Alexander Graham (inventor); Edinburgh, Scotland (1847–1922)
Bell, Quentin (author, artist); England (1910–1996)
Bellamy, Edward (author); Chicopee Falls, Mass. (1850–1898)
Bellamy, Ralph (actor); Chicago (1904–1991)
Bellini, Giovanni (painter); Venice (c. 1430–1516)
Bellow, Saul (novelist); Lachine, Que., Canada, 6/10/15
Bellows, George Wesley (painter, lithographer); Columbus, Ohio (1882–1925)
Belushi, Jim (actor); Chicago, 6/15/54
Belushi, John (comedian, actor); Chicago (1949–1982)
Benchley, Peter Bradford (novelist); New York City, 5/8/40
Benchley, Robert Charles (humorist); Worcester, Mass. (1889–1945)
Bendix, William (actor); New York City (1906–1964)
Benedict, Ruth Fulton (anthropologist); New York City (1887–1948)
Benes, Eduard (statesman); Kozlany, former Czechoslovakia (1884–1948)
Benét, Stephen Vincent (poet, story writer); Bethlehem, Pa. (1898–1943)
Benét, William Rose (poet, novelist); Ft. Hamilton, Brooklyn, N.Y. (1886–1950)
Ben-Gurion, David (David Green) (statesman); Plónsk, Poland (1886–1973)
Benigni, Roberto (actor, director, screenwriter); Misericordia, Arezzo, Italy, 10/27/52
Bening, Annette (actress); Topeka, Kans., 5/29/58
Bennett, Enoch Arnold (novelist, dramatist); Hanley, England (1867–1931)
Bennett, James Gordon (editor); Keith, Scotland (1795–1872)
Bennett, Joan (actress); Palisades, N.J. (1910–1990)
Bennett, Robert Russell (composer); Kansas City, Mo. (1894–1981)
Bennett, Tony (Anthony Benedetto) (singer); Astoria, Queens, N.Y., 8/3/26
Benny, Jack (Benjamin Kubelsky) (comedian); Chicago (1894–1974)
Benson, Robby (Robert Segal) (actor); Dallas, 1/21/56
Bentham, Jeremy Heinrich (economist); London (1748–1832)
Benton, Thomas Hart (painter); Neosho, Mo. (1889–1975)
Berendt, John (writer); Syracuse, N.Y., 12/5/39
Berenger, Tom (actor); Chicago, 5/31/50
Berg, Alban (composer); Vienna (1885–1935)
Berg, Gertrude (writer, actress); New York City (1899–1966)
Bergen, Candice (actress); Beverly Hills, Calif., 5/9/46
Bergen, Edgar (ventriloquist); Chicago (1903–1978)
Bergen, Polly (Nellie Paulina Burgin) (actress, singer); Knoxville, Tenn., 7/14/30
Bergerac, Cyrano de (poet); Paris (1619–1655)
Bergman, Ingmar (film director); Uppsala, Sweden, 7/14/18
Bergman, Ingrid (actress); Stockholm (1918–1982)
Bergson, Henri (philosopher); Paris (1859–1941)
Berkeley, Busby (William Berkeley Enos) (choreographer, director); Los Angeles (1895–1976)
Berle, Milton (Milton Berlinger) (comedian); New York City, 7/12/08
Berlin, Irving (Israel Baline) (songwriter); Temum, Russia (1888–1989)
Berlioz, Louis Hector (composer); La Côte-Saint-André, France (1803–1869)
Berman, Lazar (concert pianist); Leningrad (St. Petersburg), Russia, 2/26/30
Bernardin, Joseph Cardinal (prelate); Columbia, S.C. (1928–1996)
Bernhard, Sandra (actress, comedian); Flint, Mich., 6/6/55
Bernhardt, Sarah (Rosine Bernard) (actress); Paris (1844–1923)
Bernini, Gian Lorenzo (sculptor, painter); Naples, Italy (1598–1680)
Bernoulli, Jacques (scientist); Basel, Switzerland (1654–1705)
Bernsen, Corbin (actor); North Hollywood, Calif., 7/7/54
Bernstein, Leonard (conductor); Lawrence, Mass. (1918–1990)
Berry, Chuck (Charles Edward Berry) (singer, guitarist); St. Louis, Mo., 10/19/26
Berry, Halle (actress, model); Cleveland, Ohio, 8/14/68
Berry, Ken (actor); Moline, Ill., 11/3/30
Berry, Richard (songwriter); Extension, S.C. (1935–1997)
Berryman, John (poet); McAlester, Okla. (1914–1972)
Bertinelli, Valerie (actress); Wilmington, Del., 4/23/60
Bertolucci, Bernardo (actor); Parma, Italy, 3/16/40
Bethune, Mary McLeod (educator); Mayesville, S.C. (1875–1955)

Betjeman, Sir John (poet laureate); London **(1906–1984)**
Bettelheim, Bruno (psychoanalyst); Vienna **(1903–1990)**
Bierce, Ambrose Gwinnett (journalist); Meigs County, Ohio **(1842–1914?)**
Bikel, Theodore (actor, folk singer); Vienna, 5/2/24
Bing, Sir Rudolf (opera manager); Vienna **(1902–1997)**
Bingham, George Caleb (painter); Augusta Co., Va. **(1811–1879)**
Binoche, Juliette (actress); Paris, 3/9/64
Bishop, Joey (Joseph Gottlieb) (comedian); New York City, 2/3/19
Bismarck-Schönhausen, Prince Otto Eduard Leopold von (statesman); Schönhausen, Germany **(1815–1898)**
Bisset, Jacqueline (actress); Weybridge, England, 9/13/44
Bixby, Bill (actor); San Francisco **(1934–1993)**
Bizet, Georges (Alexandre César Léopold Bizet) (composer); Paris **(1838–1875)**
Bjoerling, Jussi (tenor); Stora Tuna, Sweden **(1911–1960)**
Björk (Björk Gudmundsdottir) (pop musician, singer); Reykjavik, Iceland, 11/21/65
Black, Clint (singer, songwriter); Long Branch, N.J., 2/4/62
Black, Karen (Karen Ziegler) (actress); Park Ridge, Ill., 7/1/42
Black, Shirley Temple (child actress, former ambassador); Santa Monica, Calif., 4/23/28
Blackstone, Sir William (jurist); London **(1723–1780)**
Blackwell, Elizabeth (physician, educator); England **(1821–1910)**
Blades, Ruben (actor, musician, composer); Panama City, Panama, 7/16/48
Blair, Tony (British prime minister); Edinburgh, Scotland, 3/6/53
Blake, Amanda (Beverly Louise Neill) (actress); Buffalo, N.Y. **(1929–1989)**
Blake, Eubie (James Hubert) (pianist); Baltimore **(1883–1983)**
Blake, Robert (Michael Gubitosi) (actor); Nutley, N.J., 9/18/33
Blake, William (poet, artist); London **(1757–1827)**
Blanc, Mel (Melvin Jerome) (actor, voice specialist); San Francisco **(1908–1989)**
Blass, Bill (fashion designer); Fort Wayne, Ind., 6/22/22
Bleeth, Yasmine (model, actress); New York City, 6/14/68
Blige, Mary J. (hip-hop singer); Bronx, N.Y., 1/11/71
Bloch, Ernest (composer); Geneva **(1880–1959)**
Bloom, Claire (actress); London, 2/15/31
Bloomgarden, Kermit (producer); Brooklyn, N.Y. **(1904–1976)**
Blume, Judy (Judy Sussman) (young adult novelist); Elizabeth, N.J., 2/12/38
Bly, Nellie (pseud. for Elizabeth Seaman) (journalist); Cochrane Mills, Pa. **(1867–1922)**
Bly, Robert (poet, critic); Madison, Minn., 12/23/26
Boccaccio, Giovanni (author); Paris **(1313–1375)**
Boccherini, Luigi (Rodolfo) (composer); Lucca, Italy **(1743–1805)**
Boccioni, Umberto (painter, sculptor); Reggio di Calabria, Italy **(1882–1916)**
Bochco, Steven (TV producer, writer); New York City, 12/16/43
Bock, Jerry (composer); New Haven, Conn., 11/23/28
Bogarde, Dirk (Derek Van den Bogaerde) (film actor, director); London **(1921–1999)**
Bogart, Humphrey DeForest (actor); New York City **(1899–1957)**
Bogdanovich, Peter (film producer, director); Kingston, N.Y., 7/30/39
Bogosian, Eric (playwright, screenwriter, actor, monologuist); Woburn, Mass., 4/24/53
Bohlen, Charles E. (diplomat); Clayton, N.Y. **(1904–1974)**
Bohr, Niels (atomic physicist); Copenhagen **(1885–1962)**
Bok, Sissela (Sissela Ann Myrdal) (scholar); Stockholm, 12/2/34
Bolger, Ray (dancer, actor); Dorchester, Mass **(1904–1987)**
Bolívar, Simón (South American liberator); Caracas, Venezuela **(1783–1830)**
Bologna, Giovanni da (sculptor); Douai, France **(1529–1608)**
Bombeck, Erma (author, columnist); Dayton, Ohio **(1927–1996)**
Bonaparte, Napoléon (Emperor of the French); Ajaccio, Corsica, France **(1769–1821)**
Bond, Julian (Georgia legislator); Nashville, Tenn., 1/14/40
Bonet, Lisa (actress); San Francisco, 11/16/67
Bonham Carter, Helena (actress); London, 5/23/66
Bon Jovi, Jon (musician, songwriter); Sayreville, N.J., 3/2/62
Bonnard, Pierre (painter); Fontenayaux-Roses, France **(1867–1947)**
Bono (Paul Hewson) (singer, songwriter); Dublin, Ireland, 5/10/60
Bono, Sonny (Salvatore Bono) (singer, politician); Detroit **(1935–1998)**
Boone, Daniel (frontiersman); nr. Reading, Pa. **(1734–1820)**
Boone, Pat (Charles Boone) (singer); Jacksonville, Fla., 6/1/34
Boone, Richard (actor); Los Angeles **(1917–1981)**
Boorstin, Daniel (historian); Atlanta, 10/1/14
Booth, Edwin Thomas (actor); Bel Air, Md. **(1833–1893)**
Booth, Evangeline Cory (religious leader); London **(1865–1950)**

Booth, John Wilkes (actor; assassin of Lincoln); Harford County, Md. **(1838–1865)**
Booth, Shirley (Thelma Booth Ford) (actress); New York City **(1907–1992)**
Borden, Lizzie (Elizabeth Andrew Borden) (accused murderer); Fall River, Mass. **(1860–1927)**
Borge, Victor (pianist, comedian); Copenhagen, 1/3/09
Borgia, Cesare (nobleman, soldier); Rome **(1476–1507)**
Borgia, Lucrezia (Duchess of Ferrara); Rome **(1480–1519)**
Borgnine, Ernest (actor); Hamden, Conn., 1/24/17
Borromini, Francesco (architect); Bissone, Italy **(1599–1667)**
Bosch, Hieronymus (Hieronymus van Aeken) (painter); Hertogenbosch, Netherlands **(c. 1450–1516)**
Bosley, Tom (actor); Chicago, 10/1/27
Bostwick, Barry (actor); San Mateo, Calif., 2/24/45
Boswell, James (diarist, biographer); Edinburgh, Scotland **(1740–1795)**
Botticelli, Sandro (Alessandro di Mariano dei Filipepi) (painter); Florence, Italy **(1444–1510)**
Bottoms, Timothy (actor); Santa Barbara, Calif., 8/30/50
Boulez, Pierre (conductor); Montbrison, France, 3/26/25
Bourke-White, Margaret (photographer); New York City **(1906–1971)**
Boutros-Ghali, Boutros (ex-secretary general of the U.N.); Cairo, Egypt, 11/14/22
Bow, Clara (actress); Brooklyn, N.Y. **(1905–1965)**
Bowen, Catherine Drinker (biographer); Haverford, Pa. **(1897–1973)**
Bowie, David (David Robert Jones) (actor, musician); London, 1/8/47
Bowie, James (soldier); Burke County, Ga. **(1799–1836)**
Bowles, Chester (diplomat); Springfield, Mass. **(1901–1986)**
Boxleitner, Bruce (actor); Elgin, Ill., 5/12/50
Boyce, William (composer); London? **(1710–1779)**
Boyd, Bill ("Hopalong Cassidy") (actor); Cambridge, Ohio **(1895–1972)**
Boyd, Stephen (Stephen Millar) (actor); Belfast, Northern Ireland **(1928–1977)**
Boyer, Charles (actor); Figeac, France **(1897–1978)**
Boy George (George Alan O'Dowd) (singer); London, 6/14/61
Boyle, Peter (actor); Philadelphia, 10/18/33
Boyle, Robert (scientist); Lismore Castle, Munster, Ireland **(1627–1691)**
Bradbury, Ray Douglas (science-fiction writer); Waukegan, Ill., 8/22/20
Bradlee, Benjamin C. (editor); Boston, 8/26/21
Bradley, Ed (broadcast journalist); Philadelphia, 6/22/41
Bradley, Omar N. (5-star general); Clark, Mo. **(1893–1981)**
Bradley, Thomas (mayor of Los Angeles); Calvert, Tex. **(1917–1998)**
Brady, Mathew (early photographer); Warren Co., N.Y. **(c. 1823–1896)**
Brahe, Tycho (astronomer); Knudstrup, Denmark **(1546–1601)**
Bragg, Billy (singer, songwriter); Barking, England, 12/20/57
Brahms, Johannes (composer); Hamburg, Germany **(1833–1897)**
Braille, Louis (teacher of blind); Coupvray, France **(1809–1862)**
Brailowsky, Alexander (pianist); Kiev, Ukraine **(1896–1976)**
Bramante, Donato D'Agnolo (architect); Monte Asdrualdo (now Fermignano), Italy **(1444–1514)**
Branagh, Kenneth (actor, director, writer, producer); Belfast, Northern Ireland, 12/10/60
Brancusi, Constantin (sculptor); Pestisansi, Romania **(1876–1957)**
Brandauer, Klaus Maria (Klaus Maria Steng) (actor); Bad Aussee, Steiermark, Austria , 6/22/44
Brando, Marlon (actor); Omaha, Neb., 4/3/24
Brandt, Willy (Herbert Frahm) (ex-chancellor); Lübeck, Germany **(1913– 1992)**
Brandy (Brandy Norwood) (actress, singer); McComb, Miss., 2/11/79
Braque, Georges (painter); Argenteuil, France **(1882–1963)**
Bratt, Benjamin (actor); San Francisco, 12/16/63
Braugher, André (actor); Chicago, 7/1/62
Braxton, Toni (R&B singer); Severn, Maryland, 10/7/67
Brazelton, T(homas) Berry II (pediatrician, writer); Waco, Tex., 5/10/18
Brecht, Bertolt (dramatist, poet); Augsburg, Bavaria **(1898–1956)**
Brel, Jacques (singer, composer); Brussels **(1929–1978)**
Brennan, Walter (actor); Lynn, Mass. **(1894–1974)**
Brennan, William J., Jr. (Supreme Court justice); Newark, N.J. **(1906–1997)**
Breslin, Jimmy (journalist); Jamaica, Queens, N.Y., 10/17/30
Breton, André (writer); Tinchebray, France **(1896–1966)**
Breuer, Marcel (architect, designer); Pécs, Hungary **(1902–1981)**

Brewster, Kingman, Jr. (ex-president of Yale); Longmeadow, Mass. **(1919–1988)**

Brezhnev, Leonid I. (Communist Party Secretary); Dneprodzerzhinsk, Ukraine **(1906–1982)**

Brice, Fanny (Fannie Borach) (comedienne); New York City **(1892–1951)**

Bridges, Beau (actor); Los Angeles, 12/9/41

Bridges, Jeff (actor); Los Angeles, 12/4/49

Bridges, Lloyd (actor); San Leandro, Calif. **(1913–1998)**

Brinkley, Christie (model, actress); Malibu, Calif., 2/2/54

Brinkley, David (TV newscaster); Wilmington, N.C., 7/10/20

Britten, Benjamin (composer); Lowestoft, England **(1913–1976)**

Broderick, Matthew (actor); New York City, 3/21/62

Brodsky, Joseph Alexandrovitch (poet); St. Petersburg, Russia **(1940–1996)**

Brody, Jane (journalist); Brooklyn, N.Y., 5/19/41

Brokaw, Tom (TV newscaster); Webster, S.D., 2/6/40

Brolin, James (actor); Los Angeles, 7/18/40

Bromfield, Louis (novelist); Mansfield, Ohio **(1896–1956)**

Bronson, Charles (Charles Buchinsky) (actor); Ehrenfield, Pa., 11/3/21

Brontë, Charlotte (novelist); Thornton, England **(1816–1855)**

Brontë, Emily Jane (novelist); Thornton, England **(1818–1848)**

Bronzino, Agnolo (painter); Monticelli, Italy **(1503–1572)**

Brook, Peter (director); London, 3/21/25

Brooke, Rupert (poet); Rugby, England **(1887–1915)**

Brooks, Albert (Albert Einstein) (actor, writer, director); Beverly Hills, Calif., 7/22/47

Brooks, Avery (actor) 4/18/49

Brooks, Gwendolyn (poet); Topeka, Kans., 6/7/17

Brooks, James L. (film and television producer); New York City, 5/9/40

Brooks, Mel (Melvin Kaminsky) (writer, film director); Brooklyn, N.Y., 6/28/26

Brosnan, Pierce (actor); County Meath, Ireland, 5/16/52

Brothers, Joyce (Bauer) (psychologist, author, radio-TV personality); New York City, 9/20/28

Broun, Matthew Heywood Campbell (journalist); Brooklyn, N.Y. **(1888–1939)**

Brown, Charles Brockden (novelist); Philadelphia **(1771–1810)**

Brown, Helen Gurley (editor, author); Green Forest, Ark., 2/18/22

Brown, James (singer); Augusta, Ga., 5/3/34

Brown, Joe E. (comedian); Holgate, Ohio **(1892–1973)**

Brown, John (abolitionist); Torrington, Conn. **(1800–1859)**

Brown, Les (band leader); Reinerton, Pa., 3/14/12

Brown, Margaret Wise (children's author); Brooklyn, N.Y. **(1910–1962)**

Brown, Trisha (choreographer); Aberdeen, Wash., 11/25/36

Browne, Jackson (singer, guitarist); Heidelberg, Germany, 10/9/48

Browning, Elizabeth Barrett (poet); Durham, England **(1806–1861)**

Browning, Robert (poet); London **(1812–1889)**

Brubeck, Dave (musician); Concord, Calif., 12/6/20

Bruce, Lenny (comedian); Long Island, N.Y. **(1926–1966)**

Bruce, Nigel (actor); Ensenada, Mexico **(1895–1953)**

Brueghel, Pieter (painter); nr. Breda, Flanders, Netherlands (c. 1520–1569)

Bruhn, Erik (Belton Evers) (ballet dancer); Copenhagen **(1928–1986)**

Brunelleschi, Filippo (architect); Florence, Italy **(1377–1446)**

Bruno, Giordano (philosopher); Nola, Italy **(1548–1600)**

Brutus, Marcus Junius (Roman politician) **(85–42 B.C.)**

Bryan, William Jennings (orator, politician); Salem, Ill. **(1860–1925)**

Bryant, Anita (singer); Barnsdall, Okla., 3/25/40

Bryant, William Cullen (poet, editor); Cummington, Mass. **(1794–1878)**

Brynner, Yul (Taidje Khan) (actor); Sakhalin Island, Russia **(1920–1985)**

Brzezinski, Zbigniew (ex-presidential adviser); Warsaw, 3/28/28

Buber, Martin (philosopher, theologian); Vienna **(1878–1965)**

Buchanan, Pat (politician); Washington, D.C., 11/2/38

Buchholz, Horst (actor); Berlin, 12/4/33

Büchner, Georg (dramatist); Goddelau, Germany **(1813–1837)**

Buchwald, Art (Arthur Buchwald) (columnist); Mount Vernon, N.Y., 10/20/25

Buck, Pearl S(ydenstricker) (author); Hillsboro, W. Va. **(1892–1973)**

Buckley, Christopher (writer); New York City, 1952

Buckley, Jeff (singer, songwriter); Orange County, Calif. **(1966–1997)**

Buckley, William F., Jr. (journalist); New York City, 11/24/25

Buffalo Bill (William Frederick Cody) (scout); Scott County, Iowa **(1846–1917)**

Buffett, Jimmy (singer, writer); Pascogoula, Miss., 12/25/46

Buffett, Warren (investment expert); Omaha, Neb., 8/30/30

Bujold, Genevieve (actress); Montreal, 7/1/42

Bujones, Fernando (ballet dancer); Miami, Fla., 3/9/55

Bulgakov, Mikhail (novelist); Kiev, Ukraine **(1891–1940)**

Bullins, Ed (playwright); Philadelphia, 7/2/35

Bullock, Sandra (actress); Washington D.C., 7/26/65

Bunche, Ralph J. (statesman); Detroit **(1904–1971)**

Bundy, McGeorge (educator); Boston **(1919–1996)**

Bundy, William Putnam (editor); Washington, D.C. **(1917–2000)**

Buñuel, Luis (film director); Calanda, Spain **(1900–1983)**

Bunyan, John (preacher, author); Elstow, England **(1628–1688)**

Burbank, Luther (horticulturist); Lancaster, Mass. **(1849–1926)**

Burke, Adm. Arleigh A. (ex-Chief of Naval Operations); Boulder, Colo. **(1901–1996)**

Burke, Billie (Mary William Ethelbert Appleton Burke) (comedienne); Washington, D.C. **(1885–1970)**

Burke, Delta (actress); Orlando, Fla., 7/30/56

Burke, Edmund (statesman); Dublin **(1729–1797)**

Burne-Jones, Edward Coley (painter); Birmingham, England **(1833–1898)**

Burnett, Carol (comedienne); San Antonio, 4/26/33

Burney, Fanny (Frances) (writer); King's Lynn, England **(1752–1840)**

Burns, Edward (actor, film director, screenwriter, producer); Long Island, N.Y., 1/29/68

Burns, George (Nathan Birnbaum) (comedian); New York City **(1896–1996)**

Burns, Ken (documentary filmmaker); Brooklyn, N.Y., 7/29/53

Burns, Robert (poet); Alloway, Scotland **(1759–1796)**

Burr, Aaron (political leader); Newark, N.J. **(1756–1836)**

Burr, Raymond (William Stacey Burr) (actor); New Westminster, B.C., Canada **(1917–1993)**

Burroughs, Edgar Rice (novelist); Chicago **(1875–1950)**

Burroughs, William S. (writer); St. Louis **(1914–1997)**

Burrows, Abe (playwright, director); New York City **(1910–1985)**

Burstyn, Ellen (Edna Rae Gillooly) (actress); Detroit, 12/7/32

Burton, LeVar (actor, director); Landsthul, Germany, 2/16/57

Burton, Richard (Richard Jenkins) (actor); Pontrhyfden, Wales **(1925–1984)**

Burton, Tim (filmmaker); Burbank, Calif., 8/25/58

Buscemi, Steve (actor); Brooklyn, N.Y., 12/13/57

Bush, George Herbert Walker (41st U.S. president); Milton, Mass., 6/12/24

Butkus, Dick (NFL linebacker, actor); Chicago, 12/9/42

Butler, Samuel (author); Langar, England **(1835–1902)**

Butterworth, Charles (actor); South Bend, Ind. **(1896–1946)**

Buttons, Red (Aaron Chwatt) (actor); New York City, 2/5/19

Buzzi, Ruth (comedienne); Westerly, R.I., 7/24/36

Byrd, Richard Evelyn (polar explorer); Winchester, Va. **(1888–1957)**

Byrne, David (composer, musician, director, actor); Dumbarton, Scotland, 5/14/52

Byrne, Gabriel (actor); Dublin, 5/12/50

Byron, George Gordon (6th Baron Byron) (poet); London **(1788–1824)**

C

Caan, James (actor); Queens, N.Y., 3/26/39

Caballé, Montserrat (soprano); Barcelona, Spain, 4/12/33

Cabot, John (Giovanni Caboto) (navigator); Genoa **(1450–1498)**

Cabot, Sebastian (navigator); Venice (c. 1476–1557)

Cadmus, Paul (painter, etcher); New York City **(1904–1999)**

Caesar, Irving (lyricist); New York City **(1895–1996)**

Caesar, Gaius Julius (statesman); Rome **(100–44 B.C.)**

Caesar, Sid (comedian); Yonkers, N.Y., 9/8/22

Cage, Nicolas (Nicolas Coppola) (actor); Long Beach, Calif., 1/7/64

Cagney, James (actor); New York City **(1899–1986)**

Cahn, Sammy (songwriter); New York City **(1913–1993)**

Caine, Michael (Maurice J. Micklewhite) (actor); London, 3/14/33

Calder, Alexander (sculptor); Lawnton, Pa. **(1898–1976)**

Calderón del la Barca, Pedro (dramatist); Madrid **(1600–1681)**

Caldwell, Erskine (novelist); White Oak, Ga. **(1903–1987)**

Caldwell, Sarah (opera director, conductor); Maryville, Mo., 3/6/24

Caldwell, Taylor (novelist); Manchester, England **(1900–1985)**

Caldwell, Zoe (actress); Hawthorn, Australia, 9/14/33

Calhoun, John Caldwell (statesman); nr. Calhoun Mills, S.C. **(1782–1850)**

Caligula Gaius Caesar (Roman emperor); Antium, Latium **(12–41)**

Calisher, Hortense (novelist); New York City, 12/20/11

Callas, Maria (Maria Calogeropoulos) (dramatic soprano); New York City **(1923–1977)**

Calloway, Cab (Cabell Calloway) (band leader); Rochester, N.Y. **(1907–1994)**

Calvin, John (Jean Chauvin) (religious reformer); Noyon, Picardy (1509–1564)

Calvin, Melvin (chemist, Nobel laureate); St. Paul, Minn. (1911–1997)

Cambridge, Godfrey (comedian); New York City (1933–1976)

Cameron, James (director); Kapuskasing, Ont., Canada, 8/16/54

Cameron, Rod (Rod Cox) (actor); Calgary, Alba., Canada (1912–1983)

Campbell, Glen (singer); nr. Delight, Ark., 4/22/38

Campbell, Naomi (model); London, England, 5/22/70

Campbell, Neve (actress); Guelph, Ont., Canada, 10/3/73

Campion, Jane (director, screenwriter); Waikanae, New Zealand, 1954

Camus, Albert (author); Mondovi, Algeria (1913–1960)

Canaletto (Giovanni Antonio Canale) (painter); Venice (1697–1768)

Candy, John (actor, comedian); Toronto (1950–1994)

Caniff, Milton (cartoonist); Hillsboro, Ohio (1907–1988)

Cannon, Dyan (Samille Diane Friesen) (actress); Tacoma, Wash., 1/4/37

Cantinflas (Mario Moreno-Reyes) (comedian); Mexico City (1911–1993)

Cantor, Eddie (Edward Iskowitz) (actor); New York City (1892–1964)

Capone, Al(fonse) (gangster); Brooklyn, N.Y. (1899–1947)

Capote, Truman (Truman Streckfus Persons) (novelist); New Orleans (1924–1984)

Capp, Al (Alfred Gerald Caplin) (cartoonist); New Haven, Conn. (1909–1979)

Capra, Frank (film producer, director); Palermo, Italy (1897–1991)

Caputo, Phil (Philip Joseph Caputo) (author, journalist); Chicago, 6/10/41

Caravaggio, Michelangelo Merisi da (painter); Caravaggio, Italy (1573–1610)

Cardin, Pierre (fashion designer); nr. Venice, 7/7/22

Cardinale, Claudia (actress); Tunis, Tunisia, 4/15/39

Carey, Drew (actor, producer); Cleveland, 5/23/58

Carey, Harry (actor); New York City (1878–1947)

Carey, Macdonald (actor); Sioux City, Iowa (1913–1994)

Carlin, George (comedian); Bronx, N.Y., 5/12/37

Carlisle, Kitty (singer, actress); New Orleans, 9/3/15

Carlyle, Robert (actor); Glasgow, Scotland, 4/14/61

Carlyle, Thomas (essayist, historian); Ecclefechan, Scotland (1795–1881)

Carmichael, Hoagy (Hoagland Howard) (songwriter); Bloomington, Ind. (1899–1981)

Carne, Judy (Joyce Botterill) (singer, actress); Northampton, England, 4/27/39

Carnegie, Andrew (industrialist); Dunfermline, Scotland (1835–1919)

Carney, Art (actor); Mt. Vernon, N.Y., 11/4/18

Caron, Leslie (actress); Paris, 7/1/31

Carpenter, Mary Chapin (singer, songwriter); Princeton, N.J., 2/21/58

Carr, Vikki (Florencia Bisenta de Casillas Martinez Cardona) (singer); El Paso, Tex., 7/19/42

Carracci, Annibale (painter); Bologna, Italy (1560–1609)

Carracci, Lodovico (painter); Bologna, Italy (1555–1619)

Carradine, David (actor); Hollywood, Calif., 12/8/36

Carradine, John (actor); New York City (1906–1988)

Carradine, Keith (actor); San Mateo, Calif., 8/8/49

Carreras, José (tenor); Barcelona, Spain, 12/5/46

Carroll, Diahann (Carol Diahann Johnson) (singer, actress); Bronx, N.Y., 7/17/35

Carroll, Leo G. (actor); Weedon, England (1892–1972)

Carroll, Lewis (Charles Lutwidge Dodgson) (author, mathematician); Daresbury, England (1832–1898)

Carson, Johnny (TV entertainer); Corning, Iowa, 10/23/25

Carson, Kit (Christopher Carson) (scout); Madison County, Ky. (1809–1868)

Carson, Rachel (biologist, author); Springdale, Pa. (1907–1964)

Carter, Betty (jazz singer, composer); Flint, Mich. (1930–1998)

Carter, Chris (television and film writer, director, producer); Bellflower, Calif., 10/13/57

Carter, Dixie (actress); McLemoresville, Tenn., 5/25/39

Carter, Jack (comedian); New York City, 6/24/23

Carter, James Earl, Jr. (39th U.S. president); Plains, Ga., 10/1/24

Carter, Lynda (actress); Phoenix, Ariz., 7/24/51

Cartier, Jacques (explorer); Saint-Malo, Brittany, France (1491–1557)

Cartier-Bresson, Henri (photographer); Chanteloup, France, 8/22/08

Cartland, Barbara (author); England (1901–2000)

Caruso, Enrico (Errico Caruso) (tenor); Naples, Italy (1873–1921)

Carver, George Washington (botanist); Diamond Grove, Mo. (1864–1943)

Cary, Arthur Joyce Lunel (novelist); Londonderry, Ireland (1888–1957)

Casals, Pablo (cellist); Vendrell, Spain (1876–1973)

Casanova de Seingalt, Giovanni Jacopo (adventurer); Venice (1725–1798)

Case, Steve (business executive); Honolulu, 8/21/58

Cash, Johnny (singer); nr. Kingsland, Ark., 2/26/32

Cass, Peggy (Mary Margaret Cass) (comedienne); Boston (1924–1999)

Cassatt, Mary (painter); Allegheny, Pa. (1844–1926)

Cassavetes, John (director); New York City (1929–1989)

Cassidy, David (singer); New York City, 4/12/50

Cassidy, Jack (actor); Richmond Hill, Queens, N.Y. (1927–1976)

Cassidy, Shaun (actor, television producer, singer); Los Angeles, 9/27/58

Cassini, Oleg (Oleg Lolewski-Cassini) (fashion designer); Paris, 4/11/13

Castagno, Andrea del (painter); San Martino a Corella, Italy (c. 1421–1457)

Castaneda, Carlos (cultural anthropologist, author); São Paulo, Brazil (1931–1998)

Castle, Irene (Irene Foote) (actress, dancer); New Rochelle, N.Y. (1893–1969)

Castle, Vernon Blythe (dancer, aviator); Norwich, England (1887–1918)

Castro Ruz, Fidel (Premier); Mayari, Oriente, Cuba, 8/13/26

Cather, Willa Sibert (novelist); Winchester, Va. (1876–1947)

Cato, Marcus Porcius (called Cato the Elder) (statesman); Tusculum, Italy (234–149 B.C.)

Catt, Carrie Lane Chapman (woman suffragist); Ripon, Wis. (1859–1947)

Catton, Bruce (historian); Petoskey, Mich. (1899–1978)

Catullus, Gaius Valerius (poet); Verona (c. 84–c. 54 B.C.)

Cavallaro, Carmen (band leader); New York City (1913–1989)

Cavett, Dick (Richard Cavett) (TV entertainer); Gibbon, Neb., 11/19/36

Ceausescu, Nicolae (head of state); Scorniscesti, Romania (1918–1989)

Céline, Louis Ferdinand (pseud. of Louis Fuch Destouches) (novelist); Paris (1894–1961)

Cellini, Benvenuto (goldsmith, sculptor); Florence, Italy (1500–1571)

Cervantes Saavedra, Miguel de (novelist); Alcalá de Henares, Spain (1547–1616)

Cézanne, Paul (painter); Aix-en-Provence, France (1839–1906)

Chagall, Marc (painter); Vitebsk, Russia (1887–1985)

Chaliapin, Feodor Ivanovitch (operatic basso); Kazan, Russia (1873–1938)

Chamberlain, Arthur Neville (statesman); Edgbaston, England (1869–1940)

Chamberlain, Richard (actor, producer); Los Angeles, 3/31/35

Champion, Gower (choreographer); Geneva, Ill. (1921–1980)

Champion, Marge (Marjorie Celeste Belcher) (actress, dancer); Los Angeles, 9/2/23

Champlain, Samuel de (explorer); nr. Rochefort, France (1567–1635)

Chan, Jackie (Chan Kwong Sang) (actor); Hong Kong, 4/7/54

Chancellor, John (TV commentator); Chicago (1927–1996)

Chandler, Jeff (Ira Grossel) (actor); Brooklyn, N.Y. (1918–1961)

Chandler, Raymond (writer); Chicago (1883–1959)

Chanel, "Coco" (Gabriel Bonheur) (fashion designer); Issoire, France (1883–1971)

Chaney, Lon (actor); Colorado Springs, Colo. (1883–1930)

Channing, Carol (actress); Seattle, 1/31/23

Channing, Stockard (Susan Stockard) (actress); New York City, 2/13/44

Chaplin, Geraldine (actress); Santa Monica, Calif., 7/31/44

Chaplin, Sir Charles (actor); London (1889–1977)

Charisse, Cyd (Tula Finklea) (dancer, actress); Amarillo, Tex., 3/8/21

Charlemagne (Holy Roman Emperor); birthplace unknown (742–814)

Charles, Ray (Ray Charles Robinson) (pianist, singer, songwriter); Albany, Ga., 9/23/30

Charo (Maria Rosario Pilar Martinez) (actress); Murcia, Spain, 1/15/51

Chase, Chevy (Cornelius Crane Chase) (comedian); New York City, 10/8/43

Chase, Lucia (founder Ballet Theatre [now American Ballet Theatre]); Waterbury, Conn. (1907–1986)

Coolidge, (John) Calvin (30th U.S. president); Plymouth, Vt. **(1872–1933)**

Coolidge, Rita (singer); Nashville, Tenn., 5/1/45

Coolio (Artis Ivey, Jr.) (rap artist); Los Angeles, Calif., 8/1/63

Cooper, Alice (Vincent Furnier) (rock musician); Detroit, 2/4/48

Cooper, Gary (Frank James Cooper) (actor); Helena, Mont. **(1901–1961)**

Cooper, Dame Gladys (actress); Lewisham, England **(1898–1971)**

Cooper, Jackie (actor, director); Los Angeles, 9/15/22

Cooper, James Fenimore (novelist); Burlington, N.J. **(1789–1851)**

Cooper, Peter (industrialist, philanthropist); New York City **(1791–1883)**

Copernicus, Nicolaus (Mikolaj Kopernik) (astronomer); Thorn, Poland **(1473–1543)**

Copland, Aaron (composer); Brooklyn, N.Y. **(1900–1990)**

Copley, John Singleton (painter); Boston **(1738–1815)**

Copperfield, David (David Kotkin) (illusionist); Metuchen, N.J., 9/16/56

Coppola, Francis Ford (film director); Detroit, 4/7/39

Corelli, Arcangelo (composer); Fusignano, Italy **(1653–1713)**

Corelli, Franco (operatic tenor); Ancona, Italy, 4/8/23

Corgan, Billy (musician); Elk Grove, Ill., 3/17/67

Corneille, Pierre (dramatist); Rouen, France **(1606–1684)**

Cornell, Katharine (actress); Berlin **(1893–1974)**

Corot, Jean Baptiste Camille (painter); Paris **(1796–1875)**

Corella, Angel (ballet dancer); Madrid, Spain, 11/8/75

Correggio, Antonio Allegri da (painter); Correggio, Italy **(1494–1534)**

Corsaro, Frank (opera director); New York harbor, 12/22/24

Cortés (or Cortez), Hernando (explorer); Medellin, Spain **(1485–1547)**

Cosby, Bill (actor); Philadelphia, 7/12/37

Cosell, Howard (Howard Cohen) (sportscaster); Winston-Salem, N.C. **(1918–1995)**

Costello, Elvis (Declan Patrick McManus) (singer, musician, songwriter); London, 1954

Costello, Lou (Louis Cristillo) (comedian); Paterson, N.J. **(1908–1959)**

Costner, Kevin (actor); Los Angeles, 1/18/55

Cotten, Joseph (actor); Petersburg, Va. **(1905–1994)**

Couperin, François (composer); Paris **(1668–1733)**

Courbet, Gustave (painter); Ornans, France **(1819–1877)**

Couric, Katie (TV host); Arlington, Va., 1/7/57

Courtenay, Tom (actor); Hull, England, 2/25/37

Cousins, Norman (publisher); Union Hill, N.J. **(1915–1990)**

Cousteau, Jacques-Yves (marine explorer); St. André-de-Cubzac, France **(1910–1997)**

Covey, Stephen R. (author); Salt Lake City, 10/24/32

Coward, Sir Noel (playwright, actor); Teddington, England **(1899–1973)**

Cowles, Gardner, Jr. (newspaper publisher); Algona, Iowa **(1903–1985)**

Cowper, William (poet); Great Berkhamstead, England **(1731–1800)**

Cox, Archibald (Watergate prosecutor); Plainfield, N.J., 5/17/12

Cox, Courteney (actress); Birmingham, Ala., 6/15/64

Coyote, Peter (actor); New York City, 10/10/41

Cozzens, James Gould (novelist); Chicago **(1903–1978)**

Crabbe, Buster (Clarence Crabbe) (actor); Oakland, Calif. **(1908–1983)**

Cranach, Lucas, the elder (painter); Kronach, Germany **(1472–1553)**

Crane, Hart (poet); Garrettsville, Ohio **(1899–1932)**

Crane, Stephen (novelist, poet); Newark, N.J. **(1871–1900)**

Cranmer, Thomas (churchman); Aslacton, England **(1489–1556)**

Craven, Wes (director, producer, screenwriter); Cleveland, 8/2/39

Crawford, Broderick (actor); Philadelphia **(1911–1986)**

Crawford, Cheryl (stage producer); Akron, Ohio **(1902–1986)**

Crawford, Cindy (model, actress); De Kalb, Illinois, 2/20/66

Crawford, Joan (Lucille LeSueur) (actress, business executive); San Antonio **(1908–1977)**

Crazy Horse (Lakota Indian leader); nr. Bear Butte, S.D. **(1840?–1877)**

Crenna, Richard (actor); Los Angeles, 11/30/27

Crespin, Régine (operatic soprano); Marseilles, France, 2/23/29

Crichton, (John) Michael (novelist, film producer); Chicago, 10/23/42

Crick, Francis Harry Compton (scientist, Nobel laureate); Northampton, England, 6/8/16

Crisp, Donald (actor); London **(1880–1974)**

Croce, Benedetto (philosopher); Peseasseroli, Aquila, Italy **(1866–1952)**

Croce, Jim (singer); Philadelphia **(1942–1973)**

Crockett, Davy (David) (frontiersman); Greene County, Tenn. **(1786–1836)**

Cromwell, Oliver (statesman); Huntingdon, England **(1599–1658)**

Cronenberg, David (film director); Toronto, Canada, 3/15/43

Cronin, A. J. (Archibald J. Cronin) (novelist); Cardross, Scotland **(1896–1981)**

Cronkite, Walter (TV newscaster); St. Joseph, Mo., 11/4/16

Cronyn, Hume (actor); London, Ont., Canada, 7/18/11

Crosby, Bing (Harry Lillis) (singer, actor); Tacoma, Wash. **(1904–1977)**

Crosby, Bob (musician); Spokane, Wash. **(1913–1993)**

Crosby, Cathy Lee (actress); Los Angeles, 12/2/48

Crosby, Norm (comedian); Boston, 9/15/27

Cross, Ben (Bernard) (actor); Paddington, England, 12/16/47

Cross, Milton (opera commentator); New York City **(1897–1975)**

Crouse, Russell (playwright); Findlay, Ohio **(1893–1966)**

Crow, Sheryl (musician, record producer); Kennett, Mo., 2/11/62

Crowe, Russell (actor, musician); Auckland, New Zealand, 4/7/64

Crudup, Billy (actor); Manhasset, N.Y., 7/8/68

Cruise, Tom (Thomas Mapother IV) (actor, producer); Syracuse, N.Y., 7/3/62

Crystal, Billy (comedian, actor); Long Beach, N.Y., 3/14/47

Cugat, Xavier (band leader); Barcelona, Spain **(1900–1990)**

Cukor, George (film director); New York City **(1899–1983)**

Culkin, Macaulay (actor); New York City, 8/26/80

Cullen, Bill (William Lawrence Cullen) (radio and TV entertainer); Pittsburgh **(1920–1990)**

Cullen, Countee (poet); New York City **(1903–1946)**

Culp, Robert (actor); Berkeley, Calif., 8/16/30

cummings, e. e. (Edward Estlin Cummings) (poet); Cambridge, Mass. **(1894–1962)**

Cummings, Robert (actor); Joplin, Mo. **(1908–1990)**

Cunningham, Merce (choreographer); Centralia, Wash., 4/16/19

Curie, Marie (Marja Sklodowska) (physical chemist, Nobel laureate); Warsaw **(1867–1934)**

Curie, Pierre (physicist); Paris **(1859–1906)**

Curtin, Jane (actress); Cambridge, Mass., 9/6/47

Curtin, Phyllis (soprano); Clarksburg, W. Va., 12/3/27

Curtis, Jamie Lee (actress); Los Angeles, 11/22/58

Curtis, Tony (Bernard Schwartz) (actor); Bronx, N.Y., 6/3/25

Curzon, Clifford (concert pianist); London **(1907–1982)**

Cusack, Joan (actress); New York City, 10/11/62

Cusack, John (actor); Chicago, 6/28/66

Custer, George Armstrong (army officer); New Rumley, Ohio **(1839–1876)**

D

Dafoe, Willem (William Dafoe, Jr.) (actor); Appleton, Wis., 7/22/55

da Gama, Vasco (explorer); Sines, Portugal **(1460–1524)**

Daguerre, Louis (photographic pioneer); nr. Paris **(1787–1851)**

Dahl, Arlene (actress); Minneapolis, 8/11/28

Dalai Lama (Tenzin Gyatso) (spiritual and temporal head of Tibet); Taktser, China, 1935

Daley, Richard J. (mayor of Chicago); Chicago **(1902–1976)**

Dali, Salvador (painter); Figueras, Spain **(1904–1989)**

Dalton, John (chemist); nr. Cockermouth, England **(1766–1844)**

Dalton, Timothy (actor); Colwyn Bay, Wales, U.K., 3/21/46

Daly, Tyne (actress); Madison, Wis., 2/21/46

d'Amboise, Jacques (ballet dancer); Dedham, Mass., 7/28/34

Damone, Vic (Vito Farinola) (singer); Brooklyn, N.Y., 6/12/28

Damrosch, Walter Johannes (orchestra conductor); Breslau, Poland **(1862–1950)**

Dana, Charles Anderson (editor); Hinsdale, N.H. **(1819–1897)**

Dandridge, Dorothy (actress); Cleveland **(1923–1965)**

Danes, Claire (actress); New York City, 4/12/79

Dangerfield, Rodney (Jacob Cohen) (actor, comedian); Babylon, N.Y., 11/22/22

Daniels, Jeff (actor); Chelsea, Mich., 2/19/55

Daniels, William (actor); Brooklyn, N.Y., 3/31/27

Danilova, Alexandra (ballet dancer); Peterhof, Russia **(1904–1997)**

Dannay, Frederic (novelist, pseudonym Ellery Queen); Brooklyn, N.Y. **(1905–1982)**

Danner, Blythe (actress); Philadelphia, 2/3/43

D'Annunzio, Gabriele (soldier, author); Francaville at Mare, Pescara, Italy **(1863–1938)**

Danson, Ted (actor); San Diego, Calif., 12/29/47

Dante (or Durante) Alighieri (poet); Florence, Italy **(1265–1321)**

Danton, Georges Jacques (French Revolutionary leader); Arcis-sur-Aube, France **(1759–1794)**

Danza, Tony (actor); Brooklyn, N.Y., 4/21/51

Darren, James (actor); Philadelphia, 6/8/36

Darrow, Clarence Seward (lawyer); Kinsman, Ohio **(1857–1938)**

Darwin, Charles Robert (naturalist); Shrewsbury, England **(1809–1882)**

Dassin, Jules (film director); Middletown, Conn., 12/18/11

Daumier, Honoré (caricaturist); Marseilles, France **(1808–1879)**

David, Jacques-Louis (painter); Paris **(1748–1825)**

David (king of Israel and Judah;) died c. 973 B.C.

Davidson, John (singer, actor); Pittsburgh, 12/13/41

Davies, Marion (Marion Douras) (actress); New York City **(1897–1961)**

Davies, (William) Robertson (writer); Thamesville, Ont., Canada **(1913–1996)**

Davis, Angela (social activist); Birmingham, Ala., 1/26/44

Davis, Ann B. (actress); Schenectady, N.Y., 5/5/26

Davis, Lt. Gen. Benjamin O., Jr. (Air Force general); Washington, D.C., 12/18/12

Davis, Brig. Gen. Benjamin O., Sr. (U.S. Army general); Washington, D.C. **(1877–1970)**

Davis, Bette (actress); Lowell, Mass. **(1908–1989)**

Davis, Geena (Virginia Davis) (actress); Wareham, Mass., 1/21/57

Davis, Jefferson (president of the Confederacy); Christian (now Todd) County, Ky. **(1808–1889)**

Davis, Judy (actress); Perth, Australia, 1955

Davis, Mac (singer); Lubbock, Tex., 1/21/42

Davis, Miles (jazz trumpeter); Alton, Ill. **(1926–1991)**

Davis, Ossie (actor, writer); Cogdell, Ga., 12/18/17

Davis, Sammy, Jr. (actor, singer); New York City **(1925–1990)**

Davis, Stuart (painter); Philadelphia **(1894–1964)**

Dawson, Richard (actor, host); Gosport, Hampshire, England, 11/20/32

Day, Doris (Doris von Kappelhoff) (singer, actress); Cincinnati, 4/3/24

Dayan, Moshe (ex-defense minister of Israel); Dagania, Palestine **(1915–1981)**

Day-Lewis, Daniel (actor); London, 4/29/58

Dean, James (actor); Marion, Ind. **(1931–1955)**

Dean, Jimmy (singer); Seth Ward, nr. Plainview, Tex., 8/10/28

De Bakey, Michael E. (heart surgeon); Lake Charles, La., 9/7/08

de Beauvoir, Simone (novelist, philosopher); Paris **(1908–1986)**

Debs, Eugene Victor (Socialist leader); Terre Haute, Ind. **(1855–1926)**

Debussy, Claude Achille (composer); St. Germain-en-Laye, France **(1862–1918)**

De Carlo, Yvonne (Peggy Yvonne Middleton) (actress); Vancouver, B.C., Canada, 9/1/24

de Chirico, Giorgio (painter); Volos, Greece **(1888–1978)**

Dee, Ruby (Ruby Ann Wallace) (actress); Cleveland, 10/27/24

Dee, Sandra (Alexandra Zuck) (actress); Bayonne, N.J., 4/23/42

Degas, Hilaire Germain Edgar (painter); Paris **(1834–1917)**

de Gaulle, Charles André Joseph Marie (soldier, statesman); Lille, France **(1890–1970)**

de Havilland, Olivia (actress); Tokyo, 7/1/16

de Kooning, Willem (artist); Rotterdam **(1904–1997)**

Delacroix, Eugène (painter); Charenton-St. Maurice, France **(1798–1863)**

Delany, Dana (actress); New York City, 3/15/56

de la Renta, Oscar (fashion designer); Santo Domingo, Dominican Republic, 7/22/32

Delaunay, Robert (painter); Paris **(1885–1941)**

De Laurentiis, Dino (film producer); Torre Annunziata, Bay of Naples, Italy, 8/8/18

della Robbia, Andrea (sculptor); Florence **(1435–1525)**

della Robbia, Luca (sculptor); Florence **(1400–1482)**

Delon, Alain (actor); Sceaux, France, 11/8/35

Del Toro, Benicio (actor); Santurce, Puerto Rico, 2/19/67

DeLuise, Dom (actor, comedian); Brooklyn, N.Y., 8/1/33

Demarest, William (actor); St. Paul, Minn. **(1892–1983)**

de Mille, Agnes (choreographer); New York City **(1905–1993)**

De Mille, Cecil Blount (film director); Ashfield, Mass. **(1881–1959)**

Demme, Jonathan (director, producer, screenwriter); Baldwin, N.Y., 2/22/44

Demosthenes (orator); Athens **(384?–322 B.C.)**

Dench, Dame Judi (film and stage actress); York, England, 12/9/34

Deneuve, Catherine (actress); Paris, 10/22/43

Deng Xiaoping (Chinese leader); Sichuan province, China **(1904–1997)**

De Niro, Robert (actor, director); New York City, 8/17/43

Dennehy, Brian (actor); Bridgeport, Conn., 7/9/39

Dennis, Sandy (actress); Hastings, Neb. **(1937–1992)**

Denny, Reginald (actor); Richmond, England **(1891–1967)**

Denver, John (Henry John Deutschendorf, Jr.) (singer, actor); Roswell, N.M. **(1943–1997)**

De Palma, Brian (film director); Newark, N.J., 9/11/40

Depp, Johnny (actor); Owensboro, Ky., 6/9/63

Derain, André (painter); Chatou, Seine-et-Oise, France **(1880–1954)**

Derek, John (Derek Harris) (actor, director); Los Angeles **(1926–1998)**

Dern, Bruce (actor); Winnetka, Ill., 6/4/36

Dern, Laura (actress); Los Angeles, 2/10/67

Dershowitz, Alan (lawyer); Brooklyn, N.Y., 9/1/38

Derrida, Jacques (philosopher); El-Biar, Algeria, 7/15/30

Descartes, René (philosopher, mathematician); La Haye, France **(1596–1650)**

De Seversky, Alexander P. (aviator); Tiflis (Tbilisi), Georgia **(1894–1974)**

De Sica, Vittorio (film director); Sora, Italy **(1901–1974)**

Desmond, Johnny (singer, composer); Detroit **(1921–1985)**

De Soto, Hernando (explorer); Barcarrota, Spain **(c. 1500–1542)**

De Valera, Eamon (ex-president of Ireland); New York City **(1882–1975)**

Devane, William (actor); Albany, N.Y., 9/5/39

Devine, Andy (actor); Flagstaff, Ariz. **(1905–1977)**

DeVito, Danny (Daniel Michael DeVito) (actor, director, producer); Neptune, N.J., 11/17/44

De Vries, Peter (novelist); Chicago **(1910–1993)**

de Waart, Edo (conductor); Amsterdam, the Netherlands, 6/1/41

Dewey, George (admiral); Montpelier, Vt. **(1837–1917)**

Dewey, John (philosopher, educator); Burlington, Vt. **(1859–1952)**

Dewey, Thomas E. (political figure); Owosso, Mich. **(1902–1971)**

Dewhurst, Colleen (actress); Montreal **(1926–1991)**

Dey, Susan (actress); Pekin, Ill., 12/10/52

Diaghilev, Sergei (ballet impressario); Novgorod, Russia **(1872–1929)**

Diamond, Neil (singer); Brooklyn, N.Y., 1/24/41

Diana (Diana Frances Spencer) (Princess of Wales); Sandringham, England **(1961–1997)**

Diaz, Cameron (actress, model); San Diego, Calif., 8/30/72

DiCaprio, Leonardo (actor); Los Angeles, 11/11/74

Dichter, Misha (pianist); Shanghai, 9/27/45

Dickens, Charles John Huffam (novelist); Portsea, England **(1812–1870)**

Dickey, James (writer); Atlanta **(1923–1997)**

Dickinson, Angie (Angeline Brown) (actress); Kulm, N.D., 9/30/31

Dickinson, Emily Elizabeth (poet); Amherst, Mass. **(1830–1886)**

Diddley, Bo (Elias McDaniel) (guitarist); McComb, Miss., 12/30/28

Diderot, Denis (encyclopedist); Langres, France **(1713–1784)**

Dietrich, Marlene (Maria Magdalena von Losch) (actress); Berlin **(1901–1992)**

DiFranco, Ani (singer, songwriter); Buffalo, N.Y., 9/23/70

Diller, Phyllis (Phyllis Driver) (comedienne); Lima, Ohio, 7/17/17

Dillon, Matt (actor); New Rochelle, N.Y., 2/18/64

Dine, Jim (painter); Cincinnati, 6/16/35

Dinesen, Isak (Karen Blixen) (author); Rungsted, Denmark **(1885–1962)**

Dinkins, David (ex-mayor of New York City); Trenton, N.J., 7/10/27

Diogenes (philosopher); Sinope, Turkey **(c. 412–323 B.C.)**

Dion (Dion DiMucci) (singer); Bronx, N.Y., 7/18/39

Dion, Celine (musician); Charlemagne, Que., Canada, 3/30/68

Dior, Christian (fashion designer); Granville, France **(1905–1957)**

Disney, Walt(er) Elias (film animator, producer); Chicago **(1901–1966)**

Disraeli, Benjamin (Earl of Beaconsfield) (statesman); London **(1804–1881)**

Dix, Dorothea (civil rights reformer); Hampden, Maine **(1802–1887)**

Dixon, Jeane (Jeane Pinckert) (seer); Medford, Wis. **(1918–1997)**

Dobbs, Mattiwilda (soprano); Atlanta, 7/11/25

Doctorow, E(dgar) L(aurence) (novelist); New York City, 1/6/31

Dogg, Snoop Doggy (Calvin Broadus) (musician); Long Beach, Calif., 10/20/72

Doherty, Shannen (actress); Memphis, Tenn., 4/21/71

Dole, Elizabeth Hanford (public official); Salisbury, N.C., 7/29/36

Dole, Robert (political figure); Russell, Kans., 7/22/23

Dolin, Anton (dancer); Slinfold, England **(1904–1983)**

Domingo, Placido (tenor); Madrid, 1/21/41

Domino, Fats (Antoine) (musician); New Orleans, 2/26/28

Donahue, Phil (TV host); Cleveland, 12/21/35

Donahue, Troy (Merle Johnson) (actor); New York City, 1/27/36

Donaldson, Sam (broadcast journalist); El Paso, Tex., 3/11/34

Donat, Robert (actor); Withington, England **(1905–1958)**

Donatello (Donato Niccolò di Betto Bardi) (sculptor); Florence **(c. 1386–1466)**

Donlevy, Brian (actor); Portadown, Ireland **(1899–1972)**

Donne, John (poet); London **(1573–1631)**

Donner, Richard (director, producer); New York City, 1939

D'Onofrio, Vincent (actor); Brooklyn, N.Y., 6/30/59

Donovan (Donovan Leitch) (singer, songwriter); Glasgow, Scotland, 2/10/46

Doolittle, James H. (ex-Air Force general); Alameda, Calif. (1896–1993)

Doohan, James (actor); Vancouver, B.C., 3/20/20

Dorati, Antal (orchestra conductor); Budapest (1906–1988)

Dorn, Michael (actor); Luling, Tex., 12/9/52

Dorris, Michael (anthropologist, writer); Louisville, Ky. (1945–1997)

Dorsey, Jimmy (band leader); Shenandoah, Pa. (1904–1957)

Dorsey, Thomas Andrew (father of gospel music); Villa Rice, Ga. (1899–1993)

Dorsey, Tommy (band leader); Mahanoy Plane, Pa. (1905–1956)

Dos Passos, John (novelist); Chicago (1896–1970)

Dostoevski, Fyodor Mikhailovich (novelist); Moscow (1821–1881)

Dotrice, Roy (actor); Guernsey, Channel Islands, England, 5/26/23

Douglas, Aaron (painter); Topeka, Kans. (1900–1979)

Douglas, Helen Gahagan (ex-representative); Boonton, N.J. (1900–1980)

Douglas, Kirk (Issur Danielovitch) (actor); Amsterdam, N.Y., 12/9/16

Douglas, Melvyn (Melvyn Hesselberg) (actor); Macon, Ga. (1901–1981)

Douglas, Michael (actor, producer); New Brunswick, N.J., 9/25/44

Douglas, Mike (Michael D. Dowd, Jr.) (TV host); Chicago, 8/11/25

Douglas, Stephen Arnold (politician); Brandon, Vt. (1813–1861)

Douglass, Frederick (abolitionist, author, orator); Tuckahoe, Md. (1817–1895)

Dow, Charles (financier); Sterling, Conn. (1851–1902)

Down, Lesley-Ann (actress); London, 3/17/54

Downey, Robert, Jr. (actor, director); New York City, 4/4/65

Downs, Hugh (broadcast journalist); Akron, Ohio, 2/14/21

Doyle, Sir Arthur Conan (novelist, spiritualist); Edinburgh, Scotland (1859–1930)

Doyle, David (actor); Lincoln, Neb. (1929–1997)

Drake, Sir Francis (navigator); Tavistock, England (1545–1596)

Dr. Dre (Andre Young) (rap singer); Los Angeles, 2/18/66

Dreiser, Theodore (writer); Terre Haute, Ind. (1871–1945)

Drescher, Fran (television and film actress); New York City, 9/30/57

Dreyfus, Alfred (French army officer); Mulhouse, France (1859–1935)

Dreyfuss, Richard (actor); Brooklyn, N.Y., 10/29/47

Drury, Allen (novelist); Houston (1918–1998)

Dryden, John (poet); Northamptonshire, England (1631–1700)

Dryer, Fred (ex-NFL player, actor); Hawthorne, Calif., 7/6/46

Dubček, Alexander (ex-president of Czechoslovakia); Uhroved, former Czechoslovakia (1921–1992)

Dubinsky, David (David Dobnievski) (labor leader); Brest-Litovsk, Belarus (1892–1982)

Du Bois, W(illiam) E(dward) B(urghardt) (scholar, civil rights activist); Great Barrington, Mass. (1868–1963)

Duchamp, Marcel (painter); Blainville, France (1887–1968)

Duchin, Eddy (pianist, bandleader); Cambridge, Mass. (1909–1951)

Duchin, Peter (pianist, band leader); New York City, 7/28/37

Duchovny, David (actor); New York City, 8/7/60

Dufay, Guillaume (composer); Cambrai, France (c. 1400–1474)

Duffy, Julia (actress); Minneapolis, Minn., 6/27/50

Dufy, Raoul (painter); Le Havre, France (1877–1953)

Dukakis, Olympia (actress); Lowell, Mass., 6/20/31

Duke, James B. (industrialist); nr. Durham, N.C. (1856–1925)

Duke, Patty (Anna Marie Duke) (actress); New York City, 12/14/46

Dulles, Allen Welsh (ex-Director of CIA); Watertown, N.Y. (1893–1969)

Dulles, John Foster (political figure); Washington, D.C. (1888–1959)

Dumas, Alexandre (called Dumas fils) (novelist); Paris (1824–1895)

Dumas, Alexandre (called Dumas père) (novelist); Villers-Cotterets, France (1802–1870)

du Maurier, Daphne (novelist); London (1907–1989)

du Maurier, George Louis Palmella Busson (novelist); Paris (1834–1896)

Dumont, Margaret (actress); Brooklyn, N.Y. (1889–1965)

Dunaway, Faye (actress); Bascom, Fla., 1/14/41

Dunbar, Paul Laurence (poet, novelist); Dayton, Ohio (1872–1906)

Duncan, Isadora (dancer); San Francisco (1878–1927)

Duncan, Michael Clarke (actor); Chicago, 12/10/57

Duncan, Sandy (actress); Henderson, Tex., 2/20/46

Dunham, Katherine (dancer, choreographer); Chicago, 6/22/09

Dunne, Irene (actress); Louisville, Ky. (1898–1990)

Duns Scotus, John (theologian); Duns, Scotland (1265–1303)

Du Pont, Pierre S. (economist); Paris (1739–1817)

Durante, Jimmy (comedian); New York City (1893–1980)

Duras, Marguerite (Donnadieu) (novelist, dramatist); Gia Dinh, Vietnam (1914–1996)

Durbin, Deanna (Edna Mae) (actress); Winnipeg, Canada, 12/4/21

Dürer, Albrecht (painter, engraver); Nürnberg, Germany (1471–1528)

Durning, Charles (actor); Highland Falls, N.Y., 2/28/23

Durrell, Lawrence George (novelist); Julundur, India (1912–1990)

Duse, Eleonora (actress); Chioggia, Italy (1859–1924)

Dussault, Nancy (actress); Pensacola, Fla., 6/30/36

Duvall, Robert (actor, director, producer); San Diego, Calif., 1/5/31

Duvall, Shelley (actress); Houston, 7/7/49

Dvořák, Antonin (composer); Nelahozeves, Czechoslovakia (1841–1904)

Dylan, Bob (Robert Zimmerman) (singer, songwriter, guitarist); Duluth, Minn., 5/24/41

Dysart, Richard (actor); Brighton, Mass., 3/30/29

E

Eakins, Thomas (painter, sculptor); Philadelphia (1844–1916)

Earhart, Amelia (aviator); Atchison, Kans. (1897–1937)

Earp, Wyatt (Berry Stapp) (sheriff, gunfighter); Monmouth, Ill. (1848–1929)

Eastman, George (camera inventor); Waterville, N.Y. (1854–1932)

Eastwood, Clint (actor, director, producer); San Francisco, 5/31/30

Ebert, Roger (film critic); Urbana, Ill., 6/18/42

Ebsen, Buddy (Christian Ebsen, Jr.) (actor); Belleville, Ill., 4/2/08

Eckstine, Billy (singer); Pittsburgh (1914–1993)

Eddy, Mary Baker (founder of Christian Science Church); Bow, N.H. (1821–1910)

Eddy, Nelson (baritone, actor); Providence, R.I. (1901–1967)

Edel, Leon (author); Pittsburgh (1907–1997)

Edelman, Marian Wright (social activist); Bennettsville, S.C., 6/6/39

Eden, Sir Anthony (Earl of Avon) (ex-prime minister); Durham, England (1897–1977)

Eden, Barbara (Barbara Huffman) (actress); Tucson, Ariz., 8/23/34

Edison, Thomas Alva (inventor); Milan, Ohio (1847–1931)

Edwards, Anthony (actor); Santa Barbara, Calif., 7/19/62

Edwards, Blake (film writer, producer); Tulsa, Okla., 7/26/22

Edwards, Jonathan (theologian); East Windsor, Conn. (1703–1758)

Edwards, Ralph (TV and radio producer); Merino, Colo., 6/13/13

Edwards, Vincent (Vincent Edward Zoino) (actor); Brooklyn, N.Y. (1928–1996)

Eglevsky, André (ballet dancer); Moscow (1917–1977)

Egoyan, Atom (film director, writer, editor); Cairo, 7/19/60

Ehrlich, Paul (bacteriologist); Strzelin, Poland (1854–1915)

Eichmann, (Karl) Adolf (Nazi, mass murderer); Solingen, Germany (1906–1962)

Eikenberry, Jill (actress); New Haven, Conn., 1/21/47

Einstein, Albert (physicist); Ulm, Germany (1879–1955)

Eisner, Michael (entertainment executive); Mt. Kisco, N.Y., 3/7/42

Eisenhower, Dwight David (34th U.S. president); Denison, Tex. (1890–1969)

Eisenhower, Milton S. (educator); Abilene, Kans. (1899–1985)

Eisenstaedt, Alfred (photographer, photojournalist); Dirschau (Prussia, now Tczew), Poland (1898–1995)

Ekland, Britt (Britt-Marie) (actress); Stockholm, 10/6/42

Electra, Carmen (Tara Patrick) (model, actress); Cincinnati, Ohio, 4/20/73

Elfman, Jenna (Jennifer Mary Butala) (actress); Los Angeles, 9/30/71

Elgar, Sir Edward (composer); Worcester, England (1857–1934)

Elgart, Larry (band leader); New London, Conn., 3/20/22

El Greco (Domenicos Theotocopoulos) (painter); Candia, Crete, Greece (c. 1541–1614)

Elion, Gertrude B. (chemist, Nobel laureate); New York City (1918–1999)

Eliot, George (Mary Ann Evans) (novelist); Chilvers Coton, England (1819–1880)

Eliot, Thomas Stearns (poet); St. Louis (1888–1965)

Elizabeth I (queen of England); Greenwich, England (1533–1603)

Elizabeth II (queen of England); London, 4/21/26

Elizondo, Hector (actor); New York City, 12/22/36

Ellington, Duke (Edward Kennedy) (jazz musician); Washington, D.C. (1899–1974)

Elliot, "Mama" Cass (Ellen Naomi Cohen) (singer); Baltimore (1941–1974)

Elliott, Sam (actor); Sacramento, Calif., 8/9/44

Ellison, Lawrence J. (computer industry executive); New York City, 1944

Ellison, Ralph (novelist); Oklahoma City, Okla. (1914–1994)

Ellsberg, Daniel (activist); Chicago, 4/7/31

Elman, Mischa (violinist); Stalnoye, Ukraine (1891–1967)

Emerson, Ralph Waldo (philosopher, poet); Boston (1803–1882)

Enesco, Georges (composer); Dorohoi, Romania (1881–1955)

Engels, Friedrich (Socialist writer); Barmen, Germany **(1820–1895)**
Englund, Robert (actor); Glendale, Calif., 6/6/49
Entremont, Philippe (concert pianist); Rheims, France, 6/7/34
Ephron, Nora (writer, director); New York City, 5/19/41
Epicurus (philosopher); Samos, Greece **(341–270 B.C.)**
Epstein, Sir Jacob (sculptor); New York City **(1880–1959)**
Erasmus, Desiderius (Gerhard Gerhards) (scholar); Rotterdam **(1469–1536)**
Erdrich, (Karen) Louise (writer); Little Falls, Minn., 7/6/54
Erickson, Leif (actor); Alameda, Calif. **(1911–1986)**
Ericsson, Leif (navigator) c. 10th century A.D.
Erikson, Erik H. (psychoanalyst); Frankfurt, Germany **(1902–1994)**
Ernst, Max (painter); Bruhl, Germany **(1891–1976)**
Erté (Romain de Tirtoff) (artist, designer); St. Petersburg, Russia **(1892–1990)**
Estevez, Emilio (actor, director, screenwriter); New York City, 5/12/62
Eszterhas, Joe (screenwriter); Csakanydoroslo, Hungary, 11/23/44
Euclid (mathematician); Megara, Greece, fl. 300 B.C.
Euler, Leonhard (mathematician); Basel, Switzerland **(1707–1783)**
Euripides (dramatist); Salamis, Greece **(c. 484–407 B.C.)**
Evangelista, Linda (model); St. Catharines, Ont., Canada, 5/10/65
Evans, Dale (born Lucille Wood Smith but raised as Frances Octavia Smith) (actress, singer); Uvalde, Tex., 10/31/12
Evans, Dame Edith (actress); London **(1888–1976)**
Evans, Linda (actress); Hartford, Conn., 11/18/42
Evans, Maurice (actor); Dorchester, England **(1901–1989)**
Everett, Chad (Raymond Lee Cramton) (actor); South Bend, Ind., 6/11/36
Everett, Rupert (actor, model, musician); Norfolk, England, 5/29/59
Everhart, Angie (model, actress); Akron, Ohio, 9/6/69
Evers, Charles (civil rights leader); Decatur, Miss., 9/14/22
Evers, Medgar (civil rights leader); Decatur, Miss. **(1925–1963)**
Evers-Williams, Myrlie (civil rights leader); Vicksburg, Miss., 3/17/33

F

Fabares, Shelley (actress); Santa Monica, Calif., 1/19/44
Fabian (Fabian Anthony Forte) (singer); Philadelphia, 2/6/43
Fabray, Nanette (Nanette Fabarés) (actress); San Diego, Calif., 10/27/22
Fahrenheit, Gabriel (German physicist); Danzig, Poland **(1686–1736)**
Fairbanks, Douglas (Douglas Ulman) (actor); Denver **(1883–1939)**
Fairbanks, Douglas, Jr. (actor); New York City **(1909–2000)**
Fairchild, Morgan (Patsy Ann McClenny) (actress); Dallas, 2/3/50
Faith, Percy (conductor); Toronto **(1908–1976)**
Falk, Peter (actor); New York City, 9/16/27
Falla, Manuel de (composer); Cadiz, Spain **(1876–1946)**
Faludi, Susan (journalist, writer); New York City, 4/18/59
Falwell, Jerry (fundamentalist preacher); Lynchburg, Va., 8/11/33
Faraday, Michael (physicist); Newington, England **(1791–1867)**
Farentino, James (actor); Brooklyn, N.Y., 2/24/38
Farley, Chris (actor, comedian); Madison, Wis. **(1964–1997)**
Farmer, James (civil rights leader); Marshall, Tex. **(1920–1999)**
Farnsworth, Richard (actor); Los Angeles, 9/1/20
Farr, Jamie (Jameel Joseph Farah) (actor); Toledo, Ohio, 7/1/34
Farrar, Geraldine (soprano, actress); Melrose, Mass. **(1882–1967)**
Farrell, Eileen (operatic soprano); Willimantic, Conn., 2/13/20
Farrell, James T. (novelist); Chicago **(1904–1979)**
Farrell, Mike (actor); St. Paul, Minn., 2/6/39
Farrell, Perry (Perry Bernstein) (lead singer); Queens, N.Y., 3/29/59
Farrell, Suzanne (Roberta Sue Ficker) (ballet dancer); Cincinnati, 8/16/45
Farrow, Mia (actress); Los Angeles, 2/9/46
Fasanella, Ralph (painter); New York City **(1914–1997)**
Fassbinder, Rainer Werner (film, stage director); Bad Wörishofen, Germany **(1946–1982)**
Fast, Howard (novelist); New York City, 11/11/14
Faubus, Orval E(ugene) (governor of Arkansas); Combs, Ark. **(1910–1994)**
Faulkner, William (novelist); New Albany, Miss. **(1897–1962)**
Fauré, Gabriel Urbain (composer); Pamiers, France **(1845–1924)**
Fawcett, Farrah (Mary Farrah Leni Fawcett) (actress); Corpus Christi, Tex., 2/2/47
Faye, Alice (Ann Leppert) (actress); New York City **(1912–1998)**
Feiffer, Jules (cartoonist); New York City, 1/26/29
Feininger, Lyonel (painter); New York City **(1871–1956)**
Feldman, Marty (actor, screenwriter, director); London **(1938–1982)**
Feldon, Barbara (actress); Pittsburgh, 3/12/41
Feliciano, José (singer); Larez, Puerto Rico, 9/10/45
Felker, Clay S. (editor, publisher); St. Louis, 10/2/25

Fell, Norman (actor); Philadelphia **(1923–1998)**
Fellini, Federico (film director); Rimini, Italy **(1920–1993)**
Fender, Freddie (Baldemar Huerta) (singer); San Benito, Tex., 6/4/37
Ferber, Edna (novelist); Kalamazoo, Mich. **(1885–1968)**
Ferguson, Maynard (jazz trumpeter); Verdun, Que., Canada, 5/4/28
Ferlinghetti, Lawrence (poet, writer, translator); Yonkers, N.Y., 3/24/19
Fermi, Enrico (atomic physicist); Rome **(1901–1954)**
Fernandel (Fernand Joseph Desire Contandin) (actor); Marseilles, France **(1903–1971)**
Ferraro, Geraldine Anne (political figure); New York City, 8/26/35
Ferrer, José (actor, director); Santurce, Puerto Rico **(1912–1992)**
Ferrer, Mel (actor); Elberon, N.J., 8/25/17
Fiedler, Arthur (conductor); Boston **(1894–1979)**
Field, Eugene (poet); St. Louis **(1850–1895)**
Field, Marshall (merchant); nr. Conway, Mass. **(1834–1906)**
Field, Sally (actress); Pasadena, Calif., 11/6/46
Fielding, Henry (novelist); nr. Glastonbury, England **(1707–1754)**
Fields, W. C. (William Claude Dukenfield) (comedian); Philadelphia **(1880–1946)**
Fiennes, Joseph (actor); Salisbury, England, 5/27/70
Fiennes, Ralph (actor); Suffolk, England, 12/22/62
Fierstein, Harvey (Forbes) (playwright, actor); Brooklyn, 6/6/54
Figgis, Mike (director, screenwriter, composer, actor); Carlisle, England, 2/28/48
Filene, Edward A. (merchant) **(1860–1937)**
Fillmore, Millard (13th U.S. president); Locke, Cayuga County, N.Y. **(1800–1874)**
Finch, Peter (actor); Kensington, England **(1916–1977)**
Finney, Albert (actor); Salford, England, 5/9/36
Fiorentino, Linda (Clorinda Fiorentino) (actress); Philadelphia, 3/9/60
Firkusny, Rudolf (pianist); Napajedia, former Czechoslovakia **(1912–1994)**
Firth, Colin (actor); Grayshot, England, 9/10/60
Fischer-Dieskau, Dietrich (baritone); Berlin, 5/28/25
Fishburne, Laurence (actor); Augusta, Ga., 7/30/61
Fisher, Carrie (actress); Los Angeles, 10/21/56
Fisher, Eddie (Edwin) (singer); Philadelphia, 8/10/28
Fitzgerald, Barry (William Joseph Shields) (actor); Dublin **(1888–1961)**
Fitzgerald, Ella (singer); Newport News, Va. **(1918–1996)**
Fitzgerald, F. Scott (Francis Scott Key Fitzgerald) (novelist); St. Paul, Minn. **(1896–1940)**
Fitzgerald, Geraldine (actress); Dublin, 11/24/14
Fitzgerald, Pegeen (radio broadcaster); Norcatur, Kans. **(1910–1989)**
Flack, Roberta (singer); Black Mountain, N.C., 2/10/40
Flagstad, Kirsten (Wagnerian soprano); Hamar, Norway **(1895–1962)**
Flatt, Lester Raymond (bluegrass musician); Overton County, Tenn. **(1914–1979)**
Flaubert, Gustave (novelist); Rouen, France **(1821–1880)**
Fleming, Sir Alexander (bacteriologist); Lochfield, Scotland **(1881–1955)**
Fletcher, John (dramatist); Rye, Sussex, England **(1579–1625)**
Flockhart, Calista (actress); Freeport, Ill., 11/11/64
Flynn, Errol (actor); Hobart, Tasmania **(1909–1959)**
Fodor, Eugene (violinist); Turkey Creek, Colo., 3/5/50
Fokine, Michel (dancer, choreographer); St. Petersburg, Russia **(1880–1942)**
Fonda, Bridget (actress); Los Angeles, 1/27/64
Fonda, Henry (actor); Grand Island, Neb. **(1905–1982)**
Fonda, Jane (actress); New York City, 12/21/37
Fonda, Peter (actor); New York City, 2/23/39
Fontaine, Frank (singer, comedian); Cambridge, Mass. **(1920–1979)**
Fontaine, Joan (Joan de Havilland) (actress); Tokyo, 10/22/17
Fontanne, Lynn (actress); London **(1887–1983)**
Fonteyn, Dame Margot (Margaret Hookham) (ballet dancer); Reigate, England **(1919–1991)**
Foote, Shelby (historian); Greenville, Miss., 11/17/16
Forbes, Malcolm S(tevenson) (publisher, sportsman); Brooklyn, N.Y. **(1919–1990)**
Ford, Gerald Rudolph (38th U.S. president); Omaha, Neb., 7/14/13
Ford, Glenn (Gwyllyn Ford) (actor); Ste.-Christine, Que., Canada, 5/1/16
Ford, Harrison (actor); Chicago, 7/13/42
Ford, Henry (industrialist); Greenfield, Mich. **(1863–1947)**
Ford, John (film director); Cape Elizabeth, Maine **(1895–1973)**

Ford, Tennessee Ernie (Ernie Jennings Ford) (singer); Bristol, Tenn. (1919–1991)
Foreman, George (boxer, actor); Marshall, Texas, 1/10/49
Forrester, Maureen (contralto); Montreal, 7/25/30
Forsythe, John (John Lincoln Freund) (actor); Penn's Grove, N.J., 1/29/18
Fosdick, Harry Emerson (clergyman); Buffalo, N.Y. (1878–1968)
Fosse, Bob (Robert Louis Fosse) (choreographer, director); Chicago (1927–1987)
Foster, Jodie (Alicia Christian Foster) (actress, director, producer); Los Angeles, 11/19/62
Foster, Stephen Collins (composer); nr. Pittsburgh (1826–1864)
Fountain, Pete (jazz musician); New Orleans, 7/3/30
Fox, Matthew (actor); Crowheart, Wyo., 7/14/66
Fox, Michael J. (actor, producer); Edmonton, Alta., Canada, 6/9/61
Foxx, Redd (John Elroy Sanford) (actor, comedian); St. Louis (1922–1991)
Foy, Eddie, Jr. (dancer, actor); New Rochelle, N.Y. (1905–1983)
Fra Angelico (Giovanni da Fiesole) (painter); Vicchio in the Mugello, Tuscany, Italy (c. 1387–1455)
Fracci, Carla (ballet dancer); Milan, Italy, 8/20/36
Fragonard, Jean Honoré (painter); Grasse, France (1732–1806)
Frakes, Jonathan (actor); Bethlehem, Pa., 8/19/52
Frampton, Peter (rock musician); Beckenham, England, 4/20/50
France, Anatole (Jacques Anatole François Thibault) (author); Paris (1844–1924)
Francescatti, Zino (violinist); Marseilles, France (1902–1991)
Franciosa, Anthony (Anthony Papaleo) (actor); New York City, 10/25/28
Francis, Anne (actress); Ossining, N.Y., 7/16/30
Francis, Connie (Concetta Franconero) (singer); Newark, N.J., 12/12/38
Francis, Genie (actress); Englewood, N.J., 5/26/62
Francis of Assisi, Saint (Giovanni Francesco Barnardone) (founder of Franciscans); Assisi, Italy (1182–1226)
Franck, César Auguste (composer); Liège, Belgium (1822–1890)
Franco Bahamonde, Francisco (chief of state); El Ferrol, Spain (1892–1975)
Frankenheimer, John (movie director, producer); New York City, 2/19/30
Frankenthaler, Helen (artist); New York City, 12/12/28
Frankl, Victor E. (psychiatrist); Vienna (1905–1997)
Franklin, Aretha (singer); Memphis, Tenn., 3/25/42
Franklin, Benjamin (statesman, scientist); Boston (1706–1790)
Franklin, Bonnie (actress); Santa Monica, Calif., 1/6/44
Franklin, John Hope (historian); Rentiesville, Okla., 1/2/15
Frann, Mary (actress); St. Louis (1943–1998)
Franz, Dennis (Dennis Schlachta) (actor); Chicago, 10/28/44
Fraser, Brendan (actor); Indianapolis, Indiana, 12/3/67
Frazer, Sir James George (anthropologist); Glasgow, Scotland (1854–1941)
Freeman, Morgan (actor); Memphis, Tenn., 6/1/37
Freud, Sigmund (psychoanalyst); Moravia, Czech Repubic (1856–1939)
Frey, Glenn (musician); Detroit, 11/6/48
Frick, Henry Clay (industrialist); Westmoreland Co., Pa. (1849–1919)
Friedan, Betty (Betty Naomi Goldstein) (feminist, writer); Peoria, Ill., 2/4/21
Fromm, Erich (psychoanalyst); Frankfurt-am-Main, Germany (1900–1980)
Frost, David (TV entertainer); Tenterden, England, 4/7/39
Frost, Robert Lee (poet); San Francisco (1874–1963)
Fry, Christopher (playwright); Bristol, England, 12/18/07
Fugard, Athol (playwright); Middleburg, South Africa, 6/11/32
Fulbright, J. William (politician); Sumner, Mo. (1905–1995)
Fuller, Charles (playwright); Philadelphia, 3/5/39
Fuller, R(ichard) Buckminster (Jr.) (architect, educator); Milton, Mass. (1895–1983)
Fulton, Robert (inventor); Lancaster County, Pa. (1765–1815)
Funicello, Annette (actress); Utica, N.Y., 10/22/42
Funt, Allen (TV producer); Brooklyn, N.Y. (1914–1999)

G

Gabin, Jean (actor); Paris (1904–1976)
Gable, (William) Clark (actor); Cadiz, Ohio (1901–1960)
Gabo, Naum (sculptor); Briansk, Russia (1890–1977)
Gabor, Eva (actress); Budapest (1920–1995)
Gabor, Zsa Zsa (Sari) (actress); Budapest, 2/6/17
Gabriel, Peter (musician); Cobham, England, 2/13/50
Gabrieli, Giovanni (composer); Venice (c. 1557–1612)
Gaddis, William (novelist); New York City (1922–1998)

Gainsborough, Thomas (painter); Sudbury, Suffolk, England (1727–1788)
Galbraith, John Kenneth (economist); Iona Station, Ont., Canada, 10/15/08
Galilei, Galileo (astronomer, physicist); Pisa, Italy (1564–1642)
Gallico, Paul (novelist); New York City (1897–1976)
Gallup, George H. (poll taker); Jefferson, Iowa (1901–1984)
Galsworthy, John (novelist, dramatist); Coombe, England (1867–1933)
Galway, James (flutist); Belfast, Northern Ireland, 12/8/39
Gambling, John A. (radio broadcaster); New York City, 1930
Gandhi, Indira (Indira Nehru) (former prime minister); Allahabad, India (1917– 1984)
Gandhi, Mohandas Karamchand (called Mahatma Gandhi) (Hindu leader); Porbandar, India (1869–1948)
Gannett, Frank E. (editor, publisher) (1876–1957)
Garagiola, Joe (Joseph Henry Garagiola) (sportscaster); St. Louis, 2/12/26
Garbo, Greta (Greta Gustafsson) (actress); Stockholm (1905–1990)
Garcia, Andy (Andres Arturo Garcia-Menendez) (actor); Havana, Cuba, 4/12/56
Garcia, Jerry (rock musician); San Francisco (1942–1995)
Garcia Lorca, Frederico (poet, dramatist); Fuente Vaqueros, Spain (1898–1936)
Garden, Mary (soprano); Aberdeen, Scotland (1874–1967)
Gardenia, Vincent (Vincente Scognamiglio) (actor); Naples, Italy (1922–1992)
Gardner, Ava (actress); Smithfield, N.C. (1922–1990)
Gardner, Erle Stanley (novelist); Malden, Mass. (1889–1970)
Garfield, James Abram (20th U.S. president); Cuyahoga County, Ohio (1831–1881)
Garfunkel, Art (Arthur) (singer); Newark, N.J., 11/5/41
Garibaldi, Giuseppe (Italian nationalist leader); Nice, France (1807–1882)
Garland, Judy (Frances Gumm) (actress, singer); Grand Rapids, Minn. (1922–1969)
Garner, Erroll (jazz pianist); Pittsburgh (1921–1977)
Garner, James (James Bumgarner) (actor); Norman, Okla., 4/7/28
Garofalo, Janeane (actress, comedienne); Newton, N.J., 9/28/64
Garr, Teri (actress); Lakewood, Ohio, 12/11/49
Garrison, William Lloyd (abolitionist); Newburyport, Mass. (1805–1879)
Garroway, Dave (TV host); Schenectady, N.Y. (1913–1982)
Garson, Greer (actress); County Down, Northern Ireland (1903–1996)
Garth, Jennie (actress); Urbana, Ill., 4/3/72
Garvey, Marcus Moziah (black nationalist leader); Jamaica (1887–1940)
Gassman, Vittorio (film actor, director); Genoa, Italy (1922–2000)
Gates, Bill (William Henry Gates III) (software pioneer); Seattle, 10/28/55
Gates, Henry Louis, Jr. (scholar); Keyser, W. Va., 9/16/50
Gaudí, Antonio (architect); Reus, Spain (1852–1926)
Gauguin, (Eugène Henri) Paul (painter); Paris (1848–1903)
Gautama Buddha (Prince Siddhartha) (philosopher); Kapilavastu, India (c. 563–c. 483 B.C.)
Gavin, John (actor, diplomat); Los Angeles, 4/8/35
Gavras, Konstantinos (Costa-Gavras) (film director); Loutra-Iraias, Greece, 2/13/33
Gaye, Marvin (singer); Washington, D.C. (1939–1984)
Gayle, Crystal (Brenda Gayle Webb) (singer); Paintsville, Ky., 1/9/51
Gaynor, Janet (actress); Philadelphia (1906–1984)
Gaynor, Mitzi (Francesca Mitzi Marlene de Czanyi von Gerber) (actress); Chicago, 9/4/31
Gazzara, Ben (Biagio Anthony Gazzara) (actor); New York City, 8/28/30
Gedda, Nicolai (tenor); Stockholm, 7/11/25
Gellar, Sarah Michelle (actress); New York City, 4/14/77
Genet, Jean (playwright); Paris (1910–1986)
Genghis Khan (Temujin) (conqueror); nr. Lake Baikal, Russia (1162–1227)
Gentry, Bobbie (Roberta Streeter) (singer); Chickasaw Co., Miss., 7/27/44
George, David Lloyd (statesman); Manchester, England (1863–1945)
George, Henry (economist, reformer); Philadelphia (1839–1897)
Gere, Richard (actor); Philadelphia, 8/29/49
Géricault, Jean Louis (painter); Rouen, France (1791–1824)
Geronimo (Goyathlay) (Apache chieftain); Arizona (1829–1909)
Gershwin, George (composer); Brooklyn, N.Y. (1898–1937)
Gershwin, Ira (lyricist); New York City (1896–1983)

Getty, J. Paul (oil executive); Minneapolis (1892–1976)
Getz, Stan (saxophonist); Philadelphia (1927–1991)
Ghiberti, Lorenzo (goldsmith, sculptor); Florence (1378–1455)
Ghostley, Alice (actress); Eve, Mo., 8/14/26
Giacometti, Alberto (sculptor); Switzerland (1901–1966)
Giannini, Giancarlo (actor); La Spezia, Italy, 8/1/42
Gibbon, Edward (historian); Putney, England (1737–1794)
Gibson, Charles Dana (illustrator); Roxbury, Mass. (1867–1944)
Gibson, Henry (actor, comedian); Germantown, Pa., 9/21/35
Gibson, Mel (actor, director, producer); Peekskill, N.Y., 1/3/56
Gide, André (author); Paris (1869–1951)
Gielgud, Sir John (actor); London (1904–2000)
Gifford, Kathie Lee (Kathie Lee Epstein) (talk show host); Paris, 8/16/53
Gilbert, Melissa (actress); Los Angeles, 5/8/64
Gilbert, Walter (chemist, Nobel laureate); Boston, 3/21/32
Gilbert, Sir William Schwenck (librettist); London (1836–1911)
Gilels, Emil (concert pianist); Odessa, Ukraine (1916–1985)
Gillespie, Dizzy (John Birks Gillespie) (jazz trumpeter); Cheraw, S.C. (1917–1993)
Gilligan, Carol (Friedman) (psychologist); New York City, 11/28/36
Gilpin, Peri (actress); Waco, Tex., 5/27/61
Gimbel, Bernard F. (merchant); Vincennes, Ind. (1885–1966)
Gingrich, Newt (politician); Harrisburg, Pa., 6/17/43
Ginsberg, Allen (poet); Newark, N.J. (1926–1997)
Giordano, Luca (painter); Naples, Italy (1632–1705)
Giorgione (painter); Castelfranco, Italy (c. 1477–1510)
Giotto di Bondone (painter); Vespignamo, Italy (c. 1266–1337)
Giovanni, Nikki (poet); Knoxville, Tenn., 6/7/43
Giroud, Françoise (French government official); Geneva, 9/21/16
Gish, Dorothy (actress); Massillon, Ohio (1898–1968)
Gish, Lillian (Lillian de Guiche) (actress); Springfield, Ohio (1893–1993)
Givenchy, Hubert (fashion designer); Beauvais, France, 2/21/27
Gladstone, William Ewart (statesman); Liverpool, England (1809–1898)
Glaser, Paul Michael (actor, director); Cambridge, Mass., 3/25/43
Glass, Philip (composer); Baltimore, 1/31/37
Gleason, Jackie (comedian); Brooklyn, N.Y. (1916–1987)
Glenn, John (legislator, astronaut); Cambridge, Ohio, 7/18/21
Gless, Sharon (actress); Los Angeles, 5/31/43
Glover, Danny (actor); San Francisco, 7/22/47
Gluck, Christoph Willibald (composer); Erasbach, Germany (1714–1787)
Gobel, George (comedian); Chicago (1920–1991)
Godard, Jean Luc (film director); Paris, 12/3/30
Goddard, Paulette (Marion Levy) (actress); Great Neck, N.Y. (1911–1990)
Goddard, Robert Hutchings (father of modern rocketry); Worcester, Mass. (1882–1945)
Godfrey, Arthur (entertainer); New York City (1903–1983)
Goebbels, Joseph Paul (Nazi leader); Rheydt, Germany (1897–1945)
Goering, Hermann (Nazi leader); Rosenheim, Germany (1893–1946)
Goethals, George Washington (engineer); Brooklyn, N.Y. (1858–1928)
Goethe, Johann Wolfgang von (poet, playwright, novelist); Frankfurt-am-Main, Germany (1749–1832)
Gogol, Nikolai Vasilievich (novelist); nr. Mirgorod, Ukraine (1809–1852)
Goldberg, Rube (cartoonist); San Francisco (1883–1970)
Goldberg, Whoopi (Caryn Johnson) (actress); New York City, 11/13/49
Goldblum, Jeff (actor); Pittsburgh, 10/22/52
Golden, Harry (Harry Goldhurst) (author); New York City (1902–1981)
Goldman, Emma (anarchist); Kovno, Lithuania (1869–1940)
Goldsmith, Oliver (dramatist, poet); County Longford, Ireland (1728–1774)
Goldwyn, Samuel (Schmuel Gelbfisz) (film producer); Warsaw (1879–1974)
Gompers, Samuel (labor leader); London (1850–1924)
Goodall, Jane (Baroness van Lawick-Goodall) (ethologist); London, 4/3/34
Gooding, Jr., Cuba (actor); Bronx, New York, 1/2/68
Goodman, Benny (clarinetist); Chicago (1909–1986)
Goodman, John (actor); St. Louis, 6/20/52
Goodwin, Doris (Helen) Kearns (historian); Rockville Center, N.Y., 1/4/43
Goodyear, Charles (inventor); New Haven, Conn. (1800–1860)
Gorbachev, Mikhail Sergeyevich (Soviet leader); Privolnoye, Russia, 3/2/31

Gordimer, Nadine (novelist, short-story writer); Springs, South Africa, 12/20/23
Gordon, Dexter (jazz musician); Los Angeles (1923–1990)
Gordon, Ruth (actress); Wollaston, Mass. (1896–1985)
Gore, Albert, Jr. (vice president of the U.S.); Washington, D.C., 3/31/48
Gordy, Berry, Jr. (record company executive); Detroit, 11/28/29
Gorey, Edward (St. John) (illustrator, author); Chicago, 2/22/25
Gorki, Maxim (Alexei Maximovich Peshkov) (author); Nizhni Novgorod, Russia (1868–1936)
Gorky, Arshile (painter); Armenia (1904–1948)
Gormé, Eydie (singer); Bronx, N.Y., 8/16/32
Gorshin, Frank (actor); Pittsburgh, 4/5/34
Gossett, Louis, Jr. (actor); Brooklyn, N.Y., 5/27/36
Gottschalk, Louis Moreau (pianist, composer); New Orleans (1829–1869)
Gould, Chester (cartoonist); Pawnee, Okla. (1900–1985)
Gould, Elliott (Elliott Goldstein) (actor); Brooklyn, N.Y., 8/29/38
Gould, Glenn (concert pianist); Toronto (1932–1982)
Gould, Morton (composer); Richmond Hill, Queens, N.Y. (1913–1996)
Gould, Stephen Jay (paleontologist, science writer); New York City, 9/10/41
Goulet, Robert (singer); Lawrence, Mass., 11/26/33
Gounod, Charles François (composer); Paris (1818–1893)
Goya y Lucientes, Francisco José de (painter); Fuendetodos, Spain (1746–1828)
Grable, Betty (actress); St. Louis (1916–1973)
Grace, Princess of Monaco (Grace Kelly) (ex-actress); Philadelphia (1929–1982)
Graham, Bill (Wolfgang Grajonca) (rock impresario); Berlin (1930–1991)
Graham, Billy (William F. Graham) (evangelist); Charlotte, N.C., 11/7/18
Graham, Katharine Meyer (newspaper publisher); New York City, 6/16/17
Graham, Martha (choreographer); Pittsburgh (1894–1991)
Grainger, Percy Aldridge (pianist, composer); Melbourne, Australia (1882–1961)
Gramm, Donald (Grambach) (bass-baritone); Milwaukee (1927–1983)
Grammer, Kelsey (actor); St. Thomas, V.I., 2/21/55
Granger, Stewart (James Stewart) (actor); London (1913–1993)
Grant, Cary (Alexander Archibald Leach) (actor); Bristol, England (1904–1986)
Grant, Hugh (actor); London, England, 9/9/60
Grant, Lee (Lyova Haskell Rosenthal) (actress); New York City, 10/31/30
Grant, Ulysses Simpson (18th U.S. president); Point Pleasant, Ohio (1822–1885)
Grass, Günter (novelist); Danzig, Poland, 10/16/27
Graves, Nancy (Stevenson) (artist); Pittsfield, Mass. (1940–1996)
Graves, Peter (Peter Aurness) (actor); Minneapolis, 3/18/26
Graves, Robert (writer); London (1895–1985)
Gray, Linda (actress); Santa Monica, Calif., 9/12/40
Gray, Thomas (poet); London (1716–1771)
Greco, José (dancer); Montorio nei Frentani, Italy, 12/23/18
Greeley, Horace (journalist, politician); Amherst, N.H. (1811–1872)
Green, Adolph (actor, lyricist); New York City, 12/2/15
Green, Al (singer); Forrest City, Ark., 4/13/46
Greene, Graham (novelist); Berkhamsted, England (1904–1991)
Greene, Lorne (actor); Ottawa, Ont., Canada (1915–1987)
Greene, Shecky (comedian, actor); Chicago, 4/8/25
Greenstreet, Sydney (actor); Sandwich, England (1879–1954)
Greenspan, Alan (chairman of the Federal Reserve); New York City, 3/6/26
Greer, Germaine (feminist, writer); Melbourne, Australia, 1/29/39
Gregory, Cynthia (ballet dancer); Los Angeles, 7/8/46
Gregory, Dick (comedian); St. Louis, 10/12/32
Gregory, Lady (Isabella) Augusta (playwright); Roxborough, Ireland (1852–1932)
Greuze, Jean-Baptiste (painter); Tournus, France (1725–1805)
Grey, Joel (Joel Katz) (actor, dancer); Cleveland, 4/11/32
Grey, Zane (author); Zanesville, Ohio (1875–1939)
Grieg, Edvard Hagerup (composer); Bergen, Norway (1843–1907)
Grier, Pam (actress); Winston-Salem, N.C., 5/26/49
Griffin, Merv (TV host, producer); San Mateo, Calif., 7/6/25
Griffith, Andy (actor); Mount Airy, N.C., 6/1/26
Griffith, David Lewelyn Wark (film producer); La Grange, Ky. (1875–1948)
Griffith, Melanie (actress); New York City, 8/9/57

Grigorovich, Yuri (choreographer); Leningrad (St. Petersburg), Russia, 1/1/27

Grimes, Tammy (actress); Lynn, Mass., 1/30/34

Grimm, Jacob (author of fairy tales); Hanau, Germany **(1785–1863)**

Grimm, Wilhelm (author of fairy tales); Hanau, Germany **(1786–1859)**

Gris, Juan (José Victoriano González) (painter); Madrid **(1887–1927)**

Grisham, John (attorney, author); Jonesboro, Ark., 2/8/55

Grodin, Charles (actor); Pittsburgh, 4/21/35

Groening, Matt (animator, producer); Portland, Ore., 2/14/54

Gromyko, Andrei A. (diplomat); Starye Gromyki, Russia **(1909–1989)**

Gropius, Walter (architect); Berlin **(1883–1969)**

Gropper, William (painter, illustrator); New York City **(1897–1977)**

Gross, Michael (actor); Chicago, 6/21/47

Grosz, George (painter); Germany **(1893–1959)**

Grove, Andrew (Andras Grof) (computer industry executive); Budapest, Hungary, 9/2/36

Grünewald, Matthias (Mathis Gothart Neithart) (painter); Würzburg, Germany **(c. 1470–1528)**

Guest, Christopher (Christopher Haden-Guest) (actor, writer, director); New York City, 2/5/48

Guggenheim, Meyer (capitalist); Langnau, Switzerland **(1828–1905)**

Guillaume, Robert (Robert Williams) (actor); St. Louis, 11/30/27

Guinness, Sir Alec (actor); London, 4/2/14

Guitry, Sacha (Alexandre Guitry) (actor, film director); St. Petersburg, Russia **(1885–1957)**

Gumbel, Bryant Charles (TV newscaster); New Orleans, 9/29/48

Gunther, John (author); Chicago **(1901–1970)**

Gutenberg, Johann (printer); Mainz, Germany **(c. 1397–1468)**

Guthrie, Arlo (singer); New York City, 7/10/47

Guthrie, Woody (folk singer, composer); Okemah, Okla. **(1912–1967)**

Gwenn, Edmund (actor); London **(1875–1959)**

Gwynne, Fred (actor); New York City **(1926–1993)**

H

Habibie, Bacharuddin, Jusuf (president of Indonesia); Pare-Pare, Indonesia, 6/25/36

Hackett, Bobby (trumpeter); Providence, R.I. **(1915–1976)**

Hackett, Buddy (Leonard Hacker) (comedian, actor); Brooklyn, N.Y., 8/31/24

Hackman, Gene (actor); San Bernardino, Calif., 1/30/31

Hagen, Uta (actress); Göttingen, Germany, 6/12/19

Haggard, Merle (songwriter, singer); Bakersfield, Calif., 4/6/37

Hagman, Larry (Larry Hageman) (actor); Weatherford, Tex., 9/21/31

Haig, Alexander Meigs, Jr. (ex-secretary of state, ex-general); Bala-Cynwyd, Pa., 12/2/24

Haile Selassie (Ras Tafari Makonnen) (ex-emperor); Ethiopia **(1892–1975)**

Hailey, Arthur (novelist); Luton, England, 4/5/20

Halberstam, David (journalist); New York City, 4/10/34

Hale, Alan (actor, director); Washington, D.C. **(1892–1950)**

Hale, Barbara (actress); DeKalb, Ill., 4/18/21

Hale, Edward Everett (clergyman, author); Boston **(1822–1909)**

Hale, Nathan (American Revolutionary officer); Coventry, Conn. **(1755–1776)**

Halevi, Judah (Jewish poet); Toledo, Spain **(1085–1140)**

Haley, Alex (writer); Ithaca, N.Y. **(1921–1992)**

Haley, Jack (actor); Boston **(1899–1979)**

Hall, Anthony Michael (Michael Anthony Thomas Charles Hall) (actor, singer); Boston, 4/14/68

Hall, Arsenio (comedian, talk-show host); Cleveland, 2/12/58

Hall, Donald (Andrew, Jr.) (poet); New Haven, Conn., 9/20/28

Hall, Huntz (actor); New York City **(1919–1999)**

Hall, Jerry (model, actress); Mesquite, Texas, 7/2/56

Hall, Monty (TV personality); Winnipeg, Canada, 8/25/23

Halley, Edmund (astronomer); London **(1656–1742)**

Hals, Frans (painter); Antwerp, Netherlands **(c. 1580–1666)**

Halsey, William Frederick, Jr. (naval officer); Elizabeth, N.J. **(1882–1959)**

Hamel, Veronica (actress); Philadelphia, 11/20/43

Hamill, Mark (actor); Oakland, 9/25/52

Hamilton, Alexander (statesman); Nevis, British West Indies **(1755–1804)**

Hamilton, Alice (physician, reformer); New York City **(1869–1970)**

Hamilton, Edith (scholar); Dresden, Germany **(1867–1963)**

Hamilton, George (actor); Memphis, Tenn., 8/12/39

Hamlin, Harry (actor); Pasadena, Calif., 10/30/51

Hamlisch, Marvin (composer, pianist); New York City, 6/2/44

Hammarskjöld, Dag (U.N. secretary-general); Jönköping, Sweden **(1905–1961)**

Hammerstein, Oscar, II (librettist, stage producer); New York City **(1895–1960)**

Hampton, Lionel (vibraharpist, band leader); Birmingham, Ala., 4/12/13

Hamsun, Knut (Knut Pedersen) (novelist); Lom, Norway **(1859–1952)**

Hancock, Herbie (jazz musician); Chicago, 4/12/40

Hancock, John (statesman); Braintree, Mass. **(1737–1793)**

Hand, Learned (jurist); Albany, N.Y. **(1872–1961)**

Handel, George Frideric (Georg Friedrich Händel) (composer); Halle, Germany **(1685–1759)**

Handy, William Christopher (blues composer); Florence, Ala. **(1873–1958)**

Hanks, Tom (actor, director, writer); Concord, Calif., 7/9/56

Hannah, Daryl (actress); Chicago, 12/19/60

Hannibal (Carthaginian general); North Africa **(247–182 B.C.)**

Hansberry, Lorraine (playwright); Chicago **(1930–1965)**

Hanson, Howard (conductor); Wahoo, Neb. **(1896–1981)**

Harburg, E. Y. "Yip" (songwriter); New York City **(1896–1981)**

Harding, Warren Gamaliel (29th U.S. president); Morrow County, Ohio **(1865–1923)**

Hardwicke, Sir Cedric (actor); Stourbridge, England **(1893–1964)**

Hardy, Oliver (comedian); Atlanta **(1892–1957)**

Hardy, Thomas (novelist); Dorsetshire, England **(1840–1928)**

Harkness, Edward S. (business executive); Cleveland **(1874–1940)**

Harlow, Jean (Harlean Carpentier) (actress); Kansas City, Mo. **(1911–1937)**

Harlow, Shalom (model, TV personality); Oshawa, Ontario, Canada, 12/5/73

Harmon, Mark (actor); Burbank, Calif., 9/2/51

Harnick, Sheldon (lyricist); Chicago, 4/30/24

Harper, Valerie (actress); Suffern, N.Y., 8/22/40

Harrell, Lynn (cellist); New York City, 1/30/44

Harrelson, Woody (actor); Midland, Tex., 7/23/61

Harriman, Pamela (ambassador); Farnborough, England **(1920–1997)**

Harriman, W. (William) Averell (ex-governor of New York); New York City **(1891–1986)**

Harrington, Pat, Jr. (actor, comedian); New York City, 8/13/29

Harris, Barbara (Sandra Markowitz) (actress); Evanston, Ill., 7/25/35

Harris, Ed (actor); Englewood, N.J., 11/28/50

Harris, Emmylou (singer); Birmingham, Ala., 4/2/47

Harris, Julie (actress); Grosse Pointe Park, Mich., 12/2/25

Harris, Phil (actor, band leader); Linton, Ind. **(1906–1995)**

Harris, Richard (actor); Limerick, Ireland, 10/1/33

Harris, Rosemary (actress); Ashby, England, 9/19/30

Harris, Roy (composer); Lincoln County, Okla. **(1898–1979)**

Harrison, Benjamin (23rd U.S. president); North Bend, Ohio **(1833–1901)**

Harrison, George (singer, songwriter); Liverpool, England, 2/25/43

Harrison, Gregory (actor); Avalon, Catalina Island, Calif., 5/31/50

Harrison, Sir Rex (Reginald Carey) (actor); Huyton, England **(1908–1990)**

Harrison, William Henry (9th U.S. president); Charles City County, Va. **(1773–1841)**

Harry, Deborah (Blondie) (musician); Miami, Fla., 7/1/45

Hart, Lorenz (lyricist); New York City **(1895–1943)**

Hart, Mary (Mary Johanna Harum) (host); Sioux Falls, S.D., 11/8/50

Hart, Melissa Joan (actress); Sayville, N.Y., 4/18/76

Hart, Moss (playwright); New York City **(1904–1961)**

Harte, Bret (Francis Brett Harte) (author); Albany, N.Y. **(1836–1902)**

Hartford, Huntington (George Huntington Hartford II) (A.&P. heir); New York City, 4/18/11

Hartford, John (singer, banjoist); New York City, 12/30/37

Hartley, Mariette (actress); New York City, 6/21/40

Hartman, David Downs (TV newscaster); Pawtucket, R.I., 5/19/35

Hartman, Phil (actor, comedian); Brantford, Ont., Canada **(1948–1998)**

Hartman Black, Lisa (actress); Houston, 6/1/56

Harvey, Laurence (Larushka Skikne) (actor); Joniskis, Lithuania **(1928–1973)**

Harvey, Polly Jean (PJ Harvey) (singer, songwriter); Yeovil, England, 10/9/69

Harvey, William (physician); Folkestone, England **(1578–1657)**

Hasselhoff, David (actor, producer); Baltimore, 7/17/52

Hatcher, Teri (actress); Sunnyvale, Calif., 12/8/64

Havel, Vaclav (political leader, dramatist, poet); Prague, 10/5/36

Havens, Richie (musician); Brooklyn, N.Y., 1/21/41

Hawke, Ethan (actor); Austin, Tex., 11/6/70

Hawking, Stephen (physicist, astronomer); Oxford, England, 1/8/42

Hawkins, Coleman (jazz musician); St. Joseph, Mo. **(1904–1969)**

Hawkins, Jack (actor); London **(1910–1973)**

Hawn, Goldie (actress, producer); Washington, D.C., 11/21/45

Haworth, Jill (actress); Sussex, England, 8/15/45

Hawthorne, Nathaniel (novelist); Salem, Mass. **(1804–1864)**

Hay, John Milton (statesman); Salem, Ind. **(1838–1905)**

Hayakawa, Sessue (actor); Honshu, Japan **(1890–1973)**

Hayden, Melissa (ballet dancer); Toronto, 4/25/23

Hayden, Sterling (Sterling Relyea Walter) (actor, writer); Montclair, N.J. **(1916–1986)**

Haydn, Franz Joseph (composer); Rohrau, Austria **(1732–1809)**

Hayek, Salma (actress); Coatzacoalcos, Mexico, 9/2/68

Hayes, Helen (Helen Hayes Brown) (actress); Washington, D.C. **(1900–1993)**

Hayes, Isaac (composer); Covington, Tenn., 8/20/42

Hayes, Peter Lind (comedian, singer); San Francisco **(1915–1998)**

Hayes, Rutherford Birchard (19th U.S. president); Delaware, Ohio **(1822–1893)**

Hayward, Leland (producer); Nebraska City, Neb. **(1902–1971)**

Hayward, Susan (Edythe Marrener) (actress); Brooklyn, N.Y. **(1918–1975)**

Hayworth, Rita (Margarita Cansino) (actress); New York City **(1918–1987)**

Head, Edith (costume designer); Los Angeles **(1907–1981)**

Heaney, Seamus (poet); Londonderry, Northern Ireland, 4/13/39

Hearst, Patricia (Campbell) (heiress); San Francisco, 2/20/54

Hearst, William Randolph (publisher); San Francisco **(1863–1951)**

Hearst, William Randolph, Jr. (publisher); New York City **(1908–1993)**

Heatherton, Joey (actress); Rockville Centre, N.Y., 9/14/44

Heche, Anne (actress); Aurora, Ohio, 5/25/69

Hecht, Ben (author); New York City **(1894–1964)**

Heckart, Eileen (actress); Columbus, Ohio, 3/29/19

Heflin, Van (Emmet Evan Heflin) (actor); Walters, Okla. **(1910–1971)**

Hefner, Hugh (publisher); Chicago, 4/9/26

Hegel, Georg Wilhelm Friedrich (philosopher); Stuttgart, Germany **(1770–1831)**

Heidegger, Martin (existentialist philosopher); Messkirch, Germany **(1889–1976)**

Heifetz, Jascha (concert violinist); Vilna, Russia **(1901–1987)**

Heine, Heinrich (Harry) (poet); Düsseldorf, Germany **(1797–1856)**

Heinemann, Gustav (ex-president of Germany); Schweim, Germany **(1899–1976)**

Heisenberg, Werner Karl (physicist); Würzburg, Germany **(1901–1976)**

Heller, Joseph (novelist); Brooklyn, N.Y. **(1923–1999)**

Hellman, Lillian (playwright); New Orleans **(1905–1984)**

Helmond, Katherine (actress); Galveston, Tex., 7/5/34

Helms, Jesse (politician); Monroe, N.C., 10/18/21

Helmsley, Harry Brakmann (business executive); New York City, 1909–1997

Hemingway, Ernest Miller (novelist); Oak Park, Ill. **(1899–1961)**

Hemingway, Margaux (actress); Portland, Ore. **(1955–1996)**

Hemmings, David (actor); Guilford, England, 11/2/41

Henderson, Florence (actress); Dale, Ind., 2/14/34

Henderson, Skitch (Lyle Russell Cedric) (conductor, pianist); Birmingham, England?, 1/27/18

Hendrix, Jimi (James Marshall Hendrix) (guitarist); Seattle **(1942–1970)**

Henley, Beth (playwright-actress); Jackson, Miss., 5/8/52

Henley, Don (musician); Linden, Tex., 7/22/47

Henner, Marilu (actress); Chicago, 4/6/52

Henning, Doug (magician, actor); Winnipeg, Canada **(1947–2000)**

Henri, Robert (painter); Cincinnati **(1865–1926)**

Henriksen, Lance (actor, screenwriter); New York City, 5/4/40

Henry VIII (king of England); Greenwich, England **(1491–1547)**

Henry, O. (William Sydney Porter) (story writer); Greensboro, N.C. **(1862–1910)**

Henry, Patrick (statesman); Hanover County, Va. **(1736–1799)**

Henson, Jim (puppeteer); Greenville, Miss. **(1936–1990)**

Hepburn, Audrey (actress); Brussels **(1929–1993)**

Hepburn, Katharine (actress); Hartford, Conn., 5/12/07

Hepplewhite, George (furniture designer); England **(?–1786)**

Hepworth, Barbara (sculptor); Wakefield, England **(1903–1975)**

Herbert, George (poet); Montgomery Castle, Wales **(1593–1633)**

Herbert, Victor (composer); Dublin **(1859–1924)**

Herblock (Herbert L. Block) (political cartoonist); Chicago, 10/13/09

Herman, Pee-wee (Paul Rubenfeld) (comedian); Peekskill, N.Y., 8/27/52

Herman, Woody (Woodrow Charles Herman) (band leader); Milwaukee **(1913–1987)**

Herod (called Herod the Great) (king of Judea) **(73–4 b.c.)**

Herodotus (historian); Halicarnassus, Asia Minor (Turkey) **(c. 484–425 b.c.)**

Herrick, Robert (poet); London **(1591–1674)**

Herschbach, Dudley Robert (chemist, Nobel laureate); San Jose, Calif., 6/18/32

Herschel, William (Frederich Wilhelm Herschel) (astronomer); Hannover, Germany **(1738–1822)**

Hershey, Barbara (Barbara Herzstein) (actress); Hollywood, Calif., 2/5/48

Herzog, Chaim (Israeli statesman); Belfast, Northern Ireland **(1918–1997)**

Hesburgh, Theodore M. (educator); Syracuse, N.Y., 5/2/17

Hesseman, Howard (actor); Salem, Ore., 2/27/40

Heston, Charlton (actor); Evanston, Ill., 10/4/24

Heyerdahl, Thor (ethnologist, explorer); Larvik, Norway, 10/6/14

Hill, Anita (lawyer, professor); Lone Tree, Okla., 7/30/56

Hill, Benny (comedian); Southampton, England **(1925–1992)**

Hill, Lauryn (actress, musician); South Orange, N.J., 5/25/75

Hillary, Sir Edmund (mountain climber); New Zealand, 7/20/19

Hillerman, John (actor); Denison, Tex., 12/20/32

Hilton, Conrad (hotelier); San Antonio, N.M. **(1887–1979)**

Hindemith, Paul (composer); Hanau, Germany **(1895–1963)**

Hindenburg, Paul von (Paul Ludwig Hans Anton von Hindenburg und Beneckendorff) (German field marshal, president); Poznan, Poland **(1847– 1934)**

Hines, Earl "Fatha" (jazz pianist); Duquesne, Pa. **(1905–1983)**

Hines, Gregory (dancer, actor); New York City, 2/14/46

Hines, Jerome (Jerome Heinz) (basso); Los Angeles, 11/8/21

Hippocrates (physician); Cos, Greece **(c. 460–c. 377 b.c.)**

Hirohito (Emperor of Japan); Tokyo **(1901–1989)**

Hiroshige, Ando (painter); Edo, Tokyo **(1797–1858)**

Hirsch, Judd (actor); New York City, 3/15/35

Hirschfeld, Al (Albert) (cartoonist); St. Louis, 6/21/03

Hirschhorn, Joseph Herman (financier, speculator, art collector); Mitau, Latvia **(1899–1981)**

Hirt, Al (trumpeter); New Orleans **(1922–1999)**

Hiss, Alger (public official); Baltimore **(1904–1996)**

Hitchcock, Alfred J. (film director); London **(1899–1980)**

Hitler, Adolf (German dictator); Braunau, Austria **(1889–1945)**

Hobbes, Thomas (philosopher); Westport, England **(1588–1679)**

Hobson, Laura Z. (Laura K. Zametkin) (novelist); New York City **(1900–1986)**

Ho Chi Minh (Nguyen That Tranh) (Vietnamese nationalist leader); Kim Lien, Vietnam **(1890–1969)**

Hockney, David (artist); Bradford, England, 7/9/37

Hodgkin, Dorothy Mary Crowfoot (chemist, Nobel laureate); Cairo, Egypt **(1910–1994)**

Hoffa, "Jimmy" James R(iddle) (labor leader); Brazil, Ind. **(1913–1975?; presumed murdered.)**

Hoffman, Dustin (actor, director); Los Angeles, 8/8/37

Hoffman, Phillip Seymour (actor); Fairport, N.Y., 1968

Hofmann, Hans (painter); Germany **(1880–1966)**

Hoffmann, Roald (chemist, Nobel laureate); Zloczow, Poland, 7/18/37

Hofstadter, Richard (historian); Buffalo, N.Y. **(1916–1970)**

Hogan, Paul (actor); Lightning Ridge, N.S.W., Australia, 10/8/39

Hogarth, William (painter, engraver); London **(1697–1764)**

Hokusai, Katsushika (artist); Yedo, Japan **(1760–1849)**

Holbein, Hans (the Elder) (painter); Augsburg, Germany **(c. 1465–1524)**

Holbein, Hans (the Younger) (painter); Augsburg, Germany **(c. 1497–1543)**

Holbrook, Hal (actor); Cleveland, 2/17/25

Holden, William (William Franklin Beedle, Jr.) (actor); O'Fallon, Ill. **(1918–1981)**

Holder, Geoffrey (dancer); Port-of-Spain, Trinidad, 8/1/30

Holiday, Billie (Eleanora Fagan) (jazz-blues singer); Baltimore **(1915–1959)**

Holliman, Earl (Anthony Numkena) (actor); Delhi, La., 9/11/28

Holly, Buddy (singer); Lubbock, Tex. **(1936–1959)**

Holly, Lauren (actress); Geneva, N.Y., 10/28/63

Holm, Celeste (actress); New York City, 4/29/19

Holmes, Katie (actress); Toledo, Ohio, 12/18/78

Holmes, Oliver Wendell (jurist); Boston **(1841–1935)**

Home, Lord (Alexander Frederick Douglas-Home) (diplomat); London, 7/2/03

Homer, Winslow (painter); Boston **(1836–1910)**

Homer (Greek poet) fl. 850 b.c.

Honegger, Arthur (composer); Le Havre, France **(1892–1955)**

Hook, Sidney (philosopher); New York City **(1902–1989)**

Hooker, John Lee (blues guitarist, singer, songwriter); Clarksdale, Miss., 8/22/20

Hoover, Herbert Clark (31st U.S. president); West Branch, Iowa **(1874–1964)**
Hoover, J. Edgar (FBI director); Washington, D.C. **(1895–1972)**
Hope, Bob (Leslie Townes Hope) (comedian); London, 5/29/03
Hopkins, Sir Anthony (actor); Port Talbot, Wales, 12/31/37
Hopkins, Gerald Manley (poet); Stratford, England **(1844–1899)**
Hopkins, Johns (financier); Anne Arundel County, Md. **(1795–1873)**
Hopper, Dennis (actor); Dodge City, Kans., 5/17/36
Hopper, Edward (painter); Nyack, N.Y. **(1882–1967)**
Horace (Quintus Horatius Flaccus) (poet); Venosa, Italy **(65– 8 B.C.)**
Horne, Lena (singer); Brooklyn, N.Y., 6/30/17
Horne, Marilyn (mezzo-soprano); Bradford, Pa., 1/16/34
Horowitz, Vladimir (pianist); Kiev, Ukraine **(1903–1989)**
Horsley, Lee (actor); Muleshoe, Tex., 5/15/55
Horton, Edward Everett (comedian); Brooklyn, N.Y. **(1887–1970)**
Hoskins, Bob (actor); Bury St. Edmunds, England, 10/26/42
Houdini, Harry (Erich Weiss) (magician); Budapest, Hungary **(1874–1926)**
Houseman, John (Jacques Haussmann) (producer, director, actor); Bucharest **(1902–1988)**
Housman, A(lfred) E(dward) (poet); Fockburg, England **(1859– 1936)**
Houston, Charles Hamilton (civil rights lawyer); Washington, D.C. **(1895–1950)**
Houston, Samuel (political leader); Rockbridge County, Va. **(1793– 1863)**
Houston, Whitney (singer); Newark, N.J., 8/9/63
Howard, Ken (actor); El Centro, Calif., 3/28/44
Howard, Leslie (Leslie Stainer) (actor); London **(1893–1943)**
Howard, Ron (actor, producer, director); Duncan, Okla., 3/1/54
Howard, Trevor (actor); Kent, England **(1916–1988)**
Howe, Elias (inventor); Spencer, Mass. **(1819–1867)**
Howe, Irving (literary critic); New York City **(1920–1993)**
Howe, Julia Ward (poet, reformer); New York City **(1819–1910)**
Hudson, Henry (English navigator) **(fl. 1607–1611)**
Hudson, Rock (born Roy Scherer, Jr.; took Roy Fitzgerald as legal name) (actor); Winnetka, Ill. **(1925–1985)**
Huggins, Nathan Irvin (historian); Chicago **(1927–1989)**
Hughes, Charles Evans (jurist); Glens Falls, N.Y. **(1862–1948)**
Hughes, Howard (industrialist, film producer); Houston **(1905–1976)**
Hughes, Langston (poet); Joplin, Mo. **(1902–1967)**
Hughes, Ted (poet); Mytholmroyd, England **(1930–1998)**
Hugo, Victor Marie (author); Besançon, France **(1802–1885)**
Hulce, Tom (actor); Detroit, 12/6/53
Hume, David (philosopher); Edinburgh, Scotland **(1711–1776)**
Hume, Kirsty (model); Glasgow, Scotland, 9/4/76
Humperdinck, Engelbert (composer); Siegburg, Germany **(1854– 1921)**
Humperdinck, Engelbert (Arnold Dorsey) (singer); Madras, India, 5/2/36
Hunt, Helen (actress); Los Angeles, 6/15/63
Hunt, Linda (actress); Morristown, N.J., 4/2/45
Hunter, Holly (actress); Atlanta, 3/20/58
Hunter, Kim (Janet Cole) (actress); Detroit, 11/12/22
Hunter, Tab (Arthur Andrew Gelien) (actor); New York City, 7/11/31
Hunter-Gault, Charlayne (activist, broadcast journalist); Due West, S.C., 2/27/42
Huntley, Chet (TV newscaster); Cardwell, Mont. **(1911–1974)**
Hurley, Elizabeth (actress, model); Backingstoke, England, 6/10/65
Hurok, Sol (Solomon Hurok) (impresario); Pogar, Russia **(1884– 1974)**
Hurst, Fannie (novelist); Hamilton, Ohio **(1889–1968)**
Hurston, Zora Neale (author); Eatonville, Fla. **(1901–1960)**
Hurt, John (actor); Shirebrook, England, 1/22/40
Hurt, William (actor); Washington, D.C., 3/20/50
Hus, Jan (Bohemian religious reformer); Husinetz, nr. Budweis, Czech Republic **(c. 1369–1415)**
Husing, Ted (sportscaster); New York City **(1901–1962)**
Hussein I (king); Jordan **(1935–1999)**
Hussein, Saddam (al-Tikriti) (Iraqi president); Tikrit, Iraq, 4/28/37
Huston, Anjelica (actress); Los Angeles, 7/8/51
Huston, John (actor, director, writer); Nevada, Mo. **(1906–1987)**
Huston, Walter (Walter Houghston) (actor); Toronto **(1884–1950)**
Hutchins, Robert M. (educator); Brooklyn, N.Y. **(1899–1977)**
Hutton, Betty (Betty Thornburg) (actress); Battle Creek, Mich., 2/26/21
Hutton, Lauren (actress, model); Charleston, S.C., 11/17/43
Hutton, Timothy (actor); Los Angeles, 8/16/60
Huxley, Aldous (author); Godalming, England **(1894–1963)**
Huxley, Sir Julian S. (biologist, author); London **(1887–1975)**
Huxley, Thomas Henry (biologist); Ealing, England **(1825–1895)**
Hynde, Chrissie (singer); Akron, Ohio, 9/7/51

I

Iacocca, Lee (Lido Anthony) (business executive); Allentown, Pa., 10/15/24
Ian, Janis (singer); New York City, 5/7/51
Ibsen, Henrik (dramatist); Skien, Norway **(1828–1906)**
Ice Cube (O'Shea Jackson) (musician, actor); Los Angeles, 6/15/69
Ice-T (Tracy Morrow) (rap musician, actor); Newark, N.J., 2/16/68
Inge, William (playwright); Independence, Kans. **(1913–1973)**
Ingres, Jean Auguste Dominique (painter); Montauban, France **(1780–1867)**
Inness, George (painter); nr. Newburgh, N.Y. **(1825–1894)**
Ionesco, Eugene (playwright); Slatina, Romania **(1912–1994)**
Ireland, Jill (actress); London **(1936–1990)**
Ireland, Kathy (model, actress); Glendale, Calif., 3/8/63
Ireland, Patricia (feminist, social activist); Oak Park, Ill., 10/19/45
Irons, Jeremy (actor); Cowes, Isle of Wight, England, 9/19/48
Irving, Amy (actress); Palo Alto, Calif., 9/10/53
Irving, John (Winslow) (writer); Exeter, N.H., 3/2/42
Irving, Washington (author); New York City **(1783–1859)**
Isaak, Chris (musician, actor); Stockton, Calif., 6/26/56
Isherwood, Christopher (novelist, playwright); nr. Dilsey and High Lane, England **(1904–1986)**
Iturbi, José (concert pianist); Valencia, Spain **(1895–1980)**
Ives, Burl (Icle Ivanhoe) (singer); Hunt, Ill. **(1909–1995)**
Ives, Charles E(dward) (composer); Danbury, Conn. **(1874–1954)**
Ivins, Molly (journalist); Monterey, Calif., 8/30/44
Ivory, James (director, producer); Berkeley, Calif., 6/7/28

J

Jackson, Andrew (7th U.S. president); Waxhaw, S.C. **(1767–1845)**
Jackson, Anne (actress); Millvale, Pa., 9/3/26
Jackson, Glenda (actress); Cheshire, England, 5/9/36
Jackson, Janet (singer); Gary, Ind., 5/16/66
Jackson, Rev. Jesse (civil rights leader); Greenville, S.C., 10/8/41
Jackson, Kate (actress); Birmingham, Ala., 10/29/49
Jackson, Mahalia (gospel singer); New Orleans **(1911–1972)**
Jackson, Maynard (mayor of Atlanta); Dallas, 3/23/38
Jackson, Michael (singer); Gary, Ind., 8/29/58
Jackson, Samuel L. (actor); Washington, D.C., 12/21/48
Jackson, Thomas Jonathan ("Stonewall") (general); Clarksburg, Va. (now W. Va.) **(1824–1863)**
Jacobi, Derek (actor); Leytonstone, England, 10/22/38
Jacobs, Jane (urbanologist); Scranton, Pa., 5/1/16
Jagger, Mick (Michael Phillip Jagger) (singer); Dartford, England, 7/26/43
James, Harry (trumpeter); Albany, Ga. **(1916–1983)**
James, Henry (novelist); New York City **(1843–1916)**
James, Jesse Woodson (outlaw); Clay County, Mo. **(1847–1882)**
James, William (psychologist); New York City **(1842–1910)**
Jameson, (Margaret) Storm (novelist); Whitby, England **(1897– 1986)**
Janis, Byron (pianist); McKeesport, Pa., 3/24/28
Janis, Conrad (actor, musician); New York City, 2/11/28
Janssen, David (David Meyer) (actor); Naponee, Neb. **(1930–1980)**
Jaworksi, Leon (Watergate special prosecutor); Waco, Tex. **(1905–1982)**
Jay, John (statesman, jurist); New York City **(1745–1829)**
Jeanmaire, Renée (dancer); Paris, 4/29/24
Jefferson, Thomas (3rd U.S. president); Shadwell, Va. **(1743– 1826)**
Jemison, Mae C. (astronaut, physician); Decatur, Ala., 10/17/56
Jenner, Edward (physician); Berkeley, England **(1749–1823)**
Jennings, Peter (news anchor); Toronto, 7/29/38
Jennings, Waylon (singer); Littlefield, Tex., 6/15/37
Jessel, George (entertainer); New York City **(1898–1981)**
Jessup, Philip C. (diplomat); New York City **(1897–1986)**
Jillian, Ann (Ann Jura Nauseda) (actress); Cambridge, Mass., 1/29/51
Joan of Arc (Jeanne d'Arc) (saint, patriot); Domremy-la-Pucelle, France **(1412–1431)**
Jobs, Steven Paul (computer industry pioneer); San Francisco, 1955
Joel, Billy (singer); New York City, 5/9/49
Joffrey, Robert (Abdullah Jaffa Bey Khan) (choreographer); Seattle **(1930–1988)**
John, Elton (Reginald Kenneth Dwight) (singer, pianist); Pinner, England, 3/25/47
Johns, Jasper (painter, sculptor); Augusta, Ga., 5/15/30
Johnson, Andrew (17th U.S. president); Raleigh, N.C. **(1808–1875)**
Johnson, Don (actor); Flatt Creek, Mo., 12/15/49

Johnson, James Weldon (author, educator); Jacksonville, Fla. **(1871–1938)**
Johnson, Lyndon Baines (36th U.S. president); Stonewall, Tex. **(1908–1973)**
Johnson, Philip Cortelyou (architect); Cleveland, 7/8/06
Johnson, Samuel (lexicographer, author); Lichfield, England **(1709–1784)**
Johnson, Van (actor); Newport, R.I., 8/20/16
Johnson, Virginia (human sexuality expert); Springfield, Mo., 2/11/25
Joliot-Curie, Frédéric (chemist, Nobel laureate); Paris **(1900–1958)**
Joliot-Curie, Irène (Irène Curie) (chemist, Nobel laureate); France **(1897–1956)**
Jolliet, Louis (Louis Joliet) (explorer); Beaupré, Canada **(1645–1700)**
Jolson, Al (Asa Yoelson) (actor, singer); St. Petersburg, Russia **(1886–1950)**
Jones, Dean (actor); Morgan County, Ala., 1/25/35
Jones, George (singer); Saratoga, Tex., 9/12/31
Jones, Inigo (architect); London **(1573–1652)**
Jones, James (novelist); Robinson, Ill. **(1921–1977)**
Jones, James Earl (actor); Arkabutla, Miss., 1/17/31
Jones, Jennifer (Phylis Isley) (actress); Tulsa, Okla., 3/2/19
Jones, John Paul (John Paul) (naval officer); Scotland **(1747–1792)**
Jones, Quincy (composer); Chicago, 3/14/33
Jones, Shirley (singer, actress); Smithtown, Pa., 3/31/34
Jones, Spike (host, orchestra leader); Long Beach, Calif. **(1911–1965)**
Jones, Tom (Thomas Jones Woodward) (singer); Pontypridd, Wales, 6/7/40
Jones, Tommy Lee (actor); San Saba, Tex., 9/15/46
Jong, Erica (writer); New York City, 3/26/42
Jonson, Ben (Benjamin Jonson) (poet, dramatist); Westminster, England **(1572–1637)**
Joplin, Janis (singer); Port Arthur, Tex. **(1943–1970)**
Joplin, Scott (ragtime pianist, composer); Texarkansas, Tex. **(1868–1917)**
Jordan, Barbara (U.S. representative); Houston **(1936–1996)**
Jordan, Neil (film director, screenwriter); Sligo, Ireland, 2/25/50
Joseph (Chief Joseph) (Nez Perce Indian leader); eastern Ore. **(1841–1904)**
Josquin des Prés (usually known as Josquin) (composer); Conde-sur-L'Escaut?, Hainaut, Belgium **(c. 1445–1521)**
Jourdan, Louis (Louis Gendre) (actor); Marseilles, France, 6/19/19
Jovovich, Milla (actress, model, singer); Kiev, Ukraine, 12/19/75
Joyce, James (novelist); Dublin **(1882–1941)**
Juárez, Benito Pablo (statesman); Guelatao, Mexico **(1806–1872)**
Judd, Ashley (actress); Los Angeles, 4/19/68
Julia, Raul (Raúl Rafael Carlos Julia y Arcelay) (actor); San Juan, P.R. **(1940–1994)**
Jung, Carl Gustav (psychoanalyst); Basel, Switzerland **(1875–1961)**

K

Kabalevsky, Dmitri (composer); St. Petersburg, Russia **(1904–1987)**
Kafka, Franz (author); Prague **(1883–1924)**
Kádár, János (Communist Party leader); Hungary **(1912–1989)**
Kahn, Gus (songwriter); Coblenz, Germany **(1886–1941)**
Kahn, Louis I. (architect); Oesel Island, Estonia **(1901–1974)**
Kahn, Madeline (actress); Boston **(1942–1999)**
Kandinsky, Wassily (painter); Moscow **(1866–1944)**
Kanin, Garson (playwright); Rochester, N.Y. **(1912–1999)**
Kant, Immanuel (philosopher); Königsberg (Kaliningrad), Russia **(1724–1804)**
Kantor, MacKinlay (novelist); Webster City, Iowa **(1904–1977)**
Kaplan, Justin (writer, editor); New York City, 9/5/25
Karan, Donna (fashion designer); Forest Hills, N.Y., 10/2/48
Karloff, Boris (William Henry Pratt) (actor); London **(1887–1969)**
Kasdan, Lawrence (film director, writer, actor, producer); Miami, 1/14/49
Kasem, Casey (disc jockey); Detroit, 4/27/32
Kaufman, Andy (actor, comedian); New York City **(1949–1984)**
Kaufman, George S. (playwright); Pittsburgh **(1889–1961)**
Kavner, Julie (actress); Los Angeles, 9/7/51
Kaye, Danny (David Daniel Kominski) (comedian); Brooklyn, N.Y. **(1913–1987)**
Kaye, Sammy (band leader); Cleveland **(1910–1987)**
Kazan, Elia (director); Constantinople, Turkey, 9/7/09
Kazan, Lainie (Levine) (singer); New York City, 5/15/40
Kazantzakis, Nikos (writer); Herakleion, Crete **(1883–1957)**
Keach, Stacy (actor); Savannah, Ga., 6/2/41

Keaton, Buster (Joseph Frank Keaton) (comedian); Piqua, Kans. **(1896–1966)**
Keaton, Diane (actress); Los Angeles, 1/5/46
Keaton, Michael (Michael Douglas) (actor); Robinson Township, Pa., 9/9/51
Keats, John (poet); London **(1795–1821)**
Keel, Howard (Harold Clifford Leek) (singer, actor); Gillespie, Ill., 4/13/19
Keeler, Ruby (Ethel Hilde Keeler) (actress, dancer); Halifax, N.S., Canada **(1910–1993)**
Keener, Catherine (actress); Miami, Fla., 1959(?)
Kefauver, Estes (legislator); Madisonville, Tenn **(1903–1963)**
Keitel, Harvey (actor); Brooklyn, N.Y., 5/13/39
Keith, Brian (Robert Brian Keith, Jr.) (actor); Bayonne, N.J. **(1921–1997)**
Keller, Helen Adams (author, educator); Tuscumbia, Ala. **(1880–1968)**
Kelley, DeForest (actor); Atlanta **(1920–1999)**
Kelly, Emmett (clown); Sedan, Kans. **(1898–1979)**
Kelly, Gene (dancer, actor); Pittsburgh **(1912–1996)**
Kelly, R. (Robert Kelly) (singer, record producer, actor); Chicago, 1969
Kempis, Thomas à (mystic); Kempis, Prussia (Germany) **(1380–1471)**
Kendall, Henry W. (physicist, Nobel laureate); Boston **(1926–1999)**
Kennan, George F. (diplomat); Milwaukee, 2/16/04
Kennedy, Arthur (actor); Worcester, Mass. **(1914–1990)**
Kennedy, Caroline Bessette (socialite); White Plains, N.Y. **(1966–1999)**
Kennedy, George (actor); New York City, 2/18/25
Kennedy, John Fitzgerald (35th U.S. president); Brookline, Mass. **(1917–1963)**
Kennedy, John F., Jr. (publisher); Washington, D.C. **(1960–1999)**
Kennedy, Joseph P. (financier); Boston **(1888–1969)**
Kennedy, Robert Francis (legislator); Brookline, Mass. **(1925–1968)**
Kennedy, Rose Fitzgerald (president's mother); Boston **(1890–1995)**
Kent, Allegra (ballet dancer); Santa Monica, Calif., 8/11/38
Kent, Rockwell (painter); Tarrytown Heights, N.Y. **(1882–1971)**
Kenton, Stan (Stanley Newcomb) (jazz musician); Wichita, Kans. **(1912–1979)**
Kepler, Johannes (astronomer); Weil, Germany **(1571–1630)**
Kercheval, Ken (actor); Wolcottville, Ind., 7/15/35
Kerensky, Alexander Fedorovich (statesman); Simbirsk, Russia **(1881–1970)**
Kern, Jerome David (composer); New York City **(1885–1945)**
Kerns, Joanna (actress); San Francisco, 2/12/53
Kerouac, Jack (Jean-Louis Kerouac) (writer); Lowell, Mass. **(1922–1969)**
Kerr, Deborah (actress); Helensburgh, Scotland, 9/30/21
Kettering, Charles F. (engineer, inventor); nr. Loudonville, Ohio **(1876–1958)**
Kevorkian, Jack (medical pathologist); Pontiac, Mich., 3/26/28
Key, Francis Scott (lawyer, author of national anthem); Frederick (Carroll) County, Md. **(1779–1843)**
Keyes, Frances Parkinson (novelist); Charlottesville, Va. **(1885–1970)**
Keynes, John Maynard (1st Baron of Tilton) (economist); Cambridge, England **(1883–1946)**
Khachaturian, Aram (composer); Tiflis, Russia **(1903–1978)**
Khomeini, Ayatollah Ruhollah (Islamic religious leader); Iran **(1900–1989)**
Khrushchev, Nikita S. (Soviet leader); Kalinovka, nr. Kursk, Ukraine **(1894–1971)**
Kidd, Michael (Milton Greenwald) (choreographer); Brooklyn, N.Y., 8/12/19
Kidd, William (called Captain Kidd) (pirate); Greenock, Scotland **(c. 1645–1701)**
Kidder, Margot (actress); Yellowknife, N.W.T., Canada, 10/17/48
Kidman, Nicole (actress); Honolulu, 6/20/67
Kiepura, Jan (tenor); Sosnowiec, Poland **(1902–1966)**
Kieran, John (writer); New York City **(1892–1981)**
Kierkegaard, Sören Aalys (philosopher); Copenhagen **(1813–1855)**
Kiesinger, Kurt Georg (diplomat); Ebingen, Germany **(1904–1988)**
Kiley, Richard (actor, singer); Chicago **(1922–1999)**
Kilmer, Alfred Joyce (poet); New Brunswick, N.J. **(1886–1918)**
Kilmer, Val (actor); Los Angeles,, 12/31/59
King, Alan (Irwin Alan Kniberg) (entertainer); Brooklyn, N.Y., 12/26/27
King, B.B. (Riley King) (guitarist); Itta Bena, Miss., 9/16/25
King, Carole (singer, songwriter); Brooklyn, N.Y., 2/9/42
King, Coretta Scott (civil rights leader); Marion, Ala., 4/27/27
King, Larry (Lawrence Harvey Zeigler) (TV host); New York City, 11/19/33

King, Martin Luther, Jr. (civil rights leader); Atlanta **(1929–1968)**

King, Stephen (writer); Portland, Maine, 9/21/47

Kingsley, Ben (Krishna Bhanji) (actor); Snainton, England, 12/31/43

Kingsley, Sidney (Sidney Kirschner) (playwright); New York City **(1906–1995)**

Kingsolver, Barbara (writer); Annapolis, Md., 4/8/55

Kingston, Maxine Hong (novelist); Stockton, Calif., 10/27/40

Kinsey, Alfred Charles (human sexuality expert); Hoboken, N.J. **(1894–1956)**

Kinski, Nastassja (Nastassja Nakszynski) (actress); West Berlin, 1/24/61

Kipling, Rudyard (author); Bombay (Mumbai) **(1865–1936)**

Kipnis, Alexander (basso); Ukraine **(1891–1978)**

Kirby, George (comedian); Chicago **(1923–1995)**

Kirchner, Ernst Ludwig (painter); Aschaffenburg, Germany **(1880–1938)**

Kirk, Grayson (educator); Jeffersonville, Ohio **(1903–1997)**

Kirkland, Gelsey (ballet dancer); Bethlehem, Pa., 12/29/52

Kirkpatrick, Jeane Jordan (educator-public affairs); Duncan, Okla., 11/19/26

Kirkpatrick, Ralph (harpsichordist); Leominster, Mass. **(1911–1984)**

Kirstein, Lincoln (dance, theater executive); Rochester, N.Y. **(1907–1996)**

Kirsten, Dorothy (soprano); Montclair, N.J. **(1910–1992)**

Kissinger, Henry (Heinz Alfred Kissinger) (ex-U.S. secretary of state); Furth, Germany, 5/27/23

Kitt, Eartha (singer); North, S.C., 1/26/28

Klee, Paul (painter); Münchenbuchsee, nr. Bern, Switzerland **(1879–1940)**

Klein, Calvin (fashion designer); Bronx, N.Y., 11/19/42

Klein, Robert (comedian); New York City, 2/8/42

Kleist, Henrich von (poet); Frankfurt an der Oder, Germany **(1777–1811)**

Klemperer, Otto (conductor); Breslau, Poland **(1885–1973)**

Klemperer, Werner (actor); Cologne, Germany, 3/22/20

Klimt, Gustav (painter); Vienna **(1862–1918)**

Kline, Kevin (actor); St. Louis, 10/24/47

Klugman, Jack (actor); Philadelphia, 4/27/22

Knight, Gladys (singer); Atlanta, 5/28/44

Knight, John S. (publisher); Bluefield, W. Va. **(1894–1981)**

Knight, Ted (Tadeus Wladyslaw Konopka) (actor); Terryville, Conn. **(1923–1986)**

Knight, Wayne (actor); Cartersville, Ga., 8/7/55

Knopf, Alfred A. (publisher); New York City **(1892–1984)**

Knopfler, Mark (musician); Glasgow, Scotland, 8/12/49

Knotts, Don (actor); Morgantown, W. Va., 7/21/24

Knox, John (religious reformer); Haddington, East Lothian, Scotland **(1505–1572)**

Koch, Robert (physician); Klausthal, Germany **(1843–1910)**

Koenig, Walter (actor); Chicago, 9/14/36

Koestler, Arthur (novelist); Budapest **(1905–1983)**

Kokoschka, Oskar (painter); Póchlarn, Austria **(1886–1980)**

Kollwitz, Käthe (graphic artist, sculptor); Königsberg, Russia **(1867–1945)**

Koop, C. Everett (ex-surgeon general); Brooklyn, N.Y., 10/14/16

Kooper, Al (singer, pianist); Brooklyn, N.Y., 2/5/44

Kopell, Bernie (actor); New York City, 6/21/33

Koppel, Ted (broadcast journalist); Lancashire, England, 2/8/40

Korman, Harvey (actor); Chicago, 2/15/27

Kosciusko, Thaddeus (Tadeusz Andrzej Bonawentura Kosciuszko) (military officer and statesman) **(1746–1817)**

Kossuth, Lajos (patriot); Monok, Hungary **(1802–1894)**

Kostelanetz, André (orchestra conductor); St. Petersburg, Russia **(1901–1980)**

Kosygin, Aleksei N. (premier); St. Petersburg, Russia **(1904–1980)**

Kotto, Yaphet (actor); New York City, 11/15/37

Koussevitzky, Serge (Sergei) Alexandrovitch (orchestra conductor); Vishni Volochek, Tver, Russia **(1874–1951)**

Kramer, Stanley E. (film producer, director); New York City, 9/29/13

Kràus, Lili (pianist); Budapest **(1905–1986)**

Kravitz, Lenny (musician); New York City, 5/26/64

Kreisler, Fritz (violinist, composer); Vienna **(1875–1962)**

Kresge, S. S. (merchant); Bald Mount, Pa. **(1867–1966)**

Krips, Josef (orchestra conductor); Vienna **(1902–1974)**

Kristofferson, Kris (singer); Brownsville, Tex., 6/22/36

Krupa, Gene (drummer); Chicago **(1909–1973)**

Krupp, Alfred (munitions magnate); Essen, Germany **(1812–1887)**

Kubelik, Rafael (conductor); Bychory, former Czechoslovakia **(1914–1996)**

Kublai Khan (Mongol conqueror) **(1216–1294)**

Kubrick, Stanley (film director, producer); New York City **(1928–1999)**

Kudrow, Lisa (actress); Encino, Calif., 7/30/63

Kuralt, Charles (TV journalist); Wilmington, N.C. **(1934–1997)**

Kurosawa, Akira (film director); Tokyo **(1910–1998)**

Kurtz, Efrem (conductor); St. Petersburg, Russia **(1900–1995)**

Kurtz, Swoosie (actress); Omaha, Neb., 9/6/44

L

LaBelle, Patti (singer, actress); Philadelphia, 5/24/44

Ladd, Cheryl (Cheryl Stoppelmoor) (actress); Huron, S.D., 7/12/51

Ladd, Diane (actress); Meridian, Miss., 11/29/32

Lafayette, Marquis de (Marie Joseph Paul Yves Roch Gilbert du Motier) (military officer); Auvergne, France **(1757–1834)**

Lafitte, Jean (pirate); Bayonne?, France **(1780–1826)**

La Follette, Robert Marin (politician); Primrose, Wis. **(1855–1925)**

La Fontaine, Jean de (poet); Château-Thierry, France **(1621–1695)**

La Guardia, Fiorello Henry (mayor of New York); New York City **(1882–1947)**

Lahti, Christine (actress, director); Birmingham, Mich., 4/4/50

Laine, Frankie (Frank Paul LoVecchio) (singer); Chicago, 3/30/13

Laird, Melvin (ex-secretary of defense); Omaha, Neb., 9/1/22

Lamarck, Chevalier de (Jean Baptiste Pierre Antoine de Monet) (naturalist); Bazantin, France **(1744–1829)**

Lamas, Lorenzo (actor); Los Angeles, 1/20/58

Lamb, Charles (Elia) (essayist); London **(1775–1834)**

L'Amour, Louis (author); Jamestown, N.D. **(1908–1988)**

Lancaster, Burt (actor); New York City **(1913–1994)**

Landau, Martin (actor); Brooklyn, N.Y., 6/20/31

Landers, Ann (Esther Pauline Friedman) (columnist); Sioux City, Iowa, 7/4/18

Landon, Michael (Eugene Maurice Orowitz) (actor, director, producer); Forest Hills, Queens, N.Y. **(1936–1991)**

Lane, Abbe (Abigail Francine Lassman) (singer); New York City, 1933

Lane, Burton (songwriter); New York City **(1912–1997)**

Lane, Nathan (Joseph Lane) (actor, singer); Jersey City, N.J., 2/3/56

Lang, Fritz (film director); Vienna **(1890–1976)**

Lange, Hope (actress); Redding Ridge, Conn., 11/28/33

Lange, Jessica (actress); Cloquet, Minn., 4/20/49

Langella, Frank (actor); Bayonne, N.J., 1/1/40

Langmuir, Irving (chemist); Brooklyn, N.Y. **(1881–1957)**

Langtry, Lillie (Emily Le Breton) (actress); Island of Jersey **(1852–1929)**

Lansbury, Angela (actress, producer); London, 10/16/25

Lansing, Robert (Robert Howell Brown) (actor); San Diego, Calif. **(1928–1994)**

Lanza, Mario (Alfred Arnold Cocozza) (singer, actor); Philadelphia **(1921–1959)**

Lao-tse (Li Erh) (philosopher); Honan Province, China **(c. 604–531 B.C.)**

Lardner, Ring (Ringgold Wilmar Lardner) (story writer); Niles, Mich. **(1885–1933)**

La Rouchefoucauld, Francois duc de (author); Paris **(1613–1680)**

Larroquette, John (actor); New Orleans, 11/25/47

Larson, Gary (cartoonist); Tacoma, Wash., 8/14/50

La Salle, Eriq (actor); Hartford, Conn., 7/23/62

La Salle, Sieur de (Robert Cavelier) (explorer); Rouen, France **(1643–1687)**

Lasch, Christopher (historian, social critic); Omaha, Neb. **(1932–1994)**

La Tour, Georges de (painter); Vic-sur-Seille, France **(1593–1652)**

Lauer, Matt (TV host); New York City, 12/20/57

Laughton, Charles (actor); Scarborough, England **(1899–1962)**

Lauper, Cyndi (singer); New York City, 6/20/53

Laurel, Stan (Arthur Jefferson) (comedian); Ulverston, England **(1890–1965)**

Laurents, Arthur (playwright); New York City, 7/14/18

Laurie, Piper (Rosetta Jacobs) (actress); Detroit, 1/22/32

Lavin, Linda (actress); Portland, Maine, 10/15/37

Lavoisier, Antoine-Laurent (chemist); Paris **(1743–1794)**

Lawford, Peter (actor); London **(1923–1984)**

Lawless, Lucy (Lucy Ryan) (actress); Auckland, New Zealand, 3/29/68

Lawrence, David Herbert (novelist); Nottingham, England **(1885–1930)**

Lawrence, Jacob (painter); Atantic City, N.J. **(1917–2000)**

Lawrence, Martin (actor); Frankfurt, Germany, 4/16/65

Lawrence, Sharon (actress); Charlotte, N.C., 6/29/62

Lawrence, Steve (Sidney Leibowitz) (singer); Brooklyn, N.Y., 7/8/35

Lawrence of Arabia (Thomas Edward Lawrence, later changed to Shaw) (author, soldier); Tremadoc, Wales **(1888–1935)**

Lawrence, Vicki (actress); Inglewood, Calif., 3/26/49

Leach, Penelope (Balchin) (child psychologist, writer); London, 11/19/37

Leach, Robin (host, producer); London, 8/29/41

Leachman, Cloris (actress); Des Moines, Iowa, 4/30/26

Leadbelly, (Huddie Ledbetter) (blues singer, guitarist); Mooringsport, La. **(1885–1949)**

Leakey, Louis Seymour Bazett (anthropologist); Kabete, Kenya **(1903–1972)**

Leakey, Mary (anthropologist); London **(1913–1996)**

Leakey, Richard (paleoanthropologist, wildlife conservationist); Kenya, 12/19/44

Lean, David (film director); Croydon, England **(1908–1991)**

Lear, Edward (nonsense poet); London **(1812–1888)**

Lear, Evelyn (Shulman) (soprano); Brooklyn, N.Y., 1/8/26

Lear, Norman (TV producer); New Haven, Conn., 7/27/22

Learned, Michael (actress); Washington, D.C., 4/9/39

Leary, Denis (actor, screenwriter, film director); Worcester, Mass., 8/18/57

Leary, Timothy (psychologist, LSD advocate); Springfield, Mass. **(1920–1996)**

Le Blanc, Matt (actor); Newton, Mass., 7/25/67

le Carré, John (David John Moore Cornwell) (novelist); Poole, England, 10/19/31

Le Corbusier (Charles Edouard Jeanneret) (architect); La Chaux-de-Fonds, Switzerland **(1887–1965)**

Lee, Ang (film director); Pingtung, Taiwan, 10/23/54

Lee, Christopher (actor); London, 5/27/22

Lee, Manfred B. (pseudonym Ellery Queen) (novelist); Brooklyn, N.Y. **(1905–1971)**

Lee, Peggy (Norma Engstrom) (singer); Jamestown, N.D., 5/26/20

Lee, Robert E(dward) (Confederate general); Stratford Estate, Va. **(1807–1870)**

Lee, Spike (Shelton Jackson Lee) (actor, director, writer, producer); Atlanta, 3/20/57

Leeuwenhoek, Anton van (zoologist); Delft, Netherlands **(1632–1723)**

Lehár, Franz (composer); Komárom, Hungary **(1870–1948)**

Lehman, Herbert H. (governor, senator); New York City **(1878–1963)**

Lehmann, Lotte (soprano); Perleberg, Germany **(1888–1976)**

Lehrer, Jim (TV newscaster); Wichita, Kans., 5/19/34

Leibniz, Gottfried W. von (scientist); Leipzig, Germany **(1646–1716)**

Leibovitz, Annie (photographer); Westbury, Conn., 10/2/49

Leigh, Janet (Jeanette Helen Morrison) (actress); Merced, Calif., 7/6/27

Leigh, Jennifer Jason (Jennifer Morrow) (actress); Los Angeles, 2/5/62

Leigh, Mike (film director, screenwriter); Manchester, England, 2/20/43

Leigh, Vivien (Vivian Mary Hartley) (actress); Darjeeling, India **(1913–1967)**

Leinsdorf, Erich (conductor); Vienna **(1912–1993)**

Lemmon, Jack (actor); Boston, 2/8/25

Lenin, Vladimir (Vladimir Ilich Ulyanov) (Soviet leader); Simbirsk, Russia **(1870–1924)**

Lennon, John (singer, songwriter); Liverpool, England **(1940–1980)**

Leno, Jay (comedian, TV host); New Rochelle, N.Y., 4/28/50

Leonard, Sheldon (Sheldon Leonard Bershad) (actor, producer); New York City **(1907–1997)**

Leonardo da Vinci, (painter, scientist); Vinci, Tuscany, Italy **(1452–1519)**

Leoni, Téa (actress); New York City, 2/25/66

Lerner, Alan Jay (lyricist); New York City **(1918–1986)**

Lerner, Max (columnist); Minsk, Russia **(1902–1992)**

Lessing, Doris (novelist); Kermanshah, Iran, 10/22/19

Leto, Jared (actor); Bossier City, La., 12/26/71

Letterman, David (TV host, producer); Indianapolis, 4/12/47

Levant, Oscar (pianist); Pittsburgh **(1906–1972)**

Levenson, Sam (humorist); New York City **(1911–1980)**

Levi, Carlo (novelist); Turin, Italy **(1902–1975)**

Levine, James (artistic director, Metropolitan Opera); Cincinnati, 6/23/43

Levine, Joseph E. (film producer); Boston **(1905–1987)**

Levinson, Barry (screenwriter, director, producer, actor); Baltimore, 4/6/42

Lewis, C(live) S(taples) (author); Belfast, Northern Ireland **(1898–1963)**

Lewis, Gilbert Newton (chemist, Nobel laureate); Weymouth, Mass. **(1875–1946)**

Lewis, Jerry (Joseph Levitch) (comedian, film director); Newark, N.J., 3/16/26

Lewis, Jerry Lee (singer); Ferriday, La., 9/29/35

Lewis, John Llewellyn (labor leader); Lucas, Iowa **(1880–1969)**

Lewis, Juliette (actress); Los Angeles, 12/21/73

Lewis, Meriwether (explorer); Albemarle Co., Va. **(1774–1809)**

Lewis, (Percy) Wyndham (artist, writer); Bay of Fundy, Maine (at sea) **(1884–1957)**

Lewis, Shari (Shari Hurwitz) (puppeteer); New York City **(1934–1998)**

Lewis, Sinclair (novelist); Sauk Centre, Minn. **(1885–1951)**

Ley, Willy (science writer); Berlin **(1906–1969)**

Liberace (Wladziu Liberace) (pianist); West Allis, Wis. **(1919–1987)**

Lichtenstein, Roy (painter); New York City **(1923–1997)**

Lie, Trygve Halvdan (first U.N. secretary-general); Oslo **(1896–1968)**

Light, Judith (actress); Trenton, N.J., 2/9/49

Lightfoot, Gordon (singer, songwriter); Orillia, Ont., Canada, 11/17/38

Limbaugh, Rush (political commentator); Cape Girardeau, Mo., 1/12/51

Lin, Maya (architect, sculptor); Athens, Ohio, 10/5/59

Lin Yutang (author); Changchow, China **(1895–1976)**

Lincoln, Abraham (16th U.S. president); Hardin (Larue) County, Ky. **(1809–1865)**

Lind, Jenny (Johanna Maria Lind) (soprano); Stockholm **(1820–1887)**

Lindbergh, Anne Morrow (author); Englewood, N.J., 6/22/06

Lindbergh, Charles A. (aviator); Detroit **(1902–1974)**

Linden, Hal (Harold Lipshitz) (actor); New York City, 3/20/31

Lindsay, Howard (playwright); Waterford, N.Y. **(1889–1968)**

Linkletter, Art (radio-TV personality); Moose Jaw, Sask., Canada, 7/17/12

Linnaeus, Carolus (Carl von Linné) (botanist); Råshult, Sweden **(1707–1778)**

Liotta, Ray (actor); Union, N.J., 12/18/55

Lipchitz, Jacques (sculptor); Druskieniki, Latvia **(1891–1973)**

Lippi, Fra Filippo (painter); Florence **(1406–1469)**

Lippmann, Walter (columnist, author, political analyst); New York City **(1889–1974)**

Lister, Joseph (1st Baron of Lyme Regis) (surgeon); Upton, England **(1827–1912)**

Liszt, Franz (composer, pianist); Raiding, Hungary **(1811–1886)**

Lithgow, John (actor); Rochester, N.Y., 6/6/45

Little, Rich (impressionist); Ottawa, Ont., Canada, 11/26/38

Livingstone, David (missionary, explorer); Lanarkshire, Scotland **(1813–1873)**

L. L. Cool J (James Todd Smith) (rap artist); New York City, 1/14/68

Llewellyn, Richard (novelist); St. David's, Wales **(1906–1983)**

Lloyd Webber, Andrew (composer); London, 3/22/48

Lloyd George, David (Earl of Dwyfor) (statesman); Manchester, England **(1863–1945)**

Lloyd, Jake (actor); Fort Collins, Colo., 3/5/89

Locke, Alain L. (philosopher); Philadelphia **(1886–1954)**

Locke, John (philosopher); Somersetshire, England **(1632–1704)**

Lockhart, June (actress); New York City, 6/25/25

Locklear, Heather (actress); Los Angeles, 9/25/61

Lodge, Henry Cabot (legislator); Boston **(1850–1924)**

Lodge, Henry Cabot, Jr. (diplomat); Nahant, Mass. **(1902–1985)**

Loesser, Frank (composer); New York City **(1910–1969)**

Loewe, Frederick (composer); Vienna **(1901–1988)**

Logan, Joshua (director, producer); Texarkana, Tex. **(1908–1988)**

Lollobrigida, Gina (Luigina Lollobrigida) (actress); Subiaco, Italy, 7/4/27

Lombard, Carole (Jane Alice Peters) (actress); Ft. Wayne, Ind. **(1908–1942)**

Lombardo, Guy (band leader); London, Ont., Canada **(1902–1977)**

London, George (baritone); Montreal **(1920–1985)**

London, Jack (John Griffith London) (novelist); San Francisco **(1876–1916)**

Long, Huey Pierce (politician); Winnfield, La. **(1893–1935)**

Long, Shelley (actress); Fort Wayne, Ind., 8/23/49

Longfellow, Henry Wadsworth (poet); Portland, Maine **(1807–1882)**

Longworth, Alice Roosevelt (social figure); New York City **(1884–1980)**

Loos, Anita (novelist); Sissons, Calif. **(1888–1981)**

Lopez, Jennifer (actress, singer); Bronx, N.Y., 12/24/70

Lopez, Trini (singer); Dallas, 5/15/37

Lopez, Vincent (band leader); Brooklyn, N.Y. **(1895–1975)**

Lord, Jack (John Joseph Ryan) (actor); New York City **(1920–1998)**

Loren, Sophia (Sofia Scicolone) (actress); Rome, 9/20/34

Lorenz, Konrad (ethologist); Vienna **(1903–1989)**

Lorre, Peter (Laszlo Löewenstein) (actor); Rosenberg, former Czechoslovakia **(1904–1964)**

Loudon, Dorothy (actress, singer); Boston, 9/17/33

Louis-Dreyfus, Julia (actress); New York City, 1/13/61

Louis XIV (King of France); St.-Germain-en-Laye, France **(1638–1715)**

Louise, Tina (actress); New York City, 2/11/37

Love, Susan (surgeon, oncologist, activist); Long Branch, N.J., 2/9/48

Lovecraft, Howard Phillips (author); Providence, R.I. **(1890–1937)**

Lovett, Lyle (country singer, songwriter); Klein, Tex., 11/1/56

Lowe, Rob (actor); Charlottesville, Va., 3/17/64

Lowell, Amy (poet); Brookline, Mass. **(1874–1925)**

Lowell, James Russell (poet); Cambridge, Mass. **(1819–1891)**

Lowell, Robert (poet); Boston **(1917–1977)**

Loy, Myrna (Myrna Williams) (actress); nr. Helena, Mont. **(1905–1993)**

Loyola, St. Ignatius of (Iñigo de Oñez y Loyola) (founder of Jesuits); Gúipuzcoa Province, Spain **(1491– 1556)**

Lubitsch, Ernst (film director); Berlin **(1892–1947)**

Lucas, George (film director); Modesto, Calif., 5/14/44

Lucci, Susan (actress); Scarsdale, N.Y., 12/23/46

Luce, Clare Boothe (playwright, former ambassador); New York City **(1903–1987)**

Luce, Henry Robinson (editor, publisher); Tengchow, China **(1898–1967)**

Ludlum, Robert (author); New York City, 5/25/27

Lugosi, Béla (Béla Blasko) (actor); Lugos, Hungary **(1888–1956)**

Lukas, J. Anthony (author); New York City **(1933–1997)**

Lukas, Paul (actor); Budapest **(1895–1971)**

Lully, Jean Baptiste (French composer); Florence **(1639–1687)**

Lumet, Sidney (director); Philadelphia, 6/25/24

Lunden, Joan (TV host); Fair Oaks, Calif., 9/19/50

Lunt, Alfred (actor); Milwaukee **(1892–1977)**

Lupino, Ida (actress, director); London **(1918–1995)**

LuPone, Patti (actress, singer); Northport, N.Y., 4/21/49

Luther, Martin (religious reformer); Eisleben, East Germany **(1483–1546)**

Lynch, David (film director); Missoula, Mont., 1/20/46

Lynn, Loretta (singer); Butcher's Hollow, Ky., 4/14/35

M

Ma, Yo-Yo (cellist); Paris, 10/7/55

Maazel, Lorin (conductor); Neuilly, France, 3/5/30

MacArthur, Charles (playwright); Scranton, Pa. **(1895–1956)**

MacArthur, Douglas (five-star general); Little Rock Barracks, Ark. **(1880–1964)**

MacArthur, James (actor); Los Angeles, 12/8/37

Macaulay, Thomas Babington (author); Rothley Temple, England **(1800–1859)**

MacDermot, Galt (composer); Montreal, 12/19/28

MacDonald, James Ramsay (statesman); Lossiemouth, Scotland **(1866–1937)**

MacDonald, Jeanette (actress, soprano); Philadelphia **(1907–1965)**

Macdonald, Ross (Kenneth Millar) (mystery writer); Los Gatos, Calif. **(1915–1983)**

MacDowell, Edward Alexander (composer); New York City **(1861–1908)**

MacDowell, Andie (Rosalie Anderson MacDowell) (actress); Gaffney, S.C., 4/21/58

MacFadden, Bernarr (physical culturist); nr. Mill Spring, Mo. **(1868–1955)**

Machaut, Guillaume de (composer); Marchault, France **(1300–1377)**

Machiavelli, Niccolò (political philosopher); Florence, Italy **(1469–1527)**

Mackie, Bob (designer); Monterey Park, Calif., 3/24/40

MacLaine, Shirley (Shirley MacLean Beaty) (actress); Richmond, Va., 4/24/34

MacLeish, Archibald (poet); Glencoe, Ill. **(1892–1982)**

Macmillan, Harold (ex-prime minister); London **(1894–1986)**

MacMurray, Fred (actor); Kankakee, Ill. **(1908–1991)**

MacNeil, Cornell (baritone); Minneapolis, 9/24/22

MacNeil, Robert (TV newscaster); Montreal, 1/19/31

MacNicol, Peter (actor); Dallas, 4/10/54

Macpherson, Elle (Eleanor Gow) (model, actress); Sydney, Australia, 3/29/64

MacRae, Gordon (singer, actor); East Orange, N.J. **(1921–1986)**

MacRae, Sheila (comedienne); London, 9/24/24

Madison, James (4th U.S. president); Port Conway, Va. **(1751–1836)**

Madonna (Madonna Louise Ciccone) (singer, actress); Bay City, Mich., 8/16/58

Maeterlinck, Count Maurice (author); Ghent, Belgium **(1862–1949)**

Magellan, Ferdinand (Fernando de Magalhaes) (navigator); Sabrosa, Portugal **(c. 1480–1521)**

Magliozzi, Ray ("Car Talk" host); Cambridge, Mass., 3/30/49

Magliozzi, Tom ("Car Talk" host); Cambridge, Mass., 6/28/37

Magritte, René (painter); Belgium **(1898–1967)**

Magsaysay, Ramón (statesman); Iba, Luzon, Philippines **(1907–1957)**

Mahan, Alfred Thayer (naval historian); West Point, N.Y. **(1840–1914)**

Mahler, Gustav (composer, conductor); Kalischt, Czechoslovakia **(1860–1911)**

Mahoney, John (actor); Manchester, England, 6/20/40

Mailer, Norman (novelist); Long Branch, N.J., 1/31/23

Maillol, Aristide (sculptor); Banyuls-sur-Mer, Rousillion, France **(1861–1944)**

Maimonides, Moses (Jewish philosopher); Cordoba, Spain **(1135–1204)**

Mainbocher (Main Rousseau Bocher) (fashion designer); Chicago **(1891–1976)**

Majors, Lee (Harvey Lee Yeary) (actor); Wyandotte, Mich., 4/23/40

Makarova, Natalia (ballet dancer); Leningrad (St. Petersburg), Russia, 11/21/40

Makeba, Miriam (singer); Johannesburg, South Africa, 3/4/32

Malamud, Bernard (novelist); Brooklyn, N.Y. **(1914–1986)**

Malcolm X (Malcolm Little; el Hajj Ma lik el-Shabazz) (Black nationalist, religious leader); Omaha, Neb. **(1925–1965)**

Malden, Karl (Karl Mladen Sekulovich) (actor); Chicago, 3/22/13

Malkovich, John (actor); Christopher, Ill., 12/9/53

Mallarmé, Stephane (poet, essayist); Paris **(1842–1898)**

Malle, Louis (director); Thumeries, France **(1932–1995)**

Malraux, André (author); Paris **(1901–1976)**

Malthus, Thomas Robert (economist); nr. Dorking, England **(1766–1834)**

Maltin, Leonard (film critic and historian); New York City, 12/18/50

Mamet, David (playwright); Chicago, 11/30/47

Manchester, Melissa (singer); Bronx, N.Y., 2/15/51

Manchester, William (writer); Attleboro, Mass., 4/1/22

Mancini, Henry (composer, conductor); Cleveland **(1924–1994)**

Mandela, Nelson (Rolihlahla) (former president of South Africa); Umtata, Transkei, 7/18/18

Mandela, Winnie (Nomzamo) (South African political activist); Pondoland district of the Transkei, 1936?

Mandrell, Barbara (singer); Houston, 12/25/48

Manet, Edouard (painter); Paris **(1832–1883)**

Mangione, Chuck (hornist, pianist, composer); Rochester, N.Y., 11/29/40

Manheim, Camryn (actress); New York City, 3/8/61

Manilow, Barry (singer); Brooklyn, N.Y., 6/17/46

Mankiewicz, Frank F. (columnist); New York City, 5/16/24

Mankiewicz, Joseph L. (film writer, director); Wilkes-Barre, Pa. **(1909–1993)**

Mann, Horace (educator); Franklin, Mass. **(1796–1859)**

Mann, Thomas (novelist); Lübeck, Germany **(1875–1955)**

Mannes, Marya (writer); New York City **(1904–1990)**

Mansfield, Jayne (Jayne Palmer) (actress); Bryn Mawr, Pa. **(1932–1967)**

Mansfield, Katherine (story writer); Wellington, New Zealand **(1888–1923)**

Manson, Marilyn (Brian Warner) (rock musician); Canton, Ohio, 1/5/69

Mantegna, Andrea (painter); Isola di Carturo, Italy **(1431–1506)**

Mantegna, Joe (actor); Chicago, 11/13/47

Mantovani, Annunzio (conductor); Venice **(1905–1980)**

Mao Zedong (Tse-tung) (Chinese leader); Shao Shan, China **(1893– 1976)**

Mapplethorpe, Robert (photographer); Floral Park, Queens, N.Y. **(1946–1989)**

Marat, Jean Paul (French revolutionist); Boudry, Neuchâtel, Switzerland **(1743–1793)**

Marceau, Marcel (mime); Strasbourg, France, 3/22/23

Marceau, Sophie (actress); Paris, 11/17/66

March, Fredric (Frederick Bickel) (actor); Racine, Wis. **(1897–1975)**

Marchand, Nancy (actress); Buffalo, N.Y. **(1928–2000)**

Marconi, Guglielmo (inventor); Bologna, Italy **(1874–1937)**

Marcus Aurelius (Marcus Annius Verus) (Roman emperor); Rome **(121–180)**

Marcus, Rudolph Arthur (chemist, Nobel laureate); Montreal, 7/21/23

Marcuse, Herbert (philosopher); Berlin **(1898–1979)**

Margaret Rose (princess of England); Glamis Castle, Angus, Scotland, 8/21/30
Margrethe II (queen of Denmark); Copenhagen, 4/16/40
Margulies, Julianna (actress); Spring Valley, N.Y., 6/8/65
Marie Antoinette (Josephe Jeanne Marie Antoinette) (queen of France); Vienna **(1755 –1793)**
Marisol (Escobar) (Venezuelan-American sculptor); Paris, 1930
Markham, Edwin (poet); Oregon City, Ore. **(1852–1940)**
Markova, Dame Alicia (Lilian Alice Marks) (ballet dancer); London, 12/1/10
Marley, Bob (singer, songwriter); Kingston, Jamaica **(1945–1981)**
Marlowe, Christopher (dramatist); Canterbury, England **(1564– 1593)**
Marquand, J(ohn) P(hillips) (novelist); Wilmington, Del. **(1893– 1960)**
Marquette, Jacques (missionary, explorer); Laon, France **(1637– 1675)**
Marriner, Neville (conductor); Lincoln, England, 4/15/24
Marsalis, Wynton (musician); New Orleans, 10/18/61
Marshall, E.G. (actor); Owatonna, Minn. **(1910–1998)**
Marshall, Garry (director, producer, screenwriter, actor); New York City, 11/13/34
Marshall, George Catlett (general); Uniontown, Pa. **(1880–1959)**
Marshall, Herbert (actor); London **(1890–1966)**
Marshall, John (jurist); nr. Germantown, Va. **(1755–1835)**
Marshall, Penny (Penny Marscharelli) (actress, director, producer); Bronx, N.Y., 10/15/42
Marshall, Thurgood (U.S. Supreme Court justice); Baltimore **(1908– 1993)**
Martin, Dean (Dino Crocetti) (singer, actor); Steubenville, Ohio **(1917–1995)**
Martin, Mary (singer, actress); Weatherford, Tex. **(1913–1990)**
Martin, Steve (actor, writer, producer); Waco, Tex., 8/14/45
Martin, Tony (Alvin Morris) (singer); San Francisco, 12/25/12
Martinelli, Giovanni (tenor); Montagnana, Italy **(1885–1969)**
Martins, Peter (dancer, choreographer); Copenhagen, 10/27/45
Marvell, Andrew (poet); Winestead, England **(1621–1678)**
Marvin, Lee (actor); New York City **(1924–1987)**
Marx, Chico (Leonard) (comedian); New York City **(1891–1961)**
Marx, Groucho (Julius) (comedian); New York City **(1890–1977)**
Marx, Harpo (Arthur) (comedian); New York City **(1893–1964)**
Marx, Karl (Socialist writer); Treves, Germany **(1818–1883)**
Marx, Zeppo (Herbert) (comedian); New York City **(1901–1979)**
Mary Stuart (Mary, Queen of Scots) (queen of Scotland); Linlithgow, Scotland **(1542–1587)**
Masaccio, (Tommaso di Giovanni di Simone Cassai) (painter); San Giovanni Valdarno, Tuscany **(1401–c. 1428)**
Masaryk, Jan Garrigue (statesman); Prague **(1886–1948)**
Masaryk, Thomas Garrigue (statesman); Hodonin, Czech Republic **(1850–1937)**
Masefield, John (poet); Ledbury, England **(1878–1967)**
Masekela, Hugh (trumpeter); Wilbank, South Africa, 4/4/39
Mason, Jackie (Jacob Moshe Maza) (comedian); Sheboygan, Wis., 6/9/31
Mason, James (actor); Huddersfield, England **(1909–1984)**
Mason, Marsha (actress); St. Louis, 4/3/42
Massenet, Jules Emile Frédéric (composer); Montaud, France **(1842–1912)**
Massine, Léonide (choreographer); Moscow **(1895–1979)**
Masters, Edgar Lee (poet); Garnett, Kans. **(1869–1950)**
Masters, William (human sexuality expert); Cleveland, 12/27/15
Masterson, Mary Stuart (actress, writer, director); New York City, 6/28/66
Mastroianni, Marcello (actor); Fontana Liri, Italy **(1924–1996)**
Mather, Cotton (clergyman); Boston **(1663–1728)**
Mathis, Johnny (singer); Gilmer, Texas, 9/30/35
Matisse, Henri (painter); Le Cateau, France **(1869–1954)**
Matthau, Walter (Walter Matuschanskayasky) (actor); New York City **(1920–2000)**
Mature, Victor (actor); Louisville, Ky. **(1915–1999)**
Maugham, W(illiam) Somerset (author); Paris **(1874–1965)**
Mauldin, Bill (political cartoonist); Mountain Park, N.M., 10/29/21
Maupassant, Henri René Albert Guy de (story writer); Normandy, France **(1850–1893)**
Maurois, André (Emile Herzog) (author); Elbauf, France **(1885– 1967)**
Maximilian (Ferdinand Maximilian Joseph) (emperor of Mexico); Vienna **(1832–1867)**
Maxwell, James Clerk (physicist); Edinburgh, Scotland **(1831– 1879)**
Maxwell, (Ian) Robert (publisher); Selo Slatina, Czechoslavakia **(1923–1991)**

May, Elaine (Elaine Berlin) (entertainer, writer); Philadelphia, 4/21/32
May, Rollo (psychologist); Ada, Ohio **(1909–1994)**
Mayer, Louis B. (movie executive); Minsk, Russia **(1885–1957)**
Mayo, Charles H. (surgeon); Rochester, Minn. **(1865–1939)**
Mayo, Charles W. (surgeon); Rochester, Minn. **(1898–1968)**
Mayo, Virginia (Jones) (actress); St. Louis, 11/30/20
Mayo, William J. (surgeon); Le Sueur, Minn. **(1861–1939)**
Mayron, Melanie (actress); Philadelphia, 10/20/52
Mazzini, Giuseppe (patriot); Genoa **(1805–1872)**
McBride, Patricia (ballet dancer); Teaneck, N.J., 8/23/42
McCallum, David (actor); Glasgow, Scotland, 9/19/33
McCambridge, Mercedes (actress); Joliet, Ill., 3/17/18
McCarthy, Eugene J. (ex-senator); Watkins, Minn., 3/29/16
McCarthy, Joseph Raymond (senator); Grand Chute, Wis. **(1908– 1957)**
McCarthy, Mary (novelist); Seattle **(1912–1989)**
McCartney, Linda (photographer, singer); New York City **(1941– 1998)**
McCartney, Paul (singer, songwriter); Liverpool, England, 6/18/42
McClanahan, Rue (actress); Healdton, Okla., 2/21/35
McClellan, George Brinton (general); Philadelphia **(1826–1885)**
McClintock, Barbara (geneticist, Nobel laureate) **(1902–1992)**
McCloy, John J. (lawyer, banker); Philadelphia **(1895–1989)**
McCormack, John (tenor); Athlone, Ireland **(1884–1945)**
McCormack, John W. (ex-Speaker of House); Boston **(1891–1980)**
McCormick, Cyrus Hall (inventor); Rockbridge County, Va. **(1809– 1884)**
McCourt, Frank (writer); Brooklyn, N.Y., 8/19/30
McCracken, James (dramatic tenor); Gary, Ind. **(1926–1988)**
McCrea, Joel (actor); Los Angeles **(1905–1990)**
McCullers, Carson (novelist); Columbus, Ga. **(1917–1967)**
McDermott, Dylan (actor); Waterbury, Conn., 10/26/62
McDormand, Frances (actress); Illinois, 6/23/57
McDowall, Roddy (actor); London **(1928–1998)**
McDowell, Malcolm (actor); Leeds, England, 6/15/43
McFadden, Gates (actress); Cuyahoga Falls, Ohio, 3/2/49
McGavin, Darren (actor); San Joaquin, Calif., 5/7/22
McGillis, Kelly (actress); Newport Beach, Calif., 7/9/57
McGinley, Phyllis (poet, writer); Ontario, Ore. **(1905–1978)**
McGoohan, Patrick (actor); Astoria, Queens, N.Y., 3/19/28
McGovern, Elizabeth (actress); Evanston, Ill., 7/18/61
McGovern, Maureen (singer); Youngstown, Ohio, 7/27/49
McGregor, Ewan (actor); Crieff, Scotland, 3/31/71
McKellen, Ian (actor); Burnley, England, 5/25/39
McKinley, William (25th U.S. president); Niles, Ohio **(1843–1901)**
McKuen, Rod (singer, composer); Oakland, Calif., 4/29/33
McLachlan, Sarah (singer, songwriter); Halifax, N.S., 1/28/68
McLaughlin, John (guitarist); Yorkshire, England, 1/4/42
McLean, Don (singer, songwriter); New Rochelle, N.Y., 10/2/45
McLuhan, Marshall (Herbert Marshall) (communications writer); Edmonton, Alta., Canada **(1911–1980)**
McMahon, Ed (TV personality); Detroit, 3/6/23
McMurtry, Larry (novelist); Wichita Falls, Tex., 6/3/36
McQueen, Butterfly (Thelma) (actress); Tampa, Fla. **(1911–1995)**
McQueen, Steve (Terence Stephen McQueen) (actor); Beech Grove, Indiana **(1930–1980)**
McRaney, Gerald (actor); Collins, Miss., 8/19/47
McTeer, Janet (actress); York, England, 1962
Mead, Margaret (anthropologist); Philadelphia **(1901–1978)**
Meadows, Audrey (actress); Wu Chang, China **(1924–1996)**
Meadows, Jayne (actress); Wu Chang, China, 9/27/26
Meaney, Colm (actor); Dublin, 5/30/53
Meany, George (labor leader); New York City **(1894–1980)**
Meara, Anne (actress); New York City, 9/20/29
Medici, Lorenzo de' (called Lorenzo the Magnificent) (Florentine ruler); Florence, Italy **(1449–1492)**
Mehta, Zubin (conductor); Bombay (Mumbai), 4/29/36
Meir, Golda (Golda Myerson, nee Mabovitz) (ex-premier of Israel); Kiev, Ukraine **(1898–1978)**
Melba, Dame Nellie (Helen Porter Mitchell) (soprano); nr. Melbourne, Australia **(1861–1931)**
Melchior, Lauritz (Lebrecht Hommel) (heroic tenor); Copenhagen **(1890–1973)**
Mellon, Andrew William (financier); Pittsburgh **(1855–1937)**
Melville, Herman (novelist); New York City **(1819–1891)**
Mencken, Henry Louis (writer); Baltimore **(1880–1956)**
Mendel, Gregor Johann (geneticist); Heinzendorf, Austrian Silesia **(1822–1884)**
Mendeleyev, Dmitri Ivanovich (chemist); Tobolsk, Russia **(1834– 1907)**

Mendelssohn-Bartholdy, Jakob Ludwig Felix (composer); Hamburg **(1809–1847)**

Mendès-France, Pierre (ex-Premier); Paris **(1905–1982)**

Mengele, Josef (Nazi, "Angel of Death"); Günzberg, Germany **(1911–1979)**

Mennin, Peter (Peter Mennini) (composer); Erie, Pa. **(1923–1983)**

Menninger, William C. (psychiatrist); Topeka, Kans. **(1899–1966)**

Menotti, Gian Carlo (composer); Cadegliano, Italy, 7/7/11

Menuhin, Yehudi (violinist, conductor); New York City **(1916–1999)**

Menzies, Robert Gordon (ex-prime minister); Jeparit, Australia **(1894–1978)**

Mercer, Johnny (songwriter); Savannah, Ga. **(1909–1976)**

Mercer, Mabel (singer); Burton-on-Trent, England **(1900–1984)**

Merchant, Ismail (Ismail Noormohamed Abdul Rehman) (film producer); Bombay (Mumbai), 12/25/36

Merchant, Natalie (singer, songwriter); Jamestown, N.Y., 10/26/63

Mercury, Freddie (Farookh Bulsara) (musician, singer); Zanzibar **(1946–1991)**

Meredith, Burgess (actor); Cleveland **(1908–1997)**

Meredith, James (author, civil-rights leader); Kosciusko, Miss., 6/26/23

Merman, Ethel (Ethel Zimmerman) (singer, actress); Astoria, Queens, N.Y. **(1909–1984)**

Merrick, David (David Margulois) (stage producer); St. Louis **(1912–2000)**

Merton, Thomas (clergyman, writer); France **(1915–1968)**

Mesmer, Franz Anton (physician); Itzmang, nr. Constance, Germany **(1733–1815)**

Mesta, Perle (social figure); Sturgis, Mich. **(1889–1975)**

Metacom, (King Philip) (Wampanoag Indian sachem); southeastern Mass. **(1640–1676)**

Metternich, Prince Klemens Wenzel Nepomuk Lothar von (statesman); Coblenz, Germany **(1773–1859)**

Mfume, Kweisi (Frizzell Gray) (politician, NAACP leader); Baltimore, 10/24/48

Michaels, Lorne (producer); Toronto, 11/17/44

Michelangelo Buonarroti (painter, sculptor, architect); Caprese, Italy **(1475–1564)**

Michener, James A. (novelist); New York City **(1907–1997)**

Mickiewicz, Adam (Polish poet); Zozie, Belorussia (Belarus) **(1798–1855)**

Midler, Bette (singer, actress, producer); Honolulu, 12/1/45

Mielziner, Jo (stage designer); Paris **(1901–1976)**

Mifune, Toshiro (actor, film producer); Tsingtao, China **(1920–1997)**

Mies van der Rohe, Ludwig (architect, designer); Aachen, Germany **(1886–1969)**

Mikoyan, Anastas I. (diplomat); Sanain, Armenia **(1895–1978)**

Milano, Alyssa (actress); Brooklyn, New York, 12/19/72

Milhaud, Darius (composer); Aix-en-Provence, France **(1892–1974)**

Mill, John Stuart (philosopher); London **(1806–1873)**

Milland, Ray (Reginald Truscott-Jones) (actor); Neath, Wales **(1907–1986)**

Millay, Edna St. Vincent (poet); Rockland, Maine **(1892–1950)**

Miller, Ann (Lucille Ann Collier) (dancer, actress); Cherino, Tex., 4/12/23

Miller, Arthur (playwright); New York City, 10/17/15

Miller, Glenn (band leader); Clarinda, Iowa **(1904–1944)**

Miller, Henry (novelist); New York City **(1891–1980)**

Miller, Jason (John Miller) (playwright, actor); New York City, 4/22/39

Miller, Mitch (Mitchell) (musician); Rochester, N.Y., 7/4/11

Miller, Roger (singer); Fort Worth **(1936–1992)**

Millet, Jean François (painter); Gruchy, France **(1814–1875)**

Millett, Kate (feminist, writer); St. Paul, Minn., 9/14/34

Millikan, Robert A. (physicist); Morrison, Ill. **(1869–1953)**

Mills, Donna (actress); Chicago, 12/11/41

Mills, Hayley (actress); London, 4/18/46

Mills, Juliet (actress); London, 11/21/41

Milne, A(lan) A(lexander) (author); London **(1882–1956)**

Milner, Martin (actor); Detroit, 12/28/31

Milnes, Sherrill (baritone); Downers Grove, Ill., 1/10/35

Milosevic, Slobodan (Yugoslav President); Pozarevac, Serbia, 8/29/41

Milstein, Nathan (concert violinist); Odessa, Ukraine **(1904–1992)**

Milton, John (poet); London **(1608–1674)**

Mingus, Charles (jazz composer); Nogales, Ariz. **(1922–1979)**

Minnelli, Liza (singer, actress); Hollywood, Calif., 3/12/46

Minnelli, Vincente (film director); Chicago **(1913–1986)**

Minuit, Peter (Governor of New Amsterdam); Wesel, Germany **(1580–1638)**

Miranda, Carmen (Maria do Carmo da Cunha) (singer, dancer); Lisbon **(1909–1955)**

Miró, Joan (painter); Barcelona **(1893–1983)**

Mirren, Helen (Ilynea Lydia Mironoff) (actress); London, 7/26/45

Mitchell, John N. (former Attorney General); Detroit **(1913–1988)**

Mitchell, Joni (Roberta Joan Anderson) (singer, songwriter); Ft. Macleod, Alb., Canada, 11/7/43

Mitchell, Margaret (novelist); Atlanta **(1900–1949)**

Mitchell, Maria (astronomer); Nantucket, Mass. **(1818–1889)**

Mitchum, Robert (actor); Bridgeport, Conn. **(1917–1997)**

Mitropoulos, Dimitri (orchestra conductor); Athens **(1896–1960)**

Mitterand, François (Maurice) (ex-prime minister of France); Jarnac, France **(1916–1996)**

Mix, Tom (actor); Mix Run, Pa. **(1880–1940)**

Mobutu Sese Seko (Zairean dictator); Lisala, Congo **(1930–1997)**

Modigliani, Amedeo (painter); Leghorn, Italy **(1884–1920)**

Moffo, Anna (soprano); Wayne, Pa., 6/27/34

Mohammed (prophet); Mecca, Saudi Arabia **(570–632)**

Molière (Jean Baptiste Poquelin) (dramatist); Paris **(1622–1673)**

Molina, Mario (chemist, Nobel laureate); Mexico City, 3/19/43

Moll, Richard (actor); Pasadena, Calif., 1/13/43?

Molnar, Ferenc (dramatist); Budapest **(1878–1952)**

Molotov, Vyacheslav M. (V. M. Skryabin) (diplomat); Kukarka, Russia **(1890–1986)**

Mondrian, Piet (painter); Amersfoort, Netherlands **(1872–1944)**

Monet, Claude (painter); Paris **(1840–1926)**

Monica Monica Arnold (singer); Atlanta, Ga., 10/24/80

Monk, Meredith (choreographer, composer, performing artist); Lima, Peru, 11/20/42

Monk, Thelonious (pianist); Rocky Mount, N.C. **(1918–1982)**

Monroe, James (5th U.S. president); Westmoreland County, Va. **(1758–1831)**

Monroe, Marilyn (Norma Jean Mortenson or Baker) (actress); Los Angeles **(1926–1962)**

Monsarrat, Nicholas (novelist); Liverpool, England **(1910–1979)**

Montaigne, Michel Eyquem de (essayist); nr. Bordeaux, France **(1533–1592)**

Montalban, Ricardo (actor); Mexico City, 11/25/20

Montand, Yves (Ivo Livi) (actor, singer); Florence, Italy **(1921–1991)**

Montesquieu, Charles-Louis de Secondat, baron de La Brède and de (philosopher); nr. Bordeaux, France **(1689–1755)**

Montessori, Maria (physician, educator); Chiaravalle, Italy **(1870–1952)**

Monteux, Pierre (conductor); Paris **(1875–1964)**

Monteverdi, Claudio (composer); Cremona Italy **(1567–1643)**

Montezuma II (Aztec emperor); Mexico **(1466–1520)**

Montgomery, Elizabeth (actress); Hollywood, Calif. **(1933–1995)**

Montgomery, Robert (Henry, Jr.) (actor); Beacon, N.Y. **(1904–1981)**

Montgomery of Alamein, 1st Viscount of Hindhead (Sir Bernard Law Montgomery) (military leader); London **(1887–1976)**

Montoya, Carlos (guitarist); Madrid **(1903–1993)**

Moore, Clayton (Jack Moore) (actor); Chicago **(1914–1999)**

Moore, Clement Clarke (author); New York City **(1779–1863)**

Moore, Demi (Demi Guynes) (actress); Roswell, N.M., 11/11/62

Moore, Dudley (actor, writer, musician); Dagenham, England, 4/19/35

Moore, Grace (soprano); Jellico, Tenn. **(1901–1947)**

Moore, Henry (sculptor); Castleford, England **(1898–1986)**

Moore, Julianne (actress); Boston, 12/3/60

Moore, Marianne (poet); Kirkwood, Mo. **(1887–1972)**

Moore, Mary Tyler (actress); Brooklyn, N.Y., 12/29/36

Moore, Melba (Beatrice) (singer, actress); New York City, 10/27/45

Moore, Roger (actor); London, 10/14/27

Moore, Thomas (poet); Dublin **(1779–1852)**

Moorehead, Agnes (actress); Clinton, Mass. **(1906–1974)**

Moranis, Rick (actor); Toronto, 4/18/53

More, Henry (philosopher); Grantham, England **(1614–1687)**

More, Sir Thomas (statesman, author); London **(1478–1535)**

Moreno, Rita (Rosita Dolores Alverio) (actress); Humacao, P.R., 12/11/31

Morgan, Harry (Harry Bratsburg) (actor); Detroit, 4/10/15

Morgan, John Pierpont (financier); Hartford, Conn. **(1837–1913)**

Moriarty, Michael (actor); Detroit, 4/5/41

Morini, Erica (concert violinist); Vienna **(1904–1995)**

Morison, Samuel Eliot (historian); Boston **(1887–1976)**

Morita, Pat (Noriyuki Morita) (actor); Berkeley, Calif., 8/28/32

Morley, Christopher Darlington (novelist); Haverford, Pa. **(1890–1957)**

Morris, Mark (choreographer); Seattle, 8/29/56

Morris, William (poet, craftsman); Walthamstow, England **(1834–1896)**

Morrison, Jim (James Douglas Morrison) (singer, songwriter); Melbourne, Fla. **(1943–1971)**

Morrison, Toni (Chloe Anthony Wofford) (novelist); Lorain, Ohio, 2/18/31

Morrison, Van (singer); Belfast, Northern Ireland, 8/31/45

Morse, Marston (mathematician); Waterville, Maine **(1892–1977)**
Morse, Samuel Finley Breese (painter, inventor); Charlestown, Mass. **(1791–1872)**
Morton, Jelly Roll (Ferdinand Joseph La Menthe) (jazz composer); New Orleans **(1890–1941)**
Moseley-Braun, Carol (U.S. Senator); Chicago, 8/16/47
Moses, Grandma (Mrs. Anna Mary Robertson Moses) (painter); Greenwich, N.Y. **(1860–1961)**
Moses, Robert (urban planner); New Haven, Conn. **(1888–1981)**
Moss, Kate (model); London, England, 1/16/74
Mostel, Zero (Samuel Joel Mostel) (actor); Brooklyn, N.Y. **(1915–1977)**
Mother Teresa (Agnes Gonxha Bojaxhiu) (nun); Skopje, Macedonia **(1910–1997)**
Motherwell, Robert (artist, "action" painter); Aberdeen, Wash. **(1915–1991)**
Mott, Lucretia (Coffin) (feminist, reformer, abolitionist); Nantucket, Mass. **(1793–1880)**
Moussorgsky, Modest Petrovich (composer); Karev, Russia **(1839–1881)**
Moyers, Bill D. (Billy Don) (journalist); Hugo, Okla., 6/5/34
Moynihan, Daniel Patrick (New York senator); Tulsa, Okla., 3/16/27
Mozart, Wolfgang Amadeus (Johannes Chrysostomus Wolfgangus Theophilus Mozart) (composer); Salzburg, Austria **(1756–1791)**
Mudd, Roger (TV newscaster); Washington, D.C., 2/9/28
Muggeridge, Malcolm (Thomas) (writer); Croydon, England **(1903–1990)**
Muhammad (founder of Islam); Mecca, Saudi Arabia **(c. 570–632)**
Muhammad, Elijah (Elijah Poole) (religious leader); Sandersville, Ga. **(1897–1975)**
Mulgrew, Kate (actress); Dubuque, Iowa, 4/29/55
Mulhare, Edward (actor); Ireland **(1923–1997)**
Mulliken, Robert Sanderson (chemist, Nobel laureate); Newburyport, Mass. **(1896–1986)**
Mulroney, Dermot (actor, musician, producer); Alexandria, Va., 10/31/63
Mumford, Lewis (cultural historian, city planner); Flushing, Queens, N.Y. **(1895–1990)**
Munch, Edvard (painter); Löten, Norway **(1863–1944)**
Munchhausen, Karl Friedrick Hieronymus, baron von (anecdotist); Hannover, Germany **(1720–1797)**
Muni, Paul (Muni Weisenfreund) (actor); Lemburg, Ukraine **(1895–1967)**
Muñoz Marín, Luis (ex-governor of Puerto Rico); San Juan, P.R. **(1898–1980)**
Munsel, Patrice (soprano); Spokane, Wash., 5/14/25
Murdoch, Iris (novelist); Dublin **(1919–1999)**
Murdoch, Rupert (publisher); Melbourne, Australia, 3/11/31
Murillo, Bartolomé Esteban (painter); Seville, Spain **(1617–1682)**
Murphy, Audie (actor, war hero); Kingston, Tex. **(1924–1971)**
Murphy, Eddie (actor, comedian); Brooklyn, N.Y., 4/3/61
Murphy, George (actor, dancer, ex-senator); New Haven, Conn. **(1902–1992)**
Murray, Arthur (dance teacher); New York City **(1895–1991)**
Murray, Bill (actor, comedian); Wilmette, Ill., 9/21/50
Murray, Kathryn (dance teacher); Jersey City, N.J. **(1906–1999)**
Murrow, Edward R. (commentator, government official); Greensboro, N.C. **(1908–1965)**
Musil, Robert (novelist); Klagenfurt, Austria **(1880–1942)**
Muskie, Edmund (political figure); Rumford, Maine **(1914–1996)**
Mussolini, Benito (Italian dictator); Dovia, Forli, Italy **(1883–1945)**
Muti, Riccardo (orchestra conductor); Naples, Italy, 7/28/41
Mutter, Anne-Sophie (violinist); Rheinfelden, Germany, 6/29/63
Myers, Mike (actor, writer, comedian); Scarborough, Ont., Canada, 5/25/63
Myerson, Bess (consumer advocate); Bronx, N.Y., 7/16/24
Myrdal, Gunnar (sociologist, economist); Gustaf Parish, Sweden **(1898–1987)**

N

Nabokov, Vladimir (novelist); St. Petersburg, Russia **(1899–1977)**
Nabors, Jim (actor, singer); Sylacauga, Ala., 6/12/32
Nader, Ralph (consumer advocate); Winsted, Conn., 2/27/34
Nair, Mira (director, screenwriter); Bhubaneswar, India, 10/15/57
Nash, Graham (singer); Blackpool, England, 1942
Nash, Ogden (poet); Rye, N.Y. **(1902–1971)**
Nasser, Gamal Abdel (statesman); Beni Mor, Egypt **(1918–1970)**
Nast, Thomas (cartoonist); Landau, Germany **(1840–1902)**
Nation, Carry Amelia (temperance leader); Garrard County, Ky. **(1846–1911)**
Natta, Giulio (chemist, Nobel laureate); Imperia, Italy **(1903–1979)**
Natwick, Mildred (actress); Baltimore **(1905–1994)**

Neagle, Anna (Marjorie Robertson) (actress); London **(1908–1986)**
Neal, Patricia (actress); Packard, Ky., 1/20/26
Neeson, Liam (William John) (actor); Ballymena, Northern Ireland, 6/7/52
Negri, Pola (Apolina Mathias-Chalupec) (actress); Bromberg, Poland **(1899–1987)**
Nehru, Jawaharlal (first prime minister of India); Allahabad, India **(1889–1964)**
Neill, Sam (Nigel Neill) (actor); Omagh, Northern Ireland, 9/14/47
Nelligan, Kate (actress); London, Ont., Canada, 3/16/51
Nelson, Barry (Robert Haakon Nielsen) (actor); San Francisco, 4/16/20
Nelson, David (actor); New York City, 10/24/36
Nelson, Harriet Hilliard (Peggy Lou Snyder) (actress); Des Moines, Iowa **(1909–1994)**
Nelson, Ozzie (Oswald) (actor); Jersey City, N.J. **(1907–1975)**
Nelson, Ricky (Eric) (singer, actor); Teaneck, N.J. **(1940–1985)**
Nelson, Viscount Horatio (naval officer); Burnham Thorpe, England **(1758–1805)**
Nelson, Willie (singer); Waco, Tex., 4/30/33
Nenni, Pietro (Socialist leader); Faenza, Italy **(1891–1980)**
Nero (Nero Claudius Caesar Drusus Germanicus) (Roman emperor); Antium, Italy **(37–68)**
Nero, Peter (pianist); New York City, 5/22/34
Netanyahu, Benjamin (Binyamin) (former Israeli prime minister); Tel Aviv, Israel, 10/21/49
Neuwirth, Bebe (Beatrice Neuwirth) (actress); Newark, N.J., 12/31/58
Nevelson, Louise (sculptor); Kiev, Russia **(1899–1988)**
Neville, Aaron (singer); New Orleans, 1/24/41
Newhart, Bob (actor); Chicago, 9/5/29
Newhouse, Samuel I. (publisher); New York City **(1895–1979)**
Newley, Anthony (actor, songwriter); London **(1931–1999)**
Newman, Edwin (news commentator); New York City, 1/25/19
Newman, John Henry (prelate); London **(1801–1890)**
Newman, Paul (actor, director); Cleveland, 1/26/25
Newman, Randy (singer); Los Angeles, 11/28/43
Newton, Huey (black activist); New Orleans **(1942–1989)**
Newton, Sir Isaac (mathematician, scientist); nr. Grantham, England **(1642–1727)**
Newton, Wayne (singer); Norfolk, Va., 4/3/42
Newton-John, Olivia (singer); Cambridge, England, 9/26/48
Nichols, Nichelle (actress); Robbins, Ill., 12/28/33
Nichols, Mike (Michael Peschkowsky) (stage and film director); Berlin, 11/6/31
Nicholson, Jack (actor, director, writer); Neptune, N.J., 4/22/37
Nicks, Stevie (Stephanie Lynn Nicks) (singer, songwriter); Phoenix, Ariz., 5/26/48
Nielsen, Leslie (actor); Regina, Sask., Canada, 2/11/26
Nietzsche, Friedrich Wilhelm (philosopher); nr. Lützen, Saxony, Germany **(1844–1900)**
Nightingale, Florence (nurse); Florence, Italy **(1820–1910)**
Nijinsky, Vaslav (ballet dancer); Warsaw **(1890–1950)**
Nilsson, Birgit (soprano); West Karup, Sweden, 5/17/23
Nilsson, Harry (singer, songwriter); Brooklyn, N.Y. **(1941–1994)**
Nimitz, Chester W. (naval officer); Fredericksburg, Tex. **(1885–1966)**
Nimoy, Leonard (actor, director, writer, producer); Boston, 3/26/31
Nin, Anais (author, diarist); Neuilly, France **(1903–1977)**
Niven, David (actor); Kirriemuir, Scotland **(1910–1983)**
Nixon, Richard Milhous (37th U.S. president); Yorba Linda, Calif. **(1913–1994)**
Nizer, Louis (lawyer, author); London **(1902–1994)**
Nobel, Alfred Bernhard (industrialist); Stockholm **(1833–1896)**
Noguchi, Isamu (sculptor); Los Angeles **(1904–1988)**
Nolan, Lloyd (actor); San Francisco **(1902–1985)**
Nolte, Nick (actor); Omaha, Neb., 2/8/40
Norell, Norman (Norman Levinson) (fashion designer); Noblesville, Ind. **(1900–1972)**
Norman, Jessye (soprano); Augusta, Ga., 9/15/45
Norman, Marsha (Marsha Williams) (playwright); Louisville, Ky., 9/21/47
Normand, Mabel (actress); Boston **(1894–1930)**
Norris, Chuck (Carlos Ray Norris) (actor, athlete); Ryan, Oklahoma, 3/10/40
Norstad, Gen. Lauris (ex-commander of NATO forces); Minneapolis **(1907–1988)**
Norton, Edward (actor); Columbia, Md., 8/18/69
North, John Ringling (circus director); Baraboo, Wis. **(1903–1985)**
North, Oliver (ex-military officer); San Antonio, 10/7/43
North, Sheree (actress); Los Angeles, 1/17/33
Norton, Eleanor Holmes (New York City government official, lawyer); Washington, D.C., 6/13/37

Nostradamus (Michel de Notredame) (astrologer); St. Rémy, France **(1503–1566)**
Novaes, Guiomar (pianist); São João de Boa Vista, Brazil **(1895–1979)**
Novak, Kim (Marilyn Novak) (actress); Chicago, 2/13/33
Novarro, Ramon (Ramon Samaniegoes) (actor); Durango, Mexico **(1899–1968)**
Novello, Ivor (actor, playwright, composer); Cardiff, Wales **(1893–1951)**
Nugent, Elliott (actor, director); Dover, Ohio **(1899–1980)**
Nureyev, Rudolf (ballet dancer); Siberia **(1938–1993)**
Nyro, Laura (singer, songwriter); Bronx, N.Y. **(1947–1997)**

O

Oakie, Jack (actor); Sedalia, Mo. **(1903–1978)**
Oakley, Annie (Phoebe Anne Oakley Mozee) (markswoman); Darke County, Ohio **(1860–1926)**
Oates, Joyce Carol (novelist); Lockport, N.Y., 6/16/38
Oberon, Merle (Estelle Merle O'Brien Thompson) (actress); Tasmania, Australia **(1911–1979)**
Oberth, Hermann (rocketry and space flight pioneer); Nagyszeben, Austria-Hungary (Sibiu, Romania) **(1894–1989)**
O'Brian, Hugh (Hugh J. Krampe) (actor); Rochester, N.Y., 4/19/25
O'Brien, Conan (TV personality); Brookline, Mass., 4/18/63
O'Brien, Edmond (actor); New York City **(1915–1985)**
O'Brien, Margaret (Angela Maxine O'Brien) (actress); San Diego, Calif., 1/15/37
O'Brien, Pat (William Joseph O'Brien, Jr.) (actor); Milwaukee **(1899–1983)**
O'Brien, Tim (novelist); Austin, Minn., 10/1/46
Obuchi, Keizo (former prime minister of Japan); Nakanojo, Japan **(1937–2000)**
O'Casey, Sean (playwright); Dublin **(1881–1964)**
Ochs, Adolph Simon (publisher); Cincinnati **(1858–1935)**
O'Connor, Carroll (actor); New York City, 8/2/24
Odets, Clifford (playwright); Philadelphia **(1906–1963)**
Odetta (Odetta Holmes) (folk singer, actress); Birmingham, Ala., 12/31/30
O'Donnell, Chris (actor); Winnetka, Ill., 6/26/70
O'Donnell, Rosie (actress, talk show host); Commack, N.Y., 3/21/62
Offenbach, Jacques (composer); Cologne, Germany **(1819–1880)**
O'Hara, John (novelist); Pottsville, Pa. **(1905–1970)**
O'Hara, Maureen (Maureen FitzSimons) (actress); Dublin, 8/17/20
Ohlsson, Garrick (pianist); Bronxville, N.Y., 4/3/48
Oistrakh, David (concert violinist); Odessa, Russia **(1908–1974)**
O'Keeffe, Georgia (painter); Sun Prairie, Wis. **(1887–1986)**
Oland, Warner (actor); Umea, Sweden **(1880–1938)**
Oldenburg, Claes (painter); Stockholm, 1/28/29
Oldman, Gary (actor, director); London, 3/21/58
Olin, Lena (actress); Stockholm, 3/22/55
Oliphant, Patrick B. (editorial cartoonist); Adelaide, Australia, 7/24/35
Olivier, Sir Laurence (actor); Dorking, England **(1907–1989)**
Olmos, Edward James (actor); East Los Angeles, 2/24/47
Olmsted, Frederick Law (landscape architect); Hartford, Conn. **(1822–1903)**
Olsen, Ole (John Sigvard Olsen) (comedian); Peru, Ind. **(1892–1963)**
Omar Khayyam (poet, astronomer); Nishapur, Iran (died c. 1123)
Onassis, Aristotle (shipping executive); Smyrna, Turkey **(1906–1975)**
Onassis, Christina (shipping executive); New York City **(1950–1988)**
Onassis, Jacqueline Kennedy (Jacqueline Bouvier) (First Lady); Southampton, N.Y. **(1929–1994)**
O'Neal, Ryan (Patrick) (actor); Los Angeles, 4/20/41
O'Neal, Tatum (actress); Los Angeles, 11/5/63
O'Neill, Eugene Gladstone (playwright); New York City **(1888–1953)**
O'Neill, Jennifer (actress); Rio de Janeiro, 2/20/49
Oppenheimer, J. Robert (nuclear physicist); New York City **(1904–1967)**
Orbach, Jerry (actor); New York City, 10/20/35
Orff, Carl (composer); Munich, Germany **(1895–1982)**
Orlando, Tony (Michael Anthony Orlando Cassavitis) (singer); New York City, 4/3/44
Ormandy, Eugene (conductor); Budapest **(1899–1985)**
Ormond, Julia (actress); Epsom, Surrey, England, 1/4/65
Orozco, José Clemente (painter); Zapotlán, Jalisco, Mexico **(1883–1949)**

Orwell, George (Eric Arthur Blair) (British author); Motihari, India **(1903–1950)**
Osborn, Paul (playwright); Evansville, Ind. **(1901–1988)**
Osborne, John (playwright); London **(1929–1994)**
Osbourne, Ozzy (John Osbourne) (singer); Birmingham, England, 12/3/48
Osler, Sir William (physician); Bondhead, Ont., Canada **(1849–1919)**
Osmond, Donny (singer, actor); Ogden, Utah, 12/9/57
Osmond, Marie (Olive Marie) (singer, actress); Ogden, Utah, 10/13/59
O'Sullivan, Maureen (actress); County Roscommon, Ireland **(1911–1998)**
Oswald, Lee Harvey (presumed assassin); New Orleans **(1939–1963)**
Otis, Elisha (inventor); Halifax, Vt. **(1811–1861)**
O'Toole, Peter (actor); Connemara, Ireland, 8/2/32
Ovid (Publius Ovidius Naso) (poet); Sulmona, Italy **(43 B.C.–A.D. 17)**
Ovitz, Michael (entertainment executive); Chicago, 12/14/46
Owens, Buck (Alvis Edgar Owens) (singer); Sherman, Tex., 8/12/29
Ozawa, Seiji (orchestra conductor); Fentian (Shenyan), Manchuria, 7/1/35

P

Paar, Jack (TV personality); Canton, Ohio, 5/1/18
Pacino, Al (Alfred) (actor); New York City, 4/25/40
Packard, Vance (author); Granville Summit, Pa. **(1914–1996)**
Paderewski, Ignace Jan (pianist, statesman); Kurylowka, Russian Podolia **(1860–1941)**
Paganini, Nicolò (violinist); Genoa, Italy **(1782–1840)**
Page, Geraldine (actress); Kirksville, Mo. **(1924–1987)**
Page, Jimmy (musician); Heston, Ireland, 1/9/44
Page, Patti (Clara Ann Fowler) (singer, entertainer); Claremore, Okla., 11/8/27
Pagels, Elaine Hiesey (religious scholar); Palo Alto, Calif., 2/13/43
Paglia, Camille (writer, social critic); Endicott, N.Y., 4/2/47
Paine, Thomas (political philosopher); Thetford, England **(1737–1809)**
Pakula, Alan J. (film director); New York City **(1928–1998)**
Palance, Jack (Walter Palanuik) (actor); Lattimer, Pa., 2/18/19
Palestrina, Giovanni Pierluigi da (composer); Palestrina, Italy **(1526–1594)**
Paley, William S. (broadcasting executive); Chicago **(1901–1990)**
Palladio, Andrea (architect); Padua or Vicenza, Italy **(1508–1580)**
Palmer, Robert (rock musician); Batley, England, 1/19/49
Palmerston, Henry John Templeton (3rd Viscount) (statesman); Broadlands, England **(1784–1865)**
Palminteri, Chazz (Calogero Lorenzo Palminteri) (actor, writer); Bronx, New York, 5/15/51
Paltrow, Gwyneth (actress); Los Angeles, 9/28/73
Papanicolaou, George N. (physician); Coumi, Greece **(1883–1962)**
Papas, Irene (Lelekou) (actress); Chiliomodian, Greece, 3/9/26
Papp, Joseph (Joseph Papirofsky) (stage producer, director); Brooklyn, N.Y. **(1921–1991)**
Paracelsus, Philippus (Aureolus Theophrastus Bombastus von Hohenheim) (physican); Einsiedeln, Switzerland **(1493–1541)**
Park, Chung Hee (ex-president of South Korea); Sangmo-ri, Korea **(1917–1979)**
Parker, Alan (director); London, 2/14/44
Parker, Charlie "Bird" (jazz musician); Kansas City, Kans. **(1920–1955)**
Parker, Dorothy (Dorothy Rothschild) (author); West End, N.J. **(1893–1967)**
Parker, Fess (actor); Fort Worth, Tex., 8/16/25
Parker, Sarah Jessica (actress); Nelsonville, Ohio, 3/25/65
Parker, Suzy (model, actress); San Antonio, 10/28/33
Parkinson, C(yril) Northcote (historian); Durham, England **(1909–1993)**
Parkman, Francis (historian); Boston **(1823–1893)**
Parks, Bert (Bert Jacobson) (entertainer); Atlanta **(1914–1992)**
Parks, Gordon (film director); Ft. Scott, Kans., 11/30/12
Parks, Rosa (civil rights activist); Tuskegee, Ala., 2/4/13
Parnell, Charles Stewart (statesman); Avondale, Ireland **(1846–1891)**
Parnis, Mollie (Mollie Parnis Livingston) (fashion designer); New York City **(1905?–1992)**
Parsons, Estelle (actress); Marblehead, Mass., 11/20/27
Parton, Dolly (singer); Locust Ridge, Tenn., 1/19/46
Pascal, Blaise (philosopher); Clermont, France **(1623–1662)**
Pasternak, Boris Leonidovich (author); Moscow **(1890–1960)**

Pasternak, Joseph (film producer); Silagy-Somlyo, Romania **(1901–1991)**

Pasteur, Louis (chemist); Dôle, France **(1822–1895)**

Pastor, Tony (Antonio) (actor, theater manager); New York City **(1837–1908)**

Pater, Walter (Horatio) (writer); London **(1839–1894)**

Patinkin, Mandy (Mandel) (actor, singer); Chicago, 11/30/52

Paton, Alan (author); Pietermaritzburg, South Africa **(1903–1988)**

Patric, Jason (actor); Queens, N.Y., 6/17/66

Patti, Adelina (soprano); Madrid **(1843–1919)**

Patton, George Smith, Jr. (general); San Gabriel, Calif. **(1885–1945)**

Paul, Alice (feminist, woman suffragist); Moorestown, N.J. **(1885–1977)**

Paul, Les (Lester William Polfus) (guitarist); Waukesha, Wis., 6/9/15

Paul VI (Giovanni Battista Montini) (Pope); Concesio, nr. Brescia, Italy **(1897–1978)**

Pauley, Jane (Margaret Jane Pauley) (TV newscaster); Indianapolis, 10/31/50

Pauling, Linus Carl (chemist, Nobel laureate); Portland, Ore. **(1901–1994)**

Pavarotti, Luciano (tenor); Modena, Italy, 10/12/35

Pavlov, Ivan Petrovich (physiologist); Ryazan district, Russia **(1849–1936)**

Pavlova, Anna (ballet dancer); St. Petersburg, Russia **(1885–1931)**

Paxton, Bill (actor); Fort Worth, Texas, 5/17/55

Peale, Norman Vincent (clergyman); Bowersville, Ohio **(1898–1993)**

Pearl, Minnie (Sarah Ophelia Colley Cannon) (comedienne, singer); Centerville, Tenn. **(1912–1996)**

Pears, Peter (tenor); Farnham, England **(1910–1986)**

Pearson, Drew (Andrew Russel Pearson) (columnist); Evanston, Ill. **(1897–1969)**

Pearson, Lester B. (statesman); Toronto **(1897–1972)**

Peary, Robert Edwin (explorer); Cresson, Pa. **(1856–1920)**

Peck, Gregory (Eldred Gregory Peck) (actor); La Jolla, Calif., 4/5/16

Peckinpah, Sam (film director); Fresno, Calif. **(1925–1984)**

Peerce, Jan (tenor); New York City **(1904–1984)**

Pegler, (James) Westbrook (columnist); Minneapolis **(1894–1969)**

Pei, I(eoh) M(ing) (architect); Canton, China, 4/26/17

Penn, Arthur (director); Philadelphia, 9/27/22

Penn, Sean (actor, filmmaker); Los Angeles, 8/17/60

Penn, William (American colonist); London **(1644–1718)**

Penney, James C. (merchant); Hamilton, Mo. **(1875–1971)**

Peppard, George (actor); Detroit **(1928–1994)**

Pepys, Samuel (diarist); Bampton, England **(1633–1703)**

Perelman, S(idney) J(oseph) (writer); Brooklyn, N.Y. **(1904–1979)**

Perez, Rosie (actress, dancer, choreographer); Brooklyn, New York, 5/16/63

Pergolesi, Giovanni Battista (composer); Jesi, Italy **(1710–1736)**

Pericles (statesman); Athens died 429 B.C.

Perkins, Anthony (actor); New York City **(1932–1992)**

Perkins, Frances (social reformer); Boston **(1882–1965)**

Perlman, Itzhak (violinist); Tel Aviv, Israel, 8/31/45

Perlman, Rhea (actress); Brooklyn, N.Y., 3/31/48

Perón, Isabel (María Estela Martínez Cartas) (former chief of state); La Rioja, Argentina, 2/4/31

Perón, Juan D. (statesman); nr. Lobos, Argentina **(1895–1974)**

Perón, Maria Eva Duarte de (political leader); Los Toldos, Argentina **(1919–1952)**

Perot, H. Ross (business executive); Texarkana, Tex., 6/27/30

Perrine, Valerie (actress, dancer); Galveston, Tex., 9/3/43

Perry, Luke (Coy Luther Perry III) (actor); Fredericktown, Ohio, 10/11/66

Perry, Matthew (actor); Williamstown, Mass., 8/19/69

Pershing, John Joseph (general); Linn County, Mo. **(1860–1948)**

Pestalozzi, Johann (educator); Zurich, Switzerland **(1746–1827)**

Peters, Bernadette (Bernadette Lazzara) (actress); New York City, 2/28/48

Peters, Brock (actor, singer); New York City, 7/2/27

Peters, Jean (actress); Canton, Ohio, 10/15/26

Peters, Roberta (Roberta Peterman) (soprano); New York City, 5/4/30

Petit, Roland (choreographer, dancer); Villemombe, France, 1924

Petrarch (Francesco Petrarca) (poet); Arezzo, Italy **(1304–1374)**

Petty, Tom (folk/rock musician); Gainesville, Fla., 10/20/50

Pfeiffer, Michelle (actress); Santa Ana, Calif., 4/29/58

Philbin, Regis (talk show host); New York City, 8/25/33

Philip (Philip Mountbatten) (Duke of Edinburgh); Corfu, Greece, 6/10/21

Phillippe, Ryan (actor); New Castle, Del., 9/10/75

Phoenix, Joaquin (actor); Puerto Rico, 10/28/74

Phoenix, River (actor); Madras, Ore. **(1970–1993)**

Piaf, Edith (Edith Gassion) (singer); Paris **(1916–1963)**

Piatigorsky, Gregor (cellist); Ekaterinoslav, Russia **(1903–1976)**

Piazza, Marguerite (soprano); New Orleans, 5/6/26

Picasso, Pablo (painter, sculptor); Málaga, Spain **(1881–1973)**

Pickett, Wilson (singer); Prattville, Ala., 3/18/41

Pickford, Mary (Gladys Mary Smith) (actress); Toronto **(1893–1979)**

Picon, Molly (actress); New York City **(1898–1992)**

Pidgeon, Walter (actor); East St. John, N.B., Canada **(1898–1984)**

Hyde Pierce, David (actor); Saratoga Springs, N.Y., 4/3/59

Pierce, Franklin (14th U.S. president); Hillsboro, N.H. **(1804–1869)**

Pileggi, Mitch (actor); Portland, Ore., 4/5/52

Pinkett-Smith, Jada (actress); Baltimore, 9/18/71

Pinsky, Robert (poet laureate of the U.S.); Long Branch, N.J., 10/20/40

Pinochet (Ugarte), Augusto (former leader of Chile's military government); Valparaiso, Chile, 11/25/15

Pinter, Harold (playwright); London, 10/10/30

Pinza, Ezio (basso); Rome **(1892–1957)**

Pirandello, Luigi (dramatist, novelist); nr. Girgenti, Italy **(1867–1936)**

Piranesi, Giambattista (artist); Mestre, Italy **(1720–1778)**

Pissaro, Camille Jacob (painter); St. Thomas, U.S. Virgin Islands **(1830–1903)**

Piston, Walter (composer); Rockland, Maine **(1894–1976)**

Pitman, Sir [Isaac] James (educator, publisher); Bath, England **(1901–1985)**

Pitt, Brad (actor); Shawnee, Okla., 12/18/63

Pitt, William ("Younger Pitt") (statesman); nr. Bromley, England **(1759–1806)**

Pitts, ZaSu (actress); Parsons, Kans. **(1898–1963)**

Pius XII (Eugenio Pacelli) (Pope); Rome **(1876–1958)**

Pizarro, Francisco (explorer); Trujillo, Spain **(c. 1476–1541)**

Planck, Max (physicist); Kiel, Germany **(1858–1947)**

Plant, Robert (musician, singer, song writer); West Bromwich, Staffordshire, England , 8/20/48

Plath, Sylvia (poet); Boston **(1932–1963)**

Plato (Aristocles) (philosopher); Athens **(c. 427–347 B.C.)**

Pleasence, Donald (actor); Worksop, England **(1919–1995)**

Pleshette, Suzanne (actress); New York City, 1/31/37

Plimpton, George (author); New York City, 3/18/27

Plimpton, Martha (actress); New York City, 11/16/70

Plisetskaya, Maya (ballet dancer); Moscow, 11/20/25

Plowright, Joan (actress); Brigg, England, 10/28/29

Plummer, Christopher (actor); Toronto, 12/13/29

Plutarch (biographer); Chaeronea, Greece **(c. 46–c. 120)**

Pocahontas (Matoaka) (American Indian princess); Virginia **(c. 1595–1617)**

Podhoretz, Norman (author); Brooklyn, N.Y., 1/16/30

Poe, Edgar Allan (poet, story writer); Boston **(1809–1849)**

Poitier, Sidney (actor, director); Miami, Fla., 2/20/24

Polanski, Roman (director); Paris, 8/18/33

Polk, James Knox (11th U.S. president); Mecklenburg County, N.C. **(1795–1849)**

Pollack, Sydney (film director, producer, actor); Lafayette, Ind., 7/1/34

Pollard, Michael J. (actor); Passaic, N.J., 5/30/39

Pollock, Jackson (painter); Cody, Wyo. **(1912–1956)**

Polo, Marco (traveler); Venice **(c. 1254–1324)**

Pol Pot (Cambodian dictator); Kompong Thom, Cambodia **(1925–1998)**

Pompadour, Mme. de (Jeanne Antoinette Poisson) (courtesan); Versailles **(1721–1764)**

Pompey (Gnaeus Pompeius Magnus) (general); Rome **(106–48 B.C.)**

Ponce de León, Juan (explorer); Servas, Spain **(c. 1460–1521)**

Pons, Lily (coloratura soprano); Cannes, France **(1904–1976)**

Ponselle, Rosa (soprano); Meriden, Conn. **(1897–1981)**

Ponti, Carlo (director); Milan, Italy, 12/11/13

Pontormo, Jacopo da (painter); Pontormo, Italy **(1492–1557)**

Pope, Alexander (poet); London **(1688–1744)**

Porter, Cole (songwriter); Peru, Ind. **(1891–1964)**

Porter, Katherine Anne (novelist); Indian Creek, Tex. **(1891–1980)**

Portman, Natalie (actress); Jerusalem, 6/9/81

Posey, Parker (actress); Baltimore, 11/8/68

Post, Wiley (aviator); Grand Plain, Tex. **(1900–1935)**

Poston, Tom (actor); Columbus, Ohio, 10/17/27

Potëmkin, Grigori Aleksandrovich, Prince (statesman); Khizovo (Khizov), Belarus **(1739–1791)**

Potok, Chaim (author); New York City, 2/17/29

Potter, (Helen) Beatrix (author, illustrator); South Kensington, Middlesex, England **(1866–1943)**

Potts, Annie (actress); Nashville, Tenn., 10/28/52

Poulenc, Francis (composer); Paris **(1899–1963)**

Pound, Ezra (poet); Hailey, Idaho **(1885–1972)**
Poussin, Nicolas (painter); Villers, France **(1594–1665)**
Powell, Adam Clayton, Jr. (congressman); New Haven, Conn. **(1908–1972)**
Powell, Colin L. (retired general); New York City, 4/5/37
Powell, Dick (actor); Mt. View, Ark. **(1904–1963)**
Powell, Eleanor (actress, tap dancer); Springfield, Mass. **(1912–1982)**
Powell, William (actor); Pittsburgh **(1892–1984)**
Power, Tyrone (actor); Cincinnati, Ohio **(1914–1958)**
Powers, Stefanie (Stefania Zofia Federkiewicz) (actress); Hollywood, Calif., 11/12/42
Praxiteles (sculptor); Athens **(c. 370–c. 330 B.C.)**
Preminger, Otto (director, producer); Vienna **(1906–1986)**
Prentiss, Paula (Paula Ragusa) (actress); San Antonio, 3/4/39
Presley, Elvis (singer, actor); Tupelo, Miss. **(1935–1977)**
Presley, Priscilla (actress); Brooklyn, N.Y., 5/24/45
Preston, Robert (Robert Preston Meservey) (actor); Newton Highlands, Mass. **(1918–1987)**
Previn, André (conductor); Berlin, 4/6/29
Price, Leontyne (Mary) (soprano); Laurel, Miss., 2/10/27
Price, Ray (country music artist); Perryville, Tex., 1/12/26
Price, Vincent (actor); St. Louis **(1911–1993)**
Pride, Charley (singer); Sledge, Miss., 3/18/38?
Priestley, Jason (actor, producer); Vancouver, B.C., Canada, 8/28/69
Priestley, J. B. (John B.) (author); Bradford, England **(1894–1984)**
Priestley, Joseph (chemist); nr. Leeds, England **(1733–1804)**
Primakov, Yevgeny (Russian political leader); Kiev, Ukraine, 10/29/29
Primrose, William (violist); Glasgow, Scotland **(1904–1982)**
Prince (Prince Rogers Nelson) (singer); Minneapolis, 6/7/58
Prince, Harold (stage producer); New York City, 1/30/28
Principal, Victoria (actress); Fukuoka, Japan, 1/3/45
Prinze, Freddie (actor); New York City **(1954–1977)**
Pritchett, V(ictor) S(awdon) (literary critic); Ipswich, England **(1900–1997)**
Procter, William (scientist); Cincinnati **(1872–1951)**
Prokofiev, Sergei Sergeevich (composer); St. Petersburg, Russia **(1891–1953)**
Proulx, E. Annie (novelist); Norwich, Conn., 8/22/35
Proust, Marcel (novelist); Paris **(1871–1922)**
Provine, Dorothy (actress); Deadwood, S.D., 1/20/37
Prowse, Juliet (actress, dancer); Bombay (Mumbai) **(1936–1996)**
Pryce, Jonathan (actor); Holywell, Wales, 6/1/47
Pryor, Richard (comedian); Peoria, Ill., 12/1/40
Ptolemy (Claudius Ptolemaeus) (astronomer, geographer); Ptolemais Hermii, Egypt, fl. 2nd cent.
Pucci, Emilio (Marchese di Barsento) (fashion designer); Naples, Italy **(1914–1992)**
Puccini, Giacomo (composer); Lucca, Italy **(1858–1924)**
Puente, Tito (band leader); New York City **(1923–2000)**
Pulaski, Casimir (military officer); Podolia, Poland **(1748–1779)**
Pulitzer, Joseph (publisher); Makó, Hungary **(1847–1911)**
Pullman, Bill (actor); Delphi, N.Y., 12/17/53
Pullman, George (inventor); Brockton, N.Y. **(1831–1897)**
Purcell, Henry (composer); London **(1658–1695)**
Pusey, Nathan M. (educator); Council Bluffs, Iowa, 4/4/07
Pushkin, Alexander Sergeevich (poet, dramatist); Moscow **(1799–1837)**
Putin, Vladimir (president of Russia); Leningrad, 1952
Puzo, Mario (novelist); New York City **(1921–1999)**
Pyle, Ernest Taylor (journalist); Dana, Ind. **(1900–1945)**
Pythagoras (mathematician, philosopher); Samos, Greece **(c. 582–c. 507A.D.)**

Q

Qaddafi, Muammar al- (Libyan leader); Libya, 1942
Quaid, Dennis (actor); Houston, 4/9/54
Quaid, Randy, (actor); Houston, 10/1/50
Quayle, Anthony (actor); Ainsdale, England **(1913–1989)**
Queen, Ellery: pen name of Frederic Dannay and Manfred B. Lee
Queen Latifah (Dana Owens) (rap musician, actress); Newark, New Jersey, 3/18/70
Queler, Eve (conductor); New York City, 1/1/36
Quennell, Sir Peter Courtney (biographer); Bromley, England **(1905–1993)**
Quindlen, Anna (writer); Philadelphia, 7/8/53
Quinn, Aidan (actor); Chicago, 3/8/59
Quinn, Anthony (Antonio Quiñones) (actor); Chihuahua, Mexico, 4/21/16

R

Rabe, David (playwright); Dubuque, Iowa, 3/10/40
Rabelais, François (satirist); nr. Chinon, France **(c. 1490–1553)**
Rabi, I(sidor) I(saac) (physicist); Rymanow, Poland **(1898–1988)**
Rabin, Yitzhak (former Israeli prime minister); Jerusalem **(1922–1995)**
Rachmaninoff, Sergei Wassilievitch (pianist, composer); Oneg Estate, Novgorod, Russia **(1873–1943)**
Racine, Jean Baptiste (dramatist); La Ferté-Milon, France **(1639–1699)**
Radner, Gilda (comedienne); Detroit **(1946–1989)**
Raft, George (actor); New York City **(1895–1980)**
Rainier III (Prince); Monaco, 5/31/23
Rains, Claude (actor); London **(1889–1967)**
Raitt, Bonnie (singer); Burbank, Calif., 11/8/49
Raitt, John (actor, singer); Santa Ana, Calif., 1/19/17
Raleigh, Sir Walter (courtier, navigator); London **(1552?–1618)**
Rambeau, Marjorie (actress); San Francisco **(1889–1970)**
Rameau, Jean-Philippe (composer); Dijon, France **(1683–1764)**
Rampal, Jean-Pierre (Louis) (flutist); Marseilles, France, 7/1/22
Rand, Ayn (novelist, philosopher); St. Petersburg, Russia **(1905–1982)**
Randall, Tony (Leonard Rosenberg) (actor); Tulsa, Okla., 2/26/20
Randolph, A(sa) Philip (labor leader); Crescent City, Fla. **(1889–1979)**
Rankin, Jeannette (politician, pacifist); Missoula, Mont. **(1880–1973)**
Raphael (Raffaello Santi) (painter, architect); Urbino, Italy **(1483–1520)**
Rasputin, Grigori Efimovich (monk); Tobolsk Province, Russia **(1872–1916)**
Rathbone, Basil (Philip St. John Basil Rathbone) (actor); Johannesburg, South Africa **(1892–1967)**
Rather, Dan (TV newscaster); Wharton, Tex., 10/31/31
Rattigan, Terence (playwright); London **(1911–1977)**
Ratzenberger, John (actor); Bridgeport, Conn., 4/6/47
Rauschenberg, Robert (painter); Port Arthur, Tex., 10/22/25
Ravel, Maurice Joseph (composer); Ciboure, France **(1875–1937)**
Ray, Aldo (DaRe) (actor); Pen Argyl, Pa. **(1926–1991)**
Ray, Gene Anthony (actor, dancer); Harlem, N.Y., 5/24/63
Ray, Man (painter); Philadelphia **(1890–1976)**
Ray, Satyajit (film director); Calcutta **(1921–1992)**
Raye, Martha (Margie Yvonne Reed) (comedienne, actress); Butte, Mont. **(1916–1994)**
Rea, Stephen (actor); Belfast, Ireland, 10/31/43
Reagan, Ronald Wilson (40th U.S. president, actor); Tampico, Ill., 2/6/11
Reasoner, Harry (TV commentator); Dakota City, Iowa **(1923–1991)**
Redding, Otis (singer); Dawson, Ga. **(1941–1967)**
Reddy, Helen (singer); Melbourne, Australia, 10/25/41
Redford, Robert (Charles Robert Redford, Jr.) (actor); Santa Monica, Calif., 8/18/37
Redgrave, Lynn (actress); London, 3/8/43
Redgrave, Sir Michael (actor); Bristol, England **(1908–1985)**
Redgrave, Vanessa (actress); London, 1/30/37
Redon, Odilon (artist); Bordeaux, France **(1840–1916)**
Reed, Donna (Donna Belle Mullenger) (actress); Denison, Iowa **(1921–1986)**
Reed, Lou (Lewis Allen Reed) (musician, guitarist, singer, song writer); Freeport, N.Y., 3/ 2/42
Reed, Rex (critic); Ft. Worth, 10/2/40
Reed, Walter (army surgeon); Belroi, Va. **(1851–1902)**
Reese, Della (Deloreese Patricia Early) (singer, actress); Detroit, 7/6/32
Reeve, Christopher (actor, activist); New York City, 9/25/52
Reeves, Jim (singer); Panola County, Tex. **(1923–1964)**
Reeves, Keanu (actor, musician); Beirut, Lebanon, 9/2/64
Reich, Robert (Clinton Cabinet Member); Scranton, Pa., 6/24/46
Reich, Steve (composer); New York City, 10/3/36
Reid, Wallace (actor); St. Louis **(1891–1923)**
Reiner, Carl (actor); New York City, 3/20/22
Reiner, Fritz (conductor); Budapest **(1888–1963)**
Reiner, Robert (actor, director, writer, producer); Bronx, N.Y., 3/6/45
Reinhardt, Max (Max Goldmann) (theater producer); nr. Vienna **(1873–1943)**
Reiser, Paul (actor, producer); New York City, 3/30/57
Remarque, Erich Maria (novelist); Osnabrük, Germany **(1898–1970)**
Rembrandt (Rembrandt Harmensz van Rijn) (painter); Leyden, Netherlands **(1605–1669)**
Remick, Lee (Ann) (actress); Boston **(1935–1991)**

Remnick, David (writer, editor); Hackensack, N.J., 10/29/58
Renfro, Brad (actor); Knoxville, Tenn., 7/25/82
Rennert, Günther (opera director, producer); Essen, Germany, 4/1/11
Rennie, Michael (actor); Bradford, England **(1909–1971)**
Reno, Janet (U.S. Attorney General); Miami, Fla., 7/21/38
Renoir, Jean (film director, writer); Paris **(1894–1979)**
Renoir, Pierre Auguste (painter); Limoges, France **(1841–1919)**
Resnais, Alain (film director); Vannes, France, 6/3/22
Resnik, Regina (mezzo-soprano); New York City, 8/30/22
Respighi, Ottorino (composer); Bologna, Italy **(1879–1936)**
Reston, James (journalist); Clydebank, Scotland **(1909–1995)**
Reuther, Walter (labor leader); Wheeling, W. Va. **(1907–1970)**
Revere, Paul (silversmith, hero of famous ride); Boston **(1735–1818)**
Revson, Charles (business executive); Boston **(1906–1975)**
Reynolds, Burt (actor, director, producer); Waycross, Ga., 2/11/36
Reynolds, Debbie (Marie Frances Reynolds) (actress); El Paso, Tex., 4/1/32
Reynolds, Sir Joshua (painter); nr. Plymouth, England **(1723–1792)**
Reynolds, Marjorie (Marjorie Goodspeed) (actress); Buhl, Idaho **(1921–1997)**
Reznor, Trent (musician); Mercer, Pa., 5/17/65
Rhodes, Cecil John (South African statesman); Bishop Stortford, England **(1853–1902)**
Ricci, Christina (actress); Santa Monica, Calif., 2/12/80
Rice, Anne (novelist); New Orleans, 10/14/41
Rice, Elmer (Elmer Leopold Reizenstein) (playwright); New York City **(1892–1967)**
Rice, Grantland (sports writer); Murfreesboro, Tenn. **(1880–1954)**
Rich, Buddy (Bernard) (drummer); Brooklyn, N.Y. **(1917–1987)**
Rich, Charlie (singer); Colt, Ark. **(1932–1995)**
Richard I the Lion-hearted (King of England); Oxford, England **(1157–1199)**
Richards, Ann (Dorothy Ann Willis) (ex-governor of Texas); Lakeview, Tex., 9/1/33
Richards, Keith (rock singer); Dartford, England, 12/18/43
Richards, Michael (actor); California, 7/21/48
Richardson, Elliot L. (ex-Cabinet member); Boston **(1920–1999)**
Richardson, Sir Ralph (actor); Cheltenham, England **(1902–1983)**
Richardson, Tony (director); Shipley, England **(1928–1991)**
Richelieu, Duc de (Armand Jean du Plessis) (cardinal); Paris **(1585–1642)**
Richie, Lionel (singer, songwriter); Tuskegee, Ala., 6/20/49
Richter, Charles Francis (seismologist); Hamilton, Ohio **(1900–1985)**
Richter, Sviatoslav (pianist); Zhitomir, Ukraine, 3/20/14
Rickenbacker, Eddie (Edward V.) (aviator); Columbus, Ohio **(1890–1973)**
Rickles, Don (comedian); New York City, 5/8/26
Rickover, Vice Admiral Hyman G. (atomic energy expert); Russia **(1900–1986)**
Riddle, Nelson (composer); Hackensack, N.J. **(1921–1985)**
Ride, Sally K(risten) (astronaut, astrophysicist); Encino, Calif., 5/26/51
Ridgway, General Matthew B. (ex-Army Chief of Staff); Ft. Monroe, Va. **(1895–1993)**
Riemenschneider, Tilman (sculptor); Osterode, Germany **(c. 1460–1531)**
Rigg, Diana (actress); Doncaster, England, 7/20/38
Riley, James Whitcomb (poet); Greenfield, Ind. **(1849–1916)**
Rilke, Rainer Maria (poet); Prague **(1875–1926)**
Rimbaud, (Jean Nicolas) Arthur (poet); Charleville, France **(1854–1891)**
Rimes, LeAnn (singer); Jackson, Miss., 8/28/82
Rimsky-Korsakov, Nikolai Andreevich (composer); Tikhvin, Russia **(1844–1908)**
Rinehart, Mary (née Roberts) (novelist); Pittsburgh **(1876–1958)**
Ringwald, Molly (actress); Sacramento, Calif., 2/18/68
Ritchard, Cyril (actor director); Sydney, Australia **(1898–1977)**
Ritter, John (Jonathan) (actor); Burbank, Calif., 9/17/48
Ritter, Tex (Woodward Maurice Ritter) (singer); Panola County, Tex. **(1905–1973)**
Ritter, Thelma (actress); Brooklyn, N.Y. **(1905–1969)**
Rivera, Chita (Dolores Conchita Figuero del Rivero) (dancer, actress, singer); Washington, D.C., 1/23/33
Rivera, Diego (painter); Guanajuato, Mexico **(1886–1957)**
Rivera, Geraldo (Miguel Rivera) (TV host); New York City, 7/4/43
Rivers, Joan (comedienne); Brooklyn, N.Y., 6/8/33
Rivers, Larry (Yitzroch Loiza Grossberg) (painter); New York City, 8/17/23
Roach, Hal (film producer); Elmira, N.Y. **(1892–1992)**
Robards, Jason, Jr. (actor); Chicago, 7/22/22

Robards, Jason, Sr. (actor); Hillsdale, Mich. **(1892–1963)**
Robbins, Harold (Harold Rubin) (novelist); New York City **(1916–1997)**
Robbins, Jerome (Jerome Rabinowitz) (choreographer); New York City **(1918–1998)**
Robbins, Marty (singer); Glendale, Ariz. **(1925–1982)**
Robbins, Tim (Timothy Francis) (actor, director); West Covina, Calif., 10/16/58
Roberts, Cokie (Mary Martha Corinne Morrison Claiborne Boggs) (broadcast journalist); New Orleans, 12/27/43
Roberts, Eric (actor); Biloxi, Miss., 4/18/56
Roberts, Julia (actress); Smyrna, Ga., 10/28/67
Roberts, Oral (Granville) (evangelist, publisher); nr. Ada, Okla., 1/24/18
Robertson, Cliff (Clifford Parker Robertson III) (actor); La Jolla, Calif., 9/9/25
Robertson, Dale (Dayle) (actor); Oklahoma City, 7/14/23
Robeson, Paul (singer, actor); Princeton, N.J. **(1898–1976)**
Robespierre, Maximilien François Marie Isidore de (French Revolutionist); Arras, France **(1758–1794)**
Robinson, Bill "Bojangles" (Luther) (dancer); Richmond, Va. **(1878–1949)**
Robinson, Edward G. (Emanuel Goldenberg) (actor); Bucharest **(1893–1973)**
Robinson, Edwin Arlington (poet); Head Tide, Maine **(1869–1935)**
Robinson Peete, Holly (Holly Robinson) (actress); Philadelphia, 9/18/64
Robinson, Robert (chemist, Nobel laureate); Chesterfield, Derbyshire, England **(1885–1975)**
Robinson, Smokey (singer, songwriter); Detroit, 2/19/40
Rock, Chris (comedian, actor); Brooklyn, New York, 2/7/66
Rockefeller, David (banker); New York City, 6/12/15
Rockefeller, John Davison (business executive); Richford, N.Y. **(1839–1937)**
Rockefeller, John Davison, Jr. (industrialist); Cleveland **(1874–1960)**
Rockefeller, John D., 3rd (philanthropist); New York City **(1906–1978)**
Rockefeller, Laurance S. (conservationist); New York City, 5/26/10
Rockwell, Norman (painter, illustrator); New York City **(1894–1978)**
Roddenberry, Gene (creator of Star Trek); El Paso, Tex. **(1921–1991)**
Rodgers, Jimmie (singer); Meridian, Miss. **(1897–1933)**
Rodgers, Richard (composer); New York City **(1902–1979)**
Rodin, François Auguste René (sculptor); Paris **(1840–1917)**
Rodzinski, Artur (conductor); Spalato, Dalmatia **(1894–1958)**
Roeg, Nicolas (film director); London, 8/15/28
Roentgen, Wilhelm Konrad (physicist); Lennep, Prussia **(1845–1923)**
Roethke, Theodore (poet); Saginaw, Mich. **(1908–1963)**
Rogers, Buddy (Charles Rogers) (actor); Olathe, Kans. **(1904–1999)**
Rogers, Carl (psychologist); Oak Park, Ill. **(1902–1987)**
Rogers, Fred (TV producer, host); Latrobe, Pa., 3/20/28
Rogers, Ginger (Virginia McMath) (dancer, actress); Independence, Mo. **(1911–1995)**
Rogers, Kenny (singer); Houston, 8/21/38
Rogers, Mimi (actress); Coral Gables, Fla., 1/27/56
Rogers, Roy (Leonard Frank Slye) (actor, singer); Cincinnati **(1911–1998)**
Rogers, Wayne (actor); Birmingham, Ala., 4/7/33
Rogers, Will (William Penn Adair Rogers) (humorist); Oologah, Okla. **(1879–1935)**
Rogers, William P. (ex-secretary of state); Norfolk, N.Y., 6/23/13
Roland, Gilbert (Luis Antonio Damaso de Alonso) (actor); Juarez, Mexico **(1905–1994)**
Rolland, Romain (author); Clamecy, France **(1866–1944)**
Rollins, Sonny (saxophonist); New York City, 9/7/30
Romberg, Sigmund (composer); Szeged, Hungary **(1887–1951)**
Rome, Harold (composer); Hartford, Conn. **(1908–1993)**
Romero, Cesar (actor); New York City **(1907–1994)**
Romney, George W. (automobile executive, governor); Chihuahua, Mexico **(1907–1995)**
Romulo, Carlos P. (diplomat, educator); Manila **(1899–1985)**
Ronsard, Pierre de (poet); La Possonnière nr. Couture, France **(1524–1585)**
Ronstadt, Linda (singer); Tucson, Ariz., 7/30/46
Rooney, Andy (TV personality); Albany, N.Y., 1/14/19
Rooney, Mickey (Joe Yule, Jr.) (actor); Brooklyn, N.Y., 9/23/20
Roosevelt, (Anna) Eleanor (reformer, humanitarian); New York City **(1884–1962)**
Roosevelt, Franklin Delano (32nd U.S. president); Hyde Park, N.Y. **(1882–1945)**

Roosevelt, Theodore (26th U.S. president); New York City **(1858–1919)**
Rorem, Ned (composer); Richmond, Ind., 10/23/23
Rose, Billy (showman); New York City **(1899–1966)**
Rose, Leonard (concert cellist); Washington, D.C. **(1918–1984)**
Roseanne (Roseanne Barr) (actress); Salt Lake City, 11/3/52
Rosenberg, Ethel (spy); New York City **(1915–1953)**
Rosenberg, Julius (spy); New York City **(1918–1953)**
Ross, Betsy (Betsey Griscom) (flagmaker); Philadelphia **(1752–1836)**
Ross, Diana (singer); Detroit, 3/26/44
Ross, Katharine (actress); Hollywood, Calif., 1/29/42
Rossellini, Isabella (model, actress); Rome, Italy, 6/18/52
Rossellini, Roberto (film director); Rome **(1906–1977)**
Rossetti, Christina Georgina (poet); London **(1830–1894)**
Rossetti, Dante Gabriel (painter, poet); London **(1828–1882)**
Rossini, Gioacchino Antonio (composer); Pesaro, Italy **(1792–1868)**
Rosten, Leo (writer); Lódz, Poland **(1908–1997)**
Rostand, Edmond (dramatist); Marseilles, France **(1868–1918)**
Rostow, Walt Whitman (economist); New York City, 10/7/16
Rostropovich, Mstislav (cellist, conductor); Baku, Azerbaijan, 3/27/27
Roth, Henry (writer); Tysmenica, Ukraine **(1906–1995)**
Roth, Philip (novelist); Newark, N.J., 3/19/33
Roth, Tim (actor); London, 5/14/64
Rothko, Mark (Marcus Rothkovich) (painter); Russia **(1903–1970)**
Rouault, Georges (painter); Paris **(1871–1958)**
Roundtree, Richard (actor); New Rochelle, N.Y., 9/7/42
Rousseau, Henri (painter); Laval, France **(1844–1910)**
Rousseau, Jean Jacques (philosopher); Geneva **(1712–1778)**
Rovere, Richard H. (journalist); Jersey City, N.J., 5/5/15
Rowan, Carl Thomas (journalist); Ravenscroft, Tenn. **(1925–2000)**
Rowan, Dan (comedian); Beggs, Okla. **(1922–1987)**
Rowlands, Gena (actress); Cambria, Wis., 6/19/30
Royko, Mike (columnist); Chicago **(1932–1997)**
Rubens, Sir Peter Paul (painter); Siegen, Germany **(1577–1640)**
Rubinstein, Arthur (concert pianist); Lódz, Poland **(1887–1982)**
Rubinstein, Helena (cosmetics executive); Kraków, Poland **(1882?–1965)**
Rubinstein, John (actor, composer); Los Angeles, 12/8/46
Rucker, Darius (musician, singer, songwriter); Charleston, S.C., 5/13/66
Rudel, Julius (conductor); Vienna, 3/6/21
Ruffo, Titta (baritone); Italy **(1878–1953)**
Runyon, (Alfred) Damon (journalist); Manhattan, Kans. **(1884–1945)**
Rushdie, (Ahmed) Salman (novelist); Bombay (Mumbai), 6/19/47
Rusk, Dean (ex-sec. of state); Cherokee County, Ga. **(1909–1994)**
Ruskin, John (art critic); London **(1819–1900)**
Russell, Keri (actress); Fountain Valley, Calif., 3/23/76
Russell, Lord Bertrand (Arthur William) (mathematician, philosopher); Trelleck, Wales **(1872–1970)**
Russell, Jane (actress); Bemidji, Minn., 6/21/21
Russell, Ken (film director); Southampton, England, 4/3/27
Russell, Kurt (actor); Springfield, Mass., 3/17/51
Russell, Leon (pianist, singer); Lawton, Okla., 4/2/41
Russell, Lillian (Helen Louise Leonard) (soprano); Clinton, Iowa **(1861–1922)**
Russell, Mark (satirist); Buffalo, N.Y., 8/23/32
Russell, Nipsy (comedian); Atlanta, 10/13/24
Russell, Rosalind (actress); Waterbury, Conn. **(1912–1976)**
Russell, Theresa (Theresa Paup) (actress); San Diego, Calif., 3/20/57
Russo, Rene (actress); Burbank, Calif., 2/17/54
Rustin, Bayard (civil rights leader); West Chester, Pa. **(1910–1987)**
Rutherford, Dame Margaret (actress); London **(1892–1972)**
Ryan, Jeri (actress); Munich, Germany, 2/22/68
Ryan, Meg (Margaret Mary Emily Anne Hyra) (actress); Fairfield, Conn., 11/19/61
Ryan, Robert (actor); Chicago **(1909–1973)**
Rydell, Bobby (Robert Ridarelli) (singer); Philadelphia, 4/26/42
Ryder, Winona (Winona Laura Horowitz) (actress); Winona, Minn., 10/29/71
Rysanek, Leonie (dramatic soprano); Vienna **(1928–1998)**

S

Saarinen, Eero (architect); Finland **(1910–1961)**
Sabin, Albert B. (polio researcher); Bialystok, Poland **(1906–1993)**
Sabu (Dastagir) (actor); Karapur, India **(1924–1963)**
Sacagawea (Shoshone Indian guide); Lemhi River valley (Idaho) **(c. 1786–1812)**

Sachs, Jeffrey D. (economist, educator); Michigan, 1954
Sadat, Anwar (former president); Egypt **(1918–1981)**
Sade, Marquis de (Donatien Alphonse François, Comte de Sade) (libertine, writer); Paris **(1740–1814)**
Safer, Morley (TV newscaster); Toronto, 11/8/31
Sagan, Carl (Edward) (astronomer, science writer); New York City **(1934–1996)**
Sagan, Françoise (novelist); Cajarc, France, 6/21/35
Sahl, Mort (Morton Lyon Sahl) (comedian); Montreal, 5/11/27
Saint, Eva Marie (actress); Newark, N.J., 7/4/24
St. Denis, Ruth (dancer, choreographer); Newark, N.J. **(1878–1968)**
St. James, Susan (Susan Miller) (actress); Los Angeles, 8/14/46
St. John, Jill (actress); Los Angeles, 8/19/40
St. Johns, Adela Rogers (journalist, author); Los Angeles **(1894–1988)**
Sainte-Marie, Buffy (Beverly) (folk singer); Craven, Sask., Canada, 2/20/41
Saint-Gaudens, Augustus (sculptor); Dublin **(1848–1907)**
Saint-Laurent, Yves (Henri Donat Mathieu) (fashion designer); Oran, Algeria, 8/1/36
Saint-Saens, Charles Camille (composer); Paris **(1835–1921)**
Sakharov, Andrei Dmitriyevich (nuclear physicist, peace activist); Russia **(1921–1989)**
Sales, Soupy (Milton Hines) (television entertainer); Franklinton, N.C., 1/6/26
Salinger, J(erome) D(avid) (novelist); New York City, 1/1/19
Salisbury, Harrison E. (journalist); Minneapolis **(1908–1993)**
Salk, Jonas (polio researcher); New York City **(1914–1995)**
Salk, Lee (psychologist); New York City **(1926–1992)**
Salomon, Haym (American Revolution financier); Leszno, Poland **(1740–1785)**
Sand, George (Amandine Lucille Aurore Dudevant, née Dupin) (novelist); Paris **(1804–1876)**
Sandburg, Carl (poet, biographer); Galesburg, Ill. **(1878–1967)**
Sanders, George (actor); St. Petersburg, Russia **(1906–1972)**
Sandler, Adam (comedian, musician, actor, screenwriter, singer); Brooklyn, N.Y., 9/9/66
Sands, Tommy (singer); Chicago, 8/27/37
Sanger, Margaret (birth-control advocate); Corning, N.Y. **(1879–1966)**
San Giacomo, Laura (actress); Hoboken, N.J., 11/14/62
Santayana, George (philosopher); Madrid **(1863–1952)**
Sappho (poet); Lesbos, Greece (610 **b.c.–580 b.c.**)
Sarandon, Susan (Susan Tomalin) (actress); New York City, 10/4/46
Sargent, John Singer (painter); Florence, Italy **(1856–1925)**
Sarnoff, David (radio executive); Minsk, Belarus **(1891–1971)**
Saroyan, William (novelist); Fresno, Calif. **(1908–1981)**
Sarto, Andrea del (Andrea Domenico d'Agnolo di Francesco) (painter); Florence, Italy **(1486–1531)**
Sartre, Jean-Paul (existentialist writer); Paris **(1905–1980)**
Sassoon, Vidal (hair stylist); London, 1/17/28
Satie, Erik (Alfred Leslie) (composer); Paris **(1866–1925)**
Saul (King of Israel) fl. 11th cent. **b.c.**
Savage, Fred (actor); Highland Park, Ill., 7/9/76
Savalas, Telly (Aristoteles) (actor); Garden City, N.Y. **(1924–1994)**
Savonarola, Girolamo (religious reformer); Ferrara, Italy **(1452–1498)**
Sawyer, Diane (broadcast journalist); Glasgow, Ky., 12/22/45
Sayão, Bidú (soprano); Rio de Janeiro **(1904–1999)**
Sayles, John (director, screenwriter, actor); Schenectady, N.Y., 9/28/50
Scarlatti, Alessandro (composer); Palermo, Italy **(1659–1725)**
Scarlatti, Domenico (composer); Naples, Italy **(1685–1757)**
Scavullo, Francesco (photographer); Staten Island, N.Y., 1/16/29
Schama, Simon (historian); London, 2/13/45
Schapiro, Meyer (Meir) (art historian); Siauliai, Lithuania **(1904–1996)**
Schary, Dore (producer, writer); Newark, N.J. **(1905–1980)**
Schell, Maximilian (actor); Vienna, 12/8/30
Schiaparelli, Elsa (fashion designer); Rome **(1890–1973)**
Schiff, Dorothy (newspaper publisher); New York City **(1903–1989)**
Schiffer, Claudia (model, actress); Rheinberg/Dusseldorf, Germany, 8/25/70
Schiller, Johann Christoph Friedrich von (dramatist, poet); Marbach, Germany **(1759–1805)**
Schipa, Tito (tenor); Lecce, Italy **(1890–1965)**
Schippers, Thomas (conductor); Kalamazoo, Mich. **(1930–1977)**
Schlegel, Friedrich von (philosopher); Hanover, Germany **(1772–1829)**
Schlesinger, Arthur M., Jr. (historian); Columbus, Ohio, 10/15/17
Schnabel, Artur (pianist, composer); Lipnik, Austria **(1882–1951)**

Schneider, Romy (Rose-Marie Albach-Retty) (actress); Vienna **(1938–1982)**
Schoenberg, Arnold (composer); Vienna **(1874–1951)**
Schomberg, Arthur (bibliophile, antiquarian); San Juan, P.R. **(1874–1938)**
Schopenhauer, Arthur (philosopher); Danzig, Poland **(1788–1860)**
Schröder, Gerhard (Chancellor of Germany); Mossenberg, Germany, 4/7/44
Schubert, Franz Peter (composer); Vienna **(1797–1828)**
Schulberg, Budd (novelist); New York City, 3/27/14
Schulz, Charles M. (cartoonist); Minneapolis **(1922–2000)**
Schumacher, Joel (film director, producer, screenwriter); New York City, 8/29/39
Schuman, Robert (statesman); Luxembourg **(1886–1963)**
Schuman, William (composer); New York City **(1910–1992)**
Schumann, Robert Alexander (composer); Zwickau, Germany **(1810–1856)**
Schwartz, Arthur (songwriter); Brooklyn, N.Y. **(1900–1984)**
Schwarzenegger, Arnold (bodybuilder, actor); Graz, Austria, 7/30/47
Schwarzkopf, Elisabeth (soprano); Poznán, Poland, 12/9/15
Schwarzkopf, H. Norman (retired general); Trenton, N.J., 8/22/34
Schweitzer, Albert (humanitarian, Nobel laureate); Kaysersburg, Upper Alsace **(1875–1965)**
Schwimmer, David (actor); New York City, 11/12/66
Scofield, Paul (actor); Hurstpierpoint, England, 1/21/22
Scorsese, Martin (actor, writer, director, producer); Flushing, N.Y., 11/17/42
Scott, George C. (actor); Wise, Va. **(1927–1999)**
Scott, Hazel (singer, pianist); Port of Spain, Trinidad **(1920–1981)**
Scott, Lizabeth (Emma Matzo) (actress); Scranton, Pa., 9/29/23
Scott, Randolph (Randolph Crane) (actor); Orange County, Va. **(1898–1987)**
Scott, Robert Falcon (explorer); Devonport, England **(1868–1912)**
Scott, Sir Walter (novelist); Edinburgh, Scotland **(1771–1832)**
Scott, Zachary (actor); Austin, Tex. **(1914–1965)**
Scotto, Renata (operatic soprano); Savona, Italy, 2/24/36
Scruggs, Earl Eugene (bluegrass musician); Cleveland County, N.C., 1/6/24
Seaborg, Glenn Theodore (chemist, Nobel laureate); Ishpeming, Mich. **(1912–1999)**
Seagal, Steven (actor); Lansing, Mich., 4/10/52
Seal (Sealhenry Olumide Samuel) (singer, songwriter); London, England, 2/19/63
Seattle (Chief Seattle) (Suquamish Indian leader); Blake Island (Wash.) **(c. 1786–1866)**
Sebastian, John (composer, singer); New York City, 3/17/44
Seberg, Jean (actress); Marshalltown, Iowa **(1938–1979)**
Sedaka, Neil (singer); Brooklyn, N.Y., 3/13/39
Sedgwick, Kyra (actress); New York City, 8/19/65
Seeger, Pete (folk singer); New York City, 5/3/19
Segal, Erich (novelist); Brooklyn, N.Y., 6/16/37
Segal, George (actor); New York City, 2/13/36
Segovia, Andrés (guitarist); Linares, Spain **(1893–1987)**
Seinfeld, Jerry (comedian); Brooklyn, N.Y., 4/29/54
Selena (Selena Quintanilla Perez) (singer); Lake Jackson, Tex. **(1971–1995)**
Selleck, Tom (actor); Detroit, 1/29/45
Sellars, Peter (theater director); Pittsburgh, 1958?
Sellers, Peter (actor); Southsea, England **(1925–1980)**
Selznick, David O. (producer); Pittsburgh **(1902–1965)**
Sendak, Maurice (Bernard) (children's book author, illustrator); Brooklyn, N.Y., 6/10/28
Sennett, Mack (Michael Sinnott) (film producer); Richmond, Que., Canada **(1880–1960)**
Sequoyah (Cherokee linguist); Taskigi, Tenn. **(c. 1770–1843)**
Serkin, Peter (pianist); New York City, 7/24/47
Serkin, Rudolf (pianist); Eger, Czech Republic **(1903–1991)**
Serling, Rod (writer, TV host); Syracuse, N.Y. **(1924–1975)**
Sessions, Roger (composer); Brooklyn, N.Y. **(1896–1985)**
Seurat, Georges (painter); Paris **(1859–1891)**
Seuss, Dr. (Theodor Seuss Geisel) (author, illustrator); Springfield, Mass. **(1904–1991)**
Sevareid, Eric (TV commentator); Velva, N.D. **(1912–1991)**
Severinsen, Doc (Carl) (band leader); Arlington, Ore., 7/7/27
Sevigny, Chlöe (actress); Darien, Conn., 1975
Sewell, Rufus (actor, musician); London, 10/29/67
Sexton, Anne (poet); Newton, Mass. **(1928–1974)**
Seymour, Jane (Joyce Penelope Wilhelmina Frankenburg) (actress); Wimbledon, England, 2/15/51
Shabazz, Betty (Betty Sanders) (civil rights activist); Detroit **(1936–1997)**
Shaffer, Peter (playwright); Liverpool, England, 5/15/26

Shaham, Gil (violinist); Urbana, Ill., 1971
Shahn, Ben(jamin) (painter); Kaunas, Lithuania **(1898–1969)**
Shakespeare, William (dramatist); Stratford on Avon, England **(1564–1616)**
Shakur, Tupac (Amaru Shakur) (singer, actor); Brooklyn, N.Y. **(1971–1996)**
Shandling, Garry (comedian, actor, producer); Chicago, 11/29/49
Shange, Ntozake (Paulette Williams) (poet, playwright); Trenton, N.J., 10/18/48
Shankar, Ravi (sitar player); Benares, India, 4/7/20
Sharif, Omar (Michael Shalhoub) (actor); Alexandria, Egypt, 4/10/32
Shatner, William (actor); Montreal, 3/22/31
Shaw, Artie (Arthur Arshawsky) (band leader); New York City, 5/23/10
Shaw, George Bernard (dramatist); Dublin **(1856–1950)**
Shaw, Irwin (novelist); Brooklyn, N.Y. **(1913–1984)**
Shaw, Robert (actor); Lancashire, England **(1927–1978)**
Shaw, Robert (chorale conductor); Red Bluff, Calif. **(1916–1999)**
Shawn, Ted (Edwin Myers Shawn) (dancer, choreographer); Kansas City, Mo. **(1891–1972)**
Shawn, Wallace (actor); New York City, 11/12/43
Shearer, Moira (ballet dancer); Dunfermline, Scotland, 1/17/26
Shearer, Norma (actress); Montreal **(1900–1983)**
Shearing, George (pianist); London, 8/13/20
Sheedy, Ally (Alexandra Sheedy) (actress, writer); New York City, 6/12/62
Sheen, Charlie (actor); Los Angeles, 3/3/65
Sheen, Fulton J. (Peter Sheen) (Roman Catholic bishop); El Paso, Ill. **(1895–1979)**
Sheen, Martin (Ramon Estevez) (actor); Dayton, Ohio, 8/3/40
Shelley, Mary Wollstonecraft Godwin (writer); London **(1797–1851)**
Shelley, Percy Bysshe (poet); nr. Horsham, England **(1792–1822)**
Shelton, Henry (chairman of the Joint Chiefs of Staff); Tarboro, N.C., 1/2/42
Shepard, Sam (Samuel Shepard Rogers) (playwright); Ft. Sheridan, Ill., 11/5/43
Shepherd, Cybill (actress); Memphis, Tenn., 2/18/50
Sheraton, Thomas (furniture designer); Stockton-on-Tees, England **(1751–1806)**
Sheridan, Ann (Clara Lou Sheridan) (actress); Denton, Tex. **(1915–1967)**
Sheridan, Philip (army officer); Albany, N.Y. **(1831–1888)**
Sheridan, Richard Brinsley (dramatist); Dublin **(1751–1816)**
Sherman, William Tecumseh (army officer); Lancaster, Ohio **(1820–1891)**
Sherwood, Robert Emmet (playwright); New Rochelle, N.Y. **(1896–1955)**
Shevardnadze, Eduard Amvrosiyevich (State Council Chairman, Georgia); Mamati, Georgia, 1/25/28
Shields, Brooke (actress); New York City, 5/31/65
Shire, Talia (Coppola) (actress); Lake Success, N.Y., 4/25/46
Shirer, William L. (journalist, historian); Chicago **(1904–1993)**
Sholokhov, Mikhail (novelist); Veshenskaya, Russia **(1905–1984)**
Shore, Dinah (Frances Rose Shore) (singer); Winchester,Tenn. **(1917–1994)**
Short, Bobby (Robert Waltrip Short) (singer, pianist); Danville, Ill., 9/15/24
Short, Martin (actor); Hamilton, Ont., Canada, 3/26/50
Shostakovich, Dmítri (composer); St. Petersburg, Russia **(1906–1975)**
Shriner, Herb (humorist, host); Toledo, Ohio **(1918–1970)**
Shriver, Maria (TV co-host); Chicago, 11/6/55
Shriver, Sargent (Robert Sargent Shriver, Jr.) (business executive); Westminster, Md., 11/9/15
Shue, Andrew (actor, soccer player); South Orange, N.J., 2/20/67
Shue, Elisabeth (actress); Wilmington, Del., 6/10/63
Shulman, Max (novelist); St. Paul, Minn. **(1919–1988)**
Sibelius, Jean (Johann Julius Christian Sibelius) (composer); Tavastehus, Finland **(1865–1957)**
Sidney, Sir Philip (poet); Penshurst, England **(1554–1586)**
Sidney, Sylvia (Sophia Kosow) (actress); New York City **(1910–1999)**
Siegfried and Roy (illusionists) **Siegfried Fischbacher;** Rosenheim, Bavaria, Germany, 1939 **Roy Uwe Ludwig Horn;** Nordenham, nr. Bremen, Germany, 1944
Siepi, Cesare (basso); Milan, Italy, 2/10/23
Signoret, Simone (Simone Kaminker) (actress); Wiesbaden, Germany **(1921–1985)**
Sihanouk, Norodom (king of Cambodia); Cambodia, 10/31/22
Sikorsky, Igor I. (inventor); Kiev, Ukraine **(1889–1972)**
Sills, Beverly (Belle Silverman) (soprano, opera director); Brooklyn, N.Y., 5/25/29

Sills, Milton (actor); Chicago **(1882–1930)**
Silone, Ignazio (Secondo Tranquilli) (novelist); Pescina del Marsi, Italy **(1900–1978)**
Silver, Ron (Ron Zimelman) (actor); New York City, 7/2/46
Silverheels, Jay (Harold J. Smith) (actor); Brantford, Ont., Canada **(1919–1980)**
Silverman, Fred (broadcasting executive); New York City, 9/13/37
Silvers, Phil (Philip Silversmith) (comedian); Brooklyn, N.Y. **(1912–1985)**
Silverstein, Shel (writer, poet); Chicago **(1932–1999)**
Silverstone, Alicia (actress); San Francisco, 10/4/76
Simenon, Georges (Georges Sim) (mystery writer); Liège, Belgium **(1903–1989)**
Simmons, Jean (actress); Crouch Hill, London, 1/31/29
Simon, Carly (singer, songwriter); New York City, 6/25/45
Simon, Neil (playwright); Bronx, N.Y., 7/4/27
Simon, Norton (business executive); Portland, Ore. **(1907–1993)**
Simon, Paul (singer, songwriter); Newark, N.J., 11/5/42
Simone, Nina (Eunice Kathleen Waymoa) (singer, pianist); Tryon, N.C., 2/21/33
Sinatra, Frank (Francis Albert Sinatra) (singer, actor); Hoboken, N.J. **(1915–1998)**
Sinbad (David Adkins) (actor, comedian); Benton Harbor, Mich., 11/10/56
Sinclair, Upton Beall (novelist); Baltimore **(1878–1968)**
Singer, Isaac Bashevis (novelist); Radzymin, Poland **(1904–1991)**
Singleton, John (writer, director); Los Angeles, 1/6/68
Sinise, Gary (actor, director); Chicago, 3/17/55
Siqueiros, David (painter); Chihuahua, Mexico **(1896–1974)**
Sirtis, Marina (actress); London, 3/29/59
Siskel, Gene (film critic); Chicago **(1946–1999)**
Sisley, Alfred (painter); Paris **(1839–1899)**
Sitting Bull (Prairie Sioux Indian Chief); on Grand River, S.D. **(c. 1835–1890)**
Skelton, Red (Richard) (comedian); Vincennes, Ind. **(1913–1997)**
Skerritt, Tom (actor); Detroit, 8/25/43
Skinner, B(urrhus) F(rederic) (psychologist); Susquehanna, Pa. **(1904–1990)**
Skinner, Otis (actor); Cambridge, Mass. **(1858–1942)**
Slater, Christian (Christopher Hawkins) (actor); New York City, 8/18/69
Slatkin, Leonard (conductor); Los Angeles, 9/1/44
Sloan, Alfred P., Jr. (industrialist); New Haven, Conn. **(1875–1965)**
Sloan, John (painter); Lock Haven, Pa. **(1871–1951)**
Smalley, Richard E. (chemist, Nobel laureate); Akron, Ohio, 6/6/43
Smetana, Bedrich (composer); Litomysl, Czech Republic **(1824–1884)**
Smith, Adam (economist); Kirkaldy, Scotland **(1723–1790)**
Smith, Alexis (actress); Penticon, Canada **(1921–1993)**
Smith, Alfred Emanuel (politician); New York City **(1873–1944)**
Smith, Bessie (blues singer); Chattanooga, Tenn. **(1894–1937)**
Smith, Sir C. Aubrey (actor); London **(1863–1948)**
Smith, David (sculptor); Decatur, Ind. **(1906–1965)**
Smith, Harry (TV co-anchor); Hammond, Ind., 8/21/51
Smith, Howard K. (TV commentator); Ferriday, La., 5/12/14
Smith, Jaclyn (actress); Houston, 10/26/47
Smith, John (American colonist); Willoughby, Lincolnshire, England **(1580–1631)**
Smith, Joseph (religious leader); Sharon, Vt. **(1805–1844)**
Smith, Kate (Kathryn) (singer); Greenville, Va. **(1909–1986)**
Smith, Kevin (director, screenwriter); Red Bank, N.J., 8/2/70
Smith, Dame Maggie (actress); Ilford, England, 12/28/34
Smith, Patti Lee (singer, songwriter); Chicago, 12/30/46
Smith, Red (Walter) (sports columnist); Green Bay, Wis. **(1905–1982)**
Smith, Will (actor, rap singer); Philadelphia, 9/25/68
Smits, Jimmy (actor); New York City, 7/9/55
Smollett, Tobias (novelist); Dalquhurn, Scotland **(1721–1771)**
Smothers, Dick (Richard) (comedian); New York City, 11/20/39
Smothers, Tom (Thomas) (comedian); New York City, 2/2/37
Snipes, Wesley (actor); Orlando, Fla., 7/31/62
Snow, Lord (Charles Percy) (author); Leicester, England **(1905–1980)**
Snowdon, Earl of (Anthony Armstrong-Jones) (photographer); London, 3/7/30
Snyder, Tom (TV personality); Milwaukee, 5/12/36
Socrates (philosopher); Athens **(469–399 B.C.)**
Soderbergh, Steven (film director, screenwriter); Baton Rouge, La., 1/14/63
Solomon (King of Israel); Jerusalem, fl. 950 B.C.
Solon (lawgiver); Salamis, Greece **(c. 630–559 B.C.)**
Solti, Sir Georg (conductor); Budapest **(1912–1997)**
Solzhenitsyn, Aleksandr (novelist); Kislovodsk, Russia, 12/11/18

Somers, Suzanne (Suzanne Mahoney) (actress); San Bruno, Calif., 10/16/46
Somes, Michael (ballet dancer); Horsley, England **(1917–1994)**
Sommer, Elke (Elke Schletz) (actress); Berlin, 11/5/42
Sondheim, Stephen (composer); New York City, 3/22/30
Sonnenfeld, Barry (cinematographer, film director); New York City, 4/1/53
Sontag, Susan (author, film director); New York City, 1/28/33
Sophocles (dramatist); nr. Athens **(c. 496–406 B.C.)**
Sorbo, Kevin (actor); Mound, Minn., 9/24/58
Sorvino, Mira (actress); Tenafly, N.J., 9/28/67
Sorvino, Paul (actor); Brooklyn, N.Y., 4/13/39
Sothern, Ann (Harriette Lake) (actress); Valley City, N.D., 1/22/09
Soul, David (David Solberg) (actor); Chicago, 8/28/43
Sousa, John Philip (composer); Washington, D.C. **(1854–1932)**
Soyer, Raphael (painter); Borisoglebsk, Russia **(1899–1987)**
Spaak, Paul-Henri (statesman); Brussels **(1899–1972)**
Spacek, Sissy (Mary Elizabeth Spacek) (actress); Quitman, Tex., 12/25/49
Spacey, Kevin (actor); South Orange, N.J., 7/28/59
Spade, David (actor; comedian); Birmingham, Mich., 7/22/65
Spader, James (actor); Boston, 2/7/60
Spark, Muriel (novelist); Edinburgh, Scotland, 2/1/18
Spector, Phil (rock producer); Bronx, N.Y., 12/25/40
Spelling, Aaron (producer); Dallas, 4/22/28
Spelling, Tori (Victoria) (actress); Los Angeles, 5/16/73
Spencer, Herbert (philosopher); Derby, England **(1820–1903)**
Spender, Stephen (poet); nr. London **(1909–1995)**
Spengler, Oswald (philosopher); Blankenburg, Germany **(1880–1936)**
Spenser, Edmund (poet); London **(1552?–1599)**
Spewack, Bella (playwright); Hungary **(1899–1990)**
Spiegel, Sam (producer); Jaroslaw, Poland **(1901–1985)**
Spielberg, Steven (director, producer, writer, actor); Cincinnati, 12/18/47
Spillane, Mickey (Frank Spillane) (mystery writer); Brooklyn, N.Y., 3/9/18
Spiner, Brent (actor); Houston, 2/2/49
Spinoza, Baruch (philosopher); Amsterdam, Netherlands **(1632–1677)**
Spitalny, Phil (orchestra leader) **(1890–1970)**
Spivak, Lawrence (TV producer); Brooklyn, N.Y. **(1900–1994)**
Spock, Benjamin (pediatrician, writer); New Haven, Conn. **(1903–1998)**
Springsteen, Bruce (singer, songwriter); Freehold, N.J., 9/23/49
Sproul, Robert G. (educator); San Francisco **(1891–1975)**
Squanto (Wampanoag Indian emissary); Patuxet (Plymouth Bay, Mass.) **(c. 1590–1622)**
Stack, Robert (Robert Modini) (actor); Los Angeles, 1/13/19
Stafford, Jo (singer); Coalinga, Calif., 11/12/18
Stahl, Lesley (broadcast journalist); Lynn, Mass., 12/16/41
Stalin, Joseph Vissarionovich (Iosif V. Dzhugashvili) (Soviet leader); nr. Tiflis (Tbilisi), Georgia **(1879–1953)**
Stallone, Sylvester (actor, writer, director); New York City, 7/6/46
Stamp, Terence (actor); London, 1938
Stander, Lionel (actor); New York City **(1908–1994)**
Stanislavski (Konstantin Sergeevich Alekseev) (stage producer); Moscow **(1863–1938)**
Stanley, Sir Henry Morton (John Rowlands) (explorer); Denbigh, Wales **(1841–1904)**
Stanley, Kim (Patricia Reid) (actress); Tularosa, N.M., 2/11/25
Stans, Maurice H. (ex-Secretary of Commerce); Shakope, Minn. **(1908–1998)**
Stanton, Elizabeth Cady (woman suffragist); Johnstown, N.Y. **(1815–1902)**
Stanton, Frank (broadcasting executive); Muskegon, Mich., 3/20/08
Stanwyck, Barbara (Ruby Stevens) (actress); Brooklyn, N.Y. **(1907–1990)**
Stapleton, Jean (Jeanne Murray) (actress); New York City, 1/19/23
Stapleton, Maureen (actress); Troy, N.Y., 6/21/25
Starker, János (cellist); Budapest, 7/5/26
Starr, Kay (Starks) (singer); Dougherty, Okla., 7/21/22
Starr, Kenneth (independent counsel for Whitewater investigation); Vernon, Tex., 7/21/46
Starr, Ringo (Richard Starkey) (singer, songwriter); Liverpool, England, 7/7/40
Stassen, Harold E. (ex-government official); West St. Paul, Minn., 4/13/07
Staudinger, Hermann (chemist, Nobel laureate); Worms, Germany **(1881–1965)**
Steber, Eleanor (soprano); Wheeling, W. Va. **(1916–1990)**
Steegmuller, Francis (biographer); New Haven, Conn. **(1906–1994)**

Steel, Danielle (Danielle Fernande Schuelein-Steel) (novelist); New York City, 8/14/47
Steele, Tommy (singer); London, 12/17/36
Stefani, Gwen (singer); Orange County, Calif., 10/3/69
Stegner, Wallace (Earle) (novelist, critic); Lake Mills, Iowa **(1909–1993)**
Steichen, Edward Jean (photographer, artist); Luxembourg **(1879–1973)**
Steiger, Rod (Rodney) (actor); Westhampton, N.Y., 4/14/25
Stein, Gertrude (author); Allegheny, Pa. **(1874–1946)**
Steinbeck, John Ernst (novelist); Salinas, Calif. **(1902–1968)**
Steinberg, David (comedian); Winnipeg, Man., Canada, 8/19/42
Steinberg, William (conductor); Cologne, Germany **(1899–1978)**
Steinem, Gloria (feminist, publisher); Toledo, Ohio, 3/25/34
Steinmetz, Charles (electrical engineer); Breslau, Poland **(1865–1923)**
Steenburgen, Mary (actress); Newport, Ark., 2/8/53
Stendhal (Marie Henri Beyle) (novelist); Grenoble, France **(1783–1842)**
Stern, Howard (radio personality); New York City, 1/2/54
Stern, Isaac (concert violinist); Kreminlecz, Russia, 7/21/20
Sterne, Laurence (novelist); Clonmel, Ireland **(1713–1768)**
Stevens, Cat (Steven Georgiou) (singer, songwriter); London, 7/21/47
Stevens, Connie (Concetta Ingolia) (singer); Brooklyn, N.Y., 8/8/38
Stevens, George (film director); Oakland, Calif. **(1905–1975)**
Stevens, Risë (mezzo-soprano); New York City, 6/11/13
Stevens, Wallace (poet); Reading, Pa. **(1879–1955)**
Stevenson, Adlai Ewing (statesman); Los Angeles **(1900–1965)**
Stevenson, McLean (actor); Bloomington, Ill. **(1929–1996)**
Stevenson, Parker (actor); Philadelphia, 6/4/52
Stevenson, Robert Louis Balfour (novelist, poet); Edinburgh, Scotland **(1850–1894)**
Stewart, James (actor); Indiana, Pa. **(1908–1997)**
Stewart, Jon (Jonathan Stewart Leibowitz) (comedian, actor); Trenton, N.J., 11/28/62
Stewart, Martha (entrepreneurial home stylist); Nutley, N.J., 8/3/41
Stewart, Patrick (actor); Mirfield, England, 7/13/40
Stewart, Rod (Roderick David) (singer); London, 1/10/45
Stieglitz, Alfred (photographer); Hoboken, N.J. **(1864–1946)**
Stiers, David Ogden (actor); Peoria, Ill., 10/31/42
Stiller, Ben (actor, director, comic); New York City, 11/30/65
Stiller, Jerry (actor); Brooklyn, N.Y., 6/8/29
Stills, Stephen (singer, songwriter); Dallas, 1/3/45
Stine, R.L. (Robert Lawrence Stine) (writer); Columbus, Ohio, 10/8/43
Sting (Gordon Matthew Sumner) (singer, composer); Wallsend, England, 10/2/51
Stipe, Michael (singer); Decatur, Ga., 1/4/60
Stockwell, Dean (actor); North Hollywood, Calif., 3/5/36
Stoker, Bram (novelist); Dublin **(1847–1912)**
Stokes, Carl (TV newscaster); Cleveland **(1927–1996)**
Stokowski, Leopold (conductor); London **(1882–1977)**
Stoltz, Eric (actor); Whittier, Calif., 9/30/61
Stone, Edward Durell (architect); Fayetteville, Ark. **(1902–1978)**
Stone, I(sidor) F(einstein) (journalist); Philadelphia **(1907–1989)**
Stone, Irving (Irving Tennenbaum) (novelist); San Francisco **(1903–1989)**
Stone, Lucy (woman suffragist); nr. West Brookfield, Mass. **(1818–1893)**
Stone, Oliver (director, writer, producer); New York City, 9/15/46
Stone, Robert (novelist); Brooklyn, N.Y., 8/21/37
Stone, Sharon (actress); Meadville, Pa., 3/10/58
Stone, Sly (Sylvester Stone) (rock musician) 1944
Stooges, The Three (comedy team) **Moe Howard** (Moses Horwitz); Brooklyn, N.Y. **(1897–1975;) Shemp Howard** (Samuel Horwitz); Brooklyn, N.Y. **(1900–1955;) Larry Fine** (Laurence Feinburg); Philadelphia **(1911–1974;) Curly Howard** (Jerome Horwitz); Brooklyn, N.Y. **(1906 –1952)**
Stoppard, Tom (Thomas Straussler) (playwright); Zlin, Slovakia, 7/3/37
Stout, Rex (mystery writer); Noblesville, Ind. **(1886–1975)**
Stowe, Harriet Elizabeth Beecher (novelist); Litchfield, Conn. **(1811–1896)**
Stowe, Madeleine (actress); Eagle Rock, Calif., 8/18/58
Strachey, (Giles) Lytton (biographer); London **(1880–1932)**
Stradivari, Antonio (violinmaker); Cremona, Italy **(1644–1737)**
Straight, Beatrice (actress); Old Westbury, N.Y., 8/2/18
Strasberg, Lee (stage director); Budanov, Austria **(1901–1982)**
Strasberg, Susan (actress); New York City **(1938–1999)**
Stratas, Teresa (soprano); Toronto, 5/26/38
Straus, Oskar (composer); Vienna **(1870–1954)**
Strauss, Johann (composer); Vienna **(1825–1899)**

Strauss, Lewis L. (naval officer, scientist); Charleston, W. Va. **(1896–1974)**
Strauss, Peter (actor); New York City, 2/20/47
Strauss, Richard (composer); Munich, Germany **(1864–1949)**
Stravinsky, Igor (composer); Orlenbaum, Russia **(1882–1971)**
Streep, Meryl (Mary Louise) (actress); Summit, N.J., 6/22/49
Streisand, Barbra (singer, actress, director, producer, writer); Brooklyn, N.Y., 4/24/42
Strindberg, (Johan) August (dramatist); Stockholm **(1849–1912)**
Stritch, Elaine (actress); Detroit, 2/2/25
Struthers, Sally Ann (actress); Portland, Ore., 7/28/48
Stuart, Gilbert Charles (painter); Rhode Island **(1755–1828)**
Stuart, Gloria (film actress); Santa Monica, Calif., 7/4/10
Stuart, James Ewell Brown (known as Jeb) (Confederate army officer; Patrick County, Va. **(1833–1864)**
Sturges, Preston (Edmond P. Biden) (director, screenwriter, playwright; Chicago **(1898–1959)**
Stuyvesant, Peter (Governor of New Amsterdam); West Friesland, Netherlands **(1592–1672)**
Styne, Jule (Julius Kerwin Stein) (songwriter); London **(1905–1994)**
Styron, William (William Clark Styron, Jr.) (novelist); Newport News, Va., 6/11/25
Suharto (President of Indonesia); Sedaju-Godean, Java, 2/20/21
Sukarno (Indonesian leader); Surabaja, Java **(1901–1970)**
Sullavan, Margaret Brooke (actress); Norfolk, Va. **(1911–1960)**
Sullivan, Sir Arthur Seymour (composer); London **(1842–1900)**
Sullivan, Barry (Patrick Barry) (actor); New York City **(1912–1994)**
Sullivan, Ed (columnist, TV personality); New York City **(1901–1974)**
Sullivan, Frank (Francis John) (humorist); Saratoga Springs, N.Y. **(1892–1976)**
Sullivan, Louis Henry (architect); Boston **(1856–1924)**
Sulzberger, Arthur Ochs (newspaper publisher); New York City, 2/5/26
Sumac, Yma (singer); Ichocan, Peru, 9/10/27
Summer, Donna (La Donna Andrea Gaines) (singer); Boston, 12/31/48
Sun Ra (Herman "Sunny" Blount) (jazz composer); Birmingham, Ala. **(1914?–1993)**
Sun Tzu (writer, military strategist); China **(fl. c. 500–320 B.C.)**
Sun Yat-sen (statesman); nr. Macao **(1866–1925)**
Susann, Jacqueline (novelist); Philadelphia **(1918–1974)**
Susskind, David (TV producer); New York City **(1920–1987)**
Sutherland, Donald (actor); St. John, N.B., Canada, 7/17/34
Sutherland, Joan (soprano); Sydney, Australia, 11/7/26
Sutherland, Kiefer (actor); London, 12/18/66
Suzuki, Pat (actress); Cressey, Calif., 1931
Swados, Elizabeth (composer, playwright); Buffalo, N.Y., 2/5/51
Swank, Hilary (actress); Bellingham, Wash., 7/30/74
Swanson, Gloria (Gloria May Josephine Svensson) (actress); Chicago **(1899–1983)**
Swarthout, Gladys (soprano); Deepwater, Mo. **(1904–1969)**
Swayze, John Cameron (news commentator); Wichita, Kans. **(1906–1995)**
Swayze, Patrick (actor, dancer); Houston, 8/18/54
Swedenborg, Emanuel (scientist, philosopher, mystic); Stockholm **(1688–1772)**
Swift, Jonathan (satirist); Dublin **(1667–1745)**
Swinburne, Algernon Charles (poet); London **(1837–1909)**
Swit, Loretta (actress); Passaic, N.J., 11/4/37
Swope, Herbert Bayard (journalist); St. Louis **(1882–1958)**
Sydow, Max von (Carl Adolf von Sydow) (actor); Lund, Sweden, 4/10/29
Symons, Arthur (poet, critic); Milford Haven, Wales **(1865–1945)**
Synge, John Millington (dramatist); nr. Dublin **(1871–1909)**
Szilard, Leo (physicist); Budapest **(1898–1964)**

T

Taft, Robert Alphonso (legislator); Cincinnati **(1889–1953)**
Taft, William Howard (27th U.S. president); Cincinnati **(1857–1930)**
Tagore, Sir Rabindranath (poet); Calcutta **(1861–1941)**
Tallchief, Maria (ballet dancer); Fairfax, Okla., 1/24/25
Talleyrand-Pèrigord, Charles Maurice de (statesman); Paris **(1754–1838)**
Talmadge, Norma (actress); Niagara Falls, N.Y. **(1897–1957)**
Talvela, Martti (basso); Hiitola, Finalnd **(1935–1989)**
Tamerlane (Timur) (Mongol conqueror); nr. Samarkand, Turkestan **(c. 1336–1405)**
Tamiroff, Akim (actor); Baku, Azerbaijan **(1899–1972)**
Tan, Amy (novelist); Oakland, Calif., 2/19/52
Tanaka, Tomoyuki (film producer); Osaka, Japan **(1910–1997)**
Tandy, Jessica (actress); London **(1909–1994)**

Tarbell, Ida Minerva (author, muckraker); Erie Co., Pa. (1857–1944)

Tarkington, (Newton) Booth (novelist); Indianapolis (1869–1946)

Tartikoff, Brandon (television executive); Freeport, N.Y. (1949–1997)

Tate, Allen (John Orley) (poet, critic); Winchester, Ky. (1899–1979)

Tate, Sharon (actress); Dallas (1943–1969)

Taylor, Deems (composer); New York City (1885–1966)

Taylor, Elizabeth (actress); London, 2/27/32

Taylor, Harold (educator); Toronto, 9/28/14

Taylor, James (singer, songwriter); Boston, 3/12/48

Taylor, Laurette (Laurette Cooney) (actress); New York City (1884–1946)

Taylor, Lili (actress); Glenco, Ill., 2/20/67

Taylor, Gen. Maxwell D. (former Army Chief of Staff); Keytesville, Mo. (1901–1987)

Taylor, Niki (model); Pembroke Pines, Fla., 3/5/75

Taylor, Paul (choreographer); Wilkinsburg, Pa., 7/29/30

Taylor, Rod (actor); Sydney, Australia, 1/11/30

Taylor, Zachary (12th U.S. president); Montebello, Orange County, Va. (1784–1850)

Tchaikovsky, Peter (Pětr) Ilich (composer); Votkinsk, Russia (1840–1893)

Teasdale, Sara (poet); St. Louis (1884–1933)

Tebaldi, Renata (lyric soprano); Pesaro, Italy, 1/2/22

Tecumseh (Shawnee Indian chief); nr. Springfield, Ohio (1768–1813)

Te Kanawa, Kiri (soprano); Gisborne, New Zealand, 3/6/44

Telemann, Georg Philipp (composer); Magdeburg, Germany (1681–1767)

Teller, Edward (atomic physicist); Budapest, 1/15/08

Templeton, Alec Andrew (pianist, composer); Cardiff, Wales (1910–1963)

Tennille, Toni (singer); Montgomery, Ala., 5/8/43

Tennyson, Alfred (1st Baron Tennyson) (poet); Somersby, England (1809–1892)

Tenskwatawa (Shawnee prophet); Old Piqua, Ohio (c. 1770–c. 1835)

Terhune, Albert Payson (novelist, journalist); Newark, N.J. (1872–1942)

Terkel, Studs (writer, interviewer); New York City, 5/16/12

Terry, Ellen Alicia (actress); Coventry, England (1848–1928)

Terry-Thomas (Thomas Terry Hoar Stevens) (actor); London (1911–1990)

Tesla, Nikola (electrical engineer, inventor); Smiljan, Croatia (1856–1943)

Thackeray, William Makepeace (novelist); Calcutta (1811–1863)

Thalberg, Irving G. (producer); Brooklyn, N.Y. (1899–1936)

Thant, U (U.N. statesman); Pantanaw, Burma (1909–1974)

Tharp, Twyla (dancer, choreographer); Portland, Ind., 7/1/42

Thatcher, Margaret (former Prime Minister); Grantham, England, 10/13/25

Thebom, Blanche (mezzo-soprano); Monessen, Pa., 9/19/19

Theodorakis, Mikis (composer); Chios, Greece, 7/29/25

Thicke, Alan (actor, composer); Kirland Lake, Ont., Canada, 3/1/47

Thieu, Nguyen Van (ex-President of South Vietnam); Trithuy, Vietnam, 4/5/23

Thomas, Danny (Amos Jacobs) (entertainer, TV producer); Deerfield, Mich. (1912–1991)

Thomas, Dylan Marials (poet); Carmarthenshire, Wales (1914–1953)

Thomas, JonathanTaylor (actor); Bethlehem, Pa., 9/8/81

Thomas, Kristen Scott (actress); Redruth, Cornwall, England, 1960

Thomas, Lowell (explorer, commentator); Woodington, Ohio (1892–1981)

Thomas, Marlo (actress); Detroit, 11/21/43

Thomas, Michael Tilson (conductor); Hollywood, Calif., 12/21/44

Thomas, Norman Mattoon (Socialist leader); Marion, Ohio (1884–1968)

Thomas, Philip Michael (actor); Columbus, Ohio, 5/26/49

Thomas, Richard (actor); New York City, 6/13/51

Thompson, Dorothy (writer); Lancaster, N.Y. (1894–1961)

Thompson, Emma (actress); London, 4/15/59

Thompson, Hunter (Stockton) (writer); Louisville, Ky., 7/18/39

Thompson, Lea (actress); Rochester, Minn., 5/31/61

Thompson, Sada (actress); Des Moines, Iowa, 9/27/29

Thomson, Virgil (Garnett) (composer); Kansas City, Mo. (1896–1989)

Thoreau, Henry David (naturalist, author); Concord, Mass. (1817–1862)

Thorndike, Dame Sybil (actress); Gainsborough, England (1882–1976)

Thorne-Smith, Courtney (actress); San Francisco, 11/8/67

Thornton, Billy Bob (actor, screenwriter); Hot Springs, Ark., 8/4/55

Thurber, James Grover (author, cartoonist); Columbus, Ohio (1894–1961)

Thurman, Robert A. F. (scholar, Indo-Tibetan Buddhist studies); New York City, 8/6/40

Thurman, Uma (actress); Boston, 4/29/70

Thurmond, (James) Strom (U.S. Senator); Edgefield, S.C., 12/5/02

Tibbett, Lawrence (baritone); Bakersfield, Calif. (1896–1960)

Tiberius Caesar Augustus (Roman emperor); Capri (42 b.c.–a.d. 37)

Tiegs, Cheryl (model, actress); Minnesota, 9/25/47

Tierney, Gene (actress); Brooklyn, N.Y. (1920–1991)

Tillich, Paul (philosopher, theologian); Starzeddel, Germany (1886–1965)

Tilly, Meg (Margaret Tilly) (actress); Texada Island, B.C., Canada, 2/14/60

Tintoretto, Il (Jacopo Robusti) (painter); Venice (1518–1594)

Tiny Tim (Herbert Khaury) (entertainer); New York City (1932–1996)

Tiomkin, Dmitri (composer); St. Petersburg, Russia (1894–1979)

Titian (Tiziano Vecelli) (painter); Pieve di Cadore, Italy (1477–1576)

Tito (Josip Broz or Brozovich) (president of Yugoslavia); Croatia (former Yugoslavia) (1892–1980)

Tocqueville, Alexis de (writer); Verneuil, France (1805–1859)

Todd, Michael (producer); Minneapolis (1907–1958)

Todd, Thelma (actress); Lawrence, Mass. (1905–1935)

Tolkien, J(ohn) R(onald) R(euel) (fantasy writer); Bloemfontein, South Africa (1892–1973)

Tolstoy, Count Leo (Lev) Nikolaevich (novelist); Tula Province, Russia (1828–1910)

Tomei, Marisa (actress); Brooklyn, N.Y., 12/4/64

Tomlin, Lily (actress, comedienne); Detroit, 9/1/36

Tone, Franchot (actor); Niagara Falls, N.Y. (1905–1968)

Tormé, Mel (Melvin) (singer); Chicago (1925–1999)

Torn, Rip (Elmore Torn, Jr.) (actor, director); Temple, Tex., 2/6/31

Torquamada, Tomásde (Spanish Inquisitor); Valladolid, Spain (1420–1498)

Toscanini, Arturo (orchestra conductor); Parma, Italy (1867–1957)

Totenberg, Nina (broadcast journalist); New York City, 1/14/44

Toulouse-Lautrec (Henri Marie Raymond de Toulouse-Lautrec Monfa) (painter); Albi, France (1864–1901)

Toynbee, Arnold J. (historian); London (1889–1975)

Tracy, Spencer (actor); Milwaukee (1900–1967)

Traubel, Helen (Wagnerian soprano); St. Louis (1903–1972)

Travanti, Daniel J. (actor); Kenosha, Wis., 3/7/40

Travolta, John (actor); Englewood, N.J., 2/18/54

Treacher, Arthur (actor); Brighton, England (1894–1975)

Tree, Sir Herbert Beerbohm (actor, manager); London (1853–1917)

Trevor, Claire (Wemlinger) (actress); New York City (1909–2000)

Trigère, Pauline (fashion designer); Paris, 11/4/12

Trilling, Diana (writer); New York City (1905–1996)

Trilling, Lionel (author, educator); New York City (1905–1975)

Trollope, Anthony (novelist); London (1815–1882)

Trotsky, Leon (Lev Davidovich Bronstein) (statesman); Elisavet-grad, Russia (1879–1940)

Troyanos, Tatiana (mezzo-soprano); New York City (1938–1993)

Trudeau, Garry (cartoonist); New York City, 1948

Trudeau, Pierre Elliott (former Prime Minister); Montreal (1919–2000)

Truffaut, François (film director); Paris (1932–1984)

Trujillo y Molina, Rafael Leonidas (dictator); San Cristóbal, Dominican Republic (1891–1961)

Truman, Harry S. (33rd U.S. president); near Lamar, Mo. (1884–1972)

Truman, Margaret (author); Independence, Mo., 2/17/24

Trump, Donald (business executive); New York City, 6/14/46

Truth, Sojourner (Isabella) (preacher, abolitionist); Ulster Co., N.Y. (c. 1797–1883)

Tryon, Thomas (actor, novelist); Hartford, Conn. (1926–1991)

Tsiolkovsky, Konstantin E. (father of cosmonautics); Izhevskoye, Russia (1857–1935)

Tsongas, Paul E. (politician); Lowell, Mass. (1941–1997)

Tubman, Harriet (Araminta) (abolitionist); Dorchester Co., Md. (c. 1820–1913)

Tuchman, Barbara (Wertheim) (historian, author); New York City (1912–1989)

Tucker, Forrest (actor); Plainfield, Ind. (1919–1986)

Tucker, Richard (tenor); New York City (1914–1975)

Tucker, Sophie (Sophia Kalish) (singer); Russia (1884–1966)

Tudor, Antony (choreographer); London (1909–1987)

Tune, Tommy (dancer, choreographer); Wichita Falls, Tex., 2/28/39

Turgenev, Ivan Sergeevich (novelist); Orel, Russia (1818–1883)

Turlington, Christy (model); San Francisco, 1/2/69

Turner, Frederick J. (historian); Portage, Wis. (1861–1932)

Turner, Ike (singer); Clarksdale, Miss., 11/5/31

Turner, Janine (actress); Lincoln, Neb., 12/6/62

Turner, Joseph M.W. (painter); London (1775–1851)

Turner, Kathleen (actress); Springfield, Mo., 6/19/54

Turner, Lana (Julia Jean Mildred Frances Turner) (actress); Wallace, Idaho **(1920–1995)**
Turner, Nat (civil rights leader); Southampton County, Va. **(1800–1831)**
Turner, Ted (business executive); Cincinnati, 11/19/38
Turner, Tina (Annie Mae Bullock) (singer); Nut Bush, Tenn., 11/26/39
Turpin, Ben (comedian); New Orleans **(1874–1940)**
Turturro, John (actor); Brooklyn, N.Y., 2/28/57
Twain, Mark (Samuel Langhorne Clemens) (author); Florida, Mo. **(1835–1910)**
Twain, Shania (Eileen Regina Twain) (country singer); Windsor, Ont., Canada, 8/28/65
Tweed, William Marcy (politician); New York City **(1823–1878)**
Twiggy (Leslie Hornby) (model); London, 9/19/49
Twining, Gen. Nathan F. (former Air Force Chief of Staff); Monroe, Wis. **(1897–1982)**
Twitty, Conway (Harold Lloyd Jenkins) (singer, guitarist); Friars Point, Miss. **(1933–1993)**
Tyler, John (10th U.S. president); Charles City County, Va. **(1790–1862)**
Tyler, Liv (actress, model); Portland, Maine, 7/1/77
Tyler, Steven (singer); New York City, 3/26/48
Tyson, Cicely (actress); New York City, 12/19/33

U

Uccello, Paolo (painter); Florence **(1397–1475)**
Udall, Stewart L. (ex-Secretary of the Interior); St. Johns, Ariz., 1/31/20
Uggams, Leslie (singer, actress); New York City, 5/25/43
Ulanova, Galina (ballet dancer); St. Petersburg, Russia **(1910–1998)**
Ullman, Tracey (actress, singer); Slough, England, 12/30/59
Ullmann, Liv (actress); Tokyo, 12/16/39
Ulrich, Skeet (actor, model); North Carolina, 1/20/70
Untermeyer, Louis (anthologist, poet); New York City **(1885–1977)**
Updike, John (novelist); Shillington, Pa., 3/18/32
Urey, Harold C. (chemist, Nobel laureate); Walkerton, Ind. **(1893–1981)**
Uris, Leon (novelist); Baltimore, 8/3/24
Ustinov, Peter (actor, producer); London, 4/16/21
Utrillo, Maurice (painter); Paris **(1883–1955)**

V

Vaccaro, Brenda (actress); Brooklyn, N.Y., 11/18/39
Vadim, Roger (Roger Vadim Plemiannikov) (film director); Paris **(1928–2000)**
Valentine, Karen (actress); Santa Rosa, Calif., 5/25/47
Valentino, Rudolph (Rodolpho d'Antonguolla) (actor); Castellaneta,. Italy **(1895–1926)**
Valentino (Valentino Garavani) (fashion designer); nr. Milan, Italy, 5/11/32
Valéry, Paul (Ambroise Toussaint Jules) (poet, critic); Sète, France **(1871–1945)**
Vallee, Rudy (Hubert Prior Rudy Vallée) (band leader, singer); Island Pond, Vt. **(1901–1986)**
Valli, Frankie (Frank Castellaccio) (singer); Newark, N.J., 5/3/37
Van Allen, James Alfred (space physicist); Mt. Pleasant, Iowa, 9/7/14
Van Buren, Abigail (Pauline Esther Friedman) (columnist); Sioux City, Iowa, 7/4/18
Van Buren, Martin (8th U.S. president); Kinderhook, N.Y. **(1782–1862)**
Vance, Vivian (Vivian Jones) (actress); Cherryvale, Kans. **(1912–1979)**
Van Der Beek, James (actor); Cheshire, Conn., 3/8/77
Vanderbilt, Alfred G. (sportsman); London **(1912–1999)**
Vanderbilt, Cornelius (financier); Port Richmond, N.Y. **(1794–1877)**
Vanderbilt, Gloria (fashion designer); New York City, 2/20/24
Van Doren, Carl (writer, educator); Hope, Ill. **(1885–1950)**
Van Doren, Mamie (actress); Rowena, S.D., 2/6/33
Vandross, Luther (R&B singer); New York City, 4/20/51
Van Dyke, Dick (actor); West Plains, Mo., 12/13/25
Vandyke (or Van Dyck), Sir Anthony (painter); Antwerp, Belgium **(1599–1641)**
Van Eyck, Jan (painter); Maeseyck, Belgium **(c. 1390–1441)**
Van Fleet, Jo (actress); Oakland, Calif. **(1915–1996)**
van Gogh, Vincent (painter); Groot Zundert, Brabant, Belgium **(1853–1890)**
van Hamel, Martine (ballet dancer); Brussels, 11/16/45

Van Heusen, Jimmy (Edward Chester Babcock) (songwriter); Syracuse, N.Y. **(1913–1990)**
Van Patten, Dick (actor); Richmond Hill, N.Y., 12/9/28
Van Peebles, Melvin (playwright); Chicago, 9/21/32
Vasari, Giorgio (art historian); Arezzo, Italy **(1511–1574)**
Vaughan, Sarah (singer); Newark, N.J. **(1924–1990)**
Vaughan Williams, Ralph (composer); Down Ampney, England **(1872–1958)**
Vaughn, Robert (actor); New York City, 11/22/32
Vaughn, Vince (actor); Minneapolis, 3/28/70
Veblen, Thorstein (economist; social critic); Cato Township, Wis. **(1857–1929)**
Veidt, Conrad (actor); Potsdam, Germany **(1893–1943)**
Velázquez, Diego Rodriguez de Silva y (painter); Seville, Spain **(1599–1660)**
Venturi, Robert (Charles) (architect); Philadelphia, 6/25/25
Verdi, Giuseppe (composer); Roncole, Italy **(1813–1901)**
Verdon, Gwen (actress); Culver City, Calif., 1/13/25
Vereen, Ben (actor, singer); Miami, Fla., 10/10/46
Verlaine, Paul (poet); Metz, France **(1844–1896)**
Vermeer, Jan (or Jan van der Meer van Delft) (painter); Delft, Netherlands **(1632–1675)**
Verne, Jules (author); Nantes, France **(1828–1905)**
Veronese, Paolo (Paolo Cagliari) (painter); Verona, Italy **(1528–1588)**
Verrazano, Giovanni da (navigator); Florence, Italy **(c. 1485–1528)**
Verrett, Shirley (mezzo-soprano); New Orleans, 5/31/33
Versace, Gianni (fashion designer); Reggio di Calabria, Italy **(1946–1997)**
Vesalius, Andreas (anatomist); Brussels **(1515–1564)**
Vespucci, Amerigo (navigator); Florence, Italy **(1454–1512)**
Vico, Giovanni Battista (philosopher); Naples, Italy **(1668–1744)**
Victoria (Queen of England); London **(1819–1901)**
Vidal, Gore (novelist); West Point, N.Y., 10/3/25
Vidor, King (film director, producer); Galveston, Tex. **(1895–1982)**
Vigoda, Abe (actor); New York City, 2/24/21
Villa, Pancho (Doroteo Arango) (revolutionary); Hacienda de Rio Grande, San Juan del Rio, Mexico **(1877–1923)**
Villella, Edward (ballet dancer); Bayside, Queens, N.Y., 10/1/36
Villon, François (François de Montcorbier) (poet); Paris **(1431–1463)**
Vinton, Bobby (singer); Canonsburg, Pa., 4/16/35
Virgil (or Vergil) (Publius Vergilius Maro) (poet); nr. Mantua, Italy **(70–19 B.C.)**
Vishnevskaya, Galina (soprano); St. Petersburg, Russia, 10/25/26
Vivaldi, Antonio (composer); Venice **(1678–1741)**
Vlaminck, Maurice de (painter); Paris **(1876–1958)**
Voight, Jon (actor); Yonkers, N.Y., 12/29/38.
Volta, Alessandro (scientist); Como, Italy **(1745–1827)**
Voltaire (François Marie Arouet) (author); Paris **(1694–1778)**
von Braun, Wernher (rocket scientist); Wirsitz, Germany **(1912–1977)**
von Furstenberg, Betsy (Elizabeth Caroline Maria Agatha Felicitas Therese von Furstenberg-Hedringen) (actress); Nelheim-Heusen, Germany, 8/16/35
von Fürstenberg, Diane (Diane Simone Michelle Halfin) (fashion designer); Brussels, 12/31/46
von Hindenburg, Paul (statesman); Posen, Poland **(1847–1934)**
von Karajan, Herbert (conductor); Salzburg, Austria **(1908–1989)**
Vonnegut, Kurt, Jr. (novelist); Indianapolis, 11/11/22
Von Stade, Frederica (mezzo-soprano); Somerville, N.J., 6/1/45
Von Stroheim, Erich Oswald Hans Carl Maria von Nordenwall (actor, director); Vienna **(1885–1957)**
Von Zell, Harry (announcer); Indianapolis **(1906–1981)**
Vreeland, Diana (Diana Da Iziel) (fashion journalist, museum consultant); Paris **(1903?–1989)**

W

Wagner, Lindsay (actress); Los Angeles, 6/22/49
Wagner, Robert (actor); Detroit, 2/10/30
Wagner, Robert F. (ex-mayor of New York City); New York City **(1910–1991)**
Wagner, Wilhelm Richard (composer); Leipzig, Germany **(1813–1883)**
Wahlberg, Mark (actor, model, musician); Dorchester, Mass., 6/5/71
Waits, Tom (blues singer); Pomona, Calif., 12/7/49
Waldheim, Kurt (ex-U.N. secretary-general); St. Andrae-Wörden, Austria, 12/21/18
Walesa, Lech (Polish labor leader and ex-president); Popowo, Poland, 9/29/43
Walken, Christopher (actor); Queens, N.Y., 3/31/43
Walker, Alice (novelist, poet); Eatonon, Ga., 2/9/44

Williams, Paul (singer, composer, actor); Omaha, Neb., 9/19/40

Williams, Robin (actor, producer); Chicago, 7/21/52

Williams, Roger (clergyman); London (1603?–1683)

Williams, Tennessee (Thomas L. Williams) (playwright); Columbus, Miss. (1911–1983)

Williams, Treat (Richard Williams) (actor); Rowayton, Conn., 12/1/51

Williams, Vanessa (actress, singer); Milwood, N.Y., 3/18/63

Williams, William Carlos (physician, poet); Rutherford, N.J. (1883–1963)

Williamson, Nicol (actor); Hamilton, Scotland, 9/14/38

Willkie, Wendell Lewis (lawyer); Elwood, Ind. (1892–1944)

Willis, Bruce (actor); Germany, 3/19/55

Willson, Meredith (composer); Mason City, Iowa (1902–1984)

Wilson, August (poet, writer, playwright); Pittsburgh, 4/27/45

Wilson, Brian (musician); Inglewood, Calif., 6/20/42

Wilson, Don (radio and TV announcer); Lincoln, Neb. (1900–1982)

Wilson, Dooley (actor, musician); Tyler, Tex. (1894–1953)

Wilson, Edmund (literary critic, author); Red Bank, N.J. (1895–1972)

Wilson, Flip (Clerow Wilson) (comedian); Jersey City, N.J. (1933–1998)

Wilson, Harold (ex-prime minister); Huddersfield, England (1916–1995)

Wilson, Nancy (singer); Chillicothe, Ohio, 2/20/37

Wilson, Sloan (novelist); Norwalk, Conn., 5/8/20

Wilson, (Thomas) Woodrow (28th U.S. president); Staunton, Va. (1856–1924)

Winchell, Walter (columnist); New York City (1897–1972)

Windsor, Duchess of (Bessie Wallis Warfield) Blue Ridge Summit, Pa. (1896–1986)

Windsor, Duke of (formerly King Edward VIII of England); Richmond Park, England (1894–1972)

Winfrey, Oprah (TV host, actress, producer); Kosciusko, Miss., 1/29/54

Winger, Debra (Mary Debra) (actress); Cleveland, 5/17/55

Winkler, Henry (actor, director, producer); New York City, 10/30/45

Winningham, Mare (actress); Phoenix, Ariz., 5/16/59

Winter, Johnny (guitarist); Leland, Miss., 2/23/44

Winters, Jonathan (comedian); Dayton, Ohio, 11/11/25

Winters, Shelley (Shirley Schrift) (actress); East St. Louis, Ill., 8/18/22

Winthrop, John (first governor, Massachusetts Bay Colony); Suffolk, England (1588–1649)

Wise, Stephen Samuel (rabbi); Budapest (1874–1949)

Withers, Jane (actress); Atlanta, 4/12/26

Witherspoon, Reese (actress); Nashville, 3/22/76

Wittig, Georg F. K. (chemist, Nobel laureate); Berlin, Germany (1897–1987)

Wittgenstein, Ludwig (Josef Johann) (philosopher); Vienna (1889–1951)

Wodehouse, P(elham) G(renville) (novelist); Guildford, England (1881–1975)

Wolf, Scott (actor); Boston, 6/4/68

Wolfe, Thomas Clayton (novelist); Asheville, N.C. (1900–1938)

Wolfe, Tom (journalist); Richmond, Va., 3/2/31

Wolff, Tobias (author); Birmingham, Ala., 6/19/45

Wolsey, Thomas (prelate, statesman); Ipswich, England (c. 1475–1530)

Wonder, Stevie (Steveland Judkins, later Steveland Morris) (singer, songwriter); Saginaw, Mich., 5/13/50

Wong, Anna May (Lu Tsong Wong) (actress); Los Angeles (1907–1961)

Woo, John (actor, film director, screenwriter); Guangzhou, Canton, China, 5/1/46

Wood, Elijah (actor); Cedar Rapids, Iowa, 1/28/81

Wood, Grant (painter); Anamosa, Iowa (1892–1942)

Wood, Natalie (Natasha Viparaeff) (actress); San Francisco (1938–1981)

Woods, James (actor); Vernal, Utah, 4/18/47

Woodhouse, Barbara (Blackburn) (dog trainer, author, TV personality); Rathfarnham, Ireland (1910–1988)

Woodruff, Judy (broadcast journalist); Tulsa, Okla., 11/20/46

Woodson, Carter G. (historian); New Canton, Va. (1875–1950)

Woodward, Edward (actor); Croydon, England, 6/1/30

Woodward, Joanne (actress); Thomasville, Ga., 2/27/30

Woodward, Robert Burns (chemist, Nobel laureate); Boston (1917–1979)

Woolf, (Adeline) Virginia (née Stephens) (novelist); London (1882–1941)

Woollcott, Alexander (author, critic); Phalanx, N.J. (1887–1943)

Woolley, Monty (Edgar Montillion Woolley) (actor); New York City (1888–1963)

Woolworth, Frank (merchant); Rodman, N.Y. (1852–1919)

Wopat, Tom (actor); Lodi, Wis., 9/9/50

Wordsworth, William (poet); Cockermouth, England (1770–1850)

Wouk, Herman (novelist); New York City, 5/27/15

Wovoka (Jack Wilson) (Paiute Indian religious leader); (western Nev.) (c. 1858–1932)

Wray, Fay (actress); nr. Cardston, Alb., Canada, 9/14/07

Wren, Sir Christopher (architect); East Knoyle, England (1632–1723)

Wright, Frank Lloyd (architect); Richland Center, Wis. (1869–1959)

Wright, Martha (singer); Seattle, 3/23/26

Wright, Orville (inventor); Dayton, Ohio (1871–1948)

Wright, Richard (novelist); nr. Natchez, Miss. (1908–1960)

Wright, Wilbur (inventor); Millville, Ind. (1867–1912)

Wyatt, Jane (actress); Campgaw, N.J., 8/12/12

Wycliffe, John (church reformer); Hipswell, England (1320–1384)

Wyeth, Andrew (painter); Chadds Ford, Pa., 7/12/17

Wyle, Noah (actor); Hollywood, Calif., 6/4/71

Wyler, William (director); Mulhouse, France (1902–1981)

Wyman, Jane (Sarah Jane Fulks) (actress); St. Joseph, Mo., 1/4/14

Wynette, Tammy (Virginia Wynette Pugh) (singer); Tupelo, Miss. (1942–1998)

Wynn, Ed (Isaiah Edwin Leopold) (comedian); Philadelphia (1886–1966)

Wynn, Keenan (actor); New York City (1916–1986)

X

Xavier, St. Francis (Jesuit missionary); Pamplona, Navarre, Spain (1506–1552)

Xenophon (soldier, historian, essayist); Athens (c. 435–c. 355 B.C.)

Xerxes, the Great (king); Persian Empire (c. 519–465 B.C.)

Y

Yeats, William Butler (poet); nr. Dublin (1865–1939)

Yeltsin, Boris (Russian president); Yekaterinburg (then Sverdlovsk), Russia, 2/1/31

Yevtushenko, Yevgeny (poet); Zima, Russia, 7/18/33

York, Michael (actor); Fulmer, England, 3/27/42

York, Susannah (Fletcher) (actress); London, 1/9/42

Yorty, Samuel W. (ex-mayor of Los Angeles); Lincoln, Neb. (1909–1998)

Yothers, Tina (actress); Whittier, Calif., 5/5/73

Young, Alan (actor); North Shield, England, 11/19/19

Young, Andrew (civil rights leader); New Orleans, 3/12/32

Young, Brigham (religious leader); Whitingham, Vt. (1801–1877)

Young, Gig (Byron Barr) (actor); St. Cloud, Minn. (1917–1978)

Young, Loretta (Gretchen Young) (actress); Salt Lake City (1913–2000)

Young, Neil (singer, songwriter); Toronto, 11/12/45

Young, Robert (actor); Chicago (1907–1998)

Youngman, Henny (comedian); Whitechapel, London (1906–1998)

Z

Zane, Billy (William George Zane, Jr.) (actor); Chicago, 2/24/66

Zanuck, Darryl F. (producer); Wahoo, Neb. (1902–1979)

Zappa, Frank (Francis Vincent Zappa, Jr.) (singer, songwriter); Baltimore (1940–1993)

Zeffirelli, Franco (director); Florence, Italy, 2/12/23

Zellweger, Renee (actress); Katy, Texas, 4/25/69

Zemeckis, Robert (filmmaker); Chicago, 1952

Zhou Enlai (premier); Huaiyin, China (1898–1976)

Ziegfeld, Florenz (theatrical producer); Chicago (1869–1932)

Ziegler, Karl (chemist, Nobel laureate); Helsa, Germany (1898–1973)

Zimbalist, Efrem (concert violinist); Rostov-on-Don, Russia (1889–1985)

Zimbalist, Efrem, Jr. (actor); New York City, 11/30/23

Zimbalist, Stephanie (actress); New York City, 10/8/56

Zinnemann, Fred (director); Vienna (1907–1997)

Zola, Emile (novelist); Paris (1840–1902)

Zoroaster (religious leader); Persian Empire (c. 628–c. 551 B.C.)

Zucker, Jerry (film producer, director, screenwriter); Milwaukee, 3/11/50

Zukerman, Pinchas (violinist); Tel Aviv, Israel, 7/16/48

Zukor, Adolph (movie executive); Risce, Hungary (1873–1976)

Zurbarán, Francisco de (painter); Fuentes de Cantos, Spain (1598–1664)

Zweig, Stefan (author); Vienna (1881–1942)

Zwingli, Huldrych (humanist); Wildaus, Switzerland (1484–1531)

Nobel Prizes

(For years not listed, no award was made. See p. 42 for 2000 winners.)

PEACE

1901	Henri Dunant (Switzerland); Frederick Passy (France)
1902	Elie Ducommun and Albert Gobat (Switzerland)
1903	Sir William R. Cremer (U.K.)
1904	Institut de Droit International (Belgium)
1905	Bertha von Suttner (Austria)
1906	Theodore Roosevelt (U.S.)
1907	Ernesto T. Moneta (Italy) and Louis Renault (France)
1908	Klas P. Arnoldson (Sweden) and Frederik Bajer (Denmark)
1909	Auguste M. F. Beernaert (Belgium) and Baron Paul H. B. B. d'Estournelles de Constant de Rebecque (France)
1910	Bureau International Permanent de la Paix (Switzerland)
1911	Tobias M. C. Asser (Holland) and Alfred H. Fried (Austria)
1912	Elihu Root (U.S.)
1913	Henri La Fontaine (Belgium)
1917	International Red Cross
1919	Woodrow Wilson (U.S.)
1920	Léon Bourgeois (France)
1921	Karl H. Branting (Sweden) and Christian L. Lange (Norway)
1922	Fridtjof Nansen (Norway)
1925	Sir Austen Chamberlain (U.K.) and Charles G. Dawes (U.S.)
1926	Aristide Briand (France) and Gustav Stresemann (Germany)
1927	Ferdinand Buisson (France) and Ludwig Quidde (Germany)
1929	Frank B. Kellogg (U.S.)
1930	Lars O. J. Söderblom (Sweden)
1931	Jane Addams and Nicholas M. Butler (U.S.)
1933	Sir Norman Angell (U.K.)
1934	Arthur Henderson (U.K.)
1935	Karl von Ossietzky (Germany)
1936	Carlos de S. Lamas (Argentina)
1937	Lord Cecil of Chelwood (U.K.)
1938	Office International Nansen pour les Réfugiés (Switzerland)
1944	International Red Cross
1945	Cordell Hull (U.S.)
1946	Emily G. Balch and John R. Mott (U.S.)
1947	American Friends Service Committee (U.S.) and British Society of Friends' Service Council (U.K.)
1949	Lord John Boyd Orr (Scotland)
1950	Ralph J. Bunche (U.S.)
1951	Léon Jouhaux (France)
1952	Albert Schweitzer (French Equatorial Africa)
1953	George C. Marshall (U.S.)
1954	Office of U.N. High Commissioner for Refugees
1957	Lester B. Pearson (Canada)
1958	Rev. Dominique Georges Henri Pire (Belgium)
1959	Philip John Noel-Baker (U.K.)
1960	Albert John Luthuli (South Africa)
1961	Dag Hammarskjöld (Sweden)
1962	Linus Pauling (U.S.)
1963	Intl. Comm. of Red Cross; League of Red Cross Societies (both Geneva)
1964	Rev. Dr. Martin Luther King, Jr. (U.S.)
1965	UNICEF (United Nations Children's Fund)
1968	René Cassin (France)
1969	International Labour Organization
1970	Norman E. Borlaug (U.S.)
1971	Willy Brandt (West Germany)
1973	Henry A. Kissinger (U.S.); Le Duc Tho (North Vietnam)[1]
1974	Eisaku Sato (Japan); Sean MacBride (Ireland)
1975	Andrei D. Sakharov (U.S.S.R.)
1976	Mairead Corrigan and Betty Williams (both Northern Ireland)
1977	Amnesty International
1978	Menachem Begin (Israel) and Anwar el-Sadat (Egypt)
1979	Mother Teresa of Calcutta (India)
1980	Adolfo Pérez Esquivel (Argentina)
1981	Office of the United Nations High Commissioner for Refugees
1982	Alva Myrdal (Sweden) and Alfonso García Robles (Mexico)
1983	Lech Walesa (Poland)
1984	Bishop Desmond Tutu (South Africa)
1985	International Physicians for the Prevention of Nuclear War
1986	Elie Wiesel (U.S.)
1987	Oscar Arias Sánchez (Costa Rica)
1988	U.N. Peacekeeping Forces
1989	Dalai Lama (Tibet)
1990	Mikhail S. Gorbachev (U.S.S.R.)
1991	Daw Aung San Suu Kyi (Burma)
1992	Rigoberta Menchú (Guatemala)
1993	F. W. de Klerk and Nelson Mandela (both South Africa)
1994	Yasir Arafat (Palestine), Shimon Peres, and Yitzhak Rabin (both Israel)
1995	Joseph Rotblat and Pugwash Conference on Science and World Affairs (U.K.)
1996	Carlos Filipe Ximenes Belo and José Ramos-Horta (East Timor)
1997	International Campaign to Ban Landmines and Jody Williams (U.S.)
1998	John Hume and David Trimble (Northern Ireland)
1999	Doctors without Borders (France)

1. Le Duc Tho refused prize, charging that peace had not yet really been established in South Vietnam.

LITERATURE

1901	René F. A. Sully Prudhomme (France)
1902	Theodor Mommsen (Germany)
1903	Björnstjerne Björnson (Norway)
1904	Frédéric Mistral (France) and José Echegaray (Spain)
1905	Henryk Sienkiewicz (Poland)

1906 Giosuè Carducci (Italy)
1907 Rudyard Kipling (U.K.)
1908 Rudolf Eucken (Germany)
1909 Selma Lagerlöf (Sweden)
1910 Paul von Heyse (Germany)
1911 Maurice Maeterlinck (Belgium)
1912 Gerhart Hauptmann (Germany)
1913 Rabindranath Tagore (India)
1915 Romain Rolland (France)
1916 Verner von Heidenstam (Sweden)
1917 Karl Gjellerup (Denmark) and Henrik Pontoppidan (Denmark)
1919 Carl Spitteler (Switzerland)
1920 Knut Hamsun (Norway)
1921 Anatole France (France)
1922 Jacinto Benavente (Spain)
1923 William B. Yeats (Ireland)
1924 Wladyslaw Reymont (Poland)
1925 George Bernard Shaw (Ireland)
1926 Grazia Deledda (Italy)
1927 Henri Bergson (France)
1928 Sigrid Undset (Norway)
1929 Thomas Mann (Germany)
1930 Sinclair Lewis (U.S.)
1931 Erik A. Karlfeldt (Sweden)
1932 John Galsworthy (U.K.)
1933 Ivan G. Bunin (Russia)
1934 Luigi Pirandello (Italy)
1936 Eugene O'Neill (U.S.)
1937 Roger Martin du Gard (France)
1938 Pearl S. Buck (U.S.)
1939 Frans Eemil Sillanpää (Finland)
1944 Johannes V. Jensen (Denmark)
1945 Gabriela Mistral (Chile)
1946 Hermann Hesse (Switzerland)
1947 André Gide (France)
1948 Thomas Stearns Eliot (U.K.)
1949 William Faulkner (U.S.)
1950 Bertrand Russell (U.K.)
1951 Pär Lagerkvist (Sweden)
1952 François Mauriac (France)
1953 Sir Winston Churchill (U.K.)
1954 Ernest Hemingway (U.S.)
1955 Halldór Kiljan Laxness (Iceland)
1956 Juan Ramón Jiménez (Spain)
1957 Albert Camus (France)
1958 Boris Pasternak (U.S.S.R.) (declined)
1959 Salvatore Quasimodo (Italy)
1960 St. John Perse (Alexis St.-Léger Léger) (France)
1961 Ivo Andric (Yugoslavia)
1962 John Steinbeck (U.S.)
1963 Giorgios Seferis (Seferiades) (Greece)
1964 Jean-Paul Sartre (France) (declined)
1965 Mikhail Sholokhov (U.S.S.R.)
1966 Shmuel Yosef Agnon (Israel) and Nelly Sachs (Sweden)
1967 Miguel Angel Asturias (Guatemala)
1968 Yasunari Kawabata (Japan)
1969 Samuel Beckett (Ireland)
1970 Aleksandr Solzhenitsyn (U.S.S.R.)
1971 Pablo Neruda (Chile)
1972 Heinrich Böll (Germany)
1973 Patrick White (Australia)
1974 Eyvind Johnson and Harry Martinson (both Sweden)
1975 Eugenio Montale (Italy)
1976 Saul Bellow (U.S.)
1977 Vicente Aleixandre (Spain)
1978 Isaac Bashevis Singer (U.S.)

1979 Odysseus Elytis (Greece)
1980 Czeslaw Milosz (U.S.)
1981 Elias Canetti (Bulgaria)
1982 Gabriel García Márquez (Colombia)
1983 William Golding (U.K.)
1984 Jaroslav Seifert (Czechoslovakia)
1985 Claude Simon (France)
1986 Wole Soyinka (Nigeria)
1987 Joseph Brodsky (U.S.)
1988 Naguib Mahfouz (Egypt)
1989 Camilo José Cela (Spain)
1990 Octavio Paz (Mexico)
1991 Nadine Gordimer (South Africa)
1992 Derek Walcott (Trinidad)
1993 Toni Morrison (U.S.)
1994 Kenzaburo Oe (Japan)
1995 Seamus Heaney (Ireland)
1996 Wislawa Szymborska (Poland)
1997 Dario Fo (Italy)
1998 José Saramago (Portugal)
1999 Günter Grass (Germany)

PHYSICS

1901 Wilhelm K. Roentgen (Germany), for discovery of Roentgen rays
1902 Hendrik A. Lorentz and Pieter Zeeman (Netherlands), for work on influence of magnetism upon radiation
1903 A. Henri Becquerel (France), for work on spontaneous radioactivity; and Pierre and Marie Curie (France), for study of radiation
1904 John Strutt (Lord Rayleigh) (U.K.), for discovery of argon in investigating gas density
1905 Philipp Lenard (Germany), for work with cathode rays
1906 Sir Joseph Thomson (U.K.), for investigations on passage of electricity through gases
1907 Albert A. Michelson (U.S.), for spectroscopic and metrologic investigations
1908 Gabriel Lippmann (France), for method of reproducing colors by photography
1909 Guglielmo Marconi (Italy) and Ferdinand Braun (Germany), for development of wireless
1910 Johannes D. van der Waals (Netherlands), for work with the equation of state for gases and liquids
1911 Wilhelm Wien (Germany), for his laws governing the radiation of heat
1912 Gustaf Dalén (Sweden), for discovery of automatic regulators used in lighting lighthouses and light buoys
1913 Heike Kamerlingh-Onnes (Netherlands), for work leading to production of liquid helium
1914 Max von Laue (Germany), for discovery of diffraction of Roentgen rays passing through crystals
1915 Sir William Bragg and William L. Bragg (U.K.), for analysis of crystal structure by X rays
1917 Charles G. Barkla (U.K.), for discovery of Roentgen radiation of the elements
1918 Max Planck (Germany), discoveries in connection with quantum theory
1919 Johannes Stark (Germany), discovery of Doppler effect in Canal rays and decomposition of spectrum lines by electric fields

1920 Charles E. Guillaume (Switzerland), for discoveries of anomalies in nickel-steel alloys

1921 Albert Einstein (Germany), for discovery of the law of the photoelectric effect

1922 Niels Bohr (Denmark), for investigation of structure of atoms and radiations emanating from them

1923 Robert A. Millikan (U.S.), for work on elementary charge of electricity and photoelectric phenomena

1924 Karl M. G. Siegbahn (Sweden), for investigations in X ray spectroscopy

1925 James Franck and Gustav Hertz (Germany), for discovery of laws governing impact of electrons upon atoms

1926 Jean B. Perrin (France), for work on discontinuous structure of matter and discovery of the equilibrium of sedimentation

1927 Arthur H. Compton (U.S.), for discovery of Compton phenomenon; and Charles T. R. Wilson (U.K.), for method of perceiving paths taken by electrically charged particles

1928 In 1929, the 1928 prize was awarded to Sir Owen Richardson (U.K.), for work on the phenomenon of thermionics and discovery of the Richardson Law

1929 Prince Louis Victor de Broglie (France), for discovery of the wave character of electrons

1930 Sir Chandrasekhara Raman (India), for work on diffusion of light and discovery of the Raman effect

1932 In 1933, the prize for 1932 was awarded to Werner Heisenberg (Germany), for creation of quantum mechanics

1933 Erwin Schrödinger (Austria) and Paul A. M. Dirac (U.K.), for discovery of new fertile forms of the atomic theory

1935 James Chadwick (U.K.), for discovery of the neutron

1936 Victor F. Hess (Austria), for discovery of cosmic radiation; and Carl D. Anderson (U.S.), for discovery of the positron

1937 Clinton J. Davisson (U.S.) and George P. Thomson (U.K.), for discovery of diffraction of electrons by crystals

1938 Enrico Fermi (Italy), for identification of new radioactivity elements and discovery of nuclear reactions effected by slow neutrons

1939 Ernest Orlando Lawrence (U.S.), for development of the cyclotron

1943 Otto Stern (U.S.), for detection of magnetic momentum of protons

1944 Isidor Isaac Rabi (U.S.), for work on magnetic movements of atomic particles

1945 Wolfgang Pauli (Austria), for work on atomic fissions

1946 Percy Williams Bridgman (U.S.), for studies and inventions in high-pressure physics

1947 Sir Edward Appleton (U.K.), for discovery of layer that reflects radio short waves in the ionosphere

1948 Patrick M. S. Blackett (U.K.), for improvement on Wilson chamber and discoveries in cosmic radiation

1949 Hideki Yukawa (Japan), for mathematical prediction, in 1935, of the meson

1950 Cecil Frank Powell (U.K.), for method of photographic study of atom nucleus, and for discoveries about mesons

1951 Sir John Douglas Cockcroft (U.K.) and Ernest T. S. Walton (Ireland), for work in 1932 on transmutation of atomic nuclei

1952 Edward Mills Purcell and Felix Bloch (U.S.), for work in measurement of magnetic fields in atomic nuclei

1953 Fritz Zernike (Netherlands), for development of "phase contrast" microscope

1954 Max Born (U.K.), for work in quantum mechanics; and Walther Bothe (Germany), for work in cosmic radiation

1955 Polykarp Kusch and Willis E. Lamb, Jr. (U.S.), for atomic measurements

1956 William Shockley, Walter H. Brattain, and John Bardeen (all U.S.), for developing electronic transistor

1957 Tsung Dao Lee and Chen Ning Yang (China), for disproving principle of conservation of parity

1958 Pavel A. Cherenkov, Ilya M. Frank, and Igor E. Tamm (all U.S.S.R.), for work resulting in development of cosmic-ray counter

1959 Emilio Segre and Owen Chamberlain (both U.S.), for demonstrating the existence of the anti-proton

1960 Donald A. Glaser (U.S.), for invention of "bubble chamber" to study subatomic particles

1961 Robert Hofstadter (U.S.), for determination of shape and size of atomic nucleus; Rudolf Mössbauer (Germany), for method of producing and measuring recoil-free gamma rays

1962 Lev D. Landau (U.S.S.R.), for his theories about condensed matter

1963 Eugene Paul Wigner, Maria Goeppert Mayer (both U.S.), and J. Hans D. Jensen (Germany), for research on structure of atom and its nucleus

1964 Charles Hard Townes (U.S.), Nikolai G. Basov, and Aleksandr M. Prochorov (both U.S.S.R.), for developing maser and laser principle of producing high-intensity radiation

1965 Richard P. Feynman, Julian S. Schwinger (both U.S.), and Shinichiro Tomonaga (Japan), for research in quantum electrodynamics

1966 Alfred Kastler (France), for work on energy levels inside atom

1967 Hans A. Bethe (U.S.), for work on energy production of stars

1968 Luis Walter Alvarez (U.S.), for study of subatomic particles

1969 Murray Gell-Mann (U.S.), for study of subatomic particles

1970 Hannes Alfvén (Sweden), for theories in plasma physics; and Louis Néel (France), for discoveries in antiferromagnetism and ferromagnetism

1971 Dennis Gabor (U.K.), for invention of holographic method of three-dimensional imagery

1972 John Bardeen, Leon N. Cooper, and John Robert Schrieffer (all U.S.), for theory of superconductivity, where electrical resistance in certain metals vanishes above absolute zero temperature

1973 Ivar Giaever (U.S.), Leo Esaki (Japan), and Brian D. Josephson (U.K.), for theories that have advanced and expanded the field of miniature electronics

1974 Antony Hewish (U.K.), for discovery of pulsars; Martin Ryle (U.K.), for using radiotelescopes to probe outer space with high degree of precision

1975 James Rainwater (U.S.), Ben Mottelson, and Aage N. Bohr (both Denmark), for showing that the atomic nucleus is asymmetrical

1976 Burton Richter and Samuel C. C. Ting (both U.S.), for discovery of subatomic particles known as J and psi

1977 Philip W. Anderson, John H. Van Vleck (both U.S.), and Nevill F. Mott (U.K.), for work underlying computer memories and electronic devices

1978 Arno A. Penzias and Robert W. Wilson (both U.S.), for work in cosmic microwave radiation; Piotr L. Kapitsa (U.S.S.R.), for basic inventions and discoveries in low-temperature physics

1979 Steven Weinberg, Sheldon L. Glashow (both U.S.), and Abdus Salam (Pakistan), for developing theory that electromagnetism and the "weak" force, which causes radioactive decay in some atomic nuclei, are facets of the same phenomenon

1980 James W. Cronin and Val L. Fitch (both U.S.), for work concerning the asymmetry of subatomic particles

1981 Nicolaas Bloembergen, Arthur L. Schawlow (both U.S.), and Kai M. Siegbahn (Sweden), for developing technologies with lasers and other devices to probe the secrets of complex forms of matter

1982 Kenneth G. Wilson (U.S.), for analysis of changes in matter under pressure and temperature

1983 Subrahmanyam Chandrasekhar and William A. Fowler (both U.S.), for complementary research on processes involved in the evolution of stars

1984 Carlo Rubbia (Italy) and Simon van der Meer (Netherlands), for their role in discovering three subatomic particles, a step toward developing a single theory to account for all natural forces

1985 Klaus von Klitzing (Germany), for developing an exact way of measuring electrical conductivity

1986 Ernst Ruska, Gerd Binnig (both Germany), and Heinrich Rohrer (Switzerland), for work on microscopes

1987 K. Alex Müller (Switzerland) and J. Georg Bednorz (Germany), for their discovery of high-temperature superconductors

1988 Leon M. Lederman, Melvin Schwartz, and Jack Steinberger (all U.S.), for research that improved the understanding of elementary particles and forces

1989 Norman F. Ramsey (U.S.), for work leading to development of the atomic clock, and Hans G. Dehmelt (U.S.) and Wolfgang Paul (Germany), for developing methods to isolate atoms and subatomic particles

1990 Richard E. Taylor (Canada), Jerome I. Friedman, and Dr. Henry W. Kendall (both U.S.), for their "breakthrough in our understanding of matter" that confirmed the reality of quarks

1991 Pierre-Gilles de Gennes (France), for his discoveries about the ordering of molecules in substances ranging from "super" glue to an exotic form of liquid helium

1992 George Charpak (France), for his inventions of particle detectors

1993 Joseph H. Taylor and Russell A. Hulse (both U.S.), for their discovery of a binary pulsar

1994 Clifford G. Shull (U.S.) and Bertram N. Brockhouse (Canada), for adapting beams of neutrons as probes to explore the atomic structure of matter

1995 Martin L. Perl and Frederick Reines (both U.S.), for their discoveries of "two of nature's most remarkable subatomic particles"—the tau and the neutrino

1996 David M. Lee, Robert C. Richardson, and Douglas D. Osheroff (all U.S.), for their discovery of superfluity in helium-3

1997 Steven Chu, William D. Phillips (both U.S.), and Claude Cohen-Tannoudji (France), for developing a method to cool and trap atoms using light from lasers

1998 Robert B. Laughlin (U.S.), Horst L. Störmer (Germany), and Daniel C. Tsui (U.S.), for their discovery of a new form of quantum fluid with fractionally charged excitations

1999 Gerardus 't Hooft (Netherlands) and Martinus J. G. Veltman (Netherlands), for their theory concerning the production of the Sun's energy

CHEMISTRY

1901 Jacobus H. van't Hoff (Netherlands), for laws of chemical dynamics and osmotic pressure in solutions

1902 Emil Fischer (Germany), for experiments in sugar and purin groups of substances

1903 Svante A. Arrhenius (Sweden), for his electrolytic theory of dissociation

1904 Sir William Ramsay (U.K.), for discovery and determination of place of inert gaseous elements in air

1905 Adolf von Baeyer (Germany), for work on organic dyes and hydroaromatic combinations

1906 Henri Moissan (France), for isolation of fluorine, and introduction of electric furnace

1907 Eduard Buchner (Germany), discovery of cell-less fermentation and investigations in biological chemistry

1908 Sir Ernest Rutherford (U.K.), for investigations into disintegration of elements

1909 Wilhelm Ostwald (Germany), for work on catalysis and investigations into chemical equilibrium and reaction rates

1910 Otto Wallach (Germany), for work in the field of alicyclic compounds

1911 Marie Curie (France), for discovery of elements radium and polonium

1912 Victor Grignard (France), for reagent discovered by him; and Paul Sabatier (France), for methods of hydrogenating organic compounds

1913 Alfred Werner (Switzerland), for linking up atoms within the molecule

1914 Theodore W. Richards (U.S.), for determining atomic weight of many chemical elements

1915 Richard Willstätter (Germany), for research into coloring matter of plants, especially chlorophyll

1918 Fritz Haber (Germany), for synthetic production of ammonia

1920 Walther Nernst (Germany), for work in thermochemistry

1921 Frederick Soddy (U.K.), for investigations into origin and nature of isotopes

1922 Francis W. Aston (U.K.), for discovery of isotopes in nonradioactive elements and for discovery of the whole number rule

1923 Fritz Pregl (Austria), for method of microanalysis of organic substances discovered by him

1925 In 1926, the 1925 prize was awarded to Richard Zsigmondy (Germany), for work on the heterogeneous nature of colloid solutions

1926 Theodor Svedberg (Sweden), for work on disperse systems

1927 In 1928, the 1927 prize was awarded to Heinrich Wieland (Germany), for investigations of bile acids and kindred substances

1928 Adolf Windaus (Germany), for investigations on constitution of the sterols and their connection with vitamins

1929 Sir Arthur Harden (U.K.) and Hans K. A. S. von Euler-Chelpin (Sweden), for research of fermentation of sugars

1930 Hans Fischer (Germany), for work on coloring matter of blood and leaves and for his synthesis of hemin

1931 Karl Bosch and Friedrich Bergius (both Germany), for invention and development of chemical high-pressure methods

1932 Irving Langmuir (U.S.), for work in realm of surface chemistry

1934 Harold C. Urey (U.S.), for discovery of heavy hydrogen

1935 Frédéric and Irène Joliot-Curie (both France), for synthesis of new radioactive elements

1936 Peter J. W. Debye (Netherlands), for investigations on dipole moments and diffraction of X rays and electrons in gases

1937 Walter N. Haworth (U.K.), for research on carbohydrates and vitamin C; and Paul Karrer (Switzerland), for work on carotenoids, flavins, and vitamins A and B

1938 Richard Kuhn (Germany), for carotenoid study and vitamin research (declined)

1939 Adolf Butenandt (Germany), for work on sexual hormones (declined the prize); and Leopold Ruzicka (Switzerland), for work with polymethylenes

1943 Georg Hevesy De Heves (Hungary), for work on use of isotopes as indicators

1944 Otto Hahn (Germany), for work on atomic fission

1945 Artturi Illmari Virtanen (Finland), for research in the field of conservation of fodder

1946 James B. Sumner (U.S.), for crystallizing enzymes; John H. Northrop and Wendell M. Stanley (both U.S.), for preparing enzymes and virus proteins in pure form

1947 Sir Robert Robinson (U.K.), for research in plant substances

1948 Arne Tiselius (Sweden), for biochemical discoveries and isolation of mouse paralysis virus

1949 William Francis Giauque (U.S.), for research in thermodynamics, especially effects of low temperature

1950 Otto Diels and Kurt Alder (both Germany), for discovery of diene synthesis enabling scientists to study structure of organic matter

1951 Glenn T. Seaborg and Edwin H. McMillan (both U.S.), for discovery of plutonium

1952 Archer John Porter Martin and Richard Laurence Millington Synge (both U.K.), for development of partition chromatography

1953 Hermann Staudinger (Germany), for research in giant molecules

1954 Linus C. Pauling (U.S.), for study of forces holding together protein and other molecules

1955 Vincent du Vigneaud (U.S.), for work on pituitary hormones

1956 Sir Cyril Hinshelwood (U.K.) and Nikolai N. Semenov (U.S.S.R.), for parallel research on chemical reaction kinetics

1957 Sir Alexander Todd (U.K.), for research with chemical compounds that are factors in heredity

1958 Frederick Sanger (U.K.), for determining molecular structure of insulin

1959 Jaroslav Heyrovsky (Czechoslovakia), for development of polarography, an electrochemical method of analysis

1960 Willard F. Libby (U.S.), for "atomic time clock" to measure age of objects by measuring their radioactivity

1961 Melvin Calvin (U.S.), for establishing chemical steps during photosynthesis

1962 Max F. Perutz and John C. Kendrew (U.K.), for mapping protein molecules with X rays

1963 Carl Ziegler (Germany) and Giulio Natta (Italy), for work in uniting simple hydrocarbons into large molecule substances

1964 Dorothy Mary Crowfoot Hodgkin (U.K.), for determining structure of compounds needed in combatting pernicious anemia

1965 Robert B. Woodward (U.S.), for work in synthesizing complicated organic compounds

1966 Robert Sanderson Mulliken (U.S.), for research on bond holding atoms together in molecule

1967 Manfred Eigen (Germany), Ronald G. W. Norrish, and George Porter (both U.K.), for work in high-speed chemical reactions

1968 Lars Onsager (U.S.), for development of system of equations in thermodynamics

1969 Derek H. R. Barton (U.K.) and Odd Hassel (Norway), for study of organic molecules

1970 Luis F. Leloir (Argentina), for discovery of sugar nucleotides and their role in biosynthesis of carbohydrates

1971 Gerhard Herzberg (Canada), for contributions to knowledge of electronic structure and geometry of molecules, particularly free radicals

1972 Christian Boehmer Anfinsen, Stanford Moore, and William Howard Stein (all U.S.), for pioneering studies in enzymes

1973 Ernst Otto Fischer (W. Germany) and Geoffrey Wilkinson (U.K.), for work that could solve problem of automobile exhaust pollution

1974 Paul J. Flory (U.S.), for developing analytic methods to study properties and molecular structure of long-chain molecules

1975 John W. Cornforth (Australia) and Vladimir Prelog (Switzerland), for research on structure of biological molecules such as antibiotics and cholesterol

1976 William N. Lipscomb, Jr. (U.S.), for work on the structure and bonding mechanisms of boranes

1977 Ilya Prigogine (Belgium), for contributions to nonequilibrium thermodynamics, particularly the theory of dissipative structures

1978 Peter Mitchell (U.K.), for contributions to the understanding of biological energy transfer

1979 Herbert C. Brown (U.S.) and Georg Wittig (West Germany), for developing a group of substances that facilitate very difficult chemical reactions

1980 Paul Berg, Walter Gilbert (both U.S.), and Frederick Sanger (U.K.), for developing methods to map the structure and function of DNA, the substance that controls the activity of the cell

1981 Roald Hoffmann (U.S.) and Kenichi Fukui (Japan), for applying quantum-mechanics theories to predict the course of chemical reactions

1982 Aaron Klug (U.K.), for research in the detailed structures of viruses and components of life

1983 Henry Taube (U.S.), for research on how electrons transfer between molecules in chemical reactions

1984 R. Bruce Merrifield (U.S.), for research that revolutionized the study of proteins

1985 Herbert A. Hauptman and Jerome Karle (both U.S.), for their outstanding achievements in the development of direct methods for the determination of crystal structures

1986 Dudley R. Herschbach, Yuan T. Lee (both U.S.), and John C. Polanyi (Canada), for their work on "reaction dynamics"

1987 Donald J. Cram, Charles J. Pedersen (both U.S.), and Jean-Marie Lehn (France), for wide-ranging research that has included the creation of artificial molecules that can mimic vital chemical reactions of the processes of life

1988 Johann Deisenhofer, Robert Huber, and Hartmut Michel (all West Germany), for unraveling the structure of proteins that play a crucial role in photosynthesis

1989 Thomas R. Cech and Sidney Altman (both U.S.), for their discovery, independently, that RNA could actively aid chemical reactions in the cells

1990 Elias James Corey (U.S.), for developing new ways to synthesize complex molecules ordinarily found in nature

1991 Richard R. Ernst (Switzerland), for refinements he developed in nuclear magnetic-resonance spectroscopy

1992 Rudolph A. Marcus (U.S.), for his mathematical analysis of how the overall energy in a system of interacting molecules changes and induces an electron to jump from one molecule to another

1993 Kary B. Mullis (U.S.) and Michael Smith (Canada), for their contributions to the science of genetics

1994 George A. Olah (U.S.), University of Southern California in Los Angeles, for research that opened new ways to break apart and rebuild compounds of carbon and hydrogen

1995 F. Sherwood Rowland, Mario Molina (both U.S.), and Paul Crutzen (Netherlands), for their pioneering work in explaining the chemical processes that deplete the earth's ozone shield

1996 Richard E. Smalley, Robert F. Curl, Jr. (both U.S.), and Harold W. Kroto (U.K.), for discovery of a new class of carbon molecule

1997 Paul D. Boyer (U.S.), Jens C. Skou (Denmark), and John E. Walker (U.K.), for discoveries about a molecule that allows the human body to store and transfer energy between cells

1998 Walter Kohn (U.S.) and John A. Pople (U.K.), for their developments in the study of properties of molecules and the chemical processes in which they are involved

1999 Ahmed H. Zewail (Egypt and U.S.), for creating the world's fastest camera, which captures atoms in motion

PHYSIOLOGY OR MEDICINE

1901 Emil A. von Behring (Germany), for work on serum therapy against diphtheria

1902 Sir Ronald Ross (U.K.), for work on malaria

1903 Niels R. Finsen (Denmark), for his treatment of lupus vulgaris with concentrated light rays

1904 Ivan P. Pavlov (U.S.S.R.), for work on the physiology of digestion

1905 Robert Koch (Germany), for work on tuberculosis

1906 Camillo Golgi (Italy) and Santiago Ramón y Cajal (Spain), for work on structure of the nervous system

1907 Charles L. A. Laveran (France), for work with protozoa in the generation of disease

1908 Paul Ehrlich (Germany) and Elie Metchnikoff (U.S.S.R.), for work on immunity

1909 Theodor Kocher (Switzerland), for work on the thyroid gland

1910 Albrecht Kossel (Germany), for achievements in the chemistry of the cell

1911 Allvar Gullstrand (Sweden), for work on the dioptrics of the eye

1912 Alexis Carrel (France), for work on vascular ligature and grafting of blood vessels and organs

1913 Charles Richet (France), for work on anaphylaxis

1914 Robert Bárány (Austria), for work on physiology and pathology of the vestibular system

1919 Jules Bordet (Belgium), for discoveries in connection with immunity

1920 August Krogh (Denmark), for discovery of regulation of capillaries' motor mechanism

1922 In 1923, the 1922 prize was shared by Archibald V. Hill (U.K.), for discovery relating to heat-production in muscles; and Otto Meyerhof (Germany), for correlation between consumption of oxygen and production of lactic acid in muscles

1923 Sir Frederick Banting (Canada) and John J. R. Macleod (Scotland), for discovery of insulin

1924 Willem Einthoven (Netherlands), for discovery of the mechanism of the electrocardiogram

1926 Johannes Fibiger (Denmark), for discovery of the Spiroptera carcinoma

1927 Julius Wagner-Jauregg (Austria), for use of malaria inoculation in treatment of dementia paralytica

1928 Charles Nicolle (France), for work on typhus exanthematicus

1929 Christiaan Eijkman (Netherlands), for discovery of the antineuritic vitamins; and Sir Frederick Hopkins (U.K.), for discovery of growth-promoting vitamins

1930 Karl Landsteiner (U.S.), for discovery of human blood groups

1931 Otto H. Warburg (Germany), for discovery of the character and mode of action of the respiratory ferment

1932 Sir Charles Sherrington (U.K.) and Edgar D. Adrian (U.S.), for discoveries of the function of the neuron

1933 Thomas H. Morgan (U.S.), for discoveries on hereditary function of the chromosomes

1934 George H. Whipple, George R. Minot, and William P. Murphy (U.S.), for discovery of liver therapy against anemias

1935 Hans Spemann (Germany), for discovery of the organizer effect in embryonic development

1936 Sir Henry Dale (U.K.) and Otto Loewi (Germany), for discoveries on chemical transmission of nerve impulses

1937 Albert Szent-Györgyi von Nagyrapolt (Hungary), for discoveries on biological combustion

1938 Corneille Heymans (Belgium), for determining importance of sinus and aorta mechanisms in the regulation of respiration

1939 Gerhard Domagk (Germany), for antibacterial effect of prontocilate

1943 Henrik Dam (Denmark) and Edward A. Doisy (U.S.), for analysis of vitamin K

1944 Joseph Erlanger and Herbert Spencer Gasser (both U.S.), for work on functions of the nerve threads

1945 Sir Alexander Fleming, Ernst Boris Chain, and Sir Howard Florey (all U.K.), for discovery of penicillin

1946 Herman J. Muller (U.S.), for hereditary effects of X rays on genes

1947 Carl F. and Gerty T. Cori (U.S.), for work on animal starch metabolism; Bernardo A. Houssay (Argentina), for study of pituitary

1948 Paul Mueller (Switzerland), for discovery of insect-killing properties of DDT

1949 Walter Rudolf Hess (Switzerland), for research on brain control of body; and Antonio Caetano de Abreu Freire Egas Moniz (Portugal), for development of brain operation

1950 Philip S. Hench, Edward C. Kendall (both U.S.), and Tadeus Reichstein (Switzerland), for discoveries about hormones of adrenal cortex

1951 Max Theiler (South Africa), for development of anti-yellow-fever vaccine

1952 Selman A. Waksman (U.S.), for codiscovery of streptomycin

1953 Fritz A. Lipmann (Germany-U.S.) and Hans Adolph Krebs (Germany-U.K.), for studies of living cells

1954 John F. Enders, Thomas H. Weller, and Frederick C. Robbins (all U.S.), for work with cultivation of polio virus

1955 Hugo Theorell (Sweden), for work on oxidation enzymes

1956 Dickinson W. Richards, Jr., André F. Cournand (both U.S.), and Werner Forssmann (Germany), for new techniques in treating heart disease

1957 Daniel Bovet (Italy), for development of drugs to relieve allergies and relax muscles during surgery

1958 Joshua Lederberg (U.S.), for work with genetic mechanisms; George W. Beadle and Edward L. Tatum (both U.S.), for discovering how genes transmit hereditary characteristics

1959 Severo Ochoa and Arthur Kornberg (both U.S.), for discoveries related to compounds within chromosomes that play a vital role in heredity

1960 Sir Macfarlane Burnet (Australia) and Peter Brian Medawar (U.K.), for discovery of acquired immunological tolerance

1961 Georg von Bekesy (U.S.), for discoveries about physical mechanisms of stimulation within cochlea

1962 James D. Watson (U.S.), Maurice H. F. Wilkins, and Francis H. C. Crick (both U.K.), for determining structure of deoxyribonucleic acid (DNA)

1963 Alan Lloyd Hodgkin, Andrew Fielding Huxley (both U.K.), and Sir John Carew Eccles (Australia), for research on nerve cells

1964 Konrad E. Bloch (U.S.) and Feodor Lynen (Germany), for research on mechanism and regulation of cholesterol and fatty-acid metabolism

1965 François Jacob, André Lwolff, and Jacques Monod (all France), for study of regulatory activities in body cells

1966 Charles Brenton Huggins (U.S.), for studies in hormone treatment of cancer of prostate; Francis Peyton Rous (U.S.), for discovery of tumor-producing viruses

1967 Haldan K. Hartline, George Wald, and Ragnar Granit (all U.S.), for work on human eye

1968 Robert W. Holley, Har Gobind Khorana, and Marshall W. Nirenberg (all U.S.), for studies of genetic code

1969 Max Delbruck, Alfred D. Hershey, and Salvador E. Luria (all U.S.), for study of mechanism of virus infection in living cells

1970 Julius Axelrod (U.S.), Ulf S. von Euler (Sweden), and Sir Bernard Katz (U.K.), for studies of how nerve impulses are transmitted within the body

1971 Earl W. Sutherland, Jr. (U.S.), for research on how hormones work

1972 Gerald M. Edelman (U.S.), and Rodney R. Porter (U.K.), for research on the chemical structure and nature of antibodies

1973 Karl von Frisch, Konrad Lorenz (both Austria), and Nikolaas Tinbergen (Netherlands), for their studies of individual and social behavior patterns

1974 George E. Palade, Christian de Duve (both U.S.), and Albert Claude (Belgium), for contributions to understanding inner workings of living cells

1975 David Baltimore, Howard M. Temin, and Renato Dulbecco (all U.S.), for work in interaction between tumor viruses and genetic material of the cell

1976 Baruch S. Blumberg and D. Carleton Gajdusek (both U.S.), for discoveries concerning new mechanisms for the origin and dissemination of infectious diseases

1977 Rosalyn S. Yalow, Roger C. L. Guillemin, and Andrew V. Schally (all U.S.), for research in role of hormones in chemistry of the body

1978 Daniel Nathans, Hamilton Smith (both U.S.), and Werner Arber (Switzerland), for discovery of restriction enzymes and their application to problems of molecular genetics

1979 Allan McLeod Cormack (U.S.) and Godfrey Newbold Hounsfield (U.K.), for developing computed axial tomography (CAT scan) X ray technique

1980 Baruj Benacerraf, George D. Snell (both U.S.), and Jean Dausset (France), for discoveries that explain how the structure of cells relates to organ transplants and diseases

1981 Roger W. Sperry, David H. Hubel (both U.S.), and Torsten N. Wiesel (Sweden), for studies vital to understanding the organization and functioning of the brain

1982 Sune Bergstrom, Bengt Samuelsson (both Sweden), and John R. Vane (U.K.), for research in prostaglandins, hormonelike substances involved in a wide range of illnesses

1983 Barbara McClintock (U.S.), for her discovery of mobile genes in the chromosomes of a plant that change the future generations of plants they produce

1984 Cesar Milstein (U.K./Argentina), Georges J. F. Kohler (West Germany), and Niels K. Jerne (U.K./Denmark), for their work in immunology

1985 Michael S. Brown and Joseph L. Goldstein (both U.S.), for their work, which has drastically widened our understanding of the cholesterol metabolism and increased our possibilities to prevent and treat atherosclerosis and heart attacks

1986 Rita Levi-Montalcini (dual U.S./Italy) and Stanley Cohen (U.S.), for their contributions to the understanding of substances that influence cell growth

1987 Susumu Tonegawa (Japan), for his discoveries of how the body can suddenly marshal its immunological defenses against millions of different disease agents that it has never encountered before

1988 Gertrude B. Elion, George H. Hitchings (both U.S.), and Sir James Black (U.K.), for their discoveries of important principles for drug treatment

1989 J. Michael Bishop and Harold E. Varmus (both U.S.), for their unifying theory of cancer development

1990 Joseph E. Murray and E. Donnall Thomas (both U.S.), for their pioneering work in transplants

1991 Erwin Neher and Bert Sakmann (both Germany), for their research, particularly for the development of a technique called patch clamp

1992 Edmond H. Fischer and Edwin G. Krebs (both U.S.), for their discovery of a regulatory mechanism affecting almost all cells

1993 Phillip A. Sharp (U.S.) and Richard J. Roberts (U.K.), for their independent discovery in 1977 of "split genes"

1994 Alfred G. Gilman and Martin Rodbell (both U.S.), for discovery of G-proteins that help cells respond to outside signals

1995 Edward B. Lewis, Eric F. Wieschaus (both U.S.), and Christiane Nüsslein-Volhard (Germany), for studies of the fruit fly that will help explain congenital malformations in humans

1996 Peter C. Doherty (Australia) and Rolf M. Zinkernagel (Switzerland), for discoveries about how the immune system recognizes virus-infected cells

1997 Stanley B. Prusiner (U.S.), for discovery of a new type of germ, called prions, that causes degenerative brain disorders

1998 Robert F. Furchgott, Louis J. Ignarro, and Ferid Murad (all U.S.), for discovering that nitric oxide acts as a signal in the cardiovascular system

1999 Günter Blobel (U.S.), for discovering that proteins have intrinsic signals that govern their transport and localization in the cell

ECONOMIC SCIENCE

1969 Ragnar Frisch (Norway) and Jan Tinbergen (Netherlands), for work in econometrics (application of mathematics and statistical methods to economic theories and problems)

1970 Paul A. Samuelson (U.S.), for efforts to raise the level of scientific analysis in economic theory

1971 Simon Kuznets (U.S.), for developing concept of using a country's gross national product to determine its economic growth

1972 Kenneth J. Arrow (U.S.) and Sir John R. Hicks (U.K.), for theories that help to assess business risk and government economic and welfare policies

1973 Wassily Leontief (U.S.), for devising the input-output technique to determine how different sectors of an economy interact

1974 Gunnar Myrdal (Sweden) and Friedrich A. von Hayek (U.K.), for pioneering analysis of the interdependence of economic, social, and institutional phenomena

1975 Leonid V. Kantorovich (U.S.S.R.) and Tjalling C. Koopmans (U.S.), for work on the theory of optimum allocation of resources

1976 Milton Friedman (U.S.), for work in consumption analysis and monetary history and theory, and for demonstration of complexity of stabilization policy

1977 Bertil Ohlin (Sweden) and James E. Meade (U.K.), for contributions to theory of international trade and international capital movements

1978 Herbert A. Simon (U.S.), for research into the decision-making process within economic organizations

1979 Sir Arthur Lewis (U.K.) and Theodore Schultz (U.S.), for work on economic problems of developing nations

1980 Lawrence R. Klein (U.S.), for developing models for forecasting economic trends and shaping policies to deal with them

1981 James Tobin (U.S.), for analyses of financial markets and their influence on spending and saving by families and businesses

1982 George J. Stigler (U.S.), for work on government regulation in the economy and the functioning of industry

1983 Gerard Debreu (U.S.), in recognition of his work on the basic economic problem of how prices operate to balance what producers supply with what buyers want

1984 Sir Richard Stone (U.K.), for his work to develop the systems widely used to measure the performance of national economics

1985 Franco Modigliani (U.S.), for his pioneering work in analyzing the behavior of household savers and the functioning of financial markets

1986 James M. Buchanan (U.S.), for his development of new methods for analyzing economic and political decision-making

1987 Robert M. Solow (U.S.), for seminal contributions to the theory of economic growth

1988 Maurice Allais (France), for his pioneering development of theories to better understand market behavior and the efficient use of resources

1989 Trygve Haavelmo (Norway), for his pioneering work in methods for testing economic theories

1990 Harry M. Markowitz, William F. Sharpe, and Merton H. Miller (all U.S.), whose work provided new tools for weighing the risks and rewards of different investments and for valuing corporate stocks and bonds

1991 Ronald Coase (U.S.), for his pioneering work in how property rights and the cost of doing business affect the economy

1992 Gary S. Becker (U.S.), for "having extended the domain of economic theory to aspects of human behavior which had previously been dealt with—if at all—by other social science disciplines"

1993 Robert W. Fogel and Douglass C. North (both U.S.), for their work in economic history

1994 John F. Nash, John C. Harsanyi (both U.S.), and Reinhard Selten (Germany), for their pioneering work in game theory

1995 Robert E. Lucas, Jr. (U.S.), for having had the greatest influence on macroeconomic research since 1970

1996 James A. Mirrlees (U.K.) and William Vickrey (U.S.), for "their fundamental contributions to the economic theory of incentives"

1997 Robert C. Merton and Myron S. Scholes (both U.S.), for developing a formula that determines the value of stock options and other derivatives

1998 Amartya Sen (India), for his contributions to welfare economics

1999 Robert A. Mundell (Canada), for his work on monetary dynamics and optimum currency areas

Pulitzer Prizes

For years not listed, no award was made.

PULITZER PRIZES IN JOURNALISM

Meritorious Public Service

1918 *New York Times;* also special award to Minna Lewinson and Henry Beetle Hough
1919 *Milwaukee Journal*
1921 *Boston Post*
1922 *New York World*
1923 *Memphis Commercial Appeal*
1924 *New York World*
1926 *Columbus* (Ga.) *Enquirer Sun*
1927 *Canton* (Ohio) *Daily News*
1928 *Indianapolis Times*
1929 *New York Evening World*
1931 *Atlanta Constitution*
1932 *Indianapolis News*
1933 *New York World-Telegram*
1934 *Medford* (Ore.) *Mail Tribune*
1935 *Sacramento Bee*
1936 *Cedar Rapids* (Iowa) *Gazette*
1937 *St. Louis Post-Dispatch*
1938 *Bismarck* (N.D.) *Tribune*
1939 *Miami Daily News*
1940 *Waterbury* (Conn.) *Republican* and *American*
1941 *St. Louis Post-Dispatch*
1942 *Los Angeles Times*
1943 *Omaha World-Herald*
1944 *New York Times*
1945 *Detroit Free Press*
1946 *Scranton* (Pa.) *Times*
1947 *Baltimore Sun*

1948 *St. Louis Post-Dispatch*
1949 *(Lincoln) Nebraska State Journal*
1950 *Chicago Daily News;* and *St. Louis Post-Dispatch*
1951 *Miami Herald;* and *Brooklyn Eagle*
1952 *St. Louis Post-Dispatch*
1953 *Whiteville* (N.C.) *News Reporter;* and *Tabor City* (N.C.) *Tribune*
1954 *Newsday* (Garden City, N.Y.)
1955 *Columbus* (Ga.) *Ledger* and *Sunday Ledger-Enquirer*
1956 *Watsonville* (Calif.) *Register-Pajaronian*
1957 *Chicago Daily News*
1958 *(Little Rock) Arkansas Gazette*
1959 *Utica* (N.Y.) *Observer Dispatch* and *Utica Daily Press*
1960 *Los Angeles Times*
1961 *Amarillo* (Tex.) *Globe-Times*
1962 *Panama City* (Fla.) *News-Herald*
1963 *Chicago Daily News*
1964 *St. Petersburg* (Fla.) *Times*
1965 *Hutchinson* (Kans.) *News*
1966 *Boston Globe*
1967 *Louisville Courier-Journal* and *Milwaukee Journal*
1968 *Riverside* (Calif.) *Press-Enterprise*
1969 *Los Angeles Times*
1970 *Newsday* (Garden City, N.Y.)
1971 *Winston–Salem* (N.C.) *Journal and Sentinel*
1972 *New York Times*
1973 *Washington Post*

1974 *Newsday* (Garden City, N.Y.)	**1950** Carl M. Saunders *(Jackson [Mich.] Citizen*
1975 *Boston Globe*	*Patriot)*
1976 *Anchorage* (Alaska) *Daily News*	**1951** William H. Fitzpatrick *(New Orleans States)*
1977 *Lufkin* (Tex.) *News*	**1952** Louis LaCoss *(St. Louis Globe-Democrat)*
1978 *Philadelphia Inquirer*	**1953** Vermont C. Royster *(Wall Street Journal)*
1979 *Point Reyes* (Calif.) *Light*	**1954** Don Murray *(Boston Herald)*
1980 Gannett News Service	**1955** Royce Howes *(Detroit Free Press)*
1981 *Charlotte* (N.C.) *Observer*	**1956** Lauren K. Soth *(Des Moines Register and*
1982 *Detroit News*	*Tribune)*
1983 *Jackson* (Miss.) *Clarion-Ledger*	**1957** Buford Boone *(Tuscaloosa [Ala.] News)*
1984 *Los Angeles Times*	**1958** Harry S. Ashmore *(Arkansas Gazette)*
1985 *The Fort Worth Star-Telegram*	**1959** Ralph McGill *(Atlanta Constitution)*
1986 *Denver Post*	**1960** Lenoir Chambers *(Virginian-Pilot)*
1987 *Pittsburgh Press,* reporting by Andrew	**1961** William J. Dorvillier *(San Juan [P.R.] Star)*
Schneider and Matthew Brelis	**1962** Thomas M. Storke *(Santa Barbara [Calif.]*
1988 *Charlotte* (N.C.) *Observer*	*News-Press)*
1989 *Anchorage Daily News*	**1963** Ira B. Harkey, Jr. *(Pascagoula [Miss.]*
1990 *Philadelphia Inquirer* and *Washington* (N.C.)	*Chronicle)*
Daily News	**1964** Hazel Brannon Smith *(Lexington [Miss.]*
1991 *Des Moines Register,* reporting by Jane	*Advertiser)*
Schorer	**1965** John R. Harrison *(Gainesville [Fla.] Daily*
1992 *Sacramento Bee* for "The Sierra in Peril"	*Sun)*
series by Tom Knudson	**1966** Robert Lasch *(St. Louis Post-Dispatch)*
1993 *Miami Herald*	**1967** Eugene Patterson *(Atlanta Constitution)*
1994 *The Akron* (Ohio) *Beacon Journal*	**1968** John S. Knight *(Knight Newspapers)*
1995 *The Virgin Islands Daily News*	**1969** Paul Greenberg *(Pine Bluff [Ark.]*
1996 *The News and Observer* (Raleigh, N.C.)	*Commercial)*
1997 *The Times-Picayune* (New Orleans, La.)	**1970** Phillip L. Geyelin *(Washington Post)*
1998 *Grand Forks* (N.D.) *Herald*	**1971** Horance G. Davis, Jr. *(Gainesville [Fla.] Sun)*
1999 *Washington Post*	**1972** John Strohmeyer *(Bethlehem [Pa.] Globe*
2000 *Washington Post*	*Times)*
	1973 Roger Bourne Linscott *(Berkshire Eagle*
Editorial	*[Pittsfield, Mass.])*
1917 *New York Tribune*	**1974** F. Gilman Spencer *(Trenton [N.J.] Trentonian)*
1918 *Louisville Courier-Journal*	**1975** John Daniell Maurice *(Charleston [W. Va.]*
1920 Harvey E. Newbranch *(Omaha Evening*	*Daily Mail)*
World-Herald)	**1976** Philip P. Kerby *(Los Angeles Times)*
1922 Frank M. O'Brien *(New York Herald)*	**1977** Warren L. Lerude, Foster Church, and
1923 William Allen White *(Emporia [Kan.] Gazette)*	Norman F. Cardoza *(Reno [Nev.] Gazette* and
1924 *Boston Herald;* special prize: Frank I. Cobb	*Nevada State Journal)*
(New York World)	**1978** Meg Greenfield *(Washington Post)*
1925 *Charleston* (S.C.) *News and Courier*	**1979** Edwin M. Yoder, Jr. *(Washington Star)*
1926 Edward M. Kingsbury *(New York Times)*	**1980** Robert L. Bartley *(Wall Street Journal)*
1927 F. Lauriston Bullard *(Boston Herald)*	**1982** Jack Rosenthal *(New York Times)*
1928 Grover Cleveland Hall *(Montgomery [Ala.]*	**1983** *Miami Herald*
Advertiser)	**1984** Albert Scardino *(Georgia Gazette)*
1929 Louis Isaac Jaffe *(Norfolk Virginian-Pilot)*	**1985** Richard Aregood *(Philadelphia Daily News)*
1931 Charles S. Ryckman *(Fremont [Neb.] Tribune)*	**1986** Jack Fuller *(Chicago Tribune)*
1933 *Kansas City* (Mo.) *Star*	**1987** Jonathan Freedman *(San Diego Tribune)*
1934 E. P. Chase *(Atlantic [Iowa] News Telegraph)*	**1988** Jane E. Healy *(Orlando Sentinel)*
1936 Felix Morley *(Washington Post);* George B.	**1989** Lois Wille *(Chicago Tribune)*
Parker (Scripps–Howard Newspapers)	**1990** Thomas J. Hylton *(Pottstown [Pa.] Mercury)*
1937 John W. Owens *(Baltimore Sun)*	**1991** Ron Casey, Harold Jackson, and Joey
1938 W. W. Waymack *(Des Moines Register and*	Kennedy *(Birmingham [Ala.] News)*
Tribune)	**1992** Maria Henson *(Lexington [Ky.] Herald-Leader)*
1939 Ronald G. Callvert *(Portland Oregonian)*	**1994** R. Bruce Dold *(Chicago Tribune)*
1940 Bart Howard *(St. Louis Post-Dispatch)*	**1995** Jeffrey Good *(St. Petersburg [Fla.] Times)*
1941 Reuben Maury *(New York Daily News)*	**1996** Robert B. Semple, Jr. *(New York Times)*
1942 Geoffrey Parsons *(New York Herald Tribune)*	**1997** Michael Gartner *(Daily Tribune [Ames, Iowa])*
1943 Forrest W. Seymour *(Des Moines Register*	**1998** Bernard L. Stein *(The Riverdale Press*
and Tribune)	*[Bronx, N.Y.])*
1944 Henry J. Haskell *(Kansas City [Mo.] Star)*	**1999** Editorial Board *(Daily News [New York, N.Y.])*
1945 George W. Potter *(Providence [R.I.]*	**2000** John C. Bersia *(The Orlando Sentinel*
Journal-Bulletin)	*[Orlando, Fla.])*
1946 Hodding Carter *([Greenville, Miss.] Delta*	
Democrat-Times)	**Correspondence**
1947 William H. Grimes *(Wall Street Journal)*	**1929** Paul Scott Mowrer *(Chicago Daily News)*
1948 Virginius Dabney *(Richmond Times-Dispatch)*	**1930** Leland Stowe *(New York Herald Tribune)*
1949 John H. Crider *(Boston Herald);* Herbert	**1931** H. R. Knickerbocker *(Philadelphia Public*
Elliston *(Washington Post)*	*Ledger* and *New York Evening Post)*

1932 Walter Duranty *(New York Times)*; Charles G. Ross *(St. Louis Post-Dispatch)*
1933 Edgar Ansel Mowrer *(Chicago Daily News)*
1934 Frederick T. Birchall *(New York Times)*
1935 Arthur Krock *(New York Times)*
1936 Wilfred C. Barber *(Chicago Tribune)*
1937 Anne O'Hare McCormick *(New York Times)*
1938 Arthur Krock *(New York Times)*
1939 Louis P. Lochner (Associated Press)
1940 Otto D. Tolischus *(New York Times)*
1941 Group award[1]
1942 Carlos P. Romulo *(Philippines Herald)*
1943 Hanson W. Baldwin *(New York Times)*
1944 Ernie Pyle (Scripps–Howard Newspaper Alliance)
1945 Harold V. (Hal) Boyle (Associated Press)
1946 Arnaldo Cortesi *(New York Times)*
1947 Brooks Atkinson *(New York Times)*

1. For the public services and the individual achievements of American news reporters in the war zones.

Editorial Cartooning

1922 Rollin Kirby *(New York World)*
1924 Jay Norwood Darling *(New York Tribune)*
1925 Rollin Kirby *(New York World)*
1926 D. R. Fitzpatrick *(St. Louis Post-Dispatch)*
1927 Nelson Harding *(Brooklyn Eagle)*
1928 Nelson Harding *(Brooklyn Eagle)*
1929 Rollin Kirby *(New York World)*
1930 Charles R. Macauley *(Brooklyn Eagle)*
1931 Edmund Duffy *(Baltimore Sun)*
1932 John T. McCutcheon *(Chicago Tribune)*
1933 H. M. Talburt *(Washington Daily News)*
1934 Edmund Duffy *(Baltimore Sun)*
1935 Ross A. Lewis *(Milwaukee Journal)*
1937 C. D. Batchelor *(New York Daily News)*
1938 Vaughn Shoemaker *(Chicago Daily News)*
1939 Charles G. Werner *(Daily Oklahoman* [Oklahoma City])
1940 Edmund Duffy *(Baltimore Sun)*
1941 Jacob Burck *(Chicago Times)*
1942 Herbert L. Block (NEA Service)
1943 Jay Norwood Darling *(New York Herald Tribune)*
1944 Clifford K. Berryman *(Washington Evening Star)*
1945 Bill Mauldin (United Features Syndicate)
1946 Bruce Alexander Russell *(Los Angeles Times)*
1947 Vaughn Shoemaker *(Chicago Daily News)*
1948 Reuben L. Goldberg *(New York Sun)*
1949 Lute Pease *(Newark Evening News)*
1950 James T. Berryman *(Washington Evening Star)*
1951 Reg (Reginald W.) Manning *(Arizona Republic* [Phoenix])
1952 Fred L. Packer *(New York Mirror)*
1953 Edward D. Kuekes *(Cleveland Plain Dealer)*
1954 Herbert L. Block *(Washington Post* and *Times-Herald)*
1955 Daniel R. Fitzpatrick *(St. Louis Post-Dispatch)*
1956 Robert York *(Louisville Times)*
1957 Tom Little *(Nashville Tennessean)*
1958 Bruce M. Shanks *(Buffalo Evening News)*
1959 Bill Mauldin *(St. Louis Post-Dispatch)*
1961 Carey Orr *(Chicago Tribune)*
1962 Edmund S. Valtman *(Hartford Times)*
1963 Frank Miller *(Des Moines Register)*
1964 Paul Conrad (formerly of *Denver Post,* later on *Los Angeles Times)*
1966 Don Wright *(Miami News)*
1967 Patrick B. Oliphant *(Denver Post)*

1968 Eugene Gray Payne *(Charlotte* [N.C.] *Observer)*
1969 John Fischetti *(Chicago Daily News)*
1970 Thomas F. Darcy *(Newsday* [Garden City, N.Y.])
1971 Paul Conrad *(Los Angeles Times)*
1972 Jeffrey K. MacNelly *(Richmond* [Va.] *News Leader)*
1974 Paul Szep *(Boston Globe)*
1975 Garry Trudeau (Universal Press Syndicate)
1976 Tony Auth *(Philadelphia Inquirer)*
1977 Paul Szep *(Boston Globe)*
1978 Jeffrey K. MacNelly *(Richmond* [Va.] *News Leader)*
1979 Herbert L. Block *(Washington Post)*
1980 Don Wright *(Miami News)*
1981 Mike Peters *(Dayton* [Ohio] *Daily News)*
1982 Ben Sargent *(Austin* [Tex.] *American-Statesman)*
1983 Richard Locher *(Chicago Tribune)*
1984 Paul Conrad *(Los Angeles Times)*
1985 Jeff MacNelly *(Chicago Tribune)*
1986 Jules Feiffer *(Village Voice)*
1987 Berke Breathed *(Washington Post* Writers Group)
1988 Doug Marlette *(Atlanta Constitution* and *Charlotte* [N.C.] *Observer)*
1989 Jack Higgins *(Chicago Sun-Times)*
1990 Tom Toles *(Buffalo News)*
1991 Jim Borgman *(Cincinnati Inquirer)*
1992 Signe Wilkinson *(Philadelphia Daily News)*
1993 Stephen R. Benson *(Arizona Republic)*
1994 Michael P. Ramirez *(The Commercial Appeal,* Memphis)
1995 Mike Luckovich *(The Atlanta Constitution)*
1996 Jim Morin *(The Miami Herald)*
1997 Walt Handelsman *(The Times-Picayune)*
1998 Stephen P. Breen *(The Asbury Park* [N.J.] *Press)*
1999 David Horsey *(Seattle Post-Intelligencer)*
2000 Joel Pett *(Lexington* [Ky.] *Herald-Leader)*

News Photography

1942 Milton Brooks *(Detroit News)*
1943 Frank Noel (Associated Press)
1944 Frank Filan (Associated Press); Earle L. Bunker *(Omaha World-Herald)*
1945 Joe Rosenthal (Associated Press)
1947 Arnold Hardy
1948 Frank Cushing *(Boston Traveler)*
1949 Nat Fein *(New York Herald Tribune)*
1950 Bill Crouch *(Oakland Tribune)*
1951 Max Desfor (Associated Press)
1952 John Robinson and Don Ultang *(Des Moines Register & Tribune)*
1953 William M. Gallagher *(Flint* [Mich.] *Journal)*
1954 Mrs. Walter M. Schau
1955 John L. Gaunt, Jr. *(Los Angeles Times)*
1956 *New York Daily News*
1957 Harry A. Trask *(Boston Traveler)*
1958 William C. Beall *(Washington Daily News)*
1959 William Seaman *(Minneapolis Star)*
1960 Andrew Lopez (United Press International)
1961 Yasushi Nagao (Mainichi Newspapers, Tokyo)
1962 Paul Vathis (Harrisburg [Pa.] bureau of Associated Press)
1963 Hector Rondon *(La Republica,* Caracas, Venezuela)
1964 Robert H. Jackson *(Dallas Times Herald)*
1965 Horst Faas (Associated Press)
1966 Kyoichi Sawada (United Press International)

1967 Jack R. Thornell (Associated Press)
1968 News: Rocco Morabito *(Jacksonville* [Fla.] *Journal);* features: Toshio Sakai (United Press International)
1969 Spot news: Edward T. Adams (Associated Press); features: Moneta Sleet, Jr.
1970 Spot news: Steve Starr (Associated Press); features: Dallas Kinney *(Palm Beach Post)*
1971 Spot news: John Paul Filo *(Valley Daily News* and *Daily Dispatch* [Tarentum and New Kensington, Pa.]); features: Jack Dykinga *(Chicago Sun-Times)*
1972 Spot news: Horst Faas and Michel Laurent (Associated Press); features: Dave Kennerly (United Press International)
1973 Spot news: Huynh Cong Ut *(Associated Press);* features: Brian Lanker *(Topeka Capital-Journal)*
1974 Spot news: Anthony K. Roberts (Associated Press); features: Slava Veder (Associated Press)
1975 Spot news: Gerald H. Gay *(Seattle Times);* features: Matthew Lewis *(Washington Post)*
1976 Spot news: Stanley J. Forman *(Boston Herald-American);* features: photographic staff of *Louisville Courier-Journal* and *Times*
1977 Spot news: Neal Ulevich (Associated Press) and Stanley J. Forman *(Boston Herald-American);* features: Robin Hood *(Chattanooga News-Free Press)*
1978 Spot news: John Blair, freelance, Evansville, Ind.; features: J. Ross Baughman (Associated Press)
1979 Spot news: Thomas J. Kelly, 3rd *(Pottstown* [Pa.] *Mercury);* features: photographic staff of *Boston Herald-American*
1980 Features: Erwin H. Hagler *(Dallas Times Herald)*
1981 Spot news: Larry C. Price *(Fort Worth Star-Telegram);* features: Taro M. Yamasaki *(Detroit Free Press)*
1982 Spot news: Ron Edmonds (Associated Press); features: John H. White *(Chicago Sun-Times)*
1983 Spot news: Bill Foley (Associated Press); features: James B. Dickman *(Dallas Times Herald)*
1984 Spot news: Stan Grossfeld *(Boston Globe);* features: Anthony Suau *(Denver Post)*
1985 Spot news: photographic staff of *Register,* Santa Ana, Calif.; features: Stan Grossfeld *(Boston Globe)*
1986 Spot news: Michel duCille and Carol Guzy *(Miami Herald);* features: Tom Gralish *(Philadelphia Inquirer)*
1987 Spot news: Kim Komenich *(San Francisco Examiner);* features: David Peterson *(Des Moines Register)*
1988 Spot news: Scott Shaw *(Odessa* [Texas] *American);* features: Michel duCille *(Miami Herald)*
1989 Spot news: Ron Olshwanger *(St. Louis Post-Dispatch);* features: Manny Crisostomo *(Detroit Free Press)*
1990 Spot news: *Oakland Tribune;* features: David C. Turnley *(Detroit Free Press)*
1991 Spot news: Greg Marinovich (Associated Press); features: William Snyder *(Dallas Morning News)*

1992 Spot news: Associated Press staff; features: John Kaplan *(Herald* [Monterey, Calif.] and *Pittsburgh Post–Gazette)*
1993 Spot news: William Snyder and Ken Geiger *(Dallas Morning News);* features: Associated Press
1994 Spot news: Paul Watson *(Toronto Star);* features: Kevin Carter, freelancer for *New York Times*
1995 Spot news: Carol Guzy *(Washington Post);* features: Associated Press Staff
1996 Spot news: Charles Porter IV, freelance photographer for Associated Press; features: Stephanie Walsh, freelance photographer for Newhouse News Service
1997 Spot news: Annie Wells *(The Press Democrat* [Santa Rosa, Calif.]); features: Alexander Zemlianichenko (Associated Press)
1998 Spot news: Martha Rial *(The Pittsburgh Post–Gazette);* features: Clarence Williams *(The Los Angeles Times)*
1999 Spot news: Associated Press photo staff; features: Associated Press photo staff
2000 Breaking news: photographic staff of *Denver Rocky Mountain News;* features: Carol Guzy, Michael Williamson, and Lucian Perkins *(Washington Post)*

National Telegraphic Reporting
1942 Louis Stark *(New York Times)*
1944 Dewey L. Fleming *(Baltimore Sun)*
1945 James Reston *(New York Times)*
1946 Edward A. Harris *(St. Louis Post-Dispatch)*
1947 Edward T. Folliard *(Washington Post)*

National Reporting
1948 Bert Andrews *(New York Herald Tribune);* Nat S. Finney *(Minneapolis Tribune)*
1949 C. P. Trussell *(New York Times)*
1950 Edwin O. Guthman *(Seattle Times)*
1952 Anthony Leviero *(New York Times)*
1953 Don Whitehead *(Associated Press)*
1954 Richard Wilson (Cowles Newspapers)
1955 Anthony Lewis *(Washington Daily News)*
1956 Charles L. Bartlett *(Chattanooga Times)*
1957 James Reston *(New York Times)*
1958 Relman Morin (Associated Press) and Clark Mollenhoff *(Des Moines Register & Tribune)*
1959 Howard Van Smith *(Miami News)*
1960 Vance Trimble (Scripps-Howard Newspaper Alliance)
1961 Edward R. Cony *(Wall Street Journal)*
1962 Nathan G. Caldwell and Gene S. Graham *(Nashville Tennessean)*
1963 Anthony Lewis *(New York Times)*
1964 Merriman Smith (United Press International)
1965 Louis M. Kohlmeier *(Wall Street Journal)*
1966 Haynes Johnson *(Washington Evening Star)*
1967 Stanley Penn and Monroe Karmin *(Wall Street Journal)*
1968 Howard James *(Christian Science Monitor);* Nathan K. (Nick) Kotz *(Des Moines Register* and *Minneapolis Tribune)*
1969 Robert Cahn *(Christian Science Monitor)*
1970 William J. Eaton *(Chicago Daily News)*
1971 Lucinda Franks and Thomas Powers (United Press International)
1972 Jack Anderson *(United Feature Syndicate)*
1973 Robert Boyd and Clark Hoyt *(Knight Newspapers)*

1974 Jack White *(Providence* [R.I.] *Journal-Bulletin);* James R. Polk *(Washington Star-News)*
1975 Donald L. Barlett and James B. Steele *(Philadelphia Inquirer)*
1976 James Risser *(Des Moines Register)*
1977 Walter Mears (Associated Press)
1978 Gaylord D. Shaw *(Los Angeles Times)*
1979 James Risser *(Des Moines Register)*
1980 Bette Swenson Orsini and Charles Stafford *(St. Petersburg Times)*
1981 John M. Crewdson *(New York Times)*
1982 Rick Atkinson *(Kansas City* [Mo.] *Times)*
1983 *Boston Globe*
1984 John N. Wilford *(New York Times)*
1985 Thomas J. Knudson *(Des Moines Register)*
1986 Craig Flournoy and George Rodrigue *(Dallas Morning News)* and Arthur Howe *(Philadelphia Inquirer)*
1987 *Miami Herald,* staff; *New York Times,* staff
1988 Tim Weiner *(Philadelphia Inquirer)*
1989 Donald L. Barlett and James B. Steele *(Philadelphia Inquirer)*
1990 Ross Anderson, Bill Dietrich, Mary Ann Gwinn, and Eric Nalder *(Seattle Times)*
1991 Marjie Lundstrom and Rochelle Sharpe (Gannett News Service)
1992 Jeff Taylor and Mike McGraw *(Kansas City Star)*
1993 David Maranniss *(Washington Post)*
1994 Eileen Welsome *(Albuquerque* [N.M.] *Tribune)*
1995 Tony Horwitz *(Wall Street Journal)*
1996 Alix M. Freedman *(Wall Street Journal)*
1997 *Wall Street Journal* staff
1998 Russell Carollo and Jeff Nesmith *(Dayton* [Ohio] *Daily News)*
1999 *New York Times* staff
2000 *Wall Street Journal* staff

International Telegraphic Reporting
1942 Laurence Edmund Allen (Associated Press)
1943 Ira Wolfert (North American Newspaper Alliance, Inc.)
1944 Daniel De Luce (Associated Press)
1945 Mark S. Watson *(Baltimore Sun)*
1946 Homer W. Bigart *(New York Herald Tribune)*
1947 Eddy Gilmore (Associated Press)

International Reporting
1948 Paul W. Ward *(Baltimore Sun)*
1949 Price Day *(Baltimore Sun)*
1950 Edmund Stevens *(Christian Science Monitor)*
1951 Keyes Beech and Fred Sparks *(Chicago Daily News);* Homer Bigart and Marguerite Higgins *(New York Herald Tribune);* Relman Morin and Don Whitehead (Associated Press)
1952 John M. Hightower (Associated Press)
1953 Austin C. Wehrwein *(Milwaukee Journal)*
1954 Jim G. Lucas (Scripps-Howard Newspapers)
1955 Harrison E. Salisbury *(New York Times)*
1956 William Randolph Hearst, Jr., and Frank Conniff (Hearst Newspapers); Kingsbury Smith (INS)
1957 Russell Jones (United Press)
1958 *New York Times*
1959 Joseph Martin and Philip Santora *(New York Daily News)*
1960 A. M. Rosenthal *(New York Times)*
1961 Lynn Heinzerling (Associated Press)
1962 Walter Lippmann (New York Herald Tribune Syndicate)

1963 Hal Hendrix *(Miami News)*
1964 Malcolm W. Browne (Associated Press); David Halberstam *(New York Times)*
1965 J. A. Livingston *(Philadelphia Bulletin)*
1966 Peter Arnett (Associated Press)
1967 R. John Hughes *(Christian Science Monitor)*
1968 Alfred Friendly *(Washington Post)*
1969 William Tuohy *(Los Angeles Times)*
1970 Seymour M. Hersh (Dispatch News Service)
1971 Jimmie Lee Hoagland *(Washington Post)*
1972 Peter R. Kann *(Wall Street Journal)*
1973 Max Frankel *(New York Times)*
1974 Hedrick Smith *(New York Times)*
1975 William Mullen and Ovie Carter *(Chicago Tribune)*
1976 Sydney H. Schanberg *(New York Times)*
1978 Henry Kamm *(New York Times)*
1979 Richard Ben Cramer *(Philadelphia Inquirer)*
1980 Joel Brinkley and Jay Mather *(Louisville Courier-Journal)*
1981 Shirley Christian *(Miami Herald)*
1982 John Darnton *(New York Times)*
1983 Thomas L. Friedman *(New York Times)*
1984 Karen E. House *(Wall Street Journal)*
1985 Josh Friedman, Dennis Bell, and Ozier Muhammad *(Newsday)*
1986 Lewis M. Simons, Pete Carey, and Katherine Ellison *(San Jose Mercury News)*
1987 Michael Parks *(Los Angeles Times)*
1988 Thomas L. Friedman *(New York Times)*
1989 Bill Keller *(New York Times);* Glenn Frankel *(Washington Post)*
1990 Nicholas D. Kristof and Sheryl WuDunn *(New York Times)*
1991 Caryle Murphy *(Washington Post);* Serge Schmemann *(New York Times)*
1992 Patrick J. Sloyan *(Newsday)*
1993 John F. Burns *(New York Times);* Roy Gutman *(Newsday)*
1994 *Dallas Morning News* team
1995 Mark Fritz (Associated Press)
1996 David Rohde *(Christian Science Monitor)*
1997 John F. Burns *(New York Times)*
1998 *New York Times* staff
1999 *Wall Street Journal* staff
2000 Mark Schoofs *(The Village Voice* [New York, N.Y.])

Reporting
1917 Herbert B. Swope *(New York World)*
1918 Harold A. Littledale *(New York Evening Post)*
1920 John J. Leary, Jr. *(New York World)*
1921 Louis Seibold *(New York World)*
1922 Kirke L. Simpson (Associated Press)
1923 Alva Johnston *(New York Times)*
1924 Magner White *(San Diego Sun)*
1925 James W. Mulroy and Alvin H. Goldstein *(Chicago Daily News)*
1926 William Burke Miller *(Louisville Courier-Journal)*
1927 John T. Rogers *(St. Louis Post-Dispatch)*
1929 Paul Y. Anderson *(St. Louis Post-Dispatch)*
1930 Russell D. Owen *(New York Times);* special award: W. O. Dapping *(Auburn* [N.Y.] *Citizen)*
1931 A. B. MacDonald *(Kansas City* [Mo.] *Star)*
1932 W. C. Richards, D. D. Martin, J. S. Pooler, F. D. Webb, and J. N. W. Sloan *(Detroit Free Press)*
1933 Francis A. Jamieson (Associated Press)
1934 Royce Brier *(San Francisco Chronicle)*
1935 William H. Taylor *(New York Herald Tribune)*

1936   Lauren D. Lyman *(New York Times)*
1937   John J. O'Neill *(New York Herald Tribune)*;
      William Leonard Laurence *(New York Times)*;
      Howard W. Blakeslee (Associated Press);
      Gobind Behari Lal (Universal Service); David
      Dietz (Scripps–Howard Newspapers)
1938   Raymond Sprigle *(Pittsburg Post-Gazette)*
1939   Thomas L. Stokes *(New York
      World-Telegram)*
1940   S. Burton Heath *(New York World-Telegram)*
1941   Westbrook Pegler *(New York
      World-Telegram)*
1942   Stanton Delaplane *(San Francisco Chronicle)*
1943   George Weller *(Chicago Daily News)*
1944   Paul Schoenstein and associates *(New York
      Journal-American)*
1945   Jack S. McDowell *(San Francisco
      Call-Bulletin)*
1946   William Leonard Laurence *(New York Times)*
1947   Frederick Woltman *(New York
      World-Telegram)*
1948   George E. Goodwin *(Atlanta Journal)*
1949   Malcolm Johnson *(New York Sun)*
1950   Meyer Berger *(New York Times)*
1951   Edward S. Montgomery *(San Francisco
      Examiner)*
1952   George de Carvalho *(San Francisco
      Chronicle)*
1953   Editorial staff *(Providence Journal and
      Evening Bulletin)*;[1] Edward J. Mowery *(New
      York World-Telegram and Sun)*[2]
1954   *Vicksburg* (Miss.) *Sunday Post-Herald*;[1] Alvin
      Scott McCoy *(Kansas City* [Mo.] *Star)*[2]
1955   Mrs. Caro Brown *(Alice* [Tex.] *Daily Echo)*;[1]
      Roland Kenneth Towery *(Cuero* [Tex.]
      Record)[2]
1956   Lee Hills *(Detroit Free Press)*;[1] Arthur Daley
      (New York Times)[2]
1957   *Salt Lake Tribune*;[1] Wallace Turner and
      William Lambert *(Portland Oregonian)*[2]
1958   *Fargo* [N.D.] *Forum*;[1] George Beveridge
      (Washington [D.C.] *Evening Star)*[2]
1959   Mary Lou Werner *(Washington* [D.C.] *Evening
      Star)*;[1] John Harold Brislin *(Scranton* [Pa.]
      Tribune & Scrantonian)[2]
1960   Jack Nelson *(Atlanta Constitution)*;[1] Miriam
      Ottenberg *(Washington Evening Star)*[2]
1961   Sanche de Gramont *(New York Herald
      Tribune)*;[1] Edgar May *(Buffalo Evening
      News)*[2]
1962   Robert D. Mullins *(Deseret News,* Salt Lake
      City);[1] George Bliss *(Chicago Tribune)*[2]
1963   Sylvan Fox, Anthony Shannon, and
      William Longgood *(New York
      World-Telegram and Sun)*;[1] Oscar
      Griffin, Jr. (former editor of *Pecos* [Tex.]
      Independent and Enterprise, now on
      staff of *Houston Chronicle)*[2]

1. Reporting under pressure of edition deadlines.
2. Reporting not under pressure of edition deadlines.

General Local Reporting

1964   Norman C. Miller *(Wall Street Journal)*
1965   Melvin H. Ruder *(Hungry Horse News,*
      Columbia Falls, Mont.)
1966   *Los Angeles Times* staff
1967   Robert V. Cox *(Chambersburg* [Pa.] *Public
      Opinion)*
1968   *Detroit Free Press* staff
1969   John Fetterman *(Louisville Times* and
      Courier-Journal)

1970   Thomas Fitzpatrick *(Chicago Sun-Times)*
1971   Akron (Ohio) *Beacon* staff
1972   Richard Cooper and John Machacek
      (Rochester [N.Y.] *Times-Union)*
1973   *Chicago Tribune*
1974   Arthur M. Petacque and Hugh F. Hough
      (Chicago Sun-Times)
1975   *Xenia* (Ohio) *Daily Gazette*
1976   Gene Miller *(Miami Herald)*
1977   Margo Huston *(Milwaukee Journal)*
1978   Richard Whitt *(Louisville Courier-Journal)*
1979   Staff of *San Diego* (Calif.) *Evening Tribune*
1980   Staff of *Philadelphia Inquirer*
1981   *Longview* (Wash.) *Daily News*
1982   *Kansas City* (Mo.) *Star* and *Kansas City*
      (Mo.) *Times*
1983   *Fort Wayne* (Ind.) *News-Sentinel*
1984   *Newsday*

General News Reporting

1985   Thomas Turcol *(Virginian-Pilot and
      Ledger-Star)*
1986   Edna Buchanan *(Miami Herald)*
1987   *Akron Beacon Journal* staff
1988   *Alabama Journal* (Montgomery) staff;
      Lawrence (Mass.) *Eagle-Tribune* staff
1989   *Louisville Courier-Journal* staff
1990   *San Jose* (Calif.) *Mercury News*

Spot News Reporting

1991   *Miami Herald* staff
1992   *New York Newsday* staff
1993   *Los Angeles Times* staff
1994   *New York Times* staff
1995   *Los Angeles Times* staff
1996   Robert D. McFadden *(New York Times)*
1997   *Newsday* staff (Long Island, N.Y.)

Breaking News Reporting

1998   *Los Angeles Times* staff
1999   *Hartford Courant* staff
2000   *Denver Post* staff

Special Local Reporting

1964   James V. Magee, Albert V. Gaudiosi, and
      Frederick A. Meyer *(Philadelphia Bulletin)*
1965   Gene Goltz *(Houston Post)*
1966   John A. Frasca *(Tampa Tribune)*
1967   Gene Miller *(Miami Herald)*
1968   J. Anthony Lukas *(New York Times)*
1969   Albert L. Delugach and Denny Walsh *(St.
      Louis Globe-Democrat)*
1970   Harold Eugene Martin *(Montgomery
      Advertiser)*
1971   William Hugh Jones *(Chicago Tribune)*
1972   Timothy Leland, Gerard N. O'Neill, Stephen
      A. Kurkjian, and Ann DeSantis *(Boston
      Globe)*
1973   Sun Newspapers of Omaha, Neb.
1974   William Sherman *(New York Daily News)*
1975   *Indianapolis Star*
1976   *Chicago Tribune*
1977   Acel Moore and Wendell Rawls, Jr.
      (Philadelphia Inquirer)
1978   Anthony R. Dolan *(Stamford* [Conn.]
      Advocate)
1979   Gilbert M. Gaul and Elliot G. Jaspin
      (Pottsville [Pa.] *Republican)*
1980   Nils J. Bruzelius, Alexander B. Hawes, Jr.,
      Stephen A. Kurkjian, Robert M. Porterfield,
      and Joan Vennochi *(Boston Globe)*

1981 Clark Hallas and Robert B. Lowe (*Arizona Daily Star,* Tucson)
1982 Paul Henderson (*Seattle Times*)
1983 Loretta Tofani (*Washington Post*)
1984 Kenneth Cooper, Joan FitzGerald, Jonathan Kaufman, Norman Lockman, Gary McMillan, Kirk Scharfenberg, and David Wessel (*Boston Globe*)

Investigative Reporting
1985 Lucy Morgan, Jack Reed (*St. Petersburg* [Fla.] *Times),* and William K. Marimow (*Philadelphia Inquirer*)
1986 Jeffrey A. Marx and Michael M. York (*Lexington* [Ky.] *Herald Leader*)
1987 Daniel R. Biddle, H. G. Bissinger, and Fredric N. Tulsky (*Philadelphia Inquirer*)
1988 Dean Baquet, William C. Gaines, and Ann Marie Lipinski (*Chicago Tribune*)
1989 Bill Dedman (*Atlanta Journal and Constitution*)
1990 Lou Kilzer and Chris Ison (*Minneapolis-St. Paul Star Tribune*)
1991 Joseph T. Hallinan and Susan M. Headden (*Indianapolis Star*)
1992 Lorraine Adams and Dan Malone (*Dallas Morning News*)
1993 Jeff Brazil and Steve Berry (*Orlando* [Fla.] *Sentinel*)
1994 *Providence* (R.I.) *Journal-Bulletin* staff
1995 Stephanie Saul and Brian Donovan (*Newsday*)
1996 *Orange County Register* staff (Santa Ana, Calif.)
1997 Eric Nalder, Deborah Nelson, and Alex Tizon (*Seattle Times*)
1998 Gary Cohn and Will Englund (*The Sun* [Baltimore, Md.])
1999 *The Miami Herald* staff
2000 Sang-Hun Choe, Charles J. Hanley, and Martha Mendoza (Associated Press)

Feature Writing
1979 Jon D. Franklin (*Baltimore Evening Sun*)
1980 Madeleine Blais (*Miami Herald*)
1981 Teresa Carpenter (*Village Voice,* New York)
1982 Saul Pett (Associated Press)
1983 Nan Robertson (*New York Times*)
1984 Peter M. Rinearson (*Seattle Times*)
1985 Alice Steinbach (*Baltimore Sun*)
1986 John Camp (*St. Paul Pioneer Press and Dispatch*)
1987 Steve Twomey (*Philadelphia Inquirer*)
1988 Jacqui Banaszynski (*St. Paul Pioneer Press Dispatch*)
1989 David Zucchino (*Philadelphia Inquirer*)
1990 Dave Curtin (*Colorado Springs Gazette Telegraph*)
1991 Sheryl James (*St. Petersburg* [Fla.] *Times*)
1992 Howell Raines (*New York Times*)
1993 George Lardner, Jr. (*Washington Post*)
1994 Isabel Wilkerson (*New York Times*)
1995 Ron Suskind (*Wall Street Journal*)
1996 Rick Bragg (*New York Times*)
1997 Lisa Pollak (*Baltimore Sun*)
1998 Thomas French (*St. Petersburg* [Fla.] *Times*)
1999 Angelo B. Henderson (*Wall Street Journal*)
2000 J. R. Moehringer (*Los Angeles Times*)

Commentary
1970 Marquis W. Childs (*St. Louis Post-Dispatch*)
1971 William A. Caldwell (*Record* [Hackensack, N.J.])
1972 Mike Royko (*Chicago Daily News*)
1973 David S. Broder (*Washington Post*)
1974 Edwin A. Roberts, Jr. (*National Observer*)
1975 Mary McGrory (*Washington Star*)
1976 Walter W. (Red) Smith (*New York Times*)
1977 George F. Will (*Washington Post* Writers Group)
1978 William Safire (*New York Times*)
1979 Russell Baker (*New York Times*)
1980 Ellen H. Goodman (*Boston Globe*)
1981 Dave Anderson (*New York Times*)
1982 Art Buchwald (*Los Angeles Times* Syndicate)
1983 Claude Sitton (*Raleigh* [N.C.] *News & Observer*)
1984 Vermont Royster (*Wall Street Journal*)
1985 Murray Kempton (*Newsday*)
1986 Jimmy Breslin (*New York Daily News*)
1987 Charles Krauthammer (*Washington Post* Writers Group)
1988 Dave Barry (*Miami Herald*)
1989 Clarence Page (*Chicago Tribune*)
1990 Jim Murray (*Los Angeles Times*)
1991 Jim Hoagland (*Washington Post*)
1992 Anna Quindlen (*New York Times*)
1993 Liz Balmaseda (*Miami Herald*)
1994 William Raspberry (*Washington Post*)
1995 Jim Dwyer (*New York Newsday*)
1996 E. R. Shipp (*New York Daily News*)
1997 Eileen McNamara (*Boston Globe*)
1998 Mike McAlary (*New York Daily News*)
1999 Maureen Dowd (*New York Times*)
2000 Paul A. Gigot (*Wall Street Journal*)

Criticism
1970 Ada Louise Huxtable (*New York Times*)
1971 Harold C. Schonberg (*New York Times*)
1972 Frank Peters, Jr. (*St. Louis Post-Dispatch*)
1973 Ronald Powers (*Chicago Sun-Times*)
1974 Emily Genauer (*Newsday* Syndicate)
1975 Roger Ebert (*Chicago Sun-Times*)
1976 Alan M. Kriegsman (*Washington Post*)
1977 William McPherson (*Washington Post*)
1978 Walter Kerr (*New York Times*)
1979 Paul Gapp (*Chicago Tribune*)
1980 William A. Henry, 3rd (*Boston Globe*)
1981 Jonathan Yardley (*Washington Star*)
1982 Martin Bernheimer (*Los Angeles Times*)
1983 Manuela Hoelterhoff (*Wall Street Journal*)
1984 Paul Goldberger (*New York Times*)
1985 Howard Rosenberg (*Los Angeles Times*)
1986 Donal Henahan (*New York Times*)
1987 Richard Eder (*Los Angeles Times*)
1988 Tom Shales (*Washington Post*)
1989 Michael Skube (*News and Observer* [Raleigh, N.C.])
1990 Allan Temko (*San Francisco Chronicle*)
1991 David Shaw (*Los Angeles Times*)
1993 Michael Dirda (*Washington Post*)
1994 Lloyd Schwartz (*Boston Phoenix*)
1995 Margo Jefferson (*New York Times*)
1996 Robert Campbell (*Boston Globe*)
1997 Tim Page (*Washington Post*)
1998 Michiko Kakutani (*New York Times*)
1999 Blair Kamin (*Chicago Tribune*)
2000 Henry Allen (*Washington Post*)

Explanatory Journalism
1985 Jon Franklin (*Baltimore Evening Sun*)
1986 *New York Times*
1987 Jeff Lyon and Peter Gorner (*Chicago Tribune*)

1988 Daniel Hertzberg and James B. Stewart *(Wall Street Journal)*
1989 David Hanners, William Snyder, and Karen Blessen *(Dallas Morning News)*
1990 David A. Vise and Coll *(Washington Post)*
1991 Susan C. Faludi *(Wall Street Journal)*
1992 Robert S. Capers and Eric Lipton *(Hartford Courant)*
1993 Mike Toner *(Atlanta Journal–Constitution)*
1994 Ronald Kotulak *(Chicago Tribune)*
1995 Leon Dash and Lucian Perkins *(Washington Post)*
1996 Laurie Garrett *(Newsday* [Long Island, N.Y.])
1997 Michael Vitez, Ron Cortes, and April Saul *(Philadelphia Inquirer)*
1998 Paul Salopek *(Chicago Tribune)*
1999 Richard Read *(Oregonian* [Portland, Ore.])
2000 Eric Newhouse *(Great Falls* [Mont.] *Tribune)*

Specialized Reporting
1985 Randall Savage and Jackie Crosby *(Macon* [Ga.] *Telegraph and News)*
1986 Andrew Schneider and Mary Pat Flaherty *(Pittsburgh Press)*
1987 Alex S. Jones *(New York Times)*
1988 Walt Bogdanich *(Wall Street Journal)*
1989 Edward Humes *(Orange County Register)*
1990 Tamar Stieber *(Albuquerque* (N.M.) *Journal)*

Beat Reporting
1991 Natalie Angier *(New York Times)*
1992 Deborah Blum *(Sacramento Bee)*
1993 Paul Ingrassia and Joseph B. White *(Wall Street Journal)*
1994 Eric Freedman and Jim Mitzelfeld *(Detroit News)*
1995 David M. Shribman *(Boston Globe)*
1996 Bob Keeler *(Newsday* [Long Island, N.Y.])
1997 Byron Acohido *(Seattle Times)*
1998 Linda Greenhouse *(New York Times)*
1999 Chuck Philips and Michael A. Hiltzik *(Los Angeles Times)*
2000 George Dohrmann *(St. Paul Pioneer Press)*

PULITZER PRIZES IN LETTERS

Fiction[1]
1918 *His Family,* Ernest Poole
1919 *The Magnificent Ambersons,* Booth Tarkington
1921 *The Age of Innocence,* Edith Wharton
1922 *Alice Adams,* Booth Tarkington
1923 *One of Ours,* Willa Cather
1924 *The Able McLaughlins,* Margaret Wilson
1925 *So Big,* Edna Ferber
1926 *Arrowsmith,* Sinclair Lewis
1927 *Early Autumn,* Louis Bromfield
1928 *The Bridge of San Luis Rey,* Thornton Wilder
1929 *Scarlet Sister Mary,* Julia Peterkin
1930 *Laughing Boy,* Oliver La Farge
1931 *Years of Grace,* Margaret Ayer Barnes
1932 *The Good Earth,* Pearl S. Buck
1933 *The Store,* T. S. Stribling
1934 *Lamb in His Bosom,* Caroline Miller
1935 *Now in November,* Josephine Winslow Johnson
1936 *Honey in the Horn,* Harold L. Davis
1937 *Gone With the Wind,* Margaret Mitchell
1938 *The Late George Apley,* John Phillips Marquand
1939 *The Yearling,* Marjorie Kinnan Rawlings
1940 *The Grapes of Wrath,* John Steinbeck
1942 *In This Our Life,* Ellen Glasgow

1943 *Dragon's Teeth,* Upton Sinclair
1944 *Journey in the Dark,* Martin Flavin
1945 *A Bell for Adano,* John Hersey
1947 *All the King's Men,* Robert Penn Warren
1948 *Tales of the South Pacific,* James A. Michener
1949 *Guard of Honor,* James Gould Cozzens
1950 *The Way West,* A. B. Guthrie, Jr.
1951 *The Town,* Conrad Richter
1952 *The Caine Mutiny,* Herman Wouk
1953 *The Old Man and the Sea,* Ernest Hemingway
1955 *A Fable,* William Faulkner
1956 *Andersonville,* MacKinlay Kantor
1958 *A Death in the Family,* James Agee
1959 *The Travels of Jaimie McPheeters,* Robert Lewis Taylor
1960 *Advise and Consent,* Allen Drury
1961 *To Kill a Mockingbird,* Harper Lee
1962 *The Edge of Sadness,* Edwin O'Connor
1963 *The Reivers,* William Faulkner
1965 *The Keepers of the House,* Shirley Ann Grau
1966 *Collected Stories of Katherine Anne Porter,* Katherine Anne Porter
1967 *The Fixer,* Bernard Malamud
1968 *The Confessions of Nat Turner,* William Styron
1969 *House Made of Dawn,* N. Scott Momaday
1970 *Collected Stories,* Jean Stafford
1972 *Angle of Repose,* Wallace Stegner
1973 *The Optimist's Daughter,* Eudora Welty
1975 *The Killer Angels,* Michael Shaara
1976 *Humboldt's Gift,* Saul Bellow
1978 *Elbow Room,* James Alan McPherson
1979 *The Stories of John Cheever,* John Cheever
1980 *The Executioner's Song,* Norman Mailer
1981 *A Confederacy of Dunces,* John Kennedy Toole
1982 *Rabbit Is Rich,* John Updike
1983 *The Color Purple,* Alice Walker
1984 *Ironweed,* William Kennedy
1985 *Foreign Affairs,* Alison Lurie
1986 *Lonesome Dove,* Larry McMurtry
1987 *A Summons to Memphis,* Peter Taylor
1988 *Beloved,* Toni Morrison
1989 *Breathing Lessons,* Anne Tyler
1990 *The Mambo Kings Play Songs of Love,* Oscar Hijuelos
1991 *Rabbit at Rest,* John Updike
1992 *A Thousand Acres,* Jane Smiley
1993 *A Good Scent From a Strange Mountain,* Robert Olen Butler
1994 *The Shipping News,* E. Annie Proulx
1995 *The Stone Diaries,* Carol Shields
1996 *Independence Day,* Richard Ford
1997 *Martin Dressler: The Tale of an American Dreamer,* Steven Millhauser
1998 *American Pastoral,* Philip Roth
1999 *The Hours,* Michael Cunningham
2000 *Interpreter of Maladies,* Jhumpa Lahiri
1. Before 1948, award was for novels only.

History of United States
1917 *With Americans of Past and Present Days,* J. J. Jusserand, Ambassador of France to United States
1918 *A History of the Civil War, 1861–1865,* James Ford Rhodes
1920 *The War With Mexico,* Justin H. Smith
1921 *The Victory at Sea,* William Sowden Sims, in collaboration with Burton J. Hendrick
1922 *The Founding of New England,* James Truslow Adams

1923 *The Supreme Court in United States History*, Charles Warren

1924 *The American Revolution—A Constitutional Interpretation*, Charles Howard McIlwain

1925 *A History of the American Frontier*, Frederic L. Paxson

1926 *The History of the United States*, Edward Channing

1927 *Pinckney's Treaty*, Samuel Flagg Bemis

1928 *Main Currents in American Thought*, Vernon Louis Parrington

1929 *The Organization and Administration of the Union Army, 1861–1865*, Fred Albert Shannon

1930 *The War of Independence*, Claude H. Van Tyne

1931 *The Coming of the War: 1914*, Bernadotte E. Schmitt

1932 *My Experiences in the World War*, John J. Pershing

1933 *The Significance of Sections in American History*, Frederick J. Turner

1934 *The People's Choice*, Herbert Agar

1935 *The Colonial Period of American History*, Charles McLean Andrews

1936 *The Constitutional History of the United States*, Andrew C. McLaughlin

1937 *The Flowering of New England*, Van Wyck Brooks

1938 *The Road to Reunion, 1865–1900*, Paul Herman Buck

1939 *A History of American Magazines*, Frank Luther Mott

1940 *Abraham Lincoln: The War Years*, Carl Sandburg

1941 *The Atlantic Migration, 1607–1860*, Marcus Lee Hansen

1942 *Reveille in Washington*, Margaret Leech

1943 *Paul Revere and the World He Lived In*, Esther Forbes

1944 *The Growth of American Thought*, Merle Curti

1945 *Unfinished Business*, Stephen Bonsal

1946 *The Age of Jackson*, Arthur M. Schlesinger, Jr.

1947 *Scientists Against Time*, James Phinney Baxter III

1948 *Across the Wide Missouri*, Bernard DeVoto

1949 *The Disruption of American Democracy*, Roy Franklin Nichols

1950 *Art and Life in America*, Oliver W. Larkin

1951 *The Old Northwest, Pioneer Period 1815–1840*, R. Carlyle Buley

1952 *The Uprooted*, Oscar Handlin

1953 *The Era of Good Feelings*, George Dangerfield

1954 *A Stillness at Appomattox*, Bruce Catton

1955 *Great River: The Rio Grande in North American History*, Paul Horgan

1956 *The Age of Reform*, Richard Hofstadter

1957 *Russia Leaves the War: Soviet–American Relations, 1917–1920*, George F. Kennan

1958 *Banks and Politics in America: From the Revolution to the Civil War*, Bray Hammond

1959 *The Republican Era: 1869–1901*, Leonard D. White, assisted by Jean Schneider

1960 *In the Days of McKinley*, Margaret Leech

1961 *Between War and Peace: The Potsdam Conference*, Herbert Feis

1962 *The Triumphant Empire: Thunder-Clouds Gather in the West*, Lawrence H. Gipson

1963 *Washington, Village and Capital, 1800–1878*, Constance McLaughlin Green

1964 *Puritan Village: The Formation of a New England Town*, Sumner Chilton Powell

1965 *The Greenback Era*, Irwin Unger

1966 *Life of the Mind in America*, Perry Miller

1967 *Exploration and Empire: The Explorer and Scientist in the Winning of the American West*, William H. Goetzmann

1968 *The Ideological Origins of the American Revolution*, Bernard Bailyn

1969 *Origins of the Fifth Amendment*, Leonard W. Levy

1970 *Present at the Creation: My Years in the State Department*, Dean Acheson

1971 *Roosevelt: The Soldier of Freedom*, James McGregor Burns

1972 *Neither Black Nor White: Slavery and Race Relations in Brazil and the United States*, Carl N. Degler

1973 *People of Paradox: An Inquiry Concerning the Origin of American Civilization*, Michael Kammen

1974 *The Americans: The Democratic Experience, Vol. 3*, Daniel J. Boorstin

1975 *Jefferson and His Time*, Dumas Malone

1976 *Lamy of Santa Fe*, Paul Horgan

1977 *The Impending Crisis: 1841–1861*, David M. Potter

1978 *The Invisible Hand: The Managerial Revolution in American Business*, Alfred D. Chandler, Jr.

1979 *The Dred Scott Case: Its Significance in Law and Politics*, Don E. Fehrenbacher

1980 *Been in the Storm So Long*, Leon F. Litwack

1981 *American Education: The National Experience; 1783–1876*, Lawrence A. Cremin

1982 *Mary Chesnut's Civil War*, C. Vann Woodward, editor

1983 *The Transformation of Virginia, 1740–1790*, Rhys L. Isaac

1985 *The Prophets of Regulation*, Thomas K. McCraw

1986 *The Heavens and the Earth: A Political History of the Space Age*, Walter A. McDougall

1987 *Voyagers to the West: A Passage in the Peopling of America on the Eve of the Revolution*, Bernard Bailyn

1988 *The Launching of Modern American Science 1846–1876*, Robert V. Bruce

1989 *Parting the Waters*, Taylor Branch; *Battle Cry of Freedom*, James M. McPherson

1990 *In Our Image: America's Empire in the Philippines*, Stanley Karnow

1991 *A Midwife's Tale: The Life of Martha Ballard, Based on Her Diary 1785–1812*, Laurel Thatcher Ulrich

1992 *The Fate of Liberty: Abraham Lincoln and Civil Liberties*, Mark E. Neely, Jr.

1993 *The Radicalism of the American Revolution*, Gordon S. Wood

1995 *No Ordinary Time: Franklin and Eleanor Roosevelt: The Home Front in World War II*, Doris Kearns Goodwin

1996 *William Cooper's Town: Power and Persuasion on the Frontier of the Early American Republic*, Alan Taylor

1997 *Original Meanings: Politics and Ideas in the Making of the Constitution*, Jack N. Rakove

1998	*Summer for the Gods: The Scopes Trial and America's Continuing Debate Over Science and Religion*, Edward J. Larson
1999	*Gotham: A History of New York City to 1898*, Edwin G. Burrows and Mike Wallace
2000	*Freedom from Fear: The American People in Depression and War, 1929–1945*, David M. Kennedy

Biography or Autobiography

1917	*Julia Ward Howe*, Laura E. Richards and Maude Howe Elliott, assisted by Florence Howe Hall
1918	*Benjamin Franklin, Self-Revealed*, William Cabell Bruce
1919	*The Education of Henry Adams*, Henry Adams
1920	*The Life of John Marshall*, Albert J. Beveridge
1921	*The Americanization of Edward Bok*, Edward Bok
1922	*A Daughter of the Middle Border*, Hamlin Garland
1923	*The Life and Letters of Walter H. Page*, Burton J. Hendrick
1924	*From Immigrant to Inventor*, Michael Idvorsky Pupin
1925	*Barrett Wendell and His Letters*, M. A. DeWolfe Howe
1926	*The Life of Sir William Osler*, Harvey Cushing
1927	*Whitman*, Emory Holloway
1928	*The American Orchestra and Theodore Thomas*, Charles Edward Russell
1929	*The Training of an American: The Earlier Life and Letters of Walter H. Page*, Burton J. Hendrick
1930	*The Raven*, Marquis James
1931	*Charles W. Eliot*, Henry James
1932	*Theodore Roosevelt*, Henry F. Pringle
1933	*Grover Cleveland*, Allan Nevins
1934	*John Hay*, Tyler Dennett
1935	*R. E. Lee*, Douglas S. Freeman
1936	*The Thought and Character of William James*, Ralph Barton Perry
1937	*Hamilton Fish*, Allan Nevins
1938	*Pedlar's Progress*, Odell Shepard; *Andrew Jackson*, Marquis James
1939	*Benjamin Franklin*, Carl Van Doren
1940	*Woodrow Wilson: Life and Letters*, Vols. VII and VIII, Ray Stannard Baker
1941	*Jonathan Edwards*, Ola E. Winslow
1942	*Crusader in Crinoline*, Forrest Wilson
1943	*Admiral of the Ocean Sea*, Samuel Eliot Morison
1944	*The American Leonardo: The Life of Samuel F. B. Morse*, Carleton Mabee
1945	*George Bancroft: Brahmin Rebel*, Russel Blaine Nye
1946	*Son of the Wilderness*, Linnie Marsh Wolfe
1947	*The Autobiography of William Allen White*
1948	*Forgotten First Citizen: John Bigelow*, Margaret Clapp
1949	*Roosevelt and Hopkins*, Robert E. Sherwood
1950	*John Quincy Adams and the Foundations of American Foreign Policy*, Samuel Flagg Bemis
1951	*John C. Calhoun: American Portrait*, Margaret Louise Coit
1952	*Charles Evans Hughes*, Merlo J. Pusey
1953	*Edmund Pendleton, 1721–1803*, David J. Mays
1954	*The Spirit of St. Louis*, Charles A. Lindbergh
1955	*The Taft Story*, William S. White
1956	*Benjamin Henry Latrobe*, Talbot F. Hamlin
1957	*Profiles in Courage*, John F. Kennedy
1958	*George Washington*, Douglas Southall Freeman (Vols. 1–6) and John Alexander Carroll and Mary Wells Ashworth (Vol. 7)
1959	*Woodrow Wilson, American Prophet*, Arthur Walworth
1960	*John Paul Jones*, Samuel Eliot Morison
1961	*Charles Sumner and the Coming of the Civil War*, David Donald
1963	*Henry James: Vol. II, The Conquest of London, 1870–1881; Vol. III, The Middle Years, 1881–1895*, Leon Edel
1964	*John Keats*, Walter Jackson Bate
1965	*Henry Adams* (3 Vols.), Ernest Samuels
1966	*A Thousand Days*, Arthur M. Schlesinger, Jr.
1967	*Mr. Clemens and Mark Twain*, Justin Kaplan
1968	*Memoirs, 1925–1950*, George F. Kennan
1969	*The Man From New York*, B. L. Reid
1970	*Huey Long*, T. Harry Williams
1971	*Robert Frost: The Years of Triumph, 1915–1938*, Lawrance Thompson
1972	*Eleanor and Franklin: The Story of Their Relationship Based on Eleanor Roosevelt's Private Papers*, Joseph P. Lash
1973	*Luce and His Empire*, W. A. Swanberg
1974	*O'Neill, Son and Artist*, Louis Sheaffer
1975	*The Power Broker: Robert Moses and the Fall of New York*, Robert A. Caro
1976	*Edith Wharton: A Biography*, Richard W. B. Lewis
1977	*A Prince of Our Disorder*, John E. Mack
1978	*Samuel Johnson*, Walter Jackson Bate
1979	*Days of Sorrow and Pain: Leo Baeck and the Berlin Jews*, Leonard Baker
1980	*The Rise of Theodore Roosevelt*, Edmund Morris
1981	*Peter the Great*, Robert K. Massie
1982	*Grant: A Biography*, William S. McFeely
1983	*Growing Up*, Russell Baker
1984	*Booker T. Washington*, Louis R. Harlan
1985	*The Life and Times of Cotton Mather*, Kenneth Silverman
1986	*Louise Bogan: A Portrait*, Elizabeth Frank
1987	*Bearing the Cross: Martin Luther King, Jr., and the Southern Christian Leadership Conference*, David J. Garrow
1988	*Look Homeward: A Life of Thomas Wolfe*, David Herbert Donald
1989	*Oscar Wilde*, Richard Ellmann
1990	*Machiavelli in Hell*, Sebastian de Grazia
1991	*Jackson Pollock: An American Saga*, Steven Naifeh and Gregory White Smith
1992	*Fortunate Son: The Healing of a Vietnam Vet*, Lewis B. Puller, Jr.
1993	*Truman*, David McCullough
1994	*W. E. B. Du Bois: Biography of a Race, 1868–1919*, David Levering Lewis
1995	*Harriet Beecher Stowe: A Life*, Joan D. Hedrick
1996	*God: A Biography*, Jack Miles
1997	*Angela's Ashes: A Memoir*, Frank McCourt
1998	*Personal History*, Katharine Graham
1999	*Lindbergh*, A. Scott Berg
2000	*Vera (Mrs. Vladimir Nabokov)*, Stacy Schiff

Poetry[1]

| 1918 | *Love Songs*, Sara Teasdale |
| 1919 | *Old Road to Paradise*, Margaret Widdemer; *Corn Huskers*, Carl Sandburg |

1922 *Collected Poems*, Edwin Arlington Robinson
1923 *The Ballad of the Harp-Weaver; A Few Figs from Thistles; eight sonnets in American Poetry, 1922, A Miscellany*, Edna St. Vincent Millay
1924 *New Hampshire: A Poem With Notes and Grace Notes*, Robert Frost
1925 *The Man Who Died Twice*, Edwin Arlington Robinson
1926 *What's O'Clock*, Amy Lowell
1927 *Fiddler's Farewell*, Leonora Speyer
1928 *Tristram*, Edwin Arlington Robinson
1929 *John Brown's Body*, Stephen Vincent Benét
1930 *Selected Poems*, Conrad Aiken
1931 *Collected Poems*, Robert Frost
1932 *The Flowering Stone*, George Dillon
1933 *Conquistador*, Archibald MacLeish
1934 *Collected Verse*, Robert Hillyer
1935 *Bright Ambush*, Audrey Wurdemann
1936 *Strange Holiness*, Robert P. T. Coffin
1937 *A Further Range*, Robert Frost
1938 *Cold Morning Sky*, Marya Zaturenska
1939 *Selected Poems*, John Gould Fletcher
1940 *Collected Poems*, Mark Van Doren
1941 *Sunderland Capture*, Leonard Bacon
1942 *The Dust Which Is God*, William Rose Benét
1943 *A Witness Tree*, Robert Frost
1944 *Western Star*, Stephen Vincent Benét
1945 *V-Letter and Other Poems*, Karl Shapiro
1947 *Lord Weary's Castle*, Robert Lowell
1948 *The Age of Anxiety*, W. H. Auden
1949 *Terror and Decorum*, Peter Viereck
1950 *Annie Allen*, Gwendolyn Brooks
1951 *Complete Poems*, Carl Sandburg
1952 *Collected Poems*, Marianne Moore
1953 *Collected Poems, 1917–1952*, Archibald MacLeish
1954 *The Waking*, Theodore Roethke
1955 *Collected Poems*, Wallace Stevens
1956 *Poems—North & South*, Elizabeth Bishop
1957 *Things of This World*, Richard Wilbur
1958 *Promises: Poems, 1954–1956*, Robert Penn Warren
1959 *Selected Poems, 1928–1958*, Stanley Kunitz
1960 *Heart's Needle*, William Snodgrass
1961 *Times Three: Selected Verse From Three Decades*, Phyllis McGinley
1962 *Poems*, Alan Dugan
1963 *Pictures From Breughel*, William Carlos Williams
1964 *At the End of the Open Road*, Louis Simpson
1965 *77 Dream Songs*, John Berryman
1966 *Selected Poems*, Richard Eberhart
1967 *Live or Die*, Anne Sexton
1968 *The Hard Hours*, Anthony Hecht
1969 *Of Being Numerous*, George Oppen
1970 *Untitled Subjects*, Richard Howard
1971 *The Carrier of Ladders*, William S. Merwin
1972 *Collected Poems*, James Wright
1973 *Up Country*, Maxine Winokur Kumin
1974 *The Dolphin*, Robert Lowell
1975 *Turtle Island*, Gary Snyder
1976 *Self-Portrait in a Convex Mirror*, John Ashbery
1977 *Divine Comedies*, James Merrill
1978 *Collected Poems*, Howard Nemerov
1979 *Now and Then: Poems, 1976–1978*, Robert Penn Warren
1980 *Selected Poems*, Donald Rodney Justice
1981 *The Morning of the Poem*, James Schuyler

1982 *The Collected Poems*, Sylvia Plath
1983 *Selected Poems*, Galway Kinnell
1984 *American Primitive*, Mary Oliver
1985 *Yin*, Carolyn Kizer
1986 *The Flying Change*, Henry Taylor
1987 *Thomas and Beulah*, Rita Dove
1988 *Partial Accounts: New and Selected Poems*, William Meredith
1989 *New and Collected Poems*, Richard Wilbur
1990 *The World Doesn't End*, Charles Simic
1991 *Near Changes*, Mona Van Duyn
1992 *Selected Poems*, James Tate
1993 *The Wild Iris*, Louise Gluck
1994 *Neon Vernacular*, Yusef Komunyakaa
1995 *Simple Truth*, Philip Levine
1996 *The Dream of the Unified Field*, Jorie Graham
1997 *Alive Together: New and Selected Poems*, Lisel Mueller
1998 *Black Zodiac*, Charles Wright
1999 *Blizzard of One*, Mark Strand
2000 *Repair*, C. K. Williams

1. The poetry prize was established in 1922. The 1918 and 1919 awards were made from gifts provided by the Poetry Society.

General Nonfiction

1962 *The Making of the President, 1960*, Theodore H. White
1963 *The Guns of August*, Barbara W. Tuchman
1964 *Anti-Intellectualism in American Life*, Richard Hofstadter
1965 *O Strange New World*, Howard Mumford Jones
1966 *Wandering Through Winter*, Edwin Way Teale
1967 *The Problem of Slavery in Western Culture*, David Brion Davis
1968 *Rousseau and Revolution*, Will and Ariel Durant
1969 *So Human an Animal*, Rene Jules Dubos; *The Armies of the Night*, Norman Mailer
1970 *Gandhi's Truth*, Erik H. Erikson
1971 *The Rising Sun*, John Toland
1972 *Stilwell and the American Experience in China, 1911–1945*, Barbara W. Tuchman
1973 *Fire in the Lake: The Vietnamese and the Americans in Vietnam*, Frances FitzGerald; *Children of Crisis* (Vols. 1 and 2), Robert M. Coles
1974 *The Denial of Death*, Ernest Becker
1975 *Pilgrim at Tinker Creek*, Annie Dillard
1976 *Why Survive? Being Old in America*, Robert N. Butler
1977 *Beautiful Swimmers: Watermen, Crabs and the Chesapeake Bay*, William W. Warner
1978 *The Dragons of Eden*, Carl Sagan
1979 *On Human Nature*, Edward O. Wilson
1980 *Gödel, Escher, Bach: An Eternal Golden Braid*, Douglas R. Hofstadter
1981 *Fin-de-Siecle Vienna: Politics and Culture*, Carl E. Schorske
1982 *The Soul of a New Machine*, Tracy Kidder
1983 *Is There No Place on Earth for Me?*, Susan Sheehan
1984 *Social Transformation of American Medicine*, Paul Starr
1985 *The Good War: An Oral History of World War II*, Studs Terkel
1986 *Move Your Shadow: South Africa, Black and White*, Joseph Lelyveld; *Common Ground: A Turbulent Decade in the Lives of Three American Families*, J. Anthony Lukas

1987 *Arab and Jew: Wounded Spirits in a Promised Land,* David K. Shipler
1988 *The Making of the Atomic Bomb,* Richard Rhodes
1989 *A Bright Shining Lie,* Neil Sheehan
1990 *And Their Children After Them,* Dale Maharidge and Michael Williamson
1991 *The Ants,* Bert Holldobler and Edward O. Wilson
1992 *The Prize: The Epic Quest for Oil, Money and Power,* Daniel Yergin
1993 *Lincoln at Gettysburg: The Words That Remade America,* Garry Wills
1994 *Lenin's Tomb: The Last Days of the Soviet Empire,* David Remick
1995 *The Beak of the Finch: A Story of Evolution in Our Time,* Jonathan Weiner
1996 *The Haunted Land: Facing Europe's Ghosts After Communism,* Tina Rosenberg
1997 *Ashes to Ashes: America's Hundred-Year Cigarette War, the Public Health, and the Unabashed Triumph of Philip Morris,* Richard Kluger
1998 *Guns, Germs, and Steel: The Fates of Human Societies,* Jared Diamond
1999 *Annals of the Former World,* John McPhee
2000 *Embracing Defeat: Japan in the Wake of World War II,* John W. Dower

PULITZER PRIZES IN MUSIC

1943 *Secular Cantata No. 2, A Free Song,* William Schuman
1944 *Symphony No. 4 (Op. 34),* Howard Hanson
1945 *Appalachian Spring,* Aaron Copland
1946 *The Canticle of the Sun,* Leo Sowerby
1947 *Symphony No. 3,* Charles Ives
1948 *Symphony No. 3,* Walter Piston
1949 *Louisiana Story* music, Virgil Thomson
1950 *The Consul,* Gian Carlo Menotti
1951 Music for opera *Giants in the Earth,* Douglas Stuart Moore
1952 *Symphony Concertante,* Gail Kubik
1954 *Concerto for Two Pianos and Orchestra,* Quincy Porter
1955 *The Saint of Bleecker Street,* Gian Carlo Menotti
1956 *Symphony No. 3,* Ernst Toch
1957 *Meditations on Ecclesiastes,* Norman Dello Joio
1958 *Vanessa,* Samuel Barber
1959 *Concerto for Piano and Orchestra,* John La Montaine
1960 *Second String Quartet,* Elliott Carter
1961 *Symphony No. 7,* Walter Piston
1962 *The Crucible,* Robert Ward
1963 *Piano Concerto No. 1,* Samuel Barber
1966 *Variations for Orchestra,* Leslie Bassett
1967 *Quartet No. 3,* Leon Kirchner
1968 *Echoes of Time and the River,* George Crumb
1969 *String Quartet No. 3,* Karel Husa
1970 *Time's Encomium,* Charles Wuorinen
1971 *Synchronisms No. 6 for Piano and Electronic Sound,* Mario Davidowsky
1972 *Windows,* Jacob Druckman
1973 *String Quartet No. 3,* Elliott Carter
1974 *Notturno,* Donald Martino
1975 *From the Diary of Virginia Woolf,* Dominick Argento
1976 *Air Music,* Ned Rorem

1977 *Visions of Terror and Wonder,* Richard Wernick
1978 *Déjà Vu for Percussion Quartet and Orchestra,* Michael Colgrass
1979 *Aftertones of Infinity,* Joseph Schwantner
1980 *In Memory of a Summer Day,* David Del Tredici
1982 *Concerto for Orchestra,* Roger Sessions
1983 *Three Movements for Orchestra,* Ellen T. Zwilich
1984 *Canti del Sole,* Bernard Rands
1985 *Symphony RiverRun,* Stephen Albert
1986 *Wind Quintet IV,* George Perle
1987 *The Flight Into Egypt,* John Harbison
1988 *12 New Etudes for Piano,* William Bolcom
1989 *Whispers Out of Time,* Roger Reynolds
1990 *Duplicates: A Concerto for Two Pianos and Orchestra,* Mel Powell
1991 *Symphony,* Shulamit Ran
1992 *The Face of the Night, The Heart of the Dark,* Wayne Peterson
1993 *Trombone Concerto,* Christopher Rouse
1994 *Of Reminiscences and Reflections,* Gunther Schuller
1995 *Stringmusic,* Morton Gould
1996 *Lilacs,* George Walker
1997 *Blood on the Field,* Wynton Marsalis
1998 *String Quartet No. 2, Musica Instrumentalis,* Aaron Jay Kernis
1999 *Concerto for Flute, Strings and Percussion,* Melinda Wagner
2000 *Life Is a Dream, Opera in Three Acts: Act II, Concert Version,* Lewis Spratlan

PULITZER PRIZES IN DRAMA

1918 *Why Marry?,* Jesse Lynch Williams
1920 *Beyond the Horizon,* Eugene O'Neill
1921 *Miss Lulu Bett,* Zona Gale
1922 *Anna Christie,* Eugene O'Neill
1923 *Icebound,* Owen Davis
1924 *Hell-Bent Fer Heaven,* Hatcher Hughes
1925 *They Knew What They Wanted,* Sidney Howard
1926 *Craig's Wife,* George Kelly
1927 *In Abraham's Bosom,* Paul Green
1928 *Strange Interlude,* Eugene O'Neill
1929 *Street Scene,* Elmer L. Rice
1930 *The Green Pastures,* Marc Connelly
1931 *Alison's House,* Susan Glaspell
1932 *Of Thee I Sing,* George S. Kaufman, Morrie Ryskind, and Ira Gershwin
1933 *Both Your Houses,* Maxwell Anderson
1934 *Men in White,* Sidney Kingsley
1935 *The Old Maid,* Zöe Akins
1936 *Idiot's Delight,* Robert E. Sherwood
1937 *You Can't Take It with You,* Moss Hart and George S. Kaufman
1938 *Our Town,* Thornton Wilder
1939 *Abe Lincoln in Illinois,* Robert E. Sherwood
1940 *The Time of Your Life,* William Saroyan
1941 *There Shall Be No Night,* Robert E. Sherwood
1943 *The Skin of Our Teeth,* Thornton Wilder
1945 *Harvey,* Mary Chase
1946 *State of the Union,* Russel Crouse and Howard Lindsay
1948 *A Streetcar Named Desire,* Tennessee Williams
1949 *Death of a Salesman,* Arthur Miller
1950 *South Pacific,* Richard Rodgers, Oscar Hammerstein II, and Joshua Logan

1952 *The Shrike,* Joseph Kramm
1953 *Picnic,* William Inge
1954 *The Teahouse of the August Moon,* John Patrick
1955 *Cat on a Hot Tin Roof,* Tennessee Williams
1956 *The Diary of Anne Frank,* Frances Goodrich and Albert Hackett
1957 *Long Day's Journey into Night,* Eugene O'Neill
1958 *Look Homeward, Angel,* Ketti Frings
1959 *J. B.,* Archibald MacLeish
1960 *Fiorello!,* George Abbott, Jerome Weidman, Jerry Bock, and Sheldon Harnick
1961 *All the Way Home,* Tad Mosel
1962 *How to Succeed in Business without Really Trying,* Frank Loesser and Abe Burrows
1965 *The Subject Was Roses,* Frank D. Gilroy
1967 *A Delicate Balance,* Edward Albee
1969 *The Great White Hope,* Howard Sackler
1970 *No Place to Be Somebody,* Charles Gordone
1971 *The Effect of Gamma Rays on Man-in-the-Moon Marigolds,* Paul Zindel
1973 *That Championship Season,* Jason Miller
1975 *Seascape,* Edward Albee
1976 *A Chorus Line,* conceived by Michael Bennett
1977 *The Shadow Box,* Michael Cristofer
1978 *The Gin Game,* Donald L. Coburn
1979 *Buried Child,* Sam Shepard
1980 *Talley's Folly,* Lanford Wilson
1981 *Crimes of the Heart,* Beth Henley
1982 *A Soldier's Play,* Charles Fuller
1983 *'Night, Mother,* Marsha Norman
1984 *Glengarry Glen Ross,* David Mamet
1985 *Sunday in the Park with George,* Stephen Sondheim and James Lapine
1987 *Fences,* August Wilson
1988 *Driving Miss Daisy,* Alfred Uhry
1989 *The Heidi Chronicles,* Wendy Wasserstein
1990 *The Piano Lesson,* August Wilson
1991 *Lost in Yonkers,* Neil Simon
1992 *The Kentucky Cycle,* Robert Schenkkan
1993 *Angels in America: Millennium Approaches,* Tony Kushner
1994 *Three Tall Women,* Edward Albee
1995 *The Young Man from Atlanta,* Horton Foote
1996 *Rent,* Jonathan Larson
1998 *How I Learned to Drive,* Paula Vogel
1999 *Wit,* Margaret Edson
2000 *Dinner with Friends,* Donald Margulies

SPECIAL CITATIONS

1938 *Edmonton* [Alberta] *Journal,* special bronze plaque for editorial leadership in defense of freedom of the press in province of Alberta
1941 New York Times, for the public educational value of its foreign news report
1944 Byron Price, director of the Office of Censorship, for the creation and administration of the newspaper and radio codes; Mrs. William Allen White, for her husband's interest and services during the past seven years as a member of the Advisory Board of the Graduate School of Journalism, Columbia University; Richard Rodgers and Oscar Hammerstein II, for their musical *Oklahoma!*

1945 The cartographers of the American press, for their war maps
1947 (Pulitzer centennial year.) Columbia University and the Graduate School of Journalism, for their efforts to maintain and advance the high standards governing the Pulitzer Prize awards; the *St. Louis Post-Dispatch,* for its unswerving adherence to the public and professional ideals of its founder and its leadership in American journalism
1948 Dr. Frank D. Fackenthal, for his interest and service
1951 Cyrus L. Sulzberger *(New York Times),* for his exclusive interview with Archbishop Stepinac in a Yugoslav prison
1952 *Kansas City Star,* for coverage of 1951 floods; Max Kase *(New York Journal–American),* for exposures of bribery in basketball
1953 *New York Times,* for its 17-year publication of "Review of the Week," and Lester Markel, its founder
1957 Kenneth Roberts, for his historical novels
1958 Walter Lippmann *(New York Herald Tribune),* for his "wisdom, perception and high sense of responsibility" in his commentary on national and international affairs
1960 Garrett Mattingly, for *The Armada*
1961 *American Heritage Picture History of the Civil War,* as a distinguished example of American book publishing
1964 Gannett Newspapers, Rochester, N.Y.
1973 James Thomas Flexner, for his biography *George Washington*
1974 Roger Sessions, for his "life's work in music"
1976 John Hohenberg, for "services for 22 years as Administrator of the Pulitzer Prizes"; Scott Joplin, for his contributions to American music
1977 Alex Haley, for his novel, *Roots*
1978 E. B. White of *New Yorker* magazine and Richard L. Strout of *The Christian Science Monitor*
1982 Milton Babbitt, "for his life's work as a distinguished and seminal American composer"
1984 Theodor Seuss Geisel (Dr. Seuss), for "books full of playful rhymes, nonsense words and strange illustrations"
1985 William Schuman, for "more than half a century of contribution to American music as a composer and educational leader"
1987 Joseph Pulitzer, Jr., "for extraordinary services to American journalism and letters during his 31 years as chairman of the Pulitzer Prize Board and for his accomplishments as an editor and publisher"
1992 *Maus,* Art Spiegelman
1996 Herb Caen *(San Francisco Chronicle),* "for his extraordinary and continuing contribution as a voice and conscience of his city"
1998 George Gershwin
1999 Edward Kennedy "Duke" Ellington, who "made an indelible contribution to art and culture"

Academy Awards (Oscars)

1928

Picture: *Wings,* Paramount
Director: Frank Borzage, *Seventh Heaven;* Lewis Milestone, *Two Arabian Nights*
Actress: Janet Gaynor, *Seventh Heaven, Street Angel, Sunrise*
Actor: Emil Jannings, *The Way of All·Flesh, The Last Command*

1929

Picture: *The Broadway Melody,* MGM
Director: Frank Lloyd, *The Divine Lady*
Actress: Mary Pickford, *Coquette*
Actor: Warner Baxter, *In Old Arizona*

1930

Picture: *All Quiet on the Western Front,* Universal
Director: Lewis Milestone, *All Quiet on the Western Front*
Actress: Norma Shearer, *The Divorcee*
Actor: George Arliss, *Disraeli*

1931

Picture: *Cimarron,* RKO Radio
Director: Norman Taurog, *Skippy*
Actress: Marie Dressler, *Min and Bill*
Actor: Lionel Barrymore, *A Free Soul*

1932

Picture: *Grand Hotel,* MGM
Director: Frank Borzage, *Bad Girl*
Actress: Helen Hayes, *The Sin of Madelon Claudet*
Actor: Fredric March, *Dr. Jekyll and Mr. Hyde,* and Wallace Beery, *The Champ*

1933

Picture: *Cavalcade,* Fox
Director: Frank Lloyd, *Cavalcade*
Actress: Katharine Hepburn, *Morning Glory*
Actor: Charles Laughton, *The Private Life of Henry VIII*

1934

Picture: *It Happened One Night,* Columbia
Director: Frank Capra, *It Happened One Night*
Actress: Claudette Colbert, *It Happened One Night*
Actor: Clark Gable, *It Happened One Night*

1935

Picture: *Mutiny on the Bounty,* MGM
Director: John Ford, *The Informer*
Actress: Bette Davis, *Dangerous*
Actor: Victor McLaglen, *The Informer*

1936

Picture: *The Great Ziegfeld,* MGM
Director: Frank Capra, *Mr. Deeds Goes to Town*
Actress: Luise Rainer, *The Great Ziegfeld*
Actor: Paul Muni, *The Story of Louis Pasteur*
Supporting Actress: Gale Sondergaard, *Anthony Adverse*
Supporting Actor: Walter Brennan, *Come and Get It*

1937

Picture: *The Life of Emile Zola,* Warner Bros.
Director: Leo McCarey, *The Awful Truth*
Actress: Luise Rainer, *The Good Earth*
Actor: Spencer Tracy, *Captains Courageous*
Supporting Actress: Alice Brady, *In Old Chicago*
Supporting Actor: Joseph Schildkraut, *The Life of Emile Zola*

1938

Picture: *You Can't Take It with You,* Columbia
Director: Frank Capra, *You Can't Take It with You*
Actress: Bette Davis, *Jezebel*
Actor: Spencer Tracy, *Boys Town*
Supporting Actress: Fay Bainter, *Jezebel*
Supporting Actor: Walter Brennan, *Kentucky*

1939

Picture: *Gone with the Wind,* Selznick MGM
Director: Victor Fleming, *Gone with the Wind*
Actress: Vivien Leigh, *Gone with the Wind*
Actor: Robert Donat, *Goodbye, Mr. Chips*
Supporting Actress: Hattie McDaniel, *Gone with the Wind*
Supporting Actor: Thomas Mitchell, *Stagecoach*

1940

Picture: *Rebecca,* Selznick-United Artists
Director: John Ford, *The Grapes of Wrath*
Actress: Ginger Rogers, *Kitty Foyle*
Actor: James Stewart, *The Philadelphia Story*
Supporting Actress: Jane Darwell, *The Grapes of Wrath*
Supporting Actor: Walter Brennan, *The Westerner*

1941

Picture: *How Green Was My Valley,* 20th Century–Fox
Director: John Ford, *How Green Was My Valley*
Actress: Joan Fontaine, *Suspicion*
Actor: Gary Cooper, *Sergeant York*
Supporting Actress: Mary Astor, *The Great Lie*
Supporting Actor: Donald Crisp, *How Green Was My Valley*

1942

Picture: *Mrs. Miniver,* MGM
Director: William Wyler, *Mrs. Miniver*
Actress: Greer Garson, *Mrs. Miniver*
Actor: James Cagney, *Yankee Doodle Dandy*
Supporting Actress: Teresa Wright, *Mrs. Miniver*
Supporting Actor: Van Heflin, *Johnny Eager*

1943

Picture: *Casablanca,* Warner Bros.
Director: Michael Curtiz, *Casablanca*
Actress: Jennifer Jones, *The Song of Bernadette*
Actor: Paul Lukas, *Watch on the Rhine*
Supporting Actress: Katina Paxinou, *For Whom the Bell Tolls*
Supporting Actor: Charles Coburn, *The More the Merrier*

1944

Picture: *Going My Way,* Paramount
Director: Leo McCarey, *Going My Way*
Actress: Ingrid Bergman, *Gaslight*
Actor: Bing Crosby, *Going My Way*
Supporting Actress: Ethel Barrymore, *None but the Lonely Heart*
Supporting Actor: Barry Fitzgerald, *Going My Way*

1945

Picture: *The Lost Weekend,* Paramount
Director: Billy Wilder, *The Lost Weekend*
Actress: Joan Crawford, *Mildred Pierce*
Actor: Ray Milland, *The Lost Weekend*
Supporting Actress: Anne Revere, *National Velvet*
Supporting Actor: James Dunn, *A Tree Grows in Brooklyn*

1946

Picture: *The Best Years of Our Lives,* Goldwyn-RKO Radio
Director: William Wyler, *The Best Years of Our Lives*
Actress: Olivia de Havilland, *To Each His Own*
Actor: Fredric March, *The Best Years of Our Lives*
Supporting Actress: Anne Baxter, *The Razor's Edge*
Supporting Actor: Harold Russell, *The Best Years of Our Lives*

1947

Picture: *Gentleman's Agreement,* 20th Century–Fox
Director: Elia Kazan, *Gentleman's Agreement*
Actress: Loretta Young, *The Farmer's Daughter*
Actor: Ronald Colman, *A Double Life*
Supporting Actress: Celeste Holm, *Gentleman's Agreement*
Supporting Actor: Edmund Gwenn, *Miracle on 34th Street*

1948
Picture: *Hamlet,* Rank-Two Cities-UI
Director: John Huston, *Treasure of Sierra Madre*
Actress: Jane Wyman, *Johnny Belinda*
Actor: Laurence Olivier, *Hamlet*
Supporting Actress: Claire Trevor, *Key Largo*
Supporting Actor: Walter Huston, *Treasure of Sierra Madre*

1949
Picture: *All the King's Men,* Rossen-Columbia
Director: Joseph L. Mankiewicz, *A Letter to Three Wives*
Actress: Olivia de Havilland, *The Heiress*
Actor: Broderick Crawford, *All the King's Men*
Supporting Actress: Mercedes McCambridge, *All the King's Men*
Supporting Actor: Dean Jagger, *Twelve O'Clock High*

1950
Picture: *All About Eve,* 20th Century–Fox
Director: Joseph L. Mankiewicz, *All About Eve*
Actress: Judy Holliday, *Born Yesterday*
Actor: José Ferrer, *Cyrano de Bergerac*
Supporting Actress: Josephine Hull, *Harvey*
Supporting Actor: George Sanders, *All About Eve*

1951
Picture: *An American in Paris,* MGM
Director: George Stevens, *A Place in the Sun*
Actress: Vivien Leigh, *A Streetcar Named Desire*
Actor: Humphrey Bogart, *The African Queen*
Supporting Actress: Kim Hunter, *A Streetcar Named Desire*
Supporting Actor: Karl Malden, *A Streetcar Named Desire*

1952
Picture: *The Greatest Show on Earth,* DeMille-Paramount
Director: John Ford, *The Quiet Man*
Actress: Shirley Booth, *Come Back, Little Sheba*
Actor: Gary Cooper, *High Noon*
Supporting Actress: Gloria Grahame, *The Bad and the Beautiful*
Supporting Actor: Anthony Quinn, *Viva Zapata!*

1953
Picture: *From Here to Eternity,* Columbia
Director: Fred Zinnemann, *From Here to Eternity*
Actress: Audrey Hepburn, *Roman Holiday*
Actor: William Holden, *Stalag 17*
Supporting Actress: Donna Reed, *From Here to Eternity*
Supporting Actor: Frank Sinatra, *From Here to Eternity*

1954
Picture: *On the Waterfront,* Horizon-American Corp., Columbia
Director: Elia Kazan, *On the Waterfront*
Actress: Grace Kelly, *The Country Girl*
Actor: Marlon Brando, *On the Waterfront*
Supporting Actress: Eva Marie Saint, *On the Waterfront*
Supporting Actor: Edmond O'Brien, *The Barefoot Contessa*

1955
Picture: *Marty,* Hecht and Lancaster, United Artists.
Director: Delbert Mann, *Marty*
Actress: Anna Magnani, *The Rose Tattoo*
Actor: Ernest Borgnine, *Marty*
Supporting Actress: Jo Van Fleet, *East of Eden*
Supporting Actor: Jack Lemmon, *Mister Roberts*

1956
Picture: *Around the World in 80 Days,* Michael Todd Co., Inc.-United Artists
Director: George Stevens, *Giant*
Actress: Ingrid Bergman, *Anastasia*
Actor: Yul Brynner, *The King and I*
Supporting Actress: Dorothy Malone, *Written on the Wind*
Supporting Actor: Anthony Quinn, *Lust for Life*

1957
Picture: *The Bridge on the River Kwai,* Horizon Films, Columbia

Director: David Lean, *The Bridge on the River Kwai*
Actress: Joanne Woodward, *The Three Faces of Eve*
Actor: Alec Guinness, *The Bridge on the River Kwai*
Supporting Actress: Miyoshi Umeki, *Sayonara*
Supporting Actor: Red Buttons, *Sayonara*

1958
Picture: *Gigi,* Arthur Freed Productions, Inc., MGM
Director: Vincente Minnelli, *Gigi*
Actress: Susan Hayward, *I Want to Live!*
Actor: David Niven, *Separate Tables*
Supporting Actress: Wendy Hiller, *Separate Tables*
Supporting Actor: Burl Ives, *The Big Country*

1959
Picture: *Ben-Hur,* MGM
Director: William Wyler, *Ben-Hur*
Actress: Simone Signoret, *Room at the Top*
Actor: Charlton Heston, *Ben-Hur*
Supporting Actress: Shelley Winters, *The Diary of Anne Frank*
Supporting Actor: Hugh Griffith, *Ben-Hur*

1960
Picture: *The Apartment,* Mirisch Co., Inc., United Artists
Director: Billy Wilder, *The Apartment*
Actress: Elizabeth Taylor, *Butterfield 8*
Actor: Burt Lancaster, *Elmer Gantry*
Supporting Actress: Shirley Jones, *Elmer Gantry*
Supporting Actor: Peter Ustinov, *Spartacus*

1961
Picture: *West Side Story,* Mirisch Pictures, Inc., and B and P Enterprises, Inc., United Artists
Director: Robert Wise and Jerome Robbins, *West Side Story*
Actress: Sophia Loren, *Two Women*
Actor: Maximillian Schell, *Judgment at Nuremberg*
Supporting Actress: Rita Moreno, *West Side Story*
Supporting Actor: George Chakiris, *West Side Story*

1962
Picture: *Lawrence of Arabia,* Horizon Pictures, Ltd.-Columbia
Director: David Lean, *Lawrence of Arabia*
Actress: Anne Bancroft, *The Miracle Worker*
Actor: Gregory Peck, *To Kill a Mockingbird*
Supporting Actress: Patty Duke, *The Miracle Worker*
Supporting Actor: Ed Begley, *Sweet Bird of Youth*

1963
Picture: *Tom Jones,* A Woodfall Production, United Artists-Lopert Pictures
Director: Tony Richardson, *Tom Jones*
Actress: Patricia Neal, *Hud*
Actor: Sidney Poitier, *Lilies of the Field*
Supporting Actress: Margaret Rutherford, *The V.I.P.s*
Supporting Actor: Melvyn Douglas, *Hud*

1964
Picture: *My Fair Lady,* Warner Bros.
Director: George Cukor, *My Fair Lady*
Actress: Julie Andrews, *Mary Poppins*
Actor: Rex Harrison, *My Fair Lady*
Supporting Actress: Lila Kedrova, *Zorba the Greek*
Supporting Actor: Peter Ustinov, *Topkapi*

1965
Picture: *The Sound of Music,* Argyle Enterprises Production, 20th Century–Fox
Director: Robert Wise, *The Sound of Music*
Actress: Julie Christie, *Darling*
Actor: Lee Marvin, *Cat Ballou*
Supporting Actress: Shelley Winters, *A Patch of Blue*
Supporting Actor: Martin Balsam, *A Thousand Clowns*

1966
Picture: *A Man for All Seasons,* Highland Films, Ltd., Production, Columbia
Director: Fred Zinnemann, *A Man for All Seasons*
Actress: Elizabeth Taylor, *Who's Afraid of Virginia Woolf?*
Actor: Paul Scofield, *A Man for All Seasons*

Supporting Actress: Sandy Dennis, *Who's Afraid of Virginia Woolf?*
Supporting Actor: Walter Matthau, *The Fortune Cookie*

1967
Picture: *In the Heat of the Night,* Mirisch Corp. Productions, United Artists
Director: Mike Nichols, *The Graduate*
Actress: Katharine Hepburn, *Guess Who's Coming to Dinner*
Actor: Rod Steiger, *In the Heat of the Night*
Supporting Actress: Estelle Parsons, *Bonnie and Clyde*
Supporting Actor: George Kennedy, *Cool Hand Luke*

1968
Picture: *Oliver!,* Columbia Pictures
Director: Sir Carol Reed, *Oliver!*
Actress: Katharine Hepburn, *The Lion in Winter* and Barbra Streisand, *Funny Girl*
Actor: Cliff Robertson, *Charly*
Supporting Actress: Ruth Gordon, *Rosemary's Baby*
Supporting Actor: Jack Albertson, *The Subject Was Roses*

1969
Picture: *Midnight Cowboy,* Jerome Hellman-John Schlesinger Production, United Artists
Director: John Schlesinger, *Midnight Cowboy*
Actress: Maggie Smith, *The Prime of Miss Jean Brodie*
Actor: John Wayne, *True Grit*
Supporting Actress: Goldie Hawn, *Cactus Flower*
Supporting Actor: Gig Young, *They Shoot Horses, Don't They?*

1970
Picture: *Patton,* Frank McCarthy-Franklin J. Schaffner Production, 20th Century–Fox
Director: Franklin J. Schaffner, *Patton*
Actress: Glenda Jackson, *Women in Love*
Actor: George C. Scott, *Patton*
Supporting Actress: Helen Hayes, *Airport*
Supporting Actor: John Mills, *Ryan's Daughter*

1971
Picture: *The French Connection,* D'Antoni Productions, 20th Century–Fox
Director: William Friedkin, *The French Connection*
Actress: Jane Fonda, *Klute*
Actor: Gene Hackman, *The French Connection*
Supporting Actress: Cloris Leachman, *The Last Picture Show*
Supporting Actor: Ben Johnson, *The Last Picture Show*

1972
Picture: *The Godfather,* Albert S. Ruddy Production, Paramount
Director: Bob Fosse, *Cabaret*
Actress: Liza Minnelli, *Cabaret*
Actor: Marlon Brando, *The Godfather*
Supporting Actress: Eileen Heckart, *Butterflies Are Free*
Supporting Actor: Joel Gray, *Cabaret*

1973
Picture: *The Sting,* Universal-Bill/Phillips-George Roy Hill Production, Universal
Director: George Roy Hill, *The Sting*
Actress: Glenda Jackson, *A Touch of Class*
Actor: Jack Lemmon, *Save the Tiger*
Supporting Actress: Tatum O'Neal, *Paper Moon*
Supporting Actor: John Houseman, *The Paper Chase*

1974
Picture: *The Godfather, Part II,* Coppola Co. Production, Paramount
Director: Francis Ford Coppola, *The Godfather, Part II*
Actress: Ellen Burstyn, *Alice Doesn't Live Here Anymore*
Actor: Art Carney, *Harry and Tonto*
Supporting Actress: Ingrid Bergman, *Murder on the Orient Express*
Supporting Actor: Robert De Niro, *The Godfather, Part II*

1975
Picture: *One Flew Over the Cuckoo's Nest,* Fantasy Films Production, United Artists
Director: Milos Forman, *One Flew Over the Cuckoo's Nest*
Actress: Louise Fletcher, *One Flew Over the Cuckoo's Nest*
Actor: Jack Nicholson, *One Flew Over the Cuckoo's Nest*
Supporting Actress: Lee Grant, *Shampoo*
Supporting Actor: George Burns, *The Sunshine Boys*

1976
Picture: *Rocky,* Robert Chartoff-Irwin Winkler Production, United Artists
Director: John G. Avildsen, *Rocky*
Actress: Faye Dunaway, *Network*
Actor: Peter Finch, *Network*
Supporting Actress: Beatrice Straight, *Network*
Supporting Actor: Jason Robards, *All the President's Men*

1977
Picture: *Annie Hall,* Jack Rollins-Charles H. Joffe Production, United Artists
Director: Woody Allen, *Annie Hall*
Actress: Diane Keaton, *Annie Hall*
Actor: Richard Dreyfuss, *The Goodbye Girl*
Supporting Actress: Vanessa Redgrave, *Julia*
Supporting Actor: Jason Robards, *Julia*

1978
Picture: *The Deer Hunter,* Michael Cimino Film Production, Universal
Director: Michael Cimino, *The Deer Hunter*
Actress: Jane Fonda, *Coming Home*
Actor: Jon Voight, *Coming Home*
Supporting Actress: Maggie Smith, *California Suite*
Supporting Actor: Christopher Walken, *The Deer Hunter*

1979
Picture: *Kramer vs. Kramer,* Stanley Jaffe Production, Columbia Pictures
Director: Robert Benton, *Kramer vs. Kramer*
Actress: Sally Field, *Norma Rae*
Actor: Dustin Hoffman, *Kramer vs. Kramer*
Supporting Actress: Meryl Streep, *Kramer vs. Kramer*
Supporting Actor: Melvyn Douglas, *Being There*

1980
Picture: *Ordinary People,* Wildwood Enterprises Production, Paramount
Director: Robert Redford, *Ordinary People*
Actress: Sissy Spacek, *Coal Miner's Daughter*
Actor: Robert De Niro, *Raging Bull*
Supporting Actress: Mary Steenburgen, *Melvin and Howard*
Supporting Actor: Timothy Hutton, *Ordinary People*

1981
Picture: *Chariots of Fire,* Enigma Productions, Ladd Company/Warner Bros.
Director: Warren Beatty, *Reds*
Actress: Katharine Hepburn, *On Golden Pond*
Actor: Henry Fonda, *On Golden Pond*
Supporting Actress: Maureen Stapleton, *Reds*
Supporting Actor: John Gielgud, *Arthur*

1982
Picture: *Gandhi,* Indo-British Films Production/Columbia
Director: Richard Attenborough, *Gandhi*
Actress: Meryl Streep, *Sophie's Choice*
Actor: Ben Kingsley, *Gandhi*
Supporting Actress: Jessica Lange, *Tootsie*
Supporting Actor: Louis Gossett, Jr., *An Officer and a Gentleman*

1983
Picture: *Terms of Endearment,* Paramount
Director: James L. Brooks, *Terms of Endearment*
Actress: Shirley MacLaine, *Terms of Endearment*
Actor: Robert Duvall, *Tender Mercies*
Supporting Actress: Linda Hunt, *The Year of Living Dangerously*
Supporting Actor: Jack Nicholson, *Terms of Endearment*

1984
Picture: *Amadeus*, Orion
Director: Milos Forman, *Amadeus*
Actress: Sally Field, *Places in the Heart*
Actor: F. Murray Abraham, *Amadeus*
Supporting Actress: Dame Peggy Ashcroft, *A Passage to India*
Supporting Actor: Haing S. Ngor, *The Killing Fields*

1985
Picture: *Out of Africa*, Universal
Director: Sydney Pollack, *Out of Africa*
Actress: Geraldine Page, *The Trip to Bountiful*
Actor: William Hurt, *Kiss of the Spider Woman*
Supporting Actress: Anjelica Huston, *Prizzi's Honor*
Supporting Actor: Don Ameche, *Cocoon*

1986
Picture: *Platoon*, Orion
Director: Oliver Stone, *Platoon*
Actress: Marlee Matlin, *Children of a Lesser God*
Actor: Paul Newman, *The Color of Money*
Supporting Actress: Dianne Wiest, *Hannah and Her Sisters*
Supporting Actor: Michael Caine, *Hannah and Her Sisters*

1987
Picture: *The Last Emperor*, Columbia Pictures
Director: Bernardo Bertolucci, *The Last Emperor*
Actress: Cher, *Moonstruck*
Actor: Michael Douglas, *Wall Street*
Supporting Actress: Olympia Dukakis, *Moonstruck*
Supporting Actor: Sean Connery, *The Untouchables*

1988
Picture: *Rain Man*, United Artists
Director: Barry Levinson, *Rain Man*
Actress: Jodie Foster, *The Accused*
Actor: Dustin Hoffman, *Rain Man*
Supporting Actress: Geena Davis, *The Accidental Tourist*
Supporting Actor: Kevin Kline, *A Fish Called Wanda*

1989
Picture: *Driving Miss Daisy*, Warner Bros.
Director: Oliver Stone, *Born on the Fourth of July*
Actress: Jessica Tandy, *Driving Miss Daisy*
Actor: Daniel Day-Lewis, *My Left Foot*
Supporting Actress: Brenda Fricker, *My Left Foot*
Supporting Actor: Denzel Washington, *Glory*

1990
Picture: *Dances With Wolves*, Orion
Director: Kevin Costner, *Dances With Wolves*
Actress: Kathy Bates, *Misery*
Actor: Jeremy Irons, *Reversal of Fortune*
Supporting Actress: Whoopi Goldberg, *Ghost*
Supporting Actor: Joe Pesci, *Goodfellas*

1991
Picture: *The Silence of the Lambs*, Orion
Director: Jonathan Demme, *The Silence of the Lambs*
Actress: Jodie Foster, *The Silence of the Lambs*
Actor: Anthony Hopkins, *The Silence of the Lambs*
Supporting Actress: Mercedes Ruehl, *The Fisher King*
Supporting Actor: Jack Palance, *City Slickers*

1992
Picture: *Unforgiven*, Warner Bros.
Director: Clint Eastwood, *Unforgiven*
Actress: Emma Thompson, *Howards End*
Actor: Al Pacino, *Scent of a Woman*
Supporting Actress: Marisa Tomei, *My Cousin Vinny*
Supporting Actor: Gene Hackman, *Unforgiven*

1993
Picture: *Schindler's List*, Universal
Director: Steven Spielberg, *Schindler's List*
Actress: Holly Hunter, *The Piano*
Actor: Tom Hanks, *Philadelphia*
Supporting Actress: Anna Paquin, *The Piano*
Supporting Actor: Tommy Lee Jones, *The Fugitive*

1994
Picture: *Forrest Gump*, Paramount
Director: Robert Zemeckis, *Forrest Gump*
Actress: Jessica Lange, *Blue Sky*
Actor: Tom Hanks, *Forrest Gump*
Supporting Actress: Dianne Wiest, *Bullets Over Broadway*
Supporting Actor: Martin Landau, *Ed Wood*

1995
Picture: *Braveheart*, Paramount
Director: Mel Gibson, *Braveheart*
Actress: Susan Sarandon, *Dead Man Walking*
Actor: Nicolas Cage, *Leaving Las Vegas*
Supporting Actress: Mira Sorvino, *Mighty Aphrodite*
Supporting Actor: Kevin Spacey, *The Usual Suspects*

1996
Picture: *The English Patient*, Miramax
Director: Anthony Minghella, *The English Patient*
Actress: Frances McDormand, *Fargo*
Actor: Geoffrey Rush, *Shine*
Supporting Actress: Juliette Binoche, *The English Patient*
Supporting Actor: Cuba Gooding, Jr., *Jerry Maguire*

1997
Picture: *Titanic*, 20th Century–Fox and Paramount
Director: James Cameron, *Titanic*
Actress: Helen Hunt, *As Good As It Gets*
Actor: Jack Nicholson, *As Good As It Gets*
Supporting Actress: Kim Basinger, *L.A. Confidential*
Supporting Actor: Robin Williams, *Good Will Hunting*

1998
Picture: *Shakespeare in Love*, Miramax
Director: Steven Spielberg, *Saving Private Ryan*
Actress: Gwyneth Paltrow, *Shakespeare in Love*
Actor: Roberto Benigni, *Life Is Beautiful*
Supporting Actress: Judi Dench, *Shakespeare in Love*
Supporting Actor: James Coburn, *Affliction*

1999
Picture: *American Beauty*, DreamWorks SKG
Director: Sam Mendes, *American Beauty*
Actress: Hilary Swank, *Boys Don't Cry*
Actor: Kevin Spacey, *American Beauty*
Supporting Actress: Angelina Jolie, *Girl, Interrupted*
Supporting Actor: Michael Caine, *The Cider House Rules*

Other Academy Awards for 1999

Art Direction: Rick Heinrichs, *Sleepy Hollow*
Cinematography: Conrad L. Hall, *American Beauty*
Costume Design: Lindy Hemming, *Topsy-Turvy*
Documentary (feature): Arthur Cohn, *One Day in September*; **(short subject):** Susan Hannah Hadary and William A. Whiteford, *King Gimp*
Editing: Zach Staenberg, *The Matrix*
Foreign-Language Film: *All about My Mother*, Spain
Makeup: Christine Blundell and Trefor Proud, *Topsy-Turvy*
Music (original score): John Corigliano, *The Red Violin*; **(original song):** Phil Collins, "You'll Be in My Heart," *Tarzan*
Adapted Screenplay: John Irving, *The Cider House Rules*
Original Screenplay: Alan Ball, *American Beauty*

Short Subject (live action): Barbara Schock and Tamara Tiehel, *My Mother Dreams the Satan's Disciples in New York*; **(animated):** Alexandre Petrov, *The Old Man and the Sea*
Sound: John Reitz, Gregg Rudloff, David Campbell, and David Lee, *The Matrix*
Sound Effects Editing: Dane A. Davis, *The Matrix*
Visual Effects: John Gaeta, Janek Sirrs, Steve Courtley, and Jon Thum, *The Matrix*
Honorary Award: Andrzej Wajda, director
Irving G. Thalberg Memorial Award: Warren Beatty, producer, director, writer, actor
Gordon E. Sawyer Award (technological contribution): Dr. Roderick T. Ryan

1999 National Society of Film Critics Awards

Best Picture (tie): *Being John Malkovich* and *Topsy-Turvy*
Best Actor: Russell Crowe, *The Insider*
Best Actress: Reese Witherspoon, *Election*
Best Supporting Actor: Christopher Plummer, *The Insider*
Best Supporting Actress: Chloë Sevigny, *Boys Don't Cry*

Best Director: Mike Leigh, *Topsy-Turvy*
Best Screenplay: Charlie Kaufman, *Being John Malkovich*
Best Cinematography: Conrad L. Hall, *American Beauty*
Best Foreign Film: *Autumn Tale*, Eric Rohmer (France)
Best Documentary: *Buena Vista Social Club*, Wim Wenders

1999 Broadcast Film Critics Association Awards

Best Picture: *American Beauty*
Best Actor: Russell Crowe, *The Insider*
Best Actress: Hilary Swank, *Boys Don't Cry*
Best Supporting Actor: Michael Clarke Duncan, *The Green Mile*
Best Supporting Actress: Angelina Jolie, *Girl, Interrupted*
Best Director: Sam Mendes, *American Beauty*
Best Original Screenplay: Alan Ball, *American Beauty*
Best Adapted Screenplay: Frank Darabont, *The Green Mile*
Best Song: "Music of My Heart," *Music of the Heart*
Best Score: Gabriel Yared, *The Talented Mr. Ripley*

Best Foreign-Language Film: *All about My Mother*, Pedro Almodóvar (Spain)
Best Documentary: *Buena Vista Social Club*
Best Animated Feature: *Toy Story 2*
Best Family Film: *October Sky*
Best Made-for-Television Movie (tie): *RKO 281* and *Tuesdays with Morrie*
Best Child Performance: Haley Joel Osment, *The Sixth Sense*
Breakthrough Performer: Spike Jonze, *Being John Malkovich* and *Three Kings*

1999 National Board of Review Awards

Best Picture: *American Beauty*
Best Actor: Russell Crowe, *The Insider*
Best Actress: Janet McTeer, *Tumbleweeds*
Best Supporting Actor: Philip Seymour Hoffman, *Magnolia* and *The Talented Mr. Ripley*
Best Supporting Actress: Julianne Moore, *Magnolia*, *An Ideal Husband*, *Cookie's Fortune*, and *A Map of the World*

Best Director: Anthony Minghella, *The Talented Mr. Ripley*
Best Foreign Film: *All about My Mother*, Pedro Almodóvar (Spain)
Best Documentary: *Buena Vista Social Club*
Career Achievement Award: Clint Eastwood
Special Achievement in Filmmaking: Tim Robbins
Freedom of Expression Award: Michael Mann, *The Insider*

1999 Golden Globe Awards

Film Awards

Best Motion Picture—Drama: *American Beauty*
Best Actress in a Drama: Hilary Swank, *Boys Don't Cry*
Best Actor in a Drama: Denzel Washington, *The Hurricane*
Best Motion Picture—Musical or Comedy: *Toy Story 2*
Best Actress in a Musical or Comedy: Janet McTeer, *Tumbleweeds*
Best Actor in a Musical or Comedy: Jim Carrey, *Man on the Moon*
Best Supporting Actress: Angelina Jolie, *Girl, Interrupted*
Best Supporting Actor: Tom Cruise, *Magnolia*
Best Director: Sam Mendes, *American Beauty*
Best Screenplay: Alan Ball, *American Beauty*
Best Original Score: Ennio Morricone, *The Legend of 1900*
Best Original Song: "You'll Be in My Heart," Phil Collins, *Tarzan*
Best Foreign Film: *All about My Mother*, Pedro Almodóvar (Spain)

Television Awards

Best Series—Drama: *The Sopranos* (HBO)
Best Actress in a Drama: Edie Falco, *The Sopranos*
Best Actor in a Drama: James Gandolfini, *The Sopranos*
Best Series—Musical or Comedy: *Sex and the City* (HBO)
Best Actress in a Musical or Comedy Series: Sarah Jessica Parker, *Sex and the City*
Best Actor in a Musical or Comedy Series: Michael J. Fox, *Spin City*
Best Miniseries or Movie Made for Television: *RKO 281* (HBO)
Best Actress in a Miniseries or Movie Made for Television: Halle Berry, *Introducing Dorothy Dandridge*
Best Actor in a Miniseries or Movie Made for Television: Jack Lemmon, *Inherit the Wind*
Best Supporting Actress in a Series, Miniseries, or Movie Made for Television: Nancy Marchand, *The Sopranos*
Best Supporting Actor in a Series, Miniseries, or Movie Made for Television: Peter Fonda, *The Passion of Ayn Rand*

2000 Tony (Antoinette Perry) Awards

Play: *Copenhagen*
Musical: *Contact*
Revival—Play: *The Real Thing*
Revival—Musical: *Kiss Me, Kate*
Actor—Play: Stephen Dillane, *The Real Thing*
Actress—Play: Jennifer Ehle, *The Real Thing*
Actor—Musical: Brian Stokes Mitchell, *Kiss Me, Kate*
Actress—Musical: Heather Headley, *Aida*
Featured Actor—Play: Roy Dotrice, *A Moon for the Misbegotten*
Featured Actress—Play: Blair Brown, *Copenhagen*
Featured Actor—Musical: Boyd Gaines, *Contact*
Featured Actress—Musical: Karen Ziemba, *Contact*
Director—Play: Michael Blakemore, *Copenhagen*
Director—Musical: Michael Blakemore, *Kiss Me, Kate*

Book—Musical: *James Joyce's The Dead*
Score—Musical: *Aida*
Orchestration: Don Sebesky, *Kiss Me, Kate*
Scenic Designer: Bob Crowley, *Aida*
Costume Designer: Martin Pakledinaz, *Kiss Me, Kate*
Choreographer: Susan Stroman, *Contact*
Lighting Designer: Natasha Katz, *Aida*
Regional Theater: The Utah Shakespearian Festival of Cedar City, Utah
Special Awards: *Dame Edna: The Royal Tour*, special Tony Award for a live theatrical event; T. Edward Hambleton, founder of the Phoenix Theatre
Excellence in Theatre: Eileen Heckart, *Encores! Great American Musicals in Concert*, Sylvia Herscher

2000 New York Drama Critics Circle Awards

Best New Play: *Jitney*
Best Musical: *James Joyce's The Dead*

Best Foreign Play: *Copenhagen*

2000 Obie Awards

The Obie Awards, presented by *The Village Voice*, honor superior off-Broadway theater.

Best Production: Ben Katcho, Michael Gordon, David Lang, Julia Wolfe, Bob McGrath, *The Carbon Copy Building*
Playwriting: Harley Granville Barker, *Waste*
Direction: Marion McClinton, *Jitney*
Performance: Colm Meaney, *The Cider House Rules: Part One, Here in St. Cloud's;* Lynne Thigpen, *Jar the Floor;* Elizabeth Marvel, *A Streetcar Named Desire;* Christopher Evan Welch, *A Streetcar Named Desire;* Charlayne Woodard, *In the Blood;* Lola Pashalinski, *Gertrude and Alice;* Dominique Dibbell, *Jet Lag;* Cynthia Hopkins, *Another Telepathic Thing;* Debra Monk, *The Time of the Cuckoo;* Eddie Korbich, *Taking a Chance on Love;* Byron Jennings, *Waste;* Eileen Heckart, *The Waverly Gallery;* the cast of *Jitney,* excellence of ensemble performance

Design: Jan Hartley, for sustained excellence of projection design; Mark Dendy, choreography for *The Wild Party;* Christopher Akerlind, for sustained excellence of lighting design; David Gallo, for sustained excellence of set design; Susan Hilferty, for sustained excellence of costume design
Special Citations: Jan Lauwers/Needcompany, *Morning Song;* Sarah E. Johnson, *Lava Love;* Joe Mantello and Marc Wolf, *Another American: Asking and Telling;* The Builders Association and Diller + Scofidio, *Jet Lag;* Jesusa Rodriguez and Liliana Felipe, *Las Horas de Belen—A Book of Hours;* Bill Talen, *The Reverend Billy;* Maria Irene Fornes, *Letters from Cuba;* Deb Margolin, sustained excellence of performance
Sustained Achievement: Ping Chong
Ross Wetzsteon Grant: The Foundry

Major Grammy Awards for Recording in 1999

Record: "Smooth," Santana featuring Rob Thomas
Album: *Supernatural,* Santana
Song: "Smooth," Itaal Shur and Rob Thomas, songwriters
New Artist: Christina Aguilera
Female Pop Vocal: "I Will Remember You," Sarah McLachlan
Male Pop Vocal: "Brand New Day," Sting
Pop Duo or Group with Vocals: "Maria Maria," Santana
Pop Collaboration with Vocals: "Smooth," Santana featuring Rob Thomas
Pop Instrumental: "El Farol," Santana
Dance Recording: "Believe," Cher
Pop Album: *Brand New Day,* Sting
Traditional Pop Album: *Bennett Sings Ellington—Hot & Cool,* Tony Bennett
Female Rock Vocal: "Sweet Child O' Mine," Sheryl Crow
Male Rock Vocal: "American Woman," Lenny Kravitz
Rock Duo or Group with Vocals: "Put Your Lights On," Santana featuring Everlast
Hard Rock: "Whiskey in the Jar," Metallica
Metal: "Iron Man," Black Sabbath
Rock Instrumental: "The Calling," Santana featuring Eric Clapton
Rock Song: "Scar Tissue," Flea, John Frusciante, Anthony Kiedis, and Chad Smith, songwriters
Rock Album: *Supernatural,* Santana
Alternative Music Performance: *Mutations,* Beck
Female R&B Vocal: "It's Not Right but It's Okay," Whitney Houston
Male R&B Vocal: "Staying Power," Barry White
R&B Duo or Group with Vocals: "No Scrubs," TLC
R&B Song: "No Scrubs," Kevin "Shekspere" Briggs, Kandi Burruss, and Tameka Cottle, songwriters
R&B Album: *Fanmail,* TLC
Traditional R&B Vocal Performance: *Staying Power,* Barry White
Rap Solo: "My Name Is," Eminem
Rap Duo or Group: "You Got Me," The Roots featuring Erykah Badu
Rap Album: *The Slim Shady LP,* Eminem
Female Country Vocal: "Man! I Feel Like a Woman!," Shania Twain
Male Country Vocal: "Choices," George Jones
Country Duo or Group with Vocals: "Ready to Run," Dixie Chicks
Country Collaboration with Vocals: "After the Gold Rush," Emmylou Harris, Linda Ronstadt, and Dolly Parton
Country Instrumental: "Bob's Breakdowns," Asleep at the Wheel featuring Tommy Allsup, Floyd Domino, Larry Franklin, Vince Gill, and Steve Wariner
Country Song: "Come on Over," Robert John "Mutt" Lange and Shania Twain, songwriters
Country Album: *Fly,* Dixie Chicks
Bluegrass Album: *Ancient Tones,* Ricky Skaggs and Kentucky Thunder
New Age Album: *Celtic Solstice,* Paul Winter & Friends
Contemporary Jazz: *Inside,* David Sanborn
Jazz Vocal: *When I Look in Your Eyes,* Diana Krall
Jazz Instrumental, Solo: "In Walked Wayne," Wayne Shorter
Jazz Instrumental, Individual or Group: *Like Minds,* Gary Burton, Chick Corea, Pat Metheny, Roy Haynes, and Dave Holland
Large Jazz Ensemble: *Serendipity 18,* The Bob Florence Limited Edition
Latin Jazz: *Latin Soul,* Poncho Sanchez
Rock Gospel Album: *Pray,* Rebecca St. James
Pop/Contemporary Gospel Album: *Speechless,* Steven Curtis Chapman
Southern Gospel, Country Gospel, or Bluegrass Gospel Album: *Kennedy Center Homecoming,* Bill & Gloria Gaither and Their Homecoming Friends
Traditional Soul Gospel Album: *Christmas with Shirley Caesar,* Shirley Caesar
Contemporary Soul Gospel Album: *Mountain High . . . Valley Low,* Yolanda Adams
Gospel Album by a Choir or Chorus: *High & Lifted Up,* The Brooklyn Tabernacle Choir; Carol Cymbala, choir director
Latin Pop: *Tiempos,* Rubén Blades
Latin Rock/Alternative: *Resurrection,* Chris Perez Band
Tropical Latin: *Mambo Birdland,* Tito Puente
Salsa: *Llego . . . Van Van: Van Van Is Here,* Los Van Van
Merengue: *Pintame,* Elvis Crespo
Mexican-American: *100 Años de Mariachi,* Plácido Domingo
Tejano: *Por Eso Te Amo,* Los Palominos
Traditional Blues: *Blues on the Bayou,* B. B. King
Contemporary Blues: *Take Your Shoes Off,* The Robert Cray Band
Traditional Folk: *Press On,* June Carter Cash
Contemporary Folk: *Mule Variations,* Tom Waits
Reggae Album: *Calling Rastafari,* Burning Spear
World Music Album: *Livro,* Caetano Veloso
Polka Album: *Polkasonic,* Brave Combo
Musical Album for Children: *The Adventures of Elmo in Grouchland,* Various Artists

Spoken Word Album for Children: *Listen to the Storyteller*, Wynton Marsalis, Graham Greene, and Kate Winslet
Spoken Word Album: *The Autobiography of Martin Luther King, Jr.*, LeVar Burton (with Martin Luther King, Jr.)
Spoken Comedy Album: *Bigger & Blacker*, Chris Rock
Musical Show Album: *Annie Get Your Gun*, New Broadway Cast, featuring Bernadette Peters and Tom Wopat
Best Soundtrack Album: *Tarzan*, Phil Collins
Instrumental Composition for a Motion Picture, Television, or Other Visual Media: *A Bug's Life*, Randy Newman, composer
Song Written Specifically for a Motion Picture or Television: "Beautiful Stranger" (from *Austin Powers: The Spy Who Shagged Me*), Madonna and William Orbit, songwriters
Instrumental Composition: "Joyful Noise Suite," Don Sebesky, composer
Instrumental Arrangement: "Chelsea Bridge," Don Sebesky, arranger
Instrumental Arrangement with Accompanying Vocals: "Lonely Town," Alan Broadbent, arranger
Best Recording Package: *Ride with Bob*, Ray Benson, Sally Carns, and Buddy Jackson, art directors
Best Album Notes: *John Coltrane—The Classic Quartet—Complete Impulse! Studio Recordings*, Bob Blumenthal, album notes writer
Historical Album: *The Duke Ellington Centennial Edition—The Complete RCA Victor Recordings (1927–1973)*
Engineered Album, Non-Classical: *When I Look in Your Eyes*, Al Schmitt, engineer
Producer, Non-Classical: Walter Afanasieff
Remixer, Non-Classical: Club 69 (Peter Rauhofer)
Engineered Album, Classical: *Stravinsky: Firebird; The Rite of Spring; Perséphone*, Markus Heiland, engineer
Classical Producer: Adam Abeshouse

Classical Album: *Stravinsky: Firebird; The Rite of Spring; Perséphone*, Michael Tilson Thomas, conductor
Orchestral Performance: *Stravinsky: Firebird; The Rite of Spring; Perséphone*, Michael Tilson Thomas, conductor
Opera: *Stravinsky: The Rake's Progress*, John Eliot Gardiner, conductor
Choral: *Britten: War Requiem*, Robert Shafer, conductor
Instrumental Soloist with Orchestra: *Prokofiev: Piano Cons. Nos. 1 & 3/Bartók: Piano Con. No. 3*, Martha Argerich, piano; Charles Dutoit, conductor
Instrumental Soloist without Orchestra: *Shostakovich: 24 Preludes & Fugues, Op. 87*, Vladimir Ashkenazy, piano
Chamber Music: *Beethoven: The Violin Sonatas (Nos. 1–3, Op. 12; Nos. 1–3, Op. 30; "Spring" Sonata, Etc.)*, Anne-Sophie Mutter, violin; Lambert Orkis, piano
Small Ensemble Performance (with or without conductor): *Colors of Love (Works of Thomas, Stucky, Tavener, Rands, Etc.)*, Chanticleer, Joseph Jennings, conductor
Classical Vocal: *Mahler: Des Knaben Wunderhorn*, Thomas Quasthoff, baritone; Anne Sofie von Otter, mezzo soprano
Classical Contemporary Composition: *Boulez: Répons*, Pierre Boulez, composer
Classical Crossover Album: *Schickele: Hornsmoke (Piano Con. No. 2 in F Maj. "Ole"; Brass Calendar; Hornsmoke—A Horse Opera)*, The Chestnut Brass Co.; Peter Schickele, piano & narrator
Music Video, Short Form: "Freak on a Leash" (Korn), Jonathan Dayton, Valerie Faris, Todd McFarlane, and Graham Morris, video directors
Music Video, Long Form: *Band of Gypsys—Live at Fillmore East* (Jimi Hendrix), Bob Smeaton, video director

1999 Country Music Association Awards

Entertainer of the Year: Shania Twain
Single of the Year: "Wide Open Spaces," Dixie Chicks
Album of the Year: *A Place in the Sun*, Tim McGraw
Song of the Year: "This Kiss," Annie Roboff, Robin Lerner and Beth Nielsen Chapman
Male Vocalist of the Year: Tim McGraw
Female Vocalist of the Year: Martina McBride
Vocal Group of the Year: Dixie Chicks

Vocal Duo of the Year: Brooks & Dunn
Vocal Event of the Year: "My Kind of Woman/My Kind of Man," Vince Gill with Patty Loveless
Horizon Award: Jo Dee Messina
Musician of the Year: Randy Scruggs
Music Video of the Year: "Wide Open Spaces," Dixie Chicks

1999 National Book Awards

Fiction: *Waiting*, Ha Jin (Pantheon)
Nonfiction: *Embracing Defeat: Japan in the Wake of World War II*, John W. Dower (W. W. Norton & Company/The New Press)

Poetry: *Vice: New and Selected Poems*, Ai (W. W. Norton & Company)
Young People's Literature: *When Zachary Beaver Came to Town*, Kimberly Willis Holt (Henry Holt and Company)

Booker Prize

Britain's most prestigious literary award, officially the "Booker McConnell Prize," honors the best full-length novel written in English by a citizen of a current or former British Commonwealth country. (Book's current publisher is listed in parentheses.)

1969 *Something to Answer For*, P. H. Newby (out of print)
1970 *The Elected Member*, Bernice Rubens (Abacus [Little Brown U.K.])
1971 *In a Free State*, V. S. Naipaul (Random House) paper
1972 *G.: A Novel*, John Berger (Vintage) paper
1973 *The Siege of Krishnapur*, J. G. Farrell (Carroll & Graf) paper
1974 (tie) *The Conservationist*, Nadine Gordimer (Viking) paper
  Holiday, Stanley Middleton (out of print)
1975 *Heat and Dust*, Ruth Prawer Jhabvala (Peter Smith)
1976 *Saville*, David Storey (Vintage)
1977 *Staying On*, Paul Scott (Univ. of Chicago Press) paper
1978 *The Sea, The Sea*, Iris Murdoch (Viking) paper
1979 *Offshore*, Penelope Fitzgerald (Mariner) paper

1980 *Rites of Passage*, William Golding (Farrar, Straus & Giroux)
1981 *Midnight's Children*, Salman Rushdie (Knopf)
1982 *Schindler's List*, Thomas Keneally (Simon & Schuster)
1983 *Life & Times of Michael K*, J. M. Coetzee (Viking) paper
1984 *Hotel du Lac*, Anita Brookner (Vintage) paper
1985 *The Bone People*, Keri Hulme (Viking) paper
1986 *The Old Devils*, Kingsley Amis (Penguin) U.K.
1987 *Moon Tiger*, Penelope Lively (Grove/Atlantic) paper
1988 *Oscar and Lucinda*, Peter Carey (Vintage) paper
1989 *The Remains of the Day*, Kazuo Ishiguro (Vintage) paper
1990 *Possession: A Romance*, A. S. Byatt (Vintage) paper
1991 *The Famished Road*, Ben Okri (Anchor) paper

1992 (tie) *The English Patient*, Michael Ondaatje (Knopf)
Sacred Hunger, Barry Unsworth (W. W. Norton & Company) paper
1993 *Paddy Clarke, Ha Ha Ha*, Roddy Doyle (Penguin USA) paper
1994 *How Late It Was, How Late*, James Kelman (Delta) paper

1995 *The Ghost Road*, Pat Barker (Dutton)
1996 *Last Orders*, Graham Swift (Knopf)
1997 *The God of Small Things*, Arundhati Roy (Random House)
1998 *Amsterdam*, Ian McEwan (Doubleday)
1999 *Disgrace*, J. M. Coetzee (Viking)

1999 National Book Critics Circle Awards

Fiction: *Motherless Brooklyn*, Jonathan Lethem (Doubleday)
General Nonfiction: *Time, Love, Memory: A Great Biologist and His Quest for the Origins of Behavior*, Jonathan Weiner (Knopf)
Biography or Autobiography: *The Hairstons: An American Family in Black and White*, Henry Wiencek (St. Martin's Press)

Poetry: *Ordinary Words*, Ruth Stone (Consortium Book Sales & Dist.)
Criticism: *Selected Non-Fictions*, Jorge Luis Borges (Viking)

Newbery Medal

The Newbery Medal is awarded annually by the American Library Association for the most distinguished contribution to American literature for children.

2000 Newbery Medal and Honor Books
Newbery Medal for Best Book: *Bud, Not Buddy*, Christopher Paul Curtis (Delacorte Press)
Newbery Honor Books: *Getting Near to Baby*, Audrey Couloumbis (G. P. Putnam's Sons); *26 Fairmount Avenue*, Tomie dePaola (G. P. Putnam's Sons); *Our Only May Amelia*, Jennifer L. Holm (HarperCollins)

1922–1999
1922 *The Story of Mankind*, Hendrick Willem Van Loon
1923 *The Voyages of Dr. Doolittle*, Hugh A. Lofting
1924 *The Dark Frigate*, Charles Boardman Hawes
1925 *Tales from Silver Lands*, Charles Joseph Finger
1926 *Shen of the Sea*, Arthur Bowie Chrisman
1927 *Smoky, the Cow Horse*, Will James
1928 *Gay-Neck, the Story of a Pigeon*, Dhan Gopal Mukerji
1929 *The Trumpeter of Krakow*, Eric P. Kelly
1930 *Hitty, Her First Hundred Years*, Rachel Field
1931 *The Cat Who Went to Heaven*, Elizabeth Jane Coatsworth
1932 *Waterless Mountain*, Laura Adams Armer
1933 *Young Fu of the Upper Yangtze*, Elizabeth Foreman Lewis
1934 *Invincible Louisa*, Cornelia Meigs
1935 *Dobry*, Monica Shannon
1936 *Caddie Woodlawn*, Carol Ryrie Brink
1937 *Roller Skates*, Ruth Sawyer
1938 *The White Stag*, Kate Seredy
1939 *Thimble Summer*, Elizabeth Enright
1940 *Daniel Boone*, James Henry Daugherty
1941 *Call it Courage*, Armstrong Sperry
1942 *The Matchlock Gun*, Walter Dumax Edmonds
1943 *Adam of the Road*, Elizabeth Janet Gray
1944 *Johnny Tremain*, Esther Forbes
1945 *Rabbit Hill*, Robert Lawson
1946 *Strawberry Girl*, Lois Lenski
1947 *Miss Hickory*, Carolyn Sherwin Bailey
1948 *The Twenty-One Balloons*, William Pène du Bois
1949 *King of the Wind*, Marguerite Henry
1950 *The Door in the Wall*, Marguerite de Angeli
1951 *Amos Fortune, Free Man*, Elizabeth Yates
1952 *Ginger Pye*, Eleanor Estes
1953 *Secret of the Andes*, Ann Nolan Clark
1954 *. . . And Now Miguel*, Joseph Krumgold
1955 *The Wheel on the School*, Meindert DeJong

1956 *Carry On, Mr. Bowditch*, Jean Lee Latham
1957 *Miracles on Maple Hill*, Virginia Eggertsen Sorensen
1958 *Rifles for Watie*, Harold Keith
1959 *The Witch of Blackbird Pond*, Elizabeth George Speare
1960 *Onion John*, Joseph Krumgold
1961 *Island of the Blue Dolphins*, Scott O'Dell
1962 *The Bronze Bow*, Elizabeth George Speare
1963 *A Wrinkle in Time*, Madeleine L'Engle
1964 *It's Like This, Cat*, Emily Cheney Neville
1965 *Shadow of a Bull*, Maia Wojciechowska
1966 *I, Juan de Pareja*, Elizabeth Borton de Treviño
1967 *Up a Road Slowly*, Irene Hunt
1968 *From the Mixed-Up Files of Mrs. Basil E. Frankweiler*, E. L. Konigsburg
1969 *The High King*, Lloyd Alexander
1970 *Sounder*, William H. Armstrong
1971 *Summer of the Swans*, Betsy Cromer Byars
1972 *Mrs. Frisby and the Rats of NIMH*, Robert C. O'Brien
1973 *Julie of the Wolves*, Jean Craighead George
1974 *The Slave Dancer*, Paula Fox
1975 *M. C. Higgins, the Great*, Virginia Hamilton
1976 *The Grey King*, Susan Cooper
1977 *Roll of Thunder, Hear My Cry*, Mildred D. Taylor
1978 *Bridge to Terabithia*, Katherine Paterson
1979 *The Westing Game*, Ellen Raskin
1980 *A Gathering of Days: A New England Girl's Journal, 1830–32*, Joan W. Blos
1981 *Jacob Have I Loved*, Katherine Paterson
1982 *A Visit to William Blake's Inn: Poems for Innocent and Experienced Travelers*, Nancy Willard
1983 *Dicey's Song*, Cynthia Voigt
1984 *Dear Mr. Henshaw*, Beverly Cleary
1985 *The Hero and the Crown*, Robin McKinley
1986 *Sarah, Plain and Tall*, Patricia MacLachlan
1987 *The Whipping Boy*, Sid Fleischman
1988 *Lincoln: A Photobiography*, Russell Freedman
1989 *Joyful Noise: Poems for Two Voices*, Paul Fleischman
1990 *Number the Stars*, Lois Lowry
1991 *Maniac Magee: a Novel*, Jerry Spinelli
1992 *Shiloh*, Phyllis Reynolds Naylor
1993 *Missing May*, Cynthia Rylant

1994	*The Giver,* Lois Lowry	1997	*The View from Saturday,* E. L. Konigsburg
1995	*Walk Two Moons,* Sharon Creech	1998	*Out of the Dust,* Karen Hesse
1996	*The Midwife's Apprentice,* Karen Cushman	1999	*Holes,* Louis Sachar

Caldecott Medal

The Caldecott Medal is awarded annually by the American Library Association for the most distinguished American picture book for children.

2000 Caldecott Medal and Honor Books

Caldecott Medal for Best Picture Book: *Joseph Had a Little Overcoat,* illustrated by Simms Taback (Viking)

Caldecott Honor Books: *Sector 7,* written and illustrated by David Wiesner (Clarion Books); *The Ugly Duckling,* adapted and illustrated by Jerry Pinkney (Morrow); *When Sophie Gets Angry—Really, Really Angry,* illustrated and written by Molly Bang (Scholastic); *A Child's Calendar,* illustrated by Trina Schart Hyman, written by John Updike (Holiday House)

1938–1999

1938 *Animals of the Bible, a Picture Book,* text selected by Helen Dean Fish, illustrated by Dorothy P. Lathrop

1939 *Mei Li,* written and illustrated by Thomas Handforth

1940 *Abraham Lincoln,* written and illustrated by Ingrid and Edgar Parin D'Aulaire

1941 *They Were Strong and Good,* written and illustrated by Robert Larson

1942 *Make Way for Ducklings,* written and illustrated by Robert McCloskey

1943 *The Little House,* written and illustrated by Virginia Lee Burton

1944 *Many Moons,* written by James Thurber, illustrated by Louis Slobodkin

1945 *Prayer for a Child,* written by Elizabeth Orton Jones

1946 *The Rooster Crows,* written and illustrated by Maud and Miska Petersham

1947 *The Little Island,* written by Golden MacDonald, illustrated by Leonard Weisgard

1948 *White Snow, Bright Snow,* written by Alvin Tresselt, illustrated by Roger Duvoisin

1949 *The Big Snow,* written and illustrated by Berta and Elmer Hader

1950 *Song of the Swallows,* written and illustrated by Leo Politi

1951 *The Egg Tree,* written and illustrated by Katherine Milhous

1952 *Finders Keepers,* written by William Lipkind, illustrated by Nicolas Mordivinoff

1953 *The Biggest Bear,* written and illustrated by Lynd Ward

1954 *Madeline's Rescue,* written and illustrated by Ludwig Bemelmans

1955 *Cinderella, or, The Little Glass Slipper,* translated and illustrated by Marcia Brown

1956 *Frog Went A-Courtin',* retold by John Langstaff, illustrated by Feodor Rojankovsky

1957 *A Tree Is Nice,* written by Janice May Udry, illustrated by Marc Simont

1958 *Time of Wonder,* written and illustrated by Robert McCloskey

1959 *Chanticleer and the Fox,* adapted and illustrated by Barbara Cooney

1960 *Nine Days to Christmas,* written by Marie Hall Ets and Aurora Labastida, illustrated by Marie Hall Ets

1961 *Baboushka and the Three Kings,* written by Ruth Robbins, illustrated by Nicolas Sidjakov

1962 *Once a Mouse,* retold and illustrated by Marcia Brown

1963 *The Snowy Day,* written and illustrated by Ezra Jack Keats

1964 *Where the Wild Things Are,* written and illustrated by Maurice Sendak

1965 *May I Bring a Friend?,* written by Beatrice Schenk de Regniers, illustrated by Beni Montresor

1966 *Always Room for One More,* written by Sorche Nic Leodhas, illustrated by Nonny Hogrogian

1967 *Sam, Bangs and Moonshine,* written and illustrated by Evaline Ness

1968 *Drummer Hoff,* written by Barbara Emberley, illustrated by Ed Emberley

1969 *The Fool of the World and the Flying Ship,* retold by Arthur Ransome, illustrated by Uri Shulevitz

1970 *Sylvester and the Magic Pebble,* written and illustrated by William Steig

1971 *A Story, A Story: An African Tale,* retold and illustrated by Gail E. Haley

1972 *One Fine Day,* written and illustrated by Nonny Hogrogian

1973 *The Funny Little Woman,* retold by Arlene Mosel, illustrated by Blair Lent

1974 *Duffy and the Devil,* retold by Harve Zemach, illustrated by Margot Zemach

1975 *Arrow to the Sun: A Pueblo Indian Tale,* adapted and illustrated by Gerald H. McDermott

1976 *Why Mosquitos Buzz in People's Ears (An African Tale),* retold by Verna Aardema, illustrated by Leo and Diane Dillon

1977 *Ashanti to Zulu: African Traditions,* written by Margaret Musgrove, illustrated by Leo and Diane Dillon

1978 *Noah's Ark,* written by Jacob Revius, illustrated by Peter Spier

1979 *The Girl Who Loved Wild Horses,* written and illustrated by Paul Goble

1980 *Ox-Cart Man,* written by Donald Hall, illustrated by Barbara Cooney

1981 *Fables,* written and illustrated by Arnold Lobel

1982 *Jumanji,* written and illustrated by Chris Van Allsburg

1983 *Shadow,* translated and illustrated by Marcia Brown

1984 *The Glorious Flight: Across the Channel with Louise Blériot,* written and illustrated by Alice and Martin Provensen

1985 *St. George and the Dragon,* retold by Margaret Hodges, illustrated by Trina Schart Hyman

1986 *The Polar Express,* written and illustrated by Chris Van Allsburg

1987 *Hey, Al,* written by Arthur Yorinks, illustrated by Richard Egielski

1988 *Owl Moon,* written by Jane Yolen, illustrated by John Schoenherr

1989	*Song and Dance Man,* written by Karen Ackerman, illustrated by Stephen Gammell	1995	*Smoky Night,* written by Eve Bunting, illustrated by David Diaz
1990	*Lon Po Po: A Red-Riding Hood Story from China,* translated and illustrated by Ed Young	1996	*Officer Buckle and Gloria,* written and illustrated by Peggy Rathmann
1991	*Black & White,* written and illustrated by David Macaulay	1997	*Golem,* written and illustrated by David Wisniewski
1992	*Tuesday,* written and illustrated by David Wiesner	1998	*Rapunzel,* illustrated and retold by Paul O. Zelinsky
1993	*Mirette on the High Wire,* written and illustrated by Emily Arnold McCully	1999	*Snowflake Bentley,* illustrated by Mary Azarian, written by Jacqueline Briggs Martin
1994	*Grandfather's Journey,* written and illustrated by Allen Say		

Other American Library Association Awards for Children's Books, 2000

2000 Coretta Scott King Award, honoring black authors and illustrators: (author): *Bud, Not Buddy,* Christopher Paul Curtis (Delacorte Press); **(illustrator):** *In the Time of the Drums,* illustrated by Brian Pinkney, written by Karen English (Jump at the Sun/Hyperion Books for Children)

2000 Coretta Scott King Honor Books: (author): *Francie,* Karen English (Farrar, Straus & Giroux); *Black Hands, White Sails: The Story of African-American Whalers,* Patricia C. and Frederick L. McKissack (Scholastic); *Monster,* Walter Dean Myers (HarperCollins); **(illustrator):** *My Rows and Piles of Coins,* E. B. Lewis (Clarion Books); *The Black Cat,* Christopher Myers (Scholastic)

2000 Michael L. Printz Award for excellence in young adult literature: *Monster,* Walter Dean Myers (HarperCollins)

2000 Michael L. Printz Honor Books: *Hard Love,* Ellen Wittlinger (Simon & Schuster); *Skellig,* David Almond (Delacorte Press); *Speak,* Laurie Halse Anderson (Farrar, Straus & Giroux)

2000 Pura Belpré Award for excellence in Latino/Latina writers and illustrators (awarded biennially): (author): *Under the Royal Palms: A Childhood in Cuba,* Alma Flor Ada (Atheneum Books); **(illustrator):** *Magic Windows,* illustrated and written by Carmen Lomas Garza (Children's Book Press)

2000 Pura Belpré Honor Awards: (author): *From the Bellybutton of the Moon and Other Summer Poems/Del Ombligo de la Luna y Otro Poemas de Verano,* written by Francisco X. Alarcón, illustrated by Maya Christina Gonzalez (Children's Book Press); *Laughing Out Loud, I Fly: Poems in English and Spanish,* written by Juan Felipe Herrera, illustrated by Karen Barbour (HarperCollins); **(illustrator):** *Barrio: José's Neighborhood,* illustrated and written by George Ancona (Harcourt Brace); *The Secret Stars,* illustrated by Felipe Dávalos, written by Joseph Slate (Marshall Cavendish); *Mama & Papa Have a Store,* illustrated and written by Amelia Lau Carling (Dial Books)

2000 Mildred L. Batchelder Award, for best book originally published in a foreign language in a foreign country: *The Baboon King,* written by Anton Quintana in Dutch and translated by John Nieuwenhuizen (Walker and Company)

2000 Margaret A. Edwards Award, lifetime achievement award for outstanding literature for young adults: Chris Crutcher

Andrew Carnegie Medal, for excellence in children's video: *Miss Nelson Has a Field Day,* produced by Paul R. Gagne for Weston Woods Studio

2000 National Magazine Awards

General Excellence:
Nest (circulation less than 100,000)
Saveur (circulation 100,000 to 400,000)
The New Yorker (circulation 400,000 to 1,000,000)
National Geographic (circulation more than 1,000,000)
Personal Service: *PC Computing*
Special Interests: *I.D. Magazine*
Reporting: *Vanity Fair*
Essays: *The Sciences*

Reviews and Criticism: *Esquire*
Profiles: *Sports Illustrated*
Feature Writing: *Sports Illustrated*
Public Interest: *The New Yorker*
Design: *Fast Company*
Fiction: *The New Yorker*
Photography: *Vanity Fair*
General Excellence in New Media: *BusinessWeek Online*

Bollingen Prize in Poetry

1949	Ezra Pound	1967	Robert Penn Warren
1950	Wallace Stevens	1969	John Berryman and Karl Shapiro
1951	John Crowe Ransom	1971	Richard Wilbur and Mona Van Duyn
1952	Marianne Moore	1973	James Merrill
1953	Archibald MacLeish and William Carlos Williams	1975	Archie Randolph Ammons
1954	W. H. Auden	1977	David Ignatow
1955	Léonie Adams and Louise Bogan	1979	W. S. Merwin
1956	Conrad Aiken	1981	Howard Nemerov and May Swenson
1957	Allen Tate	1983	Anthony Hecht and John Hollander
1958	e. e. cummings	1985	John Ashbery and Fred Chappell
1959	Theodore Roethke	1987	Stanley Kunitz
1960	Delmore Schwartz	1989	Edgar Bowers
1961	Yvor Winters	1991	Laura Riding Jackson and Donald Justice
1962	John Hall Wheelock and Richard Eberhart	1993	Mark Strand
1963	Robert Frost	1995	Kenneth Koch
1965	Horace Gregory	1997	Gary Snyder
		1999	Robert Creeley

Kingsley Tufts Poetry Prize

1993	Susan Mitchell, *Rapture*	
1994	Yusef Komunyakaa, *Neon Vernacular*	
1995	Thomas Lux, *Split Horizon*	
1996	Deborah Digges, *Rough Music*	

1997   Campbell McGrath, *Spring Comes to Chicago*
1998   John Koethe, *Falling Water*
1999   B. H. Fairchild, *The Art of the Lathe*
2000   Robert Wrigley, *Reign of Snakes: Poems*

1999 George Foster Peabody Awards for Broadcasting

Lost & Found Sound: National Public Radio and The Kitchen Sisters, Davia Nelson and Nikki Silva, with Jay Allison

The Mississippi: River of Song: Smithsonian Productions; presented on Public Radio International

Morning Edition with Bob Edwards: National Public Radio

ABC 2000: ABC News, New York

Bob Simon: International reporting for CBS News, CBS News, New York

Singled Out: WAGA-TV, Atlanta

Stadium Investigation: WCPO-TV, Cincinnati

Investigative reporting by GMA Network: Manila, Philippines

ABC News 20/20: "Those Were Our Children," ABC News, New York

BIOrhythm: MTV Networks, New York

Playing the China Card: Brook Lapping Productions for Channel 4, London; presented on PBS by WGBH-TV, Boston

Facing the Truth with Bill Moyers: Public Affairs Television; presented on PBS by Thirteen/WNET, New York

The Second World War in Colour: A TWI/Carlton co-production for TV, London, The History Channel

ESPN SportsCentury: ESPN, Bristol, Conn.

Not for Ourselves Alone: The Story of Elizabeth Cady Stanton and Susan B. Anthony: Florentine Films in association with WETA-TV, Washington, D.C.; presented on PBS

FRONTLINE: "The Lost Children of Rockdale County," a FRONTLINE co-production with 10/20 Productions; presented on PBS

Dare to Compete: The Struggle of Women in Sports: Home Box Office Sports, New York

Arguing the World: Riverside Films, New York; presented on PBS

The Valley: A Mentorn Barraclough Carey Production for Channel 4, London

Fists of Freedom: The Story of the '68 Summer Games: Home Box Office Sports, New York, in association with Black Canyon Productions

Murder in Purdah: BBC News, London

I'll Make Me a World: A Century of African-American Arts: Blackside, Inc., in association with Thirteen/WNET, New York; presented on PBS

The Life of Birds by David Attenborough: BBC, London, in association with PBS

Goodnight Moon and Other Sleepytime Tales: Home Box Office, New York

Annie: ABC, Storyline Entertainment, Columbia-Tristar Television, Inc., and Chris Montan Productions in association with Walt Disney Television

VH1 Save the Music Campaign: VH1 Public Affairs, MTV Networks, New York

The Sopranos: Home Box Office and Brillstein-Grey Entertainment

Having Our Say: The Delany Sisters' First 100 Years: CBS, Televest, Columbia-Tristar Television in association with Cosby & James Productions

Strange Justice: Showtime and Haft Entertainment

ExxonMobil Masterpiece Theatre: Lost for Words: A Yorkshire Television Production; presented on PBS by WGBH-TV, Boston

A Lesson before Dying: Home Box Office, a Spanky Pictures Production in association with Ellen M. Krass Productions

City Life: Thirteen/WNET, New York

ExxonMobil Masterpiece Theatre: A Rather English Marriage: Wall to Wall Television, Ltd., BBC, Carlton Television; presented on PBS by WGBH-TV, Boston

The West Wing: NBC, John Wells Productions in association with Warner Bros. Television

American Presidents: Life Portraits: C-SPAN, Washington, D.C.

Sheila Nevins, Home Box Office: One of the true independent spirits in television today, whose passion and vision consistently create excellence

1999 Alfred I. du Pont—Columbia University Awards in Television and Radio

GOLD BATON

Bill Moyers and Public Affairs Television for *Facing the Truth*, a two-hour documentary about the aftermath of apartheid in South Africa (PBS)

SILVER BATONS

Television Awards:

ABC News and Diane Sawyer for *20/20: The Unwanted Children of Russia*, a segment about the neglect and abuse of handicapped children in Russian orphanages

CBS News and Bob Simon for *60 Minutes II: The Shame of Srebrenica*, an account of the massacre of 8,000 Muslims by Serbs in 1995 during the Bosnian war

Frontline and WGBH-TV for *The Triumph of Evil*, a one-hour documentary about the massacre of 800,000 Tutsi people in 1994 by the Hutu majority in Rwanda (PBS)

CNN and Candy Crowley for coverage of the impeachment and trial of President Clinton

New England Cable News, Newton, Mass., for in-depth reporting on a wide range of subjects, including crime, breast cancer, and AIDS

KTVX-TV, Salt Lake City, and Chris Vanocur for investiga-

tive reporting on the Olympics bribery scandal

WTHR-TV, Indianapolis, for *Guarding the Guardians*, a series of investigative reports that revealed abuses by the guardians of elderly heiress Ruth Lilly

WMTW-TV, Auburn, Maine, and Christine Young for investigative reports on the Christian Civic League, an influential conservative lobbying group in Maine

Walter Brock and *P.O.V.* for *If I Can't Do It*, a one-hour documentary that profiled a severely disabled but independent man (PBS)

Stanley Nelson for *The Black Press: Soldier without Swords*, a history of black-owned newspapers in the United States (PBS)

Radio Awards:

Youth Radio, Berkeley, Calif., for *E-Mails from Kosovo*, a series of e-mail letters between a Californian high-school student and an Albanian schoolgirl in Kosovo (NPR)

SoundVision Productions, Berkeley, Calif., for *The DNA Files*, a nine-hour radio series about genetic science (NPR)

2000 Major Emmy Awards

Drama Series: *The West Wing* (NBC)
   Actress: Sela Ward, *Once and Again*
   Actor: James Gandolfini, *The Sopranos*
   Supporting Actress: Allison Janney, *The West Wing*
   Supporting Actor: Richard Schiff, *The West Wing*
   Guest Actor: James Whitmore, *The Practice*
   Guest Actress: Beah Richards, *The Practice*
Comedy Series: *Will & Grace* (NBC)
   Actress: Patricia Heaton, *Everybody Loves Raymond*
   Actor: Michael J. Fox, *Spin City*
   Supporting Actress: Megan Mullally, *Will & Grace*
   Supporting Actor: Sean Hayes, *Will & Grace*
   Guest Actress: Jean Smart, *Frasier*
   Guest Actor: Bruce Willis, *Friends*
Variety, Music, or Comedy Series: *Late Show with David Letterman* (CBS)
Variety, Music, or Comedy Special: *Saturday Night Live: The 25th Anniversary Special* (NBC)
Miniseries or Special: *The Corner* (HBO)
   Actress: Halle Berry, *Introducing Dorothy Dandridge*

Actor: Jack Lemmon, *Oprah Winfrey Presents: Tuesdays with Morrie*
Supporting Actress: Vanessa Redgrave, *If These Walls Could Talk 2*
Supporting Actor: Hank Azaria, *Oprah Winfrey Presents: Tuesdays with Morrie*
Made-for-TV Movie: *Oprah Winfrey Presents: Tuesdays with Morrie* (ABC)
Individual Performance, Variety or Music Program: Eddie Izzard, *Eddie Izzard: Dress to Kill*
Outstanding Nonfiction Series (possibility of one or more than one award): *American Masters*: "Hitchcock, Selznick, and the End of Hollywood" (PBS)
Outstanding Nonfiction Special: *Children in War* (HBO)
Outstanding Children's Program (possibility of one or more than one award): *The Color of Friendship* (Disney) and *Goodnight Moon and Other Sleepytime Tales* (HBO)
Outstanding Animated Program (one hour or less): *The Simpsons*: "Behind the Laughter" (Fox)

1999–2000 Daytime Emmy Awards

Outstanding Drama Series: *General Hospital* (ABC)
Lead Actor in a Drama Series: Anthony Geary, *General Hospital*
Lead Actress in a Drama Series: Susan Flannery, *The Bold and the Beautiful*
Supporting Actor in a Drama Series: Shemar Moore, *The Young and the Restless*
Supporting Actress in a Drama Series: Sarah Brown, *General Hospital*
Younger Actor in a Drama Series: David Tom, *The Young and the Restless*
Younger Actress in a Drama Series: Camryn Grimes, *The Young and the Restless*
Outstanding Children's Series: *Disney Presents: Bill Nye the Science Guy* (syndicated)
Outstanding Children's Special: *Summer's End* (Showtime)
Outstanding Children's Animated Program: *Steven Spielberg Presents: Pinky, Elmyra and the Brain* (WB)
Outstanding Children's Animated Program (special class): *Rolie Polie Olie* (Disney Channel)
Performer in a Children's Series: Shari Lewis, *Charlie Horse Music Pizza*

Performer in a Children's Special: James Earl Jones, *Summer's End*
Performer in an Animated Program: James Woods, *Disney's Hercules*
Outstanding Preschool Children's Series: *Sesame Street* (PBS)
Special Class Program: *1999 Macy's Thanksgiving Day Parade* (NBC)
Outstanding Game and Audience Participation Show: *Who Wants to Be a Millionaire* (ABC)
Outstanding Game-Show Host (tie): Bob Barker, *The Price Is Right* and Tom Bergeron, *Hollywood Squares*
Outstanding Talk Show: *The Rosie O'Donnell Show* (syndicated)
Outstanding Talk-Show Host: Rosie O'Donnell, *The Rosie O'Donnell Show*
Outstanding Service Show: *Martha Stewart Living* (syndicated)
Outstanding Service-Show Host: Christopher Lowell, *The Christopher Lowell Show*

2000 NAACP Image Awards

MOTION PICTURE

Outstanding Motion Picture: *The Best Man*
Outstanding Actress in a Motion Picture: Nia Long, *The Best Man*
Outstanding Actor in a Motion Picture: Denzel Washington, *The Hurricane*
Outstanding Supporting Actress in a Motion Picture: Angela Bassett, *Music of the Heart*
Outstanding Supporting Actor in a Motion Picture: Terrence Howard, *The Best Man*

TELEVISION

Outstanding Comedy Series: *The Steve Harvey Show* (WB)
Outstanding Actress in a Comedy Series: Tia Mowry and Tamera Mowry, *Sister, Sister*
Outstanding Actor in a Comedy Series: Steve Harvey, *The Steve Harvey Show*
Outstanding Supporting Actress in a Comedy Series: Jackee Harry, *Sister, Sister*
Outstanding Supporting Actor in a Comedy Series: Cedric the Entertainer, *The Steve Harvey Show*
Outstanding Drama Series: *Touched by an Angel* (CBS)
Outstanding Actress in a Drama Series: Della Reese, *Touched by an Angel*
Outstanding Actor in a Drama Series: Eriq La Salle, *ER*
Outstanding Supporting Actress in a Drama Series: Rosa Parks, *Touched by an Angel*
Outstanding Supporting Actor in a Drama Series: Clarence Gilyard, *Walker, Texas Ranger*

Outstanding Youth Actor/Actress: Jurnee Smollett, *Cosby*
Outstanding Television Movie/Miniseries/Dramatic Special: *Introducing Dorothy Dandridge*
Outstanding Actress in a Television Movie/Miniseries/Dramatic Special: Halle Berry, *Introducing Dorothy Dandridge*
Outstanding Actor in a Television Movie/Miniseries/Dramatic Special: Sidney Poitier, *The Simple Life of Noah Dearborn*

RECORDING

Outstanding Song: Eric Benet, "Spend My Life with You"
Outstanding Album: *The Best Man* (Soundtrack), Various Artists
Outstanding New Artist: Eve, *Ruff Ryders' First Lady*
Outstanding Female Artist: Whitney Houston, *It's Not Right but It's Okay*
Outstanding Male Artist: Brian McKnight, *Back at One*
Outstanding Duo or Group: Destiny's Child, *The Writing's on the Wall*
Outstanding Rap Artist: Will Smith, *Wild Wild West*
Outstanding Jazz Artist: Quincy Jones, *From Q, with Love*
Outstanding Gospel Artist—Traditional: Vickie Winans, *Live in Detroit 2*
Outstanding Gospel Artist—Contemporary: Yolanda Adams, *Mountain High. . .Valley Low*
Outstanding Music Video: Will Smith, "Wild Wild West"

The Spingarn Medal

The Spingarn Medal is awarded annually by the National Association for the Advancement of Colored People for outstanding achievement by a black American.

1915	Ernest E. Just	1944	Charles Drew	1973	Wilson C. Riles		
1916	Charles Young	1945	Paul Robeson	1974	Damon Keith		
1917	Harry T. Burleigh	1946	Thurgood Marshall	1975	Hank Aaron		
1918	William Stanley Braithwaite	1947	Percy Julian	1976	Alvin Ailey		
		1948	Channing H. Tobias	1977	Alex Haley		
1919	Archibald H. Grimke	1949	Ralph J. Bunche	1978	Andrew Young		
1920	W. E. B. Du Bois	1950	Charles Hamilton Houston	1979	Rosa L. Parks		
1921	Charles S. Gilpin	1951	Mabel Keaton Staupers	1980	Rayford W. Logan		
1922	Mary B. Talbert	1952	Harry T. Moore	1981	Coleman Young		
1923	George Washington Carver	1953	Paul R. Williams	1982	Benjamin E. Mays		
		1954	Theodore K. Lawless	1983	Lena Horne		
1924	Roland Hayes	1955	Carl Murphy	1984	Tom Bradley		
1925	James Weldon Johnson	1956	Jackie Robinson	1985	Bill Cosby		
1926	Carter G. Woodson	1957	Martin Luther King, Jr.	1986	Benjamin L. Hooks		
1927	Anthony Overton	1958	Daisy Bates and the Little Rock Nine	1987	Percy Ellis Sutton		
1928	Charles W. Chesnutt			1988	Frederick Douglass Patterson		
1929	Mordecai Wyatt Johnson	1959	Edward Kennedy (Duke) Ellington				
1930	Henry A. Hunt			1989	Jesse Jackson		
1931	Richard Berry Harrison	1960	Langston Hughes	1990	L. Douglas Wilder		
1932	Robert Russa Moton	1961	Kenneth B. Clark	1991	Colin T. Powell		
1933	Max Yergan	1962	Robert C. Weaver	1992	Barbara Jordan		
1934	William T. B. Williams	1963	Medgar Evers	1993	Dorothy Irene Height		
1935	Mary McLeod Bethune	1964	Roy Wilkins	1994	Maya Angelou		
1936	John Hope	1965	Leontyne Price	1995	John Hope Franklin		
1937	Walter White	1966	John H. Johnson	1996	A. Leon Higginbotham, Jr.		
1938	No award	1967	Edward W. Brooke III	1997	Carl Rowan		
1939	Marian Anderson	1968	Sammy Davis, Jr.	1998	Myrlie Evers-Williams		
1940	Louis T. Wright	1969	Clarence M. Mitchell, Jr.	1999	Earl G. Graves, Sr.		
1941	Richard Wright	1970	Jacob Lawrence	2000	Oprah Winfrey		
1942	A. Philip Randolph	1971	Leon Howard Sullivan				
1943	William H. Hastie	1972	Gordon Parks				

2000 MacArthur Foundation Awards

The MacArthur Foundation awards $500,000 over five years to each innovator.

Susan Alcock, 39, associate professor of classical archaeology and classics; Ann Arbor, Mich.

K. Christopher Beard, 38, associate curator, vertebrate paleontology; Mars, Pa.

Lucy Blake, 40, president, Sierra Business Council; Sierraville, Calif.

Anne Carson, 49, history professor, poet, and essayist; Berkeley, Calif., and Montreal

Peter Hayes, 47, executive director, Nautilus Institute for Security and Sustainable Development; Berkeley, Calif.

David Isay, 34, radio producer; New York

Alfredo Jaar, 44, artist; New York

Ben Katchor, 48, cartoonist; New York

Hideo Mabuchi, 28, assistant professor of physics; Pasadena, Calif.

Susan Marshall, 41, artistic director and choreographer; New York

Samuel Mockbee, 55, professor of architecture; Canton, Miss.

Cecilia Muñoz, 37, vice president, Office of Research, Advocacy, and Legislation, National Council of La Raza; Silver Springs, Md.

Margaret Murnane, 41, professor of physics; Boulder, Colo.

Laura Otis, 38, associate professor of English; Port Washington, N.Y.

Lucia Perillo, 41, associate professor of creative writing; Carbondale, Ill.

Matthew Rabin, 36, professor of economics; San Francisco

Carl Safina, 45, vice president, marine conservation at the National Audubon Society; Islip, N.Y.

Daniel Schrag, 34, professor of geochemistry; Cambridge, Mass.

Susan Sygall, 47, executive director, Mobility International USA; Eugene, Ore.

Gina Turrigiano, 37, assistant professor of biology; Acton, Mass.

Gary Urton, 53, professor of anthropology; Earlville, N.Y.

Patricia J. Williams, 48, law professor; New York

Deborah Willis, 52, curator of exhibitions, Center for African-American History and Culture and the Anacostia Museum at the Smithsonian Institution; Washington, D.C.

Erik Winfree, 30, assistant professor of computer science and computation and neural systems; Pasadena, Calif.

Horng-Tzer Yau, 40, professor of mathematics; New York

Presidential Medal of Freedom

The Presidential Medal of Freedom, the nation's highest civilian award, recognizes exceptional meritorious service. The medal was established by President Truman in 1945 to recognize notable service in the war. In 1963, President Kennedy reintroduced it as an honor for distinguished civilian service in peacetime. Shown below are only those medals awarded during President Clinton's administration.

1993* Arthur Ashe, Jr. (tennis professional)	1998 Robert Coles (psychiatrist and author)
1993 William J. Brennan, Jr. (jurist)	1998 Justin Dart, Jr. (founder of Americans with
1993 Marjory Stoneman Douglas (conservationist)	Disabilities Act)
1993 J. William Fulbright (public servant)	1998 James Farmer (civil-rights leader)
1993* Thurgood Marshall (jurist)	1998 Dante B. Fascell (public servant)
1993 General Colin L. Powell[1] (soldier)	1998 Zachary Fisher (philanthropist)
1993* Joseph L. Raugh, Jr. (civil-rights and labor activist)	1998 Frances Hesselbein (former leader of the Girl
1993 Martha Raye (entertainer)	Scouts of America)
1993 John Minor Wisdom (public servant)	1998 Fred Korematsu (activist redressing
1994 Herbert Block (cartoonist)	Japanese-American internment in WWII)
1994* Cesar Chavez (labor leader)	1998 Sol M. Linowitz (jurist)
1994 Arthur Flemming (government servant)	1998 Wilma Mankiller (former Cherokee Nation leader)
1994 James Grant (executive director, UNICEF)	1998 Margaret Murie (environmentalist)
1994 Dorothy Height (civil-rights leader)	1998 Mario G. Obledo (activist for Mexican-American
1994 Barbara Jordan (public servant)	civil rights)
1994 Lane Kirkland (labor leader)	1998 Elliot L. Richardson (public servant)
1994 Robert H. Michel (public servant)	1998 David Rockefeller (philanthropist)
1994 R. Sargent Shriver (government servant)	1998* Albert Shanker (educator)
1995 Peggy Charren (children's television advocate)	1998 Adm. Elmo R. Zumwalt, Jr. (soldier)
1995 William Thaddeus Coleman, Jr. (public servant and	1999 Lloyd M. Bentsen (public servant)
civil-rights advocate)	1999 Edgar M. Bronfman, Sr. (president of World Jewish
1995 Joan Ganz Cooney (children's television advocate)	Congress)
1995 John Hope Franklin (historian)	1999 President Jimmy Carter (public servant, activist)
1995 A. Leon Higginbotham, Jr. (jurist and civil-rights	1999 Rosalynn Carter (human-rights activist)
advocate)	1999 Evelyn Dubrow (lobbyist)
1995 Frank M. Johnson, Jr. (jurist)	1999 Sister Isolina Ferré (advocate for the poor)
1995 C. Everett Koop (public-health worker)	1999 President Gerald Ford (public servant)
1995 Gaylord A. Nelson (public servant and conservationist)	1999 Oliver White Hill (civil-rights lawyer)
1995 Walter P. Reuther (labor leader)	1999 Max Kampelman (arms-control expert)
1995 James W. Rouse (urban planner)	1999 Helmut Kohl (former German chancellor)
1995* William C. Velasquez (voting rights advocate)	1999 Edgar Wayburn (Sierra Club leader)
1995 Lew R. Wasserman (media executive)	2000 James Edward Burke (businessman, antidrug
1996 James Scott Brady (gun-control advocate)	activist)
1996 Cardinal Joseph Bernadin (Catholic leader)	2000* John Chafee (public servant)
1996 Millard D. Fuller (founder, Habitat for Humanity)	2000 Gen. Wesley Clark (soldier)
1996 David Alan Hamburg (physician and children's	2000 Adm. William Crowe (soldier)
advocate)	2000 Marian Wright Edelman (lawyer, president of
1996 John H. Johnson (founder, *Ebony* and *Jet*)	Children's Defense Fund)
1996 Eugene M. Lang (founder, "I Have a Dream"	2000 John Kenneth Galbraith (economist)
Foundation)	2000 Monsignor George Higgins (labor movement
1996 Jan Nowak-Jezioranski (WWII Polish resistence	advocate)
fighter)	2000 Rev. Jesse Jackson (civil-rights activist)
1996 Antonia Pantoja (Puerto Rican educational and	2000 Mildred Jeffrey (women's labor activist)
economic advocate)	2000 Mathilde Krim (AIDS researcher)
1996 Rosa Parks (civil-rights leader)	2000 George McGovern (public servant)
1996 Ginetta Sagan (advocate for political prisoners)	2000 Cruz Reynoso (lawyer, civil-rights advocate)
1996 Morris Udall (public servant)	2000 Rev. Gardner Taylor (author, civil-rights advocate)
1997 Robert Dole (public servant)	2000 Simon Wiesenthal (concentration camp survivor,
1997 William J. Perry (soldier)	Nazi hunter)
1998 Arnold Aronson (civil-rights advocate)	2000 Daniel Patrick Moynihan (public servant)
1998 Brooke Astor (philanthropist)	

1. With Distinction. NOTE: An asterisk following a year denotes a posthumous award.

Enrico Fermi Award

The $100,000 award is given in recognition of scientific and technical achievement in atomic energy. Awarded by the president, it is the U.S. government's oldest science and technology award.

1954	Enrico Fermi	1959	Glenn T. Seaborg
1956	John von Neumann	1961	Hans A. Bethe
1957	Ernest O. Lawrence	1962	Edward Teller
1958	Eugene P. Wigner	1963	J. Robert Oppenheimer

1964	Hyman G. Rickover	1986	Ernest D. Courant and M. Stanley Livingston
1966	Otto Hahn, Lise Meitner, and Fritz Strassman	1987	Luis W. Alvarez and Gerald F. Tape
1968	John A. Wheeler	1988	Richard B. Setlow and Victor F. Weisskopf
1969	Walter H. Zinn	1989	Award not given
1970	Norris E. Bradbury	1990	George A. Cowan and Robley D. Evans
1971	Shields Warren and Stafford L. Warren	1991	Award not given
1972	Manson Benedict	1992	Leon M. Lederman, Harold Brown, and John
1976	William L. Russell		S. Foster, Jr.
1978	Harold M. Agnew and Wolfgang K. H.	1993	Freeman J. Dyson and Liane B. Russell
	Panofsky	1994	Award not given
1980	Alvin M. Weinberg and Rudolf E. Peirls	1995	Ugo Fano and Martin Kamen
1981	W. Bennett Lewis	1996	Richard Garwin, Mortimer Elkind, and
1982	Herbert Anderson and Seth Neddermeyer		H. Rodney Withers
1983	Alexander Hollaender and John Lawrence	1997	Award not given
1984	Robert R. Wilson and Georges Vendryès	1998	Maurice Goldhaber and Michael E. Phelps
1985	Norman C. Rasmussen and Marshall N.		
	Rosenblath		

Fields Medal Winners

The Fields Medal has been awarded quadrennially since 1936 by the International Congress of Mathematicians in Toronto to recognize outstanding mathematics achievement.

1936 Lars Valerian Ahlfors (Harvard University) and Jesse Douglas (Massachusetts Institute of Technology)

(Fields Medals were not awarded during World War II)

1950 Laurent Schwarts (University of Nancy) and Alte Selberg (Institute for Advanced Study, Princeton)

1954 Kunihiko Kodaira (Princeton University) and Jean-Pierre Serre (University of Paris)

1958 Klaus Friedrich Roth (University of London) and René Thom (University of Strasbourgh)

1962 Lars V. Hörmander (University of Stockholm) and John Willard Milnor (Princeton University)

1966 Michael Francis Atiyah (Oxford University), Paul Joseph Cohen (Stanford University), Alexander Grothendieck (University of Paris), and Stephen Smale (University of California, Berkeley)

1970 Alan Baker (Cambridge University), Heisuke Hironaka (Harvard University), Serge P. Novikov (Moscow University), and John Griggs Thompson (Cambridge University)

1974 Enrico Bombieri (University of Pisa) and David Bryant Mumford (Harvard University)

1978 Pierre René Deligne (Institut des Hautes Études Scientifiques), Charles Louis Fefferman (Princeton University), Gregori Alexandrovitch Margulis (Moscow University), and Daniel G. Quillen (Massachusetts Institute of Technology)

1982 Alain Connes (Institut des Hautes Études Scientifiques), William P. Thurston (Princeton University), and Shing-Tung Yau (Institute for Advanced Study, Princeton)

1986 Simon Donaldson (Oxford University), Gerd Faltings (Princeton University), and Michael Freedman (University of California, San Diego)

1990 Vladimir Drinfeld (Phys. Inst. Kharkov), Vaughan Jones (University of California, Berkeley), Shigefumi Mori (University of Kyoto), and Edward Witten (Institute for Advanced Study, Princeton)

1994 Pierre-Louis Lions (Université de Paris–Dauphine), Jean-Christophe Yoccoz (Université de Paris–Sud), Jean Bourgain (Institute for Advanced Study, Princeton), and Efim Zelmanov (University of Wisconsin)

1998 Richard E. Borcherds (Cambridge University), William T. Gowers (Cambridge University), Maxim Kontsevich (Institut des Hautes Études Scientifiques and Rutgers University), and Curtis T. McMullen (Harvard University)

Recipients of Kennedy Center Honors

The Kennedy Center Honors recognize the lifetime achievements of selected American performing artists.

1978 Marian Anderson (contralto), Fred Astaire (dancer-actor), Richard Rodgers (Broadway composer), Arthur Rubinstein (pianist), George Balanchine (choreographer)

1979 Ella Fitzgerald (jazz singer), Henry Fonda (actor), Martha Graham (choreographer), Tennessee Williams (playwright), Aaron Copland (composer)

1980 James Cagney (actor), Leonard Bernstein (composer-conductor), Agnes de Mille (choreographer), Lynn Fontanne (actress), Leontyne Price (soprano)

1981 Count Basie (jazz composer-pianist), Cary Grant (actor), Helen Hayes (actress), Jerome Robbins (choreographer), Rudolf Serkin (pianist)

1982 George Abbott (Broadway producer), Lillian Gish (actress), Benny Goodman (jazz clarinetist), Gene Kelly (dancer-actor), Eugene Ormandy (conductor)

1983 Katherine Dunham (dancer-choreographer), Elia Kazan (director-author), James Stewart (actor), Virgil Thomson (music critic-composer), Frank Sinatra (singer)

1984 Lena Horne (singer), Danny Kaye (comedian-actor), Gian Carlo Menotti (composer), Arthur Miller (playwright), Isaac Stern (violinist)

1985 Merce Cunningham (dancer-choreographer), Irene Dunne (actress), Bob Hope (comedian), Alan Jay Lerner (lyricist-playwright), Frederick Loewe (composer), Beverly Sills (soprano)

1986 Lucille Ball (comedienne), Ray Charles (musician), Yehudi Menuhin (violinist), Antony Tudor (choreographer), Hume Cronyn and Jessica Tandy (husband-and-wife acting team)

1987 Perry Como (singer), Bette Davis (actress), Sammy Davis, Jr., (entertainer), Nathan Milstein (violinist), Alwin Nikolais (choreographer)

1988 Alvin Ailey (choreographer), George Burns (comedian-actor), Myrna Loy (actress), Alexander Schneider (violinist), Roger L. Stevens (theatrical producer and the Kennedy Center's founding chairman)

1989 Harry Belafonte (singer-actor), Claudette Colbert (actress), Alexandra Danilova (ballerina), Mary Martin (actress), William Schuman (composer)

1990 Dizzy Gillespie (jazz trumpeter), Katharine Hepburn (actress), Risë Stevens (mezzo-soprano), Jule Styne (composer), Billy Wilder (director)

1991 Roy Acuff (country songwriter and singer), Betty Comden and Adolph Green (co-authors of books and lyrics of musicals), the brothers Fayard and Harold Nicholas (dancers), Gregory Peck (actor), Robert Shaw (choral director)

1992 Lionel Hampton (jazz musician), Paul Newman (actor), Joanne Woodward (actress), Ginger Rogers (dancer-actress), Mstislav Rostropovich (cellist-conductor), Paul Taylor (choreographer)

1993 Johnny Carson (talk-show host), Arthur Mitchell (dancer and choreographer), Georg

Solti (conductor), Stephen Sondheim (composer and lyricist), Marion Williams (gospel singer)

1994 Kirk Douglas (actor), Aretha Franklin (singer), Morton Gould (composer), Harold Prince (producer and director), Pete Seeger (folk singer)

1995 Jacques D'Ambroise (choreographer), Marilyn Horne (mezzo soprano), B. B. King (blues singer), Sidney Poitier (actor), Neil Simon (playwright)

1996 Edward Albee (playwright), Benny Carter (jazz musician), Johnny Cash (musician), Jack Lemmon (actor), Maria Tallchief (ballerina)

1997 Lauren Bacall (actress), Bob Dylan (songwriter and singer), Charlton Heston (actor), Jessye Norman (soprano), Edward Villella (ballet dancer and director)

1998 Bill Cosby (actor and comedian), John Kander and Fred Ebb (Broadway composer and lyricist team), Willie Nelson (singer and songwriter), André Previn (composer and conductor), Shirley Temple Black (actress)

1999 Victor Borge (comedian and pianist), Sean Connery (actor), Judith Jamison (dancer and teacher), Jason Robards (actor), Stevie Wonder (singer and songwriter)

2000 Mikhail Baryshnikov (dancer), Plácido Domingo (tenor), Angela Lansbury (actress), Chuck Berry (rock 'n' roll musician), Clint Eastwood (actor, director, and producer)

Templeton Foundation Prize for Progress in Religion

The Templeton Prize, an award to encourage progress in religion, was established in 1972 by Sir John Templeton, a Tennessee-born financial analyst and Presbyterian layman, and first presented in 1973. Its value has increased over the years to nearly $1 million, depending on exchange rates.

1973 Mother Teresa of Calcutta, founder, the Missionaries of Charity

1974 Brother Roger, founder and prior, the Taize Community in France

1975 Dr. Sarvepalli Radhakrishnan, former president of India and Oxford Professor of Eastern Religions and Ethics

1976 H. E. Leon Joseph Cardinal Suenens, Archbishop of Malines-Brussels

1977 Chiara Lubich, founder of the Focolare Movement, Italy

1978 Prof. Thomas F. Torrance, president of International Academy of Religion and Sciences, Scotland

1979 Nikkyo Niwano, founder of Rissho Kosel Kai and World Conferences on Religion and Peace, Japan

1980 Prof. Ralph Wendell Burhoe, founder and editor of Zygon, Chicago

1981 Dame Cicely Saunders, originator of Modern Hospice Movement, England

1982 The Rev. Dr. Billy Graham, founder, The Billy Graham Evangelistic Association

1983 Aleksandr Solzhenitsyn, U.S.

1984 The Rev. Michael Bourdeaux, founder, Keston College, England

1985 Sir Alister Hardy, Oxford, England

1986 Rev. Dr. James McCord, Princeton, N.J.

1987 Rev. Professor Stanley L. Jaki, Priceton, N.J.

1988 Dr. Inamullah Khan, secretary-general, World Muslim Congress

1989 The Very Reverend Lord MacLeod of the Iona Community, Scotland, and Professor Carl Friedrich von Weizsäcker, Starnberg, West Germany

1990 Baba Amte, India, and Professor Charles Birch, Sydney, Australia

1991 The Rt. Hon. Lord Jakobovits, chief rabbi of Great Britain and the Commonwealth

1992 Dr. Kyung-Chik Han, founder, Seoul's Young Nak Presbyterian Church

1993 Charles W. Colson, founder, Prison Fellowship, Virginia

1994 Michael Novak, scholar at the American Enterprise Institute, Washington, D.C.

1995 Dr. Paul Davies, professor, University of Adelaide, Australia

1996 William R. "Bill" Bright, president and founder, Campus Crusade for Christ International, California

1997 Pandurang Shastri Athavale, founder and leader of Swadhyaya, a spiritual movement credited with improving the lives of 20 million people

1998 Sir Sigmund Sternberg, founder and chairman, Sternberg Centre for Judaism, London

1999 Ian Barbour, professor emeritus, Carleton College, Minnesota

2000 Freeman J. Dyson, professor emeritus, Institute for Advanced Study, Princeton, N.J.

U.S. Symphony Orchestras and Their Music Directors

(with expenses over $1,050,000)

Akron Symphony Orchestra: Jeffrey K. Sperry[1]
Alabama Symphony Ochestra: Richard Westerfield
American Composers Orchestra: Dennis Russell Davies
American Symphony Orchestra: Leon Botstein
Arkansas Symphony Orchestra: David Itkin
Aspen Chamber Symphony: David Zinman
Atlanta Symphony: Yoel Levi
Austin Symphony: Peter Bay
Baltimore Symphony: Yuri Temirkanov
Baton Rouge Symphony: Timothy Muffit
Boca Pops (Florida Symphonic Pops): Crafton Beck[2, 3]
Boston Symphony: Seiji Ozawa
Boston Symphony Chamber Players: Malcolm Lowe
Boulder Philharmonic Orchestra: Theodor Kuchar
Brooklyn Philharmonic: Robert Spano
Buffalo Philharmonic Orchestra: JoAnn Falletta
Cedar Rapids Symphony: Christian Tiemeyer[2]
Charleston Symphony: David Stahl
Charlotte Symphony: Juanita Hauk
Chattanooga Symphony & Opera Association: Robert Bernhardt
Chicago Sinfonietta: Paul Freeman
Chicago Symphony: Daniel Barenboim
Cincinnati Symphony: Jesus Lopez-Cobos
Cleveland Orchestra: Christoph von Dohnanyi
Colorado Springs Symphony: Yaacov Bergman
Columbus Symphony: Alessandro Siciliani
Dallas Symphony: Andrew Litton
Dayton Philharmonic: Neal Gittleman
Delaware Symphony: Stephen Gunzenhauser
Des Moines Symphony: Joseph Giunta
Detroit Symphony: Neeme Järvi
Elgin Symphony Orchestra: Robert L. Hanson[2]
El Paso Symphony Orchestra: Gurer Aykal
Erie Philharmonic: Peter Bay
Evansville Philharmonic Orchestra: Alfred Savia
Florida Orchestra: Jahja Ling
Florida Philharmonic Orchestra: James Judd
Florida West Coast Symphony Orchestra: Leif Bjaland[2, 3]
Fort Wayne Philharmonic: Edvard Tchivzhel
Fort Worth Symphony: John Giordano
Fresno Philharmonic Orchestra: Raymond Harvey
Grand Rapids Symphony: Catherine Comet
Grant Park Symphony (Chicago): Hugh Wolff[4]
Greensboro Symphony Orchestra: Stuart Malina
Greenville Symphony Orchestra: Edvard Tchivzhel
Handel & Haydn Society: Christopher Hogwood[3]
Harrisburg Symphony Orchestra: Richard Westerfield
Hartford Symphony: Michael Lankester
Honolulu Symphony Society: Samuel Wong
Houston Symphony: Christopher Eschenbach
Indianapolis Symphony: Raymond Leppard
Jacksonville Symphony: Roger Nierenberg
Kalamazoo Symphony Orchestra: Yoshimi Takeda
Kansas City Symphony: Anne Manson
Kennedy Center Opera House Orchestra: Heinze Frickle
Knoxville Symphony: Kirk Trevor
Little Orchestra Society of New York: Dino Anagnost
Long Beach Symphony: JoAnn Falletta
Long Island Philharmonic: Karen L. Barnes[1]
Los Angeles Chamber Orchestra: Jeffrey Kahane

Los Angeles Philharmonic: Esa-Pekka Salonen
Louisiana Philharmonic Orchestra: Klauspeter Seibel
Louisville Orchestra: Robert Fran[2]
Madison Symphony Orchestra: John De Main
Memphis Symphony: David Loebel
Milwaukee Symphony Orchestra: Andreas Delfs
Minnesota Orchestra: Eiji Oue
Mississippi Symphony: Colman Pearce
Monterey County Symphony: Kate Tamarkin
Music Academy of the West Summer Festival Orchestra: Carleen Landes[3]
Music of the Baroque: Thomas S. Wikman
Naples Philharmonic: Christopher Seaman
Nashville Symphony: Kenneth D. Schermerhorn
National Sinfonietta: Burton A. Zipser[3]
National Symphony (D.C.): Leonard Slatkin
New Haven Symphony: Michael Palmer
New Jersey Symphony: Zdenek Macal[2, 3]
New Mexico Symphony: Roger Melone[2]
New West Symphony: Boris Brott
New World Symphony (Fla.): Michael Tilson Thomas[3]
New York Chamber Symphony of the 92nd St. Y: Gerard Schwarz
New York Philharmonic: Kurt Masur
New York Pops: Skitch Henderson
North Carolina Symphony: Gerhardt Zimmermann
Northeastern Pennsylvania Philharmonic: Hugh Keelan
Ohio Chamber Orchestra: David Lockington[1]
Oklahoma City Philharmonic: Joel A. Levine
Omaha Symphony: Victor Yampolsky
Omaha Symphony Chamber Orchestra: Victor Yampolsky
Oregon Symphony: James DePreist
Pacific Symphony Orchestra (Calif.): Carl St. Clair
Palm Beach Pops: Bob Lappin
Philadelphia Orchestra: Wolfgang Sawallisch
Philharmonia Baroque Orchestra: Nicholas McGegan
Phoenix Symphony: Hermann Michael
Pittsburgh Symphony Orchestra: Mariss Jansons
Portland Symphony: Toshiyuki Shimada
Quad City Symphony Orchestra Association: Donald Schleicher
Rhode Island Philharmonic: Larry Rachleff
Richmond Symphony: Mark Russell Smith
River City Brass Band: Denis Colwell
Rochester Philharmonic: Christopher Seaman
St. Louis Symphony: Hans Vonk
St. Paul Chamber Orchestra: Hugh Wolff
San Antonio Symphony: Christopher Wilkins
San Francisco Symphony: Michael Tilson Thomas
San Jose Symphony: Leonid Grin[2]
Santa Barbara Symphony Orchestra: Gisele Ben-Dor
Santa Rosa Symphony: Jeffrey Kahane
Savannah Symphony: Philip Greenberg
Seattle Symphony: Gerard Schwarz
Shreveport Symphony: Dennis Simons
Spokane Symphony: Fabio Mechetti
Springfield Symphony (Mass.): Mark Russell Smith
Stamford Symphony Orchestra: Roger Nierenberg[2]
Symphony of United Nations: Joseph Eger
Syracuse Symphony: Fabio Mechetti
Toledo Symphony: Andrew Massey

Tucson Symphony: George Hanson
Tulsa Philharmonic: Bernard Rubenstein
Utah Symphony: Keith Lockhart
Virginia Symphony: JoAnn Falletta
Westchester Philharmonic: Paul Lustig Dunkel[2]

West Virginia Symphony: Thomas B. Conlin[3]
Wichita Symphony: Zuohuang Chen
Winston-Salem Piedmont Triad Symphony:
Peter J. Perret
Youngstown Symphony Orchestra: Isaiah Jackson

1. Executive Director. 2. Conductor. 3. Artistic Director. 4. Principal Conductor. 5. Music Conductor.

U.S. Opera Companies
(budgets $2,000,000 and over)

American Musical Theatre of San Jose (Calif.), Dianna Shuster, Art. Dir.
Arizona Opera Company (Tucson, Phoenix), David Speers, Gen. Dir.
Aspen Opera Theater Center (Colo.), Robert Harth, Pres. and CEO
Atlanta Opera, The (Ga.), William Fred Scott, Art. Dir.
Austin Lyric Opera (Tex.), Joseph McClain, Gen. Dir.
Baltimore Opera Company (Md.), Michael Harrison, Gen. Dir.
Boston Lyric Opera Company (Mass.), Janice Mancini Del Sesto, Gen. Dir.
Central City Opera House Association (Colo.), Pelham G. Pearce, Gen. Dir.
Cincinnati Opera Association (Ohio), Nicholas Muni, Art. Dir.
Civic Light Opera (Pittsburgh), Van Kaplan, Exec. Prod.
Cleveland Opera (Ohio), David Bamberger, Gen. Dir.
Dallas Opera, The (Tex.), Anthony Whitworth-Jones, Gen. Dir.
Florentine Opera Company (Milwaukee), Dennis W. Hanthorn, Gen. Dir.
Florida Grand Opera (Miami), Robert M. Heuer, Gen. Mgr. and CEO
Glimmerglass Opera (Cooperstown, N.Y.), Paul Kellogg, Art. Dir.
Goodspeed Opera House (East Haddam, Conn.), Michael Price, Exec. Dir.
Hawaii Opera Theatre (Honolulu), Henry G. Akina, Gen. Dir. and Art. Dir.
Houston Grand Opera Association (Tex.), R. David Gockley, Gen. Dir.
Kentucky Opera (Louisville), Deborah Sandler, Gen. Dir.
Long Beach Civic Light Opera (Calif.), Pegge Logefeil, Exec. Dir.
Los Angeles Music Center Opera (Calif.), Peter Hemmings, Gen. Dir.
Lyric Opera of Chicago (Ill.), William Mason, Gen. Dir.
Lyric Opera of Kansas City (Mo.), Evan R. Luskin, Gen. Dir.
Metro Lyric Opera (Allenhurst, N.J.), Era M. Tognoli, Gen. Dir. and Art. Dir.

Metropolitan Opera Association (N.Y.), James Levine, Art. Dir.
Michigan Opera Theatre (Detroit), David DiChiera, Gen. Dir.
Minnesota Opera, The (Minneapolis), Kevin Smith, Pres. and Gen. Dir.
New York City Opera (N.Y.), Paul Kellogg, Gen. Dir.
New York City Opera National Company (N.Y.), Julie Samuels, Bus. Mgr.
Ohio Light Opera (Wooster), Steven Daigle, Art. Dir.
Opera Colorado (Denver), James Robinson, Art. Dir.
Opera Company of Philadelphia (Pa.), Robert B. Driver, Gen. Dir.
Opera Festival of New Jersey (Princeton), Karen Tiller, Gen. Dir.
Opera Pacific (Irvine, Calif.), David DiChiera, Art. Dir.
Opera Theatre of St. Louis (Mo.), Charles MacKay, Gen. Dir.
Orlando Opera Company Inc. (Fla.), Robert Swedberg, Gen. Dir.
Palm Beach Opera Inc. (Fla.), Anton Guadagno, Art. Dir.
Pittsburgh Opera, Inc. (Pa.), Christopher Hahn, Art. Dir.
Portland Opera Association (Ore.), Robert Bailey, Gen. Dir.
San Diego Civic Light Opera Association (Calif.), Cinda Lucas, Pres.
San Diego Opera (Calif.), Ian D. Campbell, Gen. Dir.
San Francisco Opera (Calif.), Lotfi Mansouri, Gen. Dir.
San Francisco Opera Center (Calif.), Richard Harrell, Dir.
Santa Barbara Civic Light Opera (Calif.), Paul Iannacone, Exec. Prod.
Santa Fe Opera (N.M.), John Crosby, Gen. Dir.
Sarasota Opera Association (Fla.), Susan Danis, Exec. Dir.
Seattle Opera Association (Wash.), Speight Jenkins, Gen. Dir.
Utah Opera Company (Salt Lake City), Anne Ewers, Gen. Dir.
Virginia Opera (Norfolk), Peter Mark, Gen. Dir.
Washington Opera, The (D.C.), Plácido Domingo, Art. Dir. Designate

Most Frequently Produced Operas in the U.S.
(1994–1995 through 1999–2000)

Top 5 works	Composer/Librettist	Number of productions* (and date of first performance)
1. *Madama Butterfly*	Puccini/Giacosa and Illica	103 (Feb. 17, 1904)
2. *La Bohème*	Puccini/Giacosa and Illica	101 (May 6, 1897)
3. *La Traviata*	Verdi/Piave	98 (March 6, 1853)
4. *Carmen*	Bizet/Meilhac and Halévy	95 (March 3, 1875)
5. *Tosca*	Puccini/Giacosa and Illica	88 (Jan. 14, 1900)
Top 5 works by American artists		
1. *Porgy and Bess*	Gershwin/Heyward	22 (Oct. 10, 1935)
1. *Susannah*	Floyd/Floyd	22 (Feb. 24, 1955)
2. *Candide*	Bernstein/Hellman, Wilbur	13 (Oct. 29, 1956)
2. *Ballad of Baby Doe*	Moore/Latouche	13 (July 7, 1956)
2. *The Rake's Progress*	Stravinsky/Auden and Kallman	13 (Sept. 11, 1951)

*Represents the number of productions by professional member companies of Opera America, not the number of performances. *Source:* Opera America's Annual Season Schedule of Performances.

U.S. Dance Companies
(budgets $2,500,000 and over)

Alvin Ailey American Dance Theatre (1958): Judith Jamison, Art. Dir.
American Ballet Theatre (1940): Kevin McKenzie, Art. Dir.
Atlanta Ballet Company (1929): John McFall, Art. Dir. and CEO
Ballet Florida (1986): Marie Hale, Art. Dir.
BalletMet Columbus (1978): David Nixon, Art. Dir.
Ballet West (1968¹): Jonas Kåge, Art. Dir.
Boston Ballet (1964): Anna-Marie Holmes, Art. Dir.
Cincinnati Ballet (1955): Victoria Morgan, Art. Dir.
Cleveland San Jose Ballet (1976): Dennis Nahat, Art. Dir.
Colorado Ballet (1961): Martin Fredmann, Art. Dir.
Merce Cunningham Dance Company (1952): Merce Cunningham, Art. Dir.
Dance Theater of Harlem (1968): Arthur Mitchell, Art. Dir.
Feld Ballet New York (1974): Eliot Feld, Dir.
Martha Graham Dance Company (1926)*

Houston Ballet (1968): Ben Stevenson, Art. Dir.
Joffrey Ballet of Chicago (1954): Gerald Arpino, Art. Dir.
Bill T. Jones/Arnie Zane Dance Company (1982): Bill T. Jones, Art. Dir.
José Limón Dance Company (1946): Carla Maxwell, Art. Dir.
Miami City Ballet (1986): Edward Villella, Art. Dir.
Milwaukee Ballet (1970): Simon Dow, Art. Dir.
New York City Ballet (1948): Peter Martins, Ballet-Master-in-Chief
Ocheami-Afrikan Dance Company (1978): Kofe Anang, Art. Dir.
Pacific Northwest Ballet (1972): Kent Stowell and Francia Russell, Art. Dirs.
Pittsburgh Ballet Theater (1970): Terrence S. Orr, Art. Dir.
San Francisco Ballet (1933): Helgi Tomasson, Art. Dir.
Paul Taylor Dance Company (1954): Paul Taylor, Dir.

*The Martha Graham Dance Company suspended operations and canceled performances in May 2000 amid financial disaster and a vitriolic internal battle. Ron Protas, the company's artistic director, was fired by the board, yet has retained the rights to Graham's works. The future of the company remains in jeopardy. NOTE: Year founded appears in parentheses after name. 1. Prior company founded 1963, name changed to Ballet West in 1968.

Best-Selling Books, 1999

Source: Publishers Weekly

Hardcover Fiction

1. *The Testament*, John Grisham
2. *Hannibal*, Thomas Harris
3. *Assassins*, Jerry B. Jenkins and Tim LaHaye
4. *Star Wars: Episode 1, The Phantom Menace*, Terry Brooks
5. *Timeline*, Michael Crichton
6. *Hearts in Atlantis*, Stephen King
7. *Apollyon*, Jerry B. Jenkins and Tim LaHaye
8. *The Girl Who Loved Tom Gordon*, Stephen King
9. *Irresistible Forces*, Danielle Steel
10. *Tara Road*, Maeve Binchy

Hardcover Nonfiction

1. *Tuesdays with Morrie*, Mitch Albom
2. *The Greatest Generation*, Tom Brokaw
3. *Guinness World Records 2000 Millennium Edition*, Guinness Publishing
4. *'Tis*, Frank McCourt
5. *Who Moved My Cheese?*, Spencer Johnson
6. *The Courage to Be Rich*, Suze Orman
7. *The Greatest Generation Speaks*, Tom Brokaw
8. *Sugar Busters!*, H. Leighton Steward, Morrison C. Bethea, Sam S. Andrews, and Luis A. Balart
9. *The Art of Happiness*, Dalai Lama and Howard C. Cutler
10. *The Century*, Peter Jennings and Todd Brewster

1. Movie tie-in published in Dec. 1999.

Trade Paperbacks

1. *The Pilot's Wife*, Anita Shreve
2. *Memoirs of a Geisha*, Arthur Golden
3. *The Reader*, Bernhard Schlink
4. *Angela's Ashes*, Frank McCourt
5. *Chicken Soup for the Couple's Soul*, Jack Canfield, Mark Victor Hansen, Barbara DeAngelis, and Mark and Chrissy Donnelly
6. *Don't Sweat the Small Stuff at Work*, Richard Carlson
7. *Where the Heart Is*, Billy Letts
8. *Angela's Ashes*, Frank McCourt[1]
9. *Soul Harvest*, Jerry B. Jenkins and Tim LaHaye
10. *Nicolae*, Jerry B. Jenkins and Tim LaHaye

Mass Market Paperbacks

1. *The Street Lawyer*, John Grisham
2. *The Testament*, John Grisham
3. *Bag of Bones*, Stephen King
4. *Point of Origin*, Patricia Cornwell
5. *Rainbow Six*, Tom Clancy
6. *Jewels of the Sun*, Nora Roberts
7. *Summer Sister*, Judy Blume
8. *Southern Cross*, Patricia Cornwell
9. *Op Center VI: State of Siege*, Tom Clancy and Steve Pieczenik
10. *Homeport*, Nora Roberts

All-Time Children's Best-Selling Books
From the date of publication (in parentheses) through the end of 1995.
Source: Publishers Weekly
Hardcovers

1. *The Poky Little Puppy*, Janette Sebring Lowrey (1942)
2. *The Tale of Peter Rabbit*, Beatrix Potter (1902)
3. *Tootle*, Gertrude Crampton (1945)
4. *Saggy Baggy Elephant*, Kathryn and Byron Jackson (1955)
5. *Scuffy the Tugboat*, Gertrude Crampton (1955)
6. *Pat the Bunny*, Dorothy Kunhardt (1940)
7. *Green Eggs and Ham*, Dr. Seuss (1960)
8. *The Cat in the Hat*, Dr. Seuss (1957)
9. *The Littlest Angel*, Charles Tazewell (1946)
10. *One Fish, Two Fish, Red Fish, Blue Fish*, Dr. Seuss (1960)

Paperbacks

1. *Charlotte's Web*, E. B. White, illus. by Garth Williams (1974)
2. *The Outsiders*, S. E. Hinton (1968)
3. *Tales of a Fourth Grade Nothing*, Judy Blume (1976)
4. *Shane*, Jack Schaeffer (1983)
5. *Are You There, God? It's Me, Margaret*, Judy Blume (1972)
6. *Where the Red Fern Grows*, Wilson Rawls (1974)
7. *A Wrinkle in Time*, Madeleine L'Engle (1973)
8. *Island of the Blue Dolphins*, Scott O'Dell (1971)
9. *Little House on the Prairie*, Laura Ingalls Wilder, illus. by Garth Williams (1971)
10. *Little House in the Big Woods*, Laura Ingalls Wilder, illus. by Garth Williams (1971)

The 100 Best Novels of the 20th Century

The Board of the Modern Library, a division of Random House, published its selections in July 1998.

1. *Ulysses*, James Joyce (1922)
2. *The Great Gatsby*, F. Scott Fitzgerald (1925)
3. *A Portrait of the Artist as a Young Man*, James Joyce (1916)
4. *Lolita*, Vladimir Nabokov (1958)
5. *Brave New World*, Aldous Huxley (1932)
6. *The Sound and the Fury*, William Faulkner (1929)
7. *Catch-22*, Joseph Heller (1961)
8. *Darkness at Noon*, Arthur Koestler (1941)
9. *Sons and Lovers*, D. H. Lawrence (1913)
10. *The Grapes of Wrath*, John Steinbeck (1939)
11. *Under the Volcano*, Malcolm Lowry (1947)
12. *The Way of All Flesh*, Samuel Butler (1903)
13. *1984*, George Orwell (1949)
14. *I, Claudius*, Robert Graves (1934)
15. *To the Lighthouse*, Virginia Woolf (1927)
16. *An American Tragedy*, Theodore Dreiser (1925)
17. *The Heart Is a Lonely Hunter*, Carson McCullers (1940)
18. *Slaughterhouse-Five*, Kurt Vonnegut (1969)
19. *Invisible Man*, Ralph Ellison (1952)
20. *Native Son*, Richard Wright (1940)
21. *Henderson the Rain King*, Saul Bellow (1959)
22. *Appointment in Samarra*, John O'Hara (1934)
23. *U.S.A.* (trilogy), John Dos Passos (1937—trilogy completed)
24. *Winesburg, Ohio*, Sherwood Anderson (1919)
25. *A Passage to India*, E. M. Forster (1924)
26. *The Wings of the Dove*, Henry James (1902)
27. *The Ambassadors*, Henry James (1903)
28. *Tender Is the Night*, F. Scott Fitzgerald (1934)
29. *The Studs Lonigan Trilogy*, James T. Farrell (1935)
30. *The Good Soldier*, Ford Madox Ford (1915)
31. *Animal Farm*, George Orwell (1946)
32. *The Golden Bowl*, Henry James (1904)
33. *Sister Carrie*, Theodore Dreiser (1900)
34. *A Handful of Dust*, Evelyn Waugh (1934)
35. *As I Lay Dying*, William Faulkner (1930)
36. *All the King's Men*, Robert Penn Warren (1946)
37. *The Bridge of San Luis Rey*, Thornton Wilder (1927)
38. *Howards End*, E. M. Forster (1910)
39. *Go Tell It on the Mountain*, James Baldwin (1953)
40. *The Heart of the Matter*, Graham Greene (1948)
41. *Lord of the Flies*, William Golding (1954)
42. *Deliverance*, James Dickey (1969)
43. *A Dance to the Music of Time* (series), Anthony Powell (1975—series completed)
44. *Point Counter Point*, Aldous Huxley (1928)
45. *The Sun Also Rises*, Ernest Hemingway (1926)
46. *The Secret Agent*, Joseph Conrad (1907)
47. *Nostromo*, Joseph Conrad (1904)
48. *The Rainbow*, D. H. Lawrence (1915)
49. *Women in Love*, D. H. Lawrence (1921)
50. *Tropic of Cancer*, Henry Miller (1934)
51. *The Naked and the Dead*, Norman Mailer (1948)
52. *Portnoy's Complaint*, Philip Roth (1969)
53. *Pale Fire*, Vladimir Nabokov (1962)
54. *Light in August*, William Faulkner (1932)
55. *On the Road*, Jack Kerouac (1957)
56. *The Maltese Falcon*, Dashiell Hammett (1930)
57. *Parade's End*, Ford Madox Ford (1950)
58. *The Age of Innocence*, Edith Wharton (1920)
59. *Zuleika Dobson*, Max Beerbohm (1911)
60. *The Moviegoer*, Walker Percy (1961)
61. *Death Comes for the Archbishop*, Willa Cather (1927)
62. *From Here to Eternity*, James Jones
63. *The Wapshot Chronicles*, John Cheever
64. *The Catcher in the Rye*, J. D. Salinger
65. *A Clockwork Orange*, Anthony Burgess
66. *Of Human Bondage*, W. Somerset Maugham
67. *Heart of Darkness*, Joseph Conrad
68. *Main Street*, Sinclair Lewis
69. *The House of Mirth*, Edith Wharton (1905)
70. *The Alexandria Quartet*, Lawrence Durrell (1960—series completed)
71. *A High Wind in Jamaica*, Richard Hughes (1929)
72. *A House for Mr. Biswas*, V. S. Naipaul (1961)
73. *The Day of the Locust*, Nathanael West (1939)
74. *A Farewell to Arms*, Ernest Hemingway (1929)
75. *Scoop*, Evelyn Waugh (1938)
76. *The Prime of Miss Jean Brodie*, Muriel Spark (1961)
77. *Finnegans Wake*, James Joyce (1939)
78. *Kim*, Rudyard Kipling (1901)
79. *A Room with a View*, E. M. Forster (1908)
80. *Brideshead Revisited*, Evelyn Waugh (1945)
81. *The Adventures of Augie March*, Saul Bellow (1953)
82. *Angle of Repose*, Wallace Stegner (1971)
83. *A Bend in the River*, V. S. Naipaul (1979)
84. *The Death of the Heart*, Elizabeth Bowen (1938)
85. *Lord Jim*, Joseph Conrad (1900)
86. *Ragtime*, E. L. Doctorow (1975)
87. *The Old Wives' Tale*, Arnold Bennett (1908)
88. *The Call of the Wild*, Jack London (1903)
89. *Loving*, Henry Green (1945)
90. *Midnight's Children*, Salman Rushdie (1981)
91. *Tobacco Road*, Erskine Caldwell (1933)

92. *Ironweed*, William Kennedy (1983)
93. *The Magus*, John Fowles (1966)
94. *Wide Sargasso Sea*, Jean Rhys (1966)
95. *Under the Net*, Iris Murdoch (1954)
96. *Sophie's Choice*, William Styron (1979)
97. *The Sheltering Sky*, Paul Bowles (1949)
98. *The Postman Always Rings Twice*, James M. Cain (1934)
99. *The Ginger Man*, J. P. Donleavy (1955)
100. *The Magnificent Ambersons*, Booth Tarkington (1918)

The 100 Best Nonfiction Books of the 20th Century

The Board of the Modern Library, a division of Random House, published its selections in April 1999.

1. *The Education of Henry Adams*, Henry Adams (1906)
2. *The Varieties of Religious Experience*, William James (1902)
3. *Up from Slavery*, Booker T. Washington (1901)
4. *A Room of One's Own*, Virginia Woolf (1929)
5. *Silent Spring*, Rachel Carson (1962)
6. *Selected Essays, 1917–1932*, T. S. Eliot (1932)
7. *The Double Helix*, James D. Watson (1968)
8. *Speak, Memory*, Vladimir Nabokov (1967)
9. *The American Language*, H. L. Mencken (1919)
10. *The General Theory of Employment, Interest, and Money*, John Maynard Keynes (1935–1936)
11. *The Lives of a Cell*, Lewis Thomas (1974)
12. *The Frontier in American History*, Frederick Jackson Turner (1920)
13. *Black Boy*, Richard Wright (1945)
14. *Aspects of the Novel*, E. M. Forster (1927)
15. *The Civil War*, Shelby Foote (1958–1974)
16. *The Guns of August*, Barbara Tuchman (1962)
17. *The Proper Study of Mankind*, Isaiah Berlin (1997)
18. *The Nature and Destiny of Man*, Reinhold Niebuhr (1941–1943)
19. *Notes of a Native Son*, James Baldwin (1955)
20. *The Autobiography of Alice B. Toklas*, Gertrude Stein (1933)
21. *The Elements of Style*, William Strunk and E. B. White (1959)
22. *An American Dilemma*, Gunnar Myrdal (1944)
23. *Principia Mathematica*, Alfred North Whitehead and Bertrand Russell (1910–1913)
24. *The Mismeasure of Man*, Stephen Jay Gould (1981)
25. *The Mirror and the Lamp*, Meyer Howard Abrams (1953)
26. *The Art of the Soluble*, Peter B. Medawar (1967)
27. *The Ants*, Bert Hoelldobler and Edward O. Wilson (1990)
28. *A Theory of Justice*, John Rawls (1971)
29. *Art and Illusion*, Ernest H. Gombrich (1961)
30. *The Making of the English Working Class*, E. P. Thompson (1963)
31. *The Souls of Black Folk*, W. E. B. Du Bois (1903)
32. *Principia Ethica*, G. E. Moore (1903)
33. *Philosophy and Civilization*, John Dewey (1927)
34. *On Growth and Form*, D'Arcy Thompson (1917)
35. *Ideas and Opinions*, Albert Einstein (1954)
36. *The Age of Jackson*, Arthur Schlesinger, Jr. (1945)
37. *The Making of the Atomic Bomb*, Richard Rhodes (1986)
38. *Black Lamb and Grey Falcon*, Rebecca West (1942)
39. *Autobiographies*, W. B. Yeats (1926)
40. *Science and Civilization in China*, Joseph Needham (1954–)
41. *Goodbye to All That*, Robert Graves (1929)
42. *Homage to Catalonia*, George Orwell (1938)
43. *The Autobiography of Mark Twain*, Mark Twain (1924)
44. *Children of Crisis*, Robert Coles (1967)
45. *A Study of History*, Arnold J. Toynbee (1934-1961)
46. *The Affluent Society*, John Kenneth Galbraith (1958)
47. *Present at the Creation*, Dean Acheson (1969)
48. *The Great Bridge*, David McCullough (1972)
49. *Patriotic Gore*, Edmund Wilson (1962)
50. *Samuel Johnson*, Walter Jackson Bate (1977)
51. *The Autobiography of Malcolm X*, Alex Haley and Malcolm X (1965)
52. *The Right Stuff*, Tom Wolfe (1979)
53. *Eminent Victorians*, Lytton Strachey (1918)
54. *Working*, Studs Terkel (1974)
55. *Darkness Visible*, William Styron (1990)
56. *The Liberal Imagination*, Lionel Trilling (1950)
57. *The Second World War*, Winston Churchill (1948–1953)
58. *Out of Africa*, Isak Dinesen (1937)
59. *Jefferson and His Time*, Dumas Malone (1948–1981)
60. *In the American Grain*, William Carlos Williams (1925)
61. *Cadillac Desert*, Marc Reisner (1986)
62. *The House of Morgan*, Ron Chernow (1990)
63. *The Sweet Science*, A. J. Liebling (1956)
64. *The Open Society and Its Enemies*, Karl Popper (1945)
65. *The Art of Memory*, Frances A. Yates (1966)
66. *Religion and the Rise of Capitalism*, R. H. Tawney (1926)
67. *A Preface to Morals*, Walter Lippmann (1929)
68. *The Gate of Heavenly Peace*, Jonathan D. Spence (1981)
69. *The Structure of Scientific Revolutions*, Thomas S. Kuhn (1962)
70. *The Strange Career of Jim Crow*, C. Vann Woodward (1955)
71. *The Rise of the West*, William H. McNeill (1963)
72. *The Gnostic Gospels*, Elaine Pagels (1979)
73. *James Joyce*, Richard Ellmann (1959)
74. *Florence Nightingale*, Cecil Woodham-Smith (1950)
75. *The Great War and Modern Memory*, Paul Fussell (1975)
76. *The City in History*, Lewis Mumford (1961)
77. *Battle Cry of Freedom*, James M. McPherson (1988)
78. *Why We Can't Wait*, Martin Luther King, Jr. (1964)
79. *The Rise of Theodore Roosevelt*, Edmund Morris (1979)

80. *Studies in Iconology*, Erwin Panofsky (1939)
81. *The Face of Battle*, John Keegan (1976)
82. *The Strange Death of Liberal England*, George Dangerfield (1935)
83. *Vermeer*, Lawrence Gowing (1952)
84. *A Bright Shining Lie*, Neil Sheehan (1988)
85. *West with the Night*, Beryl Markham (1942)
86. *This Boy's Life*, Tobias Wolff (1989)
87. *A Mathematician's Apology*, G. H. Hardy (1940)
88. *Six Easy Pieces*, Richard P. Feynman (1963)
89. *Pilgrim at Tinker Creek*, Annie Dillard (1974)
90. *The Golden Bough*, James George Frazer (1922) (1 vol. ed.)
91. *Shadow and Act*, Ralph Ellison (1964)

92. *The Power Broker*, Robert A. Caro (1974)
93. *The American Political Tradition*, Richard Hofstadter (1948)
94. *The Contours of American History*, William Appleman Williams (1966)
95. *The Promise of American Life*, Herbert Croly (1909)
96. *In Cold Blood*, Truman Capote (1965)
97. *The Journalist and the Murderer*, Janet Malcolm (1990)
98. *The Taming of Chance*, Ian Hacking (1990)
99. *Operating Instructions*, Anne Lamott (1994)
100. *Melbourne*, Lord David Cecil (1939 & 1954)

Best American Journalism of the 20th Century

The following works were chosen as the 20th century's best American journalism by a panel of experts assembled by the New York University school of journalism.

1. **John Hersey:** "Hiroshima," *The New Yorker*, 1946
2. **Rachel Carson:** *Silent Spring*, book, 1962
3. **Bob Woodward and Carl Bernstein:** Investigation of the Watergate break-in, *The Washington Post*, 1972
4. **Edward R. Murrow:** *Battle of Britain*, CBS radio, 1940
5. **Ida Tarbell:** "The History of the Standard Oil Company," *McClure's*, 1902–1904
6. **Lincoln Steffens:** "The Shame of the Cities," *McClure's*, 1902–1904
7. **John Reed:** *Ten Days That Shook the World*, book, 1919
8. **H. L. Mencken:** Scopes "Monkey" trial, *The Sun* of Baltimore, 1925
9. **Ernie Pyle:** Reports from Europe and the Pacific during World War II, Scripps-Howard newspapers, 1940-45
10. **Edward R. Murrow and Fred Friendly:** Investigation of Sen. Joseph McCarthy, CBS, 1954
11. **Edward R. Murrow, David Lowe, and Fred Friendly:** documentary "Harvest of Shame," CBS television, 1960
12. **Seymour Hersh:** Investigation of massacre by American soldiers at My Lai in Vietnam, Dispatch News Service, 1969
13. **The New York Times:** Publication of the Pentagon Papers, 1971
14. **James Agee and Walker Evans:** *Let Us Now Praise Famous Men*, book, 1941
15. **W. E. B. Du Bois:** *The Souls of Black Folk*, collected articles, 1903
16. **I. F. Stone:** *I. F. Stone's Weekly*, 1953-67
17. **Henry Hampton:** "Eyes on the Prize," documentary, 1987
18. **Tom Wolfe:** *The Electric Kool-Aid Acid Test*, book, 1968
19. **Norman Mailer:** *The Armies of the Night*, book, 1968
20. **Hannah Arendt:** *Eichmann in Jerusalem: A Report on the Banality of Evil*, collected articles, 1963
21. **William Shirer:** *Berlin Diary: The Journal of a Foreign Correspondent, 1939–1941*, collected articles, 1941
22. **Truman Capote:** *In Cold Blood: A True Account of a Multiple Murder and Its Consequences*, book, 1965

23. **Joan Didion:** *Slouching Towards Bethlehem*, collected articles, 1968
24. **Tom Wolfe:** *The Kandy-Kolored Tangerine-Flake Streamline Baby*, collected articles, 1965
25. **Michael Herr:** *Dispatches*, book, 1977
26. **Theodore White:** *The Making of the President: 1960*, book, 1961
27. **Robert Capa:** Ten photographs from D-Day, 1944
28. **J. Anthony Lukas:** *Common Ground: A Turbulent Decade in the Lives of Three American Families*, book, 1985
29. **Richard Harding Davis:** Coverage of German march into Belgium, Wheeler Syndicate and magazines, 1914
30. **Dorothy Thompson:** Reports on the rise of Hitler, *Cosmopolitan* and *Saturday Evening Post*, 1931–1934
31. **John Steinbeck:** Reports on Okie migrant camp life, *The San Francisco News*, 1936
32. **A. J. Liebling:** *The Road Back to Paris*, collected articles, 1944
33. **Ernest Hemingway:** Reports on the Spanish Civil War, *The New Republic*, 1937–1938
34. **Martha Gellhorn:** *The Face of War*, collected articles, 1959
35. **James Baldwin:** *The Fire Next Time*, book, 1963
36. **Joseph Mitchell:** *Up in the Old Hotel and Other Stories*, collection of much older articles, 1992
37. **Betty Friedan:** *The Feminine Mystique*, book, 1963
38. **Ralph Nader:** *Unsafe at Any Speed: The Designed-In Dangers of the American Automobile*, book, 1965
39. **Herblock (Herbert Block):** Cartoons on McCarthyism, *The Washington Post*, 1950
40. **James Baldwin:** "Letter from the South: Nobody Knows My Name," *The Partisan Review*, 1959
41. **Nick Ut:** Photograph of a burning girl running from a napalm attack, The Associated Press, 1972
42. **Pauline Kael:** "Trash, Art, and the Movies," *Harper's*, 1969
43. **Gay Talese:** *Fame and Obscurity: Portraits by Gay Talese*, collected articles, 1970
44. **Randy Shilts:** Reports on AIDS, *The San Francisco Chronicle*, 1981–1985

45. **Janet Flanner (Genet):** *Paris Journals* chronicling Paris' emergence from the Occupation, *The New Yorker,* 1944–1945
46. **Neil Sheehan:** *A Bright Shining Lie: John Paul Vann and America in Vietnam,* book, 1988
47. **A. J. Liebling:** *The Wayward Pressman,* collected articles, 1947
48. **Tom Wolfe:** *The Right Stuff,* book, 1979
49. **Murray Kempton:** *America Comes of Middle Age: Columns 1950–1962,* collected articles, 1963
50. **Murray Kempton:** *Part of Our Time: Some Ruins and Monuments of the Thirties,* book, 1955
51. **Donald L. Barlett and James B. Steele:** "America: What Went Wrong?", *The Philadelphia Inquirer,* 1991
52. **Taylor Branch:** *Parting the Waters: America in the King Years, 1954–63,* book, 1988
53. **Harrison Salisbury:** Reporting from the Soviet Union, *The New York Times,* 1949–1954
54. **John McPhee:** *The John McPhee Reader,* collected articles, 1976
55. **ABC:** Live television broadcast of Army-McCarthy hearings, 1954
56. **Frederick Wiseman:** *Titicut Follies,* documentary, 1967
57. **David Remnick:** *Lenin's Tomb: The Last Days of the Soviet Empire,* book, 1993
58. **Richard Ben Cramer:** *What It Takes: The Way to the White House,* book, 1992
59. **Jonathan Schell:** *The Fate of the Earth,* book, 1982
60. **Russell Baker:** "Francs and Beans," *The New York Times,* 1975
61. **Homer Bigart:** Account of being over Japan in a bomber when World War II came to an end, The New York *Herald-Tribune,* 1945
62. **Ben Hecht:** *1,001 Afternoons in Chicago,* collected articles, 1922
63. **Walter Cronkite:** documentary on Vietnam, CBS television, 1968
64. **Walter Lippmann:** Early essays, *The New Republic,* 1914
65. **Margaret Bourke-White:** Photographs following the defeat of Germany, *Life* magazine, 1945
66. **Lillian Ross:** *Reporting,* collected articles, 1964
67. **Nicholas Lemann:** *The Promised Land: The Great Black Migration and How It Changed America,* book, 1991
68. **Joe Rosenthal:** Photograph of Marines raising an American flag on Mount Suribachi on the island of Iwo Jima, The Associated Press, 1945
69. **Hodding Carter Jr.:** "Go for Broke," editorial, Carter's *Delta Democrat-Times* (Greenville, Miss.), 1945
70. **The New Yorker:** *The New Yorker Book of War Pieces,* collected articles, 1947
71. **Meyer Berger:** Report on the murderer Howard Unruh, *The New York Times,* 1949
72. **Norman Mailer:** *The Executioner's Song,* book, 1979
73. **Robert Capa:** Spanish Civil War photos, *Life* magazine, 1936
74. **Susan Sontag:** "Notes on 'Camp'," *The Partisan Review,* 1964
75. **Bob Woodward and Carl Bernstein:** *All the President's Men,* book, 1974
76. **John Hersey:** *Here to Stay,* collected articles, 1963
77. **A. J. Liebling:** *The Earl of Louisiana,* book, 1961
78. **Mike Davis:** *City of Quartz: Excavating the Future in Los Angeles,* book, 1990
79. **Melissa Fay Greene:** *Praying for Sheetrock,* book, 1991
80. **J. Anthony Lukas:** "The Two Worlds of Linda Fitzpatrick," *The New York Times,* 1967
81. **Herbert Bayard Swope:** "Klan Exposed," *The New York World,* 1921
82. **William Allen White:** "To an Anxious Friend," *The Emporia* (Kan.) *Gazette,* 1922
83. **Edward R. Murrow:** Report of the liberation of Buchenwald, CBS radio, 1945
84. **Joseph Mitchell:** *McSorley's Wonderful Saloon,* collected articles, 1943
85. **Lillian Ross:** *Picture,* book, 1952
86. **Earl Brown:** Series of articles on race, *Harper's* and *Life* magazines, 1942–1944
87. **Greil Marcus:** *Mystery Train: Images of America in Rock 'n' Roll Music,* book, 1975
88. **Morley Safer:** Atrocities committed by American soldiers on the hamlet of Cam Ne in Vietnam, CBS television, 1965
89. **Ted Poston:** Coverage of the "Little Scottsboro" trial, *The New York Post,* 1949
90. **Leon Dash:** "Rosa Lee's Story," *The Washington Post,* 1994
91. **Jane Kramer:** *Europeans,* collected articles, 1988
92. **Eddie Adams and Vo Suu:** Associated Press photograph and NBC television footage of a Saigon execution, 1968
93. **Grantland Rice:** "Notre Dame's 'Four Horsemen'," The New York *Herald-Tribune,* 1924
94. **Jane Kramer:** *The Politics of Memory: Looking for Germany in the New Germany,* collected articles, 1996
95. **Frank McCourt:** *Angela's Ashes,* book, 1996
96. **Vincent Sheean:** *Personal History,* book, 1935
97. **W. E. B. Du Bois:** Columns on race during his tenure as editor of *The Crisis,* 1910–1934
98. **Damon Runyon:** Crime reporting, *The New York American,* 1926
99. **Joe McGinniss:** *The Selling of the President 1968,* book, 1969
100. **Hunter S. Thompson:** *Fear and Loathing on the Campaign Trail,* book, 1973

Poets Laureate of the United States

Robert Penn Warren	1986–1987	Mona Van Duyn	1992–1993
Richard Wilbur	1987–1988	Rita Dove	1993–1995
Howard Nemerov	1988–1990	Robert Hass	1995–1997
Mark Strand	1990–1991	Robert Pinsky	1997–2000
Joseph Brodsky	1991–1992	Stanley Kunitz	2000–

NOTE: The post was established in 1985. Appointment is for a one-year term, but is renewable.

Poets Laureate of England

Edmund Spenser	1591–1599	Laurence Eusden	1718–1730	Alfred Austin	1896–1913
Samuel Daniel	1599–1619	Colley Cibber	1730–1757	Robert Bridges	1913–1930
Ben Jonson	1619–1637	William Whitehead	1757–1785	John Masefield	1930–1967
William Davenant	1638–1668	Thomas Warton	1785–1790	Cecil Day-Lewis	1967–1972
John Dryden[1]	1670–1689	Henry James Pye	1790–1813	Sir John Betjeman	1972–1984
Thomas Shadwell	1689–1692	Robert Southey	1813–1843	Ted Hughes	1984–1998
Nahum Tate	1692–1715	William Wordsworth	1843–1850	Andrew Motion	1999–
Nicholas Rowe	1715–1718	Alfred Lord Tennyson	1850–1892		

1. First to bear the title officially.

Longest Broadway Runs

Show	Dates	Performances[1]	Show	Dates	Performances[1]
1. Cats	10/82–present	7,365	14. Beauty and the Beast	4/94–present	2,472
2. A Chorus Line	10/75–4/90	6,137	15. Annie	4/77–1/83	2,377
3. Oh! Calcutta	9/76–8/89	5,962	16. Man of La Mancha	11/65–6/71	2,329
4. Les Misérables	3/87–present	5,447	17. Abie's Irish Rose	5/22–10/27	2,327
5. The Phantom of the Opera	1/88–present	5,150	18. Oklahoma!	3/43–5/48	2,212
			19. Smokey Joe's Cafe	3/95–1/00	2,037
6. Miss Saigon	4/91–present	3,812	20. Pippin	10/72–6/77	1,944
7. 42nd Street	8/80–1/89	3,485	21. South Pacific	4/49–1/54	1,925
8. Grease	2/72–4/80	3,388	22. The Magic Show	5/74–12/78	1,920
9. Fiddler on the Roof	9/64–7/72	3,242	23. Gemini	6/77–9/81	1,819
10. Life with Father	11/39–7/47	3,224	24. Deathtrap	2/78–6/82	1,793
11. Tobacco Road	12/33–5/41	3,182	25. Harvey	11/44–1/49	1,775
12. Hello, Dolly!	1/64–12/70	2,844	26. Dancin'	3/78–6/82	1,774
13. My Fair Lady	3/56–9/62	2,717	27. La Cage Aux Folles	6/83–11/87	1,761

1. As of 5/28/00. *Source:* League of American Theatres and Producers, Inc.

Top 10 Classical Albums, 1999

1. *Aria—The Opera Album,* Andrea Bocelli (Philips/ Universal Classics Group)
2. *Viaggio Italiano,* Andrea Bocelli (Philips/Universal Classics Group)
3. *The 3 Tenors: Paris 1998,* Carreras, Domingo, Pavarotti (Levine) (Atlantic/AG)
4. *The Most Relaxing Classical Album in the World . . . Ever!,* Various Artists (Circa/Virgin/Angel Records)
5. *Simply Baroque,* Yo-Yo Ma (Sony Classical)
6. *Sacred Arias,* Andrea Bocelli (Philips/Universal Classics Group)
7. *Classic Wynton,* Wynton Marsalis (Sony Classical)
8. *Romantic Moments,* Andre Rieu (Philips/Universal Classics Group)
9. *The Mozart Effect—Music for Children, Vol I: Tune Up Your Mind,* Don Campbell (Children's Group/ Atlantic/AG)
10. *The Best Opera Album in the World . . . Ever!,* Various Artists (Circa/Virgin/Angel Records)

Source: © 2000 BPI Communications Inc. Used with permission from *Billboard* ® magazine.

Top 10 Country Singles, 1999

1. "It Don't Matter to the Sun/Lost in You," Garth Brooks as Chris Gaines (Capitol)
2. "Please Remember Me/For a Little While," Tim McGraw (Curb)
3. "I Don't Want to Miss a Thing," Mark Chesnutt (Decca/MCA Nashville)
4. "This Kiss," Faith Hill (Warner Bros./WRN)
5. "Fly (The Angel Song)," The Wilkinsons (Giant/ Warner Bros.)
6. "With You," Lila McCann (Asylum/EEG)
7. "That Don't Impress Me Much," Shania Twain (Mercury)
8. "God Must Have Spent a Little More Time on You," Alabama featuring 'N Sync (RCA/RLG)
9. "Never Been Kissed," Sherrie Austin (Arista Nashville)
10. "Big Deal," LeAnn Rimes (Curb)

Source: © 2000 BPI Communications Inc. Used with permission from *Billboard* ® magazine.

Top 10 Country Albums, 1999

1. *Come On Over,* Shania Twain (Mercury)
2. *Double Live,* Garth Brooks (Capitol)
3. *Wide Open Spaces,* Dixie Chicks (Monument/ Sony)
4. *A Place in the Sun,* Tim McGraw (Curb)
5. *Fly,* Dixie Chicks (Monument/Sony)
6. *Faith,* Faith Hill (Warner Bros.)
7. *I'm Alright,* Jo Dee Messina (Curb)
8. *Lonely Grill,* Lonestar (BNA/RLG)
9. *Hope Floats,* Soundtrack (Capitol)
10. *Always Never the Same,* George Strait (MCA/ Nashville)

Source: © 2000 BPI Communications Inc. Used with permission from *Billboard* ® magazine.

Top 10 Pop Singles, 1999

1. "Believe," Cher (Warner Bros.)
2. "No Scrubs, " TLC (LaFace/Arista)
3. "Angel of Mine," Monica (Arista).
4. "Heartbreak Hotel," Whitney Houston featuring Faith Evans & Kelly Price (Arista)
5. " . . . Baby One More Time," Britney Spears (Jive)
6. "Kiss Me," Sixpence None the Richer (Squint/Columbia)
7. "Genie in a Bottle," Christina Aguilera (RCA)
8. "Every Morning," Sugar Ray (Lava/Atlantic)
9. "Nobody's Supposed to Be Here," Deborah Cox (Arista)
10. "Livin' la Vida Loca," Ricky Martin (C2)

Source: © 2000 BPI Communications Inc. Used with permission from *Billboard* ® magazine.

Top 10 Pop Albums, 1999

1. *Millennium,* Backstreet Boys (Jive)
2. *. . . Baby One More Time,* Britney Spears (Jive)
3. *Come On Over,* Shania Twain (Mercury Nashville)
4. *'N Sync,* 'N Sync (RCA)
5. *Ricky Martin,* Ricky Martin (C2/Columbia/CRG)
6. *Double Live,* Garth Brooks (Capitol Nashville)
7. *Americana,* The Offspring (Columbia/CRG)
8. *Wide Open Spaces,* Dixie Chicks (Monument/Sony Nashville)
9. *Significant Other,* Limp Bizkit (Flip/Interscope)
10. *Fanmail,* TLC (La Face/Arista)

Source: © 2000 BPI Communications Inc. Used with permission from *Billboard* ® magazine.

Top 10 R&B/Hip-Hop Singles, 1999

1. "Nobody's Supposed to Be Here," Deborah Cox (Arista)
2. "Heartbreak Hotel," Whitney Houston featuring Faith Evans & Kelly Price (Arista)
3. "Fortunate," Maxwell (RockLand/Interscope/Columbia)
4. "Bills, Bills, Bills," Destiny's Child (Columbia)
5. "Who Dat," JT Money featuring Sole (Tony Mercedes/Freeworld/Priority)
6. "What's It Gonna Be?!" Busta Rhymes featuring Janet (FlipMode/Elektra/EEG)
7. "If You (Lovin' Me)," Silk (Elektra/EEG)
8. "808," Blaque (Track Masters/Columbia)
9. "Angel of Mine," Monica (Arista)
10. "Chante's Got a Man," Chante Moore (Silas/MCA)

Source: © 2000 BPI Communications Inc. Used with permission from *Billboard* ® magazine.

Top 10 R&B/Hip-Hop Albums, 1999

1. *400 Degreez,* Juvenile (Cash Money/Universal)
2. *Flesh of My Flesh Blood of My Blood,* DMX (Ruff Ryders/IDJMG)
3. *The Miseducation of Lauryn Hill,* Lauryn Hill (Ruffhouse/Columbia/CRG)
4. *R.,* R. Kelly (Jive)
5. *Vol. 2 . . . Hard Knock Life,* Jay-Z (Roc-A-Fella/IDJMG)
6. *Ruff Ryders: Ryde or Die, Vol. 1,* Various Artists (Ruff Ryders/Interscope)
7. *Fanmail,* TLC (LaFace/Arista)
8. *Greatest Hits,* 2Pac (Amaru/Death Row/Interscope)
9. *I Am . . . ,* NAS (Columbia/CRG)
10. *Enter the Dru,* Dru Hill (Def Soul/IDJMG)

Source: © 2000 BPI Communications Inc. Used with permission from *Billboard* ® magazine.

Top 10 Rap Singles, 1999

1. "Who Dat," JT Money featuring Sole (Tony Mercedes/Freeworld/Priority)
2. "What's It Gonna Be?!" Busta Rhymes featuring Janet (FlipMode/Elektra/EEG)
3. "It Ain't My Fault 2/Somebody Like Me," Silkk the Shocker featuring Mystikal (No Limit/Priority)
4. "Ghetto Cowboy," Mo Thugs Family featuring Bone Thugs-N-Harmony (Mo Thugs/Ruthless/Relativity)
5. "No Pigeons," Sporty Thievz featuring Mr. Woods (Roc-A-Blok/Ruffhouse/CRG)
6. "Jamboree," Naughty by Nature featuring Zhane (Arista)
7. "Holla Holla," Ja Rule (Murder Inc./Def Jam/IDJMG)
8. "Watch for the Hook," Cool Breeze featuring OutKast, Goodie Mob & Witchdoctor (Organized Noize/A&M/Interscope)
9. "I Want It All!" Warren G featuring Mack 10 (G-Funk/Restless)
10. "Hard Knock Life (Ghetto Anthem)," Jay-Z (Roc-A-Fella/IDJMG)

Source: © 2000 BPI Communications Inc. Used with permission from *Billboard* ® magazine.

Top 15 Concert Grosses of 1999

Amusement Business annually ranks domestic and international concert grosses and touring acts.

(Headliner, supporting act, dates; gross ticket sales in U.S. dollars; total attendance; venue)

1. **Woodstock '99 (7/22–7/25),** $28,864,745; 186,963; Griffiss Park, Rome, N.Y.
2. **Bruce Springsteen (7/15–8/12),** $19,000,605; 304,785; Continental Airlines Arena, East Rutherford, N.J.
3. **Bruce Springsteen (9/13–9/25),** $7,394,085; 114,922; First Union Center, Philadelphia, Pa.
4. **The Rolling Stones, Sheryl Crow (6/11–6/12),** $7,174,154; 139,962; Wembley Stadium, London, England
5. **The Three Tenors (7/17),** $6,092,944; 31,441; Tiger Stadium, Detroit, Mich.
6. **Bruce Springsteen (8/21–8/27),** $5,469,060; 98,894; FleetCenter, Boston, Mass.

7. **Celine Dion, Andre-Philippe Gagnon (12/7–12/18),** $5,070,308; 142,485; Molson Centre, Montreal, Quebec

8. **Globe (5/18–5/25),** $4,961,250; 81,000; Yoyoghi National Stadium, Tokyo, Japan

9. **Dave Matthews Band, Santana, The Roots (5/20–5/22),** $4,752,350; 133,869; Veterans Stadium, Philadelphia, Pa.

10. **Bee Gees (3/27),** $4,540,917; 56,120; Stadium Australia, Sydney, Australia

11. **The Rolling Stones, Goo Goo Dolls (3/22–3/23),** $4,403,159; 35,049; FleetCenter, Boston, Mass.

12. **Billy Joel (12/5–12/22),** $4,363,051; 114,000; Madison Square Garden, New York, N.Y.

13. **The Rolling Stones, The Corrs (3/15–3/16),** $4,293,584; 37,429; First Union Center, Philadelphia, Pa.

14. **The Rolling Stones, Bryan Adams (2/9–2/11),** $4,095,681; 32,827; Arrowhead Pond, Anaheim, Calif.

15. **The Rolling Stones, The Corrs (3/7–3/8),** $3,980,893; 35,713; MCI Center, Washington, D.C.

Source: © 2000 BPI Communications Inc. Used with permission from *Amusement Business®.*

The Recording Industry Association of America's Diamond Awards
Top-Selling Certified Albums of All Time*

The RIAA certifies recordings that sell 10,000,000 or more copies as diamond. The Diamond Awards were established in March 1999.

26 Million
Their Greatest Hits 1971–1975, Eagles (Elektra)

25 Million
Thriller, Michael Jackson (Epic)

23 Million
The Wall, Pink Floyd (Columbia)

22 Million
Led Zeppelin IV, Led Zeppelin (Swan Song)

20 Million
Greatest Hits Volumes I & II, Billy Joel (Columbia)

18 Million
Rumours, Fleetwood Mac (Warner Bros.)

17 Million
The Beatles, The Beatles (Capitol)
The Bodyguard (Soundtrack), Whitney Houston (Arista)

16 Million
Boston, Boston (Epic)
Back in Black, AC/DC (ATCO)
No Fences, Garth Brooks (Capitol Nashville)
Jagged Little Pill, Alanis Morissette (Maverick)
Cracked Rear View, Hootie & the Blowfish (Atlantic)
Come On Over, Shania Twain (Mercury Nashville)

15 Million
Physical Graffiti, Led Zeppelin (Swan Song)
Born in the U.S.A., Bruce Springsteen (Columbia)
Dark Side of the Moon, Pink Floyd (Capitol)
Appetite for Destruction, Guns 'N Roses (Geffen)
Elton John—Greatest Hits, Elton John (Rocket)
Hotel California, Eagles (Elektra)
Saturday Night Fever (Soundtrack), Bee Gees (Polydor/Atlas)

14 Million
The Beatles/1967–1970, The Beatles (Capitol)
Ropin' the Wind, Garth Brooks (Capitol Nashville)

13 Million
Bruce Springsteen & the E Street Band Live 1975–1985, (Box set), Bruce Springsteen & the E Street Band (Columbia)
The Beatles/1962–1966, The Beatles (Capitol)
Purple Rain (Soundtrack), Prince and the Revolution (Warner Bros.)
Bat Out of Hell, Meat Loaf (Epic)
Whitney Houston, Whitney Houston (Arista)

12 Million
Double Live, Garth Brooks (Capitol Nashville)
Slippery When Wet, Bon Jovi (Mercury)
II, Boyz II Men (Motown)
Kenny Rogers' Greatest Hits, Kenny Rogers (Capitol)
Breathless, Kenny G (Arista)
Hysteria, Def Leppard (Mercury)
Led Zeppelin II, Led Zeppelin (Atlantic)
Metallica, Metallica (Elektra)
Backstreet Boys, Backstreet Boys (Jive)

11 Million
Dirty Dancing (Soundtrack) (RCA)
Greatest Hits, James Taylor (Warner Bros.)
Abbey Road, The Beatles (Capitol)
Sgt. Pepper's Lonely Hearts Club Band, The Beatles (Capitol)
Candle in the Wind 1997/Something about the Way You Look Tonight (Single), Elton John (Rocket)
The Woman in Me, Shania Twain (Mercury Nashville)
CrazySexyCool, TLC (LaFace)
Ten, Pearl Jam (Epic)
Pieces of You, Jewel (Atlantic)
Houses of the Holy, Led Zeppelin (Atlantic)
Millennium, Backstreet Boys (Jive)
. . . Baby One More Time, Britney Spears (Jive)

10 Million
Life after Death, Notorious B.I.G. (Bad Boy/Arista)
Can't Slow Down, Lionel Richie (Motown)
Please Hammer Don't Hurt 'Em, Hammer (Capitol)
Tapestry, Carole King (Ode)
The Joshua Tree, U2 (Island)
The Lion King (Soundtrack) (Walt Disney)
Unplugged, Eric Clapton (Reprise)
Best of the Doobies, Doobie Brothers (Warner Bros.)
Eliminator, ZZ Top (Warner Bros.)
Van Halen, Van Halen (Warner Bros.)
Faith, George Michael (Columbia)
Music Box, Mariah Carey (Columbia)
Falling into You, Celine Dion (550 Music)
Titanic (Soundtrack) (Sony Classical)
Like a Virgin, Madonna (Sire)
The Hits, Garth Brooks (Capitol Nashville)
Daydream, Mariah Carey (Columbia)
Tragic Kingdom, No Doubt (Trauma/Interscope)
1984 (MCMLXXXIV), Van Halen (Warner Bros.)
Dookie, Green Day (Reprise)
Greatest Hits, Journey (Columbia)
Nevermind, Nirvana (DGC)
Legend, Bob Marley & the Wailers (Island)
No Jacket Required, Phil Collins (Atlantic)
Yourself or Someone Like You, Matchbox 20 (Atlantic)
Let's Talk about Love, Celine Dion (550 Music/Epic)
'N Sync, 'N Sync (RCA)

*Through January 2000.

The Country Music Hall of Fame

1961
Jimmie Rodgers
Fred Rose
Hank Williams

1962
Roy Acuff

1963
No candidate received enough votes to qualify for induction.

1964
Tex Ritter

1965
Ernest Tubb

1966
Eddy Arnold
James R. Denny
George D. Hay
Uncle Dave Macon

1967
Red Foley
J. L. Frank
Jim Reeves
Stephen H. Sholes

1968
Bob Wills

1969
Gene Autry
Bill Monroe

1970
Original Carter Family

1971
Arthur Edward Satherley

1972
Jimmie H. Davis

1973
Chet Atkins
Patsy Cline

1974
Owen Bradley
Frank "Pee Wee" King

1975
Minnie Pearl

1976
Paul Cohen
Kitty Wells

1977
Merle Travis

1978
Grandpa Jones

1979
Hubert Long
Hank Snow

1980
Johnny Cash
Connie B. Gay
Original Sons of the Pioneers

1981
Vernon Dalhart
Grant Turner

1982
Lefty Frizzell
Ray Horton
Marty Robbins

1983
Little Jimmy Dickens

1984
Ralph Sylvester Peer
Floyd Tillman

1985
Lester Flatt and Earl Scruggs

1986
Whitey Ford
Wesley H. Rose

1987
Rod Brasfield

1988
Loretta Lynn
Roy Rogers

1989
Jack Stapp
Cliffie Stone
Hank Thompson

1990
Tennessee Ernie Ford

1991
Boudleaux and Felice Bryant

1992
George Jones
Frances Williams Preston

1993
Willie Nelson

1994
Merle Haggard

1995
Roger Miller
Jo Walker-Meador

1996
Patsy Montana
Buck Owens
Ray Price

1997
Cindy Walker
Harlan Howard
Brenda Lee

1998
Tammy Wynette
Elvis Presley
George Morgan

1999
Dolly Parton
Conway Twitty
Johnny Bond

Top 10 Video Sales, 1999

1. *Austin Powers: International Man of Mystery* (New Line Home Video/Warner Home Video)
2. *Tae-Bo Workout* (Tae-Bo Retail/Ventura Distribution)
3. *Armageddon* (Touchstone Home Video/Buena Vista Home Entertainment)
4. *A Bug's Life* (Walt Disney Home Video/Buena Vista Home Entertainment)
5. *Blade* (New Line Home Video/Warner Home Video)
6. *Mulan* (Walt Disney Home Video/Buena Vista Home Entertainment)
7. *The Wedding Singer* (New Line Home Video/Warner Home Video)
8. *'N the Mix with 'N Sync* (BMG Video)
9. *You've Got Mail* (Warner Home Video)
10. *Backstreet Boys: Homecoming—Live in Orlando* (Jive/Zomba Video)

Source: © 2000 BPI Communications Inc. Used with permission from *Billboard* ® magazine.

Top 10 Video Rentals, 1999

1. *Enemy of the State* (Touchstone Home Video/Buena Vista Home Entertainment)
2. *There's Something about Mary* (FoxVideo)
3. *The Truman Show* (Paramount Home Video)
4. *Elizabeth* (USA Home Entertainment)
5. *Ronin* (MGM Home Entertainment/Warner Home Video)
6. *Armageddon* (Touchstone Home Video/Buena Vista Home Entertainment)
7. *Saving Private Ryan* (DreamWorks Home Entertainment)
8. *The Siege* (FoxVideo)
9. *Payback* (Paramount Home Video)
10. *American History X* (New Line Home Video/Warner Home Video)

Source: © 2000 BPI Communications Inc. Used with permission from *Billboard* ® magazine.

Top Television Specials, 1999–2000[1]

Rank	Program name (network) [first telecast]	Rating (% of TV households)	Rank	Program name (network) [first telecast]	Rating (% of TV households)
1.	Academy Awards (ABC) [3/26/00]	29.2%	4.	Who Wants to Be a Millionaire Special (ABC) [3/1/00]	20.7%
2.	Who Wants to Be a Millionaire Special (ABC) [5/3/00]	22.6	5.	Countdown to Oscar 2000 (ABC) [3/26/00]	20.6
3.	Who Wants to Be a Millionaire Special (ABC) [5/1/00]	22.5			

NOTES: Each rating point represents 1,008,000 households using television. Does not include sports telecasts. 1. Through May 24, 2000. *Source:* Nielsen Media Research. © 2000, Nielsen Media Research.

The Rock and Roll Hall of Fame

1986
Chuck Berry
James Brown
Ray Charles
Sam Cooke
Fats Domino
The Everly Brothers
Buddy Holly
Jerry Lee Lewis
Elvis Presley
Little Richard
Nonperformers
Alan Freed
Sam Phillips
Early Influences
Robert Johnson
Jimmie Rodgers
Jimmy Yancey
Lifetime Achievement
John Hammond

1987
The Coasters
Eddie Cochran
Bo Diddley
Aretha Franklin
Marvin Gaye
Bill Haley
B.B. King
Clyde McPhatter
Ricky Nelson
Roy Orbison
Carl Perkins
Smokey Robinson
Joe Turner
Muddy Waters
Jackie Wilson
Nonperformers
Leonard Chess
Ahmet Ertegun
Jerry Leiber and Mike Stoller
Jerry Wexler
Early Influences
Louis Jordan
T-Bone Walker
Hank Williams

1988
The Beach Boys
The Beatles
The Drifters
Bob Dylan
The Supremes
Nonperformer
Berry Gordy, Jr.
Early Influences
Woody Guthrie
Leadbelly
Les Paul

1989
Dion
Otis Redding
The Rolling Stones
The Temptations
Stevie Wonder
Nonperformer
Phil Spector
Early Influences
The Ink Spots
Bessie Smith
The Soul Stirrers

1990
Hank Ballard
Bobby Darin
The Four Seasons
The Four Tops
The Kinks
The Platters
Simon and Garfunkel
The Who
Nonperformers
Gerry Goffin and Carole King
Brian Holland, Eddie Holland, and Lamont Dozier
Early Influences
Louis Armstrong
Charlie Christian
Ma Rainey

1991
LaVern Baker
The Byrds
John Lee Hooker
The Impressions
Wilson Pickett
Jimmy Reed
Ike and Tina Turner
Nonperformers
Dave Bartholomew
Ralph Bass
Early Influence
Howlin' Wolf
Lifetime Achievement
Nesuhi Ertegun

1992
Bobby "Blue" Bland
Booker T. and the MG's
Johnny Cash
Jimi Hendrix Experience
Isley Brothers
Sam and Dave
The Yardbirds
Nonperformers
Leo Fender
Bill Graham
Doc Pomus

Early Influences
Elmore James
Professor Longhair
1993
Ruth Brown
Cream
Creedence Clearwater Revival
The Doors
Etta James
Frankie Lymon and the Teenagers
Van Morrison
Sly and the Family Stone
Nonperformers
Dick Clark
Milt Gabler
Early Influence
Dinah Washington

1994
The Animals
The Band
Duane Eddy
The Grateful Dead
Elton John
John Lennon
Bob Marley
Rod Stewart
Nonperformer
Johnny Otis
Early Influence
Willie Dixon

1995
The Allman Brothers Band
Al Green
Janis Joplin
Led Zeppelin
Martha and the Vandellas
Neil Young
Frank Zappa
Nonperformer
Paul Ackerman
Early Influence
The Orioles

1996
David Bowie
Jefferson Airplane
Little Willie John
Gladys Knight and the Pips
Pink Floyd
The Shirelles
The Velvet Underground
Nonperformer
Tom Donahue
Early Influence
Pete Seeger

1997
The Bee Gees
Buffalo Springfield
Crosby, Stills and Nash
The Jackson Five
Joni Mitchell
Parliament-Funkadelic
The (Young) Rascals
Nonperformer
Syd Nathan
Early Influences
Mahalia Jackson
Bill Monroe

1998
The Eagles
Fleetwood Mac
Mamas and Papas
Lloyd Price
Santana
Gene Vincent
Nonperformer
Allen Toussaint
Early Influence
"Jelly Roll" Morton

1999
Billy Joel
Curtis Mayfield
Paul McCartney
Del Shannon
Dusty Springfield
Bruce Springsteen
The Staple Singers
Nonperformer
George Martin
Early Influences
Charles Brown
Bob Wills and His Texas Playboys

2000
Eric Clapton
Earth, Wind, and Fire
Lovin' Spoonful
The Moonglows
Bonnie Raitt
James Taylor
Nonperformer
Clive Davis
Early Influences
Nat King Cole
Billie Holiday
Side-Men
Hal Blaine
King Curtis
James Jamerson
Scotty Moore
Earl Palmer

Top 15 Syndicated TV Programs, 1999–2000 Season[1]

Rank	Program name[2]	Rating (% of TV households)	Rank	Program name[2]	Rating (% of TV households)
1.	*Wheel of Fortune*	11.1%	9.	*Frasier* (AT)	5.2%
2.	*Jeopardy*	9.2	10.	*Hollywood Squares* (AT)	4.3
3.	*Judge Judy* (AT)	7.2	10.	*Jerry Springer* (AT)	4.3
4.	*Oprah Winfrey Show* (AT)	6.4	12.	*The X-Files* (AT)	4.2
5.	*Entertainment Tonight*	6.2	13.	*Drew Carey* (AT)	4.1
5.	*Friends* (AT)	6.2	13.	*Judge Joe Brown* (AT)	4.1
7.	*Seinfeld*	5.8	15.	*ER* (AT)	4.0
8.	*Wheel of Fortune* (Weekend)	5.3			

NOTES: Each rating point represents 1,008,000 households using television. (AT) = Additional Telecasts. 1. Aug. 30, 1999–May 30, 2000. 2. Programs airing three or less weeks have been excluded from this ranking. *Source:* Nielsen Media Research. © 2000, Nielsen Media Research.

Top 25 Regularly Scheduled Network Programs, 1999–2000[1]

Rank	Program name (network)	Rating (% of TV households)	Rank	Program name (network)	Rating (% of TV households)
1.	Who Wants to Be a Millionaire–Tues. (ABC)	18.6%	12.	Law & Order (NBC)	11.5%
2.	Who Wants to Be a Millionaire–Thu. (ABC)	17.5	13.	Everybody Loves Raymond (CBS)	11.4
3.	Who Wants to Be a Millionaire–Sun. (ABC)	17.1	13.	NFL Monday Showcase (ABC)	11.4
			15.	Jesse (NBC)	11.3
4.	ER (NBC)	16.9	16.	CBS Sunday Movie (CBS)	10.8
5.	Friends (NBC)	14.0	16.	Daddio (NBC)	10.8
6.	NFL Monday Night Football (ABC)	13.7	18.	NYPD Blue (ABC)	10.7
7.	Frasier (NBC)	13.6	18.	Stark Raving Mad (NBC)	10.7
8.	Frasier 9:30 (NBC)	12.4	20.	Dharma & Greg (ABC)	10.5
9.	60 Minutes (CBS)	12.0	21.	Becker (CBS)	10.4
10.	The Practice (ABC)	11.8	22.	Judging Amy (CBS)	10.2
11.	Touched by an Angel (CBS)	11.6	23.	JAG (CBS)	9.7
			24.	Drew Carey Show (ABC)	9.5
			25.	Providence (NBC)	9.4

NOTE: Each rating point represents 1,008,000 households using television. 1. 1999–2000 season through May 24, 2000. *Source:* Nielsen Media Research. © 2000, Nielsen Media Research.

Top 10 Sports Telecasts, 1999–2000[1]

Rank	Program name (network)	Description	Rating (% of TV households)
1.	Super Bowl XXXIV (ABC)	Tennessee vs. St. Louis	43.3%
2.	Fox NFC Championship (Fox)	Tampa Bay at St. Louis	26.9
3.	AFC Championship on CBS (CBS)	Tennessee at Jacksonville	23.2
4.	Fox NFC Championship (Fox)	Tampa Bay at St. Louis	21.4
5.	AFC Divisional Playoff (CBS)	Tennessee at Indianapolis	20.5
6.	Fox NFC Playoff (Fox)	Minnesota at St. Louis	20.4
7.	AFC Wildcard Playoff (CBS)	Miami at Seattle	20.3
8.	Fox NFC Wildcard Game (Fox)	Dallas at Minnesota	19.1
9.	NBC World Series Game 4 (NBC)	Atlanta at N.Y. Yankees	17.8
10.	Sugar Bowl (ABC)	Florida State vs. Virginia Tech	17.5

NOTE: Each rating point represents 1,008,000 households using television. 1. Through May 24, 2000. *Source:* Nielsen Media Research. © 2000, Nielsen Media Research.

Top-Rated TV Movies, 1999–2000[1]

Rank	Episode title (network)	Rating (% of TV households)	Rank	Episode title (network)	Rating (% of TV households)
1.	One Special Night (CBS)	17.5%	8.	Mary and Rhoda (ABC)	13.3%
2.	Beyond the Prairie: The True Story of Laura Ingalls Wilder (CBS)	15.3	9.	Perfect Murder, Perfect Town (CBS)	12.9
			10.	The Soul Collector (CBS)	12.4
3.	A Season for Miracles (CBS)	15.1	11.	The Test of Love (CBS)	12.3
4.	Jesus, Part 1 (CBS)	15.0	11.	Jesus, Part 2 (CBS)	12.3
5.	Annie (ABC)	14.2	13.	The Color of Love: Jacey's Story (CBS)	11.6
5.	Sarah Plain and Tall: Winter's End (CBS)	13.8	14.	Ransom (ABC)	11.5
7.	Sally Hemings: An American Scandal, Part 1 (CBS)	13.4	14.	Take Me Home: The John Denver Story (CBS)	11.5

NOTE: Each rating point represents 1,008,000 households using television. 1. Through May 24, 2000. *Source:* Nielsen Media Research. © 2000, Nielsen Media Research.

Weekly TV Viewing by Age
(in hours and minutes)

	Time per week				Time per week		
	Oct. 1999	Nov. 1998	Nov. 1997		Oct. 1999	Nov. 1998	Nov. 1997
Women 18–24	21 hr. 30 min.	22 hr. 11 min.	25 hr. 22 min.	Female teens 12–17	18 hr. 49 min.	19 hr. 40 min.	19 hr. 60 min.
Women 25–54	30 hr. 35 min.	30 hr. 35 min.	31 hr. 45 min.	Male teens 12–17	20 hr. 28 min.	20 hr. 16 min.	19 hr. 60 min.
Women 55+	41 hr. 20 min.	42 hr. 00 min.	41 hr. 50 min.	Children 2–5	21 hr. 50 min.	23 hr. 01 min.	26 hr. 02 min.
Men 18–24	20 hr. 10 min.	19 hr. 29 min.	20 hr. 30 min.	Children 6–11	18 hr. 18 min.	18 hr. 59 min.	19 hr. 49 min.
Men 25–54	27 hr. 33 min.	27 hr. 53 min.	28 hr. 44 min.				
Men 55+	36 hr. 28 min.	36 hr. 47 min.	36 hr. 17 min.				

Source: Nielsen Media Research. © 2000, Nielsen Media Research.

Television Set Ownership
Estimated total number of TV households: 100,800,000

	1950	1955	1960	1965	1970	1975	1980	1985	1990	1995	2000
% of total households:											
TV households	10	67	87	94	96	97	98	98	98	98	98
% of TV households:											
Multi-set	—	4	12	22	35	43	50	57	65	71	76
Color	—	—	—	7	41	74	83	91	98	99	99
VCR	—	—	—	—	—	—	—	14	66	79	85
Remote control	—	—	—	—	—	—	—	29	77	91	95
Wired pay cable	—	—	—	—	—	—	—	26	29	28	32
Wired cable	—	—	—	—	7	12	20	43	56	63	68

Source: Nielsen Media Research. © 2000, Nielsen Media Research.

Top 100 Daily Newspapers in the United States
By circulation, as of Sept. 30, 1999

Rank	Newspaper	Circulation	Rank	Newspaper	Circulation
1.	*Wall Street Journal* (New York, N.Y.)	1,752,693	51.	*Times* (Seattle)	219,698
2.	*USA Today* (Arlington, Va.)	1,671,539	52.	*Courant* (Hartford, Conn.)	207,511
3.	*Times* (New York, N.Y.)	1,086,293	53.	*Pioneer Press* (St. Paul, Minn.)	204,430
4.	*Times* (Los Angeles)	1,078,186	54.	*Daily Oklahoman* (Oklahoma City)	201,892
5.	*Post* (Washington, D.C.)	763,305	55.	*Daily News* (Los Angeles)	201,435
6.	*Daily News* (New York, N.Y.)	701,831	56.	*Times-Dispatch* (Richmond, Va.)	199,814
7.	*Tribune* (Chicago)	657,690	57.	*Virginian-Pilot* (Norfolk, Va.)	197,502
8.	*Newsday* (Long Island, N.Y.)	574,941	58.	*Enquirer* (Cincinnati)	195,744
9.	*Chronicle* (Houston)	542,414	59.	*Post-Intelligencer* (Seattle)	191,169
10.	*Morning News* (Dallas)	490,249	60.	*Tennessean* (Nashville)	187,618
11.	*Sun-Times* (Chicago)	468,170	61.	*American-Statesman* (Austin, Tex.)	184,825
12.	*Globe* (Boston)	462,850	62.	*Contra Costa Times* (Walnut Creek, Calif.)	182,071
13.	*Chronicle* (San Francisco)	456,742	63.	*Democrat-Gazette* (Little Rock, Ark.)	175,145
14.	*Post* (New York, N.Y.)	438,158	64.	*Democrat and Chronicle* (Rochester, N.Y.)	174,800
15.	*Arizona Republic* (Phoenix)	433,296	65.	*Times-Union* (Jacksonville, Fla.)	173,867
16.	*Star-Ledger* (Newark, N.J.)	407,129	66.	*Palm Beach Post* (W. Palm Beach, Fla.)	171,956
17.	*Inquirer* (Philadelphia)	399,339	67.	*Journal* (Providence, R.I.)	166,888
18.	*Rocky Mountain News* (Denver)	396,114	68.	*Press-Enterprise* (Riverside, Calif.)	165,043
19.	*Plain Dealer* (Cleveland)	386,312	69.	*Commercial Appeal* (Memphis)	163,134
20.	*Union-Tribune* (San Diego)	376,604	70.	*Daily News* (Philadelphia)	162,434
21.	*Post* (Denver)	376,549	71.	*Asbury Park Press* (Neptune, N.J.)	159,705
22.	*Free Press* (Detroit)	365,145	72.	*News & Observer* (Raleigh, N.C.)	159,156
23.	*Register* (Orange County, Calif.)	358,754	73.	*Register* (Des Moines, Iowa)	158,537
24.	*Herald* (Miami)	349,114	74.	*Review-Journal* (Las Vegas)	157,945
25.	*Oregonian* (Portland)	347,538	75.	*Bee* (Fresno, Calif.)	156,466
26.	*Times* (St. Petersburg, Fla.)	336,821	76.	*News* (Birmingham, Ala.)	152,007
27.	*Star Tribune* (Minneapolis)	336,510	77.	*World* (Tulsa, Okla.)	149,292
28.	*Sun* (Baltimore)	314,819	78.	*Journal News* (White Plains, N.Y.)	144,916
29.	*Constitution* (Atlanta)	307,667	79.	*Blade* (Toledo, Ohio)	144,887
30.	*Post-Dispatch* (St. Louis)	303,314	80.	*Daily Herald* (Arlington Heights, Ill.)	143,961
31.	*Bee* (Sacramento, Calif.)	291,007	81.	*Press* (Grand Rapids, Mich.)	141,643
32.	*Journal Sentinel* (Milwaukee)	286,610	82.	*Record* (Bergen County, N.J.)	141,006
33.	*Mercury News* (San Jose, Calif.)	285,848	83.	*Daily News* (Dayton, Ohio)	140,891
34.	*Star* (Kansas City, Mo.)	275,336	84.	*Beacon Journal* (Akron, Ohio)	140,329
35.	*Times-Picayune* (New Orleans)	273,076	85.	*Tribune* (Salt Lake City)	135,018
36.	*Sentinel* (Orlando, Fla.)	259,967	86.	*News Tribune* (Tacoma, Wash.)	127,901
37.	*Investor's Business Daily* (Los Angeles)	258,302	87.	*Morning Call* (Allentown, Pa.)	126,518
38.	*Sun-Sentinel* (Fort Lauderdale, Fla.)	258,118	88.	*News Journal* (Wilmington, Del.)	123,924
39.	*Herald* (Boston)	256,422	89.	*State* (Columbia, S.C.)	118,298
40.	*Dispatch* (Columbus, Ohio)	246,668	90.	*News-Sentinel* (Knoxville, Tenn.)	115,182
41.	*Observer* (Charlotte, N.C.)	243,990	91.	*Spokesman-Review* (Spokane, Wash.)	112,145
42.	*Star* (Indianapolis)	240,309	92.	*Herald-Leader* (Lexington, Ky.)	111,906
43.	*Post-Gazette* (Pittsburgh, Pa.)	239,894	93.	*Journal* (Albuquerque)	110,710
44.	*News* (Detroit)	232,434	94.	*La Opinion* (Los Angeles, Calif.)	107,897
45.	*News* (Buffalo, N.Y.)	230,287	95.	*Herald-Tribune* (Sarasota, Fla.)	107,168
46.	*Courier-Journal* (Louisville, Ky.)	227,117	96.	*Examiner* (San Francisco)	107,129
47.	*Star-Telegram* (Fort Worth, Tex.)	225,737	97.	*Telegram & Gazette* (Worcester, Mass.)	106,748
48.	*Tribune* (Tampa, Fla.)	224,972	98.	*Press-Telegram* (Long Beach, Calif.)	105,710
49.	*World-Herald* (Omaha, Neb.)	222,688	99.	*Post & Courier* (Charleston, S.C.)	105,296
50.	*Express-News* (San Antonio, Tex.)	219,837	100.	*Advertiser* (Honolulu)	101,948

Source: © ASM Communications, Inc.

Top 50 Daily Newspapers in the World by 1999 Circulation

Rank	Newspaper	Circulation	Rank	Newspaper	Circulation
1.	Yomiuri Shimbun (Japan)	10,223,923	26.	Shizuoka Shimbun (Japan)	1,449,329
2.	Asahi Shimbun (Japan)	8,321,138	27.	Sports Nippon (Japan)	1,422,215
3.	Sichuan Ribao (China)	8,000,000	28.	Sankei Sports (Japan)	1,367,734
4.	Bild (Germany)	5,674,400	29.	West Deutche Allgemeine (Germany)	1,313,400
5.	Mainichi Shimbun (Japan)	3,978,617	30.	Yangcheng Wanbao (China)	1,300,000
6.	Sun (England)	3,687,370	31.	Hokkaido Shimbun (Japan)	1,227,615
7.	Chunichi Shimbun (Japan)	3,075,320	32.	China Times (Taiwan)	1,200,000
8.	Nihon Keizai Shimbun (Japan)	2,827,662	33.	Economic Daily (China)	1,200,000
9.	Gongren Ribao (China)	2,500,000	34.	Jang Daily (Pakistan)	1,200,000
10.	Chosun Ilbo (South Korea)	2,369,211	35.	Jang Lahore (Pakistan)	1,200,000
11.	Daily Mail (England)	2,364,315	36.	United Daily News (Taiwan)	1,200,000
12.	Daily Mirror (England)	2,350,737	37.	Akhbar El Yom/Al Akhbar (Egypt)	1,158,000
13.	Dong-A Ilbo (South Korea)	2,150,000	38.	Hochi Shimbun (Japan)	1,109,309
14.	Renmin Ribao (China)	2,150,000	39.	Daily Express (England)	1,086,760
15.	Joong-Ang Ilbo (South Korea)	2,020,000	40.	New York Times (United States)	1,086,293
16.	Hankook Ilbo (South Korea)	2,000,000	41.	Los Angeles Times (United States)	1,078,186
17.	Sankei Shimbun (Japan)	1,977,122	42.	Daily Telegraph (England)	1,043,848
18.	Eleftherotypia (Greece)	1,858,316	43.	Nishi Nippon Shimbun (Japan)	1,039,293
19.	Xin Min Wan Bao (China)	1,800,000	44.	Tokyo Shimbun (Japan)	1,031,405
20.	Wall Street Journal (United States)	1,752,693	45.	Malayala Manorama (India)	1,013,590
21.	Kerala Kaumudi (India)	1,720,000	46.	Jiefangjun Ribao (China)	1,000,000
22.	Wen Hui Bao Daily (China)	1,700,000	47.	Nanfang Ribao (China)	1,000,000
23.	USA Today (United States)	1,671,539	48.	Nongmin Ribao (China)	1,000,000
24.	Rodong Sinmun (North Korea)	1,500,000	49.	Zhongguo Qingnian Ribao (China)	1,000,000
25.	Kyung-Hyang Daily News (South Korea)	1,478,537	50.	Nikkan Sports (Japan)	992,230

Source: © ASM Communications, Inc.

Top 100 Consumer Magazines, 1999

1999		Avg. Circulation[1]	1999		Avg. Circulation[1]
1.	NRTA/AARP Bulletin	20,554,989	39.	Ebony	1,768,222
2.	Modern Maturity	20,419,458	40.	Country Living	1,658,511
3.	Reader's Digest	12,962,369	41.	Men's Health	1,635,630
4.	TV Guide	11,461,612	42.	Teen People	1,604,201
5.	National Geographic Magazine	8,566,453	43.	Life	1,603,950
6.	Better Homes and Gardens	7,605,845	44.	Woman's World	1,582,861
7.	Family Circle	5,002,547	45.	Golf Digest	1,558,834
8.	Good Housekeeping	4,588,161	46.	Popular Science	1,556,148
9.	Ladies' Home Journal	4,512,930	47.	First for Women	1,531,860
10.	McCall's	4,205,992	48.	Entertainment Weekly	1,497,861
11.	Woman's Day	4,177,306	49.	Shape	1,465,455
12.	Time	4,103,799	50.	Cooking Light	1,445,374
13.	People Weekly	3,599,198	51.	Sunset	1,444,729
14.	Sports Illustrated	3,266,553	52.	Maxim	1,408,206
15.	Home & Away	3,231,059	53.	Golf Magazine	1,402,785
16.	Playboy	3,202,087	54.	In Style	1,397,218
17.	Newsweek	3,162,551	55.	Parenting Magazine	1,396,392
18.	Prevention	3,069,520	56.	Car and Driver	1,371,424
19.	Cosmopolitan	2,866,794	57.	Outdoor Life	1,364,267
20.	Westways	2,666,925	58.	Boys' Life	1,307,468
21.	The American Legion Magazine	2,664,745	59.	Motor Trend	1,289,030
22.	Via Magazine	2,551,805	60.	American Rifleman	1,269,795
23.	Southern Living	2,531,365	61.	Popular Mechanics	1,255,348
24.	Redbook	2,525,824	62.	Rolling Stone	1,251,606
25.	Seventeen	2,388,364	63.	Scholastic Parent & Child	1,230,634
26.	Martha Stewart Living	2,308,656	64.	PC Magazine	1,229,562
27.	YM	2,232,638	65.	PC World	1,220,891
28.	Glamour	2,203,773	66.	Consumers Digest	1,200,221
29.	U.S. News & World Report	2,200,651	67.	New Woman	1,187,616
30.	National Enquirer	2,169,404	68.	Endless Vacation	1,171,817
31.	Teen	2,094,532	69.	Bon Appetit	1,171,422
32.	AAA Going Places	2,040,951	70.	Discover	1,156,672
33.	Smithsonian	2,034,878	71.	Health	1,148,391
34.	Money	1,952,013	72.	Sesame Street Magazine	1,146,690
35.	Parents	1,797,064	73.	The Elks Magazine	1,145,609
36.	V.F.W. Magazine	1,795,352	74.	Mademoiselle	1,142,077
37.	Field & Stream	1,782,238	75.	Vogue	1,141,981
38.	Star	1,769,890	76.	FamilyFun	1,140,831

1999	Avg. Circulation[1]	1999	Avg. Circulation[1]
77. *Self*	1,122,947	89. *Fitness*	1,002,664
78. *The Family Handyman*	1,121,366	90. *Us*	1,001,281
79. *Weight Watchers Magazine*	1,116,586	91. *Essence*	1,000,498
80. *Soap Opera Digest*	1,102,940	92. *Travel & Leisure*	997,742
81. *Sport*	1,075,983	93. *American Homestyle & Gardening*	991,736
82. *Vanity Fair*	1,058,528	94. *Penthouse*	966,321
83. *Kiplinger's Personal Finance*	1,051,731	95. *Victoria*	965,516
84. *PC/Computing*	1,037,488	96. *The American Hunter*	955,666
85. *Scouting*	1,031,533	97. *Today's Homeowner*	953,010
86. *Michigan Living*	1,024,554	98. *Jet*	947,213
87. *Country Home*	1,019,320	99. *American Health*	934,128
88. *Home*	1,008,634	100. *Elle*	930,364

1. Figure includes subscriptions and single-copy sales. *Source:* Audit Bureau of Circulations, tabulated by Magazine Publishers of America.

American Film Institute's 50 Greatest Screen Legends

Men
1. Humphrey Bogart
2. Cary Grant
3. James Stewart
4. Marlon Brando
5. Fred Astaire
6. Henry Fonda
7. Clark Gable
8. James Cagney
9. Spencer Tracy
10. Charlie Chaplin
11. Gary Cooper
12. Gregory Peck
13. John Wayne
14. Laurence Olivier
15. Gene Kelly
16. Orson Welles
17. Kirk Douglas
18. James Dean
19. Burt Lancaster
20. The Marx Brothers
21. Buster Keaton
22. Sidney Poitier
23. Robert Mitchum
24. Edward G. Robinson
25. William Holden

Women
1. Katharine Hepburn
2. Bette Davis
3. Audrey Hepburn
4. Ingrid Bergman
5. Greta Garbo
6. Marilyn Monroe
7. Elizabeth Taylor
8. Judy Garland
9. Marlene Dietrich
10. Joan Crawford
11. Barbara Stanwyck
12. Claudette Colbert
13. Grace Kelly
14. Ginger Rogers
15. Mae West
16. Vivien Leigh
17. Lillian Gish
18. Shirley Temple
19. Rita Hayworth
20. Lauren Bacall
21. Sophia Loren
22. Jean Harlow
23. Carole Lombard
24. Mary Pickford
25. Ava Gardner

American Film Institute's Greatest 100 Movies of All Time

1. *Citizen Kane* (1941)
2. *Casablanca* (1942)
3. *The Godfather* (1972)
4. *Gone with the Wind* (1939)
5. *Lawrence of Arabia* (1962)
6. *The Wizard of Oz* (1939)
7. *The Graduate* (1967)
8. *On the Waterfront* (1954)
9. *Schindler's List* (1993)
10. *Singin' in the Rain* (1952)
11. *It's a Wonderful Life* (1946)
12. *Sunset Boulevard* (1950)
13. *The Bridge on the River Kwai* (1957)
14. *Some Like It Hot* (1959)
15. *Star Wars* (1977)
16. *All About Eve* (1950)
17. *The African Queen* (1951)
18. *Psycho* (1960)
19. *Chinatown* (1974)
20. *One Flew Over the Cuckoo's Nest* (1975)
21. *The Grapes of Wrath* (1940)
22. *2001: A Space Odyssey* (1968)
23. *The Maltese Falcon* (1941)
24. *Raging Bull* (1980)
25. *E.T.—the Extra-Terrestrial* (1982)
26. *Dr. Strangelove* (1964)
27. *Bonnie and Clyde* (1967)
28. *Apocalypse Now* (1979)
29. *Mr. Smith Goes to Washington* (1939)
30. *The Treasure of the Sierra Madre* (1948)
31. *Annie Hall* (1977)
32. *The Godfather Part II* (1974)
33. *High Noon* (1952)
34. *To Kill a Mockingbird* (1962)
35. *It Happened One Night* (1934)
36. *Midnight Cowboy* (1969)
37. *The Best Years of Our Lives* (1946)
38. *Double Indemnity* (1944)
39. *Doctor Zhivago* (1965)
40. *North by Northwest* (1959)
41. *West Side Story* (1961)
42. *Rear Window* (1954)
43. *King Kong* (1933)
44. *The Birth of a Nation* (1915)
45. *A Streetcar Named Desire* (1951)
46. *A Clockwork Orange* (1971)
47. *Taxi Driver* (1976)
48. *Jaws* (1975)
49. *Snow White and the Seven Dwarfs* (1937)
50. *Butch Cassidy and the Sundance Kid* (1969)
51. *The Philadelphia Story* (1940)
52. *From Here to Eternity* (1953)
53. *Amadeus* (1984)
54. *All Quiet on the Western Front* (1930)
55. *The Sound of Music* (1965)
56. *M*A*S*H* (1970)
57. *The Third Man* (1949)
58. *Fantasia* (1940)
59. *Rebel without a Cause* (1955)
60. *Raiders of the Lost Ark* (1981)
61. *Vertigo* (1958)
62. *Tootsie* (1982)
63. *Stagecoach* (1939)
64. *Close Encounters of the Third Kind* (1977)
65. *The Silence of the Lambs* (1991)
66. *Network* (1976)
67. *The Manchurian Candidate* (1962)
68. *An American in Paris* (1951)
69. *Shane* (1953)
70. *The French Connection* (1971)
71. *Forrest Gump* (1994)
72. *Ben-Hur* (1959)
73. *Wuthering Heights* (1939)
74. *The Gold Rush* (1925)
75. *Dances with Wolves* (1990)
76. *City Lights* (1931)
77. *American Graffiti* (1973)
78. *Rocky* (1976)
79. *The Deer Hunter* (1978)
80. *The Wild Bunch* (1969)
81. *Modern Times* (1936)
82. *Giant* (1956)
83. *Platoon* (1986)
84. *Fargo* (1996)
85. *Duck Soup* (1933)
86. *Mutiny on the Bounty* (1935)
87. *Frankenstein* (1931)
88. *Easy Rider* (1969)
89. *Patton* (1970)
90. *The Jazz Singer* (1927)
91. *My Fair Lady* (1964)
92. *A Place in the Sun* (1951)
93. *The Apartment* (1960)
94. *GoodFellas* (1990)
95. *Pulp Fiction* (1994)
96. *The Searchers* (1956)
97. *Bringing Up Baby* (1938)
98. *Unforgiven* (1992)
99. *Guess Who's Coming to Dinner* (1967)
100. *Yankee Doodle Dandy* (1942)

Movie Revenues

All-Time Box Office Grosses[1]		Top 25 Movies of 1999[4]	
1. Titanic (1997)[2]	$600,788,188	1. Star Wars: Episode One—The Phantom Menace (Fox)	$430,443,350
2. Star Wars (1977)[2]	460,998,007		
3. Star Wars: Episode One—The Phantom Menace (1999)	431,088,295	2. The Sixth Sense (Buena Vista)	276,386,495
		3. Toy Story 2 (Buena Vista)	208,768,773
4. E.T.—the Extra-Terrestrial (1982)[2]	399,804,539	4. Austin Powers: The Spy Who Shagged Me (New Line)	205,444,716
5. Jurassic Park (1993)	357,067,947		
6. Forrest Gump (1994)[2]	329,694,499	5. The Matrix (Warner Bros.)	171,383,253
7. The Lion King (1994)[2]	312,855,561	6. Tarzan (Buena Vista)	170,904,824
8. Return of the Jedi (1983)[2]	309,153,948	7. Big Daddy (Sony)	163,479,795
9. Independence Day (1996)	306,169,255	8. The Mummy (Universal)	155,270,725
10. The Sixth Sense (1999)	293,501,675	9. Runaway Bride (Paramount)	152,054,428
11. The Empire Strikes Back (1980)[2]	290,266,497	10. The Blair Witch Project (Artisan)	140,530,114
12. Home Alone (1990)	285,761,243	11. The World Is Not Enough (MGM)	117,877,025
13. Jaws (1975)[2]	260,000,000	12. Notting Hill (Universal)	116,089,678
14. Batman (1989)	251,188,924	13. Double Jeopardy (Paramount)	114,032,117
15. Men in Black (1997)	250,690,539	14. Wild Wild West (Warner Bros.)	113,745,408
16. Toy Story 2 (1999)	245,373,675[3]	15. Analyze This (Warner Bros.)	106,694,016
17. Raiders of the Lost Ark (1981)[2]	245,034,358	16. The General's Daughter (Paramount)	102,678,089
18. Twister (1996)	241,708,908	17. American Pie (Universal)	101,736,215
19. Ghostbusters (1984)[2]	238,600,000	18. Inspector Gadget (Buena Vista)	97,403,112
20. Beverly Hills Cop (1984)	234,760,478	19. Sleepy Hollow (Paramount)	92,839,722
21. The Lost World: Jurassic Park (1997)	229,086,679	20. The Haunting (DreamWorks)	91,240,529
22. Mrs. Doubtfire (1993)	219,195,243	21. Entrapment (Fox)	87,704,396
23. Ghost (1990)	217,618,602	22. Pokemon: The First Movie (Warner Bros.)	84,091,099
24. Aladdin (1992)	217,350,219	23. Payback (Paramount)	81,526,121
25. Saving Private Ryan (1998)[2]	216,173,322	24. Stuart Little (Sony)	79,403,127
		25. The Green Mile (Warner Bros.)	76,682,014

1. As of June 4, 2000. 2. Including reissues. 3. Still tracking. 4. As of Jan. 2, 2000. *Source:* Exhibitor Relations Co. Inc.

Miss America Winners

1921	Margaret Gorman, Washington, D.C.	1966	Deborah Irene Bryant, Overland Park, Kan.
1922–23	Mary Campbell, Columbus, Ohio	1967	Jane Anne Jayroe, Laverne, Okla.
1924	Ruth Malcolmson, Philadelphia, Pa.	1968	Debra Dene Barnes, Moran, Kan.
1925	Fay Lamphier, Oakland, Calif.	1969	Judith Anne Ford, Belvidere, Ill.
1926	Norma Smallwood, Tulsa, Okla.	1970	Pamela Anne Eldred, Birmingham, Mich.
1927	Lois Delaner, Joliet, Ill.	1971	Phyllis Ann George, Denton, Texas
1933	Marion Bergeron, West Haven, Conn.	1972	Laurie Lea Schaefer, Columbus, Ohio
1935	Henrietta Leaver, Pittsburgh, Pa.	1973	Terry Anne Meeuwsen, DePere, Wis.
1936	Rose Coyle, Philadelphia, Pa.	1974	Rebecca Ann King, Denver, Colo.
1937	Bette Cooper, Bertrand Island, N.J.	1975	Shirley Cothran, Fort Worth, Texas
1938	Marilyn Meseke, Marion, Ohio	1976	Tawney Elaine Godin, Yonkers, N.Y.
1939	Patricia Donnelly, Detroit, Mich.	1977	Dorothy Kathleen Benham, Edina, Minn.
1940	Frances Marie Burke, Philadelphia, Pa.	1978	Susan Perkins, Columbus, Ohio
1941	Rosemary LaPlanche, Los Angeles, Calif.	1979	Kylene Baker, Galax, Va.
1942	JoCaroll Dennison, Tyler, Texas	1980	Cheryl Prewitt, Ackerman, Miss.
1943	Jean Bartel, Los Angeles, Calif.	1981	Susan Powell, Elk City, Okla.
1944	Venus Ramey, Washington, D.C.	1982	Elizabeth Ward, Russellville, Ark.
1945	Bess Myerson, New York, N.Y.	1983	Debra Maffett, Anaheim, Calif.
1946	Marilyn Buferd, Los Angeles, Calif.	1984	Vanessa Williams, Milwood, N.Y.[1]
1947	Barbara Walker, Memphis, Tenn.	1984	Suzette Charles, Mays Landing, N.J.
1948	BeBe Shopp, Hopkins, Minn.	1985	Sharlene Wells, Salt Lake City, Utah
1949	Jacque Mercer, Litchfield, Ariz.	1986	Susan Akin, Meridian, Miss.
1951	Yolande Betbeze, Mobile, Ala.	1987	Kellye Cash, Memphis, Tenn.
1952	Coleen Kay Hutchins, Salt Lake City, Utah	1988	Kaye Lani Rae Rafko, Monroe, Mich.
1953	Neva Jane Langley, Macon, Ga.	1989	Gretchen Elizabeth Carlson, Anoka, Minn.
1954	Evelyn Margaret Ay, Ephrata, Pa.	1990	Debbye Turner, Mexico, Mo.
1955	Lee Meriwether, San Francisco, Calif.	1991	Marjorie Judith Vincent, Oak Park, Ill.
1956	Sharon Ritchie, Denver, Colo.	1992	Carolyn Suzanne Sapp, Honolulu, Hawaii
1957	Marian McKnight, Manning, S.C.	1993	Leanza Cornett, Jacksonville, Fla.
1958	Marilyn Van Derbur, Denver, Colo.	1994	Kimberly Clarice Aiken, Columbia, S.C.
1959	Mary Ann Mobley, Brandon, Miss.	1995	Heather Whitestone, Birmingham, Ala.
1960	Lynda Lee Mead, Natchez, Miss.	1996	Shawntel Smith, Muldrow, Okla.
1961	Nancy Fleming, Montague, Mich.	1997	Tara Dawn Holland, Overland Park, Kan.
1962	Maria Fletcher, Asheville, N.C.	1998	Katherine Shindle, Evanston, Ill.
1963	Jacquelyn Mayer, Sandusky, Ohio	1999	Nicole Johnson, Roanoke, Va.
1964	Donna Axum, El Dorado, Ark.		
1965	Vonda Kay Van Dyke, Phoenix, Ariz.		1. Resigned July 23, 1984.

Sticking to the Script

Some schools spell out exactly how teachers must teach. And their scores are up

By JODIE MORSE TIME

Ringed by the run-down buildings on Chicago's South Side, Harold Washington Elementary is the picture of a frayed inner-city school. Eighty-five percent of the students live below the poverty level. And a security guard keeps students inside—and intruders out—once the morning bell rings. But enter El-Roy Estes's fourth-grade classroom and you'll see a model of order. As students wearing crisp blue-and-white uniforms file in, Estes studies a three-ring binder to find out what's on tap for this morning, Day 111 of the school year. He begins the class with grammar exercises and then discusses a short story. All the while, Estes consults his lesson plan, which prods him with very specific instructions, from what to put on the board ("Write 'Realistic Fiction' on the chalkboard") to assignments for the class ("Invite students to determine point of view of the story").

Micromanaged Curriculum

Estes takes his cues from Chicago's controversial "structured curriculum," a scripted day-by-day lesson plan given to the city's 27,400 teachers by the board of education. Though the program is voluntary, administrators expect all teachers to draw on it. And they're pushing it on poorly performing teachers and the thousands of rookie teachers and substitutes who flow into the district each year, many of whom are asked to teach subjects for which they were not trained. "As a new teacher, I like it because it does all the brainstorming for you," says Estes.

PROS

■ **Scripts can raise test scores, studies show, especially among poor kids**

■ **They help ground new teachers and those asked to teach outside their specialty**

■ **They ensure that all kids will be exposed to the common skills tested on state exams**

CONS

■ **Teachers contend that the programs curb creativity and spontaneity in the classroom**

■ **Some experts say they teach only rote facts without fostering true learning**

■ **The programs are so costly that some schools find it hard to keep them going**

And proponents point to higher test scores in schools that adopt the scripted method. But critics charge that it saps teachers and students of creativity and spontaneity.

For decades teachers have enjoyed almost complete autonomy over how they get their lessons across. It's not uncommon that if two sixth-grade classes in the same school are doing a unit on, say, the American Revolution, one teacher might focus on Paul Revere's ride and another on the Declaration of Independence. But these days, states and districts are taking steps to keep all teachers on the same page. California, Texas, Virginia, and Massachusetts have adopted specified curriculums. In New York City, the United Federation of Teachers is pouring $2 million into writing a core curriculum for its members. More than 6,000 of America's 88,000 public schools have gone a step further, buying into one of a dozen or so prefab curriculums, known as whole-school reforms, that blueprint everything from textbooks to teacher training.

The appeal of the spell-it-out approach is growing because it seems to impact overall performance. Schools that have used these rigid curriculums have seen spikes in sagging test scores, especially among disadvantaged kids. Parents, anxious about the rising importance of standardized tests, like the guarantee that all students will be exposed to a uniform set of skills. "Teachers don't need creativity," says Diane Ravitch, an education official under President George Bush. "Teachers need to use methods that have proved successful."

Blueprint for Teachers

One promising method is Success for All, a tightly scripted reading program that has spread to 1,551 elementary schools in 48 states. The brainchild of husband-and-wife researchers at Johns Hopkins University in the 1980s, the program aims to get at-risk kids academically up to speed with 90 minutes of daily intensive reading. The founders specify that 80% of a school's teachers must vote to adopt the program by secret ballot. Once they do, Success for All micromanages everything down to telling teachers to write questions for the class on Post-it notes to themselves ("What do you think this word means?"). The specificity allows understaffed schools to use all faculty members, including art teachers and librarians, as teachers and to reduce class sizes.

The drill is exacting. At Anthony Bowen School in Washington, a dervish of a teacher named Nadine Broadus begins a reading lesson by tapping the classroom's "word wall" with a baton. "*Clock. Hiccup. Clapping,*" chirps a staccato chorus of first-graders. Lest she get sidetracked, a kitchen timer cues her to move on after one minute. Broadus, a physical-education teacher for 29 years, had no training in reading instruction prior to Success for All. "I had no background," she laughs. "And with this program, I had no choice." The rigor apparently pays off at test time. In a three-year University of Memphis study of local Success for All schools, scores surged past state averages. At Anthony Bowen School, administrators say the scores of more than 50% of the children have risen.

Henry James, Not Batman

There's considerably more teaching freedom in a program called Core Knowledge. It was fashioned by University of Virginia English professor E. D. Hirsch, Jr., author of the best-seller *Cultural Literacy*, on the premise that there's a canon of facts that all schoolchildren should know. In lieu of precise lesson plans, teachers are told that third-graders, for example, should study the Punic Wars and sixth-graders selections from Shakespeare. "There's been a real diffuseness in curricula," says former education secretary William Bennett, whose book *The Educated Child* lays out a grade-school curriculum based on Core Knowledge. "Kids are reading *Batman* rather than Henry James, and that's got to change."

At P.S. 137 in Brooklyn, N.Y., one of more than 1,000 Core Knowledge schools nationwide, it already has. Student imitations of Van Gogh and Jackson Pollock paintings decorate the hallways. And at neighboring P.S. 165, also a Core Knowledge school, a third-grade class has christened its pet rabbit Leonardo—after Da Vinci, not DiCaprio.

Studies Inconclusive

Scholarly studies of structured-curriculum programs, while encouraging, are by no means conclusive. Richard Venezky, a professor of education at the University of Delaware who conducted a three-year study of Success for All schools in Baltimore, found that though the lessons were developmentally sound and students made some improvement, they still lagged 2.4 years behind the national average in reading, and 25% couldn't read at all. And the programs' high price tags, coupled with administrative turnover at many struggling schools, can make it difficult to sustain them. Core Knowledge can cost as much as $60,000 in the first year and $15,000 for follow-up training.

Some teachers, who resent any challenge to their autonomy, gripe that structured curriculums merely supply rote facts while stifling creativity among teachers and students alike. "The only teaching this does is to make kids cough up answers on command," says Alfie Kohn, author of *The Schools Our Children Deserve*. Adds Linda McNeil, a professor of education at Rice University: "They'll drive out the best teachers and give the weakest a place to hide."

Back in Chicago, Estes carried out Day 111 by the book—but with a few notable exceptions. While his binder called for a bland spelling drill, Estes had the class act out the words. "It does take the first steps for you," he says, "but I still use my creativity to make them want to learn." And, as any good teacher will tell you, there's no script for that. □

International Ranks in Educational Attainment, 1996
(percent who completed secondary and higher education)

Country	Secondary education[1]	Higher education	Country	Secondary education[1]	Higher education
Canada	84.9%	20.1%	Japan[2]	90.6%	22.9%
France	74.3	12.4	United Kingdom	86.6	15.2
Germany	86.4	12.9	**United States**	86.9	26.5
Italy	52.1	8.3			

NOTES: Data applies to population ages 25–34 living in large industrialized countries. 1. Includes individuals who have completed at least secondary education. 2. Data are for 1989. *Source:* National Center for Education Statistics, U.S. Department of Education, *The Condition of Education*, 1999, Indicator 60, page 154.

Percent of Population Enrolled in School,[1] 1998

Age	Total	White, non-Hispanic	Black, non-Hispanic	Hispanic origin	Male	Female
Total, 3 to 34 years	55.8%	55.9%	59.2%	50.4%	55.9%	55.6%
3 and 4 years	52.1	54.0	58.3	39.7	53.3	50.9
5 and 6 years	95.6	96.1	95.3	93.3	95.2	95.9
7 to 9 years	98.8	98.8	98.6	98.8	98.7	98.8
10 to 13 years	99.0	99.2	98.6	99.1	99.0	99.1
14 and 15 years	98.4	98.9	98.8	96.8	98.3	98.5
16 and 17 years	93.9	95.0	92.9	89.1	93.5	94.3
18 and 19 years	62.2	66.6	61.1	40.3	60.1	64.4
20 and 21 years	44.8	49.2	39.9	25.6	42.7	47.2
22 to 24 years	24.9	26.1	20.8	16.3	24.6	25.2
25 to 29 years	11.9	11.5	13.7	8.7	10.9	12.9
30 to 34 years	6.6	6.3	8.8	5.5	5.5	7.7

NOTES: Data are based upon sample surveys of the civilian noninstitutional population. 1. Includes enrollment in any type of graded public, parochial, or other private schools. Includes nursery schools, kindergartens, elementary schools, high schools, colleges, universities, and professional schools. Attendance may be on either a full-time or part-time basis and during the day or night. Enrollments in "special" schools, such as trade schools, business colleges, or correspondence schools, are not included. *Source:* U.S. Dept. of Commerce, Bureau of the Census. From *Digest of Education Statistics 1999*.

Educational Attainment by Race and Hispanic Origin, 1960–1998
(percent of population age 25 and older)

Year	Total[1]	White	Black	Asian and Pacific Islander	Hispanic[2] Total[3]	Mexican	Puerto Rican	Cuban
Completed 4 years of high school or more								
1960	41.1%	43.2%	20.1%	—	—	—	—	—
1965	49.0	51.3	27.2	—	—	—	—	—
1970	52.3	54.5	31.4	—	32.1%	24.2%	23.4%	43.9%
1975	62.5	64.5	42.5	—	37.9	31.0	28.7	51.7
1980	66.5	68.8	51.2	—	44.0	37.6	40.1	55.3
1985	73.9	75.5	59.8	—	47.9	41.9	46.3	51.1
1990	77.6	79.1	66.2	80.4%	50.8	44.1	55.5	63.5
1994	80.9	82.0	72.9	84.8	53.3	46.7	59.4	64.1
1995[4]	81.7	83.0	73.8	—	53.4	46.5	61.3	64.7
1996[4]	81.7	82.8	74.3	83.2	53.1	46.9	60.4	63.8
1997[4]	82.1	83.0	74.9	84.9	54.7	48.6	61.1	65.2
1998[4]	82.8	83.7	76.0	—	55.5	48.3	63.8	67.8
Completed 4 years of college or more								
1960	7.7%	8.1%	3.1%	—	—	—	—	—
1965	9.4	9.9	4.7	—	—	—	—	—
1970	10.7	11.3	4.4	—	4.5%	2.5%	2.2%	11.1%
1975	13.9	14.5	6.4	—	—	—	—	—
1980	16.2	17.1	8.4	—	7.6	4.9	5.6	16.2
1985	19.4	20.0	11.1	—	8.5	5.5	7.0	13.7
1990	21.3	22.0	11.3	39.9%	9.2	5.4	9.7	20.2
1994	22.2	22.9	12.9	41.2	9.1	6.3	9.7	16.2
1995[4]	23.0	24.0	13.2	—	9.3	6.5	10.7	19.4
1996[4]	23.6	24.3	13.6	41.7	9.3	6.5	11.0	18.8
1997[4]	23.9	24.6	13.3	42.2	10.3	7.5	10.7	19.7
1998[4]	24.4	25.0	14.7	—	11.0	7.5	11.9	22.2

NOTES: (—) = not available. 1960, 1970, and 1980 as of April 1 and based on sample data from the censuses of population. Other years as of March and based on the Current Population Survey. 1. Includes other races, not shown separately. 2. Persons of Hispanic origin may be of any race. 3. Includes persons of other Hispanic origin, not shown separately. 4. Beginning 1995, persons who are high school graduates and those with a B.A. degree or higher. *Source:* U.S. Bureau of the Census, *U.S. Census of Population, U.S. Summary, Current Population Reports,* and unpublished data. From *Statistical Abstract of the United States, 1999.*

Educational Attainment by Sex, 1910–1998
(percent of population ages 25 and older)

	Both Sexes			Male			Female		
Year	Less than 5 years of elementary school	High school completion or higher[1]	4 or more years of college[2]	Less than 5 years of elementary school	High school completion or higher	4 or more years of college	Less than 5 years of elementary school	High school completion or higher	4 or more years of college
1910[3]	23.8%	13.5%	2.7%	—	—	—	—	—	—
1920[3]	22.0	16.4	3.3	—	—	—	—	—	—
1930[3]	17.5	19.1	3.9	—	—	—	—	—	—
April 1940	13.7	24.5	4.6	15.1%	22.7%	5.5%	12.4%	26.3%	3.8%
April 1950	11.1	34.3	6.2	12.2	32.6	7.3	10.0	36.0	5.2
April 1960	8.3	41.1	7.7	9.4	39.5	9.7	7.4	42.5	5.8
March 1970	5.3	55.2	11.0	5.9	55.0	14.1	4.7	55.4	8.2
March 1980	3.4	68.6	17.0	3.6	69.2	20.9	3.2	68.1	13.6
March 1985	2.7	73.9	19.4	—	—	—	—	—	—
March 1990	2.5	77.6	21.3	2.7	77.7	24.4	2.2	77.5	18.4
March 1994	1.9	80.9	22.2	2.1	81.1	25.1	1.7	80.8	19.6
March 1995	1.9	81.7	23.0	2.0	81.7	26.0	1.7	81.6	20.2
March 1996	1.8	81.7	23.6	1.9	81.9	26.0	1.7	81.6	21.4
March 1997	1.7	82.1	23.9	1.8	82.0	26.2	1.6	82.2	21.7
March 1998	1.7	82.8	24.4	1.7	82.8	26.5	1.6	82.9	22.4

NOTES: (—) = not available. Data for 1980 and subsequent years are for the noninstitutional population. 1. Data for years prior to 1993 include all persons with at least 4 years of high school. 2. Data for 1993 and later years are for persons with a bachelor's degree or higher. 3. Estimates based on Bureau of the Census retrojection of 1940 Census data on education by age. *Source:* Based on data from the U.S. Department of Commerce, Bureau of the Census, *U.S Census of Population, 1960,* Vol. 1, part 1; *Current Population Reports,* Series P-20 and unpublished data; and *1960 Census Monograph,* "Education of the American Population," by John K. Folger and Charles B. Nam. From U.S. Dept. of Education, *Digest of Education Statistics 1999.*

High School Dropout Rates by Sex, 1960–1998

Year	Total	Male	Female
1960	27.2%	27.8%	26.7%
1970	15.0	14.2	15.7
1980	14.1	15.1	13.1
1985	12.6	13.4	11.8
1990	12.1	12.3	11.8
1992	11.0	11.3	10.7
1993	11.0	11.2	10.9
1994	11.4	12.3	10.6
1995	12.0	12.2	11.7
1996	11.1	11.4	10.9
1997	11.0	11.9	10.1
1998	11.8	13.3	10.3

High School Dropout Rates by Race/Ethnicity, 1960–1998

Year	White	Black	Hispanic
1960	n.a	n.a	n.a.
1970	13.2%	27.9%	n.a.
1980	11.4	19.1	35.2%
1985	10.4	15.2	27.6
1990	9.0	13.2	32.4
1992	7.7	13.7	29.4
1993	7.9	13.6	27.5
1994	7.7	12.6	30.0
1995	8.6	12.1	30.0
1996	7.3	13.0	29.4
1997	7.6	13.4	25.3
1998	7.7	13.8	29.5

NOTE: n.a. = not available. Data apply to persons ages 16–24. Because of changes in data collection procedures, data for 1992–1998 may not be comparable with figures for earlier years. *Source:* U.S. Dept. of Education, National Center for Education Statistics, *Digest of Education Statistics 1999.*

Drugs and Violence on School Property

Type of violence or drug-related behavior	1997			
	Total	White	Black	Hispanic
Carried a weapon[1,2]	8.5%	7.8%	9.2%	10.4%
Male	12.5	12.3	10.7	15.6
Female	3.7	2.1	7.8	4.3
Threatened or injured with a weapon[3]	7.4	6.2	9.9	9.0
Male	10.2	8.2	14.0	12.7
Female	4.0	3.7	5.8	4.6
In a physical fight[3]	14.8	13.3	20.7	19.0
Male	20.0	19.1	24.6	24.7
Female	8.6	5.9	17.0	12.3
Property stolen or deliberately damaged[3]	32.9	32.6	34.0	32.1
Male	36.1	35.7	37.5	33.4
Female	29.0	28.6	30.6	30.6

Type of violence or drug-related behavior	1997			
	Total	White	Black	Hispanic
Cigarette use[1]	14.6%	15.8%	8.8%	11.9%
Male	15.9	16.5	12.4	15.3
Female	13.0	14.9	5.5	7.7
Smokeless tobacco use[4]	5.1	6.5	1.4	3.3
Male	9.0	11.3	2.5	5.8
Female	0.4	0.4	0.4	0.3
Alcohol use[1]	5.6	4.8	5.6	8.2
Male	7.2	6.3	7.3	8.7
Female	3.6	2.9	4.0	7.6
Marijuana use[1]	7.0	5.8	9.1	10.4
Male	9.0	7.3	13.0	14.1
Female	4.6	3.9	5.4	5.9
Offered, sold, or given an illegal drug[3]	31.7	31.0	25.4	41.1
Male	37.4	36.1	34.6	46.8
Female	24.7	24.5	16.7	34.4

NOTES: For American students grades 9–12. 1. On one or more of the 30 days preceding the survey. 2. Such as a gun, knife, or club. 3. One or more times during the 12 months preceding the survey. 4. Used chewing tobacco or snuff during the 30 days preceding the survey. *Source:* U.S. Dept. Health and Human Services, Centers for Disease Control and Prevention. From *Digest of Education Statistics 1999.*

Public Schools with Access to the Internet, 1994–1999

School characteristic	Percent of schools with Internet access					
	1994	1995	1996	1997	1998	1999
Total	35%	50%	65%	78%	89%	95%
Instructional level[1]:						
Elementary	30	46	61	75	88	94
Secondary	49	65	77	89	94	98
Size of enrollment:						
Less than 300	39	39	57	75	87	96
300 to 999	35	52	66	78	89	94
1,000 or more	58	69	80	89	95	96

School characteristic	Percent of schools with Internet access					
	1994	1995	1996	1997	1998	1999
Percent minority enrollment:						
Less than 6%	38%	52%	65%	84%	91%	n.a.
6% to 20%	38	58	72	87	93	n.a.
21% to 49%	38	54	65	73	91	n.a.
50% or more	27	40	56	63	82	n.a.

NOTES: n.a. = not available. Excludes special education, vocational education, and alternative based on sample and subject to sampling error. 1. Data for combined schools are included in the totals and in analyses by other school characteristics but are not shown separately. *Source:* U.S. National Center for Education Statistics, "Internet Access in U.S. Public Schools and Classrooms: 1994–1999, Feb. 2000."

Students with Disabilities

In 1995–1996, 5.6 million children (ages 0 to 21), or about 12% of public school children, were enrolled in special education programs. The number of students participating in federal programs for children with disabilities has increased at a faster rate than total public school enrollment. Between 1977 and 1995, the number of students involved in federal programs for children with disabilities increased 47%, while total public school enrollment decreased by 2%. Most students enrolled in special education programs have specific learning disabilities or language impairments, or have serious emotional disturbances.

	Percent of All Students Served by Federally Supported Programs for Students with Disabilities[1]				
Type of disability	1976–1977	1980–1981	1990–1991	1995–1996	1997–1998
All disabilities	8.33%	10.13%	11.55%	12.43%	12.80%
Specific learning disabilities	1.80	3.58	5.17	5.75	5.91
Speech or language impairments	2.94	2.86	2.39	2.28	2.30
Mental retardation	2.16	2.03	1.30	1.27	1.28
Serious emotional disturbance	0.64	0.85	0.95	0.98	0.98
Hearing impairments	0.20	0.19	0.14	0.15	0.15
Orthopedic impairments	0.20	0.14	0.12	0.14	0.15
Other health impairments	0.32	0.24	0.13	0.30	0.41
Visual impairments	0.09	0.08	0.06	0.06	0.05
Multiple disabilities	—	0.17	0.23	0.21	0.23
Deaf–blindness	—	0.01	(2)	(2)	(2)
Developmental Delay	—	—	—	—	(2)
Autism and others	—	—	—	0.09	0.12
Preschool disabled[3]	(4)	(4)	1.07	1.21	1.22

NOTES: Counts are based on reports from the 50 states and District of Columbia. Increases since 1987–1988 are due in part to legislation enacted in fall 1986, which mandates public school special education services of all handicapped children ages 3 through 5. Because of rounding, details may not add to totals. 1. Based on the enrollment in public schools, kindergarten through 12th grade, including a relatively small number of prekindergarten students. Includes students ages 0 to 21. 2. Less than .005%. 3. Includes preschool children 3–5 years and 0–5 years served under Chapter I of the Elementary and Secondary Education Act and the Individuals with Disabilities Education Act (IDEA). 4. Prior to 1987–1988, these students were included in the counts by handicapping condition. Beginning in 1987–1988, states were no longer required to report preschool handicapped students (0–5 years) by handicapping condition. *Source:* National Center for Education Statistics, U.S. Dept. of Education, *Digest of Education Statistics 1999.*

Median Annual Income by Level of Education, 1989–1998

Sex and year	Total	Less than 9th grade	9th to 12th grade, no diploma[1]	High school graduate[2]	Some college, no degree[3]	Associate degree[4]	Bachelor's degree or higher[5]
Men							
1989	$30,465	$17,555	$21,065	$26,609	$31,308	n.a.	$41,892
1990	30,733	17,394	20,902	26,653	31,734	n.a.	42,671
1991	31,613	17,623	21,402	26,779	31,663	$33,817	45,138
1992	32,057	17,294	21,274	27,280	32,103	33,433	45,802
1993	32,359	16,863	21,752	27,370	32,077	33,690	47,740
1994	33,440	17,532	22,048	28,037	32,279	35,794	49,228
1995	34,551	18,354	22,185	29,510	33,883	35,201	50,481
1996	35,622	17,962	22,717	30,709	34,845	37,131	51,436
1997	36,678	19,291	24,726	31,215	35,945	38,022	53,450
1998	37,906	19,380	23,958	31,477	36,934	40,274	56,524
Women							
1989	$20,570	$12,188	$13,923	$17,528	$21,631	n.a.	$28,799
1990	21,372	12,251	14,429	18,319	22,227	n.a.	30,377
1991	22,043	12,066	14,455	18,836	22,143	$25,000	31,310
1992	23,139	12,958	14,559	19,427	23,157	25,624	32,304
1993	23,629	12,415	15,386	19,963	23,056	25,883	34,307
1994	24,399	12,430	15,133	20,373	23,514	25,940	35,378
1995	24,875	13,577	15,825	20,463	23,997	27,311	35,259
1996	25,808	14,414	16,953	21,175	25,167	28,083	36,461
1997	26,974	14,161	16,697	22,067	26,335	28,812	38,038
1998	27,956	14,467	16,482	22,780	27,420	29,924	39,786

NOTES: n.a. = not available or not applicable. Applies to Americans working year-round, full-time. Data for 1992 and later years are based on 1990 census counts. Due to rounding, numbers may not add to totals. Data in current dollars. 1. Includes 1 to 3 years of high school for 1989 and 1990. 2. Includes 4 years of high school for 1989 and 1990, and equivalency certificates for the other years. 3. Includes 1 to 3 years of college and associate degrees for 1989 and 1990. 4. Not reported separately for 1989 and 1990. 5. Includes 4 or more years of college for 1989 and 1990. *Source:* U.S. Department of Commerce, Bureau of the Census, *Current Population Reports.*

Cost of Higher Education, 1986–1999[1]

Year	All institutions	4-year institutions	2-year institutions	Year	All institutions	4-year institutions	2-year institutions
All Institutions				1996–1997	$ 6,530	$ 7,334	$ 4,404
1986–1987	$ 5,206	$ 5,964	$3,295	1997–1998	6,813	7,673	4,509
1991–1992	7,077	8,238	4,092	1998–1999[2]	7,093	8,018	4,621
1995–1996	8,800	10,330	4,725	**Private Institutions**			
1996–1997	9,206	10,841	4,895	1986–1987	9,676	10,039	6,384
1997–1998	9,588	11,277	5,192	1991–1992	13,892	14,258	9,632
1998–1999[2]	10,007	11,834	5,276	1995–1996	17,208	17,612	11,563
Public Institutions				1996–1997	18,039	18,442	11,954
1986–1987	3,805	4,138	2,989	1997–1998	18,516	19,070	12,921
1991–1992	5,138	5,693	3,623	1998–1999[2]	19,410	19,970	13,252
1995–1996	6,256	7,014	4,217				

1. Average undergraduate tuition fees and room and board. 2. Preliminary data based on fall 1997 enrollment weights. *Source:* National Center for Education Statistics, U.S. Department of Education, *Digest of Education Statistics 1999.*

College and University Endowments, 1998–1999

Top 50, in millions of dollars

Institution	Endowment[1]	Institution	Endowment[1]	Institution	Endowment[1]
Harvard Univ.	$14,535.7	Duke Univ.	$1,759.6	Baylor Coll. of Medicine	$1,029.2
Yale Univ.	7,221.7	Dartmouth Coll.	1,710.6	Grinnell Coll.	1,020.4
Princeton Univ.	6,469.2	Mayo Foundation	1,629.2	Rockefeller Univ.	1,019.7
Stanford Univ.	6,227.0	Univ. of Southern Calif.	1,589.8	New York Univ.	999.8
Massachusetts Inst. of Tech.	4,287.7	Johns Hopkins Univ.	1,520.8	Georgia Inst. of Tech.	974.1
Washington Univ.	3,854.0	Univ. of Minnesota	1,512.8	Williams Coll.	971.3
Columbia Univ.	3,636.6	Case Western Reserve Univ.	1,434.0	Univ. of N.C.–Chapel Hill	925.8
Univ. of Pennsylvania	3,281.3	Univ. of Texas–Austin	1,355.0	St. Louis Univ.	913.1
Texas A&M Univ.	3,102.4	Univ. of Virginia	1,280.6	Boston Coll.	910.9
Northwestern Univ.	3,078.1	California Inst. of Tech.	1,270.0	Swarthmore Coll.	905.7
William Marsh Rice Univ.	2,936.6	Univ. of Calif.–Los Angeles	1,253.7	Univ. of Cincinnati	899.0
Cornell Univ.	2,776.0	Brown Univ.	1,201.2	Wellesley Coll.	887.0
Univ. of Chicago	2,755.3	Purdue Univ.	1,164.1	Smith Coll.	884.8
Univ. of Michigan	2,539.5	Univ. of Rochester	1,114.8	Univ. of Wisconsin–Madison	882.3
Univ. of Notre Dame	2,028.0	Ohio State Univ.	1,086.4	Syracuse Univ.	863.3
Univ. of Calif.–Berkeley	1,866.7	Univ. of Washington	1,034.4	Wake Forest Univ.	857.9
Vanderbilt Univ.	1,796.8			Texas Christian Univ.	834.3

NOTES: List includes only institutions that participated in the 1998–1999 Voluntary Support of Education Survey. State systems that submitted combined endowments above the current cut-off are not included. 1. Endowment is market value at fiscal year-end 1999. *Source:* 1998–1999 Voluntary Support of Education Survey. Council for Aid to Education, an independent subsidiary of RAND.

Top 50 Colleges for Black Students

Based on responses from more than 1,000 African-American professionals in higher education, *Black Enterprise* magazine has ranked the top 50 colleges and universities where African-American students are most likely to succeed. The ranking considers factors such as black population (at least 1.5%), academic strengths, social environment, and graduation rates. (Web: www.blackenterprise.com)

Ranking	Name, location	Internet address	1996–1997 Student population	(% black)
1	Spelman College, Atlanta, Ga.	www.spelman.edu	1,961	95%
2	Morehouse College, Atlanta, Ga.	www.morehouse.edu	2,889	99
3	Florida A&M University, Tallahassee, Fla.	www.famu.edu	10,306	88
4	Clark Atlanta University, Atlanta, Ga.	www.cau.edu	5,311	96
5	Howard University, Washington, D.C.	www.howard.edu	10,332	91
6	Xavier University, New Orleans, La.	www.xula.edu	3,463	90
7	Hampton University, Hampton, Va.	www.hamptonu.edu	6,035	84
8	Tuskegee University, Tuskegee, Ala.	www.tusk.edu	3,100	92
9	North Carolina A&T Univ., Greensboro, N.C.	www.ncat.edu	7,947	87
10	Stanford University, Palo Alto, Calif.	www.stanford.edu	16,003	5
11	Georgetown University, Washington, D.C.	www.georgetown.edu	12,618	6
12	Oberlin College, Oberlin, Ohio	www.oberlin.edu	2,892	8
13	Swarthmore College, Swarthmore, Pa.	www.swarthmore.edu	1,353	6
14	Vassar College, Poughkeepsie, N.Y.	www.vassar.edu	2,346	6
15	Columbia University, New York, N.Y.	www.columbia.edu	19,302	6

Ranking	Name, location	Internet address	1996–1997 Student population	(% black)
16	Emory University, Atlanta, Ga.	www.emory.edu	11,308	12%
17	Amherst College, Amherst, Mass.	www.amherst.edu	1,623	7
18	Johnson C. Smith University, Charlotte, N.C.	www.jcsu.edu	1,398	99
19	University of North Carolina, Chapel Hill, N.C.	www.unc.edu	24,439	9
20	Duke University, Durham, N.C.	www.duke.edu	11,512	7
21	Morgan State University, Baltimore, Md.	www.morgan.edu	6,016	94
22	Wesleyan University, Middletown, Conn.	www.wesleyan.edu	3,244	7
23	Fisk University, Nashville, Tenn.	www.fisk.edu	879	99
24	Tennessee State University, Nashville, Tenn.	www.tnstate.edu	8,464	65
25	Bryn Mawr College, Bryn Mawr, Pa.	www.brynmawr.edu	1,821	5
26	Florida State University, Tallahassee, Fla.	www.fsu.edu	30,155	10
27	Bethune-Cookman College, Daytona Beach, Fla.	www.bethune.cookman.edu	2,402	93
28	Harvard University, Cambridge, Mass.	www.harvard.edu	24,687	6
29	Johns Hopkins University, Baltimore, Md.	www.jhu.edu	15,765	7
30	Univ. of Southern California, Los Angeles, Calif.	www.usc.edu	27,971	6
31	North Carolina Central Univ., Durham, N.C.	www.nccu.edu	5,555	83
32	Morris Brown College, Atlanta, Ga.	www.morrisbrown.edu	2,065	96
33	Southern University, Baton Rouge, La.	www.subr.edu	10,359	93
34	University of Pennsylvania, Philadelphia, Pa.	www.upenn.edu	22,148	6
35	Williams College, Williamstown, Mass.	www.williams.edu	2,055	6
36	George Washington University, Washington, D.C.	www.gwu.edu	19,670	8
37	Dillard University, New Orleans, La.	www.dillard.edu	1,562	98
38	Jackson State University, Jackson, Miss.	www.jsums.edu	6,313	94
39	Grambling State University, Grambling, La.	www.gram.edu	6,800	95
40	Wellesley College, Wellesley, Mass.	www.wellesley.edu	2,257	6
41	Yale University, New Haven, Conn.	www.yale.edu	10,893	6
42	Univ. of California Los Angeles, Los Angeles, Calif.	www.ucla.edu	34,713	6
43	New York University, New York, N.Y.	www.nyu.edu	35,835	7
44	Smith College, Northampton, Mass.	www.smith.edu	3,189	4
45	Mass. Institute of Technology, Cambridge, Mass.	www.mit.edu	9,960	4
46	Mount Holyoke College, South Hadley, Mass.	www.mtholyoke.edu	1,896	4
47	Lincoln University, Lincoln University, Pa.	www.lincoln.edu	1,553	92
48	South Carolina State University, Orangeburg, S.C.	www.scsu.edu	4,993	92
49	Alabama A&M University, Normal, Ala.	www.aamu.edu	5,400	76
50	Cornell University, Ithaca, N.Y.	www.cornell.edu	11,865	4

Accredited U.S. Senior Colleges and Universities

Source: The Princeton Review's Complete Book of Accredited Colleges, 2001 Edition.

Schools are listed alphabetically within each state and are accredited four-year institutions offering at least a bachelor's degree. Tuition and room and board listed are average annual figures (including fees) subject to fluctuation, usually covering two semesters, two out of three trimesters, or three out of four quarters, depending on the school calendar.

Note that some schools include room and board expenses within the tuition figures rather than reporting them separately. List includes only schools for which data was provided. For further information, write to the registrar of the school concerned.

(Pr) = private; (Pu) = public.

Institution name; city, state (type)	Students	Percent Accepted	Women	Tuition In-state	Out-of-state	Room and board
ALABAMA						
Alabama A&M University; Normal, Ala. (Pu)	3,903	66%	43%			
Alabama State University; Montgomery, Ala. (Pu)	4,683	12	56		$ 5,040	$3,700
Athens State University; Athens, Ala. (Pu)	1,271			$ 1,656	3,312	4,800
Auburn University; Auburn, Ala. (Pu)	18,669	88	48	2,895	8,685	
Auburn University-Montgomery; Montgomery, Ala. (Pu)	4,539	99	62	2,577	7,731	5,034
Birmingham-Southern College; Birmingham, Ala. (Pr)	1,447	96	59	14,450	14,450	5,365
Faulkner University; Montgomery, Ala. (Pr)	1,892	81	60	7,800	7,800	3,950
Huntingdon College; Montgomery, Ala. (Pr)	705	78	62	11,000	11,000	5,500
Jacksonville State University; Jacksonville, Ala. (Pu)	6,640	89	57	2,440	4,880	3,100
Judson College; Marion, Ala. (Pr)	322	81	97	7,100	7,100	4,430
Miles College; Birmingham, Ala. (Pr)	1,453		57	4,280	4,280	2,950
Oakwood College; Huntsville, Ala. (Pr)	1,666					3,999
Samford University; Birmingham, Ala. (Pr)	2,855	88	62	10,300	10,300	4,560
Southern Christian University; Montgomery, Ala. (Pr)	97		22	7,200	7,200	
Spring Hill College; Mobile, Ala. (Pr)	1,212	89	61	15,254	15,254	5,768

Institution name; city, state (type)	Students	Percent Accepted	Women	Tuition In-state	Out-of-state	Room and board
Stillman College; Tuscaloosa, Ala. (Pr)	913					$3,100
Talladega College; Talladega, Ala. (Pr)						
Troy State University; Troy, Ala. (Pu)	4,695	74%	60%	$ 2,660	$ 5,320	3,854
Troy State University Dothan; Dothan, Ala. (Pu)	1,552		63	2,760	5,520	
Troy State University Montgomery; Montgomery, Ala. (Pu)	2,799		62	1,980	3,960	
Tuskegee University; Tuskegee, Ala. (Pr)	2,616	66	59	9,500	9,500	5,100
University of Alabama-Birmingham; Birmingham, Ala. (Pu)	10,420	89	58	2,730	5,460	6,471
University of Alabama-Huntsville; Huntsville, Ala. (Pu)	5,513	92	50	3,112	6,516	3,780
University of Alabama-Tuscaloosa; Tuscaloosa, Ala. (Pu)	14,403	94	52	2,684	7,216	3,810
University of Mobile; Mobile, Ala. (Pr)	1,772	98	70	7,710	7,710	4,280
University of Montevallo; Montevallo, Ala. (Pu)	2,678	83	68	3,040	6,080	
University of North Alabama; Florence, Ala. (Pu)	5,099		59	2,232	4,464	3,352
University of South Alabama; Mobile, Ala. (Pu)	9,360	94	57	2,475	4,950	2,883
University of West Alabama; Livingston, Ala. (Pu)	1,838			2,280	4,560	2,460
ALASKA						
Alaska Pacific University; Anchorage, Alaska (Pr)	385	80	61	13,200	13,200	5,000
Sheldon Jackson College; Sitka, Alaska (Pr)	235	50	56	7,250	7,250	5,150
University of Alaska-Anchorage; Anchorage, Alaska (Pu)	14,475		62	2,016	3,006	5,480
University of Alaska-Fairbanks; Fairbanks, Alaska (Pu)	6,028	82	59	2,460	7,380	4,150
University of Alaska-Southeast; Juneau, Alaska (Pu)	2,782			2,168	6,428	7,650
ARIZONA						
Al Collins Graphic Design School; Tempe, Ariz. (Pr)						
Arizona State University; Tempe, Ariz. (Pu)	33,948	80	53	2,188	9,340	5,010
Arizona State University East; Tempe, Ariz. (Pu)	1,105	81	35	2,188	9,340	2,440
Arizona State University West; Phoenix, Ariz. (Pu)	3,737	92	69	2,118	9,340	
DeVry Institute of Technology; Phoenix, Ariz. (Pr)	3,706		24	7,778	7,778	
Embry Riddle Aeronautical University; Prescott, Ariz. (Pr)	1,592	80	16	10,700	10,700	4,426
Grand Canyon University; Phoenix, Ariz. (Pr)	1,594	76	66	7,680	7,680	4,246
Metropolitan College of Court Reporting; Phoenix, Ariz. (Pr)	132	65		5,940	5,940	
Northern Arizona University; Flagstaff, Ariz. (Pu)	13,947	82	58	2,188	8,304	3,802
Prescott College; Prescott, Ariz. (Pr)	718			11,500	11,500	4,706
Southwestern College; Phoenix, Ariz. (Pr)	258	78	47	8,000	8,000	3,200
University of Arizona; Tucson, Ariz. (Pu)	26,258	84	53	2,188	9,340	5,548
Western International University; Phoenix, Ariz. (Pr)	820					
ARKANSAS						
Arkansas Baptist College; Little Rock, Ark. (Pr)	157	100	60	2,200	2,200	3,000
Arkansas State University; Jonesboro, Ark. (Pu)	9,398	76	58	2,352	6,024	3,020
Arkansas Tech University; Russellville, Ark. (Pu)	4,576	59	52	2,352	4,704	3,222
Central Baptist College; Conway, Ark. (Pr)	321	84	45	5,424	5,424	3,634
Harding University; Searcy, Ark. (Pr)	3,752	80	55	7,955	7,955	4,250
Henderson State University; Arkadelphia, Ark. (Pu)	3,114	93	56	2,280	4,560	2,976
Hendrix College; Conway, Ark. (Pr)	1,143	88	54	11,440	11,440	4,415
John Brown University; Siloam Springs, Ark. (Pr)	1,522	54	54	11,022	11,022	4,478
Lyon College; Batesville, Ark. (Pr)	462	81	58	10,580	10,580	4,930
Philander Smith College; Little Rock, Ark. (Pr)	918	55	64	3,360	3,360	2,746
Southern Arkansas University-Magnolia; Magnolia, Ark. (Pu)	2,602	92	57	2,112	3,240	2,800
University of Arkansas; Fayetteville, Ark. (Pu)	12,240	88	49	1,400	3,892	4,453
University of Arkansas-Little Rock; Little Rock, Ark. (Pu)	8,559			1,131	2,916	2,435
University of Arkansas-Monticello; Monticello, Ark. (Pu)	2,200			2,040	4,248	2,930
University of Arkansas-Pine Bluff; Pine Bluff, Ark. (Pu)	3,425			1,680	3,888	3,470
University of Central Arkansas; Conway, Ark. (Pu)	7,914	75	61	1,494	2,742	2,920
University of the Ozarks; Clarksville, Ark. (Pr)	573			8,830	8,830	4,080
CALIFORNIA						
Academy of Art College; San Francisco, Calif. (Pr)	5,008	65	42	12,000	12,000	8,958
American Academy of Dramatic Arts - West; Hollywood, Calif. (Pr)	104	79	53	11,700	11,700	
Art Center College of Design; Pasadena, Calif. (Pr)	1,345	65		18,890	18,890	
Art Institutes International at San Francisco; San Francisco, Calif. (Pr)	79	100	51	32,000	32,000	5,060
Azusa Pacific University; Azusa, Calif. (Pr)	3,092	80	63	14,630	14,630	4,880
Bethany College; Scotts Valley, Calif. (Pr)						4,190
Biola University; La Mirada, Calif. (Pr)	2,564	92	63	16,630	16,630	5,272
Bishop's University; Quebec, Calif. (Pu)	2,457	83	56	1,668	3,438	5,400
California Baptist University; Riverside, Calif. (Pr)	1,618	80	60	10,062	10,062	4,966
California College for Health Sciences; National City, Calif. (Pr)	4,517			3,000	3,000	
California College of Arts and Crafts; San Francisco, Calif. (Pr)	1,063	73	60	18,188	18,188	5,858
California Institute of Technology; Pasadena, Calif. (Pr)	907	18		19,743	19,743	6,180
California Institute of the Arts; Valencia, Calif. (Pr)	804	40	44	19,750	19,750	5,500
California Lutheran University; Thousand Oaks, Calif. (Pr)	1,751	78	55	16,020	16,020	6,240
California Maritime Academy of California State University; Vallejo, Calif. (Pu)	1,000	70	50	1,506	7,380	5,801
California Polytechnic State University; San Luis Obispo, Calif. (Pu)	15,503	42	44		5,904	5,553
California State Polytechnic University-Pomona; Pomona, Calif. (Pu)	16,086	71	43		7,872	6,278
California State University-Bakersfield; Bakersfield, Calif. (Pu)	4,309		62	1,506	7,380	5,801

Institution name; city, state (type)	Students	Percent Accepted	Percent Women	Tuition In-state	Tuition Out-of-state	Room and board
California State University-Chico; Chico, Calif. (Pu)	13,397	80%	54%	$ 1,428	$ 8,808	$5,860
California State University-Dominguez Hills; Carson, Calif. (Pu)	4,809	74	67	1,506	7,380	5,801
California State University-Fresno; Fresno, Calif. (Pu)	14,767	68	56	1,746	9,126	6,288
California State University-Fullerton; Fullerton, Calif. (Pu)	21,279	73	57		7,380	3,747
California State University-Hayward; Hayward, Calif. (Pu)	9,364	57	64	1,428	8,808	6,910
California State University-Long Beach; Long Beach, Calif. (Pu)	24,109	81	58		7,380	5,400
California State University-Los Angeles; Los Angeles, Calif. (Pu)	13,935		60	1,506	7,380	5,801
California State University-Northridge; Northridge, Calif. (Pu)	20,955	78	57	1,506	7,874	5,801
California State University-Sacramento; Sacramento, Calif. (Pu)	19,343	41	56	1,428	8,808	5,510
California State University-San Bernardino; San Bernardino, Calif. (Pu)	11,007			1,506	7,380	5,801
California State University-San Marcos; San Marcos, Calif. (Pu)	4,103	65	65		7,616	
California State University-Stanislaus; Turlock, Calif. (Pu)	5,048	73	64	1,799	9,179	5,769
Chapman University; Orange, Calif. (Pr)	2,594	58	56	20,724	20,724	7,928
Claremont McKenna College; Claremont, Calif. (Pr)	1,024	28		20,600	20,600	7,060
Cogswell Polytechnical College; Sunnyvale, Calif. (Pr)	500	85	13	7,800	7,800	
College of Notre Dame; Belmont, Calif. (Pr)	813		65	14,976	14,976	6,400
Columbia College-Hollywood; Tarzana, Calif. (Pr)	144	88		10,500	10,500	
Concordia University Irvine; Irvine, Calif. (Pr)	1,083	79	67	15,700	15,700	5,550
DeVry Institute of Technology-Fremont; Fremont, Calif. (Pr)	1,417		24	8,776	8,776	
DeVry Institute of Technology-Long Beach; Long Beach, Calif. (Pr)	2,627		28	7,778	7,778	
DeVry Institute of Technology-Pomona; Pomona, Calif. (Pr)	3,499		27	7,778	7,778	
DeVry Institute of Technology-West Hills; West Hills, Calif. (Pr)	366		22	7,778	7,778	
Dominican College of San Rafael; San Rafael, Calif. (Pr)	984	88	81	17,256	17,256	8,440
Emmanuel Bible College; Pasadena, Calif. (Pr)	24	74	25	4,800	4,800	
Fresno Pacific University; Fresno, Calif. (Pr)	816			12,480	12,480	4,950
Golden Gate University; San Francisco, Calif. (Pr)	1,302		58	8,592	8,592	
Harvey Mudd College; Claremont, Calif. (Pr)	703	33	27	21,584	21,584	8,017
Humboldt State University; Arcata, Calif. (Pu)	6,570	80	54		5,904	5,845
Humphreys College; Stockton, Calif. (Pr)	363	81	84	6,552	6,552	3,441
John F. Kennedy University; Orinda, Calif. (Pr)	318		80	8,172	8,172	
LIFE Bible College; San Dimas, Calif. (Pr)	496	94	53	5,550	5,550	3,200
Loyola Marymount University; Los Angeles, Calif. (Pr)	4,727		57	19,100	19,100	7,608
Master's College; Santa Clarita, Calif. (Pr)	1,037	82	52	14,100	14,100	5,800
Menlo College; Atherton, Calif. (Pr)	626	79	45	17,700	17,700	6,800
Mills College; Oakland, Calif. (Pr)	727	78		17,250	17,250	7,296
Monterey Institute of International Studies; Monterey, Calif. (Pr)	20			19,500	19,500	
Mount Saint Mary's College; Los Angeles, Calif. (Pr)	1,753	74	94	16,776	16,776	6,634
New College of California; San Francisco, Calif. (Pr)	1,402		57	8,200	8,200	
Newschool of Architecture; San Diego, Calif. (Pr)				12,600	12,600	
Occidental College; Los Angeles, Calif. (Pr)	1,570	60	56	23,532	23,532	6,880
Otis College of Art & Design; Los Angeles, Calif. (Pr)	811	68	60	18,894	18,894	
Pacific Oaks College; Pasadena, Calif. (Pr)	253		94	12,000	12,000	
Pacific Union College; Angwin, Calif. (Pr)	1,623	44	55	14,985	14,985	4,530
Pepperdine University; Malibu, Calif. (Pr)	3,230	35	60	23,000	23,000	7,010
Pitzer College; Claremont, Calif. (Pr)	930	64	64	20,880	20,880	6,214
Point Loma Nazarene University; San Diego, Calif. (Pr)	2,350	78	61	13,186	13,186	5,480
Pomona College; Claremont, Calif. (Pr)	1,450	32	48	22,940	22,940	7,750
Saint Mary's College; Moraga, Calif. (Pr)	2,863	85	61	18,120	18,120	7,560
San Diego State University; San Diego, Calif. (Pu)	25,773	77	56	1,506	8,886	7,110
San Francisco Art Institute; San Francisco, Calif. (Pr)	522	69	52	19,300	19,300	
San Francisco Conservatory of Music; San Francisco, Calif. (Pr)	158		52	18,400	18,400	
San Francisco State University; San Francisco, Calif. (Pu)	21,044	69	59	1,904	7,802	6,720
San Jose State University; San Jose, Calif. (Pu)	20,681	75	52		7,843	6,248
Santa Clara University; Santa Clara, Calif. (Pr)	4,477	70	54	18,786	18,786	7,644
Scripps College; Claremont, Calif. (Pr)	773	70		21,000	21,000	7,870
Shasta Bible College; Redding, Calif. (Pr)	212	100	63	5,300	5,300	
Simpson College and Graduate School; Redding, Calif. (Pr)	971	55	64	8,200	8,200	4,100
Sonoma State University; Rohnert Park, Calif. (Pu)	5,845	80	65		7,878	6,217
Stanford University; Stanford, Calif. (Pr)	7,784	15	51	24,441	24,441	8,030
Thomas Aquinas College; Santa Paula, Calif. (Pr)	267	85		14,900	14,900	4,300
United States International University; San Diego, Calif. (Pr)	401	59	54	12,015	12,015	5,040
University of California-Berkeley; Berkeley, Calif. (Pu)	22,261	28	50		9,384	8,122
University of California-Davis; Davis, Calif. (Pu)	19,403	66	55		13,596	5,946
University of California-Irvine; Irvine, Calif. (Pu)	14,336	63	53		9,384	5,953
University of California-Los Angeles; Los Angeles, Calif. (Pu)	24,668	29	55			7,692
University of California-Riverside; Riverside, Calif. (Pu)	10,120	84	54		9,804	6,579
University of California-San Diego; La Jolla, Calif. (Pu)	15,840	41	51	3,848	13,652	7,134
University of California-Santa Barbara; Santa Barbara, Calif. (Pu)	17,699	53	54		10,174	7,156
University of California-Santa Cruz; Santa Cruz, Calif. (Pu)	9,960	79	59	4,359	13,933	6,900
University of Judaism; Bel Air, Calif. (Pr)	105	91		14,500	14,500	7,664
University of LaVerne; La Verne, Calif. (Pr)	1,300	75	59	16,800	16,800	5,650
University of Redlands; Redlands, Calif. (Pr)	1,669	80	56	20,260	20,260	7,590
University of San Diego; San Diego, Calif. (Pr)	2,537	63	57	17,780	17,780	7,920
University of San Francisco; San Francisco, Calif. (Pr)	4,572	80	62	18,860	18,860	8,242

Institution name; city, state (type)	Students	Percent Accepted	Percent Women	Tuition In-state	Tuition Out-of-state	Room and board
University of Southern California; Los Angeles, Calif. (Pr)	15,552	45%	49%	$20,962	$20,962	$6,834
University of the Pacific; Stockton, Calif. (Pr)	2,944	82	58	20,350	20,350	6,378
University of West Los Angeles; Inglewood, Calif. (Pr)	71		76	210	210	
Vanguard University of Southern California; Costa Mesa, Calif. (Pr)	1,289	90	62	13,310	13,310	5,120
Westmont College; Santa Barbara, Calif. (Pr)	1,323	71		20,378	20,378	7,068
Whittier College; Whittier, Calif. (Pr)	1,291	92	57	19,828	19,828	6,736
Woodbury University; Burbank, Calif. (Pr)	1,035	93	54	17,540	17,540	5,790
COLORADO						
Adams State College; Alamosa, Colo. (Pu)	2,025	85	58	1,532	5,748	5,320
Art Institute of Colorado; Denver, Colo. (Pr)	1,977	99	43	12,480	12,480	6,000
Colorado Christian University; Lakewood, Colo. (Pr)	1,786	74	56	9,960	9,960	5,160
Colorado College; Colorado Springs, Colo. (Pr)	1,941	55	55	21,822	21,822	5,568
Colorado School of Mines; Golden, Colo. (Pu)	2,463	76	24	4,620	15,300	4,920
Colorado State University; Fort Collins, Colo. (Pu)	20,667	77	52	2,340	10,026	5,142
Fort Lewis College; Durango, Colo. (Pu)	4,357	91	48	1,676	8,128	4,514
Jones International University; Englewood, Colo. (Pr)	22	100		600	600	
Mesa State College; Grand Junction, Colo. (Pu)	4,926	94	56	1,576	5,966	5,048
Metropolitan State College of Denver; Denver, Colo. (Pu)	17,916	86	57	1,976	7,062	7,320
Regis University; Denver, Colo. (Pr)	1,022	84		15,600	15,600	6,200
United States Air Force Academy; Colorado Springs, Colo. (Pu)	4,161	20		0	0	0
University of Colorado-Boulder; Boulder, Colo. (Pu)	22,660	85	48	2,444	15,224	5,202
University of Colorado-Colorado Springs; Colorado Springs, Colo. (Pu)	4,957		60	2,820	11,190	5,683
University of Colorado-Denver; Denver, Colo. (Pu)	8,478	70	56	2,068	11,194	
University of Denver; Denver, Colo. (Pr)	3,809	84	58	18,936	18,936	6,165
University of Northern Colorado; Greeley, Colo. (Pu)	10,134	81	60	2,014	8,997	4,796
University of Southern Colorado; Pueblo, Colo. (Pu)	5,082	83	57	1,810	8,434	4,661
Western State College of Colorado; Gunnison, Colo. (Pu)	2,440	90	41	1,516	7,028	4,890
CONNECTICUT						
Albertus Magnus College; New Haven, Conn. (Pr)	1,720	93	66	13,908	13,908	6,512
Central Connecticut State University; New Britain, Conn. (Pu)	9,264	74	51	2,062	6,674	5,652
Charter Oak State College; New Britain, Conn. (Pu)	1,429			430	628	
Connecticut College; New London, Conn. (Pr)	1,764	32	57	26,490	26,490	
Eastern Connecticut State University; Willimantic, Conn. (Pu)	4,673	79	56	2,062	6,674	5,048
Fairfield University; Fairfield, Conn. (Pr)	4,064	61	53	21,000	21,000	7,380
Lyme Academy of Fine Arts; Old Lyme, Conn. (Pr)	171	100	64	11,200	11,200	
Mitchell College; New London, Conn. (Pr)	655	76	49	14,800	14,800	7,100
Quinnipiac College; Hamden, Conn. (Pr)	4,102	70	66	16,120	16,120	7,790
Sacred Heart University; Fairfield, Conn. (Pr)	3,920	82	62	15,257	15,257	7,530
Saint Joseph College; West Hartford, Conn. (Pr)	1,114	87	98	15,900	15,900	6,610
Southern Connecticut State University; New Haven, Conn. (Pu)	7,624	70	59		6,874	5,934
Teikyo Post University; Waterbury, Conn. (Pr)	1,422	82	66	13,125	13,125	5,900
Trinity College; Hartford, Conn. (Pr)	2,169	40	49	23,730	23,730	6,890
United States Coast Guard Academy; New London, Conn. (Pu)	838	7				
University of Bridgeport; Bridgeport, Conn. (Pr)	1,212	78	53	13,800	13,800	6,970
University of Connecticut; Storrs, Conn. (Pu)	11,715	73	52	2,079	12,676	5,544
University of Hartford; West Hartford, Conn. (Pr)	5,340	72	53	17,910	17,910	7,538
University of New Haven; West Haven, Conn. (Pr)	2,880		38	14,250	14,250	6,500
Wesleyan University; Middletown, Conn. (Pr)	2,759	29	52	25,380	25,380	6,630
Western Connecticut State University; Danbury, Conn. (Pu)	4,658	69	55	2,062	6,674	5,434
Yale University; New Haven, Conn. (Pr)	5,440	18	50	24,500	24,500	7,440
DELAWARE						
Delaware State University; Dover, Del. (Pu)	2,910		59	3,096	7,088	4,990
University of Delaware; Newark, Del. (Pr)	15,443	67	58			
Wesley College; Dover, Del.						
Wilmington College; New Castle, Del. (Pr)	4,965		74	6,060	6,060	
DISTRICT OF COLUMBIA						
American University; Washington, D.C. (Pr)	5,545	72	61	20,118	20,118	7,982
Catholic University of America; Washington, D.C. (Pr)	2,557	88	54	18,200	18,200	7,600
Corcoran College of Art and Design; Washington, D.C. (Pr)	425	58	69	14,100	14,100	
Gallaudet University; Washington, D.C. (Pr)	1,244	74	54	6,870	6,870	7,130
George Washington University; Washington, D.C. (Pr)	8,695	49	56	22,340	22,340	8,210
Georgetown University; Washington, D.C. (Pr)	6,361	23	54	23,088	23,088	8,693
Howard University; Washington, D.C. (Pr)	4,285			8,750	8,750	5,250
Mount Vernon College; Washington, D.C. (Pr)	341					7,730
Southeastern University; Washington, D.C. (Pr)	806	64		6,660	6,660	
Strayer University; Washington, D.C. (Pr)	9,111		56			
Trinity College; Washington, D.C. (Pr)	1,035	95		13,875	13,875	6,500
University of the District of Columbia; Washington, D.C. (Pu)	10,004			2,360	5,660	
FLORIDA						
Barry University; Miami Shores, Fla. (Pr)	5,468	38	66	15,530	15,530	6,220
Bethune-Cookman College; Daytona Beach, Fla. (Pr)	2,558	83	56	8,988	8,988	5,534
Clearwater Christian College; Clearwater, Fla. (Pr)	641	67	56	8,100	8,100	3,850
Eckerd College; St. Petersburg, Fla. (Pr)	1,530	76	55	18,025	18,025	4,960

Institution name; city, state (type)	Students	Percent Accepted	Percent Women	Tuition In-state	Tuition Out-of-state	Room and board
Embry-Riddle Aeronautical University; Daytona Beach, Fla. (Pr)	4,637	78%	15%	$10,700	$10,700	$5,440
Flagler College; St. Augustine, Fla. (Pr)	1,736	31	62	6,320	6,320	3,910
Florida A&M University; Tallahassee, Fla. (Pu)	10,691	70	58	1,777	7,368	3,896
Florida Atlantic University; Boca Raton, Fla. (Pu)	16,470	71	61	2,253	9,242	4,774
Florida Baptist Theological College; Graceville, Fla. (Pr)	530	90	32	3,760	3,760	3,150
Florida Gulf Coast University; Fort Myers, Fla. (Pu)	2,649	61	66	1,991	8,979	5,326
Florida Institute of Technology; Melbourne, Fla. (Pr)	1,943	87	31	17,300	17,300	5,270
Florida International University; Miami, Fla. (Pu)	25,709	56	56	2,164	9,153	6,081
Florida Memorial College; Miami, Fla. (Pr)	1,488			5,420	5,420	2,428
Florida Southern College; Lakeland, Fla. (Pr)	1,764	79	61	11,650	11,650	5,600
Florida State University; Tallahassee, Fla. (Pu)	25,965	64	55	1,697	8,685	4,951
International Academy of Design; Tampa, Fla. (Pr)	900	56	67	9,876	9,876	
International College; Naples, Fla. (Pr)	711	68		9,900	9,900	
Jacksonville University; Jacksonville, Fla. (Pr)	1,832	65	52	15,270	15,270	5,400
Johnson & Wales University; North Miami, Fla. (Pr)	1,156	77	41	12,885	12,885	
Lynn University; Boca Raton, Fla. (Pr)	1,633	80	54	17,300	17,300	6,550
New College of the University of South Florida; Sarasota, Fla. (Pu)	617	75		2,492	10,878	4,663
Northwood University, Florida Campus; West Palm Beach, Fla. (Pr)	975	76	44	11,325	11,325	6,233
Nova Southeastern University; Ft. Lauderdale, Fla. (Pr)	4,218	70	71	12,400	12,400	6,300
Palm Beach Atlantic College; West Palm Beach, Fla. (Pr)	1,838	69	60	11,040	11,040	4,470
Ringling School of Art & Design; Sarasota, Fla. (Pr)	892	39	43	14,500	14,500	7,000
Rollins College; Winter Park, Fla. (Pr)	1,519	73	60	21,250	21,250	6,700
Saint Leo University; Saint Leo, Fla. (Pr)	1,467	70	58	11,450	11,450	6,050
St. Thomas University; Miami, Fla. (Pr)	1,109	77	59	13,342	13,342	4,400
Stetson University; DeLand, Fla. (Pr)	12,304	80	93	17,475	17,475	6,070
University of Central Florida; Orlando, Fla. (Pu)	26,485	61	55	2,025	7,940	3,610
University of Florida; Gainesville, Fla. (Pu)	31,633	60	52	2,141	9,130	5,040
University of Miami; Coral Gables, Fla. (Pr)	8,391	59	54	20,960	20,960	7,782
University of North Florida; Jacksonville, Fla. (Pu)	10,267	73	58			
University of South Florida; Tampa, Fla. (Pu)	28,916	72	59	2,256	9,245	4,896
University of Tampa; Tampa, Fla. (Pr)	2,761	80	61	14,740	14,740	5,175
University of West Florida; Pensacola, Fla. (Pu)	6,414	83	58	2,294	9,282	4,532
Warner Southern College; Lake Wales, Fla. (Pr)	781	63	59	8,340	8,340	4,500
Webber College; Babson Park, Fla. (Pr)	421	48	47	9,900	9,900	3,570
GEORGIA						
Agnes Scott College; Atlanta, Ga. (Pr)	879	77		16,600	16,600	6,900
Albany State University; Albany, Ga. (Pu)	2,935	90	67	1,808	7,232	3,106
American InterContinental University; Atlanta, Ga. (Pr)	981		73		10,868	
Armstrong Atlantic State University; Savannah, Ga. (Pu)	5,157	79	68	2,098	7,522	4,460
Art Institute of Atlanta; Atlanta, Ga. (Pr)	1,939		46	12,144	12,144	
Atlanta College of Art; Atlanta, Ga. (Pr)	429	77	38	13,180	13,180	
Augusta State University; Augusta, Ga. (Pu)	4,635	64	63	1,808	7,232	
Berry College; Mount Berry, Ga. (Pr)	1,933	65	62	11,550	11,550	5,700
Brenau Women's College; Gainesville, Ga. (Pr)	633	73		11,730	11,730	6,876
Brewton-Parker College; Mt. Vernon, Ga. (Pr)	1,682			5,560	5,560	2,250
Clark Atlanta University; Atlanta, Ga. (Pr)	3,740	67	56	10,250	10,250	7,142
Clayton College & State University; Morrow, Ga.						
Columbus State University; Columbus, Ga. (Pu)	4,584		62	2,202	6,660	4,130
Covenant College; Lookout Mtn., Ga. (Pr)	1,049	78	58	15,600	15,600	4,850
DeVry Institute of Technology-Alpharetta; Alpharetta, Ga. (Pr)	1,336		31	7,778	7,778	
DeVry Institute of Technology-Decatur; Decatur, Ga. (Pr)	2,818		40	7,778	7,778	
Emmanuel College; Franklin Springs, Ga. (Pr)	837	57	54	7,165	7,165	3,600
Emory University; Atlanta, Ga. (Pr)	5,000	43	52	24,532	24,532	7,868
Fort Valley State College; Fort Valley, Ga. (Pu)	2,124					3,075
Georgia Baptist College of Nursing; Atlanta, Ga. (Pr)	337	33	98	10,050	10,050	5,035
Georgia College & State University; Milledgeville, Ga. (Pu)	7,147	54	34	1,808	7,232	4,170
Georgia Institute of Technology; Atlanta, Ga. (Pu)	10,256	69	29	2,414	9,656	4,976
Georgia Southern University; Statesboro, Ga. (Pu)	12,909	88	54	1,808	7,232	4,284
Georgia Southwestern College; Americus, Ga. (Pu)	2,071					3,130
Georgia State University; Atlanta, Ga. (Pu)	16,309	53	61	2,322	9,288	7,948
Kennesaw State College; Kennesaw, Ga. (Pu)	10,994			1,730	6,950	
LaGrange College; LaGrange, Ga. (Pr)	962					
Life University; Marietta, Ga. (Pr)	823		37			
Medical College of Georgia; Augusta, Ga. (Pu)	631		85	2,700	9,942	3,870
Mercer University-Atlanta; Atlanta, Ga. (Pr)	235			14,706	14,706	
Mercer University-Macon; Macon, Ga. (Pr)	4,092		65	16,290	16,290	5,380
Morehouse College; Atlanta, Ga. (Pr)	3,012	64		8,980	8,980	6,970
Morris Brown College; Atlanta, Ga. (Pr)	1,891					4,750
North Georgia College and State University; Dahlonega, Ga. (Pu)	3,005	80	66	2,192	7,686	3,542
Oglethorpe University; Atlanta, Ga. (Pr)	1,250	76	64	18,180	18,180	5,560
Piedmont College; Demorest, Ga. (Pr)	1,042	69	61	9,500	9,500	6,550
Reinhardt College; Waleska, Ga. (Pr)	1,190	86	63	8,000	8,000	4,750

Institution name; city, state (type)	Students	Percent Accepted	Percent Women	Tuition In-state	Tuition Out-of-state	Room and board
Savannah College of Art & Design; Savannah, Ga. (Pr)	4,431	76%	43%	$16,200	$16,200	$6,750
Savannah State University; Savannah, Ga. (Pu)	2,822					3,495
Shorter College; Rome, Ga. (Pr)	1,739	95	61	9,350	9,350	4,900
South College; Savannah, Ga. (Pr)	445		81			
Southern Polytechnic State University; Marietta, Ga. (Pu)	3,008	83	17	1,808	7,232	4,452
Spelman College; Atlanta, Ga. (Pr)	1,899			9,250	9,250	6,560
State University of West Georgia; Carrollton, Ga. (Pu)	6,772	68	62	2,250	7,674	3,806
Thomas University; Thomasville, Ga. (Pr)	589	100	64	7,500	7,500	1,500
Toccoa Falls College; Toccoa Falls, Ga. (Pr)	924		57	8,384	8,384	3,896
University of Georgia; Athens, Ga. (Pu)	24,040	63	54	2,930	9,860	4,672
Valdosta State University; Valdosta, Ga. (Pu)	7,635	61	60	2,290	7,714	3,954
Wesleyan College; Macon, Ga. (Pr)	585	76		15,450	15,450	7,150
HAWAII						
Brigham Young University; Laie Oahu, Hawaii (Pr)	2,294	47	62	2,665	2,665	4,900
Hawaii Pacific University; Honolulu, Hawaii (Pr)	6,914	78	51	8,920	8,920	8,350
University of Hawaii-Hilo; Hilo, Hawaii (Pu)	2,723			1,344	6,960	3,400
University of Hawaii-Manoa; Honolulu, Hawaii (Pu)	11,939	70	55	3,024	9,504	4,435
IDAHO						
Albertson College; Caldwell, Idaho (Pr)	3,246	83	1	16,000	16,000	4,200
Boise State University; Boise, Idaho (Pu)	13,287	87	57	2,294	8,174	3,370
Idaho State University; Pocatello, Idaho (Pu)	10,230	88	55		6,240	3,730
Lewis-Clark State College; Lewiston, Idaho (Pu)	3,151	82	59	2,204	7,476	2,960
Northwest Nazarene University; Nampa, Idaho (Pr)	1,114	46	57	12,990	12,990	4,020
University of Idaho; Moscow, Idaho (Pu)	8,591	85	46		6,000	3,952
ILLINOIS						
Augustana College; Rock Island, Ill. (Pr)	2,209	80	59	16,866	16,866	5,037
Barat College; Lake Forest, Ill. (Pr)	813	57	74	13,590	13,590	5,500
Benedictine University; Lisle, Ill. (Pr)	1,795	76	58	14,500	14,500	5,500
Blackburn College; Carlinville, Ill. (Pr)	448			7,795	7,795	3,240
Blessing-Rieman College of Nursing; Quincy, Ill. (Pr)	122	75		10,100	10,100	4,370
Bradley University; Peoria, Ill. (Pr)	4,961	81	54	13,880	13,880	5,300
Chicago State University; Chicago, Ill. (Pu)	5,585	189	73	2,957	7,253	5,825
Columbia College Chicago; Chicago, Ill. (Pr)	8,346	90	49	11,400	11,400	4,988
Concordia University-River Forest; River Forest, Ill. (Pr)	1,280	82	67	12,800	12,800	5,266
DePaul University; Chicago, Ill. (Pr)	11,776	78	59	14,670	14,670	6,300
DeVry Institute of Technology-DuPage; Addision, Ill. (Pr)	4,063		23	7,778	7,778	
DeVry Institute of Technology-Chicago; Chicago, Ill. (Pr)	4,001		33	7,778	7,778	
Dominican University; River Forest, Ill. (Pr)	1,147	78	69	14,720	14,720	5,030
Eastern Illinois University; Charleston, Ill. (Pu)	9,861	85	58	2,322	6,964	
Elmhurst College; Elmhurst, Ill. (Pr)	2,678	74	64	13,900	13,900	5,266
Eureka College; Eureka, Ill. (Pr)	502			14,540	14,540	4,400
Greenville College; Greenville, Ill. (Pr)	1,049	88	54	12,576	12,576	4,850
Harrington Institute of Interior Design; Chicago, Ill. (Pr)	512	90	87	5,738	5,738	
Illinois College; Jacksonville, Ill. (Pr)	883	81	57	10,200	10,200	4,500
Illinois Institute of Technology; Chicago, Ill. (Pr)	1,718	65	31	18,000	18,000	5,472
Illinois State University; Normal, Ill. (Pu)	17,705	75	58	3,219	9,657	4,238
Illinois Wesleyan University; Bloomington, Ill. (Pr)	2,091	64	56	20,284	20,284	5,150
Judson College; Elgin, Ill. (Pr)	975		57	12,580	12,580	5,060
Knox College; Galesburg, Ill. (Pr)	1,220	75	55	20,940	20,940	5,436
Lake Forest College; Lake Forest, Ill. (Pr)	1,241	77	57	20,900	20,900	5,000
Lewis University; Romeoville, Ill. (Pr)	4,018	70	55	13,320	13,320	6,000
Loyola University of Chicago; Chicago, Ill. (Pr)	7,669			16,074	16,074	7,000
MacMurray College; Jacksonville, Ill. (Pr)	692	76	51	13,140	13,140	4,650
McKendree College; Lebanon, Ill. (Pr)	2,061	72	63	10,500	10,500	4,170
Millikin University; Decatur, Ill. (Pr)	2,272	75	59	15,808	15,808	5,593
Monmouth College; Monmouth, Ill. (Pr)	1,057	77	57	16,370	16,370	4,450
North Central College; Naperville, Ill. (Pr)	2,179	76	58	15,096	15,096	5,250
North Park University; Chicago, Ill. (Pr)	1,589		62	16,180	16,180	5,570
Northeastern Illinois University; Chicago, Ill. (Pu)	8,205	40	61	2,858	7,382	
Northern Illinois University; DeKalb, Ill. (Pu)	16,893	73	54	4,347		5,010
Northwestern University; Evanston, Ill. (Pr)	7,842	32	52	24,648	24,648	7,320
Olivet Nazarene University; Bourbonnais, Ill. (Pr)	1,700			11,178	11,178	4,696
Principia College; Elsah, Ill. (Pr)	548	83	54	15,714	15,714	5,784
Quincy University; Quincy, Ill. (Pr)	1,051	81	55	14,300	14,300	4,780
Robert Morris College; Chicago, Ill. (Pr)	3,728	63	72			
Rush University; Chicago, Ill. (Pr)	197		86	4,000	4,000	
Saint Xavier University; Chicago, Ill. (Pr)	2,338	99	80	13,050	13,050	5,340
School of the Art Institute of Chicago; Chicago, Ill. (Pr)	1,819	73	61	19,140	19,140	
Shimer College; Waukegan, Ill. (Pr)	110	80	61	14,370	14,370	2,000
Southern Illinois University-Carbondale; Carbondale, Ill. (Pu)	17,939	74	43	2,781	8,343	3,777
Southern Illinois University-Edwardsville; Edwardsville, Ill. (Pu)	9,313	87	59	2,208	4,416	4,290
Trinity Christian College; Palos Heights, Ill. (Pr)	723	99	65	12,730	12,730	5,010
Trinity International University; Deerfield, Ill. (Pr)	945	72	52	12,840	12,840	4,800
University of Chicago; Chicago, Ill. (Pr)	3,844	48	49	23,820	23,820	7,835
University of Illinois at Chicago; Chicago, Ill. (Pu)	16,160	61	54	3,232	9,696	5,856

Institution name; city, state (type)	Students	Percent Accepted	Percent Women	Tuition In-state	Tuition Out-of-state	Room and board
University of Illinois at Urbana-Champaign; Urbana, Ill. (Pu)	28,916	71%	48%	$ 3,724	$11,172	$5,424
University of St. Francis; Joliet, Ill. (Pr)	3,153	84	84	11,670	11,670	4,740
Vandercook College of Music; Chicago, Ill. (Pr)	80		43	10,000	10,000	5,100
Western Illinois University; Macomb, Ill. (Pu)	10,434	66	52	2,812	5,624	4,506
Wheaton College; Wheaton, Ill. (Pr)	2,338	54	52	14,930	14,930	5,080
INDIANA						
Anderson University; Anderson, Ind. (Pr)						
Ball State University; Muncie, Ind. (Pu)	16,114	79	53	3,576	9,736	4,520
Bethel College; Mishawaka, Ind. (Pr)	1,552	72	66	11,950	11,950	3,950
Butler University; Indianapolis, Ind. (Pr)	3,294	86	62	18,140	18,140	6,140
DePauw University; Greencastle, Ind. (Pr)	2,216	67	56	18,530	18,530	6,080
Earlham College; Richmond, Ind. (Pr)	1,123	84	57	19,684	19,684	4,810
Franklin College of Indiana; Franklin, Ind. (Pr)	953	76	50	14,110	14,110	4,330
Goshen College; Goshen, Ind. (Pr)	1,084	98	57	12,870	12,870	4,640
Grace College and Seminary; Winona Lake, Ind. (Pr)	923	87	52	10,700	10,700	4,685
Hanover College; Hanover, Ind. (Pr)	1,123	82	53	10,700	10,700	4,655
Huntington College; Huntington, Ind. (Pr)	855	89	60	12,250	12,250	4,770
Indiana Institute of Technology; Fort Wayne, Ind. (Pr)	1,645	12	51	12,300	12,300	4,564
Indiana State University; Terre Haute, Ind. (Pu)	9,280	86	51	3,426	8,554	4,434
Indiana University-Bloomington; Bloomington, Ind. (Pu)	28,511	81	54	3,752	12,460	5,492
Indiana University East; Richmond, Ind. (Pu)	2,215	97	68	2,922	7,692	
Indiana University-Kokomo; Kokomo, Ind. (Pu)	2,326	85	72	2,922	7,692	
Indiana University Northwest; Gary, Ind. (Pu)	4,170	79	71	2,922	7,692	
Indiana University-Purdue University Fort Wayne; Fort Wayne, Ind. (Pu)	9,815	98	56	3,213	7,361	
Indiana University-Purdue University Indianapolis; Indianapolis, Ind. (Pu)	20,416	86	59	3,432	10,680	3,450
Indiana University South Bend; South Bend, Ind. (Pu)	5,702	82	63	2,975	8,259	
Indiana University Southeast; New Albany, Ind. (Pu)	5,440	94	63	2,922	7,692	
Indiana Wesleyan University; Marion, Ind. (Pr)	1,947					4,158
Manchester College; North Manchester, Ind. (Pr)	1,065	82	52	14,510	14,510	5,360
Marian College; Indianapolis, Ind. (Pr)	1,352			12,458	12,458	4,422
Oakland City University; Oakland City, Ind. (Pr)	1,258	95	50	10,410	10,410	3,146
Purdue University-Calumet; Hammond, Ind. (Pu)	8,350		55	2,262	5,688	
Purdue University-North Central; Westville, Ind. (Pu)	3,355	94	60	3,054	7,553	
Purdue University-West Lafayette; West Lafayette, Ind. (Pu)	30,835	84	43	3,724	12,348	5,500
Rose-Hulman Institute of Technology; Terre Haute, Ind. (Pr)	1,545	67	17	19,948	19,948	5,751
Saint Joseph's College; Rensselaer, Ind. (Pr)	934	77	52	14,070	14,070	5,080
Saint Mary-of-the-Woods College; Saint Mary-of-the-Woods, Ind. (Pr)	1,270	75		14,370	14,370	5,540
Saint Mary's College; Notre Dame, Ind. (Pr)	1,409	83		16,994	16,994	5,962
Taylor University; Upland, Ind. (Pr)	1,880	78	53	14,900	14,900	4,630
Taylor University, Fort Wayne Campus; Fort Wayne, Ind. (Pr)	428		57	12,550	12,550	4,230
Tri-State University; Angola, Ind. (Pr)	1,231	83	29	13,450	13,450	4,950
University of Evansville; Evansville, Ind. (Pr)	5,592	91	62	15,200	15,200	4,600
University of Indianapolis; Indianapolis, Ind. (Pr)	2,781	85	65	14,000	14,000	5,000
University of Notre Dame; Notre Dame, Ind. (Pr)	8,014	35	45			
University of Saint Francis; Fort Wayne, Ind. (Pr)	794	82	65	10,310	10,310	4,270
University of Southern Indiana; Evansville, Ind. (Pu)	8,217	97	59	2,860	7,006	4,586
Valparaiso University; Valparaiso, Ind. (Pr)	2,986	78	53	16,280	16,280	4,360
Wabash College; Crawfordsville, Ind. (Pr)	861	75		16,975	16,975	5,435
IOWA						
Allen College; Waterloo, Iowa (Pr)	219	97		7,620	7,620	
Briar Cliff College; Sioux City, Iowa (Pr)	1,001	82	65	12,690	12,690	4,071
Buena Vista University; Storm Lake, Iowa (Pr)	1,283	86	49	15,751	15,751	4,642
Central College; Pella, Iowa (Pr)	1,301	85	56	14,070	14,070	4,944
Clarke College; Dubuque, Iowa (Pr)	1,120	78	66	13,725	13,725	5,290
Coe College; Cedar Rapids, Iowa (Pr)	1,246	82	54	17,390	17,390	5,020
Cornell College; Mount Vernon, Iowa (Pr)	965	72	59	18,835	18,835	5,140
Dordt College; Sioux Center, Iowa (Pr)	1,429	95	55			3,600
Drake University; Des Moines, Iowa (Pr)	3,474	92	61	16,480	16,480	4,870
Graceland University; Lamoni, Iowa (Pr)	3,252	65	78	12,230	12,230	3,830
Grand View College; Des Moines, Iowa (Pr)	1,419	85	63	12,430	12,430	3,832
Grinnell College; Grinnell, Iowa (Pr)	1,335	67	55	19,982	19,982	5,820
Iowa State University; Ames, Iowa (Pu)	21,503	88	45	2,906	9,748	4,171
Iowa Wesleyan College; Mt. Pleasant, Iowa (Pr)	785	85	61	13,200	13,200	4,250
Loras College; Dubuque, Iowa (Pr)	1,551	81	53	15,190	15,190	5,804
Luther College; Decorah, Iowa (Pr)	2,550	87	59	18,080	18,080	3,870
Marycrest International University; Davenport, Iowa (Pr)	357		56	12,400	12,400	4,840
Morningside College; Sioux City, Iowa (Pr)	1,021	85	62	13,310	13,310	4,794
Mount Mercy College; Cedar Rapids, Iowa (Pr)	1,291	88	67	13,850	13,850	4,600
Mount Saint Clare College; Clinton, Iowa (Pr)	590	81	56	12,580	12,580	4,450
Northwestern College; Orange City, Iowa (Pr)	1,219	92	61	12,270	12,270	3,500
Saint Ambrose University; Davenport, Iowa (Pr)	2,022	88	60	13,890	13,890	5,160
Simpson College; Indianola, Iowa (Pr)	1,897	84	57	15,015	15,015	5,040

Institution name; city, state (type)	Students	Percent		Tuition		Room and board
		Accepted	Women	In-state	Out-of-state	
University of Dubuque; Dubuque, Iowa (Pr)	680	91%	42%	$12,640	$12,640	$4,340
University of Iowa; Iowa City, Iowa (Pu)	19,537	83	54	2,906	10,668	4,680
University of Northern Iowa; Cedar Falls, Iowa (Pu)	12,100	82	57	2,786	7,546	3,926
Upper Iowa University; Fayette, Iowa (Pr)	4,239	69	56	10,240	10,240	3,958
Wartburg College; Waverly, Iowa (Pr)	1,546	87	57	15,510	15,510	4,400
William Penn College; Oskaloosa, Iowa (Pr)	1,096	88	50	11,924	11,924	4,140
KANSAS						
Baker University; Baldwin City, Kans. (Pr)	1,741	82	60	11,750	11,750	4,700
Barclay College; Haviland, Kans. (Pr)	169	73	50	6,240	6,240	3,300
Benedictine College; Atchison, Kans. (Pr)	1,390	97	55	12,116	12,116	4,800
Bethany College; Lindsborg, Kans. (Pr)	587	73	45	12,154	12,154	3,660
Bethel College; North Newton, Kans. (Pr)	477	84	51	11,700	11,700	4,700
Emporia State University; Emporia, Kans. (Pu)	4,158	100	60	2,086	6,552	3,656
Fort Hays State University; Hays, Kans. (Pu)	4,412		55	2,182	6,904	3,770
Friends University; Wichita, Kans. (Pr)	2,614	93	50	11,050	11,050	3,420
Kansas State University; Manhattan, Kans. (Pu)	17,903	65	47	2,042	8,693	3,950
Kansas Wesleyan University; Salina, Kans. (Pr)	684	70	60	11,000	11,000	4,000
Manhattan Christian College; Manhattan, Kans. (Pr)	400	94	57	6,870	6,870	3,610
McPherson College; McPherson, Kans. (Pr)	494	72	45	11,500	11,500	4,900
Mid America Nazarene University; Olathe, Kans. (Pr)	1,266					4,496
Newman University; Wichita, Kans. (Pr)	1,524	84	66	10,148	10,148	3,950
Ottawa University; Ottawa, Kans. (Pr)	521	68	43	10,750	10,750	4,640
Pittsburg State University; Pittsburg, Kans. (Pu)	5,115	60	47	2,142	6,464	3,670
Saint Mary College; Leavenworth, Kans. (Pr)	839			5,695	5,695	4,300
Southwestern College; Winfield, Kans. (Pr)	810	96	51	10,600	10,600	4,170
Sterling College; Sterling, Kans. (Pr)	424	70	54	11,030	11,030	4,586
University of Kansas; Lawrence, Kans. (Pu)	19,477	69	53	2,090	8,693	3,941
Washburn University; Topeka, Kans. (Pu)	4,711	100	61	3,090	6,960	3,950
Wichita State University; Wichita, Kans. (Pu)	10,876	76	56	1,976	8,429	4,070
KENTUCKY						
Alice Lloyd College; Pippa Passes, Ky. (Pr)	452	51	58	6,360	6,360	2,680
Asbury College; Wilmore, Ky. (Pr)	1,317	87	58	13,644	13,644	3,566
Bellarmine College; Louisville, Ky. (Pr)	2,373	95	64	12,480	12,480	3,940
Berea College; Berea, Ky. (Pr)	1,522	34	57			3,871
Brescia University; Owensboro, Ky. (Pr)	720	81	64	9,390	9,390	4,240
Campbellsville University; Campbellsville, Ky. (Pr)	1,548	72	60	8,000	8,000	3,990
Centre College; Danville, Ky. (Pr)	1,022	86	51	21,350	21,350	5,300
Cumberland College; Williamsburg, Ky. (Pr)	1,540		54	9,698	9,698	4,276
Eastern Kentucky University; Richmond, Ky. (Pu)	13,478	95	57	2,190	6,030	3,396
Georgetown College; Georgetown, Ky. (Pr)	1,338	91	58	12,140	12,140	4,610
Kentucky Christian College; Grayson, Ky. (Pr)	564	88	54	6,880	6,880	3,914
Kentucky State University; Frankfort, Ky. (Pu)	2,277		58	2,020	6,060	3,446
Kentucky Wesleyan College; Owensboro, Ky. (Pr)	747	84	57	9,770	9,770	4,770
Midway College; Midway, Ky. (Pr)	974		90	9,062	9,062	4,600
Morehead State University; Morehead, Ky. (Pu)	6,638	80	59		13,470	6,310
Murray State University; Murray, Ky. (Pu)	7,288	78	56	2,256	6,600	3,570
Northern Kentucky University; Highland Heights, Ky. (Pu)	10,674	97	59	2,100	6,140	3,866
Pikeville College; Pikeville, Ky. (Pr)	735	100	69	7,500	7,500	3,175
Spalding University; Louisville, Ky. (Pr)	1,128	85	81	10,300	10,300	2,790
Thomas More College; Crestiew Hill, Ky. (Pr)	1,417		54	11,578	11,578	4,500
Transylvania University; Lexington, Ky. (Pr)	1,072	89	59	14,700	14,700	5,530
Union College; Barbourville, Ky. (Pr)	541	94	48	11,070	11,070	3,650
University of Kentucky; Lexington, Ky. (Pu)	16,841	73	52	3,110	9,330	3,722
University of Louisville; Louisville, Ky. (Pu)	14,548	89	53	2,400	7,200	4,982
Western Kentucky University; Bowling Green, Ky. (Pu)	12,912	85	58	2,150	6,450	
LOUISIANA						
Centenary College of Louisiana; Shreveport, La. (Pr)	878	83	59	14,200	14,200	4,500
Dillard University; New Orleans, La. (Pr)	1,584			8,500	8,500	4,464
Grambling State University; Grambling, La. (Pu)	6,828			2,208	7,358	2,636
Louisiana College; Pineville, La. (Pr)	1,003			6,210	6,210	3,112
Louisiana State University and A&M College; Baton Rouge, La. (Pu)	24,760	81	53	2,301	6,202	3,910
Louisiana State University-Shreveport; Shreveport, La. (Pu)	3,354			1,950	5,290	1,827
Louisiana Tech University; Ruston, La. (Pu)	8,721	99	49	2,532	5,847	2,850
Loyola University New Orleans; New Orleans, La. (Pr)	3,478	83	63	14,989	14,989	6,116
McNeese State University; Lake Charles, La. (Pu)	7,045	99	58	2,006	6,446	2,310
Nicholls State University; Thibodaux, La. (Pu)	6,596	93	62	2,117	6,389	2,850
Northwestern State University of Louisiana; Natchitoches, La. (Pu)	7,640	95	66	2,147	6,437	2,416
Saint Joseph Seminary College; St. Benedict, La. (Pr)	180	100		6,450	6,450	4,750
Southeastern Louisiana University; Hammond, La. (Pu)	13,476	88	61	2,150	6,446	2,400
Southern University and Agricultural and Mechanical College; Shreveport, La. (Pu)	1,345	100	69	1,104	2,394	
Southern University-Baton Rouge; Baton Rouge, La. (Pu)	7,976			2,065	5,852	3,228

Institution name; city, state (type)	Students	Percent Accepted	Women	Tuition In-state	Out-of-state	Room and board
Southern University of New Orleans; New Orleans, La. (Pr)	4,500					
Tulane University; New Orleans, La. (Pr)	7,163	78%	53%	$22,590	$22,590	$6,700
University of Louisiana-Lafayette; Lafayette, La. (Pu)	14,900	83	56	2,019	7,251	2,656
University of Louisiana-Monroe; Monroe, La. (Pu)	8,669	92	61		2,400	3,380
University of New Orleans; New Orleans, La. (Pu)	11,638	84	56	2,362	7,888	3,150
Xavier University of Louisiana; New Orleans, La. (Pr)	3,278	85	72	8,900	8,900	5,100
MAINE						
Bates College; Lewiston, Maine (Pr)	1,706	33		31,400	31,400	
Bowdoin College; Brunswick, Maine (Pr)	1,608	32	52	25,435	24,435	6,760
Colby College; Waterville, Maine (Pr)	1,764	33				
College of the Atlantic; Bar Harbor, Maine (Pr)	288	73	66	19,485	19,485	5,220
Husson College; Bangor, Maine (Pr)	1,613	93	65	9,480	9,480	5,150
Maine College of Art; Portland, Maine (Pr)	325	73	59	17,370	17,370	7,042
Maine Maritime Academy; Castine, Maine (Pu)	635			4,374	8,029	5,022
Saint Joseph's College; Standish, Maine (Pr)	821	75	66	13,920	13,920	6,250
Thomas College; Waterville, Maine (Pr)	759	96	58	12,480	12,480	5,700
Unity College; Unity, Maine (Pr)	512	92	31	12,330	12,330	5,300
University of Maine; Orono, Maine (Pu)	7,882	85	51	3,960	11,250	5,256
University of Maine-Augusta; Augusta, Maine (Pu)	5,611	67	74	3,090	7,590	
University of Maine-Farmington; Farmington, Maine (Pu)	2,411	75	68	3,390	8,280	4,500
University of Maine-Fort Kent; Fort Kent, Maine (Pu)	926	93	64	3,120	7,590	4,100
University of Maine-Machias; Machias, Maine (Pu)	908	91	66	3,090	7,620	4,330
University of Maine-Presque Isle; Presque Isle, Maine (Pu)	1,378	89	62	3,090	7,560	4,048
University of New England; Biddeford, Maine (Pr)	1,695	90	80	14,990	14,990	6,200
University of Southern Maine; Gorham, Maine (Pu)	8,703	69	59	3,630	10,110	4,926
Westbrook College; Portland, Maine (Pr)	458			14,320	14,320	5,820
MARYLAND						
Bowie State University; Bowie, Md. (Pu)	2,960			3,357	7,792	4,427
Capitol College; Laurel, Md. (Pr)	695	96	21	10,542	10,542	
College of Notre Dame of Maryland; Baltimore, Md. (Pr)	2,037	74	94	15,600	15,600	6,800
Columbia Union College; Tacoma Park, Md. (Pr)	1,172					4,150
Coppin State College; Baltimore, Md. (Pu)	2,931			3,012	7,392	4,884
Frostburg State University; Frostburg, Md. (Pu)	4,313	77	54	3,342	8,492	5,214
Goucher College; Baltimore, Md. (Pr)	1,131	83	72	21,000	21,000	7,650
Hood College; Fredrick, Md. (Pr)	894	74	89	18,295	18,295	6,900
Johns Hopkins University; Baltimore, Md. (Pr)	3,924	33	41	24,660	24,660	7,870
Loyola College; Baltimore, Md. (Pr)	3,381	66	55	18,310	18,310	7,600
Maryland Institute, College of Art; Baltimore, Md. (Pr)	1,254	52	57	19,800	19,800	6,540
Morgan State University; Baltimore, Md. (Pu)	5,356			1,853	4,405	5,296
Mount Saint Mary's College; Emmitsburg, Md. (Pr)	1,354	81	57	16,520	16,520	6,650
St. John's College; Annapolis, Md. (Pr)	452	78		23,290	23,290	6,360
St. Mary's College of Maryland; St Mary's City, Md. (Pu)	1,613	65	58	6,285	11,125	6,325
Salisbury State University; Salisbury, Md. (Pu)	5,536	57	57	2,972	7,366	5,590
Towson University; Towson, Md. (Pu)	13,978	69	59	3,466	9,896	5,800
United States Naval Academy; Annapolis, Md. (Pu)	4,123	15				
University of Baltimore; Baltimore, Md. (Pu)	1,925		53	1,771	5,442	
University of Maryland-Baltimore County; Baltimore, Md. (Pu)	8,854	69	50	4,046	8,518	5,694
University of Maryland-College Park; College Park, Md. (Pu)	24,657	54	48	4,172	11,704	6,216
University of Maryland-Eastern Shore; Princess Anne, Md. (Pu)	2,862			2,577	7,219	4,530
University of Maryland University College; Adelphi, Md. (Pu)	11,603	100	57	4,584	6,048	
Villa Julie College; Stevenson, Md. (Pr)	2,091	75	72	10,250	10,250	3,650
Washington College; Chestertown, Md. (Pr)	1,117	85	60	19,750	19,750	5,740
Western Maryland College; Westminster, Md. (Pr)	1,574	76	55	18,650	18,650	5,350
MASSACHUSETTS						
American International College; Springfield, Mass. (Pr)	1,426			13,600	13,600	7,112
Amherst College; Amherst, Mass. (Pr)	1,668	19		24,800	24,800	6,560
Anna Maria College; Paxton, Mass. (Pr)	694	85	64	13,495	13,495	6,200
Art Institute of Boston at Lesley; Boston, Mass. (Pr)	534	35	50	13,350	13,350	8,300
Assumption College; Worcester, Mass. (Pr)	2,352	74	65	17,950	17,950	6,980
Atlantic Union College; South Lancaster, Mass. (Pr)	1,193			12,125	12,125	3,900
Babson College; Babson Park, Mass. (Pr)	1,701	45		21,952	21,952	8,746
Bay Path College; Longmeadow, Mass. (Pr)				13,010	13,010	6,864
Bentley College; Waltham, Mass. (Pr)	4,209	57	43			
Berklee College of Music; Boston, Mass. (Pr)	2,953			16,590	16,590	8,890
Boston Architectural Center; Boston, Mass. (Pr)	795	94	39	6,682	6,682	
Boston College; Chestnut Hill, Mass. (Pr)	9,190	40		21,700	21,700	
Boston Conservatory; Boston, Mass. (Pr)	350		71	17,300	17,300	8,200
Boston University; Boston, Mass. (Pr)	18,018	55	58	24,700	24,700	8,450
Brandeis University; Waltham, Mass. (Pr)	3,112	52	56	24,421	24,421	7,040
Bridgewater State College; Bridgewater, Mass. (Pu)	7,320	70	61		7,050	4,502
Cambridge College; Cambridge, Mass.						
Clark University; Worcester, Mass. (Pr)	2,182	80	60	22,400	22,400	4,350
College of the Holy Cross; Worcester, Mass. (Pr)	2,801	44	52	23,400	23,400	7,540
Curry College; Milton, Mass. (Pr)	2,082	82	53	16,500	16,500	6,600

Institution name; city, state (type)	Students	Percent Accepted	Percent Women	Tuition In-state	Tuition Out-of-state	Room and board
Eastern Nazarene College; Quincy, Mass. (Pr)	1,508					$3,976
Elms College; Chicopee, Mass. (Pr)	836	92%	91%	$14,144	$14,144	5,566
Emerson College; Boston, Mass. (Pr)	3,135	65	58	18,816	18,816	8,734
Emmanuel College; Boston, Mass. (Pr)	1,312	78	89	15,488	15,488	3,737
Endicott College; Beverly, Mass. (Pr)	1,395	75	68	14,550	14,550	7,698
Fitchburg State College; Fitchburg, Mass. (Pu)	3,352	71	56	1,030	7,050	4,600
Framingham State College; Framingham, Mass. (Pu)	4,296	60	64	1,150	7,050	4,154
Gordon College; Wenham, Mass. (Pr)	1,487	76	65	15,740	15,740	5,050
Hampshire College; Amherst, Mass. (Pr)	1,172	61		24,984	24,984	6,622
Harvard College; Cambridge, Mass. (Pr)	6,684	11	46	22,054	22,054	7,757
Lasell College; Newton, Mass. (Pr)	706	81		14,700	14,700	7,700
Lesley College; Cambridge, Mass. (Pr)	571	82		16,300	16,300	7,520
Massachusetts College of Art; Boston, Mass. (Pu)	2,266	47	63	1,060	9,000	7,889
Massachusetts College of Liberal Arts; North Adams, Mass. (Pu)	1,392	70	61	1,090	7,050	4,290
Massachusetts College of Pharmacy and Health Sciences; Boston, Mass. (Pr)	720	79	63	16,900	16,900	7,900
Massachusetts Institute of Technology; Cambridge, Mass. (Pr)	4,300	19	41	25,000	25,000	6,900
Massachusetts Maritime Academy; Buzzards Bay, Mass. (Pu)	791	81		9,240	16,100	3,960
Merrimack College; North Andover, Mass. (Pr)	2,677	72	50			
Montserrat College of Art; Beverly, Mass. (Pr)	386	85	54	12,550	12,550	3,638
Mount Holyoke College; South Hadley, Mass. (Pr)	1,979	60	99	24,200	24,200	7,110
New England Conservatory of Music; Boston, Mass. (Pr)	387	45	50	18,750	18,750	8,600
Nichols College; Dudley, Mass. (Pr)	1,145	78	50	14,200	14,200	6,540
Northeastern University; Boston, Mass. (Pr)	12,300	62		18,675	18,675	8,610
Pine Manor College; Chestnut Hill, Mass. (Pr)	306	82	100	11,440	11,440	7,245
Regis College; Weston, Mass. (Pr)	889	94		17,500	17,500	8,100
Salem State College; Salem, Mass. (Pu)	7,336	69	62	1,150	6,450	4,086
School of the Museum of Fine Arts; Boston, Mass. (Pr)	522			17,000	17,000	
Simmons College; Boston, Mass. (Pr)	1,211	72		19,520	19,520	8,046
Simon's Rock College of Bard; Gt. Barrington, Mass. (Pr)	372	58	56	20,800	20,800	6,410
Smith College; Northampton, Mass. (Pr)	2,665	56		23,400	23,400	8,160
Springfield College; Springfield, Mass. (Pr)	2,046	59				5,856
Stonehill College; Easton, Mass. (Pr)	2,549	53	59	16,680	16,680	8,166
Suffolk University; Boston, Mass. (Pr)	3,305	77	57	14,580	14,580	9,210
Tufts University; Medford, Mass. (Pr)	4,791	33	52	23,106	23,106	7,108
University of Massachusetts-Amherst; Amherst, Mass. (Pu)	19,372	69	51	1,714	9,756	4,790
University of Massachusetts-Boston; Boston, Mass. (Pu)	10,579	62	56	1,714	9,758	
University of Massachusetts-Dartmouth; Dartmouth, Mass. (Pu)	6,162	65	53	1,417	7,845	4,992
University of Massachusetts-Lowell; Lowell, Mass. (Pu)	9,354	71	39	1,454	7,871	4,836
Wellesley College; Wellesley, Mass. (Pr)	2,333	46		23,718	23,718	7,480
Wentworth Institute of Technology; Boston, Mass. (Pr)	4,073	64	33	13,000	13,000	6,800
Western New England College; Springfield, Mass. (Pr)	3,344	77	35	14,354	14,354	7,050
Westfield State College; Westfield, Mass. (Pu)	4,282	65	54	1,090	7,050	4,174
Wheaton College; Norton, Mass. (Pr)	1,500	71	66	22,950	24,225	6,920
Wheelock College; Boston, Mass. (Pr)	632	86	96	16,740	16,740	6,615
Williams College; Williamstown, Mass. (Pr)	2,113	23	49	24,619	24,619	6,730
Worcester Polytechnic Institute; Worcester, Mass. (Pr)	2,783	78	22	21,770	21,770	6,912
Worcester State College; Worcester, Mass. (Pu)	4,465	52	63	1,090	7,050	4,484
MICHIGAN						
Adrian College; Adrian, Mich. (Pr)	1,049			13,150	13,150	4,320
Albion College; Albion, Mich. (Pr)	1,490	90	55	17,984	17,984	5,220
Alma College; Alma, Mich. (Pr)	1,383	83	57	15,734	15,734	5,726
Andrews University; Berrien Springs, Mich. (Pr)	1,847		57	11,685	11,685	3,630
Aquinas College; Grand Rapids, Mich. (Pr)	1,983	84	66	14,034	14,034	4,884
Baker College of Auburn Hills; Auburn Hills, Mich. (Pr)	1,319	50	70	7,200	7,200	
Baker College of Cadillac; Cadillac, Mich.						
Baker College of Jackson; Jackson, Mich. (Pr)	1,010		76	6,950	6,950	
Baker College of Mount Clemens; Clinton Township, Mich.						
Baker College of Muskegon; Muskegon, Mich. (Pr)	2,370	100	73	6,950	6,950	
Baker College of Owosso; Owosso, Mich.						
Baker College of Port Huron; Port Huron, Mich. (Pr)	1,098	84	78	7,200	7,200	
Calvin College; Grand Rapids, Mich. (Pr)	4,218	99	55	14,040	14,040	4,890
Center for Creative Studies; Detroit, Mich. (Pr)	1,048	70	41	15,630	15,630	5,600
Central Michigan University; Mount Pleasant, Mich. (Pu)	17,866	83	58	3,150	8,175	4,620
Cleary College; Howell, Mich. (Pr)	642		66	7,605	7,605	
Cornerstone University; Grand Rapids, Mich. (Pr)	1,219	91	61	9,700	9,700	4,830
Detroit College of Business; Dearborn, Mich. (Pr)	5,951	100	76	6,768	6,768	
Eastern Michigan University; Ypsilanti, Mich. (Pu)	18,043	80	60			
Grace Bible College; Grand Rapids, Mich. (Pr)	158	43	52	6,800	6,800	4,150
Grand Valley State University; Allendale, Mich. (Pu)	3,223	76	67	4,048	8,830	4,910
Hillsdale College; Hillsdale, Mich. (Pr)	1,167	84	52	13,600	13,600	5,700
Hope College; Holland, Mich. (Pr)	2,943	89	60	16,554	16,554	5,224
Kalamazoo College; Kalamazoo, Mich. (Pr)	1,367	77		19,188	19,188	5,787
Kendall College of Art and Design; Grand Rapids, Mich. (Pr)	527			10,500	10,500	
Kettering University; Flint, Mich. (Pr)	2,553	75		14,640	14,640	3,960

Institution name; city, state (type)	Students	Percent Accepted	Women	Tuition In-state	Out-of-state	Room and board
Lake Superior State University; Sault Ste. Marie, Mich. (Pu)	3,332		52%	$ 3,727	$ 7,320	$4,738
Lawrence Technological University; Southfield, Mich. (Pr)	3,073					4,200
Madonna University; Livonia, Mich. (Pr)	3,307	89%	78	6,610	6,610	4,676
Marygrove College; Detroit, Mich. (Pr)	991	31	80	10,140	10,140	5,200
Michigan State University; East Lansing, Mich. (Pu)	33,966	71	53	5,004	12,406	4,298
Michigan Technological University; Houghton, Mich. (Pu)	5,661	94	27	4,365	10,578	4,726
Northern Michigan University; Marquette, Mich. (Pu)	7,049	89	53		12,035	4,602
Northwood University, Michigan Campus; Midland, Mich. (Pr)	3,190	93	47	11,325	11,325	5,208
Oakland University; Rochester, Mich. (Pu)	11,624	75	65	3,864	11,258	4,715
Olivet College; Olivet, Mich. (Pr)	889	35	48	13,382	13,382	4,452
Rochester College; Rochester Hills, Mich. (Pr)	557		48	7,808	7,808	4,416
Saginaw Valley State University; University Center, Mich. (Pu)	6,658		60	3,257	6,681	4,690
Saint Mary's College; Orchard Lake, Mich. (Pr)	310	70	43	5,352	5,352	5,600
Siena Heights College; Adrian, Mich. (Pr)	993					4,630
Spring Arbor College; Spring Arbor, Mich. (Pr)	2,145	88	66	11,600	11,600	4,460
University of Detroit Mercy; Detroit, Mich. (Pr)	4,275		66	13,350	13,350	5,380
University of Michigan-Ann Arbor; Ann Arbor, Mich. (Pu)	24,493	59	50	6,550	20,270	5,614
University of Michigan-Dearborn; Dearborn, Mich. (Pu)	6,521	76	53		11,615	
University of Michigan-Flint; Flint, Mich. (Pu)	5,994	91	65	3,640	10,830	
Walsh College of Accountancy and Business Administration; Troy, Mich. (Pr)	1,179		61	2,460	2,460	
Wayne State University; Detroit, Mich. (Pu)	18,393	82	61	3,429	7,860	
Western Michigan University; Kalamazoo, Mich. (Pu)	21,829	85	54	3,342	8,388	4,831
William Tyndale College; Farmington Hills, Mich. (Pr)	637	86	53	7,050	7,050	2,800
MINNESOTA						
Augsburg College; Minneapolis, Minn. (Pr)	2,829	77	61	15,974	15,974	5,320
Bemidji State University; Bemidji, Minn. (Pu)	4,293	75	56	2,800	5,940	3,084
Bethel College; Saint Paul, Minn. (Pr)	2,721	81	63	15,300	15,300	5,410
Carleton College; Northfield, Minn. (Pr)	1,905	46	53	23,325	23,325	4,761
College of Saint Benedict; Saint Joseph, Minn. (Pr)	1,977	91	100	16,195	16,195	5,025
College of Saint Catherine; Saint Paul, Minn. (Pr)	2,545	87	100	15,456	15,456	4,550
College of Saint Scholastica; Duluth, Minn. (Pr)	1,429	93	74	15,420	15,420	4,760
Concordia College-Moorhead; Moorhead, Minn. (Pr)	2,918	90	63	13,904	13,904	3,900
Concordia College-Saint Paul; Saint Paul, Minn. (Pr)	1,027			12,658	12,658	4,726
Crown College; St. Bonifacius, Minn. (Pr)	794	93	61	9,450	9,450	4,316
Gustavus Adolphus College; Saint Peter, Minn. (Pr)	2,543	79	55	17,200	17,200	4,320
Hamline University; Saint Paul, Minn. (Pr)	1,709	85	63	15,574	15,574	5,450
Macalester College; St. Paul, Minn. (Pr)	1,791	56	57	19,673	19,673	5,593
Martin Luther College; New Ulm, Minn. (Pr)	811	89	48	4,130	4,130	2,285
Minneapolis College of Art and Design; Minneapolis, Minn. (Pr)	577	73	42	19,060	19,060	4,640
Minnesota State University-Moorhead; Moorhead, Minn. (Pu)	6,729	80	63	2,728	6,118	3,264
Minnesota State University-Mankato; Mankato, Minn. (Pu)	10,350	85	53	2,582	5,769	2,965
North Central University; Minneapolis, Minn. (Pr)	1,172	62	57			3,550
Northwestern College; Saint Paul, Minn. (Pr)	1,744	71	61	14,982	14,982	4,448
Saint Cloud State University; Saint Cloud, Minn. (Pu)	13,372	60	54	3,135	5,616	3,422
Saint John's University/College of Saint Benedict; Collegeville/ St. Joseph, Minn. (Pr)	3,803	87	53	16,195	16,195	4,930
Saint Mary's University of Minnesota; Winona, Minn. (Pr)	1,799	82	49	13,990	13,990	4,620
Saint Olaf College; Northfield, Minn. (Pr)	2,981	83	57	18,250	18,250	4,320
Southwest State University; Marshall, Minn. (Pu)	2,900			2,648	5,965	3,000
University of Minnesota-Crookston; Crookston, Minn. (Pu)	2,464	95	55	3,780	3,780	4,046
University of Minnesota-Duluth; Duluth, Minn. (Pu)	7,959	83	50	4,230	12,000	4,132
University of Minnesota-Morris; Morris, Minn. (Pu)	1,867	87	59	4,778	9,480	3,910
University of Minnesota-Twin Cities; Minneapolis, Minn. (Pu)	48,030	73	34	4,172	12,312	4,494
University of Saint Thomas; St. Paul, Minn. (Pr)	5,399	85	54	17,088	17,088	5,407
Winona State University; Winona, Minn. (Pu)	6,402	65	62	2,800	6,200	3,500
MISSISSIPPI						
Alcorn State University; Lorman, Miss. (Pu)	2,555			2,685	5,546	2,427
Belhaven College; Jackson, Miss. (Pr)	1,317	64	62	10,450	10,450	4,280
Delta State University; Cleveland, Miss. (Pu)	3,469	84	60	2,596	5,546	2,600
Jackson State University; Jackson, Miss. (Pu)	5,250			2,688	5,546	3,800
Millsaps College; Jackson, Miss. (Pr)	1,191	87	55	14,190	14,190	6,106
Mississippi College; Clinton, Miss. (Pr)	2,522	93	57	9,090	9,090	4,176
Mississippi State University; Mississippi State, Miss. (Pu)	12,879	70	45	3,017	6,119	4,835
Mississippi University for Women; Columbus, Miss. (Pu)	3,314	78	81	2,556	5,546	2,557
Mississippi Valley State University; Itta Bena, Miss. (Pu)	2,212	21	62	2,646	5,546	2,900
Rust College; Holly Springs, Miss. (Pr)	843	47	60	5,200	5,200	2,400
Tougaloo College; Tougaloo, Miss. (Pr)	967	99	72	6,400	6,400	3,060
University of Mississippi; University, Miss. (Pu)	9,222	72	52	3,053	6,155	3,414
University of Southern Mississippi; Hattiesburg, Miss. (Pu)	12,049	65	60	2,870	5,972	2,965
Wesley College; Florence, Miss. (Pr)	81		41	2,500	2,500	2,150
William Carey College; Hattiesburg, Miss. (Pr)	1,524	94	66	6,880	6,880	3,060
MISSOURI						
Avila College; Kansas City, Mo. (Pr)	1,061	96	71	11,800	11,800	4,800
Central Methodist College; Fayette, Mo. (Pr)	1,258	88	60	10,350	10,350	4,110

Institution name; city, state (type)	Students	Percent Accepted	Women	Tuition In-state	Out-of-state	Room and board
Central Missouri State University; Warrensburg, Mo. (Pu)	9,074	90%	53%	$ 3,150	$ 5,040	$4,104
College of the Ozarks; Point Lookout, Mo. (Pr)	1,429	18	53			2,500
Columbia College; Columbia, Mo. (Pr)	7,865	64	58	10,102	10,102	4,399
Culver-Stockton College; Canton, Mo. (Pr)	870	92	58	10,650	10,650	4,750
DeVry Institute of Technology; Kansas City, Mo. (Pr)	2,555		24	7,778	7,778	
Drury University; Springfield, Mo. (Pr)	1,431		53	10,150	10,150	4,050
Fontbonne College; St. Louis, Mo. (Pr)	1,362	87	72	11,686	11,686	5,500
Hannibal-LaGrange College; Hannibal, Mo. (Pr)	1,139		65	7,770	7,770	2,927
Kansas City Art Institute; Kansas City, Mo. (Pr)	590	74		16,896	16,896	
Lincoln University; Jefferson City, Mo. (Pu)	3,088	100	59		4,416	3,790
Maryville University of Saint Louis; St. Louis, Mo. (Pr)	2,530	80	71	12,880	12,880	5,600
Messenger College; Joplin, Mo. (Pr)						
Missouri Baptist College; St. Louis, Mo. (Pr)	2,714	66	65	9,090	9,090	4,480
Missouri Southern State College; Joplin, Mo. (Pu)	5,651	87	57	2,370	4,740	3,610
Missouri Valley College; Marshall, Mo. (Pr)	1,192					5,000
Missouri Western State College; Saint Joseph, Mo. (Pu)	5,157	100	61	2,622	4,830	3,374
Northwest Missouri State University; Maryville, Mo. (Pu)	5,304		55	2,723	4,733	3,890
Park University; Parkville, Mo. (Pr)	1,122	87	61	4,950	4,950	4,850
Rockhurst University; Kansas City, Mo. (Pr)	2,074	90	54	12,500	12,500	4,920
Saint Louis College of Pharmacy; Saint Louis, Mo. (Pr)	822	62	65	13,000	13,000	5,220
Saint Louis University; Saint Louis, Mo. (Pr)	9,882	69	57	17,230	17,230	5,900
Southeast Missouri State University; Cape Girardeau, Mo. (Pu)	7,443	94	58	2,979	5,559	4,080
Southwest Baptist University; Bolivar, Mo. (Pr)	2,498					2,623
Southwest Missouri State University; Springfield, Mo. (Pu)	14,515	80	55	3,180	6,360	3,846
Stephens College; Columbia, Mo. (Pr)	734	84	93	15,770	15,770	5,870
Truman State University; Kirksville, Mo. (Pu)	5,963	81	58	3,680	6,664	4,452
University of Missouri-Columbia; Columbia, Mo. (Pu)	17,346	80	53			
University of Missouri-Kansas City; Kansas City, Mo. (Pu)	6,790	68	58	3,822	10,357	4,865
University of Missouri-Rolla; Rolla, Mo. (Pu)	3,882	89	23	3,978	11,892	4,557
University of Missouri-Saint Louis; Saint Louis, Mo. (Pu)	9,615		58	4,796	12,710	4,000
Washington University; Saint Louis, Mo. (Pr)	6,509	34	51	24,500	24,500	7,724
Webster University; Saint Louis, Mo. (Pr)	3,489	62	63	12,150	12,150	5,440
Westminster College; Fulton, Mo. (Pr)	686	81	42	14,060	14,060	5,020
William Jewell College; Liberty, Mo. (Pr)	1,145	86	58	13,500	13,500	4,250
MONTANA						
Carroll College; Helena, Mont. (Pr)	1,247	96	60	11,490	11,490	4,540
Montana State University-Billings; Billings, Mont. (Pu)	3,862	79	62	2,922	7,885	4,200
Montana State University-Bozeman; Bozeman, Mont. (Pu)	10,458	87	45	2,965	8,715	4,650
Montana State University-Northern; Havre, Mont. (Pu)	1,509					3,700
Montana Tech of the University of Montana; Butte, Mont. (Pu)	2,355	95	49	2,865	8,162	4,090
Salish-Kootenai College; Pablo, Mont. (Pr)	1,075	63	60	1,620	1,620	
University of Great Falls; Great Falls, Mont. (Pr)	825	100	72	7,650	7,650	2,570
University of Montana-Missoula; Missoula, Mont. (Pu)	10,457	88	53	3,064	8,311	4,800
Western Montana College; Dillon, Mont. (Pu)	1,081	99	56	1,979	6,581	3,800
NEBRASKA						
Bellevue University; Bellevue, Nebr. (Pr)	2,486	94	51	3,960	3,960	
Chadron State College; Chadron, Nebr. (Pu)	2,483	100	59	1,875	3,750	3,300
Clarkson College; Omaha, Nebr. (Pr)	380		89	6,528	6,528	
College of Saint Mary; Omaha, Nebr. (Pr)	1,071	88		12,428	12,428	4,598
Concordia College; Seward, Nebr. (Pr)	1,087			11,310	11,310	3,786
Creighton University; Omaha, Nebr. (Pr)	3,976	91	58	12,858	12,858	5,190
Dana College; Blair, Nebr. (Pr)	532	84	51	12,150	12,150	3,880
Doane College; Crete, Nebr. (Pr)	1,608	89	53	12,010	12,010	3,730
Hastings College; Hastings, Nebr. (Pr)	1,118	86	53	11,916	11,916	3,986
Midland Lutheran College; Fremont, Nebr. (Pr)	1,033	93	58	12,800	12,800	3,450
Nebraska Wesleyan University; Lincoln, Nebr. (Pr)	1,675	94	58	12,584	12,584	3,890
Peru State College; Peru, Nebr. (Pu)	1,454	88	55	1,865	3,750	3,192
Union College; Lincoln, Nebr. (Pr)	2,042					3,120
University of Nebraska-Kearney; Kearney, Nebr. (Pu)	5,886		56	2,101	3,765	3,150
University of Nebraska-Lincoln; Lincoln, Nebr. (Pu)	17,804	92	47	2,618	7,125	4,070
University of Nebraska-Omaha; Omaha, Nebr. (Pu)	10,659	90	53	2,393	6,458	3,120
Wayne State College; Wayne, Nebr. (Pu)	3,036	100	56	1,875	3,750	3,300
York College; York, Nebr. (Pr)						
NEVADA						
Deep Springs College; Dyer, Nev. (Pr)	26	11				
Sierra Nevada College; Incline Villa, Nev. (Pr)	540			10,800	10,800	5,600
University of Nevada-Las Vegas; Las Vegas, Nev. (Pu)	16,195	78	54	2,340	9,320	5,694
University of Nevada-Reno; Reno, Nev. (Pu)	9,150			1,920	7,020	5,200
NEW HAMPSHIRE						
Colby-Sawyer College; New London, N.H. (Pr)	808	84	65	18,960	18,960	7,240
Daniel Webster College; Nashua, N.H. (Pr)	536			14,280	14,280	5,662
Dartmouth College; Hanover, N.H. (Pr)	4,057	21	48	25,497	25,497	7,557
Franklin Pierce College; Rindge, N.H. (Pr)	1,383	77	48	18,150	18,150	6,250
Keene State College; Keene, N.H. (Pu)	4,233	81	57	3,830	9,140	4,938
New England College; Henniker, N.H. (Pr)	708	91	52	18,382	18,382	6,538

Institution name; city, state (type)	Students	Percent Accepted	Women	Tuition In-state	Out-of-state	Room and board
New Hampshire College; Manchester, N.H. (Pr)	4,058	80%	52%	$15,600	$15,600	$6,790
Notre Dame College; Manchester, N.H. (Pr)	732		76	14,098	14,098	5,713
Plymouth State College; Plymouth, N.H. (Pu)	3,417	77	48	3,830	9,140	5,030
Rivier College; Nashua, N.H. (Pr)	1,546	78	81	15,210	15,210	6,100
Saint Anselm College; Manchester, N.H. (Pr)	2,003	68	56	17,300	17,300	6,520
Thomas More College of Liberal Arts; Merrimack, N.H. (Pr)	72	100		9,600	9,600	7,400
University of New Hampshire; Durham, N.H. (Pu)	10,877	81	59			
University of New Hampshire at Manchester; Manchester, N.H. (Pu)	1,123	74	61	4,630	12,190	
NEW JERSEY						
Berkeley College; West Paterson, N.J. (Pr)	1,960	93	81	12,585	12,585	
Bloomfield College; Bloomfield, N.J. (Pr)	1,958	60	71	10,300	10,300	
Caldwell College; Caldwell, N.J. (Pr)	1,816	68	69	13,100	13,100	6,250
Centenary College; Hackettstown, N.J. (Pr)	940	83	76	13,800	13,800	6,150
College of New Jersey; Ewing, N.J. (Pu)	5,930	55	60	4,445	7,762	6,330
College of Saint Elizabeth; Morristown, N.J. (Pr)	1,351	83	92			
DeVry Institute of Technology; North Brunswick, N.J. (Pr)	3,640		22	7,778	7,778	
Drew University; Madison, N.J. (Pr)	1,486	75	58	22,462	22,462	6,564
Fairleigh Dickinson University, Florham-Madison Campus; Teaneck, N.J. (Pr)	2,433	73	55	14,732	14,732	6,536
Fairleigh Dickinson University, Teaneck Campus; Teaneck, N.J. (Pr)	2,077	64	55	13,996	13,996	
Felician College; Lodi, N.J. (Pr)	978			11,010	11,010	5,960
Georgian Court College; Lakewood, N.J. (Pr)	1,582	91	90	12,742	12,742	4,700
Kean University; Union, N.J. (Pu)	9,227	57	65	3,373	5,070	5,530
Monmouth University; West Long Branch, N.J. (Pr)	4,004	87	58	15,138	15,138	6,682
Montclair State University; Upper Montclair, N.J. (Pu)	9,203	41	61	3,204	4,946	5,802
New Jersey City University; Jersey City, N.J. (Pu)	6,412	49	61	2,880	4,898	5,000
New Jersey Institute of Technology; Newark, N.J. (Pu)	5,266	64	22	5,508	9,852	7,050
Princeton University; Princeton, N.J. (Pr)	4,565	11		25,430	25,430	7,206
Ramapo College of New Jersey; Mahwah, N.J. (Pu)	4,655	47	57	3,822	6,688	6,624
Richard Stockton College of New Jersey; Pomona, N.J. (Pu)	5,975	48	57	3,280	5,312	5,368
Rider University; Lawrenceville, N.J. (Pr)	4,223	80	58	17,180	17,180	7,080
Rowan University; Glassboro, N.J. (Pu)	8,391	97	57	3,750	7,500	5,766
Rutgers University-Camden College of Arts & Sciences; Camden, N.J. (Pu)	2,813	62	59	4,762	9,692	5,322
Rutgers University-College of Nursing; Newark, N.J. (Pu)	466	26	92	4,762	9,692	6,090
Rutgers University-College of Pharmacy; New Brunswick, N.J. (Pu)	825	45	64	5,286	10,754	6,098
Rutgers University-Cook College; Piscataway, N.J. (Pu)	3,231	64	50	5,286	10,754	6,098
Rutgers University-Douglass College; Piscataway, N.J. (Pu)	3,099	68		4,762	9,692	6,098
Rutgers University-Livingston College; Piscataway, N.J. (Pu)	3,536	60	52	4,762	9,692	6,098
Rutgers University-Mason Gross School of the Arts; Piscataway, N.J. (Pu)	617	22	58	4,762	9,692	6,098
Rutgers University-Newark College of Arts & Sciences; Newark, N.J. (Pu)	3,665	57	56	4,762	9,692	6,110
Rutgers University-Rutgers College; Piscataway, N.J. (Pu)	10,993	48	51	4,762	9,692	6,098
Rutgers University-School of Engineering; Piscataway, N.J. (Pu)	2,190	68	22	5,286	10,754	6,098
Rutgers University, University College-Camden; Camden, N.J. (Pu)	724	65	57	5,602	10,326	5,322
Rutgers University, University College-Newark; Newark, N.J. (Pu)	1,645		56	4,262	8,676	5,314
Rutgers University,University College-New Brunswick; Piscataway, N.J. (Pu)	3,308	63	51	4,732	9,626	5,314
Saint Peter's College; Jersey City, N.J. (Pr)	3,211	79	57	14,100	14,100	5,060
Seton Hall University; South Orange, N.J. (Pr)	5,718	82	54	13,830	13,830	7,230
Stevens Institute of Technology; Hoboken, N.J. (Pr)	1,564	59	23	20,890	20,890	7,280
Thomas Edison State College; Trenton, N.J. (Pu)	8,399		44	2,200	3,150	
Westminster Choir College of Rider University; Princeton, N.J. (Pr)	280					6,610
William Paterson University; Wayne, N.J. (Pu)	8,270	50	58	4,690	7,360	5,760
NEW MEXICO						
College of Santa Fe; Santa Fe, N.M. (Pr)	1,500	84	63	15,750	15,000	5,000
College of the Southwest; Hobbs, N.M. (Pr)	566	71	73	4,500	4,500	3,492
Eastern New Mexico University; Portales, N.M. (Pu)	3,012		59	1,752	6,510	3,104
New Mexico Highlands University; Las Vegas, N.M. (Pu)	2,054			1,782	7,122	2,171
New Mexico Institute of Mining & Technology; Socorro, N.M. (Pu)	1,218	70	37	1,600	6,600	3,584
New Mexico State University; Las Cruces, N.M. (Pu)	12,621	69	53	2,502	8,166	3,426
St. John's College; Santa Fe, N.M. (Pr)	431	84		22,000	22,000	6,386
University of New Mexico; Albuquerque, N.M. (Pu)	16,874	92	57	2,430	9,172	4,800
Western New Mexico University; Silver City, N.M. (Pu)	1,758					2,260
NEW YORK						
Adelphi University; Garden City, N.Y. (Pr)	2,774	78	67	14,000	14,000	6,850
Albany College of Pharmacy; Albany, N.Y. (Pr)	652	77	58	11,250	11,250	
Alfred University; Alfred, N.Y. (Pr)	2,113	81	50	19,918	19,918	
Audrey Cohen College; New York, N.Y. (Pr)	1,093	78		14,160	14,160	
Bard College; Annandale-on-Hudson, N.Y. (Pr)	1,233	47	58	23,480	23,480	7,220

Institution name; city, state (type)	Students	Percent Accepted	Percent Women	Tuition In-state	Tuition Out-of-state	Room and board
Barnard College; New York, N.Y. (Pr)	2,270	36%	100%	$21,410	$21,410	$ 9,084
Berkeley College; White Plains, N.Y. (Pr)	680		75	12,585	12,585	7,800
Berkeley College of New York City; New York, N.Y. (Pr)	1,720		73	12,585	12,585	
Canisius College; Buffalo, N.Y. (Pr)	3,329	81	51	15,990	15,990	6,730
Cazenovia College; Cazenovia, N.Y. (Pr)	896	55	64	11,230	11,230	
City University of New York-Baruch College; New York, N.Y. (Pu)	12,386	19	56	3,330	6,930	
City University of New York-Brooklyn College; Brooklyn, N.Y. (Pu)	10,417	70	61	3,200	6,800	
City University of New York-City College; New York, N.Y. (Pu)	8,349	59	52	3,200	6,800	
City University of New York-College of Staten Island; Staten Island, N.Y. (Pu)	10,130		58	3,200	6,800	
City University of New York-Hunter College; New York, N.Y. (Pu)	15,568	42	70	3,200	6,800	1,840
City University of New York-John Jay College of Criminal Justice; New York, N.Y. (Pu)	9,772			2,450	5,050	
City University of New York-Lehman College; Bronx, N.Y. (Pu)	7,698			3,200	6,800	
City University of New York-Medgar Evers College; New York, N.Y. (Pu)	5,401			3,200	6,800	
City University of New York-Queens College; Flushing, N.Y. (Pu)	11,566	52	63	3,200	6,800	
City University of New York-York College; Jamaica, N.Y. (Pu)	5,362	52	71	3,200	6,800	
Clarkson University; Potsdam, N.Y. (Pr)	2,581	83	27	19,825	19,825	7,484
Colgate University; Hamilton, N.Y. (Pr)	2,866	42	52	25,565	25,565	6,330
College of Aeronautics; Flushing, N.Y. (Pr)	1,305	49	7	8,550	8,550	4,280
College of Insurance; New York, N.Y. (Pr)	338	60	52	14,252	14,252	9,140
College of Mount Saint Vincent; Riverdale, N.Y. (Pr)	1,255	73	79	14,910	14,910	7,020
College of New Rochelle; New Rochelle, N.Y. (Pr)	4,705	74	87	11,600	11,600	6,000
College of Saint Rose; Albany, N.Y. (Pr)	2,729	75	73	12,434	12,434	6,358
Columbia University; New York, N.Y. (Pr)	7,530	14	50	23,244	23,244	7,492
Concordia College; Bronxville, N.Y. (Pr)	599	82	60	12,590	12,590	5,750
Cooper Union; New York, N.Y. (Pr)	870	13	34	8,300	8,300	10,000
Cornell University; Ithaca, N.Y. (Pr)	13,669	33				7,827
Daemen College; Amherst, N.Y. (Pr)	1,630	73	75	11,100	11,100	5,800
DeVry Institute of Technology; Long Island City, N.Y. (Pr)	1,250		21	8,776	8,776	
Dominican College of Blauvelt; Orangeburg, N.Y. (Pr)	1,645	73	75	12,660	12,000	7,000
Dowling College; Oakdale, N.Y. (Pr)	2,922	88	59	11,940	11,940	2,650
D'Youville College; Buffalo, N.Y. (Pr)	1,221		74	11,580	11,580	5,120
Eastman School of Music, University of Rochester; Rochester, N.Y. (Pr)	503	29	55	20,320	20,320	7,512
Elmira College; Elmira, N.Y. (Pr)	1,640	72	69	21,960	21,960	7,280
Eugene Lang College; New York, N.Y. (Pr)	520	54	68	19,620	19,620	8,857
Fashion Institute of Technology; New York, N.Y. (Pu)				2,500	5,950	5,600
Five Towns College; Dix Hills, N.Y. (Pr)	724		25	9,300	9,300	6,500
Fordham University; New York, N.Y. (Pr)	6,578	62	59	19,200	19,200	8,240
Hamilton College; Clinton, N.Y. (Pr)	1,740	42	49	25,000	25,000	6,200
Hartwick College; Oneonta, N.Y. (Pr)	1,450	79	52	23,745	23,745	
Hilbert College; Hamburg, N.Y. (Pr)	842	86	67	10,850	10,850	4,805
Hobart and William Smith Colleges; Geneva, N.Y. (Pr)	1,830	71	52	23,865	23,865	6,882
Hofstra University; Hempstead, N.Y. (Pr)	9,300	55	54	13,750	13,750	7,060
Houghton College; Houghton, N.Y. (Pr)	1,380	89	63	14,590	14,590	5,160
Iona College; New Rochelle, N.Y. (Pr)	3,341	77	52	15,500	15,500	8,430
Ithaca College; Ithaca, N.Y. (Pr)	5,702	73	56	18,410	18,410	7,956
Juilliard School; New York, N.Y. (Pr)	665	8	52	16,000	16,000	6,850
Keuka College; Keuka Park, N.Y. (Pr)	895	94	75	12,730	12,730	6,370
Laboratory Institute of Merchandising; New York, N.Y. (Pr)	267	76		12,800	12,800	
Le Moyne College; Syracuse, N.Y. (Pr)	2,387	80	58	14,580	14,580	6,320
Long Island University-Brooklyn; Brooklyn, N.Y. (Pr)	4,193					7,620
Long Island University-C.W. Post; Brookville, N.Y. (Pr)	5,748	85	57			
Manhattan College; Riverdale, N.Y. (Pr)	2,703	70	46	15,500	15,500	7,450
Manhattan School of Music; New York, N.Y. (Pr)	400	40	47	18,200	18,200	
Manhattanville College; Purchase, N.Y. (Pr)	1,529	67	68	17,430	17,430	8,000
Mannes College of Music; New York, N.Y. (Pr)	160	31		18,000	18,000	6,875
Marist College; Poughkeepsie, N.Y. (Pr)	4,107	54	56	14,394	14,394	7,542
Marymount College; Tarrytown, N.Y. (Pr)	898	85	95	14,700	14,700	7,800
Marymount Manhattan College; New York, N.Y. (Pr)	2,455	67	81	13,050	13,050	
Medaille College; Buffalo, N.Y. (Pr)	1,302	75	70	11,190	11,190	5,300
Mercy College; Dobbs Ferry, N.Y. (Pr)	9,500			7,800	7,800	6,500
Molloy College; Rockville Centre, N.Y. (Pr)	1,920		79	11,900	11,900	
Mount Saint Mary College; Newburgh, N.Y. (Pr)	1,698	87	69	11,100	11,100	5,670
Nazareth College of Rochester; Rochester, N.Y. (Pr)	1,793	81	75	14,046	14,046	6,376
New York Institute of Technology; Old Westbury, N.Y. (Pr)	5,750		39	11,010	11,010	6,360
New York School of Interior Design; New York, N.Y. (Pr)	692		91	15,200	15,200	
New York University; New York, N.Y. (Pr)	18,204	32	59	24,336	24,336	9,226
Niagara University; Sanborn, N.Y.						
Nyack College; Nyack, N.Y. (Pr)	1,293	72	59	11,440	11,440	5,600
Pace University-White Plains; White Plains, N.Y. (Pr)						
Pace University-New York City; New York, N.Y. (Pr)	5,869	73	61	15,130	15,130	6,550
Pace University-Pleasantville/Briarcliff; Pleasantville, N.Y. (Pr)	3,446	75	59	15,130	15,130	6,550
Parsons School of Design; New York, N.Y. (Pr)	2,397	44	72	21,550	21,550	12,500

Institution name; city, state (type)	Students	Percent Accepted	Percent Women	Tuition In-state	Tuition Out-of-state	Room and board
Polytechnic University-Brooklyn; Brooklyn, N.Y. (Pr)	1,843	70%	18%	$20,312	$20,312	$ 4,600
Pratt Institute; Brooklyn, N.Y. (Pr)	2,676	50	49	19,524	19,524	7,800
Regents College; Albany, N.Y. (Pr)	17,418					
Rensselaer Polytechnic Institute; Troy, N.Y. (Pr)	4,922	78	24	22,300	22,300	7,692
Roberts Wesleyan College; Rochester, N.Y. (Pr)	1,149	93	66	13,690	13,690	4,758
Rochester Institute of Technology; Rochester, N.Y. (Pr)	10,746	77	34	17,328	17,328	6,852
Russell Sage College; Troy, N.Y. (Pr)	842	93		15,920	15,920	5,950
Saint Bonaventure University; St. Bonaventure, N.Y. (Pr)	2,200	91	52	13,888	13,888	5,800
Saint Francis College; Brooklyn Heights, N.Y. (Pr)	2,299	76	60	8,250	8,250	
Saint John Fisher College; Rochester, N.Y. (Pr)	2,118	80	61	14,690	14,690	6,300
St. John's University; Jamaica, N.Y. (Pr)	14,035	83	57	13,990	13,990	8,550
St. Joseph's College-Brooklyn; Brooklyn, N.Y. (Pr)	1,256	49	78	9,030	9,030	
St. Joseph's College-Patchogue; Patchogue, N.Y. (Pr)	2,931	78	78	8,850	8,850	
St. Lawrence University; Canton, N.Y. (Pr)	1,861	74	52	23,765	21,175	7,205
Saint Thomas Aquinas College; Sparkill, N.Y. (Pr)	2,038		58	12,500	12,500	10,840
Sarah Lawrence College; Bronxville, N.Y. (Pr)	1,178	43	73	24,810	24,810	7,991
School of Visual Arts; New York, N.Y. (Pr)	5,315	64	53	15,000	15,000	8,200
Siena College; Loudonville, N.Y. (Pr)	3,002	73	54	13,660	13,660	6,215
Skidmore College; Saratoga Springs, N.Y. (Pr)	2,540	49	60	25,210	25,210	7,270
Southampton College of Long Island University; Southampton, N.Y. (Pr)	2,649	67	60	15,340	15,340	7,390
State University of New York at Albany; Albany, N.Y. (Pu)	11,737	61	49	3,400	8,300	5,828
State University of New York at Buffalo; Buffalo, N.Y. (Pu)	16,259	74	47	3,400	8,300	5,904
State University of New York at New Paltz; New Paltz, N.Y. (Pu)	6,050	55	63	3,400	8,300	5,246
State University of New York at Plattsburgh; Plattsburgh, N.Y. (Pu)	5,326	69	57	3,400	8,300	4,850
State University of New York at Stony Brook; Stony Brook, N.Y. (Pu)	12,690	58	50	3,400	8,300	6,230
State University of New York-Binghamton University; Binghamton, N.Y. (Pu)	9,872	42	53	3,400	8,300	5,516
State University of New York-Buffalo College; Buffalo, N.Y. (Pu)	9,421			3,400	8,300	5,420
State University of New York College at Brockport; Brockport, N.Y. (Pu)	6,719	55	57	3,400	8,300	5,410
State University of New York College at Cortland; Cortland, N.Y. (Pu)	5,660	64	57	3,400	8,300	5,560
State University of New York College at Fredonia; Fredonia, N.Y. (Pu)	4,727	62	59	3,400	8,300	5,400
State University of New York College at Geneseo; Geneseo, N.Y. (Pu)	5,321	52	66	3,400	8,300	4,880
State University of New York College at Old Westbury; Old Westbury, N.Y. (Pu)	3,245	87	57	3,400	8,300	5,286
State University of New York College at Oneonta; Oneonta, N.Y. (Pu)	5,147	65	59	3,400	8,300	5,456
State University of New York College at Oswego; Oswego, N.Y. (Pu)	6,849	59	54	3,400	8,300	6,160
State University of New York College at Potsdam; Potsdam, N.Y. (Pu)	3,587	81	59	3,400	8,300	5,750
State University of New York College at Purchase; Purchase, N.Y. (Pu)	3,837	35	56	3,400	8,300	5,942
State University of New York College of A&T at Cobleskill; Cobleskill, N.Y. (Pu)	2,325	79	45	3,200	5,000	5,620
State University of New York College of A&T at Morrisville; Morrisville, N.Y. (Pu)	2,843	77	48	3,200	5,200	5,650
State University of New York College of Environmental Science and Forestry; Syracuse, N.Y. (Pu)	1,171	50	37	3,400	8,300	8,310
State University of New York College of Technology at Alfred; Alfred, N.Y. (Pu)				3,400	8,300	5,420
State University of New York College of Technology at Canton; Canton, N.Y. (Pu)	2,260	88	48	3,200	5,000	5,510
State University of New York College of Technology at Delhi; Delhi, N.Y. (Pu)	1,893		45	3,200		
State University of New York College of Technology at Farmingdale; Farmingdale, N.Y. (Pu)				3,200	5,000	5,230
State University of New York Empire State College; Saratoga, N.Y. (Pu)	7,213		52	3,400	8,300	
State University of New York Health Science Center at Brooklyn; Brooklyn, N.Y. (Pu)				3,400	8,300	5,420
State University of New York Health Science Center at Syracuse; Syracuse, N.Y. (Pu)	303		74		8,300	5,680
State University of New York Institute of Technology at Utica/Rome; Utica, N.Y. (Pu)	2,159		50	3,949	8,849	4,170
State University of New York Maritime College; Throg's Neck, N.Y. (Pu)	646			3,400	8,300	5,420
Syracuse University; Syracuse, N.Y. (Pr)	10,685	59	54	20,380	20,380	8,750
Touro College; Brooklyn, N.Y. (Pr)	6,661	74	68	9,250	9,250	
Union College; Schenectady, N.Y. (Pr)	2,150	46	47	24,750	24,750	6,639
United States Merchant Marine Academy; Kings Point, N.Y. (Pu)	940	48		1,000	1,000	
United States Military Academy; West Point, N.Y. (Pu)	4,087	14	14			

Institution name; city, state (type)	Students	Percent Accepted	Percent Women	Tuition In-state	Tuition Out-of-state	Room and board
University of Rochester; Rochester, N.Y. (Pr)	4,529	66%	48%	$23,150	$23,150	$7,740
Utica College of Syracuse University; Utica, N.Y. (Pr)	2,017	84	64	16,150	16,150	6,350
Vassar College; Poughkeepsie, N.Y. (Pr)	2,321	43	61	23,700	23,700	6,770
Wadhams Hall Seminary College; Ogdensburg, N.Y. (Pr)	22	100		5,300	5,300	4,970
Wagner College; Staten Island, N.Y. (Pr)	1,650	68	56	19,200	19,200	6,800
Webb Institute; Glen Cove, N.Y. (Pr)	81	46				6,250
Wells College; Aurora, N.Y. (Pr)	404	90	99	11,850	11,850	6,100
Yeshiva University; New York, N.Y. (Pr)	1,990			14,920	14,920	4,750
NORTH CAROLINA						
Appalachian State University; Boone, N.C. (Pu)	11,694	72	50	962	8,232	3,340
Barton College; Wilson, N.C. (Pr)	1,233	87	68	10,812	10,812	4,270
Belmont Abbey College; Belmont, N.C. (Pr)	926	98	54	11,650	11,650	6,528
Brevard College; Brevard, N.C. (Pr)	674	87	43	10,660	10,660	4,820
Campbell University; Buies Creek, N.C. (Pr)	2,274		56	11,350	11,350	4,122
Catawba College; Salisbury, N.C. (Pr)	1,195	78	50	13,330	13,330	4,980
Chowan College; Murfreesboro, N.C. (Pr)	726	90	43	11,820	11,820	4,780
Davidson College; Davidson, N.C. (Pr)	1,652	38	50	22,104	22,104	6,340
Duke University; Durham, N.C. (Pr)	6,388	28	48	23,210	23,210	7,088
East Carolina University; Greenville, N.C. (Pu)	15,246	80	58	992	8,558	4,070
Elizabeth City State College; Elizabeth City, N.C. (Pu)	1,937	72	63	1,552	7,816	4,952
Elon College; Elon College, N.C. (Pr)	3,701	59	60	12,671	12,671	4,551
Fayetteville State University; Fayetteville, N.C. (Pu)	3,249	87		900	8,028	3,400
Gardner-Webb University; Boiling Springs, N.C. (Pr)	2,369	87	64	10,780	10,780	
Greensboro College; Greensboro, N.C. (Pr)	991	72	53	11,500	11,500	4,900
Guilford College; Greensboro, N.C. (Pr)	1,245	76	53	16,400	16,400	5,610
High Point University; High Point, N.C. (Pr)	2,658	91	59	11,120	11,120	5,300
Johnson C. Smith University; Charlotte, N.C. (Pr)	1,283			8,126	8,126	3,846
Lees-McRae College; Banner Elk, N.C. (Pr)	643	86	51	11,200	11,200	4,100
Lenoir-Rhyne College; Hickory, N.C. (Pr)	1,353	86	64	12,870	12,870	4,920
Mars Hill College; Mars Hill, N.C. (Pr)	1,224	90	57	12,000	12,000	4,500
Meredith College; Raleigh, N.C. (Pr)	2,457	85		9,840	9,840	4,260
Methodist College; Fayetteville, N.C. (Pr)	1,851	94	44	12,600	12,600	4,830
Montreat College; Montreat, N.C. (Pr)	1,116	80	58			4,614
Mount Olive College; Mount Olive, N.C. (Pr)	1,822	91	53	9,100	9,100	4,000
North Carolina A&T State University; Greensboro, N.C. (Pu)	6,684	34	52	918	8,188	3,860
North Carolina Central University; Durham, N.C. (Pu)	5,580	18	63	962	8,232	3,904
North Carolina School of the Arts; Winston-Salem, N.C. (Pu)	727	47	39	1,590	10,218	4,686
North Carolina State University; Raleigh, N.C. (Pu)	21,684	62	41	1,528	10,694	4,560
North Carolina Wesleyan College; Rocky Mount, N.C. (Pr)	2,421		62			4,830
Pfeiffer University; Misenheimer, N.C. (Pr)	847			10,230	10,230	1,860
Queens College; Charlotte, N.C. (Pr)	1,115	58	79	7,200	7,200	
Saint Andrews Presbyterian College; Laurinburg, N.C. (Pr)	638	81	55	14,015	14,015	5,300
Saint Augustine's College; Raleigh, N.C. (Pr)	1,492	45	58	5,132	5,132	4,508
Salem College; Winston-Salem, N.C. (Pr)	923	88	98	13,200	13,200	7,920
Shaw University; Raleigh, N.C. (Pr)	2,529	68	63	6,272	6,272	4,342
University of North Carolina-Asheville; Asheville, N.C. (Pu)	3,125	61	58	806	7,426	4,179
University of North Carolina-Chapel Hill; Chapel Hill, N.C. (Pu)	15,434	39	61	1,528	10,694	5,280
University of North Carolina-Charlotte; Charlotte, N.C. (Pu)	14,195	70	54	962	8,232	3,816
University of North Carolina-Greensboro; Greensboro, N.C. (Pu)	10,286	77	66	1,086	9,590	4,064
University of North Carolina-Pembroke; Pembroke, N.C. (Pu)	2,649	86	61	918	8,188	3,202
University of North Carolina-Wilmington; Wilmington, N.C. (Pu)	9,067	58	59	962	8,232	4,656
Wake Forest University; Winston-Salem, N.C. (Pr)	3,990	49	52	21,420	21,420	5,900
Warren Wilson College; Asheville, N.C. (Pr)	763	80	61	14,375	14,375	4,644
Western Carolina University; Cullowhee, N.C. (Pu)	5,352	82	52	962	8,232	3,050
Wingate University; Wingate, N.C. (Pr)	1,115	91	50	12,300	12,300	5,200
Winston-Salem State University; Winston-Salem, N.C. (Pu)	2,865	80	67	1,575	7,868	
NORTH DAKOTA						
Dickinson State University; Dickinson, N.D. (Pu)	1,800	100	59	2,096	5,256	2,670
Jamestown College; Jamestown, N.D. (Pr)	1,141	100	55	7,150	7,150	3,200
Mayville State University; Mayville, N.D. (Pu)	851	99	49	1,982	5,292	3,026
Medcenter One College of Nursing; Bismarck, N.D. (Pr)	82			3,132	3,132	
Minot State University; Minot, N.D. (Pu)	2,982	97	62	2,144	5,724	2,800
North Dakota State University; Fargo, N.D. (Pu)	8,761	75	42	2,604	6,953	3,542
University of Mary; Bismarck, N.D. (Pr)	1,934	95	63	7,900	7,900	3,150
University of North Dakota; Grand Forks, N.D. (Pu)	8,680	71	49	2,362	6,306	3,243
Valley City State University; Valley City, N.D. (Pu)	1,081	95	55		5,842	2,694
OHIO						
Antioch College; Yellow Spring, Ohio (Pr)	595	85	66	21,628	21,628	4,176
Art Academy of Cincinnati; Cincinnati, Ohio (Pr)	187					
Ashland University; Ashland, Ohio (Pr)	2,850	81	64	15,134	15,134	5,610
Baldwin-Wallace College; Berea, Ohio (Pr)	4,002	81	61	15,340	15,340	5,460
Bluffton College; Bluffton, Ohio (Pr)	999	86	54	14,076	14,076	5,122
Bowling Green State University; Bowling Green, Ohio (Pu)	15,444	90	57	4,058	9,606	4,612
Bryant and Stratton College; Cleveland, Ohio						
Capital University; Columbus, Ohio (Pr)	2,807	81	63	16,880	16,880	5,170

Institution name; city, state (type)	Students	Percent Accepted	Women	Tuition In-state	Out-of-state	Room and board
Case Western Reserve University; Cleveland, Ohio (Pr)	3,598	72%	40%	$20,100	$20,100	$5,815
Cedarville College; Cedarville, Ohio (Pr)	2,762	74	55	10,608	10,608	4,788
Central State University; Wilberforce, Ohio (Pu)	998	42	57	3,318	7,293	4,695
Cincinnati Bible College and Seminary; Cincinnati, Ohio (Pr)	625	99	42	6,560	6,560	3,940
Cleveland College of Jewish Studies; Beachwood, Ohio (Pr)	14	20	79	5,600	5,600	
Cleveland Institute of Art; Cleveland, Ohio (Pr)	525	74	48	14,175	14,175	5,076
Cleveland Institute of Music; Cleveland, Ohio (Pr)	222	29		17,875	17,875	5,590
Cleveland State University; Cleveland, Ohio (Pu)	16,326	79	54	1,872	3,744	4,848
College of Mount Saint Joseph; Cincinnati, Ohio (Pr)	1,941	85	70	13,000	13,000	4,750
College of Wooster; Wooster, Ohio (Pr)	1,709	79	53	20,530	20,530	5,420
Columbus College of Art & Design; Columbus, Ohio (Pr)	1,494			14,520	14,520	6,100
Denison University; Granville, Ohio (Pr)	2,089	69	55	21,710	21,710	6,300
DeVry Institute of Technology; Columbus, Ohio (Pr)	3,369		26	7,778	7,778	
Franciscan University of Steubenville; Steubenville, Ohio (Pr)	1,694	89	60	12,690	12,690	5,070
Franklin University; Columbus, Ohio (Pr)	3,812	100	59	5,642	5,642	
Heidelberg College; Tiffin, Ohio (Pr)	1,360	86	51	16,998	16,998	5,474
Hiram College; Hiram, Ohio (Pr)	1,204	86	55	17,870	17,870	6,254
John Carroll University; University Heights, Ohio (Pr)	3,527	88	53	16,334	16,334	6,128
Kent State University; Kent, Ohio (Pu)	17,275	92	59	4,012	8,916	4,530
Kenyon College; Gambier, Ohio (Pr)	1,588	68	56	25,370	25,370	4,370
Lake Erie College; Painesville, Ohio (Pr)	509	87	74	15,140	15,140	5,420
Lourdes College; Sylvania, Ohio (Pr)	1,298	84	85	8,770	8,770	
Malone College; Canton, Ohio (Pr)	1,949	88	61	12,800	12,800	5,450
Marietta College; Marietta, Ohio (Pr)	1,219	92	51	18,010	18,010	5,196
Miami University; Oxford, Ohio (Pu)	15,288	79	55	5,052	11,706	5,330
Mount Union College; Alliance, Ohio (Pr)	1,407					3,870
Mount Vernon Nazarene College; Mount Vernon, Ohio (Pr)	1,843	51	58	11,468	11,468	4,203
Muskingum College; New Concord, Ohio (Pr)	1,564	85	52	12,250	12,250	5,100
Notre Dame College of Ohio; South Euclid, Ohio (Pr)	639	55		13,686	13,686	5,248
Oberlin College; Oberlin, Ohio (Pr)	2,951	50	59	24,096	24,096	6,178
Ohio Dominican College; Columbus, Ohio (Pr)	2,135	100	67	10,250	10,250	5,070
Ohio Northern University; Ada, Ohio (Pr)	2,381	93	49	21,435	21,435	5,265
Ohio State University-Columbus; Columbus, Ohio (Pu)	36,092	74	48	3,780	11,730	5,328
Ohio State University-Lima; Lima, Ohio (Pu)	1,166	116	58	3,528	11,097	4,278
Ohio University-Athens; Athens, Ohio (Pu)	16,554	80	55	4,800	10,101	5,484
Ohio University-Chillecothe; Chillicothe, Ohio (Pu)	1,565		37	3,102	7,581	5,800
Ohio University-Eastern; West Saint Clairsville, Ohio (Pu)	1,000		40		7,383	
Ohio University-Lancaster; Lancaster, Ohio (Pu)	1,500		41		7,383	
Ohio University-Southern; Ironton, Ohio (Pu)	1,963		63	3,087	3,219	
Ohio University-Zanesville; Zanesville, Ohio (Pu)	1,078		32		7,383	
Ohio Wesleyan University; Delaware, Ohio (Pr)	1,930	83	51			
Otterbein College; Westerville, Ohio (Pr)	2,587	89	64	16,911	16,911	5,289
Pontifical College Josephinum; Columbus, Ohio (Pr)	42					2,320
Shawnee State University; Portsmouth, Ohio (Pu)	3,613	100	63	2,745	5,148	4,431
Tiffin University; Tiffin, Ohio (Pr)	1,150	87		11,130	11,130	5,050
Union Institute; Cincinnati, Ohio (Pr)	681	62	63			
University of Akron; Akron, Ohio (Pu)	19,248	100	55	3,755	9,956	5,010
University of Cincinnati; Cincinnati, Ohio (Pu)	20,656	96	48	4,257	12,138	6,375
University of Dayton; Dayton, Ohio (Pr)	7,018	80	51	15,540	15,540	5,080
University of Findlay; Findlay, Ohio (Pr)	3,327	82	56			
University of Rio Grande; Rio Grande, Ohio (Pr)	1,971			7,593	7,593	4,612
University of Toledo; Toledo, Ohio (Pu)	16,729	95	55	4,416	10,783	
Urbana University; Urbana, Ohio (Pr)	1,113	79	49			4,350
Ursuline College; Pepper Pike, Ohio (Pr)	1,065			8,856	8,856	4,330
Walsh University; North Canton, Ohio (Pr)	1,261			10,900	10,900	5,110
Wilmington College; Wilmington, Ohio (Pr)	1,163	70	54	14,330	14,330	5,220
Wittenberg University; Springfield, Ohio (Pr)	2,100	87	56	20,406	20,406	5,376
Wright State University; Dayton, Ohio (Pu)	10,904	92	56	4,128	8,256	5,053
Xavier University; Cincinnati, Ohio (Pr)	3,958	89	60	15,680	15,680	6,680
Youngstown State University; Youngstown, Ohio (Pu)	11,025	90	54	3,762		
OKLAHOMA						
Bartlesville Wesleyan College; Bartlesville, Okla. (Pr)	571	60	64	8,200	8,200	3,800
Cameron University; Lawton, Okla. (Pu)	4,493	91	54	2,000	4,800	2,830
East Central University; Ada, Okla. (Pu)	3,786			1,106	3,323	2,200
Northeastern State University; Tahlequah, Okla. (Pu)	7,025		55	1,800	4,200	3,260
Northwestern Oklahoma State University; Alva, Okla. (Pu)	1,648	100	55	1,830	4,340	2,316
Oklahoma Baptist University; Shawnee, Okla. (Pr)	2,098	89	53	8,800	8,800	3,470
Oklahoma Christian University; Oklahoma City, Okla. (Pr)	1,593	90	47	9,700	9,700	4,200
Oklahoma City University; Oklahoma City, Okla. (Pr)	2,100	63	57	9,320	9,320	4,400
Oklahoma Panhandle State University; Goodwell, Okla. (Pu)	1,589					2,330
Oklahoma State University; Stillwater, Okla. (Pu)	16,203	89	47	1,950	6,540	4,536
Oral Roberts University; Tulsa, Okla. (Pr)	2,788			10,160	10,160	4,728
Southeastern Oklahoma State University; Durant, Okla. (Pu)	3,384	93	54	1,470	3,900	2,689
Southwestern Oklahoma State University; Weatherford, Okla. (Pu)	3,853	93	54	1,485	4,140	2,440

Institution name; city, state (type)	Students	Percent Accepted	Percent Women	Tuition In-state	Tuition Out-of-state	Room and board
University of Central Oklahoma; Edmond, Okla. (Pu)	11,476	96%	57%	$ 1,470	$ 3,990	$2,783
University of Oklahoma; Norman, Okla. (Pu)	17,245	89	48	1,890	6,225	4,384
University of Science and Arts of Oklahoma; Chickasha, Okla. (Pu)	1,393	66	63	1,485	4,140	2,320
University of Tulsa; Tulsa, Okla. (Pr)	2,924	80	52	13,400	13,400	4,660
OREGON						
Cascade College; Portland, Ore.						
Concordia University; Portland, Ore. (Pr)	910	81	63	15,500	15,500	3,820
Eastern Oregon State College; LaGrande, Ore. (Pu)	2,056	50	52	2,316	2,316	4,165
Eugene Bible College; Eugene, Ore. (Pr)	201	64	44	5,913	5,913	3,663
George Fox University; Newberg, Ore. (Pr)	1,677	93	60	17,300	17,300	5,550
Lewis & Clark College; Portland, Ore. (Pr)	1,742	69	59	20,326	20,326	6,208
Linfield College; McMinnville, Ore. (Pr)	1,550	92	55	18,450	18,450	5,350
Marylhurst University; Marylhurst, Ore. (Pr)	832	77	78	10,575	10,575	5,928
Oregon Health Sciences University; Portland, Ore. (Pu)	663		61	3,436	8,092	3,804
Oregon Institute of Technology; Klamath Falls, Ore. (Pu)	2,811		45	3,309	10,083	3,910
Oregon State University; Corvallis, Ore. (Pu)	12,783	91	46	3,549	12,393	5,394
Pacific Northwest College of Art; Portland, Ore. (Pr)	317	99	61	11,500	11,500	5,170
Pacific University; Forest Grove, Ore. (Pr)	1,082	86	61	17,300	17,300	5,295
Portland State University; Portland, Ore. (Pu)	12,696	78	56	2,694	10,887	6,150
Reed College; Portland, Ore. (Pr)	1,353	68	54	24,820	24,820	6,700
Southern Oregon University; Ashland, Ore. (Pu)	4,849	66	57	2,520	9,183	4,350
University of Oregon; Eugene, Ore. (Pu)	13,610	90	53	2,694	12,081	5,350
University of Portland; Portland, Ore. (Pr)	2,392	89	56	16,930	16,930	5,190
Warner Pacific College; Portland, Ore. (Pr)	645	79	66	14,410	14,410	4,600
Western Baptist College; Salem, Ore. (Pr)	683	87	57	13,224	13,224	4,940
Western Oregon University; Monmouth, Ore. (Pu)	3,927		60	3,198	4,410	4,410
Willamette University; Salem, Ore. (Pr)	1,725	90	55	21,700	21,700	5,700
PENNSYLVANIA						
Albright College; Reading, Pa. (Pr)	1,350	78	55	19,760	19,760	6,040
Allegheny College; Meadville, Pa. (Pr)	1,886	75	53	21,290	21,290	5,100
Allentown College of Saint Francis de Sales; Center Valley, Pa. (Pr)	1,743	75	55	14,500	14,500	6,090
Alvernia College; Reading, Pa. (Pr)	1,290	73	66	12,950	12,950	5,840
Beaver College; Glenside, Pa. (Pr)	1,635	63	74	17,550	17,550	7,740
Bloomsburg University of Pennsylvania; Bloomsburg, Pa. (Pu)	6,878	57	62	3,618	9,046	3,784
Bryn Mawr College; Bryn Mawr, Pa. (Pr)	1,316	59	98	23,520	23,520	8,340
Bucknell University; Lewisburg, Pa. (Pr)	3,403	44	48	22,740	22,740	5,469
Cabrini College; Randor, Pa. (Pr)	1,731	87	68	15,250	15,250	7,200
California University of Pennsylvania; California, Pa. (Pu)	5,041	81	54			
Carlow College; Pittsburgh, Pa. (Pr)	1,767	73	93	12,450	12,450	5,076
Carnegie Mellon University; Pittsburgh, Pa. (Pr)	5,262	38	36	22,850	22,850	7,028
Cedar Crest College; Allentown, Pa. (Pr)	1,679	90	95	17,790	17,790	6,465
Chatham College; Pittsburgh, Pa. (Pr)	580	82		17,388	17,388	6,120
Chestnut Hill College; Philadelphia, Pa. (Pr)	962	72	85	16,200	16,200	6,840
Cheyney University of Pennsylvania; Cheyney, Pa. (Pu)	1,140	78	56	3,468	8,824	4,646
Clarion University of Pennsylvania; Clarion, Pa. (Pu)	5,436	92	61	3,468	5,202	3,480
College Misericordia; Dallas, Pa. (Pr)	1,506	75	74	14,470	14,470	6,340
Delaware Valley College; Doylestown, Pa. (Pr)	1,890	80	51	16,267	16,267	6,379
Dickinson College; Carlisle, Pa. (Pr)	2,067	64	60	24,050	24,050	6,450
Drexel University; Philadelphia, Pa. (Pr)	9,530	69	37	15,927	15,927	8,320
Duquesne University; Pittsburgh, Pa. (Pr)	6,084	84	58	14,378	14,378	6,134
East Stroudsburg University of Pennsylvania; East Stroudsburg, Pa. (Pu)	4,782	67	58	3,618	9,046	3,938
Eastern College; St. Davids, Pa. (Pr)	1,902	52	66	13,200	13,200	5,654
Edinboro University of Pennsylvania; Edinboro, Pa. (Pu)	6,400	77	58	3,618	5,428	3,788
Elizabethtown College; Elizabethtown, Pa. (Pr)	1,778	78	65	19,100	19,100	5,600
Franklin & Marshall College; Lancaster, Pa. (Pr)	1,864	50	50	23,720	23,720	5,730
Gannon University; Erie, Pa. (Pr)	2,200	86	57	13,670	13,670	5,600
Geneva College; Beaver Falls, Pa. (Pr)	1,877		54	13,000	13,000	5,690
Gettysburg College; Gettysburg, Pa. (Pr)	2,123	73	52	23,922	23,922	5,346
Gratz College; Melrose Park, Pa. (Pr)	24		71			
Grove City College; Grove City, Pa. (Pr)	2,313	44	49	6,976	6,976	4,048
Gwynedd-Mercy College; Gwynedd Valley, Pa. (Pr)	1,732	36	77	14,400	14,400	6,900
Haverford College; Haverford, Pa. (Pr)	1,118	33	53			
Holy Family College; Philadelphia, Pa. (Pr)	1,927	86	76	11,500	11,500	
Immaculata College; Immaculata, Pa. (Pr)	2,360	83	82	13,950	13,950	6,800
Indiana University of Pennsylvania; Indiana, Pa. (Pu)	11,892	65	56	3,618	9,046	3,782
Juniata College; Huntingdon, Pa. (Pr)	1,268	85	56	18,940	18,940	5,290
King's College; Wilkes-Barre, Pa. (Pr)	2,091	81	54	16,000	16,000	6,890
Kutztown University of Pennsylvania; Kutztown, Pa. (Pu)	7,059	75	60	3,618	9,046	4,352
Lafayette College; Easton, Pa. (Pr)	2,283	48	48	22,844	22,844	7,106
Lancaster Bible College; Lancaster, Pa. (Pr)	652	84	53	9,100	9,100	4,300
LaRoche College; Pittsburgh, Pa. (Pr)	1,430	88	63	11,100	11,100	6,130
LaSalle University; Philadelphia, Pa. (Pr)	3,980	39	58	17,260	17,260	6,702

Institution name; city, state (type)	Students	Percent Accepted	Women	In-state	Out-of-state	Room and board
Lebanon Valley College; Annville, Pa. (Pr)	1,773	72%	59%	$17,870	$17,870	$5,680
Lehigh University; Bethlehem, Pa. (Pr)	4,605	48	40	24,000	24,000	6,860
Lincoln University; Lincoln University, Pa. (Pu)	1,576	28	57			
Lock Haven University of Pennsylvania; Lock Haven, Pa. (Pu)	3,740	83	56	3,468	6,824	3,676
Lycoming College; Williamsport, Pa. (Pr)	1,550	82	57	16,500	16,500	4,960
Mansfield University of Pennsylvania; Mansfield, Pa. (Pu)	2,892	80	59	3,618	9,046	3,852
Marywood University; Scranton, Pa. (Pr)	1,633	72	72	15,008	15,008	6,540
Mercyhurst College; Erie, Pa. (Pr)	2,832	79	57	13,190	13,190	5,364
Messiah College; Grantham, Pa. (Pr)	2,735	81	62	15,000	15,000	5,580
Millersville University of Pennsylvania; Millersville, Pa. (Pu)	6,401	69	58	3,618	9,046	4,730
Moore College of Art & Design; Philadelphia, Pa. (Pr)	495	59		15,475	15,475	6,100
Moravian College; Bethlehem, Pa. (Pr)	1,703	73	58	18,245	18,245	5,920
Mount Aloysius College; Cresson, Pa. (Pr)	1,221	53	73	9,800	9,800	4,640
Muhlenberg College; Allentown, Pa. (Pr)	2,443	55	57	20,085	20,085	5,390
Neumann College; Aston, Pa. (Pr)	1,445	98	67			
Pennslyvania State University-Abington College; Abington, Pa. (Pu)	3,219	83	51	6,058	9,418	
Pennsylvania State University-Altoona College; Altoona, Pa. (Pu)	3,842	85	50	6,058	9,418	4,690
Pennsylvania State University-Beaver College; Monaca, Pa. (Pu)	750	91	40	5,968	9,244	4,690
Pennsylvania State University-Berks College; Reading, Pa. (Pu)	2,049	88	39	6,058	9,418	4,690
Pennsylvania State University-Delaware County; Media, Pa. (Pu)	1,732	82	48	5,968	9,244	
Pennsylvania State University-DuBois; Dubois, Pa. (Pu)	1,059	93	52	5,968	9,244	
Pennsylvania State University-Erie, Behrend College; Erie, Pa. (Pu)	3,501	83	38	6,162	11,836	4,690
Pennsylvania State University-Fayette; Uniontown, Pa. (Pu)	1,040	91	54	5,968	9,244	
Pennsylvania State University-Harrisburg; Middletown, Pa. (Pu)	1,878	100	52	6,162	11,836	4,690
Pennsylvania State University-Hazleton; Hazleton, Pa. (Pu)	1,283	92	45	5,968	9,244	4,690
Pennsylvania State University-Lehigh Valley College; Fogelsville, Pa. (Pu)	639	87	41	5,968	9,244	
Pennsylvania State University-McKeesport; McKeesport, Pa. (Pu)	834	88	37	5,968	9,244	4,690
Pennsylvania State University-Mont Alto; Mont Alto, Pa. (Pu)	1,194	89	56	5,968	9,244	4,690
Pennsylvania State University-New Kensington; New Kensington, Pa. (Pu)	783	89	42	5,654	8,792	
Pennsylvania State University-Schuylkill; Schuylkill Haven, Pa. (Pu)	993	87	52	5,968	9,244	4,690
Pennsylvania State University-Shenango; Sharon, Pa. (Pu)	1,051	92	62	5,968	9,244	
Pennsylvania State University-University Park; University Park, Pa. (Pu)	34,505	49	46	6,162	13,278	4,690
Pennsylvania State University-Wilkes-Barre; Lehman, Pa. (Pu)	810	89	36	5,654	8,792	
Pennsylvania State University-Worthington Scranton; Dunmore, Pa. (Pu)	1,524	85	51	5,968	9,244	
Pennsylvania State University-York; York, Pa. (Pu)	1,775	88	43	5,968	9,244	
Philadelphia College of Bible; Langhorne, Pa. (Pr)	1,073	92	54	10,070	10,070	5,073
Philadelphia University; Philadelphia, Pa. (Pr)	2,805	79	65	14,692	14,692	6,576
Point Park College; Pittsburgh, Pa. (Pr)	2,417	89	54	12,054	12,054	5,334
Robert Morris College; Moon Township, Pa. (Pr)	3,833	91	50	8,460	8,460	6,062
Rosemont College; Rosemont, Pa. (Pr)	953	83		14,020	14,020	7,030
Saint Francis College; Loretto, Pa. (Pr)	1,486	89	63	15,040	15,040	6,480
Saint Joseph's University; Philadelphia, Pa. (Pr)	4,153	67	56	17,030	17,030	6,972
Saint Vincent College; Latrobe, Pa. (Pr)	1,186	88	51	14,725	14,725	5,114
Seton Hill College; Greensburg, Pa. (Pr)	1,085	88	84	14,500	14,500	5,050
Shippensburg University of Pennsylvania; Shippensburg, Pa. (Pu)	5,735	64	54	3,618	9,046	4,126
Slippery Rock University of Pennsylvania; Slippery Rock, Pa. (Pu)	6,130	91	57	3,618	9,046	3,810
Susquehanna University; Selinsgrove, Pa. (Pr)	1,772	75	58	20,140	20,140	5,770
Swarthmore College; Swarthmore, Pa. (Pr)	1,467	22	53	23,964	23,964	7,500
Temple University; Philadelphia, Pa. (Pu)	18,175	64	58	6,322	11,450	6,302
Thiel College; Greenville, Pa. (Pr)	980	83	53	10,732	10,732	5,674
University of Pennsylvania; Philadelphia, Pa. (Pr)	9,827	26	49	21,746	21,746	7,362
University of Pittsburgh-Bradford; Bradford, Pa. (Pu)	1,172	67	59	6,364	13,976	5,136
University of Pittsburgh-Johnstown; Johnstown, Pa. (Pu)	3,147	84	54	5,884	12,918	5,700
University of Pittsburgh-Greensburg; Greensburg, Pa. (Pu)	1,548	78	55	6,118	13,434	4,820
University of Pittsburgh-Pittsburgh; Pittsburgh, Pa. (Pu)	17,168	66	53	6,118	13,434	5,766
University of Scranton; Scranton, Pa. (Pr)	4,099	76	58	17,540	17,540	7,710
University of the Arts; Philadelphia, Pa. (Pr)	1,806	55	53	15,300	15,300	
University of the Sciences in Philadelphia; Philadelphia, Pa. (Pr)	1,137	78	62	14,800	14,800	6,800
Ursinus College; Collegeville, Pa. (Pr)	1,241	78	53	21,050	21,050	6,140
Villanova University; Villanova, Pa. (Pr)	7,130	62	51	20,555	20,555	3,040
Washington & Jefferson College; Washington, Pa. (Pr)	1,217	80	49	19,275	19,275	5,160
Waynesburg College; Waynesburg, Pa. (Pr)	1,323	78	51	11,160	11,160	4,590
West Chester University of Pennsylvania; West Chester, Pa. (Pu)	10,078	58	60	3,618	9,046 ·	4,518
Westminster College; New Wilmington, Pa. (Pr)	1,447	88	62	15,485	15,485	4,760
Widener University; Chester, Pa. (Pr)	3,587	89	55	15,750	15,750	3,400

Institution name; city, state (type)	Students	Percent Accepted	Percent Women	Tuition In-state	Tuition Out-of-state	Room and board
Wilkes University; Wilkes-Barre, Pa. (Pr)	1,752	91%	47%	$15,652	$15,652	$7,102
Wilson College; Chambersburg, Pa. (Pr)	833	93	84	13,238	13,238	6,152
York College of Pennsylvania; York, Pa. (Pr)	5,025	71	58	6,280	6,280	4,670
RHODE ISLAND						
Brown University; Providence, R.I. (Pr)	6,108	17	53	23,616	23,616	6,898
Bryant College; Smithfield, R.I. (Pr)	2,864	71	42	17,330	17,330	7,250
Johnson and Wales University; Providence, R.I. (Pr)	8,208	83	47	12,885	12,885	5,829
Providence College; Providence, R.I. (Pr)	4,630	70	60	16,980	16,980	7,125
Rhode Island College; Providence, R.I. (Pu)	6,769	73	68	2,780	7,880	5,715
Rhode Island School of Design; Providence, R.I. (Pr)	8,505					6,390
Roger Williams University; Bristol, R.I. (Pr)	3,375	86	50	17,300	17,300	8,200
Salve Regina University; Newport, R.I. (Pr)	1,800	77	66	17,200	17,200	7,750
University of Rhode Island; Kingston, R.I. (Pu)	10,483	79	56	3,282	11,286	6,166
SOUTH CAROLINA						
Anderson College; Anderson, S.C. (Pr)	1,216	76	57			
Benedict College; Columbia, S.C. (Pr)	2,208	79	53	7,284	7,284	4,182
Charleston Southern University; Charleston, S.C. (Pr)	2,226		59	9,820	9,820	3,776
Citadel, the Military College of S.C.; Charleston, S.C. (Pu)	1,955	79	6	3,404	9,426	4,350
Clemson University; Clemson, S.C. (Pu)	13,526	68	45	3,280	9,266	4,122
Coastal Carolina University; Conway, S.C. (Pu)	4,370	75	57	3,340	9,280	4,970
Coker College; Hartsville, S.C. (Pr)	935	75	71	14,352	14,352	4,718
College of Charleston; Charleston, S.C. (Pu)	9,713	44	63	3,290	6,580	3,850
Columbia College; Columbia, S.C. (Pr)	1,242	77	100	13,200	13,200	4,500
Columbia International University; Columbia, S.C. (Pr)	519	76		7,871	7,871	4,110
Converse College; Spartanburg, S.C. (Pr)	730					4,080
Erskine College; Due West, S.C. (Pr)	469	91	58	14,265	14,265	4,921
Francis Marion University; Florence, S.C. (Pu)	2,923	80	59	3,470	6,850	3,550
Furman University; Greenville, S.C. (Pr)	2,640	66	55	18,768	18,768	2,134
Johnson and Wales University; Charleston, S.C. (Pr)	1,450	84	35	11,472	11,472	
Lander University; Greenwood, S.C. (Pu)	2,431	89	64	3,735	6,723	3,732
Medical University of South Carolina; Charleston, S.C. (Pu)	422		82	5,000	13,000	
Morris College; Sumter, S.C. (Pr)	907	55	67	5,969	5,969	3,051
Newberry College; Newberry, S.C. (Pr)	750	87	46	13,602	13,602	3,960
North Greenville College; Tigerville, S.C. (Pr)	1,081		43	7,200	7,200	4,280
Presbyterian College; Clinton, S.C. (Pr)	1,119	81	52	15,870	15,870	4,900
South Carolina State University; Orangeburg, S.C. (Pu)	4,911					4,100
Southern Wesleyan University; Central, S.C. (Pr)	1,472	40	62			
University of South Carolina-Aiken; Aiken, S.C. (Pu)	3,107		65		7,544	3,890
University of South Carolina-Columbia; Columbia, S.C. (Pu)	15,551	67	55	3,640	9,714	4,167
University of South Carolina-Spartanburg; Spartanburg, S.C. (Pu)	3,492	71	64	3,250	7,776	3,950
Voorhees College; Denmark, S.C. (Pr)	932	57	62	5,860	5,860	3,190
Winthrop University; Rock Hill, S.C. (Pu)	5,840	75	70	4,106	7,414	4,022
Wofford College; Spartanburg, S.C. (Pr)	1,100	100	47	17,030	17,030	5,235
SOUTH DAKOTA						
Augustana College; Sioux Falls, S.D. (Pr)	1,728	86	65	14,492	14,492	4,260
Black Hills State University; Spearfish, S.D. (Pu)	3,469		60	1,867	5,941	2,785
Dakota State University; Madison, S.D. (Pu)	1,517		49			
Dakota Wesleyan University; Mitchell, S.D. (Pr)	661		60	9,355	9,355	3,540
Huron University; Huron, S.D. (Pr)	404			8,100	8,100	3,600
Mount Marty College; Yankton, S.D. (Pr)	949	99	71	9,248	9,248	4,020
Northern State University; Aberdeen, S.D. (Pu)	2,659	97	59	1,868	5,940	
South Dakota School of Mines & Technology; Rapid City, S.D. (Pu)	2,020	97	31	1,867	5,940	3,122
South Dakota State University; Brookings, S.D. (Pu)	7,382	94	50	1,868	5,940	2,864
University of Sioux Falls; Sioux Falls, S.D. (Pr)	914		59	11,500	11,500	3,660
University of South Dakota; Vermillion, S.D. (Pu)	5,138	100	58	1,867	5,941	2,946
TENNESSEE						
Aquinas College; Nashville, Tenn. (Pr)	329	73	77	9,000	9,000	
Austin Peay State University; Clarksville, Tenn. (Pu)	6,985	58	57	2,020	7,136	3,230
Belmont University; Nashville, Tenn. (Pr)	2,521	78	61	11,990	11,990	5,000
Bethel College; McKenzie, Tenn. (Pr)	726	65	49	7,550	7,550	4,380
Bryan College; Dayton, Tenn. (Pr)						3,950
Carson-Newman College; Jefferson City, Tenn. (Pr)	1,946	88	58	11,240	11,240	3,940
Christian Brothers University; Memphis, Tenn. (Pr)	1,598	77	53	13,140	13,140	4,080
Crichton College; Memphis, Tenn. (Pr)	821	68	59	6,600	6,600	
Cumberland University; Lebanon, Tenn. (Pr)	966	72	52	8,000	8,000	5,200
East Tennessee State University; Johnson City, Tenn. (Pu)	9,403	77	58	2,020	7,136	3,070
Fisk University; Nashville, Tenn. (Pr)	812	97	72	8,480	8,480	4,930
Freed-Hardeman University; Henderson, Tenn. (Pr)	1,420	72	55	7,328	7,328	4,400
Johnson Bible College; Knoxville, Tenn. (Pr)	388					3,200
King College; Bristol, Tenn. (Pr)	587	79	59	11,800	11,800	4,250
Lambuth University; Jackson, Tenn. (Pr)	966	70	56	7,418	7,418	4,320
Lane College; Jackson, Tenn. (Pr)	661	65	50	5,600	5,600	3,800
Lee University; Cleveland, Tenn. (Pr)	3,155	90	56	10,970	10,970	4,020

Institution name; city, state (type)	Students	Percent Accepted	Women	Tuition In-state	Out-of-state	Room and board
LeMoyne-Owen College; Memphis, Tenn. (Pr)	1,121					$3,916
Maryville College; Maryville, Tenn. (Pr)	1,001	82%	56%	$16,224	$16,224	5,310
Memphis College of Art; Memphis, Tenn. (Pr)	225		48	11,450	11,450	4,500
Middle Tennessee State University; Merfreesboro, Tenn. (Pu)	15,890			1,906	6,732	3,030
Milligan College; Milligan College, Tenn. (Pr)	796	69	59	11,900	11,900	4,200
Rhodes College; Memphis, Tenn. (Pr)	1,499	77	55	19,303	19,303	
Southern Adventist University; Collegedale, Tenn. (Pr)	1,707	80	55	10,700	10,700	3,886
Tennessee State University; Nashville, Tenn. (Pu)	7,277	68	63	2,442	7,558	3,060
Tennessee Technological University; Cookeville, Tenn. (Pu)	7,043	89	47	2,390	5,116	3,484
Tennessee Wesleyan College; Athens, Tenn. (Pr)	835	82	65	7,400	7,400	4,080
Trevecca Nazarene University; Nashville, Tenn. (Pr)	1,004	84	57	10,016	10,016	4,448
Tusculum College; Greenville, Tenn. (Pr)	1,137		54	11,800	11,800	3,900
Union University; Jackson, Tenn. (Pr)	1,916		61	9,180	9,180	3,360
University of Memphis; Memphis, Tenn. (Pu)	15,485					3,995
University of the South; Sewanee, Tenn. (Pr)	1,332	73	54	18,900	18,900	5,230
University of Tennessee-Martin; Martin, Tenn. (Pu)	5,385	80	57	2,342	7,168	3,396
University of Tennessee-Chattanooga; Chattanooga, Tenn. (Pu)	7,216	85	57	2,660	7,920	4,297
University of Tennessee-Knoxville; Knoxville, Tenn. (Pu)	20,259	67	51		6,068	4,430
Vanderbilt University; Nashville, Tenn. (Pr)	5,780	61	53	24,080	24,080	8,328
TEXAS						
Abilene Christian University; Abilene, Tex. (Pr)	4,078	79	55	9,810	9,810	4,020
Angelo State University; San Angelo, Tex. (Pu)	5,859	71	56	2,000	6,096	4,066
Arlington Baptist College; Arlington, Tex. (Pr)	219	100	47	2,520	2,520	2,150
Austin College; Sherman, Tex. (Pr)	1,233	78	54	15,094	15,094	5,891
Baylor University; Waco, Tex. (Pr)	11,472	87	58	10,650	10,650	5,238
Concordia University-Austin; Austin, Tex. (Pr)	706			9,800	9,800	5,000
Dallas Baptist University; Dallas, Tex. (Pr)	3,150	55	61	8,700	8,700	3,680
DeVry Institute of Technology; Irving, Tex. (Pr)	3,033		27	7,778	7,778	
East Texas Baptist University; Marshall, Tex. (Pr)	1,192	80	59	7,200	7,200	3,098
Hardin-Simmons University; Abilene, Tex. (Pr)	1,924	53	54	9,300	9,300	3,336
Jarvis Christian College; Hawkins, Tex. (Pr)	519	67	57	8,685	8,685	3,485
Lamar University; Beaumont, Tex. (Pu)	9,551		55	864	5,976	3,040
LeTourneau University; Longview, Tex. (Pr)	2,523	85	47	12,090	12,090	5,250
McMurry University; Abilene, Tex. (Pr)	1,339	68	49	8,100	8,100	4,244
Midwestern State University; Wichita Falls, Tex. (Pu)	5,093		57		6,804	3,534
Northwood University, Texas Campus; Cedarhill, Tex. (Pr)	1,007	95	52	11,325	11,325	5,146
Our Lady of the Lake University; San Antonio, Tex. (Pr)	2,330		77	11,150	11,150	5,040
Prairie View A&M University; Prarie View, Tex. (Pu)	4,963	96	54	2,644	9,124	4,184
Rice University; Houston, Tex. (Pr)	2,769	28	47	14,300	14,300	6,600
Saint Edward's University; Austin, Tex. (Pr)	2,957	79	56	11,438	11,438	3,400
St. Mary's University of San Antonio; San Antonio, Tex. (Pr)	2,642	86	59	11,500	11,500	4,908
Sam Houston State University; Huntsville, Tex. (Pu)	10,825	78	56	912	6,096	3,390
Schreiner College; Kerrville, Tex. (Pr)	800	72	51	11,540	11,540	6,796
Southern Methodist University; Dallas, Tex. (Pr)	5,620	90	54	15,640	15,640	6,579
Southwest Texas State University; San Marcos, Tex. (Pu)	18,856	65	55	1,200	7,680	4,349
Southwestern University; Georgetown, Tex. (Pr)	1,254	67	58	15,750	15,750	5,560
Stephen F. Austin State University; Nonacogdoches, Tex. (Pu)	10,116			1,080	7,470	4,118
Sul Ross State University; Alpine, Tex. (Pu)	2,270		53	1,080	7,470	3,480
Tarleton State University; Stephenville, Tex. (Pu)	6,102	74	54	1,860	7,470	3,570
Texas Christian University; Fort Worth, Tex. (Pr)	6,456	75	59	11,700	11,700	4,240
Texas A&M University-Galveston; Galveston, Tex. (Pu)	1,291	89	49	1,140	7,112	3,976
Texas A&M University-College Station; College Station, Tex. (Pu)	36,082	74	48	1,824	7,008	4,898
Texas A&M University-Commerce; Commerce, Tex. (Pu)	4,574	67	56	2,526	9,006	4,550
Texas A&M University-Corpus Christi; Corpus Christi, Tex. (Pu)	4,690	88	60	864	5,976	5,259
Texas Lutheran University; Seguin, Tex. (Pr)	1,547	83	52	12,500	12,500	4,120
Texas Southern University; Houston, Tex. (Pu)	8,832			2,058	7,180	4,000
Texas Tech University; Lubbock, Tex. (Pu)	20,227	75	46	1,140	7,620	4,787
Texas Wesleyan University; Fort Worth, Tex. (Pr)	2,034	84	65	8,500	9,260	3,910
Texas Woman's University; Denton, Tex. (Pu)	5,752			2,084	7,196	3,578
Trinity University; San Antonio, Tex. (Pr)	2,278	76	51	15,660	15,660	6,540
University of Dallas; Irving, Tex. (Pr)	1,157	82	58	14,450	14,450	5,562
University of Houston; Houston, Tex. (Pu)	24,268	74	53		6,096	4,513
University of Houston-Clear Lake; Houston, Tex. (Pu)	3,468					
University of Houston-Downtown; Houston, Tex. (Pu)	8,000					
University of Houston-Victoria Campus; Victoria, Tex. (Pu)	832		73	912	6,096	
University of North Texas; Denton, Tex. (Pu)	20,449	74	54	2,070	8,550	8,192
University of Saint Thomas; Houston, Tex. (Pr)	1,597	85	66	11,700	11,700	4,860
University of Texas-Arlington; Arlington, Tex. (Pu)	15,266	97	53	1,824	7,008	1,686
University of Texas-Austin; Austin, Tex. (Pu)	37,203	71	50	2,160	8,550	4,537
University of Texas-Dallas; Richardson, Tex. (Pu)	5,974	63	49	1,824	7,008	
University of Texas-El Paso; El Paso, Tex. (Pu)	12,852	87	53		7,440	
University of Texas-Houston Health Science Center; Houston, Tex. (Pu)	262		93	2,880	12,510	5,400
University of Texas Medical Branch at Galveston; Galveston, Tex. (Pu)	654	31	79	1,720	11,008	6,480

Institution name; city, state (type)	Students	Percent Accepted	Women	Tuition In-state	Out-of-state	Room and board
University of Texas-Permian Basin; Odessa, Tex. (Pu)	1,219			$ 1,776	$ 8,166	$3,934
University of Texas-San Antonio; San Antonio, Tex. (Pu)	15,796	99%	55%	2,160	8,640	5,876
University of the Incarnate Word; San Antonio, Tex. (Pr)	2,905	97	70	11,850	11,850	4,870
Wayland Baptist University; Plainview, Tex. (Pr)	4,130	100	44	7,050	7,050	3,121
West Texas A&M University; Canyon, Tex. (Pu)	5,521	77	54	1,458	6,594	3,310
UTAH						
Brigham Young University; Provo, Utah (Pr)	30,037	64	53	2,830	2,830	4,454
Southern Utah University; Cedar City, Utah (Pu)		84		1,570	5,927	2,790
University of Utah; Salt Lake City, Utah (Pu)	20,344		45	2,601	7,998	4,620
Utah State University; Logan, Utah (Pu)	17,228	86	53	2,314	7,004	3,968
Weber State University; Ogden, Utah (Pu)	14,813	100	52	1,654	5,790	3,196
Westminster College of Salt Lake City; Salt Lake City, Utah (Pr)	1,737	86	62	12,456	12,456	4,750
VERMONT						
Bennington College; Bennington, Vt. (Pr)	447	83		22,200	22,200	5,650
Burlington College; Burlington, Vt. (Pr)	160	91		8,420	8,420	
Castleton State College; Castleton, Vt. (Pu)	1,579	91	57	4,092	9,588	5,298
Champlain College; Burlington, Vt. (Pr)	2,440	81	54	10,905	10,905	7,765
College of Saint Joseph in Vermont; Rutland, Vt. (Pr)	393	97	64	11,250	11,250	6,050
Goddard College; Plainfield, Vt. (Pr)	349	93		15,218	15,218	5,288
Green Mountain College; Poultney, Vt. (Pr)	616	59	53	17,000	17,000	4,150
Johnson State College; Johnson, Vt. (Pu)	1,398	85	55	4,092	9,588	5,298
Lyndon State College; Lyndonville, Vt. (Pu)	1,138	93	45	4,092	9,588	5,298
Marlboro College; Marlboro, Vt. (Pr)	290	80	59	18,800	18,800	6,750
Middlebury College; Middlebury, Vt. (Pr)	2,265	26	51			
Norwich University; Northfield, Vt. (Pr)	2,214	94	40	14,926	14,926	5,718
Saint Michael's College; Colchester, Vt. (Pr)	2,004	71	53	18,615	18,615	7,253
Southern Vermont College; Bennington, Vt. (Pr)	515	82	64	10,990	10,990	5,450
Sterling College; Craftsbury Common, Vt. (Pr)	90	97		13,230	13,230	5,670
Trinity College of Vermont; Burlington, Vt. (Pr)	600	99	92	13,620	13,620	6,700
University of Vermont; Burlington, Vt. (Pu)	8,739	80	55	7,464	18,672	5,620
VIRGINIA						
Averett College; Danville, Va. (Pr)	1,589	76	61	12,585	12,585	4,385
Bluefield College; Bluefield, Va. (Pr)	827	100	52	6,900	6,900	4,890
Bridgewater College; Bridgewater, Va. (Pr)	1,120	89	57	14,470	14,470	6,970
Christendom College; Front Royal, Va. (Pr)	259	85	53	11,300	11,300	4,570
Christopher Newport University; Newport News, Va. (Pu)	4,978	59	60	3,056	9,078	5,350
College of William and Mary; Williamsburg, Va. (Pu)	5,552	45	58			
Eastern Mennonite University; Harrisonburg, Va. (Pr)	1,099	85	60	13,480	13,480	4,950
Emory and Henry College; Emory, Va. (Pr)	956	80	50	12,950	12,950	5,322
Ferrum College; Ferrum, Va. (Pr)	945	81	40	10,990	10,990	5,000
George Mason University; Fairfax, Va. (Pu)	15,262	59	56	2,976	11,136	5,190
Hampden-Sydney College; Hampden-Sydney, Va. (Pr)	997	74		16,048	16,048	5,898
Hampton University; Hampton, Va. (Pr)	5,435	64	60	9,490	9,490	4,754
Hollins University; Roanoke, Va. (Pr)	826	86	99	16,460	16,460	6,125
James Madison University; Harrisonburg, Va. (Pu)	14,156	65	57	3,926	9,532	5,182
Johnson and Wales University-Norfolk; Norfolk, Va. (Pr)	583	80	37	13,254	13,254	5,538
Johnson and Wales University-Vail; Norfolk, Va. (Pr)	29		48	19,935	19,935	
Liberty University; Lynchburg, Va. (Pr)	5,942	31	49	8,550	8,550	4,800
Longwood College; Farmville, Va. (Pu)	3,208	76	64	8,544	13,990	4,620
Lynchburg College; Lynchburg, Va. (Pr)	1,652	76	64	17,120	17,120	4,400
Mary Baldwin College; Staunton, Va. (Pr)	1,478	90	96	14,475	14,475	7,450
Mary Washington College; Fredericksburg, Va. (Pu)	3,965		69	1,550	7,980	5,298
Marymount University; Arlington, Va. (Pr)	1,969	78	72	13,750	13,750	6,160
Norfolk State University; Norfolk, Va. (Pu)	6,734	96	62	3,000	6,802	4,166
Old Dominion University; Norfolk, Va. (Pu)	13,065	71	56	2,184	9,774	5,114
Radford University; Radford, Va. (Pu)	7,406	46	61	1,629	7,384	4,770
Randolph-Macon College; Ashland, Va. (Pr)	1,145	74	53	17,160	17,160	4,520
Randolph-Macon Woman's College; Lynchburg, Va. (Pr)	710	84		16,730	16,730	7,010
Roanoke College; Salem, Va. (Pr)	1,731	81	60	16,655	16,655	5,450
Saint Paul's College; Lawrenceville, Va. (Pr)						3,834
Shenandoah University; Winchester, Va. (Pr)	1,285	80	65	15,080	15,080	5,150
Sweet Briar College; Sweet Briar, Va. (Pr)	710	99	97	17,174	17,174	7,016
University of Richmond; Richmond, Va. (Pr)	3,034	45	50	20,140	20,140	4,240
University of Virginia; Charlottesville, Va. (Pu)	13,570	34	54	3,046	15,519	4,589
University of Virginia-Wise; Wise, Va. (Pu)	1,554	74	53	1,885	8,379	4,748
Virginia Commonwealth University; Richmond, Va. (Pu)	15,824	74	59	2,492	11,946	4,839
Virginia Intermont College; Bristol, Va. (Pr)	795	76	76	11,700	11,700	5,200
Virginia Military Institute; Lexington, Va. (Pu)	1,335	74		3,655	11,445	4,210
Virginia State University; Petersburg, Va. (Pu)	3,369	77	58	1,588	7,132	5,096
Virginia Tech; Blacksburg, Va. (Pu)	21,479	73	41	2,792	11,016	4,776
Virginia Union University; Richmond, Va. (Pr)	1,307					3,950
Virginia Wesleyan College; Norfolk, Va. (Pr)	1,568			13,400	13,400	5,500
Washington and Lee University; Lexington, Va. (Pr)	1,729	36		16,950	16,950	5,547

Institution name; city, state (type)	Students	Percent Accepted	Percent Women	Tuition In-state	Tuition Out-of-state	Room and board
WASHINGTON						
Central Washington University; Ellensburg, Wash. (Pu)	7,729	83%	54%	$ 2,753	$ 9,781	$5,122
City University; Renton, Wash. (Pr)	2,548		46	1,860	1,860	
Cornish College of the Arts; Seattle, Wash. (Pr)	649	78	61	13,700	13,700	
Eastern Washington University; Cheney, Wash. (Pu)	7,225	88	58	2,700	9,594	4,399
Evergreen State College; Olympia, Wash. (Pu)	3,932	89	59	2,637	9,330	4,530
Gonzaga University; Spokane, Wash. (Pr)	2,747	87	54	16,710	16,710	5,350
Northwest College; Kirkland, Wash. (Pr)	848	99	57	9,672	9,672	5,030
Pacific Lutheran University; Tacoma, Wash. (Pr)	3,302	84	60	16,800	16,800	5,300
Saint Martin's College; Lacey, Wash. (Pr)	1,139	91	60	14,050	14,050	4,768
Seattle Pacific University; Seattle, Wash. (Pr)	2,636	93	66	15,381	15,381	5,895
Seattle University; Seattle, Wash. (Pr)	3,245	80	58	17,010	17,010	6,075
Trinity Western University; Blaine, Wash. (Pr)	2,379	78	56	10,350	10,350	5,990
University of Puget Sound; Tacoma, Wash. (Pr)	2,695	74	61	21,270	21,270	5,510
University of Washington; Seattle, Wash. (Pu)	25,838	77	52	3,638	12,029	5,844
Walla Walla College; College Place, Wash. (Pr)	1,535	73	49	13,806	13,806	3,021
Washington State University; Pullman, Wash. (Pu)	17,087	84	51	3,351	10,267	4,826
Western Washington University; Bellingham, Wash. (Pu)	10,914		56	2,521	8,956	4,635
Whitman College; Walla Walla, Wash. (Pr)	1,300	50	57	21,550	21,550	6,090
Whitworth College; Spokane, Wash. (Pr)	1,771	88	59	15,970	15,970	5,400
WEST VIRGINIA						
Alderson-Broaddus College; Philippi, W.Va. (Pr)	679	70	60	13,740	13,740	5,100
Bethany College; Bethany, W.Va. (Pr)	718	70	46	19,141	19,141	6,909
Bluefield State College; Bluefield, W.Va. (Pu)	2,349	96	60	2,178	5,290	
Concord College; Athens, W.Va. (Pr)	2,877	74	58	2,538	5,580	4,018
Davis & Elkins College; Elkins, W.Va. (Pr)	658	94	56	12,080	12,080	5,330
Fairmont State College; Fairmont, W.Va. (Pu)	6,712	100	56	2,244	5,228	3,882
Glenville State College; Glenville, W.Va. (Pu)	2,179					3,480
Marshall University; Huntington, W.Va. (Pu)	9,424	98	56	2,440	6,512	4,652
Ohio Valley College; Parkersburg, W.Va. (Pr)	407	55	52	6,860	6,860	4,000
Salem-Teikyo University; Salem, W.Va. (Pr)	163	70	42	12,800	12,800	4,408
Shepherd College; Shepherdstown, W.Va. (Pu)	4,597	93	60	2,228	5,348	4,139
University of Charleston; Charleston, W.Va. (Pr)	1,162	73	67	13,200	13,200	4,480
West Liberty State College; West Liberty, W.Va. (Pu)	2,397	95	55	2,190	5,630	3,100
West Virginia State College; Institute, W.Va. (Pu)	4,530			2,116	5,150	3,550
West Virginia University; Morgantown, W.Va. (Pu)	15,417	94	46	2,748	8,100	4,832
West Virginia University Institute of Technology; Montgomery, W.Va. (Pu)	2,587	100	39	2,646	6,458	4,048
West Virginia Wesleyan College; Buckhannon, W.Va. (Pr)	1,601	84	57	16,800	16,800	4,350
Wheeling Jesuit University; Wheeling, W.Va. (Pr)	1,530			15,000	15,000	5,200
WISCONSIN						
Beloit College; Beloit, Wis. (Pr)	1,258	70	59	20,220	20,220	4,628
Cardinal Stritch College; Milwaukee, Wis. (Pr)	2,955	70	66	11,000	11,000	4,410
Carroll College; Waukesha, Wis. (Pr)	2,444		66	14,740	14,740	4,600
Carthage College; Kenosha, Wis. (Pr)	2,101	91	58	21,500	21,500	4,810
Concordia University Wisconsin; Mequon, Wis. (Pr)	3,845	76	63	12,900	12,900	4,820
Edgewood College; Madison, Wis. (Pr)	1,448	77	73	11,450	11,450	4,380
Lakeland College; Sheboygan, Wis. (Pr)	3,328	74	61	11,980	11,980	4,860
Lawrence University; Appleton, Wis. (Pr)	1,246	80	54	20,882	20,882	4,697
Marian College of Fond Du Lac; Fond du Lac, Wis. (Pr)	1,571	81	67	11,966	11,966	4,364
Marquette University; Milwaukee, Wis. (Pr)	7,437	84	54	17,080	17,080	6,086
Milwaukee School of Engineering; Milwaukee, Wis. (Pr)	2,343	72	17	19,845	19,845	4,530
Mount Mary College; Milwaukee, Wis. (Pr)	1,174	83	99	11,380	11,380	3,970
Mount Senario College; Ladysmith, Wis. (Pr)	930	75	35	12,250	12,250	4,750
Northland College; Ashland, Wis. (Pr)	782	89	59	14,415	14,415	4,470
Ripon College; Ripon, Wis. (Pr)	746	87	52	18,000	18,000	4,400
St. Norbert College; De Pere, Wis. (Pr)	1,950	90	59	15,600	15,600	5,162
Silver Lake College; Manitowoc, Wis. (Pr)	700	48	69	11,150	11,150	4,365
University of Wisconsin-Eau Claire; Eau Claire, Wis. (Pu)	9,919	74	60	3,210	10,074	3,301
University of Wisconsin-Green Bay; Green Bay, Wis. (Pu)	5,274	82	64	2,594	9,458	3,235
University of Wisconsin-LaCrosse; LaCrosse, Wis. (Pu)	8,650	75	57	3,161	9,757	3,400
University of Wisconsin-Madison; Madison, Wis. (Pu)	28,984	73	53	3,650	12,400	5,250
University of Wisconsin-Milwaukee; Milwaukee, Wis. (Pu)	17,032	82	54	3,741	3,741	3,594
University of Wisconsin-Oshkosh; Oshkosh, Wis. (Pu)	9,295	89	58	2,950	9,606	3,130
University of Wisconsin-Parkside; Kenosha, Wis. (Pu)	4,486		60	2,838	9,120	3,730
University of Wisconsin-Platteville; Platteville, Wis. (Pu)	4,665			2,806	9,068	3,254
University of Wisconsin-River Falls; River Falls, Wis. (Pu)	5,399	74	62	3,102	9,936	3,350
University of Wisconsin-Stevens Point; Stevens Point, Wis. (Pu)	8,400	60	56	3,140	10,004	3,524
University of Wisconsin-Stout; Menomonie, Wis. (Pu)	6,931	80	49	2,836	9,118	3,156
University of Wisconsin-Superior; Superior, Wis. (Pu)	2,314			2,768	9,050	3,296
University of Wisconsin-Whitewater; Whitewater, Wis. (Pu)	9,537	84	53	3,000	9,113	2,800
Viterbo University; La Crosse, Wis. (Pr)	1,750	88	75	12,770	12,770	4,530
Wisconsin Lutheran College; Milwaukee, Wis. (Pr)	440	93	60	11,960	11,960	4,500
WYOMING						
University of Wyoming; Laramie, Wyo. (Pu)	8,438	97	53	2,166	7,284	4,568

The Maternal Instinct: Learning About Parenting from Mother Nature

Scientists contend that animal and human mothers share striking similarities—just ask the birds and the bees

By JEFFREY KLUGER TIME

With squalling infants in tow, she works backbreaking shifts—as long as 17 hours a day—to feed her growing family. Then she drags herself home, where she is greeted by her equally demanding older children, who expect her to referee their squabbles as they roughhouse and play. When the kids finally fall asleep, she has only a few hours to eat, clean up, and grab some shut-eye before the sun rises and she must do it all again.

Primate Parenting

Typical working mom? No, a wild baboon living on the plains of Kenya. But in ways that are deeper and more resonant than most people realize, female baboons and other nonhuman primates *are* typical working moms. They struggle with the same challenges that human mothers face and work out surprisingly similar solutions. Tamarin mothers in the Amazon Basin rely on aunts and grandmothers to tend the young while the mothers forage for food. Moms and dads among Brazil's titi monkeys take turns minding the kids and bringing home the bacon, just as in any well-adjusted two-income human family.

And it is not just primates whose parenting strategies echo our own. More and more, scientists have come to realize that among creatures as diverse as mice and seals, birds and spiders, mothering is a surprisingly consistent, remarkably familiar business. If there is a message in all this, it's that the more we understand the animals' behavior, the better we can understand our own.

Anthropology by Analogy?

Certainly, not everyone is pleased with this research. Looking to animals to study something as complex as motherhood, critics say, is little more than anthropology by analogy, relying on the worst kind of scientific reductionism to explain the highest kind of human impulses. But anthropologists view matters differently, seeing in animal and human mothers a striking commonness of purpose—and a striking commonness of grace. "All mothers face similar dilemmas," says anthropologist Sarah Blaffer Hrdy of the University of California at Davis, "no matter what their ambitions or circumstances."

Alloparenting

There are few challenges the animal families of Africa or the Amazon face that the Banzer family of Houston wouldn't understand. Stephanie Banzer is a marketing manager for Compaq Computers as well as the mother of toddler Matthew. When Stephanie gave birth, she and her husband knew they would need her income to keep the household running. Full-time mothering was thus not an option—and full-time baby-sitters were too expensive. Instead, she turned to a team of child-care providers she knew could do the job: her mother and two aunts. The three older women look after Matthew when Banzer and her husband are at work, returning the toddler well cared for at the end of the day. "These are the women who raised me," Banzer says. "He is in very loving hands."

While the Banzers may think of the work Matthew's grandmother and great-aunts do as mere baby-sitting, anthropologists know it is part of a far more primal practice called alloparenting. In all manner of animals, including bees, elephants, lions, lemurs, bats, and birds, creatures with no parental investment in offspring routinely expend enormous amounts of energy caring for their relatives' young. Alloparents are not unconditional caretakers; they won't devote scarce resources to others' offspring at the expense of their own. But when conditions allow an alloparenting deal to be made, it's a good bargain all around.

Dog-Eat-Dog World

Of course, even with a parade of alloparents, off-spring will have little chance of reaching maturity if there isn't sufficient food to keep them nourished. In the game of survival, there is nothing more critical than keeping babies' bellies full, and mothers go to great lengths to get the job done. After one type of Australian spider lays her eggs, she lives barely long enough to see her young mature. Then she positions herself among them and slowly liquefies, transforming herself into an edible goo that gives her babies a nutritional kick start in life.

Often animals don't have to go to such nurturing extremes. For all creatures, one key to successful parenting is not merely reproducing but also knowing when not to reproduce—timing births so that the supply of food and other resources stay ahead of the babies to tend.

Procreative Strategies

Heather Knotts of Chicago, a career mom, walks just this kind of parenting tightrope. Holding down a demanding job in an advertising agency, she works even harder at home, rearing a daughter and a son. If Knotts and her husband had their way, she would set aside being an adwoman and work full-time as a mom. That was what they had planned. "After our first child was born, we knew I'd have to keep working," she says, "but we thought it would be for only a couple of years."

Three years after the Knottses had their first child, however, the second came along, and the idea of halving the household income while doubling the number of children it had to support was out of the question. The best Knotts could do was cut her workweek from five days to four, taking herself out of the running for promotions she had coveted but still not getting the round-the-clock time she wants with her kids.

As procreative strategies go, this seems an odd one. If you want to devote yourself exclusively to parenting, it's better to take your reproductive chips off the table after having one child so you can maximize the resources you have to do the job. If you want a multichild family, you'd better make sure that the family bank account is full to bursting.

When it comes to reproduction, though, nothing is quite so easy. "All mother mammals are forced to make the most of the resources available while making trade-offs compatible with their own survival," says Hrdy.

When Things Go Wrong

But what happens when this resource management system breaks down? What if the mother gambles wrong and an offspring comes along when there are no resources to support it, or what if she is too young to care for it? What if the infant is sickly and seems likely to languish no matter how well it's looked after? Humans agonize over these situations, but mothers throughout the animal kingdom show a surprising willingness to abandon or even kill such luckless young rather than pour energy down a bottomless reproductive well.

An American black bear, which normally gives birth to two or three cubs at a time, may walk away from one born alone, calculating that it's better to wait for a multiple birth next year than exhaust herself with a singleton now. Mice will examine offspring after they're born and eat undersize young, improving the overall fitness of the litter and giving themselves a valuable dose of protein in the process.

Chilling Analogies

Things become truly troubling when human beings facing the same difficult circumstances start making equally brutal choices. Anthropologists report that during a three-year period of social upheaval in Bolivia in the 1930s, nearly every mother in an Ayoreo Indian village committed infanticide at least once. In India and China, selective infanticide of baby girls is still commonly, if quietly, practiced. And while there may be less of a history of such killing in the U.S., periodic cases of high-schoolers secretly giving birth and then murdering their infants are proof that such practices know no cultural boundaries.

Are the Parallels Too Pat?

Critics of the work of Hrdy and others resist drawing too many parallels between human and animal parents, insisting that the few traits that distinguish us from other species are far more important than the many things we share. In human mothers—indeed, in all animal mothers—there has always been tension between much that is sublimely good and at least a few things that aren't so good. It is humans alone, however, who have the ability to contemplate those choices—and then know which ones to make. □

Households, Families, and Married Couples, 1890–1998

	Households		Families		Married couples
Date	**Number**	**Average population per household**	**Number**	**Average population per family**	**Number**
June 1890	12,690,000	4.93	—	—	—
April 1930	29,905,000	4.11	—	—	25,174,000
April 1940	34,949,000	3.67	32,166,000	3.76	26,571,000
March 1950	43,554,000	3.37	39,303,000	3.54	34,075,000
April 1955	47,874,000	3.33	41,951,000	3.59	36,251,000
March 1960[1]	52,799,000	3.35	45,111,000	3.67	39,254,000
March 1965	57,436,000	3.32	47,956,000	3.70	41,689,000
March 1970	63,401,000	3.14	51,586,000	3.58	44,728,000
March 1975	71,120,000	2.94	55,712,000	3.42	46,951,000
March 1980	80,776,000	2.76	59,550,000	3.29	49,112,000
March 1985	86,789,000	2.69	62,706,000	3.23	50,350,000
March 1990	93,347,000	2.63	66,090,000	3.17	52,317,000
March 1995	98,990,000	2.65	69,305,000	3.19	53,858,000
March 1996	99,627,000	2.65	69,594,000	3.20	53,567,000
Dec. 1997	101,018,000	2.64	70,241,000	3.19	53,604,000
Dec. 1998	102,528,000	2.62	70,880,000	3.18	54,317,000

1. First year in which figures for Alaska and Hawaii were included. *Source:* U.S. Bureau of the Census; Web: www.census.gov.

Families by Number of Parents Present, 1970–1998

(with children under age 18)

Family type	1970	1980	1990	1991	1992	1993	1994	1995	1996	1997	1998
Total											
Two parents[1]	85%	77%	73%	72%	71%	71%	69%	69%	68%	68%	68%
Mother only[2]	11	18	22	22	23	23	23	23	24	24	23
Father only[2]	1	2	3	3	3	3	3	4	4	4	4
No parent	3	4	3	3	3	3	4	4	4	4	4
White											
Two parents[1]	90	83	79	78	77	77	76	76	75	75	74
Mother only[2]	8	14	16	17	18	17	18	18	18	18	18
Father only[2]	1	2	3	3	3	3	3	3	4	4	5
No parent	2	2	2	2	2	2	3	3	3	3	3
Black											
Two parents[1]	58	42	38	36	36	36	33	33	33	35	36
Mother only[2]	30	44	51	54	54	54	53	52	53	52	51
Father only[2]	2	2	4	4	3	3	4	4	4	5	4
No parent	10	12	8	7	7	7	10	11	9	8	9
Hispanic[3]											
Two parents[1]	78	75	67	66	65	65	63	63	62	64	64
Mother only[2]	—	20	27	27	28	28	28	28	29	27	27
Father only[2]	—	2	3	3	4	4	4	4	4	4	4
No parent	—	3	3	4	3	4	5	4	5	5	5

1. Excludes families where parents are not living as a married couple. 2. Includes some families where both parents are present in the household, but living as unmarried partners. 3. Persons of Hispanic origin may be of any race. NOTE: Data applies to U.S. families. *Source:* U.S. Bureau of the Census, *Current Population Reports.*

Female Family Householders with No Spouse Present, 1980–1998

	White			Black			Hispanic origin[1]		
	1980	1990	1998	1980	1990	1998	1980	1990	1998
Total (in thousands):	6,052	7,306	8,308	2,495	3,275	3,926	610	1,116	1,612
Marital Status:									
Never married (single)	11%	15%	22%	27%	39%	48%	23%	27%	35%
Married, spouse absent	17	16	15	29	21	16	32	29	25
Widowed	33	26	21	22	17	13	15	16	12
Divorced	40	43	42	22	23	23	30	29	28

NOTES: As of March. Covers persons 15 years old and over. 1. Persons of Hispanic origin may be of any race. *Source:* U.S. Bureau of the Census, *Current Population Reports,* P20–515, and earlier reports. From *Statistical Abstract of the United States, 1999.*

Young Adults Living at Home, 1960–1998

	Male			Female		
	Total population, 18–24 years old	Number living at home	Percent	Total population, 18–24 years old	Number living at home	Percent
1960	6,842,000	3,583,000	52%	7,876,000	2,750,000	35%
1970	10,398,000	5,641,000	54	11,959,000	4,941,000	41
1980	14,278,000	7,755,000	54	14,844,000	6,336,000	43
1985	13,695,000	8,172,000	60	14,149,000	6,758,000	48
1990	12,450,000	7,232,000	58	12,860,000	6,135,000	48
1995	12,545,000	7,328,000	58	12,613,000	5,896,000	47
1998	12,633,000	7,399,000	59	12,568,000	5,974,000	48

	Male			Female		
	Total population, 25–34 years old	Number living at home	Percent	Total population, 25–34 years old	Number living at home	Percent
1960	10,896,000	1,185,000	11%	11,587,000	853,000	7%
1970	11,929,000	1,129,000	9	12,637,000	829,000	7
1980	18,107,000	1,894,000	10	18,689,000	1,300,000	7
1985	20,184,000	2,685,000	13	20,673,000	1,661,000	8
1990	21,462,000	3,213,000	15	21,779,000	1,774,000	8
1995	20,589,000	3,166,000	15	20,800,000	1,759,000	8
1998	19,526,000	2,845,000	15	19,828,000	1,680,000	8

NOTE: Unmarried college students living in dorms are counted as living at home. *Source:* U.S. Bureau of the Census, *Current Population Reports,* March 1998.

Coresident Grandparents and Grandchildren

Source: U.S. Census Bureau, *Current Population Reports*, P23-198, May 1999

Web: www.census.gov/population/www/socdemo/grandparents.html

Researchers first began to notice an increase in the number of grandchildren living in grandparent-maintained households in the early 1990s. The U.S. Census Bureau's Current Population Report *Marital Status and Living Arrangements: March 1992* noted that the number of children under 18 living in grandparent-maintained households had increased from 2.2 million in 1970, to 2.3 million in 1980, to 3.3 million in 1992. In 1970, a little over 3 percent of all children under age 18 were living in a home maintained by their grandparents. By 1992, this percentage had increased to nearly 5 percent. More recent data show that this trend has continued. In 1997, 3.9 million children were living in homes maintained by their grandparents—5.5 percent of all children under 18.

In most cases (51%), these households have both a grandmother and a grandfather present living with the children. In most other cases (43% of the total), the household is maintained by a grandmother only, with no spouse present. Only 6% of such families

are maintained by a grandfather alone. Thus coresident grandmothers outnumber coresident grandfathers five to three. The reasons for this discrepancy may have to do with the fact that women in general are longer lived than men, and they are also more likely than men to assume a caregiving role.

Other data show that substantial increases in the number of children living in households maintained by grandparents appear to have occurred regardless of the presence or absence of the grandchildren's parents. Between 1970 and 1992, these increases were greatest among children with only one parent in the household. Between 1992 and 1997, the greatest growth occurred among grandchildren living with grandparents with no parent present.[1] The increase in grandchildren in these "skipped generation" living arrangements has been attributed to a variety of factors, including the growth in drug use among parents, teen pregnancy, divorce, the rapid rise of single-parent households, child abuse and neglect, and incarceration of parents.[2]

---

1. Fuller-Thomson, Minkler, and Driver refer to skipped-generation households as those composed of grandparents and their grandchildren with neither of the child's parents present. Fuller-Thomson, Esme, Meredith Minkler, and Diane Driver. 1997. "A Profile of Grandparents Raising Grandchildren in the United States." *The Gerontologist* 37: 406–411. 2. For a more thorough discussion of these causes see Minkler, M. 1998. "Intergenerational Households Headed by Grandparents: Demographic and Sociological Contexts." In Generations United (eds.) *Grandparents and Other Relatives Raising Children: Background Papers from Generations United's Expert Symposiums.* Washington, D.C.: Generations United.

Grandchildren Living with Their Grandparents

Percent of children under 18

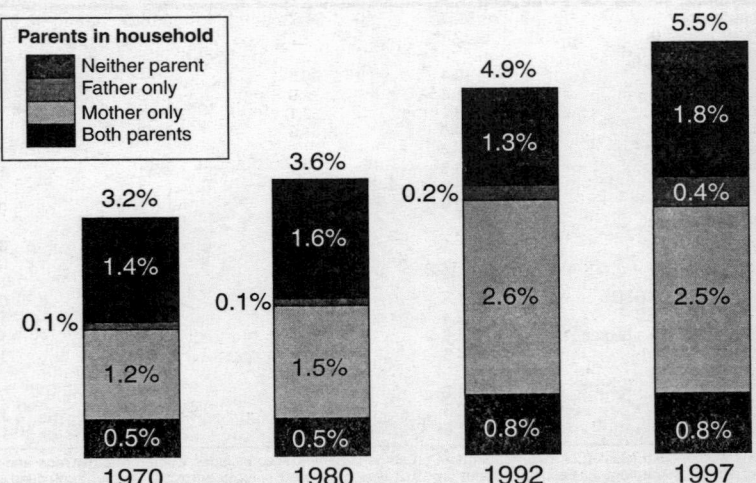

Source: U.S. Bureau of the Census, 1970 and 1980 censuses and 1992 and 1997 Current Population Surveys as reported in *Marital Status and Living Arrangements: March 1992* and *Marital Status and Living Arrangements: March 1997*.

Blended Families[1]

Characteristics of women	Number	Any child	Stepchild	Child of relative, friend, or partner	Foster child	Adopted child
Age						
18–19 years	3,508,000	1.9	—	1.6	—	—
20–24 years	9,041,000	4.3	0.8	2.4	0.1	0.1
25–29 years	9,693,000	8.2	1.6	5.2	0.8	0.3
30–34 years	11,065,000	11.1	3.4	6.7	0.6	0.5
35–39 years	11,211,000	16.0	5.7	7.3	1.7	1.7
40–44 years	10,230,000	17.5	5.7	7.8	1.2	2.0
Marital status						
Never married	17,300,000	5.2	0.0	4.1	0.3	0.1
Currently married	29,600,000	13.5	5.3	5.7	1.1	1.2
Formerly married	7,849,000	14.9	3.2	9.2	1.1	1.2
Parity						
0 birth	19,998,000	8.0	2.3	4.1	0.3	1.2
1 birth	10,502,000	12.2	4.9	5.5	0.7	0.6
2 births	13,871,000	12.9	3.7	6.9	1.1	0.8
3 or more births	10,377,000	13.5	3.3	7.4	1.7	0.5
Education at interview						
No high school diploma or GED	5,424,000	14.2	3.2	9.0	1.5	0.7
High school diploma or GED	18,169,000	14.1	4.3	7.4	0.9	0.9
Some college, no bachelor's degree	12,399,000	13.7	4.3	7.2	1.1	1.1
Bachelor's degree or higher	11,748,000	7.4	2.8	2.6	0.7	1.1
Race and Hispanic origin						
Hispanic	6,015,000	11.5	2.5	6.3	0.8	0.6
Non-Hispanic white	38,987,000	10.8	3.8	4.9	1.3	0.9
Non-Hispanic black	7,357,000	12.9	1.9	9.1	0.8	1.0
Non-Hispanic other	2,390,000	9.3	2.1	6.5	0.4	0.5

NOTE: Percents may not add to "Any child" total because some women lived and cared for more than one child not born to them. 1. Number of women 18–44 years of age and percent who have ever lived with and cared for a child to whom they did not give birth, by the child's relationship to them and selected characteristics: in the United States in 1995. Source: Health, United States, 1995.

Adoption in the U.S., 1973–1995

(Number of ever-married women 18–44 years of age and percent who have ever adopted a child)

Characteristic	1973	1982	1988	1995
All women (thousands)	30,701	34,632	36,689	37,448
Percent who ever adopted[1]	2.1%	2.2%	1.6%	1.3%
Age at interview				
18-24 years	0.4	0.6	—	0.2
25-34 years	1.8	2.0	0.5	0.4
35-39 years	3.1	2.1	2.2	1.9
40-44 years	4.0	4.3	4.3	2.5
Fecundity status at interview[2]				
Surgically sterile	3.3	2.1	2.1	1.3
Impaired fecundity	5.7	9.2	6.1	4.1
Fecund	0.8	0.8	0.2	0.5
Ever used infertility services				
Yes	—	7.5	6.6	3.7
No	—	1.0	0.6	0.6
Education at interview[3]				
No high school diploma or GED[4]	1.8	1.7	1.8	0.8
High school diploma or GED	2.4	2.4	1.5	1.2
Some college, no bachelor's degree	1.6	2.2	1.2	1.4
Bachelor's degree or higher	4.6	3.1	2.4	1.7
Race and Hispanic origin				
Hispanic	1.2	0.7	0.8	0.6
Non-Hispanic white	2.3	2.4	1.8	1.4
Non-Hispanic black	1.6	1.5	1.4	1.9

1. Total includes women with missing or inapplicable data on some variables. Also includes women of other race and ethnic origins, not shown separately. 2. Fecundity status in 1973 was measured only as surgically sterile, subfecund, and fecund. In 1982, 1988, and 1995, fecundity status differentiated surgically sterile women based on contraceptive versus noncontraceptive reasons. Fecundity status also included three subcategories of impaired fecundity—nonsurgically sterile, subfecund, and long interval. 3. Limited to women 22–44 years at interview. 4. GED is general equivalency diploma. GED was explicitly asked about in only the 1988 and 1995 surveys. Source: Centers for Disease Control and Prevention, National Center for Health Statistics. Advance Data no. 306, May 11, 1999.

Children in Foster Care

	Percent	Number		Percent	Number
Total		520,000	**Race/ethnicity**		
			White	35	182,000
Ages			Black	45	234,000
Under 1 year	4%	20,800	Hispanic[1]	13	67,600
1–5 years	27	140,400	American Indian/Alaskan Native	1	5,200
6–10 years	28	145,600	Asian/Pacific Islander	1	5,200
11–15 years	27	140,400	Unknown/unable to determine	4	20,800
16–18 years	13	67,600	**Gender**		
19 years and over	1	5,200	Male	51	265,200
			Female	49	254,800

NOTE: Data as of March 31, 1998. Percentages may not add up to 100% and numbers may not add up to totals due to rounding. 1. Hispanic can be of any race. *Source:* U.S. Dept. of Health and Human Services, Admin. for Children and Families: Adoption and Foster Care Analysis and Reporting System and American Public Human Services Association.

Child Abuse and Neglect

Based on reports alleging child abuse and neglect that were referred for investigation by the respective child-protective services agency in each state. The reporting period may be either calendar year or fiscal year. The majority of states provided duplicated counts. Also, varying number of states reported the various characteristics presented below. A substantiated case represents a type of investigation disposition that determines that there is sufficient evidence under state law to conclude that maltreatment occurred or that the child is at risk of maltreatment. An indicated case represents a type of disposition that concludes that there was a reason to suspect maltreatment had occurred.

	1990		1995		1996		1997	
Item	Number	Percent	Number	Percent	Number	Percent	Number	Percent
Types of substantiated maltreatment								
Victims, total[1, 2]	690,658	100.0%	970,285	100.0%	969,018	100.0%	798,358	100.0%
Neglect	338,770	49.1%	507,015	52.3	500,032	51.6	436,630	54.7
Physical abuse	186,801	27.0	237,840	24.5	229,332	23.7	195,517	24.5
Sexual abuse	119,506	17.3	122,964	12.7	119,397	12.3	97,425	12.2
Emotional maltreatment	45,621	6.6	42,051	4.3	55,473	5.7	49,146	6.2
Medical neglect	n.a.	n.a.	28,541	2.9	25,758	2.7	18,866	2.4
Sex of victim								
Victims, total[2]	794,101	100.0	809,634	100.0	808,370	100.0	669,057	100.0
Male	357,367	45.0	381,075	47.1	384,280	47.5	316,842	47.4
Female	405,409	51.1	425,193	52.5	419,656	51.9	349,606	52.3
Age of victim								
Victims, total[2]	807,965	100.0	808,575	100.0	807,854	100.0	668,059	100.0
1 year and younger	106,507	13.2	103,335	12.8	101,055	12.5	83,921	12.6
2 to 5 years old	192,018	23.8	215,303	26.6	208,754	25.8	167,658	25.1
6 to 9 years old	175,609	21.7	195,400	24.2	200,888	24.9	166,718	25.0
10 to 13 years old	150,507	18.6	154,682	19.1	158,247	19.6	130,840	19.6
14 to 17 years old	116,015	14.4	121,548	15.0	123,872	15.3	97,348	14.6
18 years and over	5,464	0.7	7,506	0.9	6,466	0.8	3,063	0.5

NOTE: n.a. = not available. 1. More than one type of maltreatment may be substantiated per child. Therefore, totals for this category will add up to more than 100 percent. Victim totals and maltreatment types are based on subset of states that reported both the number of child victims and maltreatment incidences by type for that year. 2. Includes other and unknown not shown separately. *Source: Statistical Abstract of the United States, 1999.*

Top 15 States for Rearing Children, 1999

Each year the Children's Rights Council, a national child advocacy organization, ranks the states (plus the District of Columbia) based upon conditions for rearing children. Criteria include abuse and neglect rates, immunization, high school dropout rate, poverty level, child death rate, infant mortality rate, prenatal care, juvenile arrests, birth rate, and divorce rate.

Rank			Rank			Rank		
1999	1998	State	1999	1998	State	1999	1998	State
1	8	Maine	6	6	North Dakota	11	2	Minnesota
2	5	Massachusetts	7	26	Maryland	12	18	Rhode Island
3	17	Connecticut	8	14	Kansas	13	11	Hawaii
4	10	Vermont	9	13	Wisconsin	14	28	Alaska
5	3	New Hampshire	10	1	Iowa	15	4	Nebraska

Source: Children's Rights Council, Washington, D.C., Web: www.gocrc.com.

Child Care for Children Under Six Years Old, 1995

Characteristic	Children Number (1,000)	Children Percent distribution	Type of nonparental arrangement Total[1]	Type of nonparental arrangement Relative care	Type of nonparental arrangement Nonrelative care	Type of nonparental arrangement Center-based program[2]	No nonparental arrangement
Total	**21,421**	**100%**	**60%**	**21%**	**18%**	**31%**	**40%**
Race-ethnicity							
White, non-Hispanic	13,996	65	62	18	21	33	38
Black, non-Hispanic	3,344	6	66	31	12	33	34
Hispanic	2,838	13	46	23	12	17	54
Other	1,243	6	58	25	13	28	42
Mother's employment status[3]							
35 or more hours per week	7,101	34	88	33	32	39	12
Less than 35 hours per week	4,034	19	75	30	26	35	25
Looking for work	1,635	8	42	16	4	25	58
Not in labor force	8,354	40	32	7	6	22	68
Household income							
Less than $10,001	4,502	21	50	22	10	25	50
$10,001 to $20,000	2,909	14	54	27	12	24	46
$20,001 to $30,000	3,385	16	53	22	14	25	47
$30,001 to $40,000	3,047	14	60	23	20	27	40
$40,001 to $50,000	2,304	11	63	19	22	32	37
$50,001 to $75,000	3,063	14	74	20	26	40	26
$75,001 or more	2,211	10	77	14	30	49	23

NOTES: Estimates are based on children under 6 years old who have yet to enter kindergarten. Based on 14,064 interviews from a sample survey of the civilian, noninstitutional population in households with telephones; see source for details. 1. Columns do not add to total because some children participated in more than one type of nonparental arrangement. 2. Center-based programs include day-care centers, head-start programs, preschool, prekindergartens, and other early childhood programs. 3. Children without mothers are not included. *Source:* U.S. National Center for Education Statistics, *Statistics in Brief,* Oct. 1995 (NCES 95-824).

Breast-Feeding by Selected Characteristics of Mother, 1972–1994

Breast-feeding, which has gone in and out of fashion over the decades, nearly doubled between 1972 and 1994 and continues to be on the rise. Breast milk contains antibodies that help protect babies against illnesses and allergies, and is considered by doctors to be more beneficial than formula.

Selected characteristics of mother	Percent of babies breast-fed 1972–74	Percent of babies breast-fed 1975–77	Percent of babies breast-fed 1978–80	Percent of babies breast-fed 1981–83	Percent of babies breast-fed 1984–86	Percent of babies breast-fed 1987–89	Percent of babies breast-fed 1990–92	Percent of babies breast-fed 1993–94
Total	**30.1%**	**36.7%**	**47.5%**	**58.1%**	**54.5%**	**52.3%**	**54.2%**	**58.1%**
Race								
White, non-Hispanic	32.5	38.9	53.2	64.3	59.7	58.3	59.1	61.2
Black, non-Hispanic	12.5	16.8	19.6	26.0	22.9	21.0	22.9	27.5
Hispanic[1]	33.1	42.9	46.3	52.8	58.9	51.3	58.8	67.4
Education[2]								
No high school diploma or GED[3]	14.0	19.4	27.6	31.4	36.8	30.0	38.6	43.0
High school diploma or GED[3]	25.0	33.6	40.2	54.3	46.7	46.6	46.0	51.2
Some college, no bachelor's degree	35.2	43.5	63.2	66.7	66.1	57.8	60.7	65.9
Bachelor's degree or higher	65.5	66.9	71.3	83.2	75.3	79.2	80.8	80.6
Geographic region								
Northeast	29.9	34.7	49.3	68.2	55.3	49.9	54.0	56.7
Midwest	22.3	30.9	34.4	46.0	50.9	50.4	51.6	49.7
South	30.6	33.1	49.5	57.9	45.3	42.5	43.6	49.7
West	47.1	54.5	66.6	69.9	70.9	69.1	70.5	79.3
Age at baby's birth								
Under 20 years	17.0	22.1	31.4	31.0	30.6	26.2	35.2	45.3
20–24 years	28.7	33.5	44.7	50.8	50.2	46.7	44.7	50.9
25–29 years	38.7	45.9	53.6	62.2	59.8	57.1	56.5	55.9
30–44 years	43.1	47.5	55.2	73.1	65.9	65.3	67.5	71.1

NOTE: Years indicate babies' birth years. Based on household interviews of samples of women ages 15–44. 1. Hispanic may be of any race. 2. For women 22–44 years of age. Education is as of year of interview. 3. General equivalency diploma. *Source:* National Center for Health Statistics.

Findings from the National Violence against Women Survey, July 2000

Domestic Violence Pervasive

According to the National Violence against Women (NVAW) survey, sponsored by the National Institute of Justice and the Centers for Disease Control and Prevention, intimate partner violence is pervasive in U.S. society. Nearly 25% of surveyed women and 7.5% of surveyed men said they were raped and/or physically assaulted by a current or former spouse, cohabiting partner, or date at some time in their lifetime. Stalking by intimates is more prevalent than previously thought, exceeding previous nonscientific "guesstimates" of stalking in the general population. Almost 5% of surveyed women and 0.6% of surveyed men reported being stalked by a current or former spouse, cohabiting partner, or date at some time in their lifetime.

Women Bear the Brunt of the Violence

Women experience more intimate partner violence than do men. The NVAW survey found that women are significantly more likely than men to report being victims of rape, physical assault, or stalking than men. Women also experience more chronic and injurious physical assaults at the hands of intimate partners. The survey found that women who were physically assaulted by an intimate partner averaged 6.9 physical assaults by the same partner, whereas men averaged 4.4 assaults.

Emotional Abuse Frequently Accompanies Physical Abuse

Violence perpetrated against women by intimates is often accompanied by emotionally abusive and controlling behavior. The survey found that women whose partners were jealous, controlling, or verbally abusive were significantly more likely to report being raped, physically assaulted, and/or stalked by their partners, even when other sociodemographic and relationship characteristics were controlled. Indeed, having a verbally abusive partner was the variable most likely to predict that a woman would be victimized by an intimate partner. These findings support the theory that violence perpetrated against women by intimates is often part of a systematic pattern of dominance and control.

Lesbian Couples

Women living with female partners experience less partner violence than women living with male partners. Slightly more than 11% of the women who had lived with a woman as part of a couple reported being raped, physically assaulted, and/or stalked by a female cohabitant, but 21.7% of the women who had married or lived with a man as part of a couple reported such violence by a husband or male cohabitant. These findings suggest that lesbian couples experience less intimate partner violence than do heterosexual couples; however, more research is needed to support or refute this conclusion.

Gay Male Couples

Men living with male partners experience more partner violence than do men who live with female partners. Approximately 23% of the men who had lived with a man as a couple reported being raped, physically assaulted, and/or stalked by a male cohabitant, while 7.4% of the men who had married or lived with a woman as a couple reported such violence by a wife or female cohabitant. These findings provide further evidence that intimate partner violence is perpetrated primarily by men, whether against male or female intimates.

Domestic Violence Underreported to Police

Most intimate partner victimizations are not reported to the police. Only approximately one-fifth of all rapes, one-quarter of all physical assaults, and one-half of all stalkings perpetrated against female respondents by intimates were reported to the police. Even fewer rapes, physical assaults, and stalkings perpetrated against male respondents by intimates were reported. The majority of victims who did not report their victimization to the police thought the police would not or could not do anything on their behalf.

Domestic Violence

Type of victimization over lifetime	Percent		Number	
	Women	Men	Women	Men
Rape	7.7%	0.3%	7,753,669	278,244
Physical assault	22.1	7.4	22,254,037	6,863,352
Rape and/or physical assault	24.8	7.6	24,972,856	7,048,848
Stalking	4.8	0.6	4,833,456	556,488
Total victimized	25.5	7.9	25,677,735	7,327,092

Survey consisted of telephone interviews with a nationally representative sample of 8,000 U.S. women and 8,000 men. **Definitions:** Rape includes completed or attempted forced vaginal, oral, or anal sex. Physical assault includes a range of behaviors from slapping and hitting to using a gun. Stalking involves repeated acts of harassment and intimidation with the victim reporting a high level of fear. *Source:* National Violence against Women survey, National Institute of Justice and Centers for Disease Control, July 2000.

Key Events in the Women's Rights Movement

1848 The first women's rights convention is held in Seneca Falls, New York. A Declaration of Sentiments, which outlines grievances and sets the agenda for the women's rights movement, is signed by 68 women and 32 men.

1850 The first National Women's Rights Convention takes place in Worcester, Mass., attracting more than 1,000 participants. National conventions are held yearly (except for 1857) through 1860.

1869 In May, Susan B. Anthony and Elizabeth Cady Stanton form the National Woman Suffrage Association. Its primary goal is to achieve voting rights for women by means of a congressional amendment to the Constitution.

In Nov. Lucy Stone, Henry Blackwell, and others form the American Woman Suffrage Association. This group focuses exclusively on gaining voting rights for women through amendments to individual state constitutions.

In Dec. the territory of Wyoming passes the first women's suffrage law. The following year, women begin serving on juries in the territory.

1890 The National Woman Suffrage Association and the American Woman Suffrage Association merge to form the National American Woman Suffrage Association (NAWSA). As the movement's mainstream organization, NAWSA wages state-by-state campaigns to obtain voting rights for women.

1893 Colorado is the first state to adopt an amendment granting women the right to vote. Utah and Idaho follow suit in 1896, Washington State in 1910, California in 1911, Oregon, Kansas, and Arizona in 1912, Alaska and Illinois in 1913, Montana and Nevada in 1914, New York in 1917, Michigan, South Dakota, and Oklahoma in 1918.

1896 The National Association of Colored Women is formed, bringing together more than 100 black women's clubs. Leaders in the black women's club movement include Josephine St. Pierre Ruffin, Mary Church Terrell, and Anna Julia Cooper.

1913 Alice Paul and Lucy Burns form the Congressional Union to work toward the passage of a federal amendment to give women the vote. The group is later renamed the National Women's Party. Members picket the White House and practice other forms of civil disobedience.

1919 The federal woman suffrage amendment, originally written by Susan B. Anthony and introduced in Congress in 1878, is passed by the House of Representatives and the Senate. It is then sent to the states for ratification.

1920 On Aug. 26, the 19th Amendment to the Constitution, granting women the right to vote, is signed into law.

1921 Margaret Sanger founds the American Birth Control League, which evolves into the Planned Parenthood Federation of America in 1942.

1936 The federal law prohibiting the dissemination of contraceptive information through the mail is modified, and birth control information is no longer classified as obscene. Throughout the 1940s and 1950s, birth control advocates are engaged in numerous legal suits.

1961 President John Kennedy establishes the President's Commission on the Status of Women and appoints Eleanor Roosevelt as chairwoman. The report issued by the commission in 1963 documents substantial discrimination against women in the workplace and urges reform, including fair hiring practices, paid maternity leave, and affordable child care.

1963 Betty Friedan publishes her highly influential book *The Feminine Mystique,* which becomes a best-seller and galvanizes the modern women's rights movement.

In June Congress passes the Equal Pay Act, making it illegal for employers to pay a woman less than what a man would receive for the same job.

1964 Title VII of the Civil Rights Act bars discrimination in employment on the basis of race and sex. At the same time it establishes the Equal Employment Opportunity Commission (EEOC) to investigate complaints and impose penalties.

1965 In *Griswold* v. *Connecticut,* the Supreme Court strikes down the one remaining state law prohibiting the use of contraceptives by married couples.

1966 The National Organization for Women (NOW) is founded. The largest women's rights group in the U.S., NOW seeks to end sexual discrimination by means of legislative lobbying, litigation, and public demonstrations.

1967 Executive Order 11375 expands President Lyndon Johnson's affirmative action policy of 1965 to cover discrimination based on gender. As a result, federal agencies and contractors must take active measures to ensure that women as well as minorities enjoy the same educational and employment opportunities as white males.

1968 The EEOC rules that sex-segregated help wanted ads in newspapers are illegal. This ruling is upheld in 1973 by the Supreme Court, opening the way for women to apply for higher-paying jobs hitherto open only to men.

1969 California becomes the first state to adopt a "no fault" divorce law, which allows couples to divorce by mutual consent. By 1985 every state has adopted a similar law. Laws are also passed regarding the equal division of common property.

1971 *Ms.* magazine is first published as a sample insert in *New York* magazine; 300,000 copies are sold out in 8 days. The first regular issue is published in July 1972. The magazine becomes the major forum for feminist voices and turns cofounder and editor Gloria Steinem into an icon of the modern feminist movement.

In *Eisenstadt* v. *Baird* the Supreme Court rules that the right to privacy includes an unmarried person's right to use contraceptives.

1972 The Equal Rights Amendment (ERA) is passed by Congress and sent to the states for ratification. Originally drafted by Alice Paul in 1923, the amendment reads: "Equality of rights under the law shall not be denied or abridged by the United States or by any State on account of sex." The amendment died in 1982 when it failed to achieve ratification by a minimum of 38 states.

Title IX of the Education Amendments bans sex discrimination in schools. As a result, the enrollment of women in athletics programs and professional schools increases dramatically.

1973 As a result of *Roe* v. *Wade,* the Supreme Court establishes a woman's legal right to abortion, overriding the antiabortion laws of many states.

1974 The Equal Credit Opportunity Act prohibits discrimination in consumer credit practices on the basis of sex, race, marital status, religion, national origin, age, or receipt of public assistance.

1978 The Pregnancy Discrimination Act bans employment discrimination against pregnant women.

1984 EMILY's List (Early Money Is Like Yeast) is established as a financial network for pro-choice Democratic women running for national political office. The organization makes a significant impact on the increasing numbers of women elected to Congress.

1986 In *Meritor Savings Bank* v. *Vinson,* the Supreme Court finds that sexual harassment is a form of illegal job discrimination.

1994 The Violence against Women Act tightens federal penalties for sex offenders, funds services for victims of rape and domestic violence, and provides for special training of police officers.

Gender of Sexual Partners in the United States

(sexually active only)

	Same gender		Both genders		Opposite genders	
	Men	Women	Men	Women	Men	Women
1988	2.3%	0.2%	0.3%	0.0%	97.4%	99.8%
1989	1.4	1.2	0.3	0.4	98.3	98.4
1990	1.1	0.5	0.9	0.0	98.0	99.5
1991	2.0	0.3	0.7	0.1	97.3	99.6
1993	1.8	1.8	0.3	0.4	97.9	97.8
1994	2.1	2.1	0.5	0.4	97.5	97.5
1996	3.5	2.1	0.6	0.9	96.0	97.0

Source: General Social Survey (GSS), National Opinion Research Center, University of Chicago, 1996.

What Is a Civil Union?

On July 1, 2000, Vermont became the first state in the country to legally recognize civil unions between gay or lesbian couples. Building on a state Supreme Court decision in Dec. 1999, which ruled that denying gay couples the benefits of marriage was unconstitutional discrimination, the ground-breaking law grants the same state benefits, civil rights, and protections to same-sex couples as to married couples.

Why Marriage Isn't a Civil Union, and Vice Versa

Same-sex unions have provoked enormous controversy on moral and philosophical grounds, but separate from these issues, they have raised a legal quagmire: can a couple of the same sex be married, given that the very definition of marriage is the legal union of a man and a woman? To solve this problem and to protect the legal institution of marriage, Vermont's legislators adopted a different term—"civil union"—to apply to same-sex marriages. Couples in a civil union would thus be entitled to the same legal rights as married couples.

Hawaii the First to Raise the Issue

Vermont was not the first state to attempt socially progressive legislation benefiting gays. In 1993, two

men in Hawaii applied for a marriage license and were turned away. The couple brought their case, *Baehr* v. *Miike,* to Hawaii's Supreme Court, which ruled in May 1993 that the denial of the license was equivalent to discrimination—a violation of the state's constitution. In 1998, the Hawaii legislature took up the issue, and passed a state constitutional amendment barring same-sex marriages, thus rendering the earlier decision by the Hawaii Supreme Court unconstitutional.

Same-Sex Marriage Ban in 32 States

The progressive Vermont law stands in stark contrast to the antigay marriage laws of more than 32 states and the federal government. Just months before passage of the Vermont law, California—with an eighth of the United States' population—voted against recognition of gay unions. Proposition 22, passed on March 7, 2000, ensures that most state benefits of married couples are not extended to same-sex couples. California is not alone. In total, 32 states have passed similar legislation, and on the federal level, the Defense of Marriage Act was passed in 1996, barring federal benefits to same-sex partners. On the other hand, several states in 2000 defeated bills that would have banned state benefits for same-sex unions, including Mississippi, New Hampshire, and New Mexico. □

The Wage Gap

The wage gap is a statistical indicator often used as an index of the status of women's earnings relative to men's. It is also used to compare the earnings of other races and ethnicities to those of white males, a group generally not subject to race- or sex-based discrimination. The wage gap is expressed as a percentage (e.g., in 1998, women earned 73% as much as men) and is calculated by dividing the median annual earnings for women by the median annual earnings for men. Since 1963, when the Equal Pay Act was signed, the closing of the wage gap between men and women has been at a rate of less than half a penny a year.

1998 Median Annual Earnings by Race and Sex

Race/gender	Earnings	Wage ratio	Race/gender	Earnings	Wage ratio
White men	$36,172	100.0%	All men	$35,345	
White women	$26,243	72.6	All women	$25,362	
Black men	$27,050	74.9	Wage gap		73.0%
Black women	$22,648	62.6			
Hispanic men	$22,285	61.6			
Hispanic women	$19,221	53.1			

Source: The National Committee on Pay Equity.

Women's Earnings as a Percentage of Men's, 1951–1998

(for year-round full-time work)

Year	Percent	Year	Percent	Year	Percent	Year	Percent	Year	Percent
1951	63.9%	1961	59.2%	1971	59.5%	1981	59.2%	1991	69.9%
1952	63.9	1962	59.3	1972	57.9	1982	61.7	1992	70.8
1953	63.9	1963	58.9	1973	56.6	1983	63.6	1993	71.5
1954	63.9	1964	59.1	1974	58.8	1984	63.7	1994	72.0
1955	63.9	1965	59.9	1975	58.8	1985	64.6	1995	71.4
1956	63.3	1966	57.6	1976	60.2	1986	64.3	1996	73.8
1957	63.8	1967	57.8	1977	58.9	1987	65.2	1997	74.2
1958	63.0	1968	58.2	1978	59.4	1988	66.0	1998	73.0
1959	61.3	1969	58.9	1979	59.7	1989	68.7		
1960	60.7	1970	59.4	1980	60.2	1990	71.6		

Source: U.S. Women's Bureau.

20 Leading Occupations of Employed Women

(1999 annual averages)

Occupations	Employed (in thousands)	Percent who are women	Women's median usual weekly earnings[1]	Ratio of women's earnings to men's earnings
Secretaries	2,741	98.6%	$443	n.a.
Managers and administrators, n.e.c.[2]	2,349	30.5	692	64.6 %
Cashiers[3]	2,321	77.0	275	92.9
Sales supervisors and proprietors	2,005	40.9	454	65.7
Registered nurses	1,978	92.9	747	94.4
Sales workers, retail, and personal services	1,849	63.9	296	70.0
Nursing aides, orderlies, and attendants	1,772	89.9	318	86.6
Elementary school teachers	1,736	83.8	697	88.8
Bookkeepers, accounting and auditing clerks	1,545	91.4	440	92.1
Waiters and waitresses	1,108	77.4	294	90.5
Receptionists	1,041	95.5	373	n.a.
Accountants and auditors	972	58.6	651	73.1
Sales workers, other commodities[4]	940	67.8	315	80.4
Cooks	914	44.0	279	88.0
Machine operators, assorted materials	899	32.6	350	71.9
Investigators and adjusters, excluding insurance	815	77.3	435	85.1
Secondary school teachers	772	57.5	722	89.9
Administrative support occupations, n.e.c.[2]	725	79.2	453	74.0
Janitors and cleaners	759	35.8	293	83.5
Hairdressers and cosmetologists	712	90.8	323	n.a.

NOTE: n.a. = not available. Median not available where base is less than 50,000 male workers 1. Wage and salary for full-time workers. 2. Not elsewhere classified. 3. Included in sales workers, personal, and retail services. 4. Includes foods, drugs, health, and other commodities. *Source:* U.S. Dept. of Labor, Bureau of Labor Statistics.

Black Schools Go White

More and more white students enroll at historically black colleges

By TAMMERLIN DRUMMOND TIME

After graduating from a St. Louis, Mo., high school where she was one of very few blacks, Elizabeth Johnson wanted to "try something different." She enrolled at Lincoln University, a historically black college founded by African-American Civil War veterans in Jefferson City, Mo. But Johnson was in for a shock when she arrived at her first class. "I was the only black face in the room," she recalls.

Johnson didn't realize that Lincoln is one of four historically black colleges and universities, out of 106, where white students are in the majority. Once revered as the black Harvard of the Middle West, Lincoln is now nearly 70% white. Overall, white enrollment at historically black colleges across the U.S. climbed 16% between 1990 and 1998. At Bluefield State College in West Virginia, more than 90% of the students are white.

Quality Education

Why? White students and parents are discovering what African Americans have known for decades—many historically black colleges offer a quality education for about half the price of comparable mainstream schools. Some black students and administrators welcome the new diversity. Others, though, argue that schools that are now predominantly white should no longer receive federal funds for their "unique mission" of educating African Americans. Most historically black colleges were founded before 1965, when African Americans were shut out of most predominantly white institutions. But today some historically black colleges with a majority of white students and faculty are at an important crossroads. Says M. Christopher Brown, a professor of higher education at the University of Illinois: "It doesn't mean they're going to disappear completely, but they will have a decidedly different shape."

Reverse Desegregation

Another reason white enrollment is growing at historically black colleges is that courts have ordered many of them to desegregate by admitting more whites. Many offer minority scholarships to white students. Given the tide of opposition to affirmative action at mainstream institutions, the whites-only scholarships have sparked an outcry. But with African-American enrollment dropping, historically black colleges have no choice but to recruit people of all races. "Lincoln is schizophrenic at this point," says Rosemary Hearn, who teaches English at the school. "There's always that real concern about how we're going to maintain our heritage."

Lincoln, which has a strong agricultural program, has reinvented itself as an open-admissions school. Anyone who graduates from a state-accredited high school is eligible for admission. So Lincoln is attracting white commuter students from nearby farm towns who probably couldn't get admitted anywhere else. But Lincoln president David Henson insists that despite changing demographics, "the university's culture is still driven for the most part by African-American standards." All incoming students must take courses on cultural diversity and African-American history.

Race Still an Issue

Yet despite the politically correct curriculum, one of the most jarring sights at Lincoln is its de facto segregation. It has even spawned the saying "White by day, black by night." That's because most white students drive home when their classes end. There's even an unofficial white student union on the fourth floor of the Martin Luther King campus building. The dorms, fraternities, sororities, and other social activities are dominated by blacks. "It's really sad," says Tanya Servick, a communications major who is African American. Josh Cleveland, a creative-writing major from St. Louis, says he commutes because he feels that whites like him aren't welcome in the dorms.

Being in the minority took a while for Kimberly McCullough, a white student on a tennis scholarship, to get used to. She is one of four whites out of 300 students in the women's dorm. "Until I made some friends, it was kind of weird at first," she says. "But then it was no big deal." In the end, it wasn't a big deal for Elizabeth Johnson either. After all, she was used to being in the minority. □

Historically Black Colleges
Student Body (1999)

	Black	White
Lincoln University (Missouri)	32%	68%
Bluefield State (West Virginia)	9%	91%
West Virginia State	15%	85%
Kentucky State University	50%	50%

Milestones in African American Education

1837 Institute for Colored Youth founded by Richard Humphreys; later became Cheyney University.

1856 Wilberforce University, the first black school of higher learning in the U.S., founded by the African Methodist Episcopal Church

1876 Meharry Medical College, the first black medical school in the U.S., founded by the Freedman's Aid Society of the Methodist Episcopal Church.

1881 Spelman College, the first college for black women in the U.S., founded by Sophia B. Packard and Harriet E. Giles.

1922 William Leo Hansberry teaches the first course in African civilization at an American university, at Howard University.

1944 Frederick Douglass Patterson establishes the United Negro College Fund to help support black colleges and black students.

1960 Black and white students form the Student Nonviolent Coordinating Committee (SNCC), dedicated to working against segregation and discrimination.

1962 James Meredith is the first black student to enroll at the University of Mississippi; on the day he enters the university, he is escorted by U.S. marshals.

1963 Despite Governor George Wallace physically blocking their way, Vivian Malone and James Hood register for classes at the University of Alabama.

1969 The Ford Foundation gives $1 million to Morgan State University, Howard University, and Yale University to help prepare faculty members to teach courses in African American studies.

Historically Black Colleges and Universities (HBCUs)

In the late 19th century, colleges for black students were started in box cars (Atlanta University) and church basements (Spelman College). Mary McLeod Bethune, one of the nation's foremost black educators, opened a college in 1904 with $1.50 and 5 students. Today, there are 106 historically black colleges and universities in the United States, who can count among their graduates such luminaries as W. E. B. Du Bois (Fisk University), Thurgood Marshall (Lincoln University and Howard University), Toni Morrison (Howard University), and Martin Luther King, Jr. (Morehouse College).

Alabama A&M University (Ala.)
Alabama State University (Ala.)
Albany State University (Ga.)
Alcorn State University (Miss.)
Allen University (S.C.)
Arkansas Baptist College (Ark.)
Barber-Scotia College (N.C.)
Benedict College (S.C.)
Bennett College (N.C.)
Bethune-Cookman College (Fla.)
Bishop State Community College (Ala.)
Bluefield State College (W.Va.)
Bowie State University (Md.)
Central State University (Ohio)
Charles Drew University of Medicine (Calif.)
Cheyney University (Pa.)
Chicago State University (Ill.)
Claflin College (S.C.)
Clark Atlanta University (Ga.)
Clinton Junior College (S.C.)
Coahoma Community College (Miss.)
Concordia College (Ala.)
Coppin State College (Md.)
Delaware State University (Del.)
Denmark Technical College (S.C.)
Dillard University (La.)
Edward Waters College (Fla.)
Elizabeth City State University (N.C.)
Fayetteville State University (N.C.)
Fisk University (Tenn.)
Florida A&M University (Fla.)
Florida Memorial College (Fla.)
Fort Valley State University (Ga.)
Grambling State University (La.)
Hampton University (Va.)
Harris-Stowe State College (Mo.)
Hinds Community College (Miss.)
Howard University (D.C.)
Huston-Tillotson College (Tex.)

Interdenominational Theological Center (Ga.)
J. F. Drake State Technical College (Ala.)
Jackson State University (Miss.)
Jarvis Christian College (Tex.)
Johnson C. Smith University (N.C.)
Kentucky State University (Ky.)
Knoxville College (Tenn.)
Lane College (Tenn.)
Langston University (Okla.)
Lawson State Community College (Ala.)
LeMoyne-Owen College (Tenn.)
Lewis College of Business (Mich.)
Lincoln University (Mo.)
Lincoln University (Pa.)
Livingstone College (N.C.)
Mary Holmes College (Miss.)
Meharry Medical College (Tenn.)
Miles College (Ala.)
Mississippi Valley State University (Miss.)
Morehouse College (Ga.)
Morehouse School of Medicine (Ga.)
Morgan State University (Md.)
Morris Brown College (Ga.)
Morris College (S.C.)
Norfolk State University (Va.)
North Carolina A&T State University (N.C.)
North Carolina Central University (N.C.)
Oakwood College (Ala.)
Paine College (Ga.)
Paul Quinn College (Tex.)
Philander Smith College (Ark.)
Prairie View A&M University (Tex.)
Rust College (Miss.)
Saint Augustine's College (N.C.)

Saint Paul's College (Va.)
Saint Philip's College (Tex.)
Savannah State University (Ga.)
Selma University (Ala.)
Shaw University (N.C.)
Shelton State Community College (Ala.)
Shorter College (Ark.)
South Carolina State University (S.C.)
Southern University and A&M College (La.)
Southern University, New Orleans (La.)
Southern University, Shreveport (La.)
Southwestern Christian College (Tex.)
Spelman College (Ga.)
Stillman College (Ala.)
Talladega College (Ala.)
Tennessee State University (Tenn.)
Texas College (Tex.)
Texas Southern University (Tex.)
Tougaloo College (Miss.)
Trenholm State Technical College (Ala.)
Tuskegee University (Ala.)
University of Arkansas at Pine Bluff (Ark.)
University of Maryland, Eastern Shore (Md.)
University of the District of Columbia (D.C.)
University of the Virgin Islands (V.I.)
Virginia State University (Va.)
Virginia Union University (Va.)
Voorhees College (S.C.)
West Virginia State College (W.Va.)
Wilberforce University (Ohio)
Wiley College (Tex.)
Winston-Salem State University (N.C.)
Xavier University of Louisiana (La.)

For a list of *Black Enterprise* magazine's "Top 50 Colleges for Black Students," *see* pp. 314–315.

Population of the United States by Race and Hispanic Origin

(as of April 2000)

	Total population	% of population		Total population	% of population
All races	272,878,000	100.0%	American Indian, Eskimo, and Aleut	2,396,000	0.9%
White	224,692,000	82.3	Asian and Pacific Islander	10,887,000	4.0
Black	34,903,000	12.8	Hispanic origin (of any race)	31,365,000	11.5

NOTE: Percentages add up to more than 100% because Hispanics may be of any race and are therefore counted under more than one category. *Source:* U.S. Census Bureau; Web: www.census.gov.

U.S. Asian Population

(Percent distribution)
Total Asians counted in the 1990 Census: 6,908,638

National origin	Percent	National origin	Percent	National origin	Percent
Chinese	23.8%	Laotian	2.2%	Bangladeshi	0.2%
Filipino	20.4	Cambodian	2.1	Malayan	0.2
Japanese	12.3	Thai	1.3	Indonesian	0.4
Asian Indian	11.8	Hmong	1.3	Pakistani	1.2
Korean	11.6	Burmese	0.1	Other Asian	2.1
Vietnamese	8.9	Sri Lankan	0.2		

Source: U.S. Census Bureau, 1990 figures.

U.S. Pacific Islander Population

(Percent distribution)
Total Pacific Islanders counted in the 1990 Census: 365,024

National origin or ancestry	Percent	National origin or ancestry	Percent	National origin or ancestry	Percent
Hawaiian	57.8%	Fijian	1.9%	Tahitian	0.3%
Samoan	17.2	Palauan	0.4	Other Pacific Islander	3.8
Guamanian	13.5	Northern Mariana	0.3		
Tongan	4.8	Islander			

Source: U.S. Census Bureau, 1990 figures.

U.S. Hispanic/Latino Population

(Percent distribution)
Total Hispanics counted in the 1990 Census: 22.3 million

National origin	Percent	National origin	Percent	National origin	Percent
Mexican	61.2%	Central American	6.0%	South American	4.7%
Puerto Rican	12.1	Salvadoran	42.7	Colombian	36.6
Cuban	4.8	Guatemalan	20.3	Ecuadorian	18.5
Dominican	2.4	Nicaraguan	15.3	Peruvian	16.9
Other Hispanic	3.9	Honduran	9.9	Argentinean	9.7
Spaniard[1]	4.4	Panamanian	7.0	Chilean	6.6
		Costa Rican	4.3	Other South American	11.7
		Other Central American	2.1		

NOTE: Hispanics may be of any race. 1. Includes those who reported "Spanish." *Source:* U.S. Census Bureau, 1990 figures.

Preference for Racial or Ethnic Terminology

Preferred term[1]	Percent	Preferred term[1]	Percent
Hispanic		**Black**	
Hispanic	57.88%	Black	44.15%
Of Spanish origin	12.34	African American	28.07
Latino	11.74	Afro-American	12.12
Some other term	7.85	Negro	3.28
No preference	10.18	Some other term	2.19
White		Colored	1.09
White	61.66%	No preference	9.11
Caucasian	16.53	**American Indian**	
European American	2.35	American Indian	49.76%
Some other term	1.97	Native American	37.35
Anglo	.96	Some other term	3.66
No preference	16.53	Alaska Native	3.51
		No preference	5.72

1. Preferred term by group of people the term is meant to represent. *Source:* U.S. Census Bureau Survey, May 1995.

U.S. Federal and State Reservations

Federal reservation
▲ State reservation

Populations of the Ten Largest Reservations

(1990 Census figures)

Name	Population
Navajo (Ariz., N.M., Utah)	143,405
Pine Ridge (Neb., S.D.)	11,182
Fort Apache (Ariz.)	9,825
Gila River (Ariz.)	9,116
Papago (Ariz.)	8,480
Rosebud (S.D.)	8,043
San Carlos (Ariz.)	7,110
Zuni Pueblo (Ariz., N.M.)	7,073
Hopi (Ariz.)	7,061
Blackfeet (Mont.)	7,025

The 218,320 American Indians living on these 10 reservations account for about half of all American Indians living on reservations and trust lands. *Source:* 1990 Census Bureau. *Map source:* Frederick E. Hoxie, ed., *Encyclopedia of North American Indians* (Boston: Houghton Mifflin, 1996). Reprinted with permission.

American Indian Tribes with Populations Greater than 10,000

(1990 U.S. Census figures)

American Indian tribe	Number	Percent distribution	American Indian tribe	Number	Percent distribution
American Indian population, total[1]	1,878,285	100.0%	Canadian and Latin American tribes	22,379	1.2%
Cherokee	308,132	16.4	Chickasaw	20,631	1.1
Navajo	219,198	11.7	Potawatomi	16,763	0.9
Chippewa	103,826	5.5	Tohono O'Odham	16,041	0.9
Sioux	103,255	5.5	Pima	14,431	0.8
Choctaw	82,299	4.4	Tlingit	13,925	0.7
Pueblo	52,939	2.8	Seminole	13,797	0.7
Apache	50,051	2.7	Alaskan Athabaskans	13,738	0.7
Iroquois	49,038	2.6	Cheyenne	11,456	0.6
Lumbee	48,444	2.6	Comanche	11,322	0.6
Creek	43,550	2.3	Paiute	11,142	0.6
Blackfoot	32,234	1.7	Puget Sound Salish	10,246	0.5

1. Includes other American Indian tribes not shown separately. *Source:* U.S. Census Bureau, *1990 Census of Population, General Population Characteristics, American Indian and Alaska Native Areas* (CP-1-1A); and press releases CB91-232 and CB92-244.

Ancestry of U.S. Population by Rank, 1990 Census

(Groups with populations exceeding one million)

1990 Rank	Ancestry group	Number	Percent	1990 Rank	Ancestry group	Number	Percent
1	German	57,947,873	23.2%	18	Welsh	2,033,893	0.8%
2	Irish	38,735,539	15.6	19	Spanish	2,024,004	0.8
3	English	32,651,788	13.1	20	Puerto Rican	1,955,323	0.8
4	African	23,777,098	9.6	21	Slovak	1,882,897	0.8
5	Italian	14,664,550	5.9	22	White	1,799,711	0.7
6	American	12,395,999	5.0	23	Danish	1,634,669	0.7
7	Mexican	11,586,983	4.7	24	Hungarian	1,582,302	0.6
8	French	10,320,935	4.1	25	Chinese	1,505,245	0.6
9	Polish	9,366,106	3.8	26	Filipino	1,450,512	0.6
10	American Indian	8,708,220	3.5	27	Czech	1,296,411	0.5
11	Dutch	6,227,089	2.5	28	Portuguese	1,153,351	0.5
12	Scotch-Irish	5,617,773	2.3	29	British	1,119,154	0.4
13	Scottish	5,393,581	2.2	30	Hispanic	1,113,259	0.4
14	Swedish	4,680,863	1.9	31	Greek	1,110,373	0.4
15	Norwegian	3,869,395	1.6	32	Swiss	1,045,495	0.4
16	Russian	2,952,987	1.2	33	Japanese	1,004,645	0.4
17	French Canadian	2,167,127	0.9				

Note: Data are based on a sample and subject to sampling variability. Since persons who reported multiple ancestries were included in more than one group, the sum of the persons reporting the ancestry is greater than the total; for example, a person reporting "English-French" was tabulated in both the "English" and "French" categories. *Source:* U.S. Census Bureau.

Persons Speaking a Language Other than English at Home

Language	Persons five years old and over who speak language	Language	Persons five years old and over who speak language	Language	Persons five years old and over who speak language
Speak only English	198,601,000	Portuguese	430,000	Armenian	150,000
Spanish	17,339,000	Japanese	428,000	Navajo	149,000
French	1,702,000	Greek	388,000	Hungarian	148,000
German	1,547,000	Arabic	355,000	Hebrew	144,000
Italian	1,309,000	Hindi (Urdu)	331,000	Dutch	143,000
Chinese	1,249,000	Russian	242,000	Mon-Khmer (Cambodian)	127,000
Tagalog	843,000	Yiddish	213,000	Gujarathi	102,000
Polish	723,000	Thai (Laotian)	206,000		
Korean	626,000	Persian	202,000		
Vietnamese	507,000	French Creole	188,000		

Source: U.S. Census Bureau, 1990 Census of Population and Housing Data Paper Listing (CPH-L-133).

The Foreign-Born Population in the United States, 1990
25 most common places of birth

1990 rank	Place of birth	Number	Percent	1990 rank	Place of birth	Number	Percent
1	Mexico	4,298,014	21.7%	14	Dominican Republic	347,858	1.8%
2	Philippines	912,674	4.6	15	Jamaica	334,140	1.7
3	Canada	744,830	3.8	16	Soviet Union	333,725	1.7
4	Cuba	736,971	3.7	17	Japan	290,128	1.5
5	Germany	711,929	3.6	18	Colombia	286,124	1.4
6	United Kingdom	640,145	3.2	19	Taiwan	244,102	1.2
7	Italy	580,592	2.9	20	Guatemala	225,739	1.1
8	Korea	568,397	2.9	21	Haiti	225,393	1.1
9	Vietnam	543,262	2.7	22	Iran	210,941	1.1
10	China	529,837	2.7	23	Portugal	210,122	1.1
11	El Salvador	465,433	2.4	24	Greece	177,398	0.9
12	India	450,406	2.3	25	Laos	171,577	0.9
13	Poland	388,328	2.0				

Source: U.S. Census Bureau.

Percent of U.S. Foreign Born: 1900 and 1990

Latin America 1.3
Asia 1.2
All other 12.6
Europe 84.9

1900

All other 10.3
Europe 22.0
Latin America 42.5
Asia 25.2

1990

Source: U.S. Census Bureau

Immigration to U.S.: 1850–1930, 1960–1990

Year	Total[1]	Region of birth reported					
		Europe	Asia	Africa	Oceania	Latin America	North America
1990	19,767,316	4,350,403	4,979,037	363,819	104,145	8,407,837	753,917
1980	14,079,906	5,149,572	2,539,777	199,723	77,577	4,372,487	853,427
1970	9,619,302	5,740,891	824,887	80,143	41,258	1,803,970	812,421
1960	9,738,091	7,256,311	490,996	35,355	34,730	908,309	952,500
1930	14,204,149	11,784,010	275,665	18,326	17,343	791,840	1,310,369
1920	13,920,692	11,916,048	237,950	16,126	14,626	588,843	1,138,174
1910	13,515,886	11,810,115	191,484	3,992	11,450	279,514	1,209,717
1900	10,341,276	8,881,548	120,248	2,538	8,820	137,458	1,179,922
1890	9,249,547	8,030,347	113,383	2,207	9,353	107,307	980,938
1880	6,679,943	5,751,823	107,630	2,204	6,859	90,073	717,286
1870	5,567,229	4,941,049	64,565	2,657	4,028	57,871	493,467
1860	4,138,697	3,807,062	36,796	526	2,140	38,315	249,970
1850	2,244,602	2,031,867	1,135	551	588	20,773	147,711

1. The sum of the regions for a particular year will not equal the total. Totals include significant numbers of immigrants for whom no region of birth was reported. *Source:* U.S. Census Bureau, March 9, 1999.

Affirmative Action Timeline

In its tumultuous 30-year history, affirmative action has been both praised and pilloried as an answer to racial inequality. The policy was introduced in 1965 by President Johnson as a method of redressing discrimination that had persisted in spite of civil rights laws and constitutional guarantees. Focusing in particular on education and jobs, affirmative action policies required active measures to ensure that blacks and other minorities enjoyed the same opportunities for promotions, salary increases, career advancement, school admissions, scholarships, and financial aid that had been the nearly exclusive province of whites. From the outset, affirmative action was envisioned as a temporary remedy that would end once there was a "level playing field" for all Americans.

By the late '70s, however, flaws in the policy began to show up amid its good intentions. Reverse discrimination became a passionate issue, epitomized by the famous *Bakke* case in 1978. A backlash against affirmative action mounted, and in the last decade the tide has turned against it in both the courts and on a state level—California and Washington have gone as far as abolishing the policy.

Yet the questions of fairness and racial equality remain troubling for most of those not positioned at the ideological poles of the issue. Even a once-adamant opponent of affirmative action like John Bunzel, president of San Jose State University, has acknowledged that "perhaps the most important lesson I've learned is that there are no airtight, completely coherent, unassailable, and holistic answers on the question of affirmative action. . . . Any intelligent person who wrestles with it is going to be vulnerable and subject to the twists and turns of unintended consequences." Serious advocates both for and against affirmative action could easily share such an estimation.

March 6, 1961: Executive Order 10925 makes the first reference to "affirmative action." President John F. Kennedy issues Executive Order 10925, which creates the Committee on Equal Employment Opportunity and mandates that projects financed with federal funds "take affirmative action" to ensure that hiring and employment practices are free of racial bias.

July 2, 1964: Civil Rights Act signed by President Lyndon Johnson. The most sweeping civil rights legislation since Reconstruction, the Civil Rights Act prohibits discrimination of all kinds based on race, color, religion, or national origin.

June 4, 1965: Speech defining concept of affirmative action. In a speech to the graduating class at Howard University, President Johnson frames the concept underlying affirmative action, asserting that civil rights laws alone are not enough to remedy discrimination: "You do not wipe away the scars of centuries by saying: 'now, you are free to go where you want, do as you desire, and choose the leaders you please.' You do not take a man who for years has been hobbled by chains, liberate him, bring him to the starting line of a race, saying, 'you are free to compete with all the others,' and still justly believe you have been completely fair. . . . This is the next and more profound stage of the battle for civil rights. We seek not just freedom but opportunity—not just legal equity but human ability—not just equality as a right and a theory, but equality as a fact and as a result."

Sept. 24, 1965: Executive Order 11246 enforces affirmative action for the first time. Issued by President Johnson, the executive order requires government contractors to "take affirmative action" toward prospective minority employees in all aspects of hiring and employment. Contractors must take specific measures to ensure equality in hiring and must document these efforts. On Oct. 13, 1967, the order was amended to cover discrimination on the basis of gender.

1969: The Philadelphia Order. Initiated by President Richard Nixon, the "Philadelphia Order" was the most forceful plan thus far to guarantee fair hiring practices in construction jobs. Philadelphia was selected as the test case because, as Assistant Secretary of Labor Arthur Fletcher explained,

"The craft unions and the construction industry are among the most egregious offenders against equal opportunity laws . . . openly hostile toward letting blacks into their closed circle." The order included definite "goals and timetables." As President Nixon asserted, "We would not impose quotas, but would require federal contractors to show 'affirmative action' to meet the goals of increasing minority employment."

June 28, 1978: *Regents of the University of California v. Bakke.* This landmark Supreme Court case imposed limitations on affirmative action to ensure that providing greater opportunities for minorities did not come at the expense of the rights of the majority—affirmative action was unfair if it led to reverse discrimination. The case involved the University of California, Davis, Medical School, which had two separate admissions pools, one for standard applicants, and another for minority and economically disadvantaged students. The school reserved 16 of its 100 places for this latter group. Allan Bakke, a white applicant, was rejected twice even though there were minority applicants admitted with significantly lower scores than his. Bakke maintained that judging him on the basis of his race was a violation of the Equal Protection Clause of the Fourteenth Amendment. The Supreme Court ruled that while race was a legitimate factor in school admissions, the use of such inflexible quotas as the medical school had set aside was not. The Supreme Court, however, was split 5–4 in its decision on the Bakke case and addressed only a minimal number of the many complex issues that had sprung up about affirmative action.

July 2, 1980: *Fullilove v. Klutznick.* While Bakke struck down strict quotas, in Fullilove the Supreme Court ruled that some modest quotas were perfectly constitutional. The Court upheld a federal law requiring that 15% of funds for public works be set aside for qualified minority contractors. The "narrowed focus and limited extent" of the affirmative action program did not violate the equal rights of nonminority contractors, according to the Court—there was no "allocation of federal funds according to inflexible percentages solely based on race or ethnicity."

May 19, 1986: *Wygant v. Jackson Board of Education.* This case challenged a school board's policy of protecting minority employees by laying off nonminority teachers first, even though the nonminority employees had seniority. The Supreme Court ruled against the school board, maintaining that the injury suffered by nonminorities affected could not justify the benefits to minorities: "We have previously expressed concern over the burden that a preferential-layoffs scheme imposes on innocent parties. In cases involving valid hiring goals, the burden to be borne by innocent individuals is diffused to a considerable extent among society generally. Though hiring goals may burden some innocent individuals, they simply do not impose the same kind of injury that layoffs impose. Denial of a future employment opportunity is not as intrusive as loss of an existing job."

Feb. 25, 1987: *United States v. Paradise.* In July 1970, a federal court found that the State of Alabama Department of Public Safety systematically discriminated against blacks in hiring: "in the thirty-seven-year history of the patrol there has never been a black trooper." The court ordered that the state reform its hiring practices to end "pervasive, systematic, and obstinate discriminatory exclusion of blacks." A full 12 years and several lawsuits later, the department still had not promoted any blacks above entry level. In response, the court ordered specific racial quotas to correct the situation. For every white hired or promoted, one black would also be hired or promoted until at least 25% of the upper ranks of the department were composed of blacks. The case challenged this use of numerical quotas. The Supreme Court, however, upheld the use of strict quotas in this case as one of the only means of combating the department's overt and defiant racism.

Jan. 23, 1989: *City of Richmond v. Croson.* Affirmative action on the state and local level was challenged in this case involving a Richmond, Va., program setting aside 30% of city construction funds for black-owned firms. For the first time, affirmative action was judged as a "highly suspect tool." The Supreme Court ruled that an "amorphous claim that there has been past discrimination in a particular industry cannot justify the use of an unyielding racial quota." It maintained that affirmative action must be subject to "strict scrutiny" and is unconstitutional unless racial discrimination can be proven to be "widespread throughout a particular industry." The Court maintained that "the purpose of strict scrutiny is to 'smoke out' illegitimate uses of race by assuring that the legislative body is pursuing a goal important enough to warrant use of a highly suspect tool. The test also ensures that the means chosen 'fit' this compelling goal so closely that there is little or no possibility that the motive for the classification was illegitimate racial prejudice or stereotype."

June 12, 1995: *Adarand Constructors, Inc. v. Peña.* What Croson was to state- and local-run affirmative action programs, Adarand was to federal programs. The Court again called for "strict scrutiny" in determining whether discrimination existed before implementing a federal affirmative action program. "Strict scrutiny" meant that affirmative action programs fulfilled a "compelling governmental interest," and were "narrowly tailored" to fit the particular situation. Although two of the judges (Scalia and Thomas) felt that there should be a complete ban on affirmative action, the majority of judges asserted that "the unhappy persistence of both the practice and the lingering effects of racial discrimination against minority groups in this country" justified the use of race-based remedial measures in certain circumstances.

July 19, 1995: White House guidelines on affirmative action. President Clinton asserted in a speech that while Adarand set "stricter standards to mandate reform of affirmative action, it actually reaffirmed the need for affirmative action and reaffirmed the continuing existence of systematic discrimination in the United States." In a White House memorandum on the same day, he called for the elimination of any program that "(a) creates a quota; (b) creates preferences for unqualified individuals; (c) creates reverse discrimination; or (d) continues even after its equal opportunity purposes have been achieved."

March 18, 1996: *Hopwood v. University of Texas Law School.* Four white law-school applicants at the University of Texas challenged the school's affirmative action program, asserting that they were rejected because of unfair preferences toward less qualified minority applicants. As a result, the 5th U.S. Court of Appeals suspended the university's affirmative action admissions program and ruled that the 1978 Bakke decision was invalid—while Bakke rejected racial quotas it maintained that race could serve as a factor in admissions. In addition to remedying past discrimination, Bakke maintained that the inclusion of minority students would create a diverse student body, and that was beneficial to the educational environment as a whole. Hopwood, however, rejected the legitimacy of diversity as a goal, asserting that "educational diversity is not recognized as a compelling state interest." The Supreme Court allowed the ruling to stand. In 1997, the Texas Attorney General announced that all "Texas public universities [should] employ race-neutral criteria."

Nov. 3, 1997: Proposition 209 enacted in California. A state ban on all forms of affirmative action was passed in California: "The state shall not discriminate against, or grant preferential treatment to, any individual or group on the basis of race, sex, color, ethnicity, or national origin in the operation of public employment, public education, or public contracting." Proposed in 1996, the controversial ban had been delayed in the courts for almost a year before it went into effect.

Dec. 3, 1998: Initiative 200 enacted in Washington State. Washington becomes the second state to abolish state affirmative action measures when it passed "I 200," which is similar to California's Proposition 209.

Feb. 22, 2000: Florida bans race as factor in college admissions. Florida legislature approves education component of Gov. Jeb Bush's "One Florida" initiative, aimed at ending affirmative action in the state.

"Ten Most Wanted" List Turns 50

It all started in 1949, when a reporter from the International News Service decided to write a story about the "toughest guys" sought by the Federal Bureau of Investigation. In response, the F.B.I. provided ten names of wanted criminals.

The article created a sensation. Delighted at the subsequent publicity, F.B.I. director J. Edgar Hoover began the "Ten Most Wanted Fugitives" program in March 1950.

Since then the list has become a standard crime-fighting tool for the F.B.I. By widely circulating the lists to media outlets and posting them in public buildings, the F.B.I. has been able to enlist public help in finding what it calls serious offenders. Of the 458 names that have appeared on the list since its inception, 429 have been apprehended, including 137 nabbed as a direct result of tips from the public. The Internet has made the list even more universal, since it can be seen all over the world in a matter of seconds.

From Car Thieves to Terrorists

The makeup of the list has reflected the changing nature of American crime. At first, bank robbers, burglars, and car thieves dominated. In the 1960s, more fugitives were charged with destruction of government property, sabotage, and kidnapping.

As international organized crime and political terrorism increased in the 1970s, the makeup of the list changed again.

Currently, organized crime figures, major international drug dealers, terrorists, and serial murderers predominate. Ramzi Ahmed Yousef, convicted of the World Trade Center bombing in 1997 and sentenced to 240 years in jail, was on the list from 1993 to 1995. Alleged mastermind in the 1998 bombing of the US Embassies in Kenya and Tanzania, Osama bin Laden, is currently on the list, as are suspected abortion clinic bomber Eric Rudolph, and alleged Boston organized crime figure James J. "Whitey" Bulger.

Dangerous to Society

The F.B.I. bureaucracy creates the list, starting with names submitted by the 56 F.B.I. field offices. In order to be listed, a suspect must be considered especially dangerous. Authorities must also believe the publicity would increase chances of apprehension.

Fugitives remain on the list until they are captured, the charges against them are dropped, or they are no longer determined to be a menace to society. Only four suspects have ever been removed for this reason. Charges have been dropped against 15 fugitives on the list since its inception.

Public Enemy Number One

People sometimes confuse the "Ten Most Wanted" list with the "public eneies" lists released by the Chicago Crime Commission in 1930, and popularized by the 1931 James Cagney movie, "The Public Enemy." The popular *Dick Tracy* comic strip; the ABC radio network program, *F.B.I., This Week;* and the Fox network TV show, *America's Most Wanted: America Fights Back,* are all used to publicize the list.

To find out who is currently on the list, visit the Web site, http://www.fbi.gov/mostwant/topten/ fugitives/fugitives.htm.

State Prison Inmates, by Most Serious Offense, 1996[1]

Most Serious Offense	Number of Prisoners	Percent
Total	326,547	100.0%
Violent offenses	96,300	29.5
Murder[2]	9,200	2.8
Negligent manslaughter	3,600	1.1
Sexual assault[3]	19,700	6.0
Robbery	29,700	9.1
Aggravated assault	28,400	8.7
Other violent	5,700	1.8
Property offenses	94,800	29.0%
Burglary	39,000	12.0
Larceny/theft	24,400	7.5
Motor vehicle theft	6,800	2.1
Fraud	13,200	4.1
Other property	11,400	3.3
Drug offenses	98,700	30.2%
Public-order offenses	34,600	10.6%
Other	2,100	0.7%

NOTE: Data may not sum to total due to rounding. 1. Includes only those with sentences of more than one year. 2. Includes nonnegligent manslaughter. 3. Includes rape and other sexual assault. *Source:* National Corrections Reporting Program, Bureau of Justice Statistics.

Federal Prison Inmates, by Most Serious Offense, 1996

Most Serious Offense	Number of Prisoners	Percent
Total	92,672	100.0%
Violent offenses	11,523	12.6%
Homicide[1]	1,084	1.2
Assault	645	0.7
Robbery	8,334	9.1
Other Violent[2]	1,460	1.6
Property offenses	7,781	8.5%
Burglary	181	0.2
Fraud[3]	5,807	6.3
Larceny/theft	1,793	2.0
Drug offenses	55,194	60.2%
Public-order offenses	17,227	18.8%
Immigration	4,476	4.9
Weapons	7,480	8.2
Escape/court	325	0.4
Other public-order	4,946	5.4

1. Includes murder, nonnegligent manslaughter, and negligent manslaughter. 2. Includes kidnapping, rape, and other sexual assault, threats against the President, and other offenses. 3. Includes embezzlement, counterfeiting, forgery, bankruptcy, and fraud (excluding tax fraud but including securities fraud). *Source:* BJS Federal Justice database.

Homicide Rate (per 100,000), 1950–1998

Year	Homicide rate	Year	Homicide rate	Year	Homicide rate	Year	Homicide rate	Year	Homicide rate
1950	4.6	1960	5.1	1970	7.9	1980	10.2	1990	9.4
1951	4.4	1961	4.8	1971	8.6	1981	9.8	1991	9.8
1952	4.6	1962	4.6	1972	9.0	1982	9.1	1992	9.3
1953	4.5	1963	4.6	1973	9.4	1983	8.3	1993	9.5
1954	4.2	1964	4.9	1974	9.8	1984	7.9	1994	9.0
1955	4.1	1965	5.1	1975	9.6	1985	7.9	1995	8.2
1956	4.1	1966	5.6	1976	8.8	1986	8.6	1996	7.4
1957	4.0	1967	6.2	1977	8.8	1987	8.3	1997	6.8
1958	4.8	1968	6.9	1978	9.0	1988	8.4	1998	6.3
1959	4.9	1969	7.3	1979	9.7	1989	8.7		

Source: FBI, Uniform Crime Reports.

Number of Persons Executed,[1] by Jurisdiction, 1930–1998

State	Number executed since 1930	1977[2]	State	Number executed since 1930	1977[2]	State	Number executed since 1930	1977[2]
Texas	461	164	Illinois	101	11	Oregon	21	2
Georgia	389	23	Missouri	94	32	Connecticut	21	—
New York	329	—	Tennessee	93	—	Delaware	20	8
California	297	5	New Jersey	74	—	Utah	18	5
North Carolina	274	11	Oklahoma	73	13	Iowa	18	—
Florida	213	43	Maryland	71	3	Kansas	15	—
South Carolina	182	20	Arizona	50	12	Montana	8	2
Ohio	172	—	Washington	50	3	Wyoming	8	1
Mississippi	158	4	Colorado	48	1	New Mexico	8	—
Louisiana	157	24	Indiana	47	6	Nebraska	7	3
Pennsylvania	154	2	District of Columbia	40	—	Idaho	4	1
Alabama	152	17	West Virginia	40	—	Vermont	4	—
Virginia	151	59	Nevada	36	7	New Hampshire	1	—
Arkansas	135	17	Federal system	33	—	South Dakota	1	—
Kentucky	104	1	Massachusetts	27	—	**U.S. total**	**4,359**	**500**

1. Executed under civil authority; military authorities carried out an additional 160 executions, 1930–97. 2. In 1972 the Supreme Court ruled that capital punishment, as it was then administered, was "cruel and unusual" and therefore unconstitutional. On July 1, 1976, however, the Court overturned the ruling by a 7–2 decision, and capital punishment was reinstated. *Source: Capital Punishment, 1998.*

Characteristics of Prisoners under Sentence of Death[1]

Characteristic	1980	1990	1996	1997	Characteristic	1980	1990	1996	1997
White	418	1,368	1,820	1,876	Marital status:				
Black and other	270	978	1,399	1,459	Never married	268	998	1,498	1,561
Under 20 years	11	8	16	14	Married	229	632	731	744
20 to 24 years	173	168	281	275	Divorced[1]	217	726	990	1,030
25 to 34 years	334	1,110	1,076	1,075	Time elapsed since sentencing:				
35 to 54 years	186	1,006	1,707	1,818	Less than 12 months	185	231	285	242
55 years and over	10	64	139	153	12 to 47 months	389	753	815	849
Years of schooling completed:					48 to 71 months	102	438	447	462
7 years or less	68	178	196	199	72 months and over	38	934	1,672	1,782
8 years	74	186	199	204	Legal status at arrest:				
9 to 11 years	204	775	1,026	1,065	Not under sentence	384	1,345	1,863	1,946
12 years	162	729	1,034	1,077	Parole or probation[2]	115	578	892	909
More than 12 years	43	209	280	286	Prison or escaped	45	128	111	114
Unknown	163	279	484	504	Unknown	170	305	353	366
					Total	**688**	**2,346**	**3,219**	**3,335**

1. Includes widows, widowers, and unknown. 2. Includes persons on mandatory conditional release, work release, leave, AWOL, or bail. Excludes prisoners under sentence of death confined in local correctional systems pending appeal or who have not been committed to prison. *Source:* U.S. Bureau of Justice Statistics, *Capital Punishment,* annual, from *Statistical Abstract of the United States, 1999.*

Methods of Execution

State	Minimum age	Method	State	Minimum age	Method
Alabama	16	Electrocution	Nevada	16	Lethal injection
Alaska	—	No death penalty	New Hampshire[6]	17	Lethal injection or hanging
Arizona[1]	none	Lethal injection or gas	New Jersey	18	Lethal injection
Arkansas[2]	14	Lethal injection or electrocution	New Mexico	18	Lethal injection
			New York	18	Lethal injection
California	18	Lethal gas or injection	North Carolina[7]	17	Lethal gas or injection
Colorado	18	Lethal injection	North Dakota	—	No death penalty
Connecticut	18	Lethal injection	Ohio	18	Electrocution or lethal injection
Delaware[3]	16	Lethal injection or hanging	Oklahoma[8]	16	Lethal injection, electrocution, or firing squad
D.C.	—	No death penalty			
Florida	16	Electrocution	Oregon	18	Lethal injection
Georgia	17	Electrocution	Pennsylvania	none	Lethal injection
Hawaii	—	No death penalty	Rhode Island	—	No death penalty
Idaho	none	Lethal injection or firing squad	South Carolina	none	Electrocution or lethal injection
Illinois	18	Lethal injection	South Dakota[9]	none	Lethal injection
Indiana	16	Lethal injection	Tennessee[10]	18	Electrocution
Iowa	—	No death penalty	Texas	17	Lethal injection
Kansas	18	Lethal injection	Utah	none	Firing squad or lethal injection
Kentucky[4]	16	Electrocution	Vermont	—	No death penalty
Louisiana	none	Lethal injection	Virginia[11]	14	Electrocution or lethal injection
Maine	—	No death penalty	Washington	18	Hanging or lethal injection
Maryland	18	Lethal injection	West Virginia	—	No death penalty
Massachusetts	—	No death penalty	Wisconsin	—	No death penalty
Michigan	—	No death penalty	Wyoming[12]	16	Lethal injection or gas
Minnesota	—	No death penalty	Federal system[13]	18	Lethal injection
Mississippi[5]	16	Lethal injection or gas	American Samoa	—	No death penalty
Missouri	16	Lethal injection or gas	Guam	—	No death penalty
Montana	none	Lethal injection	Puerto Rico	—	No death penalty
Nebraska	18	Electrocution	Virgin Islands	—	No death penalty

1. Ariz. authorizes lethal injection for persons sentenced after 11/15/92; before that date methods available are lethal injection or lethal gas. 2. Ark. authorizes lethal injection for those sentenced on or after 7/4/83; before that date, methods available are lethal injection or electrocution. 3. Del. also authorizes lethal injection for those sentenced after 6/13/86; before that date, methods available are lethal injection or hanging. 4. Ky. authorizes lethal injection for persons sentenced on or after 3/31/98; before that date methods available are lethal injection or electrocution. 5. Miss. minimum age defined by statute is 13, but the effective age is 16 based on interpretation of the Mississippi Supreme Court. 6. N.H. authorizes hanging only if lethal injection cannot be given. 7. N.C.'s minimum age is 17, unless the person was already incarcerated for murder when the subsequent murder occurred; then the minimum age is 14. 8. Okla. authorizes electrocution if lethal injection is ever held to be unconstitutional and firing squad if both lethal injection and electrocution are held unconstitutional. 9. S.D. authorizes juveniles to possibly be transferred to adult court; age can be a mitigating factor. 10. Tenn. also authorizes lethal injection for those whose capital offense occurred after 12/31/98; those who committed the offense before that date may select lethal injection or electrocution. 11. Va.'s minimum age for transfer to adult court by statute is 14, but the effective age is 16 based on interpretation of U.S. Supreme Court decisions by the State attorney general's office. 12. Wyo. authorizes lethal gas if lethal injection is ever held to be unconstitutional. 13. The method of execution of federal prisoners is lethal injection. For offenses under the Violent Crime Control and Law Enforcement Act of 1994, the method is that of the state in which the conviction took place. *Source: Capital Punishment, 1998.*

Federal Prosecutions of Public Corruption

Prosecution status	1996	1995	1994	1993	1992	1991	1990	1989	1985	1980
Total: Indicted	952	1,051	1,165	1,371	1,189	1,452	1,176	1,348	1,157	727
Convicted	878	878	969	1,362	1,081	1,194	1,084	1,149	997	602
Federal officials: Indicted	440	527	571	627	624	803	615	695	563	123
Convicted	450	438	488	595	532	665	583	610	470	131
State officials: Indicted	66	61	99	113	84	115	96	71	79	72
Convicted	55	61	97	133	92	77	79	54	66	51
Local officials: Indicted	232	236	248	309	232	242	257	269	248	247
Convicted	190	191	202	272	211	180	225	201	221	168

NOTE: Figures are latest available. *Source:* U.S. Department of Justice, *Report to Congress on the Activities and Operations of the Public Integrity Section,* annual, from *Statistical Abstract of the United States, 1998.*

Law Enforcement Officers Killed or Assaulted[1]

	1997	1996	1995	1994	1993	1992	1991	1990	1989	1988	1980
Total officers killed	132	100	130	133	129	129	122	132	144	151	164
Officers assaulted											
Firearm	1,844	1,887	2,277	3,168	4,002	4,455	3,532	3,662	3,154	2,759	3,295
Knife or cutting instrument	895	871	1,325	1,513	1,574	2,095	1,493	1,641	1,379	1,367	1,653
Other dangerous weapon	5,389	5,084	6,299	7,210	7,551	8,604	7,014	7,390	5,778	5,573	5,415
Hands, fists, feet, etc.	41,023	38,853	46,634	53,021	53,848	66,098	50,813	59,101	51,861	49,053	47,484
Total assaulted	**49,151**	**46,695**	**56,535**	**64,912**	**66,975**	**81,252**	**62,852**	**71,794**	**62,172**	**58,752**	**57,847**

1. Covers officers killed feloniously and accidentally in line of duty; includes federal officers. 1988 excludes Florida and Kentucky. NOTE: Data are latest available. *Source: Statistical Abstract of the United States, 1999.*

Total Arrests by Age, 1998

	Number of arrests	Percent distribution		Number of arrests	Percent distribution
Total, all ages	10,295,129	100.0%	16	435,282	4.2%
Total, under 18	1,855,002	18.0	15	356,161	3.5
Total, under 15	582,661	5.7	13–14	419,109	4.1
18	521,311	5.1	10–12	135,406	1.3
17	480,898	4.7	Under 10	28,146	0.3

NOTE: Because of rounding, the percentages may not add up to total. *Source:* Department of Justice, Federal Bureau of Investigation, *Uniform Crime Reports for the United States, 1998.*

A Timeline of Recent School Shootings

Feb. 2, 1996
Moses Lake, Wash. 2 students and 1 teacher killed, 1 other wounded when 14-year-old Barry Loukaitis opened fire on his algebra class.

Feb. 19, 1997
Bethel, Alaska Principal and 1 student killed, 2 others wounded by Evan Ramsey, 16.

Oct. 1, 1997
Pearl, Miss. 2 students killed and 7 wounded by a 16-year-old who was also accused of killing his mother. He and his friends were said to be outcasts who worshipped Satan.

Dec. 1, 1997
West Paducah, Ky. 3 students killed, 5 wounded by a 14-year-old boy as they participated in a prayer circle at Heath High School.

Dec. 15, 1997
Stamps, Ark. 2 students wounded. Colt Todd, 14, was hiding in the woods when he shot the students as they stood in the parking lot.

March 24, 1998
Jonesboro, Ark. 4 students and 1 teacher killed, 10 others wounded outside as Westside Middle School emptied during a false fire alarm. Mitchell Johnson, 13, and Andrew Golden, 11, shot at their classmates and teachers from the woods.

April 24, 1998
Edinboro, Pa. 1 teacher killed, 2 students wounded at a dance at James W. Parker Middle School. A 14-year-old boy was charged.

May 19, 1998
Fayetteville, Tenn. 1 student killed in the parking lot at Lincoln County High School three days before he was to graduate. The victim was dating the ex-girlfriend of his killer, 18-year-old honor student Jacob Davis.

May 21, 1998
Springfield, Ore. 2 students killed, 22 others wounded in the cafeteria at Thurston High School by 15-year-old Kip Kinkel. Kinkel had been arrested and released a day earlier for bringing a gun to school. His parents were later found dead at home.

June 15, 1998
Richmond, Va. 1 teacher and 1 guidance counselor wounded by a 14-year-old boy in the school hallway.

April 20, 1999
Littleton, Colo. 14 students (including killers) and 1 teacher killed, 23 others wounded at Columbine High School in the nation's deadliest school shooting. Eric Harris, 18, and Dylan Klebold, 17, had plotted for a year to kill at least 500 and blow up their school. At the end of their hour-long rampage, they turned their guns on themselves.

April 28, 1999
Taber, Alberta, Canada 1 student killed, 1 wounded at W. R. Myers High School in first fatal high school shooting in Canada in 20 years. The suspect, a 14-year-old boy, had dropped out of school in order to begin home schooling.

May 20, 1999
Conyers, Ga. 6 students injured at Heritage High School by 15-year-old T. J. Solomon, who was reportedly depressed after breaking up with his girlfriend.

Dec. 6, 1999
Fort Gibson, Okla. 4 students wounded as a 13-year-old boy opened fire with a 9mm semiautomatic handgun at Fort Gibson Middle School.

February 29, 2000
Mount Morris Township, Mich. 6-year-old Kayla Rolland shot dead at Buell Elementary School near Flint, Mich. The assailant is identified as a six-year-old boy with a .32-caliber handgun.

May 26, 2000
Lake Worth, Fla. 1 teacher, Barry Grunow, shot and killed at Lake Worth Middle School by 13-year-old boy with .25-caliber semiautomatic pistol on the last day of classes.

Murder: Types of Weapon Used, 1998

Type of weapon	Total no.	% distribution[1]	Type of weapon	Total no.	% distribution[1]
Firearms	9,143	64.9%	Explosives	10	0.1
Knives or cutting instruments	1,877	13.3	Fire	130	0.9
Blunt objects (clubs, hammers, etc.)	741	5.3	Narcotics	32	0.2
			Strangulation	211	1.5
Personal weapons (hands, fists, feet, etc.)[2]	949	6.7	Asphyxiation	99	0.7
			Other weapon or not stated[3]	890	6.3
Poison	6	—	Total	14,088	100.0

1. Because of rounding, percentages may not add up to 100. 2. Pushed is included in personal weapons. 3. Includes drowning. *Source: Crime in the United States,* 1998.

Use of Guns Responsible for Increased Homicides by Juveniles

According to the FBI, the increase in homicides committed by juveniles has been related to their use of guns as the murder weapon. Between 1980 and 1987, firearms were used in just over half (54%) of all homicides involving a juvenile offender. Then, firearm-related homicides began to increase, so that by 1994, most homicides by juvenile offenders (82%) involved guns. And the sharp decline in homicides by juveniles between 1994 and 1997 was attributable entirely to a decline in homicides by firearms.

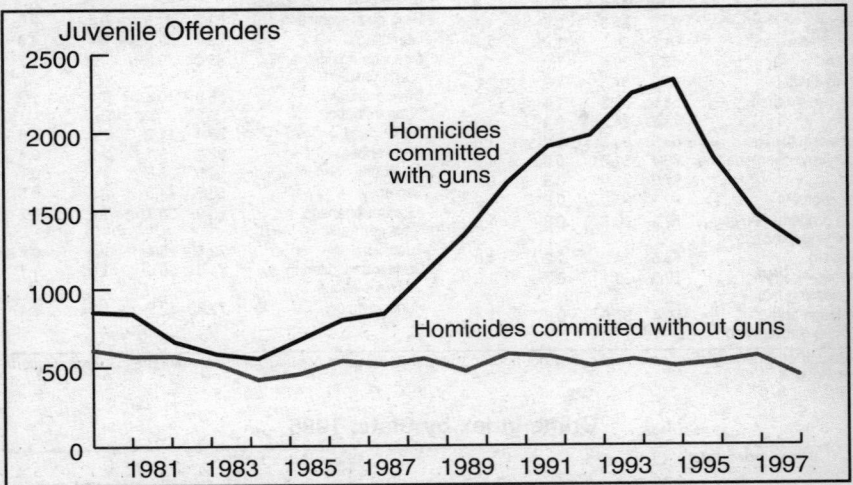

Source: Snyder, H. and Sickmund, M. *Juvenile Offenders and Victims: 1999 National Report*, p. 54. Washington, D.C.: Office of Juvenile Justice and Delinquency Prevention, 1999.

Index of Crime, United States, 1979–1998
(Rate per 100,000 inhabitants)

Year:	Crime index total	Violent crime[1]	Property crime[2]	Murder and non-negligent man-slaughter	Forcible rape	Robbery	Aggra-vated assault	Burglary	Larceny-theft	Motor vehicle theft
1979	5,565.5	548.9	5,016.6	9.7	34.7	218.4	286.0	1,511.9	2,999.1	505.6
1980	5,950.0	596.6	5,353.3	10.2	36.8	251.1	298.5	1,684.1	3,167.0	502.2
1981	5,858.2	594.3	5,263.9	9.8	36.0	258.7	289.7	1,649.5	3,139.7	474.7
1982	5,603.6	571.1	5,032.5	9.1	34.0	238.9	289.2	1,488.8	3,084.8	458.8
1983	5,175.0	537.7	4,637.4	8.3	33.7	216.5	279.2	1,337.7	2,868.9	430.8
1984	5,031.3	539.2	4,492.1	7.9	35.7	205.4	290.2	1,263.7	2,791.3	437.1
1985	5,207.1	556.6	4,650.5	8.0	37.1	208.5	302.9	1,287.3	2,901.2	462.0
1986	5,480.4	617.7	4,862.6	8.6	37.9	225.1	346.1	1,344.6	3,010.3	507.8
1987	5,550.0	609.7	4,940.3	8.3	37.4	212.7	351.3	1,329.6	3,081.3	529.4
1988	5,664.2	637.2	5,027.1	8.4	37.6	220.9	370.2	1,309.2	3,134.9	582.9
1989	5,741.0	663.1	5,077.9	8.7	38.1	233.0	383.4	1,276.3	3,171.3	630.4
1990	5,820.3	731.8	5,088.5	9.4	41.2	257.0	424.1	1,235.9	3,194.8	657.8
1991	5,897.8	758.1	5,139.7	9.8	42.3	272.7	433.3	1,252.0	3,228.8	659.0
1992	5,660.2	757.5	4,902.7	9.3	42.8	263.6	441.8	1,168.2	3,103.0	631.5
1993	5,484.4	746.8	4,737.6	9.5	41.1	255.9	440.3	1,099.2	3,032.4	606.1
1994	5,373.5	713.6	4,660.0	9.0	39.3	237.7	427.6	1,042.0	3,026.7	591.3
1995	5,275.9	684.6	4,591.3	8.2	37.1	220.9	418.3	987.1	3,043.8	560.4
1996	5,086.6	636.5	4,450.1	7.4	36.3	201.9	390.9	944.8	2,797.7	525.6
1997	4,930.0	611.3	4,318.7	6.8	35.9	186.3	382.3	919.4	2,893.4	506.0
1998	4,615.5	566.4	4,049.1	6.3	34.4	165.2	360.5	862.0	2,728.1	459.0

1. Violent crimes are offenses of murder, forcible rape, robbery, and aggravated assault. 2. Property crimes are offenses of burglary, larceny-theft, and motor vehicle theft. Data are not included for the property crime of arson. *Source*: FBI, Uniform Crime Reports.

Arrests by Race, 1998

Offense charged	Percent distribution[1]				Offense charged	Percent distribution[1]			
	White	Black	American Indian or Alaskan Native	Asian or Pacific Islander		White	Black	American Indian or Alaskan Native	Asian or Pacific Islander
Total	68.0%	29.7%	1.2%	1.1%	Sex offenses, except forcible rape and prostitution	74.8%	22.9%	1.1%	1.2%
Murder[2]	44.5	53.4	1.1	1.0					
Forcible rape	60.2	37.5	1.1	1.3	Drug abuse violation	61.5	37.3	0.5	0.6
Robbery	43.0	55.3	0.6	1.1	Gambling	29.9	65.0	0.4	4.8
Aggravated assault	61.6	36.3	1.0	1.1	Offenses against family and children	68.2	29.2	0.9	1.7
Burglary	68.3	29.5	1.0	1.2					
Larceny-theft	65.3	31.8	1.2	1.7	Driving under the influence	86.9	10.5	1.4	1.2
Motor vehicle theft	58.0	39.2	1.1	1.7					
Arson	73.7	24.2	0.9	1.2	Liquor laws	85.4	11.2	2.6	0.9
Other assaults	64.0	33.7	1.2	1.0	Drunkenness	82.1	15.1	2.3	0.4
Forgery and counterfeiting	66.4	31.8	0.6	1.2	Disorderly conduct	64.5	33.6	1.2	0.7
Fraud	67.3	31.5	0.5	0.7	Vagrancy	53.0	44.0	2.5	0.5
Embezzlement	63.1	35.0	0.6	1.2	All other offenses except traffic	63.9	33.7	1.2	1.2
Stolen property—buying, receiving, possessing	57.3	40.9	0.8	1.0					
					Suspicion	72.6	25.4	1.3	0.7
Vandalism	73.6	24.2	1.2	1.0	Curfew and loitering law violations	71.3	26.6	1.0	1.1
Weapons—carrying, possessing, etc.	59.3	39.1	0.7	1.0					
Prostitution and commercialized vice	60.4	37.6	0.6	1.4	Runaways	77.8	17.9	1.0	3.4

1. Because of rounding, the percentages may not add up to total. 2. Includes nonnegligent manslaughter. *Source: Uniform Crime Reports, 1998.*

Crime Index by State, 1998

State	Crime index total		Violent crime	Property crime	Murder[1]	State	Crime index total		Violent crime	Property crime	Murder[1]
	Number	Rate per 100,000					Number	Rate per 100,000			
Ala.	200,065	4,597.1	22,286	177,779	354	Nebr.	73,259	4,405.2	7,507	65,752	51
Alaska	29,331	4,777.0	4,015	25,316	41	Nev.	92,250	5,280.5	11,244	81,006	170
Ariz.	306,985	6,575.0	26,984	280,001	376	N.H.[2]	28,675	2,419.8	1,270	27,405	18
Ark.	108,713	4,283.4	12,442	96,271	201	N.J.	296,527	3,654.1	35,717	260,810	322
Calif.	1,418,674	4,342.8	229,883	1,188,791	2,171	N.M.	116,711	6,719.1	16,700	100,011	190
Colo.	178,197	4,487.5	15,008	163,189	183	N.Y.	652,202	3,588.5	115,915	536,287	924
Conn.	123,971	3,786.5	11,993	111,978	135	N.C.	401,615	5,322.2	43,723	357,892	612
Del.	39,902	5,363.2	5,672	34,230	21	N.D.	17,105	2,681.0	570	16,535	7
D.C.	46,210	8,835.6	8,988	37,222	260	Ohio	485,066	4,327.5	40,628	444,438	443
Fla.	1,027,123	6,886.0	140,016	887,107	967	Okla.	167,479	5,003.9	18,053	149,426	204
Ga.	417,479	5,463.0	43,762	373,717	618	Ore.	185,323	5,646.6	13,778	171,545	126
Hawaii	63,623	5,333.0	2,946	60,677	24	Pa.	392,788	3,273.0	50,470	342,318	633
Idaho	45,653	3,714.6	3,468	42,185	36	P.R.	87,020	n.a.	16,439	70,581	652
Ill.[2]	586,923	4,872.8	97,291	489,632	1,008	R.I.	34,756	3,517.8	3,084	31,672	24
Ind.	245,952	4,169.4	25,423	220,529	454	S.C.	221,607	5,777.0	34,647	186,960	306
Iowa	100,188	3,500.6	8,916	91,272	54	S.D.	19,366	2,624.1	1,139	18,227	10
Kans.[2]	127,737	4,858.8	10,438	117,299	154	Tenn.	273,420	5,034.4	38,832	234,588	460
Ky.[2]	113,725	2,889.4	11,180	102,545	182	Tex.	1,010,062	5,111.6	111,566	898,496	1,346
La.	266,435	6,098.3	34,057	232,378	560	Utah	115,624	5,505.9	6,599	109,025	65
Maine	37,826	3,040.7	1,565	36,261	25	Vt.[2]	18,552	3,139.1	628	17,924	13
Md.	275,527	5,365.7	40,903	234,624	513	Va.	248,576	3,660.4	22,115	226,461	422
Mass.	211,203	3,435.9	38,192	173,011	124	Wash.	333,799	5,867.4	24,380	309,419	224
Mich.	459,720	4,682.9	60,947	398,773	721	W.Va.	46,130	2,547.2	4,503	41,627	78
Minn.	191,197	4,046.5	14,656	176,541	121	Wisc.	185,093	3,543.1	13,009	172,084	190
Miss.	120,647	4,384.0	11,302	109,345	315	Wyo.	18,315	3,807.7	1,191	17,124	23
Mo.	262,506	4,826.4	30,222	232,284	399	**U.S. total**	12,475,634	4,615.5	1,531,044	10,944,599	16,914
Mont.[2]	35,822	4,070.7	1,221	34,601	36						

NOTE: The Crime Index is composed of the violent and property crime categories. Violent crimes are murder, forcible rape, robbery, and aggravated assault. Property crimes are burglary, larceny-theft, and auto-theft. Data are not included for the property crime of arson. 1. Includes nonnegligent manslaughter 2. Complete data were not available for the states of Illinois, Kansas, Kentucky, Montana, New Hampshire, and Vermont; therefore it was necessary that their crime counts be estimated. *Source: F.B.I. Uniform Crime Reports for the United States, 1998.*

Crime Rates for Selected Large Cities: 1997
(Offenses known to the police per 100,000 population)

City ranked by population size, 1997[1]	Crime index, total		Violent crime				Property crime	
		Murder	Forcible rape	Robbery	Aggravated assault	Burglary	Larceny-theft	Motor vehicle theft
New York, N.Y.	4,861.6	10.5	29.5	610.7	617.8	739.0	2,145.2	708.9
Los Angeles, Calif.	5,776.3	16.3	39.9	579.1	961.3	852.7	2,332.6	994.5
Chicago, Ill.	(2)	27.4	(2)	914.3	1,320.4	1,469.1	4,324.5	1,215.1
Houston, Tex.	7,263.6	14.1	43.9	452.2	664.3	1,330.5	3,604.2	1,154.4
San Diego, Calif.	4,985.6	5.7	32.5	220.2	569.4	689.9	2,553.9	914.0
Phoenix, Ariz.	9,608.0	14.9	36.5	317.7	515.8	1,793.3	5,256.5	1,673.2
Dallas, Tex.	9,335.8	19.4	69.0	522.0	773.4	1,647.3	4,693.3	1,611.4
San Antonio, Tex.	8,050.5	9.2	59.5	196.1	136.9	1,274.5	5,544.3	830.0
Detroit, Mich.	11,669.1	45.9	94.8	803.6	1,207.3	1,891.9	4,351.9	3,273.8
Honolulu, Hawaii	6,067.4	3.9	29.2	137.9	128.5	994.6	4,138.5	634.9
San Jose, Calif.	3,870.2	5.1	44.6	108.0	578.8	521.2	2,144.2	468.2
Indianapolis, Ind.	6,743.4	18.7	71.0	427.9	614.8	1,474.2	3,146.9	990.0
San Francisco, Calif.	6,893.8	7.8	30.9	610.7	484.1	948.4	3,830.5	981.5
Baltimore, Md.	10,783.3	43.4	66.7	1,199.2	1,111.1	1,772.5	5,363.2	1,227.2
Jacksonville, Fla.	8,252.6	10.7	86.3	337.2	909.1	1,756.9	4,382.6	769.8
Columbus, Ohio	9,735.9	13.1	108.5	484.0	327.9	2,097.6	5,594.9	1,109.9
Memphis, Tenn.	10,041.7	21.6	147.1	822.0	865.9	2,426.9	3,961.0	1,797.2
Milwaukee, Wisc.	7,587.0	19.4	48.8	565.3	419.4	1,084.8	4,129.5	1,319.8
El Paso, Tex.	6,960.2	3.9	36.7	174.0	576.7	530.6	5,055.5	582.8
Charlotte-Mecklenburg, N.C.	9,409.9	10.5	61.4	483.3	1,075.6	1,852.8	5,146.2	780.1
Boston, Mass.	6,817.4	7.7	63.1	491.5	858.5	774.9	3,228.7	1,392.9
Seattle, Wash.	10,350.7	9.0	39.8	380.3	485.0	1,487.4	6,655.0	1,294.2
Austin, Tex.	7,870.0	7.3	51.8	235.1	351.5	1,375.1	5,031.8	817.4
Nashville, Tenn.	11,091.4	21.1	103.4	485.6	1,136.7	1,660.8	6,147.3	1,536.5
Washington, D.C.	9,827.2	56.9	41.2	850.5	1,075.2	1,316.3	5,056.3	1,430.8
Denver, Colo.	5,803.4	13.1	67.7	238.3	353.2	1,227.9	2,806.2	1,097.0
Cleveland, Ohio	7,455.5	15.5	128.5	772.6	542.1	1,640.3	2,880.4	1,476.2
New Orleans, La.	9,355.8	54.7	78.8	813.1	773.8	1,659.5	4,055.8	1,920.1
Tucson, Ariz.	9,965.8	10.3	59.9	297.6	685.1	1,424.3	6,085.4	1,403.3
Fort Worth, Tex.	7,317.8	15.5	55.5	293.4	538.2	1,375.4	4,187.1	852.9
Portland, Ore.	11,199.6	9.7	75.0	411.2	1,108.3	1,561.8	6,492.3	1,541.1
Oklahoma City, Okla.	11,655.6	12.5	86.6	295.9	677.9	2,071.4	7,547.6	963.7
Kansas City, Kans.	10,952.1	22.1	92.2	599.7	1,181.5	1,911.4	5,502.2	1,642.9
Long Beach, Calif.	4,898.2	12.6	28.1	415.1	488.8	964.3	2,039.5	949.9
Virginia Beach, Va.	4,482.0	4.3	23.0	116.0	96.4	673.7	3,358.4	210.2
Albuquerque, N.M.	11,118.3	11.4	62.6	401.1	841.9	1,982.0	6,021.4	1,797.8
Atlanta, Ga.	13,921.6	35.6	87.0	1,128.9	1,797.0	2,181.9	6,821.4	1,869.7
Fresno, Calif.	9,480.6	15.1	48.4	452.1	689.4	1,673.2	4,796.6	1,805.8
Miami, Fla.	12,828.8	26.3	48.2	1,153.0	1,586.2	2,283.5	5,771.0	1,960.6
Sacramento, Calif.	8,890.4	10.7	41.9	482.1	433.4	1,790.2	4,501.4	1,630.5
Tulsa, Okla.	7,472.2	10.5	72.8	240.3	880.7	1,666.5	3,629.1	972.4
St. Louis, Mo.	13,576.7	40.6	59.6	946.9	1,495.4	2,676.7	6,204.6	2,152.8
Oakland, Calif.	10,100.5	26.3	81.2	924.4	1,152.7	1,572.4	5,019.7	1,323.9
Minneapolis, Minn.	11,439.5	15.9	147.3	909.0	777.9	2,263.3	5,730.7	1,595.4
Pittsburgh, Pa.	5,817.7	14.2	49.5	436.8	285.9	950.9	3,283.2	797.2
Omaha, Neb.	7,236.2	8.8	50.0	232.6	1,094.0	899.8	3,964.8	986.2
Mesa, Ariz.	7,730.1	3.7	35.9	128.4	560.5	1,218.5	4,799.6	983.5
Toledo, Ohio	8,526.5	7.7	72.0	337.6	405.9	1,789.9	4,973.8	939.7
Wichita, Kans.	8,037.9	10.1	72.2	281.9	469.1	1,510.7	4,976.4	717.5
Buffalo, N.Y.	8,095.4	14.7	73.6	702.6	493.6	1,915.4	3,656.7	1,238.8
Arlington, Tex.	6,621.7	4.0	41.8	173.6	577.9	1,007.0	4,141.5	675.8
Tampa, Fla.	12,260.1	11.7	88.4	846.7	1,717.1	2,202.6	5,983.7	1,410.0
Santa Ana, Calif.	4,035.9	9.0	30.5	327.6	308.1	537.6	1,925.2	897.9
Corpus Christi, Tex.	10,219.0	6.2	52.9	146.9	778.2	1,500.4	7,173.9	560.6
Anaheim, Calif.	4,187.9	5.2	34.5	280.3	358.0	783.7	2,045.3	680.8
Louisville, Ky.	6,906.7	22.4	46.3	559.0	484.5	1,620.9	3,150.0	1,023.6
Birmingham, Ala.	9,590.0	39.2	80.7	485.8	769.5	1,884.2	5,110.9	1,219.7
St. Paul, Minn.	7,909.7	8.9	85.2	308.3	484.2	1,487.2	4,558.6	977.3
Aurora, Colo.	6,188.4	6.4	83.5	187.7	343.5	867.1	3,890.7	809.5
Newark, N.J.	10,728.0	21.6	64.3	1,302.5	1,346.4	1,728.2	4,091.3	2,173.9
Anchorage, Alaska	5,971.4	9.0	68.1	196.0	465.9	755.4	3,944.3	532.8
St. Petersburg, Fla.	8,939.1	8.4	80.2	500.9	1,508.9	1,612.7	4,520.1	708.0
Raleigh, N.C.	7,747.3	9.3	41.0	292.4	564.8	1,468.3	4,805.9	565.6

1. Resident population estimated by the F.B.I. 2. The rates for forcible rape, violent crime, and crime index are not shown because the forcible rape figures were not in accordance with national Uniform Crime Reporting guidelines. *Source:* U.S. Federal Bureau of Investigation, *Crime in the United States,* annual.

Aye, Aye, Ma'am

The navy makes history with a woman at the helm of a warship

By MARK THOMPSON TIME

In April 2000, Commander Kathleen McGrath became the first American woman ever to take a warship to sea. Back on land, women have already smashed through ceilings that once seemed to be made of unbreakable glass, from Silicon Valley to the State Department. But change has come more slowly to the hidebound military. Only 12 of the navy's 220 admirals are women.

A Few Good Men and Women

McGrath led the USS *Jarrett* and its crew of 262 to the Middle East, where it prowled the northern reaches of the Persian Gulf. Their mission: hunting down ships smuggling Iraqi oil in violation of United Nations sanctions. It's a game of nautical cat and mouse, as U.S. spy satellites and surveillance planes pick out possible smugglers and relay their whereabouts to ships down below. The smugglers are beyond the U.N.'s reach as long as they stay in Iraqi and Iranian territorial waters. But there are a few swaths of water beyond the U.S.-recognized 12-mile limit where the *Jarrett* and other allied warships can pounce. The recent spike in oil prices has made smuggling more lucrative. During its two months on the gulf assignment, the *Jarrett*'s crew boarded approximately 30 vessels and ordered violators to friendly ports, where their ships and cargo were auctioned off.

Not long ago, McGrath's breakthrough would have seemed inconceivable. Women have served on support vessels since 1978, but it wasn't until 1994 that they were permitted, reluctantly, on warships. In 1991, Admiral Frank Kelso, then chief of naval operations, told Congress bluntly that he didn't want women on warships at all, much less in command. "There is a delicate balance between equal opportunity for men and women," he cautioned the Senate Armed Services Committee, "and maintaining combat effectiveness of our forces."

The Tailhook Albatross

But times have changed. In part it's simply a matter of the available labor pool. In these booming times, the navy can't recruit enough men for its 315 ships. The other driving force has been the navy's resolve to bleach the stain of the 1991 Tailhook Association convention, at which naval aviators sexually assaulted 83 women and then tried to cover it up. For years the navy has been fighting the perception that women are not welcome in its ranks. (In January 2000 the navy closed a chapter on the Tailhook scandal, restoring official ties with the group after exacting a pledge that the misconduct of 1991 would not recur.)

The navy has come a long way since Tailhook. Kelso, who was tarnished by the scandal, retired early. In his wake, women stormed aboard warships. They are now assigned to 155 vessels—106 of them combatants—and they account for 11,400 of the 155,000 officers and sailors afloat. Some ships have substantial numbers: the carrier *Eisenhower* has 600 women in a crew of 4,700. The *Jarrett* has only four, all officers, because the lack of berthing space has kept the enlisted ranks all male. By 2004, when nearly all vessels will be opened to women, the navy is projecting that the average crew will be 12% female.

The navy's new generation of women are not just swabbing decks. They've been moving into the highest echelons of the navy—and the Pentagon as well. Vice Admiral Patricia Tracey is a deputy assistant secretary of defense for personnel. Rear Admiral Jacquelyn Barnes directs the Pentagon's On-Site Inspection Agency, charged with verifying arms-control pacts with other nations. Rear Admiral Barbara McGann is the navy's top recruiting officer. And Rear Admiral Bonnie Potter is the Atlantic fleet's top doctor.

Battle Ready?

But sending women into battle remains controversial. Skeptics point to navy studies showing that female sailors are physically weaker than males and leave ships at more than twice the rate men do, often because they're pregnant. But officers who have commanded ships with women on board have generally brushed aside such concerns. Writing in the navy journal *Proceedings*, Commander Gerard Roncolato, former skipper of the destroyer USS *The Sullivans*, declared that there is no job on board a ship today that cannot be done by a woman because of a lack of strength or stamina.

And navy women have in fact been playing an increasing combat role. In 1996, Lieutenant Junior Grade Erica Niedermeier became the first woman to fire Tomahawk cruise missiles from a warship in combat, helping send 13 into southern Iraq. Two years later, flying her F-18 off the USS *Enterprise* in a mission over Iraq, Lieutenant Kendra Williams became the first female pilot in U.S. history to drop bombs on an enemy target.

Women Aboard

Having women aboard—and especially one in command—has changed the atmosphere on the *Jarrett*. Personnelman Second Class Eldukl Ngiraingas was worried that working with women might make the crew less efficient. "I had a different kind of bonding when I was with all guys on a carrier," he says. "We didn't have to worry about offending people—everyone swore." But then he worked with a female colleague on a fire drill. "I found out that I didn't have to yell to get her to do something," he says. Another difference: modesty prevails. "You can't walk around in your underwear anymore," notes Signalman Second Class Terry Cole.

McGrath has also brought a more inclusive spirit to the *Jarrett*. Last August she invited the ship's five newly minted chief petty officers and their spouses to her home to celebrate their promotion into the senior enlisted ranks. She and her husband cooked on the outdoor grill. McGrath's meal wasn't in keeping with a long-standing navy tradition: segregation between enlisted men and officers. Command Master Chief Mike Fulton, the *Jarrett*'s senior enlisted man, says that night was the first time in his 24-year career—spread over 13 ships—he ever attended such a mixed-rank social gathering.

Skepticism Persists

McGrath doesn't like to talk about the fact that she has just made history. "You don't get to this position by saying, 'I'm different and I'm special, so

therefore I deserve to be the C.O.,'" she says. Not all the skeptics have been won over. There are still those who object on principle to women commanders. "These are not female jobs," insists Dudley Carlson, a retired three-star admiral who once ran the navy's entire personnel system. "You can make anything work in peacetime, but the peacetime navy becomes the wartime navy in the blink of an eye."

Some of the skepticism originated right on board the *Jarrett*. "I've never worked for a woman before, so I'm not really sure what to expect in combat," says Personnelman First Class Arnell Ramos. "Being a majority-male organization," he says, "most of us would prefer to take orders from a male officer."

But as McGrath has proved herself, most of the doubters have come around. McGrath's crew seems generally impressed with her. "She's not in command because she's a woman," says her second-in-command, Lieutenant Commander Joseph Chiaravallotti. "She's in command because she's better than everyone else who's not in command." □

Women in the Navy: A Timeline

1812 First U.S. record of women at sea; they are nurses in the war

1908 U.S. Navy Nurse Corps established

1916 The Navy Reserve Act calls for the enlistment of qualified "persons," which leads Navy Secretary Josephus Daniels to ask, "Is there any law that says a Yeoman must be a man?"

1917 Shortly before the U.S. enters World War I, Navy Department authorizes enrollment of women in Naval Reserve with ratings of yeoman

1942 F.D.R. signs law creating the WAVES—Women Accepted for Volunteer Emergency Service—to fill World War II slots

1945 USS *Higbee* commissioned, the first navy warship named after a woman, Lenah S. Higbee, head of navy nurses in World War I

1948 Women permitted to enlist, although new law says they cannot make up more than 2% of the force and cannot be promoted to rank of admiral

1972 Rear Admiral Alene Duerk becomes the first woman to hold that rank

1973 Women begin navy pilot training. Lieutenant (j.g.) Judith Neuffer is first military aviatrix

1976 First women enter the Naval Academy

1978 Congress changes law, allowing women to serve aboard support ships

1990 Lieutenant Commander Darlene Iskra becomes the first woman to assume command of a ship, the USS *Opportune*

1994 The aircraft carrier USS *Eisenhower* becomes the navy's first combat ship with women in its crew

1996 Lieutenant (j.g.) Erica Niedermeier is the first woman to fire Tomahawk cruise missiles in combat

2000 Commander Kathleen McGrath is the first woman to command a warship headed into harm's way. Women now make up 14% of the navy, and are 12 of 220 admirals

Highest Ranking Officers in U.S. History

General and Commander-in-Chief[1]

George Washington (1732–1799), b. Westmoreland County, Va., unanimously voted by Congress on June 15, 1775, to the rank of general and commander-in-chief (of the Continental army).

General of the Armies[2]

John Joseph Pershing (1860–1948), b. Linn County, Mo., made permanent general of the armies, 1919.

General of the Army, General of the Air Force (Five-Stars)

George Catlett Marshall (1880–1959), b. Uniontown, Pa., promoted December, 1944.

Douglas MacArthur (1880–1964), b. Little Rock, Ark., promoted December, 1944.

Dwight David Eisenhower (1890–1969), b. Denison, Tex., promoted December, 1944.

Henry Harley Arnold (1866–1950), b. Gladwyne, Pa. Arnold had the unique distinction of being a five-star general twice—in 1944 as general of the army, and in June,

1949 as general of the air force. He is the only air force general to have held the five-star rank.

Omar Nelson Bradley (1893–1981), b. Clark, Mo., promoted September, 1950.

Fleet Admiral (Five-Star)

William Daniel Leahy (1875–1959), b. Hampton, Iowa, promoted December, 1944.

Ernest Joseph King (1878–1956), b. Lorain, Ohio, promoted December, 1944.

Chester William Nimitz (1885–1966), b. Fredericksburg, Tex., promoted December, 1944.

William Frederick Halsey (1882–1959), b. Elizabeth, N.J., promoted December, 1945.

1. On March 15, 1978, George Washington was promoted posthumously to the newly created rank of General of the Armies of the United States. Congress authorized this title to make it clear that Washington was the army's senior general. 2. General Pershing was given the option of five stars but he declined. *Source:* Department of Defense and U.S. Army Historian, Research and Analysis Center.

The Joint Chiefs of Staff (JCS)

The Joint Chiefs of Staff consist of the chairman, the vice chairman, the chief of staff of the army, the chief of naval operations, the chief of staff of the air force, and the commandant of the Marine Corps.

The collective body of the JCS is headed by the chairman (or vice chairman in the chairman's absence), who sets the agenda and presides over JCS meetings. Their responsibilities take precedence over their duties as the Chiefs of Military Services. The chairman is the principal military adviser to the president, the secretary of defense, and the National Security Council (NSC); however, all JCS members are by law military advisers, and they may respond to a request or voluntarily submit, through the chairman, advice or opinions to the president, the secretary of state, or the NSC. The Joint Chiefs of Staff have no executive authority to commit combatant forces.

In addition to their responsibilities on the JCS, the military service chiefs are responsible to the secretaries of their military departments for management of the services. The service chiefs serve for four years. By custom the vice chiefs of the services act for their chiefs in most matters having to do with day-to-day operation of the services.

Joint Chiefs of Staff, Mid-2000

Chairman of the Joint Chiefs of Staff, General Henry H. Shelton, U.S. Army; vice chairman of the Joint Chiefs of Staff, General Richard B. Myers, U.S. Air Force; General Eric K. Shinseki, chief of staff of the U.S. Army; Admiral Vernon Clark, chief of naval operations; General Michael E. Ryan, chief of staff of the U.S. Air Force; and General James L. Jones, commandant of the Marine Corps.

Past Chairmen of the JCS

General of the Army, Omar N. Bradley, 1949–1953
Adm. Arthur W. Radford, U.S. Navy, 1953–1957
Gen. Nathan F. Twining, U.S. Air Force, 1957–1960
Gen. Lyman L. Lemnitzer, U.S. Army, 1960–1962
Gen. Maxwell D. Taylor, U.S. Army, 1962–1964
Gen. Earle G. Wheeler, U.S. Air Force, 1964–1970
Adm. Thomas H. Moorer, U.S. Navy, 1970–1974
Gen. George S. Brown, U.S. Air Force, 1974–1978
Gen. David C. Jones, U.S. Air Force, 1978–1982
Gen. John W. Vessey, Jr., U.S. Army, 1982–1985
Adm. William J. Crowe, U.S. Navy, 1985–1989
Gen. Colin L. Powell, U.S. Army, 1989–1993
Gen. John M. Shalikashvili, U.S. Army, 1993–1997

Monthly Basic Pay Rates by Grade, as of Jan. 2000

Grade	<2	>2	>4	>6	>10	>14	>16	>18	>20	>26
					Years of Service					
Commissioned Officers										
O-10	$8,214.90	$8,503.80	$8,503.80	$8,503.80	$8,830.20	$9,319.50	$9,986.40	$9,986.40	$10,655.10	$11,318.40
O-9	7,280.70	7,471.50	7,630.50	7,630.50	7,824.60	8,150.10	8,830.20	8,830.20	9,319.50	9,986.40
O-8	6,594.30	6,792.30	6,953.10	6,953.10	7,471.50	7,824.60	8,150.10	8,503.80	8,830.20	9,048.00
O-7	5,479.50	5,851.80	5,851.80	6,114.60	6,468.90	6,792.30	7,471.50	7,985.40	7,985.40	7,985.40
O-6	4,061.10	4,461.60	4,754.40	4,754.40	4,754.40	4,916.10	5,693.10	5,983.80	6,114.60	7,015.50
O-5	3,248.40	3,813.90	4,077.90	4,077.90	4,200.30	4,723.80	5,077.50	5,368.20	5,531.10	5,724.60
O-4	2,737.80	3,333.90	3,556.20	3,622.20	4,040.40	4,461.60	4,658.10	4,785.90	4,785.90	4,785.90
O-3	2,544.00	2,844.30	3,364.80	3,525.90	3,850.20	4,139.10	4,139.10	4,139.10	4,139.10	4,139.10
O-2	2,218.80	2,423.10	3,009.00	3,071.10	3,071.10	3,071.10	3,071.10	3,071.10	3,071.10	3,071.10
O-1	1,926.30	2,004.90	2,423.10	2,423.10	2,423.10	2,423.10	2,423.10	2,423.10	2,423.10	2,423.10
Warrant Officers										
W-5	0.00	0.00	0.00	0.00	0.00	0.00	0.00	0.00	$4,423.80	$4,923.30
W-4	$2,592.00	$2,781.30	$2,844.30	$2,974.20	$3,235.50	$3,622.20	$3,749.40	$3,850.20	3,974.10	4,427.10
W-3	2,355.90	2,555.40	2,588.40	2,618.70	2,974.20	3,168.60	3,263.40	3,364.80	3,495.90	3,749.40
W-2	2,063.40	2,232.60	2,297.40	2,423.10	2,652.60	2,844.30	2,944.30	3,041.10	3,136.80	3,263.40
W-1	1,719.00	1,971.00	2,135.70	2,232.60	2,423.10	2,618.70	2,716.20	2,810.40	2,910.90	2,910.90
Enlisted Members										
E-9	0.00	0.00	0.00	0.00	$3,015.30	$3,152.70	$3,225.60	$3,298.20	$3,361.50	$3,882.60
E-8	0.00	0.00	0.00	0.00	2,601.60	2,739.00	2,811.60	2,875.50	2,946.30	3,467.10
E-7	$1,765.80	$1,906.20	$2,045.70	$2,115.60	2,252.70	2,427.90	2,496.90	2,566.20	2,599.50	3,119.40
E-6	1,518.90	1,655.70	1,797.60	1,865.40	2,003.40	2,172.90	2,242.80	2,277.00	2,277.00	2,277.00
E-5	1,332.60	1,450.50	1,587.30	1,691.70	1,830.00	1,932.60	1,932.60	1,932.60	1,932.60	1,932.60
E-4	1,242.90	1,312.80	1,497.30	1,556.70	1,556.70	1,556.70	1,556.70	1,556.70	1,556.70	1,556.70
E-3	1,171.50	1,235.70	1,335.90	1,355.90	1,335.90	1,335.90	1,335.90	1,335.90	1,335.90	1,335.90
E-2	1,127.40	1,127.40	1,127.40	1,127.40	1,127.40	1,127.40	1,227.40	1,227.40	1,227.40	1,227.40
E-1 >4	1,005.60	1,005.60	1,005.60	1,005.60	1,005.60	1,005.60	1,005.60	1,005.60	1,005.60	1,005.60

NOTE: E-1 with less than 4 months: $930.30. *Source:* Department of Defense, Defense Finance and Accounting Service, Executive Order 13144.

U.S. Military Pay Grades

Source: U.S. Department of Defense

Pay Grade	Army	Navy	Marines	Air Force
Commissioned Officers				
0-1	Second Lieutenant	Ensign	Second Lieutenant	Second Lieutenant
0-2	First Lieutenant	Lieutenant Junior Grade	First Lieutenant	First Lieutenant
0-3	Captain	Lieutenant	Captain	Captain
0-4	Major	Lieutenant Commander	Major	Major
0-5	Lieutenant Colonel	Commander	Lieutenant Colonel	Lieutenant Colonel
0-6	Colonel	Captain	Colonel	Colonel
0-7	Brigadier General	Rear Admiral (L)	Brigadier General	Brigadier General
0-8	Major General	Rear Admiral	Major General	Major General
0-9	Lieutenant General	Vice Admiral	Lieutenant General	Lieutenant General
0-10	General	Admiral	General	General
Special Grades[1]				
(5 stars)	General of the Army	Fleet Admiral	(none)	General of the Air Force
Warrant Officers				
W-1	Warrant Officer. Grades W-2 to W-5 Chief Warrant Officer			
Enlisted Personnel				
E-1	Private	Seaman Recruit	Private	Airman Basic
E-2	Private	Seaman Apprentice	Private First Class	Airman
E-3	Private First Class	Seaman	Lance Corporal	Airman First Class
E-4	Corporal Specialist 4	Petty Officer, Third Class	Corporal	Sergeant Senior Airman
E-5	Sergeant Specialist 5	Petty Officer, Second Class	Sergeant	Staff Sergeant
E-6	Staff Sergeant Specialist 6	Petty Officer, First Class	Staff Sergeant	Technical Sergeant
E-7	Sergeant First Class Specialist 7	Chief Petty Officer	Gunnery Sergeant	Master Sergeant
E-8	First Sergeant Master Sergeant	Senior Chief Petty Officer	First Sergeant Master Sergeant	Senior Master Sergeant
E-9	Command Sergeant Major Sergeant Major	Master Chief Petty Officer	Sergeant Major Master Gunnery Sergeant	Chief Master Sergeant
Special Grades[2]				
	Sergeant Major of the Army	Master Chief Petty Officer of the Navy	Sergeant Major of the Marine Corps	Chief Master Sergeant of the Air Force

1. There are no living five-star commissioned officers. 2. Senior enlisted advisers. There is only one for each branch of service.

Service Academies

U.S. Military Academy

Established in 1802 by an act of Congress, the U.S. Military Academy is located on the west bank of the Hudson River some 50 miles north of New York City. To gain admission a candidate must first secure a nomination from a member of Congress or the Department of the Army.

Any number of applicants can meet the requirements for a *nomination* in these categories. *Appointments* (offers of admission), however, can only be made to a much smaller number, about 1,150 to 1,200 each year. Approximately 15% of the Corps of Cadets are women.

Candidates may be nominated for vacancies during the year preceding the day of admission, which occurs in late June or early July. The best time to apply is during the spring of the junior year in high school.

Candidates must be citizens of the U.S. at time of enrollment (except foreign students admitted by agreement between the U.S. and another country), not married, pregnant, nor have a legal obligation to support a child or children, be at least 17 but not yet 23 years old on July 1 of the year admitted. Entrance requirements and procedures for appointment are described in the Admissions Bulletin and the Admissions Prospectus, available without charge from Admissions, U.S. Military Academy, West Point, N.Y. 10996-1797. Phone: 914-938-4041.

Cadets are members of the U.S. Army. As such they receive annual salaries of more than $6,500. This pay covers the cost of their uniforms, textbooks, a personal computer, and living incidentals. There is no tuition and room and board are provided. Upon successful completion of the four-year course, the graduate receives the degree of bachelor of science and is commissioned a second lieutenant in the U.S. Army with a requirement to serve as an officer on active duty for a minimum of five years.

Service Academy Web Sites

U.S. Military Academy: www.usma.edu
U.S. Air Force Academy: www.usafa.af.mil
U.S. Naval Academy: www.nadn.navy.mil
U.S. Coast Guard Academy:
   www.cga.edu
U.S. Merchant Marine Academy: www.usmma.edu

U.S. Naval Academy

The Naval School, established in 1845 at Fort Severn, Annapolis, Md., was renamed the U.S. Naval Academy in 1850. A four-year course was adopted a year later. The "Yard," as the campus is referred to, blends French Renaissance and modern architecture with many new academic, athletic, and laboratory facilities.

Nineteen majors are offered in engineering, science, mathematics, social sciences, and the humanities. Graduates are awarded the bachelor of science or bachelor of science in engineering and are commissioned as officers in the U.S. Navy or Marine Corps. The class of 2003 includes 16% women.

A nomination is required in order to receive an appointment. You can apply to congressmen, senators, and the vice president for a nomination. Alternate nomination sources are available.

To have basic eligibility for admission, candidates must be citizens of the U.S., of good moral character, at least 17 and not more than 23 years of age on July 1 of their entering year, unmarried, not pregnant, and without legal obligation to dependents.

Tuition, board, lodging, and medical and dental care are provided. Midshipmen receive $558.04 a month for books, uniforms, and personal needs. Upon being commissioned as an ensign in the navy or a second lieutenant in the Marine Corps, the commitment is at least 5 years' active duty. Aviation service commitment depends upon type of aircraft and whether you are a pilot or naval flight officer. Most aviators serve 7 years after they complete their initial flight training.

For general information or answers to specific questions, write: Director of Candidate Guidance, U.S. Naval Academy, Annapolis, Md. 21402-5018, or call 1-410-293-4361.

U.S. Air Force Academy

The bill establishing the U.S. Air Force Academy was signed by President Eisenhower on April 1, 1954. The first class of 306 cadets was sworn in on July 11, 1955, at Lowry Air Force Base, Denver, Colo., the academy's temporary location. The Cadet Wing moved into the academy's permanent home north of Colorado Springs, Colo., in 1958.

Cadets receive four years of academic, military, and physical education to prepare them for leadership as officers in the air force. The academy is authorized to enroll a total of 4,000 male and female cadets. Each new class averages 1,200. The candidates for the academy must be at least 17 and not have passed their 23rd birthday on July 1 of the year for which they enter the academy, must be a U.S. citizen, unmarried, have no dependents, be of good moral character, and be able to meet the mental and physical requirements. International students authorized admission are exempt from the U.S. citizenship requirement.

Cadets receive their entire education at government expense and, in addition, receive a monthly salary of $558.00 to pay for supplies, clothing, and personal expenses. Prior to admission, appointees deposit $2,500 to help defray the initial cost of uniforms, a personal computer, and supplies. Upon completion of the four-year program, leading to a bachelor of science degree, a cadet who meets the qualifications is commissioned a second lieutenant

Military & Veterans Web Sites

U.S. Air Force: www.af.mil
U.S. Army: www.army.mil
U.S. Navy: www.navy.mil
MarineLINK: www.usmc.mil
U.S. Coast Guard: www.uscg.mil
DefenseLink (DOD): www.defenselink.mil
Military Woman:
    www.wimsa.org (not a DOD or armed forces site)
Selective Service System: www.sss.gov
Department of Veterans Affairs (VA):
    www.va.gov
BosniaLINK: www.dtic.mil/bosnia/index.html
Gulf War Veterans: www.gulfweb.org
Vietnam Veterans: www.vva.org
WWII U.S. Veterans: ww2.vet.org
Korean War Veterans Association:
    www.kwva.org
Kosovo Peacekeeping Force: http://kforonline.com
American Legion: www.legion.org
Air America: www.air-america.org
North Atlantic Treaty Organization (NATO):
    www.nato.int

in the U.S. Air Force. For details on admissions, call 1-800-443-9266, or write: HQ USAFA/RRS, 2304 Cadet Drive, Suite 200, USAF Academy, Colorado Springs, Colo. 80840-5025.

U.S. Coast Guard Academy

The U.S. Coast Guard Academy is the only one of the four armed forces service academies that offers appointments based solely on the basis of an annual nationwide competition, with no congressional appointments or geographical quotas. Competition is open to all unmarried U.S. citizens with no dependents who have reached their 17th but not their 22nd birthday by July 1 of the entering year. There is no fee to apply, but candidates who are offered and accept an appointment to the academy must pay an entrance fee of $3,000. Cadets receive a full scholarship including room and board. In addition, they receive a monthly allowance of approximately $600 to cover the costs of uniforms, textbooks, a new laptop, and other expenses.

Upon graduation, there is a 5-year commitment to serve as a commissioned Coast Guard officer, the first two years of which are on a Coast Guard cutter.

A viewbook or video can be obtained by writing to Director of Admissions, U.S. Coast Guard Academy, 31 Mohegan Avenue, New London, Conn. 06320, or by calling 1-800-883-8724 or 860-444-8500.

U.S. Merchant Marine Academy

The U.S. Merchant Marine Academy, situated at Kings Point, N.Y., on the north shore of Long Island, was dedicated Sept. 30, 1943. It is maintained by the Department of Transportation under direction of the Maritime Administration.

The academy has an enrollment of approximately 950 men and women who represent every state, D.C., the Canal Zone, Puerto Rico, Guam, American Samoa, and the Virgin Islands. Special legislation permits the appointment of midshipmen from the Latin American republics and nations other than the United States.

Candidates are nominated by senators and members of the House of Representatives. Nominations to the academy are governed by a state and territory quota system based on population and the results of the College Entrance Examination Board tests.

A candidate must be a citizen not less than 17 and not yet 25 years of age by July 1 of the year in which admission is sought, unmarried, and without dependents. The current class of cadets includes 13% women.

The course is four years and includes one year of practical training aboard a merchant ship. Study includes marine engineering, navigation, satellite navigation and communications, electricity, ship construction, naval science and tactics, economics, business, languages, history, etc.

Upon completion of the course of study, a graduate receives a bachelor of science degree, a license as a merchant marine officer (issued by the U.S. Coast Guard), and a commission as an ensign in the Naval Reserve.

For additional information, write to Admissions Office, U.S. Merchant Marine Academy, 300 Steamboat Rd., Kings Point, N.Y. 11024, or call 516-773-5391.

Anthrax Is the Greatest Biological Threat

Source: U.S. Department of Defense (DOD)

At least ten countries, including several hostile to Western democracies—Iran, Iraq, Libya, and North Korea—are known to possess anthrax biological weapons or are developing it. It is within the reach of not only rogue nations, but also transnational terrorist groups. Anthrax tops the DOD threat list of biological weapons because it is easy to manufacture at low cost in large quantities. Anthrax is extremely stable. It can be stored almost indefinitely as a dry powder. The material can be loaded, in a freeze-dried condition, in munitions, or disseminated as an aerosol with crude sprayers.

Anthrax is produced by the bacteria *Bacillus anthracis*. A tough protective coat allows the bacteria to survive for decades as spores. It is a dangerous, silent, invisible killer. One hundred million lethal doses per gram of anthrax material is 100,000 times more deadly than the deadliest chemical warfare weapon.

If an individual inhales aerosolized anthrax, there is little chance of survival from this devastating disease. Antibiotics exist, but they must be taken before symptoms develop. However, the chance of that is minimal since aerosolized anthrax is colorless, odorless, tasteless, and very difficult to detect. By the time we determined an attack has occurred, it would most likely be too late.

There are three types of anthrax diseases: cutaneous anthrax, caused by contact with infected animals or contaminated animal products; gastrointestinal anthrax, caused by ingestion of contaminated meat (not considered a threat to U.S. forces); and inhalation anthrax, caused by inhalation of anthrax spores (the biggest threat to U.S. forces).

The symptoms of anthrax begin after a one- to six-day incubation period following the exposure. For contact or cutaneous anthrax, itching will occur at the site of exposure followed by the formation of a lesion. Untreated contact anthrax has a fatality rate of 5% to 20%, but with effective antibiotic treatment, few deaths occur.

Initial symptoms for inhalational anthrax are generally nonspecific: low-grade fever, a dry hacking cough, and weakness. The person may briefly improve after 2 to 4 days; however, within 24 hours after this brief improvement, respiratory distress occurs with shock and death following thereafter.

The current vaccine given to U.S. forces requires six doses administered over 18 months to complete the primary series. The DOD gave the following statistics about the Department of Defense's Anthrax Immunization Program to Congress on May 16, 2000. More than 1,700,000 doses of the vaccine were given to over 440,000 military personnel. Only 0.00008 percent has resulted in loss of duty. Only 0.00001 percent, or 31 people, have required hospitalization. Of these 31, only six have been determined to, more probably than not, have illnesses that have resulted from anthrax vaccination. Those persons were granted waivers not to receive future vaccinations. □

The National Guard

The National Guard consists of citizen-soldiers and airmen who serve on both a federal and a state level. The Army National Guard has units in 2,700 communities in all 50 states, the District of Columbia, Guam, Puerto Rico, and the Virgin Islands. The Air National Guard has 88 flying units at more than 170 installations nationwide. National Guard units are organized, trained, and equipped to the same standards as the U.S. Army and the U.S. Air Force.

The National Guard has two roles—one as part of the nation's military force and the other for state emergencies and community support missions. This dual state/federal role for the National Guard is based on a Constitutional mandate. The relationship is unique and sets the National Guard apart from other military reserve forces.

Currently, the Army National Guard, 350,000 strong, makes up more than one-half of the total army's ground combat forces and one-third of its support forces. Air National Guard units, with a total strength of 105,000, are closely integrated with the U.S. Air Force and perform worldwide operations on a daily basis. □

Veterans of U.S. Wars and Their Dependents
(on the VA Compensation and Pension Rolls as of July 1, 1999)

As of July 1, 1999, 3,287,477 veterans, their dependents, and survivors of deceased veterans are receiving VA benefits and services.

Veterans' benefits have existed since the origins of the nation. The last dependent of a Revolutionary War veteran died in 1911; the War of 1812's last dependent died in 1946; the Mexican War's in 1962. Some 879 children and widows of Spanish-American War veterans are receiving VA benefits. There are in fact still a few surviving widows and children of Civil War and Indian War veterans who draw VA benefits.

	Veterans	Children[1]	Parents	Surviving spouses
Civil War	—	14	—	1
Indian Wars	—	1	—	1
Spanish-American War	—	309	—	570
Mexican Border	14	27	—	254
World War I	447	6,581	2	37,568
World War II	741,783	19,647	2,319	288,742
Korean Conflict	265,220	4,400	2,041	65,681
Gulf War	272,142	7,314	369	5,053
Peacetime Veterans	557,979	8,631	2,761	36,717
Total	**2,668,186**	**62,487**	**14,590**	**542,214**

1. Children connotes a minor or a helpless adult. *Source:* Department of Veterans Affairs.

Last Living Veterans of America's Wars

American Revolution (1775–1783)
- Last veteran, Daniel F. Bakeman, died 4/5/1869, age 109
- Last widow, Catherine S. Damon, died 11/11/06, age 92
- Last dependent, Phoebe M. Palmeter, died 4/25/11, age 90

War of 1812 (1812–1815)
- Last veteran, Hiram Cronk, died 5/13/05, age 105
- Last widow, Carolina King, died 6/28/36, age unknown
- Last dependent, Esther A. H. Morgan, died 3/12/46, age 89

Indian Wars (c. 1861–1898)
- Last veteran, Fredrak Fraske, died 6/18/73, age 101

Mexican War (1846–1848)
- Last veteran, Owen Thomas Edgar, died 9/3/29, age 98
- Last widow, Lena James Theobald, died 6/20/63, age 89
- Last dependent, Jesse G. Bivens, died 11/1/62, age 94

Civil War (1861–1865)
- Last Union veteran, Albert Woolson, died 8/2/56, age 109
- Last Confederate veteran, John Salling, died 3/16/58, age 112

Spanish-American War (1898)
- Last veteran, Nathan E. Cook, died 9/10/92, age 106

Active Military Duty Personnel, 1940–2000[1]

Year	Army[2]	Air Force[2,3]	Navy	Marine Corps	Total
1940	269,023		160,997	28,345	458,365
1945	8,266,373		3,319,586	469,925	12,055,884
1950	593,167	411,277	380,739	74,279	1,459,462
1955	1,109,296	959,946	660,695	205,170	2,935,107
1960	873,078	814,752	616,987	170,621	2,475,438
1965	969,066	824,662	669,985	190,213	2,653,926
1970	1,322,548	791,349	691,126	259,737	3,064,760
1975	784,333	612,751	535,085	195,951	2,128,120
1980	777,036	557,969	527,153	188,469	2,050,627
1985	780,787	601,515	570,705	198,025	2,151,032
1990	732,403	535,233	579,417	196,652	2,043,705
1991	710,821	510,432	570,262	194,040	1,985,555
1992	610,450	470,315	541,883	184,529	1,807,177
1993	572,423	444,351	509,950	178,379	1,705,103
1994	541,343	426,327	468,662	174,158	1,610,490
1995	508,559	400,409	434,617	174,639	1,518,224
1996	491,103	389,001	416,735	174,883	1,471,722
1997	491,707	377,385	395,564	173,906	1,438,562
1998	483,880	367,470	382,338	173,142	1,406,830
1999[4]	473,595	363,449	370,343	172,369	1,379,756
2000[4]	474,205	355,891	368,440	171,701	1,370,237

1. Military personnel on extended or continued active duty. Excludes reserves on active duty for training. Prior year totals have been corrected. 2. Represents "Command Strength" prior to June 30, 1956. 3. Army Air Forces and its predecessors for period prior to Sept. 18, 1947. 4. Totals as of Sept. 30, except 1999 and 2000 totals, are for Jan. 31. Figures for 1998 through 2000 include cadets-midshipmen. *Source:* Department of Defense.

The Medal of Honor

Often called the Congressional Medal of Honor, it is the nation's highest military award for "uncommon valor" by men and women in the armed forces. It is given for actions that are above and beyond the call of duty in combat against an armed enemy. The medal was first awarded by the army on March 25, 1863. More than 3,400 men and one woman have been awarded the medal.

Recipients of the medal are awarded $400 per month for life, a right to burial at Arlington National Cemetery, admission for them or their children to a service academy (if they qualify and quotas permit), and free travel on government aircraft to almost anywhere in the world, on a space-available basis.

Medal of Honor Recipients

	Total[1]	Army	Navy	Marines	Air Force	Coast Guard
Civil War	1,520	1,195	308	17	—	—
Indian Wars (1861–1898)	428	428	—	—	—	—
Korea (1871)	15	—	9	6	—	—
Spanish-American War	109	30	64	15	—	—
Philippines/Samoa	91	70	12	9	—	—
Boxer Rebellion	59	4	22	33	—	—
Veracruz (1914)	55	—	46	9	—	—
Haiti (1915)	6	—	—	6	—	—
Dominican Republic	3	—	—	3	—	—
Haiti (1919–1920)	2	—	—	2	—	—
Nicaragua (1927–1933)	2	—	—	2	—	—
Peacetime (1865–1870)	12	—	12	—	—	—
Peacetime (1871–1898)	103	—	101	2	—	—
Peacetime (1899–1911)	51	1	48	2	—	—
Peacetime (1915–1916)	8	—	8	—	—	—
Peacetime (1920–1940)	18	2	15	1	—	—
World War I	124	96	21	7	—	—
World War II	461	322	57	81	—	1
Korean War	131	78	7	42	4	—
Vietnam War	240	156	15	57	12	—
Somalia (1993)	2	2	—	—	—	—
Unknown Soldiers	9	—	—	—	—	—
Total	**3,449**	**2,384**	**745**	**294**	**16**	**1**

1. These totals reflect the total number of Medals of Honor awarded. Nineteen (19) men received a second award. In February 2000, the medal was awarded to an army Vietnam War medic. In May 2000, the medal was awarded to 21 Asian-American army veterans for their heroism in World War II. *Source:* The Congressional Medal of Honor Society, Mt. Pleasant, S.C.

American Prisoners of War

Congress defines a former prisoner of war as a person who, while serving on active military, naval, or air service, was forcibly detained or interned in the line of duty by an enemy government or a hostile force, during a period of war or in situations comparable to war. Less than half (40%) of the Americans held prisoner in the last six conflicts are now living.

	Total	WWI	WWII	Korea	Vietnam	Persian Gulf	Somalia
Captured and interned	142,257	4,120	130,201	7,140	772	23	1
Returned to U.S. military control	125,202	3,973	116,129	4,418	658	23	1
Refused repatriation	21	0	0	21	0	0	0
Died while POW	17,034	147	14,072	2,701	144	0	0
Alive, Jan. 1998	55,999	5	52,531	2,814	625	23	1

Source: U.S. Department of Veterans Affairs.

Post-Vietnam Combat Casualties*

Place	Dates	Casualties	Place	Dates	Casualties
Lebanon	Aug. 1982–Feb. 1984	254	Persian Gulf	Aug. 1990–March 1998, Dec. 1998–present	148
Grenada	Oct.–Nov. 1983	18			
Libya	April 10–16, 1986	2	Somalia	Dec. 1992–May 1993	29
Panama	Dec. 1989–Jan. 1990	23	Haiti	Sept. 1994–April 1996	0
			Yugoslavia	March–June 1999	0

*Does not include deaths from accidents. *Source:* Defense Dept.

U.S. Casualties in the Major Wars

War	Branch of service	Numbers engaged	Battle deaths	Other deaths	Total deaths	Wounds not mortal	Total casualties[1]
Revolutionary War	Army	n.a.	4,044	n.a.	n.a.	6,004	n.a.
(1775 to 1783)	Navy	n.a.	342	n.a.	n.a.	114	n.a.
	Marines	n.a.	49	n.a.	n.a.	70	n.a.
	Total	**n.a.**	**4,435**	**n.a.**	**n.a.**	**6,188**	**n.a.**
War of 1812	Army	n.a.	1,950	n.a.	n.a.	4,000	n.a.
(1812 to 1815)	Navy	n.a.	265	n.a.	n.a.	439	n.a.
	Marines	n.a.	45	n.a.	n.a.	66	n.a.
	Total	**286,730**	**2,260**	**n.a.**	**n.a.**	**4,505**	**n.a.**
Mexican War	Army	n.a.	1,721	11,550	13,271	4,102	17,373
(1846 to 1848)	Navy	n.a.	1	n.a.	n.a.	3	n.a.
	Marines	n.a.	11	n.a.	n.a.	47	n.a.
	Total	**78,718**	**1,733**	**n.a.**	**n.a.**	**4,152**	**n.a.**
Civil War	Army	2,128,948	138,154	221,374	359,528	280,040	639,568
(1861 to 1865)[2]	Navy	84,415	2,112	2,411	4,523	1,710	6,233
	Marines		148	312	460	131	591
	Total	**2,213,363**	**140,414**	**224,097**	**364,511**	**281,881**	**646,392**
Spanish-American War	Army	280,564	369	2,061	2,430	1,594	4,024
(1898)	Navy	22,875	10	0	10	47	57
	Marines	3,321	6	0	6	21	27
	Total	**306,760**	**385**	**2,061**	**2,446**	**1,662**	**4,108**
World War I	Army	4,057,101	50,510	55,868	106,378	193,663	300,041
(1917 to 1918)	Navy	599,051	431	6,856	7,287	819	8,106
	Marines	78,839	2,461	390	2,851	9,520	12,371
	Total	**4,734,991**	**53,402**	**63,114**	**116,516**	**204,002**	**320,518**
World War II	Army[3]	11,260,000	234,874	83,400	318,274	565,861	884,135
(1941 to 1946)	Navy	4,183,466	36,950	25,664	62,614	37,778	100,392
	Marines	669,100	19,733	4,778	24,511	67,207	91,718
	Total	**16,112,566**	**291,557**	**113,842**	**405,399**	**670,846**	**1,076,245**
Korean War	Army	2,834,000	27,709	2,452	30,161	77,596	107,757
(1950 to 1953)	Navy	1,177,000	475	173	648	1,576	2,224
	Marines	424,000	4,270	339	4,609	23,744	28,353
	Air Force	1,285,000	1,198	298	1,496	368	1,864
	Total	**5,720,000**	**33,652**	**3,262**	**36,914**	**103,284**	**140,198**
War in Southeast Asia[4]	Army	4,368,000	30,914	7,275	38,189	96,802	134,991
	Navy	1,842,000	1,631	928	2,559	4,178	6,737
	Marines	794,000	13,082	1,754	14,836	51,392	66,228
	Air Force	1,740,000	1,739	844	2,583	931	3,514
	Total	**8,744,000**	**47,366**	**10,801**	**58,167**	**153,303**	**211,470**

See p. 371 for post-Vietnam casualties. NOTES: All data are subject to revision. For wars before World War I, information represents best data from available records. However, due to incomplete records and possible difference in usage of terminology, reporting systems, etc., figures should be considered estimates. n.a. = not available. 1. Excludes captured or interned and missing in action who were subsequently returned to military control. 2. Union forces only. Totals should probably be somewhat larger as data or disposition of prisoners are far from complete. Final Confederate deaths, based on incomplete returns, were 133,821, to which should be added 26,000–31,000 personnel who died in Union prisons. 178,975 blacks served in the Union army. 2,894 were killed in battle or mortally wounded, 33,953 died from other causes including 29,658 deaths from disease. 3. Army data include air force. 4. Vietnam figures provided by the U.S. Center of Military History, Reference Division, Washington, D.C., February 1994. Navy figures exclude Coast Guard, in which there were 5 battle deaths. *Source:* Department of Defense.

Merchant Marine Casualties in World War II

In 1988, the U.S. government conferred official veteran status on those who served aboard oceangoing merchant ships in World War II. The officers and crews played a key role in transporting the troops and war matériel that enabled the United States and its allies to defeat the Axis powers.

During the war, merchant seamen died as a result of enemy attacks at a rate that proportionately exceeded all branches of the armed services, with the exception of the U.S. Marine Corps.

Enemy action sank more than 700 U.S.-flag merchant ships and claimed the lives of over 6,000 civilian seafarers. Untold thousands of additional seamen were wounded or injured during these attacks, and nearly 600 were made prisoners of war.

For international military affairs, *see* p. 716.

Stormy Weather on the Sun

Every eleven years, Earth is besieged by a solar maximum

By LEON JAROFF TIME

A million miles from Earth, NASA's Advanced Composition Explorer (ACE) spacecraft suddenly found itself under assault. Late in Jan. 2000, the tiny, instrument-packed spacecraft was buffeted by an exceptionally powerful burst of particles spewed out by the Sun.

In the space-environment control room at the National Oceanic and Atmospheric Administration (NOAA) headquarters in Boulder, Colo., alarms sounded. "All of a sudden, a blast wave of solar wind showed up at the ACE spacecraft," says NOAA's Joe Hirman, "as dense as any we've seen, and, bam, 30 minutes later the Earth's magnetic field got hit hard."

A Fiery Forecast

To astronomers, this violent event signaled an approaching solar maximum, a period of enormous turbulence that roils the Sun every eleven years or so. The last solar maximum occurred in 1989, and right on schedule, the year 2000 became the next period of solar tumult.

During solar maximums, space weather becomes stormy. The normally benign Sun pounds Earth mercilessly with ultraviolet radiation, X rays, and floods of charged particles, distorting the planet's protective magnetic field and inducing powerful electric currents that can wreak havoc not only with spacecraft but also with many aspects of terrestrial life.

One 1989 solar storm knocked out Hydro-Quebec transformers, leaving 6 million people in eastern Canada and the U.S. Northeast without electricity for nine hours. The same storm disrupted shortwave radio transmissions, crippled Coast Guard loran navigation systems, and had automatic garage doors opening on their own.

Technology a Target

In the years since, we have become increasingly dependent on satellite-based communications, and even off-peak solar outbursts have caused trouble. They are suspected in damage to at least a dozen satellites and the failure of the Galaxy IV satellite during a 1998 solar storm that silenced 80% of North America's pagers. In the past four years alone, says Chris Kunstadter, of U.S. Aviation Underwriters, space losses may have exceeded $550 million.

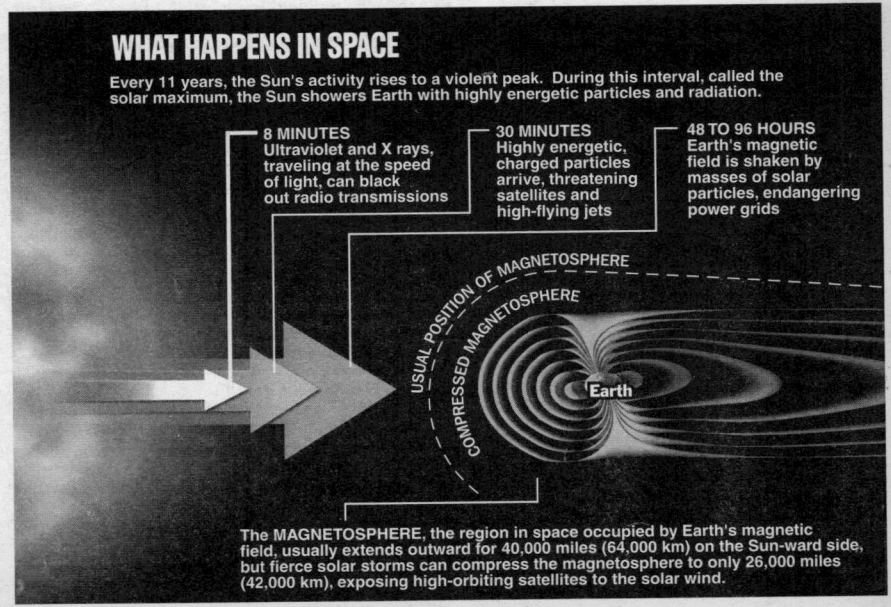

WHAT HAPPENS IN SPACE

Every 11 years, the Sun's activity rises to a violent peak. During this interval, called the solar maximum, the Sun showers Earth with highly energetic particles and radiation.

8 MINUTES
Ultraviolet and X rays, traveling at the speed of light, can black out radio transmissions

30 MINUTES
Highly energetic, charged particles arrive, threatening satellites and high-flying jets

48 TO 96 HOURS
Earth's magnetic field is shaken by masses of solar particles, endangering power grids

USUAL POSITION OF MAGNETOSPHERE

COMPRESSED MAGNETOSPHERE

Earth

The MAGNETOSPHERE, the region in space occupied by Earth's magnetic field, usually extends outward for 40,000 miles (64,000 km) on the Sun-ward side, but fierce solar storms can compress the magnetosphere to only 26,000 miles (42,000 km), exposing high-orbiting satellites to the solar wind.

Controlling the Universe

The key to the Sun's energetic fury is, in a word, magnetism. "Control magnetic energy, and you control the universe," says University of Colorado astrophysicist Daniel Baker, paraphrasing a character in the old Dick Tracy comic strip. If the Sun were a rigid body, its magnetic field might resemble Earth's, with symmetrical field lines like a bar magnet's. But as the Sun turns, its equatorial gases rotate faster than those at higher latitudes, twisting the magnetic lines "like a rubber band," explains David Hathaway, a solar physicist at NASA's Marshall Space Flight Center.

Under increasing tension, the magnetic field eventually breaks through the surface. This produces sunspots, darker magnetized regions of relatively cooler gases. When regions of opposite polarity meet, prodigious amounts of pent-up magnetic energy are released as heat. The upshot: coronal mass ejections—the spewing out of billions of tons of solar material—and giant flares.

What ACE detected in Jan. 2000 was a violent gust of "solar wind," the constant flow of charged particles from the Sun. Usually it streams past Earth at less than 1 million m.p.h., but when that wind gushed from a rare gap in the Sun's tangled magnetic web, its velocity exceeded 2 million m.p.h. and particle density was 30 times normal.

An Ill Wind Blowing

"If you can imagine yourself sitting in a chair and suddenly being sprayed by a fire hose," says NOAA's Hirman, "that's what the solar wind did to Earth that morning." Usually Earth's magnetic field acts as a shield. But the ill wind so squeezed it on Earth's Sun side that the field slipped below the orbits of many satellites and briefly exposed them.

Fortunately, no astronauts were aloft to experience the deadly particles.

Solar flares can also doom satellites. Reaching Earth in just eight minutes, their powerful UV and X rays help heat up and expand the atmosphere, thereby increasing molecular drag on low-orbiting satellites and shortening their orbital life—as happened in 1989 to the Solar Max satellite, which was designed to study the very thing that did it in.

Magnetic Mayhem

Perhaps the most spectacular effect of solar bombardments is on Earth's magnetic field. By causing it "to wobble and shake," explains NASA's Hathaway, it induces strong electric currents in the atmosphere and on the ground. In an instant, the surges destroy transformers, like Hydro-Quebec's, and overwhelm circuit breakers. The surges also corrode pipelines by weakening the metal.

Even passengers in high-flying jets, like the Concorde, which carries a radiation detector, might receive several chest X rays' worth of radiation in a solar storm. During the 1989 maximum, says Ernie Hildner, director of NOAA's Space Environment Center, "the Concorde's alarm went yellow five times. It never went red." That would have required the pilots to dive immediately to lower altitudes, seeking protection in the thicker atmosphere.

Space weather forecasting is still in its infancy, and thus far, only the ACE spacecraft has the capability of providing even an hour's notice of a solar strike. NASA hopes to launch more than 50 early-warning spacecraft in time for the next solar maximum, due in 2011. Flying fantastic solar sails, some would circle the Sun. Others would monitor the terrestrial magnetic field. Still others would stand as sentinels in high Earth orbit to spot dangerous intruders from our star. □

Astronomical Terms

Planet is the term used for a body in orbit around a star. Its origin is Greek; even in antiquity it was known that a number of "stars" did not stay in the same positions relative to the others. There were five such restless "stars" known—Mercury, Venus, Mars, Jupiter, and Saturn—and the Greeks referred to them as *planetes,* a word which means "wanderers." That Earth is one of the planets was realized later. The additional planets were discovered after the invention of the telescope.

In 1994, Dr. Alexander Wolszcan, an astronomer at Pennsylvania State University, presented convincing evidence of the first known planets to exist outside our solar system. They circle a pulsar or exploded star in the constellation *Virgo.*

In 1995, several of these *extrasolar planets* were discovered orbiting ordinary stars similar to our Sun as a result of observing gravitational variations of the stars. Swiss astronomers found a planet orbiting star 51 in the constellation *Pegasus,* about 40 light-years away. It is the first planet ever discovered to circle a normal sunlike star. Over the last five years, almost 50 planets have been discovered (*see* page 396). The nearest star to Earth known to have a planet is Epsilon Eridani, which is bright enough to be seen with the naked eye.

Satellite (or *moon*) is the term for a body in orbit around a planet. As long as our own Moon was the only moon known, there was no need for a general term for the moons of planets. But when Galileo Galilei discovered the four main moons of the planet Jupiter, Johannes Kepler (in a letter to Galileo) suggested "satellite" (from the Latin *satelles,* which means attendant) as a general term for such bodies. The word is used interchangeably with "moons": astronomers speak and write about the moons of Neptune, Saturn, etc. It is also used to describe man-made devices that are launched into orbit. A satellite may be any size.

Orbit is the term for the path traveled by a body in space. It comes from the Latin *orbis,* which means circle or circuit, and *orbita,* which means a rut or a wheel track. Theoretically, there are four mathematical figures that are possible orbits: two are open (hyperbola and parabola) and two are closed (ellipse and circle), but in reality all closed orbits are ellipses. These ellipses can be nearly circular, as are the orbits of most planets, or very elongated, as are the orbits of most comets. In these orbits, the Sun is in one focal point of the ellipse, and the other focal point is empty. In the orbits of satellites, the planet stands in one focal point of the orbit. The *primary* of an orbit is the body in the focal point. For planets, the point of the orbit closest to the Sun is the *perihelion,* and the point farthest from the Sun is the *aphelion.* For orbits around Earth, the corresponding terms are *perigee* and *apogee;* for orbits around other planets, corresponding terms are coined when necessary.

Two heavenly bodies are in *inferior* or *superior conjunction* when they have the same *right ascension,* or are in the same meridian; that is, when one is due north or south of the other. If the bodies appear near each other as seen from Earth, they will rise and set at the same time. They are in *opposition* when they are opposite each other in the heavens: when one rises as the other is setting. *Greatest elongation* is the greatest apparent angular distance from the Sun, when a planet is most favorably suited for observation. Mercury can be seen with the naked eye only at about this time. An *occultation* of a planet or star is an eclipse of it by some other body, usually the Moon.

Stars are the basic units of population in the universe. Our Sun is the nearest star. Stars are very large (our Sun has a diameter of 865,400 miles—a comparatively small star). Stars are composed of intensely hot gasses, deriving their energy from nuclear reactions going on in their interiors.

Galaxies are immense systems containing billions of stars. All that you can see in the sky (with a very few exceptions) belongs to our galaxy—a system of roughly 200 billion stars. The few exceptions are other galaxies. Our own galaxy, the rim of which we see as the "Milky Way," is about 100,000 light-years in diameter and about 10,000 light-years in thickness. Its shape is roughly that of a thick lens; more precisely it is a "spiral nebula," a term first used for other galaxies when they were discovered and before it was realized that these were separate and distinct galaxies. The spiral galaxy nearest to ours is in the constellation *Andromeda.* It is somewhat larger than our own galaxy and is visible to the naked eye. Astronomers have estimated that the universe could contain 40 to 50 billion galaxies.

A *black hole* is the theoretical end-product of the total gravitational collapse of a massive star or group of stars. Crushed even smaller than an incredibly dense neutron star, such a body may become so dense that not even light can escape its gravitational field. It has been suggested that black holes may be detectable in proximity to normal stars when they draw matter away from their visible neighbors. Strong sources of X rays in our galaxy and beyond may also indicate the presence of black holes.

Quasars ("quasi-stellar" objects), originally thought to be peculiar stars in our own galaxy, are now believed to be the most remote objects in the universe. Quasars emit tremendous amounts of light and microwave radiation. Recent Hubble Space Telescope images suggest that there may be a variety of mechanisms for "turning on" quasars. Although a number of images show collisions between pairs of galaxies, which could trigger the birth of quasars, some pictures reveal apparently normal, undisturbed galaxies possessing quasars.

Quasars are among the most baffling objects in the universe because of their small size and prodigious energy output. Quasars are not much bigger than Earth's solar system but pour out 100 to 1,000 times as much light as an entire galaxy containing a

The Milky Way, the galaxy containing our solar system, is about 100,000 light-years in diameter and about 10,000 light-years thick.

hundred billion stars. A quasar detected in March 2000 with a redshift of 5.8 is 12 billion light-years from Earth and is the most distant object ever observed to date.[1]

A super massive black hole, gobbling up stars, gas, and dust, is theorized to be the "engine" powering a quasar. Most astronomers agree that an active black hole is the only credible possibility that explains how quasars can be so compact, variable, and powerful. However, no conclusive evidence supports this assumption.

Pulsars are believed to be rapidly spinning neutron stars, so crushed by their own gravity that a million tons of their matter would hardly fill a thimble. Pulsars are so named because they emit bursts of radio waves at regular intervals.

In 1996, astronomers found strong evidence for a massive black hole at the center of the Milky Way. Recent evidence suggests that black holes are so common that they probably exist at the core of nearly all galaxies.

The existence of brown dwarfs, also called failed stars, was confirmed in Nov. 1995 when astronomers at Palomar Observatory in California took the first photograph of this mysterious object. Brown dwarfs lack the mass to generate nuclear fission like true stars but are also too massive and hot to be a planet.

Origin of the Universe

In 1999, the age of the cosmos was determined by NASA's Hubble Space Telescope Key Project Team to be about 12 billion years old (plus or minus 10%), with a maximum age of 15 billion years, depending on the number of variables. The universe began its existence as a dense, hot globule of gas expanding rapidly outward. At that time, the universe contained nothing but hydrogen and a small amount of helium. There were no stars and no planets. The first stars probably began to condense out of the primordial hydrogen when the universe was about 100 million years old and continued to form as the universe aged. The Sun arose in this way 4.6

1. Redshift is the amount by which light from a distant object is shifted toward the red end of the spectrum by the expansion of the universe. The higher the redshift, the greater the distance and the younger the universe when the light was emitted.

Astronomical Constants

Light-year (distance traveled by light in one year)	5,880,000,000,000 mi.
Parsec (parallax of one second, or stellar distances)	3.259 light-yrs.
Velocity of light	c. 186,282.4 mi./sec.
Astronomical unit (A.U.), or mean distance Earth to Sun	ca. 93,000,000 mi.[1]
Mean distance, Earth to Moon	238,860 mi.
General precession	50',.26
Obliquity of the ecliptic	23° 27'8'.26-0'.4684(t-1900)[2]
Equatorial radius of Earth	3963.34 statute mi.
Polar radius of Earth	3949.99 statute mi.
Earth's mean radius	3958.89 statute mi.
Oblateness of Earth	1/297
Equatorial horizontal parallax of the moon	57'2'.70
Earth's mean velocity in orbit	18.5 mi./sec.
Sidereal year	365d.2564
Tropical year	365d.2422
Sidereal month	27d.3217
Synodic month	29d.5306
Mean sidereal day	23h56m4s.091 of mean solar time
Mean solar day	24h3m56s.555 of sidereal time

1. Actual mean distance derived from radar bounces: 92,935,700 mi. The value of 92,897,400 mi. (based on parallax of 8".80) is used in calculations. 2. *t* refers to the year in question, for example, 2001.

billion years ago. Many stars came into being before the Sun was formed; many others formed after the Sun appeared. This process continues, and through telescopes we can now see stars forming out of compressed pockets of hydrogen in outer space.

In 1992, instruments aboard the Cosmic Background Explorer (COBE) satellite, launched in 1989, showed that 99.97% of the radiant energy of the universe was released within the first year of the primeval explosion. This evidence seems to confirm the Big Bang theory, which holds that the universe originated from a single violent explosion (a *big bang*) of a very small agglomeration of matter of extremely high density and temperatures. Astronomers also theorize that 99% of the matter in the universe is invisible or *dark matter* composed of some kind of matter that they cannot yet detect.

In March 1995, astronomers found supporting evidence for the Big Bang when they concluded that data obtained from the space shuttle's *Astro 2* observatory showed that helium was widespread in the early universe. The theory holds that hydrogen and helium were the first elements created when the universe was formed.

Birth and Death of a Star

When a star begins to form as a dense cloud of gas, the individual hydrogen atoms fall toward the center of the cloud under the force of the star's gravity. As it falls, it picks up speed, and its energy increases. The increase in energy heats the gas. When this process has continued for some millions of years, the temperature reaches about 20 million degrees Fahrenheit. At this temperature, the hydrogen within the star ignites and burns in a continuing series of nuclear reactions in which all the elements in the universe are manufactured from hydrogen and helium. The onset of these reactions marks the birth of a star. When a star begins to exhaust its hydrogen supply, its life nears an end. The first sign of old age is a swelling and reddening of its outer regions. Such an aging, swollen star is called a red giant. The Sun, a middle-aged star, will probably swell to a red giant in 5 billion years, vaporizing Earth and any

creatures that may be left on its surface. When all its fuel has been exhausted, a star cannot generate sufficient pressure at its center to balance the crushing force of gravity. The star collapses under the force of its own weight; if it is a small star, it collapses gently and remains collapsed. Such a collapsed star, at its life's end, is called a white dwarf. The Sun will probably end its life in this way. A different fate awaits a large star. Its final collapse generates a violent explosion, blowing the innards of the star out into space. There, the materials of the exploded star mix with the primeval hydrogen of the universe. Later in the history of the galaxy, other stars are formed out of this mixture. The Sun is one of these stars. It contains the debris of countless other stars that exploded before the Sun was born.

Supernovas

On Feb. 24, 1987, Canadian astronomer Ian Shelter at the Las Campanas Observatory in Chile discovered a supernova—an exploding star—from a photograph taken on Feb. 23 of the Large Magellanic Cloud, a galaxy some 160,000 light-years away from Earth. Astronomers believe that the dying star was Sanduleak −69°202, a 10-million-year-old blue supergiant.

Supernova 1987A was the closest and best-studied supernova in almost 400 years. One was previously observed by Johannes Kepler in 1604, four years before the telescope was invented.

Formation of the Solar System

The Sun's age was calculated in 1989 to be 4.49 billion years old, less than the 4.7 billion years previously believed. It was formed from a cloud of hydrogen mixed with small amounts of other substances that had been manufactured in the bodies of other stars before the Sun was born. This was the parent cloud of the solar system. The dense, hot gas at the center of the cloud gave rise to the Sun; the outer regions of the cloud—cooler and less dense—gave birth to the planets.

Our solar system consists of one star (the Sun), nine planets and all their moons, several thousand

A Star's Magnitude

Magnitude is the degree of brightness of a star. In 1856, British astronomer Norman Pogson proposed a quantitative scale of stellar magnitudes, which was adopted by the astronomical community. He noted that we receive 100 times more light from a first magnitude star as from a sixth; thus with a difference of five magnitudes, there is a 100:1 ratio of incoming light energy, which is called *luminous flux*.

Because of the nature of human perception, equal intervals of brightness are actually equal ratios of luminous flux. Pogson's proposal was that one increment in magnitude be the fifth root of 100. This means that each increment in magnitude corresponds to an increase in the amount of energy by 2.512, approximately. A fifth magnitude star is 2.512 times as bright as a sixth, and a fourth magnitude star is 6.310 times as bright as a sixth, and so on. The naked eye, upon optimum conditions, can see down to around the sixth magnitude, that is +6. Under Pogson's system, a few of the brighter stars now have negative magnitudes. For example, Sirius is –1.5. The lower the magnitude number, the brighter the object. The full moon has a magnitude of about –12.5, and the sun is a bright –26.51!

The Brightest Stars

Star	Constellation	Mag.	Dist (l.-y.)	Star	Constellation	Mag.	Dist (l.-y.)
Sirius	Canis Major	-1.6	8	Antares	Scorpius	1.2	170
Canopus	Carina	-0.9	650	Fomalhaut	Piscis Austrinus	1.3	27
Alpha Centauri	Centaurus	+0.1	4	Deneb	Cygnus	1.3	465
Vega	Lyra	0.1	23	Regulus	Leo	1.3	70
Capella	Auriga	0.2	42	Beta Crucis	Crux	1.5	465
Arcturus	Boötes	0.2	32	Eta Carinae	Carina	1-7	—
Rigel	Orion	0.3	545	Alpha-one Crucis	Crux	1.6	150
Procyon	Canis Minor	0.5	10	Castor	Gemini	1.6	44
Achernar	Eridanus	0.6	70	Gamma Crucis	Crux	1.6	—
Beta Centauri	Centaurus	0.9	130	Epsilon Canis Majoris	Canis Major	1.6	325
Altair	Aquila	0.9	18	Epsilon Ursae Majoris	Ursa Major	1.7	50
Betelgeuse	Orion	0.9	600	Bellatrix	Orion	1.7	215
Aldebaran	Taurus	1.1	54	Lambda Scorpii	Scorpius	1.7	205
Spica	Virgo	1.2	190	Epsilon Carinae	Carina	1.7	325
Pollux	Gemini	1.2	31	Mira	Cetus	2-10	250

minor planets called asteroids or planetoids, and an equally large number of comets.

The Sun

All the stars, including our Sun, are gigantic balls of superheated gas, kept hot by atomic reactions in their centers. In our Sun, this atomic reaction is hydrogen fusion: four hydrogen atoms are combined to form one helium atom. The temperature at the core of our Sun must be 20 million degrees Celsius, and the surface temperature averages 6,000° C, or about 11,000° F. The diameter of the Sun is 865,400 miles, and its surface area is approximately 12,000 times that of Earth. Compared with other stars, our Sun is just a bit below average in size and temperature, and is a yellow dwarf star. Its fuel supply (hydrogen) is estimated to be sufficient for another 5 billion years.

Our Sun is not motionless in space; in fact it has two proper motions. One is a seemingly straight-line motion in the direction of the constellation Hercules at the rate of about 12 miles per second. But since the Sun is a part of the Milky Way system and since the whole system rotates slowly around its own center, the Sun also moves at the rate of 175 miles per second as part of the rotating Milky Way system.

In addition to this motion, the Sun rotates on its axis. Observing the motion of sunspots (darkish areas that look like enormous whirling storms) and solar flares, which are usually associated with sunspots, has shown that the rotational period of the Sun is just short of 25 days. But this figure is valid for the Sun's equator only; the sections near the Sun's poles seem to have a rotational period of 34 days. Naturally, since the Sun generates its own heat and light, there is no temperature difference between poles and equator.

What we call the Sun's "surface" is technically known as the photosphere. Since the whole Sun is a ball of very hot gas, there is really no such thing as a surface; it is a question of visual impression. The next layer outside the photosphere is known as the chromosphere, which extends several thousand miles beyond the photosphere. It is in steady motion, and often enormous prominences can be seen to burst from it, extending as much as 100,000 miles into space. Outside the chromosphere is the corona. The corona consists of very tenuous gases (essentially hydrogen) and makes a magnificent sight when the Sun is eclipsed.

The mysterious behavior of solar flares may have been solved in 2000 by scientists from Montana State University and the Institute of Space and Astronautical Science in Japan. Solar flares and related outbursts called coronal mass ejections are immensely powerful, capable of hurling streams of plasma into space with the energy of a billion megatons of TNT. These solar belches occur when coiled magnetic fields on the Sun's surface release massive amounts of energy. Following such outbursts, scientists theorize, those magnetic fields still anchored on the Sun arch backward, forming new connections to the Sun and then snapping back into place like stretched rubber bands.

As the Sun ages, it gradually expands and heats. In 1994, American astrophysicists studying the eventual fate of the Sun estimated that its brilliancy will increase by 10% over the next 1.1 billion years or more and, in about 6.5 billion years hence, our aging star will have doubled its present luminosity. The extreme heat generated will cause a catastrophic greenhouse effect on Earth and our oceans will boil away, and life on Earth as we know it will end.

The Sun will eventually expand enormously to 166 times its present size and become over 2,000 times as bright. Eight billion years from now, the Sun's radius will engulf the planet Mercury and extend beyond the present orbit of Venus, causing the total destruction of Earth.

The Moon

Mercury and Venus do not have any moons. Therefore, Earth is closer to the Sun than any other planet orbited by a moon.

The next planet farther out, Mars, has two very small moons. Jupiter has four major moons and twelve minor ones. Saturn, the ringed planet, has 18 known moons (and possibly more), of which one (Titan) is larger than the planet Mercury. Uranus has at least 21 moons (four of them large) as well as rings, while Neptune has one large and seven small moons. Pluto has one moon, discovered in 1978. Some astronomers still consider Pluto to be a "runaway moon" of Neptune.

Our Moon, with a diameter of 2,160 miles, is one of the larger moons in our solar system and is especially large when compared with the planet that it orbits. In fact, the common center of gravity of the Earth–Moon system is only about 1,000 miles below Earth's surface. The closest the Moon can come to us (its perigee) is 221,463 miles; the farthest it can go away (its apogee) is 252,710 miles. The period of rotation of the Moon is equal to its period of revolution around Earth. Hence from Earth we can see only one hemisphere of the Moon. Both periods are 27 days, 7 hours, 43 minutes, and 11.47 seconds. But while the rotation of the Moon is constant, its velocity in its orbit is not, since it moves more slowly in apogee than in perigee. Consequently, some portions near the rim that are not normally visible will appear briefly. This phenomenon is called "libration," and by taking advantage of the librations, astronomers have succeeded in mapping approximately 59% of the lunar surface. The other 41% can never be seen from Earth but has been mapped by American and Russian Moon-orbiting spacecraft.

Though the Moon goes around Earth in the time mentioned, the interval from new moon to new moon is 29 days, 12 hours, 44 minutes, and 2.78 seconds. This delay of nearly two days is due to the fact that Earth is moving around the Sun, so that the Moon needs two extra days to reach a spot in its orbit where no part is illuminated by the Sun, as seen from Earth.

If the plane of Earth's orbit around the Sun (the ecliptic) and the plane of the Moon's orbit around Earth were the same, the Moon would be eclipsed by Earth every time it is full, and the Sun would be eclipsed by the Moon every time the Moon is "new" (it would be better to call it the "black moon" when it is in this position). But because the two orbits do not coincide, the Moon's shadow normally misses Earth

and Earth's shadow misses the Moon. The inclination of the two orbital planes to each other is 5°.

The tides are, of course, caused by the Moon with the help of the Sun, but in the open ocean they are surprisingly low, amounting to about one yard. The very high tides that can be observed near the shore in some places are due to funneling effects of the shorelines. At new moon and at full moon the tides raised by the Moon are reinforced by the Sun; these are the "spring tides." If the Sun's tidal power acts at right angles to that of the Moon (quarter moons) we get the low "neap tides."

The *Lunar Prospector* spacecraft, launched in January 1998, found that as much as three billion metric tons of water ice is hidden in the permanently shaded craters at the poles. The water probably came from interstellar comets that crashed into the Moon. *Lunar Prospector* also confirmed that the Moon has a small core, supporting the theory that the Moon was ripped away from the early Earth when an object the size of Mars collided with the Earth.

At the end of its mission, on July 31, 1999, the spacecraft was intentionally crashed into a permanently shadowed crater at the Moon's south pole in the hope of detecting a rising plume of water ice, but no cloud of water vapor molecules was observed by powerful Earth telescopes.

Earth

Earth, circling the Sun at an average distance of 93 million miles, is the fifth-largest planet and the third from the Sun. It orbits the Sun at a speed of 67,000 miles per hour, making one revolution in 365 days, 5 hours, 48 minutes, and 45.51 seconds. Earth completes one rotation on its axis every 23 hours, 56 minutes, and 4.09 seconds. Actually a bit pear-shaped rather than a true sphere, Earth has a diameter of 7,927 miles at the equator and a few miles less at the poles. It has an estimated mass of about 6.6 sextillion tons, with an average density of 5.52 grams per cubic centimeter. Earth's surface area encompasses 196,949,970 miles of which about three-fourths is water.

Origin of Earth

Earth, along with the other planets, is believed to have been born 4.5 billion years ago as a solidified cloud of dust and gases left over from the creation of the Sun. For perhaps 500 million years, the interior of Earth stayed solid and relatively cool, perhaps 2000° F. The main ingredients, according to the best available evidence, were iron and silicates, with small amounts of other elements, some of them radioactive. As millions of years passed, energy released by radioactive decay—mostly of uranium, thorium, and potassium—gradually heated Earth, melting some of its constituents. The iron melted before the silicates, and, being heavier, sank toward the center. This forced up the silicates that it found there. After many years, the iron reached the center, almost 4,000 miles deep, and began to accumulate. No eyes were around at that time to view the turmoil that must have taken place on the face of Earth—gigantic heaves and bubblings on the surface, exploding volcanoes, and flowing lava covering everything in sight. Finally, the iron in the center accumulated as the core. Around it, a thin but fairly stable crust of solid rock formed as Earth cooled. Depressions in the crust were natural basins in which water, rising from the interior of the planet through volcanoes and fissures, collected to form the oceans. Slowly, Earth acquired its present appearance.

Earth Today

As a result of radioactive heating over millions of years, Earth's molten *core* is probably fairly hot today, around 11,000° F. By comparison, lead melts at around 800° F. Most of Earth's 2,100-mile-thick core is liquid, but there is evidence that the center of the core is solid. The liquid outer portion, about 95% of the core, is constantly in motion, causing Earth to have a magnetic field that makes compass needles point north and south. The details are not known, but the latest evidence suggests that planets that have a magnetic field probably have a solid core or a partially liquid one.

Outside the core is Earth's *mantle,* 1,800 miles thick and extending nearly to the surface. The mantle is composed of heavy silicate rock, similar to that brought up by volcanic eruptions. It is somewhere between liquid and solid, slightly yielding, and therefore contributing to an active, moving Earth. Most of Earth's radioactive material is in the thin *crust* that covers the mantle, but some is in the mantle and continues to give off heat. The crust's thickness ranges from 5 to 25 miles.

Scientists recently discovered that Earth's core is not a perfect sphere. X ray–like images of inside Earth show that there are vast mountains six to seven miles high and deep valleys on the core. These features are in an upside-down relationship to Earth's surface.

In 1996, geophysicists discovered that Earth's solid-iron inner core rotates slightly faster than the rest of the planet and gains a quarter-turn every century. The finding may help explain how Earth's magnetic field periodically reverses its polarity.

Continental Drift

A great deal of recent evidence confirms the theory that the continents of Earth, made mostly of relatively light granite, float in the slightly yielding mantle, like logs in a pond. For many years it had been noticed that if North and South America could be pushed toward western and southern Europe and western Africa, they would fit like pieces in a jigsaw puzzle. Today, there is little question—the continents have drifted widely and continue to do so.

In 10 million years, the world as we know it may be unrecognizable, with California drifting out to sea, Florida joining South America, and Africa moving farther away from Europe and Asia.

Earth's Atmosphere

The thin blanket of atmosphere that envelops Earth extends several hundred miles into space. From sea level—the very bottom of the ocean of air—to a height of about 60 miles, the air in the atmosphere is made up of the same gases in the same ratio: about 78% nitrogen, 21% oxygen, and the remaining 1% being a mixture of argon, carbon dioxide, and tiny amounts of neon, helium, krypton, xenon, and other gases. The atmosphere becomes less dense with increasing altitude: more than three-fourths of Earth's huge envelope is concentrated in the first 5 to 10 miles above the surface. At sea level, a cubic foot of atmosphere weighs about an ounce and a quarter. The entire atmosphere weighs 5,700 trillion tons, and the force with which gravity holds it in place causes it to exert a pressure of nearly 15 pounds per square inch. Going out from Earth's surface, the atmosphere is divided into five regions. The regions, and the heights to which they extend, are: *troposphere,* 0 to 7 miles (at middle latitudes); *stratosphere,* 7 to 30 miles; *mesosphere,* 30 to 50 miles; *thermosphere,* 50 to 400 miles; and *exosphere,* above 400 miles. The boundaries between each of the regions are known respectively as the *tropopause, stratopause, mesopause,* and *thermopause.* Alternative terms often used for the layers above the troposphere are *ozonosphere* (for stratosphere) and *ionosphere* for the remaining upper layers.

The Seasons

Seasons are caused by the 23.4-degree tilt of Earth's axis, which alternately turns the North and South Poles toward the Sun. Times when the Sun's apparent path crosses the equator are known as *equinoxes.* Times when the Sun's apparent path is at the greatest distance from the equator are known as *solstices.* The lengths of the days are most extreme at each solstice. If Earth's axis were perpendicular to the plane of Earth's orbit around the Sun, there would be no seasons, and the days always would be equal in length. Since Earth's axis is at an angle, the Sun strikes Earth directly at the equator only twice a year: in March (vernal equinox) and September (autumnal equinox). In the Northern Hemisphere, spring begins at the vernal equinox, summer at the summer solstice, fall at the autumnal equinox, and winter at the winter solstice. The situation is reversed in the Southern Hemisphere.

Mercury

Mercury is the planet nearest the Sun. Appropriately named for the wing-footed Roman messenger of the gods, Mercury whizzes around the Sun at a speed of 30 miles per second, completing one circuit in 88 days. The days and nights are long on Mercury. It takes 59 Earth days for Mercury to make a single rotation. It spins at a rate of about 6 miles (about 10 kilometers) per hour, measured at the equator, as compared to Earth's spin of about 1,000 miles (about 1,600 kilometers) per hour at the equator.

The photographs *Mariner 10* (1974–1975) radioed back to Earth revealed an ancient, heavily cratered surface on Mercury, closely resembling our own Moon. The pictures showed huge cliffs, or scarps, crisscrossing the planet. These apparently were created when Mercury's interior cooled and shrank, compressing the planet's crust. The cliffs are as high as 1.2 miles (two kilometers) and as long as 932 miles (1,500 kilometers). Another unique feature is the Caloris Basin, a large impact crater about 808 miles (1,300 kilometers) in diameter.

Mercury, like Earth, appears to have a crust of light silicate rock. Scientists believe it has a heavy iron-rich core that makes up about half of its volume. Instruments onboard *Mariner 10* discovered that the planet has a weak magnetic field and a trace of atmosphere—a trillionth the density of Earth's and composed chiefly of argon, neon, and helium. The spacecraft reported temperatures ranging from 950° F (510° C) on Mercury's sunlit side to –346° F (–210° C) on the dark side. Mercury literally bakes in daylight and freezes at night.

Until the *Mariner 10* probe, little was known about the planet. Even the best telescopic views from Earth showed Mercury as an indistinct object

Largest Channel in Solar System. *Magellan* took the above image of the largest known channel on Venus. At 4,200 miles (6,800 kilometers) long and an average of 1.1 miles (1.8 kilometers) wide, it is longer than the Nile River, Earth's longest river, making it the longest known channel in the solar system. The channel was originally discovered by the Soviet *Venery 15* and *16* spacecraft orbiters. *Source: NASA.*

lacking any surface detail. The planet is so close to the Sun that it is usually lost in the Sun's glare.

Radar images taken by astronomers at Jet Propulsion Laboratories and California Institute of Technology during the summer of 1991 suggest that the polar regions of Mercury may be covered with patches of water ice. Although this seems impossible due to the planet's sizzling heat, the polar regions receive very little sunlight and may get as cold as −235° F (−148° C). The radar images showed bright patterns at the poles that are characteristic of ice reflecting radar signals. Other explanations may be offered for this unexpected discovery.

In March 2004, NASA plans to launch a spacecraft, *Messenger*, that will orbit Mercury in Sept. 2009. It will map the planet for one Earth year and search for water, a magnetic field, and other phenomena.

Mercury is a naked-eye object at morning or evening twilight when it is at greatest elongation.

Venus

Although Venus is Earth's closest neighbor, very little is known about the planet because it is permanently covered by thick clouds. In 1962, Soviet and American space probes, coupled with Earth-based radar and infrared spectroscopy, began slowly unraveling some of the mystery surrounding Venus. Twenty-eight years later, the *Magellan* spacecraft, sent by the United States, arrived at Venus in Aug. 1990 and began radar-mapping the planet's surface in greater detail.

According to the latest results, Venus's atmosphere exerts a pressure at the surface 94.5 times greater than Earth's. Walking on Venus would be as difficult as walking a half-mile beneath the ocean. Because of a thick blanket of carbon dioxide, a "greenhouse effect" exists on Venus. Venus intercepts twice as much of the Sun's light as does Earth. The light enters freely through the carbon dioxide gas and is changed to heat radiation in molecular collisions. But carbon dioxide prevents the heat from escaping. Consequently, the temperature of the surface of Venus is over 800° F (427° C), hot enough to melt lead.

The atmospheric composition of Venus is about 96% carbon dioxide, 4% nitrogen, and minor amounts of water, oxygen, and sulfur compounds. There are at least four distinct cloud and haze layers that exist at different altitudes above the planet's surface. The haze layers contain small aerosol particles, possibly droplets of sulfuric acid. A concentration of sulfur dioxide above the cloud tops has been observed to be decreasing since 1978. The source of sulfur dioxide at this altitude is unknown; it may be injected by volcanic explosions or atmospheric overturning.

Measurements of the Venusian atmosphere and its cloud patterns reveal nearly constant high-speed zonal winds, about 220 miles per hour (100 meters per second) at the equator. The winds decrease toward the poles so that the atmosphere at cloud-top level rotates almost like a solid body. The wind speeds at the equator correspond to Venus's rotation period of four to five days at most latitudes. The circulation is always in the same direction—east to west—as Venus's slow retrograde motion. Earth's winds blow from west to east, the same direction as its rotation.

Venus is quite round, very different from the other planets and from the Moon. Venus has neither polar flattening nor an equatorial bulge. The diameter of Venus is 7,519 miles (12,100 kilometers). Venus has a retrograde axial rotation period of 243.1 Earth days. The surface atmospheric pressure is 1,396 pounds per square inch (95 Earth atmospheres). The planet's mean distance from the Sun is 67.2 million miles (108.2 million kilometers). The period of its revolution around the Sun is 224.7 days.

The highest point on Venus is the summit of Maxwell Montes, 6.71 miles (10.8 kilometers) above the mean level, more than a mile higher than Mount Everest. There is some evidence that this huge mountain is an active volcano. The lowest point is in the rift valley, Diana Chasma, 1.8 miles (2.9 kilometers) below the mean level. This point is about one-fifth the greatest depth on Earth in the Marianas Trench.

Venus has an extreme lowland basin, Atalanta Planitia, which is about the size of Earth's North Atlantic Ocean basin. The smooth surface of the Atalanta Planitia resembles the mare basins of the Moon.

There are only two highland or continental masses on Venus: Ishtar Terra and Aphrodite Terra. Ishtar Terra is 6.8 miles (11 kilometers) at its highest points (the highest peaks on Venus) and those of Aphrodite Terra rise to about 3.10 miles (5 kilometers) above the planet. Ishtar Terra is about the size of the continental United States and Aphrodite Terra is about the size of Africa.

The unmanned NASA spacecraft *Magellan* was launched on May 4, 1989, from the shuttle *Atlantis* and arrived at Venus Aug. 10, 1990, to map most of the planet. Despite some problems with its radio transmissions, the results of the radar mapping delighted scientists and provided them with the sharpest images ever taken of the planet's surface. Images taken from *Magellan* show ten times more detail than ever seen before.

The radar images provided scientists with compelling evidence that the planet has been dominated by volcanism on a global scale. The photos also showed that the planet's second-highest mountain, Maat Mons, rising five miles (eight kilometers) above the Venusian plains, appears to be covered with fresh lava and is possibly an active volcano.

Magellan discovered the longest known channel in the solar system on Venus. It is 4,200 miles (6,800 kilometers) long and averages slightly over a mile (1.8 kilometers) wide. Its origin is puzzling to scientists because high-temperature lava is unlikely to have caused such a long-distance flow on the surface, and there are no known substances that could remain liquid long enough under the planet's atmospheric pressure and temperature to have carved out this snakelike feature. The channel is slightly longer than the Nile River, the longest river on Earth. *Magellan* ended its radar and emissions mapping in Sept. 1992 after covering 98% of the planet's surface.

Venus is the brightest of all the planets and is often visible in the morning or evening, when it is frequently referred to as the Morning Star or Evening Star. At its brightest, it can sometimes be seen in full daylight with the naked eye, if one knows where to look.

Mars

Mars, on the other side of Earth from Venus, is Venus's direct opposite in terms of physical proper-ties. Its atmosphere is cold, thin, and transparent, and readily permits observation of the planet's features. We know more about Mars than any other planet except Earth. Mars is a forbidding, rugged planet with huge volcanoes and deep chasms. The largest volcano, Olympus Mons (Olympic Mountain) rises 78,000 feet above the surface, higher than Mount Everest. The plains of Mars are pockmarked by the hits of thousands of meteors over the years.

Until the arrival of *Mars Pathfinder* and *Mars Global Surveyor* in 1997, most of our information about Mars came from the *Mariner* and *Viking* spacecrafts. *Mariner 9* orbited the planet in 1971 and photographed 100% of the planet, uncovering spectacular geological formations, including a Martian "Grand Canyon" that dwarfs the one on Earth. Called Valles Marineris (Mariner Valley), it stretches more than 3,000 miles along the equatorial region of Mars and is over 2.5 miles (4 kilometers) deep in places and 50–62 miles (80 to 100 kilometers) wide. The spacecraft's cameras also recorded what appeared to be dried riverbeds, suggesting the one-time presence of water on the planet. The latter idea gave encouragement to scientists looking for life on Mars, for where there is water, there may be life. However, to date, no evidence of life has been found. Temperatures range from 80° F at the equator during the day to –199° F at the poles at night.

Mars rotates upon its axis in nearly the same period as Earth—24 hours, 37 minutes—so that a Mars day is almost identical to an Earth day. Mars takes 687 days to make one trip around the Sun. Because of its eccentric orbit, Mars's distance from the Sun can vary by about 36 million miles. Its distance from Earth can vary by as much as 200 million miles. The atmosphere of Mars is much thinner than Earth's; atmospheric pressure is about 1% that of our planet. Its gravity is one-third of Earth's. Major constituents are carbon dioxide and nitrogen. Water vapor and oxygen are minor constituents. Mars's polar caps, composed mostly of frozen carbon dioxide (dry ice), recede and advance according to the Martian seasons.

Mars has four seasons like Earth, but they are much longer. For example, in the northern hemisphere, the Martian spring is 198 days, and the winter season lasts 158 days.

The *Mars Pathfinder* lander and its rover, *Sojourner*, set down on the edge of a boulder-strewn outflow channel known as *Ares Vallis* on July 4, 1997, and provided scientists with a wealth of information on the rocks, soils, and atmosphere of Mars. The lander sent back the first live pictures of the planet's topography, and its tiny rover explored a variety of rocks and analyzed their mineral composition with its cameras and on-board X-ray spectrometer.

Analysis of the reddish surface soil pointed to the presence of oxidized iron, indicating that the planet's surface is rusting. *Sojourner* samples of soil taken from several sites found their composition similar to those analyzed by the two *Viking* landers in 1976, indicating that the Martian winds have distributed the soil evenly over the planet.

Scientists were surprised to learn how rapidly the Martian temperature fluctuates due to atmospheric turbulence. It can change by as much as 30°–40° F (17°–22° C) in a matter of minutes, possibly due to strong, gusty winds bringing warm air from one region or cold air from another.

Pictures and subsequent data from *Pathfinder* give the strongest evidence that Mars had an abundance of water millions of years ago. Scientists have inferred from the variety of rocks and sediments found in the *Ares* basin that the spacecraft landed in a channel that was once awash with torrential floods greater than any known on Earth. The diversity of rocks deposited there suggests their different origins, and it appears that they were washed down from the highlands at a time when great floods moved over the surface of Mars.

Before *Pathfinder*, knowledge of the kinds of rocks present on Mars was based mostly on the Martian meteorites found on Earth. Chemical analysis of the Martian rocks and soil found at *Ares Vallis* confirmed that these rocks have compositions distinct from those of the Martian meteorites found on Earth.

In its three months of operation, the mission returned more than 16,000 images of the Martian landscape from the lander's camera and 550 images from the rover.

The *Sojourner* rover traveled a total of about 328 feet (100 meters), performed more than 16 chemical analyses of rocks and soil, and explored 820 square feet (250 square meters) of the planet's surface. Communications were lost with the lander on Sept. 27, 1997, after 83 days of relaying data.

NASA launched the *Mars Global Surveyor* spacecraft on Nov. 7, 1996, to provide detailed maps of the planet's surface, its distribution of minerals, and to monitor its weather. The spacecraft entered Mars's orbit on Sept. 11, 1997, and began mapping operations in mid-March 1999.

Surveyor discovered the first clear evidence of an ancient hydrothermal system near the equator. This implies that water was stable at or near the surface and that a thicker atmosphere existed in Mars's early history.

Most surprising to mission scientists was finding that the planet's northern hemisphere was exceptionally flat, with slopes and surface roughness increasing towards the equator.

Surveyor's three-dimensional views of the planet's northern polar ice cap showed often striking canyons and spiral troughs in the water and carbon dioxide ice that can reach depths as great as 3,600 feet below the surface. Its data also showed that large areas of the ice cap were extremely smooth, with elevations varying only a few feet over many miles.

In 1999, the *Mars Global Surveyor* discovered magnetic stripes about 100 miles (160 kilometers) wide, the remnants of the planet's ancient magnetism, running east and west on the surface of Mars. At their longest, the band-patterns of magnetic fields extend as far as 1,240 miles (1,996 kilometers) along the surface.

NASA's recent Mars exploration program suffered a setback with the loss of the *Climate Orbiter* as it entered the Martian atmosphere in Sept. 1999. The following December scientists also failed to establish contact with the *Polar Lander* after it reached Mars.

In June 2000, NASA announced that the *Mars Global Surveyor* had observed features that looked like gullies carved out by flowing water and deposits of soil and rocks that were transported by the flow. Because gullies had never been seen before on Mars, the *Surveyor* images suggest that there may be current sources of liquid water at or near the surface.

Mars was named for the Roman god of war, because when seen from Earth its distinct red color reminded the ancient people of blood. We know now that the reddish hue reflects the oxidized (rusted) iron in the surface material.

The Martian Moons

Mars has two very small elliptical-shaped moons, Deimos and Phobos—the Greek names for the companions of the god Mars: Deimos (Terror) and Phobos (Fear). They were discovered in Aug. 1877 by the American astronomer Asaph Hall (1829–1907) of the U.S. Naval Observatory in Washington, D.C.

The inner satellite, Phobos, is 16.78 miles (27 kilometers) long, and it revolves around the planet in 7.6 hours. The outer moon, Deimos, is 9.32 miles (15 kilometers) long, and it circles the planet in 30.35 hours. The short orbital period of Phobos means that the satellite travels around Mars three times in a Martian day.

Recent studies of Phobos indicate that its orbit is slowly decreasing downward; in about 40 million years, it will crash into the planet's surface.

Meteorites from Mars

Fourteen meteorites, almost certainly from Mars, have been discovered as of Feb. 2000. They are known as SNCs[1] (named for the towns where they were found: Shergotty, India, in 1865; Nakhla, Egypt, in 1911; and Chassigny, France, in 1815). This hypothesis was based largely on the composition of noble gases (particularly argon and ·xenon) trapped in the meteorites, and the shergottites in particular, which resemble measurements of the Martian atmosphere made by the *Viking* spacecraft. Major element compositions of the SNCs are also similar to Martian soil analyses made by *Viking*.

The relatively young isotopic ages of the SNC meteorites (1.3 billion years or less) suggest that Mars has been volcanically active during its recent past.

In 1991, a ninth meteorite, LEW 88516, was identified as having reached Earth from Mars some 180 million years ago. It was discovered in Dec. 1988 near Lewis Cliff in Antarctica. The meteorite is very small with a dark pitted surface and weighs less than half an ounce (13.2 grams).

A 4-pound, 7-ounce (1.9-kilogram) meteorite, ALH 84001, found in the Allen Hills of Antarctica in 1984 was reclassified in 1993 as coming from the Red Planet, making it the tenth meteorite known to have originated from Mars. In 1996, NASA announced that meteorite ALH 84001 contained fossils of ancient Martian life forms.

A 40-pound meteorite that crashed to Earth in Nigeria in 1962 has been classified as coming from Mars. It was named Zagami for the region in which it was found.

A 0.38-ounce (12-gram) meteorite (QUE 94201) found in Antarctica in 1995 became the 12th meteorite identified as having a Martian origin.

In 1997, the thirteenth known Martian meteorite, Dar al Gani 476, a 4.8-pound (2.2-kilogram) meteorite, was found in the Sahara Desert.

---

1. Pronounced "snick."

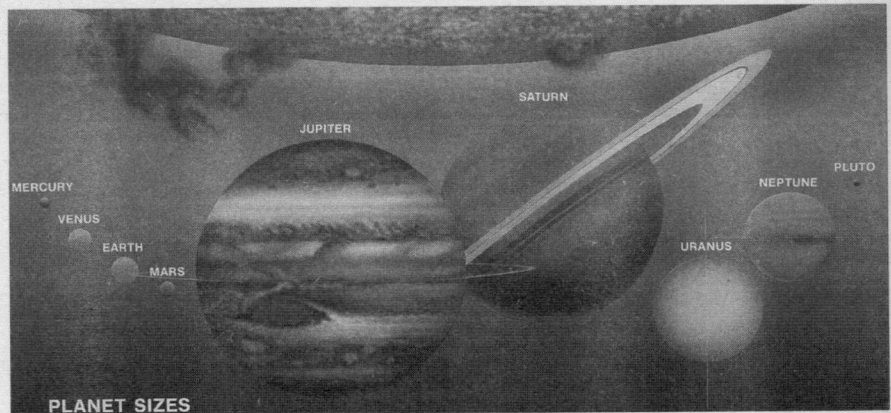

PLANET SIZES. Shown from left to right: Mercury, Venus, Earth, Mars, Jupiter, Saturn, Uranus, Neptune, and Pluto. *Copyright 1990 Hansen Planetarium, Salt Lake City, Utah. Reproduced with permission.*

Basic Planetary Data

	Mercury	Venus	Earth	Mars	Jupiter
Mean distance from Sun (millions of kilometers)	57.9	108.2	149.6	227.9	778.3
Mean distance from Sun (millions of miles)	36.0	67.24	92.9	141.71	483.88
Period of revolution	88 days	224.7 days	365.2 days	687 days	11.86 yrs
Rotation period	59 days	243 days retrograde	23 hr 56 min 4 sec	24 hr 37 min	9 hr 55 min 30 sec
Inclination of axis	Near 0°	3°	23°27′	25° 12′	3° 5′
Inclination of orbit to ecliptic	7°	3.4°	0°	1.9°	1.3°
Eccentricity of orbit	.206	.007	.017	.093	.048
Equatorial diameter (kilometers)	4,880	12,100	12,756	6,794	142,800
(miles)	3,032.4	7,519	7,926.2	4,194	88,736
Atmosphere (main components)	Virtually none	Carbon dioxide	Nitrogen oxygen	Carbon dioxide	Hydrogen helium
Satellites	0	0	1	2	17[1]
Rings	0	0	0	0	1

	Saturn	Uranus	Neptune	Pluto
Mean distance from Sun (millions of kilometers)	1,427	2,870	4,497	5,900
Mean distance from Sun (millions of miles)	887.14	1,783.98	2,796.46	3,666
Period of revolution	29.46 yrs	84 yrs	165 yrs	248 yrs
Rotation period	10 hr 40 min 24 sec	16.8 hr(?) retrograde	16 hr 11 min(?)	6 days 9 hr 18 mins retrograde
Inclination of axis	26°44′	97°55′	28°48′	60° (?)
Inclination of orbit to ecliptic	2.5°	0.8°	1.8°	17.2°
Eccentricity of orbit	.056	.047	.009	.254
Equatorial diameter (kilometers)	120,660	51,810	49,528	2,290 (?)
(miles)	74,978	32,193	30,775	1,423 (?)
Atmosphere (main components)	Hydrogen helium	Helium hydrogen methane	Hydrogen helium methane	None detected
Satellites	18[2]	21	8	1
Rings	1,000 (?)	11	4	?

1. A possible 17th moon, tentatively designated S/1999 J1 was announced in July 2000. 2. Possible additional small moons may orbit Saturn but they have not been confirmed yet. Source: Basic NASA data and other sources.

Two rock speciments weighing 8.6 ounces (245.4 grams) and 16 ounces (452.6 grams) that were found in the Mojave Desert about 20 years ago were classified in Feb. 2000 as the fourteenth Mars meteorite. The rocks are known as the Los Angeles meteorites.

Jupiter

Jupiter is the largest planet in the solar system—a gaseous world as large as 1,300 Earths. Its equatorial diameter is 88,736 miles (142,800 kilometers), while from pole to pole, Jupiter measures only 84,201 miles (133,500 kilometers). For comparison, the diameter of Earth is 7,926.2 miles (12,756 kilometers). The massive planet rotates at a dizzying speed—once every 9 hours and 55 minutes. It takes Jupiter almost 12 Earth years to complete a journey around the Sun.

The giant planet appears as a banded disk of turbulent clouds with all of its stripes running parallel to its bulging equator. Large dusky gray regions surround each pole. Darker gray or brown stripes called belts intermingle with lighter, yellow-white stripes called zones. The belts are regions of descending air masses and the zones are rising cloudy air masses. The strongest winds—up to 250 miles (400 kilometers) per hour—are found at boundaries between the belts and zones.

This uniquely colorful atmosphere is mainly 89% molecular hydrogen and 11% helium. It contains small amounts of methane, ammonia, ethane, and water.

Cloud-type lightning bolts similar to those on Earth have been found in the Jovian atmosphere. At the polar regions, auroras have been observed. A very thin ring of material less than 0.6 mile (one kilometer) in thickness and about 4,000 miles (6,000 kilometers) in radial extent has been observed circling the planet about 35,000 miles (55,000 kilometers) above the cloud tops.

The most prominent feature on Jupiter is its "Great Red Spot," an oval larger than the planet Earth. It is a tremendous atmospheric storm that rotates counterclockwise with one revolution every six days at the outer edge, while at the center almost no motion can be seen. The spot is about 16,000 miles (25,000 kilometers) on its long axis, and would cover three Earths. The outer rim shows streamline shapes of 225-mile (360-kilometer) winds.

Jupiter is circled by faint rings. They are very tenuous and contain many microscopic-sized particles. The rings are formed by dust kicked up as interplanetary meteoroids smash into the planet's four small inner moons.

Jupiter emits 67% more heat than it absorbs from the Sun. This heat is thought to have been accumulated during the planet's formation several billion years ago.

Twenty-one fragments of comet Shoemaker-Levy 9 bombarded the cloud-covered surface of Jupiter, July 16–22, 1994. It was the most violent event in the recorded history of our solar system. The cometary explosions caused towering plumes of debris and hot gas to rise from the darkened impact sites.

On Dec. 7, 1995, the *Galileo* spacecraft released a probe into Jupiter's atmosphere to study the planet's physical and chemical properties. The probe lasted 57 minutes and early results indicated a lower abundance of water than was expected.

Galileo data has shown that Jupiter has both wet and dry regions, just as Earth has tropics and deserts. This could explain why the probe found less water than anticipated. These dry spots cover less than 1% of the Jovian atmosphere.

Jovian Moons

The four great moons of Jupiter were discovered by Galileo Galilei (1564–1642) in Jan. 1610, and are called the Galilean satellites after their discoverer. Their names are Io, Europa, Ganymede, and Callisto. Like our Moon, the satellites always keep the same face turned toward the planet they circle. Jupiter has 17 known satellites.

On July 21, 2000, astronomers with the Spacewatch Project at the University of Arizona in Tucson and the Minor Planet Center at the Astrophysical Observatory in Massachusetts announced their discovery of a 17th moon designated S/1999 J1. The newly found satellite is perhaps 3 miles (0.048 kilometers) across and makes an eccentric orbit around Jupiter at an average distance of 15 million miles (24 million kilometers) every two years.

Jupiter's four largest moons all have thin atmospheres. A carbon dioxide atmosphere envelopes Callisto; Europa and Ganymede each have thin oxygen atmospheres; and Io's contains sulfur dioxide.

Ganymede

Ganymede, 3,275 miles (5,270 kilometers) in diameter, is Jupiter's largest moon, and it is also the largest satellite in the solar system. Ganymede is about one and one-half times the size of our Moon. It is heavily cratered and probably has the greatest variety of geologic process recorded on its surface. Ganymede is half water and half rock, resulting in a density about two-thirds that of Europa, an ice-coated satellite.

The first close-up photos of Ganymede taken by the *Galileo* spacecraft, during its June 1996 flyby, revealed a surface pockmarked with ancient craters and a landscape wrinkled and torn by the same forces that make mountains and move continents on Earth. *Galileo*'s findings also indicated that Ganymede is enveloped in its own magnetic field, possibly created by a molten iron core or even a thin layer of conducting salty water underneath its icy crust.

Ganymede is the first known moon with its own magnetosphere.

Europa

Europa, the brightest of Jupiter's satellites, is about 1,950 miles (3,160 kilometers) in diameter or about the size of Earth's Moon. Its density is about three times that of water. The moon is covered with a thin ice crust and is crisscrossed with an amazingly complex network of ridges. Some of the fractures on its crust are more than 1,850 miles (3,000 kilometers) long. Very few impact craters are visible on the surface.

Europea is the smoothest object in the solar system. Its mostly flat surface doesn't exceed 0.62 miles (1 kilometer) in height.

Galileo spacecraft photos taken at its closest flyby on Feb. 20, 1997, at a distance of 363 miles (586 kilometers), showed the existence of ice flows on the surface that strongly suggest that the moon has a hidden subsurface ocean of water or ice-slush. The photos revealed chunky ice rafts that appear to be floating, comparable to icebergs on Earth. The presence of water and enough heat to keep water in a

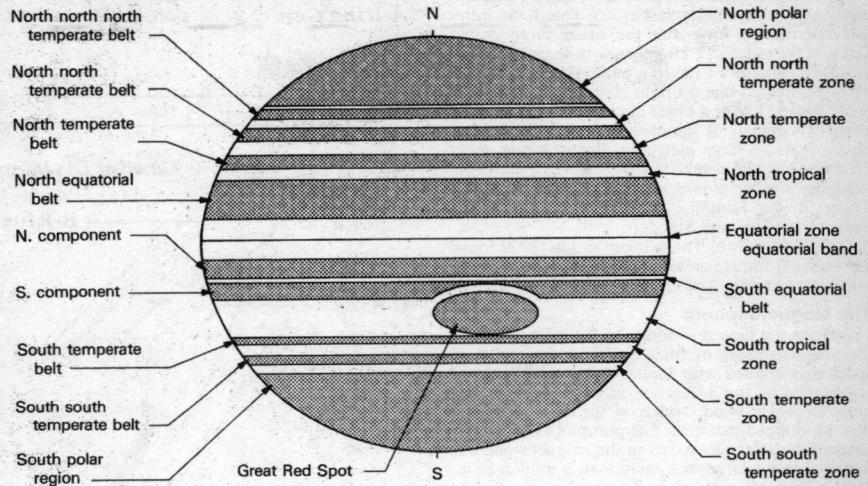

Schematic diagram of Jupiter's major features. *Source:* NASA.

liquid state on Europa enhances the possibility that it could provide an environment for some form of extraterrestrial ocean life.

New evidence that a liquid ocean lies beneath Europa's crust was found when *Galileo* visited the moon in Jan. 2000. The spacecraft detected changes in Europa's magnetic field that are best explained by an electrically conducting (salty) body of water.

Definitive answers may not be possible for another decade, however. NASA scientists had proposed sending a spacecraft called the *Europa Ice Clipper* to the moon in 2001, but the mission was scrapped due to lack of funding. The *Europa Orbiter* mission, scheduled for launch in 2004, is currently under consideration. This spacecraft would include instruments such as an ice-penetrating radar that could see through the ice to any ocean below.

Callisto

Callisto, 2,400 miles (4,800 kilometers) in diameter, is the outermost and, apparently, the least geologically active of Jupiter's four major satellites. Its density is less than twice that of water. Callisto has the oldest body and most cratered face of any body yet observed in the solar system. Like Ganymede, it seems to have a rocky core surrounded by ice. Unlike Ganymede, the surface of Callisto is completely covered with scars left by tens of thousands of meteoric impacts. Scientist estimate that it would take several billion years to accumulate the number of craters found there. So Callisto is believed to be inactive for at least that long. Although it is the darkest of the Galilean satellites, it is twice as bright as Earth's Moon.

Data from the *Galileo* spacecraft in 1998 suggest that Callisto has a salty ocean beneath its crust, similar to Europa's.

Io

Io, 2,262 miles (3,640 kilometers) in diameter, is the most spectacular of the Galilean moons. Its bril-

liant colors of red, orange, and yellow set it apart from any other moon or planet. Active volcanoes have been detected on Io, with some plumes extending up to 200 miles (320 kilometers) above the surface. The relative smoothness of Io's surface and its volcanic activity suggest that it has the youngest surface of Jupiter's moons. Its surface is composed of large amounts of sulfur and sulfur-dioxide frost, which account for the primarily yellow-orange surface color.

The volcanoes seem to eject a sufficient amount of sulfur dioxide to form a doughnut-shaped ring (torus) of ionized sulfur and oxygen atoms around Jupiter near Io's orbit. Close-up views taken in 1999 and 2000 showed that Io had more than 100 erupting volcanoes, gigantic lava flows and lava lakes, and towering, collapsing mountains. The eruptions of Loki, the most powerful volcano in the solar system, can be seen by Earth telescopes.

Observations by *Galileo* during 1998 revealed dozens of volcanic vents on Io where lava is hotter than any surface temperatures recorded on any planetary body in our solar system. At one such volcanic vent, known as Pillan Patera, two of the spacecraft's instruments indicated that the lava temperature may have been 3,140° F.

In 1996, the *Galileo* spacecraft detected a huge iron core within Io that occupies half the moon's diameter. *Galileo* also discovered evidence that Io has its own magnetic field.

Amalthea

Amalthea, Jupiter's innermost satellite, was discovered in 1892. It is so small—165 miles (265 kilometers) long and 90 miles (150 kilometers) wide—that it is extremely difficult to observe from Earth. Amalthea is an elongated, irregularly shaped satellite of reddish color. It orbits the planet every 12 hours and is in synchronous rotation, with its long axis always oriented toward Jupiter.

Amalthea is heavily cratered, with two that are especially large. The largest crater, Pan, is 56 miles (90 kilometers) long and the other large crater, Gaea, is 47 miles (75 kilometers) in length.

Galileo images of the tiny moon taken at the end of 1999 showed that a bright surface feature, previously named Ida, is a linear streak of bright material about 31 miles (50 kilometers) long. The images also revealed a large meteoroid impact crater about 25 miles (40 kilometers) across.

Jupiter's other moons are named Adrasta, Metis, Thebe, Leda, Himalia, Lysithea, Elara, Ananke, Carne, Pasiphae, and Sinope.

Galileo images of Thebe taken in Jan. 2000 found a prominent impact crater that is about 25 miles (40 kilometers) across and provisionally named Zethus.

The Magnetosphere

Perhaps the largest structure in the solar system is the magnetosphere of Jupiter. This is the region of space that is filled with Jupiter's magnetic field and is bounded by the interaction of that magnetic field with the solar wind, which is the Sun's outward flow of charged particles. The plasma of electrically charged particles that exists in the magnetosphere is flattened into a large disk more than 3 million miles (4.8 million kilometers) in diameter, is coupled to the magnetic field, and rotates around Jupiter. The Galilean satellites are located in the inner regions of the magnetosphere and are subjected to intense radiation bombardment.

The intense radiation field that surrounds Jupiter is fatal to humans. If astronauts were one day able to approach the planet as close as the *Voyager 1* spacecraft did, they would receive a dose of 400,000 rads, or roughly 1,000 times the lethal dose for humans.

Even when nearest Earth, Jupiter is still almost 400 million miles away. However, because of its size, it may rival Venus in brilliance when near. Jupiter's four large moons may be seen through field glasses, moving rapidly around Jupiter and changing their positions from night to night.

Saturn

Saturn, the second-largest planet in the solar system, is the least dense. Its mass is 95 times the mass of Earth and its density is 0.70 gram per cubic centimeter, so that it would float in an ocean if there were one big enough to hold it.

Saturn radiates about 80% more energy than it receives from the Sun. However, the excess thermal energy cannot be primarily attributed to Saturn's primordial heat loss, as is speculated for Jupiter.

Saturn's diameter is 74,978 miles (120,660 kilometers) but 10% less at the poles, a consequence of its rapid rotation. Its axis of rotation is tilted by 27 degrees and the length of its day is 10 hours, 39 minutes, and 24 seconds.

Saturn is composed primarily of liquid metallic hydrogen (about 80%) and the second most common element is believed to be helium.

Saturn's atmospheric appearance is very similar to Jupiter's with dark and light cloud markings and swirls, eddies, and curling ribbons; the belts and zones are more numerous and a thick haze mutes the markings. Temperatures recorded by *Voyager II* ranged from 82° K (–312° F) to 143° K (–202° F).

NASA illustration of the divisions in Saturn's ring system.

Winds blow at extremely high speeds on Saturn. Near the equator, the *Voyagers* measured winds of about 1,100 miles per hour (500 meters per second). The winds blow primarily in an eastward direction.

Saturn's Rings

Saturn's spectacular ring system is unique in the solar system, with uncountable billions of tiny particles of water ice (with traces of other material) in orbit around the planet. The ring particles range in size from smaller than grains of sugar to as large as a house. The main rings stretch out from about 4,350 miles (7,000 kilometers) to above the atmosphere of the planet out to the F ring, a total span of 45,984 miles (74,000 kilometers). Saturn's rings can be likened to a phonograph, rings within rings numbering in the hundreds, and spokes in the B rings, and shepherding satellites controlling the F ring.

The main rings are called the A, B, and C rings moving from outside to inside. The gap between the A and B rings is called Cassini's Division and is named for the Italian-French astronomer, Gian Domenico Cassini, who discovered four of Saturn's major moons and the dark, narrow gap, Cassini's Division, splitting the planet's rings.

Saturn's magnetic field has well-defined north and south magnetic poles, and is aligned with Saturn's axis of rotation to within one degree.

Saturn's Moons

Saturn has 18 known moons. There are several possible smaller moons around Saturn but they haven't been confirmed. The five largest moons—Tethys, Dione, Rhea, Titan, and Iapetus—range from 650 to 3,200 miles (1,060 to 5,150 kilometers) in diameter. The planet's outstanding satellite is

Titan, first discovered by the Dutch astronomer Christiaan Huygens in 1656.

Titan

Titan is remarkable because it is the only known moon in the solar system that has a substantial atmosphere—largely nitrogen with a minor amount of methane and a rich variety of other hydrocarbons. Its surface is completely hidden from view (except at infrared and radio wavelengths) by a dense, hazy atmosphere.

The diameter of Titan is 3,200 miles (5,150 kilometers), and it is the second-largest satellite in the solar system after Jupiter's Ganymede. Titan is larger than the planet Mercury.

Titan's surface temperature is about −175° C (−280° F), and its surface pressure is about 50% greater than the surface pressure of Earth. In 1990, radio telescope data showed that Titan reflects and scatters radio waves, suggesting that the satellite has a solid surface, possibly with small hydrocarbon lakes or ponds.

Infrared images of Titan taken in late 1999 by the W. M. Keck II telescope in Hawaii also revealed features that could be frozen land masses separated by frigid hydrocarbon seas and lakes. Other features might be highlands, and one dark area appeared to be a large impact crater or basin.

NASA plans to send a scientific probe to the surface of Titan in the summer of 2004 as part of its *Cassini* mission. The probe will be provided by the European Space Agency (ESA).

Other Notable Saturnian Moons

The other four largest moons of Saturn are Tethys, Dione, Rhea, and Iapetus.

Tethys is 650 miles (1,060 kilometers) in diameter. Its surface is heavily cratered, and it has a huge, globe-girdling canyon, Ithaca Chasma. Part of the canyon stretches over three-quarters of the satellite's surface. Ithaca Chasma is about 1,550 miles (2,500 kilometers) long. It has an average width of about 62 miles (100 kilometers) and a depth of 1.8 to 3.1 miles (3 to 5 kilometers).

Tethys also has a huge impact crater named Odysseus 244 miles, (4,400 kilometers) in diameter, or more than one-third of the moon's diameter.

Dione is slightly larger than Tethys, 696 miles (1,120 kilometers) in diameter, and is more than half composed of water ice. It has bright, wispy markings resembling thin veils covering its features.

Rhea, the largest of the inner satellites, is 951 miles (1,530 kilometers) in diameter. It is composed mainly of water ice, causing its reflective surface to present an almost uniform white appearance.

Iapetus is the outermost of Saturn's icy satellites. Its appearance is unique because it has one dark and one bright hemisphere. The origin of the black coating of its dark face is unknown. Iapetus has a diameter of 907 miles (1,460 kilometers).

Other notable moons of Saturn are Mimas, Enceladus, Hyperion, Phoebe, and Pan.

Mimas is small, only 244 miles (329 kilometers) in diameter. It has a huge impact crater, Herschel, nearly one-third of its diameter. The crater is about 81 miles (130 kilometers) wide and its icy peak rises almost 6.2 miles (10 kilometers) above the floor.

Mimas is believed to be composed mainly of water and ice and to contain between 20% and 50% rock.

Enceladus is remarkable in that its surface shows signs of extensive and recent geological activity. There may be active water volcanism. The surface is extremely bright, reflecting more than 90% of incident sunlight. This suggests that its surface is composed of extremely pure ice without dust or rocks to contaminate it. Enceladus has a diameter of 310 miles (500 kilometers).

Hyperion orbits between Iapetus and Titan. It is irregular in shape, measuring about 248 by 155 by 124 miles (400 by 250 by 200 kilometers). It may be a remnant of a much larger object that was shattered by impact with another space body. It appears that Hyperion is composed primarily of water ice. Hyperion orbits Saturn in a randomlike motion ("chaotic tumbling").

Phoebe is Saturn's outermost satellite. It travels in a retrograde orbit at a distance of over 6.2 million miles (10 million kilometers) away from the planet. It is the darkest moon of Saturn and is the planet's only known satellite that does not keep the same face always turned to Saturn. It has been speculated that it is an asteroid that was captured by the planet. Phoebe rotates in about nine hours and orbits Saturn in 406 days. It has a diameter of 124 miles (200 kilometers).

Pan was discovered in 1990 from *Voyager 2* photos taken in 1981. The satellite is estimated to be about 12.43 miles (20 kilometers) in diameter, which makes it the planet's smallest known moon. It orbits within the Encke Gap, a 202-mile (325-kilometer) division in Saturn's A ring. It was identified by Johann Franz Encke (1791–1865) in 1837.

The remaining eight moons range from 15 to 120 miles (25 to 190 kilometers) in diameter. They are all non-spherical in shape. Their names are Atlas, Prometheus, Pandora, Epimetheus, Janus, Telesto, Calypso, and Helene.

NASA's *Cassini* mission to Saturn, launched in Oct. 1997, will shed more light on the planet's mysteries when it arrives there in June 2004.

Saturn is the last of the planets visible to the naked eye. Saturn is never an object of overwhelming brilliance, but it looks like a bright star. The rings can be seen with a small telescope.

Uranus

Uranus, the first planet discovered in modern times by Sir William Herschel in 1781, is the seventh planet from the Sun, twice as far out as Saturn. Its mean distance from the Sun is 1,783 million miles (2,869 million kilometers). Uranus's equatorial diameter is 32,200 miles (51,810 kilometers). The axis of Uranus is tilted at 97 degrees, so it goes around the Sun nearly lying on its side.

Due to Uranus's unusual inclination, the polar regions receive more sunlight during a Uranus year of 84 Earth years. Scientists had thought that the temperature of its poles would be warmer than that at its equator, but *Voyager 2* discovered that the equatorial temperatures were similar to the temperatures at the poles, −209° C (−344° F), implying that some redistribution of heat toward the equatorial region must occur within the atmosphere. The wind patterns are much like Saturn's, flowing parallel to the equator in the direction of the planet's rotation.

Ninety-eight percent of the upper atmosphere is composed of hydrogen and helium; the remaining two percent is methane. Scientists speculate that the bulk of the lower atmosphere is composed of water (perhaps as much as 50%), methane, and ammonia. Methane is responsible for Uranus's blue-green color because it selectively absorbs red sunlight and condenses to form clouds of ice crystals in the cooler, higher regions of Uranus's atmosphere.

It was also discovered that the planet's magnetic field was 60 degrees tilted from the planet's axis of rotation and offset from the planet's center by one-third of Uranus's radius. It may be generated at a depth where water is under sufficient pressure to be electrically conductive.

The Uranian Rings

Voyager 2 also expanded the body of information pertaining to the rings and moons of Uranus. *Voyager*'s cameras obtained the first images of 9 previously known narrow rings and discovered at least 2 new rings, one narrow and one broadly diffused, bringing the total known rings to 11. It was found that a highly structured distribution of fine dust exists throughout the ring system.

The outermost (epsilon) ring contains nothing smaller than fist-sized particles. It is flanked by two small moons discovered interior to the orbit of the Uranian moon Miranda. The moons exert a shepherding influence on the epsilon ring and on the outer edges of the gamma and delta rings.

All of the rings lie within one planetary radius[1] of Uranus's cloud tops. Most of Uranus's rings are narrow, ranging in width from 0.6 to 58 miles (1 to 93 kilometers), and are only a few kilometers thick. The Uranian rings are colorless and extremely dark. The dark material may be either irradiated methane ice or organic-rich minerals mixed with water-impregnated, silicon-based compounds. There is evidence that incomplete rings, or "ring arcs," exist at Uranus.

The Uranian Moons

There are 21 known moons of Uranus. In order of decreasing distance from the planet, the moons are 1999 U3, 1999 U2, Sycorax, 1999 U1, Caliban, Oberon, Titania, Umbriel, Ariel, Miranda, Puck, 1986 U10, Belinda, Cressida, Portia, Rosalind, Desdemona, Juliet, Bianca, Ophelia, and Cordelia. Ten of the moons range in size from 16 to 67 miles (26 to 108 kilometers) in diameter and, being closer to the planet, have faster periods of revolution (8–15 hours) than their more distant relatives.

Oberon and Titania

The two largest moons, Oberon, 942 miles (1,516 kilometers) in diameter, and Titania, 982 miles (1,580 kilometers) in diameter, are less than half the diameter of Earth's moon. Titania, the reddest of Uranus's moons, may have endured global tectonics as evidenced by complex valleys and fault lines etched into its surface. Smooth sections indicate that volcanic resurfacing has taken place.

Umbriel and Ariel

Umbriel and Ariel are roughly three-fourths the size of Oberon and Titania. Umbriel is the darkest of the large moons, with huge craters peppering its surface. Umbriel has a paucity of what are known as bright ray craters, which are formed on an older darker surface when bright submerged ice is excavated and sprayed by meteoroid impacts.

In contrast, the surface of Ariel, the brightest of the Uranian moons, is relatively free of pockmarks due to volcanism that periodically erases the damage done by foreign projectiles. However, there are several extremely deep cuts on Ariel's surface.

Miranda

The smallest of Uranus's large moons, Miranda, 293 miles (472 kilometers) in diameter, has been described as "the most bizarre body in the solar system," with the most geologically complex surface. Miranda's remarkable terrain consists of rolling, heavily cratered plains (the oldest known in the Uranian system) adjoined by three huge, 120- to 180-mile (200- to 300-kilometer) oval-to-trapezoidal regions known as coronae, which are characterized by networks of concentric canyons.

Puck

Puck was the first new moon discovered by *Voyager.* It is 96 miles (154 kilometers) in diameter and makes a trip around Uranus every 18 hours. Puck is shaped somewhat like a potato with a huge impact crater marring roughly one-fourth of its surface.

Caliban and Sycorax

In 1997, two new moons, the first with irregular, non-circular orbits, were discovered around Uranus. These far distant satellites were temporarily designated U16 and U17 and later named Caliban and Sycorax, respectively. Caliban has a diameter of 37 miles (60 kilometers) and orbits Uranus at an average distance of 4.5 million miles (7.2 million kilometers). Sycorax has a diameter of 74.5 miles (120 kilometers) and a much more elliptical orbit than Caliban, bringing it as close as 3.7 million miles (6 million kilometers) to the planet.

New Uranian Moons Discovered

On May 18, 1999, the International Astronomical Union announced that Erich Karkoschka, a researcher at the Lunar and Planetary Lab of the University of Arizona in Tucson, had discovered the 18th moon orbiting Uranus.

Although the moon was found in 1999, it is designated as Satellite 1986 U10 (S/1986 U10). According to its discoverer, the satellite is approximately 25 miles (40 kilometers) in diameter, about the size of comet Hale-Bopp, and it may have a similar composition to the comet. It orbits 35,000 miles (51,000 kilometers) from Uranus, circling the planet every 15 hours and 18 minutes, similar to the planet's rotational period of about 16.8 hours.

In Sept. 1999, Cornell University astronomers announced the discovery of three more satellites, bringing the total up to 21. The yet unnamed moons are designated 1999 U1, 1999 U2, and 1999 U3. The new satellites are about 12 miles (20 kilometers) in diameter and orbit 6 to 12 miles (10 to 20 kilometers) from the planet.

Uranus can—on rare occasions—become bright enough to be seen with the naked eye, if one knows

---

1. The equatorial radius of Uranus is 15,880 miles (25,560 kilometers) at a pressure of 1 bar.

exactly where to look; normally, a good set of field glasses or a small portable telescope is required.

Neptune

Little was known about Neptune until Aug. 1989, when NASA's *Voyager 2* became the first spacecraft to observe the planet. Passing about 3,000 miles (4,950 kilometers) above Neptune's north pole, *Voyager 2* made its closest approach to any planet since leaving Earth 12 years prior. The spacecraft passed about 25,000 miles (40,000 kilometers) from Neptune's largest moon, Triton, the last solid body that *Voyager 2* will have studied.

Nearly 3 billion miles (4.5 billion kilometers) from the Sun, Neptune orbits the Sun once in 165 years, and therefore has made not quite a full circle around the Sun since it was discovered.[1]

With an equatorial diameter of 30,775 miles (49,528 kilometers), Neptune is the smallest of our solar system's four gas giants, Jupiter, Saturn, and Uranus.[2] Even so, its volume could hold nearly 60 Earths. Neptune is also denser than the other gas giants and about 64% heavier than if it were composed entirely of water.

Neptune has a blue color as a result of methane in its atmosphere. Methane preferentially absorbs the longer wavelengths of sunlight (those near the red end of the spectrum). What are left to be reflected are colors at the blue end of the spectrum. The atmosphere of Neptune is mainly composed of hydrogen, with helium and traces of methane and ammonia.

Neptune is a dynamic planet even though it receives only 3% as much sunlight as Jupiter does. *Voyager 2* discovered several large, dark spots that were prominent features on the planet. The largest spot was about the size of Earth and was designated the "Great Dark Spot" by its discoverers. It appeared to be an anticyclone similar to Jupiter's Great Red Spot. While Neptune's Great Dark Spot is comparable in size, relative to the planet, and at the same latitude (22°S latitude) as Jupiter's Great Red Spot, it was far more variable in size and shape than its Jovian counterpart. Bright, wispy "cirrus-type" clouds overlaid the Great Dark Spot at its southern and northeastern boundaries.

At about 42°S latitude, a bright, irregularly shaped, eastward-moving cloud circles much faster than did the Great Dark Spot, "scooting" around Neptune in about 16 hours. This "scooter" may have been a cloud plume rising between cloud decks.

Another spot, designated "D2," was located far to the south of the Great Dark Spot, at 55°S latitude. It is almond-shaped, with a bright central core, and moves eastward around the planet in about 16 hours.

In 1995, images taken by the Hubble Space Telescope showed that the Great Dark Spot has vanished. The great storm center has either dissipated or is obscured by other atmospheric conditions.

The atmosphere above Neptune's clouds is hotter near the equator, cooler in the mid-latitudes, and warm again at the south pole. Temperatures in the stratosphere were measured to be 750° K (900° F), while at the 100 millibar pressure level they were measured to be 55° K (−360° F).

Long, bright clouds, reminiscent of cirrus clouds on Earth, were seen high in Neptune's atmosphere. They appear to form above most of the methane, and consequently are not blue.

At northern low latitudes (27°N), *Voyager* captured images of cloud streaks casting their shadows on cloud decks estimated to be about 30 to 60 miles (50 to 100 kilometers) below. The widths of these cloud streaks range from 30 to 125 miles (50 to 200 kilometers). Cloud streaks were also seen in the southern polar regions (71°S) where the cloud heights were about 30 miles (50 kilometers).

Most of the winds on Neptune blow in a westward direction, which is retrograde, or opposite to the rotation of the planet.

In Jan. 2000, astronomers announced taking the best Earth-based infrared images of Neptune, captured by the W. M. Keck II telescope in Hawaii. They revealed giant 600-mph (966-km/hr) storms born of heat generated from the planet's still contracting core. Storm features are pulled across the face of Neptune as it whirls through its 16-hour day.

The Magnetic Field

Neptune's magnetic field is tilted 47 degrees from the planet's rotation axis, and is offset at least 0.55 radii, about 8,500 miles (13,500 kilometers) from the physical center. The dynamo electric currents produced within the planet, therefore, must be relatively closer to the surface than for Earth, Jupiter, or Saturn. Because of its unusual orientation, and the tilt of the planet's rotation axis, Neptune's magnetic field goes through dramatic changes as the planet rotates in the solar wind.

Voyager's planetary radio astronomy instrument measured the periodic radio waves generated by the magnetic field and determined that the rotation rate of the interior of Neptune is 16 hours and 7 minutes.

Voyager also detected auroras, similar to the northern and southern lights on Earth, in Neptune's atmosphere. Unlike those on Earth, due to Neptune's complex magnetic field, the auroras are extremely complicated processes that occur over wide regions of the planet, not just near the planet's magnetic poles.

Neptune's Moons

Triton

The largest of Neptune's eight known satellites, Triton is different from all other icy moons that *Voyager* has studied. Triton circles Neptune in a tilted, circular, retrograde orbit, completing an orbit in 5.875 days at an average distance of 205,000 miles (330,000 kilometers) above the planet's cloud tops.

Triton shows evidence of a remarkable geologic history, and *Voyager 2* images show active geyser-like eruptions spewing invisible nitrogen gas and dark dust particles 1 to 5 miles (2 to 8 kilometers) into space.

Triton is about three-quarters the size of Earth's Moon and has a diameter of about 1,680 miles

---

1. Astronomers have studied Neptune since Sept. 23, 1846, when Johann Gottfried Galle, of the Berlin Observatory, and Louis d'Arrest, an astronomy student, discovered the eighth planet on the basis of mathematical predictions by Urbain Jean Joseph Le Verrier. Similar predictions were made independently by John Couch Adams. Galileo Galilei had seen Neptune during several nights of observing Jupiter, in Jan. 1613, but didn't realize he was seeing a new planet.
2. These four planets are about 4 to 12 times greater in diameter than Earth. They have no solid surfaces, but possess massive atmospheres that contain substantial amounts of hydrogen and helium with traces of other gases.

(2,705 kilometers) and a mean density of about 2.066 grams per cubic centimeter. (The density of water is 1.0 grams per cubic centimeter.) This means that Triton contains more rock in its interior than the icy satellites of Saturn and Uranus.

The relatively high density and the retrograde orbit offer strong evidence that Triton did not originate near Neptune, but is a captured object.

An extremely thin atmosphere extends as much as 500 miles (800 kilometers) above the satellite's surface. Tiny nitrogen ice particles may form thin clouds a few kilometers above the surface. Triton is very bright, reflecting 60% to 95% of the sunlight that strikes it. (By comparison, Earth's Moon reflects only 11%.)

The atmospheric pressure at Triton's surface is about 14 microbars, a mere 1/70,000th the surface pressure on Earth. Temperature at the surface is about 38° K (–391° F), making it the coldest surface of any body yet visited in the solar system.

Nereid

Nereid was discovered in 1948 through Earth-based telescopes. Little is known about Nereid, which is slightly smaller than Proteus, having a diameter of 211 miles (340 kilometers). The satellite's surface reflects about 14% of the sunlight that strikes it. Nereid's orbit is the most eccentric in the solar system, ranging from about 841,100 miles (1,353,600 kilometers) to 5,980,200 miles (9,623,700 kilometers).

The Smaller Satellites

In addition to the previously known moons, Triton and Nereid, *Voyager 2* found six more satellites, making the total eight.

Proteus

Like all six of Neptune's recently discovered small satellites, it is one of the darkest objects in the solar system—"as dark as soot" is a good description. It reflects only 6% of the sunlight that strikes it. Proteus is an ellipsoid about 258 miles (416 kilometers) in diameter, larger than Nereid. It circles Neptune at a distance of about 57,700 miles (92,800 kilometers) above the cloud tops, and completes one orbit in 26 hours and 54 minutes. Scientists say that it is about as large as a satellite can be without being pulled into a spherical shape by its own gravity.

Proteus and its tiny companions are cratered and irregularly shaped—they are not round—and show no signs of any geologic modifications. All circle the planet in the same direction as Neptune rotates, and remain close to Neptune's equatorial plane.

Larissa

This object is only about 30,300 miles (48,800 kilometers) from Neptune and circles the planet in 13 hours and 18 minutes. Its diameter is 120 miles (190 kilometers).

Despina

The satellite is 17,200 miles (27,700 kilometers) from Neptune's clouds and makes one orbit every 8 hours. Its diameter is about 90 miles (150 kilometers).

Galatea

It lies 23,100 miles (37,200 kilometers) from Neptune. Its diameter is 110 miles (180 kilometers), and it completes an orbit in 10 hours and 18 minutes.

Thalassa

The satellite appears to be about 50 miles (80 kilometers) in diameter. It orbits Neptune in 7 hours and 30 minutes some 15,700 miles (25,200 kilometers) above the cloud tops.

Naiad

The last satellite discovered, it is about 37 miles (60 kilometers) in diameter and orbits Neptune about 14,400 miles (23,200 kilometers) above the clouds in 7 hours and 6 minutes.

Neptune's Rings

Voyager found four rings and evidence of ring *arcs* or incomplete rings. The "Main Ring" orbits Neptune at about 23,812.5 miles (38,100 kilometers) above the cloud tops. The "Inner Ring" is about 17,750 miles (28,400 kilometers) from Neptune's cloud tops. An "Inside Diffuse Ring"—a complete ring—is located about 10,687.5 miles (17,100 kilometers) from the planet's cloud tops. Some scientists suspect that this ring may extend all the way down to Neptune's cloud tops. An area called "the Plateau" is a broad, diffuse sheet of fine material just outside the so-called "Inner Ring." The fine material is approximately the size of smoke particles. All other rings contain a greater proportion of larger material.

Pluto

Pluto, the outermost and smallest planet in the solar system, is the only planet not visited by an exploring spacecraft. So little is known about it that it is difficult to classify. Its distance is so great that the Hubble Space Telescope cannot reveal its surface features. Appropriately named for the Roman god of the underworld, it must be frozen, dark, and dead. Pluto's mean distance from the Sun is 3,687.5 million miles (5,900 million kilometers).

In 1978, light-curve studies gave evidence of a moon revolving around Pluto within the same period as Pluto's rotation. Therefore, it stays over the same point on Pluto's surface. In addition, it keeps the same face toward the planet. The satellite was later named Charon and is estimated to be about 789 miles (1,262.4 kilometers) in diameter. Recent estimates indicate Pluto's diameter is about 1,441.6 miles (2,306.56 kilometers), making the pair more like a double planet than any other in the solar system. Previously, the Earth–Moon system held this distinction. The density of Pluto is slightly greater than that of water.

There is evidence that Pluto has an atmosphere containing methane and polar ice caps that increase and decrease in size with the planet's seasons. It is not known to have water. The Hubble Space Telescope's faint-object camera revealed light and dark regions on Pluto indicating an ice cap at the planet's north pole. It is not known if there is an ice cap at Pluto's south pole.

Pluto was predicted by calculation when Percival Lowell (1855–1916) noticed irregularities in the orbits of Uranus and Neptune. Clyde Tombaugh (1906–1997) discovered the planet in 1930, precisely where Lowell predicted it would be. The name Pluto was chosen because the first two letters represent the initials of Percival Lowell.

Pluto has the most eccentric orbit in the solar system, bringing it at times closer to the Sun than Neptune. Pluto approached the perihelion of its orbit on

The First Ten Minor Planets (Asteroids)

Name	Year of discovery	Mean distance from Sun (millions of miles)	Orbital period (years)	Diameter (miles)	Magnitude
1. Ceres	1801	257.0	4.60	485	7.4
2. Pallas	1802	257.4	4.61	304	8.0
3. Juno	1804	247.8	4.36	118	8.7
4. Vesta	1807	219.3	3.63	243	6.5
5. Astraea	1845	239.3	4.14	50	9.9
6. Hebe	1847	225.2	3.78	121	8.5
7. Iris	1847	221.4	3.68	121	8.4
8. Flora	1847	204.4	3.27	56	8.9
9. Metis	1848	221.7	3.69	78	8.9
10. Hygeia	1849	222.6	5.59	40(?)	9.5

Sept. 5, 1989, and until Feb. 1999 was closer to the Sun than Neptune. Even then, it could be seen only with a large telescope.

The Asteroids

Between the orbits of Mars and Jupiter are an estimated 30,000 pieces of rocky debris, known collectively as the asteroids, or planetoids. The first and, incidentally, the largest (Ceres), was discovered during the New Year's night of 1801 by the Italian astronomer Father Piazzi (1746–1826), and its orbit was calculated by the German mathematician Karl Friedrich Gauss (1777–1855). Gauss invented a new method of calculating orbits on that occasion. A few asteroids do not move in orbits beyond the orbit of Mars, but in orbits that cross the orbit of Mars. The first of them was named Eros because of this peculiar orbit. It had become the rule to bestow female names on the asteroids, but when it was found that Eros crossed the orbit of a major planet, it received a male name. These orbit-crossing asteroids are often referred to as the "male asteroids." A few of them—Albert, Adonis, Apollo, Amor, and Icarus—cross the orbit of Earth, and two of them may come closer than our Moon; but the crossing is like a bridge crossing a highway, not like two highways intersecting. Hence there is very little danger of collision from these bodies. They are all small, 3 to 5 miles (4.8 to 8.0 kilometers) in diameter, and therefore very difficult objects to identify, even when quite close. Some scientists believe the asteroids represent the remains of an exploded planet.

On Oct. 29, 1991, the *Galileo* spacecraft took a historic photograph of asteroid 951 Gaspra from a distance of 10,000 miles (16,000 kilometers) away. It was the first close-up photo ever taken of an asteroid in space.

Gaspra is an irregular, potato-shaped object about 12.5 miles (20 kilometers) by 7.5 miles (12 kilometers) by 7 miles (11.2 kilometers) in size. Its surface is covered with a layer of loose rubble and its terrain is covered with several dozen small craters.

Close-up photos of Asteroid 243 Ida taken by the *Galileo* spacecraft on Aug. 28, 1993, revealed that Ida had a tiny egg-shaped moon measuring 0.9 miles by 0.7 miles (1.44 by 1.12 kilometers). The moon has been named Dactyl.

NASA's *Near-Earth Asteroid Rendezvous* spacecraft was launched on Feb. 17, 1996. (Near-Earth asteroids come within 121 million miles (195 million kilometers) of the Sun. Their orbits come close enough that one could eventually hit Earth.) It flew within 750 miles (1,200 kilometers) of minor planet 253 Mathilde on June 27, 1997, and took spectacular images of the dark, crater-battered world. The asteroid's mean diameter was found to be 33 miles (52.8 kilometers). The *NEAR* spacecraft discovered that the carbon-rich Mathilde is one of the darkest objects in the solar system, only reflecting about 3% of the Sun's light, making it twice as dark as a chunk of charcoal. The asteroid is almost completely cratered, and at least five of its craters just on the lighted side are larger than 12 miles (19.2 kilometers).

The spacecraft reached asteroid 433 Eros in Dec. 1998, but aborted its mission due to engine problems. *NEAR* measured Eros to be 21 miles (33.6 kilometers) long by 8 miles (12.8 kilometers) wide and 8 miles (12.8 kilometers) deep. It rotates once every 5.27 hours and has no visible moons.

The spacecraft was renamed *NEAR Shoemaker* in honor of geologist Dr. Eugene M. Shoemaker (1928–1997), who influenced research on asteroids and comets in shaping the planets. It made a successful rendezvous with Eros on Feb. 14, 2000, and began a year-long orbit of the asteroid. *NEAR Shoemaker* data showed that the asteroid's ancient surface is covered with craters, ridges, boulders, and other complex features.

Comets

Comets, according to the noted astronomer Fred L. Whipple (1906–), are enormous "snowballs" of frozen gases (mostly carbon dioxide, methane, and water vapor) and contain very little solid material. The whole behavior of comets can then be explained as the behavior of frozen gas being heated by the Sun. When the comet Kohoutek made its first appearance to man in 1973, its behavior seemed to confirm this theory, and later the international study by five spacecraft that encountered Halley's comet in March 1986 confirmed Whipple's idea of the make-up of comets.

Since comets appear in the sky without any warning, people in classical times and especially during the Middle Ages believed that they had a special meaning, which, of course, was bad. Since a natural catastrophe of some sort or a military conflict occurs every year, it was quite simple to blame the comet that happened to be visible. But even in the past, there were some people who used logical reasoning. When, in Roman times, a comet was blamed for the loss of a battle and hence was called a "bad omen,"

Ultraviolet Death May Follow Asteroid Devastation

Source: OSU News, Oregon State University

Scientists from Oregon State University and the British Antarctic Survey reported in March 2000 that if a huge asteroid were to hit Earth, the catastrophic destruction it would cause, and even the "impact winter" that would follow, might only be a prelude to a different but very deadly phase that would start later on. They're calling it "ultraviolet spring."

Andrew Blaustein, a professor of zoology at Oregon State University, and his colleague Charles Cockell, a researcher with the British Antarctic Survey, examined secondary ecological repercussions of a major asteroid impact of a magnitude similar to the one that occurred around the Cretaceous-Tertiary, or K-T, boundary. This asteroid is believed to have hit off the Yucatán Peninsula with a force of almost one trillion megatons. At the time, there was a massive extinction of many animals, including the dinosaurs.

The immediate result of an asteroid impact would be devastating destruction and an impact winter, with widespread death of plants and the large terrestrial animals—including humans—that most directly depend on those plants for food. Such an impact would also load the atmosphere with nitric oxide, causing massive amounts of acid rain. As they became acidified, the lakes and rivers would have reduced amounts of dissolved organic carbons, thereby allowing for much greater penetration of ultraviolet light.

At first, the ultraviolet rays would be blocked by the global dust cloud that would blot out the sunlight and choke the planet in icy winter-like conditions for months. During the extended winter, animals across the biological spectrum would starve and become weaker, and many would die. The researchers calculated that the dust cloud would shield Earth from ultraviolet light for an extended period of about 390 days before the dust settled and the ultraviolet radiation returned to its level before the impact. After that, the ozone depletion would cause ultraviolet levels to at least double, about 600 days after impact.

According to their study, these factors would lead to ultraviolet-related DNA damage about 1,000 times higher than normal and general ultraviolet damage to plants about 500 times higher than normal. Ultraviolet radiation can cause mutations, cancer, and cataracts. It can kill plants or slow their growth, suppressing photosynthesis, which forms the base of the world's food chain.

The researchers said that smaller asteroid impacts, which have happened far more frequently in Earth's history, theoretically might cause similar or even worse problems with ultraviolet exposure. The ozone depletion would be less, but there would also be less of a protective dust cloud.

During the K-T event, the scientists said, many of the animals may actually have been spared most of the ultraviolet spring they envision. That impact, oddly enough, hit a portion of Earth's crust that was rich in anhydride rocks. This produced a 12-year sulfide haze that blocked much of the ultraviolet radiation. But it was a lucky shot because that type of rock covers less than one percent of Earth's surface.

Part of what the scientists are trying to stress is that with an asteroid collision, there will be many synergistic effects on the environment that go far beyond the initial impact. They warn that when the next "big one" comes, the collision will be devastating and the impact winter deadly, but it will be the ultraviolet spring that may finish off the survivors. □

---

a Roman writer observed that the victors in the battle probably did not think so.

Up until the middle of the 16th century, comets were believed to be phenomena of the upper atmosphere; they were usually "explained" as "burning vapors" which had risen from "distant swamps." That nobody had ever actually seen burning vapors rise from a swamp did not matter.

But a large comet which appeared in 1577 was carefully observed by Tycho Brahe (1546–1601), a Danish astronomer who is often, and with the best of reasons, called eccentric, but who insisted on precise measurements for everything. It was Tycho Brahe's accumulation of literally thousands of precise measurements that later enabled his younger collaborator, Johannes Kepler (1571–1630), to discover the laws of planetary motion. Measuring the motion of the comet of 1577, Brahe could show that it had been far beyond the atmosphere, even though he could not give figures for the distance. Brahe's work proved that comets were astronomical and not meteorological phenomena.

In 1682, the second Astronomer Royal of Great Britain, Dr. Edmond Halley (1656–1742), checked the orbit of a bright comet that was in the sky and then compared it with earlier comet orbits that were known in part. Halley found that the comet of 1682 was the third to move through what appeared to be the same orbit, and that the three appearances were roughly 76 years apart. Halley concluded that this was the same comet, moving around the Sun in a closed orbit, like the planets. He predicted that it would reappear in 1758 or 1759. Halley himself died in 1742, but a large comet appeared 16 years after his death as predicted and was immediately referred to as "Halley's comet."

Halley's comet appeared again in 1986, sparking a worldwide effort to study it up close. Five satellites in all took readings from the comet at various distances. Two Soviet craft, *Vega 1* and *Vega 2*, went in close to provide detailed pictures of the comet, including the first of the comet's core. The European Space Agency's craft, *Giotto*, entered the comet itself, coming to within 450 miles of the comet's center and successfully passing through its tail. In addition, two Japanese craft, the *Suisei* and the *Sakigake*, passed at a longer distance and analyzed the cloud and tail of the comet and the effect of solar radiation upon it.

Astronomers refer to comets as "periodic" or as "nonperiodic" comets, but the latter term does not mean that these comets have no period; it merely means that their period is not known. The actual periods of comets run from 3.3 years (the shortest known) to many thousands of years. Their orbits are elliptical, like those of the planets, but they are very eccentric, long, and narrow ellipses. Only comet Schwassmann-Wachmann has an orbit that has such a low eccentricity (for a cometary orbit) that it could be the orbit of a minor planet.

When a comet, coming from deep space, approaches the Sun, it is at first indistinguishable from a minor planet. Somewhere between the orbits of Mars and Jupiter, its outline becomes fuzzy; it is said to develop a "coma" (the word used here is the Latin word coma, which means "hair," not the phonetically identical Greek word that means "deep sleep"). Then, near the orbit of Mars, the comet develops its tail, which at first trails behind. This grows steadily as the comet comes closer and closer to the Sun. As it rounds the Sun (as first noticed by Girolamo Fracastoro, 1483–1553), the tail always points away from the Sun so that the comet, when moving away from the Sun, points its tail ahead like the landing lights of an airplane.

The reason for this behavior is that the tail is pushed in these directions by the radiation pressure of the Sun. It sometimes happens that a comet loses its tail at perihelion; it then grows another one. Although the tail is clearly visible against the black of the sky, it is very tenuous. It has been said that if the tail of Halley's comet could be compressed to the density of iron, it would fit into a small suitcase.

Although very low in mass, comets are among the largest members of the solar system. The nucleus of a comet may be up to 10,000 miles in diameter; its coma between 10,000 and 50,000 miles in diameter; and its tail as long as 28 million miles.

Comet Shoemaker-Levy 9 broke up into 21 fragments in July 1992 and crashed into the surface of Jupiter, July 16–22, 1994, in the most violent event in the recorded history of the solar system.

In 1951, Dutch astronomer Gerard Kuiper first suggested the existence of a disk-shaped swarm of short-period comets that begin beyond the orbit of Neptune and extend past Pluto. In 1995, the Hubble Space Telescope detected the long-sought Kuiper Belt and an estimated 200 million comets were discovered orbiting it.

Meteors and Meteorites

The term meteor for what is usually called a shooting star bears an unfortunate resemblance to the term meteorology, the science of weather and weather forecasting. This resemblance is due to an ancient misunderstanding that wrongly considered meteors an atmospheric phenomenon. Actually, the streak of light in the sky that scientists call a meteor is essentially an astronomical phenomenon: the entry of a small piece of cosmic matter into our atmosphere.

The distinction between meteors and fireballs (formerly also called bolides) is merely one of convenience; a fireball is an unusually bright meteor. Incidentally, it also means that a fireball is larger than a faint meteor.

Bodies that enter our atmosphere become visible when they are about 60 miles above the ground. The fact that they grow hot enough to emit light is not due to the "friction" of the atmosphere, as one often reads. The phenomenon responsible for the heating is one of compression. Unconfined air can-

not move faster than the speed of sound. Since the entering meteorite moves with 30 to 60 times the speed of sound, the air simply cannot get out of the way. Therefore, it is compressed like the air in the cylinder of a diesel engine and is heated by compression. This heat—or part of it—is transferred to the moving body. The details of this process are now fairly well understood as a result of re-entry tests with ballistic-missile nose cones.

The average weight of a body producing a faint shooting star is only a small fraction of an ounce. Even a bright fireball may not weigh more than 2 or 3 pounds. Naturally, the smaller bodies are worn to dust by the passage through the atmosphere; only rather large ones reach the ground. Those that are found are called meteorites. (The meteor, to repeat, is the term for the light streak in the sky.) About 1,000 meteorites fall to Earth each year.

The largest meteorite known is still embedded in the ground near Grootfontein in southwest Africa and is estimated to weigh 70 tons. The second-largest known is the 34-ton Anighito (on exhibit in the Hayden Planetarium, New York), which was found by Admiral Peary in 1892 at Cape York in Greenland. The largest meteorite found in the United States is the Willamette meteorite (found in Oregon, weight ca. 15 tons), but large portions of this meteorite weathered away before it was found. Its weight as it struck the ground may have been 20 tons.

All these are iron meteorites (an iron meteorite normally contains about 7% nickel), which form one class of meteorites. The other class consists of the stony meteorites, and between them there are the so-called stony irons. The so-called tektites consist of glass similar to our volcanic glass obsidian, and because of the similarity, there is doubt in a number of cases whether the glass is of terrestrial or of extraterrestrial origin.

Though no meteorite larger than the Grootfontein is actually known, we do know that Earth has, on occasion, been struck by much larger bodies. Evidence for such hits are the meteorite craters, of which an especially good example is located near the Cañon Diablo in Arizona. Another meteor crater in the United States is a rather old crater near Odessa, Texas. A large number of others are known, especially in eastern Canada; and for many "probables," meteoric origin has now been proved.

The 13th known lunar meteorite was found in Dec. 1993 by a team from the Antarctic Search for Meteorites project. It is approximately 2 inches long and weighs 0.75 of an ounce.

Some scientists theorize that the mass extermination of dinosaurs from the face of Earth 65 million years ago was due to a large meteor that struck our planet at that time.

Meteor showers are caused by multitudes of very small bodies traveling in swarms. Earth travels in its orbit through these swarms like a car driving through falling snow. The point from which the meteors seem to emanate is called the radiant and is named for the constellation in that area. The Perseid meteor shower in August is the most spectacular of the year, boasting, at peak, roughly 60 meteors per hour under good atmospheric conditions. The presence of a bright moon diminishes the number of visible meteors.

The 88 Recognized Constellations

In astronomical works, the Latin names of the constellations are used. The letter N or S following the Latin name indicates whether the constellation is located to the north or south of the Zodiac. The letter Z indicates that the constellation is within the Zodiac.

Latin name	Letter	English version	Latin name	Letter	English version	Latin name	Letter	English version
Andromeda	N	Andromeda	Delphinus	N	Dolphin	Pegasus	N	Pegasus
Antlia	S	Airpump	Dorado	S	Swordfish (Gold-	Perseus	N	Perseus
Apus	S	Bird of Paradise			fish)	Phoenix	S	Phoenix
Aquarius	Z	Water Bearer	Draco	N	Dragon	Pictor	S	Painter (or his
Aquila	N	Eagle	Equuleus	N	Filly			Easel)
Ara	S	Altar	Eridanus	S	Eridanus (river)	Pisces	Z	Fishes
Aries	Z	Ram	Fornax	S	Furnace	Piscis Austrinus	S	Southern Fish
Auriga	N	Charioteer	Gemini	Z	Twins	Puppis	S	Poop (of Argo)[1]
Boötes	N	Herdsmen	Grus	S	Crane	Pyxis	S	Mariner's Com-
Caelum	S	Sculptor's Tool	Hercules	N	Hercules			pass
Camelopardalis	N	Giraffe	Horologium	S	Clock	Reticulum	S	Net
Cancer	Z	Crab	Hydra	S	Sea Serpent	Sagitta	N	Arrow
Canes Venatici	N	Hunting Dogs	Hydrus	S	Water Snake	Sagittarius	Z	Archer
Canis Major	S	Great Dog	Indus	S	Indian	Scorpius	Z	Scorpion
Canis Minor	S	Little Dog	Lacerta	N	Lizard	Sculptor	S	Sculptor
Capricornus	Z	Goat (or Sea-	Leo	Z	Lion	Scutum	N	Shield
		Goat)	Leo Minor	N	Little Lion	Serpens	N	Serpent
Carina	S	Keel (of Argo)[1]	Lepus	S	Hare	Sextans	S	Sextant
Cassiopeia	N	Cassiopeia	Libra	Z	Scales	Taurus	Z	Bull
Centaurus	S	Centaur	Lupus	S	Wolf	Telescopium	S	Telescope
Cepheus	N	Cepheus	Lynx	N	Lynx	Triangulum	N	Triangle
Cetus	S	Whale	Lyra	N	Lyre (Harp)	Triangulum Aus-	S	Southern Triangle
Chameleon	S	Chameleon	Mensa	S	Table (mountain)	trale		
Circinus	S	Compasses	Microscopium	S	Microscope	Tucana	S	Toucan
Columba	S	Dove	Monoceros	S	Unicorn	Ursa Major	N	Big Dipper[2]
Coma Berenices	N	Berenice's Hair	Musca	S	Southern Fly	Ursa Minor	N	Little Dipper[3]
Corona Australis	S	Southern Crown	Norma	S	Rule (straight-	Vela	S	Sail (of Argo)[1]
Corona Borealis	N	Northern Crown			edge)	Virgo	Z	Virgin
Corvus	S	Crow (Raven)	Octans	S	Octant	Volans	S	Flying Fish
Crater	S	Cup	Ophiuchus	N	Serpent-Bearer	Vulpecula	N	Fox
Crux	S	Southern Cross	Orion	S	Orion			
Cygnus	N	Swan	Pavo	S	Peacock			

1. The original constellation Argo Navis (the Ship Argo) has been divided into Carina, Puppis, and Vela. Normally the brightest star in each constellation is designated by alpha, the first letter of the Greek alphabet, the second brightest by beta, the second letter of the Greek alphabet, and so forth. But the Greek letters run through Carina, Puppis, and Vela as if it were still one constellation. 2. The Big Dipper is only a part of the constellation Ursa Major (Great Bear) and is not a constellation by itself. 3. The Little Dipper is called Ursa Minor (Little Bear).

The Constellations

Constellations are groupings of stars that form easily recognized and remembered patterns, such as Orion and the Big Dipper. The Big Dipper is actually an asterism, not a constellation, because it is only part of the constellation Ursa Major (the Big Bear). Actually, the stars in the majority of all constellations do not "belong together." Usually they are at greatly varying distances from Earth and just happen to lie more or less in the same line of sight as seen from our solar system. But in a few cases, the stars of a constellation are actually associated; most of the bright stars of the Big Dipper travel together and form what astronomers call an *open cluster*.

If you observe a planet, say Mars, for one complete revolution, you will see that it passes successively through 12 constellations. All planets (except Pluto at certain times) can be observed only in these 12 constellations, which form the so-called zodiac, and the Sun also moves through the zodiacal signs, though the Sun's apparent movement is actually caused by the movement of Earth.

Although the constellations are due mainly to the optical accident of line of sight and have no real significance, astronomers have retained them as reference areas. It is much easier to speak of a star in Orion than to give its geometrical position in the sky. During the Astronomical Congress of 1928, it was decided to recognize 88 constellations. A description of their agreed-upon boundaries was published at Cambridge, England, in 1930, under the title *Atlas Céleste*.

The Auroras

The "northern lights" (*Aurora borealis*) as well as the "southern lights" (*Aurora australis*) are upper-atmosphere phenomena of astronomical origin. The auroras center around the magnetic (not the geographical) poles of Earth, which explains why, in the Western Hemisphere, they have been seen as far to the south as New Orleans and Florida, while the equivalent latitude in the Eastern Hemisphere never sees an aurora. The northern magnetic pole happens to be in the Western Hemisphere.

The lower limit of an aurora is at about 50 miles (80 kilometers). Upper limits have been estimated to be as high as 400 miles (640 kilometers). Since about 1880, a connection between the auroras on Earth and sunspots has been suspected and has gradually come to be accepted. It was said that the sunspots probably eject "particles" (later the word *electrons* was substituted), which on striking Earth's atmosphere cause the auroras. But this explanation suffered from certain difficulties. Sometimes a very large sunspot group on the Sun, with individual spots bigger than Earth itself, would not cause an aurora. Moreover, even if a sunspot caused an aurora, the time that passed between the appearance of the one and the occurrence of the other was highly unpredictable.

This problem of the time lag is, in all probability, solved by the discovery of the Van Allen layer by artificial satellite *Explorer I*. The Van Allen layer[1] is a double layer of charged subatomic particles around Earth. The inner layer, with its center some 1,500 miles (2,400 kilometers) from the ground, reaches from about 40°N to about 40°S and does not touch the atmosphere. The outer layer, much larger and with its center several thousand miles from the ground, does touch the atmosphere in the vicinity of the magnetic poles.

It seems probable that the "leakage" of electrons from the outer Van Allen layer causes the auroras. A new burst of electrons from the Sun seems to be caught in the outer layer first. Under the assumption that all electrons are first caught in the outer layer, the time lag can be understood. There has to be an "overflow" from the outer layer to produce an aurora.

The Atmosphere

Though reasonably transparent to visible light, the atmosphere may absorb as much as 60% of the visible and near-visible light. It is opaque to most other wavelengths, except certain fairly short radio waves. In addition to absorbing much light, our atmosphere bends light rays entering at a slant (for a given observer) so that the true position of a star close to the horizon is not what it seems to be. One effect is that we see the Sun above the horizon before it actually is. And the unsteady movement of the atmosphere causes the "twinkling" of the stars, which may be romantic, but is a nuisance when it comes to observing.

The composition of our atmosphere near the ground is 78% nitrogen and 21% oxygen, the remaining 1% consisting of other gases, most of it argon. The composition stays the same to an altitude of at least 70 miles (112 kilometers) (except that higher up two impurities, carbon dioxide and water vapor, are missing), but the pressure drops very fast. At 18,000 feet, half of the total mass of the atmosphere is below, and at 100,000 feet, 99% of the mass of the atmosphere is below. The upper limit of the atmosphere is usually given as 120 miles (192 kilometers); no definitive figure is possible, since there is no boundary line between the incredibly attenuated gases 120 miles (192 kilometers) up and space.

Some Giant Telescopes

• The world's largest fixed-dish radio telescope (1963) is located near Arecibo, Puerto Rico. It is 1,000 feet (35 meters) in diameter and spans some 25 acres.
• The Very Large Array (VLA) telescope (1980) near Socorro, N.M., is the world's most powerful radio telescope. It is Y-shaped and has 27 separate mobile antennas (each 82 feet in diameter) and is spread out over about a 25-mile (40-kilometer) area.
• One of the world's largest fully steerable radio telescopes (1972), located at Effelsberg, Germany, has a 328-foot (100-meter) dish antenna.
• The 200-inch (5-meter) Hale telescope at Mount Palomar, Calif. (1948), is the second-largest reflector in use.
• The 236-inch (6-meter) Special Astrophysical Observatory (1976) at Zelenchukskaya, on the northern slopes of the Caucasus Mountains in the

1. Named after the American physicist, James Alfred Van Allen (1914–), who discovered the broad bands of intense radiation surrounding Earth in 1958.

Russian Federation, is the world's largest reflector telescope in use. However, problems with it make it less useful than the 200-inch Hale.
• The Green Bank Telescope at the National Radio Astronomy Observatories site at Green Bank, W. Va., is considered to be the world's largest fully steerable radio telescope. Although it is described as a 328-foot (100-meter) telescope, the actual surface dimensions of its dish antenna are 328 by 360.89 feet (100 x 110 meters). It is scheduled to begin regular scientific observations in the first quarter of 2001.
• The W. M. Keck Telescope (1991) at Mauna Kea, Hawaii, is the world's most powerful reflector telescope. It has a primary mirror composed of 36 hexagonal segments, each 5.9 feet (1.8 meters) in size. The Keck Telescope has a light-gathering power four times greater than the 200-inch Hale.
• The Very Large European Space Observatory (ESO) Telescope (VLT) (construction to be completed by the end of 2000), located at Cerro Paranal, Chile, will consist of four telescopes that can work independently or in a combined mode. In the combined mode, the VLT provides the total light-collecting power of a 52.5-foot (16-meter) single telescope, making it the largest optical telescope in the world.
• The 40-inch (1.01 meter) telescope at Yerkes Observatory (1897) at Williams Bay, Wis., is the world's largest refracting telescope.
• The Sabaru 27.23-foot (8.3-meter) optical-infrared monolithic-mirror telescope (scheduled for operation in 2000) of the National Observatory of Japan (NADJ), located at Mauna Kea, Hawaii, will be the world's largest single mirror telescope.

Hubble Space Telescope

The $2 billion Edwin P. Hubble Space Telescope (HST) is the most complex and sensitive space observatory ever constructed. It was placed into orbit by the space shuttle *Discovery* on April 25, 1990. HST is 43.3 feet (13 meters) long and 14 feet (4 meters) wide, about the size of a bus or truck. Hubble weighs 25,500 pounds (11,000 kg) and orbits 335 nautical miles (536 kilometers) above Earth.

Since being lifted into orbit, HST has become the principal tool for exploring the universe.

The third Space Telescope servicing mission by the crew of *Discovery* in Dec. 1999 extended the telescope's scientific power with new instruments and repaired its optics, solar arrays, gyros, and other components. Future servicing missions are planned for 2001 and 2003.

Hubble will be decommissioned in 2010 and replaced by the Next Generation Space Telescope (NGST).   □

Breakthroughs in the Search for Extrasolar Worlds

Scientists have identified 44 new planets since 1995

Sources: W. M. Keck Observatory, European Southern Observatory, and University of California, Berkeley

Since the first extrasolar planet, or "exoplanet," was discovered around the star 51 Pegasi in 1995 by Michel Mayor and Didier Queloz, the intensive hunt for planets around other stars continues to be highly successful. The total number of known and suspected planetary companions outside our solar system is approaching 50. In March 2000, a team of astronomers announced that they had discovered for the first time two planets orbiting suns that may be smaller in mass than Saturn. The two Saturn-class planets are the smallest ones to be found outside our solar system. Saturn, our second-largest planet, is one-third the mass of Jupiter. All of the 30 extrasolar worlds previously known had been the size of Jupiter or larger. The existence of the Saturn-size candidates suggests that many stars may harbor smaller planets in addition to the Jupiter-size ones.

This discovery is important because it reinforces the theory (solar-disk/accretion theory) that planets form by a snowball effect, growing from small ones to large ones in a star-encircling dust disk. The theory predicts that there should be more small planets than large planets, and this is a trend that researchers are beginning to see in their data.

No Earth-like Planets Yet

The new findings were made by Geoffrey Marcy of San Francisco State and the University of California, Berkeley, Paul Butler of the Carnegie Institution of Washington, and Steve Vogt of the University of California, Santa Cruz, using the world's largest ground-based telescope, the 10-meter Keck I on Mauna Kea, Hawaii. The great difficulty of detecting these smaller planets was explained by Geoffrey Marcy as "like looking at a beach from a distance. Previously we only saw the large boulders, which were Jupiter-size planets or larger. Now we are seeing the 'rocks,' Saturn-size planets or smaller. We still don't have the capability of detecting Earth-like planets, which would be equivalent to seeing pebbles on the beach."

Astronomers don't actually see the new planets with their telescopes. They infer the presence of a planet around a star by a telltale wobble in the motion of a star as a result of the gravitational force exerted by the orbiting planet.

One of the new planets is orbiting 3.8 million miles from the star HD46375, 109 light-years away in the constellation Monoceros. It is at least 80% of the mass of Saturn. The other planet is orbiting 32.5 million miles from the star 79 Ceti (also known as HD16141), located 117 light-years away in the constellation Cetus.

In Nov. 1999, the team of Marcy, Butler, Vogt, and Kevin Apps of the University of Sussex, England, found six new planets orbiting nearby stars, bringing the total then to 28. The planets circle stars that are similar in size, age, and brightness to the Sun and are at distances ranging from 65 to 192 light-years from Earth. The planets themselves range in mass from slightly smaller to several times larger than the planet Jupiter (0.8 to 6.5 times the mass of Jupiter).

Water Worlds

Five of the six new worlds are located within the so-called habitable zones of their parent stars. This is the region where temperature would allow water to exist in liquid form. According to Vogt, the planets are at just the right distance, with temperatures in one case around 108° F. He also noted that if these Jupiter-size planets are similar to those in our solar system, they probably have numerous moons associated with them.

In May 2000, a team of astronomers from Geneva Observatory, Sauverny, Switzerland, reported their discovery of eight new companions to solar-type stars, upping the number of exoplanets to over 40. Their detection was made using the European Southern Observatory's telescope at La Silla, Chile. The masses of these objects range from less than that of the planet Saturn to about 15 times that of Jupiter.

Six of the new planet candidates are most likely extrasolar planets, and two of them may be low-mass brown dwarfs (objects of substellar mass without a nuclear energy source in their interior). One of the eight new worlds orbits the star HD 168746 in the constellation Scutum, located at a distance of 140 light-years. It is about 80% the size of Saturn, which makes it the third exoplanet to date with a possible sub-Saturnian mass.

The European astronomers also found that the companion of star HD 83443 in the constellation Vela is particularly remarkable, not only because of its low mass, 0.35 times the mass of Jupiter, or 1.17 that of Saturn, but because it is the one exoplanet detected so far with the shortest period (2.986 days) and the smallest distance to its central star, only 3.54 million miles (5.7 million kilometers.)

More Recent Discoveries

In Aug. 2000, a team of astronomers led by Geoffrey Marcy and Paul Butler added three new exoplanets to the list of 41 previously discovered. All the new planets were large gas giants similar to Jupiter. They were found orbiting the stars HD 12661 on the border of the constellation Aries; HD 92788 in the constellation Sextans; and HD 38529 in the constellation Orion. There is also evidence suggesting that there may be a second planet orbiting HD 38529.

Another star, 55 Cancri, around which the team found a planet four years ago, is also suspected of having a second companion. Postdoctoral fellow Debra Fisher and her team at U.C., Berkeley, studied a dozen stars with known planets for which they had at least two years of data and found that five of them exhibit unexplained wobbles that cannot be caused by a single planet. This suggests that there is a second planet at a much greater distance from the star. Up until now, only one sunlike star has been found with multiple planets, Upsilon Andromedae, which the team discovered in 1996. These new discoveries hint that many extrasolar planets could have siblings. □

Phenomena, 2001

Configurations of Sun, Moon, and Planets

NOTE: The hour listings are in Universal Time. For conversion to United States time zones, *see* Conversion of Universal Time to Civil Time, p. 399.

JANUARY

d	hr.	
2	23	FIRST QUARTER
4	09	Earth at perihelion
6	01	Saturn 2° N of Moon
6	14	Jupiter 3° N of Moon
9	20	FULL MOON (Eclipse)
10	09	Moon at perigee
13	17	Mercury 2° S of Neptune
16	13	LAST QUARTER
17	06	Venus greatest elong. E (47°)
17	20	Mars 4° S of Moon
21	04	Ceres 0°7 S of Moon (Occn.)
22	18	Mercury 0°4 S of Uranus
24	13	NEW MOON
24	19	Moon at apogee
25	15	Jupiter stationary
25	16	Saturn stationary
26	03	Mercury 3° N of Moon
26	04	Neptune in conjunction with Sun
27	11	Vesta 0°8 S of Moon (Occn.)
28	13	Mercury greatest elong. E (18°)
28	14	Venus 6° N of Moon

FEBRUARY

d	hr.	
1	14	FIRST QUARTER
2	10	Saturn 2° N of Moon
2	22	Jupiter 3° N of Moon
3	12	Mercury stationary
7	22	Moon at perigee
8	07	FULL MOON
9	12	Uranus in conjunction with Sun
13	00	Mercury in inferior conjunction
15	03	LAST QUARTER
15	10	Mars 3° S of Moon
18	07	Ceres 0°5 S of Moon (Occn.)
20	22	Moon at apogee
20	23	Neptune 2° N of Moon
21	16	Mercury 6° N of Moon
22	01	Venus greatest brilliancy
23	08	NEW MOON
24	19	Juno 0°2 S of Moon (Occn.)
25	02	Mercury stationary
25	17	Juno 1°0 N of Moon (Occn.)
26	08	Venus 11° N of Moon

MARCH

d	hr.	
1	18	Saturn 2° N of Moon
2	09	Jupiter 3° N of Moon
3	02	FIRST QUARTER
4	14	Mars 5° N of Antares
7	11	Venus stationary

d	hr.	
8	09	Moon at perigee
9	17	FULL MOON
10	11	Mercury 0°1 N of Uranus
11	06	Mercury greatest elong. W (27°)
15	21	Mars 1°8 S of Moon
16	21	LAST QUARTER
18	07	Ceres 0°5 S of Moon (Occn.)
18	22	Pluto stationary
20	08	Neptune 2°N of Moon
20	11	Moon at apogee
20	14	Equinox
21	14	Uranus 3° N of Moon
22	18	Mercury 2° N of Moon
25	01	NEW MOON
27	07	Vesta in conjunction with Sun
29	04	Saturn 1°7 N of Moon
29	21	Jupiter 2° N of Moon
30	04	Venus in inferior conjunction

APRIL

d	hr.	
1	11	FIRST QUARTER
5	10	Moon at perigee
6	21	Mercury 10° S of Venus
8	03	FULL MOON
10	02	Pallas stationary
13	02	Mars 1°3 S of Moon
15	04	Ceres 0°9 S of Moon (Occn.)
15	16	LAST QUARTER
16	14	Jupiter 5° N of Aldebaran
16	16	Neptune 3° N of Moon
17	06	Moon at apogee
17	17	Venus stationary
17	23	Uranus 3° N of Moon
20	20	Venus 10° N of Moon
23	09	Mercury in superior conjunction
23	15	NEW MOON
25	16	Saturn 1°4 N of Moon
26	13	Jupiter 1°8 N of Moon
30	02	Juno in conjunction with Sun
30	17	FIRST QUARTER

MAY

d	hr.	
2	04	Moon at perigee
4	18	Venus greatest brilliancy
7	14	FULL MOON
7	17	Mercury 4° N of Saturn
10	19	Mars 1°9 S of Moon
11	02	Neptune stationary
11	15	Mars stationary
12	10	Mercury 8° N of Aldebaran
14	00	Neptune 3° N of Moon
15	01	Moon at apogee
15	08	Uranus 3° N of Moon
15	10	LAST QUARTER

d	hr.	
16	17	Mercury 3° N of Jupiter
18	21	Ceres stationary
19	09	Venus 4° N of Moon
20	21	Vesta 0°6 S of Moon (Occn.)
22	04	Mercury greatest elong. E (22°)
23	03	NEW MOON
24	07	Jupiter 1°3 N of Moon
24	19	Mercury 3° N of Moon
25	13	Saturn in conjunction with Sun
27	07	Moon at perigee
27	18	Pallas at opposition
29	22	FIRST QUARTER
29	22	Uranus stationary

JUNE

d	hr.	
4	05	Mercury stationary
4	12	Pluto at opposition
6	02	FULL MOON
6	19	Mars 4° S of Moon
8	05	Venus greatest elong. W (46°)
10	08	Neptune 3° N of Moon
11	16	Uranus 3° N of Moon
11	20	Moon at apogee
13	08	Mars at opposition
14	03	LAST QUARTER
14	13	Jupiter in conjunction with Sun
16	13	Mercury in inferior conjunction
17	22	Venus 1°7 N of Moon
19	22	Saturn 0°9 N of Moon (Occn.)
21	08	Solstice
21	12	NEW MOON (Eclipse)
21	23	Mars closest approach
23	17	Moon at perigee
28	03	FIRST QUARTER
28	07	Mercury stationary

JULY

d	hr.	
3	10	Mars 6° S of Moon
4	14	Earth at aphelion
5	15	FULL MOON (Eclipse)
7	14	Neptune 3° N of Moon
7	19	Ceres at opposition
8	22	Uranus 3° N of Moon
9	11	Moon at apogee
9	17	Mercury greatest elong. W (21°)
12	22	Mercury 1°9 S of Jupiter
13	08	Saturn 4° N of Aldebaran
13	19	LAST QUARTER
15	01	Venus 3° N of Aldebaran
15	05	Venus 0°7 S of Saturn

d	hr.	
17	13	Saturn 0°6 N of Moon (Occn.)
17	18	Venus 0°3 S of Moon (Occn.)
19	00	Jupiter 0°2 N of Moon (Occn.)
19	13	Mercury 1°0 S of Moon (Occn.)
19	23	Mars stationary
20	20	NEW MOON
21	21	Moon at perigee
26	09	Pallas stationary
27	10	FIRST QUARTER
27	15	Mercury 6° S of Pollux
30	12	Neptune at opposition
30	14	Mars 6° S of Moon

AUGUST

d	hr.	
3	19	Neptune 3° N of Moon
4	06	FULL MOON
5	03	Uranus 3° N of Moon
5	21	Moon at apogee
5	22	Mercury in superior conjunction
6	00	Venus 1°2 S of Jupiter
12	08	LAST QUARTER
14	03	Saturn 0°2 N of Moon (Occn.)
15	15	Uranus at opposition
15	20	Jupiter 0°4 S of Moon (Occn.)
16	13	Venus 1°9 S of Moon
19	03	NEW MOON
19	06	Moon at perigee
22	13	Venus 7° S of Pollux
25	07	Pluto stationary
25	20	FIRST QUARTER
27	12	Mars 5° S of Moon
28	02	Ceres stationary
31	00	Neptune 3° N of Moon

SEPTEMBER

d	hr.	
1	07	Uranus 3° N of Moon
1	23	Moon at apogee
2	22	FULL MOON

d	hr.	
10	13	Saturn 0°2 S of Moon (Occn.)
10	19	LAST QUARTER
12	12	Jupiter 1°0 S of Moon (Occn.)
15	07	Venus 3° S of Moon
16	16	Moon at perigee
17	10	NEW MOON
18	22	Mercury greatest elong. E (27°)
19	02	Mercury 8° S of Moon
20	20	Mercury 0°9 N of Spica
20	20	Venus 0°5 N of Regulus
22	23	Equinox
24	10	FIRST QUARTER
25	01	Mars 2° S of Moon
27	03	Saturn stationary
27	05	Neptune 3° N of Moon
28	11	Uranus 3° N of Moon
29	06	Moon at apogee

OCTOBER

d	hr.	
1	20	Mercury stationary
2	14	FULL MOON
7	19	Saturn 0°5 S of Moon (Occn.)
9	18	Vesta stationary
10	00	Jupiter 1°4 S of Moon
10	04	LAST QUARTER
14	02	Mercury in inferior conjunction
14	23	Moon at perigee
15	02	Venus 4° S of Moon
16	19	NEW MOON
17	23	Neptune stationary
22	11	Mercury stationary
22	20	Mars 0°1 N of Moon (Occn.)
24	03	FIRST QUARTER
24	12	Neptune 3° N of Moon
25	17	Uranus 3° N of Moon
26	20	Moon at apogee
29	17	Mercury greatest elong. W (19°)
31	04	Uranus stationary

NOVEMBER

d	hr.	
1	06	FULL MOON
2	09	Mercury 5° N of Spica
2	12	Venus 4° N of Spica
2	17	Jupiter stationary
3	22	Saturn 0°6 S of Moon (Occn.)
4	18	Mars 2° S of Neptune
6	07	Jupiter 1°7 S of Moon
8	12	LAST QUARTER
11	17	Moon at perigee
15	07	NEW MOON
20	21	Neptune 3° N of Moon
21	19	Mars 3° N of Moon
22	02	Uranus 4° N of Moon
22	23	FIRST QUARTER
23	16	Moon at apogee
26	10	Mars 0°8 S of Uranus
27	17	Vesta at opposition
30	21	FULL MOON

DECEMBER

d	hr.	
1	02	Saturn 0°5 S of Moon (Occn.)
3	11	Jupiter 1°6 S of Moon
3	14	Saturn at opposition
4	22	Mercury in superior conjunction
6	23	Moon at perigee
7	04	Pluto in conjunction with Sun
7	20	LAST QUARTER
14	21	NEW MOON (Eclipse)
17	17	Saturn 4° N of Aldebaran
18	07	Neptune 4° N of Moon
19	12	Uranus 4° N of Moon
20	20	Mars 4° N of Moon
21	13	Moon at apogee
21	19	Solstice
22	21	FIRST QUARTER
25	21	Juno stationary
28	08	Saturn 0°2 S of Moon (Occn.)
30	11	FULL MOON (Penumbral Eclipse)
30	14	Jupiter 1°2 S of Moon (Occn.)

Some Facts about Eclipses

Source: U.S. Naval Observatory and NASA/Goddard Space Flight Center

Anaxagoras, in the 5th century B.C., is credited as the first to figure out the true cause of a lunar eclipse, but his explanation neither reached nor convinced centuries of humanity, the majority of whom would have trembled with fear and trepidation as they watched the Moon turn the color of blood. For generations, an eclipse of the Moon foretold of no good.

Lunar eclipses do not occur as frequently as total solar eclipses, but they are visible from anywhere on the side of Earth facing the Moon during the evening. A total solar eclipse can only be seen from a narrow band about a hundred miles wide at most, and while up to seven of these a year are not unusual, they frequently occur over the most inaccessible regions on the planet.

The Sun can be viewed safely with the naked eye only during the few brief seconds or minutes of a total solar eclipse. Partial eclipses, annular eclipses, and partial phases of total eclipses are *never safe to watch without taking special precautions.* Even when 99% of the Sun's surface is obscured during the partial phases of a total eclipse, the remaining photospheric crescent is intensely bright and cannot be viewed safely without eye protection. Failure to use appropriate filtration may result in permanent eye damage or blindness. □

Conversion of Universal Time (U.T.) to Civil Time

U.T.	E.D.T.[1]	E.S.T.[2]	C.S.T.[3]	M.S.T.[4]	P.S.T.[5]
00	*8P	*7P	*6P	*5P	*4P
01	*9P	*8P	*7P	*6P	*5P
02	*10P	*9P	*8P	*7P	*6P
03	*11P	*10P	*9P	*8P	*7P
04	M	*11P	*10P	*9P	*8P
05	1A	M	*11P	*10P	*9P
06	2A	1A	M	*11P	*10P
07	3A	2A	1A	M	*11P
08	4A	3A	2A	1A	M
09	5A	4A	3A	2A	1A
10	6A	5A	4A	3A	2A
11	7A	6A	5A	4A	3A
12	8A	7A	6A	5A	4A
13	9A	8A	7A	6A	5A
14	10A	9A	8A	7A	6A
15	11A	10A	9A	8A	7A
16	N	11A	10A	9A	8A
17	1P	N	11A	10A	9A
18	2P	1P	N	11A	10A
19	3P	2P	1P	N	11A
20	4P	3P	2P	1P	N
21	5P	4P	3P	2P	1P
22	6P	5P	4P	3P	2P
23	7P	6P	5P	4P	3P

NOTES: * denotes previous day. N = noon. M = midnight. 1. Eastern Daylight Time. 2. Eastern Standard Time, same as Central Daylight Time. 3. Central Standard Time, same as Mountain Daylight Time. 4. Mountain Standard Time, same as Pacific Daylight Time. 5. Pacific Standard Time.

Eclipses of the Sun and Moon, 2001

Note: The day of an eclipse is given in Universal Time (U.T.) and may start a day earlier or later depending on your time zone. (*See* Phenomena, 2001 table, pp. 397–398, to find time of eclipse.)

January 9. Total eclipse of the Moon. The beginning of the umbral phase visible in northern region of Canada, most of Alaska, Greenland, Arctic, Europe, most of Africa, Australia, western Micronesia, Asia, Queen Mary coast of Antarctica, northeastern North Atlantic Ocean, eastern South Atlantic Ocean, Indian Ocean, and western North Pacific Ocean; the end visible in northeastern North America, Greenland, Arctic, northeastern South America, Europe, Africa, coast of Antarctica near Cape Ann, Asia, Atlantic Ocean, Indian Ocean, and western Philippine Sea.

June 21. Total eclipse of the Sun. Visible in the South Atlantic Ocean, Angola, Zambia, Zimbabwe, Mozambique, Madagascar, and the Indian Ocean.

July 5. Partial eclipse of the Moon. The beginning of the umbral phase visible in Antarctica, Australia, New Zealand, eastern Asia except the far north, Aleutian Islands, Pacific Ocean except extreme east, and the eastern Indian Ocean; the end visible in Australia, Antarctica, New Zealand, Asia except the extreme northern part, eastern Africa, western Pacific Ocean, and the Indian Ocean.

December 14. Annular eclipse of the Sun. Visible in the Pacific Ocean, northwest South America, Central America, the United States, western and southern parts of Canada.

December 30. Penumbral eclipse of the Moon. The beginning of the penumbral phase visible in North America, Central America, South America except the eastern coast, Greenland, extreme northwestern Europe, northeast Asia, Arctic, most of New Zealand, North Atlantic Ocean, Pacific Ocean, eastern Philippine Sea, and Coral Sea; the end visible in North America except eastern coast, Greenland, Arctic, northern part of Central America, Asia, Indonesia, Australia, New Zealand, the North Pacific Ocean, South Pacific Ocean except southeastern part and eastern portion of the Indian Ocean.

Visibility of Planets in Morning and Evening Twilight, 2001

	Morning		Evening
Venus	April 4–December 3	Venus	January 1–March 26
Mars	January 1–June 13	Mars	June 13–December 31
Jupiter	June 29–December 31	Jupiter	January 1–May 31
Saturn	June 13–December 3	Saturn	January 1–May 7
			December 3–December 31

A Human Mission to Mars? Not Yet

We still lack the resources to put astronauts on Mars

The scientific community was intrigued by the startling announcement in June 2000 that some high-resolution images of Mars taken by the Mars *Global Surveyor* showed strong evidence of small channels and gullies that appeared to be carved by outflows of subsurface water. If significant amounts of liquid water are confirmed to be lurking in some areas below the planet's surface, it will increase the likelihood of a human Mars exploration program and the possibility of finding microscopic life there.

First Stop, Mars

Mars is the first nearby world that people from Earth will eventually visit. With its recognizable four seasons, clouds, polar ice caps, mountains, dry river beds, and dormant volcanoes, Mars is the most Earth-like planet in our solar system, and it has the greatest potential for human habitation. Although it has a very cold, dry climate, surface temperatures at the equator can reach 80°F during the summer.

Scientists believe that there were once similar conditions on Mars and Earth billions of years ago. Data from past Mars missions suggest that the planet once had a warmer, wetter climate and abundant liquid water—lakes, rivers, and even oceans—during its early history.

A detailed exploration of Mars would give us insights into the past and future of our planet. We might also learn whether Mars could sustain self-sufficient colonies that might prove to be a lifeboat for humanity's survival in the event of a distant future global calamity. Finally, exploring the planet could create new commercial opportunities and sources of income.

A Very Dangerous Mission

NASA has no current program to send humans to Mars. Any possibility of planning such a trip was set back a few decades because of long delays in assembling the International Space Station and the unexpected loss of the *Climate Orbiter* and the *Polar Lander* in 1999. Also, a human expedition cannot be attempted until extensive robotic explorations have made a detailed study of the planet, found vital sources of water, returned soil samples to Earth, and located the best landing sites. Eventually, however, NASA will develop the critical technologies for long-term survival in beyond-Earth orbits on the International Space Station, which will make it possible for humans to make such a journey.

No one knows how many billions of dollars a human mission to Mars will eventually cost, and the enormous financial burden will have to be shared by other nations. Possibly by the end of this century, a multinational crew of six humans will depart our home planet for a long sojourn on Mars. The epic endeavor will be far more dangerous and technically difficult to accomplish than it was when we sent men to the Moon over three decades ago. The Moon was only a short hop of 240,000 mi. compared to a 47-million-mi. voyage to Mars. If an Apollo 13–type disaster were to befall them, the astronauts wouldn't be able to return again to Earth.

The monumental challenge of sending humans to Mars for a lengthy stay and then returning them safely to Earth is mind-boggling. Unlike previous space missions, when these astronauts leave Earth, they will not be able to return for almost three years. The trip to Mars will take between four and six months, depending on the propulsion system used. After the interplanetary voyagers arrive on the Red Planet, they will have to remain there for approximately 18 months until the proper alignment of Earth and Mars allows them to blast off for home.

A Hypothetical Scenario

Most likely the internationally supported mission will require transporting most of the necessary supplies and equipment by unmanned spacecraft to the chosen landing area and confirming their operable condition before the first astronauts even arrive.

During their long, confined stay, the Mars pioneers may live in an inflatable modular housing unit similar to the TransHab (for "transportation and habitat") design proposed by NASA in 1997 as a possible replacement for the U.S. crew quarters on the International Space Station. The cylindrical structure would be 27 ft. (8.2 m) in diameter and have a foot-thick protective shell when inflated. The shell would be made of almost two dozen layers of material that is stronger than steel. It would also provide insulation from the extreme Martian temperatures that range from −199°F (−128.3°C) during the polar night to 80°F (26.6°C) at the equator. The module would consist of four levels, for work, health care, crew quarters, and a galley area.

The space travelers will drive for miles across the planet's diverse terrain in advanced-type roving vehicles equipped with specialized tools, drills, and analytical instruments. Much of their time will be spent searching for water and past and present evidence of Martian life forms, and conducting a wide range of scientific activities that cannot be accomplished by robotic exploration.

Survival on Mars

Because it is impossible to take all the supplies that they will need from Earth, the astronauts will probably have to live off the barren land, using the planet's raw materials to provide fuel, oxygen, and most of the food for a primarily vegetarian diet. Possibly some type of "care" packages of goodies will be sent by rocket to them from time to time to relieve the dietary monotony. The versatile explorers will even have to manufacture the special spacecraft fuel required for their return to Earth.

Their survival in the inhospitable environment will be totally dependent on their combined expertise, specialized skills, and available equipment. When unexpected problems and challenges arise, as they undoubtedly will, the spacefarers will have to solve them with little or no help from Earth. Even their radio communications with mission controllers will be difficult because of the time delay between Mars and Earth. Depending on Mars's distance from Earth, which can vary by as much as 200 million mi. (322 km), radio signals from the planet can take anywhere from 4 minutes to 21 minutes to reach Earth.

Health Issues a Priority

The physical and mental health and safety of the crew during their long, arduous months on Mars are a major concern for mission planners. How do you plan for life-threatening medical emergencies when you are trapped on a far distant world? In 1999, a doctor wintering at a South Pole station found a lump in her breast, but she couldn't be flown out for proper treatment until the end of the harsh winter. If Mars astronauts become perilously ill, they can't be "flown out" for two years.

The astronauts must also be shielded from harmful radiation while traveling in their spacecraft and when on the planet's surface. And because the gravity on Mars is only 38% of Earth's, ways to counteract any damaging effects of the weak gravity on their bodies,

such as progressive bone loss and muscle atrophy, will have to be found. Currently, there is no fully effective treatment for microgravity-induced bone loss, and counter measures against bone loss are a top space science priority.

Working Together

Finally, the multinational crews will have to learn to appreciate and understand their cultural differences if they are to live and work together in harmony during their long isolation millions of miles from Earth. The need for this training was emphasized during a six-month test of long-term spaceflight isolation begun in Dec. 1999, when four multinational volunteers living in a simulated space station encountered problems arising from their cultural differences.

In March 2000, NASA took one of the first steps necessary in preparing humans to live on Mars when it successfully tested the prototype of a device to produce pure oxygen from the carbon dioxide in a simulated Martian atmosphere. Besides providing breathable oxygen for future colonists, the unit, called the Mars In-situ Propellant Production Precursor (MIP), demonstrated that rocket fuel can be manufactured on Martian soil for the return trip to Earth. NASA hopes to send an identical MIP unit for further testing aboard the next Mars lander missions, tentatively scheduled to launch in 2003. □

Space Station Assembly Back on Track

The long-awaited Russian-built temporary living quarters and propulsion system, the *Zvezda* (meaning "star") service module, was finally launched and connected to the *Zarya* ("sunrise") component of the International Space Station (ISS) on July 25, 2000. The *Zvezda* (a.k.a. the Functional Cargo Block) was originally scheduled to be launched in April 1998, but Russian financial problems and launch failures delayed its delivery. The *Zvezda* module is also the main docking port for Russian *Progress* resupply vehicles. Russia plans to launch three *Progress* resupply craft to the space station by the end of 2000.

First Crew

Zvezda's link-up with two previously orbited modules set the stage for the arrival of the first permanent crew, consisting of space station commander Bill Shepherd (Capt. USN), *Soyuz* commander Yuri P. Gidzenko (Lt. Col. Russian AF), and flight engineer, cosmonaut Sergei K. Krikalev. The three-man crew are due to be launched aboard a *Soyuz* spacecraft on Oct. 30, 2000, for about a four-month stay. The space shuttle *Discovery* will bring a replacement crew to the station in Feb. 2001 and return the resident crew home to Earth. (In Sept. 2000, the space shuttle *Atlantis* will visit the station, and its seven-member crew will transfer supplies to outfit *Zvezda* in preparation for the arrival of the inaugural crew.)

Assembly Required

The first pieces of the ISS to be joined in orbit were the U.S.-built connecting module Node 1, named *Unity*, and the U.S.-funded and Russian-built

Zarya control module in Dec. 1998. *Unity* has six hatches that are used as docking ports, and it also serves as a passageway for station crews as they move through the connected modules.

The space shuttle *Atlantis* is tentatively scheduled to launch the U.S. Laboratory Module in Jan. 2001. It is the centerpiece of the ISS, in which unprecedented science experiments will be performed in the near-zero gravity of space.

A Space for Science

When the space station is completed in 2005, an international crew of up to seven will live and work there for between three and four months. The station's six laboratories will provide more space for research than any spacecraft ever built. Return vehicles will always be attached to the ISS to insure the safe return of all crew members in the event of an emergency.

The finished space outpost will be 356 ft. (109 m) across and 290 ft. (88 m) long and will orbit 246 by 234 statute mi. (396 by 377 km) above Earth. It will circle the globe at an inclination of 51.6° to the equator. This orbit can be reached by the launch vehicles of all international partners and provides an excellent view of 85 percent of Earth's globe.

Led by the U.S., the International Space Station is the largest and most complex international science and engineering program ever attempted. Partners in the program are Russia, Japan, Canada, and participating countries of the European Space Agency (ESA): Belgium, Denmark, France, Germany, Italy, the Netherlands, Norway, Spain, Sweden, Switzerland, and the United Kingdom. □

Major Space Explorations

Ongoing Missions

Galileo (U.S.)

Destination: Jupiter. **Launched:** Oct. 18, 1989. **Achieved Orbit:** Dec. 7, 1995. **Mission:** To study the chemical composition and physical state of the largest planet in the solar system, its atmosphere, and four of its moons, for almost two years. The spacecraft encountered the asteroid 951 Gaspera on Oct. 29, 1991, and took the first close-up photographs ever of an asteroid in space. On Aug. 28, 1993, it passed by asteroid 243 Ida and took close-up photographs, which revealed that Ida has a tiny moon. Upon arrival at Jupiter, *Galileo* released a probe into the planet's atmosphere that descended for 57 minutes before it was destroyed by the planet's extreme temperature and pressure. In 1996, *Galileo* visited and photographed Jupiter's large moons Io, Callisto, and Europa and made flybys of Io, Ganymede, Europa, and Callisto in 1997. *Galileo* was named for the Italian astronomer Galileo Galilei, who discovered the four great moons of Jupiter that were the major targets of this mission.

Galileo Europa Mission (GEM):

A two-year continuation of the original Galileo Mission, which was completed in Dec. 1997. GEM included eight flybys of Europa, four flybys of Callisto, and two flybys of Io by the end of 1999. The spacecraft also observed the smaller moons Amalthea, Thebe, and Metis on Jan. 3, 2000. GEM mission ended Jan. 31, 2000.

Galileo Millennium Mission:

An extended mission to explore Jupiter and its moons through the end of 2000. On Feb. 22, 2000, Galileo made the closest pass ever of Io at 124 mi. (200 km). Two flybys of Ganymede are planned for May 20 and Dec. 28, 2000. Galileo will embark on a joint scientific expedition with the Saturn-bound Cassini spacecraft around Dec. 2000 to make simultaneous observations of the Jupiter system from two vantage points.

Ulysses (U.S. and European Space Agency)

Destination: The Sun. **Launched:** Oct. 6, 1990. **Flew by Jupiter:** Feb. 8, 1992. **Achieved Highest Southern Latitude:** Sept. 13, 1994 (−80.2 degrees). **Achieved Highest Northern Latitude:** July 31, 1995 (+80.2 degrees). **Mission:** An international project to study the Sun and interstellar space above and below its poles. The spacecraft was put into orbit at right angles to the solar system's ecliptic plane. This special orbit enabled *Ulysses* to examine for the first time the Sun's north and south polar regions. Besides investigating the Sun, the spacecraft is also studying phenomena from the Milky Way and beyond. The spacecraft completed its first full orbit around the Sun on April 17, 1998. *Ulysses* will continue to orbit the Sun, passing over the north and south poles in 2000 and 2001.

Near-Earth Asteroid Rendezvous (NEAR) (U.S.)

Destination: Asteroid 433 Eros. **Launched:** Feb. 17, 1996. **Arrival:** Feb. 14, 2000. **Mission:** To rendezvous with Eros and orbit the asteroid for almost one year. It is taking comprehensive measurements of Eros's surface, size, volume, mass, spin, and magnetic field. *NEAR* passed by and photographed minor planet 253 Mathilde on June 27, 1997. The mission will end Feb. 2001. The spacecraft was posthumously named NEAR-Shoemaker in honor of geologist Eugene M. Shoemaker.

Mars Global Surveyor (U.S.)

Destination: Mars. **Launched:** Nov. 7, 1996. **Arrival:** Sept. 11, 1997. **Mission:** An orbiting spacecraft designed to provide detailed maps of the planet's surface and distribution of minerals, and to monitor the Martian weather. Six instruments are studying Martian surface, atmosphere, and gravitational and magnetic fields. *Surveyor*'s cameras are able to distinguish features as small as 10 ft. across.

The primary mapping mission was delayed until March 1999, due to problems with the craft's solar panels. The spacecraft will orbit Mars for 687 days, the length of one Martian year. After mapping is finished, the orbiter will act as a relay until Jan. 2003 in support of other Mars missions. The mapping operations should continue through Jan. 2001.

Cassini (U.S., the European Space Agency, and the Italian Space Agency)

Destination: Saturn. **Launched:** Oct. 15, 1997. **Arrival:** July 1, 2004. **Mission:** Will orbit Saturn for four years. Before reaching Saturn, *Cassini* will encounter Jupiter on Dec. 30, 2000, and fly down the giant planet's magnetotail, performing studies complementing the Galileo Mission. While orbiting Saturn, *Cassini* will send a small probe named *Huygens* (after the Dutch astronomer Christiaan Huygens, who discovered Titan) to the surface of Saturn's largest moon, Titan, to learn more about its dense atmosphere and its surface state and composition. After relaying data to Earth from Titan, *Cassini* will continue with orbits of Saturn and flybys of the planet's 16 or more moons. The spacecraft will also examine Saturn's equatorial zone and study the planet's polar regions. The spacecraft flew by asteroid 2685 Masursky on Jan. 23, 2000. The Cassini mission is named for the Italian-French astronomer Gian Domenico Cassini, who discovered four of Saturn's major moons.

Nozomi ("Hope") (Japan)

Destination: Mars. **Launched:** July 4, 1998, from Kagoshima Space Center. **Arrival:** Dec. 2003. Engine problems delayed its scheduled 1999 arrival at Mars until 2003. **Mission:** To send an orbiter around Mars to study the effect of the solar wind on the planet's atmosphere for one Martian year (687 days). Its cameras will provide photographic data on cloud distribution, polar haze, dust storms, polar ice, and the planet's surface. After its successful launch, the Planet-B spacecraft was renamed *Nozomi* (hope). Japan's new effort made it the third nation after the United States and Russia to conduct a mission to another planet.

Stardust (U.S.)

Destination: Comet Wild 2. **Launched:** Feb. 7, 1999. **Mission:** To fly through coma of Comet Wild 2 in 2004, capture particles spewing out of comet, and return comet dust samples to Earth in 2006. *Stardust* will be the first mission to return with comet samples. En route to Wild 2, the spacecraft collected particles from the interstellar dust stream between Feb. 22 and May 1, 2000.

Deep Space 1 (U.S.)

Launched: Oct. 24, 1998. **Mission:** First launch of NASA's New Millennium program, a series of missions to test new technologies. *Deep Space 1* is the first craft to employ an ion-propulsion system. It flew past near-Earth asteroid Braille on July 28, 1999, took photos, and collected scientific data. The primary mission ended Sept. 18, 1999, and its mission was extended to fly past comet Borrelly, Sept. 2001.

Future Missions
(Note: Dates are tentative.)

Genesis (U.S.)

Destination: The Sun. **Launch:** Jan. 2001. **Mission:** Gather samples of charged particles of the solar wind and return them to Earth in Aug. 2003 for detailed analysis. The reentry vehicle will separate from the spacecraft and parachute its sample return capsule to a location in the Utah desert. The data to be obtained are crucial for improving theories about the origin of the Sun and planets that formed from the same primordial dust cloud.

Mars Surveyor Orbiter 2001 (U.S.)

Destination: Mars. **Launch:** April 7, 2001. **Arrival:** Oct. 20, 2001. **Mission:** To conduct mineralogical mapping of the planet, study radiation risk to humans, and determine abundance of shallow subsurface water. Due to the loss of the Mars *Polar Lander* in 1999, the Mars *Surveyor Lander* 2001 was postponed until 2003. NASA decided to cancel the lander portion of the mission as part of the restructuring of the Mars Planetary Program and continue only with the orbiter portion as planned.

Mars Surveyor Rovers 2003 (U.S.)

Destination: Mars. **First launch:** May 22, 2003. **Arrival:** Jan. 2, 2004. **Second launch:** June 4, 2003. **Arrival:** Jan. 20, 2004. **Mission:** To deploy two identical large long-range rovers (larger than *Pathfinder*'s *Sojourner*) in two different locations that can trek up to 300 yards (100 m) across the surface in a Martian day. The rovers' sophisticated instruments will enable them to act as mobile field geologists, taking color pictures, analyzing soil and rocks, and searching for past and present evidence of water. The rovers are designed to operate for 90 days but could continue longer.

Contour (U.S.)

Destination: Comet Nucleus Tour. **Launch:** July 2002. **Mission:** To fly by Comet Encke at 60 mi. (100 km), followed by encounters with Comet Schwassmann-Wachmann-3 in June 2006, and Comet d'Arrest in Aug. 2008. The spacecraft will take images and spectral maps of nuclei and analyze dust flowing from them. The mission will help scientists to learn more about the composition and structure of comets, which are believed to be quite individual in their properties.

Selene SELenological and Engineering Explorer (Japan)

Destination: The Moon. **Launch:** 2003. **Mission:** An orbiting spacecraft to study the origin and evolution of the Moon for one year. It will map the entire surface and gather data on chemical and mineralogical composition, magnetic fields, and interior structure. After a year, the propulsion module of the orbiter will separate from the spacecraft and softland on the lunar surface to continue the mission for two more months.

U.S. Unstaffed Planetary and Lunar Programs

Lunar Orbiter. Series of spacecraft designed to orbit the Moon, taking pictures and obtaining data in support of the subsequent staffed *Apollo* landings. The U.S. launched five *Lunar Orbiters* between Aug. 10, 1966 and Aug. 2, 1967.

Mariner. Designation for a series of spacecraft designed to fly past or orbit the planets, particularly Mercury, Venus, and Mars. *Mariners* provided the early information on Venus and Mars. *Mariner 9,* orbiting Mars in 1971, returned the most revealing photographs of that planet and helped pave the way for a *Viking* landing in 1976. *Mariner 10* explored Venus and Mercury in 1973 and was the first probe to use a planet's gravity to propel it toward another.

Pioneer. Designation for the United States' first series of sophisticated interplanetary spacecraft. *Pioneers 10* and *11* reached Jupiter in 1973 and 1974 and continued on to explore Saturn and the other outer planets. *Pioneer 11,* renamed *Pioneer Saturn,* examined the Saturn system in Sept. 1979. Significant discoveries were the finding of a small new moon and a narrow new ring. In 1986, *Pioneer 10* was the first man-made object to escape the solar system. *Pioneer Venus 1* and *2* reached Venus in 1978 and provided detailed information about that planet's surface and atmosphere.

Ranger. NASA's earliest Moon-exploration program. Spacecraft were designed for a crash landing on the Moon, taking pictures and returning scientific data up to the moment of impact. Provided the first close-up views of the lunar surface. The *Rangers* provided more than 17,000 close-up pictures, giving us more information about the Moon in a few years than in all the time that had gone before.

Surveyor. Series of unstaffed spacecraft designed to land gently on the Moon and provide information on the surface in preparation for the staffed lunar landings. *Surveyors'* legs were instrumented to return data on the surface hardness of the Moon. *Surveyor* dispelled the fear that *Apollo* spacecraft might sink several feet or more into the lunar dust.

Viking. Designation for two spacecraft designed to conduct detailed scientific examination of the planet Mars, including a search for life. *Viking 1* landed on July 20, 1976; *Viking 2,* Sept. 3, 1976. More was learned about the red planet in a few short months than in all previous missions, but the question of whether there is life on Mars remains unresolved.

Voyager. Designation for two spacecraft designed to explore Jupiter and the other outer planets. *Voyager 1* and *Voyager 2* passed Jupiter in 1979 and sent back surprising color TV images of that planet and its moons. They took a total of about 33,000 pictures. *Voyager 1* passed Saturn in Nov. 1980. *Voyager 2* passed Saturn in Aug. 1981 and Uranus in Jan. 1986.

Voyager 2 encountered Neptune on Aug. 29, 1989, and made many discoveries. It found four rings around the planet, six new moons, a giant spot, and evidence of volcanic-like activity on its largest moon, Triton. The spacecraft sent back over 9,000 pictures of the planet and its system.

On Feb. 13, 1990, at a distance of 3.7 billion miles, *Voyager 1* took its final pictures—the Sun and six of its planets as seen from deep space. NASA released the extraordinary images to the public on June 6, 1990. Only Mercury, Mars, and Pluto were not seen.

Notable Unstaffed Lunar and Interplanetary Probes

Spacecraft	Launch date	Destination	Remarks
Pioneer 3 (U.S.)	Dec. 6, 1958	Moon	Max. alt.: 66,654 mi. Discovered outer Van Allen layer.
Luna 2 (U.S.S.R.)	Sept. 12, 1959	Moon	Impacted on Sept. 14. First space vehicle to reach Moon.
Luna 3 (U.S.S.R.)	Oct. 4, 1959	Moon	Flew around Moon and transmitted first pictures of lunar far side, Oct. 7.
Mariner 2 (U.S.)	Aug. 27, 1962	Venus	Venus probe. Successful mid-course correction. Passed 21,648 mi. from Venus Dec. 14, 1962. Reported 800°F. surface temp. Contact lost Jan. 3, 1963, at 54 million mi.
Ranger 7 (U.S.)	July 28, 1964	Moon	Impacted near Crater Guericke 68.5 hr. after launch. Sent 4,316 pictures during last 15 min. of flight as close as 1,000 ft. above lunar surface.
Mariner 4 (U.S.)	Nov. 28, 1964	Mars	Transmitted first close-up pictures on June 14, 1965, from altitude of 6,000 mi.
Luna 9 (U.S.S.R.)	Jan. 31, 1966	Moon	3,428 lb. Instrument capsule of 220 lb. soft-landed Feb. 3, 1966. Sent back about 30 pictures.
Surveyor 1 (U.S.)	May 30, 1966	Moon	Landed June 2, 1966. Sent almost 10,400 pictures, a number after surviving the 14-day lunar night.
Lunar Orbiter 1 (U.S.)	Aug. 10, 1966	Moon	Orbited Moon Aug. 14. 21 pictures sent.
Surveyor 3 (U.S.)	April 17, 1967	Moon	Soft-landed 65 hr. after launch on Oceanus Procellarum. Scooped and tested lunar soil.
Venera 4 (U.S.S.R.)	June 12, 1967	Venus	Arrived Oct. 17. Instrument capsule sent temperature and chemical data.
Surveyor 5 (U.S.)	Sept. 8, 1967	Moon	Landed near lunar equator Sept. 10. Radiological analysis of lunar soil. Mechanical claw for digging soil.
Surveyor 7 (U.S.)	Jan. 6, 1968	Moon	Landed near Crater Tycho Jan. 10. Soil analysis. Sent 3,343 pictures.
Pioneer 9 (U.S.)	Nov. 8, 1968	Sun	Achieved orbit. Six experiments returned solar radiation data.
Venera 5 (U.S.S.R.)	Jan. 5, 1969	Venus	Landed May 16, 1969. Returned atmospheric data.
Mariner 6 (U.S.)	Feb. 24, 1969	Mars	Came within 2000 mi. of Mars July 31, 1969. Sent back data and TV pictures.
Luna 16 (U.S.S.R.)	Sept. 12, 1970	Moon	Soft-landed Sept. 20, scooped up rock, returned to Earth Sept. 24.
Luna 17 (U.S.S.R.)	Nov. 10, 1970	Moon	Soft-landed on Sea of Rains Nov. 17. *Lunokhod 1,* self-propelled vehicle, used for first time. Sent TV photos, made soil analysis, etc.
Mariner 9 (U.S.)	May 30, 1971	Mars	First craft to orbit Mars, Nov. 13. 7,300 pictures, 1st close-ups of one of Mars's moons. Transmission ended Oct. 27, 1972.
Luna 20 (U.S.S.R.)	Feb. 14, 1972	Moon	Soft-landed Feb. 21 in Sea of Fertility. Returned Feb. 25 with rock samples.
Pioneer 10 (U.S.)	March 3, 1972	Jupiter	620-million-mi. flight path through asteroid belt passed Jupiter Dec. 3, 1973, to give man first close-up of planet. In 1986, it became first man-made object to escape solar system.
Luna 21 (U.S.S.R.)	Jan. 8, 1973	Moon	Soft-landed Jan. 16. *Lunokhod 2* (moon-car) scooped up soil samples, returned them to Earth Jan. 27.
Mariner 10 (U.S.)	Nov. 3, 1973	Venus, Mercury	Passed Venus Feb. 5, 1974. Arrived Mercury March 29, 1974, for man's first close-up look at planet. First time gravity of one planet (Venus) used to propel spacecraft toward another (Mercury).
Viking 1 (U.S.)	Aug. 20, 1975	Mars	Carrying life-detection labs. Landed July 20, 1976, for detailed scientific research, including pictures. Designed to work for only 90 days, it operated for almost 6½ years before it went silent in Nov. 1982.
Viking 2 (U.S.)	Sept. 9, 1975	Mars	Like Viking 1. Landed Sept. 3, 1976. Functioned 3½ years.
Luna 24 (U.S.S.R.)	Aug. 9, 1976	Moon	Soft-landed Aug. 18, 1976. Returned soil samples Aug. 22, 1976.

Spacecraft	Launch date	Destination	Remarks
Voyager 2 (U.S.)	Aug. 20, 1977	Jupiter, Saturn, Uranus	Launched before *Voyager 1.* Encountered Jupiter in July 1979; flew by Saturn Aug. 1981; passed Uranus Jan. 1986; and passed Neptune in Aug. 1989.
Voyager 1 (U.S.)	Sept. 5, 1977	Jupiter, Saturn	Fly-by mission. Reached Jupiter in March 1979; passed Saturn Nov. 1980; passed Uranus 1986.
Pioneer Venus 1 (U.S.)	May 20, 1978	Venus	Arrived Dec. 4 and orbited Venus, photographing surface and atmosphere. Crashed into planet's surface mid-Oct. 1992 after circling Venus for 14 years.
Pioneer Venus 2 (U.S.)	Aug. 8, 1978	Venus	Four-part multiprobe, landed Dec. 9.
Venera 13 (U.S.S.R.)	Oct. 30, 1981	Venus	Landed March 1, 1982. Took first X-ray fluorescence analysis of the planet's surface. Transmitted data 2 hours, 7 minutes.
VEGA 1 (U.S.S.R.)	Deployed on Venus, June 10, 1985	Halley's Comet	In flyby over Venus while en route to encounter Halley's Comet, *VEGA 1* and *2* dropped scientific capsules onto Venus to study atmosphere and surface material. Encountered Halley's Comet on March 6 and March 9, 1986. Took TV pictures and studied comet's dust particles.
VEGA 2 (U.S.S.R.)	Deployed on Venus, June 14, 1985	Halley's Comet	See *VEGA 1* above.
Suisei (Japan)	Encountered Halley's Comet March 8, 1986	Halley's Comet	Spacecraft made flyby of comet and studied atmosphere with ultraviolet camera. Observed rotation nucleus.
Sakigake (Japan)	Encountered Halley's Comet March 10, 1986	Halley's Comet	Spacecraft made flyby to study solar wind and magnetic fields. Detected plasma waves.
Giotto (E.S.A.)	Encountered Halley's Comet March 13, 1986	Halley's Comet	European Space Agency spacecraft made closest approach to comet. Studied atmosphere and magnetic fields. Sent back best pictures of nucleus. Flew by comet Grigg-Skjellerup July 10, 1992. Unable to send pictures.
Phobos Mission (U.S.S.R.)	July 7 and July 12, 1988	Mars and Phobos	Two spacecraft to probe Martian moon Phobos starting April 1989. Were to study orbit and soil chemistry, and send TV pictures and data of planet. Contact was lost with *Phobos 1* in Aug. 1988 and later with *Phobos 2* in March 1989 after it reached the Martian moon.
Magellan (U.S.)	May 4, 1989	Venus	Arrived at Venus on Aug. 10, 1990, and made a geologic map of planet with a powerful radar. Crashed into Venus Oct. 12, 1994.
Galileo (U.S.)	Oct. 18, 1989	Jupiter	To study Jupiter's atmosphere and its moons during 22-month mission.
Ulysses (U.S., E.S.A.)	Oct. 6, 1990	Sun	To study the poles of the Sun and interstellar space above and below the poles. First solar encounter was in 1994, second encounter in 1995.
Gamma-Ray Observatory (U.S.)	April 7, 1991	Earth orbit	To make first survey of gamma-ray sources across the whole sky, studying explosive energy sources such as supernovae, quasars, neutron stars, pulsars, and black holes. Mission ended; it was deorbited and crashed into Pacific Ocean, June 4, 2000.
Clementine (U.S.)	Jan. 25, 1994	Moon and asteroid Geographos 1620	Entered lunar orbit Feb. 21 and took close-up photos of lunar surface for two months. Computer malfunction prevented planned rendezvous with *Geographos.*
Mars Pathfinder (U.S.)	Dec. 5, 1996	Ares Vallis, Mars	Landed July 4, 1997. The spacecraft lander and its rover, *Sojourner,* provided a wealth of information on the Martian rocks, soil, and atmosphere. Sent back the first live pictures. All *Pathfinder*'s objectives were fulfilled and communications failed on Sept. 27, 1997.
Lunar Prospector (U.S.)	Jan. 6, 1998	Moon	Orbited Moon for one year, mapped chemical composition of lunar surface. Found frozen water at north and south poles. At end of its mission on July 31, 1999, it was intentionally crashed into south polar crater in hope of detecting plume of water ice, but no cloud of molecular water vapor was observed by powerful Earth telescopes.

U.S. Staffed Space Flight Programs

Mercury. *Project Mercury,* initiated in 1958 and completed in 1963, was the United States' first human-in-space program. It was designed to further knowledge about humanity's capabilities in space.

In April 1959, seven military-jet test pilots were introduced to the public as America's first astronauts. They were: Lt. M. Scott Carpenter, USN; Capt. L. Gordon Cooper, Jr., USAF; Lt. Col. John H. Glenn, Jr., USMC; Cap. Virgil I. Grissom, USAF; Lt. Cdr. Walter M. Schirra, Jr., USN; Lt. Cdr. Alan B. Shepard, Jr., USN; and Capt. Donald K. Slayton, USAF. Six of the original seven would make a Mercury flight. Slayton was grounded for medical reasons, but remained a director of the astronaut office. He returned to flight status in 1975 as Docking Module Pilot on the *Apollo-Soyuz* flight.

Flight Summary

Each astronaut named his capsule and added the numeral 7 to denote the teamwork of the original astronauts.

May 5, 1961. Alan B. Shepard, Jr., made a suborbital flight in *Freedom 7* and became the first American in space. Time: 15 minutes, 22 seconds.

July 21, 1961. Virgil I. Grissom made the second successful suborbital flight in *Liberty Bell 7,* but spacecraft sank shortly after splashdown. Time: 15 minutes, 37 seconds. Grissom was later killed in *Apollo 1* fire, Jan. 27, 1967.

Feb. 20, 1962. John H. Glenn, Jr., made a three-orbit flight and became the first American in orbit. Time: 4 hours, 55 minutes.

May 24, 1962. M. Scott Carpenter duplicated Glenn's flight in *Aurora 7.* Time: 4 hours, 56 minutes.

Oct. 3, 1962. Walter M. Schirra, Jr., made a six-orbit engineering test flight in *Sigma 7.* Time: 9 hours, 13 minutes.

May 15–16, 1963. L. Gordon Cooper, Jr., performed the last *Mercury* mission and completed 22 orbits in *Faith 7* to evaluate effects of one day in space. Time: 34 hours, 19 minutes.

The Women in Space Program

In 1960, NASA also tested the first female trainees for astronaut duty in the *Mercury* program. Thirteen out of America's 25 top female civilian pilots (women weren't allowed to be military pilots then) passed the same rigorous testing that male candidates underwent in the *Mercury 7* space program. Although all the pilots proved fit to become *Mercury* astronauts, NASA suddenly canceled its testing of qualified women in July 1961, claiming that they required jet test-pilot training at Edwards Air Force Base. Unfortunately, instruction at Edwards was closed to women. This new requirement ended America's chance to put the first women in space.

It is ironic that unlike her skilled American counterparts, Valentina Tereshkova, the first woman to fly in space, was a textile factory worker when she entered the Soviet space program. She had no experience as a pilot and her only qualification was that of an amateur parachute jumper before being trained as a cosmonaut in 1962.

These outstanding "Mercury 13" candidates deserve much credit for preparing the way for American women in space. They were: Jerrie Cobb, Rhea Allison, Jane Hart, Mary Wallace Funk, Jean Hixson, Myrtle Cagle, Irene Leverton, Sarah Gorelick, twins Jan and Marion Dietrich, Gene Stumbough, Bernice Steadman, and Gerry Sloan Truhill.

Gemini. *Gemini* was an extension of *Project Mercury,* to determine the effects of prolonged space flight on humans for two weeks or longer—the time it would take to reach the Moon and return. "Walks in space" provided invaluable information for astronauts' later walks on the Moon. The *Gemini* spacecraft, twice as large as the *Mercury* capsule, accommodated two astronauts. Its crew named the project *Gemini* for the third constellation of the Zodiac and its twin stars, Castor and Pollux. The capsule differed from the *Mercury* spacecrafts in that it had hatches above the capsules so that the astronauts could leave the spacecraft and perform spacewalks or extra-vehicular activities (EVAs).

There were 10 staffed flights in the *Gemini* program, starting with *Gemini 3* on March 23, 1965, and ending with the *Gemini 12* mission on Nov. 15, 1966. *Gemini 1* and *2* were unstaffed test flights of the equipment.

Apollo. *Apollo* was the designation for the United States' effort to land a person on the Moon and return him safely to Earth. The goal was successfully accomplished with *Apollo 11* on July 20, 1969, culminating eight years of rehearsal and centuries of dreaming. Astronauts Neil A. Armstrong and Col. Edwin E. Aldrin, Jr., scooped up and brought back the first lunar rocks ever seen on Earth—about 47 pounds.

Tragedy struck Jan. 27, 1967, on the launch pad during a preflight test of what would have become *Apollo 1,* the first staffed mission. Astronauts Lt. Col. Virgil "Gus" Grissom, Lt. Col. Edward H. White, and Lt. Cdr. Roger Chafee lost their lives when a fire swept through the command module.

Six *Apollo* flights followed, ending with *Apollo 17* in December 1972. The last three *Apollos* carried mechanized vehicles called lunar rovers for wide-ranging surface exploration of the Moon by astronauts. The rendezvous and docking of an *Apollo* spacecraft with a Russian *Soyuz* craft in Earth orbit on July 18, 1975, closed out the *Apollo* program.

During the Apollo project, the following 12 astronauts explored the lunar terrain: Col. Edwin E. "Buzz" Aldrin, Jr., and Neil A. Armstrong, *Apollo 11;* Cdr. Alan L. Bean and Cdr. Charles "Pete" Conrad, Jr., *Apollo 12;* Edgar D. Mitchell and Alan B. Shepard, *Apollo 14;* Lt. Col. James B. Irwin and Col. David R. Scott, *Apollo 15;* Col. Charles M. Duke, Jr., and Capt. John W. Young, *Apollo 16;* and Capt. Eugene A. Cernan and Dr. Harrison H. Schmitt, *Apollo 17.*

Apollo was a three-part spacecraft: the command module (CM), the crew's quarters and flight control section; the service modules (SM) for the propulsion and spacecraft support systems (when together, the two modules were called CSM); and the lunar module (LM) that took two of the crew to the lunar surface, supported them on the Moon, and returned them to the CSM in orbit.

The third lunar attempt, *Apollo 13,* April 11–17, 1970, 5 days, 22.9 hours, was aborted after the service module oxygen tank ruptured. The *Apollo 13* crew members were James A. Lovell, Jr., John L. Swigert, Jr., and Fred W. Haise, Jr. The mission was classified as a "successful failure" because the crew was rescued.

Skylab. America's first Earth-orbiting space station. *Project Skylab* was designed to demonstrate that men can work and live in space for prolonged periods without ill effects. Originally the spent third stage of a *Saturn 5* Moon rocket, *Skylab* measured 118 ft. from stem to stern, and carried the most varied assortment of experimental equipment ever assembled in a single spacecraft. Three three-man crews visited the space stations, spending more than 740 hours observing the Sun and bringing home more than 175,000 solar pictures. These were the first recordings of solar activity above Earth's obscuring atmosphere. *Skylab* also evaluated systems designed to gather information on Earth's resources and environmental conditions. *Skylab*'s biomedical findings indicated that humans adapt well to space for at least a period of three months, provided they have a proper diet and adequately programmed exercise, sleep, work, and recreation periods. *Skylab* orbited Earth at a distance of about 300 mi. Five years after the last *Skylab* mission, the 77-ton space station's orbit began to deteriorate faster than expected, owing to unexpectedly high sunspot activity. On July 11, 1979, the parts of *Skylab* that did not burn up in the atmosphere came crashing down on parts of Australia and the Indian Ocean. No one was hurt.

Space Shuttle. The space shuttle *Columbia* was successfully launched on April 12, 1981. It made five flights (the first four were test runs), the last completed on Nov. 16, 1982. The second shuttle, *Challenger,* made its maiden flight on April 4, 1983. The third shuttle, *Discovery,* made its first flight on Aug. 30, 1984. The fourth space shuttle, *Atlantis,* made its maiden flight on Oct. 3, 1985.

A tragedy occurred on Jan. 28, 1986, when the shuttle *Challenger* exploded, killing the crew of seven 73 seconds after takeoff. It was the world's worst space flight disaster.

The crew members who were killed were: Francis R. Scobee, shuttle commander; Cdr. Michael J. Smith, pilot; mission specialists Judith A. Resnik, Lt. Col. Ellison S. Onizuka, and Ronald E. McNair; and payload specialists Gregory B. Jarvis and Christa McAuliffe (who was to be the first civilian schoolteacher in space).

The cause of the explosion was a rupture in a seal on one of the booster rockets that let a jet of flame escape, igniting the fuel. The weakness in the seal was caused by the cold air temperature when the shuttle was launched.

The first U.S. space mission since the *Challenger* disaster was launched 32 months later, on Sept. 29, 1988, with the flight of *Discovery.* It had a crew of five and deployed a communications satellite.

The fifth and last orbiter, *Endeavour,* was built as a replacement for *Challenger.* It was named after the 16th-century British explorer James Cook's first ship. *Endeavour* was launched on its maiden voyage on May 7, 1992, with a crew of seven astronauts. They made four spacewalks and retrieved a disabled *Intelsat-6* communications satellite. During the mission, Dr. Kathryn Thornton became the second American woman to walk in space.

The shuttle *Columbia* spent a record 17 days, 15 hours in space, Nov. 19–Dec. 7, 1996.

The crew of the 50th mission aboard the *Endeavour,* launched Sept. 12, 1992, included the first black woman astronaut, Dr. Mae C. Jemison, and the first married couple to fly together in space, Air Force Lt. Col. Mark C. Lee and Dr. N. Jan Davis.

Lt. Col. Eileen M. Collins became the first woman to pilot a shuttle, *Discovery,* during the spacecraft's historic rendezvous with the Russian space station *Mir* on Feb. 6, 1995. The shuttle *Atlantis* made the first link-up with the *Mir* on June 29, 1995.

Lt. Col. Collins became the first woman to command a space shuttle when *Columbia* was launched in July 1999 on a mission to deploy the Chandra X-ray Observatory (formerly called AXAF).

Senator John Glenn, 76, the first American to orbit the Earth, flew as a payload specialist on the Oct. 1998 *Discovery* mission. He studied the effects of aging and microgravity on the human body.

Soviet Staffed Space Flight Programs

Vostok. The Soviets' first staffed capsule, roughly spherical, used to place the first six cosmonauts in Earth orbit (1961–1965).

Voskhod. Adaptation of the *Vostok* capsule to accommodate two and three cosmonauts. *Voskhod 1* orbited three persons, and *Voskhod 2* orbited two persons, performing the world's first staffed extravehicular activity.

Soyuz. Late-model staffed spacecraft with provisions for three cosmonauts and a "working compartment" accessible through a hatch. Soyuz is the Russian word for "union." The *Soyuz* spacecraft can carry three cosmonauts, and routinely brings cosmonauts and their foreign "guests" to the *Mir* space station. *Soyuz 19,* launched July 15, 1975, docked with the American *Apollo* spacecraft.

Salyut. Earth-orbiting space station intended for prolonged occupancy and revisitation by cosmonauts. They are usually launched by Soviet Proton rockets. *Salyut 1* was launched April 19, 1971. *Salyut 2,* launched April 3, 1973, malfunctioned in orbit and was never occupied. *Salyut 3* was launched June 25, 1974. *Salyut 4* was launched Dec. 26, 1974. *Salyut 5* was launched June 22, 1976. *Salyut 6* was launched on Sept. 29, 1977. *Salyut 7* was launched on April 19, 1982. A record-breaking Russian endurance flight was set (Feb. 8, 1984–Oct. 2, 1985) when Soviet astronauts spent 237 days in orbit aboard *Salyut 7*. *Salyut 7* reentered the atmosphere and crashed into the Atlantic Ocean on Feb. 6, 1991.

Mir. Soviet space station, launched into orbit on Feb. 20, 1986. The Russian government had planned to deorbit the abandoned *Mir* in early 2000 due to lack of funds, but the space station got a new lease on life when private investors provided the cash to keep the craft in orbit. The new Russian partners, MirCorp, a Netherlands-based company, funded cosmonauts Sergei Zaloytin and Alexander Kaleri's return mission to reopen and repair the *Mir,* April 4 to June 15, 2000. Russian officials hope to obtain additional funds to keep the *Mir* aloft. ☐

China's Unstaffed Spacecraft

China launched its first unstaffed spacecraft from the Jiuquan Space Center in Gansu province on Nov. 19, 1999. The space capsule, named "Shenzhou" (God Vessel, or Divine Ship), made 14 orbits of Earth in 21 hours before landing in Inner Mongolia. The automated test launch and successful recovery means that China will likely become the third nation after the U.S. and Soviet Union capable of sending people into space.

Future flights with taikonauts (Chinese astronauts) aboard the space capsule will depend on the results of additional unstaffed tests. As of Aug. 2000, no date had been set for a manned mission. ☐

Notable Staffed Space Flights

Designation and country	Date	Astronauts	Flight time (hr./min)	Remarks
Vostok 1 (U.S.S.R.)	April 12, 1961	Yuri A. Gagarin	1/48	First person in space.
MR III (U.S.)	May 5, 1961	Alan B. Shepard, Jr.	0/15	Range 486 km (302 mi.), peak 187 km (116.5 mi.); capsule recovered. First American in space.
Vostok 2 (U.S.S.R.)	Aug. 6–7, 1961	Gherman S. Titov	25/18	First long-duration flight.
MA VI (U.S.)	Feb. 20, 1962	John H. Glenn, Jr.	4/55	First American in orbit.
MA IX (U.S.)	May 15–16, 1963	L. Gordon Cooper, Jr.	34/20	Longest *Mercury* flight.
Vostok 6 (U.S.S.R.)	June 16–19, 1963	Valentina V. Tereshkova	70/50	First woman in space.
Voskhod 1 (U.S.S.R.)	Oct. 12, 1964	Vladimir M. Komarov, Konstantin P. Feoktistov, Boris G. Yegorov	24/17	First 3-person orbital flight; also first flight without space suits.
Voskhod 2 (U.S.S.R.)	March 18, 1965	Alexei A. Leonov, Pavel I. Belyayev	26/2	First "space walk" (by Leonov), 10 min.
GT III (U.S.)	March 23, 1965	Virgil I. Grissom, John W. Young	4/53	First American 2-person crew.
GT IV (U.S.)	June 3–7, 1965	James A. McDivitt, Edward H. White, II	97/48	First American "space walk" (by White), lasting slightly over 20 min.
GT VIII (U.S.)	March 16–17, 1966	Neil A. Armstrong, David R. Scott	10/42	First docking between staffed spacecraft and an unstaffed space vehicle (an orbiting *Agena* rocket).
Apollo 7 (U.S.)	Oct. 11–22, 1968	Walter M. Schirra, Jr., Donn F. Eisele, R. Walter Cunningham	260/9	First staffed test of *Apollo* command module; first live TV transmissions from orbit.
Soyuz 3 (U.S.S.R.)	Oct. 26–30, 1968	Georgi T. Bergeovoi	94/51	First staffed rendezvous and possible docking by Soviet cosmonaut.
Apollo 8 (U.S.)	Dec. 21–27, 1968	Frank Borman, James A. Lovell, Jr., William A. Anders	147/00	First spacecraft in circumlunar orbit; TV transmissions from this orbit. The three astronauts were also the first astronauts to view the whole Earth.
Apollo 9 (U.S.)	Mar. 3–13, 1969	James A. McDivitt, David R. Scott, Russell L. Schweikart	241/1	First staffed flight of Lunar Module.
Apollo 10 (U.S.)	May 18–26, 1969	Thomas P. Stafford, Eugene A. Cernan, John W. Young	192/3	First descent to within nine miles of Moon's surface by staffed craft.
Apollo 11 (U.S.)	July 16–24, 1969	Neil A. Armstrong, Edwin E. Aldrin, Jr., Michael Collins	195/18	First staffed landing and EVA on Moon; soil and rock samples collected; experiments left on lunar surface.
Soyuz 6 (U.S.S.R.)	Oct. 11–16, 1969	Gorgiy Shonin, Valriy Kabasov	118/42	Three spacecraft and seven men put into Earth orbit simultaneously for first time.
Apollo 12 (U.S.)	Nov. 14–24, 1969	Charles Conrad, Jr., Richard F. Gordon, Jr., Alan Bean	244/36	Staffed lunar landing mission; investigated *Surveyor 3* spacecraft; collected lunar samples. EVA time: 15 hr., 30 min.

Designation and country	Date	Astronauts	Flight time (hr./min)	Remarks
Apollo 13 (U.S.)	April 11–17, 1970	James A. Lovell, Jr., Fred W. Haise, Jr., John L. Swigert, Jr.	142/54	Third staffed lunar landing attempt; aborted due to pressure loss in liquid oxygen in service module and failure of fuel cells.
Apollo 14 (U.S.)	Jan. 31–Feb. 9, 1971	Alan B. Shepard, Stuart A. Roosa, Edgar D. Mitchell	216/42	Third staffed lunar landing: returned largest amount of lunar material.
Soyuz 11 (U.S.S.R.)	June 6–30, 1971	Georgiy Tomofeyevich Dobrovolskiy, Vladislav Nikolayevich Volkov, Viktor Ivanovich Patsyev	569/40	Longest stay in space. Linked up with first space station, Salyut 1. Astronauts died just before reentry due to loss of pressurization in spacecraft.
Apollo 15 (U.S.)	July 26–Aug. 7, 1971	David R. Scott, James B. Irwin, Alfred M. Worden	295/12	Fourth staffed lunar landing; first use of lunar rover propelled by Scott and Irwin; first live pictures of LM lift-off from Moon; exploration time: 18 hours.
Apollo 16 (U.S.)	April 16–27, 1972	John W. Young, Thomas K. Mattingly, Charles M. Duke, Jr.	265/51	Fifth staffed lunar landing; second use of lunar rover vehicle, propelled by Young and Duke. Total exploration time on the Moon was 20 hr., 14 min., setting new record. Mattingly's in-flight "walk in space" was 1 hr., 23 min. Approximately 213 lb of lunar rock returned.
Apollo 17 (U.S.)	Dec. 7–19, 1972	Eugene A. Cernan, Ronald E. Evans, Harrison H. Schmitt	301/51	Sixth and last staffed lunar landing; third to carry lunar rover. Cernan and Schmitt, during three EVAs, completed total of 22 hr., 05 min., 3 sec. USS Ticonderoga recovered crew and about 250 lbs of lunar samples.
Skylab SL-2 (U.S.)	May 25–June 22, 1973	Charles Conrad, Jr., Joseph P. Kerwin, Paul J. Weitz	672/50	First staffed Skylab launch. Established Skylab Orbital Assembly and conducted scientific and medical experiments.
Skylab SL-3 (U.S.)	July 28–Sept. 25, 1973	Alan L. Bean, Jr., Jack R. Lousma, Owen K. Garriott	1427/9	Second staffed Skylab launch. New crew remained in space for 59 days, continuing scientific and medical experiments and Earth observations from orbit.
Skylab SL-4 (U.S.)	Nov. 16, 1973–Feb. 8, 1974	Gerald Carr, Edward Gibson, William Pogue	2017/16	Third staffed Skylab launch; obtained medical data on crew for use in extending the duration of staffed space flight; crews "walked in space" 4 times, totaling 44 hr., 40 min. Longest space mission yet: 84 d, 1 hr., 16 min. Splashdown in Pacific, Feb. 9, 1974.
Apollo/Soyuz Test Project (U.S. and U.S.S.R.)	July 15–24, 1975 (U.S.)	U.S.: Brig. Gen. Thomas P. Stafford, Vance D. Brand, Donald K. Slayton	216/05	World's first international staffed rendezvous and docking in space; aimed at developing a space rescue capability.
Apollo/Soyuz Test Project (U.S. and U.S.S.R.)	July 15–21, 1975 (U.S.S.R.)	U.S.S.R.: Col. A. A. Leonov, V. N. Kubasov	223/35	Apollo and Soyuz docked and crewmen exchanged visits on July 17, 1975. Mission duration for Soyuz: 142 hr., 31 min. For Apollo: 217 hr., 28 min.
Columbia (U.S.)	April 12–14, 1981	Capt. Robert L. Crippen, John W. Young	54/20	Maiden voyage of space shuttle.
Mir (U.S.S.R.)	Dec. 21, 1987–Dec. 21, 1988	Col. Vladimir Titov, Musa Manarov	366 days	Set current record for Soviet team endurance flight in orbiting space station.
Endeavour (U.S.)	May 7–16, 1992	Richard J. Hieb, Maj. Thomas D. Akers, Cdr. Pierre J. Thugt	8 days, 23 hr., 17 min.	The three mission specialists remained free of the Endeavour for 8 hours and 20 minutes on May 13 during the repair of communications satellite, setting an absolute record for extravehicular duration in space. First capture of a satellite using hands only.
Endeavour (U.S.)	Dec. 2–13, 1993	Col. Richard O. Covey, Cdr. Kenneth D. Bowersox, Lt. Col. Tom Akers,* Dr. Jeffrey A. Hoffman,** Dr. Story Musgrave,** Claude Nicollier, Dr. Kathryn C. Thornton* (*two space walks; **three space walks)	10 days, 19 hr., 59 min.	Repaired Hubble Space Telescope. Replaced gyroscopes, solar arrays, camera, electronics, and hardware. Installed COSTAR corrective optics to compensate for flaw in Hubble's primary mirror. Record five space walks in a single mission.

Designation and country	Date	Astronauts	Flight time (hr./min)	Remarks
Mir-17 (Russia)	Jan. 8, 1994– Mar. 22, 1995	Dr. Valery Polyakov	439[1] days	Record single endurance flight in orbiting space station. Returned to Earth with crewmates cosmonaut Helena Kondakova and commander Alexander Viktorenko, who spent 169 days each in *Mir*.
Discovery (U.S.)	Feb. 3–11, 1995	Cdr. James D. Wetherbee, Lt. Col. Eileen M. Collins, Dr. Janice Voss, Dr. Bernard A. Harris, Jr.,* Dr. C. Michael Foale,* Russian cosmonaut Co. Vladimir G. Titov *performed spacewalks.	8 days, 6 hr., 29 min.	First rendezvous of U.S. spacecraft with a Russian space station (*Mir*), Feb. 6. Lt. Col. Collins was first female shuttle pilot. Deployed and retrieved solar observatory satellite. Extravehicular activity to test new space suit modifications and practice space station assembly techniques. EVA time: 4 hr., 35 min.
Soyuz TM-21 (Russia)	March 14–22, 1995	Russian cosmonauts Lieut. Col. Vladimir N. Dezhurov and Gennady M. Strekalov, and U.S. astronaut Dr. Norman E. Thagard		Dr. Thagard became the first American astronaut to fly aboard a *Soyuz* spacecraft with a Russian crew launched from Baikonur Space Center in Kazakhstan. He also became the first American to enter the *Mir* space station on March 16.
Atlantis (U.S.)	June 27–July 7, 1995	Lt. Col. Charles J. Precourt, Capt. Robert L. (Hoot) Gibson, Dr. Eileen S. Baker, Gregory J. Harbaugh, Dr. Bonnie Dunbar, Russian cosmonauts: *Mir-19* commander Anatoly Y. Solovyev, Nikolai M. Budarin	10 days	Marked 100th human mission in U.S. space program and first shuttle link-up with *Mir*: docked June 29, undocked July 4. Joined spacecraft held a record 10 people: 6 Americans and 4 Russians. Three *Mir* crew (*Mir-18* commander Lieut. Col. Vladimir N. Dezhurov, cosmonaut Grennady M. Strekalov, and U.S. astronaut Dr. Norman E. Thagard) returned to Earth aboard the *Atlantis*. Dr. Thagard set a U.S. space record of 112 days in space aboard *Mir*. Cosmonauts Solovyev and Budarin remained aboard *Mir*.
Atlantis (U.S.)	Nov. 12–20, 1995	Col. Kenneth D. Cameron, Lieut. Col. James D. Halsell, Jr., Col. Jerry L. Ross, Lieut. Col. William S. McArthur, Jr., Canadian Major Chris A. Hadfield, who operated the robot arm	8 days, 4 hr., 31 min.	Second docking with *Mir*. Carried 15-ft.-long Russian-made docking module and attached it to *Mir*. Brought 2 new solar-powered panels for *Mir* and also supplies and scientific equipment. U.S. and Russian astronauts spent 3 days together on *Mir* conducting experiments.
Endeavour (U.S.)	Jan. 11–20, 1996	Col. Brian Duffy, Brent Jett, Dr. Leroy Chiao,** Capt. Winston E. Scott,* Dr. Daniel T. Berry,* and Japanese astronaut Koichi Wakata, who operated robot arm (*one spacewalk; **two spacewalks)	8 days, 22 hr., 1 min.	Deployed and retrieved NASA satellite, retrieved Japanese satellite. Two spacewalks performed to test spacesuit components and practice space station construction, tools, and techniques. Total EVA time: 13 hours.
Atlantis (U.S.)	March 22–31, 1996	Col. Kevin P. Chilton, Lieut. Col. Richard A. Searfoss, Dr. Ronald M. Sega, Dr. Linda M. Goodwin, Lieut. Col. Michael R. Clifford, Shannon W. Lucid	9 days, 5 hr., 15 min.	Third link-up with *Mir* (March 22–27). Clifford and Goodwin conducted 6-hour spacewalk in shuttle cargo bay while docked with *Mir*. Lucid remained on board *Mir* for scheduled 140-day tour to conduct biomedical and material science experiments. Booster problems delayed her return until mid-September. Lucid is first American woman to live on *Mir*. On July 15, 1996, she broke the previous record for the longest U.S. manned space flight.
Endeavour (U.S.)	May 19–29, 1996	Col. John H. Casper, Lieut. Col. Curtis L. Brown, Jr., Cdr. Daniel W. Bursch, Mario Runco, Jr., Dr. Andrew S.W. Thomas, Canadian astronaut Dr. Marc Garneau	10 days, 0 hr., 40 min.	Made record of four satellite rendezvous, including three with small PAMS satellite to test the concept of a self-stabilizing satellite in orbit. Deployed and retrieved a Spartan satellite that carried an experimental inflatable antenna.
Columbia (U.S.)	June 20–July 7, 1996	Col. Terence T. Henricks, Kevin R. Kregel, Lieut. Col. Susan J. Helms, Richard M. Linnehan, Cdr. Charles E. Brady, Jr., Dr. Jean-Jacques Favier (France), Dr. Robert Brent Thirsk (Canada)	16 days, 21 hr., 48 min.	Second-longest mission to date. Studied the effects of weightlessness on people, plants, and animals, and material manufacturing in near-zero gravity.

Designation and country	Date	Astronauts	Flight time (hr./min)	Remarks
Atlantis (U.S.)	Sept. 16–26, 1996	William F. Readdy, Terrence W. Wilcutt, Thomas D. Akers, John E. Blaha, Jerome Apt, Carl E. Waltz. Download: Shannon W. Lucid	10 days, 3hr., 19 min.	Fourth Mir docking. Carried a Spacelab module. Transferred supplies and equipment to Mir. After breaking all American and women's space endurance records (188 days, 5 hr., 0 min.), Lucid returned with Atlantis crew. John E. Blaha remained on Mir for a four-month stay.
Columbia (U.S.)	Nov. 19–Dec. 7, 1996	Kenneth D. Cockrell, Cdr. Kent V. Rommgel, Tamara E. Jernigan, Thomas D. Jones, Dr. F. Story Musgrave	17 days, 15 hr., 53 min.	Deployed and recovered two free-flying satellites during mission: an ultraviolet telescope and Wake Shield (semiconductor processing) Facility. A jammed airlock hatch canceled two scheduled spacewalks. Is longest mission to date. Dr. Musgrave, 61, became first person to fly on all five space shuttles.
Atlantis (U.S.)	Jan. 12–22, 1997	Capt. Michael A. Baker, Cdr. Brent W. Jett, Jr., John M. Grunsfeld, Marsha S. Ivins, Peter J.K. Wiscoff, Dr. Jerry L. Linenger. Download: John E. Blaha	10 days, 4 hr., 6 min.	Fifth Mir docking (Jan.14–19). Carried Spacehab double module. Transferred supplies to Mir. Conducted experiments in Spacehab and Mir. John E. Blaha returned with Atlantis crew after 128 days in space, 118 aboard Mir. Jerry Linenger remained aboard Mir for 4.5-month stay.
Discovery (U.S.)	Feb. 11–21, 1997	Cdr. Kenneth Bowersox, Lt. Col. Scott J. Harowitz, Col. Mark C. Lee,* Steven A. Hawley, Gregory J. Harbaugh,* Steven L. Smith,* Joseph R. Tanner (*spacewalks)	9 days, 23 hr., 38 min.	Second space telescope servicing mission. Installed new imaging spectrograph and infrared camera. Also patched torn telescope insulating cover. Deployed telescope at higher altitude: 335 x 321 nautical mile orbit. Mission required five spacewalks totaling 33 hr., 11 min.
Atlantis (U.S.)	May 15–24,1997	Col. Charles J. Precourt, Lt. Col. Eileen M. Collins, Edward T. Lu, Maj. Carlos I. Noriega, Jean-François Clervoy (France), Elena V. Kondakova (Russia), C. Michael Foale. Download: Dr. Jerry M. Linenger	9 days, 5 hr., 20 min.	Sixth Mir docking (May 16–21). Carried a Spacehab double module. Transferred supplies and equipment. Jerry M. Linenger returned with Atlantis after 132 days in space. Michael Foale remained on Mir for a 4.5-month stay.
Atlantis (U.S.)	Sept. 25–Oct. 6, 1997	James T. Wetherbee, Michael J. Boomfield, Col. Vladimir G Titov,* Scott E. Parazynski,* Jean-Loup J.M. Chretien (France), Wendy B. Lawrence. Up: Dr. David Wolf. Down: C. Michael Foale after 145 days in space, 134 days on Mir (*spacewalks)	10 days, 19 hr., 22 min.	7th Mir docking (Sept. 27–Oct. 3). 5-hr. spacewalks (Oct.1) retrieved U.S. experimental packages from Mir for return to Earth. Transferred supplies. Tested emergency jet packs for space station workers. Dr. David Wolf replaced Michael Foale on Mir for 4-month stay.
Endeavour (U.S.)	Jan. 22–31, 1998	Lt. Col. Terrence W. Wilcutt, Joe F. Edwards, Bonnie J. Dunbar, Maj. Michael P. Anderson, James F. Reilly, II, Salizhan S. Sharipov (Kirghizia), Andrew S.W. Thomas. Down: Dr. David Wol	8 days, 19 hr., 48 min.	8th Mir docking (Jan. 24–29). Thomas replaced David Wolf after 128 days in orbit. Thomas is the seventh and last American to live aboard Mir.
Discovery (U.S.)	June 2–12, 1998	Col. Charles J. Precourt, Cmdr. Dominic L. Gorie, Cmdr. Wendy B. Lawrence, Franklin R. Chang-Diaz, Janet Kavandi, Valeriy Ruymin (Russia) Down: Andrew S.W. Thomas	9 days, 19 hr., 54 min.	Ninth and final Mir docking mission concluded the joint U.S.–Russian program as a precursor to the International Space Station partnership. Thomas returned to Earth after a 4.5-month stay.
Discovery (U.S.)	Oct. 29–Nov.7, 1998	Lt. Col. Curtis L. Brown, Maj. Steven W. Lindsey, Stephen K. Robinson, Dr. Scott E. Parazynski, Pedro Duque (Spain), Dr. Chiaki Mukai (Japan), Senator John H. Glenn, Jr.	8 days, 21 hr., 56 min.	Deployed and retrieved Spartan solar observing satellite. Did research with Hubble Telescope Optical Systems Test Platform (HOST). Studied the effects of aging and microgravity in space.

Designation and country	Date	Astronauts	Flight time (hr./min)	Remarks
Endeavour (U.S.)	Dec. 4–15, 1998	Capt. Robert D. Cabana, Capt. Frederick W. Sturckow, Lt. Col. Nancy Currie, Col. Jerry L. Ross, Jim H. Newman, Sergei K. Krikalev (Russia)	11 days, 19 hr., 18 min.	International Space Station assembly mission. Connected Node 1, "Unity," to Functional Cargo Block, "Zarya." Ross and Newman made three spacewalks, total EVA: 21 hr., 22 min.
Discovery (U.S.)	May 27–June 6, 1999	Cmdr. Ken V. Rominger, Rick D. Husband, Ellen Ochoa, Tamara E. Jernigan, Daniel T. Barry, Julie Payette (Canada), Valery Tokarev (Russia)	9 days, 19 hr., 13 min.	Docked 5 days, 18 hr. with uninhabited International Space Station. Readied it for arrival of first resident crew. Jernigan and Barry conducted space walks (7 hr., 55 min.) for assembly work.
Columbia (U.S.)	July 23–27, 1999	Lt. Col. Eileen M. Collins, Capt. Jeffrey S. Ashby, Steven A. Hawley, Lt. Col. Catherine G. Coleman, Col. Michel Tognini (France)	4 days, 22 hr., 50 min.	Deployed Chandra X-ray Observatory (formerly AXAF). Eileen Collins became the first female shuttle commander.
Discovery (U.S.)	Dec. 19–27, 1999	Col. Curtis L. Brown Jr., Lt. Cmdr. Scott J. Kelly, Steven L. Smith, C. Michael Foale, John M. Grunsfeld, Claude Nicollier (Switzerland), Jean-François Clervoy (France)	7 days, 23 hr., 10 min.	Third Hubble Space Telescope servicing mission. Three EVAs totaled 24 hr., 33 min.: Dec. 22, Smith and Grunsfeld, 8 hr., 15 min.; Dec. 23, Foale and Nicollier, 8 hr., 10 min.; Dec. 24, Smith and Grunsfeld, 8 hr., 8 min.
Endeavour (U.S.)	Feb.11–22, 2000	Cmdr. Dominic L. Pudwill Gorie, Janet Lynn Kavandi, Janet Voss, Kevin R. Kregel, Mamoru Mohri (Japan), Gerhard P. J. Thiele (Germany)	11 days, 5 hr., 38 min.	Radar mapping obtained most detailed topographical map of Earth to date.
Atlantis (U.S.)	May 19–29, 2000	Col. James D. Halsell, Jr., Lt. Col. Scott J. Horowitz, Mary Ellen Weber, Lt. Col. (Ret.) Jeffrey N. Williams, Col. James S. Voss, Lt. Col. Susan J. Helms, Yuri V. Usachev (Russia)	9 days, 20 hr., 9 min.	Docked with International Space Station May 20–26. Prepared station for arrival of *Zvezda (Star)* service module. EVAs by Voss and Williams May 21–22 totaled 6 hr., 44 min.
Atlantis (U.S.)	Tentatively Sept. 2000[2]	Lt. Col. Terance Wilcutt, Lt. Cmdr. Scott Altman, Edward Tsang Lu, Richard Mastracchio, Lt. Cmdr. Dan Burbank, Col. Yuri I. Malenchenko (Russia), Boris Morukov (Russia)	10 days, 18 hr., 41 min.	Prepare International Space Station for arrival of first resident crew. Outfit *Zvezda* module.
Discovery (U.S.)	Tentatively Oct. 2000[2]	Col. Brian Duffy, Lt. Col. Pamela A. Melroy, Koichi Wakata (Japan), Peter J. K. Wisoff, Cmdr. Michael E. Lopez-Alegria, Col. William S. McArthur, Jr.	10 days, 19 hr., 28 min.	Assemble Integrated Truss Structure on space station to allow U.S. solar arrays to be installed on *Unity* for early power.
Endeavour (U.S.).	Tentatively Nov. 2000[2]	Lt. Col. Michael J. Bloomfield, Marc Garneau (Canada), Lt. Col. Carlos I. Noriega, Joseph R. Tanner, Brent Jett	9 days	Install photovoltaic (PV) module on space station to provide power with solar arrays and batteries.

1. From launch to landing. 2. Official dates are set approximately two weeks prior to the targeted lift-off date. For recorded launch information, call 407-867-4636. NOTES: EVA = Extravehicular Activity. The letters MR stand for Mercury (capsule) and Redstone (rocket); MA, for Mercury and Atlas (rocket); GT, for Gemini (capsule) and Titan-II (rocket). The first astronaut listed in the Gemini and Apollo flights is the command pilot. The Mercury capsules had names: MR-III was *Freedom 7*, MR-IV was *Liberty Bell 7*, MA-VI was *Friendship 7*, MA-VII was *Aurora 7*, MA-VIII was *Sigma 7*, and MA-IX was *Faith 7*. The figure 7 referred to the fact that the first group of U.S. astronauts numbered seven men. Only one Gemini capsule had a name: GT-III was called *Molly Brown* (after the Broadway musical *The Unsinkable Molly Brown*); thereafter the practice of naming the capsules was discontinued.

Too Close Encounters

A rising trend of runway miscues puts pressure on the FAA to act

By SALLY B. DONNELLY TIME

Bob Dole survived the battlefields of Italy during World War II, but he almost didn't make it out of Los Angeles International Airport. It was a clear Nov. 1999 evening when Dole and his wife, Elizabeth, boarded a United Airlines flight to Washington. The 757 began its rapid roll to takeoff. Moments before, an AeroMexico jet had mistakenly begun to cross that very runway on its way to the terminal. As the United plane hurtled down the tarmac, the pilots were startled to see the AeroMexico plane wandering into their path. The United captain reacted quickly, abruptly pulling the jetliner's nose off the ground. His plane, with 133 passengers on board, avoided the AeroMexico plane by 100 feet.

Fear of Flying

It was a frightening near collision. But what is even more alarming is how much the occurrence of such incidents has grown: up 71% between 1993 and 1999. The Federal Aviation Administration says in 1999 there were 322 so-called runway incursions—incidents that present an on-the-ground collision hazard. A joint industry-government commission to study aviation safety, which used broader guidelines, put the annual number at closer to 1,000.

Uncomfortably Close

The number of reported runway incursions in the US

350
300
250
200

'94 '95 '96 '97 '98 '99

TIME Chart
Source: NTSB

Fears of plane accidents usually focus on airborne problems, but runway incursions can be just as deadly. The worst accident in flying history took place when two packed 747 jetliners collided on a runway on Tenerife in the Canary Islands in 1977, killing 583 people.

The main reason for the growing problem is simple physics: much more matter in the same amount of space. There were 100 million more passengers in 2000 than there were in 1995, but only one major new airport has opened in the 1990s. Many older, big-city airports are as jammed at rush hour as the highways leading to them. "The hard part isn't flying to Chicago, it's getting around on the ground," says a veteran airline pilot. "And the controllers are so rushed you don't ask for help." A big part of the problem is human error. The FAA says more than half of runway incursions are attributed to pilot mistakes. These include not following instructions, missing turns, even getting lost at an unfamiliar airport. An additional 25% of runway incursions result from controller miscues.

The FAA Takes Action

The FAA can take some small steps to make runways safer. Jane Garvey, director of the FAA, says a regional airport manager told her to make sure the lights in airports were washed more frequently, and she intends to do that. The FAA has installed bigger and brighter signs, embedded lights in the tarmac pavement, and painted more lines on taxiways. The FAA has also announced programs to provide refresher training for controllers and to encourage pilots to come forward to report runway incursions.

But the best solutions may be the big-ticket improvements that have proved most elusive. The FAA continues to support a sophisticated ground-radar system that is $30 million over budget and years late. Closing poorly designed airports and restricting the number of flights per hour would probably prove effective—and expensive. It comes down, says *Air Safety Week* editor David Evans, to "the classic tension between economics and safety." In this trade-off, there's a lot to be said for safety. Just ask Bob and Elizabeth Dole. □

New Women's Free-fall Record Set

A team of 118 women skydivers, known as *Jump for Cause,* created the "largest free-fall formation" in the sky over Perris, Calif., on Sept. 5, 1999. They were able to hold the formation for 3.46 seconds before breaking away. The previous record was a 100-women formation set in 1992.

According to the National Aeronautical Association, parachuting as a sport began just before World War I, when Georgia "Tiny" Broadwick, who in 1912 was the first woman to jump from an airplane, made free-fall jumps for exhibition purposes. After the war, parachuting became a popular attraction at fairs and air shows.

Forgotten Pioneers of Flight

Dec. 17, 2003, will mark the 100th anniversary of the Wright brothers' first flight at Kitty Hawk, N.C. Many inventors before the Wrights, especially in Europe, had tried to become airborne in ingenious and sometimes impractical heavier-than-air powered craft. Although their successes only amounted to short hops a few inches above the ground and never solved the problem of controlled and sustained flight, their aeronautical research did contribute significantly to the development of the modern airplane.

By far, the most important contributions to the science of aeronautics and heavier-than-air flight were made by an Englishman, **Sir George Cayley (1773–1857)**. Because of his brilliant alterations to the basic design of a man-carrying glider and his research on aerodynamic principles, Cayley is considered the father of modern aeronautics. He experimented with fixed-wing designs for lift; steering rudders and rear elevators for control; and he understood the importance of the screw propeller for powered flight. On several occasions during 1853, Cayley was able to send his coachman and a boy airborne aboard a glider he had constructed—the world's first successful fixed-wing man-carrying glider.

In 1842, another Englishman, **William Mathew Henson (1812–1888)**, patented his invention of an aircraft that appeared to be years ahead its time. His proposed flying machine, the *Aerial Steam Carriage,* resembled the designs that were later used for World War I airplanes. Henson's craft was a monoplane with a 150-ft. (46 m) wingspan, a tricycle landing gear, and two pusher-type six-bladed propellers driven by a steam engine. Henson made a model of his plane, but it was unsuccessful in tests; and he gave up on machine-powered flight.

About 1858, a Frenchman named **Felix du Temple (1823–1890)** designed and tested a model of a propeller aircraft that was driven by a small steam engine. It took off under its own power and briefly flew for a short distance in the air before gliding to a landing. This was the first successful test flight of a powered aircraft model. About 1874, he constructed a man-carrying monoplane with a forward swept wing, a tail and rudder, a lightweight steam engine, front-mounted propellers, and a retractable landing gear. However, when it was piloted down an inclined ramp, it only "hopped" into the air and failed to make a sustained flight.

In 1873, Frenchman **Clement Ader (1841–1925)** test-flew in his 45-ft. (13.7 m) bat-winged aircraft, the *Eole,* the propeller of which was driven by a lightweight steam engine. According to witnesses, the machine ascended with Ader in it and flew 8 in. (20.3 cm) above the ground for some 156 ft. (47.5 m) before landing. It was the first man-carrying heavier-than-air machine to take off and land under its own power. The French military became interested in his experiments and, encouraged with a government subsidy in 1897, he built the *Avion III,* a twin-engine monoplane that proved to be a failure. Discouraged, Ader quit designing aircraft.

In 1894, outside his residence in Kent, England, American-born British inventor **Sir Hiram S. Maxim (1840–1916)** tested his design of a huge steam-driven biplane with a crew of three aboard,

sending it zipping down a 1,800-ft. (549 m) track. The flying machine was 200 ft. (61 m) long and had a 107-ft. (33 m) wingspan. The giant aircraft's twin propellers were driven by a powerful 80-hp steam engine. During its final test, it raced ahead under full power, broke away from a protective guard rail, lifted off the track, and glided to an abrupt stop. It did not actually fly, and the damaged craft was never flown again. Forgotten as an aircraft designer, today Hiram Maxim is remembered as the inventor of the world's first machine gun, which bore his name.

In America, the Wright brothers' greatest rival, **Samuel Pierpont Langley (1834–1906)**, secretary of the Smithsonian Institution, made several successful sustained flights with a one-quarter scaled-down model of his *Aerodrome* flying machine for distances of up to 4,200 ft. (1,800 m). The U.S. War Department became interested in the possible military potential of an airplane and gave Langley a $50,000 subsidy to develop and fly a full-size man-carrying version of the *Aerodrome.*

However, the first attempt to fly the full-size aircraft with a pilot failed, as it fell into the water after it was launched by catapult from a houseboat on the Potomac River. Just two weeks before the Wright brothers made their historic flight, Professor Langley attempted a second piloted flight of his *Aerodrome,* and again it caught on its catapult during takeoff and tumbled into the river. As a result of the disaster Langley lost his financial support and was ridiculed by the press. He abandoned further attempts at flight and died a few years later.

A bizarre twist to this story occurred in 1914, when the Smithsonian took the old *Aerodrome* out of storage and made repairs and extensive modifications to the craft to make it flightworthy. This time the resurrected plane was put on pontoons rather than prepared for a catapult launch. On May 28, 1914, off Hammondsport, N.Y., the cleverly redesigned *Aerodrome* with a new engine ascended from the waters of Keuka Lake and flew for some 150 ft. (47 m) before landing safely with its pilot, aviation pioneer Glen Curtiss. Denying that they modified the plane from its original design, the Smithsonian claimed that this was proof that the original *Aerodrome,* and not the Wright brothers' Flyer, was the first craft capable of manned flight back in 1903.

Orville Wright (Wilbur died in 1912) was infuriated by this deceitful act. The brothers were eventually vindicated after photographs of Langley's 1903 machine were compared with the 1914 aircraft, proving beyond a doubt that many changes were made to the original model in order to get it into the air.

Still unhappy over their treatment by the Smithsonian, Orville Wright sent the historic Flyer to the British Science Museum in 1928. It remained there until its return to the U.S. in 1942, when the Smithsonian fully recanted its past claims about Langley's *Aerodrome* to Orville Wright's total satisfaction.

Among those who said that they flew before the Wrights, the most controversial is **Gustave A. Whitehead (1874–1927)**, who was born in Leutershausen, Germany, and immigrated to America. Modern-day supporters of the forgotten aviation pioneer are trying to prove that he made a sustained flight of 880 ft. (270 m) at a height of 50 ft. (15 m) in the early morning hours of Aug. 14, 1901, aboard his twin-propellered butterflylike-winged aircraft in Bridgeport, Conn.

Whitehead called his fragile flying machine *Number 21* because it was the 21st experimental plane that he had designed and built. Aside from its unusual body that resembled a small rowboat, the airplane had two engines designed to run on acetylene gas. One engine powered the landing gear's wooden wheels to add speed during the takeoff and the other drove the propellers.

According to *Scientific American*'s write-up of Whitehead's aircraft in June 1901, the plane's body was 16 ft. (4.8 m) long and measured 2½ ft. (0.76 m) wide and 3 ft. (1 m) deep. The machine was to be controlled during flight with its 10-ft. (3.04 m) rudder, which, like the tail of a bird, could be moved up and down, and its twin propellers, whose speed could be independently increased or decreased.

Photographs of Whitehead and his aircraft on the ground do exist, but unfortunately, there are no photographs of Whitehead's airplane in flight or blueprints of the craft. His notebooks, records, and models of his flying machines have been lost.

Although the local newspapers and *Scientific American* (which later credited the Wright brothers in 1906) reported his achievement at the time, the mostly circumstantial evidence remaining has never been completely substantiated by aviation historians, and the opinion of the Smithsonian is that none of Whitehead's planes ever actually attained true flight.

The controversy over Whitehead's aeronautical accomplishments rages on, and we may never discover for sure if Gustave Whitehead beat out the Wright brothers. □

Famous Firsts in Aviation

1783 **First balloon flight.** Jacques and Joseph Montgolfier of Annonay, France, sent up a small smoke-filled balloon about mid-November.
First hydrogen-filled balloon flight. Jacques A. C. Charles, Paris physicist, supervised construction by A. J. and M. N. Robert of a 13-ft.-in-diameter balloon that was filled with hydrogen. It got up to about 3,000 ft. and traveled about 16 mi. in a 45-min. flight (Aug. 27).
First human balloon flights. A Frenchman, Jean Pilâtre de Rozier, made the first captive-balloon ascension (Oct. 15). With the Marquis d'Arlandes, Pilâtre de Rozier, made the first free flight, reaching a peak altitude of about 500 ft., and traveling about 5½ mi. in 20 min. (Nov. 21).

1784 **First powered balloon.** Gen. Jean Baptiste Marie Meusnier developed the first propeller-driven and elliptically shaped balloon—the crew cranking three propellers on a common shaft to give the craft a speed of about 3 mph.
First balloon flight by a woman. Mme. Thible, a French opera singer (June 4).

1793 **First balloon flight in America.** Jean Pierre Blanchard, a French pilot, made it from Philadelphia to near Woodbury, N.J., in just over 45 min. (Jan. 9).

1794 **First military use of the balloon.** Jean Marie Coutelle, using a balloon built for the French Army, made two 4-hr. observation ascents. The military purpose of the ascents seems to have been to damage the enemy's morale.

1797 **First parachute jump.** André-Jacques Garnerin dropped from about 6,500 ft. over Monceau Park in Paris in a 23-ft.-diameter parachute made of white canvas with a basket attached (Oct. 22).

1843 **First air transport company.** In London, William S. Henson and John Stringfellow filed articles of incorporation for the Aerial Transit Company (March 24). It failed.

1852 **First dirigible.** Henri Giffard, a French engineer, flew in a controllable (more or less) steam-engine-powered balloon, 144 ft. long and 39 ft. in diameter, inflated with 88,000 cu. ft. of coal gas. It reached 6.7 mph on a flight from Paris to Trappe (Sept. 24).

1860 **First aerial photographers.** Samuel Archer King and William Black made two photos of Boston, which are still in existence.

1872 **First gas-engine-powered dirigible.** Paul Haenlein, a German engineer, flew in a semi-rigid-frame dirigible, powered by a 4-cylinder internal-combustion engine running on coal gas drawn from the supporting bag.

1873 **First transatlantic attempt.** *The New York Daily Graphic* sponsored the attempt with a 400,000 cu. ft. balloon carrying a lifeboat. A rip in the bag during inflation brought collapse of the balloon and the project.

1897 **First successful metal dirigible.** An all-metal dirigible, designed by David Schwarz, a Hungarian, took off from Berlin's Tempelhof Field and, powered by a 16-hp Daimler engine, got several miles before leaking gas caused it to crash (Nov. 13).

1900 **First zeppelin flight.** Germany's Count Ferdinand von Zeppelin flew the first of his long series of rigid-frame airships. It attained a speed of 18 mph and got 3½ mi. before its steering gear failed (July 2).

1903 **First successful heavier-than-air machine flight.** Aviation was really born on the sand dunes at Kitty Hawk, N.C., when Orville Wright crawled to his prone position between the wings of the biplane he and his brother Wilbur had built, opened the throttle of their home-made 12-hp engine, and took to the air. He covered 120 ft. in 12 sec. Later that day, in one of four flights, Wilbur stayed up 59 sec. and covered 852 ft. (Dec. 17).

1904 **First airplane maneuvers.** Orville Wright made the first turn with an airplane (Sept. 15); five days later his brother Wilbur made the first complete circle.

1905 **First airplane flight over half an hour.** Orville Wright kept his craft up 33 min., 17 sec. (Oct. 4).

1906 **First European airplane flight.** Alberto Santos-Dumont, a Brazilian, flew a heavier-than-air machine at Bagatelle Field, Paris (Sept. 13).

1908 **First airplane fatality.** Lt. Thomas E. Selfridge, U.S. Army Signal Corps, was in a group evaluating the Wright plane at Fort Myer, Va. He was up 75 ft. with Orville Wright when the propeller hit a bracing wire and was broken, throwing the plane out of control, killing Selfridge and seriously injuring Wright (Sept. 17).

1909 **First cross-Channel flight.** Louis Blériot flew in a 25-hp Blériot VI monoplane from Les

Baraques near Calais, France, and landed near Dover Castle, England, in a 26.61-mi. (38-km) 37-min. flight across the English Channel (July 25).

First International Aviation Competition Meeting. American Glenn Curtiss narrowly beat France's Louis Blériot in the main event and won the Gordon Bennett Cup. Meet held at Rheims, France (Aug. 22–28).

1910 **First licensed woman pilot.** Baroness Raymonde de la Roche of France, who learned to fly in 1909, received ticket No. 36 on March 8.

First flight from shipboard. Lt. Eugene Ely, USN, took a Curtiss plane off from the deck of the cruiser *Birmingham* at Hampton Roads, Va., and flew to Norfolk (Nov. 14). The following January he reversed the process, flying from Camp Selfridge to the deck of the armored cruiser *Pennsylvania* in San Francisco Bay (Jan. 18).

First aircraft to take off from water. Henri Fabrer in a Gnome-powered floatplane, at Martigues, France (March 28).

1911 **First U.S. woman pilot.** Harriet Quimby, a magazine writer, got ticket No. 37, making her the second licensed female pilot in the world.

1912 **First woman's cross-Channel flight.** Harriet Quimby flew from Dover, England, across the English Channel and landed at Hardelot, France, in a Blériot monoplane loaned to her by Louis Blériot (April 16). She was later killed in a flying accident over Dorchester Bay during a Harvard-Boston aviation meet on July 1, 1912.

First parachute jump from a powered airplane. Albert Berry jumped in a test over Jefferson Barracks military post, St. Louis (March 1). Some sources credit Grant Morton as making first jump in 1911.

1913 **First multi-engined aircraft.** Built and flown by Igor Ivan Sikorsky while still in his native Russia.

1914 **First aerial combat.** In Aug., Allied and German pilots and observers started shooting at each other with pistols and rifles—with negligible results.

1915 **First air raids on England.** German zeppelins started dropping bombs on four English communities (Jan. 19).

1918 **First U.S. air squadron.** The U.S. Army Air Corps made its first independent raids over enemy lines, in DH-4 planes (British-designed) powered with 400-hp American-designed Liberty engines (April 8).

First regular airmail service. Operated for the Post Office Department by the Army, the first regular service was inaugurated with one round trip a day (except Sunday) between Washington, D.C., and New York City (May 15).

1919 **First transatlantic flight.** The NC-4, one of four Curtiss flying boats commanded by Lt. Comdr. Albert C. Read, reached Lisbon, Portugal (May 27), after hops from Trepassy Bay, Newfoundland, to Horta, Azores (May 16–17), to Ponta Delgada (May 20). The Liberty-powered craft was piloted by Walter Hinton.

First nonstop transatlantic flight. Capt. John Alcock and Lt. Arthur Whitten Brown, British World War I flyers, made the 1,900 mi. trip from St. John's, Newfoundland, to Clifden, Ireland, in 16 hr., 12 min. in a Vickers-Vimy bomber with two 350-hp Rolls-Royce engines (June 15–16).

First lighter-than-air transatlantic flight. The British dirigible R-34, commanded by Maj. George H. Scott, left Firth of Forth, Scotland (July 2), and touched down at Mineola, L.I., 108

hr. later. The eastbound trip was made in 75 hr. (completed July 13).

First scheduled London-Paris passenger service (using airplanes). Aircraft Travel and Transport inaugurated London–Paris service (Aug. 25). Later the company started the first trans-Channel mail service on the same route (Nov. 10).

First free-fall parachute jump. Leslie Irvin jumped over McCook Field, Dayton, Ohio, to prove that one won't lose consciousness during a delayed free-fall using a manually operated parachute (April 28).

1921 **First U.S. black female pilot.** Bessie Coleman received license June 15. Was killed April 30, 1926, in flying accident.

First naval vessel sunk by aircraft. Two battleships being scrapped by treaty were sunk by bombs dropped from Army planes in demonstration put on by Brig. Gen. William S. Mitchell (July 21).

First helium balloon. The C-7, nonrigid Navy dirigible was first to use noninflammable helium as lifting gas, making a flight from Hampton Roads, Va., to Washington, D.C. (Dec. 1).

1922 **First member of Caterpillar Club.** Lt. (later Maj. Gen.) Harold Harris bailed out of a crippled plane he was testing at McCook Field, Dayton, Ohio (Oct. 20), and became the first man to join the Caterpillar Club—those whose lives have been saved by parachutes.

1923 **First nonstop transcontinental flight.** Lts. John A. Macready and Oakley Kelly flew a single-engine Fokker T-2 nonstop from New York to San Diego, a distance of just over 2,500 mi. in 26 hr., 50 min. (May 2–3).

First autogyro flight. Juan de la Cierva, a brilliant Spanish mathematician, made the first successful flight in a rotary wing aircraft in Madrid (June 9).

1924 **First round-the-world flight.** Four Douglas Cruiser biplanes of the U.S. Army Air Corps took off from Seattle under command of Maj. Frederick Martin (April 6). 175 days later, two of the planes (Lt. Lowell Smith's and Lt. Erik Nelson's) landed in Seattle after a circuitous route—one source saying 26,345 mi., another saying 27,553 mi.

1926 **First polar flight.** Then–Lt. Cmdr. Richard E. Byrd, acting as navigator, and Floyd Bennett as pilot, flew a trimotor Fokker from Kings Bay, Spitsbergen, over the North Pole and back in 15½ hr. (May 8–9).

1927 **First solo nonstop transatlantic flight.** Charles Augustus Lindbergh lifted his Wright-powered Ryan monoplane, *Spirit of St. Louis,* from

Roosevelt Field, N.Y., to stay aloft 33 hr. 39 min and travel 3,600 mi. to Le Bourget Field outside Paris (May 20–21). Although 91 persons in 13 separate flights crossed the Atlantic before him, he flew directly between two great world cities and did it alone.

First transatlantic passenger. Charles A. Levine was piloted by Clarence D. Chamberlin from Roosevelt Field, N.Y., to Eisleben, Germany, in a Wright-powered Bellanca (June 4–5).

1928 **First east-west transatlantic crossing.** Baron Guenther von Huenefeld, piloted by German Capt. Hermann Koehl and Irish Capt. James Fitzmaurice, left Dublin for New York City (April 12) in a single-engine all-metal Junkers-monoplane. Some 37 hr. later, they crashed on Greely Island, Labrador. Rescued.

First U.S.–Australia flight. Sir Charles Kingsford-Smith and Capt. Charles T. P. Ulm, Australians, and two American navigators, Harry W. Lyon and James Warner, crossed the Pacific from Oakland to Brisbane. They went via Hawaii and the Fiji Islands in a trimotor Fokker (May 31–June 8).

First transarctic flight. Sir Hubert Wilkins, an Australian explorer, and Carl Ben Eielson, who served as pilot, flew from Point Barrow, Alaska, to Spitsbergen (mid-April).

1929 **First of the endurance records.** With Air Corps Maj. Carl Spaatz in command and Capt. Ira Eaker as chief pilot, an Army Fokker, aided by refueling in the air, remained aloft 150 hr. 40 min. at Los Angeles (Jan. 1–7).

First round-the-world airship flight. The LZ-127, known as the *Graf Zeppelin*, flew 21,300 mi. in 20 days and 4 hr. Also set distance record (Aug.).

First blind flight. James H. Doolittle proved the feasibility of instrument-guided flying when he took off and landed entirely on instruments (Sept. 24).

First rocket-engine flight. Fritz von Opel, a German auto maker, stayed aloft in his small rocket-powered craft for 75 sec., covering nearly 2 mi. (Sept. 30).

First South Pole flight. Comdr. Richard E. Byrd, with Bernt Balchen as pilot, Harold I. June, radio operator, and Capt. A. C. McKinley, photographer, flew a trimotor Fokker from the Bay of Whales, Little America, over the South Pole and back (Nov. 28–29).

1930 **First Paris–New York nonstop flight.** Dieudonné Coste and Maurice Bellonte, French pilots, flew a Hispano-powered Breguet biplane from Le Bourget Field to Valley Stream, L.I., in 37 hr., 18 min. (Sept. 2–3).

1931 **First flight into the stratosphere.** Auguste Piccard, a Swiss physicist, and Charles Knipfer ascended in a balloon from Augsburg, Germany, and reached a height of 51,793 ft. in a 17-hr. flight that terminated on a glacier near Innsbruck, Austria (May 27).

First nonstop transpacific flight. Hugh Herndon and Clyde Pangborn took off from Sabishiro Beach, Japan, dropped their landing gear, and flew 4,860 mi. to near Wenatchee, Wash., in 41 hr. 13 min. (Oct. 4–5).

1932 **First woman's transatlantic solo.** Amelia Earhart, flying a Pratt & Whitney Wasp-powered Lockheed Vega, flew alone from Harbor Grace, Newfoundland, to Ireland in approximately 15 hr. (May 20–21).

First westbound transatlantic solo. James A. Mollison, a British pilot, took a de Havilland Puss Moth from Portmarnock, Ireland, to Pennfield, New Brunswick (Aug. 18).

First woman airline pilot. Ruth Rowland Nichols, first woman to hold three international records at the same time—speed, distance, and altitude—was employed by N.Y.–New England Airways.

1933 **First round-the-world solo.** Wiley Post took a Lockheed Vega, *Winnie Mae,* 15,596 mi. around the world in 7 days, 18 hr., 49½ min. (July 15–22).

1937 **First successful helicopter flight.** Hanna Reitsch, a German pilot, flew Dr. Heinrich Focke's FW-61 in free, totally controlled flight at Bremen (July 4). Ms. Reitsch was also the first woman civil and military aviation test pilot.

First woman known to fly combat. Sabiha Gokcen, Turkish female army pilot, bombed and strafed Kurdish tribesmen during a rebellion.

1939 **First turbojet flight.** Just before their invasion of Poland, the Germans flew a Heinkel He-178 plane powered by a Heinkel S3B turbojet (Aug. 27).

1940 **First wartime use of military gliders.** German commandos made a successful glider assault on Belgium's Fort Eben-Emael during WWII (May 10).

1941–1945 **Most combat missions flown by a pilot in any war.** Captain Hans-Ulrich Rudel of Germany flew 2,530 combat missions during WWII while flying a JU-87 Stuka dive bomber. He survived the war.

1942–1945 **Top-scoring fighter pilot of any war.** German Luftwaffe ace Maj. Erich Hartmann scored 352 victories all while flying a Messerschmitt BF 109 during WWII. He was involved in 800 dogfights, and flew 1,425 missions. Maj. Hartmann survived the war.

1942 **First and only enemy bombing of U.S. mainland.** During WWII, a floatplane launched from a Japanese submarine off Cape Blanco, Ore., dropped incendiary bombs on the Oregon forest in two attempts to start forest fires and terrorize American civilians, but the bombs did little damage (Sept. 9 and 29).

First American jet plane flight. Robert Stanley, chief pilot for Bell Aircraft Corp., flew the Bell XP-59 *Airacomet* at Muroc Army Base, Calif. (Oct. 1).

First woman fighter pilot to shoot down an enemy aircraft. Soviet Lieutenant Lilya Litvyak, flying a Yak-1 fighter of the women's 586th Fighter Aviation Regiment, shot down two German planes over Stalingrad on Sept. 13, 1942.

1944 **First production stage rocket-engine fighter plane.** The German Messerschmitt Me 163B *Komet* (test flown 1941) became operational in June 1944. Some 350 of these delta-wing fighters were built before WWII in Europe ended.

1947 **First piloted supersonic flight in an airplane.** Capt. Charles E. Yeager, U.S. Air Force, flew the X-1 rocket-powered research plane built by Bell Aircraft Corp., faster than the speed of sound at Muroc Air Force Base, Calif. (Oct. 14).

1949 **First round-the-world nonstop flight.** Capt. James Gallagher and USAF crew of 13 flew a Boeing B-50A Superfortress around the world nonstop from Ft. Worth, returning to same point: 23,452 mi. in 94 hr., 1 min., with four aerial refuelings en route (Feb. 27–March 2).

Active Pilot Certificates Held

Year	Total	Airline transport	Commercial	Private
1970	720,028	31,442	176,585	299,491
1980	814,667	63,652	182,097	343,276
1985	722,376	79,192	155,929	320,086
1990	702,659	107,732	149,666	299,111
1995	639,184	123,877	133,980	261,399
1996	622,261	127,486	129,187	254,002
1997	616,342	130,858	125,300	247,604
1998	618,298	134,612	122,053	247,226
1999	635,472	137,642	124,261	258,749

NOTE: Includes student (97,359), glider (9,390), recreational (343), and other pilot categories. Also nonpilot, i.e., mechanic, parachute rigger, etc. Data as of Dec. 31, 1999. *Source:* Department of Transportation, Federal Aviation Administration.

1950 First nonstop transatlantic jet flight. Col. David C. Schilling (USAF) flew 3,300 mi. from England to Limestone, Maine, in 10 hr., 1 min. (Sept. 22).

1951 First solo across North Pole. Charles F. Blair, Jr., flew a converted P-51 (May 29).

1952 First jetliner service. The De Havilland Comet flight was inaugurated by BOAC between London and Johannesburg, South Africa (May 2). Flight, including stops, took 23 hr., 38 min.
First transatlantic helicopter flight. Capt. Vincent H. McGovern and 1st Lt. Harold W. Moore piloted two Sikorsky H-19s from Westover, Mass., to Prestwick, Scotland (3,410 mi.). Trip was made in five steps, with a flying time of 42 hr., 25 min. (July 15–31).
First transatlantic round trip in same day. A British Canberra twin-jet bomber flew from Aldergrove, Northern Ireland, to Gander, Newfoundland, and back in 7 hr., 59 min. flying time (Aug. 26).

1955 First transcontinental round trip in same day. Lt. John M. Conroy piloted an F-86 Sabrejet across U.S. (Los Angeles–New York) and back—5,085 mi.—in 11 hr., 33 min., 27 sec. (May 21).

1957 First round-the-world nonstop jet plane flight. Maj. Gen. Archie J. Old, Jr., USAF, led a flight of three Boeing B-52 bombers, powered with eight 10,000-lb.-thrust Pratt & Whitney Aircraft J57 engines around the world in 45 hr., 19 min; distance 24,325 mi.; average speed 525 mph (completed Jan. 18).

1958 First transatlantic jet passenger service. BOAC, New York to London (Oct. 4). Pan American started daily service, New York to Paris (Oct. 26).
First domestic jet passenger service. National Airlines inaugurated service between New York and Miami (Dec. 10).

1968 Prototype of world's first supersonic airliner. The Soviet-designed Tupolev Tu-144 made its first flight, Dec. 31. It first achieved supersonic speed on June 5, 1969.

1973 First female pilot of a major U.S. scheduled airline. Emily H. Warner became employed by Frontier Airlines on Jan. 29 as second officer on a Boeing 737.

1976 First regularly scheduled commercial supersonic transport (SST) flights begin. Air France and British Airways inaugurated service (Jan. 21). Air France flew the Paris–Rio de Janeiro route; B.A., the London–Bahrain. Both airlines began SST service to Washington, D.C. (May 24).

1977 First successful human-powered aircraft. Paul MacCready, an aeronautical engineer from Pasadena, Calif., was awarded the Kremer Prize for creating the world's first successful human-powered aircraft. The *Gossamer Condor* was flown by Bryan Allen over the required 3-mi. course on Aug. 23.

1978 First successful transatlantic balloon flight. Three Albuquerque, N.M., men, Ben Abruzzo, Larry Newman, and Maxie Anderson, completed the crossing (Aug. 16.; landed, Aug. 17) in their helium-filled balloon, *Double Eagle II.*

1979 First man-powered aircraft to fly across the English Channel. The Kremer Prize for the Channel crossing was won by Bryan Allen, who flew the *Gossamer Albatross* from Folkestone, England, to Cap Gris-Nez, France, in 2 hr., 55 min. (June 12).

1980 First successful balloon flight over the North Pole. Sidney Conn and his wife, Eleanor, in hot-air balloon *Joy of Sound* (April 11).
First nonstop transcontinental balloon flight, and also record for longest overland voyage in a balloon. Maxie Anderson and his son, Kris, completed four-day flight from Fort Baker, Calif., to successful landing outside Matane, Quebec, on May 12 in their helium-filled balloon, *Kitty Hawk.*
First long-distance solar-powered flight. Janice Brown, a 98-lb. former teacher, flew a tiny experimental solar-powered aircraft, *Solar Challenger,* six mi. in 22 min. near Marana, Ariz. (Dec. 3). The craft was powered by a 2.75-hp engine.
First solar-powered aircraft to fly across the English Channel. Stephen R. Ptacek flew the 210-lb. *Solar Challenger* at an average speed of 30 mph from Cormeilles-en-Vexin near Paris to the Royal Manston Air Force Base on England's southeastern coast in 5 hr., 30 min. (July 7).

1984 First solo transatlantic balloon flight. Joe W. Kittinger landed Sept. 18 near Savona, Italy, in his helium-filled balloon *Rosie O'Grady's Balloon of Peace* after a flight of 3,535 mi. from Caribou, Maine.

1986 First nonstop flight around the world without refueling. From Edwards AFB, Calif., Dick Rutan and Jeana Yeager flew in *Voyager* around the world (24,986.727 mi.), returning to Edwards in 216 hr., 3 min., 44 sec. (Dec. 14–23).

1987 First transatlantic hot-air balloon flight. Richard Branson and Per Lindstrand flew 2,789.6 mi. from Sugarloaf Mt., Maine, to Ireland in the hot-air balloon *Virgin Atlantic Flyer* (July 2–4).

1991 First transpacific hot-air balloon flight. Richard Branson and Per Lindstrand flew about 6,700 mi. from Miyakonyo, Japan, to 150 mi. west of Yellowknife, Northwest Territories, Canada (Jan. 15–17).

1993 First woman to copilot a commercial supersonic plane. Barbara Harmer, British Airways, flew as first officer on the Concorde from London to New York City (March 25).

1995 First solo transpacific balloon flight. Steve Fossett made a flight of more than 5,430 mi. from Seoul, South Korea, to Leader, Saskatchewan, Canada, in a helium-filled balloon. Also set record for distance (Feb. 18–21, 1995).

1998 First U.S. female combat pilot to bomb an enemy target. On Dec. 16, Lt. Kendra Williams, USN, bombed enemy targets over Iraq during Operation Desert Fox.

Absolute World Records

(maximum performance in any class)

Source: National Aeronautic Association

Speed around the World, Nonstop, Nonrefueled

Speed (mph)	Date	Plane	Pilots	Place
115.65	Dec. 14–23, 1986	*Voyager*	Dick Rutan & Jeana Yeager (U.S.)	Edwards AFB, Calif.— Edwards AFB, Calif.

Distance, Great Circle without Landing, also Distance, Closed Circuit without Landing

Distance (mi.)	Date	Plane	Pilots	Place
24,986.727	Dec. 14–23, 1986	*Voyager*	Dick Rutan & Jeana Yeager (U.S.)	Edwards AFB, Calif.— Edwards AFB, Calif.

Speed over a Straight Course

Speed (mph)	Date	Plane type	Pilot	Place
2,193.16	July 28, 1976	Lockheed SR-71A	Capt. Eldon W. Joersz (USAF)	Beale AFB, Calif.

Speed over a Closed Circuit

Speed (mph)	Date	Plane type	Pilot	Place
2,092.294	July 27, 1976	Lockheed SR-71A	Maj. Adolphus H. Bledsoe, Jr. (USAF)	Beale AFB, Calif.

Altitude

Height (ft.)	Date	Plane type	Pilot	Place
123,523.58	Aug. 31, 1977	MIG-25, E-266M	Alexander Fedotov (U.S.S.R.)	U.S.S.R.

Altitude in Horizontal Flight

Height (ft.)	Date	Pilot	Place
85,068.997	July 28, 1976	Capt. Robert C. Helt (USAF)	Beale AFB, Calif.

Altitude, Aircraft Launched from a Carrier Airplane

Height (ft.)	Date	Plane type	Pilot	Place
314,750.00	July 17, 1962	N. American X-15-1	Maj. Robert White (USAF)	Edwards AFB, Calif.

World-Class Helicopter Records

Selected records. *Source:* National Aeronautic Association.

Great Circle Distance without Landing
International: 2,213.04 mi.; 3,561.55 km.
Robert G. Ferry (U.S.) in Hughes YOH-6A helicopter powered by Allison T-63-A-5 engine; from Culver City, Calif., to Ormond Beach, Fla., April 6–7, 1966.

Distance, Closed Circuit without Landing
International: 1,739.96 mi.; 2,800.20 km.
Jack Schweibold (U.S.) in Hughes YOH-6A helicopter powered by Allison T-62-A-5 engine; Edwards Air Force Base, Calif., March 26, 1966.

Altitude without Payload
International: 40,820 ft.; 12,442 m.
Jean Boulet (France) in Alouette SA 315-001 *Lama* powered by Artouste IIIB 735 KW engine; Istres, France, June 21, 1972.

Speed around the World, Eastbound
40.99 mph; 65.97 kph.
Joe Ronald Bower (U.S.) pilot, in Bell JetRanger III, powered by one Allison 250-C20J (317 shp), covered 23,800 mi. in 24 days, 4 hr., 36 min. June 28–July 22, 1994.

Speed around the World, Westbound
57.01 mph; 91.75 kph.
Joe Ronald Bower (U.S.) pilot, John W. Williams (U.S.), co-pilot in Bell 430 powered by 2 Allison 250–C40, (811 shp), Aug. 17–Sept. 3, 1996.

Absolute World Records, Balloons

Selected records. *Source:* National Aeronautic Association.

Altitude
113,739.9 ft.; 34,668 m.
Cmdr. M.D. Ross (U.S.) and Lt. Cmdr. V.A. Prather, *Lee Lewis Memorial*, Gulf of Mexico, May 4, 1961.

Distance
25,360 mi.; 40,814 km.
Bertrand Piccard (Switzerland) and Brian Jones (U.K.), *Cameron Balloons R-650*, Château d'Oex, Switzerland, to Dakhla, Egypt, March 1–21, 1999.

Duration
477 hrs., 47 min.
Bertrand Piccard (Switzerland) and Brian Jones (U.K.), *Cameron Balloons R-650*, Château d'Oex, Switzerland, to Dakhla, Egypt, March 1–21, 1999.

Shortest time around the world
370 hrs., 24 min.
Bertrand Piccard (Switzerland) and Brian Jones (U.K.), *Cameron Balloons R-650*, Château d'Oex, Switzerland, to Dakhla, Egypt, March 1–21, 1999.

Major Religions of the World

Judaism

Judaism is the oldest of the monotheistic faiths. It affirms the existence of one God, Yahweh, who entered into covenant with the descendants of Abraham, God's chosen people. Judaism's holy writings reveal how God has been present with them throughout their history. These writings are known as the Torah, specifically the five books of Moses, but most broadly conceived as the Hebrew Scriptures (traditionally called the Old Testament by Christians) and the compilation of oral tradition known as the Talmud (which includes the Mishnah, the oral law).

According to Scripture, the Hebrew patriarch Abraham (20th century? B.C.) founded Judaism. He obeyed the call of God to depart northern Mesopotamia and travel to Canaan. God promised to bless his descendants if they remained faithful in worship. Abraham's line descended through Isaac, then Jacob (also called Israel; his descendants came to be called

Israelites). According to Scripture, 12 families that descended from Jacob migrated to Egypt, where they were enslaved. They were led out of bondage (13th century? B.C.) by Moses, who united them in the worship of Yahweh. The Hebrews returned to Canaan after a 40-year sojourn in the desert, conquering from the local peoples the "promised land" that God had provided for them.

The 12 tribes of Israel lived in a covenant association during the period of the judges (1200?–1000? B.C.), leaders known for wisdom and heroism. Saul first established a monarchy (r. 1025?–1005? B.C.); his successor, David (r. 1005?–965? B.C.), unified the land of Israel and made Jerusalem its religious and political center. Under his son, Solomon (r. 968?–928? B.C.), a golden era culminated in the building of a temple, replacing the portable sanctuary in use until that time. Following Solomon's death, the kingdom was split into Israel in the north and Judah in the south. Political conflicts resulted in

Religious Population of the World, 1998
(in thousands)

Statistics of the world's religions are only very rough approximations. Aside from Christianity, few religions, if any, attempt to keep statistical records; and even Protestants and Catholics employ different methods of counting members.

Religion	Total	Percent distri- bution	Africa	Asia	Latin America	North America	Europe[1]	Oceania
Total population	5,929,839	100.0%	778,484	3,588,877	499,534	304,078	729,406	29,460
Christians	1,943,038	32.8%	356,277	283,734	462,965	256,882	558,729	24,451
Affiliated Christians	1,835,352	31.0%	323,782	275,836	456,919	222,678	536,092	20,045
Roman Catholics	1,026,501	17.3%	114,316	106,399	442,808	69,536	286,124	7,318
Protestants	316,445	5.3%	74,436	43,998	45,295	69,437	76,776	6,503
Orthodox	213,743	3.6%	33,660	15,232	549	4,852	158,775	675
Anglicans	63,748	1.1%	27,957	856	853	3,260	25,632	5,190
Other Christians	373,832	6.3%	74,853	143,080	44,331	83,519	25,551	2,498
Unaffiliated Christians	107,686	1.8%	32,495	7,898	6,046	34,204	22,637	4,406
Atheists	149,913	2.5%	420	121,451	2,673	1,569	23,444	356
Baha'is	6,764	0.1%	1,695	3,260	825	753	126	105
Buddhists	353,794	6.0%	138	348,806	622	2,445	1,517	266
Chinese folk religionists[2]	379,162	6.4%	33	377,795	184	839	250	61
Confucians	6,241	0.1%	—	6,207	—	—	11	23
Ethnic Religionists	248,565	4.2%	97,200	148,189	1,231	424	1,262	259
Hindus	761,689	12.8%	2,411	755,500	785	1,266	1,382	345
Jains	3,922	0.1%	65	3,850	—	7	—	—
Jews	14,111	0.2%	230	4,139	1,121	5,996	2,530	95
Mandeans	38	0.0%	—	38	—	—	—	—
Muslims	1,164,622	19.6%	315,000	812,000	1,624	4,349	31,401	248
New Religionists[3]	100,144	1.7%	27	98,548	604	759	155	51
Nonreligious[4]	759,655	12.8%	4,863	600,822	15,300	27,500	108,000	3,170
Other religionists	1,001	0.0%	68	11	95	585	233	9
Shintoists	2,789	0.0%	—	2,727	7	55	—	—
Sikhs	22,332	0.4%	53	21,531	—	498	236	14
Spiritists	11,785	0.2%	3	—	11,498	148	129	7
Zoroastrians	274		1	269	—	3	1	—

NOTES: — Represents or rounds to zero. 1. Includes Russia. 2. Persons professing no religion, nonbelievers, agnostics, freethinkers, and dereligionized secularists indifferent to all religions. 3. Followers of traditional Chinese religion. 4. Followers of Asiatic 20th-century New Religions, New Religious movements, radical new crisis religions, and non-Christian syncretistic mass religions. *Source:* Encyclopædia Britannica, Inc., Chicago, Ill., *Britannica Book of the Year.* Reprinted with permission from *Britannica Book of the Year,* 1999 © 1999 Encyclopædia Britannica, Inc.

the conquest of Israel by Assyria (721 B.C.) and the defeat of Judah by Babylon (586 B.C.). Jerusalem and its temple were destroyed, and many Judeans were exiled to Babylon.

During the era of the kings, the prophets were active in Israel and Judah. Their writings emphasize faith in Yahweh as God of Israel and of the entire universe, and they warn of the dangers of worshiping other gods. They also cry out for social justice. The Judeans were permitted to return in 539 B.C. to Judea, where they were ruled as a Persian province. Though temple and cult were restored in Jerusalem, during the exile a new class of religious leaders had emerged—the scribes. They became rivals to the temple hierarchy and would eventually evolve into the party known as the Pharisees.

Persian rule ended when Alexander the Great conquered Palestine in 332 B.C. After his death, rule of Judea alternated between Egypt and Syria. When the Syrian ruler Antiochus IV Epiphanes tried to prevent the practice of Judaism, a revolt was led by the Maccabees (a Jewish family), winning Jewish independence in 128 B.C. The Romans conquered Jerusalem in 63 B.C.

During this period the Sadducees (temple priests) and the Pharisees (teachers of the law in the synagogues) offered different interpretations of Judaism. Smaller groups that emerged were the Essenes, a religious order; the Apocalyptists, who expected divine deliverance led by the Messiah; and the Zealots, who were prepared to fight for national independence. Hellenism also influenced Judaism at this time.

When the Zealots revolted, the Roman armies destroyed Jerusalem and its temple (A.D. 70). The Jews were scattered in the Diaspora (dispersion) and experienced much persecution. Rabbinic Judaism, developed according to Pharisaic practice and centered on Torah and synagogue, became the primary expression of faith. The Scriptures became codified, and the Talmud took shape. In the 12th century Maimonides formulated the influential 13 Articles of Faith, including belief in God, God's oneness and lack of physical or other form, the changelessness of Torah, restoration of the monarchy under the Messiah, and resurrection of the dead.

Two branches of European Judaism developed during the Middle Ages: the Sephardic, based in Spain and with an affinity to Babylonian Jews; and the Ashkenazic, based in Franco-German lands and affiliated with Rome and Palestine. Two forms of Jewish mysticism also arose at this time: medieval Hasidism and attention to the Kabbalah (a mystical interpretation of Scripture).

After a respite during the 18th-century Enlightenment, anti-Semitism again plagued European Jews in the 19th century, sparking the Zionist movement that culminated in the founding of the state of Israel in 1948. The Holocaust of World War II took the lives of more than 6 million Jews.

Jews today continue synagogue worship, which includes readings from the Law and the Prophets and prayers, such as the Shema (Hear, O Israel) and the Amidah (the 18 Benedictions). Religious life is guided by the commandments of the Torah, such as circumcision and Sabbath observance.

Present-day Judaism has three main expressions: Orthodox, Conservative, and Reform. Reform movements, resulting from the Haskala (Jewish Enlightenment) of the 18th century, began in western Europe but took root in North America. Reform Jews do not hold the oral law (Talmud) to be a divine revelation, and they emphasize ethical and moral teachings. Orthodox Jews follow the traditional faith and practice with great seriousness. They follow a strict kosher diet and keep the Sabbath with care. Conservative Judaism, which developed in the mid-18th century, holds the Talmud to be authoritative and follows most traditional practices, yet tries to make Judaism relevant for each generation, believing that change and tradition can complement each other. Because the Torah assumes belief in God but does not require it, a strong secular movement also exists within Judaism, including atheist and agnostic elements.

In general, Jews do not proselytize, but they do welcome newcomers to their faith.

Christianity

Christianity is a monotheistic religion founded by the followers of Jesus of Nazareth. Jesus, a Jew, was born in about 7 B.C. and assumed his public life, probably after his 30th year, in Galilee. The New Testament Gospels describe Jesus as a teacher and miracle worker. He proclaimed the kingdom of God, a future reality that is at the same time already present. Jesus set the requirements for participation in the kingdom of God as a change of heart and repentance for sins, love of God and neighbor, and concern for justice. Circa A.D. 30 he was executed on a cross in Jerusalem, a brutal form of punishment for those considered a political threat to the Roman Empire.

After his death his followers came to believe in him as the Christ, the Messiah. The Gospels report his resurrection and how the risen Jesus was witnessed by many of his followers. The apostle Paul helped spread the new faith in his missionary travels. Historically, Christianity arose out of Judaism and claims that Jesus fulfilled many of the promises of the Hebrew Scripture (often referred to as the Old Testament).

The new religion spread rapidly throughout the Roman Empire. In its first two centuries, Christianity began to take shape as an organization, developing distinctive doctrine, liturgy, and ministry. By the fourth century the Christian church had taken root in countries stretching from Spain in the West to Persia and India in the East. Christians had been subject to persecution by the Roman state, but gained tolerance under Constantine the Great (A.D. 313). The church became favored under his successors, and in 380 the emperor Theodosius proclaimed Christianity the state religion. Other religions were suppressed.

Because differences in doctrine threatened to divide the church, a standard Christian creed was formulated by bishops at successive ecumenical councils, the first of which was held in A.D. 325 (Nicaea). Important doctrines were defined concerning the Trinity—in other words, that there is one God in three persons: Father, Son, and Holy Spirit (Constantinople, A.D. 381), and the nature of Christ as both divine and human (Chalcedon, A.D. 541). Christians came to accept both Hebrew Scripture and the New Testament as authoritative. The New Testament comprises four Gospels (narratives of Jesus' life), 21 Epistles, The Acts of the Apostles, and Revelation.

Because of differences between Christians of the East and West, the unity of the church was broken in 1054. The religious center for the Eastern Orthodox Church was Constantinople, and the Roman Catholic Church defined doctrine and practice for Christians in the West. In 1517 began the Reformation, which ultimately caused a schism in the Western church. Reformers wished to correct certain practices within the Roman church, but also came to view the Christian faith in a distinctly new way. The major Protestant denominations (Lutheran, Presbyterian, Reformed, and Anglican [Episcopalian]) thus came into being. Over the centuries, numerous denominations have broken with these major traditions, resulting in a spectrum of Christian expression.

In the 20th century, many Christians hope to regain a sense of unity through dialogue and cooperation among different traditions. The ecumenical movement led to the formation of the World Council of Churches in 1948 (Amsterdam), which has since been joined by many denominations.

Through its missionary activity Christianity has spread to most parts of the globe.

U.S. Religious Bodies with More Than 500,000 Members

Religious body (year reporting)	Members
Roman Catholic Church (1998)	62,018,436
Southern Baptist Convention (1998)	15,729,356
United Methodist Church (1998)	8,400,000
National Baptist Convention, U.S.A., Inc. (1997)	8,200,000
Church of God in Christ (1991)	5,499,875
Evangelical Lutheran Church in America (1998)	5,178,225
Church of Jesus Christ of Latter-day Saints (1997)	4,923,100
Presbyterian Church (U.S.A.) (1998)	3,574,959
National Baptist Convention of America, Inc. (1987)	3,500,000
Lutheran Church—Missouri Synod (1998)	2,594,404
Assemblies of God (1998)	2,525,812
African Methodist Episcopal Church (1999)	2,500,000
National Missionary Baptist Convention of America (1992)	2,500,000
Progressive National Baptist Convention, Inc. (1995)	2,500,000
Episcopal Church (1996)	2,364,559
Greek Orthodox Archdiocese of America (1998)	1,954,500
American Baptist Churches in the U.S.A. (1998)	1,507,400
Churches of Christ (1999)	1,500,000
Pentecostal Assemblies of the World (1998)	1,500,000
United Church of Christ (1998)	1,421,088
African Methodist Episcopal Zion Church (1998)	1,252,369
Baptist Bible Fellowship International (1997)	1,200,000
Christian Churches and Churches of Christ (1988)	1,071,616
Jehovah's Witnesses (1999)	1,040,283
Orthodox Church in America (1998)	1,000,000
Christian Church (Disciples of Christ) (1997)	879,436
Seventh-Day Adventist Church (1998)	839,915
Church of God (Cleveland, Tenn.) (1995)	753,230
Christian Methodist Episcopal Church (1983)	718,922
Church of the Nazarene (1998)	627,054

Source: Yearbook of American & Canadian Churches, 2000.

Eastern Orthodoxy

Eastern Orthodoxy comprises the faith and practices stemming from ancient churches in the eastern part of the Roman Empire. It encompasses Orthodox churches in communion with the see of Constantinople.

The Orthodox, Catholic, Apostolic Church is the direct descendant of the Byzantine state church and consists of independent national churches that are united by doctrine, liturgy, and hierarchical organization (church leaders include deacons and priests, who may either be married or be monks before ordination, and bishops, who must be celibates). The heads of these churches are called patriarchs or metropolitans. Rivalry between the pope of Rome and the patriarch of Constantinople, as well as differences that existed for centuries between the eastern and western parts of the empire, led to a schism in 1054. The mutual excommunication pronounced in that year was lifted in 1965, however, and a climate of better understanding has been created in the 20th century. Orthodox churches belong to the World Council of Churches.

The Eastern Orthodox churches recognize only the canons of the seven ecumenical councils (325–787) as binding for faith, and they reject doctrines that have been added in the West.

The central worship service is called the Liturgy, which is understood as representing God's acts of salvation. Its center is the celebration of the Eucharist, or Lord's Supper. Icons (sacred pictures) have a special place in Orthodox worship. The Mother of Christ, angels, and saints are venerated. The Orthodox Church and the Western Catholic Church recognize the same number of sacraments.

Orthodox Churches are found in Greece, Turkey, Russia, the Balkans, and other parts of the former Soviet Union. In this century Orthodox faith has spread to western Europe and other parts of the world, particularly America.

Eastern Rite Churches

These include the Uniate Churches that recognize the authority of the pope but keep their own traditional liturgies and those churches dating back to the fifth century that emancipated themselves from the Byzantine state church. They include the Melchites, Syrian Catholics, Maronites (Arab Christians in Lebanon), Catholic Copts and Ethiopians, the autonomous Nestorian Church, and others.

Roman Catholicism

Roman Catholicism comprises the belief and practice of the Roman Catholic Church. It stands under the authority of the bishop of Rome, the pope, and is led by him and bishops who are held to be, through ordination, successors of Peter and the apostles. Doctrine and sacraments are administered by the hierarchy of archbishops, bishops, priests, and deacons. As successor to Peter, the pope is considered the Vicar of Christ. Roman Catholics believe their church to be the one, holy, catholic, and apostolic church, possessing all the properties of the one, true church of Christ.

The faith of the church is understood to be identical with that taught by Christ and his apostles and contained in the Bible and tradition. New definitions of doctrines, such as the Immaculate Conception of Mary (1854) and the bodily

Assumption of Mary (1950), have been declared by popes, however. At Vatican Council I (1870) the pope was proclaimed "endowed with infallibility, *ex cathedra,* in other words, when exercising the office of pastor and teacher of all Christians."

The center of Roman Catholic worship is the celebration of the Mass, the Eucharist, which is the commemoration of Christ's sacrificial death and resurrection. Other sacraments are baptism, confirmation, penance, matrimony, anointing of the sick (formerly known as extreme unction), and holy orders. The Virgin Mary and the other saints, and their relics, are venerated, and prayers are made to them to intercede with God, in whose presence they are believed to dwell.

The Roman Catholic Church is the largest Christian organization in the world, found in most countries.

Vatican Council II (1962–1965) sought to "update" the church, bringing about changes in practice and more deeply involving the laity. The immensely popular Pope John Paul II (1978–) has taken a more conservative course and has reached out to Catholics worldwide through his extensive travels.

Protestantism

Protestantism encompasses the Christian churches that separated from Rome during the Reformation in the 16th century. This movement was initiated by an Augustinian monk, Martin Luther. The term "Protestant" was originally applied to followers of Luther, who protested at the Diet of Spires (1529) against the decree that prohibited all further ecclesiastical reforms. Other influential reformers included John Calvin, Ulrich Zwingli, and John Knox. Protestantism rejected attempts to tie God's revelation to earthly institutions and strictly adhered to the Word of God as sole authority in matters of faith and practice *(sola scriptura).* Central in the reformers' understanding of the biblical message is the justification of the sinner by faith alone. The church is understood as a fellowship, and the priesthood of all believers is stressed.

The Augsburg Confession (1530) was the principal statement of Lutheran faith and practice. It became a model for other Protestant confessions of faith. Major Protestant denominations include the Lutheran, Reformed (Calvinist), Presbyterian, and Anglican (Episcopalian). Innumerable sects and denominations sprung from these roots, including Quakers, Baptists, Pentecostals, Congregationalists, Methodists, and nondenominational assemblies. Sects that base their faith on additional revelations or insights gained in the modern period include Mormons, Christian Scientists, and Jehovah's Witnesses.

Since the latter part of the 19th century, national councils of churches have been established in many countries, for example, the Federal Council of Churches of Christ in America in 1908. Churches of a particular denomination have joined in federations and world alliances, beginning with the Anglican Lambeth Conference in 1867.

Protestant missionary activity, particularly strong in the last century, resulted in the founding of many churches in Asia and Africa. The ecumenical movement, which originated with Protestant missions, aims at unity among Christians and churches.

Islam

Islam, one of the three major monotheistic faiths, was founded in Arabia by Muhammad between 610 and 632. There are an estimated 5.5 million Muslims in North America and 1 billion Muslims worldwide.

Muhammad was born in 570 A.D. at Mecca and belonged to the Quraysh tribe, which was active in caravan trade. At the age of 25 he joined the trade from Mecca to Syria in the employment of a rich widow, Khadiji, whom he later married. Critical of the lax moral standards and polytheistic practices of the inhabitants of Mecca, he began to lead a contemplative life in the desert. In a dramatic religious vision, the angel Gabriel announced to Muhammad that he was to be a prophet. Encouraged by Khadiji, he devoted himself to the reform of religion and society. Polytheism was to be abandoned. But leaders of the Quraysh generally rejected his teaching, and Muhammad gained only a small following and suffered persecution. He eventually fled Mecca.

The Hegira *(Hijra,* meaning "emigration") of Muhammad from Mecca, where he was not honored, to Medina, where he was well received, occurred in 622 and marks the beginning of the Muslim era. After a number of military conflicts with Mecca, in 630 he marched on Mecca and conquered it. Muhammad died at Medina in 632. His grave there has since been a place of pilgrimage.

Muhammad's followers, called Muslims, revered him as the prophet of Allah (God), the only God. Muslims consider Muhammad to be the last in the line of prophets that included Abraham and Jesus. Islam spread quickly, stretching from Spain in the west to India in the east within a century after the prophet's death. Sources of the Islamic faith are the Qur'an (Koran), regarded as the uncreated, eternal Word of God, and tradition *(hadith)* regarding sayings and deeds of the prophet.

Islam means "surrender to the will of Allah," the all-powerful, who determines humanity's fate. Good deeds will be rewarded at the Last Judgment in paradise, and evil deeds will be punished in hell.

The Five Pillars, or primary duties, of Islam are profession of faith; prayer, to be performed five times a day; almsgiving to the poor and the mosque (house of worship); fasting during daylight hours in the month of Ramadan; and pilgrimage to Mecca at least once in a Muslim's lifetime, if it is physically and financially possible. The pilgrimage includes homage to the ancient shrine of the Ka'aba, the most sacred site in Islam.

Muslims gather for corporate worship on Fridays. Prayers and a sermon take place at the mosque, which is also a center for teaching of the Qur'an. The community leader, the *imam,* is considered a teacher and prayer leader.

Islam succeeded in uniting an Arab world of separate tribes and castes, but disagreements concerning the succession of the prophet caused a division in Islam between two groups, Sunnis and Shi'ites. The Shi'ites rejected the first three successors to Muhammad as usurpers, claiming the fourth, Muhammad's son-in-law Ali, as the rightful leader. The Sunnis (from the word *tradition),* the largest division of Islam (today more than 80%), believe in the legitimacy of the first three successors. Among these, other sects arose (such as the conservative

Wahhabi of Saudi Arabia), as well as different schools of theology. Another development within Islam, beginning in the eighth and ninth centuries, was Sufism, a form of mysticism. This movement was influential for many centuries and was instrumental in the spread of Islam in Asia and Africa.

Islam has expanded greatly under Muhammad's successors. It is the principal religion of the Middle East, Asia, and the northern half of Africa.

Hinduism

Hinduism is the major religion of India, practiced by more than 80% of the population. In contrast to other religions, it has no founder. Considered the oldest religion in the world, it dates back, perhaps, to prehistoric times.

No single creed or doctrine binds Hindus together. Intellectually there is complete freedom of belief, and one can be monotheist, polytheist, or atheist. Hinduism is a syncretic religion, welcoming and incorporating a variety of outside influences.

The most ancient sacred texts of the Hindu religion are written in Sanskrit and called the *Vedas* (*vedah* means "knowledge"). There are four Vedic books, of which the Rig-Veda is the oldest. It discusses multiple gods, the universe, and creation. The dates of these works are unknown (1000 B.C.?). Present-day Hindus rarely refer to these texts but do venerate them.

The Upanishads (dated 1000–300 B.C.), commentaries on the Vedic texts, speculate on the origin of the universe and the nature of deity, and *atman* (the individual soul) and its relationship to *Brahman* (the universal soul). They introduce the doctrine of *karma* and recommend meditation and the practice of yoga.

Further important sacred writings include the Epics, which contain legendary stories about gods and humans. They are the Mahabharata (composed between 200 B.C. and A.D. 200) and the Ramayana. The former includes the Bhagavad-Gita (Song of the Lord), an influential text that describes the three paths to salvation. The Puranas (stories in verse, probably written between the 6th and 13th centuries) detail myths of Hindu gods and heroes and also comment on religious practice and cosmology.

According to Hindu beliefs, Brahman is the principle and source of the universe. This divine intelligence pervades all beings, including the individual soul. Thus the many Hindu deities are manifestations of the one Brahman. Hinduism is based on the concept of reincarnation, in which all living beings, from plants on earth to gods above, are caught in a cosmic cycle of becoming and perishing.

Life is determined by the law of karma—one is reborn to a higher level of existence based on moral behavior in a previous phase of existence. Life on earth is regarded as transient and a burden. The goal of existence is liberation from the cycle of rebirth and death and entrance into the indescribable state of *moksha* (liberation).

The practice of Hinduism consists of rites and ceremonies centering on birth, marriage, and death. There are many Hindu temples, which are considered to be dwelling places of the deities and to which people bring offerings. Places of pilgrimage include Benares on the Ganges, the most sacred river in India. Of the many Hindu deities, the most popular are the cults of Vishnu, Shiva, and Shakti,

and their various incarnations. Also important is Brahma, the creator god. Hindus also venerate human saints.

Orthodox Hindu society in India was divided into four major hereditary classes: (1) the Brahmin (priestly and learned class); (2) the Kshatriya (military, professional, ruling, and governing occupations); (3) the Vaishya (landowners, merchants, and business occupations); and (4) the Sudra (artisans, laborers, and peasants). Below the Sudra was a fifth group, the Untouchables (lowest menial occupations and no social standing). The Indian government banned discrimination against the Untouchables in the constitution of India in 1950. Observance of class and caste distinctions varies throughout India.

In modern times work has been done to reform and revive Hinduism. One of the outstanding reformers was Ramakrishna (1836–1886), who inspired many followers, one of whom founded the Ramakrishna mission. The mission is active both in India and in other countries and is known for its scholarly and humanitarian works.

Buddhism

Buddhism was founded in the fourth or fifth century B.C. in northern India by a man known traditionally as Siddhartha (meaning "he who has reached the goal") Gautama, the son of a warrior prince. Some scholars believe that he lived from 563 to 483 B.C., though his exact life span is uncertain. Troubled by the inevitability of suffering in human life, he left home and a pampered life at the age of 29 to wander as an ascetic, seeking religious insight and a solution to the struggles of human existence. He passed through many trials and practiced extreme self-denial. Finally, while meditating under the bodhi tree ("tree of perfect knowledge") he reached enlightenment and taught his followers about his new spiritual understanding.

Gautama's teachings differed from the Hindu faith prevalent in India at the time. Whereas in Hinduism the Brahmin caste alone performed religious functions and attained the highest spiritual understanding, Gautama's beliefs were more egalitarian, accessible to all who wished to be enlightened. At the core of his understanding were the Four Noble Truths: (1) all living beings suffer; (2) the origin of this suffering is desire—for material possessions, power, and so on; (3) desire can be overcome; and (4) there is a path that leads to release from desire. This way is called the Noble Eightfold Path: right views, right intention, right speech, right action, right livelihood, right effort, right concentration, and right ecstasy.

Gautama promoted the concept of *anatman* (that a person has no actual self) and the idea that existence is characterized by impermanence. This realization helps one let go of desire for transient things. Still, Gautama did not recommend extreme self-denial, but rather a disciplined life called the Middle Way. Like the Hindus, he believed that existence consisted of reincarnation, a cycle of birth and death. He held that it could be broken only by reaching complete detachment from worldly cares. Then the soul could be released into *nirvana* (literally "blowing out")—an indescribable state of total transcendence. Gautama traveled to preach the *dharma* (sacred truth) and was recognized as the Buddha (enlightened one). After his death his followers continued to develop doctrine and practice, which came to center on the Three Jewels: the *dharma* (the sacred teachings of Buddhism), the *sangha* (the community of followers, which now includes nuns, monks, and laity), and the Buddha. Under the patronage of the Mauryan emperor Ashoka (third century B.C.), Buddhism spread throughout India and to other parts of Asia. Monasteries were established, as well as temples dedicated to Buddha; at shrines his relics were venerated. Though by the fourth century C.E. Buddhist presence in India had dwindled, it flourished in other parts of Asia.

Numerous Buddhist sects have emerged. The oldest, called the Theravada (Way of the Elders) tradition, interprets Buddha as a great sage but not a deity. It emphasizes meditation and ritual practices that help the individual become an *arhat*, an enlightened being. Its followers emphasize the authority of the earliest Buddhist scriptures, the Tripitaka (Three Baskets), a compilation of sermons, rules for celibates, and doctrine. This sect is prevalent in Southeast Asia and Sri Lanka. It is sometimes called the Hinayana (Lesser Vehicle) tradition (once considered a pejorative term).

Between the second century B.C. and the second century C.E., the Mahayana (Greater Vehicle) tradition refocused Buddhism to concentrate less on individual attainment of enlightenment and more on concern for humanity. It promotes the ideal of the *bodhisattva* (enlightened being), who shuns entering nirvana until all sentient beings can do so as well, willingly remaining in the painful cycle of birth and death to perform works of compassion. Members of this tradition conceive of Buddha as an eternal being to whom prayers can be made; other Buddhas are revered as well, adding a polytheistic dimension to the religion. Numerous sects have developed from the Mahayana tradition, which has been influential in China, Korea, and Japan.

A third broad tradition, variously called Vajrayana (Diamond Vehicle), Mantrayana (Vehicle of the Mantra), or Tantric Buddhism, offers a quicker, more demanding way to achieve nirvana. Because of its level of challenge—enabling one to reach enlightenment in one lifetime—it requires the guidance of a spiritual leader. It is most prominent in Tibet and Mongolia. Zen Buddhism encourages individuals to seek the Buddha nature within themselves and to practice a disciplined form of sitting meditation in order to reach *satori*—spiritual enlightenment.

Confucianism

Confucius (K'ung Fu-tzu), born in the state of Lu (northern China), lived from 551 to 479 B.C. He was a brilliant teacher, viewing education not merely as the accumulation of knowledge but as a means of self-transformation. His legacy was a system of thought emphasizing education, proper behavior, and loyalty. His effect on Chinese culture was immense.

The teachings of Confucius are contained in the *Analects*, a collection of his sayings as remembered by his students. They were further developed by philosophers such as Mencius (Meng Tse, fl. 400 B.C.). Confucianism is little concerned with metaphysical discussion of religion or with spiritual attainments. It instead emphasizes moral conduct and right relationships in the human sphere.

Cultivation of virtue is a central tenet of Confucianism. Two important virtues are *jen*, a benevolent and humanitarian attitude, and *li*, maintaining proper relationships and rituals that enhance the life of the individual, the family, and the state. The "five relations," between king and subject, father and son, man and wife, older and younger brother, and friend and friend, are of utmost importance. These relationships are reinforced by participation in rituals, including the formal procedures of court life and religious rituals such as ancestor worship.

Confucius revolutionized educational thought in China. He believed that learning was not to be focused only on attaining the skills for a particular profession, but for growth in moral judgment and self-realization. Confucius's standards for the proper conduct of government shaped the statecraft of China for centuries. Hundreds of temples in honor of Confucius testify to his stature as sage and teacher.

Confucianism is far less dominant in 20th-century China, at least on an official level. The state cult of Confucius was ended in 1911. Still, Confucian traditions and moral standards are part of the cultural essence of China and other East Asian countries.

Shinto

Shinto comprises the religious ideas and practices indigenous to Japan. Ancient Shinto focused on the worship of the *kami*, a host of supernatural beings that could be known through forms (objects of nature, remarkable people, abstract concepts such as justice) but were ultimately mysterious. Shinto has no formal dogma and no holy writ, though early collections of Japanese religious thought and practice (*Kojiki*, "Records of Ancient Matters," A.D. 712, and *Nihon shoki*, "Chronicles of Japan," A.D. 720) are highly regarded.

Shinto has been influenced by Confucianism and by Buddhism, which was introduced in Japan in the 6th century. Syncretic schools (such as Ryobu Shinto) emerged, as did other sects that decried Buddhism (such as Ise Shinto).

Under the reign of the emperor Meiji (1868–1912), Shinto became the official state religion. State Shinto, the national cult, emphasized the divinity of the emperor, whose succession was traced back to the first emperor, Jimmu (660 B.C.), and beyond him to the sun goddess Amaterasu-o-mi-kami. State Shinto was disestablished after World War II.

Sect Shinto, deriving from sects that developed during the 19th and 20th centuries, continues to thrive in Japan. Shrines dedicated to particular *kami* are visited by parishioners for prayer and traditional ceremonies, such as presenting a newborn child to the *kami*. Traditional festivals celebrated at the shrines include purification rites, presentation of food offerings, prayer, sacred music and dance, and a feast.

No particular day of the week is set aside for prayer. A person may visit a shrine at will, entering through the *torii* (gateway). It is believed that the *kami* can respond to prayer and can offer protection and guidance.

A variety of Shinto sects and practices exist today. Ten-rikyo emphasizes faith healing. Folk Shinto is characterized by veneration of roadside shrines and rites related to agriculture. Buddhist priests serve at many Shinto shrines, and many families keep a small shrine, or god-shelf, at home. Veneration of ancestors and pilgrimage are also common practices.

Taoism

Taoism, one of the major religions of China, is based on ancient philosophical works, primarily the Tao Te Ching, "Classic of Tao and Its Virtue." Traditionally, this book was thought to be the work of Lao-tzu, a quasi-historical philosopher of the 6th century B.C.; scholars now believe that the book dates from about the 3rd century B.C. The philosopher Chuang Tzu (4th–3rd centuries B.C.) also contributed to the seminal ideas of Taoism.

Tao, "the Way," is the ultimate reality of the universe, according to Taoism. It is a creative process, and humans can live in harmony with it by clearing the self of obstacles. By cultivating *wu-wei*, a type of inaction characterized by humility and prudence, a person can participate in the simplicity and spontaneity of Tao. Striving to attain virtue or achievement is counterproductive and unnecessary. Taoism values mystical contemplation and balance. The human being is viewed as a microcosm of the universe, and the Chinese principle of *yin-yang*, complementary duality, is a model of harmony.

The religious practices of Taoism emerged from these ancient philosophies and from Chinese shamanistic tradition; by the 2nd century A.D., it constituted an organized religion. Longevity and immortality were sought through regulating the energies of the body through breathing exercises, meditation, use of medicinal plants, talismans, and magical formulas. A cult of immortals, including the divinized Lao Tzu, also developed. Influenced by Buddhism, Taoists organized monastic orders. Temple worship and forms of divination, including the *I ching*, were practiced.

Since its beginnings, many sects have arisen within Taoism. All subscribe to the philosophical origins of the religion; some have emphasized faith healing, exorcism, the worship of the immortals, meditation, or alchemy. Buddhism and Confucianism influenced some sects; some operated as secret societies.

Though the present government has tried to suppress it, Taoism is still practiced in mainland China, Taiwan, and Hong Kong. It profoundly influenced Chinese art and literature, and Taoist ideas have become popular in the West during the twentieth century.

Roman Catholic Pontiffs

Name	Birthplace	Reigned		Name	Birthplace	Reigned	
		From	To			From	To
St. Peter	Bethsaida	42?	67?	St. Damasus I	Spain	366	384
St. Linus	Tuscia	c. 67	76	St. Siricius	Rome	384	399
St. Anacletus (Cletus)	Rome	76	88	St. Anastasius I	Rome	399	401
				St. Innocent I	Albano	401	417
St. Clement	Rome	88	97	St. Zozimus	Greece	417	418
St. Evaristus	Greece	97	105	St. Boniface I	Rome	418	422
St. Alexander I	Rome	105	115	St. Celestine I	Campania	422	432
St. Sixtus I	Rome	115	125	St. Sixtus III	Rome	432	440
St. Telesphorus	Greece	125	136	St. Leo I (the Great)	Tuscany	440	461
St. Hyginus	Greece	136	140				
St. Pius I	Aquileia	140	155	St. Hilary	Sardinia	461	468
St. Anicetus	Syria	155	166	St. Simplicius	Tivoli	468	483
St. Soter	Campania	166	175	St. Felix III (II)[2]	Rome	483	492
St. Eleutherius	Epirus	175	189	St. Gelasius I	Africa	492	496
St. Victor I	Africa	189	199	Anastasius II	Rome	496	498
St. Zephyrinus	Rome	199	217	St. Symmachus	Sardinia	498	514
St. Callistus I	Rome	217	222	St. Hormisdas	Frosinone	514	523
St. Urban I	Rome	222	230	St. John I	Tuscany	523	526
St. Pontian	Rome	230	235	St. Felix IV (III)	Samnium	526	530
St. Anterus	Greece	235	236	Boniface II	Rome	530	532
St. Fabian	Rome	236	250	John II	Rome	533	535
St. Cornelius	Rome	251	253	St. Agapitus I	Rome	535	536
St. Lucius I	Rome	253	254	St. Silverius	Campania	536	537
St. Stephen I	Rome	254	257	Vigilius	Rome	537	555
St. Sixtus II	Greece	257	258	Pelagius I	Rome	556	561
St. Dionysius	Unknown	259	268	John III	Rome	561	574
St. Felix I	Rome	269	274	Benedict I	Rome	575	579
St. Eutychian	Luni	275	283	Pelagius II	Rome	579	590
St. Caius	Dalmatia	283	296	St. Gregory I (the Great)	Rome	590	604
St. Marcellinus	Rome	296	304				
St. Marcellus I	Rome	308	309	Sabinianus	Tuscany	604	606
St. Eusebius	Greece	309[1]	309[1]	Boniface III	Rome	607	607
St. Meltiades	Africa	311	314	St. Boniface IV	Marsi	608	615
St. Sylvester I	Rome	314	335	St. Deusdedit (Adeodatus I)	Rome	615	618
St. Marcus	Rome	336	336				
St. Julius I	Rome	337	352	Boniface V	Naples	619	625
Liberius	Rome	352	366	Honorius I	Campania	625	638

Name	Birthplace	Reigned From	To	Name	Birthplace	Reigned From	To
Severinus	Rome	640	640	Gregory V	Saxony	996	999
John IV	Dalmatia	640	642	Sylvester II	Auvergne	999	1003
Theodore I	Greece	642	649	John XVII	Rome	1003	1003
St. Martin I	Todi	649	655	John XVIII	Rome	1004	1009
St. Eugene I[3]	Rome	654	657	Sergius IV	Rome	1009	1012
St. Vitalian	Segni	657	672	Benedict VIII	Tusculum	1012	1024
Adeodatus II	Rome	672	676	John XIX	Tusculum	1024	1032
Donus	Rome	676	678	Benedict IX[6]	Tusculum	1032	1044
St. Agatho	Sicily	678	681	Sylvester III	Rome	1045	1045
St. Leo II	Sicily	682	683	Benedict IX	Tusculum	1045	1045
St. Benedict II	Rome	684	685	(2nd time)			
John V	Syria	685	686	Gregory VI	Rome	1045	1046
Conon	Unknown	686	687	Clement II	Saxony	1046	1047
St. Sergius I	Syria	687	701	Benedict IX	Tusculum	1047	1048
John VI	Greece	701	705	(3rd time)			
John VII	Greece	705	707	Damasus II	Bavaria	1048	1048
Sisinnius	Syria	708	708	St. Leo IX	Alsace	1049	1054
Constantine	Syria	708	715	Victor II	Germany	1055	1057
St. Gregory II	Rome	715	731	Stephen IX (X)	Lorraine	1057	1058
St. Gregory III	Syria	731	741	Nicholas II	Burgundy	1059	1061
St. Zachary	Greece	741	752	Alexander II	Milan	1061	1073
Stephen II (III)[4]	Rome	752	757	St. Gregory VII	Tuscany	1073	1085
St. Paul I	Rome	757	767	Bl. Victor III	Benevento	1086	1087
Stephen III (IV)	Sicily	768	772	Bl. Urban II	France	1088	1099
Adrian I	Rome	772	795	Paschal II	Ravenna	1099	1118
St. Leo III	Rome	795	816	Gelasius II	Gaeta	1118	1119
Stephen IV (V)	Rome	816	817	Callistus II	Burgundy	1119	1124
St. Paschal I	Rome	817	824	Honorius II	Flagnano	1124	1130
Eugene II	Rome	824	827	Innocent II	Rome	1130	1143
Valentine	Rome	827	827	Celestine II	Città di Castello	1143	1144
Gregory IV	Rome	827	844	Lucius II	Bologna	1144	1145
Sergius II	Rome	844	847	Bl. Eugene III	Pisa	1145	1153
St. Leo IV	Rome	847	855	Anastasius IV	Rome	1153	1154
Benedict III	Rome	855	858	Adrian IV	England	1154	1159
St. Nicholas I	Rome	858	867	Alexander III	Siena	1159	1181
(the Great)				Lucius III	Lucca	1181	1185
Adrian II	Rome	867	872	Urban III	Milan	1185	1187
John VIII	Rome	872	882	Gregory VIII	Benevento	1187	1187
Marinus I	Gallese	882	884	Clement III	Rome	1187	1191
St. Adrian III	Rome	884	885	Celestine III	Rome	1191	1198
Stephen V (VI)	Rome	885	891	Innocent III	Anagni	1198	1216
Formosus	Portus	891	896	Honorius III	Rome	1216	1227
Boniface VI	Rome	896	896	Gregory IX	Anagni	1227	1241
Stephen VI (VII)	Rome	896	897	Celestine IV	Milan	1241	1241
Romanus	Gallese	897	897	Innocent IV	Genoa	1243	1254
Theodore II	Rome	897	897	Alexander IV	Anagni	1254	1261
John IX	Tivoli	898	900	Urban IV	Troyes	1261	1264
Benedict IV	Rome	900	903	Clement IV	France	1265	1268
Leo V	Ardea	903	903	Bl. Gregory X	Piacenza	1271	1276
Sergius III	Rome	904	911	Bl. Innocent V	Savoy	1276	1276
Anastasius III	Rome	911	913	Adrian V	Genoa	1276	1276
Landus	Sabina	913	914	John XXI[7]	Portugal	1276	1277
John X	Tossignano	914	928	Nicholas III	Rome	1277	1280
Leo VI	Rome	928	928	Martin IV[8]	France	1281	1285
Stephen VII (VIII)	Rome	928	931	Honorius IV	Rome	1285	1287
John XI	Rome	931	935	Nicholas IV	Ascoli	1288	1292
Leo VII	Rome	936	939	St. Celestine V	Isernia	1294	1294
Stephen VIII (IX)	Rome	939	942	Boniface VIII	Anagni	1294	1303
Marinus II	Rome	942	946	Bl. Benedict XI	Treviso	1303	1304
Agapitus II	Rome	946	955	Clement V	France	1305	1314
John XII[5]	Tusculum	955	964	John XXII	Cahors	1316	1334
Leo VIII[5]	Rome	963	965	Benedict XII	France	1334	1342
Benedict V[5]	Rome	964	966	Clement VI	France	1342	1352
John XIII	Rome	965	972	Innocent VI	France	1352	1362
Benedict VI	Rome	973	974	Bl. Urban V	France	1362	1370
Benedict VII	Rome	974	983	Gregory XI	France	1370	1378
John XIV	Pavia	983	984	Urban VI	Naples	1378	1389
John XV	Rome	985	996	Boniface IX	Naples	1389	1404

Name	Birthplace	Reigned From	To	Name	Birthplace	Reigned From	To
Innocent VII	Sul mona	1404	1406	Urban VIII	Florence	1623	1644
Gregory XII	Venice	1406	1415	Innocent X	Rome	1644	1655
Martin V	Rome	1417	1431	Alexander VII	Siena	1655	1667
Eugene IV	Venice	1431	1447	Clement IX	Pistoia	1667	1669
Nicholas V	Sarzana	1447	1455	Clement X	Rome	1670	1676
Callistus III	Jativa	1455	1458	Bl. Innocent XI	Como	1676	1689
Pius II	Siena	1458	1464	Alexander VIII	Venice	1689	1691
Paul II	Venice	1464	1471	Innocent XII	Spinazzola	1691	1700
Sixtus IV	Savona	1471	1484	Clement XI	Urbino	1700	1721
Innocent VIII	Genoa	1484	1492	Innocent XIII	Rome	1721	1724
Alexander VI	Jativa	1492	1503	Benedict XIII	Gravina	1724	1730
Pius III	Siena	1503	1503	Clement XII	Florence	1730	1740
Julius II	Savona	1503	1513	Benedict XIV	Bologna	1740	1758
Leo X	Florence	1513	1521	Clement XIII	Venice	1758	1769
Adrian VI	Utrecht	1522	1523	Clement XIV	Rimini	1769	1774
Clement VII	Florence	1523	1534	Pius VI	Cesena	1775	1799
Paul III	Rome	1534	1549	Pius VII	Cesena	1800	1823
Julius III	Rome	1550	1555	Leo XII	Genga	1823	1829
Marcellus II	Montepulciano	1555	1555	Pius VIII	Cingoli	1829	1830
Paul IV	Naples	1555	1559	Gregory XVI	Belluno	1831	1846
Pius IV	Milan	1559	1565	Pius IX	Senegallia	1846	1878
St. Pius V	Bosco	1566	1572	Leo XIII	Carpineto	1878	1903
Gregory XIII	Bologna	1572	1585	St. Pius X	Riese	1903	1914
Sixtus V	Grottammare	1585	1590	Benedict XV	Genoa	1914	1922
Urban VII	Rome	1590	1590	Pius XI	Desio	1922	1939
Gregory XIV	Cremona	1590	1591	Pius XII	Rome	1939	1958
Innocent IX	Bologna	1591	1591	John XXIII	Sotto il Monte	1958	1963
Clement VIII	Florence	1592	1605	Paul VI	Concesio	1963	1978
Leo XI	Florence	1605	1605	John Paul I	Forno di Canale	1978	1978
Paul V	Rome	1605	1621	John Paul II	Wadowice, Poland	1978	
Gregory XV	Bologna	1621	1623				

1. Or 310. 2. He should be called Felix II, and his successors of the same name should be numbered accordingly. The discrepancy was caused by the erroneous insertion in some lists of the name of St. Felix of Rome, Martyr. 3. He was elected during the exile of St. Martin I, who endorsed him as pope. 4. After St. Zachary died, a Roman priest named Stephen was elected but died before his consecration as bishop of Rome. His name is not included in all lists for this reason. In view of this historical confusion, the *National Catholic Almanac* lists the true Stephen II as Stephen II (III), the true Stephen III as Stephen III (IV), etc. 5. Confusion exists concerning the legitimacy of claims. If the deposition of John was invalid, Leo was an antipope until after the end of Benedict's reign. If the deposition of John was valid, Leo was the legitimate pope and Benedict an antipope. 6. If the triple removal of Benedict IX was not valid, Sylvester III, Gregory VI, and Clement II were antipopes. 7. Elimination was made of the name of John XX in an effort to rectify the numerical designation of popes named John. The error dates back to the time of John XV. 8. The names of Marinus I and Marinus II were construed as Martin. In view of these two pontificates and the earlier reign of St. Martin I, this pontiff was called Martin IV. *Source: National Catholic Almanac,* from *Annuarto Pontificio.*

Non-Christian Religious Adherents in the United States

Adherents	Year 1900	% of total pop.	Mid-1970	% of total pop.	Mid-1990	% of total pop.	Mid-1995	% of total pop.	(Projected) mid-2000	% of total pop.
Total	**2,724,800**	**3.6**	**20,789,000**	**9.9**	**37,079,000**	**14.6**	**39,077,000**	**14.6**	**41,054,000**	**14.8**
Atheists	1,000	0.0	200,000	0.1	770,000	0.3	874,000	0.3	925,000	0.3
Baha'is	2,800	0.0	138,000	0.1	600,000	0.2	683,000	0.3	750,000	0.3
Buddhists	30,000	0.0	200,000	0.1	1,680,000	0.7	1,864,000	0.7	2,000,000	0.7
Chinese folk religionists	70,000	0.1	90,000	0.0	76,000	0.0	74,000	0.0	70,000	0.0
Hindus	1,000	0.0	100,000	0.0	650,000	0.3	795,000	0.3	950,000	0.3
Jews	1,500,000	2.0	6,700,000	3.2	5,535,000	2.2	5,518,000	2.1	5,500,000	2.0
Muslims	10,000	0.0	800,000	0.4	3,600,000	1.4	3,767,000	1.4	3,950,000	1.4
Black Muslims	0	0.0	200,000	0.1	1,250,000	0.5	1,400,000	0.5	1,650,000	0.6
New-Religionists	0	0.0	110,000	0.1	575,000	0.2	603,000	0.2	675,000	0.2
Nonreligious	1,000,000	1.3	11,730,000	5.6	22,233,000	8.7	23,394,000	8.8	24,554,000	8.8
Sikhs	0	0.0	1,000	0.0	160,000	0.1	190,000	0.1	220,000	0.1
Tribal religionists	100,000	0.1	70,000	0.0	280,000	0.1	305,000	0.1	350,000	0.1
Other religionists	10,000	0.0	650,000	0.3	920,000	0.4	1,010,000	0.4	1,110,000	0.4

Non-Christians: Followers of non-Christian religions or of no religion; the 12 largest such varieties are listed. Jews: Core Jewish population relating to Judaism, excluding Jewish persons professing a different religion but including immigrants from the former U.S.S.R., Eastern Europe, Israel, and other areas. Figures for A.D. 2000 are projections based on current long-term trends. *Source:* Reprinted with permission from *1998 Britannica Book of the Year.* © 1998 Encyclopædia Britannica, Inc.

The Books of the Bible

Below is the Protestant canon of the Bible (New Revised Standard Version). The Roman Catholic canon also includes the Deuterocanonical books as part of the Old Testament (these are considered apocryphal by most Protestants). The Hebrew Bible recognizes the books referred to as the Old Testament in the Protestant Bible, but not the Apocryphal/Deuterocanonical books or the New Testament.

The Old Testament with the Apocryphal/ Deuterocanonical Books

The Hebrew Scriptures

Genesis
Exodus
Leviticus
Numbers
Deuteronomy
Joshua
Judges
Ruth
1 Samuel
2 Samuel
1 Kings
2 Kings
1 Chronicles
2 Chronicles
Ezra
Nehemiah
Esther
Job
Psalms
Proverbs
Ecclesiastes
Song of Solomon
Isaiah
Jeremiah
Lamentations
Ezekiel
Daniel
Hosea
Joel
Amos
Obadiah
Jonah
Micah
Nahum
Habakkuk
Zephaniah
Haggai
Zechariah
Malachi

The Apocryphal/ Deuterocanonical Books

Tobit
Judith
Additions to the Book of Esther
Wisdom of Solomon
Ecclesiasticus, or the Wisdom of Jesus Son of Sirach
Baruch
The Letter of Jeremiah
The Prayer of Azariah and the Song of the Three Jews
Susanna
Bel and the Dragon
1 Maccabees
2 Maccabees
1 Esdras
Prayer of Manasseh
Psalm 151
3 Maccabees
2 Esdras
4 Maccabees

The New Testament

Matthew
Mark
Luke
John
Acts of the Apostles
Romans
1 Corinthians
2 Corinthians
Galatians
Ephesians
Philippians
Colossians
1 Thessalonians
2 Thessalonians
1 Timothy
2 Timothy
Titus
Philemon
Hebrews
James
1 Peter
2 Peter
1 John
2 John
3 John
Jude
Revelation

The Ten Commandments

The Ten Commandments, also called the Decalogue (Greek, "ten words"), were divine laws revealed to Moses by God on Mt. Sinai. Appearing in both Exodus (Ex. 20: 2–17) and Deuteronomy (Deut. 5:6–21), the commandments are numbered differently depending on whether they appear in a Catholic, Protestant, or Hebrew Bible. The following is the version given in the Revised Standard Version of the Bible.

You shall have no other gods before me.

You shall not make for yourself a graven image, or any likeness of anything that is in heaven above, or that is in the earth beneath, or that is in the water under the earth; you shall not bow down to them or serve them; for I the Lord your God am a jealous God, visiting the iniquity of the fathers upon the children to the third and the fourth generation of those who hate me, but showing steadfast love to thousands of those who love me and keep my commandments.

You shall not take the name of the Lord your God in vain; for the Lord will not hold him guiltless who takes his name in vain.

Remember the Sabbath day, to keep it holy. Six days you shall labor, and do all your work; but the seventh day is a Sabbath to the Lord your God; in it you shall not do any work, you, or your son, or your daughter, your manservant, or your maidservant, or your cattle, or the sojourner who is within your gates; for in six days the Lord made heaven and earth, the sea, and all that is in them, and rested the seventh day; therefore the Lord blessed the Sabbath day and hallowed it.

Honor your father and your mother, that your days may be long in the land which the Lord your God gives you.

You shall not kill.

You shall not commit adultery.

You shall not steal.

You shall not bear false witness against your neighbor.

You shall not covet your neighbor's wife, or his manservant, or his maidservant, or his ox, or his ass, or anything that is your neighbor's.

Source: Revised Standard Version of the Bible (Ex.20: 2–17)

Religion Web Sites

About Islam and Muslims:
http://www.ummah.org.uk/what-is-islam/index.html
Academic Info: Religion:
http://www.academicinfo.net/religindex.html
Buddha Net: http://www.buddhanet.net/
Christianity Online: http://www.christianity.net/

Hartford Seminary's Internet Links:
http://www.hartsem.edu/internet.htm
Hinduism Online: http://www.hinduismtoday.kauai.hi.us/
Judaism and Jewish Resources:
http://shamash.org/trb/judaism.html
World Council of Churches:
http://www.wcc-coe.org/wcc/map/index-e.html

See Calendar and Holidays for listings of religious holidays.

2001

January
S	M	T	W	T	F	S
	1	2	3	4	5	6
7	8	9	10	11	12	13
14	15	16	17	18	19	20
21	22	23	24	25	26	27
28	29	30	31			

1—New Year's Day
6—Epiphany
15—Martin Luther King, Jr.'s Birthday

February
S	M	T	W	T	F	S
				1	2	3
4	5	6	7	8	9	10
11	12	13	14	15	16	17
18	19	20	21	22	23	24
25	26	27	28			

2—Groundhog Day
12—Lincoln's Birthday
14—Valentine's Day
19—Washington's Birthday observed
22—Washington's Birthday
28—Ash Wednesday

March
S	M	T	W	T	F	S
				1	2	3
4	5	6	7	8	9	10
11	12	13	14	15	16	17
18	19	20	21	22	23	24
25	26	27	28	29	30	31

9—Purim*
17—St. Patrick's Day

April
S	M	T	W	T	F	S
1	2	3	4	5	6	7
8	9	10	11	12	13	14
15	16	17	18	19	20	21
22	23	24	25	26	27	28
29	30					

1—Daylight Saving Time begins
8—Palm Sunday
8—1st Day of Passover*
13—Good Friday
15—Easter Sunday
15—Orthodox Easter

May
S	M	T	W	T	F	S
		1	2	3	4	5
6	7	8	9	10	11	12
13	14	15	16	17	18	19
20	21	22	23	24	25	26
27	28	29	30	31		

13—Mother's Day
28—Memorial Day observed
28—1st Day of Shavuot*

June
S	M	T	W	T	F	S
					1	2
3	4	5	6	7	8	9
10	11	12	13	14	15	16
17	18	19	20	21	22	23
24	25	26	27	28	29	30

3—Pentecost
14—Flag Day
17—Father's Day

July
S	M	T	W	T	F	S
1	2	3	4	5	6	7
8	9	10	11	12	13	14
15	16	17	18	19	20	21
22	23	24	25	26	27	28
29	30	31				

1—Canada Day
4—Independence Day

August
S	M	T	W	T	F	S
			1	2	3	4
5	6	7	8	9	10	11
12	13	14	15	16	17	18
19	20	21	22	23	24	25
26	27	28	29	30	31	

September
S	M	T	W	T	F	S
						1
2	3	4	5	6	7	8
9	10	11	12	13	14	15
16	17	18	19	20	21	22
23	24	25	26	27	28	29
30						

3—Labor Day
18—Rosh Hashanah*
27—Yom Kippur*

October
S	M	T	W	T	F	S
	1	2	3	4	5	6
7	8	9	10	11	12	13
14	15	16	17	18	19	20
21	22	23	24	25	26	27
28	29	30	31			

8—Columbus Day observed
8—Thanksgiving Day (Canada)
28—Daylight Saving Time ends
31—Halloween

November
S	M	T	W	T	F	S
				1	2	3
4	5	6	7	8	9	10
11	12	13	14	15	16	17
18	19	20	21	22	23	24
25	26	27	28	29	30	

1—All Saints' Day
6—Election Day
11—Veterans Day
17—Ramadan begins*
22—Thanksgiving Day

December
S	M	T	W	T	F	S
						1
2	3	4	5	6	7	8
9	10	11	12	13	14	15
16	17	18	19	20	21	22
23	24	25	26	27	28	29
30	31					

2—1st Sunday of Advent
10—1st Day of Hanukkah*
17—Eid al-Fitr (Ramadan ends)*
25—Christmas Day

*All Jewish and Islamic holidays begin at sundown the day before they are listed here.

Seasons for the Northern Hemisphere, 2001

Mar. 20, 8:31 A.M. EST (13:31 UT[1]), Sun enters sign of Aries; spring begins

June 21, 3:38 A.M. EDT (07:38 UT[1]), Sun enters sign of Cancer; summer begins

Sept. 22, 7:05 A.M. EDT (23:05 UT[1]), Sun enters sign of Libra; fall begins

Dec. 21, 2:22 P.M. EST (19:22 UT[1]), Sun enters sign of Capricorn; winter begins

1. Universal Time (UT), also known as Greenwich Mean Time (GMT). See p. 399 for a conversion table of Universal Time.

2000

January
S	M	T	W	T	F	S
						1
2	3	4	5	6	7	8
9	10	11	12	13	14	15
16	17	18	19	20	21	22
23	24	25	26	27	28	29
30	31					

February
S	M	T	W	T	F	S
		1	2	3	4	5
6	7	8	9	10	11	12
13	14	15	16	17	18	19
20	21	22	23	24	25	26
27	28	29				

March
S	M	T	W	T	F	S
			1	2	3	4
5	6	7	8	9	10	11
12	13	14	15	16	17	18
19	20	21	22	23	24	25
26	27	28	29	30	31	

April
S	M	T	W	T	F	S
						1
2	3	4	5	6	7	8
9	10	11	12	13	14	15
16	17	18	19	20	21	22
23	24	25	26	27	28	29
30						

May
S	M	T	W	T	F	S
	1	2	3	4	5	6
7	8	9	10	11	12	13
14	15	16	17	18	19	20
21	22	23	24	25	26	27
28	29	30	31			

June
S	M	T	W	T	F	S
				1	2	3
4	5	6	7	8	9	10
11	12	13	14	15	16	17
18	19	20	21	22	23	24
25	26	27	28	29	30	

July
S	M	T	W	T	F	S
						1
2	3	4	5	6	7	8
9	10	11	12	13	14	15
16	17	18	19	20	21	22
23	24	25	26	27	28	29
30	31					

August
S	M	T	W	T	F	S
		1	2	3	4	5
6	7	8	9	10	11	12
13	14	15	16	17	18	19
20	21	22	23	24	25	26
27	28	29	30	31		

September
S	M	T	W	T	F	S
					1	2
3	4	5	6	7	8	9
10	11	12	13	14	15	16
17	18	19	20	21	22	23
24	25	26	27	28	29	30

October
S	M	T	W	T	F	S
1	2	3	4	5	6	7
8	9	10	11	12	13	14
15	16	17	18	19	20	21
22	23	24	25	26	27	28
29	30	31				

November
S	M	T	W	T	F	S
			1	2	3	4
5	6	7	8	9	10	11
12	13	14	15	16	17	18
19	20	21	22	23	24	25
26	27	28	29	30		

December
S	M	T	W	T	F	S
					1	2
3	4	5	6	7	8	9
10	11	12	13	14	15	16
17	18	19	20	21	22	23
24	25	26	27	28	29	30
31						

2002

January
S	M	T	W	T	F	S
		1	2	3	4	5
6	7	8	9	10	11	12
13	14	15	16	17	18	19
20	21	22	23	24	25	26
27	28	29	30	31		

February
S	M	T	W	T	F	S
					1	2
3	4	5	6	7	8	9
10	11	12	13	14	15	16
17	18	19	20	21	22	23
24	25	26	27	28		

March
S	M	T	W	T	F	S
					1	2
3	4	5	6	7	8	9
10	11	12	13	14	15	16
17	18	19	20	21	22	23
24	25	26	27	28	29	30
31						

April
S	M	T	W	T	F	S
	1	2	3	4	5	6
7	8	9	10	11	12	13
14	15	16	17	18	19	20
21	22	23	24	25	26	27
28	29	30				

May
S	M	T	W	T	F	S
			1	2	3	4
5	6	7	8	9	10	11
12	13	14	15	16	17	18
19	20	21	22	23	24	25
26	27	28	29	30	31	

June
S	M	T	W	T	F	S
						1
2	3	4	5	6	7	8
9	10	11	12	13	14	15
16	17	18	19	20	21	22
23	24	25	26	27	28	29
30						

July
S	M	T	W	T	F	S
	1	2	3	4	5	6
7	8	9	10	11	12	13
14	15	16	17	18	19	20
21	22	23	24	25	26	27
28	29	30	31			

August
S	M	T	W	T	F	S
				1	2	3
4	5	6	7	8	9	10
11	12	13	14	15	16	17
18	19	20	21	22	23	24
25	26	27	28	29	30	31

September
S	M	T	W	T	F	S
1	2	3	4	5	6	7
8	9	10	11	12	13	14
15	16	17	18	19	20	21
22	23	24	25	26	27	28
29	30					

October
S	M	T	W	T	F	S
		1	2	3	4	5
6	7	8	9	10	11	12
13	14	15	16	17	18	19
20	21	22	23	24	25	26
27	28	29	30	31		

November
S	M	T	W	T	F	S
					1	2
3	4	5	6	7	8	9
10	11	12	13	14	15	16
17	18	19	20	21	22	23
24	25	26	27	28	29	30

December
S	M	T	W	T	F	S
1	2	3	4	5	6	7
8	9	10	11	12	13	14
15	16	17	18	19	20	21
22	23	24	25	26	27	28
29	30	31				

Astrological Signs

♈ **Aries (Ram):** March 21–April 19

♉ **Taurus (Bull):** April 20–May 20

♊ **Gemini (Twins):** May 21–June 20

♋ **Cancer (Crab):** June 21–July 22

♌ **Leo (Lion):** July 23–Aug. 22

♍ **Virgo (Virgin):** Aug. 23–Sept. 22

♎ **Libra (Scales):** Sept. 23–Oct. 22

♏ **Scorpio (Scorpion):** Oct. 23–Nov. 21

♐ **Sagittarius (Archer):** Nov. 22–Dec. 21

♑ **Capricorn (Goat):** Dec. 22–Jan. 19

♒ **Aquarius (Water Bearer):** Jan. 20–Feb. 18

♓ **Pisces (Fish):** Feb. 19–March 20

PERPETUAL CALENDAR

1800...4	1844...9	1888...8	1932.13	1976.12	2020.11
1801...5	1845...4	1889...3	1933...1	1977...7	2021...6
1802...6	1846...5	1890...4	1934...2	1978...1	2022...7
1803...7	1847...6	1891...5	1935...3	1979...2	2023...1
1804...8	1848.14	1892.13	1936.11	1980.10	2024...9
1805...3	1849...2	1893...1	1937...6	1981...5	2025...4
1806...4	1850...3	1894...2	1938...7	1982...6	2026...5
1807...5	1851...4	1895...3	1939...1	1983...7	2027...6
1808.13	1852.12	1896.11	1940...9	1984...8	2028.14
1809...1	1853...7	1897...6	1941...4	1985...3	2029...2
1810...2	1854...1	1898...7	1942...5	1986...4	2030...3
1811...3	1855...2	1899...1	1943...6	1987...5	2031...4
1812.11	1856.10	1900...2	1944.14	1988.13	2032.12
1813...6	1857...5	1901...3	1945...2	1989...1	2033...7
1814...7	1858...6	1902...4	1946...3	1990...2	2034...1
1815...1	1859...7	1903...5	1947...4	1991...3	2035...2
1816...9	1860...8	1904.13	1948.12	1992.11	
1817...4	1861...3	1905...1	1949...7	1993...6	
1818...5	1862...4	1906...2	1950...1	1994...7	
1819...6	1863...5	1907...3	1951...2	1995...1	
1820.14	1864.13	1908.11	1952.10	1996...9	
1821...2	1865...1	1909...6	1953...5	1997...4	
1822...3	1866...2	1910...7	1954...6	1998...5	
1823...4	1867...3	1911...1	1955...7	1999...6	
1824.12	1868.11	1912...9	1956...8	2000.14	
1825...7	1869...6	1913...4	1957...3	2001...2	
1826...1	1870...7	1914...5	1958...4	2002...3	
1827...2	1871...1	1915...6	1959...5	2003...4	
1828.10	1872...9	1916.14	1960.13	2004.12	
1829...5	1873...4	1917...2	1961...1	2005...7	
1830...6	1874...5	1918...3	1962...2	2006...1	
1831...7	1875...6	1919...4	1963...3	2007...2	
1832...8	1876.14	1920.12	1964.11	2008.10	
1833...3	1877...2	1921...7	1965...6	2009...5	
1834...4	1878...3	1922...1	1966...7	2010...6	
1835...5	1879...4	1923...2	1967...1	2011...7	
1836.13	1880.12	1924.10	1968...9	2012...8	
1837...1	1881...7	1925...5	1969...4	2013...3	
1838...2	1882...1	1926...6	1970...5	2014...4	
1839...3	1883...2	1927...7	1971...6	2015...5	
1840.11	1884.10	1928...8	1972.14	2016.13	
1841...6	1885...5	1929...3	1973...2	2017...1	
1842...7	1886...6	1930...4	1974...3	2018...2	
1843...1	1887...7	1931...5	1975...4	2019...3	

DIRECTIONS: The number given with each year in the key above is the number of the calendar to use for that year.

1

```
        JANUARY              FEBRUARY               MARCH                APRIL
  S  M  T  W  T  F  S   S  M  T  W  T  F  S   S  M  T  W  T  F  S   S  M  T  W  T  F  S
     1  2  3  4  5  6  7            1  2  3  4            1  2  3  4   1  2  3  4  5  6  7
  8  9 10 11 12 13 14   5  6  7  8  9 10 11   5  6  7  8  9 10 11   8  9 10 11 12 13 14
 15 16 17 18 19 20 21  12 13 14 15 16 17 18  12 13 14 15 16 17 18  15 16 17 18 19 20 21
 22 23 24 25 26 27 28  19 20 21 22 23 24 25  19 20 21 22 23 24 25  22 23 24 25 26 27 28
 29 30 31              26 27 28              26 27 28 29 30 31     29 30

          MAY                   JUNE                  JULY                AUGUST
  S  M  T  W  T  F  S   S  M  T  W  T  F  S   S  M  T  W  T  F  S   S  M  T  W  T  F  S
        1  2  3  4  5            1  2  3                  1  2  3            1  2  3  4  5
  7  8  9 10 11 12 13   4  5  6  7  8  9 10   2  3  4  5  6  7  8   6  7  8  9 10 11 12
 14 15 16 17 18 19 20  11 12 13 14 15 16 17   9 10 11 12 13 14 15  13 14 15 16 17 18 19
 21 22 23 24 25 26 27  18 19 20 21 22 23 24  16 17 18 19 20 21 22  20 21 22 23 24 25 26
 28 29 30 31           25 26 27 28 29 30     23 24 25 26 27 28 29  27 28 29 30 31
                                             30 31

        SEPTEMBER             OCTOBER               NOVEMBER              DECEMBER
  S  M  T  W  T  F  S   S  M  T  W  T  F  S   S  M  T  W  T  F  S   S  M  T  W  T  F  S
                 1  2   1  2  3  4  5  6  7            1  2  3  4                  1  2
  3  4  5  6  7  8  9   8  9 10 11 12 13 14   5  6  7  8  9 10 11   3  4  5  6  7  8  9
 10 11 12 13 14 15 16  15 16 17 18 19 20 21  12 13 14 15 16 17 18  10 11 12 13 14 15 16
 17 18 19 20 21 22 23  22 23 24 25 26 27 28  19 20 21 22 23 24 25  17 18 19 20 21 22 23
 24 25 26 27 28 29 30  29 30 31              26 27 28 29 30        24 25 26 27 28 29 30
                                                                   31
```

2

```
        JANUARY              FEBRUARY               MARCH                APRIL
  S  M  T  W  T  F  S   S  M  T  W  T  F  S   S  M  T  W  T  F  S   S  M  T  W  T  F  S
     1  2  3  4  5  6            1  2  3            1  2  3   1  2  3  4  5  6  7
  7  8  9 10 11 12 13   4  5  6  7  8  9 10   4  5  6  7  8  9 10   8  9 10 11 12 13 14
 14 15 16 17 18 19 20  11 12 13 14 15 16 17  11 12 13 14 15 16 17  15 16 17 18 19 20 21
 21 22 23 24 25 26 27  18 19 20 21 22 23 24  18 19 20 21 22 23 24  22 23 24 25 26 27 28
 28 29 30 31           25 26 27 28           25 26 27 28 29 30 31  29 30

          MAY                   JUNE                  JULY                AUGUST
  S  M  T  W  T  F  S   S  M  T  W  T  F  S   S  M  T  W  T  F  S   S  M  T  W  T  F  S
        1  2  3  4  5                  1  2   1  2  3  4  5  6  7            1  2  3  4
  6  7  8  9 10 11 12   3  4  5  6  7  8  9   8  9 10 11 12 13 14   5  6  7  8  9 10 11
 13 14 15 16 17 18 19  10 11 12 13 14 15 16  15 16 17 18 19 20 21  12 13 14 15 16 17 18
 20 21 22 23 24 25 26  17 18 19 20 21 22 23  22 23 24 25 26 27 28  19 20 21 22 23 24 25
 27 28 29 30 31        24 25 26 27 28 29 30  29 30 31              26 27 28 29 30 31

        SEPTEMBER             OCTOBER               NOVEMBER              DECEMBER
  S  M  T  W  T  F  S   S  M  T  W  T  F  S   S  M  T  W  T  F  S   S  M  T  W  T  F  S
                    1      1  2  3  4  5  6            1  2  3                     1
  2  3  4  5  6  7  8   7  8  9 10 11 12 13   4  5  6  7  8  9 10   2  3  4  5  6  7  8
  9 10 11 12 13 14 15  14 15 16 17 18 19 20  11 12 13 14 15 16 17   9 10 11 12 13 14 15
 16 17 18 19 20 21 22  21 22 23 24 25 26 27  18 19 20 21 22 23 24  16 17 18 19 20 21 22
 23 24 25 26 27 28 29  28 29 30 31           25 26 27 28 29 30     23 24 25 26 27 28 29
 30                                                                30 31
```

3

```
        JANUARY              FEBRUARY               MARCH                APRIL
  S  M  T  W  T  F  S   S  M  T  W  T  F  S   S  M  T  W  T  F  S   S  M  T  W  T  F  S
        1  2  3  4  5               1  2               1  2   1  2  3  4  5  6
  6  7  8  9 10 11 12   3  4  5  6  7  8  9   3  4  5  6  7  8  9   7  8  9 10 11 12 13
 13 14 15 16 17 18 19  10 11 12 13 14 15 16  10 11 12 13 14 15 16  14 15 16 17 18 19 20
 20 21 22 23 24 25 26  17 18 19 20 21 22 23  17 18 19 20 21 22 23  21 22 23 24 25 26 27
 27 28 29 30 31        24 25 26 27 28        24 25 26 27 28 29 30  28 29 30
                                             31

          MAY                   JUNE                  JULY                AUGUST
  S  M  T  W  T  F  S   S  M  T  W  T  F  S   S  M  T  W  T  F  S   S  M  T  W  T  F  S
           1  2  3  4                     1      1  2  3  4  5  6            1  2  3
  5  6  7  8  9 10 11   2  3  4  5  6  7  8   7  8  9 10 11 12 13   4  5  6  7  8  9 10
 12 13 14 15 16 17 18   9 10 11 12 13 14 15  14 15 16 17 18 19 20  11 12 13 14 15 16 17
 19 20 21 22 23 24 25  16 17 18 19 20 21 22  21 22 23 24 25 26 27  18 19 20 21 22 23 24
 26 27 28 29 30 31     23 24 25 26 27 28 29  28 29 30 31           25 26 27 28 29 30 31
                       30

        SEPTEMBER             OCTOBER               NOVEMBER              DECEMBER
  S  M  T  W  T  F  S   S  M  T  W  T  F  S   S  M  T  W  T  F  S   S  M  T  W  T  F  S
  1  2  3  4  5  6  7         1  2  3  4  5               1  2   1  2  3  4  5  6  7
  8  9 10 11 12 13 14   6  7  8  9 10 11 12   3  4  5  6  7  8  9   8  9 10 11 12 13 14
 15 16 17 18 19 20 21  13 14 15 16 17 18 19  10 11 12 13 14 15 16  15 16 17 18 19 20 21
 22 23 24 25 26 27 28  20 21 22 23 24 25 26  17 18 19 20 21 22 23  22 23 24 25 26 27 28
 29 30                 27 28 29 30 31        24 25 26 27 28 29 30  29 30 31
```

4

```
        JANUARY              FEBRUARY               MARCH                APRIL
  S  M  T  W  T  F  S   S  M  T  W  T  F  S   S  M  T  W  T  F  S   S  M  T  W  T  F  S
           1  2  3  4                     1                     1   1  2  3  4  5
  5  6  7  8  9 10 11   2  3  4  5  6  7  8   2  3  4  5  6  7  8   6  7  8  9 10 11 12
 12 13 14 15 16 17 18   9 10 11 12 13 14 15   9 10 11 12 13 14 15  13 14 15 16 17 18 19
 19 20 21 22 23 24 25  16 17 18 19 20 21 22  16 17 18 19 20 21 22  20 21 22 23 24 25 26
 26 27 28 29 30 31     23 24 25 26 27 28     23 24 25 26 27 28 29  27 28 29 30
                                             30 31

          MAY                   JUNE                  JULY                AUGUST
  S  M  T  W  T  F  S   S  M  T  W  T  F  S   S  M  T  W  T  F  S   S  M  T  W  T  F  S
           1  2  3   1  2  3  4  5  6  7         1  2  3  4  5               1  2
  4  5  6  7  8  9 10   8  9 10 11 12 13 14   6  7  8  9 10 11 12   3  4  5  6  7  8  9
 11 12 13 14 15 16 17  15 16 17 18 19 20 21  13 14 15 16 17 18 19  10 11 12 13 14 15 16
 18 19 20 21 22 23 24  22 23 24 25 26 27 28  20 21 22 23 24 25 26  17 18 19 20 21 22 23
 25 26 27 28 29 30 31  29 30                 27 28 29 30 31        24 25 26 27 28 29 30
                                                                   31

        SEPTEMBER             OCTOBER               NOVEMBER              DECEMBER
  S  M  T  W  T  F  S   S  M  T  W  T  F  S   S  M  T  W  T  F  S   S  M  T  W  T  F  S
     1  2  3  4  5  6            1  2  3  4                     1      1  2  3  4  5  6
  7  8  9 10 11 12 13   5  6  7  8  9 10 11   2  3  4  5  6  7  8   7  8  9 10 11 12 13
 14 15 16 17 18 19 20  12 13 14 15 16 17 18   9 10 11 12 13 14 15  14 15 16 17 18 19 20
 21 22 23 24 25 26 27  19 20 21 22 23 24 25  16 17 18 19 20 21 22  21 22 23 24 25 26 27
 28 29 30              26 27 28 29 30 31     23 24 25 26 27 28 29  28 29 30 31
                                             30
```

5

```
        JANUARY              FEBRUARY               MARCH                APRIL
  S  M  T  W  T  F  S   S  M  T  W  T  F  S   S  M  T  W  T  F  S   S  M  T  W  T  F  S
              1  2  3   1  2  3  4  5  6  7   1  2  3  4  5  6  7            1  2  3  4
  4  5  6  7  8  9 10   8  9 10 11 12 13 14   8  9 10 11 12 13 14   5  6  7  8  9 10 11
 11 12 13 14 15 16 17  15 16 17 18 19 20 21  15 16 17 18 19 20 21  12 13 14 15 16 17 18
 18 19 20 21 22 23 24  22 23 24 25 26 27 28  22 23 24 25 26 27 28  19 20 21 22 23 24 25
 25 26 27 28 29 30 31                        29 30 31              26 27 28 29 30

          MAY                   JUNE                  JULY                AUGUST
  S  M  T  W  T  F  S   S  M  T  W  T  F  S   S  M  T  W  T  F  S   S  M  T  W  T  F  S
                 1  2      1  2  3  4  5  6            1  2  3  4                     1
  3  4  5  6  7  8  9   7  8  9 10 11 12 13   5  6  7  8  9 10 11   2  3  4  5  6  7  8
 10 11 12 13 14 15 16  14 15 16 17 18 19 20  12 13 14 15 16 17 18   9 10 11 12 13 14 15
 17 18 19 20 21 22 23  21 22 23 24 25 26 27  19 20 21 22 23 24 25  16 17 18 19 20 21 22
 24 25 26 27 28 29 30  28 29 30              26 27 28 29 30 31     23 24 25 26 27 28 29
 31                                                                30 31

        SEPTEMBER             OCTOBER               NOVEMBER              DECEMBER
  S  M  T  W  T  F  S   S  M  T  W  T  F  S   S  M  T  W  T  F  S   S  M  T  W  T  F  S
        1  2  3  4  5               1  2  3   1  2  3  4  5  6  7         1  2  3  4  5
  6  7  8  9 10 11 12   4  5  6  7  8  9 10   8  9 10 11 12 13 14   6  7  8  9 10 11 12
 13 14 15 16 17 18 19  11 12 13 14 15 16 17  15 16 17 18 19 20 21  13 14 15 16 17 18 19
 20 21 22 23 24 25 26  18 19 20 21 22 23 24  22 23 24 25 26 27 28  20 21 22 23 24 25 26
 27 28 29 30           25 26 27 28 29 30 31  29 30                 27 28 29 30 31
```

6

```
        JANUARY              FEBRUARY               MARCH                APRIL
  S  M  T  W  T  F  S   S  M  T  W  T  F  S   S  M  T  W  T  F  S   S  M  T  W  T  F  S
                 1  2      1  2  3  4  5  6      1  2  3  4  5  6            1  2  3
  3  4  5  6  7  8  9   7  8  9 10 11 12 13   7  8  9 10 11 12 13   4  5  6  7  8  9 10
 10 11 12 13 14 15 16  14 15 16 17 18 19 20  14 15 16 17 18 19 20  11 12 13 14 15 16 17
 17 18 19 20 21 22 23  21 22 23 24 25 26 27  21 22 23 24 25 26 27  18 19 20 21 22 23 24
 24 25 26 27 28 29 30  28                    28 29 30 31           25 26 27 28 29 30
 31

          MAY                   JUNE                  JULY                AUGUST
  S  M  T  W  T  F  S   S  M  T  W  T  F  S   S  M  T  W  T  F  S   S  M  T  W  T  F  S
                    1         1  2  3  4  5               1  2  3   1  2  3  4  5  6  7
  2  3  4  5  6  7  8   6  7  8  9 10 11 12   4  5  6  7  8  9 10   8  9 10 11 12 13 14
  9 10 11 12 13 14 15  13 14 15 16 17 18 19  11 12 13 14 15 16 17  15 16 17 18 19 20 21
 16 17 18 19 20 21 22  20 21 22 23 24 25 26  18 19 20 21 22 23 24  22 23 24 25 26 27 28
 23 24 25 26 27 28 29  27 28 29 30           25 26 27 28 29 30 31  29 30 31
 30 31

        SEPTEMBER             OCTOBER               NOVEMBER              DECEMBER
  S  M  T  W  T  F  S   S  M  T  W  T  F  S   S  M  T  W  T  F  S   S  M  T  W  T  F  S
           1  2  3  4               1  2      1  2  3  4  5  6               1  2  3  4
  5  6  7  8  9 10 11   3  4  5  6  7  8  9   7  8  9 10 11 12 13   5  6  7  8  9 10 11
 12 13 14 15 16 17 18  10 11 12 13 14 15 16  14 15 16 17 18 19 20  12 13 14 15 16 17 18
 19 20 21 22 23 24 25  17 18 19 20 21 22 23  21 22 23 24 25 26 27  19 20 21 22 23 24 25
 26 27 28 29 30        24 25 26 27 28 29 30  28 29 30              26 27 28 29 30 31
                       31
```

7

JANUARY
S M T W T F S
1
2 3 4 5 6 7 8
9 10 11 12 13 14 15
16 17 18 19 20 21 22
23 24 25 26 27 28 29
30 31

FEBRUARY
S M T W T F S
1 2 3 4 5
6 7 8 9 10 11 12
13 14 15 16 17 18 19
20 21 22 23 24 25 26
27 28

MARCH
S M T W T F S
1 2 3 4 5
6 7 8 9 10 11 12
13 14 15 16 17 18 19
20 21 22 23 24 25 26
27 28 29 30 31

APRIL
S M T W T F S
1 2
3 4 5 6 7 8 9
10 11 12 13 14 15 16
17 18 19 20 21 22 23
24 25 26 27 28 29 30

MAY
S M T W T F S
1 2 3 4 5 6 7
8 9 10 11 12 13 14
15 16 17 18 19 20 21
22 23 24 25 26 27 28
29 30 31

JUNE
S M T W T F S
1 2 3 4
5 6 7 8 9 10 11
12 13 14 15 16 17 18
19 20 21 22 23 24 25
26 27 28 29 30

JULY
S M T W T F S
1 2
3 4 5 6 7 8 9
10 11 12 13 14 15 16
17 18 19 20 21 22 23
24 25 26 27 28 29 30
31

AUGUST
S M T W T F S
1 2 3 4 5 6
7 8 9 10 11 12 13
14 15 16 17 18 19 20
21 22 23 24 25 26 27
28 29 30 31

SEPTEMBER
S M T W T F S
1 2 3
4 5 6 7 8 9 10
11 12 13 14 15 16 17
18 19 20 21 22 23 24
25 26 27 28 29 30

OCTOBER
S M T W T F S
1
2 3 4 5 6 7 8
9 10 11 12 13 14 15
16 17 18 19 20 21 22
23 24 25 26 27 28 29
30 31

NOVEMBER
S M T W T F S
1 2 3 4 5
6 7 8 9 10 11 12
13 14 15 16 17 18 19
20 21 22 23 24 25 26
27 28 29 30

DECEMBER
S M T W T F S
1 2 3
4 5 6 7 8 9 10
11 12 13 14 15 16 17
18 19 20 21 22 23 24
25 26 27 28 29 30 31

8

JANUARY
S M T W T F S
1 2 3 4 5 6 7
8 9 10 11 12 13 14
15 16 17 18 19 20 21
22 23 24 25 26 27 28
29 30 31

FEBRUARY
S M T W T F S
1 2 3 4
5 6 7 8 9 10 11
12 13 14 15 16 17 18
19 20 21 22 23 24 25
26 27 28 29

MARCH
S M T W T F S
1 2 3
4 5 6 7 8 9 10
11 12 13 14 15 16 17
18 19 20 21 22 23 24
25 26 27 28 29 30 31

APRIL
S M T W T F S
1 2 3 4 5 6 7
8 9 10 11 12 13 14
15 16 17 18 19 20 21
22 23 24 25 26 27 28
29 30

MAY
S M T W T F S
1 2 3 4 5
6 7 8 9 10 11 12
13 14 15 16 17 18 19
20 21 22 23 24 25 26
27 28 29 30 31

JUNE
S M T W T F S
1 2
3 4 5 6 7 8 9
10 11 12 13 14 15 16
17 18 19 20 21 22 23
24 25 26 27 28 29 30

JULY
S M T W T F S
1 2 3 4 5 6 7
8 9 10 11 12 13 14
15 16 17 18 19 20 21
22 23 24 25 26 27 28
29 30 31

AUGUST
S M T W T F S
1 2 3 4
5 6 7 8 9 10 11
12 13 14 15 16 17 18
19 20 21 22 23 24 25
26 27 28 29 30 31

SEPTEMBER
S M T W T F S
1
2 3 4 5 6 7 8
9 10 11 12 13 14 15
16 17 18 19 20 21 22
23 24 25 26 27 28 29
30

OCTOBER
S M T W T F S
1 2 3 4 5 6
7 8 9 10 11 12 13
14 15 16 17 18 19 20
21 22 23 24 25 26 27
28 29 30 31

NOVEMBER
S M T W T F S
1 2 3
4 5 6 7 8 9 10
11 12 13 14 15 16 17
18 19 20 21 22 23 24
25 26 27 28 29 30

DECEMBER
S M T W T F S
1
2 3 4 5 6 7 8
9 10 11 12 13 14 15
16 17 18 19 20 21 22
23 24 25 26 27 28 29
30 31

9

JANUARY
S M T W T F S
1 2 3 4 5 6
7 8 9 10 11 12 13
14 15 16 17 18 19 20
21 22 23 24 25 26 27
28 29 30 31

FEBRUARY
S M T W T F S
1 2 3
4 5 6 7 8 9 10
11 12 13 14 15 16 17
18 19 20 21 22 23 24
25 26 27 28 29

MARCH
S M T W T F S
1 2
3 4 5 6 7 8 9
10 11 12 13 14 15 16
17 18 19 20 21 22 23
24 25 26 27 28 29 30
31

APRIL
S M T W T F S
1 2 3 4 5 6
7 8 9 10 11 12 13
14 15 16 17 18 19 20
21 22 23 24 25 26 27
28 29 30

MAY
S M T W T F S
1 2 3 4
5 6 7 8 9 10 11
12 13 14 15 16 17 18
19 20 21 22 23 24 25
26 27 28 29 30 31

JUNE
S M T W T F S
1
2 3 4 5 6 7 8
9 10 11 12 13 14 15
16 17 18 19 20 21 22
23 24 25 26 27 28 29
30

JULY
S M T W T F S
1 2 3 4 5 6
7 8 9 10 11 12 13
14 15 16 17 18 19 20
21 22 23 24 25 26 27
28 29 30 31

AUGUST
S M T W T F S
1 2 3
4 5 6 7 8 9 10
11 12 13 14 15 16 17
18 19 20 21 22 23 24
25 26 27 28 29 30 31

SEPTEMBER
S M T W T F S
1 2 3 4 5 6 7
8 9 10 11 12 13 14
15 16 17 18 19 20 21
22 23 24 25 26 27 28
29 30

OCTOBER
S M T W T F S
1 2 3 4 5
6 7 8 9 10 11 12
13 14 15 16 17 18 19
20 21 22 23 24 25 26
27 28 29 30 31

NOVEMBER
S M T W T F S
1 2
3 4 5 6 7 8 9
10 11 12 13 14 15 16
17 18 19 20 21 22 23
24 25 26 27 28 29 30

DECEMBER
S M T W T F S
1 2 3 4 5 6 7
8 9 10 11 12 13 14
15 16 17 18 19 20 21
22 23 24 25 26 27 28
29 30 31

10

JANUARY
S M T W T F S
1 2 3 4 5
6 7 8 9 10 11 12
13 14 15 16 17 18 19
20 21 22 23 24 25 26
27 28 29 30 31

FEBRUARY
S M T W T F S
1 2
3 4 5 6 7 8 9
10 11 12 13 14 15 16
17 18 19 20 21 22 23
24 25 26 27 28 29

MARCH
S M T W T F S
1
2 3 4 5 6 7 8
9 10 11 12 13 14 15
16 17 18 19 20 21 22
23 24 25 26 27 28 29
30 31

APRIL
S M T W T F S
1 2 3 4 5
6 7 8 9 10 11 12
13 14 15 16 17 18 19
20 21 22 23 24 25 26
27 28 29 30

MAY
S M T W T F S
1 2 3
4 5 6 7 8 9 10
11 12 13 14 15 16 17
18 19 20 21 22 23 24
25 26 27 28 29 30 31

JUNE
S M T W T F S
1 2 3 4 5 6 7
8 9 10 11 12 13 14
15 16 17 18 19 20 21
22 23 24 25 26 27 28
29 30

JULY
S M T W T F S
1 2 3 4 5
6 7 8 9 10 11 12
13 14 15 16 17 18 19
20 21 22 23 24 25 26
27 28 29 30 31

AUGUST
S M T W T F S
1 2
3 4 5 6 7 8 9
10 11 12 13 14 15 16
17 18 19 20 21 22 23
24 25 26 27 28 29 30
31

SEPTEMBER
S M T W T F S
1 2 3 4 5 6
7 8 9 10 11 12 13
14 15 16 17 18 19 20
21 22 23 24 25 26 27
28 29 30

OCTOBER
S M T W T F S
1 2 3 4
5 6 7 8 9 10 11
12 13 14 15 16 17 18
19 20 21 22 23 24 25
26 27 28 29 30 31

NOVEMBER
S M T W T F S
1
2 3 4 5 6 7 8
9 10 11 12 13 14 15
16 17 18 19 20 21 22
23 24 25 26 27 28 29
30

DECEMBER
S M T W T F S
1 2 3 4 5 6
7 8 9 10 11 12 13
14 15 16 17 18 19 20
21 22 23 24 25 26 27
28 29 30 31

11

JANUARY
S M T W T F S
1 2 3 4
5 6 7 8 9 10 11
12 13 14 15 16 17 18
19 20 21 22 23 24 25
26 27 28 29 30 31

FEBRUARY
S M T W T F S
1
2 3 4 5 6 7 8
9 10 11 12 13 14 15
16 17 18 19 20 21 22
23 24 25 26 27 28

MARCH
S M T W T F S
1
2 3 4 5 6 7 8
9 10 11 12 13 14 15
16 17 18 19 20 21 22
23 24 25 26 27 28 29
30 31

APRIL
S M T W T F S
1 2 3 4
5 6 7 8 9 10 11
12 13 14 15 16 17 18
19 20 21 22 23 24 25
26 27 28 29 30

MAY
S M T W T F S
1 2
3 4 5 6 7 8 9
10 11 12 13 14 15 16
17 18 19 20 21 22 23
24 25 26 27 28 29 30
31

JUNE
S M T W T F S
1 2 3 4 5 6
7 8 9 10 11 12 13
14 15 16 17 18 19 20
21 22 23 24 25 26 27
28 29 30

JULY
S M T W T F S
1 2 3 4
5 6 7 8 9 10 11
12 13 14 15 16 17 18
19 20 21 22 23 24 25
26 27 28 29 30 31

AUGUST
S M T W T F S
1
2 3 4 5 6 7 8
9 10 11 12 13 14 15
16 17 18 19 20 21 22
23 24 25 26 27 28 29
30 31

SEPTEMBER
S M T W T F S
1 2 3 4 5
6 7 8 9 10 11 12
13 14 15 16 17 18 19
20 21 22 23 24 25 26
27 28 29 30

OCTOBER
S M T W T F S
1 2 3
4 5 6 7 8 9 10
11 12 13 14 15 16 17
18 19 20 21 22 23 24
25 26 27 28 29 30 31

NOVEMBER
S M T W T F S
1 2 3 4 5 6 7
8 9 10 11 12 13 14
15 16 17 18 19 20 21
22 23 24 25 26 27 28
29 30

DECEMBER
S M T W T F S
1 2 3 4 5
6 7 8 9 10 11 12
13 14 15 16 17 18 19
20 21 22 23 24 25 26
27 28 29 30 31

12

JANUARY
S M T W T F S
1 2 3
4 5 6 7 8 9 10
11 12 13 14 15 16 17
18 19 20 21 22 23 24
25 26 27 28 29 30 31

FEBRUARY
S M T W T F S
1 2 3 4 5 6 7
8 9 10 11 12 13 14
15 16 17 18 19 20 21
22 23 24 25 26 27 28

MARCH
S M T W T F S
1 2 3 4 5 6
7 8 9 10 11 12 13
14 15 16 17 18 19 20
21 22 23 24 25 26 27
28 29 30 31

APRIL
S M T W T F S
1 2 3
4 5 6 7 8 9 10
11 12 13 14 15 16 17
18 19 20 21 22 23 24
25 26 27 28 29 30

MAY
S M T W T F S
1
2 3 4 5 6 7 8
9 10 11 12 13 14 15
16 17 18 19 20 21 22
23 24 25 26 27 28 29
30 31

JUNE
S M T W T F S
1 2 3 4 5
6 7 8 9 10 11 12
13 14 15 16 17 18 19
20 21 22 23 24 25 26
27 28 29 30

JULY
S M T W T F S
1 2 3
4 5 6 7 8 9 10
11 12 13 14 15 16 17
18 19 20 21 22 23 24
25 26 27 28 29 30 31

AUGUST
S M T W T F S
1 2 3 4 5 6 7
8 9 10 11 12 13 14
15 16 17 18 19 20 21
22 23 24 25 26 27 28
29 30 31

SEPTEMBER
S M T W T F S
1 2 3 4
5 6 7 8 9 10 11
12 13 14 15 16 17 18
19 20 21 22 23 24 25
26 27 28 29 30

OCTOBER
S M T W T F S
1 2
3 4 5 6 7 8 9
10 11 12 13 14 15 16
17 18 19 20 21 22 23
24 25 26 27 28 29 30
31

NOVEMBER
S M T W T F S
1 2 3 4 5 6
7 8 9 10 11 12 13
14 15 16 17 18 19 20
21 22 23 24 25 26 27
28 29 30

DECEMBER
S M T W T F S
1 2 3 4
5 6 7 8 9 10 11
12 13 14 15 16 17 18
19 20 21 22 23 24 25
26 27 28 29 30 31

13

JANUARY
S M T W T F S
1 2
3 4 5 6 7 8 9
10 11 12 13 14 15 16
17 18 19 20 21 22 23
24 25 26 27 28 29 30
31

FEBRUARY
S M T W T F S
1 2 3 4 5 6
7 8 9 10 11 12 13
14 15 16 17 18 19 20
21 22 23 24 25 26 27
28

MARCH
S M T W T F S
1 2 3 4 5
6 7 8 9 10 11 12
13 14 15 16 17 18 19
20 21 22 23 24 25 26
27 28 29 30 31

APRIL
S M T W T F S
1 2
3 4 5 6 7 8 9
10 11 12 13 14 15 16
17 18 19 20 21 22 23
24 25 26 27 28 29 30

MAY
S M T W T F S
1 2 3 4 5 6 7
8 9 10 11 12 13 14
15 16 17 18 19 20 21
22 23 24 25 26 27 28
29 30 31

JUNE
S M T W T F S
1 2 3 4
5 6 7 8 9 10 11
12 13 14 15 16 17 18
19 20 21 22 23 24 25
26 27 28 29 30

JULY
S M T W T F S
1 2
3 4 5 6 7 8 9
10 11 12 13 14 15 16
17 18 19 20 21 22 23
24 25 26 27 28 29 30
31

AUGUST
S M T W T F S
1 2 3 4 5 6
7 8 9 10 11 12 13
14 15 16 17 18 19 20
21 22 23 24 25 26 27
28 29 30 31

SEPTEMBER
S M T W T F S
1 2 3
4 5 6 7 8 9 10
11 12 13 14 15 16 17
18 19 20 21 22 23 24
25 26 27 28 29 30

OCTOBER
S M T W T F S
1
2 3 4 5 6 7 8
9 10 11 12 13 14 15
16 17 18 19 20 21 22
23 24 25 26 27 28 29
30 31

NOVEMBER
S M T W T F S
1 2 3 4 5
6 7 8 9 10 11 12
13 14 15 16 17 18 19
20 21 22 23 24 25 26
27 28 29 30

DECEMBER
S M T W T F S
1 2 3
4 5 6 7 8 9 10
11 12 13 14 15 16 17
18 19 20 21 22 23 24
25 26 27 28 29 30 31

14

JANUARY
S M T W T F S
1
2 3 4 5 6 7 8
9 10 11 12 13 14 15
16 17 18 19 20 21 22
23 24 25 26 27 28 29
30 31

FEBRUARY
S M T W T F S
1 2 3 4 5
6 7 8 9 10 11 12
13 14 15 16 17 18 19
20 21 22 23 24 25 26
27 28

MARCH
S M T W T F S
1 2 3 4
5 6 7 8 9 10 11
12 13 14 15 16 17 18
19 20 21 22 23 24 25
26 27 28 29 30 31

APRIL
S M T W T F S
1
2 3 4 5 6 7 8
9 10 11 12 13 14 15
16 17 18 19 20 21 22
23 24 25 26 27 28 29
30

MAY
S M T W T F S
1 2 3 4 5 6
7 8 9 10 11 12 13
14 15 16 17 18 19 20
21 22 23 24 25 26 27
28 29 30 31

JUNE
S M T W T F S
1 2 3
4 5 6 7 8 9 10
11 12 13 14 15 16 17
18 19 20 21 22 23 24
25 26 27 28 29 30

JULY
S M T W T F S
1
2 3 4 5 6 7 8
9 10 11 12 13 14 15
16 17 18 19 20 21 22
23 24 25 26 27 28 29
30 31

AUGUST
S M T W T F S
1 2 3 4 5
6 7 8 9 10 11 12
13 14 15 16 17 18 19
20 21 22 23 24 25 26
27 28 29 30 31

SEPTEMBER
S M T W T F S
1 2
3 4 5 6 7 8 9
10 11 12 13 14 15 16
17 18 19 20 21 22 23
24 25 26 27 28 29 30

OCTOBER
S M T W T F S
1 2 3 4 5 6 7
8 9 10 11 12 13 14
15 16 17 18 19 20 21
22 23 24 25 26 27 28
29 30 31

NOVEMBER
S M T W T F S
1 2 3 4
5 6 7 8 9 10 11
12 13 14 15 16 17 18
19 20 21 22 23 24 25
26 27 28 29 30

DECEMBER
S M T W T F S
1 2
3 4 5 6 7 8 9
10 11 12 13 14 15 16
17 18 19 20 21 22 23
24 25 26 27 28 29 30
31

History of the Calendar

The purpose of a calendar is to reckon time in advance, to show how many days have to elapse until a certain event takes place—the harvest, a religious festival, or whatever. The earliest calendars, naturally, were crude, and they must have been strongly influenced by the geographical location of the people who made them. In the Scandinavian countries, for example, where the seasons are pronounced, the concept of the year was determined by the seasons, specifically by the end of winter. The Norsemen, before becoming Christians, are said to have had a calendar consisting of 10 months of 30 days each.

But in warmer countries, where the seasons are less pronounced, the Moon became the basic unit for time reckoning; an old Jewish book actually makes the statement that "the Moon was created for the counting of the days." All the oldest calendars for which we have reliable information were lunar calendars, based on the time interval from one new moon to the next—a so-called lunation. But even in a warm climate there are annual events that pay no attention to the phases of the Moon. In some areas it was a rainy season; in Egypt it was the annual flooding of the Nile. It was, therefore, necessary to regulate daily life and religious festivals by lunations, but to take care of the annual event in some other manner.

The calendar of the Assyrians was based on the phases of the Moon. The month began with the first appearance of the lunar crescent, and since this can best be observed in the evening, the day began with sunset. They knew that a lunation was 29½ days long, so their lunar year had a duration of 354 days, falling 11 days short of the solar year.[1] After three years such a lunar calendar would be off by 33 days, or more than one lunation. We know that the Assyrians added an extra month from time to time, but we do not know whether they had developed a special rule for doing so or whether the priests proclaimed the necessity for an extra month from observation. If they made every third year a year of 13 lunations, their three-year period would cover 1,091½ days (using their value of 29½ days for one lunation), or just about 4 days too short. In one century this mistake would add up to 133 days by their reckoning (in reality closer to 134 days), requiring four extra lunations per century.

We now know that an eight-year period, consisting of five years with 12 months and three years with 13 months, would lead to a difference of only 20 days per century, but we do not know whether such a calendar was actually used.

The best approximation that was possible in antiquity was a 19-year period, with 7 of these 19 years having 13 months. This means that the period contained 235 months. This, still using the old value for a lunation, made a total of 6,932½ days, while 19 solar years added up to 6,939.7 days, a difference of just one week per period and about five weeks per century. Even the 19-year period required constant adjustment, but it was the period that became the basis of the religious calendar of the Jews. The Arabs used the same calendar at first, but Muhammad forbade shifting from 12 months to 13 months, so that the Islamic religious calendar, even today, has a lunar year of 354 days. As a result the Islamic religious festivals run through all the seasons of the year three times per century.

The Egyptians had a traditional calendar with 12 months of 30 days each. At one time they added 5 extra days at the end of every year. These turned into a 5-day festival because it was thought to be unlucky to work during that time.

When Rome emerged as a world power, the difficulties of making a calendar were well known, but the Romans complicated their lives because of their superstition that even numbers were unlucky. Hence their months were 29 or 31 days long, with the exception of February, which had 28 days. However, 4 months of 31 days, 7 months of 29 days, and 1 month of 28 days added up to only 355 days. Therefore, the Romans invented an extra month called Mercedonius of 22 or 23 days. It was added every second year.

Even with Mercedonius, the Roman calendar was so far off that Julius Caesar, advised by the astronomer Sosigenes, ordered a sweeping reform in 45 B.C. One year, made 445 days long by imperial decree, brought the calendar back in step with the seasons. Then the solar year (with the value of 365 days and 6 hours) was made the basis of the calendar. The months were 30 or 31 days in length, and to take care of the 6 hours, every fourth year was made a 366-day year. Moreover, Caesar decreed the year began with the first of January, not with the vernal equinox in late March.

This was the Julian calendar, named after Julius Caesar. It is still the calendar of the Eastern Orthodox churches. However, the year is 11½ minutes shorter than the figure written into Caesar's calendar by Sosigenes, and after a number of centuries, even 11½ minutes add up.

While Caesar could decree that the vernal equinox should not be used as the first day of the new year, the vernal equinox is still a fact of nature that could not be disregarded. One of the first (as far as we know) to become alarmed about this was Roger Bacon. He sent a memorandum to Pope Clement IV, who apparently was not impressed. But Pope Sixtus IV (who reigned from 1471 to 1484) decided that another reform was needed and called the German astronomer Regiomontanus to Rome to advise him. Regiomontanus arrived in 1475, but one year later he died in an epidemic, one of the recurrent outbreaks of the plague. The pope himself survived, but his reform plans died with Regiomontanus.

Less than a hundred years later, in 1545, the Council of Trent authorized the then pope, Paul III, to reform the calendar once more. Most of the mathematical and astronomical work was done by Father Christopher Clavius, S.J. The immediate correction, advised by Father Clavius and ordered by Pope Gregory XIII, was that Thursday, Oct. 4, 1582, was to be the last day of the Julian calendar. The next day was Friday, with the date of October 15. For long-range accuracy, a formula suggested by the

---

1. The correct figures are lunation: 29 d, 12 h, 44 min, 2.8 sec (29.530585 d); solar year: 365 d, 5 h, 48 min, 46 sec (365.242216 d); 12 lunations: 354 d, 8 h, 48 min, 34 sec (354.3671 d).

Drift of the Vernal Equinox in the Julian Calendar

Date	Julian year	Date	Julian year	Date	Julian year
March 21	A.D. 325	March 17	A.D. 837	March 13	A.D. 1349
March 20	A.D. 453	March 16	A.D. 965	March 12	A.D. 1477
March 19	A.D. 581	March 15	A.D. 1093	March 11	A.D. 1605
March 18	A.D. 709	March 14	A.D. 1221		

Vatican librarian Aloysius Giglio (latinized into Lilius) was adopted: every fourth year is a leap year *unless* it is a century year like 1700 or 1800. Century years can be leap years *only* when they are divisible by 400 (e.g., 1600). This rule eliminates three leap years in four centuries, making the calendar sufficiently correct for all ordinary purposes.

Unfortunately, all the Protestant princes in 1582 chose to ignore the papal bull; they continued with the Julian calendar. It was not until 1698 that the German professor Erhard Weigel persuaded the Protestant rulers of Germany and of the Netherlands to change to the new calendar. In England the shift took place in 1752, and in Russia it needed the revolution to introduce the Gregorian calendar in 1918.

The average year of the Gregorian calendar, in spite of the leap year rule, is about 26 seconds longer than the earth's orbital period. But this discrepancy will need 3,323 years to build up to a single day.

Modern proposals for calendar reform do not aim at a "better" calendar, but at one that is more convenient to use, especially for commercial purposes. A 365-day year cannot be divided into equal halves or quarters; the number of days per month is haphazard; the months begin or end in the middle of a week; a holiday fixed by date (e.g., the Fourth of July) will wander through a week; a holiday fixed in another manner (e.g., Easter) can fall on 35 possible dates. The Gregorian calendar, admittedly, keeps the calendar dates in reasonable unison with astronomical events, but it still is full of minor annoyances. Moreover, you need a calendar every year to look up dates; an ideal calendar should be one that you can memorize for one year and that is valid for all other years, too.

Time and Calendar

The two natural cycles on which time measurements are based are the year and the day. The year is defined as the time required for Earth to complete one revolution around the Sun, while the day is the time required for Earth to complete one turn upon its axis. Unfortunately Earth needs 365 days plus about six hours to go around the Sun once, so that the year does not consist of so and so many days; the fractional day has to be taken care of by an extra day every fourth year.

But because Earth, while turning upon its axis, also moves around the Sun, there are two kinds of days. A day may be defined as the interval between the highest point of the Sun in the sky on two successive days. This, averaged out over the year, produces the customary 24-hour day. But one might also define a day as the time interval between the moments when a certain point in the sky, say a conveniently located star, is directly overhead. This is called:

Sidereal time. Astronomers use a point which they call the "vernal equinox" for the actual determination. Such a sidereal day is somewhat shorter than the "solar day," namely by about three minutes and 56 seconds of so-called mean solar time.

Apparent solar time is the time based directly on the Sun's position in the sky. In ordinary life the day runs from midnight to midnight. It begins when the Sun is invisible by being 12 hours from its zenith. Astronomers use the so-called Julian Day, which runs from noon to noon; the concept was invented by the astronomer Joseph Scaliger, who named it after his father, Julius. To avoid the problems caused by leap-year days and so forth, Scaliger picked a conveniently remote date in the past (4713 B.C.) and suggested just counting days without regard to weeks, months, and years. The reason for having the Julian Day run from noon to noon is the practical one that astronomical observations usually extend across the midnight hour, which would require a change in date (or in the Julian Day number) if the astronomical day, like the civil day, ran from midnight to midnight.

Mean solar time, rather than apparent solar time, is what is actually used most of the time. The mean solar time is based on the position of a fictitious "mean sun." The reason why this fictitious sun has to be introduced is the following: Earth turns on its axis regularly; it needs the same number of seconds regardless of the season. But the movement of Earth around the Sun is not regular because Earth's orbit is an ellipse. This has the result (as explained in the section on the seasons below) that Earth moves faster in January and slower in July. Though it is Earth that changes velocity, it looks to us as if the Sun does. In January, when Earth moves faster, the *apparent* movement of the Sun looks faster. The mean sun of time measurements, then, is a sun that moves regularly all year round; the real Sun will be either ahead of or behind the mean sun. The difference between the real Sun and the fictitious mean sun is called the *equation of time.*

When the real Sun is west of the mean sun we have the "sun fast" condition, with the real Sun crossing the meridian ahead of the mean sun. The opposite is the "sun slow" situation, when the real Sun crosses the meridian after the mean sun. Of course, what is observed is the real Sun. The equation of time is needed to establish mean solar time, kept by the reference clocks.

But if all clocks were actually set by mean solar time we would be plagued by a welter of time differences that would be "correct" but a major nuisance. A clock on Long Island, correctly showing mean solar time for its location (this would be *local civil time*), would be slightly ahead of a clock in Newark, N.J. The Newark clock would be slightly ahead of a clock in Trenton, N.J., which, in turn, would be ahead of a clock in Philadelphia. This condition prevailed until 1884, when a system of standard time was adopted by the International Meridian Conference. Earth's surface was divided

The Names of the Days of the Week

Latin	Old English	English	German	French	Italian	Spanish
Dies Solis	Sun's Day	Sunday	Sonntag	dimanche	domenica	domingo
Dies Lunae	Moon's Day	Monday	Montag	lundi	lunedì	lunes
Dies Martis	Tiw's Day	Tuesday	Dienstag	mardi	martedì	martes
Dies Mercurii	Woden's Day	Wednesday	Mittwoch	mercredi	mercoledì	miércoles
Dies Jovis	Thor's Day	Thursday	Donnerstag	jeudi	giovedì	jueves
Dies Veneris	Frigg's Day	Friday	Freitag	vendredi	venerdì	viernes
Dies Saturni	Seterne's Day	Saturday	Samstag	samedi	sabato	sábado

NOTE: The seven-day week originated in ancient Mesopotamia and became part of the Roman calendar in A.D. 321. The names of the days are based on the seven celestial bodies (the Sun, the Moon, Mars, Mercury, Jupiter, Venus, and Saturn), believed at that time to revolve around Earth and influence its events. Most of Western Europe adopted the Roman nomenclature. The Germanic languages substituted Germanic equivalents for the names of four of the Roman gods: Tiw, the god of war, replaced Mars; Woden, the god of wisdom, replaced Mercury; Thor, the god of thunder, replaced Jupiter; and Frigg, the goddess of love, replaced Venus.

into 24 zones. The standard time of each zone is the mean astronomical time of one of 24 meridians, 15 degrees apart, beginning at the Greenwich, England, meridian and extending east and west around the globe to the International Date Line. (This system was actually put into use a year earlier by the railroad companies of the U.S. and Canada who, until then, had to contend with some 100 conflicting local sun times observed in terminals across the land.)

For practical purposes, this convention is sometimes altered. For example, Alaska, for a time, consisted of four of the eight U.S. time zones: the Pacific standard time zone (east of Juneau) and the 6th (Juneau), 7th (Anchorage), and 8th (Nome) zones, encompassing the 135°, 150°, and 165° meridians, respectively. In 1983, by act of Congress, the entire state (except the westernmost Aleutians) was united into the 6th zone, Alaska standard time.

The eight U.S. standard time zones are: Atlantic (includes Puerto Rico and the Virgin Islands), eastern, central, mountain, Pacific, Alaska, Hawaii-Aleutian (includes all of Hawaii and those Aleutians west of the Fox Islands), and Samoa standard time.

The Date Line. While the time zones are based on the natural event of the Sun crossing a meridian, the date must be an arbitrary decision. The meridians are traditionally counted from the meridian of the observatory of Greenwich, in England, which is called the zero meridian. The logical place for changing the date is 12 hours, or 180°, from Greenwich. Fortunately, the 180th meridian runs mostly through the open Pacific. The Date Line makes a zigzag in the north to incorporate the eastern tip of Siberia into the Siberian time system and then another one to incorporate a number of islands into the Hawaii-Aleutian time zone. In the south there is a similar zigzag for the purpose of tying a number of British-owned islands to the New Zealand time system. Otherwise, the Date Line is the same as 180° from Greenwich. At points to the east of the Date Line the calendar is one day earlier than at points to the west of it. A traveler going eastward across the Date Line from one island to another would not have to reset his watch because he would stay inside the time zone (provided he does so where the Date Line does *not* coincide with the 180° meridian), but it would be the same time of the *previous* day.

The Seasons

The seasons are caused by the tilt of Earth's axis (23.4°) and not by the fact that Earth's orbit around the Sun is an ellipse. The average distance of Earth from the Sun is 93 million miles; the difference between aphelion (farthest away from the Sun) and perihelion (closest to the Sun) is 3 million miles, so that perihelion is about 91.4 million miles from the Sun. Earth goes through the perihelion point a few days after New Year's Day, just when the Northern Hemisphere has winter. Aphelion is passed during the first days of July. This by itself shows that the distance from the Sun is not important within these limits. What is important is that when Earth passes through perihelion, the northern end of Earth's axis happens to tilt away from the Sun, so that the areas beyond the Tropic of Cancer receive only slanting rays from a Sun low in the sky.

The tilt of Earth's axis is responsible for four lines you find on every globe. When, say, the North Pole is tilted away from the Sun as much as possible, the farthest points in the North which can still be reached by the Sun's rays are 23.5° from the pole. This is the Arctic Circle. The Antarctic Circle is the corresponding limit 23.4° from the South Pole; the Sun's rays cannot reach beyond this point when we have midsummer in the North.

When the Sun is vertically above the equator, the day is of equal length all over Earth. This happens twice a year, and these are the "equinoxes" in March and in September. After having been over the equator in March, the Sun will seem to move northward. The northernmost point where the Sun can be straight overhead is 23.4° north of the equator. This is the Tropic of Cancer; the Sun can never be vertically overhead to the north of this line. Similarly the Sun cannot be vertically overhead to the south of a line 23.4° south of the equator—the Tropic of Capricorn.

This explains the climatic zones. In the belt (the Greek word *zone* means "belt") between the Tropic of Cancer and the Tropic of Capricorn, the Sun can be straight overhead; this is the tropical zone. The two zones where the Sun cannot be overhead but will be above the horizon every day of the year are the two temperate zones; the two areas where the Sun will not rise at all for varying lengths of time are the two polar areas, Arctic and Antarctic. ☐

The Names of the Months

January: named after Janus, protector of the gateway to heaven

February: named after Februalia, a time period when sacrifices were made to atone for sins

March: named after Mars, the god of war, presumably signifying that the campaigns interrupted by the winter could be resumed

April: from *aperire*, Latin for "to open" (buds)

May: named after Maia, the goddess of growth of plants

June: from *junius*, Latin for the goddess Juno

July: named after Julius Caesar in 44 B.C.

August: named after Augustus, the first Roman Emperor, in 8 B.C.

September: from *septem*, Latin for "seven"

October: from *octo*, Latin for "eight"

November: from *novem*, Latin for "nine"

December: from *decem*, Latin for "ten"

NOTE: The earliest Latin calendar was a 10-month one, beginning with March; thus, September was the seventh month, October, the eighth, etc. July was originally called Quintilis, meaning fifth; August was originally called Sextilis, meaning sixth.

The Islamic (Hijri) Calendar

The Islamic calendar is based on the lunar year of 354 days. The number of days each month is adjusted according to the lunar cycle, beginning about two days after the new moon. The months drift backwards over the seasons, beginning again on the same day every 32½ years. The Islamic year begins on the first day of Muharram, and is counted from the year of the Hegira *(anno Hegirae)*—the year in which Muhammad emigrated from Mecca to Medina (A.D. 622). The year 2001 translates to A.H. 1421–1422.

Months	Number of days	Months	Number of days	Months	Number of days	Months	Number of days
Muharram	29 or 30	Rabi II	29 or 30	Rajab	29 or 30	Shawwal	29 or 30
Safar	29 or 30	Jumada I	29 or 30	Sha'ban	29 or 30	Dhu'l-Qa'dah	29 or 30
Rabi I	29 or 30	Jumada II	29 or 30	Ramadan	29 or 30	Dhu'l-Hijjah	29 or 30

The Jewish Calendar

The Jewish calendar is based on both solar and lunar years. The average lunar year of 354 days is adjusted to the solar year by the addition of a leap year and an intercalary month. Nisan is considered the first month, although the new year begins with Rosh Hashanah, on the first of Tishri, which is in fact the seventh month—the calendar has different starting points for different purposes. The year 2001 translates to the Jewish year 5761–5762.

Months	Number of days	Months	Number of days	Months	Number of days
Nisan (March–April)*	30	Tishri (Sept.–Oct.)	30	Shevat (Jan.–Feb.)	30
Iyar (April–May)	29	Heshvan (Oct.–Nov.)	29	Adar (Feb.–March)	29
Sivan (May–June)	30	in some years	30	in some years	30
Tammuz (June–July)	29	Kislev (Nov.–Dec.)	29	Adar Sheni	29
Av (July–Aug.)	30	in some years	30	(intercalary month	
Elul (Aug.–Sept.)	29	Tevet (Dec.–Jan.)	29	in leap year only)	

*The months correspond approximately to those of the Gregorian calendar.

The Chinese Calendar

The Chinese lunar year is divided into 12 months of 29 or 30 days. The calendar is adjusted to the length of the solar year by the addition of extra months at regular intervals. The years are arranged in major cycles of 60 years. Each successive year is named after one of 12 animals. These 12-year cycles are continuously repeated. The Chinese New Year is celebrated at the second new moon after the winter solstice and falls between January 21 and February 19 on the Gregorian calendar. The year 2001 translates to the Chinese year 4699.

Rat	Ox	Tiger	Cat (Rabbit)	Dragon	Snake	Horse	Sheep (Goat)	Monkey	Rooster	Dog	Pig
1900	1901	1902	1903	1904	1905	1906	1907	1908	1909	1910	1911
1912	1913	1914	1915	1916	1917	1918	1919	1920	1921	1922	1923
1924	1925	1926	1927	1928	1929	1930	1931	1932	1933	1934	1935
1936	1937	1938	1939	1940	1941	1942	1943	1944	1945	1946	1947
1948	1949	1950	1951	1952	1953	1954	1955	1956	1957	1958	1959
1960	1961	1962	1963	1964	1965	1966	1967	1968	1969	1970	1971
1972	1973	1974	1975	1976	1977	1978	1979	1980	1981	1982	1983
1984	1985	1986	1987	1988	1989	1990	1991	1992	1993	1994	1995
1996	1997	1998	1999	2000	2001	2002	2003	2004	2005	2006	2007

Holidays

Religious and Secular, 2001

In the United States, there are 10 federal holidays set by law. Four are set by date (New Year's Day, Independence Day, Veterans Day, and Christmas Day). The other six are set by a day of the week and month: Martin Luther King, Jr.'s Birthday, Washington's Birthday, Memorial Day, Labor Day, Columbus Day, and Thanksgiving. All but the last are celebrated on Mondays to create three-day weekends for federal employees. All Jewish and Islamic holidays begin at sundown the day before they are listed here.

New Year's Day, Mon., Jan. 1. A federal holiday in the United States, New Year's Day has its origin in Roman times, when sacrifices were offered to Janus, the two-faced Roman deity who looked back on the past and forward to the future.

Epiphany (from Greek *epiphaneia,* "manifestation"), Sat., Jan. 6. Falls on the 12th day after Christmas and commemorates the manifestation of Jesus Christ to the Gentiles, as represented by the Magi, the baptism of Jesus, and the miracle of the wine at the marriage feast at Cana. One of the 3 major Christian festivals, along with Christmas and Easter. Epiphany originally marked the beginning of the carnival season preceding Lent, and the evening preceding it is known as Twelfth Night.

Martin Luther King, Jr.'s Birthday, Mon., Jan. 15. This year the holiday falls on the actual date of his birthday. A federal holiday observed on the third Monday in January that honors the late civil rights leader. It became a federal holiday in 1986. In 2000, South Carolina, the last holdout, became the fiftieth state to officially honor the holiday.

Groundhog Day, Fri., Feb. 2. Legend has it that if the groundhog sees his shadow, he'll return to his hole, and winter will last another six weeks.

Lincoln's Birthday, Mon., Feb. 12. A holiday in many states, this day was first formally observed in Washington, D.C., in 1866, when both houses of Congress gathered for a memorial address in tribute to the assassinated president.

St. Valentine's Day, Wed., Feb. 14. This day is the festival of two third-century martyrs, both named St. Valentine. It is not known why this day is associated with lovers. It may derive from an old pagan festival about this time of year, or it may have been inspired by the belief that birds mate on this day.

Washington's Birthday, Mon., Feb. 19. (The actual date of his birthday is Feb. 22.) A federal holiday observed the third Monday in February. It is a common misperception that the federal holiday was changed to "Presidents' Day" and now celebrates both Washington and Lincoln. Only Washington is commemorated by the federal holiday; 12 states, however, officially celebrate "Presidents' Day."

Shrove Tuesday, Feb. 27. Falls the day before Ash Wednesday and marks the end of the carnival season, which once began on Epiphany but is now usually celebrated the last three days before Lent. In France, the day is known as Mardi Gras (Fat Tuesday), and Mardi Gras celebrations are also held in several American cities, particularly in New Orleans. The day is sometimes called Pancake Tuesday by the English because fats, which were prohibited during Lent, had to be used up.

Ash Wednesday, Feb. 28. The seventh Wednesday before Easter and the first day of Lent, which lasts 40 days. Having its origin sometime before A.D. 1000, it is a day of public penance and is marked in the Roman Catholic Church by the burning of the palms blessed on the previous year's Palm Sunday. With the ashes from the palms the priest then marks a cross with his thumb upon the forehead of each worshipper. The Anglican Church and a few Protestant groups in the United States also observe the day, but generally without the use of ashes.

Purim (Feast of Lots), Fri., March 9. A day of joy and feasting celebrating the deliverance of the Jews from a massacre planned by the Persian minister Haman. According to the Book of Esther, the Jewish queen Esther interceded with her husband, King Ahasuerus, to spare the life of her uncle, Mordecai, and Haman was hanged on the same gallows he had built for Mordecai. The holiday is marked by the reading of the Book of Esther (The Megillah), and by the exchange of gifts, donations to the poor, and the presentation of Purim plays.

St. Patrick's Day, Sat., March 17. St. Patrick, patron saint of Ireland, has been honored in America since the first days of the nation. Perhaps the most notable part of the observance is the annual St. Patrick's Day parade on Fifth Avenue in New York City.

Palm Sunday, April 8. Observed the Sunday before Easter to commemorate the entry of Jesus into Jerusalem. The procession and the ceremonies introducing the benediction of palms probably had their origins in Jerusalem.

First Day of Passover (Pesach), Sun., April 8. The Feast of the Passover, also called the Feast of Unleavened Bread, commemorates the escape of the Jews from Egypt. As the Jews fled, they ate unleavened bread, and from that time the Jews have allowed no leavening in their houses during Passover, bread being replaced by matzoh.

Good Friday, April 13. The Friday before Easter, it commemorates the Crucifixion, which is retold during services from the Gospel according to St. John. A feature in Roman Catholic churches is the Liturgy of the Passion; there is no Consecration, the Host having been consecrated the previous day. The eating of hot-cross buns on this day is said to have started in England.

Easter Sunday, April 15. Observed in all Western Christian churches, Easter commemorates the Resurrection of Jesus. It is celebrated on the first day after the full moon that occurs on or next after the vernal equinox (fixed at March 21) and is therefore celebrated between March 22 and April 25 inclusive. This date was fixed by the Council of Nicaea in A.D. 325.

Orthodox Easter (Pascha), Sun., April 15. The Orthodox church uses the same formula to calculate Easter as the Western church, but bases it on the traditional Julian calendar instead of the more contemporary Gregorian calendar. For this reason Orthodox Easter generally falls on a different date than the Western Christian Easter. This year, however, the dates coincide, a circumstance which last occurred in 1990.

Mother's Day, Sun., May 13. Observed the second Sunday in May, as proposed by Anna Jarvis of Philadelphia in 1907.

Ascension Day, Thurs., May 24. The Ascension of Jesus took place in the presence of His apostles 40 days after the Resurrection. It is traditionally thought to have occurred on Mount Olivet in Bethany.

Memorial Day, Mon., May 28. Memorial Day became a federal holiday in 1971 that is observed on the last Monday in May. It originated in 1868, when Union General John A. Logan designated a day in which the graves of Civil War soldiers would be decorated. Originally known as Decoration Day, the holiday was changed to Memorial Day within twenty years, becoming a holiday dedicated to the memory of all war dead.

First Day of Shavuot (Hebrew Pentecost), Mon., May 28. This festival, sometimes called the Feast of Weeks, or of Harvest, or of the First Fruits, falls 50 days after Passover and originally celebrated the end of the seven-week grain-harvesting season. In later tradition, it also celebrated the giving of the Law to Moses on Mount Sinai.

Pentecost (Whitsunday), June 3. This day commemorates the descent of the Holy Ghost upon the apostles 50 days after the Resurrection. The sermon by the Apostle Peter, which led to the baptism of 3,000 who professed belief, originated the ceremonies that have since been followed. "Whitsunday" is believed to have come from "white Sunday" when, among the English, white robes were worn by those baptized on the day.

Flag Day, Thurs., June 14. This day commemorates the adoption by the Continental Congress on June 14, 1777, of the Stars and Stripes as the U.S. flag. Although it is a legal holiday only in Pennsylvania, President Truman, on Aug. 3, 1949, signed a bill requesting the president to call for its observance each year by proclamation.

Father's Day, Sun., June 17. Observed the third Sunday in June, it was first celebrated June 19, 1910.

Independence Day, Wed., July 4. The day of the adoption of the Declaration of Independence in 1776, celebrated in all states and territories. The observance began the next year in Philadelphia.

Labor Day, Mon., Sept. 3. A federal holiday observed the first Monday in September. Labor Day was first celebrated in New York in 1882 under the sponsorship of the Central Labor Union, following the suggestion of Peter J. McGuire, of the Knights of Labor, that the day be set aside in honor of labor.

First Day of Rosh Hashanah (Jewish New Year), Tues., Sept. 18. This day marks the beginning of the Jewish year 5762 and opens the Ten Days of Penitence, which close with Yom Kippur.

Yom Kippur (Day of Atonement), Thurs., Sept. 27. This day marks the end of the Ten Days of Penitence that began with Rosh Hashanah. It is described in Leviticus as a "Sabbath of rest," and synagogue services begin the preceding sundown, resume the following morning, and continue to sundown.

First Day of Sukkot (Feast of Tabernacles), Tues., Oct. 2. This festival, also known as the Feast of the Ingathering, originally celebrated the fruit harvest, and the name comes from the booths or tabernacles in which the Jews lived during the harvest, although one tradition traces it to the shelters used by the Jews in their wandering through the wilderness. During the festival many Jews build small huts in their backyards or on the roofs of their houses.

Columbus Day, Mon., Oct. 8. A federal holiday, observed the second Monday in October, it commemorates Christopher Columbus's landing in the New World in 1492. Quite likely the first celebration of Columbus Day was that organized in 1792 by the Society of St. Tammany, or the Columbian Order, widely known as Tammany Hall.

Simchat Torah (Rejoicing of the Law), Wed., Oct. 10. This joyous holiday falls on the eighth day of Sukkot. It marks the end of the year's reading of the Torah (Five Books of Moses) in the synagogue every Saturday and the beginning of the new cycle of reading.

Halloween, Wed., Oct. 31. Eve of All Saints' Day, formerly called All Hallows and Hallowmass. Halloween is traditionally associated in some countries with customs such as bonfires, masquerading, and the telling of ghost stories. These are old Celtic practices marking the beginning of winter.

All Saints' Day, Thurs., Nov. 1. A Roman Catholic and Anglican holiday celebrating all saints, known and unknown.

Election Day (legal holiday in certain states), Tues., Nov. 6. Since 1845, by act of Congress, the first Tuesday after the first Monday in November is the date for choosing presidential electors. State elections are also generally held on this day.

Veterans Day, Sun., Nov. 11. Armistice Day, a federal holiday, was established in 1926 to commemorate the signing in 1918 of the armistice ending World War I. On June 1, 1954, the name was changed to Veterans Day to honor all men and women who have served America in its armed forces.

First Day of Ramadan, Sat., Nov. 17. This day marks the beginning of a month-long fast that all Muslims must keep during the daylight hours. It commemorates the first revelation of the Qur'an. Following the last day of Ramadan, **Eid al-Fitr** is celebrated on Mon., Dec. 17.

Thanksgiving, Thurs., Nov. 22. A federal holiday observed the fourth Thursday in November by act of Congress (1941), it was the first such national proclamation issued by President Lincoln in 1863, on the urging of Mrs. Sarah J. Hale, editor of *Godey's Lady's Book*. Most Americans believe that the holiday dates back to the day of thanks ordered by Governor Bradford of Plymouth Colony in New England in 1621, but scholars point out that days of thanks stem from ancient times.

First Sunday of Advent, Dec. 2. Advent is the season in which the faithful must prepare themselves for the advent of the Savior on Christmas. The four Sundays before Christmas are marked by special church services.

First Day of Hanukkah (Festival of Lights), Mon., Dec. 10. This festival was instituted by Judas Maccabeus in 165 B.C. to celebrate the purification of the Temple of Jerusalem, which had been desecrated three years earlier by Antiochus Epiphanes, who set up a pagan altar and offered sacrifices to Zeus Olympius. In Jewish homes, a light is lighted on each night of the eight-day festival.

Christmas (Feast of the Nativity), Tues., Dec. 25. The most widely celebrated holiday of the Christian year, Christmas is observed as the anniversary of the birth of Jesus. Christmas customs are centuries old. The mistletoe, for example, comes from the Druids, who, in hanging the mistletoe, hoped for peace and good fortune. Use of such plants as holly comes from the ancient belief that such plants blossomed at Christmas.

Comparatively recent is the Christmas tree, first set up in Germany in the 17th century. The use of candles on trees developed from the belief that candles appeared by miracle on the trees at Christmas. Colonial Manhattan Islanders introduced the name Santa Claus, a corruption of the Dutch name St. Nicholas, who lived in fourth-century Asia Minor.

Christian and Secular Holidays, 2000–2002

Year	Ash Wednesday	Easter	Pentecost	Labor Day	Election Day	Thanksgiving	1st Sun. Advent
2000	March 8	April 23	June 11	Sept. 4	Nov. 7	Nov. 23	Dec. 3
2001	Feb. 28	April 15	June 3	Sept. 3	Nov. 6	Nov. 22	Dec. 2
2002	Feb. 13	March 31	May 19	Sept. 2	Nov. 5	Nov. 28	Dec. 1

Shrove Tuesday: 1 day before Ash Wednesday. Palm Sunday: 7 days before Easter. Maundy Thursday: 3 days before Easter. Good Friday: 2 days before Easter. Holy Saturday: 1 day before Easter. Ascension Day: 10 days before Pentecost. Trinity Sunday: 7 days after Pentecost. Corpus Christi: 11 days after Pentecost.

Orthodox Holidays, 2000–2003

Year	Great Lent Begins	Pascha (Easter)	Ascension	Pentecost	Year	Great Lent Begins	Pascha (Easter)	Ascension	Pentecost
2000	March 13	April 30	June 8	June 18	2002	March 18	May 5	June 13	June 23
2001	Feb. 26	April 15	May 24	June 3	2003	March 10	April 27	June 5	June 15

Jewish Holidays, 2000–2002

Year	Purim[1]	1st day Passover[2]	1st day Shavuot[3]	1st day Rosh Hashanah[4]	Yom Kippur[5]	1st day Sukkot[6]	Simchat Torah[7]	1st day Hanukkah[8]
2000	March 21	April 20	June 9	Sept. 30	Oct. 9	Oct. 14	Oct. 22	Dec. 22
2001	March 9	April 8	May 28	Sept. 18	Sept. 27	Oct. 2	Oct. 10	Dec. 10
2002	Feb. 26	March 28	May 17	Sept. 7	Sept. 16	Sept. 21	Sept. 29	Nov. 30

1. Feast of Lots. 2. Feast of Unleavened Bread. 3. Hebrew Pentecost; or Feast of Weeks, or of Harvest, or of First Fruits. 4. Jewish New Year. 5. Day of Atonement. 6. Feast of Tabernacles, or of the Ingathering. 7. Rejoicing of the Law. In Israel, Simchat Torah is celebrated on the day before the date given. 8. Festival of Lights.
Length of Jewish holidays (O=Orthodox, C=Conservative, R=Reform): Passover: O & C, 8 days (holy days: first 2 and last 2); R, 7 days (holy days: first and last). Shavuot: O & C, 2 days; R, 1 day. Rosh Hashanah: O & C, 2 days; R, 1 day. Yom Kippur: All groups, 1 day. Sukkot: All groups, 7 days (holy days: O & C, first 2; R, first only); O & C observe 2 additional days: Shemini Atseret (Eighth Day of the Feast) and Simchat Torah; R observes Shemini Atseret but not Simchat Torah. Hanukkah: All groups, 8 days. NOTE: All holidays begin at sundown on the evening before the date given.

Islamic Holidays, 2000–2003 (A.H. 1421–1423)

In the Year of the Hegira	Muharram (Islamic New Year)	Mawlid al-Nabi (Muhammed's Birthday)	Ramadan begins	Eid al-Fitr (Ramadan ends)	Eid al-Adha (Festival of Sacrifice)
A.H. 1421	April 6, 2000	June 15, 2000	Nov. 28, 2000	Dec. 27, 2000	March 6, 2001
A.H. 1422	March 26, 2001	June 4, 2001	Nov. 17, 2001	Dec. 17, 2001	Feb. 23, 2002
A.H. 1423	March 15, 2002	May 24, 2002	Nov. 6, 2002	Dec. 6, 2002	Feb. 12, 2003

NOTE: All holidays begin at sundown on the evening before the date given. Islamic holidays are based on the lunar calendar and thus may vary by one or two days. Dates apply to North America.

Hindu Festival Dates, 2001
Source: Indian Calendars for the 21st Century, by Pal Singh Purewal.

Jan. 13	Makar Sankranti	Aug. 4	Raksha Bandhan
Jan. 29	Vasant Panchami	Aug. 12	Sri Krishna Jayanti
Feb. 21	Maha Shivaratri Vrat (fast)	Aug. 22	Ganesh Chaturathi
March 9	Holi (last day)	Oct. 2	Saradhas begin
March 26	Chetra Navratras begin	Oct. 17	Asuj Navratras begin
March 26	Bikarami Samvat (2058 begins)	Oct. 26	Dassehra
April 2	Rama Navmi	Nov. 4	Karva Chauth Vrat (fast)
April 13	Vaisakhi (solar new year)	Nov. 14	Diwali (Festival of Lights)

Sikh Festival Dates, 2001*
Source: Indian Calendars for the 21st Century, by Pal Singh Purewal.

Jan. 2	Birthday of Guru Gobind Singh Ji	Nov. 14	Bandi Chhor Divas
Jan. 13	Maghi	Nov. 17	Installation of Holy Scriptures
March 10	Hola Muhalla		as Guru Granth Sahib Ji
April 13	Vaisakhi	Nov. 30	Birthday of Guru Nanak Dev Ji
May 26	Martyrdom of Guru Arjan Dev Ji	Dec. 19	Martyrdom of Guru Tegh Bahadur Ji
Aug. 19	First Parkash Granth Sahib Ji		

*The dates for the Sikh festivals are given according to the Bikarami (Hindu) calendar, which is based on the sidereal year. The reformed Nanakshahi (Sikh) calendar, which is based on the tropical year, has yet to be officially adopted. NOTE: Dates for Sikh and Hindu holidays are determined according to the date of their observance in India.

Chinese New Year

2000 Feb. 5	**2003** Feb. 1	**2006** Jan. 29	**2009** Jan. 26
2001 Jan. 24	**2004** Jan. 22	**2007** Feb. 18	**2010** Feb. 14
2002 Feb. 12	**2005** Feb. 9	**2008** Feb. 7	**2011** Feb. 3

State Holidays

Jan. 6, Three Kings' Day: P.R.
Jan. 8, Battle of New Orleans Day: La.
Jan. 11, De Hostos's Birthday: P.R.
Jan. 19, Robert E. Lee's Birthday: Ark., Fla., Ky., La., S.C.; **(third Mon.):** Ala., Miss.
Jan. 19, Confederate Heroes Day: Tex.
Jan. (third Mon.), Lee-Jackson-King Day: Va.
Jan. 30, F. D. Roosevelt's Birthday: Ky.
Feb. 15, Susan B. Anthony's Birthday: Fla., Minn.
March (first Tues.), Town Meeting Day: Vt.
March 2, Texas Independence Day: Tex.
March (first Mon.), Casimir Pulaski's Birthday: Ill.
March 17, Evacuation Day: Mass. (in Suffolk County)
March 20 (first day of spring), Youth Day: Okla.
March 22, Abolition Day: P.R.
March 25, Maryland Day: Md.
March 26, Prince Jonah Kuhio Kalanianaole Day: Hawaii
March (last Mon.), Seward's Day: Alaska
April 2, Pascua Florida Day: Fla.
April 13, Thomas Jefferson's Birthday: Ala., Okla.
April 16, De Diego's Birthday: P.R.
April (third Mon.), Patriots' Day: Maine, Mass.
April 21, San Jacinto Day: Tex.
April 22, Arbor Day: Nebr.
April 22, Oklahoma Day: Okla.
April 26, Confederate Memorial Day: Fla., Ga.
April (fourth Mon.), Fast Day: N.H.
April (last Mon.), Confederate Memorial Day: Ala., Miss.
May 1, Bird Day: Okla.
May 8, Truman Day: Mo.
May 11, Minnesota Day: Minn.
May 20, Mecklenburg Independence Day: N.C.

June (first Mon.), Jefferson Davis's Birthday: Ala., Miss.
June 3, Jefferson Davis's Birthday: Fla., S.C.
June 3, Confederate Memorial Day: Ky., La.
June 9, Senior Citizens Day: Okla.
June 11, King Kamehameha I Day: Hawaii
June 15, Separation Day: Del.
June 17, Bunker Hill Day: Mass. (in Suffolk County)
June 19, Emancipation Day: Tex.
June 20, West Virginia Day: W.Va.
July 17, Muñoz Rivera's Birthday: P.R.
July 24, Pioneer Day: Utah
July 25, Constitution Day: P.R.
July 27, Barbosa's Birthday: P.R.
Aug. (first Sun.), American Family Day: Ariz.
Aug. (first Mon.), Colorado Day: Colo.
Aug. (second Mon.), Victory Day: R.I.
Aug. 16, Bennington Battle Day: Vt.
Aug. (third Friday), Admission Day: Hawaii
Aug. 27, Lyndon B. Johnson's Birthday: Tex.
Aug. 30, Huey P. Long Day: La.
Sept. 9, Admission Day: Calif.
Sept. 12, Defenders' Day: Md.
Sept. 16, Cherokee Strip Day: Okla.
Sept. (first Sat. after full moon), Indian Day: Okla.
Oct. 10, Leif Eriksson Day: Minn.
Oct. 10, Oklahoma Historical Day: Okla.
Oct. 18, Alaska Day: Ala.
Oct. 31, Nevada Day: Nev.
Nov. 4, Will Rogers Day: Okla.
Nov. (week of the 16th), Oklahoma Heritage Week: Okla.
Nov. 19, Discovery Day: P.R.
Dec. 7, Delaware Day: Del.

Birthstones

Month	Stone	Month	Stone	Month	Stone
January	Garnet	June	Pearl, Alexandrite, or	October	Opal or Tourmaline
February	Amethyst		Moonstone	November	Topaz or Citrine
March	Aquamarine or Bloodstone	July	Ruby or Star Ruby	December	Turquoise, Lapis Lazuli,
April	Diamond	August	Peridot or Sardonyx		Blue Zircon, or Blue
May	Emerald	September	Sapphire or Star Sapphire		Topaz

Source: Jewelry Industry Council.

Traditional Wedding Anniversary Gift List

Anniv.	Gift	Anniv.	Gift	Anniv.	Gift	Anniv.	Gift
1st	Paper	7th	Copper, wool	13th	Lace	35th	Coral
2nd	Cotton	8th	Bronze, pottery	14th	Ivory	40th	Ruby
3rd	Leather	9th	Pottery, willow	15th	Crystal	45th	Sapphire
4th	Fruit, flowers	10th	Tin	20th	China	50th	Gold
5th	Wood	11th	Steel	25th	Silver	55th	Emerald
6th	Sugar	12th	Silk, linen	30th	Pearl	60th	Diamond

Modern Wedding Anniversary Gift List

Anniv.	Gift	Anniv.	Gift	Anniv.	Gift	Anniv.	Gift
1st	Gold jewelry	8th	Tourmaline	15th	Ruby	30th	Pearl jubilee
2nd	Garnet	9th	Lapis	16th	Peridot	35th	Emerald
3rd	Pearls	10th	Diamond jewelry	17th	Watch	40th	Ruby
4th	Blue topaz	11th	Turquoise	18th	Cat's-eye	45th	Sapphire
5th	Sapphire	12th	Jade	19th	Aquamarine	50th	Golden jubilee
6th	Amethyst	13th	Citrine	20th	Emerald	60th	Diamond jubilee
7th	Onyx	14th	Opal	25th	Silver jubilee		

Source: Jewelry Industry Council.

Selected National Holidays Around the World, 2001

Country	Date	Country	Date	Country	Date	Country	Date
Afghanistan	Aug. 19	Haiti	Jan. 1	Pakistan	March 23		
Albania	Nov. 28	Hungary	Aug. 20	Panama	Nov. 3		
Argentina	May 25	Iceland	June 17	Paraguay	May 15		
Armenia	Sept. 21	India	Jan. 26	Peru	July 28		
Australia	Jan. 26	Indonesia	Aug. 17	Philippines	June 12		
Austria	Oct. 26	Iran	Feb. 11	Poland	May 3		
Bahamas	July 10	Iraq	July 17	Portugal	June 10		
Bangladesh	March 26	Ireland	March 17	Romania	Dec. 1		
Barbados	Nov. 30	Israel	May 12[1]	Samoa	June 1		
Belgium	July 21	Italy	June 2	Saudi Arabia	Sept. 23		
Belize	Sept. 21	Jamaica	Aug. 6[2]	Senegal	April 4		
Bolivia	Aug. 6	Japan	Dec. 23	Singapore	Aug. 9		
Brazil	Sept. 7	Jordan	May 25	Slovakia	Sept. 1		
Bulgaria	March 3	Kenya	Dec. 12	Slovenia	June 25		
Canada	July 1	North Korea	Sept. 9	Somalia	Oct. 21		
Chile	Sept. 18	South Korea	Aug. 15	South Africa	April 27		
China	Oct. 1	Kuwait	Feb. 25	Spain	Oct. 12		
Colombia	July 20	Lebanon	Nov. 22	Sri Lanka	Feb. 4		
Congo, Republic of	Aug. 15	Liberia	July 26	Swaziland	Sept. 6		
Croatia	May 30	Lithuania	Feb. 16	Sweden	June 6		
Cuba	Jan. 1	Luxembourg	June 23	Switzerland	Aug. 1		
Czech Republic	Oct. 28	Macedonia	Aug. 2	Tanzania	April 26		
Denmark	April 16	Malaysia	Aug. 31	Thailand	Dec. 5		
Dominican Republic	Feb. 27	Malta	Sept. 21	Tunisia	March 20		
Ecuador	Aug. 10	Mexico	Sept. 16	Turkey	Oct. 29		
Egypt	July 23	Monaco	Nov. 19	Uganda	Oct. 9		
El Salvador	Sept. 15	Mongolia	July 11	United Arab Emirates	Dec. 2		
Ethiopia	May 28	Morocco	March 3	United Kingdom	June 9[3]		
Finland	Dec. 6	Mozambique	June 25	United States	July 4		
France	July 14	Nepal	Dec. 28	Uruguay	Aug. 25		
Gabon	Aug. 17	Netherlands	April 30	Venezuela	July 5		
Georgia	May 26	New Zealand	Feb. 6	Vietnam	Sept. 2		
Germany	Oct. 3	Nicaragua	Sept. 15	Yemen, Republic of	May 22		
Greece	March 25	Nigeria	Oct. 1	Zambia	Oct. 24		
Guatemala	Sept. 15	Norway	May 17	Zimbabwe	April 18		

1. Changes yearly according to Hebrew calendar. 2. Celebrated on first Monday in August. 3. Celebrated the second Saturday in June.

The Seven Wonders of the World

Since ancient times, people have put together many "seven wonders" lists; examples include the Seven Wonders of the Natural World, the Seven Wonders of the Modern World, and the Seven Natural Wonders of the U.S. The content of these lists tends to vary, and none is definitive. The original list of seven wonders is the Seven Wonders of the Ancient World, which is made up of a selection of ancient architectural and sculptural accomplishments. The seven wonders that are most widely agreed upon as being in the original list are outlined below. (* indicates photo can be found in the Headline History section.)

The Pyramids of Egypt. * A group of three pyramids, *Khufu, Khafra,* and *Menkaura* at Giza, outside modern Cairo, is often called the first wonder of the world. The largest pyramid, built by Khufu (Cheops), a king of the fourth dynasty, had an original estimated height of 482 ft. (now approximately 450 ft.). The base has sides 755 ft. long. It contains 2,300,000 blocks; the average weight of each is 2.5 tons. Estimated date of completion was 2680 B.C. Of all the Ancient Wonders, the pyramids alone survive.

Hanging Gardens of Babylon. Often listed as the second wonder, these gardens were supposedly built by Nebuchadnezzar around 600 B.C. to please his queen, Amuhia. They are also associated with the mythical Assyrian queen, Semiramis. Archeologists surmise that the gardens were laid out atop a vaulted building, with provisions for raising water. The terraces were said to rise from 75 to 300 ft.

The Walls of Babylon, also built by Nebuchadnezzar, are sometimes referred to as the second (or the seventh) wonder instead of the Hanging Gardens.

Statue of Zeus (Jupiter) at Olympia. The work of Phidias (5th century B.C.), this colossal figure in gold and ivory was reputedly 40 ft. high. All trace of it is lost, except for reproductions on coins.

Temple of Artemis (Diana) at Ephesus. A beautiful structure, begun about 350 B.C., in honor of a non-Hellenic goddess who later became identified with the Greek goddess of the same name. The temple, with Ionic columns 60 ft. high, was destroyed by invading Goths in A.D. 262.

Mausoleum at Halicarnassus. This famous monument was erected by Queen Artemisia in memory of her husband, King Mausolus of Caria in Asia Minor, who died in 353 B.C. Some remains of the structure are in the British Museum. This shrine is the source of the modern word "mausoleum."

Colossus at Rhodes. This bronze statue of Helios (Apollo), about 105 ft. high, was the work of the sculptor Chares, who reputedly labored for 12 years before completing it in 280 B.C. It was destroyed during an earthquake in 224 B.C.

Pharos of Alexandria. The seventh wonder was the Pharos (lighthouse) of Alexandria, built by Sostratus of Cnidus during the 3rd century B.C. on the island of Pharos off the coast of Egypt. It was destroyed by an earthquake in the 13th century.

Famous Structures

Ancient

The *Great Sphinx of Egypt,* one of the wonders of ancient Egyptian architecture, adjoins the pyramids of Giza and has a length of 240 ft. Built in the 4th dynasty, it is approximately 4,500 years old. A 10-year, $2.5 million restoration project was completed in 1998. Other Egyptian buildings of note include the *Temples of Karnak, Edfu,* and the *Tombs at Beni Hassan.*

The *Parthenon of Greece,** built on the Acropolis in Athens, was the chief temple to the goddess Athena. It was believed to have been completed by 438 B.C. The present temple remained intact until the 5th century A.D. Today, though the Parthenon is in ruins, its majestic proportions are still discernible.

Other great structures of ancient Greece were the *Temples at Paestum* (c. 540 and 420 B.C.); the famous *Erechtheum* (c. 421–405 B.C.), the *Temple of Athena Niké* (c. 426 B.C.), and the *Olympieum* (174 B.C.–A.D. 131) atop the Acropolis; the *Athenian Treasury* at Delphi (c. 515 B.C.); and the *Theater* at Epidaurus (c. 325 B.C.).

The *Colosseum (Flavian Amphitheater) of Rome,* the largest and most famous of the Roman amphitheaters, was opened for use A.D. 80. Elliptical in shape, it consisted of three stories and an upper gallery, rebuilt in stone in its present form in the third century A.D. It was principally used for gladiatorial combat and could seat between 40,000 and 50,000 spectators.

The *Pantheon* at Rome, begun by Agrippa in 27 B.C. as a temple, was rebuilt in its present circular form by Hadrian (A.D. 118–128). Literally the Pantheon was intended as a temple of "all the gods." It is remarkable for its perfect preservation today, and it has served continuously for 20 centuries as a place of worship.

Famous Roman arches, built to commemorate major military victories, include the *Arch of Titus* (c. A.D. 80) and the *Arch of Constantine* (c. A.D. 315).

Teotihuacán, located in central Mexico, was the largest city in the Americas at its height between A.D. 300 and 900. Built on a grid plan with a central avenue known as the Street of the Dead, it is the site of two enormous pyramid temples and the temple of the plumed serpent god Quetzalcoatl.

Machu Picchu is an ancient Inca fortress in the Andes Mountains of Peru. Thought to have been built and occupied from the mid-15th century, it is surrounded on three sides by stepped agricultural terraces, which are connected to the main plazas and buildings by thousands of stone steps.

Later European

St. Mark's Cathedral in Venice (1063–1071), one of the great examples of Byzantine architecture, was begun in the 9th century. Partly destroyed by fire in 976, it was later rebuilt as a Byzantine edifice.

Other famous examples of Byzantine architecture are *St. Sophia* in Istanbul (532–537); *San Vitale* in Ravenna (542); and *Assumption Cathedral* in the Kremlin, Moscow (begun in 1475).

The *Cathedral Group* at Pisa (1067–1173), one of the most celebrated groups of structures built in Romanesque-style, consists of the cathedral, the cathedral's baptistery, and the campanile (*Leaning Tower**). The campanile, a form of bell tower, is 179 ft. high and leans more than 16 ft. out of the perpendicular.

Other examples of Romanesque architecture include the *Vézelay Abbey* in France (1130) and *Durham Cathedral* in England.

The *Alhambra* (1248–1354), located in Granada, Spain, is universally esteemed as one of the greatest masterpieces of Muslim architecture. Designed as a palace and fortress for the Moorish monarchs of Granada, it is surrounded by a heavily fortified wall more than a mile in perimeter. The location of the Alhambra in the Sierra Nevada provides a magnificent setting for this jewel of Moorish Spain.

The *Tower of London* is a group of buildings and towers covering 13 acres along the north bank of the Thames. The central *White Tower*, begun in 1078 during the reign of William the Conqueror, was originally a fortress and royal residence, but was later used as a prison. The *Bloody Tower* is associated with Anne Boleyn and other notables.

Westminster Abbey, in London, was begun in 1050 and completed in 1065. It was rebuilt and enlarged in several phases, beginning in 1245. With only two exceptions (Edward V and Edward VIII), every British monarch since William the Conqueror has been crowned in the Abbey.

Notre-Dame de Paris (begun in 1163), one of the great examples of Gothic architecture, is a twin-towered church with a steeple over the crossing and immense flying buttresses supporting the masonry at the rear of the church.

Other famous Gothic structures are *Chartres Cathedral** (France; 12th century); *Sainte Chapelle* (Paris, France; 1246–1248); *Reims Cathedral* (France; 13th–14th centuries; rebuilt after its almost complete destruction in World War I); *Rouen Cathedral* (France; 13th–16th centuries); *Salisbury Cathedral* (England; 1220–1260); *York Minster* or the *Cathedral of St. Peter* (England; 1220–1472); *Milan Cathedral* (Italy; begun 1386); and *Cologne Cathedral* (Germany; 13th–19th centuries; badly damaged in World War II).

The *Duomo** (cathedral) in Florence was founded in 1296, completed by Brunelleschi, and consecrated in 1436. The oval-shaped dome dominates the entire structure.

The *Vatican* is a group of buildings in Rome comprising the official residence of the pope. The *Basilica of St. Peter*, the largest church in the Christian world, was begun in 1452, and it was rebuilt between 1506 and 1626. The *Sistine Chapel*, begun in 1473, is noted for the art masterpieces of Michelangelo, Botticelli, and others. The *Basilica of the Savior* (known as *St. John Lateran*) is the first-ranking Catholic Church in the world, for it is the cathedral of the pope.

Other examples of Renaissance architecture are the *Palazzo Riccardi*, the *Palazzo Pitti*, and the *Palazzo Strozzi* in Florence; the *Farnese Palace* in Rome; *Palazzo Grimani* (completed about 1550) in Venice; the *Escorial* (1563–93) near Madrid; the *Town Hall* of Seville (1527–32); the *Louvre*, Paris; the *Château* at Blois, France; *St. Paul's Cathedral*, London (1675–1710; badly damaged in World War II); the *École Militaire*, Paris (1752); the *Pazzi Chapel*, Florence, designed by Brunelleschi (1429); and the *Palace of Fontainebleau* and the *Château de Chambord* in France.

The *Palace of Versailles* in France, containing the famous Hall of Mirrors, was built during the reign of Louis XIV in the 17th century and served as the royal palace until 1793.

Outstanding European buildings of the 18th and 19th centuries are the *Superga* at Turin (Italy); the *Hôtel-Dieu* in Lyons; the *Belvedere Palace* at Vienna; the *Royal Palace* of Stockholm; the *Bank of England*, the *British Museum*, the *University of London*, and the *Houses of Parliament*, all in London; and the *Panthéon*, the *Church of the Madeleine*, the *Bourse*, the *Palais de Justice*, and the *Opera House*, all in Paris.

The *Eiffel Tower*, in Paris, was built for the Exposition of 1889 by Alexandre Eiffel. It is 984-ft. high (1,056 ft., including the television tower).

Asian and African

The *Taj Mahal** (1632–1650), at Agra, India, built by Shah Jahan as a tomb for his wife, is considered by some as the most perfect example of the Mogul style and by others as the most beautiful building in the world. Four slim white minarets flank the building, which is topped by a white dome; the entire structure is made of marble. Other examples of Indian architecture are the temples at Benares and Tanjore.

Among famed Muslim edifices are the *Dome of the Rock* or *Mosque of Omar*, Jerusalem (A.D. 691); the *Citadel* (1166) and the *Tombs of the Mamelukes* (15th century) in Cairo; the *Tomb of Humayun* in Delhi; the *Blue Mosque* (1468) at Tabriz; and the *Tamerlane Mausoleum* at Samarkand.

Angkor Wat, outside the city of Angkor Thom, Cambodia, is one of the most beautiful examples of Cambodian or Khmer architecture. The sanctuary was built during the 12th century.

The Great Wall of China (begun c. 214 B.C.), designed specifically as a defense against nomadic tribes, has large watch towers that could be called buildings. It was erected by Emperor Ch'in Shih Huang Ti and is 1,400 miles long. Built mainly of earth and stone, it varies in height between 18 and 30 ft.

Typical of Chinese architecture are the pagodas or temple towers. Among some of the better-known pagodas are the *Great Pagoda of the Wild Geese* at Sian (founded in 652) and *Nan t'a* (11th century) at Fang Shan.

Other well-known Chinese buildings are the *Drum Tower* (1273), the *Three Great Halls* in the Purple Forbidden City (1627), *Buddha's Perfume Tower* (19th century), the *Porcelain Pagoda*, and the *Summer Palace*, all at Beijing.

The painted wooden *Torii*, or Gateway, at Miyajima Island, Japan, stands in the tidal flats opposite the historic Itsukushima Shrine. Built in the traditional Shinto style, with two columns supporting a concave crosspiece on top, the gate serves to welcome the spirits of the dead as they come from across the Inland Sea.

Himeji Castle represents the finest example of medieval Japanese castle architecture. The complex, which survives relatively intact, was built between 1601 and 1614 and featured a six-story donjon and gates designed like mazes to confuse the enemy.

United States

The *Chrysler Building* in New York City is one of the finest examples of Art Deco style high-rise architecture. Built for the automotive magnate Walter P. Chrysler between 1928 and 1930, the building makes use of decorative elements borrowed from automobiles. At 1,046 ft. it was briefly the tallest building in the world before the Empire State Building was completed the following year.

The *Empire State Building,* one of the most popular tourist attractions in the heart of Manhattan, was constructed between 1930 and 1931. Features include a tiered structure that recalls ancient Egyptian and Aztec pyramids and a mast at the top for mooring dirigibles. Rising to 1,250 ft. (not including the mast), it remained the tallest building in the world until the 1970s.

Rockefeller Center, in New York City, extends from 5th Ave. to the Avenue of the Americas between 48th and 52nd Sts. (and halfway to 7th Ave. between 47th and 51st Sts.). It occupies more than 22 acres and has 19 buildings.

The Cathedral of St. John the Divine, at 112th St. and Amsterdam Ave. in New York City, was begun in 1892 and is now in the final stages of completion. When completed, it will be the largest cathedral in the world: 601-ft. long, 146-ft. wide at the nave, 320-ft. wide at the transept. The east end is designed in Romanesque-Byzantine style, and the nave and west end are Gothic.

The World Trade Center, in New York City, was dedicated in 1973. Its twin towers are 110 stories high (about 1,365 ft.), and the complex contains over 9-million sq ft. of office space. A restaurant is on the 107th floor of the North Tower.

The Statue of Liberty* was designed by Frédéric Auguste Bartholdi of Alsace as a gift to Americans from the people of France. The statue of a female figure holding a torch in her raised hand was accepted on Oct. 28, 1886, by President Grover Cleveland. The 225-ton, steel-reinforced copper structure stands on Liberty Island in New York Harbor. It is 152 ft. tall and stands on a 150-ft. pedestal.

The *Sears Tower* in Chicago is, at 1,450 ft., the tallest building in the U.S. Constructed between 1974 and 1976 for Sears, Roebuck and Company, the structure is composed of 75-ft. square tubes that rise to varying levels.

The *Gateway Arch,* located on the riverfront in St. Louis, Missouri, is a tapered curve of stainless steel rising to 630 ft. The tallest manmade memorial in the U.S., the Arch was designed by Finnish-born U.S. architect Eero Saarinen and built between 1963 and 1966. Visitors can ride to the top in specially devised capsule-like tram cars.

Mount Rushmore (6,000 ft.), in South Dakota, became a celebrated American landmark after sculptor Gutzon Borglum took on the project of carving into the side of it the heads of four great presidents. From 1927 until his death in 1941, Borglum worked on chiseling the 60-ft. likenesses of Washington, Jefferson, Lincoln, and Theodore Roosevelt. His son, Lincoln, finished the sculpture later that year.

San Francisco's *Golden Gate Bridge,* completed in 1937, is one of the most recognizable structures in the U.S. Designed by Joseph B. Strauss, this elegant suspension bridge has a main span of 4,200 ft.

The Seattle *Space Needle* was planned as the central structure and symbol of the 1962 Seattle World's Fair, the theme of which was "Century 21." The Needle, which is 605 ft. tall, is topped by an observation deck and a revolving restaurant.

* Photos of these structures can be found in the Headline History section.

Famous Ship Canals

Name	Location	Length (miles)[1]	Width (feet)	Depth (feet)	Locks	Year opened
Albert	Belgium	80.0	53.0	16.5	6	1939
Amsterdam-Rhine	Netherlands	45.0	164.0	41.0	3	1952
Beaumont-Port Arthur	United States	40.0	200.0	34.0	—	1916
Canal du Midi	France	149.0	n.a.	n.a.	100	1692
Chesapeake and Delaware	United States	14.0	450.0	35.0	—	1829
Erie Canal	United States	363.0	70	7	82	1825
Grand Canal	China	1,085.0	n.a.	n.a.	n.a.	7th cent.
Göta Canal	Sweden	240.0	n.a.	n.a.	58	1832
Houston	United States	50.0	(2)	40.0	—	1914
Kiel (Nord-Ostsee Kanal)	Germany	61.3	144.0	36.0	4	1895
Panama	Panama	50.7	110.0	41.0	12	1914
St. Lawrence Seaway	U.S. and Canada	2,400.0[3]	(4)	—	—	1959
Montreal to Prescott	U.S. and Canada	11.5	80.0	30.0	7	1959
Welland	Canada	27.5	80.0	27.0	8	1931
Sault Ste. Marie	Canada	1.2	60.0	16.8	1	1895
Sault Ste. Marie	United States	1.6	80.0	25.0	4	1915
Suez	Egypt	119.9[5]	1197.5	68.9	—	1869

1. Statute miles. 2. 300–400 feet. 3. From Montreal to Duluth. 4. 442–550 feet; there are 11.5 miles of locks, 80-feet wide and 30-feet deep. 5. From Port Said lighthouse to entrance channel in Suez roads. *Source:* American Society of Civil Engineers.

Notable Modern Bridges

Name	Location	Length of main span		Year completed
		feet	meters	
Suspension	**United States**			
Verrazano-Narrows	Lower New York Bay	4,260	1,298	1964
Golden Gate	San Francisco Bay	4,200	1,280	1937
Mackinac	Mackinac Straits, Mich.	3,800	1,158	1957
George Washington	Hudson River at New York City	3,500	1,067	1931
Tacoma Narrows II	Puget Sound at Tacoma, Wash.	2,800	853	1950
San Francisco–Oakland Bay[1]	San Francisco Bay	2,310	704	1936
Bronx-Whitestone	East River, New York City	2,300	701	1939
Delaware Memorial[1]	Delaware River near Wilmington, Del.	2,150	655	1951, 1968
Seaway Skyway	St. Lawrence River at Ogdensburg, N.Y.	2,150	655	1960
Walt Whitman	Delaware River at Philadelphia	2,000	610	1957
Ambassador International	Detroit River at Detroit	1,850	564	1929
Throgs Neck	East River, New York City	1,800	549	1961
Benjamin Franklin	Delaware River at Philadelphia	1,750	533	1926
Brooklyn Bridge	East River, New York City	1,596	486	1883
Royal Gorge	Arkansas River, Colo.	1,053	321	1929
Wheeling Bridge	Ohio River, Wheeling, W.Va.	1,010	308	1847
	International			
Akashi Kaikyo	Hyogo, Japan	6,529	1,990	1998
Izmit Bay	Marmara Sea, Turkey	5,472	1,668	UC
Storebælt	Denmark	5,328	1,624	1998
Humber	Humberside, England	4,626	1,410	1981
Jiangyin	Yangtze River, China	4,543	1,385	1999
Tsing Ma Bridge	Hong Kong	4,518	1,377	1997
Hardanger Fjord	Norway	4,347	1,324	n.a.
Hoga Kusten	400 km N. Stockholm, Sweden	3,970	1,210	1997
High Coast Bridge	Västernorrland, Sweden	3,969	1,210	1997
Minami Bisan-Seto	Japan	3,668	1,118	1988
Second Bosporus	Istanbul, Turkey	3,576	1,090	1988
First Bosporus	Istanbul, Turkey	3,524	1,074	1973
Third Kurushima	Japan	3,379	1,030	UC
Second Kurushima	Japan	3,346	1,020	UC
Ponte 25 de Abril	Tagus River at Lisbon, Portugal	3,323	1,013	1966
Forth Road	Queensferry, Scotland	3,300	1,006	1964
Kita Bisan-Seto	Japan	3,248	990	1988
Severn	Severn River at Beachley, England	3,240	988	1966
Yicang Bridge	Yangtze River, Hubei Province, China	3,150	960	UC
Shimotsui Straits	Japan	3,084	940	1988
Xiling Yangtze	Three Gorges Dam, China	2,952	900	1996
Tigergate (Humen)	Pearl River, Guangdon Province, China	2,913	888	1997
Ohnaruto	Japan	2,874	876	1988
Pierre Laporte	Quebec, Canada	2,190	668	1970
Cantilever	**United States**			
Commodore John Barry	Chester, Pa.	1,644	501	1974
Greater New Orleans[1]	Mississippi River, La.	1,576	480	1958
Transbay Bridge	San Francisco Bay	1,400	427	1936
	International			
Quebec Railway	Quebec, Canada	1,800	549	1917
Forth Railway[1]	Queensferry, Scotland	1,710	521	1890
Minato Ohashi	Osaka, Japan	1,673	510	1974
Howrah	Hooghly River at Calcutta, India	1,500	457	1943
Steel Arch	**United States**			
New River Gorge	Fayetteville, W. Va.	1,700	518	1977
Bayonne	Kill Van Kull at Bayonne, N.J.	1,675	510	1931
Hell Gate Bridge	East River (Hell Gate), New York City	978	298	1916
	International			
Sydney Harbor	Sydney, Australia	1,670	509	1932
Zdákov	Vltava River, Czech Republic	1,244	380	1967
Port Mann	Fraser River at Vancouver, British Columbia	1,200	366	1964
Cable-Stayed	**United States**			
Dame Point	Jacksonville, Fla.	1,300	396	1988
Houston Ship Channel	Baytown, Tex.	1,250	381	1995

Name	Location	Length of main span feet	meters	Year completed
Sidney Lanier Bridge	Brunswick River, Ga.	1,250	381	UC
Hale Boggs Memorial	Luling, La.	1,222	373	1983
Sunshine Skyway	Tampa, Fla.	1,200	366	1987
	International			
Tatara	Honshu–Shikoku, Japan	2,920	890	1999
Ponte de Normandie	Le Havre, France	2,808	856	1995
Second Nanjing	Yangtze River, Nanjing, China	2,060	628	UC
Wuhan Third Yangtze	Wuhan, Hubei Province, China	2,028	618	UC
Qingzhou Minjiang	Fuzhou, China	1,985	605	1996
Yang Pu	Shanghai, China	1,975	602	1993
Xupu	Shanghai, China	1,936	590	1997
Meiko Chuo	Aichi, Japan	1,936	590	1997
Patras Bridge	Greece	1,837	560	UC
Skarnsundet Bridge	near Trondheim, Norway	1,739	530	1991
Quishi Bridge	Guangdong Province, China	1,700	518	UC
Tsurumi Tsubasa	Kanagawa, Japan	1,673	510	1995
Jingsha Bridge	Yangtze River, Hubei Province, China	1,640	500	UC
Oresund	Denmark/Sweden	1,614	492	2000
Ikuchi	Honshu-Shikoku, Japan	1,608	490	1991
Higashi Kobe	Hyogo, Japan	1,591	485	1994
Zhanjiang Bay Bridge	Guangdong Province, China	1,575	480	1998
Ting Kau	Hong Kong	1,558	475	1997
Seohae	Korea	1,542	470	UC
Alex Fraser	Vancouver, B.C., Canada	1,525	465	1986
Yokohama-ko-odan	Kanagawa, Japan	1,509	460	1989
Second Hooghly	Calcutta, India	1,500	457	1992
Second Severn Crossing	Severn River, England	1,496	456	1996
Dartford	Thames River, Dartford, England	1,476	450	1992
Dao Kanong	Chao Phraya River, Bangkok, Thailand	1,476	450	1987
Queen Elizabeth II	Thames River, Dartford, England	1,476	450	1991
Chongqing 2nd Bridge	Sichuan Province, China	1,457	444	1996
Continuous Truss	**United States**			
Astoria	Columbia River, Ore.	1,232	376	1966
Croton Reservoir	Croton, N.Y.	1,052	321	1970
Ravenswood	Ohio River, Ravenswood, W. Va.	902	275	1981
	International			
Oshima	Oshima Island, Japan	1,066	325	1976
Tenmon	Kumamoto, Japan	984	300	1966
Kuronoseto	Nagashima-Kyushu, Japan	984	300	1974
Graf Spee	Germany	839	256	1936
Concrete Arch	**United States**			
Natchez Trace Pkwy.	Franklin, Tenn.	582	177	1994
Westinghouse	Pittsburgh, Pa.	460	140	1931
Jack's Run	Pittsburgh, Pa.	400	120	1930
Cappelen	Minneapolis, Minn.	400	120	1923
	International			
Wanxian	Wanxian, Sichuan Province, China	1,378	420	1997
Krk (I)	Krk, Croatia	1,280	390	1980
Gladesville	Parramatta River at Sydney, Australia	1,000	305	1964
Amizade	Paraná River at Foz do Iguassu, Brazil	951	290	1964
Arrábida	Porto, Portugal	886	270	1963
Sandö	Angerman River at Kramfors, Sweden	866	264	1943
Confederation Bridge	Northumberland Strait, Canada	820	250	1997
Sibenik	Sibenik, Yugoslavia	808	246	1966
Krk (II)	Krk, Croatia	800	244	1979
Fiumarella	Catanzaro, Italy	758	231	1961
Zaporozhe	Old Dnepr River, Ukraine	748	228	1952
Esla Bridge	Esla River at Zamora, Spain	645	197	1940
Segmental Construction	**United States**			
Jesse H. Jones Memorial	Houston Ship Channel, Texas	750	228	1982

NOTES: UC = under construction in 1999. n.a. = not available. 1. Twin span. *Source:* Federal Highway Administration.

World's Tallest Buildings

Building, city	Year	Stories	Height m	Height ft.	Building, city	Year	Stories	Height m	Height ft.
Petronas Tower 1, Kuala Lumpur, Malaysia	1998	88	452	1,483	SunTrust Plaza, Atlanta	1992	60	265	871
Petronas Tower 2, Kuala Lumpur, Malaysia	1998	88	452	1,483	Water Tower Place, Chicago	1976	74	262	859
Sears Tower, Chicago	1974	110	442	1,450	First Interstate Tower, Los Angeles	1974	62	262	858
Jin Mao Building, Shanghai	1999	88	421	1,380	Canada Trust Tower, Toronto	1990	51	261	856
World Trade Center One, New York	1972	110	417	1,368	Transamerica Corporate Headquarters, San Francisco	1972	48	260	853
World Trade Center Two, New York	1973	110	415	1,362	G.E. Building, New York	1933	70	259	850
Citic Plaza, Guangzhou, China	1997	80	391	1,283	One First National Plaza, Chicago	1969	60	259	850
Shun Hing Square, Shenzhen, China	1996	69	384	1,260	Two Liberty Place, Philadelphia	1990	58	258	848
Empire State Building, New York	1931	102	381	1,250	Messeturm, Frankfurt	1990	63	257	843
Central Plaza, Hong Kong	1992	78	374	1,227	USX Tower, Pittsburgh	1970	64	256	841
Bank of China Tower, Hong Kong	1989	70	369	1,209	Rinku Gate Tower, Osaka	1996	56	256	840
T & C Tower, Kaoshiung, Taiwan	1997	85	348	1,140	World Trade Center, Osaka	1995	55	252	827
Amoco Building, Chicago	1973	80	346	1,136	IBM Tower, Atlanta	1988	50	250	820
The Center, Hong Kong	1998	79	346	1,135	BNI City Tower, Jakarta	1995	46	250	820
John Hancock Center, Chicago	1969	100	344	1,127	Korea Life Insurance Company, Seoul	1985	60	249	817
Chicago Beach Tower Hotel, Dubai	1998	60	321	1,053	CitySpire, New York	1989	75	248	814
Baiyoke Tower II, Bangkok	1997	90	320	1,050	Rialto Tower, Melbourne	1985	63	248	814
Chrysler Building, New York	1930	77	319	1,046	One Chase Manhattan Plaza, New York	1961	60	248	813
NationsBank Plaza, Atlanta	1993	55	312	1,023	MetLife, New York	1963	59	246	808
Library Tower, Los Angeles	1990	75	310	1,018	Shin Kong Life Tower, Taipei, Taiwan	1993	51	244	801
AT&T Corporate Center, Chicago	1989	60	307	1,007	Malayan Bank, Kuala Lumpur, Malaysia	1988	50	244	799
Texas Commerce Tower, Houston	1982	75	305	1,000	Tokyo City Hall, Tokyo	1991	48	243	797
Two Prudential Plaza, Chicago	1990	64	303	995	Woolworth Building, New York	1913	57	241	792
Ryugyong Hotel, Pyongyang, N. Korea	1995	105	300	984	Mellon Bank Center, Philadelphia	1991	54	241	792
Commerzbank Tower, Frankfurt	1997	56	299	981	John Hancock Tower, Boston	1976	60	240	788
First Interstate Bank Plaza, Houston	1983	71	296	972	Bank One Center, Dallas	1987	60	240	787
Landmark Tower, Yokohama, Japan	1993	70	296	971	Commerce Court West, Toronto	1973	57	239	784
311 South Wacker Drive, Chicago	1990	65	293	961	Moscow State University, Moscow	1953	26	239	784
American International Building, New York	1932	67	290	952	Empire Tower, Kuala Lumpur, Malaysia	1994	62	238	781
First Canadian Place, Toronto	1975	72	290	951	NationsBank Center, Houston	1984	56	238	780
Society Tower, Cleveland	1991	57	290	950	Bank of America Center, San Francisco	1969	52	237	779
One Liberty Place, Philadelphia	1987	61	287	945	Worldwide Plaza, New York	1989	47	237	778
Columbia Seafirst Center, Seattle	1984	76	287	943	One Canada Square, London	1991	50	237	777
40 Wall Street, New York	1930	72	283	927	IDS Center, Minneapolis	1973	52	236	775
NationsBank Plaza, Dallas	1985	72	281	921	U.S. Bank Place, Minneapolis	1992	58	236	774
Overseas Union Bank Centre, Singapore	1986	66	280	919	Norwest Center, Minneapolis	1988	57	235	773
United Overseas Bank Plaza, Singapore	1992	66	280	919	Treasury Building, Singapore	1986	52	235	770
Republic Plaza, Singapore	1995	66	280	919	One Ninety One Peachtree Tower, Atlanta	1991	50	235	770
Citicorp Center, New York	1977	59	279	915	Opera City Tower, Tokyo	1997	54	234	768
Scotia Plaza, Toronto	1989	68	275	902	Shinjuku Park Tower, Tokyo	1994	52	233	764
Transco Tower, Houston	1983	64	275	901	Heritage Plaza, Houston	1987	52	232	762
Renaissance Tower, Dallas	1975	56	270	886	Kompleks Tun Abdul Razak Building, Penang, Malaysia	1985	65	232	760
900 North Michigan Ave., Chicago	1989	66	265	871	Palace of Culture and Science, Warsaw	1955	42	231	758
NationsBank Corporate Center, Charlotte	1992	60	265	871	Carnegie Hall Tower, New York	1991	60	231	757
					Three First National Plaza, Chicago	1981	57	230	753
					Equitable Tower, New York	1986	51	229	752
					MLC Centre, Sydney	1978	65	229	751
					One Penn Plaza, New York	1972	57	229	750
					1251 Avenue of the Americas, New York	1972	54	229	750

NOTE: Height is measured from sidewalk level of main entrance to structural top of building. Antennas and flag poles are not included. *Source:* Council on Tall Buildings and Urban Habitat, Lehigh University.

World's Highest Dams

Name	River, state, and country	Structural height feet	Structural height meters	Gross reservoir capacity thousands of acre feet	Gross reservoir capacity millions of cubic meters	Year completed
Rogun	Vakhsh, Tajikistan	1099	335	9,404	11,600	1985
Nurek	Vakhsh, Tajikistan	984	300	8,512	10,500	1980
Grande Dixence	Dixence, Switzerland	935	285	324	400	1962
Inguri	Inguri, Georgia	892	272	801	1,100	1984
Vaiont	Vaiont, Italy	859	262	137	169	1961
Manuel M. Torres	Grijalva, Mexico	856	261	1,346	1,660	1981
Tehri	Bhagirathi, India	856	261	2,869	3,540	UC
Alvaro Obregon	Mextiquic, Mexico	853	260	n.a.	n.a.	1926
Mauvoisin	Drance de Bagnes, Switzerland	820	250	146	180	1957
Alberto Lleras	Orinoco, Colombia	797	243	811	1,000	1989
Mica	Columbia, Canada	797	243	20,000	24,670	1972
Sayano-Shushensk	Yenisei, Russia	794	242	25,353	31,300	1980
Ertan	Yangtze/Yalong, China	787	240	4,702	5,800	1999
La Esmeralda	Batá, Colombia	778	237	661	815	1975
Kishau	Tons, India	774	236	1,946	2,400	1985
Oroville	Feather, Calif., U.S.	770	235	3,538	4,299	1968
El Cajón	Humuya, Honduras	768	234	4,580	5,650	1984
Chirkey	Sulak, Russia	764	233	2,252	2,780	1977
Bhakra	Sutlej, India	741	226	8,002	9,870	1963
Luzzone	Brenno di Luzzone, Switzerland	738	225	71	87	1963
Hoover	Colorado, Ariz./Nev., U.S.	732	223	28,500	35,154	1936
Contra	Verzasca, Switzerland	722	220	70	86	1965
Mratinje	Piva, Herzegovina	722	220	713	880	1973
Dworshak	N. Fk. Clearwater, Idaho, U.S.	717	219	3,453	4,259	1974
Glen Canyon	Colorado, Ariz., U.S.	710	216	27,000	33,304	1964

NOTES: UC = under construction in 1999. n.a. = not available. *Source: World Register of Dams 1998*, International Commission on Large Dams.

World's Largest Dams

Dam	Location	Volume (thousands) Cubic meters	Volume (thousands) Cubic yards	Year completed
Syncrude Tailings	Canada	540,000	706,320	UC
Chapetón	Argentina	296,200	311,539	UC
Pati	Argentina	238,180	274,026	UC
New Cornelia Tailings	United States	209,500	274,026	1973
Tarbela	Pakistan	121,720	159,210	1976
Kambaratinsk	Kyrgyzstan	112,200	146,758	UC
Fort Peck	Montana	96,049	125,628	1940
Lower Usuma	Nigeria	93,000	121,644	1990
Cipasang	Indonesia	90,000	117,720	UC
Atatürk	Turkey	84,500	110,522	1990
Yacyretá-Apipe	Paraguay/Argentina	81,000	105,944	UC
Guri (Raul Leoni)	Venezuela	78,000	102,014	1986
Rogun	Tajikistan	75,500	98,750	1985
Oahe	South Dakota	70,339	92,000	1963
Mangla	Pakistan	65,651	85,872	1967
Gardiner	Canada	65,440	85,592	1968
Afsluitdijk	Netherlands	63,400	82,927	1932
Oroville	California	59,639	78,008	1968
San Luis	California	59,405	77,700	1967
Nurek	Tajikistan	58,000	75,861	1980
Garrison	North Dakota	50,843	66,500	1956
Cochiti	New Mexico	48,052	62,850	1975
Tabka (Thawra)	Syria	46,000	60,168	1976
Bennett W.A.C.	Canada	43,733	57,201	1967
Tucuruí	Brazil	43,000	56,242	1984

NOTE: UC = under construction in 1999. *Source:* Department of the Interior, Bureau of Reclamation and *International Water Power and Dam Construction.*

World's Largest Hydroelectric Plants
(over 4,000 MW capacity)

Name of dam	Location	Rated capacity (MW)		Year of initial operation
		Present	Ultimate	
Itaipu	Brazil/Paraguay	12,600	14,000	1983
Guri	Venezuela	10,000	10,000	1986
Grand Coulee	Washington	6,494	6,494	1942
Sayano-Shushensk	Russia	6,400	6,400	1989
Krasnoyarsk	Russia	6,000	6,000	1968
Churchill Falls	Canada	5,428	6,528	1971
La Grande 2	Canada	5,328	5,328	1979
Bratsk	Russia	4,500	4,500	1961
Moxoto	Brazil	4,328	4,328	n.a.
Ust-Ilim	Russia	4,320	4,320	1977
Tucurui	Brazil	4,245	8,370	1984

NOTES: MW = megawatts. n.a. = not available. *Source: International Journal on Hydropower and Dams,* official journal of the International Hydropower Association, Sutton, England.

Notable Tunnels

Name	Location	Length		Year completed
		mi.	km	
Railroad, excluding subways				
Seikan	Tsugaru Strait, Japan	33.5	53.9	1988
Channel Tunnel[1]	English Channel, England–France	31.1	50.0	1994
Simplon (I and II)	Alps, Switzerland–Italy	12.3	19.8	1906 & 1922
Apennine	Bologna–Florence, Italy	11.5	18.5	1934
St. Gotthard	Swiss Alps	9.3	15.0	1880
Lötschberg	Swiss Alps	9.1	14.6	1911
Mont Cénis	French Alps	8.5[2]	13.7	1871
New Cascade	Cascade Mountains, Washington	7.8	12.6	1929
Vosges	Vosges, France	7.0	11.3	1940
Flathead	Rocky Mountains, Montana	7.0	11.3	1970
Arlberg	Austrian Alps	6.3	10.1	1884
Moffat	Rocky Mountains, Colorado	6.2	9.9	1928
Shimizu	Shimizu, Japan	6.1	9.8	1931
Rimutaka	Wairarapa, New Zealand	5.5	8.9	1955
Storebaelt	Great Belt, Denmark	5.0	8.0	1995
Vehicular				
Laerdal	Laerdal–Aurland, Norway	15.2	24.5	2000
St. Gotthard	Alps, Switzerland	10.2	16.4	1980
Mt. Blanc	Alps, France–Italy	7.0	11.3	1965
Aqualine Expressway	Tokyo Bay, Japan	5.9	9.5	1997
Mt. Ena	Japan Alps, Japan	5.3	8.5	1976[3]
Great St. Bernard	Alps, Switzerland–Italy	3.4	5.5	1964
Mount Royal	Montreal, Canada	3.2	5.1	1918
Queensway	Mersey River, Liverpool, England	2.2	3.5	1934
Brooklyn-Battery	East River, New York City	1.7	2.7	1950
Fort McHenry	Baltimore, Maryland	1.7	2.7	1985
Holland	Hudson River, New York–New Jersey	1.6	2.6	1927
Lincoln	Hudson River, New York–New Jersey	1.6	2.6	1937
Hampton Roads[4]	Norfolk, Virginia	1.4	2.3	1957
Queens-Midtown	East River, New York City	1.3	2.1	1940
Liberty Tubes	Pittsburgh, Pennsylvania	1.2	1.9	1923
Baltimore Harbor	Baltimore, Maryland	1.2	1.9	1957
Allegheny Tunnels	Pennsylvania Turnpike	1.2	1.9	1940[5]
Yerba	Yerba Buena Island, Calif.	0.5	0.8	1936

NOTE: UC = Under construction in 1999. 1. Three-tunnel system including two rail tunnels (one carries passengers from England to France, the other from France to England) and a central service tunnel. 2. Lengthened to its present 8.5 miles in 1881. 3. Parallel tunnel begun in 1976. 4. Parallel bridge-tunnel opened in 1976. 5. Parallel tunnel built in 1965, twin tunnel in 1966. *Source:* American Society of Civil Engineers and International Bridge, Tunnel & Turnpike Association, Wittiker's.

Some World-Famous Cathedrals

Cathedral	Location	Style	Date built	Height ft	m
Canterbury	Canterbury, England	various	1070–1089, 1175–1184, 1379–1503	235.0	72.0
Chartres (Notre Dame)	Chartres, France	Gothic	12th–13th centuries	375.0 350.0	114.0 107.0
Church of Christ and Blessed Mary the Virgin	Durham, England	Norman	1093–1133	n.a.	n.a.
Cologne	Cologne, Germany	Gothic	1248–1560, 1842–1880	515.0	157.0
Hagia Sophia	Istanbul, Turkey	Byzantine	532–537	184.0	56.0
Imperial	Speyer, Germany	Romanesque	c. 1030–1061	n.a.	n.a.
Lincoln	Lincoln, England	originally Norman	1075–1501	271.0	83.0
Liverpool	Liverpool, England	n.a.	1904–1978	n.a.	n.a.
Lund	Lund, Sweden	Romanesque	11th century	n.a.	n.a.
Milan	Milan, Italy	various (esp. Gothic)	1386–1813	354.0	108.0
Mosque/Cathedral of Córdoba	Cordoba, Spain	Islamic	784–786, 9th–10th centuries	300.0	90.0
Notre Dame	Amiens, France	Gothic	1220–c. 1270, 14th century, 16th century	370.0	113.0
Notre Dame	Antwerp, Belgium	Gothic	14th–16th centuries	400.0	122.0
Notre Dame	Rouen, France	Gothic	12th–15th centuries	495.0	151.0
Notre-Dame de Paris	Paris, France	Gothic	1163–14th century, 1845–	223.0	68.0
Orvieto	Orvieto, Italy	Gothic	1290–1580	n.a.	n.a.
Our Lady of Peace of Yamoussoukro Basilica	Yamoussoukro, Côte d'Ivoire	n.a.	1986–1989	489.0	149.0
Palatine Chapel of Charlemagne	Aachen, Germany	Carolingian	790–805	101.5	30.9
Reims	Reims, France	French Gothic	13th–14th centuries	n.a.	n.a.
Rochester	Rochester, England	Norman, Gothic	1125–1130	n.a.	n.a.
St. Basil the Blessed (Church of the Intercession)	Moscow, Russia	n.a.	1554–1560	n.a.	n.a.
St. David's	Saint David's, Wales	Norman	12th century	n.a.	n.a.
St.-Étienne	Caen, France	Norman Romanesque	1060s	295.0	90.0
St. Isaac's	St. Petersburg, Russia	Russian Empire	1818–1858	n.a.	n.a.
St. John the Divine	New York, N.Y.	Byzantine-Romanesque, French-Gothic	1892–	n.a.	n.a.
St. Julien du Mans	Le Mans, France	Gothic, Romanesque	11th–15th centuries	210.0	64.0
St. Patrick's	New York, N.Y.	Gothic	1858–1879	n.a.	n.a.
St. Paul's	London, England	Classical English Baroque	1675–1710	365.0	111.3
St. Peter (York Minster)	York, England	Norman, Gothic	13th–15th centuries	n.a.	n.a.
St. Peter's Basilica	Rome, Italy	n.a.	1506–1626	404.0	123.0
St. Pierre	Beauvais, France	Gothic	1227 (never completed)	157.0	48.0
St. Stephen's	Vienna, Austria	Romanesque, Gothic	1147, 1304–1450, 1952	n.a.	n.a.
Salisbury	Salisbury, England	Early English	1220–1260	404.0	123.0
San Marco Basilica	Venice, Italy	Byzantine	completed 1071	324.0	99.0
Santa Maria	Seville, Spain	Gothic, Moorish, Plateresque, Baroque	1402–1506	n.a.	n.a.
Santa Maria del Fiore	Florence, Italy	Gothic	1296–1436	138.0	42.0
Santiago	Santiago, Spain	Romanesque, Plateresque, Baroque	1078–1211	n.a.	n.a.
Siena	Siena, Italy	Italian Gothic	12th–14th centuries	n.a.	n.a.
Strasbourg	Strasbourg, France	Rhenish	1015–1439	475.0	144.0
Toledo	Toledo, Spain	Gothic	13th century	n.a.	n.a.
Ulm	Ulm, Germany	Gothic	14th century	528.0	161.0
Washington National	Washington, D.C.	English Gothic	1907–1990	n.a.	n.a.
Westminster Abbey	Westminster, England	Gothic, Perpendicular	1050–1065, 1245–16th century	n.a.	n.a.
Winchester	Winchester, England	Norman, Gothic	1093, 14th century	n.a.	n.a.
Worms	Worms, Germany	Romanesque	1018–12th century, 13th–14th centuries	n.a.	n.a.

NOTES: n.a. = not available. For more cathedrals, *see* Famous Structures on pp. 444–445.

First Aid for Crossword Puzzlers

We cannot begin to list all the odd words you might encounter in your daily and Sunday crossword puzzles, for such words run into the thousands. But we have tried to include those that turn up most frequently, as well as many others that should be of help to you when you are unable to go any further.

We do not guarantee that the definitions in your puzzle will be exactly the same as ours, although we have checked every word with a standard dictionary and have followed its definition.

In nearly every case, we have used as the key word the principal noun of the definition, rather than any adjective, adjective phrase, or noun used as an adjective. And, to simplify your searching, we have grouped the words according to the number of spaces you have to fill.

Words of Two Letters

Ambary, DA
And (French, Latin), ET
Article (Arabic), AL
 (French), LA, LE, UN
 (Spanish), EL, LA, UN
At the (French), AU
 (Spanish), AL
Behold, LO
Bird: Hawaiian, OO
Birthplace: Abraham's, UR
Bone, OS
Buddha, FO
Butterfly: Peacock, IO
Champagne, AY
Chaos, NU
Chief: Burmese, BO
Coin: Roman, AS
 Siamese, AT
Concerning, RE
Dialect: Chinese, WU
Double (Egy. relig.), KA
Drama: Japanese, NO
Egg (comb. form), OO
Esker, OS

Eye (Scottish), EE
Factor: Amplification, MU
Fifty (Greek), NU
Fish: Carplike, ID
Force, OD
Forty (Greek), MU
From (French, Latin, Spanish), DE
 (Latin prefix), AB
From the (French), DU
God: Babylonian, EA, ZU
 Egyptian sun, RA
 Hindu unknown, KA
 Semitic, EL
Goddess: Babylonian, AI
 Greek Earth, GE
Gold (heraldry), OR
Gulf: Arctic, OB
Heart (Egy. relig.), AB
Indian: South American, GE
King: Of Bashan, OG
Language: Artificial, RO
 Assamese, AO
Lava: Hawaiian, AA

Letter: Greek, MU, NU, PI, XI
 Hebrew, HE, PE
Lily: Palm, TI
Measure: Chinese, HO, HU,
 KO, LI, MU, PU, TO, TU
 Japanese, GO, JO, MO, RI,
 SE, TO
 Netherlands, EL
 Portuguese, PE
 Siamese, WA
 Swedish, AM
Type, EM, EN
 Vietnamese, LY
Monk: Buddhist, BO
Month: Jewish, AB
Mouth, OS
Mulberry: Indian, AL
Native: Burmese, WA
Note: Of scale, DO, FA, MI,
 LA, RE, TI
Of (French, Latin, Spanish), DE
Of the (French), DU

One (Scottish), AE
Pagoda: Chinese, TA
Plant: East Indian fiber, DA
Ridge: Sandy, AS, OS
River: Russian, OB
Sloth: Three-toed, AI
Soul (Egy. relig.), BA
Sound: Hindu mystic, OM
Suffix: Comparative, ER
To the: French, AU
 Spanish, AL
Tree: Buddhist sacred, BO
Tribe: Assamese, AO
Type: Jumbled, PI
Weight: Chinese, LI
 Danish, ES
 Japanese, MO
 Roman, AS
 Vietnamese, TA
Whirlwind: Faeroe Is., OE
Yes (German), JA
 (Italian, Spanish), SI
 (Russian), DA

Words of Three Letters

Adherent, IST
Again, BIS
Age, ERA
Antelope: African, GNU, KOB
Apricot: Japanese, UME
Article (German): DAS, DEM,
 DEN, DER, DES, DIE, EIN
 (French), LES, UNE
 (Spanish), LAS, LOS, UNA
Banana: Polynesian, FEI
Barge, HOY
Bass: African, IYO
Beak, NEB, NIB
Beard: Grain, AWN
Beetle: June, DOR
Being, ENS
Berry: Hawthorn, HAW
Beverage: Hawaiian, AVA
Bird: Australian, EMU
 Crowlike, JAY
 Extinct, MOA
 Fabulous, ROC
 Frigate, IWA
 Parson, POE, TUE, TUI
 Sea, AUK
Blackbird, ANI, ANO
Born, NEE
Bronze: Roman, AES
Bugle: Yellow, IVA
By way of, VIA
Canton: Swiss, URI
Cap: Turkish, FEZ
Catnip, NEP
Character: In "Faerie Queene,"
 UNA
Coin (Money of account):
 Afghan, PUL
 Albanian, LEK
 Bulgarian, LEV, LEW

French, ECU, SOU
Guyanese, BIT
Indian, PIE
Japanese, SEN, YEN
Korean, WON
Lithuanian, LIT
Macao, Timor, AVO
Palestinian, MIL
Persian, PUL
Peruvian, SOL
Rumanian, BAN, LEU, LEY
Scandinavian, ORE
Siamese, ATT
Collection: Facts, ANA
Commune: Belgian, ANS, ATH
 Netherlands, EDE, EPE
Community: Russian, MIR
Constellation: Southern, ARA
Contraction: Poetic, EEN, EER,
 OER
Covering: Apex of roof, EPI
Crab: Fiddler, UCA
Crag: Rocky, TOR
Cry: Crow, rook, raven, CAW
Cup: Wine, AMA
Cymbal, Oriental, TAL, ZEL
Disease: Silkworm, UJI
Division: Danish territorial, AMT
 Geologic, EON
Doctrine, ISM
Dowry, DOT
Dry (French), SEC
Dynasty: Chinese, CHI, HAN,
 SUI, WEI, YIN
Eagle: Sea, ERN
Earth (comb. form), GEO
Egg: Louse, NIT
Eggs: Fish, ROE
Emmet, ANT

Enzyme, ASE
Equal (comb. form), ISO
Extension: building, ELL
Far (comb. form), TEL
Farewell, AVE
Fiber: Palm, TAL
Finial, EPI
Fish: Carplike, IDE
 Pikelike, GAR
Flatfish, DAB
Fleur-de-lis, LIS, LYS
Food: Hawaiian, POI
Formerly, NEE
Friend (French), AMI
Game: Card, LOO
Garment: Camel-hair, ABA
Gateway, DAR
Gazelle: Tibetan, GOA
Genus: Ducks, AIX
 Grasses, POA
 Grasses (maize), ZEA
 Herbs or shrubs, IVA
 Lizards, UTA
 Rodents (incl. house mice),
 MUS
 Ruminants (incl. cattle), BOS
 Swine, SUS
Gibbon: Malay, LAR
God: Assyrian, SIN
 Babylonian, ABU, ANU, BEL,
 HEA, SIN, UTU
 Irish sea, LER
 Phrygian, MEN
 Polynesian, ORO
Goddess: Babylonian, AYA
 Etruscan, UNI
 Hindu, SRI, UMA, VAC
 Teutonic, RAN

Governor: Algerian, DEY
 Turkish, BEY
Grampus, ORC
Grape, UVA
Grass: Meadow, POA
Gypsy, ROM
Hail, AVE
Hare: Female, DOE
Hawthorn, HAW
Hay: Spread for drying, TED
Herb: Japanese, UDO
 Perennial, PIA
 Used for blue dye, WAD
Herd: Whales, GAM, POD
Hero: Spanish, CID
High (music), ALT
Honey (pharm.), MEL
Humorist: American, ADE
I (Latin), EGO
I love (Latin), AMO
Indian: Algonquin, FOX, SAC,
 WEA
 Chimakuan, HOH
 Keresan, SIA
 Mayan, MAM
 Shoshonean, UTE
 Siouan, KAW, OTO
 South American, ITE, ONA,
 URO, URU, YAO
 Tierra del Fuego, ONA
 Wakashan, AHT
Ingot, PIG
Inlet: Narrow, RIA
Island: Cyclades, IOS
 Dodecanese, COS, KOS
 (French), ILE
 River, AIT
Jackdaw, DAW

John (Gaelic), IAN
Keelbill, ANI, ANO
Kiln, OST
King: British legendary, LUD
Kobold, NIS
Lace: To make, TAT
Lamprey, EEL
Language: Artificial, IDO
   Bantu, ILA
   Siamese, LAO, TAI
Leaf: Palm, OLA, OLE
Leaving, ORT
Left: Cause to turn, HAW
Letter: Greek, CHI, ETA, PHI,
   PSI, RHO, TAU
   Hebrew, MEM, NUN, SIN,
   TAV, VAU
Lettuce, COS
Life (comb. form), BIO
Lily: Palm, TOI
Lizard, EFT
Louse: Young, NIT
Love (Anglo-Irish), GRA
Lute: Oriental, TAR
Macaw: Brazilian, ARA
Marble, TAW
Match: Shooting (French), TIR
Meadow, LEA
Measure: Abyssinian, TAT
   Algerian, PIK
   Arabian, DEN, SAA
   Belgian, VAT
   Bulgarian, OKA, OKE
   Chinese, FEN, TOU, YIN
   Cloth, ELL
   Cyprus, OKA, OKE, PIK
   Czech, LAN, SAH
   Danish, FOD, MIL, POT
   Dominican Republic, ONA
   Dutch, old, AAM
   East Indian, KIT
   Egyptian, APT, HEN, PIK,
   ROB
   Electric, MHO, OHM
   Energy, ERG
   English, PIN
   Estonian, TUN
   French, POT
   German, AAM
   Greek, PIK
   Hebrew, CAB, HIN, KOR,
   LOG
   Hungarian, AKO
   Icelandic, FET
   Indian, GAZ, GUZ, JOW,
   KOS
   Japanese, BOO, CHO, KEN,
   RIN, SHO, SUN, TAN
   Malabar, ADY
   Metric (land), ARE
   Netherlands, KAN, KOP,
   MUD, VAT, ZAK
   Norwegian, FOT, POT
   Persian, GAZ, GUZ, MOU,
   ZAR, ZER
   Polish, CAL
   Rangoon, DHA, LAN
   Roman, PES, URN
   Russian, FUT, LOF
   Scottish, COP

Siamese, KEN, NIU, RAI,
   SAT, SEN, SOK, WAH, YOT
Somaliland, TOP
Spanish, PIE
Straits Settlements, PAU,
   TUN
Swedish, ALN, FOT, MIL,
   REF, TUM
Swiss, POT
Tunisian, SAA
Turkish, OKA, OKE, PIK
Vietnamese, GON, MAU,
   NGU, VUO, SAO, TAO, TAT
Wire, MIL
Württemberg, IMI
Yarn, LEA
Yugoslav, OKA, RIF
Milk, LAC
Milkfish, AWA
Moccasin, PAC
Money: Yap stone, FEI
Money of Account (also Coin):
   Anglo-Saxon, ORA, ORE
   French, SOU
   Indian, LAC
   Japanese, RIN
Oman, GAJ
Virgin Islands, BIT
Monkey: Capuchin, SAI
Morsel, ORT
Mother: Peer Gynt's, ASE
Mountain: Asia Minor, IDA
Mulberry: Indian, AAL, ACH,
   AWL
Muttonbird: New Zealand, OII
Nahoor, SNA
Native: Mindanao, ATA
Neckpiece, BOA
Newt, EFT
No (Scottish), NAE
Note: Guido's highest, ELA
   Of scale, SOL
Nursemaid: Oriental, AMA, IYA
Ocher: Yellow, SIL
One (Scottish), YIN
Ornament: Pagoda, TEE
Oven: Polynesian, UMU
Ox: Tibetan, YAK
Pagoda: Chinese, TAA
Parrot: Hawk, HIA
   New Zealand, KEA
Part: Footlike, PES
Particle: Electrified, ION
Pasha, DEY
Pass: Mountain, COL
Paste: Rice, AME
Pea: Indian split, DAL
Peasant: Philippine, TAO
Penpoint, NEB, NIB
Piece out, EKE
Pigeon, NUN
Pine: Textile screw, ARA
Pistol (slang), GAT
Pit: Baking, IMU
Plant: Pepper, AVA
Play: By Capek, RUR
Poem: Old French, DIT
Porgy: Japanese, TAI
Priest: Biblical high, ELI
Prince: Ethiopian, RAS

Pseudonym: Dickens', BOZ
Queen: Fairy, MAB
Quince: Bengal, BEL
Record: Ship's, LOG
Refuse: Flax (Scottish), PAB,
   POB
Resin, LAC
Resort, SPA
Revolver (slang), GAT
Right: Cause to turn, GEE
River: Scottish or English, DEE
   (Spanish), RIO
   Swiss, AAR
Room: Harem, ODA
Rootstock: Fern, ROI
Rose (Persian), GUL
Ruff: Female, REE
Rule: Indian, RAJ
Sailor, GOB, TAR
Saint: Female (abbr.), STE
   Islamic, PIR
Salt, SAL
Sash: Japanese, OBI
Scrap, ORT
Seed: Poppy, MAW
   Small, PIP
Self, EGO
Serpent: Vedic sky, AHI
Sesame, TIL
Sheep: Female, EWE
   Indian, SHA
   Male, RAM
Sheepfold (Scottish), REE
Shelter, LEE
Shield, ECU
Shooting match (French), TIR
Shrew: European, ERD
Shrub: Evergreen, YEW
Silkworm, ERI
Snake: Asp, BOA
Soak, RET
Son-in-law: Mohammed's, ALI
Sorrel: Wood, OCA
Spade: Long, narrow, LOY
Spirit: Malignant, KER
Spot: Playing-card, PIP
Spread for drying, TED
Spring: Mineral, SPA
Sprite: Water, NIX
Statesman: Japanese, ITO
Stern: Toward, AFT
Stomach: Bird's, MAW
Street (French), RUE
Summer (French), ETE
Sun, SOL
Swamp, BOG, FEN
Swan: Male, COB
Tea: Chinese, CHA
Temple: Shinto, SHA
Thing (law), RES
Title: Etruscan, LAR
   Monk's, FRA
   Portuguese, DOM
   Spanish, DON
   Turkish, AGA, BEY
Tool: Cutting, ADZ, AXE
   Mining, GAD
   Piercing, AWL
Tree: Candlenut, AMA
   Central American, EBO

East Indian, SAJ, SAL
Evergreen, YEW
Hawaiian, KOA, KOU
Indian, BEL, DAR
Linden, LIN
New Zealand, AKE
Philippine, DAO, TUA, TUI
Rubber, ULE
South American, APA
Tribe: New Zealand, ATI
Turmeric, REA
Twice, BIS
Twin: Siamese, ENG
Uncle (dialect), EAM, EME
Veil: Chalice, AER, AIR
Vessel: Wine, AMA
Vestment: Ecclesiastical, ALB
Vetch: Bitter, ERS
Victorfish, AKU
Vine: New Zealand, AKA
   Philippine, IYO
Wallaba, APA
Wapiti, ELK
Water (French), EAU
Waterfall, LIN
Watering place: Prussian, EMS
Weave: Designating plain,
   UNI
Weight: Bulgarian, OKA, OKE
   Burmese, MOO, VIS
   Chinese, FEN, HAO, KIN,
   SSU, TAN, YIN
   Cyprus, OKA, OKE
   Danish, LOD, ORT, VOG
   East Indian, TJI
   Egyptian, KAT, OKA, OKE
   English, for wool, TOD
   German, LOT
   Greek, MNA, OKA, OKE
   Indian, SER
   Japanese, FUN, KIN, RIN,
   SHI
   Korean, KON
   Malacca, KIP
   Mongolian, LAN
   Netherlands, ONS
   Norwegian, LOD
   Polish, LUT
   Rangoon, PAI
   Roman, BES
   Russian, LOT
   Siamese, BAT, HAP, PAI
   Swedish, ASS, ORT
   Turkish, OKA, OKE
   Vietnamese, CAN
   Yugoslav, OKA, OKE
Whales: Herd, GAM, POD
Wildebeest, GNU
Wing, ALA
Witticism, MOT
Wolframite, CAL
Worm: African, LOA
Wreath: Hawaiian, LEI
Yale, ELI
Yam: Hawaiian, HOI
Yes (French), OUI
Young: Bring forth, EAN
Z (letter), ZED

Words of Four Letters

Aborigine: Borneo, DYAK
Agave, ALOE
Animal: Footless, APOD
Ant: White, ANAI, ANAY
Antelope: African, ASSE, BISA, GUIB,
   KOBA, KUDU, ORYX, POKU, PUKU,
   TOPI, TORA
Apoplexy: Plant, ESCA
Apple, POME
Apricot, ANSU
Ardor, ELAN
Armadillo, APAR, PEBA, PEVA, TATU
Ascetic: Islamic, SUFI
Association: Chinese, TONG

Astronomer: Persian, OMAR
Avatar: Of Vishnu, RAMA
Axillary, ALAR
Band: Horizontal (heraldry), FESS
Barracuda, SPET
Bark: Mulberry, TAPA
Base: Column, DADO
Bearing (heraldry), ORLE
Beer: Russian, KVAS
Beige, ECRU
Being, ESSE
Beverage: Japanese rice, SAKE
Bird: Asian, MINA, MYNA
   Egyptian sacred, IBIS

Extinct, DODO, MAMO
Flightless, KIWI
Gull-like, TERN
Hawaiian, IIWI, MAMO
Parson, KOKO
Unfledged, EYAS
Birds: As class, AVES
Black, EBON
   (French), NOIR
Blackbird: European, MERL
Boat: Flat-bottomed, DORY
Bone: Forearm, ULNA
Bones, OSSA
Box, Japanese, INRO

Bravo (rare), EUGE
Buffalo: Indian wild, ARNA
Bull (Spanish), TORO
Burden, ONUS
Cabbage: Sliced, SLAW
Caliph: Islamic, OMAR
Canoe: Malay, PRAU, PROA
Cap: Military, KEPI
Cape, NESS
Capital: Ancient Irish, TARA
Case: Article, ETUI
Cat: Wild, BALU, EYRA
Chalcedony, SARD
Chamber: Indian ceremonial, KIVA
Channel: Brain, ITER
Cheese: Dutch, EDAM
Chest: Sepulchral stone, CIST
Chieftain: Arab, EMIR
Church: Part of, APSE, NAVE
  (Scottish), KIRK
Claim (law), LIEN
Cluster: Flower, CYME
Coin: Chinese, TAEL, YUAN
  German, MARK
  Indian, ANNA
  Iranian, RIAL
  Italian, LIRA
  Moroccan, OKIA
  Siamese, BAHT
  South American, PESO
  Spanish, DURO, PESO
  Turkish, PARA
Commune: Belgian, AATH
Composition: Musical, OPUS
Compound: Chemical, DIOL
Constellation: Southern, PAVO
Council: Russian, DUMA
Counsel, REDE
Covering: Seed, ARIL
Cross: Egyptian, ANKH
Cry: Bacchanalian, EVOE
Cup (Scottish), TASS
Cupbearer, SAKI
Dagger, DIRK
  Malay, KRIS
Dam: River, WEIR
Dash, ELAN
Date: Roman, IDES
Dawn: Pertaining to, EOAN
Dean: English, INGE
Decay: In fruit, BLET
Deer: Sambar, MAHA
Disease: Skin, ACNE
Disk: Solar, ATEN
Dog: Hunting, ALAN
Drink: Hindu intoxicating, SOMA
Duck, SMEE, SMEW, TEAL
Dynasty: Chinese, CHEN, CHIN, CHOU,
  CHOW, HSIA, MING, SUNG, TANG,
  TSIN
  Mongol, YUAN
Eagle: Biblical, GIER
  Sea, ERNE
Ear: Pertaining to, OTIC
Egyptian: Christian, COPT
Entrance: Mine, ADIT
Esau, EDOM
Escutcheon: Voided, ORLE
Eskers, OSAR
Evergreen: New Zealand, TAWA
Fairy: Persian, PERI
Family: Italian, ESTE
Far (comb. form), TELE
Farewell, VALE
Father (French), PERE
Fennel: Philippine, ANIS
Fever: Malarial, AGUE
Fiber: East Indian, JUTE
Firn, NEVE
Fish: Carplike, DACE
  Hawaiian, ULUA
  Herringlike, SHAD
  Mackerellike, CERO
  Marine, HAKE
  Sea, LING, MERO, OPAH
  Spiny-finned, GOBY

Food: Tropical, TARO
Foot: Metric, IAMB
Formerly, ERST
Founder: Of Carthage, DIDO
France: Southern, MIDI
Furze, ULEX
Gaelic, ERSE
Gaiter, SPAT
Game: Card, FARO, SKAT
Garlic: European wild, MOLY
Garment: Hindu, SARI
  Roman, TOGA
Gazelle, CORA
Gem, JADE, ONYX, OPAL, RUBY
Genus: Amphibians (incl. frogs), RANA
  Amphibians (incl. tree toads), HYLA
  Antelopes, ORYX
  Auks, ALCA, URIA
  Bees, APIS
  Birds (American ostriches), RHEA
  Birds (cranes), CRUS
  Birds (magpies), PICA
  Birds (peacocks), PAVO
  Cetaceans, INIA
  Ducks (incl. mallards), ANAS
  Fishes (burbots), LOTA
  Fishes (incl. bowfins), AMIA
  Geese (snow geese), CHEN
  Gulls, XEMA
  Herbs, ARUM, GEUM
  Insects (water scorpions), NEPA
  Lilies, ALOE
  Mammals (humans), HOMO
  Orchids, DISA
  Owls, ASIO, BUBO, OTUS
  Palms, NIPA
  Sea birds, SULA
  Sheep, OVIS
  Shrubs, Eurasian, ULEX
  Shrubs (hollies), ILEX
  Shrubs (incl. Virginia Willow), ITEA
  Shrubs, tropical, EVEA
  Snakes (sand snakes), ERYX
  Swans, OLOR
  Trees, chocolate, COLA
  Trees (ebony family), MABA
  Trees (incl. maples), ACER
  Trees (olives), OLEA
  Trees, tropical, EVEA
  Turtles, EMYS
Goat: Wild, IBEX, KRAS, TAHR, TAIR,
  THAR
God: Assyrian, ASUR
  Babylonian, ADAD, ADDU, ENKI,
  ENZU, IRRA, NABU, NEBO, UTUG
  Celtic, LLEU, LLEW
  Hindu, AGNI, CIVA, DEVA, DEWA,
  KAMA, RAMA, SIVA, VAYU
  Phrygian, ATYS
  Semitic, BAAL
  Teutonic, HLER
Goddess: Babylonian, ERUA, GULA
  Hawaiian, PELE
  Hindu, DEVI, KALI, SHRI, VACH
Gooseberry: Hawaiian, POHA
Gourd, PEPO
Grafted (heraldry), ENTE
Grandfather (obsolete), AIEL
Grandparents: Pertaining to, AVAL
Grass: Hawaiian, HILO
Gray (French), GRIS
Green (heraldry), VERT
Groom: Indian, SYCE
Half (prefix), DEMI, HEMI, SEMI
Hamlet, DORP
Hammerhead: Part of, PEEN
Handle, ANSA
Harp: Japanese, KOTO
Hartebeest, ASSE, TORA
Hautboy, OBOE
Hawk: Taken from nest (falconry), EYAS
Hearing (law), OYER
Heater: For liquids, ETNA
Herb: Aromatic, ANET, DILL
  Fabulous, MOLY
  Perennial, GEUM, SEGO

Pot, WORT
Used for blue dye, WADE, WOAD
Hill: Flat-topped, MESA
  Sand, DENE, DUNE
Hoarfrost, RIME
Hog: Immature female, GILT
Holly, ILEX
House: Cow, BYRE
  (Spanish), CASA
Ice: Floating, FLOE
Image, ICON, IKON
Incarnation: Of Vishnu, RAMA
Indian: Algonquin, CREE, SAUK
  Central American, MAYA
  Iroquoian, ERIE
  Mexican, CORA
  Peruvian, CANA, INCA, MORO
  Shoshonean, HOPI
  Siouan, OTOE
  Southwestern, HOPI, PIMA, YUMA,
  ZUNI
Insect: Immature, PUPA
Instrument: Stringed, LUTE, LYRE
Ireland, EIRE, ERIN
Jacket: English, ETON
Jail (British), GAOL
Jar, OLLA
Judge: Islamic, CADI
Juniper: European, CADE
Kiln, OAST, OVEN
King: British legendary, LUDD, NUDD
Kiss, BUSS
Knife: Philippine, BOLO
Koran: Section of, SURA
Laborer: Spanish American, PEON
Lake: Mountain, TARN
  (Scottish), LOCH
Lamp: Miner's, DAVY
Landing place: Indian, GHAT
Language: Buddhist, PALI
  Japanese, AINU
  Latvian, LETT
Layer: Of iris, UVEA
Leaf: Palm, OLAY, OLLA
Legislature: Ukrainian, RADA
Lemur, LORI
Leopard, PARD
Let it stand, STET
Letter: Greek, BETA, IOTA, ZETA
  Hebrew, AYIN, BETH, CAPH, KOPH,
  RESH, SHIN, TETH, YODH
  Papal, BULL
Lily, ALOE
Literature: Hindu sacred, VEDA
Lizard, GILA
Loquat, BIWA
Magistrate: Genoese or Venetian, DOGE
Man (Latin), HOMO
Mark: Omission, DELE
Marmoset: South American, MICO
Meadow: Fertile, VEGA
Measure: Electric, VOLT, WATT
  Force, DYNE
  Hebrew, OMER
  Printing, PICA
  Spanish or Portuguese, VARA
  Swiss land, IMMI
Medley, OLIO
Merganser, SMEW
Milk (French), LAIT
Molding, GULA
  Curved, OGEE
Mongoose: Crab-eating, URVA
Monk: Tibetan, LAMA
Monkey: African, MONA, WAAG
  Ceylonese, MAHA
  Cochin-China, DOUC
  South American, SAKI, TITI
Monkshood, ATIS
Month: Jewish, ADAR, ELUL, IYAR
Mother (French), MERE
Mountain: Thessaly, OSSA
Mouse: Meadow, VOLE
Mythology: Norse, EDDA
Nail (French), CLOU

Native: Philippine, MORO
Nest: Of pheasants, NIDE
Network, RETE
No (German), NEIN
Noble: Islamic, AMIR
Notice: Death, OBIT
Novel: By Zola, NANA
Nursemaid: Oriental AMAH, AYAH, EYAH
Nut: Philippine, PILI
Oak: Holm, ILEX
Oil (comb. form), OLEO
Ostrich: American, RHEA
Oven, KILN, OAST
Owl: Barn, LULU
Ox: Celebes wild, ANOE
 Extinct wild, URUS
Palm, ATAP, NIPA, SAGO
Parliament, DIET
Parrot: New Zealand, KAKA
Pass: Indian mountain, GHAT
Passage: Closing (music), CODA
Peach: Clingstone, PAVY
Peasant: Indian, RYOT
 Old English, CARL
Pepper: Australasian, KAVA
Perfume, ATAR
Persia, IRAN
Person: Extraordinary, ONER
Pickerel or pike, ESOX
Pitcher, EWER
Plant: Aromatic, NARD
 Century, ALOE
 Indigo, ANIL
 Pepper, KAVA
Platform: Raised, DAIS
Plum: Wild, SLOE
Pods: Vegetable, OKRA, OKRO
Poem: Epic, EPOS
Poet: Persian, OMAR
 Roman, OVID
Poison, BANE
 Arrow, INEE
Porkfish, SISI
Portico: Greek, STOA
Premium, AGIO
Priest: Islamic, IMAM
Prima donna, DIVA
Prong: Fork, TINE
Pseudonym: Lamb's, ELIA
Queen: Carthaginian, DIDO
 Hindu, RANI
Rabbit, CONY
Race: Of Japan, AINU
Rail: Ducklike, COOT
 North American, SORA
Redshank, CLEE
Refuse: After pressing, MARC
Regiment: Turkish, ALAI
Reliquary, ARCA
Resort: Italian, LIDO
Ridges: Sandy, ASAR, OSAR
River: German, ELBE, ODER
 Italian, ADDA
 Siberian, LENA
Road: Roman, ITER

Abode of dead: Babylonian, ARALU
Aborigine: Borneo, DAYAK
Aftersong, EPODE
Aloe, AGAVE
Animal: Footless, APODE
Ant, EMMET
Antelope: African, ADDAX, BEISA,
 CAAMA, ELAND, GUIBA, ORIBI,
 TIANG
 Goat, GORAL, SEROW
 Indian, SASIN
 Siberian, SAIGA
Arch: Pointed, OGIVE
Armadillo, APARA, POYOU, TATOU
Arrowroot, ARARU
Artery: Trunk, AORTA
Association: Russian, ARTEL
 Secret, CABAL
Author: English, READE

Rockfish: California, RENA
Rodent: Mouselike, VOLE
 South American, PACA
Rootstock, TARO
Salamander, NEWT
Salmon: Silver, COHO
 Young, PARR
Same (Greek), HOMO
 (Latin), IDEM
Sauce: Fish, ALEC
School: English, ETON
Seaweed, AGAR, ALGA, KELP
Secular, LAIC
Sediment, SILT
Seed: Dill, ANET
 Of vetch, TARE
Serf, ILOT
Sesame, TEEL
Settlement: Eskimo, ETAH
Shark: Atlantic, GATA
 European, TOPE
Sheep: Wild, UDAD
Sheltered, ALEE
Shield, EGIS
Ship: Jason's, ARGO
 Left side of, PORT
 Two-masted, BRIG
Shrine: Buddhist, TOPE
Shrub: New Zealand, TUTU
Sign: Magic, RUNE
Silkworm, ERIA
Skin: Beaver, PLEW
Skink: Egyptian, ADDA
Slave, ESNE
Sloth: Two-toed, UNAU
Smooth, LENE
Snow: Glacial, NEVE
Soapstone, TALC
Society: African secret, EGBO, PORO
Son: Of Seth, ENOS
Song (German), LIED
 Unaccompanied, GLEE
Sound: Lung, RALE
Sour, ACID
Sow: Young, GILT
Spike: Brad-shaped, BROB
Spirit: Buddhist evil, MARA
Stake: Poker, ANTE
Star: Temporary, NOVA
Starch: East Indian, SAGO
Stone: Precious, OPAL
Strap: Bridle, REIN
Strewn (heraldry), SEME
Sweetsop, ATES, ATTA
Sword: Fencing, EPEE, FOIL
Tambourine: African, TAAR
Tapir: Brazilian, ANTA
Tax, CESS
Tea: South American, MATE
Therefore (Latin), ERGO
Thing: Extraordinary, ONER
Three (dice, cards, etc.), TREY
Thrush: Hawaiian, OMAO
Tide, NEAP

Tipster: Racing, TOUT
Tissue, TELA
Title: Etruscan, LARS
 Hindu, BABU
 Indian, RAJA
 Islamic, EMIR, IMAM
 Persian, BABA
 Spanish, DONA
 Turkish, AGHA, BABA
Toad: Largest-known, AGUA
 Tree, HYLA
Tool: Cutting, ADZE
Track: Deer, SLOT
Tract: Sandy, DENE
Tree: Apple, SORB
 Central American, EBOE
 East Indian, TEAK
 Eucalyptus, YATE
 Guyanese and Trinidadian, MORA
 Javanese, UPAS
 Linden, LIME, LINN, TEIL, TILL
 Sandarac, ARAR
 Sassafras, AGUE
 Tamarisk salt, ATLE
Tribe: Moro, SULU
Trout, CHAR
Vessel: Arab, DHOW
Vestment: Ecclesiastical, COPE
Vetch, TARE
Vine: East Indian, SOMA
Violinist: Famous, AUER
Vortex, EDDY
Wampum, PEAG
Wapiti, STAG
Waste: Allowance for, TRET
Watchman: Indian, MINA
Water (Spanish), AGUA
Waterfall, LINN
Wavy (heraldry), ONDE, UNDE
Wax, CERE
 Chinese, PELA
Weed: Biblical, TARE
Weight: Ancient, MINA
 Danish (pl.), ESER
 East Asian, TAEL
 Greek, MINA
 Siamese, BAHT
 Well done (rare), EUGE
Whale, CETE
 Killer, ORCA
 White, HUSE, HUSO
Whirlpool, EDDY
Wife: Of Geraint, ENID
Willow: Virginia, ITEA
Wine, PORT
Winged, ALAR
 (Heraldry), AILE
Wings, ALAE
Withered, SERE
Without (French), SANS
Wool: To comb, CARD
Work, OPUS
Wrong: Civil, TORT
Young: Bring forth, YEAN

Words of Five Letters

Automaton, GOLEM, ROBOT
Award: Motion-picture, OSCAR
Basket: Fishing, CREEL
Beer: Russian, KVASS
Bible: Islamic, KORAN, QUR'AN
Bird: Asian, MINAH, MYNAH
 Indian, SHAMA
 Larklike, PIPIT
 Loonlike, GREBE
 Oscine, VIREO
 South American, AGAMI
 Swimming, GREBE
Black: (French), NOIRE
 (Heraldry), SABLE
Blackbird: European, MERLE, OUSEL,
 OUZEL
Block: Glacial, SERAC
Blue (heraldry), AZURE
Boat: Eskimo, BIDAR, UMIAK

Bobwhite, COLIN, QUAIL
Bone (comb. form), OSTEO
 Leg, TIBIA
 Thigh, FEMUR
Broom: Twig, BESOM
Brother (French), FRERE
 Moses, AARON
Canoe: Eskimo, BIDAR, KAYAK
Cape: Papal, FANON, ORALE
Caravansary, SERAI
Card: Old playing, TAROT
Caterpillar: New Zealand, AWETO
Catkin, AMENT
Cavity: Stone, GEODE
Cephalopod, SQUID
Cetacean, WHALE
Chariot, ESSED
Cheek: Pertaining to, MALAR
Chieftain: Arab, EMEER

Child (Scottish), BAIRN
Cigar, CLARO
Coating: Seed, TESTA
Cockatoo: Palm, ARARA
Coin: Costa Rican, COLON
  Danish, KRONE
  Ecuadorian, SUCRE
  English, GROAT, PENCE
  French, FRANC
  German, KRONE, TALER
  Hungarian, PENGO
  Icelandic, KRONA
  Indian, RUPEE
  Iraqi, DINAR
  Norwegian, KRONE
  Polish, ZLOTY
  Russian, COPEC, KOPEK, RUBLE
  Swedish, KRONA
  Turkish, ASPER
  Yugoslav, DINAR
Collar: Papal, FANON, ORALE
  Roman, RABAT
Commune: Italian, TREIA
Composition: Choral, MOTET
Compound: Chemical, ESTER
Conceal (law), ELOIN
Council: Ecclesiastical, SYNOD
Court: Anglo-Saxon, GEMOT
  Inner, PATIO
Crest: Mountain, ARETE
Crown: Papal, TIARA
Cuttlefish, SEPIA
Date: Roman, NONES
Decree: Islamic, IRADE
  Russian, UKASE
Deposit: Loam, LOESS
Desert: Gobi, SHAMO
Devilfish, MANTA
Disease: Cereals, ERGOT
Disk, PATEN
Dog: Wild, DHOLE, DINGO
Dormouse, LEROT
Drum, TABOR
Duck: Sea, EIDER
Dynasty: Chinese, CHING, LIANG,
  SHANG
Earthquake, SEISM
Eel, ELVER, MORAY
Ermine: European, STOAT
Ether: Crystalline, APIOL
Fabric: Velvetlike, PANNE
Fabulist, AESOP
Family: Italian, CENCI
Fiber: West Indian, SISAL
Fig: Smyrna, ELEME, ELEMI
Figure: Of speech, TROPE
Finch: European, SERIN
Fish: American small, KILLY
Flower: Garden, ASTER
Friend (Spanish), AMIGO
Fruit: Tropical, MANGO
Fungus: Rye, ERGOT
Furze, GORSE
Gateway, TORAN, TORII
Gem, AGATE, BERYL, PEARL, TOPAZ
Genus: Barnacles, LEPAS
  Bears, URSUS
  Birds (loons), GAVIA
  Birds (nuthatches), SITTA
  Cats, FELIS
  Dogs, CANIS
  Fishes (chiros), ELOPS
  Fishes (perch), PERCA
  Geese, ANSER
  Grasses, STIPA
  Grasses (incl. oats), AVENA
  Gulls, LARUS
  Hares, rabbits, LEPUS
  Hawks, BUTEO
  Herbs, old world, INULA
  Herbs, trailing or climbing, APIOS
  Herbs, tropical, TACCA, URENA
  Horses, EQUUS
  Insects (olive flies), DACUS
  Lice, plant, APHIS
  Lichens, USNEA

Lizards, AGAMA
Moles, TALPA
Mollusks, OLIVA
Monkeys, CEBUS
Palms, ARECA
Pigeons, GOURA
Plants (amaryllis family), AGAVE
Ruminants (goats), CAPRA
Shrubs, Asiatic, SABIA
Shrubs (heath), ERICA
Shrubs (incl. raspberry), RUBUS
Shrubs, tropical, IXORA, TREMA,
  URENA
Ticks, ARGAS
Trees (of elm family), TREMA, ULMUS
Trees, tropical, IXORA, TREMA
Goat: Bezoar, PASAN
God: Assyrian, ASHIR, ASHUR, ASSUR
  Babylonian, DAGAN, SIRIS
  Gaelic, DAGDA
  Hindu, BHAGA, INDRA, SHIVA
  Japanese, EBISU
  Philistine, DAGON
  Phrygian, ATTIS
  Teutonic, AEGIR, GYMIR
  Welsh, DYLAN
Goddess: Babylonian, ISTAR, NANAI
  Hindu, DURGA, GAURI, SHREE
Group: Of six, HEXAD
Grove: Sacred to Diana, NEMUS
Growing out, ENATE
Guitar: Hindu, SITAR
Gull: PEWEE, PEWIT
Hartebeest, CAAMA
Headdress: Jewish or Persian, TIARA
  Liturgical, MITER, MITRE
Heath, ERICA
Herb: Grasslike marsh, SEDGE
Heron, EGRET
Hog: Young, SHOAT, SHOTE
Image, EIKON
Indian: Cariban, ARARA
  Iroquoian, HURON
  Mexican, AZTEC, OPATA, OTOMI
  Muskhogean, CREEK
  Siouan, OSAGE, TETON
  Spanish American, ARARA, CARIB
Inflorescence: Racemose, AMENT
Insect: Immature, LARVA
Intrigue, CABAL
Iris: Yellow, SEDGE
Juniper, GORSE, RETEM
Kidneys: Pertaining to, RENAL
King: British legendary, LLUDD
Kite: European, GLEDE
Kobold, NISSE
Land: Cultivated, ARADA, ARADO
Landholder (Scottish), LAIRD, THANE
Language: Dravidian, TAMIL
Lariat, LASSO, REATA
Laughing, RIANT
Lawgiver: Athenian, DRACO, SOLON
Leaf: Calyx, SEPAL
  Fern, FROND
Lemur, LORIS
Letter: English, AITCH
  Greek, ALPHA, DELTA, GAMMA,
    KAPPA, OMEGA, SIGMA, THETA
  Hebrew, ALEPH, CHETH, GIMEL,
    SADHE, ZAYIN
Lichen, USNEA
Lighthouse, PHARE
Lizard: Old World, AGAMA
Loincloth, DHOTI
Louse: Plant, APHID
Macaw: Brazilian, ARARA
Mahogany: Philippine, ALMON
Mammal: Badgerlike, RATEL
  Civetlike, GENET
  Giraffelike, OKAPI
  Raccoonlike, COATI
Man (French), HOMME
Marble, AGATE
Mark: Insertion, CARET
Market place: Greek, AGORA
Marsupial: Australian, KOALA

Measure: Electric, FARAD, HENRY
  Energy, JOULE
  Metric, LITER, STERE
  Printing, AGATE
  Russian, VERST
Mixture: Smelting, MATTE
Mohicans: Last of, UNCAS
Molding: Convex, OVOLO, TORUS
Mole, TALPA
Monkey: African, PATAS
  Capuchin, SAJOU
  Howling, ARABA
Monkshood, ATEES
Month: Jewish, NISAN, SIVAN, TEBET
Museum (French), MUSEE
Musketeer, ATHOS
Native: Aleutian, ALEUT
  New Zealand, MAORI
Neckpiece: Ecclesiastical, AMICE
Nerve (comb. form), NEURO
Nest: Eagle's or hawk's, AERIE
  Insect's, NIDUS
Net: Fishing, SEINE
Newsstand, KIOSK
Nitrogen, AZOTE
Noble: Islamic, AMEER
Nodule: Stone, GEODE
Nostrils, NARES
Notched irregularly, EROSE
Nymph: Islamic, HOURI
Official: Roman, EDILE
Oleoresin, ELEMI
Opening: Mouthlike, STOMA
Oration: Funeral, ELOGE
Ostiole, STOMA
Page: Left-hand, VERSO
  Right-hand, RECTO
Palm, ARECA, BETEL
Park: Colorado, ESTES
Perfume, ATTAR
Philosopher: Greek, PLATO
Pillar: Stone, STELA, STELE
Pinnacle: Glacial, SERAC
Plain, LLANO
Plant: Century, AGAVE
  Climbing, LIANA
  Dwarf, CUMIN
  East Asian perennial, RAMIE
  Medicinal, SENNA
  Mustard family, CRESS
Plate: Communion, PATEN
Poem: Lyric, EPODE
Point: Lowest, NADIR
Poplar, ABELE, ALAMO, ASPEN
Porridge: Spanish American, ATOLE
Post: Stair, NEWEL
Priest: Islamic, IMAUM
Protozoan, AMEBA
Queen: (French), REINE
  Hindu, RANEE
Rabbit, CONEY
Rail, CRAKE
Red (heraldry), GULES
Religion: Moslem, Muslim, ISLAM
Resin, ELEMI
Revoke (law), ADEEM
Rich man, MIDAS, NABOB
Ridge: Sandy, ESKAR, ESKER
River: French, LOIRE, SEINE
Rockfish: California, REINA
Rootstock: Fragrant, ORRIS
Ruff: Female, REEVE
Sack: Pack, KYACK
Salt: Ethereal, ESTER
Saltpeter, NITER, NITRE
Salutation: Eastern, SALAM
Sandpiper: Old World, TEREK
Scented, OLENT
School: Fish, SHOAL
  French public, LYCEE
Scriptures: Islamic, KORAN
Seaweeds, ALGAE
Seed: Aromatic, ANISE
Seraglio, HAREM, SERAI
Serf, HELOT
Sheep: Wild, AUDAD

Sheeplike, OVINE
Shield, AEGIS
Shoe: Wooden, SABOT
Shoots: Pickled bamboo, ACHAR
Shot: Billiard, CAROM, MASSE
Shrine: Buddhist, STUPA
Shrub: Burning bush, WAHOO
   Ornamental evergreen, TOYON
   Used in tanning, SUMAC
Silk: Watered, MOIRE
Sister (French), SOEUR
   (Latin), SOROR
Six: Group of, HEXAD
Skeleton: Marine, CORAL
Slave, HELOT
Snake, ABOMA, ADDER, COBRA,
   RACER
Soldier: French, POILU
   Indian, SEPOY
Sour, ACERB
Spirit: Air, ARIEL
Staff: Shepherd's, CROOK
Starwort, ASTER
Steel (German), STAHL
Stockade: Russian, ETAPE

Stop (nautical), AVAST
Storehouse, ETAPE
Subway: Parisian, METRO
Tapestry, ARRAS
Tea: Paraguayan, YERBA
Temple: Hawaiian, HEIAU
Terminal: Positive, ANODE
Theater: Greek, ODEON, ODEUM
Then (French), ALORS
Thread: Surgical, SETON
Thrush: Wilson's, VEERY
Title: Hindu, BABOO
   Indian, RAJAH, SAHEB, SAHIB
   Islamic, EMEER, IMAUM
Tree: Buddhist sacred, PIPAL
   East Indian cotton, SIMAL
   Hickory, PECAN
   Light-wooded, BALSA
   Malayan, TERAP
   Mediterranean, CAROB
   Mexican, ABETO
   Mexican pine, OCOTE
   New Zealand, MAIRE
   Philippine, ALMON
   Rain, SAMAN

South American, UMBRA
Tamarack, LARCH
Tamarisk salt, ATLEE
West Indian, ACANA
Trout, CHARR
Troy, ILION, ILIUM
Twin: Siamese, CHANG
Vestment: Ecclesiastical, STOLE
Violin: Famous, AMATI, STRAD
Volcano: Mud, SALSE
Wampum, PEAGE
War cry: Greek, ALALA
Wavy (heraldry), UNDEE
Weight: Jewish, GERAH
Wen, TALPA
Wheat, SPELT
Wheel: Persian water, NORIA
Whitefish, CISCO
Willow, OSIER
Window: Bay, ORIEL
Wine, MEDOC, RHINE, TINTA, TOKAY
Winged, ALATE
Woman (French), FEMME
Year: Excess of solar over lunar, EPACT
Zoroastrian, PARSI

Words of Six or More Letters

Agave, MAGUEY
Alkaloid: Crystalline, ESERIN, ESERINE
Alligator, CAYMAN
Amphibole, EDENITE, URALITE
Ant: White, TERMITE
Antelope: African, DIKDIK, DUIKER,
   GEMSBOK, IMPALA, KOODOO
   European, CHAMOIS
   Indian, NILGAI, NILGAU, NILGHAI,
   NILGHAU
Ape: Asian or East Indian, GIBBON
Appendage: Leaf, STIPEL, STIPULE
Armadillo: PELUDO, TATOUAY
Arrowroot, ARARAO
Ascetic: Jewish, ESSENE
Ass: Asian wild, ONAGER
Avatar: Of Vishnu, KRISHNA
Babylonian, ELAMITE
Badge: Shoulder, EPAULET
Baldness, ALOPECIA
Barracuda, SENNET
Bark: Aromatic, SINTOC
Bearlike, URSINE
Beetle, ELATER
Bible: Zoroastrian, AVESTA
Bird: Sea, PETREL
   South American, SERIEMA
   Wading, AVOCET, AVOSET
Bone: Leg, FIBULA
Branched, RAMATE
Brother (Latin), FRATER
Bunting: European, ORTOLAN
Call: Trumpet, SENNET
Canoe: Eskimo, BAIDAR, OOMIAK
Caravansary, IMARET
Cat: Asian or African, CHEETAH
   Leopardlike, OCELOT
Cenobite: Jewish, ESSENE
Centerpiece: Table, EPERGNE
Cetacean, DOLPHIN, PORPOISE
Chariot, ESSEDA, ESSEDE
Chief: Seminole, OSCEOLA
Claim: Release as (law), REMISE
Clock: Water, CLEPSYDRA
Cloud, CUMULUS, NIMBUS
Coach: French hackney, FIACRE
Coin: Czech, KORUNA
   Dutch, GUILDER
   Ethiopian, TALARI
   Finnish, MARKKA
   German, THALER
   Greek, DRACHMA
   Haitian, GOURDE
   Honduran, LEMPIRA
   Hungarian, FORINT
   Indo-Chinese, PIASTER
   Panamanian, BALBOA
   Paraguayan, GUARANI
   Portuguese, ESCUDO

Russian, COPECK, KOPECK,
   ROUBLE
   Spanish, PESETA
   Venezuelan, BOLIVAR
Communion: Last holy, VIATICUM
Conceal (law), ELOIGN
Confection, PRALINE
Construction: Sentence, SYNTAX
Convexity: Shaft of column, ENTASIS
Court: Anglo-Saxon, GEMOTE
Cow: Sea, DUGONG, MANATEE
Cylindrical, TERETE
Dagger, STILETTO
   Malay, CREESE, KREESE
Date: Roman, CALENDS, KALENDS
Deer, CARIBOU, WAPITI
Disease: Plant, ERINOSE
Doorkeeper, OSTIARY
Dragonflies: Order of, ODANATA
Drink: Of gods, NECTAR
Drum: TABOUR
   Moorish, ATABAL, ATTABAL
Duck: Fish-eating, MERGANSER
   Sea, SCOTER
Dynasty: Chinese, MANCHU
Eel, CONGER
Edit, REDACT
Envelope: Flower, PERIANTH
Eskimo, AMERIND
Ether: Crystalline, APIOLE
Excuse (law), ESSOIN
Eyespots, OCELLI
Fabric, ESTAMENE, ESTAMIN,
   ETAMINE
Falcon: European, KESTREL
Figure: Used as column, CARYATID,
   TELAMON
Fine: For punishment, AMERCE
Fish: Asian fresh-water, GOURAMI
   Pikelike, BARRACUDA
Five: Group of, PENTAD
Fly: African, TSETSE
Foot: Metric, ANAPEST, IAMBUS
Foxlike, VULPINE
Frying pan, SPIDER
Fur, KARAKUL
Galley: Greek or Roman, BIREME,
   TRIREME
Game: Card, ECARTE
Garment: Greek, CHLAMYS
Gateway: Greek, GOPURA, TORANA
Genus: Birds (ravens, crows), CORVUS
   Eels, CONGER
   Fishes, ANABAS
   Foxes, VULPES
   Herbs, ANEMONE
   Insects, CICADA
   Lemurs, GALAGO
   Mints (incl. catnip), NEPETA

Mollusks, ANOMIA, ASTARTE,
   TEREDO
Mollusks (incl. oysters), OSTREA
Monkeys (spider monkeys), ATELES
Thrushes (incl. robins), TURDUS
Trees (of elm family), CELTIS
Trees (inc. dogwood), CORNUS
Trees, tropical American, SAPOTA
Wrens, NANNUS
Gibbon, SIAMANG, WOUWOU
Gland: Salivary, RACEMOSE
Goat: Bezoar, PASANG
Goatlike, CAPRINE
God: Assyrian, ASHSHUR, ASSHUR
   Babylonian, BABBAR, MARDUK,
   MERODACH, NANNAR, NERGAL,
   SHAMASH
   Hindu, BRAHMA, KRISHNA, VISHNU
   Tahitian, TAAROA
Goddess: Babylonian, ISHTAR
   Hindu, CHANDI, HAIMAVATI,
   LAKSHMI, PARVATI, SARASVATI,
   SARASWATI
Government, POLITY
Governor: Persian, SATRAP
Grandson (Scottish), NEPOTE
Group: Of five, PENTAD
   Of nine, ENNEAD
   Of seven, HEPTAD
Hare: in first year, LEVERET
Harpsichord, SPINET
Herb: Alpine, EDELWEISS
   Chinese, GINSENG
   South African, FREESIA
Hermit, EREMITE
Hero: Legendary, PALADIN
Heron, BITTERN
Horselike, EQUINE
Hound: Short-legged, BEAGLE
House (French), MAISON
Idiot, CRETIN
Implement: Stone, NEOLITH
Incarnation: Hindu, AVATAR
Indian, APACHE, COMANCHE, PAIUTE,
   SENECA
Inn: Turkish, IMARET
Insects: Order of, DIPTERA
Instrument: Japanese banjolike,
   SAMISEN
   Musical, CLAVIER, SPINET
Interstice, AREOLA
Ironwood, COLIMA
Juniper: Old Testament, RAETAM
Kettledrum, ATABAL
King: Fairy, OBERON
Kneecap, PATELLA
Knife, MACHETE
Langur: Sumatran, SIMPAI
Legislature: Spanish, CORTES

Lemur: African, GALAGO
  Madagascar, AYEAYE
Letter: Greek, EPSILON, LAMBDA,
  OMICRON, UPSILON
  Hebrew, DALETH, LAMEDH, SAMEKH
Lighthouse, PHAROS
Lizard, IGUANA
Llama, ALPACA
Lockjaw, TETANUS
Locust, CICADA, CICALA
Macaw: Brazilian, MARACAN
Maid: Of Astolat, ELAINE
Mammal: Madagascar, TENDRAC,
  TENREC
Man (Spanish), HOMBRE
Marmoset: South American, TAMARIN
Marsupial, BANDICOOT, WOMBAT
Massacre, POGROM
Mayor: Spanish, ALCALDE
Measure: Electric, AMPERE, COULOMB,
  KILOWATT
Medicine: Quack, NOSTRUM
Member: Religious order, CENOBITE
Molasses, TREACLE
Monkey: African, GRIVET, NISNAS
  Asian, LANGUR
  Philippine, MACHIN
  South American, PINCHE, SAIMIRI,
  SAMIRI, SAPAJOU
Monster, CHIMERA, GORGON
  (Comb. form), TERATO
  Cretan, MINOTAUR
Month: Jewish, HESHVAN, KISLEV,
  SHEBAT, TAMMUZ, TISHRI, VEADAR
Mountain: Asia Minor, ARARAT
Mulct, AMERCE
Musketeer, ARAMIS, PORTHOS
Nearsighted, MYOPIC
Net, TRAMMEL
New York City, GOTHAM
Nine: Group of, ENNEAD
Nobleman: Spanish, GRANDEE
Official: Roman, AEDILE
Onyx: Mexican, TECALI
Order: Dragonflies, ODANATA
  Insects, DIPTERA
Organ: Plant, PISTIL

Ornament: Shoulder, EPAULET
Overcoat: Military, CAPOTE
Ox: Wild, BANTENG
Oxidation: Bronze or copper, PATINA
Paralysis: Incomplete, PARESIS
Pear: Alligator, AVOCADO
Persimmon: Mexican, CHAPOTE
Pipe: Peace, CALUMET
Plaid (Scottish), TARTAN
Plain, PAMPAS, STEPPE, TUNDRA
Plant: Buttercup family, ANEMONE
  Century, MAGUEY
  On rocks, LICHEN
Plowing: Fit for, ARABLE
Poem: Heroic, EPOPEE
  Six-lined, SESTET
Point: Highest, ZENITH
Potion: Love, PHILTER, PHILTRE
Protozoan, AMOEBA
Punish, AMERCE
Purple (heraldry), PURPURE
Queen: Fairy, TITANIA
Race: Skiing, SLALOM
Rat, BANDICOOT, SAPOTE
Retort, RIPOST, RIPOSTE
Ring: Harness, TERRET
  Little, ANNULET
Rodent: Jumping, JERBOA
  Spanish American, AGOUTI, AGOUTY
Sailor: East Indian, LASCAR
Salmon: Young, GRILSE
Salutation: Eastern, SALAAM
Sandpiper, PLOVER
Sandy, ARENOSE
Sapodilla, SAPOTA, SAPOTE
Saw: Surgical, TREPAN
Seven: Group of, HEPTAD
Sexes: Common to both, EPICENE
Shawl: Mexican, SERAPE
Sheathing: Flower, SPATHE
Sheep: Wild, AOUDAD, ARGALI
Shipworm, TEREDO
Shoes: Mercury's winged, TALARIA
Shortening: Syllable, SYSTOLE
Shrub, SPIRAEA
Sickle-shaped, FALCATE

Silver (heraldry), ARGENT
Snake, ANACONDA
Speech: Loss of, APHASIA
Spiral, HELICAL
Staff: Bishop's, CROSIER, CROZIER
Stalk: Plant, PETIOLE
State: Swiss, CANTON
Studio, ATELIER
Swan: Young, CYGNET
Swimming, NATANT
Sword-shaped, ENSATE
Terminal: Negative, CATHODE
Third (music), TIERCE
Thrust: Fencing, RIPOST, RIPOSTE
Tile: Pertaining to, TEGULAR
Tomb: Empty, CENOTAPH
Tooth (comb. form), ODONTO
Tower: Islamic, MINARET
Tree: African timber, BAOBAB
  Black gum, TUPELO
  East Indian, MARGOSA
  Locust, ACACIA
  Malayan, SINTOC
  Marmalade, SAPOTE
Urn: Tea, SAMOVAR
Vehicle, LANDAU, TROIKA
Verbose, PROLIX
Viceroy: Egyptian, KHEDIVE
Vulture: American, CONDOR
Warehouse (French), ENTREPOT
Whale: White, BELUGA
Whirlpool, VORTEX
Will: Addition to, CODICIL
  Having left, TESTATE
Wind, CHINOOK, MONSOON, SIMOOM,
  SIMOON, SIROCCO
Window: In roof, DORMER
Wine, BARBERA, BURGUNDY,
  CABERNET, CHABLIS, CHIANTI,
  CLARET, MUSCATEL, RIESLING,
  SAUTERNE, SHERRY, ZINFANDEL
Wolfish, LUPINE
Woman: Boisterous, TERMAGANT
Woolly, LANATE
Workshop, ATELIER
Zoroastrian, PARSEE

Old Testament Names

We do not pretend that this list is all-inclusive. We list only those names that occur most often in crossword puzzles.

Aaron: First high priest of Jews; son of Amram; brother of Miriam and Moses; father of Abihu, Eleazer, Ithamar, and Nadab.
Abel: Son of Adam and Eve; slain by Cain.
Abigail: Wife of Nabal; later, wife of David.
Abihu: Son of Aaron.
Abimelech: King of Gerar.
Abner: Commander of army of Saul and Ishbosheth; slain by Joab.
Abraham (or Abram): Patriarch; forefather of the Jews; son of Terah; husband of Sarah; father of Isaac and Ishmael.
Absalom: Son of David and Maacah; revolted against David; slain by Joab.
Achish: King of Gath; gave refuge to David.
Achsa (or Achsah): Daughter of Caleb; wife of Othniel.
Adah: Wife of Lamech.
Adam: First man; husband of Eve; father of Cain, Abel, and Seth.
Adonijah: Son of David and Haggith.
Agag: King of Amalek; spared by Saul; slain by Samuel.
Ahasuerus: King of Persia; husband of Vashti and, later, Esther; sometimes identified with Xerxes the Great.
Ahijah: Prophet; foretold accession of Jeroboam.
Ahinoam: Wife of David.
Amasa: Commander of army of David; slain by Joab.
Amnon: Son of David and Ahinoam; raped Tamar; slain by Absalom.
Amram: Husband of Jochebed; father of Aaron, Miriam and Moses.
Asenath: Wife of Joseph.
Asher: Son of Jacob and Zilpah.

Balaam: Prophet; rebuked by his donkey for cursing God.
Barak: Jewish captain; associated with Deborah.
Baruch: Secretary to Jeremiah.
Bathsheba: Wife of Uriah; later, wife of David.
Belshazzar: Crown prince of Babylon.
Benaiah: Warrior of David; proclaimed Solomon King.
Ben-Hadad: Name of several kings of Damascus.
Benjamin: Son of Jacob and Rachel.
Bezaleel: Chief architect of Tabernacle.
Bilhah: Servant of Rachel; mistress of Jacob.
Bildad: Comforter of Job.
Boaz: Husband of Ruth; father of Obed.
Cain: Son of Adam and Eve; slayer of Abel; father of Enoch.
Cainan: Son of Enos.
Caleb: Spy sent out by Moses to visit Canaan; father of Achsa.
Canaan: Son of Ham.
Chilion: Son of Elimelech; husband of Orpah.
Cush: Son of Ham; father of Nimrod.
Dan: Son of Jacob and Bilhah.
Daniel: Prophet; saved from lions by God.
Deborah: Hebrew prophetess and judge; helped Israelites conquer Canaanites.
Delilah: Mistress and betrayer of Samson.
Elam: Son of Shem.
Eleazar: Son of Aaron; succeeded him as high priest.
Eli: High priest and judge; teacher of Samuel; father of Hophni and Phinehas.
Eliakim: Chief minister of Hezekiah.
Eliezer: Servant of Abraham.
Elihu: Comforter of Job.
Elijah (or Elias): Prophet; went to heaven in chariot of fire.

Elimelech: Husband of Naomi; father of Chilion and Mahlon.
Eliphaz: Comforter of Job.
Elisha (or Eliseus): Prophet; successor of Elijah.
Elkanah: Husband of Hannah; father of Samuel.
Enoch: Son of Cain.
Enoch: Father of Methuselah.
Enos: Son of Seth; father of Cainan.
Ephraim: Son of Joseph.
Esau: Son of Isaac and Rebecca; sold his birthright to his twin brother Jacob.
Esther: Jewish wife of Ahasuerus; saved Jews from Haman's plotting.
Eve: First woman; wife of Adam.
Ezra (or Esdras): Hebrew scribe and priest.
Gad: Son of Jacob and Zilpah.
Gehazi: Servant of Elisha.
Gideon: Israelite hero; defeated Midianites.
Goliath: Philistine giant; slain by David.
Hagar: Handmaid of Sarah; concubine of Abraham; mother of Ishmael.
Haggith: Mother of Adonijah.
Ham: Son of Noah; father of Cush, Mizraim, Phut, and Canaan.
Haman: Chief minister of Ahasuerus; hanged on gallows prepared for Mordecai.
Hannah: Wife of Elkanah; mother of Samuel.
Hanun: King of Ammonites.
Haran: Brother of Abraham; father of Lot.
Hazael: King of Damascus.
Hephzi-Bah: Wife of Hezekiah; mother of Mannaseh.
Hiram: King of Tyre.
Holofernes: General of Nebuchadnezzar; slain by Judith.
Hophni: Son of Eli.
Isaac: Hebrew patriarch; son of Abraham and Sarah; half brother of Ishmael; husband of Rebecca; father of Esau and Jacob.
Ishmael: Son of Abraham and Hagar; half brother of Isaac.
Issachar: Son of Jacob and Leah.
Ithamar: Son of Aaron.
Jabal: Son of Lamech and Adah.
Jabin: King of Hazor.
Jacob: Hebrew patriarch; founder of Israel; son of Isaac and Rebecca; husband of Leah and Rachel; father of sons Asher, Benjamin, Dan, Gad, Issachar, Joseph, Judah, Levi, Naphtali, Reuben, Simeon, and Zebulun, and daughter Dinah.
Jael: Slayer of Sisera.
Japheth: Son of Noah.
Jehoiada: High priest; husband of Jehoshabeath; revolted against Athaliah and made Joash King of Judah.
Jehoshabeath (or Jehosheba): Daughter of Jehoram of Judah; wife of Jehoiada.
Jephthah: Judge in Israel; sacrificed his only daughter because of vow.
Jesse: Son of Obed; father of David.
Jethro: Midianite priest; father of Zipporah.
Jezebel: Phoenician princess; wife of Ahab; mother of Ahaziah, Athaliah, and Jehoram.
Joab: Commander in chief under David; slayer of Abner, Absalom, and Amasa.
Job: Patriarch; underwent many afflictions; comforted by Bildad, Elihu, Eliphaz and Zophar.
Jochebed: Wife of Amram.
Jonah: Prophet; cast into sea and swallowed by great fish.
Jonathan: Son of Saul; friend of David.
Joseph: Son of Jacob and Rachel; sold into slavery by his brothers; husband of Asenath; father of Ephraim and Manassah.
Joshua: Successor of Moses; son of Nun.
Jubal: Son of Lamech and Adah.
Judah: Son of Jacob and Leah.
Judith: Slayer of Holofernes.
Kish: Father of Saul.

Laban: Father of Leah and Rachel.
Lamech: Son of Methuselah; father of Noah.
Lamech: Husband of Adah and Zillah; father of Jabal, Jubal, and Tubal-Cain.
Leah: Daughter of Laban; wife of Jacob; sister of Rachel.
Levi: Son of Jacob and Leah.
Lot: Son of Haran; escaped destruction of Sodom.
Maacah: Mother of Absalom and Tamar.
Mahlon: Son of Elimelech; first husband of Ruth.
Manasseh: Son of Joseph.
Melchizedek: King of Salem.
Methuselah: Patriarch; son of Enoch; father of Lamech.
Michal: Daughter of Saul; wife of David.
Miriam: Prophetess; daughter of Amram; sister of Aaron and Moses.
Mizraim: Son of Ham.
Mordecai: Uncle of Esther; with her aid, saved Jews from Haman's plotting.
Moses: Prophet and lawgiver; son of Amram; brother of Aaron and Miriam; husband of Zipporah.
Naaman: Syrian captain; cured of leprosy by Elisha.
Nabal: Husband of Abigail.
Naboth: Owner of vineyard; stoned to death because he would not sell it to Ahab.
Nadab: Son of Aaron.
Nahor: Father of Terah.
Naomi: Wife of Elimelech; mother-in-law of Ruth.
Naphtali: Son of Jacob and Bilhah.
Nathan: Prophet; reproved David for causing Uriah's death.
Nebuchadnezzar (or Nebuchadrezzar): King of Babylon; destroyer of Jerusalem.
Nehemiah: Jewish leader; empowered by Artaxerxes to rebuild Jerusalem.
Nimrod: Mighty hunter; son of Cush.
Noah: Patriarch; son of Lamech; escaped Deluge by building Ark; father of Ham, Japheth and Shem.
Nun (or Non): Father of Joshua.
Obed: Son of Boaz; father of Jesse.
Og: King of Bashan.
Orpah: Wife of Chilion.
Othniel: Kenezite; judge of Israel; husband of Achsa.
Phinehas: Son of Eleazer.
Phinehas: Son of Eli.
Phut (or Put): Son of Ham.
Potiphar: Egyptian official; bought Joseph.
Rachel: Wife of Jacob; mother of Joseph; sister of Leah.
Rebecca (or Rebekah): Wife of Isaac; mother of Esau and Jacob.
Reuben: Son of Jacob and Leah.
Ruth: Wife of Mahlon, later of Boaz; daughter-in-law of Naomi.
Samson: Judge of Israel; famed for strength; betrayed by Delilah.
Samuel: Hebrew judge and prophet; son of Elkanah.
Sarah (or Sara, Sarai): Wife of Abraham; mother of Isaac.
Sennacherib: King of Assyria.
Seth: Son of Adam; father of Enos.
Shem: Son of Noah; father of Elam.
Simeon: Son of Jacob and Leah.
Sisera: Canaanite captain; slain by Jael.
Tamar: Daughter of David and Maachah; raped by Amnon.
Terah: Son of Nahor; father of Abraham.
Tubal-Cain: Son of Lamech and Zillah.
Uriah: Husband of Bathsheba; sent to death in battle by David.
Vashti: Wife of Ahasuerus; set aside by him.
Zadok: High priest during David's reign.
Zebulun (or Zabulon): Son of Jacob and Leah.
Zillah: Wife of Lamech.
Zilpah: Servant of Leah; mistress of Jacob.
Zipporah: Daughter of Jethro; wife of Moses.
Zophar: Comforter of Job.

Kings of Judah and Israel

Kings Before Division of Kingdom

Saul: First King of Israel; son of Kish; father of Ish-Bosheth, Jonathan and Michal.
Ish-Bosheth (or Eshbaal): King of Israel; son of Saul.
David: King of Judah; later of Israel; son of Jesse; husband of Abigail, Ahinoam, Bathsheba, Michal, etc.; father of Absalom, Adonijah, Amnon, Solomon, Tamar, etc.
Solomon: King of Israel and Judah; son of David; father of Rehoboam.
Rehoboam: Son of Solomon; during his reign the kingdom was divided into Judah and Israel.

Kings of Judah (Southern Kingdom)

Rehoboam: First King.
Abijah (or Abijam or Abia): Son of Rehoboam.
Asa: Probably son of Abijah.
Jehoshaphat: Son of Asa.
Jehoram (or Joram): Son of Jehoshaphat; husband of Athaliah.
Ahaziah: Son of Jehoram and Athaliah.
Athaliah: Daughter of King Ahab of Israel and Jezebel; wife of Jehoram; only queen to occupy the throne of Judah.
Joash (or Jehoash): Son of Ahaziah.

Amaziah: Son of Joash.
Uzziah (or Azariah): Son of Amaziah.
Jotham: Regent, later King; son of Uzziah.
Ahaz: Son of Jotham.
Hezekiah: Son of Ahaz; husband of Hephzi-Bah.
Manasseh: Son of Hezekiah and Hephzi-Bah.
Amon: Son of Manasseh.
Josiah (or Josias): Son of Amon.
Jehoahaz (or Joahaz): Son of Josiah.
Jehoiakim: Son of Josiah.
Jehoiachin: Son of Jehoiakim.
Zedekiah: Son of Josiah; kingdom overthrown by Babylonians under Nebuchadnezzar.

Kings of Israel (Northern Kingdom)

Jeroboam I: Led secession of Israel.
Nadab: Son of Jeroboam I.
Baasha: Overthrew Nadab.
Elah: Son of Baasha.
Zimri: Overthrew Elah.
Omri: Overthrew Zimri.

Ahab: Son of Omri; husband of Jezebel.
Ahaziah: Son of Ahab.
Jehoram (or Joram): Son of Ahab.
Jehu: Overthrew Jehoram.
Jehoahaz (or Joahaz): Son of Jehu.
Jehoash (or Joash): Son of Jehoahaz.
Jeroboam II: Son of Jehoash.
Zechariah: Son of Jeroboam II.
Shallum: Overthrew Zechariah.
Menahem: Overthrew Shallum.
Pekahiah: Son of Menahem.
Pekah: Overthrew Pekahiah.
Hoshea: Overthrew Pekah; kingdom overthrown by Assyrians under Sargon II.

Prophets

Major. Isaiah, Jeremiah, Ezekiel, Daniel.
Minor. Hosea, Obadiah, Nahum, Haggai, Joel, Jonah, Habakkuk, Zechariah, Amos, Micah, Zephaniah, Malachi.

Greek and Roman Mythology

Most of the Greek deities were adopted by the Romans, although in many cases there was a change of name. In the list below, information is given under the Greek name; the name in parentheses is the Roman equivalent. However, all Latin names are listed with cross-references to the Greek ones. In addition, there are several deities that are exclusively Roman. **Bold** words within entries indicate cross references.

Acheron: One of several **Rivers of Underworld.**
Achilles: Greek warrior; slew Hector at Troy; slain by Paris, who wounded him in his vulnerable heel.
Actaeon: Hunter; surprised Artemis bathing; changed by her to stag; and killed by his dogs.
Admetus: King of Thessaly; his wife, Alcestis, offered to die in his place.
Adonis: Beautiful youth loved by Aphrodite.
Aeacus: One of three judges of dead in Hades; son of Zeus.
Aeëtes: King of Colchis; father of Medea; keeper of Golden Fleece.
Aegeus: Father of Theseus; believing Theseus killed in Crete, he drowned himself; Aegean Sea named for him.
Aegisthus: Son of Thyestes; with Clytemnestra, his paramour, slew Agamemnon; slain by Orestes.
Aegyptus: Brother of Danaus; his sons, except Lynceus, slain by Danaides.
Aeneas: Trojan; son of Anchises and Aphrodite; after fall of Troy, led his followers eventually to Italy; loved and deserted Dido.
Aeolus: One of several **Winds.**
Aesculapius: *See* Asclepius.
Aeson: King of Ioclus; father of Jason; overthrown by his brother Pelias; restored to youth by Medea.
Aether: Personification of sky.
Aethra: Mother of Theseus.
Agamemnon: King of Mycenae; son of Atreus; brother of Menelaus; leader of Greeks against Troy; slain on his return home by Clytemnestra and Aegisthus.
Aglaia: One of several **Graces.**
Ajax: Greek warrior; killed himself at Troy because Achilles's armor was awarded to Odysseus.
Alcestis: Wife of Admetus; offered to die in his place but saved from death by Hercules.
Alcmene: Wife of Amphitryon; mother by Zeus of Hercules.
Alcyone: One of several **Pleiades.**
Alecto: One of several **Furies.**
Alectryon: Youth changed by Ares into cock.
Althaea: Wife of Oeneus; mother of Meleager.
Amazons: Female warriors in Asia Minor; supported Troy against Greeks.
Amor: *See* Eros.
Amphion: Musician; husband of Niobe; charmed stones to build fortifications for Thebes.
Amphitrite: Sea goddess; wife of Poseidon.
Amphitryon: Husband of Alcmene.
Anchises: Father of Aeneas.
Ancile: Sacred shield that fell from heavens; palladium of Rome.
Andraemon: Husband of Dryope.
Andromache: Wife of Hector.
Andromeda: Daughter of Cepheus; chained to cliff for monster to devour; rescued by Perseus.
Anteia: Wife of Proetus; tried to induce Bellerophon to elope with her.
Anteros: God who avenged unrequited love.

Antigone: Daughter of Oedipus; accompanied him to Colonus; performed burial rite for Polynices and hanged herself.
Antinoüs: Leader of suitors of Penelope; slain by Odysseus.
Aphrodite (Venus): Goddess of love and beauty; daughter of Zeus and Dione; mother of Eros.
Apollo: God of beauty, poetry, music; later identified with Helios as Phoebus Apollo; son of Zeus and Leto.
Aquilo: One of several **Winds.**
Arachne: Maiden who challenged Athena to weaving contest; changed to spider.
Ares (Mars): God of war; son of Zeus and Hera.
Argo: Ship in which Jason and followers sailed to Colchis for Golden Fleece.
Argus: Monster with hundred eyes; slain by Hermes; his eyes placed by Hera into peacock's tail.
Ariadne: Daughter of Minos; aided Theseus in slaying Minotaur; deserted by him on island of Naxos and married to Dionysus.
Arion: Musician; thrown overboard by pirates but saved by dolphin.
Artemis (Diana): Goddess of moon; huntress; twin sister of Apollo.
Asclepius (Aesculapius): Mortal son of Apollo; slain by Zeus for raising dead; later deified as god of medicine. Also known as Asklepios.
Astarte: Phoenician goddess of love; variously identified with Aphrodite, Selene, and Artemis.
Asterope: *See* Sterope.
Astraea: Goddess of Justice; daughter of Zeus and Themis.
Atalanta: Princess who challenged her suitors to a foot race; Hippomenes won race and married her.
Athena (Minerva): Goddess of wisdom; known poetically as Pallas Athene; sprang fully armed from head of Zeus.
Atlas: Titan; held world on his shoulders as punishment for warring against Zeus; son of Iapetus.
Atreus: King of Mycenae; father of Menelaus and Agamemnon; brother of Thyestes, three of whose sons he slew and served to him at banquet; slain by Aegisthus.
Atropos: One of several **Fates.**
Aurora: *See* Eos.
Auster: One of several **Winds.**
Avernus: Infernal regions; name derived from small vaporous lake near Vesuvius which was fabled to kill birds and vegetation.
Bacchus: *See* Dionysus.
Bellerophon: Corinthian hero; killed Chimera with aid of Pegasus; tried to reach Olympus on Pegasus and was thrown to his death.
Bellona: Roman goddess of war.
Boreas: One of several **Winds.**
Briareus: Monster of hundred hands; son of Uranus and Gaea.
Briseis: Captive maiden given to Achilles; taken by Agamemnon in exchange for loss of Chryseis, which caused Achilles to cease fighting, until death of Patroclus.
Cadmus: Brother of Europa; planter of dragon seeds from which first Thebans sprang.

Calliope: One of several **Muses.**

Calypso: Sea nymph; kept Odysseus on her island Ogygia for seven years.

Cassandra: Daughter of Priam; prophetess who was never believed; slain with Agamemnon.

Castor: One of **Dioscuri.**

Celaeno: One of several **Pleiades.**

Centaurs: Beings half man and half horse; lived in mountains of Thessaly.

Cephalus: Hunter; accidentally killed his wife Procris with his spear.

Cepheus: King of Ethiopia; father of Andromeda.

Cerberus: Three-headed dog guarding entrance to Hades.

Ceres: See Demeter.

Chaos: Formless void; personified as first of gods.

Charon: Boatman on Styx who carried souls of dead to Hades; son of Erebus.

Charybdis: Female monster; personification of whirlpool.

Chimera: Female monster with head of lion, body of goat, tail of serpent; killed by Bellerophon.

Chiron: Most famous of centaurs.

Chronos: Personification of time.

Chryseis: Captive maiden given to Agamemnon; his refusal to accept ransom from her father Chryses caused Apollo to send plague on Greeks besieging Troy.

Circe: Sorceress; daughter of Helios; changed Odysseus's men into swine.

Clio: One of several **Muses.**

Clotho: One of several **Fates.**

Clytemnestra: Wife of Agamemnon, whom she slew with aid of her paramour, Aegisthus; slain by her son Orestes.

Cocytus: One of several **Rivers of Underworld.**

Creon: Father of Jocasta; forbade burial of Polynices; ordered burial alive of Antigone.

Creüsa: Princess of Corinth, for whom Jason deserted Medea; slain by Medea, who sent her poisoned robe; also known as Glaüke.

Creusa: Wife of Aeneas; died fleeing Troy.

Cronus (Saturn): Titan; god of harvests; son of Uranus and Gaea; dethroned by his son Zeus.

Cupid: See Eros.

Cybele: Anatolian nature goddess; adopted by Greeks and identified with Rhea.

Cyclopes: Race of one-eyed giants (singular: Cyclops).

Daedalus: Athenian artificer; father of Icarus; builder of Labyrinth in Crete; devised wings attached with wax for him and Icarus to escape Crete.

Danae: Princess of Argos; mother of Perseus by Zeus, who appeared to her in form of golden shower.

Danaïdes: Daughters of Danaüs; at his command, all except Hypermnestra slew their husbands, the sons of Aegyptus.

Danaüs: Brother of Aegyptus; father of Danaïdes; slain by Lynceus.

Daphne: Nymph; pursued by Apollo; changed to laurel tree.

Decuma: One of several **Fates.**

Deino: One of several **Graeae.**

Demeter (Ceres): Goddess of agriculture; mother of Persephone.

Diana: See Artemis.

Dido: Founder and queen of Carthage; stabbed herself when deserted by Aeneas.

Diomedes: Greek hero; with Odysseus, entered Troy and carried off Palladium, sacred statue of Athena.

Diomedes: Owner of man-eating horses, which Hercules, as ninth labor, carried off.

Dione: Titan goddess; mother by Zeus of Aphrodite.

Dionysus (Bacchus): God of wine; son of Zeus and Semele.

Dioscuri: Twins Castor and Pollux; sons of Leda by Zeus.

Dis: See Pluto, Hades.

Dryads: Wood nymphs.

Dryope: Maiden changed to Hamadryad.

Echo: Nymph who fell hopelessly in love with Narcissus; faded away except for her voice.

Electra: Daughter of Agamemnon and Clytemnestra; sister of Orestes; urged Orestes to slay Clytemnestra and Aegisthus.

Electra: One of several **Pleiades.**

Elysium: Abode of blessed dead.

Endymion: Mortal loved by Selene.

Enyo: One of several **Graeae.**

Eos (Aurora): Goddess of dawn.

Epimetheus: Brother of Prometheus; husband of Pandora.

Erato: One of several **Muses.**

Erebus: Spirit of darkness; son of Chaos.

Erinyes: One of several **Furies.**

Eris: Goddess of discord.

Eros (Amor or Cupid): God of love; son of Aphrodite.

Eteocles: Son of Oedipus, whom he succeeded to rule alternately with Polynices; refused to give up throne at end of year; he and Polynices slew each other.

Eumenides: One of several **Furies.**

Euphrosyne: One of several **Graces.**

Europa: Mortal loved by Zeus, who, in form of white bull, carried her off to Crete.

Eurus: One of several **Winds.**

Euryale: One of several **Gorgons.**

Eurydice: Nymph; wife of Orpheus.

Eurystheus: King of Argos; imposed twelve labors on Hercules.

Euterpe: One of several **Muses.**

Fates: Goddesses of destiny; Clotho (Spinner of thread of life), Lachesis (Determiner of length), and Atropos (Cutter of thread); also called Moirae. Identified by Romans with their goddesses of fate; Nona, Decuma, and Morta; called Parcae.

Fauns: Roman deities of woods and groves.

Faunus: See Pan.

Favonius: One of several **Winds.**

Flora: Roman goddess of flowers.

Fortuna: Roman goddess of fortune.

Furies: Avenging spirits; Alecto, Megaera, and Tisiphone; known also as Erinyes or Eumenides.

Gaea: Goddess of earth; daughter of Chaos; mother of Titans; known also as Ge, Gea, Gaia, etc.

Galatea: Statue of maiden carved from ivory by Pygmalion; given life by Aphrodite.

Galatea: Sea nymph; loved by Polyphemus.

Ganymede: Beautiful boy; successor to Hebe as cupbearer of gods.

Glaucus: Mortal who became sea divinity by eating magic grass.

Golden Fleece: Fleece from ram that flew Phrixos to Colchis; Aeëtes placed it under guard of dragon; carried off by Jason.

Gorgons: Female monsters; Euryale, Medusa, and Stheno; had snakes for hair; their glances turned mortals to stone.

Graces: Beautiful goddesses: Aglaia (Brilliance), Euphrosyne (Joy), and Thalia (Bloom); daughters of Zeus.

Graeae: Sentinels for Gorgons; Deino, Enyo, and Pephredo; had one eye among them, which passed from one to another.

Hades (Dis): Name sometimes given Pluto; also, abode of dead, ruled by Pluto.

Haemon: Son of Creon; promised husband of Antigone; killed himself in her tomb.

Hamadryads: Tree nymphs.

Harpies: Monsters with heads of women and bodies of birds.

Hebe (Juventas): Goddess of youth; cupbearer of gods before Ganymede; daughter of Zeus and Hera.

Hecate: Goddess of sorcery and witchcraft.

Hector: Son of Priam; slayer of Patroclus; slain by Achilles.

Hecuba: Wife of Priam.

Helen: Fairest woman in world; daughter of Zeus and Leda; wife of Menelaus; carried to Troy by Paris, causing Trojan War.

Heliades: Daughters of Helios; mourned for Phaëthon and were changed to poplar trees.

Helios (Sol): God of sun; later identified with Apollo.

Helle: Sister of Phrixos; fell from ram of Golden Fleece; water where she fell named Hellespont.

Hephaestus (Vulcan): God of fire; celestial blacksmith; son of Zeus and Hera; husband of Aphrodite.

Hera (Juno): Queen of heaven; wife of Zeus.

Hercules: Hero and strong man; son of Zeus and Alcmene; performed twelve labors or deeds to be free from bondage under Eurystheus; after death, his mortal share was destroyed, and he became immortal. Also known as Herakles or Heracles. Labors: (1) killing Nemean lion; (2) killing Lernaean Hydra; (3) capturing Erymanthian boar; (4) capturing Ceryrean hind; (5) killing man-eating Stymphalian birds; (6) procuring girdle of Hippolyte; (7) cleaning Augean stables; (8) capturing Cretan bull; (9) capturing man-eating horses of Diomedes; (10) capturing cattle of Geryon; (11) procuring golden apples of Hesperides; (12) bringing Cerberus up from Hades.

Hermes (Mercury): God of physicians and thieves; messenger of gods; son of Zeus and Maia.

Hero: Priestess of Aphrodite; Leander swam Hellespont nightly to see her; drowned herself at his death.

Hesperus: Evening star.

Hestia (Vesta): Goddess of hearth; sister of Zeus.

Hippolyte: Queen of Amazons; wife of Theseus.

Hippolytus: Son of Theseus and Hippolyte; falsely accused by Phaedra of trying to kidnap her; slain by Poseidon at request of Theseus.

Hippomenes: Husband of Atalanta, whom he beat in race by dropping golden apples, which she stopped to pick up.

Hyacinthus: Beautiful youth accidentally killed by Apollo, who caused flower to spring up from his blood.

Hydra: Nine-headed monster in marsh of Lerna; slain by Hercules.

Hygeia: Personification of health.

Hyman: God of marriage.

Hyperion: Titan; early sun god; father of Helios.

Hypermnestra: Daughter of Danaüs; refused to kill her husband Lynceus.

Hypnos (Somnus): God of sleep.

Iapetus: Titan; father of Atlas, Epimetheus, and Prometheus.

Icarus: Son of Daedalus; flew too near sun with wax-attached wings and fell into sea and was drowned.

Io: Mortal maiden loved by Zeus; changed by Hera into heifer.

Iobates: King of Lycia; sent Bellerophon to slay Chimera.

Iphigenia: Daughter of Agamemnon; offered as sacrifice to Artemis at Aulis; carried by Artemis to Tauris where she became priestess; escaped from there with Orestes.

Iris: Goddess of rainbow; messenger of Zeus and Hera.

Ismene: Daughter of Oedipus; sister of Antigone.

Iulus: Son of Aeneas.

Ixion: King of Lapithae; for making love to Hera he was bound to endlessly revolving wheel in Tartarus.

Janus: Roman god of gates and doors; represented with two opposite faces.

Jason: Son of Aeson; to gain throne of Ioclus from Pelias, went to Colchis and brought back Golden Fleece; married Medea; deserted her for Creüsa.

Jocasta: Wife of Laius; mother of Oedipus; unwittingly became wife of Oedipus; hanged herself when relationship was discovered.

Juno: *See* Hera.

Jupiter: *See* Zeus.

Juventas: *See* Hebe.

Lachesis: One of several **Fates.**

Laius: Father of Oedipus, by whom he was slain.

Laocoön: Priest of Apollo at Troy; warned against bringing wooden horse into Troy; destroyed with his two sons by serpents sent by Athena.

Lares: Roman ancestral spirits protecting descendants and homes.

Latona: *See* Leto.

Lavinia: Wife of Aeneas after defeat of Turnus.

Leander: Swam Hellespont nightly to see Hero; drowned in storm.

Leda: Mortal loved by Zeus in form of swan; mother of Helen, Clytemnestra, Dioscuri.

Lethe: One of several **Rivers of Underworld.**

Leto (Latona): Mother by Zeus of Artemis and Apollo.

Lucina: Roman goddess of childbirth; identified with Juno.

Lynceus: Son of Aegyptus; husband of Hypermnestra; slew Danaüs.

Maia: Daughter of Atlas; mother of Hermes.

Maia: One of several **Pleiades.**

Manes: Souls of dead Romans, particularly of ancestors.

Mars: *See* Ares.

Marsyas: Shepherd; challenged Apollo to music contest and lost; flayed alive by Apollo.

Medea: Sorceress; daughter of Aeëtes; helped Jason obtain Golden Fleece; when deserted by him for Creüsa, killed her children and Creüsa.

Medusa: One of several **Gorgons;** slain by Perseus, who cut off her head.

Megaera: One of several **Furies.**

Meleager: Son of Althaea; his life would last as long as brand burning at his birth; Althaea quenched and saved it but destroyed it when Meleager slew his uncles.

Melpomene: One of several **Muses.**

Memnon: Ethiopian king; made immortal by Zeus; son of Tithonus and Eos.

Menelaus: King of Sparta; son of Atreus; brother of Agamemnon; husband of Helen.

Mercury: *See* Hermes.

Merope: One of several **Pleiades.** Merope is said to have hidden in shame for loving a mortal.

Mezentius: Cruel Etruscan king; ally of Turnus against Aeneas; slain by Aeneas.

Midas: King of Phrygia; given gift of turning to gold all he touched.

Minerva: *See* Athena.

Minos: King of Crete; after death, one of three judges of dead in Hades; son of Zeus and Europa.

Minotaur: Monster, half man and half beast, kept in Labyrinth in Crete; slain by Theseus.

Mnemosyne: Goddess of memory; mother by Zeus of Muses.

Moirae: One of several **Fates.**

Momus: God of ridicule.

Morpheus: God of dreams.

Mors: *See* Thanatos.

Morta: One of several **Fates.**

Muses: Goddesses presiding over arts and sciences: Calliope (epic poetry), Clio (history), Erato (lyric and love poetry), Euterpe (music), Melpomene (tragedy), Polymnia or Polyhymnia (sacred poetry), Terpsichore (choral dance and song), Thalia (comedy and bucolic poetry), Urania (astronomy); daughters of Zeus and Mnemosyne.

Naiads: Nymphs of waters, streams, and fountains.

Napaeae: Wood nymphs.

Narcissus: Beautiful youth loved by Echo; in punishment for not returning her love, he was made to fall in love with his image reflected in pool; pined away and became flower.

Nemesis: Goddess of retribution.

Neoptolemus: Son of Achilles; slew Priam; also known as Pyrrhus.

Neptune: *See* Poseidon.

Nereids: Sea nymphs; attendants on Poseidon.

Nestor: King of Pylos; noted for wise counsel in expedition against Troy.

Nike: Goddess of victory.

Niobe: Daughter of Tantalus; wife of Amphion; her children slain by Apollo and Artemis; changed to stone but continued to weep for loss.

Nona: One of several **Fates.**

Notus: One of several **Winds.**

Nox: *See* Nyx.

Nymphs: Beautiful maidens; minor deities of nature.

Nyx (Nox): Goddess of night.

Oceanids: Ocean nymphs; daughters of Oceanus.

Oceanus: Eldest of Titans; god of waters.

Odysseus (Ulysses): King of Ithaca; husband of Penelope; wandered ten years after fall of Troy before arriving home.

Oedipus: King of Thebes; son of Laius and Jocasta; unwittingly murdered Laius and married Jocasta; tore his eyes out when relationship was discovered.

Oenone: Nymph of Mount Ida; wife of Paris, who abandoned her; refused to cure him when he was poisoned by arrow of Philoctetes at Troy.

Ops: *See* Rhea.

Oreades: Mountain nymphs.

Orestes: Son of Agamemnon and Clytemnestra; brother of Electra; slew Clytemnestra and Aegisthus; pursued by Furies until his purification by Apollo.

Orion: Hunter; slain by Artemis and made heavenly constellation.

Orpheus: Famed musician; son of Apollo and Muse Calliope; husband of Eurydice.

Pales: Roman goddess of shepherds and herdsmen.

Palinurus: Aeneas' pilot; fell overboard in his sleep and was drowned.

Pan (Faunus): God of woods and fields; part goat; son of Hermes.

Pandora: Opener of box containing human ills; mortal wife of Epimetheus.

Parcae: One of several **Fates.**

Paris: Son of Priam; gave apple of discord to Aphrodite, for which she enabled him to carry off Helen; slew Achilles at Troy; slain by Philoctetes.

Patroclus: Great friend of Achilles; wore Achilles' armor and was slain by Hector.

Pegasus: Winged horse that sprang from Medusa's body at her death; ridden by Bellerophon when he slew Chimera.

Pelias: King of Ioclus; seized throne from his brother Aeson; sent Jason for Golden Fleece; slain unwittingly by his daughters at instigation of Medea.

Pelops: Son of Tantalus; his father cooked and served him to gods; restored to life; Peloponnesus named for him.

Penates: Roman household gods.

Penelope: Wife of Odysseus; waited faithfully for him for many years while putting off numerous suitors.

Pephredo: One of several **Graeae.**

Periphetes: Giant; son of Hephaestus; slain by Theseus.

Persephone (Proserpine): Queen of infernal regions; daughter of Zeus and Demeter; wife of Pluto.

Perseus: Son of Zeus and Danaë; slew Medusa; rescued Andromeda from monster and married her.

Phaedra: Daughter of Minos; wife of Theseus; caused the death of her stepson, Hippolytus.

Phaethon: Son of Helios; drove his father's sun chariot and was struck down by Zeus before he set world on fire.

Philoctetes: Greek warrior who possessed Hercules' bow and arrows; slew Paris at Troy with poisoned arrow.

Phineus: Betrothed of Andromeda; tried to slay Perseus but turned to stone by Medusa's head.

Phlegethon: One of several **Rivers of Underworld.**

Phosphor: Morning star.

Phrixos: Brother of Helle; carried by ram of Golden Fleece to Colchis.

Pirithous: Son of Ixion; friend of Theseus; tried to carry off Persephone from Hades; bound to enchanted rock by Pluto.

Pleiades: Alcyone, Celaeno, Electra, Maia, Merope, Sterope or Asterope, Taygeta; seven daughters of Atlas; transformed into heavenly constellation, of which six stars are visible (Merope is said to have hidden in shame for loving a mortal).

Pluto (Dis): God of Hades; brother of Zeus.

Plutus: God of wealth.

Pollux: One of **Dioscuri.**

Polyhymnia: See Polymnia.

Polymnia (Polyhymnia): One of several **Muses.**

Polynices: Son of Oedipus; he and his brother Eteocles killed each other; burial rite, forbidden by Creon, performed by his sister Antigone.

Polyphemus: Cyclops; devoured six of Odysseus's men; blinded by Odysseus.

Polyxena: Daughter of Priam; betrothed to Achilles, whom Paris slew at their betrothal; sacrificed to shade of Achilles.

Pomona: Roman goddess of fruits.

Pontus: Sea god; son of Gaea.

Poseidon (Neptune): God of sea; brother of Zeus.

Priam: King of Troy; husband of Hecuba; ransomed Hector's body from Achilles; slain by Neoptolemus.

Priapus: God of regeneration.

Procris: Wife of Cephalus, who accidentally slew her.

Procrustes: Giant; stretched or cut off legs of victims to make them fit iron bed; slain by Theseus.

Proetus: Husband of Anteia; sent Bellerophon to Iobates to be put to death.

Prometheus: Titan; stole fire from heaven for man. Zeus punished him by chaining him to rock in Caucasus where vultures devoured his liver daily.

Proserpine: See Persephone.

Proteus: Sea god; assumed various shapes when called on to prophesy.

Psyche: Beloved of Eros; punished by jealous Aphrodite; made immortal and united with Eros.

Pygmalion: King of Cyprus; carved ivory statue of maiden which Aphrodite gave life as Galatea.

Pyramus: Babylonian youth; made love to Thisbe through hole in wall; thinking Thisbe slain by lion, killed himself.

Python: Serpent born from slime left by Deluge; slain by Apollo.

Quirinus: Roman war god.

Remus: Brother of Romulus; slain by him.

Rhadamanthus: One of three judges of dead in Hades; son of Zeus and Europa.

Rhea (Ops): Daughter of Uranus and Gaea; wife of Cronus; mother of Zeus; identified with Cybele.

Rivers of Underworld: Acheron (woe), Cocytus (wailing), Lethe (forgetfulness), Phlegethon (fire), Styx (across which souls of dead were ferried by Charon).

Romulus: Founder of Rome; he and Remus suckled in infancy by she-wolf; slew Remus; deified by Romans.

Sarpedon: King of Lycia; son of Zeus and Europa; slain by Patroclus at Troy.

Saturn: See Cronus.

Satyrs: Hoofed demigods of woods and fields; companions of Dionysus.

Sciron: Robber; forced strangers to wash his feet, then hurled them into sea where tortoise devoured them; slain by Theseus.

Scylla: Female monster inhabiting rock opposite Charybdis; menaced passing sailors.

Selene: Goddess of moon.

Semele: Daughter of Cadmus; mother by Zeus of Dionysus; demanded Zeus appear before her in all his splendor and was destroyed by his lightning bolts.

Sibyis: Various prophetesses; most famous, Cumaean sibyl, accompanied Aeneas into Hades.

Sileni: Minor woodland deities similar to satyrs (singular: silenus). Sometimes Silenus refers to eldest of satyrs, son of Hermes or of Pan.

Silvanus: Roman god of woods and fields.

Sinis: Giant; bent pines, with which he hurled victims against side of mountain; slain by Theseus.

Sirens: Minor deities who lured sailors to destruction with their singing.

Sisyphus: King of Corinth; condemned in Tartarus to roll huge stone to top of hill; it always rolled back down again.

Sol: See Helios.

Somnus: See Hypnos.

Sphinx: Monster of Thebes; killed those who could not answer her riddle; slain by Oedipus. Name also refers to other monsters having body of lion, wings, and head and bust of woman.

Sterope (Asterope): One of several **Pleiades.**

Stheno: One of several **Gorgons.**

Styx: One of several **Rivers of Underworld.** The souls of the dead were ferried across the Styx by Charon.

Symplegades: Clashing rocks at entrance to Black Sea; Argo passed through, causing them to become forever fixed.

Syrinx: Nymph pursued by Pan; changed to reeds, from which he made his pipes.

Tantalus: Cruel king; father of Pelops and Niobe; condemned in Tartarus to stand chin-deep in lake surrounded by fruit branches; as he tried to eat or drink, water or fruit always receded.

Tartarus: Underworld below Hades; often refers to Hades.

Taygeta: One of several **Pleiades.**

Telemachus: Son of Odysseus; made unsuccessful journey to find his father.

Tellus: Roman goddess of earth.

Terminus: Roman god of boundaries and landmarks.

Terpsichore: One of several **Muses.**

Terra: Roman earth goddess.

Thalia: One of several **Graces.** Also one of several **Muses.**

Thanatos (Mors): God of death.

Themis: Titan goddess of laws of physical phenomena; daughter of Uranus; mother of Prometheus.

Theseus: Son of Aegeus; slew Minotaur; married and deserted Ariadne; later married Phaedra.

Thisbe: Beloved of Pyramus; killed herself at his death.

Thyestes: Brother of Atreus; Atreus killed three of his sons and served them to him at banquet.

Tiresias: Blind soothsayer of Thebes.

Tisiphone: One of several **Furies.**

Titans: Early gods from which Olympian gods were derived; children of Uranus and Gaea.

Tithonus: Mortal loved by Eos; changed into grasshopper.

Triton: Demigod of sea; son of Poseidon.

Turnus: King of Rutuli in Italy; betrothed to Lavinia; slain by Aeneas.

Ulysses: See Odysseus.

Urania: One of several **Muses.**

Uranus: Personification of Heaven; husband of Gaea; father of Titans; dethroned by his son Cronus.

Venus: See Aphrodite.

Vertumnus: Roman god of fruits and vegetables; husband of Pomona.

Vesta: See Hestia.

Vulcan: See Hephaestus.

Winds: Aeolus (keeper of winds), Boreas (Aquilo) (north wind), Eurus (east wind), Notus (Auster) (south wind), Zephyrus (Favonius) (west wind).

Zephyrus: One of several **Winds.**

Zeus (Jupiter): Chief of Olympian gods; son of Cronus and Rhea; husband of Hera.

Norse Mythology

Aesir: Chief gods of Asgard.

Andvari: Dwarf; robbed of gold and magic ring by Loki.

Angerbotha (Angrbotha): Giantess; mother by Loki of Fenrir, Hel, and Midgard serpent.

Asgard (Asgarth): Abode of gods.

Ask (Aske, Askr): First man; created by Odin, Hoenir, and Lothur.

Asynjur: Goddesses of Asgard.

Atli: Second husband of Gudrun; invited Gunnar and Hogni to his court, where they were slain; slain by Gudrun.

Audhumia (Audhumbla): Cow that nourished Ymir; created Buri by licking ice cliff.

Balder (Baldr, Baldur): God of light, spring, peace, joy; son of Odin; slain by Hoth at instigation of Loki.

Bifrost: Rainbow bridge connecting Midgard and Asgard.

Bragi (Brage): God of poetry; husband of Ithunn.

Branstock: Great oak in hall of Volsungs; into it, Odin thrust Gram, which only Sigmund could draw forth.

Brynhild: Valkyrie; wakened from magic sleep by Sigurd; married Gunnar; instigated death of Sigurd; killed herself and was burned on pyre beside Sigurd.

Bur (Bor): Son of Buri; father of Odin, Hoenir, and Lothur.

Buri (Bori): Progenitor of gods; father of Bur; created by Audhumla.

Embla: First woman; created by Odin, Hoenir, and Lothur.

Fafnir: Son of Rodmar, whom he slew for gold in Otter's skin; in form of dragon, guarded gold; slain by Sigurd.

Fenrir: Wolf; offspring of Loki; swallows Odin at Ragnarok and is slain by Vitharr.

Forseti: Son of Balder.

Frey (Freyr): God of fertility and crops; son of Njorth; originally one of **Vanir**.

Freya (Freyja): Goddess of love and beauty; sister of Frey; originally one of **Vanir**.

Frigg (Frigga): Goddess of sky; wife of Odin.

Garm: Watchdog of Hel; slays, and is slain by, Tyr at Ragnarok.

Gimle: Home of blessed after Ragnarok.

Giuki: King of Nibelungs; father of Gunnar, Hogni, Guttorm, and Gudrun.

Glathsehim (Gladsheim): Hall of gods in Asgard.

Gram (meaning "Angry"): Sigmund's sword; reweilded by Regin; used by Sigurd to slay Fafnir.

Greyfell: Sigmund's horse; descended from Sleipnir.

Grimhild: Mother of Gudrun; administered magic potion to Sigurd which made him forget Brynhild.

Gudrun: Daughter of Giuki; wife of Sigurd; later wife of Atli and Jonakr.

Gunnar: Son of Giuki; in his semblance Sigurd won Brynhild for him; slain at hall of Atli.

Guttorm: Son of Giuki; slew Sigurd at Brynhild's request.

Heimdall (Heimdallr): Guardian of Asgard.

Hel: Goddess of dead and queen of underworld; daughter of Loki.

Hiordis: Wife of Sigmund; mother of Sigurd.

Hoenir: One of creators of Ask and Embla; son of Bur.

Hogni: Son of Giuki; slain at hall of Atli.

Hoth (Hoder, Hodur): Blind god of night and darkness; slayer of Balder at instigation of Loki.

Ithunn (Ithun, Iduna): Keeper of golden apples of youth; wife of Bragi.

Jonakr: Third husband of Gudrun.

Jormunrek: Slayer of Swanhild; slain by sons of Gudrun.

Jotunnheim (Jotunnheim): Abode of giants.

Lif and Lifthrasir: First man and woman after Ragnarok.

Loki: God of evil and mischief; instigator of Balder's death.

Lothur (Lodur): One of creators of Ask and Embla.

Midgard (Midgarth): Abode of mankind; the earth.

Midgard Serpent: Sea monster; offspring of Loki; slays, and is slain by, Thor at Ragnarok.

Mimir: Giant; guardian of well in Jotunnheim at root of Yggdrasill; knower of past and future.

Mjollnir: Magic hammer of Thor.

Nagifar: Ship to be used by giants in attacking Asgard at Ragnarok; built from nails of dead men.

Nanna: Wife of Balder.

Nibelungs: Dwellers in northern kingdom ruled by Giuki.

Niflheim (Nifelheim): Outer region of cold and darkness; abode of Hel.

Njorth: Father of Frey and Freya; originally one of **Vanir**.

Norns: Demigoddesses of fate: Urth (Urdur) (past), Verthandi (Verdandi) (present), Skuld (future).

Odin (Othin): Head of **Aesir**; creator of world with Vili and Ve; equivalent to Woden (Wodan, Wotan) in Teutonic mythology.

Otter: Son of Rodmar; slain by Loki; his skin filled with gold hoard of Andvari to appease Rodmar.

Ragnarok: Final destruction of present world in battle between gods and giants; some minor gods will survive, and Lif and Lifthrasir will repeople world.

Regin: Blacksmith; son of Rodmar; foster-father of Sigurd.

Rerir: King of Huns; son of Sigi.

Rodmar: Father of Regin, Otter, and Fafnir; demanded Otter's skin be filled with gold; slain by Fafnir, who stole gold.

Sif: Wife of Thor.

Siggeir: King of Goths; husband of Signy; he and his sons slew Volsung and his sons, except Sigmund; slain by Sigmund and Sinflotli.

Sigi: King of Huns; son of Odin.

Sigmund: Son of Volsung; brother of Signy, who bore him Sinflotli; husband of Hiordis, who bore him Sigurd.

Signy: Daughter of Volsung; sister of Sigmund; wife of Siggeir; mother by Sigmund of Sinflotli.

Sigurd: Son of Sigmund and Hiordis; wakened Brynhild from magic sleep; married Gudrun; slain by Guttorm at instigation of Brynhild.

Sigyn: Wife of Loki.

Sinflotli: Son of Sigmund and Signy.

Skuld: One of several **Norns**.

Sleipnir (Sleipner): Eight-legged horse of Odin.

Surt (Surtr): Fire demon; slays Frey at Ragnarok.

Svartalfaheim: Abode of dwarfs.

Swanhild: Daughter of Sigurd and Gudrun; slain by Jormunrek.

Thor: God of thunder; oldest son of Odin; equivalent to Germanic deity Donar.

Tyr: God of war; son of Odin; equivalent to Tiu in Teutonic mythology.

Ull (Ullr): Son of Sif; stepson of Thor.

Urth: One of several **Norns**.

Valhalla (Valhall): Great hall in Asgard where Odin received souls of heroes killed in battle.

Vali: Odin's son; Ragnarok survivor.

Valkyries: Virgins, messengers of Odin, who selected heroes to die in battle and took them to Valhalla; generally considered as nine in number.

Vanir: Early race of gods; three survivors, Njorth, Frey, and Freya, are associated with **Aesir**.

Ve: Brother of Odin; one of creators of world.

Verthandi: One of several **Norns**.

Vili: Brother of Odin; one of creators of world.

Vingolf: Abode of goddesses in Asgard.

Vitharr (Vithar): Son of Odin; survivor of Ragnarok.

Volsung: Descendant of Odin, and father of Signy, Sigmund; his descendants were called Volsungs.

Yggdrasill: Giant ash tree springing from body of Ymir and supporting universe; its roots extended to Asgard, Jotunnheim, and Niffheim.

Ymir (Ymer): Primeval frost giant killed by Odin, Vili, and Ve; world created from his body; also, from his body sprang Yggdrasill.

Egyptian Mythology

Aaru: Abode of the blessed dead.

Amen (Amon, Ammdn): One of chief Theban deities; united with sun god under form of Amen-Ra; husband of Mut.

Amenti: Region of dead where souls were judged by Osiris.

Anubis: Guide of souls to Amenti; son of Osiris; jackal-headed.

Apis: Sacred bull, an embodiment of Ptah; identified with Osiris as Osiris-Apis or Serapis.

Geb (Keb, Seb): Earth god; father of Osiris; represented with goose on head.

Hathor (Athor): Goddess of love and mirth; cow-headed.

Horus: God of day; son of Osiris and Isis; hawk-headed.

Isis: Goddess of motherhood and fertility; sister and wife of Osiris.

Khepera: God of morning sun.

Khnemu (Khnum, Chnuphis, Chnemu, Chnum): Ram-headed god.

Khonsu (Khensu, Khuns): Son of Amen and Mut.

Mentu (Ment): Solar deity, sometimes considered god of war; falcon-headed.

Min (Khem, Chem): Principle of physical life.

Mut (Maut): Wife of Amen.

Nephthys: Goddess of the dead; sister and wife of Set.

Nu: Chaos from which world was created, personified as a god.

Nut: Goddess of heavens; consort of Geb.

Osiris: God of underworld and judge of dead; son of Geb and Nut; brother and husband of Isis.

Ptah (Phtha): Chief deity of Memphis.

Ra: God of the Sun, the supreme god; son of Nut; Pharaohs claimed descent from him; represented as lion, cat, or falcon.

Serapis: God uniting attributes of Osiris and Apis.

Set (Seth): God of darkness or evil; brother and enemy of Osiris; brother and husband of Nephthys.

Shu: Solar deity; son of Ra and Hathor.

Tem (Atmu, Atum, Tum): Solar deity.

Thoth (Dhouti): God of wisdom and magic; scribe of gods; ibis-headed.

A Concise Guide to Style

This section discusses and illustrates the basic conventions of American capitalization, italicization, and punctuation.

Capitalization

Capitalize the following:

- **Proper nouns and adjectives derived from proper nouns:**

Marie Curie   China, Chinese
Smokey Robinson   Darwin, Darwinian

But, vocabulary words derived from proper nouns are generally lowercase:

china cups   plaster of paris
french fries   vienna sausage

- **The names of geographic divisions, regions, and localities and topographical features such as rivers, lakes, and mountains:**

North Pole   Gulf States
Middle East   Atlantic Ocean
Southern Hemisphere   Rocky Mountains
the North   Lake Tahoe
Lower East Side   Erie Canal

Do not capitalize directions: She lives 10 miles north of Boston.

- **The names of nationalities, ethnic groups, tribes, and languages:**

Spanish   Bantu
Asian-American   Creole

- **Titles when preceding a name:**

President Lincoln   Aunt Mary
Queen Victoria   Doctor Johnson
Senator Kennedy   Professor Davies

Do not capitalize such terms elsewhere: a biography of the queen; the senator's speech; my aunt, Mary Wilson.

Do capitalize all references to the U.S. President and Vice President: the President's fundraising efforts; the residence of the Vice President.

- **Epithets:** Ivan the Terrible; Lincoln is known as The Great Emancipator.

- **The names of political and judicial bodies, social organizations, councils, and departments:**

U.S. Senate   Rotary Club
Democratic Party   United Negro College Fund
State Department   U.S. Supreme Court

- **The names for periods, events, and documents of historical importance:**

Middle Ages   Constitution
Renaissance   Treaty of Versailles
Battle of Waterloo   Magna Carta

- **The names for streets, buildings, and monuments:**

Fifth Avenue   World Trade Center
Broadway   Statue of Liberty

- **The names for the supreme deity and sacred works:**

God, the Father Almighty   Bible
Yaweh   Talmud
Allah   Qu'ran

- **The names for religious denominations and their members:**

Judaism, Jews
Methodist Church, Methodists
Society of Friends, Quakers

- **The days of the weeks, months of the year, holidays, and holy days:**

Thursday   Labor Day
December   Passover

- **The pronoun I:**

I told her I didn't want to go.

- **The first word in the salutation and complimentary close of a letter:**

My dear Carol . . . Very truly yours . . .

- **The first word of a sentence:**

Are you hungry? Lunch will be served soon.

- **The first word of a direct quotation, except when the quotation is split:**

I asked, "Do you really like bats?"
"Yes," said Holly, "they're so cute."

- **The first word and all the key words in the title of a literary or other artistic work:**

The Bluest Eye (novel)
"The Road Not Taken" (poem)
Starry Night (painting)
"Only the Lonely" (song)

- **The names of ships, aircraft, and space vehicles:**

U.S.S. *Maine*
The Spirit of St. Louis
space shuttle *Challenger*

- **The names of constellations, planets, and stars:**

Milky Way   Saturn
the asteroid Juno   Little Dipper

- **The names of geologic eras, periods, epochs, and names of prehistoric divisions:**

Paleozoic Era   *Pleistocene*
Quaternary Period   *Stone Age*

- **The genus but not the species name in binomial nomenclature:**

Canis familiaris (dog)
Malus pumila (apple tree)

Italicization

Italicize the following:

- **The titles of books, plays, book-length poems, magazines, and newspapers:**

  War and Peace *TIME* magazine
  Twelfth Night *National Geographic*
  Beowulf   *Miami Herald*

- **The titles of movies and radio and television programs:**

  Toy Story   *The X-Files*
  Car Talk   *Masterpiece Theater*

- **The titles of works of art, including paintings, sculptures, and major musical compositions:**

  Mona Lisa (painting)
  The Thinker (sculpture)
  Swan Lake (ballet)
  Porgy and Bess (opera)

  Do not italicize musical compositions named by number or key: Symphony No. 4; Quartet in E minor.

- **Words, letters, and numbers used as such:**

  How do you spell *ache*?
  Does your name end with a *c* or a *k*?
  The *6* looked like a *0*.

- **Foreign words and phrases that have not been assimilated into English:**

  Alex's novel is a true *Bildungsroman*.
  Ed made a *tarte au citron* for dessert.

- **Words and phrases that are being emphasized:**

  Paris was *the* place to be in the '20s.

- **The names of the plaintiff and defendant in legal citations:** *Johnson* v. *Smith.*

- **The names of ships, aircraft, and space vehicles:**

  U.S.S. *Maine*
  The Spirit of St. Louis
  space shuttle *Challenger*

- **The New Latin names of genera, species, subspecies, and varieties in botanical and zoological nomenclature:** *Quercus alba; Homo sapiens.*

Punctuation

End Marks

- **Use a period after a declarative or imperative statement:**

  I went to the library.
  Sign your name here.

- **Use a question mark after a direct question or to indicate uncertainty:**

  What is your name?
  Chaucer's dates are 1340?–1400.

  Do not use a question mark after an indirect question: I asked them what time they were leaving.

- **Use an exclamation point after an exclamatory or emphatic sentence or an interjection:**

  Give me a break!
  Hey! Ouch! Wow!

Comma

Use a comma:

- **To separate words in a list or series:**

  The baby likes grapes, bananas, and cantaloupe.

- **To separate two or more adjectives that come before a noun when *and* can be substituted without changing the meaning:**

  He had a kind, generous nature.
  The dog had thick, soft, shiny fur.

  Do not use the comma if the adjectives together express a single idea or the noun is a compound made up of an adjective and a noun:

  The kitchen had bright yellow curtains.
  A majestic bald eagle soared overheard.

- **To set off words or phrases in apposition to a noun:**

  George Eliot, the great 19th-century novelist, was born in 1819.

  Do not use commas when the appositive word or phrase is essential to the meaning of the sentence:

  The novelist George Eliot was born in 1819.

- **To set off nonessential phrases and clauses:**

  My French professor, who has an odd sense of humor, has been teaching for some 30 years.

  Do not use commas when the phrase or clause is essential to the meaning of the sentence:

  The professor who teaches my French class has an odd sense of humor.

- **To separate the independent clauses joined by a coordinating conjunction in a compound sentence:**

  He lives in New York, and she lives in London.
  Some people like golf, but others prefer tennis.

- **To set off interrupters such as *of course, however, I think,* and *by the way* from the rest of the sentence:**

  She knew, of course, that he was lying.
  By the way, I'll be away next week.

- **To set off an introductory word, phrase, or clause at the beginning of a sentence:**

  Yes, I'd like to go with you.
  After some years, we met again.
  Being tall, she often gets teased.

- **To set off a word in direct address:**

  Thanks, guys, for all your help.
  How was your trip, Kathy?

- **To set off a tag question:**

  You won't do that again, will you?

- **To introduce a short quotation:**

  The queen said, "Let them eat cake!"

- **To close the salutation in a personal letter and the complimentary close in a business or personal letter:**

  Dear Mary, . . . Sincerely, Fred

- **To set off titles and degrees:**

  Sarah Little, Ph.D. Robert Johnson, Jr.

- **To separate sentence elements that might be read incorrectly without the comma:**

  As they entered, in the shadows you could see a figure lurking.

- **To set off the month and day from the year in full dates:**

  The conference will be held on August 6, 2001.

  Do not use a comma when only the month and year appear:

  The conference will be held in August 2001.

- **To set off the city and state in an address:**

  Sam Green
  10 Joy Street
  Boston, MA 02116

  If the address is inserted into text, add a second comma after the state:

  Cincinnati, Ohio, is their home.

Colon

Use a colon:

- **To introduce a list, or words, phrases, and clauses that explain, enlarge upon, or summarize what has gone before:**

  Please provide the following: your name, address, and phone number.

  "No honest poet can ever feel quite sure of the permanent value of what he has written: He may have wasted his time and messed up his life for nothing."—T. S. Eliot

- **To introduce a long quotation:**

  In 1780 John Adams wrote: "English is destined to be in the next and succeeding centuries more generally the language of the world than Latin was in the last or French is in the present age . . . "

- **To separate hour and minute(s) in standard time notation:**

  The train arrives at 9:30.

- **To close the salutation in a business letter:**

  Dear Sir or Madam:

Semicolon

Use a semicolon:

- **To separate the independent clauses in a compound sentence not joined by a conjunction:**

  Only two seats were left; we needed three.

  The situation is hopeful; the storm may lift soon.

- **To separate two independent clauses, the second of which begins with an adverb such as *however, consequently, moreover,* and *therefore:***

  We waited an hour; however, we couldn't hang around indefinitely.

- **To separate elements already punctuated with commas:**

  Invitations were mailed to the various professors, associate professors, and assistant professors; the secretary of the department; and some of the grad students.

Dashes & Hyphens

- **Use a dash to indicate a sudden break in continuity or to set off an explanatory, defining, or** an emphatic phrase:

  The sky grew dark—where were the kids?

  Dairy foods—milk, cheese, yogurt—are a good source of calcium.

- **Use a hyphen to join the elements of a compound word or to join the elements of a compound modifier before a noun:**

  well-wisher   ice-skating rink
  fifty-three   college-age students

- **Use a hyphen to divide a word at the end of a line:**

  Rasputin is one of history's most enigmatic and intriguing figures.

Brackets & Parentheses

- **Use brackets to set off words or letters in quoted matter that have been added by someone other than the author:**

  "She [Willa Cather] is certainly one of the great American writers of the 20th century."

- **Use parentheses to set off nonessential information:**

  We spent an hour (more or less) cleaning up.

Apostrophe

Use an apostrophe to indicate:

- **The possessive case of singular and plural nouns, indefinite pronouns, and proper nouns:**

  my sister's son   somebody's lunch
  my two sisters' sons   Charles's house
  the children's toys   friends of the Rosses'

- **The plural of letters, numbers, symbols, and words used as such:**

  too many *thus*'s   ten *5*'s in a row
  spelled with two *e*'s   delete some &'s

- **Missing letters in contractions and missing numbers in dates:**

  I'm (I am)   class of '95
  ma'am (madam)   winter of '97–'98

Quotation Marks

Use quotation marks:

- **To set off direct quotations:**

  "Let's go to the beach," she suggested.

- **To set off titles of short stories, articles, chapters, essays, songs, poems, and individual radio and television programs:**

  Chapter 9, "The New Englishes"
  sang the "Star-Spangled Banner"
  "The Apparent Trap" episode of *Frasier*

- **To set off words and phrases that are being used in an unusual or questionable way or might be preceded by *so-called:***

  Mari's "fine" was a day's volunteer work.

  According to the article, bees appear to "remember" landmarks.

Forms of Address

Addressee	Address	Salutation
Clerical and religious orders		
Archbishop, Eastern Orthodox	The Most Reverend *First name*, Archbishop of *Place name*	Your Eminence
Archbishop, Roman Catholic	The Most Reverend *First name*, Archbishop of *Place name*	Your Excellency
Archdeacon, Episcopal	The Venerable *Full name*, Archdeacon of *Place name*	Dear Archdeacon *Last name*
Bishop, Episcopal	The Right Reverend *Full name*, Bishop of *Place name*	Right Reverend Sir *or* Dear Bishop *Last name*
Bishop, other Protestant	The Reverend *Full name*	Dear Bishop *Last name*
Bishop, Roman Catholic	The Most Reverend *Full name*, Bishop of *Place name*	Your Excellency *or* Dear Bishop *Last name*
Cardinal	His Eminence *First name* Cardinal *Last name*	Your Eminence
Clergyman/woman, Protestant	The Reverend *Full name or* The Reverend *Full name*, D.D.	Dear Mr./Ms. *Last name or* Dear Dr. *Last name*
Dean of a Cathedral, Episcopal	The Very Reverend *Full name*, Dean of *Place name*	Dear Dean *Last name*
Monsignor	The Right Reverend Monsignor *Full name*	Dear Monsignor
Patriarch, Greek Orthodox	His All Holiness the Patriarch of *Place name*	Your All Holiness
Patriarch, Russian Orthodox	His Holiness the Patriarch of *Place name*	Your Holiness
Pope	His Holiness The Pope	Your Holiness *or* Most Holy Father
Priest, Roman Catholic	The Reverend *Full name or* The Reverend *Full name*, S.J. (or other order)	Dear Reverend Father *or* Dear Father
Rabbi, man or woman	Rabbi *Full name or Full name*, D.D.	Dear Rabbi *Last name or* Dear Dr. *Last name*
Government officials		
Assemblyman/woman	The Honorable *Full name*	Dear Mr./Ms. *Last name*
Associate Justice, U.S. Supreme Court	The Honorable Justice *Full name*	Dear Sir/Madam *or* Justice *Last name*
Cabinet member	The Honorable *Full name*, Secretary of *Department name*	Sir/Madam *or* Dear Mr./Madam Secretary
Chief Justice, U.S. Supreme Court	The Honorable *Full name*, Chief Justice of the United States	Dear Mr./Madame Chief Justice
Commissioner	The Honorable *Full name*	Dear Mr./Mrs. *Last name*
Governor	The Honorable *Full name*, Governor of *State name*	Dear Governor *Last name*
Judge, federal	The Honorable *Full name*, Judge, United States District Court	Dear Sir/Madam *or* Judge *Last name*
Judge, state or local	The Honorable *Full name*, Judge of the Court of *Place name*	Dear Judge *Last name*
Mayor	The Honorable *Full name*, Mayor of *Place name*	Dear Mayor *Last name*
President, U.S.	The President	Dear Mr./Madam President
President, U.S., former	The Honorable *Full name*	Dear Mr./Madam *Last name*
Representative, state	The Honorable *Full name*, *State name* House of Representatives	Dear Mr./Ms. *Last name*
Representative, U.S.	The Honorable *Full name*, United States House of Representativees	Dear Mr./Mrs. *Last name*
Senator, state	The Honorable *Full name*, The State Senate, *State Capital*	Dear Senator *Last name*
Senator, U.S.	The Honorable *Full name*, United States Senate	Dear Senator *Last name*
Speaker, U.S. House of Representatives	The Honorable *Full name*, Speaker of the House of Representatives	Dear Mr./Madam Speaker
Vice President, U.S.	The Vice President of the United States	Sir/Madam *or* Dear Mr./Madam Vice President
Military and naval officers		
All ranks	*Rank Full name*, USA/USN/USCG/ USAF/USMC	Dear *Rank Last name*

Easily Confused Words

affect / effect *Effect* is usually a noun that means a result or the power to produce a result: "The sound of the falling rain had a calming effect, nearly putting me to sleep." *Affect* is usually a verb that means to have an influence on: "His loud humming was affecting my ability to concentrate." Note that *effect* can also be a verb meaning to bring about or execute: "The speaker's somber tone effected a dampening in the general mood of the audience."

all together / altogether *All together* is applied to people or things that are being treated as a group. "We put the pots and pans all together on the shelf." *All together* is the form that must be used if the sentence can be reworded so that *all* and *together* are separated by other words: "We put all the pots and pans together on the shelf." *Altogether* is used to mean entirely: "I am altogether pleased to be receiving this award."

allusion / illusion *Allusion* is a noun that means an indirect reference: "The speech made allusions to the final report." *Illusion* is a noun that means a misconception: "The policy is designed to give an illusion of reform."

alternately / alternatively *Alternately* is an adverb that means in turn; one after the other: "We alternately spun the wheel in the game." *Alternatively* is an adverb that means on the other hand; one or the other: "You can choose a large bookcase or, alternatively, you can buy two small ones."

a.m. / p.m. The abbreviation *a.m.* (from Latin *ante meridiem,* before noon) is used to refer to any hour between midnight and noon. Similarly, *p.m.* (from Latin *post meridiem,* after noon) is used to refer to any hour between noon and midnight. Midnight is 12 a.m. and noon is 12 p.m.

beside / besides *Beside* is a preposition that means next to: "Stand here beside me." *Besides* is an adverb that means also: "Besides, I need to tell you about the new products my company offers."

bimonthly / semimonthly *Bimonthly* is an adjective that means every two months: "I brought the cake for the bimonthly office party." *Bimonthly* is also a noun that means a publication issued every two months: "The company publishes several popular bimonthlies." *Semimonthly* is an adjective that means happening twice a month: "We have semimonthly meetings on the 1st and the 15th."

capital / capitol The city or town that is the seat of government is called the *capital;* the building in which the legislative assembly meets is the *capitol.* The term *capital* can also refer to an accumulation of wealth or to a capital letter.

cite / site *Cite* is a verb that means to quote as an authority or example: "I cited several eminent scholars in my study of water resources." It also means to recognize formally: "The public official was cited for service to the city." It can also mean to summon before a court of law: "Last year the company was cited for pollution violations." *Site* is a noun meaning location: "They chose a new site for the factory just outside town."

complement / compliment *Complement* is a noun or verb that means something that completes or makes up a whole: "The red sweater is a perfect complement to the outfit." *Compliment* is a noun or verb that means an expression of praise or admiration: "I received many compliments about my new outfit."

comprise / compose According to the traditional rule, the whole comprises the parts, and the parts compose the whole. Thus, the board comprises five members, whereas five members compose (or make up) the board. It is also correct to say that the board is composed (not comprised) of five members.

concurrent / consecutive *Concurrent* is an adjective that means simultaneous or happening at the same time as something else: "The concurrent strikes of several unions crippled the economy." *Consecutive* means successive or following one after the other: "The union called three consecutive strikes in one year."

connote / denote *Connote* is a verb that means to imply or suggest: "The word 'espionage' connotes mystery and intrigue." *Denote* is a verb that means to indicate or refer to specifically: "The symbol for 'pi' denotes the number 3.14159."

convince / persuade Strictly speaking, one convinces a person that something is true but persuades a person to do something. "Pointing out that I was overworked, my friends persuaded [not convinced] me to take a vacation. Now that I'm relaxing on the beach with my book, I am convinced [not persuaded] that they were right." Following this rule, *convince* should not be used with an infinitive.

council / councilor / counsel / counselor A *councilor* is a member of a *council,* which is an assembly called together for discussion or deliberation. A *counselor* is one who gives *counsel,* which is advice or guidance. More specifically, a *counselor* can be an attorney or a supervisor at camp.

discreet / discrete *Discreet* is an adjective that means prudent, circumspect, or modest: "Their discreet comments about the negotiations led the reporters to expect an early settlement." *Discrete* is an adjective that means separate or individually distinct: "Each company in the conglomerate operates as a discrete entity."

disinterested / uninterested *Disinterested* is an adjective that means unbiased or impartial: "We appealed to the disinterested mediator to facilitate the negotiations." *Uninterested* is an adjective that means not interested or indifferent: "They seemed uninterested in our offer."

emigrant / immigrant *Emigrant* is a noun that means one who leaves one's native country to settle in another: "The emigrants spent four weeks aboard ship before landing in Los Angeles." *Immigrant* is a noun that means one who enters and settles in a new country: "Most of the immigrants easily found jobs."

farther / further *Farther* is an adjective and adverb that means to or at a more distant point: "We drove 50 miles today; tomorrow, we will travel 100 miles farther." *Further* is an adjective and adverb that means to or at a greater extent or degree: "We won't be able to suggest a solution until we are further along in our evaluation of the problem." It can also mean in addition or moreover: "They stated further that they would not change the policy."

few / less *Few* is an adjective that means small in number. It is used with countable objects: "This department has few employees." *Less* is an adjective that means small in amount or degree. It is used with objects of indivisible mass: "Which jar holds less water?"

figuratively / literally *Figuratively* is an adverb that means metaphorically or symbolically: "Happening upon the shadowy figure, they figuratively jumped out of their shoes." *Literally* is an adverb that means word for word or according to the exact meaning of the words: "I translated the Latin passage literally."

foreword / forward *Foreword* is a noun that means an introductory note or preface: "In my foreword I explained my reasons for writing the book." *Forward* is an adjective or adverb that means toward the front: "I sat in the forward section of the bus. Please step forward when your name is called." *Forward* is also a verb that means to send on: "Forward the letter to the customer's new address."

flammable / inflammable These two words are actually synonyms, both meaning easily set on fire. "The highly flammable (inflammable) fuel was stored safely in a specially built tank."

flaunt / flout To *flaunt* means to show off shamelessly: "Eager to flaunt her knowledge of a wide range of topics, Helene dreamed of appearing on a TV trivia show." To *flout* means to show scorn or contempt for: "Lewis disliked boarding school and took every opportunity to flout the house rules."

founder / flounder In its primary sense *founder* means to sink below the surface of the water: "The ship foundered after colliding with an iceberg." By extension, *founder* means to fail utterly. *Flounder* means to move about clumsily, or to act or proceed with confusion. A good synonym for *flounder* is blunder: "After floundering through the first half of the course, Amy finally passed with the help of a tutor."

hanged / hung *Hanged* is the past tense and past participle of hang when the meaning is to execute by suspending by the neck: "They hanged the prisoner for treason." "The convicted killer was hanged at dawn." *Hung* is the past tense and participle of hang when the meaning is to suspend from above with no support from below: "I hung the painting on the wall." "The painting was hung at a crooked angle."

historic / historical In general usage, *historic* refers to what is important in history, while *historical* applies more broadly to whatever existed in the past whether it was important or not: "A historic summit meeting between the prime ministers; historical buildings torn down in the redevelopment."

it's / its *It's* is a contraction for it is, whereas *its* is the possessive form of it: "It's a shame that we cannot talk about its size."

laid / lain / lay *Laid* is the past tense and the past participle of the verb lay and not the past tense of lie. *Lay* is the past tense of the verb lie and *lain* is the past participle: "He laid his books down and lay down on the couch, where he has lain for an hour."

lend / loan Although some people feel *loan* should only be used as a noun, *lend* and *loan* are both acceptable as verbs in standard English: "Can you lend (loan) me a dollar?" However, only *lend* should be used in figurative senses: "Will you lend me a hand?"

principal / principle *Principal* is a noun that means a person who holds a high position or plays an important role: "The school principal has 20 years of teaching experience. The principals in the negotiations will meet tomorrow at 10 o'clock." It also means a sum of money on which interest accrues: "The depositors were guaranteed they would not lose their principal." *Principal* is also an adjective that means chief or leading: "The necessity of moving to another city was the principal reason I turned down the job offer." *Principle* is a noun that means a rule or standard: "They refused to compromise their principles."

stationary / stationery *Stationary* is an adjective that means fixed or unmoving: "They maneuvered around the stationary barrier in the road." *Stationery* is a noun that means writing materials: "We printed the letters on company stationery."

Foreign Words and Phrases

The English meanings given below are not necessarily literal translations. Foreign words and phrases should be set in italics (or underlined if written in long-hand) if their meanings are likely to be unknown to the reader. Whether the expression is familiar or unfamiliar, however, is a matter of judgment. Below, all foreign words have been italicized for the sake of emphasis.

ad absurdum (ad ab-sir′dum) [Lat.]: to the point of absurdity. "He tediously repeated his argument *ad absurdum.*"

ad infinitum (ad in-fun-eye′tum) [Lat.]: to infinity. "The lecture seemed to drone on *ad infinitum.*"

ad nauseam (ad noz′ee-um) [Lat.]: to a sickening degree. "The politician uttered one platitude after another *ad nauseam.*"

aficionado (uh-fish′ya-nah′doh) [Span.]: an ardent devotee. "I was surprised at what a baseball *aficionado* she had become."

annus mirabilis (an′us muh-ra′buh-lis) [Lat.]: wonderful year. "Last year was the *annus mirabilis* for my company."

a priori (ah pree or′ee) [Lat.]: based on theory rather than observation. "The fact that their house is in such disrepair suggests *a priori* that they are having financial difficulties."

au courant (oh′ koo-rahn′) [Fr.]: up-to-date. "The shoes, the hair, the clothes—every last detail of her dress, in fact—was utterly *au courant.*"

beau geste (boh zhest′) [Fr.]: a fine or noble gesture, often futile. "My fellow writers supported me by writing letters of protest to the publisher, but their *beau geste* could not prevent the inevitable."

beau monde (boh′ mond′) [Fr.]: high society. "Such elegant decor would impress even the *beau monde.*"

bête noire (bet nwahr′) [Fr.]: something or someone particularly disliked. "Talk of the good old college days way back when had become his *bête noire,* and he began to avoid his school friends."

bona fide (boh′na fide) [Lat.]: in good faith; genuine. "For all her reticence and modesty, it was clear that she was a *bona fide* expert in her field."

bon mot (bon moe′) [Fr.]: a witty remark or comment. "One *bon mot* after another flew out of his mouth, charming the audience."

bon vivant (bon vee-vahnt′) [Fr.]: a person who lives luxuriously and enjoys good food and drink. "It's true he's quite the *bon vivant*, but when he gets down to business he conducts himself like a Spartan."

carpe diem (kar′pay dee′um) [Lat.]: seize the day. "So what if you have an 8:00 a.m. meeting tomorrow and a full day of appointments? *Carpe diem!*"

carte blanche (kart blonsh′) [Fr.]: unrestricted power to act on one's own. "I may have *carte blanche* around the office, but at home I'm a slave to my family's demands."

cause célèbre (koz suh-leb′ruh) [Fr.]: a widely known controversial case or issue. "The Sacco and Vanzetti trial became an international *cause célèbre* during the 1920s."

caveat emptor (kav′ee-ot emp′tor) [Lat.]: let the buyer beware. "Before you leap at that real estate deal, *caveat emptor!*"

comme ci comme ça (kom see′ kom sah′) [Fr.]: so-so. "The plans for the party strike me as *comme ci comme ça.*"

comme il faut (kom eel foe′) [Fr.]: as it should be; fitting. "His end was truly *comme il faut.*"

coup de grâce (koo de grahss′) [Fr.]: finishing blow. "After an already wildly successful day, the *coup de grâce* came when she won best all-around athlete."

cri de coeur (kree′ de kur′) [Fr.]: heartfelt appeal. "About to leave the podium, he made a final *cri de coeur* to his people to end the bloodshed."

de rigueur (duh ree-gur′) [Fr.]: strictly required, as by etiquette, usage, or fashion. "Loudly proclaiming one's support for radical causes had become *de rigueur* among her crowd."

deus ex machina (day′us ex mahk′uh-nuh) [Lat.]: a contrived device to resolve a situation. "Stretching plausibility, the movie concluded with a *deus ex machina* ending in which everyone was rescued at the last minute."

dolce vita (dole′chay vee′tuh) [Ital.]: sweet life; the good life perceived as one of physical pleasure and self-indulgence. "My vacation this year is going to be two uninterrupted weeks of *dolce vita.*"

Doppelgänger* (dop′pul-gang-ur) [Ger.]: a ghostly double or counterpart of a living person. "I could not shake the sense that some shadowy *Doppelgänger* echoed my every move."

ecce homo (ek′ay ho′mo) [Lat.]: behold the man. "The painting depicted the common Renaissance theme, *ecce homo*—Christ wearing the crown of thorns."

enfant terrible (ahn-fahn′ tay-reeb′luh) [Fr.]: an incorrigible child; an outrageously outspoken or bold person. "He played the role of *enfant terrible*, jolting us with his blunt assessment."

entre nous (ahn′truh noo′) [Fr.]: between ourselves; confidentially. "*Entre nous,* their marriage is on the rocks."

ex cathedra (ex kuh-thee′druh) [Lat.]: with authority; used especially of those pronouncements of the pope that are considered infallible. "I resigned myself to obeying; my father's opinions were *ex cathedra* in our household."

ex post facto (ex′ post fak′toh) [Lat.]: retroactively. "I certainly hope that the change in policy will be honored *ex post facto.*"

fait accompli (fate ah-kom-plee′) [Fr.]: an accomplished fact, presumably irreversible. "There's no use protesting—it's a *fait accompli.*"

faux pas (foh pah′) [Fr.]: a social blunder. "Suddenly, she realized she had unwittingly committed yet another *faux pas.*"

flagrante delicto (fla-grahn′tee di-lik′toh) [Lat.]: in the act. "The detective realized that without hard evidence he had no case; he would have to catch the culprit *flagrante delicto.*"

glasnost (glaz′nohst) [Rus.]: open and frank discussion: initiated by Mikhail Gorbachev in 1985 in the Soviet Union. "Once the old chairman retired, the spirit of *glasnost* pervaded the department."

hoi polloi (hoy′ puh-loy′) [Gk.]: the common people. "Marie Antoinette recommended cake to the *hoi polloi.*"

in loco parentis (in loh′koh pa-ren′tiss) [Lat.]: in the place of a parent. "The court appointed a guardian for the children, to serve *in loco parentis.*"

in situ (in sĭt′too) [Lat.]: situated in the original or natural position. "I prefer seeing statues *in situ* rather than in the confines of a museum."

in vino veritas (in vee′no vare′i-toss) [Lat.]: in wine there is truth. "By the end of the drunken banquet, several of the guests had made a good deal of their private lives public, prompting the host to murmur to his wife, '*in vino veritas.*'"

ipso facto (ip′soh fak′toh) [Lat.]: by the fact itself. "An extremist, *ipso facto,* cannot become part of a coalition."

je ne sais quoi (zhun say kwah′) [Fr.]: I know not what; an elusive quality. "She couldn't explain it, but there was something *je ne sais quoi* about him that she found devastatingly attractive."

mano a mano (mah′no ah mah′no) [Span.]: a direct confrontation or conflict. "'Stay out of it,' he admonished his friends, 'I want to handle this guy *mano a mano.*'"

mea culpa (may′uh kul′puh) [Lat.]: I am to blame. "His *mea culpa* was so offhand that I hardly think he meant it."

memento mori (muh-men′toh more′ee) [Lat.]: a reminder that you must die. "The skull rested on the mantlepiece as a *memento mori.*"

modus operandi (moh′dus op-er-an′dee) [Lat.]: a method of operating. "Her *modus operandi* is to sugar-coat the truth so thoroughly that the news almost seems welcome."

mot juste (moh zhoost′) [Fr.]: the exact, appropriate word. "'Rats!' screamed the defiant three-year-old, immensely proud of his *mot juste.*"

ne plus ultra (nee′ plus ul′truh) [Lat.]: the most intense degree of a quality or state. "Pulling it from the box, he realized he was face to face with the *ne plus ultra* of computers."

nom de guerre (nom duh gair′) [Fr.]: pseudonym. "He went by his *nom de guerre* when frequenting trendy nightclubs."

nom de plume (nom duh ploom′) [Fr.]: pen name. "Deciding it was time to sit down and begin a novel, the would-be writer spent the first several hours deciding upon a suitably dashing *nom de plume*."

nota bene (noh′tuh ben′nee) [Ital.]: note well; take notice. "She appended her suggestions to the manuscript, underlining the words *nota bene* for added emphasis."

persona non grata (per-soh′nuh non grah′tuh) [Lat.]: unacceptable or unwelcome person. "Once I was cut out of the will, I became *persona non grata* among my relatives."

pro bono (pro boh′noh) [Lat.]: done or donated without charge; free. "The lawyer's *pro bono* work gave him a sense of value that his work on behalf of the corporation could not."

quid pro quo (kwid′ pro kwoh′) [Lat.]: something for something; an equal exchange. "She vowed that when she had the means, she would return his favors *quid pro quo*."

sans souci (sahn soo-see′) [Fr.]: carefree. "Their mood was definitely *sans souci*."

savoir-faire (sav′wahr fair′) [Fr.]: the ability to say and do the correct thing. "She presided over the gathering with impressive *savoir faire*."

sine qua non (sin′ay kwah nohn′) [Lat.]: indispensable. "Lemon is the *sine qua non* of this recipe."

terra incognita (tare′uh in-kog-nee′tuh) [Lat.]: unknown territory. "When the conversation suddenly switched from contemporary fiction to medieval Albanian playwrights, he felt himself entering *terra incognita*."

tout le monde (too luh mond′) [Fr.]: everybody; everyone of importance. "Don't miss the event; it's bound to be attended by *tout le monde*."

veni, vidi, vici (ven′ee vee′dee vee′chee) [Lat.]: I came, I saw, I conquered. "After the takeover the business mogul gloated, '*veni, vidi, vici.*'"

verboten (fer-boh′ten) [Ger.]: forbidden, as by law; prohibited. "That topic, I am afraid, is *verboten* in this household."

vox populi (voks pop′yoo-lie) [Lat.]: the voice of the people. "My sentiments echo those of the *vox populi*."

Wanderjahr* (vahn′der-yahr) [Ger.]: a year or period of travel, especially following one's schooling. "The trio took off on their *Wanderjahr* soon after they graduated, planning to circle the globe by bicycle."

Weltanschauung* (velt′an-shou′ung) [Ger.]: a comprehensive conception or image of the universe and of humanity's relation to it. "His *Weltanschauung* gradually metamorphized from a grim and pessimistic one to a sunny, but no less complex, view."

Weltschmerz* (velt′shmerts) [Ger.]: sorrow over the evils of the world. "His poetry expressed a certain *Weltschmerz*, or world-weariness."

Zeitgeist* (zite′guyst) [Ger.]: the spirit of the time; general trend of thought or feeling characteristic of a particular period of time. "She blamed it on the *Zeitgeist*, which encouraged hedonistic excess."

---

*German nouns are capitalized. A familiar German expression that is not italicized, however, should be lowercased, following the English conventions of not capitalizing common nouns. "His proclivities leaned more to the occult than to the philosophical: a poltergeist he could understand; the *Zeitgeist* he could not."

National Spelling Bee

The National Spelling Bee was launched by the Louisville, Kentucky, *Courier-Journal* in 1925. With competitions, cash prizes, and a trip to the nation's capital, it was hoped the Bee would stimulate "general interest among pupils in a dull subject."

The Scripps Howard News Service took over the Bee in 1941. Over the years the national finals have grown from a mere 9 contestants to about 250, and competition week is marked by ice-cream socials, talent shows, and other events. At the end of the 2000 activities, 12-year-old champion George Abraham Thampy took home $10,000 cash, among other prizes, for correctly spelling *demarche*. Here are the winning words that made past spellers into national champions.

1925	gladiolus	1944	NO BEE	1963	equipage	1982	psoriasis
1926	abrogate	1945	NO BEE	1964	sycophant	1983	Purim
1927	luxuriance	1946	semaphore	1965	eczema	1984	luge
1928	albumen	1947	chlorophyll	1966	ratoon	1985	milieu
1929	asceticism	1948	psychiatry	1967	chihuahua	1986	odontalgia
1930	fracas	1949	dulcimer	1968	abalone	1987	staphylococci
1931	foulard	1950	haruspex	1969	interlocutory	1988	elegiacal
1932	knack	1951	insouciant	1970	croissant	1989	spoliator
1933	propitiatory	1952	vignette	1971	shalloon	1990	fibranne
1934	deteriorating	1953	soubrette	1972	macerate	1991	antipyretic
1935	intelligible	1954	transept	1973	vouchsafe	1992	lyceum
1936	interning	1955	custaceology	1974	hydrophyte	1993	kamikaze
1937	promiscuous	1956	condominium	1975	incisor	1994	antediluvian
1938	sanitarium	1957	schappe	1976	narcolepsy	1995	xanthosis
1939	canonical	1958	syllepsis	1977	cambist	1996	vivisepulture
1940	therapy	1959	cacolet	1978	deification	1997	euonym
1941	initials	1960	troche	1979	maculature	1998	chiaroscurist
1942	sacrilegious	1961	smaragdine	1980	elucubrate	1999	logorrhea
1943	NO BEE	1962	esquamulose	1981	sarcophagus	2000	demarche

Frequently Misspelled Words

absence	descent	humorous	mischievous	receive
address	desperate	independent	misspell	rhythm
advice	device	jealous	mysterious	sacrilegious
all right	disastrous	jewelry	necessary	science
arctic	embarrass	judgment	neighbor	scissors
believe	exercise	ketchup	nuclear	separate
bicycle	fascinate	knowledge	occasion	sincerely
broccoli	February	leisure	odyssey	special
bureau	fluorescent	library	piece	thorough
calendar	foreign	license	pigeon	through
camaraderie	government	mathematics	playwright	truly
ceiling	grateful	mediocre	prejudice	until
changeable	guarantee	millennium	privilege	Wednesday
conscientious	harass	miniature	pumpkin	weird
conscious	height	miscellaneous	raspberry	you're

American Sign Language and the Manual Alphabet

Sign language for the deaf was first systematized in France during the eighteenth century by Abbot Charles-Michel l'Epée. French Sign Language (FSL) was brought to the United States in 1816 by Thomas Gallaudet, founder of the American School for the Deaf in Hartford, Connecticut. He developed American Sign Language (ASL), a language of gestures and hand symbols that express words and concepts. It is the fourth most used language in the United States today.

Along with sign language and lip reading, many deaf people communicate with the manual alphabet, which uses finger positions that correspond to the letters of the alphabet to spell out words.

"You give it to me." or "Give it to me."

"How many?" or "How many do you want?"

"What's up?"

"last year" or "one year ago"

American Manual Alphabet

Baker-Shenk, C., and Cokely, D., *American Sign Language: A Teacher's Resource Text on Grammar and Culture* (1980). Washington, D.C.: Gallaudet University Press. Copyright © 1980 Charlotte Baker and Dennis Cokely. Reprinted with permission of the publisher.

The 50 Most Widely Spoken Languages[1] in the World

Rank, language	Countries[2]	Population[3] (in millions)
1. Chinese, Mandarin	Brunei, Cambodia, China, Indonesia, Malaysia, Mongolia, Philippines, Singapore, S. Africa, Taiwan, Thailand	885.0
2. Spanish	Andorra, Argentina, Belize, Bolivia, Chile, Colombia, Costa Rica, Cuba, Dominican Rep., Ecuador, El Salvador, Eq. Guinea, Guatemala, Honduras, Mexico, Nicaragua, Panama, Paraguay, Peru, Spain, Uruguay, U.S., Venezuela	332.0
3. English	Australia, Botswana, Brunei, Cameroon, Canada, Eritrea, Ethiopia, Fiji, The Gambia, Guyana, Ireland, Israel, Lesotho, Liberia, Malaysia, Micronesia, Namibia, Nauru, New Zealand, Palau, Papua New Guinea, Samoa, Seychelles, Sierra Leone, Singapore, Solomon Islands, Somalia, S. Africa, Suriname, Swaziland, Tonga, U.K., U.S., Vanuatu, Zimbabwe, many Caribbean states	322.0
4. Bengali	Bangladesh, India, Singapore	189.0
5. Hindi	India, Nepal, Singapore, S. Africa, Uganda	182.0
6. Portuguese	Brazil, Cape Verde, France, Guinea-Bissau, Portugal, São Tomé and Príncipe	170.0
7. Russian	China, Israel, Mongolia, Russia, U.S.	170.0
8. Japanese	Japan, Singapore, Taiwan	125.0
9. German, Standard	Austria, Belgium, Bolivia, Czech Rep., Denmark, Germany, Hungary, Italy, Kazakhstan, Liechtenstein, Luxembourg, Paraguay, Poland, Romania, Slovenia, Switzerland	98.0
10. Chinese, Wu	China	77.2
11. Javanese	Indonesia, Malaysia, Singapore	75.5
12. Korean	China, Japan, N. Korea, S. Korea, Singapore, Thailand	75.0
13. French	Andorra, Belgium, Burkina Faso, Burundi, Cameroon, Canada, Comoros, Congo, Congo (Dem. Rep. of), Djibouti, France, Gabon, Guinea, Haiti, Luxembourg, Mauritania, Monaco, Rwanda, Senegal, Seychelles, Switzerland, Vanuatu	72.0
14. Vietnamese	China, Vietnam	67.7
15. Telugu	India, Singapore	66.4
16. Chinese, Yue (Cantonese)	Brunei, China, Costa Rica, Indonesia, Malaysia, Panama, Philippines, Singapore, Thailand, Vietnam	66.0
17. Marathi	India	64.8
18. Tamil	India, Malaysia, Mauritius, Singapore, S. Africa, Sri Lanka	63.1
19. Turkish	Bulgaria, Cyprus, Greece, Macedonia, Romania, Turkey, Uzbekistan	59.0
20. Urdu	Afghanistan, India, Mauritius, Pakistan, S. Africa, Thailand	58.0
21. Chinese, Min Nan	Brunei, China, Indonesia, Malaysia, Philippines, Singapore, Taiwan, Thailand	49.0
22. Chinese, Jinyu	China	45.0
23. Gujarati	India, Kenya, Pakistan, Singapore, S. Africa, Tanzania, Uganda, Zambia, Zimbabwe	44.0
24. Polish	Czech Rep., Germany, Israel, Poland, Romania, Slovakia	44.0
25. Arabic, Egyptian	Egypt	42.5
26. Ukrainian	Poland, Slovakia, Ukraine	41.0
27. Italian	Croatia, Eritrea, France, Italy, San Marino, Slovenia, Switzerland	37.0
28. Chinese, Xiang	China	36.0
29. Malayalam	India, Singapore	34.0
30. Chinese, Hakka	Brunei, China, Indonesia, Malaysia, Panama, Singapore, Suriname, Taiwan, Thailand	34.0
31. Kannada	India	33.7
32. Oriya	India	31.0
33. Panjabi, Western	India, Pakistan	30.0
34. Sunda	Indonesia	27.0
35. Panjabi, Eastern	India, Kenya, Singapore	26.0
36. Romanian	Hungary, Israel, Moldova, Romania, Serbia and Montenegro, Ukraine	26.0
37. Bhojpuri	India, Mauritius, Nepal	25.0
38. Azerbaijani, South	Afghanistan, Iran, Iraq, Syria, Turkey	24.4
39. Farsi, Western	Iran, Iraq, Oman, Qatar, Tajikistan, United Arab Emirates	24.3
40. Maithili	India, Nepal	24.3
41. Hausa	Benin, Burkina Faso, Cameroon, Ghana, Niger, Nigeria, Sudan, Togo	24.2
42. Arabic, Algerian	Algeria	22.4
43. Burmese	Bangladesh, Myanmar	22.0
44. Serbo-Croatian[4]	Bosnia and Herzegovina, Croatia, Macedonia, Serbia and Montenegro, Slovakia	21.0
45. Chinese, Gan	China	20.6
46. Awadhi	India, Nepal	20.5
47. Thai	Singapore, Thailand	20.0
48. Dutch	Belgium, France, Netherlands, Suriname	20.0
49. Yoruba	Benin, Nigeria	20.0
50. Sindhi	Afghanistan, India, Pakistan, Singapore	19.7

1. Many of the languages listed are technically dialects, not separate languages. They are listed separately because they differ from each other enough to be mutually unintelligible. 2. The countries listed under Spanish, English, Portuguese, French, and Serbo-Croatian do not include those in which less than 1% of the population speaks the language as a first language. 3. The population figures refer to first language speakers in all countries and are general estimates. 4. Serbo-Croatian is now known variously as Serbian, Croatian, or Bosnian, depending on the speaker's ethnic or political affiliation. *Source: Ethnologue,* 13th Edition, Barbara F. Grimes, Editor. © 1996, Summer Institute of Linguistics, Inc.

U.S. Societies and Associations

Source: Questionnaires to organizations. Names are listed alphabetically according to key word in title; figure in parentheses is year of founding; other figure is membership.

The following is a partial list selected for general readership interest. A comprehensive listing of approximately 23,000 national and international organizations can be found in the *Encyclopedia of Associations,* 34th ed., 2000, published by Gale Research Company, 835 Penobscot Building, 645 Griswold St., Detroit, Mich. 48226-4049, available in most public libraries.

AARP (American Association of Retired Persons) (1958): 601 E. St. N.W., Washington, D.C. 20049. 33,000,000. Phone: (800) 424-3410. www.aarp.org.

Abortion Federation, National (1977): 1755 Mass. Ave., Ste. 600, Washington, D.C. 20036. Phone: (202) 667-5881 (Communications Director) or (800) 772-9100. www.prochoice.org.

Accountants, American Institute of Certified Public (1887): 1211 Avenue of the Americas, New York, N.Y. 10036-8775. 330,000. Phone: (212) 596-6200. www.aicpa.org.

ACSM: American Congress on Surveying and Mapping (1941): 5410 Grosvenor Lane, Ste. 100, Bethesda, Md. 20814-2144. 8,000. Phone: (301) 493-0200. www.survmap.org.

Actors' Equity Association (1913): 165 W. 46th St., New York, N.Y. 10036. 40,000. Phone: (212) 869-8530. www.actorsequity.org.

Actuaries, Society of (1949): 475 N. Martingale Rd., Ste. 800, Schaumburg, Ill. 60173-2226. 16,500. Phone: (847) 706-3500. www.soa.org.

Aeronautic Association, National (1905): 1815 N. Fort Myer Dr., Ste. 700, Arlington, Va. 22209. 300,000. Phone: (703) 527-0226. www.naa.ycg.org.

African-American Institute, The (1953): 380 Lexington Ave., New York, N.Y. 10168-4298. Phone: (212) 949-5666.

AFS Intercultural Programs—USA (American Field Service) (1947): 198 Madison Avenue, 8th Flr., New York, N.Y. 10016. 100,000. Phone: (212) 299-9000 or (800) AFS-INFO. www.afs.org.

Agricultural History Society (1919): Univ. of Arkansas, 2801 University Ave., Little Rock, Ark. 72204. 1,400. Phone: (501) 569–3235. www.iastate.edu/~history_info/aghissoc.htm.

Agronomy, American Society of (1907): 677 S. Segoe Rd., Madison, Wis. 53711-1086. 11,400. Phone: (608) 273-8080; fax: (608) 273-2021. www.agronomy.org.

Air & Waste Management Association (1907): One Gateway Center, 3rd Flr., Pittsburgh, Pa. 15222. 14,000. Phone: (412) 232-3444. www.awma.org.

Aircraft Association, Experimental (1953): P.O. Box 3086, Oshkosh, Wis. 54903-3086. 170,000. Phone: (920) 426-4800. www.eaa.org.

Aircraft Owners and Pilots Association (1939): 421 Aviation Way, Frederick, Md. 21701-4798. 350,000. Phone: (301) 695-2000; fax: (301) 695-2375. www.aopa.org.

Air Force Association (1946): 1501 Lee Highway, Arlington, Va. 22209-1198. 150,000. Phone: (703) 247-5800. www.afa.org.

Air Line Pilots Association (1931): 1625 Massachusetts Ave. N.W., Washington, D.C. 20036 and 535 Herndon Pkwy., Herndon, Va. 20170. 50,000. Phone: (703) 689-2270. www.alpa.org.

Al-Anon Family Group Headquarters, Inc. For families and friends of alcoholics. (1951): 1600 Corporate Landing Pkwy., Virginia Beach, Va. 23454-5617. 33,000 groups worldwide. Phone: (757) 563-1600. www.al-anon.org.

Alcoholics Anonymous (1935): A.A. World Services, Inc., P.O. Box 459, New York, N.Y. 10163. 2,000,000. Phone: (212) 870-3400. www.aa.org.

Alexander Graham Bell Association for the Deaf (1890): 3417 Volta Place N.W., Washington, D.C. 20007-2778. 6,200. Phone: (202) 337-5220 V, 337-5221 TTY; fax: (202) 337-8314. www.agbell.org.

Alzheimer's Association (1980): 919 N. Michigan Ave., Ste. 1000, Chicago, Ill. 60611-1676. 200 chapters. Phone: (312) 335-8700; (800) 272-3900. www.alz.org.

American Academy of Allergy, Asthma and Immunology (1943): 611 E. Wells St., Milwaukee, Wis. 53202. 5,000. Phone: (414) 272-6071. www.aaaai.org.

American Alliance for Health, Physical Education, Recreation and Dance (1885): 1900 Association Dr., Reston, Va. 20191. 26,000. Phone: (703) 476-3400. www.aahperd.org.

American Automobile Association (1902): 1000 AAA Dr., Heathrow, Fla. 32746-5063. Phone: (407) 444-7000. www.aaa.com.

American Civil Liberties Union (1920): 125 Broad St., 18th Flr., New York, N.Y. 10004-2400. 275,000. www.aclu.org.

American Contract Bridge League (1927): 2990 Airways Blvd., Memphis, Tenn. 38116-3847. Phone: (800) 467-1623; fax: (901) 398-7754. www.acbl.org.

American Federation of Labor and Congress of Industrial Organizations (AFL-CIO) (1955): 815 16th St. N.W., Washington, D.C. 20006. 13,000,000. Phone: (202) 637-5000. www.aflcio.org.

American Federation of Musicians of the United States and Canada (1896): 1501 Broadway, Ste. 600, Paramount Bldg., New York, N.Y. 10036. Phone: (212) 869-1330. www.afm.org.

American Forests (1875): P.O. Box 2000, Washington, D.C. 20013. 115,000. Phone: (202) 955-4500. www.americanforests.org.

American Foundrymen's Society, Inc. (1896): 505 State St., Des Plaines, Ill. 60016-8399. 13,000. Phone: (847) 824-0181; (800) 537-4237. www.afsinc.org.

American Friends Service Committee (1917): 1501 Cherry St., Philadelphia, Pa. 19102-1479. Phone: (215) 241-7000. www.afsc.org.

American Geographical Society, The (1851): 120 Wall St., Ste. 100, New York, N.Y. 10005-3904. 1,500. Phone: (212) 422-5456; fax: (212) 422-5480. email: amgeosoc@earthlink.net. www.amergeog.org.

American Geriatrics Society (1942): 350 Fifth Ave., Ste. 801, New York, N.Y. 10118. 6,000. Phone: (212) 308-1414; fax: (212) 832-8646. www.americangeriatrics.org.

American Heart Association (1924): 7272 Greenville Ave., Dallas, Tex. 75231-4596. 4,200,000 volunteers. Phone: (800) AHA-USA1. www.americanheart.org.

American Historical Association (1884): 400 A St. S.E., Washington, D.C. 20003-3889. 15,000. Phone: (202) 544-2422. email: aha@theaha.org. www.theaha.org.

American Indian Affairs, Association on (1923): Tekakwitha Complex, Agency Road #7, Box 268,

Sisseton, S.D. 57262. 40,000. Phone: (605) 698-3998. www.indian-affairs.org.

American Jewish Committee (1906): Jacob Blaustein Building, 165 East 56th Street, New York, N.Y. 10022. 100,000. Phone: (212) 751-4000; fax: (212) 838-2120. www.ajc.org.

American Kennel Club (1884): 260 Madison Ave., New York, N.Y. 10016. 505 member clubs. Phone: (212) 696-8200; (919) 233-9767 (customer service). www.akc.org.

American Legion, The (1919): 700 N. Pennsylvania St., Indianapolis, Ind. 46206. 3,000,000. Phone: (317) 630-1200. www.legion.org.

American Legion Auxiliary (1919): 777 N. Meridian St., 3rd Flr., Indianapolis, Ind. 46204. 1,000,000. Phone: (317) 635-6291. www.legion-aux.org.

American Mensa Ltd. (1960): 1229 Corporate Drive West, Arlington, Texas 76006–6103. 50,000. Phone: (817) 607-0060. www.us.mensa.org.

American Montessori Society (1960): 281 Park Avenue South, 6th Flr., New York, N.Y. 10010-6102. Phone: (212) 358-1250; fax: (212) 358-1256. www.amshq.org.

American Museum of Natural History (1869): Central Park West at 79th St., New York, N.Y. 10024-5192. 500,000. Phone: (212) 769-5606. www.amnh.org.

American Planning Association (1917) and American Institute of Certified Planners: Administrative Offices: 122 S. Michigan Ave., Chicago, Ill. 60603. 30,000. Phone: (312) 431-9100. Headquarters: 1776 Massachusetts Ave. N.W., Washington, D.C. 20036. Phone: (202) 872-0611. www.planning.org.

Americans for Democratic Action, Inc. (1947): 1625 K St. N.W., Ste. 210, Washington, D.C. 20006. 70,000. Phone: (202) 785-5980. www.adaction.org.

American Society for Nutritional Sciences (1928): 9650 Rockville Pike, Bethesda, Md. 20814-3990. 3,600. Phone: (301) 530-7050. www.faseb.org/asns.

American Society for Public Administration (ASPA) (1939): 1120 G St. N.W., Ste. 700, Washington, D.C. 20005. 12,000. Phone: (202) 393-7878. www.aspanet.org.

American Universities, Association of (1900): 1200 New York Avenue NW, Ste. 550, Washington, D.C. 20005. Phone: (202) 408-7500. www.tulane.edu/~aau.

American Water Resources Association (1964): 4 W. Federal St., P.O. Box 1626, Middleburg, Va. 20118-1626. Phone: (540) 687-8390. www.awra.org.

Amnesty International USA (1961): 322 Eighth Ave., New York, N.Y. 10001. 300,000. Phone: (212) 807-8400. www.amnesty-usa.org.

AMVETS (American Veterans of World War II, Korea, and Vietnam) (1943): 4647 Forbes Blvd., Lanham, Md. 20706-4380. 250,000. Phone: (301) 459-9600. www.amvets.org.

Animals, The American Society for the Prevention of Cruelty to (ASPCA) (1866): 424 E. 92nd St., New York, N.Y. 10128-6804. 400,000+. Phone: (212) 876-7700. www.aspca.org.

Animals, The Fund For, Inc. (1967): 200 W. 57th St., New York, N.Y. 10019. 175,000. Phone: (212) 246-2096. www.fund.org.

Anthropological Association, American (1902): 4350 N. Fairfax Dr., Ste. 640, Arlington, Va. 22203-1620. 11,500. Phone: (703) 528-1902. www.aaanet.org.

Anti-Defamation League (1913): 823 United Nations Plaza, New York, N.Y. 10017-3560. Phone: (212) 885-7700. www.adl.org.

Anti-Vivisection Society, The American (1883): 801 Old York Rd., #204, Jenkintown, Pa. 19046-1685. 15,000. Phone: (215) 887-0816; fax: (215) 887-2088. www.aavs.org.

Appraisers, American Society of (1936): 555 Herndon Parkway, Ste. 125, Herndon, VA 20170.

6,500. Phone: (800) ASA-VALU or (703) 478-2228. www.appraisers.org.

Arboriculture, International Society of (1924): P.O. Box 3129, Champaign, Ill. 61826-3129. 8,000. Phone: (217) 355-9411; fax (217) 355-9516. email: isa@isa-arbor.com. www2.champaign.isa-arbor.com.

Archaeological Institute of America (1879): 656 Beacon St., Boston, Mass. 02215-2006. 11,000. Phone: (617) 353-9361. email: aia@bu.edu. www.archaeological.org.

Architects, The American Institute of (1857): 1735 New York Ave. N.W., Washington, D.C. 20006-5292. 59,000. Phone: (202) 626-7300. www.aiaonline.com.

Architectural Historians, Society of (1940): 1365 N. Astor St., Chicago, Ill. 60610-2144. 4,000. Phone: (312) 573-1365; fax: (312) 573-1141. www.sah.org.

Army, Association of the United States (1950): 2425 Wilson Blvd., Arlington, Va. 22201-3385. 100,000+. Phone: (703) 841-4300. www.ausa.org.

Arthritis Foundation (1948): 1330 West Peachtree St., Atlanta, Ga. 30309. Over 150 local offices. Phone: (404) 872-7100; (800) 283-7800. www.arthritis.org.

Arts, National Endowment for the (1965): 1100 Pennsylvania Ave. N.W., Washington, D.C. 20506. Phone: (202) 682-5400. arts.endow.gov.

ASM International ® (formerly the American Society for Metals) (1913): 9639 Kinsman Rd., Materials Park, Ohio 44073-0002. 44,000. Phone: (440) 338-5151; fax: (440) 338-4634. www.asm-intl.org.

Association for Investment Management and Research (1990): P.O. Box 3668, Ray C. Hunt Dr., Charlottesville, Va. 22903-0668. 36,000. Phone: (800) 247-8132. www.aimr.com.

Astronomical Society, American (1899): 2000 Florida Ave. ,Ste. 400, Washington, D.C. 20009. 6,300. Phone: (202) 328-2010. www.aas.org.

Atheists, American (1963): P.O. Box 5733, Parsippany, N.J. 07054-6733. 40,000 families. Phone: (908) 276-7300. www.atheists.org.

Audubon Society, National (1905): 700 Broadway, New York, N.Y. 10003-9562. 550,000. Phone: (212) 979-3000. www.audubon.org.

Authors League of America (1912): 330 W. 42nd St., 29th Flr., New York, N.Y. 10036-6902. 14,000. Phone: (212) 564-8350.

Autism Society of America (1965): 7910 Woodmont Ave., Ste. 300, Bethesda, Md. 20814-3015. 18,000+. Phone: (301) 657-0881; (800) 3AUTISM. www.autism-society.org.

Automobile Club, National (1924): 1151 East Hillsdale Blvd., Foster City, Calif. 94404. 200,000. Phone: (650) 294-7000. www.nationalautoclub.com.

Bar Association, American (1878): 541 N. Fairbanks Court, Chicago, Ill. 60611. 371,000. Phone: (800) 285-2211. www.abanet.org.

Barber Shop Quartet Singing in America, Society for the Preservation and Encouragement of (SPEBSQSA, Inc.) (1938): 6315 Third Ave., Kenosha, Wis. 53143. 34,000. Phone: (800) 876-SING. www.spebsqsa.org.

Better Business Bureaus, Council of (1912): 4200 Wilson Blvd., Ste. 800, Arlington, Va. 22203-1804. Phone: (703) 276-0100; fax: (703) 525-8277. www.bbb.org.

Bible Society, American (1816): 1865 Broadway, New York, N.Y. 10023-7505. Phone: (800) 32-BIBLE; (212) 408-1200. www.americanbible.org.

Biblical Literature, Society of (1880): 825 Houston Mill Road, Ste. 350, Atlanta, Ga. 30329. 7,000 members, 1,200 subscribers. Phone: (404) 727-3100; fax: (404) 727-3101. www.sbl-site.org.

Big Brothers Big Sisters of America (1977): 230 N. 13th St., Philadelphia, Pa. 19107. Phone: (215) 567-7000. www.bbbsa.org.

Biochemistry and Molecular Biology, American Society for (1906): 9650 Rockville Pike, Bethesda,

Md. 20814. 10,000. Phone: (301) 530-7145. www.faseb.org/asbmb.

Biological Sciences, American Institute of (1947): 1444 I St. N.W., Ste. 200, Washington, D.C. 20005. 6,000. Phone: (202) 628-1500. www.aibs.org.

Blind, American Council of the (1961): 1155 15th St. N.W., Ste. 1004, Washington, D.C. 20005. 40,000. Phone: (202) 467-5081. www.acb.org.

Blind, National Federation of the (1940): 1800 Johnson St., Baltimore, Md. 21230. 50,000. Phone: (410) 659-9314. www.nfb.org.

B'nai B'rith International (1843): 1640 Rhode Island Ave. N.W., Washington, D.C. 20036-3278. 500,000. Phone: (202) 857-6600. www.bnaibrith.org.

Booksellers Association, American (1900): 828 So. Broadway, Tarrytown, N.Y. 10591. 4,500. Phone: (914) 591-2665, (800) 637-0037. www.bookweb.org.

Boys & Girls Clubs of America (1906): 1230 West Peachtree St. N.W., Atlanta, Ga., 30309. 2,800,000 youth served. Phone: (404) 815-5700; fax: (404) 815-5757. www.bgca.org.

Boy Scouts of America (1910): 1325 W. Walnut Hill Lane, P.O. Box 152079, Irving, Tex. 75015-2079. 4.8 mil. Phone: (972) 580-2000. www.bsa.scouting.org.

Broadcasters, National Association of (1922): 1771 N St. N.W., Washington, D.C. 20036-2891. Phone: (202) 429-5490. www.nab.org.

Brookings Institution, The (1916): 1775 Massachusetts Ave. N.W., Washington, D.C. 20036-2188. Phone: (202) 797-6000. www.brookings.org.

Business Education Association, National (1946): 1914 Association Dr., Reston, Va. 20191-1596. 16,000. Phone: (703) 860-8300; fax: (703) 620-4483. email: nbea@nbea.org; www.nbea.org.

Business Women's Association, American (1949): 9100 Ward Parkway, P.O. Box 8728, Kansas City, Mo. 64114-0728. 80,000. Phone: (800) 228-0007. fax: (816) 361-4991. email: abwa@abwahq.org. www.abwahq.org.

Camp Fire Boys and Girls (1910): 4601 Madison Ave., Kansas City, Mo. 64112-1278. 629,000. Phone: (816) 756-1950. www.campfire.org.

Camping Association, The American (1910): 5000 State Rd. 67 N., Martinsville, Ind. 46151-7902. 5,500, 2,000+ camps. Phone: (765) 342-8456. www.acacamps.org.

Cancer Society, American (1913): 1599 Clifton Rd. N.E., Atlanta, Ga. 30329. Over 2 million volunteers. Phone: (800) ACS-2345 or check local listings. www.cancer.org.

CARE, Inc. (1945): 151 Ellis St. NE, Atlanta, Ga. 30303-2439. Programs in 62 developing countries. Phone: (800) 521-CARE. www.care.org.

Carnegie Endowment for International Peace (1910): 1779 Massachusetts Ave., N.W., Washington, D.C. 20036–2103. Phone: (202) 483-7600; fax: (202) 483-1840. www.ceip.org.

Catholic Charities USA (1910): 1731 King St., Ste. 200, Alexandria, Va. 22314. 1,400 agencies and institutions. Phone: (703) 549-1390. www.catholiccharitiesusa.org.

Catholic Daughters of the Americas (1903): 10 W. 71st St., New York, N.Y. 10023. 115,000. Phone: (212) 877-3041. www.catholicdaughters.org.

Catholic War Veterans of the U.S.A. Inc. (1935): 441 N. Lee St., Alexandria, Va. 22314. 35,000. Phone: (703) 549-3622. www.va.gov/vso/cwv.htm.

Cerebral Palsy Associations, Inc., United (1949): 1660 L St. N.W., Ste. 700, Washington, D.C. 20036. 153 affiliates. Phone: (202) 973-7197 TTY, (800) 872-5827 V. www.ucpa.org.

Chamber of Commerce of the U.S. (1912): 1615 H St. N.W., Washington, D.C. 20062. 220,000. Phone: (202) 659-6000. www.uschamber.org.

Chemical Engineers, American Institute of (1908): 3 Park Ave., New York, N.Y. 10016-5991. 52,000. Phone: (212) 591-8100; (800) 242-4363. www.aiche.org.

Chemical Society, American (1876): 1155 16th St. N.W., Washington, D.C. 20036. 151,024. Phone: (202) 872-4600. www.acs.org.

Chess Federation, United States (1939): 3054 NYS Rte. 9W, New Windsor, N.Y. 12553. 50,000+. Phone: (914) 562-8350; (800) 388-KING. www.uschess.org.

Child Labor Committee, National (1904): 1501 Broadway, Rm. 1111, New York, N.Y. 10036. Phone: (212) 840-1801. www.kapow.org.

Children's Book Council (1945): 568 Broadway, Ste. 404, New York, N.Y. 10012. 80. Phone: (212) 966-1990; fax: (212) 966-2073. email: staff@cbcbooks.org. www.cbcbooks.org.

Child Welfare League of America (1920): 440 First St. N.W., Ste. 310, Washington, D.C. 20001-2085. 1,000 agencies. Phone: (202) 638-2952. www.cwla.org.

Chiropractic Association, American (1963): 1701 Clarendon Blvd., Arlington, Va. 22209. 22,000. Phone: (703) 276-8800, (800) 986-4636; fax: (703) 243-2593. www.amerchiro.org.

Cities, National League of (1924): 1301 Pennsylvania Ave. N.W., Washington, D.C. 20004-1763. 18,000 cities and towns. Phone: (202) 626-3000. www.nlc.org.

Civil Air Patrol, National Headquarters (1941): 105 S. Hansell St., Bldg. 714, Maxwell AFB, Ala. 36112-6332. 53,000. Phone: (334) 953-4287. www.capnhq.gov.

Civil Engineers, American Society of (1852): 1801 Alexander Bell Dr., Reston, Va. 20191-4400. 123,000. Phone: (800) 548–ASCE (2723); (703) 295-6300. www.asce.org.

Clinical Pathologists, American Society of (1922): 2100 W. Harrison St., Chicago, Ill. 60612. 77,200. Phone: (312) 738-1336; fax: (312) 738-9798. www.ascp.org.

The College Fund/UNCF (1944): 8260 Willow Oaks Corporate Dr., P.O. Box 10444, Fairfax, Va. 22031. 39 member institutions. Phone: (703) 205-3400, (800) 331-2244; fax: (703) 205-3576. www.uncf.org.

Colleges and Employers, National Association of (formerly College Placement Council) (1956): 62 E. Highland Ave., Bethlehem, Pa. 18017. 3,200. Phone: (800) 544-5272. www.jobweb.org.

Common Cause (1970): 1250 Connecticut Ave. N.W., Washington, D.C. 20036. 250,000. Phone: (202) 833-1200; fax: (202) 659-3716. www.commoncause.org.

Community Cultural Center Association, American (1978): 149 Cannongate 3, Nashua, N.H. 03063. Phone: (603) 886-2748; fax: (603) 886-7944.

Composers/USA, National Association of (1933): P.O. Box 49256, Barrington Station, Los Angeles, Calif. 90049. 600. Phone: (310) 541-8213. www.music-usa.org/nacusa/.

Congress of Racial Equality (CORE) (1942): 817 Broadway, 3rd Flr., New York, N.Y. 10003. Nationwide network of chapters. Phone: (212) 598-4000; fax: (212) 598-4000. www.core-online.org.

Conscientious Objectors, Central Committee for (1948): 1515 Cherry St., Philadelphia, Pa. 19102. Phone: (215) 563-8787. 630 20th St., Oakland, Calif. 94612. Phone: (510) 465-1617. www.objector.org.

Conservation Engineers, Association of (1961): Attn: David Kempf, Missouri Dept. of Conservation. Phone: (573) 522-2323 x2236; fax: (573) 522-2324. www.conservation.state.mo.us/engineering/ace.

Consumer Federation of America (1968): 1424 16th St. N.W., Ste. 604, Washington, D.C. 20036. 260 member organizations. Phone: (202) 387-6121. www.consumerfed.org.

Consumers League, National (1899): 1701 K St. N.W., Ste. 1200, Washington, D.C. 20006. Phone: (202) 835-3323. www.natlconsumersleague.org.

Consumers Union (1936): 101 Truman Ave., Yonkers, N.Y. 10703-1057. 4.6 million subscribers to *Consumer Reports Magazine.* Phone: (914) 378-2000. www.consumersunion.org.

Country Music Association (1958): One Music Circle South, Nashville, Tenn. 37203. 7,000+. Phone: (615) 244-2840. www.cmaworld.com.

Credit Management, National Association of (1896): 8840 Columbia 100 Parkway, Columbia, Md. 21045-2158. 30,000+ members. Phone: (410) 740-5560. www.nacm.org.

Credit Union National Association (1934): P.O. Box 431, Madison, Wis. 53701-0431. 51 state leagues representing 12,400 credit unions. Phone: (800) 356-9655. www.cuna.org.

Crime and Delinquency, National Council on (1907): 685 Market St., #620, San Francisco, Calif. 94105. Criminal justice research, nationwide membership. Phone: (415) 896-6223.

CSA/USA, Celiac Sprue Association/United States of America, Inc., (1978): P.O. Box 31700, Omaha, Neb. 68131-0700. 6 regions in U.S., 74 chapters, 36 active resource units. Phone: (402) 558-0600; fax: (402) 558-1347. www.csaceliacs.org.

Dairy Council, National (1915): 10255 W. Higgins Rd., Ste. 900 Rosemont, Ill. 60018-5616. Phone: (847) 803-2000; fax: (847) 803-2077. www.nationaldairycouncil.org.

Daughters of the American Revolution, National Society (1896): 1776 D St. N.W., Washington, D.C. 20006-5392. 172,000. Phone: (202) 628-1776. www.dar.org.

Deaf, National Association of the (1880): 814 Thayer Ave., Silver Spring, Md. 20910-4500. 51 state association affiliates. Phone: (301) 587-1788 V; (301) 587-1789 TTY. www.nad.org.

Defenders of Wildlife (1947): 1101 14th St. N.W., #1400, Washington, D.C. 20005. 200,000 members and supporters. Phone: (202) 682-9400. www.defenders.org.

Dental Association, American (1859): 211 E. Chicago Ave., Chicago, Ill. 60611. 141,000. Phone: (312) 440-2500. www.ada.org.

Diabetes Association, American (1940): 1701 N. Beauregard St., Alexandria, Va. 22311. Phone: (703) 549-1500; (800) 342-2383. www.diabetes.org/default.asp.

Dignity (1969): 1500 Massachusetts Ave. N.W., Ste. 11, Washington, D.C. 20005. 5,000. Phone: (202) 861-0017 and (800) 877-8797. www.dignityusa.org.

Disabled American Veterans (1920): 807 Maine Ave. S.W., Washington, D.C. 20024. 1,400,000. Phone: (202) 554-3501. www.dav.org.

Dowsers, Inc., The American Society of (1961): P.O. Box 24, Danville, Vt. 05828. 5,000. Phone: (800) 711-9530; fax: (802) 748-8565. email: ASD@dowsers.org. www.dowsers.org.

Ducks Unlimited, Inc. (1937): One Waterfowl Way, Memphis, Tenn. 38120. 600,000. Phone: (901) 758-3825. www.ducks.org.

Earthwatch (1971): 3 Clock Tower Place, Ste. 100, Box 75, Maynard, Mass. 01754. 75,000. Phone: (978) 461-0081. www.earthwatch.org.

Eastern Star, Order of, General Grand Chapter (1876): 1618 New Hampshire Ave. N.W., Washington, D.C. 20009-2549. 1,207,301. Phone: (202) 667-4737. www.easternstar.org.

Easter Seal Society, The National (1919): 230 W. Monroe, Ste. 1800, Chicago, Ill. 60606. 109 state and local affiliate societies operating 500 service sites. Phone: (312) 726-6200; (312) 726-4258 TTY. www.easter-seals.org.

Economic Association, American (1885): 2014 Broadway, Ste. 305, Nashville, Tenn. 37203. 22,000.

5,500 inst. subscribers. Phone: (615) 322-2595. www.vanderbilt.edu/AEA.

Edison Electric Institute (1933): 701 Pennsylvania Ave. N.W., Washington, D.C. 20004-2696. www.eei.org.

Education, American Council on (ACE), (1918): One Dupont Circle N.W., Washington, D.C. 20036-1193. 1,600+ colleges and universities and 200+ higher education associations. Phone: (202) 939-9300. www.acenet.edu.

Educational Exchange, Council on International (1947): 205 E. 42nd St., New York, N.Y. 10017-5706. Phone: (212) 822-2600. www.ciee.org.

Educational Research Association, American (1916): 1230 17th St. N.W., Washington, D.C. 20036-3078. 22,000. Phone: (202) 223-9485. www.aera.net.

Education Association, National (1857): 1201 16th St. N.W., Washington, D.C. 20036-3290. 2.3 million. Phone: (202) 833-4000. www.nea.org.

Electrochemical Society, The (1902): 65 S. Main St., Pennington, N.J. 08534-2839. 7,000. Phone: (609) 737-1902; fax: (609) 737-2743. email: ecs@electrochem.org. www.electrochem.org.

Elks of the U.S.A., Benevolent and Protective Order of the (1868): 2750 N. Lakeview Ave., Chicago, Ill. 60614-1889. 1,300,000. Phone: (773) 755-4700. www.elks.org/default.cfm.

Energy Engineers, Association of (1977): 4025 Pleasantdale Rd., Ste. 420, Atlanta, Ga. 30340. 8,500. Phone: (770) 447-5083; fax: (770) 446-3969. email: info@aeecenter.org. www.aeecenter.org.

English-Speaking Union of the United States (1920): 16 E. 69th St., New York, N.Y. 10021. 18,000. Phone: (212) 879-6800. www.english-speakingunion.org.

Entomological Society of America (1889): 9301 Annapolis Rd., Lanham, Md. 20706-3115. 7,400+. Phone: (301) 731-4535; fax: (301) 731-4538. email: esa@entsoc.org. www.entsoc.org.

Esperanto League for North America, The (1952): P.O. Box 1129, El Cerrito, Calif. 94530. Over 1,000. Phone: (800) 377-3726. www.esperanto-usa.org.

Exceptional Children, The Council for (1922): 1920 Association Dr., Reston, Va. 20191-1589. 54,000. Phone: (800) CEC-SPED V; (703) 264-9446 TTY; fax: (703) 264-9494. email: cec@cec.sped.org. www.cec.sped.org.

Exploration Geophysicists, Society of (1930): P.O. Box 702740, Tulsa, Okla. 74170-2740. 16,536. Phone: (918) 497-5500. www.seg.org.

Family and Consumer Sciences, American Association of (1909): 1555 King St., Alexandria, Va. 22314. 14,500. Phone: (703) 706-4600. www.aafcs.org.

Family Campers & RVers (1949): 4804 Transit Rd., Bldg. 2, Depew, N.Y. 14043. 42,000 families. Phone: (800) 245-9755; fax: (716) 668-6242. www.fcrv.org.

Family, Career, and Community Leaders of America [evolved from Future Homemakers of America, Inc. (1945)]: 1910 Association Dr., Reston, Va. 20191-1584. 230,000. Phone: (703) 476-4900. www.fcclainc.org.

Family Physicians, American Academy of (1947): 11400 Tomahawk Creek Pkwy., Leawood, Kans. 66211-2672. 88,000. Phone: (913) 906-6000. www.aafp.org.

Family Relations, National Council on (1938): 3989 Central Ave. N.E., #550, Minneapolis, Minn. 55421. 42,000 families. Phone: (612) 781-9331. www.ncfr.com.

Farm Bureau Federation, American (1919): 225 Touhy Ave., Park Ridge, Ill. 60068. 4.7 million member families. Phone: (847) 685-8600. www.fb.com.

Federal Bar Association (1920): 2215 M St. N.W., Washington, D.C. 20037. 15,000. Phone: (202) 785-1614; fax: (202) 785-1568. www.fedbar.org.

Federal Employees, National Federation of (1917): 1016 16th St. N.W., Washington, D.C. 20036. 150,000. Phone: (202) 862-4400.

Fellowship of Reconciliation (1915): Box 271, Nyack, N.Y. 10960. 20,000. Phone: (914) 358-4601. www.forusa.org.

Female Executives, National Association for (1972): P.O. Box 469031, Escondido, Calif. 92046-9925. 150,000+. Phone: (800) 634-6233. www.nafe.com.

FFA Organization, National (1928): 1410 King St., Ste. 400, Alexandria, Va. 22314. 451,997. Phone: (800) 772-0939. www.ffa.agriculture.com.

Fire Protection Association, National (1896): One Batterymarch Park, P.O. Box 9101, Quincy, Mass. 02269-9101. 65,000+. Phone: (617) 770-3000. www.nfpa.org.

Flag Foundation, National (1968): Flag Plaza, Pittsburgh, Pa. 15219-3630. 3,000+. Phone: (412) 261-1776. www.icss.com/usflag/nff.html.

Fleet Reserve Association (1924): 125 N. West St., Alexandria, Va. 22314-2754. 162,000. Phone: (703) 683-1400; (800) 372-1924. email: news-fra@fra.org. www.fra.org.

Foreign Policy Association (1918): 470 Park Ave. So., New York, N.Y. 10016-6819. Phone: (212) 481-8100. www.fpa.org.

Foreign Relations, Council on (1921): 58 E. 68th St., New York, N.Y. 10021. 3,400. Phone: (212) 434-9400. www.foreignrelations.org.

Foreign Study, American Institute for (1964): River Plaza, 9 W. Broad St., Stamford, Conn. 06902-3788. Phone: (800) 727-2437. www.aifs.org.

Forensic Sciences, American Academy of (1948): 410 N. 21st St., Ste. 203., P.O. Box 669, Colorado Springs, Colo. 80901-0669. 4,315. Phone: (719) 636-1100; fax: (719) 636-1993. www.aafs.org.

Foresters, Society of American (1900): 5400 Grosvenor Lane, Bethesda, Md. 20814. 18,000. Phone: (301) 897-8720. www.safnet.org.

4-H Program (early 1900s): 1400 Independence Ave., S.W., Washington, D.C. 20250. 5.6 million. Phone: (202) 720-2908. www.4h-usa.org.

Freedom of Information Center (1958): 127 Neff Annex, Univ. of Missouri, Columbia, Mo. 65211. Phone: (573) 882-4856. www.missouri.edu/~foiwww/

French Institute/Alliance Française (1898): 22 E. 60th St., New York, N.Y. 10022. 9,000. Phone: (212) 355-6100. www.fiaf.org.

Friends of Animals Inc. (1957): 777 Post Rd., Darien, Conn. 06820. 120,000. Phone: (203) 656-1522. www.friendsofanimals.org/.

Friends of the Earth (1969): 1025 Vermont Ave. N.W., 3rd Flr., Washington, D.C. 20005. 35,000. Phone: (202) 783-7400. www.foe.org.

Gamblers Anonymous: Box 17173, Los Angeles, Calif. 90017. Phone: (213) 386-8789. www.gamblersanonymous.org.

Gay and Lesbian Task Force, National (1973): 1700 Kalorama Rd. N.W., Washington, D.C. 20009-2624. 35,000 members. Phone: (202) 332-6483. www.ngltf.org.

Genealogical Society, National (1903): 4527 17th St. N., Arlington, Va. 22207-2399. 17,000+. Phone: (703) 525-0050; fax: (703) 525-0052. www.ngsgenealogy.org.

Geographers, Association of American (1904): 1710 16th St. N.W., Washington, D.C. 20009-3198. 7,000. Phone: (202) 234-1450; fax: (202) 234-2744. email: gaia@aag.org. www.aag.org.

Geographic Education, National Council for (1915): 16A Leonard Hall, Indiana University of Pennsylvania, Indiana, Pa. 15705. 3,700. Phone: (724) 357-6290. www.ncge.org.

Geographic Society, National (1888): 1145 17th St. N.W., Washington, D.C. 20036-4688. 9,200,000. Phone: (800) 647-5463. www.nationalgeographic.com.

Geological Institute, American (1948): 4220 King St., Alexandria, Va. 22302-1502. 34 geoscience societies representing 100,000 geoscientists. Phone: (703) 379-2480. www.agiweb.org/.

Geological Society of America, Inc. (1888): P.O. Box 9140, Boulder, Colo. 80301-9140. 15,000. Phone: (303) 447-2020. www.geosociety.org.

German American National Congress, The (Deutsch-Amerikanischer National Kongress— D.A.N.K.) (1958): 4740 N. Western Ave., Executive Office, Chicago, Ill. 60625-2097. Phone: (773) 275-1100. www.dank.org.

Gideons International, The (1889): 2900 Lebanon Rd., Nashville, Tenn. 37214-2540. 130,000. Phone: (615) 883-8533. www.gideons.org.

Gifted, The Association for the (1958): The Council for Exceptional Children, 1920 Association Dr., Reston, Va. 20191-1589. 2,200. Phone: (703) 620-3660. education.idbsu.edu/tag

Girl Scouts of the U.S.A. (1912): 420 Fifth Ave., New York, N.Y. 10018-2798. 2,500,000. Phone: (212) 852-6559. www.gsusa.org.

Girls Incorporated (1945): 120 Wall St., 3rd. Flr., New York, N.Y. 10005. 350,000. Phone: (212) 509-2000. www.girlsinc.org.

Graphoanalysis Society, International (1929): 111 N. Canal St., Ste. 399, Chicago, Ill. 60606. 10,000. Phone: (312) 930-9446; www.igas.com.

Gray Panthers (1970): 733 15th St. N.W., Ste. 437, Washington, D.C. 20005. Over 50 chapters (networks). Phone: (202) 737-6637. www.graypanthers.org.

Greenpeace (1971): 1436 U St. N.W., Washington, D.C. 20009. 600,000. Phone: (800) 326-0959. www.greenpeaceusa.org.

Guide Dog Foundation for the Blind, Inc.® (1946): 371 E. Jericho Turnpike, Smithtown, N.Y. 11787-2976. 100,000. Phone: (631) 265-2121; (800) 548-4337; fax: (631) 361-5192. www.guidedog.org.

Hadassah, The Women's Zionist Organization of America (1912): 50 W. 58th St., New York, N.Y. 10019. 385,000. Phone: (212) 355-7900. www.hadassah.org.

Handgun Control, Inc. (1974): 1225 Eye St. N.W., Ste. 100, Washington, D.C. 20005. 380,000. Phone: (202) 898-0792. www.handguncontrol.org.

Heating, Refrigerating and Air-Conditioning Engineers, Inc., American Society of (1959): 1791 Tullie Circle N.E., Atlanta, Ga. 30329. 50,000. Phone: (404) 636-8400. www.ashrae.org.

Helicopter Association International (1948): 1635 Prince St., Alexandria, Va. 22314. Phone: (703) 683-4646; fax: (703) 683-4745. www.rotor.com.

Historians, The Organization of American (1907): Indiana Univ., 112 N. Bryan St., Bloomington, Ind. 47408-4199. 12,000. Phone: (812) 855-7311. www.oah.org.

Historic Preservation, National Trust for (1949): 1785 Massachusetts Ave. N.W., Washington, D.C. 20036. 275,000. Phone: (202) 588-6000. www.nationaltrust.org.

Horse Council, Inc., American (1969): 1700 K St. N.W., #300, Washington, D.C. 20006. More than 190 organizations and 2,400 individuals. Phone: (202) 296-4031. www.horsecouncil.org.

Horse Shows Association, Inc., American (1917): 4047 Iron Works Parkway, Lexington, Ky. 40511. 70,000+. Phone: (859) 258-2472. www.ahsa.org.

Horticultural Association, National Junior (1935): 15 Railroad Ave., Homer City, Pa. 15748. Phone: (724) 479-3254.

Horticultural Society, American (1922): 7931 East Boulevard Dr., Alexandria, Va. 22308. 22,000. Phone: (703) 768-5700 or (800) 777-7931; fax: (703) 768-8700. www.ahs.org.

Hostelling International—American Youth Hostels (1934): 733 15th St. N.W., Ste. 840, Washington,

D.C. 20005. 124,000. Phone: (202) 783-6161 for membership and reservations. www.hiayh.org.

Humane Association, American (1877): 63 Inverness Drive East, Englewood, Colo. 80112-5117. Phone: (303) 792-9900. www.americanhumane.org.

Humane Society of the United States (1954): 2100 L St. N.W., Washington, D.C. 20037. 5,000,000. Phone: (202) 452-1100. www.hsus.org.

Humanities, National Endowment for the (1965): 1100 Pennsylvania Ave. N.W., Washington, D.C. 20506. Phone: (202) 606-8400. www.neh.fed.us.

Hydrogen Energy, International Association for (1975): P.O. Box 248266, Coral Gables, Fla. 33124. 2,500. Phone: (305) 284-4666. www.iahe.org.

Industrial Engineers, Institute of (1948): 25 Technology Park/Atlanta, Norcross, Ga. 30092. 24,000. Phone: (770) 449-0460. www.iienet.org.

Izaak Walton League of America (1922): 707 Conservation Lane, Gaithersburg, Md. 20878-2983. 50,000+. Phone: (800) 453-5463. www.iwla.org.

Jewish Community Centers Association (JCC) of North America (1917): 15 E. 26th St., New York, N.Y. 10010-1579. 275+ affiliated Jewish Community Centers, YM-YWHAs, and camps serving 1 million+ members. Phone: (212) 532-4958; fax: (212) 481-4158. email: info@jcca.org. www.jcca.org.

Jewish Congress, American (1918): 15 E. 84th St., New York, N.Y. 10028. 50,000. Phone: (212) 879-4500. www.ajcongress.org.

Jewish Historical Society, American (1892): 2 Thornton Rd., Waltham, Mass. 02154. 3,500. Phone: (781) 891-8110; fax: (617) 899-9208. email: ajhs@ajhs.org. www.ajhs.org.

Jewish War Veterans of the U.S.A. (1896): 1811 R St. N.W., Washington, D.C. 20009-1659. Phone: (202) 265-6280. www.penfed.org/jwv/home.htm.

Jewish Women, National Council of (1893): 53 W. 23rd St., 6th Flr., New York, N.Y. 10010. 90,000. Phone: (212) 645-4048; fax: (212) 645-7466. www.ncjw.org.

John Birch Society (1958): P.O. Box 8040, Appleton, Wis. 54912. Under 100,000. Phone: (920) 749-3780; fax: (920) 749-5062. www.jbs.org.

Journalists, Society of Professional, (1909): 3909 N. Meridian St., Indianapolis, Ind. 46208. 13,500. Phone: (317) 927-9031. www.spj.org.

Judaism, American Council for (1943): P.O. Box 9009, Alexandria, Va. 22304. Phone: (703) 836-2546. www.acjna.org

Junior Achievement Inc. (1919): One Education Way, Colorado Springs, Colo. 80906. 3 million+. Phone: (719) 540-8000. www.ja.org.

Junior Chamber of Commerce, The United States, Jaycees (1920): 4 West 21 Street, Tulsa, Okla. 74114-1116. 113,000. Phone: (918) 584-2481; fax: (918) 584-4422. www.usjaycees.org.

Junior Leagues International, Inc., Association of (1921): 132 W. 31st St., 11th flr.; New York, N.Y. 10001-3406. 295 Leagues, 193,000+ members. Phone: (212) 683-1515. www.ajli.org.

Junior State of America (1934): 60 E. Third Ave., Ste. 320, San Mateo, Calif. 94401-4302. 15,000. Phone: (650) 347-1600 or (800) 334-5353. www.jsa.org.

Kiwanis International (1915): 3636 Woodview Trace, Indianapolis, Ind. 46268. 316,000. Phone: (317) 875-8755. email: kiwanismail@kiwanis.org. www.kiwanis.org.

Knights of Columbus (1852): One Columbus Plaza, New Haven, Conn. 06510. 1,600,000. Phone: (203) 772-2130. www.kofc.org.

Knights Templar, Grand Encampment of (1816): 5097 N. Elston Ave., Ste. 101, Chicago, Ill. 60630-2460. 220,000. Phone: (773) 777-3300. www.knightstemplar.org.

La Leche League International (1956): 1400 N. Meacham Rd., Schaumburg, Ill. 60168-4079. 50,000. Phone: (847) 519-7730. www.lalecheleague.org.

Law, American Society of International (1906): 2223 Massachusetts Ave. N.W., Washington, D.C. 20008. 4,300. Phone: (202) 939-6000. www.asil.org.

League of Women Voters of the U.S. (1920): 1730 M St. N.W., Washington, D.C. 20036-4508. Phone: (202) 429-1965; fax: (202) 429-0854. www.lwv.org.

Legal Aid and Defender Association, National (1911): 1625 K St. N.W., Ste. 800, Washington, D.C. 20006-1604. 2,400. Phone: (202) 452-0620. www.nlada.org.

Legal Professionals, National Association of (1949): 314 East 3rd St., Ste. 210, Tulsa, Okla. 74120-2409. 6,000. Phone: (918) 582-5188. www.nals.org.

Leukemia and Lymphoma Society (1949): 600 Third Ave., New York, N.Y. 10016. Phone: (212) 573-8484. www.leukemia.org.

Library Association, American (1876): 50 E. Huron St., Chicago, Il. 60611. 57,000. Phone: (312) 280-3215. www.ala.org.

Lions Clubs International (1917): 300 22nd St., Oak Brook, Ill. 60521-8842. 1,419,408. Phone: (708) 571-5466. www.lr.net/lions/lci.html.

Lung Association, American (1904): 1740 Broadway, New York, N.Y. 10019-4374. 99 constituent and affiliate associations. Phone: (800) LUNG-USA; (800) 586-4872. www.lungusa.org.

Magazine Editors, American Society of (1963): 919 Third Ave., 22nd Flr., New York, N.Y. 10022. 900. Phone: (212) 872-3700. www.asme.magazine.org

Management Accountants, Institute of (1919): 10 Paragon Dr., Montvale, N.J. 07645-1759. 80,000. Phone: (201) 573-9000. www.imanet.org

Management Association, American (1923): 1601 Broadway, New York, N.Y. 10019-7420. 70,000. Phone: (212) 586-8100. www.amanet.org.

Management Consultants, Institute of (1968): 1200 19th St. N.W., Ste. 300, Washington, D.C. 20036-2422. 25 chapters. Phone: (202) 857-5334; (800) 221-2557. www.imcusa.org/imc.html.

Manufacturers, National Association of (1895): 1331 Pennsylvania Ave. N.W., Washington, D.C. 20004-1790. Approx. 14,000. Phone: (202) 637-3000. www.nam.org.

March of Dimes Birth Defects Foundation (1938): 1275 Mamaroneck Ave., White Plains, N.Y. 10605. 104 chapters. Phone: (914) 428-7100, (888) 663-4637; tty: (914) 997-4764; fax: (914) 997-4763. email: resourcecenter@modimes.org. www.modimes.org.

Marine Conservation, Center for (1972): 1725 De Sales St. N.W., Ste. 600, Washington, D.C. 20036. 120,000. Phone: (202) 429-5609. www.cmc-ocean.org.

Marine Corps Association (1913): P.O. Box 1775, 715 Broadway, Quantico, Va. 22134. 100,723. Phone: (703) 640-6161; (800) 336-0291. www.mca-marines.org.

Marine Technology Society (1963): 1828 L St. N.W., Ste. 906, Washington, D.C. 20036. 2,000+. Phone: (202) 775-5966; fax: (202) 429-9417. www.mtsociety.org.

Masons, Royal Arch, General Grand Chapter International (1797): P.O. Box 489, Danville, Ky. 40423-0489. 230,000. Phone: (606) 236-0757. members.aol.com/GGCHAPTER/HomePage.html.

Mathematical Association of America (1915): P.O. Box 91112, Washington, D.C. 20090-1112. Phone: (800) 331-1622. www.maa.org.

Mathematical Society, American (1888): P.O. Box 6248, Providence, R.I. 02940-6248. Phone: (401) 455-4000. email: ams@ams.org. www.ams.org.

Mayflower Descendants, General Society of (1897): 4 Winslow St., P.O. Box 3297, Plymouth, Mass. 02361. 24,500+. Phone: (508) 746-3188. www.mayflower.org.

Mechanical Engineers, American Society of (1880): 3 Park Ave., New York, N.Y. 10016-5990. 125,000. Phone: (800) THE-ASME. www.asme.org.

Medical Association, American (1847): 515 N. State St., Chicago, Ill. 60610. 300,000 physicians. Phone: (312) 464-5000. www.ama-assn.org.

Mental Health Association, National (1909): 1021 Prince St., Alexandria, Va., 22314-2971. 340 affiliates. Phone: (703) 684-7722; (800) 969-NMHA; TTY (800) 433-5959; fax: (703) 684-5968. email: nmhainfo@aol.com. www.nmha.org

Meteorological Society, American (1919): 45 Beacon St., Boston, Mass. 02108-3693. 10,000+. Phone: (617) 227-2425. www.ametsoc.org/ams.

Military Chaplains Association of the U.S.A. (1925): P.O. Box 42660, Washington, D.C. 20015-0660. 1,500. Phone: (202) 574-2423.

Mining, Metallurgical, and Petroleum Engineers, The American Institute of (1871): 3 Park Ave., New York, N.Y. 10016-5998. 4 Member Societies: Society for Mining, Metallurgy and Exploration; The Minerals, Metals & Materials Society; Iron & Steel Society; Society of Petroleum Engineers. Phone: (212) 419-7679; fax: (212) 419-7671. email: AIMENY@aol.com. www.idis.com/aime.

Model Aeronautics, Academy of (1936): 5151 East Memorial Dr., Muncie, Ind. 47302. 150,000. Phone: (765) 287-1256. www.modelaircraft.org.

Modern Language Association of America (1883): 10 Astor Place, New York, N.Y. 10003-6981. 30,000+. Phone: (212) 475-9500. www.mla.org.

Moose International, Inc. (1888): Mooseheart, Ill. 60539. 1,600,000+. Phone: (630) 859-2000. www.mooseintl.org.

Mothers Against Drunk Driving (MADD) (1980): P.O. Box 541688, Dallas, Tex. 75354-1688. 3 million members and supporters. Victim hotline: (800) GET-MADD. www.madd.org.

Motion Picture Arts & Sciences, Academy of (1927): 8949 Wilshire Blvd., Beverly Hills, Calif. 90211-1972. Phone: (310) 247-3000. www.oscars.org.

Multiple Sclerosis Society, National (1946): 733 Third Ave., New York, N.Y. 10017. 350,000. Phone: (800) FIGHT-MS (344-4867). www.nmss.org.

Muscular Dystrophy Association (1950): 3300 East Sunrise Dr., Tucson, Ariz. 85718. 2,300,000 volunteers. Phone: (800) 572-1717. www.mdausa.org.

Museums, American Association of (1906): 1575 Eye St. N.W., Ste. 400, Washington, D.C. 20005. 16,000+. Phone: (202) 289-1818; fax: (202) 289-6578, TTY (202) 289-8439. www.aam-us.org.

Muzzle Loading Rifle Association, National (1933): P.O. Box 67, Friendship, Ind. 47021-0067. 25,000. Phone: (812) 667-5131. www.nmlra.org.

NAFSA: Association of International Educators (1948): 1307 New York Ave. N.W., 8th Flr., Washington, D.C. 20005-4701. 7,500. Phone: (202) 737-3699. www.nafsa.org.

National Abortion and Reproductive Rights Action League (NARAL) (1969): 1156 15th St. N.W., Washington, D.C. 20005. 500,000. Phone: (202) 973-3000. www.naral.org.

National Association for the Advancement of Colored People (1909): 4805 Mt. Hope Dr., Baltimore, Md. 21215. 500,000+. Phone: (410) 358-8900. www.naacp.org.

National Association of Insurance and Financial Advisors (1890): 2901 Telestar Court, Falls Church, Va. 22042-1205. Phone: (703) 770-8100. www.naifa.org/index.html.

National Conference for Community and Justice, The (founded as The Natl. Conf. of Christians & Jews) (1927): 475 Park Avenue South, 19th Flr., New York, N.Y. 10016-6901. Phone: (212) 545-1300. www.nccj.org.

National Cooperative Business Association (formerly Cooperative League of the U.S.A.) (1916): 1401 New York Ave. N.W., Ste. 1100, Washington, D.C. 20005. Phone: (202) 638-6222. www.cooperative.org.

National Council of La Raza (1968): 1111 19th St. N.W., Ste. 1000, Washington, D.C. 20036. 20,000+. Phone: (202) 785-1670. www.nclr.org.

National Council of the Churches of Christ in the USA (1950): 475 Riverside Drive, Rm. 850, New York, N.Y. 10115. 35 Protestant and Orthodox communions. Phone: (212) 870-2227. www.ncccusa.org.

National Grange of the Order of Patrons of Husbandry, (1867): 1616 H St. N.W., Washington, D.C. 20006-4999. 300,000. Phone: (202) 628-3507; fax: (202) 347-1091. www.grange.org.

National Press Club (1908): National Press Bldg., 529 14th St. N.W., 13th Flr., Washington, D.C. 20045. 4,200+. Phone: (202) 662-7500. npc.press.org.

National PTA (National Congress of Parents and Teachers) (1897): 330 N. Wabash Ave., Ste. 2100, Chicago, Ill. 60611. 6.5 million. Phone: (800) 307-4782. email: info@pta.org. www.pta.org.

National Rifle Association of America (1871): 11250 Waples Mill Rd., Fairfax, Va. 22030. 3,300,000. Phone: (703) 267-1000. www.nra.org.

National Urban League, Inc. (1910): 120 Wall St., New York, N.Y. 10005. 115 affiliates in 34 states and D.C. Phone: (212) 558-5300. www.nul.org.

National Wildlife Federation (1936): 8925 Leesburg Pike, Vienna, VA 22184. 4,000,000+. Phone: (703) 790-4000. www.nwf.org.

Nature Conservancy, The (1951): 4245 N. Fairfax Dr., Ste. 100, Arlington, Va. 22203-1606. 900,000. Phone: (703) 841-5300. www.tnc.org.

Naturopathic Physicians, American Association of (1986): 601 Valley St. #105, Seattle, Wash. 98109. 1,700. Phone: (206) 298-0126; fax: (206) 298-0129; http://naturopathic.org/

Naval Architects and Marine Engineers, The Society of (1893): 601 Pavonia Ave., Jersey City, N.J. 07306. 10,000+. Phone: (201) 798-4800; fax: (201) 798-4975. www.sname.org.

Naval Engineers, American Society of (1888): 1452 Duke St., Alexandria, Va. 22314. 6,800. Phone: (703) 836-6727; fax: (703) 836-7491. www.navalengineers.org.

Naval Institute, United States (1873): 291 Wood Rd., Annapolis, Md. 21402. 80,000+. Phone: (410) 268-6110. www.usni.org.

Navigation, The Institute of (1945): 1800 Diagonal Rd., Ste. 480, Alexandria, Va. 22314. 3,800. Phone: (703) 683-7101; fax: (703) 683-7105. email: membership@ion.org. www.ion.org.

Navy League of the United States (1902): 2300 Wilson Blvd., Arlington, Va. 22201-3308. 71,500. Phone: (703) 528-1775. www.navyleague.org.

NDIA (National Defense Industrial Association) (1997): 2111 Wilson Blvd., Ste. 400, Arlington, Va. 22201. 28,000 individual, 900 companies. Phone: (703) 522-1820. www.ndia.org.

Neurofibromatosis Foundation, Inc., The National (1978): 95 Pine St., 16th Flr., New York, N.Y. 10005. 38,000. Phone: (800) 323-7938; in N.Y. State (212) 344-NNFF; fax: (212) 747-0004. email: nnff@aol.com. www.nf.org.

Newspaper Association of America (1992): 1921 Gallows Rd., Ste. 600, Vienna, Va. 22182. Phone (703) 902-1600. www.naa.org.

Nondestructive Testing, Inc., The American Society for (1941): 1711 Arlingate Lane, P.O. Box 28518, Columbus, Ohio 43228-0518. 10,240. Phone: (800) 222-ASNT. www.asnt.org.

Nuclear Society, American (1954): 555 N. Kensington Ave., La Grange Park, Ill. 60526. 13,000. Phone: (708) 352-6611. www.ans.org.

Numismatic Association, American (1891): 818 N. Cascade Ave., Colorado Springs, Colo. 80903-3279. 28,000. Phone: (719) 632-2646. email: ana@money.org. www.money.org.

Nurses Association, American (1897): 600 Maryland Ave. S.W., Ste. 100, Washington, D.C. 20024. 180,000. Phone: (800) 274-4ANA. www.ana.org.

Odd Fellows, Sovereign Grand Lodge, Independent Order of (1819): 422 North Trade St., Winston-Salem, N.C. 27101. 460,000. Phone: (336) 725-5955. http://128.125.109.137/IOOF.shtml

Olympic Committee, United States (1921): One Olympic Plaza, Colorado Springs, Colo. 80909-5760. Phone: (719) 632-5551. www.olympic-usa.org.

Optimist International (1919): 4494 Lindell Blvd., St. Louis, Mo. 63108. 130,000+. Phone: (314) 371-6000. www.optimist.org.

Optometric Association, American (1898): 243 N. Lindbergh Blvd., St. Louis, Mo. 63141. 32,000. Phone: (314) 991-4100. www.aoanet.org.

Ornithologists' Union, American (1883): c/o Division of Birds, National Museum of Natural History, MRC-116, Washington, D.C. 20560. 4,000. Phone: (202) 357-2051. pica.wru.umt.edu/aou/aou.html.

Overeaters Anonymous, Inc. (1960): 6075 Zenith Court N.E., Rio Rancho, N.M. 87124. 150,000. Phone: (505) 891-2664. www.overeatersanonymous.org.

Parents, Families and Friends of Lesbians and Gays (1981): 1726 M St. N.W., Ste. 400, Washington, D.C. 20036. 77,000 households. Phone: (202) 467-8180. www.pflag.org.

Parents Without Partners (1957): 1650 South Dixie Hwy., Ste. 510, Boca Raton, Fla. 33432. 50,000. Phone: (561) 391-8833. www.parentswithoutpartners.org.

Peace Action (a merger of SANE and the Nuclear Weapons Freeze Campaign) (1957): 1819 H St. N.W., Ste. 420, Washington D.C. 20006. 55,000. Phone: (202) 862-9740. www.webcom.com/peaceact.

People For the American Way (1980): 2000 M St. N.W., Ste. 400, Washington, D.C. 20036. 300,000. Phone: (202) 467-4999. www.pfaw.org.

Petroleum Geologists, American Association of (1917): P.O. Box 979, Tulsa, Okla. 74101-0979. 31,500. Phone: (918) 584-2555. www.aapg.org.

Pharmaceutical Association, American (1852): 2215 Constitution Ave. N.W., Washington, D.C. 20037-2985. 50,000+. Phone: (202) 628-4410. www.aphanet.org.

Philatelic Society, American (1886): P.O. Box 8000, State College, Pa. 16803. 55,000+. Phone: (814) 237-3803. www.stamps.org.

Photogrammetry and Remote Sensing, American Society for (1934): 5410 Grosvenor Lane, Ste. 210, Bethesda, Md. 20814-2160. 7,000+. Phone: (301) 493-0290; fax: (301) 493-0208. email: asprs@asprs.org. www.asprs.org.

Photographic Society of America (1934): 3000 United Founders Blvd., Ste. 103, Oklahoma City, Okla. 73112-3940. Phone: (405) 843-1437. www.psa-photo.org.

Physical Society, The American (1899): One Physics Ellipse, College Park, Md. 20740-3200. 41,000. Phone: (301) 209-3200. www.aps.org.

Physical Therapy Association, American (APTA) (1921): 1111 N. Fairfax St., Alexandria, Va. 22314-1488. 75,000. Phone: (703) 684-2782. www.apta.org.

Physics, American Institute of (1931): One Physics Ellipse, College Park, Md. 20740-3843. 125,000. Phone: (301) 209-3100. www.aip.org.

Pilot International (1921): Pilot International Headquarters, 244 College St., P.O. Box 4844, Macon, Ga. 31208-4844. 25,000. Phone: (912) 743-7403. www.pilotinternational.org.

Planetary Society, The (1980): 65 N. Catalina Ave., Pasadena, Calif. 91106-2301. 100,000. Phone: (626) 793-5100. www.planetary.org.

Planned Parenthood® Federation of America, Inc., (1916): 810 Seventh Ave., New York, N.Y. 10019. 150 affiliates. Phone: (212) 541-7800; fax: (212) 261-4560. www.plannedparenthood.org.

Plastics Engineers, Society of (1942): P.O. Box 403, 14 Fairfield Dr., Brookfield, Conn. 06804-0403. 32,000+. Phone: (203) 775-0471. www.4spe.org.

Police and Concerned Citizens, American Federation of (1966): Records Center, 3801 Biscayne Blvd., Miami, Fla. 33137. 100,000. Phone: (305) 573-0070. www.aphf.org.

Police, International Association of Chiefs of (1893): 515 N. Washington St., Alexandria Va. 22314-2357. 14,000. Phone: (703) 836-6767. www.theiacp.org.

Political and Social Science, American Academy of (1889): 3937 Chestnut St., Philadelphia, Pa. 19104. Phone: (215) 386-4630. www.asc.upenn.edu/aapss.

Political Science, Academy of (1880): 475 Riverside Dr., Ste. 1274, New York, N.Y. 10115-1274. 8,500. Phone: (212) 870-2500. www.psqonline.org.

Prevent Blindness America (1908): 500 E. Remington Rd., Schaumburg, Ill. 60173. 21 affiliates and divisions. Phone: (847) 843-2020; (800) 331-2020. www.preventblindness.org.

Professional Engineers, National Society of (1934): 1420 King St., Alexandria, Va. 22314-2794. 60,000. Phone: (703) 684-2800; fax: (703) 836-4875. www.nspe.org.

Professional Photographers of America, Inc. (1880): 299 Peachtree St. N.W., #2200, Atlanta, Ga. 30303-2206. 14,000. Phone: (800) 786-6277. www.ppa.com.

Psychiatric Association, American (1844): 1400 K St. N.W., Washington, D.C. 20005. 40,537. Phone: (202) 682-6000. www.psych.org.

Psychoanalytic Association, The American (1911): 309 E. 49th St., New York, N.Y. 10017. 3,116 psychoanalysts. Phone: (212) 752-0450; fax: (212) 593-0571. email: apsaorg@compuserve.com. www.apsa.org.

Psychological Association, American (1892): 750 First St. N.E., Washington, D.C. 20002. 159,000. Phone: (202) 336-5500; (202) 336-5662 TTY. www.apa.org.

Public Health Association, American (1872): 800 I St. N.W., Washington, D.C. 20001-3710. 50,000+. Phone: (202) 777-2742. www.apha.org.

Puppeteers of America (1937): P.O. Box 29417, Parma, Ohio 44129-0417. Phone: (888) 568-6235. www.puppeteers.org

Quality, The American Society for (1946): 611 E. Wisconsin Ave., P.O. Box 3005, Milwaukee, Wis. 53201-3005. 135,000+. Phone: (414) 272-8575. www.asq.org.

Railroads, Association of American (1934): 50 F St. N.W., Washington, D.C. 20001-1564. Phone: (202) 639-2100. www.aar.org.

Recording Arts & Sciences, Inc., National Academy of (1957): 3402 Pico Blvd., Santa Monica, Calif. 90405. 13,000. Phone: (310) 392-3777. www.grammy.com.

Red Cross, American (1881): 431 18th St. N.W., Washington, D.C. 20006. Approx. 1,650 chapters. Phone: (202) 639-3520. www.redcross.org.

Rehabilitation Association, National (1925): 633 S. Washington St., Alexandria, Va. 22314. 12,000. Phone: (703) 836-0850. www.nationalrehab.org.

Reserve Officers Association of the United States (1922): 1 Constitution Ave. N.E., Washington, D.C. 20002-5655. 93,000. Phone: (202) 479-2200. www.roa.org.

Retired Federal Employees, National Association (1921): 606 N. Washington St., Alexandria, Va. 22314. 422,000+. Phone: (703) 838-7760. www.narfe.org.

Reye's Syndrome Foundation, National (1974): P.O. Box 829, Bryan, Ohio 43506-0829. Phone: (800) 233-7393; fax: (419) 636-3366. email: reyessyn@mail.bright.net. www.bright.net/~reyessyn.

RID-USA (Remove Intoxicated Drivers) (1978): Box 520, Schenectady, N.Y. 12301. Phone: (518) 372-0034/(518) 393-HELP; fax: (518) 370-4917. www.crisny.org/not-for-profit/ridusa/.

Right to Life, Committee, Inc., National (1973): 419 7th St. N.W., Ste. 500, Washington, D.C. 20004. Phone: (202) 626-8800. www.nrlc.org

Rotary International (1905): One Rotary Center, 1560 Sherman Ave., Evanston, Ill. 60201. 1.2 million in 161 countries and 35 geographical regions. Phone: (847) 866-3000. www.rotary.org.

SAE (Society of Automotive Engineers) (1905): 400 Commonweatlh Dr., Warrendale, Pa. 15096-0001. 75,000+. Phone: (724) 776-5760. www.sae.org.

Safety Council, National (1913): 1121 Spring Lake Dr., Itasca, Ill. 60143-3201. Phone: (630) 285-1121. www.nsc.org.

Salvation Army, The (1865): National Headquarters, 615 Slaters Lane, P.O. Box 269, Alexandria, Va. 22313. 453,150. Phone: (703) 684-5500. www.salvationarmy.org.

Save-the-Redwoods League (1918): 114 Sansome St., Ste. 605, San Francisco, Calif. 94104-3814. 45,000. Phone: (415) 362-2352. www.savetheredwoods.org.

Science, American Association for the Advancement of (1848): 1200 New York Ave. N.W., Washington, D.C. 20005. 143,000. Phone: (202) 326-6400. www.aaas.org.

Science and Health, American Council on (1978): 1995 Broadway, 2nd Flr., New York, N.Y. 10023-5860. Phone: (212) 362-7044; fax: (212) 362-4919. email: acsh@acsh.org. www.acsh.org.

Science Fiction Society, World (1939): P.O. Box 426159, Kendall Square Station, Cambridge, Mass. 02142. email: mpc@wsfs.org www.wsfs.org.

Scientists, Federation of American (FAS) (1945): 307 Massachusetts Ave. N.E., Washington, D.C. 20002. 4,000. Phone: (202) 546-3300. www.fas.org.

SCRABBLE® Association, National (1978): P.O. Box 700, 120 Front Street Garden, Greenport, N.Y. 11944. 10,000. Phone: (516) 477-0033. www.scrabble-assoc.com

Screen Actors Guild (1933): 5757 Wilshire Blvd., Los Angeles, Calif. 90036-3600. 96,000. Phone: (323) 954-1600. www.sag.com.

Sculpture Society, National (1893): 1177 Ave. of the Americas, New York, N.Y. 10036. 4,000. Phone: (212) 764-5645. www.nationalsculpture.org

Seeing Eye Inc., The (1929): P.O. Box 375, Morristown, N.J. 07963-0375. Phone: (973) 539-4425. www.seeingeye.org.

Senior Citizens, National Alliance of (1974): 2525 Wilson Blvd., Arlington, Va. 22201. 117,000. Fax: (703) 528-4380.

Shriners of North America and Shriners Hospitals for Children, The (1872 and 1922): 2900 Rocky Point Drive, Tampa, Fla. 33607-1400. 525,000. Phone: (813) 281-0300. www.shrinershq.org.

Sierra Club (1892): 85 2nd Street, San Francisco, Calif. 94105-3441. 600,000+. Phone: (415) 977-5500. www.sierraclub.org.

SIETAR INTERNATIONAL (The International Society for Intercultural Education, Training and Research) (1974): 5 Rue Adele, 93250, Villemomble, France. 1,500. Phone: 33-1-45-28-58-27. www.sietarinternational.org.

Simon Wiesenthal Center (1977): 9786 W. Pico Blvd., Los Angeles, Calif. 90035. 400,000 member families. Phone: (800) 900-9036. www.wiesenthal.com.

Small Business United, National (1937): 1156 15th St. N.W., Washington, D.C. 20005. 65,000+. Phone: (202) 293-8830; fax: (202) 872-8543. email: nsbu@nsbu.org. www.nsbu.org.

Social Work Education, Council on (1952): 1725 Duke St., Ste. 500, Alexandria, Va. 22314. Phone: (703) 683-8080; fax: (703) 683-8099. www.cswe.org.

Social Workers, National Association of (1955): 750 First St. N.E., Ste. 700, Washington, D.C. 20002-4241. Phone: (202) 408-8600. www.naswdc.org.

Society for Integrative and Comparative Biology (formerly the American Society of Zoologists) (1890): 1313 Dolley Madison Blvd. #402, McLean, Va. 22101-3926. 2,100. Phone: (703) 790-1745; (800) 955-1236. email: SICB@BurkInc.com www.sicb.org.

Soil and Water Conservation Society (1945): 7515 N.E. Ankeny Rd., Ankeny, Iowa 50021. 10,000. Phone: (515) 289-2331; fax: (515) 289-1227. email: swcs@swcs.org. www.swcs.org.

Songwriters Guild of America, The (1931): 1500 Harbor Blvd., Weehawken, N.J. 07087-6732. Phone: (201) 867-7603. www.songwriters.org.

Sons of Italy in America, Order (1905): 219 E St. N.E., Washington, D.C. 20002. 500,000. Phone: (202) 547-2900. www.osia.org.

Sons of the American Revolution, National Society of the (1889): 1000 S. 4th St., Louisville, Ky. 40203. 26,000. Phone: (502) 589-1776. www.sar.org.

Soroptimist International of the Americas (1921): Two Penn Center Plaza, Ste. 1000, Philadelphia, Pa. 19102-1883. 100,000. Phone: (215) 557-9300. www.siahq.com.

Southern Early Childhood Association (formerly SACUS) (1948): P.O. Box 55930, Little Rock, Ark. 72215-5930. 21,000. Phone: (800) 305-7322; fax: (501) 663-2114. email: seca@aristotle.net. www.seca50.org.

Space Education Association, U.S. (1973): Global Operations Center, 746 Turnpike Rd., Elizabethtown, Pa. 17022.

Space Society, National (1974): 600 Pennsylvania Ave. S.E., Ste. 201, Washington, D.C. 20003. Phone: (202) 543-1900; fax: (202) 546-4189. www.nss.org/.

Special Olympics International, Inc. (1968): 1325 G St. N.W., Ste. 500, Washington, D.C., 20005. 1,000,000. Phone: (202) 628-3630. www.specialolympics.org.

Speech-Language-Hearing Association, American (1925): 10801 Rockville Pike, Rockville, Md. 20852. 96,000. Phone: (800) 498-2071; TTY (301) 571-0457. www.asha.org.

Sports Car Club of America Inc. (1944): 9033 E. Easter Place, P.O. Box 3278, Englewood, Colo. 80112. 55,000. Phone: (303) 694-7222. www.scca.org/index.html.

Statistical Association, American (1839): 1429 Duke St., Alexandria, Va. 22314-3402. 19,000. www.amstat.org.

Student Association, United States (1947): 1413 K Street N.W., 9th Flr., Washington, D.C. 20005. 350 schools (3.5 million students). Phone: (202) 347-8772. www.essential.org/ussa.

Surgeons, American College of (1913): 633 North Saint Clair, Chicago, Ill. 60611-3211. 56,000+. Phone: (312) 202-5000. www.facs.org.

Symphony Orchestra League, American (1942): 1156 15th St. N.W., Ste. 800, Washington, D.C. 20005. 5,000. Phone: (202) 776-0212. www.symphony.org.

TASH: The Association for Persons with Severe Handicaps (1974): 29 W. Susquehanna Ave., Ste. 210, Baltimore, Md. 21204. 8,500. Phone: (410) 828-TASH. www.tash.org.

Teachers, American Federation of (1916): 555 New Jersey Ave. N.W., Washington, D.C., 20001. 900,000+. Phone: (202) 879-4400. www.aft.org.

Testing & Materials, American Society for (1898): 100 Barr Harbor Dr., W. Conshohocken, Pa. 19428-2959. 35,000. Phone: (610) 832-9585. www.astm.org.

The Arc (1950): 1010 Wayne Ave., Ste. 650, Silver Spring, Md. 20910. A national organization on mental retardation. 140,000 members, 1,200 state and local chapters. Phone: (301) 565-3842. www.thearc.org.

Theosophical Society in America, The (1875): P.O. Box 270, Wheaton, Ill. 60189-0270. 4,400. Phone: (630) 668-1571. www.theosophical.org.

Tin Can Sailors, Inc. (1976): P.O. Box 100, Somerset, Mass. 02726. 20,900. Phone: (800) 223-5535. www.destroyers.org.

Toastmasters International (1924): P.O. Box 9052, Mission Viejo, Calif. 92690-7052. 170,000. Phone: (949) 858-8255; fax: (949) 858-1207. email: tminfo@toastmasters.org. www.toastmasters.org.

TOUGHLOVE International (1977): P.O. Box 1069, Doylestown, Pa. 18901. 500 registered groups. Phone: (215) 348-7090. www.toughlove.org.

TransAfrica Forum (1981): 1744 R. St. N.W., Washington, D.C. 20009. Phone: (202) 797-2301; fax: (202) 797-2382. email: transforum@igc.org. www.transafricaforum.org.

Travel Agents, American Society of (ASTA) (1931): 1101 King St., Alexandria, Va. 22314. 26,500. Phone: (703) 739-2782. www.astanet.com.

Travelers Aid International (1851): 1612 K St. N.W., Ste. 506, Washington, D.C. 20006. Phone: (202) 546-1127; fax: (202) 546-1127. www.travelersaid.org.

Tuberous Sclerosis Association, Inc., National (1974): 8181 Professional Place, Ste. 110, Landover, Md. 20785-2226. 5,000. Phone: (301) 459-9888; (800) 225-6872; fax: (301) 459-0394. email: ntsa@ntsa.org. www.ntsa.org.

UFOs, National Investigations Committee on (1967): 14617 Victory Blvd., Ste. 4, Van Nuys, Calif. 91411. Phone: (818) 989-5942; fax: (818) 989-2165. www.nicufo.com.

UNICEF, U.S. Committee for (1947): 333 E. 38th St., New York, N.Y. 10016. 20,000 volunteers. Phone: (800) FOR-KIDS. www.unicefusa.org.

Union of Concerned Scientists (1969): 2 Brattle Square, Cambridge, Mass. 02238. 70,000. Phone: (617) 547-5552. www.ucsusa.org.

United Daughters of the Confederacy® (1894): 328 N. Boulevard, Richmond, Va. 23220-4057. 24,000. Phone: (804) 355-1636. www.hqudc.org.

United Jewish Communities (formerly United Jewish Appeal) (1939): Ste. 11E, 111 Eighth Ave., New York, N.Y. 10011. Phone: (212) 284-6500. www.ujc.org.

United Way of America (1918): 701 N. Fairfax St., Alexandria, Va. 22314-2045. 1,400 local United Ways. Phone: (703) 836-7100; fax: (703) 683-7840. www.unitedway.org.

University Women, American Association of (1881): 1111 16th St. N.W., Washington, D.C. 20036. 150,000. Phone: (800) 326-AAUW (2289). www.aauw.org.

USO (United Service Organizations) (1941): World Headquarters, Washington Navy Yard, 1008 Eberle Place SE, Ste. 301, Washington, D.C. 20374-5096. Phone: (800) 876-7469. www.uso.org.

Veterans Committee, American (AVC) (1944): Bethesda, Md. 20817. 15,000. Phone & fax: (301) 320-6490. www.va.gov/vso/avc.htm.

Veterans of Foreign Wars of the U.S. (1899): 406 W. 34th St., Kansas City, Mo. 64111. VFW and Auxiliary, 2.1 million. Phone: (816) 756-3390. www.vfw.org.

Veterinary Medical Association, American (1863): 1931 N. Meacham Rd., Ste. 100, Schaumburg, Ill. 60173. 62,000. Phone: (847) 925-8070. www.avma.org.

Volunteers of America (1896): 1660 Duke St., Alexandria, Va. 22314-3421. Provides human services in more than 400 communities. Phone: (703) 341-5000; (800) 899-0089. www.voa.org.

War Resisters League (1923): 339 Lafayette St., New York, N.Y. 10012. 12,000. Phone: (212) 228-0450; fax: (212) 228-6193. email: wrl@igc.apc.org. www.nonviolence.org/wrl.

Washington Legal Foundation (1977): 2009 Massachusetts Ave. N.W., Washington, D.C. 20036. 100,000. Phone: (202) 588-0302. www.wlf.org.

Water Quality Association (1974): 4151 Naperville Rd., Lisle, Ill. 60532. 2,200. Phone: (630) 505-0160; fax: (630) 505-9637. www.wqa.org.

Welding Society, American (1919): 550 N.W. LeJeune Rd., Miami, Fla. 33126. 50,000. Phone: (305) 443-9353; (800) 443-9353. www.aws.org.

Wildlife Fund (U.S.), World (1961): 1250 24th St. N.W., Washington, D.C. 20037. 1.2 million. Phone: (800) 225-5993. www.wwf.org.

Woman's Christian Temperance Union, National (1874): 1730 Chicago Ave., Evanston, Ill. 60201-4585. Under 20,000. Phone: (847) 864-1397. www.wctu.org.

Women, National Organization for (NOW) (1966): 733 15th St. N.W., 2nd fl., Washington, D.C. 20005. 500,000. Phone: (202) 628-8669. www.now.org.

Women Police, The International Association of (1915): Box 149, Deer Isle, Me. 04627-9700. 3,000. Phone: (207) 348-6976; fax: (207) 348-6171. www.iawp.org.

Women's American ORT (1927): 315 Park Ave. South, New York, N.Y. 10010. Chapters throughout the U.S. Phone: (212) 505-7700. www.waort.org.

Women's Educational and Industrial Union (1877): 356 Boylston St., Boston, Mass. 02116. 1,500. Phone: (617) 536-5651; fax: (617) 247-8826.

Women's International League for Peace and Freedom (1915): 1213 Race St., Philadelphia, Pa. 19107. 10,000. Phone: (215) 563-7110. www.wilpf.org.

World Future Society (1966): 7910 Woodmont Ave., Ste. 450, Bethesda, Md. 20814. 30,000. Phone: (301) 656-8274; fax: (301) 951-0394. www.wfs.org.

World Health, American Association for (1953): 1825 K St. N.W., Washington, D.C. 20006. Phone: (202) 466-5883, fax: (202) 466-5896. email: AAWHstaff@aol.com. www.aawhworldhealth.org.

World Peace, International Association of Educators for (1967): 2267 Sacramento St. #2, San Francisco, Calif. 94115. 25,000. Phone: (415) 567-9143. www.homeplanet.org/iaewp.

World Peace Foundation (1910): 79 John F. Kennedy St., Cambridge, Mass. 02138. Phone: (617) 496-2258; fax: (617) 491-8588. www.worldpeacefoundation.org

Worldwatch Institute (1974): 1776 Massachusetts Ave. N.W., Washington, D.C. 20036-1904. Global environmental research organization. Phone: (202) 452-1999; fax: (202) 296-296-7365. email: worldwatch@worldwatch.org. www.worldwatch.org.

Writers Union, National (1981): 113 University Place, 6th Flr., New York, N.Y. 10003. 5,500. Phone: (212) 254-0279. www.nwu.org.

YMCA of the USA (1844): 101 N. Wacker Dr., Chicago, Ill. 60606. 16.9 million. Phone: (312) 977-0031. www.ymca.net.

Young Women's Christian Association of the U.S.A. (1858 in U.S.A., 1855 in England): Empire State Building, 350 Fifth Ave., Ste. 301, New York, N.Y. 10118. 2,000,000. Phone: (212) 273-7800. www.ywca.org.

Zero Population Growth (1968): 1400 Sixteenth St. N.W., Ste. 320, Washington, D.C. 20036. 55,000. Phone: (202) 332-2200. www.zpg.org.

Zionist Organization of America (1897): 4 E. 34th St., New York, N.Y. 10016. 50,000. Phone: (212) 481-1500; fax: (212) 481-1515. www.zoa.org.

Explorations

Country or place	Event	Explorer	Date
AFRICA			
Sierra Leone	Explored	Hanno, Carthaginian seaman	c. 520 B.C.
Zaire River (Congo)	Mouth visited[1]	Diogo Cão, Portuguese explorer	c. 1484
Cape of the Good Hope	Rounded	Bartolomeu Diaz, Portuguese explorer	1488
Gambia River	Explored	Mungo Park, Scottish explorer	1795
Sahara	Crossed	Dixon Denham and Hugh Clapperton, English explorers	1822–1823
Zambezi River	Explored[1]	David Livingstone, Scottish explorer	1851
Sudan	Explored	Heinrich Barth, German explorer	1852–1855
Victoria Falls	Explored[1]	David Livingstone, Scottish explorer	1855
Lake Tanganyika	Explored[1]	Richard Burton and John Speke, British explorers	1858
Lake Victoria, identified as the source of the Nile	Explored	John Speke, British explorer	1858
Zaire River (Congo)	Traced	Sir Henry M. Stanley, British explorer	1877
ASIA			
Punjab (India)	Invaded	Alexander the Great, king of Macedonia	327 B.C.
China	Explored	Marco Polo, Italian traveler	c. 1272
Tibet	Visited	Odoric of Pordenone, Italian monk	c. 1325
Southern China	Explored	Niccolò dei Conti, Venetian traveler	c. 1440
India	Explored (Cape route)	Vasco da Gama, Portuguese navigator	1498
Japan	Visited	St. Francis Xavier of Spain, missionary	1549
Arabia	Explored	Carsten Niebuhr, German explorer	1762
China	Explored	Ferdinand Richthofen, German scientist	1868
Mongolia	Explored	Nikolai M. Przhevalsky, Russian explorer	1870–1873
Central Asia	Explored	Sven Hedin, Swedish scientist	1890–1908
EUROPE			
Shetland Islands	Visited	Pytheas of Massilia (Marseille), Greek navigator and geographer	c. 325 B.C.
North Cape	Rounded	Ottar, Norwegian explorer	c. 870
Iceland	Colonized	Norwegian noblemen	c. 890–900
NORTH AMERICA			
Greenland	Colonized	Eric the Red, Norwegian	c. 985
Labrador, Newfoundland, Nova Scotia (?)	Explored[1]	Leif Ericsson, Norse explorer	1000
West Indies	Explored[1]	Christopher Columbus, Italian	1492
North America	Coast explored[1]	Giovanni Caboto (John Cabot), for British	1497
Pacific Ocean	Sighted[1]	Vasco Núñez de Balboa, Spanish explorer	1513
Florida	Explored	Ponce de León, Spanish explorer	1513
Mexico	Conquered	Hernando Cortés, Spanish adventurer	1519–1521
St. Lawrence River	Explored[1]	Jacques Cartier, French navigator	1534
Southwest United States	Explored	Francisco Coronado, Spanish explorer	1540–1542
Colorado River	Explored[1]	Hernando de Alarcón, Spanish explorer	1540
Mississippi River	Explored[1]	Hernando de Soto, Spanish explorer	1541
Frobisher Bay	Explored[1]	Martin Frobisher, English seaman	1576
Maine Coast	Explored	Samuel de Champlain, French explorer	1604
Jamestown, Va.	Settled	John Smith, English colonist	1607
Hudson River	Explored	Henry Hudson, English navigator	1609
Hudson Bay (Canada)	Explored[1]	Henry Hudson	1610
Baffin Bay	Explored[1]	William Baffin, English navigator	1616
Lake Michigan	Navigated	Jean Nicolet, French explorer	1634
Arkansas River	Explored[1]	Jacques Marquette and Louis Jolliet, French explorers	1673
Mississippi River	Explored	Sieur de La Salle, French explorer	1682
Bering Strait	Explored[1]	Vitus Bering, Danish explorer	1728
Alaska	Explored[1]	Vitus Bering	1741
Mackenzie River (Canada)	Explored[1]	Sir Alexander Mackenzie, Scottish-Canadian explorer	1789
Northwest United States	Explored	Meriwether Lewis and William Clark, American explorers	1804–1806
Northeast Passage (Arctic Ocean)	Navigated	Nils Nordenskjöld, Swedish explorer	1879
Greenland	Explored	Robert E. Peary, American explorer	1892
Northwest Passage	Navigated	Roald Amundsen, Norwegian explorer	1906

Country or place	Event	Explorer	Date
SOUTH AMERICA			
Continent	Explored	Christopher Columbus, Italian	1498
Brazil	Explored[1]	Pedro Alvarez Cabral, Portuguese	1500
Peru	Conquered	Francisco Pizarro, Spanish explorer	1532–1533
Amazon River	Explored	Francisco Orellana, Spanish explorer	1541
Cape Horn	Explored[1]	Willem C. Schouten, Dutch navigator	1615
OCEANIA			
Papua New Guinea	Explored	Jorge de Menezes, Portuguese explorer	1526
Australia	Explored	Abel Janszoon Tasman, Dutch navigator	1642
Tasmania	Explored[1]	Abel Janszoon Tasman	1642
Australia	Crossed	John McDouall Stuart, English explorer	1862
Australia	Explored	Robert Burke and William Wills, Australian explorers	1861
New Zealand	Sighted (and named)	Abel Janszoon Tasman, Dutch navigator	1642
New Zealand	Explored	James Cook, English navigator	1769
ARCTIC, ANTARCTIC, **AND MISCELLANEOUS**			
Africa, Middle East, South and Southeast Asia, and Europe	Explored	Ibn Batuta, greatest Arab traveler	1325–1349
Ocean exploration	Expedition	Ferdinand Magellan's ships circled globe for Spain	1519–1522
Galápagos Islands	Explored	Diego de Rivadeneira, Spanish captain	1535
Spitsbergen	Explored	Willem Barents, Dutch navigator	1596
Antarctic Circle	Crossed	James Cook, English navigator	1773
Antarctica	Explored[1]	Nathaniel Palmer, American whaler (archipelago), and Fabian Gottlieb von Bellingshausen, Russian admiral (mainland)	1820–1821
Antarctica	Explored	Charles Wilkes, American explorer	1840
North Pole	Reached[2]	Robert E. Peary, American explorer	1909
South Pole	Reached	Roald Amundsen, Norwegian explorer	1911

1. First European to reach the area. 2. Admiral Peary's claim to have reached the Pole has been disputed from the beginning—as was the claim made by his former colleague, Dr. Frederick Cook, who has been generally dismissed as a charlatan. The credit ultimately went to Peary, a claim officially backed by the U.S. Congress. But recent scholarship, including evidence culled from the journals and diaries of both Cook and Peary, has cast doubt on both explorers' veracity. If it is the case that neither reached the Pole, then the credit goes to Joseph Fletcher, who landed a U.S. Air Force C-47 plane there in 1952.

The Continents

A continent is defined as a large unbroken land mass completely surrounded by water, although in some cases continents are (or were in part) connected by land bridges. The seven continents are North America, South America, Europe, Asia, Africa, Australia, and Antarctica. The island groups in the Pacific are often called Oceania but this name does *not* imply that scientists consider them the remains of a continent.

Political considerations have often overridden geographical facts when it came to naming continents: Geographically, Europe, including the British Isles, is a large western peninsula of the continent of Asia; and many geographers, when referring to Europe and Asia, speak of the Eurasian continent. But traditionally, Europe is counted as a separate continent, with the Ural and the Caucasus mountains forming the line of demarcation between Europe and Asia. To the south of Europe, Asia has an odd-shaped peninsula jutting westward, which has a large number of political subdivisions. The northern section is taken up by Turkey; to the south of Turkey there are Syria, Iraq, Israel, Jordan, Saudi Arabia, and a number of smaller Arab countries. All these are part of Asia. Traditionally, the island of Cyprus in the Mediterranean is also considered to be part of Asia.

Continental Drift and Plate-Tectonics Theory

Source: U.S. Dept. of the Interior, Geological Survey

According to the theory of continental drift, the world was made up of a single continent through most of geologic time. That continent eventually separated and drifted apart, forming into the seven continents we have today. The first comprehensive theory of continental drift was suggested by the German meteorologist Alfred Wegener in 1912. The hypothesis asserts that the continents consist of lighter rocks that rest on heavier crustal material—similar to the manner in which icebergs float on water. Wegener contended that the relative positions of the continents are not rigidly fixed but are slowly moving—at a rate of about one yard per century.

According to the generally accepted plate-tectonics theory, scientists believe that Earth's surface is broken into a number of shifting slabs or plates, which average about 50 miles in thickness. These plates move relative to one another above a hotter, deeper, more mobile zone at average rates as great as a few inches per year. Most of the world's active volcanoes are located along or near the boundaries between shifting plates and are called plate-boundary volcanoes. However, some active volcanoes are not associated with plate boundaries, and many of these so-called intra-plate volcanoes form roughly linear chains in the interior of some oceanic plates. The Hawaiian Islands provide perhaps the best example of an intra-plate volcanic chain, developed by the northwest-moving Pacific plate passing over an inferred "hot spot" that initiates the magma-generation and volcano-formation process. The peripheral areas of the Pacific Ocean Basin, containing the boundaries of several plates, are dotted by many active volcanoes that form the so-called Ring of Fire. The Ring provides excellent examples of plate-boundary volcanoes, including Mount St. Helens.

World Land Areas and Elevations

Area	Approximate land area sq. km	Approximate land area sq. mi.	Percentage of total land area	Elevation, feet and meters Highest	Elevation, feet and meters Lowest
WORLD	148,429,000	57,308,738	100.0%	Mt. Everest, Asia, 29,035 ft. (8,850 m)[1]	Dead Sea, Israel-Jordan, 1,312 ft. below sea level (–400 m)
ASIA (includes the Middle East)	44,579,000	17,212,041	30.0	Mt. Everest, Tibet-Nepal, 29,035 ft. (8,850 m)	Dead Sea, Israel-Jordan, 1,312 ft. below sea level (–400 m)
AFRICA	30,065,000	11,608,156	20.3	Mt. Kilimanjaro, Tanzania, 19,340 ft. (5,895 m)	Lake Assal, Djibouti, 512 ft. below sea level (–156 m)
NORTH AMERICA	24,256,000	9,365,290	16.3	Mt. McKinley, Alaska, 20,320 ft. (6,194 m)	Death Valley, Calif., 282 ft. below sea level (–86 m)
SOUTH AMERICA (includes Central America and the Caribbean)	17,819,000	6,879,952	8.9	Mt. Aconcagua, Argentina, 22,834 ft. (6,960 m)	Valdes Peninsula, Argentina 131 ft. below sea level (–40 m)
ANTARCTICA	13,209,000	5,100,021	8.9	Vinson Massif, Ellsworth Mts., 16,066 ft. (4,897 m)	Ice covered 8,327 ft. below sea level (–2,538 m)
EUROPE (includes the recently independent states of the former Soviet Union)	9,938,000	3,837,082	6.7	Elbrus, Russia/Georgia, 18,510 ft. (5,642 m)	Caspian Sea, Russia/Kazakhstan 92 ft. below sea level (–28 m)
AUSTRALIA (includes Oceania)	7,687,000	2,967,966	5.2	Kosciusko, Australia 7,316 ft. (2,228 m)	Lake Eyre, Australia, 52 ft. below sea level (–16 m)

1. The 1954 elevation of Everest, 29,028 ft. (8,848 m) was revised on Nov. 11, 1999, and now stands at 29,035 ft. (8,850 m). *Source:* National Geographic Society.

Volcanoes of the World

Source: U.S. Dept. of the Interior, Geological Survey

About 550 volcanoes have erupted on Earth's surface since recorded history; about 60 are active each year. Far more have erupted unobserved on the ocean floor. Most volcanoes exist at the boundaries of Earth's crustal plates, such as the famous Ring of Fire that surrounds the Pacific Ocean plate. Fifty volcanoes have erupted in the United States since recorded history, and the United States ranks third, behind Indonesia and Japan, in the number of historically active volcanoes.

The Nature of Volcanoes

Volcanoes are built by the accumulation of their own eruptive products—lava, bombs (crusted over ash flows), and tephra (airborne ash and dust). A volcano is most commonly a conical hill or mountain built around a vent that connects with reservoirs of molten rock below the surface of Earth. The term *volcano* also refers to the opening or vent through which molten rock and gases are expelled.

Driven by buoyancy and gas pressure, the molten rock, which is lighter than the surrounding solid rock, forces its way upward and may ultimately break though zones of weaknesses in Earth's crust. If so, an eruption begins, and the molten rock may pour from the vent as nonexplosive lava flows, or it may shoot violently into the air as dense clouds of lava fragments. Larger fragments fall back around the vent, and accumulations of fall-back fragments may move downslope as ash flows under the force of gravity. Some of the finer ejected materials may be carried by the wind and fall to the ground many miles away. The finest ash particles may be injected miles into the atmosphere and carried many times around the world by stratospheric winds before settling out.

Magma, Lava, and Pumice

Molten rock below the surface of Earth that rises in volcanic vents is known as magma, but after it erupts from a volcano it is called lava. Originating many tens of miles beneath the ground, the ascending magma commonly contains some crystals, fragments of surrounding (unmelted) rocks, and dissolved gases, but it is primarily a liquid composed of oxygen, silicon, aluminum, iron, magnesium, calcium, sodium, potassium, titanium, and manganese. Magmas also contain many other chemical elements in trace quantities. Upon cooling, the liquid magma may precipitate crystals of various minerals until solidification is complete to form an igneous or magmatic rock.

Lava is red-hot when it pours or blasts out of a vent but soon changes to dark red, gray, black, or some other color as it cools and solidifies. Very hot, gas-rich lava containing abundant iron and magnesium is fluid and flows like hot tar, whereas cooler, gas-poor lava high in silicon, sodium, and potassium flows sluggishly, like thick honey, or in other cases, like pasty, blocky masses.

All magmas contain dissolved gases, and as they rise to the surface to erupt, the confining pressures are reduced and the dissolved gases are liberated either quietly or explosively. If the lava is a thin fluid (not viscous), the gases may escape easily. But if the lava is thick and pasty (highly viscous), the gases will not move freely but will build up tremendous pressure and ultimately escape with explosive violence, throwing out great masses of solid rock as well as lava, dust, and ashes.

The violent separation of gas from lava may produce rock froth called pumice. Some of this froth is so light—because of the many gas bubbles—that it floats on water. In many eruptions the froth is shattered explosively into small fragments that are hurled high into the air in the form of volcanic cinders (red or black), volcanic ash (commonly tan or gray), and volcanic dust. □

Recent Volcanic Activity
(**Bold** indicates activity in 2000)

Volcano	Date of last eruption or activity	Volcano	Date of last eruption or activity
Adatara, Honshu, Japan	Sept. 7, 1997	Metis Shoal, Tonga	June 6, 1995
Akutan, Alaska	March 10, 1996	Momotombo, Nicaragua	April 4, 1996
Amukta, Alaska	Sept. 17, 1996	Monowai Seamount, Kermadec Islands	Dec. 5, 1997
Arenal, Costa Rica	**Aug. 23, 2000**	**Montserrat, West Indies**	**Sept. 11–15, 2000**
Axial Seamount	Jan. 25–28, 1998	Northern Gorda Ridge	Feb. 28, 1996
Bandai, Honshu, Japan	**Aug. 16, 2000**	**Nyamuragira, Congo**	**Jan. 30, 2000**
Barren Island, Indian Ocean	Dec. 20, 1994	Okmok, Alaska	May. 2, 1997
Bezymianny, Kamchatka, Russia	**March 15, 2000**	**Mount Oyama, Miyakejima, Japan**	**Aug. 31, 2000**
Mount Cameroon, Cameroon	**June 7, 2000**	**Pacaya, Guatemala**	**March 1, 2000**
Cerro Negro, Nicaragua	Aug. 6, 1999	Papandayan, Java, Indonesia	July 1, 1998
Chiginagak, Alaska	Nov. 7, 1997	Pavlof, Alaska	June 3, 1997
Colima, Mexico	Nov. 4, 1999	Peuet Sague, Indonesia	April 27, 1998
Copahue, Argentina & Chile	**July 16, 2000**	Piparo, Trinidad	Feb. 22, 1997
Eastern Gemini Seamount, Vanuatu	Feb. 23, 1996	**Piton de la Fournaise, Réunion, Indian Ocean**	**June 23, 2000**
Etna, Sicily, Italy	**Aug. 28, 2000**	**Popocatepetl, Mexico**	**Sept. 4, 2000**
Fernandina, Galápagos	Jan. 25, 1995	Rabaul, Papua New Guinea	May 28, 1997
Fogo, Cape Verde	April 2, 1995	Rincon de la Vieja, Costa Rica	Feb. 16, 1998
Fuego, Guatemala	**Sept. 4, 2000**	Ruapehu, New Zealand	Sept. 13, 1999
Grimsvotn Volcano, Iceland	Dec. 18–28, 1998	Ruby Seamount, Mariana Islands	Oct. 25, 1995
Guagua Pichincha, Ecuador	**July 12, 2000**	Sakura-Jima, Japan	Nov. 1, 1999
Hakkoda, Japan	July 12, 1997	**San Cristobal, Nicaragua**	**May 13, 2000**
Hekla, Iceland	**Feb. 26, 2000**	**Semeru, Java, Indonesia**	**1967–continuing**
Mount Hili Aludo, Indonesia	May 13, 1997	**Sheveluch, Kamchatka, Russia**	**Aug. 6, 2000**
Hosho, Kyushu, Japan	Oct. 12, 1995	Shin-dake, Kuchinoerabujima Island, Japan	Aug. 26, 1999
Iwate-san, Honshu, Japan	July 10, 1998	**Shishaldin, Unimak Island, Alaska**	**May 15, 2000**
Kaba, Sumatra, Indonesia	**Aug. 17, 2000**	Mount St. Helens, Washington	July 1, 1998
Mount Karangetang, Indonesia	April 19, 1997	Stromboli, Italy	Aug. 23, 1998
Karymsky, Kamchatka, Russia	**Feb. 12, 2000**	**Tavurvur, Papua New Guinea**	**Sept. 10, 2000**
Kavachi Seamount, Solomon Islands	**May 14, 2000**	Taal, Philippines	Sept. 30, 1999
Kilauea, Hawaii	1983–continuing	Telica, Nicaragua	Aug. 11, 1999
Kliuchevskoi, Kamchatka, Russia	**July 28, 2000**	Terceira, Azores	Jan. 8, 1999
Komagatake, Hokkaido, Japan	**Sept. 4, 2000**	Tonga (unnamed volcano)	Jan. 18, 1999
Korovin, Alaska	June 30, 1998	**Tungurahua, Ecuador**	**May 20, 2000**
Krakatau, Indonesia	**May 29–June 9, 2000**	**Usu, Japan**	**April 20, 2000**
		Villarrica, Chile	**Jan. 20–May 30, 2000**
Lascar, Chile	**July 20, 2000**		
Mount Lewotobi, Indonesia	July 1, 1999	**White Island, New Zealand**	**July 27, 2000– continuing**
Loihi Seamount, Hawaii	July 26, 1996		
Long Valley caldera, California	April 2, 1996	Yellowstone, Wyoming	Jan. 9, 1998
Maderas, Nicaragua	Sept. 27, 1996	Zacatecas, Mexico	June 1997
Manam, Papua New Guinea	May 28, 1997		
Masaya, Nicaragua	Nov. 22, 1999		
Mayon, Philippines	**July 30, 2000**		
McDonald Island, Australia	Dec. 1996		
Merapi, Indonesia	July 20, 1998		

Source: Volcano World, University of North Dakota (http://volcano.und.nodak.edu).

The Deadliest Volcanic Eruptions

Volcano	Year	Deaths	Major cause of deaths
Tambora, Indonesia	1815	92,000	Starvation
Krakatau, Indonesia	1883	36,417	Tsunami
Mount Pelee, Martinique	1902	29,025	Ash flows
Ruiz, Colombia	1985	25,000	Mudflows
Unzen, Japan	1792	14,300	Volcano collapse, tsunami
Laki, Iceland	1783	9,350	Starvation
Kelut, Indonesia	1919	5,110	Mudflows
Galunggung, Indonesia	1882	4,011	Mudflows
Vesuvius, Italy	1631	3,500	Mudflows, lava flows
Vesuvius, Italy	79	3,360	Ash flows and falls
Papandayan, Indonesia	1772	2,957	Ash flows
Lamington, Papua New Guinea	1951	2,942	Ash flows
El Chichon, Mexico	1982	2,000	Ash flows
Soufriere, St. Vincent	1902	1,680	Ash flows
Oshima, Japan	1741	1,475	Tsunami
Asama, Japan	1783	1,377	Ash flows, mudflows
Taal, Philippines	1911	1,335	Ash flows
Mayon, Philippines	1814	1,200	Mudflows
Agung, Indonesia	1963	1,184	Ash flows
Cotopaxi, Ecuador	1877	1,000	Mudflows
Pinatubo, Philippines	1991	800	Disease
Komagatake, Japan	1640	700	Tsunami
Ruiz, Colombia	1845	700	Mudflows
Hibok-Hibok, Philippines	1951	500	Ash flows

Source: Volcano World, University of North Dakota (http://volcano.und.nodak.edu).

Principal Types of Volcanoes

Source: U.S. Dept. of the Interior, Geological Survey

Geologists generally group volcanoes into four main kinds—cinder cones, composite volcanoes, shield volcanoes, and lava domes.

Cinder Cones

Cinder cones are the simplest type of volcano. They are built from particles and blobs of congealed lava ejected from a single vent. As the gas-charged lava is blown violently into the air, it breaks into small fragments that solidify and fall as cinders around the vent to form a circular or oval cone. Most cinder cones have a bowl-shaped crater at the summit and rarely rise more than a thousand feet or so above their surroundings. Cinder cones are numerous in western North America as well as throughout other volcanic terrains of the world.

Composite Volcanoes

Composite volcanoes, sometimes called *stratovolcanoes,* are typically deep-sided, symmetrical cones of large dimension built of alternating layers of lava flows, volcanic ash, cinders, blocks, and bombs and may rise as much as 8,000 feet above their bases. Some of the most beautiful mountains in the world are composite volcanoes, including Mount Fuji in Japan, Mount Cotopaxi in Ecuador, Mount Shasta in California, Mount Hood in Oregon, and Mount St. Helens and Mount Rainier in Washington.

Most composite volcanoes have a crater at the summit that contains a central vent or a clustered group of vents. Lavas either flow through breaks in the crater wall or issue from fissures on the flanks of the cone. Lava, solidified within the fissures, forms *dikes* that act as ribs which greatly strengthen the cone.

The essential feature of a composite volcano is a conduit system through which magma from a reservoir deep in Earth's crust rises to the surface. The volcano is built up by the accumulation of material erupted through the conduit and increases in size as lava, cinders, and ash are added to its slopes.

Shield Volcanoes

Shield volcanoes are built almost entirely of fluid lava flows. Flow after flow pours out in all directions from a central summit vent, or group of vents, building a broad, gently sloping cone of flat, domical shape, with a profile much like that of a warrior's shield. They are built up slowly by the accretion of thousands of flows of highly fluid basaltic (from *basalt,* a hard, dense dark volcanic rock) lava that spread widely over great distances, and then cool as thin, gently dipping sheets. Lavas also commonly erupt from vents along fractures (rift zones) that develop on the flanks of the cone. Some of the largest volcanoes in the world are shield volcanoes. In northern California and Oregon, many shield volcanoes have diameters of 3 or 4 miles and heights of 1,500 to 2,000 feet. The Hawaiian Islands are composed of linear chains of these volcanoes, including Kilauea and Mauna Loa on the island of Hawaii.

In some shield volcano eruptions, basaltic lava pours out quietly from long fissures instead of central vents and floods the surrounding countryside with lava flow upon lava flow, forming broad plateaus. Lava plateaus of this type can be seen in Iceland, southeastern Washington, eastern Oregon, and southern Idaho.

Lava Domes

Volcanic or lava domes are formed by relatively small, bulbous masses of lava too viscous to flow any great distance; consequently, on extrusion, the lava piles over and around its vent. A dome grows largely by expansion from within. As it grows, its outer surface cools and hardens, then shatters, spilling loose fragments down its sides. Some domes form craggy knobs or spines over the volcanic vent, whereas others form short, steep-sided lava flows known as *coulees*. Volcanic domes commonly occur within the craters or on the flanks of large composite volcanoes. The nearly circular Novarupta Dome that formed during the 1912 eruption of Katmai Volcano, Alaska, measures 800 feet across and 200 feet high. The internal structure of this dome—defined by layering of lava fanning upward and outward from the center—indicates that it grew largely by expansion from within. Mount Pelée in Martinique, West Indies, and Lassen Peak and Mono domes in California are examples of lava domes.

Submarine Volcanoes

Submarine volcanoes and volcanic vents are common features on certain zones of the ocean floor. Some are active at the present time and, in shallow water, disclose their presence by blasting steam and rock-debris high above the surface of the sea. Many others lie at such great depths that the tremendous weight of the water above them results in high, confining pressure and prevents the formation and release of steam and gases. Even very large, deep-water eruptions may not disturb the ocean floor.

The famous black sand beaches of Hawaii were created virtually instantaneously by the violent interaction between hot lava and seawater.

Earthquakes

The Severity of an Earthquake

Source: National Earthquake Information Center, U.S. Geological Survey

The severity of an earthquake can be expressed in terms of both intensity and magnitude. The two terms are quite different, however, and they are often confused. Intensity is based on the observed effects of ground shaking on people, buildings, and natural features. It varies from place to place within the disturbed region depending on the location of the observer with respect to the earthquake epicenter. Magnitude is related to the amount of seismic energy released at the hypocenter of the earthquake. It is based on the amplitude of the earthquake waves recorded on instruments, which have a common calibration. The magnitude of an earthquake is thus represented by a single, instrumentally determined value.

Earthquakes are the result of forces deep within Earth's interior that continuously affect its surface. The energy from these forces is stored in a variety of ways within the rocks. When this energy is released suddenly—by shearing movements along faults in the crust of Earth, for example—an earthquake results. The area of the fault where the sudden rupture takes place is called the focus or hypocenter of the earthquake. The point on Earth's surface directly above the focus is called the epicenter of the earthquake.

The Richter Magnitude Scale

Seismic waves are the vibrations from earthquakes that travel through Earth; they are recorded on instruments called seismographs. Seismographs record a zigzag trace that shows the varying amplitude of ground oscillations beneath the instrument. Sensitive seismographs, which greatly magnify these ground motions, can detect strong earthquakes from sources anywhere in the world. The time, location, and magnitude of an earthquake can be determined from the data recorded by seismograph stations.

The Richter magnitude scale was developed in 1935 by Charles F. Richter of the California Institute of Technology as a mathematical device to compare the size of earthquakes. The magnitude of an earthquake is determined from the logarithm of the amplitude of waves recorded by seismographs. Adjustments are included in the magnitude formula to compensate for the variation in the distance between the various seismographs and the epicenter of the earthquakes. On the Richter Scale, magnitude is expressed in whole numbers and decimal fractions. For example, a magnitude of 5.3 might be computed for a moderate earthquake, and a strong earthquake might be rated as magnitude 6.3. Because of the logarithmic basis of the scale, each whole number increase in magnitude represents a tenfold increase in measured amplitude; as an estimate of energy, each whole number step in the magnitude scale corresponds to the release of about 31 times more energy than the amount associated with the preceding whole number value. Great earthquakes, such as the 1964 Good Friday earthquake in Alaska, have magnitudes of 8.0 or higher. On average, one earthquake of such size occurs somewhere in the world each year. Although the Richter Scale has no upper limit, the largest known shocks have had magnitudes in the 8.8 to 8.9 range.

Why Are There So Many Earthquake Magnitude Scales?

Earthquake size, as measured by the Richter Scale, is a well-known, but not well understood, concept. What is even less well understood is the proliferation of magnitude scales and their relation to Richter's original magnitude scale. Richter's magnitude scale was first created for measuring the size of earthquakes occurring in southern California, using relatively high-frequency data from nearby seismograph stations. This magnitude scale was referred to as ML, with the L standing for local. This is what was to eventually become known as the Richter magnitude.

As more seismograph stations were installed around the world, it became apparent that the method developed by Richter was strictly valid only for certain frequency and distance ranges. In order to take advantage of the growing number of globally distributed seismograph stations, new magnitude scales that are an extension of Richter's original idea were developed. These include body-wave magnitude, "mb," and surface-wave magnitude, "MS." Each is valid for a particular frequency range and type of seismic signal. In its range of validity each is equivalent to the Richter magnitude.

Because of the limitations of all three magnitude scales—ML, mb, and MS—a new, more uniformly applicable extension of the magnitude scale, known as moment magnitude, or "MW," was developed. In particular, for very large earthquakes moment magnitude gives the most reliable estimate of earthquake size. New techniques that take advantage of modern telecommunications have recently been implemented, allowing reporting agencies to obtain rapid estimates of moment magnitude for significant earthquakes. So nowadays, when most seismologists announce a magnitude number, they are rarely referring to the Richter Scale.

The Modified Mercalli Intensity Scale

The effect of an earthquake on Earth's surface is called the intensity. The intensity scale consists of a series of certain key responses, such as people awakening, movement of furniture, damage to chimneys, and finally—total destruction. Although numerous intensity scales have been developed over the past several hundred years to evaluate the effects of earthquakes, the one currently used in the United States is the Modified Mercalli (MM) Intensity Scale. It was developed in 1931 by the American seismologists Harry Wood and Frank Neumann. This scale, composed of 12 increasing levels of intensity that range from imperceptible shaking to catastrophic destruction, is designated by Roman numerals. It does not have a mathematical basis; instead it is an arbitrary ranking based on observed effects. The Modified Mercalli Intensity value assigned to a specific site after an earthquake has a more meaningful measure of severity to the nonscientist than the magnitude because intensity refers to the effects actually experienced at that place.

Frequency of Earthquakes Worldwide[1]

Descriptor	Magnitude	Annual average	Descriptor	Magnitude	Annual average
Great	8 or higher	1	Light	4–4.9	c. 6,200
Major	7–7.9	18	Minor	3–3.9	c. 49,000
Strong	6–6.9	120	Very minor	2–3	c. 1,000[2]
Moderate	5–5.9	800	Very minor	1–2	c. 8,000[2]

1. Since 1900. 2. Per day. *Source:* National Earthquake Information Center, U.S. Geological Survey.

Number of Earthquakes Worldwide, 1990–2000, and Mortality Figures

Magnitude	1990	1991	1992	1993	1994	1995	1996	1997	1998	1999	2000
8.0–9.9	0	0	0	1	2	3	1	0	2	0	1
7.0–7.9	12	11	23	15	13	22	21	20	14	23	7
6.0–6.9	115	105	104	141	161	185	160	125	113	123	71
5.0–5.9	1,635	1,469	1,541	1,449	1,542	1,327	1,223	1,118	979	1,106	497
4.0–4.9	4,493	4,372	5,196	5,034	4,544	8,140	8,794	7,938	7,303	7,042	2,930
3.0–3.9	2,457	2,952	4,643	4,263	5,000	5,002	4,869	4,467	5,945	5,521	1,958
2.0–2.9	2,364	2,927	3,068	5,390	5,369	3,838	2,388	2,397	4,091	4,201	1,380
1.0–1.9	474	801	887	1,177	779	645	295	388	805	715	308
0.1–0.9	0	1	2	9	17	19	1	4	10	5	2
No magnitude	5,062	3,878	4,084	3,997	1,944	1,826	2,186	3,415	2,426	2,096	771
Total	16,612	16,516	19,548	21,476	19,371	21,007	19,938	19,872	21,688	20,832	7,925[1]
Estimated deaths	**51,916**	**2,326**	**3,814**	**10,036**	**1,038**	**7,949**	**419**	**2,907**	**8,928**	**22,711**	**155**

1. As of July 11, 2000. *Source:* National Earthquake Information Center, U.S. Geological Survey.

Major Earthquakes around the World, 2000

Date	Location	Magnitude[1]	Date	Location	Magnitude[1]
Jan. 8	Tonga Islands	7.2	May 4	Minahassa Peninsula, Sulawesi, Indonesia	7.6
Feb. 25	Vanuatu Islands region	7.1			
March 28	Volcano Islands, Japan region	7.6	May 12	Jujuy Province, Argentina	7.2
			June 4	Sumatra, Indonesia	7.9
April 23	Santiago del Estero Province, Argentina	7.0	June 18	South Indian Ocean	7.8
			Aug. 6	Bonin Islands, Japan Region	7.3

NOTE: A major earthquake is defined here as having a magnitude of 7.0 or more. 1. Unless otherwise indicated, magnitudes listed are moment magnitudes, the newest, most uniformly applicable magnitude scale. *Source:* National Earthquake Information Center, U.S. Geological Survey.

The Ten Largest Earthquakes of the 20th Century

Country or place	Date	Magnitude[1]	Country or place	Date	Magnitude[1]
Chile	May 22, 1960	9.5	Kuril Islands	Nov. 6, 1958	8.7
Alaska	March 27, 1964	9.2	Alaska	Feb. 4, 1965	8.7
Russia	Nov. 4, 1952	9.0	India	Aug. 15, 1950	8.6
Ecuador	Jan. 31, 1906	8.8	Chile	Nov. 11, 1922	8.5
Alaska	March 9, 1957	8.8	Indonesia	Feb. 1, 1938	8.5

1. Moment magnitude. *Source:* National Earthquake Information Center, U.S. Geological Survey.

The 25 Largest Earthquakes in the United States

Rank	Magnitude	Date	Location	Rank	Magnitude	Date	Location
1.	9.2	March 27, 1964	Prince William Sound, Alaska	13.	7.9	Nov. 30, 1987	Gulf of Alaska
2.	8.8	March 9, 1957	Andreanof Islands, Alaska	14.	7.8	March 26, 1872	Owens Valley, California
3.	8.7	Feb. 4, 1965	Rat Islands, Alaska	15.	7.8	Feb. 24, 1892	Imperial Valley, California
4.	8.3	Nov. 10, 1938	East of Shumagin Islands, Alaska	16.	7.7	Dec. 16, 1811	New Madrid, Missouri area
5.	8.3	July 10, 1958	Lituya Bay, Alaska	17.	7.7	April 18, 1906	San Francisco, California
6.	8.2	Sept. 10, 1899	Yakutat Bay, Alaska	18.	7.7	Oct. 3, 1915	Pleasant Valley, Nevada
7.	8.2	Sept. 4, 1899	Near Cape Yakataga, Alaska	19.	7.6	Jan. 23, 1812	New Madrid, Missouri
				20.	7.6	June 28, 1992	Landers, California
8.	8.0	May 7, 1986	Andreanof Islands, Alaska	21.	7.5	July 21, 1952	Kern County, California
9.	7.9	Feb. 7, 1812	New Madrid, Missouri	22.	7.3	Nov. 4, 1927	West of Lompoc, California
10.	7.9	Jan. 9, 1857	Fort Tejon, California				
11.	7.9	April 3, 1868	Ka'u District, Island of Hawaii	23.	7.3	Dec. 16, 1954	Dixie Valley, Nevada
				24.	7.3	Aug. 18, 1959	Hebgen Lake, Montana
12.	7.9	Oct. 9, 1900	Kodiak Island, Alaska	25.	7.3	Oct. 28, 1983	Borah Peak, Idaho

Source: National Earthquake Information Center, U.S. Geological Survey.

Everest Is Higher Than Ever

As of Nov. 11, 1999, the new official height of Mount Everest was announced as 29,035 feet, or 8,850 meters—6 feet, or 2 meters, higher than the previously accepted measurement. The new elevation was determined using satellite-based technology: the Trimble Global Positioning System (GPS). A team of seven climbers measured the mountain from the summit on May 5, 1999, collecting data from various GPS satellite receivers at the very top of Everest. It took the climbers a number of attempts over several years until they were able to successfully set up the equipment at the summit.

Everest was first measured in 1852 in the Great Trigonometrical Survey of India, which established the peak as the highest on Earth. That figure (29,002 feet above sea level) remained Everest's officially accepted height for more than one hundred years. The original 1852 measurement was remarkably accurate: in 1955 the elevation was adjusted by a mere 26 feet to 29,028 feet (8,848 meters).

The World's 14 Highest Mountain Peaks (above 8,000 meters)

All 14 of the world's 8,000-meter peaks are located in the Himalaya or the Karakoram ranges in Asia. Thus far, only six climbers have reached the summits of all 14: Reinhold Messner (Italy) was first, followed by Jerzy Kukuczka (Poland), Ehardt Loretan (Switzerland), Carlos Carsolio (Mexico), Krzysztof Wielicki (Poland), and Juan Oiarzabal (Spain).

Mountain	Height Meters	Feet	First to summit	Date	Nationality
1. Everest[1]	8,850	29,035	Edmund Hillary, Tenzing Norgay	May 29, 1953	New Zealander (U.K.) and Nepalese
2. K2 (Mount Godwin Austen)	8,611	28,250	A. Compagnoni, L. Lacedelli	July 31, 1954	Italian
3. Kangchenjunga	8,586	28,169	G. Band, J. Brown, N. Hardie, S. Streather	May 25, 1955	U.K.
4. Lhotse	8,516	27,940	F. Luchsinger, E. Reiss	May 18, 1956	Swiss
5. Makalu	8,463	27,766	J. Couzy, L. Terray, J. Franco, G. Magnone-Gialtsen, J. Bouier, S. Coupé, P. Leroux, A. Vialatte	May 15, 1955	French
6. Cho Oyu	8,201	26,906	H. Tichy, S. Jöchler, Pasang Dawa Lama	Oct. 19, 1954	Austrian
7. Dhaulagiri	8,167	26,795	A. Schelbert, E. Forrer, K. Diemberger, P. Diener, Nyima Dorji, Nawang Dorji	May 13, 1960	Swiss and Nepalese
8. Manaslu	8,163	26,781	T. Iminaschi, G. Norbu, K. Kato, M. Higeta	May 9, 1956	Japanese and Nepalese
9. Nanga Parbat	8,125	26,660	Hermann Buhl	July 3, 1953	Austrian
10. Annapurna	8,091	26,545	M. Herzog, L. Lachenal	June 3, 1950	French
11. Gasherbrum I	8,068	26,470	P. K. Schoeing, A. J. Kauffman	July 4, 1958	U.S.
12. Broad Peak	8,047	26,400	M. Schmuck, F. Wintersteller, K. Diemberger, H. Buhl	June 9, 1957	Austrian
13. Gasherbrum II	8,035	26,360	F. Moravec, S. Larch, H. Willenpart	July 7, 1956	Austrian
14. Shisha Pangma	8,013	26,289	Hsu Ching and team of 9	May 2, 1964	Chinese

1. The 1955 elevation of Everest, 29,028 ft. (8,848 m), was revised on Nov. 11, 1999, and now stands at 29,035 ft. (8,850 m).

Highest Mountain Peaks of the World (continued from p. 492)

(*See* p. 502 for U.S. peaks.)

Mountain peak	Range	Location	Height ft.	m
Annapurna II	Himalayas	Nepal	26,041	7,937
Gyachung Kang	Himalayas	Nepal	25,910	7,897
Disteghil Sar	Karakoram	Pakistan	25,858	7,882
Himalchuli	Himalayas	Nepal	25,801	7,864
Nuptse	Himalayas	Nepal	25,726	7,841
Nanda Devi	Himalayas	India	25,663	7,824
Masherbrum	Karakoram	Kashmir[1]	25,660	7,821
Rakaposhi	Karakoram	Pakistan	25,551	7,788
Kanjut Sar	Karakoram	Pakistan	25,461	7,761
Kamet	Himalayas	India/Tibet	25,446	7,756
Namcha Barwa	Himalayas	Tibet	25,445	7,756
Gurla Mandhata	Himalayas	Tibet	25,355	7,728
Ulugh Muztagh	Kunlun	Tibet	25,340	7,723
Kungur	Muztagh Ata	China	25,325	7,719
Tirich Mir	Hindu Kush	Pakistan	25,230	7,690
Saser Kangri	Karakoram	India	25,172	7,672
Makalu II	Himalayas	Nepal	25,120	7,657
Minya Konka (Gongga Shan)	Daxue Shan	China	24,900	7,590
Kula Kangri	Himalayas	Bhutan	24,783	7,554
Chang-tzu	Himalayas	Tibet	24,780	7,553
Muztagh Ata	Muztagh Ata	China	24,757	7,546
Skyang Kangri	Himalayas	Kashmir	24,750	7,544
Ismail Samani Peak (formerly Communism Peak)	Pamirs	Tajikistan	24,590	7,495
Jongsong Peak	Himalayas	Nepal	24,472	7,459
Pobeda Peak	Tien Shan	Kyrgyzstan	24,406	7,439
Sia Kangri	Himalayas	Kashmir	24,350	7,422
Haramosh Peak	Karakoram	Pakistan	24,270	7,397
Istoro Nal	Hindu Kush	Pakistan	24,240	7,388
Tent Peak	Himalayas	Nepal	24,165	7,365
Chomo Lhari	Himalayas	Tibet/Bhutan	24,040	7,327
Chamlang	Himalayas	Nepal	24,012	7,319
Kabru	Himalayas	Nepal	24,002	7,316
Alung Gangri	Himalayas	Tibet	24,000	7,315
Baltoro Kangri	Himalayas	Kashmir	23,990	7,312
Muztagh Ata (K-5)	Kunlun	China	23,890	7,282
Mana	Himalayas	India	23,860	7,273
Baruntse	Himalayas	Nepal	23,688	7,220
Nepal Peak	Himalayas	Nepal	23,500	7,163
Amne Machin	Kunlun	China	23,490	7,160

Mountain peak	Range	Location	Height ft.	m
Gauri Sankar	Himalayas	Nepal/Tibet	23,440	7,145
Badrinath	Himalayas	India	23,420	7,138
Nunkun	Himalayas	Kashmir	23,410	7,135
Lenin Peak	Pamirs	Tajikistan/ Kyrgyzstan	23,405	7,134
Pyramid	Himalayas	Nepal	23,400	7,132
Api	Himalayas	Nepal	23,399	7,132
Pauhunri	Himalayas	India/China	23,385	7,128
Trisul	Himalayas	India	23,360	7,120
Korzhenevski Peak	Pamirs	Tajikistan	23,310	7,105
Kangto	Himalayas	Tibet	23,260	7,090
Nyainqen-tanglha	Nyainqen-tanglha Shan	China	23,255	7,088
Trisuli	Himalayas	India	23,210	7,074
Dunagiri	Himalayas	India	23,184	7,066
Revolution Peak	Pamirs	Tajikistan	22,880	6,974
Aconcagua	Andes	Argentina	22,834	6,960
Ojos del Salado	Andes	Argentina/ Chile	22,664	6,908
Bonete	Andes	Argentina/ Chile	22,546	6,872
Ama Dablam	Himalayas	Nepal	22,494	6,856
Tupungato	Andes	Argentina/ Chile	22,310	6,800
Moscow Peak	Pamirs	Tajikistan	22,260	6,785
Pissis	Andes	Argentina	22,241	6,779
Mercedario	Andes	Argentina/ Chile	22,211	6,770
Huascarán	Andes	Peru	22,205	6,768
Llullaillaco	Andes	Argentina/ Chile	22,057	6,723
El Libertador	Andes	Argentina	22,047	6,720
Cachi	Andes	Argentina	22,047	6,720
Kailas	Himalayas	Tibet	22,027	6,714
Incahuasi	Andes	Argentina/ Chile	21,720	6,620
Yerupaja	Andes	Peru	21,709	6,617
Kurumda	Pamirs	Tajikistan	21,686	6,610
Galan	Andes	Argentina	21,654	6,600
El Muerto	Andes	Argentina/ Chile	21,463	6,542
Sajama	Andes	Bolivia	21,391	6,520
Nacimiento	Andes	Argentina	21,302	6,493
Illampu	Andes	Bolivia	21,276	6,485
Illimani	Andes	Bolivia	21,201	6,462
Coropuna	Andes	Peru	21,083	6,426
Laudo	Andes	Argentina	20,997	6,400
Ancohuma	Andes	Bolivia	20,958	6,388
Cuzco (Ausangate)	Andes	Peru	20,945	6,384

1. Kashmir is divided between India and Pakistan, with both countries disputing the boundaries. *Source:* National Geographic Society.

Climbing the Seven Summits

Fewer than fifty mountaineers have climbed all "Seven Summits"—the highest peak on each of the seven continents. The first was Dick Bass, an American businessman, on April 30, 1985. The seven summits are Mt. Everest (Asia) 29,035 ft., Mt. Aconcagua (South America) 22,834 ft., Mt. McKinley (North America) 20,320 ft., Mt. Kilimanjaro (Africa) 19,340 ft., Mt. Elbrus (Europe) 18,510 ft., Vinson Massif (Antarctica) 16,066 ft., and Kosciusko (Australia) 7,316 ft.

Oceans and Seas

Name	Area sq. mi.	Area sq. km	Average depth ft.	Average depth m	Greatest known depth ft.	Greatest known depth m	Place of greatest known depth
Pacific Ocean	64,000,000	165,760,000	13,215	4,028	36,198	11,033	Mariana Trench
Atlantic Ocean	31,815,000	82,400,000	12,880	3,926	30,246	9,219	Puerto Rico Trench
Indian Ocean	25,300,000	65,526,700	13,002	3,963	24,460	7,455	Sunda Trench
Arctic Ocean	5,440,200	14,090,000	3,953	1,205	18,456	5,625	77°45′N; 175°W
Mediterranean Sea[1]	1,145,100	2,965,800	4,688	1,429	15,197	4,632	Off Cape Matapan, Greece
Caribbean Sea	1,049,500	2,718,200	8,685	2,647	22,788	6,946	Off Cayman Islands
South China Sea	895,400	2,319,000	5,419	1,652	16,456	5,016	West of Luzon
Bering Sea	884,900	2,291,900	5,075	1,547	15,659	4,773	Off Buldir Island
Gulf of Mexico	615,000	1,592,800	4,874	1,486	12,425	3,787	Sigsbee Deep
Okhotsk Sea	613,800	1,589,700	2,749	838	12,001	3,658	146°10′E; 46°50′N
East China Sea	482,300	1,249,200	617	188	9,126	2,782	25°16′N; 125°E
Hudson Bay	475,800	1,232,300	420	128	600	183	Near entrance
Japan Sea	389,100	1,007,800	4,429	1,350	12,276	3,742	Central Basin
Andaman Sea	308,100	797,700	2,854	870	12,392	3,777	Off Car Nicobar Island
North Sea	222,100	575,200	308	94	2,165	660	Skagerrak
Red Sea	169,100	438,000	1,611	491	7,254	2,211	Off Port Sudan
Baltic Sea	163,000	422,200	180	55	1,380	421	Off Gotland

1. Includes Black Sea and Sea of Azov. NOTE: For Caspian Sea, *see* Large Lakes of the World.

Large Lakes of the World

(area more than 1,600 sq. miles)

Name and location	Area sq. mi.	Area km	Length mi.	Length km	Maximum depth ft.	Maximum depth m
Caspian Sea, Azerbaijan-Russia-Kazakhstan-Turkmenistan-Iran[1]	152,239	394,299	745	1,199	3,104	946
Superior, U.S.-Canada	31,820	82,414	383	616	1,333	406
Victoria, Tanzania-Uganda	26,828	69,485	200	322	270	82
Huron, U.S.-Canada	23,010	59,596	247	397	750	229
Michigan, U.S.	22,400	58,016	321	517	923	281
Aral, Kazakhstan-Uzbekistan	13,000	33,800	266	428	223	68
Tanganyika, Tanzania-Congo	12,700	32,893	420	676	4,708	1,435
Baikal, Russia	12,162	31,500	395	636	5,712	1,741
Great Bear, Canada	12,000	31,080	232	373	270	82
Nyasa, Malawi-Mozambique-Tanzania	11,600	30,044	360	579	2,316	706
Great Slave, Canada	11,170	28,930	298	480	2,015	614
Chad,[2] Chad-Niger-Nigeria	9,946	25,760	—	—	23	7
Erie, U.S.-Canada	9,930	25,719	241	388	210	64
Winnipeg, Canada	9,094	23,553	264	425	204	62
Ontario, U.S.-Canada	7,520	19,477	193	311	778	237
Balkhash, Kazakhstan	7,115	18,428	376	605	87	27
Ladoga, Russia	7,000	18,130	124	200	738	225
Onega, Russia	3,819	9,891	154	248	361	110
Titicaca, Bolivia-Peru	3,141	8,135	110	177	1,214	370
Nicaragua, Nicaragua	3,089	8,001	110	177	230	70
Athabaska, Canada	3,058	7,920	208	335	407	124
Rudolf, Kenya	2,473	6,405	154	248	—	—
Reindeer, Canada	2,444	6,330	152	245	—	—
Eyre, South Australia	2,400[3]	6,216	130	209	varies	varies
Issyk-Kul, Kyrgyzstan	2,394	6,200	113	182	2,297	700
Urmia,[2] Iran	2,317	6,001	81	130	49	15
Torrens, South Australia	2,200	5,698	130	209	—	—
Vänern, Sweden	2,141	5,545	87	140	322	98
Winnipegosis, Canada	2,086	5,403	152	245	59	18
Mobutu Sese Seko, Uganda	2,046	5,299	100	161	180	55
Nettilling, Baffin Island, Canada	1,950	5,051	70	113	—	—
Nipigon, Canada	1,870	4,843	72	116	—	—
Manitoba, Canada	1,817	4,706	140	225	22	7
Great Salt, U.S.	1,800	4,662	75	121	15–25	5–8
Kioga, Uganda	1,700	4,403	50	80	about 30	9
Koko-Nor, China	1,630	4,222	66	106	—	—

1. The Caspian Sea is called "sea" because the Romans, finding it salty, named it *Mare Caspium*. Many geographers, however, consider it a lake because it is land-locked. 2. Figures represent high-water data. 3. Varies with the rainfall of the wet season. It has been reported to dry up almost completely on occasion.

Principal Rivers of the World

(See pp. 500–501 for other U.S. rivers.)

River	Source	Outflow	mi.	km
			Approx. length	
Nile	Tributaries of Lake Victoria, Africa	Mediterranean Sea	4,180	6,690
Amazon	Glacier-fed lakes, Peru	Atlantic Ocean	3,912	6,296
Mississippi-Missouri-Red Rock	Source of Red Rock, Montana	Gulf of Mexico	3,710	5,970
Yangtze Kiang	Tibetan plateau, China	China Sea	3,602	5,797
Ob	Altai Mts., Russia	Gulf of Ob	3,459	5,567
Huang Ho (Yellow)	Eastern part of Kunlan Mts., West China	Gulf of Chihli	2,900	4,667
Yenisei	Tannu-Ola Mts., western Tuva, Russia	Arctic Ocean	2,800	4,506
Paraná	Confluence of Paranaiba and Grande rivers	Río de la Plata	2,795	4,498
Irtish	Altai Mts., Russia	Ob River	2,758	4,438
Zaire (Congo)	Confluence of Lualab and Luapula rivers, Congo	Atlantic Ocean	2,716	4,371
Heilong (Amur)	Confluence of Shilka (Russia) and Argun (Manchuria) rivers	Tatar Strait	2,704	4,352
Lena	Baikal Mts., Russia	Arctic Ocean	2,652	4,268
Mackenzie	Head of Finlay River, British Columbia, Canada	Beaufort Sea (Arctic Ocean)	2,635	4,241
Niger	Guinea	Gulf of Guinea	2,600	4,184
Mekong	Tibetan highlands	South China Sea	2,500	4,023
Mississippi	Lake Itasca, Minnesota	Gulf of Mexico	2,348	3,779
Missouri	Confluence of Jefferson, Gallatin, and Madison rivers, Montana	Mississippi River	2,315	3,726
Volga	Valdai plateau, Russia	Caspian Sea	2,291	3,687
Madeira	Confluence of Beni and Maumoré rivers, Bolivia–Brazil boundary	Amazon River	2,012	3,238
Purus	Peruvian Andes	Amazon River	1,993	3,207
São Francisco	Southwest Minas Gerais, Brazil	Atlantic Ocean	1,987	3,198
Yukon	Junction of Lewes and Pelly rivers, Yukon Territory, Canada	Bering Sea	1,979	3,185
St. Lawrence	Lake Ontario	Gulf of St. Lawrence	1,900	3,058
Rio Grande	San Juan Mts., Colorado	Gulf of Mexico	1,885	3,034
Brahmaputra	Himalayas	Ganges River	1,800	2,897
Indus	Himalayas	Arabian Sea	1,800	2,897
Danube	Black Forest, Germany	Black Sea	1,766	2,842
Euphrates	Confluence of Murat Nehri and Kara Su rivers, Turkey	Shatt-al-Arab	1,739	2,799
Darling	Central part of Eastern Highlands, Australia	Murray River	1,702	2,739
Zambezi	11°21′S, 24°22′E, Zambia	Mozambique Channel	1,700	2,736
Tocantins	Goiás, Brazil	Pará River	1,677	2,699
Murray	Australian Alps, New South Wales	Indian Ocean	1,609	2,589
Nelson	Head of Bow River, western Alberta, Canada	Hudson Bay	1,600	2,575
Paraguay	Mato Grosso, Brazil	Paraná River	1,584	2,549
Ural	Southern Ural Mts., Russia	Caspian Sea	1,574	2,533
Ganges	Himalayas	Bay of Bengal	1,557	2,506
Amu Darya (Oxus)	Nicholas Range, Pamir Mts., Turkmenistan	Aral Sea	1,500	2,414
Japurá	Andes, Colombia	Amazon River	1,500	2,414
Salween	Tibet, south of Kunlun Mts.	Gulf of Martaban	1,500	2,414
Arkansas	Central Colorado	Mississippi River	1,459	2,348
Colorado	Grand County, Colorado	Gulf of California	1,450	2,333
Dnieper	Valdai Hills, Russia	Black Sea	1,419	2,284
Ohio-Allegheny	Potter County, Pennsylvania	Mississippi River	1,306	2,102
Irrawaddy	Confluence of Nmai and Mali rivers, northeast Burma	Bay of Bengal	1,300	2,092
Orange	Lesotho	Atlantic Ocean	1,300	2,092
Orinoco	Serra Parima Mts., Venezuela	Atlantic Ocean	1,281	2,062
Pilcomayo	Andes Mts., Bolivia	Paraguay River	1,242	1,999
Xi Jiang (Si Kiang)	Eastern Yunnan Province, China	China Sea	1,236	1,989
Columbia	Columbia Lake, British Columbia, Canada	Pacific Ocean	1,232	1,983
Don	Tula, Russia	Sea of Azov	1,223	1,968
Sungari	China–North Korea boundary	Amur River	1,215	1,955
Saskatchewan	Canadian Rocky Mts.	Lake Winnipeg	1,205	1,939
Peace	Stikine Mts., British Columbia, Canada	Great Slave River	1,195	1,923
Tigris	Taurus Mts., Turkey	Shatt-al-Arab	1,180	1,899

Large Islands of the World

Island	Location and political affiliation	Area sq. mi.	Area sq. km
Greenland	North Atlantic (Danish)	839,999	2,175,597
New Guinea	Southwest Pacific (Irian Jaya, Indonesia, western part; Papua New Guinea, eastern part)	316,615	820,033
Borneo	West mid-Pacific (Indonesian, south part; Brunei and Malaysian, north part)	286,914	743,107
Madagascar	Indian Ocean (Malagasy Republic)	226,657	587,042
Baffin	North Atlantic (Canadian)	183,810	476,068
Sumatra	Northeast Indian Ocean (Indonesian)	182,859	473,605
Honshu	Sea of Japan–Pacific (Japanese)	88,925	230,316
Great Britain	Off coast of NW Europe (England, Scotland, and Wales)	88,758	229,883
Ellesmere	Arctic Ocean (Canadian)	82,119	212,688
Victoria	Arctic Ocean (Canadian)	81,930	212,199
Sulawesi (Celebes)	West mid-Pacific (Indonesian)	72,986	189,034
South Island	South Pacific (New Zealand)	58,093	150,461
Java	Indian Ocean (Indonesian)	48,990	126,884
North Island	South Pacific (New Zealand)	44,281	114,688
Cuba	Caribbean Sea (republic)	44,218	114,525
Newfoundland	North Atlantic (Canadian)	42,734	110,681
Luzon	West mid-Pacific (Philippines)	40,420	104,688
Iceland	North Atlantic (republic)	39,768	102,999
Mindanao	West mid-Pacific (Philippines)	36,537	94,631
Ireland	West of Great Britain (republic, south part; United Kingdom, north part)	32,597	84,426
Hokkaido	Sea of Japan–Pacific (Japanese)	30,372	78,663
Hispaniola	Caribbean Sea (Dominican Republic, east part; Haiti, west part)	29,355	76,029
Tasmania	South of Australia (Australian)	26,215	67,897
Sri Lanka (Ceylon)	Indian Ocean (republic)	25,332	65,610
Sakhalin (Karafuto)	North of Japan (Russian)	24,560	63,610
Banks	Arctic Ocean (Canadian)	23,230	60,166
Devon	Arctic Ocean (Canadian)	20,861	54,030
Tierra del Fuego	Southern tip of South America (Argentinian, east part; Chilean, west part)	18,605	48,187
Kyushu	Sea of Japan–Pacific (Japanese)	16,223	42,018

Highest Waterfalls of the World

Name(s) (foreign)	Location	Height Feet	Height Meters
Angel (Salto Angel)	Canaima Nat'l Park, Venezuela	3,212	979
Tugela	Natal Nat'l Park, South Africa	2,800	850
Utigord (Utigordsfoss)	Norway	2,625	800
Monge (Mongefoss)	Marstein, Norway	2,540	774
Mutarazi (Mtarazi)	Nyanga Nat'l Park, Zimbabwe	2,499	762
Yosemite	Yosemite Nat'l Park, California, U.S.	2,425	739
Espelands (Espelandsfoss)	Hardanger Fjord, Norway	2,307	703[1]
Lower Mar Valley (Østra Mardolafoss)	Eikesdal, Norway	2,151	655[2]
Tyssestrengene	Odda, Norway	2,123	647[2]
Cuquenan (Salto Kukenan)	Kukenan Tepuy, Venezuela	2,000	610
Sutherland	Milford Sound, New Zealand	1,904	580
Kjell (Kjellfossen)	Gudvanger, Norway	1,841	561
Takkakaw	Yoho Nat'l Park, B.C., Canada	1,650	503
Ribbon	Yosemite Nat'l Park, California, U.S.	1,612	491
Upper Mar Valley (Mardalsfossen)	nr. Eikesdal, Norway	1,536	468
Gavarnie	nr. Lourdes, France	1,388	423
Vettis (Vettisfoss)	Jotunheimen, Norway	1,215	370
Hunlen	British Columbia, Canada	1,198	365
Tin Mine	Kosciusko Nat'l Park, Australia	1,182	360[1]
Silver Strand (Widows' Tears)	Yosemite Nat'l Park, California, U.S.	1,170	357
Basaseachic (Salto Basaseachic)	Barance del Cobre, Mexico	1,120	311
Spray Stream (Staubbachfalle)	Lauterburnnental, Switzerland	985	300
Fachoda (Cascade de Fachoda)	Tahiti, Fr. Polynesia	985	300[1]
King Edward VIII	Guyana	850	259
Wallaman	nr. Ingham, Australia	844	257[3]
Gersoppa (Jog)	Western Ghats, India	829	253
Kaieteur	Guyana	822	251
Montezuma	nr. Rosebery, Tasmania, Australia	800	240[1]
Wollomombi	nr. Armidale, Australia	722	220[3]

1. Unofficial (estimated) height. Subject to revision. 2. Incorporated in hydroelectric scheme. Greatly diminished flow. 3. Official heights established in April 2000. *Source: Fifth Continent Australia Pty Limited.*

Polar Regions

Antarctica

The second smallest continent, mostly south of the Antarctic Circle.

Area: 14.2 million sq. km (5.5 million sq. mi.).

Geographic South Pole: Earth's southernmost point, at latitude 90°S, where all lines of longitude meet.

Magnetic South Pole: The magnetic South Pole shifts about 5 miles (km) a year and is now located at about 66°S and 139°E on the Adélie Coast of Antarctica.

Terrain: About 98% thick ice sheet and 2% barren rock; glaciers form ice shelves along about half of the coastline, and floating ice shelves constitute 11% of the area of the continent. **Ice sheet:** The continental ice sheet contains approximately 7 million cubic miles (30 million cu km) of ice, representing about 90% of the world's total. **Major ice shelves:** Amery, Filchner, Larsen, Ronne, Ross. Ice shelves make up about 10% of Antarctica's ice, and are floating sheets of ice attached to land that project out into coastal waters.

Climate: The coldest, windiest, driest continent.

Regions: East Antarctica (c. 3,000,000 sq. mi./7,770,000 sq. km), the largest portion of the continent, is a high, ice-covered plateau. West Antarctica (c. 2,500,000 sq. mi./6,475,000 sq. km), is an archipelago of mountainous islands connected by ice. A mountain range divides them.

Elevation extremes: *Lowest point:* sea level; Ice shelf −8,327 ft. below sea level (−2,538 m). *Highest point:* Vinson Massif 16,066 ft. (4,897 m), Ellsworth Mountains.

The Arctic

Region, primarily made up of the frozen Arctic Ocean, that surrounds the North Pole. Land masses include islands and the northern parts of the European, Asian, and North American continents.

Area: 14.056 million sq. km (5.4 million sq. mi.), largely frozen ocean.

Geographic North Pole: Northern end of Earth's axis, located at about latitude 90°N.

Magnetic North Pole: Continues to shift and is located at about 78°N and 104°W in the Queen Elizabeth Islands of northern Canada.

Terrain: Central surface covered by a perennial drifting polar icepack that averages about 3 meters in thickness; the icepack is surrounded by open seas during the summer, but more than doubles in size during the winter and extends to the encircling landmasses.

Climate: Polar climate characterized by persistent cold and relatively narrow annual temperature ranges; winters characterized by continuous darkness, cold and stable weather conditions, and clear skies; summers characterized by continuous daylight, damp and foggy weather, and weak cyclones with rain or snow.

Regions: The Arctic is divided by the summer isotherm, a climatic boundary between regions with summer temperatures averaging 50°F (or 10°C)—the subarctic—and colder regions (the true Arctic).

Elevation extremes: *Lowest point:* Fram Basin −4,665 m. *Highest point:* sea level 0 m.

Interesting Caves and Caverns of the World

Aggtelek. In village of same name, northern Hungary. Large stalactitic cavern about 5 mi. long.

Altamira Cave. Near Santander, Spain. Contains Stone Age animal paintings on roof and walls.

Antiparos. On island of same name in the Grecian Archipelago. Some stalactites are 20 ft. long. Brilliant colors and fantastic shapes.

Blue Grotto. On island of Capri, Italy. Sea cavern hollowed out in limestone by constant wave action. Now half filled with water because of sinking coast. Name derived from unusual blue light permeating the cave. Source of light is a submerged opening allowing light to pass through the water.

Carlsbad Caverns. Southeast New Mexico. Contains some of the largest and most impressive stalactites and stalagmites, particularly in the Lechuguilla Cave.

Fingal's Cave. On island of Staffa off coast of western Scotland. Penetrates about 200 ft. inland. Contains basaltic columns almost 40 ft. high.

Jenolan Caves. In Blue Mountain plateau, New South Wales, Australia. Beautiful stalactitic formations.

Kent's Cavern. Near Torquay, England. Source of much information on Paleolithic humans.

Lascaux Cave. Southwestern France. Features prehistoric cave paintings estimated to be tens of thousands of years old. Closed to the public.

Lubang Nasib Bagus. Sarawak, Malaysia. World's largest cave chamber: 2,300 ft. long, 1,480 ft. wide, and everywhere at least 230 ft. high.

Luray Caverns. Near Luray, Va. Has large stalactitic and stalagmitic columns of many colors.

Mogao Caves. Located along the old Silk Route in China, Mogao is composed of 492 cells and cave sanc-

tuaries that are famous for their statues and wall paintings, spanning a thousand years of Buddhist art.

Mammoth Cave. This limestone cavern in central Kentucky is the longest cave system in the world. Cave area is about 10 mi. in diameter but has 345 mi. of irregular subterranean passageways at various levels, plus underground lakes and rivers.

Peak Cavern or Devil's Hole. Derbyshire, England. About 2,250 ft. into a mountain. Lowest part is about 600 ft. below the surface.

Postojna Grotto. Postojna, Slovenia. Largest cavern in Europe; numerous beautiful stalactites. Famous example of a karst cave—grooved and irregularly eroded limestone formations carved out by underground streams. Pivka River flows through part of it.

Singing Cave. Iceland. A lava cave; name derived from echoes of people singing in it.

Waitomo Cave. North Island, New Zealand. Glowworms on cave ceiling look like thousands of stars in the night sky.

Wind Cave. In Black Hills of South Dakota. Limestone caverns with stalactites and stalagmites almost entirely missing. Variety of crystal formations called "boxwork."

Wyandotte Cave. In Crawford County, southern Indiana. A limestone cavern with five levels of passages; one of the largest in North America. "Monumental Mountain," approximately 135 ft. high, is believed to be one of the world's largest underground "mountains."

Principal Deserts of the World

Deserts are arid regions, generally receiving less than ten inches of precipitation a year, or regions where the potential evaporation rate is twice as great as the precipitation.

The world's deserts are divided into four categories. **Subtropical deserts** are the hottest, with parched terrain and rapid evaporation. Although **cool coastal deserts** are located within the same latitudes as subtropical deserts, the average temperature is much cooler because of frigid offshore ocean currents. **Cold winter deserts** are marked by stark temperature differences from season to season, ranging from 100° F (38° C) in the summer to 10° F (−12° C) in the winter. **Polar regions** are also considered to be deserts because nearly all moisture in these areas is locked up in the form of ice.

Desert	Location	Size	Topography
SUBTROPICAL DESERTS			
Sahara	Morocco, Western Sahara, Algeria, Tunisia, Libya, Egypt, Mauritania, Mali, Niger, Chad, Ethiopia, Eritrea, Somalia	3.5 million sq. mi.	70% gravel plains, sand, and dunes. Contrary to popular belief, the desert is only 30% sand. The world's largest desert gets its name from the Arabic word *Sahra'*, meaning desert
Arabian	Saudi Arabia, Kuwait, Qatar, United Arab Emirates, Oman, Yemen	1 million sq. mi.	Gravel plains, rocky highlands; one-fourth is the Rub al-Khali ("Empty Quarter"), the world's largest expanse of unbroken sand
Kalahari	Botswana, South Africa, Namibia	220,000 sq. mi.	Sand sheets, longitudinal dunes
Australian Desert			
Gibson	Australia (southern portion of the Western Desert)	120,000 sq. mi.	Sandhills, gravel, grass. These three regions of desert are collectively referred to as the Great Western Desert— otherwise known as "the Outback." Contains Ayers Rock, or Uluru, one of the world's largest monoliths
Great Sandy	Australia (northern portion of the Western Desert)	150,000 sq. mi.	
Great Victoria	Australia (southernmost portion of the Western Desert)	250,000 sq. mi.	
Simpson and Sturt Stony	Australia (eastern half of the continent)	56,000 sq. mi.	Simpson's straight, parallel sand dunes are the longest in the world—up to 125 mi. Encompasses the Stewart Stony Desert, named for the Australian explorer
Mojave	U.S.: Arizona, Colorado, Nevada, Utah, California	54,000 sq. mi.	Mountain chains, dry alkaline lake beds, calcium carbonate dunes
Sonoran	U.S.: Arizona, California; Mexico	120,000 sq. mi.	Basins and plains bordered by mountain ridges; home to the Saguaro cactus
Chihuahuan	Mexico; southwestern U.S.	175,000 sq. mi.	Shrub desert; largest in North America
Thar	India, Pakistan	175,000 sq. mi.	Rocky sand and sand dunes
COOL COASTAL DESERTS			
Namib	Angola, Namibia, South Africa	13,000 sq. mi.	Gravel plains
Atacama	Chile	54,000 sq. mi.	Salt basins, sand, lava; world's driest desert
COLD WINTER DESERTS			
Great Basin	U.S.: Nevada, Oregon, Utah	190,000 sq. mi.	Mountain ridges, valleys, 1% sand dunes
Colorado Plateau	U.S.: Arizona, Colorado, New Mexico, Utah, Wyoming	130,000 sq. mi.	Sedimentary rock, mesas, and plateaus— includes the Grand Canyon and is also called the "Painted Desert" because of the spectacular colors in its rocks and canyons
Patagonian	Argentina	260,000 sq. mi.	Gravel plains, plateaus, basalt sheets
Kara-Kum	Uzbekistan, Turkmenistan	135,000 sq. mi.	90% gray layered sand—name means "black sand"
Kyzyl-Kum	Uzbekistan, Turkmenistan, Kazakhstan	115,000 sq. mi.	Sands, rock—name means "red sand"
Iranian	Iran	100,000 sq. mi.	Salt, gravel, rock
Taklamakan	China	105,000 sq. mi.	Sand, dunes, gravel
Gobi	China, Mongolia	500,000 sq. mi.	Stony, sandy soil, steppes (dry grasslands)
POLAR			
Arctic	U.S., Canada, Greenland, Iceland, Norway, Sweden, Finland, Russia		Snow, glaciers, tundra
Antarctic	Antarctica	5.4 million sq. mi.	Ice, snow, bedrock

Latitude and Longitude of World Cities
(and time corresponding to 12:00 noon, Eastern Standard Time)

City	Latitude ° '	Longitude ° '	Time
Aberdeen, Scotland	57 9 N	2 9 W	5:00 p.m.
Adelaide, Australia	34 55 S	138 36 E	2:30 a.m.[1]
Algiers, Algeria	36 50 N	3 0 E	6:00 p.m.
Amsterdam, Netherlands	52 22 N	4 53 E	6:00 p.m.
Ankara, Turkey	39 55 N	32 55 E	7:00 p.m.
Asunción, Paraguay	25 15 S	57 40 W	1:00 p.m.
Athens, Greece	37 58 N	23 43 E	7:00 p.m.
Auckland, New Zealand	36 52 S	174 45 E	5:00 a.m.[1]
Bangkok, Thailand	13 45 N	100 30 E	midnight
Barcelona, Spain	41 23 N	2 9 E	6:00 p.m.
Beijing, China	39 55 N	116 25 E	1:00 a.m.[1]
Belém, Brazil	1 28 S	48 29 W	2:00 p.m.
Belfast, Northern Ireland	54 37 N	5 56 W	5:00 p.m.
Belgrade, Yugoslavia	44 52 N	20 32 E	6:00 p.m.
Berlin, Germany	52 30 N	13 25 E	6:00 p.m.
Birmingham, England	52 25 N	1 55 W	5:00 p.m.
Bogotá, Colombia	4 32 N	74 15 W	12:00 noon
Bombay, India	19 0 N	72 48 E	10:30 p.m.
Bordeaux, France	44 50 N	0 31 W	6:00 p.m.
Bremen, Germany	53 5 N	8 49 E	6:00 p.m.
Brisbane, Australia	27 29 S	153 8 E	3:00 a.m.[1]
Bristol, England	51 28 N	2 35 W	5:00 p.m.
Brussels, Belgium	50 52 N	4 22 E	6:00 p.m.
Bucharest, Romania	44 25 N	26 7 E	7:00 p.m.
Budapest, Hungary	47 30 N	19 5 E	6:00 p.m.
Buenos Aires, Argentina	34 35 S	58 22 W	2:00 p.m.
Cairo, Egypt	30 2 N	31 21 E	7:00 p.m.
Calcutta, India	22 34 N	88 24 E	10:30 p.m.
Canton, China	23 7 N	113 15 E	1:00 a.m.[1]
Cape Town, South Africa	33 55 S	18 22 E	7:00 p.m.
Caracas, Venezuela	10 28 N	67 2 W	1:00 p.m.
Cayenne, French Guiana	4 49 N	52 18 W	1:00 p.m.
Chihuahua, Mexico	28 37 N	106 5 W	11:00 a.m.
Chongqing, China	29 46 N	106 34 E	1:00 a.m.[1]
Copenhagen, Denmark	55 40 N	12 34 E	6:00 p.m.
Córdoba, Argentina	31 28 S	64 10 W	2:00 p.m.
Dakar, Senegal	14 40 N	17 28 W	5:00 p.m.
Darwin, Australia	12 28 S	130 51 E	2:30 a.m.[1]
Djibouti, Djibouti	11 30 N	43 3 E	8:00 p.m.
Dublin, Ireland	53 20 N	6 15 W	5:00 p.m.
Durban, South Africa	29 53 S	30 53 E	7:00 p.m.
Edinburgh, Scotland	55 55 N	3 10 W	5:00 p.m.
Frankfurt, Germany	50 7 N	8 41 E	6:00 p.m.
Georgetown, Guyana	6 45 N	58 15 W	1:15 p.m.
Glasgow, Scotland	55 50 N	4 15 W	5:00 p.m.
Guatemala City, Guatemala	14 37 N	90 31 W	11:00 a.m.
Guayaquil, Ecuador	2 10 S	79 56 W	12:00 noon
Hamburg, Germany	53 33 N	10 2 E	6:00 p.m.
Hammerfest, Norway	70 38 N	23 38 E	6:00 p.m.
Havana, Cuba	23 8 N	82 23 W	12:00 noon
Helsinki, Finland	60 10 N	25 0 E	7:00 p.m.
Hobart, Tasmania	42 52 S	147 19 E	3:00 a.m.[1]
Iquique, Chile	20 10 S	70 7 W	1:00 p.m.
Irkutsk, Russia	52 30 N	104 20 E	1:00 a.m.[1]
Jakarta, Indonesia	6 16 S	106 48 E	0:30 a.m.[1]
Johannesburg, South Africa	26 12 S	28 4 E	7:00 p.m.
Kingston, Jamaica	17 59 N	76 49 W	12:00 noon
Kinshasa, Congo	4 18 S	15 17 E	6:00 p.m.
La Paz, Bolivia	16 27 S	68 22 W	1:00 p.m.
Leeds, England	53 45 N	1 30 W	5:00 p.m.
Lima, Peru	12 0 S	77 2 W	12:00 noon
Lisbon, Portugal	38 44 N	9 9 W	5:00 p.m.
Liverpool, England	53 25 N	3 0 W	5:00 p.m.
London, England	51 32 N	0 5 W	5:00 p.m.
Lyons, France	45 45 N	4 50 E	6:00 p.m.
Madrid, Spain	40 26 N	3 42 W	6:00 p.m.
Manchester, England	53 30 N	2 15 W	5:00 p.m.
Manila, Philippines	14 35 N	120 57 E	1:00 a.m.[1]
Marseilles, France	43 20 N	5 20 E	6:00 p.m.
Mazatlán, Mexico	23 12 N	106 25 W	10:00 a.m.
Mecca, Saudi Arabia	21 29 N	39 45 E	8:00 p.m.
Melbourne, Australia	37 47 S	144 58 E	3:00 a.m.[1]
Mexico City, Mexico	19 26 N	99 7 W	11:00 a.m.
Milan, Italy	45 27 N	9 10 E	6:00 p.m.
Montevideo, Uruguay	34 53 S	56 10 W	2:00 p.m.
Moscow, Russia	55 45 N	37 36 E	8:00 p.m.
Munich, Germany	48 8 N	11 35 E	6:00 p.m.
Nagasaki, Japan	32 48 N	129 57 E	2:00 a.m.[1]
Nagoya, Japan	35 7 N	136 56 E	2:00 a.m.[1]
Nairobi, Kenya	1 25 S	36 55 E	8:00 p.m.
Nanjing (Nanking), China	32 3 N	118 53 E	1:00 a.m.[1]
Naples, Italy	40 50 N	14 15 E	6:00 p.m.
Newcastle-on-Tyne, England	54 58 N	1 37 W	5:00 p.m.
Odessa, Ukraine	46 27 N	30 48 E	8:00 p.m.
Osaka, Japan	34 32 N	135 30 E	2:00 a.m.[1]
Oslo, Norway	59 57 N	10 42 E	6:00 p.m.
Panama City, Panama	8 58 N	79 32 W	12:00 noon
Paramaribo, Suriname	5 45 N	55 15 W	1:30 p.m.
Paris, France	48 48 N	2 20 E	6:00 p.m.
Perth, Australia	31 57 S	115 52 E	1:00 a.m.[1]
Plymouth, England	50 25 N	4 5 W	5:00 p.m.
Port Moresby, Papua New Guinea	9 25 S	147 8 E	3:00 a.m.[1]
Prague, Czech Republic	50 5 N	14 26 E	6:00 p.m.
Rangoon, Myanmar	16 50 N	96 0 E	11:30 p.m.
Reykjavík, Iceland	64 4 N	21 58 W	4:00 p.m.
Rio de Janeiro, Brazil	22 57 S	43 12 W	2:00 p.m.
Rome, Italy	41 54 N	12 27 E	6:00 p.m.
Salvador, Brazil	12 56 S	38 27 W	2:00 p.m.
Santiago, Chile	33 28 S	70 45 W	1:00 p.m.
St. Petersburg, Russia	59 56 N	30 18 E	8:00 p.m.
São Paulo, Brazil	23 31 S	46 31 W	2:00 p.m.
Shanghai, China	31 10 N	121 28 E	1:00 a.m.[1]
Singapore, Singapore	1 14 N	103 55 E	0:30 a.m.[1]
Sofia, Bulgaria	42 40 N	23 20 E	7:00 p.m.
Stockholm, Sweden	59 17 N	18 3 E	6:00 p.m.
Sydney, Australia	34 0 S	151 0 E	3:00 a.m.[1]
Tananarive, Madagascar	18 50 S	47 33 E	8:00 p.m.
Teheran, Iran	35 45 N	51 45 E	8:30 p.m.
Tokyo, Japan	35 40 N	139 45 E	2:00 a.m.[1]
Tripoli, Libya	32 57 N	13 12 E	7:00 p.m.
Venice, Italy	45 26 N	12 20 E	6:00 p.m.
Veracruz, Mexico	19 10 N	96 10 W	11:00 a.m.
Vienna, Austria	48 14 N	16 20 E	6:00 p.m.
Vladivostok, Russia	43 10 N	132 0 E	3:00 a.m.[1]
Warsaw, Poland	52 14 N	21 0 E	6:00 p.m.
Wellington, New Zealand	41 17 S	174 47 E	5:00 a.m.[1]
Zürich, Switzerland	47 21 N	8 31 E	6:00 p.m.

1. On the following day.

Miscellaneous Data for the United States

Highest point: Mount McKinley, Alaska	20,320 ft. (6,198 m)
Lowest point: Death Valley, Calif.	282 ft. (86 m) below sea level
Approximate mean elevation	2,500 ft. (763 m)
Points farthest apart (50 states): Log Point, Elliot Key, Fla., and Kure Island, Hawaii	5,859 mi. (9,429 km)
Geographic center (50 states): in Butte County, S.D. (west of Castle Rock)	44°58′N lat.103°46′W long.
Geographic center (48 conterminous states): in Smith County, Kan. (near Lebanon)	39°50′N lat. 98°35′W long.
Boundaries:	
Between Alaska and Canada	1,538 mi. (2,475 km)
Between the 48 conterminous states and Canada (incl. the Great Lakes)	3,987 mi. (6,416 km)
Between the United States and Mexico	1,933 mi. (3,111 km)

Source: U.S. Geological Survey.

Extreme Points of the United States (50 States)

Extreme point	Latitude	Longitude	Distance[1] mi.	Distance[1] km
Northernmost point: Point Barrow, Alaska	71°23′ N	156°29′ W	2,507	4,034
Easternmost point: West Quoddy Head, Maine	44°49′ N	66°57′ W	1,788	2,997
Southernmost point: Ka Lae (South Cape), Hawaii	18°55′ N	155°41′ W	3,463	5,573
Westernmost point: Cape Wrangell, Alaska (Attu Island)	52°55′ N	172°27′ E	3,625	5,833

1. From geographic center of United States (incl. Alaska and Hawaii), west of Castle Rock, S.D., 44°58′ lat., 103°46′ W long. If measured from the prime meridian in Greenwich, England, Cape Wrangell, Attu Island, Alaska, would be the easternmost point.

The Continental Divide

The Continental Divide is a ridge of high ground that runs irregularly north and south through the Rocky Mountains and separates eastward-flowing from westward-flowing streams. The waters that flow eastward empty into the Atlantic Ocean, chiefly by way of the Gulf of Mexico; those that flow westward empty into the Pacific.

Rivers of the United States
(350 or more miles long)

Alabama-Coosa (600 mi.; 966 km): From junction of Oostanula and Etowah R. in Georgia to Mobile R.

Altamaha-Ocmulgee (392 mi.; 631 km): From junction of Yellow R. and South R., Newton Co. in Georgia to Atlantic Ocean.

Apalachicola-Chattahoochee (524 mi.; 843 km): From Towns Co. in Georgia to Gulf of Mexico in Florida.

Arkansas (1,459 mi.; 2,348 km): From Lake Co. in Colorado to Mississippi R. in Arkansas.

Brazos (923 mi.; 1,490 km): From junction of Salt Fork and Double Mountain Fork in Texas to Gulf of Mexico.

Canadian (906 mi.; 1,458 km): From Las Animas Co. in Colorado to Arkansas R. in Oklahoma.

Cimarron (600 mi.; 966 km): From Colfax Co. in New Mexico to Arkansas R. in Oklahoma.

Colorado (1,450 mi.; 2,333 km): From Rocky Mountain National Park in Colorado to Gulf of California in Mexico.

Colorado (862 mi.; 1,387 km): From Dawson Co. in Texas to Matagorda Bay.

Columbia (1,243 mi.; 2,000 km): From Columbia Lake in British Columbia to Pacific Ocean (entering between Oregon and Washington).

Colville (350 mi.; 563 km): From Brooks Range in Alaska to Beaufort Sea.

Connecticut (407 mi.; 655 km): From Third Connecticut Lake in New Hampshire to Long Island Sound in Connecticut.

Cumberland (720 mi.; 1,159 km): From junction of Poor and Clover Forks in Harlan Co. in Kentucky to Ohio R.

Delaware (390 mi.; 628 km): From Schoharie Co. in New York to Liston Point, Delaware Bay.

Gila (649 mi.; 1,044 km): From Catron Co. in New Mexico to Colorado R. in Arizona.

Green (360 mi.; 579 km): From Lincoln Co. in Kentucky to Ohio R. in Kentucky.

Green (730 mi.; 1,175 km): From Sublette Co. in Wyoming to Colorado R. in Utah.

Illinois (420 mi.; 676 km): From St. Joseph Co. in Indiana to Mississippi R. at Grafton in Illinois.

James (sometimes called *Dakota*) (710 mi.; 1,143 km): From Wells Co. in North Dakota to Missouri R. in South Dakota.

Kanawha-New (352 mi.; 566 km): From junction of North and South Forks of New R. in North Carolina, through Virginia and West Virginia (New R. becoming Kanawha R.), to Ohio R.

Kansas (743 mi.; 1,196 km): From source of Arikaree R. in Elbert Co., Colorado, to Missouri R. at Kansas City, Kansas.

Koyukuk (470 mi.; 756 km): From Brooks Range in Alaska to Yukon R.

Kuskokwim (724 mi.; 1,165 km): From Alaska Range in Alaska to Kuskokwim Bay.

Licking (350 mi.; 563 km): From Magoffin Co. in Kentucky to Ohio R. at Cincinnati in Ohio.

Little Missouri (560 mi.; 901 km): From Crook Co. in Wyoming to Missouri R. in North Dakota.

Milk (625 mi.; 1,006 km): From junction of forks in Alberta Province to Missouri R.

Mississippi (2,348 mi.; 3,779 km): From Lake Itasca in Minnesota to mouth of Southwest Pass in Louisiana.

Mississippi-Missouri-Red Rock (3,710 mi.; 5,970 km): From source of Red Rock R. in Montana to mouth of Southwest Pass in Louisiana.

Missouri (2,315 mi.; 3,726 km): From junction of Jefferson R., Gallatin R., and Madison R. in Montana to Mississippi R. near St. Louis.

Missouri-Red Rock (2,540 mi.; 4,090 km): From source of Red Rock R. in Montana to Mississippi R. near St. Louis.

Mobile-Alabama-Coosa (645 mi.; 1,040 km): From junction of Etowah R. and Oostanula R. in Georgia to Mobile Bay.

Neosho (460 mi.; 740 km): From Morris Co. in Kansas to Arkansas R. in Oklahoma.

Niobrara (431 mi.; 694 km): From Niobrara Co. in Wyoming to Missouri R. in Nebraska.

Noatak (350 mi.; 563 km): From Brooks Range in Alaska to Kotzebue Sound.

North Canadian (800 mi.; 1,290 km): From Union Co. in New Mexico to Canadian R. in Oklahoma.

North Platte (618 mi.; 995 km): From Jackson Co. in Colorado to junction with South Platte R. in Nebraska to form Platte R.

Ohio (981 mi.; 1,579 km): From junction of Allegheny R. and Monongahela R. at Pittsburgh to Mississippi R. between Illinois and Kentucky.

Ohio-Allegheny (1,306 mi.; 2,102 km): From Potter Co. in Pennsylvania to Mississippi R. at Cairo in Illinois.

Osage (500 mi.; 805 km): From east-central Kansas to Missouri R. near Jefferson City in Missouri.

Ouachita (605 mi.; 974 km): From Polk Co. in Arkansas to Red R. in Louisiana.

Pearl (411 mi.; 661 km): From Neshoba County in Mississippi to Gulf of Mexico (Mississippi-Louisiana).

Pecos (926 mi.; 1,490 km): From Mora Co. in New Mexico to Rio Grande in Texas.

Pee Dee-Yadkin (435 mi.; 700 km): From Watauga Co. in North Carolina to Winyah Bay in South Carolina.

Pend Oreille–Clark Fork (531 mi.; 855 km): Near Butte in Montana to Columbia R. on Washington-Canada border.

Platte (990 mi.; 1593 km): From source of Grizzly Creek in Jackson Co., Colorado, to Missouri R. south of Omaha, Nebraska.

Porcupine (569 mi.; 916 km): From Yukon Territory, Canada, to Yukon R. in Alaska.

Potomac (383 mi.; 616 km): From Garrett Co. in Maryland to Chesapeake Bay at Point Lookout in Maryland.

Powder (375 mi.; 603 km): From junction of forks in Johnson Co. in Wyoming to Yellowstone R. in Montana.

Red (1,290 mi.; 2,080 km): From source of Tierra Blanca Creek in Curry County, New Mexico, to Mississippi R. in Louisiana.

Red (also called *Red River of the North*) (545 mi.; 877 km): From junction of Otter Tail R. and Bois de Sioux R. in Minnesota to Lake Winnipeg in Manitoba, Canada.

Republican (445 mi.; 716 km): From junction of North Fork and Arikaree R. in Nebraska to junction with Smoky Hill R. in Kansas to form the Kansas R.

Rio Grande (1,900 mi.; 3,060 km): From San Juan Co. in Colorado to Gulf of Mexico.

Roanoke (380 mi.; 612 km): From junction of forks in Montgomery Co. in Virginia to Albemarle Sound in North Carolina.

Sabine (380 mi.; 612 km): From junction of forks in Hunt Co. in Texas to Sabine Lake between Texas and Louisiana.

Sacramento (377 mi.; 607 km): From Siskiyou Co. in California to Suisun Bay.

Saint Francis (425 mi.; 684 km): From Iron Co. in Missouri to Mississippi R. in Arkansas.

Salmon (420 mi.; 676 km): From Custer Co. in Idaho to Snake R.

San Joaquin (350 mi.; 563 km): From junction of forks in Madera Co. in California to Suisun Bay.

San Juan (360 mi.; 579 km): From Archuleta Co. in Colorado to Colorado R. in Utah.

Santee-Wateree-Catawba (538 mi.; 866 km): From McDowell Co. in North Carolina to Atlantic Ocean in South Carolina.

Smoky Hill (540 mi.; 869 km): From Cheyenne Co. in Colorado to junction with Republican R. in Kansas to form Kansas R.

Snake (1,038 mi.; 1,670 km): From Ocean Plateau in Wyoming to Columbia R. in Washington.

South Platte (424 mi.; 682 km): From Park Co. in Colorado to junction with North Platte R. in Nebraska to form Platte R.

Stikine (379 mi.; 610 km): From British Columbia in Canada to Stikine Strait near Wrangell, Alaska.

Susquehanna (444 mi.; 715 km): From Otsego Lake in New York to Chesapeake Bay in Maryland.

Tanana (659 mi.; 1,060 km): From Wrangell Mts. in Yukon Territory, Canada, to Yukon R. in Alaska.

Tennessee (652 mi.; 1,049 km): From junction of Holston R. and French Broad R. in Tennessee to Ohio R. in Kentucky.

Tennessee–French Broad (886 mi.; 1,417 km): From Transylvania Co. in North Carolina to Ohio R. at Paducah in Kentucky.

Tombigbee (525 mi.; 845 km): From junction of forks in Itawamba Co. in Mississippi to Mobile R. in Alabama.

Trinity (360 mi.; 579 km): From junction of forks in Dallas Co. in Texas to Galveston Bay.

Wabash (512 mi.; 824 km): From Darke Co. in Ohio to Ohio R. between Illinois and Indiana.

Washita (500 mi.; 805 km): From Hemphill Co. in Texas to Red R. in Oklahoma.

White (722 mi.; 1,160 km): From Madison Co. in Arkansas to Mississippi R.

Wisconsin (430 mi.; 692 km): From Vilas Co. in Wisconsin to Mississippi R.

Yellowstone (692 mi.; 1,110 km): From Park Co. in Wyoming to Missouri R. in North Dakota.

Yukon (1,979 mi.; 3,185 km): From source of McNeil R. in Yukon Territory, Canada, to Bering Sea in Alaska.

Coastline of the United States

State	General coastline[1] (Lengths, statute miles)	Tidal shoreline[2] (Lengths, statute miles)	State	General coastline[1] (Lengths, statute miles)	Tidal shoreline[2] (Lengths, statute miles)
Atlantic Coast:			**Gulf Coast:**		
Maine	228	3,478	Florida (Gulf)	770	5,095
New Hampshire	13	131	Alabama	53	607
Massachusetts	192	1,519	Mississippi	44	359
Rhode Island	40	384	Louisiana	397	7,721
Connecticut	—	618	Texas	367	3,359
New York	127	1,850	Total Gulf Coast	1,631	17,141
New Jersey	130	1,792	**Pacific Coast:**		
Pennsylvania	—	89	California	840	3,427
Delaware	28	381	Oregon	296	1,410
Maryland	31	3,190	Washington	157	3,026
Virginia	112	3,315	Hawaii	750	1,052
North Carolina	301	3,375	Alaska (Pacific)	5,580	31,383
South Carolina	187	2,876	Total Pacific Coast	7,623	40,298
Georgia	100	2,344	**Arctic Coast:**		
Florida (Atlantic)	580	3,331	Alaska (Arctic)	1,060	2,521
Total Atlantic Coast	2,069	28,673	Total Arctic Coast	1,060	2,521
			States Total	**12,383**	**88,633**

1. Figures are lengths of general outline of seacoast. Measurements are made with unit measure of 30 minutes of latitude on charts as near scale of 1:1,200,000 as possible. Coastline of bays and sounds is included to point where they narrow to width of unit measure, and distance across at such point is included. 2. Figures were obtained in 1939–1940 with recording instrument on the largest-scale maps and charts then available. Shoreline of outer coast, offshore islands, sounds, bays, rivers, and creeks is included to head of tidewater, or to point where tidal waters narrow to width of 100 feet. *Source:* Department of Commerce, National Oceanic and Atmospheric Administration, National Ocean Service.

Mountain Peaks in the United States Higher Than 14,000 Feet

Name	State	Height (ft.)	Name	State	Height (ft.)	Name	State	Height (ft.)
Mt. McKinley	Alaska	20,320	Castle Peak	Colo.	14,265	Mt. Eolus	Colo.	14,083
Mt. St. Elias	Alaska	18,008	Quandary Peak	Colo.	14,265	Windom Peak	Colo.	14,082
Mt. Foraker	Alaska	17,400	Mt. Evans	Colo.	14,264	Mt. Columbia	Colo.	14,073
Mt. Bona	Alaska	16,500	Longs Peak	Colo.	14,255	Mt. Augusta	Alaska	14,070
Mt. Blackburn	Alaska	16,390	Mt. Wilson	Colo.	14,246	Missouri Mtn.	Colo.	14,067
Mt. Sanford	Alaska	16,237	White Mtn.	Calif.	14,246	Humboldt Peak	Colo.	14,064
Mt. Vancouver	Alaska	15,979	North Palisade	Calif.	14,242	Mt. Bierstadt	Colo.	14,060
South Buttress	Alaska	15,885	Mt. Cameron	Colo.	14,238	Sunlight Peak	Colo.	14,059
Mt. Churchill	Alaska	15,638	Mt. Shavano	Colo.	14,229	Split Mtn.	Calif.	14,058
Mt. Fairweather	Alaska	15,300	Crestone Needle	Colo.	14,197	Handies Peak	Colo.	14,048
Mt. Hubbard	Alaska	14,950	Mt. Belford	Colo.	14,197	Culebra Peak	Colo.	14,047
Mt. Bear	Alaska	14,831	Mt. Princeton	Colo.	14,197	Mt. Lindsey	Colo.	14,042
East Buttress	Alaska	14,730	Mt. Yale	Colo.	14,196	Ellingwood Point	Colo.	14,042
Mt. Hunter	Alaska	14,573	Mt. Bross	Colo.	14,172	Middle Palisade	Calif.	14,040
Browne Tower	Alaska	14,530	Kit Carson Mtn.	Colo.	14,165	Little Bear Peak	Colo.	14,037
Mt. Alverstone	Alaska	14,500	Mt. Wrangell	Alaska	14,163	Mt. Sherman	Colo.	14,036
Mt. Whitney	Calif.	14,494[1]	Mt. Sill	Calif.	14,163	Redcloud Peak	Colo.	14,034
University Peak	Alaska	14,470	Mt. Shasta	Calif.	14,162	Mt. Langley	Calif.	14,027
Mt. Elbert	Colo.	14,433	El Diente Peak	Colo.	14,159	Conundrum Peak	Colo.	14,022
Mt. Massive	Colo.	14,421	Point Success	Wash.	14,158	Mt. Tyndall	Calif.	14,019
Mt. Harvard	Colo.	14,420	Maroon Peak	Colo.	14,156	Pyramid Peak	Colo.	14,018
Mt. Rainier	Wash.	14,410	Tabeguache Mtn.	Colo.	14,155	Wilson Peak	Colo.	14,017
Mt. Williamson	Calif.	14,370	Mt. Oxford	Colo.	14,153	Wetterhorn Peak	Colo.	14,015
La Plata Peak	Colo.	14,361	Mt. Sill	Calif.	14,153	North Maroon Peak	Colo.	14,014
Blanca Peak	Colo.	14,345	Mt. Sneffels	Colo.	14,150	San Luis Peak	Colo.	14,014
Uncompahgre Peak	Colo.	14,309	Mt. Democrat	Colo.	14,148	Middle Palisade	Calif.	14,012
Crestone Peak	Colo.	14,294	Capitol Peak	Colo.	14,130	Mt. Muir	Calif.	14,012
Mt. Lincoln	Colo.	14,286	Liberty Cap	Wash.	14,112	Mt. of the Holy Cross	Colo.	14,005
Grays Peak	Colo.	14,270	Pikes Peak	Colo.	14,110	Huron Peak	Colo.	14,003
Mt. Antero	Colo.	14,269	Snowmass Mtn.	Colo.	14,092	Thunderbolt Peak	Calif.	14,003
Torreys Peak	Colo.	14,267	Mt. Russell	Calif.	14,088	Sunshine Peak	Colo.	14,001

1. National Geodetic Survey. *Source:* U.S. Dept. of the Interior, Geological Survey.

Highest, Lowest, and Mean Elevations in the United States

State	Elevation (ft.)[1]	Highest point	Elevation (ft.)	Lowest point	Elevation (ft.)
Alabama	500	Cheaha Mountain	2,405	Gulf of Mexico	Sea level
Alaska	1,900	Mt. McKinley	20,320	Pacific Ocean	Sea level
Arizona	4,100	Humphreys Peak	12,633	Colorado River	70
Arkansas	650	Magazine Mountain	2,753	Ouachita River	55
California	2,900	Mt. Whitney	14,494	Death Valley	−282[2]
Colorado	6,800	Mt. Elbert	14,433	Arkansas River	3,350
Connecticut	500	Mt. Frissell, on south slope	2,380	Long Island Sound	Sea level
Delaware	60	Ebright Road, Del.–Pa. state line	448	Atlantic Ocean	Sea level
D.C.	150	Tenleytown, at Reno Reservoir	410	Potomac River	1
Florida	100	Sec. 30, T6N, R20W, Walton County	345	Atlantic Ocean	Sea level
Georgia	600	Brasstown Bald	4,784	Atlantic Ocean	Sea level
Hawaii	3,030	Puu Wekiu, Mauna Kea	13,796	Pacific Ocean	Sea level
Idaho	5,000	Borah Peak	12,662	Snake River	710
Illinois	600	Charles Mound	1,235	Mississippi River	279
Indiana	700	Franklin Township, Wayne County	1,257	Ohio River	320
Iowa	1,100	Sec. 29, T100N, R41W, Osceola County	1,670	Mississippi River	480
Kansas	2,000	Mt. Sunflower	4,039	Verdigris River	679
Kentucky	750	Black Mountain	4,139	Mississippi River	257
Louisiana	100	Driskill Mountain	535	New Orleans	−8[2]
Maine	600	Mt. Katahdin	5,267	Atlantic Ocean	Sea level
Maryland	350	Backbone Mountain	3,360	Atlantic Ocean	Sea level
Massachusetts	500	Mt. Greylock	3,487	Atlantic Ocean	Sea level
Michigan	900	Mt. Arvon	1,979	Lake Erie	572
Minnesota	1,200	Eagle Mountain	2,301	Lake Superior	600
Mississippi	300	Woodall Mountain	806	Gulf of Mexico	Sea level
Missouri	800	Taum Sauk Mountain	1,772	St. Francis River	230
Montana	3,400	Granite Peak	12,799	Kootenai River	1,800
Nebraska	2,600	Johnson Township, Kimball County	5,424	Missouri River	840
Nevada	5,500	Boundary Peak	13,140	Colorado River	479
New Hampshire	1,000	Mt. Washington	6,288	Atlantic Ocean	Sea level
New Jersey	250	High Point	1,803	Atlantic Ocean	Sea level
New Mexico	5,700	Wheeler Peak	13,161	Red Bluff Reservoir	2,842
New York	1,000	Mt. Marcy	5,344	Atlantic Ocean	Sea level
North Carolina	700	Mt. Mitchell	6,684	Atlantic Ocean	Sea level
North Dakota	1,900	White Butte	3,506	Red River	750
Ohio	850	Campbell Hill	1,549	Ohio River	455
Oklahoma	1,300	Black Mesa	4,973	Little River	289
Oregon	3,300	Mt. Hood	11,239	Pacific Ocean	Sea level
Pennsylvania	1,100	Mt. Davis	3,213	Delaware River	Sea level
Rhode Island	200	Jerimoth Hill	812	Atlantic Ocean	Sea level
South Carolina	350	Sassafras Mountain	3,560	Atlantic Ocean	Sea level
South Dakota	2,200	Harney Peak	7,242	Big Stone Lake	966
Tennessee	900	Clingmans Dome	6,643	Mississippi River	178
Texas	1,700	Guadalupe Peak	8,749	Gulf of Mexico	Sea level
Utah	6,100	Kings Peak	13,528	Beaverdam Wash	2,000
Vermont	1,000	Mt. Mansfield	4,393	Lake Champlain	95
Virginia	950	Mt. Rogers	5,729	Atlantic Ocean	Sea level
Washington	1,700	Mt. Rainier	14,410	Pacific Ocean	Sea level
West Virginia	1,500	Spruce Knob	4,861	Potomac River	240
Wisconsin	1,050	Timms Hill	1,951	Lake Michigan	579
Wyoming	6,700	Gannett Peak	13,804	Belle Fourche River	3,099
United States	**2,500**	**Mt. McKinley (Alaska)**	**20,320**	**Death Valley (California)**	**−282[2]**

1. Approximate mean elevation. 2. Below sea level. *Source:* U.S. Geological Survey.

Latitude and Longitude of U.S. and Canadian Cities
(and time corresponding to 12:00 noon, Eastern Standard Time)

City	Lat. °	Lat. ′	Long. °	Long. ′	Time	City	Lat. °	Lat. ′	Long. °	Long. ′	Time
Albany, N.Y.	42	40	73	45	12:00 noon	Miami, Fla.	25	46	80	12	12:00 noon
Albuquerque, N.M.	35	05	106	39	10:00 a.m.	Milwaukee, Wis.	43	2	87	55	11:00 a.m.
Amarillo, Tex.	35	11	101	50	11:00 a.m.	Minneapolis, Minn.	44	59	93	14	11:00 a.m.
Anchorage, Alaska	61	13	149	54	8:00 a.m.	Mobile, Ala.	30	42	88	3	11:00 a.m.
Atlanta, Ga.	33	45	84	23	12:00 noon	Montgomery, Ala.	32	21	86	18	11:00 a.m.
Austin, Tex.	30	16	97	44	11:00 a.m.	Montpelier, Vt.	44	15	72	32	12:00 noon
Baker, Ore.	44	47	117	50	9:00 a.m.	Montreal, Que., Can.	45	30	73	35	12:00 noon
Baltimore, Md.	39	18	76	38	12:00 noon	Moose Jaw, Sask.,	50	37	105	31	10:00 a.m.
Bangor, Maine	44	48	68	47	12:00 noon	Can.					
Birmingham, Ala.	33	30	86	50	11:00 a.m.	Nashville, Tenn.	36	10	86	47	11:00 a.m.
Bismarck, N.D.	46	48	100	47	11:00 a.m.	Nelson, B.C., Can.	49	30	117	17	9:00 a.m.
Boise, Idaho	43	36	116	13	10:00 a.m.	Newark, N.J.	40	44	74	10	12:00 noon
Boston, Mass.	42	21	71	5	12:00 noon	New Haven, Conn.	41	19	72	55	12:00 noon
Buffalo, N.Y.	42	55	78	50	12:00 noon	New Orleans, La.	29	57	90	4	11:00 a.m.
Calgary, Alba., Can.	51	1	114	1	10:00 a.m.	New York, N.Y.	40	47	73	58	12:00 noon
Carlsbad, N.M.	32	26	104	15	10:00 a.m.	Nome, Alaska	64	25	165	30	8:00 a.m.
Charleston, S.C.	32	47	79	56	12:00 noon	Oakland, Calif.	37	48	122	16	9:00 a.m.
Charleston, W. Va.	38	21	81	38	12:00 noon	Oklahoma City, Okla.	35	26	97	28	11:00 a.m.
Charlotte, N.C.	35	14	80	50	12:00 noon	Omaha, Neb.	41	15	95	56	11:00 a.m.
Cheyenne, Wyo.	41	9	104	52	10:00 a.m.	Ottawa, Ont., Can.	45	24	75	43	12:00 noon
Chicago, Ill.	41	50	87	37	11:00 a.m.	Philadelphia, Pa.	39	57	75	10	12:00 noon
Cincinnati, Ohio	39	8	84	30	12:00 noon	Phoenix, Ariz.	33	29	112	4	10:00 a.m.
Cleveland, Ohio	41	28	81	37	12:00 noon	Pierre, S.D.	44	22	100	21	11:00 a.m.
Columbia, S.C.	34	0	81	2	12:00 noon	Pittsburgh, Pa.	40	27	79	57	12:00 noon
Columbus, Ohio	40	0	83	1	12:00 noon	Port Arthur, Ont.,	48	30	89	17	12:00 noon
Dallas, Tex.	32	46	96	46	11:00 a.m.	Can.					
Denver, Colo.	39	45	105	0	10:00 a.m.	Portland, Maine	43	40	70	15	12:00 noon
Des Moines, Iowa	41	35	93	37	11:00 a.m.	Portland, Ore.	45	31	122	41	9:00 a.m.
Detroit, Mich.	42	20	83	3	12:00 noon	Providence, R.I.	41	50	71	24	12:00 noon
Dubuque, Iowa	42	31	90	40	11:00 a.m.	Quebec, Que., Can.	46	49	71	11	12:00 noon
Duluth, Minn.	46	49	92	5	11:00 a.m.	Raleigh, N.C.	35	46	78	39	12:00 noon
Eastport, Maine	44	54	67	0	12:00 noon	Reno, Nev.	39	30	119	49	9:00 a.m.
El Centro, Calif.	32	38	115	33	9:00 a.m.	Richfield, Utah	38	46	112	5	10:00 a.m.
El Paso, Tex.	31	46	106	29	10:00 a.m.	Richmond, Va.	37	33	77	29	12:00 noon
Eugene, Ore.	44	3	123	5	9:00 a.m.	Roanoke, Va.	37	17	79	57	12:00 noon
Fargo, N.D.	46	52	96	48	11:00 a.m.	Sacramento, Calif.	38	35	121	30	9:00 a.m.
Flagstaff, Ariz.	35	13	111	41	10:00 a.m.	St. John, N.B., Can.	45	18	66	10	1:00 p.m.
Fort Worth, Tex.	32	43	97	19	11:00 a.m.	St. Louis, Mo.	38	35	90	12	11:00 a.m.
Fresno, Calif.	36	44	119	48	9:00 a.m.	Salt Lake City, Utah	40	46	111	54	10:00 a.m.
Grand Junction, Colo.	39	5	108	33	10:00 a.m.	San Antonio, Tex.	29	23	98	33	11:00 a.m.
Grand Rapids, Mich.	42	58	85	40	12:00 noon	San Diego, Calif.	32	42	117	10	9:00 a.m.
Havre, Mont.	48	33	109	43	10:00 a.m.	San Francisco, Calif.	37	47	122	26	9:00 a.m.
Helena, Mont.	46	35	112	2	10:00 a.m.	San Jose, Calif.	37	20	121	53	9:00 a.m.
Honolulu, Hawaii	21	18	157	50	7:00 a.m.	San Juan, P.R.	18	30	66	10	1:00 p.m.
Hot Springs, Ark.	34	31	93	3	11:00 a.m.	Santa Fe, N.M.	35	41	105	57	10:00 a.m.
Houston, Tex.	29	45	95	21	11:00 a.m.	Savannah, Ga.	32	5	81	5	12:00 noon
Idaho Falls, Idaho	43	30	112	1	10:00 a.m.	Seattle, Wash.	47	37	122	20	9:00 a.m.
Indianapolis, Ind.	39	46	86	10	12:00 noon	Shreveport, La.	32	28	93	42	11:00 a.m.
Jackson, Miss.	32	20	90	12	11:00 a.m.	Sioux Falls, S.D.	43	33	96	44	11:00 a.m.
Jacksonville, Fla.	30	22	81	40	12:00 noon	Sitka, Alaska	57	10	135	15	8:00 a.m.
Juneau, Alaska	58	18	134	24	8:00 a.m.	Spokane, Wash.	47	40	117	26	9:00 a.m.
Kansas City, Mo.	39	6	94	35	11:00 a.m.	Springfield, Ill.	39	48	89	38	11:00 a.m.
Key West, Fla.	24	33	81	48	12:00 noon	Springfield, Mass.	42	6	72	34	12:00 noon
Kingston, Ont., Can.	44	15	76	30	12:00 noon	Springfield, Mo.	37	13	93	17	11:00 a.m.
Klamath Falls, Ore.	42	10	121	44	9:00 a.m.	Syracuse, N.Y.	43	2	76	8	12:00 noon
Knoxville, Tenn.	35	57	83	56	12:00 noon	Tampa, Fla.	27	57	82	27	12:00 noon
Las Vegas, Nev.	36	10	115	12	9:00 a.m.	Toledo, Ohio	41	39	83	33	12:00 noon
Lewiston, Idaho	46	24	117	2	9:00 a.m.	Toronto, Ont., Can.	43	40	79	24	12:00 noon
Lincoln, Neb.	40	50	96	40	11:00 a.m.	Tulsa, Okla.	36	9	95	59	11:00 a.m.
London, Ont., Can.	43	2	81	34	12:00 noon	Victoria, B.C., Can.	48	25	123	21	9:00 a.m.
Long Beach, Calif.	33	46	118	11	9:00 a.m.	Virginia Beach, Va.	36	51	75	58	12:00 noon
Los Angeles, Calif.	34	3	118	15	9:00 a.m.	Washington, D.C.	38	53	77	02	12:00 noon
Louisville, Ky.	38	15	85	46	12:00 noon	Wichita, Kan.	37	43	97	17	11:00 a.m.
Manchester, N.H.	43	0	71	30	12:00 noon	Wilmington, N.C.	34	14	77	57	12:00 noon
Memphis, Tenn.	35	9	90	3	11:00 a.m.	Winnipeg, Man., Can.	49	54	97	7	11:00 a.m.

HAPPY NEW ERA! The birth of the new millennium was a remarkable worldwide event, a rolling celebration that crossed time zones from the South Pacific to America as the clock struck midnight to end the 20th century. As the world's great cities vied to stage the most festive display, Paris' illuminated Eiffel Tower was among the memorable sights.

GORE-LIEBERMAN: Al Gore's choice for running mate, Senator Joseph Lieberman of Connecticut—an outspoken critic of Bill Clinton's behavior and the first Jew ever to run for national office—helped Gore overcome George W. Bush's longtime lead in the polls.

BUSH-CHENEY: George W. Bush turned to a veteran of his father's Administration, Dick Cheney, to bring heft and experience to the G.O.P. ticket. Cheney had served as Secretary of Defense, as Congressman from Wyoming and as Gerald Ford's chief of staff.

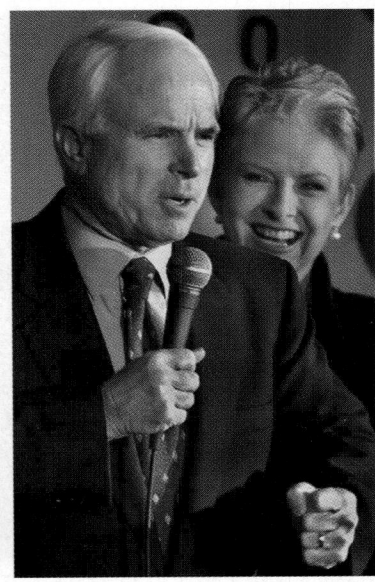

BRADLEY ON A ROLL: Former Senator Bill Bradley presented Vice President Al Gore with a strong challenge for the Democratic nomination.

MC CAIN MUTINY: Arizona Senator John McCain's race against George W. Bush for the G.O.P. nod fell short.

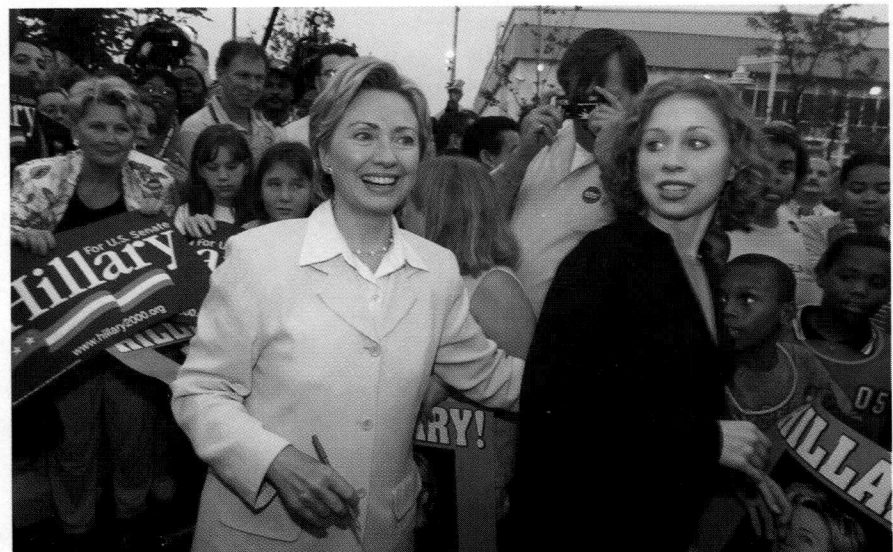

SENATE BATTLE: First Lady Hillary Clinton (above, with daughter Chelsea) continued her quest to earn a Senate seat from New York. When her presumed G.O.P. opponent, New York City Mayor Rudy Giuliani, was sidelined from the race by prostate cancer and marital problems, Long Island Congressman Rick Lazio stepped in as the Republican candidate.

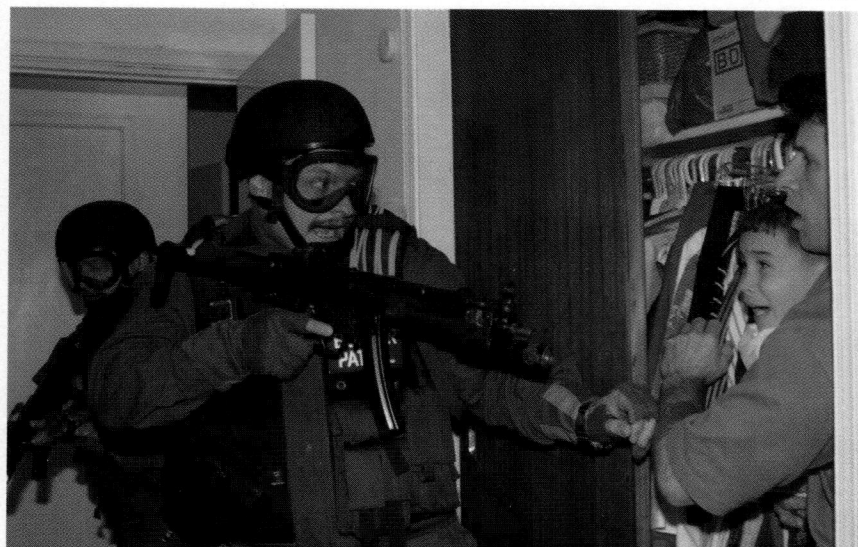

ELIAN'S SAGA: In a highly controversial raid, armed federal agents, above, remove Cuban refugee Elián González from the home of his U.S. relatives in Miami on April 22, following a federal court ruling that the six-year-old, whose mother had perished at sea as they fled Cuba, should be returned to the custody of his father, the pro-Castro Juan Miguel. In a battle of imagery, U.S. officials released a picture taken later that day, showing Elián happily reunited with his father in Maryland. The young refugee's plight inflamed the emotions of the strongly anti-Castro Cuban immigrants in the Miami area, who said the raid violated the rights of both Elián and his relatives.

FIRE! A wildfire burns perilously close to the U.S. nuclear laboratory at Los Alamos, New Mexico, on May 16. Federal agents had set the blaze in what they intended to be a controlled burn. Later in the dry summer, wildfires devastated forests across the West.

SCOUT'S HONOR: Former Eagle Scout James Dale discusses his suit against the Boy Scouts of America, who had dismissed the openly gay troop leader. In a landmark ruling, the Supreme Court held that the Scouts had the right to exclude gays from their ranks.

¡VIVA FOX! Mexicans made history by voting out the P.R.I. party after 71 years, in favor of reformer Vicente Fox and his National Action Party.

BROTHERS AGAIN? After 50 years of strife, South Korean President Kim Dae Jung, right, met North Korea's Kim Jong Il in Pyongyang, seeking to reduce the bitter conflict between the states.

NO DEAL: Israeli Prime Minister Ehud Barak, left, joined President Clinton and Palestinian leader Yasser Arafat at Camp David in July to pursue a comprehensive Middle East peace plan. The talks failed after 14 days, as the future of Jerusalem proved a sticking point.

UNDERSEA TRAGEDY: A 1999 photo shows the Russian nuclear submarine *Kursk* plying the Barents Sea. In August the enormous vessel was rocked by a series of explosions and sank, killing all 119 sailors aboard. Russia's inept, tardy rescue attempts heightened fears that its military is poorly led and in decline.

MEET THE NEW BOSS: Russia's ailing President Boris Yeltsin resigned in a dramatic Dec. 31 telecast, handing over power to his Prime Minister, former K.G.B. man Vladimir Putin. In March Yeltsin congratulated Putin following his election as the second President of Russia in its post-Soviet era.

CONCORDE CRASH:
At right, a home video camera records the last moments of Air France Flight 4590. The delta-winged Concorde aircraft caught fire and crashed just after takeoff in Paris on July 25, killing 109 aboard and five people on the ground. Weeks later, British and French authorities grounded the planes, the world's first—and only—supersonic passenger jet. Below, rescue workers inspect crash debris.

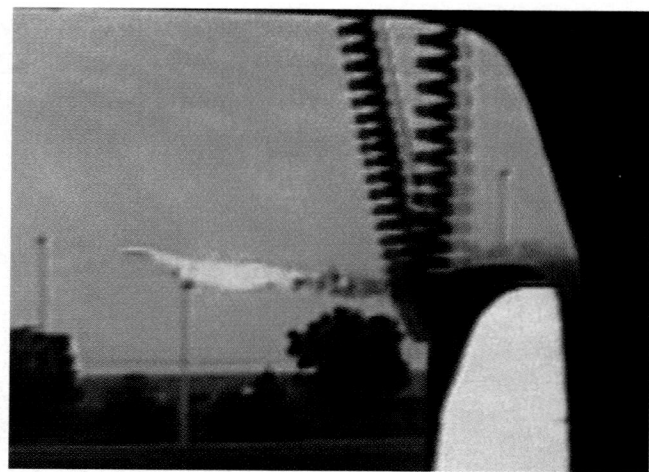

BIG DEAL: In a $160 billion merger, Steve Case, left, CEO of "new media" star America Online, agreed to acquire Time Warner, the world's largest "old media" and entertainment company, led by CEO Gerald Levin, center, and Vice Chairman Ted Turner, right.

ONE-MAN REVOLUTION: As new technologies reshaped old markets, Napster inventor Shawn Fanning, 20, hails a ruling by two federal judges allowing his popular music-trading software to remain online, despite record-company charges of copyright infringement.

TEENYBOPPER: Britney Spears, 18, led pop music's new craze: stars whose music was made by—and for—those under 20.

TV GETS REAL: The CBS hit *Survivor* stranded 16 people on a Pacific island, who then voted to evict one person each week. The $1 million winner: conniving, charming Richard Hatch, inset.

WIZARDS: Ohio boys affect the Harry Potter look to celebrate the midnight, July 7, release of *Harry Potter and the Goblet of Fire,* the fourth in British author J.K. Rowling's hit series about a schoolboy wizard. The novel sold 3 million copies in just 48 hours.

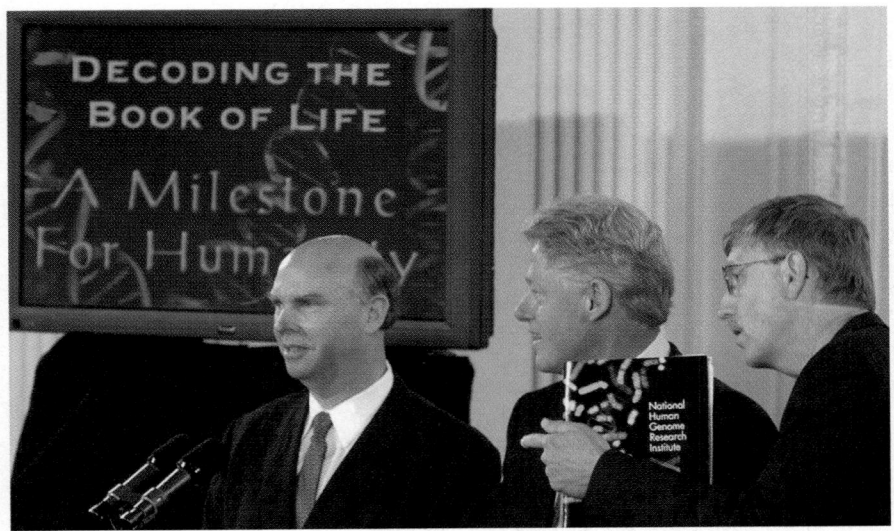

GENETIC LANDMARK: Ending a long rivalry, Dr. Craig Venter, left, of the private firm Celera Genomics, joins Dr. Francis Collins, director of federal genome research, and President Clinton, to declare the successful sequencing of the human genome and the production of the first working blueprint of the 3.4 billion "letters" of human DNA.

HOME OF THE STARS: The 87-ft.-high sphere of the Hayden Planetarium rests within the Rose Center for Earth and Space at New York City's American Museum of Natural History. Designed by James Polshek, the new structure was a breakthrough in planetarium design.

VENUS VICTORIOUS: The elder of tennis' dominant sisters celebrates her triumph at WImbledon. She also won the U.S. Open.

SHAQ ATTACK: Finally making good after years of hype, M.V.P. Shaquille O'Neal led his Los Angeles Lakers to the NBA title.

LANCE TAKES FRANCE: Lance Armstrong won cycling's prestigious Tour de France a second time after beating testicular cancer.

THE MAN: Unstoppable Tiger Woods won three of golf's major tournaments in a row: the U.S. and British Opens and the P.G.A.

LET THE GAMES BEGIN: Australian runner Cathy Freeman holds the Olympic torch aloft after lighting the cauldron to open the Summer Games in Sydney, Australia, on Sept. 15. Freeman, 27, is an Aborigine who has criticized Australia's treatment of her people.

HAFEZ ASSAD: The strongman, 69, ruled Syria with an iron hand for 30 years. His son Bashar Assad was elected President.

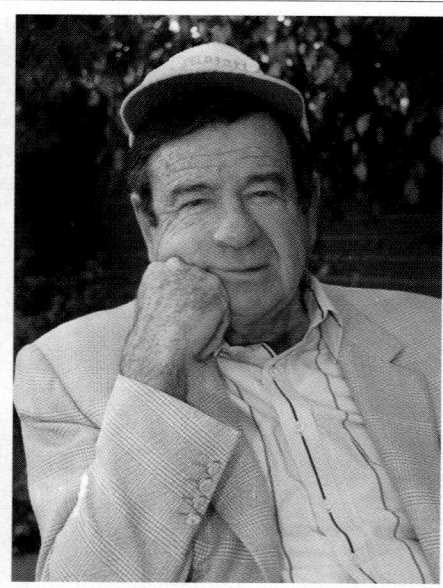

WALTER MATTHAU: The beloved comic, 79, often played an irascible grouch; he was Oscar Madison on TV's *The Odd Couple.*

JOHN CARDINAL O'CONNOR: New Yorkers of all faiths mourned the Roman Catholic prelate, 80, an apostle for ecumenism.

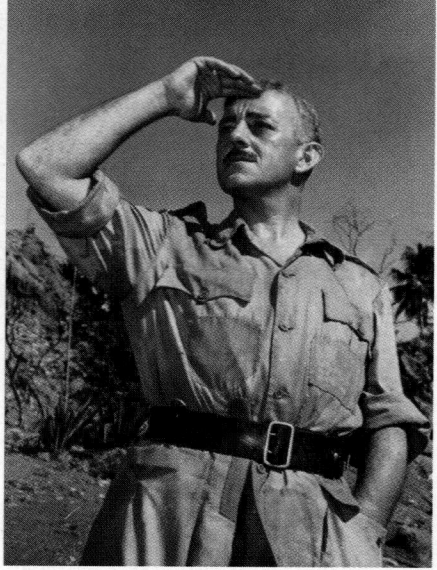

ALEC GUINNESS: The British star, 86, won an Oscar for *The Bridge on the River Kwai,* above, and was *Star Wars'* Obi-Wan Kenobi.

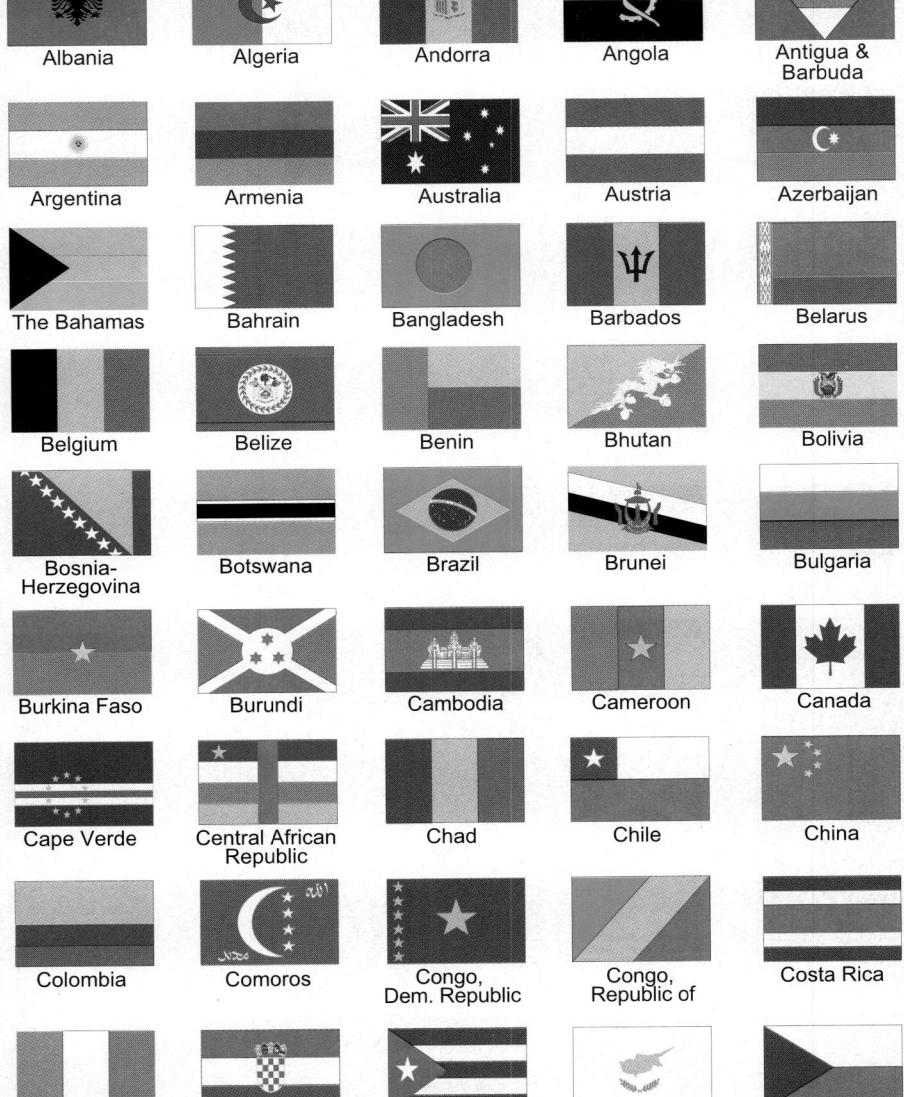

Albania	Algeria	Andorra	Angola	Antigua & Barbuda
Argentina	Armenia	Australia	Austria	Azerbaijan
The Bahamas	Bahrain	Bangladesh	Barbados	Belarus
Belgium	Belize	Benin	Bhutan	Bolivia
Bosnia-Herzegovina	Botswana	Brazil	Brunei	Bulgaria
Burkina Faso	Burundi	Cambodia	Cameroon	Canada
Cape Verde	Central African Republic	Chad	Chile	China
Colombia	Comoros	Congo, Dem. Republic	Congo, Republic of	Costa Rica
Côte d'Ivoire	Croatia	Cuba	Cyprus	Czech Republic
Denmark	Djibouti	Dominica	Dominican Rep.	Ecuador

Egypt

El Salvador

Equitorial Guinea

Eritrea

Estonia

Ethiopia

Fiji

Finland

France

Gabon

The Gambia

Georgia

Germany

Ghana

Greece

Grenada

Guatemala

Guinea

Guinea-Bissau

Guyana

Haiti

Honduras

Hungary

Iceland

India

Indonesia

Iran

Iraq

Ireland

Israel

Italy

Jamaica

Japan

Jordan

Kazakhstan

Kenya

Kiribati

Korea, North

Korea, South

Kuwait

Kyrgyzstan

Laos

Latvia

Lebanon

Lesotho

Liberia

Libya

Liechtenstein

Lithuania

Luxembourg

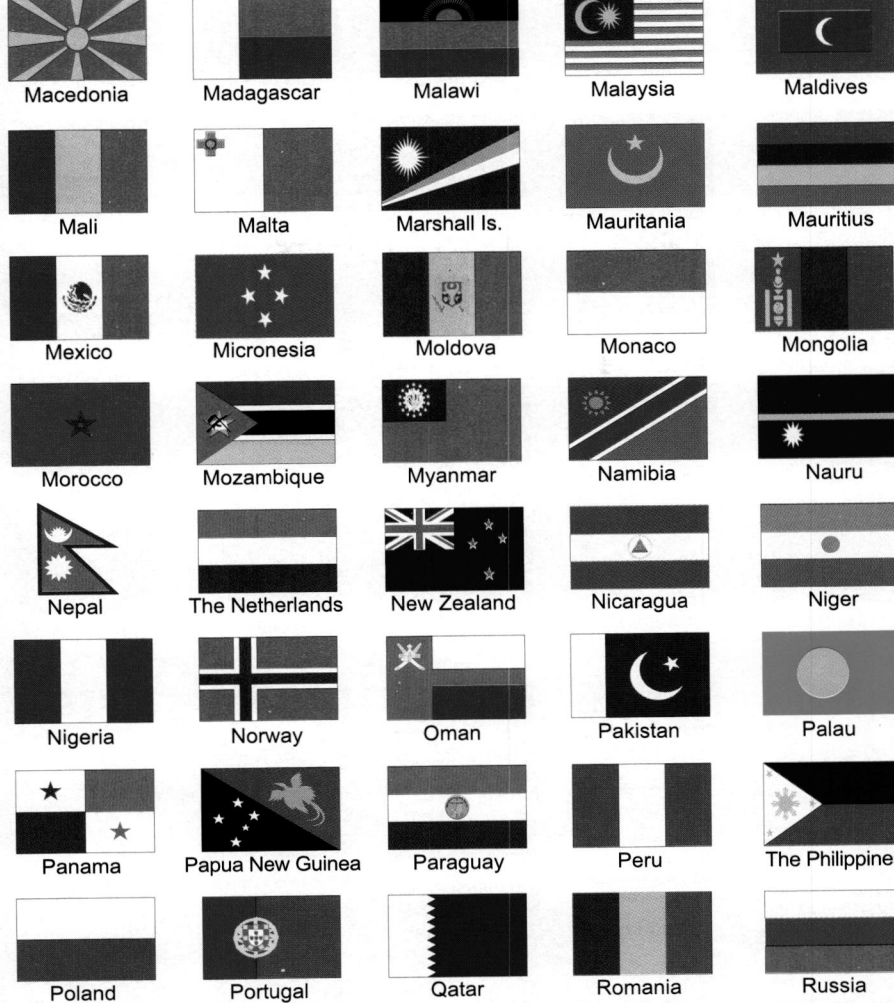

Macedonia	Madagascar	Malawi	Malaysia	Maldives
Mali	Malta	Marshall Is.	Mauritania	Mauritius
Mexico	Micronesia	Moldova	Monaco	Mongolia
Morocco	Mozambique	Myanmar	Namibia	Nauru
Nepal	The Netherlands	New Zealand	Nicaragua	Niger
Nigeria	Norway	Oman	Pakistan	Palau
Panama	Papua New Guinea	Paraguay	Peru	The Philippines
Poland	Portugal	Qatar	Romania	Russia
Rwanda	St. Kitts & Nevis	St. Lucia	St. Vincent & The Grenadines	Samoa
San Marino	São Tomé & Príncipe	Saudi Arabia	Senegal	Seychelles

Sierra Leone

Singapore

Slovakia

Slovenia

Solomon Is.

Somalia

South Africa

Spain

Sri Lanka

The Sudan

Suriname

Swaziland

Sweden

Switzerland

Syria

Taiwan

Tajikistan

Tanzania

Thailand

Togo

Tonga

Trinidad & Tobago

Tunisia

Turkey

Turkmenistan

Tuvalu

Uganda

Ukraine

United Arab Emirates

United Kingdom

United States

Uruguay

Uzbekistan

Vanuatu

Vatican City

Venezuela

Vietnam

Yemen

Yugoslavia

Zambia

Zimbabwe

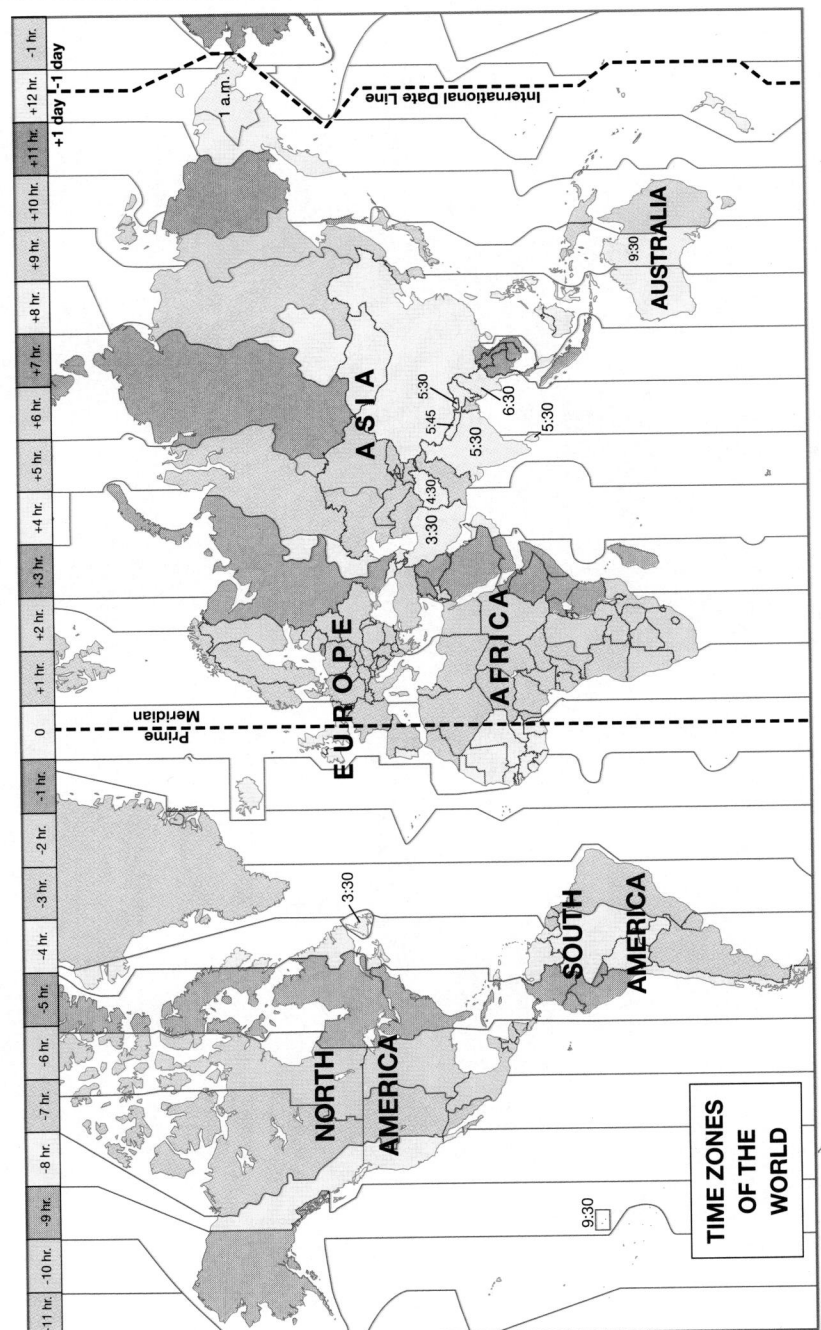

TIME ZONES OF THE WORLD

NORTH AMERICA

SOUTH AMERICA

EUROPE

AFRICA

ASIA

AUSTRALIA

Prime Meridian

International Date Line

1 a.m.

+1 day −1 day

-11 hr. | -10 hr. | -9 hr. | -8 hr. | -7 hr. | -6 hr. | -5 hr. | -4 hr. | -3 hr. | -2 hr. | -1 hr. | 0 | +1 hr. | +2 hr. | +3 hr. | +4 hr. | +5 hr. | +6 hr. | +7 hr. | +8 hr. | +9 hr. | +10 hr. | +11 hr. | +12 hr. | -1 hr.

9:30

3:30

3:30
4:30
5:45
5:30
5:30
6:30
5:30

9:30

THE WORLD (Physical)

Elevation

Meters	Feet
3,000	10,000
2,000	7,000
1,000	3,000
500	1,500
200	700
0	0

Robinson Projection
1: 191,600,000

0   1500   3000 Miles
0   1500   3000 Kilometers

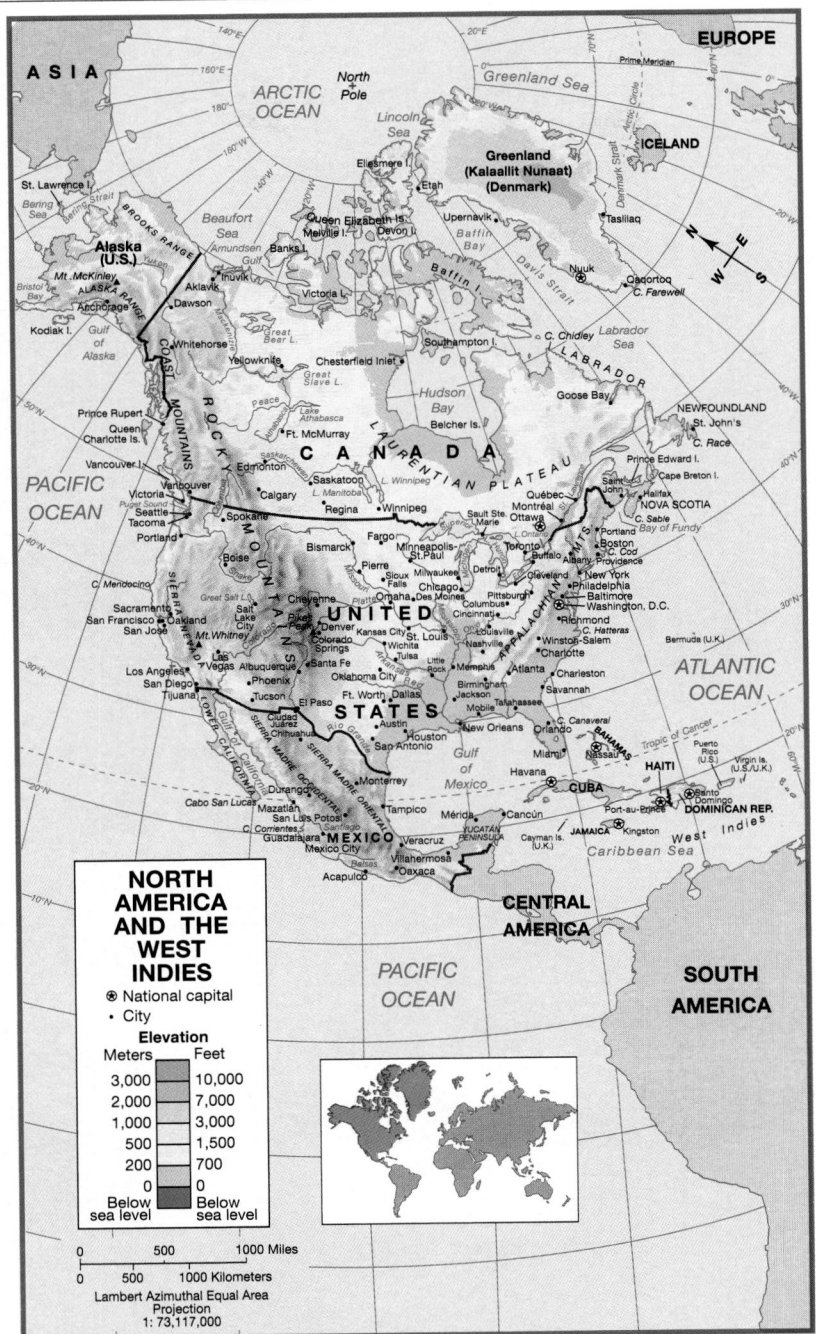

EUROPE

ASIA

ARCTIC OCEAN

North Pole

Greenland Sea

Prime Meridian

ICELAND

Lincoln Sea

Ellesmere I.

Greenland (Kalaallit Nunaat) (Denmark)

Tasiilaq

Beaufort Sea

Queen Elizabeth Is.
Melville I.
Devon I.
Banks I.

Upernavik

Baffin Bay

Etah

Alaska (U.S.)

Mt. McKinley
ALASKA RANGE
Anchorage
Kodiak I.
Bristol Bay
Gulf of Alaska

Aklavik
Inuvik
Dawson
Whitehorse

Victoria I.

Nuuk

Qaqortoq
C. Farewell

C. Chidley
Labrador Sea

Prince Rupert
Queen Charlotte Is.
Vancouver I.

Yellowknife
Great Slave L.
Great Bear L.
Chesterfield Inlet

Southampton I.

Goose Bay

NEWFOUNDLAND
St. John's
C. Race

PACIFIC OCEAN

Victoria
Vancouver
Seattle
Tacoma
Portland

Edmonton
Calgary
Saskatoon
Regina

CANADA

Hudson Bay

Belcher Is.

LAURENTIAN PLATEAU

Prince Edward I.
Cape Breton I.
NOVA SCOTIA
Halifax
C. Sable
Bay of Fundy

Boise
Spokane

Bismarck
Fargo
Pierre

Winnipeg
L. Winnipeg
L. Manitoba

Sault Ste. Marie

Québec
Montréal
Ottawa

Portland
C. Cod
Boston
Providence

San Francisco
Sacramento
Oakland
San Jose
Mt. Whitney
Great Salt L.
Salt Lake City

Cheyenne
Denver
Colorado Springs

Minneapolis-St. Paul
Sioux Falls
Omaha
Des Moines

Milwaukee
Chicago

Detroit

Toronto
Buffalo
Albany
Cleveland
Pittsburgh

New York
Philadelphia
Baltimore
Washington, D.C.

UNITED

Kansas City
Wichita
St. Louis
Louisville
Cincinnati
Columbus

Richmond
Winston-Salem
C. Hatteras

Bermuda (U.K.)

Los Angeles
San Diego
Tijuana

Las Vegas
Phoenix
Tucson

Albuquerque
Santa Fe

Oklahoma City

Tulsa
Little Rock

Memphis
Nashville

Charlotte
Charleston

ATLANTIC OCEAN

El Paso

STATES

Ft. Worth
Dallas
Austin

Birmingham
Jackson
Mobile

Atlanta
Tallahassee
Savannah

Ciudad Juárez
Chihuahua

Rio Grande

San Antonio
Houston

New Orleans
Orlando

C. Canaveral

Cabo San Lucas
Mazatlán
Durango
San Luis Potosí

Monterrey

Gulf of Mexico

Havana

Miami

BAHAMAS
Nassau

Tropic of Cancer

HAITI

Puerto Rico (U.S.)
Virgin Is. (U.S./U.K.)

C. Corrientes
Guadalajara
Mexico City

Tampico

Mérida
YUCATÁN PENINSULA

Cancún

CUBA

Port-au-Prince
Santo Domingo
DOMINICAN REP.

MEXICO
Veracruz
Acapulco
Balsas
Villahermosa
Oaxaca

Cayman Is. (U.K.)

JAMAICA
Kingston

Caribbean Sea

West Indies

CENTRAL AMERICA

PACIFIC OCEAN

SOUTH AMERICA

NORTH AMERICA AND THE WEST INDIES

⊛ National capital
• City

Elevation

Meters	Feet
3,000	10,000
2,000	7,000
1,000	3,000
500	1,500
200	700
0	0
Below sea level	Below sea level

0   500   1000 Miles

0   500   1000 Kilometers

Lambert Azimuthal Equal Area Projection
1: 73,117,000

D A

90°W 85°W 80°W 75°W 70°W 65°W 60°W

Lake Superior

Duluth
sota   Superior
St. Paul   Green Bay
apolis   Eau Claire
Rochester   **Wisconsin**   Madison
        Milwaukee Lansing
        Kenosha
Iowa   Cedar   Chicago
    Rapids Rockford   Gary Toledo
    Des   Rock Island Fort Wayne **Ohio**
    Moines Champaign Springfield
    Springfield **Illinois** Muncie Dayton
        Indianapolis Cincinnati
Missouri   **Indiana**
Kansas City   St. Louis   Frankfort Charleston
Jefferson City   Louisville Lexington
Missouri   **Kentucky**
    Springfield   Bowling
            Green Knoxville
Arkansas   Nashville
    Fort Smith   **Tennessee**
    Little Rock   Chattanooga Memphis
        Birmingham
    Shreveport   **Alabama**
Mississippi   Montgomery
Louisiana   Jackson
    Baton Rouge   Mobile Pensacola
ort Arthur   New Orleans
Galveston

Sault
Ste. Marie
Michigan
Lake Huron
Grand
Green Bay   Rapids Flint
    Detroit
Lansing
Ann Arbor

L. Ontario
Buffalo
Rochester Syracuse
L. Erie   Albany
Cleveland   **New York**
Erie **Pennsylvania**
Akron
Harrisburg
Wheeling Pittsburgh Baltimore
Clarksburg   Md.
W.   Virginia   Dover **Delaware**
Va.   Richmond   Atlantic City
    Lynchburg   Annapolis
        Washington, D.C.
    Winston-   Norfolk Virginia Beach
    Salem Durham Williamsburg
North Carolina   Chesapeake Bay
    Charlotte   Cape Hatteras
    Columbia
Athens **South Carolina**
Atlanta Augusta   Charleston
Georgia
Macon
Savannah
Albany
Jacksonville
Tallahassee St. Augustine
    Daytona Beach
Florida   Cape
Orlando   Canaveral
Tampa
St. Petersburg L. Okeechobee

L. Champlain
Maine
Augusta   Gulf of
Montpelier   Mt. Washington   Maine
Vt. **N.H.** Portland
    Manchester   Portsmouth
        Concord
    Mass. Boston Cape Cod
    Hartford Worcester
    Conn.   Providence
        R.I.
Newark   New Haven
New York   Long Island
Trenton
Reading **New Jersey**
Philadelphia

APPALACHIAN

Tennessee

Mississippi

Missouri

Ohio

APPALACHIAN MTS.

Lake Michigan

**ATLANTIC
OCEAN**

N
W   E
S

BAHAMAS

Gulf of Mexico

Fort Lauderdale
Miami

Florida Keys

Straits of Florida

CUBA

0   200   400 Miles
0   200   400 Kilometers
Albers Equal-Area Projection
1: 26,044,000

**UNITED
STATES**

⊛ National capital
★ State capital
● City

Elevation
Meters	Feet
3,000	10,000
2,000	7,000
1,000	3,000
500	1,500
200	700
0	0

Galápagos Is. (Ecuador)
I. Marchena
I. San Salvador
I. Santa Cruz
I. Fernandina
I. San Cristóbal
I. Sta.María
I. Española

WEST INDIES
Tropic of Cancer
Caribbean Sea
CENTRAL AMERICA
Neth. Antilles (Neth.)
Curaçao
I. de Margarita
Gulf of Venezuela
Gulf of Paria
Barranquilla
Cartagena
Maracaibo
Caracas
VENEZUELA
Gulf of Urabá
Montería
Cúcuta
San Cristóbal
Ciudad Bolívar
Morawhanna
Georgetown
New Amsterdam
Paramaribo
GUYANA
SURINAME
Devil's I.
Cayenne
French Guiana (Fr.)
ATLANTIC OCEAN
Medellín
Manizales
Bucaramanga
Alto Pilcomayo
C. Corrientes
Buenaventura
Bogotá
Cali
Mt. Tolima
Mt. Huila
COLOMBIA
I. Malpelo (Colombia)
Gulf of Panama
I. de Maracá
I. Caviana
Equator
ECUADOR
Quito
Mt. Cotopaxi
Mt. Chimborazo
Ambato
Guayaquil
Cuenca
Iquitos
Manaus
Belém
I. São Luís
Fortaleza
Gulf of Guayaquil
Piura
PERU
Amazon
C. São Roque
Trujillo
Mt. Huascarán
BRAZIL
Recife
Callao
Lima
Cuzco
São Francisco
Salvador
El Misti
Arequipa
La Paz
Trinidad
BOLIVIA
Brasília
Cochabamba
Santa Cruz
Sucre
Potosí
Belo Horizonte
Iquique
PACIFIC OCEAN
PARAGUAY
Paraná
C. São Tomé
Antofagasta
Asunción
São Paulo
Rio de Janeiro
Santos
Tropic of Capricorn
San Félix (Chile)
San Ambrosio (Chile)
San Miguel de Tucumán
Curitiba
I. de Santa Catarina
Mt. Ojos del Salado
Córdoba
Pôrto Alegre
CHILE
Mt. Aconcagua
Viña del Mar
Valparaíso
Mendoza
Rosario
Rivera
Salto
Paysandú
URUGUAY
L. dos Patos
Juan Fernández Is. (Chile)
Santiago
Vgl. Maipo
Buenos Aires
Montevideo
L. Mirí
I. Alejandro Selkirk
I. Robinson Crusoe
La Plata
Río de la Plata
Concepción
ARGENTINA
C. San Antonio
Mar del Plata
Negro
Bahía Blanca
Gulf of San Matías
I. de Chiloé
Pen. Valdés
Gulf of Corcovado
Archipiélago de los Chonos
Pen. Taitao
C. Tres Montes
Gulf of San Jorge
Chubut
ATLANTIC OCEAN
Gulf of Penas
Strait of Magellan
Falkland Islands (U.K.; claimed by Arg.)
Stanley
Tierra del Fuego
I. Sta. Inés
I. de los Estados
Cape Horn
South Georgia (U.K.)
ANDES

SOUTH AMERICA
⊛ National capital
• City
Elevation
Meters	Feet
3,000	10,000
2,000	7,000
1,000	3,000
500	1,500
200	700
0	0

Antarctic Circle

0 — 300 — 600 Miles
0 — 300 — 600 Kilometers

Lambert Azimuthal
Equal-Area Projection
1: 43,697,000

WESTERN EUROPE

⊗ National capital
• City

Elevation

Meters	Feet
3,000	10,000
2,000	7,000
1,000	3,000
500	1,500
200	700
0	0

0   200   400 Miles

0   200   400 Kilometers

Azimuthal Equal-Area Projection
1: 31,019,000

EASTERN EUROPE

⊕ National capital
· City

Elevation

Meters	Feet
3,000	10,000
2,000	7,000
1,000	3,000
500	1,500
200	700
0	0

0   200   400 Miles
0   200   400 Kilometers

Azimuthal Equal-Area Projection
1: 31,019,000

AFRICA

⊗ National capital
• City

Elevation

Meters	Feet
3,000	10,000
2,000	7,000
1,000	3,000
500	1,500
200	700
0	0

0	500	1000 Miles
0	500	1000 Kilometers

Mercator Projection
1: 79,200,000

NEAR AND
MIDDLE EAST

⊛ National capital
• City

Elevation
Meters   Feet
4,000   13,000
3,000   10,000
2,000   7,000
1,000   3,000
500   1,500
200   700
0   0

500 Miles

500 Kilometers

Albers Equal-Area Projection
1: 38,940,000

ASIA
⊗ National capital
• City
〜 Great Wall of China

Elevation

Meters	Feet
6,000	19,000
3,000	10,000
2,000	7,000
1,000	3,000
500	1,500
200	700
0	0

0   500   1000 Miles
0   500   1000 Kilometers
Lambert Azimuthal Equal-Area
Projection
1:61,016,000

OCEANIA

⊛ National capital
• City

Elevation

Meters	Feet
3,000	10,000
2,000	7,000
1,000	3,000
500	1,500
200	700
0	0

NORTH AMERICA

Equator

Tropic of Capricorn

Clipperton I. (Fr.)

Easter I. (Chile)

Pitcairn I. (U.K.)

Marquesas Is.

Tuamotu Arch.

Hawaiian Islands
Oahu Hawaii (U.S.)
Kauai   Hawaii

Midway Is. (U.S.)

Kingman Reef (U.S.)
Palmyra I. (U.S.)
Kiritimati (Kiribati)

Jarvis I. (U.S.)

Malden I. (Kiribati)

Starbuck I. (Kiribati)

PACIFIC OCEAN

P o l y n e s i a

Tahiti
Papeete

Society Is.
Cook Is. (N.Z.)

Tokelau Is. (N.Z.)
Apia
WESTERN SAMOA
Pago Pago
American Samoa (U.S.)
Niue (N.Z.)

International Date Line

Wake I. (U.S.)

MARSHALL ISLANDS
Majuro

K I R I B A T I

Bairiki
Tarawa I.

Funafuti
TUVALU

Wallis &
Futuna (Fr.)

Nuku'alofa
TONGA

M i c r o n e s i a

M e l a n e s i a

Yaren
NAURU

Eniwetok
Atoll

Suva
FIJI

East Cape

Auckland
North Cape

North Island
NEW ZEALAND
South Island

Wellington
Christchurch

Dunedin

ASIA

Bonin Is. (Japan)

Volcano Is. (Japan)

Northern Mariana Islands (U.S.)

Guam (U.S.)

Koror
PALAU

FEDERATED STATES OF MICRONESIA
Palikir

Admiralty Is.
New Ireland
Bismarck Arch.
New Britain

Lae
PAPUA NEW GUINEA
Port Moresby

Honiara
SOLOMON ISLANDS

Coral Sea Is. Terr. (Aust.)

Vila
VANUATU

Nouméa
New Caledonia (Fr.)

Loyalty Is.

Coral Sea

Cape York Pen.

Gulf of Carpentaria

Arafura Sea

Timor Sea

Townsville

Great Barrier Reef

GREAT DIVIDING RANGE

Brisbane

Queensland

Sydney
Canberra, A.C.T.
New South Wales

Melbourne
Victoria

Tasman Sea

Tasmania
South East Cape

AUSTRALIA

Northern Territory

Darwin

Western Australia

GREAT SANDY DESERT

GIBSON DESERT

GREAT VICTORIA DESERT

South Australia

Adelaide

Great Australian Bight

Perth

Cape Leeuwin

INDIAN OCEAN

Tropic of Cancer

Tropic of Capricorn

0   500   1,000 Miles
0 500 1,000 Kilometers

Mercator Projection
1 : 58,400,000

Conversion Factors

To change	To	Multiply by	To change	To	Multiply by
acres	square feet	43,560	liters	quarts (liquid)	1.0567
acres	square miles	.001562	meters	feet	3.2808
atmospheres	cms. of mercury	76	meters	miles	.0006214
Btu	kilowatt-hour	.0002928	meters	yards	1.0936
Btu/hour	watts	.2931	metric tons	tons (long)	.9842
bushels	cubic inches	2150.4	metric tons	tons (short)	1.1023
centimeters	inches	.3937	miles	kilometers	1.6093
centimeters	feet	.03281	miles	feet	5280
cubic feet	cubic meters	.0283	miles (nautical)	miles (statute)	1.1516
cubic meters	cubic feet	35.3145	miles (statute)	miles (nautical)	.8684
cubic meters	cubic yards	1.3079	miles/hour	feet/minute	88
cubic yards	cubic meters	.7646	millimeters	inches	.0394
fathoms	feet	6.0	ounces (avdp)	grams	28.3495
feet	meters	.3048	ounces	pounds	.0625
feet	miles (nautical)	.0001645	ounces (troy)	ounces (avdp)	1.09714
feet	miles (statute)	.0001894	pecks	liters	8.8096
feet/second	miles/hour	.6818	pints (dry)	liters	.5506
furlongs	feet	660.0	pints (liquid)	liters	.4732
furlongs	miles	.125	pounds (ap or troy)	kilograms	.3782
gallons (U.S.)	liters	3.7853	pounds (avdp)	kilograms	.4536
grains	grams	.0648	pounds	ounces	16
grams	ounces (avdp)	.0353	quarts (dry)	liters	1.1012
grams	pounds	.002205	quarts (liquid)	liters	.9463
hectares	acres	2.4710	radians	degrees	57.30
hectoliters	bushels (U.S.)	2.8378	rods	meters	5.029
horsepower	watts	745.7	rods	feet	16.5
hours	days	.04167	square feet	square meters	.0929
inches	millimeters	25.4000	square kilometers	square miles	.3861
inches	centimeters	2.5400	square meters	square feet	10.7639
kilograms	pounds (avdp or troy)	2.2046	square miles	square kilometers	2.5900
kilometers	miles	.6214	square yards	square meters	.8361
kilowatts	horsepower	1.341	tons (long)	metric tons	1.016
knots	nautical miles/hour	1.0	tons (short)	metric tons	.9072
knots	statute miles/hour	1.151	tons (long)	pounds	2240
liters	gallons (U.S.)	.2642	tons (short)	pounds	2000
liters	pints (dry)	1.8162	watts	Btu/hour	3.4129
liters	pints (liquid)	2.1134	watts	horsepower	.001341
liters	quarts (dry)	.9081	yards	meters	.9144
			yards	miles	.0005682

NOTE: avdp = avoirdupois weight, ap = apothecaries' weight. *See also* p.539.

Fahrenheit and Celsius (Centigrade) Scales

°Celsius	°Fahrenheit	°Celsius	°Fahrenheit
−273.15	−459.67	30	86
−250	−418	35	95
−200	−328	40	104
−150	−238	45	113
−100	−148	50	122
−50	−58	55	131
−40	−40	60	140
−30	−22	65	149
−20	−4	70	158
−10	14	75	167
0	32	80	176
5	41	85	185
10	50	90	194
15	59	95	203
20	68	100	212
25	77		

Zero on the Fahrenheit scale represents the temperature produced by the mixing of equal weights of snow and common salt.

	°Fahrenheit	°Celsius
Boiling point of water	212°	100°
Freezing point of water	32°	0°
Absolute zero	−459.6°	−273.1°

Absolute zero is theoretically the lowest possible temperature, the point at which all molecular motion would cease.

To convert Fahrenheit to Celsius (Centigrade), subtract 32 and multiply by .6.

To convert Celsius (Centigrade) to Fahrenheit, multiply by 1.8 and add 32.

Kelvin Scale

Absolute zero, −273.15° on the Celsius (Centigrade) scale, is 0° Kelvin. Thus, Kelvin is equivalent to Celsius plus 273.15. The freezing point of water, 0°C and 32°F, is 273.15°K. The conversion formula is $K° = C° + 273.15$.

Cardinal, Ordinal, and Nominal Numbers

Cardinal numbers, known as the "counting numbers," indicate quantity. **Ordinal numbers** indicate the order or rank of things in a set (e.g., sixth in line; fourth place). **Nominal numbers** name or identify something (e.g., a zip code or a player on a team.) They do not show quantity or rank.

Roman Numerals

Roman numerals are expressed by letters of the alphabet and are rarely used today except for formality or variety. There are four basic principles for reading Roman numerals:

1. A letter repeated once or twice repeats its value that many times (XXX = 30, CC = 200, etc.).
2. One or more letters placed after another letter of greater value increases the greater value by the amount of the smaller (VI = 6, LXX = 70, MCC = 1200, etc.).
3. A letter placed before another letter of greater value decreases the greater value by the amount of the smaller (IV = 4, XC = 90, CM = 900, etc.).
4. A bar placed on top of a letter or string of letters increases the numeral's value by 1,000 times (XV = 15, $\overline{XV}$ = 15,000).

Letter	Value	Letter	Value	Letter	Value	Letter	Value	Letter	Value
I	1	VII	7	XL	40	C	100	$\overline{C}$	100,000
II	2	VIII	8	L	50	D	500	$\overline{D}$	500,000
III	3	IX	9	LX	60	M	1,000	$\overline{M}$	1,000,000
IV	4	X	10	LXX	70	$\overline{V}$	5,000		
V	5	XX	20	LXXX	80	$\overline{X}$	10,000		
VI	6	XXX	30	XC	90	$\overline{L}$	50,000		

Mean and Median

The arithmetic mean, also called the average, of a series of quantities is obtained by finding the sum of the quantities and dividing it by the number of quantities. In the series 1, 3, 5, 18, 19, 20, 25, the mean or average is 13—in other words, 91 divided by 7.

The median of a series is that point which so divides it that half the quantities are on one side, half on the other. In the above series, the median is 18.

The median often better expresses the common-run, since it is not, as is the mean, affected by an excessively high or low figure. In the series 1, 3, 4, 7, 55, the median of 4 is a truer expression of the common-run than is the mean of 14.

Prime Numbers between 1 and 1,000

	2	3	5	7	11	13	17	19	23
29	31	37	41	43	47	53	59	61	67
71	73	79	83	89	97	101	103	107	109
113	127	131	137	139	149	151	157	163	167
173	179	181	191	193	197	199	211	223	227
229	233	239	241	251	257	263	269	271	277
281	283	293	307	311	313	317	331	337	347
349	353	359	367	373	379	383	389	397	401
409	419	421	431	433	439	443	449	457	461
463	467	479	487	491	499	503	509	521	523
541	547	557	563	569	571	577	587	593	599
601	607	613	617	619	631	641	643	647	653
659	661	673	677	683	691	701	709	719	727
733	739	743	751	757	761	769	773	787	797
809	811	821	823	827	829	839	853	857	859
863	877	881	883	887	907	911	919	929	937
941	947	953	967	971	977	983	991	997	(1009)

New Quarters and Dollar Coin

The 50 State Quarters Program Act began in 1999 and is expected to run until 2008, with five new quarters released every year over ten years. The quarters are being released in the order that the states joined the union. 700 million copies of each quarter will be produced. Each quarter will feature a different state design on the back

In 2000, a new dollar coin, featuring the Shoshone guide Sacagawea, replaced the Susan B. Anthony coin, whose reserves are running low.

State	Date of Statehood	Year of Issue	Design
Delaware	Dec. 7, 1787	1999	Caesar Rodney's horseback ride
Pennsylvania	Dec. 12, 1787	1999	Commonwealth statue, keystone, and outline of state
New Jersey	Dec. 18, 1787	1999	Washington crossing the Delaware River
Georgia	Jan. 2, 1788	1999	Peach, Live Oak, and outline of state
Connecticut	Jan. 9, 1788	1999	The Charter Oak
Massachusetts	Feb. 6, 1788	2000	Minuteman statue and outline of state
Maryland	April 28, 1788	2000	Maryland Statehouse and White Oak
South Carolina	May 23, 1788	2000	Palmetto tree, Carolina wren, and Yellow Jessamine
New Hampshire	June 21, 1788	2000	Old Man of the Mountain rock formation
Virginia	June 25, 1788	2000	First three ships to Jamestown

Portraits and Designs of U.S. Paper Currency

Currency[1]	Portrait	Design on back	Currency[1]	Portrait	Design on back
$1	Washington	ONE between obverse and reverse of Great Seal of U.S.	$50[5]	Grant	U.S. Capitol
			$100[6]	Franklin	Independence Hall
$2[2]	Jefferson	Monticello	$500	McKinley	Ornate FIVE HUNDRED
$2[3]	Jefferson	"The Signing of the Declaration of Independence"	$1,000	Cleveland	Ornate ONE THOUSAND
			$5,000	Madison	Ornate FIVE THOUSAND
$5	Lincoln	Lincoln Memorial	$10,000	Chase	Ornate TEN THOUSAND
$10	Hamilton	U.S. Treasury Building	$100,000[7]	Wilson	Ornate ONE HUNDRED THOUSAND
$20[4]	Jackson	White House			

1. Denominations of $500 and higher were discontinued in 1969. 2. Discontinued in 1966. 3. New issue, April 1976. 4. New issue, Sept. 1998. 5. New issue, fll 1997. 6. New issue, March 1996. 7. For use only in transactions between Federal Reserve System and Treasury Department.

Customary U.S. Weights and Measures

Linear Measure

12 inches (in.) = 1 foot (ft.)
3 feet = 1 yard (yd)
5½ yards = 1 rod (rd), pole, or perch (16½ ft.)
40 rods = 1 furlong (fur) = 220 yds = 660 ft.
8 furlongs = 1 statute mile (mi.) = 1,760 yds
= 5,280 ft.
3 land miles = 1 league
5,280 feet = 1 statute or land mile
6,076.11549 feet = 1 international nautical mile

Area Measure

144 square inches = 1 sq ft.
9 square feet = 1 sq yd = 1,296 sq in.
30¼ square yards = 1 sq rd = 272¼ sq ft.
160 square rods = 1 acre = 4,840 sq yds
= 43,560 sq ft.
640 acres = 1 sq mi.
1 mile square = 1 section (of land)
6 miles square = 1 township = 36 sections
= 36 sq mi.

Cubic Measure

1,728 cubic inches = 1 cu ft.
27 cubic feet = 1 cu yd

Liquid Measure

When necessary to distinguish the liquid pint or quart from the dry pint or quart, the word "liquid" or the abbreviation "liq" should be used in combination with the name or abbreviation of the liquid unit.

4 gills (gi) = 1 pint (pt) (= 28.875 cu in.)
2 pints = 1 quart (qt) (= 57.75 cu in.)
4 quarts = 1 gallon (gal) (= 231 cu in.)
= 8 pts = 32 gills

Apothecaries' Fluid Measure

60 minims (min.) = 1 fluid dram (fl dr) (= 0.2256 cu in.)
8 fluid drams = 1 fluid ounce (fl oz) (= 1.8047 cu in.)
16 fluid ounces = 1 pt (= 28.875 cu in.) = 128 fl drs
2 pints = 1 qt (= 57.75 cu in.) = 32 fl oz
= 256 fl drs
4 quarts = 1 gal (= 231 cu in.) = 128 fl oz
= 1,024 fl drs

Dry Measure

When necessary to distinguish the dry pint or quart from the liquid pint or quart, the word "dry" should be used in combination with the name or abbreviation of the dry unit.

2 pints = 1 qt (= 67.2006 cu in.)
8 quarts = 1 peck (pk) (= 537.605 cu in.) = 16 pts
4 pecks = 1 bushel (bu) (= 2,150.42 cu in.) = 32 qts

Avoirdupois Weight

When necessary to distinguish the avoirdupois dram from the apothecaries' dram, or to distinguish the avoirdupois dram or ounce from the fluid dram or ounce, or to distinguish the avoirdupois ounce or pound from the troy or apothecaries' ounce or pound, the word "avoirdupois" or the abbreviation "avdp" should be used in combination with the name or abbreviation of the avoirdupois unit. (The "grain" is the same in avoirdupois, troy, and apothecaries' weights.)

27¹¹⁄₃₂ grains = 1 dram (dr)
16 drams = 1 oz = 437½ grains
16 ounces = 1 lb = 256 drams = 7,000 grains
100 pounds = 1 hundredweight (cwt)[1]
20 hundredweights = 1 ton (tn) = 2,000 lbs[1]

In "gross" or "long" measure, the following values are recognized:

112 pounds = 1 gross or long cwt[1]
20 gross or long hundredweights = 1 gross or long ton
= 2,240 lbs[1]

1. When the terms "hundredweight" and "ton" are used unmodified, they are commonly understood to mean the 100-pound hundredweight and the 2,000-pound ton, respectively; these units may be designated "net" or "short" when necessary to distinguish them from the corresponding units in gross or long measure.

Units of Circular Measure

Second ('') = —
Minute (') = 60 seconds
Degree (°) = 60 minutes
Right angle = 90 degrees
Straight angle = 180 degrees
Circle = 360 degrees

Troy Weight

24 grains = 1 pennyweight (dwt)
20 pennyweights = 1 ounce troy (oz t) = 480 grains
12 ounces troy = 1 pound troy (lb t)
= 240 pennyweights
= 5,760 grains

Apothecaries' Weight

20 grains = 1 scruple (s ap)
3 scruples = 1 dram apothecaries' (dr ap)
= 60 grains
8 drams apothecaries' = 1 ounce apothecaries' (oz ap)
= 24 scruples = 480 grains
12 ounces apothecaries' = 1 pound apothecaries' (lb ap)
= 96 drams apothecaries'
= 288 scruples
= 5,760 grains

Gunter's or Surveyor's Chain Measure

7.92 inches = 1 link (li)
100 links = 1 chain (ch) = 4 rods = 66 ft.
80 chains = 1 statute mile = 320 rods = 5,280 ft.

The International System (Metric)

Source: Department of Commerce, National Bureau of Standards.

The International System of Units is a modernized version of the metric system, established by international agreement, that provides a logical and interconnected framework for all measurements in science, industry, and commerce. The system is built on a foundation of seven basic units, and all other units are derived from them. (Use of metric weights and measures was legalized in the United States in 1866, and our customary units of weights and measures are defined in terms of the meter and kilogram.)

Length. Meter. Up until 1983, the meter was defined as 1,650,763.73 wavelengths in a vacuum of the orange-red line of the spectrum of krypton-86. Since then, it is equal to the distance traveled by light in a vacuum in 1/299,792,45 of a second.

Time. Second. The second is defined as the duration of 9,192,631,770 cycles of the radiation associated with a specified transition of the cesium-133 atom.

Mass. Kilogram. The standard for the kilogram is a cylinder of platinum-iridium alloy kept by the International Bureau of Weights and Measures at Paris. A duplicate at the National Bureau of Standards serves as the mass standard for the United States. The kilogram is the only base unit still defined by a physical object.

Temperature. Kelvin. The Kelvin is defined as the fraction 1/273.16 of the thermodynamic temperature of the triple point of water; that is, the point at which water forms an interface of solid, liquid, and vapor. This is defined as 0.01°C on the Centigrade or Celsius scale and 32.02°F on the Fahrenheit scale. The temperature 0°K is called "absolute zero."

Electric Current. Ampere. The ampere is defined as that current that, if maintained in each of two long parallel wires separated by one meter in free space, would produce a force between the two wires (due to their magnetic fields) of 2×10^{-7} newton for each meter of length. (A newton is the unit of force that when applied to one kilogram mass would experience an acceleration of one meter per second per second.)

Luminous Intensity. Candela. The candela is defined as the luminous intensity of 1/600,000 of a square meter of a cavity at the temperature of freezing platinum (2,042°K).

Amount of Substance. Mole. The mole is the amount of substance of a system that contains as many elementary entities as there are atoms in 0.012 kilogram of carbon-12.

Tables of Metric Weights and Measures

Linear Measure

10 millimeters (mm) = 1 centimeter (cm)
10 centimeters = 1 decimeter (dm) = 100 millimeters
10 decimeters = 1 meter (m) = 1,000 millimeters
10 meters = 1 dekameter (dam)
10 dekameters = 1 hectometer (hm) = 100 meters
10 hectometers = 1 kilometer (km) = 1,000 meters

Area Measure

100 square millimeters (mm²) = 1 sq centimeter (cm²)
10,000 square centimeters = 1 sq meter (m²) =
1,000,000 sq millimeters
100 square meters = 1 are (a)
100 ares = 1 hectare (ha) =
10,000 sq meters
100 hectares = 1 sq kilometer (km²) =
1,000,000 sq meters

Volume Measure

10 milliliters (ml) = 1 centiliter (cl)
10 centiliters = 1 deciliter (dl) = 100 milliliters
10 deciliters = 1 liter (l) = 1,000 milliliters

10 liters = 1 dekaliter (dal)
10 dekaliters = 1 hectoliter (hl) = 100 liters
10 hectoliters = 1 kiloliter (kl) = 1,000 liters

Cubic Measure

1,000 cubic millimeters (mm³) = 1 cu centimeter (cm³)
1,000 cubic centimeters = 1 cu decimeter (dm³) =
1,000,000 cu millimeters
1,000 cubic decimeters = 1 cu meter (m³) =
1 stere = 1,000,000 cu
centimeters =
1,000,000,000 cu
millimeters

Weight

10 milligrams (mg) = 1 centigram (cg)
10 centigrams = 1 decigram (dg) = 100 milligrams
10 decigrams = 1 gram (g) = 1,000 milligrams
10 grams = 1 dekagram (dag)
10 dekagrams = 1 hectogram (hg) = 100 grams
10 hectograms = 1 kilogram (kg) = 1,000 grams
1,000 kilograms = 1 metric ton (t)

Metric and U.S. Equivalents

1 angstrom[1] (light wave measurement)	0.1 millimicron 0.000 1 micron 0.000 000 1 millimeter 0.000 000 004 inch
1 cable's length	120 fathoms 720 feet 219.456 meters
1 centimeter	0.3937 inch
1 decimeter	3.937 inches
1 dekameter	32.808 feet
1 fathom	6 feet 1.8288 meters
1 foot	0.3048 meter
1 furlong	10 chains (surveyor's) 660 feet 220 yards ⅛ statute mile 201.168 meters
1 inch	2.54 centimeters
1 kilometer	0.621 mile
1 league (land)	3 statute miles 4.828 kilometers
1 meter	39.37 inches 1.094 yards
1 micron	0.001 millimeter 0.000 039 37 inch
1 mil	0.001 inch 0.025 4 millimeter
1 mile (statute or land)	5,280 feet 1.609 kilometers
1 mile (nautical international)	1.852 kilometers 1.151 statute miles 0.999 U.S. nautical miles
1 millimeter	0.03937 inch
1 millimicron (m+GRKm)	0.001 micron 0.000 000 039 37 inch
1 nanometer	0.001 micrometer or 0.000 000 039 37 inch
1 point (typography)	0.013 837 inch 1/72 inch (approximately) 0.351 millimeter
1 rod, pole, or perch	16½ feet 5.0292 meters
1 yard	0.9144 meter

Areas or Surfaces

1 acre	43,560 square feet 4,840 square yards 0.405 hectare
1 are	119.599 square yards 0.025 acre
1 hectare	2.471 acres
1 square centimeter	0.155 square inch
1 square decimeter	15.5 square inches
1 square foot	929.030 square centimeters
1 square inch	6.4516 square centimeters
1 square kilometer	0.386 square mile 247.105 acres
1 square meter	1.196 square yards 10.764 square feet
1 square mile	258.999 hectares
1 square millimeter	0.002 square inch
1 square rod, square pole or square perch	25.293 square meters
1 square yard	0.836 square meters

Capacities or Volumes

1 barrel, liquid	31 to 42 gallons[2]
1 bushel (U.S.) struck measure[3]	2,150.42 cubic inches 35.238 liters
1 bushel, heaped (U.S.)	2,747.715 cubic inches 1.278 bushels, struck measure[4]
1 cord (firewood)	128 cubic feet
1 cubic centimeter	0.061 cubic inch
1 cubic decimeter	61.024 cubic inches
1 cubic foot	7.481 gallons 28.316 cubic decimeters
1 cubic inch	0.554 fluid ounce 4.433 fluid drams 16.387 cubic centimeters
1 cubic meter	1.308 cubic yards
1 cubic yard	0.765 cubic meter

1 cup, measuring	8 fluid ounces ½ liquid pint		1 teaspoon, measuring	⅓ tablespoon 1⅓ fluid drams
1 dram, fluid or liquid (U.S.)	⅛ fluid ounces 0.226 cubic inch 3.697 milliliters 1.041 British fluid drachms		1 carat	200 milligrams 3.086 grains
1 dekaliter	2.642 gallons 1.135 pecks		1 dram, apothecaries'	60 grains 3.888 grams
1 gallon (U.S.)	231 cubic inches 3.785 liters 0.833 British gallon 128 U.S. fluid ounces		1 dram, avoirdupois	27 1¹/₃₂ (=27.344) grains 1.772 grams
1 gallon (British Imperial)	277.42 cubic inches 1.201 U.S. gallons 4.546 liters 160 British fluid ounces		1 grain 1 gram	64.798 91 milligrams 15.432 grains 0.035 avoirdupois ounce
1 hectoliter	26.418 gallons 2.838 bushels		1 kilogram 1 microgram (µg— the Greek letter mu in combination with the letter g)	2.205 pounds 0.000 001 gram
1 liter	1.057 liquid quarts 0.908 dry quart 61.024 cubic inches		1 milligram	0.015 grain
1 milliliter	0.271 fluid dram 16.231 minims 0.061 cubic inch		1 ounce, avoirdupois	437.5 grains 0.911 troy or apothecaries' ounce 28.350 grams
1 ounce, fluid or liquid (U.S.)	1.805 cubic inch 29.574 milliliters 1.041 British fluid ounces		1 ounce, troy or apothecaries'	480 grains 1.097 avoirdupois ounces 31.103 grams
1 peck	8.810 liters		1 pennyweight	1.555 grams
1 pint, dry	33.600 cubic inches 0.551 liter		1 point	0.01 carat 2 milligrams
1 pint, liquid	28.875 cubic inches 0.473 liter		1 pound, avoirdupois	7,000 grains 1.215 troy or apothecaries' pounds 453.592 37 grams
1 quart, dry (U.S.)	67.201 cubic inches 1.101 liters 0.969 British quart		1 pound, troy or apothecaries'	5,760 grains 0.823 avoirdupois pound 373.242 grams
1 quart, liquid (U.S.)	57.75 cubic inches 0.946 liter 0.833 British quart		1 ton, gross or long[5]	2,240 pounds 1.12 net tons 1.016 metric tons
1 quart (British)	69.354 cubic inches 1.032 U.S. dry quarts 1.201 U.S. liquid quarts		1 ton, metric	2,204.623 pounds 0.984 gross ton 1.102 net tons
1 tablespoon, measuring	3 teaspoons 4 fluid drams ½ fluid ounce		1 ton, net or short	2,000 pounds 0.893 gross ton 0.907 metric ton

1. The angstrom is basically defined as 10⁻¹⁰ meter. 2. There is a variety of "barrels" established by law or usage. For example, federal taxes on fermented liquors are based on a barrel of 31 gallons; many state laws fix the "barrel for liquids" at 31½ gallons; one state fixes a 36-gallon barrel for cistern measurement; federal law recognizes a 40-gallon barrel for "proof spirits"; by custom, 42 gallons compose a barrel of crude oil or petroleum products for statistical purposes, and this equivalent is recognized "for liquids" by four states. 3. "Struck measure" refers to a struck, or level, bushel. It is the only official bushel measure in the U.K. 4. Frequently recognized as 1¼ bushels, struck measure. 5. The gross or long ton is used commercially in the United States to only a limited extent, usually in restricted industrial fields. These units are the same as the British "ton."

Definitions of Gold Terminology

The term "fineness" defines a gold content in parts per thousand. For example, a gold nugget containing 885 parts of pure gold, 100 parts of silver, and 15 parts of copper would be considered 885-fine.

The word "karat" indicates the proportion of solid gold in an alloy based on a total of 24 parts. Thus, 14-karat (14K) gold indicates a composition of 14 parts of gold and 10 parts of other metals.

The term "gold-filled" is used to describe articles of jewelry made of base metal that are covered on one or more surfaces with a layer of gold alloy. No article having a gold alloy portion of less than one twentieth by weight may be marked "gold-filled." Articles may be marked "rolled gold plate" provided the proportional fraction and fineness designations are also shown.

Electroplated jewelry items carrying at least 7 millionths of an inch of gold on significant surfaces may be labeled "electroplate." Plate thicknesses less than this may be marked "gold-flashed" or "gold-washed."

Bolts and Screws: Conversion from Fractions of an Inch to Millimeters

Inch	mm	Inch	mm	Inch	mm	Inch	mm
1/64	0.40	17/64	6.75	33/64	13.10	49/64	19.45
1/32	0.79	9/32	7.14	17/32	13.50	25/32	19.84
3/64	1.19	19/64	7.54	35/64	13.90	51/64	20.24
1/16	1.59	5/16	7.94	9/16	14.29	13/16	20.64
5/64	1.98	21/64	8.33	37/64	14.69	53/64	21.03
3/32	2.38	11/32	8.73	19/32	15.08	27/32	21.43
7/64	2.78	23/64	9.13	39/64	15.48	55/64	21.83
1/8	3.18	3/8	9.53	5/8	15.88	7/8	22.23
9/64	3.57	25/64	9.92	41/64	16.27	57/64	22.62
5/32	3.97	13/32	10.32	21/32	16.67	29/32	23.02
11/64	4.37	27/64	10.72	43/64	17.06	59/64	23.42
3/16	4.76	7/16	11.11	11/16	17.46	15/16	23.81
13/64	5.16	29/64	11.51	45/64	17.86	61/64	24.21
7/32	5.56	15/32	11.91	23/32	18.26	31/32	24.61
15/64	5.95	31/64	12.30	47/64	18.65	63/64	25.00
1/4	6.35	1/2	12.70	3/4	19.05	1	25.40

Cooking Measurement Equivalents

16 tablespoons = 1 cup

12 tablespoons = 3/4 cup

10 tablespoons + 2 teaspoons = 2/3 cup

8 tablespoons = 1/2 cup

6 tablespoons = 3/8 cup

5 tablespoons + 1 teaspoon = 1/3 cup

4 tablespoons = 1/4 cup

2 tablespoons = 1/8 cup

2 tablespoons + 2 teaspoons = 1/6 cup

1 tablespoon = 1/16 cup

2 cups = 1 pint

2 pints = 1 quart

3 teaspoons = 1 tablespoon

48 teaspoons = 1 cup

U.S.–Metric Cooking Conversions

U.S. to Metric

Capacity		Weight	
1/5 teaspoon	1 milliliter	1 oz	28 grams
1 teaspoon	5 ml	1 pound	454 grams
1 tablespoon	15 ml		
1 fluid oz	30 ml		
1/5 cup	47 ml		
1 cup	237 ml		
2 cups (1 pint)	473 ml		
4 cups (1 quart)	.95 liter		
4 quarts (1 gal.)	3.8 liters		

Metric to U.S.

Capacity		Weight	
1 milliliter	1/5 teaspoon	1 gram	.035 ounce
5 ml	1 teaspoon	100 grams	3.5 ounces
15 ml	1 tablespoon	500 grams	1.10 pounds
100 ml	3.4 fluid oz	1 kilogram	2.205 pounds
240 ml	1 cup		35 oz
1 liter	34 fluid oz		
	4.2 cups		
	2.1 pints		
	1.06 quarts		
	0.26 gallon		

Prefixes and Multiples

Prefix	Suffix	Equivalent	Multiple/submultiple	Prefix	Suffix	Equivalent	Multiple/submultiple
atto	a	quintillionth part	10^{-18}	deci	d	tenth part	10^{-1}
femto	f	quadrillionth part	10^{-15}	deka	da	tenfold	10
pico	p	trillionth part	10^{-12}	hecto	h	hundredfold	10^2
nano	n	billionth part	10^{-9}	kilo	k	thousandfold	10^3
micro	µ	millionth part	10^{-6}	mega	M	millionfold	10^6
milli	m	thousandth part	10^{-3}	giga	G	billionfold	10^9
centi	c	hundredth part	10^{-2}	tera	T	trillionfold	10^{12}

Common Formulas

CIRCUMFERENCE

Circle: $C = \pi d$, in which π is 3.1416 and d the diameter.

AREA

Triangle: $A = \dfrac{ab}{2}$, in which a is the base and b the height.

Square: $A = a^2$, in which a is one of the sides.

Rectangle: $A = ab$, in which a is the base and b the height.

Trapezoid: $A = \dfrac{h(a+b)}{2}$, in which h is the height, a the longer parallel side, and b the shorter.

Regular pentagon: $A = 1.720a^2$, in which a is one of the sides.

Regular hexagon: $A = 2.598a^2$, in which a is one of the sides.

Regular octagon: $A = 4.828a^2$, in which a is one of the sides.

Circle: $A = \pi r^2$, in which π is 3.1416 and r the radius.

VOLUME

Cube: $V = a^3$, in which a is one of the edges.

Rectangular prism: $V = abc$, in which a is the length, b is the width, and c the depth.

Pyramid: $V = \dfrac{Ah}{3}$, in which A is the area of the base and h the height.

Cylinder: $V = \pi r^2 h$, in which π is 3.1416, r the radius of the base, and h the height.

Cone: $V = \dfrac{\pi r^2 h}{3}$, in which π is 3.1416, r the radius of the base, and h the height.

Sphere: $V = \dfrac{4 \pi r^3}{3}$, in which π is 3.1416 and r the radius.

TEMPERATURE SCALES

Degrees Fahrenheit to Degrees Celsius:
$$T_C = \frac{5}{9}\,(T_F - 32)$$

Degrees Celsius to Degrees Fahrenheit:
$$T_F = \frac{9}{5}\,T_C + 32$$

Degrees Celsius to Kelvin:
$$T_K = T_C + 273.15$$

MISCELLANEOUS

Distance in feet traveled by falling body:
$d = 16t^2$, in which t is the time in seconds.

Speed of sound in feet per second through any given temperature of air:
$$V = \frac{1087 \sqrt{273 + t}}{16.52}$$
, in which t is the temperature Celsius.

Cost in cents of operation of electrical device:
$$C = \frac{Wtc}{1000}$$
, in which W is the number of watts, t the time in hours, and c the cost in cents per kilowatt-hour.

Conversion of matter into energy (Einstein's Theorem): $E = mc^2$, in which E is the energy in ergs, m the mass of the matter in grams, and c the speed of light in centimeters per second:
$$(c^2 = 9 \times 10^{20})$$

Decimal Equivalents of Common Fractions

½	.5000	¹⁄₁₀	.1000	²⁄₇	.2857	³⁄₁₁	.2727	⁵⁄₉	.5556	⁷⁄₁₁	.6364
⅓	.3333	¹⁄₁₁	.0909	²⁄₉	.2222	⅘	.8000	⁵⁄₁₁	.4545	⁷⁄₁₂	.5833
¼	.2500	¹⁄₁₂	.0833	²⁄₁₁	.1818	⁴⁄₇	.5714	⁵⁄₁₂	.4167	⅝	.8889
⅕	.2000	¹⁄₁₆	.0625	¾	.7500	⁴⁄₉	.4444	⁶⁄₇	.8571	⁸⁄₁₁	.7273
⅙	.1667	¹⁄₃₂	.0313	⅗	.6000	⁴⁄₁₁	.3636	⁶⁄₁₁	.5455	⁹⁄₁₀	.9000
⅐	.1429	¹⁄₆₄	.0156	³⁄₇	.4286	⅚	.8333	⅞	.8750	⁹⁄₁₁	.8182
⅛	.1250	⅔	.6667	⅜	.3750	⁵⁄₇	.7143	⁷⁄₉	.7778	¹⁰⁄₁₁	.9091
⅑	.1111	⅖	.4000	³⁄₁₀	.3000	⅝	.6250	⁷⁄₁₀	.7000	¹¹⁄₁₂	.9167

U.S. Postal Rates and Fees

Domestic Rates as of Jan. 10, 1999

Postal Information Web Sites

United States Postal Service:
http://www.usps.gov/postofc/welcome.htm
ZIP Code Look Up: http://www.usps.gov/ncsc/
U.S. Postal Service Rate Calculators:
http://www.usps.gov/business/calcs.htm

First-Class Mail

Single-Piece Letter/Flat Rates

1st ounce	$0.33
Each additional ounce	0.22

Weight not over (oz.)	Rate	Weight not over (oz.)	Rate
1*	$0.33	9	$2.09
2	0.55	10	2.31
3	0.77	11	2.53
4	0.99	12	2.75
5	1.21	13	2.97
6	1.43	Over 13 ounces, see	
7	1.65	Priority Mail.	
8	1.87		

*Nonstandard surcharge may apply to pieces weighing 1 ounce or less based on size.

Card Rates

Single postal card sold by United States Postal Service	$0.20
Double postal card sold by USPS	0.40
Single postcard (commercial)	0.20

Postcard Dimensions: Not larger than 4¼ by 6 inches by 0.016 inch thick. Not smaller than 3½ by 5 inches by 0.007 inch thick.

Periodicals

Only publishers and registered news agents approved for periodicals mailing privileges may mail at periodicals rates. Publications mailed by the public are charged at the applicable Express Mail, Priority Mail, single-piece First-Class, standard "A," or standard "B" rates.

Standard "A"

Used primarily by retailers, catalogers, and other advertisers to promote products and services. See postmaster for details. **Use**—For mailing certain items—circulars, books, catalogs, other printed matter, merchandise, seeds, cuttings, bulbs, and plants—weighing less than 16 ounces.

Express Mail

Express Mail is the postal service's fastest service. Next-day delivery by 12 noon to most destinations. Delivered 365 days a year with no extra charge for Saturday, Sunday, or holiday delivery. All packages must use an Express Mail label. Items may weigh up to 70 pounds and measure up to 108 inches in com-bined length and girth. Call 1-800-222-1811 for delivery information between ZIP codes.

Features—Express Mail envelopes, labels, and boxes are available, at no additional charge, at post offices or by calling 1-800-222-1811.

Post Office to Addressee Service

Up to 8 ounces	$11.75
Over 8 ounces, up to 2 pounds	15.75
Up to 3 pounds	17.25
Up to 4 pounds	19.40
Up to 5 pounds	21.55
Up to 6 pounds	25.40
Up to 7 pounds	26.45
Over 7 pounds, see postmaster.	

Flat-Rate Envelope—Post Office to Addressee Service

$15.00, regardless of weight or destination for matter sent in a flat-rate envelope provided by the Postal Service.

Priority Mail

Priority Mail offers two-day service to most domestic destinations. Items may weigh up to 70 pounds and measure up to 108 inches in combined length and girth.

Delivery confirmation for Priority Mail has been introduced. For mailers who apply their own bar-codes and access postal information systems for electronic confirmation, the service is free. Manual service is $0.35.

Features—Priority Mail envelopes, labels, and boxes are available, at no additional charge, at post offices or by calling 1-800-222-1811.

Single-Piece Rates[1]

Up to 2 pounds	$3.20
Up to 3 pounds	4.30
Up to 4 pounds	5.40
Up to 5 pounds	6.50
Over 5 pounds, see postmaster.	

1. A parcel weighing less than 15 pounds but measuring more than 84 inches in length and girth combined is charge-able with a minimum rate equal to that for a 15-pound par-cel for the zone to which it is addressed.

Flat-Rate Envelope

$3.00, regardless of weight or destination, for matter sent in a flat-rate envelope provided by the Postal Service.

Standard "B"

For mailing circulars, books, catalogs, other printed matter, and packages weighing 16 ounces or more. Enclosed or attached First-Class Mail is charged at First-Class rates. Packages may weigh up to 70 pounds and measure up to 108 inches in com-bined length and girth.

Parcel Post Zone Rates

For rates priced by distance and weight, see post-master.

Special Services (Domestic Mail)

Certificate of Mailing

Proves that an item was mailed. Must be purchased at time of mailing. No record kept at the post office.
Fee, in addition to postage—$0.60

Certified Mail

Provides a mailing receipt, and a record is kept at the recipient's post office. A return receipt can also be purchased for an additional fee. Available only with First-Class and Priority Mail.
Fee, in addition to postage—$1.40

Insurance

Provides coverage against loss or damage. Coverage up to $600.00 for standard "A" and standard "B" mail as well as standard "A" and standard "B" matter mailed at Priority Mail or First-Class Mail rate. Insurance up to $25,000 can be purchased by using Registered Mail. Do not insure a package for more than its value.

Liability	Fee, in addition to postage
$.01 to $50.00	$0.75
$50.01 to $100.00	1.60
$100.01 to $200.00	2.50
$200.01 to $300.00	3.40
$300.01 to $400.00	4.30
$400.01 to $500.00	5.20
$500.01 to $600.00	6.10

Money Orders

Provides safe transmission of money. Available in amounts up to $700.00.
Fee, in addition to postage—$0.80

Registered Mail

Provides maximum protection and security for valuables. Available only for Priority Mail and First-Class Mail. May be combined with COD, Restricted Delivery, or Return Receipt. Additional postal insurance available.

	Declared Value	Fee, in addition to postage
Without Insurance	$0.00	$6.00
With Insurance	$0.01 to $100	6.20
	$100.01 to $500.00	6.75
	$500.01 to $1,000.00	7.30
	$1,000.01 to $2,000.00	7.85

For higher values, consult your postmaster.

Restricted Delivery

Available only for Certified Mail, COD, Insured Mail for more than $50.00, or Registered Mail.
Fee, in addition to postage—$2.75

Return Receipt

Available only for Express Mail, Certified Mail, COD, Insured Mail for more than $50.00, or Registered Mail.
Requested at time of mailing:
Showing to whom (signature) and date delivered $1.25
Showing to whom (signature), date, and addressee's   1.50
address
Requested after mailing:
Showing to whom (signature) and date delivered   7.00

Special Delivery

Available for all classes except Express Mail. Provides preferential handling to the extent practicable in dispatch, transportation, and expedited delivery at the destination.

	Fee, in addition to postage		
Class of mail	2 lb. or less	Over 2 lb., but not over 10 lb.	Over 10 lb.
First-Class & Priority Mail	$ 9.95	$10.35	$11.15
Other classes	10.45	11.25	12.10

Collect on Delivery (COD)

Allows mailers to collect the price of goods and/or postage on merchandise ordered by addressee when it is delivered. Fees include insurance. Maximum amount $600.00; see postmaster for details.

Sizes for Domestic Mail

Mail must meet these standards:
• Thickness—No less than 0.007 inch thick. Pieces that are $1/4$ inch thick or less must be at least $3^{1}/_{2}$ inches high, 5 inches long, and rectangular in shape.
• Combined length and girth—No more than 108 inches.
• Weight—No more than 70 pounds.
Keys and identification devices are exempted from these requirements.
Additional standards apply to bulk mail and mail addressed to APOs and FPOs.

The Mail-Order Merchandise Rule

The mail-order rule adopted by the Federal Trade Commission in October 1975 provides that when you order by mail:
• You must receive the merchandise when the seller says you will.
• If you are not promised delivery within a certain time period, the seller must ship the merchandise to you no later than 30 days after your order comes in.
• If you don't receive it shortly after that 30-day period, you can cancel your order and get your money back.

ZIP Codes

The ZIP Code was instituted in 1963 and allows for electronic processing and delivery of mail. An envelope that does not include a ZIP Code in the delivery address must be manually sorted, which increases the cost of sorting the mail and causes mail to be delayed en route to the delivery address. ZIP Code directories are available for use or sale at your local post office, or you can look up ZIP Codes on-line: www.usps.gov/ncsc/.

In 1983, the Postal Service began to use an expanded ZIP Code called ZIP+4. It is composed of the original five-digit code plus a four-digit add-on. The four-digit add-on number identifies a geographic segment within the five-digit delivery area such as a city block, an office building, an individual high-volume receiver of mail, or any other unit that would aid efficient mail sorting and delivery.

International Postal Rates
As of August 1999

Letters and Letter Packages— Airmail Rates

All countries except Canada and Mexico

Weight not over (oz.)		Weight not over (oz.)	
0.5	$0.60	9.0	$ 7.40
1.0	1.00	9.5	7.80
1.5	1.40	10.0	8.20
2.0	1.80	10.5	8.60
2.5	2.20	11.0	9.00
3.0	2.60	11.5	9.40
3.5	3.00	12.0	9.80
4.0	3.40	12.5	10.20
4.5	3.80	13.0	10.60
5.0	4.20	13.5	11.00
5.5	4.60	14.0	11.40
6.0	5.00	14.5	11.80
6.5	5.40	15.0	12.20
7.0	5.80	15.5	12.60
7.5	6.20	16.0	13.00
8.0	6.60	16.5	13.40
8.5	7.00		

See postmaster for weights up to 4 lb. Maximum weight: 64 ounces.

Letters and Letter Packages— Canada and Mexico

Weight not over		Can- ada[1]	Mex -ico	Weight not over		Can- ada[1]	Mex -ico
(lb.)	(oz.)			(lb.)	(oz.)		
0	0.5	$0.48	$0.40	0	10	$2.39	$ 4.06
0	1	0.55	0.46	0	11	2.59	4.46
0	1.5	0.67	0.66	0	12	2.79	4.86
0	2	0.76	0.86	1	0	3.59	6.46
0	3	1.00	1.26	1	8	4.52	9.66
0	4	1.20	1.66	2	0	5.44	12.86
0	5	1.40	2.06	2	8	6.36	16.06
0	6	1.60	2.46	3	0	7.29	19.26
0	7	1.80	2.86	3	8	8.21	22.46
0	8	2.00	3.26	4	0	9.14	25.66
0	9	2.19	3.66				

1. A 4-pound maximum applies except for registered items sent to Canada. Canada-bound registered items may weigh up to 66 pounds. For registered items weighing over 4 pounds, the rate is $1.85 for each additional pound up to the 66-pound limit.

Postcards and Postal Rates: Canada—$0.45; Mexico—$0.40; all others—$0.55

All-Time Top 10 Most Popular Commemorative Stamps

Issue	No. saved (millions)
Elvis '93	124.0
Wildflowers '92	76.2
Rock and Roll '93	75.8
Civil War '95	46.6
Legends of the West '94	46.5
Marilyn Monroe '95	46.3
Bugs Bunny '97	45.3
Summer Olympics '92	39.6
The World of Dinosaurs	38.5
Centennial Olympic Games '96	38.1

Source: U.S.P.S., 1998. Popularity of stamps is measured by number saved, not used.

Postal Workers Bitten by Dogs, by City

City	Dog bites
1. Houston	49
2. Chicago	37
3. Miami	35
4. Los Angeles	32
5. Brooklyn	22
6. Cleveland	20
7. Buffalo, Jamaica, New York[1]	17
8. Dallas, Detroit[1]	16
9. Richmond, San Antonio, San Francisco[1]	15
10. Baltimore, Boston, Phoenix[1]	14

1. ties. *Source:* U.S.P.S., 1999. A total of 2,541 postal workers were bitten by dogs in FY1998.

State Abbreviations and State Postal Codes

State	Abbreviation	Postal code	State	Abbreviation	Postal code	State	Abbreviation	Postal code
Alabama	Ala.	AL	Kentucky	Ky.	KY	Ohio	Ohio	OH
Alaska	Alaska	AK	Louisiana	La.	LA	Oklahoma	Okla.	OK
Arizona	Ariz.	AZ	Maine	Maine	ME	Oregon	Ore.	OR
Arkansas	Ark.	AR	Maryland	Md.	MD	Pennsylvania	Pa.	PA
California	Calif.	CA	Massachusetts	Mass.	MA	Puerto Rico	P.R.	PR
Colorado	Colo.	CO	Michigan	Mich.	MI	Rhode Island	R.I.	RI
Connecticut	Conn.	CT	Minnesota	Minn.	MN	South Carolina	S.C.	SC
Delaware	Del.	DE	Mississippi	Miss.	MS	South Dakota	S.D.	SD
Dist. of Columbia	D.C.	DC	Missouri	Mo.	MO	Tennessee	Tenn.	TN
Florida	Fla.	FL	Montana	Mont.	MT	Texas	Tex.	TX
Georgia	Ga.	GA	Nebraska	Nebr.	NE	Utah	Utah	UT
Guam	Guam	GU	Nevada	Nev.	NV	Vermont	Vt.	VT
Hawaii	Hawaii	HI	New Hampshire	N.H.	NH	Virginia	Va.	VA
Idaho	Idaho	ID	New Jersey	N.J.	NJ	Virgin Islands	V.I.	VI
Illinois	Ill.	IL	New Mexico	N.M.	NM	Washington	Wash.	WA
Indiana	Ind.	IN	New York	N.Y.	NY	West Virginia	W.Va.	WV
Iowa	Iowa	IA	North Carolina	N.C.	NC	Wisconsin	Wis.	WI
Kansas	Kans.	KS	North Dakota	N.D.	ND	Wyoming	Wyo.	WY

Life-Saving Skills Summary

Skill	Adult (9 years and older)	Child (1 to 8 years)	Infant (birth to 1 year)
Rescue breathing (used when victim is not breathing)	Give 1 slow breath about every 5 seconds; about 1½ seconds per breath; 1 minute = about 10 to 12 breaths	Give 1 slow breath about every 3 seconds; about 1½ seconds per breath; 1 minute = about 20 breaths	Give 1 slow breath about every 3 seconds; about 1½ seconds per breath; 1 minute = about 20 breaths
CPR (used if victim is not breathing *and* does not have a heartbeat)	Depth of compression is about 2 inches; compressions are performed with both hands; complete 15 compressions in about 10 seconds; do cycles of 15 compressions and 2 breaths	Depth of compression is about 1½ inches; compressions are performed with 1 hand; complete 5 compressions in about 3 seconds; do cycles of 5 compressions and 1 breath	Depth of compression is about 1 inch; compressions are performed with 2 fingers; complete 5 compressions in about 3 seconds; do cycles of 5 compressions and 1 breath
Choking (conscious)	Determine if person is choking; stand behind person and deliver abdominal thrusts; repeat until object is expelled or victim loses consciousness	Determine if child is choking; stand or kneel behind child and deliver abdominal thrusts; repeat until object is expelled or child loses consciousness	Determine if infant is choking; give 5 back blows; give 5 chest thrusts; repeat until object is expelled or infant loses consciousness
Choking (unconscious)	Give 2 slow breaths; retilt head and give 2 slow breaths; give up to 5 abdominal thrusts; do finger sweep; give 2 slow breaths; repeat abdominal thrusts, finger sweep, and 2 slow breaths	Give 2 slow breaths; retilt head and give 2 slow breaths; give up to 5 abdominal thrusts; check for object in throat; do finger sweep if object is visible; give 2 slow breaths; repeat abdominal thrusts, foreign-body check/finger sweep, and 2 slow breaths	Give 2 slow breaths; retilt head and give 2 slow breaths; give 5 back blows; give 5 chest thrusts; check for object in throat; do finger sweep if object is visible; repeat back blows, chest thrusts, foreign-body check/finger sweep, and 2 slow breaths

Rescue Breathing

1. With head tilted back, pinch nose shut.

2. ADULT: Give 1 slow breath about every 5 seconds.

CHILD/INFANT: Give 1 slow breath about every 3 seconds.

CPR (Adult)

1. Find hand position.

2. Position shoulders over hands. Compress chest 15 times.

3. Give 2 slow breaths. Recheck pulse and breathing. If no pulse, continue sets of 15 compressions and 2 breaths.

Choking

If conscious but choking, give abdominal thrusts until object comes out.

If a person becomes unconscious:

Step 1. Clear any object from mouth.

Step 2. Give 2 slow breaths.

If air won't go in, give up to 5 abdominal thrusts.

Other Emergencies

Burns

First Degree: Signs/Symptoms—reddened skin. **Treatment**—Immerse quickly in cold water or apply ice until pain stops.

Second Degree: Signs/Symptoms—reddened skin, blisters. **Treatment**—(1) Cut away loose clothing. (2) Cover with several layers of cold moist dressings or, if limb is involved, immerse in cold water for relief of pain. (3) Treat for shock.

Third Degree: Signs/Symptoms—skin destroyed, tissues damaged, charring. **Treatment**—(1) Cut away loose clothing (do not remove clothing adhered to skin). (2) Cover with several layers of sterile, cold, moist dressings for relief of pain and to stop burning action. (3) Treat for shock.

Poisons

Treatment—(1) Dilute by drinking large quantities of water. (2) Induce vomiting except when poison is corrosive or a petroleum product. (3) Call the poison-control center or a doctor.

Shock

Shock may accompany any serious injury: blood loss, breathing impairment, heart failure, burns. Shock can kill—treat as soon as possible and continue until medical aid is available.

Signs/Symptoms—(1) Shallow breathing. (2) Rapid and weak pulse. (3) Nausea, collapse, vomiting. (4) Shivering. (5) Pale, moist skin. (6) Mental confusion. (7) Drooping eyelids, dilated pupils.

Treatment—(1) Establish and maintain an open airway. (2) Control bleeding. (3) Keep victim lying down. Exception: Head and chest injuries, heart attack, stroke, sun stroke. If no spine injury, victim may be more comfortable and breathe better in a semi-reclining position. If in doubt, keep the victim flat. Elevate the feet unless injury would be aggravated. Maintain normal body temperature. Place blankets under and over victim.

Frostbite

Most frequently frostbitten: toes, fingers, nose, and ears. It is caused by exposure to cold.

Signs/Symptoms—(1) Skin becomes pale or a grayish-yellow color. (2) Parts feel cold and numb. (3) Frozen parts feel doughy.

Treatment—(1) Victim should be wrapped in woolen cloth and kept dry. (2) Do not rub, chafe, or manipulate frostbitten parts. (3) Bring victim indoors. (4) Place affected parts in warm water (102° to 105°) and make sure water remains warm. Never thaw if the victim has to go back out into the cold, which may cause the affected area to be refrozen. (5) Do not use hot water bottles or a heat lamp, and do not place victim near a hot stove. (6) For serious frostbite, seek medical aid for thawing because pain will be intense and tissue damage extensive.

Heat Cramps

Affects people who work or do strenuous exercises in a hot environment. To prevent it, such people should drink large amounts of cool water and add a pinch of salt to each glass of water.

Signs/Symptoms—(1) Painful muscle cramps in legs and abdomen. (2) Faintness. (3) Profuse perspiration.

Treatment—(1) Move victim to a cool place. (2) Give victim sips of salted drinking water (one teaspoon of salt to one quart of water). (3) Apply manual pressure to the cramped muscle.

Heat Exhaustion

Signs/Symptoms—(1) Pale and clammy skin. (2) Profuse perspiration. (3) Rapid and shallow breathing. (4) Weakness, dizziness, and headache.

Treatment—(1) Care for victim as if he or she were in shock. (2) Remove victim to a cool area, do not allow chilling. (3) If body gets too cold, cover victim.

Heat Stroke

Signs/Symptoms—(1) Face is red and flushed. (2) Victim becomes rapidly unconscious. (3) Skin is hot and dry with no perspiration.

Treatment—(1) Lay victim down with head and shoulders raised. (2) Reduce the high body temperature as quickly as possible. (3) Apply cold applications to the body and head. (4) Use ice and fan if available. (5) Watch for signs of shock and treat accordingly. (6) Get medical aid as soon as possible.

The Low-Carb Diet Craze

Can you really lose weight by feasting on beef, eggs, and bacon? And should you?

By JOEL STEIN TIME

In the past few years there's been a boom in low-carb diets. These weight-loss schemes allow you to eat all the protein you want—steak, eggs, even fatty bacon—so long as you cut way down on carbohydrates like bread, pasta, and soda.

The fat-embracing diets, like so many other fads that we shouldn't have invited back, are from the '70s, when high-protein plans like the *Scarsdale Diet* and *Dr. Atkins's Diet Revolution* made fondue hip. Now the low-carb diets are back and bigger than ever. Dr. Robert Atkins, in his 70s and still the reigning guru of the movement, is back on the charts with *Dr. Atkins's New Diet Revolution.*

Other low-carb diet books jamming the shelves include *The Carbohydrate Addict's Diet* and a plateful of spin-offs by Rachael and Richard Heller, *Protein Power* by Drs. Michael and Mary Eades, *Sugar Busters!*, *The Zone*, and Suzanne Somers's *Get Skinny on Fabulous Foods*. Some probably bought the Somers book for the color picture of her licking a butterflied-lamb-slicked finger, but it still became a No. 1 best-seller, something her poetry collection (despite Johnny Carson's best efforts) never did. Even bread-loving France has had a best-selling high-protein diet book, *Eat Yourself Slim* by Michel Montignac, and Poland has the *Optimal Nourishment* plan. Russia would have one too if it had meat.

Double Whopper, Hold the Bun

It's not hard to find people talking about these diets, because the only thing people like to talk about more than eating is not eating. Celebrities and everyday folks alike are bragging about the bacon and eggs they downed for breakfast, followed by a midday repast of pork rinds. Having it your way now includes having a plate, fork, and knife included with a bunless Whopper at Burger King. In return for this unlimited meat, all the new diets ask is that you lay off the penne and rice. Who wouldn't like a diet that works at a Vegas buffet?

Turns out most mainstream doctors and professional dietitians. They're attacking these latest fad diets on CNN and making Leeza seem like the McLaughlin Group. Late in 1999, 9,000 of them met in Atlanta for a conference of the American Dietetic Association, and even though the organization hadn't scheduled any Atkins talk for its seminars, it blasted low-carb diets as "a nightmare." JoAnn Hattner, a clinical nutritionist at the UCSF Stanford University Medical Center who attended the conference, worries about the high levels of protein and fat in many of these diets, as well as their lack of fiber. "Removing fiber causes constipation, fluid dehydration, weakness, and nausea. It's a great strain on the kidneys," she says. Keith Ayoob, a professor of nutrition at Albert Einstein College of Medicine in New York City, warns about other "very unpleasant side effects—sometimes really bad breath."

But millions of people are willing to risk halitosis, or worse long-range health effects, to get rid of their obesity. The U.S. is by far the fattest country in the world, with 54% of the population overweight. If Americans didn't travel overseas, they'd think 200 lbs. was normal. They eat 7% more calories than they did 20 years ago. Even the nation's children, the ones so hyperactive they need Ritalin, are pudgy; 25% of them are overweight. To combat this, Americans, in lieu of exercise, spend $33 billion a year on the diet industry.

Pritikin and Powter Are Passé

Carb paranoia struck when people discovered that all the fat-free food they loaded up on during the last diet craze was making them fat. Diet plans like the *Pritikin Program* of the early '80s and Susan Powter's *Stop the Insanity!* in 1993 caused a run on processed low-fat food like SnackWell's and frozen yogurt. But those treats, it turned out, were chock-full of sugar and a whole mess of calories. Result: you gained weight. The reaction in recent years has been to eliminate sugar by dropping carbohydrates from the menu altogether. So instead of the 1994 book *Butter Busters,* we now have *Sugar Busters!* and a series of the most guy-embraced diets ever, regimens with Henry VIII as a role model and beef jerky as a food group.

Carbs and Ketones

The science behind these diets is less intuitive than the old fat-makes-you-fat theory and therefore easier to argue over. Each of the low-carb diets is a variation on the theme that cutting down on carbohydrates and thus decreasing blood-sugar levels will cause the pancreas to produce less of the energy catalyst insulin. With less insulin to draw on, the body is forced to burn fat reserves for energy, thus leading to a quick weight loss. Opponents argue that cause and effect have been reversed: excess insulin is caused not by too many carbs but by being too fat. The reason people lose weight on low-carb diets, they say, is simply that by cutting out carbs, these dieters are reducing their calorie intake. In response, Atkins throws out scientific terms like *ketones* (fat-burning by-products), while *The Zone* author Barry Sears talks about *eicosanoids,* which he claims are all-powerful hormones. Opponents use words like *charlatan.*

Perhaps the most appalled is *Eat More, Weigh Less* author Dr. Dean Ornish, one of the most respected of the low-fat, heart-healthy gurus and hence Atkins's natural enemy. "These books say you should eat healthy foods that won't provoke an insulin response, like bacon, as if insulin is the only mechanism that affects health," he says. "Most people eat so much sugar that when they stop eating it, they lose weight. But they're mortgaging their health in the process." Ornish, who has published studies in various medical journals, challenges the upstarts to do the same. "What's the evidence? None of these authors have ever published any data validating their claims."

The Hellers and the Oprah Factor

The hottest of the low-carb authors, the Hellers, are not medical doctors, though they pose in lab coats on their books and refer to themselves as Dr. Rachael F. Heller and Dr. Richard F. Heller. They're probably just very proud of their Ph.D.s and happen to like hospital wear. The Hellers were propelled to stardom after a guest spot on *Oprah.*

"They have actually located what they call the carbohydrate-craving gene, which is on chromosome number 11, close to the alcoholism gene and the cocaine-addiction gene," Rachael Heller says, before taking a brief talking break to join her husband in a mating dance that involves methodically removing the croutons from their chicken Caesar salad. Though her science may be suspect, her earnestness is not. During the meal, she leans over the table to confide details from her fat, ugly past. "I have stretch marks from my neck to my knees," she says, sotto voce. Her husband tells her they are battle scars. They are in love in ways that even Codependent No More never imagined.

Atkins and His Enemies

The Hellers' diet follows the basic plan of Atkins's (up with protein, down with carbohydrates) with one important concession: the Hellers allow one "reward meal" each day in which carbs are allowed. Atkins sees this as a betrayal of his science. In fact, Atkins sees most people as part of an intricate conspiracy against the truth of bacon. Twenty-seven years after publishing his trend-setting diet book, you'd think Atkins would be used to the critics by now. But sitting in his art-filled office last week in the Atkins Center for Complementary Medicine, a seven-story alternative-medicine facility in midtown Manhattan, he was angry about the spanking he had received 20 minutes earlier from the American Dietetic Association. "People in power have a tough time admitting they were wrong," he says. "The same problem exists with the American Heart Association." He is also disgusted by most other diets, which he considers either poor copies of his own or plain bad science. He has an enemies list that would impress Richard Nixon.

The Boredom Theory

One of the tricks behind these diets, detractors say, is that by cutting out one major food group, like carbohydrates, people get bored quickly. "These diets work primarily by making people feel sick," says Dr. F. Xavier Pi-Sunyer, chief of endocrinology, diabetes, and nutrition at St. Luke's–Roosevelt Hospital in New York City. "If you go on a strict high-protein diet, you feel nauseated and a little sick to your stomach after about four to five days, so you lose your appetite and eat less." By this theory an all-chocolate-and-cheese diet would work too, because eventually you'd find you can stomach only so many calories of Hershey's and Swiss each day. It would also be delicious.

Fat and Protein Zone

The Zone's Sears is defensive about having his diet, which is lower in fats and proteins, grouped with Atkins's. "Any meal that you have to take potassium supplements, there's something wrong with that," he says of the high-protein diets. He advises eating a protein portion the size of your hand, lots of vegetables and water, and treating carbs and fat like condiments. (The goal: a 40-30-30 caloric ratio of carbs to protein to fat.) Yet his diet can be boring and requires an incredible attention to detail, like eating three olives or one macadamia nut. Still, the Zone has become so popular that it has spawned a gym for devotees in Hollywood and a catering service in Los Angeles, the Delivery Zone, which serves about 120 people a day. A similar service, Perfect Balance, has started in New York City and delivers to 1,200.

Thin Thighs and Gastric Happiness

Like the Zone, Suzanne Somers's diet, which she calls Somersizing, avoids white flour and sugar, but it argues that the important thing is to combine foods in the right way. Her program (developed with endocrinologist Diana Schwarzbein, who has her own diet book) permits a meal combining protein and vegetables, but eating protein within three hours of eating carbohydrates is taboo. "The reason I used to be bloated was a gastric war between the protein and carbohydrates," says Somers. "Now I never have gas, I can proudly say. It's a great thing not to have gas." She adds that with her diet "you can even eat at McDonald's. I order two Big Macs but no buns."

Medical Evidence Slim

The medical evidence for many of these diets is flimsy, but you can find an expert somewhere to support almost every one. As long as happy dieters and supportive doctors keep going on talk shows, people with eating problems aren't going to resist a diet that lets you eat pork rinds. Sam Panayotovich, 53, the Illinois state liquor commissioner, has been following a combination of Atkins and a 1979 local diet known as the whipped-cream-and-martini diet. The diet allows fondue, bourguignon, béarnaise, fried chicken, chunks of steak, and enough alcohol for a buzz. He's lost 53 lbs. and kept it off for 11 months, a personal record. Like most Atkins adherents, the liquor commissioner talks about his diet with a mystical admiration. "When you talk about this diet, that you can drink and have a nice steak and lose weight, people look at you like you really have been drinking." And nothing cures a hangover better than a big, greasy bacon-and-eggs breakfast. □

Exploding Exercise Myths

Getting Americans off the couch and onto their feet could save an estimated 200,000 lives a year, says the surgeon general. Yet most of us are either sedentary or only minimally active. Confusion may keep many couch potatoes from getting into shape. People still ask questions like: How often should I exercise? (The more, the better, but at least 30 minutes nearly every day.) Does it have to be 30 minutes straight? (No, shorter bouts are fine.) Do I need to go to the gym? (No, walking, dancing, lawn mowing, and gardening are fine, if they're intense enough.) Still, in a world where infomercials, magazines, videos, and friends may give conflicting advice, misunderstanding abounds.

Strength-training will make women too muscular

"Many women are afraid that strength-training will make them bulky," says Miriam Nelson of the Jean Mayer U.S. Department of Agriculture Human Nutrition Research Center on Aging at Tufts University in Boston. "They think strength-training is only for men."

"Women naturally have less bone and muscle than men, so they need to take care of what they've got," says Nelson. That's why women are at greater risk of osteoporosis than men. And lost muscle puts women at greater risk of disability as they age. And don't worry about looking like a bodybuilder. "Women don't have enough testosterone to create big, bulky muscles," says Nelson. "To become a bodybuilder, women have to do a lot of weird things that most strength-training programs don't do."

Light weights on your arms or legs can boost your exercise benefit

Some people carry light (one- or two-pound) handheld weights when they walk or run. Others strap Velcro-fastened weights around their ankles. Don't bother, says exercise physiologist Ben Hurley of the University of Maryland.

"It slows you down, so you get less benefit from aerobic exercise, and it doesn't add enough weight to give you the benefits of strength-training," he explains.

To build muscle, you have to use weights that you can lift no more than eight to twelve times in a row. "If you can go beyond the twelfth repetition, the resistance is too light to stress the muscle," says Hurley. "As your muscles get stronger, you need to add more weight—or other resistance—so you can still do only eight to twelve repetitions."

With the right exercise, you can get rid of trouble spots

"Some people believe that if they exercise one area, it will cause fat to be removed from that area," says Rosemary Lindle, a University of Maryland exercise physiologist. "In our gym the men, who tend to store their fat in their abdomens, are on the ab machines, and the women are on the total hip machines for hours," she notes. "But spot-reducing is a myth."

Abdominal and hip exercises can strengthen and tone the muscles. But those muscles are *underneath* the "subcutaneous" layer of fat that gives the lovely appearance of flab. Only losing weight can get rid of excess fat, and *where* you lose the weight depends on your genes. Losing weight around the waist is easier than losing it at the hips. "I tell women to do some strength-training in their upper body to create

a better balance between upper and lower body," says Lindle. "You can build your own natural shoulder pads."

Exercise burns lots of calories

"People have the mistaken idea that exercise is a fabulous way to lose weight," says William Evans of the University of Arkansas for Medical Sciences. "But exercising doesn't burn a lot of calories." Walking or running a mile burns about 100 calories. But sitting still for the same time burns about 50 or 60 calories. "So the extra you expend isn't huge and people get discouraged at their slow rate of weight loss."

Another misconception: You keep burning considerably more calories for a long time after you stop exercising. "Calorie expenditure is elevated for the first minute or two, but by five or six minutes the extra expenditure is pretty small, and by 40 minutes post-exercise, it's back to where you started," says Evans. That doesn't mean dieters should give up on exercise. The more you exercise, the more fit you'll get. That means you'll burn more calories because you can walk briskly or run for five miles instead of one. So instead of burning 100 calories, you burn 500 (that's 250 more than if you had stayed on the couch). What's more, says Evans, "the better-conditioned you are, the more fat you burn for energy, because your muscles adapt to using an enzyme that oxidizes fat. People who are less trained burn more carbohydrates instead."

Dieters who exercise also lose less lean body mass—that is, less muscle—than dieters who just cut calories. And physical activity can help with the toughest problem: keeping weight off. Says Evans: "Studies show that after people lose weight, the best predictor of maintaining the weight loss is whether they exercise regularly."

If you don't lose weight, there's no point in exercising

What gets most people off the couch and into their walking shoes? It's that unwanted flab that motivates most of us. It shouldn't.

"Many people don't see immediate weight loss and say it's all for naught and stop," says exercise expert William Haskell of Stanford University Medical School.

In fact, exercise has a laundry list of benefits beyond any impact on your next shopping trip. Among them:

"It improves the ability of insulin to enter cells, so it lowers the risk of diabetes," says Haskell. "It also lowers the risk of heart disease by improving blood clotting mechanisms, lowering triglycerides, and raising HDL ['good'] cholesterol."

Exercise alters not only your risk of disease, but your quality of life, he adds. "In our studies, exercise improved sleep in people with modest sleep dysfunction," that is, people who take a long time to fall asleep or who wake up frequently at night.

"The psychological benefits of exercise are frequently overlooked," says Haskell. "Exercise isn't a panacea, but it has consistently been shown to relieve both depression and anxiety."

Weight gain is inevitable as you age

Most Americans get fatter as they get older . . . but they don't have to. "It's a matter of reduced physical activity levels and lower metabolic rate caused by a loss of lean body mass [muscle]," says JoAnn Manson of Harvard Medical School.

"The lifelong loss of lean body mass reduces our basal metabolic rate as we age," says Arkansas's William Evans. "It's a very subtle change that begins between ages 20 and 30. The percentage of body fat gradually increases, and it produces an ever-decreasing calorie requirement." That's because fat cells burn fewer calories than muscle cells. And a lower metabolic rate means that unless you eat *less*, you'll gain weight over the decades.

But exercise can mount a two-pronged attack on middle-age spread and muscle loss. Any activity makes you burn more calories (so you're less likely to wind up with an excess). And strength-training can offset the loss of muscle mass.

"Starting at age 40 in women and at 60 in men, we lose six to eight percent of our muscle per decade," says Maryland's Hurley. "However, after only two months of strength-training, women recover a decade of loss and men recover two decades." That's with three weekly sessions that take 40 minutes each, including warm-up, rest periods, and stretching. "The time spent doing the exercises that increase muscle mass is only about five minutes a session," says Hurley. Not a bad return on your time.

You can't be fit and fat

"The notion that all fat people are sedentary and unfit and at high risk of disease is not true," says Steven Blair of the Cooper Clinic in Dallas, Texas. "Overweight and obese individuals who are fit do not have elevated mortality rates. We need to get off those people's backs." But in Blair's study of 25,000 men who have come to the Cooper Clinic, ten percent of the normal-weight men—and half of the overweight men—were unfit.

Getting all of those unfit people—fat or thin—to move more could make a difference. In Blair's study, low fitness was as strong (or stronger) a predictor of dying as other risk factors, like high cholesterol, high blood pressure, and diabetes. Yet doctors rarely test a patient's fitness as part of a checkup. "Fitness is such an important predictor of mortality, it's inexcusable not to evaluate it as part of a person's health risk," says Blair.

No pain, no gain

"Many people still believe that you have to work at a very high intensity in order to get a benefit," says Blair. In fact, moderate-intensity exercise lowers the risk of dying just as much as high-intensity exercise. For example, says Manson, "in the Nurses' Health Study, women who regularly engaged in brisk walking reduced their risk of heart disease to the same degree as women who engaged in vigorous exercise. You don't need to run a marathon."

The trick is making sure that the exercise is at least moderate-intensity—that is, equivalent to walking at a pace of three to four miles an hour. High-intensity exercise does have one advantage: it saves time. It takes less time to burn the same number of calories at higher intensity. "You can jog for 20 minutes or walk for 40 or 45," says Blair. "You pay your money and you take your choice."

If you can't exercise regularly, why bother?

It takes ten to twelve weeks of regular exercise to become "fit"—that is, to improve your performance on a treadmill (a measure of your oxygen capacity). But your health can improve after that first brisk walk or run. "Take a 50-year-old man who is somewhat overweight and typically has moderately elevated blood sugar, triglycerides, or blood pressure," says Stanford's William Haskell. "A single bout of exercise of moderate intensity—like 30 to 40 minutes of brisk walking—will lower those numbers."

People should still try to at least follow the Center for Disease Control's modest advice to get at least 30 minutes of moderate activity on most—or preferably all—days of the week, he adds. But if you can't, don't let that stop you from taking even a single walk. "Every bout has benefits," says Haskell.

If you didn't exercise when you were younger, it could be dangerous to start when you're older

"Many people think they're too old to start an exercise program," says Tufts University's Miriam Nelson. "They think it's unsafe because they have heart disease or diabetes or because they're too out of shape to start." You're never too old to start, says Nelson. And she ought to know. In one Tufts study, the participants were frail nursing-home residents whose ages ranged from 72 to 98. After just ten weeks, strength-training improved their muscle strength, ability to climb stairs, and walking speed. "When they see what a difference it makes, they're thrilled," says Nelson. The same goes for people with chronic diseases. "People say they can't exercise because they have arthritis," she adds. "But we see some of the greatest benefits in people with arthritis. Exercise reduces pain and increases range of motion, strength, and mobility."

That doesn't mean that anyone can plunge into a bout of vigorous exercise, regardless of health history. In a recent study, ordinarily inactive people—especially men who had high cholesterol or angina or were smokers or obese—were ten times more likely to have a heart attack within an hour of exerting themselves (usually by jogging or heavy lifting) than at other times.

As for the all-too-common "I don't have time to exercise," Nelson responds, "somehow, you've got to make the time, or you're going to have medical problems like heart disease, diabetes, or osteoporosis. And it will take a lot more time to deal with them than it takes to exercise."

Source: Center for Science in the Public Interest. Reprinted/adapted from *Nutrition Action Healthletter* (1875 Connecticut Ave. N.W., Suite 300, Washington, D.C. 20009–5728. $24.00 for 10 issues).

Measuring Body Mass

The new body mass index (BMI) applies to both men and women. To determine BMI, weight in kilograms is divided by height in meters, squared. To calculate your body mass index from the table below, locate your height in inches in the left-hand column, then follow it across until you locate your weight; the number at the very top is your body mass index. A BMI of 25 to 29.9 is considered overweight and one of 30 or above is considered obese.

Body Mass Index Chart

Height (inches)	19	20	21	22	23	24	25	26	27	28	29	30	31	32	33	34	35
							Body Weight (pounds)										
58	91	96	100	105	110	115	119	124	129	134	138	143	148	153	158	162	167
59	94	99	104	109	114	119	124	128	133	138	143	148	153	158	163	168	173
60	97	102	107	112	118	123	128	133	138	143	148	153	158	163	168	174	179
61	100	106	111	116	122	127	132	137	143	148	153	158	164	169	174	180	185
62	104	109	115	120	126	131	136	142	147	153	158	164	169	175	180	186	191
63	107	113	118	124	130	135	141	146	152	158	163	169	175	180	186	191	197
64	110	116	122	128	134	140	145	151	157	163	169	174	180	186	192	197	204
65	114	120	126	132	138	144	150	156	162	168	174	180	186	192	198	204	210
66	118	124	130	136	142	148	155	161	167	173	179	186	192	198	204	210	216
67	121	127	134	140	146	153	159	166	172	178	185	191	198	204	211	217	223
68	125	131	138	144	151	158	164	171	177	184	190	197	203	210	216	223	230
69	128	135	142	149	155	162	169	176	182	189	196	203	209	216	223	230	236
70	132	139	146	153	160	167	174	181	188	195	202	209	216	222	229	236	243
71	136	143	150	157	165	172	179	186	193	200	208	215	222	229	236	243	250
72	140	147	154	162	169	177	184	191	199	206	213	221	228	235	242	250	258
73	144	151	159	166	174	182	189	197	204	212	219	227	235	242	250	257	265
74	148	155	163	171	179	186	194	202	210	218	225	233	241	249	256	264	272
75	152	160	168	176	184	192	200	208	216	224	232	240	248	256	264	272	279
76	156	164	172	180	189	197	205	213	221	230	238	246	254	263	271	279	287

Source: National Heart, Lung, and Blood Institute.

First Federal Obesity Guidelines: More Than Half of All Americans Are Too Fat

Source: National Heart, Lung, and Blood Institute

Overweight and obesity continue to be an alarming public-health problem in the United States, affecting 97 million American adults—an astonishing 55% of the population. Between 1960 and 1994, the prevalence of obesity in adults increased from nearly 13% to 22.5% of the U.S. population, with most of the increase occurring in the 1990s. These findings are recorded in the first federal guidelines on the identification, evaluation, and treatment of overweight and obesity in adults, which was released by the National Heart, Lung, and Blood Institute (NHLBI) in June 1998.

"There are several possible reasons for the increase," asserted Karen Donato, coordinator of the Obesity Education Initiative. "When people read labels, they're more likely to notice what's 'low-fat and healthy' but may not be looking at calories. Also, more people are eating out and portion sizes have increased. Another issue is decreased physical activity. So people are consuming more calories and are less active. It doesn't take much to tip the energy balance," she said.

According to the guidelines, assessment of overweight involves evaluation of three key measures—body mass index (BMI), waist circumference, and a patient's risk factors for diseases and conditions associated with obesity. Overweight is defined as having a BMI of 25 to 29.9 and obesity as a BMI of 30 and above, which is consistent with the definitions used in many other countries. BMI describes body weight relative to height and is strongly correlated with total body-fat content in adults. According to the guidelines, a BMI of 30 is about 30 pounds overweight and is equivalent to 221 pounds in a 6' person and to 186 pounds in someone who is 5'6". The BMI numbers apply to both men and women. Some very muscular people may have a high BMI without health risks.

Waist circumference, which is strongly associated with abdominal fat, is another measure of overweight—excess abdominal fat is an independent predictor of disease risk. A waist circumference of over 40 inches in men and over 35 inches in women signifies increased risk in those who have a BMI of 25 to 34.9.

According to the guidelines, the most successful strategies for weight loss include calorie reduction, increased physical activity, and behavior therapy designed to improve eating and physical activity habits.

The guidelines have been reviewed by 115 health experts at major medical and professional societies, and have been endorsed by 54 professional societies, government agencies, and consumer organizations. The published report is available on the NHLBI Web site: http://www.nhlbi.nih.gov/guidelines/obesity/ob_home.htm. Single free copies of the consumer tips referred to above are available by writing to the NHLBI Information Center, P.O. Box 30105, Bethesda, Md. 20824-0105.

Global Estimates[1] of the HIV/AIDS Epidemic as of End 1999

Western Europe 520,000

Eastern Europe & Central Asia 420,000

North America 900,000

East Asia & Pacific 530,000

North Africa & Middle East 220,000

Caribbean 360,000

South & Southeast Asia 5.6 million

Latin America 1.3 million

Sub-Saharan Africa 24.5 million

Australia & New Zealand 15,000

Global Total 34.3 million

1. Number of people currently infected with HIV/AIDS.
Source: World Health Organization, UNAIDS.

The AIDS Epidemic in the 21st Century—a Widening Gap

Source: World Health Organization, UNAIDS

As the 20th century drew to a close, some 34.3 million men, women, and children faced a future dominated by a fatal disease unknown just a few decades ago. According to new estimates from the Joint United Nations Programme on HIV/AIDS (UNAIDS) and the World Health Organization (WHO), 33 million adults and 1.3 million children were living with HIV by the end of 1999.

Global Outlook

Over the course of 1999, some 5.4 million people became infected with the human immunodeficiency virus (HIV).

The year also saw 2.8 million deaths from HIV/AIDS—a higher global total than in any year since the beginning of the epidemic, despite antiretroviral therapy which staved off AIDS and AIDS deaths in the richer countries. Deaths among those already infected would continue mounting for some years even if prevention programs managed to cut the number of new infections to zero. However, with the HIV-positive population still expanding—there were 5.4 million new infections in 1999 alone—the annual number of AIDS deaths can be expected to increase for many years before peaking.

Around half of all people who acquire HIV become infected before they turn 25 and typically die of AIDS before their 35th birthday. This age factor makes AIDS uniquely threatening to children. By the end of 1999, the epidemic had left behind a cumulative total of 13.2 million AIDS orphans, defined as those having lost their mothers before reaching the age of 15. Many of these maternal orphans have also lost their fathers.

Developing Countries

The overwhelming majority of people with HIV—some 95% of the global total—live in the developing world. That proportion is set to grow even further as infection rates continue to rise in countries where poverty, poor health systems, and limited resources for prevention and care fuel the spread of the virus.

Industrialized Countries

HIV is still a challenge in industrialized countries. There is evidence that safe sexual behavior is being eroded among gay men in some Western countries, perhaps because of complacency now that life-prolonging therapy is available. If this is the case, the complacency is misplaced. The disease remains fatal, and information from North America and Europe suggests that the decline in number of deaths due to antiretroviral therapy is tapering off.

Middle East

Injecting drug use gave the Eastern European and Central Asian region the world's steepest HIV curve in 1999. Drug-injecting is also a major concern in the industrialized countries, as it is in the Middle East, where total AIDS cases are still relatively low but where drug-injecting accounted for two-thirds of the cases in Bahrain, half in the Islamic Republic of Iran, and over a third in Tunisia.

Latin America

Some Latin American countries are managing to expand efforts to provide treatment to those infected. However, there is evidence that infections are on the rise in Central America and in the Caribbean basin—which has some of the worst HIV epidemics outside Africa.

Asia

Strong prevention programs seem to have reduced HIV risk and lowered or stabilized HIV rates in some countries of Asia, such as Thailand and the Philippines. Other Asian countries have raised warning flags after collecting new information showing that injecting drug use is spreading and that condom use is uncommon, including among clients of prostitutes and men who have sex with men. In many places prevention efforts are hampered by the shame and stigma attached to AIDS.

Sub-Saharan Africa

Sub-Saharan Africa continues to bear the brunt of HIV and AIDS, with close to 70% of the global total of HIV-positive people. Most will die in the next 10 years, joining the 13.7 million Africans already claimed by the epidemic and leaving behind shattered families and crippled prospects for development.

Because of AIDS, companies doing business in Africa are hurting and are bracing themselves for far worse as their workers sicken and die. According to a survey of commercial farms in Kenya, illness and death have already replaced old-age retirement as the leading reason why employees leave service. Retirement accounted for just 2% of employee drop-out by 1997.

New information suggests that between 12 and 13 African women are currently infected for every 10 African men. There are a number of reasons why female prevalence is higher than male in this region, including the greater efficiency of male-to-female HIV transmission through sex and the younger age at initial infection for women.

Epidemic Expands in Former States of the Soviet Union

The world's steepest HIV curve in 1999 was recorded in the newly independent states of the former Soviet Union, where the proportion of the population living with HIV doubled between end-1997 and end-1999. In the larger region comprising the former USSR as well as the remainder of Central and Eastern Europe, UNAIDS/WHO estimate that the number of infected people rose by a third over the course of 1999, reaching a total of 420,000.

The bulk of new HIV infections were caused by unsafe injection of drugs and occurred in two countries, the Russian Federation and Ukraine.

Status of the World AIDS Epidemic, End of 1999

	Total	Adults	Women	Children under 15 years
People newly infected with HIV in 1999	5.4 million	4.7 million	2.3 million	620,000
Number of people living with HIV/AIDS	34.3 million	33.0 million	15.7 million	1.3 million
AIDS deaths in 1999	2.8 million	2.3 million	1.2 million	500,000
Total number of AIDS deaths since beginning of epidemic	18.8 million	15.0 million	7.7 million	3.8 million

Source: World Health Organization; UNAIDS. Web: www.unaids.org.

Cumulative AIDS Deaths in the United States through 1998[1]

Age at death[2]	Men, cumulative total	Women, cumulative total	Cumulative total	Age at death[2]	Men, cumulative total	Women, cumulative total	Cumulative total
Under 15	2,632	2,352	4,984	45–54	63,966	7,693	71,659
15–24	6,162	2,228	8,390	55 or older	26,855	4,334	31,189
25–34	104,832	19,416	124,248	All ages	352,545	58,255	410,800
35–44	147,815	22,166	169,981				

1. Data for deaths occurring in 1998 are incomplete and not tabulated separately, but are included in the cumulative totals.
2. Data tabulated under "all ages" include 349 persons whose age at death is unknown. *Source:* Centers for Disease Control, *HIV/AIDS Surveillance Report,* vol. 10, no. 2.

Leading Causes of Mortality throughout the World

	All countries		Africa		The Americas		Eastern Mediterranean		Europe		Southeast Asia		Western Pacific	
Deaths	rank	% of total	rank	% of total	rank	% of total	rank	% of total	rank	% of total	rank	% of total	rank	% of total
Ischematic heart disease	1	13.7%	9	2.9%	1	17.9%	1	13.6%	1	25.5%	1	13.8%	3	11.1%
Cerebrovascular disease	2	9.5	7	4.7	2	10.3	5	5.3	2	13.7	4	6.5	1	14.3
Acute lower respiratory infections	3	6.4	3	8.2	3	4.2	2	9.1	4	3.6	2	9.3	4	4.0
HIV/AIDS	4	4.2	1	19.0	13	1.8	27	0.4	42	0.2	8	2.2	42	0.2
Chronic obstructive pulmonary disease	5	4.2	14	1.1	6	2.8	10	1.7	5	2.7	11	1.6	2	12.0
Diarrheal diseases	6	4.1	4	7.6	10	2.0	3	7.4	22	0.7	3	6.6	17	1.2
Perinatal conditions	7	4.0	5	5.5	7	2.6	4	7.3	13	1.2	5	6.0	10	2.2
Tuberculosis	8	2.8	11	2.2	19	1.0	7	3.7	23	0.6	6	5.1	9	2.9
Cancer of trachea/ bronchus/lung	9	2.3	38	0.3	4	3.2	20	1.0	3	4.2	15	1.2	6	3.6
Road traffic accidents	10	2.2	12	1.8	5	3.1	9	1.9	8	1.9	7	2.5	12	2.0

Source: The World Health Report, 1999.

Organ Transplant Reform

Source: Department of Health and Human Services

As of Oct. 1, 1999, the nation's organ transplantation system was reformed, ensuring that allocation of scarce organs will be based on common medical criteria, not accidents of geography.

Under the former system, organs had been first offered to the region in which they become available. If no match is found there, the organ is offered nationwide. But the emphasis on treating local transplant patients means that less ill patients may receive a transplant while patients with more urgent medical need in other locations continue to wait. Today there is a wide variation in waiting times, with patients in some areas waiting five times longer or more for an organ than in other areas. The new criteria would provide for wider sharing to ensure organs are made available to patients with greatest medical need.

The scarcity of transplant organs has remained a chronic problem in the United States. In 1996, some 20,000 Americans—about 55 each day—were able to live healthier lives through transplantation. However, more than 55,000 people are on the transplant waiting list nationwide, and some 4,000 people—10 every day—die in the U.S. while awaiting a donated organ.

For further information on organ donation, contact the U.S. Department of Health and Human Services' organ donation site: www.organdonor.gov.

National Transplant Data

Registered U.S. Patients Waiting for Transplants
(as of May 21, 2000)

Kidney	45,273	Lung	3,614	Heart-Lung	209
Liver	15,359	Kidney-Pancreas	2,278	Pancreas Islet Cell	156
Heart	4,143	Pancreas	917	Intestine	124
				Total	**69,728**

NOTE: The number of registrants may be greater than the actual number of patients, since some patients are listed with more than one transplant center. *Source:* National Organ Procurement & Transplantation Network.

Number of U.S. Transplants Per Year, 1988–1999

	1988	1990	1993	1996	1999		1988	1990	1993	1996	1999
Heart	1,676	2,107	2,297	2,345	2,185	Kidney-	170	459	661	859	1,188
Heart-Lung	74	52	60	39	48	Pancreas					
Intestine	—	5	34	45	71	Liver	1,713	2,690	3,441	4,063	4,700
Kidney	8,873	9,416	10,359	11,317	12,529	Lung	33	203	668	810	901
						Pancreas	79	69	113	165	368
						Total	**12,618**	**15,001**	**17,633**	**19,643**	**21,990**

NOTE: Kidney-pancreas transplants are counted apart from kidney transplants and pancreas transplants and do not show up in the totals for the individual organs. Double kidney, double lung, and heart-lung transplants are each counted as one transplant. All other multi-organ transplants are included in the total for each individual organ. *Source:* National Organ Procurement & Transplantation Network.

Percent of U.S. Persons Not Covered by Health Insurance, by State, 1998

State	Percent	State	Percent	State	Percent
Alabama	17.0%	Louisiana	19.0%	Oklahoma	18.3%
Alaska	17.3	Maine	12.7	Oregon	14.3
Arizona	24.2	Maryland	16.6	Pennsylvania	10.5
Arkansas	18.7	Massachusetts	10.3	Rhode Island	10.0
California	22.1	Michigan	13.2	South Carolina	15.4
Colorado	15.1	Minnesota	9.3	South Dakota	14.3
Connecticut	12.6	Mississippi	20.0	Tennessee	13.0
Delaware	14.7	Missouri	10.5	Texas	24.5
D.C.	17.0	Montana	19.6	Utah	13.9
Florida	17.5	Nebraska	9.0	Vermont	9.9
Georgia	17.5	Nevada	21.2	Virginia	14.1
Hawaii	10.0	New Hampshire	11.3	Washington	12.3
Idaho	17.7	New Jersey	16.4	West Virginia	17.2
Illinois	15.0	New Mexico	21.1	Wisconsin	11.8
Indiana	14.4	New York	17.3	Wyoming	16.9
Iowa	9.3	North Carolina	15.0	**Total U.S.**	**16.3**
Kansas	10.3	North Dakota	14.2		
Kentucky	14.1	Ohio	10.4		

NOTE: These estimates should not be used to rank the states. Results from different samplings could easily show different estimates and rankings because of small sampling sizes. For example, the high noncoverage for Texas is not statistically different from that of New Mexico. *Source:* U.S. Census Bureau, *March 1999 Current Population Survey.*

America's Best Hospitals, 2000

The annual *U.S. News & World Report* list of the United States' best hospitals is prepared by the National Opinion Research Center at the University of Chicago. The list recognizes hospitals that excel in many areas.

1. Johns Hopkins Hospital, Baltimore, Md.
2. Mayo Clinic, Rochester, Minn.
3. Massachusetts General Hospital, Boston
4. Cleveland Clinic, Ohio
5. University of California, Los Angeles Medical Center
6. Duke University Medical Center, Durham, N.C.
7. Barnes-Jewish Hospital, St. Louis, Mo.
7. Stanford University Hospital, Calif.
9. Brigham and Women's Hospital, Boston, Mass.
10. Hospital of the University of Pennsylvania, Philadelphia
11. University of California, San Francisco Medical Center
12. University of Michigan Medical Center, Ann Arbor
13. University of Washington Medical Center, Seattle
14. University of Chicago Hospitals, Ill.
15. University of Pittsburgh Medical Center, Pa.

New Cases of Cancer and Survival Rates in the U.S.

Site	Estimated new cases,[1] 1997 (thousands)			Five-year relative survival rate (percent)							
				White				Black			
	Total	Male	Female	1974–78	1979–83	1984–88	1989–92	1974–78	1979–83	1984–88	1989–92
All Sites[2]	1,382	786	597	52.6%	53.8%	57.9%	62.7%	40.4%	40.6%	42.5%	46.7%
Lung	178	98	80	13.7	14.4	14.3	15.1	11.2	12.5	11.6	10.7
Breast[3]	182	1	180	76.1	77.7	83.5	86.9	63.6	65.1	67.9	71.2
Colon and rectum	131	66	65	52.5	56.3	62.0	63.8	45.7	48.7	51.5	53.2
Prostate	335	335	n.a.	71.0	76.2	83.6	94.6	62.8	63.4	68.7	79.6
Bladder	55	40	15	74.8	78.6	81.5	83.0	50.5	58.7	60.1	63.5
Corpus uteri	35	n.a.	35	88.7	84.3	85.9	87.6	60.8	54.3	57.7	56.2
Non-Hodgkin's lymphoma[4]	54	30	23	47.8	52.0	54.1	52.3	48.2	51.1	47.1	42.0
Oral cavity and pharynx	31	21	10	55.2	55.4	56.4	55.5	36.6	32.9	35.0	32.9
Leukemia[4]	28	16	12	36.3	38.5	42.5	43.1	31.6	31.5	34.5	29.1
Melanoma of skin	40	23	17	81.0	83.1	87.1	87.6	57.9	64.2	66.0	69.5
Pancreas	28	13	14	1.9	2.7	2.7	4.1	1.8	4.3	4.8	3.5
Kidney	29	17	12	54.9	56.1	61.6	64.3	53.4	58.4	57.4	59.3
Stomach	22	14	8	15.6	16.8	18.6	19.3	16.3	17.5	19.7	21.6
Ovary	27	n.a.	27	37.6	39.8	41.7	51.0	41.6	39.2	40.8	45.0
Cervix uteri[5]	15	n.a.	15	69.9	68.8	71.5	71.2	63.6	61.4	56.5	60.6

n.a. = not applicable. 1. Estimates provided by American Cancer Society are based on rates from the National Cancer Institute's SEER program. 2. Includes other sites not shown separately. 3. Survival rates for women only. 4. All types combined. 5. Invasive cancer only. *Source:* U.S. National Institutes of Health, National Cancer Institute, *Cancer Statistics Review*, annual.

Human Carcinogens

The *Ninth Report on Carcinogens*, published May 15, 2000, lists 218 substances known or suspected to cause cancer. The *Ninth Report* added (or upgraded) 14 substances, including secondhand smoke, alcoholic beverages, excessive sun, sun lamps, and tanning beds. Saccharin, the artificial sweetener, was removed from the list of suspected carcinogens; it had been listed since 1981.

Substances Known to Be Human Carcinogens

Aflatoxins
Alcoholic Beverage Consumption
4-Aminobiphenyl (4-Aminodiphenyl)
Analgesic Mixtures Containing Phen- acetin
Arsenic and Certain Arsenic Com- pounds
Asbestos
Azathioprine
Benzene
Benzidine
bis(Chloromethyl) Ether
1,3-Butadiene
1,4-Butanediol Dimethylsulfonate
Cadmium and Cadmium Compounds
Chlorambucil
1-(2-Chloroethyl)-3-(4-methylcyclohexyl)-1-nitrosourea (MeCCNU)

Chromium Hexavalent Compounds
Coke Oven Emissions
Conjugated Estrogens
Cyclophosphamide
Cyclosporin A
Diethylstilbestrol
Dyes that Metabolize to Benzidine
  Direct Black 38
  Direct Blue 6
Environmental Tobacco Smoke
Erionite
Ethylene Oxide
Melphalan
Methoxsalen with Ultraviolet A Therapy (PUVA)
Mustard Gas
2-Naphthylamine
Radon

Silica, Crystalline (Respirable Size)
  Quartz
  Cristobalite
  Tridymite
Smokeless Tobacco
Solar Radiation and Exposure to Sun Lamps or Sunbeds
Soots
Strong Inorganic Acid Mists Contain- ing Sulfuric Acid
Tamoxifen
Tars and Mineral Oils
Thiotepa
Thorium Dioxide
Tobacco Smoking
Vinyl Chloride

Source: Ninth Report on Carcinogens, The National Institute for Environmental Health Sciences.

Overview of Mental Illness

Source: Mental Health: A Report of the Surgeon General, 1999

Mental illness is a term rooted in history that refers collectively to all of the diagnosable mental disorders. Mental disorders are characterized by abnormalities in cognition, emotion or mood, or the highest integrative aspects of behavior, such as social interactions or planning of future activities.

This overview of mental illness focuses on the most common of these disorders.

Anxiety

Anxiety is one of the most readily accessible and easily understood of the major symptoms of mental disorders. Each of us encounters anxiety in many forms throughout the course of our routine activities. Anxiety has evolved as a vitally important physiological response to dangerous situations that prepares one to evade or confront a threat in the environment. However, the mechanisms that regulate anxiety may break down in a wide variety of circumstances, leading to excessive or inappropriate expression of anxiety. Specific examples include phobias, panic attacks, and generalized anxiety. In phobias, high-level anxiety is aroused by specific situations or objects that may range from concrete entities such as snakes, to complex circumstances such as social interactions or public speaking. Panic attacks are brief and very intense episodes of anxiety that often occur without a precipitating event or stimulus. Generalized anxiety represents a more diffuse and nonspecific kind of anxiety that is most often experienced as excessive worrying, restlessness, and tension occurring with a chronic and sustained pattern. In each case, an anxiety disorder may be said to exist if the anxiety experienced is disproportionate to the circumstance, is difficult for the individual to control, or interferes with normal functioning.

In addition to these common manifestations of anxiety, obsessive-compulsive disorder and post-traumatic stress disorder are generally believed to be related to the anxiety disorders. In the case of obsessive-compulsive disorder, individuals experience a high level of anxiety that drives their obsessional thinking or compulsive behaviors. When such an individual fails to carry out a repetitive behavior such as hand washing or checking, there is an experience of severe anxiety. Post-traumatic stress disorder is produced by an intense and overwhelmingly fearful event that is often life-threatening in nature. The characteristic symptoms that result from such a traumatic event include the persistent reexperience of the event in dreams and memories, persistent avoidance of stimuli associated with the event, and increased arousal.

Psychosis

Disturbances of perception and thought process fall into a broad category of symptoms referred to as psychosis. The threshold for determining whether thought is impaired varies somewhat with the cultural context. Like anxiety, psychotic symptoms may occur in a wide variety of mental disorders. They are most characteristically associated with schizophrenia, but psychotic symptoms can also occur in severe mood disorders.

One of the most common groups of symptoms that result from disordered processing and interpretation of sensory information are hallucinations. Hallucinations are said to occur when an individual experiences a sensory impression that has no basis in reality. Hallucinations may be auditory, olfactory, gustatory, kinesthetic, tactile, or visual. For example, auditory hallucinations frequently involve the impression that one is hearing a voice. In each case, the sensory impression is falsely experienced as real.

A more complex group of symptoms resulting from disordered interpretation of information consists of delusions. A delusion is a false belief that an individual holds despite evidence to the contrary. A common example is paranoia, in which a person has delusional beliefs that others are trying to harm him or her. Attempts to convince the person that these beliefs are unfounded typically fail and may even result in the further entrenchment of the beliefs.

Hallucinations and delusions are among the most commonly observed psychotic symptoms. Symptoms of schizophrenia are divided into two broad classes: positive symptoms and negative symptoms. Positive symptoms generally involve the experience of something in consciousness that should not normally be present. For example, hallucinations and delusions represent perceptions or beliefs that should not normally be experienced. In addition to hallucinations and delusions, patients with psychotic disorders such as schizophrenia frequently have marked disturbances in the logical process of their thoughts. Specifically, psychotic thought processes are characteristically loose, disorganized, illogical, or bizarre. The severe disturbances of thought content and process that comprise the positive symptoms often are the most recognizable and striking features of psychotic disorders such as schizophrenia or manic depressive illness.

Common signs of acute anxiety
- Feelings of fear or dread
- Trembling, restlessness, and muscle tension
- Rapid heart rate
- Lightheadedness or dizziness
- Perspiration
- Cold hands/feet
- Shortness of breath

Common manifestations of schizophrenia

Positive symptoms
- Hallucinations
- Delusions
- Disorganized thoughts and behaviors
- Loose or illogical thoughts
- Agitation

Negative symptoms
- Flat or blunted affect
- Concrete thoughts
- Anhedonia (inability to experience pleasure)
- Poor motivation, spontaneity, and initiative

However, in addition to positive symptoms, patients with schizophrenia and other psychoses have been noted to exhibit major deficits in motivation and spontaneity that are referred to as negative symptoms. While positive symptoms represent the presence of something not normally experienced, negative symptoms reflect the absence of thoughts and behaviors that would otherwise be expected. Concreteness of thought represents impairment in the ability to think abstractly. Blunting of affect refers to a general reduction in the ability to express emotion. Motivational failure and inability to initiate activities represent a major source of long-term disability in schizophrenia. Anhedonia reflects a deficit in the ability to experience pleasure and to react appropriately to pleasurable situations. Positive symptoms such as hallucinations are responsible for much of the acute distress associated with schizophrenia, but negative symptoms appear to be responsible for much of the chronic and long-term disability associated with the disorder.

Disturbances of Mood

Most of us have an immediate and intuitive understanding of the notion of mood. We readily comprehend what it means to feel sad or happy. These concepts are nonetheless very difficult to formulate in a scientifically precise and quantifiable way; the challenge is greater given the cultural differences that are associated with the expression of mood. Nevertheless, dysregulation of mood and the expression of mood, or affect, represent a major category among mental disorders.

Disturbances of mood characteristically manifest themselves as a sustained feeling of sadness or sustained elevation of mood. As with anxiety and psychosis, disturbances of mood may occur in a variety of patterns associated with different mental disorders. The disorder most closely associated with persistent sadness is major depression, while that associated with sustained elevation or fluctuation of mood is bipolar disorder. Along with the prevailing feelings of sadness or elation, disorders of mood are associated with a host of related symptoms that include disturbances in appetite, sleep patterns, energy level, concentration, and memory.

Disturbances of Cognition

Cognitive function refers to the general ability to organize, process, and recall information. Progressive deterioration of cognitive function is referred to as dementia. Dementia may be caused by a number of specific conditions including Alzheimer's disease.

Common signs of mood disorders

Symptoms commonly associated with depression
- Persistent sadness or despair
- Insomnia (sometimes hypersomnia)
- Decreased appetite
- Psychomotor retardation
- Anhedonia (inability to experience pleasure)
- Irritability
- Apathy, poor motivation, social withdrawal
- Hopelessness
- Poor self-esteem, feelings of helplessness
- Suicidal ideation

Symptoms commonly associated with mania
- Persistently elevated or euphoric mood
- Grandiosity (inappropriately high self-esteem)
- Psychomotor agitation
- Decreased sleep
- Racing thoughts and distractibility
- Poor judgment and impaired impulse control
- Rapid or pressured speech

It is not uncommon to find profound disturbances of cognition in patients suffering from severe mood disturbances. More recently, cognitive deficits have been reported in schizophrenia and now have become a major new topic of research. Last, cognitive impairment frequently occurs in a host of chemical, metabolic, and infectious diseases that exert an impact on the brain.

Other Symptoms

Anxiety, psychosis, mood disturbances, and cognitive impairments are among the most common and disabling manifestations of mental disorders. It is important, however, to appreciate that mental disorders leave no aspect of human experience untouched. Other common manifestations include, for example, somatic or other physical symptoms and impairment of impulse control.

Diagnosis of Mental Illness

The standard manual used for diagnosis of mental disorders in the United States is the *Diagnostic and Statistical Manual of Mental Disorders*. Most recently revised in 1994, this manual, first published in 1952, is now in its fourth edition. *DSM-IV* organizes mental disorders into 16 major diagnostic classes. *DSM-IV* is descriptive in its listing of symptoms and does not take a position about underlying causation.

Major diagnostic classes of mental disorders *(DSM-IV)*

- Delirium, dementia, and amnestic and other cognitive disorders
- Mental disorders due to a general medical condition
- Substance-related disorders
- Schizophrenia and other psychotic disorders
- Mood disorders
- Anxiety disorders
- Somatoform disorders
- Factitious disorders
- Dissociative disorders
- Sexual and gender identity disorders
- Eating disorders
- Sleep disorders
- Impulse-control disorders
- Adjustment disorders
- Personality disorders

Caffeine Content of Selected Foods and Drugs

Product	Serving size[1]	Caffeine (mg)	Product	Serving size[1]	Caffeine (mg)
Over-the-counter			Dr. Pepper, regular		
Excedrin	2 tablets	130	or diet	12 ounces	41
Anacin	2 tablets	64	Sunkist Orange Soda	12 ounces	40
Coffees			Pepsi-Cola	12 ounces	37
Coffee, brewed	8 ounces	135	7-UP or Diet 7-UP	12 ounces	0
Coffee, instant	8 ounces	95	Minute Maid Orange		
Coffee, decaffeinated	8 ounces	5	Soda	12 ounces	0
Starbucks coffee grande	16 ounces	550	Sprite or Diet Sprite	12 ounces	0
Teas			7-Eleven Big Gulp cola	64 ounces	190
Tea, leaf or bag	8 ounces	50	**Frozen desserts and yogurt**		
Snapple Iced Tea,			Ben & Jerry's No Fat		
all varieties	16-ounce bottle	48	Coffee Fudge Frozen		
Lipton Iced Tea,			Yogurt	1 cup	85
assorted varieties	16-ounce bottle	18–40	Häagen-Dazs Coffee Ice		
Tea, green	8 ounces	30	Cream	1 cup	58
Tea, instant	8 ounces	15	Dannon Coffee Yogurt	8 ounces	45
Celestial Seasonings			Stonyfield Farm		
Herbal Tea, all varieties	8 ounces	0	Cappuccino Yogurt	8 ounces	0
Soft drinks			**Chocolates or candies**		
Mountain Dew	12 ounces	55	Hershey Bar, 1 bar	1.5 ounces	10
Diet Coke	12 ounces	47	Cocoa or hot chocolate	8 ounces	5
Coca-Cola	12 ounces	45			

1. Serving sizes are based on commonly eaten portions, pharmaceutical instructions, or the amount of the leading-selling container size. *Source:* Center for Science in the Public Interest. Reprinted/Adapted from *Nutrition Action Healthletter* (1875 Connecticut Ave., NW., Suite 300, Washington, DC 20009–5728. $24.00 for 10 issues.)

Smoking-Related Mortality

An estimated 48 million adults in the United States smoke cigarettes, even though this behavior will result in death or disability for half of all regular users. Cigarette smoking is the single most preventable cause of premature death in the United States. Each year, more than 430,000 Americans die from cigarette smoking. In fact, one in every five deaths in the United States is smoking related.

• About 10 million people in the United States have died from causes attributed to smoking (including heart disease, emphysema, and other respiratory diseases) since the first surgeon general's report on smoking and health in 1964—2 million of these deaths were the result of lung cancer alone.

• Between 1960 and 1990, deaths from lung cancer among women have increased by more than 400%—exceeding breast cancer deaths in the mid-1980s. Smoking triples the risk of dying from heart disease among middle-aged men and women.

• On average, smokers die nearly seven years earlier than nonsmokers.

• Approximately 80% of adult smokers started smoking before the age of 18. Every day, nearly 3,000 young people under the age of 18 become regular smokers.

Smoking Prevalence among U.S. Adults, 1955–1995
(as a percent of population, 18 years of age and older)

In 1995, 48 million adults 18 years of age and older (25.3 million men, 22.7 million women) were current smokers in the U.S. Smoking among adults decreased dramatically from 42% in 1965 to 26% in 1994. During this period, smoking among the adult male population declined from 52% to 28%; adult female smoking declined from 34% to 23%.

Year	Overall population	Males	Females	Whites	Blacks
1955	—	56.9%	28.4%	—	—
1965	42.4%	51.9	33.9	42.1%	45.8%
1970	37.4	44.1	31.5	37.0	41.4
1974	37.1	43.1	32.1	36.4	44.0
1978	34.1	38.1	30.7	33.9	37.7
1980	33.2	37.6	29.3	32.9	36.9
1985	30.1	32.6	27.9	29.6	34.9
1987	28.8	31.2	26.5	28.5	32.9
1988	28.1	30.8	25.7	27.8	31.7
1990	25.5	28.4	22.8	25.6	26.2
1991	25.7	28.1	23.5	25.5	29.1
1992	26.5	28.6	24.6	26.6	27.8
1993	25.0	27.7	22.5	24.9	26.1
1994	25.5	28.2	23.1	26.3	27.2
1995	24.7	27.0	22.6	24.8	25.7

Source: Office on Smoking and Health, Centers for Disease Control and Prevention.

Age of First Marijuana Use, 1965–1997

Year	Number of 1st time users (in 1000s)	Mean age	First time use (per 1,000) by age 12–17	18–25	26–34	Year	Number of 1st time users (in 1000s)	Mean age	First time use (per 1,000) by age 12–17	18–25	26–34
1965	617	18.8	9.2	13.4	4.9	1982	2080	18.2	50.5	45.8	9.1
1966	900	20.3	11.2	23.4	2.7	1983	2044	17.8	54.9	42.4	3.5
1967	1467	19.9	15.2	40.9	6.9	1984	1994	19.6	51.2	38.8	3.9
1968	1590	19.1	18.5	44.8	3.7	1985	1767	17.8	48.7	39.1	1.5
1969	2218	19.2	32.2	52.3	5.4	1986	1871	19.4	50.4	41.9	3.0
1970	2668	19.3	35.8	64.8	10.7	1987	1817	17.9	49.2	43.2	2.3
1971	2799	18.8	42.5	66.7	12.5	1988	1526	17.3	43.0	37.7	1.7
1972	2897	18.4	52.0	63.5	9.5	1989	1413	17.8	37.6	34.2	2.4
1973	2782	18.2	55.5	58.4	8.0	1990	1401	17.3	37.2	37.0	1.4
1974	3008	18.6	57.2	62.0	9.9	1991	1376	17.5	36.6	33.9	1.7
1975	3185	18.8	69.4	55.1	12.8	1992	1701	17.7	45.5	39.3	2.8
1976	2824	18.5	61.3	53.4	10.4	1993	1949	17.0	53.9	46.3	2.2
1977	2884	19.3	66.5	48.6	10.1	1994	2393	16.7	73.3	47.9	2.7
1978	2879	17.8	76.9	50.7	7.1	1995	2406	16.6	74.6	50.7	2.4
1979	2585	18.0	61.4	55.4	4.1	1996	2540	16.4	83.2	53.6	1.3
1980	2492	18.6	58.2	57.1	5.3	1997	2114	17.1	64.4	47.1	1.4
1981	2218	17.8	57.0	46.2	4.8						

Source: U.S. Substance Abuse and Mental Health Services Administration (SAMHSA), Office of Applied Studies, *National Household Survey on Drug Abuse.*

Drug Use by Americans, 12 Years and Older

Type of drug	Ever used 1979	1990	1996	Current user 1979	1990	1996
Marijuana and hashish	27.9%	30.5%	32.0%	13.2%	5.4%	4.7%
Cocaine	8.6	11.2	10.3	2.6	0.9	0.8
Inhalants	n.a.	5.7	5.6	n.a.	0.4	0.4
Hallucinogens	8.9	7.9	9.7	1.9	0.4	0.6
Heroin	1.3	0.8	1.1	0.1	—	0.1
Stimulants	n.a.	5.5	4.7	n.a.	0.6	0.4
Sedatives	n.a.	2.8	2.3	n.a.	0.2	0.1
Tranquilizers	n.a.	4.0	3.6	n.a.	0.6	0.4
Analgesics	n.a.	6.3	5.5	n.a.	0.9	0.9
Alcohol	88.5	82.2	82.6	63.2	52.6	51.0
Cigarettes	n.a.	75.4	71.6	n.a.	32.6	28.9

Current users are those who used drugs at least once within month prior to this study. *Source:* U.S. Substance Abuse and Mental Health Services Administration (SAMHSA), Office of Applied Studies, *National Household Survey on Drug Abuse.*

Heavy Alcohol Use, by Age Group, Race/Ethnicity, and Sex: 1985–1998

Demographic characteristics	1985	1990	1992	1993	1994	1995	1996	1997	1998
Total	8.3%	6.3%	6.2%	6.7%	6.2%	5.5%	5.4%	5.4%	5.9%
Age group									
12–17	9.5	4.4	3.4	3.4	2.5	2.8	2.9	3.1	2.9
18–25	13.8	14.9	15.1	14.0	13.2	12.0	12.9	11.1	13.8
26–34	11.5	8.2	8.5	8.5	8.0	7.9	7.1	7.5	7.2
≥35	5.2	3.7	3.9	5.0	4.8	3.9	3.8	4.0	4.4
Race/Ethnicity									
White	9.1	6.7	6.8	7.5	6.4	5.7	5.5	5.7	6.0
Black	3.5	4.1	3.5	3.3	4.8	4.6	5.3	3.8	4.9
Hispanic	7.1	5.9	6.3	6.0	7.3	6.3	7.2	6.3	6.5
Other	—	—	2.2	1.9	4.7	2.4	2.1	2.3	4.7
Sex									
Male	13.8	10.8	10.1	11.9	10.3	9.4	13.8	8.9	9.7
Female	3.2	2.1	2.7	1.9	2.5	2.0	1.9	2.1	2.4

NOTE: Heavy alcohol use is defined as drinking five or more drinks on the same occasion on each of five or more days in the past 30 days. *Source:* U.S. Substance Abuse and Mental Health Services Administration (SAMHSA), Office of Applied Studies, *National Household Survey on Drug Abuse.*

The Common Cold

Source: National Institute of Allergy and Infectious Diseases, National Institutes of Health

The problem. Adults average about two to four colds a year, although the range varies widely. Women, especially those aged 20–30 years, have more colds than men, possibly because of their closer contact with children. On average, individuals older than 60 have fewer than one cold a year. Colds are most prevalent among children, and seem to be related to youngsters' relative lack of resistance to infection and to contacts with other children in day-care centers and schools. Children have about 6–10 colds a year.

The causes: viruses. More than 200 different viruses are known to cause the symptoms of the common cold. **Rhinoviruses** (from the Greek *rhin,* meaning nose) cause an estimated 30 to 35 percent of all adult colds, and are most active in early fall, spring, and summer. **Coronaviruses** are believed to cause a large percentage of all adult colds. They induce colds primarily in the winter and early spring. Of the more than 30 isolated strains, three or four infect humans.

Does cold weather cause a cold? Although many people are convinced that a cold results from exposure to cold weather, or from getting chilled or overheated, these conditions in fact have little or no effect on the development or severity of a cold.

How cold viruses cause disease. Viruses cause infection by overcoming the body's complex defense system. The body's first line of defense is mucus, produced by the membranes in the nose and throat. Mucus traps the material we inhale: pollen, dust, bacteria, and viruses. When a virus penetrates the mucus and enters a cell, it commandeers the protein-making machinery to manufacture new viruses, which, in turn, attack surrounding cells.

Cold symptoms: the body fights back. Cold symptoms are probably the result of the body's immune response to the viral invasion. Virus-infected cells in the nose send out signals that recruit specialized white blood cells to the site of the infection. In turn, these cells emit a range of immune system chemicals such as kinins. These chemicals probably lead to the symptoms of the common cold by causing swelling and inflammation of the nasal membranes, leakage of proteins and fluid from capillaries and lymph vessels, and the increased production of mucus.

How colds are spread. Depending on the virus type, any or all of the following routes of transmission may be common:

• Touching infectious respiratory secretions on the skin and on environmental surfaces and then touching the eyes or nose.

• Inhaling relatively large particles of respiratory secretions transported briefly in the air.

• Inhaling droplet nuclei, smaller infectious particles suspended in the air for long periods of time.

Prevention. Handwashing is the simplest and most effective way to keep from getting rhinovirus colds. Not touching the nose or eyes is another. Individuals with colds should always sneeze or cough into a facial tissue, and promptly throw it away. If possible, one should avoid close, prolonged exposure to persons who have colds.

Treatment. Only symptomatic treatment is available for uncomplicated cases of the common cold: bed rest, plenty of fluids, gargling with warm salt water, applying petroleum jelly to a raw nose, and taking aspirin or acetaminophen to relieve headache or fever.

Nonprescription cold remedies, including decongestants and cough suppressants, may relieve some cold symptoms but will not prevent, cure, or even shorten the duration of illness. Nonprescription antihistamines may have some effect in relieving inflammatory responses such as runny nose and watery eyes.

Antibiotics do not kill viruses. These prescription drugs should be used only for rare bacterial complications, such as sinusitis or ear infections, that can develop as secondary infections.

Does vitamin C have a role? Many people are convinced that taking large quantities of vitamin C will prevent colds or relieve symptoms. To test this theory, several large-scale, controlled studies involving children and adults have been conducted. To date, no conclusive data has shown that large doses of vitamin C prevent colds. The vitamin may reduce the severity or duration of symptoms, but there is no definitive evidence.

Is It a Cold or the Flu?

Symptoms	Cold	Flu
fever	rare	characteristic, high (102–104° F); lasts 3–4 days
headache	rare	prominent
general aches, pains	slight	usual; often severe
fatigue, weakness	quite mild	can last up to 2–3 weeks
extreme exhaustion	never	early and prominent
stuffy nose	common	sometimes
sneezing	usual	sometimes
sore throat	common	sometimes
chest discomfort, cough	mild to moderate; hacking cough	common; can become severe

Source: National Institute of Allergy and Infectious Diseases.

The Genome Is Mapped: Now What?

A scientific milestone ushers in a new age of medicine

**By MICHAEL D. LEMONICK and
MATT RIDLEY** TIME

After more than a decade of dreaming, planning, and heroic number crunching, two groups that had been locked in a bitter race to solve the mystery of human genetics reached the finish line on June 26, 2000, with the joint announcement that they had deciphered essentially all the 3.4 billion biochemical "letters" of human DNA, the coded instructions for building and operating a fully functional human. The competitors—the Human Genome Project, funded by the U.S. and British governments and headed by Dr. Francis Collins, and the private firm Celera Genomics, headed by controversial researcher Dr. Craig Venter—were brought together after a diplomatic effort engineered by the White House. The two groups reached, if not a meeting of the minds, at least a workable understanding—and a framework for the historic joint announcement.

It is impossible to overstate the scientific significance of this achievement. Armed with the human genetic code, researchers can now start teasing out the secrets of human health and disease at the molecular level—secrets that will lead at the very least to a revolution in diagnosing and treating everything from Alzheimer's to heart disease to cancer, and more. In a matter of decades, the world of medicine may well be utterly transformed, and history books will mark the year 2000 as the ceremonial start of the genomic era.

Autobiography of a Species

The genome is a sort of autobiographical record, written in "genetish," of all the vicissitudes and inventions that have characterized the history of our species and its ancestors since the dawn of life. Genes have already told us that we are the closest relatives of chimpanzees; that the common ancestor of fruit flies and people was a 600 million-year-old segmented worm with the ability to learn; that the Basques are as unrelated to other Eurasians as their language implies and may be descended from indigenous European hunter-gatherers. Genes can even tell us a bit about "LUCA," the Last Universal Common Ancestor of all life, a single-celled microbe that lived about 4 billion years ago.

Unlike other autobiographies, the genome contains stories about the future as well as the past. Among the genes are clear messages about what will happen to your body as you age, a few of which we can already read. There is a gene, for example, that can alter one's susceptibility to Alzheimer's disease elevenfold, depending on whether its 334th letter is G or A. The idea of the genome as a book—longer than 800 Bibles yet so small that there are trillions of copies inside each one of us—is not a metaphor. It is literally true. A book is a piece of digital information, written in linear, one-dimensional, and one-directional form and defined by a code that transliterates a small alphabet of signs into a large lexicon of meanings through the order of their groupings. So is a genome. And the decoding of this book should give scientists a tool that will transform the way humans understand and protect their health.

Race to Decode the Genome

The two competing organizations approached their work in very different ways. The government scientists broke their DNA samples into segments of about 150 million letters long (the overall genome has some 3.1 billion letters). These were subdivided into segments of about 6,000 letters each, to be read by sequencing machines. In the final step, the pieces were reassembled into their original order on the chromosomes. Venter and the scientists at Celera, by contrast, took a more radical approach, smashing the DNA into millions of pieces, then feeding each piece into new high-speed robotic sequencers. By the end of March, Celera had all of them read, though they were not reassembled for another six weeks. So the announcement of the mapping, while historic, was a rather murky milestone, for the work is not yet really complete. What the scientists at Celera have done is sequence about 97% of the genome, and the remaining 150 million or so letters won't be deciphered anytime soon. The HGP is even further behind; unlike Celera, it hasn't put its strings of letters into proper order yet. This loose end should be cleared up in a year or two, but even then the so-called book of life will remain unreadable. That's because, explains Gerald Rubin, vice president for biomedical research at the Howard Hughes Medical Institute, "It's written in a foreign language. It's a very complicated problem. It's going to be a long time coming."

Tip of the Molecular Iceberg

Molecular biologists still know so little about the human genome, in fact, that even with some 85% of the sequence published on the HGP's GenBank Web site for every scientist in the world to see, nobody has even a ballpark figure for how many genes humans have. Before the June announcement, the betting ranged from as few as 28,000 to as many as 140,000. Now it looks more like 50,000.

Beyond that, knowing the code for a gene doesn't mean you know what protein it produces in the body, or what that protein does, or how it interacts with other proteins—vital information if you want to know how the genetic code locked in our cells ends up constructing and maintaining a fully functioning human being.

Given this seemingly overwhelming ignorance, why did everyone make such a fuss? Because laying out the biochemical code for all our genes, however many there turn out to be, and locating them within the 23 chromosomes in the human genome may turn out to be the necessary first step to solving all these mysteries. The hope is that the completed genome will enable scientists to lay bare the genetic triggers for hundreds of diseases—from Alzheimer's to diabetes to heart disease—and to devise exquisitely sensitive diagnostic tests. It will help pharmaceutical companies create drugs tailored to a patient's genetic profile, boosting effectiveness while drastically reducing side effects. It could change our very conception of what a disease is, replacing broad categories—breast cancer, for example—with precise genetic definitions that make diagnosis sure and treatment swift. And while it's true that researchers can and have sequenced individual genes, they had to use a process that was expensive and terribly laborious—like writing your own reference book before you can start any real experiments. Having the sequences laid out in advance gives the scientific world a big head start.

Those sequences are so useful, in fact, that researchers started tapping into the data long before they were complete. Scientists at drug firms, biotech companies, and university labs have taken literally hundreds of baby steps into the era of genomic medicine using an impressive array of powerful new tools: DNA chips and microarrays that let scientists see at a glance which of thousands of genes are active in a given tissue sample; sophisticated software that can organize gigabytes of genetic data; huge databases of genes, disease-tissue samples, and mRNA—the molecules that initiate the actual construction of working proteins. "The announcement of finishing the genome is to us a mini-event," says Allen Roses, worldwide director of genetics for Glaxo Wellcome. "We've been making use of the information as it has become available, and we've already done some proof of the concept that finding genes for disease and developing the right drug for the right patient will actually work."

Putting the New Findings to Work

One scientist whose work has been transformed by genomics is Dr. David Altshuler, an endocrinologist at Massachusetts General Hospital who does research at M.I.T.'s Whitehead Institute. A diabetes expert, he wanted to learn more about a gene known to be involved in adult-onset (Type II) diabetes and obesity. He knew that the gene was about 100,000 chemical letters—or base pairs—long, and that only about 2,000 of those directed the production of a protein. Hidden somewhere in the remaining 98,000 base pairs are instructions that govern how much protein gets churned out—an essential clue for developing eventual treatments for diabetics. But before the public project's data began going up on GenBank, finding the hidden code would have been, says Altshuler, "an ungodly, unacceptable amount of work."

In the spring of 2000, Altshuler simply went to the public database, fed in the 2,000 base pairs he already knew about, and asked the computer: Is the rest of the gene sequenced? "For four months," he says, "we went back every week, and the answer

was 'nope, nope, nope.' Then one week, all of a sudden, there it was," he says, "all 100,000 base pairs in a row—a year, two years' work handed to us, all before lunch." His next step was to look at the same gene in the mouse, taking advantage of the fact that the noncoding portions of the genome in man and mouse are 75% similar. Three weeks after pulling the gene's human sequence off GenBank, Altshuler lined up the mouse and man genes side by side and spotted five regions that were active in both. Now he's going to focus on these five regions as possible targets for drug design, figuring this is where the regulatory action is likely to be.

Fighting Cancer

Another Whitehead scientist, oncologist Dr. Todd Golub, is trying to improve on the primitive techniques doctors use to guide their fight against cancer. Currently, pathologists use the location of a tumor in the patient's body and its appearance under a microscope to determine what sort of malignancy is involved. It works often—but not always. Melanoma, for example, starts out as a skin cancer but may end up in the lung or breast, where it can be much more damaging than lung or breast cancer.

Proof at the genetic level that origin means more than location is coming in. Researchers at Stanford have been studying liver, breast, prostate, and lung cancers for clues to their telltale molecular fingerprints. Using microarrays to sense which genes are turned on in sample tissues, says geneticist Charles Perou, the Stanford team has discovered that most of the genes expressed by both normal breast cells and primary-breast-cancer cells are similar, and so are cells for normal lung tissue and lung cancer, normal prostate and prostate cancer, and so on—which should ultimately give doctors biochemical identifiers to guide their treatments.

What's Next?

These sorts of tightly focused studies are already beginning to make cancer treatment more effective. "Right now," says Stanford biochemist Patrick Brown, "it's like watching a movie on TV a few pixels at a time and trying to figure out the overall story. Having the complete genome sequence is something categorically different, like going from 100 scattered pixels on your screen to having the whole image. There will be a substantial increase in the rate at which discoveries are made."

Maybe too much of an increase, argues Tom Delbanco, chair of general medicine at Harvard Medical School. "Discovery is intoxicating," he says. "But the consequences of discovery are often complex, and instead of progress, it can lead to disaster." Delbanco is worried that the revolution in genetic medicine may further drain the limited amount of time that physicians have to spend with patients and add even more costs to the already expensive health-care system. Yet while Delbanco's fears may be justified—and while the genetic revolution has raised plenty of other troubling issues—its promise is so huge that putting on the brakes may be impossible. The age of genomic medicine is here; the sequencing of the human genome just marks its ceremonial beginning. □

The Nation's Highest Science and Technology Honors

The National Medal of Science

The National Medal of Science, established by Congress in 1959, is administered by the National Science Foundation. The medal honors the contributions made by outstanding individuals who have significantly advanced knowledge in the following fields: physics, biology, chemistry, mathematics, engineering, and sociology and other behavioral sciences.

The 1999 National Medal of Science and Medal of Technology recipients were announced by President Clinton on Jan. 31, 2000.

1999 National Medal of Science Recipients

David Baltimore, Nobel laureate and professor of biology and president, California Institute of Technology, for far-reaching, fundamental discoveries that dramatically altered the field of study in virology, molecular biology, and immunology, for excellence in building scientific institutions, and for fostering communication between scientists and the general public.

Jared Diamond, professor of physiology, UCLA School of Medicine, for seminal research in applying Darwinian evolutionary approaches to the disparate fields of physiology, ecology, conservation biology, and human history, and for outstanding efforts in communicating science.

Lynn Margulis, Distinguished University Professor, Department of Geosciences, University of Massachusetts, Amherst, for outstanding contributions to the understanding of the structure and evolution of living cells, and for extraordinary abilities as a teacher and communicator of science to the public.

Stuart A. Rice, Frank P. Hixon, Distinguished Service Professor, The James Franck Institute, The University of Chicago, for changing the very nature of modern physical chemistry through his research, teaching, and writing, and for using imaginative approaches to both experiment and theory that have inspired a new generation of scientists.

John Ross, professor of chemistry, Stanford University, for his enormous impact in physical chemistry, especially in molecular studies, statistical mechanics, and nonlinear kinetics, and for opening up new fields in chemical science.

Susan Solomon, senior scientist, Aeronomy Laboratory, National Oceanic and Atmospheric Administration (NOAA), Boulder, Colorado, for key insights into explaining the cause of the Antarctic ozone "hole" that changed the direction of ozone research and for providing exemplary service to worldwide public policy on ozone research.

Robert M. Solow, Nobel laureate and Institute Professor Emeritus, Massachusetts Institute of Technology, for creating the modern framework for analyzing the effects of investment and technological progress on economic growth, which has greatly influenced economics and economic policy worldwide.

Kenneth N. Stevens, C. J. LeBel Professor of Electrical Engineering, Massachusetts Institute of Technology, for pioneering contributions to the theory, mathematical methods, and analysis of acoustics in speech production, and establishing the contemporary foundations of speech science.

Felix E. Browder, Professor, Rutgers University, Piscataway, N.J., for pioneering mathematical work in the creation of nonlinear functional analysis, opening up new avenues in nonlinear problems, and for being a leader in the scientific community in broadening the range of interactions among disciplines.

Ronald R. Coifman, Phillips Professor of Mathematics, Yale University, for fundamental contributions to the field of harmonic analysis and for adapting that field to produce a family of fast, robust computational tools that have substantially benefited science and technology.

James W. Cronin, Nobel laureate and University Professor Emeritus, The Enrico Fermi Institute, The University of Chicago, for fundamental contributions to the fields of elementary particle physics and astrophysics and for leading an international effort to determine the unknown origins of very high-energy cosmic rays.

Leo P. Kadanoff, John D. and Catherine T. MacArthur Distinguished Service Professor, The James Franck Institute, The University of Chicago, for leadership in fundamental theoretical research in statistical, solid-state, and nonlinear physics, which has led to numerous and important applications in engineering, urban planning, computer science, hydrodynamics, biology, applied mathematics, and geophysics.

The National Medal of Technology

The National Medal of Technology, established by Congress in 1980, is administered by the U.S. Department of Commerce. The medal is awarded for technological innovation and the advancement of U.S. global competitiveness. The medal also recognizes groundbreaking contributions that commercialize a technology, create jobs, improve productivity, or stimulate the nation's growth and development in other ways.

1999 National Medal of Technology Recipients

Glen Jacob Culler, chief scientist and chairman of the board (retired), Culler Scientific Systems Corporation, for pioneering innovations in multiple branches of computing, including early efforts in digital speech processing, invention of the first online system for interactive graphical mathematics computing, and pioneering work on the ARPAnet.

Raymond Kurzweil, founder, chairman and chief executive officer, Kurzweil Technologies, Inc., for pioneering achievements in computer science, such as voice recognition, which have overcome many barriers and enriched the lives of disabled persons and all Americans.

Robert A. Swanson (deceased), chairman of K & E Management, Ltd., for his foresight and leadership in recognizing the commercial promise of recombinant DNA technology and his seminal role in the establishment and development of the biotechnology industry.

Robert W. Taylor, retired, for visionary leadership in the development of modern computing technology, including the ARPAnet, the personal computer, and the graphical user interface.

Symbol Technologies, Inc., for creating the global market for laser bar-code scanning and for technical innovation in and practical application of mobile computing and wireless local area network technologies.

Major Discoveries about Human Ancestors

Living and extinct human beings and their near human ancestors are called "hominids" and belong to the *Hominidae* family of primates. They are not to be confused with "hominoids," which belong to the *Hominoidea* family of primates and include apes and humans. Scientists theorize that the human and ape lines branched off from a common ancestor 8 million to 6 million years ago.

Years ago	Species	Discovered	Remarks
c. 4.4 million	*Ardipithecus ramidus*	1994 in Aramis, Ethiopia	Oldest known human ancestor. Had chimpanzee-like skull
c. 4.2 million	*Australopithecus anamensis*	1995, two sites at Lake Turkana in Kenya: Kanapoi and Allia Bay	Possible ancestor of *A. afarensis* (Lucy). Walked upright
c. 3.2 million	*Australopithecus afarensis*	1974 at Hadar in the Afar triangle of eastern Ethiopia; Laetoli, Tanzania	Nicknamed "Lucy." Her skeleton was 3.5 feet (100 cm.) tall. Had apelike skull. Walked fully upright. Lived in family groups throughout eastern Africa
c. 2.5 million	*Australopithecus africanus*	1924 at Taung, northern Cape Province, South Africa	Descendant of "Lucy." Lived in social groups
c. 2 million	*Australopithecus robustus*	1938 in Kromdraai, South Africa	Was related to *A. africanus*
c. 2 million	*Homo habilis* ("skillful man")	1960 in Olduvai Gorge, Tanzania	First brain expansion; is believed to have used stone tools
c. 1.8 million	*Homo erectus* ("upright man")	1891 at Trinil, Java, Indonesia	Brain size twice that of *australopithecine* species. Controversy exists whether "Java Man," as he was called, is a direct ancestor of *Homo sapiens* or instead developed on a separate evolutionary tract. He is, however, the first hominid to use fire and the hand ax, and to live in caves
c. 100,000(?)	*Homo sapiens* ("knowing or wise man")	1868, Cro-Magnon, France	Anatomically modern humans

Scientific Classification

Classification, or taxonomy, is a system of categorizing living things. There are seven divisions in the system: (1) Kingdom; (2) Phylum or Division; (3) Class; (4) Order; (5) Family; (6) Genus; (7) Species. Kingdom is the broadest division. There is no consensus about the number of kingdoms, though most scientists support a four-kingdom (Animalia, Plantae, Protista, and Monera) or five-kingdom (Animalia, Plantae, Protista, Monera, and Fungi) system. The lowest, most basic division is species, which consists of organisms that resemble each other and are capable of interbreeding to produce fertile offspring. Species are identified by two names (binomial nomenclature). The first is the genus, the second is the species. □

Classification of the Dinosaurs

Dinosaurs ("terrible lizards") belong to a large group of reptiles called Archosauria ("ruling reptiles"). They are classified into two distinct orders, which are distinguished by their pelvic differences.

Saurischia ("lizard hipped"). All members of this order had modern lizardlike pelvises and clawed feet. Saurischians roamed Earth from the Middle Triassic to the end of the Cretaceous period. They included carnivores and plant eaters. Members of the order included Allosaurus ("different lizard"), Apatosaurus ("deceptive lizard"), which was formerly called Brontosaurus, and Tyrannosaurus ("tyrant lizard"). The group is divided into two suborders: **Theropoda** ("beast footed") and **Sauropodomorpha** ("lizard-footed forms"). The Velociraptor ("swift robber") was a theropod.

Ornithiscia ("bird hipped"). All Ornithischian dinosaurs had pelvises similar to those of modern birds, and hoofed toes. All were herbivores. These dinosaurs lived throughout the world from the Middle Triassic to the end of the Cretaceous period. Members of the order included Iguanodon ("iguana tooth"), Stegosaurus ("plated lizard"), and Triceratops ("three-horned face"). The order is divided into four suborders: **Ornithopoda** ("bird footed"), **Stegosauria** ("plated lizards"), **Ankylosauria** ("armored lizards"), and **Certopsia** ("horned faces").

Tyrannosaurus Sue

The prehistoric giant stands again

Sue is a sensation. It's not just that she's 42 feet long and 65 million years old. She's the world's most complete, best preserved, and largest *Tyrannosaurus rex* skeleton. More than 10,000 visitors went to her May 17, 2000, debut at Chicago's Field Museum of Natural History.

Many brought their cameras—and a few brought violins. The Chicago Chamber Musicians performed a new piece, written especially for the opening, called "Tyrannosaurus Sue: A Cretaceous Concerto." (*T. rex* lived during the Cretaceous period, not the Jurassic period, as many believe.)

Rest in Pieces

Amazingly, more than 200 of Sue's bones were preserved. The skeleton includes the most complete *T. rex* tail ever found, as well as one of only two *T. rex* arms ever found. Sue's skull contains the longest (and scariest) *T. rex* tooth yet known—it's a foot long.

One amazing discovery in Sue's skeleton is that she has a wishbone, or furcula, such as you would find in most bird skeletons. This is the first wishbone found on a *T. rex*. It supports the theory that birds evolved from dinosaurs, either directly or from a common ancestor.

Even though Sue's bones are more than 65 million years old, they are so well preserved that you can see marks where muscles and tendons once lay.

Slow, But Deadly

Studies of Sue's foot bones have indicated that *T. rex* probably walked at about 6 mph and ran at not more than 15 mph, much slower than previously thought.

The lead researcher on Sue says that the way the *T. rex* moved in the movie *Jurassic Park* was probably very accurate. Most likely *T. rex* bent over so that its huge tail did not touch the ground, and walked on its toes—*T. rex* is *digitigrade,* meaning it walks on its toes like a cat. (People are *plantigrade,* meaning we walk flat-footed.)

But the movie was wrong in suggesting that *T. rex* would have to see its prey move in order to find it—from studying Sue, researchers have determined that *T. rex* had an excellent sense of smell. Sue's skull reveals that in a *T. rex* brain the olfactory nodes were much larger than the cerebrum.

Sue or Sir?

Tyrannosaurus Sue was named for Sue Hendrickson, the fossil hunter who found the skeleton in 1990. But although the skeleton is generally referred to as a "she," no one really knows whether Tyrannosaurus Sue was male or female. The skeleton's very large size could suggest that the dinosaur was female, because among birds of prey—*T. rex*'s closest ancestors—females are generally larger than males.

Senior Sue

Throughout her life Sue suffered some hard knocks, including broken ribs and an injured arm. Although scientists do not know exactly what illnesses dinosaurs had, it looks as though Sue was affected by an age-related disease much like arthritis. "Here is a very, very old dinosaur that just got sick and died after a long, active life," says John Flynn, a Field Museum paleontologist.

Just how old was she? Scientists don't know for sure how long a *T. rex* might have lived. Says Flynn, "We know turtles and crocodiles can live to 150 years, and they are cold-blooded. We know some birds, which are warm-blooded, can live for many decades. My guess is that dinosaurs could live for decades, some 100 years or more."

Queen of the Dinosaurs

For many of the researchers who have gotten to know Sue, the discovery of the massive *T. rex* was the event of a lifetime. "It's truly a dream fossil," says Tony Wentz, who worked to dig Sue out of the ground and helped prepare her skeleton for the exhibit. "It's the best of the best, the biggest, the most well-preserved. Everything you could ever want in digging a dinosaur was in Sue."

Tyrannosaurus rex Classification		
Kingdom	Animalia	animal
Phylum	Chordata	has a nerve cord ending at a brain
Class	Archosauria	has hollow teeth, special ankles, pointy head
Order	Saurischia	"lizard-hipped"
Suborder	Theropoda	walks on two feet, eats meat
Family	Tyrannosauroidea	a predator with tiny forelimbs ("arms")
Genus	Tyrannosaurus	"tyrant lizard"
Species	rex	"king"

Table of Geological Periods

It is now generally assumed that planets are formed by the accretion of gas and dust in a cosmic cloud, but there is no way of estimating the length of this process. Our Earth acquired its present size, more or less, between 4 billion and 5 billion years ago. Life on Earth originated about 2 billion years ago, but there are no good fossil remains from periods earlier than the Cambrian, which began about 550 million years ago. The largely unknown past before the Cambrian Period is referred to as the Pre-Cambrian and is subdivided into the Lower (or older) and Upper (or younger) Pre-Cambrian—also called the Archaeozoic and Proterozoic Eras.

The known geological history of Earth since the beginning of the Cambrian Period is subdivided into three eras, each of which includes a number of periods. They, in turn, are subdivided into subperiods. In a subperiod, a certain section may be especially well known because of rich fossil finds. Such a section is called a formation, and it is usually identified by a place name.

Paleozoic Era

This era began 570 million years ago and lasted for 325 million years. The name was compounded from Greek *palaios* (old) and *zoön* (animal).

Period	Duration[1]	Subperiods	Events
Cambrian (from *Cambria*, Latin name for Wales)	60	Lower Cambrian Middle Cambrian Upper Cambrian	Invertebrate sea life of many types, proliferating during this and the following period
Ordovician (from Latin *Ordovices*, people of early Britain)	70	Lower Ordovician Upper Ordovician	First known fishes
Silurian (from Latin *Silures*, people of early Wales)	30	Lower Silurian Upper Silurian	Gigantic sea scorpions
Devonian (from Devonshire in England)	50	Lower Devonian Upper Devonian	Proliferation of fishes and other forms of sea life; land still largely lifeless
Carboniferous (from Latin *carbo* = coal + *fero* = to bear)	70	Lower or Mississippian Upper or Pennsylvanian	Period of maximum coal formation in swampy forests; early insects and first known amphibians
Permian (from district of Perm in Russia)	45	Lower Permian Upper Permian	Early reptiles and mammals; earliest form of turtles

1. In millions of years.

Mesozoic Era

This era began 245 million years ago and lasted for 180 million years. The name was compounded from Greek *mesos* (middle) and *zoön* (animal). Popular name: Age of Reptiles.

Period	Duration[1]	Subperiods	Events
Triassic (from *trias* = triad)	37	Lower or Buntsandstein (from German *bunt* = colorful + *sandstein* = sandstone). Middle or Muschelkalk (from German *muschel* = shell + *kalk* = limestone). Upper or Keuper (old miner's term)	Early saurians
Jurassic (from Jura Mountains)	62	Lower or Black Jurassic, or Lias (from French *liais* = hard stone) Middle or Brown Jurassic, or Dogger (old provincial English for ironstone) Upper or White Jurassic, or Malm (Middle English for sand)	Many seagoing reptiles; early large dinosaurs; somewhat later, flying reptiles (pterosaurs), earliest known birds
Cretaceous (from Latin *creta* = chalk)	81	Lower Cretaceous Upper Cretaceous	Maximum development of dinosaurs; birds proliferating; opossumlike mammals

1. In millions of years.

Cenozoic Era

This era began 65 million years ago and includes the geological present. The name was compounded from Greek *kainos* (new) and *zoön* (animal). Popular name: Age of Mammals.

Period	Duration[1]	Subperiods	Events
Tertiary (originally thought to be the third of only three periods)	c. 65	Paleocene (from Greek *palaios* = old + *kainos* = new). Eocene (from Greek *eos* = dawn + *kainos* = new). Oligocene (from Greek *oligos* = few + *kainos* = new). Miocene (from Greek *meios* = less + *kainos* = new). Pliocene (from Greek *pleios* = more + *kainos* = new)	First mammals other than marsupials. Formation of amber, rich insect fauna, early bats, steady increase of large mammals. Mammals closely resembling present types; protohumans
Pleistocene (from Greek *pleistos* = most + *kainos* = new) (popular name: Ice Age)	2.0	Four major glaciations, named Günz, Mindel, Riss, and Würm, originally the names of rivers. Last glaciation ended 10,000 to 15,000 years ago	Various forms of early humans
Holocene (from Greek *holos* = entire + *kainos* = new)	0.01	The last 10,000 years to the present	Earliest written documents c. 3200 B.C., Sumer

1. In millions of years.

The Elements

Elements are the building blocks of nature. Water, for example, is a compound consisting of the elements hydrogen and oxygen. Each element is a pure substance that cannot be split up into any simpler pure substance.

The smallest particle of an element that can exist is an atom. An atom consists of subatomic particles. The most important of these are protons, which have positive electrical charges; electrons, which have negative electrical charges; and neutrons, which are electrically neutral.

The atomic number of an element is the number of protons in one atom of the element. Each element

has a different atomic number. For example, the atomic numbers of hydrogen and oxygen are 1 and 8, respectively.

Elements with atomic numbers 1 (hydrogen) to 94 (plutonium) occur naturally on Earth. The remaining artificial elements have been created since 1940 by using nuclear reactors and particle accelerators. Element 100 is named fermium. Elements with atomic numbers 101 onward are known as the transfermium elements. They are also known as heavy elements because their atoms have very large masses compared with atoms of hydrogen, the lightest of all elements.

Chemical Elements

Element	Symbol	Atomic no.	Atomic wt.	Specific gravity	Melting point °C	Boiling point °C	No. of isotopes[1]	Discoverer	Year
Actinium	Ac	89	227[2]	10.07[2]	1050	3200±300	11	Debierne	1899
Aluminum	Al	13	26.9815	2.6989	660.37	2467	8	Wöhler	1827
Americium	Am	95	243[6]	13.67	994±4	2607	13[3]	Seaborg et al.	1944
Antimony	Sb	51	121.75	6.61	630.74	1750	29	Early historic times	—
Argon	Ar	18	39.948	1.7837[4]	−189.2	−185.7	8	Rayleigh and Ramsay	1894
Arsenic (gray)	As	33	74.9216	5.73	817	613[5]	14	Albertus Magnus	1250?
Astatine	At	85	210	—	302	337	21	Corson et al.	1940
Barium	Ba	56	137.34	3.5	725	1640	25	Davy	1808
Berkelium	Bk	97	247[6]	14.00[7]	—	—	8[3]	Seaborg et al.	1949
Beryllium	Be	4	9.01218	1.848	1278±5	2970	6	Vauquelin	1798
Bismuth	Bi	83	208.9806	9.747	271.3	1560±5	19	Geoffroy	1753
Bohrium	Bh	107	262	—	—	—	—	Armbruster and Münzenberg	1981
Boron	B	5	10.81	2.37[8]	2300	2550[5]	6	Gay-Lussac and Thénard; Davy	1808
Bromine	Br	35	79.904	3.12[4]	−7.2	58.78	19	Balard	1826
Cadmium	Cd	48	112.40	8.65	320.9	765	22	Stromeyer	1817
Calcium	Ca	20	40.08	1.55	839±2	1484	14	Davy	1808
Californium	Cf	98	251[6]	—	—	—	12[3]	Seaborg et al.	1950
Carbon	C	6	12.011	1.8-3.5[9]	−3550	4827	7	Prehistoric	—
Cerium	Ce	58	140.12	6.771	798±3	3257	19	Berzelius and Hisinger; Klaproth	1803
Cesium	Cs	55	132.9055	1.873	28.40	678.4	22	Bunsen and Kirchoff	1860
Chlorine	Cl	17	35.453	1.56[4]	−100.98	−34.6	11	Scheele	1774
Chromium	Cr	24	51.996	7.18-7.20	1857±20	2672	9	Vauquelin	1797
Cobalt	Co	27	58.9332	8.9	1495	2870	14	Brandt	c.1735
Copper	Cu	29	63.546	8.96	1083.4±0.2	2567	11	Prehistoric	—
Curium	Cm	96	247[6]	13.51[2]	1340±40	—	13[3]	Seaborg et al.	1944
Dubnium	Db	105	262	—	—	—	—	Ghiorso et al.	1970
Dysprosium	Dy	66	162.50	8.540	1409	2335	21	Boisbaudran	1886
Einsteinium	Es	99	254[6]	—	—	—	12[3]	Ghiorso et al.	1952
Erbium	Er	68	167.26	9.045	1522	2510	16	Mosander	1843
Europium	Eu	63	151.96	5.283	822±5	1597	21	Demarcay	1896
Fermium	Fm	100	257[6]	—	—	—	10[3]	Ghiorso et al.	1953
Fluorine	F	9	18.9984	1.108[4]	−219.62	−188.14	6	Moissan	1886
Francium	Fr	87	223[6]	—	27[2]	677[2]	21	Perey	1938
Gadolinium	Gd	64	157.25	7.898	1311±1	3233	17	Marignac	1880
Gallium	Ga	31	69.72	5.904	29.78	2403	14	Boisbaudran	1875
Germanium	Ge	32	72.59	5.323	937.4	2830	17	Winkler	1886
Gold	Au	79	196.9665	19.32	1064.43	2807	21	Prehistoric	—
Hafnium	Hf	72	178.49	13.31	2227±20	4602	17	Coster and von Hevesy	1923
Hassium	Hs	108	265	—	—	—	—	Armbruster and Münzenberg	1983
Helium	He	2	4.00260	0.1785[4]	−272.2	−268.934	5	Janssen	1868
Holmium	Ho	67	164.9303	8.781	1470	2720	29	Delafontaine and Soret	1878
Hydrogen	H	1	1.0080	0.070[4]	−259.14	−252.87	3	Cavendish	1766
Indium	In	49	114.82	7.31	156.61	2080	34	Reich and Richter	1863
Iodine	I	53	126.9045	4.93	113.5	184.35	24	Cortois	1811
Iridium	Ir	77	192.22	22.42	2410	4130	25	Tennant	1803
Iron	Fe	26	55.847	7.894	1535	2750	10	Prehistoric	—
Krypton	Kr	36	83.80	3.733[4]	−156.6	−152.30±0.10	23	Ramsay and Travers	1898
Lanthanum	La	57	138.9055	6.166	920±5	3454	19	Mosander	1839
Lawrencium	Lr	103	257[6]	—	—	—	20[3]	Ghiorso et al.	1961
Lead	Pb	82	207.2	11.35	327.502	1740	29	Prehistoric	—

Element	Symbol	Atomic no.	Atomic wt.	Specific gravity	Melting point °C	Boiling point °C	No. of isotopes[1]	Discoverer	Year
Lithium	Li	3	6.941	0.534	180.54	1347	5	Arfvedson	1817
Lutetium	Lu	71	174.97	9.835	1656±5	3315	22	Urbain	1907
Magnesium	Mg	12	24.305	1.738	648.8±0.5	1090	8	Black	1755
Manganese	Mn	25	54.9380	7.21–7.44[10]	1244±3	1962	11	Gahn, Scheele, and Bergman	1774
Meitnerium	Mt	109	266	—	—	—	—	GSI, Darmstadt, West Germany	1982
Mendelevium	Md	101	256[6]	—	—	—	3[3]	Ghiorso et al.	1955
Mercury	Hg	80	200.59	13.546	−38.87	356.58	26	Prehistoric	—
Molybdenum	Mo	42	95.94	10.22	2617	4612	20	Scheele	1778
Neodymium	Nd	60	144.24	6.80 & 7.004[10]	1010	3127	16	von Welsbach	1885
Neon	Ne	10	20.179	0.89990 (g/10°C/1 atm)	−248.67	−246.048	8	Ramsay and Travers	1898
Neptunium	Np	93	237.0482	20.25	6400±1	3902	15[3]	McMillan and Abelson	1940
Nickel	Ni	28	58.71	8.902	1453	2732	11	Cronstedt	1751
Niobium (Columbium)	Nb	41	92.9064	8.57	2468±10	4742	24	Hatchett	1801
Nitrogen	N	7	14.0067	0.808[4]	−209.86	−195.8	8	Rutherford	1772
Nobelium	No	102	254[6]	—	—	—	7[3]	Ghiorso et al.	1957
Osmium	Os	76	190.2	22.57	3045±30	5027±100	19	Tennant	1803
Oxygen	O	8	15.9994	1.14[4]	−218.4	−182.962	8	Priestley	1774
Palladium	Pd	46	106.4	12.02	1552	3140	21	Wollaston	1803
Phosphorous (white)	P	15	30.9738	1.82	44.1	280	7	Brand	1669
Platinum	Pt	78	195.09	21.45	1772	3827±100	32	Ulloa	1735
Plutonium	Pu	94	244[6]	19.84	641	3232	16[3]	Seaborg et al.	1940
Polonium	Po	84	210[6]	9.32	254	962	34	Curie	1898
Potassium	K	19	39.102	0.862	63.65	774	10	Davy	1807
Praseodymium	Pr	59	140.9077	6.772	931±4	3212	15	von Weisbach	1885
Promethium	Pm	61	145[6]	≈1080	2460	14	Marinsky et al.	1945
Protactinium	Pa	91	231.0359	15.37[2]	<1600	—	14	Hahn and Meitner	1917
Radium	Ra	88	226.0254	5.0?	700	1140	15	Pierre and Marie Curie	1898
Radon	Rn	86	222[6]	4.44	−71	−61.8	20	Dorn	1900
Rhenium	Re	75	186.2	21.02	3180	5627[7]	21	Noddack, Berg, and Tacke	1925
Rhodium	Rh	45	102.9055	12.41	1966±3	3727±100	20	Wollaston	1803
Rubidium	Rb	37	85.4678	1.532	38.89	688	20	Bunsen and Kirchoff	1861
Rutherfordium	Rf	104	261	—	—	—	—	Ghiorso et al.	1969
Ruthenium	Ru	44	101.07	12.44	2310	3900	16	Klaus	1844
Samarium	Sm	62	150.4	7.536	1072±5	1778	17	Boisbaudran	1879
Scandium	Sc	21	44.9559	2.989	1539	2832	15	Nilson	1879
Seaborgium	Sg	106	263	—	—	—	—	Ghiorso et al.	1974
Selenium (gray)	Se	34	78.96	4.79	217	684.9±1	20	Berzelius	1817
Silicon	Si	14	28.086	2.33	1410	2355	8	Berzelius	1824
Silver	Ag	47	107.868	10.5	961.93	2212	27	Prehistoric	—
Sodium	Na	11	22.9898	0.971	97.81±0.03	882.9	7	Davy	1807
Strontium	Sr	38	87.62	2.54	769	1384	18	Davy	1808
Sulfur	S	16	32.06	2.07[11]	112.8	444.674	10	Prehistoric	—
Tantalum	Ta	73	180.9479	16.654	2996	5425±100	19	Ekeberg	1801
Technetium	Tc	43	98.062	11.50[2]	2172	4877	23	Perrier and Segré	1937
Tellurium	Te	52	127.60	6.24	449.5±0.3	989.8±3.8	29	von Reichenstein	1782
Terbium	Tb	65	158.9254	8.234	1360±4	3041	24	Mosander	1843
Thallium	Tl	81	204.37	11.85	303.5	1457±10	28	Crookes	1861
Thorium	Th	90	232.0381	11.72	1750	4790	12	Berzelius	1828
Thulium	Tm	69	168.9342	9.314	1545±15	1727	18	Cleve	1879
Tin (white)	Sn	50	118.69	7.31	231.9681	2270	28	Prehistoric	—
Titanium	Ti	22	47.90	4.55	1660±10	3287	9	Gregor	1791
Tungsten	W	74	183.85	19.3	3410±20	5660	22	J. and F. d'Elhuyar	1783
Uranium	U	92	238.029	19.05	1132.3±0.8	3818	15	Peligot	1841
Vanadium	V	23	50.9414	6.11	1890±10	3380	9	del Rio	1801
Xenon	Xe	54	131.30	3.52[4]	−111.9	−107.1±3	31	Ramsay and Travers	1898
Ytterbium	Yb	70	173.04	6.972	824±5	1193	16	Marignac	1878
Yttrium	Y	39	88.9059	4.457	1523±8	3337	21	Gadolin	1794
Zinc	Zn	30	65.38	7.133	419.58	907	15	Prehistoric	—
Zirconium	Zr	40	91.22	6.506[2]	1852±2	4377	20	Klaproth	1789

NOTES: Elements 110, 111, 112, 114, 116, and 118 have not yet been named and are thus not included. ≈ means "approximately." < means "less than." 1. Isotopes are different forms of the same element having the same atomic number but different atomic weights. 2. Calculated figure. 3. Artificially produced. 4. Liquid. 5. Sublimation point. 6. Mass number of the isotope of longest known life. 7. Estimated. 8. Amorphous. 9. Depending on whether amorphous, graphite, or diamond. 10. Depending on allotropic form.

Roundup of Recent Discoveries

Ice Age Haute Couture

According to recent research by archaeologists at the University of Illinois at Urbana-Champaign, the well-dressed Ice Age woman's outfit doesn't resemble anything like the crude hide and fur garments that Wilma Flintstone wore. Instead, the warm weather clothing of at least some of our ancestors included caps or snoods, belts, skirts, bandeaux (banding over the breasts), bracelets, and necklaces—all constructed of plant fibers in a great variety of woven textiles.

The finest weaves of Ice Age seamstresses are comparable not only to Neolithic but even later Bronze and Iron Age products and, in fact, to some of the thin cotton and linen worn today. The new evidence comes in part from a study of 80 textile impressions found on tiny clay fragments in the Czech Republic. The impressions are the earliest evidence for cordage and textile production in the world and reflect technologies heretofore only associated with fine garments of later periods.

Antisocial Brain Tissue Deficit

University of Southern California researchers studied 21 men who were all diagnosed with Antisocial Personality Disorder (APD), which is characterized by irresponsibility, deceitfulness, impulsiveness, irritability, lack of emotional depth and conscience, and lifelong antisocial behavior. All of the subjects had committed serious violent crimes. Using brain-imaging techniques, researchers found that the antisocial men had an 11%–14% reduction in the volume of nerve cells in the prefrontal cortex compared to normal males.

The prefrontal cortex is the brain's foremost outer portion, located right behind the eyes. This region seems to house the mental machinery that enables most people to learn moral sensibilities and to exercise self-restraint. Previous research has shown that convicted murderers and other violent offenders have poor functioning in that region. The new findings demonstrate that a physical abnormality may underlie the poor functioning in these violent antisocial men and that society may have to rethink how it regards violent crime, punishment, and the scope of free will.

New Orleans, the New Atlantis?

According to projections by the U.S. Geological Survey, the city of New Orleans may be submerged under water by the year 2100 due to subsidence (the natural sinking of land), wetland loss, predicted sea-level rise, and an absence of proper restoration programs.

Researchers at the University of New Orleans have spent years identifying the problems causing the catastrophic coastal conditions. Currently, 40% of all coastal wetlands in the United States are located in Louisiana, and 80% of all wetland loss in the nation occurs in Louisiana. From 1930 to 1990, the Mississippi River Delta lost more than 1,000 square miles of land. The current land loss rate is approximately 25 square miles (16,000 acres) of wetlands per year, and the city of New Orleans is sinking three feet per century.

Despite the city's bleak future, researchers have shown that the coastal ecosystem, while damaged, is sufficiently intact for restoration efforts to manage the problem.

Snow Falling on Water

A team of researchers have discovered that when a snowflake falls onto a body of water, it deposits a tiny amount of air just beneath the surface. Before the bubble reaches the surface and pops, it sends out a piercing sound. This sound, ranging from 50 to 200 kilohertz, is too high-pitched to be heard by human ears, which generally pick up nothing higher than 20 kilohertz. However, to porpoises and other aquatic animals that can hear the higher frequencies, the falling snowflakes create an enormous racket just below the surface. Falling snow can add 30 decibels to underwater noise levels. Beyond its deafening impact on water animals, snowflake noise can create "electronic clutter" for people who use sensitive sonar devices.

First Cloned Piglets

The U.S. staff of PPL Therapeutics, Scotland, cloned five healthy female piglets, born on March 5, 2000, in Blacksburg, Virginia. This is the first time cloned pigs have been produced from adult pig cells. Their birth marks the first step in making genetically modified pigs whose organs and cells can be successfully transplanted into humans without being rejected by the human immune system. The process of xenotransplantation (the transfer of organs from one species to another) may one day solve the worldwide organ shortage problem.

Our Tiniest Ancestor

In March 2000, a team of researchers led by Northern Illinois University paleontologist Dan Gebo announced their discovery of the fossil bones of 45-million-year-old monkeylike primates, the smallest primates ever found. The new species, named *Eosimias* ("dawn monkey"), was discovered in a limestone quarry in eastern China.

Its foot bones are the size of grains of rice, and it weighs less than a dozen paper clips. Yet the miniature "Dawn Monkey" could represent an evolutionary link between lower primates and higher primates, a group that includes apes and humans. The structure of its tiny ankle bones suggests that it could walk flat-footed, using all four legs, like advanced primates. Unlike advanced primates, however, it probably "didn't have a lot of time to be social," guesses one scientist. That's because the little animal had to spend most of its time eating to feed its high-speed metabolism—when it wasn't trying to avoid being eaten by bigger creatures. The discovery of this specimen in Asia suggests that our earliest ancestors did not live in Africa alone, as previously thought.

Snakes with Legs?

The fossil of a new species of snake with small front and hind limbs was found in 95-million-year-old deposits near Jerusalem. The site was once an ancient marine environment, suggesting a seafaring lifestyle for the fossilized snake. Dubbed *Haasiophis terrasanctus,* it is the second limbed species of primitive snake to come from there.

The first such species, *Pachyrhachis problematicus,* is thought by some paleontologists to be a transitional link between mosasaurs—gigantic swimming lizards of the Cretaceous period—and true snakes. This view of snakes originating in the sea contrasts with the traditional view that snake ancestors were small terrestrial or burrowing lizards who eventually lost their legs through evolution.

A group of scientists from the Field Museum in Chicago and the Hebrew University of Jerusalem have concluded that the new species was closely related to *Pachyrhachis.* Each of the fossil animals has a hinged upper jaw and a skull that completely surrounds the brain, feaures not found in lizards.

Our Ancestors Were Knuckle-Walkers

A new study by Brian Richmond and David Strait of George Washington University that scrutinized the fossilized wrist joints of two of our earliest known human ancestors, *A. afarensis* (best known as "Lucy") and *A. anamensis,* concluded that our earliest known human ancestors probably walked on their knuckles in a way similar to modern chimpanzees and gorillas. This discovery lends support to the theory that humans didn't evolve from tree dwellers, but from ancestors who were already adapted to walking on the ground.

The researchers compared the fossilized wrist joints from known human ancestors with the wrist joints of other primates. The wrist anatomy of Lucy and her cousins resembles that of chimpanzees and gorillas in having features that buttress the wrist joint and help to lock the wrist into a stable position so that the animal can support its weight on its fingers. It was not until the later species, *A. africanus,* at 2 to 3 million years ago, that evidence of a more humanlike, flexible wrist joint exists.

Solar "Heartbeat" Discovered

Astronomers from the National Science Foundation's National Solar Observatory have discovered a "solar heartbeat" in the motion of the layers of gas circulating beneath the Sun's surface. Their research shows that some parallel layers speed up and slow down rhythmically about every 16 months. This internal cyclic action may explain the formation of sunspots and solar flares.

The Sun is not a solid object—it is made up of layers of gas. Unlike Earth, all points on the solar surface do not rotate at the same rate. Its equatorial region rotates once every 27 days, while the regions at the Sun's poles rotate at a slower rate of once every 35 days. The "differential" rotation extends through the Sun's turbulent convective layer, located about 130,494 miles (210,000 kilometers) below the surface, nearly one-third of the distance to the solar core. At the edge of the convective layer, the rotation period varies, completing a cycle about every 15–16 days. Astronomers think that the patterns of these internal movements are connected to the cycles of eruptions seen on the surface.

New Killer Crater

Geoscientists at the Geological Survey of Western Australia and the Australian National University discovered the world's fourth-largest asteroid impact crater in western Australia. Buried beneath the redsand country east of Shark Bay, the huge crater centered on Woodleigh Station is estimated to be 75 miles (120 kilometers) in diameter. It is the result of a massive 3.1-mile- (5-kilometer-) wide asteroid that smashed into Earth some 200–360 million years ago. The impact would probably have resulted in an extinction event similar to the Chicxulub impact in the Gulf of Mexico, which has been linked to the extinction of the dinosaurs at the end of the Cretaceous period, 65 million years ago.

The Woodleigh crater's estimated age probably coincides with one of three extinction events known in the fossil record: the Late Devonian extinction (364 million years), the end of the Permian period (247 million years), or the end of the Triassic period (214 million years).

Awesome Ape-Man Find

In April 2000, scientists at the University of Witwatersrand, South Africa, announced the discovery of two early hominid fossils excavated in the Sterkfontein caves, 4 miles (7 kilometers) northwest of Johannesburg. The fossils comprise the most complete female skull ever found of her species, together with the lower jawbone of a male. The 1.5- to 2-million-year-old pair were christened Orpheus and Eurydice (after the ancient Greek mythological lovers). They were identified as *Paranthropus* ("beside man") *robustus,* a type of Australopithecine ("ape man") known for its huge teeth. They were not direct descendants of modern humans but were a line of hominids that became extinct one million years ago.

For the first time, scientists now know what a male and female *Paranthropus* looked like and what the differences were between male and female skulls. The top of the male's skull features a ridge, called a sagittal crest, to which the muscles of the lower jaw were anchored. The female, apart from being smaller than the male, has no such crest—a distinction echoed among male and female gorillas today.

Orpheus and Eurydice were largely vegetarians but may have included some meat in their diet from scavenged kills. They may even have used tools.

It's a Smaller World After All

New calculations made by University of Washington scientists for Earth's mass were reported in May 2000. According to UW physicists Jens Gundlach and Stephen Merkowitaz, Earth weighs in at 5.972 sextillion (5,972 followed by 18 zeros) metric tons. Recent textbooks list the weight as 5.98 sextillion metric tons. Either way, that's about one trillion metric tons for each person on Earth.

To make their precise measurements, the researchers used a computer-controlled device called a torsion balance that records nearly imperceptible accelerations from the gravitational effects of four 8.14-kilogram (18-pound) stainless-steel balls on a 7.62-by-3.81-centimeter (3-by-1.5-inch) gold-coated Pyrex plate just 1.5 millimeters (0.591 inches) thick.

Monster Asteroid

Astronomers using the world's most powerful radio telescope at Arecibo, Puerto Rico, have captured radar images of a giant, dog-bone–shaped asteroid located in the main asteroid belt between Mars and Jupiter. They are the first images ever made of a main-belt asteroid. The unusual space rock, named *216 Kleopatra*, measures about 135 miles (217 kilometers) long and about 58 miles (94 kilometers) wide, roughly the size of the state of New Jersey.

Although the massive asteroid was discovered in 1880, its peculiar dog-bone or distorted dumbbell-like shape was unknown until now. Its strange appearance could have been produced by an incredibly violent collision between two asteroids that did not completely shatter and disperse all the fragments. Or it may once have comprised two separate lobes in orbit around each other with empty space between them, and subsequent impacts filled in the space with debris.

Radar observations of *Kleopatra* seem to indicate that its surface is porous and loosely consolidated. Its interior appears to be composed of mostly solid metal fragments, possibly an nickel-iron alloy.

First Out-of-Africa Ancestors

A team of Georgian, German, French, and U.S. researchers reported finding a nearly complete fossil cranium and another skullcap representing the earliest known human ancestors from Eurasia, at a site in Dmanisi, Georgia. The 1.7-million-year-old fossils are the first discovered outside of Africa that show clear signs of African ancestry.

Their age and skeletal characteristics link them to the early African species *Homo ergaster*, a species that some scientists believe is the African version of *Homo erectus*. The new evidence suggests that they may have been the first hominid species to journey out of Africa.

Stone tools of the less sophisticated "pebble-chopper type," predating the Acheulean or hand-ax

tradition, were found in the sediment with the skulls, contradicting the theory that early humans didn't leave Africa until after they had invented technically advanced tools. Despite the ready availability of raw material, all of the Dmanisi artifacts found at the site are of a pre-Acheulean type that appeared in Africa as early as 2.4 million years ago. Stone Age tools featuring hand-axes, cleavers, scrapers, and sharp stone flakes are called Acheulean (from St. Acheul in France).

Rare Arctic Asteroid

On January 18, 2000, an estimated 23-foot-(7-meter-) wide, 250-metric-ton fireball as bright as the Sun streaked across the skies of western Canada and exploded with an estimated yield of 5–10 thousand tons of TNT. Scientists were able to pick up the remnants of the brilliant meteor—the first time freshly fallen meteor pieces were quickly recovered and brought to a lab untouched, on ice, and never thawed.

The Yukon meteor fragments were identified as carbonaceous chondrites, the most pristine, organically rich meteorites known. Carbonaceous chondrites are rare and difficult to recover because they are so fragile, easily breaking down during entry into Earth's atmosphere and during weathering on the ground. They comprise only about 2 percent of all meteorites known to have fallen to Earth.

Formidable Fungus

What is probably the largest living organism on Earth has been discovered by scientists in the Malheur National Forest in the Blue Ridge Mountains of eastern Oregon. A fungus living three feet underground is estimated to cover 2,200 acres. Officially known as the *Armillaria ostoyae,* or the honey mushroom, the fungus is 3.5 miles across and takes up an astonishing 1,665 football fields. The small mushrooms visible growing above ground are only the tip of the iceberg. Experts estimate that the giant mushroom is at least 2,400 years old, but possibly as old as 7,200 years. By testing samples from various locations, scientists determined that the enormous growth is all one organism. Previously, the world's largest organism was believed to be another *Armillaria ostoyae* living near Mt. Adams in Washington State.   □

Inventions & Discoveries

See also Famous Firsts in Aviation, Nobel Prizes.

Adrenaline: (isolation of) John Jacob Abel, U.S., 1897.

Aerosol can: Erik Rotheim, Norway, 1926.

Air brake: George Westinghouse, U.S., 1868.

Air conditioning: Willis Carrier, U.S., 1911.

Airship: (non-rigid) Henri Giffard, France, 1852; (rigid) Ferdinand von Zeppelin, Germany, 1900.

Aluminum manufacture: (by electrolytic action) Charles M. Hall, U.S., 1866.

Anatomy, human: (*De fabrica corporis humani,* an illustrated systematic study of the human body) Andreas Vesalius, Belgium, 1543; (comparative: parts of an organism are correlated to the functioning whole) Georges Cuvier, France, 1799–1805.

Anesthetic: (first use of anesthetic—ether—on humans) Crawford W. Long, U.S., 1842.

Antibiotics: (first demonstration of antibiotic effect) Louis Pasteur, Jules-François Joubert, France, 1887; (discovery of penicillin, first modern antibiotic) Alexander Fleming, England, 1928; (penicillin's infection-fighting properties) Howard Florey, Ernst Chain, England, 1940.

Antiseptic: (surgery) Joseph Lister, England, 1867.

Antitoxin, diphtheria: Emil von Behring, Germany, 1890.

Appliances, electric: (fan) Schuyler Wheeler, U.S., 1882; (flatiron) Henry W. Seely, U.S., 1882; (stove) Hadaway, U.S., 1896; (washing machine) Alva Fisher, U.S., 1906.

Aqualung: Jacques-Yves Cousteau, Emile Gagnan, France, 1943.

Aspirin: Dr. Felix Hoffman, Germany, 1899.

Astronomical calculator: The Antikythera device, first century B.C., Greece. Found off island of Antikythera in 1900.

Atom: (nuclear model of) Ernest Rutherford, England, 1911.

Atomic theory: (ancient) Leucippus, Democritus, Greece, c. 500 B.C.; Lucretius, Rome c.100 B.C.; (modern) John Dalton, England, 1808.

Atomic structure: (formulated nuclear model of atom, Rutherford model) Ernest Rutherford, England, 1911; (proposed current concept of atomic structure, the Bohr model) Niels Bohr, Denmark, 1913.

Automobile: (first with internal combustion engine, 250 rpm) Karl Benz, Germany, 1885; (first with practical high-speed internal combustion engine, 900 rpm) Gottlieb Daimler, Germany, 1885; (first true automobile, not carriage with motor) René Panhard, Emile Lavassor, France, 1891; (carburetor, spray) Charles E. Duryea, U.S., 1892.

Autopilot: (for aircraft) Elmer A. Sperry, U.S., c.1910, first successful test, 1912, in a Curtiss flying boat.

Avogadro's law: (equal volumes of all gases at the same temperature and pressure contain equal number of molecules) Amedeo Avogadro, Italy, 1811.

Bacteria: Anton van Leeuwenhoek, The Netherlands, 1683.

Balloon, hot-air: Joseph and Jacques Montgolfier, France, 1783.

Barbed wire: (most popular) Joseph E. Glidden, U.S., 1873.

Bar codes: (computer-scanned binary signal code): (retail trade use) Monarch Marking, U.S. 1970; (industrial use) Plessey Telecommunications, England, 1970.

Barometer: Evangelista Torricelli, Italy, 1643.

Bicycle: Karl D. von Sauerbronn, Germany, 1816; (first modern model) James Starley, England, 1884.

Big Bang theory: (the universe originated with a huge explosion) George LeMaitre, Belgium, 1927; (modified LeMaitre theory labeled "Big Bang") George A. Gamow, U.S., 1948; (cosmic microwave background radiation discovered, confirms theory) Arno A. Penzias and Robert W. Wilson, U.S., 1965.

Blood, circulation of: William Harvey, England, 1628.

Boyle's law: (relation between pressure and volume in gases) Robert Boyle, Ireland, 1662.

Braille: Louis Braille, France, 1829.

Bridges: (suspension, iron chains) James Finley, Pa., 1800; (wire suspension) Marc Seguin, Lyons, 1825; (truss) Ithiel Town, U.S., 1820.

Bullet: (conical) Claude Minié, France, 1849.

Calculating machine: (logarithms: made multiplying easier and thus calculators practical) John Napier, Scotland, 1614; (slide rule) William Oughtred, England, 1632; (digital calculator) Blaise Pascal, 1642; (multiplication machine) Gottfried Leibniz, Germany, 1671; (important 19th-century contributors to modern machine) Frank S. Baldwin, Jay R. Monroe, Dorr E. Felt, W. T. Ohdner, William Burroughs, all U.S.; ("analytical engine" design, included concepts of programming, taping) Charles Babbage, England, 1835.

Calculus: Isaac Newton, England, 1669; (differential calculus) Gottfried Leibniz, Germany, 1684.

Camera: (hand-held) George Eastman, U.S., 1888; (Polaroid Land) Edwin Land, U.S., 1948.

"Canals" of Mars: Giovanni Schiaparelli, Italy, 1877.

Carpet sweeper: Melville R. Bissell, U.S., 1876.

Car radio: William Lear, Elmer Wavering, U.S., 1929, manufactured by Galvin Manufacturing Co., "Motorola."

Cells: (word used to describe microscopic examination of cork) Robert Hooke, England, 1665; (theory: cells are common structural and functional unit of all living organisms) Theodor Schwann, Matthias Schleiden, 1838–1839.

Cement, Portland: Joseph Aspdin, England, 1824.

Chewing gum: (spruce-based) John Curtis, U.S., 1848; (chicle-based) Thomas Adams, U.S., 1870.

Cholera bacterium: Robert Koch, Germany, 1883.

Science Web Sites

National Science Foundation: www.nsf.gov
National Academy of Sciences: www.nas.edu
American Association for the Advancement of Science: www.aaas.org/
Federation of American Scientists: www.fas.org
The Franklin Institute Science Museum: sln.fi.edu
Science News Online: www.sciencenews.org
Popular Science: www.popsci.com
Periodic Table of Elements: WebElements Periodic Table: www.webelements.com
Dinosauria Online: www.dinosauria.com/
Discovery Channel Online: www.discovery.com
Fermilab: www.fnal.gov/
Argonne National Laboratory: www.anl.gov/
American Geophysical Union: www.agu.org
American Museum of Natural History: www.amnh.org
Newton (for K–12 teachers and students): www.newton.dep.anl.gov
Field Museum (Chicago): www.fmnh.org
Santa Barbara Museum of Natural History: www.sbnature.org
Inventors Hall of Fame: www.invent.org/
The Smithsonian Web: www.si.edu

Circuit, integrated: (theoretical) G.W.A. Dummer, England, 1952; (phase-shift oscillator) Jack S. Kilby, Texas Instruments, U.S., 1959.

Classification of plants: (first modern, based on comparative study of forms) Andrea Cesalpino, Italy, 1583; (classification of plants and animals by genera and species) Carolus Linnaeus, Sweden, 1737–1753.

Clock, pendulum: Christian Huygens, The Netherlands, 1656.

Coca-Cola: John Pemberton, U.S., 1886.

Combustion: (nature of) Antoine Lavoisier, France, 1777.

Compact disk: RCA, U.S., 1972.

Computers: (first design of analytical engine) Charles Babbage, 1830s; (ENIAC, Electronic Numerical Integrator and Calculator, first all-electronic, completed) 1945; (dedicated at University of Pennsylvania) 1946; (UNIVAC, Universal Automatic Computer, handled both numeric and alphabetic data) 1951.

Concrete: (reinforced) Joseph Monier, France, 1877.

Condensed milk: Gail Borden, U.S., 1853.

Conditioned reflex: Ivan Pavlov, Russia, c.1910.

Conservation of electric charge: (the total electric charge of the universe or any closed system is constant) Benjamin Franklin, U.S., 1751–1754.

Contagion theory: (infectious diseases caused by living agent transmitted from person to person) Girolamo Fracastoro, Italy, 1546.

Continental drift theory: (geographer who pieced together continents into a single landmass on maps) Antonio Snider-Pellegrini, France, 1858; (first proposed in lecture) Frank Taylor, U.S.; (first comprehensive detailed theory) Alfred Wegener, Germany, 1912.

Contraceptive, oral: Gregory Pincus, Min Chuch Chang, John Rock, Carl Djerassi, U.S., 1951.

Converter, Bessemer: William Kelly, U.S., 1851.

Cosmetics: Egypt, c. 4000 B.C.

Cosamic string theory: (first postulated) Thomas Kibble, 1976.

Cotton gin: Eli Whitney, U.S., 1793.

Crossbow: China, c. 300 B.C.

Cyclotron: Ernest O. Lawrence, U.S., 1931.

Deuterium: (heavy hydrogen) Harold Urey, U.S., 1931.

Disease: (chemicals in treatment of) crusaded by Philippus Paracelsus, 1527–1541; (germ theory) Louis Pasteur, France, 1862–1877.

DNA: (deoxyribonucleic acid) Friedrich Meischer, Germany, 1869; (determination of double-helical structure) Rosalind Elsie Franklin, F. H. Crick, England, James D. Watson, U.S., 1953.

Dye: (aniline, start of synthetic dye industry) William H. Perkin, England, 1856.

Dynamite: Alfred Nobel, Sweden, 1867.

Electric cooking utensil: (first) patented by St. George Lane-Fox, England, 1874.

Electric generator (dynamo): (laboratory model) Michael Faraday, England, 1832; Joseph Henry, U.S., c.1832; (hand-driven model) Hippolyte Pixii, France, 1833; (alternating-current generator) Nikola Tesla, U.S., 1892.

Electric lamp: (arc lamp) Sir Humphrey Davy, England, 1801; (fluorescent lamp) A.E. Becquerel, France, 1867; (incandescent lamp) Sir Joseph Swann, England, Thomas A. Edison, U.S., contemporaneously, 1870s; (carbon arc street lamp) Charles F. Brush, U.S., 1879; (first widely marketed incandescent lamp) Thomas A. Edison, U.S., 1879; (mercury vapor lamp) Peter Cooper Hewitt, U.S., 1903;

Thomas Alva Edison
(1847–1931) *Library of Congress*

(neon lamp) Georges Claude, France, 1911; (tungsten filament) Irving Langmuir, U.S., 1915.

Electrocardiography: Demonstrated by Augustus Waller, 1887; (first practical device for recording activity of heart) Willem Einthoven, 1903, Dutch physiologist.

Electromagnet: William Sturgeon, England, 1823.

Electron: Sir Joseph J. Thompson, England, 1897.

Elevator, passenger: (safety device permitting use by passengers) Elisha G. Otis, U.S., 1852; (elevator utilizing safety device) 1857.

E = mc²: (equivalence of mass and energy) Albert Einstein, Switzerland, 1907.

Engine, internal combustion: No single inventor. Fundamental theory established by Sadi Carnot, France, 1824; (two-stroke) Etienne Lenoir, France, 1860; (ideal operating cycle for four-stroke) Alphonse Beau de Roche, France, 1862; (operating four-stroke) Nikolaus Otto, Germany, 1876; (diesel) Rudolf Diesel, Germany, 1892; (rotary) Felix Wankel, Germany, 1956.

Evolution: (organic) Jean-Baptiste Lamarck, France, 1809; (by natural selection) Charles Darwin, England, 1859.

Exclusion principle: (no two electrons in an atom can occupy the same energy level) Wolfgang Pauli, Germany, 1925.

Expanding universe theory: (first proposed) George LeMaitre, Belgium, 1927; (discovered first direct evidence that the universe is expanding) Edwin P. Hubble, U.S., 1929; (Hubble constant: a measure of the rate at which the universe is expanding) Edwin P. Hubble, U.S., 1929.

Falling bodies, law of: Galileo Galilei, Italy, 1590.

Fermentation: (microorganisms as cause of) Louis Pasteur, France, c.1860.

Fiber optics: Narinder Kapany, England, 1955.

Fibers, man-made: (nitrocellulose fibers treated to change flammable nitrocellulose to harmless cellulose, precursor of rayon) Sir Joseph Swann, England, 1883; (rayon) Count Hilaire de Chardonnet, France, 1889; (Celanese)

Henry and Camille Dreyfuss, U.S., England, 1921; (research on polyesters and polyamides, basis for modern man-made fibers) U.S., England, Germany, 1930s; (nylon) Wallace H. Carothers, U.S., 1935.

Frozen food: Clarence Birdseye, U.S., 1924.

Gene transfer: (human) Steven Rosenberg, R. Michael Blaese, W. French Anderson, U.S., 1989.

Geometry, elements of: Euclid, Alexandria, Egypt, c. 300 B.C.; (analytic) René Descartes, France; and Pierre de Fermat, Switzerland, 1637.

Gravitation, law of: Sir Isaac Newton, England, c.1665 (published 1687).

Gunpowder: China, c.700.

Gyrocompass: Elmer A. Sperry, U.S., 1905.

Gyroscope: Léon Foucault, France, 1852.

Halley's Comet: Edmund Halley, England, 1705.

Heart implanted in human, permanent artificial: Dr. Robert Jarvik, U.S., 1982.

Heart, temporary artificial: Willem Kolft, 1957.

Helicopter: (double rotor) Heinrich Focke, Germany, 1936; (single rotor) Igor Sikorsky, U.S., 1939.

Helium first observed on sun: Sir Joseph Lockyer, England, 1868.

Heredity, laws of: Gregor Mendel, Austria, 1865.

Holograph: Dennis Gabor, England, 1947.

Home videotape systems (VCR): (Betamax) Sony, Japan, 1975; (VHS) Matsushita, Japan, 1975.

Ice age theory: Louis Agassiz, Swiss-American, 1840.

Induction, electric: Joseph Henry, U.S., 1828.

Insulin: (first isolated) Sir Frederick G. Banting and Charles H. Best, Canada, 1921; (discovery first published) Banting and Best, 1922; (Nobel Prize awarded for purification for use in humans) John Macleod and Banting, 1923; (first synthesized), China, 1966.

Intelligence testing: Alfred Binet, Theodore Simon, France, 1905.

Interferon: Alick Isaacs, Jean Lindemann, England, Switzerland, 1957.

Isotopes: (concept of) Frederick Soddy, England, 1912; (stable isotopes) J. J. Thompson, England, 1913; (existence demonstrated by mass spectrography) Francis W. Ashton, 1919.

Jet propulsion: (engine) Sir Frank Whittle, England, Hans von Ohain, Germany, 1936; (aircraft) *Heinkel He 178*, 1939.

Kinetic theory of gases: (molecules of a gas are in a state of rapid motion) Daniel Bernoulli, Switzerland, 1738.

Laser: (theoretical work on) Charles H. Townes, Arthur L. Schawlow, U.S., N. Basov, A. Prokhorov, U.S.S.R., 1958; (first working model) T. H. Maiman, U.S., 1960.

Lawn mower: Edwin Budding, John Ferrabee, England, 1830–1831.

LCD (liquid crystal display): Hoffmann-La Roche, Switzerland, 1970.

Lens, bifocal: Benjamin Franklin, U.S., c.1760.

Leyden jar: (prototype electrical condenser) Canon E. G. von Kleist of Kamin, Pomerania, 1745; independently evolved by Cunaeus and P. van Musschenbroek, University of Leyden, Holland, 1746, from where name originated.

Light, nature of: (wave theory) Christian Huygens, The Netherlands, 1678; (electromagnetic theory) James Clerk Maxwell, England, 1873.

Light, speed of: (theory that light has finite velocity) Olaus Roemer, Denmark, 1675.

Lightning rod: Benjamin Franklin, U.S., 1752.

Locomotive: (steam powered) Richard Trevithick, England, 1804; (first practical, due to multiple-fire-tube boiler) George Stephenson, England, 1829; (largest steam-powered) Union Pacific's "Big Boy," U.S., 1941.

Lock, cylinder: Linus Yale, U.S., 1851.

Loom: (horizontal, two-beamed) Egypt, c. 4400 B.C.; (Jacquard drawloom, pattern controlled by punch cards)

Jacques de Vaucanson, France, 1745, Joseph-Marie Jacquard, 1801; (flying shuttle) John Kay, England, 1733; (power-driven loom) Edmund Cartwright, England, 1785.

Machine gun: (hand-cranked multibarrel) Richard J. Gatling, U.S., 1862; (practical single barrel, belt-fed) Hiram S. Maxim, Anglo-American, 1884.

Magnet, Earth is: William Gilbert, England, 1600.

Match: (phosphorus) François Derosne, France, 1816; (friction) Charles Sauria, France, 1831; (safety) J. E. Lundstrom, Sweden, 1855.

Measles vaccine: John F. Enders, Thomas Peebles, U.S., 1953.

Metric system: revolutionary government of France, 1790–1801.

Microphone: Charles Wheatstone, England, 1827.

Microscope: (compound) Zacharias Janssen, The Netherlands, 1590; (electron) Vladimir Zworykin et al., U.S., Canada, Germany, 1932–1939.

Microwave oven: Percy Spencer, U.S., 1947.

Motion, laws of: Isaac Newton, England, 1687.

Motion pictures: Thomas A. Edison, U.S., 1893.

Motion pictures, sound: Product of various inventions. First picture with synchronized musical score: *Don Juan*, 1926; with spoken dialogue: *The Jazz Singer*, 1927; both Warner Bros.

Motor, electric: Michael Faraday, England, 1822; (alternating-current) Nikola Tesla, U.S., 1892.

Motorcycle: (motor tricycle) Edward Butler, England, 1884; (gasoline-engine motorcycle) Gottlieb Daimler, Germany, 1885.

Moving assembly line: Henry Ford, U.S., 1913.

Neptune: (discovery of) Johann Galle, Germany, 1846.

Neptunium: (first transuranic element, synthesis of) Edward M. McMillan, Philip H. Abelson, U.S., 1940.

Neutron: James Chadwick, England, 1932.

Neutron-induced radiation: Enrico Fermi et al., Italy, 1934.

Nitroglycerin: Ascanio Sobrero, Italy, 1846.

Nuclear fission: Otto Hahn, Fritz Strassmann, Germany, 1938.

Nuclear reactor: Enrico Fermi, Italy, et al., 1942.

Ohm's law: (relationship between strength of electric current, electromotive force, and circuit resistance) Georg S. Ohm, Germany, 1827.

Oil well: Edwin L. Drake, U.S., 1859.

Oxygen: (isolation of) Joseph Priestley, 1774; Carl Scheele, 1773.

Ozone: Christian Schönbein, Germany, 1839.

Pacemaker: (internal) Clarence W. Lillehie, Earl Bakk, U.S., 1957.

Paper China, c.100 A.D.

Parachute: Louis S. Lenormand, France, 1783.

Pen: (fountain) Lewis E. Waterman, U.S., 1884; (ball-point, for marking on rough surfaces) John H. Loud, U.S., 1888; (ball-point, for handwriting) Lazlo Biro, Argentina, 1944.

Periodic law: (that properties of elements are functions of their atomic weights) Dmitri Mendeleev, Russia, 1869.

Periodic table: (arrangement of chemical elements based on periodic law) Dmitri Mendeleev, Russia, 1869.

Phonograph: Thomas A. Edison, U.S., 1877.

Photography: (first paper negative, first photograph, on metal) Joseph Nicéphore Niepce, France, 1816–1827; (discovery of fixative powers of hyposulfite of soda) Sir John Herschel, England, 1819; (first direct positive image on silver plate, the daguerreotype) Louis Daguerre, based on work with Niepce, France, 1839; (first paper negative from which a number of positive prints could be made) William Talbot, England, 1841. Work of these four men, taken together, forms basis for all modern photography. (First color images) Alexandre Becquerel, Claude Niepce de Saint-Victor, France, 1848–1860; (commercial color film with three emulsion layers, Kodachrome) U.S., 1935.

Photovoltaic effect: (light falling on certain materials can produce electricity) Edmund Becquerel, France, 1839.

Piano: (Hammerklavier) Bartolommeo Cristofori, Italy, 1709; (pianoforte with sustaining and damper pedals) John Broadwood, England, 1873.

Planetary motion, laws of: Johannes Kepler, Germany, 1609, 1619.

Plant respiration and photosynthesis: Jan Ingenhousz, Holland, 1779.

Plastics: (first material, nitrocellulose softened by vegetable oil, camphor, precursor to Celluloid) Alexander Parkes, England, 1855; (Celluloid, involving recognition of vital effect of camphor) John W. Hyatt, U.S., 1869; (Bakelite, first completely synthetic plastic) Leo H. Baekeland, U.S., 1910; (theoretical background of macromolecules and process of polymerization on which modern plastics industry rests) Hermann Staudinger, Germany, 1922.

Plate tectonics: Alfred Wegener, Germany, 1912–1915.

Plow, forked: Mesopotamia, before 3000 B.C.

Plutonium, synthesis of: Glenn T. Seaborg, Edwin M. McMillan, Arthur C. Wahl, Joseph W. Kennedy, U.S., 1941.

Polio, vaccine: (experimentally safe dead-virus vaccine) Jonas E. Salk, U.S., 1952; (effective large-scale field trials) 1954; (officially approved) 1955; (safe oral live-virus vaccine developed) Albert B. Sabin, U.S., 1954; (available in the U.S.) 1960.

Positron: Carl D. Anderson, U.S., 1932.

Pressure cooker: (early version) Denis Papin, France, 1679.

Printing: (block) Japan, c.700; (movable type) Korea, c.1400; Johann Gutenberg, Germany, c.1450 (lithography, offset) Aloys Senefelder, Germany, 1796; (rotary press) Richard Hoe, U.S., 1844; (linotype) Ottmar Mergenthaler, U.S., 1884.

Probability theory: René Descartes, France; and Pierre de Fermat, Switzerland, 1654.

Proton: Ernest Rutherford, England, 1919.

Johann Gutenberg
(c. 1400–1468)

Prozac: (antidepressant fluoxetine) Bryan B. Malloy, Scotland, and Klaus K. Schmiegel, U.S., 1972; (released for use in U.S.) Eli Lilly & Company, 1987.

Psychoanalysis: Sigmund Freud, Austria, c.1904.

Pulsars: Antony Hewish and Jocelyn Bell Burnel, England, 1967.

Quantum theory: (general) Max Planck, Germany, 1900; (sub-atomic) Niels Bohr, Denmark, 1913; (quantum mechanics) Werner Heisenberg, Erwin Schrödinger, Germany, 1925.

Quarks: Jerome Friedman, Henry Kendall, Richard Taylor, U.S., 1967.

Quasars: Marten Schmidt, U.S., 1963.

Rabies immunization: Louis Pasteur, France, 1885.

Radar: (limited to one-mile range) Christian Hulsmeyer, Germany, 1904; (pulse modulation, used for measuring height of ionosphere) Gregory Breit, Merle Tuve, U.S., 1925; (first practical radar—radio detection and ranging) Sir Robert Watson-Watt, England, 1934–1935.

Radio: (electromagnetism, theory of) James Clerk Maxwell, England, 1873; (spark coil, generator of electromagnetic waves) Heinrich Hertz, Germany, 1886; (first practical system of wireless telegraphy) Guglielmo Marconi, Italy, 1895; (first long-distance telegraphic radio signal sent across the Atlantic) Marconi, 1901; (vacuum electron tube, basis for radio telephony) Sir John Fleming, England, 1904; (triode amplifying tube) Lee de Forest, U.S., 1906; (regenerative circuit, allowing long-distance sound reception) Edwin H. Armstrong, U.S., 1912; (frequency modulation—FM) Edwin H. Armstrong, U.S., 1933.

Radioactivity: (X-rays) Wilhelm K. Roentgen, Germany, 1895; (radioactivity of uranium) Henri Becquerel, France, 1896; (radioactive elements, radium and polonium in uranium ore) Marie Sklodowska-Curie, Pierre Curie, France, 1898; (classification of alpha and beta particle radiation) Pierre Curie, France, 1900; (gamma radiation) Paul-Ulrich Villard, France, 1900.

Radiocarbon dating, carbon-14 method: (discovered) 1947, Willard F. Libby, U.S.; (first demonstrated) U.S., 1950.

Radio signals, extraterrestrial: first known radio noise signals were received by U.S. engineer, Karl Jansky, originating from the Galactic Center, 1931.

Radio waves: (cosmic sources, led to radio astronomy) Karl Jansky, U.S., 1932.

Razor: (safety, successfully marketed) King Gillette, U.S., 1901; (electric) Jacob Schick, U.S., 1928, 1931.

Reaper: Cyrus McCormick, U.S., 1834.

Refrigerator: Alexander Twining, U.S., James Harrison, Australia, 1850; (first with a compressor device) the Domelse, Chicago, U.S., 1913.

Refrigerator ship: (first) the *Frigorifique*, cooling unit designed by Charles Teller, France, 1877.

Relativity: (special and general theories of) Albert Einstein, Switzerland, Germany, U.S., 1905–1953.

Revolver: Samuel Colt, U.S., 1835.

Richter scale: Charles F. Richter, U.S., 1935.

Rifle: (muzzle-loaded) Italy, Germany, c.1475; (breech-loaded) England, France, Germany, U.S., c.1866; (bolt-action) Paul von Mauser, Germany, 1889; (automatic) John Browning, U.S., 1918.

Rocket: (liquid-fueled) Robert Goddard, U.S., 1926.

Roller bearing: (wooden for cartwheel) Germany or France, c.100 B.C.

Rotation of Earth: Jean Bernard Foucault, France, 1851.

Royal Observatory, Greenwich: established in 1675 by Charles II of England; John Flamsteed first Astronomer Royal.

Rubber: (vulcanization process) Charles Goodyear, U.S., 1839.

Saccharin: Constantine Fuhlberg, Ira Remsen, U.S., 1879.

Safety pin: Walter Hunt, U.S., 1849.

Saturn, ring around: Christian Huygens, The Netherlands, 1659.

"Scotch" tape: Richard Drew, U.S., 1929.

Screw propeller: Sir Francis P. Smith, England, 1836; John Ericsson, England, worked independently of and simultaneously with Smith, 1837.

Seismograph: (first accurate) John Milne, England, 1880.

Sewing machine: Elias Howe, U.S., 1846; (continuous stitch) Isaac Singer, U.S., 1851.

Solar energy: First realistic application of solar energy using parabolic solar reflector to drive caloric engine on steam boiler, John Ericsson, U.S., 1860s.

Solar system, universe: (Sun-centered universe) Nicolaus Copernicus, Warsaw, 1543; (establishment of planetary orbits as elliptical) Johannes Kepler, Germany, 1609; (infinity of universe) Giordano Bruno, Italian monk, 1584.

Spectrum: (heterogeneity of light) Sir Isaac Newton, England, 1665–1666.

Spectrum analysis: Gustav Kirchhoff, Robert Bunsen, Germany, 1859.

Spermatozoa: Anton van Leeuwenhoek, The Netherlands, 1683.

Spinning: (spinning wheel) India, introduced to Europe in Middle Ages; (Saxony wheel, continuous spinning of wool or cotton yarn) England, c.1500–1600; (spinning jenny)

James Hargreaves, England, 1764; (spinning frame) Sir Richard Arkwright, England, 1769; (spinning mule, completed mechanization of spinning, permitting production of yarn to keep up with demands of modern looms) Samuel Crompton, England, 1779.

Star catalog: (first modern) Tycho Brahe, Denmark, 1572.

Steam engine: (first commercial version based on principles of French physicist Denis Papin) Thomas Savery, England, 1639; (atmospheric steam engine) Thomas Newcomen, England, 1705; (steam engine for pumping water from collieries) Savery, Newcomen, 1725; (modern condensing, double acting) James Watt, England, 1782.

Steamship: Claude de Jouffroy d'Abbans, France, 1783; James Rumsey, U.S., 1787; John Fitch, U.S., 1790. All preceded Robert Fulton, U.S., 1807, credited with launching first commercially successful steamship.

Stethoscope: René Laënnec, France, 1819.

Sulfa drugs: (parent compound, para-aminobenzenesulfanomide) Paul Gelmo, Austria, 1908; (antibacterial activity) Gerhard Domagk, Germany, 1935.

Superconductivity: (theory) Bardeen, Cooper, Scheiffer, U.S., 1957.

Symbolic logic: George Boule, 1854; (modern) Bertrand Russell, Alfred North Whitehead, England, 1910–1913.

Tank, military: Sir Ernest Swinton, England, 1914.

Tape recorder: (magnetic steel tape) Valdemar Poulsen, Denmark, 1899.

Teflon: DuPont, U.S., 1943.

Telegraph: Samuel F. B. Morse, U.S., 1837.

Telephone: Alexander Graham Bell, U.S., 1876.

Telescope: Hans Lippershey, The Netherlands, 1608; (astronomical) Galileo Galilei, Italy, 1609; (reflecting) Isaac Newton, England, 1668.

Television: (Iconoscope–T.V. camera table), Vladimir Zworkin, U.S., 1923, and also kinescope (cathode ray tube), 1928; (mechanical disk-scanning

Samuel F. B. Morse (1791–1872)
Library of Congress

method) successfully demonstrated by J.K. Baird, England, C.F. Jenkins, U.S., 1926; (first all-electric television image), 1927, Philo T. Farnsworth, U.S; (color, mechanical disk) Baird, 1928; (color, compatible with black and white) George Valensi, France, 1938; (color, sequential rotating filter) Peter Goldmark, U.S., first introduced, 1951; (color, compatible with black and white) commercially introduced in U.S., National Television Systems Committee, 1953.

Thermodynamics: (first law: energy cannot be created or destroyed, only converted from one form to another) Julius von Mayer, Germany, 1842; James Joule, England, 1843; (second law: heat cannot of itself pass from a colder to a warmer body) Rudolph Clausius, Germany, 1850; (third law: the entropy of ordered solids reaches zero at the absolute zero of temperature) Walter Nernst, Germany, 1918.

Thermometer: (open-column) Galileo Galilei, c.1593; (clinical) Santorio Santorio, Padua, c.1615; (mercury, also Fahrenheit scale) Gabriel D. Fahrenheit, Germany, 1714; (centigrade scale) Anders Celsius, Sweden, 1742; (absolute-temperature, or Kelvin, scale) William Thompson, Lord Kelvin, England, 1848.

Tire, pneumatic: Robert W. Thompson, England, 1845; (bicycle tire) John B. Dunlop, Northern Ireland, 1888.

Toilet, flush: Product of Minoan civilization, Crete, c. 2000 B.C. Alleged invention by "Thomas Crapper" is untrue.

Tractor: Benjamin Holt, U.S., 1900.

Transformer, electric: William Stanley, U.S., 1885.

Transistor: John Bardeen, Walter H. Brattain, William B. Shockley, U.S., 1947.

Tuberculosis bacterium: Robert Koch, Germany, 1882.

Typewriter: Christopher Sholes, Carlos Glidden, U.S., 1867.

Uncertainty principle: (that position and velocity of an object cannot both be measured exactly, at the same time) Werner Heisenberg, Germany, 1927.

Uranus: (first planet discovered in recorded history) William Herschel, England, 1781.

Vaccination: Edward Jenner, England, 1796.

Vacuum cleaner: (manually operated) Ives W. McGaffey, 1869; (electric) Hubert C. Booth, England, 1901; (upright) J. Murray Spangler, U.S., 1907.

Van Allen (radiation) Belt: (around Earth) James Van Allen, U.S., 1958.

Video disk: Philips Co., The Netherlands, 1972.

Vitamins: (hypothesis of disease deficiency) Sir F. G. Hopkins, Casimir Funk, England, 1912; (vitamin A) Elmer V. McCollum, M. Davis, U.S., 1912–1914; (vitamin B) McCollum, U.S., 1915–1916; (thiamin, B_1) Casimir Funk, England, 1912; (riboflavin, B_2) D. T. Smith, E. G. Hendrick, U.S., 1926; (niacin) Conrad Elvehjem, U.S., 1937; (B_6) Paul Gyorgy, U.S., 1934; (vitamin C) C. A. Hoist, T. Froelich, Norway, 1912; (vitamin D) McCollum, U.S., 1922; (folic acid) Lucy Wills, England, 1933.

Voltaic pile: (forerunner of modern battery, first source of continuous electric current) Alessandro Volta, Italy, 1800.

Wallpaper: Europe, 16th and 17th century.

Wassermann test: (for syphilis) August von Wassermann, Germany, 1906.

Wheel: (cart, solid wood) Mesopotamia, c.3800–3600 B.C.

Windmill: Persia, c.600.

World Wide Web: (developed while working at CERN) Tim Berners-Lee, England, 1989; (development of Mosaic browser makes WWW available for general use) Marc Andreeson, U.S., 1993.

Xerography: Chester Carlson, U.S., 1938.

Zero: India, c.600; (absolute zero temperature, cessation of all molecular energy) William Thompson, Lord Kelvin, England, 1848.

Zipper: W. L. Judson, U.S., 1891.

The National Inventors Hall of Fame

The Inventors Hall of Fame, located in Akron, Ohio, was established in 1973 by the National Council of Patent Law Associations, now the National Council of Intellectual Property Law Associations, and the Patent and Trademark Office of the U.S. Department of Commerce.

The 2000 Class of Inductees

Disney, Walt, 1901–1966, ART OF ANIMATION. Animation pioneer, invented the multiplane camera in 1937. This advanced camera created three-dimensional effects by giving the illusion of depth, as seen in the first full-length animated feature *Snow White and the Seven Dwarfs.* Disney went on to create many more award-winning movies filled with classic characters in addition to breaking new ground in family entertainment.

Fessenden, Reginald A., 1866–1932, APPARATUS FOR SIGNALING BY ELECTROMAGNETIC WAVES. Canadian Reginald Fessenden made history in 1906 when he broadcast the world's first radio program through wireless transmission. He is known not just for the first radio transmission of the human voice, but for over 200 additional patents, including a version of microfilm and an early form of sonar.

Free, Alfred, 1913–2000, COMPOSITION OF MATTER. Free revolutionized urinalysis by devising a dip-and-read test, CLINISTIX®, for detecting glucose in urine. Working at Miles Laboratories, he also advanced diabetes testing with the first one-minute test for blood glucose, leading to the concept of self-testing for persons with diabetes. Today, there are many different reagents and instrumentation that were inspired by his work.

Free, Helen Murray, 1923–, INDICATOR FOR DETECTING GLUCOSE. Her work in diagnostic chemistry led to the development of many tests used in urine testing, including CLINISTIX®, introduced in 1956. Early on at Miles Laboratories, she devised tests to detect glucose, ketone, and bilirubin in urine. The procedures she and her husband, Alfred Free, developed are still used. Today, Helen Free is a high-profile promoter of science education, involved in chemistry awareness programs around the world.

Hyde, J. Franklin, 1903–1999, METHOD FOR MAKING A TRANSPARENT ARTICLE OF SILICA. Hyde was with Corning Glass when he discovered a way to create an ultra-pure glass called fused silica. Fused silica has many uses, such as in spaceship windows and high-powered telescopes like the Hubble, and as the basis for the optical fiber industry. He also was a forerunner in developing silicones, which can be found in a wide range of everyday products, including lubricants, caulks, electrical insulators, and gaskets.

Kroll, William J., 1889–1973, METHOD FOR MANUFACTURING TITANIUM AND ALLOYS THEREOF. Metallurgist William Kroll invented the Kroll process, a technique for producing titanium and zirconium. His work at the U.S. Bureau of Mines increased titanium production during World War II when it was badly needed. Strong as steel but 45% lighter, titanium is used in artificial joints, bicycle frames, and golf clubs. Zirconium, which effectively resists corrosion, is found in jet engines, surgical equipment, and fiber optics.

Wozniak, Steve, 1950–, MICROCOMPUTER FOR USE WITH VIDEO DISPLAY. Wozniak is best known for inventing the first personal computer. In 1976, he cofounded Apple Computer. The following year, he introduced the Apple II, a revolutionary computer that offered the consumer a keyboard, color graphics, and a disk drive. Today he is a noted philanthropist and is dedicated to teaching and inspiring youngsters to learn.

Attack of the Love Bug

It came. It flattered. It wreaked havoc on the Internet. Why are we so vulnerable? What can be done?

By LEV GROSSMAN TIME

Anne Guepiere works in the Hong Kong office of a large U.S. company that would prefer to remain nameless. At about 4 o'clock on a Thursday in May, she received an email. It seemed innocuous enough. The subject line read ILOVEYOU. With it came an attached document labeled LOVE-LETTER-FOR-YOU.TXT.VBS. How nice. Just a couple of clicks, and her curiosity would be satisfied.

Too late. "I didn't even read the 'ILOVEYOU' part," recalled Guepiere, whom history would record as, if not Patient Zero, then surely one of the earliest victims in a global pandemic. "Only when I opened [the attachment] did I realize there was a problem." Indeed, it was a bigger problem than anybody, probably even its mischievous creator, could have imagined as computers everywhere tumbled like so many dominoes. Once again that scourge of the Internet age—a computer virus—had struck. Silently, lethally, without even a hint of a warning fever, it raced around the world at the speed of light, clogging communications and bringing both commerce and politics to a halt.

Unlovable Pandemic

Because of its implicit, fatally attractive message—*Oh, just give me a glance, I bear friendly tidings from a loving admirer!*—headline writers immediately (and irresistibly) nicknamed it the Love Bug. But there was nothing lovable about it. Before it spent itself—in its first incarnation, it was truly a 24-hour virus—it would affect tens of millions of computers, eventually ring up a toll as high as $10 billion in lost work hours, and reopen troubling questions about the safety and security of our vital electronic lifelines. By almost any measure, it was the most damaging virus ever, with at least three times the byte—as more than one punster put it—of Melissa, 1999's electronic femme fatale. This was not so much because of its ingenuity, says Finnish computer-virus hunter Mikko Hypponen, whose team was among the first to capture the bug's digital DNA, but because of its blinding speed, spreading around the world in a hypersonic two hours (versus six for Melissa). Like a real Asian influenza, the virus first emerged in Hong Kong. From there it sped westward with the Sun, lying silently in wait in corporate email accounts until unsuspecting office denizens punched in, logged on, and double-clicked on the file.

But worse was yet to come. On the other side of the world, in the offices of the German newspaper *Abendblatt* in Hamburg, system administrators watched in horror as the virus gobbled up 2,000 digital photographs in their picture archive. In Belgium ATMs were disabled, leaving citizens cashless. In Paris cosmetics maker L'Oréal shut down its email servers, as did businesses throughout the Continent. As much as 70% of the computers in Germany, the Netherlands, and Sweden were laid low. The companies affected made up a *Who's Who* of industry and finance, including Ford, Siemens, Silicon Graphics, and Fidelity Investments. Even Microsoft, whose software was the Love Bug's special target, got so badly battered that it finally severed outside email links at its Redmond, Wash., headquarters.

The Yanks didn't do any better. On Capitol Hill, crippled email systems forced an atypical silence in the halls of Congress, as well as some unusual scrambling. The bug infected 80% of all federal agencies, including both the Defense and State departments, leaving them temporarily out of email contact with their far-flung outposts.

Inside the Bug

Fiendishly created, the Love Bug struck with a one-two punch. Once you clicked open that fatal attachment and activated its deadly code, the virus either erased or moved a wide range of data files. It singled out in particular so-called .jpgs and .mp3s—digital pictures and music—and, like a natural virus, replaced them with identical copies of itself. Then, if it found the Microsoft Outlook Express email program on your computer, it raided the program's address book and sent copies of itself to everyone on that list. (The more innocent Melissa grabbed only the first 50 names.) Technically, this two-pronged approach made the Love Bug both a virus and a worm; it was a virus because it bred on a host computer's hard drive and a worm because it also reproduced over a network.

As these replicated messages spread, they created monumental jams, slowing Internet traffic to a crawl. And they quickly attracted the attention of virus hunters. At the F-Secure headquarters just outside Helsinki, Hypponen's team first got word of the virus at 9:41 a.m. local time, seven hours ahead of the Eastern U.S. That was when Bulgarian-born Katrin Tocheva, one of the few women in the tight-knit antiviral community, opened an email containing a sample of the ILOVEYOU attachment and a warning from their Norwegian field office; a U.S. client's European network had been hit and needed help. She alerted the rest of the staff, who went immediately into emergency mode.

At ICSA.net, a Pennsylvania computer-security company, chief scientist Peter Tippett was also getting warnings from his European offices. By 4 a.m., he began rounding up his 15-person antivirus SWAT team. Because of the stiff competition among antivirus-software makers, others were mobilizing too. "Our Leyden team in Holland was up and

---

How to Protect Yourself

- **Don't open email** from strangers or attachments you weren't expecting—especially attachments with .exe extensions
- **Back up important files** on floppy disks, Zip drives, or other storage devices on a regular basis, so that they can easily be replaced if a virus wipes out your hard drive
- **Install the newest antivirus software** on your computer, such as Norton Anti-Virus 2000 or McAfee Virus Scan for Windows, or Virex for Macs
- **Check your software vendor's Web site** regularly for updates that will protect against viruses and worms—like the Love Bug—released since your antiviral software was written

---

awake and began the initial research," said Ron Moritz, chief technology officer of Symantec, one of the antiviral Big Three (the other two are McAfee and Computer Associates).

Computer Genome Project

Their first challenge: nailing the bug's digital fingerprint. "Every virus, every attack has a unique pattern, a unique set of bits," said Moritz. "Once you know what that is, you can then identify it each and every time it comes in." The second challenge: identifying the perpetrator. Clues weren't hard to find. Embedded in the virus's code—or blueprint—were the alias "spyder," an email address, and the words "Manila, Philippines." The code also yielded a short sentence in broken English that provided at least the shadow of a motive: "i hate go to school." Was the world facing a cyber-Columbine? By 4:30 a.m. Eastern time, the virus fighters had linked the Love Bug to a Web site hosted by Sky Internet, an Internet service provider based in Quezon, the Philippines. They persuaded the ISP to close down the site, but the Love Bug kept on spreading.

The feds were moving as well. By 11 a.m., the National Infrastructure Protection Center, an FBI-based group created to defend against cyberattacks on crucial public and private networks, posted a virus alert on its Web page. Meanwhile, NIPC was assessing the extent of the damage at home, and the FBI launched a massive criminal investigation. Under the Computer Fraud and Abuse Act of 1986, the Love Bug's author could face a penalty of as much as five years behind bars and a $250,000 fine.

The major antivirus firms quickly posted antidotes—software to neutralize the bug—on their Web sites, but they were too late to prevent widespread chaos. Desperate for a cure, victims deluged the sites, making them all but inaccessible. McAfee received requests for help from 10,000 affected companies on the first day of the outbreak alone.

The consensus among computer-security experts is that the Love Bug was the biggest virus outbreak in history—"by at least threefold," said ICSA.net's Tippett. Agreed McAfee president and CEO Gene

Hodges: "It's clear at this point that this is the most damaging and the most widespread virus outbreak ever."

By Thursday night, more than a day after its first appearance, the Love Bug began to mutate. Either the creator or, more likely, other members of the virus-writing clan started editing the virus and reintroducing it to the Internet with some new, tilted spins. One version had the subject line "FWD: Joke." Another was written in Lithuanian. One, more devious, bore the email header "Mother's Day Order Confirmation"—posing as an email receipt for a credit-card transaction for flowers or a gift for Mom. Perhaps most diabolical of all was the version titled "Dangerous Virus Warning," with an attached file that cleansed the system of the Love Bug but substituted an equally dangerous one of its own.

Within a week, a skinny 23-year-old Filipino computer student, Onel de Guzman, emerged from hiding for a press conference at which he came close to admitting responsibility for the Love Bug onslaught. Did he unleash the virus? "It is possible," admitted Guzman, who sported dark glasses and covered his face with a handkerchief. If he did it, he insisted, it was as a result of "youthful exuberance." Guzman was later arrested and charged with "traditional crimes," theft and fraud, since the Philippines had no laws against computer hacking at the time Guzman allegedly released the virus.

An Easy Target

What kind of future is there for an Internet so fragile that a cobbled-together program can bring it to its knees? It is painfully obvious that the present network lacks any built-in immune system to defend it against malicious infections. Emmanuel Goldstein, founder of the legendary hacker journal 2600, stressed that better technology is the answer—not passing more laws or throwing more hackers in prison. "Melissa should have protected us from this," he said at a 2600 gathering on the Friday night two days after the virus had struck. "Catching the guy doesn't prevent hackers. All the legislation in the world will not stop a 12-year-old in Thailand from doing this."

Clearly, the Internet is still not ready for prime time. The next virus could be worse. Imagine what a well-designed Love Bug could do when we have become even more dependent on computer networks and those networks are wireless. An Internet outage could keep us not only from sending email but also from gassing up the car or depositing our paychecks.

The medium may be new, but human nature hasn't changed: whatever firewalls and antidotes the virus hunters come up with, virus writers will always find a way around them. As veteran hacker Goldstein put it, "If your system can be knocked out, assume it will be."

What the Love Bug attack teaches us is that if we want to become a connected society, it is not enough to defend our own backyard (i.e., our own PC). We have to clean up the streets and build an Internet in which it is safe for us to stay as intimately linked as we clearly want to be. □

Computer Virus Timeline

1949 Theories for self-replicating programs are first developed.

1981 Apple Viruses 1, 2, and 3 are some of the first viruses "in the wild," or in the public domain. Found on the Apple II operating system, the viruses spread through Texas A&M via pirated computer games.

1983 Fred Cohen, while working on his dissertation, formally defines a computer virus as "a computer program that can affect other computer programs by modifying them in such a way as to include a (possibly evolved) copy of itself."

1986 Two programmers named Basit and Amjad replace the executable code in the boot sector of a floppy disk with their own code designed to infect each 360kb floppy accessed on any drive. Infected floppies had "© Brain" for a volume label.

1988 One of the most common viruses, Jerusalem, is unleashed. Activated every Friday the 13th, the virus affects both .exe and .com files and deletes any programs run on that day.

1990 Symantec launches Norton AntiVirus, one of the first antivirus programs developed by a large company.

1991 Tequila is the first widespread polymorphic virus found in the wild. Polymorphic viruses make detection difficult for virus scanners by changing their appearance with each new infection.

1992 1300 viruses are in existence, an increase of 420% from December of 1990.

The Michelangelo scare predicts 5 million computers will crash on March 6. Only 5,000–10,000 actually go down.

1994 Good Times email hoax tears through the computer community. The hoax warns of a malicious virus that will erase an entire hard drive just by opening an email with the subject line "Good Times." Though disproved, the hoax resurfaces every six to twelve months.

1995 Word Concept becomes one of the most prevalent viruses in the mid-1990s. It is spread through Microsoft Word documents.

1998 Currently harmless and yet to be found in the wild, StrangeBrew is the first virus to infect Java files. The virus modifies CLASS files to contain a copy of itself within the middle of the file's code and to begin execution from the virus section.

The Chernobyl virus spreads quickly via .exe files. As the notoriety attached to its name would suggest, the virus is quite destructive, attacking not only files but also a certain chip within infected computers.

1999 The Melissa virus, W97M/Melissa, executes a macro in a document attached to an email, which forwards the document to 50 people in the user's Outlook address book. The virus also infects other Word documents and subsequently mails them out as attachments. Melissa spread faster than any previous virus, infecting an estimated 1 million PCs.

Bubble Boy is the first worm that does not depend on the recipient opening an attachment in order for infection to occur. As soon as the user opens the email, Bubble Boy sets to work.

2000 The Love Bug, also known as ILOVEYOU virus, sends itself out via Outlook, much like Melissa. The virus comes as a VBS attachment and deletes files, including MP3, MP2, and .JPG. It also sends usernames and passwords to the virus's author.

W97M.Resume.A, a new variation of the Melissa virus, is determined to be in the wild. The "resume" virus acts much like Melissa, using a Word macro to infect Outlook and spread itself.

The "Stages" virus, disguised as a joke email about the stages of life, spreads across the Internet. Unlike most previous viruses, Stages is hidden in an attachment with a false ".txt" extension, making it easier to lure recipients into opening it. Until now, it has generally been safe to assume that text files are safe.

What Users Do on the Internet

In February 2000 the Stanford Institute for the Quantitative Study of Society released an extensive report on Internet use. The study was based on a random sampling of more than 4,000 American Internet users. Participants were asked to identify whether they did or did not do each of the activities listed below. The resulting data show that the Internet's greatest impact has perhaps been in facilitating communications. To view the survey's additional findings on the Internet's social impact, visit http://www.stanford.edu/group/siqss/Press_Release/internetStudy.html.

Activity	Internet users (percent)	Activity	Internet users (percent)	Activity	Internet users (percent)
Email	90%	Travel information	54%	Chat rooms	24%
General information	77	Work/Business	46	Homework	21
Surfing	69	Entertainment/Games	36	Auctions	13
Reading	67	Buying	36	Banking	12
Hobbies	63	Stock quotes	27	Trading stocks	7
Product information	62	Job search	26		

Internet Users in North America, 1995–1999
(in millions)

	Aug. 1995	Apr. 1996	Jan. 1997	Sept. 1997	June 1998	Apr. 1999
Total online	18.0	34.0	51.0	58.0	79.0	92.0
Gender composition						
Female	33%	34%	42%	43%	43%	46%
Male	67%	66%	58%	57%	57%	54%

Source: Based on an April 1999 survey conducted by CommerceNet/Nielsen Media Research.

Top Web Sites, May 2000

Rank	Web site	Unique visitors (thousands)	Rank	Web site	Unique visitors (thousands)
1.	AOL Network*	59,230	14.	Go2Net Network*	12,794
2.	Microsoft sites*	49,309	15.	eBay*	12,084
3.	Yahoo sites*	48,851	16.	LookSmart*	11,602
4.	Lycos*	32,475	17.	eUniverse Network*	10,809
5.	Excite@Home*	28,751	18.	CNET Networks*	10,549
6.	GO Network*	23,065	19.	ZDNet sites*	10,113
7.	About.com sites*	17,926	20.	InfoSpace Impressions*	8,661
8.	NBC Internet*	16,489	21.	Juno	8,605
9.	Amazon*	14,972	22.	iWon.com	8,408
10.	Time Warner Online*	14,256	23.	EarthLink*	8,216
11.	AltaVista Network*	14,183	24.	Viacom Online*	8,102
12.	Ask Jeeves*	13,319	25.	FortuneCity Network*	7,829
13.	Real.com Network*	13,005			

NOTES: "Unique visitors" refers to the estimated number of total users who visited the Web site once in the given month. All unique visitors are unduplicated (only counted once). *Represents an aggregation of commonly owned/branded domain names. *Source:* Media Metrix, Inc. Web: www.mediametrix.com.

Top Shopping Sites, May 2000

Rank	Web site	Unique visitors (thousands)	Rank	Web site	Unique visitors (thousands)
1.	Amazon.com	14,040	6.	MyPoints.com	5,528
2.	Blue Mountain eCards	13,042	7.	Barnes & Noble.com	5,167
3.	eBay.com	12,046	8.	Webstakes.com	4,922
4.	AOL Shoppping Channel	11,419	9.	BizRate.com	4,908
5.	AmericanGreetings.com	7,243	10.	Priceline.com	4,768

NOTES: Includes Web and online sites and channels. "Unique visitors" refers to the estimated number of total users who visited the Web site once in the given month. All unique visitors are unduplicated (only counted once). *Source:* Media Metrix, Inc. Web: www.mediametrix.com.

Top News/Information/Entertainment Sites, May 2000

Rank	Web site	Unique visitors (thousands)	Rank	Web site	Unique visitors (thousands)
1.	ZDnet*	9,792	6.	Disney Online*	6,532
2.	CNET*	9,586	7.	FreeLotto.com	6,435
3.	About.com	9,360	8.	Sony Online*	6,143
4.	MSNBC.com	8,908	9.	iVillage sites*	6,053
5.	Weather.com	7,617	10.	LifeMinders.com	5,753

NOTES: Includes Web and online sites and channels. "Unique visitors" refers to the estimated number of total users who visited the Web site once in the given month. All unique visitors are unduplicated (only counted once). *Represents an aggregation of commonly owned/branded domain names. *Source:* Media Metrix, Inc. Web: www.mediametrix.com.

Top Education Sites, May 2000

Rank	Web site	Unique visitors (thousands)	Rank	Web site	Unique visitors (thousands)
1.	University of California, Berkeley	1,733	6.	Harvard University	1,215
2.	University of Michigan	1,550	7.	University of Tennessee	1,168
3.	University of Texas at Austin	1,455	8.	University of North Carolina at Chapel Hill	1,135
4.	Massachusetts Institute of Technology	1,331	9.	Cornell University	1,098
5.	University of Illinois at Urbana-Champaign	1,261	10.	University of Virginia	1,017

NOTES: "Unique visitors" refers to the estimated number of total users who visited the Web site once in the given month. All unique visitors are unduplicated (only counted once). *Source:* Media Metrix, Inc. Web: www.mediametrix.com.

Top Travel Sites, May 2000

Rank	Web site	Unique visitors (thousands)	Rank	Web site	Unique visitors (thousands)
1.	AOL Travel Channel	9,142	6.	Preview Travel*	1,579
2.	Expedia Travel*	6,427	7.	Lowestfare.com	1,472
3.	Travelocity.com	6,034	8.	Cheaptickets.com	1,443
4.	MapQuest.com	5,746	9.	TRIP.com Online*	1,132
5.	Internet Travel Network	1,819	10.	TravelNow.com	1,054

NOTES: Includes Web and online sites and channels. "Unique visitors" refers to the estimated number of total users who visited the Web site once in the given month. All unique visitors are unduplicated (only counted once). *Represents an aggregation of commonly owned/branded domain names. *Source:* Media Metrix, Inc. Web: www.mediametrix.com.

Top Government Sites, May 2000

Rank	Web site	Unique visitors (thousands)	Rank	Web site	Unique visitors (thousands)
1.	NASA	1,945	6.	U.S. Navy	1,192
2.	State of California	1,808	7.	U.S. Army	1,148
3.	National Institutes of Health	1,694	8.	Library of Congress	1,061
4.	National Oceanic and Atmospheric Administration	1,683	9.	National Park Service	947
5.	U.S. Department of Education	1,344	10.	U.S. Geological Survey	936

NOTES: "Unique visitors" refers to the estimated number of total users who visited the Web site once in the given month. All unique visitors are unduplicated (only counted once). *Source:* Media Metrix, Inc. Web: www.mediametrix.com.

Internet Timeline

1969 ARPA (Advanced Research Projects Agency) goes online in December, connecting four major U.S. universities. Designed for research, education, and government organizations, it provides a communications network linking the country in the event that a military attack destroys conventional communications systems.

1972 Electronic mail is introduced. Queen Elizabeth sends her first email in 1976.

1973 Transmission Control Protocol/Internet Protocol (TCP/IP) is designed and in 1983 it becomes the standard for communicating between computers over the Internet. One of these protocols, FTP (File Transfer Protocol), allows users to log onto a remote computer, list the files on that computer, and download files from that computer.

1989 The first effort to index the Internet is created by Peter Deutsch at McGill University in Montreal, who devises Archie, an archive of FTP sites. Another indexing system, WAIS (Wide Area Information Server), is developed by Brewster Kahle of Thinking Machines Corp. Tim Berners-Lee of CERN (European Laboratory for Particle Physics) develops a new technique for distributing information on the Internet, which eventually is called the World Wide Web. The Web is based on hypertext, which permits the user to connect from one document to another at different sites on the Internet via hyperlinks (specially programmed words, phrases, buttons, or graphics). Unlike other Internet protocols, such as FTP and email, the Web is accessible through a graphical user interface.

1991 Gopher, the first user-friendly interface, is created at the University of Minnesota and named after the school mascot. Gopher becomes the most popular interface for several years.

1993 Mosaic is developed by Marc Andreeson at the National Center for Supercomputing Applications (NCSA). It becomes the dominant navigating system for the World Wide Web, which at this time accounts for merely 1% of all Internet traffic.

1994 The White House launches its Web site, www.whitehouse.gov. Initial commerce sites are established and mass marketing campaigns are launched via email, introducing the term "spamming" to the Internet vocabulary.

1996 Approximately 45 million people are using the Internet, with roughly 30 million of those in North America (United States and Canada), 9 million in Europe, and 6 million in Asia/Pacific (Australia, Japan, etc.). 43.2 million (44%) of U.S. households own a personal computer, and 14 million of them are online.

1997 On July 8, 1997, Internet traffic records are broken as the NASA Web site broadcasts images taken by *Pathfinder* on Mars. The broadcast generates 46 million hits in one day.

1999 The number of Internet users worldwide reaches 150 million by the beginning of 1999. Over 50% are from the United States. "E-commerce" becomes the new buzzword as Internet shopping rapidly spreads.

2000 To the chagrin of the Internet population, deviant computer programmers begin designing and circulating viruses with greater frequency. "Love Bug" and "Stages" are two examples of self-replicating viruses that send themselves to people listed in a computer user's email address book. The heavy volume of email messages being sent and received forces many infected companies to temporarily shut down their clogged networks.

Sources for this timeline include International Data Corporation, the W3C Consortium, and the Internet Society.

Electronic Commerce Users in North America, 1999

Shopping categories	Shoppers (millions)
Total online shoppers	**55.0**
Gender composition	
Female	41%
Male	59%
Overall top shopping categories	
Cars/car parts	18.2
Books	12.6
Computers	12.4
Clothing	11.6
CDs & videos	11.4

Shopping categories	Shoppers (millions)
Top shopping categories for male users	
Cars/car parts	12.6
Computers	9.4
CDs & videos	7.0
Books	6.4
Home electronics	6.3
Top shopping categories for female users	
Clothing	6.9
Books	6.2
Cars/car parts	5.6
CDs & videos	4.4
Travel	4.0

Purchasing categories	Purchasers (millions)
Total online purchasers	**28.0**
Gender composition	
Female	38%
Male	62%
Overall top purchasing categories	
Books	9.2
CDs & videos	7.2
Computers	5.4
Clothing	4.5
Software	4.0

Purchasing categories	Purchasers (millions)
Top purchasing categories for male users	
Books	5.1
CDs & videos	4.5
Computers	4.1
Software	3.1
Clothing	2.1
Travel	2.1
Top purchasing categories for female users	
Books	4.1
CDs & videos	2.7
Clothing	2.4
Travel	1.3
Computers	1.3

NOTES: "Shoppers" is defined as people researching and comparing the price and features of products and services online, regardless of whether or not an actual online purchase was made. "Purchasers" is defined as people who actually purchase items online. Based on spring 1999 survey. *Source:* CommerceNet/Nielsen Media Research Demographics of the Internet Survey.

Internet Resource Guide

The Internet has become a convenient tool for finding information on just about anything. These days it's hard to find a company or organization that doesn't have its own home page. Because sifting through search engine returns can be more time-consuming than a trek to the library, we've compiled a list of Web sites that we've found to be especially useful and informative.

Arts and Literature
Library of Congress: *www.loc.gov*
The Louvre: *www.louvre.fr/louvrea.htm*
National Endowment for the Arts: *www.arts.endow.gov*
Smithsonian American Art Museum: *www.nmaa.si.edu*
World Wide Arts Resources: *www.wwar.com*

Business and Investing
Better Business Bureau: *www.bbb.org*
Commodity Futures Trading Commission: *www.cftc.gov*
E*TRADE: *www.etrade.com*
Nasdaq: *www.nasdaq.com*
New York Stock Exchange: *www.nyse.com*
Securities and Exchange Commission (SEC): *www.sec.gov*
Small Business Administration (SBA): *www.sba.gov*
Standard & Poor's: *www.standardpoor.com*

Computers and the Internet
CNET: *www.cnet.com*
Shareware.com: *shareware.cnet.com/*
WIRED News: *www.wired.com*
World Wide Web Consortium: *www.w3.org*
ZDNet: *www.zdnet.com*

Education
College Board Online: *www.collegeboard.org*
FamilyEducation.com: *www.familyeducation.com*
FinAid: *www.finaid.org*
Peterson's: *www.petersons.com*
Princeton Review: *www.review.com*
U.S. News Online Education Page: *www.usnews.com/usnews/edu*

Entertainment
All Music Guide: *www.allmusic.com*
Entertainment Weekly Online: *www.ew.com/ew/*
Internet Movie Database: *www.imdb.com*
Moviefone: *www.moviefone.com*
Mr. Showbiz: *www.mrshowbiz.com*
NetRadio: *www.netradio.com*
SonicNet: *www.sonicnet.com*

Government
White House: *www.whitehouse.gov*
Senate: *www.senate.gov*
House of Representatives: *www.house.gov*
Supreme Court Collection: *supct.law.cornell.edu/supct*
Department of Agriculture: *www.usda.gov*
Department of Commerce: *www.doc.gov*
Department of Defense: *www.defenselink.mil*
Department of Education: *www.ed.gov*
Department of Energy: *www.doe.gov*
Department of Health and Human Services: *www.dhhs.gov*
Department of Housing and Urban Development: *www.hud.gov*
Department of the Interior: *www.doi.gov*
Department of Justice: *www.usdoj.gov*
Department of Labor: *www.dol.gov*
Department of State: *www.state.gov*
Department of Transportation: *www.dot.gov*
Department of the Treasury: *www.ustreas.gov*
Department of Veterans' Affairs: *www.va.gov*

Other Government Resources

Census Bureau: *www.census.gov*
Central Intelligence Agency (CIA): *www.odci.gov/cia*
Consumer Product Safety Commission: *www.cpsc.gov*
Environmental Protection Agency (EPA): *www.epa.gov*
Equal Employment Opportunity Commission (EEOC):
   www.eeoc.gov
Federal Bureau of Investigation: *www.fbi.gov*
Federal Communications Commission: *www.fcc.gov*
Federal Deposit Insurance Corporation (FDIC):
   www.fdic.gov
Federal Election Commission (FEC): *www.fec.gov*
Federal Emergency Management Agency: *www.fema.gov*
Federal Housing Finance Board: *www.fhfb.gov*
Federal Reserve System (FRS), Board of Governors of
   (the Federal Reserve Board): *www.federalreserve.gov*
Federal Trade Commission (FTC): *www.ftc.gov*
National Transportation Safety Board: *www.ntsb.gov*
Postal Rate Commission: *www.prc.gov*
Social Security Administration: *www.ssa.gov*
U.S. Commission on Civil Rights: *www.usccr.gov*
U.S. International Trade Commission: *www.usitc.gov*
U.S. Postal Service: *www.usps.gov*

Health and Fitness

Centers for Disease Control and Prevention: *www.cdc.gov*
Fitness Online: *www.fitnessonline.com*
MedExplorer: *www.medexplorer.com*
National Institutes of Health: *www.nih.gov*
New England Journal of Medicine: *www.nejm.org*
President's Council on Physical Fitness and Sports:
   www.indiana.edu/~preschal/council.html
ReutersHealth: *www.reutershealth.com*
World Health Organization: *www.who.int/*

Jobs

CareerMosaic: *www.careermosaic.com*
CareerPath.com: *www.careerpath.com*
Monster Board: *www.monster.com*

Kids

Information Please Kids' Almanac: *kids.infoplease.com*
Sports Illustrated Kids: *www.sikids.com*
TIME for Kids: *www.timeforkids.com/TFK*
Yahooligans!: *www.yahooligans.com*

Labor

Federal Labor Relations Authority: *www.flra.gov*
National Labor Relations Board (NLRB): *www.nlrb.gov*
Occupational Safety and Health Review Commission:
   www.oshrc.gov
President's Committee on Employment of People with Dis-
   abilities: *www50.pcepd.gov/pcepd*

Magazines

Consumer Reports Online: *www.consumerreports.org*
Fortune: *www.fortune.com/fortune*
People: *people.aol.com/people/index.html*
Salon: *www.salon.com*
TIME: *www.time.com/time*
U.S. News & World Report:
   www.usnews.com/usnews/home.htm

Military

U.S. Marine Corps: *www.usmc.mil*
Selective Service System: *www.sss.gov*
U.S. Air Force: *www.af.mil*
U.S. Army: *www.army.mil*
U.S. Coast Guard: *www.uscg.mil*
U.S. Navy: *www.navy.mil*

News/Media

Associated Press: *wire.ap.org*
BBC TV & Radio: *www.bbc.co.uk*
CNN Interactive: *www.cnn.com*
MSNBC: *www.msnbc.com*
National Public Radio Online: *www.npr.org*
Newspapers Online: *www.newspapers.com*
New York Times: *www.nytimes.com*
Reuters: *www.reuters.com/news*
USA Today: *www.usatoday.com*
Wall Street Journal: *www.wsj.com*
The Washington Post: *www.washingtonpost.com*

Public Service

Corporation for National Service: *www.cns.gov*
Habitat for Humanity: *www.habitat.org*
Peace Corps: *www.peacecorps.gov*

Reference

Ask Jeeves: *www.ask.com*
CIA World Factbook:
   www.odci.gov/cia/publications/factbook
eHow: *www.ehow.com*
FedStats (gov't. statistics): *www.fedstats.gov*
Information Please: *www.infoplease.com*
Internet Public Library: *www.ipl.org*
MapQuest: *www.mapquest.com*

Science

National Aeronautics and Space Administration (NASA):
   www.nasa.gov
National Science Foundation (NSF): *www.nsf.gov*
Science Magazine: *www.sciencemag.org*
Scientific American Magazine: *www.scientificamerican.com*

Search Engines

AltaVista: *www.altavista.com*
Excite: *www.excite.com*
Lycos: *www.lycos.com*
Yahoo!: *www.yahoo.com*

Shopping

Amazon.com: *www.amazon.com*
CDNow: *www.cdnow.com*
eBay: *www.ebay.com*
Florists' Transworld Delivery, Inc.: *www.ftd.com*
Powell's Books: *www.powells.com*
AltaVista Shopping: *shopping.altavista.com/home.sdc*

Sports

CNN Sports Illustrated: *www.CNNSI.com*
ESPN: *espn.go.com*
Major League Baseball: *www.majorleaguebaseball.com*
Major League Soccer: *www.majorleaguesoccer.com*
National Basketball Association: *www.nba.com*
National Football League: *www.nfl.com*
National Hockey League: *www.nhl.com*
Women's National Basketball Association: *www.wnba.com*

Travel

Centers for Disease Control Home Travel Information
   Page: *www.cdc.gov/travel/*
Europe Through the Back Door: *www.ricksteves.com*
Flight Tracker:
   www.thetrip.com/ft/home/0,2096,1-1,00.shtml
Fodor's: *www.fodors.com*
Frommer's BudgetTravel Online: *www.frommers.com*
Hostelling International: *www.iyhf.org/index.html*
Lonely Planet Online: *www.lonelyplanet.com*
National Park Service: *www.nps.gov*
Priceline.com: *www.priceline.com*
Travelocity.com: *www.travelocity.com*

Weather

IntelliCast: *www.intellicast.com*
National Weather Service: *www.nws.noaa.gov*
The Weather Channel: *www.weather.com*

U.S. Households Using the Internet by Characteristic, 1998

(percent)

Characteristic	Total U.S.	Rural	Urban	Central city	Characteristic	Total U.S.	Rural	Urban	Central city
Race:					**Income:**				
White non-Hispanic	29.8%	23.7%	32.4%	32.3%	Under $5,000	8.1%	4.3%	9.1%	9.5%
Black non-Hispanic	11.2	7.1	11.7	10.2	$5,000–$9,999	6.1	2.9	7.2	6.8
AIEA non-Hispanic[1]	18.9	12.8	22.5	20.2	$10,000–$14,999	7.4	6.0	7.9	8.1
API non-Hispanic[2]	36.0	24.7	36.5	33.3	$15,000–$19,999	9.8	8.4	10.3	11.0
Hispanic	12.6	9.8	12.9	10.2	$20,000–$24,999	12.1	10.0	12.9	14.4
					$25,000–$34,999	19.1	15.4	20.4	22.5
Age:					$35,000–$49,999	29.5	26.4	30.6	31.8
Under 25 years	20.5	13.3	22.0	22.8	$50,000–$74,999	43.9	38.7	45.7	44.0
25–34 years	30.1	24.2	31.6	28.8	$75,000+	60.3	53.7	62.0	59.7
35–44 years	34.1	30.2	35.4	31.3					
45–54 years	35.0	30.8	36.5	30.7					
55+ years	14.6	12.4	15.4	13.8					

1. American Indians/Eskimos/Aleuts. 2. Asians/Pacific Islanders. *Source:* U.S. Dept. of Commerce, National Telecommunications and Information Administration. *Falling Through the Net: Defining the Digital Divide.* Web: www.ntia.doc.gov/ntiahome/fttn99/.

U.S. Computer Ownership by Characteristic, 1998

(percent)

Characteristic	Total U.S.	Rural	Urban	Central city	Characteristic	Total U.S.	Rural	Urban	Central city
Race:					**Income:**				
White non-Hispanic	46.6%	42.0%	48.5%	47.4%	Under $5,000	15.9%	11.9%	16.9%	15.7%
Black non-Hispanic	23.2	17.9	23.8	21.8	$5,000–$9,999	12.3	8.1	13.6	12.9
AIEA non-Hispanic[1]	34.3	26.8	38.7	35.6	$10,000–$14,999	15.9	13.8	16.6	17.9
API non-Hispanic[2]	55.0	40.6	55.6	50.5	$15,000–$19,999	21.2	22.1	20.8	21.8
Hispanic	25.5	23.2	25.7	21.4	$20,000–$24,999	25.7	24.7	26.1	26.6
					$25,000–$34,999	35.8	34.0	36.5	38.3
Age:					$35,000–$49,999	50.2	51.0	50.0	50.2
Under 25 years	32.3	27.7	33.3	34.0	$50,000–$74,999	66.3	64.2	67.1	65.4
25–34 years	46.0	42.4	46.9	43.5	$75,000+	79.9	76.5	80.8	77.3
35–44 years	54.9	55.2	54.8	48.5					
45–54 years	54.7	52.8	55.3	49.2					
55+ years	25.8	23.3	26.7	23.0					

1. American Indians/Eskimos/Aleuts. 2. Asians/Pacific Islanders. *Source:* U.S. Dept. of Commerce, National Telecommunications and Information Administration. *Falling through the Net: Defining the Digital Divide.* Web: www.ntia.doc.gov/ntiahome/fttn99/.

Top-Selling Software, 1999

Rank	Title	Publisher	Average price	Rank	Title	Publisher	Average price
1.	TurboTax	Intuit	$20	12.	TaxCut 1998 Deluxe Filing Edition	Block Financial	$ 16
2.	TurboTax Deluxe	Intuit	28	13.	Microsoft Encarta Encyclopedia	Microsoft	26
3.	Norton Antivirus 5.0	Symantec	18	14.	Microsoft Age of Empires II: Age of Kings	Microsoft	43
4.	Microsoft Windows 98 Upgrade Second Edition	Microsoft	89	15.	Starcraft	Havas Interactive	28
5.	Quicken Deluxe	Intuit	55	16.	Print Shop 6.0 Deluxe	Mattel Media	22
6.	MP Roller Coaster Tycoon	Hasbro Interactive	28	17.	Half-Life	Havas Interactive	32
7.	Quicken	Intuit	30	18.	QuickBooks Pro 99	Intuit	201
8.	Microsoft Windows 98 Upgrade	Microsoft	86	19.	Command & Conquer 2: Tiberian Sun	Electronic Arts	40
9.	VirusScan 4.0 Classic	Network Associates	19	20.	Microsoft Flight Simulator	Microsoft	43
10.	Sim City 3000	Electronic Arts	42				
11.	Who Wants to Be a Millionaire	Disney	19				

Source: PC Data, Reston, Va. Web: www.pcdata.com.

Top-Selling Home Education Software, 1999

Rank	Title	Publisher	Average price	Rank	Title	Publisher	Average price
1.	Pokemon Studio Blue	Mattel Interactive	$20	6.	Jumpstart Preschool	Havas Interactive	$20
2.	Jumpstart First Grade	Havas Interactive	21	7.	Jumpstart Third Grade	Havas Interactive	20
3.	Blue's ABC Time Activities	Humongous (GT Interactive)	20	8.	Rugrats Movie Activity Challenge	Mattel Interactive	29
4.	Pokemon Studio Red	Mattel Interactive	20	9.	Jumpstart Kindergarten II	Havas Interactive	20
5.	Jumpstart Second Grade	Havas Interactive	20	10.	Blue's Birthday Adventure	Humongous (GT Interactive)	20

Source: PC Data, Reston, Va. Web: www.pcdata.com.

Top-Selling Business Software, 1999

Rank	Title	Publisher	Average price	Rank	Title	Publisher	Average price
1.	Norton Antivirus 5.0	Symantec	$ 18	6.	QuickBooks 99	Intuit	$115
2.	Microsoft Windows 98 Upgrade Second Edition	Microsoft	89	7.	Norton Antivirus 2000 6.0	Symantec	36
3.	Microsoft Windows 98 Upgrade	Microsoft	86	8.	Norton System Works 2000 3.0	Symantec	53
4.	VirusScan 4.0 Classic	Network Associates	19	9.	Norton System Works 2.0	Symantec	53
5.	QuickBooks Pro 99	Intuit	201	10.	VirusScan 4.0 Deluxe	Network Associates	43

Source: PC Data, Reston, Va. Web: www.pcdata.com.

Remember Y2K?

A Nostalgic Look at the Disaster That Never Was

In 1999 talk of the "Y2K glitch" was almost as inescapable as El Niño conversations the year before. It seemed everyone had a prediction about what would happen at the first moment of the new millennium as high-tech equipment not programmed to understand dates past 1999 reacted to the switch. Thousands of people stocked up on canned goods, withdrew extra cash from ATM machines, and even built underground shelters in anticipation of power outages or worse. After all, according to the most dire news reports, computers maintained by the Russian government could potentially have launched nuclear missiles aimed at the United States.

As it turned out, the world entered 2000 quietly and the paranoia that preoccupied us the previous year was soon forgotten. Some claim the hubbub was for nothing. Others, including the International Y2K Cooperation Center (IYCC), believe the extensive preparations were essential to our escape from greater disaster.

The IYCC, a multinational organization set up to address the Y2K concern, released a report in February 2000 summarizing the actual consequences of the bug. According to the report, there were "no serious disruptions of critical services on a national, regional, or global level." The most frequent malfunctions involved date recording in many types of hospital equipment, finance and accounting program glitches, and problems in ticketing systems used by transportation and entertainment companies. Most problems were remedied by switching to manual operations while the computer equipment was quickly fixed or replaced. Below is a sampling of some of the world's more unusual (though still considered "minor") Y2K problems.

- In France, ground stations reported a communications problem due to a glitch in a military satellite.
- In Hong Kong, the police department experienced a failure in the equipment used for breath-testing suspected drunk drivers.
- Kazakhstan reported that a lack of funding prevented one hydroelectric power station from replacing non-Y2K compliant computers. As a result, technology processes were being handled manually.
- In Nigeria, some private telephone operators were forced to stop service for a few days beginning Dec. 31, 1999, after failing to comply with Y2K standards.
- Spain reported problems at two nuclear power plants on Jan. 1, 2000. One plant experienced a calculation glitch, while the other had problems accessing restricted areas. Both incidents were labeled "noncritical" and resolved quickly.
- In Tanzania, a glitch in a computer used for gathering international news led to television transmission problems in Zanzibar.
- The United States reported three Y2K-related glitches. The first was the potential for transactions involving certain credit-card companies to be recorded twice due to the companies' failure to implement Y2K-compliant software. The second involved the automated telephone system for claiming unemployment insurance benefits in Florida and Kentucky. The third, reported by the Federal Reserve Bank of Chicago, was a problem in the transfer of about $700,000 in tax payments from customers of 60 area financial institutions.
- Zambia reported that a Y2K glitch led to a telecommunications block between Zambia and Malawi.

How to Prevent a Meltdown

Answers to global warming are in the wind—and in the sunshine

By MICHAEL D. LEMONICK TIME

After decades of rancorous debate, only a handful of the most doctrinaire die-hards still dispute the idea that human activity is heating up the planet. All the signs seem to point that way: storms have become more intense and weather patterns more erratic; the 1990s was by far the hottest decade on record; and the rise in temperature has been greatest in polar regions and around cities. These facts dovetail ominously well with the theory that carbon dioxide (CO_2), released by burning coal, oil, and gasoline for heat, electricity, and transportation, is trapping excess energy from the sun. Global warming is real—and will probably get worse.

Energy Sources Must Change

The only way to slow it down, almost every scientist agrees, is to restructure the way we produce energy. Such stopgap measures as insulation, carpooling, and energy-efficient light bulbs are all useful ways to begin curbing the burning of carbon-rich fossil fuels. But in the long run, as the world's population continues to increase and living standards rise, these measures will not be enough.

That's why experiments going on in laboratories around the world are so important. At a research center outside Stuttgart, Germany, engineers at DaimlerChrysler have created a high-performance car whose tail pipe emits nothing but water vapor. In a giant wind tunnel at NASA's Ames Research Center in California, engineers are set to analyze air turbulence in order to make superefficient wind-power turbines. In Japan scientists are perfecting paper-thin solar cells that will be cheap to produce and could turn every house into its own electricity supplier. These ventures, along with many others, are beginning to draw the outlines of a world in which energy use keeps rising and, though fossil fuels remain an important power source, CO_2 levels in the atmosphere actually begin to drop.

Hydrogen-Powered Cars

Cars like the NECAR4, housed in a lab near Stuttgart, could help make that happen. This experimental vehicle, being jointly developed by Ford, DaimlerChrysler, and Canada's Ballard Power Systems, gets its energy from hydrogen—the most abundant fuel in the entire universe. Hydrogen, unlike fossil fuels, contains no carbon atoms and thus generates zero carbon dioxide.

Using hydrogen as an energy source can cause pollution, since burning hydrogen taints the atmosphere by rearranging air molecules to form nitrogen oxides and ozone. But NECAR4 doesn't burn hydrogen. Instead, it uses an onboard fuel cell, developed by Ballard, to let hydrogen combine slowly with oxygen at moderate temperatures. What comes out is plain H_2O and electricity.

Fuel cells were invented in the 1800s and adopted by NASA for generating clean power in space in the 1960s. Only in the 1990s were they made small enough to fit inside a car. The NECAR4, based on a Mercedes-Benz A-class compact sedan, accommodates five people plus luggage, reaches speeds of 90 m.p.h. (145 km/h), and goes about 280 mi. (450 km) between fill-ups. "It's comparable," says Ferdinand Panik, head of DaimlerChrysler's Fuel Cell Project, "to the impact the microchip had on computer technology."

Fuel Cell Revolution

That impact may be felt very soon. The first major field test of fuel-cell vehicles took place in California in 2000. And by 2004, DaimlerChrysler and Ford—as well as GM, Toyota, and other companies—expect to be selling fuel-cell cars directly to consumers.

Ideally, the hydrogen would be produced sustainably with renewable electricity from the sun or wind. But even under the most optimistic predictions for improvements in renewable technology, the electricity required to split H_2O into H and O would be prohibitively expensive. So the first large-scale plants will probably wrest hydrogen from old-fashioned fossil fuels.

That's extraordinarily good news for China, whose gigantic size, rapid industrialization, and huge domestic coal reserves threaten to pump cataclysmic amounts of CO_2 into the air over the next century. While scaling fuel cells down to fit inside cars and trucks has been a challenge, scaling them up or linking them together to run factories and power plants should be no problem at all.

The one danger in pulling hydrogen from fossil fuels is that it leaves carbon dioxide behind. If the CO_2 is simply vented into the atmosphere, global warming will be as big a problem as ever. There is an alternative though: pump it into the ground. In Norway, for example, the energy company Norsk Hydro is building a power plant that will be fueled with hydrogen drawn from natural gas. The CO_2 that's left over will be reinjected into an oil field on the continental shelf. Not only will this take the carbon dioxide out of circulation but it will also pressurize the field and make the remaining oil easier to pump out. In Europe and the U.S., pumping CO_2 into underground aquifers has proved an effective way of keeping it out of the atmosphere.

Fossil fuels will remain an important energy source for the foreseeable future, but they will eventually run out and the world will have to switch to what environmental visionaries have been dreaming about since the original Earth Day: endlessly renewable power from wind and sun.

Wind and Solar Power

Wind has the edge. It's fast catching up with oil and gas in cost efficiency with the help of experiments such as the one at Ames Research Center. By comparing what they learn from the wind tunnel's smooth airflow with data from the turbulent breezes at the National Renewable Energy Laboratory's test range near Golden, Colo., engineers expect to build a new generation of superefficient wind turbines with blades well over 200 ft. (60 m) across.

Efficiency doesn't help when the wind isn't blowing; you need to store energy generated during gales for use when the air is still. The best way to do that, says Robert Williams, of Princeton University's Center for Energy and Environmental Studies, is to use the excess to compress air and force it into subterranean aquifers, caves, or salt domes.

Then, when the wind dies, the compressed air can be pulled out to help drive the turbines. "The technology was originally developed in the 1960s," says Williams, "to let nuclear power plants store excess electricity during off-peak hours." Now it could permit countries rich in wind resources—including China, the U.S., Denmark, and Germany—to take advantage of a free, unlimited, and nearly pollutionless source of electricity.

Solar Cells

On the solar-power front, the visions of 1970s-era environmentalists can still be realized, at least in part, if manufacturers could find a way to produce silicon-based photovoltaic cells more efficiently and thus drive down their high cost. One strategy is to reduce the thickness of a solar cell from the current standard—about that of a piece of cardboard—to one-hundredth of that size. Such thin-film cells, whose development is furthest along in Japan, will use less raw material and be far easier to manufacture with the extraordinary purity required to make them efficient enough to be economical. Beyond that, their light weight will make installation easy, permitting them to be applied as building façades or even over windows. Because a given solar cell is sensitive to just a few colors of the many that make up sunlight, researchers are working on multilayered cells, which will trap most of the colors of the rainbow.

Since the sun doesn't shine with equal power everywhere, even a building slathered with solar cells will need another source of electricity. One possibility: a system that uses both solar cells and a two-way fuel cell. During daylight, when the solar cells are operating, excess electricity could be run through a fuel cell to produce hydrogen from water. At night, the fuel cell could use the hydrogen to produce electricity again.

Ideally, every factory, building, home, and vehicle would have its own clean, renewable power source, eliminating oil wells, coal mines, power plants, and power lines—and all the environmental disruption they cause. For now, though, the world has a more urgent mission: to stop the planet from overheating, and do it in a hurry. Thanks to the fuel-cell cars and more advanced wind turbines and solar cells that are close to fruition, the global-warming challenge seems a little less daunting than it did just a few years ago. □

World Energy Overview

Source: Energy Information Administration, Dept. of Energy. Web: www.eia.doe.gov/emeu/iea/overview.html.

World Primary Energy Production Trends

Between 1989 and 1998, the world's total output of primary energy—petroleum, natural gas, coal, and electric power (hydro, nuclear, biomass, geothermal, solar, and wind)—increased at an average annual rate of 1.1 percent. World production increased from 346 quadrillion Btu in 1989 to 382 quadrillion Btu in 1998.

In 1998, petroleum continued to be the world's most important primary energy source, accounting for 39.8 percent, or 152 quadrillion Btu, of world primary energy production. Coal ranked second, accounting for 23.2 percent of world primary energy production. Dry natural gas, which accounted for 22.4 percent of world primary energy production in 1998, ranked third.

Hydro, nuclear, and other (biomass, geothermal, solar, and wind) electric power generation ranked fourth, fifth, and seventh, respectively, as primary energy sources in 1998, accounting for 7.0, 6.4, and 0.6 percent, respectively, of world primary energy production. Hydroelectric power continued to represent the largest share of primary electric power generation, contributing 2.6 trillion kilowatthours in 1998.

In 1998, the 2.5 quadrillion Btu of biomass, geothermal energy, and solar energy produced in the United States and not used for generating electricity ranked sixth as a primary energy source, accounting for about 0.7 percent of world primary energy production.

Major Energy Producers and Consumers

In 1998, three countries—the United States, Russia, and China—were the leading producers and consumers of world energy. These three countries produced 38 percent and consumed 41 percent of the world's total energy.

The United States, Russia, China, Saudi Arabia, and Canada were the world's five largest producers of energy in 1998, supplying 48.4 percent of the world's total energy. The next five leading producers of primary energy were the United Kingdom, India, Iran, Norway, and Mexico, and together they supplied an additional 13 percent of the world's total energy. The United States supplied 72.8 quadrillion Btu of primary energy, significantly more than the 41.0 quadrillion Btu produced by Russia or the 33.1 quadrillion Btu produced by China.

The United States, China, Russia, Japan, and Germany were the world's five largest consumers of primary energy in 1998, accounting for 50.3 percent of world energy consumption. They were followed by India, Canada, France, the United Kingdom, and Brazil, which together accounted for an additional 13.8 percent of world energy consumption. The United States consumed 94.8 quadrillion Btu, more than two and three-quarter times the 33.9 quadrillion Btu consumed by China, while Russia consumed 26.0 quadrillion Btu.

Production and Consumption of Major Energy Sources

Petroleum

Global production of petroleum (crude oil and natural gas plant liquids) increased from 64.4 million barrels per day to 72.8 million barrels per day between 1989 and 1998, or 13.1 percent. Saudi Arabia, the United States, and Russia were the three largest producers of petroleum in 1998. Together, they produced 31.9 percent of the world's petroleum. Production from Iran and Mexico accounted for an additional 9.9 percent.

In 1998, the United States consumed 18.9 million barrels per day of petroleum—almost 26 percent of world consumption. Japan ranked a distant second in consumption, with 5.5 barrels per day, followed by China, Germany, and Russia.

Natural Gas

World production of dry natural gas increased from 72.1 trillion cubic feet to 83 trillion cubic feet, or 15 percent, over the period from 1989 to 1998. Russia was the leading producer in 1998 at 20.9 trillion cubic feet, followed by the United States at 18.9 trillion cubic feet. Together these two countries produced 48 percent of the world total. Canada ranked a distant third in production at 6.0 trillion cubic feet, followed by the United Kingdom and the Netherlands, with 3.2 and 2.8 trillion cubic feet, respectively. These three countries accounted for 15 percent of the world total.

In 1998, the United States, which was the leading consumer of dry natural gas at 21.3 trillion cubic feet, and Russia, which ranked second at 13.9 trillion cubic feet, together accounted for 43 percent of world consumption. Germany ranked a distant third in consumption, with 3.3 trillion cubic feet, followed by the United Kingdom and Canada, at 3.1 and 3.0 trillion cubic feet, respectively.

Energy Web Sites

U.S. Department of Energy: www.doe.gov
Energy Efficiency and Renewable Energy Network (EREN): www.eren.doe.gov
ENERGYguide:
  www.energyguide.com
Federal Energy Regulatory Commission: www.ferc.fed.us
Energy Information Administration (EIA): www.eia.doe.gov
Nuclear Regulatory Commission (NRC): www.nrc.gov
National Renewable Energy Laboratory (NREL): www.nrel.gov
Alliance to Save Energy: www.ase.org
Natural Resources Defense Council: www.nrdc.org
American Council for an Energy-Efficient Economy: www.aceee.org
Center for Renewable Energy and Sustainable Technology (CREST): www.solstice.crest.org

Coal

Coal was the only primary energy source to experience a production decline between 1989 and 1998. Production dropped from 5.33 billion short tons to 5.04 billion short tons, or 5.3 percent, over the period. China was the leading producer in 1998 at 1.35 billion short tons—equivalent to 23.1 quadrillion Btu. The United States was the second leading producer in 1998 with 1.12 billion short tons—equivalent to 23.8 quadrillion Btu. India ranked a distant third at 359 million short tons—equivalent to 6.6 quadrillion Btu, followed by Australia, at 314 million short tons—equivalent to 5.7 quadrillion Btu, and Russia at 272 million short tons—equivalent to 4.5 quadrillion Btu. Together, these five countries accounted for 68 percent of world coal production in 1998.

China was also the largest consumer of coal in 1998, using 1.31 billion short tons, followed by the United States, which consumed 1.04 billion short tons, India, Russia, and Germany. These five countries together accounted for 65 percent of world coal consumption.

Hydroelectric Power

The generation of hydroelectric power increased from 2.1 trillion kilowatthours to 2.6 trillion kilowatthours, or 22.8 percent, between 1989 and 1998. Canada, the United States, Brazil, China, and Russia, were the five largest producers of hydroelectric power in 1998. Their combined hydroelectric power generation accounted for 51 percent of the world total. Canada led the world with 329 billion kilowatthours or 3.4 quadrillion Btu. The United States was a close second with 324 billion kilowatthours or 3.3 quadrillion Btu. Brazil ranked third with 289 billion kilowatthours or 3.0 quadrillion Btu. China was fourth with 203 billion kilowatthours or 2.1 quadrillion Btu, followed by Russia with 151 billion kilowatthours or 1.6 quadrillion Btu.

Nuclear Electric Power

The generation of nuclear electric power increased from 1.8 trillion kilowatthours to 2.3 trillion kilowatthours between 1989 and 1998, or 25.7 percent. The United States led the world in nuclear electric power generation in 1998 with 674 billion kilowatthours or 7.2 quadrillion Btu. France was second with 367 billion kilowatthours or 3.8 quadrillion Btu and Japan ranked third with 318 billion kilowatthours or 3.3 quadrillion Btu. In 1998, these three countries generated 59 percent of the world's nuclear electric power.

Geothermal, Solar, and Wind Electric Power

The generation of biomass, geothermal, solar, and wind electric power increased from 117 billion kilowatthours to 196 billion kilowatthours between 1989 and 1998, or 68.1 percent. The United States led the world in biomass, geothermal, solar, and wind electric power generation in 1998 with 75.7 billion kilowatthours. Japan was second with 23.9 billion kilowatthours, followed by Germany with 10.4 billion kilowatthours, Brazil with 9.7 billion kilowatthours, and Finland with 8.4 billion kilowatthours. These five countries accounted for 65 percent of the world's biomass, geothermal, solar, and wind electric power generation in 1998.

World Energy Consumption and Carbon Emissions, 1990–2020

Region	Energy consumption (quadrillion btu)				Carbon emissions (million metric tons)			
	1990	1997	2010	2020	1990	1997	2010	2020
Industrialized nations[1]	182.8	203.7	238.7	259.9	2,850	3,039	3,563	3,928
Eastern Europe/Former Soviet Union	76.4	53.3	63.0	75.7	1,337	878	992	1,151
Developing nations								
Asia[2]	51.4	75.3	126.4	172.6	1,067	1,522	2,479	3,380
Middle East[3]	13.1	17.9	26.2	34.3	229	297	422	552
Africa	9.3	11.4	15.8	20.6	180	214	292	380
Central and South America[4]	13.7	18.3	30.1	44.7	174	225	399	617
Total developing	87.6	122.9	198.5	272.1	1,649	2,258	3,591	4,930
Total world	346.7	379.9	500.2	607.7	5,836	6,175	8,146	10,009

1. Includes the U.S., Canada, Mexico, Japan, France, Germany, Italy, the Netherlands, and the United Kingdom. 2. China, India, and South Korea are represented in developing Asia. 3. Turkey is represented in the Middle East. 4. Brazil is represented in Central and South America. *Source:* U.S. Energy Information Administration, *International Energy Outlook 2000.* Web: www.eia.doe.gov/oiaf/ieo/tbl_1.html

Renewable Energy Consumption in the U.S. by Source, 1989–1999

(quadrillion btu)

Year	Wood and waste[1]	Geothermal[2]	Conventional hydroelectric power[3, 4]	Solar[5]	Wind[6]	Total
1989	3.050	0.338	2.999	0.059	0.024	6.470
1990	2.665	0.359	3.140	0.063	0.032	6.260
1991	2.679	0.368	3.222	0.066	0.032	6.367
1992	2.826	0.379	2.863	0.068	0.030	6.167
1993	2.782	0.393	3.147	0.071	0.031	6.424
1994	2.914	0.395	2.971	0.072	0.036	6.387
1995	3.044	0.339	3.474	0.073	0.033	6.963
1996	3.104	0.352	3.915	0.075	0.035	7.482
1997	2.982	0.328	3.940	0.074	0.034	7.358
1998	2.991	0.335	3.552	0.074	0.031	6.984
1999e	3.514	0.327	3.417	0.076	0.038	7.373

NOTES: Totals may not equal sum of components due to independent rounding. 1. Wood, wood waste, black liquor, red liquor, spent sulfite liquor, pitch, wood sludge, peat, railroad ties, utility poles, municipal solid waste, landfill gas, methane, digester gas, liquid acetonitrile waste, tall oil, waste alcohol, medical waste, paper pellets, sludge waste, solid byproducts, tires, agricultural byproducts, closed looped biomass, fish oil, and straw. 2. Includes electricity imports from Mexico that are derived from geothermal energy. Includes grid-connected electricity, and geothermal heat pump and direct use energy. Excludes shaft power and remote electrical power. 3. Hydroelectricity generated by pumped storage is not included in renewable energy. 4. Includes electricity net imports from Canada that are derived from hydroelectric power. 5. Includes solar thermal and photovoltaic energy. 6. Includes only grid-connected electricity. e = estimated. *Source:* Energy Information Administration (EIA). Web: www.eia.doe.gov.

U.S. Emissions of Greenhouse Gases, 1990–1998

(million metric tons of gas)

Gas	1990	1991	1992	1993	1994	1995	1996	1997	1998[1]
Carbon dioxide	4,939.0	4,886.0	4,972.9	5,091.5	5,169.7	5,220.5	5,395.6	5,464.9	5,483.4
Methane	30.2	30.5	30.6	29.9	30.0	30.2	29.3	29.3	28.8
Nitrous oxide	1.2	1.2	1.2	1.2	1.3	1.3	1.2	1.2	1.2
Halocarbons and other gases									
CFC-11, CFC-12, CFC-113	0.2	0.2	0.1	0.1	0.1	0.1	0.1	0.0	0.0
HCFC-22	0.1	0.1	0.1	0.1	0.1	0.1	0.1	0.1	0.1
HFCs, PFCs, and SF_6	*	*	*	*	*	*	*	*	*
Methyl chloroform	0.2	0.2	0.1	0.1	0.1	*	*	*	*
Carbon monoxide	86.8	88.6	85.5	85.6	89.5	80.7	82.3	79.2	n.a.
Nitrogen oxides	21.2	21.3	21.6	21.8	22.1	21.5	21.3	21.4	n.a.
Nonmethane VOCs	18.9	19.0	18.6	18.8	19.4	18.6	17.4	17.3	n.a.

NOTES: * Less than 50,000 metric tons of gas. n.a. = not available. 1. Preliminary data. *Source:* Compiled by the U.S. Energy Information Administration. Web: www.eia.doe.gov/oiaf/1605/ggrpt/tbles1.html.

Air Quality in Selected U.S. Cities, 1983–1992

(number of PSI days greater than 100)[1]

PMSA[2]	1983	1984	1985	1986	1987	1988	1989	1990	1991	1992
Atlanta	23	8	9	17	19	15	3	16	5	4
Baltimore	60	46	21	24	28	41	7	12	20	4
Boston	37	28	9	9	10	17	5	3	7	4
Chicago	23	18	16	15	21	30	6	7	15	8
Cleveland	17	4	1	2	10	18	8	1	5	3
Dallas	20	18	19	10	10	6	4	7	7	4
Denver	69	62	39	47	37	19	12	7	7	7
Detroit	18	7	2	5	9	18	10	3	7	0
El Paso	16	20	24	34	27	13	29	20	8	11
Houston	70	49	48	45	54	48	32	48	40	29
Kansas City	4	12	3	4	3	3	2	2	1	1
Los Angeles	194	225	205	218	199	240	231	180	177	183
Miami	3	2	5	4	4	4	4	1	2	0
Minneapolis/St. Paul	36	21	21	13	7	1	6	1	0	0
New York	89	140	88	72	64	58	27	24	30	10
Philadelphia	58	39	29	24	37	43	22	17	32	8
Phoenix	72	107	82	85	40	22	30	8	4	8
Pittsburgh	27	15	9	8	13	23	9	11	3	1
San Diego	60	51	54	45	41	49	61	39	25	19
San Francisco	26	33	31	16	15	11	17	7	12	2
Seattle	11	4	27	11	13	6	4	3	0	0
St. Louis	33	22	10	14	16	17	12	8	6	2
Washington, D.C.	53	30	15	12	25	35	7	5	16	2
Total	**1,019**	**961**	**767**	**734**	**702**	**737**	**548**	**430**	**429**	**310**

1. PSI = Pollutant Standards Index. The PSI index integrates carbon monoxide and ozone data across an entire monitoring network into a single number which represents the worst daily air quality experienced in an urban area. PSI index ranges (and health effect descriptors) are as follows: 0 to 50 (good); 51 to 100 (moderate); 101 to 199 (unhealthful); 200 to 299 (very unhealthful); and 300 and above (hazardous). 2. PMSAs = Primary Metropolitan Statistical Areas. *Source:* U.S. Environmental Protection Agency, Office of Air Quality Planning & Standards. *National Air Quality and Emissions Trends Report, 1992.*

World Net Electricity Consumption by Region, 1990–2020

(billion kilowatt-hours)

Region	History		Projections					Average annual percent change, 1996–2020
	1990	1996	2000	2005	2010	2015	2020	
Industrialized countries	**6,248**	**7,194**	**7,529**	**8,298**	**9,001**	**9,749**	**10,485**	**1.6%**
United States	2,713	3,243	3,333	3,585	3,843	4,113	4,345	1.2
Eastern Europe/ Former Soviet Union	**1,908**	**1,535**	**1,396**	**1,536**	**1,673**	**1,813**	**1,965**	**1.0**
Developing countries	**2,274**	**3,324**	**3,895**	**5,033**	**6,282**	**7,695**	**9,422**	**4.4**
Developing Asia	1,268	2,002	2,350	3,105	3,937	4,918	6,122	4.8
China	551	925	1,107	1,520	2,030	2,672	3,486	5.7
India	257	378	493	644	802	981	1,192	4.9
South Korea	95	181	190	237	285	335	387	3.2
Other developing Asia	365	519	560	704	819	930	1,056	3.0
Central and South America	449	604	735	950	1,182	1,421	1,728	4.5
Total world	**10,431**	**12,053**	**12,821**	**14,868**	**16,956**	**19,257**	**21,872**	**2.5**

Sources: Energy Information Administration (EIA): *International Energy Annual 1996*, DOE/EIA-0219(96), and World Energy Projection System (1999).

Greatest Oil Reserves by Country, 2000

2000 rank	1999 rank	Country	2000 proved reserves (billion bbl)	1999 proved reserves (billion bbl)	2000 rank	1999 rank	Country	2000 proved reserves (billion bbl)	1999 proved reserves (billion bbl)
1.	1.	Saudi Arabia	261.0	259.0	6.	6.	Venezuela	72.6	72.6
2.	2.	Iraq	112.5	112.5	7.	7.	Russia	48.6	48.6
3.	3.	Kuwait	94.0	94.0	8.	9.	Libya	29.5	29.5
4.	4.	Abu Dhabi	92.2	92.2	9.	8.	Mexico	28.4	47.8
5.	5.	Iran	89.7	89.7	10.	10.	China	24.0	24.0

NOTES: Former Soviet Union figures are "explored reserves," which are understood to be proved plus some probable. All other figures are proved reserves recoverable with present technology and prices. bbl = barrels. *Source:* "Worldwide Look at Reserves and Production," *Oil & Gas Journal*, Vol. 97, No. 51 (Dec. 20, 1999), pp. 92–93. Web: http://ogj.pennnet.com.

Greatest Gas Reserves by Country, 2000

2000 rank	1999 rank	Country	2000 proved reserves (billion cu. ft.)	1999 proved reserves (billion cu. ft.)	2000 rank	1999 rank	Country	2000 proved reserves (billion cu. ft.)	1999 proved reserves (billion cu. ft.)
1.	1.	Russia	1,700,000	1,700,000	6.	6.	United States	164,041	167,223
2.	2.	Iran	812,300	812,300	7.	8.	Algeria	159,700	130,300
3.	3.	Qatar	300,000	300,000	8.	7.	Venezuela	142,500	142,500
4.	4.	Saudi Arabia	204,000	204,000	9.	9.	Nigeria	124,000	124,000
5.	5.	Abu Dhabi	196,100	196,100	10.	10.	Iraq	109,800	109,800

NOTES: Former Soviet Union figures are "explored reserves," which are understood to be proved plus some probable. All other figures are proved reserves recoverable with present technology and prices. *Source:* "Worldwide Look at Reserves and Production," *Oil & Gas Journal,* Vol. 97, No. 51 (Dec. 20, 1999), pp. 92–93. Web: http://ogj.pennnet.com.

Motor Vehicle Fuel Consumption and Travel in the U.S., 1960–1997

	1960	1965	1970	1975	1980	1985	1990	1995	1996	1997
Number registered (thousands)										
Passenger car	61,671	75,258	89,244	106,706	121,601	127,885	133,700	128,387	129,728	129,749
Total[1]	73,858	90,358	111,242	137,913	161,490	177,133	193,057	205,427	210,441	211,580
Vehicle-miles traveled (millions)										
Passenger car	587,000	723,000	917,000	1,034,000	1,112,000	1,247,000	1,408,000	1,438,000	1,470,000	1,502,000
Total[1]	719,000	888,000	1,110,000	1,328,000	1,527,000	1,775,000	2,144,000	2,423,000	2,486,000	2,560,000
Fuel consumed (million gallons)										
Passenger car	41,171	49,723	67,819	74,140	69,982	71,518	69,568	68,072	69,221	69,867
Total[1]	57,880	71,104	92,329	108,984	114,960	121,301	130,755	143,834	147,365	150,332
Average miles traveled per vehicle (thousands)										
Passenger car	9.5	9.6	10.3	9.7	9.1	9.7	10.5	11.2	11.3	11.6
Total[1]	9.7	9.8	10.0	9.6	9.5	10.0	11.1	11.8	11.8	12.1
Average miles traveled per gallon										
Passenger car	14.3	14.5	13.5	13.9	15.9	17.4	20.2	21.1	21.2	21.5
Total[1]	12.4	12.5	12.0	12.2	13.3	14.6	16.4	16.8	16.9	17.0
Average fuel consumed per vehicle (gallons)										
Passenger car	668	661	760	695	576	559	520	530	534	538
Total[1]	784	787	830	790	712	685	677	700	700	711

1. Includes personal passenger vehicles, buses, and trucks. *Source:* U.S. Department of Transportation. Web: www.dot.gov.

Major Air Pollutants

Pollutant	Sources	Effects
Ozone. A gas that can be found in two places. Near the ground (the troposphere), it is a major part of smog. Higher in the air (the stratosphere), it helps block radiation from the sun.	Ozone is not created directly, but is formed when nitrogen oxides and volatile organic compounds mix in sunlight. That is why ozone is mostly found in the summer. Nitrogen oxides come from burning gasoline, coal, or other fossil fuels. There are many types of volatile organic compounds, and they come from sources ranging from factories to trees.	Ozone near the ground can cause a number of health problems. Ozone can lead to more frequent asthma attacks in people who have asthma and can cause sore throats, coughs, and breathing difficulty. It may even lead to premature death. Ozone can also hurt plants and crops.
Carbon monoxide. A gas that comes from the burning of fossil fuels, mostly in cars. It cannot be seen or smelled.	Carbon monoxide is released when engines burn fossil fuels. Emissions are higher when engines are not tuned properly, and when fuel is not completely burned. Cars emit a lot of the carbon monoxide found outdoors. Furnaces and heaters in the home can emit high concentrations of carbon monoxide, too, if they are not properly maintained.	Carbon monoxide makes it hard for body parts to get the oxygen they need to run correctly. Exposure to carbon monoxide makes people feel dizzy and tired, and gives them headaches. Elderly people with heart disease are hospitalized more often when they are exposed to higher amounts of carbon monoxide.

Pollutant	Sources	Effects
Nitrogen dioxide. A reddish-brown gas that comes from the burning of fossil fuels. It has a strong smell at high levels.	Nitrogen dioxide mostly comes from power plants and cars. Nitrogen dioxide is formed in two ways—when nitrogen in the fuel is burned, or when nitrogen in the air reacts with oxygen at very high temperatures. Nitrogen dioxide can also react in the atmosphere to form ozone, acid rain, and particles.	High levels of nitrogen dioxide exposure can give people coughs and can make them feel short of breath. People who are exposed to nitrogen dioxide for a long time have a higher chance of getting respiratory infections. Acid rain can hurt plants and animals, and can make lakes dangerous to swim in or fish in.
Particulate matter. Solid or liquid matter that is suspended in the air. To remain in the air, particles are usually less than 0.1 mm wide, and can be as small as 0.00005 mm.	Particulate matter can be divided into two types—coarse particles and fine particles. Coarse particles are bigger than 0.002 mm, and are formed from sources like road dust, sea spray, and construction. Fine particles are smaller than 0.002 mm, and are formed when fuel is burned in automobiles and power plants.	Particulate matter that is small enough can enter the lungs and cause health problems. Some of these problems include: more frequent asthma attacks, more trips to the hospital for respiratory problems, and premature death. Particulate matter can also make clothes and other materials dirty.
Sulfur dioxide. A corrosive gas that cannot be seen or smelled at low levels but can have a "rotten egg" smell at high levels.	Sulfur dioxide mostly comes from the burning of coal or oil in power plants. It also comes from factories that make chemicals, paper, or fuel. Like nitrogen dioxide, sulfur dioxide also reacts in the atmosphere to form acid rain and particles.	Sulfur dioxide exposure can affect people who have asthma or emphysema by making it more difficult for them to breathe. It can also irritate people's eyes, noses, and throats. Sulfur dioxide can harm trees and crops, damage buildings, and make it harder for people to see long distances.
Lead. A blue-gray metal that is very toxic and is found in a number of forms and locations.	Outside, lead comes from cars in areas where unleaded gasoline is not used. Lead can also come from power plants and other industrial sources. Inside, lead paint is an important source of lead, especially in houses where paint is peeling. Lead in old pipes can also be a source of lead in drinking water.	High amounts of lead can be dangerous for small children, and can lead to lower IQs and kidney problems. For adults, exposure to lead can increase the chance of having heart attacks or strokes.
Toxic air pollutants. A large number of chemicals that are known or suspected to cause cancer. Some important pollutants in this category include arsenic, asbestos, benzene, and dioxin.	Each toxic air pollutant comes from a slightly different source, but many are created in chemical plants or are emitted when fossil fuels are burned. Some toxic air pollutants, like asbestos and formaldehyde, can be found in building materials and can lead to indoor air problems. Many toxic air pollutants can also enter the food and water supply, and people can be exposed when they eat or drink.	Toxic air pollutants can cause cancer. Some toxic air pollutants can also cause birth defects. Other effects depend on the pollutant, but can include skin and eye irritation and breathing problems.
Stratospheric ozone depleters. Chemicals that can destroy the ozone in the stratosphere. These chemicals include chlorofluorocarbons (CFCs), halons, and other compounds that include chlorine or bromine.	CFCs are used in air conditioners and refrigerators, since they work well as coolants. They can also be found in aerosol cans and fire extinguishers. Other stratospheric ozone depleters are used as solvents in industry.	If the ozone in the stratosphere is destroyed, people are exposed to more radiation from the sun (ultraviolet radiation). This can lead to skin cancer and eye problems. Higher ultraviolet radiation can also harm plants and animals.
Greenhouse gases. Gases that stay in the air for a long time, and warm up the planet by trapping sunlight. This is called the "greenhouse effect" because the gases act like the glass in a greenhouse. Some of the important greenhouse gases are carbon dioxide, methane, and nitrous oxide.	Carbon dioxide is the most important greenhouse gas, and it comes from the burning of fossil fuels in cars, power plants, houses, and industry. Methane is released during the processing of fossil fuels, and also comes from natural sources like cows and rice paddies. Nitrous oxide comes from industrial sources and decaying plants.	The greenhouse effect can lead to changes in the climate of the planet. Some of these changes might include more temperature extremes, higher sea levels, changes in forest composition, and damage to land near the coast. Human health might be affected by diseases that are related to temperature, or by damage to land and water.

Source: Jonathan Levy, Harvard School of Public Health. Based on information provided by the Environmental Protection Agency.

Largest Nuclear Power Plants in the U.S.

Plant	Operating utility	Capacity (net MWe)	Year operative
Palo Verde 3, Ariz.	Arizona Public Service	1262	1987
Palo Verde 1, Ariz.	Arizona Public Service	1258	1985
Palo Verde 2, Ariz.	Arizona Public Service	1258	1986
South Texas 1, Tex.	Houston Lighting & Power	1250	1988
South Texas 2, Tex.	Houston Lighting & Power	1250	1989
Grand Gulf 1, Miss.	System Energy Resources	1200	1984
Washington Nuclear 2, Wash.	Washington Public Power Supply System	1170	1984
Perry 1, Ohio	Cleveland Electric Illuminating	1169	1986
Vogtle 2, Ga.	Georgia Power	1169	1989
Vogtle 1, Ga.	Georgia Power	1164	1987
Wolf Creek, Kans.	Wolf Creek Nuclear Operating	1163	1985
Seabrook 1, N.H.	Public Service Co. of N.H.	1162	1990
Comanche Peak 1, Tex.	Texas Utilities Electric Co.	1150	1990
Comanche Peak 2, Tex.	Texas Utilities Electric Co.	1150	1993
Callaway 1, Mo.	Union Electric	1143	1984
Nine Mile Point 2, N.Y.	Niagara Mohawk Power Corp.	1136	1987
Catawba 1, S.C.	Duke Power Co.	1129	1985
Catawba 2, S.C.	Duke Power Co.	1129	1986
McGuire 1, N.C.	Duke Power Co.	1129	1981
McGuire 2, N.C.	Duke Power Co.	1129	1983
Byron 1, Ill.	Commonwealth Edison	1120	1985
Byron 2, Ill.	Commonwealth Edison	1120	1987
Millstone 3, Conn.	Northeast Nuclear Energy	1120	1986
Sequoyah 1, Tenn.	Tennessee Valley Authority	1119	1980
Sequoyah 2, Tenn.	Tennessee Valley Authority	1119	1981

Source: Department of Energy, Energy Information Administration.

Animals and Nature

Animal Names: Male, Female, and Young

Animal	Male	Female	Young	Animal	Male	Female	Young	Animal	Male	Female	Young
Ass	Jack	Jenny	Foal	Duck	Drake	Duck	Duckling	Sheep	Ram	Ewe	Lamb
Bear	Boar	Sow	Cub	Elephant	Bull	Cow	Calf	Swan	Cob	Pen	Cygnet
Cat	Tom	Queen	Kitten	Fox	Dog	Vixen	Cub	Swine	Boar	Sow	Piglet
Cattle	Bull	Cow	Calf	Goose	Gander	Goose	Gosling	Tiger	Tiger	Tigress	Cub
Chicken	Rooster	Hen	Chick	Horse	Stallion	Mare	Foal	Whale	Bull	Cow	Calf
Deer	Buck	Doe	Fawn	Lion	Lion	Lioness	Cub	Wolf	Dog	Bitch	Pup
Dog	Dog	Bitch	Pup	Rabbit	Buck	Doe	Bunny				

Source: James G. Doherty, General Curator, The Wildlife Conservation Society.

Gestation, Incubation, and Longevity of Certain Animals

Animal	Gestation or incubation, in days & (average)	Longevity, in years & (record exceptions)	Animal	Gestation or incubation, in days & (average)	Longevity, in years & (record exceptions)
Ass	365	18-20 (63)	Horse	329-345 (336)	20-25 (50+)
Bear	180-240[1]	15-30 (47)	Human	253-303	[2]
Cat	52-69 (63)	10-12 (26+)	Kangaroo	32-39[1]	4-6 (23)
Chicken	22	7-8 (14)	Lion	105-113 (108)	10 (29)
Cow	280	9-12 (39)	Monkey	139-270[1]	12-15[1] (29)
Deer	197-300[1]	10-15 (26)	Mouse	19-31[1]	1-3 (4)
Dog	53-71 (63)	10-12 (24)	Parakeet (Budgerigar)	17-20 (18)	8 (12+)
Duck	21-35[1] (28)	10 (15)	Pig	101-130 (115)	10 (22)
Elephant	510-730[1] (624)	30-40 (71)	Pigeon	11-19	10-12 (39)
Fox	51-63[1]	8-10 (14)	Rabbit	30-35 (31)	6-8 (15)
Goat	136-160 (151)	12 (17)	Rat	21	3 (5)
Groundhog	31-32	4-9	Sheep	144-152[1] (151)	12 (16)
Guinea pig	58-75 (68)	3 (6)	Squirrel	44	8-9 (15)
Hamster, golden	15-17	2 (8)	Whale	365-547[1]	—
Hippopotamus	220-255 (240)	30 (49+)	Wolf	60-63	10-12 (16)

1. Depending on kind. 2. For life expectancy charts, *see* Expectation of Life by Race and Sex. *Source:* James G. Doherty, General Curator, The Wildlife Conservation Society.

Animal Group Terminology

Source: James G. Doherty, General Curator, The Wildlife Conservation Society.

ants: colony
bears: sleuth, sloth
bees: grist, hive, swarm
birds: flight, volery
cattle: drove
cats: clutter, clowder
chicks: brood, clutch
clams: bed
cranes: sedge, seige
crows: murder
doves: dule
ducks: brace, team
elephants: herd
elks: gang
finches: charm

fish: school, shoal, draught
foxes: leash, skulk
geese: flock, gaggle, skein
gnats: cloud, horde
goats: trip
gorillas: band
hares: down, husk
hawks: cast
hens: brood
hogs: drift
horses: pair, team
hounds: cry, mute, pack
kangaroos: troop
kittens: kindle, litter
larks: exaltation

lions: pride
locusts: plague
magpies: tidings
mules: span
nightingales: watch
oxen: yoke
oysters: bed
parrots: company
partridges: covey
peacocks: muster, ostentation
pheasants: nest, bouquet
pigs: litter
ponies: string
quail: bevy, covey

rabbits: nest
seals: pod
sheep: drove, flock
sparrows: host
storks: mustering
swans: bevy, wedge
swine: sounder
toads: knot
turkeys: rafter
turtles: bale
vipers: nest
whales: gam, pod
wolves: pack, route
woodcocks: fall

Speed of Animals

Most of the following measurements are for maximum speeds over approximate quarter-mile distances. Exceptions—which are included to give a wide range of animals—are the lion and elephant, whose speeds were clocked in the act of charging; the whippet, which was timed over a 200-yard course; the cheetah over a 100-yard distance; humans for a 15-yard segment of a 100-yard run; and the black mamba snake, six-lined race runner, spider, giant tortoise, three-toed sloth, and garden snail, which were measured over various small distances.

Animal	Speed (mph)	Animal	Speed (mph)	Animal	Speed (mph)
Peregrine falcon	200.00+	Zebra	40.00	Cat (domestic)	30.00
Cheetah	70.00	Mongolian wild ass	40.00	Human	27.89
Pronghorn antelope	61.00	Greyhound	39.35	Elephant	25.00
Wildebeest	50.00	Whippet	35.50	Black mamba snake	20.00
Lion	50.00	Rabbit (domestic)	35.00	Six-lined race runner	18.00
Thomson's gazelle	50.00	Mule deer	35.00	Squirrel	12.00
Quarter horse	47.50	Jackal	35.00	Pig (domestic)	11.00
Elk	45.00	Reindeer	32.00	Chicken	9.00
Cape hunting dog	45.00	Giraffe	32.00	House mouse	8.00
Coyote	43.00	Kangaroo	30.00	Spider (Tegenearia atrica)	1.17
Gray fox	42.00	White-tailed deer	30.00	Giant tortoise	0.17
Ostrich	40.00	Wart hog	30.00	Three-toed sloth	0.15
Hyena	40.00	Grizzly bear	30.00	Garden snail	0.03

Source: Natural History Magazine, March 1974, copyright 1974. The American Museum of Natural History; and James G. Doherty, General Curator, The Wildlife Conservation Society.

Threatened and Endangered Species

Group	Endangered[1] U.S.	Endangered[1] Foreign	Threatened[2] U.S.	Threatened[2] Foreign	Total species[3]	Species with recovery plans
Mammals	63	251	9	16	339	47
Birds	76	176	15	6	274	76
Reptiles	14	65	22	14	115	30
Amphibians	10	8	8	1	27	12
Fishes	68	11	44	0	123	90
Clams	61	2	8	0	71	45
Snails	20	1	11	0	32	20
Insects	30	4	8	0	42	27
Arachnids	6	0	0	0	6	5
Crustaceans	18	0	3	0	21	12
Animal subtotal	367	518	128	37	1,050	364
Flowering plants	565	1	139	0	705	528
Conifers and cycads	2	0	1	2	5	2
Ferns and allies	24	0	2	0	26	26
Lichens	2	0	0	0	2	2
Plant subtotal	593	1	142	2	738	558
Total	960	519	270[4]	39	1,788	922

NOTE: As of April 30, 2000. 1. *Endangered species* are those in danger of extinction. 2. *Threatened species* are those likely to become an endangered species within the foreseeable future. 3. Species listed as both endangered and threatened are tallied only once, for the endangered population (except the olive ridley sea turtle, for which only the threatened U.S. population is tallied). Those species are the argali, leopard, gray wolf, piping plover, roseate tern, chimpanzee, green sea turtle, Stellar sea lion, saltwater crocodile, chinook salmon, sockeye salmon, and steelhead. 4. Nine U.S. species have dual status. *Source:* U.S. Fish and Wildlife Service. Web: http://ecos.fws.gov/tess/html/boxscore.html.

America's 13 Most Endangered Rivers of 2000

Each year American Rivers analyzes the condition of the nation's rivers to determine which are the most "endangered." Threats to these rivers include dams and channelizations that are harmful to fish or wildlife populations; depletion due to the rivers' use as a water supply for human populations; and coal mining operations that fill streams with coal and dirt. For more information, refer to the American Rivers web site: http://www.amrivers.org/mer00rivers.html.

Rank	River	State(s)	Threat(s)
1.	Snake River	Wash.	Four federal dams
2.	Missouri River	Mont., N.D., S.D., Neb., Iowa, Kans., Mo.	Dam operations
3.	Ventura River	Calif.	Dam
4.	Copper River Delta	Alaska	Proposed logging road
5.	Tri-State River Basin	Ala., Ga., Fla.	Water withdrawals; dams; urban growth; non-point pollution
6.	Coal River	W. Va.	Mountaintop removal mining
7.	Rio Grande	Colo., N.M., Tex., and Chihuahua and Coahuila, Mexico	Excessive diversion and overconsumption of water; flood control and irrigation projects; land development; pollution
8.	Mississippi and White Rivers	Minn., Wisc., Ill., Iowa, Mo., Ky., Tenn., Ark., Miss., La.	Flood control and navigation projects
9.	North Fork Feather River	Calif.	Hydropower dam operations; transfer of dam ownership; electric industry deregulation
10.	Clear Creek	Tex.	Flood-control project
11.	Green River	Utah, Colo.	Dam operations
12.	Presumpscot River	Maine	Dam operations
13.	Clark Fork River	Mont., Idaho	Proposed mine

Water Supply of the World

The Antarctic Icecap is the largest supply of fresh water, nearly 2% of the world's total of fresh and salt water. As can be seen from the table below, the amount of water in our atmosphere is over ten times as large as the water in all the rivers taken together. The fresh water actually available for human use in lakes and rivers and the accessible ground water amounts to only about one third of one percent of the world's total water supply.

	Surface area (square miles)	Volume (cubic miles)	Percentage of total[1]
Salt Water			
The oceans	139,500,000	317,000,000	97.2
Inland seas and saline lakes	270,000	25,000	0.008
Fresh Water			
Freshwater lakes	330,000	30,000	0.009
All rivers (average level)	—	300	0.0001
Antarctic Icecap	6,000,000	6,300,000	1.9
Arctic Icecap and glaciers	900,000	680,000	0.21
Water in the atmosphere	197,000,000	3,100	0.001
Ground water within half a mile from surface	—	1,000,000	0.31
Deep-lying ground water	—	1,000,000	0.31
Total (rounded)	—	326,000,000	100.00

1. All figures are estimated. *Source:* Department of the Interior, Geological Survey.

National Forest System, 1900–1997

Year	Number of forests	Area (million acres)	Year	Number of forests	Area (million acres)
1900	38	46.52	1960	151	180.84
1905	83	75.35	1965	154	182.14
1910	149	168.03	1970	154	182.57
1915	162	162.77	1975	155	183.28
1920	152	156.03	1980	155	183.06
1925	159	158.40	1985	156	186.32
1930	149	160.09	1992	156	187.11
1935	142	163.31	1993	155	187.23
1940	160	174.77	1994	155	187.27
1945	155	177.64	1995	155	187.24
1950	151	179.69	1996	155	187.28
1955	149	180.30	1997	155	187.42

Source: U.S. Dept. of Agriculture, Forest Service. *Land Areas of the National Forest System.*

Ten Most Visited National Park Sites, 1999

Rank	Name and location	Number of visitors	Rank	Name and location	Number of visitors
1.	Blue Ridge Parkway, Va.-N.C.	19,836,842	6.	Gateway Nat'l. Recreation Area, N.Y.-N.J.	6,813,607
2.	Golden Gate Nat'l. Recreation Area, Calif.	14,048,085	7.	Natchez Trace Parkway, Miss.-Ala.-Tenn.	6,392,961
3.	Great Smoky Mountains Nat'l. Park, Tenn.	10,283,598	8.	Statue of Liberty Nat'l. Monument, N.Y.-N.J.	5,370,015
4.	Lake Mead Nat'l. Recreation Area, Nev.-Az.	9,023,943	9.	Delaware Water Gap Nat'l. Recreation Area, Pa.-N.J.	4,953,427
5.	George Washington Memorial Parkway, Va.-M.D.-D.C.	6,946,945	10.	Cape Cod Nat'l. Seashore, Mass.	4,915,414

Source: Based on data from the National Park Service. Web: www.nps.gov.

The National Park System

Source: Department of the Interior, National Park Service.

The National Park System of the United States is administered by the National Park Service, a bureau of the Department of the Interior. Started with the establishment of Yellowstone National Park on March 1, 1872, the system includes not only the most extraordinary and spectacular scenic exhibits in the United States, but also a large number of sites distinguished either for their historic or prehistoric importance or scientific interest, or for their superior recreational assets. The National Park System is made up of 375 areas covering more than 83 million acres in every state except Delaware. It also includes areas in the District of Columbia, American Samoa, Guam, Puerto Rico, and the Virgin Islands. A list of the areas follows. Note that the National Park System does not include the Affiliated Areas, National Heritage Areas, Wild and Scenic Rivers System, and the National Trails System. See also the excellent Web site of the Park Service: www.nps.gov.

NATIONAL PARKS

Name, location, and year authorized	Acreage	Outstanding characteristics
Acadia (Maine), 1919	47,633.10	Rugged seashore on Mt. Desert Island and adjacent mainland
Arches (Utah), 1971	76,518.98	Unusual stone arches, windows, pedestals caused by erosion (Park was a National Monument 1929–1971)
Badlands (S.D.), 1978	242,755.94	Arid land of fossils, prairie, bison, deer, bighorn sheep, antelope (Park was a National Monument 1929–1978)
Big Bend (Tex.), 1935	801,163.21	Mountains and desert bordering the Rio Grande
Biscayne (Fla.), 1980	172,924.07	Aquatic, coral reef park south of Miami (Park was a National Monument, 1968–1980)
Bryce Canyon (Utah), 1924	35,835.08	Area of grotesque eroded rocks brilliantly colored
Canyonlands (Utah), 1964	337,597.83	Colorful wilderness with impressive red-rock canyons, spires, arches
Capitol Reef (Utah), 1971	241,904.26	Highly colored sedimentary rock formations in high, narrow gorges (Park was a National Monument 1937–1971)
Carlsbad Caverns (N.M.), 1930	46,766.45	One of the world's largest known caves
Channel Islands (Calif.), 1980	249,353.77	Area is rich in marine mammals, sea birds, endangered species, and archeology (Park was a National Monument 1938–1980)
Crater Lake (Ore.), 1902	183,224.05	Deep blue lake in heart of inactive volcano
Death Valley (Calif.-Nev.), 1994	3,367,627.68	Largest desert, surrounded by high mountains, containing the lowest point in the Western hemisphere (Park was a National Monument 1933–1994)
Denali (Alaska), 1917	4,740,911.72	Contains Mt. McKinley, N. America's highest mountain (20,320 ft.) (Formerly Mt. McKinley National Park, 1917–1980)
Dry Tortugas (Fla.), 1992	64,701.22	Located 70 miles off Key West. Features an underwater nature trail (Formerly Ft. Jefferson National Monument 1935–1992)
Everglades (Fla.), 1934	1,508,570.74	Subtropical area with abundant bird and animal life
Gates of the Arctic (Alaska), 1980	7,523,897.77	Diverse north central wilderness contains part of Brooks Range
Glacier (Mont.), 1910	1,013,572.42	Rocky Mountain scenery with many glaciers and lakes
Glacier Bay (Alaska), 1980	3,224,840.31	Popular for wildlife, whale-watching, glacier-calving, and scenery (Park was a National Monument 1925–1980)
Grand Canyon (Ariz.), 1919	1,217,403.32	Mile-deep gorge, 4 to 18 miles wide, 217 miles long
Grand Teton (Wyo.), 1929	309,993.51	Picturesque range of high mountain peaks
Great Basin (Nev.), 1986	77,180.00	Exceptional scenic, biologic, and geologic attractions (Formerly Lehman Caves National Monument 1922–1986)
Great Smoky Mts. (N.C.-Tenn.), 1926	521,621.15	Highest mountain range east of Black Hills; luxuriant plant life
Guadalupe Mountains (Tex.), 1966	86,415.97	Contains highest point in Texas: Guadalupe Peak (8,751 ft.)
Haleakala (Hawaii), 1916	29,823.82	World-famous 10,023-ft. Haleakala volcano (dormant) (Formerly part of Hawaii National Park. Renamed in 1960)

Name, location, and year authorized	Acreage	Outstanding characteristics
Hawaii Volcanoes (Hawaii), 1916	209,695.38	Spectacular volcanic area; luxuriant vegetation at lower levels (Formerly Hawaii National Park. Renamed in 1961)
Hot Springs (Ark.), 1921	5,549.46	47 mineral hot springs said to have therapeutic value
Isle Royale (Mich.), 1931	571,790.11	Largest wilderness island in Lake Superior; moose, wolves, lakes
Joshua Tree (Calif.), 1994	1,022,703.30	Desert region featuring Joshua trees and a great variety of plants and animals. (Park was a National Monument 1936–1994)
Katmai (Alaska), 1980	3,674,529.68	Expansion may assure brown bear's preservation. Park is known for fishing, 1912 eruption of Novarupta, bears (Park was a National Monument 1918–1980)
Kenai Fjords (Alaska), 1980	669,982.99	Mountain goats, marine mammals, birdlife are features at this seacoast park near Seward (Park was a National Monument 1978–1980)
Kings Canyon (Calif.), 1890	461,901.20	Huge canyons; high mountains; giant sequoias (Formerly General Grant National Park 1890–1940)
Kobuk Valley (Alaska), 1980	1,750,736.86	Native culture and anthropology center around the broad Kobuk River in northwest Alaska (Park was a National Monument 1978–1980)
Lake Clark (Alaska), 1980	2,619,733.22	Park provides scenic and wilderness recreation across Cook Inlet from Anchorage. (Park was a National Monument 1978–1980)
Lassen Volcanic (Calif.), 1916	106,372.36	Exhibits of impressive volcanic phenomena
Mammoth Cave (Ky.), 1926	52,830.19	Vast limestone labyrinth with underground river
Mesa Verde (Colo.), 1906	52,121.93	Best-preserved prehistoric cliff dwellings in United States
Mount Rainier (Wash.), 1899	235,625.00	Single-peak glacial system; dense forests, flowered meadows
National Park of American Samoa, 1988	9,000.00	Samoa National Park, American Samoa: two rain forest preserves and a coral reef on the island of Ofu are home to unique tropical animals. The park also includes several thousand acres on the islands of Tutuila and Ta'u
North Cascades (Wash.), 1968	504,780.94	Roadless Alpine landscape; jagged peaks; mountain lakes; glaciers
Olympic (Wash.), 1938	922,650.94	Finest Pacific Northwest rain forest; scenic mountain park
Petrified Forest (Ariz.), 1962	93,532.57	Extensive natural exhibit of petrified wood (Park was a National Monument 1906–1962)
Redwood (Calif.), 1968	110,232.40	Coastal redwood forests; contains world's tallest known tree (369.2 ft.)
Rocky Mountain (Colo.), 1915	265,722.62	Section of the Rocky Mountains; 107 named peaks over 10,000 ft.
Saguaro (Ariz.), 1994	91,443.46	Giant saguaro cacti, unique to the Sonoran Desert, sometimes reach a height of 50 ft. in this cactus forest. (Park was a National Monument 1933–1994)
Sequoia (Calif.), 1890	402,510.05	Giant sequoias; magnificent High Sierra scenery, including Mt. Whitney
Shenandoah (Va.), 1926	198,081.42	Tree-covered mountains; scenic Skyline Drive
Theodore Roosevelt (N.D.), 1978	70,446.89	Scenic valley of Little Missouri River; T.R. Ranch; wildlife (Theodore Roosevelt National Memorial Park 1947–1978)
Virgin Islands (U.S. V.I.), 1956	14,688.87	Beaches; lush hills; prehistoric Carib Indian relics
Voyageurs (Minn.), 1971	218,200.17	Wildlife, canoeing, fishing, and hiking
Wind Cave (S.D.), 1903	28,295.03	Limestone caverns in Black Hills; buffalo herd
Wrangell-St. Elias (Alaska), 1980	8,323,617.68	Largest Park System area has abundant wildlife, second highest peak in U.S. (Mt. St. Elias); adjoins Canadian park. (Park was a National Monument 1978–1980)
Yellowstone (Wyo.-Mont.-Idaho), 1872	2,219,790.71	World's greatest geyser area; abundant falls, wildlife, and canyons
Yosemite (Calif.), 1890	761,266.28	Mountains; inspiring gorges and waterfalls; giant sequoias
Zion (Utah), 1919	146,592.31	Multicolored gorge in heart of southern Utah desert

Name and location	Total acreage	Name and location	Total acreage
National Historical Parks		Colonial (Va.)	9,350.43
Appomattox Court House (Va.)	1,774.56	Cumberland Gap (Ky.-Tenn.-Va.)	20,454.02
Boston (Mass.)	41.03	Dayton Aviation Heritage (Ohio)	85.65
Cane River Creole (La.)	207.38	George Rogers Clark (Ind.)	26.17
Chaco Culture (N.M.)	33,974.29	Harpers Ferry (W.Va.-Md.)	2,343.48
Chesapeake and Ohio Canal (Md.-W.Va.-D.C.)	19,550.83	Hopewell Culture (Ohio)	1,244.84
		Independence (Pa.)	44.88

Name and location	Total acreage
Jean Lafitte (La.)	20,020.00
Kalaupapa (Hawaii)	10,778.88
Kaloko-Honokohau (Hawaii)	1,160.91
Keweenaw (Mich.)	1,900.81
Klondike Goldrush (Alaska-Wash.)	13,191.35
Lowell (Mass.)	141.07
Lyndon B. Johnson (Tex.)	1,570.15
Marsh-Billings-Rockefeller (Vt.)	643.07
Minuteman (Mass.)	965.03
Morristown (N.J.)	1,697.99
Natchez (Miss.)	108.39
New Bedford Whaling (Mass.)	34.00
New Orleans Jazz (La.)	5.13
Nez Perce (Idaho)	2,133.65
Pecos (N.M.)	6,671.42
Pu'uhonua o Honaunau (Hawaii)	181.80
Salt River Bay and Ecological Preserve (U.S. V.I.)	945.77
San Antonio Missions (Tex.)	819.19
San Francisco Maritime (Calif.)	49.86
San Juan Island (Wash.)	1,751.99
Saratoga (N.Y.)	3,392.42
Sitka (Alaska)	106.83
Tumacacori (Ariz.)	46.28
Valley Forge (Pa.)	3,466.47
War in the Pacific (Guam)	2,027.36
Women's Rights (N.Y.)	6.60

National Monuments

Name and location	Total acreage
Agate Fossil Beds (Neb.)	3,055.22
Agua Fria (Ariz.)	71,100.00
Alibates Flint Quarries (Tex.)	1,370.97
Aniakchak (Alaska)	137,176.00
Aztec Ruins (N.M.)	317.71
Bandelier (N.M.)	33,676.67
Black Canyon of the Gunnison (Colo.)	30,385.14
Booker T. Washington (Va.)	223.92
Buck Island Reef (U.S. V.I.)	880.00
Cabrillo (Calif.)	137.06
California Coastal (Calif.)	(along 840-mi. coastline)
Canyon de Chelly (Ariz.)	83,840.00
Cape Krusenstern (Alaska)	649,182.18
Capulin Volcano (N.M.)	792.84
Casa Grande Ruins (Ariz.)	472.50
Castillo de San Marcos (Fla.)	20.20
Castle Clinton (N.Y.)	1.00
Cedar Breaks (Utah)	6,154.60
Chiricahua (Ariz.)	11,984.73
Colorado (Colo.)	20,533.93
Congaree Swamp (S.C.)	21,887.53
Craters of the Moon (Idaho)	53,440.05
Devils Postpile (Calif.)	798.46
Devils Tower (Wyo.)	1,346.91
Dinosaur (Utah-Colo.)	210,277.55
Effigy Mounds (Iowa)	1,481.39
El Malpais (N.M.)	114,276.95
El Morro (N.M.)	1,278.72
Florissant Fossil Beds (Colo.)	5,998.09
Fort Frederica (Ga.)	241.42
Fort Matanzas (Fla.)	227.76
Fort McHenry (Md.)	43.26
Fort Pulaski (Ga.)	5,623.10
Fort Stanwix (N.Y.)	15.52
Fort Sumter (S.C.)	194.60
Fort Union (N.M.)	720.60
Fossil Butte (Wyo.)	8,198.00

Name and location	Total acreage
George Washington Birthplace (Va.)	550.23
George Washington Carver (Mo.)	210.00
Gila Cliff Dwellings (N.M.)	533.13
Grand Canyon–Parashant (Ariz.)	1,014,000.00
Grand Portage (Minn.)	709.97
Grand Staircase–Escalante (Utah)	1,900,000.00
Great Sand Dunes (Colo.)	38,662.18
Hagerman Fossil Beds (Idaho)	4,351.15
Hohokam Pima (Ariz.)	1,690.00
Homestead (Neb.)	195.11
Hovenweep (Utah-Colo.)	784.93
Jewel Cave (S.D.)	1,273.51
John Day Fossil Beds (Ore.)	14,056.73
Lava Beds (Calif.)	46,559.87
Little Big Horn Battlefield (Mont.)	765.34
Montezuma Castle (Ariz.)	857.69
Muir Woods (Calif.)	553.55
Natural Bridges (Utah)	7,636.49
Navajo (Ariz.)	360.00
Ocmulgee (Ga.)	701.54
Oregon Caves (Ore.)	487.98
Organ Pipe Cactus (Ariz.)	330,688.50
Petroglyph (N.M.)	7,231.61
Pinnacles (Calif.)	16,265.44
Pipe Spring (Ariz.)	40.00
Pipestone (Minn.)	281.78
Poverty Point (La.)	910.85
Rainbow Bridge (Utah)	160.00
Russell Cave (Ala.)	310.45
Salinas Pueblo Missions (N.M.)	1,071.42
Scotts Bluff (Neb.)	3,003.30
Statue of Liberty (N.Y.-N.J.)	58.38
Sunset Crater Volcano (Ariz.)	3,040.00
Timpanogos Cave (Utah)	250.00
Tonto (Ariz.)	1,120.00
Tuzigoot (Ariz.)	800.62
Walnut Canyon (Ariz.)	3,579.46
White Sands (N.M.)	143,732.92
Wupatki (Ariz.)	35,422.13
Yucca House (Colo.)	33.97

National Preserves

Name and location	Total acreage
Aniakchak (Alaska)	465,603.00
Bering Land Bridge (Alaska)	2,697,639.22
Big Cypress (Fla.)	720,570.27
Big Thicket (Tex.)	97,191.01
Denali (Alaska)	1,334,117.99
Gates of the Arctic (Alaska)	948,628.90
Glacier Bay (Alaska)	58,406.00
Katmai (Alaska)	418,699.22
Lake Clark (Alaska)	1,410,325.32
Little River Canyon (Ala.)	13,632.96
Mojave (Calif.)	1,541,662.35
Noatak (Alaska)	6,569,904.43
Tallgrass Prairie (Kans.)	10,894.00
Timucuan Ecological and Historic Preserve (Fla.)	46,019.00
Wrangell-St. Elias (Alaska)	4,852,753.24
Yukon-Charley (Alaska)	2,526,512.31

National Reserves

Name and location	Total acreage
City of Rocks (Idaho)	14,107.19
Ebey's Landing (Wash.)	19,018.64

Name and location	Total acreage
National Military Parks	
Chickamauga and Chattanooga (Ga.-Tenn.)	8,129.30
Fredericksburg and Spotsylvania (Va.)	7,923.08
Gettysburg Nat. Mil. Park (Pa.)	5,984.33
Guilford Courthouse (N.C.)	220.90
Horseshoe Bend (Ala.)	2,040.00
Kings Mountain (S.C.)	3,945.29
Pea Ridge (Ark.)	4,300.35
Shiloh Nat. Park (Tenn.)	3,972.87
Vicksburg Nat. Mil. Park (Miss.)	1,743.51
National Battlefields	
Antietam (Md.)	3,244.93
Big Hole (Mont.)	655.61
Cowpens (S.C.)	841.56
Fort Donelson (Tenn.)	551.69
Fort Necessity (Pa.)	902.80
Monocacy (Md.)	1,647.01
Moores Creek (N.C.)	87.75
Petersburg (Va.)	2,659.19
Stones River (Tenn.)	713.52
Tupelo (Miss.)	1.00
Wilson's Creek (Mo.)	1,749.91
National Battlefield Parks	
Kennesaw Mountain (Ga.)	2,884.14
Manassas (Va.)	5,071.62
Richmond (Va.)	1,718.15
National Battlefield Site	
Brices Cross Roads (Miss.)	1.00
National Historic Sites	
Abraham Lincoln Birthplace (Ky.)	116.50
Adams (Mass.)	13.82
Allegheny Portage Railroad (Pa.)	1,249.20
Andersonville (Ga.)	494.61
Andrew Johnson (Tenn.)	16.68
Bent's Old Fort (Colo.)	798.80
Boston African-American (Mass.)	0.59
Brown v. Board of Education (Kans.)	1.85
Carl Sandburg Home (N.C.)	263.65
Central High School (Ark.)	17.95
Charles Pinckney (S.C.)	28.45
Christiansted (U.S. V.I.)	27.15
Clara Barton (Md.)	8.59
Edgar Allan Poe (Pa.)	0.52
Edison (N.J.)	21.25
Eisenhower (Pa.)	690.46
Eleanor Roosevelt (N.Y.)	180.50
Eugene O'Neill (Calif.)	13.19
Ford's Theatre (Lincoln Museum) (D.C.)	0.29
Fort Bowie (Ariz.)	1,000.00
Fort Davis (Tex.)	473.87
Fort Laramie (Wyo.)	832.85
Fort Larned (Kan.)	718.39
Fort Point (Calif.)	29.00
Fort Raleigh (N.C.)	512.93
Fort Scott (Kan.)	16.69
Fort Smith (Ark.-Okla.)	75.00
Fort Union Trading Post (N.D.-Mont.)	443.80
Fort Vancouver (Wash.)	208.89
Frederick Douglass Home (D.C.)	8.53

Name and location	Total acreage
Frederick Law Olmsted (Mass.)	7.21
Friendship Hill (Pa.)	674.56
Golden Spike (Utah)	2,735.28
Grant-Kohrs Ranch (Mont.)	1,618.38
Hampton (Md.)	62.04
Harry S. Truman (Mo.)	6.67
Herbert Hoover (Iowa)	186.80
Home of F. D. Roosevelt (N.Y.)	349.26
Hopewell Furnace (Pa.)	848.06
Hubbell Trading Post (Ariz.)	160.09
James A. Garfield (Ohio)	7.82
Jimmy Carter (Ga.)	70.86
John F. Kennedy (Mass.)	0.09
John Muir (Calif.)	344.73
Knife River Indian Villages (N.D.)	1,758.35
Lincoln Home (Ill.)	12.24
Longfellow (Mass.)	1.98
Maggie L. Walker (Va.)	1.29
Manzanar (Calif.)	813.81
Martin Luther King, Jr. (Ga.)	38.38
Martin Van Buren (N.Y.)	39.79
Mary McLeod Bethune Council House (D.C.)	0.07
Nicodemus (Kans.)	161.35
Ninety Six (S.C.)	989.14
Palo Alto Battlefield (Tex.)	3,357.42
Pennsylvania Avenue (D.C.)	n.a.
Puukohola Heiau (Hawaii)	86.24
Sagamore Hill (N.Y.)	83.02
Saint-Gaudens (N.H.)	148.15
Saint Paul's Church (N.Y.)	6.13
Salem Maritime (Mass.)	9.02
San Juan (P.R.)	75.13
Saugus Iron Works (Mass.)	8.51
Springfield Armory (Mass.)	54.93
Steamtown (Pa.)	62.48
Theodore Roosevelt Birthplace (N.Y.)	0.11
Theodore Roosevelt Inaugural (N.Y.)	1.03
Thomas Stone (Md.)	328.25
Tuskegee Institute (Ala.)	57.92
Ulysses S. Grant (Mo.)	9.60
Vanderbilt Mansion (N.Y.)	211.65
Washita Battlefield (Okla.)	315.20
Weir Farms (Conn.)	74.30
Whitman Mission (Wash.)	98.15
William Howard Taft (Ohio)	3.10

Name and location	Total acreage
National Memorials	
Arkansas Post (Ark.)	746.88
Arlington House, the Robert E. Lee Memorial (Va.)	27.91
Chamizal (Tex.)	54.90
Coronado (Ariz.)	4,750.22
De Soto (Fla.)	26.84
Federal Hall (N.Y.)	0.45
Fort Caroline (Fla.)	138.39
Fort Clatsop (Ore.)	125.20
Franklin Delano Roosevelt Memorial (D.C.)	7.50
General Grant (N.Y.)	0.76
Hamilton Grange (N.Y.)	0.11
Jefferson National Expansion Memorial (Mo.)	192.83
Johnstown Flood (Pa.)	164.12
Korean War Veterans (D.C.)	2.20

Name and location	Total acreage
Lincoln Boyhood (Ind.)	199.65
Lincoln Memorial (D.C.)	107.43
Lyndon Baines Johnson Memorial Grove on the Potomac (D.C.)	17.00
Mount Rushmore (S.D.)	1,278.45
Perry's Victory and International Peace Memorial (Ohio)	25.38
Roger Williams (R.I.)	4.56
Thaddeus Kosciuszko (Pa.)	0.02
Theodore Roosevelt Island (D.C.)	88.50
Thomas Jefferson Memorial (D.C.)	18.36
USS *Arizona* Memorial (Hawaii)	10.50
Vietnam Veterans Memorial (D.C.)	2.00
Washington Monument (D.C.)	106.01
Wright Brothers (N.C.)	428.44

National Seashores

Name and location	Total acreage
Assateague Island (Md.-Va.)	39,729.60
Canaveral (Fla.)	57,661.69
Cape Cod (Mass.)	43,604.38
Cape Hatteras (N.C.)	30,321.46
Cape Lookout (N.C.)	28,243.36
Cumberland Island (Ga.)	36,415.13
Fire Island (N.Y.)	19,579.59
Gulf Islands (Fla.-Miss.)	137,457.89
Padre Island (Tex.)	130,434.27
Point Reyes (Calif.)	71,067.54

National Parkways

Name and location	Total acreage
Blue Ridge (Va.-N.C.)	88,692.56
George Washington Memorial (Va.-Md.)	7,247.63
John D. Rockefeller, Jr., Memorial (Wyo.)	23,777.22
Natchez Trace (Miss.-Tenn.-Ala.)	51,746.50

National Lakeshores

Name and location	Total acreage
Apostle Islands (Wis.)	69,371.89
Indiana Dunes (Ind.)	15,138.35
Pictured Rocks (Mich.)	73,228.37
Sleeping Bear Dunes (Mich.)	71,193.57

National Park System Rivers

Name and location	Total acreage
Alagnak Wild River (Alaska)	30,665.00
Big South Fork National River and Recreation Area (Ky.-Tenn.)	125,242.34
Bluestone National Scenic River (W. Va.)	4,309.51
Buffalo National River (Ark.)	94,292.56
Delaware National Scenic River (Pa.)	1,973.33
Great Egg Harbor Scenic and Recreational River (N.J.-Pa.)	n.a.
Mississippi National River and Recreation Area (Minn.)	53,775.00
Missouri National Recreational River (Neb.)	n.a.
New River Gorge National River (W.Va.)	69,832.96
Niobrara National Scenic Riverway (Neb.)	n.a.
Obed Wild and Scenic River (Tenn.)	5,173.42
Ozark National Scenic Riverways (Mo.)	80,785.04
Rio Grande Wild and Scenic River (Tex.)	9,600.00
St. Croix National Scenic River (Minn.-Wis.)	67,465.63
Upper Delaware Scenic and Recreational River (Pa.)	75,004.80

National Recreation Areas

Name and location	Total acreage
Amistad (Tex.)	58,500.00
Bighorn Canyon (Wyo.-Mont.)	120,296.22
Boston Harbor Islands (Mass.)	1,482.25
Chattahoochee River (Ga.)	9,205.53
Chickasaw (Okla.)	9,888.83
Curecanti (Colo.)	41,972.42
Cuyahoga Valley (Ohio)	32,859.18
Delaware Water Gap (Pa.-N.J.)	66,760.69
Gateway (N.Y.-N.J.)	26,610.38
Gauley River (W. Va.)	11,505.92
Glen Canyon (Ariz.-Utah)	1,254,306.19
Golden Gate (Calif.)	73,689.70
Lake Chelan (Wash.)	61,957.92
Lake Mead (Ariz.-Nev.)	1,495,665.69
Lake Meredith (Tex.)	44,977.63
Lake Roosevelt (Wash.)	100,390.31
Ross Lake (Wash.)	117,574.59
Santa Monica Mountains (Calif.)	153,823.52
Whiskeytown-Shasta-Trinity (Calif.)	42,503.46

National Scenic Trails

Name and location	Total acreage
Appalachian (Maine-N.H.-Vt.-Mass.-Conn.-N.Y.-N.J.- Pa.-Md.-W.Va.-Va.-N.C.-Tenn., Ga.)	214,542.34
Natchez Trace (Ala.-Miss.-Tenn.)	10,995.00
Potomac Heritage (D.C.-Md.-Va.-Pa.)	n.a.

International Historic Site

Name and location	Total acreage
Saint Croix Island (Maine)	44.90

National Cemeteries[1]

Name and location	Total acreage
Andersonville (Ga.)	494.61
Andrew Johnson (Tenn.)	16.68
Antietam (Md.)	11.36
Battleground (D.C.)	1.03
Fort Donelson (Tenn.)	15.30
Fredericksburg (Va.)	12.00
Gettysburg (Pa.)	20.58
Little Big Horn (Mont.)	765.34
Poplar Grove (Va.)	8.72
Shiloh (Tenn.)	10.05
Stones River (Tenn.)	719.81
Vicksburg (Miss.)	116.28
Yorktown (Va.)	2.91

1. The National Cemeteries are not independent areas of the National Park System; each is part of a military park, battlefield, etc., except Battleground. Their acreage is kept separately. Arlington National Cemetery is under the Department of the Army.

Other Parks

Name and location	Total acreage
Catoctin Mountain (Md.)	5,770.22
Constitution Gardens (D.C.)	52.00
Fort Washington Park (Md.)	341.00
Greenbelt (Md.)	1,175.99
National Capital Parks (D.C.)	6,543.85
National Mall (D.C.)	146.35
Piscataway (Md.)	4,485.52
Prince William Forest (Va.)	18,622.15
Rock Creek Park (D.C.)	1,754.37
White House (D.C.)	18.07
Wolf Trap Farm Park for the Performing Arts (Va.)	130.28

How People Control the Weather

It's not in ways we planned, and now we're stuck with the damage

By **J. MADELEINE NASH** TIME

Pioneering chemist Irving Langmuir once suggested that it would prove easier to change the weather to our liking than to predict its duplicitous twists and turns. The great mathematician John von Neumann even calculated what mounting an effective weather-modification effort would cost the U.S.—about as much as building the railroads, he figured, and worth incalculably more.

At the start of the 21st century, alas, all that these happy visions amount to are a few scattered cloud-seeding programs, whose modest successes, while real, have proved less than earthshaking. In fact, sunny hopes that we could somehow change the weather for the better have given way to the gloomy knowledge that we are only making things worse. It is now clear that what the world's cleverest scientists could not achieve by design, ordinary people are on the verge of accomplishing by accident. Human beings not only have the ability to alter weather patterns on local, regional, and global scales, but they are already doing it—in ways that are potentially catastrophic.

Meteorological Mischief

Consider the billions of tons of carbon dioxide that are emitted every year in the course of our daily life. Driving a car, switching on a light, working in a factory, fertilizing a field, all contribute to the atmosphere's growing burden of heat-trapping gases. Unless we start to control emissions of CO_2 and similar compounds, global mean temperatures will probably rise somewhere between 2°F and 7°F by the end of the next century; even the low end of that spectrum could set the stage for a lot of meteorological mischief. Among other things, the higher the temperature, the more rapidly moisture can evaporate from the earth's surface and condense as rain droplets in clouds, substantially increasing the risk of both drought and torrential rain. There could also be a rise in the number of severe storms.

Human activity is modifying precipitation in other dramatic ways. Satellite images show that industrial aerosols—sulfuric acid and the like—emitted by steel mills, oil refineries, and power plants are suppressing rainfall downwind of major industrial centers.

Polluted Clouds

This creates an additional conundrum. Because a polluted cloud does not rain itself out, notes University of Colorado atmospheric scientist Brian Toon, it tends to grow larger and last longer, providing a shiny white surface that bounces sunlight out to space. Indeed, one reason the earth has not yet warmed up as much as many anticipated may be due to the tug-of-war between industrial aerosols like sulfuric acid

(which reflect heat) and greenhouse gases like carbon dioxide (which trap it). Ironically, then, the cost of reducing one kind of pollution may come at the price of intensifying the effects of the other.

Deforestation has a similarly broad range of impact. One thing trees do is lock up a lot of carbon in their woody tissues, thereby preventing it from escaping into the atmosphere. Trees are also important recyclers of moisture to the atmosphere. In some parts of the Amazon basin, deforestation has reached the point where it is altering precipitation patterns. This is because so much of the moisture entrained by clouds comes from the canopy of the forest below; as large tracts of trees disappear, so do portions of the aqueous reservoir that feeds the local rainmaking machine.

Shrubs, grasses, and other vegetative covers act in much the same way, trapping water, feeding moisture into the atmosphere, and providing shade that shields the surface of the land from the drying rays of the sun. Large-scale land-clearing efforts under way around the world wipe all that out. The ongoing development of South Florida, for instance, has filled in and paved over much of the Everglades wetlands, which have long served as an important source of atmospheric moisture. As a consequence, says Colorado State University atmospheric scientist Roger Pielke Sr., South Florida in July and August has become significantly drier and hotter than it would have been a century ago under the same set of climatic conditions.

Atmospheric Interference

Scientists are just beginning to disentangle the myriad levels on which human beings and the natural climate system interact, which only increases the potential for surprise. For example, we now realize that not all the aerosols we are pumping into the atmosphere exert a cooling effect. A notable exception is soot, which is produced by wood fires and incomplete industrial combustion. Because of its dark color, soot absorbs solar energy rather than reflecting it. So when a scientific excursion to the Indian Ocean established that big soot clouds were circulating through the atmosphere, a number of scientists speculated that their presence might be raising sea-surface temperatures, potentially affecting the strength of the monsoon.

We are tampering with systems that are so complex that scientists are struggling to understand them. Climatologist Tom Wigley of the National Center for Atmospheric Research, for one, fervently believes the answer to our problems lies not just in improved knowledge of the climate system but in technological advances that could counter—and perhaps reverse—present trends. In other words, the farfetched dreams that prominent scientists like von Neumann once harbored have not died. Rather they have been transformed and, in the process, become more urgent. □

Spring 2000: Hottest on Record for the U.S.

Source: Storm Phillips, STORMFAX, Inc.

The National Climatic Data Center (NCDC) says the meteorological spring (March through May 2000) averaged 55.5°F (13°C) across the U.S. That is 0.4 degrees warmer than the previous record set in 1910. The U.S. also experienced the hottest Jan.– May in 106 years of record keeping.

Globally, land and ocean surface temperature readings were also warmer than normal, tying 1990 as the second warmest spring on record. However, satellite-derived readings measuring the lower atmosphere did not produce the same result, with colder than normal waters in the tropical Pacific Ocean holding down readings. The globally averaged temperature as measured by satellite was 0.07 degrees below normal for spring.

It is unusual to have every state in the U.S. above normal for a season. Generally, some states are above normal, some near normal, and some below normal. In addition to topping the 1910 record for spring warmth, 2000 was 3.3 degrees above average for the Jan.–May period, according to NCDC data.

For the five-month Jan.–May period, the nation's average temperature was 48.5°F (9°C). The old record of 47.4°F (8°C) was set in 1986. The heat contributed to worsening drought conditions in many areas of the U.S. Parts of the Southeast, Midwest, and Southwest were under severe to extreme drought, causing crop damage and creating the need for water rationing in many areas. Meanwhile the Northeast received above normal moisture.

It was the 24th consecutive March–May period in which temperatures were warmer than average over the Northern Hemisphere, but readings in the tropics were lower than average because of the La Niña phenomenon, a large area of colder than normal water in the Pacific Ocean. □

Costliest Hurricanes of the 20th Century

(U.S. Mainland)

Rank	Year	Name	Damage then (in millions)	Damage now (in millions)	Dead	Rank	Year	Name	Damage then (in millions)	Damage now (in millions)	Dead
1.	1926	Unnamed	$ 105	$77,490	243	6.	1938	Unnamed	$ 306	$17,821	600
2.	1992	Andrew	$26,500	$35,468	15	7.	1928	Unnamed	$ 25	$14,785	1,836
3.	1900	Unnamed (Galveston)	$ 30	$28,528	8,000	8.	1965	Betsy	$1,420	$13,326	75
						9.	1960	Donna	$ 387	$12,913	50
4.	1915	Unnamed	$ 50	$24,171	275	10.	1969	Camille	$1,421	$11,752	256
5.	1944	Unnamed	$ 63	$18,074	18						

Sources: Normalized Hurricane Damages in the United States by Roger Pielke, Jr., and Christopher Landsea; National Oceanic and Atmospheric Administration.

Most Deadly Western Hemisphere Hurricanes on Record

Hurricane	Date	Areas struck	Deaths
1. "The Great Hurricane"	Oct. 10–16, 1780	Martinique, St. Eustatius, Barbados, ships	22,000
2. Hurricane Mitch	Oct. 26–Nov. 4, 1998	Central America: Honduras, Nicaragua	11,000
3. Galveston, Texas	Sept. 8, 1900	Galveston Island	8,000
4. Hurricane Fifi	Sept. 14–19, 1974	Honduras	8,000
5. Dominican Republic	Sept. 1–6, 1930	Dominican Republic	8,000
6. Hurricane Flora	Sept. 30, 1963–Oct. 8, 1963	Haiti, Cuba	7,200
7. Martinique	Sept. 6, 1776	Point Petre Bay	6,000

Source: National Oceanic and Atmospheric Administration.

Strongest Atlantic Hurricanes on Record

Hurricane	Date	Pressure	Peak winds	Total no. of hours at Cat 5	Total no. of hours winds 155+ knots
1. Gilbert	Sept. 13, 1988	888 mb (26.22 in.)	160 knots	18 hours	6 hours
2. Florida Keys	Sept. 3, 1935	892 mb (26.34 in.)	140 knots	3 hours	0 hours
3. Allen	Aug. 7, 1980	899 mb (26.55 in.)	165 knots	24/24/12 hours[1]	3/12/3 hours[1]
4. Mitch	Oct. 26, 1998	905 mb (26.73 in.)	155 knots	33 hours	15 hours
5. Camille	Aug. 17, 1969	905 mb (26.73 in.)	165 knots	24 hours	18 hours

1. Hurricane Allen attained Category 5 status three times during its life history: first on Aug. 5, second on Aug. 7, and third on Aug. 9. *Source:* National Oceanic and Atmospheric Administration.

Climate of 100 Selected U.S. Cities

| City | Average monthly temperature (°F)[1] | | | | Precipitation | | Snowfall | |
	Jan.	April	July	Oct.	Average annual (in.)[1]	Average annual (days)[2]	Average annual (in.)[2]	Years[2]
Albany, N.Y.	21.1	46.6	71.4	50.5	35.74	134	65.5	38
Albuquerque, N.M.	34.8	55.1	78.8	57.4	8.12	59	10.6	45
Anchorage, Alaska	13.0	35.4	58.1	34.6	15.20	115	69.2	41[3]
Asheville, N.C.	36.8	55.7	73.2	56.0	47.71	124	17.5	20
Atlanta, Ga.	41.9	61.8	78.6	62.2	48.61	115	1.9	50
Atlantic City, N.J.	31.8	51.0	74.4	55.5	41.93	112	16.4	40[3]
Austin, Texas	49.1	68.7	84.7	69.8	31.50	83	0.9	43
Baltimore, Md.	32.7	54.0	76.8	56.9	41.84	113	21.8	34
Baton Rouge, La.	50.8	68.4	82.1	68.2	55.77	108	0.1	34[3]
Billings, Mont.	20.9	44.6	72.3	49.3	15.09	96	57.2	50
Birmingham, Ala.	42.9	62.8	80.1	62.6	54.52	117	1.3	41
Bismark, N.D.	6.7	42.5	70.4	46.1	15.36	96	40.3	45
Boise, Idaho	29.9	48.6	74.6	51.9	11.71	92	21.4	45
Boston, Mass.	29.6	48.7	73.5	54.8	43.81	127	41.8	49[3]
Bridgeport, Conn.	29.5	48.6	74.0	56.0	41.56	117	26.0	36
Buffalo, N.Y.	23.5	45.4	70.7	51.5	37.52	169	92.2	41
Burlington, Vt.	16.6	42.7	69.6	47.9	33.69	153	78.2	41
Caribou, Maine	10.7	37.3	65.1	43.1	36.59	160	113.3	45
Casper, Wyo.	22.2	42.1	70.9	47.1	11.43	95	80.5	34
Charleston, S.C.	47.9	64.3	80.5	65.8	51.59	113	0.6	42
Charleston, W.Va.	32.9	55.3	74.5	55.9	42.43	151	31.5	37
Charlotte, N.C.	40.5	60.3	78.5	60.7	43.16	111	6.1	45
Cheyenne, Wyo.	26.1	41.8	68.9	47.5	13.31	98	54.1	49
Chicago, Ill.	21.4	48.8	73.0	53.5	33.34	127	40.3	26
Cleveland, Ohio	25.5	48.1	71.6	53.2	35.40	156	53.6	43
Columbia, S.C.	44.7	63.8	81.0	63.4	49.12	109	1.9	37
Columbus, Ohio	27.1	51.4	73.8	53.9	36.97	137	28.3	37[3]
Concord, N.H.	19.9	44.1	69.5	48.3	36.53	125	64.5	43
Dallas-Ft. Worth, Texas	44.0	65.9	86.3	67.9	29.46	78	3.1	31
Denver, Colo.	29.5	47.4	73.4	51.9	15.31	88	59.8	50
Des Moines, Iowa	18.6	50.5	76.3	54.2	30.83	107	34.7	45
Detroit, Mich.	23.4	47.3	71.9	51.9	30.97	133	40.4	26
Dodge City, Kan.	29.5	54.3	80.0	57.7	20.66	78	19.5	42
Duluth, Minn.	6.3	38.3	65.4	44.2	29.68	135	77.4	41[3]
El Paso, Texas	44.2	63.6	82.5	63.6	7.82	47	5.2	45
Fairbanks, Alaska	-12.7	30.2	61.5	25.1	10.37	106	67.5	33
Fargo, N.D.	4.3	42.1	70.6	46.3	19.59	100	35.9	42
Grand Junction, Colo.	25.5	51.7	78.9	54.9	8.00	72	26.1	38
Grand Rapids, Mich.	22.0	46.3	71.4	50.9	34.35	143	72.4	21
Hartford, Conn.	25.2	48.8	73.4	52.4	44.39	127	50.0	30
Helena, Mont.	18.1	42.3	67.9	45.1	11.37	96	47.9	44
Honolulu, Hawaii	72.6	75.7	80.1	79.5	23.47	100	0.0	38[3]
Houston, Texas	51.4	68.7	83.1	69.7	44.76	105	0.4	50
Indianapolis, Ind.	26.0	52.4	75.1	54.8	39.12	125	23.1	53[3]
Jackson, Miss.	45.7	65.1	81.9	65.0	52.82	109	1.2	21
Jacksonville, Fla.	53.2	67.7	81.3	69.5	52.76	116	T	43
Juneau, Alaska	21.8	39.1	55.7	41.8	53.15	220	102.8	41
Kansas City, Mo.	28.4	56.9	80.9	59.6	29.27	98	20.0	43
Knoxville, Tenn.	38.2	59.6	77.6	59.5	47.29	127	12.3	42
Las Vegas, Nev.	44.5	63.5	90.2	67.5	4.19	26	1.4	36
Lexington, Ky.	31.5	55.1	75.9	56.8	45.68	131	16.3	40
Little Rock, Ark.	39.9	62.4	82.1	63.1	49.20	104	5.4	42
Long Beach, Calif.	55.2	60.9	72.8	67.5	11.54	32	T	41[3]
Los Angeles, Calif.	56.0	59.5	69.0	66.3	12.08	36	T	49
Louisville, Ky.	32.5	56.6	77.6	57.7	43.56	125	17.5	37
Madison, Wisc.	15.6	45.8	70.6	49.5	30.84	118	40.8	36
Memphis, Tenn.	39.6	62.6	82.1	62.9	51.57	107	5.5	34
Miami, Fla.	67.1	75.3	82.5	77.9	57.55	129	0.0	42
Milwaukee, Wisc.	18.7	44.6	70.5	50.9	30.94	125	47.0	44
Minneapolis–St. Paul, Minn.	11.2	46.0	73.1	49.6	26.36	115	48.9	46
Mobile, Ala.	50.8	68.0	82.2	68.5	64.64	123	0.3	43
Montgomery, Ala.	46.7	65.2	81.7	65.3	49.16	108	0.3	40
Mt. Washington, N.H.	5.1	22.4	48.7	30.5	89.92	209	246.8	52
Nashville, Tenn.	37.1	59.7	79.4	60.2	48.49	119	11.1	43
Newark, N.J.	31.2	52.1	76.8	57.2	42.34	122	28.2	43
New Orleans, La.	52.4	68.7	82.1	69.2	59.74	114	0.2	38[3]
New York, N.Y.	31.8	51.9	76.4	57.5	42.82	119	26.1	40[3]

City	Average monthly temperature (°F)[1]				Precipitation		Snowfall	
					Average annual		Average annual	
	Jan.	April	July	Oct.	(in.)[1]	(days)[2]	(in.)[2]	Years[2]
Norfolk, Va.	39.9	58.2	78.4	61.3	45.22	115	7.9	36
Oklahoma City, Okla.	35.9	60.2	82.1	62.3	30.89	82	9.0	45
Olympia, Wash.	37.2	47.3	63.0	50.1	50.96	164	18.0	43
Omaha, Neb.	20.2	52.2	77.7	54.5	30.34	98	31.1	49[3]
Philadelphia, Pa.	31.2	52.9	76.5	56.5	41.42	117	21.9	42[3]
Phoenix, Ariz.	52.3	68.1	92.3	73.4	7.11	36	T	47[3]
Pittsburgh, Pa.	26.7	50.1	72.0	52.5	36.30	154	44.6	32
Portland, Maine	21.5	42.8	68.1	48.5	43.52	128	72.4	44
Portland, Ore.	38.9	50.4	67.7	54.3	37.39	154	6.8	44
Providence, R.I.	28.2	47.9	72.5	53.2	45.32	124	37.1	31
Raleigh, N.C.	39.6	59.4	77.7	59.7	41.76	112	7.7	40
Reno, Nev.	32.2	46.4	69.5	50.3	7.49	51	25.3	42
Richmond, Va.	36.6	57.9	77.8	58.6	44.07	113	14.6	47
Roswell, N.M.	41.4	61.9	81.4	61.7	9.70	52	11.4	37[3]
Sacramento, Calif.	45.3	58.2	75.6	63.9	17.10	58	0.1	36[3]
Salt Lake City, Utah	28.6	49.2	77.5	53.0	15.31	90	59.1	56
San Antonio, Texas	50.4	69.6	84.6	70.2	29.13	81	0.4	42
San Diego, Calif.	56.8	61.2	70.3	67.5	9.32	43	T	44
San Francisco, Calif.	48.5	54.8	62.2	60.6	19.71	63	T	57
Savannah, Ga.	49.1	66.0	81.2	66.9	49.70	111	0.3	34
Seattle-Tacoma, Wash.	39.1	48.7	64.8	52.4	38.60	158	12.8	40
Sioux Falls, S.D.	12.4	46.4	74.0	49.4	24.12	96	39.9	39
Spokane, Wash.	25.7	45.8	69.7	47.5	16.71	114	51.5	37
Springfield, Ill.	24.6	53.3	76.5	56.0	33.78	114	24.5	37
St. Louis, Mo.	28.8	56.1	78.9	57.9	33.91	111	19.8	48[3]
Tampa, Fla.	59.8	71.5	82.1	74.4	46.73	107	T	38
Toledo, Ohio	23.1	47.8	71.8	51.7	31.78	137	38.3	29
Tucson, Ariz.	51.1	64.9	86.2	70.4	11.14	52	1.2	44
Tulsa, Okla.	35.2	61.0	83.2	62.6	38.77	89	9.0	46
Vero Beach, Fla.	61.9	71.7	81.1	75.2	51.41	n.a.	n.a.	0
Washington, D.C.	35.2	56.7	78.9	59.3	39.00	112	17.0	41[3]
Wichita, Kan.	29.6	56.3	81.4	59.1	28.61	85	16.4	31
Wilmington, Del.	31.2	52.4	76.0	56.3	41.38	117	20.9	37

1. Based on 30-year period 1951–80. Data latest available. 2. Data through 1984 based on number of years as indicated in Years column. 3. For snowfall data where number of years differs from that for precipitation data. T = trace. n.a. = not available. *Source:* National Oceanic and Atmospheric Administration.

Wind Chill Factors

Wind speed (mph)	Thermometer reading (°F)																
	35	30	25	20	15	10	5	0	−5	−10	−15	−20	−25	−30	−35	−40	−45
5	33	27	21	19	12	7	0	−5	−10	−15	−21	−26	−31	−36	−42	−47	−52
10	22	16	10	3	−3	−9	−15	−22	−27	−34	−40	−46	−52	−58	−64	−71	−77
15	16	9	2	−5	−11	−18	−25	−31	−38	−45	−51	−58	−65	−72	−78	−85	−92
20	12	4	−3	−10	−17	−24	−31	−39	−46	−53	−60	−67	−74	−81	−88	−95	−103
25	8	1	−7	−15	−22	−29	−36	−44	−51	−59	−66	−74	−81	−88	−96	−103	−110
30	6	−2	−10	−18	−25	−33	−41	−49	−56	−64	−71	−79	−86	−93	−101	−109	−116
35	4	−4	−12	−20	−27	−35	−43	−52	−58	−67	−74	−82	−89	−97	−105	−113	−120
40	3	−5	−13	−21	−29	−37	−45	−53	−60	−69	−76	−84	−92	−100	−107	−115	−123
45	2	−6	−14	−22	−30	−38	−46	−54	−62	−70	−78	−85	−93	−102	−109	−117	−125

NOTE: This chart gives equivalent temperatures for combinations of wind speed and temperature. For example, the combination of a temperature of 10° Fahrenheit and a wind blowing at 10 mph has a cooling power equal to −9° F. Wind speeds of higher than 45 mph have little additional cooling effect.

Recorded Weather Extremes

Highest average annual mean temperature (world): Dallol, Ethiopia (Oct. 1960–Dec. 1966), 94° F (35° C). **(U.S.):** Key West, Fla. (30-year normal), 78.2° F (25.7° C).

Lowest average annual mean temperature (world): Plateau Station, Antarctica, −70° F (−7° C). **(U.S.):** Barrow, Alaska (30-year normal), 9.3° F (−13° C).

Greatest average yearly rainfall (world): Cherrapunji, India (74-year avg), 450 in. (1,143 cm). **(U.S.):** Mt. Waialeale, Kauai, Hawaii (32-year avg), 460 in. (1,168 cm).

Minimum average yearly rainfall (world): Arica, Chile (59-year avg), 0.03 in. (0.08 cm) (no rainfall for 14 consecutive years). **(U.S.):** Death Valley, Calif. (42-year avg), 1.63 in. (4.14 cm). Bagdad, Calif., holds the U.S. record for the longest period with no measurable rain, 767 days, from Oct. 3, 1912 to Nov. 8, 1914.

Hottest summer average in Western Hemisphere (U.S.): Death Valley, Calif., 98° F (36.7° C).

Longest hot spell (world): Marble Bar, W. Australia, 100° F (38° C) (or above) for 162 consecutive days, Oct. 30, 1923 to Apr. 7, 1924.

Largest hailstone (U.S.): Coffeyville, Kans., 17.5 in. (44.5 cm), Sept. 3, 1979.

World and U.S. Extremes of Climate

Highest Recorded Temperatures

	Place	Date	Degrees Fahrenheit	Degrees Celsius
World (Africa)	El Azizia, Libya	Sept. 13, 1922	136	58
North America (U.S.)	Death Valley, Calif.	July 10, 1913	134	57
Asia	Tirat Tsvi, Israel	June 21, 1942	129	54
Australia	Cloncurry, Queensland	Jan. 16, 1889	128	53
Europe	Seville, Spain	Aug. 4, 1881	122	50
South America	Rivadavia, Argentina	Dec. 11, 1905	120	49
Canada	Midale and Yellow Grass, Saskatchewan, Canada	July 5, 1937	113	45
Persian Gulf (sea-surface)		Aug. 5, 1924	96	36
Antarctica	Vanda Station	Jan. 5, 1974	59	15
South Pole		Dec. 27, 1978	7.5	−14

Lowest Recorded Temperatures

	Place	Date	Degrees Fahrenheit	Degrees Celsius
World (Antarctica)	Vostok	July 21, 1983	−129	−89
Asia	Verkhoyansk/Oimekon	Feb. 6, 1933	−90	−68
Greenland	Northice	Jan. 9, 1954	−87	−66
North America (excl. Greenland)	Snag, Yukon, Canada	Feb. 3, 1947	−81	−63
United States	Prospect Creek, Alaska	Jan. 23, 1971	−80	−62
U.S. (excl. Alaska)	Rogers Pass, Mont.	Jan. 20, 1954	−70	−56.5
Europe	Ust 'Shchugor, Russia	n.a.	−67	−55
South America	Sarmiento, Argentina	June 1, 1907	−27	−33
Africa	Ifrane, Morocco	Feb. 11, 1935	−11	−24
Australia	Charlotte Pass, N.S.W.	June 29, 1994	−9	−22

Greatest Rainfalls

	Place	Date	Inches	Centimeters
1 minute (World)	Unionville, Md.	July 4, 1956	1.23	3.1
20 minutes (World)	Curtea-de-Arges, Romania	July 7, 1889	8.1	20.5
42 minutes (World)	Holt, Mo.	June 22, 1947	12	30.5
12 hours (World)	Grand Ilet, La Réunion	Jan. 26, 1980	46	114
24 hours (World)	Foc-Foc, La Réunion	Jan. 7–8, 1966	72	182.5
24 hours (N. Hemisphere)	Paishih, Taiwan	Sept. 10–11, 1963	49	125
24 hours (Australia)	Bellenden Ker, Queensland	Jan. 4, 1979	44	114
24 hours (U.S.)	Alvin, Tex.	July 25–26, 1979	43	109
24 hours (Canada)	Ucluelet Brynnor Mines, British Columbia	Oct. 6, 1967	19	49
5 days (World)	Commerson, La Réunion	Jan. 23–28, 1980	156	395
1 month (World)	Cherrapunji, India	July 1861	366	930
12 months (World)	Cherrapunji, India	Aug. 1860–Aug. 1861	1,042	2,647
12 months (U.S.)	Kukui, Maui, Hawaii	Dec. 1981–Dec. 1982	739	1878

Greatest Snowfalls

	Place	Date	Inches	Centimeters
1 month (U.S.)	Tamarack, Calif.	Jan. 1911	390	991
24 hours (N. America)	Silver Lake, Colo.	April 14–15, 1921	76	195.6
24 hours (Alaska)	Thompson Pass	Dec. 29, 1955	62	157.5
19 hours (France)	Bessans	April 5–6, 1969	68	173
1 storm (N. America)	Mt. Shasta Ski Bowl, Calif.	Feb. 13–19, 1959	189	480
1 storm (Alaska)	Thompson Pass	Dec. 26–31, 1955	175	445.5
1 season (N. America)	Mount Baker, Wash.	1998–1999	1,140	2,895.6
1 season (Alaska)	Thompson Pass	1952–1953	974.5	2,475
1 season (Canada)	Revelstoke Mt. Copeland, British Columbia	1971–1972	964	2,446.5

Source: U.S. Army Corps of Engineers, Engineer Topographic Laboratories.

Apparent Temperature for Values of Room Temperature and Relative Humidity

Relative Humidity (%)

Room temperature (°F)	0	10	20	30	40	50	60	70	80	90	100
75	68	69	71	72	74	75	76	76	77	78	79
74	66	68	69	71	72	73	74	75	76	77	78
73	65	67	68	70	71	72	73	74	75	76	77
72	64	65	67	68	70	71	72	73	74	75	76
71	63	64	66	67	68	70	71	72	73	74	75
70	63	64	65	66	67	68	69	70	71	72	73
69	62	63	64	65	66	67	68	69	70	71	72
68	61	62	63	64	65	66	67	68	69	70	71
67	60	61	62	63	64	65	66	67	68	68	69
66	59	60	61	62	63	64	65	66	67	67	68
65	59	60	61	61	62	63	64	65	65	66	67
64	58	59	60	60	61	62	63	64	64	65	66
63	57	58	59	59	60	61	62	62	63	64	64
62	56	57	58	58	59	60	61	61	62	63	63
61	56	57	57	58	59	59	60	60	61	61	62
60	55	56	56	57	58	58	59	59	60	60	61

Source: National Oceanic and Atmospheric Administration, Environmental Data and Information Service and National Climatic Center.

Deadliest Tornado Outbreak

Source: National Weather Service

The most expensive tornado outbreak in U.S. history and the deadliest of the year occurred May 3–4, 1999, in Oklahoma and Kansas. In less than 21 hours, a total of 74 tornadoes touched down across the two states, with as many as four tornadoes from different storms on the ground at once.

An F-5 tornado, the strongest on the Fujita Tornado Scale, moved along a 38-mi. (61-km) path, from Chickasha through south Oklahoma City and the suburbs of Bridge Creek, Newcastle, Moore, Midwest City, and Del City. With 8,000 buildings damaged, the Oklahoma City tornado is the most expensive single tornado in history, causing about a billion dollars in damage. In all, the tornadoes killed 46 people, injured 800, and caused $1.5 billion in damage.

The deadliest and most devastating U.S. tornado outbreak of the 20th century was the April 3–4, 1974, "Super Tornado Outbreak." It lasted 16 hours and produced a total of 148 tornadoes across 13 states, killing 330 people and injuring more than 5,000. □

Record Highest Temperatures by State

State	Temp. °F	Temp. °C	Date	Station	Elevation in feet
Alabama	112	44	Sept. 5, 1925	Centerville	345
Alaska	100	38	June 27, 1915	Fort Yukon	est. 420
Arizona	128	53	June 29, 1994	Lake Havasu	785
Arkansas	120	49	Aug. 10, 1936	Ozark	396
California	134	57	July 10, 1913	Greenland Ranch	-178
Colorado	118	48	July 11, 1888	Bennett	5,484
Connecticut	106	41	July 15, 1995	Danbury	457
Delaware	110	43	July 21, 1930	Millsboro	20
D.C.	106	41	July 20, 1930	Washington	410
Florida	109	43	June 29, 1931	Monticello	207
Georgia	113	45	May 27, 1978	Greenville	860
Hawaii	100	38	Apr. 27, 1931	Pahala	850
Idaho	118	48	July 28, 1934	Orofino	1,027
Illinois	117	47	July 14, 1954	E. St. Louis	410
Indiana	116	47	July 14, 1936	Collegeville	672
Iowa	118	48	July 20, 1934	Keokuk	614
Kansas	121	49	July 24, 1936*	Alton (near)	1,651
Kentucky	114	46	July 28, 1930	Greensburg	581
Louisiana	114	46	Aug. 10, 1936	Plain Dealing	268
Maine	105	41	July 10, 1911*	North Bridgton	450
Maryland	109	43	July 10, 1936*	Cumberland & Frederick	623; 325
Massachusetts	107	42	Aug. 2, 1975	New Bedford & Chester	120; 640
Michigan	112	44	July 13, 1936	Mio	963
Minnesota	114	46	July 6, 1936*	Moorhead	904
Mississippi	115	46	July 29, 1930	Holly Springs	600
Missouri	118	48	July 14, 1954*	Warsaw & Union	687; 560
Montana	117	47	July 5, 1937	Medicine Lake	1,950
Nebraska	118	48	July 24, 1936*	Minden	2,169
Nevada	125	52	June 29, 1994	Laughlin	680
New Hampshire	106	41	July 4, 1911	Nashua	125
New Jersey	110	43	July 10, 1936	Runyon	18
New Mexico	122	50	June 27, 1994	Lakewood	3,418
New York	108	42	July 22, 1926	Troy	35
North Carolina	110	43	Aug. 21, 1983	Fayetteville	81
North Dakota	121	49	July 6, 1936	Steele	1,857
Ohio	113	45	July 21, 1934*	Gallipolis (near)	673
Oklahoma	120	49	June 29, 1994*	Tipton	1,251
Oregon	119	48	Aug. 10, 1898	Pendleton	1,074
Pennsylvania	111	44	July 10, 1936*	Phoenixville	100
Rhode Island	104	40	Aug. 2, 1975	Providence	51
South Carolina	111	44	June 28, 1954*	Camden	170
South Dakota	120	49	July 5, 1936	Gannvalley	1,750
Tennessee	113	45	Aug. 9, 1930*	Perryville	377
Texas	120	49	Aug. 12, 1936	Seymour	1,291
Utah	117	47	July 5, 1895	Saint George	2,880
Vermont	105	41	July 4, 1911	Vernon	310
Virginia	110	43	July 15, 1954	Balcony Falls	725
Washington	118	48	Aug. 5, 1961*	Ice Harbor Dam	475
West Virginia	112	44	July 10, 1936*	Martinsburg	435
Wisconsin	114	46	July 13, 1936	Wisconsin Dells	900
Wyoming	114	46	July 12, 1900	Basin	3,500

* Also on earlier dates at the same or other places. *Source:* National Climatic Data Center, Asheville, N.C., and Storm Phillips, STORMFAX, INC.

Record Lowest Temperatures by State

State	Temp. °F	Temp. °C	Date	Station	Elevation in feet
Alabama	−27	−33	Jan. 30, 1966	New Market	760
Alaska	−80	−62	Jan. 23, 1971	Prospect Creek	1,100
Arizona	−40	−40	Jan. 7, 1971	Hawley Lake	8,180
Arkansas	−29	−34	Feb. 13, 1905	Pond	1,250
California	−45	−43	Jan. 20, 1937	Boca	5,532
Colorado	−61	−52	Feb. 1, 1985	Maybell	5,920
Connecticut	−32	−36	Feb. 16, 1943	Falls Village	585
Delaware	−17	−27	Jan. 17, 1893	Millsboro	20
D.C.	−15	−26	Feb. 11, 1899	Washington	410
Florida	−2	−19	Feb. 13, 1899	Tallahassee	193
Georgia	−17	−27	Jan. 27, 1940	CCC Camp F-16	est. 1,000
Hawaii	7	−14	Jan. 23, 1997	Mauna Kea	13,770
Idaho	−60	−51	Jan. 18, 1943	Island Park Dam	6,285
Illinois	−36	−38	Jan. 5, 1999	Elizabeth	880
Indiana	−36	−38	Jan. 19, 1994	New Whiteland	785
Iowa	−47	−44	Feb. 3, 1996	Elkader	745
Kansas	−40	−40	Feb. 13, 1905	Lebanon	1,812
Kentucky	−37	−38	Jan. 19, 1994	Shelbyville	730
Louisiana	−16	−27	Feb. 13, 1899	Minden	194
Maine	−48	−44	Jan. 19, 1925	Van Buren	510
Maryland	−40	−40	Jan. 13, 1912	Oakland	2,461
Massachusetts	−35	−37	Jan. 12, 1981	Chester	640
Michigan	−51	−46	Feb. 9, 1934	Vanderbilt	785
Minnesota	−60	−51	Feb. 2, 1996	Tower	1,400
Mississippi	−19	−28	Jan. 30, 1966	Corinth	420
Missouri	−40	−40	Feb. 13, 1905	Warsaw	700
Montana	−70	−57	Jan. 20, 1954	Rogers Pass	5,470
Nebraska	−47	−44	Feb. 12, 1899	Camp Clarke	3,700
Nevada	−50	−46	Jan. 8, 1937	San Jacinto	5,200
New Hampshire	−46	−43	Jan. 28, 1925	Pittsburg	1,575
New Jersey	−34	−37	Jan. 5, 1904	River Vale	70
New Mexico	−50	−46	Feb. 1, 1951	Gavilan	7,350
New York	−52	−47	Feb. 18, 1979*	Old Forge	1,720
North Carolina	−34	−37	Jan. 21, 1985	Mt. Mitchell	6,525
North Dakota	−60	−51	Feb. 15, 1936	Parshall	1,929
Ohio	−39	−39	Feb. 10, 1899	Milligan	800
Oklahoma	−27	−33	Jan. 18, 1930	Watts	958
Oregon	−54	−48	Feb. 10, 1933*	Seneca	4,700
Pennsylvania	−42	−41	Jan. 5, 1904	Smethport	est. 1,500
Rhode Island	−25	−32	Feb. 5, 1996	Greene	425
South Carolina	−20	−28	Jan. 18, 1977	Caesars Head	3,100
South Dakota	−58	−50	Feb. 17, 1936	McIntosh	2,277
Tennessee	−32	−36	Dec. 30, 1917	Mountain City	2,471
Texas	−23	−31	Feb. 8, 1933*	Seminole	3,275
Utah	−69	−56	Feb. 1, 1985	Peters Sink	8,095
Vermont	−50	−46	Dec. 30, 1933	Bloomfield	915
Virginia	−30	−34	Jan. 22, 1985	Mountain Lake	3,870
Washington	−48	−44	Dec. 30, 1968	Mazama & Winthrop	2,120; 1,765
West Virginia	−37	−38	Dec. 30, 1917	Lewisburg	2,200
Wisconsin	−54	−48	Jan. 24, 1922	Danbury	908
Wyoming	−63	−53	Feb. 9, 1933	Moran	6,770

* Also on earlier dates at the same or other places. *Source:* National Climatic Data Center, Asheville, N.C., and Storm Phillips, STORMFAX, INC.

Record Monthly High and Low Temperatures in the United States

Source: National Climatic Data Center, Asheville, N.C., and Storm Phillips, STORMFAX, Inc.

January

The highest temperature ever recorded for the month of January occurred on January 17, 1936, and again in 1954, in Laredo, Tex. (elevation 421 ft.), where the temperature reached 98° F.

The lowest temperature ever recorded for the month of January occurred on January 20, 1954, in Rogers Pass, Mont. (elevation 5,470 ft.), where the temperature fell to –70° F.

February

The highest temperature ever recorded for the month of February occurred on February 3, 1963, in Montezuma, Ariz. (elevation 735 ft.), where the temperature reached 105° F.

The lowest temperature ever recorded for the month of February occurred on February 1, 1985, at the Peters Sink station in Utah (elevation 8,095 ft.), where the temperature fell to –69° F.

March

The highest temperature ever recorded for the month of March occurred on March 31, 1954, in Rio Grande City, Tex. (elevation 168 ft.), where the temperature reached 108° F.

The lowest temperature ever recorded for the month of March occurred on March 17, 1906, in Snake River, Wyo. (elevation 6,862 ft.), where the temperature dropped to –50° F.

April

The highest temperature ever recorded for the month of April occurred on April 25, 1898, at Volcano Springs, Calif. (elevation –220 ft.), where the temperature reached 118° F.

The lowest temperature ever recorded for the month of April occurred on April 5, 1945, in Eagle Nest, N.M. (elevation 8,250 ft.), where the temperature dropped to –36° F.

May

The highest temperature ever recorded for the month of May occurred on May 27, 1896, in Salton, Calif. (elevation –263 ft.), where the temperature reached 124° F.

The lowest temperature ever recorded for the month of May occurred on May 7, 1964, in White Mountain 2, Calif. (elevation 12,470 ft.), where the temperature dropped to –15° F.

June

The highest temperature ever recorded for the month of June occurred on June 23, 1902, at Volcano Springs, Calif. (elevation –220 ft.), where the temperature reached 129° F.

The lowest temperature ever recorded for the month of June occurred on June 13, 1907, in Tamarack, Calif. (elevation 8,000 ft.), where the temperature dropped to 2° F.

July

The highest temperature ever recorded for the month of July occurred on July 10, 1913, at Greenland Ranch, Calif. (elevation –178 ft.), where the temperature reached 134° F.

The lowest temperature ever recorded for the month of July occurred on July 21, 1911, at Painter, Wyo. (elevation 6,800 ft.), where the temperature fell to 10° F.

August

The highest temperature ever recorded for the month of August occurred on August 12, 1933, at Greenland Ranch, Calif. (elevation –178 ft.), where the temperature reached 127° F.

The lowest temperature ever recorded for the month of August occurred on August 25, 1910, in Bowen, Mont. (elevation 6,080 ft.), where the temperature fell to 5° F.

September

The highest temperature ever recorded for the month of September occurred on September 2, 1950, in Mecca, Calif. (elevation –175 ft.), where the temperature reached 126° F.

The lowest temperature ever recorded for the month of September occurred on September 24, 1926, at Riverside Ranger Station, Mont. (elevation 6,700 ft.), where the temperature fell to –9° F.

October

The highest temperature ever recorded for the month of October occurred on October 5, 1917, in Sentinel, Ariz. (elevation 685 ft.), where the temperature reached 116° F.

The lowest temperature ever recorded for the month of October occurred on October 29, 1917, in Soda Butte, Wyo. (elevation 6,600 ft.), where the temperature fell to –33° F.

November

The highest temperature ever recorded for the month of November occurred on November 12, 1906, in Craftonville, Calif. (elevation 1,759 ft.), where the temperature reached 105° F.

The lowest temperature ever recorded for the month of November occurred on November 16, 1959, at Lincoln, Mont. (elevation 5,130 ft.), where the temperature fell to –53° F.

December

The highest temperature ever recorded for the month of December occurred on December 8, 1938, in La Mesa, Calif. (elevation 539 ft.), where the temperature reached 100° F.

The lowest temperature ever recorded for the month of December occurred on December 19, 1924, at Riverside Ranger Station, Mont. (elevation 6,700 ft.), where the temperature fell to –59° F.

Temperature Extremes in the United States

Source: National Oceanic and Atmospheric Administration, Environmental Data and Information Service, and National Climatic Center

The Highest Temperature Extremes

Greenland Ranch, California, with 134° F on July 10, 1913, holds the record for the highest temperature ever officially observed in the United States. This station was located in barren Death Valley, 178 feet below sea level. Death Valley is about 140 miles long, four to six miles wide, and oriented north to south in southwestern California. Much of the valley is below sea level and is flanked by towering mountain ranges with Mt. Whitney, the highest landmark in the 48 conterminous states, rising to 14,495 feet above sea level, less than 100 miles to the west. Death Valley has the hottest summers in the Western Hemisphere, and is the only known place in the United States where nighttime temperatures sometimes remain above 100° F.

The highest annual normal (1941–1970 mean) temperature in the United States, 78.2° F, and the highest summer (June–August) normal temperature, 92.8° F, are for Death Valley, California. The highest winter (December–February) normal temperature is 72.8° F for Honolulu, Hawaii.

Amazing temperature rises of 40° to 50° F in a few minutes occasionally may be brought about by chinook winds.[1]

---

1. A warm, dry wind that descends from the eastern slopes of the Rocky Mountains, causing a rapid rise in temperature.

Some Outstanding Temperature Rises

In 12 hours: 83° F, Granville, N.D., Feb. 21, 1918, from –33° F to 50° F from early morning to late afternoon.

In 15 minutes: 42° F, Fort Assiniboine, Mont., Jan. 19, 1892, from –5° F to 37° F.

In seven minutes: 34° F, Kipp, Mont., Dec. 1, 1896. The observer also reported that a total rise of 80° F occurred in a few hours and that 30 inches of snow disappeared in half a day.

In two minutes: 49° F, Spearfish, S.D., Jan. 22, 1943, from –4° F at 7:30 A.M. to 45° F at 7:32 A.M.

The Lowest Temperature Extremes

The lowest temperature on record in the United States, –79.8° F, was observed at Prospect Creek Camp in the Endicott Mountains of northern Alaska (latitude 66°48′N, longitude 150°40′W) on Jan. 23, 1971. The lowest ever recorded in the conterminous 48 states, –69.7° F, occurred at Rogers Pass, in Lewis and Clark County, Mont., on Jan. 20, 1954. Rogers Pass is in mountainous and heavily forested terrain about one half of a mile east of and 140 feet below the summit of the Continental Divide.

The lowest annual normal (1941–1970 mean) temperature in the United States is 9.3° F for Barrow, Alaska, which lies on the Arctic coast. Barrow also has the coolest summers (June–August) with a normal temperature of 36.4° F. The lowest winter (December–February) normal temperature, is –15.7° F for Barter Island on the Arctic coast of northeast Alaska.

In the 48 conterminous states, Mt. Washington, N.H. (elevation 6,262 feet), has the lowest annual normal temperature, 26.9° F, and the lowest normal summer temperature, 46.8° F. A few stations in the northeastern United States and in the upper Rocky Mountains have normal annual temperatures in the 30s; summer normal temperatures at these stations are in the low 50s. Winter normal temperatures are lowest in northeastern North Dakota, 5.6° F for Langdon Experiment Farm, and in northwestern Minnesota, 5.3° F for Hallock.

Some Outstanding Temperature Falls

In 24 hours: 100° F, Browing, Mont., Jan. 23–24, 1916, from 44° F to –56° F.

In 12 hours: 84° F, Fairfield, Mont., Dec. 24, 1924, from 63° F at noon to –21° F at midnight.

In 2 hours: 62° F, Rapid City, S.D., Jan. 12, 1911, from 49° F at 6:00 A.M. to –13° F at 8:00 A.M.

In 27 minutes: 58° F, Spearfish, S.D., Jan. 22, 1943, from 54° F at 9:00 A.M. to –4° F at 9:27 A.M.

In 15 minutes: 47° F, Rapid City, S.D., Jan. 10, 1911, from 55° F at 7:00 A.M. to 8° F. at 7:15 A.M.

Tornado Facts

Tornadoes, violently rotating columns of air extending from a thunderstorm to the ground, are among nature's most virulent storms. In an average year, 800 tornadoes are reported across the United States, resulting in 80 deaths and more than 1,500 injuries. The worst tornadoes are capable of tremendous destruction with wind speeds of 250 miles per hour or more.

Tornadoes can occur anywhere in the U.S. at any time of the year. In the southern states, the peak tornado season is March through May, while peak months in the northern states are during the summer.

Average No. of Tornado Deaths, 1950–1999

Jan.	Feb.	Mar.	Apr.	May	June	July	Aug.	Sept.	Oct.	Nov.	Dec.
3	6	13	27	19	11	1	2	2	2	3	3

Average No. of Tornadoes, 1950–1999

Jan.	Feb.	Mar.	Apr.	May	June	July	Aug.	Sept.	Oct.	Nov.	Dec.
20	22	54	109	180	171	96	60	41	29	30	17

Source: Storm Prediction Center at the National Weather Service; Web: www.spc.noaa.gov/.

GREAT DISASTERS

The following lists are not all-inclusive due to space limitations. Only disasters involving great loss of life and/or property, historical interest, or unusual circumstances are listed. Data as of late August 2000. For other disasters *see* Current Events: What Happened in 2000.

WORST UNITED STATES DISASTERS

AIRCRAFT

1979 **May 25, Chicago:** American Airlines DC-10 lost left engine upon take-off and crashed seconds later, killing all 272 persons aboard and three on the ground in worst U.S. air disaster.

DAM

1928 **March 12, Santa Paula, Calif.:** collapse of St. Francis Dam left 450 dead.

DROUGHT

1930s **Many states:** longest drought of 20th century. Peak periods were 1930, 1934, 1936, 1939, and 1940. During 1934, dry regions stretched solidly from N.Y. and Pa. across the Great Plains to the Calif. coast. A great "dust bowl" covered 50 million acres in south-central plains during winter of 1935–1936.

EARTHQUAKE

1906 **April 18, San Francisco:** earthquake accompanied by fire razed more than 4 sq mi.; more than 500 dead or missing.

EPIDEMIC

1918 **Nationwide:** Spanish influenza killed over 500,000 Americans.

EXPLOSION

1947 **April 16–18, Texas City, Tex.:** most of the city destroyed by a fire and subsequent explosion on the French freighter *Grandcamp*, which was carrying a cargo of ammonium nitrate. At least 516 were killed and over 3,000 injured.

FIRE

1871 **Oct. 8, Peshtigo, Wis.:** over 1,200 lives lost and 2 billion trees burned in forest fire.

FLOOD

1889 **May 31, Johnstown, Pa.:** more than 2,200 died in flood.

HURRICANE

1900 **Aug. 27–Sept. 15, Galveston, Tex.:** the "Galveston Hurricane" killed over 6,000 from devastation due to both winds and tidal wave.

MARINE

1865 **April 27, Mississippi River, Tenn.:** boiler explosion on Mississippi River steamboat *Sultana*, near Memphis; 1,547 killed.

MINE

1907 **Dec. 6, Monongha, W. Va.:** coal mine explosion killed 361.

OIL SPILL

1989 **Mar. 24, Prince William Sound, Alaska:** tanker *Exxon Valdez* hit an undersea reef and released 10 million plus gallons of oil into the waters.

RAILROAD

1918 **July 9, Nashville, Tenn.:** 101 killed in a two-train collision near Nashville.

SUBMARINE

1963 **April 10, North Atlantic:** atomic-powered submarine *Thresher* sank; 129 dead.

TERRORIST ATTACK

1995 **April 19, Oklahoma City:** car bomb exploded outside federal office building, collapsing wall and floors. 168 persons were killed, including 19 children and one person who died in rescue effort. Over 220 buildings sustained damage. Timothy McVeigh and Terry Nichols later convicted in the antigovernment plot to avenge the Branch Davidian standoff in Waco, Tex., exactly two years earlier. (*See* Miscellaneous Disasters.)

TORNADO

1925 **March 18, Mo., Ill., and Ind.:** great "Tri-State Tornado"; 689 deaths. Over 2,000 injured. Property damage estimated at $16.5 million.

WINTER STORM

1888 **March 11–14, East Coast:** the "Blizzard of 1888." 400 people died; as much as five feet of snow. Damage was estimated at $20 million.

EARTHQUAKES AND VOLCANIC ERUPTIONS

A.D. **79 Aug. 24, Italy:** eruption of Mt. Vesuvius buried cities of Pompeii and Herculaneum, killing thousands.

856 Dec. 22, Damghan, Iran: 200,000 were killed in one of the deadliest earthquakes on record.

893 March 23, Ardabil, Iran: earthquake killed about 150,000 people.

1138 Aug. 9, Aleppo, Syria: deadly earthquake claimed lives of 230,000 people.

1290 Sept., Chihli, China: earthquake killed about 100,000 people.

1556 Jan. 23, Shaanxi (Shensi) province, China: most deadly earthquake in history; 830,000 killed.

1667 Nov., Shemakha, Caucasia: earthquake killed about 80,000 people.

1727 Nov. 18, Tabriz, Iran: about 77,000 victims killed in deadly earthquake.

1755 Nov. 1, Portugal: one of the most severe of recorded earthquakes leveled Lisbon and was felt as far away as southern France and North Africa; 70,000 killed.

1811 Dec. 16, Mississippi Valley nr. New Madrid, Mo.: earthquake reversed the course of the Mississippi River. Fatalities unknown due to sparse population in area. Aftershocks and tremors continued into 1812. It has been estimated that three of the series of earthquakes had surface-wave magnitudes of 8.6, 8.4, and 8.8 on the Richter scale. It is the largest series of earthquakes known to have occurred in North America.

1883 Aug. 26–28, Netherlands Indies: eruption of Krakatau; violent explosions destroyed two-thirds of island, leaving an estimated 36,000 dead. Sea waves occurred as far away as Cape Horn and possibly England.

1886 **Aug. 31, Charleston, S.C.:** 60 persons killed and extensive damage to city. Earthquake's magnitude was 7.7 on the Richter scale.

1902 **May 8, Martinique, West Indies:** Mt. Pelée erupted and wiped out city of St. Pierre; 40,000 dead.

1906 **April 18, San Francisco:** earthquake accompanied by fire razed more than 4 sq mi.; more than 500 dead or missing.

1908 **Dec. 28, Messina, Sicily:** city totally destroyed by earthquake. Death toll 70,000–100,000 in Sicily and southern Italy.

1915 **Jan. 13, Avezzano, Italy:** earthquake left 29,980 dead.

1920 **Dec. 16, Gansu province, China:** magnitude 8.6 earthquake killed 100,000 in northwestern China.

1923 **Sept. 1, Japan:** earthquake destroyed one-third of Tokyo and most of Yokohama. More than 140,000 killed in magnitude 8.3 quake.

1927 **May 22, nr. Xining, China:** magnitude 8.3 earthquake claimed approximately 200,000 victims.

1932 **Dec. 25, Gansu, China:** magnitude 7.6 earthquake rattled China, killing approximately 70,000.

1933 **March 10, Long Beach, Calif.:** 117 left dead by earthquake.

1935 **May 30, Pakistan:** earthquake at Quetta killed 30,000–60,000.

1939 **Jan. 24, Chile:** earthquake razed 50,000 sq mi.; about 30,000 killed.

Dec. 27, northern Turkey: severe quakes destroyed city of Erzingan; about 100,000 casualties.

1950 **Aug. 15, India:** earthquake affected 30,000 sq mi. in Assam; 20,000–30,000 believed killed.

1964 **March 28, Alaska:** strongest earthquake ever to strike North America hit 80 miles east of Anchorage; followed by seismic wave 50 feet high that traveled 8,445 miles at 450 miles per hour; 117 killed.

1970 **May 31, Peru:** earthquake left more than 50,000 dead, 17,000 missing.

1972 **Dec. 22, Managua, Nicaragua:** earthquake devastated city, leaving up to 6,000 dead.

1976 **Feb. 4, Guatemala:** quake left over 23,000 dead.

July 28, Tangshan, China: worst earthquake to hit China in 20th century; devastated 20 sq mi. of city, leaving 242,000 confirmed dead.

Aug. 17, Mindanao, Philippines: earthquake and tidal wave left up to 8,000 dead or missing.

1978 **Sept. 16, Tabas, Iran:** earthquake destroyed city in eastern Iran, leaving 25,000 dead.

1985 **Sept. 19–20, Mexico:** earthquake registering 8.1 on Richter scale struck central and southwestern regions, devastating part of Mexico City and three coastal states; estimated 25,000 killed.

Nov. 14–16, Colombia: eruption of Nevada del Ruiz, 85 miles northwest of Bogotá. Mudslides buried most of the town of Armero and devastated Chinchiná; estimated 25,000 killed.

1988 **Dec. 7, Armenia:** earthquake measuring 6.9 on the Richter scale killed nearly 25,000, injured 15,000, and left at least 400,000 homeless.

1989 **Oct. 17, San Francisco Bay area:** earthquake measuring 7.1 on Richter scale killed 67 and injured over 3,000. Over 100,000 buildings damaged or destroyed. Damage cost city billions of dollars.

1990 **June 21, northwestern Iran:** earthquake measuring 7.7 on Richter scale destroyed cities and villages in Caspian Sea area. At least 50,000 dead, over 60,000 injured, and 400,000 homeless.

1994 **Jan. 17, San Fernando Valley, Calif.:** earthquake measuring 6.6 on Richter scale killed 61 and injured over 8,000. Damage estimated at $13–20 billion.

1995 **Jan.17, Osaka, Kyoto, and Kobe, Japan:** 5,100 killed and 26.800 injured; estimated damage $100 billion. Epicenter 12 miles under Awaji Island in the Inland Sea; magnitude: 7.2.

1997 **May 12, northeastern Iran:** severe earthquake measuring 7.1 on Richter scale left more than 1,500 people dead and at least 4,460 injured.

June–Sept., southern Montserrat: ongoing eruption of Soufriere Hills volcano since July 1995; killed 20 persons in major eruption on June 25, 1997, rendered southern two-thirds of Montserrat uninhabitable, and forced some 8,000 of the island's 12,000 residents to abandon the island.

1998 **May 30, northern Afghanistan:** magnitude 7.1 earthquake and aftershocks killed an estimated 5,000 and injured at least 1,500. A quake on Feb. 4 in same area had killed about 2,300.

1999 **Jan. 25, western Colombia:** 1,124 dead and 4,000 injured in magnitude 6 earthquake in and around the city of Armenia. More than 200,000 left homeless; city plagued by looting and violence among desperate survivors.

Aug. 17, northwestern Turkey: magnitude 7.4 quake centered near Izmit killed over 17,000 and injured about 44,000. Damage estimated at $8.5 billion.

Nov. 12, northwestern Turkey: another severe 7.2 temblor killed more than 700 in Ducze and surrounding towns.

Sept. 21, central Taiwan: severe 7.6 earthquake and aftershocks killed 2,295 and injured 8,729.

MAJOR U.S. EPIDEMICS

1793 **Philadelphia:** more than 4,000 residents died from yellow fever.

1832 **July–Aug., New York City:** over 3,000 people killed in a cholera epidemic.

Oct., New Orleans: cholera took the lives of 4,340 people.

1848 **New York City:** more than 5,000 deaths caused by cholera.

1853 **New Orleans:** yellow fever killed 7,790.

1867 **New Orleans:** 3,093 perished from yellow fever.

1878 **Southern states:** over 13,000 people died from yellow fever in lower Mississippi Valley.

1916 **Nationwide:** over 7,000 deaths occurred and 27,363 cases were reported of polio (infantile paralysis) in America's worst polio epidemic.

1918 **March–Nov., nationwide:** outbreak of Spanish influenza killed over 500,000 people in the worst single U.S. epidemic.

1949 **Nationwide:** 2,720 deaths occurred from polio, and 42,173 cases were reported.

1952 **Nationwide:** polio killed 3,300; 57,628 cases reported; worst epidemic since 1916.

1981 **1981 to Dec. 1999:** total U.S. AIDS cases reported to Centers for Disease Control: 724,656; total AIDS deaths reported: 425,357.

FLOODS, AVALANCHES, AND TIDAL WAVES

1228 **Holland:** 100,000 people reputedly drowned by sea flood in Friesland.

1642 **China:** rebels destroyed Kaifeng seawall; 300,000 drowned.

1889 **May 31, Johnstown, Pa.:** more than 2,200 died in flood.

1896 **June 15, Sanriku, Japan:** earthquake and tidal wave killed 27,000.

1954 **Jan. 31–Feb. 5, northwestern Europe:** storm followed by floods devastated North Sea coastal areas. Netherlands was hardest hit with 1,794 dead.

1959 **Dec. 2, Fréjus, France:** flood caused by collapse of Malpasset Dam left 412 dead.

1960 **Agadir, Morocco:** 10,000–12,000 dead as earthquake set off tidal wave and fire, destroying most of city.

1962 **Jan. 10, Peru:** avalanche down Huascaran, extinct Andean volcano, killed more than 3,000.

1963 **Oct. 9, Italy:** landslide into the Vaiont Dam; flood killed about 2,000.

1966 **Oct. 21, Aberfan, Wales:** avalanche of coal, waste, mud, and rocks killed 144 people, including 116 children in school.

1969 **Jan. 18–26, southern Calif.:** floods and mudslides from heavy rains caused widespread property damage; at least 100 dead. Another downpour (Feb. 23–26) caused further floods and mudslides; at least 18 dead.

1970 **Nov. 13, East Pakistan:** 200,000 killed by cyclone-driven tidal wave from Bay of Bengal. Over 100,000 missing.

1972 **Feb. 26, Man, W. Va.:** more than 118 died when slag-pile dam collapsed under pressure of torrential rains and flooded 17-mile valley.
June 9–10, Rapid City, S.D.: flash flood caused 237 deaths and $160 million in damage.
June 20, Eastern Seaboard: tropical storm Agnes, in ten-day rampage, caused widespread flash floods. Death toll 129; 115,000 left homeless; damage estimated at $3.5 billion.

1976 **Aug. 1, Loveland, Colo.:** flash flood along Route 34 in Big Thompson Canyon left 139 dead.

1988 **Aug.–Sept., Bangladesh:** heaviest monsoon in 70 years inundated three-fourths of country, killing more than 1,300 and leaving 30 million homeless. Damage estimated at over $1 billion.

1993 **June–Aug., Ill., Iowa, Kan., Ky., Minn., Mo., Neb., N.D., S.D., Wis.:** two months of heavy rain caused Mississippi River and tributaries to flood in ten states, causing almost 50 deaths and about $12 billion in damage to property and agriculture in Midwest. Almost 70,000 left homeless.

1997 **Dec. 1996–Jan. 1997, U.S. West Coast:** torrential rains and snowmelt produced severe floods in parts of Calif., Ore., Wash., Idaho, Nev., and Mont., causing 36 deaths and about $2–3 billion in damage.
March, Ohio and Mississippi Valleys: flooding and tornadoes plagued Ark., Mo., Miss., Tenn., Ill., Ind., Ky., Ohio, and W.Va. 67 were killed and damage totaled approximately $1 billion.
April, N.D., S.D., and Minn.: Grand Forks, N.D., and surrounding area devastated as the Red River swelled thirteen feet above flood level.

1998 **July 17, Papua New Guinea:** spurred by undersea earthquake, three tsunamis wiped out entire villages in the northwestern province of Sepik. One tidal wave reported by survivor to be 30 ft. high. At least 2,000 found or presumed dead. Many who were injured by the tsunamis were later killed by deadly gangrene infections.
Summer, central and northeast China: heaviest flooding of Yangtze and other rivers since 1954. More than 3,000 killed and 14 million left homeless. Estimated damages exceeded $20 billion.

1999 **Summer, Asia:** flooding plagued Asia again after weeks of torrential downpours. More than 950 killed and millions left homeless in S. Korea, China, Japan, the Philippines, and Thailand.
Oct., southwestern Mexico: over a week of heavy rains killed at least 360 people in mudslides and flood waters.
Nov. and Dec., Vietnam: devastating floods caused $285 million in damage and killed more than 700 people.
Dec. 15–16, northern Venezuela: heavy rains caused catastrophic flooding and mudslides, killing an estimated 5,000 to 20,000 people. Is country's worst modern-day natural disaster.

2000 **Feb., southeastern Africa:** weeks of rain resulted in deadly floods in Mozambique and Zimbabwe. About 700 people were killed and more than 280,000 were left homeless.

TROPICAL STORMS

Cyclones, hurricanes, and typhoons are the same kind of tropical storm but are called by different names in different areas of the world.

CYCLONES

1864 **Oct. 5, India:** most of Calcutta denuded by cyclone; 70,000 killed.

1942 **Oct. 16, India:** cyclone devastated Bengal; about 40,000 lives lost.

1960 **Oct. 10, East Pakistan:** cyclone and tidal wave killed about 6,000.

1963 **May 28–29, East Pakistan:** cyclone killed about 22,000 along coast.

1965 **May 11–12 and June 1–2, East Pakistan:** cyclones killed about 47,000.
Dec. 15, Karachi, Pakistan: cyclone killed about 10,000.

1970 **Nov. 12–13, East Pakistan:** cyclone and tidal waves killed 200,000 and another 100,000 were reported missing.

1971 **Sept. 29, Orissa state, India:** cyclone and tidal wave off the Bay of Bengal killed as many as 10,000.

1974 **Dec. 25, Darwin, Australia:** cyclone destroyed nearly the entire city, causing mass evacuation; 50 reported dead.

1977 **Nov. 19, Andhra Pradesh, India:** cyclone and tidal wave claimed lives of 20,000.

1991 **April 30, southeastern Bangladesh:** cyclone killed over 131,000 and left as many as 9 million homeless. Thousands of survivors died from hunger and water-borne disease.

1999 **Oct. 29, eastern India:** supercyclone swept in from Bay of Bengal and devastated state of Orissa, killing at least 9,573 and leaving over 10 million homeless.

U.S. HURRICANES

(U.S. deaths only, except where noted)

1776 Sept. 2–Sept. 9, N.C. to Nova Scotia: called the "Hurricane of Independence", it is believed that 4,170 in the U.S. and Canada died in the storm.

1856 Aug. 11, Last Island, La.: 400 died.

1893 Aug. 28, Savannah, Ga., Charleston, S.C., Sea Islands, S.C.: at least 1,000 died.

1900 Aug. 27–Sept. 15, Galveston, Tex. and Texas Gulf Coast: more than 8,000 died in hurricane and tidal wave. The "Galveston Hurricane" is considered the deadliest in U.S. history.

1909 Sept. 10–21, La. and Miss.: 350 deaths.

1915 Aug. 5–23, East Tex. and La.: 275 killed.

1919 Sept. 2–15, Fla., La., and Tex.: 287 deaths, and 488 deaths at sea.

1926 Sept. 11–22, Fla. and Ala.: 243 deaths.

1928 Sept. 6–20, southern Fla.: 1,836 died and 1,870 injured.

1935 Aug. 29–Sept. 10, southern Fla.: 408 killed.

1938 Sept. 10–22, Long Island and southern New England: 600 deaths; 1,764 injured.

1944 Sept. 9–16, N.C. to New England: 46 deaths, and 344 deaths at sea.

1947 Sept. 4–21, Fla. and mid-Gulf Coast: 51 killed.

1954 Aug. 25–31, N.C. to New England: "Carol" killed 60 and injured 1,000 in Long Island–New England area.

Oct. 5–18, S.C. to N.Y.: "Hazel" killed 95 in U.S.; about 400–1,000 in Haiti; 78 in Canada.

1955 Aug. 7–21, N.C. to New England: "Diane" took 184 lives.

1957 June 25–28. Tex. to Ala.: "Audrey" wiped out Cameron, La., causing 390 deaths.

1960 Aug. 29–Sept. 13, Fla. to New England: "Donna" killed 50 in the U.S. 115 deaths in Antilles—mostly from flash floods in Puerto Rico.

1961 Sept. 3–15, Tex. coast: "Carla" devastated Texas gulf cities, taking 46 lives.

1965 Aug. 27–Sept. 12, southern Fla. and La.: "Betsy" killed 75 people.

1969 Aug. 14–22, Miss., La., Ala., Va., and W. Va.: 256 killed and 68 persons missing as a result of "Camille."

1972 June 14–23, Fla. to N.Y.: "Agnes" caused 117 deaths (50 in Pa.).

1979 Aug. 25–Sept. 7, Caribbean islands to New England: "David" caused five U.S. deaths; 1,200 in the Dominican Republic.

1980 Aug. 3–10, Caribbean islands to Tex. Gulf: "Allen" killed 28 in U.S.; over 200 in Caribbean.

1985 Oct.–Nov.: "Juan" struck La. and the Southeast. Though only a category 1 hurricane, it caused severe flooding and $1.5 billion in damages; 63 lives were lost.

1989 Sept. 10–22, Caribbean Sea, S.C., and N.C.: "Hugo" claimed 49 U.S. lives (71 killed overall); $4.2 billion paid in insurance claims.

1992 Aug. 22–26, southern Fla., La., and Bahamas: Gulf Coast hurricane "Andrew," with damage estimated at $15–$20 billion, is most costly hurricane in U.S. history.

1994 Nov. 8–21, Caribbean and southern Fla.: flooding and mudslides caused by "Gordon" led to an estimated 1,122 deaths in Haiti. There were eight deaths in Fla.; total estimated U.S. damage nearly $400 million.

1995 Nov. 29, Fla. panhandle and Ala.: storm surge during "Opal" caused extensive damage to coastal areas. In U.S. death toll reached nine and damages $3 billion.

1996 Sept. 5, N.C. and Va.: "Fran," a category 3 hurricane, took 37 lives and caused $5.0 billion in damage.

1999 Sept. 14–18, Bahamas to New England: "Floyd" and associated flooding caused at least 75 deaths including one in the Bahamas. Hardest-hit N.C. suffered 49 "Floyd" related deaths. Damage estimated to be over $6 billion.

OTHER HURRICANES

1780 Oct. 10–16, Barbados, West Indies: "The Great Hurricane of 1780" killed 20–22,000 persons and completely flattened the islands of Barbados, Martinique, and St. Eustatius; is the deadliest western hemisphere hurricane on record.

1926 Oct. 20, Cuba: powerful hurricane killed 650.

1930 Sept. 3, Santo Domingo: hurricane killed about 8,000 people.

1934 Sept. 21, Japan: hurricane killed more than 4,000 on Honshu.

1955 Sept. 19, Mexico: "Hilda" took 200 lives.

Sept. 22–28, Caribbean: "Janet" killed 200 in Honduras and 300 in Mexico.

1961 Oct. 31, British Honduras: "Hattie" devastated capital Belize, killed at least 400.

1963 Oct. 2–7, Caribbean: "Flora" killed about 7,200 in Haiti and Cuba.

1966 Sept. 24–30, Caribbean area: "Inez" killed 293.

1974 Sept. 14–19, Honduras: "Fifi" struck northern part of country, leaving 8,000 dead and 100,000 homeless.

1988 Sept. 12–17, Caribbean Sea and Gulf of Mexico: "Gilbert" took at least 260 lives and caused some 39 tornados and 300 deaths.

1997 Oct. 8–10, southern Mexico: "Pauline" devastated resort city of Acapulco and villages along the coast in states of Oaxaca and Guerrero, leaving 217 dead and 20,000 homeless.

1998 Sept. 20–29, Caribbean, Fla. Keys, and Gulf Coast: "Georges" killed about 600 people, mostly in Dominican Republic. Damage estimated to be $5 billion, including $2 billion in Puerto Rico.

Oct. 26–Nov. 4, Central America (notably, Honduras and Nicaragua): "Mitch" killed more than 11,000 people in Central America, becoming the deadliest Atlantic storm in 200 years. Winds reached as high as 180 m.p.h. Two to three million people were left homeless and more than $5 billion in damage was done to crops and infrastructure in Honduras, Nicaragua, and Guatemala.

TYPHOONS

1906 Sept. 18, Hong Kong: typhoon with tsunami killed an estimated 10,000 persons.

1949 Dec. 5, off Korea: typhoon struck fishing fleet; several thousand men reported dead.

1959 Aug. 20, Fukien province, China: "Iris" killed 2,334.

Sept. 27, Honshu, Japan: "Vera" killed an estimated 4,464.

1960 June 9, Fukien province, China: "Mary" caused at least 1,600 deaths.

1984 Sept. 2–3, Philippines: "Ike" hit seven major islands, leaving 1,300 dead.

1991 Nov. 5, central Philippines: flash floods triggered by tropical storm "Thelma" killed about 3,000 people. Leyte city of Ormoc was worst hit.

RECENT HURRICANE-LIKE STORMS

1999 Dec. 26, northern Europe: sweeping killer storm with winds gusting up to 124 mph caused the deaths of more than 60 people, including 15 in Germany and 11 in Switzerland.

U.S. TORNADOES

1840 **May 6, Natchez, Miss.:** tornado struck heart of the city, killing 317 and injuring over 1,000.

1880 **April 18, Marshfield, Mo.:** series of 24 tornadoes demolished city, killing 99 people.

1884 **Feb. 19, Miss., Ala., N.C., S.C., Tenn., Ky., Ind.:** tornadoes caused estimated 800 deaths.

1896 **May 27, St. Louis, Mo.:** tornado destroyed large section of the city, killing 255.

1899 **June 12, New Richmond, Wis.:** tornado struck while circus was in town, causing 117 deaths.

1902 **May 18, Goliad, Tex.:** tornado killed 114.

1903 **June 1, Gainesville, Holland, Ga.:** twister caused 98 deaths.

1905 **May 10, Snyder, Okla.:** tornado killed 97.

1908 **April 24, Amite, La.; Purvis, Miss.:** tornado killed 143.

April 24, Natchez, Miss.: twister struck, causing 91 deaths.

1913 **March 23, Omaha, Neb.:** tornado devastated city Easter Sunday evening, killing 103.

1917 **May 26, Mattoon, Ill.:** tornado smashed area, causing 101 deaths.

1924 **June 28, Lorain, Sandusky, Ohio:** tornado swept through cities, causing 85 deaths.

1925 **March 18, Mo., Ill., Ind.:** the "Tri-State Tornado" was the most violent single twister in U.S. history. It caused the deaths of 689 people and injured over 2,000. Property damage was estimated at $16.5 million.

1927 **May 9, Poplar Bluff, Mo.:** twister killed 98.

Sept. 29, St. Louis, Mo.: a five-minute tornado ripped through the city and caused 79 deaths.

1932 **March 21, Ala., Miss., Ga., Tenn.:** outbreak of tornadoes killed 268.

1936 **April 5, Tupelo, Miss.:** tornado ripped through the town, killing 216.

April 6, Gainesville, Ga.: twister obliterated the small mill town, causing 203 deaths.

1944 **June 23, Shinnston, W.Va.:** tornadoes caused 100 deaths.

1947 **April 9, Woodward, Okla.:** tornado demolished town, killing 181.

1952 **March 21–22, Ark., Tenn., Mo., Miss., Ala., Ky.:** tornadoes caused 343 deaths.

1953 **May 11, Waco, Tex.:** a single tornado struck, killing 114.

June 8, Flint, Mich.: tornado killed 116.

June 9, Worcester, Mass.: tornado hit town, causing 90 deaths.

1955 **May 25, Udall, Kans.:** tornado killed 80.

1965 **April 11, Iowa, Ind., Ohio, Mich:** tornadoes in Iowa, Ill., Ind., Ohio, Mich., and Wis. caused 256 deaths.

1974 **April 3–4:** a series of 148 twisters comprised the deadly 1974 "Super Tornado Outbreak" that struck 13 states in the East, South, and Midwest. Before it was over, 330 died and 5,484 were injured in a damage path covering more than 2,500 miles. It was the worst tornado outbreak in U.S. history.

1999 **May 3:** unusually large twister, thought to have been a mile wide at times, killed 41 people and injured at least 748 others in Okla. A separate tornado killed another 5 and injured about 150 in Kans. Damages totaled at least $1 billion.

NUCLEAR POWER PLANT ACCIDENTS

1952 **Dec. 12, Chalk River, nr. Ottawa, Canada:** a partial meltdown of the reactor's uranium fuel core resulted after the accidental removal of four control rods. Although millions of gallons of radioactive water accumulated inside the reactor, there were no injuries.

1957 **Oct. 7, Windscale Pile No. 1, north of Liverpool, England:** fire in a graphite-cooled reactor spewed radiation over the countryside, contaminating a 200-sq.-mi. area.

South Ural Mountains: explosion of radioactive wastes at Soviet nuclear weapons factory 12 miles from city of Kyshtym forced the evacuation of over 10,000 people from a contaminated area. No casualties were reported by Soviet officials.

1976 **nr. Greifswald, East Germany:** radioactive core of reactor in the Lubmin nuclear power plant nearly melted down due to the failure of safety systems during a fire.

1979 **March 28, Three Mile Island, nr. Harrisburg, Pa.:** one of two reactors lost its coolant, which caused overheating and partial meltdown of its uranium core. Some radioactive water and gases were released.

1986 **April 26, Chernobyl, nr. Kiev, former U.S.S.R.:** explosion and fire in the graphite core of one of four reactors released radioactive material that spread over part of the Soviet Union, Eastern Europe, Scandinavia, and later Western Europe. 31 claimed dead. Total casualties are unknown and estimates run into the thousands. Worst such accident to date.

1999 **Sept. 30, Tokaimura, Japan:** uncontrolled chain reaction in a uranium-processing nuclear fuel plant spewed high levels of radioactive gas into the air, exposing 69 people, killing one worker, and seriously injuring two others. Japan's worst nuclear accident.

FIRES AND EXPLOSIONS

1666 **Sept. 2, England:** "Great Fire of London" destroyed St. Paul's Cathedral, etc. Damage £10 million.

1835 **Dec. 16, New York City:** 530 buildings destroyed by fire.

1871 **Oct. 8, Chicago:** the "Chicago Fire" burned 17,450 buildings and killed 250 persons; $196 million in damage.

1872 **Nov. 9, Boston:** fire destroyed 800 buildings; $75 million in damage.

1876 **Dec. 5, New York City:** fire in Brooklyn Theater killed more than 300.

1881 **Dec. 8, Vienna:** at least 620 died in fire at Ring Theatre.

1900 **June 30, Hoboken, N.J.:** piers of North German Lloyd Steamship line burned; 326 dead.

1903 **Dec. 30, Chicago:** Iroquois Theatre fire killed 602.

1906 **March 10, France:** explosion in coal mine in Courrières killed 1,060.

1907 **Dec. 6, Monongha, W. Va.:** coal mine explosion killed 361.

Dec. 19, Jacobs Creek, Pa.: explosion in coal mine left 239 dead.

1909 **Nov. 13, Cherry, Ill.:** explosion in coal mine killed 259.

1911 **March 25, New York City:** fire in Triangle Shirtwaist Factory fatal to 145.

1913 **Oct. 22, Dawson, N.M.:** coal mine explosion left 263 dead.

1917 **Dec. 6, Halifax Harbor, Nova Scotia:** Belgian steamer collided with ammunition ship *Mont Blanc*, which was carrying over 2,500 tons of explosives. Explosion leveled part of Halifax and left about 1,600 people dead.

1930 **April 21, Columbus, Ohio:** fire in Ohio State Penitentiary killed 320 convicts.

1937 **March 18, New London, Tex.:** explosion destroyed schoolhouse; 294 killed.

1942 **April 26, Manchuria:** explosion in Honkeiko Colliery killed 1,549.

Nov. 28, Boston, Mass.: Coconut Grove nightclub fire killed 491.

1944 **July 6, Hartford, Conn.:** fire and ensuing stampede in main tent of Ringling Brothers Circus killed 168, injured 487.

July 17, Port Chicago, Calif.: 322 killed when ammunition ships exploded.

1946 **Dec. 7, Atlanta:** fire in Winecoff Hotel killed 119.

1947 **April 16–18, Texas City, Tex.:** most of the city destroyed by a fire and subsequent explosion on the French freighter *Grandcamp*, which was carrying a cargo of ammonium nitrate. At least 516 were killed and over 3,000 injured.

1949 **Sept. 2, China:** fire on Chongqing (Chungking) waterfront killed 1,700.

1954 **May 26, off Quonset Point, R.I.:** explosion and fire aboard aircraft carrier *Bennington* killed 103 crewmen.

1956 **Aug. 7, Colombia:** about 1,100 reported killed when seven army ammunition trucks exploded at Cali.

Aug. 8, Belgium: 262 died in coal mine fire at Marcinelle.

1960 **Jan. 21, Coalbrook, South Africa:** coal mine explosion killed 437.

Nov. 13, Syria: 152 children killed in moviehouse fire.

1961 **Dec. 17, Niteroi, Brazil:** circus fire fatal to 323.

1962 **Feb. 7, Saarland, West Germany:** coal mine gas explosion killed 298.

1963 **Nov. 9, Japan:** explosion in coal mine at Omuta killed 447.

1965 **May 28, India:** coal mine fire in state of Bihar killed 375.

June 1, nr. Fukuoka, Japan: coal mine explosion killed 236.

1967 **May 22, Brussels, Belgium:** fire in L'Innovation, major department store, left 322 dead.

July 29, off North Vietnam: fire on U.S. carrier *Forrestal* killed 134.

1969 **Jan. 14, Pearl Harbor, Hawaii:** nuclear aircraft carrier *Enterprise* ripped by explosions; 27 dead, 82 injured.

1970 **Nov. 1, Saint-Laurent-du-Pont, France:** fire in dance hall killed 146 young people.

1972 **May 13, Osaka, Japan:** 118 people died in fire in nightclub on top floor of Sennichi department store.

June 6, Wankie, Rhodesia: explosion in coal mine killed 427.

1973 **Nov. 29, Kumamoto, Japan:** fire in Taiyo department store killed 101.

1974 **Feb. 1, São Paulo, Brazil:** fire in upper stories of bank building killed 189 persons, many of whom leaped to their deaths.

1975 **Dec. 27, Dhanbad, India:** explosion in coal mine followed by flooding from nearby reservoir left 372 dead.

1977 **May 28, Southgate, Ky.:** fire in Beverly Hills Supper Club; 167 dead.

1978 **July 11, Tarragona, Spain:** 140 killed at coastal campsite when tank truck carrying liquid gas overturned and exploded.

Aug. 20, Abadan, Iran: nearly 400 killed when arsonists set fire to crowded theater.

1982 **Dec. 18–21, Caracas, Venezuela:** power-plant fire left 128 dead.

1986 **Dec. 31, San Juan, P.R.:** arson fire in Dupont Plaza Hotel was set by three employees, killing 96 people.

1989 **June 3, Ural Mountains:** liquefied petroleum gas leaking from a pipeline running alongside the Trans-Siberian railway near Uta, 72 miles east of Moscow, exploded and destroyed two passing passenger trains. About 500 travelers were killed and 723 injured of an estimated 1,200 passengers on both trains.

1990 **March 25, New York City:** arson fire in the illegal Happy Land Social Club, in the Bronx, killed 87 people.

1993 **May 10, nr. Bangkok, Thailand:** fire in doll factory killed at least 187 persons and injured 500 others. World's deadliest factory fire.

1999 **March 24, Chamonix, France:** Belgian truck carrying margarine and flour broke out into flames in the Mont Blanc tunnel, trapping dozens of cars. Death toll at least 42.

WORST U.S. FOREST FIRES

1871 **Oct. 8–14, Peshtigo, Wis:** over 1,200 lives lost and 4 million acres burned in nation's worst forest fire.

1889 **June 6, Seattle, Wash.:** fire destroyed 64 acres of the city and killed 2 persons. Damage was estimated at $15 million.

1894 **Sept. 1, Minn.:** forest fires ravaged over 160,000 acres and destroyed six towns, killing 600, including 413 in town of Hinckley.

1910 **Aug. 10, Idaho:** fires burned 2 million acres of woods and killed over 70 people.

1918 **Oct. 13–15, Minn. and Wis.:** forest fire struck towns in both states; 1,000 died, including 400 in town of Cloquet, Minn. About $1 million in losses.

1947 **Oct. 25–27, Maine:** forest fire destroyed part of Bar Harbor and damaged Acadia National Park.

1956 **Nov. 25, Calif.:** raging fire destroyed 40,000 acres in Cleveland National Forest and caused 11 deaths.

1988 **Aug.–Sept., western U.S.:** fires destroyed over 1.2 million acres in Yellowstone National Park and damaged Alaska woodlands.

1991 **Oct. 20–23, Oakland-Berkeley, Calif.:** brush fire in drought-stricken area destroyed over 3,000 homes and apartments. At least 24 persons died; damage estimated at $1.5 billion.

2000 **April–May, northern N.M.:** fire started by National Park Service to clear brush from Bandelier National Monument area raged out of control on May 4 and spread to Los Alamos (May 10) destroying at least 250 homes and forcing evacuation of more than 20,000 people. Blaze

consumed an estimated 47,000 acres and threatened Los Alamos National Laboratory.
Summer, western U.S.: as of Aug. 31 nearly 6.5 million acres had burned nationwide, more than double the ten-year average. States hardest hit included Alaska, Calif., Colo., Idaho, Mont., N.M., Nev., Ore., Tex., Utah, Wash., and Wyo.

SHIPWRECKS

1833   **May 11, *Lady of the Lake:*** bound from England to Quebec, struck iceberg; 215 perished.

1853   **Sept. 29, *Annie Jane:*** emigrant vessel off coast of Scotland; 348 died.

1865   **April 27, *Sultana:*** boiler explosion on Mississippi River steamboat, near Memphis; 1,547 killed. Most of the dead were Union POWs finally heading home at the end of the Civil War.

1898   **Feb. 15, *Maine:*** U.S. battleship destroyed in Havana harbor by an explosion that killed 260 men. The incident led to the outbreak of the Spanish-American War in April 1898.

   Nov. 26, *City of Portland:* 157 died nr. Cape Cod.

1904   **June 15, *General Slocum:*** excursion steamer burned in East River, N.Y.; 1,021 perished.

1912   **March 5, *Principe de Asturias:*** Spanish steamer struck rock off Sebastien Point; 500 drowned.

   April 15, *Titanic:* supposedly unsinkable British ocean liner went down on maiden voyage after colliding with an iceberg. More than 1,500 people died.

1914   **May 29, *Empress of Ireland:*** sank after collision in St. Lawrence River; 1,024 perished.

1915   **July 24, *Eastland:*** Great Lakes excursion steamer overturned in Chicago River; 812 died.

1917   **Dec. 6, *Mont Blanc:*** French ammunition ship collided with Belgian steamer in Halifax Harbor, Canada; 1,600 people died.

1934   **Sept. 8, *Morro Castle:*** 134 killed in fire off Asbury Park, N.J.

1942   **Feb. 24, *Struma:*** steamer sunk by Soviet submarine in the Black Sea near the Bosporus. Of the 778 people aboard, mostly Romanian Jews fleeing the Holocaust, only one person survived.

   Oct. 2, *Queen Mary:* rammed and sank a British cruiser; 338 aboard the cruiser died.

1945   **Jan. 30, *Wilhelm Gustloff:*** cruise ship carrying German refugees and soldiers sunk by Soviet submarine in Baltic. It is thought that as many as 10,000 people were aboard, of which only about 900 survived.

   April 9: U.S. ship, loaded with aerial bombs, exploded at Bari, Italy; at least 360 killed.

1948   **Nov.:** unidentified Chinese troopship evacuating Nationalist troops from Manchuria sank nr. Yingkow, killing an estimated 6,000 persons.

   Dec. 3, *Kiangya:* Chinese passenger ship carrying refugees fleeing Communist troops sank off Shanghai; over 3,000 believed to have been killed.

1949   **Sept. 17, *Noronic:*** Canadian Great Lakes cruise ship burned at Toronto dock; about 130 died.

1952   **April 26, *Hobson:*** minesweeper collided with aircraft carrier *Wasp* and sank during night maneuvers in mid-Atlantic; 176 persons lost.

1953   **Jan. 9, *Chang Tyong-Ho:*** South Korean ferry foundered off Pusan; 249 reported dead.

1954   **Sept. 26, *Toya Maru:*** more than 1,000 killed when commercial ferry sank in Tsugaru Strait, Japan.

1956   **July 25, *Andrea Doria:*** Italian liner collided with Swedish liner *Stockholm* off Nantucket Island, Mass., and sank next day. At least 52 died or were unaccounted for.

1962   **April 8, *Dara:*** British liner exploded and sank in Persian Gulf; 236 dead. Caused by time bomb.

1963   **April 10, *Thresher:*** atomic-powered submarine sank in North Atlantic; 129 dead.

1968   **Late May, *Scorpion:*** nuclear submarine sank in Atlantic 400 miles southwest of Azores; 99 dead.

1983   **May 25, *10th of Ramadan:*** Nile steamer caught fire and sank in Lake Nasser, near Aswan, Egypt; 272 dead and 75 missing.

1987   **March 9:** British ferry capsized after leaving Belgian port of Zeebrugge with 500 aboard; 134 drowned. Water rushing through open bow is believed to be probable cause.

   Dec. 20.: over 4,000 killed when passenger ferry *Dona Paz* collided with oil tanker *Victor* off Mindoro Is., 110 miles south of Manila.

1990   **April 7, *Scandinavian Star:*** suspected arson fire aboard Danish-owned North Sea ferry killed at least 110 passengers in Skagerrak Strait off Norway.

1991   **Dec. 14:** ferry carrying 569 passengers sank in Red Sea off coast of Safaga, Egypt, after hitting a coral reef. Over 460 people believed drowned.

1993   **Feb. 17, *Neptune:*** triple-deck ferry capsized off southern peninsula of Haiti during a squall. Over 1,000 passengers believed drowned. About 300 survived the sinking.

1994   **Sept. 28, *Estonia:*** passenger ferry capsized off coast of southwest Finland and sank in a stormy Baltic Sea. Only about 140 of the estimated 1,040 passengers aboard survived.

1996   **Jan. 21, *Gurita:*** overloaded ferry sank off the coast of northern Sumatra, killing 340.

1999   **Feb., *Harta Rimba:*** ship sank in the South China Sea, killing about 325 people. The ship had not been licensed for passenger use.

2000   **June 29, *Cahaya Bahari:*** ferry carrying mostly Christian refugees from the island of Halmahera sank approximately 40 miles off the coast of Sulawesi. None of the 492 persons on board survived.

   Aug. 12, *Kursk:* Russian nuclear submarine sank to bottom of Barents Sea following an explosion; none of the 118 men aboard survived.

MYSTERIOUS DISAPPEARANCES

1872   ***Mary Celeste:*** the brigantine set sail from New York harbor for Genoa, Italy, on Nov. 5. A British brigantine, the *DeGratia,* discovered the ship derelict on Dec. 5 and boarded her. Everyone aboard the *Mary Celeste* had vanished—her captain, his family, and its 14-man crew. The ship was in perfect order with ample supplies and there was no sign of violence or trouble. The fate of the crew remains unknown.

1928   **Dec. 22, *Köbenhavn:*** the five-masted Danish steel barque, a sail-training ship with a crew of 75 including 45 boy cadets, sailed from the River Plate for Melbourne, Australia, on Dec. 14. The last radio contact with the ship was made on Dec. 22 and all was well. The *Köbenhavn* and its crew disappeared without a trace and no one knows what happened to it.

AIRCRAFT CRASHES

(150 deaths or more, with exceptions)

1921 Aug. 24, England: British dirigible *AR-2* broke in two on trial trip near Hull; 62 died.

1925 Sept. 3, Caldwell, Ohio: U.S. dirigible *Shenandoah* broke apart; 14 dead.

1930 Oct. 5, Beauvais, France: British dirigible *R 101* crashed, killing 47.

1933 April 4, N.J.: U.S. dirigible *Akron* crashed; 73 died.

1937 May 6, Lakehurst, N.J.: German zeppelin *Hindenburg* destroyed by fire at tower mooring; 36 killed.

1945 July 28, New York City: U.S. Army bomber B-25 crashed into Empire State Building; 13 dead.

1960 Dec. 16, New York City: United DC-8 and Trans World Super Constellation collided then crashed in two boroughs, killing 134 in air and on ground.

1961 Feb. 15, nr. Brussels, Belgium: 72 on board and farmer on ground killed in crash of Sabena plane; U.S. figure skating team wiped out.

1966 Dec. 24, Binh Thai, South Vietnam: crash of military-chartered CL-44 into village killed 129.

1971 July 30, Morioka, Japan: Japanese Boeing 727 and F-86 fighter collided in midair; 162 died.

1973 Jan. 22, Kano, Nigeria: 171 Nigerian Muslims returning from Mecca and five crewmen died in crash.

Feb. 21, Sinai: civilian Libyan Arab Airlines Boeing 727 shot down by Israeli fighters after it had strayed off course; 108 died, five survived. Officials claimed that the pilot had ignored fighters' warnings to land.

1974 March 3, Paris: Turkish DC-10 jumbo jet crashed in forest shortly after takeoff; all 346 passengers and crew killed.

Dec. 4, Colombo, Sri Lanka: Dutch DC-8 carrying Muslims to Mecca crashed on landing approach, killing all 191 persons aboard.

1975 April 4, nr. Saigon, Vietnam: Air Force Galaxy C-5A crashed after takeoff, killing 172, mostly Vietnamese children.

Aug. 3, Agadir, Morocco: chartered Boeing 707, returning Moroccan workers home after vacation in France, plunged into mountainside; all 188 aboard killed.

1976 Sept. 10, Zagreb, Yugoslavia: midair collision between British Airways Trident and Yugoslav charter DC-9 fatal to all 176 persons aboard.

1977 March 27, Santa Cruz de Tenerife, Canary Islands: Pan American and KLM Boeing 747s collided on runway. All 249 on KLM plane and 333 of 394 aboard Pan Am jet killed. Total of 582 is highest for any type of aviation disaster.

1978 Jan. 1, Bombay: Air India 747 with 213 aboard exploded and plunged into sea minutes after takeoff.

Nov. 15, Colombo, Sri Lanka: chartered Icelandic Airlines DC-8, carrying 249 Muslim pilgrims from Mecca, crashed in thunderstorm during landing approach; 183 killed.

1979 May 25, Chicago: American Airlines DC-10 lost left engine upon takeoff and crashed seconds later, killing all 272 persons aboard and three on the ground in worst U.S. air disaster.

Nov. 26, Jidda, Saudi Arabia: Pakistan International Airlines 707 carrying pilgrims returning from Mecca crashed on takeoff; all 156 aboard killed.

Nov. 28, Mt. Erebus, Antarctica: Air New Zealand DC-10 crashed on sightseeing flight; 257 killed.

1980 Aug. 19, Riyadh, Saudi Arabia: all 301 aboard Saudi Arabian jet killed when burning plane made safe landing but passengers were unable to escape.

1981 Dec. 1, Ajaccio, Corsica: Yugoslav DC-9 Super 80 carrying tourists crashed into mountain on landing approach, killing all 178 aboard.

1983 Aug. 30, nr. island of Sakhalin off Siberia: South Korean civilian jetliner Boeing 747, flight KAL-007, shot down by Soviet fighter after it strayed off course into Soviet airspace. All 269 aboard killed. Secret Soviet documents released in Oct. 1992 reveal that the plane was flying a straight course for two hours with its navigational lights on and did not take evasive action. The Soviet fighter did not give a warning by firing tracer bullets as originally claimed. Recorded conversations indicated that the crew members did not know what hit them.

1985 June 23, off coast of Ireland: Air-India Boeing 747 exploded over Atlantic; all 329 aboard were killed.

Aug. 12, Japan: Japan Air Lines Boeing 747 crashed into a mountain, killing 520 of the 524 aboard.

Dec. 12, Gander, Newfoundland: a chartered Arrow Air DC-8 bringing American soldiers home for Christmas crashed on takeoff. All 256 aboard died.

1987 Aug. 16, Detroit: Northwest Airlines McDonnell Douglas MD-30 plunged to heavily traveled boulevard, killing 156. Girl, 4, only survivor.

Nov. 29, Burma: Korean Air Boeing 747 jetliner exploded from bomb planted by North Korean agents and crashed into sea, killing all 115 aboard.

1988 July 3, Persian Gulf: U.S. Navy cruiser *Vincennes* shot down Iran Air A300 Airbus, killing 290 persons, after mistaking it for an attacking jet fighter.

Aug. 28, Ramstein Air Force Base, West Germany: three jets from Italian Air Force acrobatic team collided in midair during air show and crashed, killing 70 persons, including the pilots and spectators on the ground. It is worst air-show disaster in history.

Dec. 21, Lockerbie, Scotland: N.Y.-bound Pan-Am Boeing 747 exploded in flight from a terrorist bomb and crashed into Scottish village, killing all 259 aboard and 11 on the ground. Passengers included 35 Syracuse University students and many U.S. military personnel.

1989 June 7, Paramaribo, Suriname: a Surinam Airways DC-8 carrying 174 passengers and nine crew members crashed into the jungle while making a third attempt to land in a thick fog, killing 168 aboard.

1991 July 11, Jedda, Saudi Arabia: Canadian-chartered DC-8 carrying pilgrims returning to Nigeria crashed after takeoff, killing 261 persons.

1994 April 14, northern Iraq: two American F-15C fighter aircraft mistook two U.S. Army blackhawk helicopters for Russian-made Iraqi MI-24 helicopters and shot them down over no-fly zone, killing all 26 on board.

April 26, Nagoya, Japan: China Airlines A-300 Airbus from Taiwan crash-landed and exploded on the tarmac. Only seven of the 271 passengers aboard survived.

1995 **Dec. 20, nr. Cali, Colombia:** 160 people killed when American Airlines Boeing 757 crashed in Andean Mountains.

1996 **Jan. 8, Kinshasa, Zaire:** Russian-built Antonov-32 cargo plane crashed after takeoff from Kinshasa into the center of the city, killing over 350 people and injuring at least 470.

Feb. 5, off coast of Puerto Plata, Dominican Republic: a Boeing 737 crashed into Atlantic Ocean after takeoff, killing 189.

May 11, Everglades, Fla.: ValuJet flight went down in swamp, killing 110. Cargo fire caused by oxygen generators missing safety caps.

July 17, off coast of Long Island, N.Y.: TWA Boeing 747-100 bound for Paris from New York exploded over waters of eastern L.I. and crashed into Atlantic Ocean, killing all 230 aboard.

Nov. 12, nr. New Delhi, India: shortly after take-off, Saudi Arabian Airlines Boeing 747 collided in midair with Kazak Airlines Ilyushin 76 plane approaching the New Delhi airport. All 349 passengers and crew were killed; the world's worst midair collision.

1997 **Aug. 6, Guam:** South Korean Air Boeing 747-300 from Seoul crashed into jungle near Agana International Airport killing 227 persons; 27 survived.

Sept. 26, nr. northern Indonesia: Indonesian Garuda Airlines A-300 Airbus jetliner crashed while approaching Medan Airport, Sumatra, killing all 234 persons aboard.

1998 **Feb. 3, Mt. Cermis, Italy:** low-flying U.S. Marine surveillance jet on training flight accidentally cut ski-lift cable-car line, causing all 20 people aboard to fall some 260 feet to their deaths.

Feb. 16, Taipei, Taiwan: China Airlines Airbus 300 jumbo jet crashed while trying to land in fog at Chiang Ki-Shek International Airport, killing all 196 passengers and crew and at least six persons on the ground.

Sept. 2, Nova Scotia, Canada: Swissair flight from New York to Geneva crashed off Canadian coast, killing all 229 aboard. 136 Americans were on the McDonnell Douglas MD-11.

1999 **Oct. 31, southeast of Nantucket Island:** Egypt Air Boeing 767-300 on flight from N.Y. to Cairo crashed into the Atlantic Ocean, killing all 217 aboard.

2000 **Jan. 30, off the Ivory Coast:** Kenya Airways Airbus 310, carrying 179 passengers and crew, crashed after takeoff from Abidjan into the Atlantic Ocean. Ten persons survived.

July 25, Gonesse, France: Air France Concorde jet en route to New York crashed into a hotel just after taking off from Charles de Gaulle airport near Paris; all 109 aboard and four on the ground were killed; first Concorde jet to crash since the plane went into commercial service in 1976.

SPACE ACCIDENTS

1967 **Jan. 27, *Apollo 1*:** a fire aboard the space capsule on the ground at Cape Kennedy, Fla., killed astronauts Virgil I. Grissom, Edward H. White, and Roger Chaffee.

April 23–24, *Soyuz 1*: Vladimir M. Komarov was killed when his craft crashed after its parachute lines, released at 23,000 feet for reentry, became snarled.

1971 **June 6–30, *Soyuz 11*:** three cosmonauts, Georgi T. Dolrovolsky, Vladislav N. Volkov, and Viktor I. Patsayev, found dead in the craft after its automatic landing. Apparent cause of death was loss of pressurization in the space craft during reentry into the earth's atmosphere.

1980 **March 18, U.S.S.R.** a Vostok rocket exploded on its launch pad while being refueled, killing 50 at the Plesetsk Space Center.

1986 **Jan. 28, *Challenger* Space Shuttle:** exploded 73 seconds after liftoff, killing all seven crew members. They were: Francis R. Scobee, Michael J. Smith, Judith A. Resnick, Ronald E. McNair, Ellison S. Onizuka, Gregory B. Jarvis, and schoolteacher Christa McAuliffe. A booster leak ignited the fuel, causing the explosion.

RAILROAD ACCIDENTS

NOTE: Very few passengers were killed in a single U.S. train wreck up until 1853. These early trains ran slowly and made short trips, night travel was rare, and there were not many of them in operation.

1831 **June 17:** the boiler exploded on America's first passenger locomotive, *The Best Friend of Charleston*, killing the fireman. He was the first person in America to be killed in a railroad accident.

1833 **Nov. 8, nr. Heightstown, N.J.:** world's first train wreck and first passenger fatalities recorded. A 24-passenger Camden & Amboy train derailed due to a broken axle, killing two passengers and injuring all others. Former President John Quincy Adams and Cornelius Vanderbilt, who later made a fortune in railroads, were aboard the train.

1853 **May 6, Norwalk, Conn.:** a New Haven Railroad train ran through an open drawbridge and plunged into the Norwalk River. Forty-six passengers were crushed to death or drowned. This was the first major drawbridge accident.

1856 **July 17, Camp Hill, Pa.:** two Northern Penn trains crashed head-on. Sixty-six church-school children bound for a picnic died in the flaming wreckage.

1876 **Dec. 29, Ashtabula, Ohio:** a Lake Shore train fell into the Ashtabula River when the bridge it was crossing collapsed during a snowstorm; 92 people were killed.

1887 **Aug. 10, nr. Chatsworth, Ill.:** a burning railroad trestle collapsed while a Toledo, Peoria & Western train was crossing, killing 81 and injuring 372.

1910 **March 1, Wellington, Wash.:** two trains swept into canyon by avalanche; 96 dead.

1915 **May 22, Gretna, Scotland:** two passenger trains and troop train collided; 227 killed.

1917 **Dec. 12, Modane, France:** nearly 550 killed in derailment of troop train near mouth of Mt. Cenis tunnel.

1918 **July 9, Nashville, Tenn.:** 101 killed in a two-train collision near Nashville.

Nov. 1, New York City: derailment of subway train in Malbone St. tunnel in Brooklyn left 92 dead.

1926 **March 14, Virilla River Canyon, Costa Rica:** an overcrowded train carrying pilgrims derailed while crossing the Colima Bridge, killing over 300 people and injuring hundreds more.

1943 **Dec. 16, nr. Rennert, N.C.:** 72 killed in derailment and collision of two Atlantic Coast Line trains.

1944 **March 2, nr. Salerno, Italy:** 521 suffocated when Italian train stalled in tunnel.

1949 **Oct. 22, nr. Nowy Dwor, Poland:** more than 200 reported killed in derailment of Danzig-Warsaw express.

1950 **Nov. 22, Richmond Hill, N.Y.:** 79 died when one Long Island Railroad commuter train crashed into rear of another.

1951 **Feb. 6, Woodbridge, N.J.:** 85 died when Pennsylvania Railroad commuter train plunged through temporary overpass.

1952 **Oct. 8, Harrow-Wealdstone, England:** two express trains crashed into commuter train; 112 dead.

1957 **Sept. 1, nr. Kendal, Jamaica:** about 175 killed when train plunged into ravine.

Sept. 29, nr. Montgomery, West Pakistan: express train crashed into standing oil train; nearly 300 killed.

Dec. 4, St. John's, England: 92 killed and 187 injured as one commuter train crashed into another in fog.

1962 **May 3, nr. Tokyo:** 163 killed and 400 injured when train crashed into wreckage of collision between inbound freight train and outbound commuter train.

1963 **Nov. 9, nr. Yokohama, Japan:** two passenger trains crashed into derailed freight train, killing 162.

1970 **Feb. 4, nr. Buenos Aires:** 236 killed when express train crashed into standing commuter train.

1972 **Oct. 6, nr. Saltillo, Mexico:** train carrying religious pilgrims derailed and caught fire, killing 204 and injuring over 1,000.

Oct. 30, Chicago: two Illinois Central commuter trains collided during morning rush hour; 45 dead and over 200 injured.

1974 **Aug. 30, Zagreb, Yugoslavia:** train entering station derailed, killing 153 and injuring over 60.

1981 **June 6, nr. Mansi, India:** driver of train carrying over 500 passengers braked to avoid hitting a cow, causing train to plunge off a bridge into the Baghmati River; 268 passengers were reported killed, but at least 300 more were missing.

1982 **July 11, Tepic, Mexico:** Nogales-Guadalajara train plunged down mountain gorge, killing 120.

1989 **Jan. 15, Maizdi Khan, Bangladesh:** a train carrying Muslim pilgrims crashed head-on with a mail train, killing at least 110 persons and injuring as many as 1,000. Many people were riding on the roof of the trains and between the cars.

1990 **Jan. 4, Sangi village, Sindh province, Pakistan:** an overcrowded 16-car passenger train was switched to the wrong track and rammed into a standing freight train. At least 210 persons were killed and 700 were believed injured in what is said to be Pakistan's worst train disaster.

1993 **Sept. 22, nr. Mobile, Ala.:** Amtrak's *Sunset Limited,* en route to Miami, jumped rails on weakened bridge that had been damaged by a barge and plunged in Big Bayou Canot, killing 47 persons.

1995 **Aug. 20, Firozabad, northern India:** a speeding passenger train rammed another train that was stalled after hitting a cow. About 300 persons were killed and over 400 injured.

1997 **March 3, Punjab province, Pakistan:** passenger train crashed due to failed brakes, killing 119 and injuring at least 80 persons.

1998 **June 3, nr. Eschede, Germany:** Inter City Express passenger train traveling at 125 m.p.h. crashed into support pier of an overpass, killing 98. Is nation's worst postwar train accident. Crash may have been caused by a defective wheel.

OIL SPILLS

1978 **March 16, off Portsall, France:** wrecked supertanker *Amoco Cadiz* spilled 68 million gallons, causing widespread environmental damage over 100 miles of Brittany coast—world's largest tanker disaster.

1979 **June 3, Gulf of Mexico:** exploratory oil well Ixtoc 1 blew out, spilling an estimated 140 million gallons of crude oil into the open sea. Although it is the largest known oil spill, it had a low environmental impact.

1989 **Mar. 24, Prince William Sound, Alaska:** tanker *Exxon Valdez* hit an undersea reef and spilled 10 million plus gallons of oil into the waters, causing the worst oil spill in U.S. history.

Dec. 19, off Las Palmas, the Canary Islands: explosion in Iranian supertanker, the *Kharg-5,* tore through its hull and caused 19 million gallons of crude oil to spill out into the Atlantic

Ocean about 400 miles north of Las Palmas, forming a 100-sq-mi. oil slick.

1991 **Jan. 25, southern Kuwait:** during the Persian Gulf War, Iraq deliberately released an estimated 460 million gallons of crude oil into the Persian Gulf from tankers at Mina al-Ahmadi and Sea Island Terminal 10 miles off Kuwait. Spill had little military significance. On Jan. 27, U.S. warplanes bombed pipe systems to stop the flow of oil.

1994 **Sept. 8, Russia:** a dam built to contain oil burst and spilled oil into Kolva River tributary. U.S. Energy Department estimated spill at 2 million barrels. Russian state-owned oil company claimed spill was only 102,000 barrels.

1996 **Feb. 15, off Welsh coast:** supertanker *Sea Empress* ran aground at port of Milford Haven, Wales, spewed out 70,000 tons of crude oil, and created a 25-mile slick.

SPORTS DISASTERS

1955 **June 11, Le Mans, France:** racing car in Grand Prix hurtled into grandstand, killing 82 spectators.

1964 **May 24, Lima, Peru:** more than 300 soccer fans killed and over 500 injured during riot and panic

following unpopular ruling by referee in Peru vs. Argentina soccer game. It is worst soccer disaster on record.

1971 **Jan. 2, Glasgow, Scotland:** 66 killed in crush at Glasgow Rangers home stadium when soccer fans trying to leave encountered fans trying to return to stadium after hearing that a late goal had been scored.

1982   **Oct. 20, Moscow:** according to *Sovietsky Sport*, as many as 340 died at Lenin Stadium when exiting soccer fans collided with returning fans after final goal was scored. All the fans had been crowded into one section of stadium by police.

1985   **May 11, Bradford, England:** 56 burned to death and over 200 injured when fire engulfed main grandstand at Bradford's soccer stadium.

May 29, Brussels, Belgium: drunken group of British soccer fans supporting Liverpool club stormed stand filled with Italian supporters of Juventus team before European Champion's Cup final. While British fans attacked rival spectators at the Heysel Stadium, concrete retaining wall collapsed and 39 persons were crushed or trampled to death, 32 of them Italians. More than 400 persons were injured.

1988   **March 12, Katmandu, Nepal:** some 80 soccer fans seeking cover during a violent hail storm at the national stadium were trampled to death in a stampede because the stadium doors were locked.

1989   **April 15, Sheffield, England:** 94 killed and 170 injured at Hillsborough stadium when throngs of Liverpool soccer fans, many without tickets, collapsed a stadium barrier in a mad rush to see the game between Liverpool and Nottingham Forest. It is Britain's worst soccer disaster.

1996   **Oct. 16, Guatemala City:** at least 84 killed and 147 injured by stampeding soccer fans before a 1998 World Cup qualifying match between Guatemala and Peru held at Mateo Flores National Stadium.

TERRORIST ATTACKS IN U.S.

1920   **Sept. 16, New York City:** TNT bomb planted in unattended horse-drawn wagon exploded on Wall Street opposite House of Morgan, killing 35 persons and injuring hundreds more. Bolshevist or anarchist terrorists believed responsible, but crime never solved.

1975   **Jan. 24, New York City:** bomb set off in historical Fraunces Tavern killed four and injured more than 50 persons. Puerto Rican nationalist group (FALN) claimed responsibility and police tied 13 other bombings to it.

1993   **Feb. 26, New York City:** bomb exploded in basement garage of World Trade Center; killed six and injured at least 1,040 others. Six Middle Eastern men were later convicted in this act of vengeance for the Palestinian people. They claimed to be retaliating against U.S. support for the Israeli government.

1995   **April 19, Oklahoma City:** car bomb exploded outside federal office building, collapsing wall and floors. 168 persons were killed, including 19 children and one person who died in rescue effort. Over 220 buildings sustained damage. Timothy McVeigh and Terry Nichols later convicted in the antigovernment plot to avenge the Branch Davidian standoff in Waco, Tex., exactly two years earlier. (*See* Miscellaneous Disasters.)

WARTIME DISASTERS

1915   **May 6, off the coast of Ireland:** despite German warnings in newspapers, the Cunard Liner *Lusitania* sailed from N.Y. for Liverpool, England, on May 1st and was sunk by a German submarine. 1,198 passengers and crew, 128 of them Americans, died. Unknown to the passengers, the ship was carrying a cargo of small arms. Disaster contributed to entry of the U.S. into World War I.

1916   **Feb. 26, Mediterranean:** 3,100 people died when the French cruiser *Provence* was sunk by a German submarine.

1940   **Sept. 13, Atlantic Ocean:** luxury liner SS *City of Benares* sailed from Liverpool with over 90 British children who were being evacuated to Canada to escape harm during World War II. About 600 miles out to sea, the ship was torpedoed by a German submarine during the night and only 13 of the children survived the disaster.[1]

1941   **Dec. 7, Pearl Harbor, Hawaii:** 1,177 crewmen killed when U.S. battleship *Arizona* was sunk during a surprise attack on the American naval base by Japanese warplanes. The devastating air strike, which damaged or destroyed every battleship in the U.S. Pacific Fleet, is the worst naval catastrophe in U.S. history.

1943   **Nov. 26, Mediterranean Sea:** 1,105 U.S. soldiers died when the British troopship HMT *Rohna* was sunk by a German air-to-surface guided missile. It is the worst U.S. troopship disaster.

Dec., Bari Harbor, Italy: U.S. ship, damaged during German bombing attack, leaked mustard gas into harbor, killing 83 U.S. servicemen and nearly 1,000 civilians.

1944   **Sept. 12, South China Sea:** U.S. submarines torpedoed and sank two Japanese troopships, the *Kachidoki Maru* and the *Rakuyo Maru*. Unknown to the submarines, the Japanese, in disregard for the rules of treatment of prisoners of war, had forced 2,000 British, Australian, and American POWs into the holds of the ships, which were designed to hold only 300 troops. Later, when the subs discovered the tragedy, they sought to rescue as many survivors as possible. Japanese vessels picked up most of *Kachidoki Maru*'s prisoners but abandoned those from the *Rakuyo Maru*, taking only the Japanese survivors. Of the 1,300 POWs aboard the *Rakuyo Maru*, 159 were rescued, but only seven lived.

Oct. 24, South China Sea: the *Arisan Maru* carrying 1,800 American prisoners was torpedoed by a U.S. submarine and sunk. The Japanese destroyer escort rescued Japanese military and civilian personnel and left the POWs to their fate. It is estimated that only ten prisoners survived the disaster.

Dec. 17–18, Philippine Sea: a typhoon struck U.S. Third Fleet's Task Force 38, sank three destroyers, damaged seven other ships, destroyed 186 aircraft, and killed 800 officers and men.

---

1. During the war (1939–1945), some 10,000 children were evacuated to stay with foster parents in the United States and Canada. The sinking of the *City of Benares* ended the British government's evacuation program.

1945 **Jan. 30, Baltic Sea:** Nazi passenger ship *Wilhelm Gustloff*, carrying Germans fleeing Poland, was torpedoed by a Soviet submarine. As many as 9,000–10,000 may have died. World's largest marine disaster.

May 3: several days before World War II ended in Europe, the German passenger ship, *Cap Arcona*, carrying about 6,000, of which an estimated 5,000 were concentration camp prisoners, was sunk by British aircraft. An estimated 5,000 persons were killed.

May 4, Gearhart Mountain, south-central Ore.: six people on a picnic, including a mother and her unborn child, were the only persons ever killed by a balloon-carried bomb launched from Japan. During the war, Japan launched some 6,000 FUGO ("windship weapon") balloons to drift across the Pacific to the U.S. and Canada, each carrying bombs and incendiaries for starting forest fires and creating death and havoc. Although over 200 of the deadly balloons floated to the U.S. before the war ended, the government kept it a secret from the American people.

July 29, nr. Leyte Gulf, Philippines: heavy cruiser *Indianapolis* torpedoed and sunk by a Japanese submarine. Of the crew of 1,199 men, only 316 survived. Due to Navy blundering, the warship was not reported missing when it did not arrive at Leyte on July 31 as scheduled, and therefore no search was ever made for crew. The survivors were discovered by a Navy patrol plane 82 hours after the ship had gone down.

1991 **Feb., Kuwait:** during Persian Gulf War, Iraqi troops systematically dynamited and set fire to 650 of Kuwait's 950 oil wells, causing world's worst man-made environmental disaster. Total of 749 wells damaged. Last of oil fires extinguished on Nov. 6, 1991.

MISCELLANEOUS DISASTERS

1888 **March 11–14, East Coast:** the "Blizzard of 1888." 400 people died; as much as five feet of snow. Damage was estimated at $20 million.

1928 **March 12, Santa Paula, Calif.:** collapse of St. Francis Dam left 450 dead.

1930s **Many states:** longest drought of the 20th century. Peak periods were 1930, 1934, 1936, 1939, and 1940. During 1934, dry regions stretched solidly from N.Y. and Pa. across the Great Plains to the Calif. coast. A great "dust bowl" covered some 50 million acres in the south-central plains during the winter of 1935–1936.

1980 **June–Sept., central and eastern U.S.:** an estimated 10,000 people were killed during the summer in a long heat wave and drought. Damages totaled about $20 billion.

1981 **July 18, Kansas City, Mo.:** suspended walkway in Hyatt Regency Hotel collapsed; 113 dead, 186 injured.

1984 **Dec. 3, Bhopal, India:** toxic gas, methyl isocyanate, seeped from Union Carbide insecticide plant, killed more than 2,000, injured about 150,000.

1987 **Sept. 18. Goiânia, Brazil:** 244 people contaminated with cesium-137 that was removed from a steel cylinder taken from a cancer-therapy machine in an abandoned clinic and sold as scrap. Four people died in worst radiation disaster in Western Hemisphere.

1988 **Summer, central and eastern U.S.:** a severe drought and heat wave killed an estimated 5,000–10,000 people, including heat stress-related deaths. Damages reached $40 billion.

July 6, North Sea off Scotland: 166 workers killed in explosion and fire on Occidental Petroleum's *Piper Alpha* rig in North Sea; 64 survivors. It is the world's worst offshore oil disaster.

1991 **Nov. 29, nr. Coalinga, Calif.:** a massive traffic accident occurred during a severe dust storm involving 104 vehicles in a pileup on Interstate 5; 17 persons killed.

1993 **March 12–14, eastern U.S.:** "storm of the century" struck the eastern seaboard, killing approximately 270. Record snowfalls (with rates of 2–3 inches per hour) and high winds caused $3–6 billion in damage.

April 19, Waco, Tex.: 51-day stalemate between federal agents and members of Christian Branch Davidian cult ended in a fiery tragedy after federal agents botched their assault on the sect's compound. About 80 Branch Davidians, including at least 17 children, died when the compound burned to the ground in a suspicious blaze. Earlier, on Feb. 28, four agents were shot to death in failed attack on heavily armed compound. Jurors in the criminal trial of surviving cult members were unable to determine who fired the first shot. The incident was reopened for investigation in Aug. 1999.

1995 **July 12–17, U.S. Midwest and Northeast:** over 800 persons, including 560 in Chicago, died in record heat wave.

1996 **Jan. 6–8, eastern U.S.:** heavy snow paralyzed the Appalachians, the mid-Atlantic, and the Northeast. 187 were killed in the blizzard and in the floods that resulted after a sudden warm-up. Damages reached $3 billion.

May 10–11, Mt. Everest, Nepal: eight climbers died near summit during storm on mountain. Is worst single loss of lives to occur in a season on Mt. Everest. Another four died over the remaining course of the month.

1998 **Summer, southern U.S.:** severe heat and drought spread across Tex. and Okla., all the way to North and South Carolina. At least 200 were left dead and $6–9 billion of damage was estimated.

1999 **Summer, eastern U.S.:** rainfall shortages resulted in what was the worst drought on record for Md., Del., N.J., and R.I. The state of W.Va. was declared a disaster area. 3.81 million acres were consumed by fire as of mid-Aug. Crops were severely damaged in many states, putting losses in the mid-Atlantic region at at least $800 million.

Summer, continental U.S.: record heat continued throughout the country, resulting in drought, crop damage, and 282 deaths nationwide.

Nov. 17, College Station, Tex.: twelve Texas A&M students were killed when the 40-foot logpile they were constructing collapsed. They were preparing a bonfire for an annual celebration.

Dec. 26–28, western Europe: fierce wind and rain storms swept through Europe, killing 30 in Britain, Spain, Italy, and Switzerland, and 83 in France, which bore the brunt of the storms. 3.4 million homes were left without electricity as winds reached 124 mph.

2000 **June 18, Dover, England:** British customs officials discovered the bodies of 58 illegal immigrants in the back of a tomato truck. The victims, all from China, suffocated to death in an airless compartment.

For Dotcom Pioneers, the Gold Rush Is Over

The dotcom bubble finally bursts, in a wave of mass firings and worthless stock options. For Internet businesses, it's time to evolve

By CHRIS TAYLOR   TIME

In every revolution there comes that bitter moment when the flag-waving has to stop, the grand social theories have to adapt to reality, and a large number of the revolutionaries inevitably find themselves hauled off to the guillotine. The dotcom revolution is no different, except that, true to form, it has accelerated the process. The time it takes to go from hero on the barricades to zero with your head in a basket has shrunk to a nanosecond.

For even the truest of new-economy true believers, bloody April 2000—during which the Nasdaq stock index fell 25.3% and the initial public offering (IPO) window slammed shut—had given way to a Summer of Discontent. By July, many of the most famous names in cyberspace were substantially down for the year: Yahoo, off 50%; CMGI, down 70%; Priceline.com, off 57%; Amazon, off 70%. And when these Internet elephants begin to stumble, the mice get crushed. For every Amazon or Yahoo, there are 10,000 smaller Net companies that never got the chance to go public—and now probably never will. For those companies and their employees, who believed just as hard as Amazon's Jeff Bezos and Yahoo's Jerry Yang but got to the barricades a lot later, the business climate is drastically different. Call it the new new economy.

Reeling from Reel.com's Plunge

Consider the case of Tor Thorsen, movie reviewer and employee No. 5 at Reel.com, formerly one of the Web's largest DVD and video stores. Six months ago, Thorsen was a true believer. Three years' worth of 60-hr. weeks seemed about to pay off. He held 32,000 shares of Reel.com, which was planning to go public. And he was whooping it up at the Sundance Film Festival. A-list stars like Kevin Spacey, Nick Nolte, and Emily Watson granted interviews. "For the first time, we were really part of the film scene," recalls Thorsen. "People knew our name. They were like, 'See you next year.'"

Except there will be no next year. By July 1, Reel.com's headquarters in Emeryville, Calif., was like a ghost town. Every last one of the site's 230 employees had got a pink slip the previous week. Thorsen and 14 others remained as independent contractors, keeping the site running while its owner, Hollywood Entertainment, based in Portland, Ore., worked out the details of how to give it a decent burial.

In 1998, in the full flush of the revolution, Hollywood ponied up $100 million for Reel.com. Now, with the site's IPO canceled because of lack of interest and venture capital running dry, its e-commerce operations were halted. That left Thorsen's 32,000 shares worthless. "I used to think about buying a house and paying off my student loans," he says. "Now I'm thinking about unemployment."

When his contract runs out, Thorsen will hardly be the only dotcom refugee standing in line. This has always been a highly volatile industry, but recent events have been on the scale of a virtual earthquake. Here's a sample of the casualty list for just two days in June: More than a third of Seattle-based Hardware.com's workers went under the hammer. Furniture.com in Framingham, Mass., laid off 80 employees—that's 41% of its workforce. Streaming video site Pseudo.com axed 58 jobs in New York City. Planned IPOs were canned by firms including electronics site 800.com in Portland, Ore., and video-delivery site Kozmo.com in New York City.

Cyberspace Smacks against the Bottom Line

It's not as if the Internet economy is about to collapse. In fact, most laid-off workers are being recruited by other tech firms faster than ever. (A group of headhunters from Amazon.com arrived at Reel.com's offices a day after the firings and found the company's engineers and management had already obtained employment elsewhere.) It's just that cautious investors have finally forced Web sites to think about that once blasphemous bottom line. Talk to upper management at more mature online companies—any more than two years old, say—and you'll hear strange new words like consolidation, restructuring, streamlining, even profitability. "The downturn in the 'stupid' economy is going to precipitate a flight to quality," says Kyle Shannon, cofounder of agency.com, a business-support site that lost employees as its stock went from $98 to $17 in seven months. "I can't wait, frankly. I'm so excited."

Shannon's sentiments, if a little overenthusiastic, are fairly orthodox. You would be hard-pressed to find anyone who does not outwardly profess that a market correction and a separation of wheat from chaff are good for Internet business. But a lot of get-rich-quick dreams have died, and it would be surprising if disappointment did not manifest itself.

"Before the market tank [April's Nasdaq collapse], I could have retired, bought three houses and my dream boat, and had $150,000 a year in interest to live on. Now I'm back where I started," says a senior engineer at a West Coast Web-services company, whose stock was briefly worth $9 million and is currently underwater. That means it has sunk beneath the price at which he originally bought it.

Paper Millionaires to Pink Slips

Even more cruel, of course, is when the paycheck stops too. Just ask the 140 former employees at APBnews.com, a Wall Street–based crime-reporting Web site that hired reporters for a salary in the low $40,000s—very low for a New York City dotcom—plus a meager 500 to 1,000 options. Once again, they turned out to be worthless when the site ran out of cash. As with most dotcom firings, the end was as swift as it was ignominious.

The e-commerce struggle has also produced plenty of grizzled, cynical veterans. Take Janice Crotty, a San Francisco Web consultant. In the space of a single year, she helped give birth to two online ventures—and watched both of them pass away. In early 1999 Crotty quit her job and went without pay for five months to found a Web portal called iAuthentic.com. That failed to attract venture funding, so she joined health site wholepeople.com, which, in turn, was recently rescued by, and merged with, rival site Gaiam.com. Now Crotty is back in the consulting business with no regrets. Her only beef is with venture capitalists, the moneymen who she believes are responsible for most dotcom failures. She thinks they push sites into an early grave by forcing them to become too big, too fast. "I've been burned by the culture of stupid growth that VCs have fostered," she says. "Some businesses ought to grow organically. You can't just add water and expect to compete in the mass market."

The VCs say they're simply reacting to the demands of the market, which became far more cautious and skeptical in the first half of 2000. The game used to be about building a virtual Roman Empire, all glorious acquisitions and land grabs. Now it's about building a Monaco, a tiny but incredibly profitable niche nation. Companies that don't understand the need to change direction—in geekspeak, the phrase is "turn and burn"—are doomed. "The great thing is that people aren't throwing in the towel," says Quincy Smith, partner at the Barksdale Group, a VC firm founded by former Netscape supremo James Barksdale. "They're saying this is a fact of life. Let's get back to work."

It's fair to say the dotcom hubris of a few years ago has gone, replaced by an almost paranoid fear of being the next company to go under. Cautionary tales circulate like computer viruses.

In response to the crisis, the digital workforce has started to act in a new and strangely sensible manner. When he got bored in his last job, software engineer Jason Fisher went to a headhunter and arranged interviews with 10 small, good-looking pre-IPO companies. Each made him a higher offer than the one before, and yet Fisher chose the company—myplay.com, which copies and stores your CDs online—that made him the lowest offer. In fact, it was a pay cut. Why? "I didn't want to go anywhere that I didn't feel was going to succeed," he explains. It was a wise decision. The man Fisher interviewed with at his second-choice company is currently looking for a job himself.

While no one's taking vows of poverty, working for love more than money is clearly hip with online employers. "I'm not sure the message has got out to the masses, but the gold rush is over," says Lesley Workman, CEO of Urbanite Networks in San Francisco. "If you hire someone who's in it for the money, you can be sure they're going to get calls from 700 headhunters a week. That's not the basis of a good relationship."

In other words, Eldorado just closed its gates. That bright shining myth we became so accustomed to over the past two years, the idea that you can make your millions simply by being at the right junction of Silicon Valley's Route 101 at the right time, no longer applies. Says Tony Perkins, editor of *Red Herring* magazine: "No one is going to become a billionaire in the Internet era without deserving it anymore." Or earning, through decades of turn and burn, an inescapable engineer gravity. The revolution is dead; long live the evolution.   □

Performance of Selected Publicly Traded Dotcom Companies

Company and ticker	Total revenues (net sales)	Net income	Total stockholders' equity
Agency.com (ACOM)			
March 31, 2000	$ 38.51	$ −4.15	$ 194.90
Dec. 31, 1999	87.79	−12.88	190.69
March 31, 1999	8.92	−0.13	n.a.
Dec. 31, 1998	26.45	−2.48	2.06
Amazon.com (AMZN)			
March 31, 2000	573.89	−308.43	25.62
Dec. 31, 1999	1,639.84	−719.97	266.28
Sept. 30, 1999	355.78	−197.08	419.93
June 30, 1999	314.38	−138.01	571.05
Barnes & Noble Inc. (BKS)			
April 29, 2000	894.26	−4.14	807.27
Jan. 29, 2000	3,486.04	124.50	846.36
Oct. 30, 1999	715.90	3.39	830.66
July 31, 1999	727.17	23.54	829.39
CMGI, Inc. (CMGI)			
April 30, 2000	225.88	−428.04	6,622.14
Jan. 31, 200	153.47	−185.58	6,236.19
Oct. 31, 1999	123.73	−117.41	3,853.41
July 31, 1999	175.67	476.24	1,473.74

Company and ticker	Total revenues (net sales)	Net income	Total stockholders' equity
Doubleclick Inc. (DCLK)			
March 31, 2000	$110.06	$ −18.37	$ 956.12
Dec. 31, 1999	258.29	−55.82	361.66
Sept. 30, 1999	44.95	−5.37	131.61
June 30, 1999	30.99	−5.61	137.17
DrKoop.com, Inc. (KOOP)			
March 31, 2000	4.74	−24.76	47.94
Dec. 31, 1999	9.43	−56.14	71.32
Sept. 30, 1999	2.86	−20.60	80.71
June 30, 1999	1.02	−11.37	92.26
Priceline.com Incorporated (PCLN)			
March 31, 2000	313.80	−13.57	405.26
Dec. 31, 1999	482.41	−1,055.09	402.64
Sept. 30, 1999	152.22	−102.22	223.36
June 30, 1999	111.56	−14.26	171.31
Yahoo! Inc. (YHOO)			
March 31, 2000	228.38	77.85	1,620.81
Dec. 31, 1999	588.61	61.13	1,261.31
Sept. 30, 1999	155.08	14.86	886.01
June 30, 1999	115.24	−15.06	813.97

Economic Outlook through 2008

Source: Bureau of Labor Statistics, *Monthly Labor Review,* Nov. 1999.

Every two years, the Bureau of Labor Statistics (BLS) publishes its latest projections on the structure of the economy, labor force demographics, and future job growth. The following is a summary of the most recent BLS projections that were released at the end of 1999. They focused on occupational changes over the period 1998–2008. The full report is located on the BLS Web site: http://stats.bls.gov/opub/mls/1999/11/contents.htm.

Moderate Economic Growth Projected

Bureau of Labor Statistics (BLS) projections envision a moderately growing economy over the 1998–2008 decade, with gross domestic product (GDP) reaching $9.5 trillion in chained 1992 dollars by the end of the decade, an increase of almost $2 trillion over the period. Rising by an average annual rate of 2.4%, GDP growth is projected to be somewhat slower than the 2.6% annual rate of growth over the preceding 10-year period, from 1988 to 1998.

Slower growth of civilian household employment, from 1.3% a year during the 1988–1998 period to 1.1% from 1998 to 2008, accompanies the slowdown in GDP growth. Civilian household employment is projected to increase by almost 16 million employees over the 1998–2008 period, slightly less than the increase of 16.5 million persons experienced between 1988 and 1998. The employment projection is accompanied by an assumed unemployment rate of 4.7%, only marginally higher than the 1998 annual average of 4.5%.

Consumer Spending to Decline

Consumer demand is projected to slow over the projection period, growing at an average annual rate of 2.4% from 1998 to 2008, matching the 2.4% growth rate of GDP. As a result, consumption expenditures will amount to 68.3% of GDP in 2008, virtually the same as in 1998. The projection for real disposable income is that it will grow at a 2.5% annual rate between 1998 and 2008, 0.4 percentage point higher than the rate during 1988–1998.

Consumer durables—items with an expected life in excess of 3 years, such as motor vehicles, personal computers, and household furnishings—have a higher income elasticity than does personal consumption spending on nondurables and services. Over the next decade, with a projected rise in family income, the fastest growth sector still is expected to be durable goods, and the continued demand for computers will lead the way.

During the past three decades, expenditures for nondurable goods, such as food, clothing, and gasoline, have increased at a significantly slower pace than has spending on durable goods and consumer services. As family income rises, spending on these short-term consumable necessities also rises, up to a point. After that point is reached, spending on such items tends to increase much more slowly than rises in income, although increases in income enhance the demand for higher quality products.

Continued Trade Deficit

As the world is assumed to become more open to trade, the share of GDP of both exports and imports is expected to grow apace. With these conditions in place, the dollar is expected to remain moderately strong throughout the projection period, but not so strong as to significantly weaken anticipated export growth.

Exports are expected to grow faster than imports between 1998 and 2008. Exports are projected to grow at a 6.9% annual rate over the period, with exports of goods leading the way with a 7.4% annual rate of growth. Exports of services are expected to grow at a rate of 5.9%.

Characteristics of the Civilian Labor Force, 1988–2008
(numbers in thousands)

Group	Level			Percent change		Percent distribution		
	1988	1998	2008	1988–1998	1998–2008	1988	1998	2008
Total	121,669	137,673	154,576	13.2%	12.3%	100.0%	100.0%	100.0%
Sex								
Men	66,927	73,959	81,132	10.5	9.7	55.0	53.7	52.5
Women	54,742	63,714	73,444	16.4	15.3	45.0	46.3	47.5
Age								
16 to 24	22,536	21,894	25,210	–2.8	15.1	18.5	15.9	16.3
25 to 54	84,041	98,718	104,133	17.5	5.5	69.1	71.7	67.4
55 and older	15,092	17,062	25,233	13.1	47.9	12.4	12.4	16.3
Race								
White	104,756	115,415	126,665	10.2	9.7	86.1	83.8	81.9
Black	13,205	15,982	19,101	21.0	19.5	10.9	11.6	12.4
Asian and other[1]	3,708	6,278	8,809	69.3	40.3	3.0	4.6	5.7
Hispanic origin	8,982	14,317	19,585	59.4	36.8	7.4	10.4	12.7
Other than Hispanic origin	112,687	123,356	134,991	9.5	9.4	92.6	89.6	87.3
White non-Hispanic	96,141	101,767	109,216	5.9	7.3	79.0	73.9	70.7

NOTE: Data apply to workers aged 16 and older. 1. Includes Asians, Pacific Islanders, American Indians, and Alaska Natives. *Source:* Bureau of Labor Statistics, *Monthly Labor Review,* Nov. 1999. Web: stats.bls.gov.

Imports, on the other hand, are projected to grow at a relatively slower rate of 6.4% annually during 1998–2008, compared with the 7.7% annual rate of growth over the 1988–1998 10-year span. Imports of goods are expected to grow at 7.0% annually, and a 3.0% annual rate of growth is projected for imports of services during the 1998–2008 period.

These projections result in a trade deficit of $347.5 billion in real terms by 2008, with both exports and imports increasing their share of GDP, the former from 13.0% in 1998 to 20.2% in 2008 and the latter from 16.2% to 23.8%.

Disposable Income on the Rise

On a per capita basis, nominal disposable income is anticipated to increase at an average annual rate of 3.8% from 1998 to 2008, reaching a level of $32,400 in 2008, a gain of more than $10,000 over the projection span.

In real terms—that is, chained 1992 dollars—per capita income is projected to grow 1.6% per year from 1998 to 2008, up from a 1.2% rate of growth between 1988 and 1998. Thus, the bureau expects its projections to be characterized by a long-term

improvement in the real standard of living—at least, measured on the basis of growth in disposable personal income.

Employment Outlook

Total employment is projected to increase by 20.3 million jobs over the 1998–2008 period, rising from 140.5 million to 160.8 million, according to the latest projections of the Bureau of Labor Statistics. The projected 14.4% change in employment is less than the 17.1% increase attained during the previous 10-year period, 1988–1998, when the economy added 20.5 million jobs.

The economy will continue generating jobs for workers at all levels of education and training, although growth rates are projected to be faster, on average, for occupations requiring at least an associate's degree than for occupations requiring less training. However, most job growth will be in occupations requiring less formal education or training, even though many of these occupations are projected to have below-average growth rates. There also will be numerous job openings resulting from the need to replace workers who leave the labor force or move to other occupations.

Persons in the Labor Force, 1840–1990

Year	Labor force[1] Number (thousands)	Percent of working-age population	Percent in labor force in[2] Farm occupation	Nonfarm occupation	Year	Labor force[1] Number (thousands)	Percent of working-age population	Percent in labor force in[2] Farm occupation	Nonfarm occupation
1840	5,420	46.6%	68.6%	31.4%	1920	42,434	51.3%	27.0%	73.0%
1850	7,697	46.8	63.7	36.3	1930	48,830	49.5	21.4	78.6
1860	10,533	47.0	58.9	41.1	1940	52,789	52.2	17.4	82.6
1870	12,925	45.8	53.0	47.0	1950	60,054	53.5	11.6	88.4
1880	17,392	47.3	49.4	50.6	1960	69,877	55.3	6.0	94.0
1890	23,318	49.2	42.6	57.4	1970	82,049	58.2	3.1	96.9
1900	29,073	50.2	37.5	62.5	1980	106,085	62.0	2.2	97.8
1910	37,371	52.2	31.0	69.0	1990	125,182	65.3	1.6	98.4

1. For 1830 to 1930, the data relate to the population and gainful workers at age 10 and over. For 1940 to 1960, the data relate to the population and labor force at age 14 and over; for 1970 and 1980, the data relate to the population and labor force at age 16 and over. For 1940 to 1980, the data include the Armed Forces. 2. The farm and nonfarm percentages relate only to the experienced civilian labor force. *Source:* U.S. Bureau of the Census. Web: www.census.gov.

Fastest Growing Occupations, 1998–2008
(numbers in thousands of jobs)

Occupation	Employment 1998	2008	Change Number	Percent	Occupation	Employment 1998	2008	Change Number	Percent
Computer engineers	299	622	323	108%	Paralegals and legal assistants	136	220	84	62%
Computer support specialists	429	869	439	102	Personal care and home health aides	746	1,179	433	58
Systems analysts	617	1,194	577	94	Medical assistants	252	398	146	58
Database administrators	87	155	67	77	Social and human service assistants	268	410	141	53
Desktop publishing specialists	26	44	19	73	Physician assistants	66	98	32	48

Source: U.S. Department of Labor, Bureau of Labor Statistics, *Monthly Labor Review,* Nov. 1999. Web: stats.bls.gov.

Percent Distribution of Employed Persons by Occupation and Sex

Occupation	Total		Men		Women	
	1998	1999	1998	1999	1998	1999
Total, 16 years and over (thousands)	131,463	133,488	70,693	71,446	60,771	62,042
Percent	100.0%	100.0%	100.0%	100.0%	100.0%	100.0%
Managerial and professional specialty	29.6	30.3	28.1	28.6	31.4	32.3
Executive, administrative, and managerial	14.5	14.7	15.0	15.0	13.9	14.2
Professional specialty	15.1	15.6	13.1	13.6	17.4	18.0
Technical, sales, and administrative support	29.3	29.2	19.5	19.7	40.7	40.0
Technicians and related support	3.2	3.3	2.8	2.9	3.8	3.6
Sales occupations	12.1	12.1	11.1	11.3	13.1	13.0
Administrative support, including clerical	14.0	13.8	5.6	5.5	23.8	23.4
Service occupations	13.6	13.4	10.2	9.9	17.5	17.4
Private household	.6	.6	.1	.1	1.3	1.3
Protective service	1.8	1.8	2.8	2.8	.7	.7
Service, except private household and protective	11.1	11.0	7.3	7.1	15.4	15.4
Precision production, craft, and repair	11.0	10.9	18.7	18.6	2.0	2.1
Operators, fabricators, and laborers	13.9	13.6	19.5	19.3	7.4	7.0
Machine operators, assemblers, and inspectors	5.9	5.5	6.9	6.5	4.8	4.4
Transportation and material moving occupations	4.1	4.1	6.8	7.0	.9	.9
Handlers, equipment cleaners, helpers, and laborers	3.9	3.9	5.8	5.9	1.7	1.7
Farming, forestry, and fishing	2.7	2.6	4.0	3.8	1.1	1.1

NOTE: Beginning in Jan. 1999, data reflect revised population controls used in the household survey. *Source:* U.S. Department of Labor, Bureau of Labor Statistics. Web: stats.bls.gov.

Number of Employed and Unemployed Workers by Sex and Age, 1970–1999

(in thousands)

	1999[1]	1998[1]	1997[1]	1996[1]	1995[1]	1990[2]	1985	1980	1970
Men, 20 years and over									
Employed	67,761	67,134	66,524	64,897	64,085	61,678	56,562	53,101	45,581
Unemployed	2,433	2,580	2,826	3,147	3,239	3,239	3,715	3,353	1,638
Women, 20 years and over									
Employed	58,655	57,278	57,647	53,310	54,396	50,535	44,154	38,492	26,952
Unemployed	2,285	2,424	2,187	2,783	2,819	2,596	3,129	2,615	1,349
Total, 16 years and over									
Employed	133,488	131,463	130,785	126,707	124,900	118,793	107,150	99,303	78,678
Unemployed	5,880	6,209	5,957	7,236	7,404	7,047	8,312	7,637	4,093
Total, 16–19 years									
Employed	7,172	7,051	6,614	6,499	6,419	6,581	6,434	7,710	6,144
Unemployed	1,162	1,205	944	1,307	1,346	1,212	1,468	1,669	1,106

1. Data beginning in 1994 are not directly comparable with earlier years due to the introduction of a major redesign of the Current Population Survey. 2. Revised; data beginning in 1990 are not directly comparable with earlier years due to the introduction of 1990 census-based population controls, adjusted for the estimated under-count. *Source:* U.S. Department of Labor, Bureau of Labor Statistics. Current Population Survey. Web: stats.bls.gov.

Overall Unemployment Rate in the Civilian Labor Force, 1920–2000

Year	Rate	Year	Rate	Year	Rate	Year	Rate	Year	Rate	Year	Rate
1920	5.2%	1944	1.2%	1962	5.5%	1980	7.1%	1992	7.5%	2000	
1928	4.2	1946	3.9	1964	5.2	1982	9.7	1993	6.9	Jan.	4.0%
1930	8.7	1948	3.8	1966	3.8	1984	7.5	1994	6.1	Feb.	4.1
1932	23.6	1950	5.3	1968	3.6	1986	7.0	1995	5.6	March	4.1
1934	21.7	1952	3.0	1970	4.9	1987	6.2	1996	5.4	April	3.9
1936	16.9	1954	5.5	1972	5.6	1988	5.5	1997	4.9	May	4.1
1938	19.0	1956	4.1	1974	5.6	1989	5.3	1998	4.5	June	4.0
1940	14.6	1958	6.8	1976	7.7	1990	5.6	1999	4.2		
1942	4.7	1960	5.5	1978	6.1	1991	6.8				

NOTES: Estimates prior to 1940 are based on sources other than direct enumeration. Data prior to 1948 are for persons age 14 and over. Data beginning in 1948 are for persons age 16 and over. *Source:* U.S. Department of Labor, Bureau of Labor Statistics. Web: stats.bls.gov.

Unemployment Rate by Race, Age, and Sex, 1998–1999

Age and sex	Total		White		Black		Hispanic	
	1998	1999	1998	1999	1998	1999	1998	1999
Men, 16 years and over	4.4%	4.1%	3.9%	3.6%	8.9%	8.2%	6.4%	5.6%
Men, 20 years and over	3.7	3.5	3.2	3.0	7.4	6.7	5.4	4.7
Women, 16 years and over	4.6	4.3	3.9	3.8	9.0	7.8	8.2	7.6
Women, 20 years and over	4.1	3.8	3.4	3.3	7.9	6.8	7.1	6.6
Both sexes, 16 years and over	4.5	4.2	3.9	3.7	8.9	8.0	7.2	6.4

NOTE: Detail for race and Hispanic-origin groups will not sum to totals because data for the "other races" group are not presented and Hispanics are included in both the white and black population groups. *Source:* U.S. Department of Labor, Bureau of Labor Statistics. Web: stats.bls.gov.

Youth Employment Trends, 1996–1998

Source: U.S. Department of Labor. *Report on the Youth Labor Force,* June 2000. Based on Current Population Survey data. Web: stats.bls.gov/opub/rylf/rylfhome.htm.

How Many Youths Work?

During the 1996–1998 period, 2.9 million youths aged 15 to 17 worked during school months, and 4.0 million worked during the summer months.

Among youths, employment increased markedly with age. During the school months of 1996–1998, only 9% of 15-year-olds were employed in an average month, compared with 26% of those a year older and 39% of 17-year-olds. Youths in each age group were more likely to work in the summer, during which employment rates increased to 18%, 36%, and 48% at each age, respectively.

Despite popular perceptions that youths work more than they did in the past, the proportion of 15- to 17-year-olds who work has declined over time. Employment-population ratios declined with economic downturns in the early 1980s and 1990s. After the decline in the early 1990s, however, the rates did not return to earlier levels. During the 1996–1998 period, a quarter of youths worked during the school months, down from 30% in 1977–1979. Just over a third worked during the summer, down from 43% during the late 1970s.

How Much Do Youths Earn?

The minimum wage often is associated with young workers first entering the labor force. CPS data indicate that earnings were at or below the minimum wage for most youths, but a large proportion of youths actually earned more than minimum wage, which was $5.15 in 1998.

In 1998, median earnings of 15- to 17-year-olds combined were $5.57 per hour. In 1998, the earnings increased with age: 15-year-olds earned a median of $5.38 per hour, 16-year-olds earned $5.52, and 17-year-olds earned $5.65 per hour. Earnings varied slightly across sex and race groups. Hispanic and white males had the highest median hourly earnings; Hispanic and black females had the lowest.

Where Do Youths Work?

About 62% of youths aged 15 to 17 employed during the school months of the 1996–1998 period worked in retail trade, more than in any other major industry. Within retail trade, eating and drinking places accounted for the greatest share of employed youths, about one-third of all employed 15- to 17-year-olds. Another 1 in 4 youths was employed in service industries. In the summer, youth employment was less concentrated in retail trade and youths were employed in a wider variety of industries than during the school months. Retail trade still accounted for about half, services increased to 30%, and employment in agriculture and goods-producing industries (mining, construction, and manufacturing) increased. This seasonal pattern of employment also was present in earlier periods.

Most Popular Occupations among Youths Aged 15–17

Industry	Percent of total employed youths	Industry	Percent of total employed youths
Male		**Female**	
Stock handlers and baggers	13.4%	Cashiers	24.3%
Cooks	12.0	Food counter, fountain, and related occupations	6.5
Cashiers	9.6	Waiters and waitresses	6.4
Waiters' and waitresses' assistants	5.2	Sales workers, other commodities	5.1
Miscellaneous food preparation occupations	5.1	Child care workers, private household	4.9
Farm workers	4.7	Cooks	4.4
Janitors and cleaners	4.2	Stock handlers and baggers	3.3
Food counter, fountain, and related occupations	3.5	Sales workers, apparel	3.2
Groundskeepers and gardeners, except farm	3.3	Supervisors, food preparation and service occupations	3.1
Sales workers, other commodities	2.3	Waiters' and waitresses' assistants	2.9

NOTE: School months are January to May and September to December. *Source:* U.S. Department of Labor. *Report on the Youth Labor Force,* June 2000. Web: stats.bls.gov/opub/rylf/rylfhome.htm.

Mothers Participating in Labor Force, 1955–1999

	Percentage of mothers with children		
Year	Under 18 years	6 to 17 years	Under 6 years[1]
1955	27.0%	38.4%	18.2%
1965	35.0	45.7	25.3
1975	47.3	54.8	38.8
1980	56.6	64.3	46.8
1985	62.1	69.9	53.5
1986	62.8	70.4	54.4
1987	64.7	72.0	56.7
1988	65.1	73.3	56.1
1989	65.7	74.2	56.7
1990	66.7	74.7	58.2
1991	66.6	74.4	58.4
1992	67.2	75.9	58.0
1993	67.0	75.4	57.9
1994	68.4	76.0	60.3
1995	69.7	76.4	62.3
1996	70.2	77.2	62.3
1997	72.1	78.1	65.0
1998	71.8	77.6	64.9
1999	72.2	78.2	64.8

1. May also have older children. NOTE: 1955 data are for April; 1965 and 1975–94 data are for March. Data for 1994 and subsequent years are not directly comparable to previous years because of major revisions in the survey questionnaire and the data collection methodology, and the introduction of 1990 census-based population controls into the estimation process. *Source:* U.S. Department of Labor, Bureau of Labor Statistics. Web: stats.bls.gov.

Women in the Civilian Labor Force, 1900–1998

Year	Number[1] (thousands)	% Female population aged 16 and over[1]	% of labor force population aged 16 and over[1]
1900	5,319	18.8%	18.3%
1910	7,445	21.5	19.9
1920	8,637	21.4	20.4
1930	10,752	22.0	22.0
1940	12,845	25.4	24.3
1950	18,389	33.9	29.6
1960	23,240	37.7	33.4
1970	31,543	43.3	38.1
1980	45,487	51.5	42.5
1990[2]	56,829	57.5	45.2
1993	58,795	57.9	45.5
1994[3]	60,239	58.8	46.0
1996	61,857	59.3	46.2
1997	63,036	59.8	46.2
1998	63,714	59.8	46.3

1. For 1900–1930, data relate to population and labor force aged 10 and over; for 1940, to population and labor force aged 14 and over; beginning 1950, to civilian population and labor force aged 16 and over. 2. Data beginning in 1990 are not strictly comparable with data for prior years because population controls were adjusted. 3. Data beginning 1994 are not strictly comparable with data for prior years because of a major redesign of the Current Population Survey (household survey) questionnaire and collection methodology. *Source:* U.S. Department of Labor, Women's Bureau.

National Labor Organizations with Membership over 100,000

Members[1]	Union
760,000	United International Union of Automobile, Aerospace, and Agricultural Implement Workers of America[2]
104,875	Bakery, Confectionery, and Tobacco Workers International Union
123,041	International Association of Bridge, Structural, Ornamental, and Reinforcing Iron Workers
400,000	United Brotherhood of Carpenters and Joiners of America
630,000	Communications Workers of America
2,500,000	National Education Association (Ind.)
658,647	International Brotherhood of Electrical Workers
180,000	International Union of Electronic, Electrical, Salaried, Machine, and Furniture Workers
231,000	International Association of Fire Fighters
1,400,000	United Food and Commercial Workers International Union
600,000	American Federation of Government Employees
150,000	Graphic Communications International Union
300,000	Hotel Employees and Restaurant Employees International Union
800,000	Laborers' International Union of North America
315,000	National Association of Letter Carriers
741,000	International Association of Machinists and Aerospace Workers[2]
130,000	United Mine Workers of America
205,000	Union of Needletrades, Industrial, and Textile Employees[3]
180,000	American Nurses Association (Ind.)
130,000	Office and Professional Employees International Union
400,000	International Union of Operating Engineers
130,000	International Brotherhood of Painters and Allied Trades
320,000	Paper, Allied-Industrial, Chemical, and Energy Workers International Union[4]
291,000	United Association of Journeymen and Apprentices of the Plumbing and Pipe Fitting Industry of the United States and Canada
366,000	American Postal Workers Union
100,000	Retail, Wholesale, and Department Store Union
1,300,000	Service Employees International Union
150,000	Sheet Metal Workers' International Association
1,300,000	American Federation of State, County, and Municipal Employees
700,000	United Steelworkers of America[2]
1,000,000	American Federation of Teachers
1,500,000	International Brotherhood of Teamsters
168,000	Amalgamated Transit Union
125,000	United Transportation Union

NOTE: List is arranged alphabetically by keyword. 1. Unless otherwise noted, unions are AFL-CIO affiliated. 2. The United Int'l Union of Automobile, Aerospace, and Agricultural Implement Workers of America; the Int'l Assoc. of Machinists and Aerospace Workers; and the United Steelworkers of America announced on July 27, 1995, that they will merge over a five-year period. 3. Merger of the International Ladies Garment Workers' Union and the Amalgamated Clothing and Textile Workers Union. 4. The United Paperworkers International Union merged with the Oil, Chemical, and Atomic Workers International Union on Jan. 4, 1999. *Source:* Web sites for labor organizations.

Work Stoppages (Strikes) Involving 1,000 Workers or More

Year	Work stoppages	Workers involved (thousands)	Days idle (thousands)	Year	Work stoppages	Workers involved (thousands)	Days idle (thousands)
1950	424	1,698	30,390	1989	51	452	16,996
1960	222	896	13,260	1990	44	185	5,926
1970	381	2,468	52,761	1991	40	392	4,584
1975	235	965	17,563	1992	35	364	3,989
1980	187	795	20,844	1993	35	184	3,981
1983	81	909	17,461	1994	45	322	5,020
1984	68	391	8,499	1995	28	176	5,736
1985	61	584	7,079	1996	37	273	4,887
1986	72	900	11,861	1997	29	339	4,497
1987	46	174	4,456	1998	34	387	5,116
1988	40	118	4,381	1999	17	73	1,996

NOTE: Refers to stoppages that began in the year. Days idle is total for all stoppages in effect. Workers are counted more than once if they were involved in more than one stoppage during the year. *Source:* U.S. Department of Labor, Bureau of Labor Statistics, *Monthly Labor Review,* March 2000. Web: stats.bls.gov.

Median Weekly Earnings of Selected Occupations, 1999

Occupation	Both sexes		Men		Women	
	Number of workers (in thousands)	Median weekly earnings	Number of workers (in thousands)	Median weekly earnings	Number of workers (in thousands)	Median weekly earnings
Executive, administrative, and managerial	14,973	$ 792	7,981	$ 967	6,992	$652
Accountants and auditors	1,362	723	549	891	813	651
Architects	129	918	108	983	21	—
Computer systems analysts and scientists	1,348	1,008	959	1,079	390	907
Physicians	460	1,266	335	1,364	125	852
Teachers, college and university	638	953	397	1,038	241	859
Teachers, except college and university	4,259	688	1,130	768	3,129	659
Librarians, archivists, and curators	210	701	39	—	171	684
Psychologists	141	673	55	760	86	623
Social workers	705	601	220	661	485	579
Clergy	295	657	256	676	38	—
Lawyers	577	1,168	386	1,340	191	974
Airplane pilots and navigators	99	1,048	97	1,050	3	—
Sales workers, retail and personal services	3,324	329	1,475	423	1,849	296
Secretaries, stenographers, and typists	2,629	446	47	—	2,582	446
Mail carriers, postal service	301	697	218	714	82	646
Bank tellers	288	346	21	—	267	343
Police and detectives	1,079	657	898	681	181	574
Food preparation and service occupations	3,189	298	1,583	311	1,607	286
Hairdressers and cosmetologists	310	322	47	—	263	323
Mechanics and repairers	4,263	621	4,057	622	206	592
Electricians	739	645	723	651	17	—
Truck drivers	2,493	527	2,409	532	85	412
Taxicab drivers and chauffeurs	149	427	127	441	22	—
Farm operators and managers	72	499	61	525	11	—
Forestry and logging occupations	58	503	55	508	2	—

NOTES: Dash indicates base is less than 50,000 workers, so no data are provided. *Source:* U.S. Department of Labor, Bureau of Labor Statistics. Web: stats.bls.gov.

Median Four-Person Family Income

(in current dollars)

Year	Income	Percent change	Year	Income	Percent change	Year	Income	Percent change
1998	$56,061	3.5%	1990	$41,151	1.7%	1982	$27,619	5.1%
1997	53,350	3.6	1989	40,763	4.4	1981	26,274	8.0
1996	51,518	3.7	1988	39,051	6.1	1980	24,332	8.6
1995	49,687	5.7	1987	36,812	6.0	1979	22,395	9.6
1994	47,012	4.1	1986	34,716	5.9	1978	20,428	9.1
1993	45,161	2.1	1985	32,777	5.4	1977	18,723	8.1
1992	44,251	2.8	1984	31,097	6.6	1976	17,315	9.3
1991	43,056	3.9	1983	29,184	5.7	1975	15,848	7.5

Source: Income Statistics Branch/HHES Division, U.S. Bureau of the Census. Web: www.census.gov.

Women's Earnings in 1999

Source: U.S. Department of Labor, Bureau of Labor Statistics. *Highlights of Women's Earnings in 1999,* May 2000.
Web: stats.bls.gov.

In 1999, women earned approximately 77% as much as men did. Median weekly earnings of female full-time wage and salary workers were $473, compared to $618 for their male counterparts. In 1979, when comparable earnings data were first available, the female-to-male earnings ratio was about 63%.

Gender differences in earnings varied considerably by demographic group in 1999. Among blacks and Hispanics, for example, the female-to-male earnings ratios were 84% and 86%, respectively; for whites, the ratio was about 76%. Young women and men (those under age 25) had fairly similar earnings (young women's earnings were 91% of young men's); however, women's earnings were much lower than men's in older age groups—women 35 and over made less than 80% of what men in the same age group earned.

Women's Earnings as a Percent of Men's, 1983 and 1999

	1983			1999		
Occupation	Number of workers (thousands)	Percent women	Women's earnings as percent of men's[1]	Number of workers (thousands)	Percent women	Women's earnings as percent of men's[1]
Total, 16 years and over	**70,976**	**40.4%**	**66.6%**	**97,626**	**43.5%**	**76.5%**
Managerial and professional specialty	17,451	40.9	69.2	30,704	49.4	71.5
Executive, administrative, and managerial	8,117	34.2	64.0	14,973	46.7	67.5
Professional specialty	9,334	46.8	72.6	15,731	52.0	75.3
Technical, sales, and administrative support	21,641	62.5	64.0	27,388	61.6	68.8
Technicians and related support	2,574	44.5	70.6	3,550	49.3	72.6
Sales occupations	6,313	39.0	52.7	9,728	44.5	59.9
Administrative support, including clerical	12,755	77.7	68.7	14,109	76.5	79.1
Service occupations	7,321	49.2	67.8	10,841	52.0	75.7
Private household	278	96.0	(2)	384	95.5	(2)
Protective service	1,453	9.5	70.4	2,138	16.2	80.3
Service, except private household and protective	5,590	57.1	81.0	8,318	59.1	90.0
Precision production, craft, and repair	9,963	7.9	66.1	11,927	8.9	70.6
Operators, fabricators, and laborers	13,319	26.2	66.5	15,182	23.0	71.4
Machine operators, assemblers, and inspectors	6,990	40.8	63.3	6,814	35.9	69.7
Transportation and material-moving occupations	3,358	4.7	75.5	4,401	7.2	75.5
Handlers, equipment cleaners, helpers, and laborers	2,970	16.0	83.9	3,967	18.6	83.2
Farming, forestry, and fishing	1,280	11.2	84.2	1,583	13.8	82.8

1. These figures are computed using unrounded medians and may differ slightly from percents computed using the rounded medians displayed in this table. 2. Data not shown where base for either the numerator or denominator is less than 50,000 workers. *Source:* U.S. Department of Labor, Bureau of Labor Statistics. *Highlights of Women's Earnings in 1999,* May 2000. Web: stats.bls.gov.

Federal Minimum Wage Rates, 1955–2000

	Value of the minimum wage			Value of the minimum wage			Value of the minimum wage			Value of the minimum wage	
Year	Current dollars	Constant (1996) dollars[1]	Year	Current dollars	Constant (1996) dollars[1]	Year	Current dollars	Constant (1996) dollars[1]	Year	Current dollars	Constant (1996) dollars[1]
1955	$0.75	$4.39	1967	$1.40	$6.58	1979	$2.90	$6.27	1991	$4.25	$4.90
1956	1.00	5.77	1968	1.60	7.21	1980	3.10	5.90	1992	4.25	4.75
1957	1.00	5.58	1969	1.60	6.84	1981	3.35	5.78	1993	4.25	4.61
1958	1.00	5.43	1970	1.60	6.47	1982	3.35	5.45	1994	4.25	4.50
1959	1.00	5.39	1971	1.60	6.20	1983	3.35	5.28	1995	4.25	4.38
1960	1.00	5.30	1972	1.60	6.01	1984	3.35	5.06	1996	4.75	4.75
1961	1.15	6.03	1973	1.60	5.65	1985	3.35	4.88	1997	5.15	5.03
1962	1.15	5.97	1974	2.00	6.37	1986	3.35	4.80	1998	5.15	4.96
1963	1.25	6.41	1975	2.10	6.12	1987	3.35	4.63	1999	5.15	4.85
1964	1.25	6.33	1976	2.30	6.34	1988	3.35	4.44	2000	5.15	4.72
1965	1.25	6.23	1977	2.30	5.95	1989	3.35	4.24			
1966	1.25	6.05	1978	2.65	6.38	1990	3.80	4.56			

1. Adjusted for inflation using the CPI-U. *Source:* U.S. Employment Standards Admin. Web: www.dol.gov/esa/public/minwage.

Median Income of Households with Selected Characteristics, 1998

Characteristic	White Number (thousands)	White Median income	Black Number (thousands)	Black Median income	Hispanic origin[1] Number (thousands)	Hispanic origin[1] Median income	All races Number (thousands)	All races Median income
All households	87,212	$40,912	12,579	$25,351	9,060	$28,330	103,874	$38,885
Region								
Northeast	16,901	43,246	2,354	22,908	1,526	26,009	19,877	40,634
Midwest	21,659	42,218	2,344	24,215	651	32,365	24,489	40,609
South	29,305	38,489	6,817	25,420	3,200	27,222	36,959	35,797
West	19,347	41,122	1,064	33,040	3,684	29,193	22,549	40,983
Type of household								
Family households	60,068	49,781	8,444	30,636	7,270	30,812	71,535	47,469
Married-couple families	48,456	54,845	3,975	47,382	4,945	35,207	54,770	54,276
Single-father household	3,086	41,384	660	30,360	600	32,239	3,976	39,414
Single-mother household	8,526	27,542	3,809	17,737	1,725	18,452	12,789	24,393
Nonfamily households	27,144	24,582	4,135	16,071	1,790	16,805	32,339	23,441
Male householder	11,995	31,659	1,827	20,673	927	23,427	14,368	30,414
Living alone	9,028	27,096	1,545	18,351	644	18,358	10,966	26,021
Female householder	15,150	19,239	2,308	13,608	863	11,669	17,971	18,615
Living alone	13,148	16,960	2,087	12,397	685	9,812	15,640	16,406
Size of household								
One person	22,176	20,845	3,633	14,285	1,329	12,584	26,606	20,154
Two persons	29,897	43,218	3,339	26,506	1,972	26,522	34,262	41,512
Three persons	14,217	51,462	2,342	28,661	1,767	29,405	17,386	49,069
Four persons	12,476	58,580	1,771	37,862	1,823	32,998	15,030	55,886
Five persons	5,699	56,169	905	36,160	1,264	33,714	6,962	53,706
Six persons	1,848	52,721	348	31,752	544	33,797	2,367	49,080
Seven persons or more	898	51,915	242	31,420	361	41,343	1,261	46,646
Number of earners								
No earners	17,968	15,929	2,759	8,084	1,296	8,353	21,263	14,442
One	29,308	32,844	5,472	22,046	3,303	21,175	36,216	31,162
Two	31,477	58,524	3,453	46,905	3,234	38,288	36,501	57,388
Three	6,380	70,882	657	58,713	842	48,156	7,409	70,012
Four or more	2,080	90,049	238	74,696	386	71,630	2,485	86,676

1. Persons of Hispanic origin may be of any race. *Source:* U.S. Bureau of the Census, *Money Income in the United States: 1998.* Web: www.census.gov.

Median Income by Sex and Race, 1947–1998

	All races		White		Black[1]		Asian and Pacific Islander		Hispanic origin[2]	
Year	Men	Women	Men	Women	Men	Women	Men	Women	Men	Women
1998	$26,492	$14,430	$27,646	$14,617	$19,321	$13,137	$25,124	$15,228	$17,257	$10,862
1995	24,131	12,974	25,557	13,173	17,119	11,723	23,703	13,757	15,872	9,549
1990	25,308	12,559	26,402	12,867	16,048	10,386	24,187	13,826	16,799	9,393
1985	24,709	10,933	25,921	11,145	16,312	9,509	—	—	17,321	9,120
1980	24,816	9,744	26,397	9,798	15,862	9,071	—	—	19,130	8,724
1975	25,677	9,818	26,973	9,919	16,126	9,011	—	—	19,656	9,287
1970	26,325	8,829	27,671	8,943	16,414	8,142	—	—	—	—
1965	23,940	7,249	25,213	7,688	13,569	5,595	—	—	—	—
1960	20,653	6,383	21,747	6,844	11,440	4,237	—	—	—	—
1955	18,809	6,274	19,851	7,013	10,447	3,658	—	—	—	—
1950	15,989	5,929	16,854	6,595	9,152	2,949	—	—	—	—
1947	15,020	6,850	—	—	—	—	—	—	—	—

Median income (1998 dollars)

NOTES: Year-round, full-time workers, aged 15 years and over. Income in 1998 dollars. Dash indicates data are not available. 1. Prior to 1967, data are for blacks and other races. 2. Persons of Hispanic origin may be of any race. *Source:* Current Population Reports, Series P60, U.S. Bureau of the Census. Web: www.census.gov/hhes/income/histinc/p02.html.

Distribution of Household Income by Race

Income range	White			Black			Hispanic origin[1]		
	1972	1985	1998	1972	1985	1998	1972	1985	1998
Number of households (thousands)	60,618	76,576	87,212	6,809	9,797	12,579	2,655	5,213	9,060
Percent distribution									
Under $5,000	3.4%	3.0%	2.6%	8.0%	8.0%	7.3%	3.7%	5.0%	4.9%
$5,000 to $9,999	7.7	7.5	6.1	15.0	17.0	14.1	8.0	12.0	10.1
$10,000 to $14,999	7.3	7.4	7.4	12.7	11.2	10.6	11.7	11.5	10.9
$15,000 to $24,999	13.9	14.9	13.7	20.1	19.0	17.4	20.7	19.0	17.9
$25,000 to $34,999	14.7	14.0	13.2	15.6	13.6	13.5	20.1	15.4	16.3
$35,000 to $49,999	20.9	18.2	16.3	13.9	14.0	14.3	19.9	16.6	15.8
$50,000 to $74,999	20.0	18.9	19.3	11.4	11.3	13.2	11.4	13.0	14.0
$75,000 to $99,999	7.1	9.0	10.0	2.1	4.1	5.6	2.9	5.2	5.6
$100,000 and over	5.0	7.1	11.3	1.3	1.8	4.0	1.5	2.3	4.6
Median income	$37,347	$37,732	$40,912	$21,799	$22,449	$25,351	$28,184	$26,457	$28,330

1. Persons of Hispanic origin may be of any race. *Source:* U.S. Bureau of the Census. *Current Population Reports,* P60-206. Sept. 1999. Web: www.census.gov/hhes/www/income.html.

Per Capita Personal Income

Year	Amount	Year	Amount	Year	Amount	Year	Amount	Year	Amount	Year	Amount
1935	$ 474	1965	$2,773	1981	$10,949	1986	$15,122	1991	$19,652	1996	$24,651
1945	1,223	1970	3,893	1982	11,731	1987	15,968	1992	20,576	1997	25,924
1950	1,501	1975	5,851	1983	12,352	1988	17,052	1993	21,231	1998	27,203
1955	1,881	1979	8,638	1984	13,585	1989	18,176	1994	22,086	1999[1]	28,518
1960	2,219	1980	9,910	1985	14,427	1990	19,188	1995	23,562		

1. Preliminary. *Source:* U.S. Department of Commerce, Bureau of Economic Analysis, *Survey of Current Business.* Web: www.bea.doc.gov/bea/regional/spi/.

Per Capita Personal Income by State

State	1980	1990	1995	1999[1]	State	1980	1990	1995	1999[1]
Alabama	$ 7,465	$14,899	$19,683	$28,518	Montana	$ 8,342	$14,743	$18,764	$22,314
Alaska	13,007	20,887	25,798	28,523	Nebraska	8,895	17,379	22,196	27,437
Arizona	8,854	16,262	20,634	25,307	Nevada	10,848	20,248	25,808	30,351
Arkansas	7,113	13,779	18,546	22,114	New Hampshire	9,150	20,231	25,008	30,905
California	11,021	20,656	24,496	29,819	New Jersey	10,966	24,182	29,277	36,106
Colorado	10,143	18,818	24,865	31,678	New Mexico	7,940	14,213	18,852	22,063
Connecticut	11,532	25,426	31,947	39,167	New York	10,179	22,322	27,721	33,946
Delaware	10,059	19,719	25,391	30,685	North Carolina	7,780	16,284	21,938	26,220
Dist. of Columbia	12,251	24,643	33,045	38,228	North Dakota	8,642	15,320	19,084	23,518
Florida	9,246	18,785	23,512	28,023	Ohio	9,399	17,547	22,887	27,081
Georgia	8,021	17,121	22,230	27,198	Oklahoma	9,018	15,117	19,394	22,801
Hawaii	10,129	20,905	25,584	27,842	Oregon	9,309	17,201	22,668	27,135
Idaho	8,105	15,304	19,630	23,445	Pennsylvania	9,353	18,884	23,738	28,676
Illinois	10,454	20,159	25,643	31,278	Rhode Island	9,227	19,035	24,046	29,720
Indiana	8,914	16,815	21,845	26,092	South Carolina	7,392	15,101	19,473	23,496
Iowa	9,226	16,683	21,181	25,727	South Dakota	7,800	15,628	19,848	25,107
Kansas	9,880	17,639	21,889	26,633	Tennessee	7,711	15,903	21,800	25,581
Kentucky	7,679	14,751	19,215	23,161	Texas	9,439	16,747	21,526	26,525
Louisiana	8,412	14,279	19,541	22,792	Utah	7,671	14,063	18,858	23,356
Maine	7,760	17,041	20,240	24,960	Vermont	7,957	17,444	21,359	25,892
Maryland	10,394	22,088	26,896	32,166	Virginia	9,413	19,543	24,456	29,484
Massachusetts	10,103	22,248	28,051	35,733	Washington	10,256	19,268	23,878	30,295
Michigan	9,801	18,239	23,975	27,844	West Virginia	7,764	13,964	17,913	20,888
Minnesota	9,673	18,784	24,583	30,622	Wisconsin	9,364	17,399	22,573	27,412
Mississippi	6,573	12,578	17,185	20,506	Wyoming	11,018	16,905	21,514	26,003
Missouri	8,812	17,407	22,094	26,187	**United States**	**9,494**	**18,667**	**23,562**	**25,518**

NOTE: Per capita personal income was computed using midyear population estimates of the Bureau of the Census. 1. Preliminary. *Source:* U.S. Department of Commerce, Bureau of Economic Analysis, *Survey of Current Business.* Web: www.bea.doc.gov/bea/regional/spi/.

Per Capita Income and Personal Consumption Expenditures
(in current dollars)

Year	Gross national product	Personal income	Disposable personal income	Personal consumption expenditures			
				Durable goods	Nondurable goods	Services	Total
1950	$ 1,900	$ 1,504	$ 1,368	$ 203	$ 648	$ 416	$ 1,267
1955	2,456	1,901	1,687	235	755	570	1,560
1960	2,851	2,265	1,986	240	847	741	1,829
1965	3,268	2,840	2,505	327	987	954	2,268
1970	4,951	4,056	3,489	418	1,318	1,385	3,121
1975	7,401	6,081	5,291	627	1,927	2,135	4,689
1980	11,985	9,916	8,421	963	2,992	3,653	7,607
1985	16,776	13,895	11,861	1,555	3,807	5,622	10,985
1990	21,737	18,477	15,695	1,910	4,748	7,888	14,547
1991	22,500	19,100	16,700	1,800	5,000	8,700	15,400
1992	23,340	19,802	17,346	1,881	5,053	9,101	16,035
1993	24,576	20,810	18,153	2,083	5,185	9,683	16,951
1994	27,119	22,589	19,711	2,290	5,555	10,574	18,419
1995	28,060	23,413	20,316	2,358	5,631	11,072	19,061
1996	29,378	24,578	21,127	2,443	5,885	11,610	19,938
1997	30,634	25,686	21,871	2,538	6,001	12,268	20,807
1998	n.a.	26,240[1]	22,212[2]	2,661[2]	6,143[2]	12,581[2]	21,385[2]

NOTE: n.a. = not available. 1. Revised. 2. Preliminary. *Source:* U.S. Department of Commerce, *Survey of Current Business,* May 1998. Web: www.doc.gov.

The Rich Get Richer

In September 1999, the Center on Budget and Policy Priorities (CBPP) released a report examining the distribution of after-tax income among Americans in 1977 and 1999. The report, which is based on data from the Congressional Budget Office, shows that despite tax increases on high-income households in 1990 and 1993, this group has received large tax cuts overall since 1977. The result has been a widening of the gap between the rich and the poor.

The CBPP report breaks the U.S. population into fifths based on after-tax household income level. According to the report, the top 1% of Americans made an average gain of 115% in after-tax income between 1977 and 1999. The top one-fifth also fared well, gaining 43%. In contrast, the middle fifth made only 8% more and the bottom fifth in fact saw its average income decline by 9%. The next-to-bottom fifth did not change significantly.

Average After-Tax Income in 1977 and 1999

Income group	1999[1]		1977	
	Average income	Share of all income (percent)	Average income	Share of all income (percent)
Lowest fifth	$ 8,800	4.2%	$ 10,000	5.7%
Second fifth	20,000	9.7	22,100	11.5
Middle fifth	31,400	14.7	32,400	16.4
Fourth fifth	45,100	21.3	42,600	22.8
Highest fifth	102,300	50.4	74,000	44.2
Top one percent	515,600	12.9	234,700	7.3

NOTE: Figures rounded to nearest hundred dollars. 1. Projected. *Source:* Center on Budget and Policy Priorities. Web: www.cbpp.org. (Based on data from the Congressional Budget Office.)

Consumer Credit Outstanding[1]
(in billions of dollars; not seasonally adjusted)

	Total	Commercial banks	Finance companies	Credit unions	Savings institutions	Nonfinancial business	Pools of securitized assets[2]
1975	$ 168.7	$ 82.9	$ 32.7	$ 25.7	n.a.	n.a.	n.a.
1980	302.1	147.0	62.3	44.0	n.a.	n.a.	n.a.
1985	526.3	245.1	111.7	72.7	n.a.	n.a.	n.a.
1990	751.9	347.1	133.3	93.1	n.a.	n.a.	n.a.
1995	1,122.8	502.0	152.1	131.9	$40.1	$85.1	$211.6
1999	1,426.2	499.8	181.6	167.9	61.5	80.3	435.1

1. Covers most short- and intermediate-term credit extended to individuals, excluding loans secured by real estate. 2. Outstanding balances of pools upon which securities have been issued; these balances are no longer carried on the balance sheets of the loan originators. *Source:* Federal Reserve Board. Web http://www.bog.frb.fed.us.

Financial Debt Held by Families, 1998

Family characteristic	Any debt	Home-secured	Other residential property	Installment loans	Other lines of credit	Credit card balances	Other
Percent of families holding debt							
Total	74.1%	43.1%	5.1%	43.7%	2.3%	44.1%	8.8%
By age of head of family							
Under 35 years old	81.2	33.2	2.0	60.0	2.4	50.7	9.6
35 to 44 years old	87.6	58.7	6.7	53.3	3.6	51.3	11.4
45 to 54 years old	87.0	58.8	6.7	51.2	3.6	52.5	11.1
55 to 64 years old	76.4	49.4	7.8	37.9	1.6	45.7	8.3
65 to 74 years old	51.4	26.0	5.1	20.2	(1)	29.2	4.1
75 years old and over	24.6	11.5	1.8	4.2	(1)	11.2	2.0
By family income							
Less than $10,000	41.7	8.3	(1)	25.7	(1)	20.6	3.6
$10,000 to $24,999	63.7	21.3	1.8	34.4	1.2	37.9	7.0
$25,000 to $49,999	79.6	43.7	4.1	50.0	2.9	49.9	7.7
$50,000 to $99,999	89.4	71.0	7.7	55.0	3.3	56.7	12.2
$100,000 or more	87.8	73.4	16.4	43.2	2.6	40.4	14.8

NOTE: Percentages may not add up to 100 due to rounding. 1. Ten or fewer instances. *Source:* Board of Governors of the Federal Reserve System. *Federal Reserve Bulletin*, vol. 86 (Jan. 2000), pp. 1–29. Web: www.bog.frb.fed.us/pubs/bulletin.

Financial and Nonfinancial Assets of Families, 1989–1998

Type of financial asset	Percent distribution				Type of nonfinancial asset	Percent distribution			
	1989	1992	1995	1998		1989	1992	1995	1998
Total financial assets	100.0%	100.0%	100.0%	100.0%	**Total nonfinancial assets**	100.0%	100.0%	100.0%	100.0%
Transaction accounts	19.1	17.5	14.0	11.4					
Certificates of deposit	10.2	8.1	5.7	4.3	Vehicles	5.6	5.7	7.1	6.5
Savings bonds	1.5	1.1	1.3	0.7	Primary residence	45.9	47.0	47.4	47.1
Bonds	10.2	8.4	6.3	4.3	Other residential property	8.1	8.5	8.0	8.5
Stocks	15.0	16.5	15.7	22.7					
Mutual funds (excluding money market funds)	5.3	7.7	12.7	12.5	Equity in nonresidential property	11.0	10.9	7.9	7.7
Retirement accounts	21.5	25.5	27.9	27.5	Business equity	26.9	26.3	27.3	28.5
Cash value of life insurance	6.0	6.0	7.2	6.4	Other	2.5	1.6	2.3	1.7
Other managed assets	6.6	5.4	5.9	8.6	**Nonfinancial assets as a share of total assets**	**69.6%**	**68.5%**	**63.4%**	**59.4%**
Other	4.8	3.8	3.4	1.7					
Financial assets as a percentage of total assets	**30.4%**	**31.5%**	**36.6%**	**40.6%**					

NOTE: Percentages may not add up to 100 due to rounding. *Source:* Board of Governors of the Federal Reserve System. *Federal Reserve Bulletin*, vol. 86 (Jan. 2000), pp. 1–29. Web: www.bog.frb.fed.us/pubs/bulletin.

Poverty in the United States

Source: U.S. Bureau of the Census, *Poverty in the United States, 1998.* Web: www.census.gov.

The 1998 poverty rate of 12.7% was significantly lower than the 13.3% reported for 1997. The number of people with family incomes below their official poverty level in 1998 was 34.5 million, down from 35.6 million people in 1997.

Between 1997 and 1998, the poverty rate declined by a statistically significant amount for children, Hispanics, whites not of Hispanic origin, female unrelated individuals (women not living with any relatives), people living in the South, and people living outside metropolitan areas.

The 1998 poverty rate of 12.7% was not statistically different from the poverty rate in 1989, when the economic expansion of the 1980s reduced the poverty rate to 13.1%. For some groups, however, poverty rates were lower in 1998 than in 1989. These groups included: blacks, children (under age 18), the elderly (aged 65 or older), residents of the Midwest and South, people living outside metropolitan areas, married-couple families, female-householder families, black families, black married-couple families, and black female-householder families. Groups with poverty rates that were higher in 1998 than in 1989 included male unrelated individuals and residents of the Northeast and West.

Age

The number of poor and the poverty rate for children declined significantly; however, the child poverty rate remained significantly higher than the rates for working-age adults and the elderly. Among children, the poverty rate decreased to 18.9% in 1998, down from 19.9% in 1997. The number of poor children decreased to 13.5 million in 1998, down from 14.1 million in 1997. For people aged 18 to 64 years old and for people aged 65 and over, neither the poverty rate nor the number of poor changed.

In addition to having the highest poverty rate of all age groups, children continued to represent a large share of the poor population (39%) even though they were only about 26% of the total population.

Race and Hispanic Origin

For Hispanics and for whites not of Hispanic origin, the poverty rate declined significantly in 1998. The Hispanic poverty rate was 25.6% in 1998, down from 27.1% in 1997. Among non-Hispanic whites, the poverty rate dropped to 8.2% in 1998, from 8.6% in 1997. The number of poor Hispanics and non-Hispanic whites remained statistically unchanged: 8.1 million and 15.8 million, respectively, in 1998.

Poverty remained statistically unchanged both among blacks and among Asians and Pacific Islanders. In 1998, 9.1 million or 26.1% of blacks were poor, and 1.4 million or 12.5% of Asians and Pacific Islanders were poor.

Even though the 1998 poverty rate for blacks remained statistically unchanged from 1997, it continued to represent the lowest level since 1959, the earliest year for which poverty statistics are available. However, the lack of change in poverty among blacks in 1998 contrasts with 1997, when blacks accounted for more than one-half of the net decline in the number of poor people.

Nativity

In 1998, United States natives[1] and noncitizens experienced declines in poverty. The poverty rate for natives fell to 12.1%, down from 12.5% in 1997. Both the number of poor (3.7 million) and the poverty rate (22.2%) fell for noncitizens, down from 4.1 million and 25.0% in 1997. The poverty rate for naturalized citizens, 11.0%, was statistically unchanged from 1997 and was not statistically different from the poverty rate for natives. Since noncitizens comprised the majority (16.6 million) of the 26.4 million foreign-born individuals living in the United States, the foreign-born poverty rate is disproportionately high (18.0%, compared with 12.7% for all people).

---

1. Natives are defined as people born in the U.S., Puerto Rico, or an outlying area of the U.S., and those born in a foreign country but who had at least one parent who was a U.S. citizen. All others are foreign-born regardless of date of entry into the U.S. or citizenship status.

Families

In 1998, neither the number of poor families nor the poverty rate for families declined overall. In 1998, 7.2 million families were poor, and the family poverty rate was 10.0%.

Families with a female householder, no husband present, had the highest poverty rate in 1998 (29.9%) and comprised the majority of poor families (53%). Married-couple families, by contrast, had the lowest poverty rate (5.3%), yet still comprised a large share of poor families (40%) since they were the most common type of family.

The poverty rate for unrelated individuals (people not living with any relatives) declined in 1998 to 19.9% from 20.8% in 1997. Among female unrelated individuals, both the number of poor and the poverty rate declined. In 1998, 5.0 million, or 22.6% of female unrelated individuals, were poor, significantly lower than the 5.2 million and 24.0% reported for 1997. Unrelated individuals accounted for 25% of the poor population, compared with only 16% of the total population.

Region

The South had a substantial decline in its poverty rate and number of poor people—13.7% and 13.0 million in 1998, down from 14.6% and 13.7 million in 1997. With a 1998 poverty rate of 13.7%, the South achieved an all-time low. None of the other regions experienced significant declines in their poverty rates in 1998; the West had a poverty rate of 14.0%, the Northeast, 12.3%, and the Midwest, 10.3%.

Residence

The poverty rate and number of people in poverty outside metropolitan areas decreased in 1998 to 14.4% and 7.5 million people, from 15.9% and 8.3 million people in 1997. No significant changes occurred for those living within metropolitan areas. The poverty rate for metropolitan areas was 12.3% in 1998, but those living inside central cities had a poverty rate (18.5%) more than twice that for those living in the suburbs[2] (8.7%).

---

2. "Suburbs" refers to places within metropolitan areas but outside central cities.

Weighted Average Poverty Thresholds for Families of Specified Size, 1960–1999

| Calendar year | Individual | Families of 2 persons or more | | | | | |
		2 persons	3 persons	4 persons	5 persons	6 persons	7 persons
1960	$1,490	$ 1,924	$ 2,359	$ 3,022	$ 3,560	$ 4,002	$ 4,921[1]
1965	1,582	2,048	2,514	3,223	3,797	4,264	5,248[1]
1970	1,954	2,525	3,099	3,968	4,680	5,260	6,468[1]
1975	2,724	3,506	4,293	5,500	6,499	7,316	9,022[1]
1980	4,190	5,363	6,565	8,414	9,966	11,269	12,761
1985	5,469	6,998	8,573	10,989	13,007	14,696	16,656
1990	6,652	8,509	10,419	13,359	15,792	17,839	20,241
1995	7,763	9,933	12,158	15,569	18,408	20,804	23,552
1996	7,995	10,223	12,516	16,036	18,952	21,389	24,268
1997	8,183	10,473	12,802	16,400	19,380	21,886	24,802
1998	8,316	10,634	13,003	16,660	19,680	22,228	25,257
1999	8,500	10,869	13,290	17,028	20,115	22,719	25,815

1. For years before 1980, data are for families with seven persons or more. *Source:* U.S. Bureau of the Census. Web: www.census.gov.

Persons below Poverty Level, 1975–1998

(in thousands)

Year	All persons	White	Black	Hispanic origin[1]	Year	All persons	White	Black	Hispanic origin[1]
1975	25,877	17,770	7,545	2,991	1987	32,221	21,195	9,520	5,422
1976	24,975	16,713	7,595	2,783	1988	31,745	20,715	9,356	5,357
1977	24,720	16,416	7,726	2,700	1989	32,415	21,294	9,525	6,086
1978	24,497	16,259	7,625	2,607	1990	33,585	22,326	9,837	6,006
1979	26,072	17,214	8,050	2,921	1991	35,708	23,747	10,242	6,339
1980	29,272	19,699	8,579	3,491	1992	38,014	25,259	10,827	7,592
1981	31,822	21,553	9,173	3,713	1993	39,265	26,226	10,877	8,126
1982	34,398	23,517	9,697	4,301	1994	38,059	25,379	10,196	8,416
1983	35,303	23,984	9,882	4,633	1995	36,425	24,423	9,872	8,574
1984	33,700	22,955	9,490	4,806	1996	36,529	24,650	9,694	8,697
1985	33,064	22,860	8,926	5,236	1997	35,574	24,396	9,116	8,308
1986	32,370	22,183	8,983	5,117	1998	34,476	23,454	9,091	8,070

1. Persons of Hispanic origin may be of any race. *Source:* U.S. Bureau of the Census. Web: www.census.gov.

Characteristics of Persons below Poverty Level in 1989 and 1998

(in thousands)

	1998		1989			1998		1989	
	Number	Percent	Number	Percent		Number	Percent	Number	Percent
Total[1]	**34,476**	**12.7%**	**32,415**	**13.1%**	35 to 44 years	4,082	9.1%	3,115	8.3%
Race					45 to 54 years	2,444	6.9	1,873	7.5
White	23,454	10.5	21,294	10.2	55 to 59 years	1,165	9.2	971	9.5
Black	9,091	26.1	9,525	30.8	60 to 64 years	1,039	10.1	986	9.4
Asian and Pacific Islander	1,360	12.5	1,032	14.2	65 years and over	3,386	10.5	3,312	11.4
Hispanic origin[2]	8,070	25.6	6,086	26.3	**Region**				
Age					Northeast	6,357	12.3	5,213	10.2
Under 18 years	13,467	18.9	13,154	20.1	Midwest	6,501	10.3	7,088	12.0
18 to 24 years	4,312	16.6	4,132	15.4	South	12,992	13.7	13,277	15.6
25 to 34 years	4,582	11.9	4,873	11.2	West	8,625	14.0	6,838	12.8

1. Includes races not shown separately. 2. Persons of Hispanic origin may be of any race. *Source:* U.S. Census Bureau, *Poverty in the United States, 1998*, Sept. 1999. Web: www.census.gov.

Percent of People in Poverty by State, 1996–1998

State	3-year average 1996–1998	Average 1997–1998	Average 1996–1997	State	3-year average 1996–1998	Average 1997–1998	Average 1996–1997
United States	13.2%	13.0%	13.5%	Missouri	10.4%	10.8%	10.6%
Alabama	14.7	15.1	14.8	Montana	16.4	16.1	16.3
Alaska	8.8	9.1	8.5	Nebraska	10.8	11.1	10.0
Arizona	18.1	16.9	18.8	Nevada	9.9	10.8	9.6
Arkansas	17.2	17.2	18.4	New Hampshire	8.4	9.4	7.7
California	16.3	16.0	16.8	New Jersey	0.0	8.9	9.2
Colorado	9.3	8.7	9.4	New Mexico	22.4	20.8	23.4
Connecticut	9.9	9.0	10.1	New York	16.6	16.6	16.6
Delaware	9.5	10.0	9.1	North Carolina	12.5	12.7	11.8
D.C.	22.7	22.0	23.0	North Dakota	13.2	14.4	12.3
Florida	13.9	13.7	14.3	Ohio	11.6	11.1	11.8
Georgia	14.3	14.0	14.7	Oklahoma	14.8	13.9	15.2
Hawaii	12.3	12.4	13.0	Oregon	12.8	13.3	11.7
Idaho	13.2	13.8	13.3	Pennsylvania	11.3	11.2	11.4
Illinois	11.1	10.6	11.6	Rhode Island	11.8	12.2	11.9
Indiana	8.6	9.1	8.2	South Carolina	13.3	13.4	13.1
Iowa	9.4	9.3	9.6	South Dakota	13.0	13.7	14.1
Kansas	10.1	9.6	10.4	Tennessee	14.5	13.9	15.1
Kentucky	15.5	14.7	16.4	Texas	16.1	15.9	16.7
Louisiana	18.6	17.7	18.4	Utah	8.5	8.9	8.3
Maine	10.6	10.2	10.7	Vermont	10.6	9.6	10.9
Maryland	8.6	7.8	9.3	Virginia	11.3	10.8	12.5
Massachusetts	10.3	10.4	11.2	Washington	10.0	9.1	10.5
Michigan	10.8	10.6	10.7	West Virginia	17.6	17.1	17.5
Minnesota	9.9	10.0	9.7	Wisconsin	8.6	8.5	8.5
Mississippi	18.3	17.1	18.6	Wyoming	12.0	12.1	12.7

Source: U.S. Census Bureau, *Poverty in the United States, 1998*, Sept. 1999. Web: www.census.gov.

Social Welfare Expenditures under Public Programs
(in millions of dollars)

Item	1965	1970	1975	1980	1985	1990	1995
Amount							
Gross domestic product	$701,000	$1,023,100	$1,590,800	$2,718,900	$4,108,000	$5,682,900	$7,186,900
Total social welfare expenditures[1]	77,084	145,979	288,967	492,213	731,840	1,048,951	1,505,136
Social insurance	28,123	54,691	123,013	229,754	369,595	513,822	705,483
Public aid	6,283	16,488	41,447	72,703	98,362	146,811	253,530
Health and medical programs	6,155	10,030	16,535	26,762	38,643	61,684	85,507
Veterans' programs	6,031	9,078	17,019	21,466	27,042	30,916	39,072
Education	28,108	50,846	80,834	121,050	172,048	258,332	365,625
Housing	318	701	3,172	6,879	12,598	19,468	29,361
Other social welfare	2,066	4,145	6,947	13,599	13,552	17,918	26,558
All health and medical care[2]	9,302	24,801	51,022	99,145	170,665	274,472	435,075
As percent of gross domestic product							
Gross domestic product	100.0%	100.0%	100.0%	100.0%	100.0%	100.0%	100.0%
Total social welfare expenditures	11.0	14.3	18.2	18.1	17.8	18.5	20.9
Social insurance	4.0	5.3	7.7	8.5	9.0	9.0	9.8
Public aid	.9	1.6	2.6	2.7	2.4	2.6	3.5
Health and medical programs	.9	1.0	1.0	1.0	.9	1.1	1.2
Veterans' programs	.9	.9	1.1	.8	.7	.5	.5
Education	4.0	5.0	5.1	4.5	4.2	4.5	5.1
Housing	(3)	.1	.2	.3	.3	.3	.4
Other social welfare	.3	.4	.4	.5	.3	.3	.4
All health and medical care	1.3	2.4	3.2	3.6	4.2	4.8	6.1

NOTES: Through 1976, fiscal year ended June 30 for federal government, most states, and some localities. Beginning in 1977, federal fiscal year ended Sept. 30. 1. Represents program and administrative expenditures from federal, state, and local public revenues and trust funds under public law. Includes workers' compensation and temporary disability insurance payments made through private carriers and self-insurers. Includes capital outlay and some expenditures abroad. 2. Combines "health and medical programs" with medical services provided in connection with social insurance, public aid, veterans', and "other social welfare" categories. 3. Less than 0.05%. *Source:* Social Security Administration. Web: www.ssa.gov/statistics/Supplement/1999/tables/index.html.

Drop in Welfare Rolls, 1993–1999

	Number of families on welfare Jan. 1993	Number of families on welfare Sept. 1999	Percent reduction 1993–1999		Number of families on welfare Jan. 1993	Number of families on welfare Sept. 1999	Percent reduction 1993–1999
Alabama	51,910	19,719	−62%	Nebraska	16,637	10,780	−35%
Alaska	11,626	7,481	−36	Nevada	12,892	6,945	−46
Arizona	68,982	33,805	−51	New Hampshire	10,805	6,187	−43
Arkansas	26,897	12,178	−55	New Jersey	126,179	57,043	−55
California	844,494	591,977	−30	New Mexico	31,103	24,733	−20
Colorado	42,445	12,427	−71	New York	428,191	279,692	−35
Connecticut	56,759	31,941	−44	North Carolina	128,946	48,975	−62
Delaware	11,315	6,366	−44	North Dakota	6,577	3,061	−53
Dist. of Columbia	24,628	18,028	−27	Ohio	257,665	99,333	−61
Florida	256,145	74,428	−71	Oklahoma	50,955	15,395	−70
Georgia	142,040	56,936	−60	Oregon	42,409	16,681	−61
Guam	1,406	2,788	98	Pennsylvania	204,216	96,760	−53
Hawaii	17,869	14,843	−17	Puerto Rico	60,950	34,032	−44
Idaho	7,838	1,219	−84	Rhode Island	21,900	17,330	−21
Illinois	229,308	105,916	−54	South Carolina	54,599	17,052	−69
Indiana	73,115	37,405	−49	South Dakota	7,262	2,828	−61
Iowa	36,515	20,830	−43	Tennessee	112,159	57,339	−49
Kansas	29,818	12,733	−57	Texas	279,002	106,805	−62
Kentucky	83,320	40,242	−52	Utah	18,606	8,990	−52
Louisiana	89,931	32,077	−64	Vermont	10,081	6,469	−36
Maine	23,903	12,880	−46	Virgin Islands	1,073	895	−17
Maryland	80,256	30,471	−62	Virginia	73,446	36,061	−51
Massachusetts	113,571	50,010	−56	Washington	100,568	59,317	−41
Michigan	228,377	85,667	−62	West Virginia	41,525	11,969	−71
Minnesota	63,995	40,699	−36	Wisconsin	81,291	7,343	−91
Mississippi	60,520	14,982	−75	Wyoming	6,493	676	−90
Missouri	88,744	47,747	−46	**U.S. total**	4,963,050	2,453,068	−51
Montana	11,793	4,582	−61				

Source: U.S. Dept. of Health and Human Services, Administration for Children and Families. Web: www.acf.dhhs.gov.

Social Security

Source: Social Security Administration.

The original Social Security Act was passed in 1935 and is administered by the Social Security Administration and other agencies within the Department of Health and Human Services.

What Does Social Security Offer?

The Social Security contribution you pay gives you four different kinds of protection: (1) retirement benefits, (2) survivors' benefits, (3) disability benefits, and (4) Medicare hospital insurance benefits.

Retirement Benefits

Currently, as a worker you become eligible for the full amount of your retirement benefits at age 65. You may retire at age 62 and get 80% of your full benefit. The closer you are to age 65 when you start collecting your benefit, the larger the fraction of your full benefit you will get.

The amount of the retirement benefit you are entitled to at age 65 is the key to all other benefits under the program. The retirement benefit is based on covered earnings, which will be updated (indexed) to reflect the increases in average wages that have occurred since the earnings were paid. Your largest 35 years of adjusted earnings are averaged together and a formula is applied to the adjusted average to figure the benefit rate.

In general, the highest retirement check that can be paid to a worker who retired at 65 in January 1997 is about $1,327.60 a month. Maximum payment to the family of this retired worker is about $2,324.40 as of January 1997.

Survivor Benefits

This feature of the Social Security program gives your family valuable life-insurance protection. The amount of protection is again geared to what the worker would be entitled to if he had been age 65 when he died. Total family survivor benefits were estimated to be as high as $2,534.00 a month if the worker died in 1995. Your survivors could get:

1. A one-time cash payment of $255 for your spouse or minor children if you have enough work credits.
2. A benefit for each child until he or she reaches 18 (or 19, if the child is in full-time attendance at an elementary or secondary school), or at any age if disabled before 22. "Child" includes biological or legally adopted children, or dependent stepchildren or grandchildren.
3. A benefit for your widow(er), at any age, if she/he has your entitled children under 16 or disabled in care.
4. Your spouse or divorced spouse can get a widow's, widower's, or surviving divorced spouse's benefit starting at age 60. A widow, or widower, who first becomes entitled at 65 or later will get 100% of his or her deceased spouse's basic amount (or the amount of the deceased spouse's reduced benefits).
5. Dependent parents can sometimes collect survivors' benefits. They are usually eligible if: (a) they were getting at least half their support from the deceased worker; (b) they have reached 62; (c) they are not eligible for a greater retirement benefit based on their own earnings; and (d) they have not married since the worker's death.

Disability Benefits

Disability benefits can be paid to several groups of people:
- Disabled workers under age 65 and their families.
- Persons disabled before age 22 who continue to be disabled. These benefits are payable as early as age 18 when a parent (or step-parent or grandparent under certain circumstances) receives Social Security retirement or disability benefits or when an insured parent dies.
- Disabled widows and widowers and (under certain conditions) disabled, surviving, and divorced spouses of workers who were insured at death. These benefits are payable as early as 50. Consult your local Social Security office for the latest disability information.

The SSA determines whether or not you qualify for disability benefits based on criteria including the severity of your condition and the earnings you continue to receive after you become disabled. To be considered for disability benefits, you should file a claim with a Social Security office as soon as you become disabled. However, even if you are approved, benefits will not begin until after a waiting period of six months after the beginning of your disability.

Medicare Program

Medicare is the nation's largest health insurance program. Generally, you are eligible for Medicare if you or your spouse worked for at least 10 years in Medicare-covered employment and you are 65 years old and a citizen or permanent resident of the United States. You might also qualify for coverage if you are a younger person with a disability or with chronic kidney disease.

Medicare-covered services include:
- **Hospital insurance.** Financial assistance is available for necessary medical care and services furnished by Medicare-certified hospitals, skilled nursing facilities, home health agencies, and hospices.
- **Inpatient hospital care.** Medicare helps pay for up to 90 days of inpatient hospital care in each benefit period. Covered services include your semi-private room and meals, general nursing services, operating and recovery room costs, intensive care, drugs, laboratory tests, X rays, and all other necessary medical services and supplies.
- **Skilled nursing facility care.** You may need inpatient skilled nursing or rehabilitation services after a hospital stay. If you meet certain conditions, Medicare will help pay for up to 100 days in a participating skilled nursing facility in each benefit period.
- **Home health care.** If you meet certain conditions, Medicare pays the full approved cost of covered home health care services. This includes part-time or intermittent skilled nursing services prescribed by a physician for treatment or rehabilitation of homebound patients.
- **Hospice care.** Medicare helps pay for hospice care for terminally ill beneficiaries who select the hospice care benefit.

• **Medical insurance (Part B).** Medicare Part B helps pay for doctor's services, outpatient hospital services (including emergency room visits), ambulance transportation, diagnostic tests, laboratory services, some preventive care like mammography and Pap smear screening, outpatient therapy services, durable medical equipment and supplies, and a variety of other health services.

Additional benefits are available through the Medicare program. For further information contact the Social Security Administration at 1-800-772-1213.

Average Monthly Social Security Benefits, 1940–1998

Year	Retired workers			Disabled workers			Non-disabled widows
	Total	Men	Women	Total	Men	Women	
1940	$ 22.71	$ 23.26	$ 18.38	—	—	—	$ 20.36
1945	25.11	25.71	19.99	—	—	—	20.17
1950[1]	29.03	30.16	22.98	—	—	—	21.65
1955	69.74	75.86	56.05	—	—	—	49.68
1960	81.73	92.03	63.26	$ 91.16	$ 94.02	$ 78.91	62.12
1965[1]	82.69	90.89	68.78	93.26	97.89	80.27	73.81
1970	123.82	136.80	103.67	139.79	148.39	115.74	106.95
1975[2]	196.42	220.35	160.50	220.60	241.48	175.27	185.34
1980[2]	321.10	374.00	244.90	352.10	388.80	269.70	277.50
1985[3]	432.00	509.60	322.20	459.20	514.00	345.00	431.10
1990[3]	550.50	654.60	403.30	566.90	637.80	438.90	541.10
1995[3]	671.70	794.30	505.80	675.70	767.30	546.00	662.50
1998[3]	744.70	882.10	577.10	737.00	841.50	610.60	716.70

1. Jan.–Aug. 2. Jan.–May. 3. Jan.–Nov. *Source:* Social Security Administration, *Social Security Bulletin: Annual Statistical Supplement, 1999.*

The Federal Budget, 1995–2001

(in millions of dollars)

Description	Actual			Estimates	
	1995	1997	1999	2000	2001
Receipts by source					
Individual income taxes	$590,244	$737,466	$879,480	$951,586	$972,410
Corporate income taxes	157,004	182,293	184,680	192,395	194,770
Social insurance and retirement receipts	484,473	539,371	611,833	650,021	682,080
Excise taxes	57,484	56,924	70,414	68,384	76,676
Estate and gift taxes	14,763	19,845	27,782	30,486	32,304
Customs duties and fees	19,301	17,928	18,336	20,875	20,871
Miscellaneous receipts:					
Deposits of earnings by Federal Reserve System	23,378	19,636	25,917	32,452	29,520
All other[1]	5,183	5,829	9,012	10,053	10,400
Total receipts	1,351,830	1,579,292	1,827,454	1,956,252	2,019,031
Outlays by function					
National defense	272,066	270,505	274,873	290,636	291,202
International affairs	16,434	15,228	15,243	17,078	19,607
General science, space, and technology	16,724	17,174	18,125	18,853	19,638
Energy	4,936	1,475	912	−1,640	−651
Natural resources and environment	21,915	21,227	23,968	24,479	24,973
Agriculture	9,778	9,032	23,011	31,988	22,414
Commerce and housing credit	−17,808	−14,624	2,647	5,598	2,945
Transportation	39,350	40,767	42,531	46,709	49,532
Community and regional development	10,749	11,055	11,870	11,115	10,177
Education, training, employment, and social services	54,263	53,008	56,402	63,397	67,544
Health	115,418	123,843	141,079	154,227	166,686
Medicare	159,855	190,016	190,447	202,513	220,515
Income security	220,493	230,899	237,707	251,286	259,724
Social security	335,846	365,257	390,041	406,625	425,738
Veterans benefits and services	37,890	39,313	43,212	46,796	46,449
Administration of justice	16,216	20,173	25,924	26,771	31,408
General government	13,998	12,891	15,758	15,035	15,429
Net interest	232,169	244,016	229,735	220,314	208,312
Total outlays	1,515,837	1,601,282	1,703,040	1,789,562	1,835,033
Total surplus or deficit (−)	−164,007	−21,990	124,414	166,690	183,998

1. Beginning 1984, includes universal service fund receipts. *Source:* Department of the Treasury and Office of Management and Budget.

Receipts and Outlays of the Federal Government, 1789–2005
(in millions of dollars)

From 1789 to 1842, the federal fiscal year ended on December 31; from 1844 to 1976, on June 30; and beginning in 1977, on September 30.

Year	Total			On-budget[1]		
	Receipts	Outlays	Surplus or deficit (−)	Receipts	Outlays	Surplus or deficit (−)
1789–1849	$ 1,160	$ 1,090	$ 70	$ 1,160	$ 1,090	$ 70
1850–1900	14,462	15,453	−991	14,462	15,453	−991
1905	544	567	−23	544	567	−23
1910	676	694	−18	676	694	−18
1915	683	746	−63	683	746	−63
1920	6,649	6,358	291	6,649	6,358	291
1925	3,641	2,924	717	3,641	2,924	717
1930	4,058	3,320	738	4,058	3,320	738
1935	3,609	6,412	−2,803	3,609	6,412	−2,803
1940	6,548	9,468	−2,920	5,998	9,482	−3,484
1945	45,159	92,712	−47,553	43,849	92,569	−48,720
1950	39,443	42,562	−3,119	37,336	42,038	−4,702
1955	65,451	68,444	−2,933	60,370	64,461	−4,091
1960	92,492	92,191	301	81,851	81,341	510
1965	116,817	118,228	−1,411	100,094	101,699	−1,605
1970	192,807	195,649	−2,842	159,348	168,042	−8,694
1975	279,090	332,332	−53,242	216,633	271,892	−55,260
1980	517,112	590,947	−73,835	403,903	476,618	−72,715
1985	734,088	946,423	−212,334	547,918	769,615	−221,698
1990	1,031,969	1,253,198	−221,229	750,314	1,028,133	−277,819
1995	1,351,830	1,515,837	−164,007	1,000,751	1,227,173	−226,422
2000[2]	1,956,252	1,789,562	166,690	1,479,489	1,460,633	18,856
2005[2]	2,340,896	2,125,451	215,445	1,742,330	1,740,539	1,791

1. Excludes the Social Security surplus. For years prior to 1933, on-budget surplus was not calculated separately. 2. Estimated. *Source:* The Budget for Fiscal Year 2001.

The Public Debt

Year	Gross debt amount	Year	Gross debt amount	Year	Gross debt amount	Year	Gross debt amount
1800	$82,976,294	1855	$ 35,586,957	1910	$ 2,652,665,838	1965	$ 320,904,110,042
1805	82,312,151	1860	64,842,288	1915	3,058,136,873	1970	389,158,403,690
1810	53,173,218	1865	2,680,647,870	1920	25,952,456,406	1975	576,649,000,000[1]
1815	99,833,660	1870	2,480,672,428	1925	20,516,193,888	1980	930,210,000,000[1]
1820	91,015,566	1875	2,232,284,532	1930	16,185,309,831	1985	1,945,941,616,460
1825	83,788,433	1880	2,120,415,371	1935	28,700,892,625	1990	3,233,313,451,777
1830	48,565,407	1885	1,863,964,873	1940	42,967,531,038	1995	4,973,982,900,709
1835	33,733	1890	1,552,140,205	1945	258,682,187,410	1999	5,656,270,901,615
1840	3,573,344	1895	1,676,120,983	1950	257,357,352,351		
1845	15,925,303	1900	2,136,961,092	1955	280,768,553,189		
1850	63,452,774	1905	2,274,615,064	1960	290,216,815,242		

NOTE: Figures as of Jan. 1 for years 1800–1840; as of July 1 for years 1845–1920; as of June 30 for years 1925–1950; as of Dec. 31 for years 1955–1985; as of Sept. 30 for years 1990–present. 1. Rounded to millions. *Source:* U.S. Department of the Treasury, The Public Debt Online. Web: www.publicdebt.treas.gov/opd/opd.htm.

Gross Domestic Product or Expenditure, 1930–1999
(in billions of dollars)

Item	1930	1940	1950	1960	1970	1980	1990	1995	1999[1]
Gross domestic product	$ 91.3	$101.3	$294.3	$ 527.4	$1,039.7	$2,795.6	$5,803.2	$7,400.5	$9,248.4
Personal consumption expenditures	70.2	71.2	192.7	332.2	648.9	1,762.9	3,831.5	4,969.0	6,254.9
Gross private domestic investment	10.8	13.6	54.1	75.7	150.4	484.2	847.2	1,110.7	1,577.4
Exports of goods and services	4.4	4.8	12.3	25.3	57.0	278.9	557.2	818.6	996.3
Imports of goods and services	4.1	3.4	11.6	22.8	55.8	293.8	628.6	902.8	1,253.1
Government	10.0	15.1	46.9	113.8	237.1	569.7	1,181.4	1,372.0	1,628.7

NOTE: Government consumption expenditures and gross investment. 1. Preliminary data. *Source:* U.S. Bureau of Economic Analysis. Web: www.bea.doc.gov.

Summary of Federal Government Expenditure, by State and Territory, Fiscal Year 1999

(in millions of dollars)

State and outlying area	Total	Retirement and disability	Other direct payments	Grants	Procurement	Salaries and wages
United States, total	$1,531,627	$523,450	$328,336	$294,469	$208,094	$177,279
Alabama	26,776	9,888	5,762	4,632	3,696	2,798
Alaska	5,279	787	445	1,929	845	1,272
Arizona	26,959	9,473	5,506	4,537	4,782	2,661
Arkansas	13,631	5,815	3,619	2,614	467	1,116
California	166,050	50,686	35,466	36,370	25,795	17,733
Colorado	21,755	6,877	3,491	3,446	4,443	3,499
Connecticut	19,241	6,344	4,065	3,846	3,636	1,350
Delaware	3,766	1,537	776	825	221	406
District of Columbia	27,034	1,718	1,645	5,293	6,403	11,975
Florida	87,215	37,386	22,164	11,191	8,639	7,835
Georgia	39,215	13,247	7,775	6,752	5,150	6,292
Hawaii	8,568	2,431	1,226	1,335	1,141	2,436
Idaho	6,165	2,238	1,186	1,177	870	693
Illinois	55,836	21,018	14,752	10,586	3,480	6,000
Indiana	26,828	11,055	6,873	4,706	2,222	1,972
Iowa	15,602	5,751	5,388	2,595	898	970
Kansas	14,447	5,231	4,017	2,183	1,263	1,752
Kentucky	22,198	8,340	4,573	4,395	2,275	2,615
Louisiana	24,384	7,911	6,414	5,228	2,667	2,165
Maine	7,281	2,758	1,262	1,664	803	795
Maryland	41,990	10,805	6,513	5,744	10,584	8,346
Massachusetts	37,803	11,732	8,560	8,838	5,753	2,919
Michigan	43,872	18,141	10,969	9,764	2,065	2,932
Minnesota	21,666	7,847	5,735	4,499	1,807	1,778
Mississippi	16,488	5,656	3,807	3,387	1,939	1,699
Missouri	33,231	11,189	7,545	5,478	5,705	3,313
Montana	6,225	1,878	1,761	1,399	520	667
Nebraska	8,793	3,289	2,390	1,651	470	992
Nevada	7,942	3,457	1,532	1,249	802	903
New Hampshire	5,301	2,300	946	1,120	482	453
New Jersey	40,398	15,426	9,905	7,262	4,206	3,599
New Mexico	13,580	3,520	1,733	2,750	3,931	1,646
New York	101,809	33,997	24,648	28,870	6,773	7,521
North Carolina	37,228	14,885	7,410	7,608	2,050	5,275
North Dakota	4,535	1,218	1,435	1,009	255	618
Ohio	53,262	21,646	12,513	10,254	4,508	4,341
Oklahoma	19,189	7,256	4,272	3,231	1,670	2,761
Oregon	15,592	6,524	3,279	3,518	765	1,506
Pennsylvania	69,448	27,174	17,776	13,141	5,934	5,424
Rhode Island	6,036	2,166	1,315	1,411	421	723
South Carolina	20,833	8,087	3,886	3,879	2,540	2,441
South Dakota	4,909	1,474	1,296	1,056	524	559
Tennessee	30,867	11,092	6,637	5,900	4,520	2,718
Texas	97,988	31,507	21,810	18,370	14,502	11,798
Utah	9,239	3,163	1,345	1,994	1,268	1,469
Vermont	3,114	1,105	549	883	276	301
Virginia	57,842	15,465	6,534	4,749	19,044	12,050
Washington	31,993	11,073	5,716	5,720	4,614	4,869
West Virginia	11,028	4,713	2,288	2,490	625	911
Wisconsin	22,604	9,615	5,200	4,842	1,433	1,514
Wyoming	2,916	935	439	933	199	410
American Samoa	173	29	—	131	11	3
Fed. States of Micronesia	24	—	1	22	1	—
Guam	833	156	52	188	134	304
Marshall Islands	152	1	—	14	137	—
Northern Marianas	86	21	6	54	3	2
Palau	98	—	—	9	89	—
Puerto Rico	12,982	4,302	2,032	5,284	525	839
Virgin Islands	503	110	96	216	34	47
Undistributed	20,825	4	—	248	17,277	3,296

NOTE: Detail may not add to total due to rounding. *Source: Consolidated Federal Funds Report for Fiscal Year 1999.* www.census.gov.

U.S. Direct Investment in Other Countries, 1999
(in millions of dollars)

	All industries	Petro-leum	Manu-facturing	Wholesale trade	Banking	Finance, insurance, real estate	Services	Other industries
All countries	$1,132,622	$99,925	$318,121	$80,148	$39,937	$436,024	$68,763	$89,705
Canada	111,707	16,416	44,023	8,982	1,977	25,084	6,438	8,785
Europe	581,791	33,990	161,627	46,466	23,368	237,659	42,379	36,301
Belgium	17,285	109	7,176	3,456	365	3,728	2,593	−142
France	39,984	1,044	17,210	2,839	1,652	10,583	5,400	1,257
Germany	49,617	2,683	24,351	3,197	1,388	14,131	2,373	1,493
Ireland	19,823	(*)	8,949	235	−7	7,960	1,994	(*)
Italy	17,595	(*)	9,394	2,129	390	1,656	2,397	(*)
Luxembourg	15,263	53	2,569	(*)	228	11,700	(*)	18
Netherlands	106,436	3,296	19,508	8,498	(*)	64,199	9,031	(*)
Spain	12,456	200	7,786	1,245	2,022	435	465	304
Switzerland	51,227	271	5,702	14,289	2,844	25,684	1,865	571
United Kingdom	213,070	17,443	49,699	7,175	9,778	86,659	14,285	28,031
Latin America and Other Western Hemisphere	223,182	8,715	51,294	7,620	2,371	124,072	6,203	22,908
South America	74,839	6,364	28,491	1,761	5,595	15,365	2,222	15,041
Argentina	14,187	601	3,537	488	2,205	4,837	597	1,922
Brazil	35,003	1,703	20,225	355	2,034	5,225	848	4,613
Central America	70,774	1,288	20,265	2,534	1,342	38,395	1,599	5,350
Mexico	34,265	188	18,861	1,167	1,182	6,308	1,303	5,257
Panama	33,429	648	157	442	131	31,805	285	−38
Other Western Hemisphere	77,569	1,063	2,537	3,325	−4,567	70,312	2,382	2,516
Bermuda	45,959	(*)	(*)	1,901	0	42,367	1,657	(*)
United Kingdom Islands, Caribbean	19,948	304	1,271	743	−2,561	19,867	154	171
Africa	15,062	9,629	1,964	179	363	905	307	1,715
Middle East	11,137	3,246	2,321	335	834	2,448	777	1,177
Asia and Pacific	185,912	25,347	56,891	16,566	11,025	45,856	12,659	17,568
Australia	33,662	3,344	7,646	2,146	2,705	8,465	2,190	7,167
Hong Kong	20,848	398	3,798	4,851	1,873	5,766	1,141	3,022
Indonesia	10,504	7,378	66	8	287	287	53	2,424
Japan	47,786	4,419	13,332	5,429	608	14,928	7,132	1,938
Singapore	24,781	2,815	11,367	1,354	532	8,103	519	91

NOTES: Only countries receiving more than ten trillion dollars in 1999 are listed separately. * Suppressed to avoid disclosure of data of individual countries. *Source:* U.S. Department of Commerce, Bureau of Economic Analysis. Web: www.bea.doc.gov/bea/di/diapos_99.htm.

U.S. Contributions to International Organizations
(in millions of dollars)

Organization	1999 (est.)	1998
United Nations and affiliated agencies		
Food and Agriculture Org.	$ 81	$ 81
International Atomic Energy Agency	51	56
International Civil Aviation Org.	13	13
International Labor Org.	64	57
International Maritime Org.	1	1
International Telecommunications Union	8	7
United Nations	277	259
U.N. War Crimes Tribunals	25	14
Universal Postal Union	2	1
World Health Org.	108	107
World Intellectual Property Org.	1	1
World Meteorological Org.	12	11
Subtotal	643	607
Inter-American organizations		

Organization	1999 (est.)	1998
Inter-American Institute for Cooperation on Agriculture	$ 17	$ 17
Org. of American States	55	55
Pan American Health Org.	50	50
Subtotal	122	122
Regional organizations		
Asia Pacific Economic Cooperation	1	1
North Atlantic Assembly	1	1
North Atlantic Treaty Org.	48	36
Org. for Economic Cooperation and Development	63	55
South Pacific Commission	1	1
Subtotal	114	94
Other international organizations		
World Trade Org./General Agreement on Tariffs and Trade	14	13

Organization	1999 (est.)	1998
Customs Cooperation Council	$ 4	$ 3
International Agency for Research on Cancer	2	2
International Center for Study of Preservation & Restoration of Cultural Properties	1	1
International Bureau of Weights and Measures	1	1
International Grains Council	1	1
Interparliamentary Union	0	0
Org. for Prohibition of Chemical Weapons	17	24
Other international organizations	2	1
Subtotal	42	46
U.N. Buydown	0	19
Chemical Weapons/Biological Weapons Center	2	n.a.
Total	$922	$889
International peacekeeping activities		
U.N. Disengagement Observer Force	8	8
U.N. Interim Force in Lebanon	30	36

Organization	1999 (est.)	1998
U.N. Operations in Angola	$ 14	$ 37
U.N. Iraq–Kuwait Observer Mission	5	4
U.N. Mission for the Referendum in the Western Sahara	24	13
War Crimes Tribunal–Rwanda	12	7
U.N. Operations in the Former Yugoslavia	105	80
War Crimes Tribunal–Yugoslavia	12	7
U.N. Peacekeeping Operation in Guatemala	0	0
U.N. Observer Mission in Georgia	8	5
U.N. Mission in Haiti	0	0
U.N. Observer Mission in Liberia	0	0
U.N. Assistance Mission for Rwanda	0	0
U.N. Force in Cyprus	7	6
U.N. Mission in Tajikistan	3	5
U.N. Observer Mission in Sierra Leone	3	3
Payment of Prior Year Balances	138	78
Total	$369	$289

NOTE: All years are fiscal years. *Source:* Budget of the United States Government Fiscal Year 2000.

Exports and Imports of Goods and Services, 1978–2008

Category	Billions of chained 1992 dollars				Average annual rate of change		
	1978	1988	1998	2008[1]	1978–1988	1988–1998	1998–2008[1]
Exports of goods and services	**$273.1**	**$ 465.8**	**$ 984.7**	**$ 1,925.0**	**5.5%**	**7.8%**	**6.9%**
Goods	189.5	321.4	742.6	1,522.6	5.4	8.7	7.4
Foods, feeds, and beverages	29.2	32.4	43.1	57.2	1.0	2.9	2.9
Industrial supplies and materials	57.7	82.2	130.6	195.6	3.6	4.7	4.1
Capital goods except autos	47.3	110.3	408.4	1,224.7	8.8	14.0	11.6
Computers	.6	15.1	153.5	1,314.1	38.1	26.1	24.0
Civilian aircraft and parts	15.2	26.3	45.7	44.5	5.6	5.7	−0.3
Other	44.3	69.2	241.4	715.9	4.6	13.3	11.5
Autos and parts	31.9	36.8	68.7	106.5	1.4	6.4	4.5
Consumer goods	18.9	30.5	75.8	112.8	4.9	9.5	4.0
Other merchandise exports	11.9	29.6	39.7	61.5	9.5	3.0	4.5
Services	83.0	145.0	246.4	436.0	5.7	5.4	5.9
Residual[2]	−19.6	−1.3	−60.3	−1,118.8	—	—	—
Imports of goods and services	**$338.6**	**$ 580.2**	**$1,222.9**	**$ 2,272.5**	**5.5%**	**7.7%**	**6.4%**
Goods	274.8	463.2	1,054.4	2,076.2	5.4	8.6	7.0
Foods, feeds, and beverages	21.5	25.9	38.1	43.7	1.9	3.9	1.4
Industrial supplies and materials	128.0	125.3	210.4	282.6	−0.2	5.3	3.0
Petroleum and products	55.4	47.8	71.8	89.1	−1.5	4.1	2.2
Other	59.8	76.9	137.0	193.2	2.5	5.9	3.5
Capital goods, except autos	15.6	87.9	426.7	1,578.1	18.9	17.1	14.0
Computers	.2	12.4	202.5	1,672.5	51.1	32.2	23.5
Other	18.5	76.7	257.5	744.6	15.3	12.9	11.2
Autos and parts	50.5	95.6	138.0	197.3	6.6	3.7	3.6
Consumer goods	47.4	106.0	213.7	340.0	8.4	7.3	4.8
Other merchandise imports	9.1	25.7	57.3	99.6	10.9	8.3	5.7
Services	62.5	117.1	171.2	230.1	6.5	3.9	3.0
Residual[3]	13.7	−3.9	−64.1	−1,337.6	—	—	—
Trade deficit	**$−65.5**	**$−114.4**	**$ −238.2**	**$ −347.5**	**5.7%**	**7.6%**	**3.8%**

1. Projected. 2. The residual following the detailed categories for exports is the difference between the aggregate of "exports of goods and services" and the sum of the figures for those separate categories for exports of goods and services. 3. The residual following the detailed categories for imports is the difference between the aggregate of "imports of goods and services" and the sum of the figures for those separate categories for imports of goods and services. *Source:* Bureau of Labor Statistics, *Monthly Labor Review,* Nov. 1999.

Imports and Exports of Leading Commodities
by Principal SITC Groupings (in millions of dollars)

Item	1999 Cumulative Exports	1999 Cumulative Imports	Item	1999 Cumulative Exports	1999 Cumulative Imports
Selected commodities[1]			Liquefied propane/butane	$ 87	$ 282
ADP equipment; office machines	$16,199	$32,120	Live animals	190	615
Airplane parts	6,477	2,446	Meat and preparations	2,420	1,256
Airplanes	14,456	3,284	Metal manufactures, n.e.s.	4,542	5,763
Alcoholic beverages, distilled	160	877	Metalworking machinery	2,011	3,835
Aluminum	1,439	2,632	Metal ores; scrap	1,297	1,372
Animal feeds	1,418	222	Mineral fuels, other	958	418
Artwork/antiques	463	2,029	Natural gas	88	2,355
Basketware, etc.	1,150	1,653	Nickel	137	317
Cereal flour	515	576	Oils/fats, vegetable	532	477
Chemicals—cosmetics	1,957	1,185	Optical goods	823	1,241
Chemicals—dyeing	1,453	1,071	Paper and paperboard	3,999	5,347
Chemicals—fertilizers	1,149	750	Petroleum preparations	1,080	4,603
Chemicals—inorganic	1,806	2,000	Photographic equipment	1,355	2,138
Chemicals—medicinal	4,505	5,099	Plastic articles, n.e.s.	2,553	2,774
Chemicals—n.e.s.	4,517	2,083	Platinum	178	1,641
Chemicals—organic	5,932	8,662	Pottery	46	607
Chemicals—plastics	6,708	3,674	Power generating machinery	12,710	12,614
Cigarettes and tobacco	1,471	61	Printed materials	1,775	1,204
Clothing	3,481	20,337	Pulp and waste paper	1,318	919
Coal	927	281	Records/magnetic media	2,406	1,679
Coffee	3	1,212	Rice	425	83
Copper	447	1,236	Rubber articles, n.e.s.	565	712
Cork, wood, lumber	1,820	3,390	Rubber tires and tubes	967	1,858
Corn	2,062	134	Scientific instruments	10,257	6,706
Cotton, raw and linters	322	86	Ships, boats	624	461
Crude fertilizers	617	503	Silver and bullion	114	277
Crude oil	295	15,257	Soybeans	1,776	19
Electrical machinery	29,523	33,302	Spacecraft	240	66
Fish and preparations	1,005	3,162	Specialized industrial machinery	9,922	9,521
Footwear	300	5,674	Sugar	1	237
Furniture and bedding	1,809	6,466	Televisions, VCRs, etc.	9,508	16,974
Gem diamonds	78	3,627	Textile yarn, fabric	3,797	5,391
General industrial machinery	12,505	13,014	Tobacco, unmanufactured	740	293
Glass	873	765	Toys/games/sporting goods	1,301	6,045
Glassware	282	665	Travel goods	134	1,510
Gold, nonmonetary	1,194	1,280	Vegetables and fruits	2,879	4,461
Hides and skins	408	42	Vehicles	23,353	58,801
Iron and steel mill products	1,994	5,340	Watches/clocks/parts	136	1,150
Jewelry	414	2,048	Wheat	1,354	127
Lighting, plumbing	506	1,533	Wood manufactures	694	2,731

NOTES: SITC = Standard International Trade Classification; n.e.s. = not elsewhere specified; n.a. = not applicable. Details may not equal totals due to rounding. Data not seasonally adjusted. 1. Domestic exports. *Source:* U.S. Census Bureau, Foreign Trade Division. Web: http://www.census.gov/foreign-trade/Press-Release/current_press_release/exh15.txt.

National Income by Type
(in billions of dollars)

Type of income	1930	1940	1950	1960	1970	1980	1990	1995	1999
National income	$75.6	$81.1	$241.0	$427.5	$837.5	$2,243.0	$4,642.1	$5,876.7	$7,496.3
Compensation of employees	46.9	52.2	155.4	296.4	617.2	1,651.7	3,351.0	4,202.5	5,331.7
Wage and salary accruals	46.2	49.9	147.2	272.8	551.5	1,377.4	2,754.6	3,441.1	4,472.3
Supplements to wages and salaries	0.7	2.3	8.1	23.6	65.7	274.3	596.4	761.4	859.4
Proprietors' income[1,2]									
Farm	4.4	4.5	13.5	11.4	14.3	13.1	31.1	22.2	31.3
Nonfarm	7.3	8.4	25.1	40.4	65.5	164.5	349.9	475.5	627.3
Rental income[1]	4.9	3.4	8.7	16.2	20.3	31.3	49.1	117.9	145.9
Corporate profits[1,2]	7.3	9.5	35.4	52.3	81.6	198.5	408.6	668.8	892.7
Net interest	4.8	3.2	3.0	10.7	38.4	183.9	452.4	389.8	467.5
Personal income	76.5	78.6	229.9	412.7	841.1	2,323.9	4,903.2	6,200.9	7,791.8
Disposable personal income	74.6	76.7	210.6	366.2	736.5	2,019.8	4,293.6	5,422.6	6,639.7
Personal savings	3.2	4.5	15.2	26.4	69.5	205.6	334.3	302.4	156.3

1. Includes capital consumption adjustment. 2. Includes inventory valuation adjustment. *Source:* U.S. Department of Commerce, Bureau of Economic Analysis, *Survey of Current Business,* May 1999. Web: www.bea.doc.gov.

Producer Price Indexes by Major Commodity Groups
(1982 = 100)

Commodity	1998	1997	1995	1990	1985	1980	1975	1970
All commodities	**124.4**	**126.7**	**124.7**	**116.3**	**103.2**	**89.8**	**58.4**	**38.1**
Farm products	104.6	110.1	107.4	112.2	95.1	102.9	77.0	45.8
Processed foods and feeds	131.6	132.9	127.0	121.9	103.5	95.9	72.6	44.6
Textile products and apparel	126.7	122.5	120.8	114.9	102.9	89.7	67.4	52.4
Hides, skins, and leather products	n.a.	153.5	153.7	141.7	108.9	94.7	56.5	42.0
Fuels and related products and power	89.1	82.8	78.0	82.2	91.4	82.8	35.4	15.3
Chemicals and allied products	n.a.	143.5	142.5	123.6	103.7	89.0	62.0	35.0
Rubber and plastic products	n.a.	123.1	124.3	113.6	101.9	90.1	62.2	44.9
Lumber and wood products	179.5	181.9	178.1	129.7	106.6	101.5	62.1	39.9
Pulp, paper, and allied products	171.7	171.2	172.2	141.3	113.3	86.3	59.0	37.5
Metals and metal products	122.5	130.6	134.5	123.0	104.4	95.0	61.5	38.7
Machinery and equipment	147.2	125.4	126.6	120.7	107.2	86.0	57.9	40.0
Furniture and household durables	148.4	130.7	128.2	119.1	107.1	90.7	67.5	51.9
Nonmetallic mineral products	n.a.	133.7	129.0	114.7	108.6	88.4	54.4	35.3
Transportation equipment	141.2	141.5	139.7	121.5	107.9	82.9	56.7	41.9

NOTE: n.a. = not available. *Source:* U.S. Department of Labor, Bureau of Labor Statistics, Division of Industrial Prices and Price Indexes. Web: stats.bls.gov

Output by Major Industry Division, 1998–2008

Industry	Billions of chained 1992 dollars		Percent distribution		Average annual rate of change
	1998	2008	1998	2008	1998–2008
Total	$13,509.4	$18,241.5	100.0%	100.0%	3.0%
Goods producing	4,932.2	6,609.6	36.5	36.2	3.0
Mining	174.8	197.0	1.3	1.1	1.2
Construction	696.7	791.8	5.2	4.3	1.3
Manufacturing	4,060.7	5,650.2	30.1	31.0	3.4
Durable	2,428.0	3,813.0	18.0	20.9	4.6
Nondurable	1,632.7	1,909.2	12.1	10.5	1.6
Service producing	7,700.9	10,537.1	57.0	57.8	3.2
Transportation, communications, and utilities	1,071.7	1,502.3	7.9	8.2	3.4
Wholesale trade	820.2	1,178.3	6.1	6.5	3.7
Retail trade	1,065.4	1,393.4	7.9	7.6	2.7
Finance, insurance, and real estate	1,330.0	1,787.8	9.8	9.8	3.0
Services	2,434.3	3,566.9	18.0	19.6	3.9
Government	979.3	1,109.6	7.2	6.1	1.3
Federal government	306.6	309.0	2.3	1.7	.1
State and local government	672.6	800.5	5.0	4.4	1.8
Agriculture	267.4	308.2	2.0	1.7	1.4
Private households	11.1	10.3	.1	.1	−.8
Special industries[1]	608.9	780.5	4.5	4.3	2.5
Residual[2]	−11.1	−4.2	−.1	.0	—

1. Consists of nonproducing accounting categories to reconcile input-output system with NIPA accounts. 2. Residual is shown for the first level only. Subcategories do not necessarily add to higher categories as a byproduct of chainweighting. *Source:* U.S. Department of Labor, Bureau of Labor Statistics, *Monthly Labor Review,* Nov. 1999.

Consumer Price Index for All Urban Consumers
(1982–84 = 100)

Group	1999	1995	1990	1985	1980	1975	1970	1965	1960	1950
All items	166.6	152.4	130.7	107.6	82.4	53.8	38.8	31.5	29.6	24.1
Food and beverages	164.6	148.9	132.1	105.6	86.7	60.2	40.1	n.a.	n.a.	n.a.
Housing	163.9	148.5	128.5	107.7	81.1	50.7	36.4	n.a.	n.a.	n.a.
Apparel	131.3	132.0	124.1	105.0	90.9	72.5	59.2	47.8	45.7	40.3
Transportation	144.4	139.1	120.5	106.4	83.1	50.1	37.5	31.9	29.8	22.7
Medical care	250.6	220.5	162.8	113.5	74.9	47.5	34.0	25.2	22.3	15.1

NOTE: n.a. = not available. *Source:* U.S. Department of Labor, Bureau of Labor Statistics. Web: www.bls.gov.

Retail Prices of Selected Foods in U.S. Cities, 1890–1970

(in cents per unit indicated)

Year	Flour (5 lbs)	Bread (lb)	Round steak (lb)	Bacon (lb)	Butter (lb)	Eggs (doz.)	Milk (½ gal.)	Oranges (doz.)	Potatoes (10 lbs)	Coffee (lb)	Sugar (5 lb)
1970	58.9	24.3	130.2	94.9	86.6	61.4	65.9	86.4	89.7	91.1	64.8
1965	58.1	20.9	108.4	81.3	75.4	52.7	52.6	77.8	93.7	83.3	59.0
1960	55.4	20.3	105.5	65.5	74.9	57.3	52.0	74.8	71.8	75.3	58.2
1955	53.8	17.7	90.3	65.9	70.9	60.6	46.2	52.8	56.4	93.0	52.1
1950	49.1	14.3	93.6	63.7	72.9	60.4	41.2	49.3	46.1	79.4	48.7
1945	32.1	8.8	40.6	41.1	50.7	58.1	31.2	48.5	49.3	30.5	33.4
1940	21.5	8.0	36.4	27.3	36.0	33.1	25.6	29.1	23.9	21.2	26.0
1935	25.3	8.3	36.0	41.3	36.0	37.6	23.4	22.0	19.1	25.7	28.2
1930	23.0	8.6	42.6	42.5	46.4	44.5	28.2	57.1	36.0	39.5	30.5
1925	30.5	9.3	36.2	47.1	55.2	55.4	27.8	57.1	36.0	50.4	35.0
1920	40.5	11.5	39.5	52.3	70.1	68.1	33.4	63.2	63.0	47.0	97.0
1915	21.0	7.0	23.0	26.9	35.8	34.1	17.6	n.a.	15.0	30.0	33.0
1910	18.0	n.a.	17.4	25.5	35.9	33.7	16.8	n.a.	17.0	n.a.	30.0
1905	16.0	n.a.	14.0	18.1	29.0	27.2	14.4	n.a.	17.0	n.a.	30.0
1900	12.5	n.a.	13.2	14.3	26.1	20.7	13.6	n.a.	14.0	n.a.	30.5
1895	12.0	n.a.	12.3	13.0	24.9	20.6	13.6	n.a.	14.0	n.a.	26.5
1890	14.5	n.a.	12.3	12.5	25.5	20.8	13.6	n.a.	16.0	n.a.	34.5

NOTE: n.a. = not available. *Source:* U.S. Bureau of the Census, *Historical Statistics of the United States, Colonial Times to 1970, Bicentennial Edition, Part 2.*

Per Capita Consumption of Principal Foods[1]

(in pounds)

Food	1990	1992	1995	1998p	Food	1990	1992	1995	1998p
Red meat[2]	112.3	114.1	115.1	115.6	Vegetables	383.5	393.9	409.5	418.1
Fish[2]	15.0	14.7	14.9	14.8	Flour and cereal products	182.0	186.2	192.5	n.a.
Poultry[2]	56.3	60.8	62.9	68.4	Sugar (refined)	64.4	64.6	65.5	n.a.
Eggs	30.2	30.3	30.3	31.4	Corn sweeteners[5]	71.1	75.2	83.0	n.a.
Fluid milk and cream	233.4	230.5	223.3	218.8	Coffee (green bean equivalent)	10.3	10.0	8.0	n.a.
Cheese[3]	24.6	26.0	27.3	28.4	Cocoa (chocolate liquor equivalent)[6]	4.3	4.6	3.6	n.a.
Ice cream	15.8	16.3	15.7	16.6	Tea (dry leaf equivalent)	0.7	0.9	0.9	n.a.
Total fats and oils[4]	63.0	66.8	66.4	65.3	Peanuts (shelled)	6.0	6.2	5.7	5.9
Butter	4.4	4.4	4.5	4.2					
Margarine	10.9	11.0	9.2	8.3					
Fruits	272.6	283.8	284.8	281.4					

NOTE: n.a. = not available. p = preliminary. 1. Data are on a retail-weight basis unless otherwise indicated. 2. Boneless, trimmed equivalent. 3. Excluding cottage cheese. Natural equivalent of cheese and cheese products. 4. Fat-content basis. 5. High fructose, glucose, and dextrose. 6. Ground or bitter chocolate. *Source:* U.S. Department of Agriculture, Economic Research Service. Web: www.usda.gov.

Farm Income

(in millions of dollars)

Year	Crops[1]	Livestock, livestock products	Government payments	Gross cash income	Year	Crops[1]	Livestock, livestock products	Government payments	Gross cash income
1930	$ 5,187	$ 5,187	—	$ 9,055	1990	$80,131	$89,843	$ 9,298	$186,824
1935	2,977	4,143	$ 573	7,693	1991	82,060	86,735	8,214	184,858
1940	3,469	4,913	723	9,105	1992	84,853	86,350	9,169	188,160
1945	9,655	12,008	742	22,405	1993	87,500	90,200	13,402	200,100
1950	12,356	16,105	283	28,764	1994	93,100	88,200	7,900	198,300
1955	13,523	15,967	229	29,842	1995	101,000	87,100	7,300	205,900
1960	15,023	18,989	703	34,958	1996	106,200	93,000	7,300	217,400
1965	17,479	21,886	2,463	42,215	1997	111,100	96,500	7,500	227,500
1970	20,997	29,532	3,717	54,768	1998	102,200	94,500	12,200	222,800
1975	45,813	43,089	807	90,707	1999[2]	95,100	96,900	22,700	229,100
1980	71,746	67,991	1,285	143,295	2000[3]	93,300	96,500	17,200	221,100
1985	74,293	69,822	7,705	157,854					

1. Includes items not listed. 2. Preliminary. 3. Forecast. *Source:* U.S. Department of Agriculture, Economic Research Service. *Agricultural Income and Finance.* Web: www.usda.gov.

Agricultural Output by State, 1998 Crops

State	Corn (1,000 bu)	Wheat (1,000 bu)	Cotton[2] (1,000 ba[3])	Potatoes (1,000 cwt)	Tobacco (1,000 lb)	Cattle (1,000 head)	Swine (1,000 head)
Alabama	12,600	3,570	570	780		229	91
Arizona	5,250	15,840	604	2,284		463	9
Arkansas	21,500	45,900	1,220			21	
California	41,600	38,550	1,495			1,019	2,212
Colorado	155,150	103,710		28,230		2,417	41
Connecticut					4,573	(1)	(1)
Delaware	15,500	3,723		1,012		36 [4]	279 [4]
Florida	3,410	559	68	8,798	17,102	51	141
Georgia	22,525	10,320	1,550		92,400	359	297
Hawaii						18	37
Idaho	7,800	102,410		139,650		743	
Illinois	1,473,450	57,600		1,421		1,019	9,197
Indiana	760,350	35,750		1,600	17,000	43	6,327
Iowa	1,769,000	1,280		306		932	28,906
Kansas	418,950	494,900	13			7,541	
Kentucky	135,700	24,750			460,910	50	2,530
Louisiana	43,740	3,960	645			26	38
Maine		10,750	1,450	18,060		(1)	(1)
Maryland	43,600			1,081	9,100	(4)	(4)
Massachusetts				660	1,764	(1)	(1)
Michigan	227,550	30,780		14,725		395	
Minnesota	1,032,750	80,444		21,170		685	7,940
Mississippi	43,000	6,750					
Missouri	285,000	57,500	350	1,892	6,300	76	3,927
Montana	2,070	168,790		3,180		22	28
Nebraska	1,239,750	82,800		9,781		7,300	6,286
Nevada				2,726		1	
New Hampshire		1,240				(1)	(1)
New Jersey	9,016	2,288		702		24	96
New Mexico	14,025	7,950	101	3,204		21	3
New York	66,120	7,020	1,005	7,290		87	53
North Carolina	53,900	27,880		3,430	566,890	162	9,786
North Dakota	88,275	310,650		28,670			72
Ohio	470,940	74,240		1,200	17,934	150	1,261
Oklahoma	28,600	198,900	140			35	4,119
Oregon	6,270	57,490		26,229		15	189
Pennsylvania	116,550	9,690		3,360	15,720	959	2,428
Rhode Island				147		(1)	(1)
South Carolina	11,000	7,680	350		96,750		
South Dakota	429,550	120,884		1,248		249	4,452
Tennessee	59,520	15,170	545		117,969		
Texas	185,000	136,500	3,550	4,867		6,767	324
Utah	3,384	8,834		728			27
Vermont						(1)	(1)
Virginia	25,200	11,025	140	1,380	98,625	19	4,173
Washington	19,000	157,425		93,225		925	
West Virginia	2,720	456			2,380	14	11
Wisconsin	404,150	7,635		30,895	4,230	1,650	375
Wyoming	7,620	6,790		120		6	6
Total U.S.	9,761,085	2,550,383	13,796	477,754	1,529,647	35,465	101,029

1. The cattle and pig estimates for New England states have been aggregated. 2. Production ginned and to be ginned. 3. 480-lb net weight bales. 4. The cattle and pig totals for Maryland are included with those for Delaware. *Source:* U.S. Department of Agriculture, National Agricultural Statistics Service. Web: www.usda.gov/nass.

Farm Indexes
(1990–1992 = 100)

Year	Prices paid by farmers[1]	Prices rec'd by farmers[2]	Ratio[3]	Year	Prices paid by farmers[1]	Prices rec'd by farmers[2]	Ratio[3]
1975	47	73	155	1994	106	100	94
1980	75	98	137	1995	109	102	93
1985	86	91	106	1996	115	112	98
1990	99	104	105	1997	118	107	91
1991	100	100	99	1998	115	101	88
1992	101	98	97	1999	115	96	83
1993	104	101	97				

1. Commodities and services, interest, taxes, and wage rates. 2. All farm products. 3. Ratio of index of prices received by farmers to index of prices paid by farmers. May not compute directly due to rounding. *Source:* U.S. Department of Agriculture, National Agricultural Statistics Service. Web: www.usda.gov.

Largest U.S. Businesses

1997	1998	1999	Company	Revenues ($ millions)	1997	1998	1999	Company	Revenues ($ millions)
1	1	1	General Motors	$189,058.0	—	44	50	Bank One Corp.	$25,986.0
4	3	2	Wal-Mart Stores	166,809.0	55	47	51	USX	25,610.0
—	—	3	Exxon Mobil	163,881.0	32	41	52	Lockheed Martin	25,530.0
2	2	4	Ford Motor	162,558.0	43	39	53	Metropolitan Life Insurance	25,426.0
5	5	5	General Electric	111,630.0					
6	6	6	Intl. Business Machines Corp.	87,548.0	—	—	54	Goldman Sachs Group	25,363.0
					48	45	55	GTE	25,336.2
21	7	7	Citigroup	82,005.0	—	78	56	Dell Computer	25,265.0
10	10	8	AT&T Corp.	62,391.0	41	43	57	United Technologies	25,242.0
9	8	9	Philip Morris	61,751.0	56	52	58	BellSouth Corp.	25,224.0
11	9	10	Boeing	57,993.0	—	93	59	Cardinal Health	25,033.6
—	—	11	Bank of America Corp.	51,392.0	45	50	60	ConAgra	24,594.3
40	35	12	SBC Communications	49,489.0	58	70	61	International Paper	24,573.0
14	14	13	Hewlett-Packard	48,253.0	95	79	62	Federal Home Loan Mortgage Corp. (Freddie Mac)	24,268.0
36	36	14	Kroger	45,351.6					
13	12	15	State Farm Insurance Cos.	44,637.2					
					—	—	63	AutoNation	24,206.6
16	15	16	Sears Roebuck	41,071.0	—	—	64	Berkshire Hathaway	24,028.0
26	22	17	American International Group	40,656.1	—	—	65	Honeywell International	23,735.0
					51	53	66	Walt Disney	23,402.0
57	27	18	Enron	40,112.0	96	56	67	First Union Corp.	22,084.0
30	18	19	TIAA-CREF	39,410.2	—	62	68	Wells Fargo	21,795.0
42	28	20	Compaq Computer	38,525.0	81	81	69	Duke Energy	21,742.0
44	32	21	Home Depot	38,434.0	67	68	70	New York Life Insurance	21,679.3
37	33	22	Lucent Technologies	38,303.0	73	72	71	American Express	21,278.0
20	17	23	Procter & Gamble	38,125.0	63	60	72	Loews	20,952.6
92	92	24	Albertson's	37,478.1	85	65	73	PG&E Corp.	20,820.0
62	80	25	MCI WorldCom	37,120.0	—	—	74	Conoco	20,817.0
33	26	26	Federal Natl. Mortgage Assoc. (Fannie Mae)	36,968.6	59	57	75	Cigna	20,644.0
					31	54	76	PepsiCo	20,367.0
23	21	27	Kmart	35,925.0	70	71	77	AMR	20,262.0
12	24	28	Texaco	35,690.0	78	77	78	Bristol-Myers Squibb	20,222.0
24	19	29	Merrill Lynch	34,879.0	61	64	79	Sara Lee	20,212.0
35	29	30	Morgan Stanley Dean Witter	33,928.0	—	—	80	FleetBoston	20,000.0
					90	88	81	Sprint	19,930.0
27	23	31	Chase Manhattan Corp.	33,710.0	100	69	82	Raytheon	19,841.0
—	—	32	Target	33,702.0	68	73	83	Coca-Cola	19,805.0
28	25	33	Bell Atlantic	33,174.0	—	—	84	Microsoft	19,747.0
46	37	34	Merck	32,714.0	66	58	85	Caterpillar	19,702.0
19	38	35	Chevron	32,676.0	—	84	86	UnitedHealth Group	19,562.0
25	31	36	J.C. Penney	32,510.0	72	63	87	Xerox	19,228.0
29	34	37	Motorola	30,931.0	77	66	88	Lehman Brothers Holdings	18,989.0
—	59	38	McKesson HBOC	30,382.3					
38	40	39	Intel	29,389.0	60	75	89	Dow Chemical	18,929.0
50	48	40	Safeway	28,859.9	—	—	90	UtiliCorp United	18,621.5
79	55	41	Ingram Micro	28,068.6	88	90	91	Electronic Data Systems	18,534.2
15	16	42	E. I. du Pont de Nemours	27,892.0	74	76	92	J. P. Morgan & Co.	18,110.0
					—	99	93	CVS	18,098.3
49	51	43	Johnson & Johnson	27,471.0	75	82	94	UAL	18,027.0
53	49	44	Costco Wholesale	27,456.0	—	98	95	Walgreen	17,838.8
—	—	45	Time Warner	27,333.0	—	—	96	Georgia-Pacific	17,796.0
52	46	46	United Parcel Service	27,052.0	83	95	97	Federated Department Stores	17,716.0
39	42	47	Allstate	26,959.0					
18	20	48	Prudential Ins. Co. of America	26,618.0	94	97	98	Sysco	17,422.8
					80	86	99	Supervalu	17,420.5
71	61	49	Aetna	26,452.7	—	—	100	Bergen Brunswig	17,244.9

NOTE: Dash indicates the company was not in the top 100 for the year noted. *Source:* Fortune 500, © 2000 Time, Inc. All rights reserved. For more detailed information, visit *Fortune* on the Web, www.fortune.com/fortune500.

Women- and Minority-Owned Firms, 1987 and 1992

Geographic Area	Firms							
	Women-owned		Black-owned		Hispanic-owned		American Indian- and Asian-owned[1]	
	1992	1987	1992	1987	1992	1987	1992	1987
United States	5,888,883	4,114,787	620,912	424,165	771,708	422,373	606,426	376,711
Alabama	71,466	48,018	14,707	10,085	1,029	397	1,777	1,007
Alaska	19,380	13,976	739	507	766	502	3,916	5,034
Arizona	93,300	60,567	2,936	1,811	17,835	9,845	5,852	3,398
Arkansas	50,440	35,469	5,738	4,392	701	324	1,214	658
California	801,487	559,821	68,968	47,728	249,717	132,212	232,672	147,633
Colorado	121,659	89,411	4,372	2,871	13,817	9,516	5,788	3,543
Connecticut	79,931	60,924	5,714	4,061	4,502	2,235	3,485	2,051
Delaware	14,904	9,727	2,060	1,399	497	184	809	479
District of Columbia	14,599	10,987	10,111	8,275	1,452	762	1,393	807
Florida	352,048	221,361	40,371	25,527	118,208	64,413	17,499	8,902
Georgia	143,045	88,050	38,264	21,283	5,501	1,931	8,961	4,221
Hawaii	29,743	21,696	717	399	3,192	1,226	38,392	31,406
Idaho	29,946	18,973	152	94	1,865	974	759	513
Illinois	250,613	177,057	28,433	19,011	18,368	9,636	21,743	14,872
Indiana	125,411	89,949	8,349	5,867	2,454	1,427	3,193	1,808
Iowa	71,040	53,592	1,106	703	859	475	1,011	617
Kansas	66,429	53,505	3,078	2,323	2,396	1,541	1,842	1,366
Kentucky	74,280	53,454	5,097	3,738	752	359	1,614	899
Louisiana	76,849	55,852	20,312	15,331	4,983	2,697	4,826	2,808
Maine	35,260	23,922	235	131	427	139	483	233
Maryland	121,777	81,891	35,758	21,678	7,289	2,931	13,697	7,954
Massachusetts	147,572	111,376	7,225	4,761	6,914	2,636	7,009	3,916
Michigan	193,820	133,958	19,695	13,708	5,036	2,654	7,409	4,729
Minnesota	124,143	88,137	2,785	1,448	1,583	751	3,168	2,024
Mississippi	40,879	28,976	14,067	9,667	660	308	1,765	1,178
Missouri	117,885	87,658	9,973	7,832	2,216	1,247	3,451	2,193
Montana	25,310	17,747	113	77	568	304	845	612
Nebraska	43,637	32,285	1,350	863	1,147	619	670	451
Nevada	32,430	18,831	1,736	1,002	3,900	1,767	2,769	1,395
New Hampshire	31,492	22,713	326	229	487	244	666	333
New Jersey	164,798	117,373	20,137	14,556	22,198	12,094	23,116	12,665
New Mexico	40,636	25,397	925	587	21,586	14,299	4,608	2,155
New York	395,944	284,912	51,312	36,289	50,601	28,254	63,053	36,257
North Carolina	142,516	93,532	29,221	19,487	2,802	918	6,155	3,827
North Dakota	15,355	12,689	117	57	116	88	385	329
Ohio	224,693	154,084	22,690	15,983	4,289	1,989	7,146	4,011
Oklahoma	82,894	63,690	4,621	3,461	2,854	1,516	5,627	3,751
Oregon	87,970	58,941	1,447	848	3,538	1,598	5,414	3,340
Pennsylvania	227,500	167,362	15,917	11,728	5,186	2,650	12,053	7,189
Rhode Island	21,353	14,517	857	489	1,297	426	987	472
South Carolina	64,812	42,604	18,343	12,815	1,057	393	1,877	965
South Dakota	18,215	13,374	111	63	239	109	555	375
Tennessee	101,134	67,448	14,920	10,423	1,602	554	3,026	1,664
Texas	414,179	298,138	50,008	35,725	155,909	94,754	38,763	22,682
Utah	45,626	29,810	354	202	2,375	1,300	1,746	1,239
Vermont	21,033	13,802	139	98	351	118	274	111
Virginia	138,494	94,416	26,100	18,781	7,654	2,716	13,752	8,163
Washington	136,337	90,285	4,575	2,583	6,093	2,686	15,648	8,241
West Virginia	30,644	22,549	1,093	727	313	177	712	551
Wisconsin	99,357	69,185	3,446	2,381	1,762	894	2,486	1,451
Wyoming	14,617	10,796	97	81	766	584	362	233

1. Includes Alaska Native and Pacific Islander-owned. *Source:* U.S. Bureau of the Census. *State and Metropolitan Area Data Book 1997–1998.*

Job-Related Work at Home, 1997

| Characteristic | Total number (thousands) | Rate[1] | Percent distribution of those working at home | | | |
| | | | Wage and salary | | Self-employed[2] | |
			Paid	Unpaid	Total	Home-based business
Total, 16 years and over	21,478	17.8%	17.0%	51.5%	30.1%	19.2%
Men	11,202	17.3	15.0	50.1	33.8	19.3
Women	10,275	18.3	19.1	53.1	26.2	19.2
Occupation						
Managerial and professional specialty	13,120	36.7	14.0	61.7	23.5	13.1
Executive, administrative, and managerial	5,940	34.0	14.6	54.8	29.8	17.1
Professional specialty	7,180	39.2	13.5	67.5	18.2	9.7
Technical, sales, and administrative support	5,457	15.0	25.0	40.7	32.0	18.6
Technicians and related support	417	10.6	26.9	60.3	11.3	8.6
Sales occupations	3,356	22.4	19.1	39.1	40.4	21.5
Administrative support, including clerical	1,684	9.7	36.3	39.0	20.5	15.4
Service occupations	1,250	7.2	20.4	23.0	54.0	49.3
Precision production, craft, and repair	1,145	8.2	10.1	26.5	62.0	49.2
Operators, fabricators, and laborers	506	2.9	14.4	31.2	51.1	42.5
Industry						
Mining	73	12.3	(3)	(3)	(3)	(3)
Construction	1,330	16.2	10.3	20.0	66.8	54.6
Manufacturing	2,318	11.5	22.3	62.7	14.2	8.3
Transportation and public utilities	963	10.9	21.2	56.2	21.0	13.7
Wholesale trade	1,202	24.4	28.5	42.8	27.7	15.4
Retail trade	1,964	9.2	14.7	36.9	47.3	27.1
Finance, insurance, and real estate	2,008	25.7	16.4	48.6	33.1	14.5
Services	10,954	25.1	14.8	55.6	28.3	18.8
Public administration	666	12.3	29.5	69.2	—	—
Race and Hispanic origin						
White	19,646	19.2	17.0	50.7	30.9	19.7
Black	1,117	8.5	16.6	64.8	16.2	12.1
Hispanic origin	830	7.2	17.5	53.9	27.8	18.8

NOTES: Data refer to employed persons in nonagricultural industries who reported work at home during the survey reference week as part of their primary job. Excludes unpaid family workers, not shown separately. Detail for the above race and
Hispanic-origin groups will not sum to totals because data for the "other races" group are not presented and Hispanics are
included in both the white and black population groups. Data reflect revised population controls used in the Current Population Survey effective with January 1997 estimates. Dash represents zero. 1. Refers to the number of persons working at
home as a percent of the total at work. The calculation excludes those persons who did not respond to the questions on
work at home. 2. Includes both the incorporated and unincorporated self-employed. 3. Data not shown where the base is
less than 75,000. *Source:* U.S. Department of Labor, Bureau of Labor Statistics. Web; stats.bls.gov.

Leading Advertising Agencies
(ranked by revenues in thousands of dollars)

Rank 1998	Rank 1997	Agency	1998 revenues	Percent change	1998 billings	Percent change
1	1	McCann-Erickson World Group	$1,950,944	13.0%	$16,370,370	22.9%
2	3	BBDO Worldwide	1,868,314	11.5	14,706,635	14.0
3	2	DDB Needham Worldwide	1,780,101	11.0	13,956,250	11.9
4	5	J. Walter Thompson	1,233,000	5.2	8,458,000	5.6
5	4	Young & Rubicam	1,209,609	10.9	11,848,076	15.7
6	9	Euro RSCG Worldwide	1,151,624	11.4	9,483,353	21.6
7	6	Ogilvy & Mather Worldwide	1,118,000	8.4	9,748,000	11.8
8	7	Ammirati Puris Lintas Worldwide	1,113,871	8.4	8,357,042	9.4
9	8	Grey Advertising	1,002,300	5.0	6,685,500[1]	5.0
10	10	Leo Burnett Co.	949,800	7.2	6,810,000	7.1
11	13	TBWA	896,953	12.0	6,301,774	12.3
12	12	D'Arcy Masius Benton & Bowles	616,700	1.5	5,794,318	0.2
13	11	Foote, Cone & Belding	576,000[2]	2.9	5,905,532	2.9
14	14	The Lowe Group	553,651	10.4	4,007,212	12.6
15	16	Saatchi & Saatchi	516,000[2]	5.9	n.a.	n.a.

NOTE: n.a. = not available. 1. Capitalized figure. 2. *Adweek* Estimate. *Source: Adweek,* Top U.S.-Based Agency Networks,
April 19, 1999, edition. © 1999 *Adweek.* Used with permission of *Adweek.*

World's Largest Banks[1]
(in millions of U.S. dollars)

Rank	Bank	Assets	Rank	Bank	Assets
1	Bank of Tokyo-Mitsubishi Ltd., Japan	$691,920.3	29	JP Morgan & Co., Inc., New York, U.S.	$262,159.0
2	Deutsche Bank AG, Frankfurt, Ger.	580,069.0	30	BankAmerica Corp., San Francisco, U.S.	260,159.0
3	Sumitomo Bank Ltd., Osaka, Japan	483,730.4	31	Lloyds TSB Group Inc., London, U.K.	260,042.8
4	Credit Suisse Group, Zurich, Switz.	473,829.8	32	Sumitomo Trust & Banking Co. Ltd., Osaka, Japan	254,189.7
5	HSBC Holdings, Plc., London, U.K.	471,037.8			
6	Dai-Ichi Kangyo Bank Ltd., Tokyo, Japan	433,102.9	33	Credit Lyonnais, Paris, France	250,149.9
7	Sanwa Bank Ltd., Osaka, Japan	427,979.6	34	Bayerische Vereinsbank AG, Munich, Ger.	249,830.6
8	Credit Agricole Mutuel, Paris, France	419,763.2	35	Abbey National, Plc., London, U.K.	248,040.3
9	Fuji Bank Ltd., Tokyo, Japan	414,173.0	36	Compagnie Financiere de Paribas, Paris, France	245,061.1
10	ABN-AMRO Bank, N.V., Amsterdam, Neth.	412,771.9			
11	Societe Generale, Paris, France	410,842.2	37	Mitsui Trust & Banking Co., Ltd., Tokyo, Japan	241,916.0
12	Sakura Bank Ltd., Tokyo, Japan	399,491.5			
13	Union Bank of Switzerland, Zurich, Switz.	395,086.5	38	Bayerische Landesbank Girozentrale, Munich, Ger.	241,714.0
14	Norin Chunkin Bank, Tokyo, Japan	392,553.5			
15	Barclays Bank Plc., London, U.K.	385,950.3	39	Asahi Bank Ltd., Tokyo, Japan	219,939.4
16	Dresdner Bank, Frankfurt, Ger.	371,371.0	40	Halifax Plc., Leeds, U.K.	215,625.4
17	Industrial Bank of Japan Ltd., Tokyo, Japan	369,954.0	41	Rabobank Group, Utrecht, Neth.	208,739.6
			42	Deutsche Genossenschaftsbank, Frankfurt, Ger.	207,768.9
18	Chase Manhattan Corp., New York, U.S.	365,521.0			
19	Banque Nationale de Paris, France	339,648.2	43	Bayerische Hypotheken-und Wechsel-Bank AG, Munich, Ger.	203,567.0
20	Westdeutsche Landesbank Girozentrale, Duesseldorf, Ger.	335,816.2			
			44	Dexia Belgium, Brussels, Belgium	202,958.5
21	Citicorp, New York, U.S.	310,897.0	45	Bankgesellschaft Berlin AG, Berlin, Ger.	197,364.8
22	ING Bank, Amsterdam, Neth.	307,559.6	46	Long Term Credit Bank of Japan Ltd., Tokyo, Japan	188,497.4
23	NatWest Group, London, U.K.	304,941.8			
24	Swiss Bank Corp., Basel, Switz.	300,259.1	47	Royal Bank of Canada, Toronto, Can.	171,218.5
25	Commerzbank, Frankfurt, Ger.	286,946.6	48	Grupo Santander, Spain	170,927.0
26	Mitsubishi Trust & Banking Corp., Tokyo, Japan	269,524.4	49	Canadian Imperial Bank of Commerce, Toronto, Can.	166,472.4
27	NationsBank Corp., Charlotte, N.C., U.S.	264,562.0	50	Yasuda Trust & Banking Co., Ltd., Tokyo, Japan	165,784.2
28	Tokai Bank Ltd., Nagoya, Japan	262,423.7			

1. Based on total assets held on December 31, 1997. *Source: American Banker,* August 6, 1998. Reprinted with permission. Copyright © American Banker/Bond Buyer. Web: www.americanbanker.com.

Largest World Ports by Cargo Volume, 1998

Rank	Port	Country	Metric tons (thousands)	Rank	Port	Country	Metric tons (thousands)
1.	Singapore	Singapore	313,322	27.	Dampier	Australia	71,333
2.	Rotterdam	Netherlands	306,859	28.	Newcastle	Australia	70,942
3.	South Louisiana	U.S.	178,515	29.	Tubarao	Brazil	69,575
4.	Hong Kong	China	167,170	30.	Port Hedland	Australia	67,230
5.	Shanghai	China	166,000	31.	LeHavre	France	66,407
6.	Chiba	Japan	164,060	32.	Baton Rouge, La.	U.S.	60,673
7.	Houston, Tex.	U.S.	153,482	33.	Hampton Roads, Va.	U.S.	60,663
8.	Ulsan	South Korea	148,332	34.	Plaquemines, La.	U.S.	59,738
9.	Nagoya	Japan	133,863	35.	London	U.K.	56,374
10.	New York/New Jersey	U.S.	124,862	36.	Valdez, Alaska	U.S.	56,235
11.	Antwerp	Belgium	119,789	37.	Amsterdam	Netherlands	55,734
12.	Yokohama	Japan	117,820	38.	Beaumont, Tex.	U.S.	54,515
13.	Kwangyang	South Korea	114,964	39.	Long Beach, Calif.	U.S.	52,421
14.	Kobe	Japan	100,048	40.	Tees and Hartlepool	U.K.	51,455
15.	Kaohsiung	Taiwan	98,203	41.	Itaqui	Brazil	50,268
16.	Busan	South Korea	96,434	42.	Lake Charles, La.	U.S.	48,629
17.	Inchon	South Korea	93,948	43.	Grimsby and Imming-ham	U.K.	48,387
18.	Marseilles	France	93,421				
19.	Tokyo	Japan	88,392	44.	Tampa, Fla.	U.S.	48,316
20.	Kitayushu	Japan	87,346	45.	Pittsburgh, Pa.	U.S.	48,027
21.	Osaka	Japan	86,689	46.	Pohang	South Korea	47,552
22.	Richards Bay	South Africa	86,084	47.	Port Kelang	Malaysia	47,341
23.	New Orleans, La.	U.S.	80,584	48.	Trieste	Italy	47,217
24.	Corpus Christi, Tex.	U.S.	78,234	49.	Texas City, Tex.	U.S.	44,916
25.	Hamburg	Germany	76,263	50.	Genoa	Italy	44,874
26.	Vancouver, B.C.	Canada	71,933				

Source: American Association of Port Authorities. Web: www.aapa-ports.org.

Life Insurance in Force
(in millions of dollars)

As of Dec. 31	Ordinary	Group	Industrial	Credit	Total
1900	$ 6,124	—	$ 1,449	—	$ 7,573
1915	16,650	$ 100	4,279	—	21,029
1930	78,576	9,801	17,963	$ 73	106,413
1945	101,550	22,172	27,675	365	151,762
1950	149,116	47,793	33,415	3,844	234,168
1955	216,812	101,345	39,682	14,493	372,332
1960	341,881	175,903	39,563	29,101	586,448
1965	499,638	308,078	39,818	53,020	900,554
1970	734,730	551,357	38,644	77,392	1,402,123
1975	1,083,421	904,695	39,423	112,032	2,139,571
1980	1,760,474	1,579,355	35,994	165,215	3,541,038
1985	3,247,289	2,561,595	28,250	215,973	6,053,107
1990	5,366,982	3,753,506	24,071	248,038	9,392,597
1995	6,872,252	4,604,856	18,134	201,083	11,696,325
1998	8,505,894	5,735,273	17,365	212,917	14,471,449

Source: American Council of Life Insurance.

U.S. Light Vehicle Production by Manufacturer

Manufacturer	1985	1990	1999
Cars			
American Motors	111,138	0	0
AutoAlliance	0	184,428	165,143
BMW	0	0	48,394
Chrysler Corp..	1,266,070	726,753	431,827
Ford N.A. Mfg.	1,636,146	1,378,123	1,225,117
General Motors N.A. Mfg.	4,822,482	2,652,996	2,093,345
Honda	145,337	435,437	686,043
Mitsubishi	0	148,379	159,702
Nissan	43,810	95,844	167,742
NUMMI	64,601	205,287	210,726
Subaru Isuzu	0	32,461	93,070
Toyota	0	218,195	356,840
Volkswagen	96,459	0	0
Total car	8,186,043	6,077,903	5,637,949

Manufacturer	1985	1990	1999
Light trucks			
American Motors	236,280	0	0
BMW	0	0	2,412
Chrysler Corp.	213,930	526,502	1,528,283
Ford N.A. Mfg.	1,148,373	1,336,443	2,413,762
Freightliner	0	0	811
General Motors N.A. Mfg.	1,468,915	1,426,689	2,342,907
Mercedes Benz	0	0	77,696
Nissan	107,422	139,404	156,903
NUMMI	0	0	156,395
Subaru Isuzu	0	34,499	99,130
Toyota	0	0	176,862
Total light truck	3,174,920	3,463,537	6,955,161
Total light vehicles	11,360,963	9,541,440	12,593,110

Source: Ward's AutoInfoBank. © 2000, Ward's Communications, Southfield, Mich. 48075 USA.

Stock Ownership by Age and Income, 1989–1998

Family characteristic	Families having direct or indirect stock holdings (percent)			Median value among families with holdings (thousands of constant 1998 dollars)			Stock holdings as share of group's financial assets (percent)		
	1989	1995	1998	1989	1995	1998	1989	1995	1998
All families	31.6%	40.4%	48.8%	$10.8	$15.4	$ 25.0	27.8%	40.0%	53.9%
Age of head of family									
Under 35 years old	22.4	36.6	40.7	3.8	5.4	7.0	20.2	27.2	44.8
35 to 44 years old	38.9	46.4	56.5	6.6	10.6	20.0	29.2	39.5	54.7
45 to 54 years old	41.8	48.9	58.6	16.7	27.6	38.0	33.5	42.9	55.7
55 to 64 years old	36.2	40.0	55.9	23.4	32.9	47.0	27.6	44.4	58.3
65 to 74 years old	26.7	34.4	42.6	25.8	36.1	56.0	26.0	35.8	51.3
75 years old and over	25.9	27.9	29.4	31.8	21.2	60.0	25.0	39.8	48.7
Family income[1]									
Less than $10,000	(2)	5.4	7.7	(2)	3.2	4.0	(2)	12.9	24.8
$10,000 to $24,999	12.7	22.2	24.7	6.4	6.4	9.0	11.7	26.7	27.5
$25,000 to $49,999	31.5	45.4	52.7	6.0	8.5	11.5	16.9	30.3	39.1
$50,000 to $99,999	51.5	65.4	74.3	10.2	23.6	35.7	23.2	39.9	48.8
$100,000 and more	81.8	81.6	91.0	53.5	85.5	150.0	35.3	46.4	63.0

NOTES: Percentages may not add up to 100 due to rounding. 1. In 1998 dollars. 2. Ten or fewer observations. *Source:* Board of Governors of the Federal Reserve System, *Federal Reserve Bulletin,* vol. 86 (Jan. 2000), pp. 1–29. Web: www.bog.frb.fed.us/pubs/bulletin.

Top Stocks by Market Value

Rank 1999	Rank 1998	Company name	Shares outstanding (millions)	Market value (millions)	Rank 1999	Rank 1998	Company name	Shares outstanding (millions)	Market value (millions)
1	2	Microsoft Corp. (MSFT)	5,160	$602,433	25	—	QUALCOMM Incorporated (QCOM)	660	116,227
2	1	General Electric Co. (GE)	3,714	574,726	26	34	Hewlett-Packard Co. (HWP)	1,020	$116,198
3	11	Cisco Systems Inc. (CSCO)	3,421	366,498	27	—	Yahoo! Inc. (YHOO)	263	113,901
4	5	Exxon Mobil Corp. (XOM)	4,013	323,286	28	—	EMC Corporation (EMC)	1,005	109,793
5	7	Wal-Mart Stores, Inc. (WMT)	4,604	318,248	29	25	Bell Atlantic Corp. (BEL)	1,576	97,038
6	6	Intel Corp. (INTC)	3,341	275,004	30	—	BellSouth Corporation (BLS)	2,020	94,576
7	35	Lucent Technologies Inc. (LU)	3,072	229,805	31	—	Motorola, Inc. (MOT)	603	88,809
8	8	International Business Machines Corp. (IBM)	1,875	202,447	32	36	Time Warner Inc. (TWX)	1,195	86,588
9	3	Coca-Cola Co. (KO)	3,464	201,805	33	—	Morgan Stanley Dean Witter (MWD)	606	86,484
10	48	Citigroup Inc. (C)	3,598	199,921	34	19	Bank of America Corp. (BAC)	1,712	85,921
11	4	Merck & Co., Inc. (MRK)	2,968	199,045	35	16	Schering-Plough Corp. (SGP)	2,030	85,623
12	17	American International Group, Inc. (AIG)	1,657	179,165	36	20	Berkshire Hathaway Inc. (BRKA)	1,350	75,755
13	30	America Online, Inc. (AOL)	2,234	168,532	37	—	American Express Company (AXP)	453	75,291
14	18	SBC Communications Inc. (SBC)	3,427	167,077	38	42	DuPont Co. (DD)	1,140	75,121
15	13	AT&T Corp. (T)	3,194	162,078	39	21	Eli Lilly and Co. (LLY)	1,123	74,687
16	—	Oracle Corporation (ORCL)	1,424	159,540	40	—	BP Amoco PLC (BPA)	1,243	73,702
					41	24	Fannie Mae (FNM)	1,129	70,498
17	23	Home Depot Inc. (HD)	2,227	152,661	42	39	GTE Corp. (GTE)	998	70,408
18	14	MCI WorldCom, Inc. (WCOM)	2,838	150,608	43	—	AT&T Corp. Liberty Media Group (LMGA)	1,209	68,611
19	40	Procter & Gamble Co. (PG)	1,326	145,332	44	45	Chase Manhattan Corp. (CMB)	882	68,491
20	15	Johnson & Johnson (JNJ)	1,535	142,934	45	37	Wells Fargo & Co. (WFC)	1,687	68,211
21	12	Bristol-Myers Squibb Co. (BMY)	2,189	140,498	46	10	Philip Morris Companies Inc. (MO)	2,806	65,063
22	9	Pfizer Inc. (PFE)	4,138	134,225	47	—	Tyco International (TYC)	1,636	63,582
23	22	Dell Computer Corp. (DELL)	2,565	130,823	48	—	Amgen Inc. (AMGN)	1,020	61,258
24	—	Sun Microsystems, Inc. (SUNW)	1,547	119,820	49	41	Walt Disney Co. (DIS)	2,089	61,098
					50	32	PepsiCo, Inc. (PEP)	1,726	60,847

NOTE: Based on closing prices on December 31, 1999. *Sources:* New York Stock Exchange *1999 Fact Book;* Nasdaq Stock Market, Inc.

Dow 101

Five Fundamental Facts about the Dow Jones Industrial Average

The Index Is Not Truly Industrial

Though its name would lead you to believe it is composed of only industrial companies, in fact the DJIA contains stocks across many "industries," not all of which are industrial.

The industries represented include financial, food, technology, retail, heavy equipment, oil, chemical, pharmaceutical, consumer goods, and entertainment. Dow Jones also collects and reports data for two other sectors of the economy in its Transportation and Utilities indexes.

The DJIA Represents Only 30 Stocks

To be chosen for inclusion in the index, a stock must be a leader in its industry and must be widely held by both individual and institutional investors (i.e., pension plans, mutual funds, etc.). Together, the 30 stocks in the average represent about 20% of the market value of all U.S. stocks, so although the DJIA is not the whole stock market, it is certainly representative of the stock market as a whole.

The DJIA Is Not Really an "Average"

A simple average is calculated by adding up a value for a number of items, then dividing by the number of items. The Dow reflects the value of stock prices, but a simple average cannot accurately reflect the value of stock prices.

Here's why. When stocks become pricey, companies routinely announce stock splits to make their stocks more appealing to individual investors.

For example, a company may have 100 shares outstanding priced at $100 per share, for a market value of $10,000. If the firm announces a 2-for-1 split, the price is cut in half, and the number of shares is doubled, so there would be 200 shares outstanding, priced at $50 per share. The market value is still $10,000, but the price point is now more attractive to smaller investors.

To take into account the changes in price associated with stock splits, the Dow Jones Industrial "Average" is adjusted to account for any stock splits in each of the included companies.

The Following 30 Companies Currently Compose the Dow Industrials

- Alcoa Inc. (AA)
- American Express Co. (AXP)
- AT&T Corp. (T)
- Boeing Co. (BA)
- Caterpillar Inc. (CAT)
- Citigroup Inc. (C)
- Coca-Cola Co. (KO)
- DuPont Co. (DD)
- Eastman Kodak Co. (EK)
- Exxon Mobil Corp. (XOM)
- General Electric Co. (GE)
- General Motors Corp. (GM)
- Hewlett-Packard Co. (HWP)
- Home Depot Inc. (HD)
- Honeywell International Inc. (HON)
- Intel Corp. (INTC)
- International Business Machines Corp. (IBM)
- International Paper Co. (IP)
- J. P. Morgan & Co. (JPM)
- Johnson & Johnson (JNJ)
- McDonald's Corp. (MCD)
- Merck & Co., Inc. (MRK)
- Microsoft Corp. (MSFT)
- Minnesota Mining & Manufacturing Co. (MMM)
- Philip Morris Companies Inc. (MO)
- Procter & Gamble Co. (PG)
- SBC Communications Inc. (SBC)
- United Technologies Corp. (UTX)
- Wal-Mart Stores, Inc. (WMT)
- Walt Disney Co. (DIS)

Who Is Dow Jones?

Charles Dow and Edward Jones are two-thirds of the team that founded Dow Jones & Company in 1882. Charles Bergstresser was the "& Company," but by 1889 he was joined by 47 others as the company grew. They specialized in newsletters (the precursor to *The Wall Street Journal*) focusing on financial news. When Dow died in 1902, Clarence Barron, originally hired as a correspondent, purchased a controlling interest in the firm.

Most Active Stocks on NYSE

Rank			Share volume	Rank			Share volume
1999	1998	Company name (symbol)	(in millions)	1999	1998	Company name (symbol)	(in millions)
1	6	America Online (AOL)	3,182.5	25	(1)	Wells Fargo Co. (WFC)	810.7
2	1	Compaq Computer Corp. (CPQ)	3,026.3	26	(1)	Bank One Corp. (ONE)	797.7
3	5	AT&T Corp. (T)	2,160.2	27	24	American Home Products (AHP)	788.1
4	36	Citigroup Inc. (C)	2,119.2	28	29	Gillette Co. (G)	787.8
5	4	Lucent Technologies Inc. (LU)	1,975.7	29	44	SBC Communications Inc. (SBC)	785.8
6	2	Philip Morris Companies Inc. (MO)	1,780.2	30	(1)	Schwab (Charles) Corp. (SCH)	767.9
7	9	International Business Machines Corp. (IBM)	1,472.3	31	34	Motorola Inc. (MOT)	760.1
				32	30	DuPont Co. (DD)	753.0
8	13	Pfizer Inc. (PFE)	1,376.8	33	27	Texas Instruments (TXN)	742.1
9	20	Disney (Walt) & Co. (DIS)	1,375.0	34	(1)	Rite Aid Corp. (RAD)	741.6
10	(1)	Tyco International Ltd. (TYC)	1,339.1	35	37	Home Depot Inc. (HD)	729.4
				36		Abbott Laboratories (ABT)	720.0
11	8	Micron Technology Inc. (MU)	1,181.2	37	26	Merrill Lynch & Co. (MER)	717.1
				38	(1)	Bristol-Myers Squibb Co. (BMY)	715.9
12	23	Wal-Mart Stores, Inc. (WMT)	1,092.9	39	(1)	Schering-Plough Corp. (SGP)	715.0
13	7	General Electric Co. (GE)	1,063.9				
14	35	EMC Corporation (EMC)	1,027.2	40	(1)	Warner-Lambert Co. (WLA)	714.8
15	17	Bank of America Corp. (BAC)	988.9	41	10	Boeing Co. (BA)	686.1
16	31	Merck & Co., Inc. (MRK)	959.8	42	(1)	Time Warner Inc. (TWX)	671.4
17	21	Coca-Cola Co. (KO)	874.7	43	(1)	McDonald's Corp. (MCD)	664.9
18	(1)	Waste Management Inc. (WMI)	851.9	44	16	Schlumberger Ltd. (SLB)	655.9
				45	(1)	BellSouth Corp. (BLS)	651.1
19	3	Cendant Corp. (CD)	850.6	46	(1)	Mattel Inc. (MAT)	644.5
20	18	Exxon Mobil Corp. (XON)	844.5	47	(1)	Allstate Corp. (ALL)	625.4
21	11	PepsiCo, Inc. (PEP)	842.5	48	(1)	Medtronic Inc. (MDT)	624.7
22	15	Chase Manhattan Corp. (CMB)	824.5	49	(1)	Bell Atlantic Corp. (BEL)	623.4
23	(1)	Xerox Corp. (XRX)	817.7	50	25	Eli Lilly and Co. (LLY)	614.1
24	22	Hewlett-Packard Co. (HWP)	811.9				

NOTES: As of December 31, 1999. In case of stock splits, volume in old and new issues was combined. 1. Not ranked in top 50 in 1998. *Source:* New York Stock Exchange *1999 Fact Book.*

Investment Basics about Mutual Funds

When you buy a share in a mutual fund, you're buying both a share in an investment company and a service from that company (or more accurately, the management company that sponsors it).

The service you buy is convenient and relatively inexpensive access to the capital markets. The value of your shares in the company depends on the company's profits (how well the mutual fund invests and performs in the markets).

Structure

When people refer to mutual funds, they usually mean open-end funds which can issue an unlimited number of shares. The more money investors put into the fund, the more shares it issues. There is no limit to the size of a mutual fund: Fidelity's legendary Magellan Fund has well over $50 billion in assets under management.

Funds use shareholder money to buy assets. The stocks or bonds a fund holds comprise its portfolio, and the financial professional who decides what to buy and sell is the portfolio manager.

Market Timing

Every day the fund's accountants calculate the value of each share. This is done by totaling up the value of all assets in the fund's portfolio and dividing that figure by the number of fund shares outstanding. The resulting number is the fund's net asset value (NAV). All fund managers share one goal—to make the NAV go higher.

How does the mutual fund company make money?

Management Fees

Fund managers charge management fees, which are generally pretty small, often less than 1.5% of the money you invest. This small percentage, however, is enough to be profitable for the fund company, since so many people are investing so much money.

Types

There are four general mutual fund types:
• Stock funds buy stocks. Their investment objective is usually specific to a certain stock type—small cap, large cap, international, etc.
• Bond funds hold only bonds. As with stock funds, they can be designed to purchase particular grades of bonds.
• Balanced funds invest in a mix of stocks and bonds.
• Money market funds stick with safe, short-term debt instruments such as commercial paper, banker's acceptances, repurchase agreements, and certificates of deposit. Because they have low risk, they typically provide the lowest returns among mutual funds. Their main uses are to park money between investments, hold emergency savings, and save for short-term goals. A small investment in money markets may also reduce some risk in a long-term investment account.

Mutual Fund Choices

Funds are usually categorized by the type of assets they invest in—small cap stock, intermediate bond, etc.

Index Funds

One type of fund that bears a special mention is the Index Fund, which invests in the companies that comprise the various "indexes" (Standard & Poor's 500, Russell 2000, etc.). The fund buys a portfolio of stocks that are expected to behave almost exactly as the index does. This is called passive management, since the account doesn't change and the portfolio manager doesn't make daily investment decisions.

How to Judge Mutual Funds

Because it's not possible to predict the future, people often look at a mutual fund's historical performance to gauge how the fund might behave in times to come. While it may be tempting to focus solely on how much money the fund has earned for its investors (the return), it is also important to draw other lessons about the fund, such as the risk level of its investments, its expenses, and its style of investing. However, it is important to realize that many things change over time, including market conditions and personnel working for the mutual fund. There are countless examples of funds achieving spectacularly high returns in one year only to incur equally spectacular losses in the following year.

There are many services available to track fund performance, the best-known of which is Chicago-based Morningstar Inc.

Morningstar provides data on mutual fund expenses, management objectives, major investments, and historical returns. The company also provides the well-known "star" rating for funds—one to five stars according to performance. In advertisements, fund companies love to tout high Morningstar ratings. But as with any type of numeric or thumbs-up-thumbs-down rating, you should look beyond the rating to learn more about the fund before you invest.

Tips for Online Investing

Source: Securities and Exchange Commission

Every day, more and more Americans are investing in the stock market and many of them are doing so through the Internet. Online brokerages account for approximately 25% of all retail stock trades, and the number of online brokerage accounts is expected to exceed 10 million by the end of 1999.

The price of some stocks, especially recent "hot" IPOs and high-tech stocks, can soar and drop suddenly. In these fast markets, when many investors want to trade at the same time and prices change quickly, delays can develop across the board. Executions and confirmations slow down, while reports of prices lag behind actual prices. In these markets, investors can suffer unexpected losses very quickly.

Investors trading over the Internet, who are used to instant access to their accounts and near instantaneous executions of their trades, especially need to understand how they can protect themselves in fast-moving markets.

Trading is quick, investing takes time

With a click of the mouse, you can buy and sell stocks from more than 100 online brokers offering executions as low as $5 per transaction. Although online trading saves investors time and money, it does not take the homework out of making investment decisions. You may be able to make a trade in a nanosecond, but making wise investment decisions takes time. Before you trade, know why you are buying or selling, and the risk of your investment.

Set price limits

To avoid buying or selling a stock at a price higher or lower than you wanted, you need to place a limit order rather than a market order. A limit order is an order to buy or sell a security at a specific price. A buy limit order can only be executed at the limit price or lower, and a sell limit order can only be executed at the limit price or higher. When you place a market order, you can't control the price at which your order will be filled.

For example, if you want to buy a stock of a "hot" IPO that was initially offered at $9, but don't want to end up paying more than $20 for the stock, you can place a limit order to buy the stock at any price up to $20. By entering a limit order rather than a market order, you will not be caught buying the stock at $90 and then suffering immediate losses as the stock drops later in the day or in the weeks ahead.

Remember that your limit order may never be executed because the market price may quickly surpass your limit before your order can be filled. But by using a limit order you also protect yourself from buying the stock at too high a price.

What if you can't access your account?

Most online trading firms offer alternatives for placing trades. These alternatives may include touch-tone telephone trades, faxing your order, or doing it the low-tech way—talking to a broker over the phone. Make sure you know whether using these different options may increase your costs. And remember, if you experience delays getting online, you may experience similar delays when you turn to one of these alternatives.

Don't assume your order didn't go through

Some investors have mistakenly assumed that their orders have not been executed and place another order. They end up owning either twice as much stock as they could afford or wanted, or with sell orders, selling a stock they do not own. Talk with your firm about how you should handle a situation where you are unsure if your original order was executed.

Make sure your cancel order worked

When you cancel an online trade, it is important to make sure that your original transaction was not executed. Although you may receive an electronic receipt for the cancellation, don't assume that it means the trade was canceled. Orders can only be canceled if they have not been executed. Ask your firm about how you should check to see if a cancellation order actually worked.

A word about margin trades

Now is the time to reread your margin agreement and pay attention to the fine print. If your account has fallen below the firm's maintenance margin requirement, your broker has the legal right to sell your securities at any time without consulting you first. Some investors have been rudely surprised that "margin calls" are a courtesy, not a requirement. Brokers are not required to make margin calls to their customers.

Even when your broker offers you time to put more cash or securities into your account to meet a margin call, the broker can act without waiting for you to meet the call. In a rapidly declining market, your broker can sell your entire margin account at a substantial loss to you, because the securities in the account have declined in value.

There is no time limit to make a trade

There are no Securities and Exchange Commission regulations that require a trade to be executed within a set period of time. But if firms advertise their speed of execution, they must not exaggerate or fail to tell investors about the possibility of significant delays.

If you have a complaint

Act promptly. By law, you only have a limited time to take legal action. Follow these steps to solve your problem:

1. Talk to your broker or online firm and ask for an explanation. Take notes.
2. If you are dissatisfied with the response and believe you have been treated unfairly, ask to talk with the broker's branch manager. In the case of an online firm, go directly to step number three.
3. If you are still dissatisfied, write to the compliance department at the firm's main office. Explain your problem clearly, and tell the firm how you want it resolved. Ask the compliance office to respond in writing within 30 days.
4. If you're still dissatisfied, then send a letter of complaint to the National Association of Securities Dealers, your state securities administrator, or to the Office of Investor Education and Assistance at the SEC along with copies of the letters you've already sent to the firm. □

Glossary of Financial Terms

Adjusted gross income Amount of income which is subject to federal income tax. In addition to any other tax credits, contributions to IRAs and 401(k) plans are subtracted from the total, so that the adjusted gross income will be lower, as will the amount of tax paid.

Aggressive Relating or referring to an investment philosophy that seeks above-average returns by accepting above-average risk.

American Stock Exchange (AMEX) The second-largest exchange in the U.S., specializing in small-to-medium-size companies.

Annuity Contract issued by a life insurance company that promises to make periodic payments to the buyer over a set period of time. Payments are made to individuals, referred to as annuitants.

Appreciation An increase in value of an asset.

Balanced fund A type of mutual fund that spreads its investments among stocks and bonds. Essentially, a balanced fund is a middle-of-the-road fund that balances its portfolio to achieve both moderate income and moderate capital growth.

Bear market An extended period of general price declines in the securities market.

Bellwether A stock whose performance is indicative of the overall market direction.

Blue chip A very high-quality investment involving a lower-than-average risk of loss of principal or reduction in income.

Bond A long-term promissory note that obligates the borrower to make specified payments over a set period of time.

Bull market An extended period of general price increases in the securities market.

Capital gain The excess by which proceeds from the sale of a capital asset exceeds the cost.

Capitalization The company's stock price per share multiplied by the total number of shares outstanding. **Small-cap:** less than $1.5 billion. **Mid-cap:** between $1.5 billion and $10 billion. **Large-cap:** over $10 billion.

Certificate of deposit (CD) A receipt for a deposit of funds in a financial institution that permits the holder to receive interest plus the deposit at maturity.

Commercial paper A short-term unsecured promissory note issued by a finance company or a large industrial firm. Commonly found in money market funds.

Common stock A class of stock that has no preference as to dividends or any distribution of assets.

Compound interest Interest paid on interest from previous periods in addition to principal.

Consumer price index (CPI) A measure of the average change over time in the prices paid by urban consumers for a fixed "market basket" of day-to-day expenses.

Correction Reverse movement in the price of an individual stock, bond, commodity, or index after any long-term move. Can be a movement up or down, but usually refers to a fall in the price.

Diversification Minimizing risk by investing in a wide range of securities invested in many industries.

Dividend A share of a company's net profits distributed to a class of its stockholders.

Dollar-cost averaging Investment of an equal amount of money at regular intervals resulting in the purchase of more shares during market downturns and fewer shares during market upturns.

Dow Jones Industrial Average (DJIA) A widely quoted measure of stock market price movements of 30 large, seasoned industrial firms.

Earnings Income of a business, typically after-tax income, but it may refer to before-tax income or revenues.

Earnings per share The amount a stock will pay in income or dividends.

Emerging growth stock The common stock of a relatively young firm operating in an industry with very good growth prospects. This kind of stock offers unusually high returns and a high risk.

Emerging market Market in a country that does not have a fully developed economy. Investments in these markets are usually characterized by a high level of risk and possibility of a high return.

Federal funds Reserve balances above those required that are maintained by commercial banks in the Federal Reserve System.

Federal Reserve Board The seven governing members of the Federal Reserve System who determine the country's monetary policy.

Federal Reserve System The independent central bank that influences the U.S.'s supply of money and credit through its control of bank reserves.

Fixed annuity Annuity that guarantees fixed payments to the annuitant, either for life or for a set period of time.

401(k) plan Plan in which employees elect to contribute pretax dollars to a qualified, tax-deferred investment plan.

Global fund A mutual fund that includes at least 25% foreign securities in its portfolio.

Gross national product (GNP) The dollar output of final goods and services in the economy during a period of time.

Growth stock The stock of a firm that is expected to have above-average increases in revenues and earnings. These firms normally retain most of their earnings for reinvestment and therefore pay small dividends. Growth stocks tend to have dividend yields below that of the market average, valuation levels above the market average, and volatility above the market average. A growth fund will tend to have a greater amount of portfolio turnover (purchases and sales).

Hedge fund A very specialized, volatile investment company (mutual fund) that permits the manager to use a variety of investment techniques normally prohibited in other types of funds.

Income fund An investment company (mutual fund) whose main objective is to achieve current income for its owners; typically, the fund purchases bonds, preferred stocks, and common stocks paying high dividends.

Index Statistical composite that measures changes in the economy or in financial markets and that can be expressed in percent changes from a base year or from the previous month. Most common are the S&P and the Dow Jones Industrial Average.

Index fund A mutual fund that keeps a portfolio of securities designed to match the performance of a certain market as a whole.

Individual Retirement Account (IRA) A custodial account or trust in which individuals may set aside earned income in a tax-deferred retirement plan.

Initial Public Offering (IPO) The first sale of a corporation's stock to the investing public.

International fund A mutual fund that invests only outside the country in which it is located.

Junk bonds Debt issued by a company whose credit rating is below investment grade (BBB for S&P and Baa for Moody's). Because there is a considerable risk, the company must offer a high coupon to make the bond attractive to an investor.

Keogh plan A federally approved retirement program that permits self-employed people to set aside for savings up to $30,000 or 25% of their income, whichever is lower.

Large-capitalization stock The stock of a big company that has considerable retained earnings and a large amount of common stock outstanding, typically a market capitalization of over $3 billion.

Liquid asset A security that can easily be sold for cash.

Load The sales fee that the buyer pays in order to acquire a security, typically a mutual fund.

Long-term bonds Debt securities with maturities of 10 to 30 years. The benchmark for this asset class is the Lehman Government Long Bond Index.

Market capitalization The total value of all of a firm's outstanding shares, calculated by multiplying the market price per share times the total number of shares outstanding.

Money market fund A mutual fund that purchases short-term, high-quality securities such as treasury bills, negotiable CDs, and commercial paper.

Money market securities Low-risk, very liquid securities with maturities of one year or less. Other short-term debt that is scheduled to mature within one year may also be classified as money market securities.

Moody's A company rating service issuing ratings denoting the relative investment quality of corporate and municipal bonds.

Mutual fund An investment company that continually offers new shares and stands ready to redeem existing shares from the owners. Also an investment company.

NASDAQ The NASD's Automated Quotation marketplace, which trades shares electronically. Companies traded on the NASDAQ include many small-to-medium-size firms and many technology companies.

National Association of Securities Dealers Self-regulatory organization of broker-dealers operating under the auspices of the Securities and Exchange Commission.

Net Asset Value (NAV) The market value of an investment company's (mutual fund) asset less any liabilities divided by the number of shares outstanding. This is the value of each share if the fund sold all of its assets at their current market value and paid off any outstanding debts.

Net income Income after all expenses and taxes have been deducted.

New York Stock Exchange The oldest and most established stock exchange in the U.S., located at 11 Wall Street in New York City. Companies traded on the NYSE are typically the largest in the U.S.

No-load fund An open-end investment company (mutual fund), shares of which are sold without a sales charge.

Option A contract that permits the owner, depending on the contract, to purchase or sell a security at a fixed price until a specific date.

Over-the-counter stock Stock that is traded outside of an organized exchange, usually through telephone or electronic connections.

Preferred stock A security that shows ownership in a corporation and gives the holder a claim prior to the claim of common stockholders on earnings and also generally on assets in the event of liquidation.

Price/earnings ratio Price of a stock divided by its earnings per share.

Profit-sharing plan An agreement that allows employees to share in the corporation's profit. The company makes annual contributions to a profit-sharing fund, which is invested in stocks, bonds, or cash, and generally accumulate tax-free until the employee retires or leaves the company. Do not confuse this plan with investments of 401(k) money in a company's stock.

Prospectus A formally written document relating to a new securities offering that delineates the proposed business plan or the data relevant to an existing business plan, i.e., information necessary to make an educated decision to purchase a security or not.

Sector fund An investment company that concentrates its holdings among securities or other assets sharing a common interest.

Small-cap stocks The stock of a relatively small firm with little equity and few shares of common stock outstanding. Small-capitalization stocks tend to be subject to large fluctuations; therefore, the potential for short-term gains and losses is great.

Standard & Poor's 500 (S&P 500) An inclusive index of 500 stocks, including 400 industrial stocks, 40 utilities, 20 transportation stocks, and 40 financial stocks.

Stock An ownership share(s) in a corporation; also equity, common stock. See also **Preferred stock.**

Treasuries All bonds backed by the U.S. government that are issued through the Department of the Treasury.

Treasury bill A short-term debt security of the U.S. government that is sold in minimum amounts of $10,000 increments and multiples of $5,000 above this.

Yield to maturity The total return an investor will get by holding a long-term, interest-bearing instrument (usually a bond) until it matures.

Source: 401 Kafé, www.401kafe.com. Copyright © 1996–2000 mPower. All Rights Reserved.

The Nitty-Gritty of Mortgage Shopping

Source: The Federal Interagency Task Force on Fair Lending

A mortgage—whether it's a home purchase, a refinancing, or a home equity loan—is a product, just like a car, so the price and terms may be negotiable. You'll want to compare all the costs involved in obtaining a mortgage so that you can negotiate for the best deal. Different lenders may quote you different prices, so you should contact several lenders to make sure that you are getting the best price. You can also get a home loan through a mortgage broker. Brokers arrange transactions rather than lending money directly; in other words, they find a lender for you. Brokers are not obligated to find the best deal for you unless they have contracted with you to act as your agent. Consequently, you should consider contacting more than one broker just as you should do with banks and thrift institutions.

Whether you are dealing with a lender or a broker may not always be clear. Some financial institutions operate as both lenders and brokers. And most brokers' advertisements do not use the word *broker*. Therefore, be sure to ask whether a broker is involved. This information is important because brokers are usually paid a fee for their services that may be separate from and in addition to the lender's origination or other fees.

A broker's compensation may be in the form of "points" at closing or as an add-on to your interest rate, or both. You should ask each broker you work with how he or she will be compensated so that you can compare the different fees. Be prepared to negotiate with the brokers as well as the lenders.

Cost Information You Need

Know how much of a down payment you can afford, and find out all the costs involved in the loan. Knowing just the amount of the monthly payment or the interest rate is not enough. Ask for information about the same loan amount, loan term, and type of loan so that you can compare the information.

Rates. Ask each lender and broker for a list of their current mortgage interest rates and whether the rates being quoted are the lowest for that day or week. Ask whether the rate is fixed or adjustable. Keep in mind that when interest rates for adjustable-rate loans go up, generally so does the monthly payment. If the rate quoted is for an adjustable-rate loan, ask how your rate and loan payment will vary, including whether your loan payment will be reduced when rates go down.

Ask about the loan's annual percentage rate (APR). The APR takes into account not only the interest rate but also points, broker fees, and certain other credit charges that you may be required to pay, expressed as a yearly rate.

Points. Points are fees paid to the lender or broker for the loan and are often linked to the interest rate; usually the more points you pay, the lower the rate. Check your local newspaper for information about rates and points currently being offered. Also ask for points to be quoted to you as a dollar amount—rather than just as the number of points—so that you will actually know how much you will have to pay.

Fees. A home loan often involves many fees, such as loan origination or underwriting fees, broker fees, and transaction, settlement, and closing costs. Every lender or broker should be able to give you an estimate of its fees. Many of these fees are negotiable. Some fees are paid when you apply for a loan (such as application and appraisal fees), and others are paid at closing. In some cases, you can borrow the money needed to pay these fees, but doing so will increase your loan amount and total costs. "No cost" loans are sometimes available, but they usually involve higher rates. Inquire as to what each fee includes. Several items may be lumped into one fee. Ask for an explanation of any fee you do not understand.

Down Payments and Mortgage Insurance

Some lenders require 20 percent of the home's purchase price as a down payment. However, many lenders now offer loans that require less than 20 percent down—sometimes as little as five percent on conventional loans. If a 20 percent down payment is not made, lenders usually require the home buyer to purchase private mortgage insurance (PMI) to protect the lender in case the home buyer fails to pay. When government-assisted programs such as FHA (Federal Housing Administration), VA (Veterans Administration), or Rural Development Services are available, the down payment requirements may be substantially smaller.

Ask about the lender's requirements for a down payment, including what you need to do to verify that funds for your down payment are available. Ask your lender about special programs it may offer. If PMI is required for your loan, find out how much your monthly payment will be including the PMI premium. Ask how long you will be required to carry this insurance.

Negotiate the Best Deal

On any given day, lenders and brokers may offer different prices for the same loan terms to different consumers, even if those consumers have the same loan qualifications. The most likely reason for this difference in price is that loan officers and brokers are often allowed to keep some or all of this difference as extra compensation. Generally, the difference between the lowest available price for a loan product and any higher price that the borrower agrees to pay is called an *overage*. When overages occur, they are built into the prices quoted to consumers. They can occur in both fixed and variable-rate loans and can be in the form of points, fees, or the interest rate. Whether quoted to you by a loan officer or a broker, the price of any loan may contain overages.

Have the lender or broker write down all the costs associated with the loan. Then ask if the lender or broker will waive or reduce one or more of its fees or agree to a lower rate or fewer points. You'll want to make sure that the lender or the broker is not agreeing to lower one fee while raising another or to lower the rate while raising points. There's no harm in asking the lender or broker for better terms than the ones originally quoted.

Once you are satisfied with the terms you have negotiated, you may want to obtain a written lock-in from the lender or broker. The lock-in should include the rate that you have agreed upon, the period the lock-in lasts, and the number of points to be paid. A fee may be charged for locking in the loan rate. This fee may be refundable at closing. Lock-ins can protect you from rate increases while your loan is being processed; if rates fall, however, you could end up with a less favorable rate. Should that happen, try to negotiate a compromise with the lender or broker. □

Credit Card Use, 1989–1995

General-purpose credit cards include Mastercard, Visa, Optima, and Discover. All dollar figures are given in constant 1995 dollars based on consumer price index data as published by the U.S. Bureau of Labor Statistics.

Age of family head and family income[1]	Percent having a general-purpose credit card	Percent having a balance after last month's bills	Median balance[2]	Percent of cardholding families who:		
				Almost always pay off the balance	Sometimes pay off the balance	Hardly ever pay off the balance
1989, total	55.8%	52.0%	$1,200	53.1%	21.5%	25.4%
1992, total	62.2	52.8	1,100	52.8	19.6	27.6
1995, total	**66.4**	**56.3**	**1,500**	**51.9**	**20.4**	**27.7**
Under 35 years old	59.0	69.2	1,500	40.2	23.5	36.3
35 to 44 years old	68.5	68.1	1,900	40.7	26.9	32.4
45 to 54 years old	75.4	64.8	1,800	47.1	22.5	30.4
55 to 64 years old	71.9	48.0	1,800	59.3	18.4	22.3
65 to 74 years old	68.3	30.8	800	72.0	12.9	15.1
75 years old and over	54.6	18.2	700	85.8	2.5	11.7
Less than $10,000	26.3	55.8	1,000	56.4	12.4	31.2
$10,000 to $24,999	53.3	57.0	1,500	50.9	17.2	31.9
$25,000 to $49,999	75.0	59.2	1,500	47.6	20.9	31.5
$50,000 to $99,999	93.1	59.4	2,000	49.7	25.3	25.1
$100,000 and more	97.1	35.4	2,100	73.7	17.2	9.1

1. Families include one-person units. 2. Among families having a balance. *Source:* Board of Governors of the Federal Reserve System, *Statistical Abstract of the U.S., 1997;* www.census.gov/statab/www/.

How to Measure the Shrinking Value of the Dollar

Source: Martin Lefkowitz, economist, U.S. Chamber of Commerce

How to use this table. This table provides a method for translating dollar values from the past 52 years into 1998 dollars. For example: What weekly salary would you need to earn in 1998 to equal the purchasing power of a weekly salary of $100 in 1970? Take the 1970 multiplier, 4.20, times $100 and you would need to earn $420 a week in 1998 to achieve the same salary.

Year	Value of dollar in 1998 dollars	Year	Value of dollar in 1998 dollars	Year	Value of dollar in 1998 dollars
1946	$8.36	1964	$5.26	1982	$1.69
1947	7.00	1965	5.17	1983	1.64
1948	6.76	1966	5.03	1984	1.57
1949	6.85	1967	4.88	1985	1.51
1950	6.76	1968	4.68	1986	1.49
1951	6.27	1969	4.44	1987	1.43
1952	6.15	1970	4.20	1988	1.38
1953	6.10	1971	4.02	1989	1.31
1954	6.06	1972	3.90	1990	1.25
1955	6.08	1973	3.67	1991	1.20
1956	5.99	1974	3.31	1992	1.16
1957	5.80	1975	3.03	1993	1.13
1958	5.64	1976	2.86	1994	1.10
1959	5.60	1977	2.69	1995	1.07
1960	5.51	1978	2.50	1996	1.04
1961	5.45	1979	2.25	1997	1.02
1962	5.40	1980	1.98	1998	1.00
1963	5.33	1981	1.79		

National Consumer Organizations

NOTE: For other organizations, *see* Societies & Associations, pp. 474–483.

Alliance Against Fraud In Telemarketing & Electronic Commerce (AAFTEC), c/o National Consumers League, 1701 K St. N.W., Suite 1200, Washington, D.C. 20006; 202-835-3323; 202-835-0747 (fax).

The alliance was formed by the National Consumers League to raise public awareness about fraudulent telephone solicitations. With the increasing use of the Internet and online services for marketing, the alliance now also focuses on scams in cyberspace. AAFTEC members from the areas of government, law enforcement, consumer advocacy, and businesses are united in their commitment to combat telemarketing and Internet fraud through consumer education.

American Association of Retired Persons (AARP), Consumer Affairs Section, 601 E St. N.W., Washington, D.C. 20049; 800-424-3410; Web: www.aarp.org.

AARP's Consumer Affairs Section advocates on behalf of mid-life and older consumers, develops and distributes consumer information, and educates the private sector about the specific needs of older consumers. It offers programs and materials on housing, insurance, funeral practices, eligibility for public benefits, financial security, transportation, and consumer protection issues, with special focus on the needs and problems of older consumers.

American Council on Consumer Interests (ACCI), 240 Stanley Hall, University of Missouri, Columbia, Mo. 65211-0001; 573-882-3817; 573-884-6571 (fax); Web: www.consumerinterests.org.

A nonprofit organization dedicated to providing research-based information on topics of consumer interest. Provides information about consumer publications, policies, and resources.

American Council on Science and Health (ACSH), 1995 Broadway, 2nd Fl., New York, N.Y. 10023-5860; 212-362-7044; 212-362-4919 (fax); Web: www.acsh.org.

A consumer education consortium concerned with issues related to food, nutrition, chemicals, pharmaceuticals, lifestyle, the environment, and health. Booklets and special reports on a variety of topics are available, as is a quarterly magazine, *Priorities.*

American Savings Education Council, 2121 K Street N.W., Suite 600, Washington, D.C. 20037; 202-659-0670; Web: www.asec.org.

The council is a coalition of private and public sector institutions that undertakes initiatives to raise public awareness about what is needed to ensure long-term personal financial independence.

Center for Auto Safety (CAS), 1825 Connecticut Ave. N.W., Suite 3301, Washington, D.C. 20009; 202-328-7700; Web: www.autosafety.org.

Founded by Consumers Union and Ralph Nader in 1970 to provide consumers a voice for auto safety and quality in Washington and to help lemon owners fight back across the country.

Center for Science in the Public Interest (CSPI), 1875 Connecticut Ave., N.W. Suite 300, Washington, D.C. 20009; 202-332-9110; 202-265-4954 (fax); Web: www.cspinet.org.

A nonprofit membership organization, CSPI provides research, education, and advocacy on nutrition, health, food safety, and related issues, and publishes the monthly *Nutrition Action Healthletter* as well as other consumer materials.

Center for the Study of Services, 733 15th Street N.W., Washington, D.C. 20005; 202-347-7283; Web: www.checkbook.org.

Nonprofit organization publishes books and pamphlets to help consumers select doctors, hospitals, and health plans. Publishes pamphlets and offers services to help consumers get good prices on new cars. Also publishes information and maintains online database to help consumers shop for good prices and desired features in big-ticket products—audio-video, major appliances, sporting good tires, home office, etc.

Coalition Against Insurance Fraud, 1010 Vermont Ave. N.W., Suite 817, Washington, D.C.; 202-393-7330; Web: www.insurancefraud.org.

An independent nonprofit organization of consumers, government agencies, and insurers dedicated to combating all forms of insurance fraud through public information and advocacy.

Community Nutrition Institute (CNI), 910 17th Street N.W., Suite 413, Washington, D.C. 20006; 202-776-0595; Web: www.unidial.com/~cni.

An advocate for programs and services to enable consumers to enjoy a diet that is adequate, safe, and healthy. CNI also works to increase citizen participation in the state and federal policy and administrative processes to achieve these goals. CNI publishes *Nutrition Week,* a newsletter covering nutrition and food safety issues, as well as related legislative and regulatory actions.

Congress Watch, 215 Pennsylvania Ave. S.E., Washington, D.C. 20003; 202-546-4996; Web: www.citizen.org.

An arm of Public Citizen, Congress Watch champions consumer and citizen interest before the U.S. Congress. The organization works for consumer-related legislation,

---

The Consumer Action Handbook

Source: U.S. Office of Consumer Affairs

The *2001 Consumer Action Handbook,* published by the Federal Consumer Information Center, is 148 pages of valuable information that no consumer should be without. It provides advice on car repair, purchase and leasing, shopping from home, avoiding consumer and investment fraud, home improvement and financing, and much more. Also included is the *Consumer Assistance Directory* with thousands of useful names, addresses, phone numbers, and Web sites.

Single copies of the *Consumer Action Handbook* are available free by writing to: Handbook, Federal Consumer Information Center, Pueblo, Colo. 81009, or by calling 1-800-688-9889. The handbook can also be viewed and ordered on the FCIC Web site: www.pueblo.gsa.gov.

---

regulation, and policies in such areas as health and safety, and campaign financing. Publications are available on the issues with which it deals.

Consumer Action (CA), 717 Market St., Suite 310, San Francisco, Calif. 94103; 415-777-9635 (consumer complaint hotline); 415-777-9456 (voice/ttd); Web: consumer-action.org.

An education and advocacy organization specializing in credit, finance, and telecommunications issues, Consumer Action offers a multilingual consumer complaint hotline, free information on its surveys of banks and long-distance telephone companies, and consumer education materials in as many as eight languages.

Consumer Alert, 1001 Connecticut Ave. N.W., Suite 1128, Washington, D.C. 20036; 202-467-5809; 202-467-5814 (fax); Web: www.consumeralert.org.

Consumer Alert is a nonprofit, nonpartisan membership organization whose mission is to inform the public about the consumer benefits of competitive enterprise, and promote sound economic, scientific, and risk data on public policy decisions. A bimonthly newsletter and other materials are available.

Consumer Federation of America (CFA), 1424 16th St. N.W., Suite 604, Washington, D.C. 20036; 202-387-6121; Web: www.consumerfed.org.

Made up of more than 260 organizations representing over 50 million consumers, CFA is a consumer advocacy and education organization. CFA focuses much of its advocacy in the areas of financial service, utilities, product safety, transportation, health care, and food safety. It develops and distributes studies of various consumer issues, as well as consumer guides in book and pamphlet form, and a newsletter.

Consumers Union of U.S., Inc. (CU), 101 Truman Ave., Yonkers, N.Y. 10703-1057; 914-378-2000; Web: www.consumersunion.org.

A nonprofit, independent testing and information organization serving only consumers, CU researches and tests consumer goods and services and disseminates the results in its monthly magazine, *Consumer Reports,* as well as other publications and media.

Families USA Foundation, 1334 G St. N.W., Washington, D.C. 20005; 202-628-3030; Web: www.familiesusa.org.

A national nonprofit, nonpartisan consumer advocacy membership organization, Families USA is dedicated to the achievement of high-quality, affordable health and long-term care for all Americans.

Global Trade Watch (GTW), 215 Pennsylvania Ave. S.E., Washington, D.C. 20003; 202-546-4996; Web: www.tradewatch.org.

A division of Public Citizen headquartered at Public Citizen's Pennsylvania address, Global Trade Watch leads the way in educating the American public about the enormous impact of international trade and economic globalization on jobs, the environment, public health and safety, and democratic accountability.

HALT: An Organization of Americans for Legal Reform, 1612 K Street N.W., Suite 510, Washington, D.C. 20006; 202-887-8255, toll-free: 1-888-367-4258; 202-347-2417 (fax); Web: www.halt.org

HALT's mission is to enable Americans to handle their legal affairs affordably, equitably, and simply. HALT publishes a series of self-help legal manuals, operates a legal information clearinghouse, and advocates for legal reforms that will benefit consumers.

Health Research Group (HRG), 1600 20th St. N.W., Washington, D.C. 20009; 202-885-1000; Web: www.citizen.org/hrg.

A division of Public Citizen, HRG works for protection against unsafe foods, drugs, medical devices, and workplaces, and advocates for greater consumer control over personal health decisions. A monthly *Health Letter* and other publications are available.

Jump$tart Coalition for Personal Financial Literacy, 919 18th Street N.W., Washington, D.C. 20006; 202-466-8604, toll-free: 1-888-338-2283; Web: www.jumpstart.org.

The coalition's direct objective is to encourage curriculum enrichment to ensure that basic personal financial management skills are attained during the K–12 educational experience.

National Association of Consumer Agency Administrators (NACAA), 1010 Vermont Ave. N.W., Suite 514, Washington, D.C. 20005; 202-347-7395; Web: www.nacaanet.org.

A nonprofit association for administrators of government consumer protection agencies. NACAA members work directly with consumers to solve problems, advance relevant legislation, and support consumer outreach and education.

National Association of State Utility Consumer Advocates (NASUCA), 1133 15th St ,N.W. Suite 550, Washington, D.C. 20005; 202-727-3908; Web: www.nasuca.org.

A national organization of 41 advocate offices in 39 states and the District of Columbia, NASUCA members represent millions of consumers served by investor-owned gas, telephone, electric, and water companies. Its members represent the concerns of utility consumers by testifying before Congress.

National Coalition for Consumer Education (NCCE), c/o National Consumers League, 1701 K Street N.W., Suite 1200, Washington, D.C. 20006; 202-835-3323; Web: www.lifesmarts.org.

NCCE is a coalition coordinated by the National Consumers League. It develops and provides educational materials and resources to consumer educators through a network of state coordinators. The coalition sponsors LifeSmarts, an educational game that develops the consumer and marketplace knowledge and skill of teenagers in a fun way. LifeSmarts is open to all teens in the United States in the 9th through 12th grades.

National Community Reinvestment Coalition (NCRC), 733 15th Street N.W., Suite 540, Washington, D.C. 20005; 202-628-9800; Web: www.ncrc.org.

NCRC was founded in 1990 with the goal of ending discriminatory banking practices, and increasing the flow of private capital and credit into underserved communities across the country. NCRC has over 600 members in every state and major city in America as well as in many smaller cities and rural areas.

Better Business Bureaus

Better Business Bureaus (BBBs) are nonprofit organizations supported primarily by local business members. BBBs offer a variety of consumer services including educational materials, information on charities and other organizations seeking public donations, and mediation and arbitration services. If you need help with a consumer question or complaint, call your local BBB to ask about its services, or contact the BBB online at www.bbb.org.

National Consumer Law Center (NCLC), 18 Tremont Street, Boston, Mass. 02108; 617-523-8010; Web: www.consumerlaw.org.

NCLC is an advocacy and research organization focusing on the needs of low-income consumers. It represents the interests of consumers in court, before administrative agencies, and before legislatures. The center also publishes *Surviving Debt: A Guide for Consumers* and the Consumer Credit and Sales Legal Practice series, consisting of thirteen desk reference manuals for attorneys.

National Consumers League (NCL), 1701 K St., N.W. Suite 1201, Washington, D.C. 20006; 202-835-3323; Web: nclnet.org.

Founded in 1899, NCL is America's pioneer consumer advocacy organization. The league is a nonprofit membership organization working for consumer health and safety protection and fairness in the marketplace and workplace. NCL provides government, businesses, and other organizations with the consumer's perspective on concerns including child labor, privacy on the Internet, food safety, and medication information. The league develops and distributes consumer education materials and newsletters.

National Foundation for Consumer Credit, Inc. (NFCC), Web: www.nfcc.org.

The NFCC is a national nonprofit network of 1,450 neighborhood Financial Care Centers™ designed to provide assistance dealing with stressful financial situations.

National Fraud Information Center/Internet Fraud Watch (NFIC/IFW), P.O. Box 65868, Washington, D.C. 20035; 800-876-7060, TDD/TTY: 202-835-0778; Web: www.fraud.org.

A project of the National Consumers League, the center's toll-free hotline assists consumers with advice on avoiding telemarketing fraud and online and Internet fraud, and assists them in filing complaints.

National Institute for Consumer Education (NICE), 559 Gary M. Owen Bldg., 300 W. Michigan Ave., Ypsilanti, Mich. 48197; 734-487-2292; 734-487-7153 (fax); Web: www.nice.emich.edu.

A consumer education resource and professional development center for K–12 classroom teachers and business, government, labor, and community educators, NICE conducts training programs, develops teaching guides and resource lists, and manages a national clearinghouse of consumer education materials, including videos, software programs, textbooks, and curriculum guides.

National Senior Citizens Law Center, 1101 14th St. N.W. Suite 400, Washington, D.C. 20005; 202-289-6976; Web: www.nsclc.org.

The National Senior Citizens Law Center (NSCLC) was established in 1972 to help older Americans live their lives in dignity and freedom from poverty. NSCLC works with legal services offices and senior organizations throughout the U.S. to provide quality service and advice.

Public Citizen, Inc., 1600 20th St. N.W., Washington, D.C. 20009; 202-885-1000; Web: www.citizen.org.

A national nonprofit membership organization. Public Citizen represents consumer interests in Congress, the courts, government agencies, and the media. Primary current areas of interest include product liability, health-care delivery, safe medical devices and medications, open and ethical government, and safe and sustainable energy use.

Public Voice for Food and Health Policy, 1012 14th St. N.W., Suite 800, Washington, D.C. 20005; 202-347-6200; Web: www.publicvoicedc.com.

A national nonprofit research, education, and advocacy organization that looks at food and agriculture policy from a consumer perspective. Public Voice promotes a safer, healthier, and more affordable food supply.

United Seniors Health Cooperative (USHC), 409 Third Street S.W., Suite 200, Washington, D.C. 20024; 202-479-6973; Web: www.ushc-online.org.

USHC is a nonprofit membership organization that provides consumer-tested information to help seniors achieve good health, independence, and financial security. Publications include books on long-term care planning, managing health-care finances, and choosing an HMO. Professionals working with low-income persons of all ages will find USHC's benefit-screening software valuable for a quick, comprehensive determination of a person's eligibility for public benefits and assistance programs.

U.S. Public Interest Research Group (U.S. PIRG), 218 D St. S.E., Washington, D.C. 20003; 202-546-9707; Web: www.pirg.org.

The PIRGs are state-based advocates for the public interest that lobby and publish reports on issues such as the environment, product safety, and financial privacy and identity theft.

Copyrights

Source: Excerpted from *Copyright Basics (Circular 1),* U.S. Copyright Office

Copyright is a form of protection provided by the laws of the United States to the creators of "original works of authorship," including literary, dramatic, musical, artistic, and certain other intellectual works. This protection is available to both published and unpublished works. The 1976 Copyright Act generally gives the owner of copyright the exclusive right to do and to authorize others to do the following:

• to reproduce the copyrighted work in copies or phonorecords;

• to prepare derivative works based upon the copyrighted work;

• to distribute copies or phonorecords of the copyrighted work to the public by sale or other transfer of ownership, or by rental, lease, or lending;

• to perform the copyrighted work publicly;

• to display the copyrighted work publicly; and

• in the case of sound recordings, to perform the work publicly by means of a digital audio transmission.

It is illegal for anyone to violate these rights. However, these rights are not unlimited in scope. In some cases they are limited by the doctrine of "fair use," or by a "compulsory license" under which certain limited uses of copyrighted works are permitted in exchange for payment. For further information about the limitations of any of these rights, consult the Copyright Law or write to the Copyright Office.

Copyright protection exists from the time the work is created in fixed form. The copyright in the work of authorship immediately becomes the property of the author who created it. Only the property of the author, or those deriving their rights through the author, can rightfully claim copyright.

In the case of works made for hire, the employer and not the employee is considered the author.

The authors of a joint work are co-owners of the copyright in the work, unless there is an agreement to the contrary.

Copyright in each separate contribution to a periodical or other collective work is distinct from copyright in the collective work as a whole and vests initially with the author of the contribution.

Two General Principles:

• Mere ownership of a book, manuscript, painting, or any other copy or phonorecord does not give the possessor the copyright. The law provides that transfer of ownership of any material object that embodies a protected work does not of itself convey any rights in the copyright.

• Minors may claim copyright, but state laws may regulate the business dealings involving copyrights owned by minors. For information on relevant state laws, consult an attorney.

Copyright is secured automatically when the work is created, and a work is "created" when it is fixed in a copy or phonorecord for the first time. "Copies" are material objects from which a work can be read or visually perceived, such as books, manuscripts, sheet music, film, videotape, or microfilm. "Phonorecords" are material objects embodying fixations of sounds (excluding, by statutory definition, motion picture soundtracks), such as cassette tapes, CDs, or LPs. Thus, for example, a song (the "work") can be fixed in sheet music ("copies") or in phonograph disks ("phonorecords"), or both. If a work is prepared over a period of time, the part of the work that is fixed on a particular date constitutes the created work as of that date.

Copyright protection is available for all unpublished works, regardless of the nationality or domicile of the author. Published works are eligible for copyright protection in the United States if any one of the several conditions regarding the nationality of the authors or place of publication is met. Check with the Copyright Office for details.

What Works Are Protected

Copyright protects "original works of authorship" that are fixed in a tangible form of expression. The fixation need not be directly perceptible so long as it may be communicated with the aid of a machine or device. Categories include:

• literary works;
• musical works, including any accompanying words;
• dramatic works, including any accompanying music;
• pantomimes and choreographic works;
• pictorial, graphic, and sculptural works;
• motion pictures and other audiovisual works;
• sound recordings; and
• architectural works.

These categories should be viewed quite broadly. For example, computer programs and most "compilations" are registrable as "literary works." Maps and architectural plans are registrable as "pictorial, graphic, and sculptural works."

Several categories of material are generally not eligible for federal copyright protection. These include among others:

• works that have not been fixed in a tangible form of expression. For example, choreographic works that have not been notated or recorded, or improvisational speeches or performances that have not been written or recorded;

• titles, names, short phrases, and slogans; familiar symbols or designs; mere variations of typographic ornamentation, lettering, or coloring; mere listings of ingredients or contents;

• ideas, procedures, methods, systems, processes, concepts, principles, discoveries, or devices, as distinguished from a description, explanation, or illustration;

• works consisting entirely of information that is common property and containing no original authorship. For example, standard calendars, height and weight charts, tape measures and rulers, and lists or tables taken from public documents or other common sources.

Notice of Copyright

The use of a copyright notice is no longer required under U.S. law, although it is often beneficial. Because prior law did contain such a requirement, however, the use of notice is still relevant to the copyright status of older works. Use of the notice may be important because it informs the public that the work is protected by copyright, identifies the copyright owners, and shows the year of first publication.

Furthermore, in the event that a work is infringed, if a proper notice of copyright appears on the published copy or copies to which a defendant in a copyright infringement suit had access, then no weight shall be given to such a defendant's interposition of a defense based on innocent infringement in mitigation of actual or statutory damages, except as provided in section 504(c)(2) of the Copyright Code. Innocent infringement occurs when the infringer did not realize that the work was protected.

The use of the copyright notice is the responsibility of the copyright owner and does not require advance permission from, or registration with, the Copyright Office.

Form of Notice for Visually Perceptible Copies

The notice for visually perceptible copies should contain all of the following three elements:

1. the symbol © (the letter C in a circle), or the word "Copyright," or the abbreviation "Copr.";
2. the year of first publication of the work; and
3. the name of the owner of copyright in the work, or an abbreviation by which the name can be recognized, or a generally known alternative designation of the owner.

Example: © 2001 John Doe

Form of Notice for Sound Recordings

The copyright notice for phonorecords of sound recordings should contain the following three elements:

1. the symbol ℗ (the letter P in a circle);
2. the year of first publication of the sound recording; and
3. the name of the owner of copyright in the sound recording, or an abbreviation by which the name can be recognized, or a generally known alternative designation of the owner. If the producer of the sound recording is named on the phonorecord labels or containers, and if no other name appears in conjunction with the notice, the producer's name shall be considered a part of the notice.

Example: ℗ 2001 A.B.C., Inc.

NOTE: Since questions may arise from the use of variant forms of the notice, you may wish to seek legal advice before using any form of the notice other than those given here.

Position of Notice

The notice should be positioned so as to "give reasonable notice of the claim of copyright." The Copyright Office has issued regulations concerning the form and position of the copyright notice. For more information, contact them directly.

Publications Incorporating United States Government Works

Works by the U.S. Government are not eligible for copyright protection. For works published on or after March 1, 1989, the previous notice requirement for works that consist primarily of one or more works of the U.S. Government has been eliminated. Copies of works published before March 1, 1989, that consist mostly of one or more works of the U.S. Government should have a notice and the accompanying statement. Example:

© 2001 Jane Brown. Copyright claimed in Chapters 7–10, exclusive of U.S. Government maps.

Unpublished Works

The author or other owner of copyright may wish to place a copyright notice on any unpublished copies or phonorecords that leave his or her control. An appropriate notice for an unpublished work is "Unpublished work © 2001 Jane Doe."

Copyright Protection Endurance

Works Originally Created on or after Jan. 1, 1978

A work that is created on or after Jan. 1, 1978, is automatically protected from the moment of its creation, and is ordinarily given a term of the author's life, plus an additional 70 years after the author's death. In the case of a joint work prepared by two or more authors who did not work for hire, the term lasts for 70 years after the last surviving author's death. For works made for hire, and for anonymous and pseudonymous works (unless the author's identity is revealed in Copyright Office records), the duration of copyright will be 95 years from publication or 120 years from creation, whichever is shorter.

Works Originally Created before Jan. 1, 1978

Works that were created but not published or registered for copyright before Jan. 1, 1978, have been automatically brought under the statute and are now given federal copyright protection. The duration of copyright in these works will generally be computed in the same way as for works created on or after Jan. 1, 1978: the life-plus-70 or 95/120-year terms will apply to them as well. The law provides that in no case will the term of copyright for works in this category expire before Dec. 31, 2002, and for works published on or before Dec. 31, 2002, the term of copyright will not expire before Dec. 31, 2047. Works that were created and published or registered before Jan. 1, 1978, generally enjoy a copyright term of 75 years from the date of publication or registration. Check with the Copyright Office for details.

International Copyright Protection

There is no "international copyright" that will automatically protect an author's work throughout the entire world. Protection against unauthorized use in a particular country depends basically on the national laws of that country. However, most countries do offer protection to foreign works under certain conditions, and these conditions have been greatly simplified by international copyright treaties and conventions.

For a list of countries that maintain copyright relations with the United States, request Circular 38a from the Copyright Office.

Copyright Registration

Copyright registration makes a public record of the basic facts of a particular copyright. Even though registration is not a requirement for protection, the copyright law provides several incentives to encourage copyright owners to register. They include the following:

• Registration establishes a public record of the copyright claim;

• Before an infringement suit may be filed in court, registration is necessary for works of U.S. origin;

• If made before or within five years of publication, registration will establish *prima facie* evidence in court of the validity of the copyright and of the facts stated in the certificate;

• If registration is made within three months after publication of the work or prior to an infringement of the work, statutory damages and attorney's fees will be available to the copyright owner in court actions. Otherwise, only an award of actual damages and profits is available to the copyright owner; and

• Copyright registration allows the owner of the copyright to record the registration with the U.S. Customs Service for protection against the importation of infringing copies.

Registration may be made at any time within the life of the copyright. When a work has been registered in unpublished form, it is not necessary to make another registration when the work becomes published (although the copyright owner may register the published edition, if desired).

To register a work, send the following three elements in the same envelope or package to the Registrar of Copyrights, Copyright Office, Library of Congress, 101 Independence Ave., S.E., Washington, D.C. 20559-6000:

1. a properly completed application form;
2. a nonrefundable filing fee of $30 (effective through June 30, 2002) for each application; and
3. a nonreturnable deposit of the work that is being registered. The deposit requirements vary in particular situations. Contact the Copyright Office for current information on fees and special requirements.

A copyright registration is effective on the date the Copyright Office receives all of the required elements in acceptable form, regardless of how long it takes to process the application and mail the certificate of registration. The time the Copyright Office requires to process an application varies, depending on the amount of material the office is receiving. If you apply for copyright registration, you will not receive an acknowledgment that your application has been received, but you can expect a letter or telephone call from a Copyright Office staff member if further information is needed or a certificate of registration indicating that the work has been registered, or if the application cannot be accepted, a letter explaining why it has been rejected.

Requests to have certificates sent by Federal Express or another mail service cannot be honored. If you want to know the date that the Copyright Office receives your material, send it by registered or certified mail and request a return receipt.

For More Information

Information on registration and application forms may be obtained free of charge by writing or calling the Copyright Office. Address inquiries to the Copyright Office, Publications Section, LM-455, Library of Congress, 101 Independence Ave., S.E., Washington, D.C. 20559-6000. To speak with an information specialist, call 202-707-3000 (TTY: 202-707-6737) between 8:30 A.M. and 5:00 P.M., Eastern Time, Monday to Friday, except federal holidays. Recorded information is available 24 hours a day. Or if you know which application forms and circulars you want, request them from the Forms and Publications hotline at 202-707-3000, 24 hours a day. Leave a recorded message.

Copyright information, including the most frequently requested circulars, is available on the Web at www.loc.gov/copyright.

Trademarks

Source: Department of Commerce, Patent and Trademark Office

A trademark may be defined as a word, letter, device, or symbol, as well as any combination of these, that is used in connection with merchandise and that points distinctly to the origin of the goods.

Certificates of registration of trademarks are issued under the seal of the Patent and Trademark Office and may be registered by the owner if he or she is engaged in interstate or foreign commerce. Federal jurisdiction over trademarks arises under the commerce clause of the Constitution. Effective November 16, 1989, applications to register may also be based on a "bona fide intention to use the mark in commerce." Trademarks may be registered by foreign owners who comply with U.S. law, as well as by citizens of foreign countries with which the U.S. has treaties relating to trademarks. American citizens may register trademarks in foreign countries by complying with the laws of those coun-

tries. The right to registration and protection of trademarks in many foreign countries is guaranteed by treaties.

General jurisdiction in trademark cases involving Federal Registrations is given to federal courts. Adverse decisions of examiners on applications for registration are appealable to the Trademark Trial and Appeal Board, whose affirmances and decisions in *inter partes* proceedings are subject to court review. Before adopting a trademark, a person should make a search of prior marks to avoid unwittingly infringing upon them.

The duration of a trademark registration is 10 years, but it may be renewed indefinitely for 10-year periods, provided the trademark is still in use at the time of expiration.

The application fee for registering is $325 per class.

Patents

Source: Department of Commerce, Patent and Trademark Office

A patent, in the most general sense, is a document issued by a government, conferring some special right or privilege. The term is now restricted mainly to patents for inventions, and occasionally, land patents.

The grant of a patent for an invention gives the inventor the privilege, for a limited period of time, of excluding others from making, using, or selling a certain article.

In the U.S., the law provides that a patent may be granted, for a term of 20 years from the date of application, to any person who has invented or discovered any new and useful art, machine, manufacture, or composition of matter, as well as any new and useful improvements thereof. A patent may also be granted to a person who has invented or discovered and asexually reproduced a new and distinct variety of plant (other than a tuber-propagated one) or has invented a new, original, and ornamental design for an article of manufacture, for a term of 20 years and 14 years, respectively.

A patent is granted only upon receipt of a complete, regularly filed application and the appropriate fees, and upon determination that the invention is new, useful, and, in view of the prior art, unobvious to one skilled in the art. The disclosure must be of such nature as to enable others to reproduce the invention.

A complete application, which must be addressed to the Commissioner of Patents and Trademarks, Washington, D.C. 20231, consists of a specification with one or more claims; oath or declaration; drawing (whenever the nature of the case admits of it); and a basic filing fee of $380. The filing fee is not returned to the applicant if the patent is refused. If the patent is allowed, another fee of $660 is required before the patent is issued. The fee for design patent application is $155; the issue fee is $215. The fee for a plant patent application is $240; the issue fee is $290. Maintenance fees are required on utility patents at stipulated intervals. Phone 1-800-786-9199 for the latest fees.

Applications are ordinarily considered in the order in which they are received. Patents are not granted for printed matter, for methods of doing business, or for devices for which claims contrary to natural laws are made. Applications for a perpetual-motion machine have been made from time to time, but until a working model is presented that actually fulfills the claim, no patent will be issued.

NOTE: Fees are subject to change in October of each year.

In any broad overview of history, arbitrary compartmentalization of facts is self-defeating (and makes locating interrelated people, places, and things that much harder). Therefore, Headline History is designed as a "timeline"—a chronology that highlights both the march of time and interesting, sometimes surprising, juxtapositions.

See also related sections of the almanac, particularly Inventions and Discoveries, U.S. Government and History, and Countries of the World.

B.C.

Before Christ (B.C.) or Before the Common Era (B.C.E.)

4.5 billion B.C. Planet Earth formed.
3 billion B.C. First signs of primeval life (bacteria and blue-green algae) appear in oceans.
600 million B.C. Earliest date to which fossils can be traced.
4.4 million B.C. Earliest known hominid fossils (*Ardipithecus ramidus*) found in Aramis, Ethiopia, 1994.
4.2 million B.C. *Australopithecus anamensis* found in Lake Turkana, Kenya, 1995.
3.2 million B.C. *Australopithecus afarensis* (nicknamed "Lucy") found in Ethiopia, 1974.
2.5 million B.C. *Homo habilis* ("Skillful Man"). First brain expansion; is believed to have used stone tools.
1.8 million B.C. *Homo erectus* ("Upright Man"). Brain size twice that of *Australopithecine* species.
1.7 million B.C. *Homo erectus* leaves Africa.
100,000 B.C. First modern *Homo sapiens* in South Africa.
70,000 B.C. Neanderthal man (use of fire and advanced tools).
35,000 B.C. Neanderthal man replaced by later groups of *Homo sapiens* (i.e., Cro-Magnon man, etc.).
18,000 B.C. Cro-Magnons replaced by later cultures.
15,000 B.C. Migrations across Bering Straits into the Americas.
10,000 B.C. Semi-permanent agricultural settlements in Old World.
10,000–4,000 B.C. Development of settlements into cities and development of skills such as the wheel, pottery, and improved methods of cultivation in Mesopotamia and elsewhere.
5500–3000 B.C. Predynastic Egyptian cultures develop (5500–3100 B.C.); begin using agriculture (c. 5000 B.C.). Earliest known civilization arises in Sumer (4500–4000 B.C.). Earliest recorded date in Egyptian calendar (4241 B.C.). First year of Jewish calendar (3760 B.C.). First phonetic writing appears (c. 3500 B.C.). Sumerians develop a city-state civilization (c. 3000 B.C.). Copper used by Egyptians and Sumerians. Western Europe is neolithic, without metals or written records.
3000–2000 B.C. Pharaonic rule begins in Egypt. King Khufu (Cheops), 4th dynasty (2700–2675 B.C.), completes construction of the Great Pyramid at Giza (c. 2680 B.C.). The Great Sphinx of Giza (c. 2540 B.C.) is built by King Khafre. Earliest Egyptian mummies. Papyrus. Phoenician settlements on coast of what is now Syria and Lebanon. Semitic tribes settle in Assyria. Sargon, first Akkadian king, builds Mesopotamian empire. The Gilgamesh epic (c. 3000 B.C.). Abraham leaves Ur (c. 2000 B.C.). Systematic astronomy in Egypt, Babylon, India, China.
3000–1500 B.C. The most ancient civilization on the Indian subcontinent, the sophisticated and extensive Indus Valley civilization, flourishes in what is today Pakistan. In Britain, Stonehenge erected according to some unknown astronomical rationale. Its three main phases of construction are thought to span c. 3000–1500 B.C.
2000–1500 B.C. Hyksos invaders drive Egyptians from Lower Egypt (17th century B.C.). Amosis I frees Egypt from Hyksos (c. 1600 B.C.). Assyrians rise to power—cities of Ashur and Nineveh. Twenty-four-character alphabet in Egypt. Israelites enslaved in Egypt. Cuneiform inscriptions used by Hittites. Peak of Minoan culture on Isle of Crete—earliest form of written Greek. Hammurabi, king of Babylon, develops oldest existing code of laws (18th century B.C.).

Ra, Egyptian Sun God (3000–2000 B.C.)

The Great Pyramid at Giza (c. 2680 B.C.)

Stonehenge (c. 3000–1500 B.C.)

Pythagoras
(c. 582–c. 507 B.C.)

Buddha
(c. 563–c. 483 B.C.)

1500–1000 B.C. Ikhnaton develops monotheistic religion in Egypt (c. 1375 B.C.). His successor, Tutankhamen, returns to earlier gods. Moses leads Israelites out of Egypt into Canaan—Ten Commandments. Greeks destroy Troy (c. 1193 B.C.). End of Greek civilization in Mycenae with invasion of Dorians. Chinese civilization develops under Shang Dynasty. Olmec civilization in Mexico—stone monuments; picture writing.

1000–900 B.C. Solomon succeeds King David, builds Jerusalem temple. After Solomon's death, kingdom divided into Israel and Judah. Hebrew elders begin to write Old Testament books of Bible. Phoenicians colonize Spain with settlement at Cadiz.

900–800 B.C. Phoenicians establish Carthage (c. 810 B.C.). The *Iliad* and the *Odyssey,* perhaps composed by Greek poet Homer.

800–700 B.C. Prophets Amos, Hosea, Isaiah. First recorded Olympic games (776 B.C.). Legendary founding of Rome by Romulus (753 B.C.). Assyrian king Sargon II conquers Hittites, Chaldeans, Samaria (end of Kingdom of Israel). Earliest written music. Chariots introduced into Italy by Etruscans.

700–600 B.C. End of Assyrian Empire (616 B.C.)—Nineveh destroyed by Chaldeans (Neo-Babylonians) and Medes (612 B.C.). Founding of Byzantium by Greeks (c. 660 B.C.). Building of the Acropolis in Athens. Solon, Greek lawgiver (640–560 B.C.). Sappho of Lesbos, Greek poet (fl. 610–c. 580 B.C.). Lao-tse, Chinese philosopher and founder of Taoism (born c. 604 B.C.).

600–500 B.C. Babylonian King Nebuchadnezzar builds empire, destroys Jerusalem (586 B.C.). Babylonian Captivity of the Jews (starting 587 B.C.). Hanging Gardens of Babylon. Cyrus the Great of Persia creates great empire, conquers Babylon (539 B.C.), frees the Jews. Athenian democracy develops. Aeschylus, Greek dramatist (525–465 B.C.). Pythagoras, Greek philosopher and mathematician (c. 582–c. 507 B.C.). Confucius (551–479 B.C.) develops ethical and social philosophy in China. The *Analects* or Lun-yü ("collected sayings") are compiled by the second generation of Confucian disciples. Buddha (c. 563–c. 483 B.C.) founds Buddhism in India.

SOME ANCIENT CIVILIZATIONS

Name	Approximate dates	Location	Major cities
Akkadian	2350–2230 B.C.	Mesopotamia, parts of Syria, Asia Minor, Iran	Akkad, Ur, Erich
Assyrian	1800–889 B.C.	Mesopotamia, Syria	Assur, Nineveh, Calah
Babylonian	1728–1686 B.C. (old) 625–539 B.C. (new)	Mesopotamia, Syria, Palestine	Babylon
Cimmerian	750–500 B.C.	Caucasus, northern Asia Minor	—
Egyptian	2850–715 B.C.	Nile valley	Thebes, Memphis, Tanis
Etruscan	900–396 B.C.	Northern Italy	—
Greek	900–200 B.C.	Greece	Athens, Sparta, Thebes, Mycenae, Corinth
Hittite	1640–1200 B.C.	Asia Minor, Syria	Hattusas, Nesa
Indus Valley	3000–1500 B.C.	Pakistan, Northwestern India	—
Lydian	700–547 B.C.	Western Asia Minor	Sardis, Miletus
Mede	835–550 B.C.	Iran	Media
Minoan	3000–1100 B.C.	Crete	Knossos
Persian	559–330 B.C.	Iran, Asia Minor, Syria	Persepolis, Pasargadae
Phoenician	1100–332 B.C.	Palestine (colonies: Gibraltar, Carthage, Sardinia)	Tyre, Sidon, Byblos
Phrygian	1000–547 B.C.	Central Asia Minor	Gordion
Roman	500 B.C.–A.D. 300	Italy, Mediterranean region, Asia Minor, western Europe	Rome, Byzantium
Scythian	800–300 B.C.	Caucasus	—
Sumerian	3200–2360 B.C.	Mesopotamia	Ur, Nippur

500–400 B.C. Greeks defeat Persians: battles of Marathon (490 B.C.), Thermopylae (480 B.C.), Salamis (480 B.C.). Peloponnesian Wars between Athens and Sparta (431–404 B.C.)—Sparta victorious. Pericles comes to power in Athens (462 B.C.). Flowering of Greek culture during the Age of Pericles (450–400 B.C.). The Parthenon is built in Athens as a temple of the goddess Athena (447–432 B.C.). Ictinus and Callicrates are the architects and Phidias is responsible for the sculpture. Sophocles, Greek dramatist (496–c.406 B.C.). Hippocrates, Greek "Father of Medicine" (born 460 B.C.). Xerxes I, king of Persia (rules 485–465 B.C.).

400–300 B.C. Pentateuch—first five books of the Old Testament evolve in final form. Philip of Macedon, who believed himself to be a descendant of the Greek people, assassinated (336 B.C.) after subduing the Greek city-states; succeeded by son, Alexander the Great (356–323 B.C.), who destroys Thebes (335 B.C.), conquers Tyre and Jerusalem (332 B.C.), occupies Babylon (330 B.C.), invades India, and dies in Babylon. His empire is divided among his generals; one of them, Seleucis I, establishes Middle East empire with capitals at Antioch (Syria) and Seleucia (in Iraq). Trial and execution of Greek philosopher Socrates (399 B.C.). Dialogues recorded by his student, Plato (c. 427–348 or 347 B.C.). Euclid's work on geometry (323 B.C.). Aristotle, Greek philosopher (384–322 B.C.). Demosthenes, Greek orator (384–322 B.C.). Praxiteles, Greek sculptor (400–330 B.C.).

300–251 B.C. First Punic War (264–241 B.C.): Rome defeats the Carthaginians and begins its domination of the Mediterranean. Temple of the Sun at Teotihuacan, Mexico (c. 300 B.C.). Invention of Mayan calendar in Yucatán—more exact than older calendars. First Roman gladiatorial games (264 B.C.). Archimedes, Greek mathematician (287–212 B.C.).

250–201 B.C. Second Punic War (219–201 B.C.): Hannibal, Carthaginian general (246–142 B.C.), crosses the Alps (218 B.C.), reaches gates of Rome (211 B.C.), retreats, and is defeated by Scipio Africanus at Zama (202 B.C.). Great Wall of China built (c. 215 B.C.).

200–151 B.C. Romans defeat Seleucid King Antiochus III at Thermopylae (191 B.C.)—beginning of Roman world domination. Maccabean revolt against Seleucids (167 B.C.).

150–101 B.C. Third Punic War (149–146 B.C.): Rome destroys Carthage, killing 450,000 and enslaving the remaining 50,000 inhabitants. Roman armies conquer Macedonia, Greece, Anatolia, Balearic Islands, and southern France. Venus de Milo (c. 140 B.C.). Cicero, Roman orator (106–43 B.C.).

100–51 B.C. Julius Caesar (100–44 B.C.) invades Britain (55 B.C.) and conquers Gaul (France) (c. 50 B.C.). Spartacus leads slave revolt against Rome (71 B.C.). Romans conquer Seleucid empire. Roman general Pompey conquers Jerusalem (63 B.C.). Cleopatra on Egyptian throne (51–31 B.C.). Chinese develop use of paper (c. 100 B.C.). Virgil, Roman poet (70–19 B.C.). Horace, Roman poet (65–8 B.C.).

50–1 B.C. Caesar crosses Rubicon to fight Pompey (50 B.C.). Herod made Roman governor of Judea (37 B.C.). Caesar murdered (44 B.C.). Caesar's nephew, Octavian, defeats Mark Antony and Cleopatra at Battle of Actium (31 B.C.), and establishes Roman empire as Emperor Augustus—rules 27 B.C.–A.D. 14. Pantheon built for the first time under Agrippa, 27 B.C. Ovid, Roman poet (43 B.C.–A.D. 18).

Confucius
(551–479 B.C.)

Parthenon
(447–432 B.C.)

Plato
(c. 427–348 or 347 B.C.)

A.D.
Christian Era (A.D.) or the Common Era (C.E.)

1–49 Birth of Jesus Christ (variously given from 4 B.C. to A.D. 7). After Augustus, Tiberius becomes emperor (dies, 37), succeeded by Caligula (assassinated, 41), who is followed by Claudius. Crucifixion of Jesus (probably 30). Han dynasty in China founded by Emperor Kuang Wu Ti. Buddhism introduced to China.

50–99 Claudius poisoned (54), succeeded by Nero (commits suicide, 68). Missionary journeys of Paul the Apostle (34–60). Jews revolt against Rome; Jerusalem destroyed (70). Roman persecutions of Christians begin (64). Colosseum built in Rome (71–80). Trajan (rules 98–116); Roman empire extends to Mesopotamia, Arabia, Balkans. First Gospels of St. Mark, St. John, St. Matthew.

Roman Aqueduct
Montpellier, France

Mayan Pyramid at Chichén Itzá

Celtic Cross

Japanese Pagoda

Viking Ship (c. 900)

100–149 Hadrian rules Rome (117–138); codifies Roman law, rebuilds Pantheon, establishes postal system, builds wall between England and Scotland. Jews revolt under Bar Kokhba (122–135); final Diaspora (dispersion) of Jews begins.

150–199 Marcus Aurelius rules Rome (161–180). Oldest Mayan temples in Central America (c. 200).

200–249 Goths invade Asia Minor (c. 220). Roman persecutions of Christians increase. Persian (Sassanid) empire re-established. End of Chinese Han dynasty.

250–299 Increasing invasions of the Roman empire by Franks and Goths. Buddhism spreads in China. Classic period of Mayan civilization (250–900); develop hieroglyphic writing, advances in art, architecture, science.

300–349 Constantine the Great (rules 312–337) reunites eastern and western Roman empires, with new capital (Constantinople) on site of Byzantium (330); issues Edict of Milan legalizing Christianity (313); becomes a Christian on his deathbed (337). Council of Nicaea (325) defines orthodox Christian doctrine. First Gupta dynasty in India (c. 320).

350–399 Huns (Mongols) invade Europe (c. 360). Theodosius the Great (rules 392–395)—last emperor of a united Roman empire. Roman empire permanently divided in 395: western empire ruled from Rome; eastern empire ruled from Constantinople.

400–449 Western Roman empire disintegrates under weak emperors. Alaric, king of the Visigoths, sacks Rome (410). Attila, Hun chieftain, attacks Roman provinces (433). St. Patrick returns to Ireland (432) and brings Christianity to the island. St. Augustine's *City of God* (411).

450–499 Vandals destroy Rome (455). Western Roman empire ends as Odoacer, German chieftain, overthrows last Roman emperor, Romulus Augustulus, and becomes king of Italy (476). Ostrogothic kingdom of Italy established by Theodoric the Great (493). Clovis, ruler of the Franks, is converted to Christianity (496). First schism between western and eastern churches (484).

500–549 Eastern and western churches reconciled (519). Justinian I, the Great (483–565), becomes Byzantine emperor (527), issues his first code of civil laws (529), conquers North Africa, Italy, and part of Spain. Plague spreads through Europe (542 *et seq.*). Arthur, semi-legendary king of the Britons (killed, c. 537). Boëthius, Roman scholar (executed, 524).

550–599 Beginnings of European silk industry after Justinian's missionaries smuggle silkworms out of China (553). Mohammed, founder of Islam (570–632). Buddhism in Japan (c. 560). St. Augustine of Canterbury brings Christianity to Britain (597). After killing about half the population, plague in Europe subsides (594).

600–649 Mohammed flees from Mecca to Medina (the *Hegira*); first year of the Muslim calendar (622). Muslim empire grows (634). Arabs conquer Jerusalem (637), destroy Alexandrian library (641), conquer Persians (641). Fatima, Mohammed's daughter (606–632).

650–699 Arabs attack North Africa (670), destroy Carthage (697). Venerable Bede, English monk (672–735).

700–749 Arab empire extends from Lisbon to China (by 716). Charles Martel, Frankish leader, defeats Arabs at Tours/Poitiers, halting Arab advance in Europe (732). Charlemagne (742–814). Introduction of pagodas in Japan from China.

750–799 Charlemagne becomes king of the Franks (771). Caliph Harun al-Rashid rules Arab empire (786–809): the "golden age" of Arab culture. Vikings begin attacks on Britain (790), land in Ireland (795). City of Machu Picchu flourishes in Peru.

800–849 Charlemagne crowned first Holy Roman Emperor in Rome (800). Charlemagne dies (814), succeeded by his son, Louis the Pious, who divides France among his sons (817). Arabs conquer Crete, Sicily, and Sardinia (826–827).

850–899 Norsemen attack as far south as the Mediterranean but are thwarted (859), discover Iceland (861). Alfred the Great becomes king of Britain (871), defeats Danish invaders (878). Russian nation founded by Vikings under Prince Rurik, establishing capital at Novgorod (855–879).

900–949 Beginning of Mayan Post-Classical period (900–1519). Vikings discover Greenland (c. 900). Arab Spain under Abd ar-Rahman III becomes center of learning (912–961). Otto I becomes King of Germany (936).

950–999 Mieczyslaw I becomes first ruler of Poland (960). Eric the Red establishes first Viking colony in Greenland (982). Hugh Capet elected King of France in 987; Capetian dynasty to rule until 1328. Musical notation systematized (c.

990). Vikings and Danes attack Britain (988–999). Otto I crowned Holy Roman Emperor by Pope John XII (962).

1000–1099 (A.D.)

c. 1000–1300 Classic Pueblo period of Anasazi culture; cliff dwellings.

c.1000 Hungary and Scandinavia converted to Christianity. Viking raider Leif Eriksson discovers North America, calls it Vinland. *Beowulf,* Old English epic.

c. 1008 Murasaki Shikibu finishes *The Tale of Genji,* the world's first novel.

1009 Muslims destroy Holy Sepulchre in Jerusalem.

1013 Danes control England. Canute takes throne (1016), conquers Norway (1028), dies (1035); kingdom divided among his sons: Harold Harefoot (England), Sweyn (Norway), Hardecanute (Denmark).

1040 Macbeth murders Duncan, king of Scotland.

1053 Robert Guiscard, Norman invader, establishes kingdom in Italy, conquers Sicily (1072).

1054 Final separation between Eastern (Orthodox) and Western (Roman) churches.

1055 Seljuk Turks, Asian nomads, move west, capture Baghdad, Armenia (1064), Syria, and Palestine (1075).

1066 William of Normandy invades England, defeats last Saxon king, Harold II, at Battle of Hastings, crowned William I of England ("the Conqueror").

1068 Construction on the cathedral in Pisa, Italy, begins.

1073 Emergence of strong papacy when Gregory VII is elected. Conflict with English and French kings and German emperors will continue throughout medieval period.

1095 At Council of Clermont, Pope Urban II calls for a holy war to wrest control of Jerusalem from Muslims, which launches the First Crusade (1096), one of at least 8 European military campaigns between 1095 and 1291 to regain the Holy Land.

1100–1199 (A.D.)

1100–1300 Construction of Cathedral at Chartres, France.

1144 Second Crusade begins.

c. 1150 Angkor Wat is completed.

1150–1167 Universities of Paris and Oxford founded in France and England.

1162 Thomas á Becket named Archbishop of Canterbury, murdered by Henry II's men (1170). Troubadours (wandering minstrels) glorify romantic concepts of feudalism.

1169 Ibn-Rushd begins translating Aristotle's works.

1189 Richard I ("the Lionhearted") succeeds Henry II in England, killed in France (1199), succeeded by King John. Third Crusade.

1200–1299 (A.D.)

1200–1204 Fourth Crusade.

1211 Genghis Khan invades China, captures Peking (1214), conquers Persia (1218), invades Russia (1223), dies (1227).

1212 Children's Crusade.

1215 King John forced by barons to sign Magna Carta at Runneymede, limiting royal power.

1217 Fifth Crusade.

1228 Sixth Crusade.

**Mesa Verde
Cliff Dwellings
(c. 1000–1300)**

**Cathedral and Tower
at Pisa**

Chartres Cathedral

**King John
(1167–1216)**

THE CRUSADES (1096–1291)

In 1095 at Council of Clermont, Pope Urban II calls for war to rescue Holy Land from Muslim infidels. The *First Crusade* (1096) is assembled in response to Emperor Alexius I. The Christians capture Antioch (1098) and Jerusalem (1099). They establish the Crusader States, ruled by Europeans. It is the only successful crusade. The *Second Crusade* begins after the Seljuk Turks recapture Edessa, one of the Crusader States, in 1144. It is led by King Louis VIII of France and Holy Roman Emperor Conrad III. Crusaders perish in Asia Minor (1147).

Saladin controls Egypt (1171), unites Islam in Holy War *(Jihad)* against Christians, recaptures Jerusalem (1187). *Third Crusade* (1189) under kings of France, England, and Germany fails to reduce Saladin's power. *Fourth Crusade* (1200–1204)—French knights sack Greek Christian Constantinople, establish Latin empire in Byzantium. Greeks re-establish Orthodox faith (1262).

Children's Crusade (1212)—Only one of 30,000 French children and about 200 of 20,000 German children survive to return home. Other Crusades—*Fifth,* against Egypt (1217), *Sixth* (1228), *Seventh* (1248), *Eighth* (1270). Mamelukes conquer Acre; end of the Crusades (1291).

**Thomas Aquinas
(1225–1274)**

**The Duomo in
Florence**

**Joan of Arc
(1412–1431)**

**Michelangelo's David
(1504)**

**Balboa
(1475–1517)**

1231 The Inquisition begins as Pope Gregory IX assigns Dominicans responsibility for combating heresy. Torture used (1252). Ferdinand and Isabella establish Spanish Inquisition (1478). Tourquemada, Grand Inquisitor, forces conversion or expulsion of Spanish Jews (1492). Forced conversion of Moors (1499). Inquisition in Portugal (1531). First Protestants burned at the stake in Spain (1543). Spanish Inquisition abolished (1834).

1241 Mongols defeat Germans in Silesia, invade Poland and Hungary, withdraw from Europe after Ughetai, Mongol leader, dies.

1248 Seventh Crusade.

1251 Kublai Khan governs China, becomes ruler of Mongols (1259), establishes Yuan dynasty in China (1280), invades Burma (1287), dies (1294).

1260 Chartres cathedral consecrated.

1270 Eighth Crusade.

1271 Marco Polo of Venice travels to China, in court of Kublai Khan (1275–1292), returns to Genoa (1295) and writes *Travels.*

1273 Thomas Aquinas stops work on *Summa Theologica,* the basis of all Catholic theological teaching; never completes it.

1295 English King Edward I summons the Model Parliament.

1300–1399 (A.D.)

1312–1337 Mali Empire reaches its height in Africa under King Mansa Musa.

c.1325 The beginning of the Renaissance in Italy: writers Dante, Petrarch, Boccaccio; painter Giotto. Development of *Noh* drama in Japan. Aztecs establish Tenochtitlán on site of modern Mexico City. Peak of Muslim culture in Spain. Small cannon in use.

1337–1453 Hundred Years' War—English and French kings fight for control of France.

1347–1351 At least 25 million people die in Europe's "Black Death" (bubonic plague).

1368 Ming Dynasty begins in China.

1376–1382 John Wycliffe, pre-Reformation religious reformer, and followers translate Latin Bible into English.

1378 The Great Schism (to 1417)—rival popes in Rome and Avignon, France, fight for control of Roman Catholic Church.

c.1387 Chaucer's *Canterbury Tales.*

1399 Tamerlane begins last great conquest.

1400–1499 (A.D.)

1407 Casa di San Giorgio, one of the first public banks, founded in Genoa.

1415 Henry V defeats French at Agincourt. Jan Hus, Bohemian preacher and follower of Wycliffe, burned at stake in Constance as heretic.

1418–1460 Portugal's Prince Henry the Navigator sponsors exploration of Africa's coast.

1420 Brunelleschi begins work on the Duomo in Florence.

1428 Joan of Arc leads French against English, captured by Burgundians (1430) and turned over to the English, burned at the stake as a witch after ecclesiastical trial (1431).

1438 Incas rule in Peru.

1450 Florence becomes center of Renaissance arts and learning under the Medicis.

1453 Turks conquer Constantinople, end of the Byzantine empire, beginning of the Ottoman empire.

1455 The Wars of the Roses, civil wars between rival noble factions, begin in England (to 1485). Having invented printing with movable type at Mainz, Germany, Johann Gutenberg completes first Bible.

1462 Ivan the Great rules Russia until 1505 as first czar; ends payment of tribute to Mongols.

1492 Moors conquered in Spain by troops of Ferdinand and Isabella. Columbus becomes first European to encounter Caribbean islands, returns to Spain (1493). Second voyage to Dominica, Jamaica, Puerto Rico (1493–1496). Third voyage to Orinoco (1498). Fourth voyage to Honduras and Panama (1502–1504).

1497 Vasco da Gama sails around Africa and discovers sea route to India (1498). Establishes Portuguese colony in India (1502). John Cabot, employed by England, reaches and explores Canadian coast. Michelangelo's *Bacchus* sculpture.

1500–1599 (A.D.)

1501 First black slaves in America brought to Spanish colony of Santo Domingo.

c.1503 Leonardo da Vinci paints the *Mona Lisa.* Michelangelo sculpts the *David* (1504).

1506 St. Peter's Church started in Rome; designed and decorated by such artists and architects as Bramante, Michelangelo, da Vinci, Raphael, and Bernini before its completion in 1626.

1509 Henry VIII ascends English throne. Michelangelo paints the ceiling of the Sistine Chapel.

1513 Balboa becomes the first European to encounter the Pacific Ocean. Machiavelli's *The Prince.*

1517 Turks conquer Egypt, control Arabia. Martin Luther posts his 95 theses denouncing church abuses on church door in Wittenberg—start of the Reformation in Germany.

1519 Ulrich Zwingli begins Reformation in Switzerland. Hernando Cortes conquers Mexico for Spain. Charles I of Spain is chosen Holy Roman Emperor Charles V. Portuguese explorer Ferdinand Magellan sets out to circumnavigate the globe.

Martin Luther
(1483–1546)

1520 Luther excommunicated by Pope Leo X. Suleiman I ("the Magnificent") becomes Sultan of Turkey, invades Hungary (1521), Rhodes (1522), attacks Austria (1529), annexes Hungary (1541), Tripoli (1551), makes peace with Persia (1553), destroys Spanish fleet (1560), dies (1566). Magellan reaches the Pacific, is killed by Philippine natives (1521). One of his ships under Juan Sebastián del Cano continues around the world, reaches Spain (1522).

1524 Verrazano, sailing under the French flag, explores the New England coast and New York Bay.

1527 Troops of the Holy Roman Empire attack Rome, imprison Pope Clement VII—the end of the Italian Renaissance. Castiglione writes *The Courtier.* The Medici family expelled from Florence.

Henry VIII
(1491–1547)

1532 Pizarro marches from Panama to Peru, kills the Inca chieftain, Atahualpa, of Peru (1533). Machiavelli's *The Prince* published posthumously.

1535 Reformation begins as Henry VIII makes himself head of English Church after being excommunicated by Pope. Sir Thomas More executed as traitor for refusal to acknowledge king's religious authority. Jacques Cartier sails up the St. Lawrence River, basis of French claims to Canada.

1536 Henry VIII executes second wife, Anne Boleyn. John Calvin establishes Reformed and Presbyterian form of Protestantism in Switzerland, writes *Institutes of the Christian Religion.* Danish and Norwegian Reformations. Michelangelo's *Last Judgment.*

1541 John Knox leads Reformation in Scotland, establishes Presbyterian church there (1560).

1543 Publication of *On the Revolution of Heavenly Bodies* by Polish scholar Nicolaus Copernicus—giving his theory that the earth revolves around the sun.

1545 Council of Trent to meet intermittently until 1563 to define Catholic dogma and doctrine, reiterate papal authority.

Queen Elizabeth I
(1533–1603)

1547 Ivan IV ("the Terrible") crowned as czar of Russia, begins conquest of Astrakhan and Kazan (1552), battles nobles (boyars) for power (1564), kills his son (1580), dies, and is succeeded by his weak and feeble-minded son, Fyodor I.

1553 Roman Catholicism restored in England by Queen Mary I.

1556 Akbar the Great becomes Mogul emperor of India, conquers Afghanistan (1581), continues wars of conquest (until 1605).

1558 Queen Elizabeth I ascends the throne (rules to 1603). Restores Protestantism, establishes state Church of England (Anglicanism). Renaissance will reach height in England—Shakespeare, Marlowe, Spenser.

1561 Persecution of Huguenots in France stopped by Edict of Orleans. French religious wars begin again with massacre of Huguenots at Vassy. St. Bartholomew's Day Massacre—thousands of Huguenots murdered (1572). Amnesty granted (1573). Persecution continues periodically until Edict of Nantes (1598) gives Huguenots religious freedom (until 1685).

William Shakespeare
(1564–1616)

1568 Protestant Netherlands revolts against Catholic Spain; independence will be acknowledged by Spain in 1648. High point of Dutch Renaissance—painters Rubens, Van Dyck, Hals, and Rembrandt.

1570 Japan permits visits of foreign ships. Queen Elizabeth I excommunicated by Pope. Turks attack Cyprus and war on Venice. Turkish fleet defeated at Battle of Lepanto by Spanish and Italian fleets (1571). Peace of Constantinople (1572) ends Turkish attacks on Europe.

1580 Francis Drake returns to England after circumnavigating the globe; knighted by Queen Elizabeth I (1581). Montaigne's *Essays* published.

1582 Pope Gregory XIII implements the Gregorian calendar.

Rembrandt van Rijn
(1606–1669)

Catherine de Medici
(1519–1589)

1583 William of Orange rules the Netherlands; assassinated on orders of Philip II of Spain (1584).

1587 Mary, Queen of Scots, executed for treason by order of Queen Elizabeth I. Monteverdi's *First Book of Madrigals.*

1588 Defeat of the Spanish Armada by English. Henry, King of Navarre and Protestant leader, recognized as Henry IV, first Bourbon king of France. Converts to Roman Catholicism in 1593 in attempt to end religious wars.

1590 Henry IV enters Paris, wars on Spain (1595), marries Marie de Medici (1600), assassinated (1610). Spenser's *The Faerie Queen.* El Greco's *St. Jerome.* Galileo's experiments with falling objects.

1598 Boris Godunov becomes Russian czar. Tycho Brahe describes his astronomical experiments.

1600–1699 (A.D.)

1600 Giordano Bruno burned as a heretic. English East India Company established.

1603 Ieyasu rules Japan, moves capital to Edo (Tokyo). Shakespeare's *Hamlet.*

1605 Cervantes's *Don Quixote de la Mancha,* the first modern novel.

1607 Jamestown, Virginia, established—first permanent English colony on American mainland. Pocahontas, daughter of Chief Powhatan, saves life of John Smith.

1609 Samuel de Champlain establishes French colony of Quebec. The *Relation,* the first newspaper, debuts in Germany.

1610 Galileo sees the moons of Jupiter through his telescope.

1611 Gustavus Adolphus elected King of Sweden. King James Version of the Bible published in England. Rubens paints his *Descent from the Cross.*

1614 John Napier discovers logarithms.

1618 Start of the Thirty Years' War—Protestants revolt against Catholic oppression; Denmark, Sweden, and France will invade Germany in later phases of war. Kepler proposes last of three laws of planetary motion.

1619 A Dutch ship brings the first African slaves to British North America.

1620 Pilgrims, after three-month voyage in *Mayflower,* land at Plymouth Rock. Francis Bacon's *Novum Organum.*

1623 New Netherland founded by Dutch West India Company.

1630 Massachusetts Bay Colony.

1632 Maryland founded by Lord Baltimore.

1633 Inquisition forces Galileo to recant his belief in Copernican theory.

1642 English Civil War. Cavaliers, supporters of Charles I, against Roundheads, parliamentary forces. Oliver Cromwell defeats Royalists (1646). Parliament demands reforms. Charles I offers concessions, brought to trial (1648), beheaded (1649). Cromwell becomes Lord Protector (1653). Rembrandt paints his *Night Watch.*

1643 Taj Mahal completed.

1644 End of Ming Dynasty in China—Manchus come to power. Descartes's *Principles of Philosophy.*

1648 End of the Thirty Years' War. German population about half of what it was in 1618 because of war and pestilence.

1658 Cromwell dies; son Richard resigns and Puritan government collapses.

1660 English Parliament calls for the restoration of the monarchy; invites Charles II to return from France.

1661 Charles II is crowned King of England. Louis XIV begins personal rule as absolute monarch; starts to build Versailles.

1664 British take New Amsterdam from the Dutch. English limit "Nonconformity" with re-established Anglican Church. Isaac Newton's experiments with gravity.

1665 Great Plague in London kills 75,000.

1666 Great Fire of London. Molière's *Misanthrope.*

1667 Milton's *Paradise Lost,* widely considered the greatest epic poem in English.

1682 Pennsylvania founded by William Penn.

1683 War of European powers against the Turks (to 1699). Vienna withstands three-month Turkish siege; high point of Turkish advance in Europe.

1684 Gottfried Wilhelm Leibniz's calculus published.

1685 James II succeeds Charles II in England, calls for freedom of conscience (1687). Protestants fear restoration of Catholicism and demand "Glorious Revolution." William of Orange invited to England and James II escapes to France (1688). William III and his wife, Mary, crowned. In France, Edict of Nantes of 1598, granting freedom of worship to Huguenots, is revoked by Louis XIV; thousands of Protestants flee.

Galileo
(1564–1642)

Pocahontas
(c. 1595–1617)

Taj Mahal

John Milton
(1608–1674)

1689 Peter the Great becomes Czar of Russia—attempts to westernize nation and build Russia as a military power. Defeats Charles XII of Sweden at Poltava (1709). Beginning of the French and Indian Wars (to 1763), campaigns in America linked to a series of wars between France and England for domination of Europe.

1690 William III of England defeats former king James II and Irish rebels at Battle of the Boyne in Ireland. John Locke's *Human Understanding.*

**Sir Isaac Newton
(1642–1727)**

1700–1799 (A.D.)

1701 War of the Spanish Succession begins—the last of Louis XIV's wars for domination of the continent. The Peace of Utrecht (1714) will end the conflict and mark the rise of the British Empire. Called Queen Anne's War in America, it ends with the British taking New Foundland, Acadia, and Hudson's Bay Territory from France, and Gibraltar and Minorca from Spain.

1704 Deerfield (Mass.) Massacre of English colonists by French and Indians. Bach's first cantata. Jonathan Swift's *Tale of a Tub. Boston News Letter*—first newspaper in America.

1707 United Kingdom of Great Britain formed—England, Wales, and Scotland joined by parliamentary Act of Union.

1729 Bach's *St. Matthew Passion.* Isaac Newton's *Principia* translated from Latin into English.

1732 Benjamin Franklin begins publishing *Poor Richard's Almanack.* James Oglethorpe and others found Georgia.

**Frederick the Great
(1712–1786)**

1735 John Peter Zenger, New York editor, acquitted of libel in New York, establishing press freedom.

1740 Capt. Vitus Bering, Dane employed by Russia, discovers Alaska. Frederick II "the Great" crowned king of Prussia.

1746 British defeat Scots under Stuart Pretender Prince Charles at Culloden Moor. Last battle fought on British soil.

1751 Publication of the *Encyclopédie* begins in France, the "bible" of the Enlightenment.

1755 Samuel Johnson's *Dictionary* first published. Great earthquake in Lisbon, Portugal—over 60,000 die. U.S. postal service established.

1756 Seven Years' War (French and Indian Wars in America) (to 1763), in which Britain and Prussia defeat France, Spain, Austria, and Russia. France loses North American colonies; Spain cedes Florida to Britain in exchange for Cuba. In India, over 100 British prisoners die in "Black Hole of Calcutta."

**Samuel Johnson
(1709–1784)**

1757 Beginning of British Empire in India as Robert Clive, British commander, defeats Nawab of Bengal at Plassey.

1759 British capture Quebec from French. Voltaire's *Candide.* Haydn's *Symphony No. 1.*

1762 Catherine II ("the Great") becomes czarina of Russia. Jean Jacques Rousseau's *Social Contract.* Mozart tours Europe as six-year-old prodigy.

1765 James Watt invents the steam engine. Britain imposes the Stamp Act on the American colonists.

THE REVOLUTIONARY WAR

Conflicts increase between colonists and Britain on western frontier because of royal edict limiting western expansion (1763) and regulation of colonial trade and increased taxation of colonies (Writs of Assistance allow search for illegal shipments, 1761; Sugar Act, 1764; Currency Act, 1764; Stamp Act, 1765; Quartering Act, 1765; Duty Act, 1767). Boston Massacre (1770). Lord North attempts conciliation (1770). Boston Tea Party (1773), followed by punitive measures passed by Parliament—the "Intolerable Acts."

First Continental Congress (1774) sends "Declaration of Rights and Grievances" to King George III, urges colonies to form Continental Association. Paul Revere's ride and Lexington and Concord battle between Massachusetts Minutemen and British (1775).

Second Continental Congress (1775), while sending "olive branch" to the king, begins to raise army, appoints Washington commander-in-chief, and seeks alliance with France. Some colonial legislatures urge their delegates to vote for independence. Declaration of Independence **(July 4, 1776)**.

Major Battles of the Revolutionary War: *Long Island:* Howe defeats Putnam's division of Washington's Army in Brooklyn Heights, but Americans escape across East River (1776). *Trenton and Princeton:* Washington defeats Hessians at Trenton, British at Princeton. Winters at Morristown (1776–1777). Howe winters in Philadelphia; Washington at Valley Forge (1777–1778). Burgoyne surrenders British army to General Gates at *Saratoga* (1777).

France recognizes American independence (1778). The War moves south: Savannah captured by British (1778); Charleston occupied (1780); Americans fight successful guerrilla actions under Marion, Pickens, and Sumter. In the West, George Rogers Clark attacks Forts Kaskaskia and Vincennes (1778–1779), defeating British in the region. Cornwallis surrenders at Yorktown, Virginia **(Oct. 19, 1781).** By 1782, Britain is eager for peace because of conflicts with European nations. *Peace of Paris* (1783): Britain recognizes American independence.

**Benjamin Franklin
(1706–1790)**

**George Washington
(1732–1799)**

**Alexander Hamilton
(1755–1804)**

**Ludwig van Beethoven
(1770–1827)**

1769 Sir William Arkwright patents a spinning machine—an early step in the Industrial Revolution.

1770 The Boston Massacre.

1772 Joseph Priestley and Daniel Rutherford independently discover nitrogen. Partition of Poland—in 1772, 1793, and 1795, Austria, Prussia, and Russia divide land and people of Poland, end its independence.

1773 The Boston Tea Party.

1774 First Continental Congress drafts "Declaration of Rights and Grievances."

1775 The American Revolution begins with battle of Lexington and Concord. Second Continental Congress. Priestley discovers hydrochloric and sulfuric acids.

1776 Declaration of Independence. Gen. George Washington crosses the Delaware Christmas night. Adam Smith's *Wealth of Nations.* Edward Gibbon's *Decline and Fall of the Roman Empire.* Thomas Paine's *Common Sense.* Fragonard's *Washerwoman.* Mozart's *Haffner Serenade.*

1778 Capt. James Cook discovers Hawaii. Franz Mesmer uses hypnotism.

1781 Immanuel Kant's *Critique of Pure Reason.* Herschel discovers Uranus.

1783 Revolutionary War ends with Treaty of Paris. William Blake's poems. Beethoven's first printed works.

1784 Crimea annexed by Russia. John Wesley's *Deed of Declaration,* the basic work of Methodism.

1785 Russians settle Aleutian Islands.

1787 The Constitution of the United States signed. Lavoisier's work on chemical nomenclature. Mozart's *Don Giovanni.*

1788 French *Parlement* presents grievances to Louis XVI who agrees to convening of Estates-General in 1789—not called since 1613. Goethe's *Egmont.* Laplace's *Laws of the Planetary System.*

1789 French Revolution begins with the storming of the Bastille. In U.S., Washington elected president with all 69 votes of the Electoral College, takes oath of office in New York City. Vice President: John Adams. Secretary of State: Thomas Jefferson. Secretary of Treasury: Alexander Hamilton.

1790 H.M.S. *Bounty* mutineers settle on Pitcairn Island. Aloisio Galvani experiments on electrical stimulation of the muscles. Philadelphia temporary capital of U.S. as Congress votes to establish new capital on Potomac. U.S. population about 3,929,000, including 698,000 slaves. Lavoisier formulates *Table of 31 chemical elements.*

1791 U.S. Bill of Rights ratified. Boswell's *Life of Johnson.*

1792 Mary Wollstonecraft's *Vindication of the Rights of Woman.*

1793 Louis XVI and Marie Antoinette executed. Reign of Terror begins in France. Eli Whitney invents the cotton gin, spurring the growth of the cotton industry and helping to institutionalize slavery in the U.S. South.

1794 Kosciusko's uprising in Poland quelled by the Russians. In U.S., Whiskey Rebellion in Pennsylvania as farmers object to liquor taxes. Reign of Terror ends with execution of Robespierre.

1796 Napoléon Bonaparte, French general, defeats Austrians. In the U.S., Washington's Farewell Address (**Sept. 17**); John Adams elected president; Thomas Jefferson, vice president. Edward Jenner introduces smallpox vaccination.

1798 Napoleon extends French conquests to Rome and Egypt. U.S. Navy Department established.

FRENCH REVOLUTION (1789–1799)

Revolution begins when Third Estate (Commons) delegates swear not to disband until France has a constitution. Paris mob storms Bastille, symbol of royal power (**July 14, 1789**). National Assembly votes for Constitution, Declaration of the Rights of Man, a limited monarchy, and other reforms (1789–1790). Legislative Assembly elected, Revolutionary Commune formed, and French Republic proclaimed (1792). War of the First Coalition—Austria, Prussia, Britain, Netherlands, and Spain fight to restore French nobility (1792–1797).

Start of series of wars between France and European powers that will last, almost without interruption, for 23 years. Louis XVI and Marie Antoinette executed. Committee of Public Safety begins Reign of Terror as political control measure. Interfactional rivalry leads to mass killings. Danton and Robespierre executed. Third French Constitution sets up Directory government (1795). Napoleon abolishes the Directory, establishes the Consulate, becomes the First Consul of France (1799).

1799 Rosetta Stone discovered in Egypt. Napoleon leads coup that overthrows Directory, establishes the Consulate, becomes First Consul—one of three who rule France together.

Napoléon Bonaparte (1769–1821)

1800–1899 (A.D.)

1800 Napoleon conquers Italy, firmly establishes himself as First Consul in France. In the U.S., federal government moves to Washington, D.C. Robert Owen's social reforms in England. William Herschel discovers infrared rays. Alessandro Volta produces electricity.

1801 Austria makes temporary peace with France. United Kingdom of Great Britain and Ireland established with one monarch and one parliament; Catholics excluded from voting.

1803 U.S. negotiates Louisiana Purchase from France: for $15 million, U.S. doubles its domain, increasing its territory by 827,000 sq. mi. (2,144,500 sq km), from Mississippi River to Rockies and from Gulf of Mexico to British North America.

1804 Haiti declares independence from France; first black nation to gain freedom from European colonial rule. Napoleon transforms the Consulate of France into an empire, proclaims himself emperor of France, systematizes French law under *Code Napoleon*. In the U.S., Alexander Hamilton is mortally wounded in duel with Aaron Burr. Lewis and Clark expedition begins exploration of what is now northwestern U.S.

1805 Lord Nelson defeats the French-Spanish fleets in the Battle of Trafalgar. Napoleon victorious over Austrian and Russian forces at the Battle of Austerlitz.

Edgar Allan Poe (1809–1849)

1807 Robert Fulton makes first successful steamboat trip on *Clermont* between New York City and Albany.

1808 French armies occupy Rome and Spain, extending Napoleon's empire. Britain begins aiding Spanish guerrillas against Napoleon in Peninsular War. In the U.S., Congress bars importation of slaves. Beethoven's *Fifth* and *Sixth Symphonies* performed.

1812 Napoleon's Grand Army invades Russia in June. Forced to retreat in winter, most of Napoleon's 600,000 men are lost. In the U.S., war with Britain declared over freedom of the seas for U.S. vessels (War of 1812). USS *Constitution* sinks British frigate.

Richard Wagner (1813–1883)

1814 French defeated by allies (Britain, Austria, Russia, Prussia, Sweden, and Portugal) in War of Liberation. Napoleon exiled to Elba, off Italian coast. Bourbon king Louis XVIII takes French throne. George Stephenson builds first practical steam locomotive.

1815 Napoleon returns: "Hundred Days" begin. Napoleon defeated by Wellington at Waterloo, banished again to St. Helena in South Atlantic. Congress of Vienna: victorious allies change the map of Europe. War of 1812 ends with treaty of Ghent.

1819 Simón Bolívar liberates New Granada (now Colombia, Venezuela, and Ecuador) as Spain loses hold on South American countries; named president of Colombia.

1820 Missouri Compromise—Missouri admitted as slave state but slavery barred in rest of Louisiana Purchase north of 36°30′ N.

Harriet Beecher Stowe (1811–1896)

1821 Guatemala, Panama, and Santo Domingo proclaim independence from Spain.

1822 Greeks proclaim a republic and independence from Turkey. Turks invade Greece. Russia declares war on Turkey (1828). Greece also aided by France and Britain. War ends and Turks recognize Greek independence (1829). Brazil becomes independent of Portugal. Schubert's *Eighth Symphony* ("The Unfinished").

1823 U.S. Monroe Doctrine warns European nations not to interfere in Western Hemisphere.

1824 Mexico becomes a republic, three years after declaring independence from Spain. Bolívar liberates Peru, becomes its president. Beethoven's *Ninth Symphony*.

1825 First passenger-carrying railroad in England.

1826 Joseph-Nicéphore Niepce takes the world's first photograph.

Walt Whitman (1819–1892)

WAR OF 1812

British interference with American trade, impressment of American seamen, and "War Hawks" drive for western expansion lead to war. American attacks on Canada foiled; U.S. Commodore Perry wins battle of Lake Erie (1813). British capture and burn Washington (1814) but fail to take Fort McHenry at Baltimore. Andrew Jackson repulses assault on New Orleans after treaty of Ghent ends war (1815). War settles little but strengthens U.S. as independent nation.

**Dred Scott
(1795?–1858)**

**Charles Darwin
(1809–1882)**

**Frederick Douglass
(1817–1895)**

**Harriet Tubman
(c. 1820–1913)**

**Samuel Clemens
(Mark Twain)
(1835–1910)**

1830   French invade Algeria. Louis Philippe becomes "Citizen King" as revolution forces Charles X to abdicate. Mormon church formed in U.S. by Joseph Smith.

1831   Polish revolt against Russia fails. Belgium separates from the Netherlands. In U.S., Nat Turner leads unsuccessful slave rebellion.

1833   Slavery abolished in British Empire.

1834   Charles Babbage invents "analytical engine," precursor of computer. McCormick patents reaper.

1836   Boer farmers start "Great Trek"—Natal, Transvaal, and Orange Free State founded in South Africa. Mexican army besieges Texans in Alamo. Entire garrison, including Davy Crockett and Jim Bowie, wiped out. Texans gain independence from Mexico after winning Battle of San Jacinto. Dickens's *Pickwick Papers.*

1837   Victoria becomes queen of Great Britain. Mob kills Elijah P. Lovejoy, Illinois abolitionist publisher.

1839   First Opium War (to 1842) between Britain and China, over importation of drug into China.

1840   Lower and Upper Canada united.

1841   U.S. President Harrison dies (**April 4**) one month after inauguration; John Tyler becomes first vice president to succeed to presidency.

1842   Crawford Long uses first anesthetic (ether).

1843   Wagner's opera *The Flying Dutchman.*

1844   Democratic convention calls for annexation of Texas and acquisition of Oregon ("Fifty-four-forty-or-fight"). Five Chinese ports opened to U.S. ships. Samuel F. B. Morse patents telegraph.

1845   Congress adopts joint resolution for annexation of Texas. Edgar Allan Poe publishes *The Raven and Other Poems.*

1846   U.S. declares war on Mexico. California and New Mexico annexed by U.S. Brigham Young leads Mormons to Great Salt Lake. W. T. Morton uses ether as anesthetic. Sewing machine patented by Elias Howe. Frederick Douglass launches abolitionist newspaper *The North Star.* Failure of potato crop causes famine in Ireland.

1848   Revolt in Paris: Louis Philippe abdicates; Louis Napoleon elected president of French Republic. Revolutions in Vienna, Venice, Berlin, Milan, Rome, and Warsaw. Put down by royal troops in 1848–1849. U.S.-Mexico War ends; Mexico cedes claims to Texas, California, Arizona, New Mexico, Utah, Nevada. U.S. treaty with Britain sets Oregon Territory boundary at 49th parallel. Karl Marx and Friedrich Engels's *Communist Manifesto.* Harriet Tubman escapes from slavery and joins the Underground Railroad. Women's Rights Convention in Seneca Falls, N.Y.

1849   California gold rush begins.

1850   Henry Clay opens great debate on slavery, warns South against secession.

1851   Herman Melville's *Moby-Dick.*

1852   South African Republic established. Louis Napoleon proclaims himself Napoleon III ("Second Empire"). Harriet Beecher Stowe's *Uncle Tom's Cabin.*

1853   Crimean War begins as Turkey declares war on Russia. Commodore Perry reaches Tokyo.

1854   Britain and France join Turkey in war on Russia. In U.S., Kansas-Nebraska Act permits local option on slavery; rioting and bloodshed. Japanese allow American trade. Antislavery men in Michigan form Republican Party. Tennyson's *Charge of the Light Brigade.* Thoreau's *Walden.*

1855   Armed clashes in Kansas between pro- and anti-slavery forces. Florence Nightingale nurses wounded in Crimea. Walt Whitman's *Leaves of Grass.*

1856   Flaubert's *Madame Bovary.*

1857   Supreme Court, in Dred Scott decision, rules that a slave is not a citizen. Financial crisis in Europe and U.S. Great Mutiny (Sepoy Rebellion) begins in India. India placed under crown rule as a result.

1858   Pro-slavery constitution rejected in Kansas. Abraham Lincoln makes strong antislavery speech in Springfield, Ill.: "...this Government cannot endure permanently half slave and half free." Lincoln-Douglas debates. First trans-Atlantic telegraph cable completed by Cyrus W. Field.

1859   John Brown raids Harpers Ferry; is captured and hanged. Work begins on Suez Canal. Unification of Italy starts under leadership of Count Cavour, Sardinian premier. Joined by France in war against Austria. Jean-Joseph-Étienne Lenoir builds first practical internal-combustion engine. Edward Fitzgerald's translation of *The Rubaiyat of Omar Khayyam.* Charles Darwin's *Origin of Species.* J. S. Mill's *On Liberty.*

1860 South Carolina secedes from the Union.

1861 U.S. Civil War begins as attempts at compromise fail. Mississippi, Florida, Alabama, Georgia, Louisiana, and Texas secede; with South Carolina, they form the Confederate States of America, with Jefferson Davis as president. Virginia, Arkansas, Tennessee, North Carolina secede and join Confederacy. First Battle of Bull Run (Manassas). Congress creates Colorado, Dakota, and Nevada territories; adopts income tax; Lincoln inaugurated. Serfs emancipated in Russia. Pasteur's theory of germs. Independent Kingdom of Italy proclaimed under Sardinian king Victor Emmanuel II.

1862 Several major Civil War battles: Battle of Shiloh, Second Battle of Bull Run (Manassas), Battle of Antietam. Salon des Refusés introduces impressionism.

**Abraham Lincoln
(1809–1865)**

1863 French capture Mexico City; proclaim Archduke Maximilian of Austria emperor. Battle of Gettysburg.

1864 Gen. Sherman's Atlanta campaign and "march to the sea."

1865 Gen. Lee surrenders to Grant at Appomattox; the Civil War is over. Lincoln fatally shot at Ford's Theater by John Wilkes Booth. Vice President Johnson sworn as successor. Booth caught and dies of gunshot wounds; four conspirators are hanged. Joseph Lister begins antiseptic surgery. Gregor Mendel's *Law of Heredity.* Lewis Carroll's *Alice's Adventures in Wonderland.*

1866 Alfred Nobel invents dynamite (patented in Britain, 1867). Seven Weeks' War: Austria defeated by Prussia and Italy.

1867 Austria-Hungary Dual Monarchy established. French leave Mexico; Maximilian executed. Dominion of Canada established. U.S. buys Alaska from Russia for $7,200,000. South African diamond field discovered. Japan ends 675-year shogun rule. Volume I of Marx's *Das Kapital.* Strauss's *Blue Danube.*

**Robert E. Lee
(1807–1870)**

1868 Revolution in Spain; Queen Isabella deposed, flees to France. In U.S., Fourteenth Amendment giving civil rights to blacks is ratified. Georgia under military government after legislature expels blacks.

1869 First U.S. transcontinental rail route completed. James Fisk and Jay Gould's attempt to control gold market causes Black Friday panic. Suez Canal opens. Mendeleev's periodic table of elements.

1870 Franco-Prussian War (to 1871): Napoleon III capitulates at Sedan. Revolt in Paris; Third Republic proclaimed.

**William Tecumseh Sherman
(1820–1891)**

1871 France surrenders Alsace-Lorraine to Germany; war ends. German Empire proclaimed with Prussian King as Kaiser Wilhelm I. Fighting with Apaches begins in American West. Boss Tweed corruption exposed in New York. The Chicago Fire, with 250 deaths and $196-million damage. Stanley meets Livingstone in Africa.

1872 Congress gives amnesty to most Confederates. Jules Verne's *Around the World in 80 Days.*

THE CIVIL WAR

Apart from the matter of slavery, the Civil War arose out of both the economic and political rivalry between an agrarian South and an industrial North and the issue of the right of states to secede from the Union.

1861 After South Carolina secedes **(Dec. 20, 1860),** Mississippi, Florida, Alabama, Georgia, Louisiana, and Texas follow, forming the Confederate States of America, with Jefferson Davis as president **(Jan.– March).** War begins as Confederates fire on Fort Sumter **(April 12).** Lincoln calls for 75,000 volunteers. Southern ports blockaded by superior Union naval forces. Virginia, Arkansas, Tennessee, and North Carolina secede to complete 11-state Confederacy. Union army advancing on Richmond repulsed at first Battle of Bull Run (Manassas) **(July).**

1862 Edwin M. Stanton named Secretary of War **(Jan.).** Grant wins first important Union victory in West, at Fort Donelson; Nashville falls **(Feb.).** Ironclads, Union's *Monitor* and Confederate's *Virginia (Merrimac)* duel at Hampton Roads **(March).** New Orleans falls to Union fleet under Farragut; city occupied **(April).** Grant's army escapes defeat at Shiloh. Memphis falls as Union gunboats control upper Mississippi **(June).** Confederate General Robert E. Lee victorious at second Battle of Bull Run (Manassas) **(Aug.).** Union army under McClellan halts Lee's attack on Washington in the Battle of Antietam **(Sept.).** Lincoln removes

McClellan for lack of aggressiveness. Burnside's drive on Richmond fails at Fredericksburg **(Dec.).** Union forces under Rosecrans chase Bragg through Tennessee; battle of Murfreesboro **(Oct.–Jan. 1863).**

1863 Lee defeats Hooker at Chancellorsville; "Stonewall" Jackson, Confederate general, dies **(May).** Confederate invasion of Pennsylvania stopped at Gettysburg by George Meade—Lee loses 20,000 men—the greatest battle of the War **(July).** It and the Union victory at Vicksburg mark the war's turning point. Union general George H. Thomas, the "Rock of Chickamauga," holds Bragg's forces on Georgia-Tennessee border **(Sept.).** Sherman, Hooker, and Thomas drive Bragg back to Georgia. Tennessee restored to the Union **(Nov.).**

1864 Ulysses S. Grant named commander-in-chief of Union forces **(March).** In the Wilderness campaign, Grant forces Lee's Army of Northern Virginia back toward Richmond **(May–June).** Sherman's Atlanta campaign and "march to the sea" **(May–Sept.).** Farragut's victory at Mobile Bay **(Aug.).** Hood's Confederate army defeated at Nashville. Sherman takes Savannah **(Dec.).**

1865 Sheridan defeats Confederates at Five Forks; Confederates evacuate Richmond **(April).** On **April 9,** Lee surrenders to Grant at Appomattox.

Johannes Brahms
(1833–1897)

Chief Joseph
(c. 1840–1904)

Statue of Liberty

Marie Curie
(1867–1934)

1873 Economic crisis in Europe. U.S. establishes gold standard.

1875 First Kentucky Derby.

1876 Sioux kill Gen. George A. Custer and 264 troopers at Little Big Horn River. Alexander Graham Bell patents the telephone.

1877 After Presidential election of 1876, Electoral Commission gives disputed Electoral College votes to Rutherford B. Hayes despite Tilden's popular majority. Russo-Turkish war (ends in 1878 with power of Turkey in Europe broken). Reconstruction ends in the American South. Thomas Edison patents phonograph. The Nez Perce leader Chief Joseph is forced to surrender. Tchaikovsky's *Swan Lake*.

1878 Congress of Berlin revises Treaty of San Stefano, ending Russo-Turkish War; makes extensive redivision of southeastern Europe. First commercial telephone exchange opened in New Haven, Conn.

1879 Thomas A. Edison invents electric light.

1880 U.S.-China treaty allows U.S. to restrict immigration of Chinese labor.

1881 President Garfield fatally shot by assassin; Vice President Arthur succeeds him. Charles J. Guiteau convicted and executed (1882).

1882 Terrorism in Ireland after land evictions. Britain invades and conquers Egypt. Germany, Austria, and Italy form Triple Alliance. In U.S., Congress adopts Chinese Exclusion Act. Rockefeller's Standard Oil Trust is first industrial monopoly. In Berlin, Robert Koch announces discovery of tuberculosis germ.

1883 Congress creates Civil Service Commission. Brooklyn Bridge and Metropolitan Opera House completed.

1884 Berlin West Africa Conference held in Berlin (lasting until **Feb. 1885**), at which the major European nations discuss expansion in Africa.

1885 British Gen. Charles G. "Chinese" Gordon killed at Khartoum in Egyptian Sudan. World's first skyscraper built in Chicago.

1886 Bombing at Haymarket Square, Chicago, kills seven policemen and injures many others. Eight alleged anarchists accused—three imprisoned, one commits suicide, four hanged. (In 1893, Illinois Governor Altgeld, critical of trial, pardons three survivors.) Statue of Liberty dedicated. Geronimo, Apache Indian chief, surrenders.

1887 Queen Victoria's Golden Jubilee. Sir Arthur Conan Doyle's first Sherlock Holmes story, *A Study in Scarlet*.

1888 Historic March blizzard in Northeast U.S.—many perish, property damage exceeds $25 million. George Eastman's box camera (the Kodak). J. B. Dunlop invents pneumatic tire. Jack the Ripper murders in London.

1889 Second (Socialist) International founded in Paris. Indian Territory in Oklahoma opened to settlement. Thousands die in Johnstown, Pa. flood. Eiffel Tower built for the Paris exposition. Mark Twain's *A Connecticut Yankee in King Arthur's Court*.

1890 Congress votes to pass Sherman Antitrust Act. Sioux Chief Sitting Bull arrested and killed by police on Pine Ridge reservation; two weeks later, U.S. troops kill over 200 Sioux at Battle of Wounded Knee.

1892 Battle between steel strikers and Pinkerton guards at Homestead, Pa.; union defeated after militia intervenes. Silver mine strikers in Idaho fight non-union workers; U.S. troops dispatched. Diesel engine patented.

1893 New Zealand becomes first country in the world to grant women the vote.

1894 Sino-Japanese War begins (ends in 1895 with China's defeat). In France, Capt. Alfred Dreyfus convicted on false treason charge (pardoned in 1906). In U.S., Jacob S. Coxey of Ohio leads "Coxey's Army" of unemployed on Washington. Eugene V. Debs calls general strike of rail workers to support Pullman Company strikers; strike broken, Debs jailed for six months. Edison's kinetoscope given first public showing in New York City.

1895 X-rays discovered by German physicist Wilhelm Roentgen. Auguste and Louis Lumière premiere motion pictures at a café in Paris.

SPANISH-AMERICAN WAR (1898–1899)

War fires stoked by "jingo journalism" as American people support Cuban rebels against Spain. American business sees economic gain in Cuban trade and resources and American power zones in Latin America. Outstanding events: Submarine mine sinks U.S. battleship *Maine* in Havana Harbor (**Feb. 15**); 260 killed; responsibility never fixed. Congress declares independence of Cuba **(April 19)**. Spain declares war on U.S. **(April 24)**; Congress **(April 25)** formally declares nation has been at war with Spain since **April 21**. Commodore George Dewey wins seven-hour battle of Manila Bay **(May 1)**. Spanish fleet destroyed off Santiago, Cuba **(July 3)**; city surrenders **(July 17)**. Treaty of Paris (ratified by Senate 1899) ends war. U.S. given Guam and Puerto Rico and agrees to pay Spain $20 million for Philippines. Cuba independent of Spain; under U.S. military control for three years until **May 20, 1902**. Yellow fever is eradicated and political reforms achieved.

1896 Supreme Court's *Plessy v. Ferguson* decision—"separate but equal" doctrine. Alfred Nobel's will establishes prizes for peace, science, and literature. Marconi receives first wireless patent in Britain. William Jennings Bryan delivers "Cross of Gold" speech at Democratic Convention in Chicago. First modern Olympic games held in Athens, Greece.

1897 Theodor Herzl launches Zionist movement.

1898 Chinese "Boxers," anti-foreign organization, established. They stage uprisings against Europeans in 1900; U.S. and other Western troops relieve Peking legations. U.S. Battleship *Maine* is sunk in Havana Harbor. Spanish-American War begins. U.S. destroys Spanish fleet near Santiago, Cuba. Pierre and Marie Curie discover radium and polonium.

1899 Boer War (or South African War): conflict between British and Boers (descendants of Dutch settlers of South Africa). Causes rooted in long-standing territorial disputes and in friction over political rights for English and other "uitlanders" following 1886 discovery of vast gold deposits in Transvaal. (British victorious as war ends in 1902.) Casualties: 5,774 British dead, about 4,000 Boers. Union of South Africa established in 1908 as confederation of colonies; becomes British dominion in 1910.

Sigmund Freud
(1856–1939)

1900–1999 (A.D.)

1900 Hurricane ravages Galveston, Tex.; 6,000 drown. Fauvist movement in painting begins, led by Henri Matisse. Sigmund Freud's *The Interpretation of Dreams.* Carrie Chapman Catt succeeds Susan B. Anthony as president of National Woman Suffrage Association.

1901 Queen Victoria dies, and is succeeded by her son, Edward VII. As President McKinley begins second term, he is shot fatally by anarchist Leon Czolgosz. Theodore Roosevelt sworn in as successor.

1902 Enrico Caruso's first gramophone recording. Aswan Dam completed.

1903 Wright brothers, Orville and Wilbur, fly first powered, controlled, heavier-than-air plane at Kitty Hawk, N.C. Henry Ford organizes Ford Motor Company. The Boston Red Sox win the first World Series against the Pittsburgh Pirates. W. E. B. Du Bois publishes *The Souls of Black Folk.*

Carrie Chapman Catt
(1859–1947)

1904 Russo-Japanese War begins—competition for Korea and Manchuria. *Entente Cordiale:* Britain and France settle their international differences. General theory of radioactivity by Rutherford and Soddy. New York City subway opens.

1905 In Russo-Japanese War, Port Arthur surrenders to Japanese; Russia suffers other defeats. President Roosevelt mediates Treaty of Portsmouth, N.H., which recognizes Japan's control of Korea and restores southern Manchuria to China. The Russian Revolution of 1905 begins on "Bloody Sunday" when troops fire onto a defenseless group of demonstrators in St. Petersburg. Strikes and riots follow. Sailors on battleship *Potemkin* mutiny; reforms, including first Duma (parliament), established by Czar Nicholas II's "October Manifesto." Albert Einstein's special theory of relativity and other key theories in physics. Franz Lehar's *Merry Widow.*

1906 San Francisco earthquake and three-day fire; more than 500 dead. Roald Amundsen, Norwegian explorer, fixes magnetic North Pole.

Albert Einstein
(1879–1955)

1907 Second Hague Peace Conference, of 46 nations, adopts 10 conventions on rules of war. Financial panic of 1907 in U.S. Mahler begins work on "Song of the Earth." Oklahoma becomes 46th state. Picasso's *Les Demoiselles d'Avignon* introduces cubism.

1908 Earthquake kills 150,000 in southern Italy and Sicily. U.S. Supreme Court, in Danbury Hatters' case, outlaws secondary union boycotts. Model T produced by Ford Motor Company.

1909 North Pole reportedly reached by American explorers Robert E. Peary and Matthew Henson. The National Association for the Advancement of Colored People is founded in New York by prominent black and white intellectuals and led by W. E. B. Du Bois.

1910 Boy Scouts of America incorporated. Angel Island, in San Francisco Bay, becomes immigration center for Asians entering U.S.

Vladimir Lenin
(1870–1924)

1911 First use of aircraft as offensive weapon in Turkish-Italian War. Italy defeats Turks and annexes Tripoli and Libya. Chinese Republic proclaimed after revolution overthrows Manchu dynasty. Sun Yat-sen named president. Mexican Revolution: Porfirio Diaz, president since 1877, replaced by Francisco Madero. Triangle Shirtwaist Company fire in New York; 146 killed. Amundsen reaches South Pole. Ernest Rutherford discovers the structure of the atom. Richard Strauss's *Der Rosenkavalier.* Irving Berlin's *Alexander's Ragtime Band.*

Robert Peary
(1856–1920)

W. E. B. Du Bois
(1868–1963)

Woodrow Wilson
(1856–1924)

Bessie Smith
(1894–1937)

1912 Balkan Wars (1912–1913) resulting from territorial disputes: Turkey defeated by alliance of Bulgaria, Serbia, Greece, and Montenegro; London peace treaty (1913) partitions most of European Turkey among the victors. In second war (1913), Bulgaria attacks Serbia and Greece and is defeated after Romania intervenes and Turks recapture Adrianople. *Titanic* sinks on maiden voyage; over 1,500 drown. New Mexico and Arizona admitted as states.

1913 Suffragettes demonstrate in London. Garment workers strike in New York and Boston; win pay raise and shorter hours. Henry Ford develops first moving assembly line. 16th Amendment (income tax) and 17th (popular election of U.S. senators) adopted. Bill creating U.S. Federal Reserve System becomes law. Stravinsky's *The Rite of Spring*. Woodrow Wilson becomes 28th U.S. president. Armory Show introduces modern art to U.S.; Duchamp's *Nude Descending a Staircase* shocks public.

1914 World War I begins: Austrian Archduke Francis Ferdinand and wife Sophie are assassinated; Austria declares war on Serbia, Germany on Russia and France, Britain on Germany. Panama Canal officially opened. Congress sets up Federal Trade Commission, passes Clayton Antitrust Act. U.S. Marines occupy Veracruz, Mexico, intervening in civil war to protect American interests.

1915 *Lusitania* sunk by German submarine. Second Battle of Ypres. U.S. banks lend $500 million to France and Britain. Genocide of estimated 600,000 to 1 million Armenians by Turkish soldiers. D. W. Griffith's film *Birth of a Nation*. Albert Einstein's *General Theory of Relativity*.

1916 Congress expands armed forces. Battle of Verdun. Battle of the Somme. Tom Mooney arrested for San Francisco bombing (pardoned in 1939). Pershing fails in raid into Mexico in quest of rebel Pancho Villa. U.S. buys Virgin Islands from Denmark for $25 million. President Wilson re-elected with "he kept us out of war" slogan. "Black Tom" explosion at munitions dock in Jersey City, N.J., $40,000,000 damages; traced to German saboteurs. Margaret Sanger opens first birth control clinic. Easter Rebellion in Ireland put down by British troops. Jeannette Rankin becomes first woman elected to Congress.

1917 First U.S. combat troops in France as U.S. declares war on Germany **(April 6)**. Third Battle of Ypres. Russian Revolution of 1917—climax of long unrest under czars. February Revolution—Nicholas II forced to abdicate, liberal government created. Kerensky becomes prime minister and forms provisional government **(July)**. In October Revolution, Bolsheviks seize power in armed coup d'état led by Lenin and Trotsky. Kerensky flees. Balfour Declaration promises Jewish homeland in Palestine. U.S. declares war on Austria-Hungary **(Dec. 7)**. Armistice between

---

WORLD WAR I (1914–1918)

Imperial, territorial, and economic rivalries led to the "Great War" between the Central Powers (Austria-Hungary, Germany, Bulgaria, and Turkey) and the Allies (U.S., Britain, France, Russia, Belgium, Serbia, Greece, Romania, Montenegro, Portugal, Italy, Japan). About 10 million combatants killed, 20 million wounded.

1914 Austrian Archduke Francis Ferdinand and wife assassinated in Sarajevo by Serbian nationalist, Gavrilo Princip **(June 28)**. Austria declares war on Serbia **(July 28)**. Germany declares war on Russia **(Aug. 1)**, on France **(Aug. 3)**, invades Belgium **(Aug. 4)**. Britain declares war on Germany **(Aug. 4)**. Germans defeat Russians in Battle of Tannenberg on Eastern Front **(Aug.)**. First Battle of the Marne **(Sept.)**. German drive stopped 25 miles from Paris. By end of year, war on the Western Front is "positional" in the trenches.

1915 German submarine blockade of Great Britain begins **(Feb.)**. Dardanelles Campaign—British land in Turkey **(April)**, withdraw from Gallipoli **(Dec.–Jan. 1916)**. Germans use gas at second Battle of Ypres **(April–May)**. *Lusitania* sunk by German submarine—1,198 lost, including 128 Americans **(May 7)**. On Eastern Front, German and Austrian "great offensive" conquers all of Poland and Lithuania; Russians lose 1 million men (by **Sept. 6**). "Great Fall Offensive" by Allies results in little change from 1914 **(Sept.–Oct.)**. Britain and France declare war on Bulgaria **(Oct. 14)**.

1916 Battle of Verdun—Germans and French each lose about 350,000 men **(Feb.)**. Extended submarine

warfare begins **(March)**. British-German sea battle of Jutland **(May)**; British lose more ships, but German fleet never ventures forth again. On Eastern Front, the Brusilov offensive demoralizes Russians, costs them 1 million men **(June–Sept.)**. Battle of the Somme—British lose over 400,000; French, 200,000; Germans, about 450,000; all with no strategic results **(July–Nov.)**. Romania declares war on Austria-Hungary **(Aug. 27)**. Bucharest captured **(Dec.)**.

1917 U.S. declares war on Germany **(April 6)**. Submarine warfare at peak **(April)**. On Italian Front, Battle of Caporetto—Italians retreat, losing 600,000 prisoners and deserters **(Oct.–Dec.)**. On Western Front, Battles of Arras, Champagne, Ypres (third battle), etc. First large British tank attack **(Nov.)**. U.S. declares war on Austria-Hungary **(Dec. 7)**. Armistice between new Russian Bolshevik government and Germans **(Dec. 15)**.

1918 Great offensive by Germans **(March–June)**. Americans' first important battle role at Château-Thierry—as they and French stop German advance **(June)**. Second Battle of the Marne **(July–Aug.)**—start of Allied offensive at Amiens, St. Mihiel, etc. Battles of the Argonne and Ypres panic German leadership **(Sept.–Oct.)**. British offensive in Palestine **(Sept.)**. Germans ask for armistice **(Oct. 4)**. British armistice with Turkey **(Oct.)**. German Kaiser abdicates **(Nov.)**. Hostilities cease on Western Front **(Nov. 11)**.

new Russian Bolshevik government and Germans (**Dec. 15**). Sigmund Freud's *Introduction to Psychoanalysis*.

1918 Russian revolutionaries execute the former czar and his family. Russian Civil War between Reds (Bolsheviks) and Whites (anti-Bolsheviks); Reds win in 1920. Allied troops (U.S., British, French) intervene (**March**); leave in 1919. Second Battle of the Marne (**July–Aug.**) German Kaiser abdicates (**Nov.**); hostilities cease on the Western Front. Japanese hold Vladivostok until 1922. World-wide influenza epidemic strikes; by 1920, nearly 20 million are dead. In U.S. alone, 500,000 perish.

1919 Third International (Comintern) establishes Soviet control over international Communist movements. Paris peace conference. Versailles Treaty, incorporating Woodrow Wilson's draft Covenant of League of Nations, signed by Allies and Germany; rejected by U.S. Senate. Congress formally ends war in 1921. 18th (Prohibition) Amendment adopted. Alcock and Brown make first trans-Atlantic non-stop flight. Mahatma Gandhi initiates satyagraha ("truth force") campaigns, beginning his nonviolent resistance movement against British rule in India.

**Mahatma Gandhi
(1869–1948)**

1920 League of Nations holds first meeting at Geneva, Switzerland. U.S. Dept. of Justice "red hunt" nets thousands of radicals; aliens deported. Women's suffrage (19th) amendment ratified. Treaty of Sèvres dissolves Ottoman Empire. First Agatha Christie mystery. Sinclair Lewis's *Main Street*.

1921 Reparations Commission fixes German liability at 132 billion gold marks. German inflation begins. Major treaties signed at Washington Disarmament Conference limit naval tonnage and pledge to respect territorial integrity of China. In U.S., Nicola Sacco and Bartolomeo Vanzetti, Italian-born anarchists, convicted of armed robbery murder; case stirs world-wide protests; they are executed in 1927.

**William Butler Yeats
(1865–1939)**

1922 Mussolini marches on Rome; forms Fascist government. Irish Free State, a self-governing dominion of British Empire, officially proclaimed. Kemal Atatürk, founder of modern Turkey, overthrows last sultan. James Joyce's *Ulysses*.

1923 Adolf Hitler's "Beer Hall Putsch" in Munich fails; in 1924 he is sentenced to five years in prison where he writes *Mein Kampf;* released after eight months. Occupation of Ruhr by French and Belgian troops to enforce reparations payments. Widespread Ku Klux Klan violence in U.S. Earthquake destroys third of Tokyo. George Gershwin's *Rhapsody in Blue*. Bessie Smith, known as "the Empress of the Blues," makes her first record. Irish poet William Butler Yeats wins Nobel Prize in Literature.

**Robert Frost
(1874–1963)**

1924 Death of Lenin; Stalin wins power struggle, rules as Soviet dictator until death in 1953. Italian Fascists murder Socialist leader Giacomo Matteotti. Interior Secretary Albert B. Fall and oilmen Harry Sinclair and Edward L. Doheny are charged with conspiracy and bribery in the Teapot Dome scandal, involving fraudulent leases of naval oil reserves. In 1931, Fall is sentenced to year in prison; Doheny and Sinclair acquitted of bribery. Nathan Leopold and Richard Loeb convicted in "thrill killing" of Bobby Franks in Chicago; defended by Clarence Darrow; sentenced to life imprisonment. (Loeb killed by fellow convict in 1936; Leopold paroled in 1958, dies in 1971.) Robert Frost wins first of four Pulitzers.

**Pablo Picasso
(1881–1973)**

1925 Nellie Tayloe Ross elected governor of Wyoming; first woman governor elected in U.S. Locarno conferences seek to secure European peace by mutual guarantees. John T. Scopes convicted and fined for teaching evolution in a public school in Tennessee "Monkey Trial"; sentence set aside. John Logie Baird, Scottish inventor, transmits human features by television. Hitler publishes Volume I of *Mein Kampf*.

1926 General strike in Britain brings nation's activities to standstill. U.S. marines dispatched to Nicaragua during revolt; they remain until 1933. Gertrude Ederle of U.S. is first woman to swim English Channel. Ernest Hemingway's *The Sun Also Rises*.

1927 German economy collapses. Socialists riot in Vienna; general strike follows acquittal of Nazis for political murder. Trotsky expelled from Russian Communist Party. Charles A. Lindbergh flies first successful solo non-stop flight from New York to Paris. Ruth Snyder and Judd Gray convicted of murder of Albert Snyder; they are executed at Sing Sing prison in 1928. Philo T. Farnsworth demonstrates working television model. Georges Lemaître proposes Big Bang Theory. Babe Ruth hits 60 home runs in the season; record stands for next 34 years. *The Jazz Singer*, with Al Jolson, first part-talking motion picture.

**Babe Ruth
(George Herman Ruth)
(1895–1948)**

Benito Mussolini
(1883–1945)

Joseph Stalin
(1879–1953)

Adolf Hitler
(1889–1945)

1928 Kellogg-Briand Pact, outlawing war, signed in Paris by 65 nations. Alexander Fleming discovers penicillin. Richard E. Byrd starts expedition to Antarctic; returns in 1930. Anthropologist Margaret Mead publishes *Coming of Age in Samoa*. *Oxford English Dictionary* published after 44 years of research.

1929 Trotsky expelled from U.S.S.R. Lateran Treaty establishes independent Vatican City. In U.S., stock market prices collapse, with U.S. securities losing $26 billion—first phase of Depression and world economic crisis. St. Valentine's Day gangland massacre in Chicago. Edwin Powell Hubble proposes theory of expanding universe.

1930 Britain, U.S., Japan, France, and Italy sign naval disarmament treaty. Nazis gain in German elections. Cyclotron developed by Ernest O. Lawrence, U.S. physicist. Pluto discovered by astronomers.

1931 Spain becomes a republic with overthrow of King Alfonso XIII. German industrialists finance 800,000-strong Nazi party. British parliament enacts statute of Westminster, legalizing dominion equality with Britain. Mukden Incident begins Japanese occupation of Manchuria. In U.S., Hoover proposes one-year moratorium of war debts. Harold C. Urey discovers heavy hydrogen. Gangster Al Capone sentenced to 11 years in prison for tax evasion (freed in 1939; dies in 1947). Notorious Scottsboro trial begins, exposing depth of Southern racism. "The Star Spangled Banner" officially becomes national anthem.

1932 Nazis lead in German elections with 230 Reichstag seats. Famine in U.S.S.R. In U.S., Congress sets up Reconstruction Finance Corporation to stimulate economy. Veterans march on Washington—most leave after Senate rejects payment of cash bonuses; others removed by troops under Douglas MacArthur. U.S. protests Japanese aggression in Manchuria. Amelia Earhart is first woman to fly Atlantic solo. Charles A. Lindbergh's baby son kidnapped, killed. (Bruno Richard Hauptmann arrested in 1934, convicted in 1935, executed in 1936.)

1933 Hitler appointed German chancellor, gets dictatorial powers. Reichstag fire in Berlin; Nazi terror begins. Germany and Japan withdraw from League of Nations. Giuseppe Zangara executed for attempted assassination of president-elect Roosevelt in which Chicago mayor Cermak is fatally shot. Roosevelt inaugurated ("the only thing we have to fear is fear itself"); launches New Deal. Prohibition repealed. U.S.S.R. recognized by U.S.

1934 Chancellor Dollfuss of Austria assassinated by Nazis. Hitler becomes führer. U.S.S.R. admitted to League of Nations. Dionne sisters, first quintuplets to survive beyond infancy, born in Canada. Mao Zedong begins the Long March north with 100,000 soldiers.

1935 Saar incorporated into Germany after plebiscite. Nazis repudiate Versailles Treaty, introduce compulsory military service. Mussolini invades Ethiopia; League of Nations invokes sanctions. Roosevelt opens second phase of

---

THE HOLOCAUST (1933–1945)

"Holocaust" is the term describing the Nazi annihilation of about 6 million Jews (two thirds of the pre-World War II European Jewish population), including 4,500,000 from Russia, Poland, and the Baltic; 750,000 from Hungary and Romania; 290,000 from Germany and Austria; 105,000 from The Netherlands; 90,000 from France; 54,000 from Greece.

The Holocaust was unique in its being *genocide*—the systematic destruction of a people solely because of religion, race, ethnicity, nationality, or sexual preference—on an unmatched scale. Along with the Jews, another 9 to 10 million people—Gypsies, Slavs (Poles, Ukrainians, and Belarussians), homosexuals, and the disabled—were exterminated.

1933 Hitler named German Chancellor **(Jan.)**. Dachau, first concentration camp, established **(March)**. Boycotts against Jews begin **(April)**.

1935 Anti-Semitic Nuremberg Laws passed by Reichstag; Jews lose citizenship and civil rights **(Sept.)**.

1937 Buchenwald concentration camp opens **(July)**.

1938 Extension of anti-Semitic laws to Austria after annexation **(March)**. *Kristallnacht* (Night of Broken Glass)—anti-Semitic riots and destruction of Jewish institutions in Germany and Austria **(Nov. 9)**. 26,000 Jews sent to concentration camps; Jewish children expelled from schools **(Nov. 9–10)**. Expropriation of Jewish property and businesses **(Dec.)**.

1940 As war continues, Einsatzgruppen (mobile killing squads) follow German army into conquered lands, rounding up and massacring Jews and other "undesirables."

1941 Goering instructs Heydrich to carry out the "final solution to the Jewish question" **(July 31)**. Deportation of German Jews begins; massacres of Jews in Odessa and Kiev **(Nov.)**; and in Riga and Vilna **(Dec.)**.

1942 Mass killings using Zyklon-B begin at Auschwitz-Birkenau **(Jan.)**. Nazi leaders attend Wannsee Conference to coordinate the "final solution" **(Jan. 20)**. 100,000 Jews from Warsaw Ghetto deported to Treblinka death camp **(July)**.

1943 Warsaw Ghetto uprisings **(Jan. and April)**; Ghetto exterminated **(May)**.

1944 476,000 Hungarian Jews sent to Auschwitz **(May–June)**. D-day **(June 6)**. Soviet Army liberates Maidanek death camp **(July)**. Nazis try to hide evidence of death camps **(Nov.)**.

1945 As Allies advance, Nazis force concentration camp inmates on death marches. Americans liberate Buchenwald and British liberate Bergen-Belsen camps **(April)**. Nuremberg War Crimes Trial **(Nov. 1945–Oct. 1946)**.

New Deal in U.S., calling for social security, better housing, equitable taxation, and farm assistance. Huey Long assassinated in Louisiana.

1936 Germans occupy Rhineland. Italy annexes Ethiopia. Rome-Berlin Axis proclaimed (Japan to join in 1940). Trotsky exiled to Mexico. King George V dies; succeeded by son, Edward VIII, who soon abdicates to marry an American-born divorcée, and is succeeded by brother, George VI. Spanish civil war begins. Hundreds of Americans join the "Lincoln Brigades." (Franco's fascist forces defeat Loyalist forces by 1939, when Madrid falls.) War between China and Japan begins, to continue through World War II. Japan and Germany sign anti-Comintern pact; joined by Italy in 1937.

1937 Hitler repudiates war guilt clause of Versailles Treaty; continues to build German power. Italy withdraws from League of Nations. U.S. gunboat *Panay* sunk by Japanese in Yangtze River. Japan invades China, conquers most of coastal area. Amelia Earhart lost somewhere in Pacific on round-the-world flight. Picasso's *Guernica* mural.

1938 Hitler marches into Austria; political and geographical union of Germany and Austria proclaimed. Munich Pact—Britain, France, and Italy agree to let Germany partition Czechoslovakia. Douglas "Wrong-Way" Corrigan flies from New York to Dublin. Fair Labor Standards Act establishes minimum wage. Orson Welles's radio broadcast *War of the Worlds*.

1939 Germany invades Poland; occupies Bohemia and Moravia; renounces pact with England and concludes 10-year non-aggression pact with U.S.S.R. Russo-Finnish War begins; Finns to lose one-tenth of territory in 1940 peace treaty. World War II begins. In U.S., Roosevelt submits $1,319-million defense budget, proclaims U.S. neutrality, and declares limited emergency. Einstein writes FDR about feasibility of atomic bomb. New York World's Fair opens. DAR refuses to allow Marian Anderson to perform. *Gone with the Wind* premieres.

Dorothea Lange's photo "Migrant Mother" (1936) documented the Great Depression (1929–1940)

Amelia Earhart (1897–1937)

WORLD WAR II (1939–1945)

Axis powers (Germany, Italy, Japan, Hungary, Romania, Bulgaria) *versus* Allies (U.S., Britain, France, U.S.S.R., Australia, Belgium, Brazil, Canada, China, Denmark, Greece, Netherlands, New Zealand, Norway, Poland, South Africa, Yugoslavia).

1939 Germany invades Poland and annexes Danzig; Britain and France give Hitler ultimatum (Sept. 1), declare war (Sept. 3). Disabled German pocket battleship *Admiral Graf Spee* blown up off Montevideo, Uruguay, on Hitler's orders (Dec. 17). Limited activity ("Sitzkrieg") on Western Front.

1940 Nazis invade Netherlands, Belgium, and Luxembourg (May 10). Chamberlain resigns as Britain's prime minister; Churchill takes over (May 10). Germans cross French frontier (May 12) using air/tank/infantry "Blitzkrieg" tactics. Dunkerque evacuation—about 335,000 out of 400,000 Allied soldiers rescued from Belgium by British civilian and naval craft (May 26–June 3). Italy declares war on France and Britain; invades France (June 10). Germans enter Paris; city undefended (June 14). France and Germany sign armistice at Compiègne (June 22). Nazis bomb Coventry, England (Nov. 14).

1941 Germans launch attacks in Balkans. Yugoslavia surrenders—General Mihajlovic continues guerrilla warfare; Tito leads left-wing guerrillas (April 17). Nazi tanks enter Athens; remnants of British Army quit Greece (April 27). Hitler attacks Russia (June 22). Atlantic Charter—FDR and Churchill agree on war aims (Aug. 14). Japanese attacks on Pearl Harbor, Philippines, Guam force U.S. into war; U.S. Pacific fleet crippled (Dec. 7). U.S. and Britain declare war on Japan. Germany and Italy declare war on U.S.; Congress declares war on those countries (Dec. 11).

1942 British surrender Singapore to Japanese (Feb. 15). Roosevelt orders Japanese and Japanese Americans in western U.S. to be exiled to "relocation centers," many for the remainder of the war (Feb. 19). U.S. forces on Bataan peninsula in Philippines surrender (April 9). U.S. and Filipino troops on Corregidor island in Manila Bay surrender to Japanese (May 6). Village of Lidice in Czechoslovakia razed by Nazis

(June 10). U.S. and Britain land in French North Africa (Nov. 8).

1943 Casablanca Conference—Churchill and FDR agree on unconditional surrender goal (Jan. 14–24). German 6th Army surrenders at Stalingrad—turning point of war in Russia (Feb. 1–2). Remnants of Nazis trapped on Cape Bon, ending war in Africa (May 12). Mussolini deposed; Badoglio named premier (July 25). Allied troops land on Italian mainland after conquest of Sicily (Sept. 3). Italy surrenders (Sept. 8). Nazis seize Rome (Sept. 10). Cairo Conference: FDR, Churchill, Chiang Kai-shek pledge defeat of Japan, free Korea (Nov. 22–26). Teheran Conference: FDR, Churchill, Stalin agree on invasion plans (Nov. 28–Dec. 1).

1944 U.S. and British troops land at Anzio on west Italian coast and hold beachhead (Jan. 22). U.S. and British troops enter Rome (June 4). D-Day—Allies launch Normandy invasion (June 6). Hitler wounded in bomb plot (July 20). Paris liberated (Aug. 25). Athens freed by Allies (Oct. 13). Americans invade Philippines (Oct. 20). Germans launch counteroffensive in Belgium—Battle of the Bulge (Dec. 16).

1945 Yalta Agreement signed by FDR, Churchill, Stalin—establishes basis for occupation of Germany, returns to Soviet Union lands taken by Germany and Japan; U.S.S.R. agrees to friendship pact with China (Feb. 11). Mussolini killed at Lake Como (April 28). Admiral Doenitz takes command in Germany; suicide of Hitler announced (May 1). Berlin falls (May 2). Germany signs unconditional surrender terms at Rheims (May 7). Allies declare V-E Day (May 8). Potsdam Conference—Truman, Churchill, Atlee (after July 28), Stalin establish council of foreign ministers to prepare peace treaties; plan German postwar government and reparations (July 17–Aug. 2). A-bomb dropped on Hiroshima by U.S. (Aug. 6). U.S.S.R. declares war on Japan (Aug. 8). Nagasaki hit by A-bomb (Aug. 9). Japan agrees to surrender (Aug. 14). V-J Day—Japanese sign surrender terms aboard battleship *Missouri* (Sept. 2).

Franklin Delano Roosevelt (1882–1945)

Winston Churchill (1874–1965)

Harry S. Truman (1884–1972)

Atomic Bomb

Anne Frank (1929–1945)

1940 Hitler invades Norway, Denmark (**April 9**), the Netherlands, Belgium, Luxembourg (**May 10**), and France (**May 12**). Churchill becomes Britain's prime minister. Trotsky assassinated in Mexico (**Aug. 20**). Estonia, Latvia, and Lithuania annexed by U.S.S.R. U.S. trades 50 destroyers for leases on British bases in Western Hemisphere. Selective Service Act signed. The first official network television broadcast is put out by NBC.

1941 Germany attacks the Balkans and Russia. Japanese surprise attack on U.S. fleet at Pearl Harbor brings U.S. into World War II; U.S. and Britain declare war on Japan. Manhattan Project (atomic bomb research) begins. Roosevelt enunciates "four freedoms," signs Lend-Lease Act, declares national emergency, promises aid to U.S.S.R. Orson Welles's *Citizen Kane*.

1942 Declaration of United Nations signed in Washington (**Jan. 1**). Nazi leaders attend Wannsee Conference to coordinate the "final solution to the Jewish question," the systematic genocide of Jews known as the Holocaust. Women's military services established. Enrico Fermi achieves nuclear chain reaction. More than 120,000 Japanese and persons of Japanese ancestry living in western U.S. moved to "relocation centers," some for the duration of the war (Executive Order 9066). Coconut Grove nightclub fire in Boston kills 492 (**Nov. 28**).

1943 Churchill and Roosevelt hold Casablanca Conference (**Jan. 14–23**). Mussolini deposed. President freezes prices, salaries, and wages to prevent inflation. Income tax withholding introduced.

1944 Allies invade Normandy on D-Day (**June 6**). G.I. Bill of Rights enacted. Bretton Woods Conference creates International Monetary Fund and World Bank (**July 1–22**). Dumbarton Oaks Conference—U.S., British Commonwealth, and U.S.S.R. propose establishment of United Nations (**Aug. 21–Oct. 7**). Battle of the Bulge (**Dec. 16**). Gunnar Myrdal's *An American Dilemma*.

1945 Yalta Conference (Roosevelt, Churchill, Stalin) plans final defeat of Germany (**Feb. 4–11**). FDR dies (**April 12**). Hitler commits suicide (**April 30**); Germany surrenders (**May 7**); **May 8** is declared V-E Day. Potsdam Conference (Truman, Churchill, Stalin) establishes basis of German reconstruction (**July–Aug.**). U.S. drops atomic bombs on Japanese cities of Hiroshima (**Aug. 6**) and Nagasaki (**Aug. 9**). Japan signs official surrender on V-J Day (**Sept. 2**). United Nations established (**Oct. 24**). First electronic computer, ENIAC, built.

1946 First meeting of UN General Assembly opens in London (**Jan. 10**). Winston Churchill's "Iron Curtain" speech warns of Soviet expansion (**March 5**). League of Nations dissolved (**April**). Italy abolishes monarchy (**June**). Verdict in Nuremberg war trial: 12 Nazi leaders (including 1 tried in absentia) sentenced to hang; 7 imprisoned; 3 acquitted (**Oct. 1**). Goering commits suicide a few hours before 10 other Nazis are executed (**Oct. 15**). Juan Perón becomes president of Argentina. Benjamin Spock's childcare classic published.

1947 Britain nationalizes coal mines (**Jan. 1**). Peace treaties for Italy, Romania, Bulgaria, Hungary, Finland signed in Paris (**Feb. 10**). Soviet Union rejects U.S. plan for UN atomic-energy control (**March 4**). Truman proposes Truman Doctrine, which was to aid Greece and Turkey in resisting communist expansion (**March 12**). Marshall Plan for European recovery proposed—a coordinated program to help European nations recover from ravages of war (**June**). (By the time it ended in 1951, this "European Recovery Program" had cost $13 billion.) India and Pakistan gain independence from Britain (**Aug. 15**). U.S. Air Force pilot Chuck Yeager becomes first person to break the sound barrier (**Oct. 14**). Jackie Robinson joins the Brooklyn Dodgers. Anne Frank's *The Diary of a Young Girl* published.

1948 Gandhi assassinated in New Delhi by Hindu fanatic (**Jan. 30**). Burma (**Jan. 4**) and Ceylon (**Feb. 4**) granted independence by Britain. Communists seize power in Czechoslovakia (**Feb. 23–25**). Organization of American States (OAS) Charter signed at Bogotá, Colombia (**April 30**). Nation of Israel proclaimed; British end mandate at midnight; Arab armies attack (**May 14**). Berlin blockade begins (**June 24**), prompting Allied airlift (**June 26**). (Blockade ends **May 12, 1949**; airlift continues until **Sept. 30, 1949**.) Stalin and Tito break (**June 28**). Independent Republic of Korea is proclaimed, following election supervised by UN (**Aug. 15**). Verdict in Japanese war trial: 18 imprisoned (**Nov. 12**); Tojo and six others hanged (**Dec. 23**). United States of Indonesia established as Dutch and Indonesians settle conflict. (**Dec. 27**). Alger Hiss, former

U.S. State Department official, indicted on perjury charges after denying passing secret documents to communist spy ring; convicted in second trial (1950) and sentenced to five-year prison term. Truman ends racial segregation in military. Alfred Kinsey publishes *Sexual Behavior in the American Male.* Tennessee Williams's *A Streetcar Named Desire* wins Pulitzer.

1949 Cease-fire in Palestine (**Jan. 7**). Truman proposes Point Four Program to help world's less developed areas (**Jan. 20**). Israel signs armistice with Egypt (**Feb. 24**). Start of North Atlantic Treaty Organization (NATO)—treaty signed by 12 nations (**April 4**). Federal Republic of Germany (West Germany) established (**May 23**). First successful Soviet atomic test (**July 14**). Communist People's Republic of China formally proclaimed by Chairman Mao Zedong (**Oct. 1**). German Democratic Republic (East Germany) established under Soviet rule (**Oct. 7**). South Africa institutionalizes apartheid.

Tennessee Williams
(1911–1983)

1950 Brink's robbery in Boston; almost $3 million stolen (**Jan. 17**). Truman orders development of hydrogen bomb (**Jan. 31**). Robert Schuman proposes Schuman Plan to pool European coal and steel (**May 9**). Korean War begins when North Korean Communist forces invade South Korea (**June 25**). Assassination attempt on President Truman by Puerto Rican nationalists (**Nov. 1**). McCarthyism begins.

1951 Julius and Ethel Rosenberg sentenced to death for passing atomic secrets to Russians (**March**). Spurred by Schuman Plan, six nations form European Coal and Steel Community (**April**); effective 1952. Japanese peace treaty signed in San Francisco by 49 nations (**Sept. 8**). Color television introduced in U.S. Libya gains independence (**Dec. 24**).

Woody Guthrie
(1912–1967)

1952 George VI dies; his daughter becomes Elizabeth II (**Feb. 6**). AEC announces "satisfactory" experiments in hydrogen-weapons research; eyewitnesses tell of blasts near Enewetak (**Nov.**). Ralph Ellison's *The Invisible Man.*

1953 Gen. Dwight D. Eisenhower inaugurated president of United States (**Jan. 20**). Stalin dies (**March 5**). Malenkov becomes Soviet premier; Beria, minister of interior; Molotov, foreign minister (**March 6**). Dag Hammarskjöld begins term as UN secretary-general (**April 10**). James Watson and Francis Crick publish their discovery of the molecular model of DNA (**April–May**). Edmund Hillary of New Zealand and Tenzing Norgay of Nepal reach top of Mt. Everest (**May 29**). East Berliners rise against Communist rule; quelled by tanks (**June 17**). Egypt becomes republic ruled by military junta (**June 18**). Julius and Ethel Rosenberg executed in Sing Sing prison (**June 19**). Korean armistice signed (**July 27**). Moscow announces explosion of hydrogen bomb (**Aug. 20**). Tito becomes president of Yugoslavia. James Watson, Francis Crick, and Rosalind Franklin discover structure of DNA. Ernest Hemingway wins Pulitzer for *The Old Man and the Sea.*

Dwight D. Eisenhower
(1890–1969)

1954 First atomic submarine *Nautilus* launched (**Jan. 21**). Five U.S. congressmen shot on floor of House as Puerto Rican nationalists fire from spectators' gallery; all five recover (**March 1**). Soviet Union grants sovereignty to East Germany (**March 23**). *Army* v. *McCarthy* inquiry—Senate subcommittee report blames both sides (**April 22–June 17**). Dien Bien Phu, French military outpost in Vietnam, falls to Vietminh army (**May 7**). U.S. Supreme Court (in *Brown* v. *Board of Education of Topeka*) unanimously bans racial segregation in public schools (**May 17**). Eisenhower launches world atomic pool without Soviet Union (**Sept. 6**). Eight-nation Southeast Asia defense treaty (SEATO) signed at Manila (**Sept. 8**). Dr. Jonas Salk starts inoculating children against polio. Algerian War of Independence against France begins (**Nov.**); France struggles to maintain colonial rule until 1962 when it agrees to Algeria's independence. William Faulkner's *A Fable* wins Pulitzer.

Dag Hammarskjöld
(1905–1961)

KOREAN WAR (1950–1953)

1950 North Korean Communist forces invade South Korea (**June 25**). UN calls for cease-fire and asks UN members to assist South Korea (**June 27**). Truman orders U.S. forces into Korea (**June 27**). North Koreans capture Seoul (**June 28**). Gen. Douglas MacArthur designated commander of unified UN forces (**July 8**). Pusan Beachhead—UN forces counterattack and capture Seoul (**Aug.–Sept.**), capture Pyongyang, North Korean capital (**Oct.**). Chinese Communists enter war (**Oct. 26**), force UN retreat toward 39th parallel (**Dec.**).

1951 Gen. Matthew B. Ridgeway replaces MacArthur after he threatens Chinese with massive retaliation (**April 11**). Armistice negotiations (**July**) continue with interruptions until **June 1953**.

1953 Armistice signed (**July 27**). Chinese troops withdraw from North Korea (**Oct. 26, 1958**), but over 200 violations of armistice noted to **1959**.

Fidel Castro
(1926–)

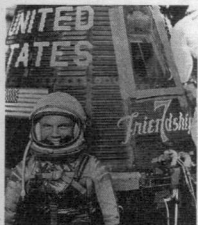

John H. Glenn, Jr.
(1921–)

Martin Luther King, Jr.
(1929–1968)

John F. Kennedy
(1917–1963)

1955 Nikolai A. Bulganin becomes Soviet premier, replacing Malenkov (**Feb. 8**). Churchill resigns; Anthony Eden succeeds him (**April 6**). West Germany becomes a sovereign state (**May 5**). Western European Union (WEU) comes into being (**May 6**). Warsaw Pact, east European mutual defense agreement, signed (**May 14**). Argentina ousts Perón (**Sept. 19**). President Eisenhower suffers coronary thrombosis in Denver (**Sept. 24**). Rosa Parks refuses to sit at the back of the bus. Martin Luther King, Jr., leads black boycott of Montgomery, Ala., bus system (**Dec. 1**); desegregated service begins **Dec. 21, 1956.** AFL and CIO become one organization—AFL-CIO (**Dec. 5**). Tennessee Williams's *Cat on a Hot Tin Roof* wins Pulitzer.

1956 Nikita Khrushchev, First Secretary of U.S.S.R. Communist Party, denounces Stalin's excesses (**Feb. 24**). First aerial H-bomb tested over Namu islet, Bikini Atoll—10 million tons TNT equivalent (**May 21**). Workers' uprising against Communist rule in Poznan, Poland, is crushed (**June 28–30**); rebellion inspires Hungarian students to stage a protest against Communism in Budapest (**Oct. 23**). Egypt takes control of Suez Canal (**July 26**). Hungarian rebellion forces Soviet troops to withdraw from Budapest (**Oct.**). Israel launches attack on Egypt's Sinai peninsula and drives toward Suez Canal (**Oct. 29**). Imre Nagy announces Hungary's withdrawal from Warsaw Pact (**Nov. 1**); Soviet troops enter and reclaim Budapest (**Nov. 4**). British and French invade Port Said on the Suez Canal (**Nov. 5**). Cease-fire forced by U.S. pressure stops British, French, and Israeli advance (**Nov. 6**). Morocco gains independence. Ingmar Bergman's *The Seventh Seal*. Woody Guthrie composes "This Land is Your Land." Allen Ginsberg's *Howl*.

1957 Eisenhower Doctrine calls for aid to Mideast countries which resist armed aggression from Communist-controlled nations (**Jan. 5**). The "Little Rock Nine" integrate Arkansas high school. Eisenhower sends troops to quell mob and protect school integration (**Sept. 24**). Russians launch *Sputnik I*, first earth-orbiting satellite—the Space Age begins (**Oct. 4**).

1958 European Economic Community (Common Market) becomes effective (**Jan. 1**). Army's Jupiter-C rocket fires first U.S. earth satellite, *Explorer I*, into orbit (**Jan. 31**). Egypt and Syria merge into United Arab Republic (**Feb. 1**). Khrushchev becomes premier of Soviet Union as Bulganin resigns (**Mar. 27**). Gen. Charles de Gaulle becomes French premier (**June 1**), remaining in power until 1969. Eisenhower orders U.S. Marines into Lebanon at request of President Chamoun, who fears overthrow (**July 15**). New French constitution adopted (**Sept. 28**), de Gaulle elected president of 5th Republic (**Dec. 21**).

1959 Cuban President Batista resigns and flees—Castro takes over (**Jan. 1**). Tibet's Dalai Lama escapes to India (**Mar. 31**). St. Lawrence Seaway opens, allowing ocean ships to reach Midwest (**April 25**). Alaska and Hawaii become states. Leakeys discover hominid fossils.

1960 American U-2 spy plane, piloted by Francis Gary Powers, shot down over Russia (**May 1**). Khrushchev kills Paris summit conference because of U-2 (**May 16**). Top Nazi murderer of Jews, Adolf Eichmann, captured by Israelis in Argentina (**May 23**)—executed in Israel in 1962. Powers sentenced to prison for 10 years (**Aug. 19**)—freed in **February 1962** in exchange for Soviet spy. Communist China and Soviet Union split in conflict over Communist ideology. Senegal, Ghana, Nigeria, Madagascar, and Zaire (Belgian Congo) gain independence. Cuba begins confiscation of $770 million of U.S. property (**Aug. 7**). There are 900 U.S. military advisers in South Vietnam.

1961 U.S. breaks diplomatic relations with Cuba (**Jan. 3**). Robert Frost recites "The Gift Outright" at John F. Kennedy's inauguration as president of U.S. (**Jan. 20**). Moscow announces putting first man in orbit around earth, Maj. Yuri A. Gagarin (**April 12**). Cuba invaded at Bay of Pigs by an estimated 1,200 anti-Castro exiles aided by U.S.; invasion crushed (**April 17**). First U.S. spaceman, Navy Cmdr. Alan B. Shepard, Jr., rockets 116.5 miles up in 302-mile trip (**May 5**). Virgil Grissom becomes second American astronaut, making 118-mile-high, 303-mile-long rocket flight over Atlantic (**July 21**). Gherman Stepanovich Titov is launched in Soviet spaceship *Vostok II:* makes 17½ orbits in 25 hours, covering 434,960 miles before landing safely (**Aug. 6**). East Germans erect Berlin Wall between East and West Berlin to halt flood of refugees (**Aug. 13**). U.S.S.R. fires 50-megaton hydrogen bomb, biggest explosion in history (**Oct. 29**). There are 2,000 U.S. military advisers in South Vietnam.

1962 Lt. Col. John H. Glenn, Jr., is first American to orbit Earth—three times in 4 hr 55 min **(Feb. 20)**. France transfers sovereignty to new republic of Algeria **(July 3)**. Cuban missile crisis—U.S.S.R. to build missile bases in Cuba; Kennedy orders Cuban blockade, lifts blockade after Russians back down **(Aug.–Nov.)**. James H. Meredith, escorted by federal marshals, registers at University of Mississippi **(Oct. 1)**. Pope John XXIII opens Second Vatican Council **(Oct. 11)**—Council holds four sessions, finally closing **Dec. 8, 1965**. Cuba releases 1,113 prisoners of 1961 invasion attempt **(Dec. 24)**. Burundi, Jamaica, Western Samoa, Uganda, and Trinidad and Tobago become independent. William Faulkner wins Pulitzer for *The Reivers*. Rachel Carson's *Silent Spring*.

**James H. Meredith
(1933–)**

1963 France and West Germany sign treaty of cooperation ending four centuries of conflict **(Jan. 22)**. Michael E. De Bakey implants artificial heart in human for first time at Houston hospital; plastic device functions and patient lives for four days **(April 21)**. Pope John XXIII dies **(June 3)**—succeeded **June 21** by Cardinal Montini, who becomes Paul VI. U.S. Supreme Court rules no locality may require recitation of Lord's Prayer or Bible verses in public schools **(June 17)**. U.K.'s Profumo scandal **(June)**. Civil rights rally held by 200,000 blacks and whites in Washington, D.C.; Martin Luther King delivers "I have a dream" speech **(Aug. 28)**. Washington-to-Moscow "hot line" communications link opens, designed to reduce risk of accidental war **(Aug. 30)**. President Kennedy shot and killed by sniper in Dallas, Tex. Lyndon B. Johnson becomes President same day **(Nov. 22)**. Lee Harvey Oswald, accused assassin of President Kennedy, is shot and killed by Jack Ruby, Dallas nightclub owner **(Nov. 24)**. Kenya achieves independence. Betty Friedan publishes *The Feminine Mystique*. There are 15,000 U.S. military advisers in South Vietnam.

**Betty Friedan
(1921–)**

VIETNAM WAR (1950–1975)

U.S., South Vietnam, and Allies versus North Vietnam and National Liberation Front (Viet Cong).

1950 President Truman sends 35-man military advisory group to aid French fighting to maintain colonial power in Vietnam.

1954 After defeat of French at Dien Bien Phu, Geneva Agreements **(July)** provide for withdrawal of French and Vietminh to either side of demarcation zone (DMZ) pending reunification elections, which are never held. Presidents Eisenhower and Kennedy (from 1954 onward) send civilian advisers and, later, military personnel to train South Vietnamese.

1960 Communists form National Liberation Front in South.

1960–1963 U.S. military advisers in South Vietnam rise from 900 to 15,000.

1963 Ngo Dinh Diem, South Vietnam's premier, slain in coup **(Nov. 1)**.

1964 North Vietnamese torpedo boats reportedly attack U.S. destroyers in Gulf of Tonkin **(Aug. 2)**. President Johnson orders retaliatory air strikes. Congress approves Gulf of Tonkin resolution **(Aug. 7)** authorizing president to take "all necessary measures" to win in Vietnam, allowing for the war's expansion.

1965 U.S. planes begin combat missions over South Vietnam. In **June**, 23,000 American advisers committed to combat. By end of year over 184,000 U.S. troops in area.

1966 B-52s bomb DMZ, reportedly used by North Vietnam for entry into South **(July 31)**.

1967 South Vietnam National Assembly approves election of Nguyen Van Thieu as president **(Oct. 21)**.

1968 U.S. has almost 525,000 men in Vietnam. In Tet offensive **(Jan.–Feb.)**, Viet Cong guerrillas attack Saigon, Hue, and some provincial capitals. In My Lai massacre, American soldiers kill 300 Vietnamese villagers **(March 16)**. President Johnson orders halt to U.S. bombardment of North Vietnam **(Oct. 31)**. Saigon and N.L.F. join U.S. and North Vietnam in Paris peace talks.

1969 President Nixon announces Vietnam peace offer **(May 14)**—begins troop withdrawals **(June)**. Viet Cong forms Provisional Revolutionary Government. U.S. Senate calls for curb on commitments **(June 25)**. Ho Chi Minh, 79, North Vietnam president, dies **(Sept. 3)**; collective leadership chosen. Some 6,000 U.S. troops pulled back from Thailand and 1,000 marines from Vietnam (announced **Sept. 30)**. Massive demonstrations in U.S. protest or support war policies **(Oct. 15)**.

1970 U.S. troops invade Cambodia in order to destroy North Vietnamese sanctuaries **(May 1)**.

1971 Congress bars use of combat troops, but not air power, in Laos and Cambodia **(Jan. 1)**. South Vietnamese troops, with U.S. air cover, fail in Laos thrust. Many American ground forces withdrawn from Vietnam combat. *New York Times* publishes Pentagon papers, classified material on expansion of war **(June)**.

1972 Nixon responds to North Vietnamese drive across DMZ by ordering mining of North Vietnam ports and heavy bombing of Hanoi-Haiphong area **(April 1)**. Nixon orders "Christmas bombing" of North to get North Vietnamese back to conference table **(Dec.)**.

1973 President orders halt to offensive operations in North Vietnam **(Jan. 15)**. Representatives of North and South Vietnam, U.S., and N.L.F. sign peace pacts in Paris, ending longest war in U.S. history **(Jan. 27)**. Last American troops departed in their entirety **(March 29)**.

1974 Both sides accuse each other of frequent violations of cease-fire agreement.

1975 Full-scale warfare resumes. South Vietnam premier Nguyen Van Thieu resigns **(April 21)**. South Vietnamese government surrenders to North Vietnam; U.S. Marine embassy guards and U.S. civilians and dependents evacuated **(April 30)**. More than 140,000 Vietnamese refugees leave by air and sea, many to settle in U.S. Provisional Revolutionary Government takes control **(June 6)**.

1976 Election of National Assembly paves way for reunification of North and South.

The Beatles

**Malcolm X
(1925–1965)**

**Thurgood Marshall
(1908–1993)**

**Lyndon B. Johnson
(1908–1973)**

**Richard Nixon
(1913–1994)**

1964 U.S. Supreme Court rules that Congressional districts should be roughly equal in population (**Feb. 17**). Jack Ruby convicted of murder in slaying of Lee Harvey Oswald; sentenced to death by Dallas jury (**March 14**)—conviction reversed **Oct. 5, 1966**; Ruby dies **Jan. 3, 1967**, before second trial can be held. Three civil rights workers—Schwerner, Goodman, and Cheney—murdered in Mississippi (**June**). Twenty-one arrests result in trial and conviction of seven by federal jury. Nelson Mandela sentenced to life imprisonment (**June 11**). Congress approves Gulf of Tonkin resolution (**Aug. 7**). President's Commission on the Assassination of President Kennedy issues Warren Report concluding that Lee Harvey Oswald acted alone. The Beatles appear on *The Ed Sullivan Show.*

1965 Rev. Dr. Martin Luther King, Jr., and more than 2,600 other blacks arrested in Selma, Ala., during three-day demonstrations against voter-registration rules (**Feb. 1**). Malcolm X, black-nationalist leader, shot to death at Harlem rally in New York City (**Feb. 21**). U.S. Marines land in Dominican Republic as fighting persists between rebels and Dominican army (**April 28**). Medicare, senior citizens' government medical assistance program, begins (**July 1**). Blacks riot for six days in Watts section of Los Angeles: 34 dead, over 1,000 injured, nearly 4,000 arrested, fire damage put at $175 million (**Aug. 11–16**). Power failure in Ontario plant blacks out parts of eight northeastern states of U.S. and two provinces of southeastern Canada (**Nov. 9**). Ralph Nader's *Unsafe at Any Speed.*

1966 Black teenagers riot in Watts, Los Angeles; two men killed and at least 25 injured (**March 15**). Supreme Court decides *Miranda* v. *Arizona.*

1967 Three Apollo astronauts—Col. Virgil I. Grissom, Col. Edward White II, and Lt. Cmdr. Roger B. Chaffee—killed in spacecraft fire during simulated launch (**Jan. 27**). Biafra secedes from Nigeria (**May**). Israeli and Arab forces battle; six-day war ends with Israel occupying Sinai Peninsula, Golan Heights, Gaza Strip, and east bank of Suez Canal (**June 5**). Red China announces explosion of its first hydrogen bomb (**June 17**). Racial violence in Detroit; 7,000 National Guardsmen aid police after night of rioting. Similar outbreaks occur in New York City's Spanish Harlem, Rochester, N.Y., Birmingham, Ala., and New Britain, Conn. (**July 23**). Thurgood Marshall sworn in as first black U.S. Supreme Court justice (**Oct. 2**). Dr. Christiaan N. Barnard and team of South African surgeons perform world's first successful human heart transplant (**Dec. 3**)—patient dies 18 days later.

1968 North Korea seizes U.S. Navy ship *Pueblo;* holds 83 on board as spies (**Jan. 23**). Tet offensive, turning point in Vietnam war (**Jan.–Feb.**). My Lai massacre (**March 16**). President Johnson announces he will not seek or accept presidential renomination (**March 31**). Martin Luther King, Jr., civil rights leader, is slain in Memphis (**April 4**)—James Earl Ray, indicted in murder, captured in London on **June 8**. In 1969 Ray pleads guilty and is sentenced to 99 years. Sen. Robert F. Kennedy is shot and critically wounded in Los Angeles hotel after winning California primary (**June 5**)—dies **June 6**. Sirhan B. Sirhan convicted 1969. Czechoslovakia is invaded by Russians and Warsaw Pact forces to crush liberal regime (**Aug. 20**).

1969 Richard M. Nixon is inaugurated 37th president of the U.S. (**Jan. 20**). Stonewall riot in New York City marks beginning of gay rights movement (**June 28**). Apollo 11 astronauts—Neil A. Armstrong, Edwin E. Aldrin, Jr., and Michael Collins—take man's first walk on moon (**July 20**). Sen. Edward M. Kennedy pleads guilty to leaving scene of fatal accident at Chappaquiddick, Mass. (**July 18**), in which Mary Jo Kopechne was drowned—gets two-month suspended sentence (**July 25**). Woodstock Festival (**Aug.**). *Sesame Street* debuts. Internet (ARPA) goes online.

1970 Biafra surrenders after 32-month fight for independence from Nigeria (**Jan. 12**). Rhodesia severs last tie with British crown and declares itself a racially segregated republic (**March 1**). U.S. troops invade Cambodia (**May 1**). Four students at Kent State University in Ohio slain by National Guardsmen at demonstration protesting incursion into Cambodia (**May 4**). Senate repeals Gulf of Tonkin resolution (**June 24**).

1971 Supreme Court rules unanimously that busing of students may be ordered to achieve racial desegregation (**April 20**). Anti-war militants attempt to disrupt government business in Washington (**May 3**)—police and military units arrest as many as 12,000; most are later released. *Pentagon Papers* published **(June)**. Twenty-sixth Amendment to U.S. Constitution lowers voting age to 18. UN seats Communist China and expels Nationalist China **(Oct. 25)**.

1972 President Nixon makes unprecedented eight-day visit to Communist China and meets with Mao Zedong **(Feb.)**. Britain takes over direct rule of Northern Ireland in bid for peace **(March 24)**. Gov. George C. Wallace of Alabama is shot by Arthur H. Bremer at Laurel, Md., political rally **(May 15)**. Five men are apprehended by police in attempt to bug Democratic National Committee headquarters in Washington, D.C.'s Watergate complex—start of the Watergate scandal **(June 17)**. Supreme Court rules that death penalty is unconstitutional **(June 29)**. Eleven Israeli athletes at Olympic Games in Munich are killed after eight members of an Arab terrorist group invade Olympic Village; five guerrillas and one policeman are also killed **(Sept. 5)**. "Christmas bombing" of North Vietnam **(Dec.)**.

Mao Zedong
(1893–1976)

1973 Great Britain, Ireland, and Denmark enter European Economic Community **(Jan. 1)**. Vietnam War ends with signing of peace pacts **(Jan. 27)**. Nixon, on national TV, accepts responsibility, but not blame, for Watergate; accepts resignations of advisers H. R. Haldeman and John D. Ehrlichman, fires John W. Dean III as counsel **(April 30)**. Greek military junta abolishes monarchy and proclaims republic **(June 1)**. U.S. bombing of Cambodia ends, marking official halt to 12 years of combat activity in Southeast Asia **(Aug. 15)**. Chile's Marxist president, Salvadore Allende, is overthrown **(Sept. 11)**. Fourth and biggest Arab-Israeli conflict begins as Egyptian and Syrian forces attack Israel as Jews mark Yom Kippur, holiest day in their calendar **(Oct. 6)**. Spiro T. Agnew resigns as vice president and then, in federal court in Baltimore, pleads no contest to charges of evasion of income taxes on $29,500 he received in 1967, while governor of Maryland. He is fined $10,000 and put on three years' probation **(Oct. 10)**. In the "Saturday Night Massacre," Nixon fires special Watergate prosecutor Archibald Cox and Deputy Attorney General William D. Ruckelshaus; Attorney General Elliot L. Richardson resigns **(Oct. 20)**. Egypt and Israel sign U.S.-sponsored cease-fire accord **(Nov. 11)**. Supreme Court rules on *Roe* v. *Wade*. Duke Ellington's autobiography, *Music Is My Mistress,* is published.

Duke Ellington
(1899–1974)

1974 Patricia Hearst, 19-year-old daughter of publisher Randolph Hearst, kidnapped by Symbionese Liberation Army **(Feb. 5)**. House Judiciary Committee adopts three articles of impeachment charging President Nixon with obstruction of justice, failure to uphold laws, and refusal to produce material subpoenaed by the committee **(July 30)**. Richard M. Nixon announces he will resign the next day, the first president to do so **(Aug. 8)**. Vice President Gerald R. Ford of Michigan is sworn in as 38th president of the U.S. **(Aug. 9)**. Ford grants "full, free, and absolute pardon" to ex-president Nixon **(Sept. 8)**.

Gerald R. Ford
(1913–)

1975 John N. Mitchell, H. R. Haldeman, John D. Ehrlichman found guilty of Watergate cover-up **(Jan. 1)**; sentenced to 30 months to 8 years in jail **(Feb. 21)**. Pol Pot and Khmer Rouge take over Cambodia **(April)**. American merchant ship *Mayaguez,* seized by Cambodian forces, is rescued in operation by U.S. Navy and Marines, 38 of whom are killed **(May 15)**. *Apollo* and *Soyuz* spacecraft take off for U.S.-Soviet link-up in space **(July 15)**. President Ford escapes assassination attempt in Sacramento, Calif. **(Sept. 5)**. President Ford escapes second assassination attempt in 17 days **(Sept. 22)**.

Jimmy Carter
(1924–)

1976 Supreme Court rules that blacks and other minorities are entitled to retroactive job seniority **(March 24)**. Ford signs Federal Election Campaign Act **(May 11)**. Supreme Court rules that death penalty is not inherently cruel or unusual and is a constitutionally acceptable form of punishment **(July 3)**. Nation celebrates bicentennial **(July 4)**. Israeli airborne commandos attack Uganda's Entebbe Airport and free 103 hostages held by pro-Palestinian hijackers of Air France plane; one Israeli and several Ugandan soldiers killed in raid **(July 4)**. Mysterious disease that eventually claims 29 lives strikes American Legion convention in Philadelphia **(Aug. 4)**. Jimmy Carter elected U.S. president **(Nov. 2)**.

1977 First woman Episcopal priest ordained **(Jan. 1)**. Scientists identify previously unknown bacterium as cause of mysterious "legionnaire's disease" **(Jan. 18)**. Carter pardons Vietnam draft evaders **(Jan. 21)**. Scientists report using bacteria in lab to make insulin **(May 23)**. Supreme

Pope John Paul II
(1920–)

Anwar Sadat
(1918–1981)

Ayatollah Ruhollah
Khomeini
(1900–1989)

Ronald Reagan
(1911–)

Sandra Day O'Connor
(1930–)

Court rules that states are not required to spend Medicaid funds on elective abortions (**June 20**). Deng Xiaoping, purged Chinese leader, restored to power as "Gang of Four" is expelled from Communist Party (**July 22**). South African activist Stephen Biko dies in police custody (**Sept. 12**). Nuclear-proliferation pact, curbing spread of nuclear weapons, signed by 15 countries, including U.S. and U.S.S.R. (**Sept. 21**).

1978 President chooses Federal Appeals Court Judge William H. Webster as F.B.I. Director (**Jan. 19**). Rhodesia's prime minister Ian D. Smith and three black leaders agree on transfer to black majority rule (**Feb. 15**). U.S. Senate approves Panama Canal neutrality treaty (**March 16**); votes treaty to turn canal over to Panama by year 2000 (**April 18**). Former Italian premier Aldo Moro kidnapped by left wing terrorists, who kill five bodyguards (**March 16**); he is found slain (**May 9**). Californians in referendum approve Proposition 13 for nearly 60% slash in property tax revenues (**June 6**). Supreme Court, in Bakke case, bars quota systems in college admissions but affirms constitutionality of programs giving advantage to minorities (**June 28**). Pope Paul VI, dead at 80, mourned (**Aug. 6**); new Pope, John Paul I, 65, dies unexpectedly after 34 days in office (**Sept. 28**); succeeded by Karol Cardinal Wojtyla of Poland as John Paul II (**Oct. 16**). "Framework for Peace" in Middle East signed by Egypt's president Anwar Sadat and Israeli premier Menachem Begin after 13-day conference at Camp David led by President Carter (**Sept. 17**). Jim Jones's followers commit mass suicide in Jonestown, Guyana (**Nov. 18**).

1979 Oil spills pollute ocean waters in Atlantic and Gulf of Mexico (**Jan. 1, June 8, July 21**). Ohio agrees to pay $675,000 to families of dead and injured in Kent State University shootings (**Jan. 4**). Vietnam and Vietnam-backed Cambodian insurgents announce fall of Phnom Penh, Cambodian capital, and collapse of Pol Pot regime (**Jan. 7**). Shah leaves Iran after year of turmoil (**Jan. 16**); revolutionary forces under Muslim leader, Ayatollah Ruhollah Khomeini, take over (**Feb. 1** *et seq.*). Conservatives win British election; Margaret Thatcher new prime minister (**March 28**). Nuclear power plant accident at Three Mile Island, Pa., releases radiation (**March 28**). Carter and Brezhnev sign SALT II agreement (**June 14**). Nicaraguan president Gen. Anastasio Somoza Debayle resigns and flees to Miami (**July 17**); Sandinistas form government (**July 19**). Earl Mountbatten of Burma, 79, British World War II hero, and three others killed by blast on fishing boat off Irish coast (**Aug. 27**); two I.R.A. members accused (**Aug. 30**). Iranian militants seize U.S. embassy in Teheran and hold hostages (**Nov. 4**). Soviet invasion of Afghanistan stirs world protests (**Dec. 27**).

1980 Six U.S. embassy aides escape from Iran with Canadian help (**Jan. 29**). F.B.I.'s undercover operation "Abscam" (for Arab scam) implicates public officials (**Feb. 2**). U.S. breaks diplomatic ties with Iran (**April 7**). Eight U.S. servicemen are killed and five are injured as helicopter and cargo plane collide in abortive desert raid to rescue American hostages in Teheran (**April 25**). Supreme Court upholds limits on federal aid for abortions (**June 30**). Shah of Iran dies at 60 (**July 27**). Anastasio Somoza Debayle, ousted Nicaragua ruler, and two aides assassinated in Asunción, Paraguay capital (**Sept. 17**). Iraq troops hold 90 square miles of Iran after invasion; 8-year Iran-Iraq war begins (**Sept. 19**). Ronald Reagan elected president in Republican sweep (**Nov. 4**). Three U.S. nuns and lay worker found shot in El Salvador (**Dec. 4**). John Lennon of the Beatles shot dead in New York City (**Dec. 8**). Smallpox eradicated.

1981 Ronald Reagan takes oath as 40th president (**Jan. 20**). U.S.-Iran agreement frees 52 hostages held in Teheran since 1979 (**Jan. 20**); hostages welcomed back in U.S. (**Jan. 25**). President Reagan wounded by gunman, with press secretary and two law-enforcement officers (**March 30**). Pope John Paul II wounded by gunman (**May 14**). Supreme Court rules, 4–4, that former president Nixon and three top aides may be required to pay monetary damages for unconstitutional wiretap of home telephone of former national security aide (**June 22**). Reagan nominates Judge Sandra Day O'Connor, 51, of Arizona, as first woman on Supreme Court (**July 7**). More than 110 die in collapse of aerial walkways in lobby of Hyatt Regency Hotel in Kansas City; 188 injured (**July 18**). Air controllers strike, disrupting flights (**Aug. 3**); government dismisses strikers (**Aug. 11**). AIDS is first identified.

1982 British overcome Argentina in Falklands war **(April 2–June 15).** Israel invades Lebanon in attack on P.L.O. **(June 4).** John W. Hinckley, Jr. found not guilty because of insanity in shooting of President Reagan **(June 21).** Alexander M. Haig, Jr., resigns as secretary of state **(June 25).** Equal Rights Amendment fails ratification **(June 30).** Princess Grace, 52, dies of injuries when car plunges off mountain road; daughter Stephanie, 17, suffers serious injuries **(Sept. 14).** Lebanese Christian Phalangists kill hundreds of people in two Palestinian refugee camps in West Beirut **(Sept. 15).** Leonid Brezhnev, Soviet leader, dies at 75 **(Nov. 10).** Yuri V. Andropov, 68, chosen as successor **(Nov. 15).** Permanent artificial heart implanted in human for first time in Dr. Barney B. Clark, 61, at University of Utah Medical Center in Salt Lake City **(Dec. 2).**

Indira Gandhi
(1917–1984)

1983 Pope John Paul II signs new Roman Catholic code incorporating changes brought about by Second Vatican Council **(Jan. 25).** Second space shuttle, *Challenger*, makes successful maiden voyage, which includes the first U.S. space walk in nine years **(April 4).** U.S. Supreme Court declares many local abortion restrictions unconstitutional **(June 15).** Sally K. Ride, 32, first U.S. woman astronaut in space as a crew member aboard space shuttle *Challenger* **(June 18).** U.S. admits shielding former Nazi Gestapo chief Klaus Barbie, 69, the "butcher of Lyon," wanted in France for war crimes **(Aug. 15).** Benigno S. Aquino, Jr., 50, political rival of Philippines president Marcos, slain in Manila **(Aug. 21).** South Korean Boeing 747 jetliner bound for Seoul apparently strays into Soviet airspace and is shot down by a Soviet SU-15 fighter after it had tracked the airliner for two hours; all 269 aboard are killed, including 61 Americans **(Aug. 30).** Terrorist explosion kills 237 U.S. Marines in Beirut **(Oct. 23).** U.S. and Caribbean allies invade Grenada **(Oct. 25).**

Corazon Aquino
(1933–)

1984 Bell System broken up **(Jan. 1).** France gets first deliveries of Soviet natural gas **(Jan. 1).** Syria frees captured U.S. Navy pilot, Lieut. Robert C. Goodman, Jr. **(Jan. 3).** U.S. and Vatican exchange diplomats after 116-year hiatus **(Jan. 10).** Reagan orders U.S. Marines withdrawn from Beirut international peacekeeping force **(Feb. 7).** Yuri V. Andropov dies at 69; Konstantin U. Chernenko, 72, named Soviet Union leader **(Feb. 9).** Italy and Vatican agree to end Roman Catholicism as state religion **(Feb. 18).** Reagan ends U.S. role in Beirut by relieving Sixth Fleet from peacekeeping force **(March 30).** Congress rebukes President Reagan on use of federal funds for mining Nicaraguan harbors **(April 10).** Soviet Union withdraws from summer Olympic games in U.S., and other bloc nations follow **(May 7 et seq.).** José Napoleón Duarte, moderate, elected president of El Salvador **(May 11).** Three hundred slain as Indian Army occupies Sikh Golden Temple in Amritsar **(June 6).** Thirty-ninth Democratic National Convention, in San Francisco, nominates Walter F. Mondale and Geraldine A. Ferraro **(July 16–19).** Thirty-third Republican National Convention, at Dallas, renominates President Reagan and Vice President Bush **(Aug. 20–25).** Brian Mulroney and Conservative party win Canadian election in landslide **(Sept. 4).** Indian prime minister Indira Gandhi assassinated by two Sikh bodyguards; 1,000 killed in anti-Sikh riots; son Rajiv succeeds her **(Oct. 31).** President Reagan re-elected in landslide with 59% of vote **(Nov. 7).** Toxic gas leaks from Union Carbide plant in Bhopal, India, killing 2,000 and injuring 150,000 **(Dec. 3).**

Mikhail S. Gorbachev
(1931–)

1985 Ronald Reagan, 73, takes oath for second term as 40th president **(Jan. 20).** General Westmoreland settles libel action against CBS **(Feb. 18).** Prime Minister Margaret Thatcher addresses Congress, endorsing Reagan's policies **(Feb. 20).** U.S.S.R. leader Chernenko dies at 73 and is replaced by Mikhail Gorbachev, 54 **(March 11).** Two Shi'ite Muslim gunmen capture TWA airliner with 133 aboard, 104 of them Americans **(June 14);** 39 remaining hostages freed in Beirut **(June 30).** Supreme Court, 5–4, bars public school teachers from parochial schools **(July 1).** Arthur James Walker, 50, retired naval officer, convicted by federal judge of participating in Soviet spy ring operated by his brother, John Walker **(Aug. 9).** P.L.O. terrorists hijack *Achille Lauro,* Italian cruise ship, with 80 passengers, plus crew **(Oct. 7);** American, Leon Klinghoffer, killed **(Oct. 8);** Italian government toppled by political crisis over hijacking **(Oct. 16).** John A. Walker and son, Michael I. Walker, 22, sentenced in Navy espionage case **(Oct. 28).** Reagan and Gorbachev meet at summit **(Nov. 19);** agree to step up arms control talks and renew cultural contacts **(Nov. 21).** Terrorists seize Egyptian Boeing 737 airliner after take-off from Athens **(Nov. 23);** 59 dead as Egyptian forces storm plane on Malta **(Nov. 24).** U.S. budget-balancing bill enacted **(Dec. 12).**

Margaret Thatcher
(1925–)

Sally K. Ride
(1951–)

**William Rehnquist
(1924–)**

**George Bush
(1924–)**

**Benazir Bhutto
(1953–)**

1986 Spain and Portugal join European Economic Community (**Jan. 1**). President freezes Libyan assets in U.S. (**Jan. 8**). Supreme Court bars racial bias in trial jury selection (**Jan. 14**). *Voyager 2* spacecraft reports secrets of Uranus (**Jan. 26**). Space shuttle *Challenger* explodes after launch at Cape Canaveral, Fla., killing all seven aboard (**Jan. 28**). Haiti president Jean-Claude Duvalier flees to France (**Feb. 7**). President Marcos flees Philippines after ruling 20 years, as newly elected Corazon Aquino succeeds him (**Feb. 26**). Prime Minister Olof Palme of Sweden shot dead (**Feb. 28**). Austrian president Kurt Waldheim's service as Nazi army officer revealed (**March 3**). Union Carbide agrees to settlement with victims of Bhopal gas leak in India (**March 22**). Halley's comet yields information on return visit (**April 10**). U.S. planes attack Libyan "terrorist centers" (**April 14**). Desmond Tutu elected archbishop in South Africa (**April 14**). Major nuclear accident at Soviet Union's Chernobyl power station alarms world (**April 26** *et seq.*). Ex-Navy analyst, Jonathan Jay Pollard, 31, guilty as spy for Israel (**June 4**). Supreme Court reaffirms abortion rights (**June 11**). World Court rules U.S. broke international law in mining Nicaraguan waters (**June 27**). Supreme Court voids automatic provisions of budget-balancing law (**July 7**). Jerry A. Whitworth, ex-Navy radioman, convicted as spy (**July 24**); he is also part of Walker family spy ring. Muslim captors release Rev. Lawrence Martin Jenco (**July 26**). Senate Judiciary Committee approves William H. Rehnquist as Chief Justice of U.S. (**Aug. 14**). House votes arms appropriations bill rejecting administration's "star wars" policy (**Aug. 15**). Three Lutheran church groups in U.S. set to merge (**Aug. 29**). Congress overrides Reagan veto of stiff sanctions against South Africa (**Sept. 29** and **Oct. 2**). Congress approves immigration bill barring hiring of illegal aliens, with amnesty provision (**Oct. 17**). Reagan signs $11.7-billion budget reduction measure (**Oct. 21**). He approves sweeping revision of U.S. tax code (**Oct. 22**). Democrats triumph in elections, gaining eight seats to win Senate majority (**Nov. 4**). Secret initiative to send arms to Iran revealed (**Nov. 6** *et seq.*); Reagan denies exchanging arms for hostages and halts arms sales (**Nov. 19**); diversion of funds from arms sales to Nicaraguan Contras revealed (**Nov. 25**).

1987 William Buckley, U.S. hostage in Lebanon, reported slain (**Jan. 20**). Supreme Court rules Rotary Clubs must admit women (**May 4**). Iraqi missiles kill 37 in attack on U.S. frigate *Stark* in Persian Gulf (**May 17**); Iraqi president apologizes (**May 18**). Prime Minister Thatcher wins rare third term in Britain (**June 11**). Supreme Court Justice Lewis F. Powell, Jr., retires (**June 26**). Klaus Barbie, 73, Gestapo wartime chief in Lyon, sentenced to life by French court for war crimes (**July 4**). Oliver North, Jr., tells congressional inquiry higher officials approved his secret Iran-Contra operations (**July 7–10**). Admiral John M. Poindexter, former National Security Adviser, testifies he authorized use of Iran arms sale profits to aid Contras (**July 15–22**). George P. Shultz testifies he was deceived repeatedly on Iran-Contra affair (**July 23–24**). Defense Secretary Caspar W. Weinberger tells inquiry of official deception and intrigue (**July 31, Aug. 3**). Reagan says Iran arms-Contra policy went astray and accepts responsibility (**Aug. 12**). Severe earthquake strikes Los Angeles, leaving 100 injured and six dead (**Oct. 1**). Senate, 58–42, rejects Robert H. Bork as Supreme Court justice (**Oct. 23**).

1988 U.S. and Canada reach free trade agreement (**Jan. 2**). Robert C. McFarlane, former National Security Adviser, pleads guilty in Iran-Contra case (**March 11**). U.S. Navy ship shoots down Iranian airliner in Persian Gulf, mistaking it for jet fighter; 290 killed (**July 3**). Terrorists kill nine tourists on Aegean cruise (**July 11**). Democratic convention nominates Gov. Michael Dukakis of Massachusetts for president and Texas senator Lloyd Bentsen for vice president (**July 17** *et seq.*). Republicans nominate George Bush for president and Indiana senator Dan Quayle for vice president (**Aug. 15** *et seq.*). Plane blast kills Pakistani president Mohammad Zia ul-Haq (**Aug. 17**). Republicans sweep 40 states in election. Bush beats Dukakis (**Nov. 8**). Benazir Bhutto, first Islamic woman prime minister, chosen to lead Pakistan (**Dec. 1**). Pan-Am 747 explodes from terrorist bomb and crashes in Lockerbie, Scotland, killing all 259 aboard and 11 on ground (**Dec. 21**).

1989 U.S. planes shoot down two Libyan fighters over international waters in Mediterranean (**Jan. 4**). Emperor Hirohito of Japan dead at 87 (**Jan. 7**). George Herbert Walker Bush inaugurated as 41st U.S. President (**Jan. 20**). Iran's Ayatollah Khomeini declares author Salman Rushdie's book *The Satanic Verses* offensive and sentences him to death (**Feb. 14**). Ruptured tanker *Exxon Valdez* sends 11 million gallons of crude oil into Alaska's Prince William Sound (**March 24**). Tens of thousands of Chinese students take over Beijing's Tiananmen Square in rally for democracy (**April 19** *et seq.*). U.S. jury convicts Oliver North in Iran-Contra affair (**May 4**). More than one million in Beijing demonstrate for democracy; chaos spreads across nation (**mid-May** *et seq.*). Mikhail S. Gorbachev named Soviet president (**May 25**). Thousands killed in Tiananmen Square as Chinese leaders take hard line toward demonstrators (**June 4** *et seq.*). Army Gen. Colin R. Powell is first black chairman of Joint Chiefs of Staff (**Aug. 9**). P. W. Botha quits as South Africa's president (**Aug. 14**). *Voyager 2* spacecraft speeds by Neptune after making startling discoveries about the planet and its moons (**Aug. 29**). Deng Xiaoping resigns from China's leadership (**Nov. 9**). After 28 years, Berlin Wall is open to West (**Nov. 11**). Czech Parliament ends Communists' dominant role (**Nov. 30**). Romanian uprising overthrows Communist government (**Dec. 15** *et seq.*); President Ceausescu and wife executed (**Dec. 25**). U.S. troops invade Panama, seeking capture of Gen. Manuel Noriega (**Dec. 20**); resistance to U.S. collapses (**Dec. 24**). Dalai Lama wins Nobel Peace Prize.

François Mitterrand
(1916–1996)

General Colin Powell
(1937–)

1990 Gen. Manuel Noriega surrenders in Panama (**Jan. 3**). Yugoslav Communists end 45-year monopoly of power (**Jan. 22**). Soviet Communists relinquish sole power (**Feb. 7**). South Africa frees Nelson Mandela, imprisoned 27½ years (**Feb. 11**). Violeta Barrios de Chamorro inaugurated as Nicaraguan president. Hubble Space Telescope launched (**April 25**). U.S.-Soviet summit reaches accord on armaments (**June 1**). Supreme Court upsets law banning flag burning (**June 11**). Western Alliance ends Cold War and proposes joint action with Soviet Union and Eastern Europe (**July 6**). U.S. Appeals Court overturns Oliver North's Iran-Contra conviction (**July 20**). Iraqi troops invade Kuwait and seize petroleum reserves, setting off Persian Gulf War (**Aug. 2** *et seq.*) East and West Germany reunited.(**Oct. 3**). Republicans set back in midterm elections (**Nov. 8**). Gorbachev assumes emergency powers (**Nov. 17**). Leaders of 34 nations in Europe and North America proclaim a united Europe (**Nov. 21**). Margaret Thatcher resigns as British prime minister (**Nov. 22**); John Major succeeds her (**Nov. 28**). Lech Walesa wins Poland's runoff presidential election (**Dec. 9**). Haiti elects leftist priest as president in first democratic election (**Dec. 17**).

Saddam Hussein
(1937–)

1991 U.S. and Allies at war with Iraq (**Jan. 15**). Warsaw Pact dissolves military alliance (**Feb. 25**). Cease-fire ends Persian Gulf War; UN forces are victorious (**April 3**). Europeans end sanctions on South Africa (**April 15**). Supreme Court limits death row appeals (**April 16**). Winnie Mandela sentenced in kidnapping (**May 13**). William H. Webster retires as director of

---

THE PERSIAN GULF WAR (Aug. 2, 1990–April 6, 1991)

1990 Iraq invades its tiny neighbor, Kuwait, after talks break down over oil production and debt repayment. Iraqi president Saddam Hussein later annexes Kuwait and declares it a 19th province of Iraq (**Aug. 2**). President Bush believes that Iraq intends to invade Saudi Arabia and take control of the region's oil supplies. He begins organizing a multi-national coalition to seek Kuwait's freedom and restoration of its legitimate government. The UN Security Council authorizes economic sanctions against Iraq. Bush orders U.S. troops to protect Saudi Arabia at the Saudis' request and "Operation Desert Shield" begins (**Aug. 6**). 230,000 American troops arrive in Saudi Arabia to take defensive action, but when Iraq continues a huge military buildup in Kuwait, the President orders an additional 200,000 troops deployed to prepare for a possible offensive action by the U.S.-led coalition forces. He subsequently obtains a UN Security Council resolution setting a **Jan. 15, 1991** deadline for Iraq to withdraw unconditionally from Kuwait (**Nov. 8**).

1991 Bush wins Congressional approval for his position with the most devastating air assault in history against military targets in Iraq and Kuwait (**Jan. 16**). He rejects a Soviet-Iraq peace plan for a gradual withdrawal that does not comply with all the UN resolutions and gives Iraq an ultimatum to withdraw from Kuwait by noon **Feb. 23** (**Feb. 22**). The president orders the ground war to begin (**Feb. 24**). In a brilliant and lightning-fast campaign, U.S. and coalition forces smash through Iraq's defenses and defeat Saddam Hussein's troops in only four days of combat. Allies enter Kuwait City (**Feb. 26**). Iraqi army sets fire to over 500 of Kuwait's oil wells as final act of destruction to Kuwait's infrastructure. Bush orders a unilateral cease-fire 100 hours after the ground offensive started (**Feb. 27**). Allied and Iraqi military leaders meet on battlefield to discuss terms for a formal cease-fire to end the Gulf War. Iraq agrees to abide by all of the UN resolutions (**Mar. 3**). The first Allied prisoners of war are released (**Mar. 4**). Official cease-fire accepted and signed (**April 6**). 532,000 U.S. forces served in Operation Desert Storm. There were a total of 148 U.S. battle deaths during the Gulf War, 145 nonbattle deaths, and 467 wounded in action.

Hubble Space Telescope

**Lech Walesa
(1943–)**

**Toni Morrison
(1931–)**

**Ruth Bader Ginsburg
(1933–)**

CIA; Robert H. Gates succeeds him (**May 14**). France agrees to sign 1968 treaty banning spread of atomic weapons (**June 3**). Communist government of Albania resigns (**June 4**). Jiang Qing, widow of Mao, commits suicide (**June 4**). South African Parliament repeals apartheid laws (**June 5**). Warsaw Pact dissolved (**July 1**). Boris N. Yeltsin inaugurated as first freely elected president of Russian Republic (**July 10**). Bush-Gorbachev summit negotiates strategic arms reduction treaty (**July 31**). China accepts nuclear nonproliferation treaty (**Aug. 10**). Lithuania, Estonia, and Latvia win independence (**Aug. 25**); Bush recognizes them (**Sept. 2**). Haitian troops seize president in uprising (**Sept. 30**). U.S. suspends assistance to Haiti (**Oct. 1**). Professor Anita Hill accuses Judge Clarence Thomas of sexual harassment (**Oct. 6**); Senate, 52–48, confirms Thomas for Supreme Court after stormy hearings (**Oct. 15**). Israel and Soviet Union resume relations after 24 years (**Oct. 18**). U.S. indicts two Libyans in 1988 bombing of Pan Am Flight 103 over Lockerbie, Scotland (**Nov. 15**). Anglican envoy Terry Waite and U.S. Prof. Thomas M. Sutherland freed by Lebanese (**Nov. 18**). Last three U.S. hostages freed in Lebanon (**Dec. 2–4**). Soviet Union breaks up after President Gorbachev's resignation; constituent republics form Commonwealth of Independent States (**Dec. 25**).

1992 A text-based Web browser is made available to the public (**Jan.**); within a few years, millions of people become regular users of the World Wide Web. Yugoslav Federation broken up (**Jan. 15**). Bush and Yeltsin proclaim formal end to Cold War (**Feb. 1**). U.S. lifts trade sanctions against China (**Feb. 21**). U.S. recognizes three former Yugoslav republics (**April 7**). Gen. Noriega, former Panama leader, convicted in U.S. court (**April 9**). Four police officers acquitted in Los Angeles beating of Rodney King; rioting erupts in South-Central Los Angeles (**April 29** *et seq.*). Caspar W. Weinberger indicted in Iran-Contra affair (**June 16**). Last Western hostages freed in Lebanon (**June 17**). Supreme Court reaffirms right to abortion (**June 29**). Democrats nominate Bill Clinton and Al Gore (**July 1**). Gen. Noriega sentenced to 40 years on drug charges (**July 10**). Court clears *Exxon Valdez* skipper (**July 10**). Israeli Parliament approves Yitzhak Rabin's coalition government, dominated by Labor Party (**July 13**). Police officers acquitted in April on criminal charges in Rodney King beating are indicted on federal civil rights charges (**Aug. 5**). North American trade compact announced (**Aug. 12**). Republicans renominate Bush and Quayle (**Aug. 20**). UN expels Serbian-dominated Yugoslavia (**Sept. 22**). Senate ratifies second Strategic Arms Limitation Treaty (**Oct. 1**). Top Japanese leader, Shin Kanemaru, resigns in scandal (**Oct. 14**). Bill Clinton elected president, Al Gore vice president; Democrats keep control of Congress (**Nov. 3**). Russian Parliament approves START treaty (**Nov. 4**). U.S. forces leave Philippines, ending nearly a century of American military presence (**Nov. 24**). Czechoslovak Parliament approves separation into two nations (**Nov. 25**). UN approves U.S.-led force to guard food for Somalia (**Dec. 3**). Prince and Princess of Wales agree to separate (**Dec. 9**). Bush pardons former Reagan administration officials involved in Iran-Contra affair (**Dec. 24**).

1993 Vaclav Havel elected as Czech president (**Jan. 26**). Clinton agrees to compromise on military's ban on homosexuals (**Jan. 29**). U.S. begins airlift of supplies to besieged Bosnia towns (**Feb. 28**). Federal agents besiege Texas Branch Davidian religious cult after six are killed in raid (**March 1** *et seq.*). Five arrested, sixth sought in bombing of World Trade Center in New York (**March 29**). Two police officers convicted on federal civil rights charges in Rodney King beating (**April 17**); sentenced **Aug. 4**. Fire kills 72 as cult standoff in Texas ends with federal assault (**April 19**). President of Sri Lanka assassinated (**May 1**). British Commons approves European unity pact (**May 20**). Twenty-two UN troops killed in Somalia (**June 5**). Ruth Bader Ginsburg appointed to Supreme Court (**June 14**). Iraq accepts UN weapons monitoring (**July 19**). Vincent W. Foster, Jr., senior White House lawyer, commits suicide (**July 22**). Midwest flood damage expected to exceed $10 billion (**July 24**). Israeli-Palestinian accord reached (**Aug. 28**). U.S. agents blamed in Waco, Tex., siege (**Oct. 1**). Yeltsin's forces crush revolt in Russian Parliament (**Oct. 4** *et seq.*). China breaks nuclear test moratorium (**Oct. 5**). Canada's opposition Liberal Party regains power in landslide (**Oct. 25**). Europe's Maastricht Treaty takes effect, creating European Union (**Nov. 1**). Jean Chretien sworn in as Canada's 20th prime minister (**Nov. 4**). House of Representatives approves North American Free Trade Agreement (**Nov. 17**); Senate follows (**Nov.**

21). South Africa adopts majority rule constitution (**Nov. 18**). Clinton signs Brady bill regulating firearms purchases (**Nov. 30**). Toni Morrison wins Nobel prize for literature.

1994 Serbs' heavy weapons pound Sarajevo (**Jan. 5–6**). Olympic figure skater Nancy Kerrigan attacked (**Jan. 6**); three arrested in attack (**Jan. 13**). Major earthquake jolts Los Angeles; 51 dead (**Jan. 17** *et seq.*). Clinton ends trade embargo on Vietnam (**Feb. 9**). Aldrich Ames, high C.I.A. official, charged with spying for Soviets (**Feb. 22**). Four convicted in World Trade Center bombing (**March 4**). Mexican presidential candidate assassinated (**March 23**). Rwandan genocide of Tutsis by Hutus begins; estimated 800,000 slaughtered in c. 100 days (**April 6**). South Africa holds first interracial national election (**April 29**); Nelson Mandela elected president. Israel and Palestinians sign accord (**May 4**). Clinton accused of sexual harassment while governor of Arkansas (**May 6**). Congress votes protection for women's health clinics (**May 12**). Jacqueline Kennedy Onassis dies (**May 20**). O. J. Simpson arrested in killings of wife, Nicole Brown Simpson, and friend, Ronald Goldman (**June 18**). Supreme Court approves limit on abortion protests (**June 30**). Senate confirms Stephen G. Breyer for Supreme Court (**July 29**). Women's health clinic doctor shot dead outside Florida clinic (**July 29**). Major league baseball players strike (**Aug. 13**). "Carlos the Jackal," international terrorist, captured (**Aug. 15**). I.R.A. declares cease-fire in Northern Ireland (**Aug. 31**). Small plane crashes against White House (**Sept. 12**). Baseball owners end season and cancel World Series (**Sept. 14**). Powerful earthquake strikes Japan (**Oct. 4**). Aristide returns to joyous Haiti (**Oct. 4**). U.S. sends forces to Persian Gulf (**Oct. 7**). Ulster Protestants declare cease-fire (**Oct. 13**). Israel and Jordan sign peace treaty (**Oct. 17**). Reagan, 83, reveals Alzheimer's disease (**Nov. 6**). G.O.P. wins control of House and Senate (**Nov. 8**). Aristide forms Haitian government with prime minister and full Cabinet (**Nov. 9**). Clinton orders Bosnian arms embargo ended (**Nov. 10**). Killer of women's health doctor sentenced twice (**Dec. 2**). Newt Gingrich named House Speaker (**Dec. 5**). Bentsen resigns as Treasury Secretary (**Dec. 6**). Russians attack secessionist Republic of Chechnya (**Dec. 11** *et seq.*). John Salvi kills two at Massachusetts Planned Parenthood clinic (**Dec. 30**).

1995 Republicans take control of Congress (**Jan. 4**). More than 5,000 dead in Japanese earthquake (**Jan. 17** *et seq.*). Criminal trial of O. J. Simpson opens in California (**Jan. 24**). U.S. rescues Mexico's economy with $20-billion aid program (**Feb. 21**). Senate rejects balanced-budget amendment (**March 2**). Nerve gas attack in Tokyo subway kills eight and injures thousands. The Aum Shinrikyo ("Supreme Truth") cult is to blame (**March 20**). Major League Baseball strike ends (**April 2**). Appeals court upholds woman's plea to enter Citadel military academy (**April 13**). UN Council votes easier sanctions for Iraq (**April 14**). Scores killed as terrorist's car bomb blows up block-long Oklahoma City federal building (**April 19**); Timothy McVeigh, 27, Army veteran, arrested as suspect (**April 21**); authorities seek second suspect, link right-wing paramilitary groups to bombing (**April 22**). Death toll 2,000 in Rwanda massacre (**April 22**). Fighting escalates in Bosnia and Croatia (**May 1**). U.S. shuttle docks with Russian space station (**June 27**). F.B.I. suspends four in Idaho siege inquiry (**Aug. 11**). France explodes nuclear device in Pacific; wide protests ensue (**Sept. 5**). Senator Bob Packwood of Oregon resigns under pressure for sexual and official misconduct (**Sept. 6**). Israelis and Palestinians agree on transferring West Bank to Arabs (**Sept. 24**). Los Angeles jury finds O. J. Simpson not guilty of murder charges (**Oct. 3**). Pope John Paul II visits U.S. on whirlwind tour (**Oct. 4–8**). Warring parties agree on cease-fire in Bosnia (**Oct. 5**). Million Man March draws hundreds of thousands of black men to capital (**Oct. 16**). Quebec narrowly rejects independence from Canada (**Oct. 30**). Israel prime minister Yitzhak Rabin slain by Jewish extremist at peace rally (**Nov. 4**). U.S. servicemen admit rape of Japanese schoolgirl in Okinawa (**Nov. 7**). Nigeria hangs writer Ken Saro-Wiwa and eight other minority rights advocates (**Nov. 10**). Irish voters approve end to constitutional ban on divorce (**Nov. 24**). Combatants sign Bosnia peace treaty (**Dec. 14**). House move stalls Congress-White House negotiations to avert government shutdown (**Dec. 20**). Seamus Heaney wins Nobel prize for literature.

Nelson Mandela
(1918–)

Jean-Bertrand Aristide
(1953–)

Dalai Lama
(1935–)

Yitzhak Rabin
(1922–1995)

Seamus Heaney
(1939–)

**Ella Fitzgerald
(1918–1996)**

**Madeleine Albright
(1937–)**

**Kofi Annan
(1938–)**

Hale-Bopp Comet

1996 U.S. budget crisis in fourth month (**Jan 3**). Clinton approves resumption of many government operations (**Jan. 6**). Senate ratifies major arms reduction treaty (**Jan. 26**). France announces end to nuclear tests (**Jan. 29**). At least 73 dead in Sri Lankan suicide bombing (**Feb. 1**). Suicide bombers kill 59 in Israel (**March 4**). Bob Dole sweeps Republican primaries (**March 5**). Britain alarmed by deadly cow disease (**March 20** *et seq.*). UN tribunal charges war crimes by Bosnian Muslims and Croats (**March 22**). Commerce Secretary Ronald H. Brown, 54, killed in plane crash (**April 3**). F.B.I. arrests suspected Unabomber (**April 3**). Clinton signs line-item veto bill (**April 9**). President blocks ban on late-term abortions (**April 10**). Valujet crashes in Everglades; all 110 aboard killed (**May 11**). Chechnya peace treaty signed (**May 27**). Israel elects Benjamin Netanyahu as prime minister (**May 31**). China agrees to world ban on atomic testing (**June 6**). Leaders in Balkans sign accord on arms limits (**June 14**). Jazz great Ella Fitzgerald dies (**June 15**). Truck bomb kills 19 at U.S. base in Saudi Arabia (**June 25**). Boris Yeltsin is reelected in Russian election (**July 3**). Prince Charles and Princess Diana agree on divorce (**July 12**). 747 airliner crashes in Atlantic off Long Island; all 230 aboard perish (**July 17**). Bomb mars Summer Olympic games in Atlanta (**July 25**). Clinton signs bill to raise minimum wage (**Aug. 2**). Congress passes welfare reform bill (**Aug. 2**); approved by Clinton (**Aug. 22**). Republican convention opens in San Diego (**Aug. 12**); Bob Dole and Jack Kemp nominated (**Aug. 14**). Democrats convene in Chicago (**Aug. 26**). Iraqis strike at Kurdish enclave (**Aug. 31**); after warning, U.S. attacks Iraq's southern air defenses (**Sept. 2–3**); Iraq halts attacks on U.S. planes enforcing flight exclusion zones in north and south (**Sept. 13**). Violence flares in Jerusalem over Israel opening tourist tunnel (**Sept. 24**). Taliban Muslim fundamentalists capture Afghan capital (**Sept. 27**). Ethnic violence breaks out in Zairian refugee camps (**Oct. 13**); thousands of refugees from Rwanda and Burundi abandon camps (**Oct. 21**). Clinton-Gore ticket wins national election; Republicans retain control of Congress (**Nov. 5**). Mid-air collision in India kills 342 (**Nov. 12**). Texaco settles racial bias suit (**Nov. 15**). Hundreds of thousands of Hutu refugees return to Rwanda (**Nov. 15–18**). Clinton appoints Madeleine Albright as first female U.S. secretary of state (**Dec. 5**). Kofi Annan named UN secretary-general (**Dec. 13**). F.B.I. agent charged with spying for Moscow (**Dec. 18**). Thousands march in Belgrade in continuing protest against president's annulment of election results (**Dec. 26**).

1997 Two Hutu sentenced to death in Rwandan genocide (**Jan. 3**). Floods cause wide damage in U.S. West (**Jan. 5**). Newt Gingrich re-elected as House Speaker (**Jan. 7**). Hebron agreement signed; Israel gives up large part of West Bank city of Hebron (**Jan. 16**). U.S. shuttle joins Russian space station (**Jan. 17**). Gingrich found guilty of ethics violations (**Jan. 17**). President Clinton starts second term (**Jan. 20**). U.S., U.K., and France agree to freeze Nazis' gold loot (**Feb. 3**). O. J. Simpson found liable in civil suit (**Feb. 5**). Deng Xiaoping, Chinese leader, dead at 92 (**Feb. 19**). Israeli government approves establishment of Jewish settlement in East Jerusalem, a setback in Middle East peace process (**Feb. 26**). Tornadoes wreak havoc in Arkansas, Ohio, and Kentucky (**March 3**). Senate dooms balanced-budget amendment (**March 4**). State of anarchy in Albania when third of population loses savings because of pyramid schemes (**March 13**). Hale-Bopp comet is the closest it will be to Earth until 4397 (**March 22**). Heaven's Gate cult members commit mass suicide in California (**March 27**). U.S. Appeals Court upholds California ban on affirmative action (**April 8**). U.S. judge upholds California marijuana law (**April 11**). Tiger Woods breaks multiple records in Masters golf tournament (**April 13**). Fire kills 300 pilgrims outside Mecca (**April 15**). Senate, 74–26, approves chemical-weapons treaty (**April 24**). Thousands flee North Dakota flood (**April 27**). UN tribunal convicts Bosnian Serb for killings and tortures (**May 7**). Sergeant Major of the Army, Gene C. McKinney, charged in sex cases (**May 7**). Russian President Yeltsin signs Chechnya peace treaty (**May 12**). U.S.-Russian spaceship linkup in orbit ends (**May 21**). U.S. jobless rate for May reported 4.8%, lowest since 1973 (**June 6**). European Union bolsters currency merger (**June 16**). Congress votes major tax cuts (**June 26**). Hong Kong returns to Chinese rule (**June 30**). U.S. spacecraft begins exploration of Mars (**July 4**). Andrew Cunanan murders fashion designer Gianni Versace (**July 15**). Khmer Rouge hold trial of longtime leader Pol Pot

(**July 25**). White House and G.O.P. agree on measure to balance budget (**July 28**). U.S. spacecraft transmits thousands of pictures from Mars (**Aug. 8**). Clinton exercises new line-item veto (**Aug. 11**). Timothy J. McVeigh sentenced to death for Oklahoma City bombing (**Aug. 14**). Princess Diana, 36, killed with two others in Paris car crash (**Aug. 31**). Three Islamic suicide bombers kill four persons in Jerusalem (**Sept. 4**). Mother Teresa dead at 87 (**Sept. 5**). Swiss plan first payment to Holocaust victims (**Sept. 17**). U.S. space shuttle docks with Russian *Mir*, bringing new astronaut (**Sept. 27**). Militant Taliban leaders seize Kabul (**Sept. 27**). Israeli prime minister Netanyahu center of controversy over failed attempt to assassinate militant Islamic leader (**Oct. 6**). Iraq expels all U.S. members of UN arms-inspection team (**Oct. 29**). G.O.P. victorious in off-year elections (**Nov. 4**). Pakistani convicted in 1993 C.I.A. killings (**Nov. 10**). Two convicted in New York Trade Center bombing (**Nov. 12**). Egyptian Islamic militants kill 62 at Luxor tourist site (**Nov. 17**). F.B.I. ends 16-month investigation of crash of Flight 800 off Long Island; denies sabotage (**Nov. 18**). Attorney General exonerates Clinton and Gore on fund-raising calls (**Dec. 2**). European Union plans to admit six nations (**Dec. 13**). Gunmen kill 45 in raid on Indian village in Mexico (**Dec. 22**). U.S. company launches first commercial spy satellite (**Dec. 24**). Paris court convicts "Carlos the Jackal" of murder (**Dec. 24**).

Mother Teresa
(1910–1997)

1998 Floods and freezing rain cripple Northeast (**Jan. 9**). Ramzi Ahmed Yousef sentenced to life for 1993 World Trade Center bombing (**Jan. 9**). Iraq blocks UN weapons inspection (**Jan. 13**). Pope John Paul II visits Cuba (**Jan. 21–25**). President accused in White House sex scandal; denies allegations of affair with White House intern, Monica Lewinsky (**Jan. 21** *et seq.*). President outlines first balanced budget in 30 years (**Feb. 3**). U.S. plane cuts ski cable in Italy and sends car plunging; 20 killed (**Feb. 3**). Thousands dead in Afghanistan quake (**Feb. 4** *et seq.*). U.S. court rules line-item veto unconstitutional (**Feb. 12**). Serbs battle ethnic Albanians in Kosovo (**March 5** *et seq.*). U.S. drops condemnation of China's human rights record (**March 13**). Sergeant Major Gene C. McKinney acquitted on sex charges (**March 13**). Vatican regrets inaction in Holocaust (**March 16**). Presbyterians keep ban on gay clergy (**March 18**). Hindu nationalist Vajpayee becomes India's prime minister (**March 19**). Clinton acclaimed on visit to Africa (**March 23** *et seq.*). F.D.A. approves Viagra, male impotence drug (**March 27**). Federal judge in Arkansas throws out Paula Jones case (**April 1**). Landmark peace settlement, the Good Friday Accord, reached in Northern Ireland (**April 10**). U.S. trade deficit biggest in decade (**April 17**). Irish Parliament backs peace agreement (**April 22**). Russian Parliament approves prime minister appointee, Sergei Kiriyenko (**April 24**). Europeans agree on single currency, the euro (**May 3**). Unabomber, Theodore Kaczynski, sentenced to four life terms (**May 4**). India conducts three atomic tests despite worldwide disapproval (**May 11, 13**). Indonesian dictator Suharto steps down after 32 years in power (**May 21**). Pakistan stages five nuclear tests in response to India's (**May 29, 30**). Serbs renew attack on Kosovo rebels (**June 1**). Life sentence meted out to Terry Nichols, convicted in Oklahoma City bombing fatal to 168 (**June 4**). Nigerian dictator Sani Abacha dies (**June 8**). Chinese use of U.S. satellites reported (**June 12**). President Clinton visits China (**June 25** *et seq.*). Congress votes to overhaul I.R.S. (**July 9**). Japanese voters oust ruling party (**July 12**). Independent counsel Kenneth Starr subpoenas Clinton to testify in Grand Jury investigation of reported White House sex scandal (**July 25**). Iraq ends cooperation with UN arms inspectors (**Aug. 5**). Monica Lewinsky testifies before grand jury about affair with Clinton (**Aug. 6**). U.S. embassies in Kenya and Tanzania bombed (**Aug. 7**). Clinton admits to affair with White House intern in televised address to nation (**Aug. 17**). Russia fights to avert financial collapse (**Aug. 17**). U.S. cruise missiles hit suspected terrorist bases in Sudan and Afghanistan (**Aug. 20**). North Korea fires missile across Japan (**Aug. 31**). UN tribunal convicts Rwandan in genocide; first such verdict ever (**Sept. 2**). Swissair jet crashes; kills 229 (**Sept. 2**). Starr Report by independent counsel outlines case for impeachment proceedings against president (**Sept. 11**). Senate sustains veto of bill to outlaw late-term abortions (**Sept. 18**). Iran lifts death threat against Salman Rushdie (**Sept. 24**). German chancellor Helmut Kohl defeated by Gerhard Schröder (**Sept. 27**). U.S. budget surplus largest in three decades. House Judiciary Committee votes to investigate

Princess Diana
(1961–1997)

Mars Sojourner Rover

Euro 100

William J. Clinton
(1946–)

Boris Yeltsin
(1931–)

Eileen Collins
(1956–)

possible impeachment of president (**Oct. 5**). China signs international accord to improve human rights (**Oct. 5**). Matthew Shepard, gay Wyoming student, fatally beaten in hate crime (**Oct. 6**). NATO, on verge of air strikes, reaches settlement with Milosevic on Kosovo (**Oct. 12**). Former Chilean dictator Pinochet arrested in London (**Oct. 16**). Wye Mills Agreement between Netanyahu and Arafat moves Middle East peace talks forward (**Oct. 23**). More than 10,000 die in Central American hurricane, Mitch (**Nov. 1**). Democrats unexpectedly gain five House seats in national election; Republicans keep control of House and Senate (**Nov. 3**). Astronaut John Glenn returns to Earth after encore space mission (**Nov. 7**). House Speaker Gingrich to step down (**Nov. 9**). House panel drafts impeachment charges; votes along party lines to approve four articles (**Dec. 11–12**). Osama bin Laden, Islamic extremist, reported to plot terrorist attacks on U.S. targets in Persian Gulf (**Dec. 15**). Clinton orders air strikes on Iraq (**Dec. 16–19**). House impeaches President Clinton along party lines on two charges, perjury and obstruction of justice. Senators divide on plan for trial or censure (**Dec. 19**).

1999   U.S. agrees to ease restrictions on Cuba (**Jan. 4**). U.S. warplanes fire on Iraqi jets over Iraqi no-fly zone (**Jan. 5**). Dennis Hastert elected to replace Newt Gingrich as Speaker of the House (**Jan. 6**). NBA ends 191-day labor dispute (**Jan. 6**). Michael Jordan retires from the Chicago Bulls (**Jan. 13**). Female genital mutliation banned in Senegal (**Jan. 14**). International Olympic Committee expels six members as bribery scandal widens (**Jan. 24**). King Hussein of Jordan dies at age 65 (**Feb. 7**). Senate acquits President Clinton of impeachment charges (**Feb. 12**). Gen. Olusegun Obasanjo elected president of Nigeria (**Feb. 28**). First nonstop balloon flight around world completed in 20 days (**March 1–20**). Marine pilot acquitted in killing of 20 in 1998 Italian ski gondola accident; Italians outraged (**March 4**). U.S. accuses China of stealing nuclear secrets (**March 5**). Joe DiMaggio dies at age 84 (**March 8**). Czech Republic, Poland, and Hungary join NATO (**March 12**). NATO launches air strikes on Serbia to end attacks against ethnic Albanians in Kosovo (**March 24**). Dr. Jack Kevorkian convicted of second-degree murder in assisted-suicide case (**March 26**). "Melissa" computer virus spreads through the Internet (**March 27**). Ore. jury orders Philip Morris to pay $81 million to family of lung cancer victim (**March 30**). Libya hands over two suspects in 1988 Pan Am jet bombing (**April 5**). Former Pakistani prime minister Benazir Bhutto imprisoned for taking kickbacks while in office (**April 15**). Two Colo. students go on shooting spree in Columbine High School, killing 15, including themselves (**April 20**). NATO bombs mistakenly hit Chinese embassy in Belgrade (**May 7**). Citadel graduates its first woman (**May 8**). Crime rate in U.S. falls for seventh consecutive year (**May 16**). Ehud Barak defeats Benjamin Netanyahu in Israeli prime minister election (**May 17**). Russian Parliament confirms new prime minister, Sergei Stepashin (**May 19**). U.S. inspects suspected nuclear weapons site in North Korea, finds nothing (**May 20–24**). Indian jets strike guerrillas in disputed Kashmir territory (**May 26**). Yugoslav president Slobodan Milosevic charged with crimes against humanity by Hague tribunal (**May 27**). Scientists announce discovery of two new elements, atomic numbers 116 and 118 (**June 7**). Serbs sign agreement to pull troops out of Kosovo after 11 weeks of NATO air attacks (**June 9**). Nelson Mandela retires as president of South Africa; succeeded by African National Congress member Thabo Mbeki (**June 16**). Prince Edward marries Sophie Rhys-Jones (**June 19**). Kurd leader Abdullah Ocalan sentenced to death for treason in Turkey (**June 29**). White supremacist goes on shooting spree in Midwest, killing 3 including self and wounding eight (**July 2–5**). U.S. soccer team tops China for women's World Cup (**July 10**). Taiwanese leader Lee Teng-hui challenges "One China" policy (**July 11**). Serial killer Rafael Reséndez-Ramirez surrenders himself to U.S. authorities (**July 13**). John F. Kennedy, Jr., wife Carolyn Bessette Kennedy, and sister-in-law Lauren Bessette killed in plane crash off coast of Martha's Vineyard (**July 16**). Col. Eileen Collins becomes first female to head a space shuttle mission (**July 16**). Falun Gong meditation sect banned by Chinese government (**July 22**). King Hassan II of Morocco dies at 70 (**July 23**). New York Stock Exchange and Nasdaq markets announce intent to become public companies (**July 23**). Suspect confesses to three killings in Feb. and one in July near Yosemite National Park (**July 26**). Day-trader kills 9 and wounds 13 in two Atlanta brokerage offices before committing suicide (**July 29**). China launches long-range missile (**Aug. 2**). Yeltsin replaces Prime Minister Stepashin with Vladimir Putin in fourth government shake-up in 17 months (**Aug. 9**). India downs unarmed Pakistani plane near disputed border (**Aug. 10**). Islamic militants declare independence for Dagestan and announce holy war against Russia (**Aug. 10**). White supremacist opens fire at Jewish community center in L.A., wounding five and killing one as he flees (**Aug. 10**). More than 15,600 people die in 7.4 earthquake in Turkey (**Aug. 17**). Attorney General Janet Reno reopens investigation of 1993 Waco, Tex., stand-off after new evidence shows F.B.I. may have started blaze that killed more than 80 Branch Davidians (**Aug. 25**). Last full crew leaves 13-year-old Russian space station *Mir* (**Aug. 28**). People of East Timor vote for independence from Indonesia (**Aug. 31**). Israeli prime minister Ehud Barak and PLO leader Yasir Arafat announce peace accord (**Sept. 4**). Gunman goes on rampage in Tex. church, killing seven before committing suicide (**Sept. 15**). NASA accidentally loses $125 million spacecraft as it orbits Mars (**Sept. 23**). Dozens of people exposed to radiation in Japan's worst nuclear accident (**Sept. 30**). Russia sends ground troops to Chechnya as conflict with Isalamic militants intensifies (**Oct. 1**). U.S. conducts missile defense system test over Pacific (**Oct. 2**). Train crash in London kills 31 (**Oct. 5**). Prime Minister Atal Bihari Vajpayee wins reelection in India (**Oct. 7**). World population reaches six billion milestone (**Oct. 11**). Military coup led by Gen. Pervaiz Musharraf overthrows Pakistani government (**Oct. 12**). Tobacco companies admit to harm caused by cigarette smoking (**Oct. 13**). Grand jury closes 1996 JonBenet Ramsey murder case due to lack of evidence (**Oct. 13**). Senate rejects 1996 nuclear test-ban treaty; international leaders scold U.S. (**Oct. 13**). Indonesia elects Muslim leader Abdurrahman Wahid president in nation's first democratic transfer of power (**Oct. 20**). Pro golfer Payne Stewart and five others killed in plane crash (**Oct. 25**). EgyptAir flight crashes over Atlantic, killing all 217 on board (**Oct. 31**). Judge finds Microsoft to be a monopoly (**Nov. 5**). U.S. and China reach landmark trade agreement (**Nov. 15**). China launches first spacecraft (**Nov. 21**). First Lady Hillary Rodham Clinton declares run for Senate in 2000 (**Nov. 23**). Five-year-old Cuban refugee gets caught in politically charged custody battle (**Nov. 25**). World Trade Organization conference disrupted by violent protests in Seattle (**Nov. 29** *et seq.*). New Northern Ireland government begins self-rule for first time in 25 years (**Dec. 2**). Muslim terrorists hijack Indian Airlines jet with 189 on board (**Dec. 24**).

PICTURE CREDITS

The editors wish to thank the following organizations and individuals who have contributed illustrations to Headline History.

Agence France Press/Archive Photos: **Mao Zedong;** AIP Niels Bohr Library: **Marie Curie, Albert Einstein;** AMW Pressedienst/Archive Photos: **Nelson Mandela;** Archive Photos: **Richard Wagner, William Butler Yeats, Pablo Picasso, Anne Frank, Woody Guthrie, Robert Frost, William Faulkner, The Beatles, Mahatma Gandhi, Duke Ellington, Tennessee Williams, Toni Morrison, Seamus Heaney, Ella Fitzgerald, Lech Walesa, Princess Diana, Pope John Paul, Mother Teresa, Yitzhak Rabin, Malcolm X, William Rehnquist, Anwar Sadat;** Linda J. Barnes: **the Duomo in Florence;** British Information Services: **Margaret Thatcher;** Consolidated News/Archive Photos: **Jean-Bertrand Aristide;** Tina Diodati: **Aqueduct, Parthenon;** Embassy of the Philippines: **Corazon Aquino;** The French Consulate, Boston: **François Mitterrand;** Gerald R. Ford Library: **Gerald Ford;** Peter F. Harrington: **Stonehenge;** Erik Hjortshoj: **Pagoda;** Imapress/Archive Photos: **Boris Yeltsin;** INA/Reuters/Archive Photos: **Saddam Hussein;** John Fitzgerald Kennedy Library, Boston: **John F. Kennedy;** Priscilla Lee: **Dalai Lama;** Leo Baeck Inst./Archive Photos: **Sigmund Freud;** Jimmy Carter Library: **Jimmy Carter;** The Library of Congress Picture Collection: **Pocahontas, Taj Mahal, Edgar Allan Poe, Harriet Tubman, Walt Whitman, Dred Scott, Samuel Clemens (Mark Twain), Henri Matisse, W. E. B. Du Bois, Woodrow Wilson, Bessie Smith, Dorothea Lange photo, Amelia Earhart, Harry S. Truman, John H. Glenn, Jr., James H. Meredith, Betty Friedan, Richard Nixon, Lyndon B. Johnson;** Pete Maio: **Mesa Verde;** Muzammil Paha/Reuters/Archive Photos: **Benazir Bhutto;** National Archives and Records Admin.: **Frederick Douglass, Harriet Beecher Stowe, Abraham Lincoln, Robert E. Lee, William Tecumseh Sherman, Chief Joseph, Benito Mussolini, Franklin Delano Roosevelt, Adolf Hitler, Winston Churchill, Atomic Bomb, Dwight D. Eisenhower, Rev. Martin Luther King, Jr.;** NASA: **Eileen Collins, Hubble Space Telescope;** NASA/JPL/Caltech: **Mars Sojourner Rover;** Novosti Photos: **Vladimir Lenin, Mikhail S. Gorbachev;** Elaine Ouellette: **Pantheon in Rome;** The Permanent Mission of India to the UN: **Indira Gandhi;** Permanent Mission of Islamic Republic of Iran to the UN: **Ayatollah Ruhollah Khomeini;** Renée Scott: **Celtic Cross, Mayan Pyramid;** The Republican National Committee: **Ronald Reagan, George Bush;** Kim Storm: **Egyptian Pyramid;** United Nations: **Dag Hammarskjöld, Fidel Castro, Kofi Annan;** U.S. Army Photos: **Joseph Stalin, Yalta Conference, General Colin Powell;** U.S. State Department: **Madeleine Albright;** U.S. Supreme Court: **Ruth Bader Ginsburg, Thurgood Marshall, Sandra Day O'Connor;** Tasha Vincent: **Cathedral and Tower at Pisa, Chartres Cathedral, Michelangelo's David, Statue of Liberty;** The White House: **William J. Clinton.**

The Big Population Crunch

Some encouraging news about demographics

By JEFFREY KLUGER TIME

Odds are you'll never meet any of the estimated 247 human beings who were born in the past minute. In a population of 6 billion, 247 is a demographic hiccup. In the minute before last, however, there were another 247. In the minutes to come there will be another, then another, then another. By next year at this time, all those minutes will have produced nearly 130 million newcomers to the great human mosh pit. That kind of crowd is awfully hard to miss.

Troubling Statistics

For folks inclined to fret that the earth is heading for the environmental abyss, the population problem has always been one of the biggest causes for worry—and with good reason. The last time humanity celebrated a new century there were 1.6 billion people here for the party—or a quarter as many as this time. In 1900 the average life expectancy was, in some places, as low as 23 years; in 2000 it was 65, meaning the extra billions are staying around longer and demanding more from the planet. The 130 million or so births registered annually—even after subtracting the 52 million deaths—is still the equivalent of adding nearly one new Germany to the world's population each year.

But things may not be as bleak as they seem. Lately demographers have come to the conclusion that the population locomotive—while still cannon-balling ahead—may be chugging toward a stop. In country after country, birthrates are easing, and the population growth rate is falling.

Bringing Down Birth Rates

To be sure, this kind of success is uneven. For every region in the world that has brought its population under control, there's another where things are still exploding. For every country that has figured out the art of sustainable agriculture, there are others that have worked their land to exhaustion. The population bomb may yet go off before governments can snuff the fuse, but for now, the news is better than it's been in a long time. "We could have an end in sight to population growth in the next century," says Carl Haub, a demographer with the nonprofit Population Research Bureau. "That's a major change." As cheering as the population reports are becoming today, for much of the past 50 years, demographers were bearers of mostly bad tidings. In census after census, they reported that humanity was not just settling the planet but smothering it.

WHAT HAPPENS TO THE NUMBER OF HUMANS ...

(in billions)

World population is expected to reach somewhere between 7.3 billion and 10.7 billion by 2050

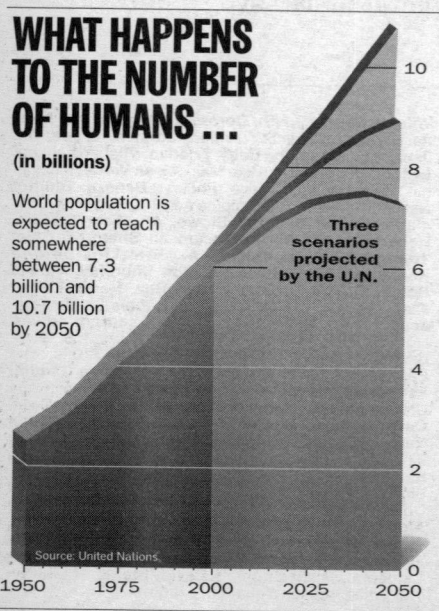

Three scenarios projected by the U.N.

Source: United Nations

... DEPENDS ON HOW FAST FERTILITY RATES FALL

(babies born per woman)

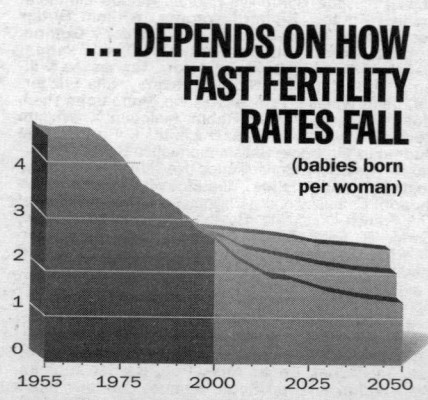

2.7 Children

It was not until the century was nearly two-thirds over that scientists and governments finally bestirred themselves to do something about it. The first great brake on population growth came in the early 1960s, with the development of the birth-control pill, a magic pharmacological bullet that made contraception easier—not to mention tidier—than it had ever been before. In 1969 the United Nations got in on the population game, creating the U.N. Population Fund, a global organization dedicated to bringing family-planning techniques to women who would not otherwise have them.

Such efforts have paid off in a big way. According to U.N. head counters, the average number of children produced per couple in the developing world—a figure that reached a whopping 4.9 earlier this century—has plunged to just 2.7. In many countries, including Spain, Slovenia, Greece, and Germany, the fertility rate is well below 1.5, meaning parents are producing 25% fewer offspring than would be needed to replace themselves—in effect, throwing the census into reverse. A little more than 30 years ago, global population growth was 2.04% a year, the highest in human history. In 2000, it was just 1.3%. "It was a remarkable century," says Joseph Chamie of the U.N. Population Division. "We quadrupled the population in 100 years, but that's not going to happen again."

As sunny as the global averages look, however, things get a lot darker when you break them down by region. In parts of the Middle East and Africa, the fertility rate exceeds seven babies per woman. In India, nearly 16 million births are registered each year, for a growth rate of 1.8%. While Europe's population was three times that of Africa in 1950, in 2000 the two continents had about the same count. At the current rate, Africa will triple Europe by 2050.

Forced Family Planning

Many of the countries in the deepest demographic trouble have imposed aggressive family-planning programs, only to see them go badly—even criminally—awry. In the 1970s, Indian prime minister Indira Gandhi tried to reduce the national birthrate by offering men cash and transistor radios if they would undergo vasectomies. In the communities in which those sweeteners failed, the government resorted to coercion, putting millions of males—from teenage boys to elderly men—on the operating table. Amid the popular backlash that followed, Gandhi's government was turned out of office, and the public rejected family planning.

China's similarly notorious one-child policy has done a better job of slowing population growth, but not without problems. In a country that values boys over girls, one-child rules have led to abandonments, abortions, and infanticides, as couples limited to a single offspring keep spinning the reproductive wheel until it comes up male.

Success Stories

That strategy has worked in many countries that once had runaway population growth. Mexico, one of Latin America's population success stories, has made government-subsidized contraception widely available and at the same time launched public-

information campaigns to teach people the value of using it. A series of ads aimed at men made the powerful point that there is more machismo in clothing and feeding offspring than in conceiving and leaving them. In the past 30 years, the average number of children born to a Mexican woman has plunged from seven to just 2.5. Many developing nations are starting to recognize the importance of educating women and letting them—not just their husbands—have a say in how many children they will have.

But bringing down birthrates loses some of its effectiveness as mortality rates also fall. At the same time Mexico reduced its children-per-mother figure, for example, it also boosted its average life expectancy from 50 years to 72—a wonderful accomplishment, but one that offsets part of the gain achieved by reducing the number of births.

Life Expectancy Lengthening

When people live longer, populations grow not just bigger but also older and frailer. In the U.S. there has been no end of hand wringing over what will happen when baby boomers—who owe their very existence to the procreative free-for-all that followed World War II—retire, leaving themselves to be supported by the much smaller generation they produced. In Germany there are currently four workers for every retired person. Before long that ratio will be down to just 2 to 1.

World Population Milestones

• 1 billion in 1804		
• 2 billion in 1927	(123 years later)	
• 3 billion in 1960	(33 years later)	
• 4 billion in 1974	(14 years later)	
• 5 billion in 1987	(13 years later)	
• 6 billion in 1999	(12 years later)	

For now, the only answer may be to tough things out for a while, waiting for the billions of people born during the great population booms to live out their long life, while at the same time continuing to reduce birthrates further so that things don't get thrown so far out of kilter again. But there's no telling if the earth—already worked to exhaustion feeding the 6 billion people currently here—can take much more. People in the richest countries consume a disproportionate share of the world's resources, and as poorer nations push to catch up, pressure on the planet will keep growing. "An ecologist looks at the population size relative to the carrying capacity of Earth," says Lester Brown, president of the Worldwatch Institute. "Looking at it that way, things are much worse than we expected them to be 20 years ago."

How much better they'll get will be decided in the next half-century. According to three scenarios published by the U.N., the global population in the year 2050 will be somewhere between 7.3 billion and 10.7 billion, depending on how fast the fertility rate falls. The difference between the high scenario and the low scenario? Just one child per couple. With the species poised on that kind of demographic knife edge, it pays for those couples to make their choices carefully. □

Total Population of the World by Decade, 1950–2050
(historical and projected)

Year	Total world population (mid-year figures)	Ten-year growth rate (%)	Year	Total world population (mid-year figures)	Ten-year growth rate (%)
1950	2,556,000,053	18.9%	2010	6,848,932,929	10.7%
1960	3,039,451,023	22.0	2020	7,584,821,144	8.7
1970	3,706,618,163	20.2	2030	8,246,619,341	7.3
1980	4,453,831,714	18.5	2040	8,850,045,889	5.6
1990	5,278,639,789	15.2	2050	9,346,399,468	—
2000	6,082,966,429	12.6			

Source: U.S. Bureau of the Census, International Database.

World's 50 Most Populous Countries: 2000

Rank	Country	Population	Rank	Country	Population	Rank	Country	Population
1.	China	1,261,832,482	18.	Ethiopia	64,117,452	34.	Canada	31,278,097
2.	India	1,014,003,817	19.	Thailand	61,230,874	35.	Algeria	31,193,917
3.	United States	275,562,673	20.	United Kingdom	59,508,382	36.	Kenya	30,339,770
4.	Indonesia	224,784,210	21.	France	59,329,691	37.	Morocco	30,122,350
5.	Brazil	172,860,370	22.	Italy	57,634,327	38.	Peru	27,012,899
6.	Russia	146,001,176	23.	Congo, Dem. Rep. of	51,964,999	39.	Afghanistan	25,888,797
7.	Pakistan	141,553,775				40.	Uzbekistan	24,755,519
8.	Bangladesh	129,194,224	24.	Ukraine	49,153,027	41.	Nepal	24,702,119
9.	Japan	126,549,976	25.	South Korea	47,470,969	42.	Venezuela	23,542,649
10.	Nigeria	123,337,822	26.	South Africa	43,421,021	43.	Uganda	23,317,560
11.	Mexico	100,349,766	27.	Burma	41,734,853	44.	Iraq	22,675,617
12.	Germany	82,797,408	28.	Spain	39,996,671	45.	Romania	22,411,121
13.	Philippines	81,159,644	29.	Colombia	39,685,655	46.	Taiwan	22,191,087
14.	Vietnam	78,773,873	30.	Poland	38,646,023	47.	Saudi Arabia	22,023,506
15.	Egypt	68,359,979	31.	Argentina	36,955,182	48.	Malaysia	21,793,293
16.	Turkey	65,666,677	32.	Tanzania	35,306,126	49.	North Korea	21,687,550
17.	Iran	65,619,636	33.	Sudan	35,079,814	50.	Ghana	19,533,560

Source: U.S. Department of Commerce, U.S. Census Bureau, International Database.

World's 50 Most Populous Cities[1]

Name	Country	Est. population (in millions)	Name	Country	Est. population (in millions)
1. Tokyo	Japan	34.8	26. Beijing	China	8.5
2. New York	USA	20.2	27. Taipei	Taiwan	7.7
3. Seoul	South Korea	19.9	28. Lima	Peru	7.5
4. Mexico City	Mexico	19.8	29. Washington, D.C.	USA	7.5
5. São Paulo	Brazil	17.9	30. Bogotá	Colombia	7.4
6. Bombay (Mumbai)	India	17.9	31. Bangkok	Thailand	7.2
7. Osaka	Japan	17.9	32. San Francisco	USA	6.9
8. Los Angeles	USA	16.2	33. Hong Kong	China	6.8
9. Cairo	Egypt	14.4	34. Madras (Chennai)	India	6.6
10. Manila	Philippines	13.5	35. Hyderabad	India	6.5
11. Buenos Aires	Argentina	13.3	36. Lahore	Pakistan	6.4
12. Moscow	Russia	13.2	37. Essen	Germany	6.1
13. Lagos	Nigeria	13.1	38. Kinshasa	Congo, Dem. Rep. of	6.1
14. Calcutta	India	12.9	39. Philadelphia	USA	6.1
15. Jakarta	Indonesia	12.3	40. Johannesburg	South Africa	5.7
16. Karachi	Pakistan	12.1	41. Boston	USA	5.7
17. London	U.K.	11.8	42. St. Petersburg	Russia	5.6
18. Shanghai	China	11.8	43. Bangalore	India	5.5
19. Delhi	India	11.5	44. Detroit	USA	5.4
20. Rio de Janeiro	Brazil	10.7	45. Santiago	Chile	5.4
21. Teheran	Iran	10.4	46. Tianjin	China	5.4
22. Istanbul	Turkey	10.3	47. Nagoya	Japan	5.1
23. Paris	France	10.2	48. Madrid	Spain	5.1
24. Dhaka	Bangladesh	9.6	49. Dallas	USA	5.0
25. Chicago	USA	8.9	50. Baghdad	Iraq	4.9

1. Includes surrounding urban agglomerations. Agglomerations include a central city and bordering urban areas. Some agglomerations have more than one central city (e.g., Washington, D.C. includes Baltimore; Tokyo includes Yokohama and Kawasaki). NOTE: The definitions of agglomerations vary significantly from city to city, hence the difficulty of compiling an accurate, comparative list of the world's most populous cities. *Source:* Thomas Brinkhoff, *Principal Agglomerations and Cities of the World.* http://www.citypopulation.de, 4.6.00.

Country Statistics at a Glance

Country rankings of the type presented below cannot pretend to be definitive; instead they aspire only to provide the reader with a general approximation of the high and low ends on a particular scale. Country data vary enormously depending on the sources, and the absence of reliable data on some countries requires their omission, which further skews the results.

LARGEST COUNTRIES[1] (in sq. mi.): 1999

(1)	Russia	6,592,800
(2)	Canada	3,851,809
(3)	China	3,691,521
(4)	United States	3,536,341
(5)	Brazil	3,286,470
(6)	Australia	2,966,150
(7)	India	1,229,737
(8)	Argentina	1,072,067
(9)	Kazakhstan	1,049,000
(10)	Sudan	967,491

SMALLEST COUNTRIES[1] (in sq. mi.): 1999

(1)	Vatican City	0.17
(2)	Monaco	0.73
(3)	Nauru	8.2
(4)	Tuvalu	10.0
(5)	San Marino	23.6
(6)	Liechtenstein	61.0
(7)	Marshall Islands	70.0
(8)	St. Kitts & Nevis	100.0
(9)	Maldives	115.0
(10)	Malta	122.0

HIGHEST POPULATION DENSITY[2] (per sq. mi.): 1999

(1)	Monaco	44,040
(2)	Singapore	14,315
(3)	Malta	3,128
(4)	Maldives	2,621
(5)	Bahrain	2,611
(6)	Bangladesh	2,286
(7)	Taiwan	1,591
(8)	Barbados	1,561
(9)	Mauritius	1,502
(10)	Nauru	1,293

LOWEST POPULATION DENSITY[2] (per sq. mi.): 1999

(1)	Greenland	0.1
(2)	Western Sahara	1.5
(3)	Mongolia	4.0
(4)	Namibia	5.0
(5)	Australia	6.0
	Botswana	6.0
	Mauritania	6.0
(8)	Iceland	7.0
	Libya	7.0
	Suriname	7.0

HIGHEST GDP PER CAPITA[3] (PPP in US dollars): 1998

(1)	Luxembourg	$32,700
(2)	United States	31,500
(3)	Switzerland	26,400
(4)	Singapore	26,300
(5)	Monaco	25,000
(6)	Norway	24,700
(7)	Belgium	23,400
(8)	Denmark	23,300
(9)	Japan	23,100
(10)	Liechtenstein	23,000

LOWEST GDP PER CAPITA[3] (PPP in US dollars): 1998

(1)	Sierra Leone	$530
(2)	Ethiopia	560
(3)	Somalia	600
(4)	Eritrea	660
(5)	Rwanda	690
(6)	Cambodia	700
	Comoros	700
(8)	Congo, Dem. Rep. of	710
(9)	Madagascar	730
	Tanzania	730

HIGHEST INFLATION:[3] 1998

(1)	Afghanistan	240.0%
(2)	Belarus	182.0
(3)	Congo, Dem. Rep. of	147.0
(4)	Laos	112.0
(5)	Angola	90.0
(6)	Cyprus (Turkish)	87.5
(7)	Russia	84.0
(8)	Malawi[4]	83.4
(9)	Indonesia	77.0
(10)	Turkey	70.0

LOWEST INFLATION:[3] 1998

(1)	Azerbaijan	−7.6%
(2)	Nauru[5]	−3.6
(3)	Mozambique	−1.3
(4)	Antigua and Barbuda	−1.1
(5)	China	−0.8
(6)	Kiribati	−0.6
(7)	Belize	−0.5
	Singapore	−0.5
(9)	Bahrain	−0.2
	Oman	−0.2
	Saudi Arabia	−0.2

HIGHEST INFANT MORTALITY RATE:[2] 1998 (deaths per 1,000 births)

(1)	Angola	195.78
(2)	Afghanistan	149.28
(3)	Sierra Leone	148.66
(4)	Mozambique	139.86
(5)	Liberia	134.63
(6)	Western Sahara	133.59
(7)	Guinea	130.98
(8)	Somalia	125.77
(9)	Niger	124.90
(10)	Mali	123.25

LOWEST INFANT MORTALITY RATE:[2] 1998 (deaths per 1,000 births)

(1)	Sweden	3.49
(2)	Singapore	3.64
(3)	Finland	3.82
(4)	Japan	3.91
(5)	Norway	3.98
(6)	Andorra	4.08
(7)	Netherlands	4.42
(8)	Austria	4.50
(9)	France	4.51
(10)	Switzerland	4.53

HIGHEST LIFE EXPECTANCY[2] (in years): 1998

(1)	Andorra	83.46
(2)	San Marino	81.14
(3)	Japan	80.70
(4)	Singapore	80.05
(5)	Australia	79.75
(6)	Switzerland	79.60
(7)	Sweden	79.58
(8)	Canada	79.43
(9)	Iceland	79.39
(10)	Italy	79.03

LOWEST LIFE EXPECTANCY[2] (in years): 1998

(1)	Mozambique	37.52
(2)	Malawi	37.58
(3)	Zimbabwe	37.78
(4)	Angola	38.31
(5)	Botswana	39.27
(6)	Rwanda	39.34
(7)	Swaziland	40.44
(8)	Niger	41.27
(9)	Namibia	42.46
(10)	Uganda	42.93

Sources: 1. Information Please Database. 2. U.S. Bureau of the Census, International Database. 3. *The World Factbook, 1999.* 4. Figure is for 1995. 5. Figure is for 1993. Note: Only countries for which statistics were available in sources 1, 2, or 3 figure in these lists.

Area and Population of Countries

(mid-2000 estimates)

Country	Area (in sq. km)	Population	Country	Area (in sq. km)	Population
Afghanistan	647,500	25,888,797	Ghana	238,540	19,533,560
Albania	28,750	3,490,435	Greece	131,940	10,601,527
Algeria	2,381,740	31,193,917	Grenada	340	89,312
Andorra	450	66,824	Guatemala	108,890	12,639,939
Angola	1,246,700	10,145,267	Guinea	245,860	7,466,200
Antigua and Barbuda	440	66,464	Guinea-Bissau	36,120	1,285,715
Argentina	2,766,890	36,955,182	Guyana	214,970	697,286
Armenia	29,800	3,344,336	Haiti	27,750	6,867,995
Australia	7,686,850	19,164,620	Honduras	112,090	6,249,598
Austria	83,858	8,131,111	Hungary	93,030	10,138,844
Azerbaijan	86,600	7,748,163	Iceland	103,000	276,365
The Bahamas	13,940	294,982	India	3,287,590	1,014,003,817
Bahrain	620	634,137	Indonesia	1,919,440	224,784,210
Bangladesh	144,000	129,194,224	Iran	1,648,000	65,619,636
Barbados	430	274,059	Iraq	437,072	22,675,617
Belarus	207,600	10,366,719	Ireland	70,280	3,797,257
Belgium	30,510	10,241,506	Israel	20,770	5,842,454
Belize	22,960	249,183	Italy	301,230	57,634,327
Benin	112,620	6,395,919	Jamaica	10,990	2,652,689
Bhutan	47,000	2,005,222	Japan	377,835	126,549,976
Bolivia	1,098,580	8,152,620	Jordan	89,213	4,998,564
Bosnia and Herzegovina	51,233	3,835,777	Kazakhstan	2,717,300	16,733,227
Botswana	600,370	1,576,470	Kenya	582,650	30,339,770
Brazil	8,511,965	172,860,370	Kiribati	717	91,985
Brunei	5,770	336,376	North Korea	120,540	21,687,550
Bulgaria	110,910	7,796,694	South Korea	98,480	47,470,969
Burkina Faso	274,200	11,946,065	Kuwait	17,820	1,973,572
Burma (Myanmar)	678,500	41,734,853	Kyrgyzstan	198,500	4,685,230
Burundi	27,830	6,054,714	Laos	236,800	5,497,459
Cambodia	181,040	12,212,306	Latvia	64,100	2,404,926
Cameroon	475,440	15,421,937	Lebanon	10,400	3,578,036
Canada	9,976,140	31,278,097	Lesotho	30,350	2,143,141
Cape Verde	4,030	401,343	Liberia	111,370	3,164,156
Central African Republic	622,980	3,512,751	Libya	1,759,540	5,115,450
Chad	1,284,000	8,424,504	Liechtenstein	160	32,204
Chile	756,950	15,153,797	Lithuania	65,200	3,620,756
China, People's Republic of	9,596,960	1,261,832,482	Luxembourg	2,586	437,389
Colombia	1,138,910	39,685,655	Macedonia	25,333	2,041,467
Comoros	2,170	578,400	Madagascar	587,040	15,506,472
Republic of Congo	342,000	2,830,961	Malawi	118,480	10,385,849
Democratic Republic of the Congo (formerly Zaire)	2,345,410	51,964,999	Malaysia	329,750	21,793,293
			Maldives	300	301,475
Costa Rica	51,100	3,710,558	Mali	1,240,000	10,685,948
Côte d'Ivoire	322,460	15,980,950	Malta	320	391,670
Croatia	56,538	4,282,216	Marshall Islands	181.3	68,126
Cuba	110,860	11,141,997	Mauritania	1,030,700	2,667,859
Cyprus	9,250	758,363	Mauritius	1,860	1,179,368
Czech Republic	78,703	10,272,179	Mexico	1,972,550	100,349,766
Denmark	43,094	5,336,394	Micronesia	702	133,144
Djibouti	22,000	451,442	Moldova	33,700	4,430,654
Dominica	750	71,540	Monaco	1.95	31,693
Dominican Republic	48,730	8,442,533	Mongolia	1,565,000	2,616,383
Ecuador	283,560	12,920,092	Morocco	446,550	30,122,350
Egypt	1,001,450	68,359,979	Mozambique	801,590	19,104,696
El Salvador	21,040	6,122,515	Namibia	825,418	1,771,327
Equatorial Guinea	28,050	474,214	Nauru	21	11,845
Eritrea	121,320	4,135,933	Nepal	140,800	24,702,119
Estonia	45,226	1,431,471	Netherlands	41,526	15,892,237
Ethiopia	1,127,127	64,117,452	New Zealand	268,680	3,819,762
Fiji	18,270	832,494	Nicaragua	129,494	4,812,569
Finland	337,030	5,167,486	Niger	1,267,000	10,075,511
France	547,030	59,329,691	Nigeria	923,770	123,337,822
Gabon	267,670	1,208,436	Norway	324,220	4,481,162
The Gambia	11,300	1,367,124	Oman	212,460	2,533,389
Georgia	69,700	5,019,538	Pakistan	803,940	141,553,775
Germany	356,910	82,797,408	Palau	458	18,766

Country	Area (in sq. km)	Population	Country	Area (in sq. km)	Population
Panama	78,200	2,808,268	Suriname	163,270	431,303
Papua New Guinea	461,690	4,926,984	Swaziland	17,360	1,083,289
Paraguay	406,750	5,585,828	Sweden	449,964	8,873,052
Peru	1,285,220	27,012,899	Switzerland	41,290	7,262,372
Philippines	300,000	81,159,644	Syria	185,180	16,305,659
Poland	312,683	38,646,023	Taiwan	35,980	22,191,087
Portugal	92,391	10,048,232	Tajikistan	143,100	6,440,732
Qatar	11,437	744,483	Tanzania	945,090	35,306,126
Romania	237,500	22,411,121	Thailand	514,000	61,230,874
Russia	17,075,200	146,001,176	Togo	56,790	5,018,502
Rwanda	26,340	7,229,129	Tonga	748	102,321
Saint Kitts and Nevis	269	38,819	Trinidad and Tobago	5,130	1,175,523
Saint Lucia	620	156,260	Tunisia	163,610	9,593,402
Saint Vincent and Grenadines	340	115,461	Turkey	780,580	65,666,677
Samoa	2,860	179,466	Turkmenistan	488,100	4,518,268
San Marino	60	26,937	Tuvalu	26	10,838
São Tomé and Príncipe	960	159,883	Uganda	236,040	23,317,560
Saudi Arabia	1,960,582	22,023,506	Ukraine	603,700	49,153,027
Senegal	196,190	9,987,494	United Arab Emirates	82,880	2,369,153
Serbia and Montenegro	102,350	9,981,929	United Kingdom	244,820	59,508,382
Seychelles	455	79,326	United States	9,629,091	275,562,673
Sierra Leone	71,740	5,232,624	Uruguay	176,220	3,334,074
Singapore	647.5	4,151,720	Uzbekistan	447,400	24,755,519
Slovakia	48,845	5,407,956	Vanuatu	14,760	189,618
Slovenia	20,256	1,927,593	Vatican City	.44	850
Solomon Islands	28,450	466,194	Venezuela	912,050	23,542,649
Somalia	637,660	7,253,137	Vietnam	329,560	78,773,873
South Africa	1,219,912	43,421,021	Western Sahara	266,000	244,943
Spain	504,750	39,996,671	Yemen	527,970	17,479,206
Sri Lanka	65,610	19,238,575	Zambia	752,610	9,582,418
Sudan	2,505,810	35,079,814	Zimbabwe	390,580	11,342,521

Source: U.S. Census Bureau, International Database and *The World Factbook, 1999.*

Crude Marriage Rates for Selected Countries
(per 1,000 population)

Country	1998	1997	1990	Country	1998	1997	1990	Country	1998	1997	1990
Australia	—	5.8	6.9	Hungary	4.5	4.6	6.4	Portugal	6.7	6.5	7.3
Austria	4.8	5.1	5.8	Ireland	—	4.3	5.0	Romania	6.4	6.5	8.3
Belgium	4.4	4.7	6.6	Israel	—	5.6	7.0	Russia	5.8	6.3	8.9
Bulgaria	4.3	4.1	6.7	Italy	—	4.8	5.4	Sweden	3.5	3.7	4.7
Czech Republic[1]	5.4	5.6	8.4	Japan	6.3	6.2	5.8	Switzerland	—	5.3	6.9
Denmark	6.5	6.4	6.1	Luxembourg	—	4.8	6.2	United Kingdom	—		6.8
Finland	4.5	4.6	4.8	Netherlands	—	5.5	6.4	United States	—	8.9	9.8
France	4.8	4.8	5.1	New Zealand	—	5.3	7.0	Yugoslavia[3]	5.0	5.3	6.2
Germany[2]	5.1	5.2	6.5	Norway	—	—	5.2				
Greece	5.5	5.7	5.8	Poland	5.4	5.3	6.7				

1. Data prior to 1993 pertain to the former Czechoslovakia. 2. All data pertaining to Germany prior to 1990 are for West Germany. 3. Beginning January 1992, data refer to the Federal Republic of Yugoslavia. Prior to that date, data refer to the Socialist Federal Republic of Yugoslavia. *Source:* United Nations, *Monthly Bulletin of Statistics, May 1999.*

Percentage of Divorces in Selected Countries

Country	Divorces (as % of marriages) 1996	Country	Divorces (as % of marriages) 1996	Country	Divorces (as % of marriages) 1996	Country	Divorces (as % of marriages) 1996
Belarus	68%	United States	49%	Denmark	35%	Spain	17%
Russian Federation	65	Hungary	46	Slovakia	34	Azerbaijan	15
Sweden	64	Canada	45	Bulgaria	28	Croatia	15
Latvia	63	Norway	43	Israel	26	Cyprus	13
Ukraine	63	France	43	Slovenia	26	Tajikistan	13
Czech Republic	61	Germany	41	Kyrgyzstan	25	Georgia	12
Belgium	56	Netherlands	41	Romania	24	Italy	12
Finland	56	Switzerland	40	Portugal	21	Uzbekistan	12
Lithuania	55	Iceland	39	Poland	19	Albania	7
United Kingdom	53	Kazakhstan	39	Armenia	18	Turkey	6
Moldova	52	Luxembourg	39	Greece	18	Macedonia	5
		Austria	38	Turkmenistan	18		

Source: Human Development Report, 1999, United Nations.

Infant Mortality and Life Expectancy for Selected Countries, 1999

Country	Infant mortality[1]	Life expectancy[2]	Country	Infant mortality[1]	Life expectancy[2]	Country	Infant mortality[1]	Life expectancy[2]
Albania	42.90	69.00	Germany	5.14	77.17	Poland	12.76	73.06
Australia	5.11	80.14	Greece	7.13	78.43	Portugal	6.73	75.88
Austria	5.10	77.48	Guatemala	46.15	66.45	Russia	23.00	65.12
Bangladesh	69.68	60.60	Hungary	9.46	71.18	Slovakia	9.48	73.46
Belgium	6.17	77.53	India	60.81	63.40	S. Africa	51.99	54.76
Brazil	35.37	64.06	Iran	29.73	69.76	S. Korea	7.57	74.30
Canada	5.47	79.37	Ireland	5.94	76.39	Spain	6.41	77.71
Chile	10.02	75.46	Israel	7.78	78.61	Sri Lanka	16.12	72.67
China	43.31	69.92	Italy	6.30	78.51	Sweden	3.91	79.29
Costa Rica	12.89	76.04	Japan	4.07	80.11	Switzerland	4.87	78.99
Cyprus	7.68	77.10	Kenya	59.07	47.02	Syria	36.42	68.09
Czech Rep.	6.67	74.35	Mexico	24.62	72.00	Trinidad	18.56	70.66
Denmark	5.11	76.51	N.Z.	6.22	77.82	U.K.	5.78	77.37
Ecuador	30.69	72.16	Norway	4.96	78.36	U.S.	6.33	76.23
Egypt	67.46	62.39	Pakistan	91.86	59.38	Uruguay	13.49	75.83
Finland	3.80	77.32	Panama	23.35	74.66	Venezuela	26.51	72.95
France	5.62	78.63	Peru	38.97	70.38			

1. Infant deaths per 1,000 live births. 2. Life expectancy at birth, in years. *Source:* U.S. Census Bureau, International Database.

Crude Birth and Death Rates for Selected Countries
(per 1,000 population)

Country	Birth rate						Death rate					
	1998	1994	1990	1985	1980	1975	1998	1994	1990	1985	1980	1975
Australia	13.47	14.5	15.4	15.7	15.3	16.9	6.89	7.1	7.0	7.5	7.4	7.9
Austria	9.89	11.5	11.6	11.6	12.0	12.5	10.05	10.0	10.6	11.9	12.2	12.8
Belgium	10.21	11.6	12.6	11.5	12.7	12.2	10.41	10.4	10.6	11.2	11.6	12.2
Czech Republic[1]	8.96	10.3	13.4	14.5	16.4	19.6	10.92	11.3	11.7	11.8	12.1	11.5
France	11.68	12.3	13.5	13.9	14.8	14.1	9.12	9.0	9.3	10.1	10.2	10.6
Germany[2]	8.84	9.5	11.4	9.6	10.0	9.7	10.77	10.9	11.2	11.5	11.6	12.1
Greece	9.65	9.9	10.2	11.7	15.4	15.7	9.37	9.4	9.3	9.4	9.1	8.9
Ireland	13.49	13.4	15.1	17.6	21.9	21.5	8.51	8.6	9.1	9.4	9.7	10.6
Israel	19.99	21.2	22.2	23.5	24.1	28.2	6.19	6.3	6.2	6.6	6.7	7.1
Italy	9.13	9.2	9.8	10.1	11.2	14.8	10.18	9.6	9.4	9.5	9.7	9.9
Japan	10.26	9.9	9.9	11.9	13.7	17.2	7.94	7.0	6.7	6.2	6.2	6.4
Mauritius	18.64	19.6	21.0	18.8	27.0	25.1	6.69	6.7	6.5	6.8	7.2	8.1
Netherlands	11.62	12.7	13.3	12.3	12.8	13.0	8.69	8.7	8.6	8.5	8.1	8.3
New Zealand	14.89	16.3	18.0	15.6	—	18.4	7.60	7.8	7.9	8.4	—	8.1
Norway	12.90	13.6	14.3	12.3	12.5	14.1	10.17	10.1	10.7	10.7	10.1	9.9
Panama	21.99	21.7	23.9	26.6	26.8	32.3	5.14	—	—	—	—	—
Poland	9.79	12.5	14.3	18.2	19.5	18.9	9.76	10.1	10.2	10.3	9.8	8.7
Portugal	10.63	10.7	11.8	12.8	16.4	19.1	10.26	9.9	10.4	9.6	9.9	10.4
Romania	9.33	11.0	13.6	15.8	—	—	11.62	11.6	10.6	10.9	—	—
Switzerland	10.81	11.9	12.5	11.6	11.3	12.3	9.03	8.9	9.5	9.2	9.2	8.7
Tunisia	20.07	22.7	25.8	31.3	35.2	36.6	5.06	—	—	—	—	—
United Kingdom	12.01	12.9	13.9	13.3	13.5	12.5	10.72	10.7	11.2	11.8	11.8	11.9
United States	14.40	15.2	16.7	15.7	16.2	14.0	8.80	8.8	8.6	8.7	8.9	8.9

1. Data prior to 1994 pertain to the former Czechoslovakia. 2. All data pertaining to Germany prior to 1990 are for West Germany. NOTE: (—) = not available. *Source:* United Nations, *Monthly Bulletin of Statistics, June 1997.* Data for 1998 from the U.S. Bureau of the Census, International Database.

Legal Abortions in Selected Countries

Country	1985	1990	1995	Country	1985	1990	1995
Bulgaria	132,041	144,644	97,023	Israel	18,406	15,509	—
Canada	60,956	71,092	70,549	Italy	210,192	161,285	134,137
Cuba	138,671	147,530	83,963	Japan	550,127	456,797	343,024
Finland	13,832	12,232	9,884	New Z.	7,130	11,173	—
France	173,335	161,129	—	Norway	14,599	15,551	13,672
Germany[1]	—	145,267	97,937	Poland	135,564	59,417	559
Greece	180	1,216	—	Russia	—	4,103,425	2,766,362
Hungary	81,970	90,394	76,957	Sweden	30,838	37,489	—
Iceland	705	714	807	U.K.	180,983	184,092	167,297
India	583,704	596,345	—	U.S.	1,588,600	1,429,577	1,210,883

1. Figures for Germany represent those available after the unification of the Federal Republic of Germany and the German Democratic Republic in Oct. 1990. *Source:* United Nations, *Demographic Yearbook, 1997.*

Prevalence of Contraceptive Use in Selected Countries[1]

Country	Year of data	Contra- ceptive use[2]	Country	Year of data	Contra- ceptive use[2]	Country	Year of data	Contra- ceptive use[2]
Australia	1986	76.1%	India	1992–1993	40.7	Romania	1993	57.3
Bangladesh	1993–1994	44.6	Indonesia	1994	54.7	Russia	1994	66.8
Brazil	1996	76.7	Iran	1992	65.0	South Africa	1988	49.7
Canada	1984	73.1	Jamaica	1993	62.0	South Korea	1991	79.0
China	1992	76.9	Japan	1992	64.0	Switzerland	1994–1995	81.9
Colombia	1995	72.2	Jordan	1990	34.9	Thailand	1987	65.5
Costa Rica	1993	75.0	Kenya	1993	33.0	Turkey	1993	62.6
Denmark	1988	78.0	Mexico	1987	52.7	United Kingdom	1989	72.0
Egypt	1995	47.9	New Zealand	1976	69.5	United States	1990	70.7
El Salvador	1993	53.3	Nigeria	1990	6.0	Uzbekistan	1996	55.6
Ethiopia	1990	4.3	Pakistan	1990–1991	11.8	Venezuela	1977	60.3
France	1994	75.1	Peru	1996	64.2			

1. Data refer to currently married women, 15–49. 2. Contraception includes use of the birth control pill, the IUD (intra-uterine device), condoms, male and female sterilization, and other modern methods, as well as traditional methods. 3. Less than 0.5%. n.a. = not available. *Source: World Population Profile: 1998,* U.S. Census Bureau.

The Death Penalty Worldwide

Death Penalty Outlawed (year)

Andorra (1990)
Angola (1992)
Australia (1985)
Austria (1968)
Azerbaijan (1998)
Belgium (1996)
Bulgaria (1998)
Cambodia (1989)
Canada (1998)
Cape Verde (1981)
Colombia (1910)
Costa Rica (1877)
Croatia (1990)
Czech Republic (1990)
Denmark (1978)
Dominican Republic (1966)
East Timor (1999)
Ecuador (1906)
Estonia (1998)
Finland (1972)
France (1981)
Georgia (1997)
Germany (1987)
Greece (1993)
Guinea-Bissau (1993)
Haiti (1987)
Honduras (1956)
Hungary (1990)
Iceland (1928)
Ireland (1990)
Italy (1994)
Kiribati (1979)
Liechtenstein (1987)
Lithuania (1998)
Luxembourg (1979)
Macedonia (n.a.)
Marshall Islands (1986)
Mauritius (1995)
Micronesia (1986)
Moldova (1995)

Monaco (1962)
Mozambique (1990)
Namibia (1990)
Nepal (1997)
Netherlands (1982)
New Zealand (1989)
Nicaragua (1979)
Norway (1979)
Palau (n.a.)
Panama (1903)
Paraguay (1992)
Poland (1997)
Portugal (1976)
Romania (1989)
San Marino (1865)
São Tomé and Príncipe (1990)
Seychelles (1993)
Slovak Republic (1990)
Slovenia (1989)
Solomon Islands (1966)
South Africa (1997)
Spain (1995)
Sweden (1972)
Switzerland (1992)
Turkmenistan (1999)
Tuvalu (1978)
Ukraine (1999)
United Kingdom (1998)
Uruguay (1907)
Vanuatu (1980)
Vatican City State (1969)
Venezuela (1863)

Death Penalty Permitted in Exceptional Cases[1]

Argentina
Bolivia
Bosnia-Herzegovina
Brazil

Cook Islands
Cyprus
El Salvador
Fiji
Israel
Latvia
Malta
Mexico
Peru
United Kingdom

De Facto Ban on Death Penalty[2]

Albania (n.a.)
Bermuda (1977)
Bhutan (1964) [3]
Brunei Darussalam (1957)[3]
Central African Republic (1981)
Congo (Republic) (1982)
Côte d'Ivoire (n.a.)
Djibouti (1977)[3]
Gambia (1981)
Grenada (1978)
Madagascar (1958)[3]
Maldives (1952)[3]
Mali (1980)
Nauru (1968)
Niger (1976)[3]
Papua New Guinea (1950)
Samoa (1962)
Senegal (1967)
Sri Lanka (1976)
Suriname (1982)
Togo (n.a.)
Tonga (1982)
Turkey (1984)

Death Penalty Permitted

Afghanistan
Algeria
Antigua and Barbuda

Armenia
Bahamas
Bahrain
Bangladesh
Barbados
Belarus
Belize
Benin
Botswana
Burkina Faso
Burundi
Cameroon
Chad
Chile
China (People's Republic)
Comoros
Congo (Democratic Republic)
Cuba
Dominica
Egypt
Equatorial Guinea
Eritrea
Ethiopia
Gabon
Ghana
Guatemala
Guinea
Guyana
India
Indonesia
Iran
Iraq
Jamaica
Japan
Jordan
Kazakhstan
Kenya
Korea, North
Korea, South
Kuwait
Kyrgyzstan
Laos
Lebanon

Lesotho
Liberia
Libya
Malawi
Malaysia
Mauritania
Mongolia
Morocco
Myanmar
Nigeria
Oman
Pakistan
Palestinian Authority
Philippines
Qatar
Russian Federation
Rwanda
St. Kitts and Nevis
St. Lucia
St. Vincent and the Grenadines
Saudi Arabia
Sierra Leone
Singapore
Somalia
Sudan
Swaziland
Syria
Taiwan
Tajikistan
Tanzania
Thailand
Trinidad and Tobago
Tunisia
Turkey
Uganda
United Arab Emirates
United States of America
Uzbekistan
Vietnam
Yemen
Yugoslavia
Zambia
Zimbabwe

NOTE: There were 1,625 executions in 1998. Of those, 80% were in China (1,067), Dem. Rep. of the Congo (100), the United States (68), and Iran (66). n.a. = date not available. 1. Exceptional crimes include some committed under military law or crimes committed in wartime. 2. Death penalty is sanctioned by law but has not been the practice for 10 or more years (year of last execution). 3. Year of last known execution. *Source:* Amnesty International, Dec. 1999.

Most and Least Livable Countries: UN Human Development Index, 2000

The Human Development Index (HDI), published annually by the UN, ranks nations according to their citizens' quality of life rather than strictly by a nation's traditional economic figures. The criteria for calculating rankings include life expectancy, adult literacy, school enrollment, educational attainment, and per capita GDP.

Most Livable Countries, 1999		Least Livable Countries, 1999	
1. Canada	14. Germany	1. Sierra Leone	14. Gambia
2. Norway	15. Denmark	2. Niger	15. Angola
3. United States	16. Austria	3. Burkina Faso	16. Eritrea
4. Australia	17. Luxembourg	4. Ethiopia	17. Uganda
5. Iceland	18. Ireland	5. Burundi	18. Benin
6. Sweden	19. Italy	6. Guinea-Bissau	19. Tanzania
7. Belgium	20. New Zealand	7. Mozambique	20. Senegal
8. Netherlands	21. Spain	8. Chad	21. Côte d'Ivoire
9. Japan	22. Cyprus	9. Central African Republic	22. Zambia
10. United Kingdom	23. Israel	10. Mali	23. Congo, Dem. Rep. of
11. Finland	24. Singapore	11. Rwanda	24. Nigeria
12. France	25. Greece	12. Malawi	25. Haiti
13. Switzerland		13. Guinea	

Source: Human Development Report, 1999, United Nations.

The 2000 Transparency International Corruption Perceptions Index (CPI)

According to the annual survey by the Berlin-based organization Transparency International, which ranks countries based on the degree to which corruption is perceived to exist among public officials and politicians, the world's least corrupt country is Finland and its most corrupt is Nigeria.

Country rank	Country	2000 CPI Score	Country rank	Country	2000 CPI Score	Country rank	Country	2000 CPI Score
1.	Finland	10.0		Namibia	5.4		Ethiopia	3.2
2.	Denmark	9.8	32.	Hungary	5.2		Thailand	3.2
3.	New Zealand	9.4		Tunisia	5.2	63.	China	3.1
	Sweden	9.4	34.	South Africa	5.0		Egypt	3.1
5.	Canada	9.2	35.	Greece	4.9	65.	Burkina Faso	3.0
6.	Iceland	9.1	36.	Malaysia	4.8		Kazakhstan	3.0
	Norway	9.1	37.	Mauritius	4.7		Zimbabwe	3.0
	Singapore	9.1		Morocco	4.7	68.	Romania	2.9
9.	Netherlands	8.9	39.	Italy	4.6	69.	India	2.8
10.	United Kingdom	8.7		Jordan	4.6		Philippines	2.8
11.	Luxembourg	8.6	41.	Peru	4.4	71.	Bolivia	2.7
	Switzerland	8.6	42.	Czech Republic	4.3		Côte d'Ivoire	2.7
13.	Australia	8.3	43.	Belarus	4.1		Venezuela	2.7
14.	United States	7.8		El Salvador	4.1	74.	Ecuador	2.6
15.	Austria	7.7		Lithuania	4.1		Moldova	2.6
	Hong Kong	7.7		Malawi	4.1	76.	Armenia	2.5
17.	Germany	7.6		Poland	4.1		Tanzania	2.5
18.	Chile	7.4	48.	South Korea	4.0		Vietnam	2.5
19.	Ireland	7.2	49.	Brazil	3.9	79.	Uzbekistan	2.4
20.	Spain	7.0	50.	Turkey	3.8	80.	Uganda	2.3
21.	France	6.7	51.	Croatia	3.7	81.	Mozambique	2.2
22.	Israel	6.6	52.	Argentina	3.5	82.	Kenya	2.1
23.	Japan	6.4		Bulgaria	3.5		Russia	2.1
	Portugal	6.4		Ghana	3.5	84.	Cameroon	2.0
25.	Belgium	6.1		Senegal	3.5	85.	Angola	1.7
26.	Botswana	6.0		Slovak Republic	3.5		Indonesia	1.7
27.	Estonia	5.7	57.	Latvia	3.4	87.	Azerbaijan	1.5
28.	Slovenia	5.5		Zambia	3.4		Ukraine	1.5
	Taiwan	5.5	59.	Mexico	3.3	89.	Yugoslavia	1.3
30.	Costa Rica	5.4	60.	Colombia	3.2	90.	Nigeria	1.2

Source: Transparency International, 2000. Web: www.transparency.de

The 1999 Bribe Payers' Index

The Bribe Payers' Index (BPI) ranks the 19 leading exporting countries according to the degree to which their companies are perceived to be paying bribes abroad to senior public officials. According to the survey published by Transparency International in 1999, the countries most likely to offer bribes—from most to least likely—were China, South Korea, Taiwan, Italy, Malaysia, Japan, France, Spain, Singapore, United States, Germany, Belgium, United Kingdom, Netherlands, Switzerland, Austria, Canada, Australia, and Sweden.

Territories, Colonies, and Dependencies

Source: The World Factbook, 1999.

The following is a list of dependencies—territories under the jurisdiction of another country.

Under Australian Jurisdiction (6)
Ashmore and Cartier Islands
Christmas Island
Cocos (Keeling) Islands
Coral Sea Islands
Heard Island and McDonald Islands
Norfolk Island

Under Danish Jurisdiction (2)
Faeroe Islands
Greenland

Under Dutch Jurisdiction (2)
Aruba
Netherlands Antilles

Under French Jurisdiction (16)
Bassas da India
Clipperton Island
Europa Island
French Guiana
French Polynesia
French Southern and Antarctic Lands
Glorioso Islands
Guadeloupe
Juan de Nova Island

Martinique
Mayotte
New Caledonia
Réunion
Saint Pierre and Miquelon
Tromelin Island
Wallis and Futuna

Under New Zealand Jurisdiction (3)
Cook Islands
Niue
Tokelau

Under Norwegian Jurisdiction (3)
Bouvet Island
Jan Mayen
Svalbard

Under UK Jurisdiction (15)
Anguilla
Bermuda
British Indian Ocean Territory
British Virgin Islands
Cayman Islands
Falkland Islands

Gibraltar
Guernsey
Jersey
Isle of Man
Montserrat
Pitcairn Islands
Saint Helena
South Georgia and the South Sandwich Islands
Turks and Caicos Islands

Under U.S. Jurisdiction (14)
American Samoa
Baker Island
Guam
Howland Island
Jarvis Island
Johnston Atoll
Kingman Reef
Midway Islands
Navassa Island
Northern Mariana Islands
Palmyra Atoll
Puerto Rico
Virgin Islands
Wake Island

Disputed Territories (6): Antarctica, Gaza Strip, Paracel Islands, Spratly Islands, West Bank, Western Sahara

Kingdoms and Monarchs of the World

Country	Monarch	Type of monarchy	Country	Monarch	Type of monarchy
Bahrain	Sheik Hamad bin Isa al-Khalifa	Traditional	Monaco	Prince Rainier III	Constitutional principality
Belgium	King Albert II	Constitutional	Morocco	King Muhammad VI	Constitutional
Bhutan	King Jigme Singye Wangchuck	Constitutional	Nepal	King Birendra Bir Bikram Shah Deva	Constitutional
Brunei	Sultan Haji Hassanal Bolkiah	Constitutional	Netherlands	Queen Beatrix	Constitutional
			Norway	King Harald V	Constitutional
Cambodia	King Norodom Sihanouk	Constitutional	Oman	Sultan Qabus ibn Sa'id	Absolute
Denmark	Queen Margrethe II	Constitutional	Qatar	Emir Sheik Hamad bin Khalifa al-Thani	Traditional
Japan	Emperor Akihito	Constitutional			
Jordan	King Abdullah II	Constitutional	Saudi Arabia	King Fahd bin 'Abdulaziz	Absolute
Kuwait	Sheik Jaber al-Ahmad al-Sabah	Constitutional	Spain	King Juan Carlos I	Parliamentary
			Swaziland	King Mswati III	Near-absolute
Lesotho	King Letsie III	Constitutional	Sweden	King Carl XVI Gustaf	Constitutional
Liechtenstein	Prince Hans Adam II	Constitutional	Thailand	King Bhumibol Adulyadej	Constitutional
Luxembourg	Grand Duke Jean	Constitutional	Tonga	King Taufa'ahau Tupou IV	Constitutional
Malaysia	Tuanku Salehuddin Abdul Aziz Shah ibni al-Marhum Hisamuddin Alam Shah	Constitutional	United Kingdom	Queen Elizabeth II[1]	Constitutional[2]

1. Queen Elizabeth II is also the Sovereign of 15 countries in the Commonwealth of Nations: Antigua and Barbuda, Australia, the Bahamas, Barbados, Belize, Canada, Grenada, Jamaica, New Zealand, Papua New Guinea, St. Kitts and Nevis, St. Lucia, St. Vincent and the Grenadines, the Solomon Islands, and Tuvalu. 2. Also parliamentary democracy.

Countries with Nuclear Weapons Capability

Acknowledged Nuclear Weapons Capability

Britain	France	Pakistan	United States
China	India	Russia	

Unacknowledged Nuclear Weapons Capability
Israel

Seeking Nuclear Weapons Capability

Iran	Iraq

Abandoned Nuclear Weapons Development

North Korea—An accord was reached with the North Korean government in 1994 to freeze and dismantle nuclear weapons development.

South Africa—Constructed but then voluntarily dismantled 6 uranium bombs.

Belarus, Kazakhstan, Ukraine—When Soviet Union broke up, these former states possessed nuclear warheads that they have since given up.

Source: U.S. State Department, *Time Magazine.*

Top 30 Countries with Highest Military Expenditures, 1997

Rank	Country	In millions of dollars	Rank	Country	In millions of dollars	Rank	Country	In millions of dollars
1.	United States	$276,300	11.	Brazil	$14,150	22.	Poland	$6,698
2.	China, People's Rep. of	74,910	12.	Taiwan	13,060	23.	Sweden	5,550
			13.	India	10,850	24.	Greece	5,533
3.	Russia	41,730	14.	Israel	9,335	25.	Indonesia	4,812
4.	France	41,520	15.	Australia	8,463	26.	Iran	4,726
5.	Japan	40,840	16.	Canada	7,800	27.	Mexico	4,294
6.	United Kingdom	35,290	17.	Turkey	7,792	28.	Ukraine	4,285
7.	Germany	32,870	18.	Spain	7,670	29.	Switzerland	3,859
8.	Italy	22,720	19.	Netherlands	6,839	30.	Argentina	3,701
9.	Saudi Arabia	21,150	20.	North Korea	6,000			
10.	South Korea	15,020	21.	Singapore	5,664			

Source: U.S. Arms Control and Disarmament Agency, *World Military Expenditures and Arms Transfers, 1997.*

Top 30 Countries with Highest Military Expenditures Ranked by Percent of Country's GNP, 1997

Rank	Country	Percentage	Rank	Country	Percentage	Rank	Country	Percentage
1.	Burma	n.a.	10.	Russia	30.9	20.	Qatar	n.a.
2.	Sudan	53.8 %	11.	Liberia	n.a.	21.	Uganda	23.9
3.	United Arab Emirates	46.5	12.	Central African Republic	27.7	22.	Taiwan	23.8
4.	Congo, Dem. Rep. of	41.4	13.	Kuwait	26.8	23.	Rwanda	22.2
5.	Oman	36.4	14.	Burundi	25.8	24.	Sri Lanka	21.2
6.	Angola	36.3		Cambodia	25.8	25.	Israel	20.9
7.	Saudi Arabia	35.8	16.	Jordan	25.0	26.	Ecuador	20.3
8.	Sierra Leone	33.0	17.	Bahrain	24.9	27.	Croatia	20.1
9.	North Korea	n.a.	18.	Pakistan	24.2	28.	Colombia	19.9
			19.	Syria	n.a.	29.	Singapore	19.4
						30.	Eritrea	18.1

Source: U.S. Arms Control and Disarmament Agency, *World Military Expenditures and Arms Transfers, 1997.*

Worldwide Armed Conflicts, 1999

An armed conflict is defined as a political conflict involving armed combat by the military forces of at least one state (or one or more armed factions seeking to gain control of all or part of the state), and in which at least 1,000 people have been killed during the fighting. In 1999 there were 40 armed conflicts fought on the territories of 36 countries. According to *The Armed Conflicts Report 2000*, six new conflicts erupted in 1999: Eritrea/Ethiopia, Andhra Pradesh state in India, Molucca Islands in Indonesia, Nigeria, Chechnya Republic in Russia, and Senegal. Two conflicts that were included in earlier reports have been removed from the report: the Punjab state of India and the Kurdish conflict in Iran.

	No. of conflicts in region	No. of countries hosting conflicts	Percentage of world conflicts
Africa	16	17	40%
Asia	14	9	35%
Europe	2	2	5%
The Americas	2	2	5%
Middle East	6	6	15%
World Total	**40**	**36**	**100%**

Source: The Armed Conflicts 2000 Report, Project Ploughshares, Institute of Peace and Conflict Studies, Conrad Grebel College; Waterloo, Ontario, Canada. www.ploughshares.ca

Worldwide Refugees and Asylum Seekers,[1] 1998

Group or country of origin	Number	Group or country of origin	Number	Group or country of origin	Number
Palestinians	3,753,000	Angola	250,000	Sri Lanka	110,000
Afghanistan	2,616,000	Burundi	250,000	Georgia	100,000
Iraq	602,400	Azerbaijan	236,000	Western Sahara	85,000
Sierra Leone	450,000	El Salvador	202,500	Cambodia	51,000
Somalia	400,000	Myanmar (Burma)	198,000	Uzbekistan	46,000
Sudan	350,000	Armenia	188,000	Congo, Rep. of	40,000
Croatia	326,000	Yugoslavia	144,300	Ethiopia	40,000
Eritrea	320,000	Guatemala	140,600	Mauritania	40,000
Bosnia and Herzegovina	311,300	China (Tibet)	130,000	Rwanda	40,000
Vietnam	281,000	Congo, Dem. Rep. of	130,000	Tajikistan	30,000
Liberia	270,000	Bhutan	115,000	Iran	29,000

1. Table is limited to refugee populations exceeding 15,000. NOTE: In part because asylum seekers do not always report country-of-origin data, this table understates the number of refugees and asylum seekers from many countries. The total number of refugees and asylum seekers throughout the world in 1998 was estimated to be 12.3 million. Nearly half were either Palestinians or Afghans. One of the world's largest new refugee outflows was from Sierra Leone. *Source:* U.S. Committee for Refugees.

Economic Statistics by Country, 1998

Country	GDP/PPP	GDP/PPP per capita	Real growth rate	Inflation	Country	GDP/PPP	GDP/PPP per capita	Real growth rate	Inflation
Afghanistan	20.0 billion	800	n.a.	240%[1]	Ghana	33.6 billion	1,800	3%	27.7%[2]
Albania	5 billion	1,490	7%	40%[2]	Greece	143 billion	13,400	3%	3.9%
Algeria	140.2 billion	4,600	3.2%	9%	Grenada	340 million	3,500	5%	1.4%
Andorra	1.2 billion[3]	18,000[3]	n.a.	n.a.	Guatemala	45.7 billion	3,800	5%	6.4%
Angola	11 billion	1,000	0.5%	90%	Guinea	8.8 billion	1,180	4.9%	3.5%
Antigua	503 million	7,900	6%	1.1%[2]	Guinea-Bis.	1.2 billion	1,000	3.5%	25.6%[2]
Argentina	374 billion	10,300	4.3%	1%	Guyana	1.8 billion	2,500	1.8%	4.1%
Armenia	9.2 billion	2,700	6%	10%	Haiti	8.9 billion	1,300	3%	8%
Australia	393.9 billion	21,200	4.5%	1%	Honduras	14.4 billion	2,400	3%	14.5%
Austria	184.5 billion	22,700	2.9%	0.9%	Hungary	75.4 billion	7,400	5%	14%
Azerbaijan	12.9 billion	1,640	10%	7.6%	Iceland	6.06 billion	22,400	5.1%	1.7%
Bahamas	5.63 billion	20,100	4%	0.4%[2]	India	1.689 trillion	1,720	5.4%	14%
Bahrain	8.2 billion	13,100	2%	0.2%[1]	Indonesia	602 billion	2,830	13.7%	77%
Bangladesh	175.5 billion	1,380	4%	7%	Iran	339.7 billion	5,000	2.1%	24%
Barbados	2.9 billion	11,200	3%	3.6%[2]	Iraq	52.3 billion	2,400	10%	n.a.
Belarus	53.7 billion	5,200	7%	182%	Ireland	67.1 billion	18,600	9.5%	2.4%
Belgium	236 billion	23,400	2.8%	1%	Israel	101.9 billion	18,100	1.9%	5.4%
Belize	700 million	3,000	0.5%	0.5%	Italy	1.181 trillion	20,800	1.5%	1.8%
Benin	7.6 billion	1,300	4.4%	5.6%	Jamaica	8.8 billion	3,300	2%	9.9%
Bhutan	1.9 billion	1,000	6.5%	7.4%[2]	Japan	2.903 trillion	23,100	2.6%	0.9%
Bolivia	23.4 billion	3,000	4.7%	4.4%	Jordan	15.5 billion	3,500	2.2%	4%
Bosnia	5.8 billion	1,720	30%	n.a.	Kazakhstan	52.9 billion	3,100	2.5%	10%
Botswana	5.25 billion	3,600	3%	9%[2]	Kenya	43.9 billion	1,550	1.6%	2.5%
Brazil	1.0352 trillion	6,100	0.5%	2%	Kiribati	62 million[1]	800[1]	1.9%	0.6%
Brunei	5.4 billion	17,000	1%	2%[2]	Korea, North	21.8 billion	1,000	5%	n.a.
Bulgaria	33.6 billion	4,100	4%	1%	Korea, South	584.7 billion	12,600	6.8%	7.5%
Burkina Faso	11.6 billion	1,000	6%	2.5%	Kuwait	43.7 billion	22,700	5%	1%[2]
Burundi	4.1 billion	740	4.5%	17%	Kyrgyzstan	9.8 billion	2,200	1.8%	18.4%
Cambodia	7.8 billion	700	0%	15%	Laos	6.6 billion	1,260	4%	112%
Cameroon	29.6 billion	2,000	5%	2.5%	Latvia	9.7 billion	4,100	3.6%	4.7%
Canada	688.3 billion	22,400	3%	0.9%	Lebanon	15.8 billion	4,500	3%	5%
Cape Verde	581 million	1,450	7%	4.3%	Lesotho	5.1 billion[2]	2,400[2]	10%	8%[2]
Central African Republic	5.5 billion	1,640	5.5%	2.6%	Liberia	2.8 billion	1,000	n.a.	n.a.
					Libya	38 billion	6,700	1%	24.2%
Chad	7.5 billion	1,000	2.9%	15%[2]	Liechtenstein	730 million	23,000	n.a.	0.5%[2]
Chile	184.6 billion	12,500	3.5%	4.7%	Lithuania	17.6 billion	4,900	4.5%	5.1%
China	4.42 trillion	3,600	7.8%	0.8%	Luxembourg	13.9 billion	32,700	2.9%	1.4%
Colombia	254.7 billion	6,600	0.2%	16.7%	Macedonia	2.1 billion	1,050	4.5%	3%
Comoros	400 million[2]	700[2]	3.5%	2.5%[2]	Madagascar	10.3 billion[2]	730[2]	3%	4.5%[2]
Congo, Rep. of	3.9 billion	1,500	2.5%	5%[2]	Malawi	8.9 billion	940	3.2%	83.4%[3]
					Malaysia	215.4 billion	10,300	7%	5.3%
Congo, Dem. Rep. of	34.9 billion	710	3.5%	147%	Maldives	500 million	1,840	5.8%	6.3%[1]
					Mali	8 billion	790	4.6%	5%
Costa Rica	24 billion	6,700	5.5%	12%	Malta	5 billion	13,000	4%	2.8%[2]
Côte d'Ivoire	24.2 billion	1,680	6%	6%	Marshall Is.	91 million	1,450	5%	5%[2]
Croatia	23.6 billion	5,100	3%	5.4%	Mauritania	4.7 billion	1,890	4.2%	4.7%[1]
Cuba	17.3 billion	1,560	1.2%	n.a.	Mauritius	11.7 billion	10,000	5%	6.8%[2]
Cyprus	10 billion[2]	13,000[2]	2.3%	2.3%, 87.5%[4]	Mexico	815.3 billion	8,300	4.8%	18.6%
					Micronesia	220 million[1]	1,760[1]	1%	4%
Czech Rep.	116.7 billion	11,300	1.5%	10.7%	Moldova	10 billion	2,200	8.6%	18.3%
Denmark	124.4 billion	23,300	2.6%	1.8%	Monaco	800 million[1]	25,000[1]	n.a.	n.a.
Djibouti	530 million	1,200	0.6%	3%[2]	Mongolia	5.8 billion	2,250	3.5%	6%
Dominica	216 million[2]	3,300[2]	1.8%	2.2%	Morocco	107 billion	3,200	6.8%	2%–3%
Dom. Rep.	39.8 billion	5,000	7%	6%	Mozambique	16.8 billion	900	11%	1.3%
Ecuador	58.7 billion	4,800	1%	43%	Myanmar	56.1 billion	1,200	1.1%	50%
Egypt	188 billion	2,850	5%	3.6%	Namibia	6.6 billion	4,100	2%	7%[1]
El Salvador	17.5 billion	3,000	3.7%	2.6%	Nauru	100 million[5]	10,000[5]	n.a.	3.6%[5]
Eq. Guinea	660 million[2]	1,500[2]	n.a.	6%[1]	Nepal	26.2 billion	1,100	4.9%	7.8%
Eritrea	2.5 billion	660	5%	8%	Netherlands	348.6 billion	22,200	3.7%	2%
Estonia	7.8 billion	5,500	5.5%	6.5%	New Zealand	61.1 billion	17,000	0.2%	1.1%
Ethiopia	32.9 billion	560	6%	3.9%	Nicaragua	11.6 billion	2,500	4%	16%
Fiji	5.4 billion	6,700	2.4%	3%[2]	Niger	9.4 billion	970	4.5%	4.8%
Finland	103.6 billion	20,100	5.1%	1.5%	Nigeria	106.2 billion	960	1.6%	15%
France	1.32 trillion	22,600	3%	0.7%	Norway	109 billion	24,700	2.4%	2.3%
Gabon	7.7 billion	6,400	1.7%	1%	Oman	18.6 billion	7,900	8.5%	0.2%[2]
Gambia, The	1.3 billion	1,000	3.8%	3%	Pakistan	270 billion	2,000	5%	7.8%[6]
Georgia	11.2 billion	2,200	4%	10.5%	Palau	160 million[2]	8,800[2]	10%	n.a.
Germany	1.813 trillion	22,100	2.7%	0.9%	Panama	19.9 billion	7,300	2.7%	1.4%

Country	GDP/PPP	GDP/PPP per capita	Real growth rate	Inflation	Country	GDP/PPP	GDP/PPP per capita	Real growth rate	Inflation
Papua New Guinea	11.1 billion	2,400	1.6%	12%[6]	Suriname	1.48 billion	3,500	2%	20%
Paraguay	19.8 billion	3,700	0.5%	14.6%	Swaziland	4 billion	4,200	2.6%	8%
Peru	111.8 billion	4,300	1.8%	6.7%[2]	Sweden	175 billion	19,700	2.9%	2%
Philippines	270.5 billion	3,500	0.5%	9.7%	Switzerland	191.8 billion	26,400	2%	0%
Poland	263 billion	6,800	5.6%	11%	Syria	41.7 billion[2]	2,500[2]	2%	2.3%[7]
Portugal	144.8 billion	14,600	4.2%	2.8%	Taiwan	362 billion	16,500	4.8%	2.1%
Qatar	12 billion	17,100	3%	7.4%[1]	Tajikistan	6 billion	990	5.3%	46.3%
Romania	90.6 billion	4,050	7.3%	41%	Tanzania	22.1 billion	730	3.8%	13.5%
Russia	593.4 billion	4,000	5%	84%	Thailand	369 billion	6,100	8.5%	4.3%
Rwanda	5.5 billion	690	10.5%	10%	Togo	8.2 billion	1,670	3.8%	7.2%[2]
St. Kitts	235 million[2]	6,000[2]	6.3%[2]	11.3%[2]	Tonga	232 million[6]	2,100[6]	1.5%[6]	2%[2]
St. Lucia	625 million[2]	4,100[2]	2.2%[2]	1.9%[2]	Trinidad	8.85 billion	8,000	4.3%	3.7%[2]
St. Vincent	289 million	2,400	4%	3.6%[1]	Tunisia	49 billion	5,200	5%	3.3%
Samoa	470 million[2]	2,100[2]	3.4%[2]	2.2%	Turkey	425.4 billion	6,600	2.8%	70%
San Marino	500 million[2]	20,000[2]	n.a.	5.3%[3]	Turkmenistan	7 billion	1,630	5%	19.8%
São Tomé	164 million	1,100	2.5%	21%	Tuvalu	7.8 million[3]	800[3]	8.7%[3]	3.9%[5]
Saudi Arabia	186 billion	9,000	10.8%	0.2%	Uganda	22.7 billion	1,020	5.5%	2.6%
Senegal	15.6 billion	1,600	5.7%	1.8%	Ukraine	108.5 billion	2,200	1.7%	20%
Seychelles	550 million[2]	7,000[2]	4.3%[2]	0.6%[2]	U.A.E.	40 billion	17,400	5%	5%[2]
Sierra Leone	2.7 billion	530	0.7%	37.4%	U.K.	1.252 trillion	21,200	2.6%	2.7%
Singapore	91.7 billion	26,300	1.3%	0.5%	U.S.A.	8.511 trillion	31,500	3.8%	1.6%
Slovakia	44.5 billion	8,300	5%	7.4%	Uruguay	28.4 billion	8,600	3%	8.6%
Slovenia	20.4 billion	10,300	3.6%	8%	Uzbekistan	59.2 billion	2,500	1%	40%
Solomon Is.	1.15 billion	2,600	10%	11.8%[1]	Vanuatu	240 million[2]	1,300[2]	n.a.	2.2%[2]
Somalia	4 billion	600	n.a.	n.a.	Venezuela	194.5 billion	8,500	0.9%	29.9%
South Africa	290.6 billion	6,800	0.3%	9%	Vietnam	134.8 billion	1,770	4%	9%
Spain	645.6 billion	16,500	3.5%	2%	Yemen	12.1 billion	740	1.8%	11%
Sri Lanka	48.1 billion	2,500	4.7%	9.3%	Yugoslavia	25.4 billion	2,300	3.5%	48%
Sudan	31.2 billion	930	6.1%	27%[2]	Zambia	8.3 billion	880	2%	43.9%[1]
					Zimbabwe	26.2 billion	2,400	1.5%	32%

1. 1996 est. 2. 1997 est. 3. 1995 est. 4. The first figure is for the Greek Cypriot area; the second figure (1997 est.) is for the Turkish Cypriot area. 5. 1993 est. 6. FY97/98 est. 7. 1999 est. Definitions: Gross domestic product (GDP): The value of all goods and services produced domestically. Purchasing power parity (PPP): The PPP method involves the use of standard-ized international dollar price weights, which are applied to the GDP produced in a given economy. The data derived from the 1998 method provide a better comparison of economic well-being between countries than conversions at official currency exchange rates. *Source:* U.S. Census Bureau, International Database; and *The World Factbook, 1999.*

Communications in Selected Countries

Country	Main telephone lines per 1,000 people 1996	Televisions per 1,000 people 1996	Personal computers per 1,000 people 1996	Internet hosts per 1,000 people 1998	Number of daily newspapers 1996
Argentina	174	345[1]	34.1	1.75	181
Australia	519	666	311.3	42.70	65
Bulgaria	313	361	29.8[1]	0.81	17
Chile	156	277	45.1	2.07	52
China	45	252	3.0	0.00	39
Colombia	118	185	23.3	0.52	37
Egypt	50	126[1]	5.8	0.05	17
France	564	598[1]	150.7	7.87	117
Greece	509	442[1]	35.3	3.89	156
India	15	64	1.5	0.01	—
Indonesia	21	232	4.8	0.10	69
Israel	441	300[1]	116.3	14.20	34
Japan	489	700	128.0	11.00	122
Mexico	95	193[1]	29.0	0.92	295
Norway	555	569	284.5	71.80	83
Russian Federation	175	386	23.7	1.05	285
Saudi Arabia	106	263[1]	37.2	0.01	13
South Africa	100	123	37.7	3.82	17
Switzerland	640	493	408.5	27.90	88
Thailand	70	167	16.7	0.03	30
Turkey	224	309	13.8	0.54	57
Uganda	2	26	0.5	0.01	2
United Kingdom	528	612[1]	192.6	23.30	99
United States	640	806[1]	362.4	88.90	1,520
Vietnam	16	180	3.3	—	10
Zimbabwe	15	29[1]	6.7	0.07	2

. Data refer to 1995. *Source: Human Development Report, 1999*, United Nations.

Major sources: Questionnaires to the individual countries; C.I.A. *World Factbook 1999;* Center for International Research, Bureau of the Census; *The Columbia Encyclopedia; The World Book Encyclopedia; Encyclopædia Britannica;* U.S. State Dept., and various newspapers.
(information as of Sept. 2000)

Definitions: Gross domestic product (GDP): The value of all goods and services produced domestically; Purchasing power parity (PPP): The PPP method involves the use of standardized international dollar price weights, which are applied to the GDP produced in a given economy. The data derived from the PPP method provide a better comparison of economic well-being between countries than conversions at official currency exchange rates. Literacy rates and population figures are supplied by the U.S. Census Bureau.

Afghanistan

ISLAMIC EMIRATE OF AFGHANISTAN

National name: Dowlat-e Eslami-ye Afghanestan
Head of State: Mullah Mohammad Omar (1996)
Area: 250,000 sq. mi. (647,500 sq. km)
Population (2000 est.): 25,888,797 (average annual rate of natural increase: 2.4%); birth rate: 41.8/1000; infant mortality rate: 149.3/1000; density per sq. mi.: 104
Capital (2000 est.): Kabul, 2,450,000. **Largest cities (2000 est.):** Mazare Sharif, 2,500,000; Kandahar, 225,500; Herat, 177,300. **Monetary unit:** Afghani.
Languages: Pushtu, Dari Persian, other Turkic and minor languages. **Ethnicity/race:** Pashtun 38%, Tajik 25%, Uzbek 6%, Hazara 19%, minor ethnic groups (Chahar Aimaks, Turkmen, Baloch, and others).
Religion: Islam (Sunni, 84%; Shi'ite, 15%; other 1%).
Literacy rate: 29% (1990)
Economic summary: GDP/PPP (1998 est.): $20.0 billion; $800 per capita. **Real growth rate:** n.a. **Inflation:** 240% (1996 est.). **Arable land:** 12%. **Products:** wheat, fruit, nuts, karakul pelts, wool, mutton. **Labor force:** 7.1 million: agriculture and animal husbandry, 67.8%; industry, 10.2%; construction, 6.3%; commerce, 5%; services and other, 10.7% (1980 est.). **Unemployment:** 8% (1995 est.). **Industries:** textiles, soap, furniture, shoes, fertilizer, cement, handwoven carpets, natural gas, oil, coal, copper. **Agriculture:** wheat, fruit, nuts, karakul pelts, wool, mutton. **Natural resources:** natural gas, petroleum, coal, copper, talc, barites, sulfur, lead, zinc, iron ore, salt, precious and semiprecious stones. **Exports:** $80 million (1996 est.): fruit and nuts, handwoven carpets, wool, cotton, hides and pelts, precious and semiprecious gems. **Imports:** $150 million (1996 est.): food and petroleum products, most consumer goods. **Major trading partners:** Former Soviet Union, Pakistan, Iran, Japan, Singapore, India, U.K., Belgium, Luxembourg, Czech Republic, South Korea, Germany.

Geography Afghanistan, approximately the size of Texas, is bordered on the north by Turkmenistan, Uzbekistan, and Tajikistan, on the extreme northeast by China, on the east and south by Pakistan, and by Iran on the west. The country is split east to west by the Hindu Kush mountain range, rising in the east to heights of 24,000 feet (7,315 m). With the exception of the southwest, most of the country is covered by high snow-capped mountains and is traversed by deep valleys.

Government On Sept. 27, 1996, the ruling members of the Afghan government were displaced by members of the Islamic Taliban movement, who have declared themselves the legitimate government of Afghanistan. The U.N. has deferred a decision on the question of legitimacy. Mullah Mohammad Omar, known as the Emir al-Momineen (Leader of the Faithful), has served as the de facto leader since the Taliban came to power in 1996.

History Darius I and Alexander the Great were the first to use Afghanistan as the gateway to India. Islamic conquerors arrived in the 7th century, and Genghis Khan and Tamerlane followed in the 13th and 14th centuries.

In the 19th century, Afghanistan became a battleground in the rivalry of imperial Britain and czarist Russia for control of Central Asia. Three Anglo-Afghan Wars (1839–42, 1878–80, and 1919) ended inconclusively. In 1893 Britain established an unofficial border, the Durand Line, separating Afghanistan from British India, and London granted full independence in 1919. Emir Amanullah founded an Afghan monarchy in 1926.

During the cold war, King Mohammed Zahir Shah developed close ties with the Soviet Union, accepting extensive economic assistance from Moscow. He was overthrown in 1973 by his cousin Mohammed Daoud, who was himself ousted in a 1978 coup by Noor Taraki. Taraki and his successor, Babrak Karmal, attempted to create a Marxist state. However, the new leadership was criticized by armed insurgents who bitterly opposed communism and hoped to create an Islamic state in Afghanistan. Fearing his government was on the verge of collapse, Karmal called for Soviet troops. Moscow responded with a full-scale invasion of the country in Dec. 1979.

The Soviets were met with fierce resistance from groups already energized by opposition to the Karmal government. The guerrilla forces, calling themselves *mujahedeen*, pledged a jihad, or holy war, to expel the invaders. Initially armed with outdated weapons, the mujahedeen became a focus of U.S. cold war strategy against the Soviet Union, and with Pakistan's help, Washington began funneling sophisticated arms to the resistance. Moscow's troops were soon bogged down in a no-win conflict with determined Afghan fighters. In April 1988 the U.S.S.R., U.S., Afghanistan, and Pakistan signed accords calling for an end to outside aid to the warring factions. In return, a Soviet withdrawal took place in Feb. 1989, but the pro-Soviet government of President Najibullah was left in the capital, Kabul.

By mid-April 1992 Najibullah was ousted as Islamic rebels advanced on the capital. Almost immediately, the various rebel groups began fighting one another for control. Amid the chaos of competing factions, a group calling itself the Taliban—consisting of Islamic students—seized control of Kabul in Sept. 1996. It imposed harsh fundamentalist laws, including stoning for adultery and severing hands for theft. Women were prohibited from work and school, and they were required to cover themselves in public from head to toe. By fall 1998 the Taliban controlled about 90% of the country.

On Aug. 20, 1998, U.S. cruise missiles struck a terrorism training complex in Afghanistan believed to have been financed by Osama bin Laden, a wealthy

Islamic radical sheltered by the Taliban. The U.S. asked for the deportation of bin Laden, whom they believed was involved in the bombing of the U.S. embassies in Kenya and Tanzania on Aug. 7, 1998.

In 1999, the Taliban concentrated on defeating the forces of Ahmed Shah Masood, their last significant hurdle in gaining complete control of Afghanistan. The Taliban's scorched-earth tactics and human rights abuses have further isolated it from the international community. Only three governments—Pakistan, Saudi Arabia, and the U.A.R.—recognize the Taliban as Afghanistan's legitimate government.

The Taliban did improve its public relations image in Dec. 1999 after successfully mediating a deal between the Indian government and hijackers, widely believed to be Muslim extremists, who had commandeered an Indian Airlines plane.

Albania

THE REPUBLIC OF ALBANIA

National name: Republika E Shqiperise
President: Rexhep Mejdani (1997)
Prime Minister: Ilir Meta (1999)
Area: 11,100 sq. mi. (28,750 sq. km)
Population (2000 est.): 3,490,435 (average annual rate of natural increase: 1.3%); birth rate: 19.5/1000; infant mortality rate: 41.3/1000; density per sq. mi.: 314
Capital and largest city (1991 est.): Tiranë, 300,000.
  Monetary unit: Lek. **Languages:** Albanian, Greek.
  Ethnicity/race: Albanian 95%, Greeks 3%, other 2%: Vlachs, Gypsies, Serbs, and Bulgarians (1989 est.).
  Religions (1980): Muslim, 70%; Albanian Orthodox, 20%; Roman Catholic, 10%. **Literacy rate:** 72% (1955)
Economic summary: GDP/PPP (1998 est.): $5 billion; $1,490 per capita. **Real growth rate:** 7%. **Inflation:** (1997 est.) 40%. **Unemployment:** 14%. **Arable land:** 21%. **Agriculture:** wide range of temperate-zone crops and livestock. **Labor force:** 1.692 million (1994 est.): agriculture, 49.5%; private sector, 22.2%; state sector, 28.3%. **Industries:** food processing, textiles and clothing, lumber, oil, cement, chemicals, mining, basic metals, hydropower. **Natural resources:** petroleum, natural gas, coal, chromium, copper, timber, nickel. **Exports:** $212 million (f.o.b., 1998 est.): asphalt, metals and metallic ores, electricity, crude oil, vegetables, fruit, and tobacco. **Imports:** $791 million (f.o.b., 1998 est.): machinery, consumer goods, grains. **Major trading partners:** Italy, Greece, Germany, Belgium, U.S., Bulgaria, Turkey, Macedonia.

Geography Albania is situated on the eastern shore of the Adriatic Sea, with Montenegro and Serbia to the north, Macedonia to the east, and Greece to the south. Slightly larger than Maryland, Albania may be divided into two major regions: a mountainous highland region (north, east, and south) constituting 70% of the land area, and a western coastal lowland region that contains nearly all of the country's agricultural lands and is the most densely populated part of Albania.

Government Emerging democracy.

History A part of Illyria in ancient times, and later of the Roman Empire, Albania was ruled by the Byzantine Empire from A.D. 535 to 1204. An alliance (1444–66) of Albanian chiefs failed to halt the advance of the Ottoman Turks, and the country remained under at least nominal Turkish rule for more than four centuries, until it proclaimed its independence on Nov. 28, 1912.

Largely agricultural, Albania is one of the poorest countries in Europe. A battlefield in World War I, after the war it became a republic in which a conservative Muslim landlord, Ahmed Zogu, proclaimed himself president in 1925, and king (Zog I) in 1928. He ruled until Italy annexed Albania in 1939. Communist guerrillas under Enver Hoxha seized power in 1944, near the end of World War II. Hoxha was a devotee of Stalin, emulating the Soviet leader's repressive tactics, imprisoning or executing landowners and others who did not conform to the socialist ideal. Hoxha eventually broke with Soviet communism in 1961 because of differences with Khrushchev, and then aligned himself with Chinese communism, which he also abandoned in 1978 after the death of Mao. From then on Albania went its own way to forge its individual version of the socialist state, and became one of the most isolated countries in the world. Hoxha was succeeded by Ramiz Alia in 1982.

The elections in March 1991 gave the Communists a decisive majority. But a general strike and street demonstrations soon forced the all-Communist cabinet to resign. In June 1991 the Communist Party of Labor renamed itself the Socialist Party and renounced its past ideology. The opposition Democratic Party won a landslide victory in the 1992 elections.

But Albania's experiment with democratic reform and a free-market economy went disastrously awry in March 1997, when large numbers of its citizens invested in shady, get-rich-quick pyramid schemes. When five of these schemes collapsed in the beginning of the year, robbing Albanians of an estimated $1.2 billion in savings, their rage turned against the government, which appeared to have sanctioned the nationwide swindle. Rioting broke out, the country's fragile infrastructure collapsed, and gangsters and rebels overran the country, plunging it into virtual anarchy. A multinational protection force eventually restored order and set up the elections that formally ousted President Sali Berisha.

In spring 1999, Albania was heavily involved in the affairs of its fellow ethnic Albanians to the north, in Kosovo. Albania served as an outpost for NATO troops, and took in approximately 440,000 Kosovar refugees, about half the total number of ethnic Albanians who were driven from their homes in Kosovo.

Ilir Meta, elected prime minister in 1999 at age 30, rapidly moved forward in his first year, modernizing the economy, privatizing business, fighting crime, and reforming the judiciary and tax systems.

Algeria

DEMOCRATIC AND POPULAR REPUBLIC OF ALGERIA

National name: Al Jumhuriyah al Jaza'iriyah ad Dimuqratiyah ash Shabiyah
President: Abdel-Aziz Bouteflika (1999)
Prime Minister: Ahmed Benbitour (1999)
Area: 919,595 sq. mi. (2,381,740 sq. km)
Population (2000 est.): 31,193,917 (average annual rate of natural increase: 1.8%); birth rate: 23.1/1000; infant mortality rate: 42/1000; density per sq. mi.: 34
Capital: Algiers. **Largest cities (1987):** Algiers, 1,507,241; Oran, 628,558; Constantine, 440,842; Annaba, 305,526. **Monetary unit:** Dinar. **Languages:** Arabic (official), French, Berber dialects. **Ethnicity/ race:** Arab-Berber 99%, European less than 1%. **Religion:** 99% Islam (Sunni). **Literacy rate:** 57% (1990)
Economic summary: GDP/PPP (1998 est.): $140.2

billion; $4,600 per capita. **Real growth rate:** 3.2%. **Inflation:** 9%. **Unemployment:** 30% (1998 est.). **Arable land:** 3%. **Agriculture:** wheat, barley, oats, grapes, citrus, fruit, olives, livestock. **Labor force:** 7.8 million (1996 est.): government, 29.5%; agriculture, 22%; construction and public works, 16.2%; industry, 13.6%; commerce and services, 13.5%; transportation and communication, 5.2% (1989). **Industries:** petroleum, natural gas, light industries, mining, electrical, petrochemical, food processing. **Natural resources:** petroleum, natural gas, iron ore, phosphates, uranium, lead, zinc. **Exports:** $14 billion (f.o.b., 1997 est.): petroleum and natural gas, 97%. **Imports:** $8.5 billion (f.o.b., 1997 est.): capital goods, food and beverages, consumer goods. **Major trading partners:** Italy, U.S., France, Spain, Germany.

Geography Nearly four times the size of Texas, Algeria is bordered on the west by Morocco and Western Sahara and on the east by Tunisia and Libya. To the south are Mauritania, Mali, and Niger. The Saharan region, which is 85% of the country, is almost completely uninhabited. The highest point is Mount Tahat in the Sahara, which rises 9,850 feet (3,000 m).

Government Parliamentary republic.

History Excavations in Algeria have indicated that *Homo erectus* resided there between 500,000 and 700,000 years ago. Phoenician traders settled on the coast in the 1st millennium B.C. As ancient Numidia, Algeria became a Roman colony, part of what was called Mauretania Caesariensis, at the close of the Punic Wars (145 B.C.). Conquered by the Vandals about A.D. 440, it fell from a high state of civilization to virtual barbarism, from which it partly recovered after an invasion by Arabs about 650. Christian during its Roman period, the indigenous Berbers were then converted to Islam. Falling under control of the Ottoman Empire by 1536, Algiers served for three centuries as the headquarters of the Barbary pirates. Ostensibly to rid the region of the pirates, the French occupied Algeria in 1830 and made it a part of France in 1848.

Algerian independence movements led to the uprisings of 1954–55, which developed into full-scale war. In 1962, French president Charles de Gaulle began the peace negotiations, and on July 5, 1962, Algeria was proclaimed independent. In Oct. 1963, Ahmed Ben Bella was elected president, and the country became socialist. He began to nationalize foreign holdings and aroused opposition. He was overthrown in a military coup on June 19, 1965, by Col. Houari Boumediène, who suspended the constitution and sought to restore financial stability.

In Dec. 1991 in the first parliamentary elections ever held in Algeria, the fundamentalist Islamic Salvation Front (Front Islamique du Salut; FIS) won the largest number of votes. To thwart the electoral results, the army cancelled the general election, which plunged the country into a bloody civil war. An estimated 100,000 people have been massacred by Islamic terrorists since war began in Jan. 1992.

The undeclared civil war escalated in 1997–98 in its brutality and senselessness. Islamic extremists, who had originally focused their attacks on government officials and then shifted to intellectuals and journalists, abandoned political motivations entirely and targeted defenseless villagers. The mass slaughters were as savage as they were random, and the government was markedly ineffectual in stemming the violence. There is some evidence that the army in fact looked the other way while its civilians were slaughtered. Algeria refused international mediation, and kept the outside world largely in the dark about the war within its borders.

After President Zeroual announced he would retire early, elections were held in April 1999. Six of the seven candidates withdrew at the last minute in protest of election fraud. The lone remaining candidate, Abdel-Aziz Bouteflika, won 73.8% of the vote. Bouteflika is attempting to implement a plan of national reconciliation that includes an amnesty for Islamic militants not convicted of murder or rape. The Sept. 1999 referendum on his peace plan passed with 98% of the vote.

Andorra

PRINCIPALITY OF ANDORRA

National name: Valls d'Andorra
Head of Government: Marc Forné Molné (1994)
Area: 175 sq. mi. (450 sq. km)
Population (2000 est.): 66,824 (average annual growth rate: 0.5%); birth rate: 10.6/1000; infant mortality rate: 4.1/1000; density per sq. mi.: 382
Capital and largest city (1993 est.): Andorra la Vella, 22,390. **Monetary units:** French franc and Spanish peseta. **Languages:** Catalán (official), French, Spanish. **Ethnicity/race:** Spanish 61%, Andorran 30%, French 6%, other 3%. **Religion:** Roman Catholic. **Literacy rate:** 100%
Economic summary: GDP/PPP (1995 est.): $1.2 billion; $18,000 per capita. **Real growth rate:** n.a. **Inflation:** n.a. **Unemployment:** 0%. **Arable land:** 2%. **Agriculture:** tobacco, rye, wheat, barley, oats, vegetables, sheep. **Labor force:** n.a. **Industries:** tourism, sheep, timber, tobacco, banking. **Natural resources:** water power, mineral water, timber, iron ore, lead. **Exports:** $47 million (f.o.b., 1995): electricity, tobacco products, furniture. **Imports:** $1 billion (1995): consumer goods, food. **Major trading partners:** France, Spain, U.S.

Geography Andorra is nestled high in the Pyrenees Mountains on the French-Spanish border.

Government A parliamentary coprincipality composed of the bishop of Urgel (Spain) and the president of France.

History An autonomous and semi-independent coprincipality, Andorra has been under the joint suzerainty of the French state and the Spanish bishops of Urgel since 1278. In the late 20th century, Andorra became a popular tourist destination and an important international retail center because of its opportunities for various winter sports, low taxes, and lack of customs duties. In 1990 Andorra approved a customs union treaty with the EU permitting free movement of industrial goods between the two, but Andorra would apply the EU's external tariffs to third countries. This treaty went into effect on July 1, 1991. Andorra became a member of the U.N. in 1993 and a member of the Council of Europe in 1994.

Angola

REPUBLIC OF ANGOLA

President: José Eduardo dos Santos (1979)
Area: 481,350 sq. mi. (1,246,700 sq. km)
Population (2000 est.): 10,145,267 (average annual rate of natural increase: 2.2%); birth rate: 46.9/1000; infant mortality rate: 195.8/1000; density per sq. mi.: 21
Capital and largest city (1993): Luanda, 2,000,000. **Other large cities (1993 est.):** Huambo, 400,000; Lubango, 105,000. **Monetary unit:** Kwanza.

Languages: Bantu, Portuguese (official). **Ethnicity/race:** Ovimbundu 37%, Kimbundu 25%, Bakongo 13%, mestico (mixed European and Native African) 2%, European 1%, other 22%. **Religions:** Roman Catholic, 47%; Protestant, 38%; Indigenous, 15%. **Literacy rate:** 42% (1990)
Economic summary: GDP/PPP (1998 est.): $11 billion; $1,000 per capita. **Real growth rate:** 0.5%. **Inflation:** 90% (1998 est.). **Unemployment:** extensive. (1997 est.) **Arable land:** 2%. **Agriculture:** bananas, sugarcane, coffee, sisal, corn, cotton, manioc (tapioca), tobacco, vegetables, plantains, livestock, forest products, fish. **Labor force:** 5 million: agriculture, 85%; industry and services, 15% (1997 est.). **Industries:** petroleum, diamonds, iron ore, phosphates, feldspar, bauxite, uranium, gold, cement, basic metal products, fish processing, food processing, brewing, tobacco products, sugar, textiles. **Natural resources:** petroleum, diamonds, iron ore, phosphates, copper, feldspar, gold, bauxite, uranium. **Exports:** $3.4 billion (f.o.b., 1998 est.): crude oil, diamonds, refined petroleum products, gas, coffee, sisal, fish and fish products, timber, cotton. **Imports:** $2.2 billion (f.o.b., 1998 est.): machinery and electrical equipment, vehicles and spare parts, medicines, food, textiles and clothing, substantial military supplies. **Major trading partners:** U.S., EU, China, Portugal, France, South Africa.

Geography Angola, more than three times the size of California, extends for more than 1,000 miles (1,609 km) along the South Atlantic in southwestern Africa. The Democratic Republic of the Congo and the Republic of Congo are to the north and east, Zambia is to the east, and Namibia is to the south. A plateau averaging 6,000 feet (1,829 m) above sea level rises abruptly from the coastal lowlands. Nearly all the land is desert or savanna, with hardwood forests in the northeast.

Government Angola underwent a transition from a one-party socialist state to a nominally multiparty democracy in 1992.

History The original inhabitants of Angola are thought to have been Khoisan speakers. After A.D. 1000, large numbers of Bantu speakers migrated to the region and became the dominant group. Angola derives its name from the Bantu kingdom of Ndongo, whose name for its king is *ngola*.

Explored by the Portuguese navigator Diego Cão in 1482, Angola became a link in trade with India and Southeast Asia. Later it was a major source of slaves for Portugal's New World colony of Brazil. Development of the interior began after the Berlin Conference in 1885 fixed the colony's borders, and British and Portuguese investment fostered mining, railways, and agriculture.

Following World War II, independence movements began but were sternly suppressed by Portuguese military force. The major nationalist organizations were the Popular Movement for the Liberation of Angola (MPLA), a Marxist party, National Front for the Liberation of Angola (FNLA), and the National Union for the Total Independence of Angola (UNITA). After 14 years of war, Portugal finally granted independence to Angola in 1975. The MPLA, which had led the independence movement, has controlled the government ever since. But after its long war for independence, the new country has yet to experience an extended period of peace. UNITA disputed the MPLA's ascendancy, and civil war broke out almost immediately. With the Soviet Union and Cuba supporting the Marxist MPLA, and the United States and South Africa supporting the anticommunist UNITA, the country became a cold war battleground.

With the waning of the cold war and the withdrawal of Cuban troops in 1989, the MPLA began to make the transition to a multiparty democracy. Despite shifting ideologies, the civil war continued for more than 30 years, with UNITA's charismatic rebel leader, Jonas Savimbi, armed and sustained by his control of approximately 80% of the country's diamond trade. Free elections took place in 1992, with incumbent president José Eduardo dos Santos and the MPLA winning the U.N.-certified election over Savimbi and UNITA. Savimbi then withdrew, charging election fraud, and the civil war resumed.

In 1997 Angola played a crucial role in the civil wars of both the Republic of Congo and the Democratic Republic of the Congo. By aiding in the overthrow of these countries' leaders, Pascal Lissouba and Mobutu Sese Seko, the Angolan government was also able to destroy the UNITA strongholds within the borders of these countries. Angola again came to the aid of the Democratic Republic of the Congo's new leader, Laurent Kabila, in 1998, helping to fight the rebellion against his shaky post-administration.

Four years of relative peace took place between 1994 and 1998 when the United Nations, at a cost of $1.6 billion, oversaw the 1994 Lusaka peace accord. In 1997 it was agreed that a coalition government with UNITA would be implemented. But Savimbi violated the accord repeatedly by refusing to give up his strongholds, failing to demobilize his army, and retaking territory. As a result, the government suspended coalition rule in Sept. 1998, and the country again plunged into civil war, which, analysts say, neither side had the military power to win. Meanwhile, Angola's citizens continue to suffer. The hostilities affect an estimated four million people, about a third of the total population, and there are almost two million refugees.

Antigua and Barbuda

Sovereign: Queen Elizabeth II (1952)
Governor-General: James Beethoven Carlisle (1993)
Prime Minister: Lester Bryant Bird (1994)
Land area: 171 sq. mi. (440 sq. km)
Population (2000 est.): 66,422 (average annual growth rate: 1.4%); birth rate: 19.6/1000; infant mortality rate: 23.1/1000; density per sq. mi.: 388
Capital and largest city (1991): St. John's, 21,514; Codrington (capital of Barbuda), est. pop. 1,000.
Monetary unit: East Caribbean dollar. **Language:** English. **Ethnicity/race:** black, British, Portuguese, Lebanese, Syrian. **Religions:** Anglican and Roman Catholic. **Literacy rate:** 4% (1965)
Economic summary: GDP/PPP (1998 est.): $503 million; per capita $7,900. **Real growth rate:** 6%. **Inflation:** −1.1% (1997). **Unemployment:** 9% (1997 est.). **Arable land:** 18%. **Agriculture:** cotton, fruit, vegetables, bananas, coconuts, cucumbers, mangoes, sugarcane, livestock. **Labor force:** 30,000: industry, 7%; commerce and services, 82%; agriculture, 11% (1983). **Industries:** tourism, construction, light manufacturing (clothing, alcohol, household appliances). **Exports:** $37.8 million (1997): petroleum products, manufactures, food and live animals, machinery and transport equipment. **Imports:** $325.5 million (1997): food and live animals, machinery and transport equipment, manufactures, chemicals, oil.
Major trading partners: Organization of Eastern Caribbean States, Barbados, Guyana, Trinidad and Tobago, U.S., U.K., Canada. **Member of Commonwealth of Nations**

Geography Antigua, the larger of the two main islands located 295 miles (420 km) south-southeast of San Juan, P.R., is low-lying except for a range of hills in the south that rise to their highest point at Boggy Peak (1,330 ft.; 405 m). Well-wooded Antigua is 108 sq. miles (280 sq. km); the island dependencies of Redonda (an uninhabited rocky islet) and Barbuda (a coral island formerly known as Dulcina) are 0.5 sq. miles (1.30 sq. km) and 62 sq. miles (161 sq. km), respectively.

Government Parliamentary democracy.

History Antigua was explored by Christopher Columbus in 1493 and named for the Church of Santa Maria de la Antigua in Seville. Antigua was colonized by Britain in 1632; Barbuda was first colonized in 1678. The country joined the West Indies Federation in 1958. With the breakup of the federation, it became one of the West Indies Associated States in 1967, self-governing its internal affairs. Full independence was granted Nov. 1, 1981.

The Bird family has controlled the islands since Vere C. Bird founded the Antigua Labor Party in the mid-1940s. Bird, the former prime minister, and his sons, one of whom is the current prime minister, have a history of corruption that includes money laundering, arms sales, drug trafficking, and extortion. In recent years the Russian Mafia has gained a foothold on the island. The U.K. and the U.S. have increased their pressure on Antigua to halt its illegal activities—the U.S. State Department bluntly called the island "one of the most attractive centers in the Caribbean for money launderers."

Argentina

ARGENTINE REPUBLIC

National name: República Argentina.
President: Fernando de la Rúa (1999)
Area: 1,072,067 sq. mi. (2,766,890 sq. km)
Population (2000 est.): 36,955,182 (average annual rate of natural increase: 1.1%); birth rate: 18.6/1000; infant mortality rate: 18.3/1000; density per sq. mi.: 34
Capital and largest city (2000 est.): Buenos Aires, 13,250,000 (metro. area). **Other large cities (1999 est.):** Córdoba, 1,200,000; Rosario, 950,000; Mar del Plata, 900,000; Mendoza, 400,000. **Monetary unit:** Peso. **Languages:** Spanish, English, Italian, German, French. **Ethnicity/race:** European 97% (mostly of Spanish and Italian descent), 3% other (mostly Indian or mestizo). **Religions:** Roman Catholic 92%, Protestant 2%, Jewish 2%, other 4%. **Literacy rate:** 96% (1991)
Economic summary: GDP/PPP (1998 est.): $374 billion; $10,300 per capita. **Real growth rate:** 4.3%. **Inflation:** 1%. **Unemployment:** 15% (Aug. 1999). **Arable land:** 9%. **Agriculture:** sunflower seeds, lemons, soybeans, grapes, corn, tobacco, peanuts, tea, wheat, livestock. **Labor force:** 14 million (1997): industry, 31%; agriculture, 12%; services, 57% (1985 est.). **Industries:** food processing, motor vehicles, consumer durables, textiles, chemicals and petrochemicals, printing, metallurgy, steel. **Natural resources:** fertile plains of pampas, lead, zinc, tin, copper, iron ore, manganese, petroleum, uranium. **Exports:** $26 billion (f.o.b., 1998 est.): cereals, feed, motor vehicles, crude petroleum, steel manufactures. **Imports:** $32 billion (c.i.f., 1998 est.): motor vehicles, motor vehicle parts, organic chemicals, telecommunications equipment, plastics. **Major trading partners:** Brazil, U.S., Chile, Italy, Germany, France, China, Uruguay.

Geography Second in South America only to Brazil in size and population, Argentina is a plain, rising from the Atlantic to the Chilean border and the towering Andes peaks. Aconcagua (23,034 ft.; 7,021 m) is the highest peak in the world outside Asia. Argentina is also bordered by Bolivia and Paraguay on the north, and by Uruguay and Brazil on the east. The northern area is the swampy and partly wooded Gran Chaco, bordering on Bolivia and Paraguay. South of that are the rolling, fertile Pampas, which are rich in agriculture and sheep- and cattle-grazing and support most of the population. Next southward is Patagonia, a region of cool, arid steppes with some wooded and fertile sections.

Government Republic.

History First explored in 1516 by Juan Díaz de Solis, Argentina developed slowly under Spanish colonial rule. Buenos Aires was settled in 1580; the cattle industry was thriving as early as 1600. Invading British forces were expelled in 1806–07, and after Napoléon conquered Spain (1808), the Argentinians set up their own government in 1810. On July 9, 1816, independence was formally declared.

As it had in World War I, Argentina proclaimed neutrality at the outbreak of World War II, but in the closing phase declared war on the Axis powers on March 27, 1945. Juan D. Perón, an army colonel, emerged as the strongman of the postwar era, winning the presidential elections of 1946 and 1951. Perón's political strength was reinforced by his second wife—Eva Duarte de Perón (Evita)—and her popularity with the working classes. Although she never held a government post, Evita acted as de facto minister of health and labor, establishing a national charitable organization, and awarding generous wage increases to the unions, who responded with political support for Perón. Opposition to Perón's increasing authoritarianism led to a coup by the armed forces, which sent Perón into exile in 1955, three years after Evita's death. Argentina entered a long period of military dictatorships with brief intervals of constitutional government.

The former dictator returned to power in 1973 and his third wife, Isabel Martínez de Perón, was elected vice president. After Perón's death in 1974, she became the hemisphere's first woman chief of state. Already hampered by a small personal following and limited political experience, Isabel Perón assumed control of a deeply divided nation teetering on economic and political collapse. In 1975, terrorist acts by left- and right-wing groups killed some 700 people. The cost of living rose 355 percent, while strikes and demonstrations were constant. The Peronist Party itself was intensely divided, and Perón appeared unable to govern. After a series of cabinet crises and an attempted air force rebellion, a military junta led by army commander Lt. Gen. Jorge Rafael Videla seized power on March 24, 1976. The junta dismissed the legislature, imposed martial law, and ruled by decree.

The military quickly began the "Dirty War," an aggressive campaign to restore order and eradicate its opponents. The Argentine Commission for Human Rights, in Geneva, has charged the junta with 2,300 political murders, over 10,000 political arrests, and the disappearances of 20,000 to 30,000 people. While violence declined, the economy remained in chaos, and the junta was unstable. In March 1981 Field Marshal Roberto Viola deposed Videla, who in turn was succeeded by Lt. Gen. Leopoldo Galtieri.

On April 2, 1982, Galtieri landed thousands of troops on the British-held Falkland Islands, known as Las Islas Malvinas (Malvinas Islands) in Spanish. Argentine nationalists had long been irritated by British possession of the islands, and the invasion was widely viewed as an attempt by the junta to increase its popularity. The war, which rapidly turned into a disaster for Argentina, had the opposite effect. The British quickly dispatched more than 5,000 marines and paratroopers to the Falklands, and with the help of intelligence supplied by Chile, decisively defeated Argentina. Galtieri resigned in disgrace three days after Argentina's surrender. Major General Reynaldo Bignone took over June 14. Ironically, the Falklands victory turned into a triumph for British prime minister Margaret Thatcher, but was the last straw for an Argentine public disillusioned with military rule. Demands for a return to democracy intensified. Meanwhile the economy continued to deteriorate. As the 1983 elections approached, inflation hit 900% and Argentina's crippling foreign debt reached unprecedented levels.

In the presidential election of Oct. 1983, Raúl Alfonsín, leader of the middle-class Radical Civic Union, handed the Peronist Party its first defeat since its founding. However, the twin economic problems of growing unemployment and quadruple-digit inflation led to a Peronist victory in the elections of May 1989. Inflation of food prices provoked riots that induced Alfonsín to step down in June 1989, six months early, in favor of the new Peronist president, Carlos Menem.

In 1991, President Menem hammered out a vast deregulation of the economy designed to reverse decades of state intervention and protectionism. The president and his ruling Peronist Party saw their popularity dramatically fall in 1997 as the result of increasing social disturbances, a scandal over presidential links to an alleged mobster, and a high unemployment rate. Menem had the constitution changed in 1994 to allow him to serve for a second term; in 1998 he planned to change it again to allow for a third term but abandoned the idea after threats of civil disobedience.

Throughout the 1990s, the Argentine government continued to demonstrate economic credibility through further economic adjustment and conclusion of a new arrangement with the International Monetary Fund at the end of 1997. Beginning in Sept. 1998, however, Argentina faced its worst recession in a decade, and the ever-rising unemployment rate hit 15% in Aug. 1999. The economic woes of its trading partner Brazil have exacerbated Argentina's problems. Brazil, which traditionally bought almost one-third of Argentina's exports, bought 30% less in 1999. Unrest in the provinces—where unemployment is legion—led to riots in late summer.

In 1999 and 2000, highly publicized attempts to try former Chilean president Augusto Pinochet for alleged war crimes prompted renewed interest in Argentina in bringing to trial members of the military junta that ran the country from 1976 to 1983.

Armenia

President: Robert Kocharian (1998)
Prime Minister: Andranik Markarian (2000)
Area: 11,500 sq. mi. (29,800 sq. km)
Population (2000 est.): 3,344,336 (average annual rate of increase: 0.1%) (Armenian, 93%; others, Kurds, Ukrainians, and Russians); birth rate: 11/1000; infant mortality rate: 41.5/1000, density per sq. mi.: 291
Capital and largest city (1998 est.): Yerevan,

1,226,000. **Other large cities (1998 est.):** Gyumri (Leninakan), 121,000; Vanadzor, 74,000; Abovian, 54,000. **Monetary unit:** Dram. **Language:** Armenian. **Ethnicity/race:** Armenian 93%, Azeri 3%, Russian 2%, other (mostly Yezidi Kurds) 2% (1989) Note: as of the end of 1993, virtually all Azeris had emigrated from Armenia. **Religion:** Armenian Orthodox, 94%. **Literacy rate:** 99% (1989)
Economic summary: GDP/PPP (1998 est.): $9.2 billion; $2,700 per capita. **Real growth rate:** 6%. **Inflation:** 10%. **Unemployment:** 20% (1998 est.). **Arable land:** 17%. **Agriculture:** fruit (especially grapes), vegetables, livestock. **Labor force:** 1.6 million (1997): manufacturing, mining, and construction, 25%; agriculture, 38%; services, 37%. **Industries:** much of industry is shut down; metal-cutting machine tools, forging-pressing machines, electric motors, tires, knitted wear, hosiery, shoes, silk fabric, washing machines, chemicals, trucks, watches, instruments, microelectronics. **Exports:** $230 million (f.o.b., 1998 est.): gold and jewelry, aluminum, transport equipment, electrical equipment, scrap metal. **Imports:** $840 million (c.i.f., 1998 est.): grain, other food, fuel, other energy. **Major trading partners:** Iran, Russia, Turkmenistan, Georgia, U.S., EU.

Geography Armenia is located in the southern Caucasus and is the smallest of the former Soviet republics. It is bounded by Georgia on the north, Azerbaijan on the east, Iran on the south, and Turkey on the west. Contemporary Armenia is a fraction of the size of ancient Armenia. A land of rugged mountains and extinct volcanoes, its highest point is Mount Aragats, 13,435 ft. (4,095 m).

Government Republic.

History One of the world's oldest civilizations, Armenia once included Mount Ararat, which biblical tradition identifies as the mountain that Noah's ark rested on after the flood. It was the first country in the world to officially embrace Christianity as its religion (c. 300).

In the 6th century B.C., Armenians settled in the kingdom of Urartu (the Assyrian name for Ararat), which was in decline. Under Tigrane the Great (fl. 95–55 B.C.) the Armenian empire reached its height and became one of the most powerful in Asia, stretching from the Caspian to the Mediterranean Seas. Throughout most of its long history, however, Armenia has been invaded by a succession of empires. Under constant threat of domination by foreign forces, Armenians became both cosmopolitan as well as fierce protectors of their culture and tradition.

Over the centuries Armenia was conquered by Greeks, Romans, Persians, Byzantines, Mongols, Arabs, Ottoman Turks, and Russians. From the 16th century through World War I major portions of Armenia were controlled by their most brutal invader, the Ottoman Turks, under whom they experienced discrimination, religious persecution, heavy taxation, and armed attacks. In response to Armenian nationalist stirrings, the Turks massacred thousands of Armenians in 1894 and 1896. The most horrific massacre took place in April 1915 during World War I, when the Turks ordered the deportation of the Armenian population to the deserts of Syria and Mesopotamia. According to the majority of historians, between 600,000 and 1.5 million Armenians were murdered or died of starvation. The Armenian massacre is considered the first genocide in the 20th century. Turkey denies that a genocide took place, and claims that a much smaller number died in a civil war.

After the Turkish defeat in World War I, the independent Republic of Armenia was established on May 28, 1918, but survived only until Nov. 29, 1920, when it was annexed by the Soviet Army. On March 12, 1922, the Soviets joined Georgia, Armenia, and Azerbaijan to form the Transcaucasian Soviet Socialist Republic, which became part of the U.S.S.R. In 1936, after a reorganization, Armenia became a separate constituent republic of the U.S.S.R. Since 1988, Armenia has been involved in a territorial dispute with Azerbaijan over the enclave of Nagorno-Karabakh, to which both lay claim. Also in 1988, a devastating earthquake killed thousands and wreaked economic havoc.

Armenia declared its independence from the collapsing Soviet Union on Sept. 23, 1991. In the years that followed, Armenia successfully fought Azerbaijan for control of Nagorno-Karabakh. The majority population of the enclave are Armenian Christians who want to secede from Azerbaijan and join Armenia. A cease-fire agreement was reached between the two countries in 1994, but the fate of Nagorno-Karabakh remains unresolved. Azerbaijan has offered broad autonomy to the enclave in exchange for the withdrawal of Armenian troops from Azeri lands. But the enclave wants either full independence or annexation to Armenia.

An Armenian diaspora has existed throughout the nation's history, and Armenian emigration has been particularly heavy since independence from the Soviet Union. An estimated 60% of the total eight million Armenians worldwide live outside the country, with one million each in the U.S. and Russia. Significant Armenian communities are located in Georgia, France, Iran, Lebanon, Syria, Argentina, and Canada.

Prime Minister Vazgen Sarkisian and six others were assassinated Oct. 27, 1999, when gunmen broke into Parliament and began firing. The prime minister's brother, Aras Sarkisian, was appointed to succeed him, but in May 2000 President Kocharian replaced Sarkisian, a political rival, with a new prime minister, Andranik Markarian.

Australia

COMMONWEALTH OF AUSTRALIA

Sovereign: Queen Elizabeth II (1952)
Governor-General: Sir William Deane (1996)
Prime Minister: John Howard (1996)
Area: 2,966,150 sq. mi. (7,686,850 sq. km)
Population (2000 est.): 19,169,083 (average annual rate of natural increase: 0.6%; birth rate: 13.1/1000; infant mortality rate: 5/1000; density per sq. mi.: 6
Capital (1996 est.): Canberra, 307,700. **Largest cities (1993 est.):** Sydney, 3,713,500; Melbourne, 3,189,200; Brisbane, 1,520,600; Perth, 1,295,100; Adelaide, 1,079,200; . **Monetary unit:** Australian dollar.
Language: English. **Ethnicity/race:** Caucasian 95%, Asian 4%, aboriginal (353,000) and other 1%.
Religions: Anglican 26.1%, Roman Catholic 26.0%, other Christian 24.3%. **Literacy rate:** 100% (1980)
Economic summary: GDP/PPP (1998 est.): $393.9 billion; $21,200 per capita. **Real growth rate:** 4.5%. **Inflation:** 1%. **Unemployment:** 8.1% (1998). **Arable land:** 6%. **Agriculture:** wheat, barley, sugarcane, fruit, cattle, sheep, poultry. **Labor force:** 9.2 million (Dec. 1997); services, 73%; industry, 22%; agriculture, 5% (1997 est.). **Industries:** mining, industrial and transportation equipment, food processing, chemicals, steel. **Natural resources:** bauxite, coal, iron ore, copper, tin, silver, uranium, nickel, tungsten, mineral sands, lead, zinc, diamonds, natural gas, petroleum.
Exports: $56 billion (f.o.b, 1998 est.): coal, gold, meat, wool, alumina, iron ore, wheat, machinery and transport equipment. **Imports:** $61 billion (f.o.b, 1998 est.): machinery and transport equipment, computers and office machines, telecommunication equipment and parts, crude oil and petroleum products. **Major trading partners:** Japan, Association of Southeast Asian Nations, EU, South Korea, U.S., New Zealand, U.K., Taiwan, Hong Kong, China. **Member of Commonwealth of Nations**

Geography The continent of Australia, with the island state of Tasmania, is approximately equal in area to the United States (excluding Alaska and Hawaii). Mountain ranges run from north to south along the east coast, reaching their highest point in Mount Kosciusko (7,308 ft.; 2,228 m). The western half of the continent is occupied by a desert plateau that rises into barren, rolling hills near the west coast. It includes the Great Victoria Desert to the south and the Great Sandy Desert to the north. The Great Barrier Reef, extending about 1,245 miles (2,000 km), lies along the northeast coast. The island of Tasmania (26,178 sq. mi.; 67,800 sq. km) is off the southeastern coast.

Government Democracy. Symbolic executive power is vested in the British monarch, who is represented throughout Australia by the governor-general.

History The first inhabitants of Australia were the Aborigines, who migrated there at least 40,000 years ago from Southeast Asia. There may have been between a half million to a full million Aborigines at the time of European settlement; today there are about 350,000.

Dutch, Portuguese, and Spanish ships sighted Australia in the 17th century; the Dutch landed at the Gulf of Carpentaria in 1606. In 1616 the territory became known as New Holland. The British arrived in 1688, but it was not until Captain James Cook's voyage in 1770 that Great Britain claimed possession of the vast island, calling it New South Wales. A British penal colony was set up at Port Jackson (what is now Sydney) in 1788, and about 161,000 transported English convicts were settled there until the system was suspended in 1839.

Free settlers established six colonies: New South Wales (1786), Tasmania (then Van Diemen's Land) (1825), Western Australia (1829), South Australia (1834), Victoria (1851), and Queensland (1859). Various gold rushes attracted settlers, as did the mining of other minerals. Sheep farming and grain soon became important economic enterprises. The six colonies became states and in 1901 federated into the Commonwealth of Australia with a constitution that incorporated British parliamentary and U.S. federal traditions. Australia became known for its liberal legislation: free compulsory education, protected trade unionism with industrial conciliation and arbitration, the secret ballot, women's suffrage, maternity allowances, and sickness and old-age pensions.

Australia fought alongside Britain in World War I, notably with the Australia and New Zealand Army Corps (ANZAC) in the Dardanelles campaign (1915). Participation in World War II brought Australia closer to the United States. Parliamentary power in the second half of the 20th century shifted between three political parties: the Australian Labour Party, the Liberal Party, and the National Party. Australia relaxed its discriminatory immigration laws in the 1960s and

1970s, which favored Northern Europeans. Thereafter, about 40% of its immigrants came from Asia, diversifying a population that was predominantly of English and Irish heritage.

In March 1996 the opposition Liberal Party–National Party coalition easily won the national elections, removing the Labour Party after 13 years in power. Pressure from the new, conservative One Nation Party threatened to reduce the gains made by Aborigines and to limit immigration. An Aboriginal movement had grown in the 1960s that gained full citizenship and improved education for the country's poorest socioeconomic group.

In Sept. 1999, Australia led the international peacekeeping force sent to restore order in East Timor, Indonesia. Pro-Indonesian militias had begun massacring civilians following a U.N.-sponsored referendum that overwhelmingly called for East Timor's independence.

In Nov. 1999, Australia's 11.6 million voters rejected a referendum that would have ended Australia's formal allegiance to the British Crown. The referendum would have replaced the British governor-general with an Australian president chosen by Parliament. Although the vast majority of Australians do not consider themselves monarchists, they rejected the referendum because it did not provide for direct, popular elections but gave Parliament the power to select the president. Sydney hosted the 2000 Summer Olympic games from Sept. 15–Oct.1, 2000.

Australian External Territories

Norfolk Island (13 sq. mi.; 36.3 sq. km) was placed under Australian administration in 1914. Population 1,892 (2000). A former penal colony, Norfolk Island became home to the entire population of Pitcairn Island in 1856. The 194 residents of tiny Pitcairn—all of whom were the descendants of the mutineers from the HMS *Bounty* and their Tahitian wives—embarked on the 3,700-mile journey to Norfolk because of overpopulation. Many Norfolk residents can trace their genealogy directly to the adventurers from *Bounty*.

The Ashmore and Cartier Islands (0.8 sq. mi.), situated in the Indian Ocean off the northwest coast of Australia, came under Australian administration in 1934.

The Australian Antarctic Territory (2,360,000 sq. mi.; 6,112,400 sq. km) is made up of all the islands and territories, other than Adélie Land, situated south of lat. 60°S and lying between long. 160° and 45°E. It came under Australian administration in 1936.

Heard Island and the McDonald Islands (158 sq. mi.; 409.2 sq. km), lying in the sub-Antarctic, were placed under Australian administration in 1947. The islands are uninhabited.

Christmas Island (52 sq. mi.; 134.7 sq. km) is situated in the Indian Ocean. It came under Australian administration in 1958. Most of the island's residents had been phosphate miners until the 1990s, when the Australian-based Casinos Austria International Ltd. built a $45 million casino on Christmas Island. As a result, the population has more than doubled, to 2,564 (2000).

Coral Sea Islands (400,000 sq. mi.; 1,036,000 sq. km, but only a few sq. mi. of land) became a territory of Australia in 1969. There is no permanent population on the islands.

Cocos (Keeling) Islands are made up of a group of 27 small coral islands in two separate atolls in the Indian Ocean, 1,721 miles (2,768 km) northwest of Perth. West Island is the largest, about 6.2 miles (10 km) long. The islands became an Australian territory in 1955. In April 1984 the residents voted to merge with Australia. The population of the Cocos is 604 (July 1995).

Austria

REPUBLIC OF AUSTRIA

National name: Republik Österreich
President: Thomas Klestil (1992)
Chancellor: Wolfgang Schüssel (2000)
Area: 32,375 sq. mi. (83,850 sq. km)
Population (2000 est.): 8,131,111 (average annual rate of natural increase: –0.001%); birth rate 9.9/1000; infant mortality rate: 4.5/1000; density per sq. mi.: 251
Capital and largest city (1991 est.): Vienna, 1,600,000. **Other large cities (1995 est.):** Graz, 237,150; Linz, 203,000; Salzburg, 144,000; Innsbruck, 118,000.
Monetary units: Schilling and euro. **Languages:** German 98% (small Slovene, Croatian, and Hungarian-speaking minorities). **Ethnicity/race:** German 99.4%, Croatian 0.3%, Slovene 0.2%.
Religions: Roman Catholic 85%, Protestant 6%, other 9%. **Literacy rate:** 99% (1974)
Economic summary: GDP/PPP (1998 est.): $184.5 billion; $22,700 per capita. **Real growth rate:** 2.9%. **Inflation:** 0.9%. **Unemployment:** 7% (1999 est.). **Arable land:** 17%. **Agriculture:** grains, potatoes, sugar beets, wine, fruit, dairy products, cattle, pigs, poultry, lumber. **Labor force:** 3.7 million (1998): services, 67.7%; industry and crafts, 29%; agriculture and forestry, 0.7% (1997 est.). **Industries:** construction, machinery, vehicles and parts, food, chemicals, lumber and wood processing, paper and paperboard, communications equipment, tourism. **Natural resources:** iron ore, oil, timber, magnesite, lead, coal, lignite, copper, hydropower. **Exports:** $62.5 billion (1998): vehicles, machinery and equipment, paper and paperboard, metal goods, iron and steel, telecommunications equipment, textiles, medical and pharmaceutical products. **Imports:** $65.8 billion (1998): vehicles, machinery and equipment, apparel, metal goods, oil and oil products, office and data-processing machinery, medical and pharmaceutical products, telecommunication equipment, textiles. **Major trading partners:** EU (mostly Germany and Italy), central and eastern Europe, Japan, U.S., Asia.

Geography Slightly smaller than Maine, Austria includes much of the mountainous territory of the eastern Alps (about 75% of the area). The country contains many snowfields, glaciers, and snowcapped peaks, the highest being the Grossglockner (12,530 ft.; 3,819 m). The Danube is the principal river. Forests and woodlands cover about 40% of the land.

Government Federal republic.

History Settled in prehistoric times, the central European land that is now Austria was overrun in pre-Roman times by various tribes, including the Celts. After the fall of the Roman Empire, of which Austria was part, the area was invaded by Bavarians and Slavic Avars. Charlemagne conquered the area in A.D. 788 and encouraged colonization and Christianity. In 1252, Ottokar, king of Bohemia, gained possession, only to lose the territories to Rudolf of Hapsburg in 1278. Thereafter, until World War I, Austria's history was largely that of its ruling house, the Hapsburgs. Austria emerged from the Congress of Vienna in 1815 as the continent's dominant power. The *Ausgleich* of 1867 provided for a dual sovereignty, the empire of Austria and the kingdom of Hungary, under Franz Joseph I, who ruled until his death on Nov. 21, 1916. The Austrian-Hungarian minority rule of this immensely diverse empire became increasingly difficult in an age of emerging nationalist movements. When Archduke Francis Ferdinand was assassinated by a Serbian nationalist in Sarajevo in 1914, World War I, as well as the destruction of the Austro-Hungarian Empire, began.

During World War I, Austria-Hungary was one of the Central powers with Germany, Bulgaria, and Turkey, and the conflict left the country in political chaos and economic ruin. Austria, shorn of Hungary, was proclaimed a republic in 1918, and the monarchy was dissolved in 1919. A parliamentary democracy was set up by the constitution of Nov. 10, 1920. To check the power of Nazis advocating union with Germany, Chancellor Engelbert Dolfuss in 1933 established a dictatorship, but was assassinated by the Nazis on July 25, 1934. Kurt von Schuschnigg, his successor, struggled to keep Austria independent, but on March 12, 1938, German troops occupied the country, and Hitler proclaimed its *Anschluss* (union) with Germany, annexing it to the Third Reich.

After World War II, the U.S. and Britain declared the Austrians a "liberated" people. But the Russians prolonged the occupation. Finally Austria concluded a state treaty with the U.S.S.R. and the other occupying powers and regained its independence on May 15, 1955. The second Austrian republic, established Dec. 19, 1945, on the basis of the 1920 constitution (amended in 1929), was declared by the federal Parliament to be permanently neutral.

On June 8, 1986, former U.N. Secretary-General Kurt Waldheim was elected to the ceremonial office of president in a campaign marked by controversy over his alleged links to Nazi war crimes in Yugoslavia (he was replaced by diplomat Thomas Klestil in 1992). On Jan. 1, 1995, Austria became a member of the European Union. Despite the membership, it retained its strict constitutional neutrality and forbade the stationing of foreign troops on its soil.

In 1998, Austria discussed the return of hundreds of art objects now owned by Austria that had been confiscated by the Nazi regime from their former, primarily Jewish, owners. Deadly avalanches struck several Austrian villages in Feb. 1999, the worst avalanches in the Alps since 1970. In Aug. 1999, Austrian police arrested Gen. Momir Talic, the highest-ranking Bosnian Serb military official, wanted by the U.N. on war crimes charges.

In Feb. 2000 the conservative People's Party formed a coalition with the far-right Freedom Party, headed by Jörg Haider. A nationalist against immigration, Haider had made several controversial remarks praising some Nazi policies, which he has since recanted. His gradual rise to power—from 5% in 1983 to 28% in the October 1999 election—was credited to voters weary of decades of stasis under the rule of the Social Democrats. The European Union condemned Austria's new coalition, froze diplomatic contacts, and imposed sanctions, accusing Haider of being a racist, xenophobe, and Nazi-sympathizer. Austria responded angrily by criticizing the EU for interfering in the affairs of a democratically elected government. Large demonstrations in Austria and throughout Europe followed. Haider did not join the government, but he was expected to wield influence from the sidelines. In Feb., however, he resigned from the party, claiming he would concentrate on his role as governor of the Carinthia province. In Sept. 2000, the EU lifted sanctions against Austria.

Azerbaijan

REPUBLIC OF AZERBAIJAN

President: Heydar Aliyev (1993)
Prime Minister: Artur Rasizade (1996)
Area: 33,400 sq. mi. (86,600 sq. km)
Population (2000 est.): 7,748,163 (average annual rate of natural increase: 0.9%). Birth rate: 18.1/1000; infant mortality rate: 83.4/1000; density per sq. mi.: 232
Capital and largest city (1991): Baku, 1,713,300, a port on the Caspian Sea.. **Other large cities:** Ganja (1989), 278,000; Sumgait, 231,000. **Monetary unit:** Manat. **Languages:** Azerbaijani Turkic, 82%; Russian, 7%; Armenian, 2%. **Ethnicity/race:** Azeri 90%, Dagestani 3.2%, Russian 2.5%, Armenian 2.3%, other 2% (1995 est.). Note: almost all Armenians live in the separatist Nagorno-Karabakh region. **Religions:** Muslim, 87%; Russian Orthodox, 5.6%; Armenian Orthodox, 2%.. **Literacy rate:** 97% (1989)
Economic summary: GDP/PPP (1998 est.): $12.9 billion; $1,640 per capita. **Real growth rate:** 10%. **Inflation:** –7.6%. **Unemployment:** 20% (1996 est.). **Arable land:** 18%. **Agriculture:** cotton, grain, rice, grapes, fruit, vegetables, tea, tobacco, cattle, pigs, sheep, goats. **Labor force:** 2.9 million (1997): services, 53%; agriculture and forestry, 32%; industry and construction, 15% (1997). **Industries:** petroleum and natural gas, petroleum products, oilfield equipment, steel, iron ore, cement, chemicals and petrochemicals, textiles. **Exports:** $781 million (f.o.b., 1997 est.): oil and gas, chemicals, oilfield equipment, textiles, cotton. **Imports:** $794 million (c.i.f., 1997 est.): machinery and parts, consumer durables, foodstuffs, textiles. **Major trading partners:** C.I.S., European countries, Turkey.

Geography   Azerbaijan is located on the western shore of the Caspian Sea at the southeastern extremity of the Caucasus. The region is a mountainous country. About 7% of it is arable land. The Kura River Valley is the area's major agricultural zone.

Government   Constitutional republic.

History   Azerbaijan was known in ancient times as Albania. The area was the site of many conflicts involving Arabs, Kazars, and Turks. After the 11th century, the territory became dominated by Turks and eventually a stronghold of the Shi'ite Muslim religion and Islamic culture. The territory of Soviet Azerbaijan was acquired by Russia from Persia through the Treaty of Gulistan in 1813 and the Treaty of Turkamanchai in 1828.

After the Bolshevik Revolution, Azerbaijan declared its independence from Russia in May 1918. The republic was reconquered by the Red Army in 1920, and was annexed into the Transcaucasian Soviet Socialist Republic in 1922. It was later reestablished as a separate Soviet Republic on Dec. 5, 1936. Azerbaijan declared independence from the collapsing Soviet Union on Aug. 30, 1991.

Since 1988, Azerbaijan and Armenia have been feuding over the enclave of Nagorno-Karabakh. The majority of the enclave's inhabitants are Armenian Christians agitating to secede from the predominantly Muslim Azerbaijan and join with Armenia. War broke out in 1988 when Nagorno-Karabakh tried to break away and annex itself to Armenia, and since then Armenia has controlled Nagorno-Karabakh. A cease-fire agreement was reached between the two countries in 1994, with Armenia retaining its hold over the disputed enclave. Azerbaijan has offered broad autonomy to the enclave in exchange for the withdrawal of Armenian troops from Azeri lands, but the enclave wants either full independence or annexation to Armenia. In July and Aug. 1999 the presidents of Azerbaijan and Armenia met to negotiate a settlement on the disputed enclave, but none of the results of the ongoing discussions have been announced.

The country's economic troubles are expected to be transformed through Western investment in Azerbaijan's oil resources, an untapped reserve whose estimated worth is trillions of dollars. Since 1994, the Azerbaijan state oil company (SOCAR) has signed several billion-dollar agreements with international oil companies. A total of 15 production-sharing agreements have been signed; only one, run by BP-led Azerbaijan International Operating Company (AIOC) is thus far producing crude oil. Azerbaijan's pro-Western stance and its careful economic management have made it the most attractive of the oil-rich Caspian countries for foreign investment. In the years since its independence, the country has undergone rapid privatization and the IMF has given it high marks as one of the most successful economic overhauls ever.

But difficult negotiations over the route of the pipeline have stalled Azerbaijan's potential oil boom. Routes through Russia, Turkey, Georgia, and Iran have been proposed, and U.S., Russian, British, Iranian, and Chinese contenders in the "pipeline war" are all vying for dominance. In the volatile Caucasus region the options are complex, since all the proposed routes must pass through an unstable field of political, ethnic, religious, and environmental land mines.

Bahamas

COMMONWEALTH OF THE BAHAMAS

Sovereign: Queen Elizabeth II (1952)
Governor-General: Sir Orville Alton Turnquest (1995)
Prime Minister: Hubert Ingraham (1992)
Area: 5,380 sq. mi. (13,940 sq. km)
Population (2000 est.): 294,982 (average annual rate of natural increase: 1.3%); birth rate: 19.5/1000; infant mortality rate: 17/1000; density per sq. mi.: 55
Capital and largest city (1991 census): Nassau, 171,542. **Monetary unit:** Bahamian dollar. **Language:** English. **Ethnicity/race:** black 85%, white 15%. **Religions:** Baptist, 29%; Anglican, 23%; Roman Catholic, 22%, others. **Literacy rate:** 90% (1963)
Economic summary: GDP/PPP (1998 est.): $5.63 billion; $20,100 per capita. **Real growth rate:** 4%. **Inflation:** 0.4% (1997). **Unemployment:** 9% (1998 est.). **Labor force:** 148,000 (1996): tourism, 40%; government, 30%; business services, 10%; agriculture, 5% (1995 est.). **Agriculture:** citrus, vegetables, poultry. **Industries:** tourism, banking, cement, oil refining and transshipment, salt production, rum, aragonite, pharmaceuticals, spiral-welded steel pipe. **Natural resources:** salt, aragonite, timber. **Exports:** $300 million (1998): pharmaceuticals, cement; rum, crawfish, refined petroleum products. **Imports:** $1.37 billion (1998): foodstuffs, manufactured goods, crude oil, vehicles, electronics. **Major trading partners:** U.S., EU, U.K., Japan, Russia. **Member of Commonwealth of Nations**

Geography The Bahamas are an archipelago of about 700 islands and 2,400 uninhabited islets and cays lying 50 miles off the east coast of Florida. They extend for about 760 miles (1,223 km). Only about 30 of the islands are inhabited; the most important is New Providence (80 sq. mi.; 207 sq. km), on which the capital, Nassau, is situated. Other islands include Grand Bahama, Abaco, Eleuthera, Andros, Cat Island, and San Salvador (or Watling's Island).

Government Commonwealth.

History The Arawak Indians were the first inhabitants of the Bahamas. Columbus's first encounter with the New World on Oct. 12, 1492, was the Bahamian island of San Salvador. The British first built settlements on the islands in the 17th century. In the early 18th century, the Bahamas were a favorite pirate haunt.

The Bahamas were a crown colony from 1717 until they were granted internal self-government in 1964. The islands moved toward greater autonomy in 1968 after the overwhelming victory in general elections of the Progressive Liberal Party, led by Prime Minister Lynden O. Pindling, over the predominately white United Bahamians Party. With its new mandate from the 85% black population, Pindling's government negotiated a new constitution with Britain under which the colony became the Commonwealth of the Bahama Islands in 1969. On July 10, 1973, the Bahamas became an independent nation.

Hubert A. Ingraham, of the Free National Movement Party, was sworn in as prime minister on Aug. 20, 1992, ending 25 years of rule by the Progressive Liberal Party. In Sept. 1999, Hurricane Floyd caused severe damage throughout the archipelago.

Bahrain

STATE OF BAHRAIN

Emir: Sheik Hamad bin Isa al-Khalifa (1999)
Prime Minister: Sheik Khalifah ibn Sulman al-Khalifa (1970)
Area: 240 sq. mi. (620 sq. km)
Population (2000 est.): 634,137 (average annual rate of natural increase: 1.7%); birth rate: 20.6/1000; infant mortality rate: 20.5/1000; density per sq. mi.: 2,642
Capital (1992 est.): Al-Manámah, 140,401. **Monetary unit:** Bahraini dinar. **Languages:** Arabic (official), English, Farsi, Urdu. **Ethnicity/race:** Bahraini 63%, Asian 13%, other Arab 10%, Iranian 8%, other 6%. **Religion:** Islam. **Literacy rate:** 77% (1990)
Economic summary: GDP/PPP (1998 est.): $8.2 billion; $13,100 per capita. **Real growth rate:** −2%. **Inflation:** −0.2% (1996 est.). **Unemployment:** 15% (1996 est.). **Labor force:** 150,000 (1997 est.)[1]: industry, commerce, and service, 79%; government, 20%; agriculture, 1% (1997 est.). **Arable land:** 1%. **Agriculture:** fruit, vegetables, poultry, dairy products, shrimp, fish. **Industries:** petroleum processing and refining, aluminum smelting, offshore banking, ship repairing, tourism. **Natural resources:** oil, associated and nonassociated natural gas, fish. **Exports:** $4.7 billion (f.o.b., 1997): petroleum and petroleum products, 61%; aluminum, 7%. **Imports:** $4.4 billion (f.o.b., 1997): nonoil, 59%; crude oil, 41%. **Major trading partners:** India, Japan, Saudi Arabia, South Korea, U.A.E., U.S., U.K., Germany.

1. 44% of the population in the 15–64 age group is nonnational (July 1998 est.).

Geography Bahrain is an archipelago in the Persian Gulf off the coast of Saudi Arabia. The islands for the most part are level expanses of sand and rock. A causeway connects Bahrain to Saudi Arabia.

Government Traditional monarchy.

History Known in ancient times as Dilmun, Bahrain was an important center of trade by the 3rd millennium B.C. The islands were ruled by the Persians in the 4th century A.D., and then by Arabs until 1541, when the Portuguese invaded them. Persia again claimed Bahrain in 1602. In 1783 Ahmad ibn al-Khalifah took over, and the al-Khalifahs remain the ruling family today. Bahrain became a British protectorate in 1820. It did not gain full independence until Aug. 14, 1971.

Although oil was discovered in Bahrain in the 1930s, it was relatively little compared to other Gulf states, and the wells are expected to be the first in the region to dry up. Sheik Isa ibn-Sulman al-Khalifa, who became emir in 1961, was determined to diversify his country's economy, and set about establishing Bahrain as a major financial center. The country provides its people with free medical care, education, and old-age pensions.

Conflicts between the Shi'ites and Sunnis are a continuing problem in Bahrain. The Sunni minority, to which the ruling al-Khalifa family belongs, controls nearly all the power and wealth in the country. Shi'ite Muslims have continued to agitate for more representation in government, and minor violent clashes, including several bombings, have led to about two dozen deaths since 1994.

Bahrain has been an important Western ally, serving as a Western air base during the Persian Gulf War in 1991, and continuing to serve as the base of the United States' Fifth Fleet, which patrols the Gulf. After ruling for four decades, Sheik Isa ibn-Sulman al-Khalifah died on March 6, 1999. He was succeeded by his son, Sheik Hamad bin Isa al-Khalifa, who is said to share his father's pro-Western policies.

Bangladesh

PEOPLE'S REPUBLIC OF BANGLADESH

President: Shahabuddin Ahmed (1996)
Prime Minister: Sheik Hasina Wazed (1996)
Area: 55,598 sq. mi. (144,000 sq. km)
Population (2000 est.): 129,194,224 (average annual rate of natural increase: 1.7%); birth rate: 25.4/1000; infant mortality rate: 71.7/1000; density per sq. mi.: 2,324
Capital and largest city (2000 est.): Dhaka, 9,600,000 (metro. area). **Other large cities (est. mid-1994):** Chittagong, 3,000,000; Khulna, 2,000,000. **Monetary unit:** Taka. **Principal languages:** Bangla (official), English. **Ethnicity/race:** Bengali 98%, Biharis 250,000, tribals less than 1 million. **Religions:** Muslim 83%, Hindu 16%, Buddhist, Christian, other. **Literacy rate:** 36% (1991)
Economic summary: GDP/PPP (1998 est.): $175.5 billion; $1,380 per capita. **Real growth rate:** 4%. **Inflation:** 7% (1998). **Unemployment:** 35.2% (1996). **Arable land:** 73%. **Agriculture:** rice, jute, tea, wheat, sugarcane, potatoes, beef, milk, poultry. **Labor force:** 56 million: agriculture, 65%; services, 25%; industry and mining, 10% (1996). **Industries:** jute manufacturing, cotton textiles, food processing, steel, fertilizer. **Natural resources:** natural gas, arable land, timber. **Exports:** $4.4 billion (1997): garments, jute and jute goods, leather, frozen fish and seafood. **Imports:** $7.1 billion (1997): capital goods, textiles, food, petroleum products. **Major trading partners:** western Europe, U.S., Hong Kong, Japan, India, China, Singapore. **Member of Commonwealth of Nations**

Geography Bangladesh, on the northern coast of the Bay of Bengal, is surrounded by India, with a small common border with Burma in the southeast. It is approximately the size of Wisconsin. The country is low-lying riverine land traversed by the many branches and tributaries of the Ganges and Brahmaputra Rivers. Elevations average less than 600 feet (183 m) above sea level. Tropical monsoons and frequent floods and cyclones inflict heavy damage in the delta region.

Government Republic within the British Commonwealth.

History What is now called Bangladesh is part of the historic region of Bengal, the northeastern portion of the Indian subcontinent. The earliest reference to the region was to a kingdom called Vanga, or Banga (c.1000 B.C.). Buddhists ruled for centuries, but by the 10th century Bengal was primarily Hindu. In 1576, Bengal became part of the Mogul Empire, and the majority of East Bengalis converted to Islam. Bengal was ruled by British India from 1757 until Britain withdrew in 1947, and Pakistan was founded out of the two predominantly Muslim regions of the Indian subcontinent. West Pakistan and East Pakistan were united by religion (Islam), but their peoples were separated by culture, physical features, and 1,000 miles of Indian territory. Bangladesh consists primarily of East Bengal (West Bengal is part of India and its people are primarily Hindu) plus the Sylhet district of the Indian state of Assam. For almost 25 years after independence from Britain, its history was part of Pakistan's (*see* Pakistan).

Tension between East and West Pakistan developed from the outset because of their vast geographic, economic, and cultural differences. East Pakistan's Awami League, a political party founded by the Bengali nationalist Sheik Mujibur Rahman in 1949, sought independence from West Pakistan. Although 56% of the population resided in East Pakistan, the West held the lion's share of political and economic power. In 1970 East Pakistanis secured a majority of the seats in the National Assembly. President Yahya Khan postponed the opening of the National Assembly in an attempt to circumvent East Pakistan's demand for greater autonomy. As a consequence East Pakistan seceded, and the independent state of Bangladesh, or Bengali nation, was proclaimed on March 26, 1971. Civil war broke out, and with the help of Indian troops in the last few weeks of the war, East Pakistan defeated West Pakistan on Dec. 16, 1971. An estimated one million Bengalis were killed in the fighting or later slaughtered. Ten million more took refuge in India. In Feb. 1974, Pakistan agreed to recognize the independent state of Bangladesh.

Founding president Sheikh Mujibur was assassinated in 1975, as was the next president, Zia ur-Rahman. On March 24, 1982, Gen. Hossain Mohammad Ershad, army chief of staff, took control in a bloodless coup but was forced to resign on Dec. 6, 1990, amid violent protests and numerous allegations of corruption. A succession of prime ministers governed in the 1990s, including Khaleda Zia, wife of the assassinated president Zia ur-Rahman, and the current prime minister and leader of the liberal Awami League, Hasina Wazed, the daughter of Sheik Mujibur. Disastrous floods in 1998 stranded nearly eight million people and damaged crops and structures.

Bangladesh is facing a catastrophic public health crisis today. Dangerous levels of arsenic have been found in groundwater, the result of a safe-water program sponsored by UNICEF, the government, and other aid organizations 25 years ago. To save people from drinking contaminated river and pond water, between 3 and 4 million wells were built throughout the country. In the past few years, however, it was discovered that arsenic naturally occurring in the ground has seeped into the water, causing slow poisoning over many years. The World Bank has estimated that as many as 18 million people may be affected.

In March 2000 President Clinton became the first U.S. president to visit the country.

Barbados

Sovereign: Queen Elizabeth II (1952)
Governor-General: Sir Clifford Husbands (June 1996)
Prime Minister: Owen Arthur (1994)
Area: 166 sq. mi. (430 sq. km)
Population (2000 est.): 274,540; (average annual rate of natural increase: 0.6%); birth rate: 14.5/1000; infant mortality rate: 12.4/1000; density per sq. mi.: 1,654
Capital and largest city (1990): Bridgetown, 6,700. **Monetary unit:** Barbados dollar. **Language:** English. **Ethnicity/race:** African 80%, European 4%, other 16%. **Religions:** Anglican, 40%; Methodist, 7%; Pentecostal, 8%; Roman Catholic, 4%. **Literacy rate:** 99% (1970)
Economic summary: GDP/PPP (1998 est.): $2.9 billion; $11,200 per capita. **Real growth rate:** 3%. **Inflation:** 3.6% (1997). **Unemployment:** 12% (1998 est.). **Arable land:** 37%. **Agriculture:** sugarcane, vegetables, cotton. **Industries:** tourism, sugar, light manufacturing, component assembly for export. **Labor force:** 136,000 (1998 est.): services, 75%; industry, 15%; agriculture, 10% (1996 est.). **Exports:** $280 million (1997): sugar and molasses, rum, other food and beverages, chemicals, electrical components, clothing. **Imports:** $982 million (1997): consumer goods, machinery, foodstuffs, construction materials, chemicals, fuel, electrical components. **Major trading partners:** Caricom, U.S., U.K., Canada. **Member of Commonwealth of Nations**

Geography An island in the Atlantic about 300 miles (483 km) north of Venezuela, Barbados is only 21 miles long (34 km) and 14 miles across (23 km) at its widest point. It is circled by fine beaches and narrow coastal plains. The highest point is Mount Hillaby (1,105 ft.; 337 m) in the north central area.

Government Parliamentary democracy.

History Barbados is thought to have been originally inhabited by Arawak Indians. By the time Europeans explored the island, however, it was uninhabited.

Barbados was settled by the British in 1627. Slaves were brought in from Africa to work sugar plantations, and from the time of its settlement, the population was about 90% black. Slavery was abolished in the British Empire in 1834, and in 1838 slaves on the island gained their freedom.

Barbados became a crown colony in 1885 and was a member of the Federation of the West Indies from 1958 to 1962. Britain granted the colony independence on Nov. 30, 1966, and it became a parliamentary democracy within the Commonwealth.

Since independence, Barbados has been politically stable. However, local anger over rulings by the final appeals court, appointed by Queen Elizabeth, led to the creation in 1997 of a constitutional commission to consider abandoning all ties to Great Britain. President Arthur, who has seen Barbados's unemployment fall from 22% to 11%, was reelected in 1999 by a landslide.

Belarus

REPUBLIC OF BELARUS

President: Alyaksandr Lukashenka (1994)
Prime Minister: Uladzimir Yarmoshyn (2000)
Area: 80,200 sq. mi. (207,600 sq. km)
Population (2000 est.): 10,366,719 (average annual rate of natural increase: –0.5%) (in 1989: Belarussian, 77.9%; Russian, 13.2%; Polish, 4.1%; Ukrainian, 2.9%; Jewish, 1.1%); birth rate: 9.3/1000; infant mortality rate: 14.6/1000; density per sq. mi.: 129
Capital (1992 est.): Mensk (Minsk), 1,666,000. **Other large cities (1992 est.):** Gomel, 517,300; Vitebsk, 373,000; Mogilyov, 364,000; Grodno, 291,800; Brest, 284,000; Bobruysk, 224,000. **Monetary unit:** Belarussian ruble. **Language:** Belarussian (White Russian). **Ethnicity/race:** Belarussian 77.9%, Russian 13.2%, Polish 4.1%, Ukrainian 2.9%, other 1.9%. **Religion:** Orthodoxy is predominant. **Literacy rate:** 100% (1979)
Economic summary: GDP/PPP (1998 est.): $53.7 billion; $5,200 per capita. **Real growth rate:** 7%. **Inflation:** 182%. **Unemployment:** 2.3% officially registered unemployed (Dec. 1998); large number of underemployed workers. **Arable land:** 29%. **Agriculture:** grain, potatoes, vegetables, sugar beets, flax, beef, milk. **Labor force:** 4.3 million (1998 est.): industry and construction, 40%; agriculture and forestry, 19%; services, 41% (1997 est.). **Industries:** tractors, metal-cutting machine tools, off-highway dump trucks up to 110-metric-ton load capacity, wheel-type earth movers for construction and mining, eight-wheel-drive, high-flotation trucks with cargo capacity of 25 metric tons for use in tundra and roadless areas, equipment for animal husbandry and livestock feeding, motorcycles, television sets, chemical fibers, fertilizer, linen fabric, wool fabric, radios, refrigerators, other consumer goods. **Exports:** $7 billion (f.o.b., 1998): machinery and transport equipment, chemicals, foodstuffs. **Imports:** $8.5 billion (c.i.f., 1998): fuel, natural gas, industrial raw materials, textiles, sugar, foodstuffs. **Major trading partners:** Russia, Ukraine, Poland, Germany.

Geography Much of Belarus (formerly the Belarussian Soviet Socialist Republic of the U.S.S.R., and then Byelorussia) is a hilly lowland with forests, swamps, and numerous rivers and lakes. There are wide rivers emptying into the Baltic and Black Seas. Its forests cover over one-third of the land and its peat marshes are a valuable natural resource. The largest lake is Narach, 31 sq. mi. (79.6 sq. km).

Government Republic.

History In the 5th century, Belarus (also known as White Russia) was colonized by east Slavic tribes. Kiev dominated it from the 9th to 12th centuries. After the destruction of Kiev by the Mongols in the 13th century, the territory was conquered by the dukes of Lithuania, although it retained an amount of autonomy. Belarus became part of the Grand Duchy of Lithuania, which merged with Poland in 1569. Following the partitions of Poland in 1772, 1793, and 1795, in which Poland was divided among Russia, Prussia, and Austria, Belarus became part of the Russian empire.

Following World War I, Belarus proclaimed itself a republic, only to find itself occupied by the Red Army soon after its March 1918 announcement. The Polish-Soviet War of 1918–21 was fought to decide the fate of Belarus. West Belarus was ceded to Poland; the larger eastern part formed the Belorussian S.S.R., and was then joined to the U.S.S.R. in 1922. In 1939, the

Soviet Union took back West Belarus from Poland under the secret protocol of the Nazi-Soviet Nonaggression Pact and incorporated it into the Belarussian Soviet Socialist Republic. Occupied by the Nazis in World War II, Belarus was one of the most devastated battlefields.

Belarus declared its sovereignty in July 1990 and its independence in Aug. 1991. The Chernobyl nuclear power plant in Ukraine exploded in 1986, and 70% of its radioactivity fell on Belarus. Cancer and other illnesses have multiplied as a result.

The Belarus president, Nikolai Dementei, a communist hard-liner, was forced to resign under pressure following the Aug. 1991 attempted coup, and Stanislav S. Shushkevich, first deputy chairman of the Parliament, assumed leadership of the country. Belarus became a cofounder of the Commonwealth of Independent States (C.I.S.) in Dec. 1991. In Jan. 1994, the country's Parliament ousted its reform-minded leader in protest against his support for market economics. In March 1994, Parliament adopted a new constitution, creating a presidency and reconstructing the 260-seat Parliament.

With much fanfare, Belarus and Russia signed a treaty in April 1997 aimed at significantly increasing cooperation between the two states, stopping just short of union. In 1999, there was discussion of a pan-Slav union, uniting the rump Yugoslavia under Milosevic, with Russia and Belarus. This also came to nothing.

The Russian financial crisis that began in fall 1998 severely affected Belarus's Soviet-style planned economy. Belarus is almost completely dependent on Russia, which buys 70% of its exports.

Critics continue to denounce the increasingly oppressive political atmosphere and human rights violations in Belarus under the Soviet-style authoritarianism of President Alyaksandr Lukashenko. In 1999, the year President Lukashenko was to step down, he held what international opinion widely believed to have been a rigged national referendum, which changed the constitution and allowed him to cancel the elections and remain president. Over the past several years, opposition leaders have been jailed or have simply disappeared. In June 2000, the Kremlin urged Lukashenko to permit free elections in the fall.

Belgium

KINGDOM OF BELGIUM

National name: Royaume de Belgique—Koninkrijk van België
Sovereign: King Albert II (1993)
Prime Minister: Guy Verhofstadt (1999)
Area: 11,781 sq. mi. (30,510 sq. km)
Population (2000 est.): 10,241,506 (average annual rate of natural increase: 0.1%; birth rate: 10.9/1000; infant mortality rate: 4.8/1000; density per sq. mi.: 869
Capital and largest city (1994): Brussels, 949,070 (metro area). **Other large cities (1994):** Antwerp, 476,044; Ghent, 229,900; Liège, 207,496; Charleroi, 206,898; Bruges, 116,724. **Monetary units:** Belgian franc and euro. **Languages:** Dutch (Flemish), 57%; French, 32%; bilingual (Brussels), 10%; German, 0.7%. **Ethnicity/race:** Fleming 55%, Walloon 33%, mixed or other 12%. **Religion:** Roman Catholic, 75%. **Literacy rate:** 99% (1980)
Economic summary: GDP/PPP (1998 est.): $236 billion; $23,400 per capita. **Real growth rate:** 2.8%. **Inflation:** 1%. **Unemployment:** 12% (1998). **Arable land:** 24%. **Agriculture:** sugar beets, fresh

vegetables, fruit, grain, tobacco, beef, veal, pork, milk. **Labor force:** 4.283 million (1997): services, 69.7%; industry, 27.7%; agriculture, 2.6% (1992). **Industries:** engineering and metal products, motor vehicle assembly, processed food and beverages, chemicals, basic metals, textiles, glass, petroleum, coal. **Exports:** $145.1 billion (f.o.b., 1998): iron and steel, transportation equipment, tractors, diamonds, petroleum products. **Imports:** $137.1 billion (f.o.b., 1998): fuel, grains, chemicals, foodstuffs. **Major trading partners:** EU, U.S.

Geography Located in western Europe, Belgium has about 40 miles of seacoast on the North Sea, at the Strait of Dover, and is approximately the size of Maryland. The Meuse and the Schelde, Belgium's principal rivers, are important commercial arteries.

Government Parliamentary democracy under a constitutional monarch. Under the 1994 constitution, autonomy was granted to the Walloon region (Wallonia), the Flemish region (Flanders), and the bilingual Brussels-Capital region; autonomy was also guaranteed for the Flemish-, French-, and German-speaking "communities." The central government retains responsibility for foreign policy, defense, taxation, and social security.

History Belgium occupied part of the Roman province of Belgica, named after the Belgae, a people of ancient Gaul. The area was conquered by Julius Caesar in 57–50 B.C., then was overrun by the Franks in the 5th century. It was part of Charlemagne's empire in the 8th century, then in the next century was absorbed into Lotharingia and later into the duchy of Lower Lorraine. In the 12th century it was partitioned into the duchies of Brabant and Luxembourg, the bishopric of Liège, and the domain of the count of Hainaut, which included Flanders. In the 16th century, Belgium, with most of the area of the low countries, passed to the duchy of Burgundy and was inherited by Charles V, who incorporated it into his Holy Roman Empire. Then, in 1555, the low countries were united with Spain. By the Treaty of Utrecht in 1713, the country's sovereignty passed to Austria. During the wars that followed the French Revolution, Belgium was occupied and later annexed to France. But with the downfall of Napoléon, the Congress of Vienna in 1815 gave the country to the Netherlands. The Belgians revolted in 1830 and declared their independence.

Germany's invasion of Belgium in 1914 set off World War I. The Treaty of Versailles (1919) gave the areas of Eupen, Malmédy, and Moresnet to Belgium. Leopold III succeeded Albert, king during World War I, in 1934. In World War II, Belgium was overwhelmed by Nazi Germany, and Leopold III was held prisoner. When he attempted to return in 1950, socialists and liberals revolted. He abdicated July 16, 1951, and his son, Baudouin, became king. Because of growing opposition to Belgian rule in its African colonies, Belgium granted independence to Congo (now Democratic Republic of the Congo) in 1960 and to Ruanda-Urundi (now the nations of Rwanda and Burundi) in 1962.

Divisions between Flemings and Walloons grew, and linguistic regionalization increased, culminating in the revised constitution of 1994, which granted more autonomy to Belgium's three regions and language "communities."

In the 1990s the Belgian government was involved in numerous scandals that tainted it with a reputation for incompetence and corruption. In 1991, a deputy prime minister was murdered in a contract killing that remained unsolved. In 1998, Belgian statesman and former NATO secretary-general Willy Claes was convicted of bribery. International relations fared no better. Belgian peacekeeping troops abandoned Rwanda, a former colony, at the height of the 1994 genocide against the Tutsis. The discovery of the Dutroux child-sex-and-murder ring in 1996 led to further national outrage that was compounded by disclosures that official negligence and corruption had resulted in even more children's deaths. As the scandal continued into 1997, it fueled pressure for reform of the political, judicial, and police systems.

It was evident that little had changed, however, when Belgium stumbled into its next crisis in spring 1999. Dioxin, a cancer-causing chemical, was leaked into batches of chicken feed, contaminating the country's poultry and dairy products. Government ministers admitted to keeping the public in the dark for months after they realized the public health danger. Prime Minister Jean-Luc Dehaene resigned under the weight of the scandal. Dehaene has been credited with having reduced the budget deficit from 7% in 1993 to 1% in 1999, and for reducing the public debt by 20% during the same period—it had been 135% of the GDP.

The new prime minister, Guy Verhofstadt of the right-leaning Liberal party, cobbled together a coalition of six political parties in June 1999. Verhofstadt has promised a series of reforms aimed at the legal system and the civil service.

Belize

Sovereign: Queen Elizabeth II (1952)
Governor-General: Colville Young (1993)
Prime Minister: Said Musa (1998)
Area: 8,867 sq. mi. (22,960 sq. km)
Population (2000 est.): 249,183 (average annual rate of natural increase: 2.8%); birth rate: 32.3/1000; infant mortality rate: 26/1000; density per sq. mi.: 28
Capital (1997 est.): Belmopan, 5,845. **Largest city (1997 est.):** Belize City, 52,500. **Monetary unit:** Belize dollar. **Languages:** English (official), Creole, Spanish, Garifuna, Mayan. **Ethnicity/race:** mestizo 44%, Creole 30%, Maya 11%, Garifuna 7%, other 8%. **Religions:** Roman Catholic, 62%; Protestant, 30%. **Literacy rate:** 91% (1970)
Economic summary: GDP/PPP (1998 est.): $700 million; $3,000 per capita. **Real growth rate:** 0.5%. **Inflation:** −0.5%. **Unemployment:** 13% (1997 est.). **Arable land:** 2%. **Agriculture:** bananas, coca, citrus, sugarcane, lumber, fish, cultured shrimp. **Labor force:** 71,000: agriculture, 30%; services, 16%; government, 15.4%; commerce, 11.2%; manufacturing, 10.3% (1997 est.). **Industries:** garment production, food processing, tourism, construction. **Natural resources:** arable land potential, timber, fish. **Exports:** $95.3 million (f.o.b., 1998): sugar, 46%; bananas, 26%; citrus fruit, clothing, fish products, molasses, wood. **Imports:** $149.7 million (c.i.f., 1998): machinery and transportation equipment, food, manufactured goods, fuel, chemicals, pharmaceuticals. **Major trading partners:** U.S., U.K., Mexico, Canada. **Member of Commonwealth of Nations**

Geography   Belize is situated on the Caribbean Sea south of Mexico and east and north of Guatemala in Central America. In area, it is about the size of New Hampshire. Most of the country is heavily forested with various hardwoods. Mangrove swamps and cays along the coast give way to hills and mountains in the interior. The highest point is Victoria Peak, 3,681 feet (1,122 m).

Government   Parliamentary democracy within the British Commonwealth.

History   The Mayan civilization spread into the area of Belize between 1500 B.C. and A.D. 300 and flourished until about A.D. 1200. Several major archeological sites—notably Caracol, Lamanai, Lubaantun, Altun Ha, and Xunantunich—reflect the advanced civilization and much denser population of that period. European contact began in 1502 when Columbus sailed along the coast. The first recorded European settlement was begun by shipwrecked English seamen in 1638. Over the next 150 years, more English settlements were established. This period was also marked by piracy, indiscriminate logging, and sporadic attacks by Indians and neighboring Spanish settlements. Great Britain first sent an official representative to the area in the late 18th century, but Belize was not formally termed the Colony of British Honduras until 1840. It became a crown colony in 1862. Subsequently, several constitutional changes were enacted to expand representative government. Full internal self-government under a ministerial system was granted in Jan. 1964.

Guatemala had long made claims on Honduran territory. Although the dispute between Guatemala and Great Britain remained unresolved, Belize became independent on Sept. 21, 1981, after having been self-governing since 1964. Guatemala recognized Belize's sovereignty in Sept. 1991. However, Guatemala still claims more than half of Belize's territory. At talks held in Washington, D.C., in March 2000, Belize and Guatemala agreed to an agenda for formal negotiations to resolve the dispute.

Benin

REPUBLIC OF BENIN

National name: Republique du Benin
President: Mathieu Kérékou (1996)
Area: 43,483 sq. mi. (112,620 sq. km)
Population (2000 est.): 6,395,919 (average annual rate of natural increase: 3.03%); birth rate: 44.9/1000; infant mortality rate: 90.8/1000; density per sq. mi.: 147
Capital and largest city (1996): Porto-Novo (official), 177,660; Cotonou (de facto capital) 33,212. **Other large city (1992):** Djougou, 132,192. **Monetary unit:** Franc CFA. **Languages:** French, African languages. **Ethnicity/race:** African 99% (42 ethnic groups, most important being Fon, Adja, Yoruba, Bariba), Europeans 5,500. **Religions:** indigenous, 70%; Christian, 15%; Islam, 15%. **Literacy rate:** 23% (1990)
Economic summary: GDP/PPP (1998 est.): $7.6 billion; $1,300 per capita. **Real growth rate:** 4.4%. **Inflation:** 5.6%. **Unemployment:** n.a. **Arable land:** 13%. **Agriculture:** corn, sorghum, cassava (tapioca), yams, beans, rice, cotton, palm oil, peanuts, poultry, livestock. **Labor force:** n.a. **Industries:** textiles, cigarettes, beverages, food, construction materials, petroleum. **Exports:** $250 million (f.o.b., 1998): cotton, crude oil, palm products, cocoa. **Imports:** $314 million (f.o.b., 1998): foodstuffs, beverages, tobacco, petroleum products, intermediate goods, capital goods, light consumer goods. **Major trading partners:** Brazil, Portugal, Morocco, Libya, France, U.K., Thailand, Hong Kong, China.

Geography   This West African nation on the Gulf of Guinea, between Togo on the west and Nigeria on the east, is about the size of Tennessee. It is bounded also by Burkina Faso and Niger on the north. The land consists of a narrow coastal strip that rises to a swampy, forested plateau and then to highlands in the north. A hot and humid climate blankets the entire country.

Government Republic under a multiparty democratic rule.

History The Abomey kingdom of the Dahomey, or Fon, peoples was established in 1625. A rich cultural life flourished, and Benin's wooden masks, bronze statues, tapestries, and pottery are world renowned. One of the smallest and most densely populated states in Africa, Benin was annexed by the French in 1893 and incorporated into French West Africa in 1904. It became an autonomous republic within the French Community in 1958, and on Aug. 1, 1960, Dahomey was granted its independence within the community.

Gen. Christophe Soglo deposed the first president, Hubert Maga, in an army coup in 1963. He dismissed the civilian government in 1965, proclaiming himself chief of state. A group of young army officers seized power in Dec. 1967, deposing Soglo. In Dec. 1969, Benin had its fifth coup of the decade, with the army again taking power. In May 1970, a three-man presidential commission with a six-year term was created to take over the government. In May 1972, yet another army coup ousted the triumvirate and installed Lt. Col. Mathieu Kerekou as president. Between 1974 and 1989 Dahomey embraced socialism, and changed its name to the People's Republic of Benin. The name *Benin* commemorates an African kingdom that flourished from the 15th to the 17th century in what is now southwestern Nigeria. In 1990 Benin abandoned Marxist ideology, began moving toward multiparty democracy, and changed its name again, to the Republic of Benin.

By the end of the 1980s, Benin's economy was near collapse. As its oil boom ended, Nigeria expelled 100,000 Beninese migrant workers, and closed the border with Benin. Kérékou's socialist collectivization of Benin's agriculture and the ballooning bureaucracy further damaged the economy. By 1988, international financial institutions feared Benin would default on its loans and pressured Kérékou to make financial reforms.

Kérékou subsequently embarked on a major privatization campaign, cut the government payroll, and reduced social services, prompting student and labor union unrest. Fearing a revolution, Kérékou agreed to a new constitution and free elections. In 1991, Nicéphore Soglo, an economist and former director of the International Bank for Reconstruction and Development, was elected president with 67% of the vote.

Although he enjoyed widespread support at first, Soglo gradually became unpopular as austerity measures reduced living standards, and a 50% currency devaluation in 1994 caused inflation. Kérékou defeated Soglo in the 1996 elections, with 52.5% of the vote. In 1998 Prime Minister Adrien Houngbedji resigned, prompting Kérékou to reshuffle the cabinet. Soglo's party increased its strength in the National Assembly in 1999 legislative elections. In presidential elections set for March 2001, Soglo and Houngbedji have joined forces to lead a coalition of ten parties seeking to oust Kérékou, whom they charge with corruption in the sale of former government-owned companies.

In recognition that reforms have produced increased economic growth and greater stability, in July 2000 the World Bank and the International Monetary Fund announced Benin has qualified for $460 million in debt relief under the Heavily Indebted Poor Countries Initiative.

Bhutan

KINGDOM OF BHUTAN

National name: Druk-yul
Ruler: King Jigme Singye Wangchuck (1972)
Area: 18,000 sq. mi. (47,000 sq. km)
Population (2000 est.): 2,005,222 (average annual rate of natural increase: 2.2%); birth rate: 36.2/1000; infant mortality rate: 111/1000; density per sq. mi.: 111
Capital and largest city (1993): Thimphu (official), 30,340. **Monetary unit:** Ngultrum. **Language:** Dzongkha (official). **Ethnicity/race:** Bhote 50%, ethnic Nepali 35%, indigenous or migrant tribes 15%.
Religions: Buddhist, 75%; Hindu, 25%. **Literacy rate:** 42% (1995)
Economic summary: GDP/PPP (1998 est.): $1.9 billion; $1,000 per capita. **Real growth rate:** 6.5%. **Inflation:** 7.4% (1997 est.). **Unemployment:** n.a. **Arable land:** 2%. **Labor force:** n.a.: agriculture, 93%; services, 5%; industry and commerce, 2%. **Agriculture:** rice, corn, root crops, citrus, foodgrains, dairy products, eggs. **Industries:** cement, wood products, processed fruit, alcoholic beverages, calcium carbide. **Natural resources:** timber, hydropower, gypsum, calcium carbide. **Exports:** $99 million (f.o.b., 1997 est.): cardamom, gypsum, timber, handicrafts, cement, fruit, electricity (to India), precious stones, spices. **Imports:** $131 million (c.i.f., 1997 est.): fuel and lubricants, grain, machinery and parts, vehicles, fabrics, rice. **Major trading partners:** India, Bangladesh, Japan, U.K., Germany, U.S.

Geography Mountainous Bhutan, half the size of Indiana, is situated on the southeast slope of the Himalayas, bordered on the north and east by Tibet and on the south and west and east by India. The landscape consists of a succession of lofty and rugged mountains running generally from north to south and separated by deep valleys. In the north, towering peaks reach a height of 24,000 feet (7,315 m).

Government In the 1990s, the king gradually gave up absolute rule, transforming his kingdom into a constitutional monarchy.

History Although archeological exploration of Bhutan has been limited, evidence of civilization in the region dates back to at least 2000 B.C. Aboriginal Bhutanese, known as Monpa, are believed to have migrated from Tibet. The traditional name of the country since the 17th century has been Drukyul, Land of the Drokpa (Dragon People), a reference to the dominant branch of Tibetan Buddhism that is still practiced in the Himalayan kingdom.

British troops invaded the region in 1865 and negotiated an agreement under which Britain agreed to pay an annual allowance to the Bhutanese monarchy on condition of good behavior. A treaty between India and the seat of government, Thimphu, in 1949 increased this subsidy and placed Bhutan's foreign affairs under Indian control. Until the 1960s Bhutan was largely isolated from the rest of the world, and its people carried on a tranquil, traditional way of life of farming and trading that had remained intact for centuries. After China invaded Tibet, however, Bhutan strengthened its ties and contact with India in an effort to avoid Tibet's fate. New roads and other connections to India began to end its isolation. In the 1960s Bhutan also undertook social modernization, abolishing slavery and the caste system, emancipating women, and enacting land reform. In 1985, Bhutan made its first diplomatic links with non-Asian countries.

A pro-democracy campaign emerged in 1991 that the government claimed was composed largely of

Nepali immigrants. As a result of the campaign, some 100,000 Nepali civil servants were either evicted or encouraged to emigrate. Most of them crossed the border back into Nepal, where they were housed in U.N.-administered refugee camps. The mass exodus prompted the International Red Cross to investigate charges of human rights violations in 1993. By 1995, discussions with Nepal over the problem had borne little fruit, with Thimphu insisting that the refugees had left of their own free will or were Nepali nationals wanting to immigrate to Bhutan.

In 1998, King Jigme Singye Wangchuck voluntarily curtailed his powerful monarchy by yielding to the formerly rubber-stamp legislature, giving it the right to remove him from leadership and appoint his cabinet. The move was the largest step to date in a gradual program to dilute the monarchy after nearly a century of absolute rule. Income tax was introduced, with tax forms due for the first time in Feb. 2000.

Bolivia

REPUBLIC OF BOLIVIA

National name: República de Bolivia
President: Hugo Banzer Suárez (1997)
Area: 424,162 sq. mi. (1,098,580 sq. km)
Population (2000 est.): 8,152,620 (average annual rate of natural increase: 2%); birth rate: 28.2/1000; infant mortality rate: 60.4/1000; density per sq. mi.: 19
Historic and judicial capital (1997 est.): Sucre, 131,800; **Administrative capital and largest city (1997 est.):** La Paz, 713,400. **Other large cities (1997 est.):** Santa Cruz, 697,000; Cochabamba, 407,800; El Alto, 405,500; Oruro, 184,000. **Monetary unit:** Boliviano. **Languages:** Spanish (official), Quechua, Aymara, Guarani. **Ethnicity/race:** Quechua 30%, Aymara 25%, mestizo (mixed European and Indian ancestry) 25%–30%, European 5%–15%. **Religion:** Roman Catholic, 85%. **Literacy rate:** 82% (1992)
Economic summary: GDP/PPP (1998 est.): $23.4 billion; $3,000 per capita. **Real growth rate:** 4.7%. **Inflation:** 4.4%. **Unemployment:** 11.4% (1997). **Arable land:** 2%. **Agriculture:** soybeans, coffee, coca, cotton, corn, sugarcane, rice, potatoes, timber. **Industries:** mining, smelting, petroleum, food and beverages, tobacco, handicrafts, clothing. **Labor force:** 2.5 million: agriculture, n.a.; services and utilities, n.a.; manufacturing, mining, and construction, n.a. **Natural resources:** tin, natural gas, petroleum, zinc, tungsten, antimony, silver, iron, lead, gold, timber. **Exports:** $1.1 billion (f.o.b., 1998 est.): metals, 34%; natural gas, 9.4%; soybeans, 8.4%; jewelry, 11%; wood, 6.9%. **Imports:** $1.7 billion (c.i.f., 1998): capital goods, 48%; chemicals, 11%; petroleum, 5%; food, 5% (1993 est.). **Major trading partners:** U.S., U.K., Colombia, Peru, Argentina, Japan, Brazil, Chile.

Geography Landlocked Bolivia is equal in size to California and Texas combined. Brazil forms its eastern border; its other neighbors are Peru and Chile on the west and Argentina and Paraguay on the south. The western part, enclosed by two chains of the Andes, is a great plateau—the Altiplano, with an average altitude of 12,000 ft. (3,658 m). Almost half the population lives on the plateau, which contains Oruro, Potosí, and La Paz. At an altitude of 11,910 feet (3,630 m), La Paz is the highest administrative capital city in the world. The Oriente, a lowland region ranging from rain forests to grasslands, comprises the northern and eastern two-thirds of the country. Lake Titicaca, at an altitude of 12,507 ft. (3,812 m), is the highest commercially navigable body of water in the world.

Government Republic.

History Famous since Spanish colonial days for its mineral wealth, modern Bolivia was once a part of the ancient Incan empire. After the Spaniards defeated the Incas in the 16th century, Bolivia's predominantly Indian population was reduced to slavery. The remoteness of the Andes helped protect the Bolivian Indians from the European diseases that decimated other South American Indians. But the existence of a large indigenous group forced to live under the thumb of their colonizers created a stratified society of haves and have-nots that continues to this day.

By the end of the 17th century the mineral wealth had begun to dry up. The country won its independence in 1825 and was named after Simón Bolívar, the famous liberator. Hampered by internal strife, Bolivia lost great slices of territory to three neighboring nations. Several thousand square miles and its outlet to the Pacific were taken by Chile after the War of the Pacific (1879–84). In 1903, a piece of Bolivia's Acre province, rich in rubber, was ceded to Brazil. And in 1938, after losing the Chaco War of 1932–35 to Paraguay, Bolivia gave up its claim to nearly 100,000 square miles of the Gran Chaco. Political instability ensued.

In 1965, a guerrilla movement mounted from Cuba and headed by Maj. Ernesto (Ché) Guevara began a revolutionary war. With the aid of U.S. military advisers, the Bolivian army smashed the guerrilla movement, capturing and killing Guevara on Oct. 8, 1967. Faltering steps toward restoration of civilian government were halted abruptly on July 17, 1980, when Gen. Luis Garcia Meza Tejada seized power. A series of military leaders followed before the military returned the government to civilian rule in 1982, when Hernán Siles Zuazo became president. Under Siles's left-of-center government, the country was regularly shut down by work stoppages, and the bulk of Bolivia's natural resources—natural gas, gold, lithium, potassium, and tungsten—were either sold on the black market or left in the ground. The country also had the lowest per capita income in South America, and inflation approached 3000%. In 1985, Siles decided he was unable to carry on and quit a year early.

Since 1985, Bolivia has implemented economic changes that have been phenomenally successful. Still at the bottom of the South American economic ladder, its economy has steadily improved over the past fifteen years. Political stability has helped. The standard joke about Bolivia's instability was to compare it to a long-playing record: "33 revolutions a minute."

In June 1993 Gonzalo Sánchez de Lozada was elected president, running on a platform calling for free-market policies and privatization. Former general Hugo Bánzer was elected president for the second time in Aug. 1997. Bánzer pledged to wipe out illicit coca production and drug trafficking in Bolivia by the end of his term in 2002. He has also initiated a rural literacy campaign and is implementing a plan for the poor to acquire loans.

Bosnia and Herzegovina

THE FEDERATION OF BOSNIA AND HERZEGOVINA

President: Ante Jelavic (Bosnian Croat) (1999)
Co-Prime Ministers: Alija Izetbegovic (Bosnian Muslim, and chairman) and Zivko Radisic (Bosnian Serb)
Area: 19,741 sq. mi. (51,233 sq. km)
Population (2000 est.): 3,835,777 (all data dealing with population is subject to considerable error because of

the dislocations caused by military action and ethnic cleansing); (average annual rate of natural increase: 0.5%); birth rate: 12.9/1000; infant mortality rate: 25.2/1000; density per sq. mi.: 194

Capital and largest city (1998 est.): Sarajevo, 387,876 (unofficial). **Other large cities:** Banja Luka, 220,407; Mostar, 208,904; Tuzla 118,500. **Monetary unit:** Dinar. **Language:** The language that used to be known as Serbo-Croatian but is now known as Serbian, Croatian, or Bosnian, depending on the speaker's ethnic and political affiliation. It is written in Latin and Cyrillic. **Ethnicity/race:** Serb 40%, Muslim 38%, Croat 22% (1998 est.). **Religions:** Slavic Muslim, 44%; Orthodox, 31%; Catholic, 15%; Protestant, 4%, other, 6%.

Economic summary: GDP/PPP (1998 est.): $5.8 billion; $1,720 per capita. **Real growth rate:** 30%, **Inflation:** n.a. **Unemployment:** 40%–50% (1996 est.) **Labor force:** 1,026,254. **Industries:** steel, coal, iron ore, lead, zinc, manganese, bauxite, vehicle assembly, textiles, tobacco products, wooden furniture, tank and aircraft assembly, domestic appliances, oil refining (much of capacity damaged or shut down) [1995]. **Agriculture:** wheat, corn, fruit, vegetables, livestock. **Exports:** $152 million (1995 est.). **Imports:** $1.1 billion (1995 est.). **Major trading partners:** n.a.

Geography Bosnia and Herzegovina make up a triangular-shaped republic, about half the size of Kentucky, on the Balkan peninsula. The Bosnian region in the north is mountainous and covered with thick forests. The Herzegovina region in the south is largely a rugged and flat farmland. It has a narrow coastline without natural harbors stretching 13 miles (20 km) along the Adriatic Sea.

Government Parliamentary democracy. Following the postwar general elections in 1996, a three-person multiethnic rotating presidency was formed.

History Since the time of the Roman Empire, the Balkans has been a crossroads of religions and civilizations. The ethnic groups now known as Bosnians, Croats, and Serbs are largely the result of different religious and cultural identities created by contact with neighboring empires that expanded and contracted in the Balkans over centuries. With minor differences, they speak the same language, called Serbo-Croatian or sometimes Bosnian.

Called Illyricum in ancient times, the Romans conquered the area now called Bosnia and Herzegovina in the 2nd and 1st centuries B.C. and folded it into the Roman province of Dalmatia. In the 4th and 5th centuries A.D. Goths overran that portion of the declining Roman Empire and occupied the area until the 6th century, when the Byzantine Empire claimed it. Slavs began settling the region during the 7th century A.D. Around 1200, Bosnia won independence from Hungary and endured as an independent Christian state for some 260 years.

The expansion of the Ottoman Empire into the Balkans introduced another cultural, political, and religious framework. The Turks defeated the Serbs at the famous battle of Kosovo in 1389. They conquered Bosnia in 1463. During the roughly 450 years Bosnian and Herzegovina were under Ottoman rule, many Christian Slavs became Muslim. A Bosnian Islamic elite gradually developed and ruled the country on behalf of the Turkish overlords. As the borders of the Ottoman Empire began to shrink in the 19th century, Muslims from elsewhere in the Balkans migrated to Bosnia. Bosnia also developed a sizable Jewish population, with many Jews settling in Sarajevo after their expulsion from Spain in 1492. However, through the 19th century the term "Bosnian" commonly included residents of all faiths. A relatively secular society, intermarriage among religious groups was not unknown.

Neighboring Serbia and Montenegro fought against the Ottoman Empire in 1876, and were aided by the Russians, their fellow Slavs. At the Congress of Berlin in 1878 following the end of the Russo-Turkish War (1877–78), Austria-Hungary was given a mandate to occupy and govern Bosnia and Herzegovina, in an effort by Europe to ensure that Russia did not dominate the Balkans. Although the provinces were still officially part of the Ottoman Empire, they were annexed by the Austro-Hungarian Empire on Oct. 7, 1908. As a result, relations with Serbia, which had claims on Bosnia and Herzegovina, became embittered. The hostility between the two countries climaxed in the assassination of Austrian Archduke Franz Ferdinand in Sarajevo on June 28, 1914, by a Serbian nationalist. This event precipitated the start of World War I (1914–18). Bosnia and Herzegovina were annexed to Serbia as part of the newly formed Kingdom of Serbs, Croats, and Slovenes on Oct. 26, 1918. The name was later changed to Yugoslavia in 1929.

When Germany invaded Yugoslavia in 1941, Bosnia and Herzegovina were made part of Nazi-controlled Croatia. During the German and Italian occupation, Bosnian and Herzegovinian resistance fighters fought a fierce guerrilla war against the Ustachi, the Croatian Fascist troops. At the end of World War II, Bosnia and Herzegovina were reunited into a single state as one of the six republics of the newly reestablished Communist Yugoslavia, under Marshall Tito. His authoritarian control kept the ethnic enmities of his patchwork nation in check. Tito died in 1980, and with growing economic dissatisfaction and the fall of the iron curtain over the next decade, Yugoslavia began to splinter.

In Dec. 1991, Bosnia and Herzegovina declared independence from Yugoslavia and asked for recognition by the European Union (EU). In a March 1992 referendum, Bosnian voters chose independence, and President Izetbegovic declared the nation an independent state. Unlike the other former Yugoslav states, which were generally composed of a dominant ethnic group, Bosnia was an ethnic tangle of Muslims (44%), Serbs (31%), and Croats (17%), and this mix contributed to the duration and savagery of its fight for independence.

Both the Croatian and Serbian presidents had planned to partition Bosnia between themselves. Attempting to carve out their own enclaves, the Serbian minority, with the help of the Serbian Yugoslav army, took the offensive and laid siege, particularly on Sarajevo, and began its ruthless campaigns of ethnic cleansing, which involved the expulsion or massacre of Muslims. Croats also began carving out their own communities. By the end of Aug. 1992, rebel Bosnian Serbs had conquered over 60% of Bosnia. The war did not begin to wane until NATO stepped in, bombing Serb positions in Bosnia in Aug. and Sept. 1995. This was followed by a joint offensive by Bosnian Muslim and Croatian forces that took back a significant amount of critical Bosnian territory.

U.S.-sponsored peace talks in Dayton, Ohio, led to an agreement in 1995 that called for a Muslim-Croat federation and a Serb entity within the larger federation of Bosnia. Sixty thousand NATO troops were to supervise its implementation. Fighting abated and orderly elections were held in Sept. 1996. President Alija Izetbegovic, a Bosnian Muslim, or Bosniac, won the majority of votes to become the leader of the three-member presidency, each representing one of the three ethnic groups.

But this alliance of unreconstructed enemies had little success in creating a working government or keeping violent clashes in check. The terms of the Dec. 1995 Dayton Peace Accord were largely ignored by Bosnian Serbs, with its former president, arch-nationalist Radovan Karadzic, still in de facto control of the Serbian enclave. Many indicted war criminals, including Karadzic, remain at large. Despite NATO's pledge in Oct. 1997 to remain in Bosnia beyond the 1998 mandate, the peacekeeping force remained mired in chronic ambivalence, unable to decide whether to jump into the fray or remain passive, hoping its presence was enough to spawn peace.

The crucial priorities facing postwar Bosnian leaders were rebuilding the economy, resettling the estimated one million refugees still displaced, and establishing a working government. Progress on these goals has been minimal, and a massive corruption scandal uncovered in 1999 severely tested the goodwill of the international community. Millions of dollars from international aid projects earmarked for reconstruction and humanitarian purposes had been pilfered by Bosnian officials, according to an American-led international antifraud unit. The country had received $5.1 billion in aid since 1995 by a hopeful international community supporting the dream that the quagmire of the Balkans could be surmounted.

In Aug. 2000 U.N. officials reported that a record 25,000 refugees returned to their homes since the start of the year. The situation remains somewhat unstable, however, with ethnic attacks still being reported. Land mines scattered through the country remain a threat and mass graves are occasionally uncovered.

Botswana

REPUBLIC OF BOTSWANA

President: Festus Mogae (1998)
Area: 231,800 sq. mi. (600,370 sq. km)
Population (2000 est.): 1,576,470 (average annual rate of natural increase: 0.8%); birth rate: 29.6/1000; infant mortality rate: 61.7/1000; density per sq. mi.: 7
Capital and largest city (1992 est.): Gaborone, 138,000. **Monetary unit:** Pula. **Languages:** English, Setswana. **Ethnicity/race:** Batswana 95%, Kalanga, Basarwa, and Kgalagadi 4%, white 1%. **Religions:** indigenous beliefs, 50%; Christian, 50%. **Literacy rate:** 69% (1993)
Economic summary: GDP/PPP (1998 est.): $5.25 billion; $3,600 per capita. **Real growth rate:** 3%. **Inflation:** 9% (1997 est.). **Unemployment:** 20%–40% (1997 est.). **Arable land:** 1%. **Agriculture:** sorghum, maize, millet, pulses, groundnuts (peanuts), beans, cowpeas, sunflower seed, livestock. **Labor force:** 235,000 formal sector employees; 100,000 public sector; 135,000 private sector, including 14,300 who are employed in various mines in South Africa; most others engaged in cattle raising and subsistence agriculture (1995 est.). **Industries:** diamonds, copper, nickel, coal, salt, soda ash, potash, livestock processing. **Natural resources:** diamonds, copper, nickel, salt, soda ash, potash, coal, iron ore, silver. **Exports:** $2.25 billion (f.o.b., 1998 est.): diamonds, 76%; nickel, 4%; copper, meat (1997). **Imports:** $2.43 billion (f.o.b., 1998 est.): foodstuffs, vehicles and transport equipment, textiles, petroleum products. **Major trading partners:** EU, Southern African Customs Union (SACU), Zimbabwe. **Member of Commonwealth of Nations**

Geography Twice the size of Arizona, Botswana is in south-central Africa, bounded by Namibia, Zambia, Zimbabwe, and South Africa. Most of the country is near-desert, with the Kalahari occupying the western part of the country. The eastern part is hilly, with salt lakes in the north.

Government Parliamentary democracy.

History The earliest inhabitants of the region were the San, who were followed by the Tswana. About half the country today is ethnic Tswana. The term for the country's people, *Batswana*, refers to national rather than ethnic origin.

Encroachment by the Zulu in the 1820s and by Boers from Transvaal in the 1870s and 1880s threatened the peace of the region. In 1885 Britain established the area as a protectorate, then known as Bechuanaland. In 1961, Britain granted a constitution to the country. Self-government began in 1965, and on Sept. 30, 1966, the country became independent. Botswana is Africa's oldest democracy.

The new country maintained good relations with its white-ruled neighbors, but gradually changed its policies, harboring rebel groups from South Rhodesia as well as some from South Africa.

Although Botswana is rich in diamonds, it has high unemployment and stratified socioeconomic classes. In 1999 it suffered its first budget deficit in 16 years because of a slump in the international diamond market. Yet it remains one of the wealthiest as well as most stable countries on the continent.

After 17 years in power, President Ketumile Masire retired in 1997, and Festus Mogae, an Oxford-educated economist, became the new president. Mogae has won high marks from the international financial community for continuing to privatize Botswana's mining and industrial operations. Botswana has also benefited from increased trade with South Africa, which was allowed to join the Southern African Development Community, a regional trade bloc, in 1994 when it adopted majority rule. AIDS, however, poses a major threat to Botswana, where some estimates indicate that 36% of its total population is infected, the highest rate in the world. In Aug. 2000 Mogae said health facilities around the nation would soon make AIDS drugs available and free to all who need them.

Brazil

FEDERATIVE REPUBLIC OF BRAZIL

National name: República Federativa do Brasil
President: Fernando Henrique Cardoso (1995)
Area: 3,286,470 sq. mi. (8,511,965 sq. km)
Population (2000 est.): 172,860,370 (average annual rate of natural increase: 0.95%); birth rate: 18.8/1000; infant mortality rate: 38/1000; density per sq. mi.: 53
Capital (1997 est.): Brasilia, 1,800,000. **Largest cities:** São Paulo (2000 est.), 17,900,000 (metro. area); Rio de Janeiro (2000 est.), 10,650,000 (metro. area); Porto Alegre, 3,000,000; Recife, 2,900,999; Salvador, 2,600,000; Belo Horizonte, 2,600,000. **Monetary unit:** Real. **Language:** Portuguese. **Ethnicity/race:** white (includes Portuguese, German, Italian, Spanish, Polish) 55%, mixed white and African 38%, African 6%, other (includes Japanese, Arab, Amerindian) 1%. **Religion:** Roman Catholic, 90% (nominal). **Literacy rate:** 81% (1990)
Economic summary: GDP/PPP (1998 est.): $1.0352 trillion; $6,100 per capita. **Real growth rate:** 0.5%. **Inflation:** 2%. **Unemployment:** 8.5%. **Arable land:** 5%. **Agriculture:** coffee, soybeans, wheat, rice, corn,

sugarcane, cocoa, citrus, beef. **Labor force:** 57 million (1989 est.): services, 42%; agriculture, 31%; industry, 27%. **Industries:** textiles, shoes, chemicals, cement, lumber, iron ore, tin, steel, aircraft, motor vehicles and parts, other machinery and equipment. **Natural resources:** bauxite, gold, iron ore, manganese, nickel, phosphates, platinum, tin, uranium, petroleum, hydropower, timber. **Exports:** $51 billion (f.o.b., 1998): iron ore, soybean bran, orange juice, footwear, coffee, motor vehicle parts. **Imports:** $57.6 billion (f.o.b., 1998): crude oil, capital goods, chemical products, foodstuffs, coal. **Major trading partners:** EU, Latin America, U.S., Argentina, Japan.

Geography Brazil covers nearly half of South America and is the continent's largest nation. It extends 2,965 miles (4,772 km) north-south, 2,691 miles (4,331 km) east-west, and borders every nation on the continent except Chile and Ecuador. Brazil may be divided into the Brazilian Highlands, or plateau, in the south and the Amazon River Basin in the north. More than a third of Brazil is drained by the Amazon and its more than 200 tributaries. The Amazon is navigable for ocean steamers to Iquitos, Peru, 2,300 miles (3,700 km) upstream. Southern Brazil is drained by the Plata system—the Paraguay, Uruguay, and Paraná Rivers. The most important stream entirely within Brazil is the São Francisco, navigable for 1,000 miles (1,903 km), but broken near its mouth by the 275-foot (84 m) Paulo Afonso Falls.

Government Federal republic.

History Brazil is the only Latin American nation that derives its language and culture from Portugal. The native inhabitants mostly consisted of the nomadic Tupí-Guaraní Indians. Adm. Pedro Alvares Cabral claimed the territory for Portugal in 1500. The early explorers brought back a wood that produced a red dye, *pau-brasil,* from which the land received its name. Portugal began colonization in 1532 and made the area a royal colony in 1549.

During the Napoleonic Wars, King João VI, fearing the advancing French armies, fled the country in 1808 and set up his court in Rio de Janeiro. João was drawn home in 1820 by a revolution, leaving his son as regent. When Portugal sought to reduce Brazil again to colonial status, the prince declared Brazil's independence on Sept. 7, 1822, and became Pedro I, emperor of Brazil. Harassed by his Parliament, Pedro I abdicated in 1831 in favor of his five-year-old son, who became emperor in 1840 (Pedro II). The son was a popular monarch, but discontent built up and, in 1889, following a military revolt, he had to abdicate. Although a republic was proclaimed, Brazil was ruled by military dictatorships until a revolt permitted a gradual return to stability under civilian presidents.

President Wenceslau Braz cooperated with the Allies and declared war on Germany during World War I. In World War II, Brazil again cooperated with the Allies, welcoming Allied air bases, patrolling the South Atlantic, and joining the invasion of Italy after declaring war on the Axis powers.

In the last of a long series of military coups, Gen. João Baptista de Oliveira Figueiredo became president in 1979 and pledged a return to democracy in 1985. The election of Tancredo Neves on Jan. 15, 1985, the first civilian president since 1964, brought a nationwide wave of optimism, but when Neves died on April 21, Vice President Sarney became president. Sarney was widely distrusted because he had previously been a member of the military regime's political party. Collor de Mello won the election of late

1989, pledging to lower the chronic hyperinflation by following the path of free-market economics. When Collor faced impeachment by Congress because of a corruption scandal in Dec. 1992 and resigned, Vice President Itamar Franco assumed the presidency.

A former finance minister, Fernando Cardoso won the presidency in the Oct. 1994 election with 54% of the vote. Cardoso has engineered the disposal of inefficient government-owned monopolies in the telecommunication, electrical power, port, mining, railway, and banking industries. In his short time in office Cardoso's economic acumen has made a measurable dent in Brazil's poverty level.

In Jan. 1999, the Asian economic crisis spread to Brazil. Rather than prop up the currency through financial markets, Brazil opted to let the currency float, which sent the real plummeting—at one time as much as 40%. Cardoso has been highly praised by the international community for quickly turning around his country's economic crisis. He has shown strong political courage in forcing belt-tightening measures on the economy, causing short-term misery and discontent in an effort to reap long-term stability and growth.

In 2000 Brazil's economy rebounded strongly from the slump. However, thousands of landless rural poor continued to stage large rallies to protest the government's austerity plan. In Aug. 2000, 50 people died and 120,000 fled their homes when torrential rains in Brazil's northeast submerged whole towns and caused severe mudslides.

Brunei Darussalam

STATE OF BRUNEI DARUSSALAM

Sultan: Haji Hassanal Bolkiah (1967)
Area: 2,226 sq. mi. (5,770 sq. km)
Population (2000 est.): 336,376 (annual rate of natural increase: 1.7%); birth rate: 20.8/1000; infant mortality rate: 14.8/1000; density per sq. mi.: 151
Capital and largest city (1991 est.): Bandar Seri Begawan, 52,300. **Other large cities:** Seria 23,511, Kuala Belait 19,335. **Monetary unit:** Brunei dollar.
Languages: Malay (official), Chinese, English.
Ethnicity/race: Malay 64%, Chinese 20%, other 16%.
Religions: Islam (official religion), 67%; Buddhist, 12%; Christian, 9%; indigenous beliefs and other, 12%. **Literacy rate:** 80% (1981)
Economic summary: GDP/PPP (1998 est.): $5.4 billion; $17,000 per capita. **Real growth rate:** -1%. **Inflation:** 2% (1997 est.). **Unemployment:** 4.8% (1994 est.).
Arable land: 1%. **Agriculture:** rice, cassava (tapioca), bananas, water buffalo. **Labor force:** 144,000 (1995 est.) (includes foreign workers and military personnel; temporary residents make up 41% of labor force [1991]); government, 48%; production of oil, natural gas, services, and construction, 42%; agriculture, forestry, and fishing, 4%; other, 6% (1986 est.). **Industries:** petroleum, petroleum refining, liquefied natural gas, construction. **Natural resources:** petroleum, natural gas, timber. **Exports:** $2.62 billion (f.o.b., 1996 est.): crude oil, liquefied natural gas, petroleum products. **Imports:** $2.65 billion (c.i.f., 1996 est.): machinery and transport equipment, manufactured goods, food, chemicals. **Major trading partners:** Association of Southeast Asian Nations (ASEAN), Japan, South Korea, U.K., Taiwan, Singapore, U.S., Malaysia

Geography About the size of Delaware, Brunei is an independent sultanate on the northwest coast of the island of Borneo in the South China Sea, wedged between the Malaysian states of Sabah and Sarawak.

Three-quarters of the thinly populated country is covered with tropical rain forest; there are rich oil and gas deposits.

Government Constitutional sultanate.

History Brunei (pronounced broon-eye) was trading with China during the 6th century A.D., and, through allegiance to the Javanese Majapahit kingdom (13th to 15th century), it came under Hindu influence. In the early 15th century, with the decline of the Majapahit kingdom and widespread conversion to Islam, Brunei became an independent sultanate. Brunei was a powerful state from the 16th to the 19th century, ruling over the northern part of Borneo and adjacent island chains. But it fell into decay and lost Sarawak in 1841, becoming a British protectorate in 1888 and a British dependency in 1905. Japan occupied Brunei during World War II; it was liberated by Australia in 1945.

The sultan regained control over internal affairs in 1959, but Britain retained responsibility for the state's defense and foreign affairs until 1984, when the sultanate became fully independent. Sultan Bolkiah was crowned in 1968 at the age of 22, succeeding his father, Sir Omar Ali Saifuddin, who had abdicated. During his reign, exploitation of the rich Seria oilfield had made the sultanate wealthy. Brunei has one of the highest per capita incomes in Asia, and the sultan is believed to be the richest man in the world after Microsoft's Bill Gates. In recent years, a sex scandal involving the royal family has rocked the nation and the sultan has had to punish his wayward younger brother, Prince Jefri, for squandering billions of dollars. In Feb. 2000, Prince Jefri was charged with misappropriation of state funds. During his tenure as finance minister and head of the Brunei Investment Agency, Jefri allegedly squandered about $15 billion on personal items and extravagant pet projects. In Aug. 1998, Oxford-educated Prince Al-Muhtadee Billah was inaugurated as heir to the 500-year-old monarchy.

Bulgaria

REPUBLIC OF BULGARIA

National name: Narodna Republika Bulgariya
President: Petur Stoyanov (1997)
Prime Minister: Ivan Kostov (1997)
Area: 42,823 sq. mi. (110,910 sq. km)
Population (2000 est.): 7,796,694 (average annual rate of natural increase: –0.7%); birth rate: 8.1/1000; infant mortality rate: 15.1/1000; density per sq. mi.: 182
Capital and largest city (1994 est.): Sofia, 1,113,674. **Largest cities (1994 est.):** Plovdiv, 345,205; Varna, 307,200; Burgas, 198,439; Ruse, 170,209. **Monetary unit:** Lev. **Language:** Bulgarian. **Ethnicity/race:** Bulgarian 85.3%, Turk 8.5%, Gypsy 2.6%, Macedonian 2.5%, Armenian 0.3%, Russian 0.2%, other 0.6%. **Religions:** Bulgarian Orthodox 85%, Muslim 13%, Jewish 0.8%, Roman Catholic 0.5%, Uniate Catholic 0.2%, Protestant, Gregorian-Armenian, and other 0.5%. **Literacy rate:** 93% (1970)
Economic summary: GDP/PPP (1998 est.): $33.6 billion; $4,100 per capita. **Real growth rate:** 4%. **Inflation:** 1%. **Unemployment:** 12.2%. **Arable land:** 37%. **Agriculture:** grain, oilseed, vegetables, fruit, tobacco, livestock. **Labor force:** 3.57 million (1996 est.). **Industries:** machine building and metal working, food processing, chemicals, textiles, construction materials, ferrous and nonferrous metals. **Exports:** $4.5 billion (f.o.b., 1998): machinery and equipment, metals, minerals, fuel, chemicals, plastics, food,

textiles. **Imports:** $4.6 billion (f.o.b., 1998 est.): fuel, minerals, raw materials, machinery and equipment, metals, ores, chemicals, plastics, food, textiles. **Major trading partners:** Italy, Germany, Turkey, Greece, Russia, U.S.

Geography Two mountain ranges and two great valleys mark the topography of Bulgaria, a country the size of Tennessee and situated on the Black Sea. The Balkan Mountains cross the center of the country, rising to a height of 6,888 feet (2,100 m). The Rhodope, Rila, and Pirin Mountains are to the west and south. The Maritsa is Bulgaria's principal river, and the Danube also flows through the country, forming most of the northern boundary with Romania.

Government Democratic republic.

History The Thracians lived in what is now known as Bulgaria from about 3500 B.C. They were incorporated into the Roman Empire by the first century A.D. At the decline of the empire, the Goths, Huns, Bulgars, and Avars invaded. The Bulgars, who crossed the Danube from the north in A.D. 679, took control of the region. Although the country bears the name of the Bulgars, the Bulgar language and culture died out, replaced by a Slavic language, writing, and religion. In 865, Boris I adopted Orthodox Christianity. The Bulgars twice conquered most of the Balkan peninsula between 893 and 1280. But in 1396 they were invaded by the Ottoman Empire, which made Bulgaria a Turkish province until 1878. Ottoman rule was harsh and inescapable, given Bulgaria's proximity to its oppressor. In 1878, Russia forced Turkey to give Bulgaria its independence after the Russo-Turkish War (1877–78), but the European powers, fearing Russia's and Bulgaria's dominance in the Balkans, intervened at the Congress of Berlin (1878), limited Bulgaria's territory, and fashioned it into a small principality ruled by the nephew of the Russian czar, Alexander of Battenburg.

Alexander was succeeded in 1887 by Prince Ferdinand of Saxe-Coburg-Gotha, who declared a kingdom independent of Russia on Oct. 5, 1908. In the First Balkan War (1912–13), Bulgaria and the other members of the Balkan League fought against Turkey to regain Balkan territory. Angered by the small portion of Macedonia it received after the battle—it considered Macedonia an integral part of Bulgaria—the country instigated the Second Balkan War (June–Aug. 1913) against Turkey as well as its former allies. Bulgaria lost the war and all the territory it had gained in the First Balkan War. Bulgaria joined Germany in World War I in the hope of again gaining Macedonia. After this second failure, Ferdinand abdicated in favor of his son in 1918. Boris III squandered Bulgaria's resources and assumed dictatorial powers in 1934–35. Bulgaria fought on the side of the Nazis in World War II, but after Russia declared war on Bulgaria on Sept. 5, 1944, Bulgaria switched sides. Three days later, on Sept. 9, 1944, a Communist coalition took control of the country and set up a government under Kimon Georgiev.

A Soviet-style People's Republic was established in 1947 and Bulgaria acquired the reputation of being the most slavishly loyal to Moscow of all the East European communist countries. The general secretary of the Bulgarian Communist Party, Todor Zhikov, resigned in 1989 after 35 years in power. His successor, Peter Mladenov, purged the Politburo, ended the Communist monopoly on power, and held free elections in May 1990 that led to a surprising victory for the Communists, renamed the Bulgarian Socialist Party (BSP). Mladenov was forced to resign in July 1990.

In Oct. 1991, the Union of Democratic Forces won, forming Bulgaria's first non-Communist government since 1946. Power has shifted back and forth between the pro-Western Union of Democratic Forces (UDF) and the BSP during the 1990s. The economy continued to deteriorate amid growing concern over the spread of organized crime. The new UDF government, led by Prime Minister Ivan Kostov, was elected in 1997 to overhaul the economic system and institute reforms aimed at stopping the rise of public corruption.

Burkina Faso

National name: Burkina Faso
President: Blaise Compaore (1991)
Prime Minister: Kadre Desire Ouedraogo (1996)
Area: 105,870 sq. mi. (274,200 sq. km)
Population (2000 est.): 11,946,065 (average annual rate of natural increase: 2.8%); birth rate: 45.3/1000; infant mortality rate: 108.5/1000; density per sq. mi.: 113
Capital and largest city (1994 est.): Ouagadougou, 500,000. **Monetary unit:** Franc CFA. **Languages:** French, tribal languages. **Ethnicity/race:** Mossi (about 24%), Gurunsi, Senufo, Lobi, Bobo, Mande, Fulani. **Religions:** Muslim, 50%; Christian (mainly Roman Catholic), 10%; indigenous beliefs, 40%. **Literacy rate:** 18% (1990)
Economic summary: GDP/PPP (1998 est.): $11.6 billion; $1,000 per capita. **Real growth rate:** 6%. **Inflation:** 2.5%. **Unemployment:** n.a. **Arable land:** 13%. **Agriculture:** peanuts, shea nuts, sesame, cotton, sorghum, millet, corn, rice, livestock. **Labor force:** 4.679 million (persons 10 years old and over, according to a sample survey taken in 1991): agriculture, 85%; industry, commerce, services, government (1998). **Industries:** cotton lint, beverages, agricultural processing, soap, cigarettes, textiles, gold. **Natural resources:** manganese, limestone, marble, gold, antimony, copper, nickel, bauxite, lead, phosphates, zinc, silver. **Exports:** 400 million (f.o.b., 1997 est.): cotton, animal products, gold. **Imports:** $700 million (f.o.b., 1997 est.): machinery, food products, petroleum. **Major trading partners:** Côte d'Ivoire, France, Italy, Mali, Togo, Nigeria.

Geography Slightly larger than Colorado, Burkina Faso, formerly known as Upper Volta, is a landlocked country in West Africa. Its neighbors are Côte d'Ivoire, Mali, Niger, Benin, Togo, and Ghana. The country consists of extensive plains, low hills, high savannas, and a desert area in the north.

Government Military rule since independence.

History Burkina Faso was originally inhabited by the Bobo, Lobi, and Gurunsi peoples, with the Mossi and Gurma peoples immigrating to the region in the 14th century. The lands of the Mossi empire became a French protectorate in 1897, and by 1903 France had subjugated the other ethnic groups. Called Upper Volta by the French, it became a separate colony in 1919, was partitioned among Niger, the Sudan, and Côte d'Ivoire in 1932, and was reconstituted in 1947. An autonomous republic within the French Community, Upper Volta became independent on Aug. 5, 1960.

President Maurice Yameogo was deposed on Jan. 3, 1966, by a military coup led by Col. Sangoulé Lamizana, who dissolved the National Assembly and suspended the constitution. Constitutional rule returned in 1978 with the election of an Assembly and a presidential vote in June in which Gen. Lamizana won by a narrow margin over three other candidates.

On Nov. 25, 1980, Col. Sayé Zerbo led a bloodless coup that toppled Lamizana. In turn, Maj. Jean-Baptist Ouedraogo ousted Zerbo on Nov. 7, 1982. But the real revolutionary change occurred the following year when a 33-year-old flight commander, Thomas Sankara, took control. A Marxist-Leninist, he challenged the traditional Mossi chiefs, advocated women's liberation, and allied with North Korea, Libya, and Cuba. To sever ties to the colonial past, Sankara changed the name of the country in 1984 to Burkina Faso, which combines two of the nation's languages and means "the land of upright men."

While Sankara's investments in schools, food production, and clinics brought some improvement in living standards, foreign investment declined, many businesses left the country, and unhappy labor unions began strikes. On Oct. 15, 1987, formerly loyal soldiers assassinated Sankara. His best friend and ally Blaise Compaoré became president. Compaoré immediately set about "rectifying" Sankara's revolution. In 1991 he agreed to economic reforms proposed by the World Bank. A new constitution paved the way for elections in 1991, which Compaoré won easily, although opposition parties boycotted.

In July 2000, the World Bank and the International Monetary Fund announced that Burkina Faso qualified for $700 million in debt relief under the Heavily Indebted Poor Countries Initiative. While Burkina Faso is considered one of the world's poorest countries, it has nevertheless avoided the vicious civil wars that have plagued many African countries.

Burma (Myanmar)

SEE MYANMAR.

Burundi

REPUBLIC OF BURUNDI

National name: Republika Y'Uburundi
President: Pierre Buyoya (1996)
Prime Minister: Frederic Bamvuginyumvira (1998)
Area: 10,747 sq. mi. (27,830 sq. km)
Population (2000 est.): 6,054,714 (average annual rate of natural increase: 2.4%); birth rate: 40.5/1000; infant mortality rate: 71.5/1000; density per sq. mi.: 563
Capital and largest city (1994 est.): Bujumbura, 300,000. **Other large city (est. 1982):** Gitega, 101,827. **Monetary unit:** Burundi franc. **Languages:** Kirundi and French (official), Swahili. **Ethnicity/race:** Hutu (Bantu) 85%, Tutsi (Hamitic) 14%, Twa (Pygmy) 1%. **Religions:** Roman Catholic, 62%; Protestant, 5%; indigenous, 32%. **Literacy rate:** 41% (1990)
Economic summary: GDP/PPP (1998 est.): $4.1 billion; $740 per capita. **Real growth rate:** 4.5%. **Inflation:** 17%. **Unemployment:** n.a. **Arable land:** 44%. **Agriculture:** coffee, cotton, tea, corn, sorghum, sweet potatoes, bananas, manioc (tapioca), beef, milk, hides. **Labor force:** 1.9 million: agriculture, 93%; government, 4%; industry and commerce, 1.5%; services, 1.5% (1983 est.). **Industries:** light consumer goods such as blankets, shoes, soap, assembly of imported components, public works construction, food processing. **Natural resources:** nickel, uranium, rare earth oxides, peat, cobalt, copper, unexploited platinum, vanadium. **Exports:** $49 million (f.o.b., 1998): coffee, tea, cotton, hides. **Imports:** $102 million (f.o.b., 1998): capital goods, petroleum products, foodstuffs, consumer goods. **Major trading partners:** U.K., Germany, Benelux, Switzerland, France, Japan.

Geography Wedged between Tanzania, the Democratic Republic of the Congo, and Rwanda in east-central Africa, Burundi occupies a high plateau divided by several deep valleys. It is equal in size to Maryland.

Government Republic.

History The original inhabitants of Burundi were the Twa, a Pygmy people who now make up only 1% of the population. While the Hutu and Tutsi are considered to be two separate ethnic groups, scholars point out that they speak the same language, have a history of intermarriage, and share many cultural characteristics. Traditionally, the differences between the two groups were occupational rather than ethnic. Agricultural people were considered Hutu, while the cattle-owning elite were identified as Tutsi. Supposedly Tutsi were tall and thin, while Hutu were short and square, but in fact it is often impossible to tell one from the other. The 1933 requirement by the Belgians that everyone carry an identity card indicating tribal ethnicity as Tutsi or Hutu increased the distinction. Since independence, repeated violence in both Burundi and Rwanda has increased ethnic differentiation between the groups. Since independence, the land-owning Tutsi aristocracy has dominated Burundi.

Burundi was once part of German East Africa. Belgium won a League of Nations mandate in 1923, and subsequently Burundi, with Rwanda, was transferred to the status of a United Nations trust territory. In 1962, Burundi gained independence and became a kingdom under Mwami Mwambutsa IV, a Tutsi. A Hutu rebellion took place in 1965, leading to brutal Tutsi retaliations. Mwambutsa was deposed by his son, Ntaré V, in 1966. Ntaré in turn was overthrown the same year in a military coup by Premier Michel Micombero, also a Tutsi. In 1970–71, a civil war erupted, leaving more than 100,000 Hutu dead.

On Nov. 1, 1976, Lt. Col. Jean-Baptiste Bagaza led a coup and assumed the presidency. He suspended the constitution and announced that a 30-member Supreme Revolutionary Council would be the governing body. In Sept. 1987 Bagaza was overthrown by Maj. Pierre Buyoya, who became president. Ethnic hatred again flared in Aug. 1988, and about 20,000 Hutu were slaughtered. Buyoya, however, began reforms to heal the country's ethnic rift. The Burundi Democracy Front's candidate, Melchior Ndadaye, won the country's first democratic presidential elections, held on June 2, 1993. Ndadaye, the first Hutu to assume power in Burundi, was killed within months during a coup. The second Hutu president, Cyprien Ntaryamira, was killed on April 6, 1994, when a plane carrying him and the Rwandan president was shot down. As a result, Hutu youth gangs began massacring Tutsi; the Tutsi-controlled army retaliated by killing Hutus.

The frequency of ethnic clashes increased, developing into a low-intensity civil war. A six-nation regional proposal to send troops into Burundi to maintain peace and order was devised in July 1996. Distrustful of the scheme, the Tutsi-dominated army led a coup deposing the Hutu president and installed Maj. Pierre Buyoya that month. More than 200,000 people have been killed since the conflict began, and both the Tutsi-dominated army and the Hutu rebel forces are responsible for the continuing slaughter. Nelson Mandela was appointed the new mediator for the civil war in early 2000.

Cambodia

King: Norodom Sihanouk (1991)
Prime Minister: Hun Sen (1993)
Area: 69,884 sq. mi. (181,040 sq. km)
Population (2000 est.): 12,212,306 (average annual rate of natural increase: 2.3%); birth rate: 33.5/1000; infant mortality rate: 66.8/1000; density per sq. mi.: 175
Capital and largest city (1991 est.): Phnom Penh, 900,000. **Monetary unit:** Riel. **Languages:** Khmer (official), French, English. **Ethnicity/race:** Khmer 90%, Vietnamese 5%, Chinese 1%, other 4%. **Religions:** 95% Theravada Buddhist, 5% others. **Literacy rate:** 69% (1996)
Economic summary: GDP/PPP (1998 est.): $7.8 billion; $700 per capita. **Real growth rate:** 0%. **Inflation:** 15%. **Arable land:** 13%. **Agriculture:** rice, rubber, corn, vegetables. **Labor force:** 2.5–3.0 million: agriculture, 80% (1997 est.). **Unemployment:** n.a. **Industries:** rice milling, fishing, wood and wood products, rubber, cement, gem mining, textiles. **Natural resources:** timber, gemstones, iron ore, manganese, phosphate, hydropower potential. **Exports:** $736 million (f.o.b., 1997 est.): timber, garments, rubber, soybeans, sesame. **Imports:** $1.1 billion (f.o.b., 1997 est.): cigarettes, gold, construction materials, petroleum products, machinery, motor vehicles. **Major trading partners:** Singapore, Japan, Thailand, Hong Kong, Indonesia, Malaysia, U.S., Vietnam, Australia.

Geography Situated on the Indochinese peninsula, Cambodia is bordered by Thailand and Laos on the north and Vietnam on the east and south. The Gulf of Siam is off the western coast. The country, the size of Missouri, consists chiefly of a large alluvial plain ringed by mountains and on the east by the Mekong River. The plain is centered on Lake Tonle Sap, which is a natural storage basin of the Mekong.

Government Constitutional monarchy.

History The area that is present-day Cambodia came under Khmer rule about A.D. 600, when the region was at the center of a vast empire that stretched over most of Southeast Asia. Under the Khmers, who were Hindus, a magnificent temple complex was constructed at Angkor. Buddhism was introduced in the 12th century during the rule of Jayavaram VII. However, the kingdom, then known as Kambuja, fell into decline after Jayavaram's reign and was nearly annihilated by Thai and Vietnamese invaders. Its power steadily diminished until 1863, when France colonized the region, joining Cambodia, Laos, and Vietnam into a single protectorate known as French Indochina.

The French quickly usurped all but ceremonial powers from the monarch, Norodom. When he died in 1904, the French passed over his sons and handed the throne to his brother, Sisowath. Sisowath and his son ruled until 1941, when Norodom Sihanouk was elevated to power. Sihanouk's coronation, along with the Japanese occupation during the war, worked to reinforce a sentiment among Cambodians that the region should be free from outside control. After World War II, Cambodians sought independence, but France was reluctant to part with its colony. Cambodia was granted independence within the French Union in 1949. But the French-Indochinese War provided an opportunity for Sihanouk to gain full military control of the country. He abdicated in 1955 in favor of his parents, remaining head of the government, and when his father died in 1960, became chief of state without returning to the throne. In 1963, he sought a guarantee of Cambodia's neutrality from all parties to the Vietnam War.

However, North Vietnamese and Vietcong troops had begun using eastern Cambodia as a safe haven from which to launch attacks into South Vietnam, making it increasingly difficult to stay out of the war. An indigenous Communist guerrilla movement known as the Khmer Rouge also began to put pressure on the government in Phnom Penh. On March 18, 1970, while Sihanouk was abroad, anti-Vietnamese riots broke out and Sihanouk was overthrown by Gen. Lon Nol. The Vietnam peace agreement of 1973 stipulated withdrawal of foreign forces from Cambodia, but fighting continued between Hanoi-backed insurgents and U.S.-supplied government troops.

Combat climaxed in April 1975 when the Lon Nol regime was overthrown by Pol Pot, leader of the Khmer Rouge forces. The four years of nightmarish Khmer Rouge rule led to the state-sponsored extermination of citizens by its own government. Between 1 million and 2 million people were massacred on the "killing fields" of Cambodia or worked to death through forced labor. Pol Pot's radical vision of transforming the country into a Marxist agrarian society led to the virtual extermination of the country's professional and technical class.

Pol Pot was ousted by Vietnamese forces on Jan. 8, 1979, and a new pro-Hanoi government led by Heng Samrin was installed. Pol Pot and 35,000 Khmer Rouge fighters fled into the hills of western Cambodia, where they were joined by forces loyal to the ousted Sihanouk in a guerrilla movement aimed at overthrowing the Heng Samrin government. The Vietnamese plan originally called for a withdrawal by early 1990 and a negotiated political settlement. The talks became protracted, however, and a U.N. agreement was not signed until 1992, when Sihanouk was appointed leader of an interim Supreme National Council to run the country until elections could be held in 1993.

Free elections in May 1993 saw the defeat of Heng Samrin's successor, Hun Sen, who refused to accept the outcome of the vote and insisted instead on a power-sharing agreement. Under the arrangement, Hun Sen and Sihanouk's son, Prince Norodom Ranariddh, would act as co–prime ministers.

The Khmer Rouge stronghold in the western jungles splintered in 1997, with factions either battling each other or defecting. Ranariddh and Hun Sen both courted Khmer Rouge factions in an effort to shore up their power. In early July, Hun Sen took advantage of the charged political atmosphere to depose Ranariddh, officially the first prime minister and the country's only popularly elected leader. Hun Sen later launched a brutal purge, executing more than 40 political opponents. Skirmishes between Ranariddh's forces and Hun Sen's troops continued through the fall. Meanwhile, King Norodom Sihanouk, a beloved but ineffectual figurehead, was unable to broker peace between Hun Sen and his son, Prince Ranariddh.

Shortly after the July coup, the Khmer Rouge organized a show trial of their notorious leader, Pol Pot, in an apparent bid to distance themselves from the bloody history of his regime. Visibly enfeebled from reported bouts with malaria, Pol Pot had not been seen by the West in more than two decades. He was sentenced to house arrest for his crimes against humanity. On April 15, 1998, Pol Pot died and his body was quickly cremated by former Khmer Rouge comrades.

In the July 1998 election, Hun Sen was victorious over opposition leaders Sam Rainsy and Prince Ranariddh, but the opposition parties accused him of voter fraud. Rainsy organized protests that turned into violent riots. Although Hun Sen's CCP Party won the most seats, it needed a coalition with Ranariddh's FUNCINPEC Party to reach the two-thirds majority needed to form a government. After months in limbo, a coalition government was formed in Nov. 1998, with Hun Sen as sole prime minister and Ranariddh accepting the lesser role of president of the National Assembly. With the election resolved, Cambodia was able to regain its U.N. seat, lost nearly a year earlier following Hun Sen's coup.

In 1999 and 2000, the government and U.N. officials held negotiations regarding a war crimes tribunal for senior Khmer Rouge officials. The U.N. is skeptical about the fairness of such a trial, given Hun Sen's foot-dragging and Cambodia's corrupt judicial system. In 1999 Cambodia arrested the last Khmer Rouge guerrilla at large, Ta Mok, as well as Kang Kech Iev, alias Duch, who ran the notorious Tuol Sleng prison. Numerous other high-ranking members of the Khmer Rouge (notably Ieng Sary and Khieu Samphan) live openly in Cambodia.

Cameroon

REPUBLIC OF CAMEROON

National name: République du Cameroun
President: Paul Biya (1988)
Prime Minister: Peter Musonge Mafani (1996)
Area: 183,569 sq. mi. (475,440 sq. km)
Population (2000 est.): 15,421,937 (average annual rate of natural increase: 2.5%); birth rate: 36.6/1000; infant mortality rate: 70.9/1000; density per sq. mi.: 84
Capital: Yaoundé. **Largest cities (1991 est.):** Douala, 908,000; Yaoundé, 730,000. **Monetary unit:** Franc CFA. **Languages:** French and English (both official); 24 major African language groups. **Ethnicity/race:** Cameroon Highlanders 31%, Equatorial Bantu 19%, Kirdi 11%, Fulani 10%, Northwestern Bantu 8%, Eastern Nigritic 7%, other African 13%, non-African less than 1%. **Religions:** 51% indigenous beliefs, 33% Christian, 16% Muslim. **Literacy rate:** 54% (1990)
Economic summary: GDP/PPP (1998 est.): $29.6 billion; $2,000 per capita. **Real growth rate:** 5%. **Inflation:** 2.5%. **Unemployment:** 30%. **Arable land:** 13%. **Agriculture:** coffee, cocoa, cotton, rubber, bananas, oilseed, grains, root starches, livestock, timber. **Labor force:** n.a. **Industries:** petroleum production and refining, food processing, light consumer goods, textiles, lumber. **Natural resources:** petroleum, bauxite, iron ore, timber, hydropower. **Exports:** $1.6 billion (f.o.b., 1998): crude oil and petroleum products, lumber, cocoa beans, aluminum, coffee, cotton. **Imports:** $1.3 billion (f.o.b., 1998): machines and electrical equipment, transport equipment, fuel, food. **Major trading partners:** Italy, Spain, France, Netherlands, Nigeria, U.S., Germany.

Geography Cameroon is a Central African nation on the Gulf of Guinea, bordered by Nigeria, Chad, the Central African Republic, the Republic of Congo, Equatorial Guinea, and Gabon. It is nearly twice the size of Oregon. Mount Cameroon (13,350 ft.; 4,069 m), near the coast, is the highest elevation in the country. The main rivers are the Benue, Nyong, and Sanaga.

Government After a 1972 plebiscite, a unitary nation was formed out of East and West Cameroon to replace the former federal republic.

History Bantu speakers were among the first groups to settle Cameroon, followed by the Muslim Fulani in the 18th and 19th centuries. The land escaped colonial rule until 1884, when treaties with tribal chiefs brought the area under German domination. After World War I, the League of Nations gave the French a mandate over 80% of the area, and the British 20% adjacent to Nigeria. After World War II, when the country came under a U.N. trusteeship in 1946, self-government was granted, and the Cameroon People's Union emerged as the dominant party by campaigning for reunification of French and British Cameroon and for independence. Accused of being under Communist control, the party waged a campaign of revolutionary terror from 1955 to 1958, when it was crushed. In British Cameroon, unification was also promoted by the leading party, the Kamerun National Democratic Party, led by John Foncha.

France set up Cameroon as an autonomous state in 1957, and the next year its legislative assembly voted for independence by 1960. In 1959 a fully autonomous government of Cameroon was formed under Ahmadou Ahidjo. Cameroon became an independent republic on Jan. 1, 1960. In 1961 the southern part of the British territory joined the new Federal Republic of Cameroon and the northern section voted for unification with Nigeria. The president of Cameroon since independence, Ahmadou Ahidjo, was replaced in 1982 by the prime minister, Paul Biya. Both administrations were characterized by authoritarian rule.

Calls for reform eventually resulted in the adoption of a new constitution in 1996, which gave the president considerable power, although it did mandate regional and local elections. In 1997 Biya was not challenged for reelection. With the expansion of oil, timber, and coffee exports, the economy has continued to improve, although corruption is prevalent, and environmental degradation remains a concern. In June 2000 the World Bank agreed to provide more than $200 million to build a $3.7 billion pipeline connecting the oil fields in neighboring Chad with the Cameroon coast.

Canada

Sovereign: Queen Elizabeth II (1952)
Governor-General: Adrienne Clarkson (1999)
Prime Minister: Jean Chrétien (1993)
Area: 3,851,809 sq. mi. (9,976,140 sq. km)
Population (2000 est.): 31,281,092. Average annual rate of natural increase: 0.4%; birth rate: 11.4/1000; infant mortality rate: 5.1/1000; density per sq. mi.: 8
Capital: Ottawa, Ontario. **Largest cities (1996 census; metropolitan areas):** Toronto, 4,263,757; Montreal, 3,326,510; Vancouver, 1,831,665; Ottawa/Hull, 1,010,498; Edmonton, 862,597; Calgary, 821,628; Quebec, 671,889; Winnipeg, 667,209; Hamilton, 624,360; London, 398,616. **Monetary unit:** Canadian dollar. **Languages:** English, French (both official). **Ethnicity/race:** British Isles origin 40%, French origin 27%, other European 20%, indigenous Indian and Inuit 1.5%, other, mostly Asian 11.5%. **Religions:** 46% Roman Catholic, 16% United Church, 10% Anglican. **Literacy rate:** 96% (1986)
Economic summary: GDP/PPP (1998 est.): $688.3 billion; $22,400 per capita. **Real growth rate:** 3%. **Inflation:** 0.9%. **Unemployment:** 7.8% (Dec. 1999). **Arable land:** 5%. **Agriculture:** wheat, barley, oilseed, tobacco, fruit, vegetables, dairy products, forest products, fish. **Labor force:** 15.8 million (1998): services, 75%; manufacturing, 16%; construction, 5%; agriculture, 3%; other, 1% (1997). **Industries:** processed and unprocessed minerals, food products, wood and paper products, transportation equipment, chemicals, fish products, petroleum and natural gas. **Exports:** $210.7 billion (f.o.b., 1998): motor vehicles and parts, newsprint, wood pulp, timber, crude petroleum, machinery, natural gas, aluminum, telecommunications equipment. **Natural resources:** nickel, zinc, copper, gold, lead, molybdenum, potash, silver, fish, timber, wildlife, coal, petroleum, natural gas. **Imports:** $202.7 billion (f.o.b., 1998): machinery and equipment, crude oil, chemicals, motor vehicles and parts, durable consumer goods. **Major trading partners:** U.S., Japan, U.K., Germany, South Korea, Netherlands, China, France, Mexico, Taiwan.

Geography Covering most of the northern part of the North American continent and with an area larger than that of the United States, Canada has an extremely varied topography. In the east the mountainous maritime provinces have an irregular coastline on the Gulf of St. Lawrence and the Atlantic. The St. Lawrence plain, covering most of southern Quebec and Ontario, and the interior continental plain, covering southern Manitoba and Saskatchewan and most of Alberta, are the principal cultivable areas. They are separated by a forested plateau rising from Lakes Superior and Huron.

Westward toward the Pacific, most of British Columbia, Yukon, and part of western Alberta are covered by parallel mountain ranges, including the Rockies. The Pacific border of the coast range is ragged with fjords and channels. The highest point in Canada is Mount Logan (19,850 ft.; 6,050 m), which is in the Yukon. The two principal river systems are the Mackenzie and the St. Lawrence. The St. Lawrence, with its tributaries, is navigable for over 1,900 miles (3,058 km).

Government Canada is a federation of 10 provinces (Alberta, British Columbia, Manitoba, New Brunswick, Newfoundland, Nova Scotia, Ontario, Prince Edward Island, Quebec, and Saskatchewan) and three territories (Northwest Territories, Yukon, and as of April 1, 1999, Nunavut), most of whose powers were spelled out in the British North America Act of 1867. With the passing of the Constitutional Act of 1982, the act and the constitutional amending power were transferred from the British Parliament to Canada so that the Canadian constitution is now entirely in the hands of Canadians.

While the governor-general is officially the representative of Queen Elizabeth II, in reality the

Population by Provinces and Territories

Province	1998	1999
	(in thousands)	
Alberta	2,914.5	2,964.7
British Columbia	4,008.9	4,023.1
Manitoba	1,138.6	1,143.5
New Brunswick	752.9	755.0
Newfoundland	543.8	541.0
Nova Scotia	934.2	939.8
Ontario	11,413.6	11,513.8
Prince Edward Island	136.5	138.0
Quebec	7,334.5	7,345.4
Saskatchewan	1,024.2	1,027.8
Northwest Territories	67.3	41.6
Yukon Territory	31.7	30.6
Nunavut	25.0	27.0

Source: Statistics Canada.

Canadian Prime Ministers since 1867

Term	Prime Minister	Party	Term	Prime Minister	Party
1867–1873	Sir John A. Macdonald	Conservative	1926–1930	W. L. Mackenzie King	Liberal
1873–1878	Alexander Mackenzie	Liberal	1930–1935	Richard B. Bennett	Conservative
1878–1891	Sir John A. Macdonald	Conservative	1935–1948	W. L. Mackenzie King	Liberal
1891–1892	Sir John J. C. Abbott	Conservative	1948–1957	Louis S. St. Laurent	Liberal
1892–1894	Sir John S. D. Thompson	Conservative	1957–1963	John G. Diefenbaker	Conservative
1894–1896	Sir Mackenzie Bowell	Conservative	1963–1968	Lester B. Pearson	Liberal
1896	Sir Charles Tupper	Conservative	1968–1979	Pierre Elliott Trudeau	Liberal
1896–1911	Sir Wilfrid Laurier	Liberal	1979–1980	Charles Joseph Clark	Conservative
1911–1917	Sir Robert L. Borden	Conservative	1980–1984	Pierre Elliott Trudeau	Liberal
1917–1920	Sir Robert L. Borden	Unionist	1984–1984	John Turner	Liberal
1920–1921	Arthur Meighen	Unionist	1984–1993	Brian Mulroney	Conservative
1921–1926	W. L. Mackenzie King	Liberal	1993–1993	Kim Campbell	Conservative
1926	Arthur Meighen	Conservative	1993–	Jean Chrétien	Liberal

governor-general acts only upon the advice of the Canadian prime minister.

History The first inhabitants of Canada were native Indian peoples, primarily the Inuit (Eskimo). The Norse explorer Leif Eriksson probably reached the shores of Canada (Labrador or Nova Scotia) in A.D. 1000, but the history of the white man in the country actually began in 1497, when John Cabot, an Italian in the service of Henry VII of England, reached Newfoundland or Nova Scotia. Canada was taken for France in 1534 by Jacques Cartier. The actual settlement of New France, as it was then called, began in 1604 at Port Royal in what is now Nova Scotia; in 1608, Quebec was founded. France's colonization efforts were not very successful, but French explorers by the end of the 17th century had penetrated beyond the Great Lakes to the western prairies and south along the Mississippi to the Gulf of Mexico. Meanwhile, the English Hudson's Bay Company had been established in 1670. Because of the valuable fisheries and fur trade, a conflict developed between the French and English; in 1713, Newfoundland, Hudson Bay, and Nova Scotia (Acadia) were lost to England. During the Seven Years' War (1756–63), England extended its conquest, and the British Maj. Gen. James Wolfe won his famous victory over Gen. Louis Montcalm outside Quebec on Sept. 13, 1759. The Treaty of Paris in 1763 gave England control.

At that time the population of Canada was almost entirely French, but in the next few decades, thousands of British colonists emigrated to Canada from the British Isles and from the American colonies. In 1849, the right of Canada to self-government was recognized. By the British North America Act of 1867, the dominion of Canada was created through the confederation of Upper and Lower Canada, Nova Scotia, and New Brunswick. Prince Edward Island joined the dominion in 1873. In 1869, Canada purchased from the Hudson's Bay Company the vast middle west (Rupert's Land) from which the provinces of Manitoba (1870), Alberta (1905), and Saskatchewan (1905) were later formed. In 1871, British Columbia joined the dominion. The country was linked from coast to coast in 1885 by the Canadian Pacific Railway.

During the formative years between 1866 and 1896, the Conservative Party, led by Sir John A. Macdonald, governed the country, except during the years 1873–78. In 1896, the Liberal Party took over and, under Sir Wilfrid Laurier, an eminent French Canadian, ruled until 1911. By the Statute of Westminster in 1931 the British dominions, including Canada, were formally declared to be partner nations with Britain, "equal in status, in no way subordinate to each other," and bound together only by allegiance to a common Crown.

Newfoundland became Canada's 10th province on March 31, 1949, following a plebiscite. Canada also includes three territories—the Yukon Territory, the Northwest Territories, and the newest territory, Nunavut. This area includes all of the Arctic north of the mainland, Norway having recognized Canadian sovereignty over the Svendrup Islands in the Arctic in 1931.

The Liberal Party, led by William Lyon Mackenzie King, dominated Canadian politics from 1921 until 1957, when it was succeeded by the Progressive Conservatives. The Liberals, under the leadership of Lester B. Pearson, returned to power in 1963. Pearson remained prime minister until 1968, when he retired and was replaced by a former law professor, Pierre Elliott Trudeau. Trudeau maintained Canada's defensive alliance with the United States, but began moving toward a more independent policy in world affairs. Trudeau's election was considered in part a response to the most serious problem confronting the country, the division between French- and English-speaking Canadians, which had led to a separatist movement in the predominantly French province of Quebec. In 1974, the provincial government voted to make French the official language of Quebec. In Dec. 1979, the Quebec law making French the exclusive official language of the province was voided by the Canadian Supreme Court. Resolving a dispute that had occupied Trudeau since the beginning of his tenure, Queen Elizabeth II, in Ottawa on April 17, 1982, signed the Constitution Act, cutting the last legal tie between Canada and Britain. The constitution retains Queen Elizabeth as queen of Canada and keeps Canada's membership in the Commonwealth.

In the national election on Sept. 4, 1984, the Progressive Conservative Party scored an overwhelming victory, fundamentally changing the country's political landscape. The Conservatives, led by Brian Mulroney, won the highest political majority in Canadian history. The dominant foreign issue was a free-trade pact with the U.S., a treaty bitterly opposed by the Liberal and New Democratic Parties. The conflict led to elections in Nov. 1988 that solidly reelected Mulroney and gave him a mandate to proceed with the agreement.

The issue of separatist sentiments in French-speaking Quebec flared up again in 1990 with the failure of the Meech Lake Accord. The accord was designed to ease the Quebecers' fear of losing their identity within the English-speaking majority by giving Quebec constitutional status as a "distinct society." In an attempt to keep Canada united, the three major political parties came to an agreement in Feb. 1992 on constitutional reforms. Voters in the Northwest Territories authorized the division of their region in two, creating a homeland for Canadian Eskimos, the Inuits, which in April 1999 became the territory of Nunavut. Also in 1992, Canada announced its decision to withdraw its combat units from NATO command. The economy continued to be mired in a long recession that many blamed on the free-trade agreement. A national referendum was held in Oct. 1992 on the proposal to change the constitution to ensure greater representation in Parliament for the more populous regions and thereby the French-speaking Quebecers. The referendum, however was defeated.

Brian Mulroney's popularity continued to decline, causing him to resign before the next election. In June 1993 the governing Progressive Conservative Party chose Defense Minister Kim Campbell as its leader, making her the first female prime minister in Canadian history. The national election in Oct. 1993 resulted in the reemergence of the Liberal Party and the installation of Jean Chrétien as prime minister.

The Quebec referendum on secession in Oct. 1995 yielded a narrow rejection of the proposal. But separatists vowed to try again. Early parliamentary elections in June 1997 gave a reduced majority to the ruling Liberals. The Reform Party, based largely in the West, replaced the Bloc Quebecois as the official opposition.

On April 1, 1999, the Northwest Territories were officially divided to create a new territory in the east that would be governed by Canada's Inuits, who make up 85% of the area's population. Composed of 770,000 square miles of mostly snow and ice reaching well to the north of the Arctic Circle, the 25,000 residents of Nunavut will be governed from the new capital, Iqaluit.

In July 2000, Stockwell Day of the newly formed Canadian Alliance Party unexpectedly emerged as the leader of Canada's opposition. Running on a strongly conservative platform, he is expected to oppose Prime Minister Jean Chrétien in elections scheduled for spring 2001.

Cape Verde

REPUBLIC OF CAPE VERDE

National name: República de Cabo Verde
President: Antonio Mascarenhas Monteiro (1991)
Prime Minister: Guaberto do Rosário (2000)
Area: 1,557 sq. mi. (4,030 sq. km)
Population: (1999 est.): 401,343 (average annual rate of natural increase: 2.2%); birth rate: 29.7/1000; infant mortality rate: 54.6/1000; density per sq. mi.: 258
Capital (1990): Praia, 61,797. **Other large city (est. 1982):** Mindelo, 50,000. **Monetary unit:** Cape Verdean escudo. **Languages:** Portuguese, Criuolo.
Ethnicity/race: Creole (mulatto) 71%, African 28%, European 1%. **Religion:** Roman Catholic fused with indigenous beliefs. **Literacy rate:** 67% (1989)
Economic summary: GDP/PPP (1998 est.): $581 million; $1,450 per capita. **Real growth rate:** 7%. **Inflation:** 4.3%. **Unemployment:** n.a. **Arable land:** 11%. **Agriculture:** bananas, corn, beans, sweet potatoes, sugarcane, coffee, peanuts, fish. **Labor force:** n.a. **Industries:** food and beverages, fish processing, shoes and garments, salt mining, ship repair. **Natural resources:** salt, basalt rock, pozzuolana (volcanic ash used to produce hydraulic

cement), limestone, kaolin, fish. **Exports:** $43 million (f.o.b., 1997 est.): shoes, garments, fish, bananas, hides. **Imports:** $215 million (f.o.b., 1997 est.): foodstuffs, consumer goods, industrial products, transport equipment, fuel. **Major trading partners:** Portugal, Germany, Spain, France, U.K., Malaysia, Netherlands, U.S.

Geography Cape Verde, only slightly larger than Rhode Island, is an archipelago in the Atlantic 385 miles (500 km) west of Senegal.

The islands are divided into two groups: Barlavento in the north, composed of Santo Antão (291 sq. mi.; 754 sq. km), Boa Vista (240 sq. mi.; 622 sq. km), São Nicolau (132 sq. mi.; 342 sq. km), São Vicente (88 sq. mi.; 246 sq. km), Sal (83 sq. mi.; 298 sq. km), and Santa Luzia (13 sq. mi.; 34 sq. km); and Sotavento in the south, consisting of São Tiago (383 sq. mi.; 992 sq. km), Fogo (184 sq. mi.; 477 sq. km), Maio (103 sq. mi.; 267 sq. km), and Brava (25 sq. mi.; 65 sq. km). The islands are mostly mountainous, with the land deeply scarred by erosion. There is an active volcano on Fogo.

Government Republic.

History Uninhabited upon their discovery in 1456, the Cape Verde islands became part of the Portuguese empire in 1495. A majority of their modern inhabitants are of mixed Portuguese and African ancestry.

Positioned on the great trade routes between Africa, Europe, and the New World, the islands became a prosperous center for the slave trade, but suffered economic decline after the slave trade was abolished in 1876. In the 20th century Cape Verde served as a shipping port.

In 1951 Cape Verde's status changed from a Portuguese colony to an overseas province, and in 1961 the inhabitants became full Portuguese citizens. An independence movement led by the African Party for the Independence of Guinea-Bissau (another former Portuguese colony) and Cape Verde (PAIGC) was founded in 1956, and on July 5, 1975, the islands became independent.

Elections on Jan. 13, 1991, the first free elections since independence, resulted in the ruling African Party for the Independence of Cape Verde losing its majority to the Movement for Democracy Party, whose candidate, Antonio Monteiro, won the subsequent presidential election. Monteiro handily won reelection in 1996.

In an effort to take advantage of its proximity to cross-Atlantic sea and air lanes, the government has embarked on a major expansion of its port and airport capacities. It is also modernizing the fishing fleet and enhancing its fish processing industry. These projects are being partly paid for by the European Community and the World Bank, making Cape Verde one of the largest per capita aid recipients in the world.

Central African Republic

National name: République Centrafricaine
Head of Government: Gen. André Kolingba (1986)
President: Ange-Félix Patassé (1993)
Prime Minister: Anicet Georges Dologuele (1999)
Area: 241,313 sq. mi. (622,980 sq. km)
Population (2000 est.): 3,512,751 (average annual rate of natural increase: 1.9%); birth rate: 37.5/1000; infant mortality rate: 106.7/1000; density per sq. mi.: 15
Capital and largest city (1990 est.): Bangui, 706,000.
Monetary unit: Franc CFA. **Languages:** French (official), Sangho, Arabic, Hansa, Swahili. **Ethnicity/**

race: Baya 34%, Banda 27%, Sara 10%, Mandjia 21%, Mboum 4%, M'Baka 4%, Europeans 6,500 (including 3,600 French). **Religions:** 24% indigenous beliefs, 50% Protestant and Roman Catholic with animist influence, 15% Muslim, 11% other. **Literacy rate:** 38% (1990)

Economic summary: GDP/PPP (1998 est.): $5.5 billion; $1,640 per capita. **Real growth rate:** 5.5%. **Inflation:** 2.6%. **Unemployment:** 6% (1993). **Arable land:** 3%. **Agriculture:** cotton, coffee, tobacco, manioc (tapioca), yams, millet, corn, bananas, timber. **Labor force:** n.a. **Industries:** diamond mining, sawmills, breweries, textiles, footwear, assembly of bicycles and motorcycles. **Natural resources:** diamonds, uranium, timber, gold, oil. **Exports:** $182 million (f.o.b., 1998): diamonds, timber, cotton, coffee, tobacco. **Imports:** $155 million (f.o.b., 1998): food, textiles, petroleum products, machinery, electrical equipment, motor vehicles, chemicals, pharmaceuticals, consumer goods, industrial products. **Major trading partners:** Belgium-Luxembourg, Côte d'Ivoire, Spain, Egypt, France, Cameroon, Germany, Japan.

Geography Situated about 500 miles (805 km) north of the equator, the Central African Republic is a landlocked nation bordered by Cameroon, Chad, the Sudan, the Democratic Republic of the Congo, and the Republic of Congo.

Twice the size of New Mexico, it is covered by tropical forests in the south and semidesert land in the east. The Ubangi and the Shari are the largest of many rivers.

Government Multiparty republic since 1991.

History From the 16th to 19th centuries, the people of this region were ravaged by slave traders. The Banda, Baya, Ngbandi, and Azande make up the largest ethnic groups.

The French occupied the region in 1894. As the colony of Ubangi-Shari, what is now the Central African Republic was united with Chad in 1905. In 1910 it was joined with Gabon and the Middle Congo to become French Equatorial Africa. After World War II a rebellion in 1946 forced the French to grant self-government. In 1958 the territory voted to become an autonomous republic within the French Community, and on Aug. 13, 1960, President David Dacko proclaimed the republic's independence from France. Dacko moved the country into Beijing's orbit, but was overthrown in a coup on Dec. 31, 1965, by Col. Jean-Bédel Bokassa, army chief of staff.

On Dec. 4, 1976, the Central African Republic became the Central African Empire. Marshal Jean-Bédel Bokassa, who had ruled the republic since he took power in 1965, was declared Emperor Bokassa I. Brutality and excess characterized his regime. He was overthrown in a coup on Sept. 20, 1979. Former president David Dacko returned to power and changed the country's name back to the Central African Republic. An army coup on Sept. 1, 1981, deposed President Dacko again.

In 1991, President André Kolingba, under pressure, announced a move toward parliamentary democracy. In elections held in Aug. 1993, Prime Minister Ange-Félix Patassé defeated Kolingba. Part of Patassé's popularity rested on his pledge to pay the back salaries of the military and civil servants.

A 1994 economic upturn was too small to effectively improve the catastrophic financial condition of the nation. Patassé was unable to pay the salaries due government workers and the military revolted in 1996. At Patassé's request, French troops suppressed the uprising. In 1998 the United Nations sent an all-African peacekeeping force to the country. In elections held in Sept. 1999, amid widespread charges of massive fraud, Patassé easily defeated Kolingba, and several other candidates.

Chad

REPUBLIC OF CHAD

National name: République du Tchad
President: Lieut. Gen. Idriss Déby (1990)
Prime Minister: Nagoum Yamassoum (1999)
Area: 495,752 sq. mi. (1,284,000 sq. km)
Population (2000 est.): 8,424,504 (average annual rate of natural increase, 3.3%); birth rate: 48.8/1000; infant mortality rate: 96.7/1000; density per sq. mi.: 17
Capital and largest city (1993): N'Djamena, 529,555.
Monetary unit: Franc CFA. **Languages:** French and Arabic (official), more than 100 tribal languages.
Ethnicity/race: North and center: Muslims (Arabs, Toubou, Hadjerai, Fulbe, Kotoko, Kanembou, Baguirmi, Boulala, Zaghawa, and Maba); South: non-Muslims (Sara [the largest ethnic group, 25% of the population], Ngambaye, Mbaye, Goulaye, Moundang, Moussei, Massa). **Religions:** Islam, 44%; Christian, 33%; traditional, 23%. **Literacy rate:** 30% (1990)
Economic summary: GDP/PPP (1998 est.): $7.5 billion; $1,000 per capita. **Real growth rate:** 2.9%. **Inflation:** 15% (1997 est.). **Unemployment:** n.a. **Arable land:** 3%. **Agriculture:** cotton, sorghum, millet, peanuts, rice, potatoes, manioc (tapioca), cattle, sheep, goats, camels. **Labor force:** n.a.: agriculture, 85%. **Industries:** cotton textiles, meat packing, beer brewing, natron (sodium carbonate), soap, cigarettes, construction materials. **Natural resources:** petroleum, uranium, natron, kaolin, fish. **Exports:** $220 million (f.o.b., 1998 est.): cotton, cattle, textiles. **Imports:** $252 million (f.o.b., 1998 est.): machinery and transportation equipment, industrial goods, petroleum products, foodstuffs, textiles. **Major trading partners:** Portugal, Germany, Thailand, Costa Rica, South Africa, France, Nigeria, Cameroon, India.

Geography A landlocked country in north-central Africa, Chad is about 85% the size of Alaska. Its neighbors are Niger, Libya, the Sudan, the Central African Republic, Cameroon, and Nigeria. Lake Chad, from which the country gets its name, lies on the western border with Niger and Nigeria. In the north is a desert that runs into the Sahara.

Government Republic.

History The area around Lake Chad has been inhabited since at least 500 B.C. In the 8th century A.D. Berbers began migrating to the area. Islam arrived in 1085, and by the 16th century a trio of rival kingdoms flourished: the Kanem-Bornu, the Baguirmi, and Ouaddaï. In 1883–93, all three kingdoms came under the rule of the Sudanese conqueror Rabih al-Zubayr. In 1900, Rabih was overthrown by the French, who absorbed these kingdoms into the colony of French Equatorial Africa, as part of Ubangi-Shari, in 1910.

France began the country's development after 1920, when it became a separate colony. In 1946, French Equatorial Africa was admitted to the French Union, and in 1958 the Chad territory became an autonomous republic within the French Union. An independence movement led by the first premier and president, François (later Ngarta) Tombalbaye, achieved complete independence on Aug. 11, 1960. Tombalbaye was killed in the 1975 coup and succeeded by Gen. Félix Malloum, who faced a Libyan-financed civil war throughout his tenure in office. In

1977 Libya seized a strip of Chadian land and launched an invasion two years later.

Nine rival groups meeting in Lagos, Nigeria, in March 1979 agreed to form a provisional government headed by Goukouni Oueddei, a former rebel leader. Fighting broke out again in Chad in March 1980, when Defense Minister Hissen Habré challenged Goukouni and seized the capital. Libyan president Muammar al-Qaddafi in Jan. 1981 proposed a merger of Chad with Libya. The Libyan proposal was rejected and Libyan troops withdrew from Chad that year, but in 1983 they poured back into the northern part of the country in support of Goukouni. France, in turn, sent troops into southern Chad in support of Habré. Government troops then launched an offensive in early 1987 that drove the Libyans out of most of the country.

In 1990 Idriss Déby, a former defense minister and head of a rebel group, the Patriotic Salvation Movement, overthrew Habré, suspended the constitution, and dissolved the legislature. In 1994 a new constitution was drafted and an amnesty for political prisoners was declared. Déby won multiparty elections in 1996 and his party won legislative elections the following year. International observers said the elections were fair, although Déby's opponents charged voter fraud.

Chad continues to grapple with insurgencies in both the southern and northern parts of the country, as well as with massive economic and environmental problems. In June 2000 the World Bank agreed to provide more than $200 million to build a $3.7 billion pipeline connecting the oil fields in neighboring Chad with the Cameroon coast.

Chile

REPUBLIC OF CHILE

National name: República de Chile
President: Ricardo Lagos (2000)
Area: 292,132 sq. mi. (756,950 sq. km)
Population (2000 est.): 15,153,797 (average annual rate of natural increase: 1.2%); birth rate: 17.2/1000; infant mortality rate: 9.6/1000; density per sq. mi.: 52
Capital and largest city (2000 est.): Santiago, 5,400,000 (metro. area). **Other large cities (1996 est.):** Concepción, 356,371; Viña del Mar, 326,448; Valparaíso, 282,850; Talcahuano, 265,060; Temuco, 246,304. **Monetary unit:** Peso. **Language:** Spanish. **Ethnicity/race:** European and European-Indian 95%, Indian 3%, other 2%. **Religions:** Roman Catholic, 89%; Protestant, 11%; small Jewish and Muslim populations. **Literacy rate:** 95% (1992)
Economic summary: GDP/PPP (1998 est.): $184.6 billion; $12,500 per capita. **Real growth rate:** 3.5%. **Inflation:** 4.7%. **Unemployment:** 6.4%. **Arable land:** 5%. **Agriculture:** wheat, corn, grapes, beans, sugar beets, potatoes, fruit, beef, poultry, wool, timber, fish. **Labor force:** 5.8 million (1998 est.): services, 38.3%; industry and commerce, 33.8%; agriculture, forestry, and fishing, 19.2%; mining, 2.3%; construction, 6.4% (1990). **Industries:** copper, other minerals, foodstuffs, fish processing, iron and steel, wood and wood products, transport equipment, cement, textiles. **Natural resources:** copper, timber, iron ore, nitrates, precious metals, molybdenum. **Exports:** $14.9 billion (f.o.b., 1998): copper, other metals and minerals, wood products, fish and fishmeal, fruit (1994). **Imports:** $17.5 billion (f.o.b., 1998): capital goods, spare parts, raw materials, petroleum, foodstuffs (1994). **Major trading partners:** EU, U.S., Asia, Latin America.

Geography Situated south of Peru and west of Bolivia and Argentina, Chile fills a narrow 1,800-mile (2,897 km) strip between the Andes and the Pacific. Its area is nearly twice that of Montana. One-third of Chile is covered by the towering ranges of the Andes. In the north is the driest place on Earth, the Atacama Desert, and in the center is a 700-mile-long (1,127 km), thickly populated valley with most of Chile's arable land. At the southern tip of Chile's mainland is Punta Arenas, the southernmost city in the world, and beyond that lies the Strait of Magellan and Tierra del Fuego, an island divided between Chile and Argentina. The southernmost point of South America is Cape Horn, a 1,390-foot (424-m) rock on Horn Island in the Wollaston group, which belongs to Chile. Chile also claims sovereignty over 482,628 sq. mi. (1,250,000 sq. km) of Antarctic territory, the Juan Fernández Islands, about 400 miles (644 km) west of the mainland, and Easter Island, about 2,000 miles (3,219 km) west.

Government Republic.

History Chile was originally under the control of the Incas in the north and the nomadic Araucanos in the south. In 1541, a Spaniard, Pedro de Valdivia, founded Santiago. Chile won its independence from Spain in 1818 under Bernardo O'Higgins and an Argentinian, José de San Martín. O'Higgins, dictator until 1823, laid the foundations of the modern state with a two-party system and a centralized government.

The dictator from 1830 to 1837, Diego Portales, fought a war with Peru in 1836–39 that expanded Chilean territory. Chile fought the War of the Pacific with Peru and Bolivia from 1879 to 1883, winning Antofagasta, Bolivia's only outlet to the sea, and extensive areas from Peru. A revolt in 1890 led by Pedro Montt overthrew, in 1891, José Balmaceda and established a parliamentary dictatorship that existed until a new constitution was adopted in 1925. Industrialization began before World War I and led to the formation of Marxist groups. Juan Antonio Ríos, president during World War II, was originally pro-Nazi but in 1944 led his country into the war on the side of the Allies.

A small abortive army uprising in 1969 raised the fear of military intervention in preventing a Marxist, Salvador Allende Gossens, from taking office after his election to the presidency on Sept. 4, 1970. Dr. Allende was the first president in a non-Communist country freely elected on a Marxist-Leninist program. Allende quickly established relations with Cuba and the People's Republic of China and nationalized several American companies. Allende's overthrow and death in an army assault on the presidential palace in Sept. 1973 ended a 46-year era of constitutional government in Chile.

The takeover was led by a four-man junta headed by Army Chief of Staff Augusto Pinochet Ugarte, who assumed the office of president. Committed to "exterminat[ing] Marxism," the junta embarked on a right-wing dictatorship. It suspended Parliament, banned political activity, and broke relations with Cuba. In 1977, Pinochet, in a speech marking his fourth year in power, promised elections by 1985 if conditions warranted. Earlier, he had abolished DINA, the secret police, and decreed an amnesty for political prisoners. Pinochet was inaugurated on March 11, 1981, for an eight-year term as president, at the end of which, according to the constitution adopted six months earlier, the junta would nominate a civilian as successor. He stepped down in Jan. 1990 in favor of Patricio Aylwin, who was elected in Dec. 1989 as the head of a 17-party coalition. The election of Dec. 1993 saw the reemergence of a member of the Frei family, with Eduardo Frei Ruiz-Tagle, the candidate of a center-left coalition, winning the presidency. His father had been president from 1964 to 1970.

In March 1998, Pinochet retired as army commander in chief. In Oct. 1998 he was arrested and detained in England where he was undergoing medical treatment. A Spanish judge sought Pinochet in connection with the disappearance of Spanish citizens during his rule. British courts ultimately denied his extradition to Spain and awarded him legal costs. Pinochet returned to Chile in March 2000. The Chilean Supreme Court stripped Pinochet of his immunity from prosecution in June 2000. He faces possible trial in connection with a death squad operating in 1973.

Ricardo Lagos was elected president in Jan. 2000, the first socialist to run the country since Allende.

China

PEOPLE'S REPUBLIC OF CHINA

National name: Zhonghua Renmin Gongheguo
President: Jiang Zemin (1993)
Premier: Zhu Rongji (1998)
Area: 3,691,521 sq. mi. (9,596,960 sq. km)[1]
Population (2000 est.): 1,261,832,482 (average rate of natural increase: 0.9%); birth rate: 16.1/1000; infant mortality rate: 28.9/1000; density per sq. mi.: 342. China has 56 ethnic groups. In 1991, the Han people accounted for 92% of the population
Capital (2000 est.): Beijing, 8,450,000 (metro. area).
Largest cities (1990 est.): Shanghai (2000 est.), 11,800,000 (metro. area); Hong Kong (Xianggang) (2000 est.), 6,750,000 (metro. area); Tianjin (Tientsin) (2000 est.), 5,350,000 (metro. area); Shenyang (Mukden), 4,669,737; Wuhan, 4,040,113; Guangzhou, 3,935,193; Chungking (Chongquing) 3,127,178; Haerbin, 2,990,921; Chengdu, 2,954,872; Xian, 2,872,539. **Monetary unit:** Yuan. **Languages:** Chinese, Mandarin, also local dialects. **Ethnicity/race:** Han Chinese 91.9%, Zhuang, Uygur, Hui, Yi, Tibetan, Miao, Manchu, Mongol, Buyi, Korean, and other nationalities 8.1%. **Religions:** Officially atheist but traditional religion contains elements of Confucianism, Taoism, Buddhism. **Literacy rate:** 84% (1995)
Economic summary: GDP/PPP (1998 est.): $4.42 trillion; $3,600 per capita. **Real growth rate:** 7.8%. **Inflation:** –0.8%. **Unemployment:** officially 3% in urban areas; probably 8%–10%; substantial unemployment and underemployment in rural areas. **Arable land:** 10%. **Agriculture:** rice, wheat, potatoes, sorghum, peanuts, tea, millet, barley, cotton, oilseed, pork, fish. **Labor force:** 696 million: agriculture, 50%; industry, 24%; services, 26% (1997). **Industries:** iron and steel, coal, machine building, armaments, textiles and apparel, petroleum, cement, chemical fertilizers, footwear, toys, food processing, autos, consumer electronics, telecommunications. **Exports:** $183.8 billion (f.o.b., 1998): electrical machinery and equipment, machinery and mechanical appliances, woven apparel, knit apparel, footwear, toys and sporting goods. **Imports:** $140.17 billion (c.i.f., 1998): electrical machinery and equipment, machinery and mechanical appliances, plastics, iron and steel, scientific and photograph equipment, paper and paperboard. **Major trading partners:** Hong Kong, U.S., Japan, Germany, South Korea, Netherlands, U.K., Singapore, Taiwan, Russia.

1. Including Manchuria and Tibet.

Geography China is slightly larger in area than the U.S. The greater part of the country is mountainous. Its principal ranges are the Tien Shan, the Kunlun chain, and the Trans-Himalaya. In the southwest is Tibet, which China annexed in 1950. The Gobi Desert lies to the north. China proper consists of three great river systems: the Yellow River (Huang Ho), 2,109 miles (5,464 km) long; the Chang Jiang (Yangtze Kiang), the third-longest river in the world at 2,432 miles (6,300 km); and the Zhujiang (Si Kiang), 848 miles (2,197 km) long.

Government Communist state.

History The earliest recorded human settlements in what is today called China were discovered in the Huang Ho basin and date from about 5000 B.C. During the Shang Dynasty (1500–1000 B.C.), the precursor of modern China's ideographic writing system developed, allowing the emerging feudal states of the era to achieve an advanced stage of civilization, rivaling in sophistication anything found at the time in Europe, the Middle East, or the Americas. It was following this initial flourishing of civilization, in a period known as the Chou Dynasty (1122–249 B.C.), that Lao-tse, Confucius, Mo Ti, and Mencius laid the foundation of Chinese philosophical thought.

The feudal states, often at war with one another, were first united under Emperor Ch'in Shih Huang Ti, during whose reign (246–210 B.C.) work was begun on the Great Wall of China, a monumental bulwark against invasion from the West. Although the Great Wall symbolized China's desire to protect itself from the outside world, under the Han Dynasty (206 B.C.– A.D. 220), the civilization opened extensive commercial trading with the West.

In the T'ang Dynasty (618–907), often called the golden age of Chinese history, painting, sculpture, and poetry flourished, and woodblock printing, which enabled the mass production of books, made its earliest known appearance. The Mings, last of the native rulers (1368–1644), overthrew the Mongol, or Yuan, Dynasty (1271–1368) established by Kublai Khan. The Mings in turn were overthrown in 1644 by invaders from the north, the Manchus.

China remained largely isolated from the rest of the world's civilizations, closely restricting foreign activities. By the end of the 18th century only Canton (location of modern-day Hong Kong) and the Portuguese port of Macao were open to European merchants. But with the first Anglo-Chinese War in 1839–42, a long period of instability and concessions to Western colonial powers began. Following the war, several ports were opened up for trading, and Hong Kong was ceded to Britain. Treaties signed after further hostilities (1856–60) weakened Chinese sovereignty and gave foreigners immunity from Chinese jurisdiction. European powers took advantage of the disastrous Sino-Japanese War of 1894–95 to gain further trading concessions from China. Peking's response, the Boxer Rebellion (1900), was suppressed by an international force.

The death of Empress Dowager Tzu Hsi in 1908 and the accession of the infant emperor Hsüan T'ung (Pu-Yi) were followed by a nationwide rebellion led by Dr. Sun Yat-sen, who overthrew the Manchus and became the first president of the Provisional Chinese Republic in 1911. Dr. Sun resigned in favor of Yuan Shih-k'ai, who suppressed the Republicans in a bid to consolidate his power. Yuan's death in June 1916 was followed by years of civil war between rival militarists and Dr. Sun's Republicans. Nationalist forces, led by General Chiang Kai-shek and with the advice of Communist experts, soon occupied most of China, setting up a Kuomintang regime in 1928. Internal strife continued, however, and Chiang eventually broke with the Communists.

On Sept. 18, 1931, Japan launched an invasion of Manchuria, capturing the province. Tokyo set up a puppet state dubbed Manchukuo and installed the last Manchu emperor, Henry Pu-Yi (Hsüan T'ung), as its nominal leader. Japanese troops moved to seize China's northern provinces in July 1937, but were resisted by Chiang, who had been able to use the Japanese invasion to unite most of China behind him. Within two years, however, Japan had seized most of the nation's eastern ports and railways. The Kuomintang government retreated first to Hankow and then to Chungking, while the Japanese set up a puppet government at Nanking, headed by Wang Jingwei.

Japan's surrender in 1945 touched off civil war between the Kuomintang forces under Chiang and Communists led by Mao Zedong, who had been battling since the 1930s for control of China. Despite U.S. aid, the Kuomintang were overcome by the Soviet-supported Communists, and Chiang and his followers were forced to flee the mainland, establishing a government-in-exile on the island of Formosa (Taiwan). The Mao regime proclaimed the People's Republic of China on Oct. 1, 1949, with Beijing as the new capital and Zhou Enlai as premier.

After the Korean War began in June 1950, China led the Communist bloc in supporting North Korea, and on Nov. 26, 1950, the Mao regime sent troops to assist the North in its efforts to capture the South.

In an attempt to restructure China's primarily agrarian economy, Mao undertook the "Great Leap Forward" campaign in 1958, a disastrous program that aimed to combine the establishment of rural communes with a crash program of village industrialization. The Great Leap forced the abandonment of farming activities, leading to widespread famine in which more than 20 million people died of malnutrition.

In 1959, a failed uprising against China's invasion and occupation of Tibet forced Tibetan Buddhism's spiritual leader, the Dalai Lama, and 100,000 of his followers to flee to India. The invasion of Tibet, as well as border disputes between China and India—with whom Moscow had warm relations—and a perceived rivalry for the leadership of the world Communist movement caused a serious souring of relations between China and the U.S.S.R., former allies.

The failure of the Great Leap Forward touched off a power struggle within the Chinese Communist Party between Mao and his supporters, and a reformist faction, including future premier Deng Xiaoping. Mao moved to Shanghai, and from that base he and his supporters waged what they called the Cultural Revolution. Beginning in the spring of 1966, Mao ordered the closing of schools and the formation of ideologically pure Red Guard units, dominated by youths and students. The Red Guards campaigned against "old ideas, old culture, old habits, and old customs." Millions died as a series of violent purges were carried out. By early 1967, the Cultural Revolution had succeeded in bolstering Mao's position as China's paramount leader.

Anxious to exploit the Sino-Soviet rift, the Nixon administration made a dramatic announcement in July 1971 that National Security Adviser Henry Kissinger had secretly visited Beijing and reached an agreement whereby Nixon would visit China. The movement toward reconciliation, which signaled the end of the U.S. containment policy toward China, provided momentum for China's admission to the U.N. Despite U.S. opposition to expelling Taiwan (Nationalist China), the world body overwhelmingly voted to oust Taiwan in favor of Beijing's Communist government.

President Nixon went to Beijing for a week early in 1972, meeting Mao as well as Zhou. The summit ended with a historic communiqué on Feb. 28, in which both nations promised to work toward improved relations. Full diplomatic relations were barred by China as long as the U.S. continued to recognize the legitimacy of Nationalist China.

Following Zhou's death on Jan. 8, 1976, his successor, Vice Premier Deng Xiaoping, was supplanted within a month by Hua Guofeng, former minister of public security. Hua became permanent premier in April. In Oct. he was named successor to Mao as chairman of the Communist Party. But Mao's death on Sept. 10 unleashed the bitter intraparty rivalries that had been suppressed since the Cultural Revolution. Old opponents of Mao launched a campaign against his widow, Jiang Qing, and three of her "radical" colleagues. The so-called Gang of Four was denounced for having undermined the party, the government, and the economy. They were tried and convicted in 1981. Meanwhile, in 1977 Deng Xiaoping was reinstated as deputy premier, chief of staff of the army, and member of the Central Committee of the Politburo.

Beijing and Washington announced full diplomatic relations on Jan. 1, 1979, and the Carter administration abrogated the Taiwan defense treaty. Deputy Premier Deng sealed the agreement with a visit to the U.S. that coincided with the opening of embassies in both capitals on March 1. On Deng's return from the U.S., Chinese troops invaded and briefly occupied an area along Vietnam's northern border. The action was seen as a response to Vietnam's invasion of Cambodia and ouster of the Khmer Rouge government, which China had supported.

In 1981, Deng protégé Hu Yaobang replaced Hua Guofeng as party chairman. Deng became chairman of the committee's military commission, giving him control over the army. The body's 215 members concluded the session with a statement holding Mao Zedong responsible for the "grave blunder" of the Cultural Revolution.

Under Deng Xiaoping's leadership, meanwhile, China's Communist ideology went through a massive reinterpretation, and sweeping economic changes were set in motion in the early 1980s. The Chinese scrapped the personality cult that idolized Mao Zedong, muted Mao's old call for class struggle and exportation of the Communist revolution, and imported Western technology and management techniques to replace the Marxist tenets that had slowed modernization. Deng concluded an agreement for the return of Hong Kong following the expiration of Britain's 99-year lease on the territory on July 1, 1997.

The removal of Hu Yaobang as party chairman in Jan. 1987 signaled a hard-line resurgence within the party. Hu—who had become a hero to many reform-minded Chinese—was replaced by former premier Zhao Ziyang. With the death of Hu in April 1989, the ideological struggle spilled into the streets of the capital, as student demonstrators occupied Beijing's Tiananmen Square in May, calling for democratic reforms. Less than a month later, the demonstrations were crushed in a bloody crackdown as troops and tanks moved into the square and fired on protesters, killing several hundred.

In annual sessions of the rubber-stamp National People's Congress in 1992 and 1993, the government called for accelerating the drive for economic reform, but the sessions were widely seen as an effort to maintain China's moves toward a market economy while retaining political authoritarianism. At the session in 1993, Communist Party leader Jiang Zemin was elected president, while hard-liner Li Peng was reelected to another five-year term as prime minister. Since 1993, the Chinese economy has continued to grow rapidly. In Nov. 1993 the Central Committee adopted a resolution envisaging the conversion of state-owned enterprises into joint-stock companies, and the creation of a central bank and modern tax system.

Deng Xiaoping's death in Feb. 1997 left a younger generation in charge of managing the enormous country. Hong Kong's reversion to Chinese rule on July 1 was watched with studied concern by the international community for signs of future developments within other parts of China. In 1998, Prime Minister Zhu Rongji introduced a sweeping program to privatize state-run businesses and further liberalize the nation's economy, a move lauded by Western economists.

After two years of painstaking negotiation, authorities of Britain and the People's Republic of China agreed in 1984 that Hong Kong would return to Chinese sovereignty on July 1, 1997, when Britain's lease on the New Territories expired. They also agreed that the vibrant capitalist enclave on China's coast would retain its status as a free port, with its laws remaining unchanged for 50 years.

The chief executive under the new government, Tung Chee Hwa, formulated a policy agenda based upon the concept of "one country, two systems," thus preserving Hong Kong's economic freedom. Hong Kong will continue to have its own finances and issue its own travel documents, and Beijing will not levy taxes. In early 1998, Hong Kong fell into a deep recession, with unprecedented unemployment and sharply falling prices, but by spring 1999 the financial center's economy began to rebound.

Chinese-U.S. relations in May 1999 were severely strained when Congress accused China of stealing U.S. nuclear secrets over the past two decades. Relations eroded even further, when a month later, the U.S. mistakenly bombed the Chinese embassy in Belgrade during Operation Allied Force, killing three Chinese journalists and wounding 20 others. The accidental nature of the bombing struck the Chinese government as highly implausible.

In July 1999 Taiwan's prime minister Lee Teng-hui infuriated China by announcing he was abandoning the longstanding "One China" policy, a tacit declaration of Taiwan's independence. China, which considers Taiwan a renegade province that will eventually be united with the mainland, has announced it will use force should Taiwan continue issuing incendiary statements. In Aug. 1999, China rounded up thousands of members of the Falun Gong sect, a highly popular religious movement that combines elements of Buddhism, Taoism, and martial arts. China, which has now outlawed the sect, was thought to consider the apolitical spiritual group threatening because its numbers exceeded the membership of the Chinese Communist Party.

The oldest permanent European settlement in Asia, Macao returned to Chinese administration on Dec. 20, 1999.

In March 2000, relations with Taiwan nearly reached a boiling point when Chen Shui-bian was elected president of Taiwan in March. Chen and his

Democratic Progressive Party had previously called for independence from mainland China, but he softened his stance days before the election. The move stabilized the growing threat of armed conflict, and China adapted a "wait and see" attitude and signaled it was open to talks with Chen.

After an intense lobbying effort by President Clinton, the U.S. House voted 237–197 to grant Beijing permanent normal trading relations. The agreement drastically reduces Chinese tariffs on many farm and industrial goods and gives some U.S. industries, such as banking and telecommunications, access to Chinese markets. The move also ends Congress's annual review of China's trade status and will allow China to enjoy full trading privileges when it joins the World Trade Organization.

Hong Kong

Status: Special Administrative Region of China
Chief Executive: Tung Chee Hwa (1997)
Area: 416 sq. mi. (1,077 sq. km)
Population (2000 est.): 7,116,302 (average annual rate of natural increase: 0.5%); birth rate: 11.3/1000; infant mortality rate: 5.9/1000; density per sq. mi.: 17,106

Hong Kong consists of the island of Hong Kong (32 sq. mi.; 83 sq. km), Stonecutters' Island, Kowloon Peninsula, and the New Territories on the adjoining mainland. The island of Hong Kong was ceded to Britain in 1841. Stonecutters' Island and Kowloon were annexed in 1860, and the New Territories, which are mainly agricultural lands, were leased from China in 1898 for 99 years. In 1994, Britain and the People's Republic of China agreed that Hong Kong would return to Chinese sovereignty on July 1, 1997, when Britain's lease on the New Territories expired. They also agreed that the vibrant capitalist enclave on China's coast would retain its status as a free port, with its laws remaining unchanged for 50 years. The chief executive under the new government, Tung Chee Hwa, formulated a policy agenda based upon the concept of "one country, two systems," thus preserving Hong Kong's economic independence.

Macau

Status: Special Administrative Region of China
Chief Executive: Edmund Ho (1999)
Area: 6 sq. mi. (15.5 sq. km)
Population (2000 est.): 445,594 (average annual growth rate: 0.89%); birth rate: 12.5/1000; infant mortality rate: 4.5/1000; density per sq. mi.: 74,266

Colonized by the Portuguese in 1557, Macao was the oldest European outpost in China. In 1987, Portugal and China reached an agreement to return Macau to Chinese rule on Dec. 20, 1999. They agreed upon provisions to insure the autonomy of Macau, including its right to elect local leaders, the right of its residents to travel freely, and the right to maintain its way of life for 50 years after the start of Chinese rule.

Colombia

REPUBLIC OF COLOMBIA

National name: República de Colombia
President: Andrés Pastrana Arango (1998)
Area: 439,735 sq. mi. (1,138,910 sq. km)
Population (2000 est.): 39,685,655 (average annual rate of natural increase, 1.7%); birth rate: 22.8/1000; infant

mortality rate: 24.7/1000; density per sq. mi.: 90
Capital and largest city (2000 est.): Santafé de
Bogotá, 7,350,000 (metro. area). **Largest cities (1995
est.):** Cali, 1,718,871; Medellín, 1,621,356;
Barranquilla, 1,064,255; Cartagena, 745,689.
Monetary unit: Peso. **Language:** Spanish. **Ethnicity/
race:** mestizo 58%, white 20%, mulatto 14%, black
4%, mixed black-Indian 3%, Indian 1%. **Religion:** 95%
Roman Catholic. **Literacy rate:** 87% (1990)
Economic summary: GDP/PPP (1998 est.): $254.7
billion; $6,600 per capita. **Real growth rate:** 0.2%.
Inflation: 16.7%. **Unemployment:** 15.7%. **Arable
land:** 4%. **Agriculture:** coffee, cut flowers, bananas,
rice, tobacco, corn, sugarcane, cocoa beans, oilseed,
vegetables, forest products, shrimp. **Labor force:** 16.8
million (1997 est.): services, 46%; agriculture, 30%;
industry, 24% (1990). **Industries:** food processing, oil,
clothing and footwear, beverages, chemicals, cement,
gold, coal, emeralds. **Natural resources:** petroleum,
natural gas, coal, iron ore, nickel, gold, copper,
emeralds. **Exports:** $11.3 billion (f.o.b., 1998 est.):
petroleum, coffee, coal, gold, bananas, cut flowers.
Imports: $14.4 billion (f.o.b., 1998 est.): industrial
equipment, transportation equipment, consumer
goods, chemicals, paper products, fuel. **Major trading
partners:** U.S., EU, Andean Community, Japan.

Geography Colombia, in the northwestern part of
South America, is the only country on that continent
that borders both the Atlantic and Pacific Oceans. It is
nearly equal in size to the combined areas of California and Texas. Colombia is bordered by Panama on
the northwest, on the east by Venezuela and Brazil,
and on the southwest by Peru and Ecuador. Through
the western half of the country, three Andean ranges
run north and south, merging into one at the Ecuador-
ean border. The eastern half is a low, jungle-covered
plain, drained by spurs of the Amazon and Orinoco
Rivers, inhabited mostly by isolated, tropical-forest
Indian tribes. The fertile plateau and valley of the
eastern range are the most densely populated parts of
the country.

Government Republic.

History Little is known about the various Indian
tribes who inhabited Colombia before the Spanish
arrived. In 1510 Spaniards founded Darien, the first
permanent European settlement on the American
mainland. In 1538 they established the colony of New
Granada, the area's name until 1861.

After a 14-year struggle, in which Simón Bolívar's
Venezuelan troops won the battle of Boyacá in
Colombia on Aug. 7, 1819, independence was
attained in 1824. Bolívar united Colombia, Venezuela, Panama, and Ecuador in the Republic of Greater
Colombia (1819–30), but lost Venezuela and Ecuador
to separatists. Two political parties dominated the
region: the Conservatives believed in a strong central
government and a powerful church; the Liberals
believed in a decentralized government, strong
regional power, and a less influential role for the
church. Bolívar was himself a Conservative, while his
vice president, Francisco de Paula Santander, was the
founder of the Liberal Party.

Santander served as president between 1832 and
1836, a period of relative stability, but by 1840 civil
war erupted. Other periods of Liberal dominance
(1849–57 and 1861–80), which sought to disestablish
the Roman Catholic Church, were marked by insurrection. Nine different governments followed, each
rewriting the constitution. In 1861, the country was
called the United States of New Granada; in 1863 it
became the United States of Colombia; and in 1885,

it became the Republic of Colombia. In 1899 a brutal
civil war broke out, the War of a Thousand Days, that
lasted until 1902. The following year, Colombia lost
its claims to Panama because it refused to ratify the
lease to the U.S. of the Canal Zone. Panama declared
its independence in 1903 and went ahead with the
creation of the U.S. deal.

The Conservatives held power until 1930, when
revolutionary pressure put the Liberals back in power.
The Liberal administrations of Enrique Olaya Herrera
and Alfonso López (1930–38) were marked by social
reforms that failed to solve the country's problems,
and in 1946, insurrection and banditry broke out,
claiming hundreds of thousands of lives by 1958.
Laureano Gómez (1950–53); the army chief of staff,
Gen. Gustavo Rojas Pinilla (1953–56); and a military
junta (1956–57) sought to curb disorder by repression.

The Liberals won a solid majority in 1982, but a
party split enabled Belisario Betancur Cuartas, the
Conservative candidate, to win the presidency on
May 31. After his inauguration, he ended the state of
siege that had existed almost continuously for 34
years. In an official war against drug trafficking,
Colombia became a public battleground with bombs,
killings, and kidnappings. In 1989 a leading presidential candidate, Luis Carlos Galán, was murdered. In
an effort to quell the terror, President Gaviria proposed lenient punishment in exchange for surrender
by the leading drug dealers. In addition, in 1991 the
constitutional convention voted to ban extradition. In
July 1992 Pablo Escobar of the Medellín drug cartel
escaped from prison in an operation that left six dead.
He died the next year, but the Medellín drug cartel
continues to operate.

In the country's closest presidential contest in 24
years, Ernesto Samper, the candidate of the Liberal
Party, won 50% of the vote in June 1994. Amid allegations of having accepted campaign contributions
from drug traffickers, Samper in May 1996 ordered
emergency security measures in southern Colombia to
fight leftist rebels, but the House of Representatives
absolved him of the charges by a 111–43 vote. In
1997 a constitutional amendment that allowed for
nonretroactive extradition was passed.

Andrés Pastrana Arango was elected president in
1998, pledging to clean up corruption. In Dec. 1999
the Colombian military reported that 2,787 people—
the largest number in the world—were kidnapped that
year, and blamed rebels. The murder rate soared in
1999, with some 23,000 people reported killed by
leftist guerrillas, right-wing paramilitaries, drug traffickers, and common criminals. The violence has created more than 100,000 refugees, while two million
Colombians have left the country in the past two
years.

In June 2000, an oil field containing as much as
300 million barrels was discovered southwest of
Bogotá. In Aug. 2000, the U.S. government approved
$1.3 billion in antidrug trafficking aid, and President
Clinton visited the country.

Comoros

UNION OF COMOROS ISLANDS

President: Col. Azaly Assoumani (1999)
Area: 690 sq. mi. (2,170 sq. km)
Population (2000 est.): 578,400 (average annual rate of
natural increase: 3.05%); birth rate: 40.1/1000; infant
mortality rate: 86.3/1000; density per sq. mi.: 838
Capital and largest city (1990 est.): Moroni (on Grande

Comoro), 23,432. **Monetary unit:** Franc CFA.
Languages: Shaafi Islam (Swahili dialect), Malagasu,
French, Arabic. **Ethnicity/race:** Antalote, Cafre,
Makoa, Oimatsaha, Sakalava. **Religions:** Sunni
Muslim, 86%; Roman Catholic, 14%. **Literacy rate:**
48% (1980)
Economic summary: GDP/PPP (1997 est.): $400
million; $700 per capita. **Real growth rate:** 3.5%.
Inflation: 2.5% (1997). **Unemployment:** 20% (1996
est.). **Arable land:** 35%. **Agriculture:** vanilla, cloves,
perfume essences, copra, coconuts, bananas,
cassava (tapioca). **Labor force:** 144,500 (1996 est.);
agriculture, 80%; government, 3%. **Industries:**
tourism, perfume distillation, textiles, furniture, jewelry,
construction materials, soft drinks. **Exports:** $11.4
million (f.o.b., 1996 est.): vanilla, ylang-ylang, cloves,
perfume oil, copra. **Imports:** $70 million (f.o.b., 1996
est.): rice and other foodstuffs, consumer goods,
petroleum products, cement, transport equipment.
Major trading partners: France, U.S., Germany,
South Africa, Kenya.

Geography The Comoros Islands—Grande
Comoro (Ngazidja), Anjouan, Mohéli, and Mayotte
(which is not part of the country and retains ties to
France)—are an archipelago of volcanic origin in the
Indian Ocean, 190 miles off the coast of Mozam-
bique.

Government Islamic republic run by a military
junta.

History Comoros had been visited by travelers from
Africa, Madagascar, Indonesia, and Arabia before the
first Europeans encountered the islands. Arabic influence has been the strongest.

Under French rule since 1886, the Comoros
declared themselves independent on July 6, 1975.
However, Mayotte, with a Christian majority, voted
against joining the other, mainly Islamic, islands, in
the move to independence. It remains a French overseas territory.

A month after independence, Justice Minister Ali
Soilih staged a coup with the help of a group of white
mercenaries known as Les Affreux (The Terrible
Ones), overthrowing the new nation's first president,
Ahmed Abdallah. He was himself overthrown on
May 13, 1978. In 1989 another coup took place.

A slump in world prices during the 1990s for
Comoros's main exports, vanilla and ylang-ylang,
exacerbated the country's poverty—the annual per
capita income is less than $700.

The island of Anjouan declared independence on
Aug. 3, 1997, after months of protests and clashes
with security forces. The secessionists wanted a
return to French rule, contending that independence
from France has brought economic disaster and political chaos. Mohéli, the smallest island, also seceded.
But France refused to support the secession of either
island.

In Sept. 1997, President Mohamed Taki's forces
attempted to retake Anjouan, but failed. Taki then
declared a state of emergency. Peace talks in spring
1999 ended inconclusively when all other Anjouan
representatives failed to sign a peace agreement that
the other two islands had agreed to. Anti-Anjouan
riots took place on Grande Comoros, and on April 30,
1999, Col. Azaly Assoumani led a coup, overthrowing interim president Tadjidine. He promised interim
military rule would end in a year. This was the first of
Comoros's four coups to be carried out by the Como-
rian army itself rather than mercenaries. The other
three were led by the notorious French mercenary

leader, "Colonel" Bob Denard. The island of Anjouan
continued to fight against the government on Grande
Comoro throughout 1999.

In March 2000 the Organization of African Unity
cut communications with Anjouan in an effort to end
the rebellion. The OAU has demanded that Assoumani return the Comoros to civilian rule. In July
2000, meanwhile, 70% of voters on the island of
Mayotte opted to accept greater autonomy but remain
a part of France.

Congo

REPUBLIC OF CONGO

National name: République Populaire du Congo
President: Denis Sassou-Nguesso (1997)
Area: 132,046 sq. mi. (342,000 sq. km)
Population (2000 est.): 2,830,961 (average annual rate
of natural increase: 2.2%); birth rate: 38.6/1000; infant
mortality rate: 101.6/1000; density per sq. mi.: 21
Capital and largest city (1992 est.): Brazzaville,
937,580. **Other large city (1992 est.):** Pointe-Noire,
576,206. **Monetary unit:** Franc CFA. **Languages:**
French, Lingala, Kikongo, others. **Ethnicity/race:**
south: Kongo 48%; north: Sangha 20%, M'Bochi 12%;
center: Teke 17%, Europeans 8,500 (mostly French).
Religions: 50% Christian, 48% animist, 2% Muslim.
Literacy rate: 57% (1990)
Economic summary: GDP/PPP (1998 est.): $3.9 billion;
$1,500 per capita. **Real growth rate:** 2.5%. **Inflation:**
5% (1997 est.). **Unemployment rate:** n.a. **Arable
land:** 0%. **Agriculture:** cassava (tapioca), sugar, rice,
corn, peanuts, vegetables, coffee, cocoa, forest
products. **Labor force:** n.a. **Industries:** petroleum
extraction, cement kilning, lumbering, brewing, sugar
milling, palm oil, soap, cigarette making. **Natural
resources:** petroleum, timber, potash, lead, zinc,
uranium, copper, phosphates, natural gas. **Exports:**
$1.7 billion (f.o.b., 1997): petroleum, lumber, plywood,
sugar, cocoa, coffee, diamonds. **Imports:** $803 million
(f.o.b., 1997): intermediate manufactures, capital
equipment, construction materials, foodstuffs,
petroleum products. **Major trading partners:** U.S.,
Belgium, Luxembourg, Taiwan, China, France, Italy,
U.K.

Geography The Congo is situated in west-central
Africa astride the equator. It borders Gabon, Cameroon, the Central African Republic, the Democratic
Republic of the Congo, and the Angola exclave of
Cabinda, with a short stretch of coast on the South
Atlantic. Its area is nearly three times that of Pennsylvania. Most of the inland is tropical rain forest,
drained by tributaries of the Congo River, which
flows south along the eastern border with the Democratic Republic of the Congo to Stanley Pool. The
narrow coastal plain rises to highlands separated from
the inland plateaus by the 200-mile-wide Niari River
valley, which gives passage to the coast.

Government Republic.

History In precolonial times, the region now called
the Republic of Congo was dominated by three kingdoms: Kongo (originating about A.D. 1000), the
Loango (flourishing in the 17th century), and Tio.
After the Portuguese located the Congo River in
1482, commerce was carried on with the tribes, especially the slave trade.

The Frenchman Pierre Savorgnan de Brazza signed
a treaty with Makoko, ruler of the Bateke people, in
1880, thus establishing French control. It was first
called French Congo, and after 1905 Middle Congo.
With Gabon and Ubangi-Shari, it became the colony

of French Equatorial Africa in 1910. Abuse of laborers led to public outcry against the French colonialists as well as rebellions among the Congolese, but the exploitation of the native workers continued until 1930. During World War II the colony joined Chad in supporting the Free French cause against the Vichy government. The Congo proclaimed its independence without leaving the French Community in 1960, calling itself the Republic of Congo.

Congo's second president, Alphonse Massemba-Débat, instituted a Marxist-Leninist government. In 1968, Maj. Marien Ngouabi overthrew him but kept Congo on a socialist course. He was sworn in for a second five-year term in 1975. A four-man commando squad assassinated Ngouabi on March 18, 1977. Col. Joachim Yhombi-Opango, army chief of staff, assumed the presidency on April 4. Yhombi-Opango resigned on Feb. 4, 1979, and was replaced by Col. Denis Sassou-Nguesso.

In July 1990 the leaders of the ruling party voted to end the one-party system. A national political conference, hailed as a model for sub-Saharan Africa, renounced Marxism in 1991, and scheduled the country's first free elections for 1992. The national conference ending in June 1991 rewrote the constitution.

Political and ethnic tensions intensified in 1993 after legislative elections in May and runoffs in June. The opposition's rejection of the results developed into violence. A peace agreement was achieved between the government and the opposition in Aug. 1994. A four-month civil war (June 5–Oct. 15, 1997) devastated Brazzaville, the capital. Buttressed by military aid from Angola, former Marxist dictator Denis Sassou-Nguesso overthrew President Pascal Lissouba, the country's first democratically elected president. In late 1999 a peace agreement was signed between Sassou-Nguesso, who comes from the north, and the rebels representing the populous south. An indication that the truce was holding, the 310-mile rail link between Brazzaville and the main port city of Pointe Noire was due to reopen in the summer of 2000.

Congo, Democratic Republic of the

DEMOCRATIC REPUBLIC OF THE CONGO

President: Laurent Kabila (1997)
Area: 905,365 sq. mi. (2,345,410 sq. km)
Population (2000 est.): 51,964,999 (average annual rate of natural increase: 3.1%); birth rate: 46.4/1000; infant mortality rate: 101.7/1000; density per sq. mi.: 57
Capital and largest city (2000 est.): Kinshasa, 6,050,000 (metro. area). **Other large cities:** Lubumbashi, 851,381; Mbuji-Mayi, 806,475; Kisangani, 417,517; Kolwezi, 417,810. **Monetary unit:** Congolese franc. **Languages:** French (official), Swahili, Lingala, Ishiluba, and Kikongo, others. **Ethnicity/race:** over 200 African ethnic groups, the majority are Bantu; the four largest tribes—Mongo, Luba, Kongo (all Bantu), and the Mangbetu-Azande (Hamitic)—make up about 45% of the population. **Religions:** Roman Catholic 50%, Protestant 20%, Kimbanguist 10%, Islam 10%; syncretic and traditional, 10%. **Literacy rate:** 72% (1990)
Economic summary: GDP/PPP (1998 est.): $34.9 billion; $710 per capita. **Real growth rate:** –3.5%. **Inflation:** 147%. **Unemployment:** n.a. **Arable land:** 3%. **Agriculture:** coffee, sugar, palm oil, rubber, tea, quinine, cassava (tapioca), bananas, root crops, corn, fruit, wood products. **Labor force:** 14.51 million (1993 est.): agriculture, 65%; industry, 16%; services, 19%

(1991 est.). **Industries:** mining, mineral processing, consumer products (including textiles, footwear, cigarettes, processed food and beverages), cement, diamonds. **Natural resources:** copper, cobalt, cadmium, petroleum, industrial and gem diamonds, gold, silver, zinc, managenese, tin, germanium, uranium, radium, bauxite, iron ore, coal, hydropower potential, timber. **Exports:** $1.6 billion (f.o.b., 1998 est.): diamonds, copper, coffee, cobalt, crude oil. **Imports:** $819 million (f.o.b., 1998 est.): consumer goods, foodstuffs, mining and other machinery, transport equipment, fuel. **Major trading partners:** Benelux, U.S., South Africa, France, Germany, Italy, U.K., Japan, China, Netherlands.

Geography Congo, in west-central Africa, is bordered by the Congo Republic, the Central African Republic, the Sudan, Uganda, Rwanda, Burundi, Tanzania, Zambia, Angola, and the Atlantic Ocean. It is one-quarter the size of the U.S. The principal rivers are the Ubangi and Bomu in the north and the Congo in the west, which flows into the Atlantic. The entire length of Lake Tanganyika lies along the eastern border with Tanzania and Burundi.

Government Dictatorship.

History Formerly the Belgian Congo, this territory was inhabited by ancient Negrito peoples (Pygmies), who were pushed into the mountains by Bantu and Nilotic invaders. The American correspondent Henry M. Stanley navigated the Congo River in 1877 and opened the interior to exploration. Commissioned by King Leopold II of the Belgians, Stanley made treaties with native chiefs that enabled the king to obtain personal title to the territory at the Berlin Conference of 1885.

Leopold accumulated a vast personal fortune from ivory and rubber through Congolese slave labor; 10 million people are estimated to have died from forced labor, starvation, and outright extermination during Leopold's colonial rule. His brutal exploitation of the Congo eventually became an international cause célèbre, prompting Belgium to take over administration of the Congo, which remained a colony until agitation for independence forced Brussels to grant freedom on June 30, 1960. The Katanga Province seceded from the new republic on July 11, and another mining province, South Kasai, followed. Belgium sent paratroopers to quell the civil war, and with President Joseph Kasavubu and Premier Patrice Lumumba of the national government in conflict, the United Nations flew in a peacekeeping force.

Kasavubu staged an army coup in 1960 and handed Lumumba over to the Katangan forces. A U.N. investigating commission found that Lumumba had been killed by a Belgian mercenary in the presence of Tshombe. Dag Hammarskjold, U.N. secretary-general, died in a plane crash en route to a peace conference with Tshombe on Sept. 17, 1961.

U.N. Secretary-General U Thant submitted a national reconciliation plan in 1962 that Tshombe rejected. Tshombe's troops fired on the U.N. force in Dec., and in the ensuing conflict Tshombe capitulated on Jan. 14, 1963. The peacekeeping force withdrew, and, in a complete about-face, Kasavubu named Tshombe premier in order to fight a spreading rebellion. Tshombe used foreign mercenaries, and with the help of Belgian paratroops airlifted by U.S. planes, defeated the most serious opposition, a Communist-backed regime in the northeast.

Kasavubu abruptly dismissed Tshombe in 1965 and was himself ousted by Gen. Joseph-Desiré Mobutu, army chief of staff. The new president nationalized the Union Minière, the Belgian copper mining enterprise that had been a dominant force in the Congo since colonial days. The plane carrying the exiled Tshombe was hijacked in 1967 and he was held prisoner in Algeria until his death from a heart attack, which was announced on June 29, 1969.

Mobutu eliminated opposition to win the election in 1970. In 1975, he nationalized much of the economy, barred religious instruction in schools, and decreed the adoption of African names. On March 8, 1977, invaders from Angola calling themselves the Congolese National Liberation Front pushed into Shaba and threatened the important mining center of Kolwezi. France and Belgium responded to Mobutu's pleas for help with weapons, but the U.S. gave only nonmilitary supplies. In April, France flew 1,500 Moroccan troops to Shaba to defeat the invaders, who were, Mobutu charged, Soviet-inspired and Cuban-led. U.S. intelligence sources, however, confirmed Soviet and Cuban denials of any participation and identified the rebels as former Katanga gendarmes who had fled to Angola after their 1963 defeat.

In April 1990 Mobutu announced he intended to introduce multiparty democracy but that elections in Jan. 1991 would reduce the number of political parties to two besides his own. Opposition leaders denounced the scheme as giving Mobutu's party an unfair advantage.

In early 1993 Mobutu rejected Western demands that he yield power and announced plans to regroup his one-party Parliament, dismissing the main opposition leader, Prime Minister Tshisekedi. In Jan. 1994 Mobutu dissolved Parliament and dismissed his prime minister, which led to a general strike in the capital.

Mobutu Sese Seko was overthrown in May 1997, ending one of the world's most corrupt and megalomaniacal regimes. The last of the CIA-nurtured cold war despots, Mobutu deftly courted France and the U.S., which used Zaire as a launching pad for covert operations against bordering countries, particularly Marxist Angola. Mobutu's disastrous policies drove his country to economic collapse while he siphoned off millions of dollars for himself.

Laurent Kabila and his long-standing but little-known guerrilla movement launched a seven-month campaign that ousted Mobutu. The country was renamed the Democratic Republic of the Congo, its name before Mobutu changed it to Zaire in 1971. Mobutu's downfall began in Oct. 1996, when he planned to banish the Zairian Tutsis who had lived for centuries in eastern Zaire. Neighboring Rwanda's Tutsi-led government came to their aid, as did other rebel groups, one of which was led by Kabila. After conquering eastern Zaire, Kabila earned the support of a host of Mobutu's enemies, including Uganda, Burundi, Tanzania, Zambia, Zimbabwe, and Angola. His troops swept through the country, encountering little resistance. Mobutu fled in exile to Morocco on May 16, where he died of cancer in Sept.

Elation over Mobutu's downfall faded as Kabila's own autocratic style emerged and he seemed devoid of a clear plan for reconstructing the country. He stymied U.N. human rights investigations into the alleged massacres of Hutu refugees and continued to depend on foreign troops for border skirmishes rather than establish a strong national army. Many Congolese dismissed him as a puppet ruler who allowed his country to be overrun by outsiders, particularly the Rwandans. At the same time he has alienated many of his former supporters, including Rwanda and Uganda.

In Aug. 1998, Congolese rebel forces, led by ethnic Tutsis in eastern Congo, who are backed by Rwanda and Uganda, began attacking Kabila's forces. The rebels gained control of a large portion of the country until Angolan, Namibian, and Zimbabwean troops came to Kabila's aid and pushed the rebels back.

In July 1999 a cease-fire agreement was signed by all six of the countries involved, but it has not held. Further complicating the situation, the rebel force, the Congolese Rally for Democracy, RCD, split in May 1999 and have at times fought against each other.

Costa Rica
REPUBLIC OF COSTA RICA

National name: República de Costa Rica
President: Miguel Angel Rodríguez (1998)
Area: 19,652 sq. mi. (51,100 sq. km)
Population (2000 est.): 3,710,558 (average annual rate of natural increase: 1.6%); birth rate: 20.7/1000; infant mortality rate: 11.5/1000; density per sq. mi.: 189
Capital and largest city (1994 est.): San José, 315,909. **Monetary unit:** Colón. **Language:** Spanish. **Ethnicity/race:** white (including mestizo) 96%, black 2%, Indian 1%, Chinese 1%. **Religion:** 95% Roman Catholic. **Literacy rate:** 93% (1990)
Economic summary: GDP/PPP (1998 est.): $24 billion; $6,700 per capita. **Real growth rate:** 5.5%. **Inflation:** 12%. **Unemployment:** 5.6%; much underemployment. **Arable land:** 6%. **Agriculture:** coffee, bananas, sugar, corn, rice, beans, potatoes, beef, timber. **Labor force:** 868,300: industry and commerce, 23.3%; government and services, 55.1%; agriculture, 21.6% (1996 est.). **Industries:** food processing, textiles and clothing, construction materials, fertilizer, plastic products. **Natural resources:** hydropower potential. **Exports:** $3.9 billion (f.o.b., 1998): manufactured products, coffee, bananas, textiles, sugar. **Imports:** $4.5 billion (c.i.f., 1998): raw materials, consumer goods, capital equipment, petroleum. **Major trading partners:** U.S., Benelux, Germany, Italy, Guatemala, El Salvador, Netherlands, U.K., France, Japan, Mexico, Venezuela.

Geography This Central American country lies between Nicaragua to the north and Panama to the south. Its area slightly exceeds that of Vermont and New Hampshire combined. It has a narrow Pacific coastal region. Cocos Island (10 sq. mi.; 26 sq. km), about 300 miles (483 km) off the Pacific Coast, is under Costa Rican sovereignty.

Government Democratic republic.

History Costa Rica was inhabited by 25,000 Indians when Columbus explored it in 1502. Few of the Indians survived the Spanish conquest, which began in 1563. The region grew slowly and was administered as a Spanish province. Costa Rica achieved independence in 1821 but was absorbed for two years by Agustín de Iturbide in his Mexican empire. It became a republic in 1848. Except for the military dictatorship of Tomás Guardia from 1870 to 1882, Costa Rica has enjoyed one of the most democratic governments in Latin America.

Rodrigo Carazo Odio became president in 1978. His tenure was marked by a disastrous decline in the economy. Oscar Arias Sanchez, who became president in 1986, prevented the neighboring Nicaraguan Contra rebels from using Costa Rican territory as a safe haven, and played a central role in negotiating settlements in both the Nicaraguan and the Salvadoran civil wars. He was awarded the Nobel Peace Prize in 1987.

José Maria Figueres Olsen of the National Liberation Party became president in 1994. He favored greater government intervention in the economy and other measures that the International Monetary Fund disagreed with. As a result, the World Bank withheld $100 million of financing. In 1998, Miguel Angel Rodríguez of the Social Christian Unity Party became president.

A border dispute with Nicaragua has threatened Costa Rica's tourism industry in the ecologically rich San Juan River area. Talks between the two nations regarding the border issue began in mid-1999.

In April 2000 a court ruled against a plan to partially privatize the state-owned telecommunications and electricity industries. Rodriguez said the proposal was necessary to modernize the economy. But unions bitterly opposed it, staging violent protests and a general strike that paralyzed much of the country for several days.

Côte d'Ivoire

REPUBLIC OF CÔTE D'IVOIRE

National name: République de la Côte d'Ivoire
President: Gen. Robert Guei (1999)
Prime Minister: Seydou Elimane Diarra (2000)
Area: 124,502 sq. mi. (322,460 sq. km)
Population (2000 est.): 15,980,950 (average annual rate of natural increase: 2.4%); birth rate: 40.8/1000; infant mortality rate: 95.1/1000; density per sq. mi.: 128
Capital (1988): Yamoussoukro (official); Abidjan (administrative) (since March 1983), 106,786. **Largest city (est. 1988):** Abidjan, 2,797,000. **Monetary unit:** Franc CFA. **Languages:** French and African languages (Diaula esp.). **Ethnicity/race:** Baoule 23%, Bete 18%, Senoufou 15%, Malinke 11%, Agni, foreign Africans (mostly Burkinabe and Malians, about 3 million). **Religions:** 60% indigenous, 23% Islam, 17% Christian. **Literacy rate:** 54% (1990)
Economic summary: GDP/PPP (1998 est.): $24.2 billion; $1,680 per capita. **Real growth rate:** 6%. **Inflation:** 6%. **Unemployment:** n.a. **Arable land:** 8%. **Agriculture:** coffee, cocoa beans, bananas, palm kernels, corn, rice, manioc (tapioca), sweet potatoes, sugar, cotton, rubber, timber. **Labor force:** n.a. **Industries:** foodstuffs, beverages, wood products, oil refining, automobile assembly, textiles, fertilizer, construction materials, electricity. **Natural resources:** petroleum, diamonds, manganese, iron ore, cobalt, bauxite, copper. **Exports:** $4.3 billion (f.o.b., 1998): cocoa, coffee, tropical woods, petroleum, cotton, bananas, pineapples, palm oil, fish. **Imports:** $2.5 billion (f.o.b., 1998): food, consumer goods, capital goods, fuel, transport equipment. **Major trading partners:** Netherlands, France, Germany, U.S., Italy, Nigeria.

Geography Côte d'Ivoire (also known as the Ivory Coast), in western Africa on the Gulf of Guinea is a little larger than New Mexico. Its neighbors are Liberia, Guinea, Mali, Burkina Faso, and Ghana. The country consists of a coastal strip in the south, dense forests in the interior, and savannas in the north.

Government Presidential/parliamentary democracy until Dec. 1999, when a coup installed a military dictatorship.

History Côte d'Ivoire was originally made up of numerous isolated settlements; today it represents more than sixty distinct tribes, including the Beti, Senufo, Baule, Anyi, Malinke, Dan, and Lobi. Côte d'Ivoire attracted both French and Portuguese merchants in the 15th century who were in search of ivory

and slaves. French traders set up establishments early in the 19th century, and in 1842, the French obtained territorial concessions from local tribes, gradually extending their influence along the coast and inland. The area was organized as a territory in 1893, became an autonomous republic in the French Union after World War II, and achieved independence on Aug. 7, 1960. Côte d'Ivoire formed a customs union in 1959 with Dahomey (Benin), Niger, and Burkina Faso. The nation's economy is one of the most developed in sub-Saharan Africa. It is the world's largest exporter of cocoa and one of the largest exporters of coffee.

From independence until his death in 1993, Felix Houphouët-Boigny served as president. Massive protests by students, farmers, and professionals forced the president to legalize opposition parties and hold the first contested presidential election in Oct. 1990, which Houphouët-Boigny won with 81% of the vote. Beginning in Sept. 1998, thousands of demonstrators protested a constitutional revision that granted President Henri Konan Bédié greatly enhanced powers. Bédié has also promoted the concept of *ivoirité*, which, roughly translated, means "pure Ivoirian pride." He has done so to disqualify his chief political rival, Alassane D. Ouattara, from elections—Ouattara was born in Burkina Faso, not Côte d'Ivoire, and his support comes largely from Muslims in the north. Although its defenders describe *ivoirité* as a term of positive national pride, it has led to a dangerous xenophobia, with numerous ethnic Malians and Burkinans being driven out of the country in 1999.

President Bédié was overthrown in the country's first military coup in Dec. 1999, and General Robert Guei assumed control of the country. As a result, the majority of foreign aid to the country has ceased. Guei, who had promised to stay in power only to "sweep the house clean," instead decided to run for president in October 2000 elections.

Croatia

REPUBLIC OF CROATIA

President: Stipe Mesic (2000)
Prime Minister: Ivica Racan (2000)
Area: 21,829 sq. mi. (56,538 sq. km)
Population (2000 est.): 4,282,216 (average annual rate of natural increase: 0.1%); Birth rate: 12.8/1000; infant mortality rate: 7.4/1000; density per sq. mi.: 196
Capital (1991): Zagreb, 930,753. **Other large cities (1991):** Split, 189,444; Rijeka, 167,757; Osijek, 129,792. **Monetary unit:** Kuna (May 1994). **Language:** Croatian. **Ethnicity/race:** Croat 78%, Serb 12%, Muslim 0.9%, Hungarian 0.5%, Slovenian 0.5%, others 8.1% (1991). **Religions:** Catholic 76.5%, Orthodox 11.1%, Slavic Muslim 1.2%, Protestant 0.4%, others 10.8%. **Literacy rate:** 97% (1991)
Economic summary: GDP/PPP (1998 est.): $23.6 billion; $5,100 per capita. **Real growth rate:** 3%. **Inflation:** 5.4%. **Unemployment:** 18.6% (year end 1998). **Labor force:** 1.63 million (1998): industry and mining, 31.1%; agriculture, 4.3%; government, 19.1% (including education and health); other, 45.5% (1993). **Industries:** chemicals and plastics, machine tools, fabricated metals, electronics, pig iron and rolled-steel products, aluminum, paper, wood products, construction materials, textiles, shipbuilding, petroleum and petroleum refining, food and beverages, tourism. **Agriculture:** wheat, corn, sugar beets, sunflower seed, alfalfa, clover, olives, citrus, grapes, vegetables, livestock, dairy products. **Exports:** $4.5 billion (f.o.b., 1998): machinery and transport equipment,

miscellaneous manufactures, chemicals, food and live animals, raw materials, fuel and lubricants, beverages and tobacco. **Imports:** $8.4 billion (c.i.f., 1998): machinery and transport equipment, fuel and lubricants, food and live animals, chemicals, miscellaneous manufactured articles, raw materials, beverages and tobacco. **Major trading partners:** Germany, Italy, Slovenia.

Geography Croatia is a former Yugoslav republic on the Adriatic Sea; it is about the size of West Virginia. Part of Croatia is a barren, rocky region lying in the Dinaric Alps. The Zagorje region north of the capital, Zagreb, is a land of rolling hills, and the fertile agricultural region of the Pannonian Plain is bordered by the Drava, Danube, and Sava Rivers in the east. Over one-third of Croatia is forested.

Government Parliamentary democracy.

History The original home of the Slavic Croats was in an area that was part of the Republic of Ukraine. During the 6th century A.D., other tribes arrived in the region, which was then part of the Roman province of Pannonia. The Croats converted to Christianity between the 7th and 9th centuries and adopted the Roman alphabet under the suzerainty of Charlemagne. In A.D. 925, the Croats defeated Byzantine and Frankish invaders and established their own independent kingdom, which reached its peak during the 11th century. A civil war ensued in 1089, which later led to the country being conquered by the Hungarians in 1091. The signing of the *Pacta Conventa* by Croatian tribal chiefs and the Hungarian king in 1102 united the two nations politically under the Hungarian monarch, but Croatia retained its autonomy.

When the Hungarians were defeated by the Turks in 1526, most of Croatia fell under Ottoman rule until the end of the 17th century. It maintained its Catholicism (the religion of about 80% of the country) during the centuries of Muslim rule, and its religion has always been one of Croatia's defining characteristics, distinguishing it from the other Balkan states. The rest of Croatia elected Ferdinand of Austria as its king and became associated with the Hapsburgs of Austria. After the establishment of the Austro-Hungarian kingdom in 1867, Croatia and Slovenia became part of Hungary until the collapse of Austria-Hungary in 1918 following its defeat in World War I. On Oct. 29, 1918, Croatia proclaimed its independence and joined in union with Montenegro, Serbia, and Slovenia to form the Kingdom of Serbs, Croats, and Slovenes. The name was changed to Yugoslavia in 1929.

When Germany invaded Yugoslavia in 1941, Croatia became a Nazi puppet state. Croatian Fascists, the Ustachi, slaughtered countless Serbs and Jews during the war. After Germany was defeated in 1945, Croatia was made into a republic of the newly reestablished Communist nation of Yugoslavia. In June 1991, the Croatian Parliament passed a declaration of independence from Yugoslavia. A six-month civil war followed with the Serbian-dominated Yugoslavian army. The war claimed thousands of lives and wrought mass destruction.

A U.N. cease-fire was arranged on Jan. 2, 1992. The Security Council in Feb. approved sending a 14,000-member peacekeeping force to monitor the cease-fire and protect the minority Serbs in Croatia. In a 1993 referendum the Serb-occupied portion of Croatia (Krajina) resoundingly voted for integration with Serbs in Bosnia and Serbia proper. Although the Zagreb government and representatives of Krajina signed a cease-fire in March 1994, further negotiations broke down.

In a lightning-quick operation, the Croatian army retook western Slavonia in May 1995. Similarly, in Aug. the central Croatian region of Krajina, held by Serbs, was returned to Zagreb's control.

Announcing on television in 1999 that "national issues are more important than democracy," President Tudjman continued to alienate Croatians with his authoritarian rule, out-of-touch nationalism, and disastrous handling of the war-shattered economy. In Dec. 1999, Tudjman died, and was succeeded by Stipe Mesic, a reformer. One of his first acts in office was to invite back the 300,000 ethnic Serbs who had been banished from the country under Tudjman.

Cuba

REPUBLIC OF CUBA

National name: República de Cuba
President: Fidel Castro (1976)
Area: 42,843 sq. mi. (110,860 sq. km)
Population (2000 est.): 11,141,997 (average annual rate of natural increase: 0.5%); birth rate: 12.7/1000; infant mortality rate: 7.5/1000; density per sq. mi.: 260
Capital and largest city (1994 est.): Havana, 2,241,000. **Other large cities (1994 est.):** Santiago de Cuba, 440,084; Camagüey, 293,961; Holguin, 242,085; Guantánamo, 207,796; Santa Clara, 205,400. **Monetary unit:** Peso. **Language:** Spanish. **Ethnicity/race:** mulatto 51%, white 37%, black 11%, Chinese 1%. **Religion:** at least 85% nominally Roman Catholic before Castro assumed power. **Literacy rate:** 94% (1990)
Economic summary: GDP/PPP (1998 est.): $17.3 billion; $1,560 per capita. **Real growth rate:** 1.2%. **Inflation:** n.a. **Unemployment:** 6.8% (1997 est.). **Arable land:** 24%. **Agriculture:** sugarcane, tobacco, citrus, coffee, rice, potatoes, beans, livestock. **Labor force:** 4.5 million (1996 est.): services and government, 30%; industry, 22%; agriculture, 20%; commerce, 11%; construction, 10%; transportation and communications, 7% (June 1990). **Industries:** sugar, petroleum, food, tobacco, textiles, chemicals, paper and wood products, metals (particularly nickel), cement, fertilizers, consumer goods, agricultural machinery. **Natural resources:** cobalt, nickel, iron ore, copper, manganese, salt, timber, silica, petroleum. **Exports:** $1.4 billion (f.o.b., 1998 est.): sugar, nickel, tobacco, shellfish, medical products, citrus, coffee. **Imports:** $3 billion (c.i.f., 1998 est.): petroleum, food, machinery, chemicals. **Major trading partners:** Russia, Canada, Spain, France.

Geography The largest island of the West Indies group (equal in area to Pennsylvania), Cuba is also the westernmost—just west of Hispaniola (Haiti and the Dominican Republic), and 90 miles (145 km) south of Key West, Florida, at the entrance to the Gulf of Mexico. The island is mountainous in the southeast and south-central area (Sierra Maestra). It is flat or rolling elsewhere. Cuba also includes numerous smaller islands, islets, and cays.

Government Communist state.

History Arawak (or Taino) Indians inhabiting Cuba when Columbus landed on the island in 1492 died off from diseases brought by sailors and settlers. By 1511, Spaniards under Diego Velásquez were founding settlements that served as bases for Spanish exploration. Cuba also became an assembly point for treasure looted by the conquistadores, attracting French and English pirates.

Black slaves and free laborers were imported to work sugar and tobacco plantations, and waves of chiefly Spanish immigrants maintained a European character in the island's culture. Early slave rebellions and conflicts between colonials and Spanish rulers laid the foundation for an independence movement that turned into open warfare from 1867 to 1878. Slavery was abolished in 1886. In 1895, the poet José Marti led the struggle that finally ended Spanish rule, thanks largely to U.S. intervention in 1898 after the sinking of the battleship *Maine* in Havana harbor.

A treaty in 1899 made Cuba an independent republic under U.S. protection. The U.S. occupation, which ended in 1902, suppressed yellow fever and brought large American investments. From 1906 to 1909, Washington invoked the Platt Amendment to the treaty, which gave the U.S. the right to intervene in order to suppress any revolt. U.S. troops came back in 1912 and again in 1917 to restore order. The Platt Amendment was abrogated in 1934.

Fulgencio Batista, an army sergeant, led a revolt in 1933 that overthrew the regime of President Gerado Machado. Batista's Cuba was a police state. Corrupt officials used intimidation and took payoffs from American gamblers who operated casinos, demanded bribes from Cubans for various public services, and enriched themselves with raids on the public treasury.

Fidel Castro Ruz, a tall, bearded attorney in his thirties who had been in exile in Mexico, landed in Cuba on Christmas Day 1956 with a band of 12 fellow revolutionaries, evaded Batista's soldiers, and set up headquarters in the jungled hills of the Sierra Maestra range. By 1958 his force had grown to about 2,000 guerrillas, for the most part young and middle-class. Castro's brother Raul, and Ernesto (Ché) Guevara, an Argentine physician, were his top lieutenants. Businessmen and landowners who opposed the Batista regime gave financial support to the rebels. The United States, meanwhile, cut off arms shipments to Batista's army. The beginning of the end for Batista came when the rebels routed 3,000 government troops and captured Santa Clara, capital of Las Villas province 150 miles from Havana, and a trainload of Batista reinforcements refused to get out of their railroad cars. On New Year's Day 1959, Batista flew to exile in the Dominican Republic and Castro took over the government. Crowds cheered the revolutionaries on their seven-day march to the capital.

The United States initially welcomed what looked like the prospect for a democratic Cuba, but a rude awakening came within a few months when Castro established military tribunals for political opponents, jailed hundreds, and began to veer leftward. Castro disavowed Cuba's 1952 military pact with the U.S. He confiscated U.S. investments in banks and industries and seized large U.S. landholdings, turning them first into collective farms and then into Soviet-type state farms. The United States broke relations with Cuba on Jan. 3, 1961. Castro forged an alliance with the Soviet Union.

From the ranks of the Cuban exiles who had fled to the U.S., the Central Intelligence Agency recruited and trained an expeditionary force, numbering less than 2,000 men, to invade Cuba, with the expectation that the invasion would spark an uprising of the Cuban populace against Castro. Planned under the Eisenhower administration, President John F. Kennedy gave the go-ahead for the invasion in early 1961, but rejected a CIA proposal for U.S. planes to provide air support. The landing at the Bay of Pigs on April 17, 1961, was a fiasco. Not only did the invaders fail to receive any support from the populace, but Castro's tanks and artillery made short work of the small force.

A Soviet attempt to change the global power balance by installing medium-range missiles in Cuba—capable of striking targets in the United States with nuclear warheads—provoked a crisis between the superpowers in 1962 that had the potential of touching off World War III. Denouncing the Soviets for "deliberate deception," President Kennedy on Oct. 22 announced that the U.S. Navy would enforce a "quarantine" of shipping to Cuba and search Soviet-bloc ships to prevent the missiles themselves from reaching the island. After six days of tough public statements on both sides and secret diplomacy, Soviet premier Nikita Khrushchev on Oct. 28 ordered the missile sites dismantled and shipped back to the Soviet Union, in return for a U.S. pledge not to attack Cuba.

A Soviet satellite in the 1960s and 1970s, Cuba helped spread the Communist revolution in the Western hemisphere. The U.S. established limited diplomatic ties with Cuba on Sept. 1, 1977. Emigration increased dramatically after April 1, 1980, when Castro, irritated by the granting of asylum to would-be refugees by the Peruvian embassy in Havana, removed guards and allowed 10,000 Cubans to swarm into the embassy grounds.

As an airlift began taking the refugees to Costa Rica, Castro opened the port of Mariel to a "freedom flotilla" of ships and yachts from the United States, many of them owned or chartered by Cuban-Americans to bring out relatives. It wasn't until after the refugees had reached the United States that it was discovered that the regime had opened prisons and mental hospitals to permit criminals, homosexuals, and others unwanted by the Cuban government to join the refugees.

For most of President Ronald Reagan's first term, U.S.-Cuban relations were frozen. But late in 1984, an agreement was reached between the two countries. Cuba would take back more than 2,700 Cubans who had come to the United States in the Mariel exodus but were not eligible to stay in the country under U.S. immigration law because of criminal or psychiatric disqualification. Castro canceled the agreement when the U.S. began the Radio Marti broadcasts in May 1985 to bring a non-Communist viewpoint to the Cuban people.

With the collapse of communism in eastern Europe, Cuba's foreign trade plummeted as did aid from Russia, producing the worst economic crisis in the island's history. The government moved slightly toward a mixed economy in 1993 by permitting limited private enterprise in a number of trades and services and allowing Cubans to possess convertible currencies. In March 1996, the U.S. passed the Helms-Burton Act, which further extended the U.S. trade embargo on Cuba by penalizing non-U.S. companies doing business with Cuba. Reaction to the measure was widespread international condemnation by countries that included the U.S.'s North American neighbors, Canada, Mexico, and the Caribbean nations. Christmas was declared an official holiday in Cuba in 1997, for the first time since the revolution, in preparation for Pope John Paul II's historic visit to Cuba in Jan. 1998. By Castro's allowing the pope's visit, he raised hopes that the gesture signaled a new openness, easing of restrictions, and increased religious freedom for Cubans.

In mid-1999, the U.S. sent negotiators to Havana to begin talks on better communication between the U.S. and Cuba regarding drug shipments in the Caribbean, despite protests from some Cuban-Americans. The U.S. government stated that the action was not part of an effort to normalize relations with Cuba.

In June 2000 Castro won a publicity bonanza when the Clinton administration sent Elian Gonzalez back to Cuba. The young boy, who was found clinging to an inner tube floating off the Florida coast in Nov. 1999, became the subject of an international dispute. The U.S. Cuban community demanded that the boy remain in Miami rather than be returned to his father in Cuba. By many accounts, the influential Cuban-Americans lost public sympathy by pitting political ideology against familial bonds.

Cyprus

REPUBLIC OF CYPRUS

National name: Kypriaki Dimokratia—Kibris Cumhuriyeti
President: Glafcos Klerides (1993)
Area: 3,572 sq. mi (9,250 sq. km)
Population (1998 est.): 758,363; (average annual rate of natural increase: 0.6%; birth rate: 13.3/1000; infant mortality rate: 8.1/1000; density per sq. mi.: 212
Capital and largest city (1993): Lefkosia (Nicosia) (in government-controlled area), 186,400. **Monetary unit:** Cyprus pound. **Languages:** Greek, Turkish (official), English is widely spoken. **Ethnicity/race:** total: Greek 78% (99.5% of the Greeks live in the Greek area, 0.5% live in the Turkish area), Turkish 18% (1.3% live in the Greek area, 98.7% live in the Turkish area), other 4%. **Religions (1993 est.):** Greek Orthodox, 78%; Sunni Muslim, 18%; Maronite, Armenian, Apostolic, Latin and others, 4%. **Literacy rate:** 94% (1987)
Economic summary: GDP/PPP (1997 est.): $10 billion; $13,000 per capita. **Real growth rate:** 2.3%. **Inflation:** Greek Cypriot area: 2.3% (1998 est.); Turkish Cypriot area: 87.5% (1997 est.). **Unemployment:** Greek Cypriot area: 3.3% (1998 est.); Turkish Cypriot area: 6.4% (1996). **Arable land:** 12%. **Agriculture:** potatoes, citrus, vegetables, barley, grapes, olives, vegetables. **Labor force:** Greek Cypriot area: 299,700: services, 62%; industry, 25%; agriculture, 13% (1995). Turkish Cypriot area: 76,500 (1996): services, 66%; industry, 11%; agriculture, 23% (1995). **Industries:** food, beverages, textiles, chemicals, metal products, tourism, wood products. **Natural resources:** copper, pyrites, asbestos, gypsum, timber, salt, marble, clay earth pigment. **Exports:** Greek Cypriot area: $1.2 billion (f.o.b., 1998 est.): citrus, potatoes, grapes, wine, cement, clothing and shoes; Turkish Cypriot area: $70.5 million (f.o.b., 1996): citrus, potatoes, textiles. **Imports:** Greek Cypriot area: $3.8 billion (f.o.b., 1998 est.): consumer goods, petroleum and lubricants, food and feed grains, machinery; Turkish Cypriot area: $318.4 million (f.o.b., 1996): food, minerals, chemicals, machinery. **Major trading partners:** Greek Cypriot area: Russia, Bulgaria, U.K., Greece, Germany, U.S., Italy; Turkish Cypriot area: Turkey, U.K., other EU. **Member of Commonwealth of Nations**

Geography The third-largest island in the Mediterranean (one and one-half times the size of Delaware), Cyprus lies off the southern coast of Turkey and the western shore of Syria. The highest peak is Mount Olympus at 6,406 feet (1,953 m).

Government Republic. Mediation efforts by the U.N. seek to achieve reunification of the island under one federated system of government.

History Cyprus was the site of early Phoenician and Greek colonies. For centuries its rule passed through many hands. It fell to the Turks in 1571, and a large Turkish colony settled on the island.

In World War I, at the outbreak of hostilities with Turkey, Britain annexed the island. It was declared a crown colony in 1925. For centuries the Greek population, regarding Greece as its mother country, has sought self-determination and reunion with Greece (enosis). The resulting quarrel with Turkey threatened NATO. Cyprus became an independent nation on Aug. 16, 1960, with Britain, Greece, and Turkey as guarantor powers.

Archbishop Makarios, president since 1959, was overthrown on July 15, 1974, by a military coup led by the Cypriot National Guard. The new regime named Nikos Giorgiades Sampson as president and Bishop Gennadios as head of the Cypriot Church to replace Makarios. Diplomacy failed to resolve the crisis. Turkey invaded Cyprus by sea and air on July 20, 1974, asserting its right to protect the Turkish Cypriot minority. Geneva talks involving Greece, Turkey, Britain, and the two Cypriot factions failed in mid-Aug., and the Turks subsequently gained control of 40% of the island. Some 180,000 Greek Cypriots were uprooted by the Turkish troops. Greece made no armed response to the superior Turkish force, but bitterly suspended military participation in the NATO alliance. The tension continued after Makarios returned to become president on Dec. 7, 1974. He offered self-government to the Turkish minority, but rejected any solution "involving transfer of populations and amounting to partition of Cyprus."

Turkish Cypriots proclaimed a separate state under Rauf Denktas in the northern part of the island on Nov. 15, 1983, naming it the "Turkish Republic of Northern Cyprus." The U.N. Security Council, in its Resolution 541 of Nov. 18, 1983, declared this action legally invalid and called for withdrawal. No country except Turkey has recognized this illegal entity.

In 1988, George Vassiliou, a conservative and critic of U.N. proposals to reunify Cyprus, became president. The purchase of missiles capable of reaching the Turkish coast evoked threats of retaliation from Turkey in 1997, and Cyprus's plans to deploy more missiles in Aug. 1999 again raised Turkey's ire.

Czech Republic

President: Vaclav Havel (1993)
Prime Minister: Milos Zeman (1998)
Area: 30,464 sq. mi. (78,703 sq. km)
Population (2000 est.): 10,272,179 (average annual rate of natural increase: −0.2%); birth rate: 9.1/1000; infant mortality rate: 5.6/1000; density per sq. mi.: 337
Capital and largest city (Jan. 1, 1994): Prague, 1,215,771. **Other large cities:** Brno, 389,727; Ostrava, 326,396; Plzen, 172,402; Olomouc, 106,003. **Monetary unit:** Koruna. **Languages:** Czech; Slovak minority. **Ethnicity/race:** Czech 94.4%, Slovak 3%, Polish 0.6%, German 0.5%, Roma (Gypsy) 0.3%, Hungarian 0.2%, other 1%. **Religions:** atheist 39.8%, Roman Catholic 39.2%, Protestant 4.6%, Orthodox 3%, other 13.4%. **Literacy rate:** 99%
Economic summary: GDP/PPP: (1998 est.): $116.7 billion; $11,300 per capita. **Real growth rate:** −1.5%. **Inflation:** 10.7%. **Unemployment:** 7%. **Natural resources:** hard coal, soft coal, kaolin, clay, graphite. **Industries:** fuel, ferrous metallurgy, machinery and equipment, coal, motor vehicles, glass, armaments. **Agriculture:** grains, potatoes, sugar beets, hops, fruit, pigs, cattle, poultry, forest products. **Labor force:**

3.655 million: services 43.7%; industry, 33.1%; construction, 9.1%; transport and communications, 7.2%; agriculture, 6.9% (1994). **Exports:** $23.8 billion (f.o.b., 1998): manufactured goods, machinery and transport equipment, chemicals, raw materials and fuel. **Imports:** $26.8 billion (f.o.b., 1998): machinery and transport equipment, manufactured goods, raw materials and fuel, chemicals, food. **Major trading partners:** Germany, Slovakia, Austria, Poland, Russia, Italy, France, F.S.U., U.K.

Geography The Czech Republic's central European landscape is dominated by the Bohemian Massif, which rises to heights of 3,000 feet (900 m) above sea level. This ring of mountains encircles a large elevated basin, the Bohemian Plateau. The principal rivers are the Elbe and the Vltava.

Government Parliamentary democracy.

History Probably about the 5th century A.D., Slavic tribes from the Vistula basin settled in the region of the traditional Czech lands of Bohemia, Moravia, and Silesia. The Czechs founded the kingdom of Bohemia and the Premyslide dynasty, which ruled Bohemia and Moravia from the 10th to the 16th century. One of the Bohemian kings, Charles IV, holy Roman emperor, made Prague an imperial capital and a center of Latin scholarship. The Hussite movement founded by Jan Hus (1369?–1415) linked the Slavs to the Reformation and revived Czech nationalism, previously under German domination. A Hapsburg, Ferdinand I, ascended the throne in 1526. The Czechs rebelled in 1618, precipitating the Thirty Years' War (1618–48). Defeated in 1620, they were ruled for the next 300 years as part of the Austrian empire. Full independence from the Hapsburgs was not achieved until the end of World War I, following the collapse of the Austrian-Hungarian Empire.

A union of the Czech lands and Slovakia was proclaimed in Prague on Nov. 14, 1918, and the Czech nation became one of the two component parts of the newly formed Czechoslovakian state. In March 1939, German troops occupied Czechoslovakia, and Czech Bohemia and Moravia became German protectorates for the duration of World War II. The former government returned in April 1945 when the war ended and the country's pre-1938 boundaries were restored. When elections were held in 1946, Communists became the dominant political party and gained control of the Czechoslovakian government in 1948. Thereafter, the former democracy was turned into a Soviet-style state.

Nearly 42 years of Communist rule ended when Vaclav Havel, a highly respected writer and dissident, was elected president of Czechoslovakia in 1989. The return of democratic political reform saw a strong Slovak nationalist movement emerge by the end of 1991, which sought independence for Slovakia. When the general elections of June 1992 failed to resolve the continuing coexistence of the two republics within the federation, Czech and Slovak political leaders agreed to separate their states into two fully independent nations. On Jan. 1, 1993, the Czechoslovakian federation was dissolved and two separate independent countries were established—the Czech Republic and Slovakia.

In March 1999, the Czech Republic joined NATO. The country's next goal in international relations is to gain entrance into the European Union.

Denmark

KINGDOM OF DENMARK

National name: Kongeriget Danmark
Sovereign: Queen Margrethe II (1972)
Prime Minister: Poul Nyrup Rasmussen (1993)
Area: 16,833 sq. mi. (43,094 sq. km)[1]
Population (2000 est.): 5,336,394 (average annual rate of natural increase: .12%); birth rate: 12.2/1000; infant mortality rate: 5.1/1000; density per sq. mi.: 317
Capital and largest city (1992): Copenhagen, 1,339,395. **Other large cities (1992):** Århus, 204,139; Odense, 140,886; Ålborg, 114,970. **Monetary unit:** Krone. **Languages:** Danish, Faeroese, Greenlandic (an Inuit dialect), small German-speaking minority. **Ethnicity/race:** Scandinavian, Eskimo, Faeroese, German. **Religions:** Evangelical Lutheran 91%, other Protestant and Roman Catholic 2%, other 7%. **Literacy rate:** 99% (1980)
Economic summary: GDP/PPP (1998 est.): $124.4 billion; $23,300 per capita. **Real growth rate:** 2.6%. **Inflation:** 1.8%. **Unemployment:** 6.5%. **Arable land:** 60%. **Agriculture:** grain, potatoes, rape, sugar beets, beef, dairy products, fish. **Labor force:** 2,895,950: private services, 40%; government services, 30%; manufacturing and mining, 19%; construction, 6%; agriculture, forestry, and fishing, 5% (1995). **Industries:** food processing, machinery and equipment, textiles and clothing, chemical products, electronics, construction, furniture and other wood products, shipbuilding. **Natural resources:** petroleum, natural gas, fish, salt, limestone, stone, gravel, sand. **Exports:** $48.8 billion (f.o.b., 1998): machinery and instruments, meat and meat products, fuel, dairy products, ships, fish, chemicals. **Imports:** $46.1 billion (f.o.b., 1998): machinery and equipment, petroleum, chemicals, grain and foodstuffs, textiles, paper. **Major trading partners:** Germany, Sweden, U.K., Norway, France, U.S., Netherlands, Japan.

1. Excluding Faeroe Islands and Greenland.

Geography Smallest of the Scandinavian countries (half the size of Maine), Denmark occupies the Jutland peninsula, a lowland area. The country also consists of several islands in the Baltic Sea; the two largest are Sjælland, the site of Copenhagen, and Fyn.

Government Constitutional monarchy.

History From 10,000 to 1500 B.C., the population of present-day Denmark evolved from a society of hunters and fishers into an agricultural one. Called Jutland by the end of the 8th century, its mariners belonged to the Vikings, or Norsemen, who raided western Europe and the British Isles from the 9th to 11th century.

The country was Christianized by Saint Ansgar and Harald Blaatand (Bluetooth)—the first Christian king—in the 10th century. Harald's son, Sweyn, conquered England in 1013. His son, Canute the Great, who reigned from 1014 to 1035, united Denmark, England, and Norway under his rule; the southern tip of Sweden was part of Denmark until the 17th century. On Canute's death, civil war tore apart the country until Waldemar I (1157–82) reestablished Danish hegemony over the north.

In 1282, the nobles won the Great Charter, and Eric V was forced to share power with Parliament and a Council of Nobles. Waldemar IV (1340–75) restored Danish power, checked only by the Hanseatic League of north German cities allied with ports from Holland to Poland. Denmark, Norway, and Sweden united under the rule of his daughter Margrethe in 1397. But

Sweden later achieved autonomy and in 1523, under Gustavus I, independence.

Denmark supported Napoléon, for which it was punished at the Congress of Vienna in 1815 by the loss of Norway to Sweden. In 1864, the Prussians, under Bismarck, and the Austrians made war on Denmark as an initial step in the unification of Germany. Denmark was neutral in World War I.

In 1940, Denmark was invaded by the Nazis. King Christian X reluctantly cautioned his fellow Danes to accept the occupation, but there was widespread resistance against the Nazis. Denmark was the only occupied country in World War II to save all its Jews from extermination, by smuggling them out of the country.

Beginning in 1944, Denmark's relationship with its territories changed substantially. In that year, Iceland declared its independence from Denmark, ending a union that had existed since 1380. In 1948, the Faeroe Islands, which had also belonged to Denmark since 1380, were granted home rule, and in 1953, Greenland officially became a territory of Denmark.

A referendum on the Maastricht Accord, which paved the way for greater EU economic integration, passed in May 1993. Denmark has been a member of the EC (now the EU) since 1973. On Sept. 28, 2000, Denmark voted to reject adoption of the euro, the European common currency.

Outlying Territories of Denmark

Faeroe Islands

Status: Autonomous part of Denmark
Chief of State: Queen Margrethe II (1972)
High Commissioner: Vibeke Larsen (1995)
Prime Minister: Anfinn Kallsberg (1998)
Area: 540 sq. mi. (1,399 sq. km)
Population (2000 est.): 45,296 (average annual growth rate: 0.49%); birth rate: 13.6/1000; infant mortality rate: 6.9/1000; density per sq. mi.: 84
Capital and largest city (1993 est.): Tórshavn, 16,100.
Monetary unit: Faeroese krone. **Languages:** Faeroese, Danish (both official). **Ethnicity/race:** Scandinavian. **Literacy rate:** 99%

This group of 18 islands, of which 17 are inhabited, are located in the North Atlantic about 200 miles (322 km) northwest of the Shetland Islands. They were settled by the Vikings, the ancestors of the modern-day Faeroese, in the 8th century. The Faeroese language is derived from Old Norse. The islands joined Denmark in 1386 and have been part of the Danish kingdom ever since. The Faeroes have had home rule, under Danish authority, since 1948.

Greenland

Status: Autonomous part of Denmark
Chief of State: Queen Margrethe II (1972)
High Commissioner: Gunnar Martens (1995)
Premier: Jonathan Motzfeldt (1997)
Area: 840,000 sq. mi. (incl. 708,069 sq. mi. covered by icecap) (2,175,600 sq. km)
Population (2000 est.): 56,309 (average annual growth rate: 0.93%); birth rate: 16.9/1000; infant mortality rate: 18.3/1000; density per sq. mi.: 0.07.
Capital and largest city (1995 est.): Godthaab, 12,723.
Monetary unit: Krone. **Ethnicity/race:** Greenlander 87% (Eskimos and Greenland-born whites), Danish and other13%. **Literacy rate:** 99%

The Inuit are believed to have crossed from North America to northwest Greenland, the world's largest island, between 4000 B.C. and A.D. 1000. Greenland was colonized in A.D. 985–86 by Eric the Red. The Norse settlements declined in the 14th century, how-

ever, mainly as a result of a cooling in Greenland's climate, and in the 15th century they became extinct. In 1721, Greenland was recolonized by the Royal Greenland Trading Company of Denmark.

Greenland was under U.S. protection during World War II, but maintained Danish sovereignty. A definitive agreement for the joint defense of Greenland within the framework of NATO was signed in 1951. A large U.S. air base at Thule in the far north was completed in 1953.

Under 1953 amendments to the Danish constitution, Greenland became part of Denmark, with two representatives in the Danish Folketing. On May 1, 1979, Greenland gained home rule, with its own local Parliament (Landsting). In Feb. 1982, Greenlanders voted to withdraw from the European Union, which they had joined as part of Denmark in 1973.

Djibouti

REPUBLIC OF DJIBOUTI

National name: Jumhouriyya Djibouti
President: Ismail Omar Guelleh (1999)
Prime Minister: Barkat Gourad Hamadou (1978)
Area: 8,878 sq. mi. (22,000 sq. km)
Population (2000 est.): 451,442 (average annual rate of natural increase: 2.6%); birth rate: 41/1000; infant mortality rate: 103.3/1000; density per sq. mi.: 51
Capital (1992 est.): Djibouti, 395,000. **Monetary unit:** Djibouti franc. **Languages:** Arabic, French, Afar, Somali. **Ethnicity/race:** Somali 60%, Afar 35%, French, Arab, Ethiopian, and Italian 5%. **Religions:** Muslim, 94%; Christian, 6%. **Literacy rate:** 46% (1995)
Economic summary: GDP/PPP (1998 est.): $530 million; $1,200 per capita. **Real growth rate:** 0.6%. **Inflation:** 3% (1997 est.). **Unemployment:** 40%–50% (1996 est.). **Arable land:** n.a. **Agriculture:** fruit, vegetables; goats, sheep, camels. **Labor force:** 282,000: agriculture, 75%; services, 14%; industry, 11% (1991 est.). **Industries:** limited to a few small-scale enterprises, such as dairy products and mineral-water bottling. **Natural resources:** geothermal areas. **Exports:** $39.6 million (f.o.b., 1996 est.): hides and skins, coffee (in transit). **Imports:** $200.5 million (f.o.b., 1996 est.): food, beverages, transport equipment, chemicals, petroleum products. **Major trading partners:** Ethiopia, Somalia, Yemen, Saudi Arabia, France, Italy, Thailand.

Geography Djibouti lies in northeastern Africa on the Gulf of Aden at the southern entrance to the Red Sea. It borders on Ethiopia, Eritrea, and Somalia. The country, the size of Massachusetts, is mainly a stony desert, with scattered plateaus and highlands.

Government Republic with a unicameral legislature.

History Ablé immigrants from Arabia migrated to what is now Djibouti in about the 3rd century B.C. Their descendants are the Afars, one of the two main ethnic groups that make up Djibouti today. Somali Issas arrived thereafter. Islam came to the region in A.D. 825.

Djibouti was acquired by France between 1843 and 1886 by treaties with the Somali sultans. Small, arid, and sparsely populated, it is important chiefly because of the capital city's port, the terminal of the Djibouti–Addis Ababa railway that carries 60% of Ethiopia's foreign trade. Originally known as French Somaliland, the colony voted in 1958 and 1967 to remain under French rule. It was renamed the Territory of the Afars and Issas in 1967 and took the name of its capital city on attaining independence. On June 27, 1977, France transferred sovereignty to the new nation of Djibouti. On Sept. 4, 1992, voters approved in referendum a new multiparty constitution. In 1991 conflict between the Afars and the Issa-dominated government erupted and the continued warfare has ravaged the country.

The dictatorial president, Hassan Gouled Aptidon, who had run the country since its independence, finally stepped aside in 1999 and Ismail Omar Gulleh was elected president. In March 2000, the main Afars rebel group signed a peace accord with the government.

Dominica

COMMONWEALTH OF DOMINICA

President: Vernon Shaw (1998)
Prime Minister: Pierre Charles (2000)
Area: 290 sq. mi. (750 sq. km)
Population (2000 est.): 71,540 (average annual rate of natural increase: 1.1%); birth rate: 18.3/1000; infant mortality rate: 17.1/1000; density per sq. mi.: 247
Capital and largest city (1991): Roseau, 15,853.
Monetary unit: East Caribbean dollar. **Languages:** English and French patois. **Ethnicity/race:** black, Carib Indians. **Religions:** Roman Catholic, 77%; Protestant, 15%. **Literacy rate:** 94% (1970)
Economic summary: GDP/PPP (1997 est.): $216 million; $3,300 per capita. **Real growth rate:** 1.8%. **Inflation:** 2.2%. **Unemployment:** 15% (1992 est.). **Arable land:** 9%. **Agriculture:** bananas, citrus, mangoes, root crops, coconuts; forest and fishery potential not exploited. **Labor force:** 25,000: agriculture, 40%; industry and commerce, 32%; services, 28%. **Industries:** soap, coconut oil, tourism, copra, furniture, cement blocks, shoes. **Exports:** $50.4 million (1997): bananas, soap, bay oil, vegetables, grapefruit, oranges. **Imports:** $104.2 million (1997): manufactured goods, machinery and equipment, food, chemicals. **Major trading partners:** Caricom countries, U.K., U.S., Netherlands, Canada. **Member of Commonwealth of Nations**

Geography Dominica is a mountainous island of volcanic origin of the Lesser Antilles in the Caribbean south of Guadeloupe and north of Martinique.

Government Republic.

History Explored by Columbus in 1493, Dominica was claimed by Britain and France until 1763, when it was formally ceded to Britain. Along with other Windward Isles, it became a self-governing member of the West Indies Associated States in free association with Britain in 1967.

Dissatisfaction over the slow pace of reconstruction after Hurricane David devastated the island in Sept. 1979 brought a landslide victory for the Freedom Party in July 1980. The vote gave the prime ministership to Mary Eugenia Charles, a strong advocate of free enterprise. The Freedom Party won again in 1985 and 1990, and the government pursued a policy of divesting itself of state enterprises. The opposition United Workers' Party captured the general election of June 1995. In 1997 Dominica became the first Caribbean country to participate in the work of Green Globe, aiming to make Dominica a model ecotourism destination.

On Oct. 3, Pierre Charles, previously Communications and Works Minister, became the country's sixth prime minister. He succeeded Roosevelt Douglas, who died suddenly.

Dominican Republic

National name: República Dominicana
President: Hipólito Mejía (2000)
Area: 18,704 sq. mi. (48,730 sq. km)
Population (2000 est.): 8,442,533 (average annual rate of natural increase: 2.04%); birth rate: 25.2/1000; infant mortality rate: 35.9/1000; density per sq. mi.: 451
Capital and largest city (1993): Santo Domingo, 2,100,000. **Other large city (1993):** Santiago de los Caballeros, 690,000. **Monetary unit:** Peso.
Languages: Spanish, English widely spoken.
Ethnicity/race: white 16%, black 11%, mixed 73%.
Religion: 90% Roman Catholic. **Literacy rate:** 84% (1990)
Economic summary: GDP/PPP (1998 est.): $39.8 billion; $5,000 per capita. **Real growth rate:** 7%. **Inflation:** 6%. **Unemployment:** 16% (1997 est.). **Arable land:** 21%. **Agriculture:** sugarcane, coffee, cotton, cocoa, tobacco, rice, beans, potatoes, corn, bananas, cattle, pigs, dairy products, beef, eggs. **Labor force:** 2.3–2.6 million: agriculture, 50%; services and government, 32%; industry, 18% (1991 est.). **Industries:** tourism, sugar processing, ferronickel and gold mining, textiles, cement, tobacco. **Natural resources:** nickel, bauxite, gold, silver. **Exports:** $997 million (1997 est.): ferronickel, sugar, gold, coffee, cocoa. **Imports:** $3.6 billion (1998): foodstuffs, petroleum, cotton and fabrics, chemicals and pharmaceuticals. **Major trading partners:** U.S., EU, Canada, South Korea, Venezuela, Netherlands Antilles, Mexico, Japan.

Geography The Dominican Republic in the West Indies occupies the eastern two-thirds of the island of Hispaniola, which it shares with Haiti. Its area equals that of Vermont and New Hampshire combined. Duarte Peak, at 10,417 feet (3,175 m), is the highest point in the West Indies.

Government Republic.

History The Dominican Republic was explored by Columbus on his first voyage in 1492. He named it La Española, and his son, Diego, was its first viceroy. The capital, Santo Domingo, founded in 1496, is the oldest European settlement in the Western Hemisphere.

Spain ceded the colony to France in 1795, and Haitian blacks under Toussaint L'Ouverture conquered it in 1801. In 1808 the people revolted and captured Santo Domingo the next year, setting up the first republic. Spain regained title to the colony in 1814. In 1821 Spanish rule was overthrown, but in 1822 the colony was again reconquered by the Haitians. In 1844 the Haitians were thrown out, and the Dominican Republic was established, headed by Pedro Santana. Uprisings and Haitian attacks led Santana to make the country a province of Spain from 1861 to 1865.

President Buenaventura Báez, faced with an economy in shambles, attempted to have the country annexed to the U.S. in 1870, but the U.S. Senate refused to ratify a treaty of annexation. Disorder continued until the dictatorship of Ulíses Heureaux; in 1916, when chaos broke out again, the U.S. sent in a contingent of marines, who remained until 1934.

A sergeant in the Dominican army trained by the marines, Rafaél Leonides Trujillo Molina, overthrew Horacio Vásquez in 1930 and established a dictatorship that lasted until his assassination 31 years later.

Leftists rebelled on April 24, 1965, and U.S. president Lyndon Johnson sent in marines and troops. After a cease-fire on May 6, a compromise installed

Hector Garcia-Godoy as provisional president. Joaquin Balaguer won in free elections in 1966 against Bosch, and a peacekeeping force of 9,000 U.S. troops and 2,000 from other countries withdrew. Balaguer restored political and economic stability.

In 1978, the army suspended the counting of ballots when Balaguer trailed in a fourth-term bid. After a warning from President Jimmy Carter, however, Balaguer accepted the victory of Antonio Guzmán of the opposition Dominican Revolutionary Party. Salvador Jorge Blanco of the Dominican Revolutionary Party was elected president on May 16, 1982, defeating Balaguer and Bosch. Balaguer was again elected president in May 1986 and remained in office for the next ten years.

In 1996, U.S.-raised Leonel Fernandez secured more than 51% of the vote through an alliance with Balaguer. The first item on the president's agenda was the partial sale of a number of state-owned enterprises. Fernandez was praised for changing his country's decades-long isolationist stance and for improving diplomatic relations with other Caribbean countries, but he has been criticized for doing little to reform corruption and alleviate the poverty that affects 60% of the population.

In Aug. 2000, the country's newly elected president, Hipolito Mejia, was sworn into office. The center-left Mejia takes office amid growing discontent over repeated power outages from the recently privatized electric industry. He pledged to fight corruption and expand the economy.

Ecuador

REPUBLIC OF ECUADOR

National name: República del Ecuador
President: Gustavo Noboa (2000)
Area: 106,822 sq. mi (283,560 sq. km)
Population (2000 est.): 12,920,092 (average annual rate of natural increase: 2.1%); birth rate: 26.5/1000; infant mortality rate: 35.1/1000; density per sq. mi.: 121
Capital (1998 est.): Quito, 1,500,000. **Other large cities (1998 est.):** Guayaquil, 2,000,000; Cuenca, 200,000.
Monetary unit: Sucre. **Languages:** Spanish (by 90% of population), Quéchua. **Ethnicity/race:** mestizo (mixed Indian and Spanish) 55%, Indian 25%, Spanish 10%, black 10%. **Religion:** Roman Catholic, 95%.
Literacy rate: 90% (1990)
Economic summary: GDP/PPP (1998 est.): $58.7 billion; $4,800 per capita. **Real growth rate:** 1%. **Inflation:** 43%. **Unemployment:** 12% (Nov. 1998 est.). **Arable land:** 6%. **Agriculture:** bananas, coffee, cocoa, rice, potatoes, manioc (tapioca), plantains, sugarcane, cattle, sheep, pigs, beef, pork, dairy products, balsa wood, fish, shrimp. **Labor force:** 4.2 million: services and other activities, 38%; agriculture, 29%; manufacturing, 18%; commerce, 15% (1990).
Industries: petroleum, food processing, textiles, metal working, paper products, wood products, chemicals, plastics, fishing, lumber. **Exports:** $3.4 billion (f.o.b., 1997): petroleum, bananas, shrimp, cut flowers, fish. **Imports:** $2.9 billion (c.i.f., 1997): transport equipment, consumer goods, vehicles, machinery, chemicals. **Major trading partners:** U.S., Latin America, EU, Asia.

Geography Ecuador, about equal in area to Nevada, is in the northwest part of South America fronting on the Pacific. To the north is Colombia and to the east and south is Peru. Two high and parallel ranges of the Andes, traversing the country from north to south, are topped by tall volcanic peaks. The highest is Chimborazo at 20,577 feet (6,272 m). The

Galápagos Islands (or Colón Archipelago; 3,029 sq. mi.; 7,845 sq. km), in the Pacific Ocean about 600 miles (966 km) west of the South American mainland, became part of Ecuador in 1832.

Government Republic.

History The tribes in the northern highlands of Ecuador formed the Kingdom of Quito around A.D. 1000. It was absorbed, by conquest and marriage, into the Inca empire. Spanish conquistador Francisco Pizarro conquered the land in 1532, and through the 17th century a thriving colony was built by exploitation of the Indians. The first revolt against Spain occurred in 1809. Ecuador then joined Venezuela, Colombia, and Panama in a confederacy known as Greater Colombia.

On the collapse of this union in 1830, Ecuador became independent. Revolts and dictatorships followed; it had 48 presidents during the first 131 years of the republic. Conservatives ruled until the revolution of 1895 ushered in nearly a half century of Radical Liberal rule, during which the church was disestablished and freedom of worship, speech, and press was introduced. Although it was under military rule in the 1970s, the country did not experience the violence and repression characteristic of other Latin American military regimes. Its last twenty years of democracy, however, have been largely ineffectual because of a weak executive branch and a strong, fractious Congress. In 1997, former president Abdala Bucaram was removed from office for mental instability.

Peru invaded Ecuador in 1941 and was able to seize a large tract of Ecuadorian territory in the disputed Amazonian area; the volatile situation flared up into war again in 1981 and 1995. In May 1999, the presidents of Ecuador and Peru signed a treaty ending a nearly 60-year border dispute involving the stretch of Amazon jungle.

In 1998, Ecuador experienced one of its worst economic crises. El Nino had inflicted about $3 billion in damages, the price of its principal export, oil, plunged, and its inflation rate, 43%, was the highest in Latin America. In 1999, the government was near bankruptcy and the currency lost 40% of its value against the dollar. The president's economic austerity plan was protested with massive strikes in March.

President Jamil Mahuad was overthrown in Jan. 2000, the first military coup in Latin America in a decade. The junta quickly turned over power to the vice president, Gustavo Noboa. Noboa restructured Ecuador's foreign debt, adopted the U.S. dollar as the national currency, and continued privatization of state-owned industries. The measures generated enormous congressional and public opposition.

Egypt

ARAB REPUBLIC OF EGYPT

President: Hosni Mubarak (1981)
Prime Minister: Atef Ebeid (1999)
Area: 386,900 sq. mi. (1,001,450 sq. km)
Population (2000 est.): 68,359,979 (average annual rate of natural increase: 1.8%); birth rate: 25.4/1000; infant mortality rate: 62.3/1000; density per sq. mi.: 177
Capital and largest city (2000 est.): Cairo, 14,350,000 (metro. area). **Other large cities (1992 est.):** Alexandria, 3,380,000; Giza, 2,144,000 (part of Cairo metro. area); Shubra el Khema, 834,000 (part of Cairo metro. area); El Mahalla el Kubra, 408,000. **Monetary unit:** Egyptian pound. **Language:** Arabic. **Ethnicity/**

race: Eastern Hamitic stock (Egyptians, Bedouins, and Berbers) 99%, Greek, Nubian, Armenian, other European (primarily Italian and French) 1%. **Religions:** Islam, 94%; Christian (mostly Coptic), 6%. **Literacy rate:** 48% (1990)
Economic summary: GDP/PPP (1998 est.): $188 billion; $2,850 per capita. **Real growth rate:** 5%. **Inflation:** 3.6%. **Unemployment:** 10%. **Arable land:** 2%. **Agriculture:** cotton, rice, corn, wheat, beans, fruit, vegetables, cattle, water buffalo, sheep, goats, fish. **Labor force:** 17.4 million (1998 est.): agriculture, 40%; services, including government, 38%; industry, 22% (1990 est.). **Industries:** textiles, food processing, tourism, chemicals, petroleum, construction, cement, metals. **Natural resources:** petroleum, natural gas, iron ore, phosphates, manganese, limestone, gypsum, talc, asbestos, lead, zinc. **Exports:** $5.5 billion (f.o.b., FY97/98 est.): crude oil and petroleum products, cotton yarn, raw cotton, textiles, metal products, chemicals. **Imports:** $16.7 billion (c.i.f., FY97/98 est.): machinery and equipment, food, fertilizers, wood products, durable consumer goods, capital goods. **Major trading partners:** EU, U.S., Japan.

Geography Egypt, at the northeast corner of Africa on the Mediterranean Sea, is bordered on the west by Libya, on the south by the Sudan, and on the east by the Red Sea and Israel. It is nearly one and one-half times the size of Texas. Egypt is divided into two unequal, extremely arid regions by the landscape's dominant feature, the northward-flowing Nile River. The Nile starts 100 miles (161 km) south of the Mediterranean and fans out to a sea front of 155 miles between the cities of Alexandria and Port Said.

Government Republic.

History Egyptian history dates back to about 4000 B.C., when the kingdoms of upper and lower Egypt, already highly sophisticated, were united. Egypt's "Golden Age" coincided with the 18th and 19th dynasties (16th to 13th century B.C.), during which the empire was established. Persia conquered Egypt in 525 B.C., Alexander the Great subdued it in 332 B.C., and then the dynasty of the Ptolemies ruled the land until 30 B.C., when Cleopatra, last of the line, committed suicide and Egypt became a Roman, then Byzantine, province. Arab caliphs ruled Egypt from 641 until 1517, when the Turks took it for their Ottoman Empire.
Napoléon's armies occupied the country from 1798 to 1801. In 1805, Mohammed Ali, leader of a band of Albanian soldiers, became pasha of Egypt. After completion of the Suez Canal in 1869, the French and British took increasing interest in Egypt. British troops occupied Egypt in 1882, and British resident agents became its actual administrators, though it remained under nominal Turkish sovereignty. In 1914, this fiction was ended, and Egypt became a protectorate of Britain.
Egyptian nationalism forced Britain to declare Egypt an independent, sovereign state on Feb. 28, 1922, although the British reserved rights for the protection of the Suez Canal and the defense of Egypt. In 1936, by an Anglo-Egyptian treaty of alliance, all British troops and officials were to be withdrawn, except from the Suez Canal Zone. When World War II started, Egypt remained neutral. British imperial troops finally ended the Nazi threat to Suez in 1942 in the battle of El Alamein, west of Alexandria. In 1951, Egypt abrogated the 1936 treaty and the 1899 Anglo-Egyptian condominium of the Sudan. Rioting and attacks on British troops in the Suez Canal Zone

followed, reaching a climax in Jan. 1952. The army, led by Gen. Mohammed Naguib, seized power on July 23, 1952. Three days later, King Farouk abdicated in favor of his infant son. The monarchy was abolished and a republic proclaimed on June 18, 1953, with Naguib holding the posts of provisional president and premier. He relinquished the latter in 1954 to Gamal Abdel Nasser, leader of the ruling military junta, who was confirmed as president in a referendum on June 23, 1956.
Nasser's policies embroiled his country in continual conflict. In 1956, the U.S. and Britain withdrew their pledges of financial aid for the building of the Aswan High Dam. In response, Nasser nationalized the Suez Canal and expelled British oil and embassy officials. Israel, barred from the canal and exasperated by terrorist raids, invaded the Gaza Strip and the Sinai Peninsula. Britain and France, after demanding Egyptian evacuation of the canal zone, attacked Egypt on Oct. 31, 1956. Worldwide pressure forced Britain, France, and Israel to halt the hostilities. A U.N. emergency force occupied the canal zone, and all troops were evacuated in the spring of 1957.
On June 5, 1967, Israel invaded the Sinai Peninsula, the East Bank of the Jordan River, and the zone around the Gulf of Aqaba. A U.N. cease-fire on June 10 saved the Arabs from complete rout. Nasser declared the 1967 cease-fire void along the canal in April 1969 and began a war of attrition. The U.S. peace plan of June 19, 1970, resulted in Egypt's agreement to reinstate the cease-fire for at least three months, (from Aug.) and to accept Israel's existence within "recognized and secure" frontiers that might emerge from U.N.-mediated talks. In return, Israel accepted the principle of withdrawing from occupied territories. On Sept. 28, 1970, Nasser died of a heart attack. Anwar el-Sadat, an associate of Nasser and a former newspaper editor, became the next president.
In July 1972, Sadat ordered the expulsion of Soviet "advisers and experts" from Egypt because the Russians had not provided the sophisticated weapons he felt were needed to retake territory lost to Israel in 1967. The fourth Arab-Israeli War broke out on Oct. 6, 1973, during the Jewish holiday of Yom Kippur. Egypt swept deep into the Sinai, while Syria strove to throw Israel off the Golan Heights. A U.N.-sponsored truce was accepted on Oct. 22. In Jan. 1974, both sides agreed to a settlement negotiated by U.S. Secretary of State Henry A. Kissinger that gave Egypt a narrow strip along the entire Sinai bank of the Suez Canal. In June, President Nixon made the first visit by a U.S. president to Egypt and full diplomatic relations were established. The Suez Canal was cleared and reopened on June 5, 1975.
In the most audacious act of his career, Sadat flew to Jerusalem at the invitation of Prime Minister Menachem Begin and pleaded before Israel's Knesset for a permanent peace settlement. The Arab world reacted with fury—only Morocco, Tunisia, Sudan, and Oman approved. Egypt and Israel signed a formal peace treaty on March 26, 1979. The pact ended 30 years of war and established diplomatic and commercial relations.
Egyptian and Israeli officials met in the Sinai desert on April 26, 1979, to implement the peace treaty calling for the phased withdrawal of occupation forces from the peninsula. By mid-1980, two-thirds of the Sinai was transferred, but progress was not matched elsewhere—the negotiation of Arab autonomy in the Gaza Strip and the West Bank remained stymied. Sadat halted further talks in Aug. 1980 because of

continued Israeli settlement of the West Bank. On Oct. 6, 1981, Sadat was assassinated by extremist Muslim soldiers at a parade in Cairo. Vice President Hosni Mubarak, a former air force chief of staff, succeeded him. Israel completed the return of the Sinai to Egyptian control on April 25, 1982. Israel's invasion of Lebanon in June brought a marked cooling in Egyptian-Israeli relations, but not a disavowal of the peace treaty.

While President Mubarak's stand during the Persian Gulf War won wide praise in the West, domestically this position proved far less popular. A presidential referendum in Oct. 1993 supported Mubarak's bid for a third term, although only a third of the population registered to vote. The government has concentrated much of its time and attention in recent years combating Islamic extremism, particularly attacks against Copts (Egyptian Christians).

El Salvador

REPUBLIC OF EL SALVADOR

National name: República de El Salvador
President: Francisco Guillermo Flores Pérez (1999)
Area: 8,260 sq. mi. (21,040 sq. km)
Population (2000 est.): 6,122,515 (average annual rate of natural increase: 2.3%); birth rate: 29/1000; infant mortality rate: 29.2/1000; density per sq. mi.: 741
Capital and largest city (1993 est.): San Salvador, 972,810. **Other large cities (1993 est.):** Santa Ana, 208,322; San Miguel, 161,156; Zacatecoluca, 81,035.
Monetary unit: Colón. **Language:** Spanish. **Ethnicity/race:** mestizo 94%, Indian 5%, white 1%. **Religion:** Roman Catholic. **Literacy rate:** 73% (1990)
Economic summary: GDP/PPP (1998 est.): $17.5 billion; $3,000 per capita. **Real growth rate:** 3.7%. **Inflation:** 2.6%. **Unemployment:** 7.7% (1997 est.). **Arable land:** 27%. **Agriculture:** coffee, sugarcane, corn, rice, beans, oilseed, cotton, sorghum, beef, dairy products, shrimp. **Labor force:** 2.26 million (1997 est.): agriculture, 40%; commerce, 16%; manufacturing, 15%; government, 13%; financial services, 9%; transportation, 6%; other, 1%. **Industries:** food processing, beverages, petroleum, chemicals, fertilizer, textiles, furniture, light metals. **Natural resources:** hydropower, geothermal power, petroleum. **Exports:** $1.96 billion (f.o.b., 1997 est.): coffee, sugar, shrimp, textiles. **Imports:** $3.5 billion (c.i.f., 1997 est.): raw materials, consumer goods, capital goods, fuel. **Major trading partners:** U.S., Guatemala, Germany, Costa Rica, Honduras, Mexico, Panama, Venezuela, Japan.

Geography Situated on the Pacific coast of Central America, El Salvador has Guatemala to the west and Honduras to the north and east. It is the smallest of the Central American countries, its area equal to that of Massachusetts, and the only one without an Atlantic coastline. Most of the country is on a fertile volcanic plateau about 2,000 feet (607 m) high.

Government Republic.

History The Pipil Indians, descendants of the Aztecs, were the first inhabitants of El Salvador. They were thought to have migrated to the region in the 11th century. The first Europeans to arrive were the Spanish in 1524. A year later, Pedro de Alvarado, a lieutenant of Cortés, conquered El Salvador.

El Salvador, with the other countries of Central America, declared its independence from Spain on Sept. 15, 1821, and was part of a federation of Central American states until that union was dissolved in 1838. For decades after its independence, El Salvador

experienced numerous revolutions and wars against other Central American republics. From 1931 to 1979 El Salvador was ruled by a series of military dictatorships.

In the 1970s discontent with societal inequalities, a poor economy, and the repressive measures of dictatorship led to civil war between the government, the right-wing ARENA party, and leftist antigovernment guerrilla units, whose leading group was the Farabundo Martí National Liberation Front (FMLN). The U.S., extending its cold-war policy to Central America, intervened on the side of the military, despite its scores of human rights violations. The presidency of José Napoleón Duarte, a moderate civilian, from 1984–89, offered an alternative to the stark political extremes of right and left, but Duarte was unable to end the war and was not reelected. In 1989, Alfredo Cristiani of ARENA was elected.

On Jan. 16, 1992, the government signed a peace treaty with the guerrilla forces, formally ending the 12-year civil war that had claimed the lives of 75,000. Since then, El Salvador's presidents have been members of the ARENA party, including the current president, Francisco Flores, who took office in 1999.

To stimulate the economy, El Salvador, along with Guatemala and Honduras, signed a free trade agreement with Mexico in June 2000. Flores also won parliamentary approval for a U.S. military base in El Salvador over intense opposition by former Marxist rebels who feared U.S. intervention in the country's internal affairs. The base will fight drug trafficking and replaces facilities lost when the U.S. left the Panama Canal last year.

Equatorial Guinea

REPUBLIC OF EQUATORIAL GUINEA

National name: République de Guinea Ecuatorial
President: Col. Teodoro Obiang Nguema Mbasogo (1979)
Prime Minister: Angel Serafin Seriche Dougan (1996)
Area: 10,830 sq. mi. (28,050 sq. km)
Population (2000 est.): 474,214 (average annual rate of natural increase: 2.5%); birth rate: 38.1/1000; infant mortality rate: 94.8/1000; density per sq. mi.: 44
Capital and largest city (1983): Malabo, 30,418.
Monetary unit: CFA Franc. **Languages:** Spanish (official), French (2nd official) pidgin English, Fang, Bubi, Creole. **Ethnicity/race:** Bioko (primarily Bubi, some Fernandinos), Rio Muni (primarily Fang), Europeans less than 1,000, mostly Spanish. **Religions:** Roman Catholic, Protestant, traditional. **Literacy rate:** 50% (1990)
Economic summary: GDP/PPP (1997 est.): $660 million; $1,500 per capita. **Real growth rate:** n.a. **Inflation:** 6% (1996 est.). **Unemployment:** 30% (1998 est.). **Arable land:** 5%. **Agriculture:** coffee, cocoa, rice, yams, cassava (tapioca), bananas, palm oil nuts, manioc (tapioca), livestock, timber. **Labor force:** n.a. **Industries:** petroleum, fishing, sawmilling, natural gas. **Natural resources:** timber, petroleum, small unexploited deposits of gold, manganese, uranium. **Exports:** $197 million (f.o.b., 1996 est.): petroleum, timber, cocoa. **Imports:** $248 million (c.i.f., 1996 est.): petroleum, food, beverages, clothing, machinery. **Major trading partners:** U.S., Japan, Spain, China, Nigeria, Cameroon, France.

Geography Equatorial Guinea, formerly Spanish Guinea, consists of Rio Muni (10,045 sq. mi.; 26,117 sq. km), on the western coast of Africa, and several islands in the Gulf of Guinea, the largest of which is Bioko (formerly Fernando Po) (785 sq. mi.; 2,033 sq.

km). The other islands are Annobón, Corisco, Elobey Grande, and Elobey Chico. The total area is twice that of Connecticut.

Government   President with a 17-member Supreme Military Council since a 1979 coup.

History   The mainland was originally inhabited by Pygmies. The Fang and Bubi migrated there in the 17th century and to the main island of Fernando Po (now called Bioko) in the 19th century. In the 18th century, the Portuguese ceded land to the Spanish that included Equatorial Guinea. From 1827 to 1844, Britain administered Fernando Po, but it was then reclaimed by Spain. Río Muni, the mainland, was not occupied by the Spanish until 1926. Spanish Guinea, as it was then called, gained independence from Spain on Oct. 12, 1968. It is Africa's only Spanish-speaking country.

From the outset, President Francisco Macías Nguema, considered the father of independence, began a brutal reign, destroying the economy of the fledgling country and abusing human rights. Calling himself the "Unique Miracle," Nguema is considered one of the worst despots in African history. In 1971, the U.S. State Department reported that his regime was "characterized by abandonment of all government functions except internal security, which was accomplished by terror; this led to the death or exile of up to one-third of the population."

On Aug. 3, 1979, Nguema was overthrown and executed by his nephew, Lieut. Col. Teodoro Obiang Nguema Mbasogo. Obiang has been gradually modernizing the country, but has retained many of his uncle's dictatorial practices, including the amassing of personal wealth by siphoning it from the public coffers. A recent petroleum bonanza promises to boost the country's standard of living, but the president's family is believed to control the industry.

Eritrea

President: Isaias Afwerki (1993)
Area: 45,754 sq. mi. (121,320 sq. km)
Population (2000 est.): 4,135,933 (of which 0.5 million are refugees awaiting repatriation). Average annual rate of natural increase: 3.04%; birth rate: 42.7/1000; infant mortality rate: 76.7/1000; density per sq. mi.: 90
Capital and largest city (1993): Asmara, 400,000.
Other major cities: the ports of Massawa and Assab.
Monetary unit: Birr. **Languages:** Afar, Bilen, Kunama, Nara, Arabic, Tobedawi, Saho, Tigre, Tigrinya.
Ethnicity/race: ethnic Tigrinya 50%, Tigre and Kunama 40%, Afar 4%, Saho (Red Sea coast dwellers) 3%. **Religions:** Islam and Eritrean Orthodox Christianity. **Literacy rate:** 20%
Economic summary: GDP/PPP (1998 est.): $2.5 billion; $660 per capita. **Real growth rate:** 5%. **Inflation:** 8%. **Unemployment:** n.a. **Labor force:** n.a. **Industries:** food processing, beverages, clothing and textiles. **Agriculture:** sorghum, lentils, vegetables, maize, cotton, tobacco, coffee, sisal, livestock, goats, fish. **Natural resources:** gold, potash, zinc, copper, salt, probably oil and natural gas, fish. **Exports:** $95 million (1996 est.): livestock, sorghum, textiles, food, small manufactures. **Imports:** $514 million (1996 est.): processed goods, machinery, petroleum products. **Major trading partners:** Ethiopia, Sudan, U.S., Italy, Saudi Arabia, Yemen, U.A.E.

Geography   Eritrea was formerly the northernmost province of Ethiopia and is about the size of Indiana. Much of the country is mountainous. Its narrow Red Sea coastal plain is one of the hottest and driest places in Africa. The cooler central highlands have fertile valleys that support agriculture. Eritrea is bordered by the Sudan on the north and west, the Red Sea on the north and east, and Ethiopia and Djibouti on the south.

Government   A transitional government committed to a democratic system.

History   Eritrea was part of the first Ethiopian kingdom of Aksum until its decline in the 8th century A.D. It came under the control of the Ottoman Empire in the 16th century, and later of the Egyptians. The Italians captured the coastal areas in 1885, and the Treaty of Uccialli (May 2, 1889) gave Italy sovereignty over part of Eritrea. The Italians named their colony after the Roman name for the Red Sea—*Mare Erythraeum*—and ruled it up until World War II. The British captured Eritrea in 1941 and later administered it as a U.N. Trust Territory until it became federated with Ethiopia on Sept. 15, 1952. It was made an Ethiopian province on Nov. 14, 1962. A civil war broke out against the Ethiopian government led by rebel groups who opposed the union and wanted independence for Eritrea. The bitter conflict raged on for 17 years against the hard-line Communist regime of the Ethiopian dictator, Mengistu Haile Mariam, until he was overthrown in May 1991.

The Eritrean People's Liberation Front (EPLF) took control of Eritrea and shared power in a multiparty government in Addis Ababa with the Ethiopian People's Revolutionary Democratic Front (EPRDF). They agreed to hold a referendum on Eritrean independence within two years and on April 23–25, 1993, Eritrean voters almost unanimously opted for an independent republic. Ethiopia recognized Eritrea's sovereignty on May 3, 1993, and sought a new era of cooperation between the two countries.

While relations with Ethiopia remained good in 1995, those with the Sudan deteriorated. In Nov. 1996 Eritrea accused the Sudan of plotting to assassinate the president. The mission was thwarted by a Sudanese antigovernment group. Sudan denied the charge, although Eritrea provided specific names and dates of those allegedly involved.

Since Eritrea's independence, Eritrea and Ethiopia had disagreed about the exact demarcation of their borders, and in May 1998 border clashes broke out between them. After an eight-month lull that both sides used to reinforce their 600-mile common border, civil war broke out again in earnest. Both impoverished countries have spent millions of dollars on warplanes and weapons, tens of thousands of soldiers have died, and refugees are legion. In Sept. 1999 peace talks were under way, but broke down when Ethiopia refused to go along with the terms.

A cease-fire was agreed to in June 2000 and the United Nations agreed to provide between two and four thousand troops to patrol the buffer zone between the two nations until a permanent border could be agreed upon. Tens of thousands of people were killed in the two-year conflict.

Estonia

REPUBLIC OF ESTONIA

National name: Eesti
President: Lennart Meri (1992)
Prime Minister: Mart Laar (1999)
Area: 17,666 sq. mi. (45,226 sq. km)
Population (2000 est.): 1,431,471 (average annual rate of natural increase: –0.5%); birth rate: 8.5/1000; infant mortality rate: 12.9/1000; density per sq. mi.: 81
Capital and largest city (1992 est.): Tallinn, 471,608.
Other large city (1992 est.): Tartu, 113,400.
Monetary unit: Kroon. **Languages:** Estonian (official), Russian, Finnish, English. **Ethnicity/race:** Estonian 61.5%, Russian 30.3%, Ukrainian 3.2%, Belorussian 1.8%, Finn 1.1%, other 2.1% (1989). **Religions:** Lutheran, 78%; Orthodox, 19%. **Literacy:** 100% (1989)
Economic summary: GDP/PPP (1998 est.): $7.8 billion; $5,500 per capita. **Real growth rate:** 5.5%. **Inflation:** 6.5%. **Unemployment:** 9.6%. **Labor force** 717,000 (1997 est.): services, 47%; industry, 42%; agriculture and forestry, 11% (1996 est.). **Industries:** oil shale, shipbuilding, phosphates, electric motors, excavators, cement, furniture, clothing, textiles, paper, shoes, apparel. **Natural resources:** oil shale (kukersite), peat, phosphorite, amber, cambrian blue clay. **Agriculture:** potatoes, fruit, vegetables, livestock and dairy products, fish. **Exports:** $2.6 billion (f.o.b., 1998): machinery and equipment, 17%; textiles, 16%; food products, 8%; transport equipment, 8%; mineral products, 8%; chemical products, 8% (1997). **Imports:** $3.9 billion (c.i.f., 1998): machinery and equipment, 21%; transport equipment, 12%; foodstuffs, 10%; minerals, 9%; textiles, 8%; metals, 8%; chemical products, 8% (1997). **Major trading partners:** Finland, Russia, Sweden, Germany, Latvia, Japan, U.S.

Geography Estonia is mainly a lowland country that borders on the Baltic Sea. It has numerous lakes and forests and many rivers, most draining northward into the Gulf of Finland or eastward into Lake Peipus. Lake Peipus is Estonia's largest lake and is important to the fishing and shipping industries.

Government Parliamentary democracy.

History Born out of World War I, this small Baltic state enjoyed a mere two short decades of independence before it was absorbed again by its powerful neighbor, the Soviet Union. Estonians were able to resist assaults by Vikings, Danes, Swedes and Russians before the 13th century. In 1346 the Danes, who possessed northern Estonia, sold the land to the Teutonic Knights of Germany, who already possessed Livonia (southern Estonia and Latvia). The Teutonic Knights reduced the Estonians to serfdom. In 1526, the Swedes took over, and the power of the German (Balt) landowning class was reduced. But after 1721, when Russia succeeded Sweden as the ruling power under the Peace of Nystad, the Estonians were subject to a double bondage—the Balts and the czarist officials. The oppression lasted until the closing months of World War I, when Estonia finally achieved independence after a victorious war (1918–20). Shortly after the start of World War II, the nation was occupied by Russian troops and incorporated as the 16th republic of the U.S.S.R. in 1940. Germany occupied the nation from 1941 to 1944, when it was retaken by the Soviets.

Estonia declared independence from the Soviet Union in March 1990. Soviet resistance ensued, but by 1991, after recognition by European and other countries, the Soviet Union recognized Estonian nationhood on Sept. 6, 1991. U.N. membership followed on Sept. 17, 1991. The newly independent nation embraced free-market reforms. Fueled by foreign investments, economic advances continued unabated in 1997. This prompted the European Commission (EC) to recommend that Estonia begin accession talks for membership in the European Union.

At the end of 1998, Estonia relaxed the strict citizenship requirements that kept the country's 1.5 million Russian speakers—about one-third of the population—from gaining citizenship. In an attempt to foster Estonian language and culture after 50 years of Soviet domination, Estonia instituted policies of reverse discrimination, denying citizenship to those who could not speak Estonian. Estonia's reforms have granted citizenship to children born in Estonia of Russian-speaking parents, a change that has eased the way for Estonia's entry into the European Union.

Ethiopia

FEDERAL DEMOCRATIC REPUBLIC OF ETHIOPIA

President: Negasso Gidada (1995)
Prime Minister: Meles Zenawi (1995)
Area: 446,952 sq. mi. (1,127,127 sq. km)
Population (2000 est.): 64,117,452 (average annual rate of natural increase: 2.8%); birth rate: 45.1/1000; infant mortality rate: 101.3/1000; density per sq. mi.: 143
Capital and largest city (1993 est.): Addis Ababa, 2,200,186. **Monetary unit:** Birr. **Languages:** Amharic (official), English, Orominga, Tigrigna, over 70 languages spoken. **Ethnicity/race:** Oromo 40%, Amhara and Tigrean 32%, Sidamo 9%, Shankella 6%, Somali 6%, Afar 4%, Gurage 2%, other 1%. **Religions:** Ethiopian Orthodox, 35%–40%; Islam, 40%–45%; animist, 15%–20%; other, 5%. **Literacy rate:** 28% (1984)
Economic summary: GDP/PPP (1998 est.): $32.9 billion; $560 per capita. **Real growth rate:** 6%. **Inflation::** 3.9%. **Unemployment:** n.a. **Arable land:** 12%. **Agriculture:** cereals, pulses, coffee, oilseed, sugarcane, potatoes, hides, cattle, sheep, goats. **Industries:** food processing, beverages, textiles, chemicals, metals processing, cement. **Natural resources:** small reserves of gold, platinum, copper, potash, natural gas. **Labor force:** n.a.: agriculture and animal husbandry, 80%; government and services, 12%; industry and construction, 8% (1985). **Exports:** $550 million (f.o.b., 1998): coffee, leather products, gold, oilseed. **Imports:** $1.3 billion (f.o.b., 1998 est.): food and live animals, petroleum and petroleum products, chemicals, machinery, motor vehicles and aircraft. **Major trading partners:** Germany, Japan, Italy, U.K., Djibouti, Saudi Arabia, U.S.

Geography Ethiopia is in east-central Africa, bordered on the west by the Sudan, the east by Somalia and Djibouti, the south by Kenya, and the northeast by Eritrea. It is nearly three times the size of California. Over its main plateau land, Ethiopia has several high mountains, the highest of which is Ras Dashan at 15,158 feet (4,620 m). The Blue Nile, or Abbai, rises in the northwest and flows in a great semicircle east, south, and northwest before entering the Sudan. Its chief reservoir, Lake Tana, lies in the northwestern part of the plateau.

Government Federal republic.

History Archeologists have found the oldest known human ancestors in Ethiopia, including *Ardipithecus ramidus* (c. 4.4 million years old) and *Australopithecus afarensis* (c. 3.2 million years old). Originally called Abyssinia, Ethiopia is sub-Saharan Africa's oldest state, and its Solomonic dynasty claims descent from King Menelik I, traditionally believed to have been the son of the queen of Sheba and King Solomon. The current nation is a consolidation of smaller kingdoms that owed feudal allegiance to the Ethiopian emperor.

Hamitic peoples migrated to Ethiopia from Asia Minor in prehistoric times. Semitic traders from Arabia penetrated the region in the 7th century B.C. Its Red Sea ports were important to the Roman and Byzantine Empires. Coptic Christianity was brought to the region in A.D. 341, and a variant of it became Ethiopia's state religion. Ancient Ethiopia reached its peak in the 5th century, then was isolated by the rise of Islam and weakened by feudal wars.

Modern Ethiopia emerged under Emperor Menelik II, who established its independence by routing an Italian invasion in 1896. He expanded Ethiopia by conquest. Disorders that followed Menelik's death brought his daughter to the throne in 1917, with his cousin, Tafari Makonnen, as regent and heir apparent. When the empress died in 1930, Tafari was crowned Emperor Haile Selassie I.

Haile Selassie, called the "Lion of Judah," outlawed slavery and tried to centralize his scattered realm, in which 70 languages were spoken. In 1931, he created a constitution, revised in 1955, that called for a Parliament with an appointed senate and an elected chamber of deputies, and a system of courts. But basic power remained with the emperor.

Fascist Italy invaded Ethiopia on Oct. 3, 1935, forcing Haile Selassie into exile in May 1936. Ethiopia was annexed to Eritrea, then an Italian colony, and to Italian Somaliland, forming Italian East Africa. In 1941, British troops routed the Italians, and Haile Selassie returned to Addis Ababa. In 1952, Eritrea was incorporated into Ethiopia.

On Sept. 12, 1974, Haile Selassie was deposed, the constitution suspended, and Ethiopia proclaimed a socialist state under a collective military dictatorship called the Provisional Military Administrative Council (PMAC), also known as the Derg. U.S. aid stopped, and Cuban and Soviet aid began. Lt. Col. Mengistu Haile Mariam became head of state in 1977. During this period Ethiopia fought against Eritrean secessionists as well as Somali rebels, and the government fought against its own people in a campaign called the "red terror." Mengistu remained leader until 1991, when his greatest supporter, the Soviet Union, dismantled itself.

A group called the Ethiopian People's Revolutionary Democratic Front seized the capital in 1991, and in May a separatist guerrilla organization, the Eritrean People's Liberation Front, took control of the province of Eritrea. The two groups agreed that Eritrea would have an internationally supervised referendum on independence. This election took place in April 1993 with almost unanimous support for Eritrean independence. Ethiopia accepted and recognized Eritrea as an independent state within a few days. Sixty-eight leaders of the former military government were put on trial in April 1996 on charges that included genocide and crimes against humanity.

Since Eritrea's independence, Eritrea and Ethiopia had disagreed about the exact demarcation of their borders, and in May 1998 Eritrea initiated border clashes that developed into a full-scale war that left tens of thousands dead and further destroyed both countries' ailing economies. In Aug. 1999, the countries began peace negotiations, which quickly broke down and were replaced by continued fighting.

A cease-fire was agreed to in June 2000 and the United Nations provided between two and four thousand troops to patrol the buffer zone between the two nations until a permanent border could be agreed upon.

Fiji

REPUBLIC OF FIJI
Head, Interim Military Government: Commodore Josaia Voreqe Bainimarama

President: Ratu Josefa Iloilo (2000) (interim)
Area: 7,078 sq. mi. (18,270 sq. km)
Population (2000 est.): 832,494 (average annual rate of natural increase: 1.8%); birth rate: 23.5/1000; infant mortality rate: 14.5/1000; density per sq. mi.: 118
Capital (1990 est.): Suva (on Viti Levu), 200,000.
Monetary unit: Fiji dollar. **Languages:** Fijian, Hindustani, English (official). **Ethnicity/race:** Fijian 49%, Indian 46%, European, other Pacific Islanders, overseas Chinese, and other 5%. **Religions:** Christian, 52%; Hindu, 38%; Islam, 8%; other, 2%. **Literacy rate:** 79% (1976)
Economic summary: GDP/PPP (1998 est.): $5.4 billion; $6,700 per capita. **Real growth rate:** 2.4%. **Inflation:** 3% (1997 est.). **Unemployment:** 6% (1997 est.). **Arable land:** 10%. **Agriculture:** sugarcane, coconuts, cassava (tapioca), rice, sweet potatoes, bananas, cattle, pigs, horses, goats, fish. **Labor force:** 235,000: subsistence agriculture, 67%; wage earners, 18%; salary earners, 15% (1987). **Industries:** sugar, tourism, copra, gold, silver, clothing, lumber, small cottage industries. **Natural resources:** timber, fish, gold, copper, offshore oil potential. **Exports:** $6355 million (f.o.b., 1996): sugar, clothing, gold, processed fish, lumber. **Imports:** $838 million (f.o.b., 1996): machinery and transport equipment, petroleum products, food, chemicals. **Major trading partners:** Australia, U.K., New Zealand, U.S., Japan, Singapore.

Geography Fiji consists of 332 islands in the southwestern Pacific Ocean about 1,960 miles (3,152 km) from Sydney, Australia. About 110 of these islands are inhabited. The two largest are Viti Levu (4,109 sq. mi.; 10,642 sq. km) and Vanua Levu (2,242 sq. mi.; 5,807 sq. km). The island of Rotuma (18 sq. mi.; 47 sq. km), about 400 miles (644 km) to the north, is a province of Fiji. The largest islands in the group are mountainous and volcanic, with the tallest peak being Mount Victoria (4,341 ft.; 1,323 m) on Viti Levu.

Government Republic until May 2000, when coup installed interim military dictatorship.

History Fiji, which had been inhabited since the second millennium B.C., was explored by the Dutch and the British in the 17th and 18th centuries. In 1874, an offer of cession by the Fijian chiefs was accepted, and Fiji was proclaimed a possession and dependency of the British Crown. In the 1880s large-scale cultivation of sugarcane began. During World War II, the archipelago was an important port and naval station on the route from the U.S. and Hawaii to Australia and New Zealand.

Fiji became independent on Oct. 10, 1970. The next year it joined the five-island South Pacific Forum, which intends to become a permanent regional group to promote collective diplomacy of the newly independent members. In Oct. 1987, Brig. Gen. Sitiveni Rabuka, staged a coup, declared Fiji a republic, and removed it from the British Commonwealth. The military coup caused an exodus of thousands of Fijians of Indian origin who suffered ethnic discrimination at the hands of the government.

In July 1997, the Parliament unanimously approved a new constitution for Fiji. The new constitution, which took effect in July 1998, provided for a multiracial cabinet and raised the prospect of a coalition government. The previous constitution, from 1990, guaranteed the dominance to ethnic Fijians over ethnic Indians. Following the approval of the new constitution, Fiji was readmitted to the Commonwealth of Nations. In 1999, Fiji's first ethnic Indian prime minister, Mahendra Chaudhry, took office.

However, continuing ethnic differences, partly fueled by economic problems, plunged Fiji into a national nightmare in 2000. On May 19, a group of armed soldiers entered the parliament building, taking some three dozen people hostage, including the country's ethnic Indian prime minister. George Speight, a part-Fijian businessman, led the insurrection. He demanded the 1997 constitution be rewritten to allow dominance of ethnic Fijians. While negotiations with Speight continued, commander of the armed forces, Commodore Voreque Bainimarama, declared martial law. Under heavy pressure from India, and mounting international concern over the situation, the British Commonwealth suspended Fiji's participation in the commonwealth's councils, a step short of expelling Fiji altogether. In July 2000, Speight and other coup lears were taken into custody and charged with treason.

Finland

REPUBLIC OF FINLAND

National name: Suomen Tasavalta—Republiken Finland
President: Tarja Halonen (2000)
Prime Minister: Paavo Lipponen (1995)
Area: 130,558 sq. mi. (337,030 sq. km)
Population (2000 est.): 5,167,486 (average annual rate of natural increase: 0.1%); birth rate: 10.8/1000; infant mortality rate: 3.8/1000; density per sq. mi.: 40
Capital and largest city (1995 est.): Helsinki, 515,765.
Other large cities (1995 est.): Espoo, 186,507; Tampere, 179,251; Vantaa, 164,376; Turku, 162,370.
Monetary units: Markka and euro. **Languages:** Finnish, Swedish (both official); small Sami- (Lapp) and Russian-speaking minorities. **Ethnicity/race:** Finn 93%, Swede 6%, Sami (Lapp) 0.11%, Romany (Gypsy) 0.12%, Tatar 0.02%. **Religions:** Evangelical Lutheran, 90%; Greek Orthodox, 1.2%; none, 9%; other, 1%. **Literacy rate:** 100% (1980)
Economic summary: GDP/PPP (1998 est.): $103.6 billion; $20,100 per capita. **Real growth rate:** 5.1%. **Inflation:** 1.5%. **Unemployment:** 12%. **Arable land:** 8%. **Agriculture:** cereals, sugar beets, potatoes, dairy cattle, fish. **Labor force:** 2.533 million: public services, 30.4%; industry, 20.9%; commerce, 15%; finance, insurance, and business services, 10.2%; agriculture and forestry, 8.6%; transport and communications, 7.7%; construction, 7.2%. **Industries:** metal products, shipbuilding, pulp and paper, copper refining, foodstuffs, chemicals, textiles, clothing. **Natural resources:** timber, copper, zinc, iron ore, silver. **Exports:** $43 billion (f.o.b., 1998): machinery and equipment, chemicals, metals, timber, paper, and pulp. **Imports:** $30.7 billion (f.o.b., 1998): foodstuffs, petroleum and petroleum products, chemicals, transport equipment, iron and steel, machinery, textile yarn and fabrics, fodder grains. **Major trading partners:** Germany, U.K., Sweden, U.S., Russia, France, Japan.

Geography Finland is three times the size of Ohio. It is heavily forested and contains thousands of lakes, numerous rivers, and extensive areas of marshland. Except for a small highland region in the extreme northwest, the country is a lowland less than 600 feet (180 m) above sea level. Off the southwest coast are the Swedish-populated Åland Islands (581 sq. mi.; 1,505 sq. km), which have had an autonomous status since 1921.

Government Republic.

History The first inhabitants of Finland were the Sami (Lapp) people. When Finnish speakers migrated to Finland in the first millennium B.C., the Sami were forced to move northward to the arctic regions, with which they are traditionally associated. The Finns' repeated raids on the Scandinavian coast impelled Eric IX, the Swedish king, to conquer the country in 1157. It was made a part of the Swedish kingdom and converted to Christianity.

By 1809 the whole of Finland was conquered by Alexander I of Russia, who set up Finland as a grand duchy. The period of Russification (1809–1914) sapped Finnish political power and made Russian the country's official language. When Russia became engulfed by the March Revolution of 1917, Finland seized the opportunity to declare independence on Dec. 6, 1917.

The U.S.S.R. attacked Finland on Nov. 30, 1939, after Finland refused to give into Soviet territorial demands. The Finns staged a strong defense for three months before capitulating. They were forced to cede the Soviets 16,000 square miles (41,440 sq. km) to the U.S.S.R. Under German pressure, the Finns joined the Nazis against Russia in 1941, but were defeated again and ceded the Petsamo area to the U.S.S.R. In 1948, a treaty of friendship and mutual assistance was signed by the two nations. Finland continued to pursue a foreign policy of nonalignment throughout the cold war era.

Running on a platform to revitalize the economy, Ahtisaari, a Social Democrat, won the country's first direct presidential election in a runoff in Feb. 1994. Previously, presidents had been chosen by electors. Finland became a member of the European Union in Jan. 1995, but made it clear it would not become a full member of the western European Union. Showing concern over NATO expansion eastward, Russian president Yeltsin in March 1997 iterated his view that Finnish membership in the military alliance was unacceptable, due to Finland's policy of nonalignment. On Jan. 1, 1999, Finland, along with ten other European countries, adopted the euro as its currency. In 2000, Tarja Halonen, who had been Finland's foreign minister, became its first woman president.

France

FRENCH REPUBLIC

National name: République Française
President: Jacques Chirac (1995)
Prime Minister: Lionel Jospin (1997)
Area: 211,208 sq. mi. (547,030 sq. km)
Population (2000 est.): 59,329,691 (average annual rate of natural increase: 0.3%); birth rate: 12.3/1000; infant mortality rate: 4.5/1000; density per sq. mi.: 281
Capital and largest city (2000 est.): Paris, 10,150,000 (metro. area). **Other large cities:** Marseille, 801,000; Lyon, 415,000; Toulouse, 359,000; Nice, 342,000; Strasbourg, 252,000; Nantes, 245,000; Bordeaux,

201,000. Monetary units: French Franc and euro.
Languages: French, declining regional dialects
(Provençal, Breton, Alsatian, Corsican). **Ethnicity/
race:** Celtic and Latin with Teutonic, Slavic, North
African, Southeast Asian, and Basque minorities.
Religions: Roman Catholic, 81%; Protestant, 1.7%;
Muslim, 6.9%; Jewish, 1.3%. **Literacy rate:** 99%
(1980)
Economic summary: GDP/PPP (1998 est.): $1.32
trillion; $22,600 per capita. **Real growth rate:** 3%.
Inflation: 0.7%. **Unemployment:** 11.5%. **Arable land:**
33%. **Agriculture:** wheat, cereals, sugar beets,
potatoes, wine grapes, beef, dairy products, fish.
Labor force: 25.4 million: services, 69%; industry,
26%; agriculture, 5% (1995). **Industries:** steel,
machinery, chemicals, automobiles, metallurgy,
aircraft, electronics, mining, textiles, food processing,
tourism. **Natural resources:** coal, iron ore, bauxite,
fish, timber, zinc, potash. **Exports:** $289 billion (f.o.b.,
1998): machinery and transportation equipment,
chemicals, foodstuffs, agricultural products, iron and
steel products, textiles and clothing. **Imports:** $255
billion (f.o.b., 1998): crude oil, machinery and
equipment, agricultural products, chemicals, iron and
steel products. **Major trading partners:** Germany,
U.K., Italy, Spain, Belgium, Luxembourg, U.S.,
Netherlands, Japan, Russia, China.

Geography France is about 80% the size of Texas.
In the Alps near the Italian and Swiss borders is western Europe's highest point—Mont Blanc (15,781 ft.;
4,810 m). The forest-covered Vosges Mountains are
in the northeast, and the Pyrénées are along the Spanish border. Except for extreme northern France, the
country may be described as four river basins and a
plateau. Three of the streams flow west—the Seine
into the English Channel, the Loire into the Atlantic,
and the Garonne into the Bay of Biscay. The Rhône
flows south into the Mediterranean. For about 100
miles (161 km), the Rhine is France's eastern border.
In the Mediterranean, about 115 miles (185 km) east-
southeast of Nice, is the island of Corsica (3,367 sq.
mi.; 8,721 sq. km).

Government Fifth republic.

History Archeological excavations indicate that
France has been continuously settled since Paleolithic
times. The Celts, who were later called *Gauls* by the
Romans, migrated from the Rhine valley into what is
now France. In about 600 B.C. Greeks and Phoenicians established settlements along the Mediterranean, most notably at Marseille. Julius Caesar conquered part of Gaul in 57–52 B.C., and it remained
Roman until Franks invaded in the 5th century.

The Treaty of Verdun (A.D. 843) divided the territories corresponding roughly to France, Germany, and
Italy among the three grandsons of Charlemagne.
Charles the Bald inherited *Francia Occidentalis,*
which became an increasingly feudalized kingdom.
By A.D. 987, the crown passed to Hugh Capet, a
princeling who controlled only the Ile-de-France, the
region surrounding Paris. For 350 years, an unbroken
Capetian line added to its domain and consolidated
royal authority until the accession in 1328 of Philip
VI, first of the Valois line. France was then the most
powerful nation in Europe, with a population of 15
million.

The missing pieces in Philip Valois's domain were
the French provinces still held by the Plantagenet
kings of England, who also claimed the French
crown. Beginning in 1338, the Hundred Years' War
eventually settled the contest. After France's victory
in the final battle, Castillon (1453), the Valois were

the ruling family, and the English had no French possessions left except Calais. Once Burgundy and Brittany were added, the Valois's holdings resembled
modern France. Protestantism spread throughout
France in the 16th century and led to civil wars.
Henry IV, of the Bourbon dynasty, issued the Edict of
Nantes (1598), granting religious tolerance to the
Huguenots (French Protestants). Absolute monarchy
reached its apogee in the reign of Louis XIV (1643–
1715), the Sun King, whose brilliant court was the
center of the Western world.

After a series of costly foreign wars that weakened
the government, the French Revolution plunged
France into a bloodbath beginning in 1789 with the
establishment of the First Republic and ending with a
new authoritarianism under Napoléon Bonaparte, who
had successfully defended the infant republic from
foreign attack and then made himself first consul in
1799 and emperor in 1804. The Congress of Vienna
(1815) sought to restore the pre-Napoléonic order in
the person of Louis XVIII, but industrialization and
the middle class, both fostered under Napoléon, built
pressure for change, and a revolution in 1848 drove
Louis Philippe, last of the Bourbons, into exile.
Prince Louis Napoléon, a nephew of Napoléon I's,
declared the Second Empire in 1852 and took the
throne as Napoléon III. His opposition to the rising
power of Prussia ignited the Franco-Prussian War
(1870–71), ending in his defeat, his abdication, and
the creation of the Third Republic.

A new France emerged from World War I as the
continent's dominant power. But four years of hostile
occupation had reduced northeast France to ruins.
Beginning in 1919, French foreign policy aimed at
keeping Germany weak through a system of alliances,
but it failed to halt the rise of Adolf Hitler and the
Nazi war machine. On May 10, 1940, Nazi troops
attacked, and, as they approached Paris, Italy joined
with Germany. The Germans marched into an undefended Paris and Marshal Henri Philippe Pétain
signed an armistice on June 22. France was split into
an occupied north and an unoccupied south, Vichy
France, the latter becoming a totalitarian German
puppet state with Pétain as its chief. Allied armies
liberated France in Aug. 1944, and a provisional government in Paris headed by Gen. Charles de Gaulle
was established. The Fourth Republic was born on
Dec. 24, 1946. The empire became the French Union;
the National Assembly was strengthened and the
presidency weakened; and France joined NATO. A
war against Communist insurgents in French
Indochina, now Vietnam, was abandoned after the
defeat of French forces at Dien Bien Phu in 1954. A
new rebellion in Algeria threatened a military coup,
and on June 1, 1958, the assembly invited de Gaulle
to return as premier with extraordinary powers. He
drafted a new constitution for a Fifth Republic,
adopted on Sept. 28, which strengthened the presidency and reduced legislative power. He was elected
president on Dec. 21, 1958.

France next turned its attention to decolonization
in Africa; the French protectorates of Morocco and
Tunisia had received independence in 1956. French
West Africa was partitioned and the new nations were
granted independence in 1960. Algeria, after a long
civil war, finally became independent in 1962. Relations with most of the former colonies remained amicable. De Gaulle took France out of the NATO military command in 1967 and expelled all foreign-
controlled troops from the country. De Gaulle's
government was weakened by massive protests in

Rulers of France

Name	Born	Ruled[1]	Name	Born	Ruled[1]
Carolingian Dynasty			Louis XV the Well-Beloved	1710	1715–1774
Pepin the Short	c. 714	751–768	Louis XVI	1754	1774–1792[13]
Charlemagne[2]	742	768–814	Louis XVII (Louis Charles de	1785	1793–1795
Louis I the Pious[3]	778	814–840	France)[14]		
Charles I the Bald[4]	823	840–877	**First Republic**		
Louis II the Stammerer	846	877–879	National Convention	—	1792–1795
Louis III[5]	c. 863	879–882	Directory (Directoire)	—	1795–1799
Carloman[5]	?	879–884	**Consulate**		
Charles II the Fat[6]	839	884–887[7]	Napoléon Bonaparte[15]	1769	1799–1804
Eudes (Odo), count of Paris	?	888–898	**First Empire**		
Charles III the Simple[8]	879	893–923[9]	Napoléon I	1769	1804–1815[16]
Robert I[10]	c. 865	922–923	**Restoration of House of Bourbon**		
Rudolf (Raoul), duke of Burgundy	?	923–936	Louis XVIII le Désiré	1755	1814–1824
Louis IV d'Outremer	c. 921	936–954	Charles X	1757	1824–1830[17]
Lothair	941	954–986	**Bourbon-Orleans Line**		
Louis V the Sluggard	c. 967	986–987	Louis Philippe ("Citizen King")	1773	1830–1848[18]
Capetian Dynasty			**Second Republic**		
Hugh Capet	c. 940	987–996	Louis Napoléon[19]	1808	1848–1852
Robert II the Pious[11]	c. 970	996–1031	**Second Empire**		
Henry I	1008	1031–1060	Napoléon III (Louis Napoléon)	1808	1852–1870[20]
Philip I	1052	1060–1108	**Third Republic (Presidents)**		
Louis VI the Fat	1081	1108–1137	Louis Adolphe Thiers	1797	1871–1873
Louis VII the Young	c.1121	1137–1180	Marie E. P. M. de MacMahon	1808	1873–1879
Philip II (Philip Augustus)	1165	1180–1223	François P. J. Grévy	1807	1879–1887
Louis VIII the Lion	1187	1223–1226	Sadi Carnot	1837	1887–1894
Louis IX (St. Louis)	1214	1226–1270	Jean Casimir-Périer	1847	1894–1895
Philip III the Bold	1245	1270–1285	François Félix Faure	1841	1895–1899
Philip IV the Fair	1268	1285–1314	Émile Loubet	1838	1899–1906
Louis X the Quarreler	1289	1314–1316	Clement Armand Fallières	1841	1906–1913
John I[12]	1316	1316	Raymond Poincaré	1860	1913–1920
Philip V the Tall	1294	1316–1322	Paul E. L. Deschanel	1856	1920–1920
Charles IV the Fair	1294	1322–1328	Alexandre Millerand	1859	1920–1924
House of Valois			Gaston Doumergue	1863	1924–1931
Philip VI	1293	1328–1350	Paul Doumer	1857	1931–1932
John II the Good	1319	1350–1364	Albert Lebrun	1871	1932–1940
Charles V the Wise	1337	1364–1380	**Vichy Government (Chief of State)**		
Charles VI the Well-Beloved	1368	1380–1422	Henri Philippe Pétain	1856	1940–1944
Charles VII	1403	1422–1461	**Provisional Government (Presidents)**		
Louis XI	1423	1461–1483	Charles de Gaulle	1890	1944–1946
Charles VIII	1470	1483–1498	Félix Gouin	1884	1946–1946
Louis XII the Father of the People	1462	1498–1515	Georges Bidault	1899	1946–1947
Francis I	1494	1515–1547	**Fourth Republic (Presidents)**		
Henry II	1519	1547–1559	Vincent Auriol	1884	1947–1954
Francis II	1544	1559–1560	René Coty	1882	1954–1959
Charles IX	1550	1560–1574	**Fifth Republic (Presidents)**		
Henry III	1551	1574–1589	Charles de Gaulle	1890	1959–1969
House of Bourbon			Georges Pompidou	1911	1969–1974
Henry IV of Navarre	1553	1589–1610	Valéry Giscard d'Estaing	1926	1974–1981
Louis XIII	1601	1610–1643	François Mitterrand	1916	1981–1995
Louis XIV the Great	1638	1643–1715	Jacques Chirac	1932	1995–

1. For kings and emperors through the Second Empire, year of end of rule is also that of death, unless otherwise indicated. 2. Crowned Emperor of the West in 800. His brother, Carloman, ruled as king of the Eastern Franks from 768 until his death in 771. 3. Holy Roman Emperor, 814–840. 4. Holy Roman Emperor, 875–877 as Charles II. 5. Ruled jointly, 879–882. 6. Holy Roman Emperor, 881–887, as Charles III. 7. Died 888. 8. King, 893–898, in opposition to Eudes. 9. Died 929. 10. Not counted in regular line of kings of France by some authorities. Elected by nobles but killed in Battle of Soissons. 11. Sometimes called Robert I. 12. Posthumous son of Louis X; lived for only five days. 13. Executed 1793. 14. Titular king only. He died in prison according to official reports, but many pretenders appeared during the Bourbon restoration. 15. As first consul, Napoléon held the power of government. In 1804, he became emperor. 16. Abdicated first time, June 1814. Reentered Paris, March 1815, after escape from Elba; abdicated second time, June 1815. He named as his successor his son, Napoléon II, who was not acceptable to the Allies. He died 1821. 17. Died 1836. 18. Died 1850. 19. President; became emperor in 1852. 20. Died 1873.

May 1968 when student rallies became violent and millions of factory workers engaged in wildcat strikes across France. After normalcy was reestablished by 1969, de Gaulle's successor, Georges Pompidou, modified Gaullist policies to include a classical laissez-faire attitude toward domestic economic

affairs. The conservative, pro-business climate contributed to the election of Valéry Giscard d'Estaing as president in 1974.

Socialist François Mitterrand attained a stunning victory in the May 10, 1981, presidential election. The victors immediately moved to carry out campaign pledges to nationalize major industries, halt nuclear testing, suspend nuclear power plant construction, and impose new taxes on the rich. The Socialists' policies during Mitterrand's first two years created a 12% inflation rate, a huge trade deficit, and devaluations of the franc. In March 1986, a center-right coalition led by Jacques Chirac won a slim majority in legislative elections. Chirac became prime minister, initiating a period of "cohabitation" between him and the Socialist president, Mitterrand. Mitterrand's decisive reelection in 1988 led to Chirac being replaced as premier by Michel Rocard, a Socialist. Relations, however, cooled with Rocard, and in May 1991 he was replaced with Edith Cresson, France's first female prime minister and, like Mitterrand, a Socialist. But Cresson's unpopularity forced Mitterrand to replace Cresson with a more well-liked Socialist, Pierre Bérégovoy, who eventually was embroiled in a scandal and committed suicide. Mitterrand did succeed in helping draft the Maastricht Treaty and, after winning a slim victory in a referendum, confirming close economic and security ties between France and the European Union (EU).

On his third try Chirac won the presidency in May 1995, campaigning vigorously on a platform to reduce unemployment. He moved quickly to cement ties with Germany and the rest of the EU. Elections for the National Assembly in 1997 gave the Socialist coalition a majority. Shortly after becoming president, Chirac resumed France's nuclear testing in the South Pacific, despite widespread international protests as well as rioting in the countries affected by it. Socialist leader Lionel Jospin became prime minister in 1997. On Jan. 1, 1999, France adopted the euro as its currency. In the spring of 1999, the country took part in the NATO airstrikes in Kosovo, despite some internal opposition.

In the fall of 1999, Britain and France argued heatedly about France's refusal to allow the importation of British beef. France remained leery of the possibility of infection from bovine spongiform encephalopathy (BSE), commonly known as mad cow disease, despite the fact that the EU had lifted the three-year ban on British beef in Aug. 1999. European protests over rising fuel prices originated in France on Sept. 4, 2000, when truckers blockaded refineries and service stations. The blockades succeeded in forcing the government to issue a tax break, which spurred other European countries on to attempt similar protests.

Overseas Departments

Overseas Departments elect representatives to the National Assembly, and the same administrative organization as that of continental France applies to them.

French Guiana (including Inini)
Status: Overseas Department
Prefect: Henri Masse (1999)
Area: 32,253 sq. mi. (83,534 sq. km)
Population (2000 est.): 172,605 (average annual growth rate: 1.77%); birth rate 22.4/1000; infant mortality rate 14/1000; density per sq. mi.: 5
Capital and largest city (1995 est.): Cayenne, 41,659.
Monetary unit: Franc. **Language:** French. **Ethnicity/race:** black or mulatto 66%, white 12%, East Indian, Chinese, Amerindian 12%, other 10%. **Religion:** Roman Catholic. **Literacy rate:** 80% (1982)
Economic summary: GDP/PPP (1998 est.): $1 billion; $6,000 per capita. **Real growth rate:** n.a. **Inflation:** (1992) 2.5%. **Unemployment:** 25.7% (1997 est.). **Arable land:** 0%. **Agriculture:** sugar, rice, corn, manioc (tapioca), cocoa, vegetables, bananas, cattle,

pigs, poultry. **Labor force** 58,800 (1997): services, government, and commerce, 60.6%; industry, 21.2%; agriculture, 18.2% (1980). **Industries:** construction, shrimp processing, forestry products, rum, gold mining. **Natural resources:** bauxite, timber, cinnabar, kaolin. **Exports:** $148 million (f.o.b., 1997): shrimp, timber, gold, rum, rosewood essence, clothing. **Imports:** $600 million (c.i.f., 1997): food (grains, processed meat), machinery and transport equipment, fuel and chemicals. **Major trading partners:** France, EU, Germany, Belgium, Luxembourg, U.S.

French Guiana, lying north of Brazil and east of Suriname on the northeast coast of South America, was variously settled by the Spanish, Dutch, and French. The Treaty of Breda awarded France the territory in 1667. The French used it as a penal colony between 1852 and 1939, which included the infamous Devil's Island. In 1958 it became an Overseas Department of the French Republic, which sends two elected representatives to France's National Assembly and one to the Senate. Since then, many indigenous French Guianians have called for increased autonomy, although only around 5% favor independence from France, partly due to the vast subsidies from the French government. The European Space Center at Kourou has brought a corner of French Guiana into the modern world and attracted a sizable expatriate workforce.

Guadeloupe
Status: Overseas Department
Prefect: Jean-François Carenco (1999)
Area: 327 sq. mi. (1,848 sq. km)
Population (2000 est.): 426,493 (average annual growth rate: 1.12%); birth rate: 17.3/1000; infant mortality rate: 9.8/1000; density per sq. mi.: 1,304
Capital (1990): Basse-Terre, 14,000. **Largest city (1990):** Pointe-à-Pitre, over 26,029. **Monetary unit:** Franc. **Languages:** French, Creole patois. **Ethnicity/race:** black or mulatto 90%, white 5%, East Indian, Lebanese, Chinese less than 5%. **Religion:** Roman Catholic. **Literacy rate:** 91% (1982)
Economic summary: GDP/PPP (1996 est.): $3.7 billion; $9,000 per capita. **Real growth rate:** n.a. **Inflation:** (1990), 3.7%. **Unemployment:** 29.5% (1997). **Arable land:** 14%. **Agriculture:** bananas, sugarcane, tropical fruit and vegetables, cattle, pigs, goats. **Labor force:** 128,000: services, 65%; industry, 20%; agriculture, 15% (1993). **Industries:** construction, cement, rum, sugar, tourism. **Exports:** $133 million (f.o.b., 1997): bananas, sugar, rum. **Imports:** $1.7 billion (c.i.f., 1997): foodstuffs, fuel, vehicles, clothing and other consumer goods, construction materials. **Major trading partners:** France, Martinique, EU, U.S., Japan.

Guadeloupe, in the West Indies about 300 miles (483 km) southeast of Puerto Rico, was explored by Columbus in 1493. It consists of the twin islands of Basse-Terre and Grande-Terre and five dependencies—Marie-Galante, Les Saintes, La Désirade, St. Barthélemy, and the northern three-fifths of St. Martin. The volcano Soufrière (4,813 ft.; 1,467 m), also called La Grande Soufrière, is the highest point on Guadeloupe. Violent activity in 1976 and 1977 caused thousands to flee their homes. French colonization began in 1635, and in 1674 Guadeloupe became part of the domain of France. In 1958, Guadeloupe voted in favor of the new constitution of the French Fifth Republic and remained an Overseas Department of the French Republic. It is represented in the French National Assembly by four deputies and in the French Senate by two senators.

Martinique

Status: Overseas Department
Prefect: Dominique Bellion (1998)
Area: 436 sq. mi. (1,128 sq. km)
Population (2000 est.): 414,516 (average annual growth rate: 0.97%); birth rate: 16.1/1000; infant mortality rate: 8/1000; density per sq. mi.: 951
Capital and largest city (1990): Fort-de-France, 100,072. **Other cities (1990):** Le Lamentin, 30,026; Schoelcher, 19,683; Sainte-Marie, 19,683. **Monetary unit:** Franc. **Languages:** French, Creole patois. **Ethnicity/race:** African and African-white-Indian mixture 90%, white 5%, East Indian, Lebanese, Chinese less than 5%. **Religion:** Roman Catholic. **Literacy rate:** 100% (1983)
Economic summary: GDP/PPP (1996 est.): $4.24 billion; $10,700 per capita. **Real growth rate:** n.a. **Inflation:** (1990), 3.9%. **Unemployment:** 24% (1997). **Arable land:** 8%. **Agriculture:** pineapples, avocados, bananas, flowers, vegetables, sugarcane. **Labor force:** 160,000: services, 73%; industry, 17%; agriculture, 10% (1997). **Industries:** construction, rum, cement, oil refining, sugar, tourism. **Natural resources:** coastal scenery and beaches, cultivable land. **Exports:** $200 million (f.o.b., 1997): refined petroleum products, bananas, rum, pineapples. **Imports:** $1.6 billion (c.i.f., 1997): petroleum products, crude oil, foodstuffs, construction materials, vehicles, clothing and other consumer goods. **Major trading partners:** France, Guadeloupe, French Guiana, U.K., Italy, Germany, Japan, U.S.

Martinique, a mountainous island lying in the Lesser Antilles about 300 miles (483 km) northeast of Venezuela, was probably explored by Columbus in 1502 and was taken for France in 1635. Martinique became a domain of the French crown in 1674. In 1958, Martinique voted in favor of the new constitution of the French Fifth Republic and remained an Overseas Department of the French Republic, sending four deputies to the French National Assembly and two senators to the French Senate. Martinique's young people continue to emigrate heavily, mostly to France.

Réunion

Status: Overseas Department
Prefect: Jean Doubigny (1998)
Area: 970 sq. mi. (2,512 sq. km)
Population (2000 est.): 720,934 (average annual growth rate: 1.63%); birth rate: 21.8/1000; infant mortality rate: 8.7/1000; density per sq. mi.: 743
Capital and largest city (1993): Saint-Denis, 121,999. **Other cities (est. 1993):** Saint-Paul, 71,667; Saint-Pierre, 58,846; Le Tampon, 47,598. **Monetary unit:** Franc. **Languages:** French, Creole. **Ethnicity/race:** French, African, Malagasy, Chinese, Pakistani, Indian. **Religion:** Roman Catholic, 70%. **Literacy rate:** 70% (1982)
Economic summary: GDP/PPP (1998 est.): $3.4 billion; $4,800 per capita. **Real growth rate:** 3.8%. **Inflation:** n.a. **Unemployment:** 35% (1994). **Arable land:** 17%. **Agriculture:** sugarcane, vanilla, tobacco, tropical fruit, vegetables, corn. **Labor force:** 261,000 (1995): services, 73%; industry, 19%; agriculture, 8% (1990). **Industries:** sugar, rum, cigarettes, handicraft items, flower oil extraction. **Natural resources:** fish, arable land. **Exports:** $171.78 million (f.o.b., 1994): sugar, rum and molasses, perfume essences, lobster. **Imports:** $2.35 billion (c.i.f., 1994): manufactured goods, food, beverages, tobacco, machinery and transportation equipment, raw materials, petroleum products. **Major trading partners:** France, Japan, Comoros, Bahrain, Italy.

Of volcanic origin, Réunion consists mostly of rugged mountains in an advanced state of dissection by short torrential rivers. It is located about 450 miles (724 km) east of Madagascar, in the Indian Ocean. First explored by Portuguese navigators in the 16th century, the island of Réunion, then uninhabited, was taken as a French possession in 1642. African slaves were imported first to work coffee and then sugar plantations; with the abolition of slavery in 1848, indentured laborers from Indochina, India, and East Africa were brought in. In 1958, Réunion approved the constitution of the Fifth French Republic and remained an Overseas Department of the French Republic. Réunion elects five deputies to the French National Assembly and three to the Senate. The island is administered by an appointed prefect and a general council composed of 44 elected members.

Overseas Territories

Overseas Territories are comparable to Departments, except that their administrative organization includes a locally elected government.

French Polynesia

Status: Overseas Territory
High Commissioner: Jean Aribaud (1999)
Area: 1,609 sq. mi. (4,167 sq. km)
Population (2000 est.): 249,110 (average annual growth rate: 1.5%); birth rate: 19/1000; infant mortality rate: 9.3/1000; density per sq. mi.: 155
Capital (1988): Papeete (on Tahiti), 23,555. **Monetary unit:** Pacific financial community franc. **Language:** French. **Ethnicity/race:** Polynesian 78%, Chinese 12%, local French 6%, metropolitan French 4%. **Religions:** Protestant, 55%; Roman Catholic, 30%; Other, 16%. **Literacy rate:** 98% (1977)
Economic summary: GDP/PPP (1997 est.): $2.6 billion; $10,800 per capita. **Real growth rate:** n.a. **Inflation:** 1.5% (1994). **Labor force:** 118,744 (1988): services, 68%; industry, 19%; agriculture, 13% (1997). **Unemployment:** 15% (1992 est.). **Agriculture:** coconuts, vanilla, vegetables, fruit, poultry, beef, dairy products. **Industries:** tourism, pearls, agricultural processing, handicrafts. **Exports:** $212 million (f.o.b., 1996): cultured pearls, coconut products, mother-of-pearl, vanilla, shark meat. **Imports:** $860 million (c.i.f., 1996): fuel, foodstuffs, equipment. **Major trading partners:** France, U.S.

The term French Polynesia is applied to the scattered French possessions in the South Pacific—Mangareva (Gambier), Makatea, the Marquesas Islands, Rapa, Rurutu, Rimatara, the Society Islands, the Tuamotu Archipelago, Tubuai, Raivavae, and the island of Clipperton—which were organized into a single colony in 1903. There are 120 islands, of which 25 are uninhabited.

The president of the Territorial Government is assisted by a Council of Government and a popularly elected Territorial Assembly. The principal and most populous island—Tahiti, in the Society group—was claimed as French in 1768. In 1958, French Polynesia voted in favor of the new constitution of the French Fifth Republic and remained an Overseas Territory of the French Republic. The indigenous people are mostly Maoris.

The Pacific Nuclear Test Center on the atoll of Mururoa, 744 miles (1,200 km) from Tahiti, was completed in 1966. In 1975 worldwide opposition forced the French to move the testing underground on Fangataufa. To compensate the residents for the nuclear weapons tests in 1995–96, France offered a 10-year $194-million annual compensation package. An independence movement continues to flourish in French Polynesia.

New Caledonia and Dependencies

Status: Overseas Territory
High Commissioner: Thierry Lataste (1998)
Area: 7,374 sq. mi. (19,103 sq. km)
Population (2000 est.): 201,816 (average annual growth rate: 1.52%); birth rate 20.8/1000; infant mortality rate: 8.6/1000; density per sq. mi.: 27
Capital (1989): Nouméa, 65,110. **Monetary unit:** Pacific financial community franc. **Languages:** French, Melanesian and Polynesian dialects. **Ethnicity/race:** Kanak (Melanesian) 42.5%, European 37.1%, Wallisian 8.4%, Polynesian 3.8%, Indonesian 3.6%, Vietnamese 1.6%, other 3%. **Religions:** Roman Catholic, 60%; Protestant, 30%. **Literacy rate:** 91% (1976)
Economic summary: GDP/PPP (1996 est.): $2.1 billion; $11,400 per capita; **Real growth rate:** n.a. **Inflation:** 1.7% (1996 est.). **Unemployment:** 15% (1994). **Agriculture:** vegetables, beef, other livestock products. **Industries:** nickel mining and smelting. **Natural resources:** nickel, chrome, iron, cobalt, manganese, silver, gold, lead, copper. **Labor force:** 70,044 (1988): services, 60%; agriculture, 20%; industry, 16%; mining, 4% (1996). **Exports:** $500 million (f.o.b., 1996): ferronickels, nickel ore. **Imports:** $845 million (c.i.f., 1996): food, transport equipment, machinery and electrical equipment, fuel, minerals. **Major trading partners:** Japan, France, U.S., Australia, Taiwan, Singapore, New Zealand.

New Caledonia (6,466 sq. mi.; 16,747 sq. km), about 1,070 miles (1,722 km) northeast of Sydney, Australia, was explored by Capt. James Cook in 1774 and annexed by France in 1853. The government also administers the Isle of Pines, the Loyalty Islands (Uvéa, Lifu, and Maré), the Belep Islands, the Huon Island group, and Chesterfield Islands. The native people are Melanesians called the Kanak. In 1984, the French National Assembly passed a law that granted internal autonomy to New Caledonia. In 1998 the Nouméa Accords postponed discussions about independence for the territory until at least 2013.

Southern and Antarctic Lands

Status: Overseas Territory
Administrator: Brigitte Girardin (1998)
Area: 3,004 sq. mi. (7,781 sq. km, excluding Adélie Land)
Capital: Port-au-Français
This territory is uninhabited except for the personnel of scientific bases. It consists of Adélie Land (166,752 sq. mi.; 431,888 sq. km) on the Antarctic mainland (which the U.S. does not recognize) and the following islands in the southern Indian Ocean: the Kerguelen and Crozet archipelagos and the islands of Saint-Paul and New Amsterdam.

Wallis and Futuna Islands

Status: Overseas Territory
Administrator: Christian Dors (1998)
Area: 106 sq. mi. (274 sq. km)
Population (2000 est.): 15,283 (average annual growth rate 1.71%); birth rate 21.7/1000; infant mortality rate 18.3/1000; density per sq. mi.: 144
Capital (1983): Mata-Utu. **Languages:** French, Wallisian. **Ethnicity/race:** Polynesian. **Religion:** Roman Catholic. **Literacy rate:** 50% (1969)
Economic summary: GDP/PPP (1995 est.): $28.7 million; $2,000 per capita. **Real growth rate:** n.a.

Inflation: n.a. **Unemployment:** n.a. **Industries:** copra, handicrafts, fishing, lumber. **Agriculture:** breadfruit, yams, taro, bananas, pigs, goats. **Labor force:** n.a.; agriculture, livestock, fishing, government. **Exports:** $370,000 (f.o.b., 1995 est.): copra, handicrafts. **Imports:** $13.5 million (c.i.f., 1995 est.): foodstuffs, manufactured goods, transportation equipment, fuel, clothing. **Major trading partners:** France, Australia, New Zealand.

The two island groups in the South Pacific between Fiji and Samoa were settled by French missionaries at the beginning of the 19th century. A protectorate was established in the 1880s. There is a French-appointed high administrator, a 20-member Territorial Assembly, and a deputy and a senator to the French national Parliament. The three traditional Polynesian kings also help decide internal policy matters. Following a referendum by the Polynesian inhabitants, the status was changed to that of an Overseas Territory in 1961.

Territorial Collectivities

The Territorial Collectivity status was created in 1976 for Mayotte; it was conceived as being midway between an Overseas Territory and an Overseas Department.

Saint Pierre and Miquelon

Status: Territorial Collectivity
Prefect: Francis Spitzer (1999)
Area: 93 sq. mi. (242 sq. km)
Population (2000 est.): 6,896 (average annual growth rate 0.986%); birth rate 16.5/1000; infant mortality rate 8.6/1000; density per sq. mi.: 74
Capital (1990): Saint Pierre, 5,683. **Ethnicity/race:** Basques and Bretons (French fishermen). **Literacy rate:** 99% (1982)
Economic summary: GDP/PPP (1996 est.): $74 million; $11,000 per capita. **Real growth rate:** n.a. **Inflation:** n.a. **Unemployment:** 9.8% (1997). **Agriculture:** vegetables, cattle, sheep, pigs, fish. **Industries:** fish processing and supply base for fishing fleets, tourism. **Labor force:** 3,000 (1996). **Exports:** $1.2 million (f.o.b., 1996): fish and fish products, fox and mink pelts. **Imports:** $60.5 million (c.i.f., 1996): meat, clothing, fuel, electrical equipment, machinery, building materials. **Major trading partners:** U.S., France, U.K., Canada, Portugal, Netherlands.

The sole remnant of the French colonial empire in North America, these islands were first occupied by the French in 1604. Their only importance arises from proximity to the Grand Banks, located 10 miles south of Newfoundland, making them the center of the French Atlantic cod fisheries. On July 19, 1976, the islands became an Overseas Department of the French Republic. In May 1985, the archipelago was given a new status with a new name, Territorial Collectivity, because the former departmental arrangement conflicted with the tariff structure of the European Economic Community (now European Union), to which France belongs.

Mayotte

Status: Territorial Collectivity
Prefect: Pierre Bayle (1998)
Area: 146 sq. mi. (378 sq. km)
Population (2000 est.): 155,911 (average annual rate of natural increase 3.6%); birth rate 45.3/1000; infant mortality rate 71.3/1000; density per sq. mi.: 1,068
Capital and largest city (1991): Mamoudzou (Dzaoudzi), 20,450
Economic summary: GDP/PPP (1998 est.): $85 million,

$600 per capita. **Real growth rate:** n.a. **Inflation:** n.a. **Unemployment:** 38% (1991 est.). **Industries:** lobster and shrimp. **Agriculture:** vanilla, ylang-ylang (perfume essence), coffee, copra. **Labor force:** n.a. **Natural resources:** negl. **Exports:** $3.64 million (f.o.b., 1996): ylang-ylang (perfume essence), vanilla, copra. **Imports:** $131.5 million (f.o.b., 1996): building materials, machinery and transportation equipment, metals, chemicals, rice, clothing, flour. **Major trading partners:** France, Comoros, Réunion, Africa, Southeast Asia.

France gained colonial control over Mayotte in 1843. It is the most populous of the four Comoros Islands in the Indian Ocean off Mozambique in Africa. Mayotte chose to remain a French dependency rather than join the other Comoran islands in declaring independence in 1975. Comoros laid claim to Mayotte shortly after independence and continues to do so. In July 2000, 70% of voters opted to accept greater autonomy but remain a part of France.

Gabon

GABONESE REPUBLIC

National name: République Gabonaise
President: Omar Bongo (1967)
Premier: Jean-François Ntoutoume (1999)
Area: 103,346 sq. mi. (267,670 sq. km)
Population (2000 est.): 1,208,436 (average annual rate of natural increase 1.08%); birth rate: 27.6/1000; infant mortality rate: 96.3/1000; density per sq. mi.: 12
Capital and largest city (1994): Libreville, 419,596.
  Other cities (1994): Port-Gentil, 80,000; Franceville, 42,000. **Monetary unit:** Franc CFA. **Language:** French (official). **Ethnicity/race:** (1993) Bantu tribes, including six major tribal groupings: Fang 25%, Punu 23%, Nzeiby 13%, Mbede (Obamba/Bateke) 9%, Kota 7%, and Myene 5%; Pygmies 0.7%, naturalized population 0.3%, foreigners 15%. **Religions:** Catholic 75%, Protestant 20%, Animist 4%. **Literacy rate:** 61% (1990)
Economic summary: GDP/PPP (1998 est.): $7.7 billion; $6,400 per capita. **Real growth rate:** 1.7%. **Inflation:** 1%. **Unemployment:** 21% (1997 est.). **Arable land:** 1%. **Agriculture:** cocoa, coffee, sugar, palm oil, rubber; cattle, okoume (a tropical softwood), fish. **Labor force:** n.a.: agriculture, 65%; industry and commerce, services. **Industries:** food and beverage, textiles, lumbering and plywood, cement, petroleum extraction and refining, manganese, uranium, and gold mining, chemicals, ship repair. **Natural resources:** petroleum, manganese, uranium, gold, timber, iron ore. **Exports:** $2.1 billion (f.o.b., 1998 est.): crude oil, timber, manganese, uranium. **Imports:** $890 million (f.o.b., 1998 est.): machinery and equipment, foodstuffs, chemicals, petroleum products, construction materials. **Major trading partners:** U.S., China, France, Japan, Cameroon, Netherlands, Côte d'Ivoire.
Member of French Community

Geography This West African country with the Atlantic as its western border is also bounded by Equatorial Guinea, Cameroon, and the Congo. Its area is slightly less than Colorado's. Most of the country is covered by a dense tropical forest.

Government Republic.

History The earliest humans in Gabon were believed to be the Babinga, or Pygmies, dating back to 7000 B.C., who were later followed by Bantu groups from southern and eastern Africa. Now there are many tribal groups in the country, the largest being the Fang peoples, who constitute 25% of the population.

Gabon was first explored by the Portuguese navigator Diego Cam in the 15th century. In 1472 the Por-

tuguese explorers encountered the mouth of the Como River, and named it "Rio de Gabao," river of Gabon, which later became the name of the country. The Dutch began arriving in 1593, and the French in 1630. In 1839, the French founded their first settlement on the left bank of the Gabon estuary and gradually occupied the hinterland during the second half of the 19th century. It was organized as a French territory in 1888 and became an autonomous republic within the French Union after World War II, and an independent republic on Aug. 17, 1960.

After his conversion to Islam in 1973, President Bongo changed his given name, Albert Bernard, to Omar. He has been reelected every five years since 1967. Strikes and riots led to a transitional constitution in May 1990 legalizing political parties and calling for free elections. In its first multiparty election in Dec. 1993, the incumbent president received just over 51% of the vote, while the opposition candidate refused to accept defeat; he alleged fraud and tried to establish a rival government.

In Dec. 1998, President Bongo, who has ruled the country for 31 years, was elected for an additional seven. Gabon lacks roads, schools, and adequate health care, yet the oil-rich country has lined the pockets of its ruler, who, according to the French weekly *L'Autre Afrique*, is said to own more real estate in Paris than any other foreign leader. Despite his reputation for corruption and authoritarianism, however, Bongo has a strong national following.

Gambia, The

REPUBLIC OF THE GAMBIA

President: Colonel Yahya A. J. J. Jammeh (1997)
Area: 4,093 sq. mi. (11,300 sq. km)
Population (2000 est.): 1,367,124 (average annual rate of natural increase: 2.9%); birth rate: 42.3/1000; infant mortality rate: 79.3/1000; density per sq. mi.: 334
Capital (1986): Banjul, 44,188. **Monetary unit:** Dalasi.
  Languages: Native tongues, English (official). **Ethnicity/race:** African 99% (Mandinka 42%, Fula 18%, Wolof 16%, Jola 10%, Serahuli 9%, other 4%), non-Gambian 1%. **Religions:** Islam, 90%; Christian, 9%; traditional, 1%. **Literacy rate:** 27% (1990)
Economic summary: GDP/PPP (1998 est.): $1.3 billion; $1,000 per capita. **Real growth rate:** 3.8%. **Inflation:** 3%. **Unemployment:** n.a. **Arable land:** 18%. **Agriculture:** peanuts, millet, sorghum, rice, corn, cassava (tapioca), palm kernels, cattle, sheep, goats; forest and fishery resources not fully exploited. **Labor force:** n.a.: agriculture, 75%; industry, commerce, and services, 19%; government, 6%. **Industries:** processing peanuts, fish, and hides, tourism, beverages, agricultural machinery assembly, wood working, metal working, clothing. **Natural resources:** fish. **Exports:** $120 million (f.o.b., 1997): peanuts and peanut products, fish, cotton lint, palm kernels. **Imports:** $207 million (f.o.b., 1997): foodstuffs, manufactures, raw materials, fuel, machinery and transport equipment. **Major trading partners:** Belgium, Japan, Senegal, Hong Kong, France, Switzerland, U.K., U.S., Indonesia, Côte d'Ivoire, Germany, Netherlands.
Member of Commonwealth of Nations

Geography Situated on the Atlantic coast in westernmost Africa and surrounded on three sides by Senegal, Gambia is twice the size of Delaware. The Gambia River flows for 200 miles (322 km) through Gambia on its way to the Atlantic. The country, the smallest on the continent, averages only 20 miles (32 km) in width.

Government Republic.

History Since the 13th century, the Wolof, Malinke, and Fulani peoples settled in what is now The Gambia. The Portuguese were the first European explorers, encountering the Gambia River in 1455, and in 1681 the French founded an enclave at Albredabut. During the 17th century, Gambia was settled by various companies of English merchants. Slavery was the chief source of revenue before it was abolished in 1807. Gambia became a crown colony in 1843 and an independent nation within the Commonwealth of Nations on Feb. 18, 1965. Full independence was approved in a 1970 referendum, and on April 24 of that year Gambia proclaimed itself a republic.

Elections of April 29, 1992, returned President Jawara for a fifth term. His People's Progressive Party won 25 of the 36 seats in the House of Representatives. A military coup led by Capt. Yahya Jammeh deposed the president in July 1994, suspended the constitution, and banned political parties. Jammeh promised new elections, which were held in Sept. 1996, and he won 55% of the vote against his nearest rival, Ousseynou Darboe. In April 1997 he completed the promised return to civilian rule. Censorship of the press and a ban on some opposition parties, however, continue to mar the country's transition to democracy.

Unrest plagued Gambia throughout much of 2000. In January Jammeh crushed a coup attempt staged by some of his own bodyguards, and in April violent student protests rocked the country. The peanut export system collapsed in the same year from mismanagement, leaving farmers unpaid and unable to sell a bumper crop of the country's main commodity.

Georgia

GEORGIA

National Name: Sakartvelo
President: Eduard Shevardnadze (1992)
Secretary of State: Giorgi Arsenishvili (2000)
Area: 26,900 sq. mi. (69,700 sq. km)
Population (2000 est.): 5,019,538; average annual rate of natural increase: −0.4%; birth rate: 10.9/1000; infant mortality rate: 52.9/1000; density per sq. mi.: 187
Capital and largest city (1991): Tbilisi, 1,279,000. .
Other cities (1989): Kutaisi, 235,000; Batoumi, 136,000; and Sokhumi, 121,000. **Monetary unit:** Lari.
Languages: Georgian (official), 71%; Russian, 9%; Armenian, 7%; Azerbaijani, 6%. **Ethnicity/race:** Georgian 70.1%, Armenian 8.1%, Russian 6.3%, Azeri 5.7%, Ossetian 3%, Abkhaz 1.8%, other 5%.
Religions: Georgian Orthodox, 65%; Russian Orthodox, 10%; Armenian Orthodox, 8%; Muslim, 11%. **Literacy rate:** 99% (1989)
Economic summary: GDP/PPP (1998 est.): $11.2 billion; $2,200 per capita. **Real growth rate:** 4%. **Inflation:** 10.5%. **Unemployment:** 16% (1996 est.). **Labor force:** 3.08 million (1997): industry and construction, 31%; agriculture and forestry, 25%; other, 44% (1990). **Industries:** steel, aircraft, machine tools, foundry equipment, electric locomotives, tower cranes, electric welding equipment, machinery for food preparation and meat packing, electric motors, process control equipment, trucks, tractors, textiles, shoes, chemicals, wood products, wine. **Agriculture:** citrus, grapes, tea, vegetables, potatoes, livestock. **Exports:** $230 million (f.o.b., 1997 est.): citrus fruit, tea, wine, other agricultural products, diverse kinds of machinery, ferrous and nonferrous metals, textiles, chemicals, fuel reexports. **Imports:** $931 million (c.i.f., 1997 est.): fuel, grain and other food, machinery and parts, transport equipment. **Major trading partners:** Russia, Turkey, Azerbaijan, Ukraine, Armenia, Bulgaria, Turkey, U.S., U.K., Italy, Germany, Romania.

Geography Georgia is bordered by the Black Sea in the west, by Turkey and Armenia in the south, by Azerbaijan in the east, and Russia in the north. The republic also includes the Abkhaz and Adzhar autonomous republics and the Yugo-Ossetian Autonomous Oblast. Mount Elbrus (Lalbuzi in Georgian) at 18,841 feet is the highest peak in Europe.

Government Republic.

History Georgia became a kingdom about 4 B.C. and Christianity was introduced in A.D. 337. During the reign of Queen Tamara (1184–1213), its territory included the whole of Transcaucasia. During the 13th century, Tamerlane and the Mongols decimated its population. From the 16th century on, the country was the scene of a struggle between Persia and Turkey. In the 18th century it became a vassal to Russia in exchange for protection from the Turks and Persians.

Georgia joined Azerbaijan and Armenia in 1917 to establish the anti-Bolshevik Transcaucasian Federation, and upon its dissolution, proclaimed its independence in 1918. In 1922, Georgia, Armenia, and Azerbaijan were annexed by the U.S.S.R. and formed the Transcaucasian Soviet Socialist Republic. In 1936, it became a separate Soviet republic. Under Soviet rule Georgia was transformed from an agrarian country to a largely industrial, urban society.

Georgia proclaimed its independence from the U.S.S.R. on April 6, 1991. In Jan. 1992, its leader Zviad Gamsakhurdia was sacked, and later accused of dictatorial policies, the jailing of opposition leaders, human rights abuses, and clamping down on the media. A ruling military council was established by the opposition until a civilian authority could be restored. In 1992, Eduard Shevardnadze, the Soviet Union's foreign minister under Gorbachev, became president.

In 1992–93, the government engaged in armed conflict with separatists in the breakaway province of Abkhazia. In 1994, Russia and Georgia signed a cooperation treaty that authorized Russia to keep three military bases in Georgia and allowed Russians to train and equip the Georgian army. In 1996, Georgia and its breakaway region of South Ossetia agreed to a cessation of hostilities in their six-year conflict. With little progress in resolving the Abkhazia situation, however, Parliament in April 1997 voted overwhelmingly to threaten Russia with loss of its military bases should it fail to extend Russian military control over the separatist region. In 1998 the U.S. and Britain began an operation to remove nuclear material from Georgia, dangerous remains from its Soviet years. In the 2000 presidential elections, incumbent Shevardnadze won 80% of the vote.

Germany

FEDERAL REPUBLIC OF GERMANY

National name: Bundesrepublik Deutschland
President: Johannes Rau (1999)
Chancellor: Gerhard Schröder (1998)
Area: 137,826 sq. mi. (356,910 sq. km)
Population (2000 est.): 82,797,408 (average annual growth rate: −0.11%); birth rate: 9.4/1000; infant mortality rate: 4.8/1000; density per sq. mi.: 601
Capital and largest city (1995 est.): Berlin (capital since Oct. 3, 1990), 3,471,418. **Other large cities (1997):** Hamburg, 1,703,800; Munich, 1,251,100; Cologne, 963,300; Frankfurt, 656,200; Essen, 619,600; Dortmund, 601,500; Stuttgart, 592,000;

Düsseldorf, 573,100; Bremen, 551,000; Hanover, 526,400; Duisberg, 536,500. **Monetary units:** Deutsche Mark and euro. **Language:** German. **Ethnicity/race:** German 91.5%, Turkish 2.4%, Italians 0.7%, Greeks 0.4%, Poles 0.4%, Other 4.6%. **Religions:** Protestant 38%, Roman Catholic 34%, Muslim 1.7%, Unaffiliated or other 26.3%. **Literacy rate:** 99% (1977)

Economic summary GDP/PPP (1998 est.): $1.813 trillion; $22,100 per capita. **Real growth rate:** 2.7%. **Inflation:** 0.9%. **Unemployment:** 10.6%. **Labor force:** 38.2 million (1998): services, 63.6%; industry, 33.7%; agriculture, 2.7%. **Exports:** $510 billion (f.o.b., 1998 est.): machinery, 31%; vehicles, 17%; chemicals, 13%; metals and manufactures, foodstuffs, textiles (1997). **Imports:** $426 billion (f.o.b., 1998 est.): machinery, 22%; vehicles, 10%; chemicals, 9%; foodstuffs, 8%; textiles, metals (1997). **Industries:** western: among world's largest and technologically advanced producers of iron, steel, coal, cement, chemicals, machinery, vehicles, machine tools, electronics, food and beverages; eastern: metal fabrication, chemicals, brown coal, shipbuilding, machine building, food and beverages, textiles, petroleum refining. **Agriculture:** western: potatoes, wheat, barley, sugar beets, fruit, cabbages, cattle, pigs, poultry; eastern: wheat, rye, barley, potatoes, sugar beets, fruit, pork, beef, chicken, milk, hides. **Natural resources:** iron ore, coal, potash, timber, lignite, uranium, copper, natural gas, salt, nickel. **Major trading partners:** EU (France, U.K., Italy, Netherlands, Belgium, Luxembourg), U.S., Japan.

Geography Located in central Europe, Germany is made up of the North German Plain, the Central German Uplands (Mittelgebirge), and the Southern German Highlands. The Bavarian plateau in the southwest averages 1,600 feet (488 m) above sea level, but it reaches 9,721 feet (2,962 m) in the Zugspitze Mountains, the highest point in the country. Germany's major rivers are the Danube, the Elbe, the Oder, the Weser, and the Rhine. Germany is about the size of Montana.

Government Parliamentary democracy.

History The Celts are believed to have been the first inhabitants of Germany. They were followed by German tribes at the end of the 2nd century B.C. German invasions destroyed the declining Roman Empire in the 4th and 5th centuries A.D. One of the tribes, the Franks, attained supremacy in western Europe under Charlemagne, who was crowned Holy Roman Emperor in A.D. 800. By the Treaty of Verdun (843), Charlemagne's lands east of the Rhine were ceded to the German Prince Louis. Additional territory acquired by the Treaty of Mersen (870) gave Germany approximately the area it maintained throughout the Middle Ages. For several centuries after Otto the Great was crowned king in 936, German rulers were also usually heads of the Holy Roman Empire.

By the 14th century, the Holy Roman Empire was little more than a loose federation of the German princes who elected the Holy Roman Emperor. In 1438, Albert of Hapsburg became emperor, and for the next several centuries the Hapsburg line ruled the Holy Roman Empire until its decline in 1806. Relations between state and church were changed by the Reformation, which began with Martin Luther's 95 theses, and came to a head in 1547, when Charles V scattered the forces of the Protestant League at Mühlberg. Freedom of worship was guaranteed by the Peace of Augsburg (1555), but the Counter Reformation took place later, and a dispute over the succession to the Bohemian throne brought on the Thirty Years' War (1618–48), which devastated Germany and left the empire divided into hundreds of small principalities virtually independent of the emperor.

Meanwhile, Prussia was developing into a state of considerable strength. Frederick the Great (1740–86) reorganized the Prussian army and defeated Maria Theresa of Austria in a struggle over Silesia. After the defeat of Napoléon at Waterloo (1815), the struggle between Austria and Prussia for supremacy in Germany continued, reaching its climax in the defeat of Austria in the Seven Weeks' War (1866) and the formation of the Prussian-dominated North German Confederation (1867). The architect of this new German unity was Otto von Bismarck, a conservative, monarchist, and militaristic Prussian prime minister. He unified all of Germany in a series of three wars against Denmark (1864), Austria (1866), and France (1870–71). On Jan. 18, 1871, King Wilhelm I of Prussia was proclaimed German emperor in the Hall of Mirrors at Versailles. The North German Confederation, created in 1867, was abolished, and the Second German Reich, consisting of the North and South German states, was born. With a powerful army, an efficient bureaucracy, and a loyal bourgeoisie, Chancellor Bismarck consolidated a powerful centralized state.

Wilhelm II dismissed Bismarck in 1890 and embarked upon a "New Course," stressing an intensified colonialism and a powerful navy. His chaotic foreign policy culminated in the diplomatic isolation of Germany and the disastrous defeat in World War I (1914–18). The Second German Empire collapsed following the defeat of the German armies in 1918, the naval mutiny at Kiel, and the flight of the kaiser to the Netherlands. The Social Democrats, led by Friedrich Ebert and Philipp Scheidemann, crushed the Communists and established a moderate state, known as the Weimar Republic, with Ebert as president. President Ebert died on Feb. 28, 1925, and on April 26, Field Marshal Paul von Hindenburg was elected president. The mass of Germans regarded the Weimar Republic as a child of defeat, imposed upon a Germany whose legitimate aspirations to world leadership had been thwarted by a world conspiracy. Added to this were a crippling currency debacle, a tremendous burden of reparations, and acute economic distress.

Adolf Hitler, an Austrian war veteran and a fanatical nationalist, fanned discontent by promising a Greater Germany, abrogation of the Treaty of Versailles, restoration of Germany's lost colonies, and the destruction of the Jews, whom he scapegoated as the reason for Germany's downfall and depressed economy. When the Social Democrats and the Communists refused to combine against the Nazi threat, President von Hindenburg made Hitler the chancellor on Jan. 30, 1933. With the death of von Hindenburg on Aug. 2, 1934, Hitler repudiated the Treaty of Versailles and began full-scale rearmament. In 1935 he withdrew Germany from the League of Nations, and the next year he reoccupied the Rhineland and signed the anti-Comintern pact with Japan, at the same time strengthening relations with Italy. Austria was annexed in March 1938. By the Munich agreement in Sept. 1938, he gained the Czech Sudetenland, and in violation of this agreement he completed the dismemberment of Czechoslovakia in March 1939. His invasion of Poland on Sept. 1, 1939, precipitated World War II.

Hitler established death camps to carry out "the final solution to the Jewish question." By the end of the war, Hitler's Holocaust had killed 6 million Jews, as well as Gypsies, homosexuals, Communists, the handicapped, and others not fitting the Aryan ideal. After some dazzling initial successes in 1939–42, Germany surrendered unconditionally to Allied and Soviet military commanders on May 8, 1945. On June 5 the four-nation Allied Control Council became the de facto government of Germany.

(For details of World War II and of the Holocaust, *see* Headline History, World War II.)

At the Berlin (or Potsdam) Conference (July 17–Aug. 2, 1945) President Truman, Premier Stalin, and Prime Minister Clement Attlee of Britain set forth the guiding principles of the Allied Control Council: Germany's complete disarmament and demilitarization, destruction of its war potential, rigid control of industry, and decentralization of the political and economic structure. Pending final determination of territorial questions at a peace conference, the three victors agreed to the ultimate transfer of the city of Königsberg (now Kaliningrad) and its adjacent area to the U.S.S.R. and to the administration by Poland of former German territories lying generally east of the Oder-Neisse Line. For purposes of control, Germany was divided into four national occupation zones.

The Western powers were unable to agree with the U.S.S.R. on any fundamental issues. Work of the Allied Control Council was hamstrung by repeated Soviet vetoes; and finally, on March 20, 1948, Russia walked out of the council. Meanwhile, the U.S. and Britain had taken steps to merge their zones economically (Bizone); and on May 31, 1948, the U.S., Britain, France, and the Benelux countries agreed to set up a German state comprising the three Western Zones. The U.S.S.R. reacted by clamping a blockade on all ground communications between the Western Zones and West Berlin, an enclave in the Soviet Zone. The Western Allies countered by organizing a gigantic airlift to fly supplies into the beleaguered city, assigning 60,000 men to it. The U.S.S.R. was finally forced to lift the blockade on May 12, 1949.

The Federal Republic of Germany was proclaimed on May 23, 1949, with its capital at Bonn. In free elections, West German voters gave a majority in the Constituent Assembly to the Christian Democrats, with the Social Democrats largely making up the opposition. Konrad Adenauer became chancellor, and Theodor Heuss of the Free Democrats was elected first president.

The East German states adopted a more centralized constitution for the Democratic Republic of Germany, put into effect on Oct. 7, 1949. The U.S.S.R. thereupon dissolved its occupation zone but Soviet troops remained. The Western Allies declared that the East German Republic was a Soviet creation undertaken without self-determination and refused to recognize it. Soviet forces created a state controlled by the secret police with a single party, the Socialist Unity (Communist) Party.

Agreements in Paris in 1954 giving the Federal Republic full independence and complete sovereignty came into force on May 5, 1955. Under the agreement, West Germany and Italy became members of the Brussels treaty organization created in 1948 and renamed the Western European Union. West Germany also became a member of NATO. In 1955 the U.S.S.R. recognized the Federal Republic. The Saar territory, under an agreement between France and West Germany, held a plebiscite and despite economic links to France, elected to rejoin West Germany on Jan. 1, 1957.

The division between West Germany and East Germany was intensified when the Communists erected the Berlin Wall in 1961. In 1968, the East German Communist leader, Walter Ulbricht, imposed restrictions on West German movements into West Berlin. The Soviet-bloc invasion of Czechoslovakia in Aug. 1968 added to the tension. West Germany in 1970 signed a treaty with Poland, renouncing force and setting Poland's western border as the Oder-Neisse Line. It subsequently resumed formal relations with Czechoslovakia in a pact that "voided" the Munich treaty that gave Nazi Germany the Sudetenland. By 1973, normal relations were established between East and West Germany and the two states entered the United Nations.

Willy Brandt, winner of a Nobel Peace Prize for his foreign policies, was forced to resign in 1974 when an East German spy was discovered to be one of his top staff members. Succeeding him was a moderate Social Democrat, Helmut Schmidt. Schmidt staunchly backed U.S. military strategy in Europe, staking his political fate on the strategy of placing U.S. nuclear missiles in Germany unless the Soviet Union reduced its arsenal of intermediate missiles. The chancellor also strongly opposed nuclear freeze proposals.

Helmut Kohl of the Christian Democrat Party became chancellor in 1982. An economic upswing in 1986 led to Kohl's reelection. The fall of the Communist government in East Germany left only Soviet objections to German reunification to be dealt with. This was resolved in July 1990. On Oct. 3, 1989, the German Democratic Republic acceded to the Federal Republic and Germany became a united and sovereign state for the first time since 1945.

Following unification, the Federal Republic became the second-largest country in Europe after the Soviet Union. A reunited Berlin serves as the official capital, although the government would continue to have administrative functions in Bonn during the 12-year transition period. The issue of the cost of reunification and the modernization of the former East Germany were serious considerations facing the reunified nation. Germany ratified the Maastricht Treaty in Oct. 1993, being the last of the 12 EU members to do so. Voters in the relatively new state of Brandenburg in the east rejected in May 1996 a proposal to merge with Berlin, dramatizing a lingering psychological division between eastern and western Germany.

Owing to a budget deficit that threatened the country's eligibility for introducing the future common European currency, the government in June 1997 proposed to revalue its foreign exchange holdings. Germany's other main challenge was to render Germany competitively attractive as an industrial location by radically reducing taxes so as to attract investment capital, foreign and domestic, within the EU, and thus lower the high rate of unemployment.

In its most important election in decades, on Sept. 27, 1998, Germans chose Social Democrat Gerhard Schröder as chancellor over Christian Democrat incumbent Helmut Kohl, ending a 16-year-long rule that oversaw the reunification of Germany and symbolized the end of the cold war in Europe. A centrist in the style of Clinton and Blair, Schröder campaigned for "the new middle" and promised to rectify Germany's high unemployment rate of 10.6%.

Tension between the old-style left-wing and the more pro-business pragmatists within Schröder's government came to a head with the abrupt resignation of Finance Minister Oskar Lafontaine in March 1999, who was also chairman of the ruling Social Democratic Party. Lafontaine's plans to raise taxes on industry and raise German wages—already nearly the highest in the world—went against the more centrist policies of Schröder. Hans Eichel was chosen to become the next finance minister. Germany had one of the slowest rates of economic growth in western Europe—on par with Italy—and the most that was expected in 1999 was mild improvement. But in June Schröder presented an ambitious reform package that cut billions from the federal budget and offered lower corporate taxes. In Sept. 1999, the German Parliament returned to its historic seat in Berlin.

Germany joined the other NATO allies in the military conflict in Kosovo in 1999. Before the Kosovo crisis, Germans had not participated in an armed conflict since World War II. It agreed to take 40,000 Kosovar refugees, the most of any NATO country.

In Dec. 1999, former chancellor Helmut Kohl and other high officials in the Christian Democrat party, including his successor, Wolfgang Schäuble, admitted accepting tens of millions of dollars in illegal donations during the 1980s and 1990s. The enormity of the scandal led to the virtual dismemberment of the CDU in early 2000, a party that had long been a stable conservative force in German politics.

In July 2000, Schröder managed to pass significant tax reforms that would lower the top income-tax rate from 51% to 42% by 2005. He also eliminated the capital gains tax on companies selling shares in other companies, a measure that was expected to spur mergers. In an effort to stem rising neo-Nazi violence, Schröder has contemplated banning the far-right National Democratic Party (NPD).

Ghana

REPUBLIC OF GHANA

President: Jerry John Rawlings (1981)
Area: 92,100 sq. mi. (238,540 sq. km)
Population (2000 est.): 19,533,560 (average annual rate of natural increase: 1.96%); birth rate: 29.8/1000; infant mortality rate: 57.4/1000; density per sq. mi.: 212
Capital: Accra. **Largest cities (est. 1988):** Accra, 949,100; Kumasi, 385,200; Tamale, 151,100.
Monetary unit: Cedi. **Languages:** English (official), Native tongues (Brong Ahafo, Twi, Fanti, Ga, Ewe, Dagbani). **Ethnicity/race:** black African 99.8% (major tribes: Akan 44%, Moshi-Dagomba 16%, Ewe 13%, Ga 8%), European and other 0.2%. **Religions:** indigenous beliefs, 38%; Islam, 30%; Christian, 24%. **Literacy rate:** 60% (1990)
Economic summary: GDP/PPP (1998 est.): $33.6 billion; $1,800 per capita. **Real growth rate:** 3%. **Inflation:** 27.7% (1997 est.). **Unemployment:** 20% (1997 est.). **Arable land:** 12%. **Agriculture:** cocoa, rice, coffee, cassava (tapioca), peanuts, corn, shea nuts, bananas, timber. **Labor force:** n.a.: agriculture and fishing, 61%; services, 29%; industry, 10% (1996 est.). **Industries:** mining, lumbering, light manufacturing, aluminum smelting, food processing. **Natural resources:** gold, timber, industrial diamonds, bauxite, manganese, fish, rubber. **Exports:** $1.5 billion (f.o.b., 1997): gold, 39%; cocoa, 35%; timber, 9.4%; tuna, bauxite, aluminum, manganese ore, and diamonds (1996 est.). **Imports:** $2.1 billion (f.o.b., 1997): capital equipment, petroleum, consumer goods, food, intermediate goods. **Major trading partners:** U.K., Germany, U.S., Netherlands, Japan, Nigeria.
Member of Commonwealth of Nations

Geography A West African country bordering on the Gulf of Guinea, Ghana is bounded by Côte d'Ivoire to the west, Burkina Faso to the north, Togo to the east,

and the Atlantic Ocean to the south. It compares in size to Oregon, and its largest river is the Volta.

Government Republic.

History Several major civilizations flourished in the general region of what is now Ghana. The ancient empire of Ghana (located 500 miles northwest of the contemporary state) reigned until the 13th century. The Akan peoples established the next major civilization, beginning in the 13th century, and then the Ashanti empire flourished in the 18th and 19th centuries.

Called the Gold Coast, the area was first seen by Portuguese traders in 1470. They were followed by the English (1553), the Dutch (1595), and the Swedes (1640). British rule over the Gold Coast began in 1820, but it was not until after quelling the severe resistance of the Ashanti in 1901 that it was firmly established. British Togoland, formerly a colony of Germany, was incorporated into Ghana by referendum in 1956. Created as an independent country on March 6, 1957, Ghana, as the result of a plebiscite, became a republic on July 1, 1960.

Premier Kwame Nkrumah attempted to take leadership of the Pan-African Movement, holding the All-African People's Congress in its capital, Accra, in 1958 and organizing the Union of African States with Guinea and Mali in 1961. But he oriented his country toward the Soviet Union and China and built an autocratic rule over all aspects of Ghanaian life. In Feb. 1966, while Nkrumah was visiting Beijing and Hanoi, he was deposed by a military coup led by Gen. Emmanuel K. Kotoka.

A series of military coups followed and on June 4, 1979, Flight Lieutenant Jerry Rawlings overthrew Lt. Gen. Frederick Akuffo's military rule. Rawlings permitted the election of a civilian president to go ahead as scheduled the following month, and Hilla Limann, candidate of the People's National Party, took office. Charging the civilian government with corruption and repression, Rawlings staged another coup on Dec. 31, 1981. As chairman of the Provisional National Defense Council, Rawlings instituted an austerity program and reduced budget deficits. Rawlings was reelected in 1982 and again in 1996.

A major cocoa producer, Ghana has been hurt by several year-long slumps in cocoa prices. In July 2000 Ghana and neighboring countries began destroying massive amounts of cocoa to drive up the price.

Greece

HELLENIC REPUBLIC

National name: Elliniki Dimokratia
President: Kostis Stephanopoulos (1995)
Prime Minister: Kostas Simitis (1996)
Area: 50,961 sq. mi. (131,940 sq. km)
Population (2000 est.): 10,601,527 (average annual rate of natural increase: 0.02%); birth rate: 9.8/1000; infant mortality rate: 6.5/1000; density per sq. mi.: 208
Capital: Athens. **Largest cities (1991 est.):** Athens, 3,000,000; Thessaloníki, 720,000; Piraeus, 170,000; Patras, 155,000. **Monetary unit:** Drachma.
Language: Greek. **Ethnicity/race:** Greek 98%, other 2% note: the Greek government states there are no ethnic divisions in Greece. **Religions:** Greek Orthodox, 98%; Muslim, 1.3%; Other, 0.7%. **Literacy rate:** 93% (1990)
Economic summary: GDP/PPP (1998 est.): $143 billion; $13,400 per capita. **Real growth rate:** 3%. **Inflation:** 3.9%. **Unemployment:** 10%. **Arable land:** 19%. **Agriculture:** wheat, corn, barley, sugar beets, olives, tomatoes, wine, tobacco, potatoes, beef, dairy

products. **Labor force** 4.28 million (1998): services, 59.2%; industry, 21%; agriculture, 19.8%. **Industries:** tourism, food and tobacco processing, textiles, chemicals, metal products, mining, petroleum. **Natural resources:** bauxite, lignite, magnesite, petroleum, marble. **Exports:** $12.4 billion (f.o.b., 1998): manufactured goods, foodstuffs, fuel. **Imports:** $27.7 billion (c.i.f., 1998): manufactured goods, foodstuffs, fuel, chemicals. **Major trading partners:** EU, U.S.

Geography Located in southern Europe, Greece forms an irregular-shaped peninsula in the Mediterranean with two additional large peninsulas projecting from it: the Chalcidice and the Peloponnese. The Greek Islands are generally subdivided into two groups, according to location: the Ionian Islands (including Corfu, Cephalonia, and Leucas) west of the mainland and the Aegean Islands (including Euboea, Samos, Chios, Lesbos, and Crete) to the east and south. North-central Greece, Epirus, and western Macedonia all are mountainous. The main chain of the Pindus Mountains extends from northwestern Greece to the Peloponnese. Mount Olympus, rising to 9,570 feet (2,909 m), is the highest point in the country.

Government Ceremonial executive power is held by the president; the prime minister heads the government and is responsible to a 300-member unicameral Parliament.

History Indo-European peoples, including the Mycenaeans, began entering Greece about 2000 B.C. and set up sophisticated civilizations. About 1200 B.C. the Dorians, another Indo-European people, invaded Greece, and a dark age followed, known mostly through the Homeric epics. At the end of this time, classical Greece began to emerge (c. 750 B.C.) as a loose composite of city-states with a heavy involvement in maritime trade and a devotion to art, literature, politics, and philosophy. Greece reached the peak of its glory in the 5th century B.C., but the Peloponnesian War (431–404 B.C.) weakened the nation and it was conquered by Philip II and his son Alexander the Great of Macedonia, who considered themselves Greek. By the middle of the 2nd century B.C., Greece had declined to the status of a Roman province. It remained within the eastern Roman Empire until Constantinople fell to the Crusaders in 1204. In 1453, the Turks took Constantinople and by 1460, Greece was a Turkish province with its Orthodox Church intact. The insurrection made famous by the poet Lord Byron broke out in 1821, and in 1827 Greece won independence with sovereignty guaranteed by Britain, France, and Russia.

The protecting powers chose Prince Otto of Bavaria as the first king of modern Greece in 1832 to reign over an area only slightly larger than the Peloponnese peninsula. Chiefly under the next king, George I, chosen by the protecting powers in 1863, Greece acquired much of its present territory. During his 57-year reign, a period in which he encouraged parliamentary democracy, Thessaly, Epirus, Macedonia, Crete, and most of the Aegean islands were added from the disintegrating Turkish empire. Unfavorable economic conditions forced about one-sixth of the entire Greek population to emigrate (mostly to the U.S.) in the late 19th and early 20th centuries. An unsuccessful war against Turkey after World War I brought down the monarchy, to be replaced by a republic in 1923.

Two military dictatorships and a financial crisis brought George II back from exile, but only until 1941, when Italian and German invaders defeated tough Greek resistance. After British and Greek troops liberated the country in Oct. 1944, Communist guerrillas staged a long military campaign against the government; the Greek civil war, infamous for its brutality, began in Dec. 1944 and continued until Oct. 16, 1949, when the Communist guerrillas conceded defeat. The Greek government received U.S. aid under the Truman Doctrine, the predecessor of the Marshall Plan, to fight against the Communists.

Greece was a charter member of the UN, and became a member of the North Atlantic Treaty Organization (NATO) in 1951. A military junta seized power in April 1967, sending young King Constantine II into exile. Col. George Papadopoulos, a leader of the junta, gradually attempted to re-vamp his hardline, right-wing image: first, by giving up his military post for that of prime minister in 1973, and later, as president, by ending martial law. A coup ousted Papadopoulos in Nov. 1973. The seven-year regime of the "colonels," infamous for torturing and exiling opponents, and scoffing at human rights, collapsed entirely a year later, after having bungled an attempt to seize Cyprus.

A referendum in Dec. 1974, five months after the demise of the military dictatorship, ended the Greek monarchy and established a republic. Former premier Karamanlis returned from exile to become premier of Greece's first civilian government since 1967. Greece has continued to be ruled by freely elected civilian governments ever since. On Jan. 1, 1981, Greece became the 10th member of the European Union. Anreas Papandreou, son of former premier George Papandeou, founded the Panhellenic Socialist Movement (PASOK) and became Greece's first socialist premier (1981–1989).

The Greeks were the most vocal dissenters within the NATO alliance regarding the 1999 intervention in Kosovo. They were both wary of the economic and political instability that would accompany a large influx of refugees and reluctant to ignore an Eastern Orthodox religious history shared with the Serbs.

Greece continued to experience tensions with Turkey over a disputed, unpopulated 10-acre island and over Cyprus, which is divided into Greek and Turkish sectors. Turkey's severe earthquake in Aug. 1999, however, moved Greece to provide humanitarian assistance, and brought about a slight thaw in relations.

Costas Simitis, premier since 1996, is credited with reviving the Greek economy, and the country is expected to join the European single currency in 2001. Still, *The Economist* magazine estimates it will be at least 15 years before the per capita GDP in Greece comes close to the current EU average.

Grenada

STATE OF GRENADA

Sovereign: Queen Elizabeth II (1952)
Governor-General: Daniel Williams (1996)
Prime Minister: Keith C. Mitchell (1995)
Area: 133 sq. mi. (340 sq. km)
Population (2000 est.): 89,018 (average annual growth rate 1.29%); birth rate: 21/1000; infant mortality rate: 14.6/1000; density per sq. mi.: 669
Capital and largest city (1991): St. George's, 4,439.
Monetary unit: East Caribbean dollar. **Language:** English. **Ethnicity/race:** black African descent 85%, mixed 11%, white, other 0.3%. **Religions:** Roman Catholic, 64%; Anglican, 21%. **Literacy rate:** 98% (1970)

Economic summary: GDP/PPP (1998 est.): $340 million; $3,500 per capita. **Real growth rate:** 5%. **Inflation:** 1.4%. **Unemployment:** 20% (Oct. 1996). **Arable land:** 15%. **Agriculture:** bananas, cocoa, nutmeg, mace, citrus, avocados, root crops, sugarcane, corn, vegetables. **Labor force:** 36,000: services, 31%; agriculture, 24%; construction, 8%; manufacturing, 5%; other, 32% (1985). **Industries:** food and beverages, textiles, light assembly operations, tourism, construction. **Natural resources:** timber, tropical fruit, deepwater harbors. **Exports:** $22 million (1997): bananas, cocoa, nutmeg, fruit and vegetables, clothing, mace. **Imports:** $166.5 million (1997): food, manufactured goods, machinery, chemicals, fuel. **Major trading partners:** Caricom, U.K., U.S., Netherlands, Japan. **Member of Commonwealth of Nations**

Geography Grenada (the first "a" is a long vowel) is the most southerly of the Windward Islands, about 100 miles (161 km) from the Venezuelan coast. It is a volcanic island traversed by a mountain range, the highest peak of which is Mount St. Catherine (2,756 ft.; 840 m).

Government Parliamentary democracy. A governor-general represents the sovereign, Elizabeth II.

History The Arawak Indians were the first to inhabit Grenada, but they were all eventually massacred by the belligerent Carib Indians. When Columbus arrived on the island in 1498 he encountered the Caribs, who in fact continued to rule over the island for another 150 years. The French gained control of the island in 1672 and held on to it until 1762, when British forces invaded. The black slaves, who had been shipped to the island to work on the plantations, were granted freedom in 1833. After more than 200 years of British rule, most recently as part of the West Indies Associated States, Grenada became independent on Feb. 7, 1974, with Eric M. Gairy as prime minister.

In 1979 the Marxist New Jewel Movement staged a coup, and its leader, Maurice Bishop, became prime minister. Bishop, a protégé of Cuba's President Castro, was killed in a military coup on Oct. 19, 1983.

In an effort to establish order on the island and eliminate the Cuban military presence, U.S. president Ronald Reagan ordered an invasion of Grenada on Oct. 25 involving over 1,900 U.S. troops and a small military force from Barbados, Dominica, Jamaica, St. Lucia, and St. Vincent. The troops met strong resistance from Cuban military personnel on the island but soon occupied it. After a gradual withdrawal of peacekeeping forces, a centrist coalition led by Herbert A. Blaize, a 66-year-old lawyer, won a parliamentary majority in 1984. Parliamentary elections in June 1995 gave the opposition New National Party a majority of seats and allowed its leader, Dr. Keith C. Mitchell, to form a new government. Mitchell flew to Cuba in April 1997 to meet with Castro and signed an economic cooperation agreement. In 1998 Castro made his first official state visit to the island. In 1999, Prime Minister Mitchell became one of only two prime ministers in Grenada's history to be reelected.

Guatemala

REPUBLIC OF GUATEMALA

National name: República de Guatemala
President: Alfonso Portillo Cabrera (2000)
Area: 42,042 sq. mi. (108,890 sq. km)
Population (2000 est.): 12,639,939 (average annual rate

of natural increase: 2.8%); birth rate: 35.1/1000; infant mortality rate: 47/1000; density per sq. mi.: 301
Capital and largest city (1994 est.): Guatemala City, 1,150,452. **Other large cities (1994 est.):** Mixco, 413,002; Villa Nueva, 154,508. **Monetary unit:** Quetzal. **Languages:** Spanish, Indian languages. **Ethnicity/race:** Mestizo—mixed Amerindian-Spanish ancestry (in local Spanish called Ladino) 56%, Amerindian or predominantly Amerindian 44%. **Religions:** Roman Catholic, Protestant, Mayan. **Literacy rate:** 55% (1990)
Economic summary: GDP/PPP (1998 est.): $45.7 billion; $3,800 per capita. **Real growth rate:** 5%. **Inflation:** 6.4%. **Unemployment:** 5.2% (1997 est.). **Arable land:** 12%. **Agriculture:** sugarcane, corn, bananas, coffee, beans, cardamom, cattle, sheep, pigs, chickens. **Labor force:** 3.32 million (1997 est.): agriculture, 58%; services, 14%; manufacturing, 14%; commerce, 7%; construction, 4%; transport, 2.6%; utilities, 0.3%; mining, 0.1% (1995). **Industries:** sugar, textiles and clothing, furniture, chemicals, petroleum, metals, rubber, tourism. **Natural resources:** petroleum, nickel, rare woods, fish, chicle. **Exports:** $2.9 billion (f.o.b., 1997 est.): coffee, sugar, bananas, cardamom, petroleum. **Imports:** $3.3 billion (c.i.f., 1997 est.): fuel and petroleum products, machinery, grain, fertilizers, motor vehicles. **Major trading partners:** U.S., El Salvador, Honduras, Costa Rica, Germany, Mexico, Venezuela, Japan.

Geography The northernmost of the Central American nations, Guatemala is the size of Tennessee. Its neighbors are Mexico on the north and west, and Belize, Honduras, and El Salvador on the east. The country consists of three main regions—the cool highlands with the heaviest population, the tropical area along the Pacific and Caribbean coasts, and the tropical jungle in the northern lowlands (known as the Petén). The principal mountain range rises to the highest elevation in Central America and contains many volcanic peaks. Volcanic eruptions are frequent.

Government Republic.

History Once the site of the impressive ancient Mayan civilization, Guatemala was conquered by Spanish conquistador Pedro de Alvarado in 1524 and set itself up as a republic in 1839 after the United Provinces of Central America collapsed. From 1898 to 1920, the dictator Manuel Estrada Cabrera ran the country and welcomed U.S. investment, and from 1931 to 1944, Gen. Jorge Ubico Castaneda served as strongman.

After Ubico's overthrow in 1944, liberal-democratic coalitions led by Juan José Arévalo (1945–51) and Jacobo Arbenz Guzmán (1951–54) instituted sweeping social and political reforms that strengthened the peasantry and urban workers at the expense of the military and big landowners like the United Fruit Company. With covert U.S. backing, a revolt was led by Col. Carlos Castillo Armas, and Arbenz took refuge in Mexico.

A 36-year civil war followed between a succession of right-wing governments led by the military and leftist rebels. The administration of Gen. Romeo Lucas Garcia was charged by Amnesty International with responsibility for at least 5,000 political murders in a reign of brutality and corruption that brought a cutoff of U.S. military aid in 1978.

More military leaders followed until civilian Marco Vinicio Cerezo Arévalo took office in 1986. He was followed by Jorge Serrano Elías in 1991. In 1993, Serrano moved to dissolve Congress and the Supreme

Court and suspend constitutional rights, but the military deposed Serrano and allowed the inauguration of de Leon Carpio, the former attorney general of human rights. A peace agreement was signed in Dec. 1996 ending the longest civil war in Latin American history. By the time the war had run its course, an estimated 150,000 died and 50,000 were missing. In June 1997, the new president Álvaro Arzú Irigoyen and the guerrilla movement leader Ricardo Ramirez were awarded the UNESCO Houphouet-Boigny Peace Prize.

In an effort toward national reconciliation, a Guatemalan truth commission issued a report on Feb. 25, 1999, detailing the numerous human rights abuses committed during the war. The report charged that the army was responsible for 93% of the atrocities and that the rebels (the Guatemalan National Revolutionary Unit) were responsible for 3%. As a consequence, the former guerrillas apologized for their crimes, and President Clinton apologized for U.S. support of the right-wing military governments. The army, however, has not acknowledged its guilt.

In June 1999, Cuba's state-owned airline began direct flights to Guatemala. Guatemala had reestablished diplomatic relations with Cuba in Jan. 1998, 37 years after the country's conservative government broke off ties with Castro's government.

A new president, Alfonso Portillo Cabrera, took office in Jan. 2000. Although he had campaigned with former president Efrain Rios Montt, under whose government some of the worst human rights atrocities occurred, Portillo apologized for the government's abuses in Aug. 2000. He pledged to prosecute those responsible and compensate victims, to the relief of human rights activists frustrated by Guatemala's continued unwillingness to confront the issue.

Guinea

REPUBLIC OF GUINEA

National name: République de Guinée
President: Lansana Conté (1984)
Premier: Lamine Sidime (1999)
Area: 94,925 sq. mi. (245,860 sq. km)
Population (2000 est.): 7,466,200 (average annual rate of natural increase: 2.2%); birth rate: 40.1/1000; infant mortality rate: 131/1000; density per sq. mi.: 79
Capital and largest city (1995 est.): Conakry, 1,508,000. **Monetary unit:** Guinean franc.
Languages: French (official), native tongues (Malinké, Susu, Fulani). **Ethnicity/race:** Peuhl 40%, Malinke 30%, Soussou 20%, smaller tribes 10%. **Religions:** Islam, 85%; 7% indigenous, 8% Christian. **Literacy rate:** 24% in French; 48% in local languages (1990)
Economic summary: GDP/PPP (1998 est.): $8.8 billion; $1,180 per capita. **Real growth rate:** 4.9%. **Inflation:** 3.5%. **Arable land:** 2%. **Agriculture:** rice, coffee, pineapples, palm kernels, cassava (tapioca), bananas, sweet potatoes, cattle, sheep, goats, timber.
Unemployment: n.a. **Labor force:** 2.4 million (1983): agriculture, 80%; industry and commerce, 11%; services, 5.4%; civil service, 3.6%. **Industries:** bauxite, gold, diamonds, alumina refining, light manufacturing and agricultural processing. **Natural resources:** bauxite, iron ore, diamonds, gold, uranium, hydropower, fish. **Exports:** $695 million (f.o.b., 1998 est.): bauxite, alumina, diamonds, gold, coffee, fish, agricultural products. **Imports:** $560 million (f.o.b., 1998 est.): petroleum products, metals, machinery, transport equipment, textiles, grain and other foodstuffs (1997). **Major trading partners:** Russia, U.S., Belgium, Ukraine, Ireland, Spain, France, Côte d'Ivoire, Hong Kong.

Geography Guinea, in West Africa on the Atlantic, is also bordered by Guinea-Bissau, Senegal, Mali, Côte d'Ivoire, Liberia, and Sierra Leone. Slightly smaller than Oregon, the country consists of a coastal plain, a mountainous region, a savanna interior, and a forest area in the Guinea Highlands. The highest peak is Mount Nimba at 5,748 ft. (1,752 m).

Government Republic.

History Beginning in A.D. 900, the Soussou migrated from the north and began settling in the area that is now Guinea. The Soussou civilization reached its height in the 13th century. Today the Soussou make up about 20% of Guinea's population. From the 16th to the 19th century, the Fulani empire dominated the region. In 1849, the French claimed it as a protectorate. First called Rivières du Sud, the protectorate was rechristened French Guinea, and finally, in 1895, it became part of French West Africa.

Guinea achieved independence on Oct. 2, 1958, and became an independent state with Sékou Touré as president. Under Touré, the country became the first avowedly Marxist state in Africa. Diplomatic relations with France were suspended in 1965, with the Soviet Union replacing France as the country's chief source of economic and technical assistance.

Prosperity came in 1960 after the start of exploitation of bauxite deposits. Touré was reelected to a seven-year term in 1974 and again in 1981. Touré died after 26 years as president in March 1984. A week later, a military regime headed by Col. Lansana Conté took power. Conté became president and his coconspirator in the coup, Col. Diara Traoré, became prime minister, but Conté later demoted Traoré to education minister. Traoré tried to seize power on July 4, 1985, while Conté was out of the country, but his attempted coup was crushed by troops loyal to Conté.

In 1989, President Conté announced that Guinea would move to a multiparty democracy. A new constitution approved in a nationwide referendum in Dec. 1990 provided for the establishment of a directly elected multiparty Parliament (five-year terms) and a popularly elected president for a maximum of two five-year terms, and a judiciary independent of either the presidency or the legislature. A transitional Committee for National Recovery (CTRN) replaced the military committee to guide implementation of the new constitution.

In 1991 voters approved a new constitution that would lead the country to democracy. Under mounting popular pressure Conté declared in April 1992 that constitutional rule would begin. In Dec. 1993 elections, the president's Unity and Progress Party took almost 51% of the vote cast. In Feb. 1996 rebellious soldiers demanding pay in arrears besieged the presidential palace. Loyal troops repulsed the attacks.

Guinea has had ongoing difficulties with its neighbor Liberia, which was embroiled in a long civil war during the 1990s. The fighting in Liberia spilled over the border into Guinea on several occasions, and border skirmishes continued after the civil war subsided.

Already burdened by an inadequate infrastructure and a weak economy, nearly 300,000 refugees fleeing the civil war in Sierra Leone have overwhelmed Guinea. Renewed fighting in Sierra Leone in Aug. 2000 sent several thousand more hungry, desperate people into Guinea.

Guinea-Bissau

REPUBLIC OF GUINEA-BISSAU

National name: Républica da Guiné-Bissau
President: Kumba Yalá (2000)
Prime Minister: Caetano N'Tchama (2000)
Area: 13,948 sq. mi. (36,120 sq. km)
Population (2000 est.): 1,285,715 (average annual rate of natural increase: 2.4%); birth rate: 39.6/1000; infant mortality rate: 112.3/1000; density per sq. mi.: 92
Capital and largest city (1991 est.): Bissau, 200,000.
Monetary unit: Guinea-Bissau peso. **Languages:** Portuguese Criolo, African languages. **Ethnicity/race:** African 99% (Balanta 30%, Fula 20%, Manjaca 14%, Mandinga 13%, Papel 7%), European and mulatto less than 1%. **Religions:** traditional, 65%; Islam, 30%; Christian, 5%. **Literacy rate:** 37% (1990)
Economic summary: GDP/PPP (1998 est.): $1.2 billion; $1,000 per capita. **Real growth rate:** 3.5%. **Inflation:** 25.6% (1997). **Unemployment:** n.a. **Labor force:** 480,000. **Arable land:** 11%. **Agriculture:** rice, corn, beans, cassava (tapioca), cashew nuts, peanuts, palm kernels, cotton, timber, fish. **Industries:** agricultural products processing, beer, soft drinks. **Natural resources:** fish, timber, phosphates, bauxite, unexploited deposits of petroleum. **Exports:** $25.8 million (f.o.b., 1996 est.): cashews, fish, peanuts, palm kernels, sawn lumber. **Imports:** $63 million (f.o.b., 1996 est.): foodstuffs, transport equipment, petroleum products, machinery and equipment. **Major trading partners:** Spain, India, Thailand, Italy, Portugal, Netherlands, U.S.

Geography A neighbor of Senegal and Guinea in West Africa, on the Atlantic coast, Guinea-Bissau is about half the size of South Carolina. The country is a low-lying coastal region of swamps, rain forests, and mangrove-covered wetlands, with about 25 islands off the coast. The Bijagos archipelago extends 30 miles (48 km) out to sea.

Government Republic.

History The land now known as Guinea-Bissau was once the kingdom of Gabú, which was part of the larger Mali empire. After 1546 Gabú became more autonomous, and at least portions of the kingdom existed until 1867. The first European to encounter Guinea-Bissau was the Portuguese explorer Nuño Tristão in 1446; colonists in the Cape Verde Islands obtained trading rights in the territory, and it became a center of the Portuguese slave trade. In 1879 the connection with the islands was broken.

The African Party for the Independence of Guinea-Bissau and Cape Verde (another Portuguese colony) was founded in 1956 and guerrilla warfare by nationalists grew increasingly effective. By 1974 the rebels controlled most of the countryside, where they formed a government that was soon recognized by scores of countries. The military coup in Portugal in April 1974 brightened the prospects for freedom, and in Aug. the Lisbon government signed an agreement granting independence to the province. The new republic took the name Guinea-Bissau.

In Nov. 1980, Prémier João Bernardo Vieira headed a military coup that deposed Luis Cabral, president since 1974. In his 19 years of rule, Vieira was criticized for crony capitalism and corruption and for failing to alleviate the poverty of Guinea-Bissau, one of the world's poorest countries. Vieira also brought in troops from Senegal and the Republic of Guinea to help fight against an insurgency movement, a highly unpopular move. The rebels managed to gain control of most of the country and part of the capital in 1998

before a Nov. peace deal halted the fighting. But in May 1999, after the presidential guard refused to disarm, the rebels deposed Vieira.

Following a period of military rule, presidential elections were held in Jan. 2000. Kumba Yala, a former teacher and popular leader of Guinea-Bissau's independence movement, was elected with 72% of the vote in the second round of balloting.

Guyana

COOPERATIVE REPUBLIC OF GUYANA

President: Bharrat Jagdeo (1999)
Prime Minister: Samuel Hinds (1997)
Area: 83,000 sq. mi. (214,970 sq. km)
Population (2000 est.): 697,286 (average annual rate of natural increase: 0.95%); birth rate: 17.9/1000; infant mortality rate: 39.1/1000; density per sq. mi.: 8
Capital and largest city (1992 est.): Georgetown, 248,500. **Monetary unit:** Guyana dollar. **Languages:** English (official), Amerindian dialects. **Ethnicity/race:** East Indian 51%, black and mixed 43%, Amerindian 4%, European and Chinese 2%. **Religions:** Hindu, 34%; Protestant, 18%; Islam, 9%; Roman Catholic, 18%; Anglican, 16%. **Literacy rate:** 96% (1990)
Economic summary: GDP/PPP (1998 est.): $1.8 billion; $2,500 per capita. **Real growth rate:** –1.8%. **Inflation:** 4.1%. **Unemployment (1992 est.):** 12%. **Labor force** 245,492 (1992): agriculture, hunting, and forestry, 30.2%; commerce, 16%; manufacturing, 11%. **Arable land:** 2%. **Agriculture:** sugar, rice, wheat, vegetable oils, beef, pork, poultry, dairy products; forest and fishery potential not exploited. **Industries:** bauxite, sugar, rice milling, timber, fishing (shrimp), textiles, gold mining. **Natural resources:** bauxite, gold, diamonds, hardwood timber, shrimp, fish. **Exports:** $593.4 million (1997 est.): sugar, gold, bauxite/alumina, rice, shrimp, molasses. **Imports:** $641.6 million (1997 est.): manufactures, machinery, petroleum, food. **Major trading partners:** Canada, U.S., U.K., Netherlands Antilles, Germany, Trinidad and Tobago, Japan. **Member of Commonwealth of Nations**

Geography Guyana is the size of Idaho and is situated on the northern coast of South America east of Venezuela, west of Suriname, and north of Brazil. The country consists of a low coastal area and the Guyana Highlands, a tropical forest zone covering more than 80% of the country, in the south. There is an extensive north-south network of rivers.

Government Republic.

History The Dutch, English, and French established colonies in what is now known as Guyana, but by the early 17th century the majority of the settlements were Dutch. During the Napoleonic wars Britain took over the Dutch colonies of Berbice, Demerara, and Essequibo, which became British Guiana in 1831.

Slavery was outlawed in 1834, and the great need for plantation workers led to a large wave of immigration, primarily of East Indians. Today, about half of the population is of East Indian descent and about 43% are of African descent.

British Guiana was made a crown colony in 1928, and in 1953 it was granted home rule. In 1950, Forbes Burnham and Cheddi Jagan, the former black and the latter East Indian, created the colony's first political party, which was dedicated to gaining the colony's independence. The two leaders split in 1955, creating separate parties. The leftist Jagan and the more moderate Burnham were to dominate Guyanan politics for decades to come. On May 26, 1966, the country gained independence, and resumed its traditional name, Guyana.

Burnham and his People's National Congress ruled Guyana for 21 years, until Burnham's death in 1985. In 1992, Jagan's People's Progressive Party won a majority in the general election. Jagan, who had served as prime minister in the 1960s while Guyana was still a colony, became president.

The current president, former finance minister Bharrat Jagdeo, assumed the presidency in Aug. 1999.

Guyana's potential economic development was hurt in 2000 as border disputes with both Venezuela to the west and Suriname to the east heated up. Suriname and Guyana have been unable to resolve the border dispute in an oil-rich coastal area. Venezuela's president Hugo Chavez has revived a 19th-century claim to more than half of Guyana's territory.

Haiti

REPUBLIC OF HAITI

National name: République d'Haïti
President: René García Préval (1996)
Prime Minister: Jacques-Edouard Alexis (1999)
Area: 10,714 sq. mi. (27,750 sq. km)
Population (2000 est.): 6,867,995 (average annual rate of natural increase: 1.7%); birth rate: 32/1000; infant mortality rate: 97.1/1000; density per sq. mi.: 641
Capital and largest city (1993 est.): Port-au-Prince, 1.5 million. **Monetary unit:** Gourde. **Languages:** Creole, French. **Ethnicity/race:** black 95%, mulatto and European 5%. **Religions:** Roman Catholic, 80%; Protestant, 16%; Vaudou, 95%. **Literacy rate:** 53% (1990)
Economic summary: GDP/PPP (1998 est.): $8.9 billion; $1,300 per capita. **Real growth rate:** 3%. **Inflation:** 8%. **Unemployment:** 60% (1996 est.). **Arable land:** 20%. **Agriculture:** coffee, mangoes, sugarcane, rice, corn, sorghum, wood. **Labor force:** 3.6 million (1995): agriculture, 66%; services, 25%; industry, 9%. **Industries:** sugar refining, flour milling, textiles, cement, tourism, light assembly industries based on imported parts. **Natural resources:** none. **Exports:** $110 million (f.o.b., 1997): light manufactures, coffee, other agriculture. **Imports:** $486 million (f.o.b., 1997): machines and manufactures, food and beverages, petroleum products, chemicals, fats and oils. **Major trading partners:** U.S., EU.

Geography Haiti, in the West Indies, occupies the western third of the island of Hispaniola, which it shares with the Dominican Republic. About the size of Maryland, Haiti is two-thirds mountainous, with the rest of the country marked by great valleys, extensive plateaus, and small plains.

Government Republic.

History Visited by Columbus on Dec. 6, 1492, Haiti's native Arawaks fell victim to Spanish rule. In 1697 Haiti became a French possession known as Saint-Dominique. An insurrection among a slave population of 480,000 in 1791 ended with a declaration of independence by Pierre-Dominique Toussaint l'Ouverture in 1801. Napoléon Bonaparte suppressed the independence movement, but it eventually triumphed in 1804 under Jean-Jacques Dessalines, who gave the new nation the Arawak name Haiti.

Its prosperity was hampered by internal strife as well as disputes with neighboring Santo Domingo during a succession of 19th-century dictatorships; a bankrupt Haiti accepted a U.S. customs receivership from 1905 to 1941. Occupation by U.S. Marines from 1915 to 1934 brought a measure of stability and a population growth that made Haiti the most densely populated nation in the hemisphere.

In 1949, after four years of democratic rule by President Dumarsais Estimé, dictatorship returned under Gen. Paul Magloire, who was succeeded by François Duvalier, nicknamed "Papa Doc," in 1957. Duvalier established a dictatorship based on secret police, known as the "Tontons Macoutes," who gunned down opponents of the regime. Duvalier's son, Jean-Claude, or "Baby Doc," succeeded his father in 1971 as ruler of the poorest nation in the Western Hemisphere. His infamous dictatorship, marked by pervasive corruption and repression, rivaled that of his father's. Duvalier fled the country in 1986 amid strong protests and the country remained under military rule.

Throughout the 1990s the international community devoted considerable effort to establishing democracy in Haiti. The country's first elected chief executive, Jean-Betrand Aristide, a Roman Catholic priest, was sworn in as president on Feb. 7, 1991. The military, however, then took control. A multinational peacekeeping force, led by the U.S. but under the auspices of the U.N., Operation Uphold Democracy, arrived in 1994. Aristide was restored to office and René Preval became his successor in Feb. 1996 elections.

U.S. soldiers left in 2000, but U.N. peacekeepers remain. In May 2000, the Lavalas Family Party won legislative and local elections, which were considered fraudulent by many observers. The U.S. and other countries have threatened Haiti, already one of the world's poorest countries, with sanctions unless democratic procedures are strengthened for the presidential elections set for Nov. 2000.

With unemployment of at least 50%, Haiti has turned into a major drug shipment point between Colombia and the U.S. A steady of flow of refugees has been arriving in the U.S., often in leaky boats. Despite the international emphasis on democracy, Haiti's government is paralyzed, and lacks the rudiments of a modern civil society, such as an independent court system, parliament, and administrative bureaucracy.

Honduras

REPUBLIC OF HONDURAS

National name: República de Honduras
President: Carlos Roberto Flores Facusse (1998)
Area: 43,872 sq. mi. (112,090 sq. km)
Population (2000 est.): 6,249,598 (average annual rate of natural increase: 2.7%); birth rate: 32.7/1000; infant mortality rate: 31.3/1000; density per sq. mi.: 142
Capital and largest city (1995): Tegucigalpa, 1,500,000. **Monetary unit:** Lempira. **Languages:** Spanish (official), English widely spoken in business. **Ethnicity/race:** mestizo (mixed Indian and European) 90%, Indian 7%, black 2%, white 1%. **Religions:** Roman Catholic, 94%, Protestant minority. **Literacy rate:** 73% (1990)
Economic summary: GDP/PPP (1998 est.): $14.4 billion; $2,400 per capita. **Real growth rate:** 3%. **Inflation:** 14.5%. **Unemployment:** 6.3%; underemployed, 30% (1997). **Arable land:** 15%. **Agriculture:** bananas, coffee, citrus, beef, timber, shrimp. **Labor force:** 1.3 million (1997 est.): services, 39%; agriculture, 37%; industry, 24% (1996). **Industries:** sugar, coffee, textiles, clothing, wood products. **Natural resources:** timber, gold, silver,

copper, lead, zinc, iron ore, antimony, coal, fish.
Exports: $1.3 billion (f.o.b., 1996): bananas, coffee,
shrimp, lobster, minerals, meat, lumber. **Imports:** $1.8
billion (c.i.f., 1996): machinery and transport
equipment, industrial raw materials, chemical products,
manufactured goods, fuel and oil, foodstuffs. **Major
trading partners:** U.S., Germany, Belgium, Japan,
Spain, Guatemala, Mexico, El Salvador.

Geography Honduras, in the north-central part of
Central America, has a 400-mile (644-km) Caribbean
coastline and a 40-mile (64-km) Pacific frontage. Its
neighbors are Guatemala to the west, El Salvador to
the south, and Nicaragua to the east. The second-
largest country in Central America, Honduras is
slightly larger than Tennessee. Generally mountainous, the country is marked by fertile plateaus, river
valleys, and narrow coastal plains.

Government Republic.

History Honduras was part of the Mayan civilization during the first millennium, and its cultural vortex was Copàn. Columbus explored the country on
his last voyage in 1502. Honduras, with four other
countries of Central America, declared its independence from Spain in 1821 and was part of a federation of Central American states until 1838. In that
year it seceded from the federation and became a
completely independent country. Political unrest
rocked the country in the early 20th century, including an occupation by U.S. Marines, until it was
quelled by the dictatorship of General Tiburcio Carias
Andino in 1932.

In July 1969, El Salvador invaded Honduras after
Honduran landowners had deported several thousand
Salvadorans. By threatening economic sanctions and
military intervention, the OAS induced El Salvador to
withdraw. Although parliamentary democracy
returned with the election of Roberto Suazo Córdova
as president in 1982 after a decade of military rule,
Honduras faced severe economic problems and tensions along its border with Nicaragua. "Contra"
rebels, waging a guerrilla war against the Sandinista
regime in Nicaragua, used Honduras as a training and
staging area. At the same time, the United States used
Honduras as a site for military exercises and built
bases to train both Honduran and Salvadoran troops.

The lack of a final resolution of a maritime border
dispute with Nicaragua led to incidents in 1997 in
which Nicaraguan and Honduran gunboats exchanged
fire in the disputed waters. In Nov. 1997 Carlos
Flores Facussé of the Liberal Party was elected president. Honduras suffers from rapid population growth,
high unemployment, inflation, a lack of basic services, and economic dependence on coffee and
bananas, which are subject to sharp price fluctuations.
But upon taking office on Jan. 27, 1998, Flores inaugurated programs of reform and modernization of the
Honduran government and economy, with emphasis
on helping Honduras's poorest citizens while maintaining the country's fiscal health and improving
international competitiveness.

In Oct. 1998, Hurricane Mitch caused devastating
destruction in Honduras. More than 13,000 Hondu-
rans were killed by the hurricane, 2 million were left
homeless, and damages to housing and infrastructure
alone exceeded $5 billion.

The U.N. sent food aid to southern Honduras in the
summer of 2000 because of severe drought. Much of
the region had still not fully recovered from Hurricane Mitch. To stimulate the economy, Honduras,
along with Guatemala and El Salvador, signed a free

trade agreement with Mexico in June 2000. Flores
also launched a major initiative to halt the escalating
crime rate. In Aug. 2000 Honduras agreed to allow
the U.S. military to conduct antidrug trafficking
patrols in the country.

Hungary

REPUBLIC OF HUNGARY

National name: Magyar Köztársaság
President: Ferenc Mádl (2000)
Premier: Viktor Orbán (1998)
Area: 35,919 sq. mi. (93,030 sq. km)
Population (2000 est.): 10,138,844 (average annual rate
of natural increase: −0.4%); birth rate: 9.3/1000; infant
mortality rate: 9.2/1000; density per sq. mi.: 282
Capital and largest city (1995 est.): Budapest,
2,008,546. **Other large cities (1995 est.):** Debrecen,
210,000; Miskolc, 182,000; Szeged, 169,000; Pécs,
163,000. **Monetary unit:** Forint. **Languages:** Magyar
(Hungarian), 98.2%; Other, 1.8%. **Ethnicity/race:**
Hungarian 89.9%, Gypsy 4%, German 2.6%, Serb 2%,
Slovak 0.8%, Romanian 0.7%. **Religions:** Roman
Catholic, 67.5%; Protestant, 25%; atheist and others,
7.5%. **Literacy rate:** 98% (1980)
Economic summary: GDP/PPP (1998 est.): $75.4
billion; $7,400 per capita. **Real growth rate:** 5%.
Inflation: 14%. **Unemployment:** 10.8% (1997).
Arable land: 51%. **Agriculture:** wheat, corn,
sunflower seed, potatoes, sugar beets, pigs, cattle,
poultry, dairy products. **Labor force:** 4.2 million
(1997): services, 65%; industry, 26.7%; agriculture,
8.3% (1996). **Industries:** mining, metallurgy,
construction materials, processed food, textiles,
chemicals (especially pharmaceuticals), motor
vehicles. **Natural resources:** bauxite, coal, natural
gas, fertile soils. **Exports:** $20.7 billion (f.o.b., 1998):
machinery and equipment, other manufactures,
agriculture and food products, raw materials, fuel and
electricity. **Imports:** $22.9 billion (f.o.b., 1998):
machinery and equipment, other manufactures, fuel
and electricity, agricultural and food products, raw
materials. **Major trading partners:** Germany, Austria,
Italy, Russia.

Geography This central European country is the
size of Indiana. Most of Hungary is a fertile, rolling
plain lying east of the Danube River, and drained by
the Danube and Tisza Rivers. In the extreme northwest is the Little Hungarian Plain. South of that area
is Lake Balaton (250 sq. mi.; 648 sq. km).

Government Republic.

History By 14 B.C., western Hungary was part of the
Roman Empire's provinces of Pannonia and Dacia.
The area east of the Danube was never a part of the
Roman Empire and was largely occupied by various
Germanic and Asiatic peoples. In A.D. 896 all of Hungary was invaded by the Magyars, who founded a
kingdom. Christianity was accepted during the reign
of Stephen I (Saint Stephen), 977–1038. A devastating invasion by the Mongols killed half of Hungary's
population in 1241. The peak of Hungary's great
period of medieval power came during the reign of
Louis I the Great (1342–82), whose dominions
touched the Baltic, Black, and Mediterranean Seas.
War with the Turks broke out in 1389, and for more
than 100 years the Turks advanced through the Balkans. When the Turks smashed a Hungarian army in
1526, western and northern Hungary accepted Hapsburg rule to escape Turkish occupation. Transylvania
became independent under Hungarian princes. Intermittent war with the Turks was waged until a peace
treaty was signed in 1699.

After the suppression of the 1848 revolt against Hapsburg rule, led by Louis Kossuth, the dual monarchy of Austria-Hungary was set up in 1867. The dual monarchy was defeated with the other Central Powers in World War I. After a short-lived republic in 1918, the chaotic Communist rule of 1919 under Béla Kun ended with the Romanians occupying Budapest on Aug. 4, 1919. When the Romanians left, Adm. Nicholas Horthy entered the capital with a national army. The Treaty of Trianon of June 4, 1920, cost Hungary 68% of its land and 58% of its population. Meanwhile, the National Assembly had restored the legal continuity of the old monarchy and, on March 1, 1920, Horthy was elected regent. Following the German invasion of Russia on June 22, 1941, Hungary joined the attack against the Soviet Union, but the war was not popular and Hungarian troops were almost entirely withdrawn from the eastern front by May 1943. German occupation troops set up a puppet government after Horthy's appeal for an armistice with advancing Soviet troops on Oct. 15, 1944, had resulted in his overthrow. The German regime soon fled the capital, however, and on Dec. 23 a provisional government was formed in Soviet-occupied eastern Hungary. On Jan. 20, 1945, the government signed an armistice in Moscow. Early the next year, the National Assembly approved a constitutional law abolishing the thousand-year-old monarchy and establishing a republic.

By the Treaty of Paris (1947), Hungary had to give up all territory it had acquired since 1937 and to pay $300 million reparations to the U.S.S.R., Czechoslovakia, and Yugoslavia. In 1948 the Communist Party, with the support of Soviet troops, seized control. Hungary was proclaimed a People's Republic and one-party state in 1949. Industry was nationalized, the land collectivized into state farms, and the opposition terrorized by the secret police. The terror, modeled after that of the U.S.S.R., reached its height with the trial and life imprisonment of József Cardinal Mindszenty, the leader of Hungary's Roman Catholics, in 1948. On Oct. 23, 1956, an anti-Communist revolution broke out in Budapest. To cope with it, the Communists set up a coalition government and called former premier Imre Nagy back to head the government. But he and most of his ministers were swept by the logic of events into the anti-Communist opposition, and he declared Hungary a neutral power, withdrawing from the Warsaw Treaty and appealing to the United Nations for help. One of his ministers, János Kádár, established a counterregime and asked the U.S.S.R. to send in military power. Soviet troops and tanks suppressed the revolution in bloody fighting after 190,000 people had fled the country. Under Kádár (1956–88), Communist Hungary henceforth maintained more liberal policies in the economic and cultural spheres, and Hungary became the most liberal of the Soviet-bloc nations of eastern Europe. Continuing his program of national reconciliation, Kádár emptied prisons, reformed the secret police, and eased travel restrictions.

Hungary's Communists abandoned their monopoly on power in 1989 voluntarily, and the constitution was amended in Oct. 1989 to allow for a 'multiparty state. The last Soviet troops left Hungary in June 1991, thereby ending almost 47 years of military presence. The transition to a market economy proved difficult. Hungary strengthened its ties with Poland and Czechoslovakia but grew concerned about the fate of ethnic Hungarians in neighboring countries. Hungary normalized relations with the Catholic Church in 1997 by signing an agreement concerning restitution or compensation for property seized during the Communist era.

In April 1999, Hungary became part of NATO, along with the Czech Republic and Poland. Only weeks after officially joining NATO, the country was called upon to stand up to its former ally, Russia, by blocking a shipment of Russian fuel and food destined for Yugoslavia during the Kosovo crisis.

Iceland

REPUBLIC OF ICELAND

National name: Lydveldid Island
President: Olafur Ragnar Grimsson (1996)
Prime Minister: David Oddsson (1991)
Area: 39,709 sq. mi. (103,000 sq. km)[1]
Population (2000 est.): 276,365 (average annual rate of natural increase: 0.8%); birth rate: 14.9/1000; infant mortality rate: 3.6/1000; density per sq. mi.: 7
Capital and largest city (1994 est.): Reykjavik, 103,036. **Monetary unit:** Icelandic króna. **Language:** Icelandic. **Ethnicity/race:** homogeneous mixture of descendants of Norwegians and Celts. **Religions:** Church of Iceland (Evangelical Lutheran) 96%, other Protestant and Roman Catholic 3%, none 1%. **Literacy rate:** 100% (1976)
Economic summary: GDP/PPP (1998 est.): $6.06 billion; $22,400 per capita. **Real growth rate:** 5.1%. **Inflation:** 1.7%. **Unemployment:** 3%. **Arable land:** 0%. **Agriculture:** potatoes, turnips, cattle, sheep, fish. **Labor force:** 130,000 (1998 est.): manufacturing, 12.9%; fishing and fish processing, 11.8%; construction, 10.7%; agriculture, 5.1%; other services, 59.5% (1996 est.). **Industries:** fish processing, aluminum smelting, ferrosilicon production, geothermal power, tourism. **Natural resources:** fish, hydropower, geothermal power, diatomite. **Exports:** $1.9 billion (f.o.b., 1998): fish and fish products, animal products, aluminum, diatomite and ferrosilicon. **Imports:** $2.4 billion (f.o.b., 1998): machinery and transportation equipment, petroleum products, foodstuffs, textiles. **Major trading partners:** EU (U.K., Germany, France, Denmark, Norway, Sweden), U.S.

1. Including some offshore islands.

Geography Iceland, an island about the size of Kentucky, lies in the north Atlantic Ocean east of Greenland and just touches the Arctic Circle. It is one of the most volcanic regions in the world. The island is dotted with small freshwater lakes, and there are many natural phenomena, including hot springs, geysers, sulfur beds, canyons, waterfalls, and swift rivers. More than 13% of the area is covered by snowfields and glaciers, and most of the people live in the 7% of the island that is made up of fertile coastland. The Gulf stream keeps Iceland's climate milder than one would expect from an island near the Arctic Circle.

Government Constitutional republic.

History The earliest inhabitants of Iceland were Irish hermits, who left the island upon the arrival of the pagan Norse people in the late 9th century A.D. A constitution drawn up c. 930 created a form of democracy and provided for an *Althing*, the world's oldest practicing legislative assembly. The island's early history was preserved in the Icelandic sagas of the 13th century.

In 1262–64, Iceland came under Norwegian rule and passed to ultimate Danish control through the unification of the kingdoms of Norway, Sweden, and Denmark (the Kalmar Union) in 1397.

In 1874, Icelanders obtained their own constitution, and in 1918, Denmark recognized Iceland, via the Act of Union, as a separate state with unlimited sovereignty. It remained, however, nominally under the Danish monarchy.

During the German occupation of Denmark during World War II, British, then American, troops occupied Iceland and used it for a strategic air base. While officially neutral, Iceland cooperated with the Allies throughout the conflict. On June 17, 1944, after a popular referendum, the Althing proclaimed Iceland an independent republic.

The country joined the North Atlantic Treaty Organization in 1949, and subsequently received an American air force base in 1951. In 1970, it was admitted to the European Free Trade Association. Iceland unilaterally extended its territorial fishing limit from 3 to 200 nautical miles in 1972, precipitating a dispute with the U.K. known as the "cod wars," which ended in 1976, when the U.K. recognized the new limits. In 1980, the Icelanders elected a woman to the office of the presidency, the first elected female chief of state (i.e., president as distinct from prime minister) in the world.

After the recession of the early 1990s, Iceland began strengthening its economy. Government projections in mid-1997 showed that the country would have a large budget surplus for the year owing to fiscal management and a healthy economy. The government hoped to cut public spending further and boost the surplus.

India

REPUBLIC OF INDIA

National name: Bharat
President: K. R. Narayanan (1997)
Prime Minister: Atal Bihari Vajpayee (1998)
Area: 1,229,737 sq. mi. (3,287,590 sq. km)
Population (2000 est.): 1,014,003,817 (average annual rate of natural increase: 1.6%); birth rate: 24.8/1000; infant mortality rate: 64.9/1000; density per sq. mi.: 825
Capital (2000 est.): Delhi, 11,500,000 (metro. area).
   Largest cities: Bombay (Mumbai) (2000 est.), 17,850,000 (metro. area); Calcutta (2000 est.), 12,900,000 (metro. area); Madras (Chennai) (2000 est.), 6,600,000 (metro. area); Hyderabad (2000 est.), 6,650,000 (metro. area); Bangalore (2000 est.), 5,500,000 (metro. area); Ahmedabad, 4,150,000; Kanpur, 1,874,409. **Monetary unit:** Rupee. **Principal languages:** Hindi (official), English (official), Bengali, Gujarati, Kashmiri, Malayalam, Marathi, Oriya, Punjabi, Tamil, Telugu, Urdu, Kannada, Assamese, Sanskrit, Sindhi (all recognized by the constitution). Dialects, 1,652. **Ethnicity/race:** Indo-Aryan 72%, Dravidian 25%, Mongoloid and other 3%. **Religions:** Hindu, 82.6%; Islam, 11.3%; Christian, 2.4%; Sikh, 2%; Buddhists, 0.71%; Jains, 0.48%. **Literacy rate:** 52% (1991)
Economic summary: GDP/PPP (1998 est.): $1.689 trillion; $1,720 per capita. **Real growth rate:** 5.4%. **Inflation:** 14%. **Unemployment:** n.a. **Arable land:** 56%. **Agriculture:** rice, wheat, oilseed, cotton, jute, tea, sugarcane, potatoes, cattle, water buffalo, sheep, goats, poultry, fish. **Labor force:** n.a.: agriculture, 67%; services, 18%; industry, 15% (1995 est.). **Industries:** textiles, chemicals, food processing, steel, transportation equipment, cement, mining, petroleum, machinery. **Natural resources:** coal, iron ore, manganese, mica, bauxite, titanium ore, chromite, natural gas, diamonds, petroleum, limestone. **Exports:** $32.17 billion (f.o.b., 1998): textile goods, gems and jewelry, engineering goods, chemicals, leather manufactures. **Imports:** $41.34 billion (c.i.f., 1998): crude oil and petroleum products, machinery, gems, fertilizer, chemicals. **Major trading partners:** U.S., Hong Kong, U.K., Japan, Germany, Belgium, Saudi Arabia. **Member of Commonwealth of Nations**

Geography One-third the area of the United States, the Republic of India occupies most of the subcontinent of India in south Asia. It borders on China in the northeast. Other neighbors are Pakistan on the west, Nepal and Bhutan on the north, and Burma and Bangladesh on the east.

The country can be divided into three distinct geographic regions: the Himalayan region in the north, which contains some of the highest mountains in the world, the Gangetic Plain, and the plateau region in the south and central part. Its three great river systems have extensive deltas and all rising in the Himalayas: the Ganges, 1,540 miles (2,478 km), the Indus, and the Brahmaputra.

India includes several groups of islands—the Laccadives (14 islands) in the Arabian Sea and the Andamans (204 islands) and the Nicobars (19 islands) in the Bay of Bengal.

Government Federal republic.

History One of the earliest civilizations, the Indus Valley civilization, flourished on the Indian subcontinent from c. 2600 B.C. to c. 2000 B.C. The Aryans who invaded India c. 1500 B.C. from the northwest found a land that was already home to an advanced civilization. They introduced Sanskrit and the Vedic religion, a forerunner of Hinduism, to the area. Buddhism was founded in the 6th century B.C. and spread throughout northern India, most notably by one of the great ancient kings of the Mauryan dynasty, Asoka (c. 269–232 B.C.), who also unified most of the Indian subcontinent for the first time.

In 1526, Muslim invaders founded the great Mogul empire, centered on Delhi, which lasted, at least in name, until 1857. Akbar the Great (1542–1605) strengthened and consolidated this empire. The long reign of his great-grandson, Aurangzeb (1618–1707), represents both the greatest extent of the Mogul empire and the beginning of its decay.

Vasco da Gama, the Portuguese explorer, visited India first in 1498, and for the next 100 years the Portuguese had a virtual monopoly on trade with the subcontinent. Meanwhile, the English founded the East India Company, which set up its first factory at Surat in 1612 and began expanding its influence, fighting the Indian rulers and the French, Dutch, and Portuguese traders simultaneously.

Bombay, taken from the Portuguese, became the seat of English rule in 1687. The defeat of French and Mogul armies by Lord Clive in 1757 laid the foundation of the British Empire in India. The East India Company continued to suppress native uprisings and extend British rule until 1858, when the administration of India was formally transferred to the British Crown following the Sepoy Mutiny of native troops in 1857–58.

After World War I, in which the Indian states sent more than 6 million troops to fight beside the Allies, Indian nationalist unrest rose to new heights under the leadership of a Hindu lawyer, Mohandas K. Gandhi, called Mahatma Gandhi. His philosophy of civil disobedience called for nonviolent noncooperation against British authority. He soon became the leading spirit of the Indian National Congress Party, which was the spearhead of revolt. In 1919 the British gave added responsibility to Indian officials, and in 1935 India was given a federal form of government and a measure of self-rule.

In 1942, with the Japanese pressing hard on the eastern borders of India, the British War Cabinet tried and failed to reach a political settlement with nationalist leaders. The Congress Party took the position that the British must quit India. In 1942, fearing mass civil disobedience, the government of India carried out widespread arrests of Congress leaders, including Gandhi.

Gandhi was released in 1944 and negotiations for a settlement were resumed. Finally, in Aug. 1947, India gained full independence. The victory was soured, however, by the partitioning of the predominantly Muslim regions of the north into the separate nation of Pakistan. The Muslim League, led by Mohammed Ali Jinnah, demanded a separate nation for the Muslim minority to prevent Hindu political and social domination. Indian Hindus, however, had hoped for a unified rather than balkanized Indian subcontinent. Lord Mountbatten as viceroy partitioned India along religious lines and split the provinces of Bengal and the Punjab, which both nations claimed. The partition of Pakistan and India led to the largest migration in human history, with 17 million people fleeing across the borders in both directions to escape the bloody riots occurring among sectarian groups. Armed conflict also broke out over rival claims to the princely states of Jammu and Kashmir.

Jawaharlal Nehru, nationalist leader and head of the Congress Party, was made prime minister. In 1949 a constitution, along the lines of the U.S. Constitution, was approved making India a sovereign republic. Under a federal structure the states were organized on linguistic lines. The dominance of the Congress Party contributed to stability. In 1956 the republic absorbed the former French settlements. Five years later, the republic forcibly annexed the Portuguese enclaves of Goa, Damao, and Diu.

Nehru died in 1964. His successor, Lal Bahadur Shastri, died on Jan. 10, 1966. Nehru's daughter, Indira Gandhi, became prime minister, and she continued his policy of nonalignment.

In 1971 the Pakistani army moved in to quash the independence movement in East Pakistan that was supported by India, and some 10 million Bengali refugees poured across the border into India, creating social, economic, and health problems. After numerous border incidents, India invaded East Pakistan and in two weeks forced the surrender of the Pakistani army. East Pakistan was established as an independent state and renamed Bangladesh.

In the summer of 1975, the world's largest democracy veered suddenly toward authoritarianism when a judge in Allahabad, Mrs. Gandhi's home constituency, found Gandhi's landslide victory in the 1971 elections invalid because civil servants had illegally aided her campaign. Amid demands for her resignation, Mrs. Gandhi decreed a state of emergency on June 26 and ordered mass arrests of her critics, including all opposition party leaders except the Communists.

Despite strong opposition to her repressive measures, particularly resentment against compulsory birth control programs, Mrs. Gandhi in 1977 announced parliamentary elections for March. At the same time, she freed most political prisoners. The landslide victory of Morarji R. Desai unseated Mrs. Gandhi, but she staged a spectacular comeback in the elections of Jan. 1980.

In 1984, she ordered the Indian army to root out a band of Sikh holy men and gunmen who were using the most sacred shrine of the Sikh religion, the Golden Temple in Amritsar, as a base for terrorist raids in a violent campaign for greater political autonomy in the strategic Punjab border state. The perceived sacrilege to the Golden Temple kindled outrage among many of India's 14 million Sikhs and brought a spasm of mutinies and desertions by Sikh officers and soldiers in the army.

On Oct. 31, 1984, Mrs. Gandhi was assassinated by two men identified by police as Sikh members of her bodyguard. The ruling Congress Party chose her older son, Rajiv Gandhi, to succeed her as prime minister for four years. While running for reelection, former prime minister Rajiv Gandhi was assassinated on May 22, 1991, by Tamil militants who objected to India's mediation of the civil war in Sri Lanka. Final phases of the election were postponed for a month. When they were resumed, the Congress Party and its allies won 236 seats in the lower house, 20 short of a majority. P. V. Narasimha Rao was chosen to form a new government.

The ruling Congress Party lost the parliamentary elections of May 1996, and its waning has resulted in a period of political instability. The Hindu nationalist Bharatiya Janata Party's leader, Atal Bihari Vajpayee, became prime minister in May 1996, but his government lasted only 13 days. H. D. Deve Gowda of the United Front coalition became the next prime minister. Losing the support of the Congress Party, Prime Minister Deve Gowda lost a confidence vote in April 1997. Foreign Minister Inder Gujral was sworn in later that month, only to be replaced by Atal Vajpayee in March 1998, his second time as prime minister (his first term lasting less than two weeks). Vajpayee is the first Hindu nationalist to become prime minister, and the chauvinistic ideology of his party has made a number of Muslims and moderate Hindus uneasy.

In May 1998 India set off five nuclear tests, surprising the international community, which widely condemned India's pro-nuclear stance. Despite international urging for restraint, Pakistan responded by conducting several nuclear tests of its own two weeks later. India has resisted signing the Comprehensive Test Ban Treaty for nuclear weapons and has been slapped with sanctions by the U.S. and other countries. Less than a year later, in April 1999, both India and Pakistan tested nuclear-capable ballistic missiles. On April 17, Prime Minister Atal Bihari Vajpayee's government lost a confidence vote, leaving India's government in disarray.

India and Pakistan have held various talks about the disputed territory of Kashmir, which is the issue at the base of their chronic antagonism as well as their recent displays of nuclear strength. India controls two-thirds of this Himalayan region, which is the only Indian state that is predominantly Muslim.

The Indian Air Force launched air strikes on May 26, 1999, and later sent in ground troops against Islamic guerrilla forces in Kashmir. India blamed Pakistan for orchestrating the Kashmiri attacks by sending soldiers and mercenaries across the so-called Line of Control that divides Kashmir between India and Pakistan. Pakistan countered that the guerrillas are independent Kashmiri freedom fighters struggling for India's ouster from the region. Most international sources agreed with India's assumption that Pakistan was arming the soldiers. In Aug. Pakistan was forced to withdraw, but fighting continued sporadically during the coming year.

An unexpected unilateral cease-fire was declared in July 2000 by Hizbul Mujahideen, an influential anti-India militant group that is composed mostly of Islamic Kashmiris who want the state to become part of Pakistan. But the cease-fire came to an abrupt end weeks after it was called when India refused to include Pakistan in talks proposed by Hizbul. Several deadly assaults in Kashmir immediately followed.

Native States Most of the 560-odd native states and subdivisions of pre-1947 India acceded to the new nation, and the central government pursued a vigorous policy of integration. This took three forms: merger into adjacent provinces, conversion into centrally administered areas, and grouping into unions of states. Finally, under a controversial reorganization plan effective on Nov. 1, 1956, the unions of states were abolished and India became a union of 15 states and 8 centrally administered areas. A 16th state was added in 1962, and in 1966, the Punjab was partitioned into two states. Today India consists of 25 states and 7 Union Territories.

In April 1975, the Indian Parliament voted to make the 300-year-old kingdom of Sikkim a full-fledged Indian state, and the annexation took effect on May 16. Situated in the Himalayas, Sikkim was a virtual dependency of Tibet until the early 19th century. Under an 1890 treaty between China and Great Britain, it became a British protectorate, and was made an Indian protectorate after Britain quit the subcontinent.

Indonesia

REPUBLIC OF INDONESIA

National name: Republik Indonesia
President: Abdurrahman Wahid (1999)
Area: 735,268 sq. mi. (1,919,440 sq. km)[1]
Population (2000 est.): 224,784,210 (average annual rate of natural increase: 1.6%); birth rate: 22.6/1000; infant mortality rate: 42.2/1000; density per sq. mi.: 306
Capital and largest city (2000 est.): Jakarta, 12,300,000 (metro. area). **Other large cities (1995 est.):** Surabaya, 2,701,300; Bandung, 2,368,200; Medan, 1,909,700; Semarang, 1,366,500. **Monetary unit:** Rupiah. **Languages:** Bahasa Indonesia (official), Dutch, English, and more than 583 languages and dialects. **Ethnicity/race:** Javanese 45%, Sundanese 14%, Madurese 7.5%, coastal Malays 7.5%, other 26%. **Religions:** Islam, 87%; Christian, 9%; Hindu, 2%; other, 2%. **Literacy rate:** 84% (1990)
Economic summary: GDP/PPP (1998 est.): $602 billion; $2,830 per capita. **Real growth rate:** –13.7%. **Inflation:** 77%. **Unemployment:** 15%–20%. **Arable land:** 10%. **Agriculture:** rice, cassava (tapioca), peanuts, rubber, cocoa, coffee, palm oil, copra, poultry, beef, pork; eggs. **Labor force:** 87 million (1997 est.): agriculture, 41%; trade, restaurant, and hotel, 19.8%; manufacturing, 14%; construction, 4.8%; transport and communications, 4.75%; other, 15.65% (1997). **Industries:** petroleum and natural gas, textiles, apparel, footwear, mining, cement, chemical fertilizers, plywood, rubber, food, tourism. **Natural resources:** petroleum, tin, natural gas, nickel, timber, bauxite, copper, fertile soils, coal, gold, silver. **Exports:** $49 billion (f.o.b., 1998 est.): garments, textiles, gas, electrical appliances, pulp and paper, oil, plywood. **Imports:** $24 billion (f.o.b., 1998 est.): manufactures, raw materials, foodstuffs, fuel. **Major trading partners:** Japan, EU, U.S., Singapore, Germany, South Korea, Hong Kong, China, Taiwan, Australia.

1. Includes West Irian (former Netherlands New Guinea), renamed Irian Jaya in March 1973 (159,355 sq. mi.; 421,981 sq. km), and former Portuguese Timor (5,763 sq. mi.; 14,874 sq. km), annexed in 1976.

Geography Indonesia is an archipelago in Southeast Asia consisting of 17,000 islands (6,000 inhabited) and straddles the equator. The largest islands are Sumatra, Java (the most populous), Bali, Kalimantan (Indonesia's part of Borneo), Sulawesi (Celebes), the Nusa Tenggara islands, the Maluku Islands, and Irian Jaya (western part of New Guinea), which in 1999 was renamed Papua, the name preferred by its inhabitants. Its neighbor to the north is Malaysia and to the east is Papua New Guinea.

Indonesia, part of the "ring of fire," has the largest number of active volcanoes in the world. Earthquakes are frequent. The "Wallace Line," a zoological demarcation between Asian and Australian flora and fauna, divides Indonesia.

Government Republic.

History The 17,000 islands that make up Indonesia were home to a diversity of cultures and indigenous beliefs when the islands came under the influence of Hindu priests and traders in the first and second centuries A.D. Muslim invasions began in the 13th century, and most of the archipelago had converted to Islam by the 15th. Portuguese traders arrived early in the next century but were ousted by the Dutch around 1595. The Dutch United East India Company established posts on the island of Java, in an effort to control the spice trade.

After Napoléon subjugated the Netherlands in 1811, the British seized the islands but returned them to the Dutch in 1816. In 1922 Indonesia was made an integral part of the Dutch kingdom. During World War II, Japan seized the islands. Tokyo was primarily interested in Indonesia's oil, which was vital to the war effort, and tolerated fledgling nationalists such as Sukarno and Mohammed Hatta. After Japan's surrender, Sukarno and Hatta proclaimed Indonesian independence on Aug. 17, 1945. Allied troops, mostly British Indian forces, fought nationalist militia to reassert the prewar status quo until the arrival of Dutch troops.

In Nov. 1946, a draft agreement on forming a Netherlands-Indonesian Union was reached, but differences in interpretation resulted in more fighting between Dutch and nationalist forces. Following a bitter war for independence, leaders on both sides agreed to terms of a union on Nov. 2, 1949. The transfer of sovereignty took place at Amsterdam on Dec. 27, 1949. In Feb. of 1956 Indonesia abrogated the union, and began seizing Dutch property in the islands.

In 1963, Netherlands New Guinea (the Dutch portion of the island of New Guinea) was transferred to Indonesia and renamed West Irian, which became Irian Jaya in 1973. Hatta and Sukarno, the cofathers of Indonesian independence, split over Sukarno's concept of "guided democracy," and under Sukarno's rule the Indonesian Communist Party (PKI) steadily increased its influence.

Three years later, Sukarno was named president for life. Sukarno enjoyed mass support for his policies, but a growing power struggle between the military and the PKI loomed over his government. After an attempted military coup was put down by army chief of staff General Suharto and officers loyal to him, Suharto's forces killed hundreds of thousands of suspected Communists in a massive purge aimed at undermining Sukarno's rule.

Suharto took over the reins of government and gradually eased Sukarno out of office, completing his consolidation of power in 1967. Under Suharto the military assumed an overarching role in national affairs, and relations with the West were enhanced. Indonesia's economy improved dramatically and national elections were permitted, although the opposition was so tightly controlled as to virtually choke off dissent.

In 1975, Indonesia invaded the former Portuguese half of the island of Timor and seized the territory in 1976. A separatist movement developed at once. Unlike the rest of Indonesia, which had been a Dutch colony, East Timor was governed by the Portuguese for 400 years, and although 90% of Indonesians are Muslim, the East Timorese are primarily Catholic. More than 200,000 Timorese are reported to have died from famine, disease, and fighting since the annexation. East Timor has received international attention for human rights abuses, and in 1996 two East Timorese resistance activists, Bishop Carlos Filipe Ximenes Belo and José Ramos-Horta, received the Nobel Peace Prize.

In the summer of 1997, Indonesia suffered a major economic setback along with most other Asian economies. Banks failed and the value of Indonesia's currency, the rupiah, plummeted. Antigovernment demonstrations took to the streets and riots broke out, directed mainly at the country's prosperous ethnic Chinese. As the economic crisis deepened, student demonstrators occupied the national Parliament, demanding Suharto's ouster. On May 21, 1998, Suharto stepped down, ending 32 years of rule and handing over power to Vice President B. J. Habibie. The Asian economic crisis hit Indonesia the hardest, and in 1998 one in five jobs was lost. Student unrest continued after Suharto's downfall, although the students' agenda for reform was vague.

June 7, 1999, marked Indonesia's first free parliamentary election since 1955. The ruling Golkar Party took a backseat to the Indonesian Democracy Party-Struggle (PDI-P), led by Megawati Sukarnoputri, the daughter of Sukarno, Indonesia's first president. She had been the head of the PDI in 1994 until Suharto had her removed.

The provinces of Aceh, Ambon (in the Moluccas), Borneo, and Irian Jaya saw rioting and violence in 1999. But nowhere was the violence more brutal and unjust than in East Timor. Habibie at first showed a softening of Indonesia's position on East Timor, unexpectedly announcing in Feb. 1999 that he was willing to hold a referendum on East Timorese independence. Despite the good news, the sudden Indonesian about-face was accompanied by heightened fighting between separatist guerrillas and pro-Indonesian paramilitary forces, who were armed by the Indonesian military. Twice rescheduled because of violence, a U.N.-organized referendum took place on Aug. 30, 1999, with 79% of the population voting to secede from Indonesia. In the days following the election, pro-Indonesian militias and Indonesian soldiers massacred civilians and forced a third of the population out of the region. Despite repeated assurances that order would be restored to the region, Habibie and the head of the military, General Wiranto, were either unwilling or unable to stop the violent rampage. After enormous international pressure, Indonesia finally agreed to allow U.N. forces into East Timor on Sept. 12. Led by Australia, an international peacekeeping force began restoring order to the ravaged region.

In a surprising upset, the Indonesian parliament elected Abdurrahman Wahid as the new president of Indonesia on October 20, 1999. Wahid's election over Megawati Sukarnoputiri was devastating for the tens of thousands of Indonesian Democratic Party-Struggle (PDI-P) supporters. Habibie, the incumbent, dropped out of the race days before the election after losing the confidence of his party after his involvement in a banking scandal was uncovered. Wahid, commonly known as Gus Dur, is a highly respected Sufi cleric as well as an adept politician with a reputation for honesty and moderation.

The northern Sumatran province of Aceh became the next troubled region of Indonesia, with Aceh separatists stepping up protests and demands for independence. A devoutly Muslim province of 4.5 million people, Aceh in many ways has more in common with its neighbor Malaysia than it does with Jakarta. President Wahid has proposed a referendum on permitting Islamic law in Aceh, but staunchly refused to discuss independence for the oil-rich province.

Rioting, bombing, and growing unrest continued to plague Indonesia in 2000. In Feb. 2000, President Wahid suspended the powerful General Wiranto from the Indonesian cabinet because he is being investigated for war crimes during the East Timor crisis. On June 4, 2000, separatists declared West Papua, the western half of Papua New Guinea, formerly called Irian Jaya, an independent state. Wahid has flatly opposed independence for West Papua, which contains sizable copper and gold mines. Unlike East Timor, there is little international support for an independent West Papua. Elsewhere in Indonesia, fighting between Christians and Muslims in the Moluccas Islands has killed 2,500 people since the end of 1998.

In fall 2000, Suharto failed twice to show up in court to face corruption charges of embezzling $570 million in state funds for himself, but his lawyers insist he is too ill to stand trial. Wahid insists that Suharto be tried, but he will issue Suharto a pardon if he returns his illegal fortune to the nation. In Sept. 2000 Suharto's playboy son, Hutomo "Tommy" Mandala Putra, was arrested in connection with a spate of bombings, the most serious of which left 15 dead at the Jakarta Stock Exchange.

Iran

ISLAMIC REPUBLIC OF IRAN

Chief of State: Ayatollah Khamenei (1989)
President: Mohammad Khatami (1997)
Area: 636,293 sq. mi. (1,648,000 sq. km)
Population (2000 est.): 65,619,636 (average annual rate of natural increase: 1.3%); birth rate: 18.3/1000; infant mortality rate: 30/1000; density per sq. mi.: 103
Capital and largest city (1994 est.): Teheran, 10,400,000 (metro. area). **Largest cities (1994 est.):** Mashad, 1,964,489; Isfahan, 1,220,595; Tabriz, 1,166,203. **Monetary unit:** Rial. **Languages:** Farsi (Persian), Azari, Kurdish, Arabic. **Ethnicity/race:** Persian 51%, Azerbaijani 24%, Gilaki and Mazandarani 8%, Kurd 7%, Arab 3%, Lur 2%, Baloch 2%, Turkmen 2%, other 1%. **Religions:** Shi'ite Muslim, 95%; Sunni Muslim, 4%. **Literacy rate:** 54% (1990)
Economic summary: GDP/PPP (1998 est.): $339.7 billion; $5,000 per capita. **Real growth rate:** –2.1%. **Inflation:** 24%. **Unemployment:** over 30% (1/98 est.). **Arable land:** 10%. **Agriculture:** wheat, rice, other grains, sugar beets, fruit, nuts, cotton, dairy products, wool, caviar. **Labor force:** 15.4 million: agriculture, 33%; manufacturing, 21% (1988 est.). **Industries:** petroleum, petrochemicals, textiles, cement and other construction materials, food processing (particularly sugar refining and vegetable oil production), metal fabricating, armaments. **Natural resources:** petroleum, natural gas, coal, chromium, copper, iron ore, lead,

manganese, zinc, sulfur. **Exports:** $12.2 billion (f.o.b., 1998 est.): petroleum, 80%; carpets, fruit, nuts, hides, iron, steel. **Imports:** $13.8 billion (f.o.b., 1998 est.): machinery, military supplies, metal working, foodstuffs, pharmaceuticals, technical services, refined oil products. **Major trading partners:** Japan, Italy, Greece, France, Spain, South Korea, Germany, U.A.E., U.K., Belgium.

Geography Iran, a Middle Eastern country south of the Caspian Sea and north of the Persian Gulf, is three times the size of Arizona. It shares borders with Iraq, Turkey, Azerbaijan, Turkmenistan, Armenia, Afghanistan, and Pakistan.

In general, the country is a plateau averaging 4,000 feet (1,219 m) in elevation. There are also maritime lowlands along the Persian Gulf and the Caspian Sea. The Elburz Mountains in the north rise to 18,603 feet (5,670 m) at Mount Damavend. From northwest to southeast, the country is crossed by a desert 800 miles (1,287 km) long.

Government Iran has been an Islamic theocracy since the Pahlavi monarchy regime was overthrown on Feb. 11, 1979.

History The region now called Iran was occupied by the Medes and the Persians in the 1500s B.C., until the Persian king Cyrus the Great overthrew the Medes and became ruler of the Achaemenid (Persian) Empire, which reached from the Indus to the Nile at its zenith in 525 B.C. Persia fell to Alexander in 331–330 B.C., and a succession of other rulers: the Seleucids (312–302 B.C.), the Greek-speaking Parthians (247 B.C.–A.D. 226), the Sasanians, and the Arab Muslims (in 641). By the mid-800s Persia had become an international scientific and cultural center. In the 12th century it was invaded by the Mongols. The Safavid dynasty (1501–1722), under whom the dominant religion became Shi'ite Islam, followed, and was then replaced by the Qajar Dynasty (1794–1925).

During the Qajar dynasty, the Russians and the British fought for economic control of the area, and during World War I Iran's neutrality did not stop it from becoming a battlefield for Russian and British troops. A coup in 1921 brought Reza Kahn to power. In 1925 he became shah and changed his name to Reza Shah Pahlavi. He subsequently did much to modernize the country and abolished all foreign extraterritorial rights.

The country's pro-Axis allegiance in World War II led to Anglo-Russian occupation of Iran in 1941 and deposition of the shah in favor of his son, Mohammed Reza Pahlavi. Pahlavi's Westernization programs alienated the clergy, and his authoritarian rule led to massive demonstrations during the 1970s, until the shah responded with the imposition of martial law in Sept. 1978. The shah and his family fled Iran on Jan. 16, 1979, and the exiled cleric Ayatollah Ruhollah Khomeini returned to establish an Islamic theocracy. Khomeini proceeded with his plans for revitalizing Islamic traditions. He urged women to return to the veil, banned alcohol, Western music, and mixed bathing, shut down the media, closed universities, and eliminated political parties.

Revolutionary militants invaded the U.S. embassy in Teheran on Nov. 4, 1979, seized staff members as hostages, and precipitated an international crisis. Khomeini refused all appeals, even a unanimous vote by the U.N. Security Council demanding immediate release of the hostages. Iranian hostility toward Washington was reinforced by the Carter administra-

tion's economic boycott and deportation order against Iranian students in the U.S., the break in diplomatic relations, and ultimately an aborted U.S. raid in April aimed at rescuing the hostages.

As the first anniversary of the embassy seizure neared, Khomeini and his followers insisted on their original conditions: guarantee by the U.S. not to interfere in Iran's affairs, cancellation of U.S. damage claims against Iran, release of $8 billion in frozen Iranian assets, an apology, and the return of the assets held by the former imperial family. These conditions were largely met and the 52 American hostages were released on Jan. 20, 1980, ending 444 days in captivity.

The sporadic war with Iraq regained momentum in 1982, as Iran launched an offensive in March and regained much of the border area occupied by Iraq in late 1980. The stalemated war with Iraq dragged on well into 1988. Although Iran expressed its willingness to cease fighting, Iran stated that it would not stop the war until Iraq agreed to pay for war damages, and to punish the Iraqi government leaders involved in the conflict. On July 20, 1988, Khomeini, after a series of Iranian military reverses, agreed to cease-fire negotiations with Iraq. A cease-fire went into effect on Aug. 20, 1988. Khomeini died in June 1989 and Ayotollah Khamenei succeeded him as the supreme leader.

By early 1991 the Islamic revolution appeared to have lost much of its militancy. Attempting to revive a stagnant economy, President Rafsanjani took measures to decentralize the command system and introduce free-market mechanisms.

Mohammad Khatami, a little-known moderate cleric, former newspaperman, and national librarian, won the presidential election with 70% of the vote on May 23, 1997, a stunning victory over the conservative ruling elite. Khatami has supported greater social and political freedoms, and has made overtures for friendlier relations with the West.

His steps at liberalizing the strict clerical rule governing the country has put him at odds with the supreme leader, Ayatollah Khamenei. In 1998, Tehran mayor Gholam-Hossein Karbaschi, a strong supporter of Khatami's liberalization process, was sentenced to prison for embezzlement. Many saw this as a politically motivated attack aimed at Khatami.

In Sept. 1998 Iran deployed thousands of troops on its border with Afghanistan after the Taliban admitted killing eight Iranian diplomats and a journalist. Iran, mainly Shi'ite, supports the rebels fighting against the extremist Sunni Taliban.

In July 1999, pro-democracy students held a demonstration to protest the closure of a reformist newspaper. Once security forces entered the fray, however, the demonstration turned into six days of rioting, leading to the arrest of more than 1,000 students.

While students and other liberals have been pressuring President Khatami to implement greater freedoms, Iran's military, the Revolutionary Guard, has expressed their growing impatience with his reformist measures. Khatami has struggled to keep Iran on a middle course, and his stated goal is to ensure that Iran eventually emerges as a nation of "lasting pluralism and Islamic democracy."

Signaling a sea change in Iran's political environment, in Feb. 2000 reform candidates and supporters of President Khatami won 170 seats in the 290-seat parliament, thereby gaining control of the parliament, which had been run by hard-liners since the 1979 Islamic revolution. Hard-liners won a mere 44 seats.

By Aug. 2000, however, the hard-line judiciary had succeeded in closing down every reformist newspaper in the country. Despite its slightly warmer relations with Iran, the U.S. continues to be concerned about Iran's efforts to develop a nuclear missile program.

Iraq

REPUBLIC OF IRAQ

National name: Jumhouriyat Al Iraq
President: Saddam Hussein (1979)
Area: 167,920 sq. mi. (437,072 sq. km)
Population (2000 est.): 22,675,617 (average annual rate of natural increase: 2.9%); birth rate: 35/1000; infant mortality rate: 62.5/1000; density per sq. mi.: 135
Capital and largest city (2000 est.): Baghdad, 4,850,000 (metro. area). **Largest cities (est. 1987):** Mosul, 664,221; Irbil, 485,968; Karkuk (Kirkuk), 418,624; Basra, 406,296. **Monetary unit:** Iraqi dinar.
Languages: Arabic (official) and Kurdish. **Ethnicity/ race:** Arab 75%–80%, Kurdish 15%–20%, Turkoman, Assyrian or other 5%. **Religions:** Muslim 97% (Shi'ite 60%–65%, Sunni 32%–37%), Christian or other 3%.
Literacy rate: 60% (1990)
Economic summary: GDP/PPP (1998 est.): $52.3 billion; $2,400 per capita. **Real growth rate:** 10%. **Inflation:** n.a. **Unemployment:** n.a. **Arable land:** 12%. **Agriculture:** wheat, barley, rice, vegetables, dates, cotton, cattle, sheep. **Labor force:** 4.4 million (1989): services, 48%; agriculture, 30%; industry, 22%. **Industries:** petroleum, chemicals, textiles, construction materials, food processing. **Exports:** $5 billion (1998 est.): crude oil. **Imports:** $3 billion (1998 est.): food, medicine, manufactures. **Major trading partners:** Russia, France, China, Turkey, Jordan, Australia.

Geography Iraq, a triangle of mountains, desert, and fertile river valley, is bounded on the east by Iran, on the north by Turkey, on the west by Syria and Jordan, and on the south by Saudi Arabia and Kuwait. It is twice the size of Idaho. The country has arid desert land west of the Euphrates, a broad central valley between the Euphrates and Tigris, and mountains in the northeast.

Government One-party republic.

History From earliest times Iraq was known as Mesopotamia—the land between the rivers—for it embraces a large part of the alluvial plains of the Tigris and Euphrates Rivers.

An advanced civilization existed by 4000 B.C. Sometime after 2000 B.C. the land became the center of the ancient Babylonian and Assyrian Empires. Mesopotamia was conquered by Cyrus the Great of Persia in 538 B.C., and by Alexander in 331 B.C. After an Arab conquest in A.D. 637–40, Baghdad became capital of the ruling caliphate. The country was cruelly pillaged by the Mongols in 1258, and during the 16th, 17th, and 18th centuries was the object of repeated Turkish-Persian competition.

Nominal Turkish suzerainty imposed in 1638 was replaced by direct Turkish rule in 1831. In World War I, Britain occupied most of Mesopotamia and was given a mandate over the area in 1920. The British renamed the area Iraq and recognized it as a kingdom in 1922. In 1932 the monarchy achieved full independence. Britain again occupied Iraq during World War II because of its pro-Axis stance in the initial years of the war.

Iraq became a charter member of the Arab League in 1945, and Iraqi troops took part in the Arab invasion of Palestine in 1948.

King Faisal II, born on May 2, 1935, succeeded his father, Ghazi I, who was killed in an automobile accident on April 4, 1939. Faisal and his uncle, Crown Prince Abdul-Illah, were assassinated in July 1958 in a swift revolutionary coup that ended the monarchy and brought to power a military junta headed by Abdul Karem Kassim. Kassim reversed the monarchy's pro-Western policies, attempted to rectify the economic disparities between rich and poor, and began to form alliances with Communist countries.

Kassim was overthrown and killed in a coup staged on March 8, 1963, by the Ba'ath Socialist Party. Abdel Salam Arif, a leader in the 1958 coup, staged another coup in Nov. 1963, driving the Ba'ath members of the revolutionary council from power. He adopted a new constitution in 1964. In 1966, he, two cabinet members, and other supporters died in a helicopter crash. His brother, Gen. Abdel Rahman Arif, assumed the presidency, crushed the opposition, and won an indefinite extension of his term in 1967.

His regime was ousted in July 1968 by a junta led by Maj. Gen. Ahmed Hassan al-Bakr of the Ba'ath Party. Bakr and his second-in-command, Saddam Hussein, imposed authoritarian rule in an effort to end the decades of political instability that followed World War II.

One of the world's leading producers of oil, Iraq's oil revenues were used to develop one of the strongest military forces in the region. On July 16, 1979, President Bakr was succeeded by Saddam Hussein, whose regime eventually developed an international reputation for repression, human rights abuses, and terrorism.

A long-standing territorial dispute over control of the Shatt-al-Arab waterway between Iraq and Iran broke into full-scale war on Sept. 20, 1980. Iraqi planes attacked Iranian airfields and the Abadan refinery, and Iraqi ground forces moved into Iran. Despite the smaller size of its armed forces, Iraq took and held the initiative by seizing Abadan and Khurramshahr together with substantial Iranian territory by Dec., and beating back Iranian counterattacks in Jan.

In 1982, the Iraqis fell back to their own country and dug themselves in behind sandbagged defensive fortifications. From the beginning of the war in Sept. 1980 to Sept. 1984, foreign military analysts estimated that more than 150,000 Iraqis had been killed. The Iraqis clearly wanted to end the war, but the Iranians refused. In Feb. 1986, Iranian forces gained on two fronts; but Iraq retook most of the lost ground in 1988 and a cease-fire took effect that Aug.

In July 1990, President Hussein claimed that Kuwait was flooding world markets with oil and forcing down prices. A mediation attempt by Arab leaders failed, and on Aug. 2, 1990, over this and territorial claims, Iraqi troops invaded Kuwait and set up a puppet government. On Jan. 18, 1991, U.N. forces, under the leadership of U.S. General Norman Schwarzkopf, launched Operation Desert Storm, liberating Kuwait in less than a week.

Despite rebellions by both Shi'ites and Kurds following Iraq's crushing defeat in the Gulf War, Saddam Hussein maintained his draconian grip on Iraq. The U.N. Security Council has barred Iraq from selling oil except in exchange for food and medicine. Despite the debilitating effects of U.N. sanctions, Hussein continued to defy the terms of the cease-fire agreement, waging a propaganda campaign that blamed the U.S. for the starvation and poverty suffered by the Iraqi people rather than his own refusal to meet the terms required to remove sanctions.

On Nov. 13, 1997, Iraq expelled the American members of the U.N. inspection team mandated to ascertain that Iraq had destroyed all its nuclear, chemical, biological, and ballistic arms. Under the 1991 cease-fire resolution, the U.N. would not lift sanctions until Iraq fully complied. The standoff stretched on over months, and as tensions rose, the U.S. began a military buildup in the Gulf. In Feb. 1998 U.N. secretary-general Kofi Annan brokered a peaceful solution to the standoff. Over the next months Baghdad continued to impede the U.N. inspection team, demanding that sanctions be lifted. Finally, in Aug. 1998 Hussein put a complete halt to the inspections. This time, the U.S. opted for diplomatic arm-twisting rather than military threats, and in Sept. the U.N. Security Council voted unanimously that the lifting of sanctions would not be discussed until cooperation with U.N. arms inspectors resumed.

On Oct. 31, 1998, the United States and Britain threatened Iraq with the possibility of a military strike if it did not begin cooperating. On Nov. 14 Iraq agreed to unconditional cooperation with the U.N. inspectors, and the United States and Britain called off planned military action. But on Dec. 15, chief U.N. weapons inspector Richard Butler reported that Iraq had not lived up to its promise. The following day the United States and Britain began four days of air strikes. The attacks focused on command centers, missile factories, and airfields—targets that the Pentagon believed would damage Iraq's weapons stores. Since then, the U.S. and Britain have waged a war of attrition against Iraq, conducting hundreds of air strikes of Iraqi targets within the no-fly zones, which were established after the 1991 Gulf War. The aim of the British and American military appeared to be to continue the sustained, low-level warfare in an effort to erode Iraqi military strength and, if fortunate, drive Hussein from power.

In 2000, the original U.N. inspections team, UNSCOM, was replaced with UNMOVIC, after the Clinton administration admitted that it had received intelligence reports from UNSCOM's weapons inspectors. In fall 2000, however, Baghdad was still refusing to let the new inspections team into the country, claiming it would not cooperate with inspectors until the sanctions had been lifted and U.S. and British forces stopped patrolling the no-fly zones.

Ireland

National name: Ireland, or Eire in the Irish language
President: Mary McAleese (1997)
Taoiseach (Prime Minister): Bertie Ahern (1997)
Area: 27,136 sq. mi. (70,280 sq. km)
Population (2000 est.): 3,797,257 (average annual rate of natural increase: 0.6%); birth rate: 14.5/1000; infant mortality rate: 5.7/1000; density per sq. mi.: 140
Capital: Dublin. **Largest cities (1991):** Dublin, 1,056,666; Cork, 293,254; Galway, 131,503; Limerick, 112,975. **Monetary units:** Irish pound (punt) and euro. **Languages:** English, Irish Gaelic. **Ethnicity/race:** Celtic, English. **Religions:** Roman Catholic 93%, Anglican 3%, none 1%, unknown 2%, other 1%. **Literacy rate:** 98% (1981)
Economic summary: GDP/PPP (1998 est.): $67.1 billion; $18,600 per capita. **Real growth rate:** 9.5%. **Inflation:** 2.4%. **Unemployment:** 7.7%. **Arable land:** 13%. **Agriculture:** turnips, barley, potatoes, sugar beets, wheat, beef, dairy products. **Labor force:** 1.52 million (1997 est.): services, 62.1%; manufacturing and construction, 27%; agriculture, forestry, and fishing, 10%; utilities, 0.9% (1996 est.). **Industries:**

food products, brewing, textiles, clothing, chemicals, pharmaceuticals, machinery, transportation equipment, glass and crystal. **Natural resources:** zinc, lead, natural gas, barite, copper, gypsum, limestone, dolomite, peat, silver. **Exports:** $60.9 billion (f.o.b., 1998): chemicals, data processing equipment, industrial machinery, live animals, animal products. **Imports:** $43.7 billion (c.i.f., 1998): food, animal feed, data processing equipment, petroleum and petroleum products, machinery, textiles, clothing. **Major trading partners:** EU (U.K., Germany, France), U.S.

Geography Ireland is situated in the Atlantic Ocean and separated from Great Britain by the Irish Sea. Half the size of Arkansas, it occupies the entire island except for the six counties that make up Northern Ireland. Ireland resembles a basin—a central plain rimmed with mountains, except in the Dublin region. The mountains are low, with the highest peak, Carrantuohill in County Kerry, rising to 3,415 feet (1,041 m). The principal river is the Shannon, which begins in the north-central area, flows south and southwest for about 240 miles (386 km), and empties into the Atlantic.

Government Republic.

History In the Stone and Bronze Ages, Ireland was inhabited by Picts in the north and a people called the Erainn in the south, the same stock, apparently, as in all the isles before the Anglo-Saxon invasion of Britain. About the 4th century B.C., tall, red-haired Celts arrived from Gaul or Galicia. They subdued and assimilated the inhabitants and established a Gaelic civilization. By the beginning of the Christian Era, Ireland was divided into five kingdoms—Ulster, Connacht, Leinster, Meath, and Munster. Saint Patrick introduced Christianity in A.D. 432 and the country developed into a center of Gaelic and Latin learning. Irish monasteries, the equivalent of universities, attracted intellectuals as well as the pious and sent out missionaries to many parts of Europe and, some believe, to North America.

Norse depredations along the coasts, starting in 795, ended in 1014 with Norse defeat at the Battle of Clontarf by forces under Brian Boru. In the 12th century, the pope gave all of Ireland to the English Crown as a papal fief. In 1171, Henry II of England was acknowledged "Lord of Ireland," but local sectional rule continued for centuries, and English control over the whole island was not reasonably absolute until the 17th century. In the Battle of the Boyne (1690), the Catholic King James II and his French supporters were defeated by the Protestant King William III (of Orange).

By the Act of Union (1801), England and Ireland became the "United Kingdom of Great Britain and Ireland." A steady decline in the Irish economy followed in the next decades. The population had reached 8.25 million when the great potato famine of 1846–48 took many lives and drove more than 2 million people to immigrate to North America.

In the meantime, anti-British agitation continued along with demands for Irish home rule. The advent of World War I delayed the institution of home rule and resulted in the Easter Rebellion in Dublin (April 24–29, 1916), in which Irish nationalists unsuccessfully attempted to throw off British rule. Guerrilla warfare against British forces followed proclamation of a republic by the rebels in 1919. The Irish Free State was established as a dominion on Dec. 6, 1922, with the six northern counties remaining as part of the

United Kingdom. The constitution of 1937 changed the nation's name to Éire. Ireland was neutral in World War II.

In 1948, Eamon de Valera, American-born leader of the Sinn Fein, who had won the establishment of the Free State in 1921 in negotiations with Britain's David Lloyd George, was defeated by John A. Costello, who demanded final independence from Britain. The Republic of Ireland was proclaimed on April 18, 1949. It withdrew from the Commonwealth, but in 1955 Ireland entered the United Nations. Throughout the 1960s, two antagonistic currents dominated Irish politics. One sought to bind the wounds of the rebellion and civil war. The other was the effort of the outlawed Irish Republican Army to bring Northern Ireland into the republic.

Under the First Programme for Economic Expansion (1958–63), economic protection was dismantled and foreign investment encouraged. This prosperity brought profound social and cultural changes to what had been one of the poorest and least technologically advanced countries in Europe. Ireland joined the European Economic Community (now the EU) in 1973. In the 1990 presidential election, Mary Robinson was elected the republic's first woman president. The election of a candidate with socialist and feminist sympathies was regarded as a watershed in Irish political life, reflecting the changes taking place in Irish society. Irish voters approved the Maastricht Treaty, which paved the way for the establishment of the EU, by a large majority in a referendum held in 1992. In 1993, the Irish and British governments signed a joint peace initiative (the Downing Street Declaration), in which they pledged to seek mutually agreeable political structures in Northern Ireland and between the two islands. A referendum on allowing divorce under certain conditions—hitherto constitutionally forbidden—was held in Nov. 1995 and narrowly passed.

In 1998 hope for a solution to the troubles in Northern Ireland seemed palpable. A landmark settlement, the Good Friday Accord of April 10, 1998, came after 22 months of intensive negotiations that involved eight of the ten Northern Irish political parties. Chaired by former U.S. senator George Mitchell, the talks were advanced by a high-profile set of mediators, including British prime minister Tony Blair, Irish prime minister Bertie Ahern, and President Bill Clinton. The accord called for Protestants to share political power with the minority Catholics, and gave the Republic of Ireland a voice in Northern Irish affairs. The resounding commitment to the settlement was demonstrated in a dual referendum on May 22: the North approved the accord by a vote of 71% to 29%, and in the Irish Republic 94% favored it. Although the process of forming the new coalition government proceeded over the course of the year, it came crashing down in July 1999, the very month the nascent government was to assemble for the first time. The sticking point was the timetable for the I.R.A.'s disarmament: Sinn Fein insisted the I.R.A. give up its illegal weapons after the new government formed; Unionists demanded disarmament first. On May 30, 2000, Britain returned home rule powers to the Northern Ireland Assembly after the I.R.A. announced it had put its arms "beyond use."

See also Northern Ireland, under United Kingdom.

Israel

STATE OF ISRAEL

National name: Medinat Yisra'el
President: Moshe Katzav (2000)
Prime Minister: Ehud Barak (1999)
Area: 8,020 sq. mi. (20,770 sq. km)
Population (2000 est.): 5,842,454[1] (average annual rate of natural increase: 1.3%); birth rate: 19.3/1000; infant mortality rate: 7.9/1000; density per sq. mi.: 728
Capital and largest city (1993 est.): Jerusalem[2], 550,500. **Other large cities (1993 est.):** Tel Aviv, 355,900; Haifa, 250,000. **Monetary unit:** Shekel.
Languages: Hebrew, Arabic, English. **Ethnicity/race:** Jewish 82% (Israel-born 50%, Europe/Americas/Oceania-born 20%, Africa-born 7%, Asia-born 5%), non-Jewish 18% (mostly Arab) (1993 est.). **Religions:** Judaism, 82%; Islam, 14%; Christian, 2%; others, 2%.
Literacy rate: 92% (1983)
Economic summary: GDP/PPP (1998 est.): $101.9 billion; $18,100 per capita. **Real growth rate:** 1.9%. **Inflation:** 5.4%. **Unemployment:** 8.7%. **Arable land:** 17%. **Agriculture:** citrus, vegetables, cotton, beef, poultry, dairy products. **Labor force:** 2.3 million (1997): public services, 31.2%; manufacturing, 20.2%; finance and business, 13.1%; commerce, 12.8%; construction, 7.5%; personal and other services, 6.4%; transport, storage, and communications, 6.2%; agriculture, forestry, and fishing, 2.6% (1996). **Industries:** food processing, diamond cutting and polishing, textiles and apparel, chemicals, metal products, military equipment, transport equipment, electrical equipment, potash mining, high-technology electronics, tourism. **Natural resources:** copper, phosphates, bromide, potash, clay, sand, sulfur, asphalt, manganese, small amounts of natural gas and crude oil. **Exports:** $22.1 billion (f.o.b., 1998): machinery and equipment, cut diamonds, chemicals, textiles and apparel, agricultural products, metals. **Imports:** $26.1 billion (f.o.b., 1998): raw materials, military equipment, investment goods, rough diamonds, oil, consumer goods. **Major trading partners:** U.S., U.K., Hong Kong, Benelux, Japan, Netherlands, Germany, Italy, Switzerland.

1. Includes West Bank, Gaza Strip, East Jerusalem. 2. Not recognized by U.S., which recognizes Tel Aviv.

Geography Israel, slightly larger than Massachusetts, lies at the eastern end of the Mediterranean Sea. It is bordered by Egypt on the west, Syria and Jordan on the east, and Lebanon on the north. Northern Israel is largely a plateau traversed from north to south by mountains and broken by great depressions, also running from north to south.

The maritime plain of Israel is remarkably fertile. The southern Negev region, which comprises almost half the total area, is largely a wide desert steppe area. Parts of it have been irrigated and cultivated. The Jordan, the only important river, flows from the north through Lake Hule (Waters of Merom) and Lake Kinneret (Sea of Galilee or Sea of Tiberias), finally entering the Dead Sea, 1,312 feet (400 m) below sea level. This "sea," which is actually a salt lake (394 sq. mi.; 1,020 sq. km), has no outlet, its water balance being maintained by evaporation.

Government Republic.

History Palestine, considered a holy land by Jews, Muslims, and Christians, and homeland of the modern state of Israel, was known as Canaan to the ancient Hebrews. Palestine's name derives from the Philistines, a people who occupied the southern coastal part of the country in the 12th century B.C.

A Hebrew kingdom established in 1000 B.C. was later split into the kingdoms of Judah and Israel; they were subsequently invaded by Assyrians, Babylonians, Egyptians, Persians, Romans, and Alexander the Great of Macedonia. By A.D. 135, few Jews were left in Palestine; most lived in the scattered and tenacious communities of the Diaspora. Palestine became a center of Christian pilgrimage after the emperor Constantine converted to that faith. The Arabs took Palestine from the Byzantine empire in A.D. 634–40. Interrupted only by Christian Crusaders, Muslims ruled Palestine until the 20th century (Turkish rule from 1516). During World War I, British forces defeated the Turks in Palestine and governed the area under a League of Nations mandate from 1923.

As part of the 19th-century Zionist movement, Jews had begun settling in Palestine as early as 1820. This effort to establish a Jewish homeland had received British approval in the Balfour Declaration of 1917. During the 1930s, Jews persecuted by the Hitler regime poured into Palestine. The postwar acknowledgment of the Holocaust—Hitler's genocide of 6 million Jews—increased international interest in and sympathy for the cause of Zionism. However, Arabs in Palestine and surrounding countries bitterly opposed prewar and postwar proposals to partition Palestine into Arab and Jewish sectors. The British mandate to govern Palestine ended after the war, and in 1947 the U.N. voted to partition Palestine. When the British officially withdrew on May 14, 1948, the Jewish National Council proclaimed the State of Israel

U.S. recognition came within hours. The next day, Arab forces from Egypt, Jordan, Syria, Lebanon, and Iraq invaded the new nation. By the cease-fire on Jan. 7, 1949, Israel had increased its original territory by 50%, taking western Galilee, a broad corridor through central Palestine to Jerusalem, and part of modern Jerusalem. Chaim Weizmann and David Ben-Gurion became Israel's first president and prime minister. The new government was admitted to the U.N. on May 11, 1949.

The next clash with Arab neighbors came when Egypt nationalized the Suez Canal in 1956 and barred Israeli shipping. Coordinating with an Anglo-French force, Israeli troops seized the Gaza Strip and drove through the Sinai to the east bank of the Suez Canal, but withdrew under U.S. and U.N. pressure. In the Six-Day War of 1967, Israel made simultaneous air attacks against Syrian, Jordanian, and Egyptian air bases, totally defeating the Arabs. Expanding its territory by 200%, Israel at the cease-fire held the Golan Heights, the West Bank of the Jordan River, Jerusalem's Old City, and all of the Sinai and the east bank of the Suez Canal.

In the face of Israeli reluctance even to discuss the return of occupied territories, the fourth Arab-Israeli War erupted on Oct. 6, 1973, with a surprise Egyptian and Syrian assault on the Jewish high holy day of Yom Kippur. Initial Arab gains were reversed when a cease-fire took effect two weeks later, but Israel suffered heavy losses.

A dramatic breakthrough in the tortuous history of Mideast peace efforts occurred on Nov. 9, 1977, when Egypt's president Anwar Sadat declared his willingness to go anywhere to talk peace. Prime Minister Menachem Begin on Nov. 15 extended an invitation to the Egyptian leader to address the Knesset. Sadat's arrival in Israel four days later raised worldwide hopes, but a peace agreement between Egypt and Israel was long in coming. On March 14, 1979, the

Knesset approved a final peace treaty, and 12 days later Begin and Sadat signed the document, together with President Jimmy Carter, in a White House ceremony. Israel began its withdrawal from the Sinai, which it had annexed from Egypt, on May 25, and the two countries opened their border on May 29.

Although Israel withdrew its last settlers from the Sinai in April 1982, the fragile Mideast peace was shattered on June 9 by a massive Israeli assault on southern Lebanon, where the Palestinian Liberation Organization was entrenched. The PLO had long plagued Israelis with terrorist actions. Israel destroyed PLO strongholds in Tyre and Sidon and reached the suburbs of Beirut on June 10. A U.S.-mediated accord between Lebanon and Israel, signed on May 17, 1983, provided for Israeli withdrawal from Lebanon. Israel eventually withdrew its troops from the Beirut area, but kept them in southern Lebanon, where occasional skirmishes would continue. Lebanon, under pressure from Syria, canceled the accord in March 1984.

A continual source of tension has been the relationship between the Jews and the Palestinians living within Israeli territories. Most Arabs fled the region when the state of Israel was declared, but those who remain now make up almost one-fifth of the population of Israel. They are about two-thirds Muslim, as well as Christian and Druze. Palestinians living on the West Bank and the Gaza Strip fomented the riots begun in 1987, known as the *Intifadeh*. Violence heightened as Israeli police cracked down and Palestinians retaliated. Continuing Jewish settlement of lands designated for Palestinians has added to the unrest.

In 1989 the leader of the PLO, Yasir Arafat, reversed decades of PLO polemic by acknowledging Israel's right to exist. He stated his willingness to enter negotiations to create a Palestinian political entity that would coexist with the Israeli state.

In 1991 Israel was struck by Iraqi missiles during the Persian Gulf War. The Israelis did not retaliate in order to preserve the international coalition against Iraq. In 1992 Yitzhak Rabin became prime minister. He halted the disputed Israeli settlement of the occupied territories. Highly secretive talks in Norway resulted in an agreement between the PLO and the Israeli government (the Oslo agreement, 1993). The accord stipulated a five-year plan in which Palestinians of the West Bank and the Gaza Strip would gradually become self-governing. In 1994 Israel signed a peace treaty with Jordan. Israel has no formal peace agreement with Syria or Lebanon.

On Nov. 4, 1995, Prime Minister Rabin was slain by a Jewish extremist, jeopardizing the tenuous progress toward peace. Shimon Peres succeeded him until May 1996 elections for the Knesset gave Israel a new hard-line prime minister, Benjamin Netanyahu, by a razor-thin margin. Netanyahu reversed or stymied much of the Oslo agreement, contending that it offered too many concessions too fast and jeopardized Israelis' safety. Elections for seats on the Palestinian Council and for its president took place in Jan. 1996. Yasir Arafat obtained an easy victory as president.

Israeli-Palestinian peace negotiations in 1997 were repeatedly undermined by both sides. Although the Hebron accord was signed in Jan., calling for the withdrawal of Israeli troops from the city, the construction of new Jewish settlements on the West Bank in March profoundly upset progress toward peace. Some Jews cited the influx of immigration from Russia (since the collapse of the Soviet Union, more than 700,000 Russian Jews have arrived in Israel) as necessitating the additional settlements. Others believe that Netanyahu wishes to curb Palestinian expectations raised by the Oslo agreement.

Terrorism erupted again in 1997 when radical Hamas suicide bombers claimed the lives of more than 20 Israeli civilians. Netanyahu, accusing Palestinian Authority president Arafat of lax security, retaliated with draconian sanctions against Palestinians working in Israel, including the withholding of millions of dollars in tax revenue, a blatant violation of the Oslo agreements. Netanyahu persisted in authorizing right-wing Israelis to build new settlements in mostly Arab East Jerusalem. Arafat, meanwhile, seemed unwilling or unable to curb the violence of extremist Arabs.

An Oct. 1998 summit at Wye Mills, Md., generated the first real progress in the stymied Middle East peace talks in 19 months, with Israeli prime minister Benjamin Netanyahu and Palestinian president Yasir Arafat settling several important interim issues called for by the 1993 Oslo Peace Accords. The Palestinians agreed to remove language from their founding charter that called for the dismantling of the Jewish state; Israelis agreed to cede an additional 13% of the West Bank.

Although Israel completed the first of three withdrawals from the West Bank on Nov. 20, released 250 Palestinian prisoners, and authorized the opening of the Gaza airport, the peace accord began unraveling almost immediately. Disagreement over the Israeli release of Palestinian prisoners led to violence in the West Bank and Gaza, for which each side blamed the other. To buttress the flagging accord, President Clinton visited the Gaza Strip on Dec. 15, becoming the first American president to set foot on Palestinian-occupied land. The visit coincided with the vote of the Palestine National Council to formally eliminate language from the organization's charter that calls for the destruction of Israel.

Netanyahu found himself attacked from both sides of the political spectrum—the left accused him of intentionally thwarting the peace process and the right accused him of betrayal, having elected him in the belief that he would never give up Israeli territory. In mid-Dec. Parliament voted to dissolve Netanyahu's government and hold elections in the spring, putting the peace negotiations on hold.

By the end of April 1999, Israel had made 41 air raids on Hezbollah guerrillas in Lebanon. The guerrillas were fighting against Israeli troops and their allies, the South Lebanon Army militia, who have occupied a security zone set up in 1985 to guard Israel's borders. Public pressure in Israel to withdraw the troops grew, and the issue dominated the Israeli election campaign in spring 1999. Ehud Barak of the Labour Party won the election with 55.9% of the vote, against 43.9% for incumbent Benjamin Netanyahu of Likud. Yasir Arafat originally planned to declare Palestinian statehood on May 4, but postponed that decision until an undefined time after the election, so as not to provoke Israeli hard-liners and lessen the chance of resuming the peace talks.

Barak created a broad coalition government and on his inauguration (July 6, 1999) announced that "nothing is more important in my view than . . . putting an end to the 100-year conflict in the Middle East." By this he meant not only pursuing peace with the Palestinians, but establishing relations with Syria and ending the low-grade war in Southern Lebanon with the Iranian-armed Hezbollah guerrillas. Syria has more

than 30,000 troops in Lebanon, and Iran uses Syria as its conduit for delivering weapons to Hezbollah.

In Sept. 1999, Israel moved ahead with the 1998 Wye Accord, ceding an additional 7% of territory to the Palestinians.

No thaw with Syria seemed forthcoming until Dec., when Israeli-Syrian talks resumed after a nearly four-year hiatus. From Syria's point of view, normalization of relations between the two countries would largely depend on Israel's withdrawal from the Golan Heights, which was territory that Israel had captured from Syria during the Middle East war of 1967. From Israel's point of view, relinquishing the Golan Heights, which serves as a buffer zone between the two nations, could not occur without a guarantee of Israel's security from Syria. By Jan. 2000, however, talks had broken down when Syria demanded a detailed discussion of the return of all of the Golan Heights.

In Feb., new Hezbollah attacks on Israeli troops in southern Lebanon led to Israel's retaliatory bombing as well as Barak's decision to pull out of Lebanon by July, whether or not an agreement had been reached with Syria. Israeli troops pulled out of Lebanon on May 24, 2000, after 22 years of occupation.

Peace talks in July 2000 at Camp David between Ehud Barak and Yasir Arafat ended unsuccessfully, despite President Clinton's strongest efforts—the status of Jerusalem was the primary sticking point. Clinton blamed Arafat's intransigence, but Palestinian supporters praised his strong stand. Barak, on the other hand, returned to a volatile political situation, with conservatives angered by his concessions and threatening to abandon his fragile parliamentary coalition.

Italy

ITALIAN REPUBLIC

National name: Repubblica Italiana
President: Carlo Azeglio Ciampi (1999)
Prime Minister: Giuliano Amato (2000)
Area: 116,500 sq. mi. (301,230 sq. km)
Population (2000 est.): 57,634,327 (average annual rate of natural increase: −0.9%); birth rate: 9.1/1000; infant mortality rate: 5.9/1000; density per sq. mi.: 495
Capital and largest city (1994 est.): Rome, 2,693,383.
Other large cities: Milan, 1,561,438; Naples, 1,204,149; Turin, 952,736; Genoa, 706,754; Palermo, 694,749; Florence, 460,924; Bologna, 394,969; Catania, 372,212; Bari, 355,352; Venice, 306,439.
Monetary units: Lira and euro. **Languages:** Italian; small German-, French-, and Slovene-speaking minorities. **Ethnicity/race:** Italian (includes small clusters of German-, French-, and Slovene-Italians in the north and Albanian-Italians and Greek-Italians in the south), Sicilians, Sardinians. **Religions:** Roman Catholic 98%, other 2%. **Literacy rate:** 97% (1990)
Economic summary: GDP/PPP (1998 est.): $1.181 trillion; $20,800 per capita. **Real growth rate:** 1.5%. **Inflation:** 1.8%. **Unemployment:** 12.5%. **Arable land:** 31%. **Agriculture:** fruit, vegetables, grapes, potatoes, sugar beets, soybeans, grain, olives, beef, dairy products, fish. **Labor force:** 23.193 million: services, 61%; industry, 32%; agriculture, 7% (1996).
Industries: tourism, machinery, iron and steel, chemicals, food processing, textiles, motor vehicles, clothing, footwear, ceramics. **Natural resources:** mercury, potash, marble, sulfur, dwindling natural gas and crude oil reserves, fish, coal. **Exports:** $243 billion (f.o.b., 1998): engineering products, textiles and clothing, production machinery, motor vehicles, transport equipment, chemicals, food, beverages,

tobacco, minerals and nonferrous metals. **Imports:** $202 billion (f.o.b., 1998): engineering products, chemicals, transport equipment, energy products, minerals and nonferrous metals, textiles and clothing; food, beverages, tobacco. **Major trading partners:** Germany, France, U.S., U.K., Spain, Netherlands, Belgium, Luxembourg.

Geography Italy, slightly larger than Arizona, is a long peninsula shaped like a boot bounded on the west by the Tyrrhenian Sea and on the east by the Adriatic. Approximately 600 of Italy's 708 miles (1,139 km) of length are in the long peninsula that projects into the Mediterranean from the fertile basin of the Po River. The Apennine Mountains, branching off from the Alps between Nice and Genoa, form the peninsula's backbone, and rise to a maximum height of 9,560 feet (2,912 m) at the Gran Sasso d'Italia (Corno). The Alps form Italy's northern boundary.

Italy has many northern lakes, lying below the snow-covered peaks of the Alps. The largest are Garda (143 sq. mi.; 370 sq. km), Maggiore (83 sq. mi.; 215 sq. km), and Como (55 sq. mi.; 142 sq. km). The Po, the principal river, flows from the Alps on Italy's western border and crosses the Lombard plain to the Adriatic Sea.

Several islands form part of Italy. Sicily (9,926 sq. mi.; 25,708 sq. km) lies off the toe of the boot, across the Strait of Messina, with a steep and rockbound northern coast and gentler slopes to the sea in the west and south. Mount Etna, an active volcano, rises to 10,741 feet (3,274 m), and most of Sicily is more than 500 feet (3,274 m) in elevation. Sixty-two miles (100 km) southwest of Sicily lies Pantelleria (45 sq. mi.; 117 sq. km), and south of that are Lampedusa and Linosa. Sardinia (9,301 sq. mi.; 24,090 sq. km), which is just south of Corsica and about 125 miles (200 km) west of the mainland, is mountainous, stony, and unproductive.

Government Republic.

History The migrations of Indo-European peoples into Italy probably began about 2000 B.C. and continued down to 1000 B.C. From about the 9th century B.C. until it was overthrown by the Romans in the 3rd century B.C., the Etruscan civilization dominated the area. By 264 B.C. all Italy south of Cisalpine Gaul was under the leadership of Rome. For the next seven centuries, until the barbarian invasions destroyed the western Roman Empire in the 4th and 5th centuries A.D., the history of Italy was largely the history of Rome. From A.D. 800 on, the Holy Roman Emperors, Roman Catholic popes, Normans, and Saracens all vied for control over various segments of the Italian peninsula. Numerous city-states, such as Venice and Genoa, whose political and commercial rivalries were intense, and many small principalities flourished in the late Middle Ages. Although Italy remained politically fragmented for centuries, it became the cultural center of the Western world from the 13th to the 16th century.

In 1713, after the War of the Spanish Succession, Milan, Naples, and Sardinia were handed over to the Hapsburgs of Austria, which lost some of its Italian territories in 1735. After 1800, Italy was unified by Napoléon, who crowned himself king of Italy in 1805; but with the Congress of Vienna in 1815, Austria once again became the dominant power in a disunited Italy. Austrian armies crushed Italian uprisings in 1820–21 and 1831. In the 1830s Giuseppe Mazzini, brilliant liberal nationalist, organized the Risorgimento (Resurrection), which laid the founda-

tion for Italian unity. Disappointed Italian patriots looked to the House of Savoy for leadership. Count Camille di Cavour (1810–61), premier of Sardinia in 1852 and the architect of a united Italy, joined England and France in the Crimean War (1853–56), and in 1859, helped France in a war against Austria, thereby obtaining Lombardy. By plebiscite in 1860, Modena, Parma, Tuscany, and the Romagna voted to join Sardinia. In 1860, Giuseppe Garibaldi conquered Sicily and Naples and turned them over to Sardinia. Victor Emmanuel II, king of Sardinia, was proclaimed king of Italy in 1861. The annexation of Venetia in 1866 and of papal Rome in 1870 marked the complete unification of peninsular Italy into one nation under a constitutional monarchy.

Italy declared its neutrality upon the outbreak of World War I on the ground that Germany had embarked upon an offensive war. In 1915, Italy entered the war on the side of the Allies but obtained less territory than it expected in the postwar settlement. Benito ("Il Duce") Mussolini, a former socialist, organized discontented Italians in 1919 into the Fascist Party to "rescue Italy from Bolshevism." He led his Black Shirts in a march on Rome and, on Oct. 28, 1922, became premier. He transformed Italy into a dictatorship, embarking on an expansionist foreign policy with the invasion and annexation of Ethiopia in 1935 and allying himself with Adolf Hitler in the Rome-Berlin Axis in 1936. When the Allies invaded Italy in 1943, Mussolini's dictatorship collapsed; he was executed by Partisans on April 28, 1945, at Dongo on Lake Como. Following the armistice with the Allies (Sept. 3, 1943), Italy joined the war against Germany as a cobelligerent. A June 1946 plebiscite rejected monarchy and a republic was proclaimed. The peace treaty of Sept. 15, 1947, required Italian renunciation of all claims in Ethiopia and Greece and the cession of the Dodecanese to Greece and of five small Alpine areas to France. The Trieste area west of the new Yugoslav territory was made a free territory (until 1954, when the city and a 90-square-mile zone were transferred to Italy and the rest to Yugoslavia).

Italy became an integral member of NATO and the European Economic Community (later the EU) as it successfully rebuilt its postwar economy. A prolonged outbreak of terrorist activities by the left-wing Red Brigades threatened domestic stability in the 1970s, but by the early 1980s the terrorist groups had been suppressed. Scandal brought the long reign of the Christian Democrats to an end when Italy's 40th premier since World War II, Arnaldo Forlani, was forced to resign in the wake of disclosure that many high-ranking Christian Democrats and civil servants belonged to a secret Masonic lodge known as "P-2." During 1993, the nation was riveted by a political scandal of a seemingly ever-growing size involving the Mafia and many government leaders. In a referendum, voters approved changing the proportional system of representation in the Senate for one utilizing majority voting. This series of scandals led to the collapse of the post–World War II party system and new parties filled the political vacuum. In 1996, Italians elected a government dominated by a center-left coalition for the first time since the proclamation of the Italian Republic. In 1997, Italian forces assumed leadership of a military mission to protect international aid reaching strife-torn Albania. The Communists, Italy's single largest party, refused to support the operation but refrained from withdrawing support from the government.

Italy adopted the euro as its currency in Jan. 1999. Treasury Secretary Carlo Ciampi, who is credited with the economic reforms that permitted Italy to enter the European Monetary Union, was elected president in May 1999. Italy joined its NATO partners in the Kosovo crisis. Aviano Air Base in northern Italy was a crucial base for launching air strikes into Kosovo and Yugoslavia.

In April 2000, Giuliano Amato became prime minister of the 58th "revolving door" government in postwar Italy.

Jamaica

Sovereign: Queen Elizabeth II (1952)
Governor-General: Howard F. H. Cooke (1991)
Prime Minister: Percival J. Patterson (1992)
Area: 4,411 sq. mi. (10,990 sq. km)
Population (2000 est.): 2,652,689 (average annual rate of natural increase: 1.3%); birth rate: 18.5/1000; infant mortality rate: 14.6/1000; density per sq. mi.: 601
Capital and largest city (1991 est.): Kingston, 104,000.
Monetary unit: Jamaican dollar. **Languages:** English, Jamaican Creole. **Ethnicity/race:** African 76.3%, Afro-European 15.1%, East Indian and Afro-East Indian 3%, white 3.2%, Chinese and Afro-Chinese 1.2%, other 1.2%. **Religions:** Protestant, 55.9%; Roman Catholic, 5%; other, 39.1%. **Literacy rate:** 98% (1990)
Economic summary: GDP/PPP (1998 est.): $8.8 billion; $3,300 per capita. **Real growth rate:** −2%. **Inflation:** 9.9%. **Unemployment:** 16.5% (1997 est.). **Arable land:** 14%. **Agriculture:** sugarcane, bananas, coffee, citrus, potatoes, vegetables, poultry, goats, milk. **Labor force:** 1.14 million (1996): services, 41%; agriculture, 22.5%; industry, 19% (1989). **Industries:** tourism, bauxite, textiles, food processing, light manufactures. **Natural resources:** bauxite, gypsum, limestone. **Exports:** $1.7 billion (1997): alumina, bauxite, sugar, bananas, rum. **Imports:** $2.8 billion (1997): machinery and transport equipment, construction materials, fuel, food, chemicals. **Major trading partners:** U.S., EU (excluding U.K. and Norway), Canada, U.K., Norway, Caricom, Latin America. **Member of Commonwealth of Nations**

Geography Jamaica is an island in the West Indies, 90 miles (145 km) south of Cuba and 100 miles (161 km) west of Haiti. It is a little smaller than Connecticut. The island is made up of coastal lowlands, a limestone plateau, and the Blue Mountains, a group of volcanic hills, in the east. Blue Mountain (7,402 ft.; 2,256 m) is the tallest peak.

Government Parliamentary democracy.

History Jamaica was inhabited by Arawak Indians when Columbus explored it in 1494 and named it St. Iago. It remained under Spanish rule until 1655, when it became a British possession. The island prospered from wealth brought by buccaneers to their base, Port Royal, the capital, until the city disappeared into the sea in 1692 after an earthquake. The Arawaks died off from disease and exploitation, and slaves, mostly black, were imported to work sugar plantations. During the 17th and 18th centuries the British were consistently harassed and attacked by the Maroons, armed and organized freed slaves who operated from rural Jamaica. Abolition of the slave trade (1807), emancipation of the slaves (1833), and a gradual drop in sugar prices led to depressed economic conditions that resulted in an uprising in 1865. The following year Jamaica's status was changed to that of a crown colony, and conditions improved considerably. Intro-

duction of banana cultivation made the island less dependent on the sugar crop for its well-being.

On May 5, 1953, Jamaica attained internal autonomy, and in 1958 it led in organizing the West Indies federation. This effort at Caribbean unification failed. A nationalist labor leader, Sir Alexander Bustamente, led a campaign for withdrawal from the federation. As the result of a popular referendum in 1961, Jamaica became independent on Aug. 6, 1962. Michael Manley, of the People's National Party, became prime minister in 1972 and initiated a socialist program.

The Labour Party defeated Manley's People's National Party in 1980 and its capitalist-oriented leader, Edward P. G. Seaga, became prime minister. He instituted measures to encourage private investment. Like other Caribbean countries, Jamaica was hard-hit by the 1981–82 recession. By 1984, austerity measures that Seaga instituted in the hope of bringing the economy back into balance included elimination of government subsidies. Devaluation of the Jamaican dollar made Jamaican products more competitive on the world market and Jamaica achieved record growth in tourism and agriculture. While manufacturing also grew, the cost of much food went up 50% to 75% and thousands of Jamaicans fell deeper into poverty.

In 1989, Manley swept back into power with a clear-cut victory. He indicated that he would pursue more centrist policies than he did in his previous administration. Manley stepped down in 1992 for reasons of health, and was replaced by P. J. Patterson. In May 1997 the government signed a "Ship-rider Agreement" allowing U.S. authorities, in an effort to curb drug trafficking, to enter Jamaican waters and search vessels with the Jamaican government's permission.

Japan

National name: Nippon
Emperor: Akihito (1989)
Prime Minister: Yoshiro Mori (2000)
Area: 145,874 sq. mi. (377,835 sq. km)
Population (2000 est.): 126,549,976 (average annual rate of natural increase: 0.2%); birth rate: 10/1000; infant mortality rate: 3.9/1000; density per sq. mi.: 868
Capital and largest city (2000 est.): Tokyo, 34,750,000 (metro. area). **Other large cities:** Osaka (2000 est.), 17,800,000 (metro. area); Yokohama, 3,307,136 (part of Tokyo metro. area); Nagoya (2000 est.), 5,100,000 (metro. area); Sapporo, 1,719,000; Kobe, 1,501,000 (part of Osaka metro. area); Kyoto, 1,456,000 (part of Osaka metro. area); Fukuoka, 1,263,000; Kawasaki, 1,196,000 (part of Tokyo metro. area); Hiroshima, 1,099,000. **Monetary unit:** Yen. **Language:** Japanese. **Ethnicity/race:** Japanese 99.4%, other 0.6% (mostly Korean). **Religions:** Shintoist, 111.8 million; Buddhist, 93.1 million; Christian, 1.4 million; other, 11.4 million. **Literacy rate:** 99% (1970)
Economic summary: GDP/PPP (1998 est.): $2.903 trillion; $23,100 per capita. **Real growth rate:** −2.6%. **Inflation:** 0.9%. **Unemployment:** 4.4% (Nov. 1998). **Arable land:** 11%. **Agriculture:** rice, sugar beets, vegetables, fruit, pork, poultry, dairy products, eggs, fish. **Labor force:** 67.72 million (Nov. 1998): trade and services, 50%; manufacturing, mining, and construction, 33%; utilities and communication, 7%; agriculture, forestry, and fishing, 6%; government, 3% (1994). **Industries:** among world's largest and technologically advanced producers of steel and nonferrous metallurgy, heavy electrical equipment, construction and mining equipment, motor vehicles and parts, electronic and telecommunication

equipment, machine tools, automated production systems, locomotives and railroad rolling stock, ships, chemicals, textiles, processed food. **Exports:** $440 billion (f.o.b., 1998): manufactures (including machinery, motor vehicles, consumer electronics). **Imports:** $319 billion (c.i.f., 1998): manufactures, foodstuffs and raw materials, fossil fuel. **Major trading partners:** U.S., EU, Southeast Asia, China.

Geography An archipelago extending in an arc more than 1,744 miles (2,790 km) from northeast to southwest in the Pacific, Japan is separated from the east coast of Asia by the Sea of Japan. It is approximately the size of Montana.

Japan's four main islands are Honshu, Hokkaido, Kyushu, and Shikoku. The Ryukyu chain to the southwest was U.S.-occupied from 1945 to 1972, when it reverted to Japanese control, and the Kurils to the northeast are Russian-occupied. The surface of the main islands consists largely of mountains separated by narrow valleys.

Located within a geologically active region, Japan sustains approximately 1,000 earthquakes per year, though most are minor. Offshore earthquakes can produce tsunamis, massive ocean waves that can wreak destruction along the Pacific shore. Several of Japan's mountains are active volcanoes.

Government Constitutional monarchy.

History Legend attributes creation of Japan to the sun goddess, from whom the emperors were descended. The first of them was Jimmu, supposed to have ascended the throne in 660 B.C., a tradition that constituted official doctrine until 1945.

Recorded Japanese history begins in approximately A.D. 400, when the Yamato clan, eventually based in Kyoto, managed to exact a loose control of the other family groups of central and western Japan. Contact with Korea introduced Buddhism to Japan at about this time. Through the 700s Japan was much influenced by China, and the Yamato clan set up an imperial court similar to that of China. In the ensuing centuries, the authority of the imperial court was undermined as powerful gentry families vied for control.

At the same time, warrior clans were rising to prominence as a distinct class known as samurai. In 1192 the Minamoto clan set up a military government under their leader, Yoritomo. He was designated shogun (military dictator). For the following 700 years, shoguns from a succession of clans ruled in Japan, while the imperial court existed in relative obscurity.

First contact with the West came in about 1542, when a Portuguese ship off course arrived in Japanese waters. Portuguese traders, Jesuit missionaries, and Spanish, Dutch, and English traders followed. Suspicious of Christianity and of Portuguese support of a local Japanese revolt, the shoguns of the Tokugawa period (1603–1867) prohibited all trade with foreign countries; only a Dutch trading post at Nagasaki was permitted. Western attempts to renew trading relations failed until 1853, when Commodore Matthew Perry sailed an American fleet into Tokyo Bay. Trade with the West was forced upon Japan under terms less than favorable to the Japanese. Strife caused by these actions brought down the feudal world of the shoguns. In 1868 the emperor Meiji came to the throne, and the shogun system was abolished.

Japan quickly made the transition from a medieval to a modern power. An imperial army was established with conscription, and parliamentary government was formed in 1889. The Japanese began to take steps to extend their empire. After a brief war with China in 1894–95, Japan acquired Formosa (Taiwan), the Pescadores Islands, and part of southern Manchuria. China also recognized the independence of Korea (Chosen), which Japan later annexed (1910).

In 1904–05, Japan defeated Russia in the Russo-Japanese War, gaining the territory of southern Sakhalin (Karafuto) and Russia's port and rail rights in Manchuria. In World War I Japan seized Germany's Pacific islands and leased areas in China. The Treaty of Versailles then awarded it a mandate over the islands.

At the Washington Conference of 1921–22, Japan agreed to respect Chinese national integrity, but in 1931 invaded Manchuria. The following year, Japan set up this area as a puppet state, "Manchukuo," under Emperor Henry Pu-Yi, the last of China's Manchu Dynasty. On Nov. 25, 1936, Japan joined the Axis. The invasion of China came the next year followed by the Pearl Harbor attack on the U.S. on Dec. 7, 1941. Japan won its first military engagements during the war, extending its power over a vast area of the Pacific. Yet after 1942 the Japanese were forced to retreat, island by island, to their own country. The dropping of atomic bombs on the cities of Hiroshima and Nagasaki in 1945 by the United States finally brought the government to admit defeat. Japan surrendered formally on Sept. 2, 1945, aboard the battleship *Missouri* in Tokyo Bay. Southern Sakhalin and the Kuril Islands reverted to the U.S.S.R., and Formosa (Taiwan) and Manchuria to China. The Pacific islands remained under U.S. occupation.

Gen. Douglas MacArthur was appointed supreme commander of the U.S. occupation of postwar Japan (1945–52). In 1947 a new constitution took effect. The emperor became largely a symbolic head of state. The U.S. and Japan signed a security treaty in 1951, allowing for U.S. troops to be stationed in Japan. In 1952 Japan regained full sovereignty, and in 1972 the U.S. returned to Japan the Ryuku Islands, including Okinawa.

Japan's postwar economic recovery was nothing short of remarkable. New technologies and manufacturing were undertaken with great success. A shrewd trade policy gave Japan larger shares in many Western markets, an imbalance that caused some tensions with the U.S. The close involvement of Japanese government in the country's banking and industry produced accusations of protectionism. Yet economic growth continued through the 1970s and 1980s, eventually making Japan the world's second-largest economy (after the U.S.).

Japan has also been criticized for hesitation to take an active role in world affairs. Its failure to join the international coalition in the Persian Gulf War in 1991 was a case in point. Japanese prime minister Toshiki Kaifu pledged to provide $9 billion to the U.S. to help defray the expense of the latter's operations in the Persian Gulf. The government attempted to push legislation that would have permitted Japan to send a military contingent to the Gulf in noncombat roles. This was defeated amid public outcry against it.

During the 1990s, Japan has suffered an economic downturn marked by scandals involving government officials, bankers, and leaders of industry. Banks have closed under the weight of bad loans, unemployment has risen, real estate values have dropped, and many businesses have failed. Japan, the world's second-largest economy behind the United States, succumbed to the Asian economic crisis in 1998, experiencing its worst recession since World War II. These setbacks led to the resignation of Prime Minister Ryutaro Hashimoto in July 1998. He was replaced by Keizo Obuchi. In 1999 Japan seemed to make slight progress in an economic recovery. The International Monetary Fund reported in Sept. 1999 that "several signals point to a limited recovery of the Japanese economy."

Prime Minister Obuchi died of a stroke in May 2000 and was succeeded by Yoshiro Mori, whose administration was dogged by scandal and blunders from the get-go. In June elections, the ruling Liberal Democratic Party nearly lost control of parliament and two of Mori's ministers were unseated. Then two financial scandals involving top administration officials broke within a week of each other, further imperiling Mori's government.

Jordan

THE HASHEMITE KINGDOM OF JORDAN

National name: Al Mamlaka al Urduniya al Hashemiyah
Ruler: King Abdullah II (1999)
Prime Minister: Ali Abu al-Ragheb (2000)
Area: 34,573 sq. mi (89,213 sq. km) excludes West Bank
Population (2000 est.): 4,998,564 (average annual rate of natural increase: 2.4%); birth rate: 26.2/1000; infant mortality rate: 21.1/1000; density per sq. mi.: 145
Capital and largest city (1994 est.): Amman, 963,490. **Largest cities (1994 est.):** Zarka, 420,900 (1990); Irbid, 208,201; As-Salt, 187,014. **Monetary unit:** Jordanian dinar. **Languages:** Arabic (official), English. **Ethnicity/race:** Arab 98%, Circassian 1%, Armenian 1%. **Religions:** Islam, 92%; Christian, 6%; Other, 2%. **Literacy rate:** 86% (1994)
Economic summary: GDP/PPP (1998 est.): $15.5 billion; $3,500 per capita. **Real growth rate:** 2.2%. **Inflation:** 4%. **Unemployment:** 15% [official rate; actual rate, 25%–30% (1998 est.)]. **Arable land:** 4%. **Agriculture:** wheat, barley, citrus, tomatoes, melons, olives, sheep, goats, poultry. **Labor force:** 1.5 million (1997 est.): industry, 11.4%; commerce, restaurants, and hotels, 10.5%; construction, 10%; transport and communications, 8.7%; agriculture, 7.4%; other services, 52% (1992). **Industries:** phosphate mining, petroleum refining, cement, potash, light manufacturing. **Natural resources:** phosphates, potash, shale oil. **Exports:** $1.5 billion (f.o.b., 1997 est.): phosphates, fertilizers, potash, agricultural products, manufactures. **Imports:** $3.9 billion (c.i.f., 1997 est.): crude oil, machinery, transport equipment, food, live animals, manufactured goods. **Major trading partners:** Iraq, India, Saudi Arabia, EU, Indonesia, U.A.E., Syria, Ethiopia, U.S., Japan, Turkey, Malaysia, China.

Geography The Middle East kingdom of Jordan is bordered on the west by Israel and the Dead Sea, on the north by Syria, on the east by Iraq, and on the south Saudi Arabia. It is comparable in size to Indiana. Arid hills and mountains make up most of the country. The southern section of the Jordan River flows through the country.

Government Constitutional hereditary monarchy.

History In biblical times, the country that is now Jordan contained the lands of Edom, Moab, Ammon, and Bashan. Together with other Middle Eastern territories, Jordan passed in turn to the Assyrians, the Babylonians, the Persians, and, about 330 B.C., the Seleucids. Conflict between the Seleucids and the Ptolemies enabled the Arabic-speaking Nabataeans to create a kingdom in southeastern Jordan. In A.D. 106

it became part of the Roman province of Arabia and in 633–36 was conquered by the Arabs. In the 16th century, Jordan submitted to Ottoman Turkish rule and was administered from Damascus. Taken from the Turks by the British in World War I, Jordan (formerly known as Transjordan) was separated from the Palestine mandate in 1920, and in 1921, placed under the rule of Abdullah ibn Hussein.

In 1923, Britain recognized Jordan's independence, subject to the mandate. In 1946, grateful for Jordan's loyalty in World War II, Britain abolished the mandate. That part of Palestine occupied by Jordanian troops was formally incorporated by action of the Jordanian Parliament in 1950. King Abdullah was assassinated in 1951. His son Talal was deposed as mentally ill the next year. Talal's son Hussein, born on Nov. 14, 1935, succeeded him.

From the beginning of his reign, Hussein had to steer a careful course between his powerful neighbor to the west, Israel, and rising Arab nationalism, frequently a direct threat to his throne. Riots erupted when he joined the Central Treaty Organization (the Baghdad Pact) in 1955, and he incurred further unpopularity when Britain, France, and Israel attacked the Suez Canal in 1956, forcing him to place his army under nominal command of the United Arab Republic of Egypt and Syria. The 1961 breakup of the UAR eased Arab national pressure on Hussein, who was the first to recognize Syria after it reclaimed its independence. Jordan was swept into the 1967 Arab-Israeli War, however, and lost the old city of Jerusalem and all of its territory west of the Jordan river, the West Bank. Embittered Palestinian guerrilla forces virtually took over sections of Jordan in the aftermath of defeat, and open warfare broke out between the Palestinians and government forces in 1970.

Despite intervention of Syrian tanks, Hussein's Bedouin army defeated the Palestinians. The Jordanians drove out the Syrians and 12,000 Iraqi troops who had been in the country since the 1967 war. Ignoring protests from other Arab states, Hussein, by mid-1971, crushed Palestinian strength in Jordan and shifted the problem to Lebanon, where many of the guerrillas had fled. As Egypt and Israel neared final agreement on a peace treaty early in 1979, Hussein met with Yasir Arafat, the PLO leader, on March 17 and issued a joint statement of opposition. Although the U.S. pressed Jordan to break Arab ranks on the issue, Hussein elected to side with the great majority, cutting ties with Cairo and joining the boycott against Egypt.

Jordan's stance during the Persian Gulf War strained relations with the U.S. and led to the termination of U.S. aid. The signing of a national charter by King Hussein and leaders of the main political groups in June 1991 meant political parties were permitted in exchange for acceptance of the constitution and the monarchy. King Hussein's decision to join the Middle East peace talks in mid-1991 helped restore his country's relations with the U.S.

In July 1994 King Hussein and the Israeli prime minister signed a declaration ending the state of belligerency between the two countries. A peace agreement between the two countries was signed on Oct. 26, 1994, although a clause in it calling the king the "custodian" of Islamic holy shrines in Jerusalem angered the PLO. In the wake of the agreement Jordan's relations with the U.S. and with the moderate Arab states, including Saudi Arabia, warmed. In 1997, Jordan began negotiating with the United States about membership in the World Trade Organization, determined to attract foreign investment. On Feb. 7, 1999, King Hussein died of cancer after 46 years on the throne, sending the Middle East and much of the world into mourning for the influential Middle East statesman. Just weeks earlier, on Jan. 26, King Hussein unexpectedly deposed his brother, Prince Hassan, who had been heir apparent for 34 years, and named his eldest son, Abdullah, 37, as the new crown prince. King Abdullah II, a popular military leader with little political experience, was crowned on Feb. 7, 2000. In June King Abdullah dismissed conservative prime minister Abdul Raouf al-Rawabdeh and replaced him with Ali Abu al-Ragheb, a liberal with strong business ties.

Kazakhstan

REPUBLIC OF KAZAKHSTAN

President: Nursultan A. Nazarbayev (1990)
Prime Minister: Kasymzhomart Tokayev (1999)
Area: 1,049,000 sq. mi. (2,717,300 sq. km)
Population (2000 est.): 16,733,227; average annual rate of natural increase: 0.6%; birth rate: 16.8/1000; infant mortality rate: 59.4/1000; density per sq. mi.: 16
Capital (1995 est.): Astana, 280,200 (capital since 1997) . **Largest cities (1991):** Almaty (former capital), 1,200,000; Karaganda, 608,600; Shymkent, 438,000; Ust-Kamenogorsk, 332,900; Taraz, 312,300; Aqmola, 287,000; Aqtöbe, 266,600. **Monetary unit:** Tenge.
Languages: Kazak (Qazaq), official language spoken by over 40% of population; Russian, official language spoken by two-thirds of population and used in everyday business. **Ethnicity/race:** Kazak (Qazaq) 46%, Russian 34.7%, Ukrainian 4.9%, German 3.1%, Uzbek 2.3%, Tatar 1.9%, other 7.1% (1996).
Religions: Muslim, 47%; Russian Orthodox 44%, Protestant 2%, other 7%. **Literacy rate:** 98% (1989)
Economic summary: GDP/PPP (1998 est.): $52.9 billion; $3,100 per capita. **Real growth rate:** –2.5%. **Inflation:** 10%. **Unemployment:** 13.7%. **Labor force:** 8.8 million (1997): industry, 27%; agriculture and forestry, 23%; other, 50% (1996). **Industries:** oil, coal, iron ore, manganese, chromite, lead, zinc, copper, titanium, bauxite, gold, silver, phosphates, sulfur, iron and steel, nonferrous metal, tractors and other agricultural machinery, electric motors, construction materials; much of industrial capacity is shut down and/or is in need of repair. **Agriculture:** grain (mostly spring wheat), cotton, wool, livestock. **Exports:** $6.3 billion (1998 est.): oil, ferrous and nonferrous metals, chemicals, grain, wool, meat, coal. **Imports:** $7.4 billion (1998 est.): machinery and parts, industrial materials, oil and gas, consumer goods. **Major trading partners:** Russia, U.K., Ukraine, Uzbekistan, Netherlands, China, Italy, Germany, U.S., Turkey, South Korea.

Geography Kazakhstan lies in the north of the central Asian republics and is bounded by Russia in the north, China in the east, the Kyrgyzstan and Uzbekistan in the south, and the Caspian Sea and part of Turkmenistan in the west. It has almost 15,000 miles (24,000 km) of coastline on the Caspian Sea. Kazakhstan is slightly more than twice the size of Texas. The territory is mostly steppe land with hilly plains and plateaus.

Government Republic.

History The indigenous Kazakhs were a nomadic Turkic people who belonged to several divisions of Kazakh hordes. They grouped together in settlements and lived in dome-shaped tents made of felt called "yurts." Their tribes migrated seasonally to find pastures for their herds of sheep, horses, and goats. Although they had chiefs, the Kazakhs were rarely united as a single nation under one great leader. Their tribes fell under Mongol rule in the 13th century and they were dominated by Tartar khanates until the area was conquered by Russia in the 18th century.

The area became part of the Kirgiz Autonomous Republic formed by the Soviet authorities in 1920, and in 1925 this entity's name was changed to the Kazakh Autonomous Soviet Socialist Republic (Kazakh A.S.S.R.). After 1927, the Soviet government began forcing the nomadic Kazakhs to settle on collective and state farms, and the Soviets continued the czarist policy of encouraging large numbers of Russians and other Slavs to settle in the region.

Owing to the region's intensive agricultural development and its use as a testing ground for nuclear weapons by the Soviet government, serious environmental problems developed by the late 20th century. Along with the other central Asian republics, Kazakhstan obtained its independence from the collapsing Soviet Union in 1991. Kazakhstan proclaimed its membership in the Commonwealth of Independent States on Dec. 21, 1991, along with ten other former Soviet republics. In 1993, the country overwhelmingly approved the Nuclear Non-Proliferation Treaty. In 1994, the Kazakh government resolved to transfer the national capital from Almaty to Aqmola by 2000. The president restructured and consolidated many operations of the government in 1997, eliminating a third of the government ministries and agencies.

In Jan. 1999, Nursultan Nazarbayev was sworn into office for another seven years, although the election was widely criticized because an opposition leader was disqualified from running on a technicality. Despite his authoritarianism, Nazarbayev, who has ruled Kazakhstan since 1989 when it was still part of the Soviet Union, is a widely popular leader. Kazakhstan has the potential for becoming one of central Asia's richest countries because of its huge mineral resources and its liberalized economy, which encourages Western investment.

Kenya

REPUBLIC OF KENYA

National name: Jamhuri ya Kenya
President: Daniel arap Moi (1978)
Area: 224,960 sq. mi. (582,650 sq. km)
Population (2000 est.): 30,339,770 (average annual rate of natural increase: 1.5%; birth rate: 29.4/1000; infant mortality rate: 68.7/1000; density per sq. mi.: 135
Capital and largest city (1991 est.): Nairobi, 2,000,000.
Other large city: Mombasa, 600,000. **Monetary unit:** Kenyan shilling. **Languages:** English (official), Swahili (national), and several other languages spoken by 25 ethnic groups. **Ethnicity/race:** Kikuyu 22%, Luhya 14%, Luo 13%, Kalenjin 12%, Kamba 11%, Kisii 6%, Meru 6%, Asian, European, and Arab 1%, other 15%. **Religions:** Protestant, 40%; Roman Catholic, 36%; traditional, 6%; Islam, 16%, others, 2%. **Literacy rate:** 69% (1990)
Economic summary: GDP/PPP (1998 est.): $43.9 billion; $1,550 per capita. **Real growth rate:** 1.6%. **Inflation:** 2.5%. **Unemployment:** 50%. **Arable land:** 7%.
Agriculture: coffee, tea, corn, wheat, sugarcane, fruit, vegetables, dairy products, beef, pork, poultry, eggs.
Labor force: 9.2 million (1998 est.): agriculture, 75%–80%; nonagriculture, 20%–25%. **Industries:** small-scale consumer goods (plastic, furniture, batteries, textiles, soap, cigarettes, flour), agricultural products processing, oil refining, cement, tourism. **Natural resources:** gold,

limestone, soda ash, salt barytes, rubies, fluorspar, garnets, wildlife. **Exports:** $2 billion (f.o.b., 1998): tea, coffee, petroleum products. **Imports:** $3.05 billion (f.o.b., 1998): machinery and transportation equipment, consumer goods, petroleum products. **Major trading partners:** Uganda, Tanzania, U.K., Germany, U.A.E., South Africa. **Member of Commonwealth of Nations**

Geography Kenya lies across the equator in east-central Africa on the coast of the Indian Ocean. It is twice the size of Nevada. Kenya borders Somalia to the east, Ethiopia to the north, Tanzania to the south, Uganda to the west, and Sudan to the northwest. In the north, the land is arid; the southwestern corner is in the fertile Lake Victoria basin; and a length of the eastern depression of Great Rift Valley separates western highlands from those that rise from the lowland coastal strip. Large game reserves have been developed.

Government Republic.

History Paleontologists believe people may first have inhabited Kenya about 2 million years ago. In the 700s Arab seafarers established settlements along the coast, and the Portuguese took control of the area in the early 1500s. More than 40 ethnic groups reside in Kenya. Its largest group, the Kikuyu, migrated to the region at the beginning of the 18th century.

The land became a British protectorate in 1890 and a crown colony in 1920, when it went by the name British East Africa. Nationalist stirrings began in 1940s, and in 1952 the Mau Mau movement, made up of Kikuyu militants, rebelled against the government. The fighting lasted until 1956.

On Dec. 12, 1963, Kenya became fully independent. Jomo Kenyatta, a nationalist leader during the independence struggle who had been jailed by the British, became its first president. From 1964 to 1992 the country was ruled as a one-party state by the Kenya African National Union (KANU), first under Kenyatta and then under Daniel arap Moi. Demonstrations and riots pressured Moi to allow for multi-party elections in 1992.

The economy has not flourished under Daniel arap Moi's rule. In the 1990s Kenya's infrastructure began disintegrating and official graft was rampant, contributing to the withdrawal of much foreign aid. In early 1995 President Moi moved against the opposition, and ordered the arrest of anyone who insulted him. In June the renowned paleontologist Richard Leakey registered a new political party in protest of the government's policies.

A series of disasters plagued Kenya in 1997 and 1998: severe flooding destroyed roads, bridges, and crops; epidemics of malaria and cholera overwhelmed the ineffectual health care system; and ethnic clashes erupted between the Kikuyu and Kalenjin ethnic groups in the Rift Valley.

On Aug. 7, 1998, the U.S. embassy in Nairobi was bombed by terrorists, killing 243 and injuring more than 1,000. The embassy in neighboring Tanzania was bombed the same day, killing 10.

In a surprising decision, President Moi appointed his critic and political opponent Richard Leakey as cabinet secretary and head of the civil service. Some believe the president is not serious about reform but wishes to give the appearance of cleaning up Kenya's corrupt bureaucracy, hence the high profile appointment of Leakey. This third-generation white Kenyan, son of paleontologists Louis and Mary Leakey, was highly effective as head of the Kenya Wildlife Service, and is expected to introduce a greater amount of efficiency and fairness into the Kenyan government. In July 2000 the World Bank resumed loans to Kenya following a three-year suspension.

Kiribati

REPUBLIC OF KIRIBATI

President: Teburoro Tito (1994)
Area: 280 sq. mi. (717 sq. km)
Population (2000 est.): 91,985 (average annual growth rate: 2.34%); birth rate: 32.4/1000; infant mortality rate: 55.4/1000; density per sq. mi.: 329
Capital (1990): Tarawa, 25,154. **Monetary unit:** Australian dollar. **Languages:** English (official), I-Kiribati (Gilbertese). **Ethnicity/race:** Micronesian. **Religions:** Roman Catholic, 52.6%; Protestant, 40.9%. **Literacy rate:** 90%
Economic summary: GDP/PPP (1996 est.): $62 million; $800 per capita. **Real growth rate:** 1.9%. **Inflation:** –0.6%. **Unemployment:** 2%; underemployment, 70% (1992 est.). **Arable land:** n.a. **Agriculture:** copra, taro, breadfruit, sweet potatoes, vegetables, fish. **Labor force:** 7,870 economically active, not including subsistence farmers (1985 est.). **Industries:** fishing, handicrafts. **Exports:** $6.7 million (f.o.b., 1996 est.): copra, seaweed, fish. **Imports:** $37.4 million (c.i.f., 1996 est.): foodstuffs, machinery and equipment, miscellaneous manufactured goods, fuel. **Major trading partners:** U.S., Australia, New Zealand, Fiji, Japan. **Member of Commonwealth of Nations**

Geography Kiribati, formerly the Gilbert Islands, consists of three widely separated main groups of southwest Pacific islands, the Gilberts on the equator, the Phoenix Islands to the east, and the Line Islands farther east. Ocean Island, producer of phosphates until it was mined out in 1981, is also included in the 2 million square miles of ocean. Most of the islands of Kiribati are low-lying coral atolls built on a submerged volcanic chain and encircled by reefs.

Government Republic.

History Kiribati was first settled by early Austronesian-speaking peoples long before the 1st century A.D. Fijians and Tongans arrived about the 14th century and subsequently merged with the older groups to form the traditional I-Kiribati Micronesian society and culture. The islands were first sighted by British and American ships in the late 18th and early 19th centuries and the first British settlers arrived in 1837. A British protectorate since 1892, the Gilbert and Ellice Islands became a crown colony in 1915–16. Kiritimati (Christmas) Atoll became a part of the colony in 1919, the Phoenix Islands in 1937.

Tarawa and others of the Gilbert group were occupied by Japan during World War II. Tarawa was the site of one of the bloodiest battles in U.S. Marine Corps history when Marines landed in Nov. 1943 to dislodge the Japanese defenders. The Gilbert Islands and Ellice Islands (now Tuvalu) were separated in 1975 and granted internal self-government by Britain. Kiribati became independent on July 12, 1979.

Kiribati's 1995 act of moving the international date line far to the east, so that it encompassed Kiribati's Line Islands group, courted controversy. The move, which fulfilled one of President Tito's campaign promises, was intended to enable Kiribati to become the first country to reach midnight on Dec. 31, 1999 and welcome the new millennium—an event of significance for tourism. In 1999, Kiribati gained U.N. membership.

Korea, North

DEMOCRATIC PEOPLE'S REPUBLIC OF KOREA

National name: Choson Minjujuui Inmin Konghwaguk
Head of State: Kim Jong Il (1994)
Premier: Hong Song Nam (1997)
Area: 46,768 sq. mi. (120,540 sq. km)
Population (2000 est.): 21,687,550 (average annual rate of natural increase: 1.4%); birth rate: 20.4/1000; infant mortality rate: 24.3/1000; density per sq. mi.: 464
Capital and largest city (1993): Pyongyang, 2,741,260.
Monetary unit: Won. **Language:** Korean. **Ethnicity/ race:** racially homogeneous. **Religions:** Buddhism and Confucianism, religious activities almost nonexistent. **Literacy rate:** 100% (1979)
Economic summary: GDP/PPP (1998 est.): $21.8 billion; $1,000 per capita. **Real growth rate:** –5%. **Inflation:** n.a. **Unemployment:** n.a. **Arable land:** 14%. **Agriculture:** rice, corn, potatoes, soybeans, pulses, cattle, pigs, pork, eggs. **Labor force:** 9.615 million: agricultural, 36%; nonagricultural, 64%. **Industries:** military products, machine building, electric power, chemicals, mining (coal, iron ore, magnesite, graphite, copper, zinc, lead, and precious metals), metallurgy, textiles, food processing. **Natural resources:** coal, lead, tungsten, zinc, graphite, magnesite, iron ore, copper, gold, pyrites, salt, fluorspar, hydropower. **Exports:** $743 million (f.o.b., 1997 est.): minerals, metallurgical products, agricultural and fishery products, manufactures (including armaments). **Imports:** $1.83 billion (c.i.f., 1997 est.): petroleum, grain, coking coal, machinery and equipment, consumer goods. **Major trading partners:** Japan, South Korea, China, Germany, Russia.

Geography Korea is a 600-mile (966 km) peninsula jutting out from Manchuria and China (and a small portion of the U.S.S.R.) into the Sea of Japan and the Yellow Sea off eastern Asia. North Korea occupies an area slightly smaller than Pennsylvania north of the 38th parallel.

The country is almost completely covered by a series of north-south mountain ranges separated by narrow valleys. The Yalu River forms part of the northern border with Manchuria.

Government Communist dictatorship.

History The ancient history of the Korean peninsula can be traced to the Neolithic Age, when Turkic-Manchurian-Mongol peoples migrated into the region from China. The first agriculturally based settlements appeared around 6000 B.C. Some of the larger communities of this era were established along the Han-gang River near modern-day Seoul, others near Pyongyang and Pusan. According to ancient lore, Korea's earliest civilization, known as Choson, was founded in 2333 B.C. by Tan-gun.

In the 17th century, Korea became a vassal state of China and was cut off from outside contact until the Sino-Japanese War of 1894–95. Following Japan's victory, Korea was granted independence. By 1910 Korea had been annexed by Japan, which developed the country but never won over the Korean nationalists who continued to agitate for independence.

After Japan's surrender at the conclusion of World War II, the Korean peninsula was partitioned into two occupation zones, divided at the 38th parallel. The U.S.S.R. controlled the north, with the U.S. taking charge of the south. In 1948, the division was made permanent with the establishment of the separate regimes of North and South Korea. The Democratic People's Republic of Korea (North Korea) was established on May 1, 1948, with Kim Il Sung as president.

Hoping to unify the Koreas under a single Communist government, the North launched a surprise invasion of South Korea on June 25, 1950. In the following days, the U.N. Security Council condemned the attack and demanded an immediate withdrawal.

President Harry S. Truman ordered U.S. air and naval units into action to enforce the U.N. order. The British government followed suit, and soon a U.N. multinational command was set up to aid the South Koreans.

The North Korean invaders swiftly seized Seoul and surrounded the allied forces in the peninsula's southeast corner near Pusan. In a desperate bid to reverse the military situation, U.N. Commander Gen. Douglas MacArthur ordered an amphibious landing at Inchon on Sept. 15 and routed the North Korean army. MacArthur's forces pushed north across the 38th parallel, approaching the Yalu River.

Prompted by this successful counteroffensive, Communist China entered the war, forcing the U.N. troops into a headlong retreat. Seoul was lost again, then regained; ultimately the war stabilized near the 38th parallel but dragged on for two years while negotiations took place. An armistice was agreed to on July 27, 1953.

By early 1994 tensions had mounted over international inspection of North Korea's nuclear sites. Kim Il Sung's death on July 8, 1994 introduced a period of uncertainty, as his son, Kim Jong Il assumed the leadership mantle. Negotiations over the country's suspected atomic weapons dragged on, but an agreement was reached in June 1995 which included a provision for providing the North with a South Korean nuclear reactor.

The nuclear crises that characterized the mid-1990s were overshadowed when famine struck the nation's 24 million inhabitants. Two years of floods were followed by severe droughts in 1997 and 1998, causing devastating crop failures. Although international relief programs saved many people, the situation was still considered serious in 1998, with aid agencies warning that North Korea's nationalized food distribution program had virtually shut down, forcing many people to rely on bark and wild plants to sustain themselves. The severity of the famine continued in 1999. Because of lack of fuel and machinery parts, and weather conditions that have encouraged parasites, only 10% of North Korea's rice fields have been worked. Despite the staggering food crisis, hermetic North Korea remains one of the world's few remaining hard-line Communist regimes.

In Sept. 1998 North Korea launched a test missile over Japan, claiming it was simply a scientific satellite. This launch alarmed Japan and much of the rest of the world about North Korea's intentions regarding reentry into the nuclear arms race. In 1999, North Korea agreed to allow the United States to conduct ongoing inspections of a suspected nuclear development site, Kumchangri, which North Korea admits has been devised for "a sensitive military purpose." In exchange, the U.S. would increase food aid and initiate a program for bringing potato production to the country.

Antagonism between North and South Korea erupted into open aggression twice in six months in late 1998 and 1999, with South Korea hitting one North Korean vessel and sinking two others that were discovered trespassing in South Korean waters. In late summer 1999, there were signs that North Korea might test a new version of the long-range rocket it launched over Japan a year earlier.

In the fall of 1999, North Korea's four years of severe famine, which claimed an estimated 2 million to 3 million between 1995 and 1998, had begun to wane. Tension with South Korea eased dramatically in June 2000, when South Korea's president, Kim Dae Jung, met with President Kim Jong Il in Pyongyang. The summit marked the first ever meeting of the countries' two leaders. The officials signed a hopeful, yet vague, agreement that outlined plans for unification and peace, reunions of separated families, open communication between the leaders, and a visit to South Korea by Kim Jong Il.

In Aug. 2000, 100 North Koreans were reunited with family members in Seoul in the first of several planned reunions. In a July meeting with Russia's president, Vladimir Putin, President Kim said he would abandon the country's long-range missile program if other countries provided North Korea with the rockets it needs to launch satellites into space. Western nations were skeptical, though interested, in the proposal. In Sept. defense ministers from the two nations met to discuss a range of military issues, including the restoration of rail links between the north and south, which would require the clearance of thousands of landmines. Despite the thaw in tensions, U.S. military sources report North Korea has fortified its border defenses with artillery and rocket launchers in the past year.

Korea, South

REPUBLIC OF KOREA

National name: Taehan Min'guk
President: Kim Dae Jung (1998)
Prime Minister: Lee Han Dong (2000)
Area: 38,031 sq. mi. (98,480 sq. km)
Population (2000 est.): 47,470,969 (average annual rate of natural increase: 0.9%); birth rate: 15.1/1000; infant mortality rate: 7.9/1000; density per sq. mi.: 1,248
Capital and largest city (2000 est.): Seoul, 19,850,000 (metro. area). **Other large cities:** Pusan, 3,814,235; Taegu, 2,449,000; Inchon, 2,308,000 (part of Seoul metro. area). **Monetary unit:** Won. **Language:** Korean. **Ethnicity/race:** homogeneous (except for about 20,000 Chinese). **Religions (est. mid-1996):** Christian, 48.2%; Buddhist, 48.8%; Confucianist, 0.8%; Chondogyo (religion of the Heavenly Way), 0.2%; Other, 2%. **Literacy rate:** 98% (1995)
Economic summary: GDP/PPP (1998 est.): $584.7 billion; $12,600 per capita. **Real growth rate:** –6.8%. **Inflation:** 7.5% (1998). **Unemployment:** 7.9%. **Arable land:** 19%. **Agriculture:** rice, root crops, barley, vegetables, fruit, cattle, pigs, chickens, milk, eggs, fish. **Labor force:** 20 million: services and other, 52%; mining and manufacturing, 27%; agriculture, fishing, and forestry, 21% (1991). **Industries:** electronics, automobile production, chemicals, shipbuilding, steel, textiles, clothing, footwear, food processing. **Natural resources:** coal, tungsten, graphite, molybdenum, lead, hydropower. **Exports:** $133 billion (f.o.b., 1998): electronic and electrical equipment, machinery, steel, automobiles, ships, textiles, clothing, footwear, fish. **Imports:** $94 billion (c.i.f., 1998): machinery, electronics and electronic equipment, oil, steel, transport equipment, textiles, organic chemicals, grains. **Major trading partners:** U.S., EU, Japan.

Geography Slightly larger than Indiana, South Korea lies below the 38th parallel on the Korean peninsula, bordering the East Sea and the Yellow Sea. It is mountainous in the east; in the west and south are many harbors on the mainland and offshore islands.

Government Republic.

History South Korea came into being after World War II, the result of a 1945 agreement reached by the Allies at the Potsdam Conference, making the 38th parallel the boundary between a northern zone of the Korean peninsula to be occupied by the U.S.S.R. and southern zone to be controlled by U.S. forces. (For details, see Korea, North.)

Elections were held in the U.S. zone in 1948 for a national assembly, which adopted a republican constitution and elected Syngman Rhee as the nation's president. The new republic was proclaimed on Aug. 15 and was recognized as the legal government of Korea by the U.N. on Dec. 12, 1948.

On June 25, 1950, North Korean Communist forces launched a massive surprise attack on South Korea, quickly overrunning the capital, Seoul. U.S. armed intervention was ordered on June 27 by President Harry S. Truman, and on the same day the U.N. invoked military sanctions against North Korea. Gen. Douglas MacArthur was named commander of the U.N. forces. U.S. and South Korean troops fought a heroic holding action, but by the first week of Aug. were forced back to a 4,000-square-mile beachhead in southeast Korea. There they stood off superior North Korean forces until Sept. 15, when a major U.N. amphibious assault was launched deep behind Communist lines at Inchon, the port of Seoul.

By Sept. 30, U.N. forces were in complete control of South Korea. They then crossed the 38th parallel and pursued retreating Communist forces into North Korea. In late October, as U.N. forces neared the Sino-Korean border, several hundred thousand Chinese Communist troops entered the conflict, pushing MacArthur's forces back to the border between North and South Korea. By the time truce talks began on July 10, 1951, U.N. forces had crossed over the parallel again and were driving back into North Korea. Cease-fire negotiations dragged on for two years before an armistice was finally signed at Panmunjom on July 27, 1953, leaving a devastated Korea in need of large-scale rehabilitation. No official peace treaty has ever been signed between the former combatants.

Rhee, after 12 years in office, was forced to resign in 1960 amid rising discontent with his autocratic leadership. Po Sun Yun was elected to succeed him, but political instability continued. In 1961, Gen. Park Chung Hee seized power and subsequently began a program of economic reforms designed to stimulate the nation's economy. The U.S. stepped up military aid, strengthening South Korea's armed forces to 600,000 men. Park's assassination on Oct. 26, 1979, by Kim Jae Kyu, head of the Korean Central Intelligence Agency, brought a liberalizing trend as new president Choi Kyu Hah freed imprisoned dissidents.

The release of opposition leader Kim Dae Jung in Feb. 1980 sparked antigovernment demonstrations that turned into riots, which were brutally suppressed by authorities. Kim, the most visible leader of the opposition, was imprisoned again. Choi resigned on Aug. 16. Chun Doo Hwan, head of a military Special Committee for National Security Measures, was the sole candidate as the electoral college confirmed him as president on Aug. 27. In 1986–87, South Korea's opposition demanded the president be selected by direct popular vote. After weeks of protest and rioting,

Chun agreed to the demand. A split in the opposition led to Roh Tae Woo's election on Dec. 16, 1987.

In Aug. of 1996 Roh was convicted on bribery charges and Chun was convicted for bribery as well as his role in the 1979 coup and the 1980 crackdown on rioters. In 1997, an accumulation of corrupt business practices, and bad loans led to a series of bankruptcies and a massive devaluation of South Korea's currency. The political instability that followed helped former dissident Kim Dae Jung become the first South Korean president ever to be elected from the political opposition.

In 1998 the Asian economic crisis bottomed out in South Korea, and it began rebounding in 1999—the only sizable Asian economy to do so.

Antagonism between North and South Korea erupted into open aggression twice in six months in late 1998 and 1999, with South Korea hitting one North Korean vessel and sinking two others that were discovered trespassing in South Korean waters. Tensions eased dramatically in June 2000, when President Kim Dae Jung met with the North's president, Kim Jong Il, in Pyongyang. The summit marked the first ever meeting of the countries' leaders. The officials signed a hopeful, yet vague, agreement that outlined plans for unification and peace, reunions of separated families, open communication between the leaders, and a visit to South Korea by Kim Jong Il.

Prime Minister Park Tae Joon resigned in May 2000 over a financial scandal. In Aug., North and South Korean families separated since the war were reunited in Seoul. Further reunions are planned. In Sept. defense ministers from the two nations met to discuss a range of military issues, including the restoration of rail links between the north and south, which would require the clearance of thousands of landmines.

Kuwait

STATE OF KUWAIT

National name: Dawlat al Kuwayt
Emir: Sheik Jaber al-Ahmad al-Sabah (1977)
Prime Minister: Sheik Saad al-Abdullah al-Sabah (1978)
Area: 6,880 sq. mi. (17,820 sq. km)
Population (2000 est.): 1,973,572 (average annual rate of natural increase: 1.96%); birth rate: 22/1000; infant mortality rate: 11.6/1000; density per sq. mi.: 287
Capital (1990 est.): Kuwait, 151,060. **Other large city (1993 est.):** as-Salimiyah, 116,104. **Monetary unit:** Kuwaiti dinar. **Languages:** Arabic and English. **Ethnicity/race:** Kuwaiti 45%, other Arab 35%, South Asian 9%, Iranian 4%, other 7%. **Religions:** Islam 85% (Shi'ite 30%, Sunni 45%, other 10%); Christian, Hindu, Parsi, and other 15% (1990). **Literacy rate:** 73% (1990)
Economic summary: GDP/PPP (1998 est.): $43.7 billion; $22,700 per capita. **Real growth rate:** –5%. **Inflation:** 1% (1997 est.). **Unemployment:** 1.8% (official 1996 est.). **Agriculture:** practically no crops; fish. **Labor force:** 1.1 million (1996 est.): government and social services, 50%; services, 40%; industry and agriculture, 10%. **Industries:** petroleum, petrochemicals, desalination, food processing, construction materials, salt, construction. **Natural resources:** petroleum, fish, shrimp, natural gas. **Exports:** $14.3 billion (f.o.b., 1997): oil and refined products, fertilizers. **Imports:** $7.8 billion (f.o.b., 1996): food, construction materials, vehicles and parts, clothing. **Major trading partners:** U.S., Japan, India, South Korea, Singapore, U.K., Germany, Italy.

Geography Kuwait is situated northeast of Saudi Arabia at the northern end of the Persian Gulf, south of Iraq. It is slightly larger than Hawaii. The low-lying desert land is mainly sandy and barren.

Government Kuwait is a constitutional monarchy, governed by the al-Sabah family.

History Kuwait is believed to have been part of an early civilization in the 3rd millennium B.C. and to have traded with Mesopotamian cities. Archeological and historical traces disappeared around the first millennium B.C. At the beginning of the 18th century A.D., the 'Anizah tribe of central Arabia founded Kuwait City, which became its autonomous sheikdom by 1756. 'Abd Rahim of the Al Sabah became the first sheik, and his descendants continue to rule Kuwait today. In the late 18th and early 19th century the sheikdom belonged to the fringes of the Ottoman Empire. Kuwait obtained British protection in 1897 when the sheik feared that the Turks would expand their hold over the area. In 1961, Britain ended the protectorate, giving Kuwait independence, but agreed to give military aid on request. Iraq immediately threatened to occupy the area, and the British sent troops to defend Kuwait. Soon afterward the Arab League sent in troops, replacing the British. Iraq's claim was dropped when the Arab League recognized Kuwait's independence on July 20, 1961. Kuwait typically followed a neutral and mediatory policy among Arab states.

Oil was discovered there in the 1930s, and Kuwait proved to have 20% of the world's known oil resources. Since 1946 it has been the world's second-largest oil exporter. The sheik, who receives half the profits, devotes most of them to the education, welfare, and modernization of his kingdom. In 1966, Sheik Sabah designated a relative, Jaber al-Ahmad al-Sabah, as his successor. By 1968, the sheikdom had established a model welfare state, and it sought to establish dominance among the sheikdoms and emirates of the Persian Gulf.

In July 1990, Iraqi president Hussein blamed Kuwait for falling oil prices. After a failed Arab mediation attempt to solve the dispute peacefully, Iraq invaded Kuwait on Aug. 2, 1990, set up a pro-Iraqi provisional government, and drained Kuwait of its economic resources. A coalition of Arab and Western military forces drove Iraqi troops from Kuwait in a mere four days, from Feb. 23–27, ending the Persian Gulf War. The emir returned to his country from Saudi Arabia in mid-March. Martial law, in effect since the end of the Gulf War, ended in late June. The U.S. sent 2,400 troops to the country in Aug. 1992 as part of a training exercise but this was widely interpreted as a show of strength to Saddam Hussein.

The general election of Oct. 1992 was a success for supporters of a return to Islamic law. A political independent was named speaker of the Parliament, and the opposition held 31 of the 50 seats. Iraqi "training" maneuvers near the Kuwaiti border in Oct. 1994 renewed fears of aggression in the country. A Kuwaiti appeal brought the quick deployment of U.S. and British troops and equipment. In 1999, the emir gave women the right to vote and run for Parliament, the only country on the conservative Arabian peninsula to do so besides Qatar, which gave women the vote in the same year. Later in 1999, however, Parliament defeated the ruler's decree.

Kyrgyzstan

THE KYRGYZ REPUBLIC

President: Askar Akaev (1990)
Prime Minister: Amangeldy Muraliyev (1999)
Area: 76,000 sq. mi. (198,500 sq. km)
Population (2000 est.): 4,685,230; (Kyrgyz, 52%; Russian, 21%; Uzbek, 13%, other, 14%); average annual rate of natural increase: 1.7%; birth rate: 26.3/1000; infant mortality rate: 77.1/1000; density per sq. mi.: 62
Capital and largest city (1994): Bishkek (formerly Frunze), 631,000. **Other large city (1994):** Osh 213,000. **Monetary unit:** Som. **Languages:** Kyrgyz (official); Russian is de facto second language of communication. **Ethnicity/race:** Kirghiz 52.4%, Russian 18%, Uzbek 12.9%, Ukrainian 2.5%, German 2.4%, other 11.8%. **Religions:** Muslim 75%, Russian Orthodox 20%, other 5%. **Literacy rate:** 97% (1989)
Economic summary: GDP/PPP (1998 est.): $9.8 billion; $2,200 per capita. **Real growth rate:** 1.8%. **Inflation:** 18.4%. **Unemployment:** 6%. **Natural resources:** abundant hydroelectric potential, significant deposits of gold and rare earth metals, locally exploitable coal, oil, and natural gas, other deposits of nepheline, mercury, bismuth, lead, and zinc. **Industries:** small machinery, textiles, food processing, cement, shoes, sawn logs, refrigerators, furniture, electric motors, gold, rare earth metals. **Agriculture:** tobacco, cotton, potatoes, vegetables, grapes, fruit and berries, sheep, goats, cattle, wool. **Labor force:** 1.7 million: agriculture and forestry, 40%; industry and construction, 19%; other, 41% (1995 est.). **Exports:** $630 million (1998 est.): cotton, wool, meat, tobacco, gold, mercury, uranium, hydropower, machinery, shoes. **Imports:** $670 million (1998 est.): grain, lumber, industrial products, ferrous metals, fuel, machinery, textiles, footwear. **Major trading partners:** China, U.K., F.S.U., Turkey, Cuba, U.S., Germany.

Geography Kyrgyzstan (formerly Kirghizia) is a rugged country with the Tien Shan mountain range covering approximately 95% of the whole territory. The mountaintops are covered with perennial snow and glaciers. Kyrgyzstan borders Kazakhstan on the north and northwest, Uzbekistan in the southwest, Tajikistan in the south, and China in the southeast. The republic is the same size in area as the state of Nebraska.

Government Constitutional republic.

History The native Kyrgyz are a Turkic people who in ancient times first settled in the Tien Shan mountains. They were traditionally pastoral nomads. There was extensive Russian colonization in the 1900s and Russian settlers were given much of the best agricultural land. This led to an unsuccessful and disastrous revolt by the Kyrgyz people in 1916. Kyrgyzstan became part of the Soviet Federated Socialist Republic in 1924, and was made an autonomous republic in 1926. It became a constituent republic of the U.S.S.R. in 1936. The Soviets forced the Kyrgyz to abandon their nomadic culture and brought modern farming and industrial production techniques into their society. It has greatly changed their traditional way of life.

Kyrgyzstan proclaimed its independence from the Soviet Union on Aug. 31, 1991. On Dec. 21, 1991, Kyrgyzstan joined the Commonwealth of Independent States. The country joined the U.N. and the IMF in 1992 and adopted a shock-therapy economic program. Voters endorsed market reforms in a referendum held in Jan. 1994, and in 1996, referendum voters overwhelmingly endorsed proposed constitutional changes that enhanced the power of the president. Representatives of the country along with those of Russia, China, Kazakhstan, and Tajikistan signed a non-aggression agreement in April 1996. In March 1997, Russian border control was extended until the end of the year as authorities in Kyrgyzstan grew increasingly concerned about the growth of the illegal narcotics trade in the country.

Since 1999, several groups of radical Islamic gunmen, believed to be from Uzbekistan or Tajikistan, have led raids and kidnappings from camps in Kyrgyzstan's mountains.

Laos

LAO PEOPLE'S DEMOCRATIC REPUBLIC

President: Khamtai Siphandon (1998)
Prime Minister: Sisavat Keobounphan (1998)
Area: 91,429 sq. mi. (236,800 sq. km)
Population (2000 est.): 5,497,459 (average annual rate of natural increase: 2.5%); birth rate: 38.3/1000; infant mortality rate: 94.8/1000; density per sq. mi.: 60
Capital and largest city (1990): Vientiane, 442,000.
Monetary unit: Kip. **Languages:** Lao (official), French, English. **Ethnicity/race:** Lao Loum (lowland) 68%, Lao Theung (upland) 22%, Lao Soung (highland) including the Hmong ("Meo") and the Yao (Mien) 9%, ethnic Vietnamese/Chinese 1%. **Religions:** Buddhist, 85%; animist and other, 15%. **Literacy rate:** 45% (1988)
Economic summary: GDP/PPP (1998 est.): $6.6 billion; $1,260 per capita. **Real growth rate:** 4%. **Inflation:** 112%. **Unemployment:** 5.7% (1997 est.). **Arable land:** 3%. **Agriculture:** sweet potatoes, vegetables, corn, coffee, sugarcane, tobacco, cotton, water buffalo, pigs, cattle, poultry. **Labor force:** 1–1.5 million: agriculture, 80% (1997 est.). **Industries:** tin and gypsum mining, timber, electric power, agricultural processing, construction, clothing. **Natural resources:** timber, hydropower, gypsum, tin, gold, gemstones. **Exports:** $330 million (f.o.b., 1998): wood products, clothing, electricity, coffee, tin. **Imports:** $630 million (c.i.f., 1998): machinery and equipment, vehicles, fuel. **Major trading partners:** Vietnam, Thailand, Germany, France, Japan, China, Singapore.

Geography A landlocked nation in Southeast Asia occupying the northwestern portion of the Indochinese peninsula, Laos is surrounded by China, Vietnam, Cambodia, Thailand, and Burma. It is twice the size of Pennsylvania.

Laos is a mountainous country, especially in the north, where peaks rise above 9,000 feet (2,800 m). Dense forests cover the northern and eastern areas. The Mekong River, which forms the boundary with Burma and Thailand, flows entirely through the country for 932 miles (1,500 km) of its course.

Government Communist state.

History The Lao people migrated into Laos from southern China from the 8th century A.D. onward. In the 14th century the first Laotian state was founded, the Lan Xang kingdom, which ruled Laos until it split into three separate kingdoms in 1713. During the 18th century the three kingdoms came under Siamese (Thai) rule, and in 1893 became a French protectorate. Its territory was incorporated into the union of Indochina. A strong nationalist movement developed during World War II, but France reestablished control in 1946 and made the king of Luang Prabang constitutional monarch of all Laos. France granted semiautonomy in 1949 and then, spurred by the Viet Minh rebellion in Vietnam, full independence within the French Union in 1950.

In 1951, Prince Souphanouvong organized the Pathet Lao, a Communist independence movement, in North Vietnam. Viet Minh and Pathet Lao forces invaded central Laos, and civil war resulted. By the Geneva agreements of 1954 and an armistice of 1955, two northern provinces were given to the Pathet Lao; the rest went to the royal regime. Full sovereignty was given to the kingdom by the Paris agreements of Dec. 29, 1954. In 1957, Prince Souvanna Phouma, the royal premier, and the Pathet Lao leader, Prince Souphanouvong, the premier's half-brother, agreed to reestablishment of a unified government, with Pathet Lao participation and integration of Pathet Lao forces into the royal army. The agreement broke down in 1959, and armed conflict began anew.

In 1960, the struggle became three-way as Gen. Phoumi Nosavan, controlling the bulk of the royal army, set up in the south a pro-Western revolutionary government headed by Prince Boun Gum. General Phoumi took Vientiane in December, driving Souvanna Phouma into exile in Cambodia. The Soviet bloc supported Souvanna Phouma. In 1961, a cease-fire was arranged and the three princes agreed to a coalition government headed by Souvanna Phouma.

But North Vietnam, the U.S. (in the form of Central Intelligence Agency personnel), and China remained active in Laos after the settlement. North Vietnam used a supply line (Ho Chi Minh Trail) running down the mountain valleys of eastern Laos into Cambodia and South Vietnam, particularly after the U.S.–South Vietnamese incursion into Cambodia in 1970 stopped supplies via Cambodian seaports.

An agreement reached in 1973 revived coalition government. The Communist Pathet Lao seized complete power in 1975, installing Souphanouvong as president and Kaysone Phomvihane as premier. Since then other parties and political groups have been moribund and most of their leaders have fled the country. The monarchy was abolished on Dec. 2, 1975, when the Pathet Lao ousted a coalition government and King Sisavang Vatthana abdicated.

The Supreme People's Assembly in Aug. 1991 adopted a new constitution that dropped all references to socialism but retained the one-party state. In addition to implementing market-oriented policies, the country has passed laws governing property, inheritance, and contracts.

During 1995 the country began making more diplomatic overtures toward its neighbors. Economic agreements were reached with Burma, and Laos's border disputes with Thailand in the 1980s gave way to warmer relations. The U.S. announced a lifting of its ban on aid to the nation.

By most international estimates, Laos is one of the ten poorest countries in the world. The subsistence farmers who make up more than 80% of the population have been plagued with bad agricultural conditions—alternately flood or drought—since 1993.

Latvia

THE REPUBLIC OF LATVIA

National name: Latvija
President: Vaira Vike-Freiberga (1999)
Prime Minister: Andris Berzins (2000)
Area: 25,400 sq. mi. (64,100 sq. km)
Population (2000 est.): 2,404,926; average annual rate of natural increase: –0.7%; birth rate: 7.8/1000; infant mortality rate: 15.7/1000; density per sq. mi.: 95

Capital and largest city (1993 est.): Riga, 874,000.
Other large cities: Daugavpils, 125,000; Liepaja, 108,000. **Monetary unit:** Lats. **Language:** Latvian.
Ethnicity/race: Latvian 51.8%, Russian 33.8%, Belarussian 4.5%, Ukrainian 3.4%, Polish 2.3%, other 4.2%. **Religions:** Lutheran, Catholic, and Baptist.
Literacy: 99% (1989)
Economic summary: GDP/PPP (1998 est.): $9.7 billion; $4,100 per capita. **Real growth rate:** 3.6%. **Inflation:** 4.7%. **Unemployment:** 9.2%. **Labor force:** 1.4 million (1997): services, 43%; industry, 41%; agriculture and forestry, 16% (1990). **Industries:** buses, vans, street and railroad cars, synthetic fibers, agricultural machinery, fertilizers, washing machines, radios, electronics, pharmaceuticals, processed food, textiles; dependent on imports for energy, raw materials, and intermediate products. **Agriculture:** grain, sugar beets, potatoes, vegetables, beef, milk, eggs, fish.
Natural resources: amber, peat, limestone, dolomite.
Exports: $1.9 billion (f.o.b., 1998): wood and wood products, machinery and equipment, textiles, foodstuffs. **Imports:** $3.1 billion (f.o.b., 1998): fuel, machinery and equipment, chemicals. **Major trading partners:** Russia, Germany, U.K., Sweden, Finland.

Geography Latvia borders Estonia on the north, Lithuania in the south, the Baltic Sea with the Gulf of Riga in the west, Russia in the east, and Belarus in the southeast. Latvia is largely a fertile lowland with numerous lakes and hills to the east.

Government Parliamentary democracy.

History Baltic tribespeople settled along the Baltic Sea, and lacking a centralized government, fell prey to more powerful peoples. In the 13th century they were overcome by the Livonian Brothers of the Sword, a German order of knights whose mission was to conquer and Christianize the Baltic region. The land became part of the state of Livonia until 1561. Germans made up the ruling class of Livonia and Baltic tribes made up the peasantry, and German became the official language of the region.

Poland conquered the territory in 1562, until Sweden took over the land in 1629, and ruled over it until 1721. Then the land passed to Russia. From that time until 1918, the Latvians remained Russian subjects, although they preserved their language, customs, and folklore.

The Russian Revolution of 1917 gave them their opportunity for freedom, and the Latvian republic was proclaimed on Nov. 18, 1918. The republic lasted little more than 20 years. Plagued by political instability, Latvia essentially became a dictatorship under President Karlis Ulmanis. It was occupied by Russian troops in 1939 and incorporated into the Soviet Union in 1940. Latvia allied itself with Germany in World War II, and German armies occupied the nation from 1941 to 1943–44. Of the 70,000 Jews living in Latvia during the war, 95% were massacred. In 1944, Russia again took control of Latvia.

Latvia was one of the most economically well-off and industrialized parts of the Soviet Union. When a coup against Soviet president Mikhail Gorbachev failed in 1991, the Baltic nations saw an opportunity to free themselves from Soviet domination and, following the actions of Lithuania and Estonia, Latvia declared its independence on Aug. 21, 1991. European and most other nations quickly recognized their independence, and on Sept. 2, 1991, President Bush announced full diplomatic recognition for Latvia, Estonia, and Lithuania. The Soviet Union recognized Latvia's independence on Sept. 6, and U.N. membership followed on Sept. 17, 1991.

Because Latvians' ethnic identity had been quashed throughout its history by foreign rulers, the new Latvian republic set up strict citizenship laws, limiting citizenship to ethnic Latvians and to those who had lived in the region before Soviet rule in 1940. This denied about 452,000 of the country's 740,000 ethnic Russians of citizenship.

Latvia's bid to join the European Union was not accepted in talks that began in 1997. In addition to improving its administrative systems, Latvia was told that it had to speed up naturalization of minorities, in particular its large number of Russians. In 1998, a referendum passed easing the citizenship rules, although it was still necessary to be competent in the Latvian language, which many believe is unreasonable to expect of older or poorly educated ethnic Russians. Latvia's admission to the EU and NATO was still under consideration in 1999.

Lebanon

REPUBLIC OF LEBANON

National name: Al-Joumhouriya al-Lubnaniya
President: Émile Lahoud (1998)
Premier: Selim al-Hoss (1998)
Area: 4,015 sq. mi. (10,400 sq. km)
Population (2000 est.): 3,578,036 (average annual rate of natural increase: 1.4%); birth rate: 20.3/1000; infant mortality rate: 29.3/1000; density per sq. mi.: 891
Capital and largest city (1991 est.): Beirut, 1,100,000.
Other large cities: Tripoli, 240,000; Sidon, 100,000.
Monetary unit: Lebanese pound. **Languages:** Arabic (official), French, English. **Ethnicity/race:** Arab 95%, Armenian 4%, other 1%. **Religions:** Islam, 60%; Christian, 40% (17 recognized sects); Judaism negl. (1 sect). **Literacy rate:** 80% (1990)
Economic summary: GDP/PPP (1998 est.): $15.8 billion; $4,500 per capita. **Real growth rate:** 3%. **Inflation:** 5%. **Unemployment:** 18% (1997 est.). **Arable land:** 21%. **Agriculture:** citrus, grapes, tomatoes, apples, vegetables, potatoes, olives, tobacco, hemp (hashish), sheep, goats. **Labor force:** 1 million, plus as many as 1 million foreign workers (1996 est.): services, 62%; industry, 31%; agriculture, 7% (1997 est.). **Industries:** banking, food processing, jewelry, cement, textiles, mineral and chemical products, wood and furniture products, oil refining, metal fabricating. **Exports:** $711 million (f.o.b. 1997): foodstuffs and tobacco, 20%; textiles, 12%; chemicals, 11%; metal and metal products, 11%; electrical equipment and products, 10%; jewelry, 10%; paper and paper products, 8%. **Imports:** $7.5 billion (c.i.f. 1997): foodstuffs, 29%; machinery and transport equipment, 28%; consumer goods, 18%; chemicals, 9%; textiles, 5%; metals, 5%; fuel, 3%; agricultural food, 3%. **Major trading partners:** Saudi Arabia, U.A.E., France, Syria, U.S., Kuwait, Jordan, Turkey, Italy, Germany, Switzerland, Japan, U.K.

Geography Lebanon lies at the eastern end of the Mediterranean Sea north of Israel and west of Syria. It is four-fifths the size of Connecticut.

The Lebanon Mountains, which parallel the coast on the west, cover most of the country, while on the eastern border is the Anti-Lebanon range. Between the two lies the Bekaa Valley, the principal agricultural area.

Government Republic.

History After World War I, France was given a League of Nations mandate over Lebanon and its neighbor Syria, which together had previously been a single political unit in the Ottoman Empire. France divided them in 1920 into separate colonial administrations, drawing a border that separated predominantly Muslim Syria from the kaleidoscope of religious communities in Lebanon where Maronite Christians were then dominant. After 20 years of the French mandate regime, Lebanon's independence was proclaimed on Nov. 26, 1941, but full independence came in stages. Under an agreement between representatives of Lebanon and the French National Committee of Liberation, most of the powers exercised by France were transferred to the Lebanese government on Jan. 1, 1944. The evacuation of French troops was completed in 1946.

According to the National Pact, different religious communities are represented in the government by having a Maronite Christian president, a Sunni Muslim prime minister, and a Shi'ite National Assembly speaker. The arrangement worked for two decades. Civil war broke out in 1958, with Muslim factions led by Kamal Jumblat and Saeb Salam rising in insurrection against the Lebanese government headed by President Camille Chamoun, a Maronite Christian favoring close ties to the West. At Chamoun's request, President Eisenhower on July 15 sent U.S. troops to reestablish the government's authority.

Clan warfare between various religious factions in Lebanon goes back centuries. The hodgepodge includes Maronite Christians, who since independence have dominated the government; Sunni Muslims, who have prospered in business and shared political power; the Druze, who hold a faith incorporating aspects of Islam and Gnosticism; and Shi'ite Muslims.

A new—and bloodier—Lebanese civil war that broke out in 1975 resulted in the addition of still another ingredient in the brew—the Syrians. In the fighting between Lebanese factions, 40,000 Lebanese were estimated to have been killed and 100,000 wounded between March 1975 and Nov. 1976. At that point, a Syrian-dominated Arab Deterrent Force intervened and brought large-scale fighting to a halt.

Palestinian guerrillas staging raids on Israel from Lebanese territory drew punitive Israeli raids on Lebanon, and two large-scale Israeli invasions. The Israelis withdrew in June after the U.N. Security Council created a 6,000-man peacekeeping force for the area, called UNIFIL. As they departed, the Israelis turned their strong points over to a Christian militia that they had organized, instead of to the U.N. force.

The second Israeli invasion came on June 6, 1982, and this time it was total. It was in response to an assassination attempt by Palestinian terrorists on the Israeli ambassador in London. As a stronghold of the PLO, Lebanon became the Israelis' target. Israel's government had complained that Lebanon had countenanced the presence of these militant Palestinians.

A U.S. envoy negotiated the dispersal of most of the PLO to other Arab nations and Israel pulled back some of its forces. The violence seemed to have come to an end when, on Sept. 14, Bashir Gemayel, the 34-year-old president-elect, was killed by a bomb that destroyed the headquarters of his Christian Phalangist Party.

The day after Gemayel's assassination, Israeli troops moved into West Beirut in force. On Sept. 17 it was revealed that Christian militiamen had massacred hundreds of Palestinians in two refugee camps, but Israel denied responsibility. On Sept. 20, Amin Gemayel, older brother of Bashir Gemayel, was elected president by the Parliament.

The massacre in the refugee camps prompted the return of a multinational peacekeeping force composed of U.S. Marines and British, French, and Italian soldiers. Their mandate was to support the central Lebanese government, but they soon found themselves drawn into the struggle for power between different Lebanese factions. During their stay in Lebanon, 260 U.S. Marines and about 60 French soldiers were killed, most of them in suicide bombings of the Marine and French army compounds on Oct. 23, 1983. The multinational force left in the spring of 1984.

In July 1986, Syrian observers took position in Beirut to monitor a peacekeeping agreement. The agreement broke down and fighting between Shi'ite and Druze militia in West Beirut became so intense that Syrian troops moved in force in Feb. 1987, suppressing militia resistance.

In early 1991 the Lebanese government, backed by Syria, attempted to regain control over the south and disband all private militias, thereby ending the 16-year civil war. These conflicts destroyed much of the infrastructure and industry of Lebanon.

In the general elections of Aug. 1992 most Christians abstained from voting, demanding that Syrian forces first leave the country. The new legislature consisted of mostly pro-Syrian members. The largest Christian party was further weakened when in Jan. 1993 it appeared to split into two factions.

In June 1999, just before Israeli prime minister Benjamin Netanyahu left office, Israel bombed Southern Lebanon, its most severe attack on the country since 1996. In May 2000, the new prime minister, Ehud Barak, withdrew Israeli troops after 22 years of occupation.

In Sept. 2000, opposition party candidates allied with former prime minister Rafik Hariri won a landslide victory in parliamentary elections, in which Lebanon's severe recession was a major issue. The results removed Prime Minister Salim Hoss from office and increased chances that Hariri will replace him. Hoss agreed to support Hariri on Sept. 12, but President Emile Lahoud, who appoints the prime minister, has continued to oppose Hariri. Hariri stepped down as prime minister two years ago during a power struggle with Lahoud. Syria is unlikely to oppose Hariri, a construction billionaire with large holdings in Syria, and a personal friend of Syrian president Assad.

Lesotho

KINGDOM OF LESOTHO

Sovereign: King Letsie III (1990)
Prime Minister: Pakalitha Mosisili (1998)
Area: 11,720 sq. mi. (30,350 sq. km)
Population (2000 est.): 2,143,141 (average annual rate of natural increase: 1.7%); birth rate: 31.7/1000; infant mortality rate: 83/1000; density per sq. mi.: 183
Capital and largest city (1992): Maseru (1992), 170,000. **Monetary unit:** Loti. **Languages:** English and Sesotho (official); also Zulu and Xhosa. **Ethnicity/race:** Sotho 99.7%, Europeans 1,600, Asians 800. **Religions:** Christian, 80%; indigenous beliefs; Muslim; and Bahai. **Literacy rate:** 56% (1966)
Economic summary: GDP/PPP (1997 est.): $5.1 billion; $2,400 per capita. **Real growth rate:** 10%. **Inflation:** 8% (1997 est.). **Unemployment:** substantial unemployment and underemployment affecting more than half of the labor force (1996 est.). **Arable land:** 11%. **Agriculture:** corn, wheat, pulses, sorghum, barley, livestock. **Labor force:** 689,000: subsistence agriculture, 86%. **Natural resources:** water, agricultural and grazing land, some diamonds and other minerals. **Industries:** food, beverages, textiles, handicrafts, construction, tourism. **Exports:** $200 million (f.o.b., 1997 est.): manufactures, 65% (clothing, footwear, road vehicles); wool and mohair, 7%; food and live animals, 7%. **Imports:** $880 million (f.o.b., 1997 est.): food, building materials, vehicles, machinery, medicines, petroleum products. **Major trading partners:** Southern African Customs Union (SACU), North America, EU, Asia. **Member of Commonwealth of Nations**

Geography Mountainous Lesotho, the size of Maryland, is surrounded by the Republic of South Africa in the east-central part of that country except for short borders on the east and south with two discontinuous units of the Republic of Transkei. The Drakensberg Mountains in the east are Lesotho's principal chain. Elsewhere the region consists of rocky tableland.

Government Constitutional monarchy.

History

Lesotho (formerly Basutoland) was constituted a native state under British protection by a treaty signed with the native chief Moshoeshoe in 1843. It was annexed to Cape Colony in 1871, but in 1884 it was restored to direct control by the Crown. The colony of Basutoland became the independent nation of Lesotho on Oct. 4, 1966, with King Moshoeshoe II as sovereign.

In the 1970 elections, Ntsu Mokhehle, head of the Basutoland Congress Party, claimed a victory, but Prime Minister Leabua Jonathan declared a state of emergency, suspended the constitution, and arrested Mokhehle. King Moshoeshoe II returned after a compromise with Jonathan in which the new constitution would name him head of state but forbid his participation in politics.

After the king refused to approve the replacement in Feb. 1990 of individuals dismissed by Justin Metsino Lekhanya, the chairman of the Military Council, the latter stripped the king of his executive power. Then in early March Lekhanya sent the king into exile. In November the king was dethroned, and his son was sworn in as King Letsie III.

Lekhanya was forced to resign in April 1991, and Col. Ramaema became the new chairman in May. In Jan. 1995 the crown reverted to the father of Letsie III, Moshoeshoe II. Letsie again became crown prince. In 1996, however, King Moshoeshoe died in an automobile accident, and Letsie again assumed the throne.

In fall 1998, hundreds of demonstrators protested for weeks in front of the king's palace, claiming voting fraud in the May elections that put Prime Minister Pakalitha Mosisili in power. They demanded that the government step down and hold new elections. Troops from South African and Botswana entered the country to stop the riots and put down an army mutiny.

In Feb. 2000 King Letsie III married a commoner, Karabo Motsoeneng, in a lavish $1.5 million ceremony.

Liberia

REPUBLIC OF LIBERIA

President: Charles Taylor (1997)
Area: 43,000 sq. mi. (111,370 sq. km)
Population (2000 est.): 3,164,156 (average annual rate of natural increase: 3.06%); birth rate: 47.2/1000; infant mortality rate: 134.6/1000; density per sq. mi.: 74

Capital and largest city (1993 est.): Monrovia, 1,000,000. **Monetary unit:** Liberian dollar. **Languages:** English (official) and tribal dialects. **Ethnicity/race:** indigenous African tribes 95% (including Kpelle, Bassa, Gio, Kru, Grebo, Mano, Krahn, Gola, Gbandi, Loma, Kissi, Vai, and Bella), Americo-Liberians 5% (descendants of former slaves). **Religions:** traditional, 70%; Christian, 10%; Islam, 20%. **Literacy rate:** 40% (1990) **Economic summary: GDP/PPP** (1998 est.): $2.8 billion; $1,000 per capita. **Real growth rate:** n.a. **Inflation:** n.a. **Unemployment:** 70%. **Arable land:** 1%. **Agriculture:** rubber, coffee, cocoa, rice, cassava (tapioca), palm oil, sugarcane, bananas, sheep, goats, timber. **Labor force:** agriculture, 70%. **Industries:** rubber processing, palm oil processing, diamonds. **Natural resources:** iron ore, timber, diamonds, gold. **Exports:** $1.1 billion (f.o.b., 1998 est.): diamonds, iron ore, rubber, timber, coffee. **Imports:** $3.65 billion (f.o.b., 1998 est.): fuel, chemicals, machinery, transportation equipment, manufactured goods, rice and other foodstuffs. **Major trading partners:** Belgium, Norway, Ukraine, Singapore, South Korea, Japan, Italy.

Geography Lying on the Atlantic in the southern part of West Africa, Liberia is bordered by Sierra Leone, Guinea, and Côte d'Ivoire. It is comparable in size to Tennessee.

Most of the country is a plateau covered by dense tropical forests, which thrive under an annual rainfall of about 160 inches a year.

Government Republic.

History Africa's first republic, Liberia was founded in 1822 as a result of the efforts of the American Colonization Society to settle freed American slaves in West Africa. The society contended that the immigration of blacks to Africa was an answer to the problem of slavery as well as to what they felt was the incompatibility of the races. Over the course of forty years, about 12,000 slaves were voluntarily relocated. Originally called Monrovia, the colony became the Free and Independent Republic of Liberia in 1847.

The English-speaking Americo-Liberians, descendants of former American slaves, make up only 5% of the population, but have historically dominated the intellectual and ruling class. Liberia's indigenous population is primarily composed of Mande, Kwa, and Mel peoples.

The government of Africa's first republic was modeled after that of the United States, and Joseph Jenkins Roberts of Virginia was elected the first president. Ironically, Liberia's constitution denied indigenous Liberians equal rights with the lighter-skinned American emigrants and their descendants.

After 1920, considerable progress was made toward opening up the interior, a process that was spurred in 1951 by the establishment of a 43-mile (69-km) railroad to the Bomi Hills from Monrovia. In July 1971, while serving his sixth term as president, William V. S. Tubman died following surgery and was succeeded by his long-time associate, Vice President William R. Tolbert, Jr.

Tolbert was ousted in a military coup carried out April 12, 1980, by Master Sgt. Samuel K. Doe, who was backed by the U.S. government. A rebellion led by Charles Taylor, a former Doe aide, started in Dec. 1989 and, with the help of Côte d'Ivoire and Burkina Faso, took control of Liberia's key population and economic centers by mid-July 1990. His three attempts to take the capital failed, however, and the bloody civil war continued. By mid-April 1996 factional fighting by the country's warlords had destroyed any last vestige of normality and civil society.

In what was considered by international observers a free election, Charles Taylor won 75.3% of the presidential vote in July 1997. Since then, however, Taylor's government has focused more on armed security rather than reconstruction of the country after its seven-year civil war. While Taylor attempts to fashion himself as a democratic political leader, his behavior remains that of a militia rebel. Heavy fighting continued during the summer of 2000, destabilizing northern Liberia.

Libya

SOCIALIST PEOPLE'S LIBYAN ARAB JAMAHIRIYA

National name: Socialist People's Libyan Arab Jamahiriya
Head of State: Col. Muammar al-Qaddafi (1969)
Secretary of the General People's Committee: Mubarak Abdallah al-Shamikh (2000)
Area: 679,536 sq. mi. (1,759,540 sq. km)
Population (2000 est.): 5,115,450; (average annual rate of natural increase: 2.4%); birth rate: 27.7/1000; infant mortality rate: 30.1/1000; density per sq. mi.: 8
Capital: Tripoli. **Largest cities (est. 1988):** Tripoli, 591,062; Benghazi, 446,250. **Monetary unit:** Libyan dinar. **Languages:** Arabic, Italian and English widely understood in major cities. **Ethnicity/race:** Berber and Arab 97%, Greeks, Maltese, Italians, Egyptians, Pakistanis, Turks, Indians, Tunisians. **Religion:** Islam. Literacy rate: 64% (1990)
Economic summary: GDP/PPP (1998 est.): $38 billion; $6,700 per capita. **Real growth rate:** –1%. **Inflation:** 24.2%. **Unemployment:** 30%. **Arable land:** 1%. **Agriculture:** wheat, barley, olives, dates, citrus, vegetables, peanuts, beef, eggs. **Labor force:** 1 million: industry, 31%; services, 27%; government, 24%; agriculture, 18%. **Industries:** petroleum, food processing, textiles, handicrafts, cement. **Natural resources:** petroleum, natural gas, gypsum. **Exports:** $6.8 billion (f.o.b., 1998 est.): crude oil, refined petroleum products, natural gas. **Imports:** $6.9 billion (c.i.f., 1998 est.): machinery, transport equipment, food, manufactured goods. **Major trading partners:** Italy, Germany, Spain, France, Turkey, Greece, Egypt, U.K., Tunisia, eastern Europe.

Geography Libya stretches along the northeastern coast of Africa between Tunisia and Algeria on the west and Egypt on the east; to the south are the Sudan, Chad, and Niger. It is one-sixth larger than Alaska. A greater part of the country lies within the Sahara. Along the Mediterranean coast and farther inland is arable plateau land.

Government Military dictatorship.

History The first inhabitants of Libya were Berber tribes. In the 7th century B.C., Phoenicians colonized the eastern section of Libya, called Tripolitania, and Greeks colonized the western portion, called Cyrenaica. Tripolitania was for a time under Carthaginian control. It became part of the Roman empire from 46 B.C. to A.D. 436, after which it was sacked by the Vandals. Cyrenaica belonged to the Roman empire from the 1st century B.C. until its decline, after which it was invaded by Arab forces in A.D. 642. Beginning in the 16th century, both Tripolitania and Cyrenaica nominally became part of the Ottoman Empire.

Tripolitania was one of the outposts for the Barbary pirates who raided Mediterranean merchant ships or required them to pay tribute. In 1801 the pasha of Tripoli raised the price of tribute, which led to the

Tripolitan war with the United States. When the peace treaty was signed on June 4, 1805, U.S. ships no longer had to pay tribute to Tripoli.

Following the outbreak of hostilities between Italy and Turkey in 1911, Italian troops occupied Tripoli. Italian sovereignty was recognized in 1912. Libyans continued to fight the Italians until 1914, by which time Italy controlled most of the land. Italy formally united Tripolitania and Cyrenaica in 1934 as the colony of Libya.

Libya was the scene of much desert fighting during World War II. After the fall of Tripoli on Jan. 23, 1943, it came under Allied administration. In 1949, the U.N. voted that Libya should become independent, and in 1951 it became the United Kingdom of Libya. Oil was discovered in the impoverished country in 1958, and eventually transformed its economy.

On Sept. 1, 1969, 27-year-old Colonel Muammar al-Qaddafi deposed the king and revolutionized the country, making it a pro-Arabic, anti-Western, Islamic republic with socialist leanings. It was also rabidly anti-Israeli. A notorious firebrand, Qaddafi aligned himself with dictators, such as Uganda's Idi Amin, and fostered anti-Western terrorism.

On Aug. 19, 1981, two U.S. Navy F-14s shot down two Soviet-made SU-22s of the Libyan air force that had attacked them in air space above the Gulf of Sidra. On March 24, 1986, U.S. and Libyan forces skirmished in the Gulf of Sidra, and two Libyan patrol boats were sunk. Qaddafi's troops also supported rebels in Chad but suffered major military reverses in 1987. A two-year-old U.S. covert policy to destabilize the Libyan government ended in failure in Dec. 1990.

On Dec. 21, 1988, a Boeing 747 exploded in flight over Lockerbie, Scotland, the result of a terrorist bomb, killing all 259 people aboard and 11 on the ground. Two Libyan intelligence agents were indicted, but Qaddafi refused to hand them over, leading to U.N.-approved trade and air traffic embargoes in 1992. On April 5, 1999, after years of negotiations, Libya surrendered the two men. The suspects, Abdel Basset Ali al-Megrahi and Lamen Khalifa Fhimah, will be tried in the Netherlands, though it will be considered Scottish soil for the duration of the trial. As a result of Libya's cooperation, the United Nations lifted sanctions against the nation, which had severely affected the Libyan economy. European companies almost immediately began to court the oil-rich nation once again.

Liechtenstein

PRINCIPALITY OF LIECHTENSTEIN

Ruler: Prince Hans Adam II (1989)
Prime Minister: Mario Frick (1993)
Area: 61 sq. mi. (160 sq. km)
Population (2000 est.): 32,207 (average annual growth rate: 0.5%); birth rate: 11.8/1000; infant mortality rate: 5.1/1000; density per sq. mi.: 528
Capital and largest city (1994): Vaduz, 5,067.
   Monetary unit: Swiss franc. **Languages:** German (official), Alemmanic dialect. **Ethnicity/race:** Alemannic 87.5%; Italian, Turkish, and other 12.5% . **Religions:** Roman Catholic 80%, Protestant 6.9%, unknown 5.6%, other 7.5%. **Literacy rate:** 100% (1981)
Economic summary: GDP/PPP (1998 est.): $730 million; $23,000 per capita. **Real growth rate:** n.a. **Inflation:** 0.5% (1997 est.). **Unemployment:** 1.6% (1997). **Arable land:** 25%. **Agriculture:** wheat, barley, maize, potatoes, livestock, dairy products. **Labor force:** 22,891 (including 13,847 foreigners): industry, trade, and building, 45%; services, 53%; agriculture, fishing, forestry, and

horticulture, 2% (1997 est.). **Industries:** electronics, metal manufacturing, textiles, ceramics, pharmaceuticals, food products, precision instruments, tourism. **Natural resources:** hydroelectric potential. **Exports:** $2.47 billion (1996): small specialty machinery, dental products, stamps, hardware, pottery. **Imports:** $917.3 million (1996): machinery, metal goods, textiles, foodstuffs, motor vehicles. **Major trading partners:** EU, EFTA (European Free Trade Association), Switzerland.

Geography Tiny Liechtenstein, not quite as large as Washington, D.C., lies on the east bank of the Rhine River south of Lake Constance between Austria and Switzerland. It consists of low valley land and Alpine peaks. Falknis (8,401 ft.; 2,561 m) and Naafkopf (8,432 ft.; 2,570 m) are the tallest.

Government Constitutional monarchy.

History The Liechtensteiners are descended from the Alemanni tribe that came into the region after A.D. 500. Founded in 1719, Liechtenstein was a member of the German Confederation from 1815 to 1866, when it became an independent principality. It abolished its army in 1868 and has managed to stay neutral and undamaged in all European wars since then. Liechtenstein still claims 1,600 sq. km of Czech territory (the royal family's ancestral home) confiscated in 1918; the Czech Republic insists that restitution does not go back before Feb. 1948, when the Communists seized power. In a referendum on July 1, 1984, male voters granted women the right to vote in national (but not local) elections—a victory for Prince Hans Adam. A treaty negotiated between EFTA (European Free Trade Association) and the EU linking the two as the European Economic Area was ratified in a Dec. 1993 vote, but Switzerland rejected it. After renegotiation the treaty was again subjected to a referendum in April 1995 and approved. Liechtenstein won a special concession limiting immigration.

Lithuania

REPUBLIC OF LITHUANIA

National name: Lietuva
President: Valdas Adamkus (1998)
Prime Minister: Andrius Kubilius (1999)
Area: 25,212 sq. mi. (65,200 sq. km)
Population (1998 est.): 3,620,756; (average annual rate of natural increase: –0.3%); birth rate: 9.8/1000; infant mortality rate: 14.7/1000; density per sq. mi.: 144
Capital and largest city (1993 est.): Vilnius, 590,100.
   Other large cities: Kaunas, 429,000; Klaipéda, 206,400. **Monetary unit:** Litas. **Languages:** Lithuanian (official), Polish, Russian. **Ethnicity/race:** Lithuanian 80.1%, Russian 8.6%, Polish 7.7%, Belarussian 1.5%, other 2.1%. **Religions:** Catholic, 85%; others include Lutheran, Russian Orthodox, Protestant, evangelical Christian Baptist, Islam, Judaism. **Literacy:** 98% (1989)
Economic summary: GDP/PPP (1998 est.): $17.6 billion; $4,900 per capita. **Real growth rate:** 4.5%. **Inflation:** 5.1%. **Unemployment:** 6.7% (Jan. 1998). **Labor force:** 1.8 million: industry and construction, 42%; agriculture and forestry, 20%; other, 38% (1997). **Natural resources:** peat. **Industries:** metal-cutting machine tools, electric motors, television sets, refrigerators and freezers, petroleum refining, shipbuilding (small ships), furniture making, textiles, food processing, fertilizers, agricultural machinery, optical equipment, electronic components, computers, amber. **Agriculture:** grain, potatoes, sugar beets, flax, vegetables, beef, milk, eggs, fish. **Exports:** $4.2 billion (f.o.b., 1998): machinery and equipment, mineral products, textiles, chemicals, foodstuffs. **Imports:** $5.9

billion (f.o.b., 1998): machinery and equipment, mineral products, chemicals, textiles, foodstuffs. **Major trading partners:** Russia, Germany, Belarus, Latvia, Ukraine, Poland, Denmark, Finland.

Geography Lithuania is situated on the eastern shore of the Baltic Sea and borders Latvia on the north, Belarus on the east and south, Poland and the Kaliningrad region of Russia on the southwest. It is a country of gently rolling hills, many forests, rivers and streams, and lakes. Its principal natural resource is agricultural land.

Government Parliamentary democracy.

History The Liths, or Lithuanians, united in the 12th century under the rule of Mindaugas, who became king in 1251. Through marriage, one of the later Lithuanian rulers became the king of Poland (Ladislaus II) in 1386, uniting the countries. In 1410, the Poles and Lithuanians defeated the powerful Teutonic Knights at Tannenberg. From the 14th to the 16th century, Poland and Lithuania made up one of medieval Europe's largest empires, stretching from the Black Sea almost to Moscow. The two countries formed a confederation for almost 200 years, and in 1569 they formally united. Russia, Prussia, and Austria partitioned Poland in 1772, 1792, and 1795. As a consequence, Lithuania came under Russian rule after the last partition. Russia attempted to emerse Lithuania in Russian culture and language, but anti-Russian sentiment continued to grow. Following World War I and the collapse of Russia, Lithuania declared independence (1918), under German protection.

The republic was then annexed by the Soviet Union in 1940. From June 1941 to 1944 it was occupied by German troops, with whom Lithuania served in World War II. Some 240,000 Jews were massacred in Lithuania during the Nazi years. In 1944 Russian again annexed Lithuania.

The Lithuanian independence movement reemerged in 1988. In 1990, Vytautas Landsbergis, the non-Communist head of the largest Lithuanian popular movement (Sajudis), was elected president. On the same day, the Supreme Council rejected Soviet rule and declared the restoration of Lithuania's independence, the first Baltic republic to take this action. Confrontation with the Soviet Union ensued along with economic sanctions, but they were lifted after both sides agreed to a face-saving compromise. Lithuania's independence was quickly recognized by major European and other nations, including the United States. The Soviet Union finally recognized the independence of the Baltic states on Sept. 6, 1991. U.N. admittance followed on Sept. 17, 1991. Successful implementation of structural and legislative reforms in Lithuania attracted greater foreign direct investments by the mid-1990s.

Luxembourg
GRAND DUCHY OF LUXEMBOURG

National name: Grand-Duché de Luxembourg
Ruler: Grand Duke Henri (2000)
Premier: Jean-Claude Juncker (1995)
Area: 999 sq. mi. (2,586 sq. km)
Population (2000 est.): 437,389 (average annual rate of natural increase: 0.4%); birth rate: 12.5/1000; infant mortality rate: 4.8/1000; density per sq. mi.: 438
Capital and largest city (1991): Luxembourg, 75,622.
Monetary units: Luxembourg franc and euro.
Languages: Luxermbourgish, French, German.
Ethnicity/race: Celtic base (with French and German

blend), Portuguese, Italian, and European (guest and worker residents). **Religions:** Roman Catholic 97%, Protestant and Jewish 3%. **Literacy rate:** 100% (1980)
Economic summary: GDP/PPP (1998 est.): $13.9 billion; $32,700 per capita. **Real growth rate:** 2.9%. **Inflation:** 1.4%. **Unemployment:** 3%. **Arable land:** 24%. **Agriculture:** barley, oats, potatoes, wheat, fruit, wine grapes, livestock products. **Labor force:** 226,500 (one-third of labor force is foreign workers, mostly from Portugal, Italy, France, Belgium, and Germany): services, 83.2%; industry, 14.3%; agriculture, 2.5%. **Industries:** banking, iron and steel, food processing, chemicals, metal products, engineering, tires, glass, aluminum. **Natural resources:** Iron ore (no longer exploited). **Exports:** $7.1 billion (f.o.b., 1996): finished steel products, chemicals, rubber products, glass, aluminum, other industrial products. **Imports:** $9.4 million (c.i.f., 1996): minerals, metals, foodstuffs, quality consumer goods. **Major trading partners:** Germany, France, Belgium, U.K., Netherlands.

Geography Luxembourg is about half the size of Delaware. The Ardennes Mountains extend from Belgium into the northern section of Luxembourg. The rolling plateau of the fertile Bon Pays is in the south.

Government Constitutional monarchy.

History Luxembourg, once part of Charlemagne's empire, became an independent state in A.D. 963, when Siegfried, count of Ardennes, became sovereign of Lucilinburhuc ("Little Fortress"). In 1060, Conrad, a descendant of Siegfried, took the title count of Luxembourg. From the 15th to the 18th century, Spain, France, and Austria held it in turn. The Congress of Vienna in 1815 made it a Grand Duchy and gave it to William I, king of the Netherlands. In 1839 the Treaty of London ceded the western part of Luxembourg to Belgium. The eastern part, continuing in personal union with the Netherlands and a member of the German Confederation, became autonomous in 1848 and a neutral territory by decision of the London Conference of 1867, governed by its grand duke. Germany occupied the duchy in World Wars I and II. Allied troops liberated the enclave in 1944.

Luxembourg joined NATO in 1949, the Benelux Economic Union (with Belgium and the Netherlands) in 1948, and the European Economic Community (later the EU) in 1957. In 1961, Prince Jean, son and heir of Grand Duchess Charlotte, was made head of state, acting for his mother. She abdicated in 1964, and Prince Jean became grand duke. Grand Duchess Charlotte died in 1985. Luxembourg's Parliament approved the "Maastricht Accord," paving the way for the economic unity of the EU in July 1992. Crown Prince Henri was to be sworn in as grand duke in Oct. 2000, replacing his father, Jean, who had been head of state for 26 years.

Macedonia
REPUBLIC OF MACEDONIA[1]

National Name: Republica Makedonija
President: Boris Trajkovski (1999)
Prime Minister: Ljupco Georgievski (1998)
Area: 9,928 sq. mi. (25,333 sq. km)
Population (2000 est.): 2,041,467 (average annual rate of natural increase: 0.6%); birth rate: 13.7/1000; infant mortality rate: 13.4/1000; density per sq. mi.: 203
Capital and largest city (1994 est.): Skopje, 444,229.
Other large cities: Bitola, 84,002; Prelep, 70,152; Kumanovo, 68,148. **Monetary unit:** Denar.
Languages: Macedonian, which uses the Cyrillic

alphabet, 70%; Albanian, 21%; Turkish, 3%; other, 6%.
Ethnicity/race: Macedonian 65%, Albanian 22%, Turkish 4%, Serb 2%, Rom (Gypsy) 3%, other 4%.
Religions (1994): Eastern Orthodox, 67%; Muslim, 30%
Economic summary: GDP/PPP (1998 est.): $2.1 billion; $1,050 per capita. **Real growth rate:** 4.5%. **Inflation:** 3%. **Unemployment:** 30%. **Labor force:** 591,773 (June 1994): manufacturing and mining, 40% (1992). **Industries:** coal, metallic chromium, lead, zinc, ferronickel, textiles, wood products, tobacco. **Agriculture:** rice, tobacco, wheat, corn, millet, cotton, sesame, mulberry leaves, citrus, vegetables, beef, pork, poultry, mutton. **Exports:** $1.2 billion (f.o.b., 1997): food, beverages, tobacco, machinery and transport equipment, other manufactured goods. **Imports:** $1.6 billion (c.i.f., 1997): machinery and equipment, chemicals, fuel. **Major trading partners:** Bulgaria, other former Yugoslav republics, Germany, Italy, Austria.

1. The U.N. recognized the Republic of Macedonia on April 8, 1993, under the temporary name the Former Yugoslav Republic of Macedonia. The U.S. recognized Macedonia as a state in Feb. 1994.

Geography Macedonia is a landlocked state in the heart of the Balkans and is slightly smaller than the state of Vermont. It is a mountainous country with small basins of agricultural land linked by rivers. The three major rivers are the Aliakmon, the Vardar, and the Strymon. The Vardar is the largest and most important river.

Government Republic.

History The Republic of Macedonia occupies the western half of the ancient Kingdom of Macedonia. Historic Macedonia was defeated by Rome and became a Roman province in 148 B.C. After the Roman Empire was divided in A.D. 395, Macedonia was intermittently ruled by the Byzantine Empire until Turkey took possession of the land in 1389. The Ottoman Turks dominated Macedonia for the next five centuries, up until 1913. During the 19th and 20th centuries, there was a constant struggle by the Balkan powers to possess Macedonia for its economic and strategic military corridors. The Treaty of San Stefano in 1878 ending the Russo-Turkish War gave the largest part of Macedonia to Bulgaria. Bulgaria lost much of its Macedonian territory when it was defeated by the Greeks and Serbs in the Second Balkan War of 1913. Most of Macedonia went to Serbia and the remainder was divided among Greece and Bulgaria.

In 1914, Serbia, which included Macedonia, joined in union with Croatia, Slovenia, and Montenegro to form the kingdom of Serbs, Croats, and Slovenes, which was renamed Yugoslavia in 1929. Bulgaria joined the Axis powers in World War II and occupied parts of Yugoslavia including Macedonia in 1941. During the occupation of their country, Macedonian resistance fighters fought a guerrilla war against the invading troops. The Yugoslavian republic was reestablished after the defeat of Germany in 1945, and in 1946, the government removed Macedonia from Serbian control and made it an autonomous Yugoslavian republic. Later, when President Tito recognized the Macedonian people as a separate nation, the Macedonians strove to develop their own culture and language separate from Bulgaria and Serbia.

In Jan. 1992, Macedonia declared its independence from Yugoslavia and asked for recognition from the European Union nations. It became a member of the UN in 1993 under the provisional name of the Former Yugoslav Republic of Macedonia (FYROM) because Greece vociferously protested Macedonia's right to the name, which is also the name of a large northern province of Greece. To Greece, the appropriation of the name implies Macedonia's interest in territorial expansion into the Greek province. Greece has imposed two trade embargoes against the country as a result.

The Macedonian government, in 1997, urged NATO to extend its peacekeeping role in the Balkans beyond its mid-1998 mandate, saying NATO troops provided a stabilizing role. Ethnic tensions between ethnic Albanians and Macedonians continued to rise during the Kosovo crisis, during which more than 140,000 refugees streamed into the country from neighboring Kosovo.

In 2000 Macedonian prime minister Ljubco Georgievski predicted that the dispute with Greece over the name Macedonia would resolve itself in the near future.

Madagascar

REPUBLIC OF MADAGASCAR

National name: Repoblikan'i Madagasikara
President and Head of State: Didier Ratsiraka (1997)
Prime Minister: Tantely Andrianarivo (1998)
Area: 226,660 sq. mi. (587,040 sq. km)
Population (2000 est.): 15,506,472 (average annual rate of natural increase: 3%); birth rate: 42.9/1000; infant mortality rate: 85.3/1000; density per sq. mi.: 68
Capital and largest city (1993 est.): Antananarivo, 1,000,000. **Monetary unit:** Malagasy franc.
Languages: Malagasy, French. **Ethnicity/race:** Malayo-Indonesian (Merina and related Betsileo), Cotiers (mixed African, Malayo-Indonesian, and Arab ancestry—Betsimisaraka, Tsimihety, Antaisaka, Sakalava), French, Indian, Creole, Comoran.
Religions: traditional, 52%; Christian, 41%; Islam, 7%.
Literacy rate: 80% (1990)
Economic summary: GDP/PPP (1997 est.): $10.3 billion; $730 per capita. **Real growth rate:** 3%. **Inflation:** 4.5% (1997). **Unemployment:** n.a. **Arable land:** 4%. **Agriculture:** coffee, vanilla, sugarcane, cloves, cocoa, rice, cassava (tapioca), beans, bananas, peanuts, livestock products. **Labor force:** 7 million (1995). **Industries:** meat processing, soap, breweries, tanneries, sugar, textiles, glassware, cement, automobile assembly plant, paper, petroleum, tourism. **Natural resources:** graphite, chromite, coal, bauxite, salt, quartz, tar sands, semiprecious stones, mica, fish. **Exports:** $170 million (f.o.b., 1997): coffee, vanilla, cloves, shellfish, sugar, petroleum products. **Imports:** $477 million (f.o.b., 1997): intermediate manufactures, capital goods, petroleum, consumer goods, food. **Major trading partners:** France, Japan, Germany, Réunion, Iran, South Africa, U.S.

Geography Madagascar lies in the Indian Ocean off the southeast coast of Africa opposite Mozambique. The world's fourth-largest island, it is twice the size of Arizona. The country's low-lying coastal area gives way to a central plateau. The once densely wooded interior has largely been cut down.

Government Multiparty republic.

History The Malagasy are of mixed Malayo-Indonesian and African-Arab ancestry. Indonesians are believed to have migrated about A.D. 700. King Andrianampoinimerina (1787–1810) ruled the major kingdom on the island, and his son, Radama I (1810–28) unified much of the island. The French made the island a protectorate in 1885, and then in 1894–95 ended the monarchy, exiling Queen Rànavàlona III to Algiers. A colonial administration was set up, to which the Comoro Islands were attached in 1908, and other territories later. In World War II, the British occupied Madagascar, which retained ties to Vichy France.

An autonomous republic within the French Community since 1958, Madagascar became an independent member of the community in 1960. In May 1973, an army coup led by Maj. Gen. Gabriel Ramanantsoa ousted Philibert Tsiranana, president since 1959. Comdr. Didier Ratsiraka, named president on June 15, 1975, announced that he would follow a socialist course and, after nationalizing banks and insurance companies, declared all mineral resources nationalized. Repression and censorship characterized his regime. Ratsiraka was reelected in 1989 in a suspicious election that led to riots as well as the formation of a multiparty system in 1990. In 1991 Ratsiraka agreed to share power with democratically minded opposition leader, Albert Zafy, who then overwhelmingly won the presidential elections in Feb. 1993. But Zafy was impeached by Parliament for abusing his constitutional powers during an economic crisis and lost the 1996 presidential election to Ratsiraka, who became president in Feb. 1997.

A succession of violent tropical storms battered Madagascar in the spring of 2000 causing massive flooding and destroying half of the vanilla crop, a major export. More than 40,000 people were left homeless and 1,300 died from a subsequent cholera epidemic.

Malawi

REPUBLIC OF MALAWI

President: Bakili Muluzi (1994)
Area: 45,747 sq. mi. (118,480 sq. km)
Population (2000 est.): 10,385,849 (average annual rate of natural increase: 1.6%); birth rate: 38.5/1000; infant mortality rate: 122.3/1000; density per sq. mi.: 227
Capital (1993 est.): Lilongwe, 260,000. **Largest city (1993 est.):** Blantyre, 399,000. **Monetary unit:** Kwacha. **Languages:** English and Chichewa (National). **Ethnicity/race:** Chewa, Nyanja, Tumbuko, Yao, Lomwe, Sena, Tonga, Ngoni, Ngonde, Asian, European. **Religions:** Christian, 75%; Islam, 20%. **Literacy rate:** 49% (1987)
Economic summary: GDP/PPP (1998 est.): $8.9 billion; $940 per capita. **Real growth rate:** 3.2%. **Inflation:** 83.4% (1995). **Unemployment:** n.a. **Arable land:** 18%. **Agriculture:** tobacco, sugarcane, cotton, tea, corn, potatoes, cassava (tapioca), sorghum, pulses, cattle, goats. **Labor force:** 3.5 million: agriculture, 86%; wage earners, 14% (1990 est.). **Industries:** tea, tobacco, sugar, sawmill products, cement, consumer goods. **Natural resources:** limestone, uranium, coal, bauxite. **Exports:** $405 million (f.o.b., 1995): tobacco, tea, sugar, coffee, peanuts, wood products. **Imports:** $475 million (f.o.b., 1995): food, petroleum products, semimanufactures, consumer goods, transportation equipment. **Major trading partners:** U.S., South Africa, Germany, Japan, Zimbabwe, U.K. **Member of Commonwealth of Nations**

Geography Malawi is a landlocked country the size of Pennsylvania in southeastern Africa, surrounded by Mozambique, Zambia, and Tanzania. Lake Malawi, formerly Lake Nyasa, occupies most of the country's eastern border. The north-south Rift Valley is flanked by mountain ranges and high plateau areas.

Government Multiparty democracy.

History Early human inhabitants of what is now Malawi date to 8000–2000 B.C. Bantu-speaking peoples migrated there between the 1st and 4th centuries A.D. A large slave trade took place in the 18th and 19th centuries, and brought Islam to the region. At the same time, missionaries introduced Christianity. Several major kingdoms were established in the precolonial period: the Maravi in 1480, the Ngonde in 1600, and in the Chikulamayembe in the 18th century.

The first European to make extensive explorations in the area was David Livingstone in the 1850s and 1860s. In 1884, Cecil Rhodes's British South African Company received a charter to develop the country. The company came into conflict with the Arab slavers in 1887–89. Britain annexed what was then called the Nyasaland territory in 1891 and made it a protectorate in 1892. Sir Harry Johnstone, the first high commissioner, used Royal Navy gunboats to wipe out the slavers.

Between 1951 and 1953 Britain combined Nyasaland with the colonies of Northern and Southern Rhodesia to form a federation, a move protested by black Africans who were wary of alignment with the ultraconservative white-minority rule in South Rhodesia.

On July 6, 1964, Nyasaland became the independent nation of Malawi. Two years later, it became a republic within the Commonwealth of Nations. Dr. Hastings K. Banda, Malawi's first prime minister, became its first president. In 1971 he became president for life, further consolidating his authoritarian rule. In addition to allowing former colonialists to retain considerable power in the country, he maintained warm relations with the white-minority government of South Africa. These policies drew heavy criticism from Malawian citizens and other African nations. In 1992 Banda faced violent protests.

Bakili Muluzi of the United Democratic Front (UDF) won the country's first free election in May 1994, ending Banda's 30-year rule. In 1999 Muluzi was reelected.

Malaysia

Paramount Ruler: His Majesty Tuanku Salehuddin Abdul Aziz Shah ibni al-Marhum Hisamuddin Alam Shah (1999)
Prime Minister: Mahathir bin Mohamad (1981)
Area: 128,328 sq. mi. (339,750 sq. km)
Population (2000 est.): 21,793,293 (average annual rate of natural increase: 2%); birth rate: 25.3/1000; infant mortality rate: 20.1/1000; density per sq. mi.: 170
Capital and largest city (1991 est.): Kuala Lumpur, 1,145,000. **Largest cities (1991 est.):** Georgetown (Pinang), 220,000; Ipoh, 382,600. **Monetary unit:** Ringgit. **Languages:** Malay (official), Chinese, Tamil, English. **Ethnicity/race:** Malay and other indigenous 59%, Chinese 32%, Indian 9%. **Religions:** Malays (all Muslims), Chinese (predominantly Buddhists), Indians (predominantly Hindus). **Literacy rate:** 78% (1990)
Economic summary: GDP/PPP (1998 est.): $215.4 billion; $10,300 per capita. **Real growth rate:** -7%. **Inflation:** 5.3%. **Unemployment:** 2.6% (1996 est.). **Arable land:** 3%. **Agriculture:** Peninsular Malaysia: rubber, palm oil, rice; Sabah: subsistence crops, rubber, timber, coconuts, rice; Sarawak: rubber, pepper, timber. **Labor force:** 8.398 million (1996 est.): manufacturing, 25%; agriculture, forestry, and fisheries, 21%; local trade and tourism, 17%; services, 12%; government, 11%; construction, 8%. **Industries:** Peninsular Malaysia: rubber and oil palm processing and manufacturing, light manufacturing industry, electronics, tin mining and smelting, logging and processing timber; Sabah: logging, petroleum production; Sarawak: agriculture processing,

petroleum production and refining, logging. **Natural resources:** tin, petroleum, timber, copper, iron ore, natural gas, bauxite. **Exports:** $74.3 billion (f.o.b., 1998): electronic equipment, petroleum and petroleum products, palm oil, wood and wood products, rubber, textiles. **Imports:** $59.3 billion (f.o.b., 1998): machinery and equipment, chemicals, food. **Major trading partners:** U.S., Singapore, Japan, Hong Kong, U.K., Thailand, Germany, Taiwan, South Korea. **Member of Commonwealth of Nations**

Geography Malaysia is on the Malay Peninsula in southeast Asia. The nation also includes Sabah and Sarawak on the island of Borneo to the east. Its area slightly exceeds that of New Mexico.

Most of Malaysia is covered by forest, with a mountain range running the length of the peninsula. Extensive forests provide ebony, sandalwood, teak, and other woods.

Government Constitutional monarchy.

History The ancestors of the people that now inhabit the Malaysian peninsula first migrated to the area between 2500 and 1500 B.C. Those living in the coastal regions had early contact with Chinese and Indians; seafaring traders from India brought with them Hinduism, which was blended with the local animist beliefs. As Muslims conquered India, they spread the religion of Islam to Malaysia. In the 15th century A.D., Islam acquired a firm hold on the region when the Hindu ruler of the powerful city-state of Malacca, Parameswara Dewa Shah, was overthrown by his Muslim half-brother, Mudzaffar Shah.

British and Dutch interest in the region grew in the 1800s, with the British East India Company establishing a trading settlement on the island of Singapore. Trade soared, with Singapore's population growing from only 5,000 in 1820 to nearly 100,000 in just 50 years. In the 1880s, Britain formally established protectorates in Malaysia. At about the same time, rubber trees were introduced from Brazil. With the mass production of automobiles, rubber became a valuable export, and laborers were brought in from India to work the rubber plantations.

Following the Japanese occupation of Malaysia during World War II, a growing nationalist movement prompted the British to establish the semi-autonomous Federation of Malaya in 1948. But Communist guerrillas took to the jungles to begin a war of national liberation against the British, who declared a state of emergency to quell the insurgency, which lasted until 1960.

The independent state of Malaysia came into existence on Sept. 16, 1963, as a federation of Malaya, Singapore, Sabah (North Borneo), and Sarawak. In 1965, Singapore withdrew from the federation to become a separate nation. Since 1966, the 11 states of former Malaya have been known as West Malaysia, and Sabah and Sarawak have been known as East Malaysia.

By the late 1960s Malaysia was torn by communal rioting directed against Chinese and Indians, who controlled a disproportionate share of the country's wealth. Beginning in 1968, the government moved to achieve greater economic balance through a national economic policy.

Malaysia was significantly affected in 1978 by the "boat people" fleeing Vietnam. Because the refugees were mostly ethnic Chinese, the government was apprehensive about any increase in a minority that previously had been the source of internal conflict in the country. In April 1988, it announced that within the year it would cease accepting refugees.

In the 1980s, Dr. Mohamed Mahathir succeeded Datuk Hussein as prime minister. Mahathir instituted economic reforms that would transform Malaysia into one of the so-called Asian Tigers. Throughout the 1990s, Mahathir embarked on a massive project to build a new capital from scratch in an attempt to bypass congested Kuala Lumpur.

Beginning in 1997 and continuing through the next year, Malaysia suffered from the Asian currency crisis, with the Malaysian ringgit plummeting. Mahathir blamed market speculators for the crisis, and many of his ambitious building projects had to be placed on hold as a result of the economic downturn. Instead of following the economic prescriptions of the International Monetary Fund and World Bank, the prime minister went his own way, opting for fixed exchange rates and capital controls. In late 1999, Malyasia was on the road to economic recovery, and it appeared Mahathir's measures were working.

In Sept. 1998 Prime Minister Mahathir bin Mohamad sacked his heir apparent, Anwar Ibrahim, from his posts as deputy prime minister and finance minister, after a disagreement over how to deal with the country's economic problems. In defiance, Anwar launched a reform movement attacking the government. The prime minister then jailed Anwar, who was beaten and charged with trumped-up corruption and sex crimes. In April 1999, after the longest trial in Malaysian history, Ibrahim was sentenced to an unexpectedly severe six-year jail sentence. Protests followed in Malaysia and international condemnation was swift. Another trial was held in 2000, this time for sodomy, for which Anwar received an additional nine years.

Maldives

REPUBLIC OF MALDIVES

President: Maumoon Abdul Gayoom (1978)
Area: 115 sq. mi. (300 sq. km)
Population (2000 est.): 301,475 (average annual rate of natural increase: 3.1%); birth rate: 39/1000; infant mortality rate: 65.5/1000; density per sq. mi.: 2,622
Capital and largest city (1995 census): Malé, 62,973.
Monetary unit: Maldivian Rufiyaa. **Languages:** Dhivehi (official); Arabic, Hindi, and English are also spoken. **Ethnicity/race:** Sinhalese, Dravidian, Arab, African. **Religion:** Islam (Sunni Muslim). **Literacy rate:** 91% (1985)
Economic summary: GDP/PPP: (1998 est.): $500 million; $1,840 per capita. **Real growth rate:** 5.8%. **Inflation:** 6.3% (1996). **Unemployment:** negl. %. **Arable land:** 10%. **Agriculture:** coconuts, corn, sweet potatoes, fish. **Labor force:** 56,435 (1990 est.): fishing industry and agriculture, 25%; services, 21%; manufacturing and construction, 21%; trade, restaurants, and hotels, 16%; transportation and communication, 10%; other, 7%. **Industries:** fish processing, tourism, shipping, boat building, coconut processing, garments, woven mats, rope, handicrafts, coral and sand mining. **Natural resources:** fish. **Exports:** $59 million (f.o.b., 1996): fish, clothing. **Imports:** $302 million (f.o.b., 1996): consumer goods, intermediate and capital goods, petroleum products. **Major trading partners:** Sri Lanka, U.S., Germany, Singapore, U.K., India, Hong Kong, Japan, Thailand.

Geography The Republic of Maldives is a group of atolls in the Indian Ocean about 417 miles (671 km) southwest of Sri Lanka. Its 1,190 coral islets stretch over an area of 35,200 square miles (90,000 sq. km). With concerns over global warming and the shrinking of the polar ice caps, Maldives feels directly threatened, as none of its islands rises more than six feet above sea level.

Government Republic.

History The Maldives (formerly called the Maldive Islands) were first settled in the 5th century B.C. by Buddhist seafarers from India and Sri Lanka. According to tradition, Islam was adopted in A.D. 1153. Originally the islands were under the suzerainty of Ceylon (now Sri Lanka). They came under British protection in 1887 and were a dependency of the then-colony of Ceylon until 1948. The independence agreement with Britain was signed July 26, 1965. For centuries a sultanate, the islands adopted a republican form of government in 1952, but the sultanate was restored in 1954. In 1968, however, as the result of a referendum, a republic was again established in the recently independent country. Ibrahim Nasir, president since 1968, was removed from office by the Majlis in Nov. 1978 and replaced by Maumoon Abdul Gayoom. President Gayoom was elected to a fourth five-year term in Oct. 1993. Ever concerned with the possibility of rising sea levels, the Maldives, one of the world's poorest nations, has constructed, with Japanese aid, a line of concrete breakwaters along the capital's southern coast.

Mali

REPUBLIC OF MALI

National name: République de Mali
President of the Republic: Alpha Oumar Konaré (1992)
Prime Minister: Mande Sidibe (2000)
Area: 478,819 sq. mi. (1,240,000 sq. km)
Population (2000 est.): 10,685,948 (average annual rate of natural increase: 3%); birth rate: 49.2/1000; infant mortality rate: 123.3/1000; density per sq. mi.: 22
Capital and largest city (1992 est.): Bamako, 746,000.
Monetary unit: Franc CFA. **Languages:** French (official), African languages. **Ethnicity/race:** Mande 50% (Bambara, Malinke, Sarakole), Peul 17%, Voltaic 12%, Songhai 6%, Tuareg and Moor 10%, other 5%.
Religions: Islam, 90%; traditional, 9%; Christian, 1%.
Literacy rate: 32% (1990)
Economic summary: GDP/PPP (1998 est.): $8 billion; $790 per capita. **Real growth rate:** 4.6%. **Inflation:** 5%. **Unemployment:** n.a. **Arable land:** 2%.
Agriculture: cotton, millet, rice, corn, vegetables, peanuts, cattle, sheep, goats. **Labor force:** n.a.: agriculture and fishing, 80% (1998 est.). **Industries:** minor local consumer goods production and food processing, construction, phosphate and gold mining. **Natural resources:** gold, phosphates, kaolin, salt, limestone, uranium, bauxite, iron ore, manganese, tin, and copper deposits are known but not exploited.
Exports: $590 million (f.o.b., 1998 est.): cotton, gold, livestock. **Imports:** $600 million (f.o.b., 1998 est.): machinery and equipment, construction materials, petroleum, foodstuffs, textiles. **Major trading partners:** Thailand, Italy, China, Brazil, Côte d'Ivoire, France, Franc Zone, and EU.

Geography Most of Mali, in West Africa, lies in the Sahara. A landlocked country four-fifths the size of Alaska, it is bordered by Guinea, Senegal, Mauritania, Algeria, Niger, Burkina Faso, and the Côte d'Ivoire. The only fertile area is in the south, where the Niger and Senegal Rivers provide irrigation.

Government Republic.

History Caravan routes have passed through Mali since A.D. 300. The Malinke empire ruled regions of Mali from the 12th to 16th centuries, and the Songhai

empire reigned over the Timbuktu-Gao region in the 15th century. Morocco conquered Timbuktu in 1591, and ruled over it for two centuries. Subjugated by France by the end of the 19th century, the land became a colony in 1904 (named French Sudan in 1920) and in 1946 became part of the French Union. On June 20, 1960, it became independent and, under the name of Sudanese Republic, was federated with the Republic of Senegal in the Mali federation. However, Senegal seceded from the Federation on Aug. 20, 1960, and the Sudanese Republic then changed its name to the Republic of Mali on Sept. 22.

In the 1960s, Mali concentrated on economic development, continuing to accept aid from both Soviet bloc and Western nations, as well as international agencies. In the late 1960s, it began retreating from close ties with China. But a purge of conservative opponents brought greater power to President Modibo Keita, and in 1968 the influence of the Chinese and their Malian sympathizers increased. The army overthrew the government on Nov. 19, 1968, and until 1991, Mali was under a military dictatorship. Mali and Burkina Faso fought a brief border war from Dec. 25th to 29th, 1985. Mali's second multiparty national elections took place in May 1997, with President Konaré winning reelection.

Konaré has won international praise for his efforts to revive Mali's faltering economy. His adherence to International Monetary Fund guidelines has increased foreign investment and helped make Mali the second largest cotton producer in Africa.

Malta

MALTA

President: Guido de Marco (1999)
Prime Minister: Eddie Fenech Adami (1998)
Area: 122 sq. mi. (320 sq. km)
Population (2000 est.): 391,670 (average annual rate of natural increase: 0.51%); birth rate: 12.8/1000; infant mortality rate: 5.9/1000; density per sq. mi.: 3,210
Capital (1992 est.): Valletta, 9,183. **Largest city (est. 1990):** Sliema, 13,541. **Monetary unit:** Maltese lira.
Languages: Maltese and English (both official).
Ethnicity/race: Maltese (descendants of ancient Carthaginians and Phoenicians, with strong elements of Italian and other Mediterranean stock), Spanish, English, Arab. **Religion:** Roman Catholic, 98%.
Literacy rate: 88% (1985)
Economic summary: GDP/PPP (1998 est.): $5 billion; $13,000 per capita. **Real growth rate:** 4%. **Inflation:** 2.8% (1997 est.). **Unemployment:** 5% (1997). **Arable land:** 38%. **Agriculture:** potatoes, cauliflowers, grapes, wheat, barley, tomatoes, citrus, cut flowers, green peppers, pork, milk, poultry, eggs. **Labor force:** 148,085 (Sept. 1996): public services, 34%; other services, 32%; manufacturing and construction, 22%; agriculture, 2% (1996). **Industries:** tourism, electronics, ship building and repair, construction, food and beverages, textiles, footwear, clothing, tobacco. **Natural resources:** limestone, salt. **Exports:** $1.7 billion (f.o.b., 1997): machinery and transport equipment, manufactures. **Imports:** $2.3 billion (f.o.b., 1997): machinery and transport equipment, manufactured goods, food, drink, and tobacco. **Major trading partners:** France, US, Germany, U.K., Italy. **Member of Commonwealth of Nations**

Geography The five Maltese islands—Malta, Gozo, Comino, Comminotto, and Filflawith—have a combined land area smaller than Philadelphia. Malta is located in the Mediterranean Sea, about 60 miles (97 km) south of the southeastern tip of Sicily.

History The strategic importance of Malta was recognized by the Phoenicians, who occupied it, as did, in turn, the Greeks, Carthaginians, and Romans. The apostle Paul was shipwrecked there in A.D. 60. With the division of the Roman Empire in A.D. 395, Malta was assigned to the eastern portion dominated by Constantinople. Between 870 and 1090, it came under Arab rule. In 1091 the Norman noble Roger I, then ruler of Sicily, came to Malta with a small retinue and defeated the Arabs. The Knights of St. John (Malta), who obtained the three habitable Maltese islands of Malta, Gozo, and Comino from Charles V in 1530, reached their highest fame when they withstood an attack by superior Turkish forces in 1565. Napoléon seized Malta in 1798, but the French forces were ousted by British troops the next year, and British rule was confirmed by the Treaty of Paris in 1814.

Malta was heavily attacked by German and Italian aircraft during World War II but was never invaded by the Axis powers. Malta became an independent nation on Sept. 21, 1964, and a republic on Dec. 13, 1974, but remained in the British Commonwealth. In 1979, when its alliance with Great Britain ended, Malta sought to guarantee its neutrality through agreements with other countries. Although Malta applied for membership in the European Union, when the Labour Party won the election in Oct. 1996, it froze Malta's EU application and withdrew from the NATO Partnership for Peace program in an effort to maintain its neutrality. When the Nationalist Party won the Sept. 1998 elections, however, it revived the EU accession bid.

Marshall Islands

REPUBLIC OF THE MARSHALL ISLANDS

President: Kessai H. Note (2000)
Total land area: 70 sq. mi (181.3 sq. km), includes the atolls of Bikini, Eniwetok, and Kwajalein
Population (2000 est.): 68,126; average annual rate of natural increase 3.9%; birth rate 45.2/1000; infant mortality rate 40.1/1000; density per sq. mi.: 973
Capital and largest city (1990 est.): Majuro, 20,000.
Languages: Both Marshallese and English are official languages. Marshallese is a language in the Malayo-Polynesian family. **Ethnicity/race:** Micronesian. **Religions:** predominantly Christian, mostly Protestant. **Literacy rate:** 91% (1980)
Economic summary: GDP/PPP (1998 est.): $91 million; $1,450 per capita. **Real growth rate:** −5%. **Inflation:** 5% (1997). **Unemployment:** 16% (1991 est.).
Agriculture: coconuts, cacao, taro, breadfruit, fruit, pigs, chickens. **Labor force:** n.a. **Industries:** copra, fish, tourism, craft items from shell, wood, and pearls, offshore banking (embryonic). **Natural resources:** phosphate deposits, marine products, deep seabed minerals. **Exports:** $17.5 million (f.o.b., 1996 est.): coconut oil, fish, trochus shells. **Imports:** $71.8 million (c.i.f., 1996 est.): foodstuffs, machinery and equipment, fuel, beverages and tobacco. **Major trading partners:** U.S., Japan, Australia, New Zealand.

Geography The Marshall Islands, east of the Carolines, are divided into two chains: the western, or Ralik, group, including the atolls Jaluit, Kwajalein, Wotho, Bikini, and Eniwetok; and the eastern, or Ratak, group, including the atolls Mili, Majuro, Maloelap, Wotje, and Likiep. The islands are of the coral-reef type and rise only a few feet above sea level. The Marshall Islands comprise an area slightly larger than Washington, D.C.

Government Constitutional government in free association with the U.S.

History Micronesian peoples were the first inhabitants of the archipelago. The islands were explored by the Spanish in the 16th century and were named for a British captain in 1788. Germany unsuccessfully attempted to colonize the islands in 1885. Japan claimed them in 1914, but after several battles during World War II, the U.S. seized them from the Japanese. In 1947, the U.N. made the island group, along with the Mariana and Caroline archipelagos, a U.S. trust territory.

U.S. nuclear testing took place between 1946–58 on the islands of Bikini and Enewetak. The people of Bikini were removed to another island, and a total of 23 U.S. atomic and hydrogen bomb tests were conducted. Despite clean-up attempts, the islands remain uninhabited today because of nuclear contamination. The U.S. paid the islands $183.7 million in damages in 1983. The United States and the Marshall Islands signed a Compact of Free Association in 1986, which meant the islands became self-governing but would receive U.S. military and economic aid. The Marshall Islands were admitted to the U.N. on Sept. 17, 1991.

In 1997, President Kabua deferred plans for a feasibility study of a controversial proposal to develop Bikini as a commercial nuclear-waste dump for radioactive material produced by Asian power plants. The Compact of Free Association with the U.S. and the associated economic aid are scheduled to expire in 2001. In 1999 the U.S. approved a one-time $3.8-million payment to the relocated people of Bikini atoll.

Mauritania

ISLAMIC REPUBLIC OF MAURITANIA

National name: République Islamique de Mauritanie
President: Col. Maaouye Ould Sidi Ahmed Taya (1984)
Prime Minister: Cheikh El Afia Ould Mohamed Khouna (1996)
Area: 397,953 sq. mi. (1,030,700 sq. km)
Population (2000 est.): 2,667,859 (average annual rate of natural increase: 2.9%); birth rate 43.4/1000; infant mortality rate: 78.2/1000; density per sq. mi.: 7
Capital and largest city (1992 est.): Nouakchott, 480,000. **Monetary unit:** Ouguiya. **Languages:** Arabic (official) and French. **Ethnicity/race:** mixed Maur/black 40%, Maur 30%, black 30%. **Religion:** Islam. **Literacy rate:** 34% (1990)
Economic summary: GDP/PPP (1998 est.): $4.7 billion; $1,890 per capita. **Real growth rate:** 4.2%. **Inflation:** 4.7% (1996). **Unemployment:** 23% (1995 est.). **Arable land:** 0%. **Agriculture:** dates, millet, sorghum, root crops, cattle, sheep, fish products. **Labor force:** 465,000 (1981 est.), 45,000 wage earners (1980): agriculture, 47%; services, 29%; industry and commerce, 14%; government, 10%. **Industries:** fish processing, mining of iron ore and gypsum. **Natural resources:** copper, iron ore, gypsum, fish, phosphate. **Exports:** $562 million (f.o.b., 1997): fish and fish products, iron ore, gold. **Imports:** $552 million (f.o.b., 1997): foodstuffs, consumer goods, petroleum products, capital goods. **Major trading partners:** Japan, Italy, France, Algeria, Spain, China, U.S.

Geography Mauritania, three times the size of Arizona, is situated in northwest Africa with about 350 miles (592 km) of coastline on the Atlantic Ocean. It is bordered by Morocco on the north, Algeria and

Mali on the east, and Senegal on the south. The country is mostly desert, with the exception of the fertile Senegal River valley in the south and grazing land in the north.

Government   Military government. The legal system is based on Islam.

History   Mauritania was first inhabited by blacks and Berbers, and it became a center for the Berber Almoravid movement, which sought to spread Islam through western Africa. It was first explored by the Portuguese in the 15th century, but by the 19th century the French gained control. They organized the area into a territory in 1904, and made it part of French West Africa.

Mauritania became an independent nation on Nov. 28, 1960, and was admitted to the United Nations in 1961 over the strenuous opposition of Morocco, which claimed the territory. With Moors, Arabs, Berbers, and blacks frequently in conflict, the government in the late 1960s sought to make Arab culture dominant to unify the country.

Mauritania acquired administrative control of the southern part of the former Spanish Sahara when the colonial administration withdrew in 1975, under an agreement with Morocco and Spain. Increased military spending and rising casualties in Western Sahara helped bring down the civilian government of Ould Daddah in 1978. A succession of military rulers followed.

In 1984 Col. Maaouye Ould Sidi Ahmed Taya took control of the government. He relaxed Islamic law, fought corruption, instituted economic reforms urged by the International Monetary Fund, and held the country's first multiparty parliamentary elections in 1986. Although the 1991 constitution set up a multiparty democracy, politics remains based on ethnic and racial lines. The primary conflict is between blacks that dominate southern regions, and the Moorish-Arabic north, which runs the country. Racial tensions reached a peak in 1989 when Mauritania went to war with Senegal in a dispute over the border. As each country repatriated citizens of the other, critics accused Mauritania of taking the opportunity to expel thousands of blacks. Human rights activists have also charged Mauritania with tolerating the enslavement of blacks by ethnic Moors.

In 1992 Taya won the nation's first multiparty presidential election, which opponents charged was rigged. Parliamentary elections were held in 1996 and 1997, with opposition parties winning some seats despite calls for government opponents to boycott the elections. Economically, Mauritania remains hostage to the fluctuating price of iron ore, which provides nearly half its export earnings. The country's first deepwater port opened near Nouakchott in 1986. Taya's attempts to restructure the economy provoke periodic protests, the most serious of which were the bread riots in Nouakchott in 1995. Economic development remains hampered by large-scale deforestation, over-exploitation of its rich fishing grounds, and chronic water shortages.

Mauritius

President: Cassam Uteem (1992)
Prime Minister: Sir Anerood Jugnauth (2000)
Area: 787 sq. mi. (1,860 sq. km)
Population (2000 est.): 1,179,368 (average annual rate of natural increase: 1%); birth rate: 16.7/1000; infant mortality rate: 17.7/1000; density per sq. mi.: 1,499

Capital and largest city (1993 est.): Port Louis, 134,516. **Monetary unit:** Mauritian rupee.
Languages: English (official), French, Creole, Hindi, Urdu, Hakka, Bojpoori. **Ethnicity/race:** Indo-Mauritian 68%, Creole 27%, Sino-Mauritian 3%, Franco-Mauritian 2%. **Religions:** Hindu, 52%, Christian, 28.3%; Islam, 16.6%; other, 3.1%. **Literacy rate:** 81% (1990)
Economic summary: GDP/PPP (1998 est.): $11.7 billion; $10,000 per capita. **Real growth rate:** 5%. **Inflation:** 6.8% (1997). **Unemployment:** 2% (1996 est.). **Arable land:** 49%. **Agriculture:** sugarcane, tea, corn, potatoes, bananas, pulses, cattle, goats, fish. **Labor force:** 514,000 (1995): construction and industry, 36%; services, 24%; trade, restaurants, and hotels, 16%; agriculture and fishing, 14%; transportation and communication, 7%; finance, 3%. **Natural resources:** arable land, fish. **Industries:** food processing (largely sugar milling), textiles, clothing, chemicals, metal products, transport equipment, nonelectrical machinery, tourism. **Exports:** $1.6 billion (f.o.b., 1997): clothing and textiles, sugar. **Imports:** $2.3 billion (c.i.f., 1997): manufactured goods, capital equipment, foodstuffs, petroleum products, chemicals. **Major trading partners:** U.K., France, U.S., Germany, Italy, South Africa, India. **Member of Commonwealth of Nations**

Geography   Mauritius is a mountainous island in the Indian Ocean east of Madagascar.

Government   Republic within the British Commonwealth.

History   After a brief Dutch settlement, French immigrants who came in 1715 named the island Île de France and established the first road and harbor infrastructure, as well as the sugar industry, under the leadership of Gov. Mahe de Labourdonnais. Blacks from Africa and Madagascar came as slaves to work in the cane fields. In 1810, the British captured the island and in 1814, by the Treaty of Paris, it was ceded to Great Britain along with its dependencies.

Indian immigration, which followed the abolition of slavery in 1835, rapidly changed the fabric of Mauritian society, and the country flourished with the increased cultivation of sugarcane. The opening of the Suez Canal in 1869 heralded the decline of Mauritius as a port-of-call for ships rounding the southern tip of Africa, bound for South and East Asia. The economic instability of the price of sugar, the main crop, in the first half of the 20th century brought civil unrest, then economic, administrative, and political reforms. Mauritius became independent on March 12, 1968.

The effects of Cyclone Claudette in 1979, and of falling world sugar prices in the early 1980s, led the government to initiate a vigorous program of agricultural diversification and to develop the processing of imported goods for the export market. The country formally broke ties with the British Crown in March 1992, becoming a republic within the Commonwealth.

In addition to sugar cane, textile production and tourism are the leading industries. Primary education is free, and Mauritius boasts one of the highest literacy rates in sub-Saharan Africa.

Dr. Navinchandra Ramgoolam became prime minister in an unstable coalition government in 1995. The administration has embraced free-market reforms, resulting in an economic expansion through the 1990s. In Sept. 2000 an opposition alliance defeated Ramgoolam, winning 50 of the 70 seats in parliament. The office of prime minister is to rotate: Anerood Jugnath, leader of the Socialist Militant Party, will serve for three years, followed by Paul Berenger, of the Militant Movement. Berenger will be the first non Hindu to hold office since Mauritius won independence in 1968. With a complicated ethnic mix—about 30% of the population is of African descent, the remainder is of Indian descent, both Hindu and Muslim—racial unrest continues to gnaw at the country.

Mexico

UNITED MEXICAN STATES

Official name: Estados Unidos Mexicanos
President: Vicente Fox Quesada (2000)
Area: 761,600 sq. mi. (1,972,550 sq. km)
Population (2000 est.): 100,349,766 (average annual rate of natural increase: 1.8%); birth rate: 23.2/1000; infant mortality rate: 26.2/1000; density per sq. mi.: 132
Capital and largest city (2000 est.): Mexico City, 19,750,000 (metro. area). **Other large cities (1995):** Guadalajara, 2,178,000; Monterrey, 1,702,000; Ecatepec, 1,456,438 (part of Mexico City metro. area); Nezahualcóyotl, 1,259,543 (part of Mexico City metro. area); Puebla, 1,222,177. **Monetary unit:** Peso.
Languages: Spanish, Indian languages. **Ethnicity/ race:** mestizo (Indian-Spanish) 60%, Amerindian or predominantly Amerindian 30%, Caucasian or predominantly Caucasian 9%, other 1%. **Religions:** nominally Roman Catholic, 97%; Protestant, 3%.
Literacy rate: 87% (1990)
Economic summary: GDP/PPP (1998 est.): $815.3 billion; $8,300 per capita. **Real growth rate:** 4.8%. **Inflation:** 18.6%. **Unemployment:** 2.6% (1998) (urban; plus considerable underemployment.) **Arable land:** 12%. **Agriculture:** corn, wheat, soybeans, rice, beans, cotton, coffee, fruit, tomatoes, beef, poultry, dairy products, wood products. **Labor force:** 37.5 million (1998): services, 28.8%; agriculture, forestry, hunting, and fishing, 21.8%; commerce, 17.1%; manufacturing, 16.1%; construction, 5.2%; public administration and national defense, 4.4%; transportation and communications, 4.1%. **Industries:** food and beverages, tobacco, chemicals, iron and steel, petroleum, mining, textiles, clothing, motor vehicles, consumer durables, tourism. **Natural resources:** petroleum, silver, copper, gold, lead, zinc, natural gas, timber. **Exports:** $117.5 billion (f.o.b., 1998): crude oil, oil products, coffee, silver, engines, motor vehicles, cotton, consumer electronics. **Imports:** $111.5 billion (f.o.b., 1998): metal-working machines, steel mill products, agricultural machinery, electrical equipment, car parts for assembly, repair parts for motor vehicles, aircraft, and aircraft parts. **Major trading partners:** U.S., Canada, Japan, Spain, Chile, Brazil, Germany, South Korea, Italy, France.

Geography Mexico is bordered by the United States to the north, Belize and Guatemala to the southeast; Mexico is about one-fifth the size of the United States. Baja California in the west is an 800-mile (1,287-km) peninsula and forms the Gulf of California. In the east are the Gulf of Mexico and the Bay of Campeche, which is formed by Mexico's other peninsula, the Yucatán. The center of Mexico is a great, high plateau, open to the north, with mountain chains on the east and west and with ocean-front lowlands lying outside of them.

Government Federal republic.

History At least three great civilizations—the Mayas, the Olmecs, and later the Toltecs—preceded the wealthy Aztec empire, conquered in 1519–21 by the Spanish under Hernando Cortés. Spain ruled Mexico as part of the viceroyalty of New Spain for the next 300 years until Sept. 16, 1810, when the Mexicans first revolted. They continued the struggle and finally won independence in 1821.

From 1821 to 1877, there were two emperors, several dictators, and enough presidents and provisional executives to make a new government on the average of every nine months. Mexico lost Texas (1836), and after defeat in the war with the U.S. (1846–48) it lost the area made up of the present states of California, Nevada, and Utah, most of Arizona and New Mexico, and parts of Wyoming and Colorado under the Treaty of Guadalupe Hidalgo. In 1855, the Indian patriot Benito Juárez began a series of liberal reforms, including the disestablishment of the Catholic Church, which had acquired vast property. A subsequent civil war was interrupted by the French invasion of Mexico (1861), the crowning of Maximilian of Austria as emperor (1864), and then his overthrow and execution by forces under Juárez, who again became president in 1867.

The years after the fall of the Dictator Porfirio Diaz (1877–80 and 1884–1911) were marked by bloody political-military strife and trouble with the U.S., culminating in the punitive U.S. expedition into northern Mexico (1916–17) in unsuccessful pursuit of the revolutionary Pancho Villa. Since a brief period of civil war in 1920, Mexico has enjoyed a period of gradual agricultural, political, and social reforms. The Partido Nacional Revolucionario (PNR; National Revolutionary Party), dominated by revolutionary and reformist politicians from northern Mexico, was established in 1929; it continued to control Mexico throughout the 20th century and was renamed the Partido Revolucionario Institucional (PRI; Institutional Revolutionary Party) in 1946. Relations with the U.S. were again disturbed in 1938 when all foreign oil wells were expropriated, but an agreement on compensation was finally reached in 1941.

Following World War II, the government placed heavy emphasis on economic growth. During the mid-1970s, under the leadership of President José López Portillo, Mexico emerged as one of the world's major petroleum-producing countries. By the end of Portillo's term, however, Mexico had accumulated a huge external debt because of the government's unrestrained borrowing on the strength of its petroleum revenues. The collapse of oil prices in 1986 cut into Mexico's export earnings and worsened the situation. In Jan. 1994, Mexico joined Canada and the United States in the North American Free Trade Agreement (NAFTA), which will phase out all tariffs over a 15-year period, and in Jan. 1996, it became a founding member of the World Trade Organization (WTO).

In 1994, the leading presidential candidate was shot and killed in Tijuana. The campaign manager was then selected to be the party's presidential candidate. Zedillo won the election by more than 20%, and the PRI party retained its majority in both legislative houses. In Feb. 1995, agreement was reached with the U.S. to prevent the collapse of Mexico's private banks. The strict provisions, however, gave the U.S. virtual veto power over key elements in Mexico's economic policy. Elections in July 1997 brought a stunning upset for the long ruling PRI, which lost control of the lower legislative house and the mayoralty of Mexico City, in what observers called the freest election in the country's history. To make Mexico's election system more democratic, President Zedillo announced in March 1999 that he would discontinue the practice of the "dedazo," in which the president designates his party's nominee for the upcoming election. In Nov. 1999 Mexico held its first presidential primary. Former Interior Secretary Francisco Labastida, Zedillo's closest ally among those running, was the clear winner.

In elections held July 2, 2000, the PRI lost the presidency, ending 71 years of one-party rule. Vicente Fox Quesada, of the center-right National Action Party (PAN), won a resounding victory. Fox took 43% of the vote to Labastida's 36%. Although PAN picked up seats in both the Chamber of Deputies and the Senate, it failed to win a majority in either. It will have to form coalitions with other parties to pass legislation. Fox has pledged a more honest, business-like administration. He wants to improve the economy, reform taxes, overhaul the justice system, and give state governments more power.

Micronesia

FEDERATED STATES OF MICRONESIA

President: Leo A. Falcam (1999)
Total area: 271 sq. mi (702 sq. km). Land area, same (includes islands of Pohnpei, Yap, Chuuk, and Kosrae)
Population (2000 est.): 133,144 (average annual rate of natural increase: 2.1%); birth rate: 27.1/1000; infant mortality rate: 33.5/1000; density per sq. mi.: 491
Capital: Palikir. **Languages:** English is the official and common language; major indigenous languages are Chukese, Pohnpeian, Yapase, and Kosrean.
Ethnicity/race: nine ethnic Micronesian and Polynesian groups. **Literacy rate:** 85% (1980)
Economic summary: GDP/PPP: (1996 est.), $220 million; $1,760 per capita. **Real growth rate:** 1%. **Inflation:** 4%. **Unemployment:** 27% (1989).
Agriculture: black pepper, tropical fruit and vegetables, coconuts, cassava (tapioca), sweet potatoes, pigs, chickens. **Labor force:** n.a.; two-thirds are government employees. **Industries:** tourism, construction, fish processing, craft items from shell, wood, and pearls. **Natural resources:** forests, marine products, deep-seabed minerals. **Exports:** $73 million (f.o.b., 1996 est.): fish, garments, bananas, black pepper. **Imports:** $168 million (c.i.f., 1996 est.): food, manufactured goods, machinery and equipment, beverages. **Major trading partners:** Japan, U.S., Guam, Australia.

Geography The Federated States of Micronesia is composed of the island states of Yap, Chuuk (Truk), Pohnpei (Ponape), and Kosrae, all in the Caroline Islands. The islands vary geologically from high mountainous islands to low, coral atolls, with volcanic outcroppings on Pohnpei, Kosrae, and Chuuk. They are located 3,200 miles (5,150 km) west-southwest of Hawaii, in the north Pacific Ocean.

Government Constitutional government in free association with the United States since Nov. 1986.

History The islands, inhabited by Micronesian and Polynesian peoples, were colonized by Spain in the 17th century. Germany purchased them from Spain in 1898. They were occupied by the Japanese in 1914, but American forces seized them from the Japanese during World War II. On April 2, 1947, the United Nations Security Council created the Trust Territory of the Pacific Islands. The trust placed the Northern Mariana, Caroline, and Marshall Islands under the administration of the United States.

The Micronesian Federation became self-governing in 1979. In 1983, the F.M.A. voted to accept a Compact of Free Association with the U.S., and in Nov. 1986, the U.S. government declared the Trust Terri-

tory agreements no longer in effect—thereby granting the Federated States of Micronesia full independence.

The F.M.A. was admitted to the United Nations on Sept. 17, 1991. In July 1993, the country became a member of the International Monetary Fund. Micronesia, as well as many other South Pacific countries, is alarmed by the effect continued global warming will have on their islands—the consequent rise in the level of the oceans threatens low-lying islands with flooding and, eventually, with submergence.

Moldova

REPUBLIC OF MOLDOVA

President: Petru Lucinschi (1997)
Prime Minister: Dumitru Braghis (1999)
Area: 13,000 sq. mi. (33,700 sq. km)
Population (2000 est.): 4,430,654 (average annual rate of natural increase: 0.03%); birth rate: 12.9/1000; infant mortality rate: 43.3/1000, density per sq. mi.: 341
Capital and largest city (1991): Chisinau, 676,700.
Other large cities (1991 est.): Tiraspol, 186,000; Beltsy, 165,000; Bendery (Tighina), 141,500.
Monetary unit: Moldovan Lem. **Languages:** Moldovan (official; virtually the same as Romanian), Russian, Gagauz (a Turkish dialect). **Ethnicity/race:** Moldavian/Romanian 64.5%, Ukrainian 13.8%, Russian 13%, Gagauz 3.5%, Jewish 1.5%, Bulgarian 2%, other 1.7% (1989 figures) . **Religions (1991):** Eastern Orthodox 98.5%, Jewish 1.5%, Baptist (only about 1,000 members). **Literacy rate:** 97% (1989)
Economic summary: GDP/PPP (1998 est.): $10 billion; $2,200 per capita. **Real growth rate:** –8.6%. **Inflation:** 18.3%. **Unemployment:** 2% (includes only officially registered unemployed; large numbers of underemployed workers). **Arable land:** 53%. **Agriculture:** vegetables, fruit, wine, grain, sugar beets, sunflower seed, tobacco, beef, milk. **Labor force:** 1.7 million (1998): agriculture, 40.2%; industry, 14.3%; other, 45.5%. **Industries:** food processing, agricultural machinery, foundry equipment, refrigerators and freezers, washing machines, hosiery, sugar, vegetable oil, shoes, textiles. **Natural resources:** lignite, phosphorites, gypsum. **Exports:** $633 million (f.o.b., 1998): foodstuffs, wine, tobacco, textiles and footwear, machinery. **Imports:** $1.02 billion (f.o.b., 1998): oil, gas, coal, steel, machinery, chemical products, metals, metal products, foodstuffs, automobiles, other consumer durables. **Major trading partners:** Russia, Kazakhstan, Ukraine, Belarus, Romania, U.S., Germany, Italy.

Geography Moldova (formerly Moldavia) is a landlocked republic of hilly plains lying west of the Carpathian Mountains between the Prut and Dneister (Dnestr) Rivers. The country is sandwiched between Romania and Ukraine. The area is a very fertile region with rich black soil (chernozem) covering three-quarters of the territory.

Government Democratic republic.

History Most of what is now Moldova was the independent principality of Moldavia in the 14th century. In the 16th century it came under Ottoman Turkish rule. Russia acquired Moldavian territory in 1791, and again in 1812 (the Treaty of Bucharest) when Turkey gave up the province of Bessarabia[1] to Russia. Turkey held the rest of Moldavia but it was passed to Romania in 1918. Russia did not recognize the cession of this territory.

In 1924, the U.S.S.R. established Moldavia as an Autonomous Soviet Socialist Republic. As a result of the Nazi-Soviet Nonaggression Pact of 1939, Romania was forced to cede all of Bessarabia to the Soviet

Union in 1940. The Soviets merged the Moldavia A.S.S.R. with the Romanian-speaking districts of Bessarabia to form the Moldavian Soviet Socialist Republic. During World War II, Romania joined Germany in the attack on the Soviet Union and reconquered Bessarabia. But Soviet troops retook the territory in 1944 and reestablished the Moldavian S.S.R.

For many years, Romania and the U.S.S.R. disputed each other's territorial claims over Bessarabia. Following the aborted coup against Soviet president Mikhail Gorbachev, Moldavia proclaimed its independence in Sept. 1991, and changed its name to the Romanian spelling, Moldova.

Conflict between ethnic Romanians and the Russian-Ukrainian majority in Trans-Dniester erupted upon independence. Trans-Dniester separatists (primarily ethnic Russians and Ukrainians) fought for independence from Moldova, and in the early 1990s the Russian army offered the separatists military aid and occupied the region. In the south, another breakaway republic attempted to secede—Gagauzia—which is composed mostly of Turkic Christians.

In Aug. 1994, Moldova adopted a new constitution which emphasized the country's independent identity from Romania, which had always considered it Romanian in essence.

By 1995, the dispute with Gagauzia had dissolved, and in May 1997, Moldova and Trans-Dniester signed a document in Moscow agreeing to the integrity of the country and calling for the removal of Russian troops upon the conclusion of a definite peace settlement. The Russian financial crisis in fall 1998 severely affected Moldova, which relies on Russia for 60% of its foreign trade. Economic disaster caused an exodus of an estimated 600,000 Moldovans since then. In addition to economic stagnation, corruption and organized crime are legion in this desperately poor nation.

1. The area between the Prut and Dniester Rivers.

Monaco

PRINCIPALITY OF MONACO

National name: Principauté de Monaco
Ruler: Prince Rainier III (1949)
Minister of State: Patrick Leclercq (2000)
Area: 0.73 sq. mi. (465 acres) (1.95 sq. km)
Population (2000 est.): 31,693 (average annual growth rate: –0.3%); birth rate 10/1000; infant mortality rate: 5.9/1000; density per sq. mi.: 43,415
Capital and largest city (1995 est.): Monaco, 30,400.
Monetary unit: French franc. **Languages:** French (official), English, Italian, Monégasque. **Ethnicity/race:** French 47%, Monegasque 16%, Italian 16%, other 21%. **Religion:** Roman Catholic, 95%. **Literacy rate:** 99%
Economic summary: GDP/PPP (1996 est.): $800 million; $25,000 per capita. **Real growth rate:** n.a. **Inflation:** n.a. **Unemployment:** 3.1% (1994). **Agriculture:** none. **Labor force:** 30,540 (Jan. 1994). **Natural resources:** none. **Exports:** n.a. **Imports:** n.a. Full customs integration with France, which collects and rebates Monegasque trade duties; also participates in EU.

Geography Monaco is a tiny, hilly wedge driven into the French Mediterranean coast; it is nine miles east of Nice, France.

Government Constitutional monarchy.

History The Phoenicians, and after them the Greeks, had a temple on the Monacan headland honoring Hercules. From *Monoikos*, the Greek surname for this mythological strong man, the principality took its name. After being independent for 800 years, Monaco was annexed to France in 1793 and was placed under Sardinia's protection in 1815. By the Franco-Monegasque treaty of 1861, Monaco went under French guardianship but continued to be independent. A treaty made with France in 1918 contained a clause providing that, in the event that the male Grimaldi dynasty should die out, Monaco would become an autonomous state under French protection.

Monaco has a tourist business that runs as high as 1.5 million visitors a year and is famous for its beaches and casinos. It had gaming tables as early as 1856. Five years later, a 50-year concession to operate the games was granted to François Blanc, of Bad Homburg. This concession passed into the hands of a private company in 1898.

Prince Rainier III, born on May 31, 1923, succeeded his grandfather, Louis II, on the latter's death, May 9, 1949. Rainier was married, in 1956, to U.S. actress Grace Kelly and they subsequently had three children. Their son, Prince Albert Louis Pierre (b. 1958) is heir to the throne. Immensely popular, Princess Grace died on Sept. 14, 1982, of injuries received in a car accident near Monte Carlo. She was 52.

Monaco's practice of providing a tax shelter for French businessmen resulted in a 1962 dispute between the countries. A compromise was reached by which French citizens with less than five years residence in Monaco were taxed at French rates, and taxes were imposed on Monegasque companies doing more than 25% of their business outside the principality. In 1967, Rainier took control of the Société des Bains de Mer, operator of the famous Monte Carlo gambling casino, in a program to increase hotel and convention space. The country was admitted to the U.N. in May 1993, making it the smallest country represented there. The country celebrated the 700th anniversary of the Grimaldi reign during 1997.

Mongolia

MONGOLIA

President: Ntsaagiyn Bagabandi (1997)
Prime Minister: Nambaryn Enkhbayar (2000)
Area: 604,250 sq. mi. (1,565,000 sq. km)
Population (2000 est.): 2,650,952 (average annual rate of natural increase: 1.5%); birth rate: 21.5/1000; infant mortality rate: 41.2/1000; density per sq. mi.: 4
Capital and largest city (1993 est.): Ulan Bator, 619,000.
Monetary unit: Tugrik. **Languages:** Mongolian, 90%; also Turkic, Russian, and Chinese. **Ethnicity/race:** Mongol 90%, Kazak 4%, Chinese 2%, Russian 2%, other 2%. **Religions:** predominantly Tibetan Buddhist; Islam about 4%. **Literacy rate:** 97% (1989)
Economic summary: GDP/PPP (1998 est.): $5.8 billion; $2,250 per capita. **Real growth rate:** 3.5%. **Inflation:** 6%. **Unemployment:** 4.5%. **Labor force:** 1.115 million (mid-1993 est.): primarily herding/agricultural. **Arable land:** 1%. **Agriculture:** wheat, barley, potatoes, forage crops, sheep, goats, cattle, camels, horses. **Industries:** copper, construction materials, mining (particularly coal), food and beverage, processing of animal products. **Natural resources:** oil, coal, copper, molybdenum, tungsten, phosphates, tin, nickel, zinc, wolfram, fluorspar, gold. **Exports:** $316.8 million (f.o.b., 1998): copper, livestock, animal products, cashmere, wool, hides, fluorspar, other nonferrous metals. **Imports:** $472.4 million (f.o.b., 1998): machinery and equipment, fuel, food products, industrial consumer goods, chemicals, building materials, sugar, tea. **Major trading partners:** China, Switzerland, Russia, South Korea, U.S., Japan.

Geography Mongolia lies in central Asia between Siberia on the north and China on the south. It is slightly larger than Alaska.

The productive regions of Mongolia—a tableland ranging from 3,000 to 5,000 feet (914 to 1,524 m) in elevation—are in the north, which is well drained by numerous rivers, including the Hovd, Onon, Selenga, and Tula. Much of the Gobi Desert falls within Mongolia.

Government Independent sovereign republic now in transition from Communism.

History Nomadic tribes that periodically plundered agriculturally based China from the west are recorded in Chinese history dating back more than 2,000 years. It was to protect China from these marauding peoples that the Great Wall was constructed around 200 B.C. The name *Mongol* comes from a small tribe whose leader, Ghengis Khan, began a conquest that would eventually encompass an enormous empire stretching from Asia to Europe, as far west as the Black Sea and as far south as India and the Himalayas. However, by the 14th century, the kingdom was in serious decline, with invasions from a resurgent China and internecine warfare.

The State of Mongolia was formerly known as Outer Mongolia. It contains the original homeland of the historic Mongols, whose power reached its zenith during the 13th century under Kublai Khan. The area accepted Manchu rule in 1689, but after the Chinese Revolution of 1911 and the fall of the Manchus in 1912, the northern Mongol princes expelled the Chinese officials and declared independence under the Khutukhtu, or "Living Buddha."

In 1921 Soviet troops entered the country, and facilitated the establishment of a republic by Mongolian revolutionaries in 1924. China also made a claim to the region, but was too weak to assert it. Under the 1945 Chinese-Russian Treaty, China agreed to give up Outer Mongolia, which, after a plebiscite, became a nominally independent country.

Allied with the U.S.S.R. in its dispute with China, Mongolia began mobilizing troops along its borders in 1968 when the two powers became involved in border clashes on the Kazakh-Sinkiang frontier to the west and at the Amur and Ussuri Rivers. A 20-year treaty of friendship and cooperation, signed in 1966, entitled Mongolia to call upon the U.S.S.R. for military aid in the event of invasion.

In 1989, the Mongolian democratic revolution began, led by Sanjaasurengiyn Zorig. Free elections held in Aug. 1990 produced a multiparty government, though it was still largely Communist. As a result, Mongolia has moved only gradually toward a market economy. With the collapse of the U.S.S.R., however, Mongolia was deprived of Soviet aid. Many of the country's factories were forced to shut down, and unemployment rose to 30%. Primarily in reaction to the economic turmoil, the Communist Mongolian People's Revolutionary Party (MPRP) won a significant majority in parliamentary elections in 1992. In 1996, however, the Democratic Alliance, an electoral coalition, defeated the MPRP, breaking with Communist rule for the first time since 1921. But in 1997, a former Communist and chairman of the People's Revolutionary Party, Ntsaagiyn Bagabandi, was elected president, further strengthening the hand of the antireformers.

Disagreement within Mongolia's ruling coalition over the pace and direction of market reforms in April 1998 caused a shake-up that thrust Tsakhiagiyn Elbe-

gdorj, a proreform politician, into the prime minister's position. But parliamentary cross-purposes led to his resignation, and a succession of prime ministers followed.

In July 2000, the Monogolian People's Revolutionary Party (formerly the Communist Party) nearly swept parliamentary elections, winning 72 out of 76 seats. MPRP leader Nambariin Enkhbayar said that although he planned to slow reforms and privatization, the country would not revert to Communism.

Morocco

KINGDOM OF MOROCCO

National name: al-Mamlaka al-Maghrebia
Ruler: King Muhammad VI (1999)
Prime Minister: Abderrahmane El Youssoufi (1998)
Area: 172,413 sq. mi. (446,550 sq. km)
Population (2000 est.): 30,122,350 (average annual rate of natural increase: 1.9%); birth rate: 24.6/1000; infant mortality rate: 49.7/1000; density per sq. mi.: 175
Capital (1993 est.): Rabat, 1,220,000. **Largest cities:** Casablanca, 2,943,000; Marrakech, 602,000; Fez, 564,000; Salé, 521,000. **Monetary unit:** Dirham.
Languages: Arabic, French, Berber dialects, Spanish.
Ethnicity/race: Arab-Berber 99.1%, other 0.7%, Jewish 0.2%. **Religions:** Islam, 98.7%, Christian, 1.1%; Jewish, 0.2%. **Literacy rate:** 50% (1990)
Economic summary: GDP/PPP (1998 est.): $107 billion; $3,200 per capita. **Real growth rate:** 6.8%. **Inflation:** 2%–3%. **Unemployment:** 19%. **Arable land:** 21%. **Agriculture:** barley, wheat, citrus, wine, vegetables, olives, livestock. **Labor force:** 11 million (1997 est.): agriculture, 50%; services, 26%; industry, 15%; other, 9% (1985). **Industries:** phosphate rock mining and processing, food processing, leather goods, textiles, construction, tourism. **Natural resources:** phosphates, iron ore, zinc, fish, salt, lead, manganese. **Exports:** $7 billion (f.o.b., 1997): food and beverages, semiprocessed goods, consumer goods, phosphates. **Imports:** $10 billion (c.i.f., 1997): semiprocessed goods, capital goods, food and beverages, fuel and lubricants, consumer goods, raw materials. **Major trading partners:** EU, Japan, India, U.S., Libya, Saudi Arabia, Brazil.

Geography Morocco, about one-tenth larger than California, lies across the Strait of Gibraltar on the Mediterranean and looks out on the Atlantic from the northwest shoulder of Africa. Algeria is to the east and Mauritania to the south. On the Atlantic coast there is a fertile plain. The Mediterranean coast is mountainous. The Atlas Mountains, running northeastward from the south to the Algerian frontier, average 11,000 feet (3,353 m) in elevation.

Government Constitutional monarchy.

History Morocco has been the home of the Berbers since the second millennium B.C. In A.D. 46, Morocco was annexed by Rome as part of the province of Mauritania until the Vandals overran this portion of the declining empire in the 5th century. The Arabs invaded circa 685, bringing Islam. The Berbers joined them in invading Spain in A.D. 711, but then revolted against them, resenting their secondary status. In 1086, Berbers took control of large areas of Moorish Spain until they were expelled in the 13th century.

The land was rarely unified, and was usually ruled by small tribal states. Conflicts between Berbers and Arabs were chronic. Portugal and Spain began invading Morocco, which helped to unify the land in defense. In 1660 Morocco came under the control of the Alawite dynasty. It is a sherif dynasty—descended from the prophet Muhammad—and rules Morocco to this day.

During the 17th and 18th centuries Morocco was one of the Barbary states, the headquarters of pirates who pillaged Mediterranean traders. European powers became interested in colonizing the country beginning in 1840, and there were frequent clashes with the French and Spanish. Finally, in 1904, France and Spain concluded a secret agreement that divided Morocco into zones of French and Spanish influence, with France controlling almost all of Morocco and Spain controlling the small southwestern portion, which became known as Spanish Sahara. Morocco became an even greater object of European rivalry by the turn of the century, leading almost to a European war in 1905 when Germany attempted to gain a foothold in the mineral-rich country. By terms of the Algeciras Conference (1906), the sultan of Morocco maintained control of his lands and France's privileges were curtailed. The conference was an telling indication of what was to come in World War I, with Germany and Austria-Hungary lining up on one side of the territorial dispute, and France, Britain, and the United States on the other.

In 1912, the sultan of Morocco, Moulay Abd al-Hafid, permitted French protectorate status. Nationalism began to grow during World War II. Sultan Mohammed V was deposed by the French in 1953 and replaced by his uncle, but nationalist agitation forced his return in 1955. On his death on Feb. 26, 1961, his son, Hassan, became king. France and Spain recognized the independence and sovereignty of Morocco in 1956. Sultan Sidi Muhammad formed a constitutional government, and in 1961 Moulay Hassan succeeded his father as Hassan II.

Maintaining excellent relations with the West, King Hassan became the second Arab leader to meet with an Israeli leader when, on July 21, 1986, Prime Minister Shimon Peres came to Morocco. Morocco was also the first Arab state to condemn the 1990 Iraqi invasion of Kuwait. In the 1990s King Hassan promulgated "Hassanian democracy," which allowed for significant political freedom while at the same time retaining ultimate power for the monarch. In Aug. 1999, King Hassan II died after 38 years on the throne and his son, Prince Sidi Muhammad, was crowned King Muhammad VI. Since then Muhammad VI has pledged to make the political system more open, to allow freedom of expression, and to support economic reform. He has also advocated giving more rights to women, which has been opposed by Islamic fundamentalists. The entrenched political elite and the military have also been leery of some reform proposals. With about 20% of the population living in dire poverty, economic expansion is a prime goal. In July 2001 Morocco, Mauritania, and Senegal held talks to discuss a highway linking Dakar, Senegal, with Tangier, Morocco, to facilitate trade and travel.

Morocco's occupation of Western Sahara has been repeatedly criticized by the international community. In the 1970s, tens of thousands of Moroccans crossed the border into Spanish Sahara to back their government's contention that the northern part of the territory was historically part of Morocco. Spain, which had controlled the territory since 1912, withdrew in 1976, creating a power vacuum that was filled by Morocco in the north and Mauritania in the south. When Mauritania withdrew in Aug. 1979, Morocco overran the remainder of the territory. A rebel group, the Polisario

Front, has fought against Morocco since 1976 for the independence of Western Sahara on behalf of the indigenous Saharawis. In 1981, King Hassan agreed to a cease-fire with a referendum under international supervision to decide the fate of the Sahara territory, but the dispute remains unresolved.

Mozambique

REPUBLIC OF MOZAMBIQUE

National name: República de Moçambique
President: Joaquim Chissanó (1986)
Prime Minister: Pascoal Mocumbi (1994)
Area: 303,073 sq. mi. (801,590 sq. km)
Population (2000 est.): 19,104,696 (average annual rate of natural increase: 1.5%); birth rate: 38/1000; infant mortality rate: 139.9/1000; density per sq. mi.: 63
Capital and largest city (1996 est.): Maputo, 1,095,300. **Monetary unit:** Metical. **Languages:** Portuguese (official), Bantu languages. **Ethnicity/race:** indigenous tribal groups 99.6% (Shangaan, Chokwe, Manyika, Sena, Makua, and others), Europeans 0.06%, Euro-Africans 0.2%, Indians 0.08%. **Religions:** traditional, 60%; Christian, 30%; Islam, 10%. **Literacy rate:** 33% (1990)
Economic summary: GDP/PPP (1998 est.): $16.8 billion; $900 per capita. **Real growth rate:** 11%. **Inflation:** −1.3%. **Unemployment:** n.a. **Arable land:** 4%. **Agriculture:** cotton, cashew nuts, sugarcane, tea, cassava (tapioca), corn, rice, tropical fruit, beef, poultry. **Labor force:** n.a.: agriculture, 80%; industry, 9.5%; services, 5.5%; wage earners working abroad, 5% (1993 est.). **Industries:** food, beverages, chemicals (fertilizer, soap, paints), petroleum products, textiles, cement, glass, asbestos, tobacco. **Natural resources:** coal, titanium, natural gas. **Exports:** $295 million (f.o.b., 1998 est.): shrimp, cashews, cotton, sugar, copra, citrus. **Imports:** $965 million (c.i.f., 1998 est.): food, clothing, farm equipment, petroleum. **Major trading partners:** Spain, South Africa, Portugal, U.S., Japan, Malawi, India, Zimbabwe, Saudi Arabia.

Geography Mozambique stretches for 1,535 miles (2,470 km) along Africa's southeast coast. It is nearly twice the size of California. Tanzania is to the north; Malawi, Zambia, and Zimbabwe to the west; and South Africa and Swaziland to the south.

The country is generally a low-lying plateau broken up by 25 sizable rivers that flow into the Indian Ocean. The largest is the Zambezi, which provides access to central Africa. The principal ports are Maputo, Beira, and Nacala.

Government Multiparty republic.

History Bantu-speakers migrated to Mozambique in the first millennium, and Arab and Swahili traders settled the region thereafter. It was explored by Vasco da Gama in 1498, and first colonized by Portugal in 1505. By 1510, the Portuguese had control of all the former Arab sultanates on the east African coast. Mozambique was administered as part of Goa, in India, until 1752, when it received its own captain-general. Portuguese colonial rule was repressive.

Guerrilla activity began in 1963 and became so effective by 1973 that Portugal was forced to dispatch 40,000 troops to fight the rebels. A cease-fire was signed in Sept. 1974, and after having been under Portuguese colonial rule for 470 years, Mozambique became independent on June 25, 1975. The first president, Samora Moises Machel, had been the head of the National Front for the Liberation of Mozambique

(FRELIMO) in its 10-year guerrilla war for independence. He died in a plane crash on Oct. 19, 1986, and was succeeded by his foreign minister, Joaquim Chissano.

On Jan. 25, 1985, after a decade of independence, the government was locked in a five-year-old paralyzing war with antigovernment guerrillas, known as the MNR, backed by the white minority government in South Africa. The guerrilla movement weakened President Chissano's attempts to institute socialism, which he then decided to abandon in 1989. A new constitution was drafted calling for three branches of government and granting civil liberties. A cease-fire agreement was signed in Oct. 1992 between the government and the MNR, ending 16 years of civil war.

In April 1994 the president announced that a multiparty general election would be held in late October. The incumbent won. In Nov. 1995 the country was the first non-former-British colony to become a member of the British Commonwealth. The president's disciplined economic plan has been extremely successful, winning the country foreign confidence and aid.

While Mozambique posted some of the world's largest economic growth rates in the late 1990s, there has been some discontent over the decline in cashew nut exports, a major crop. The high rate of AIDS remains a concern, and torrential rains caused devastating floods in Feb. 2000, leaving more than 200,000 people homeless.

Myanmar

UNION OF MYANMAR

National name: Pyidaungsu Myanmar Naingngandau
Head of State (Chairman): Senior Gen. Than Shwe (1992)
Area: 265,039 sq. mi. (678,500 sq. km)
Population (2000 est.): 41,734,853 (average annual rate of natural increase: 0.8%; birth rate: 20.6/1000; infant mortality rate: 75.3/1000; density per sq. mi.: 157
Capital: Rangoon (Yangon). **Largest cities (est. 1983):** Rangoon (Yangon), 2,458,712; Mandalay, 532,895.
Monetary unit: Kyat. **Languages:** Burmese, minority languages. **Ethnicity/race:** Burman 68%, Shan 9%, Karen 7%, Rakhine 4%, Chinese 3%, Mon 2%, Indian 2%, other 5%. **Religions:** Buddhist 89.5%, Christian 4.9%, Muslim 3.8%, Hindu 0.05%, Animist 1.3%.
Literacy rate: 81% (1990)
Economic summary: GDP/PPP (1998 est.): $56.1 billion; $1,200 per capita. **Real growth rate:** 1.1%. **Inflation:** 50%. **Arable land:** 15%. **Agriculture:** paddy rice, corn, oilseed, sugarcane, pulses, hardwood. **Unemployment:** n.a. **Labor force:** 18.8 million (FY 95/96 est.): agriculture, 65.2%; industry, 14.3%; trade, 10.1%; government, 6.3%; other, 4.1% (FY 88/89 est.). **Industries:** agricultural processing, textiles and footwear, wood and wood products, copper, tin, tungsten, iron, construction materials, pharmaceuticals, fertilizer. **Natural resources:** petroleum, timber, tin, antimony, zinc, copper, tungsten, lead, coal, marble, limestone, precious stones, natural gas. **Exports** $940 million (1997): pulses and beans, teak, rice, rubber, hardwood. **Imports** $2.2 billion (1997): machinery, transport equipment, construction materials, food products. **Major trading partners:** India, Singapore, China, Thailand, Japan, Malaysia.

Geography Slightly smaller than Texas, Myanmar occupies the northwest portion of the Indochinese peninsula. India lies to the northwest and China to the northeast. Bangladesh, Laos, and Thailand are also neighbors. The Bay of Bengal touches the southwestern coast. The fertile delta of the Irrawaddy in the south contains a network of intercommunicating canals and nine principal river mouths.

Government Military regime. In 1989, the military government changed the name of Burma to Myanmar. The U.S. State Department does not recognize the name Myanmar or the military regime that represents it.

History The ethnic origins of modern Myanmar (known historically as Burma) are a mixture of Indo-Aryans, who began pushing into the area around 700 B.C., and the Mongolian invaders under Kublai Khan who penetrated the region in the 13th century. Anawrahta (1044–77) was the first great unifier of Myanmar.

In 1612 the British East India Company sent agents to Burma,, but the Burmese doggedly resisted efforts of British, Dutch, and Portuguese traders to establish posts on the Bay of Bengal. Through the Anglo-Burmese War in 1824–26 and two subsequent wars, the British East India Company expanded to the whole of Burma by 1886. Myanmar was annexed to India, then became a separate colony in 1937.

During World War II, Burma was a key battleground; the 800-mile Burma Road was the Allies' vital supply line to China. The Japanese invaded the country in Dec. 1941, and by May 1942 had occupied most of it, cutting off the Burma Road. After one of the most difficult campaigns of the war, Allied forces liberated most of Burma prior to the Japanese surrender in Aug. 1945.

Burma became independent on Jan. 4, 1948. In 1951 and 1952, the socialists achieved power. In 1968, after the government had made headway against communist and separatist rebels, the military regime adopted a policy of strict nonalignment and set out to follow "the Burmese Way" to socialism. But the insurgents continued to be active.

The civilian government was overthrown in Sept. 1988 by a military junta led by Gen. Saw Maung, an associate of U Ne Win. Virtually the entire country protested the takeover, but demonstrations were brutally quashed. The military government officially changed the name of the country to Myanmar in 1989. When the new government held elections in May 1990, the opposition National League for Democracy won in a landslide. But the military, or SLORC (State Law and Order Restoration Council), refused to recognize the election results. The leader of the opposition, Aung San Suu Kyi, was awarded the Nobel Peace Prize in 1991, which focused world attention on SLORC's repressive policies. Daughter of the assassinated general Aung San, who was revered as the father of Burmese independence, Suu Kyi remained under house arrest from 1989 until July 10, 1995. A new constitution was drafted in 1994 that called for an elected executive branch but appeared designed specifically to forbid Suu Kyi from becoming president. Suu Kyi continued to protest against the government, but almost every move she made was answered with a counterblow from SLORC.

Although the ruling junta has maintained a tight grip on Myanmar since 1988, it has not been able to subdue an insurgency in the country's south that has gone on for decades. The ethnic Karen movement has sought an independent homeland along Myanmar's southern border with Thailand. The economy has been in a state of collapse except for the junta-controlled heroin trade, the universities remained closed, and the AIDS epidemic, unrecognized by the junta, has gripped the country.

In April 1997 the U.S. government imposed sanctions intended to prevent U.S. private investment in Myanmar. In 1998, Suu Kyi's party set a deadline of Aug. 21 for the convening of the 1990 Parliament, which was never allowed to meet after its election. Suu Kyi also challenged the unofficial ban on her leaving the capital, a move that brought retaliation against many of her supporters. In the boldest protests since 1998, opposition politicians, headed by Suu Kyi, declared in Sept. 1998 that they would act as the country's Parliament and announced that the ruling junta was illegitimate. Thereafter, the government detained hundreds of opposition members and staged several huge artificial demonstrations in which participants called for the deportation of Suu Kyi.

Junta officials began reopening universities over the summer of 2000, allowing about 60,000 students (out of approximately 350,000) back to class, but not without conditions. Students and their parents had to pledge allegiance to the junta and vow to refrain from political activity.

In Jan. 2000, God's Army, a ragtag group of Karen dissidents under the command of twin 12-year-olds Johnny and Luther Htoo, seized a Thai hospital in Ratchaburi, taking 800 hostages.

In Sept. 2000 Suu Kyi was prevented from leaving Rangoon to investigate reports that the government was cracking down on her supporters. She was then placed under house arrest, prompting condemnation by a number of world leaders.

Namibia

REPUBLIC OF NAMIBIA

President: Sam Nujoma (1990)
Prime Minister: Hage Geingob (1990)
Status: Independent Country
Area: 318,261 sq. mi. (825,418 sq. km)
Population (2000 est.): 1,771,327 (average annual growth rate: 1.6%); birth rate: 35.2/1000; infant mortality rate: 70.9/1000; density per sq. mi.: 6
Capital and largest city (1992 est.): Windhoek, 161,000
Summer capital (est. 1980): Swakopmund, 17,500.
Monetary unit: Namibian dollars. **Languages:** Afrikaans, German, English (official), several indigenous. **Ethnicity/race:** black 86%, white 6.6%, mixed 7.4%. Note: about 50% of the population belong to the Ovambo tribe and 9% to the Kavangos tribe; other ethnic groups are: Herero 7%, Damara 7%, Nama 5%, Caprivian 4%, Bushmen 3%, Baster 2%, Tswana 0.5%. **Religion:** Predominantly Christian. Literacy rate: 38% (1960)
Economic summary: GDP/PPP (1998 est.): $6.6 billion; $4,100 per capita. **Real growth rate:** 2%. **Inflation:** 7% (1996 est.). **Unemployment:** 30%–40% including underemployment (1997). **Arable land:** 1%. **Agriculture:** millet, sorghum, peanuts, livestock, fish. **Labor force:** 500,000: agriculture, 49%; industry and commerce, 25%; government, 18%; services, 5%; mining, 3% (1994 est.). **Industries:** meat packing, fish processing, dairy products, mining (diamond, lead, zinc, tin, silver, tungsten, uranium, copper). **Natural resources:** diamonds, copper, uranium, gold, lead, tin, lithium, cadmium, zinc, salt, vanadium, natural gas, fish, suspected deposits of oil, natural gas, coal, iron ore. **Exports:** $1.44 billion (f.o.b., 1998 est.): diamonds, copper, gold, zinc, lead, uranium, cattle, processed fish, karakul skins. **Imports:** $1.48 billion (f.o.b., 1998 est.): foodstuffs, petroleum products and fuel, machinery and equipment, chemicals. **Major trading partners:** U.K., South Africa, Spain, Japan, Germany, U.S.

Geography Namibia, bounded on the north by Angola and Zambia and on the east by Botswana and South Africa in the south. It is for the most part a portion of the high plateau of southern Africa with a general elevation of from 3,000 to 4,000 feet.

Government Republic.

History The San peoples may have inhabited what is now Namibia more than 2000 years ago. The Bantu-speaking Herero migrated there in the 1600s. The Ovambo, the largest ethnic group today, migrated there in the 1800s.

In the late 15th century, the Portuguese explorer Bartolomeu Dias became the first European to visit Namibia. Formerly called South-West Africa, the territory became a German colony in 1884. In 1908 German troops massacred the majority of the Herero population. The land was taken by South African forces in 1915, becoming a South African mandate by the terms of the Treaty of Versailles in 1920.

South Africa's application for incorporation of the territory was rejected by the U.N. General Assembly in 1946 and South Africa was invited to prepare a trusteeship agreement instead. By a law passed in 1949, however, the territory was brought into much closer association with South Africa—including representation in its Parliament.

In 1968, the U.N. called for South Africa's withdrawal from the territory, which was given the name *Namibia*. When South Africa refused, the UN Security Council and the International Court of Justice condemned it. Under a 1974 Security Council resolution, South Africa was required to begin the transfer of power to the Namibians by May 30, 1975, or face U.N. action. Prime Minister Balthazar J. Vorster rejected U.N. supervision, claiming that his government was prepared to negotiate Namibian independence, but not with the South-West African People's Organization (SWAPO), the principal black separatist group. Meanwhile, the all-white legislature of South-West Africa eased several laws on apartheid in public places.

Despite international opposition, the Turnhalle Conference in Windhoek drafted a constitution to organize an interim government based on racial divisions, a proposal overwhelmingly endorsed by white voters in the territory in 1977. At the urging of ambassadors of the five Western members of the Security Council, South Africa on June 11 announced rejection of the Turnhalle constitution and acceptance of the Western proposal to include the South-West African People's Organization in negotiations.

As policemen wielding riot sticks charged demonstrators in a black South-West Africa township, South Africa handed over limited powers to a new, multiracial administration in the former German colony on June 17, 1985. Installation of the new government ended South Africa's direct rule, but South Africa retained an effective veto over the new government's decisions along with responsibility for the territory's defense and foreign policy.

An agreement between South Africa, Angola, and Cuba arranged for elections for a constituent assembly in Nov. 1989 to establish a new government. SWAPO won 57% of the vote, a majority but not enough to dictate a constitution unilaterally. In Feb. 1990, SWAPO leader Sam Nujoma was elected president and took office when Namibia became independent on March 21, 1990.

Nujoma was reelected in 1994, and again in 1999, after the constitution was amended to allow him to seek a third term. In Sept. 1999, fighting took place between Namibian troops and separatists from the Caprivi Strip, a narrow corridor jutting out of Namibia that provides the country with access to the Zambezi River.

A big obstacle to economic development is the country's uneven rainfall. Steps have been taken to desalinate seawater and drain water from the Okavango River. A pipeline from the Congo River far to the north has also been considered. A plan to build Africa's highest hydroelectric dam on the Kunene River has been criticized by environmentalists and the inhabitants of the area.

Nauru
REPUBLIC OF NAURU

President: Bernard Dowiyogo (2000)
Area: 8.2 sq. mi. (21 sq. km)
Population (2000 est.): 11,845; average annual growth rate: 2.1%; birth rate 27.9/1000; infant mortality rate 10.9/1000; density per sq. mi.: 1,445
Capital (1983): Yaren, 559. **Monetary unit:** Australian dollar. **Languages:** Nauruan and English. **Ethnicity/race:** Nauruan 58%, other Pacific Islander 26%, Chinese 8%, European 8%. **Religions:** Protestant, 58%; Roman Catholic, 24%; Confucian and Taoist, 8%. **Literacy rate:** 99%
Economic summary: GDP/PPP (1993 est.): $100 million; $10,000 per capita. **Real growth rate:** n.a. **Inflation:** -3.6% (1993). **Unemployment:** 0%. **Agriculture:** coconuts predominate. **Labor force:** employed in mining phosphates, public administration, education, and transportation. **Industries:** phosphate mining, financial services, coconut products. **Natural resources:** phosphates. **Exports:** $25.3 million (f.o.b., 1991): phosphates. **Imports:** $21.1 million (c.i.f., 1991): food, fuel, manufactures, building materials, machinery. **Major trading partners:** Australia, New Zealand, U.K., Japan. **Special relationship within the Commonwealth of Nations**

Geography Nauru (pronounced NAH-oo-roo) is an island in the Pacific just south of the equator, about 2,500 miles (4,023 km) southwest of Honolulu.

Government Republic.

History In 1798, a British navigator became the first European to visit the island. Germany annexed it in 1888, and by the turn of the century, phosphate, a lucrative fertilizer, began to be mined. The island was placed under joint Australian, New Zealand, and British mandate after World War I. The Japanese occupied the island during World War II, and forced 1,200 Nauruans—roughly two-thirds of the population—to relocate. In 1947, it became a U.N. trusteeship administered by Australia. By 1967, the phosphate mining industry finally came under control of the islanders, and on Jan. 31, 1968, Nauru became one of the world's smallest independent republics.

Devastated by almost a century of phosphate strip mining by foreign companies, Nauru appealed to the International Court of Justice. In 1993, Australia offered Nauru an out-of-court settlement for damages, agreeing to pay $2.5 million Australian dollars for 20 years. New Zealand and the U.K. additionally agreed to pay a one-time settlement of $12 million each. Declining phosphate prices, the high cost of maintaining an international airline, and investments that did not perform well combined to make the economy flounder in the late 1990s. In 1999, Nauru gained membership in the United Nations. In 2000, the U.S. put pressure on the country to review its banking system, which is believed to be used by Russian criminals for money laundering.

Nepal
KINGDOM OF NEPAL

Ruler: King Birendra Bir Bikram Shah Deva (1972)
Prime Minister: Girija Prasad Koirala (2000)
Area: 54,463 sq. mi. (140,800 sq. km)
Population (2000 est.): 24,702,119 (average annual rate of natural growth: 2.3%); birth rate: 33.8/1000; infant mortality rate: 75.9/1000; density per sq. mi.: 454
Capital and largest city (1993): Kathmandu, 535,000. **Other large cities:** Lalitpur, 190,000; Biratnagar, 132,000. **Monetary unit:** Nepalese rupee. **Languages:** Nepali (official), Newari, Bhutia, Maithali. **Ethnicity/race:** Newars, Indians, Tibetans, Gurungs, Magars, Tamangs, Bhotias, Rais, Limbus, Sherpas. **Religions:** Hindu, 90%; Buddhist, 5%; Islam, 3%. **Literacy rate:** 38% (1993)
Economic summary: GDP/PPP (1998 est.): $26.2 billion; $1,100 per capita. **Real growth rate:** 4.9%. **Inflation:** 7.8%. **Unemployment:** n.a.; substantial underemployment (1996). **Arable land:** 17%. **Agriculture:** rice, corn, wheat, sugarcane, root crops, milk, water buffalo meat. **Labor force:** 10 million (1996 est.): agriculture, 81%; services, 16%; industry, 3% (note: severe lack of skilled labor). **Industries:** tourism, carpet, textile, small rice, jute, sugar, and oilseed mills, cigarettes, cement and brick production. **Natural resources:** quartz, water, timber, hydropower potential, scenic beauty, small deposits of lignite, copper, cobalt, iron ore. **Exports:** $394 million (f.o.b., 1997 est., but does not include unrecorded border trade with India): carpets, clothing, leather goods, jute goods, grain. **Imports:** $1.7 billion (c.i.f., 1997 est.): petroleum products, fertilizer, machinery. **Major trading partners:** India, U.S., Germany, U.K., Singapore, Japan.

Geography A landlocked country the size of Arkansas, lying between India and the Tibetan Autonomous Region of China, Nepal contains Mount Everest (29,035 ft.; 8,850 m), the tallest mountain in the world. Along its southern border, Nepal has a strip of level land that is partly forested, partly cultivated. North of that is the slope of the main section of the Himalayan range, including Everest and many other peaks higher than 8,000 m.

Government In Nov. 1990, King Birendra promulgated a new constitution and introduced a multiparty democracy in Nepal.

History The first civilizations in Nepal, which flourished around the 6th century B.C., were confined to the fertile Kathmandu Valley where the present-day capital of the same name is located today. It was in this region that Prince Siddhartha Gautama was born circa 563 B.C. Gautama achieved enlightenment as Buddha, and spawned Buddhist belief.

Nepali rulers' early patronage of Buddhism largely gave way to Hinduism, reflecting the increased influence of India, around the 12th century A.D. Though the successive dynasties of the Gopalas, the Kiratis, and the Licchavis expanded their rule, it was not until the reign of the Malla kings from A.D. 1200–1769 that Nepal assumed the approximate dimensions of the modern state.

The kingdom of Nepal was unified in 1768 by King Prithvi Narayan Shah, who had fled India following the Moghul conquests of the subcontinent. Under

Shah and his successors Nepal's borders expanded as far west as Kashmir and as far east as Sikkim (now part of India). A commercial treaty was signed with Britain in 1792, and again in 1816 after more than a year of hostilities with the British East India Company.

In 1923, Britain recognized the absolute independence of Nepal. Between 1846 and 1951, the country was ruled by the Rana family, which always held the office of prime minister. In 1951, however, the king took over all power and proclaimed a constitutional monarchy. Mahendra Bir Bikram Shah became king in 1955. After Mahendra died of a heart attack in 1972, Prince Birendra, at 26, succeeded to the throne.

In 1990, a pro-democracy movement forced King Birendra to lift the ban on political parties and appoint an opposition leader to head an interim government as prime minister. The first free election in three decades provided a victory for the liberal Nepali Congress Party in 1991, although the Communists made a strong showing. A small Maoist guerrilla movement has been operating in the countryside since 1996.

In its ten years of democracy, Nepal has been led by seven different prime ministers, as one government after another failed. Parliament has been characterized by fragile alliances and mercurial coalitions. As a Nepali economist put it, "Democracy has more or less meant multiparty chaos. Coalitions of odd bedfellows with no ideological compatibility have been running things." In addition, corruption among MPs has been legion. Government officials belong to what has been called the "Pajero culture," a reference to the expensive Japanese cars, on which the king's courtiers and MPs do not pay the heavy import taxes that ordinary Nepalese are subject to. Because Parliament has been in constant flux, many MPs have lined their pockets as quickly as possible, knowing they may be out of a job at any moment. Voter accountability is nil.

In 1999, the political scene changed when Nepalis gave the majority of the seats in Parliament to the Nepali Congress Party, thereby giving one party enough security to attempt to effectively govern. Krishna Prasad Bhattarai, a famous Nepali freedom fighter who was imprisoned for 14 years by the king's government, became prime minister.

Throughout 2000, Maoist rebels maintained their violent campaign to overthrow the constitutional monarchy and install a communist government. In their four-year war, the Communist Party of Nepal-Maoist has targeted members of rival political parties and police stations. More than 1,300 people have been slain, nearly 200 of them were officers.

The Netherlands

KINGDOM OF THE NETHERLANDS

National name: Koninkrijk der Nederlanden
Sovereign: Queen Beatrix (1980)
Premier: Wim Kok (1994)
Area: 16,221 sq. mi. (41,526 sq. km)
Population (2000 est.): 15,892,237 (average annual rate of natural increase: 0.3%); birth rate: 12.1/1000; infant mortality rate: 4.4/1000; density per sq. mi.: 980
Capital and largest city (1994 est.): Amsterdam (official), 724,096; The Hague (administrative capital), 445,279. **Other large cities (1994 est.):** Rotterdam, 598,521; Utrecht, 234,106; Eindhoven, 196,130.
Monetary units: Guilder and euro. **Language:** Dutch, Frisian. **Ethnicity/race:** Dutch 96%, Moroccans, Turks, and other 4% (1988). **Religions:** Roman Catholic

34%, Protestant 25%, Muslim 3%, other 2%, unaffiliated 36%. **Literacy rate:** 99% (1979)
Economic summary: GDP/PPP (1998 est.): $348.6 billion; $22,200 per capita. **Real growth rate:** 3.7%. **Inflation:** 2%. **Unemployment:** 4.1%. **Arable land:** 27%. **Agriculture:** grains, potatoes, sugar beets, fruit, vegetables, livestock. **Labor force:** 7 million: services, 73%; manufacturing and construction, 23%; agriculture, 4%. **Industries:** agroindustries, metal and engineering products, electrical machinery and equipment, chemicals, petroleum, construction, microelectronics, fishing. **Natural resources:** natural gas, petroleum, fertile soil. **Exports:** $160 billion (f.o.b., 1998): machinery and equipment, chemicals, fuel, food and tobacco. **Imports:** $142 billion (f.o.b., 1998): machinery and transport equipment, chemicals, foodstuffs, fuel, consumer goods. **Major trading partners:** EU, central and eastern Europe, U.S.

Geography The Netherlands, on the coast of the North Sea, is twice the size of New Jersey. Part of the great plain of north and west Europe, the Netherlands has maximum dimensions of 190 by 160 miles (360 by 257 km) and is low and flat except in Limburg in the southeast, where some hills rise to 300 feet (92 m). About half the country's area is below sea level, making the famous Dutch dikes a requisite to the use of much land. Reclamation of land from the sea through dikes has continued through recent times. All drainage reaches the North Sea, and the principal rivers—Rhine, Maas (Meuse), and Schelde—have their sources outside the country.

Government Constitutional monarchy.

History Julius Caesar found the low-lying Netherlands inhabited by Germanic tribes—the Nervii, Frisii, and Batavi. The Batavi on the Roman frontier did not submit to Rome's rule until 13 B.C., and then only as allies.

The Franks controlled the region from the 4th to the 8th century, and it became part of Charlemagne's empire in the 8th and 9th centuries A.D. The area later passed into the hands of Burgundy and the Austrian Hapsburgs, and finally in the 16th century came under Spanish rule.

When Philip II of Spain suppressed political liberties and the growing Protestant movement in the Netherlands, a revolt led by William of Orange broke out in 1568. Under the Union of Utrecht (1579), the seven northern provinces became the United Provinces of the Netherlands. War between the United Provinces and Spain continued into the 17th century, but in 1648 Spain finally recognized Dutch independence.

The Dutch East India Company was established in 1602, and by the end of the 17th century Holland was one of the great sea and colonial powers of Europe.

The nation's independence was not completely established until after the Thirty Years' War (1618–48), when the country's rise as a commercial and maritime power began. In 1688, the English Parliament invited William of Orange, stadtholder, and his wife, Mary Stuart, to rule England as William III and Mary II. William then used the combined resources of England and the Netherlands to wage war on Louis XIV's France. In 1814, all the provinces of Holland and Belgium were merged into one kingdom, but in 1830 the southern provinces broke away to form the kingdom of Belgium. A liberal constitution was adopted by the Netherlands in 1848. The country remained neutral during World War I.

In spite of its neutrality in World War II, the Netherlands was invaded by the Nazis in May 1940, and the Dutch East Indies were later taken by the Japanese. The nation was liberated in May 1945. In 1948, after a reign of 50 years, Queen Wilhelmina abdicated and was succeeded by her daughter Juliana.

In 1949, after a four-year war, the Netherlands granted independence to the Dutch East Indies, which became the Republic of Indonesia. The Netherlands also joined NATO that year. The Netherlands joined the European Economic Community (later, the EU) in 1958. In 1999, it adopted the single European currency, the euro.

In 1963, it turned over the western half of New Guinea to Indonesia, ending 300 years of Dutch presence in Asia. Attainment of independence by Suriname on Nov. 25, 1975, left the Netherlands Antilles and Aruba as the country's only overseas territories.

Although prostitution is legal, the government moved in July 1997 to permit the operation of brothels as a means of regulating the former. Only those with a valid resident's permit would be permitted to be employed in the brothels. In 1999, the Netherlands again defied convention by preparing to legalize euthanasia. In Sept. 2000, the Netherlands became the first nation in the world to legalize same-sex marriages.

Two Libyan intelligence agents accused of the 1988 bombing of Pan Am flight 103 over Lockerbie, Scotland, went on trial in the Netherlands, though the court will be considered to be Scottish soil for the duration of the trial.

The Sovereign, Queen Beatrix Wilhelmina Armgard, born on Jan. 31, 1938, assumed the throne in 1980. In 1967, Beatrix gave birth to a son, Willem-Alexander Claus George Ferdinand, the first male heir to the throne since 1884.

Netherlands Autonomous Countries

Netherlands Antilles
Status: Part of the Kingdom of the Netherlands
Governor: J. M. Saleh (1990)
Prime Minister: Miguel A. Pourier (2000)
Area: 313 sq. mi. (800 sq. km)
Population (2000 est.): 210,134 (average annual growth rate: 1.1%); birth rate: 16.9/1000; infant mortality rate: 11.7/1000; density per sq. mi.: 671. **Ethnicity/race:** mixed African 85%, Carib Indian, European, Latin, Asian
Capital and largest city (1993 est.): Willemstad, 197,019. **Literacy rate:** 94% (1981)
Economic summary: GDP/PPP (1997 est.): $2.4 billion; $11,500 per capita. **Real growth rate:** −1.8%. **Inflation:** 3.3%. **Unemployment:** 14.9% (1998 est.). **Arable land:** 10%. **Agriculture:** aloes, sorghum, peanuts, vegetables, tropical fruit. **Labor force:** 89,000: government, 65%; industry and commerce, 28% (1983). **Industries:** tourism (Curacao, Sint Maarten, and Bonaire), petroleum refining (Curacao), petroleum transshipment facilities (Curacao and Bonaire), light manufacturing (Curacao). **Exports:** $268.2 million (f.o.b., 1997): petroleum products. **Imports:** $1.4 billion (c.i.f., 1997): crude petroleum, food, manufactures. **Major trading partners:** U.S., Honduras, Belgium-Luxembourg, Italy, Guatemala, Costa Rica, Venezuela, Mexico, Netherlands, Brazil.

The Netherlands Antilles are composed of two groups of Caribbean islands 500 miles (805 km) apart: Curaçao (173 sq. mi.; 448 sq. km) and Bonaire (95 sq. mi.; 246 sq. km) are located about 40 miles (64 km) off the Venezuelan coast.

Originally inhabited by Arawak Indians, these two islands as well as Aruba were claimed by Spain in

1527, and then by the Dutch in 1643. The Dutch Lesser Antilles to the north—Sint Eustatius, the southern part of Saint Martin (Dutch: Sint Maarten), and Saba—make up the remainder of the island federation. First inhabited by the Carib Indians, Saint Martin was explored by Columbus in 1493. In 1845 the six islands (then including Aruba) officially formed the Netherlands Antilles. In 1994 the islands voted to preserve their federation with the Netherlands.

Aruba
Status: Part of the Kingdom of the Netherlands
Governor: Olindo Koolman (1992)
Prime Minister: Henny Eman (1994)
Area: 75 sq. mi. (193 sq. km)
Population (2000 est.): 69,539; growth rate 0.7%; birth rate: 13.1/1000; infant mortality rate: 6.5/1000; density per sq. mi.: 927
Capital and largest city (1991 est.): Oranjestad, 20,050. **Ethnicity/race:** mixed European/Caribbean Indian 80%. **Literacy rate:** 95%
Economic summary: GDP/PPP (1997 est.): $1.5 billion; $22,000 per capita. **Real growth rate:** 6%. **Inflation:** 3% (1997). **Unemployment:** 0.6% (1996 est.). **Agriculture:** aloes, livestock, fish. **Labor force:** n.a.: most employment is in the tourist industry (1996). **Industries:** tourism, transshipment facilities, oil refining. **Exports:** $1.73 billion (1997, including oil reexports): mostly refined petroleum products. **Imports:** $2.12 billion (1997): food, consumer goods, manufactures, petroleum products, crude oil for refining and reexport. **Major trading partners:** U.S., EU, Netherlands, Japan.

Aruba, an island slightly larger than Washington D.C., lies 18 miles (28.9 km) off the coast of Venezuela in the southern Caribbean.

The Arawak Indians were the first inhabitants of Aruba. Spain explored the island in 1499, and more than a century later the Netherlands (1636) claimed the island. After a brief rule by the British, the Dutch again took control of the island in 1816, and it officially became part of the Netherlands Antilles in 1846.

On Jan. 1, 1986, Aruba seceded from the federation, but decided in 1994 to indefinitely postpone the transition to full independence. The Netherlands controls Aruba's defense and foreign affairs, but all internal affairs are handled by an island government directing its own civil service, judiciary, revenue, and currency.

New Zealand
Sovereign: Queen Elizabeth II (1952)
Governor-General: Sir Michael Hardie Boys (1996)
Prime Minister: Helen Clark (1999)
Area: 103,884 sq. mi. (268,680 sq. km) (excluding dependencies)
Population (2000 est.): 3,819,762 (average annual growth rate: 0.7%); birth rate: 14.3/1000; infant mortality rate: 6.4/1000; density per sq. mi.: 37
Capital: Wellington. **Largest cities (est. 1995):** Auckland, 952,600; Wellington, 331,100; Christchurch, 324,400. **Monetary unit:** New Zealand dollar.
Languages: English, Maori. **Ethnicity/race:** European 88%, Maori 8.9%, Pacific Islander 2.9%, other 0.2%.
Religions: Christian, 81%; none or unspecified, 18%; Hindu, Confucian, and other, 1% (1980) **Literacy rate:** 99%
Economic summary: GDP/PPP (1998 est.): $61.1 billion; $17,000 per capita. **Real growth rate:** −0.2%. **Inflation:** 1.1%. **Unemployment:** 7.6%. **Arable land:** 9%. **Agriculture:** wheat, barley, potatoes, pulses, fruit, vegetables, wool, beef, dairy products, fish. **Labor force:** 1.86 million (1998): services, 65.1%; industry,

25.1%; agriculture, 9.8% (1995). **Industries:** food processing, wood and paper products, textiles, machinery, transportation equipment, banking and insurance, tourism, mining. **Natural resources:** natural gas, iron ore, sand, coal, timber, hydropower, gold, limestone. **Exports:** $12.9 billion (1998 est.): wool, lamb, mutton, beef, fish, cheese, chemicals, forestry products, fruit and vegetables, manufactures, dairy products, wood. **Imports:** $13 billion (1998 est.): machinery and equipment, vehicles and aircraft, petroleum, consumer goods, plastics. **Major trading partners:** Australia, Japan, U.S., U.K. **Member of Commonwealth of Nations**

Geography New Zealand, about 1,250 miles (2,012 km) southeast of Australia, consists of two main islands and a number of smaller, outlying islands so scattered that they range from the tropical to the antarctic. The country is the size of Colorado. New Zealand's two main components are North Island and South Island, separated by Cook Strait, which varies from 16 to 190 miles (26 to 396 km) in width. North Island (44,281 sq. mi.; 115,777 sq. km) is 515 miles (829 km) long and volcanic in its south-central part. This area contains many hot springs and beautiful geysers. South Island (58,093 sq. mi.; 151,215 sq. km) has the Southern Alps along its west coast, with Mount Cook (12,283.3 ft.; 3,754 m) the highest point. The largest of the outlying islands are the Auckland Islands (234 sq. mi.; 606 sq. km), Campbell Island (44 sq. mi.; 114 sq. km), the Antipodes Islands (24 sq. mi.; 62 sq. km), and the Kermadec Islands (13 sq. mi.; 34 sq. km).

Government Parliamentary democracy.

History Maoris were the first inhabitants of New Zealand, arriving on the islands in about A.D. 1000. Maori oral history maintains the Maoris came to the island in seven canoes from other parts of Polynesia. In 1642 New Zealand was explored by Abel Tasman, a Dutch navigator. British captain James Cook made three voyages to the islands, beginning in 1769. Britain formally annexed the islands in 1840.

The Treaty of Waitangi (Feb. 6, 1840) between the British and several Maori tribes promised to protect Maori land if the Maoris recognized British rule. Encroachment upon the land by European settlers was relentless, however, and skirmishes between the two groups intensified.

From the outset, the country has been in the forefront in instituting social welfare legislation. New Zealand was the world's first country to give women the right to vote (1893). It adopted old age pensions (1898); a national child welfare program (1907); social security for the aged, widows, and orphans, along with family benefit payments; minimum wages; a 40-hour work week and unemployment and health insurance (1938); and socialized medicine (1941).

New Zealand fought with the Allies in both world wars as well as in Korea. In 1999, it became part of the U.N. peacekeeping force sent to East Timor to restore order after the bloody rampage of pro-Indonesian militias, who took revenge on the province for voting for independence from Indonesia.

Cook Islands and Overseas Territories

The Cook Islands (93 sq. mi.; 241 sq. km) were placed under New Zealand administration in 1901. They achieved self-governing status in association with New Zealand in 1965. **Population (2000 est.):** 20,407; growth rate 1.7%; birth rate: 22.2/1000;

infant mortality rate: 24.7/1000; density per square mile: 219. The seat of government is on Rarotonga Island. **Economic summary: GDP/PPP** (1994 est.): $79 million; $4,000 per capita. **Exports:** $4.2 million (f.o.b., 1994 est.): copra, fresh and canned citrus fruit, coffee, fish, pearls and pearl shells, clothing. **Imports:** $85 million (c.i.f., 1994): foodstuffs, textiles, fuel, timber, capital goods. **Major trading partners:** New Zealand, Japan, Hong Kong, Italy, Australia.

Niue (100 sq. mi.; 259 sq. km) was formerly administered as part of the Cook Islands. It was placed under separate New Zealand administration in 1901 and achieved self-governing status in association with New Zealand in 1974. The capital is Alofi. **Population (1998 est.):** 1,837; growth rate –3.65%. **Economic summary: GDP/PPP** (1993 est.): $2.4 million; per capita, $1,200. **Exports:** $117,500 (f.o.b., 1989): canned coconut cream, copra, honey, passion fruit products, pawpaw, root crops, limes, footballs, stamps, handicrafts. **Imports:** $4.1 million (c.i.f., 1989): food, live animals, manufactured goods, machinery, fuel, chemicals, lubricants, drugs. **Major trading partners:** New Zealand, Fiji, Cook Islands, Australia, Japan, Samoa, U.S.

The Ross Dependency (160,000 sq. mi.; 414,400 sq. km), an Antarctic region, was placed under New Zealand administration in 1923.

Tokelau (4 sq. mi.; 10 sq. km) was formerly administered as part of the Gilbert and Ellice Islands colony. It was placed under New Zealand administration in 1925. Its population is about 1,443 (July 1998 est.).

Nicaragua

REPUBLIC OF NICARAGUA

National name: República de Nicaragua
President: Arnoldo Alemán (1997)
Area: 50,180 sq. mi. (129,494 sq. km)
Population (2000 est.): 4,812,569 (average annual rate of natural increase: 2.3%); birth rate: 28.3/1000; infant mortality rate: 34.8/1000; density per sq. mi.: 96
Capital and largest city (1992 est.): Managua, 974,000. **Monetary unit:** Cordoba. **Language:** Spanish. **Ethnicity/race:** mestizo (mixed Amerindian and white) 69%, white 17%, black 9%, Indian 5%. **Religions:** Roman Catholic, 95%; Protestant, 5%. **Literacy rate:** 57% (1971)
Economic summary: GDP/PPP (1998 est.): $11.6 billion; $2,500 per capita. **Real growth rate:** 4%. **Inflation:** 16%. **Unemployment:** 14%; underemployment, 36% (1997 est.). **Arable land:** 9%. **Agriculture:** coffee, bananas, sugarcane, cotton, rice, corn, cassava (tapioca), citrus, beans, beef, veal, pork, poultry, dairy products. **Labor force:** 1.5 million: services, 54%; agriculture, 31%; industry, 15% (1995 est.). **Industries:** food processing, chemicals, metal products, textiles, clothing, petroleum refining and distribution, beverages, footwear. **Natural resources:** gold, silver, copper, tungsten, lead, zinc, timber, fish. **Exports:** $704 million (f.o.b., 1997): coffee, seafood, meat, sugar, gold, bananas. **Imports:** $1.45 billion (c.i.f., 1997): consumer goods, machinery and equipment, petroleum products. **Major trading partners:** U.S., Central America, Germany, Canada, Venezuela, Japan.

Geography Largest but most sparsely populated of the Central American nations, Nicaragua borders on Honduras to the north and Costa Rica to the south. It is slightly larger than New York State. Nicaragua is mountainous in the west, with fertile valleys. A plateau slopes eastward toward the Caribbean. Two big lakes—Nicaragua, about 100 miles long (161 km), and Managua, about 38 miles long (61 km)—are connected by the Tipitapa River. The Pacific coast is volcanic and very fertile. The Caribbean coast, swampy and indented, is aptly called the "Mosquito Coast."

Government Republic.

History Nicaragua, which derives its name from the chief of the area's leading Indian tribe during the Spanish Conquest, was first settled by the Spanish in 1522. The country achieved independence from Spain in 1838. For the next century, Nicaragua's politics were dominated by the competition for power between the Liberals, who were centered in the city of León, and the Conservatives, centered in Granada.

To back up its support of the new Conservative government in 1909, the U.S. sent a small detachment of Marines to Nicaragua and kept them there from 1912 to 1925. The Bryan-Chamorro Treaty of 1916 (terminated in 1970) gave the U.S. an option on a canal route through Nicaragua, and naval bases. Disorder after the 1924 elections brought in the U.S. Marines again. A guerrilla leader, Gen. César Augusto Sandino, began fighting the occupation force in 1927. He fought the U.S. troops until their withdrawal in 1933.

Gen. Anastasio Somoza García emerged, after ordering the assassination of Sandino, and ruled as dictator from 1936 until his assassination in 1956. He was succeeded by his son Luis, who alternated with trusted family friends in the presidency until his death in 1967. Another son, Maj. Gen. Anastasio Somoza Debayle, became president in 1967. The Somozas ruled Nicaragua with an iron fist, making Nicaragua less dependent on banana income, exiling political foes, and amassing a great family fortune.

Sandinista guerrillas, leftists who took their name from Gen. Sandino, launched an offensive in May 1979. After seven weeks of fighting, Somoza fled the country on July 17, 1979. The Sandinistas assumed power on July 19, promising to maintain a mixed economy, a nonaligned foreign policy, and a pluralist political system. On Jan. 23, 1981, the Reagan administration suspended U.S. aid, charging that Nicaragua, with the aid of Cuba and the Soviet Union, was supplying arms to rebels in El Salvador. The Sandinistas denied the charges. Later that year, Nicaraguan guerrillas known as "Contras," began a war to overthrow the Sandinistas. The elections were finally held on Nov. 4, 1984, with Daniel Ortega, the Sandinista junta coordinator, winning the presidency. The war intensified in 1986–87, with the resupplied Contras establishing themselves inside the country. Negotiations sponsored by the Contadora (neutral Latin American) nations foundered, but a peace plan sponsored by Arias, the Costa Rican president, led to a treaty that was signed by the Central American leaders in Aug. 1987.

Violetta Barrios de Chamorro, owner of the opposition paper *La Prensa*, led a broad anti-Sandinista coalition to victory in the presidential and legislative elections of 1990, ending 11 years of Sandinista rule. After a year in office, however, President Chamorro found herself besieged. Business groups were dissatisfied with the pace of reforms; Sandinistas, upset with what they regarded as the dismantling of their earlier achievements, threatened to take up arms again. In Feb. 1991 the president brought the military under her direct command. By early 1993 relations between the president and the coalition that backed her had soured over charges of corruption and the continuing influence of the Sandinistas on the government and the army. Former Managua mayor and Conservative candidate Arnoldo Aleman won the 1996 election. His closest rival was former president and Sandinista Daniel Ortega.

In 1998, Hurricane Mitch devastated Nicaragua, killing more than 9,000 people, leaving 2 million people homeless, and causing $10 billion in damages. Many Nicaraguans fled to the U.S., which had extended an immigration amnesty program, lasting until July 1999, to Nicaraguans.

Nicaragua remains one of the poorest countries in the Western Hemisphere. Disputes over who owns land and businesses have slowed attempts to improve the economy. Property is often caught in a three-way battle between those who owned it before the Sandinistas came to power; cooperatives set up by the Sandinistas; and former Contra rebels who claim they were promised land for joining the anti-Sandinista forces. In June 2000 Nicaragua resolved its border dispute with Costa Rica.

Niger

REPUBLIC OF NIGER

National name: République du Niger
President: Tandja Mamadou (1999)
Prime Minister: Hama Amadou (1999)
Area: 489,206 sq. mi. (1,267,000 sq. km)
Population (2000 est.): 10,075,511 (average annual rate of natural increase: 2.8%); birth rate: 51.5/1000; infant mortality rate: 124.9/1000; density per sq. mi.: 21
Capital and largest city (1988): Niamey, 398,265.
  Other large cities: Zinder, 120,900; Maradi, 112,970.
  Monetary unit: Franc CFA. **Ethnicity/race:** Hausa 56%, Djerma 22%, Fula 8.5%, Tuareg 8%, Beri Beri (Kanouri) 4.3%, Arab, Toubou, and Gourmantche 1.2%, about 4,000 French expatriates. **Languages:** French (official); Hausa; Songhai; Arabic. **Religions:** Islam, 80%; Animist and Christian, 20%. **Literacy rate:** 28% (1990)
Economic summary: GDP/PPP (1998 est.): $9.4 billion; $970 per capita. **Real growth rate:** 4.5%. **Inflation:** 4.8%. **Unemployment rate:** n.a. **Arable land:** 3%. **Agriculture:** cowpeas, cotton, peanuts, millet, sorghum, cassava (tapioca), rice, cattle, sheep, goats, camels, donkeys, horses, poultry. **Labor force:** 70,000: agriculture, 90%; industry and commerce, 6%; government, 4%. **Industries:** cement, brick, textiles, food processing, chemicals, slaughterhouses, a few other small light industries, uranium mining. **Natural resources:** uranium, coal, iron ore, tin, phosphates, gold, petroleum. **Exports:** $269 million (f.o.b. 1997): uranium ore, livestock products, cowpeas, onions. **Imports:** $295 million (c.i.f., 1997): consumer goods, primary materials, machinery, vehicles and parts, petroleum, cereals. **Major trading partners:** Greece, Canada, France, Nigeria, Côte d'Ivoire, U.S., Belgium-Luxembourg.

Geography Niger, in West Africa's Sahara region, is four-fifths the size of Alaska. It is surrounded by Mali, Algeria, Libya, Chad, Nigeria, Benin, and Burkina Faso. The Niger River in the southwest flows through the country's only fertile area. Elsewhere the land is semiarid.

Government Military rule.

History The nomadic Tuaregs were the first inhabitants in the Sahara region. The Hausa (14th century), the Zerma (17th century), the Gobir (18th century), and Fulani also established themselves in the region now called Niger.

Niger was incorporated into French West Africa in 1896. There were frequent rebellions, but when order was restored in 1922, the French made the area a colony. In 1958, the voters approved the French constitution and voted to make the territory an autonomous republic within the French community. The republic adopted a constitution in 1959 but the next year withdrew from the community, proclaiming its independence.

During the 1970s the country's economy flourished from uranium production, but when uranium prices fell in the 1980s, its brief period of prosperity ended. The 1974 army coup ousted President Hamani Diori, who had held office since 1960. An estimated 2 million people were starving in Niger, but 200,000 tons of imported food, half U.S.-supplied, substantially ended famine conditions by the year's end. The new president, Lt. Col. Seyni Kountché, chief of staff of the army, installed a 12-man military government. A predominantly civilian government was formed by Kountché in 1976.

In 1993 the country's first multiparty election resulted in the presidency of Ousmane Mahamane, who was then deposed in a Jan. 1996 coup. The constitution was suspended and the president arrested. In July the military leader of the coup, Ibrahim Baré Maïnassara, was declared president in a rigged election.

A cease-fire between the government and Tuareg rebels (Revolutionary Armed Forces of the Sahara) went into effect in 1995, and in June 1997, the Democratic Renewal Front, a hold-out Tuareg rebel group, also agreed to sign a peace accord. The nomadic Tuaregs, of Berber and Arab descent, have a fiercely insular culture and share little affinity with the black African majority of Niger. The impoverished Tuaregs have received little of the economic aid they were promised, which is not surprising given Niger's political instability and desperate poverty.

President Ibrahim Baré Maïnassara, considered a corrupt and ineffectual leader, was assassinated in April 1999 by his own guards. Ever since he had overthrown Niger's only democratically elected president, political unrest had dogged his presidency. The prime minister was retained, and the National Reconciliation Council, responsible for the coup, promised that elections would follow in nine months. In Nov. 1999, democratic elections were held, Tandja Mamadou was elected president, and foreign aid, primarily from France, was restored.

Nigeria

FEDERAL REPUBLIC OF NIGERIA

President: Olusegun Obasanjo (1999)
Area: 356,700 sq. mi. (923,770 sq. km)
Population (2000 est.): 123,337,822; average annual rate of natural increase: 2.6%; birth rate: 40.2/1000; infant mortality rate: 74.2/1000; density per sq. mi.: 480
Capital (1995 est.): Abuja, 339,000. **Largest cities:** Lagos (2000 est.), 13,050,000 (metro. area); Ibadan, 1,365,000; Ogbomosho, 711,900; Kano, 657,300.
Monetary unit: Naira. **Languages:** English (official), Hausa, Yoruba, Ibo, and more than 200 others.
Ethnicity/race: Hausa, Fulani, Yoruba, Ibo, Kanuri, Ibibio, Tiv, Ijaw. **Religions:** Islam, 50%; Christian, 40%; indigenous, 10%. **Literacy rate:** 51% (1990)
Economic summary: GDP/PPP (1998 est.): $106.2

billion; $960 per capita. **Real growth rate:** 1.6%. **Inflation:** 15%. **Unemployment:** 28% (1992 est.). **Arable land:** 33%. **Agriculture:** cocoa, peanuts, palm oil, corn, rice, sorghum, millet, cassava (tapioca), yams, rubber, cattle, sheep, goats, pigs, timber, fish. **Labor force:** 42.844 million: agriculture, 54%; industry, commerce, and services, 19%; government, 15%. **Industries:** crude oil, coal, tin, columbite, palm oil, peanuts, cotton, rubber, wood, hides and skins, textiles, cement and other construction materials, food products, footwear, chemicals, fertilizer, printing, ceramics, steel. **Natural resources:** petroleum, tin, columbite, iron ore, coal, limestone, lead, zinc, natural gas. **Exports:** $9.7 billion (f.o.b., 1998): petroleum and petroleum products, cocoa, rubber. **Imports:** $9.8 billion (f.o.b., 1998): machinery, chemicals, transportation equipment, manufactured goods, food and animals. **Major trading partners:** U.S., Spain, Italy, France, U.K., Germany, Netherlands. **Member of Commonwealth of Nations**

Geography Nigeria, one-third larger than Texas and the most populous country in Africa, is situated on the Gulf of Guinea in West Africa. Its neighbors are Benin, Niger, Cameroon, and Chad. The lower course of the Niger River flows south through the western part of the country into the Gulf of Guinea. Swamps and mangrove forests border the southern coast; inland are hardwood forests.

Government Multiparty government.

History The first inhabitants of what is now Nigeria were thought to have been the Nok people (500 B.C.– circa A.D. 200). The Kanuri, Hausa, and Fulani peoples subsequently migrated there. Islam was introduced in the 13th century, and the empire of Kanem controlled the area from the end of the 11th century to the 14th.

The Fulani empire ruled the region from the beginning of the 19th century until the British annexed Lagos in 1851 and seized control of the rest of the region by 1886. It formally became the Colony and Protectorate of Nigeria in 1914. During World War I, native troops of the West African frontier force joined with French forces to defeat the German garrison in the Cameroons.

On Oct. 1, 1960, Nigeria gained independence, becoming a member of the Commonwealth of Nations and joining the United Nations. Organized as a loose federation of self-governing states, the independent nation faced an overwhelming task of unifying a country with 250 ethnic and linguistic groups.

Rioting broke out in 1966, and military leaders, primarily of Ibo ethnicity, seized control. In July, a second military coup put Col. Yakubu Gowon in power, a choice unacceptable to the Ibos. Also in that year, the Muslim Hausas in the north massacred the predominantly Christian Ibos in the east, many of whom had been driven from the north. Thousands of Ibos took refuge in the eastern region, which declared its independence as the Republic of Biafra on May 30, 1967. Civil war broke out. In Jan. 1970, after 31 months of civil war, Biafra surrendered to the federal government.

Gowon's nine-year rule was ended in 1975 by a bloodless coup that made Army Brigadier Muritala Rufai Mohammed the new chief of state. The return of civilian leadership was established with the election of Alhaji Shehu Shagari as president in 1979. An oil boom in the 1970s buoyed the economy and by the 1980s Nigeria was considered an exemplar of African democracy and economic well-being.

The military again seized power in 1984, only to be followed by another military coup the following year. Maj. Gen. Ibrahim Babangida announced that the country would be returned to civilian rule, but after the presidential election of June 12, 1993, he voided the results. Nevertheless, Babangida resigned as president in Aug. In Nov. the military, headed by defense minister Sani Abacha, seized power again.

Corruption and notorious governmental inefficiency as well as a harshly repressive military regime characterized Abacha's reign over this oil-rich country. A U.N. fact-finding mission in 1996 reported that Nigeria's "problems of human rights are terrible and the political problems are terrifying." During the 1970s Nigeria had the 33rd highest per-capita income in the world, but by 1997 it had dropped to the 13th poorest.

Nigeria has established itself as West Africa's superpower through its military interventions in the civil wars of Liberia and Sierra Leone. Although Nigeria was unsuccessful in its attempt to defeat Charles Taylor's invasion of Liberia, in Sierra Leone Nigerian troops played a major role in overthrowing the military junta in 1998 and restoring its democratically elected president to power. In Sept. 1999, however, its troops, called ECOMOG, pulled out of Sierra Leone, leaving its fragile president to forge peace with the rebels. Nigeria's costly war efforts have been unpopular with its own people, who feel Nigeria's dire economic situation is being unnecessarily drained.

Under military rule for all but ten years since independence from Britain, the military has reneged on its promises to give up power eight times. Despite international pressure to institute democratic rule, the notoriously authoritarian Gen. Sani Abacha, whose formidable security forces kept a tight reign over the country, refused to loosen his absolute grip on political and military power. Abacha's repressive rule turned Nigeria into an international pariah. The hanging of writer Ken Saro-Wiwa in 1995 because he protested against the government was condemned around the world.

Abacha died of a heart attack on June 8, 1998, and was succeeded by another military ruler, Gen. Abdulsalam Abubakar, who also pledged to step aside for an elected leader by May 1999. Abubakar's freeing of political prisoners and other gestures of easing the military's iron-clad rule have shown some signs of hope for Nigeria. However, the sudden and some believe suspicious death of opposition leader Mashood Abiola, who had been imprisoned by the military ever since he legally won the 1993 presidential election, was a crushing blow to democratic proponents. In Feb. 1999 free presidential elections led to an overwhelming victory for General Olusegu Obasanjo, a former member of the military elite who was imprisoned for three years for criticizing the military rule, and released just eight months before his election.

Obasanjo's commitment to democracy, his anti-corruption drives, and his desire to recover billions allegedly stolen by the family and cronies of Abacha were generally popular. However, Nigeria's stability is threatened by fighting between fundamentalist Muslims and Christians over the spread of Islamic law, sharia, across the heavily Muslim north. In addition, the Ogoni people and international environmentalists continue to protest oil drilling near the south coast. Nigeria has the 11th largest oil reserves in the world, with estimated reserves of 22.5 billion barrels.

Norway

KINGDOM OF NORWAY

National name: Kongeriket Norge
Sovereign: King Harald V (1991)
Prime Minister: Jens Stoltenberg (2000)
Area: 125,049 sq. mi. (324,220 sq. km)
Population (2000 est.): 4,481,162 (average annual growth rate: 0.3%); birth rate: 12.8/1000; infant mortality rate: 4/1000; density per sq. mi.: 36
Capital and largest city (1995): Oslo, 483,401. **Other large cities:** Bergen, 221,717; Trondheim, 142,927; Stavanger, 103,946. **Monetary unit:** Krone.
Languages: Two official forms of Norwegian: Bokmål and Nynorsk. **Ethnicity/race:** Germanic (Nordic, Alpine, Baltic), Lapps (Sami). **Religions:** Evangelical Lutheran 87.8% (state church), other Protestant and Roman Catholic 3.8%, none 3.2%, unknown 5.2%.
Literacy rate: 99% (1976)
Economic summary: GDP/PPP (1998 est.): $109 billion; $24,700 per capita. **Real growth rate:** 2.4%. **Inflation:** 2.3%. **Unemployment:** 2.6% (year end 1997). **Arable land:** 3%. **Agriculture:** oats, other grains, beef, milk, fish. **Labor force:** 2.3 million (1998 est.): services, 71%; industry, 23%; agriculture, forestry, and fishing, 6% (1993). **Industries:** petroleum and gas, food processing, shipbuilding, pulp and paper products, metals, chemicals, timber, mining, textiles, fishing. **Natural resources:** petroleum, copper, natural gas, pyrites, nickel, iron ore, zinc, lead, fish, timber, hydropower. **Exports:** $39.8 billion (f.o.b., 1998): petroleum and petroleum products, machinery and equipment, metals, chemicals, ships, fish. **Imports:** $37.1 billion (f.o.b., 1998): machinery and equipment, chemicals, metals, foodstuffs. **Major trading partners:** EU, U.S., Japan.

Geography Norway is situated in the western part of the Scandinavian peninsula. It extends about 1,100 miles (1,770 km) from the North Sea along the Norwegian Sea to more than 300 miles (483 km) above the Arctic Circle, the farthest north of any European country. It is slightly larger than New Mexico. Nearly 70% of Norway is uninhabitable and covered by mountains, glaciers, moors, and rivers. The hundreds of deep fjords that cut into the coastline give Norway an overall oceanfront of more than 12,000 miles (19,312 km). Galdhø Peak, at 8,100 feet (2,469 m), is Norway's highest point and the Glåma (Glomma) is the principal river, at 372 miles (598 km) long.

Government Constitutional monarchy.

History Norwegians, like the Danes and Swedes, are of Teutonic origin. The Norsemen, also known as Vikings, ravaged the coasts of northwestern Europe from the 8th to the 11th century and were ruled by local chieftains. Olaf II Haraldsson became the first effective king of all Norway in 1015 and began converting the Norwegians to Christianity. After 1442, Norway was ruled by Danish kings until 1814, when it was united with Sweden—although retaining a degree of independence and receiving a new constitution—in an uneasy partnership. In 1905, the Norwegian Parliament arranged a peaceful separation and invited a Danish prince to the Norwegian throne—King Haakon VII. A treaty with Sweden provided that all disputes be settled by arbitration and that no fortifications be erected on the common frontier.

When World War I broke out, Norway joined with Sweden and Denmark in a decision to remain neutral and to cooperate in the joint interest of the three countries. In World War II, Norway was invaded by the Germans on April 9, 1940. It resisted for two months before the Nazis took complete control. King Haakon and his government fled to London, where they established a government-in-exile. Maj. Vidkun Quisling, who served as Norway's premier during the war, was the most notorious of the Nazi collaborators. The word for traitor, *quisling,* bears his name. He was executed by the Norwegians on Oct. 24, 1945.

Despite severe losses in the war, Norway recovered quickly as its economy expanded. The country led the world in social experimentation. It entered the North Atlantic Treaty Organization in 1949. In the late 20th century, the Labor Party and the Conservative Party seesawed for control, each sometimes having to lead minority governments. An important debate has been over Norway's membership in the European Union. In an advisory referendum held in Nov. 1994, voters rejected seeking membership for their nation in the EU. The country became the second-largest net oil exporter after Saudi Arabia in 1995. Norway continued to experience rapid economic growth into the new millennium.

In Sept. 2000, Norwegian truckers held a blockade of oil terminals in protest of high gas prices. The blockade failed, however, to gain concessions from the government. Norwegians pay among the highest gas prices in Europe, 70% of which is tax.

Dependencies of Norway

Svalbard (24,208 sq. mi.; 62,700 sq. km), in the Arctic Ocean about 360 miles north of Norway, consists of the Spitsbergen group and several smaller islands, including Bear Island, Hope Island, King Charles Land, and White Island (or Gillis Land). The capital is Longyearbyen. It came under Norwegian administration in 1925. Population: 2,594 (July 1998 est.); growth rate: –3.55%. 62% of the population is Russian and Ukrainian; 38% are Norwegian. Coal mining is major economic activity. There is also some trapping of seal, polar bear, fox, and walrus. **Bouvet Island** (23 sq. mi.; 60 sq. km), an island nature reserve in the South Atlantic about 1,600 miles southsouthwest of the Cape of Good Hope, came under Norwegian administration in 1928. It is uninhabited. **Jan Mayen Island** (147 sq. mi.; 380 sq. km), in the Arctic Ocean between Norway and Greenland, came under Norwegian administration in 1929. There are no permanent inhabitants, just workers at the navigation base and weather/radio station. **Peter I Island** (96 sq. mi.; 249 sq. km), lying off Antarctica in the Bellinghausen Sea, came under Norwegian administration in 1931. **Queen Maud Land,** a section of Antarctica, came under Norwegian administration in 1939.

Oman

SULTANATE OF OMAN

National name: Saltonat Uman
Sultan: Qabus ibn Sa'id (1970)
Area: 82,030 sq. mi. (212,460 sq. km)[1]
Population (2000 est.): 2,533,389 (average annual rate of natural increase: 3.4%); birth rate: 38.1/1000; infant mortality rate: 23.3/1000; density per sq. mi.: 31
Capital and largest city (1991 est.): Muscat, 350,000.
Monetary unit: Languages: Arabic (official); also English and Indian languages. **Ethnicity/race:** Arab, Baluchi, South Asian (Indian, Pakistani, Sri Lankan, Bangladeshi), African. **Religion:** Islam, 95%.
Literacy rate: 80%
Economic summary: GDP/PPP (1998 est.): $18.6

billion; $7,900 per capita. **Real growth rate:** –8.5%. **Inflation:** –0.2% (1997 est.).
Unemployment: n.a. **Agriculture:** dates, limes, bananas, alfalfa, vegetables, camels, cattle, fish.
Labor force: 850,000 (1997 est.). **Industries:** crude oil production and refining, natural gas production, construction, cement, copper. **Natural resources:** petroleum, copper, asbestos, some marble, limestone, chromium, gypsum, natural gas.
Exports: $7.6 billion (f.o.b., 1997 est.): petroleum, reexports, fish, metals, textiles. **Imports:** $4 billion (f.o.b., 1997): machinery, transport equipment, manufactured goods, food, livestock, lubricants.
Major trading partners: Japan, China, Thailand, South Korea, U.S., U.K., Germany.

1. Excluding the Kuria Muria Islands.

Geography Oman is a 1,000-mile-long (1,700-km) coastal plain at the southeastern tip of the Arabian peninsula lying on the Arabian Sea and the Gulf of Oman. The interior is a plateau. The country is the size of Kansas.

Government Absolute monarchy.

History Arabs migrated to Oman from the 9th century B.C. onward, and conversion to Islam occurred in the 7th century A.D. Muscat, the capital of the geographical area known as Oman, was occupied by the Portuguese from 1508 to 1648. Then it fell to Ottoman Turks, but in 1741 Ahmad ibn Sa'id forced them out. The descendants of Sultan Ahmad rule Oman today.

He expanded his empire to East Africa, and for a time the Omani capital was in Zanzibar. After 1861, however, Zanzibar fell from Omani control.

The sultans and imams of Oman clashed continuously throughout the 20th century until 1959, when the last Ibadi imam was evicted from the country. In a palace coup on July 23, 1970, the sultan, Sa'id bin Taimur, who had ruled since 1932, was overthrown by his son, who promised to establish a modern government and use newfound oil wealth to aid the people of this very isolated state. Oman joined the Arab League and the United Nations in 1971.

A long border dispute with Yemen ended in late Oct. 1992 when the sultan signed an agreement with the Yemeni president. In 1997, Oman and Yemen signed maps defining the border between the two countries.

In 1997, Sultan Qabus granted women the right to be elected to the country's consultative body, the Shura Council (Majlis al-Shura). The council has no formal powers, but advises the sultan on economic matters and public policy. Two women were elected to the council in 1997 as well as in 2000.

Pakistan

ISLAMIC REPUBLIC OF PAKISTAN

Head of State: Gen. Pervez Musharraf (1999)
President: Mohammad Rafiq Tarar (1998)
Area: 310,400 sq. mi. (803,940 sq. km)[1]
Population (2000 est.): 141,553,775 (average annual growth rate: 2.3%); birth rate: 32.1/1000; infant mortality rate: 82.5/1000; density per sq. mi.: 456
Capital (1981 census): Islamabad, 201,000. **Largest cities:** Karachi (2000 est.), 12,100,000 (metro. area); Lahore (2000 est.), 6,350,000 (metro. area); Faisalabad (Lyallpur), 1,920,000; Rawalpindi, 920,000; Hyderabad, 795,000. **Monetary unit:** Pakistan rupee.
Principal languages: Punjabi 48%, Sindhi 12%, Siraiki (a Punjabi variant) 10%, Pashtu 8%, Urdu

(official) 8%, Balochi 3%, Hindko 2%, Brahui 1%, English, Burushaski, and others. **Ethnicity/race:** Punjabi, Sindhi, Pashtun (Pathan), Baloch, Muhajir (immigrants from India and their descendants). **Religions:** Islam, 97%; Hindu, Christian, Buddhist, Parsi. **Literacy rate:** 35% (1990)
Economic summary GNP/PPP: (1998 est.): $270 billion; $2,000 per capita. **Real growth rate:** 5%. **Inflation:** 7.8% (FY97/98). **Unemployment:** n.a. **Arable land:** 27%. **Agriculture:** cotton, wheat, rice, sugarcane, fruit, vegetables, milk, beef, mutton, eggs. **Labor force:** 37.8 million (1998): agriculture, 47%; mining and manufacturing, 17%; services, 17%; other, 19%. **Industries:** textiles, food processing, beverages, construction materials, clothing, paper products, shrimp. **Natural resources:** land, extensive natural gas reserves, limited petroleum, poor quality coal, iron ore, copper, salt, limestone. **Exports:** $8.5 billion (FY97/98): cotton, textiles, clothing, rice, leather, carpets. **Imports:** $10.1 billion (FY97/98): petroleum, petroleum products, machinery, transportation equipment, vegetable oils, animal fats, chemicals. **Major trading partners:** EU, U.S., Hong Kong, Japan, China.

1. Excluding Kashmir and Jammu.

Geography Pakistan is situated in the western part of the Indian subcontinent, with Afghanistan and Iran on the west, India on the east, and the Arabian Sea on the south. The name "Pakistan" is derived from the Urdu words "Pak" (meaning pure) and "stan" (meaning country). It is nearly twice the size of California.

The northern and western highlands of Pakistan contain the towering Karakoram and Pamir mountain ranges, which include some of the world's highest peaks: K2 (28,250 ft. [8,611 m]) and Nanga Parbat (26,660 ft. [8,126 m]). The Baluchistan Plateau lies to the west, and the Thar Desert and an expanse of alluvial plains, the Punjab and Sind, lie to the east. The 1,000-mile-long (1,609 km) Indus River and its tributaries flow through the country from the Kashmir region to the Arabian Sea.

Government Military rule was instituted Oct. 1999.

History Pakistan was one of the two original successor states to British India, which was partitioned along religious lines in 1947. For almost 25 years following independence, it consisted of two separate regions, East and West Pakistan, but now is made up only of the western sector. Both India and Pakistan have laid claim to the Kashmir region, and this territorial dispute led to war in 1949, and again in 1965, 1971, and 1999, and remains unresolved today.

What is now Pakistan was in prehistoric times the Indus Valley civilization (c. 2500–1700 B.C.). A series of invaders—Aryans, Persians, Greeks, Arabs, Turks, and others—controlled the region for the next several thousand years. Islam, the dominant religion, was introduced in A.D. 711. In 1526, the land became part of the Mogul Empire, which ruled most of the Indian subcontinent from the 16th to the mid-18th century. By 1857 the British became the dominant power in the region. With Hindus holding most of the economic, social, and political advantages, the Muslim minority's dissatisfaction grew, leading to the formation of the nationalist Muslim League in 1906 by Mohammed Ali Jinnah (1876–1949). The league supported Britain in the Second World War while the Hindu nationalist leaders, Nehru and Gandhi, refused. In return for the league's support of Britain, Jinnah expected British backing for Muslim autonomy. Britain agreed to the formation of Pakistan as a separate

dominion within the Commonwealth in Aug. 1947, a bitter disappointment to India's dream of a unified subcontinent. Jinnah became governor-general. The partition of Pakistan and India along religious lines resulted in the largest migration in human history, with 17 million people fleeing across the borders in both directions to escape the sectarian violence accompanying the partition.

Pakistan became a republic on March 3, 1956, with Major General Iskander Mirza becoming the first president. Military rule prevailed for the next two decades. Tensions between East and West Pakistan existed from the outset. Separated by more than a thousand miles, the two regions shared few cultural and social traditions other than religion. To the growing resentment of East Pakistan, the West monopolized the country's political and economic power. In 1970, East Pakistan's Awami League, led by the Bengali leader Sheik Mujibur Rahman, secured a majority of the seats in the National Assembly. President Yahya Khan postponed the opening of the National Assembly to skirt East Pakistan's demand for greater autonomy, provoking civil war. The independent state of Bangladesh, or Bengali nation, was proclaimed on March 26, 1971. Indian troops entered the war in its last weeks fighting on the side of the new state. Pakistan was defeated on Dec. 16, 1971, and President Yahya Khan stepped down. Zulfikar Ali Bhutto took over Pakistan and accepted Bangladesh as an independent entity. In 1976 formal relations between India and Pakistan resumed.

Pakistan's first elections under civilian rule took place in March 1977, and the overwhelming victory of Bhutto's Pakistan People's Party (PPP) was denounced as fraudulent. A rising tide of violent protest and political deadlock led to a military takeover on July 5 by Gen. Mohammed Zia ul-Haq. Bhutto was tried and convicted for the 1974 murder of a political opponent, and despite worldwide protests was executed on April 4, 1979, touching off riots by his supporters. Zia declared himself president on Sept. 16, 1978, and ruled by martial law until Dec. 30, 1985, when a measure of representative government was restored. On Aug. 19, 1988, President Zia was killed in a mid-air explosion of a Pakistani Air Force plane. Elections at the end of 1988 brought longtime Zia opponent Benazir Bhutto, daughter of Zulfikar Bhutto, into office as prime minister.

In the 1990s, Pakistan saw a shaky succession of governments—Benazir Bhutto was prime minister twice and Nawaz Sharif three times, until he was deposed in a coup on Oct. 12, 1999 by Gen. Pervez Musharraf. The Pakistani public, familiar with military rule for 25 of the nation's 52-year history, generally viewed the coup as a positive step, and hoped it would bring a badly needed economic upswing.

Former prime minister Sharif was convicted in April 2000 of hijacking and terrorism and sentenced to two life terms in prison. The charges stem from the Oct. 1999 incident in which Sharif refused to allow a passenger plane, which was carrying 198 passengers, including Gen. Pervez Musharraf, to land in Karachi. In July 2000, the deposed prime minister was sentenced to an additional 14 years in jail on charges of tax evasion. In Aug., Musharaff said local, nonparty elections would be held by mid-2001. He has not yet set a timetable for national elections.

India went ahead with five nuclear tests in May 1998 near Pakistan's borders, which further deteriorated fragile relations between Pakistan and India. In an act of nuclear brinkmanship, Pakistan evened the score by conducting nuclear tests of its own on May 28th and May 30th. In the fall of 1998, Pakistan indicated a willingness to sign a nuclear test-ban treaty to rid itself of Western sanctions, which had been imposed since the nuclear testing.

Fighting with India again broke out in the disputed territory of Kashmir in May 1999. The territory has been a major source of antagonism between the countries since their independence, when a 1949 U.N. cease-fire divided it into regions of Indian and Pakistani control. Pakistan controls one-third of Kashmir, which is a predominantly Muslim territory.

Palau

REPUBLIC OF PALAU

President: Kuniwo Nakamura (1993)
Total area: 177 sq. mi. (458 sq. km)
Population (2000 est.): 18,766 (average rate of natural increase: 1.3%); birth rate: 19.9/1000; infant mortality rate: 17.1/1000; density per sq. mi.: 106
Capital and largest city (1995): Koror, 12,299.
Monetary unit: U.S. dollar used. **Languages:** Palauan is the official language, though English is commonplace. **Ethnicity/race:** Palauans are a composite of Polynesian, Malayan, and Melanesian races. **Religions:** Christian. About one-third of the islanders observe Modekngei religion, indigenous to Palau. **Literacy rate:** 86% (1980)
Economic summary: GDP/PPP: (1997 est.) $160 million (note: GDP numbers reflect U.S. spending), $8,800 per capita. **Real growth rate:** 10%. **Inflation rate:** n.a. **Unemployment:** 7%. **Agriculture:** coconuts, copra, cassava (tapioca), sweet potatoes. **Labor force:** n.a. **Industries:** tourism, craft items (from shell, wood, pearls), some commercial fishing and agriculture. **Natural resources:** forests, minerals (especially gold), marine products, deep-seabed minerals. **Exports:** $14.3 million (f.o.b., 1996): trochus (type of shellfish), tuna, copra, handicrafts. **Imports:** $72.4 million (f.o.b., 1996). **Major trading partners:** U.S., Japan.

Geography The Palau island chain consists of about 200 islands located in the western Pacific Ocean 528 mi. (650 km) southeast of the Philippines. Only eight of the islands are permanently inhabited.

Government Republic.

History The original settlers of Palau are believed to have arrived from Indonesia as early as 2500 B.C. The Palau islands' position on the western threshold of Oceania and their proximity to Southeast Asia have led to the population being a mixture of Malay, Melanesian, Filipino, and Polynesian ancestry.

Explored by the Spanish navigator Ruy López de Villalobos in 1543, the islands remained under nominal Spanish ownership for more than 300 years before Spain sold them to Germany in 1899. Japan occupied Palau during World War I and received a mandate over them from the League of Nations in 1920. They remained in Japanese control and served as an important naval base until the U.S. seized them during World War II. After the war they became a U.N. trusteeship (1947), administered by the U.S. Palau signed a compact of free association with the U.S. in 1992, requiring the U.S. to provide economic aid in exchange for the right to build and maintain U.S. military facilities in Palau. Palau became a sovereign state in 1994.

Palestinian State (proposed)

WEST BANK AND GAZA STRIP

President: Yasir Arafat (1996)
Area: West Bank: 2,263 sq. mi. (5,860 sq. km); Gaza Strip 139 sq. mi. (360 sq. km)
Population (2000 est.): West Bank: 2,020,298, Gaza Strip: 1,132,063 (average annual rate of natural increase: West Bank: 3.2%, Gaza Strip: 3.9%); birth rate: West Bank: 36.7/1000, Gaza Strip: 43.1/1000; infant mortality rate: West Bank: 22.3/1,000, Gaza Strip: 26/1000; density per sq. mi.: West Bank: 893, Gaza Strip: 8,144
Capital: Undetermined. **Largest cities (1996 est.):** Hebron, 294,116; Nablus, 217,935. **Monetary units:** New Israeli shekels, Jordanian dinars, U.S. dollars. **Languages:** Arabic, Hebrew, English, French. **Ethnicity/race:** West Bank: Palestinian Arab and other 83%, Jewish 17%; Gaza Strip: Palestinian Arab and other 99.4%, Jewish 0.6%. **Religions:** West Bank: Muslim 75%, Jewish 17%, Christian and other 8%; Gaza Strip: Muslim 98.7%, Christian 0.7%, Jewish 0.6%
Economic summary: Gaza Strip: GDP/PPP (1998 est.): $1.1 billion; $1,000 per capita. **Real growth rate:** 2.2%. **Inflation:** 8.8% (1997 est.). **Unemployment:** 26.8% (1997 est.). **Arable land:** 24%. **Agriculture:** olives, citrus, vegetables; beef, dairy products. **Labor force:** n.a.; services, 66%; industry, 21%; agriculture, 13% (1996). **Industries:** generally small family businesses that produce cement, textiles, soap, olive-wood carvings, and mother-of-pearl souvenirs; the Israelis have established some small-scale modern industries in an industrial center (includes West Bank). **Natural resources:** negl. **Exports:** $781 million (f.o.b., 1997 est.) (includes West Bank): citrus. **Imports:** $2.1 billion (c.i.f., 1997 est.) (includes West Bank): food, consumer goods, construction materials. **Major trading partners:** Israel, Egypt, West Bank. **West Bank:** GDP/PPP (1998 est.): $3.1 billion; $2,000 per capita. **Real growth rate:** 2.2%. **Inflation:** 7.6% (1997 est.). **Unemployment:** 17.3% (1997 est.). **Arable land:** 27%. **Agriculture:** olives, citrus, vegetables; beef, dairy products. **Labor force:** n.a.; agriculture, 13%; industry, 13%; commerce, restaurants, and hotels, 12%; construction, 8%; other services, 54% (1996). **Natural resources:** negl. **Major trading partners:** Israel, Jordan.

Geography The West Bank is mostly composed of limestone hills (conventionally called the Samarian Hills north of Jerusalem and the Judaean Hills south of Jerusalem) having an average height of 2,300 to 3,000 feet (700 to 900 m). The Gaza Strip is located between Israel and Egypt on the Mediterranean coast. It is a flat to rolling sand- and dune-covered coastal plain.

Government The Palestinian Authority (PA), with Arafat its elected leader, took control of the newly non-Israeli-occupied areas, assuming all governmental duties in 1994. Permanent peace talks and implementation of Palestinian self-rule in the West Bank and Gaza Strip are still ongoing.

History The history of the proposed modern Palestinian state, which is expected to be formed from the territories of the West Bank and Gaza strip, began with the British Mandate of Palestine. From Sept. 29 1923, until May 14, 1948, Britain controlled the region, but by 1947 Britain appealed to the U.N. to solve the complex problem of competing Palestinia and Jewish claims to the land. In Aug. 1947, the U.N. proposed dividing Palestine into a Jewish state, an Arab state, and a small international zone. Arabs rejected the idea. As soon as Britain pulled out of Palestine in 1948, neighboring Arab nations invaded, intent on crushing the newly declared State of Israel. Israel emerged victorious, affirming its sovereignty. The remaining areas of Palestine were divided between Transjordan (now Jordan), which annexed the West Bank, and Egypt, which gained control of the Gaza Strip.

Through a series of political and social policies, Jordan sought to consolidate its control over the political future of Palestinians and to become their speaker. Jordan even extended citizenship to Palestinians in 1949—Palestinians constituted about two-thirds of the country's population. In the Gaza Strip, administered by Egypt from 1948–67, poverty and unemployment were high, and most of the Palestinians lived in refugee camps.

In the Arab-Israeli war of 1967, Israel, over a period of six days, defeated the military forces of Egypt, Syria, and Jordan and annexed the territories of East Jerusalem, the Golan Heights, the West Bank, the Gaza Strip, and all of the Sinai peninsula. The Palestinian Liberation Organization (PLO), formed in 1964, was a terrorist organization bent on Israel's annihilation. Palestinian rioting, demonstrations, and terrorist acts against Israelis became chronic. In 1974, PLO leader Yasir Arafat addressed the U.N. general assembly, the first stateless government to do so. Violence again escalated in 1987 during the *intifada* ("shaking off"), a new era in Palestinian mass mobilization. In 1988, PLO leader Yasir Arafat proclaimed the independence of the Palestinian State (including the West Bank and Gaza Strip), as a government-in-exile, and publicly eschewed terrorism.

In 1993, highly secretive talks in Norway between the PLO and the Israeli government resulted in the Oslo agreement. The accord stipulated a five-year plan in which Palestinians of the West Bank and the Gaza Strip would gradually become self-governing. On Sept. 13, 1993, Arafat and Israeli prime minister Yitzak Rabin signed the historic "Declaration of Principles." As part of the agreement, Israel pulled out of the Gaza Strip and Jericho in the West Bank in 1994.

The Palestinian Authority (PA), with Arafat as its elected leader, took control of the newly non-Israeli-occupied areas, assuming all governmental duties. Permanent peace talks and implementation of Palestinian self-rule in the West Bank and Gaza Strip are still ongoing after seven years. The election in 1999 of Israeli prime minister Ehud Barak was viewed by moderate Palestinians as a positive step toward peace.

But despite intensive negotiations between Barak and Arafat in the summer and fall of 2000, the two leaders remained deadlocked over Israeli-occupied East Jerusalem, which Arafat insists must be the capital of the future Palestinian state. Arafat, however, allowed his Sept. 13 deadline for declaring a Palestinian state to pass in the interest of continued negotiations with Israel.

Panama

REPUBLIC OF PANAMA

National name: República de Panamá
President: Mireya Moscoso (1999)
Area: 29,761 sq. mi. (78,200 sq. km)
Population (2000 est.): 2,808,268 (average annual rate of natural increase: 1.5%); birth rate: 19.5/1000; infant

mortality rate: 20.8/1000; density per sq. mi.: 94
Capital and largest city (1993 est.): Panama City, 450,668. **Other large cities:** San Miguelito, 293,564; Colón, 137,825. **Monetary unit:** Balboa. **Languages:** Spanish (official); many bilingual in English. **Ethnicity/race:** mestizo (mixed Indian and European ancestry) 70%, West Indian 14%, white 10%, Indian 6%. **Religions:** Roman Catholic, over 93%; Protestant, 6%. **Literacy rate:** 89% (1990)
Economic summary: GDP/PPP (1998 est.): $19.9 billion; $7,300 per capita. **Real growth rate:** 2.7% (1998 est.). **Inflation:** 1.4% (1998 est.). **Unemployment:** 13.1% (1997 est.). **Arable land:** 7%. **Agriculture:** bananas, rice, corn, coffee, sugarcane, vegetables, livestock, shrimp. **Labor force:** 1.044 million (1997 est.): government and community services, 31.8%; agriculture, hunting, and fishing, 26.8%; commerce, restaurants, and hotels, 16.4%; manufacturing and mining, 9.4%; transportation and communications, 6.2%; finance, insurance, and real estate, 4.3%; construction, 3.2%. **Industries:** construction, petroleum refining, brewing, cement and other construction materials, sugar milling. **Natural resources:** copper, mahogany forests, shrimp. **Exports:** $6.68 billion (f.o.b., 1997): bananas, shrimp, sugar, clothing, coffee. **Imports:** $7.38 billion (f.o.b., 1997): capital goods, crude oil, foodstuffs, consumer goods, chemicals. **Major trading partners:** U.S., EU, Central America and Caribbean, Japan.

Geography The southernmost of the Central American nations, Panama is south of Costa Rica and north of Colombia. The Panama Canal bisects the isthmus at its narrowest and lowest point, allowing passage from the Caribbean Sea to the Pacific Ocean. Panama is slightly smaller than South Carolina. It is marked by a chain of mountains in the west, moderate hills in the interior, and a low range on the east coast. There are extensive forests in the fertile Caribbean area.

Government Republic.

History Explored by Columbus in 1502 on his fourth voyage and explored by Balboa in 1513, Panama was the principal shipment point for supplies to and from South and Central America in colonial days. In 1821, when Central America revolted against Spain, Panama joined Colombia, which had already declared its independence. For the next 82 years, Panama attempted unsuccessfully to break away from Colombia. Between 1850 and 1900 Panama had 40 administrations, 50 riots, 5 attempted secessions, and 13 U.S. interventions. After U.S. proposals for canal rights over the narrow isthmus had been rejected by Colombia, Panama proclaimed its independence from Colombia with U.S. backing in 1903.

For canal rights in perpetuity, the U.S. paid Panama $10 million and agreed to pay $250,000 each year, which was increased to $430,000 in 1933. It was further increased under a revised treaty signed in 1955. In exchange, the U.S. got the Canal Zone—a 10-mile-wide strip across the isthmus—and a considerable degree of influence in Panama's affairs.

Panama and the U.S. agreed in 1974 to negotiate the eventual reversion of the canal to Panama, despite strongly expressed opposition in the U.S. Congress. The texts of two treaties—one governing the transfer of the canal and the other guaranteeing its neutrality after transfer—were signed by President Omar Torrijos Herara and President Carter in Washington on Sept. 7.

The treaties provided for gradual transfer of the operations of the canal to Panamanians, the phasing out of U.S. military bases, and reversion of lands and waters used in the management of the canal. Similarly, Panama was to assume jurisdiction over the zone by degrees. A second pact promised an open and neutral canal in peace and war for all nations. The transfer was to be completed by Dec. 31, 1999. A Panamanian referendum approved the treaties in Oct., but further changes were insisted upon by the U.S. Senate. The principal change specified that although only Panama would maintain forces in its territory after Dec. 31, 1999, the U.S. would have the right to use military force to keep the canal operating if it should become obstructed. The U.S. Senate approved the treaties in March–April 1978.

Nicolas Ardito Barletta, Panama's first directly elected president in 16 years, was inaugurated on Oct. 11, 1984, for a five-year term. He was a puppet of behind-the-scenes strongman Gen. Manuel Noriega and was replaced by vice president Eric Arturo Delvalle, another Noriega supporter, a year later. In 1988, Noriega was indicted in the U.S. for drug trafficking, but when Delvalle attempted to fire him, he forced the National Assembly to replace Delvalle with Manuel Solis Palma. In Dec. 1989, the assembly named Noriega the "maximum leader" and declared the U.S. and Panama to be in a state of war. In Dec. 1989, 24,000 U.S. troops seized control of Panama City in an attempt to capture Noriega after a U.S. soldier was killed in Panama. On Jan. 3, 1990, Noriega surrendered himself to U.S. custody and was transported to Miami to stand trial for drug trafficking (he was subsequently convicted). Guillermo Endara, who probably would have won the election suppressed by Noriega, was installed as president.

Ernesto Pérez Balladares of the Democratic Revolutionary Party, whose elections invoked memories of the party's founder, Omar Torrijos, won the May 1994 elections, the first since the U.S. ousted Noriega. In May 1999, Panama elected its first woman president, Mireya Moscoso. She is the widow of former president Arnulfo Arias, who served in the 1960s.

On Dec. 31, 1999, the U.S. formally handed over control of the Panama Canal to Panama. In June 2000, the country's open banking laws again came under international fire, as the Financial Action Task Force created by the seven leading industrialized nations, the Group of 7, blacklisted Panama. The task force charged that Panama is one of 15 nations to allow its banking system to recycle money made by international criminal activity.

Panama Canal. The idea of building the canal first came about in 1524, when King Charles V of Spain ordered a survey of a waterway across the isthmus. In 1878, the Colombian government gave a construction concession to the French Canal Company. The effort ended in bankruptcy nine years later, and the United States ultimately paid the French $40 million for their rights and assets. The U.S. project, built on territory controlled by the United States, began in 1904 and was completed in 1914.

Papua New Guinea

Sovereign: Queen Elizabeth II (1952)
Governor General: Silas Atopare (1997)
Prime Minister: Mekere Morauta (1999)
Area: 178,704 sq. mi. (461,690 sq. km)
Population (2000 est.): 4,926,984 (average annual rate of natural increase: 2.5%); birth rate: 32.7/1000; infant mortality rate: 59.9/1000; density per sq. mi.: 28
Capital and largest city (1994 est.): Port Moresby, 250,000. **Monetary unit:** Kina. **Languages:** English, Tok Pisin (a Melanesian Creole English), Hiri Motu,

and 717 distinct native languages. **Ethnicity/race:** Papuan, Melanesian, Negrito, Micronesian, Polynesian. **Religions:** over half are Christian, remainder indigenous. **Literacy rate:** 50% (1990)
Economic summary: GDP/PPP (1998 est.): $11.1 billion; $2,400 per capita. **Real growth rate:** 1.6% (1998 est.). **Inflation:** 12% (FY97/98 est.). **Unemployment:** n.a. **Agriculture:** coffee, cocoa, coconuts, palm kernels, tea, rubber, sweet potatoes, fruit, vegetables, poultry, pork. **Labor force:** 1.941 million: agriculture, 64% (1993 est.). **Industries:** copra crushing, palm oil processing, plywood production, wood chip production, mining of gold, silver, and copper, crude oil production, construction, tourism. **Natural resources:** copper, gold, silver, timber, natural gas, oil, fisheries. **Exports:** $2.2 billion (f.o.b., 1997): gold, copper ore, oil, logs, palm oil, coffee, cocoa, crayfish and prawns. **Imports:** $1.5 billion (c.i.f., 1997): machinery and transport equipment, manufactured goods, food, fuel, chemicals. **Major trading partners:** Australia, Japan, Germany, U.K., South Korea, China, Singapore, U.S., New Zealand, Malaysia. **Member of Commonwealth of Nations**

Geography Papua New Guinea occupies the eastern half of the island of New Guinea, just north of Australia, and many outlying islands. The Indonesian province of Irian Jaya is to the west. To the north and east are the islands of Manus, New Britain, New Ireland, and Bougainville, all part of Papua New Guinea. About one-tenth larger than California, its mountainous interior has only recently been explored. Two major rivers, the Sepik and the Fly, are navigable for shallow-draft vessels.

Government Parliamentary democracy.

History The first inhabitants of the island New Guinea were Papuan, Melanesian, and Negrito tribes, who altogether spoke more than 700 distinct languages. The eastern half of New Guinea was first explored by Spanish and Portuguese explorers in the 16th century. In 1828, the Dutch formally took possession of the western half of the island (now the province of Irian Jaya, Indonesia). In 1885, Germany formally annexed the northern coast and Britain took similar action in the south. In 1906, Britain transferred its rights to British New Guinea to a newly independent Australia, and the name of the territory was changed to the Territory of Papua. Australian troops invaded German New Guinea (called Kaiser-Wilhelmsland) in World War I and gained control of the territory under a League of Nations mandate. New Guinea and some of Papua were invaded by Japanese forces in 1942. After being liberated by the Australians in 1945, it became a United Nations trusteeship, administered by Australia. The territories were combined and called the Territory of Papua and New Guinea.

Australia granted limited home rule in 1951. Autonomy in internal affairs came nine years later, and in Sept. 1975, Papua New Guinea achieved complete independence from Britain.

A violent nine-year secessionist movement took place on the island of Bougainville. In 1989, guerrillas of the Bougainville Revolutionary Army (BRA) shut down the island's Australian-owned copper mine, a major source of revenue for the country. The rebels believed that Bougainville deserved a greater share of the earnings for its copper. In 1990, the BRA declared Bougainville's independence, whereupon the government blockaded the island until Jan. 1991, when a peace treaty was signed. In 1997, Papua New

Guinea's government hired South African mercenary soldiers to fight on Bougainville in order to end the long-running crisis, but this action led to massive demonstrations and the mercenary contract was rescinded. In April 1998, a cease-fire was declared.

On July 17, 1998, an earthquake-triggered tsunami (tidal wave) off the northern coast of Papua New Guinea killed at least 1,500 people and left thousands more injured and homeless.

Paraguay

REPUBLIC OF PARAGUAY

National name: República del Paraguay
President: Luis Ángel González Macchi (1999)
Area: 157,047 sq. mi. (406,750 sq. km)
Population (2000 est.): 5,585,828 (average annual rate of natural increase: 2.6%); birth rate: 31.3/1000; infant mortality rate: 30.1/1000; density per sq. mi.: 36
Capital and largest city (1992): Asunción, 502,426.
Other large cities (1992): Ciudad del Este, 133,893; San Lorenzo, 133,311. **Monetary unit:** Guaraní.
Languages: Spanish (official), Guaraní. **Ethnicity/race:** mestizo (mixed Spanish and Indian) 95%, whites plus Amerindians 5%. **Religion:** Roman Catholic, 90%. **Literacy rate:** 90% (1990)
Economic summary: GDP/PPP (1998 est.): $19.8 billion; $3,700 per capita. **Real growth rate:** –0.5%. **Inflation:** 14.6% (1998 est.). **Unemployment:** 8.2% (urban 1996 est.). **Arable land:** 6%. **Agriculture:** cotton, sugarcane, soybeans, corn, wheat, tobacco, cassava (tapioca), fruit, vegetables, beef, pork, eggs, milk, timber. **Labor force:** 1.8 million (1995 est.): agriculture, 45%. **Industries:** meat packing, oilseed crushing, milling, brewing, textiles, other light consumer goods, cement, construction. **Natural resources:** iron ore, timber, manganese, limestone, hydropower. **Exports:** $1.1 billion (f.o.b., 1997 est.): cotton; soybeans, timber, vegetable oils, meat products, coffee, tung oil. **Imports:** $2.5 billion (c.i.f., 1996 est.): capital goods, consumer goods, foodstuffs, raw materials, fuel. **Major trading partners:** Brazil, Netherlands, Argentina, U.S., Uruguay, Chile, Hong Kong.

Geography California-size Paraguay is surrounded by Brazil, Bolivia, and Argentina in south-central South America. Eastern Paraguay, between the Paraná and Paraguay Rivers, is upland country with the thickest population settled on the grassy slope that inclines toward the Paraguay River. The greater part of the Chaco region to the west is covered with marshes, lagoons, dense forests, and jungles.

Government Republic.

History Indians speaking Guaraní—the most common language in Paraguay today, after Spanish—were the country's first inhabitants. In 1526 and again in 1529, Sebastian Cabot explored Paraguay when he sailed up the Paraná and Paraguay Rivers. From 1608 until their expulsion from the Spanish dominions in 1767, the Jesuits maintained an extensive establishment in the south and east of Paraguay. In 1811, Paraguay revolted against Spanish rule and became a nominal republic under two consuls.

Paraguay was governed by three dictators during the first 60 years of independence. The third, Francisco López, waged war against Brazil and Argentina in 1865–70, a conflict in which the male population was almost wiped out. A new constitution in 1870, designed to prevent dictatorships and internal strife, failed to do so, and not until 1912 did a period of comparative economic and political stability begin. The Chaco War (1932–35) with Bolivia won Paraguay more western territory.

After World War II, politics became particularly unstable. Alfredo Stroessner ruled as dictator from 1954 until 1989, during which he was responsible for the torture and murder of thousands of political opponents. Although the Stroessner regime was criticized by the U.S. during the Carter administration for violating human rights, Paraguay did not suffer cuts in U.S. military aid—the U.S.'s conditional support of Stroessner's dictatorship was part of its cold war policy in South America to stamp out communism. Only five officials in Paraguay have been convicted for torture and killing during Stroessner's regime, and Stroessner himself lives in asylum in neighboring Brazil.

Stroessner was overthrown by an army leader, Gen. Andres Rodriguez, in 1989. Rodriguez won in Paraguay's first multi-candidate election in decades. Paraguay's new constitution went into effect in 1992. In 1993, Juan Carlos Wasmosy, a wealthy businessman and the candidate of the governing Colorado Party, won a five-year term in freely held elections. In June 1997, a banking crisis struck Paraguay, involving the president, his entire government, and the central bank president. Raúl Cubas Grau was elected president in May 1998.

Vice President Luis María Argaña was assassinated in March 1999. On March 28 President Cubas was forced out of office because of his alleged involvement in the assassination—the vice president had been critical of the president's refusal to jail his mentor, Gen. Lino Oviedo, who was convicted of leading a failed 1996 coup against President Wasmosy.

The new president, Luis Ángel González Macchi, has begun to substantially overhaul the government, and for the first time since Stroessner was overthrown in 1989, political and economic power is no longer entirely within the hands of the corrupt and military-backed Colorado Party. The U.S. has accused the Colorado Party of smuggling, money laundering, trafficking Bolivian cocaine, and supporting international terrorist organizations.

In Aug. 2000 the opposition Liberal Party won its first major victory in more than 50 years with the election of Julio Cesar Franco as vice president. He narrowly defeated the son of the previous vice president, Argaña. The same month authorities ordered the country's top anti-corruption official to remain in Paraguay and face fraud, blackmailing, and other charges.

Peru

REPUBLIC OF PERU

National name: República del Perú
President: Alberto Fujimori (1990)
Prime Minister: Federico Salas Guevara (2000)
Area: 496,222 sq. mi. (1,285,220 sq. km)
Population (2000 est.): 27,012,899 (average annual rate of natural increase: 1.9%); birth rate: 24.5/1000; infant mortality rate: 40.6/1000; density per sq. mi.: 54
Capital and largest city (2000 est.): Lima, 7,450,000 (metro. area). **Other large cities:** Arequipa, 939,800; Callao, 648,000; Trujillo, 1,287,000; Chiclayo, 951,000. **Monetary unit:** Nuevo Sol (1991). **Languages:** Spanish, Quéchua, Aymara, and other native languages. **Ethnicity/race:** Indian 45%, mestizo (mixed Indian and European ancestry) 37%, white 15%, black, Japanese, Chinese, and other 3%. **Religion:** Roman Catholic. **Literacy rate:** 85% (1990)
Economic summary: GDP/PPP (1998 est.): $111.8 billion; $4,300 per capita. **Real growth rate:** 1.8% (1998 est.). **Inflation:** 6.7% (1997). **Unemployment:** 8.2%,

extensive underemployment (1996). **Arable land:** 3%. **Agriculture:** coffee, cotton, sugarcane, rice, wheat, potatoes, plantains, coca, poultry, beef, dairy products, wool, fish. **Labor force:** 7.6 million (1996 est.): agriculture, mining and quarrying, manufacturing, construction, transport, services. **Industries:** mining of metals, petroleum, fishing, textiles, clothing, food processing, cement, auto assembly, steel, shipbuilding, metal fabrication. **Natural resources:** copper, silver, gold, petroleum, timber, fish, iron ore, coal, phosphate, potash. **Exports:** $6.8 billion (f.o.b., 1997): copper, zinc, fishmeal, crude petroleum and byproducts, lead, refined silver, coffee, cotton. **Imports:** $10.3 billion (c.i.f., 1997): machinery, transport equipment, foodstuffs, petroleum, iron and steel, chemicals, pharmaceuticals. **Major trading partners:** U.S., Japan, U.K., China, Germany, Colombia, Chile, Venezuela.

Geography Peru, in western South America, extends for nearly 1,500 miles (2,414 km) along the Pacific Ocean. Colombia and Ecuador are to the north, Brazil and Bolivia to the east, and Chile to the south. Five-sixths the size of Alaska, Peru is divided by the Andes Mountains into three sharply differentiated zones. To the west is the coastline, much of it arid, extending 50 to 100 miles (80 to 160 km) inland. The mountain area, with peaks over 20,000 feet (6,096 m), lofty plateaus, and deep valleys, lies centrally. Beyond the mountains to the east is the heavily forested slope leading to the Amazonian plains.

Government Republic.

History Peru was once part of the great Incan empire and later the major vice-royalty of Spanish South America. It was conquered in 1531–33 by Francisco Pizarro. On July 28, 1821, Peru proclaimed its independence, but the Spanish were not finally defeated until 1824. For a hundred years thereafter, revolutions were frequent; a new war was fought with Spain in 1864–66, and unsuccessful war was fought with Chile from 1879 to 1883 (the War of the Pacific).

Peru emerged from 20 years of dictatorship in 1945 with the inauguration of President José Luis Bustamente y Rivero after the first free election in many decades. But he served for only three years and was succeeded in turn by Gen. Manual A. Odria, Manuel Prado y Ugarteche, and Fernando Belaúnde Terry. On Oct. 3, 1968, Belaúnde was overthrown by Gen. Juan Velasco Alvarado. Velasco nationalized the nation's second-biggest bank and turned two large newspapers over to Marxists in 1970, but he also allowed a new agreement with a copper-mining consortium of four American firms. In 1975, Velasco was replaced in a bloodless coup by his premier, Gen. Francisco Morales Bermudez, who promised to restore civilian government. In elections held on May 18, 1980, Belaúnde Terry, the last previous civilian president and the candidate of the conservative parties that have traditionally ruled Peru, was elected president again.

Peru's fragile democracy survived this period of stress. In 1985, Belaúnde Terry was the first elected president to turn over power to a constitutionally elected successor since 1945. Alberto Fujimori won the 1990 elections. Citing continuing terrorism, drug trafficking, and corruption, Fujimori in April 1992 dissolved Congress, suspended the constitution, and imposed censorship. A new constitution was approved in 1993. In Jan. 1995 fighting flared once again along part of the disputed border with Ecuador, as it had in 1941 and 1981. In April, President Fujimori was reelected, and his party (Change 90–New Majority) obtained a majority in the legislature.

In Dec. 1996, Tupac Amaru rebels seized control of the diplomatic compound of the Japanese ambassador's residence in Lima, holding 72 hostages. The standoff continued until April when government forces successfully stormed the residence, freeing the hostages. In the months that followed Fujimori came under fire for his increasingly authoritarian style. In 1997, the disastrous effects of El Niño caused the failure of the fish harvest and a severe drought in Peru.

In May 1999, the presidents of Ecuador and Peru signed a treaty ending the nearly 60-year border dispute involving a stretch of Amazon jungle. The two countries have fought three wars and numerous smaller skirmishes over the border.

Fujimori was easily reelected in May 2000 to a third five-year term, after his opponent, Alejandro Toledo, withdrew from the election charging election fraud. The Organization of American States (OAS) has been investigating voting irregularities.

In Sept. 2000, after Fujimori's intelligence chief, Vladimiro Montesinos, was caught on videotape bribing an opposition congressman, Fujimori called for new elections, declared he would step down, and announced he would dismantle the powerful National Intelligence Service, which, according to the group Human Rights Watch, is a corrupt "system of bribes, threats, extortion, privileges, and surveillance by which this government has preserved and accumulated power."

The Philippines

REPUBLIC OF THE PHILIPPINES

National name: Republika ng Pilipinas
President: Joseph Estrada (1998)
Area: 115,830 sq. mi. (300,000 sq. km)
Population (2000 est.): 81,159,644 (average annual rate of natural increase: 2.2%); birth rate: 27.9/1000; infant mortality rate: 29.5/1000; density per sq. mi.: 701
Capital and largest city (2000 est.): Manila, 13,450,000 (metro. area). **Other large cities:** Quezon City, 1,669,776 (part of Manila metro. area); Cebu, 610,415.
Monetary unit: Peso. **Languages:** Filipino (based on Tagalog), English; regional languages: Tagalog, Ilocano, Cebuano, others. **Ethnicity/race:** Christian Malay 91.5%, Muslim Malay 4%, Chinese 1.5%, other 3%. **Religions:** Roman Catholic, 84%; Protestant, 10%; Islam, 5%; Buddhist and other, 3%. **Literacy rate:** 94% (1990)
Economic summary: GDP/PPP (1998 est.): $270.5 billion; $3,500 per capita. **Real growth rate:** –0.5% (1998 est.). **Inflation:** 9.7% (1998 est.). **Unemployment:** 9.6% (October 1998). **Arable land:** 19%. **Agriculture:** rice, coconuts, corn, sugarcane, bananas, pineapples, mangoes, pork, eggs, beef, fish. **Labor force** 31.3 million (1998 est.): agriculture, 39.8%; government and social services, 19.4%; services, 17.7%; manufacturing, 9.8%; construction, 5.8%; other, 7.5%. **Industries:** textiles, pharmaceuticals, chemicals, wood products, food processing, electronics assembly, petroleum refining, fishing. **Natural resources:** timber, petroleum, nickel, cobalt, silver, gold, salt, copper. **Exports:** $25 billion (f.o.b., 1998 est.): electronics and telecommunications, machinery and transport, garments, other. **Imports:** $29 billion (f.o.b., 1998 est.): raw materials and intermediate goods, capital goods, consumer goods, fuel. **Major trading partners:** U.S., Japan, EU, Association of Southeast Asian Nations (ASEAN), Hong Kong, Taiwan, Saudi Arabia.

Geography The Philippine Islands are an archipelago of over 7,000 islands lying about 500 miles (805 km) off the southeast coast of Asia. The overall land area is comparable to that of Arizona. Only about 7% of the islands are larger than one square mile, and only one-third have names. The largest are Luzon in the north (40,420 sq. mi.; 104,687 sq. km), Mindanao in the south (36,537 sq. mi.; 94,631 sq. km), and Samar (5,124 sq. mi.; 13,271 sq. km). The islands are of volcanic origin, with the larger ones crossed by mountain ranges. The highest peak is Mount Apo (9,690 ft.; 2,954 m) on Mindanao.

Government Republic.

History Ferdinand Magellan, the Portuguese navigator in the service of Spain, explored the Philippines in 1521. Twenty-one years later, a Spanish exploration party named the group of islands in honor of Prince Philip, who was later to become Philip II of Spain. Spain retained possession of the islands for the next 350 years.

The Philippines were ceded to the U.S. in 1899 by the Treaty of Paris after the Spanish-American War. Meanwhile, the Filipinos, led by Emilio Aguinaldo, had declared their independence. They initiated guerrilla warfare against U.S. troops that persisted until the capture of Aguinaldo in 1901. By 1902, peace was established except among the Islamic Moros on the southern island of Mindanao.

The first U.S. civilian governor-general was William Howard Taft (1901–04). The Jones Law (1916) provided for the establishment of a Philippine Legislature composed of an elective Senate and House of Representatives. The Tydings-McDuffie Act (1934) provided for a transitional period until 1946, at which time the Philippines would become completely independent. Under a constitution approved by the people of the Philippines in 1935, the Commonwealth of the Philippines came into being with Manuel Quezon y Molina as president.

On Dec. 8, 1941, the islands were invaded by Japanese troops. Following the fall of Gen. Douglas MacArthur's forces at Bataan and Corregidor, Quezon established a government-in-exile that he headed until his death in 1944. He was succeeded by Vice President Sergio Osmeña. U.S. forces under MacArthur reinvaded the Philippines in Oct. 1944 and, after the liberation of Manila in Feb. 1945, Osmeña reestablished the government.

The Philippines achieved full independence on July 4, 1946. Manual A. Roxas y Acuña was elected its first president, succeeded by Elpidio Quirino (1948–53), Ramón Magsaysay (1953–57). Carlos P. García (1957–61), Diosdado Macapagal (1961–65), and Ferdinand E. Marcos (1965–86).

Under Marcos, civil unrest broke out in opposition to the leader's despotic rule. Martial law was declared on Sept. 21, 1972, and Marcos proclaimed a new constitution that ensconced himself as president. Martial law was officially lifted on Jan. 17, 1981, but Marcos and his wife Imelda retained broad powers.

Despite warnings that his life would be endangered, opposition leader Benigno S. Aquino returned to the Philippines from self-exile on Aug. 21, 1983. He was shot to death as he was being escorted from his plane by military police at Manila International Airport. There was widespread suspicion that Marcos had ordered Aquino's assassination. The event became a watershed in modern Filipino political history, acting as a catalyst for opposition groups and the "People Power" movement, led by the late leader's widow, Corazon Aquino.

In an attempt to resecure American support, Marcos set presidential elections for Feb. 7, 1986. With the support of the Catholic Church, Corazon Aquino declared her candidacy. Marcos was declared the official winner, but independent observers reported widespread election fraud and vote-rigging. Anti-Marcos protests exploded in the capital Manila, Defense Minister Juan Enrile and Lt. Gen. Fidel Ramos defected to the opposition, and Marcos lost virtually all support; he was forced to flee into exile and entered the U.S. on Feb. 25, 1986.

The Aquino government survived coup attempts by Marcos supporters and other right-wing elements, including one in Nov. by Enrile. Legislative elections on May 11, 1987, gave pro-Aquino candidates a large majority. Negotiations on renewal of leases for U.S. military bases threatened to sour relations between the two countries. Volcanic eruptions from Mount Pinatubo, however, severely damaged Clark Air Base, and in July 1991 the U.S. decided simply to abandon it.

In elections in May 1992, Gen. Fidel Ramos, who had the support of outgoing Aquino, won the presidency in a seven-way race. In Sept. of that year, the U.S. Navy turned over the Subic Bay naval base to the Philippines, ending a long-standing U.S. military presence. Meanwhile, the separatist Moro National Liberation Front was fighting a protracted war for an Islamic homeland on Mindanao, the southernmost of the two main islands. In 1996, the group agreed to a government plan designed to grant it a greater degree of political autonomy. An administrative body, headed by the former rebel chief, was established to oversee development on the southern islands. Although frequent and violent clashes continue between the army and another rebel group, the Moro Islamic Liberation Front, separate peace talks were ongoing in 1998.

Even as the Philippines experienced a somewhat lower rate of growth than many of its Asian neighbors throughout the 1990s, it was also spared the brunt of the region's financial crisis following a wave of currency devaluations sparked in July 1997. In May 1998, 61-year-old former action film star Joseph Estrada was elected president of the Philippines, succeeding Fidel Ramos, who declined to contest elections.

In the spring of 2000 the government clashed with the Moro Islamic Liberation Front, which held several groups of hostages and was blamed for several bombings in various Filipino cities. Some hostages were freed by the Philippine military. In April, Abu Sayyaf, a smaller, separate group of guerrillas, captured 21 tourists from various nations and held them at their fortified camp on Jolo Island, 560 miles south of Manila. The guerrillas asked for between $15 and $20 million in exchange for releasing the captives. A loose federation of armed groups, Abu Sayyaf is fighting for an independent Islamic state and for protection of local fishing rights. The government halted negotiations with the group after more kidnapping took place. On Sept. 16, 2000, government troops launched a massive but unsuccessful rescue attempt to free the remaining hostages.

Poland

REPUBLIC OF POLAND

National name: Rzeczpospolita Polska
President: Aleksander Kwasniewski (1995)
Prime Minister: Jerzy Buzek (1997)
Area: 120,727 sq. mi. (312,683 sq. km)
Population (2000 est.): 38,646,023 (average annual rate of natural increase: 0.01%); birth rate: 10.1/1000; infant mortality rate: 9.6/1000; density per sq. mi.: 320
Capital and largest city (1994 est.): Warsaw, 1,642,700. **Other large cities:** Lodz, 833,700; Krakow, 745,100; Wroclaw, 642,300; Poznan, 582,800; Gdansk, 463,100; Szczecin, 417,700. **Monetary unit:** Zloty. **Language:** Polish. **Ethnicity/race:** Polish 97.6%, German 1.3%, Ukrainian 0.6%, Belarussian 0.5% (1990 est.). **Religions:** Roman Catholic, 95% (about 75% practicing); Russian Orthodox, Protestant, and other, 5%. **Literacy rate:** 98% (1978)
Economic summary: GDP/PPP (1998 est.): $263 billion; $6,800 per capita. **Real growth rate:** 5.6% (1998 est.). **Inflation:** 11% (1998 est.). **Unemployment:** 10% (1998 est.). **Arable land:** 47%. **Agriculture:** potatoes, fruit, vegetables, wheat, poultry, eggs, pork, beef, milk, cheese. **Labor force:** 17.4 million (1998 est.): services, 44.1%; industry and construction, 29.9%; agriculture, 26% (1996). **Industries:** machine building, iron and steel, coal mining, chemicals, shipbuilding, food processing, glass, beverages, textiles. **Natural resources:** coal, sulfur, copper, natural gas, silver, lead, salt. **Exports:** $27.2 billion (f.o.b., 1997): manufactured goods, chemicals, machinery and equipment, mineral fuel, food and live animals. **Imports:** $38.5 billion (1997): manufactured goods, chemicals, machinery and equipment, food and live animals, mineral fuel. **Major trading partners:** Germany, Russia, Italy, Ukraine, Netherlands, France, U.K., U.S.

Geography Poland, a country the size of New Mexico, is in north-central Europe. Most of the country is a plain with no natural boundaries except the Carpathian Mountains in the south and the Oder and Neisse Rivers in the west. Other major rivers, which are important to commerce, are the Vistula, Warta, and Bug.

Government Democratic state.

History Great (north) Poland was founded in A.D. 966 by Mieszko I, who belonged to the Piast dynasty. The tribes of southern Poland then united to form Little Poland. In A.D. 1047 both Great Poland and Little Poland united under the rule of Casimir I the Restorer. Poland merged with Lithuania by royal marriage in 1386. The Polish-Lithuanian state reached the peak of its power between the 14th and 16th century, scoring military successes against the (Germanic) Knights of the Teutonic Order, the Russians, and the Ottoman Turks.

Lack of a strong monarchy enabled Russia, Prussia, and Austria to carry out a first partition of the country in 1772, a second in 1792, and a third in 1795. For more than a century thereafter, there was no Polish state, just Austrian, Prussian, and Russian sectors, but the Poles never ceased their efforts to regain their independence. The Polish people revolted against Russian, Prussian, and Austrian dominance throughout the 19th century. Poland was formally reconstituted in Nov. 1918, with Marshal Josef Pilsudski as chief of state. In 1919, Ignace Paderewski, the famous pianist and patriot, became the first premier. In 1926, Pilsudski seized complete power in a coup and ruled dictatorially until his death on May 12, 1935.

Despite a 10-year nonaggression pact signed in 1934, Hitler attacked Poland on Sept. 1, 1939. Soviet troops invaded from the east on Sept. 17, and on Sept. 28 a German-Soviet agreement divided Poland between the U.S.S.R. and Germany. Wladyslaw Raczkiewicz formed a government-in-exile in France, which moved to London after France's defeat in 1940. All of Poland was occupied by Germany after the Nazi attack on the U.S.S.R. in June 1941. Nazi Germany's occupation policy in Poland was designed to eradicate Polish culture through mass executions and to exterminate the country's large Jewish minority.

The Polish government-in-exile was replaced with the Communist-dominated Polish Committee of National Liberation by the Soviet Union in 1944. Moving to Lublin after that city's liberation, it proclaimed itself the Provisional Government of Poland. Some former members of the Polish government in London joined with the Lublin government to form the Polish Government of National Unity, which Britain and the U.S. recognized. On Aug. 2, 1945, in Berlin, President Harry S. Truman, Joseph Stalin, and Prime Minister Clement Attlee of Britain established a new de facto western frontier for Poland along the Oder and Neisse Rivers. (The border was finally agreed to by West Germany in a nonaggression pact signed on Dec. 7, 1970.) On Aug. 16, 1945, the U.S.S.R. and Poland signed a treaty delimiting the Soviet-Polish frontier. Under these agreements, Poland was shifted westward. In the east it lost 69,860 square miles (180,934 sq. km); in the west it gained (subject to final peace-conference approval) 38,986 square miles (100,973 sq. km).

A new constitution in 1952 made Poland a "people's democracy" of the Soviet type. In 1955, Poland became a member of the Warsaw Treaty Organization, and its foreign policy became identical to that of the U.S.S.R. The government undertook persecution of the Roman Catholic Church as a remaining source of opposition. Wladyslaw Gomulka was elected leader of the United Workers (Communist) Party in 1956. He denounced the Stalinist terror, ousted many Stalinists, and improved relations with the church. Most collective farms were dissolved, and the press became freer. A strike that began in shipyards and spread to other industries in August 1980 produced a stunning victory for workers when the economically hard-pressed government accepted for the first time in a Marxist state the right of workers to organize in independent unions.

Led by Solidarity, a free union founded by Lech Walesa, workers launched a drive for liberty and improved conditions. A national strike for a five-day work week in Jan. 1981 led to the dismissal of Premier Pinkowski and the naming of the fourth premier in less than a year, Gen. Wojciech Jaruzelski. Martial law was declared on Dec. 13, when Walesa and other Solidarity leaders were arrested. It formally ended in 1984 but the government retained emergency powers. Increasing opposition to the government because of the failing economy led to a new wave of strikes in 1988. Unable to totally quell the dissent, the government relegalized Solidarity and allowed it to compete in elections.

Solidarity members won a stunning victory in 1989, taking almost all the seats in the Senate and all of the 169 seats they were allowed to contest in the Sejm. This gave them substantial influence in the new government. Tadeusz Mazowiecki was appointed prime minister. Solidarity leader Lech Walesa won the presidential election of 1990 with 74% of the vote. In 1991, the first fully free parliamentary election since World War II resulted in representation for 29 political parties. In the second democratic parliamentary election of Sept. 1993, voters returned power to ex-Communists and their allies. In 1995, Aleksander Kwasniewski, leader of the successor to the Communist Party, won the presidency over Walesa, despite strong support for Walesa from the church. In 1997, the Solidarity Electoral Action (AWS), a loose coalition of some 30 right-wing groups dominated by the Solidarity trade union, handily defeated the former Communists. Also in 1997, the Polish parliament voted to abolish the death penalty. The pope visited Poland in 1999, which some believe may be his last visit to his homeland.

In 1999, Poland became part of NATO, along with the Czech Republic and Hungary. Poland is expected to become the next country accepted into the European Union (EU), though membership is not expected before 2005 or 2006.

Portugal

REPUBLIC OF PORTUGAL

National name: República Portuguesa
President: Jorge Sampaio (1996)
Prime Minister: Antonio Guterres (1995)
Area: 36,090 sq. mi. (92,391 sq. km)
Population (2000 est.): 10,048,232 (average annual rate of natural increase: 0.1%); birth rate: 11.5/1000; infant mortality rate: 6.1/1000; density per sq. mi.: 278
Capital and largest city (1991): Lisbon, 677,790. **Other large city (1991):** Oporto, 350,000. **Monetary units:** Escudo and euro. **Language:** Portuguese. **Ethnicity/race:** Homogeneous Mediterranean stock in mainland, Azores, Madeira Islands; citizens of black African descent who immigrated to mainland during decolonization number less than 100,000. **Religions:** Roman Catholic 97%, 1% Protestant, 2% other. **Literacy rate:** 85% (1991)
Economic summary: GDP/PPP (1998 est.): $144.8 billion; $14,600 per capita. **Real growth rate:** 4.2% (1998 est.). **Inflation:** 2.8% (1998 est.). **Unemployment:** 5% (Aug. 1998). **Arable land:** 26%. **Agriculture:** grain, potatoes, olives, grapes, sheep, cattle, goats, poultry, beef, dairy products. **Labor force** 4.75 million (1998 est.): services, 56%; manufacturing, 22%; agriculture, forestry, and fisheries, 12%; construction, 9%; mining, 1%. **Industries:** textiles and footwear, wood pulp, paper, and cork, metalworking, oil refining, chemicals, fish canning, wine, tourism. **Natural resources:** fish, forests (cork), tungsten, iron ore, uranium ore, marble. **Exports:** $25 billion (f.o.b., 1998): clothing and footwear, machinery, chemicals, cork and paper products, hides. **Imports:** $34.9 billion (f.o.b., 1998): machinery and transport equipment, chemicals, petroleum, textiles, agricultural products. **Major trading partners:** EU, U.S., Japan.

Geography Portugal occupies the western part of the Iberian Peninsula and is slightly smaller than Indiana. The country is crossed by three large rivers that rise in Spain, flow into the Atlantic, and divide the country into three geographic areas. The Minho River, part of the northern boundary, cuts through a mountainous area that extends south to the vicinity of the Douro River. South of the Douro, the mountains slope to the plains around the Tejo River. The remaining division is the southern one of Alentejo. The Azores stretch over 340 miles (547 km) in the Atlantic, and consist of nine islands with a total area of 902 square miles (2,335 sq. km). Madeira, consisting of two inhabited islands, Madeira and Porto Santo, and two groups of uninhabited islands, lie in the Atlantic about 535 miles (861 km) southwest of Lisbon.

Government Republic.

History An early Celtic tribe, the Lusitanians, are believed to have been the first inhabitants of Portugal. The Roman Empire conquered the region in about 140 B.C. Toward the end of the Roman Empire, the Visigoths had invaded the entire Iberian peninsula.

In the middle of the 12th century, Portugal was a part of Moorish Spain until it won its independence King John I (1385–1433) unified his country at the expense of the Castilians and the Moors of Morocco. The expansion of Portugal was brilliantly coordinated by John's son, Prince Henry the Navigator. In 1488, Bartolomeu Dias reached the Cape of Good Hope, proving that Asia was accessible by sea. In 1498, Vasco da Gama reached the west coast of India. By the middle of the 16th century, the Portuguese Empire extended to West and East Africa, Brazil, Persia, Indochina, and Malaya.

In 1581, Philip II of Spain invaded Portugal and held it for 60 years, precipitating a catastrophic decline in Portuguese commerce. Courageous and shrewd explorers, the Portuguese proved to be inefficient and corrupt colonizers. By the time the Portuguese monarchy was restored in 1640, Dutch, English, and French competitors began to seize the lion's share of the world's colonies and commerce. Portugal retained Angola and Mozambique in Africa, and Brazil (until 1822).

The corrupt King Carlos, who ascended the throne in 1889, made Joao Franco the premier with dictatorial power in 1906. In 1908, Carlos and his heir were shot dead on the streets of Lisbon. The new king, Manoel II, was driven from the throne in the revolution of 1910 and Portugal became a French-style republic. Traditionally friendly to Britain, Portugal fought in World War I on the Allied side in Africa as well as on the Western Front. Weak postwar governments and a revolution in 1926 brought Antonio Oliveira Salazar to power. As minister of finance (1928–40) and premier (1932–68), Salazar ruled Portugal as a virtual dictator. He kept Portugal neutral in World War II but gave the Allies naval and air bases after 1943. Portugal joined NATO as a founding member in 1949 but did not gain admission to the United Nations until 1955.

Portugal's foreign and colonial policies met with increasing difficulty both at home and abroad beginning in the 1950s—the bloodiest and most protracted wars against colonialism in Africa were fought against the Portuguese. Portugal lost the tiny remnants of its Indian empire—Goa, Daman, and Diu—to Indian military occupation in 1961, the year an insurrection broke out in Angola. For the next 13 years, Salazar, who died in 1970, and his successor, Marcello Caetano, fought independence movements amid growing world criticism. Leftists in the armed forces, weary of a losing battle, launched a successful revolution on April 25, 1974. After the 1974 revolution, the new military junta gave up its territories, beginning with Portuguese Guinea in Sept. 1974, which became the Republic of Guinea-Bissau. The decolonization of the Cape Verde Islands and Mozambique was effected in July 1975. Angola achieved independence later that same year, thus ending a colonial involvement in that continent that had begun in 1415. Full-scale, internationalized civil war, however, followed Portugal's departure from Angola, and Indonesia forcibly annexed independent East Timor. Also in that year, the government nationalized banking, transport, heavy industries, and the media. Portugal continued to experience social, economic, and political upheavals for the next decade.

Portugal was admitted to the European Economic Community (now European Union) on Jan. 1, 1986, and on Feb. 16, Mario Soares became the country's first civilian president in 60 years. Aníbal Cavaço Silva, an advocate of free-market economics and the Social Democratic candidate, was elected as prime minister in 1985, signaling a more politically stable era. General elections in Oct. 1995 went to the Socialist Party, which fell just short of an absolute majority in the assembly. Lisbon mayor Jorge Sampaio, a socialist, won the race for president in Jan. 1996. Portugal's socialist government continued to take advantage of rosy economic conditions in 1997, and in 1999 it became a founding member of the European Economic and Monetary Union (EMU). After Portugal's former territory, East Timor, was plunged into violence when its people voted to separate from Indonesia in Aug. 1999, Portugal was in the forefront of urging the U.N. to send in an armed, international peacekeeping force to protect the East Timorese from pro-Indonesian militia groups.

Portugal gave up its last colony, Macao, on Dec. 20, 1999, turning the small Asian seaport over to China.

Qatar

STATE OF QATAR

Emir: Sheik Hamad bin Khalifa al-Thani (1995)
Prime Minister: Abdullah bin Khalifa al-Thani (1996)
Area: 4,468 sq. mi. (11,439 sq. km)
Population (2000 est.): 744,483 (average annual rate of natural increase: 1.2%); birth rate: 16.1/1000; infant mortality rate: 22.1/1000; density per sq. mi.: 167
Capital (1990 est.): Doha, 300,000. **Monetary unit:** Qatari riyal. **Languages:** Arabic; English is also widely spoken. **Ethnicity/race:** Arab 40%, Pakistani 18%, Indian 18%, Iranian 10%, other 14%. **Religion:** Islam, 95%. **Literacy rate:** 76% (1986)
Economic summary: GDP/PPP (1998 est.): $12 billion; $17,100 per capita. **Real growth rate:** –3% (1998 est.). **Inflation:** 7.4% (1996). **Unemployment:** n.a. **Agriculture:** fruit, vegetables, poultry, dairy products, beef, fish. **Labor force:** 233,000 (1993 est.). **Industries:** crude oil production and refining, fertilizers, petrochemicals, steel reinforcing bars, cement. **Natural resources:** petroleum, natural gas, fish. **Exports:** $5.6 billion (f.o.b., 1997 est.): petroleum products, fertilizers, steel. **Imports:** $4.4 billion (f.o.b., 1997 est.): machinery and equipment, consumer goods, food, chemicals. **Major trading partners:** Japan, Singapore, South Korea, Thailand, U.S., Italy, U.K., France.

Geography Qatar occupies a small peninsula that extends into the Persian Gulf from the east side of the Arabian Peninsula. Saudi Arabia is to the west and the United Arab Emirates to the south. The country is mainly barren.

Government Traditional monarchy.

History Qatar was once controlled by the sheikhs of Bahrain, but in 1867 war broke out between the people and their absentee rulers. To keep the peace in the Gulf, the British installed Muhammad ibn Thani Al Thani, head of a leading Qatari family, as the region's ruler. In 1893, the Ottoman Turks made incursions into Qatar, but the emir successfully deflected them. In 1916, the emir agreed to allow Qatar to become a British protectorate.

Oil was discovered in the 1940s, bringing wealth to the country in the 1950s and 1960s. About 85% of Qatar's income from exports comes from oil. Its people have one of the highest per capita incomes in the world. In 1971, Qatar was to join the other emirates of the Trucial Coast to become part of the United Arab Emirates. But both Qatar and Bahrain decided against the merger and instead became independent nations.

Qatar permitted the international forces to use Qatar as a base during the 1991 Persian Gulf War. A border dispute erupted with Saudi Arabia that was settled in Dec. 1992. A territorial dispute with Bahrain over the Hawar Islands remains unresolved, however. In 1994, Qatar signed a defense pact with the U.S., becoming the third Gulf state to do so.

In June 1995 Crown Prince Hamad bin Khalifa al-Thani deposed his father, primarily because the king was out-of-step with the country's economic reforms. The emir was not stripped of his title, and much of the power was already in his son's hands. The new emir has lifted press censorship and instituted other liberal reforms, including the first democratic election in its history. Although the 1999 election—for the 29-member municipal council—was a minor election, it involved major political change: women were permitted to vote in the election as well as run for office.

Romania

REPUBLIC OF ROMANIA

President: Emil Constantinescu (1996)
Prime Minister: Mugur Isarescu (1999)
Area: 91,700 sq. mi. (237,500 sq. km)
Population (2000 est.): 22,411,121 (average annual rate of natural increase: –0.15%); birth rate: 10.8/1000; infant mortality rate: 19.8/1000; density per sq. mi.: 244
Capital and largest city (1992): Bucharest, 2,351,000.
Largest cities (1992): Constanta, 350,476; Iasi, 342,994; Timisoara, 334,278; Cluj-Napoca, 328,008; Galati, 325,788; Brasov, 323,835. **Monetary unit:** Leu.
Languages: Romanian (official); Hungarian- and German-speaking minorities. **Ethnicity/race:** Romanian 89.1%, Hungarian 8.9%, German 0.4%, Ukrainian, Serb, Croat, Russian, Turk, and Gypsy 1.6%. **Religions:** Romanian Orthodox 70%, Roman Catholic 6% (of which 3% are Uniate), Protestant 6%, unaffiliated 18%. **Literacy rate:** 96% (1992)
Economic summary: GDP/PPP (1998 est.): $90.6 billion; $4,050 per capita. **Real growth rate:** –7.3% (1998 est.). **Inflation:** 41% (1998 est.). **Unemployment:** 9% (1998 est.). **Arable land:** 41%. **Agriculture:** wheat, corn, sugar beets, sunflower seed, potatoes, grapes, milk, eggs, beef. **Labor force:** 10.1 million (1996 est.). **Industries:** mining, timber, construction materials, metallurgy, chemicals, machine building, food processing, petroleum production and refining. **Natural resources:** petroleum (reserves declining), timber, natural gas, coal, iron ore, salt. **Exports:** $8.2 billion (f.o.b., 1998 est.): textiles and footwear, metals and metal products, machinery and equipment, chemicals. **Imports:** $10.8 billion (f.o.b., 1998 est.): machinery and equipment, fuel and minerals, chemicals, foodstuffs. **Major trading partners:** Italy, Germany, France, Turkey, Russia.

Geography Romania is in southeastern Europe, and is slightly smaller than Oregon. The Carpathian Mountains divide Romania's upper half from north to south and connect near the center of the country with the Transylvanian Alps, running east and west. North and west of these ranges lies the Transylvanian plateau, and to the south and east are the plains of Moldavia and Walachia. In its last 190 miles (306 km), the Danube River flows through Romania only. It enters the Black Sea in northern Dobruja, just south of the border with the Ukraine.

Government Republic.

History Most of Romania was the Roman province of Dacia from about A.D. 100 to 271. From the 3rd to the 12th century, wave after wave of barbarian conquerors overran the native Daco-Roman population. Subjection to the first Bulgarian empire (8th–10th century) brought Eastern Orthodox Christianity to the Romanians. In the 11th century, Transylvania was absorbed into the Hungarian empire. By the 16th century, the main Romanian principalities of Moldavia and Walachia had become satellites within the Ottoman Empire, although they retained much independence. After the Russo-Turkish War of 1828–29, they became Russian protectorates. The nation became a kingdom in 1881 after the Congress of Berlin.

At the start of World War I, Romania proclaimed its neutrality, but later joined the Allied side and in 1916 declared war on the Central Powers. The armistice of Nov. 11, 1918, gave Romania vast territories from Russia and the Austro-Hungarian Empire, doubling its size. The areas acquired included Bessarabia, Transylvania, and Bukovina. The Banat, a Hungarian area, was divided with Yugoslavia. King Carol II was crowned in 1930 and transformed the throne into a royal dictatorship. In 1938, he abolished the democratic constitution of 1923. In 1940, the country was reorganized along Fascist lines, and the Fascist Iron Guard became the nucleus of the new totalitarian party. On June 27, the Soviet Union occupied Bessarabia and northern Bukovina. King Carol II dissolved Parliament, granted the new premier, Ion Antonescu, full power, abdicated his throne, and went into exile.

Romania subsequently signed the Axis Pact on Nov. 23, 1940, and the following June joined in Germany's attack on the Soviet Union, reoccupying Bessarabia. About 270,000 Jews were massacred in Fascist Romania. Following the invasion of Romania by the Red Army in Aug. 1944, King Michael led a coup that ousted the Antonescu government. An armistice with the Soviet Union was signed in Moscow on Sept. 12, 1944. A Communist-dominated government bloc won elections in 1946, Michael abdicated on Dec. 30, 1947, and in 1955 Romania joined the Warsaw Treaty Organization and the United Nations.

Nikolae Ceausescu, famous for his secret police's brutality, ruled from 1965 to 1989, when he was overthrown by a coup rising from opposition to his repressive domestic policies. Ceausescu instituted a rigorous austerity program in the 1980s to pay for the huge foreign debt that Romania had accumulated in the 1970s; as a result, the Romanians saw their standard of living plummet. An army-assisted rebellion in Dec. 1989 led to Ceausescu's overthrow, trial, and execution. The May 1990 elections were won by the National Salvation Front, whose formerly Communist leaders called for a gradual and controlled transition to a free-market economy in Romania.

The country applied for membership in the EU in June 1995 and much legislation that year was crafted in hopes of meeting that objective. Nevertheless, the reform process proceeded slowly. Growing dissatisfaction with the government's inefficiencies and economic policies led to a wave of protests by workers, students, and others that peaked in 1997, and again in 1999, when coal miners striked.

Russia

RUSSIAN FEDERATION

President: Vladimir Putin (2000)
Prime Minister: Mikhail Kasyanov (2000)
Area: 6,592,800 sq. mi. (17,075,200 sq. km)
Population (2000 est.): 146,001,176 (average annual rate of natural increase: –0.5%); birth rate: 9/1000; infant mortality rate: 20.3/1000; density per sq. mi.: 22
Capital and largest city (2000 est.): Moscow, 13,200,000 (metro. area). **Other large cities:** St. Petersburg (2000 est.), 5,550,000 (metro. area); Novosibirsk, 1,418,200; Samara, 1,222,500; Chelyabinsk, 1,124,500; Yekaterinburg, 1,347,000; Nizhny Novgorod, 1,424,600; Kazau, 1,092,300; Perm, 1,086,100; Ufa, 1,091,800; Volgograd, 1,000,400.
Monetary unit: Ruble. **Languages:** Russian, others. **Ethnicity/race:** Russian 81.5%, Tatar 3.8%, Ukrainian 3%, Chuvash 1.2%, Bashkir 0.9%, Byelorussian 0.8%, Moldavian 0.7%, other 8.1%. **Religions:** Russian Orthodox, Muslim, others. **Literacy rate:** 98% (1989)
Economic summary: GDP/PPP (1998 est.): $593.4 billion; $4,000 per capita. **Real growth rate:** –5% (1998 est.). **Inflation:** 84% (1998 est.). **Unemployment:** 11.5% with considerable additional underemployment (1998 est.). **Agriculture:** grain, sugar beets, sunflower seed, vegetables, fruit, beef, milk. **Labor force:** 66 million (1997). **Industries:** complete range of mining and extractive industries producing coal, oil, gas, chemicals, and metals, all forms of machine building from rolling mills to high-performance aircraft and space vehicles, shipbuilding, road and rail transportation equipment, communications equipment, agricultural machinery, tractors, and construction equipment, electric power generating and transmitting equipment, medical and scientific instruments, consumer durables, textiles, foodstuffs, handicrafts. **Natural resources:** oil, natural gas, coal, strategic minerals, timber. **Exports:** $71.8 billion (1998 est.): petroleum and petroleum products, natural gas, wood and wood products, metals, chemicals, and a wide variety of civilian and military manufactures. **Imports:** $58.5 billion (1998 est.): machinery and equipment, consumer goods, medicines, meat, grain, sugar, semifinished metal products. **Major trading partners:** Ukraine, Germany, U.S., Belarus, Japan, other Western and less developed countries.

Geography The Russian Federation is the largest republic of the Commonwealth of Independent States. It occupies an area about one and four-fifths of the size of the United States and occupies most of eastern Europe and north Asia. Russia stretches from the Baltic Sea in the west to the Pacific Ocean in the east and from the Arctic Ocean in the north to the Black Sea and the Caucasus, the Altai, and Sayan Mountains, and the Amur and Ussuri Rivers in the south. It is bordered by Norway and Finland in the northwest, Estonia, Latvia, Belarus, and Ukraine in the west, Georgia and Azerbaijan in the southwest, and Kazakhstan, Mongolia, and China along the southern border. The federation is composed of 21 republics.

Government Constitutional republic.

History Tradition says the Viking Rurik came to Russia in A.D. 862 and founded the first Russian dynasty in Novgorod. The various tribes were united by the spread of Christianity in the 10th and 11th centuries; Vladimir "the Saint" was converted in 988. During the 11th century, the grand dukes of Kiev held such centralizing power as existed. In 1240, Kiev was destroyed by the Mongols, and the Russian territory was split into numerous smaller dukedoms. Early dukes of Moscow extended their dominion over other Russian cities through their office of tribute collector for the Mongols and because of Moscow's role as an administrative and trade center.

In the late 15th century, Duke Ivan III acquired Novgorod and Tver and threw off the Mongol yoke. Ivan IV, the Terrible (1533–84), first Muscovite czar, is considered to have founded the Russian state. He crushed the power of rival princes and boyars (great landowners), but Russia remained largely medieval until the reign of Peter the Great (1689–1725), grandson of the first Romanov czar, Michael (1613–45). Peter made extensive reforms aimed at Westernization and, through his defeat of Charles XII of Sweden at the Battle of Poltava in 1709, he extended Russia's boundaries to the west. Catherine the Great (1762–96) continued Peter's Westernization program and also expanded Russian territory, acquiring the Crimea, Ukraine, and part of Poland. During the reign of Alexander I (1801–25), Napoléon's attempt to subdue Russia was defeated (1812–13), and new territory was gained, including Finland (1809) and Bessarabia (1812). Alexander originated the Holy Alliance, which for a time crushed Europe's rising liberal movement.

Alexander II (1855–81) pushed Russia's borders to the Pacific and into central Asia. Serfdom was abolished in 1861, but heavy restrictions were imposed on the emancipated class. Revolutionary strikes, following Russia's defeat in the war with Japan, forced Nicholas II (1894–1917) to grant a representative national body (Duma), elected by narrowly limited suffrage. It met for the first time in 1906, little influencing Nicholas in his reactionary course.

World War I demonstrated czarist corruption and inefficiency and only patriotism held the poorly equipped army together for a time. Disorders broke out in Petrograd (renamed Leningrad and now St. Petersburg) in March 1917, and defection of the Petrograd garrison launched the revolution. Nicholas II was forced to abdicate on March 15, 1917, and he and his family were killed by revolutionists on July 16, 1918. A provisional government under the successive premierships of Prince Lvov and a moderate, Alexander Kerensky, lost ground to the radical, or Bolshevik, wing of the Socialist Democratic Labor Party. On Nov. 7, 1917, the Bolshevik Revolution, engineered by N. Lenin[1] and Leon Trotsky, overthrew the Kerensky government and authority was vested in a Council of People's Commissars, with Lenin as premier.

The humiliating Treaty of Brest-Litovsk (March 3, 1918) concluded the war with Germany, but civil war and foreign intervention delayed Communist control of all Russia until 1920. A brief war with Poland in 1920 resulted in Russian defeat.

Emergence of the U.S.S.R.
The Union of Soviet Socialist Republics was established as a federation on Dec. 30, 1922. The death of Lenin on Jan. 21, 1924, precipitated an intraparty struggle between Joseph Stalin, general secretary of the party, and Trotsky, who favored swifter socialization at home and fomentation of revolution abroad. Trotsky was dismissed as commissar of war in 1925 and banished from the Soviet Union in 1929. He was murdered in Mexico City on Aug. 21, 1940, by a political agent. Stalin further consolidated his power by a series of purges in the late 1930s, liquidating prominent party leaders and military officers. Stalin assumed the premiership on May 6, 1941.

Soviet foreign policy, at first friendly toward Germany and antagonistic toward Britain and France and then, after Hitler's rise to power in 1933, becoming anti-Fascist and pro-League of Nations, took an abrupt turn on Aug. 24, 1939, with the signing of a nonaggression pact with Nazi Germany. The next month, Moscow joined in the German attack on Poland, seizing territory later incorporated into the Ukrainian and Belarussian S.S.R.'s. The Russo-Finnish War (1939–40) added territory to the Karelian S.S.R. set up on March 31, 1940; the annexation of Bessarabia and Bukovina from Romania became part of the new Moldavian S.S.R. on Aug. 2, 1940; and the annexation of the Baltic republics of Estonia, Latvia, and Lithuania in June 1940 created the 14th, 15th, and 16th Soviet republics. The illegal annexation of the Baltic republics was never acknowledged by the U.S. for the 51 years leading up to Soviet recognition of Estonia, Latvia, and Lithuania's independence on Sept. 6, 1991. The Soviet-German collaboration ended abruptly with a lightning attack by Hitler on June 22, 1941, which seized 500,000 square miles of Russian territory before Soviet defenses, aided by U.S. and British arms, could halt it. The Soviet resurgence at Stalingrad from Nov. 1942 to Feb. 1943 marked the turning point in a long battle, ending in the final offensive of Jan. 1945. Then, after denouncing a 1941 nonaggression pact with Japan in April 1945, when Allied forces were nearing victory in the Pacific, the Soviet Union declared war on Japan on Aug. 8, 1945, and quickly occupied Manchuria, Karafuto, and the Kuril Islands.

The U.S.S.R. built a cordon of Communist states running from Poland in the north to Albania and Bulgaria in the south, including East Germany, Czechoslovakia, Hungary, and Romania, which composed the territories the Soviet troops occupied at the war's end. With its eastern front solidified, the Soviet Union launched a political offensive against the non-Communist West, moving first to block the Western access to Berlin. The Western powers countered with an airlift, completed unification of West Germany, and organized the defense of western Europe in the North Atlantic Treaty Organization (NATO). Stalin died on March 6, 1953, and was succeeded the next day by G. M. Malenkov as premier.

The new power in the Kremlin was Nikita S. Khrushchev, first secretary of the party. Khrushchev formalized the eastern European system into a Council for Mutual Economic Assistance (Comecon) and a Warsaw Pact Treaty Organization as a counterweight to NATO. The Soviet Union exploded a hydrogen bomb in 1953, developed an intercontinental ballistic missile by 1957, sent the first satellite into space (Sputnik I) in 1957, and put Yuri Gagarin in the first orbital flight around Earth in 1961. Khrushchev's downfall stemmed from his decision to place Soviet nuclear missiles in Cuba and then, when challenged by the U.S., backing down and removing the weapons. He was also blamed for the ideological break with China after 1963. Khrushchev was forced into retirement on Oct. 15, 1964, and was replaced by Leonid I. Brezhnev as first secretary of the party and Aleksei N. Kosygin as premier.

U.S. presidents Jimmy Carter and Brezhnev signed the SALT II treaty in Vienna on June 18, 1979, setting ceilings on each nation's arsenal of intercontinental ballistic missiles. The U.S. Senate refused to

---

1. N. Lenin was the pseudonym taken by Vladimir Ilich Ulyanov. It is sometimes given as Nikolai Lenin or V. Lenin.

Rulers of Russia since 1533

Name	Born	Ruled [1]	Name	Born	Ruled [1]
Ivan IV the Terrible	1530	1533–1584	Alexander II	1818	1855–1881
Theodore I	1557	1584–1598	Alexander III	1845	1881–1894
Boris Godunov	c.1551	1598–1605	Nicholas II	1868	1894–1917[7]
Theodore II	1589	1605–1605	**PROVISIONAL GOVERNMENT (PREMIERS)**		
Demetrius I[2]	?	1605–1606	Prince Georgi Lvov	1861	1917–1917
Basil IV Shuiski	?	1606–1610[3]	Alexander Kerensky	1881	1917–1917
"Time of Troubles"	—	1610–1613	**POLITICAL LEADERS OF U.S.S.R.**		
Michael Romanov	1596	1613–1645	Vladimir Ilyich Lenin	1870	1917–1924
Alexis I	1629	1645–1676	Aleksei Rykov	1881	1924–1930
Theodore III	1656	1676–1682	Vyacheslav Molotov	1890	1930–1941
Ivan V[4]	1666	1682–1689[5]	Joseph Stalin[8]	1879	1941–1953
Peter I the Great[4]	1672	1682–1725	Georgi M. Malenkov	1902	1953–1955
Catherine I	c.1684	1725–1727	Nikolai A. Bulganin	1895	1955–1958
Peter II	1715	1727–1730	Nikita S. Khrushchev	1894	1958–1964
Anna	1693	1730–1740	Leonid I. Brezhnev	1906	1964–1982
Ivan VI	1740	1740–1741[6]	Yuri V. Andropov	1914	1982–1984
Elizabeth	1709	1741–1762	Konstantin U. Chernenko	1912	1984–1985
Peter III	1728	1762–1762	Mikhail S. Gorbachev	1931	1985–1991
Catherine II the Great	1729	1762–1796	**PRESIDENT OF RUSSIA**		
Paul I	1754	1796–1801	Boris Yeltsin	1931	1991–1999
Alexander I	1777	1801–1825	Vladimir Putin	1952	2000–
Nicholas I	1796	1825–1855			

1. For czars through Nicholas II, year of end of rule is also that of death, unless otherwise indicated. 2. Also known as Pseudo-Demetrius. 3. Died 1612. 4. Ruled jointly until 1689, when Ivan was deposed. 5. Died 1696. 6. Died 1764. 7. Killed 1918. 8. General secretary of Communist Party, 1924–53.

atify the treaty because of the invasion of Afghanistan by Soviet troops on Dec. 27, 1979. On Nov. 10, 1982, Soviet radio and television announced the death of Leonid Brezhnev. Yuri Andropov, who had formerly headed the K.G.B., became his successor, but died less than two years later, on Feb. 1984. Konstantin U. Chernenko, a 72-year-old party stalwart who had been close to Brezhnev, succeeded him.

In the months following Chernenko's assumption of power, the Kremlin took on a hostile mood toward the West of a kind rarely seen since the height of the cold war 30 years before. Led by Moscow, all the Soviet bloc countries except Romania boycotted the 1984 summer Olympic Games in Los Angeles—tit-for-tat for the U.S.-led boycott of the 1980 Moscow Games, in the view of most observers. After 13 months in office, Chernenko died on March 10, 1985. He had been ill much of the time and left only a minor imprint on Soviet leadership. Chosen to succeed him as Soviet leader was Mikhail S. Gorbachev, who led the Soviet Union in its long-awaited shift to a new generation of leadership. Unlike his immediate predecessors, Gorbachev did not also assume the title of president but wielded power from the post of party general secretary.

The Soviet Union took much criticism in early 1986 over the April 24 meltdown at the Chernobyl nuclear plant and its reluctance to give out any information on the accident.

In June 1987, Gorbachev obtained the support of the Central Committee for proposals that would loosen some government controls over the economy and in June 1988, an unusually open party conference approved several resolutions reforming the Soviet system. These included a shift of some power from the party to local soviets, and a ten-year limit in the terms of elected government and party officials. Gorbachev was elected president in 1989. The elections to the Congress were the first competitive elections in the Soviet Union since 1917. Dissident candidates won a surprisingly large minority though pro-government deputies maintained a strong lock on the Supreme Soviet.

Dissolution of the U.S.S.R. The possible beginning of the fragmentation of the Communist Party took place when Boris Yeltsin, leader of the Russian S.S.R. who urged faster reform, left the Communist Party along with other radicals. In March 1991, the Soviet people were asked to vote on a referendum on national unity engineered by Gorbachev. The resultant victory for the federal government was tempered by the separate approval in Russia for the creation of a popularly elected presidency of the Russian republics. The bitter election contest for the Russian presidency, principally between Yeltsin and a Communist loyalist, resulted in a major victory for Yeltsin. He took the oath of office for the new position on July 10, 1991.

Reversing his relative hard-line position, Gorbachev together with leaders of nine Soviet republics signed an accord called the Union Treaty, which was meant to preserve the unity of the nation. In exchange the federal government would have turned over control of industrial and natural resources to the individual republics. An attempted coup d'état took place on Aug. 19, 1991, orchestrated by a group of eight senior officials calling itself the State Committee on the State of Emergency. Boris Yeltsin, barricaded in the Russian Parliament building, defiantly called for a general strike. The next day huge crowds demonstrated in Leningrad, and Yeltsin supporters fortified barricades surrounding the Parliament building. On Aug. 21 the coup committee disbanded, and at least some of its members attempted to flee Moscow. The Soviet Parliament formally reinstated Gorbachev as president. Two days later he resigned from his position as general-secretary of the Communist Party and recommended that its Central Committee be disbanded. On Aug. 29 the Parliament approved the suspension of all Communist Party activities pending an investigation of its role in the failed coup. At the time of the attempted coup, the republic's president, Boris Yeltsin, was the most popular political figure in the former Soviet Union. A leading reformer, he became the first directly elected leader in Russian history and received 60% of the vote for president of the Russian Republic.

Yeltsin championed the cause for national reconstruction and the adoption of a Union Treaty with the other republics to create a free-market economic association. On Dec. 12, 1991, the Russian Parliament ratified Yeltsin's plea to establish a new commonwealth of independent nations open to all former members of the Soviet Union. The new union was created with the governments of Ukraine and Belarus who along with Russia were the three original cofounders of the Soviet Union in 1922. After the end of the Soviet Union, Russia and ten other Soviet republics joined in a Commonwealth of Independent States on Dec. 21, 1991.

At the start of 1992, Russia embarked on a series of dramatic economic reforms, including the freeing of prices on most goods, which led to an immediate downturn. A national referendum on confidence in Yeltsin and his economic program took place in April 1993. To the surprise of many, the president and his shock-therapy program won by a resounding margin. In Sept., Yeltsin dissolved the legislative bodies left over from the Soviet era. The impasse between the executive and the legislature resulted in an armed conflict on Oct. 3. Yeltsin prevailed largely through the support of the military and other forces.

The southern republic of Chechnya's president accelerated his region's drive for independence in 1994. In Dec., Russian troops closed the borders and sought to squelch the independence drive. The Russian military forces met firm and costly resistance. Shortly before the scheduled presidential election of June 1996, a cease-fire was arranged in Chechnya. Yeltsin started the year with slim chances for reelection. But bolstered by favorable media attention, fear of a Communist resurgence, and vigorous campaigning, he won the second round of voting in July against a Communist opponent. In May 1997, the two-year war formally ended with the signing of a peace treaty that adroitly avoided the issue of Chechen independence.

Yeltsin bounded back into the political fray in March 1997 after eight months' absence caused by sickness. His first action was to reshuffle the cabinet to include new ministers with strong reform credentials. The "young reformers" announced plans to overhaul taxation, housing, and welfare; restore central control over headstrong regional leaders; and curb the power of Russia's monopolies (natural gas, electricity, and railways). These plans for reform, however, went awry.

In March 1998 Yeltsin dismissed his entire government and replaced Prime Minister Viktor Chernomyrdin with the young and little known fuel and energy minister Sergei Kiriyenko. On Aug. 28, 1998, amid the Russian stock market's free fall, the Russian government halted trading of the ruble on international currency markets. This financial crisis led to a long-term economic downturn and to political upheaval. President Boris Yeltsin then sacked Prime Minister Kiriyenko and reappointed Chernomyrdin. The Duma rejected Chernomyrdin and on Sept. 11 elected foreign minister Yevgeny Primakov as prime minister. The repercussions of Russia's financial emergency were felt throughout the Commonwealth of Independent States.

Impatient with Yeltsin's chronic illnesses and increasingly erratic behavior, the Duma attempted to impeach him in May 1999 on five charges: provoking the 1991 fall of the Soviet Union, using force to dissolve the Parliament in 1993, starting the ill-conceived 1994–96 war in Chechnya, ruining the nation's military, and impoverishing the Russian people through ruinous economic policies—the charge regarding Chechnya was considered the only one with a chance of approval. But the impeachment motion was quickly quashed and soon Yeltsin was on the ascendancy again. In keeping with his capricious style, Yeltsin dismissed Prime Minister Yevgeny Primakov and replaced him with Interior Minister Sergei Stepashin. Just three months later, however, Yeltsin ousted Stepashin and replaced him with Vladimir Putin on Aug. 9, 1999, announcing that in addition to serving as prime minister, the former KGB agent was his choice as a successor in the 2000 presidential election.

During the Kosovo crisis, Russia sided with its Slavic allies, the Serbs. Regularly calling for a halt to NATO bombing, Yeltsin seemed almost more upset about his marginal role in the conflict than the fact that Serbia was under attack. Russia regularly claimed to be able to finesse a peace deal with the Serbs, yet little diplomatic progress emerged from their efforts. When NATO peacekeeping troops moved into Kosovo, Russia insisted that it take part yet refused to take orders from NATO.

Militant rebels in Dagestan, a Russian republic next to Chechnya, announced a jihad against Russia in Aug. 1999, and in an effort to create an Islamic state in Dagestan, began fighting against Russian troops. Russia subdued the Dagestanis and then turned its ire on Chechnya in Sept., provoked by several terrorist bombings in Moscow and other cities that were assumed to have been planted by Islamic militants. Just three years after the bloody 1994–96 Chechen-Russian war ended in devastation and stalemate, the fighting started again, with Russia launching air strikes and following up with ground troops. By the end of Nov., Russian troops had surrounded Chechnya's capital, Grozny, and about 215,000 Chechen refugees had fled to neighboring Ingushetia.

Russia maintained that a political solution was impossible until Islamic militants in Chechnya had been vanquished. In Dec. the Kremlin issued an ultimatum that all residents of Grozny must evacuate the city. An estimated 10,000–40,000 civilians were virtually trapped in the city, fearful of fleeing Grozny amid the constant barrage of shelling.

The ultimatum was eventually softened, in part because of the West's strong condemnation of Russia's handling of Chechnya. At its summit in Dec., the EU declared that "the European Council does not question the right of Russia to preserve its territorial integrity nor its right to fight terrorism. However, the fight against terrorism cannot . . . warrant the destruction of cities, nor that they be emptied of their inhabitants, nor that a whole population be considered as terrorists." Yet Russians themselves remained overwhelmingly in favor of the assault on Chechnya, demonstrated by the strong showing for the pro-government Unity party in Dec.'s parliamentary elections.

In a decision that took Russia and the world by surprise, Boris Yeltisin resigned on Dec. 31, 1999, and Vladimir Putin became the acting president. One of Putin's first acts was to grant Yeltsin immunity from prosecution (Yeltsin and family members had been accused of corruption and financial misconduct).

On Feb. 6, 2000, after almost five months of fighting, Russian troops captured Grozny, the Chechen capital. Although the war continues, the control of Grozny is a political as well as a military victory for

Putin, whose hard-line stance against Chechnya has greatly contributed to his political popularity.

On March 26, 2000, Putin won the presidential election with about 53% of the vote. Since then Putin has moved to centralize power in Moscow and has attempted to limit the power and influence of both the regional governors and wealthy business leaders. In July, Putin pushed through legislation that denies the 89 regional governors and local legislative leaders automatic seats in parliament. Instead, local legislatures will elect senators to the Federation Council, the upper house of parliament. In addition, the law gives Putin the authority to remove governors and dissolve local legislatures if they violate the law. In June, media tycoon Vladimir Gusinsky, who owns Russia's only independent television network, which had been critical of the Kremlin and the war in Chechnya, was arrested for allegedly embezzling millions in government property. He was held for four days before being released pending trial. Gusinsky was just one tycoon under investigation. Other oligarchs in the oil, metals, and auto industries have been under the microscope by tax investigators and state prosecutors. In Aug. 2000 the Russian government was severely criticized for its handling of the Kursk disaster, a nuclear submarine accident that left 118 sailors dead.

Rwanda

. **RWANDESE REPUBLIC**

National name: Republika y'u Rwanda
President: Paul Kagame (2000)
Prime Minister: Bernard Makuza (2000)
Area: 10,169 sq. mi. (26,340 sq. km)
Population (2000 est.): 7,229,129 (average annual rate of natural increase: 1.4%); birth rate: 34.8/1000; infant mortality rate: 120.1/1000; density per sq. mi.: 711
Capital and largest city (1991): Kigali, 232,733.
Monetary unit: Rwanda franc. **Languages:** Kinyarwanda, French, Swahili, English. **Ethnicity/race:** Hutu 80%, Tutsi 19%, Twa (Pygmoid) 1%.
Religions: Roman Catholic, 56%; Protestant, 18%; Islam, 1%; Animist, 25%. **Literacy rate:** 50% (1990)
Economic summary: GDP/PPP (1998 est.): $5.5 billion; $690 per capita. **Real growth rate:** 10.5% (1998 est.). **Inflation:** 10% (1998 est.). **Unemployment:** n.a. **Arable land:** 35%. **Agriculture:** coffee, tea, pyrethrum (insecticide made from chrysanthemums), bananas, beans, sorghum, potatoes, livestock. **Labor force:** 3.6 million: agriculture, 90%; government and services, industry and commerce. **Industries:** production of cement, processing of agricultural products, small-scale beverage production, manufacture of soap, furniture, shoes, plastic goods, textiles, cigarettes. **Natural resources:** gold, cassiterite (tin ore), wolframite (tungsten ore), natural gas, hydropower. **Exports:** $82.1 million (f.o.b., 1998 est.): coffee, tea, hides, tin ore. **Imports:** $326 million (f.o.b., 1998 est.): foodstuffs, machinery and equipment, steel, petroleum products, cement and construction material. **Major trading partners:** Brazil, Germany, U.S., Netherlands, U.K., Italy, Kenya, Tanzania, Belgium-Luxembourg.

Geography Rwanda, in east-central Africa, is surrounded by Congo, Uganda, Tanzania, and Burundi. It is slightly smaller than Maryland. Steep mountains and deep valleys cover most of the country. Lake Kivu in the northwest, at an altitude of 4,829 feet (1,472 m) is the highest lake in Africa. Extending north of it are the Virunga Mountains, which include the volcano Karisimbi (14,187 ft.; 4,324 m), Rwanda's highest point.

Government Republic.

History The original inhabitants of Rwanda were the Twa, a Pygmy people who now make up only 1% of the population. While the Hutu and Tutsi are often considered to be two separate ethnic groups, scholars point out that they speak the same language, have a history of intermarriage, and share many cultural characteristics. Traditionally, the differences between the two groups were occupational rather than ethnic. Agricultural people were considered Hutu, while the cattle-owning elite were identified as Tutsi. Supposedly Tutsi were tall and thin, while Hutu were short and square, but it is often impossible to tell one from the other. The 1933 requirement by the Belgians that everyone carry an identity card indicating tribal ethnicity as Tutsi or Hutu increased the distinction. Since independence, repeated violence in both Rwanda and Burundi has increased ethnic differentiation between the groups.

Rwanda, which became a part of German East Africa in 1890, was first visited by European explorers in 1854. During World War I, it was occupied in 1916 by Belgian troops. After the war, it became a Belgian League of Nations mandate, along with Burundi, under the name of Ruanda-Urundi. The mandate was made a U.N. trust territory in 1946. Until the Belgian Congo achieved independence in 1960, Ruanda-Urundi was administered as part of that colony. Belgium at first maintained Tutsi dominance but eventually encouraged power sharing between Hutu and Tutsi. Ethnic tensions led to civil war, forcing many Tutsi into exile. When Ruanda became the independent nation of Rwanda on July 1, 1962, it was under Hutu rule.

In Oct. 1990 rebel Tutsi (RPF) in exile in Uganda invaded. Peace accords were signed in Aug. 1993, calling for a coalition government. After the downing of an aircraft in April 1994 carrying the presidents of Rwanda and Burundi, both of whom died in the crash, deep-seated ethnic hatred erupted, and Hutus slaughtered an estimated 800,000 Tutsi civilians. It is believed that the plane was shot down by Hutu extremists who rejected the Hutu-Tutsi power-sharing plan proposed by President Juvénal Habyarimana, a Hutu moderate. Although the genocidal slaughter seemed a spontaneous eruption of hatred, it has in fact been shown to have been carefully orchestrated. In response, Tutsi rebels swept across the country in a 14-week civil war, routing the largely Hutu government. In the immediate aftermath an estimated 1.7 million Hutu fled across the border into neighboring Zaire (now the Democratic Republic of the Congo), creating an international humanitarian problem. Although the Tutsi rebel force, the Rwandan Patriotic Front, took control of the government, it permitted a Hutu to serve as president, to deflect accusations of a resurgence in Tutsi elitism and foster national unity. Paul Kagame, the Tutsi rebel leader, became vice president and minister of defense.

Amid the legitimate refugees from the genocide were Hutu militiamen who began waging guerrilla warfare from Zaire. The Hutu guerrillas in Zaire, as well as Zaire's threat to exile their own ethnic Tutsi, led to Rwanda's support of rebel forces bent on overthrowing Mobutu Sese Seko's Zaire. But Rwanda's support for the new regime of Laurent Kabila in the Democratic Republic of the Congo soon turned to disenchantment. The Kabila government was not able to prevent the raids from Hutu guerrillas that continued to traumatize the country and destabilize the region. In Aug. 1998, a little more than a year after Kabila took over, a rebellion began against his reign.

Despite their denials, it is believed to have been instigated by Rwanda and Uganda.

Refugee problems, continued massacres, and the scars of genocide continued to haunt the national psyche. In Sept. 1998, a U.N. tribunal sentenced Jean Kambanda, a former prime minister of Rwanda, to life in prison for his part in the 1994 genocide. He became the first person in history to be convicted for the crime of genocide, first defined in the 1948 Genocide Convention after World War II. In Dec. 1999, an independent report, commissioned by the U.N., took Kofi Annan and other U.N. officials to task for not intervening effectively in the genocide.

In April 2000, President Bizimungu resigned and Vice President Paul Kagame became the first Tutsi president of the nation.

St. Kitts and Nevis

FEDERATION OF ST. KITTS AND NEVIS

Sovereign: Queen Elizabeth II (1952)
Governor General: Sir Cuthbert Sebastian (1996)
Prime Minister: Denzil Douglas (1995)
Area: St. Kitts 65 sq. mi. (169 sq. km); Nevis 35 sq. mi. (100 sq. km)
Population (2000 est.): 38,819 (average annual rate of natural increase: 0.97%); birth rate: 19.1/1000; infant mortality rate: 16.7/1000; density per sq. mi.: 388
Capital: Basseterre (on St. Kitts), 19,000. **Largest town on Nevis:** Charlestown, 1,771. **Monetary unit:** East Caribbean dollar. **Ethnicity/race:** black African. **Literacy rate:** 98% (1970)
Economic summary: GDP/PPP (1997 est.): $235 million; $6,000 per capita. **Real growth rate:** 6.3% (1997 est.). **Inflation:** 11.3% (1997 est.). **Unemployment:** 4% (1997 est.). **Arable land:** 22%. **Agriculture:** sugarcane, rice, yams, vegetables, bananas, fish. **Labor force:** 18,172 (June 1995): services, 69%; manufacturing, 31%. **Industries:** sugar processing, tourism, cotton, salt, copra, clothing, footwear, beverages. **Exports:** $43.7 million (1997): machinery, food, electronics, beverages and tobacco. **Imports:** $129.6 million (1997): machinery, manufactures, food, fuel. **Major trading partners:** U.S., U.K., Caricom nations.

Geography St. Kitts and Nevis are related physiographically by a volcanic mountain chain that dominates the central core of both islands. St. Kitts is roughly oval in shape except for a long, narrow peninsula to the southeast. St. Kitts' highest point is Mount Liamuiga (3,792 feet [1,156 m]), which has a lake in its forested crater. The Narrows, a 2-mile- (3-kilometer-) wide channel, separates the two islands. The circularly shaped Nevis is surrounded by coral reefs and the island is almost entirely a single mountain, Nevis Peak (3,232 feet [985 m]).

Government Constitutional monarchy.

History When Christopher Columbus visited the islands in 1493, they were inhabited by the Carib people. St. Kitts, formerly St. Christopher, was settled by the British in 1623; Nevis in 1628. The French settled on St. Kitts in 1627, and an Anglo-French rivalry lasted for more than 100 years. After a decisive British victory over the French at Brimstone Hill in 1782, the islands came under permanent British control. The islands, including nearby Anguilla, were united in 1882. They joined the West Indies federation in 1958 and remained in that association until its dissolution in 1962. St. Kitts-Nevis-Anguilla became an associated state of the United Kingdom in 1967.

Anguilla seceded in 1980, and St. Kitts and Nevis became independent on Sept. 19, 1983.

A drop in world sugar prices hurt the nation's economy through the mid-1980s, and the government sought to reduce the islands' dependence on sugar production and to diversify the economy. In 1990, the premier of Nevis announced that he intended to seek an end to the federation with St. Kitts by 1992, but a local election in June 1992 put the idea on hold. In Aug. 1998, 62% of Nevis voters favored a referendum permitting Nevis to secede, but the vote fell short of the two-thirds majority required.

St. Lucia

Sovereign: Queen Elizabeth II (1952)
Governor-General: Pearlette Louisy (1997)
Prime Minister: Kenny D. Anthony (1997)
Area: 238 sq. mi. (620 sq. km)
Population (2000 est.): 156,260 (average annual rate of natural increase: 1.7%); birth rate: 22.2/1000; infant mortality rate: 15.6/1000; density per sq. mi.: 657
Capital and largest city (1992 est.): Castries, 13,600.
Monetary unit: East Caribbean dollar. **Languages:** English and patois. **Ethnicity/race:** African descent 90.3%, mixed 5.5%, East Indian 3.2%, white 0.8%. **Religions:** Roman Catholic, 90%; Protestant, 7%; Anglican, 3%. **Literacy rate:** 67% (1980)
Economic summary: GDP/PPP (1997 est.): $625 million; $4,100 per capita. **Real growth rate:** 2.2% (1997 est.). **Inflation:** 1.9% (1997 est.). **Unemployment:** 15% (1996 est.). **Labor force:** 43,800: agriculture, 43.4%; services, 38.9%; industry and commerce, 17.7% (1983 est.). **Arable land:** 8%. **Agriculture:** bananas, coconuts, vegetables, citrus, root crops, cocoa. **Industries:** clothing, assembly of electronic components, beverages, corrugated cardboard boxes, tourism, lime processing, coconut processing. **Exports:** $70.1 million (1997): bananas, clothing, cocoa, vegetables, fruit, coconut oil. **Imports:** $292.4 million (1997): food, manufactured goods, machinery and transportation equipment, chemicals, fuel. **Major trading partners:** U.K., U.S., Caricom countries, Japan, Canada. **Member of Commonwealth of Nations**

Geography One of the Windward Islands of the eastern Caribbean, St. Lucia lies just south of Martinique. It is of volcanic origin. A chain of wooded mountains runs from north to south, and from them flow many streams into fertile valleys.

Government Parliamentary democracy. A governor-general represents the sovereign, Queen Elizabeth II.

History The first inhabitants of St. Lucia were the Arawak Indians, who were forced off the island by the Caribs. Explored by Spain and then France, St. Lucia became a British territory in 1814 and one of the Windward Islands in 1871. With other Windward Islands, St. Lucia was granted home rule in 1967 as one of the West Indies Associated States. On Feb. 22, 1979, St. Lucia achieved full independence in ceremonies boycotted by the opposition St. Lucia Labour Party, which had advocated a referendum before cutting ties with Britain. The United Workers Party (UWP), then in power, called for new elections and was defeated by the St. Lucia Labour Party (SLP). The UWP was returned to power in the elections of 1982, 1987, and 1992.

Parliamentary elections in May 1997 gave the opposition St. Lucia Labour Party 16 of the 17 seats. The SLP had stressed economic issues and corruption, but the United Workers Party denied the corruption charges.

St. Vincent and The Grenadines

Sovereign: Queen Elizabeth II (1952)
Governor-General: Sir Charles Antrobus (1996)
Prime Minister: Sir James Fitz-Allen Mitchell (1984)
Area: 150 sq. mi. (340 sq. km)
Population (2000 est.): 115,461 (average annual rate of natural increase: 1.2%); birth rate: 18.3/1000; infant mortality rate: 17.1/1000; density per sq. mi.: 770
Capital and largest city (1992 est.): Kingstown, 15,466.
  Monetary unit: East Caribbean dollar. **Languages:** English (official), French patois. **Ethnicity/race:** African descent, white, East Indian, Carib Indian. **Religions:** Anglican, 47%; Methodist, 28%; Roman Catholic, 13%. **Literacy rate:** 96% (1970)
Economic summary: GDP/PPP (1998 est.): $289 million; $2,400 per capita. **Real growth rate:** 4% (1998 est.). **Inflation:** 3.6% (1996). **Unemployment:** 35%–40% (1994 est.). **Arable land:** 10%; **Agriculture:** bananas, coconuts, sweet potatoes, spices, fish, small numbers of cattle, sheep, pigs, goats. **Labor force:** 67,000 (1984 est.): services, 57%; agriculture, 26%; industry, 17% (1980 est.). **Industries:** food processing, cement, furniture, clothing, starch. **Exports:** $47.3 million (1997): bananas, eddoes and dasheen (taro), arrowroot starch, tennis racquets. **Imports:** $158.8 million (1997): foodstuffs, machinery and equipment, chemicals and fertilizers, minerals and fuel. **Major trading partners:** Caricom countries, U.K., U.S. **Member of Commonwealth of Nations**

Geography St. Vincent, chief island of the chain, is 18 miles (29 km) long and 11 miles (18 km) wide, and is located 100 miles (161 km) west of Barbados. The island is mountainous and well forested. St. Vincent is dominated by the volcano Mount Soufrière, which rises to 4,048 feet (1,234 m). The Grenadines, a chain of nearly 600 islets with a total area of only 17 square miles (27 sq. km), extend for 60 miles (96 km) between St. Vincent and Grenada. The main islands in the Grenadines are Bequia, Balliceau, Canouan, Mayreau, Mustique, Isle D'Quatre, Petit Saint Vincent, and Union Island.

Government Constitutional monarchy.

History The Carib Indians were the first inhabitants of St. Vincent before the Europeans arrived and the island still sports a sizable number of Carib artifacts. Explored by Columbus in 1498, and alternately claimed by Britain and France, St. Vincent became a British colony by the Treaty of Paris in 1763. In 1773, the island was divided between the Caribs and the British, but conflicts between the groups persisted. In 1776, the Caribs revolted and were subdued. Thereafter the British deported most of them to islands in the Gulf of Honduras. Sugarcane cultivation brought thousands of African slaves and, later, Portuguese and East Indian laborers.

The islands won home rule in 1969 as part of the West Indies Associated States, after being part of the federation of the West Indies from 1958 until its dissolution in 1962, and achieved full independence Oct. 26, 1979. Prime Minister Milton Cato's government quelled a brief rebellion on Dec. 8, 1979, attributed to economic problems following the eruption of La Soufrière in April 1979 (which had caused the evacuation of the northern two-thirds of the island). The eruption, followed by Hurricane Allen in 1980, seriously damaged the nation's economy, particularly the important banana crop, in the 1980s. But by the 1990s the economy had begun to rebound, and the small tourism industry began to grow. In 1996, St. Vincent and the Grenadines signed agreements with the U.S. that allowed U.S. Coast Guard personnel to pursue suspected drug smugglers into their territorial waters and provided for extradition of criminals. In 1997, the country's permanent representative to the Organization of American States assumed the chairmanship of that body's Permanent Council.

Samoa

INDEPENDENT STATE OF SAMOA

Head of State: Malietoa Tanumafili II (1962)
Prime Minister: Tuilaepa Sailele Malielegaoi (1998)
Area: 1,093 sq. mi. (2,860 sq. km)
Population (2000 est.): 179,466 (average annual growth rate: 0.9%); birth rate: 15.6/1000; infant mortality rate: 32.8/1000; density per sq. mi.: 164
Capital and largest city (1991): Apia, 32,859.
  Monetary unit: Tala. **Languages:** Samoan and English. **Ethnicity/race:** Samoan 92.6%, Euronesians 7% (persons of European and Polynesian blood), Europeans 0.4%. **Religions:** Christian, 99.7%. **Literacy rate:** 98% (1971)
Economic summary: GDP: (1997 est.) $470 million; $2,100 per capita. **Real growth rate:** 3.4% (1997 est.). **Inflation:** 2.2% (1998 est.). **Unemployment:** n.a. **Arable land:** 19%. **Agriculture:** coconuts, bananas, taro, yams. **Labor force:** 82,500 (1991 est.): agriculture, 65%; services, 30%; industry, 5% (1995 est.). **Industries:** timber, tourism, food processing, fishing. **Natural resources:** timber. **Exports:** $14.6 million (f.o.b., 1997): coconut oil and cream, copra, fish, beer. **Imports:** $99.7 million (f.o.b., 1997): intermediate goods, food, capital goods. **Major trading partners:** Australia, New Zealand, Slovakia, Germany, American Samoa, Japan, Fiji, U.S. **Member of Commonwealth of Nations.**

Geography Samoa, formerly Western Samoa, is in the South Pacific Ocean about 2,200 miles (3,540 km) south of Hawaii. The larger islands in the Samoan chain, Upolu and Savai'i, are mountainous and of volcanic origin. There is little level land except in the coastal areas, where most cultivation takes place.

Government Constitutional monarchy.

History Polynesians, possibly from Tonga, first settled in the Samoan islands about 1000 B.C. Samoa was explored by Dutch and French traders in the 18th century. Toward the end of the 19th century, conflicting interests of the U.S., Britain, and Germany resulted in an 1899 treaty that recognized the paramount interests of the U.S. in those islands west of 171° W (American Samoa) and Germany's interests in the other islands (Western Samoa).

New Zealand seized Western Samoa from Germany in 1914, and in 1946 it became a U.N. trust territory administered by New Zealand.

A resistance movement to New Zealand rule, known as the *Mau* ("strongly held view") movement, helped to edge the islands toward independence on Jan. 1, 1962. A constitutional monarchy, Samoa has a legislative assembly whose members are from the *matai*, or titled class.

Barraged regularly by cyclones that have wreaked havoc on the country's primarily agrarian economy, Samoa has begun stepping up its tourism industry—not such a difficult undertaking in this archetypical South Pacific paradise.

A referendum in 1990 gave most women the right to vote for the first time. In 1997, a new constitutional amendment changed the country's name to Samoa.

San Marino

MOST SERENE REPUBLIC OF SAN MARINO

National name: Repubblica di San Marino
Captains Regent: Gian Franco Terenzi and Enzo Colombini (2000)
Area: 23.4 sq. mi. (60 sq. km)
Population (2000 est.): 26,937 (average annual growth rate 0.3%); birth rate: 10.9/1000; infant mortality rate: 6.3/1000; density per sq. mi.: 1,151
Capital and largest city (1992 est.): San Marino, 2,397.
Monetary unit: Italian lira. **Language:** Italian.
Ethnicity/race: Sammarinese, Italian. **Religion:** Roman Catholic. **Literacy rate:** 96% (1976)
Economic summary: GDP/PPP (1997 est.): $500 million; $20,000 per capita. **Real growth rate:** n.a.
Inflation: 5.3% (1995). **Unemployment:** 3.6% (April 1996). **Arable land:** 17%. **Agriculture:** wheat, grapes, maize, olives, cattle, pigs, horses, beef, cheese, hides.
Labor force: 15,600 (1995): services, 55%; industry, 43%; agriculture, 2% (1995). **Industries:** tourism, textiles, electronics, ceramics, cement, wine. **Exports:** (trade data are included with the statistics for Italy): building stone, lime, wood, chestnuts, wheat, wine, baked goods, hides, and ceramics. **Imports:** (trade data are included with the statistics for Italy): wide variety of consumer manufactures, food.

Geography One-tenth the size of New York City, San Marino is surrounded by Italy. It is situated in the Apennines, a little inland from the Adriatic Sea near Rimini.

Government Republic.

History According to tradition, San Marino was founded about A.D. 350 and had the good luck for centuries to stay out of the many wars and feuds on the Italian peninsula. It is the oldest republic in the world. San Marino has survived, completely intact, attacks by other self-governing Italian city-states, the Napoleonic Wars, the unification of Italy, and two world wars. Those born in San Marino remain citizens and can vote no matter where they live. Throughout the 1990s San Marino has taken a more active role in international diplomacy, establishing strong diplomatic and economic ties to a host of other countries.

São Tomé and Príncipe

DEMOCRATIC REPUBLIC OF SÃO TOMÉ AND PRÍNCIPE

President: Miguel Trovoada (1991)
Prime Minister: Guilherme Posser da Costa (1999)
Area: 370 sq. mi. (960 sq. km)
Population (2000 est.): 159,883 (average annual growth rate: 3.5%); birth rate: 43/1000; infant mortality rate: 50.4/1000; density per sq. mi.: 432
Capital and largest city (1990 est.): São Tomé, 43,420.
Monetary unit: Dobra. **Language:** Portuguese.
Ethnicity/race: mestico, angolares (descendants of Angolan slaves), forros (descendants of freed slaves), servicais (contract laborers from Angola, Mozambique, and Cape Verde), tongas (children of servicais born on the islands), Europeans (primarily Portuguese).
Religions: Roman Catholic, Evangelical Protestant, Seventh-Day Adventist. **Literacy rate:** 57% (1981)
Economic summary: GDP/PPP (1998 est.): $164 million; $1,100 per capita. **Real growth rate:** 2.5% (1998 est.). **Inflation:** 21% (1998 est.).
Unemployment: 50% in the formal business sector (1998 est.). **Arable land:** 2%. **Agriculture:** cocoa, coconuts, palm kernels, copra, cinnamon, pepper, coffee, bananas, papayas, beans, poultry, fish. **Labor force:** Most engaged in subsistence agriculture and fishing. Shortages of skilled workers. **Industries:** light construction, textiles, soap, beer, fish processing, timber. **Exports:** $5.3 million (f.o.b., 1997 est.): cocoa, coffee, copra, palm oil. **Imports:** $19.2 million (f.o.b., 1997 est.): machinery and electrical equipment, food products, petroleum products. **Major trading partners:** Netherlands, Germany, Portugal, France, Angola, Belgium, Japan.

Geography The tiny volcanic islands of São Tomé and Príncipe lie in the Gulf of Guinea about 150 miles (240 km) off West Africa. São Tomé (about 330 sq. mi.; 859 sq. km) is covered by a dense mountainous jungle, out of which have been carved large plantations. Príncipe (about 40 sq. mi.; 142 sq. km) consists of jagged mountains. Other islands in the republic are Pedras Tinhosas and Rolas. About 95% of the population lives on São Tomé.

Government Republic.

History São Tomé and Príncipe, believed to have been originally uninhabited, were explored by Portuguese navigators in 1471 and settled by the end of the century. Intensive cultivation by slave labor made the islands a major producer of sugar during the 17th century but output declined until the introduction of coffee and cacao in the 19th century brought new prosperity. The island of São Tomé was the world's largest producer of cacao in 1908 and the crop is still the most important. Working conditions for laborers, however, were horrendous, and in 1909 British and German chocolate manufacturers boycotted São Tomé cocoa in protest. An exile liberation movement was formed in 1953 after Portuguese landowners quelled labor riots by killing several hundred African workers.

The Portuguese revolution of 1974 brought the end of the overseas empire and the new Lisbon government transferred power to the liberation movement on July 12, 1975. A former prime minister and dissident, Miguel Trovoada, was elected president in March 1991 after the withdrawal of the two other candidates.

In April 1995 Príncipe became autonomous. In Aug. a bloodless military coup was reversed through Angolan mediation. In Dec. an agreement was struck on forming a coalition government. President Trovoada won reelection in July 1996 against challenger and former president Manuel Pinto da Costa. Protests erupted in April 1997 when the government, in response to its inability to pay for imported oil, raised gasoline prices 140% in order to stem demand. After his center-left party won a majority of parliamentary seats in November 1998, Guilherma Posser da Costa, became the new prime minister. The government has made economic improvement a major goal, including the expansion of agriculture and the exploration of potential offshore oil reserves.

Saudi Arabia

KINGDOM OF SAUDI ARABIA

National name: Al-Mamlaka al-'Arabiya as-Sa'udiya
King and Prime Minister: King Fahd bin 'Abdulaziz (1982)
Area: 865,000 sq. mi. (1,960,582 sq. km)
Population (2000 est.): 22,023,506 (average annual rate of natural increase: 3.1%); birth rate: 37.5/1000; infant mortality rate: 52.9/1000; density per sq. mi.: 25
Capital: Riyadh. **Largest cities (1993):** Riyadh, 3,000,000; Jeddah, 2,500,000; Makkah (Mecca) (1994 est.), 550,000. **Monetary unit:** Riyal. **Languages:** Arabic, English widely spoken. **Ethnicity/race:** Arab

90%, Afro-Asian 10%. **Religion:** Islam, 100%.
Literacy rate: 62% (1990)
Economic summary: GDP/PPP (1998 est.): $186
billion; $9,000 per capita. **Real growth rate:** –10.8%
(1998 est.). **Inflation:** –0.2% (1998 est.).
Unemployment: n.a. **Arable land:** 2%. **Agriculture:**
wheat, barley, tomatoes, melons, dates, citrus; mutton,
chickens, eggs, milk. **Labor force:** 7 million (35% of
the population in the 15–64 age group is nonnational):
government, 40%; services, 30%; industry,
construction, and oil, 25%; agriculture, 5%.
Industries: crude oil production, petroleum refining,
basic petrochemicals, cement, two small steel-rolling
mills, construction, fertilizer, plastics. **Natural
resources:** oil, natural gas, iron ore. **Exports:** $59.7
billion (f.o.b., 1997): petroleum and petroleum
products, 90%. **Imports:** $26.2 billion (f.o.b., 1997):
machinery and equipment, foodstuffs, chemicals,
motor vehicles, textiles. **Major trading partners:**
Japan, U.S., South Korea, Singapore, India, Germany,
Italy, U.K.

Geography Saudi Arabia occupies most of the Ara-
bian Peninsula, with the Red Sea and the Gulf of
Aqaba to the west, the Arabian Gulf to the east.
Neighboring countries are Jordan, Iraq, Kuwait,
Qatar, the United Arab Emirates, the Sultanate of
Oman, Yemen, and Bahrain, connected to the Saudi
mainland by a causeway. Saudi Arabia contains the
world's largest continuous sand desert, the Rub
Al-Khali, or Empty Quarter. Its oil region lies prima-
rily in the eastern province along the Arabian Gulf.

Government Saudi Arabia was an absolute monarchy until 1992, at which time the Sa'ud royal
family introduced the country's first constitution.
The legal system is based on the Sharia (Islamic
law).

History Saudi Arabia is not only the homeland of
the Arab peoples—it is thought that the first Arabs
originated on the Arabian peninsula—but the
homeland of Islam, the world's second largest
religion. Muhammad founded Islam there and it is
the location of the two holy pilgrimage cities of
Mecca and Medina. The Islamic calendar begins
in 622, the year of the hegira, or Muhammad's
flight from Mecca. A succession of invaders
attempted to control the peninsula, but by 1517
the Ottoman Empire dominated, and in the middle
of the 18th century, it was divided into separate
principalities. In 1745 Muhammad ibn 'Abd
al-Wahhab began calling for the purification and
reform of Islam, and the Wahhabi movement
swept across Arabia. By 1811, Wahhabi leaders
had waged a jihad—a holy war—against other
forms of Islam on the peninsula, and succeeded in
uniting much of it. By 1818, however, the Wah-
habis had been driven out of power again by the
Ottomans and their Egyptian allies.

The kingdom of Saudi Arabia is almost entirely the
creation of King Ibn Saud (1882–1953). A descendant
of Wahhabi leaders, he seized Riyadh in 1901 and set
himself up as leader of the Arab nationalist movement. By 1906 he had established Wahhabi dominance in Nejd and conquered Hejaz in 1924–25.
Hejaz and Nejd were merged to form the kingdom of
Saudi Arabia in 1932, which was an absolute monarchy ruled by *sharia*, Islamic law. A year later the
region of Asir was incorporated into the kingdom.

Oil was discovered in 1936, and commercial production began during World War II. Its wealth
allowed the country to provide free health care and

education while not collecting any taxes from its
people. Saudi Arabia was neutral until nearly the end
of the war, but it was permitted to be a charter
member of the United Nations. The country joined
the Arab League in 1945 and took part in the 1948–49
war against Israel. Saudi Arabia still does not recognize the state of Israel. On Ibn Saud's death in 1953,
his eldest son, Saud, began an 11-year reign marked
by an increasing hostility toward the radical Arabism
of Egypt's Gamal Abdel Nasser. In 1964, the ailing
Saud was deposed and replaced by the premier,
Crown Prince Faisal, who gave vocal support but no
military help to Egypt in the 1967 Arab-Israeli War.

Faisal's assassination by a deranged kinsman in
1975 shook the Middle East, but failed to alter his
kingdom's course. His successor was his brother,
Prince Khalid. Khalid gave influential support to
Egypt during negotiations on Israeli withdrawal from
the Sinai Desert. King Khalid died of a heart attack in
1982, and was succeeded by his half-brother, Prince
Fahd bin 'Abdulaziz, who had exercised the real
power throughout Khalid's reign. King Fahd, a pro-
Western modernist, chose his 58-year-old half-
brother, Abdullah, as Crown Prince.

Saudi Arabia and the smaller, oil-rich Arab states
on the Persian Gulf, fearful that they might become
Ayatollah Ruhollah Khomeini's next targets if Iran
conquered Iraq, made large financial contributions to
the Iraqi war effort during the 1980s. At the same
time, cheating by other members of the Organization
of Petroleum Exporting Countries (OPEC), competition from nonmember oil producers, and conservation
efforts by consuming nations combined to drive down
the world price of oil. Saudi Arabia has one-third of
all known oil reserves, but falling demand and rising
production outside OPEC combined to reduce its oil
revenues from $120 billion in 1980 to less than $25
billion in 1985, threatening the country with domestic
unrest and undermining its influence in the Gulf area.

At the start of 1996, King Fahd passed authority to
Crown Prince Abdullah, saying he needed rest.
Although not an abdication, it was unclear how long
the king would be absent. In 1998 the country's oil
income fell by 40% because of a worldwide decline
in prices, and entered its first recession in 6 years.

In 2000, Saudi Arabia, along with other OPEC
nations experiencing a recession, decided to reduce
production to raise oil prices. The price hit nearly $35
per barrel in Sept. 2000, the highest level since 1990.
General uncertainty over Iraq and its tensions with
Kuwait also edged prices upward. Experts point out,
however, that OPEC controls a smaller amount of
world supply than it did during the 1970s oil crisis,
and that the world supply remains adequate.

Senegal

REPUBLIC OF SENEGAL

National name: République du Sénégal
President: Abdoulaye Wade (2000)
Prime Minister: Moustapha Niasse (2000)
Area: 75,954 sq. mi. (196,190 sq. km)
Population (2000 est.): 9,987,494 (average annual rate
of natural increase: 2.9%); birth rate: 37.9/1000; infant
mortality rate: 58.1/1000; density per sq. mi.: 131
Capital and largest city (1994 est.): Dakar, 1,729,823.
   Monetary unit: Franc CFA. **Ethnicity/race:** Wolof
36%, Fulani 17%, Serer 17%, Toucouleur 9%, Diola
9%, Mandingo 9%, European and Lebanese 1%, other
2%. **Languages:** French (official); Wolof, Serer, other
ethnic dialects. **Religions:** Islam, 92%; indigenous,
6%; Christian, 2%. **Literacy rate:** 38% (1990)

Economic summary: GDP/PPP (1998 est.): $15.6 billion; $1,600 per capita. **Real growth rate:** 5.7% (1998 est.). **Inflation:** 1.8% (1998 est.). **Unemployment:** n.a.; urban youth, 40%. **Arable land:** 12%. **Agriculture:** peanuts, millet, corn, sorghum, rice, cotton, tomatoes, green vegetables, cattle, poultry, pigs, fish. **Labor force:** n.a.; agriculture, 60%. **Industries:** agricultural and fish processing, phosphate mining, fertilizer production, petroleum refining, construction materials. **Natural resources:** fish, phosphate, iron ore. **Exports:** $925 million (f.o.b., 1998): fish, groundnuts (peanuts), petroleum products, phosphates, cotton. **Imports:** $1.2 billion (f.o.b., 1998): food and beverages, consumer goods, capital goods, petroleum products. **Major trading partners:** France, EU, India, Côte d'Ivoire, Mali, Nigeria, Cameroon, Algeria, U.S., China, Japan.

Geography The capital of Senegal, Dakar, is the westernmost point in Africa. The country, slightly smaller than South Dakota, surrounds Gambia on three sides and is bordered on the north by Mauritania, on the east by Mali, and on the south by Guinea and Guinea-Bissau.

Senegal is mainly a low-lying country, with a semi-desert area in the north and northeast and forests in the southwest. The largest rivers include the Senegal in the north and the Casamance in the south tropical climate region.

Government Parliamentary democracy with socialist leanings.

History The Toucouleur people, among the early inhabitants of Senegal, converted to Islam in the 11th century, although their religious beliefs retained strong elements of animism. The Portuguese had some stations on the banks of the Senegal River in the 15th century, and the first French settlement was made at Saint-Louis in 1659. Gorée Island became a major center for the Atlantic slave trade through the 1700s, and millions of Africans were shipped from there to the New World. The British took parts of Senegal at various times, but the French gained possession in 1840 and made it part of French West Africa in 1895. In 1946, together with other parts of French West Africa, Senegal became an overseas territory of France. On June 20, 1960, it became an independent republic federated with Mali, but the federation collapsed within four months.

Although Senegal is neither a large nor a strategically located country, it has nonetheless played a prominent role in African politics since its independence. As a black nation that is more than 90% Muslim, Senegal has been a diplomatic and cultural bridge between the Islamic and black African worlds. Senegal has also maintained closer economic, political, and cultural ties to France than probably any other former French African colony.

Senegal's first president, Léopold Sédar Senghor, towered over the country's political life until his voluntary retirement in 1981. He replaced multiparty democracy with an authoritarian regime. Senghor tried to become both French and African, which he discovered was impossible. As an acclaimed poet, Senghor sought to become a "black-skinned Frenchman," a quest he ultimately rejected. An advocate of "African socialism," Senghor increased government involvement in the economy through a series of Four Year plans.

In 1973 Senegal and six other nations created the West African Economic Community. When rising oil prices and fluctuations in the price of peanuts, a major

export crop, ruined the economy in the 1970s, Senghor reversed course. He emphasized new industries such as tourism and fishing. Politically, the so-called passive revolution allowed limited opposition.

When the economy continued to stagnate, and with it Senghor's popularity, he resigned in favor of his protégé, Abdou Diouf. Economic and political liberalization continued, including the sale of government companies, and the legalization of all political parties. Opposition party challenger Abdoulaye Wade won 60% of the vote in honest elections in March 2000. Diouf graciously accepted the results and stepped aside in what was hailed as a rare smooth transition of power in Africa. The economic crisis and the continuing rebellion in the southern Casmance region of the country are likely to dominate Senegal's political discourse for the foreseeable future.

Serbia and Montenegro

SEE YUGOSLAVIA.

Seychelles

REPUBLIC OF SEYCHELLES

President: France-Albert René (1977)
Area: 175 sq. mi. (455 sq. km)
Population (2000 est.): 79,326 (average annual rate of natural increase: 1.1%); birth rate: 18/1000; infant mortality rate: 17.7/1000; density per sq. mi.: 453
Capital and largest city (1993 est.): Victoria, 25,000.
Monetary unit: Seychelles rupee. **Languages:** English, French, and Seselwa (a creole). **Ethnicity/race:** Seychellois (mixture of Asians, Africans, Europeans). **Religions:** Roman Catholic, 90%; Anglican, 8%. **Literacy rate:** 58% (1971)
Economic summary: GDP/PPP (1997 est.): $550 million; $7,000 per capita. **Real growth rate:** 4.3% (1997 est.). **Inflation:** 0.6% (1997 est.). **Unemployment:** n.a. **Arable land:** 2%. **Agriculture:** coconuts, cinnamon, vanilla, sweet potatoes, cassava (tapioca), bananas, broiler chickens, tuna fish. **Labor force:** 26,000 (1996): services, 76%; industry, 19%; government, 14%; agriculture, forestry, and fishing, 10% (1989). **Industries:** fishing, tourism, processing of coconuts and vanilla, coir (coconut fiber) rope, boat building, printing, furniture, beverages. **Exports:** $53 million (f.o.b., 1995): fish, cinnamon bark, copra, petroleum products (reexports). **Imports:** $340 million (c.i.f., 1997): manufactured goods, food, petroleum products, tobacco, beverages, machinery and transportation equipment. **Major trading partners:** France, U.K., China, Germany, Japan, Singapore, South Africa. **Member of Commonwealth of Nations**

Geography Seychelles consists of an archipelago of about 100 islands in the Indian Ocean northeast of Madagascar. The principal islands are Mahé (55 sq. mi.; 142 sq. km), Praslin (15 sq. mi.; 38 sq. km), and La Digue (4 sq. mi.; 10 sq. km). The Aldabra, Farquhar, and Desroches groups are included in the territory of the republic.

Government Socialist multiparty state.

History The Seychelles were uninhabited when the British East India Company became the first visitors to the archipelago in 1609. Thereafter, it became a favorite pirate haven. The French claimed the islands in 1756 and administered them as part of the colony of Mauritius. The British gained control of the islands through the

Treaty of Paris (1814), and changed the islands' name from the French Séchelles to the Anglicized Seychelles.

The islands became self-governing in 1975, and independent on June 29, 1976. It has remained a member of the Commonwealth of Nations. Its first president, James Mancham, was overthrown in 1977 by the prime minister, France-Albert René. At first René created a socialist state with a one-party system, but later reintroduced a multiparty system as well as various reforms.

To increase revenue the government in 1996 quietly initiated an Economic Citizenship Program that provides foreigners with the opportunity to obtain a Seychelles passport upon payment of $25,000. A new law in late 1995 granted immunity from criminal prosecution to anyone investing $10 million in the country.

In elections held in March 1998, President France-Albert René was reelected with 66.6% of the vote.

In an effort to boost trade, the Seychelles has made future plans to join the Southern Africa Development Community, a trading bloc of Southern African nations.

Sierra Leone

REPUBLIC OF SIERRA LEONE
President: Ahmad Tejan Kabbah (1998)
Area: 27,925 sq. mi (71,740 sq. km)
Population (2000 est.): 5,232,624 (average annual rate of natural increase: 2.6%); birth rate: 45.6/1000; infant mortality rate: 148.7/1000; density per sq. mi.: 187
Capital and largest city (1994 est.): Freetown, 1,300,000. **Monetary unit:** Leone. **Languages:** English (official), Mende, Temne, Krio. **Ethnicity/race:** 18 native African tribes 99% (Temne 30%, Mende 30%, other 39%), Creole, European, Lebanese, and Asian 1%. **Religions:** Islam, 40%, Christian, 35%; Indigenous, 20%. **Literacy rate:** 21% (1990)
Economic summary: GDP/PPP (1998 est.): $2.7 billion; $530 per capita. **Real growth rate:** 5.0% (1998 est.). **Inflation:** 37.4% (1998 est.). **Unemployment:** n.a. **Arable land:** 7%. **Agriculture:** rice, coffee, cocoa, palm kernels, palm oil, peanuts, poultry, cattle, sheep, pigs, fish. **Labor force:** 1.369 million (1981 est.): agriculture, 65%; industry, 19%; services, 16% (1981 est.). **Industries:** mining (diamonds), small-scale manufacturing (beverages, textiles, cigarettes, footwear), petroleum refining. **Natural resources:** diamonds, bauxite, iron ore. **Exports:** $41 million (f.o.b., 1998): diamonds, rutile, cocoa, coffee, fish. **Imports:** $166 million (f.o.b., 1998): foodstuffs, machinery and equipment, fuel and lubricants. **Major trading partners:** Belgium, Spain, U.S., U.K., Côte d'Ivoire, Belgium-Luxembourg. **Member of Commonwealth of Nations**

Geography Sierra Leone, on the Atlantic Ocean in West Africa, is half the size of Illinois. Guinea, in the north and east, and Liberia, in the south, are its neighbors. Mangrove swamps lie along the coast, with wooded hills and a plateau in the interior. The eastern region is mountainous.

Government Constitutional democracy.

History The Bulom people were thought to have been the earliest inhabitants of Sierra Leone, followed by the Mende and Temne peoples in the 15th century, and thereafter the Fulani. The Portuguese were the first Europeans to explore the land, and gave Sierra Leone its name, which means "lion mountains." Free-

town, on the coast, was ceded to English settlers in 1787 as a home for blacks discharged from the British armed forces and also for runaway slaves who had found asylum in London. In 1808 the coastal area became a British colony, and in 1896 a British protectorate was proclaimed over the hinterland.

Sierra Leone became an independent nation on April 27, 1961. A military coup overthrew the civilian government in 1967, which was in turn replaced by civilian rule a year later. The country declared itself a republic on April 19, 1971.

A coup attempt early in 1971 led to then prime minister Siaka Stevens calling in troops from neighboring Guinea's army who remained for two years. Stevens turned the government into a one-party state under the aegis of the All People's Congress Party in April 1978. In 1992 rebel soldiers overthrew Stevens's successor, Joseph Momoh, calling for a return to a multi-party system. In 1996, another military coup ousted the country's military leader and president. Nevertheless, a multiparty presidential election proceeded in 1996, and People's Party candidate Ahmed Tejan Kabbah won with 59.4% of the vote, becoming Sierra Leone's first democratically elected president.

But a violent military coup ousted President Kabbah's civilian government in May 1997, and in June the leader of the coup, Lieut. Col. Johnny Paul Koroma, assumed the title "Head of the Armed Forces Revolutionary Council" (AFRC). Koroma began a reign of terror, destroying the economy and murdering enemies. The Commonwealth of Nations demanded the reinstatement of Kabbah and Nigerian troops intervened to this end.

After ten months in exile, Kabbah resumed his rule over Sierra Leone on March 10, 1998, although the ousted junta and other rebel forces continued to wage attacks, many of which included brutal maimings of civilians. In Jan. 1999, rebels and Liberian mercenaries stormed the capital in spite of the Nigerian-led coalition of troops, known as ECOMOG, who are protecting the government. The rebels called for the ousting of Kabbah and the release of imprisoned rebel leader Foday Sankoh. ECOMOG regained control of Freetown but President Kabbah later released Sankoh so he could participate in peace negotiations.

In July 1999 a fragile peace treaty was signed requiring the government to share power with the Revolutionary United Front (RUF), and Koroma's AFRC. While the AFRC has remained loyal to the government, the RUF has continued fighting in the north. Meanwhile, Sankoh was captured and remains in government custody, where he awaits trial for war crimes. In Aug. 2000 the U.N. Security Council approved the creation of a tribunal to try those accused of war crimes in Sierra Leone.

Singapore

REPUBLIC OF SINGAPORE
President: S. R. Nathan (1999)
Prime Minister: Goh Chok Tong (1990)
Area: 252.9 sq. mi. (647.5 sq. km)
Population (2000 est.): 4,151,264 (average annual rate of natural increase: 0.86%); birth rate: 12.8/1000; infant mortality rate: 3.7/1000; density per sq. mi.: 16,415
Capital (1996 est.): Singapore, 3,044,000. **Monetary unit:** Singapore dollar. **Languages:** Malay, Chinese (Mandarin), Tamil, English. **Ethnicity/race:** Chinese 76.4%, Malay 14.9%, Indian 6.4%, other 2.3%. **Religions:** Islam, Christian, Buddhist, Hindu, Taoist. **Literacy rate:** 90% (1990)

Economic summary: GDP/PPP (1998 est.): $91.7 billion; $26,300 per capita. **Real growth rate:** 1.3% (1998 est.). **Inflation:** −0.5% (1998 est.). **Unemployment:** 5% (1999 est.). **Arable land:** 2%. **Agriculture:** rubber, copra, fruit, vegetables, poultry. **Labor force:** 1.856 million (1997 est.): financial and business services, 33.5%; manufacturing, 25.6%; commerce, 22.9%; construction, 6.6%, other 11.4% (1994). **Industries:** electronics, financial services, oil drilling equipment, petroleum refining, rubber processing and rubber products, processed food and beverages, ship repair, entrepôt trade, biotechnology. **Exports:** $128 billion (1998 est.): computer equipment, rubber and rubber products, petroleum products, telecommunications equipment. **Imports:** $133.9 billion (1997 est.): aircraft, petroleum, chemicals, foodstuffs. **Major trading partners:** Malaysia, U.S., Hong Kong, Japan, Thailand, Taiwan, South Korea. **Member of Commonwealth of Nations**

Geography The Republic of Singapore consists of the main island of Singapore, off the southern tip of the Malay Peninsula between the South China Sea and the Indian Ocean, and 58 nearby islands.

Government Republic.

History Inhabitants of the Malaysian peninsula and the island of Singapore first migrated to the area between 2500 and 1500 B.C. (*see* Malaysia). British and Dutch interest in the region grew with the spice trade, and the trading post of Singapore was founded in 1819 by Sir Stamford Raffles. It was made a separate crown colony of Britain in 1946, when the former colony of the Straits Settlements was dissolved. The other two settlements on the peninsula—Penang and Malacca—became part of the Union of Malaya, and the small island of Labuan was transferred to North Borneo. The Cocos (or Keeling) Islands and Christmas Island were transferred to Australia in 1955 and in 1958, respectively.

Singapore attained full internal self-government in 1959, and Lee Kwan Yew, an economic visionary with an authoritarian streak, took the helm as prime minister. On Sept. 16, 1963, Singapore joined Malaya, Sabah (North Borneo), and Sarawak in the Federation of Malaysia. It withdrew from the Federation on Aug. 9, 1965, and a month later proclaimed itself a republic.

Under Lee, Singapore developed into one of the cleanest, safest, and most economically prosperous cities in Asia. However, Singapore's strict rules of civil obedience also drew criticism from those who said the nation's prosperity was achieved at the expense of individual freedoms. In 1990, Lee stepped down as prime minister but remained "senior minister" with considerable influence over his successor, Goh Chok Tong, who continued to preside over Singapore through difficult economic times in 1998.

The first direct presidential election took place in Aug. 1993. Ong Teng Cheong faced what initially appeared to be only token opposition but which ultimately took 40% of the vote.

In 1998, Singapore and Malaysia's often-strained relations soured again against the backdrop of the Asian financial crisis, which was taking a heavy toll on both economies. Singaporean leaders accused Malaysia of using a newly built $2.3 billion international airport at Kuala Lumpur to supplant the island nation as a regional air hub.

S. R. Nathan was declared president without an election when he was certified as the only candidate eligible to run in the elections originally scheduled for Aug. 28, 1999.

Slovakia

REPUBLIC OF SLOVAKIA

President: Rudolf Schuster (1999)
Prime Minister: Mikulás Dzurinda (1998)
Area: 18,917 sq. mi. (48,845 sq. km)
Population (2000 est.): 5,407,956 (average annual rate of natural increase: 0.07%); birth rate: 10/1000; infant mortality rate: 9.2/1000; density per sq. mi.: 286
Capital and largest city (1993 est.): Bratislava, 446,600. **Other large city** (1993 est.): Kosice, 237,300. **Monetary unit:** Koruna (SKK). **Languages:** Slovak (official), Hungarian. **Ethnicity/race:** Slovak 85.7%, Hungarian 10.7%, Gypsy 1.5%, Czech 1%, Ruthenian 0.3%, Ukrainian 0.3%, German 0.1%, Polish 0.1%. **Religions:** Roman Catholic, 60.3%; atheist, 9.7%; Protestant, 8.4%; Orthodox, 4.1%; other, 17.5%. **Literacy rate:** 99%
Economic summary: GDP/PPP (1998 est.): $44.5 billion; $8,300 per capita. **Real growth rate:** 5% (1998 est.). **Inflation:** 7.4% (1998 est.). **Unemployment:** 14% (1998 est.). **Arable land:** 31%. **Industries:** metal and metal products, food and beverages, electricity, gas, coke, oil and nuclear fuel, chemicals and manmade fibers, machinery; paper and printing, earthenware and ceramics, transport vehicles, textiles, electrical and optical apparatus, rubber products. **Labor force:** 3.32 million (1997): services, 45.6%; industry, 29.3%; agriculture, 8.9%; transport and communication, 8.2%; construction, 8% (1994). **Agriculture:** grains, potatoes, sugar beets, hops, fruit, pigs, cattle, poultry, forest products. **Exports:** $10.7 billion (f.o.b., 1998): machinery and transport equipment, intermediate manufactured goods, miscellaneous manufactured goods, chemicals, raw materials. **Imports:** $12.9 billion (f.o.b., 1998): machinery and transport equipment, intermediate manufactured goods, fuel, chemicals, miscellaneous manufactured goods. **Major trading partners:** EU, Czech Republic, Austria, Poland, Russia, Italy.

Geography Slovakia is located in central Europe. The land has rugged mountains, rich in mineral resources, with vast forests and pastures. The Carpathian Mountains dominate the topography of Slovakia, with lowland areas in the southern region. Slovakia is about twice the size of the state of Maryland.

Government Parliamentary democracy.

History Present-day Slovakia was settled by Slavic Slovaks about the 6th century A.D. They were politically united in the Moravian empire in the 9th century. In 907, the Germans and the Magyars conquered the Moravian state and the Slovaks fell under Hungarian control from the 10th century up until 1918. When the Hapsburg-ruled empire collapsed in 1918 following World War I, the Slovaks joined the Czech lands of Bohemia, Moravia, and part of Silesia to form the new joint state of Czechoslovakia. In March 1939, Germany occupied Czechoslovakia, established a German "protectorate," and created a puppet state out of Slovakia with Monsignor Josef Tiso as premier. The country was liberated from the Germans by the Soviet army in the spring of 1945, and Slovakia was restored to its prewar status and rejoined to a new Czechoslovakian state.

After the Communist Party took power in Feb. 1948, Slovakia was again subjected to a centralized Czech-dominated government and antagonism between the two republics developed. On Jan. 1969, the nation became the Slovak Socialist Republic of Czechoslovakia.

Nearly 42 years of Communist rule for Slovakia ended when Vaclav Havel became president of

Czechoslovakia in 1989 and democratic political reform began. However, with the demise of Communist power, a strong Slovak nationalist movement resurfaced and the rival relationship between the two states increased. By the end of 1991, discussions between Slovak and Czech political leaders turned to whether the Czech and Slovak republics should continue to coexist within the federal structure or be divided into two independent states.

After the general election in June 1992, it was decided that two fully independent republics would be created. The Republic of Slovakia came into existence on Jan. 1, 1993. The Parliament in February elected Michal Kovac as president.

Vladimir Meciar, who served three times as Slovakia's prime minister, exhibited increasingly authoritarian behavior, and was cited as the reason Slovakia was eliminated from consideration for both the EU and NATO. A referendum in May 1997 on whether the country should join NATO was boycotted by 90% of the electorate after it turned into a showdown between the prime minister and the president, who wanted a question about direct election of the president placed on the ballot. For more than a year, Slovakia was without a president after Michael Kovac finished his term. Finally, the constitution was changed to allow for direct vote, and Rudolf Schuster was elected in May 1999.

Populist prime minister Meciar was unseated in 1998 elections by the reformist government of Mikulás Dzurinda. Meciar has been blamed for Slovakia's very low influx of foreign capital because of his government's lack of transparency. In April 2000 Mecia was arrested and charged with paying illegal bonuses to his cabinet ministers while in office. A three-week standoff with police preceded the arrest, ending only when masked police commandos blew open the door on Meciar's house and seized him. He was also questioned about his alleged involvement in the 1995 kidnapping of the son of Slovakia's former president, Michal Kovac.

Slovenia

REPUBLIC OF SLOVENIA

President: Milan Kucan (1990)
Prime Minister: Andrej Bajuk (2000)
Area: 7,819 sq. mi. (20,256 sq. km)
Population (2000 est.): 1,927,593 (average annual rate of natural increase: –0.06%); birth rate: 9.4/1000; infant mortality rate: 4.6/1000; density per sq. mi.: 247
Capital and largest city (1996 est.): Ljubljana, 330,000. **Other large city:** Maribor, 103,512. **Monetary unit:** Slovenian tolar. **Languages:** Slovenian; most can also speak Serbo-Croatian. **Ethnicity/race:** Slovene 91%, Serbo-Croation 6%, other 3%. **Religions:** Roman Catholic, 70.8% (including 2% Uniate); Lutheran, 1%; Muslim, 1%; other, 27.2%. **Literacy rate:** 99%
Economic summary: GDP/PPP (1998 est.): $20.4 billion; $10,300 per capita. **Real growth rate:** 3.6% (1998 est.). **Inflation:** 8% (1998 est.). **Unemployment:** 7.1% (1997 est.). **Arable land:** 12%. **Industries:** ferrous metallurgy and rolling mill products, aluminum reduction and rolled products, lead and zinc smelting, electronics (including military electronics), trucks, electric power equipment, wood products, textiles, chemicals, machine tools. **Labor force:** 857,400. **Agriculture:** potatoes, hops, wheat, sugar beets, corn, grapes, cattle, sheep, poultry. **Exports:** $9.2 billion (f.o.b., 1998): manufactured goods, machinery and transport equipment, chemicals, food. **Imports:** $9.9 billion (f.o.b., 1998): machinery and transport equipment, manufactured goods, chemicals, fuel and lubricants, food. **Major trading partners:** Germany, Italy, Croatia, France, Austria, U.S., Hungary.

Geography Slovenia occupies an area about the size of the state of Massachusetts. It is largely a mountainous republic and almost half of the land is forested, with hilly plains spread across the central and eastern regions. Mount Triglav, the highest peak, rises to 9,393 ft. (2,864 m).

Government Parliamentary democracy.

History Slovenia was originally settled by Illyrian and Celtic peoples. It became part of the Roman empire in the first century B.C.

The Slovenes were a south Slavic group that settled in the region during the 6th century A.D. During the 7th century, the Slavs established the Slavic state of Samu, which owed its allegiance to the Avars, who dominated the Hungarian plain until Charlemagne defeated them in the late 8th century.

In the 11th century, Slovenia was a separate province of the kingdom of Hungary. When the Hungarians were defeated by the Turks in 1526, Hungary accepted Austrian Hapsburg rule in order to escape Turkish domination. Thus, Slovenia and Croatia became part of the Austro-Hungarian kingdom when the dual-monarchy was established in 1857. Like Croatia and unlike the other Balkan states, it is primarily Roman Catholic.

Following the defeat and collapse of Austria-Hungary in World War I, Slovenia declared its independence. It formally joined with Montenegro, Serbia, and Croatia on Dec. 4, 1918, to form the new nation called the Kingdom of the Serbs, Croats, and Slovenes. The name was later changed to Yugoslavia in 1929.

During World War II, Germany occupied Yugoslavia and Slovenia was divided among Germany, Italy, and Hungary. For the duration of the war many Slovenes fought a guerrilla war against the Nazis under the leadership of the Croatian-born Communist resistance leader, Marshal Tito. After the final defeat of the Axis powers in 1945, Slovenia was again made into a republic of the newly established Communist nation of Yugoslavia.

In the 1980s, Slovenia agitated for greater autonomy and occasionally threatened to secede. It introduced a multiparty system and in 1990 elected a non-communist government. Slovenia declared its independence from Yugoslavia on June 25, 1991. The Serbian-dominated Yugoslavian army tried to keep Slovenia in line and some brief fighting took place, but the army then withdrew its forces. Unlike Croatia and Bosnia, Slovenia was able to sever itself from Yugoslavia with relatively little violence. With recognition of its independence granted by the European Community in 1992, the country began realigning its economy and society toward western Europe.

Slovenia is considered one of the most promising candidates for EU admission and expects to join by 2003. In 2000, after eight years as prime minister, center-left prime minister Janez Drnovsek was unseated by the conservative government of Andrej Bajuk.

Solomon Islands

Sovereign: Queen Elizabeth II (1952)
Governor-General: John Lapli (1999)
Prime Minister: Manasseh Sogavare (2000)
Area: 11,500 sq. mi. (28,450 sq. km)
Population (2000 est.): 466,194 (average annual rate of natural increase: 3%); birth rate: 34.8/1000; infant mortality rate: 25.3/1000; density per sq. mi.: 41
Capital and largest city (1990 est.): Honiara (on Guadalcanal), 35,288. **Monetary unit:** Solomon Islands dollar. **Languages:** English, Solomon Pijin (an English pidgin), over 60 indigenous Melanesian languages. **Ethnicity/race:** Melanesian 93%, Polynesian 4%, Micronesian 1.5%, European 0.8%, Chinese 0.3%, other 0.4%. **Religions:** Anglican; Roman Catholic; South Seas Evangelical; Seventh-Day Adventist, United (Methodist) Church, other Protestant. **Literacy rate:** 30%
Economic summary: GDP/PPP (1998 est.): $1.15 billion; $2,600 per capita. **Real growth rate:** −10% (1998 est.). **Inflation:** 11.8% (1996). **Unemployment:** n.a. **Arable land:** 1%. **Agriculture:** cocoa, beans, coconuts, palm kernels, rice, potatoes, vegetables, fruit, cattle, pigs, timber, fish. **Labor force:** 26,842: services, 41.5%; agriculture, forestry, and fishing, 23.7%; commerce, transport, and finance, 21.7%; construction, manufacturing, and mining, 13.1% (1992 est.). **Industries:** copra, fish (tuna). **Natural resources:** fish, timber, gold, bauxite. **Exports:** $184 million (f.o.b., 1996): timber, fish, palm oil, cocoa, copra. **Imports:** $151 million (c.i.f., 1996 est.): plant and equipment, manufactured goods, food and live animals, fuel. **Major trading partners:** Japan, Spain, U.K., Thailand, Australia, Singapore, New Zealand, U.S. **Member of British Commonwealth**

Geography A scattered archipelago of mountainous islands and low-lying coral atolls, the Solomon Islands lie east of Papua New Guinea and northeast of Australia in the south Pacific. The islands include Guadalcanal, Malaita, Santa Isabel, San Cristóbal, Choiseul, New Georgia, the Santa Cruz group, and numerous smaller islands.

Government Parliamentary monarchy.

History It is thought that people have lived in the Solomon Islands since at least 2000 B.C. Explored in 1568 by Alvaro de Mendana of Spain, the Solomons were not visited again for about 200 years. In 1886, Great Britain and Germany divided the islands between them, but later Britain was given control of the entire territory. The Japanese invaded the islands in World War II, and they became the scene of some of the bloodiest battles in the Pacific theater, most famously the battle of Guadalcanal. The British gained control of the island again in 1945. In 1976 the islands became self-governing, and gained independence in 1978.

The border with Papua New Guinea (PNG) remained a source of tension in the 1990s. Incursions into Solomon Islands territory by PNG forces, who were countering secessionist action on neighboring Bougainville Island, gave rise to formal protests in mid-1997.

Since early 1999, the Isatabus, natives of Guadalcanal, have expelled more than 20,000 Malaitans from the island. The Malaitans had migrated from nearby Malaita, and many secured jobs in the capital, Honiara, stirring resentment among Isatabus that has grown steadily since independence. Ethnic tensions reached their height in June 2000, when the Malaita Eagle Force stole police weapons, forced Prime Min-

ister Bartholomew Ulufa'alu to resign, and seized control of Honiara. The rival groups agreed to a ceasefire in June 2000, barely averting a civil war. Legislators elected opposition leader Mannasseh Sogavare prime minister on June 30, 2000.

Somalia

SOMALI DEMOCRATIC REPUBLIC

National name: Al Jumhouriya As-Somalya al-Dimocradia
President: Abdiqasim Salad Hassan (2000)
Prime Minister: Ali Khalif Galaid (2000)
Area: 246,199 sq. mi. (637,660 sq. km)
Population (2000 est.): 7,253,137 (average annual rate of natural increase: 2.9%); birth rate: 47.7/1000; infant mortality rate: 125.8/1000; density per sq. mi.: 29
Capital and largest city (1990 est.): Mogadishu, 900,000. **Monetary unit:** Somali shilling. **Languages:** Somali (official), Arabic, English, Italian. **Ethnicity/race:** Somali 85%, Bantu, Arabs. **Religion:** Islam (Sunni). **Literacy rate:** 24% (1990)
Economic summary: As of early 1999, ongoing civil disturbances in Mogadishu and outlying areas are interfering with any substantial economic advance. **GDP/PPP** (1998 est.): $4 billion; $600 per capita. **Real growth rate:** n.a. **Inflation:** n.a. **Unemployment:** n.a. **Arable land:** 2%. **Agriculture:** bananas, sorghum, corn, sugarcane, mangoes, sesame seeds, beans, cattle, sheep, goats, fish. **Labor force:** 3.7 million (1993 est.), very few are skilled laborers: agriculture, 71%; industry and services, 29%. **Natural resources:** uranium. **Industries:** a few small industries, including sugar refining, textiles, petroleum refining (mostly shut down). **Exports:** $123 million (f.o.b., 1995 est.): livestock, bananas, hides, fish. **Imports:** $60 million (f.o.b., 1995 est.): manufactures, petroleum products, foodstuffs, construction materials. **Major trading partners:** Saudi Arabia, Yemen, Italy, U.A.E., U.S., Kenya, Djibouti, Brazil, Pakistan.

Geography Somalia, situated in the Horn of Africa, lies along the Gulf of Aden and the Indian Ocean. It is bounded by Djibouti in the northwest, Ethiopia in the west, and Kenya in the southwest. In area it is slightly smaller than Texas. Generally arid and barren, Somalia has two chief rivers, the Shebelle and the Juba.

Government Between Jan. 1991 and Aug. 2000, Somalia had no working government. A fragile parliamentary government was formed Aug. 22.

History From the 7th to the 10th century, Arab and Persian trading posts were established along the coast of present-day Somalia. Nomadic tribes occupied the interior, occasionally pushing into Ethiopian territory. In the 16th century, Turkish rule extended to the northern coast and the Sultans of Zanzibar gained control in the south.

After British occupation of Aden in 1839, the Somali coast became its source of food. The French established a coal mining station in 1862 at the site of Djibouti and the Italians planted a settlement in Eritrea. Egypt, which for a time claimed Turkish rights in the area, was succeeded by Britain. By 1920, a British protectorate and an Italian protectorate occupied what is now Somalia. The British ruled the entire area after 1941, with Italy returning in 1950 to serve as United Nations trustee for its former territory.

By 1960, Britain and Italy granted independence to their respective sectors, enabling the two to join as the Republic of Somalia on July 1, 1960. Somalia broke diplomatic relations with Britain in 1963 when the British granted the Somali-populated Northern Frontier District of Kenya to the Republic of Kenya.

On Oct. 15, 1969, President Abdi Rashid Ali Shermarke was assassinated and the army seized power, dissolving the legislature and arresting all government leaders. Maj. Gen. Mohamed Siad Barre, as president of a renamed Somali Democratic Republic, leaned heavily toward the U.S.S.R. In 1977, Somalia openly backed rebels in the easternmost area of Ethiopia, the Ogaden Desert, which had been seized by Ethiopia at the turn of the century. Somalia acknowledged defeat in an eight-month war against the Ethiopians that year, having lost much of its 32,000-man army and most of its tanks and planes. President Siad Barre fled the country in late Jan. 1991. His departure left Somalia in the hands of a number of clan-based guerrilla groups, none of which trusted each other.

Africa's worst drought occurred in 1992, and coupled with the devastation of civil war, Somalia was plunged into a severe famine—an estimated one-third of the population was in danger of dying from starvation. U.S. troops were sent in to protect the delivery of food in Dec. 1992. In May the U.N. took control of the relief efforts from the U.S. The warlord Mohamed Farah Aidid ambushed U.N. troops and dragged American bodies through the streets, causing an about-face in America's willingness to involve itself in the fate of this anarchic country. Peace talks in Kenya appeared to be moving slowly but steadily toward an agreement on an interim government, at least in principle, when on March 23, 1994, they collapsed. The last of the U.S. troops left in late March, leaving 19,000 U.N. troops behind.

Since 1991 Somalia has been engulfed in anarchy. Over the past seven years peace negotiations between the various factions have been fruitless, and no attempt has been made to rebuild the government. In 1991, a breakaway nation, the Somaliland Republic, proclaimed its independence. Since then several warlords have begun to set up their own ministates—Colonel Abdullahi Yussuf Ahmed is president of breakaway Puntland and Mohamed "General Morgan" Said Hersi began setting up Jubaland in the fall of 1998.

In Aug. 2000, a parliament convened in nearby Djibouti and elected a new president, Abdulkassim Salat Hassana. While neighboring countries were quick to recognize the new government, some Somali warlords operating out of Mogadishu, as well as the leaders of the breakaway regions of Somaliland and Puntland, oppose the parliament, and it was uncertain whether the new government—Somalia's first in nearly a decade—would actually be permitted to govern.

South Africa

REPUBLIC OF SOUTH AFRICA

National name: Republic of South Africa
President: Thabo Mbeki (1999)
Area: 471,440 sq. mi. (1,219,912 sq. km)
Population (2000 est.): 43,421,021 (average annual rate of natural increase: 0.69%); birth rate: 21.6/1000; infant mortality rate: 58.9/1000; density per sq. mi.: 92
Administrative capital: Pretoria; **Legislative capital:** Cape Town; **Judicial capital:** Bloemfontein. No decision has been made to relocate the seat of government. South Africa is demarcated into nine provinces, consisting of the Gauteng, Northern Province, Mpumalanga, North West, KwaZulu/Natal, Eastern Cape, Western Cape, Northern Cape, and Free State. Each province has its own capital. **Largest metropolitan areas (1995):** Johannesburg (2000 est.), 5,700,000 (metro. area); Cape Peninsula, 2,350,157; East Rand, 1,378,792 (part of Johannesburg metro. area); Durban/Pinetown, 1,137,378; Pretoria, 1,080,187. **Monetary unit:** Rand. **Languages:** English, Afrikaans, Ndebele, Sesotho sa Leboa, Sesotho, Swati, Xitsonga, Setswana, Tshivenda, Xhosa and Zulu are the official languages of the interim period. **Ethnicity/race:** black 75.2%, white 13.6%, Colored 8.6%, Indian 2.6%. **Religions:** Christian; Hindu; Islam. **Literacy rate:** 60% (1980)
Economic summary: GDP/PPP (1998 est.): $290.6 billion; $6,800 per capita. **Real growth rate:** 0.3% (1998 est.). **Inflation:** 9% (1998 est.). **Unemployment:** 30% (1998 est.). **Arable land:** 10%. **Agriculture:** corn, wheat, sugarcane, fruit, vegetables, beef, poultry, mutton, wool, dairy products. **Labor force:** 15 million economically active (1997): services, 35%; agriculture, 30%; industry, 20%; mining, 9%; other, 6%. **Industries:** mining (world's largest producer of platinum, gold, chromium), automobile assembly, metalworking, machinery, textile, iron and steel, chemical, fertilizer, foodstuffs. **Natural resources:** gold, diamonds, platinum, uranium, coal, iron ore, phosphates, manganese. **Exports:** $28.7 billion (f.o.b., 1998): gold, other minerals and metals, food, chemicals. **Imports:** $27.2 billion (f.o.b., 1998): machinery, transport equipment, chemicals, petroleum products, textiles, scientific instruments. **Major trading partners:** U.K., Italy, Japan, U.S., Germany.

Geography South Africa, on the continent's southern tip, is bordered by the Atlantic Ocean on the west and by the Indian Ocean on the south and east. Its neighbors are Namibia in the northwest, Zimbabwe and Botswana in the north, and Mozambique and Swaziland in the northeast. The kingdom of Lesotho forms an enclave within the southeastern part of South Africa, which occupies an area nearly three times that of California.

The southernmost point of Africa is Cape Agulhas, located in the Western Cape Province about 100 miles (161 km) southeast of the Cape of Good Hope.

Government Republic.

History The San people were the first settlers. The Dutch East India Company landed the first European settlers on the Cape of Good Hope in 1652, launching a colony that by the end of the 18th century numbered only about 15,000. Known as Boers or Afrikaners, speaking a Dutch dialect known as Afrikaans, the settlers as early as 1795 tried to establish an independent republic.

After occupying the Cape Colony in that year, Britain took permanent possession in 1814 at the end of the Napoleonic Wars, bringing in 5,000 settlers. Anglicization of government and the freeing of slaves in 1833 drove about 12,000 Afrikaners to make the "great trek" north and east into African tribal territory, where they established the republics of the Transvaal and the Orange Free State.

The discovery of diamonds in 1867 and gold nine years later brought an influx of "outlanders" into the republics and spurred Cape Colony prime minister Cecil Rhodes to plot annexation. Rhodes's scheme of sparking an "outlander" rebellion to which an armed party under Leander Starr Jameson would ride to the rescue misfired in 1895, forcing Rhodes to resign. What British expansionists called the "inevitable" war with the Boers eventually broke out on Oct. 11, 1899. The defeat of the Boers in 1902 led in 1910 to the Union of South Africa, composed of four provinces, the two former republics, and the old Cape and Natal colonies. Louis Botha, a Boer, became the first prime minister. Organized political activity among Africans started with the establishment of the African National Congress in 1912.

Jan Christiaan Smuts brought the nation into World War II on the Allied side against Nationalist opposition, and South Africa became a charter member of the United Nations in 1945, but refused to sign the Universal Declaration of Human Rights. Apartheid—racial separation—dominated domestic politics as the Nationalists gained power and imposed greater restrictions on Bantus, Asians, and Coloreds (in South Africa the term meant any nonwhite person). African voters were removed from the voter rolls in 1936.

Afrikaner hostility to Britain triumphed in 1961 with the declaration on May 31 of the Republic of South Africa and the severing of ties with the Commonwealth. Nationalist prime minister H. F. Verwoerd's government in 1963 asserted the power to restrict the freedom of those who opposed rigid racial laws. Three years later, amid increasing racial tension and criticism from the outside world, Verwoerd was assassinated. His Nationalist successor, Balthazar J. Vorster, launched a campaign of conciliation toward conservative black African states, offering development loans and trade concessions.

Elections on May 7, 1987, increased the power of President Botha's Nationalist Party while enabling the far-right Conservative Party to replace the liberal Progressives as the official opposition. The results of the whites-only vote indicated a strong conservative reaction against Botha's policy of limited reform.

A stroke led Botha to step down as leader of his party in 1989 in favor of F. W. de Klerk. De Klerk accelerated the pace of reform. He removed the ban from the African National Congress, the principal anti-apartheid organization, and released Nelson Mandela, the ANC deputy president, after 27 years of imprisonment. Negotiations between the government and the ANC commenced.

On June 5, 1991, the Parliament scrapped the country's apartheid laws concerning property ownership. On June 17 the Parliament did the same for the Population Registration Act of 1950, which classified all South Africans at birth by race. In Feb. 1993 the ANC approved a plan that would allow minority parties to participate in the government for five years after the end of white rule. Also in February, the first nonwhites entered the cabinet in an apparent bid to broaden the base of the ruling National Party.

The 1994 election, as expected, resulted in a massive victory for Mandela and his ANC. The new government included six ministers from the National Party and three from the Inkatha Freedom Party.

In 1997 the Truth and Reconciliation Commission, chaired by Desmond Tutu, began hearings regarding human rights violations between 1960 and 1993. The commission promised amnesty to those who confessed their crimes under the apartheid system. In 1998 F. W. de Klerk, P. W. Botha, and leaders of the ANC appeared before the commission, and the nation continued to grapple with its enlightened but often painful and divisive process of national recovery.

Nelson Mandela, whose term as president cemented his reputation as one of the world's most enlightened statesmen, retired in 1999. On June 2, 1999, Thabo Mbeki, the pragmatic deputy president of South Africa and leader of the African National Congress, was elected president in a landslide, having already assumed many of Mandela's governing responsibilities. In 2000, Mbeki wrestled with a slumping economy, caused in part by fluctuating commodity prices on the world market; a skyrocketing crime rate; and a rising AIDS epidemic.

Spain

KINGDOM OF SPAIN

National name: Reino de España
Ruler: King Juan Carlos I (1975)
Prime Minister: José María Aznar (1996)
Area: 195,364.5 sq. mi. (504,750 sq. km)[1]
Population (2000 est.): 39,996,671 (average annual growth rate: 0.02%); birth rate: 9.2/1000; infant mortality rate: 5/1000; density per sq. mi.: 205
Capital and largest city (2000 est.): Madrid, 5,050,000 (metro. area). **Other large cities:** Barcelona, 1,630,867; Valencia, 764,293; Seville, 714,148.
Monetary units: Peseta and euro. **Languages:** Castilian Spanish 74%, Catalan 17%, Galician 7%, Basque 2%. **Ethnicity/race:** composite of Mediterranean and Nordic types. **Religion:** Roman Catholic, 99%. **Literacy rate:** 95% (1991)
Economic summary: GDP/PPP (1998 est.): $645.6 billion; $16,500 per capita. **Real growth rate:** 3.5% (1998 est.). **Inflation:** 2% (1998 est.). **Unemployment:** 20% (1998 est.). **Arable land:** 30%. **Agriculture:** grain, vegetables, olives, wine grapes, sugar beets, citrus, beef, pork, poultry, dairy products, fish. **Labor force:** 16.2 million: services, 64%; manufacturing, mining, and construction, 28%; agriculture, 8% (1997 est.). **Industries:** textiles and apparel (including footwear), food and beverages, metals and metal manufactures, chemicals, shipbuilding, automobiles, machine tools, tourism. **Natural resources:** coal, lignite, water power, uranium, mercury, pyrites, fluorospar, gypsum, iron ore, zinc, lead, tungsten, copper. **Exports:** $111.1 billion (f.o.b., 1998 est.): cars and trucks, other machinery and manufactured goods, foodstuffs, and other consumer goods. **Imports:** $132.3 billion (f.o.b., 1998 est.): machinery, transport equipment, fuel, semifinished goods, foodstuffs, consumer goods, chemicals. **Major trading partners:** EU, U.S., Japan.

1. Including the Balearic and Canary Islands.

Geography Spain occupies 85% of the Iberian Peninsula, which it shares with Portugal, in southwestern Europe. Africa is less than 10 miles (16 km) south at the Strait of Gibraltar. A broad central plateau slopes to the south and east, crossed by a series of mountain ranges and river valleys. Principal rivers are the Ebro in the northeast, the Tajo in the central region, and the Guadalquivir in the south. Off Spain's east coast in the Mediterranean are the Balearic Islands (1,936 sq. mi.; 5,014 sq. km), the largest of which is Majorca. Sixty miles (97 km) west of Africa are the Canary Islands (2,808 sq. mi.; 7,273 sq. km).

Government Parliamentary monarchy.

History Spain, originally inhabited by Celts, Iberians, and Basques, became a part of the Roman Empire in 206 B.C., when it was conquered by Scipio Africanus. In A.D. 412, the barbarian Visigothic leader Ataulf crossed the Pyrenees and ruled Spain, first in the name of the Roman emperor and then independently. In 711, the Muslims under Tariq entered Spain from Africa and within a few years completed the subjugation of the country. In 732, the Franks, led by Charles Martel, defeated the Muslims near Poitiers, thus preventing the further expansion of Islam in southern Europe. Internal dissension of Spanish Islam invited a steady Christian conquest from the north.

Aragon and Castile were the most important Spanish states from the 12th to the 15th century, consolidated by the marriage of Ferdinand II and Isabella I in 1469. The last Muslim stronghold, Granada, was captured in 1492. Roman Catholicism was established as the official state religion and most Jews (1492) and Muslims (1502) were expelled. In the era of exploration, discovery, and colonization, Spain amassed tremendous wealth and a vast colonial empire through the conquest of Peru by Pizarro (1532–33) and of Mexico by Cortés (1519–21). The Spanish Hapsburg monarchy became for a time the most powerful in the world. In 1588, Philip II sent his invincible Armada to invade England, but its destruction cost Spain its supremacy on the seas and paved the way for England's colonization of America. Spain then sank rapidly to the status of a second-rate power under the rule of weak Hapsburg kings, and never again played a major role in European politics. The War of the Spanish Succession (1701–14) resulted in Spain's loss of Belgium, Luxembourg, Milan, Sardinia, and Naples. Its colonial empire in the Americas and the Philippines vanished in wars and revolutions during the 18th and 19th centuries.

In World War I, Spain maintained a position of neutrality. In 1923, Gen. Miguel Primo de Rivera became dictator. In 1930, King Alfonso XIII revoked the dictatorship, but a strong antimonarchist and republican movement led to his leaving Spain in 1931. The new constitution declared Spain a workers' republic, broke up the large estates, separated church and state, and secularized the schools. The elections held in 1936 returned a strong Popular Front majority, with Manuel Azaña as president.

On July 18, 1936, a conservative army officer in Morocco, Francisco Franco Bahamonde, led a mutiny against the government. The civil war that followed lasted three years and cost the lives of nearly a million people. Franco was aided by Fascist Italy and Nazi Germany, while Soviet Russia helped the Loyalist side. Several hundred leftist Americans served in the Abraham Lincoln Brigade on the side of the republic. The war ended when Franco took Madrid on March 28, 1939. Franco became head of the state, national chief of the Falange Party (the governing party), and premier and caudillo (leader). In a referendum in 1947, the Spanish people approved a Franco-drafted succession law declaring Spain a monarchy again. Franco, however, continued as chief of state.

In 1969, Franco and the Cortes designated Prince Juan Carlos Alfonso Víctor María de Borbón (who married Princess Sophia of Greece on May 14, 1962) to become king of Spain when the provisional government headed by Franco came to an end. Franco died of a heart attack on Nov. 20, 1975, after more than a year of ill health, and Juan Carlos was proclaimed king seven days later.

Under pressure from Catalonian and Basque nationalists, Premier Adolfo Suárez granted home rule to these regions in 1979. Basque separatists committed hundreds of terrorist bombings and kidnappings that continue to the present. With the overwhelming election of Prime Minister Felipe González Márquez and his Spanish Socialist Workers Party in the Oct. 20, 1982, parliamentary elections, the Franco past was finally buried.

Spain entered NATO in 1982. A treaty admitting Spain, along with Portugal, to the European Eco-

nomic Community, now the European Union, took effect on Jan. 1, 1986. Later that year, Spain voted to remain in NATO, but outside of its military command. General elections in March 1996 produced a victory for the conservative Popular Party, which, although lacking an absolute majority in the Cortes, received the backing of regional parties for a coalition government with José María Aznar as prime minister.

On Oct. 16, 1998, Spain issued a warrant for the extradition of former Chilean dictator Augusto Pinochet, charging him with the genocide, torture, and kidnapping of thousands of people, including Spanish nationals, during his 17-year rule. While the extradition was contested, Pinochet remained under house arrest in England, where he had been receiving medical treatment at the time of his arrest. Eventually, Pinochet was returned to Chile after he was deemed unfit to stand trial.

In March 2000, Prime Minister Aznar and the center-right People's Party won easily in the general election.

Sri Lanka

DEMOCRATIC SOCIALIST REPUBLIC OF SRI LANKA

President: Chandrika B. Kumaratunga (1994)
Prime Minister: Ratnasiri Wickremanayake (2000)
Area: 25,332 sq. mi. (65,610 sq. km)
Population (2000 est.): 19,238,575 (average annual rate of natural increase: 1.04%; birth rate: 16.8/1000; infant mortality rate: 16.5/1000; density per sq. mi.: 759
Capitals and largest city (1992 est.): Colombo (official) 1,994,000; Sri Jayawardenepura Kotte (legislative and judicial), 107,000 (1988 est.). **Other large cities (1992 est.):** Gampaha, 1,543,000; Kurunegala, 1,445,000; Kandy, 1,257,000. **Monetary unit:** Sri Lanka rupee.
Languages: Sinhala, Tamil, English. **Ethnicity/race:** Sinhalese 74%, Tamil 18%, Moor 7%, Burgher, Malay, and Vedda 1%. **Religions:** Buddhist, 69%; Hindu, 15%; Islam, 8%; Christian, 8%. **Literacy rate:** 88% (1990)
Economic summary: GDP/PPP (1998 est.): $48.1 billion; $2,500 per capita. **Real growth rate:** 4.7% (1998 est.). **Inflation:** 9.3% (1998 est.).
Unemployment: 11% (1997 est.). **Arable land:** 14%. **Agriculture:** rice, sugarcane, grains, oilseed, pulses, spices, tea, rubber, coconuts, milk, eggs, hides, meat. **Labor force:** 6.2 million (1997): services, 46%; agriculture, 37%; industry, 17% (1994). **Industries:** rubber processing, tea, coconuts, textiles, cement, petroleum refining, tobacco. **Natural resources:** limestone, graphite, gems. **Exports:** $4.5 billion (f.o.b., 1998): coconut products, textiles, tea, rubber, petroleum products, gems and jewelry. **Imports:** $5.3 billion (f.o.b., 1998): machinery and equipment, textiles, petroleum, building materials, sugar (1997). **Major trading partners:** U.S., U.K., Germany, Japan, India, Iran, Taiwan, Luxembourg, Hong Kong, China, South Korea. **Member of Commonwealth of Nations**

Geography An island in the Indian Ocean off the southeast tip of India, Sri Lanka is about half the size of Alabama. Most of the land is flat and rolling; mountains in the south-central region rise to over 8,000 feet (2,438 m).

Government Republic.

History Indo-Aryan emigration from India in the 5th century B.C. came to form the largest ethnic group on Sri Lanka today, the Sinhalese. Tamils, the second-largest ethnic group on the island, were originally from the Tamil region of India, and emigrated between the 3rd century B.C. and A.D. 1200. Until colonial powers controlled Ceylon (the country's name until 1972), Sinhalese and Tamil rulers fought for dominance over the island. The Tamils, primarily Hindus, claimed the northern section of the island and the Sinhalese, who are predominantly Buddhist, controlled the south. In 1505 the Portuguese took possession of Ceylon until the Dutch India Company usurped control (1658–1796). The British took over in 1796, and Ceylon became an English crown colony in 1802. The British developed coffee, tea, and rubber plantations. On Feb. 4, 1948, after pressure from Ceylonese nationalist leaders (which briefly unified the Tamil and Sinhalese), Ceylon became a self-governing dominion of the Commonwealth of Nations.

S. W. R. D. Bandaranaike became prime minister in 1956 and championed Sinhalese nationalism, making Sinhala the country's only official language and including state support of Buddhism, further marginalizing the Tamil minority. He was assassinated in 1959 by a Buddhist monk. His widow, Sirimavo Bandaranaike, became the world's first female prime minister in 1960. The name *Ceylon* was changed to Sri Lanka on May 22, 1972, which was its original name and means "resplendent island."

The Tamil minority's mounting resentment toward the Sinhalese majority's monopoly on political and economic power, exacerbated by cultural and religious differences, erupted in bloody violence in 1983. The civil war continues today. Tamils make up about 18% of the population in Sri Lanka, whereas approximately three-quarters of Sri Lanka's 18 million people are Sinhalese. Tamil rebel groups, the strongest of which are the Liberation Tigers of Tamil Eelam, or Tamil Tigers, are fighting for a separate nation.

India had sent a peacekeeping force in July 1987 to help maintain an accord granting the Tamil minority limited autonomy. The agreement failed, and Indian troops withdrew at the end of 1989.

President Ranasinghe Premadasa was assassinated at a May Day political rally in 1993 when a Tamil rebel detonated explosives strapped to himself. Tamil extremists have frequently resorted to terrorist attacks against civilians and are renowned for suicide bombers that target government officials. President Kumaratunga was reelected in Dec. 1999, three days after she was wounded by such an attack.

By early 2000, nearly 17 years of war had claimed the lives of more than 60,000, most of whom were civilians, and turned one out of every 18 people into a refugee. President Kumaratunga attempted to push through parliament a new constitution that she hoped would end the brutal war by giving broader autonomy to the minority Hindu Tamils. But she postponed voting in Aug. 2000, when it was clear the new constitution did not have the support of a two-thirds majority in parliament.

Sudan

REPUBLIC OF THE SUDAN

National name: Jamhuryat es-Sudan
President: Lt. Gen. Omar Hassan Ahmad al-Bashir (1993)
Area: 967,491 sq. mi. (2,505,810 sq. km)
Population (2000 est.): 35,079,814 (average annual rate of natural increase: 2.8%); birth rate: 38.6/1000; infant mortality rate: 70.2/1000; density per sq. mi.: 36
Capital (1993 est.): Khartoum, 924,505. **Largest cities:** Omdurman, 1,267,077; Port Sudan, 305,385.
Monetary unit: Sudanese pound. **Languages:** Arabic, English, tribal dialects. **Ethnicity/race:** black 52%, Arab 39%, Beja 6%, foreigners 2%, other 1%. **Religions:** Islam (Sunni), 70%; indigenous, 20%; Christian, 5%. **Literacy rate:** 27% (1990)
Economic summary: GDP/PPP (1998 est.): $31.2 billion; $930 per capita. **Real growth rate:** 6.1% (1998 est.). **Inflation:** 27% (mid-1997 est.). **Unemployment:** 30% (FY 92/93 est.). **Arable land:** 5%. **Agriculture:** cotton, groundnuts (peanuts), sorghum, millet, wheat, gum arabic, sesame, sheep. **Labor force:** 11 million: agriculture, 80%; industry and commerce, 10%; government, 6% (note: labor shortages for almost all categories of skilled employment) (1983 est.). **Industries:** cotton ginning, textiles, cement, edible oils, sugar, soap distilling, shoes, petroleum refining. **Natural resources:** crude oil, some iron ore, copper, chrome, industrial metals. **Exports:** $594 million (f.o.b., 1997): cotton, sesame, livestock/meat, gum arabic. **Imports:** $1.42 billion (f.o.b., 1997): foodstuffs, petroleum products, manufactured goods, machinery and equipment, medicines and chemicals, textiles. **Major trading partners:** Saudi Arabia, U.K., China, Italy, South Korea, Germany, Egypt.

Geography The Sudan, in northeast Africa, is the largest country on the continent, measuring about one-fourth the size of the United States. Its neighbors are Chad and the Central African Republic on the west, Egypt and Libya on the north, Ethiopia and Eritrea on the east, and Kenya, Uganda, and Democratic Republic of the Congo on the south. The Red Sea washes about 500 miles of the eastern coast. It is traversed from north to south by the Nile, all of whose great tributaries are partly or entirely within its borders.

Government Military government. Headed by President Omar Hassan Ahmad al-Bashir, the de facto ruler of the country is Hassan el-Turabi, a cleric and political leader who is a major figure in the pan-Arabic Islamic fundamentalist resurgence.

History What is now northern Sudan was in ancient times the kingdom of Nubia, which came under Egyptian rule after 2600 B.C. An Egyptian and Nubian civilization called Kush flourished until A.D. 350. Missionaries converted the region to Christianity in the 6th century, but an influx of Muslim Arabs, who had already conquered Egypt, eventually controlled the area and replaced Christianity with Islam. During the 1500s a people called the Funj conquered much of Sudan, and several other black African groups settled in the south, including the Dinka, Shilluk, Nuer, and Azande. Egyptians again conquered the Sudan in 1874, and after Britain occupied Egypt in 1882, it took over Sudan in 1898, ruling the country in conjunction with Egypt. It was known as the Anglo-Egyptian Sudan between 1898 and 1955.

The 20th century saw the growth of Sudanese nationalism, and in 1953 Egypt and Britain granted the Sudan self-government. Independence was proclaimed on Jan. 1, 1956. Since independence, the Sudan has been ruled by a series of unstable parliamentary governments and military regimes. Under Maj. Gen. Gaafar Mohamed Nimeiri, the Sudan instituted fundamentalist Islamic law in 1983. This exacerbated the rift between the Arab North, the seat of the government, and the black African animists and Christians in the South. Differences in language, religion, ethnicity, and political power erupted in an unending civil war between government forces, strongly influenced by the National Islamic Front (NIF), and the southern rebels, whose most influential faction is the Sudanese People's Liberation Army. Neither side has gained the upper hand, and more than an estimated 1 million people have died in battle or from famines and disease resulting from war. Human rights violations, religious persecution, and allegations that the Sudan has been a safe haven for terrorists have isolated the country from most of the international community.

On Aug. 20, 1998, the United States launched cruise missiles that destroyed a pharmaceutical manufacturing facility in Khartoum that allegedly manufactured chemical weapons. Sudan has close ties with Iraq, which has thwarted the U.N. inspections of its weapons stockpiles that are thought to include biological weapons. The U.S. contended that the Sudanese factory was financed by the wealthy Islamic militant, Osama bin Laden.

Since 1999 international attention has been focused on evidence that slavery is widespread throughout Sudan. Arab raiders from the north of the country have enslaved thousands of southerners, who are black. The Dinka people have been the hardest hit. Some sources point out that the raids intensified in the 1980s along with the civil war between north and south. Since the early 1990s, several international human rights organizations have engaged in the controversial practice of buying back slaves from the traders. Some contend this may inadvertently encourage slavery since slave redemption has become profitable. The anti-slavery organizations counter that in the absence of a political solution, buying back slaves is the only hope for thousands of Sudanese.

Suriname

REPUBLIC OF SURINAME

President: Ronald Venetiaan (2000)
Prime Minister: Jules Ajodhia (2000)
Area: 63,251 sq. mi. (163,270 sq. km)
Population (2000 est.): 431,303 (average annual rate of natural increase: 1.5%; birth rate: 21.1/1000; infant mortality rate: 25.1/1000; density per sq. mi.: 7
Capital and largest city (1993 est.): Paramaribo, 200,970. **Monetary unit:** Suriname guilder.
Languages: Dutch, Surinamese (lingua franca), English widely spoken. **Ethnicity/race:** Hindustani (also known locally as "East" Indians; their ancestors emigrated from northern India in the latter part of the 19th century) 37%, Creole (mixed European and African ancestry) 31%, Javanese 15.3%, "Bush Black" (also known as "Bush Creole" whose ancestors were brought to the country in the 17th and 18th centuries as slaves) 10.3%, Amerindian 2.6%, Chinese 1.7%, Europeans 1%, other 1.1%. **Religions:** Protestant, 25.2%; Roman Catholic, 22.8%; Hindu, 27.4%; Islam, 19.6%; indigenous, about 5%. **Literacy rate:** 95% (1990)
Economic summary: GDP/PPP (1998 est.): $1.48 billion; $3,500 per capita. **Real growth rate:** 2% (1998 est.). **Inflation:** 20% (1998 est.). **Unemployment:** 20% (1997). **Arable land:** 0%. **Agriculture:** paddy rice, bananas, palm kernels, coconuts, plantains, peanuts, beef, chickens, forest products, shrimp. **Labor force:** n.a. **Industries:** bauxite and gold mining, alumina and aluminum production, lumbering, food processing, fishing. **Natural resources:** bauxite, iron ore, timber, fish, shrimp. **Exports:** $548.84 million (1997): alumina, aluminum, crude oil, lumber, shrimp and fish, rice, bananas. **Imports:** $551.8 million (1997): capital equipment, petroleum, foodstuffs, cotton, consumer goods. **Major trading partners:** Norway, Netherlands, U.S., France, Japan, U.K.

Geography Suriname lies on the northeast coast of South America, with Guyana to the west, French Guiana to the east, and Brazil to the south. It is about one-tenth larger than Michigan. The principal rivers are the Corantijn on the Guyana border, the Marowijne in the east, and the Suriname, on which the capital city of Paramaribo is situated.

Government Republic.

History Suriname's earliest inhabitants were the Surinen Indians, after whom the country is named. By the 16th century they had been supplanted by other South American Indians. Spain explored Suriname in 1593, but by 1602 the Dutch began to settle the land, followed by the English. The English transferred sovereignty to the Dutch in 1667 (the Treaty of Breda) in exchange for New Amsterdam (New York). Colonization was confined to a narrow coastal strip, and until the abolition of slavery in 1863, African slaves furnished the labor for the coffee and sugarcane plantation economy. Escaped African slaves fled into the interior, reconstituted their western African culture and government, and came to be called "Bush Negroes" by the Dutch. After 1870, laborers were imported from British India and the Dutch East Indies.

Known as Dutch Guiana, the colony was integrated into the kingdom of the Netherlands in 1948. Two years later Dutch Guiana was granted full home rule in matters other than foreign affairs and defense. After race rioting over unemployment and inflation, the Netherlands granted Suriname complete independence on Nov. 25, 1975. A coup d'état in 1980 brought military rule. During much of the 1980s Suriname was under the control of Lieut. Col. Dési Bouterse, who in late Dec. 1990 resigned as commander of the armed forces. A guerrilla insurgency by the Jungle Commando (a Bush Negro guerrilla group) furthered disruption in the country, and the instability in the region caused some foreign governments to withhold economic aid. Free elections were held on May 25, 1991, depriving the military of much of its political power. In 1992 a peace treaty was signed between the government and several guerrilla groups. In March 1997, the president announced new economic measures, including eliminating import tariffs on most basic goods coupled with strict price controls. Later that year, the Netherlands declared that it would prosecute the former military dictator of Suriname, Dési Bouterse, for large-scale cocaine trafficking.

With 70% inflation, there has been considerable public discontent over the economy, prompting President Jules Wijdenbosch to hold elections one year ahead of schedule.

Wijdenbosch was defeated in the elections, which were held May 25, 2000, by the New Front for Democracy and Development, a coalition led by former President Ronald Venetiaan. New Front won 33 of the 51 seats in parliament, one seat short of a two-thirds majority. New Front also beat another coalition led by Bouterse. Venetiaan had served as president from 1991 until 1996, until his defeat by Wijdenbosch.

Suriname has been unable to resolve its dispute with neighboring Guyana over an oil-rich coastal region. With 10% of its territory, mostly jungle in the Amazon basin in the south, already declared a nature reserve, Suriname has tried to bolster its economy with tourism.

Swaziland

KINGDOM OF SWAZILAND

Ruler: King Mswati III (1986)
Prime Minister: Barnabas Sibusiso Dlamini (1996)
Area: 6,704 sq. mi. (17,360 sq. km)
Population (2000 est.): 1,083,289 (average annual rate of natural increase: 2.02%); birth rate: 40.6/1000; infant mortality rate: 108.9/1000; density per sq. mi.: 162
Capital and largest city (1990 est.): Mbabane 47,020.
Monetary unit: Lilangeni. **Languages:** English and Swazi (official). **Ethnicity/race:** African 97%, European 3%. **Religions:** Christian, 60%; indigenous, 40%.
Literacy rate: 70% (1986)
Economic summary: GDP/PPP (1998 est.): $4 billion; $4,200 per capita. **Real growth rate:** 2.6% (1998 est.). **Inflation:** 8% (1998 est.). **Unemployment:** 22% (1995 est.). **Arable land:** 11%. **Agriculture:** sugarcane, cotton, maize, tobacco, rice, citrus, pineapples, corn, sorghum, peanuts, cattle, goats, sheep. **Labor force:** n.a.: private sector, 70%; public sector, 30%. **Industries:** mining (coal and asbestos), wood pulp, sugar, soft drink concentrates. **Natural resources:** asbestos, diamonds. **Exports:** $972 million (f.o.b., 1998): soft drink concentrates, sugar, wood pulp, cotton yarn, citrus and canned fruit. **Imports:** $1.2 billion (f.o.b., 1998): motor vehicles, machinery, transport equipment, foodstuffs, petroleum products, chemicals. **Major trading partners:** South Africa, EU, Mozambique, North Korea, Japan, U.K., Singapore. **Member of Commonwealth of Nations**

Geography Swaziland, which is about 85% the size of New Jersey, is surrounded by South Africa and Mozambique. The country consists of a high veld in the west and a series of plateaus descending from 6,000 feet (1,829 m) to a low veld of 1,500 feet (457 m).

Government Monarchy.

History Bantu peoples migrated southwest to the area of Mozambique in the 16th century. A number of clans broke away from the main body in the 18th century and settled in Swaziland. In the 19th century these clans organized as a tribe, partly because they were in constant conflict with the Zulu. Their ruler, Mswazi, appealed to the British in the 1840s for help against the Zulu. The British and the Transvaal governments guaranteed the independence of Swaziland in 1881.

South Africa held Swaziland as a protectorate from 1894 to 1899, but after the Boer War, in 1902, Swaziland was transferred to British administration. The paramount chief was recognized as the native authority in 1941. In 1963, the territory was constituted a protectorate, and on Sept. 6, 1968, it became the independent nation of Swaziland.

Since 1986, King Mswati III has ruled as sub-Saharan Africa's last absolute monarch. Political parties are banned and the king appoints 10 of the 65 members of Parliament as well as the prime minister. King Mswati can veto any law passed by the legislature and frequently rules by decree.

With a modern infrastructure, Swaziland boasts one of the largest per capita manufacturing sectors in Africa. It is one of the few countries on the continent never to face an economic crisis severe enough to warrant imposition of a World Bank adjustment program. Many of the businesses in Swaziland moved there from South Africa in the 1980s in an effort to avoid international sanctions against apartheid.

In 2000, AIDS remains a serious threat to Swaziland. An estimated 120,000 people are infected and 50,000 people have died of the disease in the past two years. King Mswati has ordered his subjects to follow the example of himself and his seven wives, and undergo routine AIDS tests.

Sweden

KINGDOM OF SWEDEN

National name: Konungariket Sverige
Sovereign: King Carl XVI Gustaf (1973)
Prime Minister: Göran Persson (1996)
Area: 173,800 sq. mi. (449,964 sq. km)
Population (2000 est.): 8,873,052 (average annual rate of natural increase –0.06%); birth rate: 10/1000; infant mortality rate: 3.5/1000; density per sq. mi.: 51
Capital and largest city (1994): Stockholm, 703,627.
Largest cities: Göteborg, 444,553; Malmö, 242,706; Uppsala, 181,191. **Monetary unit:** Krona. **Language:** Swedish. **Ethnicity/race:** white, 88%; Lapp (Sami), foreign-born or first-generation immigrants (Finns, Yugoslavs, Danes, Norwegians, Greeks, Turks) 12%.
Religions: Evangelical Lutheran, 94%; Roman Catholic, 1.5%; Pentecostal, 1%; other, 3.5%. **Literacy rate:** 99% (1979)
Economic summary: GDP/PPP (1998 est.): $175 billion; $19,700 per capita. **Real growth rate:** 2.9% (1998 est.). **Inflation:** 2% (1998 est.).
Unemployment: 6.3% plus about 5% in training programs (1998 est.). **Arable land:** 7%. **Agriculture:** grains, sugar beets, potatoes, meat, milk. **Labor force:** 4.552 million (1992): community, social, and personal services, 38.3%; mining and manufacturing, 21.2%; commerce, hotels and restaurants, 14.1%; banking and insurance, 9%; communications, 7.2%; construction, 7%; agriculture, fishing, and forestry, 3.2% (1991). **Industries:** iron and steel, precision equipment (bearings, radio and telephone parts, armaments), wood pulp and paper products, processed food, motor vehicles. **Natural resources:** forests, iron ore, hydroelectric power, zinc, uranium. **Exports:** $85.5 billion (f.o.b., 1998): machinery, motor vehicles, paper products, pulp and wood, iron and steel products, chemicals. **Imports:** $66.6 billion (f.o.b., 1998): machinery, petroleum and petroleum products, chemicals, motor vehicles, foodstuffs, iron and steel, clothing. **Major trading partners:** EU, Norway, U.S.

Geography Sweden, which occupies the eastern part of the Scandinavian peninsula, is the fourth-largest country in Europe, and is one-tenth larger than California. The country slopes eastward and southward from the Kjölen Mountains along the Norwegian border, where the peak elevation is Kebnekaise at 6,965 feet (2,123 m) in Lapland. In the north are mountains and many lakes. To the south and east are central lowlands and south of them are fertile areas of forest, valley, and plain. Along Sweden's rocky coast, chopped up by bays and inlets, are many islands, the largest of which are Gotland and Öland.

Government Constitutional monarchy.

History The earliest historical mention of Sweden is found in Tacitus's *Germania*, where reference is made to the powerful king and strong fleet of the Sviones. In the 11th century, Olaf Sköttkonung became the first Swedish king to be baptized as a Christian. Around 1400, an attempt was made to unite Sweden, Norway, and Denmark into one kingdom, but this led to bitter strife between the Danes and the Swedes. In 1520, the Danish king Christian II conquered Sweden and in the "Stockholm Bloodbath" put leading Swedish personages to death. Gustavus Vasa (1523–60) broke away from Denmark and fashioned the modern Swedish state. He also confiscated property from the Roman Catholic Church in Sweden to pay Sweden's war debts. The king justified his actions on the basis of Martin Luther's doctrines, which were being accepted nationwide with royal encouragement. The Lutheran Swedish church was eventually adopted as the state church.

Sweden played a leading role in the second phase (1630–35) of the Thirty Years' War (1618–48). By the Treaty of Westphalia (1648), Sweden had obtained western Pomerania and some neighboring territory on the Baltic. In 1700, a coalition of Russia, Poland, and Denmark united against Sweden and by the Peace of Nystad (1721) forced it to relinquish Livonia, Ingria, Estonia, and parts of Finland. Sweden emerged from the Napoleonic Wars with the acquisition of Norway from Denmark and with a new royal dynasty stemming from Marshal Jean Bernadotte of France, who became King Charles XIV (1818–44). The artificial union between Sweden and Norway led to an uneasy relationship, and the union was finally dissolved in 1905. Sweden maintained a position of neutrality in both world wars.

An elaborate structure of welfare legislation, imitated by many larger nations, began with the establishment of old-age pensions in 1911. Economic prosperity based on its neutralist policy enabled Sweden, together with Norway, to pioneer in public health, housing, and job security programs. Forty-four years of Socialist government were ended in 1976 with the election of a conservative coalition headed by Thorbjörn Fälldin. The Socialists were returned to power in the election of 1982, but Prime Minister Olof Palme, a Socialist, was assassinated by a gunman on Feb. 28, 1986, leaving Sweden stunned. Palme's Socialist domestic policies were carried out by his successor, Ingvar Carlsson. Elections in Sept. 1991 ousted the Social Democrats (Socialists) from power. The new coalition of four conservative parties pledged to reduce taxes and cut back on the welfare state but not alter Sweden's traditional neutrality. In Sept. 1994 the Social Democrats emerged again after three years as the opposition party.

In a 1994 referendum voters approved joining the European Union. Although supportive of a European monetary union, Sweden announced in 1997 that it would not adopt the euro when it debuted in 1999.

In July 2000, Sweden and Denmark were connected by 10-mile bridge and tunnel, making it possible to drive between Copenhagen and Malmo, Sweden, Sweden's third-largest city.

Switzerland

SWISS CONFEDERATION

National name: Schweiz/Suisse/Svizzera/Svizra
President: Adolf Ogi (2000)
Area: 15,941 sq. mi. (41,290 sq. km)
Population (2000 est.): 7,262,372 (average annual rate of natural increase: 0.17%); birth rate: 10.4/1000; infant mortality rate: 4.5/1000; density per sq. mi.: 456
Capital (1994 est.): Bern, 129,423. **Largest cities:** Zurich, 343,045; Basel, 176,220; Geneva, 171,744; Lausanne, 117,153. **Monetary unit:** Swiss franc.
Languages: German, French, Italian, Romansch.
Ethnicity/race: German 65%, French 18%, Italian 10%, Romansch 1%, other 6%. **Religions:** Roman Catholic, 49%; Protestant, 40%; other, 5%; no religion, 8.3%. **Literacy rate:** 99% (1980)
Economic summary: GDP/PPP (1998 est.): $191.8 billion; $26,400 per capita. **Real growth rate:** 2%

(1998 est.). **Inflation:** 0% (1998 est.).
Unemployment: 1.8% (2000 est.). **Arable land:** 10%.
Agriculture: grains, fruit, vegetables, meat, eggs.
Labor force: 3.8 million (850,000 foreign workers): services, 67%; manufacturing and construction, 29%; agriculture and forestry, 4% (1995). **Industries:** machinery, chemicals, watches, textiles, precision instruments. **Natural resources:** water power, timber, salt. **Exports:** $94.4 billion (f.o.b., 1998): machinery, chemicals, metals, watches, agricultural products.
Imports: $95.5 billion (f.o.b., 1998): machinery, chemicals, vehicles, metals, agricultural products, textiles. **Major trading partners:** EU, U.S., Japan.

Geography Switzerland, in central Europe, is the land of the Alps. Its tallest peak is the Dufourspitze at 15,203 feet (4,634 m) on the Swiss side of the Italian border, one of 10 summits of the Monte Rosa massif. The tallest peak in all of the Alps, Mont Blanc (15,771 ft.; 4,807 m), is actually in France. Most of Switzerland is composed of a mountainous plateau bordered by the great bulk of the Alps on the south and by the Jura Mountains on the northwest. The country's largest lakes—Geneva, Constance (Bodensee), and Maggiore—straddle the French, German-Austrian, and Italian borders, respectively. The Rhine, navigable from Basel to the North Sea, is the principal inland waterway. Switzerland is twice the size of New Jersey.

Government Federal republic.

History Called Helvetia in ancient times, Switzerland in 1291 was a league of cantons in the Holy Roman Empire. Fashioned around the nucleus of three German forest districts of Schwyz, Uri, and Unterwalden, the Swiss Confederation slowly added new cantons. In 1648 the Treaty of Westphalia gave Switzerland its independence from the Holy Roman Empire.

French revolutionary troops occupied the country in 1798 and named it the Helvetic Republic, but Napoleon in 1803 restored its federal government. By 1815, the French- and Italian-speaking peoples of Switzerland had been granted political equality.

In 1815, the Congress of Vienna guaranteed the neutrality and recognized the independence of Switzerland. In the revolutionary period of 1847, the Catholic cantons seceded and organized a separate union called the *Sonderbund*, but were defeated and rejoined the federation.

In 1848, the new Swiss constitution established a union modeled upon that of the U.S. The federal constitution of 1874 established a strong central government while maintaining large powers of control in each canton. National unity and political conservatism grew as the country prospered from its neutrality. Its banking system became the world's leading repository for international accounts. Strict neutrality was its policy in both world wars. Geneva was the seat of the League of Nations (later the European headquarters of the United Nations) and of a number of international organizations.

Allegations in the 1990s concerning secret assets of Jewish Holocaust victims deposited in Swiss banks led to international criticism and the establishment of a fund to reimburse them and their families.

Surprisingly, women were not given the right to vote or to hold office until 1971. Switzerland's first woman president—as well as the first Jew to assume the position—was Ruth Dreifuss in 1999.

In Sept. 2000, the Swiss voted against a plan to cut the number of foreigners in the country to 18% of the population (in 2000 foreigners made up 19.3%). Since 1970, four similar anti-immigration plans have failed. With unemployment at 1.8%, the lowest in eight years, few Swiss feel threatened by the economic repercussions of foreign workers.

Syria

SYRIAN ARAB REPUBLIC

National name: Al-Jamhouriya al Arabiya As-Souriya
President: Bashar al-Assad (2000)
Prime Minister: Muhammad Mustafa Miro (2000)
Area: 71,498 sq. mi. (185,180 sq. km)
Population (2000 est.): 16,305,659 (average annual rate of natural increase: 2.6%); birth rate: 31.1/1000; infant mortality rate: 34.9/1000; density per sq. mi.: 228
Capital (1994 est.): Damascus, 1,549,932. **Largest cities:** Aleppo, 1,591,400; Homs, 644,204; Latakia, 306,535; Hama, 229,000. **Monetary unit:** Syrian pound. **Languages:** Arabic (official), French and English widely understood. **Ethnicity/race:** Arab 90.3%, Kurds, Armenians, and other 9.7%. **Religions:** Islam, 90%; Christian, 10%. **Literacy rate:** 65% (1990)
Economic summary: GDP/PPP (1997 est.): $41.7 billion; $2,500 per capita. **Real growth rate:** 2% (1998 est.). **Inflation:** 15%–20% (1997 est.). **Unemployment:** 12%–15% (1998 est.). **Arable land:** 28%. **Agriculture:** wheat, barley, cotton, lentils, chickpeas, olives, sugar beets, beef, mutton, eggs, poultry, milk. **Labor force:** 4.7 million (1998 est.): services, 40%; agriculture, 40%; industry, 20% (1996 est.). **Industries:** petroleum, textiles, food processing, beverages, tobacco, phosphate rock mining. **Natural resources:** chrome, manganese, asphalt, iron ore, rock salt, phosphate, oil, gypsum. **Exports:** $4.2 billion (f.o.b., 1998 est.): petroleum, textiles, food and live animals, manufactures. **Imports:** $5.7 billion (c.i.f., 1997): machinery and equipment, foodstuffs/animals, metal and metal products, textiles, chemicals, consumer goods. **Major trading partners:** Italy, Germany, France, Turkey, Lebanon, Spain, South Korea, Japan, U.S.

Geography Slightly larger than North Dakota, Syria lies at the eastern end of the Mediterranean Sea. It is bordered by Lebanon and Israel on the west, Turkey on the north, Iraq on the east, and Jordan on the south. Coastal Syria is a narrow plain, in back of which is a range of coastal mountains, and still farther inland is a steppe area. In the east is the Syrian Desert, and in the south is the Jebel Druze Range. The highest point in Syria is Mount Hermon (9,232 ft.; 2,814 m) on the Lebanese border.

Government Republic under a military regime since March 1963.

History Ancient Syria was conquered by Egypt about 1500 B.C., and after that by Hebrews, Assyrians, Chaldeans, Persians, and Alexander the Great of Macedonia. From 64 B.C. until the Arab conquest in A.D. 636, it was part of the Roman Empire except during brief periods. The Arabs made it a trade center for their extensive empire, but it suffered severely from the Mongol invasion in 1260 and fell to the Ottoman Turks in 1516. Syria remained a Turkish province until World War I.

A secret Anglo-French pact of 1916 put Syria in the French zone of influence. The League of Nations gave France a mandate over Syria after World War I, but the French were forced to put down several nationalist uprisings. In 1930, France recognized Syria as an independent republic, but still subject to the mandate. After nationalist demonstrations in 1939, the French high commissioner suspended the Syrian constitution. In 1941, British and Free French forces invaded Syria to eliminate Vichy control. During the rest of World War II, Syria was an Allied base. Again in 1945, nationalist demonstrations broke into actual fighting, and British troops had to restore order. Syrian forces met a series of reverses while participating in the Arab invasion of Palestine in 1948. In 1958, Egypt and Syria formed the United Arab Republic, with Gamal Abdel Nasser of Egypt as president. However, Syria became independent again on Sept. 29, 1961, following a revolution.

In the Arab-Israeli War of 1967, Israel quickly vanquished the Syrian army. Before acceding to the U.N. cease-fire, the Israeli forces took control of the fortified Golan Heights. Syria joined Egypt in attacking Israel in Oct. 1973 in the fourth Arab-Israeli war, but was pushed back from initial successes on the Golan Heights and ended up losing more land. However, in the settlement worked out by U.S. Secretary of State Henry A. Kissinger in 1974, the Syrians recovered all the territory lost in 1973 and a token amount of territory, including the deserted town of Quneitra, lost in 1967.

In the mid-1970s Syria sent some 20,000 troops to support Muslim Lebanese in their armed conflict with Christian militants supported by Israel during the civil war in Lebanon. Syrian troops frequently clashed with Israeli troops during Israel's 1982 invasion of Lebanon and remained thereafter as occupiers of large portions of Lebanon.

The first Arab country to condemn Iraq's invasion of Kuwait, Syria sent troops to help defend Saudi Arabia from possible Iraqi attack. After the Gulf War, hope for peace negotiations between Israel and Arab states, particularly Syria, rose but then foundered. In 1990, President Assad ruled out any possibility of legalizing opposition political parties. In Dec. 1991 voters approved a fourth term for Assad, giving him 99.98% of the vote.

In the 1990s, the slowdown in the Israeli-Palestinian peace process was echoed in the lack of progress in Israeli-Syrian relations. Confronted with a steadily strengthening strategic partnership between Israel and Turkey, Syria took steps to construct a countervailing alliance by improving relations with Iraq, strengthening ties with Iran, and collaborating more closely with Saudi Arabia. The defeat of conservative Israeli prime minister Netanyahu and the election of the Labor Party's Ehud Barak marked a shift in Syrian-Israeli relations. The new Israeli prime minister announced that one of his major goals was to broker peace with Syria and end the low-grade war in Southern Lebanon with the Syrian-backed Hezbollah guerrillas.

In Dec. 1999, Israeli-Syrian talks resumed after a nearly four-year hiatus, with the aging Assad (who would die seven months later) attempting to shore up his legacy. From Syria's point of view, normalization of relations between the two countries largely depended on Israel's withdrawal from the Golan Heights, which was territory that Israel had captured from Syria during the Arab-Israeli War of 1967. From Israel's point of view, relinquishing the Golan Heights, which served as a buffer zone between the two nations, could not occur without a guarantee of Israel's national security. Water rights and the Hezbollah guerrillas fighting Israel in Lebanon—who are essentially controlled by Syria—were also on the agenda. By Jan. 2000, however, talks broke down when Syria demanded a detailed discussion about the return of the entire Golan Heights. Most commentators believe this is only a temporary setback.

On June 10, 2000, President Hafez al-Assad died. He had ruled with an iron fist since taking power in a military coup in 1970. His son, Bashar al-Assad, an ophthalmologist by training, had been groomed in recent years to succeed him.

Taiwan

REPUBLIC OF CHINA

President: Chen Shui-bian (2000)
Prime Minister: Chang Chun-hsiung (2000)
Area: 13,895 sq. mi. (35,980 sq. km)
Population (2000 est.): 22,191,087 (average annual rate of natural increase: 0.85%); birth rate: 14.4/1000; infant mortality rate: 7.1/1000; density per sq. mi.: 1,597
Capital and largest city (2000 est.): Taipei, 7,700,000 (metro. area). **Largest cities:** Kaohsiung, 1,423,163; Tai Chung, 848,320; Tainan, 705,565; Keelung, 367,668. **Monetary unit:** New Taiwan dollar.
Language: Chinese (Mandarin). **Ethnicity/race:** Taiwanese 84%, mainland Chinese 14%, aborigine 2%. **Religions:** Buddhist, 4.86 million; Taoist, 3.3 million; Protestant, 422,000; Catholic, 304,000.
Literacy rate: 92% (1990)
Economic summary: GNP/PPP (1998 est.): $362 billion; $16,500 per capita income. **Real growth rate:** 4.8% (1998 est.). **Inflation:** 2.1% (1998 est.).
Unemployment: 2.7% (1998). **Arable land:** 24%.
Agriculture: rice, wheat, corn, soybeans, vegetables, fruit, tea, pigs, poultry, beef, milk, fish. **Labor force:** 9.4 million (1997): services, 52%; industry, 38%; agriculture, 10% (1996). **Industries:** electronics, textiles, chemicals, clothing, food processing, plywood, sugar milling, cement, shipbuilding, petroleum refining. **Natural resources:** coal, natural gas, limestone, marble. **Exports:** $122.1 billion (f.o.b., 1997): machinery and electrical equipment, electronic products, information/communications, textile products. **Imports:** $114.4 billion (c.i.f., 1997): machinery and electrical equipment, electronic products, chemicals, precision instruments. **Major trading partners:** U.S., Hong Kong, Europe, Japan.

Geography The Republic of China today consists of the island of Taiwan, an island 100 miles (161 km) off the Asian mainland in the Pacific; two offshore islands, Kinmen (Quemoy) and Matsu; and the nearby islets of the Pescadores chain. It is slightly larger than the combined areas of Massachusetts and Connecticut. Taiwan is divided by a central mountain range that runs from north to south, rising sharply on the east coast and descending gradually to a broad western plain, where cultivation is concentrated.

Government Multiparty democracy.

History Taiwan was inhabited by aborigines of Malayan descent when Chinese from the areas now designated as Fukien and Kwangtung began settling in in the 7th century, becoming the majority. The Portuguese explored the area in 1590, naming it "the Beautiful" (Formosa). In 1624 the Dutch set up forts in the south, the Spanish in the north. The Dutch forced out the Spanish in 1641 and controlled the island until

1661, when Chinese General Koxinga took it over and established an independent kingdom. The Manchus seized the island in 1683 and held it until 1895, when it passed to Japan after the first Sino-Japanese War. Japan developed and exploited Formosa. It was the target of heavy American bombing during World War II, and at the close of the war the island was restored to China.

After the defeat of its armies on the mainland, the Nationalist government of Generalissimo Chiang Kai-shek retreated to Taiwan in Dec. 1949. Chiang dominated the island, even though only 15% of the population consisted of the 1949 immigrants, the Kuomintang. He maintained a 600,000-man army in the hope of eventually recovering the mainland. Beijing viewed the Taiwanese government with suspicion and anger, referring to Taiwan as a breakaway province of China.

The U.N. seat representing all of China was held by the Nationalists for over two decades before being lost in Oct. 1971, when the People's Republic of China was admitted and Taiwan was forced to abdicate its seat to Beijing.

Chiang died at 87 of a heart attack on April 5, 1975. His son, Chiang Ching-kuo, continued as premier and was a dominant figure in the Taipei regime. In April 1991, President Lee Teng-hui formally declared an end to emergency rule, which had existed since Chiang's forces originally occupied the island. In the first full election in many decades, the governing Kuomintang in Dec. 1991 won 71% of the vote, affirming the island's opposition to reunification with China. In Feb. 1993 the president, himself a native Taiwanese, nominated Lien Chan, another native, to be prime minister, marking a further generational shift away from the mainland exiles.

In the island's first free presidential election voters defied mainland intimidation and gave 54% of the vote to incumbent President Lee Teng-hui. The second-place finisher, with 21%, advocated complete independence from China. The ruling Nationalists successfully defeated numerous no-confidence motions raised in response to a crime wave in May 1997. The president made a public apology and promised a new cabinet would be formed. In 1998, Taiwan renewed its push for a separate U.N. seat—its sixth attempt in recent years. The move has been blocked each time by the Beijing government.

President Lee Teng-hui sorely rankled mainland China by announcing in July 1999 that he was abandoning the longstanding "One China" policy that has kept the peace between the small island and its powerful neighbor, and would from now on deal with China on a "state-to-state basis."

On March 18, 2000, Taiwan held its second free presidential elections in history. Voters elected pro-independence candidate Chen Shui-bian of the Democratic Progressive Party, ending more than 50 years of Nationalist rule of Taiwan. China stated in response that it will be keeping a close eye on Chen and reiterated that "Taiwanese independence, in whatever form, will never be allowed."

In October 2000, Vice-Premier Chang Chun-hsiung was named prime minister, following the resignation of Tang Fei. While he officially resigned because of ill health, Tang Fei had strongly disagreed with President Chen Shui-bian over proceeding with construction of a controversial nuclear power plant.

Tajikistan

REPUBLIC OF TAJIKISTAN

President: Imomali Rakhmonov (1992)
Prime Minister: Akil Akilov (1999)
Area: 55,300 sq. mi. (143,100 sq. km)
Population (2000 est.): 6,440,732 (average annual rate of natural increase: 2.5%); birth rate, 33.6/1000; infant mortality rate: 117.4/1000; density per sq. mi.: 116
Capital and largest city (1994 est.): Dushanbe, 524,000.
Other large city: Khodzhent (Leninabad), 164,500.
Monetary unit: Tajik ruble. **Language:** Tajik. **Ethnicity/race:** Tajik 64.9%, Uzbek 25%, Russian 3.5% (declining because of emigration), other 6.6%. **Religion:** Sunni Muslim, 80%. **Literacy rate:** 98% (1989)
Economic summary: GNP/PPP (1998 est.): $6 billion; $990 per capita. **Real growth rate:** 5.3% (1998 est.). **Inflation:** 46.3% (1998 est.). **Unemployment:** 5.7%; includes only officially registered unemployed; also large numbers of underemployed workers and unregistered unemployed people (Dec. 1998). **Arable land:** 6%. **Labor force:** 1.9 million (1996): agriculture and forestry, 52%; services, 31%; manufacturing, mining, and construction, 17% (1995). **Industries:** aluminum, zinc, lead, chemicals and fertilizers, cement, vegetable oil, metal-cutting machine tools, refrigerators and freezers. **Agriculture:** cotton, grain, fruit, grapes, vegetables, cattle, sheep, goats. **Exports:** $740 million (1998 est.): cotton, aluminum, fruit, vegetable oil, textiles. **Imports:** $810 million (1998 est.): fuel, chemicals, machinery and transport equipment, textiles, foodstuffs. **Major trading partners:** Former Soviet Union, Netherlands, Switzerland, U.K.

Geography Ninety-three percent of Tajikistan's territory is mountainous and the mountain glaciers are the source of its rivers. Tajikistan is an earthquake-prone area. The republic is bounded by China in the east, Afghanistan to the south, Uzbekistan and Kirghizia to the west and north. The central Asian republic also includes the Gorno-Badakh Shan Autonomous region. Tajikistan is slightly larger than the state of Illinois.

Government Republic.

History The Tajiks, whose language is nearly identical with Persian, were part of the ancient Persian empire that was ruled by Darius I and later conquered by Alexander the Great (333 B.C.). In the 7th and 8th centuries, Arabs conquered the region and brought Islam. The Tajiks were successively ruled by Uzbeks and then Afghans until claimed by Russia in the 1860s. In 1924, Tajikistan was consolidated into a newly formed Tajik Autonomous Soviet Socialist Republic, which was administratively part of the Uzbek S.S.R. until the Tajik A.S.S.R. gained full-fledged republic status in 1929.

Tajikistan declared its sovereignty in Aug. 1990. In 1991, the republic's Communist leadership supported the attempted coup against Soviet president Mikhail Gorbachev. Tajikistan joined with ten other former Soviet republics in the Commonwealth of Independent States on Dec. 21, 1991. A parliamentary republic was proclaimed and presidential rule abolished on Nov. 1992. After independence, Tajikistan experienced sporadic conflict as the Communist-dominated government struggled to combat an insurgency by Islamic and democratic opposition forces. Despite continued international efforts to end the civil war, periodic fighting continued. Tajikistan's civil war ended officially on June 27, 1997, with the signing in Moscow of peace accords between the government of President Imomali Rakhmonov and

the United Tajik Opposition (UTO), a coalition of largely Islamic groups. Since then, however, peace has been tenuous, marred regularly by killing sprees by various opposition groups.

In 2000, Tajikistan has allowed approximately 25,000 Russian troops into the country to help stem the violence by helping to patrol the border with Taliban-run Afghanistan. Tajikistan has also agreed to allow for the establishment of a Russian military base in the country.

Tanzania

UNITED REPUBLIC OF TANZANIA

President: Benjamin William Mkapa (1995)
Prime Minister: Frederick Tluway Sumaye (1995)
Area: 364,879 sq. mi. (945,090 sq. km)[1]
Population (2000 est.): 35,306,126 (average annual rate of natural increase: 2.7%); birth rate: 40.2/1000; infant mortality rate: 90/1000; density per sq. mi.: 97
Capitals and largest city (1988): Dar es Salaam (administrative), 1,360,850; Dodoma (official), 45,807 (1978). **Monetary unit:** Tanzanian shilling.
Languages: Swahili, English, local languages.
Ethnicity/race: mainland: native African (95% Bantu, consisting of well over 100 tribes) 99%, Asian, European, and Arab 1%. Zanzibar: Arab, mixed Arab and native African, native African. **Religions:** Christian, 40%; Muslim, 33%. **Literacy rate:** 52% (1988)
Economic summary: GDP/PPP (1998 est.): $22.1 billion; $730 per capita. **Real growth rate:** 3.8% (1998 est.). **Inflation:** 13.5% (1998 est.). **Unemployment:** n.a. **Arable land:** 3%. **Agriculture:** coffee, sisal, tea, cotton, pyrethrum (insecticide made from chrysanthemums), cashew nuts, tobacco, cloves (Zanzibar), corn, wheat, cassava (tapioca), bananas, fruit, vegetables, cattle, sheep, goats. **Labor force:** 13.495 million: agriculture, 90%; industry and commerce, 10% (1995 est.). **Industries:** primarily agricultural processing (sugar, beer, cigarettes, sisal twine), diamond and gold mining, oil refining, shoes, cement, textiles, wood products, fertilizer, salt. **Natural resources:** hydroelectric potential, phosphates, iron, and coal. **Exports:** $952 million (f.o.b., 1998 est.): coffee, manufactured goods, cotton, cashew nuts, minerals, tobacco, sisal. **Imports:** $1.46 billion (f.o.b., 1998 est.): consumer goods, machinery and transportation equipment, industrial raw materials, crude oil. **Major trading partners:** India, Germany, Japan, Malaysia, Rwanda, Netherlands, South Africa, Kenya, U.K., Saudi Arabia, China. **Member of Commonwealth of Nations**

1. Including Zanzibar.

Geography Tanzania is in East Africa on the Indian Ocean. To the north are Uganda and Kenya; to the west, Burundi, Rwanda, and Congo; and to the south, Mozambique, Zambia, and Malawi. Its area is three times that of New Mexico. Tanzania contains three of Africa's best-known lakes—Victoria in the north, Tanganyika in the west, and Nyasa in the south. Mount Kilimanjaro in the north, 19,340 feet (5,895 m), is the highest point on the continent. The island of Zanzibar is separated from the mainland by a 22-mile channel.

Government Republic.

History Arab traders first began to colonize the area in A.D. 700. Portuguese explorers reached the coastal regions in 1500 and held some control until the 17th century, when the sultan of Oman took power. With what are now Burundi and Rwanda, Tanganyika became the colony of German East Africa in 1885. After World War I, it was administered by Britain under a League of Nations mandate and later as a U.N. trust territory.

Although not mentioned in old histories until the 12th century, Zanzibar was always believed to have had connections with southern Arabia. The Portuguese made it one of their tributaries in 1503 and later established a trading post, but they were driven from Oman by Arabs in 1698. Zanzibar was declared independent of Oman in 1861 and, in 1890, it became a British protectorate.

Tanganyika became independent on Dec. 9, 1961; Zanzibar on Dec. 10, 1963. On April 26, 1964, the two nations merged into the United Republic of Tanganyika and Zanzibar. The name was changed to Tanzania six months later.

An invasion by Ugandan troops in Nov. 1978 was followed by a counterattack in Jan. 1979, in which 5,000 Tanzanian troops were joined by 3,000 Ugandan exiles opposed to President Idi Amin. Within a month, full-scale war developed. Tanzanian president Julius Nyerere kept troops in Uganda in open support of former Ugandan president Milton Obote, despite protests from opposition groups, until the national elections in Dec. 1980.

In Nov. 1985, Nyerere stepped down as president. Ali Hassan Mwinyi, his vice president, succeeded him. Running unopposed, Mwinyi was elected president in October. Shortly thereafter plans were announced to study the benefits of instituting a multiparty democracy.

The crisis in Rwanda in 1994 sent hundreds of thousands of refugees fleeing into Tanzania, taxing the already-meager resources of the country. The government immediately appealed for international aid. In Oct. 1995 the country's first multiparty elections since independence took place.

On Aug. 7, 1998, the U.S. embassy in Dar es Salaam was bombed by terrorists, killing 10. The same day an even more devastating explosion destroyed the U.S. embassy in neighboring Kenya.

Presidential elections were set for Oct. 2000. Incumbent President Benjamin William Mkapa faced three challengers. Since taking office in 1995 Mkapa has sought to increase economic productivity while dealing with serious pollution problems and deforestation. With more than one million people infected with HIV, AIDS care and prevention have been major public health issues. On foreign policy, Tanzania has taken a leading role in bringing peace to East Africa, hosting peace talks for the factions fighting in neighboring Burundi.

Thailand

KINGDOM OF THAILAND

Ruler: King Bhumibol Adulyadej (1946)
Prime Minister: Chuan Leekpai (1997)
Area: 198,455 sq. mi. (514,000 sq. km)
Population (2000 est.): 61,230,874 (average annual rate of natural increase 0.9%); birth rate: 16.9/1000; infant mortality rate: 31.5/1000; density per sq. mi.: 309
Capital and largest city (2000 est.): Bangkok, 7,200,000 (metro. area). **Other large cities:** Nonthanburi, 261,335; Chiang Mai, 170,397.
Monetary unit: baht. **Languages:** Thai (Siamese), Chinese, English. **Ethnicity/race:** Thai 75%, Chinese 14%, other 11%. **Religions:** Buddhist, 94.4%; Islam, 4%; Hindu, 1.1%; Christian, 0.5%. **Literacy rate:** 93% (1990)
Economic summary: GDP/PPP (1998 est.): $369 billion; $6,100 per capita. **Real growth rate:** –8.5% (1998 est.). **Inflation:** 4.3% (1998 est.).

Unemployment: 4.5% (1998 est.). **Arable land:** 34%. **Agriculture:** rice, cassava (tapioca), rubber, corn, sugarcane, coconuts, soybeans. **Labor force:** 32.6 million (1997 est.): services (including government), 31%; agriculture, 54%; industry, 15% (1996 est.). **Industries:** tourism, textiles and garments, agricultural processing, beverages, tobacco, cement, light manufacturing (such as jewelry), electric appliances and components, computers and parts, integrated circuits, furniture, plastics, world's second-largest tungsten producer and third-largest tin producer. **Natural resources:** fish, natural gas, forests, fluorite, tin, tungsten. **Exports:** $51.6 billion (f.o.b., 1997): manufactures (including computers and parts), agricultural products, and fisheries. **Imports:** $73.5 billion (c.i.f., 1996): capital goods, intermediate goods and raw materials, consumer goods, fuel. **Major trading partners:** Japan, Singapore, Hong Kong, Malaysia, U.K., U.S., Taiwan, Germany.

Geography Thailand occupies the western half of the Indochinese peninsula and the northern two-thirds of the Malay Peninsula in southeast Asia. Its neighbors are Burma (Myanmar) on the north and west, Laos on the north and northeast, Cambodia on the east, and Malaysia on the south. Thailand is about the size of France.

Government Constitutional monarchy.

History The Thais first began settling their present homeland from the Asian continent in the 6th century A.D., and by the end of the 13th century ruled most of the western portion. During the next 400 years, they fought sporadically with the Cambodians to the east and Burmese to the west. Formerly called Siam, Thailand has never experienced foreign rule. The British gained a colonial foothold in the region in 1824, but by 1896 an Anglo-French accord guaranteed the independence of Thailand. A coup in 1932 demoted the monarchy to titular status and established representative government with universal suffrage.

At the outbreak of World War II, Japanese forces attacked Thailand. After five hours of token resistance Thailand yielded to Japan on Dec. 8, 1941, subsequently becoming a staging area for the Japanese campaign against Malaya. Following the demise of a pro-Japanese puppet government in July 1944, Thailand repudiated the declaration of war it had been forced to make in 1942 against Britain and the U.S.

By the late 1960s the nation's problems largely stemmed from conflicts brewing in neighboring Cambodia and Vietnam. Although Thailand had received $2 billion in U.S. economic and military aid since 1950, and had sent troops (paid by the U.S.) to Vietnam while permitting U.S. bomber bases on its territory, the collapse of South Vietnam and Cambodia in spring 1975 brought rapid changes in the country's diplomatic posture. At the Thai government's insistence, the U.S. agreed to withdraw all 23,000 U.S. military personnel remaining in Thailand by March 1976.

Three years of civilian government ended with a military coup on Oct. 6, 1976. Political parties, banned after the coup, gained limited freedom in 1980. The same year, the National Assembly elected Gen. Prem Tinsulanonda as prime minister. General elections held on April 18, 1983, and July 27, 1986, resulted in Prem continuing as prime minister over a coalition government.

Fleeing from Laos, Vietnam, and the genocidal regime of Cambodia's Pol Pot, refugees flooded into Thailand in 1978 and 1979. Despite efforts by the United States and other Western countries to resettle them, a total of 130,000 Laotians and Vietnamese were living in camps along the Cambodian border in mid-1980.

On April 3, 1981, a military coup against the Prem government failed. Another coup attempt on Sept. 9, 1985, was crushed by loyal troops after 10 hours of fighting in Bangkok. In Feb. 1991 a bloodless putsch led by Gen. Suchinda Kraprayoon overthrew the democratic government on charges of corruption. The new junta declared a state of emergency; under martial law, the houses of Parliament were dismissed and the constitution abolished. Parliamentary elections in March 1992 gave more than half the seats at stake to pro-military parties. In April, the top military commander was appointed prime minister. A scandal over a land-reform program caused the fall of the government in May 1995. The prime minister dissolved Parliament and set a date for new elections. Voters in early July gave the largest number of seats in Parliament to the Thai Nation Party, whose leader moved quickly to form a coalition government. A new draft constitution, calling for cabinet ministers to relinquish their parliamentary seats, came under fire in the early months of 1997 from a number of politicians.

Following several years of unprecedented economic growth, Thailand's economy, once one of the strongest in the region, collapsed under the weight of foreign debt in 1997. The Thai economy's downfall set off a chain reaction in the region, sparking the Asian currency crisis. Although one of the first Asian economies to be ravaged by the currency crisis, the Thai government quickly accepted restructuring guidelines as a condition of the International Monetary Fund's $17 billion bailout. By 1998, Thailand's economy, while far from completely recovered, appeared to be in better condition than that of many of its Asian neighbors, and continued to improve in 1999.

Togo

REPUBLIC OF TOGO

National name: République Togolaise
President: Gen. Gnassingbé Eyadema (1967)
Prime Minister: Agbeyome Messan Kodjo (2000)
Area: 21,925 sq. mi. (56,790 sq. km)
Population (2000 est.): 5,018,502 (average annual rate of natural increase: 2.7%); birth rate: 38/1000; infant mortality rate: 71.6/1000; density per sq. mi.: 229
Capital and largest city (1983): Lomé, 366,476.
Monetary unit: Franc CFA. **Languages:** Ewé, Mina (south), Kabyé, Cotocoli (north), French (official), and many dialects. **Ethnicity/race:** native African (37 tribes; largest and most important are Ewe, Mina, and Kabre) 99%, European and Syrian-Lebanese less than 1%. **Religions:** Indigenous beliefs, 70%; Christian, 20%; Islam, 10%. **Literacy rate:** 43% (1990)
Economic summary: GDP/PPP (1998 est.): $8.2 billion; $1,670 per capita. **Real growth rate:** 3.8% (1998 est.). **Inflation:** 7.2% (1997). **Unemployment:** n.a. **Arable land:** 38%. **Agriculture:** coffee, cocoa, cotton, yams, cassava (tapioca), corn, beans, rice, millet, sorghum, livestock, fish. **Labor force:** 1.538 million (1993 est.): agriculture, 65%; services, 30%; industry, 5% (1998 est.). **Industries:** phosphate mining, agricultural processing, cement, handicrafts, textiles, beverages. **Natural resources:** marble, phosphate, limestone. **Exports:** $345 million (f.o.b., 1997): cotton, phosphates, coffee, cocoa. **Imports:** $400 million (f.o.b., 1997): machinery and equipment, consumer goods, petroleum products. **Major trading partners:** Canada, Taiwan, Nigeria, South Africa, Ghana, France, China, Cameroon.

Geography Togo, twice the size of Maryland, is on the south coast of West Africa bordering on Ghana to the west, Burkina Faso to the north and Benin to the east. The Gulf of Guinea coastline, only 32 miles long (51 km), is low and sandy. The only port is at Lomé. The Togo hills traverse the central section.

Government Republic.

History The Voltaic peoples and the Kwa were the earliest known inhabitants. The Ewe followed in the 14th century, and the Ane in the 18th century. The Danish claimed the land in the 18th century, but by 1884 it was established as a German colony (Togoland). The area was split between the British and the French under League of Nations mandates after World War I and subsequently administered as U.N. trusteeships. The British portion voted for incorporation with Ghana. The French portion became Togo, which declared its independence on April 27, 1960.

The government of Nicolas Grunitzky was overthrown in a bloodless coup on Jan. 13, 1967, led by Lt. Col. Etienne Eyadema (now Gen. Gnassingbé Eyadema). A National Reconciliation Committee was set up to rule the country. In April, however, Eyadema dissolved the committee and took over as president. The presidential election held in Aug. 1993 gave Eyadema more than 96% of the vote, but only 36% of the electorate went to the polls. Many of the major opposition candidates withdrew prior to the election. In Aug. 1996 Prime Minister Edem Kodjo resigned. The planning minister, Kwassi Klutse, was then appointed prime minister.

In 1998 Eyadema was reelected to another five-year presidential term amid rioting and ongoing protests against alleged military harassment of opposition leaders. The Togolese economy improved in the late 1990s, but the government was broke in the summer of 2000, with wages for many federal employees several months in arrears.

Tonga

KINGDOM OF TONGA

Sovereign: King Taufa'ahau Tupou IV (1965)
Prime Minister: Prince Lavaka Ata Ulukalala (2000)
Area: 290 sq. mi. (748 sq. km)
Population (2000 est.): 102,321 (average annual rate of natural increase: 1.9%); birth rate: 24.9/1000; infant mortality rate: 14.5/1000; density per sq. mi.: 353
Capital and largest city (1990 est.): Nuku'alofa, 34,000. **Monetary unit:** Pa'anga. **Languages:** Tongan (an Austronesian language), English. **Ethnicity/race:** Polynesian, European (about 300). **Religions:** Christian; Free Wesleyan Church claims over 30,000 adherents. **Literacy rate:** 47% (1976)
Economic summary: GDP/PPP (FY97/98 est.): $232 million; $2,100 per capita. **Real growth rate:** −1.5% (FY97/98 est.). **Inflation:** 2% (1997 est.). **Arable land:** 24%. **Agriculture:** squash, coconuts, copra, bananas, vanilla beans, cocoa, coffee, ginger, black pepper, fish. **Unemployment:** 11.8% (FY93/94). **Labor force:** 36,665 (1994): agriculture, 65% (1997 est.). **Industries:** tourism, fishing. **Natural resources:** fish, copra. **Exports:** $11.9 million (f.o.b., FY97/98): squash, fish, vanilla, root crops, coconut oil. **Imports:** $78.9 million (f.o.b., FY97/98): food products, live animals, machinery and transport equipment, manufactures, fuel, chemicals. **Major trading partners:** Japan, U.S., Canada, New Zealand, Australia, U.K. **Member of Commonwealth of Nations**

Geography Situated east of the Fiji Islands in the South Pacific, Tonga (also called the Friendly Islands) consists of some 150 islands, of which 36 are inhabited. Most of the islands contain active volcanic craters; others are coral atolls.

Government Constitutional monarchy.

History Polynesians have lived on Tonga for at least 3,000 years. The Dutch were the first to explore the islands, landing on Tafahi in 1616. The current royal dynasty of Tonga was founded in 1831 by Taufa'ahau Tupou, who took the name George I. He consolidated the kingdom by conquest and in 1875 granted a constitution. In 1900, his great-grandson, George II, signed a treaty of friendship with Britain, and the country became a British protected state. The treaty was revised in 1959. Tonga became independent on June 4, 1970.

The continuing challenge to the government—largely controlled by the king, his nominees, and a small group of hereditary nobles—posed by the pro-democracy movement was institutionalized in Sept. 1994 with the formation of the Tonga Democratic Party. In March 1997, Cyclone Hina caused damage to crops and buildings, mostly on Tongatapu; one person was reported killed. In 1999, Tonga gained U.N. membership.

Trinidad and Tobago

REPUBLIC OF TRINIDAD AND TOBAGO
President: A. N. R. Robinson (1997)
Prime Minister: Basdeo Panday (1995)
Area: 1,980 sq. mi. (5,130 sq. km)
Population (2000 est.): 1,175,523 (average annual rate of natural increase: 0.5%); birth rate: 13.8/1000; infant mortality rate: 25.8/1000; density per sq. mi.: 594
Capital and largest city (1995): Port-of-Spain, 52,451.
Monetary unit: Trinidad and Tobago dollar.
Languages: English (official), Hindi, French, Spanish.
Ethnicity/race: black 43%, East Indian (a local term—primarily immigrants from northern India) 40%, mixed 14%, white 1%, Chinese 1%, other 1%.
Religions: Roman Catholic, 33%; Hindu, 25%; Anglican, 15%; other Christian, 14%; Muslim, 6%.
Literacy rate: 95% (1980)
Economic summary: GDP/PPP (1998 est.): $8.85 billion; $8,000 per capita. **Real growth rate:** 4.3% (1998 est.). **Inflation:** 3.7% (1997). **Unemployment:** 14% (June 1998). **Arable land:** 15%. **Agriculture:** cocoa, sugarcane, rice, citrus, coffee, vegetables, poultry. **Labor force** 541,000 (1997 est.): services, 64.1%; manufacturing, mining, and quarrying, 14%; construction and utilities, 12.4%; agriculture, 9.5%. **Industries:** petroleum, chemicals, tourism, food processing, cement, beverage, cotton textiles. **Exports:** $2.4 billion (f.o.b., 1997): petroleum and petroleum products, chemicals, steel products, fertilizer, sugar, cocoa, coffee, citrus, flowers. **Imports:** $3.3 billion (c.i.f., 1997): machinery, transportation equipment, manufactured goods, food, live animals. **Major trading partners:** U.S., Caricom countries, Latin America, EU, Japan. **Member of Commonwealth of Nations**

Geography Trinidad and Tobago lie in the Caribbean Sea off the northeast coast of Venezuela. Trinidad, the larger at 1,864 sq. mi. (4,828 sq. km), is mainly flat and rolling, with mountains in the north that reach a height of 3,085 feet (940 m) at Mount Aripo. Tobago, at just 116 sq. mi. (300 sq. km), is heavily forested with hardwood trees.

Government Parliamentary democracy.

History When Trinidad was explored by Columbus in 1498, it was inhabited by the Arawaks; the Carib Indians inhabited Tobago. Trinidad remained in Span-

ish possession, despite raids by other European nations, until it capitulated to the British in 1797 during a war between Britain and Spain. Trinidad was officially ceded to Britain in 1802. Tobago passed between Britain and France several times before it was ultimately ceded to Britain in 1814. In 1845, the immigration of indentured workers from India for the sugarcane plantations began; it continued until 1917. In 1889 Tobago was administratively combined with Trinidad.

Partial self-government was instituted in 1925, and from 1958 to 1962 the nation was part of the West Indies Federation. On Aug. 31, 1962, it became independent and on Aug. 1, 1976, Trinidad and Tobago became a republic, remaining within the Commonwealth. The People's National Movement (PNM) won six consecutive elections and held power from 1956 to 1986. In Dec. 1986 the National Alliance for Reconstruction (NAR), a coalition party, won the majority of parliamentary seats, promising divestment of most state-owned companies, reorganization of the civil service, and structural readjustment of the economy in the light of shrinking oil revenues.

In July 1990 a small, radical Muslim group attempted a coup in which several ministers, including the prime minister, were held hostage for six days.

The NAR was defeated in elections in Dec. 1991, and the PNM returned to power. In the 1995 elections, the United National Congress (UNC), led by Basdeo Panday, teamed up with the NAR and formed a coalition government.

Trinidad hanged several members of a gang of murderers in June 1999, its first executions in five years. There has been a growing support for capital punishment among Caribbean commonwealth members, and anger against Britain, their former colonizer, for urging them to outlaw the death penalty.

Tunisia

REPUBLIC OF TUNISIA

National name: Al-Joumhouria Attunisia
President: Zine al-Abidine Ben Ali (1987)
Prime Minister: Mohamed Ghannouchi (1999)
Area: 63,170 sq. mi. (163,610 sq. km)
Population (2000 est.): 9,593,402 (average annual rate of natural increase: 1.2%); birth rate: 17.4/1000; infant mortality rate: 30.1/1000; density per sq. mi.: 152
Capital and largest city (1994): Tunis, 887,800.
Monetary unit: Tunisian dinar. **Languages:** Arabic, French. **Ethnicity/race:** Arab-Berber 98%, European 1%, Jewish less than 1%. **Religions:** Islam (Sunni), 98%; Christian, 1%; Jewish, less than 1%. **Literacy rate:** 65% (1990)
Economic summary: GDP/PPP (1998 est.): $49 billion; $5,200 per capita. **Real growth rate:** 5% (1998 est.). **Inflation:** 3.3% (1998 est.). **Unemployment:** 15.6% (1998 est.). **Arable land:** 19%. **Agriculture:** olives, dates, oranges, almonds, grain, sugar beets, grapes, poultry, beef, dairy products. **Labor force:** 3.3 million (1995 est.): services, 55%; industry, 23%; agriculture, 22% (1995 est.). **Industries:** petroleum, mining (particularly phosphate and iron ore), tourism, textiles, footwear, food, beverages. **Exports:** $5.4 billion (f.o.b., 1997 est.): hydrocarbons, textiles, agricultural products, phosphates and chemicals. **Imports:** $7.9 billion (c.i.f., 1997 est.): industrial goods and equipment, hydrocarbons, food, consumer goods. **Major trading partners:** EU, North African countries, Asia, U.S.

Geography Tunisia, at the northernmost bulge of Africa, thrusts out toward Sicily to mark the division between the eastern and western Mediterranean Sea. Twice the size of South Carolina, it is bordered on the west by Algeria and by Libya on the south. Coastal plains on the east rise to a north-south escarpment that slopes gently to the west. The Sahara Desert lies in the most southern part. Tunisia is more mountainous in the north, where the Atlas range continues from Algeria.

Government Republic.

History Tunisia was settled by the Phoenicians in the twelfth century B.C. By the sixth and fifth centuries B.C., the great city-state of Carthage (derived from the Phoenician name for "new city") dominated much of the western Mediterranean. The three Punic Wars between Rome and Carthage (the second was the most famous, pitting the Roman general Scipio Africanus against Carthage's Hannibal), led to the complete destruction of Carthage by 146 B.C.

Except for an interval of Vandal conquest in A.D. 439–533, Carthage was part of the Roman Empire until the Arab conquest of 648–69. It was then ruled by various Arab and Berber dynasties until the Turks took it in 1570–74 and made it part of the Ottoman Empire until the nineteenth century. In the late 16th century, it was a stronghold for the Barbary pirates. French troops occupied the country in 1881, and the bey, the local Tunisian ruler, signed a treaty acknowledging a French protectorate.

Nationalist agitation forced France to recognize Tunisian independence and sovereignty in 1956. The Constituent Assembly deposed the bey on July 25, 1957, declared Tunisia a republic, and elected Habib Bourguiba as president. Bourguiba maintained a pro-Western foreign policy that earned him enemies. Tunisia refused to break relations with the U.S. during the Arab-Israeli War in June 1967. Concerned with Islamic fundamentalist plots against the state, the government stepped up efforts to eradicate the movement, including censorship and frequent detention of suspects.

In 1987, the aged Bourguiba was declared mentally unfit to continue as president and was removed from office. He was succeeded as president by General Zine al-Abidine Ben Ali, whose tenure was marked by a rise in Islamic fundamentalism and growing anti-Western sentiments among the populace.

Ben Ali was reelected in Oct. 1999 with 99% of the vote in an election criticized by many human rights observers. In May 2000 Ben Ali's Constitutional Democratic Assembly Party swept local elections with 92% of the vote, in a contest many opposition leaders boycotted. However, Tunisia's economy continued to improve in the late 1990s, making the country one of the most attractive in Africa for foreign investors.

Turkey
REPUBLIC OF TURKEY

National name: Türkiye Cumhuriyeti
President: Ahmet Necdet Sezer (2000)
Prime Minister: Bülent Ecevit (1999)
Area: 300,947 sq. mi. (incl. 9,121 in Europe) (780,580 sq. km)
Population (2000 est.): 65,666,677; average annual rate of natural increase 1.3%; birth rate: 18.7/1000; infant mortality rate: 48.9/1000; density per sq. mi.: 218
Capital (1996 est.): Ankara, 2,890,025. **Largest cities:**

Istanbul (2000 est.), 10,250,000 (metro. area); Izmir, 1,920,807; Adana, 1,010,363; Bursa, 949,810; Gaziantep, 683,557. **Monetary unit:** Turkish lira.
Language: Turkish. **Ethnicity/race:** Turkish 80%, Kurdish 20%. **Religion:** Islam (mostly Sunni), 98%.
Literacy rate: 81% (1990)
Economic summary: GDP/PPP (1998 est.): $425.4 billion; $6,600 per capita. **Real growth rate:** 2.8% (1998 est.). **Inflation:** 70% (1998 est.).
Unemployment: 10% (1998 est.). **Arable land:** 32%.
Agriculture: tobacco, cotton, grain, olives, sugar beets, pulse, citrus, livestock. **Labor force:** 22.7 million (April 1998). [Note: about 1.5 million Turks work abroad (1994)]: agriculture, 42.5%; services, 34.5%; industry, 23% (1996). **Industries:** textiles, food processing, autos, mining (coal, chromite, copper, boron), steel, petroleum, construction, lumber, paper.
Natural resources: coal, chromite, copper, borate, sulfur, petroleum. **Exports:** $31 billion (f.o.b., 1998): textiles and apparel, foodstuffs, iron and steel products. **Imports:** $47 billion (f.o.b., 1998): machinery and equipment, fuel, minerals, foodstuffs. **Major trading partners:** Germany, U.S., Russia, U.K., Italy, France.

Geography Turkey is at the northeastern end of the Mediterranean Sea in southeast Europe and southwest Asia. To the north is the Black Sea and to the west is the Aegean Sea. Its neighbors are Greece and Bulgaria to the west, Russia and Ukraine to the north (through the Black Sea), Georgia, Armenia, Azerbaijan, and Iran to the east, and Syria and Iraq to the south. The Dardanelles, the Sea of Marmara, and the Bosporus divide the country. Turkey in Europe comprises an area about equal to the state of Massachusetts. It is hilly country drained by the Maritsa River and its tributaries. Turkey in Asia, or Anatolia, is about the size of Texas. Its center is a treeless plateau rimmed by mountains.

Government Parliamentary democracy.

History Anatolia (Turkey in Asia) was occupied in about 1900 B.C. by the Indo-European Hittites and after the Hittite empire's collapse in 1200 B.C., by Phrygians and Lydians. The Persian Empire occupied the area in the 6th century B.C., giving way to the Roman Empire, then later the Byzantine Empire. The Ottoman Turks first appeared in the early 13th century, subjugating Turkish and Mongol bands pressing against the eastern borders of Byzantium and making the Christian Balkan states their vassals. They gradually spread through the Near East and Balkans, capturing Constantinople in 1453 and storming the gates of Vienna two centuries later. At its height, the Ottoman Empire stretched from the Persian Gulf to western Algeria. Lasting for 600 years, the Ottoman Empire was not only one of the most powerful empires in the history of the Mediterranean region, but generated a great cultural outpouring of Islamic art, architecture, and literature.

After the reign of Sultan Süleyman I the Magnificent (1494–1566), the Ottoman Empire began to decline politically, administratively, and economically. By the 18th century, Russia was seeking to establish itself as the protector of Christians in Turkey's Balkan territories. Russian ambitions were checked by Britain and France in the Crimean War (1854–56), but the Russo-Turkish War (1877–78) gave Bulgaria virtual independence and Romania and Serbia liberation from their nominal allegiance to the sultan. Turkish weakness stimulated a revolt of young liberals known as the Young Turks in 1909. They forced Sultan Abdul Hamid to grant a constitution and install a liberal government. However, reforms were no barrier to further defeats in a war with Italy (1911–12) and the Balkan Wars (1912–13). Under the influence of German military advisers, Turkey signed a secret alliance with Germany on Aug. 2, 1914, that led to a declaration of war by the Allied powers and the ultimate humiliation of the occupation of Turkish territory by Greek and other Allied troops.

Turkey's current boundaries were drawn in 1923 at the Conference of Lausanne, and Turkey became a republic with Kemal Atatürk as the first president. The Ottoman sultanate and caliphate were abolished, and modernization, reform, and industrialization began under Atatürk's direction. He secularized Turkish society, reducing Islam's dominant role and replacing Arabic with the Latin alphabet for writing the Turkish language. After Atatürk's death in 1938, parliamentary government and a multiparty system gradually took root in Turkey, despite periods of instability and brief intervals of military rule. Neutral during most of World War II, Turkey, on Feb. 23, 1945, declared war on Germany and Japan, but took no active part in the conflict. Turkey became a full member of NATO in 1952, was a signatory in the Balkan Entente (1953), joined the Baghdad Pact (1955; later CENTO), joined the Organization for European Economic Cooperation (OEEC) and the Council of Europe, and became an associate member of the European Common Market in 1963.

Turkey invaded Cyprus by sea and air on July 20, 1974, following the failure of diplomatic efforts to resolve conflicts between Turkish and Greek Cypriots. Turkey unilaterally announced a ceasefire on August 16, after having gained control of 40% of the island. Turkish Cypriots established their own state in the north on Feb. 13, 1975. In July 1975, after a 30-day warning, Turkey took control of all the U.S. installations except the big joint defense base at Incirlik, which it reserved for "NATO tasks alone."

The establishment of military government in Sept. 1980 stopped the slide toward anarchy and brought some improvement in the economy. A Constituent Assembly, consisting of the six-member National Security Council and members appointed by them, drafted a new constitution that was approved by an overwhelming (91.5%) majority of the voters in a Nov. 6, 1982, referendum. Martial law was gradually lifted.

About 12 million Kurds, roughly 20% of Turkey's population, live in the southeast region of Turkey. Turkey, however, does not officially recognize Kurds as a minority group and is therefore exempted from protecting their rights. Oppression of Kurds and Kurdish culture led to the emergence in 1984 of the Kurdistan Workers' Party (PKK), a militant Kurdish terrorist campaign under the leadership of Abdullah Ocalan. Although the guerrilla movement sought independence at first, by the late 1980s the rebel Kurds were willing to accept an autonomous state or a federation with Turkey. In March 1995, Turkish troops moved into northern Iraq seeking to root out Kurdish rebels, who had used Iraq as a base. About 35,000 have died in clashes between the military and the PKK during the 1980s and '90s. On Feb. 16, 1999, Kurd leader and terrorist Abdullah Ocalan was captured, tried, and convicted of treason and separatism on June 2, 1999, and sentenced to death.

On August 17, 1999, western Turkey was devastated by an earthquake (magnitude 7.4) that left more than 17,000 dead and 200,000 homeless. The government was decried for lax control of builders whose faulty construction increased the destruction and added to the death toll. On Nov. 12, another huge earthquake (magnitude 7.2) struck another section of western Turkey, leaving hundreds dead and thousands injured.

The Turkish government hopes an oil pipeline running from Azerbaijan to the Mediterranean port city of Ceyhan, Turkey, will bolster the economy. Approved in 1999, the 1,000-mile pipeline will cost some $2.4 billion. The project also symbolizes the Turkish desire for greater economic, social, and political cooperation with the former Soviet republics in Central Asia, including Azerbaijan, which share similar Turkic ethnic roots. However, the potential for Turkish leadership of a "Turkic bloc" of nations has not been fulfilled, since the Central Asian states in general have not had smooth transitions to democracy nor to market economies. There is also some Central Asian reluctance to ally with Turkey.

Turkmenistan

TURKMENISTAN

President-for-life: Saparmurad A. Niyazov (1990)
Area: 188,500 sq. mi. (488,100 sq. km)
Population (2000 est.): 4,518,268 (average annual rate of natural increase: 2%); birth rate: 28.9/1000; infant mortality rate: 73.3/1000; density per sq. mi.: 24
Capital and largest city (1994 est.): Ashgabat, 518,000. **Other large cities:** Chardzhou, 166,400; Tashauz, 117,000. **Monetary unit:** Manat.
Languages: Turkmen, 72%; Russian, 12%; Uzbek, 9%. **Ethnicity/race (1995):** Turkmen 77%, Uzbek 9.2%, Russian 6.7%, Kazak 2%, other 5.1%.
Religions: Muslim 89%, Eastern Orthodox 9%, unknown 2%. **Literacy rate:** 98% (1989)
Economic summary: GDP/PPP (1998 est.): $7 billion; $1,630 per capita. **Real growth rate:** 5% (1998 est.). **Inflation:** 19.8% (1998 est.). **Unemployment:** n.a. **Arable land:** 3%. **Labor force:** 2.34 million (1996): agriculture and forestry, 44%; industry and construction, 19%; other, 37% (1996). **Industries:** natural gas, oil, petroleum products, textiles, food processing. **Agriculture:** cotton, grain, livestock. **Exports:** $689 million (1997 est.): natural gas, cotton, petroleum products, textiles, electricity, carpets. **Imports:** $1.1 billion (1997 est.): machinery and parts, grain and food, plastics and rubber, consumer durables, textiles. **Major trading partners:** Former Soviet Union, Hong Kong, Switzerland, U.S., Germany, Turkey, Cyprus.

Geography Turkmenistan (formerly Turkmenia) is bounded by the Caspian Sea in the west, Kazakhstan in the north, Uzbekistan in the east, and Iran and Afghanistan in the south. About nine-tenths of Turkmenistan is desert, chiefly the Kara-Kum; this is one of the world's largest sand deserts at approximately 138,966 sq. mi. (360,000 sq. km) in area. Many irrigation canals and reservoirs have been built, including the Kara-Kum Canal, which runs from the Amu Darya River westward to the Caspian Sea for a distance of 870 miles (1,400 km).

Government Republic.

History Turkmenistan was once part of the ancient Persian empire. The Turkmen people were originally pastoral nomads and some of them continued this way of life up into the 20th century, living in transportable dome-shaped felt tents. The territory was ruled by the Seljuk Turks in the 11th century. The

Mongols of Ghenghis Khan conquered the land in the 13th century and dominated the area for the next two centuries until they were deposed in the late 15th century by invading Uzbeks. Prior to the 19th century, Turkmenia was divided into two lands, one belonging to the khanate of Khiva and the other belonging to the khanate of Bukhara. In 1868, the khanate of Khiva was made part of the Russian empire and Turkmenia became known as the Transcaspia Region of Russian Turkistan. Turkmenistan was later formed out of the Turkistan Autonomous Soviet Socialist Republic, founded in 1922, and was made an independent Soviet Socialist Republic on May 13, 1925.

Turkmenistan declared its sovereignty in Aug. 1990 and became a member of the Commonwealth of Independent States on Dec. 21, 1991, together with ten other former Soviet republics. It established a government more authoritarian than those functioning in the other newly independent central Asian republics. President Saparmurad A. Niyazov, also called the Turkmenbashy (Leader of All Turkmens), has attempted to create a cult of personality through heavy-handed self-promotion. Protests against his authoritarian rule and practices notwithstanding, Niyazov was declared president-for-life in 2000.

Along with Azerbaijan and Kazakhstan, Turkmenistan is one of the fortunate countries bordering the Caspian Sea, which is estimated to hold 10% of the world's potential oil reserves. In the 1990s, Turkmenistan exported gas through a Russian pipeline, bringing in about $1 billion per year. But in 1993, Russia closed down Turkmenistan's only pipeline because it competed with Russia's own gas exportation. Turkmenistan was limited to exporting gas to its impoverished central Asian neighbors, who were unable to pay their bills. Turkmenistan then opened a pipeline route to Iran, generally agreed to be the most economical route for exporting Caspian oil, and thus ruffled the feathers of Iran's enemy, the U.S. So far, the new plan has not brought in money, and the country is living off loans from Western countries such as Germany who hope to partner up with the oil-rich, money-poor country.

Tuvalu

Sovereign: Queen Elizabeth II (1952)
Governor-General: Tomasi Puapua (1998)
Prime Minister: Ionatana Ionatana (1999)
Area: 10 sq. mi. (26 sq. km)
Population (2000 est.): 10,838; growth rate: 1.4%; birth rate: 21.8/1000; infant mortality rate: 23.3/1000; density per sq. mi.: 1,084
Capital and largest city (1991): Funafuti, 3,839.
Monetary unit: Tuvaluan dollar, Australian dollar.
Languages: Tuvaluan, English. **Ethnicity/race:** Polynesian 96%. **Religion:** Church of Tuvalu (Congregationalist), 97%. **Literacy rate:** less than 50%
Economic summary: GDP/PPP (1995 est.): $7.8 million; $800 per capita. **Real growth rate:** 8.7% (1995). **Inflation:** 3.9% (average 1985–93).
Unemployment: n.a. **Arable land:** 0%. **Agriculture:** coconuts, fish. **Labor force:** n.a.; people make a living mainly through exploitation of the sea, reefs, and atolls and from wages sent home by those working abroad (mostly workers in the phosphate industry and sailors).
Industries: fishing, tourism, copra. **Exports:** $165,000 (f.o.b., 1989): copra. **Imports:** $4.4 million (c.i.f.,

1989): food, animals, mineral fuel, machinery, manufactured goods. **Major trading partners:** Fiji, Australia, New Zealand. **Member of Commonwealth of Nations**

Geography Tuvalu consists of nine small islands scattered over 500,000 square miles of the western Pacific, just south of the equator. The islands include Niulakita, Nukulaelae, Funafuti, Nukufetau, Vaitupu, Nui, Niutao, Nanumaga (Nanumanga), and Nanumea.

Government Constitutional democracy.

History Formerly the Ellice Islands, Tuvalu's first Polynesian settlers were probably Samoans or Tongans. The Ellice Islands became a British protectorate in 1892 and were annexed by Britain in 1915–16 as part of the Gilbert and Ellice Islands Colony. The Ellice Islands were separated from the Gilberts in 1975, given home rule, and renamed Tuvalu. Full independence was granted on Sept. 30, 1978, but it remained part of the Commonwealth.

In 1979, the U.S. gave Tuvalu four islands that had been U.S. territory. In 1997, the government adopted a strong stance on the need to control emissions of greenhouse gases in order to ensure the survival of low-lying island nations.

In 2000, Tuvalu became a member of the United Nations.

Uganda
REPUBLIC OF UGANDA

President: Yoweri Museveni (1986)
Prime Minister: Apolo Nsibambi (1999)
Area: 91,459 sq. mi. (236,040 sq. km)
Population (2000 est.): 23,317,560 (average annual rate of natural increase: 3%); birth rate: 48/1000; infant mortality rate: 93.3/1000; density per sq. mi.: 255
Capital and largest city (1991 est.): Kampala, 773,463.
Monetary unit: Ugandan shilling. **Languages:** English (official), Swahili, Luganda, Ateso, Luo. **Ethnicity/race:** Baganda 17%, Karamojong 12%, Basogo 8%, Iteso 8%, Langi 6%, Rwanda 6%, Bagisu 5%, Acholi 4%, Lugbara 4%, Bunyoro 3%, Batobo 3%, European, Asian, Arab 1%, other 23%. **Religions:** Christian, 66%; Islam, 16%. **Literacy rate:** 54% (1991)
Economic summary: GDP/PPP (1998 est.): $22.7 billion; $1,020 per capita. **Real growth rate:** 5.5% (1998 est.). **Inflation:** 2.6% (1998 est.).
Unemployment: n.a. **Arable land:** 25%. **Agriculture:** coffee, tea, cotton, tobacco, cassava (tapioca), potatoes, corn, millet, pulses, beef, goat meat, milk, poultry. **Labor force:** 8.361 million (1993 est.): agriculture, 86%; services, 10%; industry, 4% (1980 est.). **Industries:** sugar, brewing, tobacco, cotton textiles, cement. **Natural resources:** copper, cobalt, limestone, salt. **Exports:** $476 million (f.o.b., 1998): coffee, gold, fish and fish products, cotton, tea, corn. **Imports:** $1.4 billion (c.i.f., 1998): transportation equipment, petroleum, medical supplies, iron and steel (1996). **Major trading partners:** Spain, Germany, Netherlands, France, Italy, Kenya, U.K., Japan, India, South Africa. **Member of the Commonwealth of Nations**

Geography Uganda, twice the size of Pennsylvania, is in East Africa. It is bordered on the west by Congo, on the north by the Sudan, on the east by Kenya, and on the south by Tanzania and Rwanda. The country, which lies across the equator, is divided into three main areas—swampy lowlands, a fertile plateau with wooded hills, and a desert region. Lake Victoria forms part of the southern border.

Government Multiparty democracy.

History About 500 B.C. Bantu-speaking peoples migrated to the area now called Uganda. By the 14th century, three kingdoms dominated, Buganda (meaning "state of the Gandas"), Bunyoro, and Ankole. Uganda was first explored by Europeans as well as Arab traders in 1844. An Anglo-German agreement of 1890 declared it to be in the British sphere of influence in Africa, and the Imperial British East Africa Company was chartered to develop the area. The company did not prosper financially, and in 1894 a British protectorate was proclaimed. Few Europeans permanently settled in Uganda, but it attracted Indians, Pakistanis, and Goans, who became important players in Ugandan commerce.

Uganda became independent on Oct. 9, 1962, and Sir Edward Mutesa, the king of Buganda (Mutesa II), was elected the first president and Milton Obote the first prime minister of the newly independent country. With the help of a young army officer, Col. Idi Amin, Prime Minister Obote seized control of the government from President Mutesa four years later.

On Jan. 25, 1971, Col. Amin deposed president Obote. Obote went into exile in Tanzania. Amin expelled Asian residents and launched a reign of terror against Ugandan opponents, torturing and killing tens of thousands. In 1976, he had himself proclaimed "President for Life." In 1977, Amnesty International estimated that 300,000 may have died under his rule, including church leaders and recalcitrant cabinet ministers.

After Amin held military exercises on the Tanzanian border, angering Tanzania's president Julius Nyerere, a combined force of Tanzanian troops and Ugandan exiles loyal to former president Obote invaded Uganda and chased Amin into exile in Saudi Arabia. After a series of interim administrations, President Obote led his People's Congress Party to victory in 1980 elections that opponents charged were rigged. On July 27, 1985, army troops staged a coup and took over the government. Obote fled into exile. The military regime installed Gen. Tito Okello as chief of state.

The National Resistance Army (NRA), an anti-Obote group led by Yoweri Museveni, kept fighting after it had been excluded from the new regime. They seized Kampala on Jan. 29, 1986, and Museveni was declared president. Museveni has transformed the ruins of Idi Amin and Milton Obote's Uganda into an economic miracle, preaching a philosophy of self-sufficiency and anticorruption. Western countries have flocked to assist him in the country's transformation. Nevertheless, it remains one of Africa's poorest countries. A ban on political parties was lifted in 1996, and the incumbent Museveni won 72% of the vote, reflecting his popularity due to the country's economic recovery.

Uganda continues to battle the extremist Lord's Resistance Army based in Sudan. Close ties with Rwanda (many Rwandan Tutsi exiles helped Museveni come to power) led to the assistance of Uganda and Rwanda in the ousting of Zaire's Mobutu Sese Seko in 1997, and a year later, in efforts to unseat his successor, Laurent Kabila, whom both countries originally supported but from whom they grew estranged. In Aug. 1999, both Uganda and Rwanda signed the Congo peace agreement, along with Kabila, his foreign allies, and the rebel groups who fought against him.

But despite the peace agreement, fighting in the Congo soon resumed. The rebels split apart in 1999 and have subsequently fought each other. Since Uganda and Rwanda each support rival rebel factions, the fighting has ended Uganda's earlier alliance with Rwanda. However, Uganda has scored a victory in the fight against AIDS, reducing the rate of new infections through an intensive public health campaign.

Ukraine

UKRAINE

President: Leonid D. Kuchma (1994)
Prime Minister: Viktor Yushchenko (1999)
Area: 233,000 sq. mi. (603,700 sq. km)
Population (2000 est.): 49,153,027 (average annual rate of natural increase: –0.7%): birth rate: 9/1000; infant mortality rate: 21.7/1000; density per sq. mi.: 211
Capital: Kyiv (Kiev), 2,637,000. **Other large cities:** Kharkiv, 1,622,000; Donetske, 1,121,000; Odessa, 1,104,000; Lviv, 803,000. **Monetary unit:** Hryvnia (since Sept. 2, 1996). **Language:** Ukrainian. **Ethnicity/race:** Ukrainian 73%, Russian 22%, Jewish 1%, other 4%. **Religions:** Orthodox, 76%; Ukrainian Catholic (Uniate), 13.5%; Jewish, 2.3%; Baptist, Mennonite, Protestant, and Muslim, 8.2%. **Literacy rate:** 100% (1979)
Economic summary: GDP/PPP (1998 est.): $108.5 billion; $2,200 per capita. **Real growth rate:** –1.7% (1998 est.). **Inflation:** 20% (year end 1998 est.). **Unemployment:** 3.7% officially registered; large number of unregistered or underemployed workers (Dec. 1998). **Arable land:** 58%. **Labor force:** 22.8 million (year end 1997): industry and construction, 32%; agriculture and forestry, 24%; health, education, and culture, 17%; trade and distribution, 8%; transport and communication, 7%; other, 12% (1996). **Natural resources:** iron ore, coal, manganese, natural gas, oil, salt, sulfur, graphite, titanium, magnesium, kaolin, nickel, mercury, and timber. **Agriculture:** grain, sugar beets, sunflower seeds, vegetables, beef, milk. **Industries:** coal, electric power, ferrous and nonferrous metals, machinery and transport equipment, chemicals, food processing (especially sugar). **Exports:** $11.3 billion (1998 est.): ferrous and nonferrous metals, chemicals, machinery and transport equipment, food products. **Imports:** $13.1 billion (1998 est.): energy, machinery and parts, transportation equipment, chemicals, plastics, and rubber. **Major trading partners:** Russia, China, Turkey, Germany, Belarus, U.S., Poland, Italy.

Geography Located in southeastern Europe, the country consists largely of fertile black soil steppes. Mountainous areas include the Carpathians in the southwest and the Crimean chain in the south. There are forest lakes in the north. Ukraine is bordered by Belarus on the north, by Russia on the north, northeast, and east, by the Sea of Azov and the Black Sea on the south, by Moldova and Romania on the southwest, and by Hungary, Slovakia, and Poland on the west.

Government Constitutional republic.

History Ukraine was known as "Kievan Rus" (from which Russia is a derivative) up until the 16th century. In the 9th century, Kiev was the major political and cultural center in eastern Europe. Kievan Rus reached the height of its power in the 10th century and adopted Byzantine Christianity, the Church

Slavonic written language, and the Cyrillic alphabet during that period. The Mongol conquest in 1240 ended Kievan power. From the 13th to the 16th century, Kiev was under the influence of Poland and western Europe. The negotiation of the Union of Brest-Litovsk in 1596 divided the Ukrainians into Orthodox and Ukrainian Catholic faithful. In 1654, Ukraine asked the czar of Moscovy for protection against Poland and the Treaty of Pereyasav signed that year recognized the suzerainty of Moscow. The agreement was interpreted by Moscow as an invitation to take over Kiev and the Ukrainian state was eventually absorbed into the Russian empire.

After the Russian Revolution, Ukraine declared its independence from Russia on Jan. 28, 1918, and several years of warfare ensued with several groups. The Red Army finally was victorious over Kiev and in 1920 Ukraine became a Soviet republic. In 1922, Ukraine became one of the founders of the United Soviet Socialist Republics. In the 1930s, the Soviet government's enforcement of collectivization met with peasant resistance, which in turn prompted the confiscation of grain from Ukrainian farmers by Soviet authorities; the resulting famine took an estimated 5 million lives. Ukraine was one of the most devastated Soviet republics during World War II. (For details on World War II, see Headline History, World War II.) On April 26, 1986, the nation's nuclear power plant at Chernobyl was the site of the world's worst nuclear accident. On Oct. 29, 1991, the Ukrainian Parliament voted to shut down the reactor within two years' time and asked for international assistance in dismantling it.

When President Leonid Kravchuk was elected by the Ukrainian Parliament in 1990, he vowed to seek Ukrainian sovereignty. Ukraine declared its independence on Aug. 24, 1991. In Dec. 1991, Ukrainian, Russian, and Belarussian leaders cofounded a new Commonwealth of Independent States with the new capital to be situated in Minsk, Belarus. The new country's government was slow to reform the Soviet-era state-run economy, which was plagued by declining production, rising inflation, and widespread unemployment in the years following independence. The U.S. announced in Jan. 1994 that an agreement had been reached with Russia and Ukraine for the destruction of Ukraine's entire nuclear arsenal. In Oct. 1994, Ukraine began a program of economic liberalization and moved to reestablish central authority over Crimea. In 1995, Crimea's separatist leader was removed and the Crimean constitution revoked.

In June 1996, the last strategic nuclear warhead was removed to Russia. Also that month Parliament approved a new constitution that allows for private ownership of land. An agreement was signed in May 1997 on the future of the Black Sea fleet, by which Ukrainian and Russian ships will share the port of Sevastopol for 20 years. Ukraine and Russia also signed a 10-year political treaty three days later, by which, among other provisions, Russia recognized the political and territorial integrity of Ukraine, including the Crimean Peninsula.

The Russian financial crisis in fall 1998 led to severe problems for the Ukrainian economy, which is dependent on Russia for 40% of its foreign trade. Ukraine remains saddled with its Soviet-era economy, and all of its major industries are still under state control. Western investors have shown only minimal interest. The election of the reform-minded Viktor Yushchenko as prime minister in Dec. 1999, however, was greeted by much of the West with optimism.

United Arab Emirates

President: Sheikh Zayed Bin Sultan Al-Nahyan (1971)
Prime Minister: Sheikh Maktoum Bin Rashid Al-Maktoum (1990)
Area: 32,375 sq. mi. (82,880 sq. km)
Population (2000 est.): 2,369,153 (average annual rate of natural increase: 1.4%); birth rate: 18/1000; infant mortality rate: 17.2/1000; density per sq. mi.: 73
Capital and largest city (1989 est.): Abu Dhabi, 363,432. **Monetary unit:** U.A.E. dirham. **Languages:** Arabic, English as a second language. **Ethnicity/race:** Emiri 19%, other Arab and Iranian 23%, South Asian 50%, other expatriates (includes Westerners and East Asians) 8% (1982). **Religions:** Islam (Sunni 80%, Shi'ite 16%), others 4%. **Literacy rate:** 68% (1980)
Economic summary: GDP/PPP (1998 est.): $40 billion; $17,400 per capita. **Real growth rate:** –5% (1998 est.). **Inflation:** 5% (1997 est.). **Unemployment:** n.a. **Arable land:** 0%. **Agriculture:** dates, vegetables, watermelons, poultry, eggs, dairy products, fish. **Labor force:** 1.3 million (1997 est.). [Note: 75% of the population in the 15–64 age group is nonnational (July 1998 est.).]: services, 60%; industry, 32%; agriculture, 8% (1996 est.). **Industries:** petroleum, fishing, petrochemicals, construction materials, some boat building, handicrafts, pearling. **Natural resources:** oil. **Exports:** $38 billion (f.o.b., 1997 est.): crude oil, natural gas, reexports, dried fish, dates. **Imports:** $29.7 billion (f.o.b., 1997 est.): manufactured goods, machinery and transport equipment, chemicals, food. **Major trading partners:** Japan, South Korea, Singapore, India, Oman, U.S., U.K., Germany.

Geography The United Arab Emirates, in the eastern part of the Arabian Peninsula, extends along part of the Gulf of Oman and the southern coast of the Persian Gulf. The nation is the size of Maine. Its neighbors are Saudi Arabia to the west and south, Qatar to the north, and Oman to the east. Most of the land is barren and sandy.

Government Federation formed in 1971 by seven emirates known as the Trucial States—Abu Dhabi (the largest), Dubai, Sharjah, Ajman, Fujairah, Ras al Khaimah, and Umm al-Qaiwain.

History Originally the area was inhabited by a seafaring people who were converted to Islam in the 7th century. Later, a dissident sect, the Carmathians, established a powerful sheikdom, and its army conquered Mecca. After the sheikdom disintegrated, its people became pirates. Threatening the Sultanate of Muscat and Oman early in the 19th century, the pirates provoked the intervention of the British, who in 1820 enforced a partial truce and in 1853 a permanent truce. Thus what had been called the Pirate Coast was renamed the Trucial Coast. The British provided the nine Trucial states with protection but did not formally administer them as a colony.

The British withdrew from the Persian Gulf in 1971, and the Trucial states became a federation called the United Arab Emirates (U.A.E.). Two of the Trucial states, Bahrain and Oman, chose not to join the federation, reducing the number of states to seven.

The country signed a military defense agreement with the U.S. in 1994 and one with France in 1995. In 1997, U.A.E. officials protested Iranian military activities in the Persian Gulf, especially in regard to the ownership of three Gulf islands, which had been the subjects of disputes for many years.

In 2000, one of the biggest arms deals in history took place, with the United Arab Emirates buying 80 fighter jets and missles from Lockheed Martin for nearly $8 billion.

United Kingdom

UNITED KINGDOM OF GREAT BRITAIN AND NORTHERN IRELAND

Sovereign: Queen Elizabeth II (1952)
Prime Minister: Tony Blair (1997)
Area: 94,247 sq. mi. (244,820 sq. km)
Population (2000 est.): 59,511,464 (average annual rate of natural increase: 0.1%); birth rate: 11.8/1000; infant mortality rate: 5.6/1000; density per sq. mi.: 631
Capital and largest city (2000 est.): London, 11,800,000 (metro. area). **Other large cities:** Birmingham, 1,009,100; Leeds, 721,800; Glasgow, 681,470; Liverpool, 479,000; Bradford, 477,500; Edinburgh, 441,620; Manchester, 434,600; Bristol, 396,600. **Monetary unit:** Pound sterling (£).
Languages: English, Welsh, Scots Gaelic. **Ethnicity/race:** English 81.5%; Scottish 9.6%; Irish 2.4%; Welsh 1.9%; Ulster 1.8%; West Indian, Indian, Pakistani, and other 2.8%. **Religions:** Church of England (established church); Church of Wales (disestablished); Church of Scotland (established church—Presbyterian); Church of Ireland (disestablished); Roman Catholic; Methodist; Congregational; Baptist; Jewish. **Literacy rate:** 99% (1978)
Economic summary: GDP/PPP (1998 est.): $1.252 trillion; $21,200 per capita. **Real growth rate:** 2.6% (1998 est.). **Inflation:** 2.7% (1998 est.). **Unemployment:** 7.5% (1998 est.). **Arable land:** 25%. **Agriculture:** cereals, oilseed, potatoes, vegetables, cattle, sheep, poultry, fish. **Labor force:** 28.8 million (1998): services, 68.9%; manufacturing and construction, 17.5%; government, 11.3%; energy, 1.2%; agriculture, 1.1% (1996). **Industries:** production machinery including machine tools, electric power equipment, automation equipment, railroad equipment, shipbuilding, aircraft, motor vehicles and parts, electronics and communications equipment, metals, chemicals, coal, petroleum, paper and paper products, food processing, textiles, clothing, and other consumer goods. **Natural resources:** coal, oil, gas. **Exports:** $271 billion (f.o.b, 1998): manufactured goods, fuel, chemicals, food, beverages, tobacco. **Imports:** $304 billion (f.o.b, 1998): manufactured goods, machinery, fuel, foodstuffs. **Major trading partners:** EU, U.S.

Geography The United Kingdom, consisting of England, Wales, Scotland, and Northern Ireland, is twice the size of New York State. England, in the southeast part of the British Isles, is separated from Scotland on the north by the granite Cheviot Hills; from them the Pennine chain of uplands extends south through the center of England, reaching its highest point in the Lake District in the northwest. To the west along the border of Wales—a land of steep hills and valleys—are the Cambrian Mountains, while the Cotswolds, a range of hills in Gloucestershire, extend into the surrounding shires.

Important rivers flowing into the North Sea are the Thames, Humber, Tees, and Tyne. In the west are the Severn and Wye, which empty into the Bristol Channel and are navigable, as are the Mersey and Ribble.

Government The United Kingdom is a constitutional monarchy and parliamentary democracy, with a queen and a Parliament that has two houses: the House of Lords, with 574 life peers, 92 hereditary peers, 26 bishops, and the House of Commons, which has 651 popularly elected members. Supreme legislative power is vested in Parliament, which sits for five years unless sooner dissolved. The House of Lords was stripped of most of its power in 1911, and now its main function is to revise legislation. In Nov. 1999 hundreds of hereditary peers were expelled in an effort to make the body more democratic. The executive power of the Crown is exercised by the cabinet, headed by the prime minister.

Ruler Queen Elizabeth II, born April 21, 1926, elder daughter of King George VI and Queen Elizabeth, succeeded to the throne on the death of her father on Feb. 6, 1952. On Nov. 20, 1947, she married Prince Philip, duke of Edinburgh, born June 10, 1921. Their children are Prince Charles[1] (heir presumptive), born Nov. 14, 1948; Princess Anne, born Aug. 15, 1950; Prince Andrew, born Feb. 19, 1960; and Prince Edward, born March 10, 1964. Prince William Arthur Philip Louis, son of Prince Charles and the late princess of Wales and second in line to the throne, was born June 21, 1982. A second son, Prince Henry Charles Albert David, was born Sept. 15, 1984, and is third in line.

History Stonehenge and other examples of prehistoric culture are what remains of the earliest inhabitants of Britain. Celtic peoples followed. Roman invasions of the 1st century B.C. brought Britain into contact with continental Europe. When the Roman legions withdrew in the 5th century A.D., Britain fell easy prey to the invading hordes of Angles, Saxons, and Jutes from Scandinavia and the Low Countries. The invasions had little effect on the Celtic peoples of Wales and Scotland. Seven large Anglo-Saxon kingdoms were established, and the original Britons were forced into Wales and Scotland. It was not until the 10th century that the country finally became united under the kings of Wessex. Following the death of Edward the Confessor (1066), a dispute about the succession arose, and William, duke of Normandy, invaded England, defeating the Saxon king, Harold II, at the Battle of Hastings (1066). The Norman conquest introduced Norman French law and feudalism.

The reign of Henry II (1154–89), first of the Plantagenets, saw an increasing centralization of royal power at the expense of the nobles, but in 1215 John (1199–1216) was forced to sign the Magna Carta, which awarded the people, especially the nobles, certain basic rights. Edward I (1272–1307) continued the conquest of Ireland, reduced Wales to subjection, and made some gains in Scotland. In 1314, however, English forces led by Edward II were ousted from Scotland after the Battle of Bannockburn. The late 13th and early 14th centuries saw the development of a separate House of Commons with tax-raising powers. Edward III's claim to the throne of France led to the Hundred Years' War (1338–1453) and the loss of almost all the large English territory in France. In England, the great poverty and discontent caused by the war were intensified by the Black Death, a plague that reduced the population by about one-third. The Wars of the Roses (1455–85), a struggle for the throne between the House of York and the House of Lancaster, ended in the victory of Henry Tudor (Henry VII) at Bosworth Field (1485).

1. The title Prince of Wales, which is not inherited, was conferred on Prince Charles by his mother on July 26, 1958. The investiture ceremony took place on July 1, 1969. The previous Prince of Wales was Prince Edward Albert, who held the title from 1911 to 1936 before he became Edward VIII.

Rulers of England and Great Britain

Name	Born	Ruled[1]	Name	Born	Ruled[1]
SAXONS[2]			Henry VI	1421	1422–1461[5]
Egbert[3]	c. 775	802–839	**HOUSE OF YORK**		
Ethelwulf	?	839–858	Edward IV	1442	1461–1483[5]
Ethelbald	?	858–860	Edward V	1470	1483–1483
Ethelbert	?	860–865	Richard III	1452	1483–1485
Ethelred I	?	865–871	**HOUSE OF TUDOR**		
Alfred the Great	849	871–899	Henry VII	1457	1485–1509
Edward the Elder	c. 870	899–924	Henry VIII	1491	1509–1547
Athelstan	895	924–939	Edward VI	1537	1547–1553
Edmund I the Deed-doer	921	939–946	Jane (Lady Jane Grey)[6]	1537	1553–1553
Edred	c. 925	946–955	Mary I ("Bloody Mary")	1516	1553–1558
Edwy the Fair	c. 943	955–959	Elizabeth I	1533	1558–1603
Edgar the Peaceful	943	959–975	**HOUSE OF STUART**		
Edward the Martyr	c. 962	975–978	James I[7]	1566	1603–1625
Ethelred II the Unready	968	978–1016	Charles I	1600	1625–1649
Edmund II Ironside	c. 993	1016	**COMMONWEALTH**		
DANES			Council of State	—	1649–1653
Canute	995	1016–1035	Oliver Cromwell[8]	1599	1653–1658
Harold I Harefoot	c.1016	1035–1040	Richard Cromwell[8]	1626	1658–1659[9]
Hardecanute	c.1018	1040–1042	**RESTORATION OF HOUSE OF STUART**		
SAXONS			Charles II	1630	1660–1685
Edward the Confessor	c.1004	1042–1066	James II	1633	1685–
Harold II	c.1020	1066			1688[10]
HOUSE OF NORMANDY			William III[11]	1650	1689–1702
William I the Conqueror	1027	1066–1087	Mary II[11]	1662	1689–1694
William II Rufus	c.1056	1087–1100	Anne	1665	1702–1714
Henry I Beauclerc	1068	1100–1135	**HOUSE OF HANOVER**		
Stephen of Boulogne	c.1100	1135–1154	George I	1660	1714–1727
HOUSE OF PLANTAGENET			George II	1683	1727–1760
Henry II	1133	1154–1189	George III	1738	1760–1820
Richard I Coeur de Lion	1157	1189–1199	George IV	1762	1820–1830
John Lackland	1167	1199–1216	William IV	1765	1830–1837
Henry III	1207	1216–1272	Victoria	1819	1837–1901
Edward I Longshanks	1239	1272–1307	**HOUSE OF SAXE-COBURG[12]**		
Edward II	1284	1307–1327	Edward VII	1841	1901–1910
Edward III	1312	1327–1377	**HOUSE OF WINDSOR[12]**		
Richard II	1367	1377–1399[4]	George V	1865	1910–1936
HOUSE OF LANCASTER			Edward VIII	1894	1936[13]
Henry IV Bolingbroke	1367	1399–1413	George VI	1895	1936–1952
Henry V	1387	1413–1422	Elizabeth II	1926	1952–

1. Year of end of rule is also that of death, unless otherwise indicated. 2. Dates for Saxon kings are still subject of controversy. 3. Became king of West Saxons in 802; considered (from 828) first king of all England. 4. Died 1400. 5. Henry VI reigned again briefly 1470–71. 6. Nominal queen for 9 days; not counted as queen by some authorities. She was beheaded in 1554. 7. Ruled in Scotland as James VI (1567–1625). 8. Lord Protector. 9. Died 1712. 10. Died 1701. 11. Joint rulers (1689–1694). 12. Name changed from Saxe-Coburg to Windsor in 1917. 13. Was known after his abdication as the Duke of Windsor, died 1972.

During the reign of Henry VIII (1509–47), the church in England asserted its independence from the Roman Catholic Church. Under Edward VI and Mary, the two extremes of religious fanaticism were reached, and it remained for Henry's daughter, Elizabeth I (1558–1603), to set up the Church of England on a moderate basis. In 1588, the Spanish Armada, a fleet sent out by Catholic King Philip II of Spain, was defeated by the English and destroyed during a storm. During Elizabeth's reign, England became a world power. Elizabeth's heir was a Stuart—James VI of Scotland—who joined the two crowns as James I (1603–25). The Stuart kings incurred large debts and were forced either to depend on Parliament for taxes or to raise money by illegal means. In 1642, war broke out between Charles I and a large segment of the Parliament; Charles was defeated and executed in 1649, and the monarchy was abolished. After the death in 1658 of Oliver Cromwell, the lord protector, the Puritan Commonwealth fell to pieces and Charles II was placed on the throne in 1660. The struggle

between the king and Parliament continued, but Charles II knew when to compromise. His brother, James II (1685–88), possessed none of his ability and was ousted by the Revolution of 1688, which confirmed the primacy of Parliament. James's daughter, Mary, and her husband, William of Orange, then became the rulers.

Queen Anne's reign (1702–14) was marked by the Duke of Marlborough's victories over France at Blenheim, Oudenarde, and Malplaquet in the War of the Spanish Succession. England and Scotland meanwhile were joined by the Act of Union (1707). Upon the death of Anne, the distant claims of the Elector of Hanover were recognized, and he became king of Great Britain and Ireland as George I. The unwillingness of the Hanoverian kings to rule resulted in the formation by the royal ministers of a cabinet, headed by a prime minister, which directed all public business. Abroad, the constant wars with France expanded the British Empire all over the globe, particularly in North America and India. This imperial

British Prime Ministers since 1770

Name	Term	Name	Term
Lord North (Tory)	1770–1782	William E. Gladstone (Liberal)	1886–1886
Marquis of Rockingham (Whig)	1782–1782	Marquis of Salisbury (Conservative)	1886–1892
Earl of Shelburne (Whig)	1782–1783	William E. Gladstone (Liberal)	1892–1894
Duke of Portland (Coalition)	1783–1783	Earl of Rosebery (Liberal)	1894–1895
William Pitt, the Younger (Tory)	1783–1801	Marquis of Salisbury (Conservative)	1895–1902
Henry Addington (Tory)	1801–1804	Arthur James Balfour (Conservative)	1902–1905
William Pitt, the Younger (Tory)	1804–1806	Sir H. Campbell-Bannerman (Liberal)	1905–1908
Baron Grenville (Whig)	1806–1807	Herbert H. Asquith (Liberal)	1908–1915
Duke of Portland (Tory)	1807–1809	Herbert H. Asquith (Coalition)	1915–1916
Spencer Perceval (Tory)	1809–1812	David Lloyd George (Coalition)	1916–1922
Earl of Liverpool (Tory)	1812–1827	Andrew Bonar Law (Conservative)	1922–1923
George Canning (Tory)	1827–1827	Stanley Baldwin (Conservative)	1923–1924
Viscount Goderich (Tory)	1827–1828	James Ramsay MacDonald (Labor)	1924–1924
Duke of Wellington (Tory)	1828–1830	Stanley Baldwin (Conservative)	1924–1929
Earl Grey (Whig)	1830–1834	James Ramsay MacDonald (Labor)	1929–1931
Viscount Melbourne (Whig)	1834–1834	James Ramsay MacDonald (Coalition)	1931–1935
Sir Robert Peel (Tory)	1834–1835	Stanley Baldwin (Coalition)	1935–1937
Viscount Melbourne (Whig)	1835–1841	Neville Chamberlain (Coalition)	1937–1940
Sir Robert Peel (Tory)	1841–1846	Winston Churchill (Coalition)	1940–1945
Earl Russell (Whig)	1846–1852	Clement R. Attlee (Labor)	1945–1951
Earl of Derby (Tory)	1852–1852	Sir Winston Churchill (Conservative)	1951–1955
Earl of Aberdeen (Coalition)	1852–1855	Sir Anthony Eden (Conservative)	1955–1957
Viscount Palmerston (Liberal)	1855–1858	Harold Macmillan (Conservative)	1957–1963
Earl of Derby (Conservative)	1858–1859	Sir Alec Frederick Douglas-Home (Conservative)	1963–1964
Viscount Palmerston (Liberal)	1859–1865		
Earl Russell (Liberal)	1865–1866	Harold Wilson (Labor)	1964–1970
Earl of Derby (Conservative)	1866–1868	Edward Heath (Conservative)	1970–1974
Benjamin Disraeli (Conservative)	1868–1868	Harold Wilson (Labor)	1974–1976
William E. Gladstone (Liberal)	1868–1874	James Callaghan (Labor)	1976–1979
Benjamin Disraeli (Conservative)	1874–1880	Margaret Thatcher (Conservative)	1979–1990
William E. Gladstone (Liberal)	1880–1885	John Major (Conservative)	1990–1997
Marquis of Salisbury (Conservative)	1885–1886	Tony Blair (Labor)	1997–

growth was checked by the revolt of the American colonies (1775–81). Struggles with France broke out again in 1793 and during the Napoleonic Wars, which ended at Waterloo in 1815.

The Victorian era, named after Queen Victoria (1837–1901), saw the growth of a democratic system of government that had begun with the Reform Bill of 1832. The two important wars in Victoria's reign were the Crimean War against Russia (1853–56) and the Boer War (1899–1902), the latter enormously extending Britain's influence in Africa. Increasing uneasiness at home and abroad marked the reign of Edward VII (1901–10). Within four years after the accession of George V in 1910, Britain entered World War I when Germany invaded Belgium. The nation was led by coalition cabinets, headed first by Herbert Asquith and then, starting in 1916, by the Welsh statesman David Lloyd George. Postwar labor unrest culminated in the general strike of 1926.

King Edward VIII succeeded to the throne on Jan. 20, 1936, at his father's death, but abdicated on Dec. 11, 1936, (in order to marry an American divorcee, Wallis Warfield Simpson) in favor of his brother, who became George VI.

The efforts of Prime Minister Neville Chamberlain to stem the rising threat of Nazism in Germany failed with the German invasion of Poland on Sept. 1, 1939, which was followed by Britain's entry into World War II on Sept. 3. Allied reverses in the spring of 1940 led to Chamberlain's resignation and the formation of another coalition war cabinet by the Conservative leader, Winston Churchill, who led Britain through most of World War II. Churchill resigned shortly after V-E Day, May 7, 1945, but then formed a "caretaker" government that remained in office until after the parliamentary elections in July, which the Labor Party won overwhelmingly. The new government, formed by Clement R. Attlee, began a moderate socialist program.

(For details of World War II, see Headline History, World War II.)

In 1951, Churchill again became prime minister at the head of a Conservative government. George VI died on Feb. 6, 1952, and was succeeded by his daughter Elizabeth II. Churchill stepped down in 1955 in favor of Sir Anthony Eden, who resigned on grounds of ill health in 1957, and was succeeded by Harold Macmillan and Sir Alec Douglas-Home. In 1964, Harold Wilson led the Labor Party to victory. A lagging economy brought the Conservatives back to power in 1970. Prime Minister Edward Heath won Britain's admission to the European Community. Margaret Thatcher became Britain's first woman prime minister as the Conservatives won 339 seats on May 3, 1979.

An Argentine invasion of the Falkland Islands on April 2, 1982, involved Britain in a war 8,000 miles from the home islands. Although Argentina had long claimed the Falklands, known as the *Malvinas* in Spanish, negotiations were in progress until a month before the invasion. When more than 11,000 Argentine troops on the Falklands surrendered on June 14, 1982, Thatcher declared her intention to garrison the islands indefinitely, together with a naval presence. Although there were continuing economic problems and foreign policy disputes, an upswing in the economy in 1986–87 led Thatcher to call elections for June 11 in which she won a near-unprecedented third consecutive term. Through much, if not all, of 1990 the Conservatives were losing the confidence of the electorate. The unpopularity of her poll tax together with an uncompromising position toward further European integration eroded support within her own party. When John Major won the Conservative Party leadership in November, Thatcher resigned, paving the way for the queen to ask Mr. Major to form a government.

In the middle of a long recession John Major called a national election for April 1992. Confounding many political observers, the Conservatives won but by a far narrower margin than previously. After months of political maneuvering the U.K. ratified the Maastrict Treaty in Aug. 1993.

Eighteen years of Conservative rule ended in May 1997 when Tony Blair and the Labour Party triumphed in the British elections. Blair has been compared to U.S. president Bill Clinton for his youthful, telegenic personality and centrist views. He produced constitutional reform that partially decentralized the U.K., leading to the formation of separate Parliaments in Wales and Scotland by 1999. Britain turned over its colony Hong Kong to China in July 1997.

Blair's controversial meeting in October 1997 with Sinn Fein's president, Gerry Adams, was the first meeting in 76 years between a British prime minister and a Sinn Fein leader. It infuriated numerous factions but was a symbolic gesture in support of the nascent peace talks in Northern Ireland. In 1998 the Good Friday Agreement, strongly supported by Tony Blair, held out the promise of peace between Catholics and Protestants, but talks ran aground in 1999.

Along with the U.S., Britain launched air strikes against Iraq in Dec. 1998 after Saddam Hussein expelled U.N. arms inspectors. Low-grade bombings of Iraq continued throughout 1999. In the spring of 1999, Britain spearheaded the NATO operation in Kosovo, which resulted in Yugoslavian president Slobodan Milosevic's withdrawal from the territory. British peacekeeping forces remain in Kosovo.

In the fall of 1999, Britain and France argued heatedly about France's refusal to allow the importation of British beef. France remained leery of the possibility of infection from bovine spongiform encephalopathy (BSE), commonly known as mad cow disease, despite the fact that the EU had lifted the three-year ban on British beef in August.

In Sept. 2000, as world oil prices hit $35 per barrel, protests by French truck drivers spread to Great Britain. Truck and taxi drivers, joined by farmers, blockaded oil refineries and major roads, demanding that Britain's fuel tax be reduced. They received considerable public support and the protests grew, leading to the closure of 3,000 gas stations around the country. Caught off-guard by the protests, Blair refused to cut the fuel tax and his popularity sank to new lows, with some observers predicting he would be vulnerable in the next election. Government ministers did invoke emergency powers to ration fuel to those who needed it most, and by mid-September the protests diminished.

Northern Ireland

Status: Part of United Kingdom
Area: 5,452 sq. mi. (14,121 sq. km)
Population (1998 est.): 1,688,600
Capital and largest city (1992): Belfast, 287,500.
Monetary unit: British pound sterling (£). **Language:** English. **Religions:** Presbyterian, Church of Ireland, Roman Catholic, Methodist.

Geography Northern Ireland is composed of 26 districts, derived from the boroughs of Belfast and Londonderry and the counties of Antrim, Armagh, Down, Fermanagh, Londonderry, and Tyrone. Together they are commonly called Ulster, though the territory does not include the entire ancient province of Ulster. Predominantly Protestant, it forms the northern part of the island of Ireland, westernmost of the British Isles. It is slightly larger than Connecticut.

Government Northern Ireland is an integral part of the United Kingdom (it has 12 representatives in the British House of Commons), but under the terms of the Government of Ireland Act in 1920, it had a semiautonomous government. In 1972, however, after three years of sectarian violence between Protestants and Catholics that resulted in more than 400 dead and thousands injured, Britain suspended the Ulster Parliament. The Ulster counties became governed directly from London after an attempt to return certain powers to an elected assembly in Belfast.

As a result of the Good Friday Agreement of 1998, a coalition government was to be formed by July 16, 1999, after which the transfer of legislative powers from the British Parliament to the assembly was to take place on the 17th, thereby ending three decades of direct rule from London. Peace talks broke down once again just before the government was to be formed. David Trimble, Protestant leader of the Ulster Unionist Party (UUP) and winner of the 1998 Nobel Peace Prize, was to have been first minister.

History Ulster was part of Catholic Ireland until the reign of Elizabeth I (1558–1603) when, after suppressing three Irish rebellions, the crown confiscated lands in Ireland and settled the Scots Presbyterians in Ulster. Another rebellion in 1641–51, brutally crushed by Oliver Cromwell, resulted in the settlement of Anglican Englishmen in Ulster. Subsequent political policy favoring Protestants and disadvantaging Catholics encouraged further Protestant settlement in Northern Ireland.

Northern Ireland did not separate from the South until William Gladstone presented, in 1886, his proposal for home rule in Ireland. The Protestants in the North feared domination by the Catholic majority. Industry, moreover, was concentrated in the North and dependent on the British market. When World War I began, civil war threatened between the regions. Northern Ireland, however, did not become a political entity until the six counties accepted the Home Rule Bill of 1920. This set up a semiautonomous Parliament in Belfast and a crown-appointed governor advised by a cabinet of the prime minister and eight ministers, as well as a 12-member representation in the House of Commons in London.

When the Republic of Ireland gained sovereignty in 1922, relations improved between North and South, although the Irish Republican Army (I.R.A.), outlawed in recent years, continued the struggle to end the partition of Ireland. In 1966–69, rioting and street fighting between Protestants and Catholics occurred in Londonderry, fomented by extremist nationalist Protestants, who feared the Catholics might attain a local majority, and by Catholics demonstrating for civil rights. These confrontations became known as "the Troubles."

The religious communities, Catholic and Protestant, became hostile armed camps. British troops were brought in to separate them, but themselves became a target of Catholics, particularly by the I.R.A., which by this time had turned into a full-fledged terrorist movement. The goal of the I.R.A. was to eject the British and unify Northern Ireland with the Irish Republic to the south. The Protestants remained tenaciously loyal to the United Kingdom, and various Protestant terrorist organizations pursued the Unionist cause through violence. Various attempts at representational government and power-sharing foundered during the 1970s, and both sides were further polarized. Direct rule from London and the presence of British troops failed to stop the violence.

In Oct. 1977, the 1976 Nobel Peace Prize was awarded to Mairead Corrigan and Betty Williams, founders of the Community of Peace People, a nonsectarian organization dedicated to creating peace in Northern Ireland. Intermittent violence continued, however, and on Aug. 27, 1979, an I.R.A. bomb killed Lord Mountbatten as he was sailing off southern Ireland, heightening tensions. Catholic protests over the death of I.R.A. hunger striker Bobby Sands in 1981 fueled more violence. Riots, sniper fire, and terrorist attacks killed more than 3,200 people between 1969 and 1998. Among the attempts at reconciliation undertaken during the 1980s was the Anglo-Irish Agreement (1985), which, to the dismay of Unionists, marked the first time the Republic of Ireland had been given an official consultative role in the affairs of the province.

In 1997, Northern Ireland made a significant step in the direction of stemming sectarian strife. The first formal peace talks began on Oct. 6 with representatives of eight major Northern Irish political parties participating, a feat that in itself required three years of negotiations. Two smaller Protestant parties, including hard-liner Ian Paisley's Democratic Unionists, boycotted the talks. For the first time, Sinn Fein, the political wing of the I.R.A., won two seats in the British Parliament, which went to Sinn Fein president Gerry Adams and second-in-command Martin McGuinness. Although the election strengthened the I.R.A.'s political legitimacy, it was the I.R.A.'s resumption of the 17-month ceasefire, which had collapsed in Feb. 1996, that gained them a place at the negotiating table.

A landmark settlement, the Good Friday Agreement of April 10, 1998, came after 19 months of intensive negotiations that involved eight of the ten Northern Irish political parties. Chaired by former U.S. senator George Mitchell, the talks were advanced by a high-profile set of mediators, including British prime minister Tony Blair, Irish prime minister Bertie Ahern, and U.S. president Bill Clinton. Two participating groups, the Protestant Ulster Democratic Party and Sinn Fein, were temporarily suspended from the talks because of continued paramilitary activities. The accord called for Protestants to share political power with the minority Catholics, and gave the Republic of Ireland a voice in Northern Irish affairs. In turn, Catholics were to suspend the goal of a united Ireland—a territorial claim that was the raison d'être of the I.R.A. and was written into the Irish Republic's constitution—unless the largely Protestant North voted in favor of such an arrangement, an unlikely occurrence.

The resounding commitment to the settlement was demonstrated in a dual referendum on May 22, 1998: the North approved the accord by a vote of 71% to 29%, and in the Irish Republic 94% favored it. But the deaths of three Catholic boys in July 1998 during the traditional Protestant marches through Catholic neighborhoods was an appalling reminder of the fragility of peace. In October, the Nobel Peace Prize was awarded to John Hume and David Trimble, leaders of

the largest Catholic and Protestant political parties, an incentive for all sides to ensure that this time the peace would last.

In Dec. 1998 the rival Northern Ireland politicians agreed on the organization and contents of the new coalition government, but in June 1999 the peace process again hit an impasse when the I.R.A. refused to disarm prior to the assembly of Northern Ireland's new provincial cabinet. Sinn Fein insisted the I.R.A. would only begin giving up its illegal weapons after the formation of the new government; Unionists demanded disarmament first. As a result, the Ulster Unionists boycotted the assembly session that would have nominated the cabinet to run the new coalition government. The nascent Northern Irish government was stillborn in July 1999.

Subsequent talks on the agreement, which would have ended three decades of direct rule from London, seemed to go nowhere, despite the last-ditch intervention of George Mitchell, who helped engineer the Good Friday Agreement. Finally, at the end of November, David Trimble, leader of the Ulster Unionists, abandoned the seemingly sacrosanct "no guns, no government" position, and took a difficult leap of faith in agreeing to form a government prior to Sinn Fein's disarmament. If the IRA did not begin the destruction of their weapons by Jan. 31, 2000, however, the Ulster Unionists threatened they would withdraw from the Northern Irish Parliament, shutting down the new government. With this compromise in place, the new government was quickly formed, and on Dec. 2, 1999, the British government formally transferred governing power to the Northern Irish parliament. Two leaders of Sinn Fein, Gerry Adams and Martin McGuinness, received seats in the four party, 12-member parliament. By the deadline, Sinn Fein had made little progress toward disarmament, and claimed it had not made any such commitment. As a consequence, the British government suspended the Northern Irish parliament on Feb. 12, 2000. Finally, in May the IRA pledged to begin disarming if the power-sharing was resumed. Protestants agreed, and Britain restored powers to the new government on May 30, 2000, after the I.R.A. announced it had put its arms "beyond use."

Scotland

Status: Part of United Kingdom
First Minister: Jim Wallace (acting) (2000)
Area: 30,414 sq. mi. (78,772 sq. km)
Population (1996 est.): 5,128,000; density per sq. mi.: 168.6
Capital (1995 est.): Edinburgh, 441,620. **Largest City:** Glasgow, 681,470. **Monetary unit:** British pound sterling (£). **Languages:** English, Scots Gaelic. **Religions:** Church of Scotland (established church—Presbyterian), Roman Catholic, Scottish Episcopal Church, Baptist, Methodist

Geography Scotland occupies the northern third of the island of Great Britain. It is bounded by England in the south and on the other three sides by water: by the Atlantic Ocean on the west and north and by the North Sea on the east. Scotland is divided into three physical regions—the Highlands; the Central Lowlands, containing two-thirds of the population; and the Southern Uplands. The western Highland coast is intersected throughout by long, narrow sea lochs, or fjords. Scotland also includes the Outer and Inner Hebrides and other islands off the west coast and the Orkney and Shetland Islands off the north coast. The famous Scottish Highlands include a series of lochs (or lakes), the largest of which is Loch Ness, famous for its mythical monster.

Government England and Scotland have shared a monarch since 1603 and a Parliament since 1707, but in May 1999, Scotland elected its own Parliament for the first time in three centuries. The new Scottish legislature was in part the result of British prime minister Tony Blair's campaign promise to permit devolution, the transfer of local powers from London to Edinburgh. In a Sept. 1997 referendum, 74% of Scotland voted in favor of their own Parliament, which would control most domestic affairs, including health, education, and transportation, and will have powers to legislate and raise taxes. Queen Elizabeth opened the new Parliament on July 2, 1999.

History The first inhabitants of Scotland were the Picts, a Celtic tribe. Between A.D. 82 and A.D. 208, the Romans invaded Scotland, naming it Caledonia. Roman influence over the land, however, was minimal.

The Scots, a Celtic tribe from Ireland, migrated to the west coast of Scotland in about 500. Kenneth McAlpin, King of the Scots, ascended the throne of the Pictish kingdom in about 843, thereby uniting the various Scots and Pictish tribes under one kingdom called Alba. By the 11th century, the monarchy had extended its borders to include much of what is Scotland today.

English influence on the region expanded when Malcolm III, king of Scotland from 1057–93, married an English princess. England's appetite for Scottish land began to grow over 12th and 13th centuries, and in 1296 King Edward I of England successfully invaded Scotland in 1296. The following year Robert the Bruce led a revolt for independence, was crowned king of Scotland (Robert I) in 1306, and after years of battle, defeated the English in 1314 at the Battle of Bannockburn. In 1328 the English finally recognized Scottish independence.

In the 16th century John Knox introduced the Scottish reformation, and the Presbyterian church replaced Catholicism as the official religion. In 1567, Mary, Queen of Scots, a Catholic, was forced to abdicate the Scottish throne, and was later executed by Elizabeth I of England. Mary's son, James VI, was raised as a Protestant, and in 1603, he succeeded Elizabeth on the English throne, as King James I of England. James thus became ruler of both Scotland and England, though the countries remained separate. In 1707, after a century of turmoil, Scotland and England passed the Act of Union, which united Scotland, England, and Wales under one rule as the Kingdom of Great Britain. The House of Hanover replaced the Stuart lineage on the throne in 1714, which caused a rebellion among Scots who still supported the Stuarts. The Jacobites, as the rebels were called, led two uprisings, in 1715 and again in 1745.

With the advent of the Industrial Revolution, Scotland, whose chief product had been textiles, began developing in the industries of shipbuilding, coal mining, iron, and steel. In the late 20th century Scotland concentrated on electronics and high-tech industries. The North Sea has also become an important source of oil and gas.

In May 1999, Scotland elected their first separate Parliament in three centuries. Labour won the largest number of seats in Parliament, defeating the Scottish National Party (SNP), which supports Scotland's independence from Britain. A year later, however, the new Parliament had not lived up to its new promise—a BBC poll found that only 27% of the populace thought Parliament's performance had been good, and 31% considered it poor. At the same time, however, 62% said they wanted Parliament to have even greater powers.

Wales

Status: Part of United Kingdom
First Secretary: Rhodri Morgan (2000)
Area: 8,019 sq. mi. (20,768 sq. km)
Population (1993 est.): 2,906,500
Capital and largest city (1996 est.): Cardiff, 306,600.
 Monetary unit: British pound sterling (£). **Languages:** English, Welsh. **Religions:** Calvinistic Methodist, Church of Wales (disestablished—Anglican), Roman Catholic

Geography Wales lies west of England and is separated from England by the Cambrian Mountains. It is bordered on the northwest, west, and south by the Irish Sea and on the northeast and east by England. Wales is generally hilly; the Snowdon range in the northern part culminates in Mount Snowdon (3,560 ft., 1,085 m), Wales's highest peak.

Government Until 1999, Wales was ruled solely by the U.K. government and a secretary of state. In the referendum of Sept. 18, 1997, Welsh citizens voted to establish a National Assembly. Wales will remain part of the U.K. and the secretary of state for Wales and members of Parliament from Welsh constituencies will continue to have seats in Parliament. Although Wales will control most of its local affairs, unlike Scotland, which in 1999 voted to have its own Parliament, the National Assembly will not be able to legislate and raise taxes. The Welsh assembly officially opened on July 1, 1999.

History The prehistoric peoples of Wales left behind megaliths and other impressive monuments. They were followed by settlements of Celts in the region. The Romans occupied the region from the 1st to the 5th century A.D. Thereafter Angles, Saxons, and Jutes invaded the British island, but left Wales virtually untouched. Beginning in the 8th century, the various Welsh tribes fought with their Anglo-Saxon neighbors to the east, but the Welsh were able to thwart attempted invasions. After William the Conqueror subdued England in 1066, however, his Norman armies marched into Wales in 1093 and occupied portions of it. By 1282, the English conquest of Wales was complete, and in 1284, the Statute of Rhuddlan formalized England's sovereignty over Wales. In 1301, King Edward I gave his son, who later became Edward II, the title Prince of Wales, a gesture meant to indicate the unity and relationship between the two lands. With the exception of Edward II, all subsequent British monarchs have given this title to their eldest son.

In 1400, the Welsh prince Owen Glendower led a revolt against the English, expelling them from much of Wales in just four years. By 1410, however, his rebellion was crushed. In 1485, Henry VII became king of England. A Welshman and the first in the Tudor line, Henry's reign, and that of subsequent Tudors, made English rule more palatable to the Welsh. His son, King Henry VIII, joined England and Wales under the Act of Union in 1536.

The Industrial Revolution of the 19th century transformed Wales and threatened the traditional livelihood of farmers and shepards. In the 20th century, the economy of Wales was based primarily on coal production. After World War I, coal prices dropped; this, coupled with the Great Depression, fueled high unemployment rates and economic uncertainty.

In recent years, a resurgence of the Welsh language and culture demonstrated a stronger national identity among the Welsh, and politically the country moved toward greater self-government (devolution). In 1999, with the strong support of Britain's prime minister Tony Blair, Wales opened the Welsh National Assembly, the first real self-government Wales has had in more than six hundred years.

Dependencies of the United Kingdom

Anguilla

Status: Dependency
Governor: Peter Johnstone (2000)
Chief Minister: Osbourne Fleming (2000)
Area: 35 sq. mi. (91 sq. km)
Population (2000 est.): 11,797; average annual rate of natural increase: 0.96%; birth rate: 15.3/1000; infant mortality rate: 25.4/1000; density per sq. mi.: 337
Capital (1992): The Valley, 1,400. **Monetary unit:** East Caribbean dollar. **Ethnicity/race:** black African.
Literacy: 95% (1984)
Economic summary: GDP/PPP (1997 est.): $81 million; $7,300 per capita. **Real growth rate:** 6.5% (1997 est.). **Inflation:** 0.6% (1997 est.). **Unemployment:** 7% (1992 est.). **Agriculture:** pigeon peas, corn, sweet potatoes, sheep, goats, pigs, cattle, poultry, fish, lobsters. **Labor force** (1992): 4,400; commerce, 36%; services, 29%; construction, 18%; transportation and utilities, 10%; agriculture/forestry/fishing/mining, 4%; manufacturing, 3%. **Industries:** tourism, boat building, offshore financial services. **Exports:** $1.6 million (1997): lobster, fish, livestock, salt. **Imports:** $54.2 million (1997); n.a. **Major trading partners:** n.a.

Anguilla was first colonized in 1650 by English settlers from St. Christopher (St. Kitts) and has since remained a British territory. It was originally part of the West Indies Associated States as a component of the St. Kitts-Nevis-Anguilla Federation. In 1967, Anguilla declared its independence from the federation but Britain did not recognize this action. In Feb. 1969, Anguilla voted to cut all ties with Britain and become an independent republic. In March, Britain landed troops on the island and, on March 30, a truce was signed. In July 1971, Anguilla became a dependency of Britain and two months later Britain ordered the withdrawal of all its troops. A new constitution for Anguilla, effective in Feb. 1976, provided for separate administration and a government of elected representatives. The Associated State of St. Kitts-Nevis-Anguilla ended in 1980 and in 1982 a new Anguillan constitution took effect. In 1997, Anguilla announced that it would build a new airport, with almost double the present runway length, in an effort to increase tourism.

Bermuda

Status: Self-governing dependency
Governor: Thorold Masefield (1997)
Premier: Jennifer Smith (1998)
Area: 20 sq. mi. (52 sq. km)
Population (2000 est.): 62,997; average annual rate of natural increase: 0.5%; birth rate: 12.2/1000; infant mortality rate: 9.8/1000; density per sq. mi.: 3,150
Capital (1994 est.): Hamilton, 1,100. **Monetary unit:** Bermuda dollar. **Ethnicity/race:** black African 61%, white and other 39%. **Literacy rate:** 98% (1970)
Economic summary: GDP/PPP (1997 est.): $1.9 billion; $30,000 per capita. **Real growth rate:** 3% (1997 est.). **Unemployment:** negl. 2% (1995). **Inflation:** 2.1% (1997). **Arable land:** n.a. **Agriculture:** bananas, vegetables, citrus, flowers, dairy products. **Labor force:** 35,296 (1997): clerical, 23%; services, 22%; laborers, 17%; professional and technical, 17%; administrative and managerial, 12%; sales, 7%; agriculture and fishing, 2% (1996). **Industries:** tourism, finance, insurance, structural concrete products, paints, perfumes, pharmaceuticals, ship repairing. **Natural resources:** limestone, sandy beaches, and clear water. **Exports:** $57 million (1997): reexports of pharmaceuticals. **Imports:** $617 million (1997): miscellaneous manufactured articles, machinery and transport equipment, food and live animals, chemicals. **Major trading partners:** Netherlands, Brazil, Canada, U.S., U.K.

Bermuda is an archipelago of about 360 small islands, 580 miles (934 km) east of North Carolina. The largest is (Great) Bermuda, or Main Island. Explored by Juan de Bermúdez, a Spaniard, early in the 16th century, the islands were settled in 1612 by an offshoot of the Virginia Company. Bermuda became a crown colony in 1684.

In 1968, Bermuda was granted a new constitution, its first prime minister, and autonomy, except for foreign relations, defense, and internal security. The predominantly white United Bermuda Party has retained power in four elections against the opposition—the black-led Progressive Labor Party—although Bermuda's population is 61% black. U.S. air and navy bases, which had been leased in 1941 for 99-year terms, closed in 1995, along with Canadian, British army, and Royal Navy. In a referendum held in Aug. 1995, nearly three-fourths of those voting opposed independence. The prime minister's unexpected resignation in March 1997 led the ruling United Bermuda Party to name Pamela Gordon the country's first female and youngest premier. She was succeeded in 1998 by Jennifer Smith.

British Antarctic Territory

Status: Dependency
Commissioner: Peter M. Newton (1992)
Area: 500,000 sq. mi. (1,395,000 sq. km)
Population: no permanent residents

The British Antarctic Territory consists of the South Shetland Islands, South Orkney Islands, and nearby Graham Land on the Antarctic continent, largely uninhabited. They are dependencies of the British crown colony of the Falkland Islands but received a separate administration in 1962, being governed by a British-appointed high commissioner who is governor of the Falklands.

British Indian Ocean Territory

Status: Dependency
Commissioner: David Ross MacLennan (1994)
Administrative headquarters: Victoria, Seychelles
Area: 85 sq. mi. (220 sq. km)

This dependency, consisting of the Chagos Archipelago and other small island groups, was formed in 1965 by agreement with Mauritius and the Seychelles. There is no permanent civilian population in the territory. One of its islands, Diego Garcia (17 sq. mi.), is a joint U.S.-U.K. refueling and support station that was used during the Persian Gulf War (1991).

British Virgin Islands

VIRGIN ISLANDS
Status: Dependency
Governor: Frank Savage (1998)
Chief Minister: Ralph O'Neal (1995)
Area: 59 sq. mi. (153 sq. km)

Population (2000 est.): 19,615; average annual rate of natural increase: 1.1%; birth rate: 15.9/1000; infant mortality rate: 21.1/1000; density per sq. mi.: 332
Capital (1991 census): Road Town (on Tortola): 3,983.
Monetary unit: U.S. dollar. **Literacy rate:** 98% (1970)
Economic summary: GDP/PPP (1997 est.): $183 million; $10,000 per capita. **Real growth rate:** 4.7% (1997). **Inflation:** 6.5% (1997). **Unemployment:** 3% (1995). **Labor force:** 4,911 (1980): tourism, n.a.
Exports: $23.9 million (1996): rum, fresh fish, fruit, animals, gravel, sand. **Imports:** $121.5 million (1996): building materials, automobiles, foodstuffs, machinery.
Major trading partners: Virgin Islands (U.S.), Puerto Rico, U.S.

Some 36 islands (more than 20 are uninhabited) in the Caribbean Sea northeast of Puerto Rico and west of the Leeward Islands, the British Virgin Islands are economically interdependent with the U.S. Virgin Islands to the south. The principal islands are Tortola, Virgin Gorda, Anegada, and Jost Van Dyke. When Christopher Columbus explored the islands in 1493, he found the Carib people living there. By 1596 most of the Caribs had fled or been killed.

The British Virgin Islands were annexed in 1672. The English planters' slave-based sugar plantations declined after slavery was abolished in the first half of the 19th century. The islands received a separate administration in 1956 as a crown colony. In 1997, the British Virgin Islands' government decided to spend $25 million on a three-year development plan to increase tourist facilities. Tourism is the islands' mainstay.

Cayman Islands

Status: Dependency
Governor: Peter Smith (1999)
Area: 118 sq. mi. (190 sq. km)
Population (2000 est.): 34,763; average annual rate of natural increase: 0.9%; birth rate: 14.2/1000; infant mortality rate: 10.4/1000; density per sq. mi.: 348
Capital (1992 est.): George Town (on Grand Cayman), 15,000. **Monetary unit:** Cayman Islands dollar.
Literacy rate: 98% (1970)
Economic summary: GDP/PPP (1997 est.): $930 million; $24,500 per capita. **Inflation:** 2.7% (1997).
Unemployment: 5.1% (1996). **Exports:** $2.65 million (1996): turtle products, manufactured consumer goods. **Imports:** $379.4 million (1996): foodstuffs, manufactured goods. **Major trading partners:** U.S., Trinidad and Tobago, U.K., Netherlands Antilles, Japan.

The Caymans consist of three islands—Grand Cayman (76 sq. mi.; 197 sq. km), Cayman Brac (22 sq. mi.; 57 sq. km), and Little Cayman (20 sq. mi.; 52 sq. km)—situated about 180 miles (290 km) northwest of Jamaica. They were dependencies of Jamaica until 1959, when they became a unit territory within the Federation of the West Indies. In 1962, upon the dissolution of the federation, the Cayman Islands became a British dependency, and a new constitution approved in 1972 provided for a greater degree of autonomy. Tourism and finance are the Cayman Islands' major industries; tourism increased eightfold between the mid-1970s and the early 1990s and there are more than 500 licensed banks and trust companies on the islands.

Channel Islands

Status: Crown dependencies
Lieutenant Governor of Jersey: Sir Michael Wilkes (1995)
Lieutenant Governor of Guernsey: Vice Adm. Sir John Coward (1994)
Area: 120 sq. mi. (311 sq. km)

Populations (2000 est.): Jersey, 88,915; Guernsey, 64,080
Capital of Jersey (1991): St. Helier, 28,123
Capital of Guernsey (1991): St. Peter Port, 16,648.
Monetary units: Guernsey pound; Jersey pound

This group of islands, lying in the English Channel off the northwest coast of France, belonged to the Duchy of Normandy until it passed to the English Crown with the Norman conquest of 1066. It was the only British possession occupied by Germany during World War II. English and French are commonly spoken (though use of the latter is declining), and a Norman-French patois survives.

For administrative purposes, the islands are divided into the Bailiwick of Jersey (45 sq. mi.; 117 sq. km), including the Ecrehous rocks and Les Minquiers, and the Bailiwick of Guernsey (30 sq. mi.; 78 sq. km), including Alderney (3 sq. mi.; 7.8 sq. km); Sark (2 sq. mi.; 5.2 sq. km), Herm, Jethou, Brechou, and other smaller islands. The Channel Islands enjoy tax sovereignty, and their exports are protected by British tariff barriers. Financial services, tourism, market gardening, and dairy farming are important industries.

Falkland Islands and Dependencies

Status: Dependency
Governor: Donald Lamont (1999)
Chief Executive: R. Sampson
Area: 4,700 sq. mi. (12,173 sq. km)
Population (1998 est.): 2,805
Capital (1991): Stanley (on East Falkland), 1,643.
Monetary unit: Falkland Island pound
Exports: $7.6 million (1995): wool, hides, meat. **Imports:** $24.7 million (1995): fuel, food and drink, building materials, clothing. **Major trading partners:** U.K., Netherlands, Japan, Netherland Antilles.

This sparsely inhabited dependency consists of a group of islands in the South Atlantic, about 250 miles (402 km) east of the South American mainland. The largest islands are East Falkland and West Falkland. The English captain John Strong made the first recorded landing in the Falklands in 1690. The islands passed between the French, Spanish, and British until 1820, when the Argentine government proclaimed its sovereignty. In 1833 a British force expelled the few remaining Argentine officials from the island without firing a shot, and in 1841 a British civilian lieutenant-governor was appointed for the Falklands. Colonial status was granted to the Falklands in 1892. Argentina, calling the islands *Las Islas Malvinas*, regularly protested Britain's occupation of the islands. On April 2, 1982, Argentina's military government invaded the Falklands. The Falkland Islands war ended 10 weeks later with the surrender of the Argentine forces at Stanley to British troops, who had forcibly reoccupied the islands. Argentina still claims the islands. But an agreement between Argentina and the United Kingdom in 1995 sought to defuse licensing and sovereignty conflicts that would dampen foreign interest in exploiting the Falkland Islands' potential oil reserves.

The Falkland Islands' dependencies are South Georgia Island (1,450 sq. mi.; 3,756 sq. mi.), the South Sandwich Islands, and other islets. Three former dependencies—Graham Land, the South Shetland Islands, and the South Orkney Islands—were established as a new British dependency, the British Antarctic Territory, in 1962.

Gibraltar

Status: Self-governing dependency
Governor: David Durie (2000)
Chief Minister: Peter Caruana (1996)
Area: 2.25 sq. mi. (5.8 sq. km)
Population (2000 est.): 29,481; average annual rate of natural increase: 0.57%; birth rate: 14.1/1000; infant mortality rate: 5.6/1000; density per sq. mi.: 13,103.
Monetary unit: Gibraltar pound. **Literacy rate:** 99%
Economic summary: GDP/PPP (1997 est.): $500 million; $17,500 per capita. **Exports:** $83.7 million (f.o.b., 1995): reexports of petroleum, manufactured goods, other. **Imports:** $778 million (c.i.f., 1995): fuel, manufactured goods, and foodstuffs. **Major trading partners:** U.K, Morocco, Portugal, Netherlands, Spain, U.S., Germany, Japan.

Gibraltar, at the south end of the Iberian Peninsula, is a rocky promontory commanding the western entrance to the Mediterranean. Aside from its strategic importance, it is also a free port, naval base, and coaling station. It was captured by the Moorish leader Tarik, crossing from Africa into Spain in A.D. 711, and its name is derived from the Arabic, *Jabal-al-Tarik* (Mount of Tarik). In the 15th century, it passed to the Moorish ruler of Granada and later became Spanish. It was captured by an Anglo-Dutch force in 1704 during the War of the Spanish Succession and passed to Great Britain by the Treaty of Utrecht in 1713. Since then Spain has continually laid claims to it. Most of the inhabitants of Gibraltar are of Spanish, Italian, and Maltese descent, and in 1981 Gibraltarians were granted full British citizenship.

Spanish efforts to recover Gibraltar culminated in a referendum in 1967 in which the residents voted overwhelmingly to retain their link with Britain. In response, Spain sealed Gibraltar's land border between 1969 and 1985. The last British military battalion on the "Rock" was withdrawn in March 1991.

Isle of Man

Status: Self-governing crown dependency
Lieutenant Governor: Ian David Macfadyen (2000)
Chief Minister: Donald James Gelling (1996)
Area: 221 sq. mi. (572 sq. km)
Population (2000 est.): 73,117; average annual rate of natural increase: −0.03%; birth rate: 11.7/1000; infant mortality rate: 6.5/1000; density per sq. mi.: 331
Capital (1991): Douglas, 22,214. **Monetary unit:** Isle of Man pound

The Isle of Man is situated in the Irish Sea, equidistant from Scotland, Ireland, and England. Among its earliest inhabitants were Celts, and their language, Manx, which is closely related to Irish and Scottish Gaelic, remained the everyday speech of the people until the first half of the 19th century. Manx now has no native speakers. Norse (Viking) invasions began about A.D. 800, and the island was a dependency of Norway until 1266. During this period the Isle of Man came under a Scandinavian system of government that has remained practically unchanged ever since. The island came under the control of England in 1341. After allowing a succession of feudal lords rule the island, the British Parliament purchased sovereignty over the island in 1765. The Isle of Man continues to be administered according to its own laws by a government composed of the lieutenant-governor, a legislative council, and a House of Keys, one of the most ancient legislative assemblies in the world.

Leeward Islands

SEE BRITISH VIRGIN ISLANDS; MONTSERRAT.

Montserrat

Status: Dependency
Governor: Tony Abbot (1997)
Chief Minister: David Brandt (1997)
Area: 38 sq. mi. (98 sq. km)
Population (2000 est.): 6,409; average annual rate of natural increase: 0.9%; birth rate: 17.5/1000; infant mortality rate: 9.1/1000; density per sq. mi.: 169
Capital (1991 est.): Plymouth, 2,500. **Monetary unit:** East Caribbean dollar
Economic summary: GDP/PPP (1997 est.): $36 million; per capita n.a. **Real growth rate:** −18.5% (1997 est.). **Inflation:** 5% (1997 est.). **Labor force:** 4,521. [Note: later substantially lowered by flight of people from volcanic activity]. **Exports:** $8.2 million (1997): electronic components, plastic bags, apparel, hot peppers, live plants, cattle. **Imports:** $26.1 million (1997): machinery and transportation equipment, foodstuffs, manufactured goods, fuel, lubricants, and related materials.

The island of Montserrat is in the Lesser Antilles of the West Indies. Until 1956, it was a division of the Leeward Islands. In 1958 Montserrat joined the Federation of the West Indies, remaining a member until that organization's dissolution in 1962. Unlike most other British West Indies possessions, Montserrat, with its weak economy, has not vigorously sought independence. The Soufrière Hills volcano began erupting in 1995 and the situation continued to worsen through 1998, with the capital, Plymouth, destroyed and the southern and central parts of the British colony having been evacuated. Only about 4,000 people were left in the northern "safe zone" in 1998 after thousands had moved to nearby Antigua, Britain, or other parts of the Caribbean.

Pitcairn Island

Status: Dependency
Governor: Martin Williams (nonresident) (1998)
Island Magistrate: Jay Warren (1993)
Area: 1.75 sq. mi. (4.5 sq. km)
Population (July 1998 est.): 50; density per sq. mi.: 30
Capital: Adamstown

Pitcairn Island, in the South Pacific about midway between Australia and South America, consists of the island of Pitcairn and the three uninhabited islands of Henderson, Duicie, and Oeno. Pitcairn was settled in 1790 by British mutineers from the ship *Bounty*, commanded by Capt. William Bligh. One of the most remote islands in the world, it was annexed as a British colony in 1838. Overpopulation forced removal of the settlement to Norfolk Island in 1856, but about 40 persons soon returned.

The descendants of First Mate Fletcher Christian, the 8 other mutineers, and the dozen or so Tahitians who accompanied them still inhabit the island. In addition to English, the residents of Pitcairn speak a dialect that is a mixture of Tahitian and 18th-century English.

St. Helena

Status: Dependency
Governor: David Hollamby (1999)
Area: 158 sq. mi. (410 sq. km)
Population (2000 est.): 7,212; average annual rate of natural increase: 0.76%; birth rate: 13.7/1000; infant mortality rate: 23.2/1000; density per sq. mi.: 46
Capital (1987): Jamestown, 1,332. **Monetary unit:** Pound sterling. **Literacy rate:** 97% (1987)

St. Helena is a remote volcanic island in the South Atlantic about 1,100 miles (1,770 km) from the west coast of Africa. It is famous as Napoleon's place of exile (1815–21). The island was discovered in 1502 by João da Nova, a Spanish navigator in the service of Portugal. It was taken for England in 1659 by the East India Company and was brought under the direct government of the crown in 1834. After the opening of the Suez Canal, in 1870, St. Helena's importance as a port of call diminished. About two-thirds of the colony's budget is provided by the United Kingdom in the form of a subsidy.

St. Helena has two dependencies: Ascension (34 sq. mi.; 88 sq. km), an island about 700 miles (1,127 km) northwest of St. Helena; and Tristan da Cunha (40 sq. mi.; 104 sq. km), a group of six islands about 1,500 miles (2,414 km) south-southwest of St. Helena.

Turks and Caicos Islands
Status: Dependency
Governor: Mervyn Jones (2000)
Chief Minister: Derek H. Taylor (1995)
Area: 193 sq. mi. (500 sq. km)
Population (2000 est.): 17,502; average annual rate of natural increase: 2.1%; birth rate: 25.7/1000; infant mortality rate: 18.7/1000; density per sq. mi.: 91
Capital (1990): Cockburn Town, 3,720. **Monetary unit:** U.S. dollar. **Literacy rate:** 98% (1970)
Economic summary: GDP/PPP (1997 est.): $117 million; $7,700 per capita. **Real growth rate:** 4% (1997 est.).
Labor force: 4,848 (1990 est.): government, 33%; agriculture and fishing, 20%; significant numbers in tourism and financial and other services (1997 est.).
Exports: $4.7 million (1993): lobster, dried and fresh conch, conch shells. **Imports:** $46.6 million (1993): food and beverages, tobacco, clothing, manufactures, construction materials. **Major trading partners:** U.S., U.K.

These two groups of islands are near the Bahamas in the Caribbean. The principal islands in the Turks group are Grand Turk and Salt Cay; the principal islands in the Caicos group are South Caicos, East Caicos, Middle (or Grand) Caicos, North Caicos, Providenciales, and West Caicos. The islands were not settled by Europeans until 1678, when British colonists from Bermuda established a salt-panning industry. The islands were at first placed under the Bahamas government, but in 1874 they became dependencies of the colony of Jamaica. Following Jamaica's independence, they became a British crown colony. The salt production industry, the islands' economic mainstay, ceased in 1964 and gave way to tourism, offshore financial services, and fishing.

United States
THE UNITED STATES OF AMERICA
President: William J. Clinton (1993)
Vice President: Albert A. Gore, Jr. (1993)
Land area: 3,761,363 sq. mi. (9,629,091 sq. km)
Resident population (2000 est.): 275,562,673; average annual rate of natural increase: 0.55%); birth rate: 14.2/1000; infant mortality rate: 6.8/1000; density per sq. mi.: 73
(1990 census): 248,709,873 (change 1980–1990: 9.8%). White: 199,686,070 (80.3%); Black: 29,986,060 (12.1%); American Indian, Eskimo, or Aleut: 1,959,234 (0.8%); Asian or Pacific Islander: 7,273,662 (2.9%); Other Race: 9,804,847 (3.9%); Hispanic origin[1]: 22,354,059 (9.0%); (average annual rate of natural increase: 0.55%); birth rate: 14.3/1000; infant mortality rate: 6.3/1000; density per sq. mi.: 77

Capital (1990 census.): Washington, D.C., 606,900.
Largest cities (1998 est.): New York: city proper, 7,420,166; metro. area (2000 est.), 20,250,000; Los Angeles: city proper, 3,597,556; metro. area (2000 est.), 16,150,000; Chicago, 2,802,079; Houston, 1,786,691; Philadelphia, 1,436,287; San Diego, 1,220,666; Phoenix, 1,198,064; San Antonio, 1,114,130; Dallas, 1,075,894; Detroit, 970,196.
Monetary unit: dollar. **Languages:** predominantly English, sizable Spanish-speaking minority. **Ethnicity/race:** white 83.4%, black 12.4%, Asian 3.3%, Native American 0.8% (1992). **Religions:** Protestant, 61%; Roman Catholic, 25%; Jewish, 2%; other, 5%; none, 7%. **Literacy rate:** 97% (1980)
Economic summary: GDP/PPP (1998 est.): $8.511 trillion; $31,500 per capita. **Real growth rate:** 3.8%. **Inflation:** 1.6%. **Unemployment:** 4.5%. **Arable land:** 19%. **Agriculture:** wheat, other grains, corn, fruit, vegetables, cotton, beef, pork, poultry, dairy products, forest products, fish. **Labor force:** 137.7 million (includes unemployed, 1998): managerial and professional, 29.6%; technical, sales, and administrative support, 29.3%; manufacturing, mining, transportation, and crafts, 24.8%; services, 13.6%; farming, forestry, and fishing, 2.7%. **Industries:** leading industrial power in the world, highly diversified and technologically advanced; petroleum, steel, motor vehicles, aerospace, telecommunications, chemicals, electronics, food processing, consumer goods, lumber, mining. **Natural resources:** coal, oil, copper, gold, silver, minerals, timber. **Exports:** $663 billion (f.o.b., 1998 est.): capital goods, automobiles, industrial supplies and raw materials, consumer goods, agricultural products. **Imports:** $912 billion (c.i.f., 1998 est.): crude oil and refined petroleum products, machinery, automobiles, consumer goods, industrial raw materials, food and beverages. **Major trading partners:** Canada, western Europe, Japan, Mexico, China.

1. Persons of Hispanic origin can be of any race.

Government Federal republic.

The president is elected for a four-year term and may be reelected only once. The bicameral Congress consists of the 100-member Senate, elected to a six-year term with one-third of the seats becoming vacant every two years, and the 435-member House of Representatives, elected every two years. The minimum voting age is 18. (*See also* Profile of the United States, U.S. States, U.S. Cities, U.S. Statistics, and U.S. Government and History.)

U.S. Territories and Outlying Areas

Puerto Rico
COMMONWEALTH OF PUERTO RICO
Governor: Pedro Rosselló, New Progressive Party (1993; reelected 1997)
Capital and largest city (1990 pop.): San Juan, 437,745. **Other large cities (1990 pop.):** Bayamón, 220,262; Ponce, 190,900; Carolina, 177,806
Land area: 3,459 sq. mi. (8,959 sq. km)
2000 est. population: 3,915,798; average annual rate of natural increase: 0.8%; birth rate: 15.5/1000; infant mortality rate: 9.7/1000; density per sq. mi.: 1,132
Currency: U.S. dollars. **Languages:** Spanish and English (both official). **Ethnicity/race:** Almost entirely Hispanic. **Religions:** Roman Catholic, 85%; Protestant denominations and other, 15%. **Literacy rate:** 89% (1980)
Economic summary: GDP/PPP (1998 est.): $34.7 billion; $9,000 per capita. **Real growth rate:** 3.1% (1998 est.). **Inflation:** 5.7% (1998 est.).

Unemployment: 13% (FY96/97 est.). **Agriculture:** sugarcane, coffee, pineapples, plantains, bananas, livestock products, chickens. **Labor force:** 1.3 million (1996): government, 19%; trade, 17%; manufacturing, 13%; construction, 5%; other, 32%. **Industries:** pharmaceuticals, electronics, apparel, food products, tourism. **Natural resources:** some copper and nickel, potential for onshore and offshore oil. **Exports:** $30.3 billion (f.o.b., 1998): pharmaceuticals, electronics, apparel, canned tuna, rum, beverage concentrates, medical equipment. **Imports:** $21.8 billion (c.i.f., 1996): chemicals, machinery and equipment, clothing, food, fish, petroleum products. **Major trading partner:** U.S.

The Commonwealth of Puerto Rico is located in the Caribbean Sea, about 1,000 miles east-southeast of Miami, Fla. A possession of the United States, it consists of the island of Puerto Rico plus the adjacent islets of Vieques, Culebra, and Mona. Puerto Rico has a mountainous tropical ecosystem with very little flat land and few mineral resources.

Puerto Rico's executive power resides in the governor, who is elected directly for a term of four years. A bicameral legislature consists of a 27-member Senate and a 51-member House of Representatives, all elected for four-year terms. From 1940 to 1968, Puerto Rican politics was dominated by a party advocating voluntary association with the U.S. Since then, the New Progressive Party, a party favoring U.S. statehood, has won five of the last eight gubernatorial elections. Puerto Ricans have twice voted to determine their political status. In 1967, the outcome was Commonwealth 60%; statehood 39%; independence 1%. In 1993, Commonwealth dropped to 48.6%; statehood rose to 46.3%; independence polled 4.4%; and 0.6% of the ballots were blank or spoiled.

Under the Commonwealth formula, residents of Puerto Rico lack voting representation in Congress and the right to participate in presidential elections. Also, funding caps limit their access to several key federal programs. As U.S. citizens, Puerto Ricans are subject to military service and most federal laws. Residents of the Commonwealth pay no federal income tax on locally generated earnings, but Puerto Rico government income-tax rates are set at a level that closely parallels federal-plus-state levies on the mainland.

When Christopher Columbus arrived there in 1493, the island was inhabited by the peaceful Arawak Indians, who were being challenged by the warlike Carib Indians. Puerto Rico remained economically undeveloped until 1830, when the island gradually developed a plantation economy founded on three export crops: sugarcane, coffee, and tobacco. After Puerto Ricans began to press for political independence, the island was granted broad powers of self-government by Spain in 1897. But during the Spanish-American War of 1898 American troops invaded the island and Spain ceded it to the U.S. Since then, Puerto Rico has remained an unincorporated U.S. territory. Its people were granted American citizenship under the Jones Act in 1917; were permitted to elect their own governor, beginning in 1948; and now fully administer their internal affairs under a constitution approved by the U.S. Congress in 1952. In spite of broad popular support for the autonomy of the Commonwealth government and a rapidly modernizing industrial society, there were expressions of dissatisfaction. Puerto Rican extremists dramatized their desire for independence with an attempt to assassinate President Tru-

man on Nov. 1, 1950, and on March 1, 1954, they wounded five congressmen in an attack in the U.S. Capitol.

A self-help program of economic development and social welfare (called "Operation Bootstrap") was forged in the 1940s by Puerto Rican leader and subsequent four-time governor Luis Muñoz Marín. In a little more than four decades, much of the island's crushing poverty was eliminated. This was done partly through emphasis on the development of manufacturing and service industries, the latter related to an enormous growth in tourism. Also during this period, many Puerto Ricans migrated to large cities on the mainland U.S.

Puerto Rico is a major hub of Caribbean commerce, finance, tourism, and communications. San Juan is one of the world's busiest cruise-ship ports, and Puerto Rico's standard of living continues to be among the highest in the hemisphere. Its future political status, however, remains unclear. On March 4, 1998, the U.S. House of Representatives passed a bill that called for binding elections in Puerto Rico to decide the island's permanent political status.

Guam

TERRITORY OF GUAM

Governor: Carl T. C. Gutierrez (1995)
Capital: Agaña; population (1990) 1,139
Land area: 212 sq. mi. (549 sq. km)
2000 est. population: 154,623; average annual rate of natural increase: 2.2%; birth rate: 26.2/1000; infant mortality rate: 6.8/1000; density per sq. mi.: 729. **1996 est. net migration:** 3 migrants per 1,000 population.
Languages: English and Chamorro, most residents are bilingual; Japanese also widely spoken. **Ethnicity/race:** Chamorro 47%, Filipino 25%, Caucasian 10%, Chinese, Japanese, Korean, and other, 18%.
Religions: Roman Catholic, 98% and other 2%.
Literacy rate: 96% (1980). **Currency:** U.S. dollars
Economic summary: GDP/PPP (1996 est.): $3 billion; $19,000 per capita. **Real growth rate:** n.a. **Inflation:** 4% (1992 est.). **Unemployment:** 2% (1992 est.).
Labor force: 65,660 (1995): services, 33%; federal and territorial government, 31%; trade, 21%; construction, 12%; other, 3%. **Industries:** U.S. military, tourism, construction, transshipment services, concrete products, printing and publishing, food processing, textiles. **Exports:** $86.1 million (f.o.b., 1992): mostly transshipments of refined petroleum products, construction materials, fish, food and beverage products. **Imports:** $202.4 million (c.i.f., 1992): petroleum and petroleum products, food, manufactured goods. **Major trading partners:** U.S., Japan.

Guam is the largest and southernmost island in the Marianas Archipelago. The island is sharply divided into a northern coralline limestone plateau and a southern chain of volcanic hills. Today Guam is an unincorporated, organized territory of the United States. The people of Guam have been U.S. citizens since 1950. They have been represented in the U.S. Congress since 1973 by a nonvoting delegate, but do not participate in presidential elections. The executive branch includes a popularly elected governor, who serves a four-year term. The legislative branch is a 21-member unicameral legislature whose members are elected every two years.

Guam was probably visited by the Portuguese navigator Ferdinand Magellan (sailing for Spain) in 1521. The island was formally claimed by Spain in 1565, and its people were forced into submission and conversion to Roman Catholicism, beginning in 1668. After the Spanish-American War of 1898, Spain ceded Guam to the United States. From 1899 to 1949, the U.S. Navy administered Guam, except during 1941–44, when Japanese forces seized and occupied the island. Guam was liberated by American military forces in the summer of 1944. Guam's economy is based on two main sources of revenue: tourism and U.S. military spending (U.S. naval and air force bases occupy one-third of the land on Guam).

U.S. Virgin Islands
VIRGIN ISLANDS OF THE UNITED STATES

Governor: Charles Turnbull (1998)
Capital: Charlotte Amalie (on St. Thomas), population (1990): 12,331
Land area: 140 sq. mi (363 sq. km): St. Croix, 84 sq. mi. (218 sq. km); St. Thomas, 32 sq. mi (83 sq. km); St. John, 20 sq. mi. (52 sq. km)
Population 2000: 120,917; average annual rate of natural increase: 1.1%; birth rate: 16/1000; infant mortality rate: 9.6/1000; density per sq. mi.: 864. **Languages:** English (official), but Spanish and French are also spoken. **Ethnicity/race:** West Indian 74% (45% born in the Virgin Islands and 29% born elsewhere in the West Indies), U.S. mainland 13%, Puerto Rican 5%, other 8%, black 80%, white 15%, other 5%, 14% of Hispanic origin. **Religions:** Baptist, 42%; Roman Catholic, 34%; Episcopalian, 17%; other, 7%. **Literacy rate:** 90%. **Currency:** U.S. dollars
Economic summary: GDP/PPP (1987): $1.2 billion; $12,500 per capita. **Real growth rate:** n.a. **Inflation:** n.a. **Unemployment:** 6.2% (March 1994). **Labor force:** 47,443 (1990): services, 62%; industry, 20%; agriculture, 1%; other, 17%. **Agriculture:** truck garden products, fruit, vegetables, sorghum, Senepol cattle. **Industries:** tourism, petroleum refining, watch assembly, rum distilling, construction, pharmaceuticals, textiles, electronics. **Exports:** $1.8 billion (f.o.b., 1992): refined petroleum products. **Imports:** $2.2 billion (c.i.f., 1992): crude oil, foodstuffs, consumer goods, building materials. **Major trading partners:** U.S., Puerto Rico.

The Virgin Islands, consisting of nine main islands and some 75 islets, were explored by Columbus in 1493. They were originally inhabited by the Carib Indians. Since 1666, England has held six of the main islands; the remaining three (St. Croix, St. Thomas, and St. John), as well as about 50 of the islets, were eventually acquired by Denmark, which named them the Danish West Indies. In 1917, these islands were purchased by the U.S. from Denmark for $25 million.

Congress granted U.S. citizenship to Virgin Islanders in 1927. Universal suffrage was given in 1936 to all persons who could read and write the English language. The governor was elected by popular vote for the first time in 1970; previously he had been appointed by the president of the U.S. A unicameral 15-person legislature serves the Virgin Islands, and congressional legislation gave the islands a nonvoting representative in Congress. Residents of the islands substantially enjoy the same rights as those enjoyed by mainlanders with one important exception: citizens of the U.S. Virgin Islands who are residents may not vote in presidential elections. Independence appears not to be the goal for the islands, and statehood continues to be only a remote possibility.

Tourism is the primary economic activity, accounting for most of the GDP and 70% of employment. All goods made in the Virgin Islands qualify for duty-free entry into the United States.

American Samoa
TERRITORY OF AMERICAN SAMOA

Governor: Tauese Pita Sunia (1997)
Capital: Pago Pago, population 1990: 3,519
Land area: 77 sq. mi (199 sq. km)
Population (2000 est.): 65,446; average rate of natural increase: 2.2%; birth rate 25.8/1000; infant mortality rate: 10.6/1000; density per sq. mi.: 850. **Languages:** Samoan (closely related to Hawaiian and other Polynesian languages) and English; most people are bilingual. **Ethnicity/race:** Samoan (Polynesian) 89%, Tongan 4%, Caucasian 2%, other 6%. **Religions:** Christian Congregationalist, 50%; Roman Catholic, 20%; Protestant denominations and other,30%. **Literacy rate:** 97% (1980). **Currency:** U.S. dollars
Economic summary: GDP/PPP (1995): $150 million; $2,600 per capita. **Real growth rate:** n.a. **Inflation:** n.a. **Unemployment:** 12% (1991). **Agriculture:** bananas, coconuts, vegetables, taro, breadfruit, yams, copra, pineapples, papayas, dairy products, livestock. **Labor force:** 13,949 (1996): tuna canneries, 34%; government, 33%; other, 33% (1990). **Industries:** tuna canneries (largely dependent on foreign fishing vessels), handicrafts. **Exports:** $313 million (1996): canned tuna. **Imports:** $471 million (1996): materials for canneries, food, petroleum products, machinery and parts. **Major trading partners:** U.S., Japan, New Zealand, Australia, Fiji.

American Samoa, a group of five volcanic islands and two coral atolls located some 2,600 miles south of Hawaii in the South Pacific, is an unincorporated, unorganized territory of the U.S. It includes the eastern Samoan islands of Tutuila, Aunu'u, and Rose; three islands (Ta'u, Olosega, and Ofu) of the Manu'a group; and Swains Island. Around 1000 B.C. Protopolynesians established themselves in the islands, and their descendants are one of the few remaining societies of Polynesians. The Dutch navigator Jacob Roggeveen sighted the Manu'a Islands in 1722. American Samoa has been a territory of the United States since April 17, 1900, when the High Chiefs of Tutuila signed the first of two Deeds of Cession for the islands to the U.S. (Congress ratified the Deeds in 1929). Swains Island, which is privately owned, came under U.S. administration in 1925.

Until World War II the United States operated a coaling station and naval base in Pago Pago. During the war, the islands were an important U.S. Marines staging area. In 1960 American Samoa ratified its territorial constitution and has since developed a modern, self-governing political system. American Samoans elect a governor, lieutenant governor, and legislature. The legislature (Fono) consists of two houses: the Senate, selected by village chiefs (matai) for four-year terms, and the House of Representatives, elected by the general population for two-year terms. The people of American Samoa are U.S. nationals, not U.S. citizens, but many have become naturalized American citizens. Economic activity is strongly linked to the U.S., with which American Samoa does 80%–90% of its foreign trade. Tuna fishing and tuna processing plants are the backbone of the private sector, with canned tuna the primary export ($300 million annually). Transfers from the U.S. government add substantially to American Samoa's economic well-being.

Northern Mariana Islands

THE COMMONWEALTH OF THE NORTHERN MARIANA ISLANDS, OR CNMI

Governor: Pedro P. Tenorio (1998)
Capital: Chalan Kanoa (on Saipan)
Total area: 184.17 sq. mi. (477 sq. km)
Population (2000 est.): 71,912; average annual rate of natural increase: 1.8%; birth rate: 20.9/1000; infant mortality: 5.8/1000; density per sq. mi.: 390. Most reside on Saipan, which is also the seat of government; Rota, Agrihan, and Tinian are also inhabited. About half the population are U.S. citizens; the remainder are temporary alien workers. **Languages:** English (official), Chamorro, Carolinian. **Ethnicity/race:** Chamorro, Carolinians, other Micronesians, Caucasian, Japanese, Chinese, Korean. **Religion:** Primarily Roman Catholic. **Literacy rate:** 97% (1980). **Currency:** U.S. dollars
Economic summary: The government of the CNMI benefits substantially from U.S. financial assistance. **GDP/PPP** (1996 est.): $524 million; $9,300 per capita. **Labor force:** 6,006 total indigenous labor force; 2,699 unemployed; 28,717 foreign workers (1995). **Exports:** $1 billion (1998) mostly garments to the U.S. **Imports:** n.a. **Major trading partners:** U.S., Japan.

The Northern Mariana Islands, east of the Philippines and south of Japan, include the islands of Rota, Saipan, Tinian, Pagan, Guguan, Agrihan, and Aguijan. Although sighted by Ferdinand Magellan in 1521 as he sailed for Spain, the islands were not settled by Europeans until 1668, when missionaries converted the indigenous Chamorro people to Catholicism. They were ruled successively by Spain, Germany, and Japan before they became a U.N. Trusteeship (administered by the U.S.) after World War II. The Commonwealth of the Northern Mariana Islands (CNMI) became part of the United States on Nov. 1986. Spanish cultural traditions are still strong.

In recent years, Saipan's garment industry has been accused of luring thousands of Asians to the island with promises of good pay. Once there, the workers find themselves virtual prisoners forced to work in squalid sweat shops. Because of Saipan's territorial status, it is able to pay low wages and at the same time claim its clothing is "Made in the USA," sidestepping import duties and tariffs.

Midway Islands

Total area: 2 sq. mi. (5 sq. km)
Population (1995 est.): no indigenous inhabitants; 453 U.S. military personnel.

The Midway Islands consist of a circular atoll, 6 miles in diameter, that encloses two islands. Lying about 1,150 miles west-northwest of Hawaii, the islands were first explored by Captain N. C. Brooks on July 5, 1859, in the name of the United States. The atoll was formally declared a U.S. possession in 1867, and in 1903 Theodore Roosevelt made it a naval reservation. The island was renamed "Midway" by the U.S. Navy in recognition of its geographic location on the route between California and Japan. Air traffic across the Pacific increased the island's importance in the mid-1930s; the San Francisco–Manila mail route included a regular stop on Midway. Its military importance was soon recognized, and the navy began building an air and submarine base there in 1940. The Battle of Midway, which took place from June 3–6, 1942, was considered a turning point in World War II. After the war, the strategic importance of the island declined; the Midway stop for commercial air traffic was eliminated in 1950, and the air base closed in 1992.

Wake Island

Total area: 2.5 sq. mi. (6.5 sq. km)
Comparative size: about 11 times the size of the Mall in Washington, D.C.
Population (1995 est.): no indigenous inhabitants; 302 U.S. military personnel and civilian contractors.
Economy: The economic activity is limited to providing services to U.S. military personnel and contractors on the island. All food and manufactured goods must be imported.

Wake Island, about halfway between Midway and Guam, is an atoll consisting of the three islets of Wilkes, Peale, and Wake. They were discovered by the British in 1796 and annexed by the U.S. in 1899. In 1938, Pan American Airways established a seaplane base, and Wake Island was used as a commercial base for several years. On Dec. 8, 1941, it was attacked by the Japanese, who finally took possession on Dec. 23. It was surrendered by the Japanese on Sept. 4, 1945.

Johnston Atoll

Land area: 1.08 sq. mi. (2.8 sq. km); density per sq. mi.: 1,111
Population (July 1997 est.): no indigenous inhabitants; 1,200 U.S. military and civilian personnel

Johnston is a coral atoll about 700 miles southwest of Hawaii. It consists of four small islands—Johnston Island, Sand Island, Hikina Island, and Akau Island—which lie on a 9-mile-long reef. The atoll was discovered by Capt. Charles James Johnston of HMS *Cornwallis* in 1807. In 1858 it was claimed by Hawaii, and later became a U.S. possession. Johnston Atoll is a Naval Defensive Sea Area and Airspace Reservation and is closed to the public. In the early 1990s, the U.S. government opened a facility for destroying chemical weapons on Johnston Atoll.

Baker, Howland, and Jarvis Islands

These Pacific islands were claimed by the United States under the Guano Act of 1856 on May 13, 1936. Guano, composed of phosphates, was used as fertilizer in the 19th century, and its collection was a highly lucrative business. Through the Guano Act the U.S. gained a total of 79 tiny territories around the world; it still controls eight of them. Baker Island is a saucer-shaped atoll with an area of approximately one square mile about 1,650 miles from Hawaii. Howland Island, 36 miles to the northwest, is 1 mile long and half a mile wide. Howland Island is related to the disappearance of Amelia Earhart and Fred J. Noonan during their round-the-world flight in 1937—Howland Island was the destination they were headed for when they disappeared. Jarvis Island is several hundred miles to the east.

Kingman Reef

Kingman Reef, located about 1,000 miles south of Hawaii, was discovered by Capt. E. Fanning in 1798, but named for Capt. W. E. Kingman, who rediscovered it in 1853. Triangular in shape, it is about 9.5 miles long. A United States possession since 1922, Kingman Reef is a Naval Defensive Sea Area and Airspace Reservation, and is closed to the public.

Navassa Island

Navassa Island is located in the Caribbean Sea, 99.4 miles (160 km) south of the U.S. naval base at Guantanamo, Cuba, between Cuba, Haiti, and Jamaica. The island has a total area of 2 sq. mi. (5.2 sq. km). It was claimed for the U.S. under the Guano Act in 1857. The Navassa Phosphate Company mined the island until 1900, enlisting hundreds of freed American slaves to dig out several tons of guano. Working conditions were so brutal that the laborers finally revolted in 1889, killing their supervisors. The island is also claimed by Haiti.

Palmyra Atoll

Palmyra Atoll is an incorporated territory of the U.S. and privately owned. The atoll has a total area of 4.6 sq. mi. (11.9 sq. km) and is located in the North Pacific Ocean, 994 miles (1,600 km) southwest of Honolulu. It was used as a military base by the U.S. during World War II but was not attacked.

Uruguay

ORIENTAL REPUBLIC OF URUGUAY

National name: República Oriental del Uruguay
President: Jorge Batlle (2000)
Area: 68,040 sq. mi. (176,220 sq. km)
Population (2000 est.): 3,334,074; average annual rate of natural increase: 0.8%; birth rate: 17.4/1000; infant mortality rate: 15.1/1000; density per sq. mi.: 49
Capital and largest city (1998): Montevideo, 1,330,440.
Monetary unit: Peso. **Language:** Spanish. **Ethnicity/race:** white 88%, mestizo 8%, black 4%. **Religions:** Roman Catholic, 66%; Protestant, 2%; Jewish, 2%.
Literacy rate: 96% (1990)
Economic summary: GDP/PPP (1998 est.): $28.4 billion; $8,600 per capita. **Real growth rate:** 3% (1998 est.). **Inflation:** 8.6% (1998 est.). **Unemployment:** 10.5% (Nov. 1998). **Arable land:** 7%. **Agriculture:** wheat, rice, corn, sorghum, livestock, fish. **Labor force:** 1.38 million (1997 est.): government, 25%; manufacturing, 19%; commerce, 12%; utilities, construction, transport, and communications, 12%; agriculture, 11%; other services, 21% (1988 est.). **Industries:** meat processing, wool and hides, sugar, textiles, footwear, leather apparel, tires, cement, petroleum refining, wine. **Natural resources:** hydroelectric power potential. **Exports:** $2.7 billion (f.o.b., 1997): wool and textile manufactures, beef and other animal products, rice, fish and shellfish, chemicals. **Imports:** $3.7 billion (c.i.f., 1997): machinery and equipment, vehicles, chemicals, minerals, plastics, oil. **Major trading partners:** Brazil, Argentina, U.S., Germany, Italy, U.K., France, Spain.

Geography Uruguay, on the east coast of South America south of Brazil and east of Argentina, is comparable in size to Oklahoma. The country consists of a low, rolling plain in the south and a low plateau in the north. It has a 120-mile (193 km) Atlantic shoreline, a 235-mile (378 km) frontage on the Rio de la Plata, and 270 miles (435 km) on the Uruguay River, its western boundary.

Government Republic.

History Prior to European settlement, Uruguay was inhabited by groups of indigenous peoples collectively known as the Charrúas. Juan Díaz de Solis, a Spaniard, visited Uruguay in 1516, but the Portuguese were first to settle it when they founded the town of Colonia del Sacramento in 1680. After a long struggle, Spain wrested the country from Portugal in

1778, by which time almost all of the indigenous people had been exterminated. Uruguay revolted against Spain in 1811, only to be conquered in 1817 by the Portuguese from Brazil. Independence was reasserted with Argentine help in 1825, and the republic was set up in 1828.

Independence, however, did not restore order, and a revolt in 1836 touched off nearly 50 years of factional strife, including an inconclusive civil war (1839–51) and a war with Paraguay (1865–70), accompanied by occasional armed intervention by Argentina and Brazil. Uruguay, made prosperous by meat and wool exports, founded a welfare state early in the 20th century under President José Batlle y Ordóñez, who ruled from 1903 to 1929. A decline began in the 1950s as successive governments struggled to maintain a large bureaucracy and costly social benefits. Economic stagnation and left-wing terrorist activity followed.

A military coup ousted the civilian government in 1973. The military dictatorship that followed used fear and terror to demoralize the population, taking thousands of political prisoners. After ruling for 12 years, the brutal military regime permitted election of a civilian government in Nov. 1984 and relinquished rule in March 1985; full political and civil rights were then restored.

Subsequent leaders contended with high inflation and a mammoth national debt. Presidential and legislative elections in Nov. 1994 resulted in a narrow victory for the center-right Colorado Party and its presidential candidate Julio Sanguinetti Cairolo, who had been president in 1985–90. The new president pushed for constitutional and economic reforms aimed at reducing inflation and the size of the public sector, partially through tax increases and privatization. In Nov. 1999 Jorge Batlle, of the center-right Colorado Party, won the presidency. In Aug. 2000 a commission began investigating the disappearances of 160 people who vanished during the military regime.

Uzbekistan

REPUBLIC OF UZBEKISTAN

National name: Uzbekiston Respublikasi
President: Islam A. Karimov (1990)
Prime Minister: Otkir Sultonov (1995)
Area: 172,700 sq. mi. (447,400 sq. km)
Population (2000 est.): 24,755,519; (average annual rate of natural increase: 1.8%); birth rate: 26.2/1000; infant mortality rate: 72.1/1000; density per sq. mi.: 143
Capital and largest city (1992 est.): Tashkent, 2,106,000. **Other large cities:** Samarkand, 372,000; Andijon, 302,000. **Languages:** Uzbek 74.3%, Russian 14.2%, Tajik 4.4%, other 7.1%. **Ethnicity/race (1996 est.):** Uzbek 80%, Russian 5.5%, Tajik 5%, Kazak 3%, Karakalpak 2.5%, Tatar 1.5%, other 2.5%. **Religions:** Muslim (mostly Sunnis), 88%; Eastern Orthodox, 9%; other, 3%. **Literacy rate:** 99% (1996)
Economic summary: GDP/PPP (1998 est.): $59.2 billion; $2,500 per capita. **Real growth rate:** 1% (1998 est.). **Inflation:** 40% (1998 est.). **Unemployment:** 5% plus another 10% underemployed (Dec. 1996 est.). **Arable land:** 9%. **Labor force:** 11.9 million (1998 est.): services, 36%; agriculture and forestry, 44%; industry, 20% (1995). **Natural resources:** natural gas, petroleum, coal, gold, uranium, silver, copper, lead and zinc, tungsten, molybdenum. **Agriculture:** cotton, vegetables, fruit, grain, livestock. **Industries:** textiles, food processing, machine building, metallurgy, natural gas. **Exports:** $3.8 billion (1998): cotton, gold, natural gas, mineral fertilizers, ferrous metals, textiles, food products, autos. **Imports:** $4.1 billion (1998): grain,

machinery and parts, consumer durables, other food.
Major trading partners: Russia, Ukraine, eastern
Europe, western Europe, F.S.U., Czech Republic.

Geography Uzbekistan is situated in central Asia
between the Amu Darya and Syr Darya Rivers, the
Aral Sea, and the slopes of the Tien Shan Mountains.
It is bounded by Kazakhstan in the north and northwest, Kyrgyzstan and Tajikistan in the east and southeast, and Turkmenistan in the southwest. The republic
also includes the Karakalpakstan Autonomous Republic with its capital, Nukus (1992 est. pop., 182,000).
The country is about one-tenth larger in area than the
state of California.

Government Republic; authoritarian presidential
rule.

History The Uzbekistan land was once part of the
ancient Persian empire and was later conquered by
Alexander the Great in the 4th century B.C. During the
8th century, the nomadic Turkic tribes living there
were converted to Islam by invading Arab forces who
dominated the area. The Mongols under Ghengis
Khan took over the region from the Seljuk Turks in
the 13th century and it later became part of Tamerlane
the Great's empire and his successors until the 16th
century. The Uzbeks invaded the territory in the early
16th century and merged with the other inhabitants in
the area. Their empire broke up into separate Uzbek
principalities, the khanates of Khiva, Bukhara, and
Kokand. These city-states resisted Russian expansion
into the area but were conquered by the Russian
forces in the mid-19th century.

The territory was made into the Uzbek Republic in
1924 and became the independent Uzbekistan Soviet
Socialist Republic in 1925. Under Soviet rule,
Uzbekistan concentrated on growing cotton with the
help of irrigation, mechanization, and chemical fertilizers and pesticides, causing serious environmental
damage.

In June 1990, Uzbekistan became the first central
Asian republic to declare that its own laws had sovereignty over those of the central Soviet government.
Uzbekistan became fully independent and joined with
ten other former Soviet republics on Dec. 21, 1991, in
the Commonwealth of Independent States.

Vozrozhdeniye, an island in the Aral Sea, was a
secret test site for biological weapons during the
Soviet era. In 1988, the Soviets attempted to bury the
evidence on the island, a frightening legacy that
Uzbekistan inherited upon independence. U.S. scientists have confirmed that the island contains live
anthrax and other deadly poisons.

In Feb. 1992, President Karimov, a former Communist Party boss, affirmed his commitment to
democracy and human rights, but effectively suppressed opposition parties in mid-1993. The criminal
code was amended to impose stricter penalties for
antigovernment activity. Opposition groups were
largely excluded in future elections while the ruling
party continued to post decisive victories.

In 1999, the country battled against militant Islamic
groups bent on the overthrow of the secular government. In Feb. 1999, a series of bomb blasts killed 16
and injured hundreds in the capital, Tashkent. Militant
Islamic gunmen remain stationed across the border in
southern Kyrgyzstan, and Uzbek fighter planes have
been unable to rout them. In 2000, Russia offered to
help Uzbekistan "liquidate" the Islamic extremists,
and Russia has also offered to send at least $30 mil-
lion worth of weapons.

Vanuatu

REPUBLIC OF VANUATU

President: John Bani (1999)
Prime Minister: Barak Sopé (1999)
Area: 5,700 sq. mi. (14,760 sq. km)
Population (2000 est.): 189,618 (average annual rate of
natural increase: 1.7%); birth rate: 25.9/1000; infant
mortality rate: 62.5/1000; density per sq. mi.: 33
Capital and largest city (1993 est.): Port Vila, 26,100.
Monetary unit: Vatu. **Languages:** Bislama (a
Melanesian pidgin English), English, French (all 3
official). **Ethnicity/race:** indigenous Melanesian 94%,
French 4%, Vietnamese, Chinese, other Pacific
Islanders. **Religions:** Presbyterian, 36.7%; Roman
Catholic, 15%; Anglican, 15%; other Christian, 10%;
indigenous beliefs, 7.6%; other, 15.7%. **Literacy rate:**
55% (1979)
Economic summary: GDP/PPP (1997 est.): $240
million; $1,300 per capita. **Real growth rate:** n.a.
Inflation: 2.2% (1997 est.). **Labor force:** n.a.;
agriculture, 65%; services, 32%; industry, 3% (1995
est.). **Unemployment:** n.a. **Arable land:** 2%.
Agriculture: copra, coconuts, cocoa, coffee, taro,
yams, fruit, vegetables, fish, beef. **Industries:** food
and fish freezing, wood processing, meat canning.
Exports: $30 million (f.o.b., 1996): copra, beef, cocoa,
timber, coffee. **Imports:** $97 million (f.o.b., 1996):
machines and vehicles, food and beverages, basic
manufactures, raw materials and fuel, chemicals.
Major trading partners: Japan, Spain, Germany,
U.K., Côte d'Ivoire, Australia, New Caledonia,
Singapore, New Zealand, France, Fiji.

Geography Vanuatu is an archipelago of 83 islands
lying between New Caledonia and Fiji in the South
Pacific. Largest of the islands is Espiritu Santo (875
sq. mi.; 2,266 sq. km); others are Efate, Malekula,
Malo, Pentecost, and Tanna.

Government Republic.

History The first settlers were believed to have
arrived approximately 3,500 years ago from New
Guinea and the Solomon Islands by canoe. The islands
were sighted by Pedro Fernandes de Queiros of Portugal in 1606 and were charted by the British navigator
James Cook in 1774, who named the archipelago New
Hebrides, after the northern Scottish islands. Competing British and French claims to the islands led to the
formation of a condominium government, allowing for
joint British-French rule in 1906. The islands' plantation economy, based on imported Vietnamese labor,
was prosperous until the 1920s, when markets for its
products declined. Diseases brought by missionaries,
sandalwood traders, and others helped reduce the
population from approximately 1 million in 1800 to
45,000 in 1935. The islands served as a major Allied
base in World War II. After World War II, the indigenous Melanesians' began lobbying for independence.
In 1980 the country achieved independence and was
renamed Vanuatu.

A brief rebellion by French settlers and plantation
workers on Espiritu Santo took place in May 1980.
Britain sent a company of Royal Marines and France
a contingent of 50 policemen to quell the revolt,
which the new government said was financed by the
Phoenix Foundation, a right-wing U.S. group.

Papua New Guinea also sent aid, and in August the
secessionist movement was subdued.

When French nuclear testing resumed in 1995,
Vanuatu refused to join the other members of the
South Pacific Forum in their condemnation, on the
grounds that it was France's domestic matter.

Vatican City (Holy See)

National name: Stato della Città del Vaticano
Ruler: Pope John Paul II (1978)
Area: 0.17 sq. mi. (0.44 sq. km)
Population (July 1998 est.): 860; population growth rate: 1.15%; density per sq. mi.: 5,059. **Monetary unit:** Lira.
Languages: Latin, Italian, and various other languages.
Ethnicity/race: Italians, Swiss. **Religion:** Roman Catholic.
Labor force: dignitaries, priests, nuns, guards, and 3,000 lay workers who live outside the Vatican.
Budget (1994): Revenues: $175.5 million; Expenditures: $175 million, including capital expenditures.

Geography The Vatican City State is situated on the Vatican hill, on the right bank of the Tiber River, within the city of Rome.

Government The pope has full legal, executive, and judicial powers. Executive power over the area is in the hands of a commission of cardinals appointed by the pope. The college of Cardinals is the pope's chief advisory body, and upon his death the cardinals elect his successor for life.

History The Vatican City State, sovereign and independent, is the survivor of the papal states that in 1859 comprised an area of some 17,000 square miles (44,030 sq. km). During the struggle for Italian unification, from 1860 to 1870, most of this area became part of Italy. By an Italian law of May 13, 1871, the temporal power of the pope was abrogated, and the territory of the papacy was confined to the Vatican and Lateran palaces and the villa of Castel Gandolfo. The popes consistently refused to recognize this arrangement and, by the Lateran Treaty of Feb. 11, 1929, between the Vatican and the kingdom of Italy, the exclusive dominion and sovereign jurisdiction of the Holy See over the city of the Vatican was again recognized, thus restoring the pope's temporal authority over the area.

The first session of Ecumenical Council Vatican II was opened by John XXIII on Oct. 11, 1962, to plan and set policies for the modernization of the Roman Catholic Church. Pope Paul VI continued the council, opening the second session on Sept. 29, 1963.

On Aug. 26, 1978, Cardinal Albino Luciani was chosen by the college of cardinals to succeed Paul VI, who had died of a heart attack on Aug. 6. The new pope took the name John Paul I. (For a listing of all the popes, *see* the table in Religion.) Only 34 days after his election, John Paul I died of a heart attack, ending the shortest reign in 373 years. On Oct. 16, Cardinal Karol Wojtyla, 58, was chosen pope and took the name John Paul II.

On May 13, 1981, a Turkish terrorist shot the pope in St. Peter's Square, the first assassination attempt against the pontiff in modern times. On June 3, 1985, the Vatican and Italy ratified a new church-state treaty, known as a concordat, replacing the Lateran Pact of 1929. The new accord affirmed the independence of Vatican City but ended a number of privileges the Catholic Church had in Italy, including its status as the state religion. The treaty ended Rome's status as a "sacred city." Relations, diplomatic and ecclesiastical, with eastern Europe have improved dramatically with the fall of communism. Relations with Russia, while improving, have not yet reached the ambassadorial level. Diplomatic ties were established in March 1994 with Jordan and full relations were established with Israel in June. Six months earlier the two nations had accorded each other mutual recognition. The Holy See, calling for closer relations with Orthodoxy, was scheduled to meet with Russian Patriarch Alexy II in June 1997, but differences prevented the encounter from taking place. In Jan. 1998, Pope John Paul II made a historic visit to Cuba, hoping to promote religious freedom in that communist nation. Iranian president Mohammad Khatami met with the pope in 1999, the first state visit by an Iranian leader to a western nation since Iran's 1979 Islamic revolution.

In March 2000, the pope issued an apology for sins committed by Catholics over the past 2,000 years, including religious persecutions and discrimination against women. Several groups criticized the vagueness of the apology, wishing the pope had specified the church's particularly egregious sins.

Venezuela

REPUBLIC OF VENEZUELA

National name: Republica de Venezuela
President: Hugo Chavez (1999)
Area: 352,143 sq. mi. (912,050 sq. km)
Population (2000 est.): 23,542,649 (average annual rate of natural increase: 1.6%); birth rate: 21.1/1000; infant mortality rate: 26.2/1000; density per sq. mile: 67
Capital: Caracas. **Largest cities (1990 est.):** Caracas, city, 1,824,892, metro area, 2,784,042; Maracaibo, 1,206,726; Valencia, 616,000; Barquisimeto, 723,587.
Monetary unit: bolivar. **Languages:** Spanish, various indigenous languages in the remote interior. **Ethnicity/race:** mestizo 67%, white 21%, black 10%, Amerindian 2%. **Religions:** Roman Catholic, 96%; Protestant, 2%. **Literacy rate:** 91% (1990)
Economic summary: GDP (1998 est.): $194.5 billion; $8,500 per capita. **Real growth rate:** −0.9% (1998 est.). **Inflation:** 29.9% (1998 est.). **Unemployment:** 11.5% (1997 est.). **Arable land:** 4%. **Agriculture:** corn, sorghum, sugarcane, rice, bananas, vegetables, coffee, beef, pork, milk, eggs, fish. **Labor force:** 9.2 million: services, 64%; industry, 23%; agriculture, 13% (1997 est.). **Industries:** petroleum, iron ore mining, construction materials, food processing, textiles, steel, aluminum, motor vehicle assembly. **Natural resources:** petroleum, natural gas, iron ore, hydroelectric power. **Exports:** $16.9 billion (f.o.b., 1998): petroleum, bauxite and aluminum, steel, chemicals, agricultural products, basic manufactures. **Imports:** $12.4 billion (f.o.b., 1998): raw materials, machinery and equipment, transport equipment, construction materials. **Major trading partners:** U.S., Puerto Rico, Colombia, Brazil, Japan, Italy, Germany.

Geography Venezuela, a third larger than Texas, occupies most of the northern coast of South America on the Caribbean Sea. It is bordered by Colombia to the west, Guyana to the east, and Brazil to the south. Mountain systems break Venezuela into four distinct areas: (1) the Maracaibo lowlands; (2) the mountainous region in the north and northwest; (3) the Orinoco basin, with the llanos (vast grass-covered plains) on its northern border and great forest areas in the south and southeast; (4) the Guiana Highlands, south of the Orinoco, accounting for nearly half the national territory.

Government Federal republic.

History The Arawak and Carib Indians were the first inhabitants of Venezuela. Columbus explored Venezuela on his third voyage in 1498. A subsequent Spanish explorer gave the country its name, meaning "Little Venice." There were no important settlements until Caracas was founded in 1567. Simón Bolívar, who led the liberation of much of the continent from Spain, was born in Caracas in 1783. With Bolívar taking part, Venezuela was one of the first South American colonies to revolt against Spain in 1810, but it was not until 1821 that independence was won. Federated at first with Colombia and Ecuador as the Republic of Greater Colombia, the country set up a republic in 1830 and then sank for many decades into a condition of revolt, dictatorship, and corruption.

From 1908 to 1935, Gen. Juan Vicente Gómez was an absolute dictator. A military junta ruled after his death in 1935. Dr. Rómulo Betancourt and the liberal Acción Democrática Party won a majority of seats in a constituent assembly to draft a new constitution in 1946. A well-known writer, Rómulo Gallegos, candidate of Betancourt's party, easily won the presidential election of 1947. But the army ousted Gallegos the following year and instituted a military junta.

The country overthrew the dictatorship of Marcos Peréz Jiménez in 1958 and thereafter enjoyed a series of stable, democratically elected governments, beginning with that of Rómulo Betancourt, who served from 1959–64. Rafael Caldera Rodríguez, president from 1969 to 1974, legalized the Communist Party and established diplomatic relations with Moscow.

In 1974, President Carlos Andrés Pérez took office, and in 1976 Venezuela nationalized 21 oil companies, mostly subsidiaries of U.S. firms, offering compensation of $1.28 billion. Venezuela's developing market economy (Venezuela has the highest GNP per capita of any country in South America) continues to be supported mainly by the exploitation of petroleum, natural gas, and mineral reserves. President Pérez was reelected to a non-consecutive term in 1988. Venezuela experienced political turbulence in response to a 1989 economic austerity program launched by President Pérez. Disgruntled military officers unsuccessfully mounted two coup attempts in 1992 and in 1993 Congress impeached Pérez on corruption charges. President Rafael Caldera was elected in Dec. 1993. His administration's primary concerns were economic problems. In June 1994, approximately half of the country's banking sector collapsed and the government dealt with falling oil prices, foreign debt repayment, and high inflation in the mid-1990s. In 1997, the government announced that it planned to permit large-scale gold and diamond mining in the Imataca reserve in order to reap large tax revenues and create new, badly needed jobs. The creation of jobs was still an issue during the first quarter of 1999, when Venezuela's economy shrunk by nearly 10%, mostly due to falling oil prices. President Chavez, who took office on Feb. 2, 1999, made the idea of a new constitution the centerpiece of his governing agenda. Members of a constituent assembly formed to rewrite the constitution on July 25, 1999. In August a constitutional assembly made up of Chavez allies replaced the existing democratically elected congress. Popular with voters, who have been clamoring for the reform of their ailing economy and a stop to the growing chasm between rich and poor, Chavez has gradually garnered more and more power. His critics predict the emergence of a left-wing dictatorship.

With strong support from the poor, Chavez won a six-year term in July 2000. Troops were called in to quell serious protests over the election in several cities. Chavez pledged to end the deep recession and see the poor receive a larger share of the country's vast oil wealth. In 1999 the economy contracted 7% and billions of dollars have been sent out of the country. Business leaders and the affluent in general are increasingly jittery about Chavez's leftist rhetoric, his ties with Cuba, and his use of the military. In Aug. 2000 Chavez visited other OPEC countries, including Iran, Libya, and Iraq. The first foreign head of state to visit Iraq since the 1991 Gulf War, Chavez brushed aside strong U.S. criticism of the trip.

In Venezuela's worst natural disaster in centuries, mudslides and flooding that began on Dec. 15, 1999, killed at least 10,000, and forced the evacuation of about 70,000 others.

Vietnam

SOCIALIST REPUBLIC OF VIETNAM

National name: Công Hòa Xa Hội Chú Nghia Việt Nam
President: Tran Duc Luong (1997)
Prime Minister: Phan Van Khai (1997)
Area: 127,246 sq. mi. (329,560 sq. km)
Population (2000 est.): 78,773,873 (average annual rate of natural increase: 1.5%); birth rate: 21.6/1000; infant mortality rate: 31.1/1000; density per sq. mi.: 619
Capital: Hanoi. **Largest cities (1992 est.):** Ho Chi Minh City (Saigon), 3,015,743; Hanoi, 1,073,760. Other large cities (1989): Haiphong, 456,049; Da Nang, 370,670; Nha Trang, 213,687; Qui Nho'n, 160,091; Hué 211,085. **Monetary unit:** Dong. **Languages:** Vietnamese (official), French, English, Khmer, Chinese. **Ethnicity/race:** Vietnamese 85%–90%, Chinese 3%, Muong, Thai, Meo, Khmer, Man, Cham. **Religions:** Buddhist, Roman Catholic, Islam, Taoist, Confucian, Animist. **Literacy rate:** 94% (1995)
Economic summary: GDP/PPP (1998 est.): $134.8 billion; $1,770 per capita. **Real growth rate:** 4% (1998 est.). **Inflation:** 9% (1998 est.). **Unemployment:** 25% (1995 est.). **Arable land:** 17%. **Agriculture:** paddy rice, corn, potatoes, rubber, soybeans, coffee, tea, bananas, poultry, pigs, fish. **Labor force:** 32.7 million: agriculture, 65%; industry and services, 35% (1990 est.). **Industries:** food processing, garments, shoes, machine building, mining, cement, chemical fertilizer, glass, tires, oil, coal, steel, paper. **Natural resources:** phosphates, forests, coal. **Exports:** $9.4 billion (f.o.b., 1998 est.): crude oil, marine products, rice, coffee, rubber, tea, garments, shoes. **Imports:** $11.4 billion (f.o.b., 1998 est.): machinery and equipment, petroleum products, fertilizer, steel products, raw cotton, grain, cement, motorcycles. **Major trading partners:** Japan, Germany, Singapore, Taiwan, Hong Kong, France, South Korea.

Geography Vietnam occupies the eastern and southern part of the Indochinese peninsula in Southeast Asia, with the South China Sea along its entire coast. China is to the north and Laos and Cambodia to the west. Long and narrow on a north-south axis, Vietnam is about twice the size of Arizona. The Mekong River delta lies in the south.

Government Communist state.

History The Vietnamese are descendants of nomadic Mongols from China and migrants from Indonesia. According to mythology, the first ruler of Vietnam was Hung Vuong, who founded the nation in 2879 B.C. China ruled the nation then known as Nam Viet as a vassal state from 111 B.C. until the 15th century, an era of nationalistic expansion, when Cambodians were pushed out of the southern area of what is now Vietnam.

A century later, the Portuguese were the first Europeans to enter the area. France established its influence early in the 19th century, and within 80 years conquered the three regions into which the country was then divided—Cochin-China in the south, Annam in the central region, and Tonkin in the north.

France first unified Vietnam in 1887, when a single governor-generalship was created, followed by the first physical links between north and south—a rail and road system. Even at the beginning of World War II, however, there were internal differences among the three regions. Japan took over military bases in Vietnam in 1940 and a pro-Vichy French administration remained until 1945. Veteran Communist leader Ho Chi Minh organized an independence movement known as the Vietminh to exploit the confusion surrounding France's weakened influence in the region. At the end of the war, Ho's followers seized Hanoi and declared a short-lived republic, which ended with the arrival of French forces in 1946.

Paris proposed a unified government within the French Union under the former Annamite emperor, Bao Dai. Cochin-China and Annam accepted the proposal, and Bao Dai was proclaimed emperor of all Vietnam in 1949. Ho and the Vietminh withheld support, and the revolution in China gave them the outside help needed for a war of resistance against French and Vietnamese troops armed largely by a United States worried about cold war Communist expansion.

A bitter defeat at Dien Bien Phu in northwest Vietnam on May 5, 1954, broke the French military campaign and resulted in the division of Vietnam. In the new South, Ngo Dinh Diem, premier under Bao Dai, deposed the monarch in 1955 and made himself president. Diem used strong U.S. backing to create an authoritarian regime that suppressed all opposition but could not eradicate the Northern-supplied Communist Viet Cong.

Skirmishing grew into a full-scale war, with escalating U.S. involvement. A military coup, U.S.-inspired in the view of many, ousted Diem on Nov. 1, 1963, and a kaleidoscope of military governments followed. The most savage fighting of the war occurred in early 1968 during the Vietnamese New Year, known as Tet. Although the so-called Tet Offensive ended in a military defeat for the North, its psychological impact changed the course of the war.

U.S. bombing and an invasion of Cambodia in the summer of 1970—an effort to destroy Viet Cong bases in the neighboring state—marked the end of major U.S. participation in the fighting. Most American ground troops were withdrawn from combat by mid-1971 when the U.S. conducted heavy bombing raids on the Ho Chi Minh Trail—a crucial North Vietnamese supply line. In 1972, secret peace negotiations led by Secretary of State Henry A. Kissinger took place, and a peace settlement was signed in Paris on Jan. 27, 1973.

By April 9, 1975, Hanoi's troops marched within 40 miles of Saigon, the South's capital. South Vietnam's president Thieu resigned on April 21 and fled. Gen. Duong Van Minh, the new president, surrendered Saigon on April 30, ending a war that claimed the lives of 1.3 million Vietnamese and 58,000 Americans.

In 1977, border clashes between Vietnam and Cambodia intensified, as well as accusations by its former ally Beijing that Chinese residents of Vietnam were being subjected to persecution. Beijing cut off all aid and withdrew 800 technicians.

Hanoi was also preoccupied with a continuing war in Cambodia, where 60,000 Vietnamese troops had invaded and overthrown the country's Communist leader Pol Pot and his pro-Chinese regime. In early 1979, Vietnam was conducting a two-front war: defending its northern border against a Chinese invasion, and supporting its army in Cambodia, which was still fighting Pol Pot's Khmer Rouge guerrillas. Hanoi's Marxist policies combined with the destruction of the country's infrastructure during the decades of fighting devastated Vietnam's economy. However, it started to pick up in 1986 under *do Maui* (economic renovation), an effort at limited privatization. Vietnamese troops began limited withdrawals from Laos and Cambodia in 1988, and Vietnam supported the Cambodian peace agreement signed in Oct. 1991.

The U.S. lifted a Vietnamese trade embargo in Feb. 1994 that had been in place since its involvement in the war. Full diplomatic relations were announced between the two countries in July 1995. In April 1997, a pact was signed with the U.S. concerning repayment of the $146 million wartime debt incurred by the South Vietnamese government, and the following year the nation began a drive to eliminate inefficient bureaucrats and streamline the approval process for direct foreign investment. Although reform-minded officials have in recent years won key roles in government, Vietnam's ruling Communist Party has adamantly resisted political changes, even as major economic restructuring has been set in motion

(For a Vietnam War chronology, *see* Headline History.)

Western Sahara

WESTERN SAHARA

Head of State: none

Area: 165,185 sq. mi. (266,000 sq. km)

Population (1999): 244,943; growth rate: 2.9%; birth rate: 45.1/1000; infant mortality rate: 133.6/1000; density per sq. mi.: 1.5

Largest cities (1991): El Aaiun (20,010). **Monetary unit:** Moroccan dirham (DH). **Languages:** Hassaniya Arabic, Moroccan Arabic. **Ethnicity/race:** Saharawi, Arab, Berber. **Religion:** Muslim

Economic summary: GDP/PPP: n.a. **Labor force:** 12,000: animal husbandry and subsistence farming, 50%. **Agriculture:** fruit and vegetables (grown in the few oases), camels, sheep, goats (kept by nomads). **Industries:** phosphate mining, handicrafts. **Major trading partners:** Morocco claims and administers Western Sahara, so trade partners are included in overall Moroccan accounts.

Geography Located in northern Africa on the Atlantic Ocean, Western Sahara is surrounded by Algeria to the east, Morocco to the north, and Mauritania to the south. About the size of Colorado, it is mostly low, flat desert with some small mountains in the south and northeast.

Government Legal status of the territory is disputed and sovereignty unresolved; a U.N. referendum on the issue is planned. The territory is contested by Morocco and the Polisario Front, which in Feb. 1976 formerly proclaimed a government-in-exile of the Saharawi Arab Democratic Republic, now officially recognized by about 70 countries.

History Little is known about Western Sahara until the 4th century B.C. when trade with Europe began. During the Middle Ages it was occupied first by Berbers and then by the Arabic-speaking Muslim Bedouins. In the 19th century the Spanish laid claim to the southern coastal region, called Rio de Oro, and later occupied the northern interior region, Saguia el Hamra, in 1934. The Spanish formally united the two regions, and it became known as Spanish Sahara in 1958. Both Morocco and Mauritania sought to control the territory, and when the Spanish departed in 1976 they divided the territory between them. In the meantime, the indigenous Saharawis began fighting for independence. In 1976, the insurgents, called the Polisario Front, declared a government-in-exile (the Saharawi Arab Democratic Republic) from their base in Algeria. Mauritania reached a peace agreement with the Polisario in 1979, but Morocco then seized the land given up by Mauritania and now exerts administrative control over the entire region. The U.N. is attempting to hold a referendum on the issue, and a U.N.-administered cease-fire has been in effect since Sept. 1991, but the issue remains unresolved.

Yemen

REPUBLIC OF YEMEN

National name: Al Jumhuriyahal Yamaniyah
President: Ali Abdullah Saleh
Prime Minister: Abdul Karim al-Iryani (1998)
Area: 203,850 sq. mi. (527,970 sq. km)
Population (2000 est.): 17,479,206 (average annual rate of natural increase: 3.4%); birth rate: 43.4/1000; infant mortality rate: 70.3/1000; density per sq. mi.: 86
Capital (1995): Sanaá 972,011. **Largest cities (1995):** Tiaz, 2,205,947; Hodiedah, 1,749,944; Aden, 562,162.
Monetary unit: Rial. **Language:** Arabic. **Ethnicity/race:** predominantly Arab; Afro-Arab concentrations in western coastal locations; South Asians in southern regions; small European communities in major metropolitan areas. **Religion:** Islam (Sunni and Shi'ite). **Literacy rate:** 39% (1990)
Economic summary: GDP/PPP (1998 est.): $12.1 billion; $740 per capita. **Real growth rate:** 1.8% (1998 est.). **Inflation:** 11% (1998 est.). **Unemployment:** 30% (1995 est.). **Labor force:** most people are employed in agriculture and herding or as expatriate laborers; services, construction, industry, and commerce account for less than one-half of the labor force. **Arable land:** 3%. **Agriculture:** grain, fruit, vegetables, qat (mildly narcotic shrub), coffee, cotton, dairy products, poultry, beef, fish. **Industries:** crude oil production and petroleum refining, small-scale production of cotton textiles and leather goods, food processing, handicrafts, small aluminum products factory, cement. **Exports:** $1.6 billion (f.o.b., 1998 est.): crude oil, cotton, coffee, dried and salted fish. **Imports:** $2.8 billion (c.i.f., 1998 est.): food and live animals, machinery and equipment, manufactured goods. **Major trading partners:** China, South Korea, Thailand, Brazil, Japan, U.A.E., Saudi Arabia, U.S., France.

Geography Formerly known as the states of People's Democratic Republic of Yemen and the Yemen Arab Republic, the Republic of Yemen occupies the southwestern tip of the Arabian Peninsula on the Red Sea opposite Ethiopia, and extends along the southern part of the Arabian Peninsula on the Gulf of Aden and the Indian Ocean. Saudi Arabia is to the north and Oman to the east. The country is about the size of France. A 700-mile (1,130-km) narrow coastal plain in the south gives way to a mountainous region and then a plateau area. Some of the interior highlands in the west attain a height of 12,000 feet (3,660 m).

Government Parliamentary.

History The history of Yemen dates back to the Minaean (1200–650 B.C.) and Sabaean (750–115 B.C.) kingdoms. Ancient Yemen (centered around the port of Aden) engaged in the lucrative myrrh and frankincense trade. It was invaded by the Romans (1st century A.D.) as well as the Ethiopians and Persians (6th century A.D.). In A.D. 628 it converted to Islam and in

the 10th century came under the control of the Rassite dynasty of the Zaidi sect, which remained involved in North Yemeni politics until 1962. The Ottoman Turks nominally occupied the area from 1538 to the decline of their empire in 1918.

The northern portion of Yemen was ruled by imams until a pro-Egyptian military coup took place in 1962. The junta proclaimed the Yemen Arab Republic, and after a civil war in which Egypt's Nasser and the U.S.S.R. supported the revolutionaries, and King Saud of Saudi Arabia and King Hussein of Jordan supported the royalists, the royalists were finally defeated in mid-1969.

The southern port of Aden, strategically located at the opening of the Red Sea, was colonized by Britain in 1839, and by 1937, with an expansion of its territory, it was known as the Aden Protectorate. In the 1960s the Nationalist Liberation Front (NLF) fought against British rule, which led to the establishment of the People's Republic of Southern Yemen on Nov. 30, 1967. In 1979, under strong Soviet influence, the country became the only Marxist state in the Arab world.

The Republic of Yemen was established on May 22, 1990, when pro-Western Yemen and Marxist Yemen Arab Republic merged after 300 years of separation to form the new nation. The poverty and decline in Soviet economic support in the South was an important incentive for the merger. The new president, Ali Abdullah Saleh, was elected by the parliaments of both countries.

Differences over power sharing and the pace of integration between the north and the south came to a head in 1994, resulting in a civil war. The north's superior forces quickly overwhelmed the south in May and early June despite the south's brief declaration of succession. The victorious north presented a reconciliation plan providing for a general amnesty and pledges to protect political democracy.

The president's party, the General People's Congress, won an enormous victory in the April 1997 parliamentary elections, the first since the civil war. In 1998–99, a militant Islamic group, the Aden-Abyan Islamic Army, kidnapped several groups of Western tourists, which led to the deaths of several during a poorly orchestrated rescue attempt. The group's leader, Zein Al-Abidine al-Mihdar, threatened to continue attacks on tourists and government officials. The goal of the militants is to overthrow the government and turn Yemen into an Islamic state.

Yugoslavia

FEDERAL REPUBLIC OF YUGOSLAVIA

National name: Srbija-Crna Gora
President: Vojislav Kostunica (2000)
Prime Minister: Open
Area: 39,449 sq. mi. (102,350 sq. km)
Population (2000 est.): 10,662,087 (Montenegro: 680,158, Serbia: 9,981,929) (average annual rate of natural increase: Montenegro: 0.7%, Serbia: 0.1%); birth rate: Montenegro: 14.9/1000, Serbia: 12.2/1000; infant mortality rate: Montenegro: 11/1000, Serbia: 20.1/1000; density per sq. mi.: 270
Capital and largest city (1994 est.): Belgrade, 1,168,454. **Other large cities:** Novi Sad, 179,626; Nis, 175,391; Pristina, 155,499. **Monetary unit:** Yugoslav new dinar. **Languages:** Serbo-Croatian 95%, Albanian 5%. **Ethnicity/race:** Serbs 63%, Albanians 14%, Montenegrins 6%, Hungarians 4%, other 13%. **Religions:** Orthodox 65%, Muslim 19%, Roman Catholic 4%, Protestant 1%, other 11%.
Literacy rate: 91%

Economic summary: GDP/PPP (1998 est.): $25.4 billion; per capita $2,300. **Real growth rate:** 3.5% (1998 est.). **Inflation:** 48% (1998 est.). **Unemployment:** more than 35% (1995 est.). **Arable land:** n.a. **Agriculture:** cereals, fruit, vegetables, tobacco, olives, cattle, sheep, goats. **Labor force:** n.a.: industry, 41%; services, 35%; trade and tourism, 12%; transportation and communication, 7%; agriculture, 5% (1994). **Industries:** machine building (aircraft, trucks, and automobiles, tanks and weapons, electrical equipment, agricultural machinery), metallurgy (steel, aluminum, copper, lead, zinc, chromium, antimony, bismuth, cadmium), mining (coal, bauxite, nonferrous ore, iron ore, limestone), consumer goods (textiles, footwear, foodstuffs, appliances), electronics, petroleum products, chemicals, and pharmaceuticals. **Exports:** $2.3 billion (1998 est.): manufactured goods, food and live animals, raw materials. **Imports:** $3.9 billion (1998 est.): machinery and transport equipment, fuel and lubricants, manufactured goods, chemicals, food and live animals, raw materials. **Major trading partners:** Bosnia and Herzegovina, Italy, the Former Yugoslav Republic of Macedonia, Germany, Russia.

Geography Serbia and Montenegro are about the size of the state of Kentucky and largely mountainous. The northeastern section of Serbia is part of the rich, fertile Danubian Plain drained by the Danube, Tisa, Sava, and Morava River systems. Montenegro is a jumbled mass of mountains, containing also some grassy slopes and fertile river valleys.

Government The current federation is the third state to call itself by the name Yugoslavia, officially referring to itself as the Federal Republic of Yugoslavia. The United States, however, does not recognize it by that name because the U.S. does not consider the Serbian and Montenegrin federation the successor state of Yugoslavia. Serbia and Montenegro are a federal republic.

History Yugoslavia was formed on Dec. 4, 1918, from the patchwork of Balkan states and territories. World War I began there with the assassination of Archduke Franz Ferdinand of Austria at Sarajevo on June 28, 1914. The new kingdom of Serbs, Croats, and Slovenes included the former kingdoms of Serbia and Montenegro; Bosnia-Herzegovina, previously administered jointly by Austria and Hungary; Croatia-Slavonia, a semiautonomous region of Hungary; and Dalmatia, formerly administered by Austria. King Peter I of Serbia became the first monarch; his son, Alexander I, succeeded him on Aug. 16, 1921. Croatian demands for a federal state forced Alexander to assume dictatorial powers in 1929 and to change the country's name to Yugoslavia. Serbian dominance continued despite his efforts, amid the resentment of other regions. A Macedonian associated with Croatian dissidents assassinated Alexander in Marseilles, France, on Oct. 9, 1934, and his cousin, Prince Paul, became regent for the king's son, Prince Peter.

Paul's pro-Axis policy brought Yugoslavia to sign the Axis Pact on March 25, 1941, and opponents overthrew the government two days later. On April 6 the Nazis occupied the country, and the young king and his government fled. Two guerrilla armies—the Chetniks under Draza Mihajlovic supporting the monarchy, and the Partisans under Tito (Josip Broz) leaning toward the U.S.S.R.—fought the Nazis for the duration of the war. In 1943, Tito established an Executive National Committee of Liberation to function as a provisional government. Tito won the election held in the fall of 1945, as monarchists boycotted the vote. A new Assembly abolished the monarchy and proclaimed the Federal People's Republic of Yugoslavia, with Tito as prime minister. Tito ruthlessly eliminated the opposition and broke with the Soviet bloc in 1948. Yugoslavia followed a middle road, combining orthodox Communist control of politics and general overall economic policy with a varying degree of freedom in the arts, travel, and individual enterprise. Tito became president in 1953 and president-for-life under a revised constitution adopted in 1963.

After Tito's death on May 4, 1980, a rotating presidency designed to avoid internal dissension was put into effect immediately, and the feared clash of Yugoslavia's multiple nationalities and regions appeared to have been averted. In May 1991 Croatian voters supported a referendum calling for their republic to become an independent nation. A similar referendum passed in December in Slovenia. In June the respective Parliaments in both republics passed declarations of independence. Ethnic violence flared almost immediately. The largely Serbian-led Yugoslav military pounded breakaway Bosnia and Herzegovina, leading the U.N. Security Council in May 1992 to impose economic sanctions on the Belgrade government.

Despite rampant inflation reaching approximately 3,000% per month in Dec. 1993, the Serbian government of Slobodan Milosevic maintained its effective control over the rump Yugoslavia. Trade sanctions were lifted in Dec. 1995 following the signing of the Dayton Accords. In June 1996, the U.N. Security Council lifted its heavy weapons embargo. Large groups of demonstrators in 1996–97 engaged in several months of daily protests after Slobodan Milosevic refused to recognize opposition victories in local elections and in elections in Montenegro. Constitutionally barred from another term as president of Serbia, Milosevic became president of the Federal Republic of Yugoslavia (Serbia and Montenegro) in July 1997.

The situation in Serbia's provinces of Montenegro and Kosovo grew divisive in 1997 and 1998. In May 1998, Montenegro elected the reform-minded Milo Djukanovic as president. Not only is he an outspoken critic of Yugoslav president Slobodan Milosevic but he has openly contemplated secession.

Since Feb. 1998 the Yugoslav army and Serbian police have fought against the separatist Kosovo Liberation Army, but their scorched-earth tactics were concentrated on ethnic Albanian civilians—Muslims who make up 90% of Kosovo's population. More than 900 Kosovars were killed in the fighting, and the hundreds of thousands forced to flee their homes were without adequate food and shelter. Although Serbs make up only 10% of Kosovo's population, the region figures strongly in Serbian nationalist mythology.

NATO was reluctant to intervene because Kosovo—unlike Bosnia in 1992—was legally a province of Yugoslavia. The proof of civilian massacres finally gave NATO the impetus to intervene for the first time ever in the dealings of a sovereign nation with its own people. In an Oct. 12, 1998, truce brokered by American diplomat Richard Holbrooke, and under the threat of a military air strike—for which there was little enthusiasm among several NATO countries—Pres. Slobodan Milosevic agreed to the withdrawal of military forces. Fighting continued, however, and neither side accepted Washington's proposal for the province—Kosovars demanded full independence while Serb leaders would agree only to limited autonomy.

After negotiations in February and March 1999 went nowhere, on March 24, 1999, NATO began launching air strikes. Weeks of daily bombings destroyed significant Serbian military targets, yet Milosevic showed no signs of relenting. In fact, Serbian militia stepped up civilian massacres and deportations in Kosovo—by the end of the conflict, the U.N. high commissioner for refugees estimated that at least 850,000 people had fled Kosovo. The refugee crisis put a heavy burden on neighboring countries such as Albania and Macedonia. Many wondered whether the NATO strikes had actually exacerbated the violence. As effective as NATO airpower might be against Serbian targets, it was utterly helpless in preventing Serb soldiers and paramilitaries from wreaking havoc on Kosovo's civilians.

World opinion was divided over the effectiveness of conducting airstrikes without the support of ground troops, but NATO countries remained reluctant to do so, fearing that the inevitable casualties would dampen the public's support for troops on foreign soil. The initial reason NATO gave for involvement in Kosovo was to avoid a wider Balkan war, but once Serbia began accelerating their campaign of ethnic cleansing in Kosovo, NATO's reason for fighting changed to preventing a human rights calamity. Yet without a concomitant change in military strategy—sending in ground troops—many wondered whether there would be any Kosovars left to save. NATO's hesitation in committing to a land battle—and therefore putting its troops at greater risk—ultimately paid off. Serbia finally agreed to sign a U.N.-approved peace agreement with NATO on June 3, ending the 11-week war. As Serbian forces withdrew, a five-nation NATO peacekeeping force entered Kosovo and began monitoring the return of refugees. Russia complicated NATO's efforts by demanding a role as a peacekeeper yet refusing to answer to NATO. A new group of refugees, Kosovar's Serbs, began fleeing the province, fearing vengeance from ethnic Albanians. Milosevic, who was indicted as a war criminal by the U.N. tribunal for the deportation of ethnic Albanians from Kosovo, held fast to the presidency as opposition groups remained disorganized and focused on internecine politics.

In Feb. 2000 fighting broke out between Serbs and Albanians in Mitrovica, Kosovo. NATO peacekeepers struggled to contain the violence.

Despite widespread reports of fraud and voter intimidation by pro-Milosevic forces, opposition candidate Vojislav Kostunica nevertheless won the presidential election held in Sept. 2000. When Milosevic refused to honor the results and demanded a runoff election, the country erupted. A massive general strike was declared and some one million protesters deluged Belgrade, taking over some TV stations and the Parliament building. Many in the security forces either fled or joined the demonstrators. On Oct. 5, Milosevic stepped aside and Kostunica assumed power. The U.S. and the European Union soon began to lift economic sanctions against Yugoslavia. Kostunica faced a daunting task, however, in reenergizing the nation's shattered economy, and in rebuilding the infrastructure destroyed during the 1999 NATO bombing.

Zaire

SEE CONGO, DEMOCRATIC REPUBLIC OF.

Zambia

REPUBLIC OF ZAMBIA

President: Frederick T. J. Chiluba (1991)
Area: 290,586 sq. mi. (752,610 sq. km)
Population (2000 est.): 9,582,418 (average annual rate of natural increase: 2%); birth rate: 41.9/1000; infant mortality rate: 92.4/1000; density per sq. mi.: 33
Capital: Lusaka. **Largest cities (1997):** Lusaka, 1.6 million; (1990 est.) Kitwe, 338,207; Ndola, 376,311; Chingola, 167,954. **Monetary unit:** Kwacha.
Languages: English and local dialects. **Ethnicity/race:** African 98.7%, European 1.1%, other 0.2%.
Religions: Christian, 50–75%; Islam and Hindu, 24–49%; remainder indigenous beliefs. **Literacy rate:** 73% (1990)
Economic summary: GDP/PPP (1998 est.): $8.3 billion; $880 per capita. **Real growth rate:** –2% (1998 est.). **Inflation:** 43.9% (1996). **Unemployment:** 22% (1991). **Arable land:** 7%. **Agriculture:** corn, sorghum, rice, peanuts, sunflower seed, tobacco, cotton, sugarcane, cassava (tapioca); cattle, goats, pigs, poultry, beef, pork, poultry meat, milk, eggs, hides. **Labor force:** 3.4 million: agriculture, 85%; transport and services 9%; mining, manufacturing, and construction 6%. **Industries:** copper mining and processing, construction, foodstuffs, beverages, chemicals, textiles, fertilizer. **Natural resources:** copper, zinc, lead, cobalt, coal. **Exports:** $905 million (f.o.b., 1998 est.): copper, cobalt, zinc, lead, tobacco. **Imports:** $1.1 billion (f.o.b., 1998 est.): machinery, transportation equipment, foodstuffs, fuel, petroleum products, electricity, fertilizer. **Major trading partners:** Japan, South Africa, U.S., Saudi Arabia, India, Thailand, Malaysia, U.K., Zimbabwe. **Member of Commonwealth of Nations.**

Geography Zambia, a landlocked country in south-central Africa, is about one-tenth larger than Texas. It is surrounded by Angola, Zaire, Tanzania, Malawi, Mozambique, Zimbabwe, Botswana, and Namibia. The country is mostly a plateau that rises to 8,000 feet (2,434 m) in the east.

Government Republic.

History Early humans inhabited present-day Zambia between one and two million years ago. Today the country is made up almost entirely of Bantu-speaking peoples. Empire builder Cecil Rhodes obtained mining concessions in 1889 from King Lewanika of the Barotse and sent settlers to the area soon thereafter. The region was ruled by the British South Africa Company, which he established, until 1924, when the British government took over the administration.

From 1953 to 1964, Northern Rhodesia was federated with Southern Rhodesia and Nyasaland (now Malawi) in the Federation of Rhodesia and Nyasaland. On Oct. 24, 1964, Northern Rhodesia became the independent nation of Zambia.

Kenneth Kaunda, the first president, kept Zambia within the Commonwealth of Nations. The country's economy, dependent on copper exports, was threatened when Rhodesia declared its independence from British rule in 1965 and defied U.N. sanctions, which Zambia supported, an action that deprived Zambia of its trade route through Rhodesia. The U.S., Britain, and Canada organized an airlift in 1966 to ship gasoline into Zambia. In 1967, Britain agreed to finance new trade routes for Zambia.

Kaunda visited China in 1967, and China later agreed to finance a 1,000-mile railroad from the copper fields to Dar es Salaam in Tanzania. A pipeline was opened in 1968 from Ndola in Zambia's copper belt to the Indian Ocean at Dar es Salaam, ending the three-year oil drought. In 1969, Kaunda announced the nationalization of the foreign copper-mining industry, with Zambia to take 51% (over $1 billion, estimated). He then announced a similar takeover of foreign oil producers.

With a soaring debt and inflation rate in 1991, riots took place in Lusaka, resulting in a number of killings. Mounting domestic pressure forced Kaunda to move Zambia toward multiparty democracy.

National elections on Oct. 31, 1991, brought a stunning defeat to long-serving President Kaunda and a repudiation of his persistent belief in a one-party state. The newly elected chief executive, Frederick Chiluba, called for sweeping economic reforms, including privatization and the establishment of a stock market. Parliament passed a bill in May 1996 that stated a president may serve only two terms, thus preventing any possible political return of Kenneth Kaunda, a measure criticized by opposition parties. General elections in Nov. 1996 saw the reelection of President Chiluba with 70% of the vote.

Chiluba declared martial law in 1997 and arrested Kaunda following a failed coup attempt. The 1999 slump in world copper prices depressed the economy since copper provides 80% of Zambia's export earnings. The government has begun to privatize the copper industry. In 1999 Angola accused Zambia of support the UNITA rebels fighting the Angolan government. Zambia denied the charges, saying it simply refused to allow Angola to fight the rebels within Zambian territory. Zambian presidential elections have been set for 2001.

Zimbabwe

REPUBLIC OF ZIMBABWE

President: Robert Mugabe (1987)
Area: 150,698 sq. mi. (390,580 sq. km)
Population (2000 est.): 11,342,521 (average annual rate of natural increase: 0.26%); birth rate: 25/1000; infant mortality rate: 62.2/1000; density per sq. mi.: 75
Capital and largest city (1992): Harare, 1,184,169.
Other large cities: Bulawayo, 621,000; Chitungwiza, 274,035. **Monetary unit:** Zimbabwean dollar.
Languages: English (official), Ndebele, Shona (85%).
Ethnicity/race: African 98% (Shona 71%, Ndebele 16%, other 11%), white 1%, mixed and Asian 1%.
Religions: Christian, 25%; Animist, 24%; Syncretic, 50%. **Literacy rate:** 80% (1992)
Economic summary: GDP/PPP (1998 est.): $26.2 billion; $2,400 per capita. **Real growth rate:** 1.5% (1998 est.). **Inflation:** 32% (1998 est.).
Unemployment: at least 45% (1994 est.). **Arable land:** 7%. **Agriculture:** corn, cotton, tobacco, wheat, coffee, sugarcane, peanuts, cattle, sheep, goats, pigs. **Labor force:** 5 million (1997 est.). **Industries:** mining (coal, clay, numerous metallic and nonmetallic ores), copper, steel, nickel, tin, wood products, cement, chemicals, fertilizer, clothing and footwear, foodstuffs, beverages. **Natural resources:** gold, copper, chrome, nickel, tin, asbestos. **Exports:** $1.7 billion (f.o.b. 1998 est.): tobacco, gold, ferroalloys, cotton. **Imports:** $2 billion (f.o.b., 1998 est.): machinery and transport equipment, 39%; other manufactures, 18%; chemicals, 15%; fuels, 10% (1997 est.). **Major trading partners:** South Africa, U.K., Germany, Japan, U.S.

Geography Zimbabwe, a landlocked country in south-central Africa, is slightly smaller than California. It is bordered by Botswana on the west, Zambia on the north, Mozambique on the east, and South Africa on the south.

Government Parliamentary democracy.

History The remains of early humans, dating back 500,000 years, have been discovered in present-day Zimbabwe. The land's earliest settlers, the Khoisan, date back to 200 B.C. After a period of Bantu domination, the Shona people ruled, followed by the Nguni and Zulu peoples. By the mid–19th century the descendants of the Nguni and Zulu, the Ndebele, had established a powerful warrior kingdom.

The first British explorers, colonists, and missionaries arrived in the 1850s, and the massive influx of foreigners led to the establishment of the territory Rhodesia, named after Cecil Rhodes of the British South Africa Company. In 1923, European settlers voted to become the self-governing British colony of Southern Rhodesia. After a brief federation with Northern Rhodesia and Nyasaland (now Malawi) in the post–World War II period, Southern Rhodesia (also known as Rhodesia) chose to remain a colony when its two partners voted for independence in 1963.

On Nov. 11, 1965, the conservative white-minority government of Rhodesia declared its independence from Britain. The country resisted the demands of black Africans, and Prime Minister Ian Smith withstood British pressure, economic sanctions, and guerrilla attacks to uphold white supremacy. On March 1, 1970, Rhodesia formally proclaimed itself a republic. Heightened guerrilla war and a withdrawal of South African military aid in 1976 marked the beginning of the collapse of Smith's 11 years of resistance.

Black nationalist movements were led by Bishop Abel Muzorewa of the African National Congress and Ndabaningi Sithole, who were moderates, and guerrilla leaders Robert Mugabe of the Zimbabwe African National Union (ZANU) and Joshua Nkomo of the Zimbabwe African People's Union (ZAPU), who advocated revolution.

On March 3, 1978, Smith, Muzorewa, Sithole, and Chief Jeremiah Chirau signed an agreement to transfer power to the black majority by Dec. 31, 1978. They constituted themselves an Executive Council, with chairmanship rotating but with Smith retaining the title of prime minister. Blacks were named to each cabinet ministry, serving as co-ministers with the whites already holding these posts. African nations and rebel leaders immediately denounced the action, but Western governments were more reserved, although none granted recognition to the new regime.

The white minority finally consented to hold multiracial elections in 1980, and Robert Mugabe won a landslide victory. The country achieved independence on April 17, 1980, under the name Zimbabwe. Mugabe eventually established a one-party socialist state, but by 1990 he instituted multiparty elections and in 1991 deleted all references to Marxism-Leninism and scientific socialism from the constitution. Parliamentary elections in April 1995 gave Mugabe's party a stunning victory with 63 of the 65 contested seats, and in 1996 Mugabe won another six-year term as president.

One-third of Zimbabwe's arable land is owned by 4,000 white farmers. In Feb. 2000 President Mugabe's government lost a referendum on a constitutional amendment that would have allowed the seizure of this land without compensation. Despite the defeat, the government supported the landtaking. Veterans of Zimbabwe's war for independence in the 1970s began squatting on the land and attacking the whites in an effort to reclaim land taken under British colonization. Mugabe's support for the squatters has led to foreign sanctions against Zimbabwe.

United Nations

Preamble of the United Nations Charter

The Charter of the United Nations was adopted at the San Francisco Conference of 1945. The complete text is available on the UN Web site, www.un.org/aboutun/charter.

We the peoples of the United Nations determined to save succeeding generations from the scourge of war, which twice in our lifetime has brought untold sorrow to mankind, and

To reaffirm faith in fundamental human rights, in the dignity and worth of the human person, in the equal rights of men and women and of nations large and small, and

To establish conditions under which justice and respect for the obligations arising from treaties and other sources of international law can be maintained, and

To promote social progress and better standards of life in larger freedom, and for these ends

To practice tolerance and live together in peace with one another as good neighbors, and

To unite our strength to maintain international peace and security, and

To insure, by the acceptance of principles and the institution of methods, that armed force shall not be used, save in the common interest, and

To employ international machinery for the promotion of the economic and social advancement of all peoples, have resolved to combine our efforts to accomplish these aims.

Accordingly, our respective Governments, through representatives assembled in the city of San Francisco, who have exhibited their full powers found to be in good and due form, have agreed to the present Charter of the United Nations and do hereby establish an international organization to be known as the United Nations.

Principal Organs of the United Nations

Secretariat

This is the directorate on UN operations, apart from political decisions. The staff works under the Secretary-General, whom it assists and advises.

Secretaries-General

Kofi Annan, Ghana, Jan. 1, 1997.
Boutros Boutros-Ghali, Egypt, Jan. 1, 1992–Dec. 31, 1996.
Javier Pérez de Cuéllar, Peru, Jan. 1, 1982–Dec. 31, 1991.
Kurt Waldheim, Austria, Jan. 1, 1972–Dec. 31, 1981.
U Thant, Burma (Myanmar), Nov. 3, 1961–Dec. 31, 1971.
Dag Hammarskjöld, Sweden, April 11, 1953–Sept. 17, 1961.
Trygve Lie, Norway, Feb. 1, 1946–April 10, 1953.

General Assembly

The General Assembly is the world's forum for discussing matters affecting world peace and security, and for making recommendations concerning them. It has no power of its own to enforce decisions. It is composed of the 51 original member nations and those admitted since, a total of 185. On important questions including international peace and security, a two-thirds majority of those present and voting is required. Decisions on other questions are made by a simple majority. Emphasis is given on questions relating to international peace and security brought before it by any member, the Security Council, or nonmembers. It also maintains a broad program of international cooperation in eco-

nomic, social, cultural, educational, and health fields, and for assisting in human rights and freedoms.

Security Council

The Security Council is the primary instrument for establishing and maintaining international peace. Its main purpose is to prevent war by settling disputes between nations. Under the charter, the council is permitted to dispatch a UN force to stop aggression. All member nations undertake to make available armed forces, assistance, and facilities to maintain international peace and security.

The Security Council has 15 members. There are five permanent members: the United States, the Russian Federation, Britain, France, and China; and 10 temporary members elected by the General Assembly for two-year terms, from five different regions of the world. Voting on procedural matters requires a nine-vote majority to carry. However, on questions of substance, the vote of each of the five permanent members is required. The ten non-permanent members of the council in 2000 are Argentina (2001), Bangladesh (2001), Canada (2000), Jamaica (2001), Malaysia (2000), Mali (2001), Namibia (2000), Netherlands (2000), Tunisia (2001), and Ukraine (2001).

Economic and Social Council

This council is composed of 54 members elected by the General Assembly to 3-year terms. It works closely with the General Assembly as a link with groups formed within the UN to help peoples in such fields as education, health, and human rights.

Agencies of the United Nations

- The International Labor Organization (ILO)
- The Food and Agriculture Organization of the UN (FAO)
- The UN Educational, Scientific and Cultural Organization (UNESCO)
- The World Health Organization (WHO)
- The World Bank
- The International Monetary Fund (IMF)
- The International Civil Aviation Organization (ICAO)
- The Universal Postal Union (UPU)
- The International Telecommunication Union (ITU)
- The World Meteorological Organization (WMO)
- The International Maritime Organization (IMO)
- The World Intellectual Property Organization (WIPO)
- The International Fund for Agricultural Development (IFAD)
- The UN Industrial Development Organization (UNIDO)
- The International Atomic Energy Agency (IAEA)
- The UN and the World Trade Organization (WTO)

UN Peacekeeping Missions

Since 1948 there have been 49 UN peacekeeping operations; 17 are currently under way. Thus far, 118 nations have contributed personnel at various times; 77 are currently providing peacekeepers. As of Aug. 31, 1998, the top contributors of troops to current missions were: Poland (1,034 soldiers); Bangladesh (886); Austria (792); Ghana (788); Finland (777); Ireland (727); and Norway (727). The small island nation of Fiji has taken part in virtually every UN peacekeeping operation, as has Canada.

Current UN Peacekeeping Operations

Region/Country	Duration	Region/Country	Duration
AFRICA		**ASIA**	
Western Sahara	April 1991–present	India/Pakistan	Jan. 1949–present
Sierra Leone	Oct. 1999–present	Tajikistan	Dec. 1994–present
Democratic Republic of the Congo	Nov. 1999–present	East Timor	Oct. 1999–present
		EUROPE	
		Cyprus	March 1964–present
MIDDLE EAST		Georgia	Aug. 1993–present
Middle East	June 1948–present	Bosnia & Herzegovina	Dec. 1995–present
Golan Heights	June 1974–present	Croatia	Jan. 1996–present
Lebanon	March 1978–present	Kosovo	June 1999–present
Iraq/Kuwait	April 1991–present		

Completed UN Peacekeeping Operations

Region/Country	Duration	Region/Country	Duration
AFRICA		**AMERICAS**	
Congo	July 1960–June 1964	Dominican Republic	May 1965–Oct. 1966
Angola	Jan. 1989–June 1991	Central America	Nov. 1989–Jan. 1992
Namibia	April 1989–March 1990	Observer Group	
Angola	June 1991–Feb. 1995	El Salvador	July 1991–April 1995
Somalia	April 1992–March 1993	Haiti	Sept. 1993–June 1996
Mozambique	Dec. 1992–Dec. 1994	Haiti	July 1996–July 1997
Somalia	March 1993–March 1995	Guatemala	Jan.–May 1997
Rwanda/Uganda	June 1993–Sept. 1994	Haiti	Aug.–Nov. 1997
Rwanda	Oct. 1993–March 1996	Haiti	Dec. 1997–March 2000
Chad/Libya	May–June 1994	**ASIA**	
Angola	Feb. 1995–June 1997	West New Guinea	Oct. 1962–April 1963
Angola	July 1997–Feb. 1999	India/Pakistan	Sept. 1965–March 1966
Sierra Leone	July 1998–Oct. 1999	Afghanistan/Pakistan	April 1988–March 1990
		Cambodia	Oct. 1991–March 1992
		Cambodia	March 1992–Sept. 1993
MIDEAST			
Middle East—1st UN Emergency Force	Nov. 1956–June 1967	**EUROPE**	
		Former Yugoslavia	March 1992–Dec. 1995
Lebanon	June–Dec. 1958	Croatia	March 1995–Jan. 1996
Yemen	July 1963–Sept. 1964	Former Yugoslavia Rep. of Macedonia	March 1995–Feb. 1999
Middle East—2nd UN Emergency Force	Oct. 1973–July 1979	Croatia	Jan. 1996–Jan. 1998
Iran/Iraq	Aug. 1988–Feb. 1991	Croatia	Jan. 1998–Oct. 1998

Source: United Nations Dept. of Public Information.

Members of the United Nations (189 nations)

Country	Joined UN[1]	Country	Joined UN[1]	Country	Joined UN[1]
Afghanistan	1946	Germany	1973	Oman	1971
Albania	1955	Ghana	1957	Pakistan	1947
Algeria	1962	Greece	1945	Palau	1994
Andorra	1993	Grenada	1974	Panama	1945
Angola	1976	Guatemala	1945	Papua New Guinea	1975
Antigua and Barbuda	1981	Guinea	1958	Paraguay	1945
Argentina	1945	Guinea-Bissau	1974	Peru	1945
Armenia	1992	Guyana	1966	Philippines	1945
Australia	1945	Haiti	1945	Poland	1945
Austria	1955	Honduras	1945	Portugal	1955
Azerbaijan	1992	Hungary	1955	Qatar	1971
Bahamas	1973	Iceland	1946	Romania	1955
Bahrain	1971	India	1945	Russian Federation	1945
Bangladesh	1974	Indonesia	1950	Rwanda	1962
Barbados	1966	Iran	1945	St. Kitts and Nevis	1983
Belarus	1945	Iraq	1945	St. Lucia	1979
Belgium	1945	Ireland	1955	St. Vincent and the	
Belize	1981	Israel	1949	Grenadines	1980
Benin	1960	Italy	1955	Samoa, Western	1976
Bhutan	1971	Jamaica	1962	San Marino	1992
Bolivia	1945	Japan	1956	São Tomé and Príncipe	1975
Bosnia and Herzegovina	1992	Jordan	1955	Saudi Arabia	1945
Botswana	1966	Kazakhstan	1992	Senegal	1960
Brazil	1945	Kenya	1963	Seychelles	1976
Brunei Darussalam	1984	Kiribati	1999	Sierra Leone	1961
Bulgaria	1955	North Korea	1991	Singapore	1965
Burkina Faso	1960	South Korea	1991	Slovakia[4]	1993
Burma (Myanmar)	1948	Kuwait	1963	Slovenia	1992
Burundi	1962	Kyrgyzstan	1992	Solomon Islands	1978
Cambodia	1955	Laos	1955	Somalia	1960
Cameroon	1960	Latvia	1991	South Africa	1945
Canada	1945	Lebanon	1945	Spain	1955
Cape Verde	1975	Lesotho	1966	Sri Lanka	1955
Central African Republic	1960	Liberia	1945	Sudan	1956
Chad	1960	Libya	1955	Suriname	1975
Chile	1945	Liechtenstein	1990	Swaziland	1968
China[2]	1945	Lithuania	1991	Sweden	1946
Colombia	1945	Luxembourg	1945	Syria	1945
Comoros	1975	Macedonia[3]	1993	Tajikistan	1992
Congo	1960	Madagascar	1960	Tanzania	1961
Congo, Dem. Rep.	1960	Malawi	1964	Thailand	1946
Costa Rica	1945	Malaysia	1957	Togo	1960
Côte d'Ivoire	1960	Maldives	1965	Tonga	1999
Croatia	1992	Mali	1960	Trinidad and Tobago	1962
Cuba	1945	Malta	1964	Tunisia	1956
Cyprus	1960	Marshall Islands	1991	Turkey	1945
Czech Republic[4]	1993	Mauritania	1961	Turkmenistan	1992
Denmark	1945	Mauritius	1968	Tuvalu[5]	2000
Djibouti	1977	Mexico	1945	Uganda	1962
Dominica	1978	Micronesia	1991	Ukraine	1945
Dominican Republic	1945	Moldova	1992	United Arab Emirates	1971
Ecuador	1945	Monaco	1993	United Kingdom	1945
Egypt	1945	Mongolia	1961	United States	1945
El Salvador	1945	Morocco	1956	Uruguay	1945
Equatorial Guinea	1968	Mozambique	1975	Uzbekistan	1992
Eritrea	1993	Namibia	1990	Vanuatu	1981
Estonia	1991	Nauru	1999	Venezuela	1945
Ethiopia	1945	Nepal	1955	Viet Nam	1977
Fiji	1970	Netherlands	1945	Yemen, Republic of	1947
Finland	1955	New Zealand	1945	Yugoslavia	1945
France	1945	Nicaragua	1945	Zambia	1964
Gabon	1960	Niger	1960	Zimbabwe	1980
Gambia	1965	Nigeria	1960		
Georgia	1992	Norway	1945		

1. The UN officially came into existence on Oct. 24, 1945. 2. On Oct. 25, 1971, the UN voted membership to the People's Republic of China, which replaced the Republic of China (Taiwan) in the world body. 3. The General Assembly on April 8, 1993, decided to admit the state provisionally being referred to as "The Former Yugoslav Republic of Macedonia" pending settlement of the difference that has arisen over its name. 4. Czechoslovakia was an original member of the United Nations from Oct. 24, 1945. As of Dec. 31, 1992, it ceased to exist and the Czech Republic and Slovakia as successor states were admitted Jan. 19, 1993. 5. Tuvalu became the newest member of the UN on Sept. 5, 2000.

U.S. Representatives to the United Nations

Year	Ambassador	Year	Ambassador
1946	Edward R. Stettinius, Jr.	1975–76	Daniel P. Moynihan
1946–47	Herschel V. Johnson (acting)	1976–77	William W. Scranton
1947–53	Warren R. Austin	1977–79	Andrew Young
1953–60	Henry Cabot Lodge Jr.	1979–81	Donald McHenry
1960–61	James J. Wadsworth	1981–85	Jeane J. Kirkpatrick
1961–65	Adlai E. Stevenson	1985–89	Vernon A. Walters
1965–68	Arthur J. Goldberg	1989–92	Thomas J. Pickering
1968	George W. Ball	1992–93	Edward J. Perkins
1968–69	James Russell Wiggins	1993–96	Madeleine K. Albright
1969–71	Charles W. Yost	1997–98	Bill Richardson
1971–73	George Bush	1999–	Richard Holbrooke
1973–75	John A. Scali		

Selected International Organizations

Arab League (AL)
Members: (21 plus the Palestine Liberation Organization) Algeria, Bahrain, Comoros, Djibouti, Egypt, Iraq, Jordan, Kuwait, Lebanon, Libya, Mauritania, Morocco, Oman, Qatar, Saudi Arabia, Somalia, Sudan, Syria, Tunisia, UAE, Yemen, Palestine Liberation Organization

Association of Southeast Asian Nations (ASEAN)
Members: (10) Brunei, Burma, Cambodia, Indonesia, Laos, Malaysia, Philippines, Singapore, Thailand, Vietnam
Observers: (1) Papua New Guinea
Consultative partners: (2) China, Russia

Big Seven and Group of 7 (G-7)
Members: (7) Big Six (Canada, France, Germany, Italy, Japan, U.K.) plus the U.S.

Group of 8 (G-8)
Members: (9) Canada, EU (as one member), France, Germany, Italy, Japan, Russia, U.K., U.S.

Commonwealth of Nations
Members: (53) Antigua and Barbuda, Australia, the Bahamas, Bangladesh, Barbados, Belize, Botswana, Brunei, Cameroon, Canada, Cyprus, Dominica, Fiji, the Gambia, Ghana, Grenada, Guyana, India, Jamaica, Kenya, Kiribati, Lesotho, Malawi, Malaysia, Maldives, Malta, Mauritius, Mozambique, Namibia, Nauru, New Zealand., Nigeria, Pakistan (suspended), Papua New Guinea, Saint Kitts and Nevis, Saint Lucia, Saint Vincent and the Grenadines, Samoa, Seychelles, Sierra Leone, Singapore, Solomon Islands, South Africa, Sri Lanka, Swaziland, Tanzania, Tonga, Trinidad and Tobago, Uganda, U.K., Vanuatu, Zambia, Zimbabwe
Special members: (1) Tuvalu

Commonwealth of Independent States (CIS)
Members: (12) Armenia, Azerbaijan, Belarus, Georgia, Kazakhstan, Kyrgyzstan, Moldova, Russia, Tajikistan, Turkmenistan, Ukraine, Uzbekistan

European Union (EU)
Members: (15) Austria, Belgium, Denmark, Finland, France, Germany, Greece, Ireland, Italy, Luxembourg, Netherlands, Portugal, Spain, Sweden, U.K.
Membership applicants: (13) Bulgaria, Cyprus, Czech Republic, Estonia, Hungary, Latvia, Lithuania, Malta, Poland, Romania, Slovakia, Slovenia, Turkey

North Atlantic Treaty Organization (NATO)
Members: (19) Belgium, Canada, Czech Republic, Denmark, France, Germany, Greece, Hungary, Iceland, Italy, Luxembourg, Netherlands, Norway, Poland, Portugal, Spain, Turkey, U.K., U.S.

Organization of Petroleum Exporting Countries (OPEC)
Members: (11) Algeria, Indonesia, Iran, Iraq, Kuwait, Libya, Nigeria, Qatar, Saudi Arabia, UAE, Venezuela

Foreign Embassies in the United States

Source: U.S. Department of State.

Embassy of the Republic of Albania, 2100 S St., N.W., Washington, D.C. 20008. Phone: 202-223-4942.

Embassy of the Democratic & Popular Republic of Algeria, 2118 Kalorama Rd., N.W., Washington, D.C. 20008. Phone: 202-265-2800.

Embassy of Andorra, 2 United Nations Plaza, 25th flr. New York, N.Y. 10017. Phone: 212-750-8064.

Embassy of the Republic of Angola, 1615 M St., N.W., Suite 900, Washington, D.C. 20036. Phone: 202-785-1156.

Embassy of Antigua & Barbuda, 3216 New Mexico Ave., N.W., Washington, D.C. 20016. Phone: 202-362-5211, 5166, 5122.

Embassy of the Argentine Republic, 1600 New Hampshire Ave., N.W., Washington, D.C. 20009. Phone: 202-238-6400.

Embassy of the Republic of Armenia, 2225 R Street, N.W., Washington, D.C. 20008. Phone: 202-319-1976.

Embassy of Australia, 1601 Massachusetts Ave., N.W., Washington, D.C. 20036. Phone: 202-797-3000.

Embassy of Austria, 3524 International Court, N.W., Washington, D.C. 20008. Phone: 202-895-6700.

Embassy of the Republic of Azerbaijan, 927- 15th St., N.W., Suite 700, P.O. Box 28790, Washington, D.C. 20005. Phone: 202-842-0001.

Embassy of the Commonwealth of the Bahamas, 2220 Massachusetts Ave., N.W., Washington, D.C. 20008. Phone: 202-319-2660.

Embassy of the State of Bahrain, 3502 International Dr., N.W., Washington, D.C. 20008. Phone: 202-342-0741, 0742.

Embassy of the People's Republic of Bangladesh, 2201 Wisconsin Ave., N.W., Suite 300, Washington, D.C. 20007. Phone: 202-342-8372 to 8376.

Embassy of Barbados, 2144 Wyoming Ave., N.W., Washington, D.C. 20008. Phone: 202-939-9200 to 9202.

Embassy of the Republic of Belarus, 1619 New Hampshire Ave., N.W., Washington, D.C. 20009. Phone: 202-986-1604.

Embassy of Belgium, 3330 Garfield St., N.W., Washington, D.C. 20008. Phone: 202-333-6900.

Embassy of Belize, 2535 Massachusetts Ave., N.W., Washington, D.C. 20008. Phone: 202-332-9636.

Embassy of the Republic of Benin, 2737 Cathedral Ave., N.W., Washington, D.C. 20008. Phone: 202-232-6656 to 6658.

Embassy of the Republic of Bolivia, 3014 Massachusetts Ave., N.W., Washington, D.C. 20008. Phone: 202-483-4410, 4412.

Embassy of the Republic of Bosnia and Herzegovina, 2109 E St. N.W., Washington, D.C. 20037. Phone: 202-337-1500.

Embassy of the Republic of Botswana, 1531–1533 New Hampshire Ave., N.W., Washington, D.C. 20036. Phone: 202-244-4990, 4991.

Brazilian Embassy, 3006 Massachusetts Ave., N.W., Washington, D.C. 20008. Phone: 202-238-2700.

Embassy of the State of Brunei Darussalam, 3520 International Court, N.W., Washington, D.C. 2008. Phone: 202-342-0159.

Embassy of the Republic of Bulgaria, 1621-22nd St., N.W., Washington, D.C. 20008. Phone: 202-387-7969.

Embassy of Burkina Faso, 2340 Massachusetts Ave., N.W., Washington, D.C. 20008. Phone: 202-332-5577.

Embassy of the Union of Burma, 2300 S St., N.W., Washington, D.C. 20008. Phone: 202-332-9044, 9045.

Embassy of the Republic of Burundi, 2233 Wisconsin Ave., N.W., Suite 212, Washington, D.C. 20007. Phone: 202-342-2574.

Embassy of the Kingdom of Cambodia, 4500- 16th St., N.W., Washington, D.C. 20011. Phone: 202-726-7742.

Embassy of the Republic of Cameroon, 2349 Massachusetts Ave., N.W., Washington, D.C. 20008. Phone: 202-265-8790.

Embassy of Canada, 501 Pennsylvania Ave., N.W., Washington, D.C. 20001. Phone: 202-682-1740.

Embassy of the Republic of Cape Verde, 3415 Massachusetts Ave., N.W., Washington, D.C. 20007. Phone: 202-965-6820.

Embassy of Central African Republic, 1618-22nd St. N.W., Washington, D.C. 20008. Phone: 202-483-7800, 7801.

Embassy of the Republic of Chad, 2002 R St., N.W., Washington, D.C. 20009. Phone: 202-462-4009.

Embassy of Chile, 1732 Massachusetts Ave., N.W., Washington, D.C. 20036. Phone: 202-785-1746.

Embassy of the People's Republic of China, 2300 Connecticut Ave., N.W., Washington, D.C. 20008. Phone: 202-328-2500 to 2502.

Embassy of Colombia, 2118 Leroy Pl., N.W., Washington, D.C. 20008. Phone: 202-387-8338.

Embassy of the Federal and Islamic Republic of Comoros, c/o Permanent Mission of the Federal and Islamic Republic of Comoros to the United Nations, 420 E. 50th St., New York, N.Y. 10022. Phone: 212-972-8010.

Embassy of the Democratic Republic of Congo, 1800 New Hampshire Ave., N.W., Washington, D.C. 20009. Phone: 202-234-7690, 7691.

Embassy of the Republic of Congo, 4891 Colorado Ave., N.W., Washington, D.C. 20011. Phone: 202-726-5500.

Embassy of Costa Rica, 2114 S St., N.W., Washington, D.C. 20008. Phone: 202-234-2945.

Embassy of the Republic of Côte d'Ivoire, 3421 Massachusetts Ave., N.W., Washington, D.C. 20007. Phone: 202-797-0300.

Embassy of the Republic of Croatia, 2343 Massachusetts Ave., N.W., Washington, D.C. 20008. Phone: 202-588-5899.

Cuban Interests Section, 2630- 16th St., N.W., Washington, D.C. 20009. Phone: 202-797-8518 to 8520.

Embassy of the Republic of Cyprus, 2211 R St. N.W., Washington, D.C. 20008. Phone: 202-462-5772.

Embassy of the Czech Republic, 3900 Spring of Freedom St., N.W., Washington, D.C. 20008. Phone: 202-274-9100.

Royal Danish Embassy, 3200 Whitehaven St., N.W., Washington, D.C. 20008. Phone: 202-234-4300.

Embassy of the Republic of Djibouti, 1156-15th St., N.W., Suite 515, Washington, D.C. 20005. Phone: 202-331-0270.

Embassy of the Commonwealth of Dominica, 3216 New Mexico Ave., N.W., Washington, D.C. 20016. Phone: 202-364-6781.

Embassy of the Dominican Republic, 1715-22nd St., N.W., Washington, D.C. 20008. Phone: 202-332-6280, 6281.

Embassy of Ecuador, 2535-15th St., N.W., Washington, D.C. 20009. Phone: 202-234-7200.

Embassy of the Arab Republic of Egypt, 3521 International Court, N.W., Washington, D.C. 20008. Phone: 202-895-5400.

Embassy of El Salvador, 2308 California St., N.W., Washington, D.C. 20008. Phone: 202-265-9671, 9672.

Embassy of Equatorial Guinea, 2020- 16th St., N.W., Washington, D.C. 20009. Phone: 202-518-5700.

Embassy of the State of Eritrea, 1708 New Hampshire Ave., N.W., Washington, D.C., 20009. Phone: 202-319-1991.

Embassy of Estonia, 2131 Massachusetts Ave., Washington, D.C. 20008. Phone: 202-588-0101.

Embassy of Ethiopia, 3506 International Dr., N.W., Washington, D.C. 20008. Phone: 202-364-1200.

Embassy of the Republic of Fiji, 2233 Wisconsin Ave., N.W., Suite 240, Washington, D.C. 20007. Phone: 202-337-8320.

Embassy of Finland, 3301 Massachusetts Ave., N.W., Washington, D.C. 20008. Phone: 202-298-5800.

Embassy of France, 4101 Reservoir Rd., N.W., Washington, D.C. 20007. Phone: 202-944-6000.

Embassy of the Gabonese Republic, 2034-20th St., N.W., Suite 200, Washington, D.C. 20009. Phone: 202-797-1000.

Embassy of the Gambia, 1155-15th St., N.W., Suite 1000, Washington, D.C. 20005. Phone: 202-785-1399, 1379, 1425.

Embassy of the Republic of Georgia, 1615 New Hampshire Ave., N.W., Suite 300, Washington, D.C. 20009. Phone: 202-387-2390.

Embassy of the Federal Republic of Germany, 4645 Reservoir Rd., N.W., Washington, D.C. 20007. Phone: 202-298-8141.

Embassy of Ghana, 3512 International Dr., N.W., Washington, D.C. 20008. Phone: 202-686-4520.

Embassy of Greece, 2221 Massachusetts Ave., N.W., Washington, D.C. 20008. Phone: 202-939-5800.

Embassy of Grenada, 1701 New Hampshire Ave., N.W., Washington, D.C. 20009. Phone: 202-265-2561.

Embassy of Guatemala, 2220 R St., N.W., Washington, D.C. 20008. Phone: 202-745-4952 to 4954.

Embassy of the Republic of Guinea, 2112 Leroy Pl., N.W., Washington, D.C. 20008. Phone: 202-483-9420.

Embassy of the Republic of Guinea-Bissau, 1511 K St., N.W., Suite 519, Washington, D.C. 20005. Phone: 202-347-3950.

Embassy of Guyana, 2490 Tracy Pl., N.W., Washington, D.C. 20008. Phone: 202-265-6900, 6901.

Embassy of the Republic of Haiti, 2311 Massachusetts Ave., N.W., Washington, D.C. 20008. Phone: 202-332-4090 to 4092.

Apostolic Nunciature of the Holy See, 3339 Massachusetts Ave., N.W., Washington, D.C. 20008. Phone: 202-333-7121.

Embassy of Honduras, 3007 Tilden St., N.W., Suite 4-M, Washington, D.C. 20008. Phone: 202-966-7702, 2604, 5008, 4596.

Embassy of the Republic of Hungary, 3910 Shoemaker St., N.W., Washington, D.C. 20008. Phone: 202-362-6730.

Embassy of Iceland, 1156-15th St., N.W., Suite 1200, Washington, D.C. 20005. Phone: 202-265-6653 to 6655.

Embassy of India, 2107 Massachusetts Ave., N.W., Washington, D.C. 20008. Phone: 202-939-7000.

Embassy of the Republic of Indonesia, 2020 Massachusetts Ave., N.W., Washington, D.C. 20036. Phone: 202-775-5200.

Iranian Interests Section, 2209 Wisconsin Ave., N.W., Washington, D.C. 20007. Phone: 202-965-4990.

Iraqi Interests Section, 1801 P St., N.W., Washington, D.C. 20036. Phone: 202-483-7500.

Embassy of Ireland, 2234 Massachusetts Ave., N.W., Washington, D.C. 20008. Phone: 202-462-3939.

Embassy of Israel, 3514 International Dr., N.W., Washington, D.C. 20008. Phone: 202-364-5500.

Embassy of Italy, 1601 Fuller St., N.W., Washington, D.C. 20009. Phone: 202-328-5500.

Embassy of Jamaica, 1520 New Hampshire Ave., N.W., Washington, D.C. 20036. Phone: 202-452-0660.

Embassy of Japan, 2520 Massachusetts Ave., N.W., Washington, D.C. 20008. Phone: 202-238-6700.

Embassy of the Hashemite Kingdom of Jordan, 3504 International Dr., N.W., Washington, D.C. 20008. Phone: 202-966-2664.

Embassy of the Republic of Kazakhstan, (temporary) 1401- 16th St., N.W., Washington, D.C. 20036. Phone: 202-232-5488.

Embassy of the Republic of Kenya, 2249 R St., N.W., Washington, D.C. 20008. Phone: 202-387-6101.

Embassy of the Republic of Korea, 2450 Massachusetts Ave., N.W., Washington, D.C. 20008. Phone: 202-939-5600.

Embassy of the State of Kuwait, 2940 Tilden St., N.W., Washington, D.C. 20008. Phone: 202-966-0702.

Embassy of the Kyrgyz Republic, 1732 Wisconsin Ave., Washington, D.C. 20007. Phone: 202-338-5141.

Embassy of the Lao People's Democratic Republic, 2222 S St., N.W., Washington, D.C. 20008. Phone: 202-332-6416.

Embassy of Latvia, 4325-17th St., N.W., Washington, D.C. 20011. Phone: 202-726-8213, 8214.

Embassy of Lebanon, 2560-28th St., N.W., Washington, D.C. 20008. Phone: 202-939-6300.

Embassy of the Kingdom of Lesotho, 2511 Massachusetts Ave., N.W., Washington, D.C. 20008. Phone: 202-797-5533 to 5536.

Embassy of the Republic of Liberia, 5201- 16th St., N.W., Washington, D.C. 20011. Phone: 202-723-0437.

Embassy of the Republic of Lithuania, 2622- 16th St., N.W., Washington, D.C. 20009. Phone: 202-234-5860.

Embassy of the Grand Duchy of Luxembourg, 2200 Massachusetts Ave., N.W., Washington, D.C. 20008. Phone: 202-265-4171.

Embassy of the Former Yugoslav Republic of Macedonia, 3050 K St., N.W., Suite 210, Washington, D.C. 20007. Phone: 202-337-3063.

Embassy of the Republic of Madagascar, 2374 Massachusetts Ave., N.W., Washington, D.C. 20008. Phone: 202-265-5525, 5526.

Embassy of Malawi, 1400- 20th St., N.W., Washington, D.C. 20036. Phone: 202-223-4814.

Embassy of Malaysia, 2401 Massachusetts Ave., N.W., Washington, D.C. 20008. Phone: 202-328-2700.

Embassy of the Republic of Mali, 2130 R St., N.W., Washington, D.C. 20008. Phone: 202-332-2249.

Embassy of Malta, 2017 Connecticut Ave., N.W., Washington, D.C. 20008. Phone: 202-462-3611, 3612.

Embassy of the Republic of the Marshall Islands, 2433 Massachusetts Ave., N.W., Washington, D.C. 20008. Phone: 202-234-5414.

Embassy of the Islamic Republic of Mauritania, 2129 Leroy Pl., N.W., Washington, D.C. 20008. Phone: 202-232-5700.

Embassy of the Republic of Mauritius, 4301 Connecticut Ave. N.W., Suite 441, Washington, D.C. 20008. Phone: 202-244-1491, 1492.

Embassy of Mexico, 1911 Pennsylvania Ave., N.W., Washington, D.C. 20006. Phone: 202-728-1600.

Embassy of the Federated States of Micronesia, 1725 N St., N.W., Washington, D.C. 20036. Phone: 202-223-4383.

Embassy of the Republic of Moldova, 2101 S St., N.W., Washington, D.C. 20008. Phone: 202-667-1130.

Embassy of Mongolia, 2833 M St., N.W., Washington, D.C. 20007. Phone: 202-333-7117.

Embassy of the Kingdom of Morocco, 1601- 21st St., N.W., Washington, D.C. 20009. Phone: 202-462-7979 to 7982, inclusive.

Embassy of the Republic of Mozambique, 1990 M St., N.W., Suite 570, Washington, D.C. 20036. Phone: 202-293-7146.

Embassy of the Union of Myanmar, 2300 S St., N.W., Washington, D.C. 20008. Phone: 202-332-9044, 9045.

Embassy of the Republic of Namibia, 1605 New Hampshire Ave., N.W., Washington, D.C. 20009. Phone: 202-986-0540.

Royal Nepalese Embassy, 2131 Leroy Pl., N.W., Washington, D.C. 20008. Phone: 202-667-4550.

Royal Netherlands Embassy, 4200 Linnean Ave., N.W., Washington, D.C. 20008. Phone: 202-244-5300; after 6 p.m. 202-494-8594.

Embassy of New Zealand, 37 Observatory Circle, N.W., Washington, D.C. 20008. Phone: 202-328-4800.

Embassy of Nicaragua, 1627 New Hampshire Ave., N.W., Washington, D.C. 20009. Phone: 202-939-6570.

Embassy of the Republic of Niger, 2204 R St., N.W., Washington, D.C. 20008. Phone: 202-483-4224 to 4227, inclusive.

Embassy of the Federal Republic of Nigeria, 2201 M St., N.W., Washington, D.C. Phone: 202-986-8400.

Royal Norwegian Embassy, 2720- 34th St., N.W., Washington, D.C. 20008. Phone: 202-333-6000.

Embassy of the Sultanate of Oman, 2535 Belmont Rd., N.W., Washington, D.C. 20008. Phone: 202-387-1980, 1981, 1982.

Embassy of Pakistan, 2315 Massachusetts Ave., N.W., Washington, D.C. 20008. Phone: 202-939-6200.

Embassy of the Republic of Palau, 1150- 18th St., N.W., Suite 750, Washington, D.C. 20036. Phone: 202-452-6814.

Embassy of the Republic of Panama, 2862 McGill Terrace, N.W., Washington, D.C. 20008. Phone: 202-483-1407.

Embassy of Papua New Guinea, 1779 Massachusetts Ave., N.W., Suite 805, Washington, D.C. 20036. Phone: 202-745-3680.

Embassy of Paraguay, 2400 Massachusetts Ave., N.W., Washington, D.C. 20008. Phone: 202-483-6960 to 6962.

Embassy of Peru, 1700 Massachusetts Ave., N.W., Washington, D.C. 20036. Phone: 202-833-9860 to 9869.

Embassy of the Philippines, 1600 Massachusetts Ave., N.W., Washington, D.C. 20036. Phone: 202-467-9300.

Embassy of the Republic of Poland, 2640- 16th St., N.W., Washington, D.C. 20009. Phone: 202-234-3800 to 3802.

Embassy of Portugal, 2125 Kalorama Rd., N.W., Washington, D.C. 20008. Phone: 202-328-8610.

Embassy of the State of Qatar, 4200 Wisconsin Ave., N.W., Washington, D.C. 20016. Phone: 202-274-1603.

Embassy of Romania, 1607- 23rd St., N.W., Washington, D.C. 20008. Phone: 202-332-4846, 4848, 3694.

Embassy of the Russian Federation, 2650 Wisconsin Ave., N.W., Washington, D.C. 20007. Phone: 202-298-5700, 5701, 5704.

Embassy of the Republic of Rwanda, 1714 New Hampshire Ave., N.W., Washington, D.C. 20009. Phone: 202-232-2882.

Embassy of Saint Kitts and Nevis, 3216 New Mexico Ave., N.W., Washington, D.C. 20016. Phone: 202-686-2636.

Embassy of Saint Lucia, 3216 New Mexico Ave., N.W., Washington, D.C. 20016. Phone: 202-364-6792 to 6795.

Embassy of Saint Vincent and the Grenadines, 3216 New Mexico Ave., N.W., Washington, D.C. 20016. Phone: 202-364-6730.

Embassy of the Independent State of Samoa, 800 Second Ave., Suite 400D, New York, N.Y. 10017. Phone: 212-599-6196, 6197.

Embassy of Saudi Arabia, 601 New Hampshire Ave., N.W., Washington, D.C. 20037. Phone: 202-342-3800.

Embassy of the Republic of Senegal, 2112 Wyoming Ave., N.W., Washington, D.C. 20008. Phone: 202-234-0540, 0541.

Embassy of the Republic of Seychelles, 800 Second Ave., Suite 400C, New York, N.Y. 10017. Phone: 212-972-1785.

Embassy of Sierra Leone, 1701- 19th St., N.W., Washington, D.C. 20009. Phone: 202-939-9261, 9263.

Embassy of the Republic of Singapore, 3501 International Pl., N.W., Washington, D.C. 20008. Phone: 202-537-3100.

Embassy of the Slovak Republic, 2201 Wisconsin Ave., N.W., Suite 250, Washington, D.C. 20007. Phone: 202-965-5161.

Embassy of the Republic of Slovenia, 1525 New Hampshire Ave., N.W., Washington, D.C. 20036. Phone: 202-667-5363.

Embassy of the Solomon Islands, 800 Second Ave., Suite 400L, New York, N.Y. 10017. Phone: 212-599-6192, 6193.

Embassy of the Republic of South Africa, 3051 Massachusetts Ave., N.W., Washington, D.C. 20008. Phone: 202-232-4400.

Embassy of Spain, 2375 Pennsylvania Ave., N.W., Washington, D.C. 20037. Phone: 202-728-2332.

Embassy of the Democratic Socialist Republic of Sri Lanka, 2148 Wyoming Ave., N.W., Washington, D.C. 20008. Phone: 202-483-4026 to 4028.

Embassy of the Republic of the Sudan, 2210 Massachusetts Ave., N.W., Washington, D.C. 20008. Phone: 202-338-8565.

Embassy of the Republic of Suriname, 4301 Connecticut Ave., N.W., Suite 460, Washington, D.C. 20008. Phone: 202-244-7488.

Embassy of the Kingdom of Swaziland, 3400 International Drive, N.W., Washington, D.C. 20008. Phone: 202-362-6683, 6685.

Embassy of Sweden, 1501 M St., N.W., Washington, D.C. 20005. Phone: 202-467-2600.

Embassy of Switzerland, 2900 Cathedral Ave., N.W., Washington, D.C. 20008. Phone: 202-745-7900.

Embassy of the Syrian Arab Republic, 2215 Wyoming Ave., N.W., Washington, D.C. 20008. Phone: 202-232-6313.

Embassy of the United Republic of Tanzania, 2139 R St., N.W., Washington, D.C. 20008. Phone: 202-939-6125.

Royal Thai Embassy, 1024 Wisconsin Ave., N.W., Washington, D.C. 20007. Phone: 202-944-3600.

Embassy of the Republic of Togo, 2208 Massachusetts Ave., N.W., Washington, D.C. 20008. Phone: 202-234-4212.

Embassy of Trinidad and Tobago, 1708 Massachusetts Ave., N.W., Washington, D.C. 20036. Phone: 202-467-6490.

Embassy of Tunisia, 1515 Massachusetts Ave., N.W., Washington, D.C. 20005. Phone: 202-862-1850.

Embassy of the Republic of Turkey, 2525 Massachusetts Ave., N.W., Washington, D.C. 20008. Phone: 202-612-6700.

Embassy of Turkmenistan, 2207 Massachusetts Ave., N.W., Washington, D.C. 20008. Phone: 202-588-1500.

Embassy of the Republic of Uganda, 5911-16th St., N.W., Washington, D.C. 20011. Phone: 202-726-7100.

Embassy of Ukraine, 3350 M St., N.W., Washington, D.C. 20007. Phone: 202-333-7507.

Embassy of the United Arab Emirates, 1255- 22nd St., N.W., Suite 700, Washington, D.C. 20007. Phone: 202-955-7999.

United Kingdom of Great Britain & Northern Ireland—British Embassy, 3100 Massachusetts Ave., N.W., Washington, D.C. 20008. Phone: 202-588-6500.

Embassy of Uruguay, 2715 M St., N.W., Washington, D.C. 20007. Phone: 202-331-1313.

Embassy of the Republic of Uzbekistan, 1746 Massachusetts Ave., N.W., Washington, D.C. 20036. Phone: 202-887-5300.

Embassy of the Republic of Venezuela, 1099- 30th St., N.W., Washington D.C. 20007. Phone: 202-342-2214.

Embassy of Vietnam, 1233- 20th St., N.W., Washington, D.C. 20036. Phone: 202-861-0737.

Embassy of the Republic of Yemen, 2600 Virginia Ave., N.W., Suite 705, Washington, D.C. 20037. Phone: 202-965-4760, 4761.

Embassy of the Republic of Zambia, 2419 Massachusetts Ave., N.W., Washington, D.C. 20008. Phone: 202-265-9717 to 9719.

Embassy of the Republic of Zimbabwe, 1608 New Hampshire Ave., N.W., Washington, D.C. 20009. Phone: 202-332-7100.

Diplomatic Personnel to and from the U.S.

Country	U.S. Representative to[1]	Rank	Representative from[1]	Rank
Albania	Joseph Limprecht	Amb.	Petrit Bushati	Amb.
Algeria	Cameron R. Hume	Amb.	Driss Jazairy	Amb.
Andorra	Edward L. Romero	Amb.	Juli Minoves-Triquell	Amb.
Angola	Joseph G. Sullivan	Amb.	Antonio dos Santos Franca	Amb.
Antigua and Barbuda[2]	E. William Crotty	Amb.	Lionel Hurst	Amb.
Argentina	Manuel Rocha	Amb.	Guillermo Gonzalez	Amb.
Armenia	Michael Craig Lemmon	Amb.	Arman Kirakosian	Amb.
Australia	Genta Hawkins Holmes	Amb.	Michael Thawley	Amb.
Austria	Kathryn Walt Hall	Amb.	Peter Moser	Amb.
Azerbaijan	Stanley T. Escudero	Amb.	Hafiz Pashayev	Amb.
Bahamas	Arthur L. Schechter	Amb.	Joshua Sears	Amb.
Bahrain	Johnny Young	Amb.	Muhammad Abd Al-Ghaffar Abdallah	Amb.
Bangladesh	John C. Holzman	Amb.	Khwaja Mohammad Shehabuddin	Amb.
Barbados[2]	E. William Crotty	Amb.	Courtney Blackman	Amb.
Belarus	Daniel V. Speckhard	Amb.	Valeriy Tsepkalo	Amb.
Belgium	Paul L. Cejas	Amb.	Alexis Reyn	Amb.
Belize	Carolyn Curiel	Amb.	James Schofield Murphy	Amb.
Benin	Robert C. Felder	Amb.	Lucien Tonoukouin	Amb.
Bolivia	Donna Hrinak	Amb.	Marlene Fernandez	Amb.
Bosnia-Herzegovina	Thomas J. Miller	Amb.	Igor Davidovic	Amb.
Botswana	John E. Lange	Amb.	Kgosi Seepapitso IV	Amb.
Brazil	Anthony S. Harrington	Amb.	Rubens Antonio Barbosa	Amb.
Brunei	Sylvia Gaye Stanfield	Amb.	Puteh ibni Mohammad Alam	Amb.
Bulgaria	Richard Miles	Amb.	Filip Dimitrov	Amb.
Burkina Faso	Jimmy J. Kolker	Amb.	Bruno Zidouemba	Amb.
Burma (Myanmar)	Priscilla A. Clapp	Cd'A	Tin Winn	Amb.
Burundi	Mary C. Yates	Amb.	—	—
Cambodia	Kent M. Wiedemann	Amb.	Roland Eng	Amb.
Cameroon	John M. Yates	Amb.	Jerome Mendouga	Amb.
Canada	Gordon Giffin	Amb.	Raymond Chretien	Amb.
Cape Verde	Michael D. Metelits	Amb.	Amilcar Spencer Lopes	Amb.
Central African Republic	Robert C. Perry	Amb.	Henri Koba	Amb.
Chad	Christopher E. Goldthwait	Amb.	Ahmat Hassaballah Soubiane	Amb.
Chile	John O'Leary	Amb.	Mario Artaza	Amb.
China	Joseph W. Prueher	Amb.	Li Zhaoxing	Amb.
Colombia	Curtis W. Kamman	Amb.	Luiz Alberto Mejia Moreno	Amb.
Comoros	Mark W. Erwin	Amb.	Ahmed Djabir	Amb.
Congo, Dem. Rep. of	William L. Swing	Amb.	Faida Mitifu	Amb.
Congo, Rep. of	David H. Kaeuper	Amb.	—	—
Costa Rica	Thomas J. Dodd	Amb.	Jaime Rosenstein Daremblum	Amb.
Côte d'Ivoire	George Mu	Amb.	Youssouf Bamba	Amb.
Croatia	William Dale Montgomery	Amb.	Miomir Zuzul	Amb.
Cuba	Michael Kozak	P.O.	—	—
Cyprus	Donald Bandler	Amb.	Erato Kozakou-Marcoullis	Amb.
Czech Republic	John Shattuck	Amb.	Aleksandr Vondra	Amb.
Denmark	Richard Swett	Amb.	Knud-Erik Tygesen	Amb.
Djibouti	Lange Schermerhorn	Amb.	Olhaye Oudine Roble	Amb.
Dominica[2]	E. William Crotty	Amb.	—	—
Dominican Republic	Charles Manatt	Amb.	Roberto Saladin-Selin	Amb.
Ecuador	Gwen C. Clare	Amb.	Ivonne A-Baki	Amb.
Egypt	Daniel C. Kurtzer	Amb.	Nabil Fahmy	Amb.
El Salvador	Anne W. Patterson	Amb.	Rene Antonio Rodriguez Leon	Amb.
Equatorial Guinea	John M. Yates	Amb.	Pastor Micha Ondo Bile	Amb.
Eritrea	William D. Clarke	Amb.	Russom Semere	Amb.
Estonia	Melissa Wells	Amb.	Sven Juergenson	Amb.
Ethiopia	Tibor P. Nagy, Jr.	Amb.	Berhane Gebre-Christos	Amb.
Fiji [3]	M. Osman Siddique	Amb.	Napolioni Masirewa	Amb.
Finland	Eric Edelman	Amb.	Jaakko Laajava	Amb.
France	Felix George Rohatyn	Amb.	François Bujon de l'Estang	Amb.
Gabon	James V. Ledesma	Amb.	Paul Boundoukou-Latha	Amb.
Gambia, The	George W. Haley	Amb.	—	—
Georgia	Kenneth Spencer Yalowitz	Amb.	Tedo Japaridze	Amb.
Germany	John C. Kornblum	Amb.	Juergen Chrobog	Amb.
Ghana	Kathryn Dee Robinson	Amb.	Kobena Koomson	Amb.
Greece	R. Nicholas Burns	Amb.	Alexandros Philon	Amb.
Grenada[2]	E. William Crotty	Amb.	—	—
Guatemala	Prudence Bushnell	Amb.	—	—
Guinea	Joyce E. Leader	Amb.	Mohamed Thiam	Amb.

Country	U.S. Representative to[1]	Rank	Representative from[1]	Rank
Guinea-Bissau	—	—	Mario Lopes da Rosa	Amb.
Haiti	Donald K. Steinberg	Amb.	—	—
Holy See	Corrine Claiborne Boggs	Amb.	Gabriel Montalvo	Pap. Nun.
Honduras	Frank Almaguer	Amb.	Hugo Noe Pino	Amb.
Hong Kong	Michael Klosson	C.G.	—	—
Hungary	Peter Tufo	Amb.	Geza Jeszenszky	Amb.
Iceland	Day Olin Mount	Amb.	Jon Baldvin Hannibalsson	Amb.
India	Richard F. Celeste	Amb.	Naresh Chandra	Amb.
Indonesia	Robert S. Gelbard	Amb.	Dorodjatun Kutoro-Jakti	Amb.
Iran	—	—	Faramarz Fath-Nejad	Rep.[4]
Iraq	Francis J. Ricciardone	Rep.[5]	Akram Jasim al-Duri	Rep.[4]
Ireland	Michael J. Sullivan	Amb.	Sean O'Huiginn	Amb.
Israel	Martin S. Indyk	Amb.	David Ivry	Amb.
Italy	Thomas M. Foglietta	Amb.	Ferdinando Salleo	Amb.
Jamaica	Stan McLelland	Amb.	Richard Bernal	Amb.
Japan	Thomas S. Foley	Amb.	Shunji Yanai	Amb.
Jerusalem	John E. Herbst	C.G.	—	—
Jordan	William Joseph Burns	Amb.	Marwan Muasher	Amb.
Kazakhstan	Richard Henry Jones	Amb.	Bolat Nurgaliyev	Amb.
Kenya	Johnnie Carson	Amb.	Samuel Chemai	Amb.
Kiribati, Republic of	Joan M. Plaisted	Amb.	—	—
Korea, South	Stephen W. Bosworth	Amb.	Hong-ku Yi	Amb.
Kuwait	James A. Larocco	Amb.	Muhammad al-Sabah al-Salim Al Sabah	Amb.
Kyrgyzstan	Anne Marie Sigmund	Amb.	Bakyt Abdrisayev	Amb.
Laos	Wendy J. Chamberlin	Amb.	Vang Rattanavong	Amb.
Latvia	James Howard Holmes	Amb.	Aivis Ronis	Amb.
Lebanon	David M. Satterfield	Amb.	Mohamad Chatah	Amb.
Lesotho	Katherine H. Peterson	Amb.	Lebohang Kenneth Moleko	Amb.
Liberia	Bismarck Myrick	Amb.	William Bull	Amb.
Liechtenstein	Madeline May Kunin	Amb.	—	—
Lithuania	Keith C. Smith	Amb.	Stasys Sakalauskas	Amb.
Luxembourg	James C. Hormel	Amb.	Arlette Conzemius	Amb.
Macedonia	Michael Einik	Amb.	Ljubica Acevska	Amb.
Madagascar	Shirley E. Barnes	Amb.	Zina Andrianarivelo-Razafy	Amb.
Malawi	A. Ellen Shippy	Amb.	Paul Tony Steven Kandiero	Amb.
Malaysia	B. Lynn Pascoe	Amb.	Dali Mahmud Hashim	Amb.
Maldives, Republic of	Shaun E. Donnelly	Amb.	—	—
Mali	Michael E. Ranneberger	Amb.	Cheick Oumar Diarrah	Amb.
Malta	Kathryn Linda Haycock Proffitt	Amb.	George Saliba	Amb.
Marshall Islands	Joan M. Plaisted	Amb.	Banny de Brum	Amb.
Mauritania	Timberlake Foster	Amb.	Ahmed Ben Khalifa Ben Jidou	Amb.
Mauritius	Mark W. Erwin	Amb.	Chitmansing Jesseramsing	Amb.
Mexico	Jeffrey Davidow	Amb.	Jesus Gonzalez Garza Reyes Heroles	Amb.
Micronesia	Diane Edith Watson	Amb.	Jesse Marehalau	Amb.
Moldova	Rudolf Vilemk Perina	Amb.	Ceslav Ciobanu	Amb.
Mongolia	Alphonso F. La Porta	Amb.	Jalbuugiyn Choinhor	Amb.
Morocco	Edward M. Gabriel	Amb.	—	—
Mozambique	Brian D. Curran	Amb.	Marcos Geraldo Namashulua	Amb.
Namibia	Jeffrey A. Bader	Amb.	Leonard Iipumbu	Amb.
Nepal	Ralph Frank	Amb.	Bekh Bahadur Thapa	Amb.
Netherlands	Cynthia P. Schneider	Amb.	Joris Vos	Amb.
New Zealand	Carol Moseley Braun	Amb.	James Bolger	Amb.
Nicaragua	Oliver Garza	Amb.	Francisco Sacasa Aguirre	Amb.
Niger	Barbro A. Owens-Kirkpatrick	Amb.	—	—
Nigeria	William H. Twaddell	Amb.	—	—
Norway	David B. Hermelin	Amb.	Tom Vraalsen	Amb.
Oman	John Bruce Craig	Amb.	Abdallah bin Muhammad bin Aqil al-Dhahab	Amb.
Pakistan	William B. Milam	Amb.	Maleeha Lodhi	Amb.
Palau	Thomas C. Hubbard	Amb.	Hersey Kyota	Amb.
Panama	Simon Ferro	Amb.	Guillermo Ford	Amb.
Papua New Guinea	Arma Jane Karaer	Amb.	Nagora Bogan	Amb.
Paraguay	Maura Harty	Amb.	—	—
Peru	John R. Hamilton	Amb.	Alfonso Monsalve Rivero	Amb.
Philippines	Thomas C. Hubbard	Amb.	Ernesto Maceda	Amb.
Poland	Daniel Fried	Amb.	Jerzy Kozminski	Amb.
Portugal	Gerald S. McGowan	Amb.	Fernando Antonio De Lacerda Andresen Guimaraes	Amb.

Country	U.S. Representative to[1]	Rank	Representative from[1]	Rank
Qatar	Elizabeth D. McKune	Amb.	Saad Muhammad al-Kubaysi	Amb.
Romania	James Carew Rosapepe	Amb.	Mircea Geoana	Amb.
Russia	James Collins	Amb.	Yuriy Viktorovich Ushakov	Amb.
Rwanda	George M. Staples	Amb.	Theogene Rudasingwa	Amb.
Saint Kitts and Nevis[2]	E. William Crotty	Amb.	Osbert Liburd	Amb.
Saint Lucia[2]	E. William Crotty	Amb.	Sonia Johnny	Amb.
Saint Vincent and the Grenadines[2]	E. William Crotty	Amb.	Kingsley C.A. Layne	Amb.
Samoa, Western	Carol Moseley Braun	Amb.	Tuiloma Neroni Slade	Amb.
Sao Tome and Principe, Dem. Rep. of	James V. Ledesma	Amb.	—	
Saudi Arabia	Wyche Fowler, Jr.	Amb.	Bandar bin Sultan bin Abd al-Aziz Al Saud	Amb.
Senegal	Harriet L. Elam-Thomas	Amb.	Mamadou Mansour Seck	Amb.
Serbia Montenegro	Richard Miles	Cd'A	—	—
Seychelles	Mark W. Erwin	Amb.	Claude Morel	Amb.
Sierra Leone	Joseph H. Melrose, Jr.	Amb.	John Ernest Leigh	Amb.
Singapore	Steven Jay Green	Amb.	Heng Chee Chan	Amb.
Slovakia	Ralph Johnson	Amb.	Martin Butora	Amb.
Slovenia	Nancy Ely-Raphel	Amb.	—	—
Solomon Islands	Arma Jane Karaer	Amb.	Rex Horoi	Amb.
South Africa	Delano Eugene Lewis, Sr.	Amb.	Sheila Sisulu	Amb.
Spain	Edward L. Romero	Amb.	Antonio Marchesi Oyarzabal	Amb.
Sri Lanka	Shaun E. Donnelly	Amb.	Warnasena Rasaputram	Amb.
Sudan	—	—	Mahdi Ibrahim Mahammad	Amb.
Suriname	Dennis K. Hays	Amb.	Arnold Halfhide	Amb.
Swaziland	Gregory L. Johnson	Amb.	Mary Madzandza Kanya	Amb.
Sweden	Lyndon L. Olson, Jr.	Amb.	Rolf Ekeus	Amb.
Switzerland	Madeleine May Kunin	Amb.	Alfred Defago	Amb.
Syria	Ryan C. Crocker	Amb.	Walid Mualem	Amb.
Tajikistan	Robert P. J. Finn	Amb.	—	—
Tanzania	Charles R. Stith	Amb.	Mustafa Salim Nyang'anyi	Amb.
Thailand	Richard E. Hecklinger	Amb.	Tet Bunnak	Amb.
Togo	Brenda Brown Schoonover	Amb.	Akoussoulelou Bodjona	Amb.
Trinidad and Tobago	Edward E. Shumaker III	Amb.	Michael Arneaud	Amb.
Tunisia	Robin Lynn Raphel	Amb.	Noureddine Mejdoub	Amb.
Turkey	Mark Robert Parris	Amb.	Baki Ilkin	Amb.
Turkmenistan	Steven R. Mann	Amb.	Halil Ugur	Amb.
Uganda	Martin G. Brennan	Amb.	Edith Grace Ssempala	Amb.
Ukraine	Steven Karl Pifer	Amb.	Konstantin Hryshchenko	Amb.
United Arab Emirates	Theodore E. Kattouf	Amb.	Muhammad bin Husayn al-Shaali	Amb.
United Kingdom	Philip J. Lader	Amb.	Christopher Meyer	Amb.
Uruguay	Christopher Ashby	Amb.	Hugo Fernandez Faingold	Amb.
Uzbekistan	Joe Presel	Amb.	Sadik Safayev	Amb.
Vanuatu	Arma Jane Karaer	Amb.	—	—
Venezuela	John Francis Maisto	Amb.	Alfredo Hardy Toro	Amb.
Vietnam	Douglas Peterson	Amb.	Le Van Bang	Amb.
Yemen	Barbara K. Bodine	Amb.	Abd al-Wahhab Abdallah al-Hajri	Amb.
Zambia	David B. Dunn	Amb.	Dunstan Weston Kamana	Amb.
Zimbabwe	Thomas McDonald	Amb.	Simbi Yeke Mubako	Amb.

1. As of spring 1999. 2. The U.S. Embassy in Barbados currently serves seven independent nations of the Eastern Caribbean (Barbados, Antigua and Barbuda, Dominica, Grenada, St. Kitts and Nevis, St. Lucia, and St. Vincent and the Grenadines) and provides consular services to American citizens in the nearby European dependent territories. 3. Ambassador to Fiji, Nauru, Tonga, and Tuvalu. 4. Head of Interests Section in U.S. 5. Special Representative for Transition in Iraq. NOTE: Amb.=Ambassador; Cd'A=Charge d'Affaires; C.G.=Consul General; Pap. Nun.=Papal Nuncio; P.O.=Principal Officer. *Source:* U.S. Department of State.

Rogue Nations become "States of Concern"

The U.S. State Department has labeled the following countries state sponsors of international terrorism: Cuba, Iran, Iraq, Libya, North Korea, Sudan, and Syria.

In 2000, the State Department officially stopped referring to these nations by the term "rogue nations" and instead identified them as "states of concern." According to the State Department, "some places that were described [as rogue] have embarked upon a more democratic internal life." Examples cited were Libya's decision to turn over the two suspects in the Lockerbie bombing, Iran's election of overwhelmingly reformist parliamentary candidates, and North Korea's halting of missile testing as well as its diplomatic overtures toward South Korea.

Football

The pastime of kicking around a ball goes back beyond the limits of recorded history. Ancient savage tribes played football of a primitive kind. There was a ball-kicking game played by Athenians, Spartans, and Corinthians 2500 years ago, which the Greeks called *Episkuros*. The Romans had a somewhat similar game called *Harpastum* and are supposed to have carried the game with them when they invaded the British Isles in the First Century, B.C.

Undoubtedly the game known in the United States as football traces directly to the English game of rugby, though the modifications have been many. Informal football was played on college lawns well over a century ago, and an annual freshman-sophomore series of "scrimmages" began at Yale in 1840. The first formal intercollegiate football game was the Princeton-Rutgers contest at New Brunswick, N.J., on Nov. 6, 1869, with Rutgers winning by 6 goals to 4.

In those days, games were played with 25, 20, 15, or 11 men on a side. In 1880, there was a convention at which Walter Camp of Yale persuaded the delegates to agree to a rule calling for 11 players on a side.

The first professional game was played in 1895 at Latrobe, Pa. The National Football League was founded in 1921. The All-American Conference went into action in 1946. At the end of the 1949 season the two circuits merged, retaining the name of the older league. In 1960, the American Football League began operations. In 1970, the leagues merged. The United States Football League played its first season in 1983, from March to July. It suspended spring operations after the 1985 season, and planned a 1986 move to fall, but suspended operations again.

In 1991, another effort at spring football was launched, but this time it had the backing of the National Football League. The World League of American Football debuted in March 1991 with ten teams. Three of them were in Europe. The other seven were in North America, including the Montreal Machine in Canada. With television contracts signed with ABC and USA Cable Network, the league seemed to be on sound footing. But after just two seasons, it was suspended. The league returned in 1995, with six teams in Europe. In 1998, it was renamed the NFL Europe League.

In Feb. 2000, the World Wrestling Federation announced the formation of XFL, a new professional league, scheduled to begin play Feb. 3, 2001.

College Football

NATIONAL COLLEGE FOOTBALL CHAMPIONS

The "National Collegiate Athletic Association Football Guide" recognizes as unofficial national champion the team selected each year by press association polls of writers and coaches.

Year	Champion	Year	Champion	Year	Champion	Year	Champion	Year	Champion
1936	Minnesota	1951	Tennessee	1964	Alabama	1975	Oklahoma	1989	Miami
1937	Pittsburgh	1952	Mich. State	1965	Alabama and Mich. State	1976	Pittsburgh	1990	Colorado and Georgia Tech
1938	Texas Christian	1953	Maryland	1966	Notre Dame	1977	Notre Dame	1991	Miami and Washington
1939	Texas A & M	1954	Ohio State and UCLA	1967	So. Calif.	1978	Alabama and So. Calif.	1992	Alabama
1940	Minnesota			1968	Ohio State	1979	Alabama	1993	Florida State
1941	Minnesota	1955	Oklahoma	1969	Texas	1980	Georgia	1994	Nebraska
1942	Ohio State	1956	Oklahoma	1970	Texas and Nebraska	1981	Clemson	1995	Nebraska
1943	Notre Dame	1957	Auburn and Ohio State			1982	Penn State	1996	Univ. of Florida
1944	Army			1971	Nebraska	1983	Miami	1997	Michigan and Nebraska
1945	Army	1958	Louisiana State	1972	So. Calif.	1984	Brigham Young		
1946	Notre Dame	1959	Syracuse	1973	Notre Dame and U. of Ala.	1985	Oklahoma	1998	Tennessee
1947	Notre Dame	1960	Minnesota			1986	Penn State	1999	Florida State
1948	Michigan	1961	Alabama	1974	Oklahoma and So. Calif.	1987	Miami		
1949	Notre Dame	1962	So. Calif.			1988	Notre Dame		
1950	Oklahoma	1963	Texas						

RECORD OF ANNUAL MAJOR COLLEGE FOOTBALL BOWL GAMES

Rose Bowl (At Pasadena, Calif.)

Year	Result	Year	Result	Year	Result
1902	Michigan 49, Stanford 0	1924	Navy 14, Washington 14	1938	California 13, Alabama 0
1916	Washington State 14, Brown 0	1925	Notre Dame 27, Stanford 10	1939	So. Calif. 7, Duke 3
1917	Oregon 14, Pennsylvania 0	1926	Alabama 20, Washington 19	1940	So. Calif. 14, Tennessee 0
1918	Mare Island Marines 19, Camp Lewis 7	1927	Alabama 7, Stanford 7	1941	Stanford 21, Nebraska 13
		1928	Stanford 7, Pittsburgh 6	1942	Oregon State 20, Duke 16[1]
1919	Great Lakes 17, Mare Island Marines 0	1929	Georgia Tech 8, California 7	1943	Georgia 9, UCLA 0
		1930	So. Calif. 47, Pittsburgh 14	1944	So. Calif. 29, Washington 0
1920	Harvard 7, Oregon 6	1931	Alabama 24, Wash. State 0	1945	So. Calif. 25, Tennessee 0
1921	California 28, Ohio State 0	1932	So. Calif. 21, Tulane 12	1946	Alabama 34, So. Calif. 14
1922	Washington and Jefferson 0, California 0	1933	So. Calif. 35, Pittsburgh 0	1947	Illinois 45, UCLA 14
		1934	Columbia 7, Stanford 0	1948	Michigan 49, So. Calif. 0
1923	So. Calif. 14, Penn State 3	1935	Alabama 29, Stanford 13	1949	Northwestern 20, California 14
		1936	Stanford 7, So. Methodist 0	1950	Ohio State 17, California 14
		1937	Pittsburgh 21, Washington 0	1951	Michigan 14, California 6

1952	Illinois 40, Stanford 7
1953	So. Calif. 7, Wisconsin 0
1954	Michigan State 28, UCLA 20
1955	Ohio State 20, So. Calif. 7
1956	Michigan State 17, UCLA 14
1957	Iowa 35, Oregon State 19
1958	Ohio State 10, Oregon 7
1959	Iowa 38, California 12
1960	Washington 44, Wisconsin 8
1961	Washington 17, Minnesota 7
1962	Minnesota 21, UCLA 3
1963	So. Calif. 42, Wisconsin 37
1964	Illinois 17, Washington 7
1965	Michigan 34, Oregon State 7
1966	UCLA 14, Michigan State 12
1967	Purdue 14, So. Calif. 13
1968	So. Calif. 14, Indiana 3
1969	Ohio State 27, So. Calif. 16
1970	So. Calif. 10, Michigan 3
1971	Stanford 27, Ohio State 17
1972	Stanford 13, Michigan 12
1973	So. Calif. 42, Ohio State 17
1974	Ohio State 42, So. Calif. 21
1975	So. Calif. 18, Ohio State 17
1976	UCLA 23, Ohio State 10
1977	So. Calif. 14, Michigan 6
1978	Washington 27, Michigan 20
1979	So. Calif. 17, Michigan 10
1980	So. Calif. 17, Ohio State 16
1981	Michigan 23, Washington 6
1982	Washington 28, Iowa 0
1983	UCLA 24, Michigan 14
1984	UCLA 45, Illinois 9
1985	So. Calif. 20, Ohio St. 17
1986	UCLA 45, Iowa 28
1987	Arizona State 22, Michigan 15
1988	Michigan State 20, So. Calif. 17
1989	Michigan 22, So. Calif. 14
1990	So. Calif. 17, Michigan 10
1991	Washington 46, Iowa 34
1992	Washington 34, Michigan 14
1993	Michigan 38, Washington 31
1994	Wisconsin 21, UCLA 16
1995	Penn State 38, Oregon 20
1996	So. Calif. 41, Northwestern 32
1997	Ohio State 20, Arizona State 17
1998	Michigan 21, Washington State 16
1999	Wisconsin 38, UCLA 31
2000	Wisconsin 17, Stanford 9

1. Played at Durham, N.C.

Orange Bowl (At Miami)

1933	Miami (Fla.) 7, Manhattan 0
1934	Duquesne 33, Miami (Fla.) 7
1935	Bucknell 26, Miami (Fla.) 0
1936	Catholic 20, Mississippi 19
1937	Duquesne 13, Mississippi State 12
1938	Auburn 6, Michigan State 0
1939	Tennessee 17, Oklahoma 0
1940	Georgia Tech 21, Missouri 7
1941	Mississippi State 14, Georgetown 7
1942	Georgia 40, Texas Christian 26
1943	Alabama 37, Boston College 21
1944	Louisiana State 19, Texas A & M 14
1945	Tulsa 26, Georgia Tech 12
1946	Miami (Fla.) 13, Holy Cross 6
1947	Rice 8, Tennessee 0
1948	Georgia Tech 20, Kansas 14
1949	Texas 41, Georgia 28

1950	Santa Clara 21, Kentucky 13
1951	Clemson 15, Miami (Fla.) 14
1952	Georgia Tech 17, Baylor 14
1953	Alabama 61, Syracuse 6
1954	Oklahoma 7, Maryland 0
1955	Duke 34, Nebraska 7
1956	Oklahoma 20, Maryland 6
1957	Colorado 27, Clemson 21
1958	Oklahoma 48, Duke 21
1959	Oklahoma 21, Syracuse 6
1960	Georgia 14, Missouri 0
1961	Missouri 21, Navy 14
1962	Louisiana State 25, Colorado 7
1963	Alabama 17, Oklahoma 0
1964	Nebraska 13, Auburn 7
1965	Texas 21, Alabama 17
1966	Alabama 39, Nebraska 28
1967	Florida 27, Georgia Tech 12
1968	Oklahoma 26, Tennessee 24
1969	Penn State 15, Kansas 14
1970	Penn State 10, Missouri 3
1971	Nebraska 17, Louisiana State 12
1972	Nebraska 38, Alabama 6
1973	Nebraska 40, Notre Dame 6
1974	Penn State 16, Louisiana State 9
1975	Notre Dame 13, Alabama 11
1976	Oklahoma 14, Michigan 6
1977	Ohio State 27, Colorado 10
1978	Arkansas 31, Oklahoma 6
1979	Oklahoma 31, Nebraska 24
1980	Oklahoma 24, Florida State 7
1981	Oklahoma 18, Florida State 17
1982	Clemson 22, Nebraska 15
1983	Nebraska 21, Louisiana State 20
1984	Miami (Fla.) 31, Nebraska 30
1985	Washington 28, Oklahoma 17
1986	Oklahoma 25, Penn State 10
1987	Oklahoma 42, Arkansas 8
1988	Miami (Fla.) 20, Oklahoma 14
1989	Miami (Fla.) 23, Nebraska 3
1990	Notre Dame 21, Colorado 6
1991	Colorado 10, Notre Dame 9
1992	Miami (Fla.) 22, Nebraska 0
1993	Florida State 27, Nebraska 14
1994	Florida State 18, Nebraska 16
1995	Nebraska 24, Miami (Fla.) 17
1996	Florida State 31, Notre Dame 26
1997	Nebraska 41, Virginia Tech 21
1998	Nebraska 42, Tennessee 17
1999	Florida 31, Syracuse 10
2000	Michigan 35, Alabama 34

Sugar Bowl (At New Orleans)

1935	Tulane 20, Temple 14
1936	Texas Christian 3, Louisiana State 2
1937	Santa Clara 21, Louisiana State 14
1938	Santa Clara 6, Louisiana State 0
1939	Texas Christian 15, Carnegie Tech 7
1940	Texas A & M 14, Tulane 13
1941	Boston College 19, Tennessee 13
1942	Fordham 2, Missouri 0
1943	Tennessee 14, Tulsa 7
1944	Georgia Tech 20, Tulsa 18
1945	Duke 29, Alabama 26

1946	Oklahoma A & M 33, St. Mary's (Calif.) 13
1947	Georgia 20, North Carolina 10
1948	Texas 27, Alabama 7
1949	Oklahoma 14, North Carolina 6
1950	Oklahoma 35, Louisiana State 0
1951	Kentucky 13, Oklahoma 7
1952	Maryland 28, Tennessee 13
1953	Georgia Tech 24, Mississippi 7
1954	Georgia Tech 42, West Virginia 19
1955	Navy 21, Mississippi 0
1956	Georgia Tech 7, Pittsburgh 0
1957	Baylor 13, Tennessee 7
1958	Mississippi 39, Texas 7
1959	Louisiana State 7, Clemson 0
1960	Mississippi 21, Louisiana State 0
1961	Mississippi 14, Rice 6
1962	Alabama 10, Arkansas 3
1963	Mississippi 17, Arkansas 13
1964	Alabama 12, Mississippi 7
1965	Louisiana State 13, Syracuse 10
1966	Missouri 20, Florida 18
1967	Alabama 34, Nebraska 7
1968	Louisiana State 20, Wyoming 13
1969	Arkansas 16, Georgia 2
1970	Mississippi 27, Arkansas 22
1971	Tennessee 34, Air Force Academy 13
1972	Oklahoma 40, Auburn 22
1973	Oklahoma 14, Penn State 0
1974	Notre Dame 24, Alabama 23
1975	Nebraska 13, Florida 10
1976	Alabama 13, Penn State 6
1977	Pittsburgh 27, Georgia 3
1978	Alabama 35, Ohio State 6
1979	Alabama 14, Penn State 7
1980	Alabama 24, Arkansas 9
1981	Georgia 17, Notre Dame 10
1982	Pittsburgh 24, Georgia 20
1983	Penn State 27, Georgia 23
1984	Auburn 9, Michigan 7
1985	Nebraska 28, Louisiana State 10
1986	Tennessee 35, Miami (Fla.) 7
1987	Nebraska 30, Louisiana State 15
1988	Syracuse 16, Auburn 16 (tie)
1989	Florida State 13, Auburn 7
1990	Miami (Fla.) 33, Alabama 25
1991	Tennessee 23, Virginia 22
1992	Notre Dame 39, Florida 28
1993	Alabama 34, Miami (Fla.) 13
1994	Florida 41, West Virginia 7
1995	Florida State 23, Florida 17
1996	Virginia Tech 28, Texas 10
1997	Florida 52, Florida State 20
1998	Florida State 31, Ohio State 14
1999	Ohio State 24, Texas A & M 14
2000	Florida State 46, Virginia Tech. 29

Cotton Bowl (At Dallas)

1937	Texas Christian 16, Marquette 6
1938	Rice 28, Colorado 14
1939	St. Mary's (Calif.) 20, Texas Tech. 13
1940	Clemson 6, Boston College 3
1941	Texas A & M 13, Fordham 12
1942	Alabama 29, Texas A & M 21
1943	Texas 14, Georgia Tech 7

1944	Randolph Field 7, Texas 7
1945	Oklahoma A & M 34, Texas Christian 0
1946	Texas 40, Missouri 27
1947	Louisiana State 0, Arkansas 0
1948	So. Methodist 13, Penn State 13
1949	So. Methodist 21, Oregon 13
1950	Rice 27, North Carolina 13
1951	Tennessee 20, Texas 14
1952	Kentucky 20, Texas Christian 7
1953	Texas 16, Tennessee 0
1954	Rice 28, Alabama 6
1955	Georgia Tech 14, Arkansas 6
1956	Mississippi 14, Texas Christian 13
1957	Texas Christian 28, Syracuse 27
1958	Navy 20, Rice 7
1959	Air Force 0, Texas Christian 0
1960	Syracuse 23, Texas 14
1961	Duke 7, Arkansas 6
1962	Texas 12, Mississippi 7
1963	Louisiana State 13, Texas 0
1964	Texas 28, Navy 6
1965	Arkansas 10, Nebraska 7
1966	Louisiana State 14, Arkansas 7
1967	Georgia 24, So. Methodist 9
1968	Texas A & M 20, Alabama 16
1969	Texas 36, Tennessee 13
1970	Texas 21, Notre Dame 17
1971	Notre Dame 24, Texas 11
1972	Penn State 30, Texas 6
1973	Texas 17, Alabama 13
1974	Nebraska 19, Texas 3
1975	Penn State 41, Baylor 20
1976	Arkansas 31, Georgia 10
1977	Houston 30, Maryland 21
1978	Notre Dame 38, Texas 10
1979	Notre Dame 35, Houston 34
1980	Houston 17, Nebraska 14
1981	Alabama 30, Baylor 2

1982	Texas 14, Alabama 12
1983	So. Meth. 7, Pittsburgh 3
1984	Georgia 10, Texas 9
1985	Boston College 45, Houston 28
1986	Texas A & M 36, Auburn 16
1987	Ohio State 28, Texas A & M 12
1988	Texas A & M 35, Notre Dame 10
1989	UCLA 17, Arkansas 3
1990	Tennessee 31, Arkansas 27
1991	Miami (Fla.) 46, Texas 3
1992	Florida State 10, Texas A & M 2
1993	Notre Dame 28, Texas A & M 3
1994	Notre Dame 24, Texas A & M 21
1995	So. Calif. 55, Texas Tech 14
1996	Colorado 38, Oregon 6
1997	Brigham Young 19, Kansas State 15
1998	UCLA 29, Texas A & M 23
1999	Texas 38, Mississippi State 11
2000	Arkansas 27, Texas 6

Gator Bowl (At Jacksonville, Fla.)

1953	Florida 14, Tulsa 13
1954	Texas Tech 35, Auburn 13
1955	Auburn 33, Baylor 13
1956	Vanderbilt 25, Auburn 13
1957	Georgia Tech 21, Pittsburgh 14
1958	Tennessee 3, Texas A & M 0
1959	Mississippi 7, Florida 3
1960	Arkansas 14, Georgia Tech 7
1961	Florida 13, Baylor 12
1962	Penn State 30, Georgia Tech 15
1963	Florida 17, Penn State 7
1964	No. Carolina 14, Air Force 0
1965	Florida State 36, Oklahoma 19
1966	Georgia Tech 31, Texas Tech 21
1967	Tennessee 18, Syracuse 12

1968	Penn State 17, Florida State 17 (tie)
1969	Missouri 35, Alabama 10
1970	Florida 14, Tennessee 13
1971	Auburn 35, Mississippi 28
1972	Georgia 7, North Carolina 3
1973	Auburn 24, Colorado 3
1974	Texas Tech 28, Tennessee 19
1975	Auburn 27, Texas 3
1976	Maryland 13, Florida 0
1977	Notre Dame 20, Penn State 9
1978	Pittsburgh 34, Clemson 3
1979	Clemson 17, Ohio State 15
1980	North Carolina 17, Michigan 15
1981	Pittsburgh 37, South Carolina 9
1982	North Carolina 31, Arkansas 27
1983	Florida State 31, West Virginia 12
1984	Florida 14, Iowa 6
1985	Oklahoma State 21, South Carolina 14
1986	Florida State 34, Oklahoma State 23
1987	Clemson 27, Stanford 21
1988	Louisiana State 30, South Carolina 13
1989	Georgia 34, Mich. State 27
1990	Clemson 27, West Virginia 7
1991	Michigan 35, Mississippi 3
1992	Oklahoma 38, Virginia 14
1993	Florida 27, No. Carolina St. 10
1994	Alabama 24, No. Carolina 10
1995	Tennessee 45, Virginia Tech 23
1996	Syracuse 41, Clemson 0
1997	North Carolina 20, West Virginia 13
1998	North Carolina 42, Virginia Tech 3
1999	Georgia Tech 35, Notre Dame 28
2000	Miami (Fla.) 28, Georgia Tech 13

RESULTS OF OTHER 1999–2000 BOWL GAMES

Alamo (Dec. 28, 1999)—Penn State 24, Texas A&M 0

Aloha (Dec. 25, 1999)—Wake Forest 23, Arizona State 3

Citrus (Jan. 1, 2000)—Michigan State 37, Florida 34

Fiesta (Jan. 2, 2000)—Tennessee 21, Nebraska 31

Holiday (Dec. 29, 1999)—Washington 20, Kansas State 24

Humanitarian (Dec. 30, 1999)—Louisville 31, Boise State 34

Independence (Dec. 31, 1999)—Mississippi 27, Oklahoma 25

Insight.com (Dec. 31, 1999)—Colorado 62, Boston College 28

Las Vegas (Dec. 18, 1999)—Fresno State 16, Utah 17

Liberty (Dec. 31, 1999)—Colorado State 17, Southern Mississippi 23

Motor City (Dec. 27, 1999)—Brigham Young 3, Marshall 21

Music City (Dec. 29, 1999)—Syracuse 20, Kentucky 13

Oahu (Dec. 25, 1999)—Hawaii 23, Oregon State 17

Outback (Jan. 1, 2000)—Purdue 25, Georgia 28

PC (Dec. 30, 1999)—Illinois 63, Virginia 21

Peach (Dec. 30, 1999)—Clemson 7, Mississippi State 17

Sun (Dec. 31, 1999)—Minnesota 20, Oregon 24

HEISMAN MEMORIAL TROPHY WINNERS

The Heisman Memorial Trophy is presented annually by the Downtown Athletic Club of New York City to the nation's outstanding college football player, as determined by a poll of sportswriters and sportscasters.

1935	Jay Berwanger, Chicago
1936	Larry Kelley, Yale
1937	Clinton Frank, Yale
1938	Davey O'Brien, Texas Christian
1939	Nile Kinnick, Iowa
1940	Tom Harmon, Michigan
1941	Bruce Smith, Minnesota
1942	Frank Sinkwich, Georgia
1943	Angelo Bertelli, Notre Dame
1944	Leslie Horvath, Ohio State
1945	Felix Blanchard, Army
1946	Glenn Davis, Army
1947	Johnny Lujack, Notre Dame

1948	Doak Walker, So. Methodist
1949	Leon Hart, Notre Dame
1950	Vic Janowicz, Ohio State
1951	Dick Kazmaier, Princeton
1952	Billy Vessels, Oklahoma
1953	Johnny Lattner, Notre Dame
1954	Alan Ameche, Wisconsin
1955	Howard Cassady, Ohio State
1956	Paul Hornung, Notre Dame
1957	John Crow, Texas A & M
1958	Pete Dawkins, Army
1959	Billy Cannon, Louisiana State
1960	Joe Bellino, Navy

1961	Ernie Davis, Syracuse
1962	Terry Baker, Oregon State
1963	Roger Staubach, Navy
1964	John Huarte, Notre Dame
1965	Mike Garrett, So. Calif.
1966	Steve Spurrier, Florida
1967	Gary Beban, UCLA
1968	O.J. Simpson, So. Calif.
1969	Steve Owens, Oklahoma
1970	Jim Plunkett, Stanford
1971	Pat Sullivan, Auburn
1972	Johnny Rodgers, Nebraska
1973	John Cappelletti, Penn State

1974-75 Archie Griffin, Ohio State
1976 Tony Dorsett, Pittsburgh
1977 Earl Campbell, Texas
1978 Billy Sims, Oklahoma
1979 Charles White, So. Calif.
1980 George Rogers, South Carolina
1981 Marcus Allen, So. Calif.
1982 Herschel Walker, Georgia
1983 Mike Rozier, Nebraska

1984 Doug Flutie, Boston College
1985 Bo Jackson, Auburn
1986 Vinny Testaverde, Miami
1987 Tim Brown, Notre Dame
1988 Barry Sanders, Oklahoma State
1989 Andre Ware, Houston
1990 Ty Detmer, Brigham Young
1991 Desmond Howard, Michigan
1992 Gino Torretta, Miami

1993 Charlie Ward, Florida State
1994 Rashaan Salaam, Colorado
1995 Eddie George, Ohio State
1996 Danny Wuerffel, Florida
1997 Charles Woodson, Michigan
1998 Ricky Williams, Texas
1999 Ron Dayne, Wisconsin

1999 N.C.A.A. CHAMPIONSHIP PLAYOFFS

DIVISION I-AA
Quarterfinals
(Dec. 4, 1999)
Illinois State 37, Hofstra 20
Georgia Southern 38, Massachusetts 21
Youngstown State 41, North Carolina A&T 3
Florida A&M 17, Troy State 10
Semifinals
(Dec. 11, 1999)
Georgia Southern 28, Illinois State 17
Youngstown State 27, Florida A&M 24
Championship
(Dec. 18, 1999)
Georgia Southern 59, Youngstown State 24

DIVISION II
Quarterfinals
(Nov. 27, 1999)
Carson-Newman (Tenn.) 28, Catawba 25
Indiana (Pa.) 26, Millersville (Pa.) 21
Northwest Missouri State 41, Northern Colorado 35
Northeastern State (Okla.) 19, UC Davis 14
Semifinals
(Dec. 4, 1999)
Northwest Missouri State 20, Indiana (Pa.) 12
Carson-Newman (Tenn.) 42, Northeastern State (Okla.) 7
Championship
(Dec. 11, 1999)
Northwest Missouri State 58, Carson-Newman (Tenn.) 52

DIVISION III
Quarterfinals
(Dec. 4, 1999)
Mount Union 56, Ohio Northern 31
Rowan 42, Montclair State 13
Pacific Lutheran 19, St. John's (Minn.) 9
Trinity (Texas) 40, Hardin-Simmons 33
Semifinals
(Dec. 11, 1999)
Rowan 24, Mount Union 17 (OT)
Pacific Lutheran 49, Trinity (Texas) 28
Championship
(Dec. 18, 1999)
Pacific Lutheran 42, Rowan 13

1999 NATIONAL ASSOCIATION OF INTERCOLLEGIATE ATHLETICS CHAMPIONSHIPS

Quarterfinals
(Nov. 27, 1999)
Georgetown (Ky.) 55, Taylor (Ind.) 3
Univ. of Mary (N.D.) 7, Rocky Mountain (Mont.) 3
Northwestern Oklahoma State 56, Lambuth (Tenn.) 13
Azusa Pacific (Calif.) 38, Hastings (Neb.) 35

Semifinals
(Dec. 4, 1999)
Northwestern Oklahoma State 21, Univ. of Mary (N.D.) 6
Georgetown (Ky.) 66, Azusa Pacific (Calif.) 35
Championship
(Dec. 18, 1999)
Northwestern Oklahoma State 34, Georgetown (Ky.) 26

COLLEGE FOOTBALL HALL OF FAME

(P.O. Box 11146, South Bend, Indiana)
NOTE: Date given is player's last year of competition.

Players
Abell, Earl—Colgate, 1915
Agase, Alex—Purdue/Illinois, 1946
Agganis, Harry—Boston Univ., 1952
Albert, Frank—Stanford, 1941
Aldrich, Chas. (Ki)—Texas Christian, 1938
Aldrich, Malcolm—Yale, 1921
Alexander, Joseph—Syracuse, 1920
Allen, Marcus—So. Calif., 1981
Alworth, Lance—Arkansas, 1961
Ameche, Alan (Horse)—Wisconsin, 1954
Amling, Warren—Ohio State, 1946
Anderson, Dick—Colorado, 1967
Anderson, Donny—Texas Tech, 1965
Anderson, H. (Hunk)—Notre Dame, 1921
Atkins, Doug—Tennessee, 1952
Babich, Bob—Miami-Ohio, 1968
Bacon, C. Everett—Wesleyan, 1912
Bagnell, Francis (Reds)—Pennsylvania, 1950
Baker, Hobart (Hobey)—Princeton, 1913
Baker, John—So. Calif., 1931
Baker, Terry—Oregon State, 1962
Ballin, Harold—Princeton, 1914

Banker, Bill—Tulane, 1929
Banonis, Vince—Detroit, 1941
Barnes, Stanley—So. Calif., 1921
Barrett, Charles—Cornell, 1915
Baston, Bert—Minnesota, 1916
Battles, Cliff—W. Va. Wesleyan, 1931
Baugh, Sammy—Texas Christian, 1936
Baughan, Maxie—Georgia Tech, 1959
Bausch, James—Kansas, 1930
Beagle, Ron—Navy, 1955
Beban, Gary—UCLA, 1967
Bechtol, Hub—Texas Tech, 1946
Beck, Ray—Georgia Tech, 1951
Beckett, John—Oregon, 1913
Bednarik, Chuck—Pennsylvania 1948
Behm, Forrest—Nebraska, 1940
Bell, Bobby—Minnesota, 1962
Bellino, Joe—Navy, 1960
Below, Marty—Wisconsin, 1923
Benbrook, A.—Michigan, 1911
Bentrim, Jeff—North Dakota State, 1986
Bertelli, A.—Notre Dame, 1943
Berry, Charlie—Lafayette, 1924
Berwanger, John (Jay)—Chicago, 1935

Bettencourt, Larry—St. Mary's, 1927
Biletnikoff, Fred—Florida State, 1964
Blanchard, Felix (Doc)—Army, 1946
Bock, Ed—Iowa State, 1938
Bomar, Lynn—Vanderbilt, 1924
Bomeisler, Doug (Bo)—Yale, 1913
Booth, Albie—Yale, 1931
Bork, George—Northern Illinois, 1963
Borries, Fred—Navy, 1934
Bosely, Bruce—West Virginia, 1955
Bosseler, Don—Miami (Fla.), 1956
Bottari, Vic—California, 1939
Boynton, Ben—Williams, 1920
Bozis, Al—Georgetown, 1941
Bradshaw, Terry—Louisiana Tech, 1969
Brewer, Charles—Harvard, 1895
Bright, John—Drake, 1951
Brodie, John—Stanford, 1956
Brooke, George—Pennsylvania, 1895
Brosky, Al—Illinois, 1952
Brown, Bob—Nebraska, 1963
Brown, George—Navy/San Diego State, 1947
Brown, Gordon—Yale, 1900

Johnson, Ron—Michigan, 1968
Jones, Calvin—Iowa, 1955
Jones, Gormer—Ohio State, 1935
Jones, Stan—Maryland, 1953
Jordan, Lee Roy—Alabama, 1962
Juhan, Frank—Univ. of South, 1910
Justice, Charlie—North Carolina, 1949
Kaer, Mort—So. Calif., 1926
Karras, Alex—Iowa, 1957
Kavanaugh, Kenneth—Louisiana State, 1939
Kaw, Edgar—Cornell, 1922
Kazmaier, Richard—Princeton, 1951
Keck, James—Princeton, 1921
Kelley, Larry—Yale, 1936
Kelly, William—Montana, 1926
Kenna, Ed—Syracuse, 1966
Kern, George—Boston College, 1941
Ketcham, Henry—Yale, 1913
Keyes, Leroy—Purdue, 1968
Killinger, William—Penn State, 1922
Kilmer, Billy—UCLA, 1960
Kimbrough, John—Texas A & M, 1940
Kinard, Frank—Mississippi, 1937
Kiner, Steve—Tennessee, 1969
King, Philip—Princeton, 1893
Kinnick, Nile—Iowa, 1939
Kipke, Harry—Michigan, 1923
Kirkpatrick, John Reed—Yale, 1910
Kitzmiller, John—Oregon, 1929
Koch, Barton—Baylor, 1931
Kitner, Malcolm—Texas, 1942
Kramer, Ron—Michigan, 1956
Kroll, Alex—Rutgers, 1961
Krueger, Charlie—Texas A & M, 1957
Kwalick, Ted—Penn State, 1968
Lach, Steve—Duke, 1941
Lane, Myles—Dartmouth, 1927
Lattner, Joseph J.—Notre Dame, 1953
Lauricella, Hank—Tennessee, 1952
Lautenschlaeger—Tulane, 1925
Layden, Elmer—Notre Dame, 1924
Layne, Bobby—Texas, 1947
Lea, Langdon—Princeton, 1895
LeBaron, Eddie—Univ. of Pacific, 1949
LeClair, Jim—North Dakota, 1971
Leech, James—Va. Mil. Inst., 1920
Lester, Darrell—Texas Christian, 1935
Lilly, Bob—Texas Christian, 1960
Little, Floyd—Syracuse, 1966
Lio, Augie—Georgetown, 1940
Locke, Gordon—Iowa, 1922
Lomax, Neil—Portland (Ore.) State, 1980
Long, Chuck—Iowa, 1985
Long, Mel—Toledo, 1971
Loria, Frank—Virginia Tech, 1967
Lourie, Don—Princeton, 1921
Lucas, Richard—Penn State, 1959
Luckman, Sid—Columbia, 1938
Lujack, John—Notre Dame, 1947
Lund, J.L. (Pug)—Minnesota, 1934
Lynch, Jim—Notre Dame, 1966
MacAfee, Ken—Notre Dame, 1977
Macomber, Bart—Illinois, 1915
MacLeod, Robert—Dartmouth, 1938
Maegle, Dick—Rice, 1954
Mahan, Edward W.—Harvard, 1915
Majors, John—Tennessee, 1956
Mallory, William—Yale, 1893
Mancha, Vaughn—Alabama, 1947
Mann, Gerald—So. Methodist, 1927
Manning, Archie—Mississippi, 1970
Manske, Edgar—Northwestern, 1933
Marinaro, Ed—Cornell, 1971
Markov, Vic—Washington, 1937
Marshall, Robert—Minnesota, 1907
Martin, Jim—Notre Dame, 1949
Matson, Ollie—San Fran. U., 1952
Matthews, Ray—Texas Christian, 1928
Maulbetsch, John—Michigan, 1914
Mauthe, J.L. (Pete)—Penn State, 1912
Maxwell, Robert—Chicago/Swarthmore, 1906

McAfee, George—Duke, 1939
McClung, Thomas L.—Yale, 1891
McColl, William F.—Stanford, 1951
McCormick, James B.—Princeton, 1907
McDonald, Tom—Oklahoma, 1956
McDowall, Jack—No. Carolina State, 1927
McElhenny, Hugh—Washington, 1951
McEver, Gene—Tennessee, 1931
McEwan, John—Minn./Army, 1916
McFadden, J.B.—Clemson, 1939
McFadin, Bud—Texas, 1950
McGee, Mike—Duke, 1959
McGinley, Edward—Pennsylvania, 1924
McGovern, J.—Minnesota, 1910
McGraw, Thurman—Colorado State, 1949
McGriff, Tyrone—Florida A & M, 1979
McKeever, Mike—So. Calif., 1960
McLaren, George—Pittsburgh, 1918
McMahon, Jim—Brigham Young, 1981
McMillan, Dan—So. Calif./California, 1922
McMillin, A.N. (Bo)—Centre, 1921
McWhorter, Robert—Georgia, 1913
Mercer, Leroy—Pennsylvania, 1912
Meredith, Don—So. Methodist, 1959
Merritt, Frank—Army, 1943
Metzger, Bert—Notre Dame, 1930
Meyland, Wayne—Nebraska, 1967
Michaels, Lou—Kentucky, 1957
Michels, John—Tennessee, 1952
Mickal, Abe—Louisiana State, 1935
Miller, Creighton—Notre Dame, 1943
Miller, Don—Notre Dame, 1925
Miller, Edgar (Rip)—Notre Dame, 1924
Miller, Eugene—Penn State, 1913
Miller, Fred—Notre Dame, 1928
Millner, Wayne—Notre Dame, 1935
Milstead, Century—Wabash/Yale, 1923
Minds, John—Pennsylvania, 1897
Minisi, Anthony—Navy/Pennsylvania, 1947
Modzelewski, Dick—Maryland, 1952
Moffatt, Alex—Princeton, 1884
Molinski, Ed—Tennessee, 1940
Montgomery, Cliff—Columbia, 1933
Montgomery, Wilbert—Abilene Christian, 1976
Moomaw, Donn—UCLA, 1952
Morley, William—Columbia, 1903
Morris, George—Georgia Tech, 1952
Morris, Larry—Georgia Tech, 1954
Morton, Craig—California, 1964
Morton, William—Dartmouth, 1931
Moscrip, Monk—Stanford, 1935
Muller, Harold (Brick)—Calif., 1922
Musso, Johnny—Alabama, 1971
Nagurski, Bronko—Minnesota, 1929
Nevers, Ernie—Stanford, 1925
Newell, Marshall—Harvard, 1893
Newman, Harry—Michigan, 1932
Newsome, Ozzie—Alabama, 1977
Nielsen, Gifford—Brigham Young, 1976
Nobis, Tommy—Texas, 1965
Nomellini, Leo—Minnesota, 1949
Oberland, Andrew—Dartmouth, 1925
O'Brien, Davey—Texas Christian, 1938
O'Brien, Ken—Cal.-Davis, 1982
O'Dea, Pat—Wisconsin, 1899
Odell, Robert—Pennsylvania, 1943
O'Hearn, J.—Cornell, 1915
Olds, Robin—Army, 1942
Oliphant, Elmer—Purdue/Army, 1917
Olsen, Merlin—Utah State, 1961
Onkotz, Dennis—Penn State, 1969
Oosterbaan, Ben—Michigan, 1927
O'Rourke, Charles—Boston College, 1940
Orsi, John—Colgate, 1931
Osgood, W.D.—Cornell/Pennsylvania, 1895
Osmanski, William—Holy Cross, 1938
Owen, George—Harvard, 1922

Owens, Jim—Oklahoma, 1949
Owens, Steve—Oklahoma, 1969
Page, Alan—Notre Dame, 1966
Palumbo, Joe—U. of Virginia, 1951
Pardee, Jack—Texas A & M, 1956
Parilli, Vito (Babe)—Kentucky, 1951
Parker, Clarence (Ace)—Duke, 1936
Parker, Jackie—Miss. State, 1953
Parker, James—Ohio State, 1956
Payton, Walter—Jackson State, 1974
Pazzetti, V.J.—Wesleyan/Lehigh, 1912
Peabody, Endicott—Harvard, 1941
Peck, Robert—Pittsburgh, 1916
Pellegrini, Bob—Maryland, 1955
Pennock, Stanley B.—Harvard, 1914
Pfann, George—Cornell, 1923
Phillips, H.D.—Univ. of South, 1904
Phillips, Loyd—Arkansas, 1966
Pingel, John—Michigan State, 1938
Pihos, Pete—Indiana, 1945
Pinckert, Ernie—So. Calif., 1931
Plunkett, Jim—Stanford, 1970
Poe, Arthur—Princeton, 1899
Pollard, Fritz—Brown, 1916
Poole, Barney—Miss./Army, 1947
Powell, Marvin—So. Calif., 1976
Pregulman, Merv—Michigan, 1943
Price, Eddie—Tulane, 1949
Pruitt, Greg—Oklahoma, 1972
Pugh, Larry—Westminster, Pa., 1964
Pund, Henry—Georgia Tech, 1928
Ramsey, Gerrard—Wm. & Mary, 1942
Reasons, Gary—Northwestern State (La.), 1983
Redman, Rick—Washington, 1964
Reeds, Claude—Oklahoma, 1913
Reid, Mike—Penn State, 1970
Reid, Steve—Northwestern, 1936
Reid, William—Harvard, 1900
Reifsnyder, Bob—Navy, 1958
Renfro, Mel—Oregon, 1963
Rentner, Ernest—Northwestern, 1932
Reynolds, Robert—Nebraska, 1952
Reynolds, Robert—Stanford, 1935
Rhome, Jerry—Tulsa, 1964
Richter, Les—California, 1951
Richter, Pat—Wisconsin, 1962
Riley, John—Northwestern, 1931
Rimington, Dave—Nebraska, 1982
Rinehart, Charles—Lafayette, 1897
Ritchie, Richard—Texas A & M, 1977
Ritcher, Jim—No. Carolina St., 1979
Roberts, J.D.—Oklahoma, 1953
Robeson, Paul—Rutgers, 1918
Robinson, Dave—Penn State, 1962
Robinson, Jerry—UCLA, 1978
Rodgers, Ira—West Virginia, 1919
Rodgers, Johnny—Nebraska, 1972
Rogers, Edward L.—Minnesota, 1903
Rogers, George—South Carolina, 1980
Roland, Johnny—Missouri, 1965
Romig, Joe—Colorado, 1961
Rosenberg, Aaron—So. Calif., 1934
Rote, Kyle—So. Methodist, 1950
Routt, Joe—Texas A & M, 1937
Salmon, Louis—Notre Dame, 1904
Sarkisian, Alex—Northwestern, 1948
Sauer, George—Nebraska, 1933
Savitsky, George—Pennsylvania, 1947
Saxon, Jimmy—Texas, 1961
Sayers Gale—Kansas, 1964
Scarbath, Jack—Maryland, 1952
Scarlett, Hunter—Pennsylvania, 1909
Schloredt, Bob—Washington, 1960
Schmidt, Joe—Pittsburgh, 1952
Schoonover, Wear—Arkansas, 1929
Schreiner, Dave—Wisconsin, 1942
Schultz, Adolf (Germany)—Mich., 1908
Schwab, Frank—Lafayette, 1922
Schwartz, Marchmont—Notre Dame, 1931
Schwegler, Paul—Washington, 1931
Scott, Clyde—Arkansas, 1949

Scott, Richard—Navy, 1947
Scott, Tom—Virginia, 1953
Seibels, Henry—Sewanee, 1899
Sellers, Ron—Florida State, 1968
Sewell, Harley—Texas, 1952
Shakespeare, Bill—Notre Dame, 1935
Shell, Donnie—So. Carolina St., 1973
Shelton, Murray—Cornell, 1915
Shevlin, Tom—Yale, 1905
Shively, Bernie—Illinois, 1926
Simons, Claude—Tulane, 1934
Sims, Billy—Oklahoma, 1979
Simpson, O.J.—So. Calif., 1968
Singletary, Mike—Baylor, 1980
Sington, Fred—Alabama, 1930
Sinkwich, Frank—Georgia, 1942
Sitko, Emil—Notre Dame, 1949
Skladany, Joe—Pittsburgh, 1933
Slater, F.F. (Duke)—Iowa, 1921
Smith, Billy Ray—Arkansas, 1982
Smith, Bruce—Minnesota, 1941
Smith, Bubba—Michigan State, 1966
Smith, Ernie—So. Calif., 1932
Smith, Harry—So. Calif., 1939
Smith, Jim Ray—Baylor, 1954
Smith, John (Clipper)—Notre Dame, 1927
Smith, Riley—Alabama, 1935
Smith, Vernon—Georgia, 1931
Snow, Neil—Michigan, 1901
Sparlis, Al—UCLA, 1945
Spears, Clarence W.—Dartmouth, 1915
Spears, W.D.—Vanderbilt, 1927
Sprackling, William—Brown, 1911
Sprague, M. (Bud)—Texas/Army, 1928
Spurrier, Steve—Florida, 1966
Stafford, Harrison—Texas, 1932
Stagg, Amos Alonzo—Yale, 1889
Stanfill, Bill—Georgia, 1968
Starcevich, Max—Washington, 1936
Staubach, Roger—Navy, 1963
Steffen, Walter—Chicago, 1908
Steffy, Joe—Army, 1947
Stein, Herbert—Pittsburgh, 1921
Steuber, Robert—Missouri, 1943
Stevens, Mal—Yale, 1923
Stevenson, Vincent—Pennsylvania, 1905
Stillwagon, Jim—Ohio State, 1970
Stinchcomb, Gaylord—Ohio State, 1920
Strom, Brock—Air Force, 1959

Strong, Ken—New York Univ., 1928
Strupper, George—Georgia Tech, 1917
Stuhldreher, Harry—Notre Dame, 1924
Stydahar, Joe—West Virginia, 1935
Suffridge, Robert—Tennessee, 1940
Suhey, Steve—Penn State, 1947
Sullivan, Pat—Auburn, 1971
Sundstrom, Frank—Cornell, 1923
Swann, Lynn—So. Calif., 1973
Swanson, Clarence—Nebraska, 1921
Swiacki, Bill—Holy Cross/Colombia, 1947
Swink, Jim—Texas Christian, 1956
Talboom, Eddie—Wyoming, 1950
Taliafarro, George—Indiana, 1948
Tarkenton, Fran—Georgia, 1960
Tavener, John—Indiana, 1944
Taylor, Bruce—Boston Univ., 1969
Taylor, Charles—Stanford, 1942
Thomas, Aurelius—Ohio State, 1957
Thompson, Joe—Pittsburgh, 1907
Thomsen, Lynn—Austana, 1986
Thorne, Samuel B.—Yale, 1906
Thorpe, Jim—Carlisle, 1912
Ticknor, Ben—Harvard, 1930
Tigert, John—Vanderbilt, 1904
Tinsley, Gaynell—Louisiana State, 1936
Tipton, Eric—Duke, 1938
Tonnemaker, Clayton—Minnesota, 1949
Torrey, Robert—Pennsylvania, 1906
Trautman, Randy—Boise State, 1981
Travis, Ed Tarkio—Missouri, 1920
Trippi, Charles—Georgia, 1946
Tryon, J. Edward—Colgate, 1925
Tubbs, Jerry—Oklahoma, 1956
Utay, Joe—Texas A & M, 1907
Van Brocklin, Norm—Oregon, 1948
Van Sickel, Dale—Florida, 1929
Van Surdam, Henderson—Wesleyan, 1905
Very, Dexter—Penn State, 1912
Vessels, Billy—Oklahoma, 1952
Vick, Ernie—Michigan, 1921
Wagner, Huber—Pittsburgh, 1913
Walker, Doak—So. Methodist, 1949
Walker, Herschel—Georgia, 1982
Wallace, Bill—Rice, 1935
Walsh, Adam—Notre Dame, 1924
Warburton, I. (Cotton)—So. Calif., 1934
Ward, Robert (Bob)—Maryland, 1951

Warner, William—Cornell, 1903
Washington, Ken—UCLA, 1939
Weatherall, Jim—Oklahoma, 1951
Webster, George—Mich. State, 1966
Wedemeyer, Herman J.—St. Mary's, 1947
Weekes, Harold—Columbia, 1902
Weiner, Art—North Carolina, 1949
Weir, Ed—Nebraska, 1925
Welch, Gus—Carlisle, 1914
Weller, John—Princeton, 1935
Wendell, Percy—Harvard, 1913
West, D. Belford—Colgate, 1919
Westfall, Bob—Michigan, 1941
Weyand, Alex—Army, 1915
Wharton, Charles—Pennsylvania, 1896
Wheeler, Arthur—Princeton, 1894
White, Byron (Whizzer)—Colorado, 1937
White, Charles—So. Calif., 1979
White, Danny—Arizona State, 1973
White, Ed—California-Berkeley, 1968
White, Randy—Maryland, 1974
Whitmire, Don—Alabama/Navy, 1944
Wickhorst, Frank—Navy, 1926
Widseth, Ed—Minnesota, 1936
Wildung, Richard—Minnesota, 1942
Williams, Bob—Notre Dame, 1950
Williams, James—Rice, 1949
Willis, William—Ohio State, 1945
Wilson, George—Washington, 1925
Wilson, George—Lafayette, 1928
Wilson, Harry—Penn State/Army, 1923
Wilson, Marc—Brigham Young, 1979
Wistert, Albert A.—Michigan, 1942
Wistert, Al—Michigan, 1942
Wistert, Frank (Whitey)—Michigan, 1933
Wood, Barry—Harvard, 1931
Wojciechowicz, Alex—Fordham, 1936
Wyant, Andrew—Bucknell/Chicago, 1894
Wyatt, Bowden—Tennessee, 1938
Wyckoff, Clint—Cornell, 1896
Yarr, Tom—Notre Dame, 1931
Yary, Ron—So. Calif., 1968
Yoder, Lloyd—Carnegie Tech, 1926
Young, Claude (Buddy)—Illinois, 1946
Young, Harry—Wash. & Lee, 1916
Young, Walter—Oklahoma, 1938
Youngblood, Jack—Florida, 1970
Youngblood, Jim—Tennessee, 1972
Zarnas, Gus—Ohio State, 1937

Coaches

Bill Alexander
Dr. Ed Anderson
Ike Armstrong
Earl Banks
Harry Baujan
Matty Bell
Hugo Bezdek
Dana X. Bible
Bernie Bierman
Bob Blackman
Earl (Red) Blaik
Frank Broyles
Paul "Bear" Bryant
Harold Burry
Jim Butterfield
James "Wally" Butts
Charles W. Caldwell
Walter Camp
Len Casanova
Frank Cavanaugh
Jerry Claiborne
Richard Colman
Don Coryell
Fritz Crisler
Duffy Daugherty
Bob Devaney
Dan Devine
Gil Dobie
Bobby Dodd

Terry Donahue
Michael Donohue
Vince Dooley
Gus Dorais
Bill Edwards
Charles (Rip) Engle
Forest Evashevski
Don Faurot
Jake Gaither
Sid Gillman
Ernest Godfrey
Ray Graves
Andy Gustafson
Jack Harding
Edward K. Hall
Richard Harlow
Jesse Harper
Percy Haughton
Woody Hayes
John W. Heisman
R.A. (Bob) Higgins
Paul Hoernemann
Orin E. Hollingberry
Frank Howard
William Ingram
Don James
Morley Jennings
Howard Jones

L. (Biff) Jones
Thomas (Tad) Jones
Ralph (Shug) Jordan
Bob Keade
Andy Kerr
Chuck Klausing
Frank Kush
Frank Leahy
George E. Little
Lou Little
El (Slip) Madigan
Dave Maurer
Charley McClendon
Herbert McCracken
Daniel McGugin
John McKay
Allyn McKeen
DeOrmond (Tuss) McLaughry
John Merritt
L.R. (Dutch) Meyer
Bernie Moore
Scrappy Moore
Jack Mollenkopf
Ray Morrison
George A. Munger
Clarence Munn
Frank Murray

William Murray
Ed (Hooks) Mylin
Earle (Greasy) Neale
Jess Neely
David Nelson
Robert Neyland
Billy Nicks
Homer Norton
Frank (Buck) O'Neill
Tom Osborne
Bennie Owen
Ara Parseghian
Doyt Perry
James Phalea
Tommy Prothro
John Ralston
E.N. Robinson
Knute Rockne
E.L. (Dick) Romney
William W. Roper
Darrell Royal
Ad Rutschman
Henry (Red) Sanders
George F. Sanford
Bo Schembechler
Francis A. Schmidt
Floyd (Ben) Schwartzwalder

Clark Shaughnessy
Buck Shaw
Edgar Sherman
Andrew L. Smith
Carl Snavely
Jim Sochor
Amos A. Stagg
Gilbert Steinke
Jock Sutherland
James Tatum
Frank W. Thomas
Lee Tressell
Thad Vann
John H. Vaught
Wallace Wade
Lynn Waldorf
Glenn (Pop) Warner
E.E. (Tad) Wieman
John W. Wilce
Bud Wilkinson
Henry L. Williams
George W. Woodruff
Warren Woodson
Bowden Wyatt
Fielding H. Yost
Jim Young
Robert Zuppke

Professional Football

NATIONAL FOOTBALL LEAGUE FINAL STANDINGS 1999

AMERICAN FOOTBALL CONFERENCE

Eastern Division

	W	L	T	Pct	PF	PA
Indianapolis Colts[1]	13	3	0	.813	423	333
Buffalo Bills[2]	11	5	0	.688	320	229
Miami Dolphins[2]	9	7	0	.563	326	336
New York Jets	8	8	0	.500	308	309
New England Patriots	8	8	0	.500	299	284

Central Division

	W	L	T	Pct	PF	PA
Jacksonville Jaguars[1]	14	2	0	.875	396	217
Tennessee Oilers[2]	13	3	0	.813	392	324
Baltimore Ravens	8	8	0	.500	324	277
Pittsburgh Steelers	6	10	0	.375	317	320
Cincinnati Bengals	4	12	0	.250	283	460
Cleveland Browns	2	14	0	.125	217	437

Western Division

	W	L	T	Pct	PF	PA
Seattle Seahawks[1]	9	7	0	.563	338	298
Kansas City Chiefs	9	7	0	.563	390	322
San Diego Chargers	8	8	0	.500	269	316
Oakland Raiders	8	8	0	.500	390	329
Denver Broncos	6	10	0	.375	314	318

1. Division champion. 2. Wild card qualifier for playoffs. **Wild card:** Tennessee 22, Buffalo 16; Miami 20, Seattle 17. **Division:** Jacksonville 62, Miami 7; Tennessee 19, Indianapolis 16. **Conference:** Tennessee 33, Jacksonville 14.

NATIONAL FOOTBALL CONFERENCE

Eastern Division

	W	L	T	Pct	PF	PA
Washington Redskins[1]	10	6	0	.625	443	377
Dallas Cowboys[2]	8	8	0	.500	352	276
New York Giants	7	9	0	.438	299	358
Arizona Cardinals	6	10	0	.375	245	382
Philadelphia Eagles	5	11	0	.313	272	357

Central Division

	W	L	T	Pct	PF	PA
Tampa Bay Buccaneers[1]	11	5	0	.688	270	235
Minnesota Vikings[2]	10	6	0	.625	399	335
Detroit Lions[2]	8	8	0	.500	322	323
Green Bay Packers	8	8	0	.500	357	341
Chicago Bears	6	10	0	.375	272	341

Western Division

	W	L	T	Pct	PF	PA
St. Louis Rams[1]	13	3	0	.813	526	242
Carolina Panthers	8	8	0	.500	421	381
Atlanta Falcons	5	11	0	.313	285	380
San Francisco 49ers	4	12	0	.250	295	453
New Orleans Saints	3	13	0	.188	260	434

1. Division champion. 2. Wild card qualifier for playoffs. **Wild card:** Washington 27, Detroit 13; Minnesota 27, Dallas 10. **Division:** Tampa Bay 14, Washington 13; St. Louis 49, Minnesota 37. **Conference:** Tampa Bay 6, St. Louis 11.

LEAGUE CHAMPIONSHIP—SUPER BOWL XXXIV

(Jan. 30, 2000, Georgia Dome, Atlanta, Ga. Attendance: 72,625. Time: 3:28)

Scoring

	1st Q	2nd Q	3rd Q	4th Q	Final
St. Louis Rams	3	6	7	7	**23**
Tennessee Oilers	0	0	6	10	**16**

1st: STL—Jeff Wilkins 27-yd FG, 12:00. Drive: 54 yds in 6 plays. Key plays: Warner 32-yd pass to Holt to TEN 42; Warner 17-yd pass to Faulk to TEN 14.

2nd: STL—Jeff Wilkins 29-yd FG, 10:44. Drive: 73 yds in 11 plays. Key plays: Warner 11-yd pass to Bruce to STL 27; Warner 15-yd pass to Bruce to TEN 45; Warner 13-yd pass to Holt to TEN 32; Warner 15-yd pass to Holt to TEN 16. STL—Jeff Wilkins 28-yd FG, 14:45. Drive: 67 yds in 13 plays. Key plays: Warner 16-yd pass to Holt on 3rd-and-13 to STL 36; Warner 18-yd pass to Holt to STL 47; Warner 15-yd pass to Bruce to TEN 38; Warner 17-yd pass to Hakim to TEN 21.

3rd: STL—Torry Holt 9-yd pass from Kurt Warner (Jeff Wilkins kick), 7:40. Drive: 68 yds in 8 plays. Key plays: Warner 8-yd pass to Faulk on 3rd-and-7 to STL 43; Warner 31-yd pass to Bruce to TEN 27; Warner 16-yd pass to Conwell to TEN 10. TEN—Eddie George 1-yd run (2-pt conversion failed), 14:46. Drive: 66 yds in 12 plays. Key plays: George 9-yd run to TEN 48; McNair 5-yd pass to Wycheck on 3rd-and-3 to TEN 40; McNair 7-yd pass to Wycheck to STL 31; McNair 2-yd run on 3rd-and-1 to STL 29; McNair 23-yd run to STL 2.

4th: TEN—Eddie George 2-yd run (Al Del Greco kick), 7:39. Drive: 79 yds in 13 plays. Key plays: McNair 9-yd pass to Dyson on 3rd-and-6 to TEN 34; McNair 2-yd run on 4th-and-1 to TEN 45; McNair 21-yd pass to Byrd to STL 24; McNair 21-yd pass to Harris to STL 3. TEN—Al Del Greco 43-yd FG, 12:48. Drive: 28 yds in 8 plays. Key plays: McNair 11-yd run to STL 42; McNair 6-yd pass to Harris on 3rd-and-2 to STL 28; Byrd recovery of Harris fumble at STL 28. STL—Isaac Bruce 73-yd pass from Kurt Warner (Jeff Wilkins kick), 13:06. Drive: 73 yds in 1 play.

Individual Statistics

Rushing: ST. LOUIS: M. Faulk 10–17, R. Holcombe 1–11, K. Warner 1–1, M. Horan 1–0. TENNESSEE: E. George 28–95, S. McNair 8–64.

Passing: ST. LOUIS: K. Warner 24–45 for 414 yds. TENNESSEE: S. McNair 22–36 for 214 yds.

Receiving: ST. LOUIS: T. Holt 7–109, I. Bruce 6–162, M. Faulk 5–90, A. Hakim 1–17, E. Conwell 1–16, R. Proehl 1–11, R. Williams 1–9, R. Holcombe 1–1, F. Miller 1–minus 1. TENNESSEE: J. Harris 7–64, F. Wycheck 5–35, K. Dyson 4–41, E. George 2–35, I. Byrd 2–21, D. Mason 2–18.

MVP: Kurt Warner, St. Louis quarterback, 24–45 for 414 yds, 2 touchdowns, 0 interceptions.

Statistics of the Game

	St. Louis	Tennessee
Touchdowns	2	2
Time of possession	23:34	36:26
First downs	23	27
Total offense (net yards)	436	367
Plays	59	73
Average gain	7.4	5.0
Rushing yards	29	159
Rushes	13	36
Avg. per rush	2.2	4.4
Passing yards	407	208
Completions/attempts	24/45	22/36
Yards per pass	8.8	5.8
Times sacked/yards lost	1/7	1/6
Return yardage	63	121
Fumbles/lost	2/0	1/0
Penalties/yards	8/60	7/45

SUPER BOWLS I-XXXIV

Game	Date	Winner	Loser	Site	Attendance
XXXIV	Jan. 30, 2000	St. Louis (NFC) 23	Tennessee (AFC) 16	Georgia Dome, Atlanta, Ga.	72,625
XXXIII	Jan. 31, 1999	Denver (AFC) 34	Atlanta (NFC) 19	Pro Player Stadium, Miami, Fla.	74,803
XXXII	Jan. 25, 1998	Denver (AFC) 31	Green Bay (NFC) 24	Qualcomm Stadium, San Diego, Calif.	68,912
XXXI	Jan. 26, 1997	Green Bay (NFC) 35	New England (AFC) 21	Superdome, New Orleans, La.	72,301
XXX	Jan. 28, 1996	Dallas (NFC) 27	Pittsburgh (AFC) 17	Sun Devil Stadium, Tempe, Ariz.	76,347
XXIX	Jan. 29, 1995	San Francisco (NFC) 49	San Diego (AFC) 26	Joe Robbie Stadium, Miami, Fla.	74,107
XXVIII	Jan. 30, 1994	Dallas (NFC) 30	Buffalo (AFC) 13	Georgia Dome, Atlanta, Ga.	72,817
XXVII	Jan. 31, 1993	Dallas (NFC) 52	Buffalo (AFC) 17	Rose Bowl, Pasadena, Calif.	98,374
XXVI	Jan. 26, 1992	Washington (NFC) 37	Buffalo (AFC) 24	Metrodome, Minneapolis, Minn.	63,130
XXV	Jan. 27, 1991	Giants (NFC) 20	Buffalo (AFC) 19	Tampa Stadium, Tampa, Fla.	73,813
XXIV	Jan. 28, 1990	San Francisco (NFC) 55	Denver (AFC) 10	Superdome, New Orleans	72,919
XXIII	Jan. 22, 1989	San Francisco (NFC) 20	Cincinnati (AFC) 16	Joe Robbie Stadium, Miami, Fla.	75,179
XXII	Jan. 31, 1988	Washington (NFC) 42	Denver (AFC) 10	Jack Murphy Stadium, San Diego, Calif.	73,302
XXI	Jan. 25, 1987	Giants (NFC) 39	Denver (AFC) 20	Rose Bowl, Pasadena, Calif.	101,063
XX	Jan. 26, 1986	Chicago (NFC) 46	New England (AFC) 10	Superdome, New Orleans	73,818
XIX	Jan. 20, 1985	San Francisco (NFC) 38	Miami (AFC) 16	Stanford Stadium, Palo Alto, Calif.	84,059
XVIII	Jan. 22, 1984	Los Angeles Raiders (AFC) 38	Washington (NFC) 9	Tampa Stadium, Tampa, Fla	72,920
XVII	Jan. 30, 1983	Washington (NFC) 27	Miami (AFC) 17	Rose Bowl, Pasadena, Calif.	103,667
XVI	Jan. 24, 1982	San Francisco (NFC) 26	Cincinnati (AFC) 21	Silverdome, Pontiac, Mich.	81,270
XV	Jan. 25, 1981	Oakland (AFC) 27	Philadelphia (NFC) 10	Superdome, New Orleans	75,500
XIV	Jan. 20, 1980	Pittsburgh (AFC) 31	Los Angeles (NFC) 19	Rose Bowl, Pasadena	103,985
XIII	Jan. 21, 1979	Pittsburgh (AFC) 35	Dallas (NFC) 31	Orange Bowl, Miami	79,484
XII	Jan. 15, 1978	Dallas (NFC) 27	Denver (AFC) 10	Superdome, New Orleans	75,583
XI	Jan. 9, 1977	Oakland (AFC) 32	Minnesota (NFC) 14	Rose Bowl, Pasadena	103,424
X	Jan. 18, 1976	Pittsburgh (AFC) 21	Dallas (NFC) 17	Orange Bowl, Miami	80,187
IX	Jan. 12, 1975	Pittsburgh (AFC) 16	Minnesota (NFC) 6	Tulane Stadium, New Orleans	80,997
VIII	Jan. 13, 1974	Miami (AFC) 24	Minnesota (NFC) 7	Rice Stadium, Houston	71,882
VII	Jan. 14, 1973	Miami (AFC) 14	Washington (NFC) 7	Memorial Coliseum, Los Angeles	90,182
VI	Jan. 16, 1972	Dallas (NFC) 24	Miami (AFC) 3	Tulane Stadium, New Orleans	81,591
V	Jan. 17, 1971	Baltimore (AFC) 16	Dallas (NFC) 13	Orange Bowl, Miami	79,204
IV	Jan. 11, 1970	Kansas City (AFL) 23	Minnesota (NFL) 7	Tulane Stadium, New Orleans	80,562
III	Jan. 12, 1969	New York (AFL) 16	Baltimore (NFL) 7	Orange Bowl, Miami	75,389
II	Jan. 14, 1968	Green Bay (NFL) 33	Oakland (AFL) 14	Orange Bowl, Miami	75,546
I	Jan. 15, 1967	Green Bay (NFL) 35	Kansas City (AFL) 10	Memorial Coliseum, Los Angeles	61,946

NOTE: Super Bowls I to IV were played before the American Football League and National Football League merged into the NFL, which was divided into two conferences, the NFC and AFC.

NATIONAL LEAGUE CHAMPIONS

Year	Champion	(W-L-T)	Year	Champion	(W-L-T)	Year	Champion	(W-L-T)
1921	Chicago Bears (Staley's)	(10-1-1)	1926	Frankford Yellow Jackets	(14-1-1)	1930	Green Bay Packers	(10-3-1)
1922	Canton Bulldogs	(10-0-2)	1927	New York Giants	(11-1-1)	1931	Green Bay Packers	(12-2-0)
1923	Canton Bulldogs	(11-0-1)	1928	Providence Steamrollers	(8-1-2)	1932	Chicago Bears	(7-1-6)
1924	Cleveland Indians	(7-1-1)	1929	Green Bay Packers	(12-0-1)			
1925	Chicago Cardinals	(11-2-1)						

Year	Eastern Conference winners (W-L-T)	Western Conference winners (W-L-T)	League champion playoff results
1933	New York Giants (11-3-0)	Chicago Bears (10-2-1)	Chicago Bears 23, New York 21
1934	New York Giants (8-5-0)	Chicago Bears (13-0-0)	New York 30, Chicago Bears 13
1935	New York Giants (9-3-0)	Detroit Lions (7-3-2)	Detroit 26, New York 7
1936	Boston Redskins (7-5-0)	Green Bay Packers (10-1-1)	Green Bay 21, Boston 6
1937	Washington Redskins (8-3-0)	Chicago Bears (9-1-1)	Washington 28, Chicago Bears 21
1938	New York Giants (8-2-1)	Green Bay Packers (8-3-0)	New York 23, Green Bay 17
1939	New York Giants (9-1-1)	Green Bay Packers (9-2-0)	Green Bay 27, New York 0
1940	Washington Redskins (9-2-0)	Chicago Bears (8-3-0)	Chicago Bears 73, Washington 0
1941	New York Giants (8-3-0)	Chicago Bears (10-1-1)[2]	Chicago Bears 37, New York 9
1942	Washington Redskins (10-1-1)	Chicago Bears (11-0-0)	Washington 14, Chicago Bears 6
1943	Washington Redskins (6-3-1)[2]	Chicago Bears (8-1-1)	Chicago Bears 41, Washington 21
1944	New York Giants (8-1-1)	Green Bay Packers (8-2-0)	Green Bay 14, New York 7
1945	Washington Redskins (8-2-0)	Cleveland Rams (9-1-0)	Cleveland 15, Washington 14
1946	New York Giants (7-3-1)	Chicago Bears (8-2-1)	Chicago Bears 24, New York 14
1947	Philadelphia Eagles (8-4-0)[2]	Chicago Cardinals (9-3-0)	Chicago Cardinals 28, Philadelphia 21
1948	Philadelphia Eagles (9-2-1)	Chicago Cardinals (11-1-0)	Philadelphia 7, Chicago Cardinals 0
1949	Philadelphia Eagles (11-1-0)	Los Angeles Rams (8-2-2)	Philadelphia 14, Los Angeles 0
1950[1]	Cleveland Browns (10-2-0)[2, 3]	Los Angeles Rams (9-3-0)[2]	Cleveland 30, Los Angeles 28
1951[1]	Cleveland Browns (11-1-0)	Los Angeles Rams (8-4-0)	Los Angeles 24, Cleveland 17
1952[1]	Cleveland Browns (8-4-0)	Detroit Lions (9-3-0)[2]	Detroit 17, Cleveland 7
1953	Cleveland Browns (11-1-0)	Detroit Lions (10-2-0)	Detroit 17, Cleveland 16

Year	Eastern Conference winners (W-L-T)	Western Conference winners (W-L-T)	League champion playoff results
1954	Cleveland Browns (9-3-0)	Detroit Lions (9-2-1)	Cleveland 56, Detroit 10
1955	Cleveland Browns (9-2-1)	Los Angeles Rams (8-3-1)	Cleveland 38, Los Angeles 14
1956	New York Giants (8-3-1)	Chicago Bears (9-2-1)	New York 47, Chicago Bears 7
1957	Cleveland Browns (9-2-1)	Detroit Lions (8-4-0)[2]	Detroit 59, Cleveland 14
1958	New York Giants (9-3-0)[2]	Baltimore Colts (9-3-0)	Baltimore 23, New York 17[4]
1959	New York Giants (10-2-0)	Baltimore Colts (9-3-0)	Baltimore 31, New York 16
1960	Philadelphia Eagles (10-2-0)	Green Bay Packers (8-4-0)	Philadelphia 17, Green Bay 13
1961	New York Giants (10-3-1)	Green Bay Packers (11-3-0)	Green Bay 37, New York 0
1962	New York Giants (12-2-0)	Green Bay Packers (13-1-0)	Green Bay 16, New York 7
1963	New York Giants (11-3-0)	Chicago Bears (11-1-2)	Chicago 14, New York 10
1964	Cleveland Browns (10-3-1)	Baltimore Colts (12-2-0)	Cleveland 27, Baltimore 0
1965	Cleveland Browns (11-3-0)	Green Bay Packers (11-3-1)[2]	Green Bay 23, Cleveland 12
1966	Dallas Cowboys (10-3-1)	Green Bay Packers (12-2-0)	Green Bay 34, Dallas 27
1967	Dallas Cowboys (9-5-0)	Green Bay Packers (9-4-1)[2]	Green Bay 21, Dallas 17
1968	Cleveland Browns (10-4-0)[2]	Baltimore Colts (13-1-0)[2]	Baltimore 34, Cleveland 0
1969	Cleveland Browns (10-3-1)[2]	Minnesota Vikings (12-2-0)[2]	Minnesota 27, Cleveland 7

1. League was divided into American and National Conferences, 1950-52 and again in 1970, when leagues merged. 2. Won divisional playoff. 3. Cleveland Browns and San Francisco 49ers joined league after All-America Football Conference (1946–1949) folded. 4. Won at 8:15 of sudden death overtime period.

NATIONAL CONFERENCE CHAMPIONS

Year	Eastern Division	Central Division	Western Division	Champion
1970	Dallas Cowboys (10-4-0)	Minnesota Vikings (12-2-0)	San Francisco 49ers (10-3-1)	Dallas
1971	Dallas Cowboys (11-3-0)	Minnesota Vikings (11-3-0)	San Francisco 49ers (9-5-0)	Dallas
1972	Washington Redskins (11-3-0)	Green Bay Packers (10-4-0)	San Francisco 49ers (8-5-1)	Washington
1973	Dallas Cowboys (10-4-0)	Minnesota Vikings (12-2-0)	Los Angeles Rams (12-2-0)	Minnesota
1974	St. Louis Cardinals (10-4-0)	Minnesota Vikings (10-4-0)	Los Angeles Rams (10-4-0)	Minnesota
1975	St. Louis Cardinals (11-3-0)	Minnesota Vikings (12-2-0)	Los Angeles Rams (10-4-0)	Dallas[1]
1976	Dallas Cowboys (11-3-0)	Minnesota Vikings (11-2-1)	Los Angeles Rams (10-3-1)	Minnesota
1977	Dallas Cowboys (12-2-0)	Minnesota Vikings (9-5-0)	Los Angeles Rams (10-4-0)	Dallas
1978	Dallas Cowboys (12-4-0)	Minnesota Vikings (8-7-1)	Los Angeles Rams (12-4-0)	Dallas
1979	Dallas Cowboys (11-5-0)	Tampa Bay Buccaneers (10-6-0)	Los Angeles Rams (9-7-0)	Los Angeles
1980	Philadelphia Eagles (12-4-0)	Minnesota Vikings (9-7-0)	Atlanta Falcons (12-4-0)	Philadelphia
1981	Dallas Cowboys (12-4-0)	Tampa Bay Buccaneers (9-7-0)	San Francisco 49ers (13-3-0)	San Francisco
1982[2]				
1983	Washington Redskins (14-2-0)	Detroit Lions (8-8-0)	San Francisco 49ers (10-6-0)	Washington
1984	Washington Redskins (11-5-0)	Chicago Bears (10-6-0)	San Francisco 49ers (15-1-0)	San Francisco
1985	Dallas Cowboys (10-6-0)	Chicago Bears (15-1-0)	Los Angeles Rams (11-5-0)	Chicago
1986	New York Giants (14-2-0)	Chicago Bears (14-2-0)	San Francisco 49ers (10-5-1)	New York
1987	Washington Redskins (11-4-0)	Chicago Bears (11-4-0)	San Francisco 49ers (13-2-0)	Washington
1988	Philadelphia Eagles (10-6-0)	Chicago Bears (12-4-0)	San Francisco 49ers (10-6-0)	San Francisco
1989	New York Giants (12-4-0)	Minnesota Vikings (10-6-0)	San Francisco 49ers (14-2-0)	San Francisco
1990	New York Giants (13-3-0)	Chicago Bears (11-5-0)	San Francisco 49ers (14-2-0)	New York
1991	Washington (14-2-0)	Detroit Lions (12-4-0)	New Orleans Saints (11-5-0)	Washington
1992	Dallas Cowboys (13-3-0)	Minnesota Vikings (11-5-0)	San Francisco 49ers (14-2-0)	Dallas
1993	Dallas Cowboys (12-4-0)	Detroit Lions (10-6-0)	San Francisco 49ers (10-6-0)	Dallas
1994	Dallas Cowboys (12-4-0)	Minnesota Vikings (10-6-0)	San Francisco 49ers (13-3-0)	San Francisco
1995	Dallas Cowboys (12-4-0)	Green Bay Packers (11-5-0)	San Francisco 49ers (11-5-0)	Dallas
1996	Dallas Cowboys (10-6-0)	Green Bay Packers (13-3-0)	Carolina Panthers (12-4-0)	Green Bay
1997	New York Giants (10-5-1)	Green Bay Packers (13-3-0)	San Francisco 49ers (13-3-0)	Green Bay
1998	Dallas Cowboys (10-6-0)	Minnesota Vikings (15-1-0)	Atlanta Falcons (14-2-0)	Atlanta
1999	Washington Redskins (10-6-0)	Tampa Bay Buccaneers (11-5-0)	St. Louis Rams (13-3-0)	St. Louis

1. Wild card. 2. Schedule reduced to 9 games from usual 16, with no standings kept in Eastern, Central, and Western Divisions, because of 57-day player strike. Washington Redskins won conference title and also had best regular-season record (8-1-0).

AMERICAN LEAGUE CHAMPIONS

Year	Eastern Division (W-L-T)	Western Division (W-L-T)	League champion, playoff results
1960	Houston Oilers (10-4-0)	Los Angeles Chargers (10-4-0)	Houston 24, Los Angeles 16
1961	Houston Oilers (10-3-1)	San Diego Chargers (12-2-0)	Houston 10, San Diego 3
1962	Houston Oilers (11-3-0)	Dallas Texans (11-3-0)	Dallas 20, Houston 17[1]
1963	Boston Patriots (8-6-1)[2]	San Diego Chargers (11-3-0)	San Diego 51, Boston 10
1964	Buffalo Bills (12-2-0)	San Diego Chargers (8-5-1)	Buffalo 20, San Diego 7
1965	Buffalo Bills (10-3-1)	San Diego Chargers (9-2-3)	Buffalo 23, San Diego 0
1966	Buffalo Bills (9-4-1)	Kansas City Chiefs (11-2-1)	Kansas City 31, Buffalo 7
1967	Houston Oilers (9-4-1)	Oakland Raiders (13-1-0)	Oakland 40, Houston 7
1968	New York Jets (11-3-0)	Oakland Raiders (12-2-0)[2]	New York 27, Oakland 23
1969	New York Jets (10-4-0)	Oakland Raiders (12-1-1)	Kansas City 17, Oakland 7[3]

1. Won at 2:45 of second sudden death overtime period. 2. Won divisional playoff. 3. Kansas City defeated New York, 13-6, and Oakland defeated Houston, 56-7, in interdivisional playoffs.

AMERICAN CONFERENCE CHAMPIONS

Year	Eastern Division	Central Division	Western Division	Champion
1970	Baltimore Colts (11-2-1)	Cincinnati Bengals (8-6-0)	Oakland Raiders (8-4-2)	Baltimore
1971	Miami Dolphins (10-3-1)	Cleveland Browns (9-5-0)	Kansas City Chiefs (10-3-1)	Miami
1972	Miami Dolphins (14-0-0)	Pittsburgh Steelers (11-3-0)	Oakland Raiders (10-3-1)	Miami
1973	Miami Dolphins (12-2-0)	Cincinnati Bengals (10-4-0)	Oakland Raiders (9-4-1)	Miami
1974	Miami Dolphins (11-3-0)	Pittsburgh Steelers (10-3-1)	Oakland Raiders (12-2-0)	Pittsburgh
1975	Baltimore Colts (10-4-0)	Pittsburgh Steelers (12-2-0)	Oakland Raiders (12-2-0)	Pittsburgh
1976	Baltimore Colts (11-3-0)	Pittsburgh Steelers (10-4-0)	Oakland Raiders (13-1-0)	Oakland
1977	Baltimore Colts (10-4-0)	Pittsburgh Steelers (9-5-0)	Denver Broncos (12-2-0)	Denver
1978	New England Patriots (11-5-0)	Pittsburgh Steelers (14-2-0)	Denver Broncos (10-6-0)	Pittsburgh
1979	Miami Dolphins (10-6-0)	Pittsburgh Steelers (12-4-0)	San Diego Chargers (12-4-0)	Pittsburgh
1980	Buffalo Bills (11-5-0)	Cleveland Browns (11-5-0)	San Diego Chargers (11-5-0)	Oakland[1]
1981	Miami Dolphins (11-4-1)	Cincinnati Bengals (12-4-0)	San Diego Chargers (10-6-0)	Cincinnati
1982[2]	Miami Dolphins won the conference title, but the Los Angeles Raiders had best regular-season record (8-1-0).			
1983	Miami Dolphins (12-4-0)	Pittsburgh Steelers (10-6-0)	Los Angeles Raiders (12-4-0)	Los Angeles
1984	Miami Dolphins (14-2-0)	Pittsburgh Steelers (9-7-0)	Denver Broncos (13-3-0)	Miami
1985	Miami Dolphins (12-4-0)	Cleveland Browns (8-8)	Los Angeles Raiders (12-4-0)	New England[1]
1986	New England Patriots (11-5-0)	Cleveland Browns (12-4-0)	Denver Broncos (11-5-0)	Denver
1987	Indianapolis Colts (9-6-0)	Cleveland Browns (10-5-0)	Denver Broncos (10-4-1)	Denver
1988	Buffalo Bills (12-4-0)	Cincinnati Bengals (12-4-0)	Seattle Seahawks (9-7-0)	Cincinnati
1989	Buffalo Bills (9-7-0)	Cleveland Browns (9-6-1)	Denver Broncos (11-5-0)	Denver
1990	Buffalo Bills (13-3-0)	Cincinnati Bengals (9-7-0)	Los Angeles Raiders (12-4-0)	Buffalo
1991	Buffalo Bills (13-3-0)	Houston Oilers (11-5-0)	Denver Broncos (12-4-0)	Buffalo
1992	Miami Dolphins (11-5-0)	Pittsburgh Steelers (11-5-0)	San Diego Chargers (11-5-0)	Buffalo[1]
1993	Buffalo Bills (12-4-0)	Houston Oilers (12-4-0)	Kansas City Chiefs (11-5-0)	Buffalo
1994	Miami Dolphins (10-6-0)	Pittsburgh Steelers (12-4-0)	San Diego Chargers (11-5-0)	San Diego
1995	Buffalo Bills (10-6-0)	Pittsburgh Steelers (11-5-0)	Kansas City Chiefs (13-3-0)	Pittsburgh
1996	New England Patriots (11-5-0)	Pittsburgh Steelers (10-6-0)	Denver Broncos (13-3-0)	New England
1997	New England Patriots (10-6-0)	Pittsburgh Steelers (11-5-0)	Kansas City Chiefs (13-3-0)	Denver[1]
1998	New York Jets (12-4-0)	Jacksonville Jaguars (11-5-0)	Denver Broncos (14-2-0)	Denver
1999	Indianapolis Colts (13-3-0)	Jacksonville Jaguars (14-2-0)	Seattle Seahawks (9-7-0)	Tennessee[1]

1. Wild card. 2. Schedule reduced to 9 games from usual 16, with no standings kept in Eastern, Central, and Western Divisions, because of 57-day player strike.

PRO FOOTBALL HALL OF FAME

(National Football Museum, Canton, Ohio)

Teams named are those with which player is best identified; figures in parentheses indicate number of playing years.

Adderley, Herb, defensive back, Packers, Cowboys (12)	1961–72
Alworth, Lance, wide receiver, Chargers, Cowboys (12)	1961–72
Atkins, Doug, defensive end, Browns, Bears, Saints (17)	1953–69
Badgro, Morris, end, N.Y. Yankees, Giants, Brooklyn Dodgers (8)	1927, 1930–36
Barney, Lem, defensive back, Lions (11)	1967–78
Battles, Cliff, back, Redskins (6)	1932–37
Baugh, Sammy, quarterback, Redskins (16)	1936–52
Bednarik, Chuck, center-linebacker, Eagles (14)	1949–62
Bell, Bert, NFL founder, Eagles and Steelers, NFL Commissioner	1946–59
Bell, Bobby, linebacker, Chiefs (12)	1963–74
Berry, Raymond, end, Colts (13)	1955–67
Bidwell, Charles W., owner, Chicago Cardinals	1933–47
Biletnikoff, Fred, wide receiver, Raiders (14)	1965–78
Blanda, George, quarterback-kicker, Bears, Oilers, Raiders (27)	1949–75
Blount, Mel, cornerback, Pittsburgh Steelers (14)	1970–83
Bradshaw, Terry, quarterback, Pittsburgh Steelers (14)	1970–83
Brown, Jim, fullback, Browns (9)	1957–65
Brown, Paul E., coach, Browns (1946–62), Bengals (1968–75)	1946–75
Brown, Roosevelt, tackle, Giants (13)	1953–65
Brown, Willie, cornerback, Broncos, Raiders (16)	1963–78
Buchanan, Buck, tackle, Chiefs (11)	1963–73
Butkus, Dick, linebacker, Bears (9)	1965–73
Campbell, Earl, running back, Oilers, Saints (8)	1978–85
Canadeo, Tony, back, Packers (11)	1941–52
Carr, Joe, NFL president (18)	1921–39
Chamberlin, Guy, end, 4 teams (9)	1919–27
Christiansen, Jack, defensive back, Lions (8)	1951–58
Clark, Earl (Dutch), quarterback, Spartans, Lions (7)	1931–38
Connor, George, tackle, linebacker, Bears (8)	1948–55
Conzelman, Jimmy, quarterback, 5 teams (10), owner, Detroit Panthers	1921–48
Creekmur, Lou, offensive tackle/guard, Lions (10)	1950–59
Csonka, Larry, back, Dolphins, Giants (11)	1968–79
Davis, Al, owner, Raiders, coach, general manager	1963–
Davis, Willie, defensive end, Packers (10)	1960–69
Dawson, Len, quarterback, Steelers, Browns, Texans, Chiefs (19)	1957–75
Dickerson, Eric, running back, Rams, Colts, Raiders, Falcons (11)	1983–93
Dierdorf, Dan, tackle/center, Cardinals (13)	1971–83
Ditka, Mike, tight end, Bears, Eagles, Cowboys (12)	1961–72
Donovan, Art, defensive tackle, Colts (12)	1950–61
Dorsett, Tony, running back, Cowboys, Broncos (12)	1977–88
Driscoll, John (Paddy), quarterback, Cards, Bears (11)	1919–29
Dudley, Bill, back, Steelers, Lions, Redskins (9)	1942–53
Edwards, Albert Glen (Turk), tackle, Redskins (9)	1932–40
Ewbank, Weeb, coach, Colts, Jets (20)	1954–73
Fears, Tom, end, Rams (9); coach, Saints	1948–56
Finks, Jim, administrator/general manager, Vikings, Bears, Saints	1964–93
Flaherty, Ray, end, Yankees, Giants (9); coach, Redskins, Yankees (14)	1928–49
Ford, Len, end, defensive end, Browns, Packers (11)	1948–58
Fouts, Dan, quarterback, Chargers (15)	1973–87
Fortmann, Daniel J., guard, Bears (8)	1936–43
Gatski, Frank, offensive lineman, Browns (12)	1946–57
George, Bill, linebacker, Bears, Rams (15)	1952–66
Gibbs, Joe, coach, Redskins (11)	1981–92
Gifford, Frank, back, Giants (12)	1952–64
Gillman, Sid, coach, Rams, Chargers, Oilers (18)	1955–70, 73–74
Graham, Otto, quarterback, Browns (10)	1946–55

Grange, Harold (Red), back, Bears, Yankees (9)   1925–34
Grant, Bud, coach, Vikings (18)   1967–85
Greene, Joe, defensive tackle, Steelers (13)   1968–81
Gregg, Forrest, tackle, Packers (15)   1956–71
Griese, Bob, quarterback, Dolphins (14)   1967–80
Groza, Lou, place-kicker, tackle, Browns (21)   1946–67
Guyon, Joe, back, 6 teams (8)   1919–27
Halas, George, NFL founder, owner and coach, Staleys
    and Bears, end (11)   1919–27
Ham, Jack, linebacker, Steelers (13)   1970–82
Hannah, John, guard, Patriots (13)   1973–85
Harris, Franco, running back, Steelers, Seahawks (13)   1972–84
Haynes, Mike, defensive back, Patriots, Raiders (10)   1976–85
Healey, Ed, tackle, Bears (8)   1920–27
Hein, Mel, center, Giants (15)   1931–45
Hendricks, Ted, linebacker, Colts, Packers, Raiders (15)   1969–83
Henry, Wilbur (Pete), tackle, Bulldogs, Giants (8)   1920–28
Herber, Arnie, quarterback, Packers, Giants (13)   1930–45
Hewitt, Bill, end, Bears, Eagles (9)   1932–43
Hinkle, Clarke, fullback, Packers (10)   1932–41
Hirsch, Elroy (Crazy Legs), back, end, Rams (12)   1946–57
Hornung, Paul, running back, Packers (9)   1957–62, 64–66
Houston, Ken, defensive back, Oilers, Redskins (14)   1967–80
Hubbard, R. (Cal), tackle, Giants, Packers (9)   1927–36
Huff, Sam, linebacker, Giants, Redskins (13)   1956–67, 1969
Hunt, Lamar, founder A.F.L., owner Texans, Chiefs   1959–
Hutson, Don, end, Packers (11)   1935–45
Johnson, John Henry, back, 49ers, Lions,
    Steelers, Oilers (13)   1954–66
Johnson, Jimmy, cornerback, 49ers (16)   1961–76
Joiner, Charlie, receiver, Oilers, Bengals, Chargers (18)   1969–86
Jones, David (Deacon), defensive end, Rams,
    Chargers, Redskins (14)   1961–74
Jones, Stan, defensive tackle, Bears, Redskins (14)   1954–66
Jordan, Henry, defensive tackle, Browns, Packers (13)   1957–69
Jurgensen, Sonny, quarterback, Eagles, Redskins (18)   1957–74
Kelly, Leroy, running back, Browns (10)   1964–73
Kiesling, Walt, guard, 6 teams (13)   1926–38
Kinard, Frank (Bruiser), tackle, Dodgers (9)   1938–47
Krause, Paul, safety, Redskins, Vikings (16)   1964–79
Lambeau, Earl (Curly), NFL founder, coach,
    end, back, Packers (11)   1919–53
Lambert, Jack, linebacker, Steelers (11)   1974–84
Landry, Tom, coach, Cowboys (29)   1960–88
Lane, Richard (Night Train), defensive back,
    Rams, Cardinals, Lions (14)   1952–65
Langer, Jim, center, Dolphins, Vikings (12)   1970–81
Lanier, Willie, linebacker, Chiefs (11)   1967–77
Largent, Steve, receiver, Seahawks (14)   1976–89
Lary, Yale, defensive back, punter, Lions (11)   1952–64
Laveill, Dante, end, Browns (11)   1946–56
Layne, Bobby, quarterback, Bears, Lions, Steelers (15)   1948–62
Leemans, Alphonse (Tuffy), back, Giants (8)   1936–43
Lilly, Bob, defensive tackle, Cowboys (14)   1961–74
Little, Larry, guard, Dolphins, Chargers (14)   1967–80
Lombardi, Vince, coach, Packers, Redskins (11)   1959–70
Long, Howie, defensive end, Raiders (13)   1981–93
Lott, Ronnie, cornerback, safety, 49ers, Raiders, Jets (14)   1981–94
Luckman, Sid, quarterback, Bears (12)   1939–50
Lyman, Roy (Link), tackle, Bulldogs, Bears (11)   1922–34
Mack, Tom, guard, Rams (13)   1966–78
Mackey, John, tight end, Colts, Chargers (10)   1963–72
Mara, Tim, NFL founder, owner, Giants   1925–59
Mara, Wellington, NFL executive, owner, Giants   1937–
Marchetti, Gino, defensive end, Colts (14)   1952–66
Marshall, George P., NFL founder, owner, Redskins   1932–65
Matson, Ollie, back, Cardinals, Rams, Lions, Eagles (14)   1952–66
Maynard, Don, receiver, Giants, Jets, Cardinals (15)   1958–73
McAfee, George, back, Bears (8)   1940–50
McCormack, Mike, tackle, N.Y. Yankees,
    Cleveland Browns (10)   1951–62
McDonald, Tommy, wide receiver, Eagles, Cowboys,
    Rams, Falcons, Browns (12)   1957–68
McElhenny, Hugh, back, 49ers, Vikings, Giants (13)   1952–64
McNally, John (Blood), back, 7 teams (15)   1925–39
Michalske, August, guard, Yankees, Packers (11)   1926–37
Millner, Wayne, end, Redskins (7)   1936–45
Mitchell, Bobby, wide receiver, Browns, Redskins (11)   1958–68

Mix, Ron, tackle, Chargers (11)   1960–71
Montana, Joe, quarterback, 49ers, Chiefs (15)   1979–94
Moore, Lenny, back, Colts (12)   1956–67
Motley, Marion, fullback, Browns, Steelers (9)   1946–55
Munoz, Anthony, tackle, Bengals (13)   1980–92
Musso, George, guard-tackle, Bears (12)   1933–44
Nagurski, Bronko, fullback, Bears (9)   1930–43
Namath, Joe, quarterback, Jets, Rams (13)   1965–77
Neale, Earle (Greasy), coach, Eagles   1941–50
Nevers, Ernie, fullback, Chicago Cardinals (5)   1926–31
Newsome, Ozzie, tight end, Browns (13)   1978–90
Nitschke, Ray, linebacker, Packers (15)   1958–72
Noll, Chuck, coach, Steelers (23)   1969–81
Nomellini, Leo, defensive tackle, 49ers (14)   1950–63
Olsen, Merlin, defensive tackle, Rams (15)   1962–76
Otto, Jim, center, Raiders (15)   1960–74
Owen, Steve, tackle, Giants (9), coach, Giants (13)   1924–53
Page, Alan, defensive tackle, Vikings, Bears (15)   1967–81
Parker, Clarence (Ace), quarterback, Dodgers (7)   1937–46
Parker, Jim, guard, tackle, Colts (11)   1957–67
Payton, Walter, running back, Bears (13)   1977–89
Perry, Joe, fullback, 49ers, Colts (16)   1948–63
Pihos, Pete, end, Eagles (9)   1947–55
Ray, Hugh (Shorty), NFL advisor   1938–52
Reeves, Dan, owner, Rams   1941–71
Renfro, Mel, cornerback, safety, Cowboys (14)   1964–77
Riggins, John, running back, Jets, Redskins (14)   1971–84
Ringo, Jim, center, Packers (15)   1953–67
Robustelli, Andy, defensive end, Rams, Giants (14)   1951–64
Rooney, Art, NFL founder, owner, Steelers   1933–88
Rooney, Dan, contributor, Steelers   1955–
Rozelle, Pete, commissioner, NFL   1960–89
St. Claire, Bob, tackle, 49ers (11)   1953–63
Sayers, Gale, back, Bears (7)   1965–71
Schmidt, Joe, linebacker, Lions (13)   1953–65
Schramm, Tex, administrator, Rams, Cowboys (42)   1947–89
Selmon, Lee Roy, defensive end, Buccaneers (13)   1976–84
Shaw, Billy, guard, Bills (9)   1961–69
Shell, Art, tackle, Raiders (15)   1968–82
Shula, Don, coach, Colts, Dolphins (33)   1963–95
Simpson, O.J., back, Bills, 49ers (11)   1969–79
Singletary, Mike, linebacker, Bears (12)   1981–92
Smith, Jackie, tight end, Cardinals, Cowboys (16)   1963–78
Starr, Bart, quarterback, coach, Packers (16)   1956–71
Staubach, Roger, quarterback, Cowboys (11)   1969–79
Stautner, Ernie, defensive tackle, Steelres (14)   1950–63
Stenerud, Jan, placekicker, Chiefs, Packers, Vikings (19)   1967–85
Stephenson, Dwight, center, Dolphins (8)   1980–87
Strong, Ken, back, Giants, Yankees (14)   1929–47
Stydahar, Joe, tackle, Bears (9); coach, Rams, Cardinals (5)   1936–54
Tarkenton, Fran, quarterback, Vikings, Giants (18)   1961–78
Taylor, Charlie, wide receiver, Redskins (14)   1964–77
Taylor, Jim, fullback, Packers, Saints (10)   1958–67
Taylor, Lawrence, linebacker, Giants (13)   1981–93
Thorpe, Jim, back, 7 teams (12)   1915–28
Tittle, Y.A., quarterback, Colts, 49ers, Giants (17)   1948–64
Trafton, George, center, Bears (13)   1920–32
Trippi, Charley, back, Chicago Cardinals (9)   1947–55
Tunnell, Emlen, defensive back, Giants, Packers (14)   1948–61
Turner, Clyde (Bulldog), center, Bears (13)   1940–52
Unitas, John, quarterback, Colts (18)   1956–73
Upshaw, Gene, guard, Raiders (15)   1967–81
Van Brocklin, Norm, quarterback, Rams, Eagles (12)   1949–60
Van Buren, Steve, back, Eagles (9)   1944–51
Walker, Doak, running back, def. back, kicker, Lions (6)   1950–55
Walsh, Bill, coach, 49ers (10)   1979–88
Warfield, Paul, wide receiver, Browns, Dolphins (13)   1964–74, 76–77
Waterfield, Bob, quarterback, Rams (8)   1945–52
Webster, Mike, center, Steelers, Chiefs (17)   1974–90
Weinmeister, Arnie, tackle, N.Y. Yankees, Giants (6)   1948–53
White, Randy, defensive tackle, Cowboys (15)   1975–88
Wilcox, Dave, linebacker, 49ers (11)   1964–74
Willis, Bill, guard, Browns (8)   1946–53
Wilson, Larry, defensive back, Cardinals (13)   1960–72
Winslow, Kellen, tight end, Chargers (9)   1979–87
Wood, Willie, safety, Packers (12)   1960–71
Wojciechowicz, Alex, center, Lions, Eagles (13)   1938–50

N.F.L. INDIVIDUAL LIFETIME, SEASON, AND GAME RECORDS

(American Football League records were incorporated into NFL records after merger of the leagues.)
Players listed in boldface were active during the 1999 season. The NFL does not recognize records from
the All-American Football Conference (AAFC) which existed from 1946 to 1949. The 49ers, Browns, and
Colts merged with the NFL in 1949.

All-Time Leading Touchdown Scorers (Through 1999)

		Yrs	Rush	Rec	Ret	Total
1	**Jerry Rice**	15	10	169	1	180
2	**Emmitt Smith**	10	136	11	0	147
3	Marcus Allen	16	123	21	1	145
4	Jim Brown	9	106	20	0	126
5	Walter Payton	13	110	15	0	125
6	John Riggins	14	104	12	0	116
7	**Cris Carter**	13	0	114	1	115
8	Lenny Moore	12	63	48	2	113
9	Barry Sanders	10	99	10	0	109
10	Don Hutson	11	3	99	3	105
11	Steve Largent	14	1	100	0	101
12	Franco Harris	13	91	9	0	100
13	Eric Dickerson	11	90	6	0	96
14	Jim Taylor	10	83	10	0	93
15	Tony Dorsett	12	77	13	1	91
	Bobby Mitchell	11	18	65	8	91

All-Time Leading Receivers (Through 1999)

		Yrs	No	Yards	Avg	TD
1	**Jerry Rice**	15	1,200	18,299	15.2	169
2	Andre Reed	15	941	13,095	13.9	86
3	Art Monk	16	940	12,721	13.5	68
4	**Cris Carter**	13	924	11,688	12.5	114
5	Steve Largent	14	819	13,089	16.0	100
6	Henry Ellard	16	814	13,777	16.9	65
7	Irving Fryar	16	810	12,237	15.1	79
8	**Tim Brown**	12	770	10,944	14.2	75
9	James Lofton	16	764	14,004	18.3	75
10	Charlie Joiner	18	750	12,146	16.2	65
	Michael Irvin	12	750	11,904	15.9	65
12	Andre Rison	11	702	9,599	13.7	78
13	Gary Clark	11	699	10,856	15.5	65
14	Ozzie Newsome	13	662	7,980	12.1	47
15	Charley Taylor	13	649	9,110	14.0	79

All-Time Leading Passers (Minimum 1,500 attempts. Through 1999)

		Yrs	Att	Cmp	Cmp%	Yards	Avg Gain	TD	TD%	Int	Int%	Rating
1	**Steve Young**	15	4,149	2,667	64.4%	33,124	7.98	232	5.6%	107	2.6%	96.8
2	Joe Montana	15	5,391	3,409	63.2	40,551	7.52	273	5.1	139	2.6	92.3
3	**Brett Favre**	9	4,352	2,659	61.1	30,894	7.10	235	5.4	141	3.2	87.1
4	Dan Marino	17	8,358	4,967	59.4	61,361	7.34	420	5.0	252	3.0	86.4
5	**Mark Brunell**	7	2,160	1,297	60.1	15,572	7.21	86	4.0	52	2.4	85.4
6	Jim Kelly	11	4,779	2,874	60.1	35,467	7.42	237	5.0	175	3.7	84.4
7	Roger Staubach	11	2,958	1,685	57.0	22,700	7.67	153	5.2	109	3.7	83.4
8	Neil Lomax	8	3,153	1,817	57.6	22,771	7.22	136	4.3	90	2.9	82.7
9	**Troy Aikman**	11	4,453	2,742	61.6	31,310	7.03	158	3.5	127	2.9	82.6
10	Sonny Jurgensen	18	4,262	2,433	57.1	32,224	7.56	255	6.0	189	4.4	82.6
11	Len Dawson	19	3,741	2,136	57.1	28,711	7.67	239	6.4	183	4.9	82.5
12	Neil O'Donnell	10	3,057	1,766	57.8	20,408	6.68	114	3.7	62	2.0	82.0
13	Ken Anderson	16	4,475	2,654	59.3	32,838	7.34	197	4.4	160	3.6	81.9
14	Bernie Kosar	12	3,365	1,994	59.3	23,301	6.92	124	3.7	87	2.6	81.8
15	Danny White	13	2,950	1,761	59.7	21,959	7.44	155	5.3	132	4.5	81.7

Note: If the NFL recognized records from the AAFC, **Otto Graham** would rank 4th (after Favre) with the following stats: 10 Yrs; 2,626 Att; 1,464 Comp; 55.8 Comp Pct; 23,584 Yards; 8.98 Avg Gain; 174 TD; 6.6 TD Pct; 135 Int; 5.1 Int Pct; and 86.6 Rating Pts.

All-Time Leading Scorers (Through 1999)

		Yrs	TD	FG	PAT	Total
1	George Blanda	26	9	335	943	2,002
2	**Gary Anderson**	18	0	439	631	1,948
3	**Morten Andersen**	18	0	416	592	1,840
4	Norm Johnson	18	0	366	638	1,736
5	Nick Lowery	18	0	383	562	1,711
6	Jan Stenerud	19	0	373	580	1,699
7	**Eddie Murray**	18	0	344	531	1,563
8	Pat Leahy	18	0	304	558	1,470
9	**Al Del Greco**	16	0	320	506	1,466
10	Jim Turner	16	1	304	521	1,439
11	Matt Bahr	17	0	300	522	1,422
12	Mark Moseley	16	0	300	482	1,382
13	Jim Bakken	17	0	282	534	1,380
14	Fred Cox	15	0	282	519	1,365
15	Lou Groza	17	1	234	641	1,349

All-Time Leading Rushers (Through 1999)

		Yrs	Car	Yards	Avg	TD
1	Walter Payton	13	3,838	16,726	4.4	110
2	Barry Sanders	10	3,062	15,269	5.0	99
3	**Emmitt Smith**	10	3,242	13,963	4.3	136
4	Eric Dickerson	11	2,996	13,259	4.4	90
5	Tony Dorsett	12	2,936	12,739	4.3	77
6	Jim Brown	9	2,359	12,312	5.2	106
7	Marcus Allen	16	3,022	12,243	4.1	123
8	Franco Harris	13	2,949	12,120	4.1	91
9	**Thurman Thomas**	12	2,849	11,938	4.2	65
10	John Riggins	14	2,916	11,352	3.9	104
11	O.J. Simpson	11	2,404	11,236	4.7	61
12	Ottis Anderson	14	2,562	10,273	4.0	81
13	Earl Campbell	8	2,187	9,407	4.3	74
14	**Ricky Watters**	8	2,272	9,083	4.0	70
15	Jim Taylor	10	1,941	8,597	4.4	83

Scoring

Most points scored, lifetime—2,002, George Blanda, Chicago Bears, 1949-58; Baltimore, 1950; Houston, 1960–66; Oakland, 1967–75 (9 tds, 943 pat, 335 fg).

Most points, season—176, Paul Hornung, Green Bay, 1960 (15 td, 41 pat, 15 fg).

Most points, game—40, Ernie Nevers, Chicago Cardinals, 1929 (6 td, 4 pat).

Most touchdowns, lifetime—180, Jerry Rice, San Francisco, 1985–99.

Most touchdowns, season—25, Emmitt Smith, Dallas, 1995.

Most points after touchdown, lifetime—943, George Blanda, Chicago Bears, 1949-58; Baltimore, 1950; Houston, 1960–66; Oakland, 1967–75.

Most points after touchdown, game—9, Pat Harder, Cardinals, 1948; Bob Waterfield, Los Angeles Rams, 1950; Charlie Gogolak, Washington, 1966.

Most field goals, lifetime—439, Gary Anderson, Pittsburgh, 1982–94; Philadelphia, 1995–96; San Francisco, 1997; Minnesota, 1998–99.

Most field goals, season—39, Olindo Mare, Miami, 1999.

Most field goals, game—7, Jim Bakken, St. Louis, 1967; Rich Karlis, Minnesota, 1989; and Chris Boniol, Dallas, 1996.

Longest field goal—63 yards, Tom Dempsey, New Orleans, 1970; Jason Elam, Denver, 1998.

Rushing

Most yards gained, lifetime—16,726, Walter Payton, Chicago Bears, 1975–87.

Most yards gained, season—2,105, Eric Dickerson, Los Angeles, 1984.

Most yards gained, game—275, Walter Payton, Chicago Bears, 1977.

Most touchdowns, lifetime—123, Marcus Allen, Los Angeles Raiders, 1982–93; Kansas City Chiefs, 1993–98.

Most touchdowns, season—25, Emmitt Smith, Dallas, 1995.

Most touchdowns, game—6, Ernie Nevers, Chicago Cardinals, 1929.

Longest run from scrimmage—99 yards, Tony Dorsett, Dallas, 1983.

Receiving

Most pass receptions, lifetime—1,200, Jerry Rice, San Francisco, 1985–99.

Most pass receptions, season—123, Herman Moore, Detroit, 1995.

Most pass receptions, game—18, Tom Fears, Los Angeles, 1950.

Most yards gained, pass receptions, lifetime—18,299, Jerry Rice, San Francisco, 1985–99.

Most yards gained, receptions, season—1,848, Jerry Rice, San Francisco, 1995.

Most yards gained, receptions, game—336, Flipper Anderson, Los Angeles Rams, 1989.

Most touchdown receptions, lifetime—169, Jerry Rice, San Francisco, 1985–99.

Most touchdown pass receptions, season—22, Jerry Rice, San Francisco, 1987.

Most touchdown pass receptions, game—5, Bob Shaw, Chicago Cards, 1950; Kellen Winslow, San Diego, 1981; Jerry Rice, San Francisco, 1990.

Interceptions

Most pass interceptions, lifetime—81, Paul Krause, Washington, 1964-67; Minnesota, 1968–79.

Most pass interceptions, season—14, Richard (Night Train) Lane, Detroit, 1952.

Most pass interceptions, game—4, by 17 players.

Longest pass interception return—104 yards, James Willis, Philadelphia, 1996.

Kicking

Highest average punting, lifetime—45.1 yards, Sammy Baugh, Washington, 1937–52.

Longest punt return—103 yards, Robert Bailey, L.A. Rams, 1994.

Longest kick-off return—106 yards, Roy Green, St. Louis, 1979; Al Carmichael, Green Bay, 1956; Noland Smith, Kansas City, 1967.

Passing

Most touchdown passes, season—48, Dan Marino, Miami, 1984.

Most touchdown passes, game—7, Sid Luckman, Chicago Bears, 1943; Adrian Burk, Philadelphia, 1954; George Blanda, Houston, 1961; Y. A. Tittle, N.Y. Giants, 1962; Joe Kapp, Minnesota, 1969.

Longest pass completion—99 yards, Frank Filchock (to Andy Farkas), Washington, 1939; George Izo (to Bob Mitchell), Washington, 1963; Karl Sweetan (to Pat Studstill), Detroit, 1966; Sonny Jurgensen (to Gerry Allen), Washington, 1968; Jim Plunkett (to Cliff Branch) L.A. Raiders, 1983; Ron Jaworski (to Mike Quick), Philadelphia, 1985; Stan Humphries (to Tony Martin), San Diego, 1994; Brett Favre (to Robert Brooks), Green Bay, 1995.

Most passes completed, lifetime—4,967, Dan Marino, Miami, 1983–99.

Most passes completed, season—404, Warren Moon, 1991.

Most passes completed, game—45, Drew Bledsoe, New England, 1994.

Most touchdown passes, lifetime—420, Dan Marino, Miami, 1983–99.

Most yards gained, lifetime—61,361, Dan Marino, Miami, 1983–99.

Most yards gained, season—5,084, Dan Marino, Miami, 1984.

Most yards gained, game—554, Norm Van Brocklin, Los Angeles, 1951.

Sports Personalities

A name in parentheses is the original name or form of name. Localities are places of birth. Dates of birth appear as month/day/year. **Boldface** years in parentheses are dates of (**birth–death**).

Information has been gathered from many sources, including the individuals themselves. However, the almanac cannot guarantee the accuracy of every individual item.

Aaron, Hank (Henry) (baseball); Mobile, Ala., 2/5/34
Abdul-Jabbar, Kareem (Lewis Ferdinand Alcindor, Jr.) (basketball); New York City, 4/16/47
Affleck, Francis (auto racing) **(1951–1985)**
Agassi, Andre (tennis); Las Vegas, Nev., 4/29/70
Aikman, Troy (football); Henryetta, Okla., 11/21/66
Ali, Muhammad (Cassius Clay) (boxing); Louisville, Ky., 1/18/42
Allen, Dick (Richard Anthony) (baseball); Wampum, Pa., 3/8/42
Allen, George (football) **(1918–1990)**
Allison, Bobby (Robert Arthur) (auto racing); Hueytown, Ala., 12/3/37
Allison, Davey (auto racing); Hueytown, Ala. **(1961–1993)**
Alston, Walter (baseball); Venice, Ohio **(1911–1984)**
Alworth, Lance (football); Houston, 8/3/40
Ameche, Alan (football); Houston, Tex. **(1933–1988)**

Anderson, Sparky (George) (baseball); Bridgewater, S.D., 2/22/34
Andretti, Mario (auto racing); Montona, Trieste, Italy, 2/28/40
Anthony, Earl (bowling); Kent, Wash., 4/27/38
Appling, Luke (baseball); High Point, N.C **(1907–1990)**
Arcaro, Eddie (George Edward) (jockey); Cincinnati **(1916–1997)**
Ashe, Arthur (tennis); Richmond, Va. **(1943–1993)**
Ashford, Evelyn (track & field); Shreveport, La., 4/15/57
Austin, Tracy (tennis); Rolling Hills, Calif., 12/2/62
Averill, Earl (baseball); Everett, Wash. **(1915–1983)**
Babashoff, Shirley (swimming); Whittier, Calif., 1/31/57
Baer, Max (boxing); Omaha, Neb. **(1909–1959)**
Bailey, Donovan (track); Canada, 12/16/67
Banks, Ernie (baseball); Dallas, 1/31/31
Bannister, Roger (runner); Harrow, England, 3/24/29

Barkley, Charles (basketball); Leeds, Ala., 2/20/63
Barry, Rick (Richard) (basketball); Elizabeth, N.J., 3/28/44
Bauer, Hank (Henry) (baseball); East St. Louis, Ill., 7/31/22
Baugh, Sammy (football); Temple, Tex., 3/17/14
Baylor, Elgin (basketball); Washington, D.C., 9/16/34
Beamon, Bob (long jumper); New York City, 8/2/46
Becker, Boris (tennis); Leiman, W. Germany, 11/22/67
Bee, Clair (basketball); Cleveland, Ohio **(1896–1983)**
Beliveau, Jean (hockey); Three Rivers, Quebec, Canada, 8/31/31
Belle, Albert (baseball); Shreveport, La., 8/25/66
Beman, Deane (golf); Washington, D.C., 4/22/38
Bench, Johnny (Johnny Lee) (baseball); Oklahoma City, 12/7/47
Berg, Patty (Patricia Jane) (golf); Minneapolis, 2/13/18
Berra, Yogi (Lawrence) (baseball); St. Louis, 5/12/25
Biletnikoff, Frederick (football); Erie, Pa., 2/23/43
Bing, Dave (basketball); Washington, D.C., 11/24/43
Bird, Larry (basketball); French Lick, Ind., 12/7/56
Blaik, Earl H. (football); Detroit **(1897–1989)**
Blanda, George Frederick (football); Youngwood, Pa., 9/17/27
Bledsoe, Drew (football); Walla Walla, Wash., 2/14/72
Blue, Vida (baseball); Mansfield, La., 7/28/49
Bodine, Brett (auto racing); Chemung, N.Y., 1/11/59
Bodine, Geoff (auto racing); Chemung, N.Y., 4/18/49
Boggs, Wade (baseball); Omaha, Neb., 6/15/58
Bonds, Barry (baseball); Riverside, Calif., 7/24/64
Borg, Björn (tennis); Stockholm, Sweden, 6/6/56
Boros, Julius (golf); Fairfield, Conn. **(1920–1994)**
Bossy, Mike (hockey); Montreal, 1/22/57
Boston, Ralph (long jumper); Laurel, Miss., 5/9/39
Bourque, Ray (hockey); Montreal, Que., 12/28/60
Bradley, Bill (William Warren) (basketball); Crystal City, Mo., 7/28/43
Bradley, Pat (golf); Westford, Mass., 3/24/51
Bradshaw, Terry (football); Shreveport, La., 9/2/48
Breedlove, Craig (Norman) (speed driving); Los Angeles, 3/23/38
Brett, George (baseball); Glendale, W. Va., 5/15/53
Brock, Louis Clark (baseball); El Dorado, Ark., 6/18/39
Brown, Jim (football); St. Simon Island, Ga., 2/17/36
Brumel, Valeri (high jumper); Tolbuzino, Siberia, 4/14/42
Bryant, Paul "Bear" (football); Morro Bottom, Ark. **(1913–1983)**
Bryant, Rosalyn Evette (track); Chicago, 1/7/56
Burton, Michael (swimming); Des Moines, Iowa, 7/3/47
Butkus, Dick (Richard Marvin) (football); Chicago, 12/9/42
Calipari, John (basketball); Moon, Pa., 2/10/59
Campanella, Roy (baseball); Homestead, Pa. **(1921–1993)**
Campbell, Earl (football); Tyler, Tex., 3/29/55
Canseco, Jose (baseball); Havana, Cuba, 7/2/64
Caponi, Donna Maria (golf); Detroit, 1/29/45
Cappelletti, Gino (football); Keewatin, Minn., 3/26/34
Carew, Rod (Rodney Cline) (baseball); Gatun, Panama, 10/1/45
Carlos, John (sprinter); New York City, 6/5/45
Carlton, Steven Norman (baseball); Miami, Fla., 12/22/44
Carner, Joanne Gunderson, Mrs. Don (golf); Kirkland, Wash., 3/4/39
Casals, Rosemary (tennis); San Francisco, 9/16/48
Casper, Billy (golf); San Diego, Calif., 6/24/31
Caulkins, Tracy (swimming); Winona, Minn., 1/11/63
Cauthen, Steve (jockey); Covington, Ky., 5/1/60
Chamberlain, Wilt (Wilton) (basketball); Philadelphia **(1936–1999)**
Chandler, A.B. (Happy) (baseball); Louisville, Ky. **(1899–1991)**
Chandler, Spud (baseball); Commerce, Ga. **(1907–1990)**
Chang, Michael (tennis); Hoboken, N.J., 2/22/72
Chapot, Frank (equestrian); Camden, N.J., 2/24/34
Chastain, Brandi (soccer); San Jose, Calif., 7/21/68
Chinaglia, Giorgio (soccer); Carrara, Italy, 1/24/47
Clarke, Bobby (Robert Earle) (hockey); Flin Flon, Manitoba, Canada, 8/13/49
Clemens, Roger (baseball); Dayton, Ohio, 8/4/62
Clemente, Roberto Walker (baseball); Carolina, Puerto Rico **(1934– 1972)**
Cobb, Ty (Tyrus Raymond) (baseball); Narrows, Ga. **(1886–1961)**
Cochran, Barbara Ann (skiing); Claremont, N.H., 1/14/51
Cochran, Marilyn (skiing); Burlington, Vt., 2/7/50
Cochran, Robert (skiing); Claremont, N.H., 12/11/51
Coe, Sebastian Newbold (track); London, England, 9/29/56
Coffey, Paul (hockey); Weston, Ont., 6/1/61
Colavito, Rocky (Rocco Domenico) (baseball); New York City, 8/10/33
Coleman, Derrick (basketball); Mobile, Ala., 6/21/67
Comaneci, Nadia (gymnast); Onesti, Romania, 11/12/61
Conigliaro, Tony (baseball); Revere, Mass. **(1945–1990)**
Connors, Jimmy (James Scott) (tennis); East St. Louis, Ill., 9/2/52
Cooper, Cynthia (basketball); Chicago, Ill., 4/14/63
Cordero, Angel (jockey); Santurce, Puerto Rico, 5/8/42
Cosell, Howard (broadcaster); Winston-Salem, N.C. **(1918–1995)**
Courier, Jim (tennis); Sanford, Fla., 8/17/70
Cournoyer, Yvan Serge (hockey); Drummondville, Quebec, Canada, 11/22/43
Court, Margaret Smith (tennis); Albury, New South Wales, Australia, 7/16/42

Cousy, Bob (basketball); New York City, 8/9/28
Crabbe, Buster (swimming); Scottsdale, Ariz. **(1908–1983)**
Crenshaw, Ben (golf); Austin, Tex., 1/11/52
Cronin, Joe (baseball executive); San Francisco **(1906–1984)**
Cruyff, Johan (soccer); Amsterdam, Netherlands, 4/25/47
Csonka, Larry (Lawrence Richard) (football); Stow, Ohio, 12/25/46
Dancer, Stanley (harness racing); New Egypt, N.J., 7/25/27
Dark, Alvin (baseball); Comanche, Okla., 1/7/22
Davenport, Willie (track); Troy, Ala., 6/6/43
Dawson, Andre (baseball); Miami, Fla., 7/10/54
Dawson, Leonard Ray (football); Alliance, Ohio, 6/20/35
Dean, Dizzy (Jay Hanna) (baseball); Lucas, Ark. **(1911–1974)**
DeBusschere, Dave (basketball); Detroit, 10/16/40
De La Hoya, Oscar (boxing); East Los Angeles, Calif., 2/4/73
Delvecchio, Alex Peter (hockey); Fort William, Ontario, Canada, 12/4/31
Demaret, Jim (golf); Houston **(1910–1983)**
Dempsey, Jack (William H.) (boxing); Manassa, Colo. **(1895–1983)**
DeVicenzo, Roberto (golf); Buenos Aires, 4/14/23
Dibbs, Edward George (tennis); Brooklyn, New York, 2/23/51
Dietz, James W. (rowing); New York, N.Y., 1/12/49
DiMaggio, Joe (baseball); Martinez, Calif. **(1914–1999)**
Dionne, Marcel (hockey); Drummondville, Quebec, Canada, 8/3/51
Dorsett, Tony (football); Rochester, Pa., 4/7/54
Dryden, Kenneth (hockey); Hamilton, Ontario, Canada, 8/4/47
Drysdale, Don (baseball); Van Nuys, Calif. **(1936–1993)**
Duran, Roberto (boxing); Panama City, 6/16/51
Durocher, Leo (baseball); West Springfield, Mass. **(1906–1991)**
Durr, Francois (tennis); Algiers, Algeria, 12/25/42
Eckersley, Dennis (baseball); Oakland, Calif., 10/3/54
Elder, Lee (golf); Dallas, 7/14/34
Elway, John (football); Port Angeles, Wash., 6/28/60
Emerson, Roy (tennis); Kingsway, Australia, 11/3/36
Ender, Kornelia (swimming); Plauen, East Germany, 10/25/58
Erving, Julius ("Dr. J") (basketball); Roosevelt, N.Y., 2/22/50
Esposito, Phil (Philip Anthony) (hockey); Sault Ste. Marie, Ontario, Canada, 2/20/42
Evans, Lee (runner); Mandena, Calif., 2/25/47
Evert, Chris (Christine Marie) (tennis); Fort Lauderdale, Fla., 12/21/54
Ewbank, Weeb (football); Richmond, Ind. **(1907–1998)**
Ewing, Patrick (basketball); Kingston, Jamaica, 8/5/62
Favre, Brett (football); Gulfport, Miss., 10/10/69
Feller, Robert (Bob) (baseball); Van Meter, Iowa, 11/3/18
Feuerbach, Allan Dean (track); Preston, Iowa, 1/12/48
Finley, Charles O. (sportsman); Ensley, Ala. **(1918–1996)**
Fischer, Bobby (chess); Chicago, 3/9/43
Fitzsimmons, Bob (Robert Prometheus) (boxing); Cornwall, England **(1862–1917)**
Fleming, Peggy Gale (ice skating); San Jose, Calif., 7/27/48
Ford, Whitey (Edward) (baseball); New York City, 10/21/28
Foreman, George (boxing); Marshall, Tex., 1/10/49
Fosbury, Richard (high jumper); Portland, Ore., 3/6/47
Fox, Nellie (Jacob Nelson) (baseball); St. Thomas, Pa. **(1927–1975)**
Foxx, James Emory (baseball); Sudlersville, Md. **(1907–1967)**
Foyt, A. J. (auto racing); Houston, 1/16/35
Frazier, Joe (boxing); Beauford, S.C., 1/17/44
Frazier, Walt (basketball); Atlanta, 3/29/45
Freeman, Cathy (track & field); Mackay, Queensland, Australia, 2/16/73
Frick, Ford C. (baseball); Wawaka, Ind. **(1894–1978)**
Furniss, Bruce (swimming); Fresno, Calif., 5/27/57
Gable, Dan (wrestling); Waterloo, Iowa, 10/25/45
Gabriel, Roman (football); Wilmington, N.C., 8/5/40
Gallagher, Michael Donald (skiing); Yonkers, N.Y., 10/3/41
Garvey, Steve (baseball); Tampa, Fla., 12/22/48
Gehrig, Lou (Henry Louis) (baseball); New York City **(1903–1941)**
Gehringer, Charlie (baseball); Fowlerville, Mich. **(1903–1993)**
Geoffrion, "Boom Boom" (Bernie) (hockey); Montreal, 2/14/31
Gerulaitis, Vitas (tennis); Brooklyn, N.Y. **(1954–1994)**
Gervin, George (basketball); Long Beach, Calif., 4/27/52
Giacomin, Ed (hockey); Sudbury, Ontario, Canada, 6/6/39
Giamatti, A. Bartlett (baseball); South Hadley, Mass. **(1938–1989)**
Gibson, Bob (baseball); Omaha, Neb., 11/9/35
Gifford, Frank (football); Santa Monica, Calif., 8/16/30
Gilbert, Rod (Rodrique) (hockey); Montreal, 7/1/41
Gilmore, Artis (basketball); Chipley, Fla., 9/21/49
Glance, Harvey (track); Phenix City, Ala., 3/28/57
Gonzalez, Pancho (tennis); Los Angeles **(1928–1995)**
Goodell, Brian Stuart (swimming); Stockton, Calif., 4/2/59
Gooden, Dwight (baseball); Tampa, Fla., 11/16/64
Goodrich, Gail (basketball); Los Angeles, 4/23/43
Goolagong, Cawley, Evonne (tennis); Griffith, Australia, 7/31/51
Gordon, Jeff (auto racing); Vallejo, Calif., 8/4/71
Gossage, "Goose" (Rich) (baseball); Colorado Springs, Colo., 4/5/51
Graf, Steffi (tennis); Mannheim, W. Germany, 6/14/69
Graham, David (golf); Windson, Australia, 5/23/46
Graham, Otto Everett (football); Waukegan, Ill., 12/6/21
Grange, Red (Harold) (football); Forksville, Pa. **(1904–1991)**

Green, Hubert (golf); Birmingham, Ala., 12/28/46
Greene, Charles E. (sprinter); Pine Bluff, Ark., 3/21/45
Greene, "Mean" (Joe) (football); Temple, Tex., 9/24/46
Gretzky, Wayne (hockey); Brantford, Ont., 1/26/61
Griese, Bob (Robert Allen) (football); Evansville, Ind., 2/3/45
Griffey, Ken, Jr. (baseball); Donora, Pa., 11/21/69
Grove, Lefty (Robert Moses) (baseball); Lonaconing, Md. **(1900–1975)**
Groza, Lou (football); Martins Ferry Ohio, 1/25/24
Guidry, Ronald Ames (baseball); Lafayette, La., 8/28/50
Gwynn, Tony (baseball); Los Angeles, Calif., 5/9/60
Halas, George (football); Chicago **(1895–1983)**
Hall, Gary (swimming); Fayetteville, N.C., 8/7/51
Hamill, Dorothy (figure skating); Chicago, 7/26/56
Hamilton, Scott (figure skating); Bowling Green, Ohio, 8/28/58
Hamm, Mia (soccer); Selma, Ala., 3/17/72
Hammond, Kathy (runner); Sacramento, Calif., 11/2/51
Hardaway, Anfernee (basketball); Memphis, Tenn., 7/18/72
Harding, Tonya (figure skating); Portland, Ore., 11/12/70
Harris, Franco (football); Ft. Dix, N.J., 3/7/50
Hartack, William, Jr. (jockey); Colver, Pa., 12/9/32
Hasek, Dominik (hockey); Pardubice, Czechoslovakia, 1/29/65
Haughton, William (harness racing); Gloversville, N.Y. **(1923–1986)**
Havlicek, John (basketball); Martins Ferry, Ohio, 4/8/40
Hayes, Elvin (basketball); Rayville, La., 11/17/45
Hayes, Woody (football); Upper Arlington, Ohio **(1913–1987)**
Heiden, Eric (speed skating); Madison, Wis., 6/14/58
Hencken, John (swimming); Culver City, Calif., 5/29/54
Henderson, Rickey (baseball); Chicago, 12/25/58
Henie, Sonja (ice skater); Oslo **(1912–1969)**
Herman, Floyd Caves (Babe) (baseball); Buffalo, N.Y. **(1903–1987)**
Hernandez, Keith (baseball); San Francisco, 10/20/53
Hershiser, Orel (baseball); Buffalo, N.Y., 9/16/58
Hickcox, Charles (swimming); Phoenix, Ariz., 2/6/47
Hines, James (sprinter); Dumas, Ark., 9/10/46
Hingis, Martina (tennis); Kosice, Slovakia, 9/30/80
Hodges, Gil (baseball); Princeton, Ind. **(1924–1972)**
Hogan, Ben (golf); Dublin, Tex. **(1912–1997)**
Holmes, Larry (boxing); Cuthert, Ga., 11/3/49
Holyfield, Evander (boxing); Atlanta, Ga., 10/19/62
Hornsby, Rogers (baseball); Winters, Tex. **(1896–1963)**
Hornung, Paul (football); Louisville, Ky., 12/23/35
Houk, Ralph (baseball); Lawrence, Kan., 8/9/19
Howard, Elston (baseball); St. Louis **(1929–1980)**
Howe, Gordon (hockey); Floral, Sask., Canada, 3/31/28
Howell, Jim Lee (football); Lonoke, Ark. **(1914–1995)**
Howser, Dick (baseball); Miami, Fla. **(1937–1987)**
Hubbell, Carl (baseball); Carthage, Mo. **(1903–1988)**
Huff, Sam (Robert Lee) (football); Morgantown, W. Va., 10/4/34
Hull, Bobby (hockey); Point Anne, Ontario, Canada, 1/3/39
Hunter, "Catfish" (Jim) (baseball); Hertford, N.C. **(1946–1999)**
Hutson, Donald (football); Pine Bluff, Ark. **(1913–1997)**
Irwin, Hale (golf); Joplin, Mo., 6/3/45
Jacobs, Helen Hull (tennis); Globe, Ariz. **(1908–1997)**
Jackson, Phil (basketball coach); Deer Lodge, Mont., 9/17/45
Jackson, Reggie (baseball); Wyncote, Pa., 5/18/46
Jagr, Jaromir (hockey); Kladno, Czechoslovakia, 2/15/72
Jeffries, James J. (boxing); Carroll, Ohio **(1875–1953)**
Jenkins, Ferguson Arthur (baseball); Chatham, Ontario, Canada, 12/13/43
Jenner, (W.) Bruce (track); Mt. Kisco, N.Y., 10/28/49
Jezek, Linda (swimming); Palo Alto, Calif., 3/10/60
Johnson, "Magic" (Earvin) (basketball); E. Lansing, Mich., 8/14/59
Johnson, Anthony (rowing); Washington, D.C., 11/16/40
Johnson, Jack (John Arthur) (boxing); Galveston, Tex. **(1876–1946)**
Johnson, Jimmy (football); Port Arthur, Tex., 8/14/43
Johnson, Michael (track); Dallas, Tex., 9/13/67
Johnson, Rafer (decathlon); Hillsboro, Tex., 8/18/35
Johnson, Randy (baseball); Walnut Creek, Calif., 9/10/63
Johnson, Wilham Julius (Judy) (baseball); Wilmington, Del. **(1899–1989)**
Jones, Cobi (soccer); Detroit, Mich., 6/16/70
Jones, Deacon (David) (football); Eatonville, Fla., 12/9/38
Jones, Marion (track & field); Los Angeles, Calif., 10/12/75
Jordan, Michael (basketball); Brooklyn, N.Y., 2/17/63
Joyner, Florence Griffith (sprinter); Mojave Desert, Calif. **(1959–1998)**
Joyner-Kersee, Jackie (track); East St. Louis, Ill., 3/3/62
Juantoreno, Alberto (track); Santiago, Cuba, 12/3/51
Jurgensen, Sonny (football); Wilmington, N.C., 8/23/34
Justice, Dave (baseball); Cincinnati, Ohio, 4/14/66
Kaat, Jim (baseball); Zeeland, Mich., 11/7/38
Kaline, Al (Albert) (baseball); Baltimore, 12/19/34
Keino, Kipchoge (runner); Kapchemoiymo, Kenya, 1/17/40
Kelly, Leroy (football); Philadelphia, 5/20/42
Kelly, Red (Leonard Patrick) (hockey); Simcoe, Ontario, Canada, 7/9/27
Kerrigan, Nancy (figure skating); Woburn, Mass., 10/13/69
Killebrew, Harmon (baseball); Payette, Idaho, 6/29/36
Killy, Jean-Claude (skiing); Saint-Cloud, France, 8/30/43

Kilmer, Bill (William Orland) (football); Topeka, Kan., 9/5/39
King, Bille Jean (Bille Jean Moffitt) (tennis); Long Beach, Calif., 11/22/43
Kinsella, John (swimming); Oak Park, Ill., 8/26/52
Kluszewski, Ted (baseball); Argo, Ill. **(1924–1988)**
Kodes, Jan (tennis); Prague, 3/1/46
Kolb, Claudia (swimming); Hayward, Calif., 12/19/49
Korbut, Olga (gymnast); Grodno, Byelorussia, U.S.S.R., 5/16/55
Koufax, Sandy (Sanford) (baseball); Brooklyn, N.Y., 12/30/35
Kramer, Jack (tennis); Las Vegas, Nev., 8/1/21
Kramer, Jerry (football); Jordan, Mont., 1/23/36
Krayzelburg, Lenny (swimming); Odessa, Ukraine, 9/28/75
Kuenn, Harvey (baseball); West Allis, Wis. **(1930–1988)**
Kuhn, Bowie Kent (baseball); Takoma Park, Md., 10/28/26
Kwan, Michelle (figure skating); Torrance, Calif., 7/7/80
Lafleur, Guy Damien (hockey); Thurson, Quebec, Canada, 8/20/51
Laird, Ronald (walker); Louisville, Ky., 5/31/35
Lalas, Alexi (soccer); Birmingham, Mich., 6/1/70
Lamonica, Daryle (football); Fresno, Calif., 7/17/41
Landis, Kenesaw Mountain (1st baseball commissioner); Millville, Ohio **(1866–1944)**
Landry, Tom (football); Mission, Tex. **(1924–2000)**
Landy, John (runner); Australia, 4/4/30
Larrieu, Francie (track); Palo Alto, Calif., 11/28/52
La Russa, Tony (baseball); Tampa, Fla., 10/4/44
Lasorda, Tom (baseball); Norristown, Pa., 9/22/27
Laver, Rod (tennis); Rockhampton, Australia, 8/9/38
Layne, Bobby (football); Lubbock, Texas **(1927–1986)**
Leetch, Brian (hockey); Corpus Christi, Tex., 3/3/68
Lemieux, Mario (hockey); Montreal, Quebec, Canada, 10/5/65
Lendl, Ivan (tennis); Prague, 3/7/60
Leonard, Benny (Benjamin Leiner) (boxing); New York City **(1896–1947)**
Leonard, Sugar Ray (boxing); Wilmington, N.C., 5/17/56
Lewis, Carl (track); Willingboro, N.J., 7/1/61
Lindros, Eric (hockey); London, Ont., 2/28/73
Lipinski, Tara (figure skating); Philadelphia, Pa., 6/10/82
Liquori, Marty (runner); Montclair, N.J., 9/11/49
Little, Lou (football); Leominster, Mass. **(1893–1979)**
Littler, Gene (golf); La Jolla, Calif., 7/21/30
Lobo, Rebecca (basketball); Southwick, Mass., 10/6/73
Lombardi, Vince (football); Brooklyn, N.Y. **(1913–1970)**
Longden, Johnny (horse racing); Wakefield, England, 2/14/07
Lopat, Eddie (baseball); New York, N.Y. **(1918–1992)**
Lopez, Al (baseball); Tampa, Fla., 8/20/08
Lopez, Nancy (golf); Torrance, Calif., 1/6/57
Louis, Joe (Joe Louis Barrow) (boxing); Lafayette, Ala. **(1914–1981)**
Lukas, D. Wayne (horse racing); Antigo, Wis., 9/2/35
Lynn, Frederic Michael (baseball); Chicago, Ill., 2/3/52
Lynn, Janet (figure skating); Rockford, Ill., 4/6/53
Mack, Connie (Cornelius Alexander McGillicuddy) (baseball executive); East Brookfield, Mass. **(1862–1956)**
Mackey, John (football); New York City, 9/24/41
Maddux, Greg (baseball); San Angelo, Texas, 4/15/67
Mahovlich, Frank (Francis William) (hockey); Timmins, Ontario, Canada, 1/10/38
Mahre, Phil (skiing); White Pass, Wash., 5/10/57
Malone, Karl (basketball); Summerfield, La., 7/24/63
Malone, Moses (basketball); Petersburg, Va., 3/23/55
Mandlikova, Hana (tennis); Prague, Czechoslovakia, 2/62
Mann, Carol (golf); Buffalo, N.Y., 2/3/41
Manning, Madeline (runner); Cleveland, 1/11/48
Mantle, Mickey Charles (baseball); Spavinaw, Okla. **(1931–1995)**
Maravich, "Pistol Pete" (Peter) Aliquippa, Pa. **(1948–1988)**
Marble, Alice (tennis); Palm Springs, Calif. **(1913–1990)**
Marciano, Rocky (boxing); Brockton, Mass. **(1923–1969)**
Marichal, Juan (baseball); Laguna Verde, Montecristi, Dominican Republic, 10/20/37
Marino, Dan (football); Pittsburgh, Pa., 9/15/61
Maris, Roger (baseball); Hibbing, Minn. **(1934–1985)**
Martin, Billy (Alfred Manuel) (baseball); Berkeley, Calif. **(1928–1989)**
Martin, Christy (boxing); Mullers, W.Va.,
Martin, Rick (Richard Lionel) (hockey); Verdun, Quebec, Canada, 7/26/51
Mathews, Ed (Edwin) (baseball); Texarkana, Tex., 10/13/31
Mattingly, Don (baseball); Evansville, Ind., 4/20/61
Matson, Randy (shot putter); Kilgore, Tex., 3/5/45
Mays, Willie (baseball); Westfield, Ala., 5/6/31
McAdoo, Bob (basketball); Greensboro, N.C., 9/25/51
McCarthy, Joe (Joseph Vincent) (baseball); Philadelphia **(1887–1978)**
McCovey, Willie Lee (baseball); Mobile, Ala., 1/10/38
McDonald, Lanny (hockey); Hanna, Alberta, Canada, 2/16/53
McDowell, Jack (baseball); Van Nuys, Calif., 1/16/66
McEnroe, John Patrick, Jr. (tennis); Wiesbaden, Germany, 2/16/59
McGraw, John Joseph (baseball); Truxton, N.Y. **(1873–1934)**
McGwire, Mark (baseball); Pomona, Calif., 10/1/63
McLain, Dennis (baseball); Chicago, 3/24/44

McMillan, Kathy Laverne (track); Raeford, N.C., 11/7/57

Merrill, Janice (track); New London, Conn., 6/18/62

Messier, Mark (hockey); Edmonton, Alberta, Canada, 1/18/61

Meyer, Deborah (swimming); Haddonfield, N.J., 8/14/52

Meyers, Anne (basketball); San Diego, Calif., 3/26/55

Middlecoff, Cary (golf); Halls, Tenn. **(1921–1998)**

Mikita, Stan (hockey); Sokolce, Czechoslovakia, 5/20/40

Milburn, Rodney, Jr. (hurdler); Opelousas, La., 5/18/50

Miller, Cheryl (basketball); Riverside, Calif., 1/3/64

Miller, Johnny (golf); San Francisco, 4/29/47

Miller, Reggie (basketball); Riverside, Calif., 8/24/65

Montana, Joe (football); New Eagle, Pa., 6/11/56

Montgomery, Jim (swimming); Madison, Wis., 1/24/55

Moody, Helen Wills (tennis); Centerville, Calif. **(1906–1998)**

Moore, Archie (boxing); Benoit, Miss. **(1916–1998)**

Morgan, Joe Leonard (baseball); Bonham, Tex., 9/19/43

Morrall, Earl (football); Muskegon, Mich., 5/17/34

Morton, Craig L. (football); Flint, Mich., 2/5/43

Mosconi, Wilie (pocket billiards); Philadelphia **(1913–1993)**

Moses, Edwin Corley (track); Dayton, Ohio, 8/31/58

Mungo, Van Lingo (baseball); Pageland, S.C. **(1911–1985)**

Munson, Thurman (baseball); Akron, Ohio **(1947–1979)**

Murphy, Calvin (basketball); Norwalk, Conn., 5/9/48

Murray, Eddie (baseball); Los Angeles, Calif., 2/24/56

Musial, Stan (baseball); Donora, Pa., 11/21/20

Myers, Linda (archery); York, Pa., 6/19/47

Naber, John (swimming); Evanston, Ill., 1/20/56

Namath, Joe (Joseph William) (football); Beaver Falls, Pa., 5/31/43

Nastase, Ilie (tennis); Bucharest, 7/19/46

Navratilova, Martina (tennis); Prague, 10/18/56

Nehemiah, Renaldo (track); Newark, N.J., 3/24/59

Nelson, Cindy (skiing); Lutsen, Minn., 8/19/55

Newcombe, John (tennis); Sydney, Australia, 5/23/43

Niekro, Phil (baseball); Lansing, Ohio, 4/1/39

Nicklaus, Jack (golf); Columbus, Ohio, 1/21/40

Norman, Gregory (golf); Mount Isa, Australia, 2/10/55

Oerter, Al (discus thrower); New York City, 9/19/36

Olajuwon, Hakeem (basketball); Lagos, Nigeria, 1/21/63

Oldfield, Barney (racing driver); Fulton County, Ohio **(1878–1946)**

Oliva, Tony (Pedro) (baseball); Pinar Del Rio, Cuba, 7/20/40

Olsen, Merlin Jay (football); Logan, Utah, 9/15/40

O'Malley, Walter (baseball executive); New York City **(1903–1979)**

O'Neal, Shaquille (basketball); Newark, N.J., 3/6/72

Orantes, Manuel (tennis); Granada, Spain, 2/6/49

Orr, Bobby (hockey); Parry Sound, Ontario, Canada, 3/20/48

Ovett, Steve (track); Brighton, England, 10/9/55

Owens, Jesse (track); Decatur, Ala. **(1914–1980)**

Paige, Satchel (Leroy) (baseball); Mobile, Ala. **(1906–1982)**

Palmer, Arnold (golf); Latrobe, Pa., 9/10/29

Palmer, James Alvin (baseball); New York City, 10/15/45

Parcells, Bill (football coach); Englewood, N.J. 8/22/41

Parent, Bernard Marcel (hockey); Montreal, 4/3/45

Park, Brad (Douglas Bradford) (hockey); Toronto, Ontario, Canada, 7/6/48

Parseghian, Ara (football); Akron, Ohio, 5/21/23

Pasarell, Charles (tennis); San Juan, Puerto Rico, 2/12/44

Patterson, Floyd (boxing); Waco, N.C., 1/4/35

Peete, Calvin (golf); Detroit, Mich., 7/18/43

Pelé (Edson Arantes do Nascimento) (soccer); Tres Coracoes, Brazil, 10/23/40

Perry, Gaylord (baseball); Williamston, N.C., 9/15/38

Perry, Jim (baseball); Williamston, N.C., 10/30/36

Pettit, Bob (basketball); Baton Rouge, La., 12/12/32

Petty, Richard Lee (auto racing); Randleman, N.C., 7/2/37

Pincay, Laffit, Jr. (jockey); Panama City, Panama, 12/29/46

Pippen, Scottie (basketball); Trenton, N.J., 9/25/65

Plager, Barclay (ice hockey); Kirkland Lake, Ontario **(1941–1988)**

Plante, Jacques (hockey); Sahwinigan Falls, Quebec, Canada, 1/17/29

Player, Gary (golf); Johannesburg, South Africa, 11/1/35

Plunkett, Jim (football); San Jose, Calif., 12/5/47

Potvin, Denis Charles (hockey); Hull, Quebec, Canada, 10/29/53

Powell, Boog (John) (baseball); Lakeland, Fla., 8/17/41

Powell, Mike (track); Philadelphia, 11/10/63

Prefontaine, Steve Roland (runner); Coos Bay, Ore. **(1951–1975)**

Prince, Bob (baseball announcer); Pittsburgh **(1917–1985)**

Proell, Annemarie Moser (Alpine skier); Kleinarl, Austria, 3/27/53

Rafter, Patrick (tennis); Brisbane, Australia, 12/28/72

Ralston, Dennis (tennis); Bakersfield, Calif., 7/27/42

Rankin, Judy Torluemke (golf); St. Louis, Mo., 2/18/45

Raschi, Vic (baseball); West Springfield, Mass. **(1919–1988)**

Ratelle, Jean (Joseph Gilbert Yvon Jean) (hockey); St. Jean, Quebec, Canada, 10/29/53

Rawls, Betsy (Elizabeth Earle) (golf); Spartanburg, S.C., 5/4/28

Reed, Willis (basketball); Hico, La., 6/25/42

Reese, Pee Wee (Harold) (baseball); Ekron, Ky. **(1919–1999)**

Resch, Glenn "Chico" (hockey); Moose Jaw, Saskatchewan, Canada, 7/10/48

Rice, Jerry (football); Crawford, Miss., 10/13/62

Richard, Maurice (hockey); Montreal, 8/14/24

Riessen, Martin (tennis); Hinsdale, Ill., 12/4/41

Rigney, William (baseball); Alameda, Calif., 1/29/18

Rios, Marcelo (tennis); Santiago, Chile, 12/26/75

Ripken, Cal, Jr. (baseball); Havre de Grace, Md., 8/24/60

Rizzuto, Phil (baseball); New York City, 9/25/18

Robertson, Oscar (basketball); Charlotte, Tenn., 11/24/38

Robinson, Arnie (track); San Diego, Calif., 4/7/48

Robinson, Brooks (baseball); Little Rock, Ark., 5/18/37

Robinson, David (basketball); Key West, Fla., 8/6/65

Robinson, Frank (baseball); Beaumont, Tex., 8/31/35

Robinson, Jackie (baseball); Cairo, Ga. **(1919–1972)**

Robinson, Larry Clark (hockey); Marvelville, Ontario, Canada, 6/2/51

Robinson, "Sugar" Ray (boxing); Detroit **(1920–1989)**

Rockne, Knute Kenneth (football); Voss, Norway **(1888–1931)**

Rockwell, Martha (skiing); Providence, R.I., 4/26/44

Rodman, Dennis (basketball); Trenton, N.J., 5/13/61

Ronaldo (soccer); Bento Ribeiro, Brazil, 9/22/76

Rono, Harry (track); Kiptaragon, Kenya, 2/12/52

Rooney, Art (football); Pittsburgh, Pa. **(1901–1988)**

Rose, Pete (Peter Edward) (baseball); Cincinnati, 4/14/41

Rosenbloom, Maxie (boxing); New York City **(1904–1976)**

Rosewall, Ken (tennis); Sydney, Australia, 11/2/34

Rote, Kyle (football); San Antonio, 10/27/28

Roush, Edd (baseball); Oakland City, Ind. **(1893–1988)**

Rozelle, Pete (Alvin Ray) (commissioner of National Football League); South Gate, Calif. **(1926–1996)**

Rudolph, Wilma Glodean (sprinter); St. Bethlehem, Tenn. **(1940–1994)**

Russell, Bill (basketball); Monroe, La., 2/12/34

Ruth, Babe (George Herman Ruth) (baseball); Baltimore **(1895–1948)**

Rutherford, Johnny (auto racing); Fort Worth, 3/12/38

Ryan, Nolan (Lynn Nolan, Jr.) (baseball); Refugio, Tex., 1/31/47

Ryon, Luann (archery); Long Beach, Calif., 1/13/53

Ryun, Jim (runner); Wichita, Kan., 4/29/47

Salazar, Alberto (track); Havana, 8/7/58

Sampras, Pete (tennis); Washington, D.C., 8/12/71

Samuels, Howard (horse racing soccer); New York City **(1920–1984)**

Sanders, Barry (football); Wichita, Kan., 7/16/68

Sanders, Deion (baseball/football); Ft. Myers, Fla., 8/9/67

Santana, Manuel (Manuel Santana Martinez) (tennis); Chamartin, Spain, 5/10/38

Sayers, Gale (football); Wichita, Kan., 5/30/43

Schmidt, Mike (baseball); Dayton, Ohio, 9/27/49

Schoendienst, Red (Albert) (baseball); Germantown, Ill., 2/2/23

Schollander, Donald (swimming); Charlotte, N.C., 4/30/46

Scurry, Briana (soccer); Minneapolis, Minn., 9/7/71

Seagren, Bob (Robert Lloyd) (pole vaulter); Pomona, Calif., 10/17/46

Seau, Junior (football); Oceanside, Calif., 1/19/69

Seaver, Tom (baseball); Fresno, Calif., 11/17/44

Seidler, Maren (track); Brooklyn, N.Y., 6/11/62

Seles, Monica (tennis); Novi Sad, Yugoslavia, 12/2/73

Selke, Frank (ice hockey); Canada **(1893–1985)**

Sewell, Joe (baseball); Titus, Ala. **(1898–1990)**

Shepherd, Lee (auto racing) **(1945–1985)**

Shero, Fred (hockey); Camden, N.J. **(1925–1990)**

Shoemaker, Willie (jockey); Fabens, Tex., 8/19/31

Shore, Eddie (ice hockey); Saskatchewan, Canada **(1902–1985)**

Shorter, Frank (runner); Munich, Germany, 10/31/47

Shriver, Pam (tennis); Baltimore, 7/4/62

Shula, Don (Donald Francis) (football); Grand River, Ohio, 1/4/30

Silvester, Jay (discus thrower); Tremonton, Utah, 2/27/37

Simpson, O.J. (Orenthal James) (football); San Francisco, 7/9/47

Sims, Billy (football); St. Louis, 9/18/55

Smith, Bubba (Charles Aaron) (football); Orange, Tex., 2/28/45

Smith, Emmitt (football); Pensacola, Fla., 5/15/69

Smith, Ozzie (baseball); Mobile, Ala., 12/26/54

Smith, Ronnie Ray (sprinter); Los Angeles, 3/28/49

Smith, Stanley Roger (tennis); Pasadena, Calif., 12/14/46

Smith, Tommie (sprinter); Clarksville, Tex., 6/5/44

Smoke, Marcia Jones (canoeing); Oklahoma City, 7/18/41

Snead, Sam (golf); Hot Springs, Va., 5/27/12

Sneva, Tom (auto racing); Spokane, Wash., 6/1/48

Snider, Duke (Edwin) (baseball); Los Angeles, 9/19/26

Solomon, Harold (tennis); Washington, D.C., 9/17/52

Sosa, Sammy (Samuel) (baseball); San Pedro de Macoris, Dominican Republic, 11/12/68

Spahn, Warren (baseball); Buffalo, N.Y., 4/23/21

Speaker, Tristram (baseball); Hubbard City, Tex. **(1888–1958)**

Spencer, Brian (ice hockey); Fort St. James, British Columbia **(1949–1988)**

Spinks, Leon (boxing); St. Louis, 7/11/53

Spitz, Mark (swimming); Modesto, Calif., 2/10/50

Stabler, Kenneth (football); Foley, Ala., 12/25/45

Stagg, Amos Alonzo (football); West Orange, N.J. **(1862–1965)**

Stargell, Willie (Wilver Dornell) (baseball); Earlsboro, Okla., 3/6/41

Starr, Bart (football); Montgomery, Ala., 1/9/34

Staub, "Rusty" (Daniel) (baseball); New Orleans, 4/4/44
Staubach, Roger (football); Cincinnati, 2/5/42
Steinkraus, William C. (equestrian); Cleveland, 10/12/25
Stenerud, Jan (football); Fetsund, Norway, 11/26/42
Stengel, Casey (Charles Dillon) (baseball); Kansas City, Mo. **(1891–1975)**
Stenmark, Ingemar (Alpine skier); Tarnaby, Sweden, 3/18/56
Stevens, Scott (hockey); Completon, New Brunswick, 5/4/66
Stockton, Richard LaClede (tennis); New York City, 2/18/51
Stones, Dwight Edwin (track); Los Angeles, 12/6/53
Strawberry, Darryl (baseball); Los Angeles, 3/12/62
Street, Picabo (skiing); Triumph, Idaho, 4/3/71
Sullivan, John Lawrence (boxing); Boston **(1858–1918)**
Summitt, Pat (basketball); Henrietta, Tenn., 6/14/52
Sutton, Don (Donald Howard) (baseball); Clio, Ala., 4/2/45
Swann, Lynn (football); Alcoa, Tenn., 3/7/52
Swoopes, Sheryl (basketball); Brownfield, Tex., 3/25/71
Tanner, Leonard Roscoe III (tennis); Chattanooga, Tenn., 10/15/51
Tarkenton, Fran (Francis) (football); Richmond, Va., 2/3/40
Tebbetts, Birdie (George R.) (baseball); Nashua, N.H. **(1914–1999)**
Theismann, Joe (football); New Brunswick, N.J., 9/9/46
Thomas, Frank (baseball); Columbus, Ga., 5/27/68
Thomas, Isiah (basketball); Chicago, Ill., 4/30/61
Thomas, Thurman (football); Houston, Texas, 5/16/66
Thompson, David (basketball); Shelby, N.C., 7/13/54
Thorpe, Ian (swimming); Sydney, New South Wales, Australia, 10/13/82
Thorpe, Jim (James Francis) (all-around athlete); nr. Prague, Okla. **(1888–1953)**
Tilden, William Tatem II (tennis); Philadelphia **(1893–1953)**
Tittle, Y. A. (Yelberton Abraham) (football); Marshall, Tex., 10/24/26
Toomey, Bill (decathlon); Philadelphia, 1/10/39
Trevino, Lee (golf); Dallas, 12/1/39
Trottier, Bryan (hockey); Val Marie, Sask., Canada, 7/17/56
Tunney, Gene (James J.) (boxing); New York City **(1898–1978)**
Tyson, Mike (boxing); Brooklyn, N.Y., 6/30/66
Tyus, Wyomia (runner); Griffin, Ga., 8/29/45
Ueberroth, Peter (baseball); Evanston, Ill., 9/2/37
Unitas, John (football); Pittsburgh, 5/7/33
Unser, Al (auto racing); Albuquerque, N. Mex., 5/29/39
Unser, Bobby (auto racing); Albuquerque, N. Mex., 2/20/34
Valenzuela, Fernando (baseball); Sonora, Mexico, 11/1/60
Valvano, Jim (basketball); New York, N.Y. **(1946–1993)**
Van Brocklin, Norm (football); Eagle Butte, S. Dak. **(1926–1983)**
Vaughn, Mo (baseball); Norwalk, Conn., 12/15/67
Vilas, Guillermo (tennis); Mar del Plata, Argentina, 8/17/52

Viola, Frank (baseball); Hempstead, N.Y., 4/19/60
Viren, Lasse (track); Myrskyla, Finland, 7/12/49
Vitale, Dick (basketball); E. Rutherford, N.J., 6/9/39
Wade, Virginia (tennis); Bournemouth, England, 7/10/45
Wagner, Honus (John Peter Honus) (baseball); Carnegie, Pa. **(1867–1955)**
Waitz, Grete (Andersen) (running); Oslo, Norway, 10/1/53
Walcott, Jersey Joe (Arnold Cream) (boxing); Merchantville, N.J. **(1914–1994)**
Wallace, Rusty (auto racing); St. Louis, Mo., 8/14/56
Walsh, Adam (football) **(1902–1985)**
Walton, Bill (basketball); La Mesa, Calif., 11/5/52
Waterfield, Bob (football); Burbank, Calif. **(1921–1983)**
Watson, Martha Rae (track); Long Beach, Calif., 8/19/46
Watson, Tom (golf); Kansas City, Mo., 9/4/49
Weaver, Earl (baseball); St. Louis, 8/14/30
Weiskopf, Tom (golf); Massillon, Ohio, 11/9/42
Weiss, George (baseball executive); New Haven, Conn. **(1895–1972)**
Weissmuller, Johnny (swimmer and actor); Windber, Pa. **(1904–1984)**
West, Jerry (basketball); Cheylan, W. Va., 5/28/38
White, Reggie (football); Chattanooga, Tenn., 12/19/61
White, Willye B. (long jumper); Money, Miss., 1/1/36
Whitworth, Kathy (golf); Monahans, Tex., 9/27/39
Wilkens, Mac Maurice (track); Eugene, Ore., 11/15/50
Wilkins, Lennie (basketball) 11/25/37
Wilkinson, Bud (football); Minneapolis **(1916–1994)**
Williams, Dick (baseball); St. Louis, 5/7/29
Williams, Serena (tennis); Saginaw, Mich., 9/26/81
Williams, Ted (baseball); San Diego, Calif., 8/30/18
Williams, Venus (tennis); Lynnwood, Calif., 6/17/80
Wills, Maury (baseball); Washington, D.C., 10/2/32
Winfield, Dave (baseball); St. Paul, Minn., 10/3/51
Wohlhuter, Richard C. (runner); Geneva, Ill., 12/23/45
Wood, "Smokey Joe" (Joseph) (baseball); Kansas City, Mo. **(1890–1985)**
Woods, Tiger (Eldrick) (golf); Long Beach, Calif., 12/30/75
Wottle, David James (runner); Canton, Ohio, 8/7/50
Wright, Mickey (Mary Kathryn) (golf); San Diego, Calif., 2/14/35
Yarborough, Cale (William Caleb) (auto racing); Timmonsville, S.C., 3/27/39
Yastrzemski, Carl (baseball); Southampton, N.Y., 8/22/39
Young, Cy (Denton True) (baseball); Gilmore, Ohio **(1867–1955)**
Young, Sheila (speed skater, bicycle racer); Detroit, 10/14/50
Young, Steve (football); Salt Lake City, Utah, 10/11/61
Zaharias, Babe Didrikson (golf); Port Arthur, Tex. **(1913–1956)**

Basketball

Basketball may be the one sport whose exact origin is definitely known. In the winter of 1891–92, Dr. James Naismith, an instructor in the Y.M.C.A. Training College (now Springfield College) at Springfield, Mass., deliberately invented the game of basketball in order to provide indoor exercise and competition for the students between the closing of the football season and the opening of the baseball season. He affixed peach baskets overhead on the walls at opposite ends of the gymnasium and organized teams to play his new game in which the purpose was to toss an association (soccer) ball into one basket and prevent the opponents from tossing the ball into the other basket. Because Dr. Naismith had eighteen available players when he invented the game, the first rule was: "There shall be nine players on each side." Later the number of players became optional, depending upon the size of the available court, but the five-player standard was adopted when the game spread over the country. United States soldiers brought basketball to Europe in World War I, and it soon became a world-wide sport.

College Basketball
NATIONAL COLLEGIATE A.A. CHAMPIONS

1938 Temple	1953 Indiana	1974 No. Carolina State	1989 Michigan
1939 Oregon	1954 La Salle	1975 UCLA	1990 UNLV
1940 Indiana & USC	1955 San Francisco	1976 Indiana	1991 Duke
1941 Wisconsin	1956 San Francisco	1977 Marquette	1992 Duke
1942 Stanford	1957 North Carolina	1978 Kentucky	1993 North Carolina
1943 Wyoming	1958 Kentucky	1979 Michigan State	1994 Arkansas
1944 Utah	1959 California	1980 Louisville	1995 UCLA
1945 Oklahoma A & M	1960 Ohio State	1981 Indiana	1996 Kentucky
1946 Oklahoma A & M	1961 Cincinnati	1982 North Carolina	1997 Arizona
1947 Holy Cross	1962 Cincinnati	1983 North Carolina State	1998 Kentucky
1948 Kentucky	1963 Loyola (Chicago)	1984 Georgetown	1999 Connecticut
1949 Kentucky	1964 UCLA	1985 Villanova	2000 Michigan State
1950 C.C.N.Y.	1965 UCLA	1986 Louisville	
1951 Kentucky	1966 Texas Western	1987 Indiana	
1952 Kansas	1967–73 UCLA	1988 Kansas	

NATIONAL INVITATION TOURNAMENT (NIT) CHAMPIONS

1938 Temple	1955 Duquesne	1971 North Carolina	1987 So. Mississippi
1939 Long Island U.	1956 Louisville	1972 Maryland	1988 Connecticut
1940 Colorado	1957 Bradley	1973 Virginia Tech	1989 St. John's (N.Y.C.)
1941 Long Island U.	1958 Xavier (Cincinnati)	1974 Purdue	1990 Vanderbilt
1942 West Virginia	1959 St. John's (N.Y.C.)	1975 Princeton	1991 Stanford
1943–44 St. John's (N.Y.C.)	1960 Bradley	1976 Kentucky	1992 Virginia
1945 DePaul	1961 Providence	1977 St. Bonaventure	1993 Minnesota
1946 Kentucky	1962 Dayton	1978 Texas	1994 Villanova
1947 Utah	1963 Providence	1979 Indiana	1995 Virginia Tech
1948 St. Louis	1964 Bradley	1980 Virginia	1996 Nebraska
1949 San Francisco	1965 St. John's (N.Y.C.)	1981 Tulsa	1997 Michigan
1950 C.C.N.Y.	1966 Brigham Young	1982 Bradley	1998 Minnesota
1951 Brigham Young	1967 So. Illinois	1983 Fresno State	1999 California
1952 La Salle	1968 Dayton	1984 Michigan	2000 Wake Forest
1953 Seton Hall	1969 Temple	1985 UCLA	
1954 Holy Cross	1970 Marquette	1986 Ohio State	

N.C.A.A. DIVISION I INDIVIDUAL CAREER RECORDS

SCORING—TOTAL POINTS

	Yrs	Last	Gm	Pts
Pete Maravich, LSU	3	1970	83	3,667
Freeman Williams, Port. St.	4	1978	106	3,249
Lionel Simmons, La Salle	4	1990	131	3,217
Alphonzo Ford, Miss. Val. St.	4	1993	109	3,165
Harry Kelly, Texas Southern	4	1983	110	3,066
Hersey Hawkins, Bradley	4	1988	125	3,008
Oscar Robertson, Cincinnati	3	1960	88	2,973
Danny Manning, Kansas	4	1988	147	2,951
Alfredrick Hughes, Loyola-Ill.	4	1985	120	2,914
Elvin Hayes, Houston	3	1968	93	2,884

SCORING—AVERAGE POINTS

	Yrs	Last	Pts	Avg
Pete Maravich, LSU	3	1970	3,667	44.2
Austin Carr, Notre Dame	3	1971	2,560	34.6
Oscar Robertson, Cin.	3	1960	2,973	33.8
Calvin Murphy, Niagara	3	1970	2,548	33.1
Dwight Lamar, SW La.	2	1973	1,862	32.7
Frank Selvy, Furman	3	1954	2,538	32.5
Rick Mount, Purdue	3	1970	2,323	32.3
Darrell Floyd, Furman	3	1956	2,281	32.1
Nick Werkman, Seton Hall	3	1964	2,273	32.0
Willie Humes, Idaho St.	2	1971	1,510	31.5

REBOUNDS—TOTAL, BEFORE 1973

	Yrs	Last	Gm	No
Tom Gola, La Salle	4	1955	118	2,201
Joe Holup, G. Washington	4	1956	104	2,030
Charlie Slack, Marshall	4	1956	88	1,916
Ed Conlin, Fordham	4	1955	102	1,884
Dickie Hemric, Wake Forest	4	1955	104	1,802
Paul Silas, Creighton	3	1964	81	1,751
Art Quimby, Connecticut	4	1955	80	1,716
Jerry Harper, Alabama	4	1956	93	1,688
Jeff Cohen, Wm. & Mary	4	1961	103	1,679
Steve Hamilton, Morehead St.	4	1958	102	1,675

REBOUNDS—TOTAL, SINCE 1973

	Yrs	Last	Gm	No
Tim Duncan, Wake Forest	4	1997	128	1,570
Derrick Coleman, Syracuse	4	1990	143	1,537
Malik Rose, Drexel	4	1996	120	1,514
Ralph Sampson, Virginia	4	1983	132	1,511
Pete Padgett, Nevada-Reno	4	1976	104	1,464
Lionel Simmons, La Salle	4	1990	131	1,429
Anthony Bonner, St. Louis	4	1990	133	1,424
Tyrone Hill, Xavier-Ohio	4	1990	126	1,380
Popeye Jones, Murray St.	4	1992	123	1,374
Michael Brooks, La Salle	4	1980	114	1,372

ASSISTS—TOTAL

	Yrs	Last	Gm	No
Bobby Hurley, Duke	4	1993	140	1,076
Chris Corchiani, N.C. State	4	1991	124	1,038
Ed Cota, N. Carolina	4	2000	138	1,030
Keith Jennings, E. Tenn. St.	4	1991	127	983
Sherman Douglas, Syracuse	4	1989	138	960
Tony Miller, Marquette	4	1995	123	956
Greg Anthony, Portland/UNLV	4	1991	138	950
Doug Gottlieb, ND/Okla St.	4	2000	124	947
Gary Payton, Oregon St.	4	1990	120	938
Orlando Smart, San Fran	4	1994	116	902

BLOCKED SHOTS—AVERAGE

	Yrs	Last	No	Avg
Keith Closs, Cen. Conn. St.	2	1996	317	5.87
Adonal Foyle, Colgate	3	1997	492	5.66
David Robinson, Navy	2	1987	351	5.24
Shaquille O'Neal, LSU	3	1992	412	4.58
Jerome James, Fla. A&M	3	1998	363	4.48

Note: minimum 225 blocked shots.

STEALS—AVERAGE

	Yrs	Last	No	Avg
Mookie Blaylock, Oklahoma	2	1989	281	3.80
Ronn McMahon, Eastern Wash	3	1990	225	3.52
Eric Murdock, Providence	4	1991	376	3.21
Van Usher, Tennessee Tech	3	1992	270	3.18
Pepe Sanchez, Temple	4	2000	365	3.15

Note: minimum 225 steals.

N.C.A.A. DIVISION I SINGLE-GAME SCORING MARKS

	Year	Pts		Year	Pts
Kevin Bradshaw, US Int'l vs Loyola-CA	1991	72	Anthony Roberts, Oral Rbts. vs N.C. A.&T.	1977	66
Pete Maravich, LSU vs Alabama	1970	69	Scott Haffner, Evansville vs Dayton	1989	65
Calvin Murphy, Niagara vs Syracuse	1969	68	Pete Maravich, LSU vs Kentucky	1970	64
Jay Handlan, Wash. & Lee vs Furman	1951	66	Johnny Neumann, Ole Miss vs LSU	1971	63
Pete Maravich, LSU vs Tulane	1969	66	Hersey Hawkins, Bradley vs Detroit	1988	63

MEN'S N.C.A.A. BASKETBALL CHAMPIONSHIPS—2000

Division I

First Round—East
Oregon 71, Seton Hall 72
Temple 73, Lafayette 47
Oklahoma State 86, Hofstra 66
Indiana 57, Pepperdine 77
Illinois 68, Penn 58
Florida 69, Butler 68 (OT)
Kansas 81, DePaul 77 (OT)
Duke 82, Lamar 55
First Round—West
Texas 77, Indiana State 61
Louisiana State 64, Southeast
   Missouri State 61
Arizona 71, Jackson State 47
Wisconsin 66, Fresno State 56
Oklahoma 74, Winthrop 50
Purdue 62, Dayton 61
Louisville 66, Gonzaga 77
St. John's 61, Northern Arizona 56
First Round—Midwest
Kentucky 85, St. Bonaventure 80
   (2OT)
Syracuse 79, Samford 65
Michigan State 65, Valparaiso 38
Utah 48, St. Louis 45
Auburn 72, Creighton 69
Iowa State 88, Central Conn.
   State 78
Maryland 74, Iona 59
UCLA 65, Ball State 57
First Round—South
Cincinnati 64, North Carolina–
   Wilmington 47

Tulsa 89, UNLV 62
Ohio State 87, Appalachian State 61
Miami 75, Arkansas 71
Tennessee 63, Louisiana–
   Lafayette 58
Connecticut 75, Utah State 67
North Carolina 84, Missouri 70
Stanford 84, S. Carolina State 65
Second Round—East
Pepperdine 67, Oklahoma State 75
Seton Hall 67, Temple 65 (OT)
Florida 93, Illinois 76
Duke 69, Kansas 64
Second Round—West
Texas 67, Louisiana State 72
Arizona 59, Wisconsin 66
Purdue 66, Oklahoma 62
Gonzaga 82, St. John's 76
Second Round—Midwest
Kentucky 50, Syracuse 52
Michigan State 73, Utah 61
Auburn 60, Iowa State 79
UCLA 105, Maryland 70
Second Round—South
Tulsa 69, Cincinnati 61
Miami 75, Ohio State 62
Stanford 53, North Carolina 60
Connecticut 51, Tennessee 65
Third Round—East
Florida 87, Duke 78
Oklahoma State 68, Seton Hall 66
Third Round—West
Purdue 75, Gonzaga 66
Louisiana State 48, Wisconsin 61

Third Round—Midwest
Syracuse 58, Michigan State 75
Iowa State 80, UCLA 56
Third Round—South
Tulsa 80, Miami 71
North Carolina 74, Tennessee 69
Regional Finals
East—Oklahoma State 65, Florida 77
West—Purdue 60, Wisconsin 64
Midwest—Iowa State 64, Michigan
   State 75
South—Tulsa 55, North Carolina 59
National Semifinals
(April 1, 2000, Indianapolis, Ind.)
Michigan State 53, Wisconsin 41
Florida 71, North Carolina 59
National Final
(April 3, 2000, Indianapolis, Ind.)
Florida 76, Michigan State 89

Division II

Semifinals
Missouri Southern 74, Metro State 75
Seattle Pacific 81, Kentucky
   Wesleyan 87
Championship
Kentucky Wesleyan 79, Metro
   State 97

WOMEN'S N.C.A.A. CHAMPIONSHIPS—2000

Division I

First Round—East
Xavier 72, Stephen F. Austin 73
Louisiana State 77, Liberty 54
Drake 50, Clemson 64
Connecticut 116, Hampton 45
Oklahoma 86, Brigham Young 81
Purdue 70, Dartmouth 64
Marquette 65, Western Kentucky 68
Duke 71, Campbell 42
First Round—Mideast
Boston College 93, Nebraska 76
Virginia 74, Pepperdine 68
George Washington 79, UCLA 72
Notre Dame 87, San Diego 61
Tulane 65, Vermont 60
Texas Tech 83, Tennessee Tech 54
Arizona 73, Kent 61
Tennessee 89, Furman 38
First Round—Midwest
Illinois 73, Utah 58
Iowa State 92, St. Francis 63
Auburn 78, Southwest Missouri
   State 72
Penn State 83, Youngstown State 63
North Carolina State 63, Southern
   Methodist 64
Old Dominion 94, Wisconsin–
   Green Bay 85
Louisiana Tech 95, Alcorn State 53
Kansas 69, Vanderbilt 71 (2OT)
First Round—West
Texas 48, St. Joseph's 69
Rutgers 91, Holy Cross 70

Mississippi State 94, St. Peter's 60
Oregon 79, Alabama-Birmingham 80
   (OT)
Georgia 74, Montana 46
Michigan 74, Stanford 81
North Carolina 62, Maine 57
U.C.-Santa Barbara 64, Rice 67
Second Round—East
Louisiana State 57, Stephen F.
   Austin 45
Clemson 45, Connecticut 83
Oklahoma 76, Purdue 74
Western Kentucky 70, Duke 90
Second Round—Mideast
Boston College 70, Virginia 74
George Washington 60, Notre
   Dame 95
Tulane 59, Texas Tech 76
Arizona 60, Tennessee 75
Second Round—Midwest
Illinois 68, Iowa State 79
Auburn 69, Penn State 75
Southern Methodist 76, Old
   Dominion 96
Louisiana Tech 66, Vanderbilt 65
Second Round—West
St. Joseph's 39, Rutgers 59
Mississippi State 72, Alabama-
   Birmingham 78
Georgia 83, Stanford 64
North Carolina 83, Rice 50
Third Round—East
Louisiana State 79, Duke 66
Connecticut 102, Oklahoma 80

Third Round—Mideast
Tennessee 77, Virginia 56
Texas Tech 69, Notre Dame 65
Third Round—Midwest
Louisiana Tech 86, Old Dominion 74
Iowa State 65, Penn State 66
Third Round—West
Georgia 83, North Carolina 57
Alabama-Birmingham 45, Rutgers 60
Regional Finals
East—Louisiana State 71,
   Connecticut 86
Mideast—Texas Tech 44,
   Tennessee 57
Midwest—Louisiana Tech 65,
   Penn State 86
West—Georgia 51, Rutgers 59
National Semifinals
(March 31, 2000, Philadelphia, Pa.)
Tennessee 64, Rutgers 54
Connecticut 89, Penn State 67
National Championship
(April 2, 2000, Philadelphia, Pa.)
Tennessee 52, Connecticut 71

Division II

Semifinals
North Dakota State 72, Columbus
   State 56
Western Washington 74, Northern
   Kentucky 80
Championship
North Dakota State 62, Northern
   Kentucky 71 (OT)

LEADING N.C.A.A. DIVISION I MEN—1999–2000

SCORING

	Gm	Pts	Avg
Courtney Alexander, Fresno State	26	658	25.3
Sirvaliant Brown, George Washington	30	738	24.6
Ronnie McCollum, Centenary	28	667	23.8
Harold Arceneaux, Weber State	28	651	23.3
Marcus Fizer, Iowa State	32	742	23.2
Rashad Phillips, Detroit	32	735	23.0
Demond Stewart, Niagara	29	665	22.9
Craig Claxton, Hofstra	30	686	22.9
Troy Murphy, Notre Dame	32	729	22.8
Chris Tote, Troy State	2	45	22.5

REBOUNDING

	Gm	No	Avg
Darren Phillip, Fairfield	29	405	14.0
Darrell Neal, Norfolk State	27	354	13.1
Larry Abney, Fresno State	33	394	11.9
Josh Sankes, Holy Cross	28	334	11.9
Shaun Stonerook, Ohio	33	387	11.7
Troy Murphy, Notre Dame	32	346	10.8
Jarrett Stephens, Penn State	30	321	10.7
Chris Mihm, Texas	31	327	10.6
Darren Fenn, Canisius	30	314	10.5
Matt Williams, Montana	28	287	10.3

ASSISTS

	Gm	No	Avg
Mark Dickel, Nevada-Las Vegas	30	274	9.1
Doug Gottlieb, Oklahoma State	30	254	8.5
Chico Fletcher, Arkansas State	28	232	8.3
Brandon Granville, Southern Calif.	30	248	8.3
Ed Cota, North Carolina	30	242	8.1

	Gm	No	Avg
Juan Pepe Sanchez, Temple	23	180	7.8
Mateen Cleaves, Michigan State	19	146	7.7
Casey Rogers, Western Carolina	28	213	7.6
Cornelius Jackson, Marshall	29	213	7.3
Elliott Prasse-Freeman, Harvard	27	196	7.3

LEADING N.C.A.A. DIVISION I WOMEN—1999–2000

SCORING

	Gm	Pts	Avg
Jackie Stiles, Southwest	31	860	27.7
Diana Caramanico, Pennsylvania	28	694	24.8
Jess Zinobile, St. Francis (Pa.)	30	697	23.2
Linda Frohlich, Nevada-Las Vegas	28	604	21.6
Edwina Brown, Texas	33	708	21.5
Rhonda Smith, Long Beach	29	619	21.3
Katie Douglas, Purdue	28	597	21.3
Jamie Cassidy, Maine	30	638	21.3
Grace Daley, Tulane	30	638	21.3
Jennifer Crow, Oklahoma State	30	633	21.1

REBOUNDING

	Gm	No	Avg
Malveata Johnson, North Carolina A & T	27	363	13.4
Elise James, Robert Morris	28	367	13.1
Diana Caramanico, Pennsylvania	28	334	11.9
Deanna Jackson, Alabama-Birmingham	30	357	11.9
Jess Zinobile, St. Francis (Pa.)	30	357	11.9
Mercy Aghedo, St. Peter's	29	342	11.8
Nekesha Jewell, Grambling	30	350	11.7
Gail Strumpf, Fairfield	32	368	11.5
Linda Frohlich, Nevada-Las Vegas	28	319	11.4
Andrea Gardner, Howard	28	316	11.3

ASSISTS

	Gm	No	Avg
Angela Zampella, St. Joseph's	29	233	8.0
Helen Darling, Penn State	30	230	7.7
Michele Koclanes, Richmond	27	204	7.6
Sharin Milner, Troy State	27	202	7.5
Rochelle Luckett, Va. Commonwealth	30	214	7.1

	Gm	No	Avg
Clarissa Tomlinson, Samford	29	201	6.9
Shala Crook, Ball State	29	197	6.8
Tricia Brenitsky, Canisius	29	197	6.8
Amy Vachon, Maine	30	201	6.7
Lindsay Logan, Fresno State	29	192	6.6

OTHER TOURNAMENTS: 1999–2000

MEN

NIT—Wake Forest 71, Notre Dame 61
NAIA Div. I—Life (Ga.) 61, Georgetown College (Ky.) 59
NAIA Div. II—Embry-Riddle (Fla.) 75, College of the Ozarks (Mo.) 63

WOMEN

NIT—Wisconsin 75, Florida 74
NAIA Div. I—Oklahoma City 64, Simon Fraser (B.C.) 55
NAIA Div. II—University of Mary (N.D.) 59, Northwestern College (Iowa) 49

Professional Basketball

NATIONAL BASKETBALL ASSOCIATION CHAMPIONS

The National Basketball Association was originally the Basketball Association of America. It took its current name in 1949 when it merged with the National Basketball League.

Year	Eastern Conference	Western Conference	Winner (Series)
1947	Philadelphia Warriors	Chicago Stags	Philadelphia Warriors (4–1)
1948	Philadelphia Warriors	Baltimore Bullets	Baltimore Bullets (4–2)
1949	Washington Capitols	Minneapolis Lakers	Minneapolis Lakers (4–2)
1950	Syracuse Nationals	Minneapolis Lakers	Minneapolis Lakers (4–2)
1951	New York Knickerbockers	Rochester Royals	Rochester Royals (4–3)
1952	New York Knickerbockers	Minneapolis Lakers	Minneapolis Lakers (4–3)
1953	New York Knickerbockers	Minneapolis Lakers	Minneapolis Lakers (4–1)
1954	Syracuse Nationals	Minneapolis Lakers	Minneapolis Lakers (4–3)
1955	Syracuse Nationals	Ft. Wayne Pistons	Syracuse Nationals (4–3)

Year	Eastern Conference	Western Conference	Winner (Series)
1956	Philadelphia Warriors	Ft. Wayne Pistons	Philadelphia Warriors (4–1)
1957	Boston Celtics	St. Louis Hawks	Boston Celtics (4–3)
1958	Boston Celtics	St. Louis Hawks	St. Louis Hawks (4–2)
1959	Boston Celtics	Minneapolis Lakers	Boston Celtics (4–0)
1960	Boston Celtics	St. Louis Hawks	Boston Celtics (4–3)
1961	Boston Celtics	St. Louis Hawks	Boston Celtics (4–1)
1962	Boston Celtics	Los Angeles Lakers	Boston Celtics (4–3)
1963	Boston Celtics	Los Angeles Lakers	Boston Celtics (4–2)
1964	Boston Celtics	San Francisco Warriors	Boston Celtics (4–1)
1965	Boston Celtics	Los Angeles Lakers	Boston Celtics (4–1)
1966	Boston Celtics	Los Angeles Lakers	Boston Celtics (4–3)
1967	Philadelphia 76ers	SF Warriors	Philadelphia 76ers (4–2)
1968	Boston Celtics	Los Angeles Lakers	Boston Celtics (4–2)
1969	Boston Celtics	Los Angeles Lakers	Boston Celtics (4–3)
1970	New York Knickerbockers	Los Angeles Lakers	New York Knickerbockers (4–3)
1971	Baltimore Bullets	Milwaukee Bucks	Milwaukee Bucks (4–0)
1972	New York Knickerbockers	Los Angeles Lakers	Los Angeles Lakers (4–1)
1973	New York Knickerbockers	Los Angeles Lakers	New York Knickerbockers (4–1)
1974	Boston Celtics	Milwaukee Bucks	Boston Celtics (4–3)
1975	Washington Bullets	Golden State Warriors	Golden State Warriors (4–0)
1976	Boston Celtics	Phoenix Suns	Boston Celtics (4–2)
1977	Philadelphia 76ers	Portland Trail Blazers	Portland Trail Blazers (4–2)
1978	Washington Bullets	Seattle SuperSonics	Washington Bullets (4–3)
1979	Washington Bullets	Seattle SuperSonics	Seattle SuperSonics (4–1)
1980	Philadelphia 76ers	Los Angeles Lakers	Los Angeles Lakers (4–2)
1981	Boston Celtics	Houston Rockets	Boston Celtics (4–2)
1982	Philadelphia 76ers	Los Angeles Lakers	Los Angeles Lakers (4–2)
1983	Philadelphia 76ers	Los Angeles Lakers	Philadelphia 76ers (4–0)
1984	Boston Celtics	Los Angeles Lakers	Boston Celtics (4–3)
1985	Boston Celtics	Los Angeles Lakers	Los Angeles Lakers (4–2)
1986	Boston Celtics	Houston Rockets	Boston Celtics (4–2)
1987	Boston Celtics	Los Angeles Lakers	Los Angeles Lakers (4–2)
1988	Detroit Pistons	Los Angeles Lakers	Los Angeles Lakers (4–3)
1989	Detroit Pistons	Los Angeles Lakers	Detroit Pistons (4–0)
1990	Detroit Pistons	Portland Trail Blazers	Detroit Pistons (4–1)
1991	Chicago Bulls	Los Angeles Lakers	Chicago Bulls (4–1)
1992	Chicago Bulls	Portland Trail Blazers	Chicago Bulls (4–2)
1993	Chicago Bulls	Phoenix Suns	Chicago Bulls (4–2)
1994	New York Knickerbockers	Houston Rockets	Houston Rockets (4–3)
1995	Orlando Magic	Houston Rockets	Houston Rockets (4–0)
1996	Chicago Bulls	Seattle SuperSonics	Chicago Bulls (4–2)
1997	Chicago Bulls	Utah Jazz	Chicago Bulls (4–2)
1998	Chicago Bulls	Utah Jazz	Chicago Bulls (4–2)
1999	New York Knickerbockers	San Antonio Spurs	San Antonio Spurs (4–1)
2000	Indiana Pacers	Los Angeles Lakers	Los Angeles Lakers (4–2)

INDIVIDUAL N.B.A. SCORING CHAMPIONS

Season	Player, Team	G	FG	FT	Pts	Avg
1953–54	Neil Johnston, Philadelphia Warriors	72	591	577	1,759	24.4
1954–55	Neil Johnston, Philadelphia Warriors	72	521	589	1,631	22.7
1955–56	Bob Pettit, St. Louis Hawks	72	646	557	1,849	25.7
1956–57	Paul Arizin, Philadelphia Warriors	71	613	591	1,817	25.6
1957–58	George Yardley, Detroit Pistons	72	673	655	2,001	27.8
1958–59	Bob Pettit, St. Louis Hawks	72	719	667	2,105	29.2
1959–60	Wilt Chamberlain, Philadelphia Warriors	72	1,065	577	2,707	37.6
1960–61	Wilt Chamberlain, Philadelphia Warriors	79	1,251	531	3,033	38.4
1961–62	Wilt Chamberlain, Philadelphia Warriors	80	1,597	835	4,029	50.4
1962–63	Wilt Chamberlain, San Francisco Warriors	80	1,463	660	3,586	44.8
1963–64	Wilt Chamberlain, San Francisco Warriors	80	1,204	540	2,948	36.9
1964–65	Wilt Chamberlain, San Francisco Warriors/Phila. 76ers	73	1,063	408	2,534	34.7
1965–66	Wilt Chamberlain, Philadelphia 76ers	79	1,074	501	2,649	33.5
1966–67	Rick Barry, San Francisco Warriors	78	1,011	753	2,775	35.6
1967–68	Dave Bing, Detroit Pistons	79	835	472	2,142	27.1
1968–69	Elvin Hayes, San Diego Rockets	82	930	467	2,327	28.4
1969–70	Jerry West, Los Angeles Lakers	74	831	647	2,309	31.2
1970–71	Lew Alcindor,[1] Milwaukee Bucks	82	1,063	470	2,596	31.7
1971–72	Kareem Abdul-Jabbar, Milwaukee Bucks	81	1,159	504	2,822	34.8
1972–73	Nate Archibald, Kansas City/Omaha Kings	80	1,028	663	2,719	34.0
1973–74	Bob McAdoo, Buffalo Braves	74	901	459	2,261	30.8

Season	Player, Team	G	FG	FT	Pts	Avg
1974–75	Bob McAdoo, Buffalo Braves	82	1,095	641	2,831	34.5
1975–76	Bob McAdoo, Buffalo Braves	78	934	559	2,427	31.1
1976–77	Pete Maravich, New Orleans Jazz	73	886	501	2,273	31.1
1977–78	George Gervin, San Antonio Spurs	82	864	504	2,232	27.2
1978–79	George Gervin, San Antonio Spurs	80	947	471	2,365	29.6
1979–80	George Gervin, San Antonio Spurs	78	1,024	505	2,585	33.1
1980–81	Adrian Dantley, Utah Jazz	80	909	632	2,452	30.7
1981–82	George Gervin, San Antonio Spurs	79	993	555	2,551	32.3
1982–83	Alex English, Denver Nuggets	82	959	406	2,326	28.4
1983–84	Adrian Dantley, Utah Jazz	79	802	813	2,418	30.6
1984–85	Bernard King, New York Knicks	55	691	426	1,809	32.9
1985–86	Dominique Wilkins, Atlanta Hawks	78	888	527	2,366	30.3
1986–87	Michael Jordan, Chicago Bulls[2]	82	1,098	833	3,041	37.1
1987–88	Michael Jordan, Chicago Bulls[3]	82	1,069	723	2,868	35.0
1988–89	Michael Jordan, Chicago Bulls[4]	81	966	674	2,633	32.5
1989–90	Michael Jordan, Chicago Bulls[5]	82	1,034	593	2,753	33.6
1990–91	Michael Jordan, Chicago Bulls[6]	82	990	571	2,580	31.5
1991–92	Michael Jordan, Chicago Bulls[7]	80	943	491	2,404	30.1
1992–93	Michael Jordan, Chicago Bulls[8]	78	992	476	2,541	32.6
1993–94	David Robinson, San Antonio Spurs[9]	80	840	693	2,383	29.8
1994–95	Shaquille O'Neal, Orlando Magic[10]	79	930	455	2,315	29.3
1995–96	Michael Jordan, Chicago Bulls[11]	82	916	548	2,491	30.4
1996–97	Michael Jordan, Chicago Bulls[11]	82	920	480	2,431	29.6
1997–98	Michael Jordan, Chicago Bulls[12]	82	881	565	2,357	28.7
1998–99	Allen Iverson, Philadelphia 76ers[13]	48	435	356	1,284	26.8
1999–2000	Shaquille O'Neal, L.A. Lakers	79	956	432	2,344	29.7

1. (Kareem Abdul-Jabbar). 2. Also had 12 3-point field goals. 3. Also had 7 3-point field goals. 4. Also had 27 3-point field goals. 5. Also had 92 3-point field goals. 6. Also had 29 3-point field goals. 7. Attempted 27 3-point field goals. 8. Also had 81 3-point field goals. 9. Also had 10 3-point field goals. 10. O'Neal scored no 3-point field goals in 1994–1995. 11. Also had 111 3-point field goals in both 1995–96 and 1996–97. 12. Also had 30 3-point field goals. 13. Also had 58 3-point field goals.

N.B.A. MOST VALUABLE PLAYERS

1956 Bob Pettit, St. Louis
1957 Bob Cousy, Boston
1958 Bill Russell, Boston
1959 Bob Pettit, St. Louis
1960 Wilt Chamberlain, Philadelphia
1961–63 Bill Russell, Boston
1964 Oscar Robertson, Cincinnati
1965 Bill Russell, Boston
1966–68 Wilt Chamberlain, Philadelphia
1969 Wes Unseld, Baltimore
1970 Willis Reed, New York
1971–72 Lew Alcindor (Kareem Abdul-Jabbar), Milwaukee
1973 Dave Cowens, Boston

1974 Kareem Abdul-Jabbar, Milwaukee
1975 Bob McAdoo, Buffalo
1976–77 Kareem Abdul-Jabbar, L.A. Lakers
1978 Bill Walton, Portland
1979 Moses Malone, Houston
1980 Kareem Abdul-Jabbar, L.A. Lakers
1981 Julius Erving, Philadelphia
1982 Moses Malone, Houston
1983 Moses Malone, Philadelphia
1984 Larry Bird, Boston
1985 Larry Bird, Boston
1986 Larry Bird, Boston

1987 Earvin Johnson, L.A. Lakers
1988 Michael Jordan, Chicago
1989 Earvin Johnson, L.A. Lakers
1990 Earvin Johnson, L.A. Lakers
1991 Michael Jordan, Chicago
1992 Michael Jordan, Chicago
1993 Charles Barkley, Phoenix
1994 Hakeem Olajuwon, Houston
1995 David Robinson, San Antonio
1996 Michael Jordan, Chicago
1997 Karl Malone, Utah
1998 Michael Jordan, Chicago
1999 Karl Malone, Utah
2000 Shaquille O'Neal, Los Angeles

N.B.A. LIFETIME LEADERS

(Through 2000 season)
Players in bold face active in 1999–2000 season

POINTS

	Yrs	Gm	Pts	Avg
Kareem Abdul-Jabbar	20	1,560	38,387	24.6
Wilt Chamberlain	14	1,045	31,419	30.1
Karl Malone	15	1,192	31,041	26.0
Michael Jordan	13	930	29,277	31.5
Moses Malone	19	1,329	27,409	20.6
Elvin Hayes	16	1,303	27,313	21.0
Oscar Robertson	14	1,040	26,710	25.7
Dominique Wilkins	15	1,074	26,668	24.8
John Havlicek	16	1,270	26,395	20.8
Hakeem Olajuwon	16	1,119	25,822	23.1

SCORING AVERAGE
Minimum of 400 games and 10,000 points.

	Yrs	Gm	Pts	Avg
Michael Jordan	13	930	29,277	31.5
Wilt Chamberlain	14	1,045	31,419	30.1
Shaquille O'Neal	8	534	14,687	27.5
Elgin Baylor	14	846	23,149	27.4
Jerry West	14	932	25,192	27.0
Bob Pettit	11	792	20,880	26.4
George Gervin	10	791	20,708	26.2
Karl Malone	15	1,192	31,041	26.0
Oscar Robertson	14	1,040	26,710	25.7
Dominique Wilkins	15	1,074	26,668	24.8

FIELD GOALS

	Yrs	FG	Att	Pct
Kareem Abdul-Jabbar	20	15,837	28,307	.559
Wilt Chamberlain	14	12,681	23,497	.540
Karl Malone	15	11,432	21,777	.525
Elvin Hayes	16	10,976	24,272	.452
Michael Jordan	13	10,958	21,686	.505
Alex English	15	10,659	21,036	.507
John Havlicek	16	10,513	23,930	.439
Hakeem Olajuwon	16	10,272	21,036	.511
Dominique Wilkins	15	9,963	21,589	.461
Robert Parrish	21	9,614	17,914	.537

FREE THROWS

	Yrs	FT	Att	Pct
Moses Malone	19	8,531	11,090	.769
Karl Malone	15	8,100	11,027	.735
Oscar Robertson	14	7,694	9,185	.838
Jerry West	14	7,160	8,801	.814
Dolph Schayes	16	6,979	8,273	.844
Adrian Dantley	15	6,832	8,351	.818
Michael Jordan	13	6,798	8,115	.838
Kareem Abdul-Jabbar	20	6,712	9,304	.721
Charles Barkley	16	6,349	8,643	.734
Bob Petit	11	6,182	8,119	.761

MOST GAMES PLAYED

Robert Parish	1,611
Kareem Abdul-Jabbar	1,560
Moses Malone	1,329
Buck Williams	1,307
Elvin Hayes	1,303

PERSONAL FOULS

Kareem Abdul-Jabbar	4,657
Robert Parish	4,443
Buck Williams	4,267
Elvin Hayes	4,193
Hakeem Olajuwon	4,095

BLOCKED SHOTS

Hakeem Olajuwon	3,652
Kareem Abdul-Jabbar	3,189
Mark Eaton	3,064
Patrick Ewing	2,758
Tree Rollins	2,542

STEALS

John Stockton	2,844
Maurice Cheeks	2,310
Michael Jordan	2,306
Clyde Drexler	2,207
Alvin Robertson	2,112

REBOUNDS

Wilt Chamberlain	23,924	Robert Parish	14,715
Bill Russell	21,620	Nate Thurmond	14,464
Kareem Abdul-Jabbar	17,440	Walt Bellamy	14,241
Elvin Hayes	16,279	Wes Unseld	13,769
Moses Malone	16,212	Buck Williams	13,017

ASSISTS

John Stockton	13,790	Maurice Cheeks	7,392
Magic Johnson	10,141	Lenny Wilkens	7,211
Oscar Robertson	9,887	Bob Cousy	6,955
Isiah Thomas	9,061	Guy Rodgers	6,917
Mark Jackson	8,574	**Kevin Johnson**	6,711

N.B.A. INDIVIDUAL RECORDS, GAME

(Through 1999–2000 season)

Most points, game—100, Wilt Chamberlain, Philadelphia vs. New York, 1962

Most free throws, game—28, Wilt Chamberlain, Philadelphia vs. New York, 1962; 28, Adrian Dantley, Utah vs. Houston, 1984

Most field goals, game—36, Wilt Chamberlain, Philadelphia vs. New York, 1962

Most assists, game—30, Scott Skiles, Orlando vs. Denver, 1990

Most rebounds, game—55, Wilt Chamberlain, Philadelphia vs. Boston, 1960

Most 3-pt. field goals, game—11, Dennis Scott, Orlando vs. Atlanta, 1996

Most blocked shots, game—17, Elmore Smith, Los Angeles vs. Portland, 1973

Most steals, game—11, Larry Kenon, San Antonio vs. Kansas City, 1976; 11, Kendall Gill, New Jersey vs. Miami, 1999

NATIONAL BASKETBALL ASSOCIATION FINAL STANDINGS: 1999–2000

EASTERN CONFERENCE

Atlantic Division

	W	L	Pct	GB
Miami Heat[1]	52	30	.634	—
New York Knicks[2]	50	32	.610	2
Philadelphia 76ers[2]	49	33	.598	3
Orlando Magic	41	41	.500	11
Boston Celtics	35	47	.427	17
New Jersey Nets	31	51	.378	21
Washington Wizards	29	53	.354	23

Central Division

	W	L	Pct	GB
Indiana Pacers[1]	56	26	.683	—
Charlotte Hornets[2]	49	33	.598	7
Toronto Raptors[2]	45	37	.549	11
Detroit Pistons[2]	42	40	.512	14
Milwaukee Bucks[2]	42	40	.512	14
Cleveland Cavaliers	32	50	.390	24
Atlanta Hawks	28	54	.341	28
Chicago Bulls	17	65	.207	39

WESTERN CONFERENCE

Midwest Division

	W	L	Pct	GB
Utah Jazz[1]	55	27	.671	—
San Antonio Spurs[2]	53	29	.646	2
Minnesota Timberwolves[2]	50	32	.610	5
Dallas Mavericks	40	42	.488	15
Denver Nuggets	35	47	.427	20
Houston Rockets	34	48	.415	21
Vancouver Grizzlies	22	60	.268	33

Pacific Division

	W	L	Pct	GB
L.A. Lakers[1]	67	15	.817	—
Portland Trail Blazers[2]	59	23	.720	8
Phoenix Suns[2]	53	29	.646	14
Seattle SuperSonics[2]	45	37	.549	22
Sacramento Kings[2]	44	38	.537	23
Golden State Warriors	19	63	.232	48
L.A. Clippers	15	67	.183	52

1. Division champion. 2. Playoff qualifier.

N.B.A. PLAYOFFS—2000
(All caps denotes home team)

EASTERN CONFERENCE
First Round
(Best of 5)
Indiana defeated Milwaukee, 3 games to 2
New York defeated Toronto, 3 games to 0
Miami defeated Detroit, 3 games to 0
Philadelphia defeated Charlotte, 3 games to 1

Second Round
(Best of 7)
New York defeated Miami, 4 games to 3
Indiana defeated Philadelphia, 4 games to 2

Conference Finals
(Best of 7)
Indiana defeated New York, 4 games to 2
May 23—INDIANA 102, New York 88
May 25—INDIANA 88, New York 84
May 27—NEW YORK 98, Indiana 95
May 29—NEW YORK 91, Indiana 89
May 31—INDIANA 88, New York 79
June 2—Indiana 93, NEW YORK 80

WESTERN CONFERENCE
First Round
(Best of 5)
L.A. Lakers defeated Sacramento, 3 games to 2
Utah defeated Seattle, 3 games to 2
Portland defeated Minnesota, 3 games to 1
Phoenix defeated San Antonio, 3 games to 1

Second Round
(Best of 7)
Portland defeated Utah, 4 games to 1
L.A. Lakers defeated Phoenix, 4 games to 1

Conference Finals
(Best of 7)
Los Angeles defeated Portland, 4 games to 3
May 20—LOS ANGELES 109, Portland 94
May 22—Portland 106, LOS ANGELES 77
May 26—Los Angeles 93, PORTLAND 91
May 28—Los Angeles 103, PORTLAND 91
May 30—Portland 96, LOS ANGELES 88
June 2—PORTLAND 103, Los Angeles 93
June 4—LOS ANGELES 89, Portland 84

CHAMPIONSHIP
Los Angeles Lakers defeated Indiana Pacers, 4 games to 2
Shaquille O'Neal, Los Angeles, named Finals MVP

June 7—LOS ANGELES 104, Indianapolis 87
June 9—LOS ANGELES 111, Indianapolis 104
June 11—INDIANAPOLIS 100, Los Angeles 91

June 14—Los Angeles 120, INDIANAPOLIS 118
June 16—INDIANAPOLIS 120, Los Angeles 87
June 19—LOS ANGELES 116, Indianapolis 111

N.B.A. INDIVIDUAL LEADERS, 1999–2000 SEASON

POINTS PER GAME
Minimum of 49 games played

	Gm	Pts	PPG
Shaquille O'Neal, L.A. Lakers	79	2,344	29.7
Allen Iverson, Philadelphia	70	1,989	28.4
Grant Hill, Detroit	74	1,906	25.8
Vince Carter, Toronto	82	2,107	25.7
Karl Malone, Utah	82	2,095	25.5
Chris Webber, Sacramento	75	1,834	24.5
Gary Payton, Seattle	82	1,982	24.2
Jerry Stackhouse, Detroit	82	1,939	23.6
Tim Duncan, San Antonio	74	1,716	23.2
Kevin Garnett, Minnesota	81	1,857	22.9
Michael Finley, Dallas	82	1,855	22.6
Kobe Bryant, L.A. Lakers	66	1,485	22.5
Stephon Marbury, New Jersey	74	1,640	22.2
Ray Allen, Milwaukee	82	1,809	22.1
Alonzo Mourning, Miami	79	1,718	21.7

REBOUNDS PER GAME
Minimum of 49 games played

	Gm	Reb	RPG
Dikembe Mutombo, Atlanta	82	1,157	14.1
Shaquille O'Neal, L.A. Lakers	79	1,078	13.6
Tim Duncan, San Antonio	74	918	12.4
Kevin Garnett, Minnesota	81	956	11.8
Chris Webber, Sacramento	75	787	10.5
Shareef Abdur-Rahim, Vancouver	82	825	10.1
Elton Brand, Chicago	81	810	10.0
Dale Davis, Indiana	74	729	9.9
David Robinson, San Antonio	80	770	9.6
Jerome Williams, Detroit	82	789	9.6
Karl Malone, Utah	82	779	9.5
Alonzo Mourning, Miami	79	753	9.5
Jamie Feick, New Jersey	81	755	9.3
Antonio Davis, Toronto	79	696	8.8
Shawn Kemp, Cleveland	82	725	8.8

ASSISTS PER GAME
Minimum of 49 games played

	Gm	Ast	Avg
Jason Kidd, Phoenix	67	678	10.1
Sam Cassell, Milwaukee	81	729	9.0
Nick Van Exel, Denver	79	714	9.0
Terrell Brandon, Minnesota	71	629	8.9
Gary Payton, Seattle	82	732	8.9
John Stockton, Utah	82	703	8.6
Stephon Marbury, New Jersey	74	622	8.4
Mike Bibby, Vancouver	82	665	8.1
Mark Jackson, Indiana	81	650	8.0
Eric Snow, Philadelphia	82	624	7.6

FIELD GOAL PERCENTAGE
Minimum of 288 field goals made

	FGM	FGA	Pct
Shaquille O'Neal, L.A. Lakers	956	1,665	.574
Dikembe Mutombo, Atlanta	322	573	.562
Alonzo Mourning, Miami	652	1,184	.551
Ruben Patterson, Seattle	354	661	.536
Rasheed Wallace, Portland	542	1,045	.519
David Robinson, San Antonio	528	1,031	.512
Wally Szczerbiak, Minnesota	342	669	.511
Karl Malone, Utah	752	1,476	.509
Antonio McDyess, Denver	614	1,211	.507
Othella Harrington, Vancouver	420	830	.506

FREE-THROW PERCENTAGE
Minimum of 120 free throws made

	FTM	FTA	Pct
Jeff Hornacek, Utah	171	180	.950
Reggie Miller, Indiana	373	406	.919
Darrell Armstrong, Orlando	225	247	.911
Terrell Brandon, Minnesota	187	208	.899
Ray Allen, Milwaukee	353	398	.887
Predrag Stojakovic, Sacramento	135	153	.882
Derek Anderson, L.A. Clippers	271	309	.877
Jim Jackson, Atlanta	186	212	.877
Sam Cassell, Milwaukee	390	445	.876
Mitch Richmond, Washington	298	340	.876

3-POINT FIELD GOAL PERCENTAGE
Minimum of 65 3-point field goals made

	3FGM	3FGA	Pct
Hubert Davis, Dallas	82	167	.491
Jeff Hornacek, Utah	66	138	.478
Matt Bullard, Houston	79	177	.446
Rodney Rogers, Phoenix	115	262	.439
Allan Houston, New York	106	243	.436
Terry Porter, San Antonio	90	207	.435
Lindsey Hunter, Detroit	168	389	.432
Tracy Murray, Washington	113	263	.430
Jon Barry, Sacramento	66	154	.429
Wesley Person, Cleveland	106	250	.424

BLOCKED-SHOTS
Minimum of 49 games played or 96 block shots

	Gm	Blk	Avg
Alonzo Mourning, Miami	79	294	3.72
Dikembe Mutombo, Atlanta	82	269	3.28
Shaquille O'Neal, L.A. Lakers	79	239	3.03
Theo Ratliff, Philadelphia	57	171	3.00
Shawn Bradley, Dallas	77	190	2.47
David Robinson, San Antonio	80	183	2.29
Tim Duncan, San Antonio	74	165	2.23
Raef LaFrentz, Denver	81	180	2.22
Greg Ostertag, Utah	81	172	2.12
Marcus Camby, New York	59	116	1.97

STEALS
Minimum of 49 games played or 120 steals

	Gm	Stl	Avg
Eddie Jones, Charlotte	72	192	2.67
Paul Pierce, Boston	73	152	2.08
Darrell Armstrong, Orlando	82	169	2.06
Allen Iverson, Philadelphia	70	144	2.06
Mookie Blaylock, Golden State	73	146	2.00
Jason Kidd, Phoenix	67	134	2.00
Terrell Brandon, Minnesota	71	134	1.89
Gary Payton, Seattle	82	153	1.87
Kendall Gill, New Jersey	76	139	1.83
John Stockton, Utah	82	143	1.74

Women's Professional Basketball

WOMEN'S NATIONAL BASKETBALL ASSOCIATION—2000 SEASON

Eastern Conference

	W	L	Pct	GB	Home	Road
x-New York Liberty	20	12	.625	—	12–4	8–8
x-Cleveland Rockers	17	15	.531	3	13–3	4–12
x-Orlando Miracle	16	16	.500	4	11–5	7–9
x-Washington Mystics	14	18	.438	6	7–9	7–9
Detroit Shock	14	18	.438	6	8–8	6–10
Miami Sol	13	19	.406	7	9–7	4–12
Indiana Fever	9	23	.281	11	5–11	4–12
Charlotte Sting	8	24	.250	12	5–11	3–13

Western Conference

	W	L	Pct	GB	Home	Road
x-Los Angeles Sparks	28	4	.875	—	15–1	13–3
x-Houston Comets	27	5	.844	1	14–2	13–3
x-Sacramento Monarchs	21	11	.656	7	13–3	8–8
x-Phoenix Mercury	20	12	.625	8	11–5	9–7
Utah Starzz	18	14	.563	10	12–4	6–10
Minnesota Lynx	15	17	.469	13	8–8	7–9
Portland Fire	10	22	.313	18	6–10	4–12
Seattle Storm	6	26	.188	22	4–12	2–14

NOTES: x—clinched playoff qualifier. GB refers to Games Behind leader.

Conference Championship Series (Best of 3)

EASTERN CONFERENCE

Date	Result
Aug. 17	at Cleveland 56, New York 43
Aug. 20	at New York 51, Cleveland 45
Aug. 21	at New York 81, Cleveland 67
	New York wins series, 2–1

WESTERN CONFERENCE

Date	Result
Aug. 17	at Houston 77, Los Angeles 56
Aug. 20	Houston 74, at Los Angeles 69
	Houston wins series, 2–0

League Championship Series (Best of 3)
Houston wins championship, 2 games to 0

Date	Result
Aug. 24	Houston 59, at New York 52
Aug. 26	at Houston 79, New York 73

WNBA ANNUAL AWARDS—2000 SEASON

Most Valuable Player: Sheryl Swoopes, Houston
Defensive Player of the Year: Sheryl Swoopes, Houston
Sportsmanship Award: Suzie McConnell Serio, Cleveland

Coach of the Year: Michael Cooper, Los Angeles
Most Improved Player of the Year: Tari Phillips, New York
Rookie of the Year: Betty Lennox, Minnesota

2000 WNBA LEAGUE LEADERS

POINTS PER GAME

	Gm	Pts	PPG
Sheryl Swoopes, Houston	31	643	20.7
Katie Smith, Minnesota	32	646	20.2
Brandy Reed, Phoenix	32	608	19.0
Natalie Williams, Utah	29	543	18.7
Lisa Leslie, Los Angeles	32	570	17.8
Cynthia Cooper, Houston	31	550	17.7
Andrea Stinson, Charlotte	32	565	17.7
Chamique Holdsclaw, Washington	32	561	17.5
Adrienne Goodson, Utah	29	498	17.2
Betty Lennox, Minnesota	32	541	16.9
Tina Thompson, Houston	32	540	16.9

REBOUNDS PER GAME

	Gm	Reb	RPG
Natalie Williams, Utah	29	336	11.6
Yolanda Griffith, Sacramento	32	331	10.3
Lisa Leslie, Los Angeles	32	306	9.6
Tari Phillips, New York	31	247	8.0
Tina Thompson, Houston	32	245	7.7
Taj McWilliams, Orlando	32	244	7.6
Chamique Holdsclaw, Washington	32	240	7.5
Marlies Askamp, Miami	32	231	7.2
Rhonda Mapp, Charlotte	30	205	6.8
Wendy Palmer, Detroit	32	219	6.8

ASSISTS PER GAME

	Gm	Ast	APG
Ticha Penicheiro, Sacramento	30	236	7.9
Teresa Weatherspoon, New York	32	205	6.4
Dawn Staley, Charlotte	32	190	5.9
Shannon Johnson, Orlando	32	169	5.3
Andrea Nagy, Washington	23	118	5.1

BLOCKS PER GAME

	Gm	Blk	BPG
Margo Dydek, Utah	32	96	3.00
Lisa Leslie, Los Angeles	32	74	2.31
Tangela Smith, Sacramento	32	64	2.00
Cintia Dos Santos, Orlando	32	63	1.97
Yolanda Griffith, Sacramento	32	61	1.91

STEALS PER GAME

	Gm	Stl	Avg
Sheryl Swoopes, Houston	31	87	2.81
Yolanda Griffith, Sacramento	32	83	2.59
Rita Williams, Indiana	32	76	2.38
Ticha Penicheiro, Sacramento	30	70	2.33
Brandy Reed, Phoenix	32	66	2.06

AMERICAN BASKETBALL LEAGUE

The American Basketball League suspended operations Dec. 22, 1998

LEAGUE CHAMPIONS

Year	Champions	Head Coach	Series	Runners-up	Head Coach
1997	Columbus Quest	Brian Agler	3-2	Richmond Rage	Lisa Boyer
1998	Columbus Quest	Brian Agler	3-2	Long Beach StingRays	Maura McHugh
1999	league folded				

Hockey

Ice hockey, by birth and upbringing a Canadian game, is an offshoot of field hockey. Some historians say that the first ice hockey game was played in Montreal in December 1879 between two teams composed almost exclusively of McGill University students, but others assert that earlier hockey games took place in Kingston, Ontario, or Halifax, Nova Scotia. In the Montreal game of 1879, there were fifteen players on a side, who used an assortment of crude sticks to keep the puck in motion. Early rules allowed nine men on a side, but the number was reduced to seven in 1886 and later to six.

The first governing body of the sport was the Amateur Hockey Association of Canada, organized in 1887. In the winter of 1894–1895, a group of college students from the United States visited Canada and saw hockey played. They became enthused over the game and introduced it as a winter sport when they returned home. The first professional league was the International Hockey League, which operated in northern Michigan in 1904–1906.

Until 1910, professionals and amateurs were allowed to play together on "mixed teams," but this arrangement ended with the formation of the first "big league," the National Hockey Association, in eastern Canada in 1910. The Pacific Coast League was organized in 1911 for western Canadian hockey. The league included Seattle and later other American cities. The National Hockey League replaced the National Hockey Association in 1917. Boston, in 1924, was the first American city to join that circuit. The league expanded to include western cities in 1967. The Stanley Cup was competed for by "mixed teams" from 1894 to 1910, thereafter by professionals. It was awarded to the winner of the NHL playoffs from 1926–1967 and now to the league champion. The World Hockey Association was organized in October 1972 and was dissolved after the 1978–1979 season when the NHL absorbed four of the teams.

Rule changes have been implemented to steer the league from its violent reputation in order to better showcase the world's most talented stars.

Hockey, once considered a cold-weather sport, has taken major strides in increasing its fan base to the southern and western part of the United States as well. In the 1995–1996 season, Florida and Colorado battled in the Stanley Cup Finals, the San Jose Sharks sold out all 41 of their home games, and the second team in two years (Winnipeg) migrated from Canada to the Southwest region of the U.S. (Phoenix).

The league continued to expand when the Nashville Predators joined the league in the 1998–1999 season. In 1999–2000, the Atlanta Thrashers had its inaugural season, and the Columbus Blue Jackets and the Minnesota Wild start in the 2000–2001 season.

STANLEY CUP WINNERS

Emblematic of World Professional Championship; N.H.L. Championship after 1967

1893 Montreal A.A.A.	1924 Montreal Canadiens	1956–60 Montreal Canadiens
1894 Montreal A.A.A.	1925 Victoria Cougars	1961 Chicago Black Hawks
1895 Montreal Victorias	1926 Montreal Maroons	1962–64 Toronto Maple Leafs
1896 (Feb.) Winnipeg Victorias	1927 Ottawa Senators	1965–66 Montreal Canadiens
1896 (Dec.) Montreal Victorias	1928 N.Y. Rangers	1967 Toronto Maple Leafs
1897–99 Montreal Victorias	1929 Boston Bruins	1968–69 Montreal Canadiens
1899–1900 Montreal Shamrocks	1930–31 Montreal Canadiens	1970 Boston Bruins
1901 Winnipeg Victorias	1932 Toronto Maple Leafs	1971 Montreal Canadiens
1902 Montreal A.A.A.	1933 N.Y. Rangers	1972 Boston Bruins
1903–05 Ottawa Silver Seven	1934 Chicago Black Hawks	1973 Montreal Canadiens
1906 Montreal Wanderers	1935 Montreal Maroons	1974–75 Philadelphia Flyers
1907 (Jan.) Kenora Thistles	1936–37 Detroit Red Wings	1976–79 Montreal Canadiens
1907 (March) Montreal Wanderers	1938 Chicago Red Hawks	1980–83 N.Y. Islanders
1908 Montreal Wanderers	1939 Boston Bruins	1984–85 Edmonton Oilers
1909 Ottawa Senators	1940 N.Y. Rangers	1986 Montreal Canadiens
1910 Montreal Wanderers	1941 Boston Bruins	1987–88 Edmonton Oilers
1911 Ottawa Senators	1942 Toronto Maple Leafs	1989 Calgary Flames
1912–13 Quebec Bulldogs	1943 Detroit Red Wings	1990 Edmonton Oilers
1914 Toronto Blueshirts	1944 Montreal Canadiens	1991–92 Pittsburgh Penguins
1915 Vancouver Millionaires	1945 Toronto Maple Leafs	1993 Montreal Canadiens
1916 Montreal Canadiens	1946 Montreal Canadiens	1994 N.Y. Rangers
1917 Seattle Metropolitans	1947–49 Toronto Maple Leafs	1995 N.J. Devils
1918 Toronto Arenas	1950 Detroit Red Wings	1996 Colorado Avalanche
1919 No champion	1951 Toronto Maple Leafs	1997–98 Detroit Red Wings
1920–21 Ottawa Senators	1952 Detroit Red Wings	1999 Dallas Stars
1922 Toronto St. Patricks	1953 Montreal Canadiens	2000 N.J. Devils
1923 Ottawa Senators	1954–55 Detroit Red Wings	

N.H.L. CHAMPIONS

Wales Trophy	1958–62 Montreal	1971–72 Boston	1982–84 N.Y.	1993 Montreal
1939–41 Boston	1963 Toronto	1973 Montreal	Islanders	1994 N.Y. Rangers
1942 New York	1964 Montreal	1974 Boston	1985 Philadelphia	1995 New Jersey
1943 Detroit	1965 Detroit	**Eastern Conference[1]**	1986 Montreal	1996 Florida
1944–47 Montreal	1966 Montreal	1975 Buffalo	1987 Philadelphia	1997 Philadelphia
1948 Toronto	1967 Chicago	1976–79 Montreal	1988 Boston	1998 Washington
1948–55 Detroit	**Eastern Division**	1980 Buffalo	1989 Montreal	1999 Buffalo
1956 Montreal	1968–69 Montreal	1981 Montreal	1990 Boston	2000 New Jersey
1957 Detroit	1970 Chicago		1991–92 Pittsburgh	

1. Prior to 1994 was the Wales Conference.

CAMPBELL BOWL

Western Division	1978–79 N.Y. Islanders	1989 Calgary	1995 Detroit
1968–70 St. Louis	1980 Philadelphia	1990 Edmonton	1996 Colorado
1971–73 Chicago	1981 N.Y. Islanders	1991 Minnesota	1997–98 Detroit
1974 Philadelphia	1982–85 Edmonton	1992 Chicago	1999–2000 Dallas
Western Conference[2]	1986 Calgary	1993 Los Angeles	
1975–77 Philadelphia	1987–88 Edmonton	1994 Vancouver	

2. Prior to 1994 was the Campbell Conference.

NATIONAL HOCKEY LEAGUE YEARLY TROPHY WINNERS

The Hart Trophy—Most Valuable Player	1937 Babe Siebert, Montreal Canadiens	1951 Milt Schmidt, Boston
1924 Frank Nighbor, Ottawa	1938 Eddie Shore, Boston	1952–53 Gordie Howe, Detroit
1925 Billy Burch, Hamilton	1939 Toe Blake, Montreal Canadiens	1954 Al Rollins, Chicago
1926 Nels Stewart, Montreal Maroons	1940 Ebbie Goodfellow, Detroit	1955 Ted Kennedy, Toronto
1927 Herb Gardiner, Montreal Canadiens	1941 Bill Cowley, Boston	1956 Jean Belveau, Montreal Canadiens
1928 Howie Morenz, Montreal Canadiens	1942 Tommy Anderson, N.Y. Americans	1957–58 Gordie Howe, Detroit
1929 Roy Worters, N.Y. Americans	1943 Bill Cowley, Boston	1959 Andy Bathgate, N.Y. Rangers
1930 Nels Stewart, Montreal Maroons	1944 Babe Pratt, Toronto	1960 Gordie Howe, Detroit
1931–32 Howie Morenz, Montreal Canadiens	1945 Elmer Lach, Montreal Canadiens	1961 Bernie Geoffrion, Montreal Canadiens
1933 Eddie Shore, Boston	1946 Max Bentley, Chicago	1962 Jacques Plante, Montreal Canadiens
1934 Aurel Joliat, Montreal Canadiens	1947 Maurice Richard, Montreal Canadiens	1963 Gordon Howe, Detroit
1935–36 Eddie Shore, Boston	1948 Buddy O'Connor, N.Y. Rangers	1964 Jean Beliveau, Montreal Canadiens
	1949 Sid Abel, Detroit	1965–66 Bobby Hull, Chicago
	1950 Chuck Rayner, N.Y. Rangers	1967–68 Stan Mikita, Chicago

1969 Phil Esposito, Boston
1970–72 Bobby Orr, Boston
1973 Bobby Clarke, Philadelphia
1974 Phil Esposito, Boston
1975–76 Bobby Clarke, Philadelphia
1977–78 Guy Lafleur, Montreal
1979 Bryan Trottier, N.Y. Islanders
1980–87 Wayne Gretzky, Edmonton
1988 Mario Lemieux, Pittsburgh
1989 Wayne Gretzky, Los Angeles
1990 Mark Messier, Edmonton
1991 Brett Hull, St. Louis
1992 Mark Messier, N.Y. Rangers
1993 Mario Lemieux, Pittsburgh
1994 Sergei Fedorov, Detroit
1995 Eric Lindros, Philadelphia
1996 Mario Lemieux, Pittsburgh
1997–98 Dominik Hasek, Buffalo
1999 Jaromir Jagr, Pittsburgh
2000 Chris Pronger, St. Louis

Vezina Trophy—Leading Goalkeeper

1956–60 Jacques Plante, Montreal
1961 Johnny Bower, Toronto
1962 Jacques Plante, Montreal
1963 Glenn Hall, Chicago
1964 Charlie Hodge, Montreal
1965 Terry Sawchuk—Johnny Bower, Toronto
1966 Gump Worsley—Charlie Hodge, Montreal
1967 Glen Hall—Denis Dejordy, Chicago
1968 Gump Worsley—Rogie Vachon, Montreal
1969 Glenn Hall—Jacques Plante, St. Louis
1970 Tony Esposito, Chicago
1971 Ed Giacomin—Gilles Villemure, N.Y. Rangers
1972 Tony Esposito—Gary Smith, Chicago
1973 Ken Dryden, Montreal
1974 Bernie Parent, Philadelphia and Tony Esposito, Chicago
1975 Bernie Parent, Philadelphia
1976 Ken Dryden, Montreal
1977–79 Ken Dryden—Bunny Larocque, Montreal
1980 Bob Sauve—Don Edwards, Buffalo
1981 Richard Sevigny—Denis Herron—Bunny Larocque, Montreal
1982 Billy Smith, N.Y. Islanders
1983 Pete Peeters, Boston
1984 Tom Barrasso, Buffalo
1985 Pelle Lindbergh, Philadelphia
1986 John Vanbiesbrouck, N.Y. Rangers
1987 Ron Hextall, Philadelphia
1988 Grant Fuhr, Edmonton
1989–90 Patrick Roy, Montreal
1991 Ed Belfour, Chicago
1992 Patrick Roy, Montreal
1993 Ed Belfour, Chicago
1994–95 Dominik Hasek, Buffalo
1996 Jim Carey, Washington
1997–99 Dominik Hasek, Buffalo
2000 Olaf Kolzig, Washington

James Norris Trophy— Defenseman

1954 Red Kelly, Detroit
1955–58 Doug Harvey, Montreal
1959 Tom Johnson, Montreal
1960–62 Doug Harvey, Montreal, N.Y. Rangers (62)
1963–65 Pierre Pilote, Chicago
1966 Jacques Laperriere, Montreal
1967 Harry Howell, N.Y. Rangers
1968–75 Bobby Orr, Boston
1976 Denis Potvin, N.Y. Islanders
1977 Larry Robinson, Montreal
1978–79 Denis Potvin, N.Y. Islanders
1980 Larry Robinson, Montreal
1981 Randy Carlyle, Pittsburgh
1982 Doug Wilson, Chicago
1983–84 Rod Langway, Washington
1985–86 Paul Coffey, Edmonton
1987–88 Ray Bourque, Boston
1989 Chris Chelios, Montreal
1990–91 Ray Bourque, Boston
1992 Brian Leetch, N.Y. Rangers
1993 Chris Chelios, Chicago
1994 Ray Bourque, Boston
1995 Paul Coffey, Detroit
1996 Chris Chelios, Chicago
1997 Brian Leetch, N.Y. Rangers
1998 Rob Blake, Los Angeles
1999 Al MacInnis, St. Louis
2000 Chris Pronger, St. Louis

Lady Byng Trophy— Sportsmanship

1960 Don McKenney, Boston
1961 Red Kelly, Toronto
1962–63 Dave Keon, Toronto
1964 Ken Wharram, Chicago
1965 Bobby Hull, Chicago
1966 Alex Delvecchio, Detroit
1967–68 Stan Mikita, Chicago
1969 Alex Delvecchio, Detroit
1970 Phil Goyette, St. Louis
1971 Johnny Bucyk, Boston
1972 Jean Ratelle, N.Y. Rangers
1973 Gilbert Perreault, Buffalo
1974 Johnny Bucyk, Boston
1975 Marcel Dionne, Detroit
1976 Jean Ratelle, N.Y. Rangers, Boston
1977 Marcel Dionne, Los Angeles
1978 Butch Goring, Los Angeles
1979 Bob MacMillan, Atlanta
1980 Wayne Gretzky, Edmonton
1981 Rick Kehoe, Pittsburgh
1982 Rick Middleton, Boston
1983–84 Mike Bossy, N.Y. Islanders
1985 Jari Kurri, Edmonton
1986 Mike Bossy, N.Y. Islanders
1987 Joey Mullen, Calgary
1988 Mats Naslund, Montreal
1989 Joey Mullen, Calgary
1990 Brett Hull, St. Louis
1991–92 Wayne Gretzky, Los Angeles
1993 Pierre Turgeon, N.Y. Islanders
1994 Wayne Gretzky, Los Angeles
1995 Ron Francis, Pittsburgh
1996–97 Paul Kariya, Anaheim
1998 Ron Francis, Pittsburgh
1999 Wayne Gretzky, N.Y. Rangers
2000 Pavol Demitra, St. Louis

Calder Trophy—Rookie

1962 Bobby Rousseau, Montreal
1963 Kent Douglas, Toronto
1964 Jacques Laperriere, Montreal
1965 Roger Crozier, Detroit
1966 Brit Selby, Toronto
1967 Bobby Orr, Boston
1968 Derek Sanderson, Boston
1969 Danny Grant, Minnesota
1970 Tony Esposito, Chicago
1971 Gilbert Perreault, Buffalo
1972 Ken Dryden, Montreal
1973 Steve Vickers, N.Y. Rangers
1974 Denis Potvin, N.Y. Islanders
1975 Eric Vail, Atlanta
1976 Bryan Trottier, N.Y. Islanders
1977 Willi Plett, Atlanta
1978 Mike Bossy, N.Y. Islanders
1979 Bobby Smith, Minnesota
1980 Ray Bourque, Boston
1981 Peter Stastny, Quebec
1982 Dale Hawerchuk, Winnipeg
1983 Steve Larmer, Chicago
1984 Tom Barrasso, Buffalo
1985 Mario Lemieux, Pittsburgh
1986 Gary Suter, Calgary
1987 Luc Robitaille, Los Angeles
1988 Joe Nieuwendyk, Calgary
1989 Brian Leetch, N.Y. Rangers
1990 Sergei Makarov, Calgary
1991 Ed Belfour, Chicago
1992 Pavel Bure, Vancouver
1993 Teemu Selanne, Winnipeg
1994 Martin Brodeur, N.J. Devils
1995 Peter Forsberg, Quebec
1996 Daniel Alfredsson, Ottawa
1997 Bryan Berard, N.Y. Islanders
1998 Sergei Samsonov, Boston
1999 Chris Drury, Colorado
2000 Scott Gomez, New Jersey

Art Ross Trophy—Leading Scorer

1955 Bernie Geoffrion, Montreal
1956 Jean Beliveau, Montreal
1957 Gordie Howe, Detroit
1958–59 Dickie Moore, Montreal
1960 Bobby Hull, Chicago
1961 Bernie Geoffrion, Montreal
1962 Bobby Hull, Chicago
1963 Gordie Howe, Detroit
1964–65 Stan Mikita, Chicago
1966 Bobby Hull, Chicago
1967–68 Stan Mikita, Chicago
1969 Phil Esposito, Boston
1970 Bobby Orr, Boston
1971–74 Phil Esposito, Boston
1975 Bobby Orr, Boston
1976–78 Guy Lafleur, Montreal
1979 Bryan Trottier, N.Y. Islanders
1980 Marcel Dionne, Los Angeles
1981–87 Wayne Gretzky, Edmonton
1988–89 Mario Lemieux, Pittsburgh
1990–91 Wayne Gretzky, Los Angeles
1992–93 Mario Lemieux, Pittsburgh
1994 Wayne Gretzky, Los Angeles
1995 Jaromir Jagr, Pittsburgh
1996–97 Mario Lemieux, Pittsburgh
1998–2000 Jaromir Jagr, Pittsburgh

STANLEY CUP PLAYOFFS—2000
NOTE: Home teams are in capitals.

EASTERN CONFERENCE

Quarterfinals
Philadelphia Flyers defeated Buffalo Sabres,
4 games to 1
New Jersey Devils defeated Florida Panthers,
4 games to 0
Pittsburgh Penguins defeated Washington Capitals,
4 games to 1
Toronto Maple Leafs defeated Ottawa Senators,
4 games to 2

Semifinals
Philadelphia Flyers defeated Pittsburgh Penguins,
4 games to 2
New Jersey Devils defeated Toronto Maple Leafs,
4 games to 2

Finals
New Jersey Devils defeated Philadelphia Flyers,
4 games to 3
May 14—New Jersey 4, PHILADELPHIA 1
May 16—PHILADELPHIA 4, New Jersey 3
May 18—Philadelphia 4, NEW JERSEY 2
May 20—Philadelphia 3, NEW JERSEY 1
May 22—New Jersey 4, PHILADELPHIA 1
May 24—NEW JERSEY 2, Philadelphia 1
May 26—New Jersey 2, PHILADELPHIA 1

WESTERN CONFERENCE

Quarterfinals
Detroit Red Wings defeated Los Angeles Kings,
4 games to 0
Dallas Stars defeated Edmonton Oilers,
4 games to 1
Colorado Avalanche defeated Phoenix Coyotes,
4 games to 1
San Jose Sharks defeated St. Louis Blues,
4 games to 3

Semifinals
Dallas Stars defeated San Jose Sharks,
4 games to 1
Colorado Avalanche defeated Detroit Red Wings,
4 games to 1

Finals
Dallas Stars defeated Colorado Avalanche,
4 games to 3
May 13—Colorado 2, DALLAS 0
May 15—DALLAS 3, Colorado 2
May 19—COLORADO 2, Dallas 0
May 21—Dallas 4, COLORADO 1
May 23—DALLAS 3, Colorado 2 (OT)
May 25—COLORADO 2, Dallas 1
May 27—DALLAS 3, Colorado 2

STANLEY CUP CHAMPIONSHIP FINALS
New Jersey Devils defeated Dallas Stars, 4 games to 2

May 30—NEW JERSEY 7, Dallas 3
June 1—Dallas 2, NEW JERSEY 1
June 3—New Jersey 2, DALLAS 1

June 5—New Jersey 3, DALLAS 1
June 8—Dallas 1, NEW JERSEY 0 (3 OT)
June 10—New Jersey 2, DALLAS 1 (2 OT)

Conn Smythe Trophy for most valuable player in the playoffs: Scott Stevens, New Jersey

OTHER N.H.L. AWARDS—2000

Frank Selke Trophy (Top defensive forward)—Steve Yzerman, Detroit
King Clancy Trophy (Humanitarian community involvement)—Curtis Joseph, Toronto

Jack Adams Award (Coach of the Year)—Joel Quenneville, St. Louis
Bill Masterson Trophy (Perseverance, sportsmanship, and dedication to hockey)—Ken Daneyko, New Jersey

NATIONAL HOCKEY LEAGUE FINAL STANDINGS OF THE CLUBS: 1999–2000

EASTERN CONFERENCE

Northeast Division

	W	L	T	Pts	GF	GA
Toronto Maple Leafs[1]	45	30	7	100	246	222
Ottawa Senators[2]	41	30	11	95	244	210
Buffalo Sabres[2]	35	36	11	85	213	204
Montreal Canadiens	35	38	9	83	196	194
Boston Bruins	24	39	19	73	210	248

Atlantic Division

	W	L	T	Pts	GF	GA
Philadelphia Flyers[1]	45	25	12	105	237	179
New Jersey Devils[2]	45	29	8	103	251	203
Pittsburgh Penguins[2]	37	37	8	88	241	236
N.Y. Rangers	29	41	12	73	218	246
N.Y. Islanders	24	49	9	58	194	275

Southeast Division

	W	L	T	Pts	GF	GA
Washington Capitals[1]	44	26	12	102	227	194
Florida Panthers[2]	43	33	6	98	244	209
Carolina Hurricanes	37	35	10	84	217	216
Tampa Bay Lightning	19	54	9	54	204	310
Atlanta Thrashers	14	61	7	39	170	313

1. Division champion. 2. Playoff qualifier.

WESTERN CONFERENCE

Central Division

	W	L	T	Pts	GF	GA
St. Louis Blues[1]	51	20	11	114	248	165
Detroit Red Wings[2]	48	24	10	108	278	210
Chicago Blackhawks	33	39	10	78	242	245
Nashville Predators	28	47	7	70	199	240

Pacific Division

	W	L	T	Pts	GF	GA
[1]Dallas Stars	43	29	10	102	211	184
[2]Los Angeles Kings	39	31	12	94	245	228
[2]Phoenix Coyotes	39	35	8	90	232	228
[2]San Jose Sharks	35	37	10	87	225	214
Anaheim Mighty Ducks	34	36	12	83	217	227

Northwest Division

	W	L	T	Pts	GF	GA
[1]Colorado Avalanche	42	29	11	96	233	201
[2]Edmonton Oilers	32	34	16	88	226	212
Vancouver Canucks	30	37	15	83	227	237
Calgary Flames	31	41	10	77	211	256

N.H.L. LEADING SCORERS: 1999–2000

	GP	G	A	Pts
Jaromir Jagr, Pittsburgh	63	42	54	96
Pavel Bure, Florida	74	58	36	94
Mark Recchi, Philadelphia	82	28	63	91
Paul Kariya, Anaheim	74	42	44	86
Tony Amonte, Chicago	82	43	42	85
Teemu Selanne, Anaheim	79	33	52	85
Owen Nolan, San Jose	78	44	40	84
Joe Sakic, Colorado	60	28	54	82
Mike Modano, Dallas	77	38	43	81
Steve Yzerman, Detroit	78	35	44	79

N.H.L. LEADING GOALTENDERS: 1999–2000

(Minimum 1,500 minutes played)

	GP	Min	GA	GAA	Pct
Brian Boucher, Philadelphia	35	2,038	65	1.91	.918
Roman Turek, St. Louis	67	3,961	129	1.95	.912
Jose Theodore, Montreal	30	1,655	58	2.10	.919
Ed Belfour, Dallas	62	3,620	127	2.10	.919
John Vanbiesbrouck, Philadelphia	50	2,950	108	2.20	.906
Dominik Hasek, Buffalo	35	2,066	76	2.21	.919
Olaf Kolzig, Washington	73	4,371	163	2.24	.917
Martin Brodeur, New Jersey	72	4,312	161	2.24	.910
Patrick Roy, Colorado	63	3,704	141	2.28	.914
Patrick Lalime, Ottawa	38	2,038	79	2.33	.905

N.H.L. CAREER SCORING LEADERS

(Through 1999–2000 season)

		Yrs	Gm	G	A	Pts
1	Wayne Gretzky	20	1,487	894	1,963	2,857
2	Gordie Howe	26	1,767	801	1,049	1,850
3	Marcel Dionne	18	1,348	731	1,040	1,771
4	**Mark Messier**	21	1,479	627	1,087	1,714
5	Phil Esposito	18	1,282	717	873	1,590
6	**Steve Yzerman**	17	1,256	627	935	1,562
7	**Ron Francis**	19	1,407	472	1,087	1,559
8	**Paul Coffey**	20	1,391	396	1,131	1,527
9	**Ray Bourque**	21	1,532	403	1,117	1,520
10	Mario Lemieux	12	745	613	881	1,494

Players active during 1999–2000 season in **bold** type.

N.H.L. CAREER GOALTENDING LEADERS

(Through 1999–2000 season)

		Yrs	Gm	W	L	T	Pct
1	Terry Sawchuk	21	971	447	330	172	.562
2	**Patrick Roy**	16	841	444	264	103	.611
3	Jacques Plante	18	837	434	247	146	.614
4	Tony Esposito	16	886	423	306	152	.566
5	Glenn Hall	18	906	407	326	163	.545
6	**Grant Fuhr**	19	868	403	295	114	.567
7	Andy Moog	18	713	372	209	88	.622
8	**Mike Vernon**	17	722	371	241	86	.593
9	**J. Vanbiesbrouck**	18	829	358	318	114	.525
10	Rogie Vachon	16	795	355	291	127	.541

Players active during 1999–2000 season in **bold** type.

Chess

WORLD CHAMPIONS

1894–1921	Emanuel Lasker, Germany
1921–27	Jose R. Capablanca, Cuba
1927–35	Alexander A. Alekhine, U.S.S.R.
1935–37	Dr. Max Euwe, Netherlands
1937–46	Alexander A. Alekhine, U.S.S.R.[1]
1948–57	Mikhail Botvinnik, U.S.S.R.
1957–58	Vassily Smyslov, U.S.S.R.
1958–60	Mikhail Botvinnik, U.S.S.R.
1960–61	Mikhail Tal, U.S.S.R.
1961–63	Mikhail Botvinnik, U.S.S.R.
1963–68	Tigran Petrosian, U.S.S.R.
1969–71	Boris Spassky, U.S.S.R.
1972–74	Bobby Fischer, United States
1975	Bobby Fischer, United States[2]; Anatoly Karpov, U.S.S.R.
1976–85	Anatoly Karpov, U.S.S.R.[3]
1985–	Garry Kasparov, Russia[4]
1993–99	Anatoly Karpov, Russia[5]
1999–	Alexander Khalifman, Russia[5]
2000	Championship begins Nov. 25

1. Alekhine, a French citizen, died while champion. 2. Relinquished title. 3. In 1978, Karpov defeated Viktor Korchnoi 6 games to 5. 4. PCA (Professional Chess Association) world champion after 1993. 5. FIDE (International Chess Federation) world champion.

UNITED STATES CHAMPIONS

1909–36	Frank J. Marshall, New York
1936–44	Samuel Reshevsky, New York[1]
1944–46	Arnold S. Denker, New York
1946	Samuel Reshevsky, Boston
1948	Herman Steiner, Los Angeles
1951–52	Larry Evans, New York
1954–57	Arthur Bisguier, New York
1958–61	Bobby Fischer, Brooklyn, N.Y.
1962	Larry Evans, New York
1963–67	Bobby Fischer, New York
1968	Larry Evans, New York
1969–71	Samuel Reshevsky, Spring Valley, N.Y.
1972	Robert Byrne, Ossining, N.Y.
1973	Lubomir Kavelek, Washington; John Grefe, San Francisco
1974–77	Walter Browne, Berkeley, Calif.
1978–79	Lubomir Kavalek, New York
1980	Tie, Walter Browne, Berkeley, Calif. Larry Christiansen, Modesto, Calif. Larry Evans, Reno, Nev.
1981–82[2]	Tie, Walter Browne, Berkeley, Calif. Yasser Seirawan, Seattle, Wash.
1983	Tie, Walter Browne, Berkeley, Calif. Larry Christiansen, Los Angeles, Calif., Roman Dzindzichashvili, Corona, N.Y.
1984–85	Lev Alburt, New York City
1986	Yasser Seirawan, Seattle, Wash.
1987	Tie, Nick Defirmian, San Francisco Joel Benjamin, Brooklyn, N.Y.
1988	Michael Wilder, Princeton, N.J.
1989	Tie, Stuart Rachels, Birmingham, Ala. Yasser Seirawan, Seattle, Wash. Roman Dzindzichashvili, New York, N.Y.
1990–91	Lev Alburt, New York, N.Y.

1992	Gata Kamsky, Brooklyn, N.Y.	1997	Esther Epstein, Mass. (women)
	Patrick Wolff, Somerville, Mass.		Joel Benjamin, N.Y. (men)
1993	Tie, Alexander Shabalov, Pittsburgh, Pa.	1998	Irina Krush, Brooklyn, N.Y. (women)
	Alex Yermolinski, Edison, N.J.		Nick de Firmian, New York City (men)
1994	Boris Gulko, Fairlawn, N.J.	1999	Anjelina Belakovskaia, Brooklyn, N.Y. (women)
1995	Patrick Wolff, Somerville, Mass.		Boris Gulko, Fairlawn, N.J. (men)
1996	Alex Yurmolinsky, Cleveland, Ohio		Marcel Martinez, Miami, Fla. (junior)

1. In 1942, Isaac I. Kashdan of New York was co-champion for a while because of a tie with Reshevsky in that year's tournament. Reshevsky won the play-off. 2. Championship not contested in 1982.

Bowling

The game of bowling in the United States is an indoor development of the more ancient outdoor game that survives as lawn bowling. The outdoor game is prehistoric in origin and probably goes back to primitive man and round stones that were rolled at some target. It is believed that a game something like nine-pins was popular among the Dutch, Swiss, and Germans as long ago as A.D. 1200. The game was played outdoors with an alley consisting of a single plank 12 to 18 inches wide, along which a ball was rolled toward three rows of three pins each placed at the far end of the alley. When the first indoor alleys were built and how the game was modified from time to time are matters of dispute.

It is supposed that the early settlers of New Amsterdam (New York City), being Dutch, brought their two bowling games with them. About a century ago the game of nine-pins was flourishing in the United States but so corrupted by gambling on matches that it was barred by law in New York and Connecticut. Since the law specifically barred "nine-pins," it was eventually evaded by adding another pin and thus legally making it a new game.

Various organizations were formed to make rules for bowling and supervise competition in the United States but none was successful until the American Bowling Congress, organized Sept. 9, 1895, became the ruling body.

AMERICAN BOWLING CONGRESS CHAMPIONS

Year	Singles	All-events	Year	Singles	All-events
1959	Ed Lubanski	Ed Lubanski	1981	Rob Vital	Rod Toft
1960	Paul Kulbaga	Vince Lucci	1982	Bruce Bohm	Rich Wonders
1961	Lyle Spooner	Luke Karen	1983	Rick Kendrick	Tony Cariello
1962	Andy Renaldo	Billy Young	1984	Bob Antczak and Neal Young (tie)	Bob Goike
1963	Fred Delello	Bus Owalt	1985	Glen Harbison	Barry Asher
1964	Jim Stefanich	Les Zikes, Jr.	1986	Jess Mackey	Ed Marazka
1965	Ken Roeth	Tom Hathaway	1987	Terry Taylor	Ryan Schafer
1966	Don Chapman	John Wilcox	1988	Steve Hutkowski	Rick Steelsmith
1967	Frank Perry	Gary Lewis	1989	Paul Tetreault	George Hall
1968	Wayne Kowalski	Vince Mazzanti	1990	Bob Hochrein	Mike Neumann
1969	Greg Campbell	Eddie Jackson	1991	Ed Deines	Tom Howery
1970	Jake Yoder	Mike Berlin	1992	Bob Youker and Gary Blatchford (tie)	Mike Tucker
1971	Al Cohn	Al Cohn			
1972	Bill Pointer	Mac Lowry	1993	Dan Bock	Jeff Nimke
1973	Ed Thompson	Ron Woolet	1994	John Weltzien	Thomas Holt
1974	Gene Krause	Bob Hart	1995	Matt Surina	Jeff Kwiatkowski
1975	Jim Setser	Bobby Meadows	1996	Donald Scudder, Jr.	Scott Kurtz
1976	Mike Putzer	Jim Lindquist	1997	John Socha	Jeff Richgels
1977	Frank Gadaleto	Bud Debenham	1998	John Gaines	Chris Barnes
1978	Rich Mersek	Chris Cobus	1999	Dan Winter	Thomas A. Jones
1979	Rick Peters	Bob Basacchi	2000	Garran Hein	Roy Daniels
1980	Mike Eaton	Steve Fehr			

PROFESSIONAL BOWLERS ASSOCIATION

National Championship Tournament

1960	Don Carter	1971	Mike Lemongello	1982	Earl Anthony	1993	Ron Palombi
1961	Dave Soutar	1972	Johnny Guenther	1983	Earl Anthony	1994	David Traber
1962	Carmen Salvino	1973	Earl Anthony	1984	Bob Chamberlain	1995	Scott Alexander
1963	Billy Hardwick	1974	Earl Anthony	1985	Mike Aulby	1996	Butch Soper
1964	Bob Strampe	1975	Earl Anthony	1986	Tom Crites	1997	Rich Steelsmith
1965	Dave Davis	1976	Paul Colwell	1987	Randy Pedersen	1998	Pete Weber
1966	Wayne Zahn	1977	Tommy Hudson	1988	Brian Voss	1999	Tim Criss
1967	Dave Davis	1978	Warren Nelson	1989	Pete Weber	2000	Norm Duke
1968	Wayne Zahn	1979	Mike Aulby	1990	Jim Pencak		
1969	Mike McGrath	1980	Johnny Petraglia	1991	Mike Miller		
1970	Mike McGrath	1981	Earl Anthony	1992	Eric Forkel		

BOWLING PROPRIETORS' ASSOCIATION OF AMERICA—MEN

United States Open[1]

1971 Mike Lemongello	1979 Joe Berardi	1987 Del Ballard	1995 Dave Husted
1972 Don Johnson	1980 Steve Martin	1988 Pete Weber	1996 Dave Husted
1973 Mike McGrath	1981 Marshall Holman	1989 Mike Aulby	1997 Not held
1974 Larry Laub	1982 Dave Husted	1990 Ron Palumbi, Jr.	1998 Walter Ray Williams, Jr.
1975 Steve Neff	1983 Gary Dickinson	1991 Pete Weber	
1976 Paul Moser	1984 Mark Roth	1992 Robert Lawrence	1999 Bob Learn, Jr.
1977 Johnny Petraglia	1985 Marshall Holman	1993 Del Ballard, Jr.	2000 Robert Smith
1978 Nelson Burton, Jr.	1986 Steve Cook	1994 Justin Hromek	

1. Replaced All-Star tournament and is rolled as part of B.P.A. tour.

WOMEN'S INTERNATIONAL BOWLING CONGRESS CHAMPIONS

Year	Singles	All events	Year	Singles	All events
1959	Mae Bolt	Pat McBride	1982	Gracie Freeman	Aleta Rzepecki
1960	Marge McDaniels	Judy Roberts	1983	Aleta Rzepecki	Virginia Norton
1961	Elaine Newton	Evelyn Teal	1984	Freida Gates	Shinobu Saitoh
1962	Martha Hoffman	Flossie Argent	1985	Polly Schwarzel	Aleta Sill
1963	Dot Wilkinson	Helen Shablis	1986	Dana Stewart	Robin Romeo and Maria Lewis (tie)
1964	Jean Havlish	Jean Havlish			
1965	Doris Rudell	Donna Zimmerman	1987	Regi Junak	Leanne Barrette
1966	Gloria Bouvia	Kate Helbig	1988	Michelle Meyer-Welty	Lisa Wagner
1967	Gloria Paeth	Carol Miller	1989	Lorraine Anderson	Nancy Fehn
1968	Norma Parks	Susie Reichley	1990	Dana Miller-Mackie and Paula Carter (tie)	Carol Norman
1969	Joan Bender	Helen Duval			
1970	Dorothy Fothergill	Dorothy Fothergill	1991	Debbie Kuhn	Debbie Kuhn
1971	Mary Scruggs	Lorrie Nichols	1992	Patty Ann	Mitsuko Tokimoto
1972	D. D. Jacobson	Mildred Martorella	1993	Karen Collurs and Kari Murph (tie)	Bertha Blackshur and Sharon Davis (tie)
1973	Bobby Buffaloe	Toni Calvery			
1974	Shirley Garms	Judy C. Soutar	1994	Vicki Fifield	Wendy Macpherson-Papanos
1975	Barbara Leicht	Virginia Norton			
1976	Bev Shonk	Betty Morris	1995	Beth Owen	Beth Owen
1977	Akiko Yamaga	Akiko Yamaga	1996	Cindy Berlanga	Lorrie Nichols
1978	Mae Bolt	Annese Kelly	1997	Jean Schmidt	Kendra Cameron
1979	Betty Morris	Betty Morris	1998	Nellie Glandon	Liz Johnson
1980	Betty Morris	Cheryl Robinson	1999	Maggie Matheson	Marlene Walls
1981	Virginia Norton	Virginia Norton	2000	Cathy Krasner	Carolyn Dorin-Ballard

BOWLING PROPRIETORS' ASSOCIATION OF AMERICA—WOMEN

United States Open

1971 Paula Carter	1979 Diana Silva	1987 Carol Nurman	1995 Tish Johnson
1972 Lorrie Nichols	1980 Pat Costello (Calif.)	1988 Lisa Wagner	1996 Liz Johnson
1973 Mildred Martorella	1981 Donna Adamek	1989 Robin Romeo	1997 Not held
1974 Pat Costello (Calif.)	1982 Shinobu Saitoh	1990 Dana Miller-Mackie	1998 Aleta Sill
1975 Paula Carter	1983 Dana Miller	1991 Anne Marie Duggan	1999 Kim Adler
1976 Patty Costello (Pa.)	1984 Karen Ellingsworth	1992 Tish Johnson	2000 Tennelle Grijalva
1977 Betty Morris	1985 Pat Mercatanti	1993 Dede Davidson	
1978 Donna Adamek	1986 Wendy Macpherson	1994 Aleta Sill	

WIBC QUEENS TOURNAMENT CHAMPIONS

1961 Janet Harman	1972 Dorothy Fothergill	1983 Aleta Rzepecki	1994 Anne Marie Duggan
1962 Dorothy Wilkinson	1973 Dorothy Fothergill	1984 Kazue Inahashi	1995 Sandy Postma
1963 Irene Monterosso	1974 Judy Soutar	1985 Aleta Sill	1996 Lisa Wagner
1964 D.D. Jacobson	1975 Cindy Powell	1986 Cora Fiebig	1997 Sandra-Jo Shiery-Odom
1965 Betty Kuczynski	1976 Pamela Buckner	1987 Cathy Almeida	
1966 Judy Lee	1977 Dana Stewart	1988 Wendy Macpherson	1998 Lynda Norry
1967 Mildred Martorella	1978 Loa Boxberger	1989 Carol Gianotti	1999 Leanne Barrette
1968 Phyllis Massey	1979 Donna Adamek	1990 Patty Ann	2000 Wendy Macpherson
1969 Ann Feigel	1980 Donna Adamek	1991 Dede Davidson	
1970 Mildred Martorella	1981 Katsuko Sugimoto	1992 Cindy Coburn-Carroll	
1971 Mildred Martorella	1982 Katsuko Sugimoto	1993 Jan Schmidt	

PROFESSIONAL BOWLERS ASSOCIATION CHAMPIONSHIP—2000

(Feb. 13–19, 2000, Toledo, Ohio)

Winner—Norm Duke, Clermont, Fla., defeated Jason Couch, Clermont, Fla., 214–198 in title match.

3. Jess Stayrook, San Diego, Calif.

4. Dale Traber, Cedarburg, Wis.

5. Chris Barnes, Wichita, Kan.

AMERICAN BOWLING CONGRESS TOURNAMENT—2000

(Feb. 12–June 19, 2000, Albuquerque, N.M.)

Regular Division

Singles— Goran Hein, Brea, Calif.	811
Doubles— Billy Seprodi, Indianapolis, and Jim O'Connor, Greenwood, Inc.	1,534
All Events—Roy Daniels, El Paso, Tex.	2,181
Team—8 Ball, Medford, Ore.	3,513

WOMEN'S INTERNATIONAL BOWLING CONGRESS TOURNAMENT—2000

(March 11–July 8, 2000, Reno, Nev.)

Singles— Cathy Krasner, Baltimore, Md.	729
Doubles— Cindy Kesterson, Council Bluffs, Iowa, and Judy Gurney, Percival, Iowa	1,340
All Events— Carolyn Dorin-Ballard, Fort Worth, Tex.	2,147
Team— High Roller, Cherry Hill, N.J.	3,234

BOWLING PROPRIETORS' ASSOCIATION OF AMERICA U.S. OPEN—2000

(July 20, 2000, Phoenix, Ariz.)

Men

Robert Smith, Simi Valley, Calif., defeated Norm Duke, Clermont, Fla, 202–201 in final match.

3. Jeff Lizzi, Sandusky, Ohio

Women

Tennelle Grijalva, Orange, Calif., defeated Kelly Kulick, Union, N.J., 239–155 in final match.

3. Carol Gianotti, Australia

Skiing

HISTORY OF SKIING IN THE UNITED STATES

Skis were devised for utility, to aid those who had to travel over snow. The Norwegians, Swedes, Lapps, and other inhabitants of northern lands used skis for many centuries before skiing became a sport. Emigrants from these countries brought skis to the United States with them. The first skier of record in the United States was a mailman by the name of "Snowshoe" Thompson, born and raised in Telemarken, Norway, who came to the United States and, beginning in 1850, used skis through 20 suc-

cessive winters in carrying mail from Northern California to Carson Valley, Idaho.

Ski clubs sprang up over 100 years ago where there were Norwegian and Swedish settlers in Wisconsin and Minnesota and ski contests were held in that territory in 1886. On Feb. 21, 1904, at Ishpenning, Mich., a small group of skiers organized the National Ski Association. In 1961 it was renamed the United States Ski Association.

ALPINE SKIING

2000 United States Alpine Championships

(March 24–29, 2000, Jackson Hole, Wyo.)

Men

Downhill—1. Chris Puckett, Boulder, Colo; 2. Darin McBeath, Canada; 3. Kevin Wert, Canada

Slalom—1. Erik Schlopy, Park City, Utah; 2. Bode Miller, Franconia, N.H.; 3. Sacha Gros, Vail, Colo.

Giant Slalom—1. Casey Puckett, Crested Butte, Colo.; 2. Erik Schlopy, Park City, Utah; 3. Daron Rahlves, Truckee, Calif.

Super G—1. Daron Rahlves, Truckee, Calif.; 2. Casey Puckett, Crested Butte, Colo.; 3. Bode Miller, Franconia, N.H.

Combined (4 events)—1. Casey Puckett, Crested Butte, Colo.; 2. Bode Miller, Franconia, N.H.; 3. Josh Transue, Hunter, N.Y.

Women

Downhill—1. Kirsten Clark, Raymond, Maine; 2. Lindsey Kildow, Vail, Colo.; 3. Caroline Lalive, Steamboat Springs, Colo.

Slalom—1. Caroline Lalive, Steamboat Springs, Colo.; 2. Kristina Koznick, Burnsville, Minn.; 3. Sarah Schleper, Vail, Colo.

Giant Slalom—Cancelled because of weather

Super G—1. Kirsten Clark, Raymond, Maine; 2. Julia Mancuso, Tahoe City, Calif.; 3. Caroline Lalive; Steamboat Springs, Colo.

Combined (3 events)—1. Caroline Lalive, Steamboat Springs, Colo.; 2. Julia Mancuso, Tahoe City, Calif.; 3. Mia Cullman, Vail, Colo.

2000 Alpine World Cup Champions

Men	Pts	Women	Pts
Overall—Hermann Maier, Austria	2,000	Overall—Renate Götschl, Austria	1,631
Downhill—Hermann Maier, Austria	800	Downhill—Regina Häusl, Germany	529
Slalom—Kjetil-André Aamodt, Norway	598	Slalom—Spela Pretnar, Slovenia	645
Giant Slalom—Hermann Maier, Austria	520	Giant Slalom—Michaela Dorfmeister, Austria	684
Super G—Hermann Maier, Austria	540	Super G—Renate Götschl, Austria	554
Combined—Kjetil-André Aamodt, Norway	200	Combined—Renate Götschl, Austria	100

2000 Disabled Alpine World Cup Champions

Men

Downhill—**Blind:** Chris Williamson, Canada; **Sitting:** Karl Lotz, Germany; **Standing:** Hans Burn, Switzerland

Slalom—**Blind:** Chris Williamson, Canada; **Sitting:** Daniel Wesley, Canada; **Standing:** Gerd Schönfelder, Germany

Giant Slalom—**Blind:** Chris Williamson, Canada; **Sitting:** Christopher Waddell, United States; **Standing:** Romain Riboud, France

Super G—**Blind:** Gianmaria Dal Maistro, Italy.; **Sitting:** Karl Lotz, Germany; **Standing:** Gerd Schönfelder, Germany

Overall—**Blind:** Chris Williamson, Canada and Bart Bunting, Austria; **Sitting:** Karl Lotz, Germany; Christopher Waddell, United States;, and Daniel Wesley, Canada; **Standing:** Gerd Schönfelder, Germany and Hans Burn, Switzerland

Women

Downhill—**Blind:** Katerina Tepla, Czech Republic; **Sitting:** Sarah Will, United States; **Standing:** Sarah Billmeier, United States

Slalom—**Blind:** Katerina Tepla, Czech Republic; **Sitting:** Sarah Will, United States; **Standing:** Lauren Woolstencroft, Canada

Giant Slalom—**Blind:** Katerina Tepla, Czech Republic; **Sitting:** Sarah Will, United States; **Standing:** Lauren Woolstencroft, Canada

Super G—**Blind:** Katerina Tepla, Czech Republic; **Sitting:** Vreni Stöckli, Switzerland; **Standing:** Mary Riddell, United States

Overall—**Blind:** Katerina Tepla, Czech Republic; **Sitting:** Sarah Will, United States; Vreni Stöckli, Switzerland; and Muffy Davis, United States; **Standing:** Ramona Hoh, Canada; Mary Riddell, United States; and Lauren Woolstencroft, Canada

NORDIC SKIING/SKI JUMPING/CROSS COUNTRY

2000 U.S. Ski Jumping/Nordic Combined Championships

(March 24–26, 2000, Steamboat Springs, Colo.)

Men

Large Hill (K112m)—1. Clint Jones, Steamboat Springs, Colo.; 2. Todd Lodwick, Steamboat Springs, Colo.; 3. Brendan Doran, Steamboat Springs, Colo.

Normal Hill (K88m)—1. Brendan Doran, Steamboat Springs, Colo.; 2. Vladimir Glyvka, Ukraine; 3. Todd Lodwick, Steamboat Springs, Colo.

Nordic Combined (K88m jumping–10k race)—1. Todd Lodwick, Steamboat Springs, Colo.; 2. Bill Demong, Vermontville, N.Y.; 3. Carl Van Loan, Webster, N.H.

Women

Normal Hill (K88m)—1. Lindsey Van, Park City, Utah; 2. Karla Keck, Oconomowoc, Wis.; 3. Liz Szotyori, Saugerties, N.Y.

Large Hill (K112 m)—1. Lindsey Van, Park City, Utah; 2. Karla Keck, Oconomowoc, Wis.; 3. Liz Szotyori, Saugerties, N.Y.

2000 Cross Country U.S. Nationals

(Jan. 8–15, 2000, Midway, Utah)

Men

Sprint—Marcus Nash, Fryeburg, Maine
10k Classic—Marcus Nash, Fryeburg, Maine
15k Classic—Marcus Nash, Fryeburg, Maine
30k Classic—Donald Farley, Canada
50k Classic—Carl Swenson, Boulder, Colo.

Women

Sprint—Beckie Scott, Canada
5k Freestyle—Beckie Scott, Canada
10k Classic—Beckie Scott, Canada
15k Classic—Beckie Scott, Canada
30k Freestyle—Nina Kemppel, Anchorage, Alaska

FREESTYLE SKIING

2000 Freestyle Skiing World Cup Champions

Men

Moguls—Janne Lahtela, Finland
Dual Moguls—Janne Lahtela, Finland
Aerials—Nicolas Fontaine, Canada

Women

Moguls—Ann Battelle, United States
Dual Moguls—Kari Traa, Norway
Aerials—Jacqui Cooper, Austria

2000 U.S. Freestyle Championships

(March 24–26, 2000, Sunday River, Maine)

Men

Acro—Ian Edmondson, Birmingham, Mich.
Aerials—Eric Bergoust, Missoula, Mont.
Moguls—Evan Dybvig, Tunbridge, Vt.
Dual Moguls—Garth Hager, Bothell, Wash.

Women

Acro—Lara Rosenbaum, Portsmouth, R.I.
Aerials—Kelly Hilliman, Tonawanda, N.Y.
Moguls—Hannah Hardaway, Moultonborough, N.H.
Dual Moguls—Hannah Hardaway, Moultonborough, N.H.

SNOWBOARDING

2000 World Cup Snowboard Champions

Men

Parallel Slalom—Matthieu Bozzetto, France
Snowboardcross—Pontus Stahlkloo, Sweden
Giant Slalom—Stefan Kaltschuetz, Austria
Halfpipe—Thomas Johansson, Sweden

Women

Parallel Slalom—Isabelle Blanc, France
Snowboardcross—Sandra Farmand, Germany
Giant Slalom—Margherita Parini, Italy
Halfpipe—Sabine Wehr-Hasler, Germany

2000 U.S. Snowboard Championships

(March 23–26, 2000, Ludlow, Vt.)

Men

Slalom—Anton Pogue, Hood River, Ore.
Giant Slalom—Jasey Jay Anderson, Canada
Halfpipe—Adam Petraska, Chester, Vt.
Snowboardcross—Seth Wescott, Farmington, Maine

Women

Slalom—Rosey Fletcher, Girdwood, Alaska
Giant Slalom—Sondra Van Ert, Ketchum, Idaho
Halfpipe—Kim Stacey, Stratton Mt., Vt.
Snowboardcross—Kelly Clark, Mt. Snow, Vt.

JAMES E. SULLIVAN MEMORIAL AWARD WINNERS
(Amateur Athlete of the Year Chosen in Amateur Athletic Union Poll)

1930	Robert Tyre Jones, Jr.	Golf	1965	Bill Bradley	Basketball
1931	Bernard E. Berlinger	Track and field	1966	Jim Ryun	Track and field
1932	James A. Bausch	Track and field	1967	Randy Matson	Track and field
1933	Glenn Cunningham	Track and field	1968	Debbie Meyer	Swimming
1934	William R. Bonthron	Track and field	1969	Bill Toomey	Decathlon
1935	W. Lawson Little, Jr.	Golf	1970	John Kinsella	Swimming
1936	Glenn Morris	Track and field	1971	Mark Spitz	Swimming
1937	J. Donald Budge	Tennis	1972	Frank Shorter	Marathon
1938	Donald R. Lash	Track and field	1973	Bill Walton	Basketball
1939	Joseph W. Burk	Rowing	1974	Rick Wohlhuter	Track and field
1940	J. Gregory Rice	Track and field	1975	Tim Shaw	Swimming
1941	Leslie MacMitchell	Track and field	1976	Bruce Jenner	Track and field
1942	Cornelius Warmerdam	Track and field	1977	John Naber	Swimming
1943	Gilbert L. Dodds	Track and field	1978	Tracy Caulkins	Swimming
1944	Ann Curtis	Swimming	1979	Kurt Thomas	Gymnastics
1945	Felix (Doc) Blanchard	Football	1980	Eric Heiden	Speed skating
1946	Y. Arnold Tucker	Football	1981	Carl Lewis	Track and field
1947	John B. Kelly, Jr.	Rowing	1982	Mary Decker Tabb	Track and field
1948	Robert B. Mathias	Track and field	1983	Edwin Moses	Track and field
1949	Richard T. Button	Figure skating	1984	Greg Louganis	Diving
1950	Fred Wilt	Track and field	1985	Joan Benoit-Samuelson	Marathon
1951	Robert E. Richards	Track and field	1986	Jackie Joyner-Kersee	Heptathlon
1952	Horace Ashenfelter	Track and field	1987	Jim Abbott	Baseball
1953	Sammy Lee	Diving	1988	Florence Griffith-Joyner	Track and field
1954	Malvin Whitfield	Track and field	1989	Janet Evans	Swimming
1955	Harrison Dillard	Track and field	1990	John Smith	Wrestling
1956	Patricia McCormick	Diving	1991	Mike Powell	Track and field
1957	Bobby Jo Morrow	Track and field	1992	Bonnie Blair	Speed skating
1958	Glenn Davis	Track and field	1993	Charles Ward	Football/Basketball
1959	Parry O'Brien	Track and field	1994	Dan Jansen	Speed skating
1960	Rafer Johnson	Track and field	1995	Bruce Baumgartner	Wrestling
1961	Wilma Rudolph Ward	Track and field	1996	Michael Johnson	Track and field
1962	Jim Beatty	Track and field	1997	Peyton Manning	Football
1963	John Pennel	Track and field	1998	Chamique Holdsclaw	Basketball
1964	Don Schollander	Swimming	1999	Kelly and Coco Miller	Basketball

Speed Skating

WORLD SPEED SKATING RECORDS (LONG TRACK)

Distance	Time	Skater	Place	Date
Men				
500m	34.63	Jeremy Wotherspoon, Canada	Calgary, Canada	Jan. 29, 2000
1,000m	1:08.35	Jeremy Wotherspoon, Canada	Calgary, Canada	March 18, 2000
1,500m	1:45.56	Jakko Jan Leeuwangh, Netherlands	Calgary, Canada	Jan. 29, 2000
3,000m	3:43.76	Steven Elm, Canada	Calgary, Canada	March 17, 2000
5,000m	6:18.72	Gianni Romme, Netherlands	Calgary, Canada	Jan. 30, 2000
10,000m	13:08.71	Gianni Romme, Netherlands	Calgary, Canada	March 29, 1998
Women				
500m	37.55	Catriona LeMay Doan, Canada	Calgary, Canada	Dec. 29, 1997
1,000m	1:14.61	Monique Garbrecht, Germany	Calgary, Canada	Feb. 21, 1999
1,500m	1:55.50	Annamarie Thomas, Netherlands	Calgary, Canada	March 20, 1999
3,000m	4:00.51	Gunda Niemann-Stirnemann, Germany	Calgary, Canada	Jan. 30, 2000
5,000m	6:56.84	Gunda Niemann-Stirnemann, Germany	Hamar, Norway	Jan. 16, 2000

WORLD SPRINT CHAMPIONSHIPS—2000
(Feb. 26–27, 2000, Seoul, Korea)

Men	Times	Women	Times
500m—Jeremy Wotherspoon, Canada	35.59, 35.54	500m—Monique Garbrecht, Germany	38.81, 38.67
1,000m—Jan Bos, Netherlands	1:10.49, 1:10.88	1,000m—Chris Witty, United States	1:17.31, 1:17.25

Men Overall standings:
1. Jeremy Wotherspoon, Canada
2. Michael Ireland, Canada
3. Hiroyasu Shimizu, Japan

Women Overall standings:
1. Monique Garbrecht, Germany
2. Chris Witty, United States
3. Marianne Timmer, Netherlands

WORLD SPEED SKATING CHAMPIONS

(Feb. 5, 2000, Milwaukee, Wisconsin)

Men		Women	
500m	Jaebong Choi, Korea	500m	Edel Therese Hoiseth, Norway
1,500m	Ådne Søndrål, Norway	1,500m	Maki Tabata, Japan
5,000m	Gianni Romme, Netherlands	3,000m	Claudia Pechstein, Germany
10,000m	Gianni Romme, Netherlands	5,000m	Gunda Neimann-Stimemann, Germany

WORLD SHORT TRACK CHAMPIONSHIPS—2000

(March 10–12, 2000, Sheffield, England)

Men	Time	Women	Time
500m—Eric Bedard, Canada	42.009	500m—Evgenia Radanova, Bulgaria	44.626
1,000m—JiaJun Li, China	1:31.098	1,000m—Yang Yang (A), China	1:40.363
1,500m—Ryoung Min, Korea	2:23.098	1,500m—Yang Yang (A), China	2:32.707
3,000m—Ryoung Min, Korea	5:02.496	3,000m—Sang-Mi An, Korea	5:24.372
Relay—China	7:09.387	Relay—China	4:28.267

Figure Skating

WORLD CHAMPIONS

Men

1960	Alain Giletti, France	1993	Kurt Browning, Canada	1979	Linda Fratianne, United States
1961	No competition	1994–95	Elvis Stojko, Canada	1980	Anett Poetzsch, East Germany
1962	Donald Jackson, Canada	1996	Todd Eldredge, United States	1981	Denise Beillmann, Switzerland
1963	Don McPherson, Canada	1997	Elvis Stojko, Canada	1982	Elaine Zayak, United States
1964	Manfred Schnelldorfer, West Germany	1998–2000	Alexei Yagudin, Russia	1983	Rosalynn Sumners, United States
1965	Alain Calmat, France			1984–85	Katarina Witt, East Germany

Women

1966–68	Emmerich Danzer, Austria	1956–60	Carol Heiss, United States
1969–70	Tim Wood, United States	1961	No competition
1971–73	Ondrej Nepela, Czechoslovakia	1962–64	Sjoukje Dijkstra, Netherlands
1974	Jan Hoffman, East Germany	1965	Petra Burka, Canada
1975	Sergei Yolkov, U.S.S.R.	1966–68	Peggy Fleming, United States
1976	John Curry, Britain	1969–70	Gabriele Seyfert, East Germany
1977	Vladimir Kovalev, U.S.S.R.	1971–72	Beatrix Schuba, Austria
1978	Charles Tickner, United States	1973	Karen Magnusson, Canada
1979	Vladimir Kovalev, U.S.S.R.	1974	Christine Errath, East Germany
1980	Jan Hoffman, East Germany	1975	Dianne de Leeuw, Netherlands
1981–84	Scott Hamilton, United States	1976	Dorothy Hamill, United States
1985	Alexandr Fadeev, U.S.S.R.	1977	Linda Fratianne, United States
1986	Brian Boitano, United States	1978	Anett Poetzsch, East Germany
1987	Brian Orser, Canada		
1988	Brian Boitano, United States		
1989–91	Kurt Browning, Canada		
1992	Viktor Petrenko, Unified Team		

1986	Debi Thomas, United States
1987–88	Katarina Witt, East Germany
1989	Midori Ito, Japan
1990	Jill Trenary, United States
1991–92	Kristi Yamaguchi, United States
1993	Oksana Baiul, Ukraine
1994	Yuka Sato, Japan
1995	Chen Lu, China
1996	Michelle Kwan, United States
1997	Tara Lipinski, United States
1998	Michelle Kwan, United States
1999	Maria Butyrskaya, Russia
2000	Michelle Kwan, United States

U.S. CHAMPIONS

Men

1946–52	Richard Button	1973–75	Gordon McKellen
1953–56	Hayes Jenkins	1976	Terry Kubicka
1957–60	David Jenkins	1977–80	Charles Tickner
1961	Bradley Lord	1981–84	Scott Hamilton
1962	Monty Hoyt	1985–88	Brian Boitano
1963	Tommy Liz	1989	Christopher Bowman
1964	Scott Allen	1990–91	Todd Eldredge
1965	Gary Visconti	1992	Christopher Bowman
1966	Scott Allen	1993–94	Scott Davis
1967	Gary Visconti	1995	Todd Eldredge
1968–70	Tim Wood	1996	Rudy Galindo
1971	John M. Petkevich	1997–98	Todd Eldredge
1972	Ken Shelley	1999–2000	Michael Weiss

Women

1943–48	Gretchen Merrill
1949–50	Yvonne Sherman
1951	Sonya Klopfer
1952–56	Tenley Albright
1957–60	Carol Heiss
1961	Laurence Owen
1962	Barbara Roles Pursley
1963	Lorraine Hanlon
1964–68	Peggy Fleming
1969–73	Janet Lynn
1974–76	Dorothy Hamill
1977–80	Linda Fratianne

1981	Elaine Zayak	1988	Debi Thomas	1994	Tonya Harding
1982–84	Rosalynn Sumners	1989–90	Jill Trenary	1995	Nicole Bobek
1985	Tiffany Chin	1991	Tonya Harding	1996	Michelle Kwan
1986	Debi Thomas	1992	Kristi Yamaguchi	1997	Tara Lipinski
1987	Jill Trenary	1993	Nancy Kerrigan	1998–2000	Michelle Kwan

2000 UNITED STATES CHAMPIONSHIPS

Feb. 6–13, 2000, Cleveland, Ohio

Men's singles
1. Michael Weiss, Fairfax, Va.
2. Timothy Goebel, Rolling Meadows, Ill.
2. Trifun Zivanovic, Los Angeles, Calif.

Women's singles
1. Michelle Kwan, Lake Arrowhead, Calif.
2. Sasha Cohen, Laguna Niguel, Calif.
3. Sarah Hughes, Great Neck, N.Y.

Pairs
1. Kyoko Ina, Guttenberg, N.J., and John Zimmerman, Birmingham, Ala.
2. Tiffany Scott, Hanson, Mass., and Philip Dulebohn, Germantown, Md.
3. Larisa Spielberg, East Lansing, Mich., and Craig Joeright, Cleveland, Ohio

Dance
1. Naomi Lang, Allegan, Mich., and Peter Tchernyshev, Waterford, Mich.
2. Jamie Silverstein, Bloomfield Hills, Mich., and Justin Pekarek, Auburn Hills, Mich.
3. Deborah Koegel, Phoenixville, Pa., and Oleg Fediukov, Brookhaven, Pa.

2000 WORLD CHAMPIONSHIPS

March 26–April 2, 2000, Nice, France

Men's singles
1. Alexei Yagudin, Russia
2. Elvis Stojko, Canada
3. Michael Weiss, United States

Women's singles
1. Michelle Kwan, United States
2. Irina Slutskaya, Russia
3. Maria Butyrskaya, Russia

Pairs
1. Maria Petrova and Alexei Tikhonov, Russia
2. Xue Shen and Hongbo Zhao, China
3. Sarah Abitbol and Stephane Bernadis, France

Dance
1. Marina Anissina and Gwendal Peizerat, France
2. Barbara Fusar-Poli and Maurizio Margaglio, Italy
3. Margarita Drobiazko and Povilas Vanagas, Lithuania

Swimming

WORLD RECORDS—MEN

(Through Sept. 23, 2000)

Distance	Record	Holder	Country	Date
Freestyle				
50 m	0:21.64	Alexander Popov	Russia	June 16, 2000
100 m	0:47.84	Pieter van den Hoogenband	Netherlands	Sept. 19, 2000
200 m	1:45.35	Pieter van den Hoogenband	Netherlands	Sept. 17, 2000
400 m	3:40.59	Ian Thorpe	Australia	Sept. 16, 2000
800 m	7:46.00	Kieren Perkins	Australia	Aug. 24, 1994
1,500 m	14:41.66	Kieren Perkins	Australia	Aug. 24, 1994
Backstroke				
50 m	0:24.99	Lenny Krayzelburg	United States	Aug. 28, 1999
100 m	0:53.60	Lenny Krayzelburg	United States	Aug. 24, 1999
200 m	1:55.87	Lenny Krayzelburg	United States	Aug. 27, 1999
Breaststroke				
50 m	0:27.61	Alexander Dzhaburiya	Ukraine	Apr. 27, 1996
100 m	1:00.36	Roman Sloudnov	Russia	June 15, 2000
200 m	2:10.16	Mike Barrowman	United States	July 29, 1992
Butterfly				
50 m	0:23.60	Geoffrey Huegill	Australia	May 14, 2000
100 m	0:51.81	Michael Klim	Australia	Dec. 12, 1999
200 m	1:55.18	Tom A. Malchow	United States	June 17, 2000
Individual medley				
200 m	1:58.16	Jani Sievinen	Finland	Sept. 11, 1994
400 m	4:11.76	Tom Dolan	United States	Sept. 17, 2000
Medley relay				
400 m	3:33.73	Olympic Team	United States	Sept. 23, 2000
Freestyle relay				
400 m	3:13.67	Olympic Team	Australia	Sept. 16, 2000
800 m	7:07.05	Olympic Team	Australia	Sept. 19, 2000

Approved by the International Swimming Federation (F.I.N.A.). (F.I.N.A. discontinued acceptance of records in yards in 1968). *Source:* www.olympics.com.

WORLD RECORDS—WOMEN
(Through Sept. 23, 2000)

Distance	Record	Holder	Country	Date
Freestyle				
50 m	0:24.13	Inge de Bruijn	Netherlands	Sept. 22, 2000
100 m	0:53.77	Inge de Bruijn	Netherlands	Sept. 20, 2000
200 m	1:56.78	Franziska van Almsick	Germany	Sept. 6, 1994
400 m	4:03.85	Janet Evans	United States	Sept. 22, 1988
800 m	8:16.22	Janet Evans	United States	Aug. 20, 1989
1,500 m	15:52.10	Janet Evans	United States	March 26, 1988
Backstroke				
50 m	0:28.67	Mai Nakamura	Japan	April 23, 2000
100 m	1:00.16	Cihong He	China	Sept. 10, 1994
200 m	2:06.62	Kristina Egerszegi	Hungary	Aug. 25, 1991
Breaststroke				
50 m	0:30.83	Penny Heyns	South Africa	Aug. 28, 1999
100 m	1:06.52	Penny Heyns	South Africa	Aug. 23, 1999
200 m	2:23.64	Penny Heyns	South Africa	Aug. 27, 1999
Butterfly				
50 m	0:25.64	Inge de Bruijn	Netherlands	May 26, 2000
100 m	0:56.61	Inge de Bruijn	Netherlands	Sept. 17, 2000
200 m	2:05.81	Susann O'Neill	Australia	May 17, 2000
Individual medley				
200 m	2:09.72	Yanyan Wu	China	Oct. 17, 1997
400 m	4:33.59	Yana Klochkova	Ukraine	Sept. 16, 2000
Medley relay				
400 m	3:58.30	Olympic Team	United States	Sept. 23, 2000
Freestyle relay				
400 m	3:36.61	Olympic Team	United States	Sept. 16, 2000
800 m	7:55.47	National Team	East Germany	Aug. 18, 1987

Approved by the International Swimming Federation (F.I.N.A.). (F.I.N.A. discontinued acceptance of records in yards in 1968). *Source:* www.olympics.com.

AMERICAN SWIMMING RECORDS
(Through Sept. 23, 2000)

Distance	Record	Holder	Date	Distance	Record	Holder	Date
MEN				**WOMEN**			
Freestyle				**Freestyle**			
50 m	0:21.81	Tom Jager	March 24, 1990	50 m	0:24.63	Dara Torres	Sept. 23, 2000
100 m	0:48.42	Matt Biondi	Aug. 10, 1988	100 m	0:54.27	Jenny Thompson	July 14, 2000
200 m	1:46.73	Josh Davis	Sept. 18, 2000	200 m	1:57.90	Nicole Haislett	July 27, 1992
400 m	3:47.00	Klete Keller	Sept. 16, 2000	400 m	4:03.85	Janet Evans	Sept. 22, 1988
800 m	7:52.45	Sean Killion	July 27, 1987	800 m	8:16.22	Janet Evans	Aug. 20, 1989
1,500 m	14:56.81	Chris Thompson	Sept. 23, 2000	1,500 m	15:52.10	Janet Evans	March 26, 1988
Backstroke				**Backstroke**			
50 m	24.99	Lenny Krayzelburg	Aug. 28, 1999	50 m	29.01	Natalie Coughlin	Aug. 6, 1998
100 m	0:53.60	Lenny Krayzelburg	Aug. 28, 1999	100 m	1:00.77	Lea Maurer	Jan. 14, 1998
200 m	1:55.87	Lenny Krayzelburg	Aug. 27, 1999	200 m	2:08.60	Betsy Mitchell	June 27, 1986
Breaststroke				**Breaststroke**			
50 m	28.24	Jay Schindler	Apr. 1, 1999	50 m	0:31.55	Megan Quann	June 10, 2000
100 m	1:00.73	Ed Moses	Sept. 17, 2000	100 m	1:07.05	Megan Quann	Sept. 18, 2000
200 m	2:10.16	Mike Barrowman	July 29, 1992	200 m	2:24.56	Kristy Kowal	Sept. 21, 2000
Butterfly				**Butterfly**			
50 m	23.89	Neil Walker	Aug. 12, 1997	50 m	26.55	Amy Van Dyken	May 17, 1996
100 m	0:52.76	Neil Walker	Aug. 12, 1997	100 m	0:57.88	Jennifer Thompson	Aug. 23, 1999
200 m	1:55.18	Tom Malchow	June 17, 2000	200 m	2:05.88	Misty Hyman	Sept. 20, 2000
Individual medley				**Individual medley**			
200 m	1:59.77	Tom Dolan	Sept. 21, 2000	200 m	2:11.91	Summer Sanders	July 30, 1992
400 m	4:11.76	Tom Dolan	Sept. 17, 2000	400 m	4:37.58	Summer Sanders	July 26, 1992
Medley relay				**Medley relay**			
400 m	3:33.73	U.S. Olympic Team	Sept. 22, 2000	400 m	3:58.30	U.S. Olympic Team	Sept. 22, 2000
Freestyle relay				**Freestyle relay**			
400 m	3:13.86	U.S. Olympic Team	Sept. 16, 2000	400 m	3:36.61	U.S. Olympic Team	Sept. 16, 2000
800 m	7:12.51	U.S. National Team	Sept. 21, 1988	800 m	7:57.61	U.S. National Team	Aug. 26, 1999

Source: United States Swim Team.

NATIONAL SWIMMING CHAMPIONSHIPS

(March 28–April 1, 2000, Federal Way, Wash.)

Men	Time
50-meter freestyle—Neil Walker, Verona, Wis.	0:22.10
100-meter freestyle—Neil Walker, Verona, Wis.	0:49.02
200-meter freestyle—Josh Davis, San Antonio, Tex.	1:47.94
400-meter freestyle—Tom Dolan, Arlington, Va.	3:49.59
800-meter freestyle—Tom Dolan, Arlington, Va.	7:56.65
1,500-meter freestyle—Graeme Smith, Great Britain	15:10.35
100-meter backstroke—Neil Walker, Verona, Wis.	0:54.58
200-meter backstroke—Aaron Peirsol, Irvine, Calif.	1:57.03
100-meter breaststroke—Ed Moses, Burke, Va.	1:01.43
200-meter breaststroke—Ed Moses, Burke, Va.	2:13.86
100-meter butterfly—Zsolt Gasper, Hungary	0:52.93
200-meter butterfly—Stephen Parry, Liverpool, England	1:56.34
200-meter individual medley—Tom Wilkens, Middletown, N.J.	2:00.67
400-meter individual medley—Tom Wilkens, Middletown, N.J.	4:13.84
400-meter freestyle relay—Baywatch Hawaii (S. Muhammad, D. Jenkins, L. Rojas, G. Phillips)	3:23.58
400-meter medley relay—Irvine Nova (A. Peirsol, B. Middleton, M. Cavic, J. Lezak)	3:43.51

Women	Time
50-meter freestyle—Dara Torres, Beverly Hills, Calif.	0:25.09
100-meter freestyle—Dara Torres, Beverly Hills, Calif.	0:54.98
200-meter freestyle—Martina Moravcova, Dallas, Tex.	1:59.28
400-meter freestyle—Diana Munz, Chagrin Falls, Ohio	4:08.56
800-meter freestyle—Diana Munz, Chagrin Falls, Ohio	8:29.11
1,500-meter freestyle—Diana Munz, Chagrin Falls, Ohio	16:03.30
100-meter backstroke—Lea Maurer, Crestwood, N.Y.	1:01.47
200-meter backstroke—Jamie Reid, Puyallup, Wash.	2:12.00
100-meter breaststroke—Megan Quann, Puyallup, Wash.	1:07.54
200-meter breaststroke—Kristy Kowal, Reading, Pa.	2:25.74
100-meter butterfly—Martina Moravcova, Slovakia	0:58.41
200-meter butterfly—Margaretha Peddar, Great Britain	2:10.57
200-meter individual medley—Martina Moravcova, Dallas, Tex./Slovakia	2:14.44
400-meter individual medley—Kaitlin Sandeno, Lake Forest, Calif.	4:42.74
400-meter freestyle relay—Southern Methodist (L.Wanberg, L. Wanberg, A. Wimer, K. Inskeep)	3:51.69
400-meter medley relay—Dallas Mustangs (C. Patterson, K. McClelland, M. Moravcova, N. Imoto)	4:11.99

FINA WORLD CUP, 2000

Men	Points
50-meter freestyle—Lorenzo Vismara, Italy	100
100-meter freestyle—Bela Szabados, Hungary	94
200-meter freestyle—Bela Szabados, Hungary	146
400-meter freestyle—Chad Carvin, United States	142
1,500-meter freestyle—Chad Carvin, United States	125
50-meter backstroke—Tomislav Karlo, Croatia	114
100-meter backstroke—Lenny Krayzelburg, United States	121
200-meter backstroke—Lenny Krayzelburg, United States	125
50-meter breaststroke—Mark Warnecke, Germany	92
100-meter breaststroke—Phil Rogers, Australia	92
200-meter breaststroke—Phil Rogers, Australia	97
50-meter butterfly—Mike Mintenko, Canada	89
100-meter butterfly—Mike Mintenko, Canada	85
200-meter butterfly—Massimiliano Eroli, Italy	115
100-meter individual medley—Xufeng Xie, China	103
200-meter individual medley—Xufeng Xie, China	85
400-meter individual medley—Massimiliano Eroli, Italy	122

Women	Points
50-meter freestyle—Jenny Thompson, United States	100
100-meter freestyle—Jenny Thompson, United States	100
200-meter freestyle—Yu Yang, China	121
400-meter freestyle—Rebecca Cooke, Great Britain	72
800-meter freestyle—Rebecca Cooke, Great Britain	87
50-meter backstroke—Nina Zhivanevskaya, Spain	111
100-meter backstroke—Dyana Calub, Australia	121
200-meter backstroke—Kelly Stefanyshyn, Canada	135
50-meter breaststroke—Janne Schäfer, Germany	118
100-meter breaststroke—Alicja Peczak, Poland	124
200-meter breaststroke—Alicja Peczak, Poland	133
50-meter butterfly—Jenny Thompson, United States	100
100-meter butterfly—Yi Ruan, China	121
200-meter butterfly—Jennifer Button, Canada	85
100-meter individual medley—Jenny Thompson, United States	75
200-meter individual medley—Beatrice Caslaru, Romania	121
400-meter individual medley—Beatrice Caslaru, Romania	121

Boxing

Whether it be called pugilism, prize fighting, or boxing, there is no tracing "the Sweet Science" to any definite source. Tales of rivals exchanging blows for fun, fame, or money go back to earliest recorded history and classical legend. There was a mixture of boxing and wrestling called the "pancratium" in the ancient Olympic Games; in such contests rivals belabored one another with hands fortified by heavy leather wrappings that were sometimes studded with metal. More than one Olympic competitor lost his life in this brutal exercise.

There was little law or order in pugilism until Jack Broughton, one of the early champions of England, drew up a set of rules for the game in 1743. Broughton, called "the father of English boxing," also is credited with having invented boxing gloves. However, these gloves—or "mufflers" as they were called—were used only in teaching "the manly art of self-defense" or in training bouts. All professional championship fights were contested with bare knuckles until 1892, when John L. Sullivan lost the heavyweight championship of the world to James J. Corbett in New Orleans in a bout in which both contestants wore regulation gloves.

The Broughton Rules were superseded by the London Prize Ring Rules of 1838. In 1884 the eighth marquis of Queensberry, with the help of John G. Chambers, put forward the Queensberry Rules, a code that called for gloved contests. Amateurs took to the Queensberry Rules more quickly than the professionals did.

HISTORY OF WORLD HEAVYWEIGHT CHAMPIONSHIP FIGHTS

(Bouts in which a new champion was crowned)

Date	Where held	Winner, weight, age	Loser, weight, age	Rounds
Sept. 7, 1892	New Orleans, La.	James J. Corbett, 178 (26)	John L. Sullivan, 212 (33)	21
March 17, 1897	Carson City, Nev.	Bob Fitzsimmons, 167 (34)	James J. Corbett, 183 (30)	KO 14
June 9, 1899	Coney Island, N.Y.	James J. Jeffries, 206 (24)[1]	Bob Fitzsimmons, 167 (37)	KO 11
Feb. 23, 1906	Los Angeles	Tommy Burns, 180 (24)[2]	Marvin Hart, 188 (29)	20
Dec. 26, 1908	Sydney, Australia	Jack Johnson, 196 (30)	Tommy Burns, 176 (29)	KO 14
April 5, 1915	Havana, Cuba	Jess Willard, 230 (33)	Jack Johnson, 205½ (37)	KO 26
July 4, 1919	Toledo, Ohio	Jack Dempsey, 187 (24)	Jess Willard, 245 (37)	KO 3
Sept. 23, 1926	Philadelphia	Gene Tunney, 189 (28)[3]	Jack Dempsey, 190 (31)	10
June 12, 1930	New York	Max Schmeling, 188 (24)	Jack Sharkey, 197 (27)	WF 4
June 21, 1932	Long Island City	Jack Sharkey, 205 (29)	Max Schmeling, 188 (26)	15
June 29, 1933	Long Island City	Primo Carnera, 260½ (26)	Jack Sharkey, 201 (30)	KO 6
June 14, 1934	Long Island City	Max Baer, 209½ (25)	Primo Carnera, 263¼ (27)	KO 11
June 13, 1935	Long Island City	Jim Braddock, 193¾ (29)	Max Baer, 209½ (26)	15
June 22, 1937	Chicago	Joe Louis, 197¼ (23)	Jim Braddock, 197 (31)	KO 8
June 22, 1949	Chicago	Ezzard Charles, 181¾ (27)[4]	Joe Walcott, 195½ (35)	15
Sept. 27, 1950	New York	Ezzard Charles, 184½ (29)[5]	Joe Louis, 218 (36)	15
July 18, 1951	Pittsburgh	Joe Walcott, 194 (37)	Ezzard Charles, 182 (30)	KO 7
Sept. 23, 1952	Philadelphia	Rocky Marciano, 184 (29)[6]	Joe Walcott, 196 (38)	KO13
Nov. 30, 1956	Chicago	Floyd Patterson, 182¼ (21)	Archie Moore, 187¾ (42)	KO 5
June 26, 1959	New York	Ingemar Johansson, 196 (26)	Floyd Patterson, 182 (24)	KO 3
June 20, 1960	New York	Floyd Patterson, 190 (25)	Ingemar Johansson, 194¾ (27)	KO 5
Sept. 25, 1962	Chicago	Sonny Liston, 214 (28)	Floyd Patterson, 189 (27)	KO 1
Feb. 25, 1964	Miami Beach, Fla.	Cassius Clay (Muhammad Ali), 210 (22)[7]	Sonny Liston, 218 (30)	KO 7
March 4, 1968	New York	Joe Frazier, 204½ (24)[8]	Buster Mathis, 243½ (23)	KO 11
April 27, 1968	Oakland, Calif.	Jimmy Ellis, 197 (28)[9]	Jerry Quarry, 195 (22)	15
Feb. 16, 1970	New York	Joe Frazier, 205 (26)[10]	Jimmy Ellis, 201 (29)	KO 5
Jan. 22, 1973	Kingston, Jamaica	George Foreman, 217½ (24)	Joe Frazier, 214 (29)	KO 2
Oct. 30, 1974	Kinshasa, Zaire	Muhammad Ali, 216½ (32)	George Foreman, 220 (26)	KO 8
Feb. 15, 1978	Las Vegas, Nev.	Leon Spinks, 197 (25)	Muhammad Ali, 224½ (36)	15
June 9, 1978	Las Vegas, Nev.	Larry Holmes, 212 (28)[11]	Ken Norton, 220 (32)	15
Sept. 15, 1978	New Orleans	Muhammad Ali, 221 (36)[12]	Leon Spinks, 201 (25)	15
Oct. 20, 1979	Pretoria, S. Africa	John Tate, 240 (24)[13]	Gerrie Coetzee, 222 (24)	15
March 31, 1980	Knoxville, Tenn.	Mike Weaver, 207½ (27)	John Tate, 232 (25)	KO 15
Dec. 10, 1982	Las Vegas, Nev.	Michael Dokes, 216 (24)	Mike Weaver, 209½ (30)	KO 1
Sept. 23, 1983	Richfield, Ohio	Gerrie Coetzee, 215 (28)	Michael Dokes, 217 (25)	KO 10
March 9, 1984	Las Vegas, Nev.	Tim Witherspoon, 220½ (26)[14]	Greg Page, 239½ (25)	12
Aug. 31, 1984	Las Vegas, Nev.	Pinklon Thomas, 216 (26)	Tim Witherspoon, 216 (26)	12
Nov. 9, 1984	Las Vegas, Nev.	Larry Holmes, 221½ (35)[15]	James Smith, 227 (31)	KO 12
Dec. 1, 1984	Sun City, S. Africa	Greg Page, 236 (25)[16]	Gerry Coetzee, 217 (29)	KO 8
April 29, 1985	Buffalo, N.Y.	Tony Tubbs, 229 (26)[16]	Greg Page, 239½ (26)	15
Sept. 21,1985	Las Vegas, Nev.	Michael Spinks, 200 (29)	Larry Holmes, 221 (35)	15
Jan. 17, 1986	Atlanta, Ga.	Tim Witherspoon, 227 (28)	Tony Tubbs, 229 (27)	15
Nov. 23, 1986	Las Vegas, Nev.	Mike Tyson, 217 (20)[17]	Trevor Berbick, 220 (29)	KO 2
Dec. 12, 1986	New York, N.Y.	James Smith, 230 (33)[16]	Tim Witherspoon, 218 (29)	KO 1
March 7, 1987	Las Vegas, Nev.	Mike Tyson, 217 (20)[16]	James Smith, 230 (33)	12
Feb. 10, 1990	Tokyo	James "Buster" Douglas, 231½ (29)[18]	Mike Tyson, (220) (23)	KO 10

Date	Where held	Winner, weight, age	Loser, weight, age	Rounds
Oct. 25, 1990	Las Vegas, Nev.	Evander Holyfield, 208 (28)	James "Buster" Douglas, 246 (30)	KO 3
Nov. 13, 1992	Las Vegas, Nev.	Riddick Bowe,[19] 235 (25)	Evander Holyfield, 205 (30)	12
Nov. 6, 1993	Las Vegas, Nev.	Evander Holyfield, 217 (30)	Riddick Bowe, 246 (26)	12
April 22, 1994	Las Vegas, Nev.	Michael Moorer, 214 (26)	Evander Holyfield,[20] 214 (31)	12
Sept 24, 1994	London	Oliver McCall,[21] 228 (29)	Lennox Lewis, 238 (28)	2
Nov. 5, 1994	Las Vegas, Nev.	George Foreman,[22] 250 (45)	Michael Moorer, 222 (26)	10
April 8, 1995	Las Vegas, Nev.	Bruce Seldon,[23] 232 (28)	Tony Tucker, 238 (36)	7
Dec. 9, 1995	Stuttgart, Ger.	Frans Botha,[24] 227 (28)	Axel Schulz, 222 (27)	12
March 16, 1996	Las Vegas, Nev.	Mike Tyson,[25] 220 (29)	Frank Bruno, 247 (34)	3
June 22, 1996	Dortmund, Ger.	Michael Moorer, 222 (29)	Axel Schulz, 222 (27)	12
Sept. 7, 1996	Las Vegas, Nev.	Mike Tyson, 219 (30)	Bruce Seldon, 229 (29)	1
Nov. 9, 1996	Las Vegas, Nev.	Evander Holyfield,[23] 215 (34)	Mike Tyson, 222 (30)	11
Feb. 7, 1997	Las Vegas, Nev.	Lennox Lewis,[25] 251 (31)	Oliver McCall, 237 (30)	5
Nov. 8, 1997	Las Vegas, Nev.	Evander Holyfield,[26] 214 (35)	Michael Moorer, 223 (30)	8
Nov. 13, 1999	Las Vegas, Nev.	Lennox Lewis,[23, 27] 240 (33)	Evander Holyfield, 217 (36)	12
Aug. 13, 2000	Las Vegas, Nev.	Evander Holyfield,[23] 221 (37)	John Ruiz, 224 (24)	12

1. Jeffries retired as champion in March 1905. He named Marvin Hart and Jack Root as leading contenders and agreed to referee their fight in Reno, Nev., on July 3, 1905, with the stipulation that he would term the winner the champion. Hart, 190 (28), knocked out Root, 171 (29), in the 12th round. 2. Burns claimed the title after defeating Hart. 3. Tunney retired as champion after defeating Tom Heeney on July 26, 1928. 4. After Louis announced his retirement as champion on March 1, 1949, Charles won recognition from the National Boxing Association as champion by defeating Walcott. 5. Charles gained undisputed recognition as champion by defeating Louis, who came out of retirement. 6. Retired as champion April 27, 1956. 7. The World Boxing Association (WBA) later withdrew its recognition of Clay as champion and declared the winner of a bout between Ernie Terrell and Eddie Machen would gain its version of the title. Terrell, 199 (25), won a 15-round decision from Machen, 192 (32), in Chicago on March 5, 1965. Clay, 212¼ (25) and Terrell, 212½ (27), met in Houston on Feb. 6, 1967, Clay winning a 15-round decision. 8. Winner recognized by N.Y., Mass., Maine, Ill., Tex. and Pa. to fill vacated title when Clay was stripped of championship for failing to accept U.S. Induction. 9. Bout was final of eight-man tournament to fill Clay's place and is recognized by World Boxing Association. 10. Bout settled controversy over title. 11. Holmes won World Boxing Council title after WBC had withdrawn recognition of Spinks, March 18, 1978, and awarded its title to Norton. WBC said Spinks had reneged on agreement to fight Norton. 12. Ali regained World Boxing Association championship. 13. Tate won WBA title after Ali retired and left it vacant. 14. Tim Witherspoon and Greg Page fought for the WBC heavyweight title vacated by Larry Holmes, who could not come to agreement on a deal to fight Page, the No. 1 contender. Holmes declared he would fight under the banner of the International Boxing Federation (IBF). Several dates were set and postponed for fights between Holmes and Gerry Coetzee, the WBA champ, the latest being Nov. 16, 1984. 15. First fight under banner of International Boxing Federation. 16. New WBA champion. 17. New WBC champion. 18. New undisputed champion. 19. The WBC stripped Bowe of its version of the title in December 1992 and named Lennox Lewis champion. 20. After the loss, Holyfield retired. 21. New WBC champion. Lennox Lewis had been champion in 1992 and had won three title defenses before losing to McCall. 22. For combined WBA/IBF titles. Later WBA stripped Foreman of title for failing to fight no. 1 contender Tony Tucker. IBF also stripped Foreman on June 29, 1995. 23. New WBA champion. 24. Botha later tested positive for steroids and was stripped of the title. 25. New WBC champion. 26. New IBF champion. 27. Surrendered WBA title to fight Michael Grant in unsanctioned bout.

OTHER WORLD BOXING TITLEHOLDERS
(Through Sept. 2, 2000)

Light Heavyweight

1903	Jack Root, George Gardner	1971	Vicente Rondon (WBA), Bob Foster (WBC)	1982	Dwight Braxton (WBC), Michael Spinks (WBA)
1903–05	Bob Fitzsimmons	1972–73	Bob Foster (WBA, WBC)	1983	Michael Spinks (undisputed)
1905–12	Philadelphia Jack O'Brien[1]	1974	John Conteh (WBA), Bob Foster (WBC)[1, 4]	1984	Michael Spinks (undisputed)
1912–16	Jack Dillon	1975–76	Victor Galindez (WBA), John Conteh (WBC)	1985	Michael Spinks (undisputed)[5]
1916–20	Battling Levinsky	1977	Victor Galindez (WBA), John Conteh (WBC),[4] Miguel Cuello (WBC)	1986	Marvin Johnson (WBA), Dennis Andries (WBC)
1920–22	Georges Carpentier				
1923	Battling Siki				
1923–25	Mike McTigue	1978	Victor Galindez (WBA), Mike Rossman (WBA), Miguel Cuello (WBC), Mate Parlov (WBC), Marvin Johnson (WBC)	1987	Thomas Hearns (WBA), Virgil Hill (WBA), Bobby Czyz (IBF)
1925–26	Paul Berlenbach				
1926–27	Jack Delaney[2]				
1927	Mike McTigue				
1927–29	Tommy Loughran			1988	Charles Williams (IBF), Virgil Hill (WBA), Donny LaLonde (WBC), Sugar Ray Leonard (WBC)
1930	Jimmy Slattery	1979	Mike Rossman (WBA), Victor Galindez (WBA), Marvin Johnson (WBA), Matthew (Franklin) Saad Muhammad (WBC)		
1930–34	Maxie Rosenbloom				
1934–35	Bob Olin				
1935–39	John Henry Lewis			1989	Dennis Andries (WBC), Virgil Hill (WBA), Charles Williams (IBF), Jeff Harding (WBC)
1939	Melio Bettina	1980	Matthew Saad Muhammad (WBC), Marvin Johnson (WBA), Eddie (Gregory) Mustafa Muhammad (WBA)		
1939–41	Billy Conn[2]				
1941	Anton Christoforidis (NBA)				
1941–48	Gus Lesnevich			1990	Virgil Hill (WBA), Charles Williams (IBF), Jeff Harding (WBC), Dennis Andries (WBC)
1948–50	Freddie Mills				
1950–52	Joey Maxim				
1952–61	Archie Moore[3]	1981	Matthew Saad Muhammad (WBC), Eddie Mustafa Muhammad (WBA), Michael Spinks (WBA), Dwight Braxton (WBC)		
1961–63	Harold Johnson			1991	Virgil Hill (WBA), Thomas Hearns (WBA), Dennis Andries (WBC), Charles Williams (IBF)
1963–65	Willie Pastrano				
1965–66	José Torres				
1966–67	Dick Tiger				
1968	Dick Tiger, Bob Foster				
1969–70	Bob Foster				

1992	Charles Williams (IBF), James Waring (IBF), Jeff Harding (WBC)
1993	Virgil Hill (WBA), Jeff Harding (WBC), Henry Maske (IBF)
1994	Virgil Hill (WBA), Mike McCallum (WBC), Henry Maske (IBF)
1995	Virgil Hill (WBA), Fabio Tiozzo (WBC), Henry Maske (IBF)
1996–97	Virgil Hill (WBA), Fabio Tiozzo (WBC), Henry Maske (IBF)
1998	Roy Jones (WBA, WBC), Reggie Johnson (IBF)
1999–2000	Roy Jones (WBA, WBC, IBF)

1. Retired. 2. Abandoned title. 3. NBA withdrew recognition in 1961, New York Commission in 1962; recognized thereafter only by California and Europe. 4. WBC withdrew recognition. 5. Spinks relinquished title in 1985 to fight for heavyweight title.

Middleweight

1867–72	Tom Chandler
1872–81	George Rooke
1881–82	Mike Donovan[1]
1884–91	Jack (Nonpareil) Dempsey
1891–97	Bob Fitzsimmons[2]
1908	Stanley Ketchel, Billy Papke
1908–10	Stanley Ketchel[3]
1913	Frank Klaus
1913–14	George Chip
1914–17	Al McCoy
1917–20	Mike O'Dowd
1920–23	Johnny Wilson
1923–26	Harry Greb
1926	Tiger Flowers
1926–31	Mickey Walker[2]
1931–41	Gorilla Jones, Ben Jeby, Marcel Thil, Lou Brouillard, Vince Dundee, Teddy Yarosz, Babe Risko, Freddy Steele, Al Hostak, Solly Kreiger, Fred Apostoli, Cerferino Garcia, Ken Overlin, Billy Soose, Tony Zale[4]
1941–47	Tony Zale
1947–48	Rocky Graziano
1948	Tony Zale
1948–49	Marcel Cerdan
1949–51	Jake LaMotta
1951–52	Ray Robinson[1]
1952	Ray Robinson, Randy Turpin
1953–55	Carl Olson
1955–57	Ray Robinson[5]
1957	Gene Fullmer, Ray Robinson
1957–58	Carmen Basilio
1958–60	Ray Robinson[6]
1959–62	Gene Fullmer (NBA)
1960–61	Paul Pender[7]
1961–62	Terry Downes[1]
1962	Paul Pender[1]
1962–63	Dick Tiger
1963–65	Joey Giardello
1965–66	Dick Tiger
1966	Emile Griffith
1967	Nino Benvenuti, Emile Griffith
1968	Emile Griffith, Nino Benvenuti
1969	Nino Benvenuti
1970	Nino Benvenuti, Carlos Monzon
1971–73	Carlos Monzon
1974–75	Carlos Monzon (WBA), Rodrigo Valdez (WBC)
1976	Carlos Monzon (WBA, WBC), Rodrigo Valdez (WBC)
1977	Carlos Monzon (WBA, WBC),[1] Rodrigo Valdez (WBA, WBC)
1978	Rodrigo Valdez, Hugo Corro
1979	Hugo Corro, Vito Antuofermo
1980	Vito Antuofermo, Alan Minter, Marvin Hagler
1981	Marvin Hagler
1982–86	Marvin Hagler (undisputed)
1987	Marvin Hagler (undisputed), Sugar Ray Leonard (undisputed)
1988	Sumbu Kalambay (WBA), Thomas Hearns (WBC), Iran Barkley (WBC), Frank Tate (IBF), Michael Nunn (IBF), James Kinchen (NABF)
1989	Michael Nunn (IBF), Mike McCallum (WBA), Iran Barkley (WBC), Roberto Duran (WBC)
1990	Michael McCallum (WBA), Michael Nunn (IBF), Iran Barkley (WBC)
1991	Michael Nunn (IBF), James Toney (IBF), Michael McCallum (WBA)
1992	James Toney (IBF), Julian Jackson (WBC), Reggie Johnson (WBA)
1993	Reggie Johnson (WBA), Gerald McClellan (WBA), Roy Jones (IBF)
1994	Julian Jackson (WBA), Gerald McClellan (WBA), Roy Jones (IBF)
1995	Jorge Castro (WBA), Julian Jackson (WBC), Bernard Hopkins (IBF)
1996	William Joppy (WBA), Keith Holmes (WBC), Bernard Hopkins (IBF)
1997	Shinji Takehara (WBA), Quincy Taylor (WBC), Bernard Hopkins (IBF)
1998	William Joppy (WBA), Hassine Cherifi (WBC), Bernard Hopkins (IBF)
1999–2000	William Joppy (WBA), Keith Holmes (WBC), Bernard Hopkins (IBF)

1. Retired. 2. Abandoned title. 3. Died. 4. National Boxing Association and New York Commission disagreed on champions. Those listed were accepted by one or the other until Zale gained world-wide recognition. 5. Ended retirement in 1954. 6. NBA withdrew recognition. 7. Recognized by New York, Massachusetts, and Europe.

Welterweight

1892–94	Mysterious Billy Smith
1894–96	Tommy Ryan
1896	Kid McCoy[1]
1896–1900	Mysterious Billy Smith
1900	Rube Ferns
1900–01	Matty Matthews
1901	Ruby Ferns
1901–04	Joe Walcott
1904	Dixie Kid[1]
1904–06	Joe Walcott
1906–07	Honey Mellody
1907	Mike (Twin) Sullivan[1]
1915–19	Ted Lewis
1919–22	Jack Britton
1922–26	Mickey Walker
1926–27	Pete Latzo
1927–29	Joe Dundee
1929–30	Jackie Fields
1930	Young Jack Thompson
1930–31	Tommy Freeman
1931	Young Jack Thompson
1931–32	Lou Brouillard
1932–33	Jackie Fields
1933	Young Corbett 3rd
1933–34	Jimmy McLarnin, Barney Ross
1934–35	Jimmy McLarnin
1935–38	Barney Ross
1938–40	Henry Armstrong
1940–41	Fritzie Zivic
1941–46	Freddie Cochrane
1946	Marty Servo[2]
1946–51	Ray Robinson[1]
1951	Johnny Bratton (NBA)
1951–54	Kid Gavilan
1954–55	Johnny Saxton
1955	Tony DeMarco
1955–56	Carmen Basilio
1956	Johnny Saxton
1956–57	Carmen Basilio[1]
1958	Virgil Akins
1959–60	Don Jordan
1960–61	Benny (Kid) Paret
1961	Emile Griffith
1961–62	Benny (Kid) Paret
1962–63	Emile Griffith, Luis Rodriguez
1963–66	Emile Griffith[1]
1966–69	Curtis Cokes
1969	Curtis Cokes, José Napoles
1970	José Napoles, Billy Backus
1971	Billy Backus, José Napoles
1972–74	José Napoles
1975	José Napoles (WBA, WBC),[3] Angel Espada (WBA), John Stracey (WBC)
1976	Angel Espada (WBA), José Cuevas (WBA), John Stracey (WBC), Carlos Palomino
1977–78	José Cuevas (WBA), Carlos Palomino (WBC)
1979	José Cuevas (WBA), Carlos Palomino (WBC), Wilfredo Benitez (WBC)
1980	José Cuevas (WBA), Ray Leonard (WBC), Roberto Duran (WBC), Thomas Hearns (WBA)
1981	Ray Leonard (WBC), Thomas Hearns (WBA), Ray Leonard (WBC, WBA)
1982	Ray Leonard
1983–85	Donald Curry (WBA), Milton McCrory (WBC)
1985–86	Donald Curry (undisputed)
1987	Mark Breland (WBA), Marlon Starling (WBA), Lloyd Honeyghan (IBF)
1988	Marlon Starling (WBA), Tomas Molinares (WBA), Lloyd Honeyghan (WBC), Simon Brown (IBF)

1989	Mark Breland (WBA), Marlon Starling (WBC), Simon Brown (IBF)	
1990	Mark Breland (WBA), Aaron Davis (WBA), Simon Brown (IBF), Marlon Starling (WBC), Maurice Blocker (WBC)	
1991	Meldrick Taylor (WBA), Simon Brown (IBF, WBC)	
1992	Meldrick Taylor (WBA), James "Buddy" McGirt (WBC), Maurice Blocker (IBF)	
1993	Cristiano Espana (WBA), Pernell Whitaker (WBC), Felix Trinidad (IBF)	
1994	Ike Quartey (WBA), Pernell Whitaker (WBC), Felix Trinidad (IBF)	
1995	Ike Quartey (WBA), Pernell Whitaker (WBC), Felix Trinidad (IBF)	
1996–97	Ike Quartey (WBA), Pernell Whitaker (WBC), Felix Trinidad (IBF)	
1998	Ike Quartey (WBA), Oscar De La Hoya (WBC), Felix Trinidad (IBF)	
1999	James Page (WBA), Oscar De La Hoya (WBC), Felix Trinidad (IBF, WBC)	
2000	James Page (WBA), Shane Mosley (WBC), Vacant (IBF)	

1. Retired. 2. Abandoned title. 3. WBA withdrew recognition.

Lightweight

1869–99	Kid Lavigne
1899–	
1902	Frank Erne
1902–08	Joe Gans
1908–10	Battling Nelson
1910–12	Ad Wolgast
1912–14	Willie Ritchie
1914–17	Freddy Welsh
1917–25	Benny Leonard[1]
1925	Jimmy Goodrich
1925–26	Rocky Kansas
1926–30	Sammy Mandell
1930	Al Singer
1930–33	Tony Canzoneri
1933–35	Barney Ross[2]
1935–36	Tony Canzoneri
1936–38	Lou Ambers
1938–39	Henry Armstrong
1939–40	Lou Ambers
1940–41	Lew Jenkins
1941–42	Sammy Angott[1]
1943–47	Beau Jack (N.Y.), Bob Montgomery (N.Y.), Sammy Angott (NBA), Juan Zurita (NBA), Ike Williams (NBA)
1947–51	Ike Williams
1951–52	James Carter
1952	Lauro Salas
1952–54	James Carter
1954	Paddy DeMarco
1954–55	James Carter
1955–56	Wallace Smith
1956–62	Joe Brown
1962–65	Carlos Ortiz
1965	Ismael Laguna
1965–68	Carlos Ortiz
1968	Teo Cruz
1969	Teo Cruz, Mando Ramos
1970	Mando Ramos, Ismael Laguna, Ken Buchanan
1971	Ken Buchanan (WBA), Mando Ramos (WBC), Pedro Carrasco (WBC)
1972	Ken Buchanan (WBA), Roberto Duran (WBA), Pedro Carrasco (WBC), Mando Ramos (WBC), Chango Carmona (WBC), Rodolfo Gonzalez (WBC)
1973	Roberto Duran (WBA), Rodolfo Gonzalez (WBC)
1974	Rodolfo Gonzalez (WBC), Guts Ishimatsu (WBC)
1975	Roberto Duran (WBA), Guts Ishimatsu (WBC)
1976	Roberto Duran (WBA), Guts Ishimatsu (WBC), Esteban De Jesus (WBC)
1977	Roberto Duran (WBA), Esteban De Jesus (WBC)
1978	Roberto Duran (WBA, WBC)
1979	Roberto Duran,[2] Jim Watt (WBC), Ernesto Espana (WBA)
1980	Ernesto Espana (WBA), Hilmer Kenty (WBA), Jim Watt (WBC)
1981	Hilmer Kenty (WBA), Sean O'Grady (WBA), James Watt (WBC), Alexis Arguello (WBC), Arturo Frias (WBA)
1982	Arturo Frias (WBA), Ray Mancini (WBA), Alexis Arguello (WBC)
1983	Edwin Rosario (WBC), Ray Mancini (WBA)
1984	Edwin Rosario (WBC), Livingstone Bramble (WBA)
1985	Jose Luis Ramirez (WBC), Hector Camacho (WBC), Livingstone Bramble (WBA)
1986	Hector Camacho (WBC), Livingstone Bramble (WBA), Jim Paul (IBF)
1987	Edwin Rosario (WBA), Jose Luis Ramirez (WBC), Greg Haugen (IBF)
1988	Jose Luis Ramirez (WBC), Julio Cesar Chavez (WBA), Greg Haugen (IBF), Julio Cesar Chavez (WBC & WBA title unified)
1989	Pernell Whitaker (IBF, WBC), Edwin Rosario (WBA)
1990	Pernell Whitaker (IBF, WBC), Juan Nazario (WBA)
1991	Pernell Whitaker (IBF, WBA, WBC)
1992	Pernell Whitaker (IBF, WBA, WBC),[3] Joey Gamache (WBA)
1993	Dingaan Thobela (WBA), Angel Gonzalez (WBC), Freddie Pendleton (IBF)
1994	Orzubek Nazarov (WBA), Angel Gonzalez (WBC), Rafael Ruelas (IBF)
1995	Orzubek Nazarov (WBA), Angel Gonzalez (WBC), Oscar De La Hoya (IBF)
1996	Gusshie Nazarov (WBA), Jean Baptiste Mendy (WBC), Phillip Holiday (IBF)
1997	Orzubek Nazarov (WBA), Jean Baptiste Mendy (WBC), Philip Holiday (IBF)
1998	Jean Baptiste Mendy (WBA), Cesar Bazan (WBC), Shane Mosley (IBF)
1999	Stefano Zoff (WBA), Stevie Johnston (WBC), Paul Spadafora (IBF)
2000	Takanori Hatakeyama (WBA), Jose Luis Castillo (WBC), Paul Spadafora (IBF)

1. Retired. 2. Abandoned title. 3. Moving up in weight class, so resigned titles.

Featherweight

1889	Dal Hawkins[1]
1890	Billy Murphy
1892–	
1900	George Dixon
1900–01	Terry McGovern
1901	Young Corbett[1]
1901–12	Abe Attell
1912–23	Johnny Kilbane
1923	Eugene Criqui
1923–25	Johnny Dundee[1]
1925–27	Louis (Kid) Kaplan[1]
1927–28	Benny Bass
1928	Tony Canzoneri
1928–29	Andre Routis
1929–32	Battling Battalino[1]
1932	Tommy Paul (NBA), Kid Chocolate (N.Y.)
1933–36	Freddie Miller
1936–37	Petey Sarron
1937–38	Henry Armstrong[1]
1938–40	Joey Archibald
1940–41	Harry Jefra, Joey Archibald
1941–42	Chalky Wright
1942–48	Willie Pep
1948–49	Sandy Saddler[2]
1949–50	Willie Pep
1950–57	Sandy Saddler
1957–59	Kid Bassey
1959–63	Davey Moore
1963–64	Sugar Ramos
1964–67	Vicente Saldivar[2]
1968	Howard Winstone, José Legra,[3] Paul Rojas (WBA), Sho Saijo (WBA)
1969	Sho Saijo (WBA), Johnny Famechon[3]
1970	Sho Saijo (WBA), Johnny Famechon,[3] Vicente Salvidar,[3] Kuniaki Shibata[3]
1971	Sho Saijo (WBA), Antonio Gomez (WBA), Kuniaki Shibata (WBC)
1972	Antonio Gomez (WBA), Ernesto Marcel (WBA), Kuniaki Shibata (WBC), Clemente Sanchez (WBC), José Legra (WBC)
1973	Ernesto Marcel (WBA), José Legra (WBC), Eder Jofre (WBC)
1974	Ernesto Marcel (WBA),[2] Ruben Olivares (WBA), Alexis Arguello (WBA), Eder Jofre (WBC), Bobby Chacon (WBC)
1975	Alexis Arguello (WBA), Bobby Chacon (WBC), Ruben Olivares (WBC), David Kotey (WBC)

950   S P O R T S — BOXING

1976	Alexis Arguello (WBA),[2]
	David Kotey (WBC),
	Danny Lopez (WBC)
1977	Rafael Ortega (WBA),
	Danny Lopez (WBC)
1978	Rafael Ortega (WBA),
	Cecilio Lastra (WBA),
	Eusebio Pedroza (WBA),
	Danny Lopez (WBC)
1979	Eusebio Pedroza (WBA),
	Danny Lopez (WBC)
1980	Eusebio Pedroza (WBA),
	Danny Lopez (WBC),
	Salvador Sanchez (WBC)
1981	Eusebio Pedroza (WBA),
	Salvador Sanchez (WBC)
1982	Eusebio Pedroza (WBA),
	Salvador Sanchez (WBC)[4]
1983	Juan Laporte (WBC),
	Eusebio Pedroza (WBA)
1984	Wilfred Gomez (WBC),
	Eusebio Pedroza (WBA)
1985	Eusebio Pedroza (WBA),
	Barry McGuigan (WBA),
	Azumah Nelson (WBC)
1986	Barry McGuigan (WBA),
	Stevie Cruz (WBA),
	Azumah Nelson (WBC)
1987	Azumah Nelson (WBC),
	Antonio Esparragoza (WBA)
1988	Calvin Grove (IBF),
	Jorge Paez (IBF),
	Antonio Esparragoza (WBA),
	Jeff Fenech (WBC)
1989	Jorge Paez (IBF),
	Antonio Esparragoza (WBA),
	Jeff Fenech (WBC)
1990	Marcos Villasana (WBC),
	Antonio Esparragoza (WBA),
	Jorge Paez (IBF)
1991	Yung-Kyun Park (WBA),
	Troy Dorsey (IBF),
	Marcos Villagana (WBC)
1992	Paul Hodkinson (WBC),
	Manuel Medina (IBF),
	Yung-Kyun Park (WBA)
1993	Yung-Kyun Park (WBA),
	Goyo Vargas (WBC),
	Tom Johnson (IBF)
1994	Eloy Rojas (WBA),
	Kevin Kelley (WBC),
	Tom Johnson (IBF)
1995	Eloy Rojas (WBA),
	Alejandro Gonzalez (WBC),
	Tom Johnson (IBF)
1996	Wilfredo Vázquez (WBA),
	Luisto Espinoza (WBC),
	Tom Johnson (IBF)
1997	Elroy Rojas (WBA),
	Luisito Espinoza (WBC),
	Tom Johnson (IBF)
1998	Vacant (WBA),
	Luisito Espinoza (WBC),
	Manuel Medina (IBF)
1999	Freddie Norwood (WBA),
	Cesar Soto (WBC),
	Manuel Medina (IBF)
2000	Freddie Norwood (WBA),
	Guty Espadas (WBC),
	Paul Ingle (IBF)

1. Abandoned title. 2. Retired. 3. Recognized in Europe, Mexico, and Orient. 4. Killed in auto accident.

Bantamweight

1890–92	George Dixon[1]
1894–99	Jimmy Barry[2]
1899–	
1900	Terry McGovern[1]
1901	Harry Harris[1]
1902–03	Harry Forbes
1903–04	Frankie Neil
1904	Joe Bowker[1]
1905–07	Jimmy Walsh[1]
1910–14	Johnny Coulon
1914–17	Kid Williams
1917–20	Pete Herman
1920	Joe Lynch
1920–21	Joe Lynch,
	Pete Herman,
	Johnny Buff
1922	Johnny Buff,
	Joe Lynch
1923	Joe Lynch
1924	Joe Lynch,
	Abe Goldstein, Eddie "Cannonball" Martin
1925	Eddie "Cannonball" Martin, Charlie (Phil) Rosenberg[3]
1927–28	Bud Taylor (NBA)[1]
1929–34	Al Brown
1935	Al Brown,
	Baltazar Sangchili
1936	Baltazar Sangchili,
	Tony Marino,
	Sixto Escobar
1937	Sixto Escobar,
	Harry Jeffra
1938	Harry Jeffra,
	Sixto Escobar
1939–40	Sixto Escobar[2]
1940–42	Lou Salica
1942–46	Manuel Ortiz
1947	Manuel Ortiz,
	Harold Dade
1948–50	Manuel Ortiz
1950–52	Vic Toweel
1952–54	Jimmy Carruthers[2]
1954–55	Robert Cohen
1956	Robert Cohen,
	Mario D'Agata,
	Raul Macias (NBA)
1957	Mario D'Agata,
	Alphonse Halimi
1958–59	Alphonse Halimi
1959–60	Jose Becerra[2]
1960–61	Alphonse Halimi[4]
1961–62	Johnny Caldwell[4]
1961–65	Eder Jofre
1965–68	Masahika "Fighting" Harada
1968	Masahika "Fighting" Harada, Lionel Rose
1969	Lionel Rose, Ruben Olivares
1970	Ruben Olivares, Chucho Castillo
1971	Chucho Castillo, Ruben Olivares
1972	Ruben Olivares, Rafael Herrera, Enrique Pinder
1973	Enrique Pinder (WBA), Romeo Anaya (WBA), Arnold Taylor (WBA), Rodolfo Martinez (WBC), Rafael Herrera

1974	Arnold Taylor (WBA),
	Soo Hwan Hong (WBA),
	Rafael Herrera (WBC),
	Rodolfo Martinez (WBC)
1975	Soo Hwan Hong (WBA),
	Alfonso Zamora (WBA),
	Rodolfo Martinez (WBC)
1976	Alfonso Zamora (WBA),
	Rodolfo Martinez (WBC),
	Carlos Zarate (WBC)
1977	Alfonso Zamora (WBA),
	Jorge Lujan (WBA),
	Carlos Zarate (WBC)
1978	Jorge Lujan (WBA),
	Carlos Zarate (WBC)
1979	Jorge Lujan (WBA),
	Carlos Zarate (WBC),
	Lupe Pintor (WBC)
1980	Jorge Lujan (WBA),
	Lupe Pintor (WBC),
	Julian Solis (WBA),
	Jeff Chandler (WBA)
1981	Lupe Pintor (WBC),
	Jeff Chandler (WBA)
1982	Lupe Pintor (WBC),
	Jeff Chandler (WBA)
1983	Jeff Chandler (WBA),
	Albert Dauila (WBC)
1984	Richie Sandqual (WBA),
	Albert Dauila (WBC)
1985	Richard Sandoval (WBA),
	Daniel Zaragoza (WBC),
	Miguel Lora (WBC)
1986	Richard Sandoval (WBA),
	Bernardo Pinango (WBA),
	Jeff Fenech (IBF)
1987	Bernardo Pinango (WBA),
	Takuya Muguruma (WBA),
	Miguel Lora (WBC)
1988	Wilfredo Vásquez (WBA),
	Jibaro Perez (WBA),
	Moon Sung-gil (WBA),
	Orlando Canizales (IBF)
1989	Jibaro Perez (WBA),
	Moon Sung-gil (WBA),
	Orlando Canizales (IBF),
	Kaokor Galaxy (WBA),
	Luis Espinosa (WBA)
1990	Orlando Canizales (IBF),
	Jibaro Perez (WBC),
	Luis Espinosa (WBA)
1991	Greg Richardson (WBC),
	Orlando Canizales (IBF),
	Luis Espinosa (WBA)
1992	Joichiro Tatsuyoshi (WBC),
	Victor Manuel Rabanales (WBC),
	Eddie Cook (WBA),
	Orlando Gonzales (IBF)
1993	Jorge Julio (WBA),
	Byun-Jong-il (WBC),
	Orlando Canizales (IBF)
1994	John Michael Johnson (WBA),
	Yasuei Yakushiji (WBC),
	Orlando Canizales (IBF)
1995	Daorun Chuwatang (WBA),
	Yasuei Yakushiji (WBC),
	Mbulelo Botile (IBF)
1996–97	Nana Konadu (WBA),
	Wayne McCullough (WBC),
	Mbulelo Botile (IBF)
1998	Nana Konadu (WBA),
	Joichiro Tatsuyoshi (WBC),
	Tim Austin (IBF)
1999 –2000	Paulie Ayala (WBA),
	Veeraphol Sahaprom (WBC),
	Tim Austin (IBF)

1. Abandoned title. 2. Retired. 3. Deprived of title for failing to make weight. 4. Recognized in Europe.

Horse Racing

Ancient drawings on stone and bone prove that horse racing is at least 3,000 years old, but thoroughbred racing is a modern development. Practically every thoroughbred in training today traces its registered ancestry back to one or more of three sires that arrived in England about 1728 from the Near East and became known, from the names of their owners, as the Byerly Turk, the Darley Arabian, and the Godolphin Arabian. The Jockey Club (English) was founded at Newmarket in 1750 or 1751 and became the custodian of the Stud Book as well as the court of last resort in deciding turf affairs.

Horse racing took place in this country before the Revolution, but the great lift to the breeding industry came with the importation in 1798, by Col. John Hoomes of Virginia, of Diomed, winner of the Epsom Derby of 1780. Diomed's lineal descendants included such famous stars of the American turf as American Eclipse and Lexington. From 1800 to the time of the Civil War there were race courses and breeding establishments plentifully scattered through Virginia, North Carolina, South Carolina, Tennessee, Kentucky, and Louisiana.

The oldest stake event in North America is the Queen's Plate, a Canadian fixture that was first run in the Province of Quebec in 1836. The oldest stake event in the United States is the Travers, which was first run at Saratoga in 1864. The gambling that goes with horse racing and trickery by jockeys, trainers, owners, and track officials caused attacks on the sport by reformers and a demand among horse racing enthusiasts for an honest and effective control of some kind, but nothing of lasting value to racing came of this until the formation in 1894 of the Jockey Club (American).

"TRIPLE CROWN" WINNERS IN THE UNITED STATES
(Kentucky Derby, Preakness and Belmont Stakes)

Year	Horse	Owner	Year	Horse	Owner
1919	Sir Barton	J. K. L. Ross	1946	Assault	Robert J. Kleberg
1930	Gallant Fox	William Woodward	1948	Citation	Warren Wright
1935	Omaha	William Woodward	1973	Secretariat	Meadow Stable
1937	War Admiral	Samuel D. Riddle	1977	Seattle Slew	Karen Taylor
1941	Whirlaway	Warren Wright	1978	Affirmed	Louis Wolfson
1943	Count Fleet	Mrs. John Hertz			

KENTUCKY DERBY
Churchill Downs; 3-year-olds; 1¼ miles.

Year	Winner	Jockey	Wt.	Win val.	Year	Winner	Jockey	Wt.	Win val.
1919	Sir Barton	J. Loftus	112½	$20,825	1953	Dark Star	H. Moreno	126	$90,050
1920	Paul Jones	T. Rice	126	30,375	1954	Determine	R. York	126	102,050
1921	Behave Yourself	C. Thompson	126	38,450	1955	Swaps	W. Shoemaker	126	108,400
1922	Morvich	A. Johnson	126	46,775	1956	Needles	D. Erb	126	123,450
1923	Zev	E. Sande	126	53,600	1957	Iron Liege	W. Hartack	126	107,950
1924	Black Gold	J. D. Mooney	126	52,775	1958	Tim Tam	I. Valenzuela	126	116,400
1925	Flying Ebony	E. Sande	126	52,950	1959	Tomy Lee	W. Shoemaker	126	119,650
1926	Bubbling Over	A. Johnson	126	50,075	1960	Venetian Way	W. Hartack	126	114,850
1927	Whiskery	L. McAtee	126	51,000	1961	Carry Back	J. Sellers	126	120,500
1928	Reigh Count	C. Lang	126	55,375	1962	Decidedly	W. Hartack	126	119,650
1929	Clyde Van Dusen	L. McAtee	126	53,950	1963	Chateaugay	B. Baeza	126	108,900
1930	Gallant Fox	E. Sande	126	50,725	1964	Northern Dancer	W. Hartack	126	114,300
1931	Twenty Grand	C. Kurtsinger	126	48,725	1965	Lucky Debonair	W. Shoemaker	126	112,000
1932	Burgoo King	E. James	126	52,350	1966	Kauai King	D. Brumfield	126	120,500
1933	Brokers Tip	D. Meade	126	48,925	1967	Proud Clarion	R. Ussery	126	119,700
1934	Cavalcade	M. Garner	126	28,175	1968	Forward Pass[1]	I. Valenzuela	126	122,600
1935	Omaha	W. Saunders	126	39,525	1969	Majestic Prince	W. Hartack	126	113,200
1936	Bold Venture	I. Hanford	126	37,725	1970	Dust Commander	M. Manganello	126	127,800
1937	War Admiral	C. Kurtsinger	126	52,050	1971	Canonero II	G. Avila	126	145,500
1938	Lawrin	E. Arcaro	126	47,050	1972	Riva Ridge	R. Turcotte	126	140,300
1939	Johnstown	J. Stout	126	46,350	1973	Secretariat	R. Turcotte	126	155,050
1940	Gallahadion	C. Bierman	126	60,150	1974	Cannonade	A. Cordero, Jr.	126	274,000
1941	Whirlaway	E. Arcaro	126	61,275	1975	Foolish Pleasure	J. Vasquez	126	209,600
1942	Shut Out	W. D. Wright	126	64,225	1976	Bold Forbes	A. Cordero, Jr.	126	165,200
1943	Count Fleet	J. Longden	126	60,725	1977	Seattle Slew	J. Cruguet	126	214,700
1944	Pensive	C. McCreary	126	64,675	1978	Affirmed	S. Cauthen	126	186,900
1945	Hoop Jr.	E. Arcaro	126	64,850	1979	Spectacular Bid	R. Franklin	126	228,650
1946	Assault	W. Mehrtens	126	96,400	1980	Genuine Risk	J. Vasquez	121	250,550
1947	Jet Pilot	E. Guerin	126	92,160	1981	Pleasant Colony	J. Velasquez	126	317,200
1948	Citation	E. Arcaro	126	83,400	1982	Gato del Sol	E. Delahoussaye	126	417,600
1949	Ponder	S. Brooks	126	91,600	1983	Sunny's Halo	E. Delahoussaye	126	426,000
1950	Middleground	W. Boland	126	92,650	1984	Swale	L. Pincay, Jr.	126	537,400
1951	Count Turf	C. McCreary	126	98,050	1985	Spend a Buck	A. Cordero, Jr.	126	406,800
1952	Hill Gail	E. Arcaro	126	96,300	1986	Ferdinand	W. Shoemaker	126	609,400

Year	Winner	Jockey	Wt.	Win val.	Year	Winner	Jockey	Wt.	Win val.
1987	Alysheba	C. McCarron	126	$618,600	1994	Go For Gin	C. McCarron	126	$628,800
1988	Winning Colors	G. Stevens	121	611,200	1995	Thunder Gulch	G. Stevens	126	707,400
1989	Sunday Silence	P. Valenzuela	126	574,200	1996	Grindstone	J. Bailey	126	869,800
1990	Unbridled	C. Perret	126	581,000	1997	Silver Charm	G. Stevens	126	700,000
1991	Strike the Gold	C. Antley	126	655,800	1998	Real Quiet	K. Desormeaux	126	738,800
1992	Lil E. Tee	P. Day	126	724,800	1999	Charismatic	C. Antley	126	886,200
1993	Sea Hero	J. Bailey	126	735,900	2000	Fusaichi Pegasus	K. Desormeaux	126	888,400

1. Dancer's Image finished first but was disqualified after traces of drug were found in his system.

PREAKNESS STAKES
Pimlico; 3-year-olds; 1¾₁₆ miles.

Year	Winner	Jockey	Wt.	Win val.	Year	Winner	Jockey	Wt.	Win val.
1919	Sir Barton	J. Loftus	126	$24,500	1961	Carry Back	J. Sellers	126	$126,200
1920	Man o' War	C. Kummer	126	(¹)	1962	Greek Money	J. Rotz	126	135,800
1921	Broomspun	F. Coltiletti	126	(¹)	1963	Candy Spots	W. Shoemaker	126	127,500
1922	Pillory	L. Morris	126	(¹)	1964	Northern Dancer	W. Hartack	126	124,200
1923	Vigil	B. Marinelli	126	(¹)	1965	Tom Rolfe	R. Turcotte	126	128,100
1924	Nellie Morse	J. Merimee	126	(¹)	1966	Kauai King	D. Brumfield	126	129,000
1925	Coventry	C. Kummer	126	(¹)	1967	Damascus	W. Shoemaker	126	141,500
1926	Display	J. Maiben	126	(¹)	1968	Forward Pass	I. Valenzuela	126	142,700
1927	Bostonian	W. Abel	126	(¹)	1969	Majestic Prince	W. Hartack	126	129,500
1928	Victorian	S. Workman	126	(¹)	1970	Personality	E. Belmonte	126	151,300
1929	Dr. Freeland	L. Schaefer	126	(¹)	1971	Canonero II	G. Avila	126	137,400
1930	Gallant Fox	E. Sande	126	51,925	1972	Bee Bee Bee	E. Nelson	126	135,300
1931	Mate	G. Ellis	126	48,225	1973	Secretariat	R. Turcotte	126	129,900
1932	Burgoo King	E. James	126	50,375	1974	Little Current	M. Rivera	126	156,000
1933	Head Play	C. Kurtsinger	126	26,850	1975	Master Derby	D. McHargue	126	158,100
1934	High Quest	R. Jones	126	25,175	1976	Elocutionist	J. Lively	126	129,700
1935	Omaha	W. Saunders	126	25,325	1977	Seattle Slew	J. Cruguet	126	138,600
1936	Bold Venture	G. Woolf	126	27,325	1978	Affirmed	S. Cauthen	126	136,200
1937	War Admiral	C. Kurtsinger	126	45,600	1979	Spectacular Bid	R. Franklin	126	165,300
1938	Dauber	M. Peters	126	51,875	1980	Codex	A. Cordero	126	180,600
1939	Challedon	G. Seabo	126	53,710	1981	Pleasant Colony	J. Velasquez	126	270,800
1940	Bimelech	F.A. Smith	126	53,230	1982	Aloma's Ruler	J. Kaenel	126	209,900
1941	Whirlaway	E. Arcaro	126	49,365	1983	Deputed	D. Miller	126	251,200
1942	Alsab	B. James	126	58,175		Testamony			
1943	Count Fleet	J. Longden	126	43,190	1984	Gate Dancer	A. Cordero	126	243,600
1944	Pensive	C. McCreary	126	60,075	1985	Tank's Prospect	P. Day	126	423,200
1945	Polynesian	W.D. Wright	126	66,170	1986	Snow Chief	A. Solis	126	411,900
1946	Assault	W. Mehrtens	126	96,620	1987	Alysheba	C. McCarron	126	421,100
1947	Faultless	D. Dodson	126	98,005	1988	Risen Star	E. Delahoussaye	126	413,700
1948	Citation	E. Arcaro	126	91,870	1989	Sunday Silence	P. Valenzuela	126	438,230
1949	Capot	T. Atkinson	126	79,985	1990	Summer Squall	P. Day	126	445,900
1950	Hill Prince	E. Arcaro	126	56,115	1991	Hansel	J. Bailey	126	432,770
1951	Bold	E. Arcaro	126	83,110	1992	Pine Bluff	C. McCarron	126	484,120
1952	Blue Man	C. McCreary	126	86,135	1993	Prairie Bayou	M. Smith	126	471,835
1953	Native Dancer	E. Guerin	126	65,200	1994	Tabasco Cat	P. Day	126	447,720
1954	Hasty Road	J. Adams	126	91,600	1995	Timber Country	P. Day	126	446,810
1955	Nashua	E. Arcaro	126	67,550	1996	Louis Quatorze	P. Day	126	458,120
1956	Fabius	W. Hartack	126	84,250	1997	Silver Charm	G. Stevens	126	488,150
1957	Bold Ruler	E. Arcaro	126	65,250	1998	Real Quiet	K. Desormeaux	126	650,000
1958	Tim Tam	I. Valenzuela	126	97,900	1999	Charismatic	C. Antley	126	650,000
1959	Royal Orbit	W. Harmatz	126	136,200	2000	Red Bullet	J. Bailey	126	650,000
1960	Bally Ache	R. Ussery	126	121,000					

1. Data not available.

BELMONT STAKES
Belmont Park; 3-year-olds; 1½ miles.

Run at Jerome Park 1867 to 1890; at Morris Park 1890–94; at Belmont Park 1905–62; at Aqueduct 1963–67. Distance 1⅝ miles prior to 1874; reduced to 1½ miles, 1874; reduced to 1¼ miles, 1890; reduced to 1⅛ miles, 1893; increased to 1¼ miles, 1895; increased to 1⅜ miles, 1896; reduced to 1¼ miles in 1904; increased to 1½ miles, 1926.

Year	Winner	Jockey	Wt.	Win val.	Year	Winner	Jockey	Wt.	Win val.
1919	Sir Barton	J. Loftus	126	$11,950	1923	Zev	E. Sande	126	(¹)
1920	Man o' War	C. Kummer	126	(¹)	1924	Mad Play	E. Sande	126	(¹)
1921	Grey Lag	E. Sande	126	(¹)	1925	American Flag	A. Johnson	126	(¹)
1922	Pillory	C.H. Miller	126	(¹)	1926	Crusader	A. Johnson	126	(¹)

Year	Winner	Jockey	Wt.	Win val.	Year	Winner	Jockey	Wt.	Win val.
1927	Chance Shot	E. Sande	126	(¹)	1966	Amberoid	W. Boland	126	$117,700
1928	Vito	C. Kummer	126	(¹)	1967	Damascus	W. Shoemaker	126	104,950
1929	Blue Larkspur	M. Garner	126	(¹)	1968	Stage Door	H. Gustines	126	117,700
1930	Gallant Fox	E. Sande	126	$66,040		Johnny			
1931	Twenty Grand	C. Kurtsinger	126	58,770	1969	Arts and Letters	B. Baeza	126	104,050
1932	Faireno	T. Malley	126	55,120	1970	High Echelon	J. Rotz	126	115,000
1933	Hurryoff	M. Garner	126	49,490	1971	Pass Catcher	R. Blum	126	97,710
1934	Peace Chance	W.D. Wright	126	43,410	1972	Riva Ridge	R. Turcotte	126	93,540
1935	Omaha	W. Saunders	126	35,480	1973	Secretariat	R. Turcotte	126	90,120
1936	Granville	J. Stout	126	29,800	1974	Little Current	M. Rivera	126	101,970
1937	War Admiral	C. Kurtsinger	126	38,020	1975	Avatar	W. Shoemaker	126	116,160
1938	Pasteurized	J. Stout	126	34,530	1976	Bold Forbes	A. Cordero, Jr.	126	117,000
1939	Johnstown	J. Stout	126	37,020	1977	Seattle Slew	J. Cruguet	126	109,080
1940	Bimelech	F.A. Smith	126	35,030	1978	Affirmed	S. Cauthen	126	110,580
1941	Whirlaway	E. Arcaro	126	39,770	1979	Coastal	R. Hernandez	126	161,400
1942	Shut Out	E. Arcaro	126	44,520	1980	Temperence Hill	E. Maple	126	176,220
1943	Count Fleet	J. Longden	126	35,340	1981	Summing	G. Martens	126	170,580
1944	Bounding Home	G.L. Smith	126	55,000	1982	Conquistador	L. Pincay, Jr.	126	159,720
1945	Pavot	E. Arcaro	126	56,675		Cielo			
1946	Assault	W. Mehrtens	126	75,400	1983	Caveat	L. Pincay, Jr.	126	215,100
1947	Phalanx	R. Donoso	126	78,900	1984	Swale	L. Pincay, Jr.	126	310,020
1948	Citation	E. Arcaro	126	77,700	1985	Creme Fraiche	E. Maple	126	307,740
1949	Capot	T. Atkinson	126	60,900	1986	Danzig	C. McCarron	126	338,640
1950	Middleground	W. Boland	126	61,350		Connection			
1951	Counterpoint	D. Gorman	126	82,000	1987	Bet Twice	C. Perret	126	329,160
1952	One Count	E. Arcaro	126	82,400	1988	Risen Star	E. Delahoussaye	126	303,720
1953	Native Dancer	E. Guerin	126	82,500	1989	Easy Goer	P. Day	126	413,520
1954	High Gun	E. Guerin	126	89,000	1990	Go And Go	M. Kinane	126	411,600
1955	Nashua	E. Arcaro	126	83,700	1991	Hansel	J. Bailey	126	417,480
1956	Needles	D. Erb	126	83,600	1992	A.P. Indy	E. Delahoussaye	126	458,880
1957	Gallant Man	W. Shoemaker	126	77,300	1993	Colonial Affair	J. Krone	126	444,450
1958	Cavan	P. Anderson	126	73,440	1994	Tabasco Cat	P. Day	126	392,280
1959	Sword Dancer	W. Shoemaker	126	93,525	1995	Thunder Gulch	G.Stevens	126	415,440
1960	Celtic Ash	W. Hartack	126	96,785	1996	Editor's Note	R. Douglas	126	437,880
1961	Sherluck	B. Baeza	126	104,900	1997	Touch Gold	C. McCarron	126	432,600
1962	Jaipur	W. Shoemaker	126	109,550	1998	Victory Gallop	G. Stevens	126	600,000
1963	Chateauguay	B. Baeza	126	101,700	1999	Lemon Drop Kid	J. Santos	126	600,000
1964	Quadrangle	M. Ycaza	126	110,850	2000	Commendable	P. Day	126	600,000
1965	Hail to All	J. Sellers	126	104,150					

1. Data not available.

TRIPLE CROWN RACES—2000

Kentucky Derby (Churchill Downs, Louisville, Ky., May 6, 2000). Gross purse: $1,000,000. Distance: 1¼ miles. Order of finish: 1. Fusaichi Pegasus (Desormeaux), mutuel returns: $6.60, $5.60, $4.00. 2. Aptitude (Solis), $9.80, $5.80. 3. Impeachment (Perret), $4.00. 4. More than Ready (Velazquez). 5. Wheelaway (Migliore). 6. China Visit (Dettori). 7. Curule (St. Julien). 8. Captain Steve (Albarado). 9. War Chant (Bailey). 10. Deputy Warlock (Guidry). 11. Trippi (Chavez). 12. Exchange Rate (Borel). 13. Anees (Nakatani). 14. The Deputy (McCarron). 15. High Yield (Day). 16. Hal's Hope (Velez). 17. Commendable (Prado). 18. Ronton (Blanc). 19. Graeme Hall (Sellers). Winner's purse: $886,400. Margin of victory: 1½ lengths. Time of race: 2.01.12.

Preakness Stakes (Pimlico, Baltimore, Md., May 20, 2000). Gross purse: $1,000,000. Distance: 1 3/16 miles. Order of finish: 1. Red Bullet (Bailey), mutuel returns: $14.40, $3.20, $2.80. 2. Fusaichi Pegasus (Desormeaux), $2.60, $2.20. 3. Impeachment (Perret), $3.60. 4. Captain Steve (Albarado). 5. Snuck In (Asmussen). 6. Hugh Hefner (Espinoza). 7. High Yield (Day). 8. Hal's Hope (Velez). Winner's purse: $650,000. Margin of victory: 3¾ lengths. Time of race: 1:56.

Belmont Stakes (Belmont Park, Belmont, N.Y., June 10, 2000). Gross purse: $1,000,000. Distance: 1½ miles. Order of finish: 1. Commendable (Day), mutuel returns: $39.60, $12.80, $6.30. 2. Aptitude (Solis), $3.80, $2.80. 3. Unshaded (Sellers), $4.40. 4. Wheelaway (Migliore). 5.

Impeachment (Perret). 6. Appearing Now (Luzzi). 7. Postponed (Prado). 8. Hugh Hefner (Chavez). 9. Tahkodha Hills (Coa). 10. Globalize (Smith). 11. Curule (Bailey). Winner's purse: $600,000. Margin of victory: 1½ lengths. Time of race: 2:31.

ECLIPSE AWARDS—1999

(Presented Jan. 23, 2000)

Horse of the Year	Charismatic
2-year-old male	Anees
2-year-old female	Chilukki
3-year-old male	Charismatic
3-year-old female	Silverbulletday
Older male horse	Victory Gallop
Older female horse	Beautiful Pleasure
Sprinter	Artax
Male turf horse	Daylami
Female turf horse	Soaring Softly
Steeplechaser	Lonesome Glory
Owner	Frank Stronach
Breeders	William S. Farish and Partners
Trainer	Bob Baffert
Jockey	Jorge Chavez
Apprentice jockey	Ariel Smith

(Based on vote by the Thoroughbred Racing Associations, the *Daily Racing Form*, and the National Turf Writers Association.)

Track and Field

WORLD RECORDS—MEN

(Through Aug. 16, 2000)

Recognized by the International Athletic Federation. The I.A.A.F. decided late in 1976 not to recognize records in yards except for the one-mile run.

The I.A.A.F. also requires automatic timing for all records for races of 400 meters or less.

Event	Record	Holder	Home country	Where made	Date
Running					
100 m	0:09.79	Maurice Greene	United States	Athens, Greece	June 16, 1999
200 m	0:19.32	Michael Johnson	United States	Atlanta, Ga.	Aug. 1, 1996
400 m	0:43.18	Michael Johnson	United States	Seville, Spain	Aug. 26, 1999
800 m	1:41.11	Wilson Kipketer	Denmark	Köln, Germany	Aug. 24, 1997
1,000 m	2:12.18	Sebastian Coe	England	Oslo, Norway	July 11, 1981
1,500 m	3:26.00	Hicham El Guerrouj	Morocco	Rome, Italy	July 14, 1998
1 mile	3:43.13	Hicham El Guerrouj	Morocco	Rome, Italy	July 7, 1999
2,000 m	4:47.88	Noureddine Morceli	Algeria	Paris, France	July 3, 1995
3,000 m	7:20.67	Daniel Komen	Kenya	Rieti, Italy	Sept. 1, 1996
3,000 m steeplechase	7:55.72	Bernard Barmasai	Kenya	Köln, Germany	Aug. 24, 1997
5,000 m	12:39.36	Haile Gebrselassie	Ethiopia	Helsinki, Finland	June 13, 1998
10,000 m	26:22.75	Haile Gebrselassie	Ethiopia	Hengelo, Netherlands	June 1, 1998
20,000 m	56:55.60	Arturo Barrios	Mexico	La Fleche, France	March 30, 1991
25,000 m	1:13:55.80	Toshihiko Seko	Japan	Christchurch, N.Z.	March 22, 1981
30,000 m	1:29:18.80	Toshihiko Seko	Japan	Christchurch, N.Z.	March 22, 1981
1 hour	21,101 m	Arturo Barrios	Mexico	La Fleche, France	March 30, 1991
Marathon[1]	2:06.05	Ronaldo Da Costa	Brazil	Berlin, Germany	Sept. 20, 1998
Walking					
20,000 m	1:17:25.60	Bernardo Segura	Mexico	Bergen, Norway	May 7, 1994
30,000 m	2:01:44.10	Maurizio Damilano	Italy	Cuneo, Italy	Oct. 3, 1992
50,000 m	3:40:57.90	Thierry Toutain	France	Héricourt, France	Sept. 29, 1996
2 hours	29,572 m	Maurizio Damilano	Italy	Cuneo, Italy	Oct. 3, 1992
Hurdles					
110 m	0:12.91	Colin Jackson	Great Britain	Stuttgart, Germany	Aug. 20, 1993
400 m	0:46.78	Kevin Young	United States	Barcelona, Spain	Aug. 6, 1992
Relay races					
400 m (4 × 100)	0:37.40	National Team	United States	Barcelona, Spain	Aug. 8, 1992
	0:37.40	National Team	United States	Stuttgart, Germany	Aug. 21, 1993
800 m (4 × 200)	1:18.68	Santa Monica T.C.	United States	Walnut, Calif.	April 17, 1994
1,600 m (4 × 400)	2:54.20	National Team	United States	New York, N.Y.	July 22, 1998
3,200 m (4 × 800)	7:03.89	National Team	Britain	London	Aug. 30, 1982
Field events					
High jump	2.45 m	Javier Sotomayor	Cuba	Salamanca, Spain	July 27, 1993
Long jump	8.95 m	Mike Powell	United States	Tokyo, Japan	Aug. 30, 1991
Triple jump	18.29 m	Jonathan Edwards	Great Britain	Goteborg, Sweden	Aug. 7, 1995
Pole vault	6.14 m	Sergey Bubka	Ukraine	Sestriere, Italy	July 31, 1994
Shot-put	23.12 m	Randy Barnes	United States	Los Angeles	May 20, 1990
Discus throw	74.08 m	Jürgen Schult	East Germany	Neubrandenburg, E. Germany	June 6, 1986
Hammer throw	86.74 m	Yuriy Sedykh	U.S.S.R.	Stuttgart, Germany	Aug. 30, 1986
Javelin throw	98.48 m	Jan Zelezny	Czech Republic	Jena, Germany	May 25, 1996
Decathlon	8,994 pts.	Tomás Dvorák	Czech Republic	Prague, Czech Republic	July 4,1999

1. Not recognized by I.A.A.F. as world record, but considered to be "world best performance."

WORLD RECORDS—WOMEN

(Through Aug. 16, 2000)

Event	Record	Holder	Home country	Where made	Date
Running					
100 m	0:10.49	Florence Griffith-Joyner	United States	Indianapolis, Ind.	July 16, 1988
200 m	0:21.34	Florence Griffith-Joyner	United States	Seoul, South Korea	Sept. 29, 1988
400 m	0:47.60	Martina Koch	East Germany	Canberra, Australia	Oct. 6, 1985
800 m	1:53.28	Jarmila Kratochvilova	Czechoslovakia	Munich, W. Germany	July 26, 1983
1000 m	2:28.98	Svetlana Masterkova	Russia	Brussels, Belgium	Aug. 23, 1996
1,500 m	3:50.46	Qu Yunxia	China	Beijing, China	Sept. 11, 1993
1 mile	4:12.56	Svetlana Masterkova	Russia	Zurich, Switzerland	Aug. 14, 1996
2,000 m	5:25.36	Sonia O'Sullivan	Ireland	Edinburgh, Scotland	July 8, 1994
3,000 m	8:06.11	Wang Junxia	China	Beijing, China	Sept. 13, 1993
5,000 m	14:28.09	Jiang Bo	China	Shanghai, China	Oct. 23, 1997
10,000 m	29:31.78	Wang Junxia	China	Beijing, China	Sept. 8, 1993
20,000 m	1:06:48.80	Izumi Maki	Japan	Amagasaki, Japan	Sept. 19, 1993

Event	Record	Holder	Home country	Where made	Date
25,000 m	1:29:29.20	Karolina Szabo	Hungary	Budapest, Hungary	April 22, 1988
30,000 m	1:47:05.60	Karolina Szabo	Hungary	Budapest, Hungary	April 22, 1988
1 hour	18.340	Tegla Loroupe	Kenya	Borgholzhausen, Germany	July 8, 1999
Marathon[1]	2:20:47.0	Tegla Loroupe	Kenya	Rotterdam, The Netherlands	April 19 1999
Walking					
5,000 m	20:13.26	Kerry Saxby-Junna	Australia	Hobart, Australia	Feb. 25, 1996
10,000 m	41:56.23	Nadezhda Ryashkina	Russia	Seattle, Wash.	July 24, 1990
Hurdles					
100-m hurdles	0:12.21	Yordanka Donkova	Bulgaria	Stara Zagora, Bulgaria	Aug. 20, 1988
400 m	0:52.61	Kim Batten	United States	Goteborg, Sweden	Aug. 11, 1995
Relay races					
400 m (4 × 100)	0:41.37	East Germany	E. Germany	Canberra, Australia	Oct. 6, 1985
800 m (4 × 200)	1:27.46	United States "Blue"	United States	Philadelphia, Pa.	April 29, 2000
1,600 m (4 × 400)	3:15.17	U.S.S.R.	U.S.S.R.	Seoul, South Korea	Oct. 1, 1988
3,200 m (4 × 800)	7:50.17	U.S.S.R.	U.S.S.R.	Moscow, U.S.S.R.	Aug. 5, 1984
Field events					
High jump	2.09 m	Stefka Kostadinova	Bulgaria	Rome, Italy	Aug. 30, 1987
Pole vault	4.62 m	Stacy Dragila	United States	Phoenix, Ariz.	May 27, 2000
Long jump	7.52 m	Galina Chistyakova	U.S.S.R.	Leningrad, Russia	June 11, 1988
Triple jump	15.50 m	Inessa Kravets	Ukraine	Goteborg, Sweden	Aug. 10, 1995
Shot-put	22.63 m	Natalya Lisovskaya	U.S.S.R.	Moscow, Russia	June 7, 1987
Discus throw	76.80 m	Gabriele Reinsch	East Germany	Neubrandenburg, E. Ger.	July 9, 1988
Hammer	75.97 m	Mihaela Melinte	Romania	Clermont-Ferrand, France	May 13, 1999
Javelin throw	68.19 m	Trine Solberg-Hattestad	Norway	Bergen, Norway	July 28, 1999
Heptathlon	7,291 pts	Jackie Joyner-Kersee	United States	Seoul, South Korea	Sept. 24, 1988

1. Not recognized by I.A.A.F. as world record, but considered to be "world best performance."

AMERICAN RECORDS—MEN

(Through Aug. 16, 2000)

Event	Record	Holder	Where Made	Date
Running				
100 m	0:09.79	Maurice Greene	Athens, Greece	June 16, 1999
200 m	0:19.32	Michael Johnson	Atlanta, Ga.	Aug. 1, 1996
400 m	0:43.18	Michael Johnson	Seville, Spain	Aug. 26, 1999
800 m	1:42.60	Johnny Gray	Koblenz, W. Ger.	Aug. 29, 1985
1,000 m	2:13.90	Richard Wohlhuter	Oslo, Norway	July 30, 1974
1,500 m	3:29.77	Sydney Maree	Cologne, W. Ger.	Aug. 25, 1985
1 mile	3:47.69	Steve Scott	Oslo, Norway	July 7, 1982
2,000 m	4:54.71	Steve Scott	Ingelhelm, W. Ger.	Aug. 31, 1982
3,000 m	7:31.69	Bob Kennedy	Brussels, Belgium	Aug. 23, 1996
5,000 m	12:58.21	Bob Kennedy	Zurich, Switzerland	Aug. 14, 1996
10,000 m	27:20.56	Mark Nenow	Brussels	Sept. 5, 1986
20,000 m	58:15.00	Bill Rodgers	Boston, Mass.	Aug. 9, 1977
25,000 m	1:14:11.80	Bill Rodgers	Saratoga, Cal.	Feb. 21, 1979
30,000 m	1:31:49.00	Bill Rodgers	Saratoga, Cal.	Feb. 21, 1979
1 hour	12 mi., 1,351 yds	Bill Rodgers	Boston, Mass.	Aug. 9, 1977
3,000-m steeplechase	8:09.17	Henry Marsh	Koblenz, W. Ger.	Aug. 29, 1985
Marathon	2:09:32	David Morris	Chicago, Ill.	Oct. 24, 1999
Hurdles				
110 m	0:12.92	Roger Kingdom	Berlin	Aug. 16, 1989
		Allen Johnson	Brussels, Belgium	Aug. 23, 1996
400 m	0:46.78	Kevin Young	Barcelona	Aug. 6, 1992
Relay races				
400 m (4 × 100)	0:37.40	USA National Team	Stuttgart, Germany	Aug. 21, 1993
800 m (4 × 200)	1:18.68	Santa Monica T.C.	Walnut, Calif.	April 17, 1994
1,600 m (4 × 400)	2:54.20	USA National Team	New York, N.Y.	July 22, 1998
3,200 m (4 × 800)	7:06.50	Santa Monica T.C.	Walnut, Calif.	Apr. 26, 1986
Field events				
High jump	7 ft. 10½ in.	Charles Austin	Zurich	Aug. 7, 1991
Long jump	29 ft. 4½ in.	Mike Powell	Tokyo, Japan	Aug. 30, 1991
Triple jump	59 ft. 4 in.	Kenny Harrison	Atlanta, Ga.	July 27, 1996
Pole vault	19 ft. 9 ¼in.	Jeff Hartwig	Jonesboro, Ark.	June 14, 2000
Shot-put	75 ft. 10¼ in.	Randy Barnes	Los Angeles	May 20, 1990
Discus throw	237 ft. 4 in.	Ben Plucknett	Stockholm, Swe.	July 7, 1981
Javelin throw	285 ft. 10 in.	Tom Pukstys	Jena	May 25, 1997
Hammer throw	270 ft. 9 in.	Lance Deal	Milan, Italy	July 9, 1996
Decathlon	8,891 pts	Dan O'Brien	Talence, France	Sept. 4–5, 1992

AMERICAN RECORDS—WOMEN

(Through Aug. 16, 2000)

Event	Record	Holder	Where Made	Date
Running				
100 m	0:10.49	Florence Griffith-Joyner	Indianapolis, Ind.	July 16, 1988
200 m	0:21.56	Florence Griffith-Joyner	Seoul, South Korea	Oct. 1, 1988
400 m	0:48.83	Valerie Brisco-Hooks	Los Angeles, Cal.	Aug. 6, 1984
800 m	1:56.40	Jearl Miles-Clark	Zürich, Switzerland	Aug. 11, 1999
1,500 m	3:57.12	Mary Decker Slaney	Stockholm, Swe.	July 26, 1983
1,000 m	2:34.8	Mary Decker Slaney	Eugene, Ore.	July 4, 1985
1 mile	4:16.71	Mary Decker Slaney	Zurich	Aug. 21, 1985
3,000 m	8:29.69	Mary Decker Slaney	Cologne	Aug. 25, 1985
5,000 m	14:52.49	Regina Jacobs	Brunswick, Maine	July 4, 1998
10,000 m	31:28.92	Francie L. Smith	Austin, Texas	April 4, 1991
Marathon	2:21:21	Joan Samuelson	Chicago, Ill.	Oct. 20, 1985
Hurdles				
100 m hurdles	0:12.37	Gail Devers	Seville, Spain	Aug. 28, 1999
400 m hurdles	0:52.61	Kim Batten	Gothenburg, Sweden	Aug. 11, 1995
Relay races				
400 m (4 × 100)	41.47	U.S.A. National Team	Athens, Greece	Aug. 9, 1997
800 m (4 × 200)	1:30.20	Nike International	Philadelphia, Pa.	Apr. 26, 1997
1,600 m (4 × 400)	3:15.51	U.S. Olympic Team	Seoul, South Korea	Oct. 1, 1988
Field events				
Pole vault	15 ft. 2 in.	Stacy Dragila	Phoenix, Ariz.	May 27, 2000
High jump	6 ft. 8 in.	Louise Ritter	Austin, Tex.	July 9, 1988
Long jump	24 ft. 7 in.	Jackie Joyner-Kersee	New York, N.Y.	May 22, 1994
Triple jump	47 ft. 3½ in.	Sheila Hudson	Stockholm, Sweden	July 8, 1996
Shot-put	66 ft. 2½ in.	Ramon Pagel	San Diego, Calif.	June 25, 1988
Discus throw	230 ft. 2 in.	Dawn Ellerbe	Laramie, Wyo.	May 15, 1999
Hammer throw	210 ft. 8 in.	Dawn Ellerbe	Walnut, Calif.	April 19, 1997
Javelin throw	227 ft. 5 in.	Kate Schmidt	Furth, W. Ger.	Sept. 10, 1977
Heptathlon	7,291 pts	Jackie Joyner-Kersee	Seoul, South Korea	Sept. 23–24, 1988

HISTORY OF THE RECORD FOR THE MILE RUN

(Under 4 minutes) *Source:* USA Track & Field

Time	Athlete	Country	Year	Location
3:59.4	Roger Bannister	England	1954	Oxford, England
3:58.0	John Landy	Australia	1954	Turku, Finland
3:57.2	Derek Ibbotson	England	1957	London
3:54.5	Herb Elliott	Australia	1958	Dublin
3:54.4	Peter Snell	New Zealand	1962	Wanganui, N.Z.
3:54.1	Peter Snell	New Zealand	1964	Auckland, N.Z.
3:53.6	Michel Jazy	France	1965	Rennes, France
3:51.3	Jim Ryun	United States	1966	Berkeley, Calif.
3:51.1	Jim Ryun	United States	1967	Bakersfield, Calif.
3:51.0	Filbert Bayi	Tanzania	1975	Kingston, Jamaica
3:49.4	John Walker	New Zealand	1975	Goteborg, Sweden
3:49.0	Sebastian Coe	England	1979	Oslo
3:48.8	Steve Ovett	England	1980	Oslo
3:48.53	Sebastian Coe	England	1981	Zurich, Switzerland
3:48.40	Steve Ovett	England	1981	Koblenz, W. Ger.
3:47.33	Sebastian Coe	England	1981	Brussels
3:46.31	Steve Cram	England	1985	Oslo
3:44.39	Noureddine Morceli	Algeria	1993	Rieti, Italy
3:43.13	Hicham El Guerrouj	Morocco	1999	Rome, Italy

TOP TEN WORLD'S FASTEST OUTDOOR MILES

Source: USA Track & Field

Time	Athlete	Country	Date	Location
3:43.13	Hicham El Guerrouj	Morocco	July 27, 1999	Rome, Italy
3:44.39	Nouraddine Morceli	Algeria	Sept. 5, 1993	Rieti, Italy
3:46.31	Steve Cram	England	July 27, 1985	Oslo
3:47.33	Sebastian Coe	England	Aug. 28, 1981	Brussels
3:47.69	Steve Scott	United States	July 7, 1982	Oslo
3:47.79	Jose Gonzalez	Spain	July 27, 1985	Oslo
3:48.40	Steve Ovett	England	Aug. 26, 1981	Koblenz, W. Ger.
3:48.53	Sebastian Coe	England	Aug. 19, 1981	Zurich
3:48.53	Steve Scott	United States	June 26, 1982	Oslo
3:48.8	Steve Ovett	England	July 1, 1980	Oslo

NOTE: Professional marks not included.

TOP TEN WORLD'S FASTEST INDOOR MILES

Source: USA Track & Field

Time	Athlete	Country	Date	Location
3:48.45	Hicham El Guerrouj	Morocco	Feb, 12, 1997	Gent, Netherlands
3:49.78	Eamonn Coghlan	Ireland	Feb. 27, 1983	East Rutherford, N.J.
3:50.6	Eamonn Coghlan	Ireland	Feb. 20, 1981	San Diego
3:50.7	Noureddine Morceli	Algeria	Feb. 20, 1993	Birmingham, England
3:50.94	Marcus O'Sullivan	Ireland	Feb. 13, 1988	East Rutherford, N.J.
3:51.2	Ray Flynn[1]	Ireland	Feb. 27, 1983	East Rutherford, N.J.
3:51.66	Marcus O'Sullivan	Ireland	Feb. 10, 1989	East Rutherford, N.J.
3:51.8	Steve Scott[1]	United States	Feb. 20, 1981	San Diego
3:52.28	Steve Scott[2]	United States	Feb. 27, 1983	East Rutherford, N.J.
3:52.30	Frank O'Mara	Ireland	Feb. 1986	New York

1. Finished second. 2. Finished third.

IAAF WORLD CROSS COUNTRY CHAMPIONSHIPS

(Vilamoura, Portugal, March 18–19, 2000)

Men's Events

Long Race—Mohammed Mourhit, Belgium	35:00
Short Race—John Kibowen, Kenya	11:11
Junior Race—Robert Kipchumba, Kenya	22:49

Cross Challenge Standing: 1. Paul Tergat, Kenya; 2. Patrick Ivuti, Kenya; 3. Assefa Mezgebu, Ethiopia

Women's Events

Long Race—Derartu Tulu, Ethiopia	25:42
Short Race—Kutre Dulecha, Ethiopia	13:00
Junior Race—Vivian Cheruiyot, Kenya	20:34

Cross Challenge Standings: 1. Lydia Cheromei, Kenya; 2. Gete Wami, Ethiopia; 3. Ayelech Worku, Ethiopia

2000 USA OUTDOOR CHAMPIONSHIPS

(Atlanta, Ga., March 3–March 4, 2000)

Men's Events

60 m dash—Jon Drummond, Nike	6.46
200 m dash—Chris Chandler, Nebraska	20.84
400 m dash—James Davis, Goldwin International	45.54
800 m run—Bryan Woodward, Reebok	1:48.69
1 mile run—Jason Pyrah, Unattached	3:57.83
3,000 m run ATC—John Mayes, Atlanta Track Club	8:28.76
3,000 m run—Ray Appenheimer, Nike Farm Team	7:56.22
60 m hurdles—Terrence Trammel, South Carolina	7.57
4 x 400 m relay—Bronx International	3:09.64
High jump—Matt Hemingway, Team U.S. West	2.38 m
Pole vault—Lawrence Johnson, Adidas	5.81 m
Long jump—Savante Stringfellow, Mississppi	7.94 m
Triple jump—LaVar Anderson, Unattached	16.90 m
Shot put—Andrew Bloom, Nike	21.60 m
Weight throw—Lance Deal, New York Athletic Club	23.89 m
Heptathlon—Tom Pappas, Adidas	5,933 pts.
5,000 m race walk—Tim Seaman, New York Athletic Club	19.32.11

Women's Events

	Time
60 m dash—Carlette Guidry, Adidas	7.12
200 m dash—Nanceen Perry, Mizuno Track Club	22.65
400 m dash—Suziann Reid, Adidas	52.20
800 m run—Hazel Clark, Nike	2:03.40
1 mile run—Regina Jacobs, New York Athletic Club	4:25.92
3,000 m run—Marla Runyan, Asics	9:01.29
60 m hurdles—Melissa Morrison, Reebok	7.86
4 x 400 m relay—Nebraska	3:35.49
High jump—Tisha Waller, Nike	1.96 m
Pole vault—Stacy Dragila, Reebok	4.62 m
Long jump—Adrien Sawyer, Nike	6.54 m
Triple jump—Tiombe Hurd, Nike	14.06 m
Shot put—Connie Price-Smith, Nike	18.70 m
Weight throw—Dawn Ellerbe, New York Athletic Club	23.60 m
3,000 m race walk—Michelle Rohl, Moving Com	12:51.17

Tennis

Lawn tennis is a comparatively modern modification of the ancient game of court tennis. Major Walter Clopton Wingfield thought that something like court tennis might be played outdoors on lawns, and in December, 1873, at Nantclwyd, Wales, he introduced his new game under the name of *Sphairistike* at a lawn party. The game was a success and spread rapidly, but the name was a total failure and almost immediately disappeared when all the play-ers and spectators began to refer to the new game as "lawn tennis." In the early part of 1874, a young lady named Mary Ewing Outerbridge returned from Bermuda to New York, bringing with her the implements and necessary equipment of the new game, which she had obtained from a British Army supply store in Bermuda. Miss Outerbridge and friends played the first game of lawn tennis in the United States on the grounds of the Staten Island Cricket and Baseball Club in the spring of 1874.

For a few years, the new game went along in haphazard fashion until about 1880, when standard measurements for the court and standard equipment within definite limits became the rule. In 1881, the U.S. Lawn Tennis Association (whose name was changed in 1975 to U.S. Tennis Association) was formed and conducted the first national championship at Newport, R.I. The international matches for the Davis Cup began with a series between the British and United States players on the courts of the Longwood Cricket Club, Chestnut Hill, Mass., in 1900, with the home players winning.

Professional tennis, which got its start in 1926 when the French star Suzanne Lenglen was paid $50,000 for a tour, received full recognition in 1968. Staid old Wimbledon, the London home of what are considered the world championships, let the pros compete. This decision ended a long controversy over open tennis and changed the format of the competition. The United States championships were also opened to the pros and the site of the event, long held at Forest Hills, N.Y., was shifted to the National Tennis Center in Flushing Meadows, N.Y., in 1978. Pro tours for men and women became worldwide in play that continued throughout the year.

DAVIS CUP CHAMPIONSHIPS

No matches in 1901, 1910, 1915–18, and 1940–45.

1900 United States 3, British Isles 0	1936 Great Britain 3, Australia 2	1971 United States 3, Romania 2
1902 United States 3, British Isles 2	1937 United States 4, Great Britain 1	1972 United States 3, Romania 2
1903 British Isles 4, United States 1	1938 United States 3, Australia 2	1973 Australia 5, United States 0
1904 British Isles 5, Belgium 0	1939 Australia 3, United States 2	1974 South Africa (Default by India)
1905 British Isles 5, United States 0	1946 United States 5, Australia 0	1975 Sweden 3, Czechoslovakia 2
1906 British Isles 5, United States 0	1947 United States 4, Australia 1	1976 Italy 4, Chile 1
1907 Australasia 3, British Isles 2	1948 United States 5, Australia 0	1977 Australia 3, Italy 1
1908 Australasia 3, United States 2	1949 United States 4, Australia 1	1978 United States 4, Britain 1
1909 Australasia 5, United States 0	1950 Australia 4, United States 1	1979 United States 5, Italy 0
1911 Australasia 5, United States 0	1951 Australia 3, United States 2	1980 Czechoslovakia 3, Italy 2
1912 British Isles 3, Australasia 2	1952 Australia 4, United States 1	1981 United States 3, Argentina 1
1913 United States 3, British Isles 2	1953 Australia 3, United States 2	1982 United States 3, France 0
1914 Australasia 3, United States 2	1954 United States 3, Australia 2	1983 Australia 3, Sweden 2
1919 Australasia 4, British Isles 1	1955 Australia 5, United States 0	1984 Sweden 4, United States 1
1920 United States 5, Australasia 0	1956 Australia 5, United States 0	1985 Sweden 3, West Germany 2
1921 United States 5, Japan 0	1957 Australia 3, United States 2	1986 Australia 3, Sweden 2
1922 United States 4, Australasia 1	1958 United States 3, Australia 2	1987 Sweden 5, India 0
1923 United States 4, Australasia 1	1959 Australia 3, United States 2	1988 West Germany 4, Sweden 1
1924 United States 5, Australasia 0	1960 Australia 4, Italy 1	1989 West Germany 3, Sweden 2
1925 United States 5, France 0	1961 Australia 5, Italy 0	1990 United States 3, Australia 2
1926 United States 4, France 1	1962 Australia 5, Mexico 0	1991 France 3, United States 1
1927 France 3, United States 2	1963 United States 3, Australia 2	1992 United States 3, Switzerland 1
1928 France 4, United States 1	1964 Australia 3, United States 2	1993 Germany 4, Australia 1
1929 France 3, United States 2	1965 Australia 4, Spain 1	1994 Sweden 4, Russia 1
1930 France 4, United States 1	1966 Australia 4, India 1	1995 United States 3, Russia 1
1931 France 3, Great Britain 2	1967 Australia 4, Spain 1	1996 France 3, Sweden 2
1932 France 3, United States 2	1968 United States 4, Australia 1	1997 Sweden 5, United States 0
1933 Great Britain 3, France 2	1969 United States 5, Romania 0	1998 Sweden 4, Italy 1
1934 Great Britain 4, United States 1	1970 United States 5, West	1999 Australia 3, France 2
1935 Great Britain 5, United States 0	Germany 0	

FEDERATION CUP CHAMPIONSHIPS

World team competition for women conducted by International Lawn Tennis Federation.

1963 United States 2, Australia 1	1977 United States 2, Australia 1	1988 Czechoslovakia 2, Soviet Union 1
1964 Australia 2, United States 1	1978 United States 2, Australia 1	1989 United States 3, Spain 0
1965 Australia 2, United States 1	1979 United States 3, Australia 0	1990 United States 2, Soviet Union 1
1966 United States 3, West Germany 0	1980 United States 3, Australia 0	1991 Spain 2, United States 1
1967 United States 2, Britain 0	1981 United States 3, Britain 0	1992 Germany 2, Spain 1
1968 Australia 3, Netherlands 0	1982 United States 3, West Germany 0	1993 Spain 3, Australia 0
1969 United States 2, Australia 1	1983 Czechoslovakia 2, West	1994 Spain 3, United States 0
1970 Australia 3, West Germany 0	Germany 1	1995 Spain 3, United States 2
1971 Australia 3, Britain 0	1984 Czechoslovakia 2, Australia 1	1996 United States 5, Spain 0
1972 South Africa 2, Britain 1	1985 Czechoslovakia 2, United	1997 France 4, Netherlands 1
1973 Australia 3, South Africa 0	States 1	1998 Spain 3, Switzerland 2
1974 Australia 2, United States 1	1986 United States 3,	1999 United States 4, Russia 1
1975 Czechoslovakia 3, Australia 0	Czechoslovakia 0	
1976 United States 2, Australia 1	1987 West Germany 2, United States 1	

U.S. NATIONAL AND OPEN CHAMPIONS

SINGLES—MEN

NATIONAL

1881–87	Richard D. Sears	1926–27	Jean Rene Lacoste	1957	Mal Anderson
1888–89	Henry Slocum, Jr.	1928	Henri Cochet	1958	Ashley Cooper
1890–92	Oliver S. Campbell	1929	Bill Tilden	1959–60	Neale Fraser
1893–94	Robert D. Wrenn	1930	John H. Doeg	1961	Roy Emerson
1895	Fred H. Hovey	1931–32	Ellsworth Vines	1962	Rod Laver
1896–97	Robert D. Wrenn	1933–34	Fred J. Perry	1963	Rafael Osuna
1898–		1935	Wilmer L. Allison	1964	Roy Emerson
1900	Malcolm Whitman	1936	Fred J. Perry	1965	Manuel Santana
1901–02	William A. Larned	1937–38	Don Budge	1966	Fred Stolle
1903	Hugh L. Doherty	1939	Robert L. Riggs	1967	John Newcombe
1904	Holcombe Ward	1940	Donald McNeill	1968	Arthur Ashe
1905	Beals C. Wright	1941	Robert L. Riggs	1969	Rod Laver
1906	William J. Clothier	1942	Fred Schroeder		
1907–11	William A. Larned	1943	Joseph Hunt	**OPEN**	
	Maurice McLough-	1944–45	Frank Parker	1968	Arthur Ashe
1912–13	lin[1]	1946–47	Jack Kramer	1969	Rod Laver
1914	R. N. Williams II	1948–49	Richard Gonzales	1970	Ken Rosewall
1915	William Johnston	1950	Arthur Larsen	1971	Stan Smith
1916	R. N. William II	1951–52	Frank Sedgman	1972	Ilie Nastase
1917–18	R. Lindley Murray[2]	1953	Tony Trabert	1973	John Newcombe
1919	William Johnston	1954	Vic Seixas	1974	Jimmy Connors
1920–25	Bill Tilden	1955	Tony Trabert	1975	Manuel Orantes
		1956	Ken Rosewall	1976	Jimmy Connors

1977	Guillermo Vilas
1978	Jimmy Connors
1979	John McEnroe
1980–81	John McEnroe
1982	Jimmy Connors
1983	Jimmy Connors
1984	John McEnroe
1985–87	Ivan Lendl
1988	Mats Wilander
1989	Boris Becker
1990	Pete Sampras
1991	Stefan Edberg
1992	Stefan Edberg
1993	Pete Sampras
1994	Andre Agassi
1995	Pete Sampras
1996	Pete Sampras
1997–98	Patrick Rafter
1999	Andre Agassi
2000	Marat Safin

1. Challenge Round Abandoned in 1912. 2. Patriotic Tournament in 1917.

SINGLES—WOMEN

NATIONAL

1887	Ellen F. Hansel	1912–14	Mary K. Browne	1948–50	Margaret Osborne
1888–89	Bertha Townsend	1915–18	Molla Bjurstedt		duPont
1890	Ellen C. Roosevelt	1919	Hazel Hotchkiss	1951–53	Maureen Connolly
1891–92	Mabel E. Cahill		Wightman	1954–55	Doris Hart
1893	Aline M. Terry	1920–22	Molla Bjurstedt	1956	Shirley Fry
1894	Helen R. Helwig		Mallory	1957–58	Althea Gibson
1895	Juliette P. Atkinson	1923–25	Helen N. Wills	1959	Maria Bueno
1896	Elisabeth H. Moore	1926	Molla B. Mallory	1960–61	Darlene Hard
1897–98	Juliette P. Atkinson	1927–29	Helen N. Wills	1962	Margaret Smith
1899	Marion Jones	1930	Betty Nuthall	1963–64	Maria Bueno
1900	Myrtle McAteer	1931	Helen Wills Moody	1965	Margaret Smith
1901	Elisabeth H. Moore	1932–35	Helen Jacobs	1966	Maria Bueno
1902	Marion Jones	1936	Alice Marble	1967	Billie Jean King
1903	Elisabeth H. Moore	1937	Anita Lizana	1968–69	Margaret Smith
1904	May Sutton	1938–40	Alice Marble		Court[1]
1905	Elisabeth H. Moore	1941	Sarah Palfrey		
1906	Helen Homans		Cooke	**OPEN**	
1907	Evelyn Sears	1942–44	Pauline Betz	1968	Virginia Wade
1908	Maud	1945	Sarah Cooke	1969–70	Margaret Court
	Bargar-Wallach	1946	Pauline Betz	1971–72	Billie Jean King
1909–11	Hazel V. Hotchkiss	1947	Louise Brough	1973	Margaret Court
				1974	Billie Jean King

1975–78	Chris Evert
1979	Tracy Austin
1980	Chris Evert-Lloyd
1981	Tracy Austin
1982	Chris Evert-Lloyd
1983–84	Martina Navratilova
1985	Hana Mandlikova
1986–87	Martina Navratilova
1988	Steffi Graf
1989	Steffi Graf
1990	Grabriela Sabatini
1991	Monica Seles
1992	Monica Seles
1993	Steffi Graf
1994	Arantxa Sanchez Vicario
1995	Steffi Graf
1996	Steffi Graf
1997	Martina Hingis
1998	Lindsay Davenport
1999	Serena Williams
2000	Venus Williams

1. With the inaugural of the Open Tournament in 1968, the United States Lawn Tennis Association held a championship at Longwood, Chestnut Hill, Mass. which barred contract professionals in 1968 and 1969.

DOUBLES—MEN

NATIONAL

1920	Bill Johnston–C. J. Griffin	1935	W. L. Allison–John Van Ryn	1948	Gardnar Mulloy–Bill Talbert
1921–22	Bill Tilden–Vincent Richards	1936	Don Budge–Gene Mako	1949	John Bromwich–William Sidwell
1923	Bill Tilden–B. I. C. Norton	1937	G. von Cramm–H. Henkel		
1924	H. O. Kinsey–R. G. Kinsey	1938	Don Budge–Gene Mako	1950	John Bromwich–Frank Sedgman
1925–26	Vincent Richards–R. N. Williams II	1939	A. K. Quist–J. E. Bromwich		
		1940–41	Jack Kramer–F. R. Schroeder	1951	Frank Sedgman–Ken McGregor
1927	Bill Tilden–Frank Hunter	1942	Gardnar Mulloy–Bill Talbert	1952	Vic Seixas–Mervyn Rose
1928	G. M. Lott, Jr.–V. Hennessy	1943	Jack Kramer–Frank Parker	1953	Mervyn Rose–Rex Hartwig
1929–30	G. M. Lott, Jr.–J. H. Doeg	1944	Don McNeill–Bob Falkenburg	1954	Vic Seixas–Tony Trabert
1931	W. L. Allison–John Van Ryn	1945	Gardnar Mulloy–Bill Talbert	1955	Kosei Kamo–Atsushi Miyagi
1932	E. H. Vines, Jr.–Keith Gledh	1946	Gardnar Mulloy–Bill Talbert	1956	Lewis Hoad–Ken Rosewall
1933–34	G. M. Lott, Jr.–L. R. Stoefen	1947	Jack Kramer–Fred Schroeder	1957	Ashley Cooper–Neale Fraser

1958	Ham Richardson–Alex Olmedo	1972	Cliff Drysdale–Roger Taylor	1987	Stefan Edberg–Anders Jarryd
1959–60	Neale Fraser–Roy Emerson	1973	John Newcombe–Owen Davidson	1988	Sergio Casal–Emilio Sanchez
1961	Chuck McKinley–Dennis Ralston	1974	Bob Lutz–Stan Smith	1989	John McEnroe–Mark Woodforde
1962	Rafael Osuna–Antonio Palafox	1975	Jimmy Connors–Ilie Nastase	1990	Pieter Aldrich–Danie Visser
1963–64	Chuck McKinley–Dennis Ralston	1976	Marty Riessen–Tom Okker	1991	John Fitzgerald–Anders Jarryd
1965–66	Fred Stolle–Roy Emerson	1977	Frew McMillan–Bob Hewitt	1992	Jim Grabb–Richey Reneberg
1967	John Newcombe–Tony Roche	1978	Bob Lutz–Stan Smith	1993	Ken Flach–Rick Leach
1968	Stan Smith–Bob Lutz[1]	1979	John McEnroe–Peter Fleming	1994	Jacco Hingh–Paul Haarhuis
1969	Richard Crealy–Allan Stone[1]	1980	Stan Smith–Bob Lutz	1995–96	Todd Woodbridge–Mark Woodforde
OPEN		1981	John McEnroe–Peter Fleming	1997	Yevgeny Kafelnikov–Daniel Vacek
1968	Stan Smith–Bob Lutz	1982	Kevin Curren–Steve Denton	1998	Sandon Stolle–Cyril Zuk
1969	Fred Stolle–Ken Rosewall	1983	John McEnroe–Peter Fleming	1999	Sebastien Lareau–Alex O'Brien
1970	Nikki Pilic–Fred Barthes	1984	John Fitzgerald–Tomas Smid	2000	Lleyton Hewitt–Max Mirnyi
1971	John Newcombe–Roger Taylor	1985	Ken Flach–Robert Seguso		
		1986	Andres Gomez–Slobodan Zivojinovic		

1. With the inaugural of the Open Tournament in 1968, the United States Lawn Tennis Association held a national championship at Longwood, Chestnut Hill, Mass. which barred contract professionals in 1968 and 1969.

DOUBLES—WOMEN

NATIONAL		1962	Darlene Hard–Maria Bueno	1980	Billie Jean King–Martina Navratilova
1924	G. W. Wightman–Helen Wills	1963	Margaret Smith–Robyn Ebbern	1981	Kathy Jordan–Anne Smith
1925	Mary K. Browne–Helen Wills	1964	Karen Hantze Susman–Billie Jean Moffitt	1982	Rosemary Casals–Wendy Turnbull
1926	Elizabeth Ryan–Eleanor Goss	1965	Nancy Richey–Carole Caldwell Graebner	1983–84	Martina Navratilova–Pam Shriver
1927	L. A. Godfree–Ermyntrude Harvey	1966	Nancy Richey–Maria Bueno	1985	Claudia Khode-Kilsch–Helena Sukova
1928	Hazel Hotchkiss Wightman–Helen Wills	1967	Billie Jean King–Rosemary Casals	1986–87	Martina Navratilova–Pam Shriver
1929	Phoebe Watson–L. R. C. Michell	1968	Margaret Court–Maria Bueno[1]	1988	Gigi Fernandez–Robin White
1930	Betty Nuthall–Sarah Palfrey	1969	Margaret Court–Virginia Wade[1]	1989	Hana Mandlikova–Martina Navratilova
1931	Betty Nuthall–E. B. Wittingstall			1990	Gigi Fernandez–Martina Navratilova
1932	Helen Jacobs–Sarah Palfrey	**OPEN**			
1933	Betty Nuthall–Freda James	1968	Maria Bueno–Margaret Court	1991	Pam Shriver–Natalia Zvereva
1934	Helen Jacobs–Sarah Palfrey	1969	Darlene Hard–Francoise Durr	1992	Gigi Fernandez–Natalia Zvereva
1935	Helen Jacobs–Sarah Palfrey Fabyan	1970	Margaret Court–Judy Dalton	1993	Arantxa Sanchez Vicario–Helena Sukova
1936	Marjorie G. Van Ryn–Carolin Babcock	1971	Rosemary Casals–Judy Dalton	1994	Jana Novotna–Arantxa Sanchez Vicario
1937–40	Sarah Palfrey Fabyan–Alice Marble	1972	Francoise Durr–Betty Stove	1995	Gigi Fernandez–Natasha Zvereva
1941	Sarah Palfrey Cooke–Margaret Osborne	1973	Margaret Court–Virginia Wade	1996	Gigi Fernandez–Natasha Zvereva
1942–47	A. Louise Brough–Margaret Osborne	1974	Billie Jean King–Rosemary Casals	1997	Lindsay Davenport–Jana Novotna
1948–50	A. Louise Brough–Margaret O. duPont	1975	Margaret Court–Virginia Wade	1998	Martina Hingis–Jana Novotna
1951–54	Doris Hart–Shirley Fry	1976	Linky Boshoff–Ilana Kloss	1999	Serena Williams–Venus Williams
1955–57	A. Louise Brough–Margaret O. duPont	1977	Martina Navratilova–Betty Stove	2000	Julie-Halard Decugis–Ai Sugiyama
1958–59	Darlene Hard–Jeanne Arth	1978	Billie Jean King–Martina Navratilova		
1960	Darlene Hard–Maria Bueno	1979	Betty Stove–Wendy Turnbull		
1961	Darlene Hard–Lesley Turner				

1. With the inaugural of the Open Tournament in 1968, the United States Lawn Tennis Association held a national championship at Longwood, Chestnut Hill, Mass. which barred contract professionals in 1968 and 1969.

U.S. OPEN CHAMPIONS—2000
United States Open
(Flushing Meadow, N.Y., Aug. 28–Sept. 10, 2000)

Men's singles—Marat Safin defeated Pete Sampras, 6–4, 6–3, 6–3.

Women's singles—Venus Williams defeated Lindsay Davenport, 6–4, 7–5.

Men's doubles—Lleyton Hewitt and Max Mirnyi defeated Ellis Ferreira and Rick Leach, 6–4, 5–7, 7–6 (7–5).

Women's doubles—Julie Halard-Decugis and Ai Sugiyama defeated Cara Black and Elena Likhovtseva, 6–0, 1–6, 6–1.

Mixed doubles—Arantxa Sanchez-Vicario and Jared Palmer defeated Anna Kournikova and Max Mirnyi, 6–4, 6–3.

BRITISH (WIMBLEDON) CHAMPIONS

(Amateur from inception in 1877 through 1967)

SINGLES—MEN

1908–09	Arthur Gore	1932	Ellsworth Vines	1956–57	Lewis Hoad	1976–80	Bjorn Borg
1910–13	A. F. Wilding	1933	J. H. Crawford	1958	Ashley Cooper	1981	John McEnroe
1914	N. E. Brookes	1934–36	Fred Perry	1959	Alex Olmedo	1982	Jimmy Connors
1919	G. L. Patterson	1937–38	Don Budge	1960	Neale Fraser	1983–84	John McEnroe
1920–21	Bill Tilden	1939	Robert L. Riggs	1961–62	Rod Laver	1985–86	Boris Becker
1922	G. L. Patterson	1946	Yvon Petra	1963	Chuck McKinley	1987	Pat Cash
1923	William Johnston	1947	Jack Kramer	1964–65	Roy Emerson	1988	Stefan Edberg
1924	Jean Borotra	1948	R. Falkenburg	1966	Manuel Santana	1989	Boris Becker
1925	Rene Lacoste	1949	Fred Schroeder	1967	John Newcombe	1990	Stefan Edberg
1926	Jean Borotra	1950	Budge Patty	1968–69	Rod Laver	1991	Michael Stich
1927	Henri Cochet	1951	Richard Savitt	1970–71	John Newcombe	1992	Andre Agassi
1928	Rene Lacoste	1952	Frank Sedgman	1972	Stan Smith	1993–95	Pete Sampras
1929	Jean Cochet	1953	Vic Seixas	1973	Jan Kodes	1996	Richard Krajicek
1930	Bill Tilden	1954	Jaroslav Drobny	1974	Jimmy Connors	1997–	Pete Sampras
1931	S. B. Wood	1955	Tony Trabert	1975	Arthur Ashe	2000	

SINGLES—WOMEN

1919–23	Suzanne Lenglen	1946	Pauline M. Betz	1966–67	Billie Jean King	1982–87	Martina Navratilova
1924	Kathleen McKane	1947	Margaret Osborne	1968	Billie Jean King	1988–89	Steffi Graf
1925	Suzanne Lenglen	1948–50	A. Louise Brough	1969	Ann Jones	1990	Martina Navratilova
1926	Kathleen Godfree	1951	Doris Hart	1970	Margaret Court	1991	Steffi Graf
1927–29	Helen Wills	1952–54	Maureen Connolly	1971	Evonne Goolagong	1992	Steffi Graf
1930	Helen Wills Moody	1955	A. Louise Brough	1972–73	Billie Jean King	1993	Steffi Graf
1931	Frl. C. Aussen	1956	Shirley Fry	1974	Chris Evert	1994	Conchita Martinez
1932–33	Helen Wills Moody	1957–58	Althea Gibson	1975	Billie Jean King	1995	Steffi Graf
1934	D. E. Round	1959–60	Maria Bueno	1976	Chris Evert	1996	Steffi Graf
1935	Helen Wills Moody	1961	Angela Mortimer	1977	Virginia Wade	1997	Martina Hingis
1936	Helen Jacobs	1962	Karen Susman	1978–79	Martina Navratilova	1998	Jana Novotna
1937	D. E. Round	1963	Margaret Smith	1980	Evonne Goolagong	1999	Lindsay Davenport
1938	Helen Wills Moody	1964	Maria Bueno		Cawley	2000	Venus Williams
1939	Alice Marble	1965	Margaret Smith	1981	Chris Evert-Lloyd		

DOUBLES—MEN

1953	K. Rosewall–L. Hoad	1971	Rod Laver–Roy Emerson	1985	Heinz Gunthardt–Balazs Taroczy
1954	R. Hartwig–M. Rose	1972	Bob Hewitt–Frew McMillan		
1955	R. Hartwig–L. Hoad	1973	Jimmy Connors–Ilie Nastase	1986	Joakim Nystrom–Mats Wilander
1956	L. Hoad–K. Rosewall	1974	John Newcombe–Tony Roche		
1957	Gardnar Mulloy–Budge Patty			1987	Ken Flach–Robert Seguso
1958	Sven Davidson–Ulf Schmidt	1975	Vitas Gerulaitis–Sandy Mayer	1988	Ken Flach–Robert Seguso
1959	Roy Emerson–Neale Fraser			1989	John Fitzgerald–Anders Jarryd
1960	Dennis Ralston–Rafael Osuna	1976	Brian Gottfried–Raul Ramirez		
				1990	Rick Leach–Jim Pugh
1961	Roy Emerson–Neale Fraser	1977	Ross Case–Geoff Masters	1991	Anders Jarryd–John Fitzgerald
1962	Fred Stolle–Bob Hewitt	1978	Fred McMillan–Bob Hewitt		
1963	Rafael Osuna–Antonio Palafox	1979	Peter Fleming–John McEnroe	1992	John McEnroe–Michael Stich
1964	Fred Stolle–Bob Hewitt	1980	Peter McNamara–Paul McNamee	1993–97	Todd Woodbridge–Mark Woodforde
1965	John Newcombe–Tony Roche	1981	John McEnroe–Peter Fleming	1998	Jacco Eltingh–Paul Haarhuis
1966	John Newcombe–Ken Fletcher	1982	Paul McNamee–Peter McNamara	1999	Mahesh Bhupathi–Leander Paes
1967	Bob Hewitt–Frew McMillan	1983–84	John McEnroe–Peter Fleming	2000	Todd Woodbridge–Mark Woodforde
1968–70	John Newcombe–Tony Roche				

DOUBLES—WOMEN

1956	Althea Gibson–Angela Buxton	1962	Karen Hantze Susman–Billie Jean Moffitt	1967–68	Billie Jean King–Rosemary Casals
1957	Althea Gibson–Darlene Hard	1963	Darlene Hard–Maria Bueno	1969	Margaret Court–Judy Tegart
1958	Althea Gibson–Maria Bueno	1964	Margaret Smith–Les Turnerley	1970–71	Billie Jean King–Rosemary Casals
1959	Darlene Hard–Jeanne Arth				
1960	Darlene Hard–Maria Bueno	1965	Billie Jean Moffitt–Maria Bueno	1972	Billie Jean King–Betty Stove
1961	Karen Hantze–Billie Jean Moffitt	1966	Nancy Richey–Maria Bueno	1973	Billie Jean King–Rosemary Casals

1974	Evonne Goolagong–Peggy Michel	1985	Kathy Jordan–Elizabeth Smylie	1993	Gigi Fernandez–Natalia Zvereva
1975	Ann Kiyomura–Kazuko Sawamatsu	1986	Pam Shriver–Martina Navratilova	1994	Gigi Fernandez–Natalia Zvereva
1976	Chris Evert–Martina Navratilova	1987	Claudia Khode-Kilsch–Helena Sukova	1995	Jana Novotna–Arantxa Sanchez Vicario
1977	Helen Cawley–JoAnne Russell	1988	Steffi Graf–Gabriela Sabatini	1996	Martina Hingis–Helena Sukova
1978	Wendy Turnbull–Kerry Reid	1989	Jana Novotna–Helena Sukova	1997	Gigi Fernandez–Natasha Zvereva
1979	Billie Jean King–Martina Navratilova	1990	Jana Novotna–Helena Sukova	1998	Martina Hingis–Jana Novotna
1980	Kathy Jordan–Anne Smith	1991	Pam Shriver–Natalia Zvereva	1999	Lindsay Davenport–Corina Morariu
1981	Martina Navratilova–Pam Shriver	1992	Gigi Fernandez–Natalia Zvereva	2000	Venus Williams–Serena Williams
1982–84	Pam Shriver–Martina Navratilova				

OTHER 2000 CHAMPIONS

Wimbledon Open
(Wimbledon, England, June 26–July 9, 2000)

Men's singles—Pete Sampras defeated Patrick Rafter, 6–7 (10–12), 7–6 (7–5), 6–4, 6–2.
Women's singles—Venus Williams defeated Lindsay Davenport, 6–3, 7–6 (7–3).
Men's doubles—Mark Woodforde and Todd Woodbridge defeated Paul Haarhuis and Sandon Stolle, 6–3, 6–4, 6–1.
Women's doubles—Venus Williams and Serena Williams defeated Julie Halard-Decugis and Ai Sugiyama, 6–3, 6–2.
Mixed doubles—Donald Johnson and Kimberly Po defeated Lleyton Hewitt and Kim Clijsters, 6–4, 7–6 (7–3).

French Open
(Paris, May 29–June 11, 2000)

Men's singles—Gustavo Kuerten defeated Magnus Norman, 6–2, 6–3, 2–6, 7–6 (8–6).
Women's singles—Mary Pierce defeated Conchita Martinez, 6–2, 7–5.
Men's doubles—Mark Woodforde and Todd Woodbridge defeated Paul Haarhuis and Sandon Stolle, 7–6 (9–7), 6–4.
Women's doubles—Martina Hingis and Mary Pierce defeated Virginia Ruano-Pascual and Paola Suarez, 6–2, 6–4.
Mixed doubles—Mariaan de Swardt and David Adams defeated Rennae Stubbs and Todd Woodbridge, 6–3, 3–6, 6–3.

Australian Open
(Melbourne, Australia, Jan. 17–30, 2000)

Men's singles—Andre Agassi defeated Yevgeny Kafelnikov, 3–6, 6–3, 6–2, 6–4.
Women's singles—Lindsay Davenport defeated Martina Hingis, 6–1, 7–5.
Men's doubles—Ellis Ferreira and Rick Leach defeated Wayne Black and Andrew Kratzmann, 6–4, 3–6, 6–3, 3–6, 18–16.
Women's doubles—Lisa Raymond and Rennae Stubbs defeated Martina Hingis and Mary Pierce, 6–4, 5–7, 6–4.
Mixed doubles—Jared Palmer and Rennae Stubbs defeated Todd Woodbridge and Arantxa Sanchez-Vicario, 7–5, 7–6 (7–3).

MEN'S MONEY WINNERS—2000
(through Oct. 2, 2000)

1.	Marat Safin, Russia	$2,180,869
2.	Pete Sampras, United States	1,924,598
3.	Gustavo Kuerten, Brazil	1,846,070
4.	Magnus Norman, Sweden	1,388,029
5.	Yevgeny Kafelnikov, Russia	1,201,609
6.	Lleyton Hewitt, Australia	1,150,172
7.	Alex Corretja, Spain	1,101,325
8.	Thomas Enqvist, Sweden	1,073,920
9.	Andre Agassi, United States	987,793
10.	Dominik Hrbaty, Slovakia	936,637
11.	Cedric Pioline, France	817,039
12.	Tim Henman, Great Britain	707,923
13.	Wayne Ferreira, South Africa	699,624
14.	Patrick Rafter, Australia	679,686
15.	Todd Woodbridge, Australia	662,871
16.	Franco Squillari, Argentina	660,658
17.	Mark Woodforde, Australia	647,160
18.	Juan Carlos Ferrero, Spain	613,676
19.	Jiri Novak, Czech Republic	593,243
20.	Max Mirnyi, Bulgaria	578,948

Source: www.atptour.com.

WOMEN'S MONEY WINNERS—2000
(through Oct. 2, 2000)

1.	Venus Williams, United States	$2,030,650
2.	Lindsay Davenport, United States	1,995,484
3.	Martina Hingis, Switzerland	1,988,474
4.	Mary Pierce, France	1,208,018
5.	Conchita Martinez, Spain	941,730
6.	Monica Seles, United States	846,850
7.	Serena Williams, United States	839,818
8.	Arantxa Sanchez-Vicario, Spain	696,639
9.	Julie Halard-Decugis, France	673,470
10.	Ai Sugiyama, Japan	620,535
11.	Sandrine Testud, France	507,384
12.	Nathalie Tauziat, France	503,261
13.	Anna Kournikova, Russia	493,605
14.	Lisa Raymond, United States	491,574
15.	Anke Huber, Germany	447,441
16.	Amanda Coetzer, South Africa	447,407
17.	Elena Dementieva, Russia	434,277
18.	Elena Likhovtseva, Russia	407,464
19.	Chanda Rubin, United States	394,145
20.	Jennifer Capriati, United States	377,261

Source: Sanex WTA tour.

Rowing

Rowing goes back so far in history that there is no possibility of tracing it to any particular aboriginal source. The oldest rowing race still on the calendar is the "Doggett's Coat and Badge" contest among professional watermen of the Thames (England) that began in 1715. The first Oxford-Cambridge race was held at Henley in 1829. Competitive rowing in the United States began with matches between boats rowed by professional oarsmen of the New York waterfront. They were oarsmen who rowed the small boats that plied as ferries from Manhattan Island to Brooklyn and return, or who rowed salesmen down the harbor to meet ships arriving from Europe. Since the first salesman to meet an incoming ship had some advantage over his rivals, there was keen competition in the bidding for fast boats and the best oarsmen. This gave rise to match races.

Amateur boat clubs sprang up in the United States between 1820 and 1830 and seven students of Yale joined together to purchase a four-oared lap-streak gig in 1843. The first Harvard-Yale race was held Aug. 3, 1852, on Lake Winnepesaukee, N.H. The first time an American college crew went abroad was in 1869 when Harvard challenged Oxford and was defeated on the Thames. There were early college rowing races on Lake Quinsigamond, near Worcester, Mass., and on Saratoga Lake, N.Y., but the Intercollegiate Rowing Association in 1895 settled on the Hudson, at Poughkeepsie, as the setting for the annual "Poughkeepsie Regatta." In 1950 the I.R.A. shifted its classic to Marietta, Ohio, and in 1952 it was moved to Syracuse, N.Y. The National Association of Amateur Oarsmen, organized in 1872, has conducted annual championship regattas since that time.

INTERCOLLEGIATE ROWING ASSOCIATION REGATTA

(Varsity Eight-Oared Shells)

Rowed at 4 miles, Poughkeepsie, N.Y., 1895–97, 1899–1916, 1925–32, 1934–41. Rowed at 3 miles, Saratoga, N.Y., 1898; Poughkeepsie, 1921–24, 1947–49; Syracuse, N.Y., 1952–1963, 1965–67. Rowed at 2,000 meters, Syracuse, N.Y., 1964 and 1968–1994. Rowed at Camden, N.J., 1995–present. Rowed at 2 miles, Ithaca, N.Y., 1920; Marietta, Ohio, 1950–51. Suspended 1917–19, 1933, 1942–46.

Year	Time	First	Second
1895	21:25	Columbia	Cornell
1896	19:59	Cornell	Harvard
1897	20:47 4/5	Cornell	Columbia
1898	15:51 1/2	Pennsylvania	Cornell
1899	20:04	Pennsylvania	Wisconsin
1900	19:44 3/5	Pennsylvania	Wisconsin
1901	18:53 1/5	Cornell	Columbia
1902	19:03 3/5	Cornell	Wisconsin
1903	18:57	Cornell	Georgetown
1904	20:22 3/5	Syracuse	Cornell
1905	20:29	Cornell	Syracuse
1906	19:36 4/5	Cornell	Pennsylvania
1907	20:02 3/5	Cornell	Columbia
1908	19:24 1/5	Syracuse	Columbia
1909	19:02	Cornell	Columbia
1910	20:42 1/5	Cornell	Pennsylvania
1911	20:10 4/5	Cornell	Columbia
1912	19:31 2/5	Cornell	Wisconsin
1913	19:28 3/5	Syracuse	Cornell
1914	19:37 4/5	Columbia	Pennsylvania
1915	19:36 3/5	Cornell	Stanford
1916	20:15 2/5	Syracuse	Cornell
1920	11:02 3/5	Syracuse	Cornell
1921	14:07	Navy	California
1922	13:33 3/5	Navy	Washington
1923	14:03 1/5	Washington	Navy
1924	15:02	Washington	Wisconsin
1925	19:24 4/5	Navy	Washington
1926	19:28 3/5	Washington	Navy
1927	20:57	Columbia	Washington
1928	18:35 4/5	California	Columbia
1929	22:58	Columbia	Washington
1930	21:42	Cornell	Syracuse
1931	18:54 1/5	Navy	Cornell
1932	19:55	California	Cornell
1934	19:44	California	Washington
1935	18:52	California	Cornell
1936	19:09 3/5	Washington	California
1937	18:33 3/5	Washington	Navy
1938	18:19	Navy	California

Year	Time	First	Second
1939	18:12 3/5	California	Washington
1940	22:42	Washington	Cornell
1941	18:53 3/10	Washington	California
1947	13:59 1/5	Navy	Cornell
1948	14:06 2/5	Washington	California
1949	14:42 3/5	California	Washington
1950	8:07.5	Washington	California
1951	7:50.5	Wisconsin	Washington
1952	15:08.1	Navy	Princeton
1953	15:29.6	Navy	Cornell
1954	16:04.4	Navy[1]	Cornell
1955	15:49.9	Cornell	Pennsylvania
1956	16:22.4	Cornell	Navy
1957	15:26.6	Cornell	Pennsylvania
1958	17:12.1	Cornell	Navy
1959	18:01.7	Wisconsin	Syracuse
1960	15:57	California	Navy
1961	16:49.2	California	Cornell
1962	17:02.9	Cornell	Washington
1963	17:24	Cornell	Navy
1964	6:31.1	California	Washington
1965	16:51.3	Navy	Cornell
1966	16:03.4	Wisconsin	Navy
1967	16:13.9	Pennsylvania	Wisconsin
1968	6:15.6	Pennsylvania	Washington
1969	6:30.4	Pennsylvania	Dartmouth
1970	6:39.3	Washington	Wisconsin
1971	6:06	Cornell	Washington
1972	6:22.6	Pennsylvania	Brown
1973	6:21	Wisconsin	Brown
1974	6:33	Wisconsin	M.I.T.
1975	6:08.2	Wisconsin	M.I.T.
1976	6:31	California	Princeton
1977	6:32.4	Cornell	Pennsylvania
1978	6:39.5	Syracuse	Brown
1979	6:26.4	Brown	Wisconsin
1980	6:46	Navy	Northeastern
1981	5:57.3	Cornell	Navy
1982	5:57.5	Cornell	Princeton

Year	Time	First	Second	Year	Time	First	Second
1983	6:14.4	Brown	Navy	1992	6:10.5	Dartmouth	Harvard
1984	5:54.7	Navy	Pennsylvania	1993	5:59.1	Brown	Pennsylvania
1985	5:49.9	Princeton	Brown	1994	5:54.4	Brown	Princeton
1986	5:50.2	Brown	Pennsylvania	1995	5:31.3	Brown	Navy
1987	6:02.9	Brown	Wisconsin	1996	5:29.6	Princeton	Washington
1988	6:14.0	Northeastern	Brown	1997	5:51.0	Washington	Brown
1989	5:56.0	Penn	Wisconsin	1998	5:31.48	Princeton	Washington
1990	5:55.5	Wisconsin	Pennsylvania	1999	5:23.60[2]	California	Princeton
1991	6:05.2	Northeastern	Pennsylvania	2000	5:39.58	California	Brown

1. Disqualified. 2. New course record.

Harness Racing

Oliver Wendell Holmes, the famous Autocrat of the Breakfast Table, wrote that the running horse was a gambling toy but the trotting horse was useful and, furthermore, "horse-racing is not a republican institution; horse-trotting is." Oliver Wendell Holmes was a born-and-bred New Englander, and New England was the nursery of the harness racing sport in America. Pacers and trotters were matters of local pride and prejudice in Colonial New England, and, shortly after the Revolution, the Messenger and Justin Morgan strains produced many winners in harness racing "matches" along the turnpikes of New York, Connecticut, Rhode Island, Massachusetts, Vermont, and New Hampshire.

There was English thoroughbred blood in Messenger and Justin Morgan, and, many years later, it was blended in Rysdyk's Hambletonian, foaled in 1849. Hambletonian was not particularly fast under harness but his descendants have had almost a monopoly of prizes, titles, and records in the harness racing game. Hambletonian was purchased as a foal with its dam for a total of $124 by William Rysdyk of Goshen, N.Y., and made a modest fortune for the purchaser.

Trotters and pacers often were raced under saddle in the old days, and, in fact, the custom still survives in some places in Europe. Dexter, the great trotter that lowered the mile record from 2:19 ¾ to 2:17 ¼ in 1867, was said to handle just as well under saddle as when pulling a sulky. But as sulkies were lightened in weight and improved in design, trotting under saddle became less common and finally faded out in this country.

HISTORY OF TRADITIONAL HARNESS RACING STAKES

THE HAMBLETONIAN

Year	Winner	Driver	Best time	Total purse
1967	Speedy Streak	Del Cameron	2:00	$122,650
1968	Nevele Pride	Stanley Dancer	1:59.2	116,190
1969	Lindy's Pride	Howard Beissinger	1:57 .3	124,910
1970	Timothy T.	John Simpson, Jr.	1:58.2[1]	143,630
1971	Speedy Crown	Howard Beissinger	1:57.2	129,770
1972	Super Bowl	Stanley Dancer	1:56.2	119,090
1973	Flirth	Ralph Baldwin	1:57.1	144,710
1974	Christopher T	Billy Haughton	1:58.3	160,150
1975	Bonefish	Stanley Dancer	1:59[2]	232,192
1976	Steve Lobell	Billy Haughton	1:56.2	263,524
1977	Green Speed	Billy Haughton	1:55.3	284,131
1978	Speedy Somolli	Howard Beissinger	1:55[3]	241,280
1979	Legend Hanover	George Sholty	1:56.1	300,000
1980	Burgomeister	Billy Haughton	1:56.3	293,570
1981	Shiaway St. Pat	Ray Remmen	2:01.1[4]	838,000
1982	Speed Bowl	Tommy Haughton	1:56.4	875,750
1983	Duenna	Stanley Dancer	1:57.2	1,000,000
1984	Historic Freight	Ben Webster	1:56.2[5]	1,219,000
1985	Prakas	Bill O'Donnell	1:54.3	1,272,000
1986	Nuclear Kosmos	Ulf Thoresen	1:55.2[6]	1,172,082
1987	Mack Lobell	John Campbell	1:53.3	1,046,300
1988	Armbro Goal	John Campbell	1:54.3	1,156,800
1989	Park Avenue Joe and Probe*	Ron Wayples Bill Fahy	1:54.3	1,131,000
1990	Harmonious	John Campbell	1:54.1	1,346,000
1991	Giant Victory	Jack Moiseyev	1:54.4	1,238,000
1992	Alf Palema	Mickey McNichol	1:56.2[7]	1,288,000
1993	American Winner	Ron Pierce	1:53.1	1,200,000

Year	Winner	Driver	Best time	Total purse
1994	Victory Dream	Michel Lachance	1:53.4	1,200,000
1995	Tagliabue	John Campbell	1:54.4	1,200,000
1996	Continentalvictory	Michel La Chance	1:52.1	1,200,000
1997	Malabar Man	Malvern Burroughs	1:53.4	1,000,000
1998	Muscles Yankee	John Campbell	1:52.2	1,000,000
1999	Self Possessed	Mike La Chance	1:51.3	1,000,000
2000	Yankee Paco	Travor Ritchie	1:53.2	1,000,000

Three-year-old trotters. One mile. Guy McKinney won first race at Syracuse in 1926; held at Goshen, N.Y., 1930–1942, 1944–1956; at Yonkers, N.Y., 1943; at Du Quoin, Ill., 1957–1980. Since 1981, the race has been held at The Meadowlands in East Rutherford, N.J. *Co-winners. Fastest heat won by: 1. By Formal Notice. 2. By Yankee Bambino. 3. By Speedy Somolli and Florida Pro. 4. By Super Juan. 5. Delvin G. Hanover. 6. Royal Prestige. 7. Baltic Sonata.

LITTLE BROWN JUG

Year	Winner	Driver	Best time	Total purse
1967	Best of All	Jim Hackett	1:59[1]	$84,778
1968	Rum Customer	Billy Haughton	1:59.3	104,226
1969	Laverne Hanover	Billy Haughton	2:00.2	109,731
1970	Most Happy Fella	Stanley Dancer	1:57.1	100,110
1971	Nansemond	Herve Filion	1:57.2	102,994
1972	Strike Out	Keith Waples	1:56.3	104,916
1973	Melvin's Woe	Joe O'Brien	1:57.3	120,000
1974	Ambro Omaha	Billy Haughton	1:57	132,630
1975	Seatrain	Ben Webster	1:57[2]	147,813
1976	Keystone Ore	Stanley Dancer	1:56.4[3]	153,799
1977	Governor Skipper	John Chapman	1:56.1	150,000
1978	Happy Escort	William Popfinger	1:55.2[4]	186,760
1979	Hot Hitter	Herve Filion	1:55.3	226,455
1980	Niatross	Clint Galbraith	1:54.4	207,361
1981	Fan Hanover	Glen Garnsey	1:56[5]	243,799
1982	Merger	John Campbell	1:56.3	328,900
1983	Ralph Hanover	Ron Waples	1:55.3	358,800
1984	Colt 46	Norman Boring	1:53.3	366,717
1985	Nihilator	Bill O'Donnell	1:52.1	350,730
1986	Barberry Spur	Bill O'Donnell	1:52.4	407,684
1987	Jaguar Spur	Richard Stillings	1:55.3	412,330
1988	B.J. Scoot	Michel Lachance	1:52.3	486,050
1989	Goalie Jeff	Michel Lachance	1:54.1	500,200
1990	Beach Towel	Ray Remmen	1:53.3	253,049
1991	Precious Bunny	Jack Moiseyev	1:54.1	575,150
1992	Fake Left	Ron Waples	1:54.2	556,210
1993	Life Sign	John Campbell	1:52	465,500
1994	Magical Mike	Michel LaChance	1:52.3	512,830
1995	Nick's Fantasy	John Campbell	1:51.2	543,670
1996	Armbro Operative	Michel La Chance	1:52.3	542,220
1997	Western Dreamer	Michel La Chance	1:51.1	605,210
1998	Shady Character	Ron Pierce	1:52.3	566,630
1999	Blissfull Hall	Ron Pierce	1:55.3	543,980
2000	Astreos	Chris Christoforou	1:55.3	$547,972

Three-year-old pacers. One Mile. Raced at Delaware County Fair Grounds, Delaware, Ohio. 1. By Nardin's Byrd. 2. By Albert's Star. 3. By Armbro Ranger. 4. By Falcon Almahurst. 5. By Seahawk Hanover.

HARNESS HORSE OF THE YEAR

1959	Bye Bye Byrd, Pacer	1976	Keystone Ore, Pacer	1990	Beach Towell
1960–61	Adios Butler, Pacer	1977	Green Speed, Trotter	1991	Precious Bunny
1962	Su Mac Lad, Trotter	1978	Abercrombie, Pacer	1992	Artsplace
1963	Speedy Scot, Trotter	1979–80	Niatross, Pacer	1993	Staying Together
1964–66	Bret Hanover, Pacer	1981	Fan Hanover, Pacer	1994	Cam's Card Shark
1967–69	Nevele Pride, Trotter	1982–83	Cam Fella, Pacer	1995	CR Kay Suzie
1970	Fresh Yankee, Trotter	1984	Fancy Crown, Trotter	1996	Continentalvictory
1971–72	Albatross, Pacer	1985	Nihilator, Trotter	1997	Malabar Man
1973	Sir Dalrae, Pacer	1986	Forrest Skipper	1998–	Moni Maker
1974	Delmonica Hanover, Trotter	1987–88	Mack Lobell	1999	
1975	Savoir, Trotter	1989	Matt's Scooter		

Chosen in poll conducted by United States Trotting Association in conjunction with the U.S. Harness Writers Assn.

Golf

It may be that golf originated in Holland—historians believe it did—but certainly Scotland fostered the game and is famous for it. In fact, in 1457 the Scottish Parliament, disturbed because football and golf had lured young Scots from the more soldierly exercise of archery, passed an ordinance that "futeball and golf be utterly cryit doun and nocht usit." James I and Charles I of the royal line of Stuarts were golf enthusiasts, whereby the game came to be known as "the royal and ancient game of golf."

The golf balls used in the early games were leather-covered and stuffed with feathers. Clubs of all kinds were fashioned by hand to suit individual players. The great step in spreading the game came with the change from the feather ball to the gutta-percha ball about 1850. In 1860, formal competition began with the establishment of an annual tournament for the British Open championship. There are records of "golf clubs" in the United States as far back as colonial days but no proof of actual play before John Reid and some friends laid out six holes on the Reid lawn in Yonkers, N.Y., in 1888 and played there with golf balls and clubs brought over from Scotland by Robert Lockhart. This group then formed the St. Andrews Golf Club of Yonkers, and golf was established in this country.

However, it remained a rather sedate and almost aristocratic pastime until a 20-year-old ex-caddy, Francis Ouimet of Boston, defeated two great British professionals, Harry Vardon and Ted Ray, in the United States Open championship at Brookline, Mass., in 1913. This feat put the game and Francis Ouimet on the front pages of the newspapers and stirred a wave of enthusiasm for the sport. The greatest feat so far in golf history is that of Robert Tyre Jones, Jr., of Atlanta, who won the British Open, the British Amateur, the U.S. Open, and the U.S. Amateur titles in one year, 1930.

THE MASTERS TOURNAMENT WINNERS

Augusta National Golf Club, Augusta, Ga.

Year	Winner	Score	Year	Winner	Score	Year	Winner	Score
1934	Horton Smith	284	1958	Arnold Palmer	284	1980	Severiano Ballesteros	275
1935	Gene Sarazen[1]	282	1959	Art Wall, Jr.	284	1981	Tom Watson	280
1936	Horton Smith	285	1960	Arnold Palmer	282	1982	Craig Stadler[1]	284
1937	Byron Nelson	283	1961	Gary Player	280	1983	Severiano Ballesteros	280
1938	Henry Picard	285	1962	Arnold Palmer[1]	280	1984	Ben Crenshaw	277
1939	Ralph Guldahl	279	1963	Jack Nicklaus	286	1985	Bernhard Langer	282
1940	Jimmy Demaret	280	1964	Arnold Palmer	276	1986	Jack Nicklaus	279
1941	Craig Wood	280	1965	Jack Nicklaus	271	1987	Larry Mize[1]	285
1942	Byron Nelson[1]	280	1966	Jack Nicklaus[1]	288	1988	Sandy Lyle	281
1943–45	No Tournaments		1967	Gay Brewer, Jr.	280	1989	Nick Faldo[1]	283
1946	Herman Keiser	282	1968	Bob Goalby	277	1990	Nick Faldo	278
1947	Jimmy Demaret	281	1969	George Archer	281	1991	Ian Woosnam	277
1948	Claude Harmon	279	1970	Billy Casper[1]	279	1992	Fred Couples	275
1949	Sam Snead	282	1971	Charles Coody	279	1993	Bernard Langer	277
1950	Jimmy Demaret	283	1972	Jack Nicklaus	286	1994	Jose Maria Olazabal	279
1951	Ben Hogan	280	1973	Tommy Aaron	283	1995	Ben Crenshaw	274
1952	Sam Snead	286	1974	Gary Player	278	1996	Nick Faldo	276
1953	Ben Hogan	274	1975	Jack Nicklaus	276	1997	Tiger Woods	270
1954	Sam Snead[1]	289	1976	Ray Floyd	271	1998	Mark O'Meara	279
1955	Cary Middlecoff	279	1977	Tom Watson	276	1999	Jose Maria Olazabal	280
1956	Jack Burke	289	1978	Gary Player	277	2000	Vijay Singh	278
1957	Doug Ford	283	1979	Fuzzy Zoeller[1]	280			

1. Winner in playoff.

U.S. OPEN CHAMPIONS

Year	Winner	Score	Where played	Year	Winner	Score	Where played
1895	Horace Rawlins	173	Newport	1910	Alex Smith[1]	298	Philadelphia
1896	James Foulis	152	Shinnecock Hills	1911	John McDermott[1]	307	Chicago
1897	Joe Lloyd	162	Chicago	1912	John McDermott	294	Buffalo
1898[3]	Fred Herd	328	Myopia	1913	Francis Ouimet[1] [2]	304	Brookline
1899	Willie Smith	315	Baltimore	1914	Walter Hagen	290	Midlothian
1900	Harry Vardon	313	Chicago	1915	Jerome D. Travers[2]	297	Baltusrol
1901	Willie Anderson[1]	331	Myopia	1916	Charles Evans, Jr.[2]	286	Minikahda
1902	Laurie Auchterlonie	307	Garden City	1917–18	No tournaments[4]		
1903	Willie Anderson[1]	307	Baltusrol	1919	Walter Hagen[2]	301	Brae Burn
1904	Willie Anderson	303	Glen View	1920	Edward Ray	295	Inverness
1905	Willie Anderson	314	Myopia	1921	Jim Barnes	289	Columbia
1906	Alex Smith	295	Onwentsia	1922	Gene Sarazen	288	Skokie
1907	Alex Ross	302	Philadelphia	1923	R. T. Jones, Jr.[1] [2]	296	Inwood
1908	Fred McLeod[1]	322	Myopia	1924	Cyril Walker	297	Oakland Hills
1909	George Sargent	290	Englewood	1925	Willie Macfarlane[1]	291	Worcester

Year	Winner	Score	Where played
1926	R. T. Jones, Jr.[2]	293	Scioto
1927	Tommy Armour[1]	301	Oakmont
1928	Johnny Farrell[1]	294	Olympia Fields
1929	R. T. Jones, Jr.[1,2]	294	Winged Foot
1930	R. T. Jones, Jr.[2]	287	Interlachen
1931	Billy Burke[1]	292	Inverness
1932	Gene Sarazen	286	Fresh Meadow
1933	John Goodman[2]	287	North Shore
1934	Olin Dutra	293	Merion
1935	Sam Parks, Jr.	299	Oakmont
1936	Tony Manero	282	Baltusrol
1937	Ralph Guldahl	281	Oakland Hills
1938	Ralph Guldahl	284	Cherry Hills
1939	Byron Nelson[1]	284	Philadelphia
1940	Lawson Little[1]	287	Canterbury
1941	Craig Wood	284	Colonial
1942–45	No tournaments[5]		
1946	Lloyd Mangrum[1]	284	Canterbury
1947	Lew Worsham[1]	282	St. Louis
1948	Ben Hogan	276	Riviera
1949	Cary Middlecoff	286	Medinah
1950	Ben Hogan[1]	287	Merion
1951	Ben Hogan	287	Oakland Hills
1952	Julius Boros	281	Northwood
1953	Ben Hogan	283	Oakmont
1954	Ed Furgol	284	Baltusrol
1955	Jack Fleck[1]	287	Olympic
1956	Cary Middlecoff	281	Oak Hill
1957	Dick Mayer[1]	298	Inverness
1958	Tommy Bolt	283	Southern Hills
1959	Bill Casper, Jr.	282	Winged Foot
1960	Arnold Palmer	280	Cherry Hills
1961	Gene Littler	281	Oakland Hills
1962	Jack Nicklaus[1]	283	Oakmont
1963	Julius Boros[1]	293	Country Club
1964	Ken Venturi	278	Congressional
1965	Gary Player[1]	282	Bellerive
1966	Bill Casper[1]	278	Olympic
1967	Jack Nicklaus	275	Baltusrol
1968	Lee Trevino	275	Oak Hill
1969	Orville Moody	281	Champions G.C.
1970	Tony Jacklin	281	Hazeltine
1971	Lee Trevino[1]	280	Merion
1972	Jack Nicklaus	290	Pebble Beach
1973	Johnny Miller	279	Oakmont
1974	Hale Irwin	287	Winged Foot
1975	Lou Graham[1]	287	Medinah
1976	Jerry Pate	277	Atlanta A.C.
1977	Hubert Green	278	Southern Hills
1978	Andy North	285	Cherry Hills
1979	Hale Irwin	284	Inverness
1980	Jack Nicklaus	272	Baltusrol
1981	David Graham	273	Merion
1982	Tom Watson	282	Pebble Beach
1983	Larry Nelson	280	Oakmont
1984	Fuzzy Zoeller[1]	276	Winged Foot
1985	Andy North	279	Oakland Hills
1986	Ray Floyd	279	Shinnecock Hills
1987	Scott Simpson	277	Olympic Golf Club
1988	Curtis Strange[1]	278	The Country Club
1989	Curtis Strange	278	Oak Hill Country Club
1990	Hale Irwin[1]	280	Medinah C.C.
1991	Payne Stewart[1]	282	Hazeltine
1992	Tom Kite	285	Pebble Beach
1993	Lee Janzen	272	Baltusrol
1994	Ernie Els	279	Oakmont
1995	Corey Pavin	280	Shinnecock Hills
1996	Steve Jones	278	Oakland Hills
1997	Ernie Els	276	Congressional C.C.
1998	Lee Janzen	280	Olympic Country Club
1999	Payne Stewart	279	Pinehurst
2000	Tiger Woods	272	Pebble Beach

1. Winner in playoff. 2. Amateur. 3. In 1898, competition was extended to 72 holes. 4. In 1917, Jock Hutchison, with a 292, won an Open Patriotic Tournament for the benefit of the American Red Cross at Whitemarsh Valley Country Club. 5. In 1942, Ben Hogan, with a 271 won a Hale American National Open Tournament for the benefit of the Navy Relief Society and USO at Ridgemoor Country Club.

U.S. AMATEUR CHAMPIONS

Year	Winner	Year	Winner
1895	Charles B. Macdonald	1954	Arnold Palmer
1896–97	H. J. Whigham	1955–56	Harvie Ward
1898	Findlay S. Douglas	1957	Hillman Robbins
1899	H. M. Harriman	1958	Charles Coe
1900–01	Walter J. Travis	1959	Jack Nicklaus
1902	Louis N. James	1960	Deane Beman
1903	Walter J. Travis	1961	Jack Nicklaus
1904–05	H. Chandler Egan	1962	Labron Harris, Jr.
1906	Eben M. Byers	1963	Deane Beman
1907–08	Jerome D. Travers	1964	Bill Campbell
1909	Robert A. Gardner	1965[2]	Robert Murphy, Jr.
1910	W. C. Fownes, Jr.	1966	Gary Cowan[1]
1911	Harold H. Hilton	1967	Bob Dickson
1912–13	Jerome D. Travers	1968	Bruce Fleisher
1914	Francis Ouimet	1969	Steven Melnyk
1915	Robert A. Gardner	1970	Lanny Wadkins
1916	Charles Evans, Jr.	1971	Gary Cowan
1919	S. D. Herron	1972	Vinny Giles 3d
1920	Charles Evans, Jr.	1973[3]	Craig Stadler
1921	Jesse P. Guilford	1974	Jerry Pate
1922	Jess W. Sweetser	1975	Fred Ridley
1923	Max R. Marston	1976	Bill Sander
1924–25	R. T. Jones, Jr.	1977	John Fought
1926	George Von Elm	1978	John Cook
1927–28	R. T. Jones, Jr.	1979	Mark O'Meara
1929	H. R. Johnston	1980	Hal Sutton
1930	R. T. Jones, Jr.	1981	Nathaniel Crosby
1931	Francis Ouimet	1982	Jay Sigel
1932	Ross Somerville	1983	Jay Sigel
1933	G. T. Dunlap, Jr.	1984	Scott Verplank
1934–35	Lawson Little	1985	Sam Randolph
1936	John W. Fischer	1986	Buddy Alexander
1937	John Goodman	1987	Bill Mayfair
1938	Willie Turnesa	1988	Eric Meeks
1939	Marvin H. Ward	1989	Chris Patton
1940	R. D. Chapman	1990	Phil Mickelson
1941	Marvin H. Ward	1991	Mitch Voges
1946	Ted Bishop	1992	Justin Leonard
1947	Robert Riegel	1993	John Harris
1948	Willie Turnesa	1994–96	Tiger Woods
1949	Charles Coe	1997	Matthew Kuchar
1950	Sam Urzetta	1998	Hank Kuehne
1951	Billy Maxwell	1999	David Gossett
1952	Jack Westland	2000	Jeff Quinney
1953	Gene Littler		

1. Winner in playoff. 2. Tourney switched to medal play through 1972. 3. Return to match play.

U.S. P.G.A. CHAMPIONS

Year	Winner	Year	Winner	Year	Winner	Year	Winner
1916	Jim Barnes	1944	Bob Hamilton	1963	Jack Nicklaus	1982	Ray Floyd
1919	Jim Barnes	1945	Byron Nelson	1964	Bobby Nichols	1983	Hal Sutton
1920	Jock Hutchison	1946	Ben Hogan	1965	Dave Marr	1984	Lee Trevino
1921	Walter Hagen	1947	Jim Ferrier	1966	Al Geiberger	1985	Hubert Green
1922–23	Gene Sarazen	1948	Ben Hogan	1967	Don January[1]	1986	Bob Tway
1924–27	Walter Hagen	1949	Sam Snead	1968	Julius Boros	1987	Larry Nelson
1928–29	Leo Diegel	1950	Chandler Harper	1969	Ray Floyd	1988	Jeff Sluman
1930	Tommy Armour	1951	Sam Snead	1970	Dave Stockton	1989	Payne Stewart
1931	Tom Creavy	1952	Jim Turnesa	1971	Jack Nicklaus	1990	Wayne Grady
1932	Olin Dutra	1953	Walter Burkemo	1972	Gary Player	1991	John Daly
1933	Gene Sarazen	1954	Chick Harbert	1973	Jack Nicklaus	1992	Nick Price
1934	Paul Runyan	1955	Doug Ford	1974	Lee Trevino	1993	Paul Azinger[1]
1935	Johnny Revolta	1956	Jack Burke, Jr.	1975	Jack Nicklaus	1994	Nick Price
1936–37	Denny Shute	1957	Lionel Hebert	1976	Dave Stockton	1995	Steve Elkington
1938	Paul Runyan	1958[2]	Dow Finsterwald	1977	Lanny Wadkins[1]	1996	Mark Brooks[1]
1939	Henry Picard	1959	Bob Rosburg	1978	John Mahaffey	1997	Davis Love III
1940	Byron Nelson	1960	Jay Hebert	1979	David Graham[1]	1998	Vijay Singh
1941	Victor Ghezzi	1961	Jerry Barber[1]	1980	Jack Nicklaus	1999–	Tiger Woods
1942	Sam Snead	1962	Gary Player	1981	Larry Nelson	2000	

1. Winner in playoff. 2. Switched to medal play.

U.S. WOMEN'S AMATEUR CHAMPIONS

Year	Winner	Year	Winner	Year	Winner	Year	Winner
1916	Alexa Stirling	1946	Mildred Zaharias	1965	Jean Ashley	1984	Deb Richard
1919–20	Alexa Stirling	1947	Louise Suggs	1966	JoAnne Gunderson	1985	Michiko Hattori
1921	Marion Hollins	1948	Grace Lenczyk	1967	Lou Dill	1986	Kay Cockerill
1922	Glenna Collett	1949	Mrs. D. G. Porter	1968	JoAnne G. Carner	1987	Kay Cockerill
1923	Edith Cummings	1950	Beverly Hanson	1969	Catherine LaCoste	1988	Pearl Sinn
1924	Dorothy Campbell Hurd	1951	Dorothy Kirby	1970	Martha Wilkinson	1989	Vicki Goetze
1925	Glenna Collett	1952	Jacqueline Pung	1971	Laura Baugh	1990	Pat Hurst
1926	Helen Stetson	1953	Mary Lena Faulk	1972	Mary Ann Budke	1991	Amy Fruhwirth
1927	Mrs. M. B. Horn	1954	Barbara Romack	1973	Carol Semple	1992	Vicki Goetze
1928–30	Glenna Collett	1955	Patricia Lesser	1974	Cynthia Hill	1993	Jill McGill
1931	Helen Hicks	1956	Marlene Stewart	1975	Beth Daniel	1994	Wendy Ward
1932–34	Virginia Van Wie	1957	JoAnne Gunderson	1976	Donna Horton	1995	Kelli Kuehne
1935	Glenna Collett Vare	1958	Anne Quast	1977	Beth Daniel	1996	Kelli Kuehne
1936	Pamela Barton	1959	Barbara McIntire	1978	Cathy Sherk	1997	Silvia Cavalleri
1937	Mrs. J. A. Page, Jr.	1960	JoAnne Gunderson	1979	Carolyn Hill	1998	Grace Park
1938	Patty Berg	1961	Anne Quast Decker	1980	Juli Inkster	1999	Dorothy Delasin
1939–40	Betty Jameson	1962	JoAnne Gunderson	1981	Juli Inkster	2000	Marcy Newton
1941	Mrs. Frank Newell	1963	Anne Quast Welts	1982	Juli Inkster		
		1964	Barbara McIntire	1983	Joanne Pacillo		

U.S. WOMEN'S OPEN CHAMPIONS

Year	Winner	Score	Year	Winner	Score	Year	Winner	Score
1946	Patty Berg (match play)	—	1964	Mickey Wright[1]	290	1983	Jan Stephenson	290
			1965	Carol Mann	290	1984	Hollis Stacy	290
1947	Betty Jameson	295	1966	Sandra Spuzich	297	1985	Kathy Baker	280
1948	Mildred D. Zaharias	300	1967	Catherine LaCoste[2]	294	1986	Jane Geddes[1]	287
1949	Louise Suggs	291	1968	Susie Berning	289	1987	Laura Davies[1]	285
1950	Mildred D. Zaharias	291	1969	Donna Caponi	294	1988	Liselotte Neumann	277
1951	Betsy Rawls	293	1970	Donna Caponi	287	1989	Betsy King	278
1952	Louise Suggs	284	1971	JoAnne Carner	288	1990	Betsy King	284
1953	Betsy Rawls[1]	302	1972	Susie Berning	299	1991	Meg Mallon	283
1954	Mildred D. Zaharias	291	1973	Susie Berning	290	1992	Patty Sheehan	280
1955	Fay Crocker	299	1974	Sandra Haynie	295	1993	Lauri Merten	280
1956	Katherine Cornelius[1]	302	1975	Sandra Palmer	295	1994	Patty Sheehan	277
1957	Betsy Rawls	299	1976	JoAnne Carner[1]	292	1995	Annika Sorenstam	278
1958	Mickey Wright	290	1977	Hollis Stacy	292	1996	Annika Sorenstam	272
1959	Mickey Wright	287	1978	Hollis Stacy	289	1997	Alison Nicholas	274
1960	Betsy Rawls	291	1979	Jerilyn Britz	284	1998	Se Ri Pak	290
1961	Mickey Wright	293	1980	Amy Alcott	280	1999	Juli Inkster	272
1962	Murle Lindstrom	301	1981	Pat Bradley	279	2000	Karrie Webb	282
1963	Mary Mills	289	1982	Janet Alex	283			

1. Winner in playoff. 2. Amateur.

BRITISH OPEN CHAMPIONS

(First tournament, held in 1860, was won by Willie Park, Sr.)

Year	Winner	Score	Year	Winner	Score	Year	Winner	Score
1920	George Duncan	303	1951	Max Faulkner	285	1976	Johnny Miller	279
1921	Jock Hutchison[1]	296	1952	Bobby Locke	287	1977	Tom Watson	268
1922	Walter Hagen	300	1953	Ben Hogan	282	1978	Jack Nicklaus	281
1923	A. G. Havers	295	1954	Peter Thomson	283	1979	Severiano Ballesteros	283
1924	Walter Hagen	301	1955	Peter Thomson	281	1980	Tom Watson	271
1925	Jim Barnes	300	1956	Peter Thomson	286	1981	Bill Rogers	276
1926	R. T. Jones, Jr.	291	1957	Bobby Locke	279	1982	Tom Watson	284
1927	R. T. Jones, Jr.	285	1958	Peter Thomson[1]	278	1983	Tom Watson	275
1928	Walter Hagen	292	1959	Gary Player	284	1984	Severiano Ballesteros	276
1929	Walter Hagen	292	1960	Kel Nagle	278	1985	Sandy Lyle	282
1930	R. T. Jones, Jr.	291	1961	Arnold Palmer	284	1986	Greg Norman	280
1931	Tommy Armour	296	1962	Arnold Palmer	276	1987	Nick Faldo	279
1932	Gene Sarazen	283	1963	Bob Charles[1]	277	1988	Seve Ballesteros	273
1933	Denny Shute[1]	292	1964	Tony Lema	279	1989	Mark Calcavecchia	275
1934	Henry Cotton	283	1965	Peter Thomson	285	1990	Nick Faldo	270
1935	A. Perry	283	1966	Jack Nicklaus	282	1991	Ian Baker-Finch	272
1936	A. H. Padgham	287	1967	Roberto de Vicenzo	278	1992	Nick Faldo	272
1937	Henry Cotton	290	1968	Gary Player	289	1993	Greg Norman	267
1938	R. A. Whitcombe	295	1969	Tony Jacklin	280	1994	Nick Price	268
1939	R. Burton	290	1970	Jack Nicklaus[1]	283	1995	John Daly	282
1940	Sam Snead	290	1971	Lee Trevino	278	1996	Tom Lehman	271
1947	Fred Daly	294	1972	Lee Trevino	278	1997	Justin Leonard	272
1948	Henry Cotton	283	1973	Tom Weiskopf	276	1998	Mark O'Meara	280
1949	Bobby Locke[1]	283	1974	Gary Player	282	1999	Paul Lawrie	290
1950	Bobby Locke	279	1975	Tom Watson[1]	279	2000	Tiger Woods	269

OTHER 2000 PGA TOUR WINNERS

(Through Sept. 10, 2000)

Mercedes Championships—Tiger Woods	$522,000
SONY Open—Paul Azinger	522,000
Bob Hope Chrysler Classic—Jesper Parnevik	540,000
Phoenix Open—Tom Lehman	576,000
AT&T Pebble Beach National Pro-Am—Tiger Woods	720,000
Buick Invitational—Phil Mickelson	540,000
Nissan Open—Kirk Triplett	558,000
Touchstone Energy Tucson Open—Jim Carter	540,000
Andersen Consulting Match Play Championship—Darren Clarke	1,000,000
Doral-Ryder Open—Jim Furyk	540,000
Honda Classic—Dudley Hart	522,000
Bay Hill Invitational—Tiger Woods	540,000
The Players Championship—Hal Sutton	1,080,000
BellSouth Classic—Phil Mickelson	504,000
GTE Byron Nelson Classic—Jesper Parnevik	720,000
MasterCard Colonial—Phil Mickelson	594,000
Memorial Tournament—Tiger Woods	558,000
The INTERNATIONAL—Ernie Els	630,000
NEC Invitational—Tiger Woods	1,000,000
Canadian Open—Tiger Woods	558,000

OTHER 2000 LPGA TOUR WINNERS

(Through Sept. 10, 2000)

Subaru Memorial of Naples—Nancy Scranton	$127,500
Australian Ladies Masters—Karrie Webb	112,500
Takefuji Classic—Karrie Webb	120,000
Welch's/Circle K Championship—Annika Sörenstam	105,000
Standard Register PING—Charlotta Sörenstam	127,500
Nabisco Championship—Karrie Webb	187,500
Chick-fil-A Charity Championship—Sophie Gustafson	135,000
Electrolux U.S.A. Championship—Pat Hurst	120,000
Corning Classic—Betsy King	120,000
Wegmans Rochester International—Meg Mallon	150,000
Evian Masters—Annika Sörenstam	270,000
McDonald's LPGA Championship—Juli Inkster	210,000
ShopRite LPGA Classic—Janice Moodie	165,000
Jamie Farr Kroger Classic—Annika Sörenstam	150,000
JAL Big Apple Classic—Annika Sörenstam	135,000
Giant Eagle LPGA Classic—Dorothy Delasin	150,000
du Maurier Classic—Meg Mallon	180,000
Michelob Light Classic—Lorie Kane	120,000
Weetabix Women's British Open—Sophie Gustafson	178,800
State Farm Rail Classic—Laurel Kean	135,000

Auto Racing

INDIANAPOLIS 500

Year	Winner	Car	Time	mph	Second place
1911	Ray Harroun	Marmon	6:42:08.000	74.590	Ralph Mulford
1912	Joe Dawson	National	6:21:06.000	78.720	Teddy Tetzloff
1913	Jules Goux	Peugeot	6:35:05.000	75.930	Spencer Wishart
1914	René Thomas	Delage	6:03:45.000	82.470	Arthur Duray
1915	Ralph DePalma	Mercedes	5:33:55.510	89.840	Dario Resta
1916[1]	Dario Resta	Peugeot	3:34:17.000	84.000	Wilbur D'Alene
1919	Howard Wilcox	Peugeot	5:40:42.870	88.050	Eddie Hearne
1920	Gaston Chevrolet	Monroe	5:38:32.000	88.620	René Thomas
1921	Tommy Milton	Frontenac	5:34:44.650	89.620	Roscoe Sarles
1922	Jimmy Murphy	Murphy Special	5:17:30.790	94.480	Harry Hartz

Year	Winner	Car	Time	mph	Second place
1923	Tommy Milton	H. C. S. Special	5:29.50.170	90.950	Harry Hartz
1924	L. L. Corum-Joe Boyer	Dusenberg Special	5:05:23.510	98.230	Earl Cooper
1925	Peter DePaolo	Dusenberg Special	4:56:39.450	101.130	Dave Lewis
1926[2]	Frank Lockhart	Miller Special	4:10:14.950	95.904	Harry Hartz
1927	George Souders	Dusenberg Special	5:07:33.080	97.540	Earl DeVore
1928	Louis Meyer	Miller Special	5:01:33.750	99.480	Lou Moore
1929	Ray Keech	Simplex Special	5:07:25.420	97.580	Louis Meyer
1930	Billy Arnold	Miller-Hartz Special	4:58:39.720	100.448	Shorty Cantlon
1931	Louis Schneider	Bowes Special	5:10:27.930	96.629	Fred Frame
1932	Fred Frame	Miller-Hartz Special	4:48:03.790	104.144	Howard Wilcox
1933	Louis Meyer	Tydol Special	4:48:00.750	104.162	Wilbur Shaw
1934	Bill Cummings	Boyle Products Special	4:46:05.200	104.863	Mauri Rose
1935	Kelly Petillo	Gilmore Special	4:42:22.710	106.240	Wilbur Shaw
1936	Louis Meyer	Ring Free Special	4:35:03.390	109.069	Ted Horn
1937	Wilbur Shaw	Shaw-Gilmore Special	4:24:07.800	113.580	Ralph Hepburn
1938	Floyd Roberts	Burd Piston Ring Special	4:15:58.400	117.200	Wilbur Shaw
1939	Wilbur Shaw	Boyle Special	4:20:47.390	115.035	Jimmy Snyder
1940	Wilbur Shaw	Boyle Special	4:22:31.170	114.277	Rex Mays
1941	Floyd Davis-Mauri Rose	Noc-Out Hose Clamp Special	4:20:36.240	115.117	Rex Mays
1946	George Robson	Thorne Engineering Special	4:21:26.710	114.820	Jimmy Jackson
1947	Mauri Rose	Blue Crown Special	4:17:52.170	116.338	Bill Holland
1948	Mauri Rose	Blue Crown Special	4:10:23.330	119.814	Bill Holland
1949	Bill Holland	Blue Crown Special	4:07:15.970	121.327	Johnny Parsons
1950[3]	Johnnie Parsons	Wynn's Friction Proof Special	2:46:55.970	124.002	Bill Holland
1951	Lee Wallard	Belanger Special	3:57:38.050	126.244	Mike Nazaruk
1952	Troy Ruttman	Agajanian Special	3:52:41.880	128.922	Jim Rathmann
1953	Bill Vukovich	Fuel Injection Special	3:53:01.690	128.740	Art Cross
1954	Bill Vukovich	Fuel Injection Special	3:49:17.270	130.840	Jim Bryan
1955	Bob Sweikert	John Zink Special	3:53:59.13	128.209	Tony Bettenhausen
1956	Pat Flaherty	John Zink Special	3:53:28.840	128.490	Sam Hanks
1957	Sam Hanks	Belond Exhaust Special	3:41:14.250	135.601	Jim Rathmann
1958	Jimmy Bryan	Belond A-P Special	3:44:13.800	133.791	George Amick
1959	Rodger Ward	Leader Card 500 Roadster	3:40:49.200	135.857	Jim Rathmann
1960	Jim Rathmann	Ken-Paul Special	3:36:11.360	138.767	Rodger Ward
1961	A. J. Foyt	Bowes Special	3:35:37.490	139.130	Eddie Sachs
1962	Rodger Ward	Leader Card Special	3:33:50.330	140.293	Len Sutton
1963	Parnelli Jones	Agajanian Special	3:29:35.400	143.137	Jim Clark
1964	A. J. Foyt	Sheraton-Thompson Spl.	3:23:35.830	147.350	Rodger Ward
1965	Jim Clark	Lotus-Ford	3:19:05.340	150.686	Parnelli Jones
1966	Graham Hill	Red Ball Lola-Ford	3:27:52.530	144.317	Jim Clark
1967[4]	A. J. Foyt	Sheraton-Thompson Coyote-Ford	3:18:24.220	151.207	Al Unser
1968	Bobby Unser	Rislone Eagle-Offenhauser	3:16:13.760	152.882	Dan Gurney
1969	Mario Andretti	STP Hawk-Ford	3:11:14.710	156.867	Dan Gurney
1970	Al Unser	Johnny Lightning P. J. Colt-Ford	3:12:37.040	155.749	Mark Donohue
1971	Al Unser	Johnny Lightning P. J. Colt-Ford	3:10:11.560	157.735	Peter Revson
1972	Mark Donohue	Sunoco McLaren-Offenhauser	3:04:05.540	162.962	Al Unser
1973[5]	Gordon Johncock	STP Eagle-Offenhauser	2:05:26.590	159.036	Bill Vukovich, Jr.
1974	Johnny Rutherford	McLaren-Offenhauser	3:09:10.060	158.589	Bobby Unser
1975[6]	Bobby Unser	Jorgensen Eagle-Offenhauser	2:54:55.080	149.213	Johnny Rutherford
1976[7]	Johnny Rutherford	Hy-gain McLaren-Offenhauser	1:42:52.480	148.725	A. J. Foyt
1977	A. J. Foyt	Gilmore Coyote-Foyt	3:05:57.160	161.331	Tom Sneva
1978	Al Unser	1st Nat'l City Lola-Cosworth	3:05:54.990	161.363	Tom Sneva
1979	Rick Mears	Gould Penske-Cosworth	3:08:27.970	158.899	A. J. Foyt
1980	Johnny Rutherford	Pennzoil Chaparral-Cosworth	3:29:59.560	142.862	Tom Sneva
1981[8]	Bobby Unser	Norton Penske-Cosworth	3:35:41.780	139.029	Mario Andretti
1982	Gordon Johncock	STP Wildcat-Cosworth	3:05:09.140	162.029	Rick Mears
1983	Tom Sneva	Texaco Star March-Cosworth	3:05:03.060	162.117	Al Unser
1984	Rick Mears	Pennzoil March-Cosworth	3:03:21.000	162.962	Roberto Guerrero
1985	Danny Sullivan	Miller March-Cosworth	3:16:06.069	152.982	Mario Andretti
1986	Bobby Rahal	Budweiser March-Cosworth	2:55:43.480	170.722	Kevin Cogan
1987	Al Unser, Sr.	Cummins March-Cosworth	3:04:59.147	162.175	Roberto Guerrero
1988	Rick Mears	Pennzoil Penske P.C.17-Chevrolet	3:27:10.204	144.809	Emerson Fittipaldi
1989	Emerson Fittipaldi	Marlboro Penske-Cosworth	2:59:01.040	167.581	Al Unser, Jr.
1990	Arie Luyendyk	Domino's Pizza Lola-Cosworth	2:41:18.248	185.987	Bobby Rahal
1991	Rick Mears	Marlboro Penske-Cosworth	2:50:01.018	176.460	Michael Andretti
1992	Al Unser, Jr.	Valvoline-Chevrolet	3:43:05.148	134.477	Scott Goodyear
1993	Emerson Fittipaldi	Penske-Chevrolet	3:10:49.860	157.207	Arie Luyendyk
1994	Al Unser, Jr.	Penske-Mercedes	3:06:29.006	160.872	Jacques Villeneuve
1995	Jacques Villeneuve	Reynard-Ford	3:15:17.561	156.616	Christian Fittipaldi
1996	Buddy Lazier	Reynard-Ford	3:22:45.753	147.956	Davy Jones

Year	Winner	Car	Time	mph	Second place
1997	Arie Luyendyk	G Force-Aurora	3:25:43.388	145.827	Scott Goodyear
1998	Eddie Cheever	Dallara-Aurora	3:26:40.524	145.155	Buddy Lazier
1999	Kenny Brack	Dallara-Aurora-Goodyear	3:15:51.182	153.176	Jeff Ward
2000	Juan Montoya	GForce-Aurora-Firestone	2:58:59.431	167.607	Buddy Lazier

1. 300 miles. 2. Race ended at 400 miles because of rain. 3. Race ended at 345 miles because of rain. 4. Race, postponed after 18 laps because of rain on May 30, was finished on May 31. 5. Race postponed May 28 and 29 was cut to 332.5 miles because of rain, May 30. 6. Race ended at 435 miles because of rain. 7. Race ended at 255 miles because of rain. 8. Andretti was awarded the victory the day after the race after Bobby Unser, whose car finished first, was penalized one lap and dropped from first place to second for passing other cars illegally under a yellow caution flag. Unser appealed the decision to the U.S. Auto Club and was upheld. A panel ruled the penalty was too severe and instead fined Unser $40,000, but restored the victory to him.

2000 NASCAR WINSTON CUP RACES

Date	Race	Raceway	Winner
Feb. 13	Bud Shootout	Daytona International Speedway	Dale Jarrett
Feb. 20	Daytona 500	Daytona International Speedway	Dale Jarrett
Feb. 27	Dura Lube/Kmart 400	North Carolina Speedway	Bobby Labonte
March 5	CarsDirect.com 400	Las Vegas Motor Speedway	Jeff Burton
March 12	Cracker Barrel 500	Atlanta Motor Speedway	Dale Earnhardt
March 19	Mall.com 400	Darlington Raceway	Ward Burton
March 26	Food City 500	Bristol Motor Speedway	Rusty Wallace
April 2	DIRECTV 500	Texas Motor Speedway	Dale Earnhardt, Jr.
April 9	Goody's Body Pain 500	Martinsville Speedway	Mark Martin
April 16	DieHard 500	Talladega Superspeedway	Jeff Gordon
April 30	NAPA Auto Parts 500	California Speedway	Jeremy Mayfield
May 6	Pontiac Excitement 400	Richmond International Raceway	Dale Earnhardt, Jr.
May 20	The Winston	Lowe's Motor Speedway	Dale Earnhardt, Jr.
May 28	Coca-Cola 600	Lowe's Motor Speedway	Matt Kenseth
June 4	MBNA Platinum 400	Dover Downs International Raceway	Tony Stewart
June 11	Kmart 400	Michigan International Speedway	Tony Stewart
June 17	Pocono 500	Pocono Raceway	Jeremy Mayfield
June 25	Save Mart/Kragen 350	Sears Point Raceway	Jeff Gordon
July 1	Pepsi 400	Daytona International Speedway	Jeff Burton
July 9	thatlook.com 300	New Hampshire International Speedway	Tony Stewart
July 23	Pennsylvania 500	Pocono Raceway	Rusty Wallace
Aug. 5	Brickyard 400	Indianapolis Motor Speedway	Bobby Labonte
Aug. 14	Global Crossing @ The Glen	Watkins Glen International	Steve Park
Aug. 20	Pepsi 400 presented by Meijer	Michigan International Speedway	Rusty Wallace
Aug. 27	goracing.com 500	Bristol Motor Speedway	Rusty Wallace
Sept. 3	Pepsi Southern 500	Darlington Raceway	Bobby Labonte
Sept. 9	Chevy Monte Carlo 400	Richmond International Speedway	Jeff Gordon
Sept. 17	Dura Lube 300	New Hampshire International Speedway	Jeff Burton
Sept. 24	MBNA.com 400	Dover Downs International Speedway	Tony Stewart
Oct. 1	NAPA AutoCare 500	Martinsville Speedway	Tony Stewart

NATIONAL ASSOCIATION FOR STOCK CAR AUTO RACING
WINSTON CUP CHAMPIONS

1949	Red Byron	1962–63	Joe Weatherly	1979	Richard Petty	1990	Dale Earnhardt
1950	Bill Rexford	1964	Richard Petty	1980	Dale Earnhardt	1991	Dale Earnhardt
1951	Herb Thomas	1965	Ned Jarrett	1981	Darrell Waltrip	1992	Alan Kulwicki
1952	Tim Flock	1966	David Pearson	1982	Darrell Waltrip	1993	Dale Earnhardt
1953	Herb Thomas	1967	Richard Petty	1983	Bobby Allison	1994	Dale Earnhardt
1954	Lee Petty	1968–69	David Pearson	1984	Terry Labonte	1995	Jeff Gordon
1955	Tim Flock	1970	Bobby Isaac	1985	Darrell Waltrip	1996	Terry Labonte
1956–57	Buck Baker	1971–72	Richard Petty	1986	Dale Earnhardt	1997–98	Jeff Gordon
1958–59	Lee Petty	1973	Benny Parsons	1987	Dale Earnhardt	1999	Dale Jarrett
1960	Rex White	1974–75	Richard Petty	1988	Bill Elliott	2000[1]	Bobby Labonte
1961	Ned Jarrett	1976–78	Cale Yarborough	1989	Rusty Wallace		

1. As of Oct. 1, 2000.

INDYCAR NATIONAL CHAMPIONS

1910	Ray Harroun	1920	Gaston Chevrolet	1931	Louis Schneider	1946–48	Ted Horn
1911	Ralph Mulford	1921	Tommy Milton	1932	Bob Carey	1949	Johnnie Parsons
1912	Ralph DePalma	1922	James Murphy	1933	Louis Meyer	1950	Henry Banks
1913	Earl Cooper	1923	Eddie Hearne	1934	Bill Cummings	1951	Tony Betten-
1914	Ralph DePalma	1924	James Murphy	1935	Kelly Petillo		hausen
1915	Earl Cooper	1925	Peter DePaolo	1936	Mauri Rose	1952	Chuck Stevenson
1916	Dario Resta	1926	Harry Hartz	1937	Wilbur Shaw	1953	Sam Hanks
1917	Earl Cooper	1927	Peter DePaolo	1938	Floyd Roberts	1954	Jimmy Bryan
1918	Ralph Mulford	1928–29	Louis Meyer	1939	Wilbur Shaw	1955	Bob Sweikert
1919	Howard Wilcox	1930	Billy Arnold	1940–41	Rex Mays	1956–57	Jimmy Bryan

1958	Tony Betten-hausen	1971–72	Joe Leonard	1981–82	Rick Mears	1993	Nigel Mansell
1959	Rodger Ward	1973	Roger McCluskey	1983	Al Unser	1994	Al Unser, Jr.
1960–61	A. J. Foyt	1974	Bobby Unser	1984	Mario Andretti	1995	Jacques Ville-
1962	Rodger Ward	1975	A. J. Foyt	1985	Al Unser		neuve
1963–64	A. J. Foyt	1976	Gordon Johncock	1986–87	Bobby Rahal	1996	Jimmy Vasser
1965–66	Mario Andretti	1977–78	Tom Sneva	1988	Danny Sullivan	1997–98	Alessandro
1967	A. J. Foyt	1979	Rick Mears	1989	Emerson Fitti-		Zanardi
1968	Bobby Unser		(CART), A.J. Foyt		paldi	1999	Juan Montoya
1969	Mario Andretti		(USAC)[1]	1990	Al Unser, Jr.	2000[2]	Gil de Ferran
1970	Al Unser	1980	Johnny Ruther-	1991	Michael Andretti		
			ford	1992	Bobby Rahal		

1. Two separate series were held in 1979. 2. As of Oct. 1, 2000. NOTE: There have been three sanctioning bodies for the series: the Automobile Association of America (1909–1955), the U.S. Auto Club (1956–1979), and the Championship Auto Racing Team (CART), 1979–present.

2000 INDY RACING LEAGUE LEADING POINT WINNERS
(as of Aug. 27, 2000)

Driver	Pts	Driver	Pts	Driver	Pts
1. Buddy Lazier	258	9. Al Unser, Jr.	173	17. Jeret Schroeder	122
2. Scott Goodyear	220	10. Robby McGehee	168	18. Tyce Carlson	117
3. Eddie Cheever	217	11. Greg Ray	165	19. Sam Hornish, Jr.	107
4. Mark Dismore	186	12. Stephan Gregoire	161	20. Sarah Fisher	105
5. Eliseo Salazar	180	13. Jeff Ward	151	21. Jaques Lazier	92
6. Scott Sharp	179	14. Bill Boat	146	22. Davey Hamilton	87
7. Robbie Buhl	178	15. Airton Dare	124	23. Shigeaki Hattori	83
8. Donnie Beechler	174	16. Buzz Calkins	123	24. Jimmy Kite	70

2000 NASCAR LEADING POINT WINNERS
(as of Oct. 1, 2000)

Driver	Pts	Winnings	Driver	Pts	Winnings
1. Bobby Labonte	4,225	3,405,046	11. Mike Skinner	3,135	1,675,084
2. Dale Earnhardt	4,012	2,230,366	12. Steve Park	3,105	1,668,707
3. Jeff Burton	3,998	4,577,509	13. Matt Kenseth	3,066	1,843,839
4. Dale Jarrett	3,974	4,762,514	14. Johnny Benson	3,053	1,362,734
5. Tony Stewart	3,812	2,594,426	15. Ken Schrader	2,949	1,320,754
6. Ricky Rudd	3,797	1,979,424	16. Dale Earnhardt, Jr.	2,914	2,338,236
7. Rusty Wallace	3,703	2,666,186	17. Sterling Martin	2,844	1,542,774
8. Mark Martin	3,693	2,292,936	18. Terry Labonte	2,830	1,716,894
9. Jeff Gordon	3,513	2,220,131	19. Joe Nemechek	2,826	1,573,661
10. Ward Burton	3,431	1,995,626	20. Bill Elliott	2,678	2,163,958

WORLD GRAND PRIX DRIVER CHAMPIONS

1950	Giuseppe Farina, Italy, Alfa Romeo	1976	James Hunt, Britain, McLaren-Ford
1951	Juan Fangio, Argentina, Alfa Romeo	1977	Niki Lauda, Austria, Ferrari
1952	Alberto Ascari, Italy, Ferrari	1978	Mario Andretti, United States, Lotus
1953	Alberto Ascari, Italy, Ferrari	1979	Jody Scheckter, South Africa, Ferrari
1954	Juan Fangio, Argentina, Maserati, Mercedes-Benz	1980	Alan Jones, Australia, Williams-Ford
1955	Juan Fangio, Argentina, Mercedes-Benz	1981	Nelson Piquet, Brazil, Brabham-Ford
1956	Juan Fangio, Argentina, Lancia-Ferrari	1982	Keke Rosberg, Finland, Williams-Ford
1957	Juan Fangio, Argentina, Maserati	1983	Nelson Piquet, Brazil. Brabham-BMW
1958	Mike Hawthorn, England, Ferrari	1984	Nikki Lauda, Austria, McLaren-Porsche
1959	Jack Brabham, Australia, Cooper	1985	Alain Prost, France, McLaren-Porsche
1960	Jack Brabham, Australia, Cooper	1986	Alain Prost, France, McLaren-Porsche
1961	Phil Hill, United States, Ferrari	1987	Nelson Piquet, Brazil, Williams-Honda
1962	Graham Hill, England, BRM	1988	Aryton Senna, Brazil, McLaren-Honda
1963	Jim Clark, Scotland, Lotus-Ford	1989	Alain Prost, France, McLaren-Honda
1964	John Surtees, England, Ferrari	1990	Aryton Senna, Brazil, McLaren-Honda
1965	Jim Clark, Scotland, Lotus-Ford	1991	Aryton Senna, Brazil, McLaren-Honda
1966	Jack Brabham, Australia, Brabham-Repco	1992	Nigel Mansell, Britain, Williams-Renault
1967	Denis Hulme, New Zealand, Brabham-Repco	1993	Alain Prost, France, Williams-Renault
1968	Graham Hill, England, Lotus-Ford	1994	Michael Schumacher, Germany, Benetton
1969	Jackie Stewart, Scotland, Matra-Ford	1995	Michael Schumacher, Germany, Benetton Renault
1970	Jochen Rindt, Austria, Lotus-Ford	1996	Damon Hill, Britain, Williams
1971	Jackie Stewart, Scotland, Tyrrell-Ford	1997	Jacques Villeneuve, Canada, Williams-Renault
1972	Emerson Fittipaldi, Brazil, Lotus-Ford	1998	Mika Hakkinen, Finland, McLaren-Mercedes
1973	Jackie Stewart, Scotland, Tyrrell-Ford	1999	Mika Hakkinen, Finland, McLaren-Mercedes
1974	Emerson Fittipaldi, Brazil, McLaren-Ford	2000[1]	Michael Schumacher, Germany, Ferrari
1975	Niki Lauda, Austria, Ferrari		

1. As of Sept. 24, 2000.

Yachting

AMERICA'S CUP RECORD

First race in 1851 around Isle of Wight, Cowes, England. First defense and all others through 1920 held 30 miles off New York Bay. Races since 1930 held 30 miles off Newport, R.I. Conducted as one race only in 1851 and 1870; best four-of-seven basis, 1871; best two-of-three, 1876–1887; best three-of-five, 1893–1901; best four-of-seven, since 1930. Figures in parentheses indicate number of races won.

Year	Winner and owner	Loser and owner
1851	AMERICA (1), John C. Stevens, U.S.	AURORA, T. Le Marchant, England[1]
1870	MAGIC (1), Franklin Osgood, U.S.	CAMBRIA, James Ashbury, England[2]
1871	COLUMBIA (2), Franklin Osgood, U.S.[3]	LIVONIA (1), James Ashbury, England
	SAPPHO (2), William P. Douglas, U.S.	
1876	MADELEINE (2), John S. Dickerson, U.S.	COUNTESS OF DUFFERIN, Chas. Gifford, Canada
1881	MISCHIEF (2), J. R. Busk, U.S.	ATALANTA, Alexander Cuthbert, Canada
1885	PURITAN (2), J. M. Forbes-Gen. Charles Paine, U.S.	GENESTA, Sir Richard Sutton, England
1886	MAYFLOWER (2), Gen. Charles Paine, U.S.	GALATEA, Lt. William Henn, England
1887	VOLUNTEER (2), Gen. Charles Paine, U.S.	THISTLE, James Bell et al., Scotland
1893	VIGILANT (3), C. Oliver Iselin et al., U.S.	VALKYRIE II, Lord Dunraven, England
1895	DEFENDER (3), C. O. Iselin–W. K. Vanderbilt–E. D. Morgan, U.S.	VALKYRIE III, Lord Dunraven–Lord Lonsdale–Lord Wolverton, England
1899	COLUMBIA (3), J. P. Morgan–C. O. Iselin, U.S.	SHAMROCK I, Sir Thomas Lipton, Ireland
1901	COLUMBIA (3), Edwin D. Morgan, U.S.	SHAMROCK II, Sir Thomas Lipton, Ireland
1903	RELIANCE (3), Cornelius Vanderbilt et al., U.S.	SHAMROCK III, Sir Thomas Lipton, Ireland
1920	RESOLUTE (3), Henry Walters et al., U.S.	SHAMROCK IV (2), Sir Thomas Lipton, Ireland
1930	ENTERPRISE (4), Harold S. Vanderbilt et al., U.S.	SHAMROCK V, Sir Thomas Lipton, Ireland
1934	RAINBOW (4), Harold S. Vanderbilt, U.S.	ENDEAVOUR (2), T. O. M. Sopwith, England
1937	RANGER (4), Harold S. Vanderbilt, U.S.	ENDEAVOUR II, T. O. M. Sopwith, England
1958	COLUMBIA (4), Henry Sears et al., U.S.	SCEPTRE, Hugh Goodson et al., England
1962	WEATHERLY (4), Henry D. Mercer et al., U.S.	GRETEL (1), Sir Frank Packer et al., Australia
1964	CONSTELLATION (4), New York Y.C. Syndicate, U.S.	SOVEREIGN (0), J. Anthony Bowden, England
1967	INTREPID (4), New York Y.C. Syndicate, U.S.	DAME PATTIE (0), Sydney (Aust.) Syndicate
1970	INTREPID (4), New York Y.C. Syndicate, U.S.	GRETEL II (1), Sydney (Aust.) Syndicate
1974	COURAGEOUS (4), New York, N.Y. Syndicate, U.S.	SOUTHERN CROSS (0), Sydney (Aust.) Syndicate
1977	COURAGEOUS (4), New York, N.Y. Syndicate, U.S.	AUSTRALIA (0), Sun City (Aust.) Syndicate
1980	FREEDOM (4), New York, N.Y. Syndicate, U.S.	AUSTRALIA (1), Alan Bond et al, Australia
1983	AUSTRALIA II (4), Alan Bond et al., Australia	LIBERTY, (3) New York, N.Y. Syndicate, U.S.
1987	STARS & STRIPES (4), Dennis Conner et al., United States	KOOKABURRA III (0), Iain Murray et al., Australia
1988[4]	STARS & STRIPES, Dennis Conner, et al., United States	NEW ZEALAND, Michael Fay, et al., New Zealand
1992	AMERICA 3, Bill Koch, et al., United States	IL MORO DI VENEZIA, Paul Cayard, et al., Italy
1995	BLACK MAGIC, Peter Blake, et al., New Zealand	YOUNG AMERICA, Dennis Conner, et al., United States
2000	NEW ZEALAND, Peter Blake, et al., New Zealand	LUNA ROSSA, Patrizio Bertelli, et al., Italy

1. Fourteen British yachts started against America; Aurora finished second. 2. Cambria sailed against 23 U.S. yachts and finished tenth. 3. Columbia was disabled in the third race, after winning the first two; Sappho substituted and won the fourth and fifth. 4. Shortly after Dennis Conner and his 60-foot, twin-hulled catamaran easily defeated the challenge of the New Zealand, a 133-foot, single-hulled yacht in the waters off San Diego in early September 1988, a New York State Supreme Court judge ruled that the Americans did not live up to the America's Cup Deed of Gift, which means competing boats must be similar. The judge ruled that the Americans had an unfair advantage over the monohulled ship, and awarded the Cup to New Zealand. However, an Appeal awarded the Cup to the United States.

Bicycling

TOUR DE FRANCE–2000

(July 1–23, 2000)

	Team	Behind			Team	Behind
1. Lance Armstrong, United States	U.S. Postal	(1)	6. Richard Virenque, France		Polti	13:26
2. Jan Ullrich, Germany	Deutsche Telekom	6:02	7. Santiago Botero, Colombia		Kelme	17:21
3. Joseba Beloki, Spain	Festina	10:04	8. Fernando Escartin, Spain		Kelme	17:21
4. Christophe Moreau, France	Festina	10:34	9. Francis Mancebo, Spain		Banesto	18:09
5. Roberto Heras, Spain	Kelme	11:50	10. Daniele Nardello, Italy		Mapei	18:25

1. Completed course in 92 hours, 33 minutes, 8 seconds.

Marathons

BOSTON MARATHON
(April 17, 2000)

Men	Time
1. Elijah Lagat, Kenya	2:09:47
2. Gezahenge Abera, Ethiopia	2:09:47
3. Moses Tanui, Kenya	2:09:50
4. Ondoro Osoro, Kenya	2:10:29
5. David Busienei, Kenya	2:11:26
Wheelchair—Franz Nietlispach, Switzerland	1:33:32

Women	Time
1. Catherine Ndereba, Kenya	2:26:11
2. Irina Bogacheva, Kyrgyzstan	2:26:27
3. Fatuma Roba, Ethiopia	2:26:27
4. Anuta Catuna, Romania	2:29:46
5. Lornah Kiplagat, Kenya	2:30:12
Wheelchair—Jean Driscoll, United States	2:00:52

OTHER 1999–2000 MARATHONS

Tokyo (Feb. 13, 2000)

Men	Time
Japhet Kosgei, Kenya	2:07:15
No women's division	

Los Angeles (March 5, 2000)

Men	Time
Mutisya Mbithi, Kenya	2:11:55
Women	
Jane Salumae, Estonia	2:23:33

Paris (April 1, 2000)

Men	Time
Mohammed Ouaadi, France	2:08:49
Women	
Marleen Renders, Belgium	2:23:44

London (April 16, 2000)

Men	Time
Antonio Pinto, Portugal	2:06:36
Women	
Tegla Loroupe, Kenya	2:24:38

Rotterdam (April 17, 2000)

Men	Time
Kenneth Cheruiyot, Kenya	2:08:22
Women	
Ana Isabel Alonso, Spain	2:30:21

New York City (Nov. 7, 1999)

Men	Time
Joseph Chebet, Kenya	2:09:14
Women	
Adriana Fernandez, Mexico	2:25:06

Little League

LITTLE LEAGUE WORLD SERIES CHAMPIONS

Year	Champion	Runner-up	Score	Year	Champion	Runner-up	Score
1947	Williamsport, Pa.	Lock Haven, Pa.	16–7	1976	Tokyo, Japan	Campbell, Calif.	10–3
1948	Lock Haven, Pa.	St. Petersburg, Fla.	6–5	1977	Kao Hsiung, Taiwan	El Cajon, Calif.	7–2
1949	Hammontown, N.J.	Pensacola, Fla.	5–0	1978	Pin-Tung, Taiwan	Danville, Calif.	11–1
1950	Houston, Tex.	Bridgeport, Conn.	2–1	1979	Hsien, Taiwan	Campbell, Calif.	2–1
1951	Stamford, Conn.	Austin, Tex.	3–0	1980	Hua Lian, Taiwan	Tampa, Fla.	4–3
1952	Norwalk, Conn.	Monongahela, Pa.	4–3	1981	Tai-Chung, Taiwan	Tampa, Fla.	4–2
1953	Birmingham, Ala.	Schenectady, N.Y.	1–0	1982	Kirkland, Wash.	Hsien, Taiwan	6–0
1954	Schenectady, N.Y.	Colton, Calif.	7–5	1983	Marietta, Ga.	Barahona, D. Rep.	3–1
1955	Morrisville, Pa.	Merchantville, N.J.	4–3	1984	Seoul, S. Korea	Altamonte Springs, Fla.	6–2
1956	Roswell, N.M.	Merchantville, N.J.	3–1	1985	Seoul, S. Korea	Mexicali, Mex.	7–1
1957	Monterrey, Mex.	LaMesa, Calif.	4–0	1986	Tianan Park, Taiwan	Tucson, Ariz.	12–0
1958	Monterrey, Mex.	Kankakee, Ill.	10–1	1987	Hua Lian, Taiwan	Irvine, Calif.	21–1
1959	Hamtramck, Mich.	Auburn, Calif.	12–0	1988	Tai-Chung, Taiwan	Pearl City, Haw.	10–0
1960	Levittown, Pa.	Ft. Worth, Tex.	5–0	1989	Trumbull, Conn.	Kaohsiung, Taiwan	5–2
1961	El Cajon, Calif.	El Campo, Tex.	4–2	1990	Taipei, Taiwan	Shippensburg, Pa.	9–0
1962	San Jose, Calif.	Kankakee, Ill.	3–0	1991	Tai-Chung, Taiwan	San Ramon Valley, Calif.	11–0
1963	Granada Hills, Calif.	Stratford, Conn.	2–1				
1964	Staten Island, N.Y.	Monterrey, Mex.	4–0	1992*	Long Beach, Calif.	Zamboanga, Phil.	6–0
1965	Windsor Locks, Conn.	Stoney Creek, Can.	3–1	1993	Long Beach, Calif.	David Chiriqui, Pan.	3–2
1966	Houston, Tex.	W. New York, N.J.	8–2	1994	Maracaibo, Venezuela	Northridge, Calif.	4–3
1967	West Tokyo, Japan	Chicago, Ill.	4–1	1995	Tainan, Taiwan	Spring, Texas	17–3
1968	Osaka, Japan	Richmond, Va.	1–0	1996	Kao-Hsuing City, Taipei	Cranston, R.I.	13–3
1969	Taipei, Taiwan	Santa Clara, Calif.	5–0	1997	Guadalupe, Mexico	South Mission Viejo, Calif.	5–4
1970	Wayne, N.J.	Campbell, Calif.	2–0				
1971	Tainan, Taiwan	Gary, Ind.	12–3	1998	Toms River, N.J.	Kashima, Japan	12–9
1972	Taipei, Taiwan	Hammond, Ind.	6–0	1999	Hirakata, Osaka, Japan	Phenix City, Ala.	5–0
1973	Tainan City, Taiwan	Tucson, Ariz.	12–0				
1974	Kao Hsiung, Taiwan	El Cajon, Calif.	7–2	2000	Maracaibo, Venezuela	Bellaire, Tex.	3–2
1975	Lakewood, N.J.	Tampa, Fla.	4–3				

* Long Beach declared a 6–0 winner after the international tournament committee determined that Zamboanga City had used players that were not within its city limits.

The Olympic Games

1896 Athens, Greece	1948 St. Moritz, Switzerland (W)	1980 Lake Placid, United States (W)
1900 Paris, France	1948 London, Great Britain (S)	1980 Moscow, USSR (S)
1904 St. Louis, United States	1952 Oslo, Norway (W)	1984 Sarajevo, Yugoslavia (W)
1906 Athens, Greece	1952 Helsinki, Finland (S)	1984 Los Angeles, United States (S)
1908 London, Great Britain	1956 Cortina d'Ampezzo, Italy (W)	1988 Calgary, Canada (W)
1912 Stockholm, Sweden	1956 Melbourne, Australia (S)	1988 Seoul, South Korea (S)
1920 Antwerp, Belgium	1960 Squaw Valley, United States (W)	1992 Albertville, France (W)
1924 Chamonix, France(W)	1960 Rome, Italy (S)	1992 Barcelona, Spain (S)
1924 Paris, France (S)	1964 Innsbruck, Austria (W)	1994 Lillehammer, Norway (W)
1928 St. Moritz, Switzerland (W)	1964 Tokyo, Japan (S)	1996 Atlanta, United States (S)
1928 Amsterdam, Netherlands (S)	1968 Grenoble, France (W)	1998 Nagano, Japan (W)
1932 Lake Placid, United States (W)	1968 Mexico City, Mexico (S)	2000 Sydney, Australia (S)
1932 Los Angeles, United States (S)	1972 Sapporo, Japan (W)	2002 Salt Lake City, United States (W)
1936 Garmisch-Partenkirchen, Germany (W)	1972 Munich, Germany (S)	2004 Athens, Greece (S)
1936 Berlin, Germany (S)	1976 Innsbruck, Austria (W)	2006 Turin, Italy (W)
	1976 Montreal, Canada (S)	

(W)—Site of Winter Games. (S)—Site of Summer Games

The first Olympic Games of which there is record were held in 776 B.C., and consisted of one event, a great foot race of about 200 yards held on a plain by the River Alpheus (now the Ruphia) just outside the little town of Olympia in Greece. It was from that date the Greeks began to keep their calendar by "Olympiads," the four-year spans between the celebrations of the famous games.

The modern Olympic Games, which started in Athens in 1896, are the result of the devotion of a French educator, Baron Pierre de Coubertin, to the idea that, since young people and athletics have gone together through the ages, education and athletics might go hand-in-hand toward a better international understanding.

The principal organization responsible for the staging of the Games is the International Olympic Committee (IOC). Other important roles are played by the National Olympic Committees in each participating country, international sports federations, and the organizing committee of the host city.

The Olympic motto is "Citius, Altius, Fortius,"—"Faster, Higher, Stronger." The Olympic symbol is five interlocking circles colored blue, yellow, black, green, and red, on a white background, representing the five continents. At least one of those colors appears in the national flag of every country.

Beginning in 1994, the IOC decided to change the format of having both the Summer and Winter Games in the same year. Summer and Winter Olympics now alternate every two years.

In Feb. 1998 the IOC announced that new sports added to the games must include women's events..

Summer Games: Gold Medals

TRACK AND FIELD–MEN

100-Meter Dash

1896 Thomas Burke, United States	12.00
1900 Francis W. Jarvis, United States	10.80
1904 Archie Hahn, United States	11.00
1906 Archie Hahn, United States	11.20
1908 Reginald Walker, South Africa	10.80
1912 Ralph Craig, United States	10.80
1920 Charles Paddock, United States	10.80
1924 Harold Abrahams, Great Britain	10.60
1928 Percy Williams, Canada	10.80
1932 Eddie Tolan, United States	10.30
1936 Jesse Owens, United States	10.30[1]
1948 Harrison Dillard, United States	10.30
1952 Lindy Remigino, United States	10.40
1956 Bobby Morrow, United States	10.50
1960 Armin Hary, Germany	10.20
1964 Robert Hayes, United States	10.00
1968 James Hines, United States	09.90
1972 Valery Borzov, U.S.S.R.	10.14
1976 Hasely Crawford, Trinidad and Tobago	10.06
1980 Allan Wells, Britain	10.25
1984 Carl Lewis, United States	09.99
1988 Carl Lewis, United States	09.92[2]
1992 Linford Christie, Great Britain	09.96
1996 Donovan Bailey, Canada	09.84[3]
2000 Maurice Greene, United States	09.87

1. Wind assisted. 2. Lewis was awarded the gold medal when Ben Johnson of Canada, the original winner in 09.79s, was stripped of the medal after testing positive for steroid use. 3. World record.

200-Meter Dash

1900 John Tewksbury, United States	22.20
1904 Archie Hahn, United States	21.60
1908 Robert Kerr, Canada	22.60
1912 Ralph Craig, United States	21.70
1920 Allan Woodring, United States	22.00
1924 Jackson Scholz, United States	21.60
1928 Percy Williams, Canada	21.80
1932 Eddie Tolan, United States	21.20
1936 Jesse Owens, United States	20.70
1948 Melvin E. Patton, United States	21.10
1952 Andrew Stanfield, United States	20.70
1956 Bobby Morrow, United States	20.60
1960 Livio Berruti, Italy	20.50
1964 Henry Carr, United States	20.30
1968 Tommie Smith, United States	19.80
1972 Vallery Borzov, U.S.S.R.	20.00
1976 Don Quarrie, Jamaica	20.23
1980 Pietro Mennea, Italy	20.19
1984 Carl Lewis, United States	19.80
1988 Joe DeLoach, United States	19.75
1992 Mike Marsh, United States	20.01
1996 Michael Johnson, United States	19.32[1]
2000 Konstantinos Kenteris, Greece	20.09

1. World record.

400-Meter Dash

1896 Thomas Burke, United States	54.20
1900 Maxwell Long, United States	49.40
1904 Harry Hillman, United States	49.20
1906 Paul Pilgrim, United States	53.20

1908	Wyndham Halswelle, Great Britain (walkover)	50.00
1912	Charles Reidpath, United States	48.20
1920	Bevil Rudd, South Africa	49.60
1924	Eric Liddell, Great Britain	47.60
1928	Ray Barbuti, United States	47.80
1932	William Carr, United States	46.20
1936	Archie Williams, United States	46.50
1948	Arthur Wint, Jamaica, B.W.I.	46.20
1952	George Rhoden, Jamaica, B.W.I.	45.90
1956	Charles Jenkins, United States	46.70
1960	Otis Davis, United States	44.90
1964	Mike Larrabee, United States	45.10
1968	Lee Evans, United States	43.80
1972	Vincent Matthews, United States	44.66
1976	Alberto Juantorena, Cuba	44.26
1980	Viktor Markin, U.S.S.R.	44.60
1984	Alonzo Babers, United States	44.27
1988	Steve Lewis, United States	43.87
1992	Quincy Watts, United States	43.50
1996	Michael Johnson, United States	43.49
2000	Michael Johnson, United States	43.84

800-Meter Run

1896	Edwin Flack, Australia	2:11.00
1900	Alfred Tysoe, Great Britain	2:01.40
1904	James Lightbody, United States	1:56.00
1906	Paul Pilgrim, United States	2:01.20
1908	Mel Sheppard, United states	1:52.80
1912	Ted Meredith, United States	1:51.90
1920	Albert Hill, Great Britain	1:53.40
1924	Douglas Lowe, Great Britain	1:52.40
1928	Douglas Lowe, Great Britain	1:51.80
1932	Thomas Hampson, Great Britain	1:49.80
1936	John Woodruff, United States	1:52.90
1948	Malvin Whitfield, United States	1:49.20
1952	Malvin Whitfield, United States	1:49.20
1956	Tom Courtney, United States	1:47.70
1960	Peter Snell, New Zealand	1:46.30
1964	Peter Snell, New Zealand	1:45.10
1968	Ralph Doubell, Australia	1:44.30
1972	David Wottle, United States	1:45.90
1976	Alberto Juantorena, Cuba	1:43.50
1980	Steve Ovett, Britain	1:45.40
1984	Joaquin Cruz, Brazil	1:43.00
1988	Paul Ereng, Kenya	1:43.45
1992	William Tanui, Kenya	1:43.66
1996	Vebjoern Rodal, Norway	1:42.58
2000	Nils Schumann, Germany	1:45.08

1,500-Meter Run

1896	Edwin Flack, Australia	4:33.20
1900	Charles Bennett, Great Britain	4:06.00
1904	James Lightbody, United States	4:05.40
1906	James Lightbody, United States	4:12.00
1908	Mel Sheppard, United States	4:03.40
1912	Arnold Jackson, Great Britain	3:56.80
1920	Albert Hill, Great Britain	4:01.80
1924	Paavo Nurmi, Finland	3:53.60
1928	Harry Larva, Finland	3:53.20
1932	Luigi Becali, Italy	3:51.20
1936	Jack Lovelock, New Zealand	3:47.80
1948	Henri Eriksson, Sweden	3:49.80
1952	Joseph Barthel, Luxembourg	3:45.20
1956	Ron Delany, Ireland	3:41.20
1960	Herb Elliott, Australia	3:35.60
1964	Peter Snell, New Zealand	3:38.10
1968	Kipchoge Keino, Kenya	3:34.90
1972	Pekka Vasala, Finland	3:36.30
1976	John Walker, New Zealand	3:39.17
1980	Sebastian Coe, Britain	3:38.40
1984	Sebastian Coe, Britain	3:32.53
1988	Peter Rono, Kenya	3:35.96
1992	Fermin Cacho Ruiz, Spain	3:40.12

1996	Noureddine Morceli, Algeria	3:35.78
2000	Noah Ngeny, Kenya	3:32.07

5,000-Meter Run

1912	Hannes Kolehmainen, Finland	14:36.60
1920	Joseph Guillemot, France	14:55.60
1024	Paavo Nurmi, Finland	14:31.20
1928	Willie Ritola, Finland	14:38.00
1932	Lauri Lehtinen, Finland	14:30.00
1936	Gunnar Hockert, Finland	14:22.20
1948	Gaston Reiff, Belgium	14:17.60
1952	Emil Zatopek, Czechoslovakia	14:06.60
1956	Vladimir Kuts, U.S.S.R.	13:39.60
1960	Murray Halberg, New Zealand	13:43.40
1964	Bob Schul, United States	13:48.80
1968	Mohamed Gammoudi, Tunisia	14:05.00
1972	Lasse Viren, Finland	13:26.40
1976	Lasse Viren, Finland	13:24.76
1980	Miruts Yifter, Ethiopia	13:21.00
1984	Saud Aouita, Morocco	13:05.59
1988	John Ngugi, Kenya	13:11.70
1992	Dieter Baumann, Germany	13:12.52
1996	Venuste Niyongabo, Burundi	13:07.96
2000	Millon Wolde, Ethiopia	13:35.49

10,000-Meter Run

1912	Hannes Kolehmainen, Finland	31:20.80
1920	Paavo Nurmi, Finland	31:45.80
1924	Willie Ritola, Finland	30:23.20
1928	Paavo Nurmi, Finland	30:18.80
1932	Janusz Kusocinski, Poland	30:11.40
1936	Ilmari Salminen, Finland	30:15.40
1948	Emil Zatopek, Czechoslovakia	29:59.60
1952	Emil Zatopek, Czechoslovakia	29:17.00
1956	Vladimir Kuts, U.S.S.R.	28:45.60
1960	Peter Bolotnikov, U.S.S.R.	28:32.20
1964	Billy Mills, United States	28:24.40
1968	Nartali Temu, Kenya	29:27.40
1972	Lasse Viren, Finland	27:38.40
1976	Lasse Viren, Finland	27:40.38
1980	Miruts Yifter, Ethiopia	27:42.70
1984	Alberto Cova, Italy	27:47.50
1988	Mly Brahim Boutaib, Morocco	27:21.46
1992	Khalid Skah, Morocco	27:47.70
1996	Haile Gebrselassie, Ethiopia	27:07.34
2000	Haile Gebrselassie, Ethiopia	21:18.20

Marathon

1896	Spiridon Loues, Greece	2:58:50.00
1900	Michel Teato, France	2:59:45.00
1904	Thomas Hicks, United States	3:28:53.00
1906	William J. Sherring, Canada	2:51:23.65
1908	John J. Hayes, United States	2:55:18.40
1912	Kenneth McArthur, South Africa	2:36:54.80
1920	Hannes Kolehmainen, Finland	2:32:35.80
1924	Albin Stenroos, Finland	2:41:22.60
1928	A.B. El Ouafi, France	2:32:57.00
1932	Juan Zabala, Argentina	2:31:36.00
1936	Kitei Son, Japan	2:29:19.20
1948	Delfo Cabrera, Argentina	2:34:51.60
1952	Emil Zatopek, Czechoslovakia	2:23:30.20
1956	Alain Mimoun, France	2:25:00.00
1960	Abebe Bikila, Ethiopia	2:15:16.20
1964	Abebe Bikila, Ethiopia	2:12:11.20
1968	Mamo Wold, Ethiopia	2:20:26.40
1972	Frank Shorter, United States	2:12:19.80
1976	Walter Cierpinski, East Germany	2:09:55.00
1980	Walter Cierpinski, East Germany	2:11:30.00
1984	Carlos Lopes, Portugal	2:09:21.00
1988	Gelindo Bordin, Italy	2:10:47.00
1992	Hwang Young-Cho, South Korea	2:13:23.00
1996	Josia Thugwane, South Africa	2:12:36.00
2000	Gezahgne Abera, Ethiopia	2:10:11.00

110-Meter Hurdles

1896	Thomas Curtis, United States	17.60
1900	Alvin Kraenzlein, United States	15.40
1904	Frederick Schule, United States	16.00
1906	R.G. Leavitt, United States	16.20
1908	Forrest Smithson, United States	15.00
1912	Frederick Kelly, United States	15.10
1920	Earl Thomson, Canada	14.80
1924	Daniel Kinsey, United States	15.00
1928	Sydney Atkinson, South Africa	14.80
1932	George Saling, United States	14.60
1936	Forrest Towns, United States	14.20
1948	William Porter, United States	13.90
1952	Harrison Dillard, United States	13.70
1956	Lee Calhoun, United States	13.50
1960	Lee Calhoun, United States	13.80
1964	Hayes Jones, United States	13.60
1968	Willie Davenport, United States	13.30
1972	Rodney Milburn, United States	13.24
1976	Guy Drut, France	13.30
1980	Thomas Munkelt, East Germany	13.20
1984	Roger Kingdom, United States	13.20
1988	Roger Kingdom, United States	12.98
1992	Mark McCoy, Canada	13.12
1996	Allen Johnson, United States	12.95
2000	Anier Garcia, Cuba	13.00

200-Meter Hurdles

1900	Alvin Kraenzlein, United States	25.40
1904	Harry Hillman, United States	24.60

400-Meter Hurdles

1900	John Tewksbury, United States	57.60
1904	Harry Hillman, United States	53.00
1908	Charles Bacon, United States	55.00
1920	Frank Loomis, United States	54.00
1924	F. Morgan Taylor, United States	52.60
1928	Lord David Burghley, Great Britain	53.40
1932	Robert Tisdall, Ireland	51.80[1]
1936	Glenn Hardin, United States	52.40
1948	Roy Cochran, United States	51.10
1952	Charles Moore, United States	50.80
1956	Glenn Davis, United States	50.10
1960	Glenn Davis, United States	49.30
1964	Rex Cawley, United States	49.60
1968	David Hemery, Great Britain	48.10
1972	John Akii-Bua, Uganda	47.80
1976	Edwin Moses, United States	47.64
1980	Volker Beck, East Germany	48.70
1984	Edwin Moses, United States	47.75
1988	Andre Phillips, United States	47.19
1992	Kevin Young, United States	46.78
1996	Derrick Adkins, United States	47.54
2000	Angelo Taylor, United States	47.50

1. Record not allowed.

2,500-Meter Steeplechase

1900	George Orton, United States	7:34.00
1904	James Lightbody, United States	7:39.60

3,000-Meter Steeplechase

1920	Percy Hodge, Great Britain	10:00.40
1924	Willie Ritola, Finland	09:33.60
1928	Toivo Loukola, Finland	09:21.80
1932	Volmari Iso-Hollo, Finland	10:33.40[1]
1936	Volmari Iso-Hollo, Finland	09:03.80
1948	Thure Sjoestrand, Sweden	09:04.60
1952	Horace Ashenfelter, United States	08:45.40
1956	Chris Brasher, Great Britain	08:41.20
1960	Zdzislaw Krzyskowiak, Poland	08:34.20
1964	Gaston Roelants, Belgium	08:30.80
1968	Amos Biwott, Kenya	08:51.00
1972	Kipchoge Keino, Kenya	08:23.60
1976	Anders Gardervd, Sweden	08:08.02
1980	Bronislaw Malinowski, Poland	08:09.70

1984	Julius Korir, Kenya	08:11.80
1988	Julius Karluki, Kenya	08:05.51
1992	Matthew Birir, Kenya	08:08.84
1996	Joseph Keter, Kenya	08:07.12
2000	Reuben Kosgei, Kenya	08:21.43

1. About 3,450 meters-extra lap by error.

10,000-Meter Walk

1912	George Goulding, Canada	46:28.40
1920	Ugo Frigerio, Italy	48:06.20
1924	Ugo Frigerio, Italy	47:49.00
1948	John Mikaelsson, Sweden	45:13.20
1952	John Mikaelsson, Sweden	45:02.80

20,000-Meter Walk

1956	Leonid Spirin, U.S.S.R.	1:31:27.40
1960	Vladimir Golubnichy, U.S.S.R.	1:34:07.20
1964	Ken Mathews, Great Britain	1:29:34.00
1968	Vladimir Golubnichy, U.S.S.R.	1:33:58.40
1972	Peter Frenkel, East Germany	1:26:42.40
1976	Daniel Bautista, Mexico	1:24:40.60
1980	Maurizio Damiliano, Italy	1:23:35.50
1984	Ernesto Conto, Mexico	1:23.13.00
1988	Jozef Pribilinec, Czechoslovakia	1:19:57.00
1992	Daniel Plaza, Spain	1:21:45.00
1996	Jefferson Perez, Ecuador	1:20:07.00
2000	Robert Korzeniowski, Poland	1:18.59.00

50,000-Meter Walk

1932	Thomas W. Green, Great Britain	4:50:10.00
1936	Harold Whitlock, Great Britain	4:30:41.10
1948	John Ljunggren, Sweden	4:41:52.00
1952	Giuseppe Dordoni, Italy	4:28:07.80
1956	Norman Read, New Zealand	4:30:42.80
1960	Donald Thompson, Great Britain	4:25:30.00
1964	Abdon Pamich, Italy	4:11:12.40
1968	Christoph Hohne, East Germany	4:20:13.60
1972	Bern Kannernberg, West Germany	3:56:11.60
1980	Hartwig Guader, East Germany	3:49:24.00
1984	Raul Gonzalez, Mexico	3:37:26.00
1988	Viacheslau Ivanenko, U.S.S.R.	3:48:29.00
1992	Andrei Perlov, Unified Team[1]	3:50:13.00
1996	Robert Korzeniowski, Poland	3:43:30.00
2000	Robert Korzeniowski, Poland	3:42:22.00

1. Former Soviet Union team.

400-Meter Relay (4x100)

1912	Great Britain	42.40
1920	United States	42.20
1924	United States	41.00
1928	United States	41.00
1932	United States	40.00
1936	United States	39.80
1948	United States	40.60
1952	United States	40.10
1956	United States	39.50
1960	Germany	39.50
1964	United States	39.00
1968	United States	38.20
1972	United States	38.19
1976	United States	38.33
1980	U.S.S.R.	38.26
1984	United States	37.83
1988	U.S.S.R.	38.19
1992	United States	37.40[1]
1996	Canada	37.69
2000	United States	37.61

1. World record.

1,600-Meter Relay (4x400)

1912	United States	3:16.60
1920	Great Britain	3:22.20
1924	United States	3:16.00
1928	United States	3:14.20
1932	United States	3:08.20
1936	Great Britain	3:09.00

1948	United States	3:10.40
1952	Jamaica, B.W.I.	3:03.90
1956	United States	3:04.80
1960	United States	3:02.20
1964	United States	3:00.70
1968	United States	2:56.10
1972	Kenya	2:59.80
1976	United States	2:58.65
1980	U.S.S.R.	3:01.10
1984	United States	2:57.91
1988	United States	2:56.16
1992	United States	2:55.74[1]
1996	United States	2:55.99
2000	United States	2:56.35

1. World record.

Team Race

		Pts
1900	Great Britain (5,000 meters)	26
1904	United States (4 miles)	27
1908	Great Britain (3 miles)	6
1912	United States (3,000 meters)	9
1920	United States (3,000 meters)	10
1924	Finland (3,000 meters)	9

Standing High Jump

1900	Ray Ewry, United States	5 ft. 5 in.
1904	Ray Ewry, United States	4 ft. 11 in.
1906	Ray Ewry, United States	5 ft. 1⅝ in.
1908	Ray Ewry, United States	5 ft. 2 in.
1912	Platt Adams, United States	5 ft. 4⅛ in.

Running High Jump

1896	Ellery Clark, United States	5 ft. 11¼ in.
1900	Irving Baxter, United States	6 ft. 2¾ in.
1904	Samuel Jones, United States	5 ft. 11 in.
1906	Con Leahy, Ireland	5 ft. 9⅞ in.
1908	Harry Porter, United States	6 ft. 3 in.
1912	Alma Richards, United States	6 ft. 4 in.
1920	Richmond Landon, United States	6 ft. 4¼ in.
1924	Harold Osborn, United States	6 ft. 5¹⁵⁄₁₆ in.
1928	Robert W. King, United States	6 ft. 4⅜ in.
1932	Duncan McNaughton, Canada	6 ft. 5⅝ in.
1936	Cornelius Johnson, United States	6 ft. 7¹⁵⁄₁₆ in.
1948	John Winter, Australia	6 ft. 6 in.
1952	Walter David, United States	6 ft. 8¹⁵⁄₁₆ in.
1956	Charles Damas, United States	6 ft. 11¼ in.
1960	Robert Shavlakadze, U.S.S.R.	7 ft. 1 in.
1964	Valeri Brumel, U.S.S.R.	7 ft. 1¾ in.
1968	Dick Fosbury, United States	7 ft. 4¼ in.
1972	Yuri Tarmak, U.S.S.R.	7 ft. 3¾ in.
1976	Jacek Wszola, Poland	7 ft. 4½ in.
1980	Gerd Wessig, East Germany	7 ft. 8¾ in.
1984	Dietmar Mogenburg, West Germany	7 ft. 8½ in.
1988	Guennadi Avdeenko, U.S.S.R.	7 ft. ½ in.
1992	Javier Sotomayer, Cuba	7 ft. 8½ in.
1996	Charles Austin, United States	7 ft. 10 in.
2000	Sergey Kliugin, Russia	7 ft. 8½ in.

Long Jump

1896	Ellery Clark, United States	20 ft. 9¾ in.
1900	Alvin Kraenzlein, United States	23 ft. 6⅞ in.
1904	Myer Prinstein, United States	24 ft. 1 in.
1906	Myer Prinstein, United States	23 ft. 7½ in.
1908	Frank Irons, United States	24 ft. 6½ in.
1912	Albert Gutterson, United States	24 ft. 11¼ in.
1920	William Petterssen, Sweden	23 ft. 5½ in.
1924	DeHart Hubbard, United States	24 ft. 5⅛ in.
1928	Edward B. Hamm, United States	25 ft. 4¾ in.
1932	Edward Gordon, United States	25 ft. ¾ in.
1936	Jesse Owens, United States	26 ft. 5⅝ in.
1948	Willie Steele, United States	25 ft. 8 in.
1952	Jerome Biffle, United States	24 ft. 10 in.
1956	Gregory Bell, United States	25 ft. 8¼ in.
1960	Ralph Boston, United States	26 ft. 7¾ in.
1964	Lynn Davies, Great Britain	26 ft. 5¾ in.

1968	Bob Beamon, United States	29 ft. 2½ in.
1972	Randy Williams, United States	27 ft. ½ in.
1976	Arnie Robinson, United States	24 ft. 7¾ in.
1980	Lutz Dombrowski, E. Germany	28 ft. ¼ in.
1984	Carl Lewis, United States	28 ft. ¼ in.
1988	Carl Lewis, United States	28 ft. 7¼ in.
1992	Carl Lewis, United States	28 ft. 5½ in.
1996	Carl Lewis, United States	27 ft. 10¾ in.
2000	Ivan Pedroso, Cuba	28 ft. ¾ in.

Triple Jump

1896	James B. Connolly, United States	45 ft.
1900	Myer Prinstein, United States	47 ft. 4¼ in.
1904	Myer Prinstein, United States	47 ft.
1906	P.G. O'Connor, Ireland	46 ft. 2 in.
1908	Timothy Ahearne, Great Britain	48 ft. 1¼ in.
1912	Gustaf Lindblom, Sweden	48 ft. 5⅛ in.
1920	Vilho Tuulos, Finland	47 ft. 6⅞ in.
1924	Archie Winter, Australia	50 ft. 11⅛ in.
1928	Mikio Oda, Japan	49 ft. 10¹³⁄₁₆ in.
1932	Chuhei Nambu, Japan	51 ft. 7 in.
1936	Naoto Tajima, Japan	52 ft. 5⅞ in.
1948	Arne Ahman, Sweden	50 ft. 6¼ in.
1952	Adhemar da Silva, Brazil	53 ft. 2½ in.
1956	Adhemar da Silva, Brazil	53 ft. 7½ in.
1960	Jozef Schmidt, Poland	55 ft. 1¾ in.
1964	Jozef Schmidt, Poland	55 ft. 3¼ in.
1968	Viktor Saneyev, U.S.S.R.	57 ft. ¾ in.
1972	Viktor Saneyev, U.S.S.R.	56 ft. 11 in.
1976	Viktor Saneyev, U.S.S.R.	56 ft. 8¾ in.
1980	Jaak Uudmae, U.S.S.R.	56 ft. 11⅛ in.
1984	Al Joyner, United States	56 ft. 7½ in.
1988	Hristo Markov, Bulgaria	57 ft. 9¼ in.
1992	Mike Conley, United States	59 ft. 7½ in.
1996	Kenny Harrison, United States	59 ft. 4¼ in.
2000	Jonathan Edwards, Great Britain	58 ft. 1¼ in.

Pole Vault

1896	William Hoyt, United States	10 ft. 9¾ in.
1900	Irving Baxter, United States	10 ft. 9⅞ in.
1904	Charles Dvorak, United States	11 ft. 6 in.
1906	Fernand Gouder, France	11 ft. 6 in.
1908	Alfred Gilbert, United States, and Edward Cook, United States (tie)	12 ft. 2 in.
1912	Harry Babcock, United States	12 ft. 11½ in.
1920	Frank Foss, United States	13 ft. 5 ⁹⁄₁₆ in.
1924	Lee Barnes, United States	12 ft. 11½ in.
1928	Sabin W. Carr, United States	13 ft. 9⅜ in.
1932	William Miller, United States	14 ft. 1⅞ in.
1936	Earle Meadows, United States	14 ft. 3¼ in.
1948	Guinn Smith, United States	14 ft. ¼ in.
1952	Robert Richards, United States	14 ft. 11⅛ in.
1956	Robert Richards, United States	14 ft. 11½ in.
1960	Don Bragg, United States	15 ft. 5⅛ in.
1964	Fred Hansen, United States	16 ft. 8¾ in.
1968	Bob Seagren, United States	17 ft. 8½ in.
1972	Wolfgang Nordwig, East Germany	18 ft. ½ in.
1976	Tadeusz Slusarski, Poland	18 ft. ½ in.
1980	Wladyslaw Kozakiewics, Poland	18 ft. 11½ in.
1984	Pierre Quinon, France	18 ft. 10¼ in.
1988	Sergei Bubka, U.S.S.R.	18 ft. 4¼ in.
1992	Maxim Tarassov, Unified Team[1]	19 ft. 0¼ in.
1996	Jean Galfione, France	19 ft. 5¼ in.
2000	Nick Hysong, United States	19 ft. 4¼ in.

1. Former Soviet Union team.

16-lb Shot-Put

1896	Robert Garrett, United States	36 ft. 9¾ in.
1900	Richard Sheldon, United States	46 ft. 3⅛ in.
1904	Ralph Rose, United States	48 ft. 7 in.
1906	Martin Sheridan, United States	40 ft. 4⅘ in.
1908	Ralph Rose, United States	46 ft. 7½ in.
1912	Pat McDonald, United States	50 ft. 4 in.
1920	Ville Porhola, Finland	48 ft. 7⅛ in.

1924	Clarence Houser, United States	49 ft. 2½ in.
1928	John Kuck, United States	52 ft. 11¹¹⁄₁₆ in.
1932	Leo Sexton, United States	52 ft. 6³⁄₁₆ in.
1936	Hans Woellke, Germany	53 ft. 1¾ in.
1948	Wilbur Thompson, United States	56 ft. 2 in.
1952	Parry O'Brien, United States	57 ft. 1½ in.
1956	Parry O'Brien, United States	60 ft. 11 in.
1960	Bill Nieder, United States	64 ft. 6¾ in.
1964	Dallas Long, United States	66 ft. 8¼ in.
1968	Randy Matson, United States	67 ft. 4¾ in.
1972	Wladyslaw Komar, Poland	69 ft. 6 in.
1976	Udo Beyer, East Germany	69 ft. ¾ in.
1980	Vladmir Klselyov, U.S.S.R.	70 ft. ½ in.
1984	Alessandro Andrei, Italy	69 ft. 9 in.
1988	Uhf Timmerman, East Germany	73 ft. 8¾ in.
1992	Michael Stulze, Germany	71 ft. 2½ in.
1996	Randy Barnes, United States	70 ft. 11¼ in.
2000	Arsi Harju, Finland	69 ft. 10¼ in.

Discus Throw

1896	Robert Garrett, United States	95 ft. 7½ in.
1900	Rudolf Bauer, Hungary	118 ft. 2⅞ in.
1904	Martin Sheridan, United States	128 ft. 10½ in.
1906	Martin Sheridan, United States	136 ft. ⅓ in.
1908	Martin Sheridan, United States	134 ft. 2 in.
1912	Armas Taipale, Finland	145 ft. ⁹⁄₁₆ in.
1920	Elmer Niklander, Finland	146 ft. 7 in.
1924	Clarence Houser, United States	151 ft. 5¼ in.
1928	Clarence Houser, United States	155 ft. 2⅘ in.
1932	John Anderson, United States	162 ft. 4⅞ in.
1936	Ken Carpenter, United States	165 ft. 7⅜ in.
1948	Adolfo Consolini, Italy	173 ft. 2 in.
1952	Simeon Iness, United States	180 ft. 6½ in.
1956	Al Oerter, United States	184 ft. 10½ in.
1960	Al Oerter, United States	194 ft. 2 in.
1964	Al Oerter, United States	200 ft. 1½ in.
1968	Al Oerter, United States	212 ft. 6 in.
1972	Ludvik Danek, Czechoslovakia	211 ft. 3 in.
1976	Mac Wilkins, United States	221 ft. 5 in.
1980	Viktor Rashchupkin, U.S.S.R.	218 ft. 8 in.
1984	Rolf Dannenberg, West Germany	218 ft. 6 in.
1988	Jurgen Schult, East Germany	225 ft. 9¼ in.
1992	Romas Ubartas, Lithuania	213 ft. 7¾ in.
1996	Lars Riedel, Germany	227 ft. 8 in.
2000	Virgilijus Alekna, Lithuana	227 ft. 4in.

Javelin Throw

1906	Eric Lemming, Sweden	175 ft. 6 in.
1908	Eric Lemming, Sweden	179 ft. 10½ in.
1912	Eric Lemming, Sweden	198 ft. 11¼ in.
1920	Jonni Myyra, Finland	215 ft. 9¾ in.
1924	Jonni Myyra, Finland	206 ft. 6¾ in.
1928	Eric Lundquist, Sweden	218 ft. 6⅛ in.
1932	Matti Jarvinen, Finland	238 ft. 7 in.
1936	Gerhard Stoeck, Germany	235 ft. 8⁵⁄₁₆ in.
1948	Kaj Rautavaara, Finland	228 ft. 10½ in.
1952	Cy Young, United States	242 ft.¾ in.
1956	Egil Danielsen, Norway	281 ft. 2¼ in.
1960	Viktor Tsibuelnko, U.S.S.R.	277 ft. 8⅜ in.
1964	Pauli Nevala, Finland	271 ft. 2¼ in.
1968	Janis Lusis, U.S.S.R.	295 ft. 7 in.
1972	Klaus Wolfermann, West Germany	296 ft. 10 in.
1976	Miklos Nemeth, Hungary	310 ft. 4 in.
1980	Dainis Kula, U.S.S.R.	299 ft. 2⅜ in.
1984	Arto Haerkoenen, Finland	284 ft. 8 in.
1988	Tapio Korjus, Finland	276 ft. 6 in.
1992	Jan Zelezny, Czechoslovakia	294 ft. 2 in.
1996	Jan Zelezny, Czech Republic	289 ft. 3 in.
2000	Jan Zelezny, Czech Republic	295 ft. 9½ in.

16-lb Hammer Throw

1900	John Flanagan, United States	167 ft. 4 in.
1904	John Flanagan, United States	168 ft. 1 in.
1908	John Flanagan, United States	170 ft. 4¼ in.
1912	Matt McGrath, United States	179 ft. 7⅛ in.
1920	Pat Ryan, United States	173 ft. 5⅝ in.
1924	Fred Tootell, United States	174 ft. 10¼ in.
1928	Patrick O'Callaghan, Ireland	168 ft. 7½ in.
1932	Patrick O'Callaghan, Ireland	176 ft. 11⅛ in.
1936	Karl Hein, Germany	185 ft. 4 in.
1948	Imre Nemeth, Hungary	183 ft. 11½ in.
1952	Jozsef Csermak, Hungary	197 ft. 11⁹⁄₁₆ in.
1956	Harold Connolly, United States	207 ft. 2¾ in.
1960	Vasily Rudenkov, U.S.S.R.	220 ft. 1⅝ in.
1964	Romuald Klim, U.S.S.R.	228 ft. 9½ in.
1968	Gyula Zsivotzky, Hungary	240 ft. 8 in.
1972	Anatoly Bondarchuk, U.S.S.R.	247 ft. 8½ in.
1976	Yuri Sedykh, U.S.S.R.	254 ft. 4 in.
1980	Yuri Sedykh, U.S.S.R. (81.80m)	268 ft. 4½ in.
1984	Juha Tiainen, Finland	256 ft. 2 in.
1988	Sergei Litvinov, U.S.S.R.	278 ft. 2½ in.
1992	Andrey Abduvaliyev, Unified Team[1]	270 ft. 9½ in.
1996	Balasz Kiss, Hungary	266 ft. 6 in.
2000	Szymon Ziolkowski, Poland	262 ft. 6 in.

1. Former Soviet Union team.

Decathlon

1912	Jim Thorpe, United States	—
	Hugo Wieslander, Sweden	—
1920	Helge Lovland, Norway	6,804.35 pts.
1924	Harold Osborn, United States	7,710.775 pts.
1928	Paavo Yrjola, Finland	8,053.29 pts.
1932	James Bausch, United States	8,462.23 pts.
1936	Glenn Morris, United States	7,900 pts.[1]
1948	Robert B. Mathias, United States	7,139 pts.
1952	Robert B. Mathias, United States	7,887 pts.
1956	Milton Campbell, United States	7,937 pts.
1960	Rafer Johnson, United States	8,392 pts.
1964	Willi Holdorf, Germany	7,887 pts.[1]
1968	Bill Toomey, United States	8,193 pts.
1972	Nikolai Avilov, U.S.S.R.	8,454 pts.
1976	Bruce Jenner, United States	8,618 pts.
1980	Daley Thompson, Britain	8,495 pts.
1984	Daley Thompson, Britain	8,797 pts.
1988	Christian Schenk, East Germany	8,488 pts.
1992	Robert Zmelik, Czechoslovakia	8,611 pts.
1996	Dan O'Brien, United States	8,824 pts.
2000	Erki Nool, Estonia	8,641 pts.

1. Point system revised.

TRACK AND FIELD–WOMEN

100-Meter Dash

1928	Elizabeth Robinson, United States	12.20
1932	Stella Walsh, Poland	11.90
1936	Helen Stephens, United States	11.50
1948	Fanny Blankers-Koen, Netherlands	11.90
1952	Marjorie Jackson, Australia	11.50
1956	Betty Cuthbert, Australia	11.50
1960	Wilma Rudolph, United States	11.00
1964	Wyomia Tyus, United States	11.40
1968	Wyomia Tyus, United States	11.00
1972	Renate Stecher, East Germany	11.07
1976	Annegret Richter, West Germany	11.08
1980	Lyudmila Kondratyeva, U.S.S.R.	11.06
1984	Evelyn Ashford, United States	10.97
1988	Florence Griffith-Joyner, United States	10.54
1992	Gail Devers, United States	10.82
1996	Gail Devers, United States	10.94
2000	Marion Jones, United States	10.75

200-Meter Dash

1948	Fanny Blankers-Koen, Netherlands	24.40
1952	Marjorie Jackson, Australia	23.70
1956	Betty Cuthbert, Australia	23.40
1960	Wilma Rudolph, United States	24.00
1964	Edith McGuire, United States	23.00
1968	Irena Szewinska, Poland	22.50

1972	Renate Stecher, East Germany	22.40
1976	Baerbel Eckert, East Germany	22.37
1980	Barbara Wockel, East Germany	22.03
1984	Valerie Brisco-Hooks, United States	21.81
1988	Florence Griffith-Joyner, United States	21.34
1992	Gwen Torrence, United States	21.81
1996	Marie-Jose Perec, France	22.12
2000	Marion Jones, United States	21.84

400-Meter Dash

1964	Betty Cuthbert, Australia	52.00
1968	Colette Besson, France	52.00
1972	Monika Zehrt, East Germany	51.08
1976	Irena Szewinska, Poland	49.29
1980	Marita Koch, East Germany	48.88
1984	Valerie Brisco-Hooks, United States	48.83
1988	Olga Bryzguina, U.S.S.R.	48.65
1992	Marie Jose-Perec, France	48.83
1996	Marie Jose-Perec, France	48.25
2000	Cathy Freeman, Australia	49.11

800-Meter Run

1928	Lina Radke, Germany	2:16.80
1960	Ljudmila Shevcova, U.S.S.R.	2:04.30
1964	Ann Packer, Great Britain	2:01.10
1968	Madeline Manning, United States	2:00.90
1972	Hildegard Falck, West Germany	1:58.60
1976	Tatiana Kazankina, U.S.S.R.	1:54.94
1980	Nadezhda Olizarenko, U.S.S.R.	1:53.50
1984	Doina Melinte, Romania	1:57.60
1988	Sigrun Wodars, East Germany	1:56.10
1992	Ellen Van Langen, Netherlands	1:55.54
1996	Svetlana Masterkova, Russia	1:57.73
2000	Maria Mutola, Mozambique	1:56.15

1,500-Meter Run

1972	Ludmila Bragina, U.S.S.R.	4:01.40
1976	Tatiana Kazankina, U.S.S.R.	4:05.48
1980	Tatiana Kazankina, U.S.S.R.	3:56.60
1984	Gabriella Dorio, Italy	4:03.25
1988	Paula Ivan, Romania	3:53.96
1992	Hassiba Boulmerka, Algeria	3:55.30
1996	Svetlana Masterkova, Russia	4:00.83
2000	Nouria Merah-Benida, Algeria	4:05.10

5,000-Meter Run

1996	Wang, Jun-Xia, China	14:59.88
2000	Gabriela Szabo, Romania	14:40.79

10,000-Meter Run

1992	Derartu Tulu, Ethiopia	31:60.02
1996	Fernanda Ribeiro, Portugal	31:01.63
2000	Derartu Tulu, Ethiopia	30:17.49

80-Meter Hurdles

1932	Mildred Didrikson, United States	11.70
1936	Trebisonda Valla, Italy	11.70
1948	Fanny Blankers-Koen, Netherlands	11.20
1952	Shirley S. de la Hunty, Australia	10.90
1956	Shirley S. de la Hunty, Australia	10.70
1960	Irina Press, U.S.S.R.	10.80
1964	Karin Balzer, Germany	10.50[1]
1968	Maureen Caird, Australia	10.30

1. Wind assisted.

100-Meter Hurdles

1972	Annelie Ehrhardt, East Germany	12.59
1976	Johanna Schaller, East Germany	12.77
1980	Vera Komisova, U.S.S.R.	12.56
1984	Benita Fitzgerald-Brown, United States	12.84
1988	Jordanka Donkova, Bulgaria	12.38
1992	Paraskevi Patoulidou, Greece	12.64
1996	Ludmila Engquist, Sweden	12.58
2000	Olga Shishigina, Kazakhstan	12.65

400-Meter Hurdles

1984	Nawai El Moutawakel, Morocco	54.61
1988	Debra Flintoff-King, Australia	53.17
1992	Sally Gunnell, Great Britain	53.23

1996	Deon Hemmings, Jamaica	52.82
2000	Irina Privalova, Russia	53.02

400-Meter Relay

1928	Canada	48.40
1932	United States	47.00
1936	United States	46.90
1948	Netherlands	47.50
1952	United States	45.90
1956	Australia	44.50
1960	United States	44.50
1964	Poland	43.60
1968	United States	42.80
1972	West Germany	42.81
1976	East Germany	42.50
1980	East Germany	41.60
1984	United States	41.65
1988	United States	41.98
1992	United States	42.11
1996	United States	41.95
2000	Bahamas	41.95

1,600-Meter Relay

1972	East Germany	3:23.00
1976	East Germany	3:19.23
1980	U.S.S.R.	3:20.20
1984	United States	3:18.29
1988	U.S.S.R.	3:15.18
1992	Unified Team[1]	3:20.20
1996	United States	3:20.91
2000	United States	3:22.62

1. Former Soviet Union team.

10,000-Meter Walk

1992	ChenYue-Ling, China	44:32
1996	Yelena Nikolayeva, Russia	41:49

20,000-Meter Walk

2000	Liping Wang, China	1:29.05

Marathon

1984	Joan Benoit, United States	2:24:52
1988	Rose Mota, Portugal	2:25.40
1992	Valentina Yegorova, Unified Team	2:32.41
1996	Fatuma Roba, Ethiopia	2:26.05
2000	Naoko Takahashi, Japan	2:23.14

Running High Jump

1928	Ethel Catherwood, Canada	5 ft. 3 in.
1932	Jean Shiley, United States	5 ft. 5¼ in.
1936	Ibolya Csak, Hungary	5 ft. 3 in.
1948	Alice Coachman, United States	5 ft. 6⅛ in.
1952	Ester Brand, South Africa	5 ft. 5¾ in.
1956	Mildred McDaniel, United States	5 ft. 9¼ in.
1960	Iolanda Balas, Romania	6 ft. ¾ in.
1964	Iolanda Balas, Romania	6 ft. 2¾ in.
1968	Miloslava Rezkova, Czechoslovakia	5 ft. 11¾ in.
1972	Ulrike Meyfarth, West Germany	6 ft. 3⅜ in.
1976	Rosemarie Ackerman, E. Germany	6 ft. 4 in.
1980	Sara Simeoni, Italy	6 ft. 5½ in.
1984	Ulrike Meyfarth, West Germany	6 ft. 7½ in.
1988	Louise Ritter, United States	6 ft. 8 in.
1992	Heike Henkel, Germany	6 ft. 7½ in.
1996	Stefka Kostadinova, Bulgaria	6 ft. 8¾ in.
2000	Yelena Yelesina, Russia	6 ft. 7 in.

Long Jump

1948	Olga Gyarmati, Hungary	18 ft. 8¼ in.
1952	Yvette Williams, New Zealand	20 ft. 5¾ in.
1956	Elzbieta Krzesinska, Poland	20 ft. 9¾ in.
1960	Vera Krepkina, U.S.S.R.	20 ft. 10¾ in.
1964	Mary Rand, Great Britain	22 ft. 2 in.
1968	Viorica Ciscopoleanu, Romania	22 ft. 4½ in.
1972	Heidemarie Rosendahl, West Germany	22 ft. 3 in.
1976	Angela Voigt, East Germany	22 ft. ½ in.
1980	Tatiana Kolpakova, U.S.S.R.	23 ft. 2 in.
1984	Anisoara Stanciu, Romania	22 ft. 10 in.
1988	Jackie Joyner-Kersee, United States	24 ft. 3½ in.

1992 Heike Drechsler, Germany	23 ft. 5¼ in.
1996 Chioma Ajunwa, Nigeria	23 ft. 4½ in.
2000 Heike Drechsler, Germany	22 ft. 11¼ in.

Triple Jump

1996 Inessa Kravets, Ukraine	50 ft. 3½ in.
2000 Tereza Marinova, Belarus	49 ft. 10 ½ in.

Shot-Put

1948 Micheline Ostermeyer, France	45 ft. 1½ in.
1952 Galina Zybina, U.S.S.R.	50 ft. 1½ in.
1956 Tamara Tishkyevich, U.S.S.R.	54 ft. 5 in.
1960 Tamara Press, U.S.S.R.	56 ft. 9⅞ in.
1964 Tamara Press, U.S.S.R.	59 ft. 6 in.
1968 Margitta Gummel, East Germany	64 ft. 4 in.
1972 Nadezhda Chizhova, U.S.S.R.	69 ft.
1976 Ivanka Christova, Bulgaria	69 ft. 5 in.
1980 Ilona Sluplanek, East Germany	73 ft. 6 in.
1984 Claudia Losch, West Germany	67 ft. 2¼ in.
1988 Natalya Lisovskaya, U.S.S.R.	72 ft. 11½ in.
1992 Svetlana Kriveleva, Unified Team[1]	69 ft. 1¼ in.
1996 Astrid Kumbernuss, Germany	67 ft. 5½ in.
2000 Yanina Korolchik, Belarus	67 ft. 5½ in.
1. Former Soviet Union team.	

Discus Throw

1928 Helena Konopacka, Poland	129 ft. 11⅞ in.
1932 Lillian Copeland, United States	133 ft. 2 in.
1936 Gisela Mauermayer, Germany	156 ft. 3³⁄₁₆ in.
1948 Micheline Ostermeyer, France	137 ft. 6½ in.
1956 Olga Fikotova, Czechoslovakia	176 ft. 1½ in.
1960 Nina Ponomareva, U.S.S.R.	180 ft. 8¼ in.
1964 Tamara Press, U.S.S.R.	187 ft. 10¾ in.
1968 Lia Manoliu, Romania	191 ft. 2½ in.
1972 Faina Melnik, U.S.S.R.	218 ft. 7 in.
1976 Evelin Schlaak, East Germany	226 ft. 4 in.
1980 Evelin Jahl, East Germany	229 ft. 6½ in.
1984 Ria Stalman, Netherlands	214 ft. 5 in.
1988 Martina Hellmann, East Germany	237 ft. 2¼ in.
1992 Maritza Marten, Cuba	229 ft. 10¼ in.
1996 Ilke Wyludda, Germany	228 ft. 6½ in.
2000 Ellina Zvereva, Belarus	224 ft. 5 in.

Javelin Throw

1932 Mildred Didrikson, United States	143 ft. 4 in.
1936 Tilly Fleischer, Germany	148 ft. 2¾ in.
1948 Herma Bauma, Austria	149 ft. 6 in.
1952 Dana Zatopek, Czechoslovakia	165 ft. 7 in.
1956 Inessa Janzeme, U.S.S.R.	176 ft. 8 in.
1960 Elvira Ozolina, U.S.S.R.	183 ft. 8 in.
1964 Mihaela Penes, Romania	198 ft. 7½ in.
1968 Angela Nemeth, Hungary	198 ft.
1972 Ruth Fuchs, East Germany	209 ft. 7 in.
1976 Ruth Fuchs, East Germany	216 ft. 4 in.
1980 Maria Colon, Cuba	224 ft. 5 in.
1984 Tessa Sanderson, Britain	228 ft. 2 in.
1988 Petra Felke, East Germany	245 ft.
1992 Silke Renke, Germany	224 ft. 2½ in.
1996 Heli Rantanen, Finland	222 ft. 11 in.
2000 Trine Hattestad, Norway	226 ft. 1 in.

Hammer Throw

2000 Kamila Skolimowska, Poland	233 ft. 5 ¾ in.

Pole Vault

2000 Stacy Dragila, United States	15 ft. 1 in.

Pentathlon

1964 Irina Press, U.S.S.R.	5,246 pts.
1968 Ingrid Becker, West Germany	5,098 pts.
1972 Mary Peters, Britain	4,801 pts.
1976 Siegrun Siegl, East Germany	4,745 pts.
1980 Nadyezhda Tkachenko, U.S.S.R.	5,083 pts.
1984 Daniele Masala, Italy	5,469 pts.
1988 Jackie Joyner-Kersee, United States	7,291 pts.

Heptathlon

1992 Jackie Joyner-Kersee, United States	7,044 pts.
1996 Ghada Shouaa, Syria	6,780 pts.
2000 Denise Lewis, Great Britain	6,584 pts.

SWIMMING—MEN

50-Meter Freestyle

1988 Matt Biondi, United States	22.14
1992 Alexander Popov, Unified Team[1]	21.91
1996 Alexander Popov, Russia	22.13
2000 Anthony Ervin and Gary Hall, Jr., United States	21.98
1. Former Soviet Union team.	

100-Meter Freestyle

1896 Alfred Hajos, Hungary	1:22.20
1904 Zoltan de Halmay, Hungary	1:02.80[1]
1906 Charles Daniels, United States	1:13.00
1908 Charles Daniels, United States	1:05.60
1912 Duke P. Kahanamoku, United States	1:03.40
1920 Duke P. Kahanamoku, United States	1:01.40
1924 John Weissmuller, United States	0:59.00
1928 John Weissmuller, United States	0:58.60
1932 Yasuji Miyazaki, Japan	0:58.20
1936 Ferenc Csik, Hungary	0:57.60
1948 Walter Ris, United States	0:57.30
1952 Clarke Scholes, United States	0:57.40
1956 Jon Henricks, Australia	0:55.40
1960 John Devitt, Australia	0:55.20
1964 Don Schollander, United States	0:53.40
1968 Michael Wenden, Australia	0:52.20
1972 Mark Spitz, United States	0:51.22
1976 Jim Montgomery, United States	0:49.99
1980 Jorg Woithe, East Germany	0:50.40
1984 Rowdy Gaines, United States	0:49.80
1988 Matt Biondi, United States	0:48.63
1992 Alexander Popov, Unified Team[2]	0:49.02
1996 Alexander Popov, Russia	0:48.74
2000 Pieter van den Hoogenband, Netherlands	0:48.30
1. 100 yards. 2. Former Soviet Union team.	

200-Meter Freestyle

1900 Frederick Lane, Australia	2:25.20
1904 Charles Daniels, United States	2:44.20[1]
1968 Michael Wenden, Australia	1:55.20
1972 Mark Spitz, United States	1:52.78
1976 Bruce Furniss, United States	1:50.29
1980 Sergei Kopiliakov, U.S.S.R.	1:49.81
1984 Michael Gross, West Germany	1:47.44
1988 Duncan Armstrong, Australia	1:47.25
1992 Evgueni Sadovyi, Unified Team[2]	1:46.70
1996 Danyon Loader, New Zealand	1:47.63
2000 Pieter van den Hoogenband, Netherlands	1:45.35[3]
1. 220 yards 2. Former Soviet Union team. 3. World record.	

400-Meter Freestyle

1896 Paul Neumann, Austria	8:12.60[1]
1904 Charles Daniels, United States	6:16.20[2]
1906 Otto Sheff, Austria	6:23.80
1908 Henry Taylor, Great Britain	5:36.80
1912 George Hodgson, Canada	5:24.40
1920 Norman Ross, United States	5:26.80
1926 John Weissmuller, United States	5:04.20
1928 Albert Zorilla, Argentina	5:01.60
1932 Clarence Crabbe, United States	4:48.40
1936 Jack Medica, United States	4:44.50
1948 William Smith, United States	4:41.00
1952 Jean Boiteux, France	4:30.70
1956 Murray Rose, Australia	4:27.30
1960 Murray Rose, Australia	4:18.30
1964 Don Schollander, United States	4:12.20
1968 Mike Burton, United States	4:09.00
1972 Bradford Cooper, Australia	4:00.27[3]
1976 Brian Goodell, United States	3:51.93

1980	Vladimir Salnikov, U.S.S.R.	3:51.31
1984	George DiCarlo, United States	3:51.23
1988	Uwe Dassier, East Germany	3:46.95
1992	Evgueni Sadovyi, Unified Team	3:45.00[4]
1996	Danyon Loader, New Zealand	3:47.97
2000	Ian Thorpe, Australia	3:40.59[4]

1. 500 meters. 2. 440 yards. 3. Rich DeMont, United States,
won but was disqualified following day for medical reasons.
4. World record.

1,500-Meter Freestyle

1904	Emil Rausch, Germany	27:18.20[1]
1906	Henry Taylor, Great Britain	28:28.00[2]
1908	Henry Taylor, Great Britain	22:48.40
1912	George Hodgson, Canada	22:00.00
1920	Norman Ross, United States	22:23.20
1924	Andrew Charlton, Australia	20:06.60
1928	Arne Borg, Sweden	19:51.80
1932	Kusuo Kitamura, Japan	19:12.40
1936	Noboru Terada, Japan	19:13.70
1948	James McLane, United States	19:18.50
1952	Ford Konno, United States	18:30.00
1956	Murray Rose, Australia	17:58.90
1960	Jon Konrads, Australia	17:19.60
1964	Robert Windle, Australia	17:01.70
1968	Michael Burton, United States	16:38.90
1972	Michael Burton, United States	15:52.58
1976	Brian Goodell, United States	15:02.40
1980	Vladimir Salnikov, U.S.S.R.	14:58.27
1984	Michael O'Brien, United States	15:05.20
1988	Vladimir Salnikov, U.S.S.R.	15:00.40
1992	Kieren Perkins, Australia	14:43.48
1996	Kieren Perkins, Australia	14:56.40
2000	Grant Hackett, Australia	14:48.33

1. One mile. 2. 1,600 meters

100-Meter Backstroke

1904	Walter Brack, Germany	1:16.80[1]
1908	Arno Bieberstein, Germany	1:24.60
1912	Harry Hebner, United States	1:21.20
1920	Warren Kealoha, United States	1:15.20
1924	Warren Kealoha, United States	1:13.20
1928	George Kojac, United States	1:08.20
1932	Masaji Kiyokawa, Japan	1:08.60
1936	Adolph Kiefer, United States	1:05.90
1948	Allen Stack, United States	1:06.40
1952	Yoshinobu Oyakawa, United States	1:05.40
1956	David Thiele, Australia	1:02.20
1960	David Thiele, Australia	1:01.90
1968	Roland Matthes, East Germany	0:58.70
1972	Roland Matthes, East Germany	0:56.58
1976	John Naber, United States	0:55.49
1980	Bengt Baron, Sweden	0:56.53
1984	Rick Carey, United States	0:55.79
1988	Daichi Suzuki, Japan	0:55.05
1992	Mark Tewksbury, Canada	0:53.98
1996	Jeff Rouse, United States	0:54.10
2000	Lenny Krayzelburg, United States	0:53.72

1. 100 yards

200-Meter Backstroke

1900	Ernst Hoppenberg, Germany	2:47.00
1964	Jed Graef, United States	2:10.30
1968	Roland Matthes, East Germany	2:09.60
1972	Roland Matthes, East Germany	2:02.82
1976	John Naber, United States	1:59.19
1980	Sandor Wladar, Hungary	2:01.93
1984	Rick Carey, United States	2:00.23
1988	Igor Polianski, U.S.S.R.	1:59.37
1992	Martin Lopez Zubero, Spain	1:58.47
1996	Brad Bridgewater, United States	1:58.54
2000	Lenny Krayzelburg, United States	1:56.76

100-Meter Breaststroke

1968	Donald McKenzie, United States	1:07.70

1972	Nobutaka Taguchi, Japan	1:04.94
1976	John Hencken, United States	1:03.11
1980	Duncan Goodhew, Britain	1:03.34
1984	Steve Lindquist, United States	1:01.65
1988	Adrian Moorhouse, Great Britain	1:02.04
1992	Nelson Diebel, United States	1:01.50
1996	Fred Deburghgraeve, Belgium	1:00.60[1]
2000	Domenico Fioravanti, Italy	1:00.46

1. World record.

200-Meter Breaststroke

1908	Frederick Holman, Great Britain	3:09.20
1912	Walter Bathe, Germany	3:01.80
1920	Haken Malmroth, Sweden	3:04.40
1924	Robert Skelton, United States	2:56.60
1928	Yoshiyuki Tsuruta, Japan	2:48.80
1932	Yoshiyuki Tsuruta, Japan	2:45.40
1936	Tetsuo Hamuro, Japan	2:41.50
1948	Joseph Verdeur, United States	2:39.30
1952	John Davies, Australia	2:34.40
1956	Masaura Furukawa, Japan	2:34.70
1960	Bill Muliken, United States	2:37.40
1964	Ian O'Brien, Australia	2:07.80
1968	Felipe Munoz, Mexico	2:28.70
1972	John Hencken, United States	2:21.55
1976	David Willkie, Britain	2:15.11
1980	Robertas Zulpa, U.S.S.R.	2:15.85
1984	Victor Davis, Canada	2:13.34
1988	Jozef Szabo, Hungary	2:13.52
1992	Mike Barrowman, United States	2:10.16
1996	Norbert Rozsa, Hungary	2:12.57
2000	Domenico Fioravanti, Italy	2:10.87

100-Meter Butterfly

1968	Douglas Russell, United States	55.90
1972	Mark Spitz, United States	54.27
1976	Matt Vogel, United States	54.35
1980	Par Arvidsson, Sweden	54.92
1984	Michael Gross, West Germany	53.08
1988	Anthony Nesty, Surinam	53.00
1992	Pablo Morales, United States	53.32
1996	Denis Pankratov, Russia	52.27[1]
2000	Lars Froelander, Sweden	52.00

1. World record.

200-Meter Butterfly

1956	Bill Yorzyk, United States	2:19.30
1960	Mike Troy, United States	2:12.80
1964	Kevin Berry, Australia	2:06.60
1968	Carl Robie, United States	2:08.70
1972	Mark Spitz, United States	2:00.70
1976	Mike Bruner, United States	1:59.23
1980	Sergei Fesenko, U.S.S.R.	1:59.76
1984	Jon Sieben, Australia	1:57.00
1988	Michael Gross, East Germany	1:56.94
1992	Mel Stewart, United States	1:56.26
1996	Denis Pankratov, Russia	1:56.51
2000	Tom Malchow, United States	1:55.35

200-Meter Individual Medley

1968	Charles Hickcox, United States	2:12.00
1972	Gunnar Larsson, Sweden	2:07.17
1988	Tamas Darnyi, Hungary	2:00.17
1992	Tamas Darnyi, Hungary	2:00.76
1996	Attila Czene, Hungary	1:59.91
2000	Massimiliano Rosolino, Italy	1:58.98

400-Meter Individual Medley

1964	Dick Roth, United States	4:45.40
1968	Charles Hickox, United States	4:48.40
1972	Gunnar Larsson, Sweden	4:31.98
1976	Rod Strachan, United States	4:23.68
1980	Aleksandr Sidorenko, U.S.S.R.	4:22.80
1984	Alex Baumann, Canada	4:17.41
1988	Tamas Darnyi, Hungary	4:14.75
1992	Tamas Darnyi, Hungary	4:14.23

1996	Tom Dolan, United States	4:14.90
2000	Tom Dolan, United States	4:11.76[1]

1. World record.

400-Meter Freestyle Relay

1964	United States	3:32.20
1968	United States	3:31.70
1972	United States	3:26.42
1988	United States	3:16.52
1992	United States	3:16.74
1996	United States	3:15.41
2000	Australia	3:13.67[1]

1. World record.

800-Meter Freestyle Relay

1908	Great Britain	10:55.60
1912	Australia	10:11.20
1920	United States	10:04.40
1924	United States	09:53.40
1928	United States	09:36.20
1932	Japan	08:58.40
1936	Japan	08:51.50
1948	United States	08:46.10
1952	United States	08:31.10
1956	Australia	08:23.60
1960	United States	08:10.20
1964	United States	07:52.10
1968	United States	07:52.30
1972	United States	07:35.78
1976	United States	07:23.22
1980	U.S.S.R.	07:23.50
1984	United States	07:16.59
1988	United States	07:12.51
1992	Unified Team[1]	07:11.95
1996	United States	07:14.84
2000	Australia	07:07.05[2]

1. Former Soviet Union team. 2. World record.

400-Meter Medley Relay

1960	United States	4:05.40
1964	United States	3:58.40
1968	United States	3:54.90
1972	United States	3:48.16
1976	United States	3:42.22
1980	Australia	3:45.70
1984	United States	3:39.30
1988	United States	3:36.93
1992	United States	3:36.93
1996	United States	3:34.84
2000	United States	3:33.73[1]

1. World record.

Springboard Dive

		Points
1908	Albert Zuerner, Germany	85.50
1912	Paul Guenther, Germany	79.23
1920	Louis Kuehn, United States	675.00
1924	Albert White, United States	696.40
1928	Pete Desjardins, United States	185.04
1932	Michael Galitzen, United States	161.38
1936	Richard Degener, United States	163.57
1948	Bruce Harlan, United States	163.64
1952	David Browning, United States	205.59
1956	Robert Clotworthy, United States	159.56
1960	Gary Tobian, United States	170.00
1964	Ken Sitzberger, United States	159.90
1968	Bernard Wrightson, United States	170.15
1972	Vladimir Vasin, U.S.S.R.	594.09
1976	Phil Boggs, United States	619.05
1980	Alexsandr Portnov, U.S.S.R.	905.02
1984	Greg Louganis, United States	754.41
1988	Greg Louganis, United States	730.80
1992	Mark Lenzi, United States	676.53
1996	Xiong Ni, China	701.46
2000	Xiong Ni, China	708.72

Platform Dive

		Points
1904	G.E. Sheldon, United States	12.75
1906	Gottlob Walz, Germany	156.00
1908	Hjalmar Johansson, Sweden	83.75
1912	Erik Adlerz, Sweden	73.94
1920	Clarence Pinkston, United States	100.67
1924	Albert White, United States	487.30
1928	Pete Desjardins, United States	98.74
1932	Harold Smith, United States	124.80
1936	Marshall Wayne, United States	113.58
1948	Samuel Lee, United States	130.05
1952	Samuel Lee, United States	156.28
1956	Joaquin Capilla, Mexico	152.44
1960	Bob Webster, United States	165.56
1964	Bob Webster, United States	148.58
1968	Klaus Dibiasi, Italy	164.18
1972	Klaus Dibiasi, Italy	504.12
1976	Klaus Dibiasi, Italy	600.51
1980	Falk Hoffman, E. Germany	835.65
1984	Greg Louganis, United States	710.91
1988	Greg Louganis, United States	638.61
1992	Sun, Shu-Wei, China	677.31
1996	Dmitri Saoutine, Russia	692.34
2000	Tian Liang, China	724.53

Synchronized 3m Springboard Dive

		Points
2000	Xiao Hailiang and Xiong Ni, China	365.58

Synchronized 10m Platform Dive

		Points
2000	Igor Loukachine and Dmitri Saoutine, Russia	365.04

SWIMMING–WOMEN

50-Meter Freestyle

1988	Kristin Otto, East Germany	25.49
1992	Yang, Wen-Yi, China	24.79
1996	Amy Van Dyken, United States	24.87
2000	Inge de Bruijn, Netherlands	24.32

100-Meter Freestyle

1912	Fanny Durack, Australia	1:22.20
1920	Ethelda Bleibtrey, United States	1:13.60
1924	Ethel Lackie, United States	1:12.40
1928	Albina Osipowich, United States	1:11.00
1932	Helene Madison, United States	1:06.80
1936	Hendrika Mastenbroek, Netherlands	1:05.90
1948	Greta Andersen, Denmark	1:06.30
1952	Katalin Szoke, Hungary	1:06.80
1956	Dawn Fraser, Australia	1:02.00
1960	Dawn Fraser, Australia	1:01.20
1964	Dawn Fraser, Australia	0:59.50
1968	Marge Jan Henne, United States	1:00.00
1972	Sandra Neilson, United States	0:58.59
1976	Kornelia Ender, East Germany	0:55.65
1980	Barbara Krause, East Germany	0:54.79
1984	Carrie Steinseifer, United States	0:55.92
1988	Kristin Otto, East Germany	0:54.93
1992	Zhuang Yong, China	0:54.64
1996	Le Jingyi, China	0:54.50
2000	Inge de Bruijn, Netherlands	0:58.83

200-Meter Freestyle

1968	Debbie Meyer, United States	2:10.50
1972	Shane Gould, Australia	2:03.56
1976	Kornelia Ender, East Germany	1:59.26
1980	Barbara Krause, East Germany	1:58.33
1984	Mary Wayle, United States	1:59.23
1988	Heike Friedrich, East Germany	1:57.65
1992	Nicole Haislett, United States	1:57.90
1996	Claudia Poll, Costa Rica	1:58.16
2000	Susie O'Neill, Australia	1:58.24

400-Meter Freestyle

1920	Ethelda Bleibtrey, United States	4:34.00[1]
1924	Martha Norelius, United States	6:02.20
1928	Martha Norelius, United States	5:42.80

1932	Helene Madison, United States	5:28.50
1936	Hendrika Mastenbroek, Netherlands	5:26.40
1948	Ann Curtis, United States	5:17.80
1952	Valerie Gyenge, Hungary	5:12.10
1956	Lorraine Crapp, Australia	4:54.60
1960	Chris von Saltza, United States	4:50.60
1964	Ginny Duenkel, United States	4:43.30
1968	Debbie Meyer, United States	4:31.80
1972	Shane Gould, Australia	4:19.04
1976	Petra Thumer, East Germany	4:09.89
1980	Ines Diers, East Germany	4:08.76
1984	Tiffany Cohen, United States	4:07.10
1988	Janet Evans, United States	4:03.85
1992	Dagmar Hase, Germany	4:07.18
1996	Michelle Smith, Ireland	4:07.25
2000	Brooke Bennett, United States	4:05.80

1. 300 meters.

800-Meter Freestyle

1968	Debbie Meyer, United States	9:24.00
1972	Keena Rothhammer, United States	8:53.68
1976	Petra Thumer, East Germany	8:37.14
1980	Michelle Ford, Australia	8:28.90
1984	Tiffany Cohen, United States	8:24.95
1988	Janet Evans, United States	8:20.20
1992	Janet Evans, Unites States	8:25.52
1996	Brooke Bennett, Unites States	8:27.89
2000	Brooke Bennett, United States	8:19.67

100-Meter Backstroke

1924	Sybil Bauer, United States	1:23.20
1928	Marie Braun, Netherlands	1:22.00
1932	Eleanor Holm, United States	1:19.40
1936	Dina Senff, Netherlands	1:18.90
1948	Karen Harup, Denmark	1:14.40
1952	Joan Harrison, South Africa	1:14.30
1956	Judy Grinham, Great Britain	1:12.90
1960	Lynn Burke, United States	1:09.30
1964	Cathy Ferguson, United States	1:07.70
1968	Kaye Hall, United States	1:06.20
1972	Melissa Belote, United States	1:05.78
1976	Ulrike Richter, East Germany	1:01.83
1980	Rica Reinisch, East Germany	1:00.86
1984	Theresa Andrews, United States	1:02.55
1988	Kristin Otto, East Germany	1:00.89
1992	Krisztina Egerszegi, Hungary	1:00.68
1996	Beth Botsford, United States	1:01.19
2000	Diana Mocanu, Romania	1:00.21

200-Meter Backstroke

1968	Pokey Watson, United States	2:24.80
1972	Melissa Belote, United States	2:19.19
1976	Ulrike Richter, East Germany	2:13.43
1980	Rica Reinisch, East Germany	2:11.77
1984	Jolanda DeRover, Netherlands	2:12.38
1988	Krisztina Egerszegi, Hungary	2:09.29
1992	Krisztina Egerszegi, Hungary	2:07.06
1996	Krisztina Egerszegi, Hungary	2:07.83
2000	Diana Mocanu, Romania	2:08.16

100-Meter Breaststroke

1968	Djurdjica Bjedov, Yugoslavia	1:15.80
1972	Catherine Carr, United States	1:13.58
1976	Hannelore Anke, East Germany	1:11.16
1980	Ute Geweniger, East Germany	1:10.22
1984	Petra Van Staveren, Netherlands	1:09.88
1988	Tainia Dangalakova, Bulgaria	1:07.95
1992	Elena Roudkovskaia, Unified Team	1:08.00
1996	Penny Heyns, South Africa	1:07.73
2000	Megan Quann, United States	1:07.05

200-Meter Breaststroke

1924	Lucy Morton, Great Britain	3:33.20
1928	Hilde Schrader, Germany	3:12.60
1932	Clare Dennis, Australia	3:06.30
1936	Hideko Maehata, Japan	3:03.60

1948	Nel van Vliet, Netherlands	2:57.20
1952	Eva Szekely, Hungary	2:51.70
1956	Ursala Happe, Germany	2:53.10
1960	Anita Lonsbrough, Great Britain	2:49.50
1964	Galina Prozumenschikova, U.S.S.R.	2:46.40
1968	Sharon Wichman, United States	2:44.40
1972	Beverly Whitfield, Australia	2:41.71
1976	Marina Koshevaia, U.S.S.R.	2:33.35
1980	Lina Kachushite, U.S.S.R.	2:29.54
1984	Anne Ottenbrite, Canada	2:30.38
1988	Silke Hoerner, East Germany	2:26.71
1992	Kyoko Iwasaki, Japan	2:26.65
1996	Penny Heyns, South Africa	2:25.41
2000	Agnes Kovacs, Hungary	2:24.35

100-Meter Butterfly

1956	Shelley Mann, United States	1:11.00
1960	Carolyn Schuler, United States	1:09.50
1964	Sharon Stouder, United States	1:04.70
1968	Lynn McClements, Australia	1:05.50
1972	Mayumi Aoki, Japan	1:03.34
1976	Kornelia Ender, East Germany	1:00.13
1980	Caren Metschuck, East Germany	1:00.42
1984	Mary Meagher, United States	0:59.26
1988	Kristin Otto, East Germany	0:59.00
1992	Qian Hong, China	0:58.62
1996	Amy Van Dyken, United States	0:59.13
2000	Inge de Bruijn, Netherlands	0:56.61[1]

1. World record.

200-Meter Butterfly

1968	Ada Kok, Netherlands	2:24.70
1972	Karen Moe, United States	2:15.57
1976	Andrea Pollack, East Germany	2:11.41
1980	Ines Geissler, East Germany	2:10.44
1984	Mary Meagher, United States	2:06.90
1988	Kathleen Nord, East Germany	2:09.51
1992	Summer Sanders, United States	2:06.67
1996	Susan O'Neill, Australia	2:07.76
2000	Misty Hyman, United States	2:05.88

200-Meter Individual Medley

1968	Claudia Kolb, United States	2:24.70
1972	Shane Gould, Australia	2:23.07
1984	Tracy Caulkins, United States	2:12.64
1988	Daniela Hunger, East Germany	2:12.59
1992	Lin Lee, China	2:11.55[1]
1996	Michelle Smith, Ireland	2:13.93
2000	Yana Klochkova, Ukraine	2:10.68

1. World record.

400-Meter Individual Medley

1964	Donna de Varona, United States	5:18.70
1968	Claudia Kolk, United States	5:08.50
1972	Gail Neall, Australia	5:02.97
1976	Ulrike Tauber, East Germany	4:42.77
1980	Petra Schneider, East Germany	4:36.29
1984	Tracy Caulkins, United States	4:39.21
1988	Janet Evans, United States	4:37.76
1992	Krisztina Egerszegi, Hungary	4:36.54
1996	Michelle Smith, Ireland	4:39.18
2000	Yana Klochkova, Ukraine	4:33.59[1]

1. World record.

400-Meter Freestyle Relay

1912	Great Britain	5:52.80
1920	United States	5:11.60
1924	United States	4:58.80
1928	United States	4:47.60
1932	United States	4:38.00
1936	Netherlands	4:36.00
1948	United States	4:29.20
1952	Hungary	4:24.40
1956	Australia	4:17.10
1960	United States	4:08.90
1964	United States	4:03.80

1968	United States	4:02.50
1972	United States	3:55.19
1976	United States	3:44.82
1980	East Germany	3:42.71
1984	United States	3:44.43
1988	East Germany	3:40.63
1992	United States	3:39.46
1996	United States	3:39.29
2000	United States	3:36.61[1]

1. World record.

800-Meter Freestyle Relay

1996	United States	7:59.87
2000	United States	7:57.80

400-Meter Medley Relay

1960	United States	4:41.10
1964	United States	4:33.90
1968	United States	4:28.30
1972	United States	4:20.75
1976	East Germany	4:07.95
1980	East Germany	4:06.67
1984	United States	4:08.34
1988	East Germany	4:03.74
1992	United States	4:02.54
1996	United States	4:02.88
2000	United States	3:58.30[1]

1. World record.

Springboard Dive

		Points
1920	Aileen Riggin, United States	539.90
1924	Elizabeth Becker, United States	474.50
1928	Helen Meany, United States	78.62
1932	Georgia Coleman, United States	87.52
1936	Marjorie Gestring, United States	89.27
1948	Victoria M. Draves, United States	108.74
1952	Patricia McCormick, United States	147.30
1956	Patricia McCormick, United States	142.36
1960	Ingrid Kramer, Germany	155.81
1964	Ingrid Kramer Engel, Germany	145.00
1968	Sue Gossick, United States	150.77
1972	Micki King, United States	450.03
1976	Jennifer Chandler, United States	506.19
1980	Irina Kalinina, U.S.S.R.	725.91
1984	Sylvie Bernier, Canada	530.70
1988	Gao Min, China	580.23
1992	Gao Min, China	572.40
1996	Fu Ming-Xia, China	547.68
2000	Fu Mingxia, China	609.42

Platform Dive

		Points
1912	Greta Johansson, Sweden	39.90
1920	Stefani Fryland, Denmark	34.60
1924	Caroline Smith, United States	166.00
1928	Elizabeth B. Pinkston, United States	31.60
1932	Dorothy Poynton, United States	40.26
1936	Dorothy Poynton Hill, United States	33.92
1948	Victoria M. Draves, United States	68.87
1952	Patricia McCormick, United States	79.37
1956	Patricia McCormick, United States	84.85
1960	Ingrid Kramer, Germany	91.28
1964	Lesley Bush, United States	99.80
1968	Milena Duchkova, Czechoslovakia	109.59
1972	Ulrika Knape, Sweden	390.00
1976	Elena Vaytsekhovskaia, U.S.S.R.	406.59
1980	Martina Jaschke, East Germany	596.25
1984	Zhou Ji-Hong, China	435.51
1988	Xu Yan-Mei, China	445.20
1992	Fu Ming-Xia, China	461.43
1996	Fu Ming-Xia, China	521.58
2000	Laura Wilkinson, United States	543.75

Synchronized 3m Springboard Dive

		Points
2000	Vera Ilina and Ioulia Pakhalina, Russia	332.64

Synchronized 10m Platform Dive

		Points
2000	Li Na and Sang Xue, China	345.12

BASKETBALL—MEN

1904	United States		1972	U.S.S.R.
1936	United States		1976	United States
1948	United States		1980	Yugoslavia
1952	United States		1984	United States
1956	United States		1988	U.S.S.R.
1960	United States		1992	United States
1964	United States		1996	United States
1968	United States		2000	United States

BASKETBALL—WOMEN

1976	U.S.S.R.		1992	Unified Team[1]
1980	U.S.S.R.		1996	United States
1984	United States		2000	United States
1988	United States			

1. Former Soviet Union team.

BOXING

(U.S. winners only)

NOTE: U.S. boycotted Olympics in 1980.

Flyweight-112 pounds (51 kilograms)

1904	George Finnegan		1952	Nate Brooks
1920	Frank De Genaro		1976	Leo Randolph
1924	Fidel La Barba		1984	Steve McCrory

Bantamweight-119 (54 kg)

1904	O.L. Kirk		1988	Kennedy McKinney

Featherweight-126 pounds (57 kg)

1904	O.L. Kirk		1984	Meldrick Taylor
1924	Jackie Fields			

Lightweight-132 pounds (60 kg)

1904	H.J. Spanger		1976	Howard Davis
1920	Samuel Mosberg		1984	Pernell Whitaker
1968	Ronnie Harris		1992	Oscar De La Hoya

Light Welterweight-140 pounds (63.5 kg)

1952	Charles Adkins		1976	Ray Leonard
1972	Ray Seales		1984	Jerry Page

Welterweight-148 pounds (67 kg)

1904	Al Young		1984	Mark Breland
1932	Edward Flynn			

Light Middleweight-157 pounds (71 kg)

1960	Wilbert McClure		1996	David Reid
1984	Frank Tate			

Middleweight-165 pounds (75 kg)

1904	Charles Mayer		1960	Eddie Cook
1932	Carmen Barth		1976	Michael Spinks
1952	Floyd Patterson			

Light Heavyweight-179 pounds (81 kg)

1920	Edward Eagan		1960	Cassius Clay
1952	Norvel Lee		1976	Leon Spinks
1956	James Boyd		1988	Andrew Maynard

Heavyweight-201 pounds

1904	Sam Berger		1968	George Foreman
1952	Edward Sanders		1984	Henry Tilman
1956	Pete Rademacher		1988	Ray Mercer
1964	Joe Frazier			

Super Heavyweight (unlimited)

1984	Tyrell Biggs

DISTRIBUTION OF MEDALS—2000 SUMMER GAMES

Country	Gold	Silver	Bronze	Total	Country	Gold	Silver	Bronze	Total
United States	39	25	33	97	Iran	3	0	1	4
Russia	32	28	28	88	Turkey	3	0	1	4
China	28	16	15	59	Finland	2	1	1	4
Australia	16	25	17	58	Uzbekistan	1	1	2	4
Germany	14	17	26	57	New Zealand	1	0	3	4
France	13	14	11	38	Argentina	0	2	2	4
Italy	13	8	13	34	Korea	0	1	3	4
Cuba	11	11	7	29	Austria	2	1	0	3
Great Britain	11	10	7	28	Azerbaijan	2	0	1	3
Korea	8	9	11	28	Latvia	1	1	1	3
Romania	11	6	9	26	Yugoslavia	1	1	1	3
Netherlands	12	9	4	25	Estonia	1	0	2	3
Ukraine	3	10	10	23	Thailand	1	0	2	3
Japan	5	8	5	18	Nigeria	0	3	0	3
Hungary	8	6	3	17	Slovenia	2	0	0	2
Belarus	3	3	11	17	Bahamas	1	1	0	2
Poland	6	5	3	14	Croatia	1	0	1	2
Canada	3	3	8	14	Saudi Arabia	0	1	1	2
Bulgaria	5	6	2	13	Moldova	0	1	1	2
Greece	4	6	3	13	Trinidad & Tobago	0	1	1	2
Sweden	4	5	3	12	Costa Rica	0	0	2	2
Brazil	0	6	6	12	Portugal	0	0	2	2
Spain	3	3	5	11	Cameroon	1	0	0	1
Norway	4	3	3	10	Colombia	1	0	0	1
Switzerland	1	6	2	9	Mozambique	1	0	0	1
Ethiopia	4	1	3	8	Ireland	0	1	0	1
Czech Republic	2	3	3	8	Uruguay	0	1	0	1
Kazakhstan	3	4	0	7	Vietnam	0	1	0	1
Kenya	2	3	2	7	Armenia	0	0	1	1
Jamaica	0	4	3	7	Barbados	0	0	1	1
Denmark	2	3	1	6	Chile	0	0	1	1
Indonesia	1	3	2	6	India	0	0	1	1
Mexico	1	2	3	6	Iceland	0	0	1	1
Georgia	0	0	6	6	Israel	0	0	1	1
Lithuania	2	0	3	5	Kyrgyzstan	0	0	1	1
Slovakia	1	3	1	5	Kuwait	0	0	1	1
Algeria	1	1	3	5	Macedonia	0	0	1	1
Belgium	0	2	3	5	Qatar	0	0	1	1
South Africa	0	2	3	5	Sri Lanka	0	0	1	1
Morocco	0	1	4	5	**Total**	**301**	**299**	**328**	**928**
Chinese Taipei	0	1	4	5					

Other 2000 Summer Olympic Games Champions

Archery
Women's individual—Yun Mi-jin, South Korea
Women's team—South Korea
Men's individual—Simon Fairweather, Australia
Men's team—South Korea

Badminton
Men's singles—Ji Xinpeng, China
Men's doubles—Indonesia (Tony Gunawan, Candra Wijaya)
Women's singles—Gong Zhichao, China
Women's doubles—China (Ge Fei, Gu Jun)
Mixed doubles—China (Jun Zhang, Ling Gao)

Baseball
Men—United States

Beach Volleyball
Women—Australia (Natalie Cook, Kerri Pottharst)

Men—United States (Dain Blanton, Eric Fonoimoana)

Boxing
Light flyweight—Brahim Asloum, France
Flyweight—Wijan Ponlid, Thailand
Bantamweight—Guillermo Rigondeaux, Cuba
Featherweight—Bekzat Sattarkhanov, Kazakhstan
Lightweight—Mario Kindelan, Cuba
Light welterweight—Mahamadkadyz Abdullaev, Uzbekistan
Welterweight—Oleg Saitov, Russia
Light middleweight—Yermakhan Ibraimov, Kazakhstan
Middleweight—Jorge Gutierrez, Cuba
Light heavyweight—Alexander Lebziak, Russia
Heavyweight—Felix Savon, Cuba
Super heavyweight—Audley Harrison, Great Britain

Cycling—Men
1 km time trial (track)—Jason Queally, Great Britain
Individual pursuit (track)—Robert Bartko, Germany
Team pursuit (track)—Germany
Individual points race (track)—Juan Llaneras, Spain
Individual sprint (track)—Marty Nothstein, United States
Olympic sprint (track)—France
Madison (track)—Australia
Keirin (track)—Florian Rousseau, France
Mountain bike—Miguel Martinez, France
Individual road race—Jan Ullrich, Germany
Individual time trial (road)—Viacheslav Ekimov, Russia

Cycling—Women
500m time trial (track)—Felicia Ballanger, France
Individual pursuit (track)—Leontien Zijlaard, Netherlands
Sprint (track)—Felicia Ballanger, France
Points race (track)—Antonella Bellutti, Italy
Mountain bike—Paola Pezzo, Italy
Road race—Leontien Zijlaard, Netherlands
Individual time trial (road)—Leontien Zijlaard, Netherlands

Equestrian
Individual three-day—David O'Connor, United States
Three-day team event—Australia
Individual dressage—Anky van Grunsven, Netherlands
Team dressage—Germany
Individual jumping—Jeroen Dubbeldam, Netherlands
Team jumping—Germany

Fencing—Men
Individual epee—Pavel Kolobkov, Russia
Individual foil—Kim Young-ho, South Korea
Individual sabre—Mihai Claudiu Covaliu, Romania
Team epee—Italy
Team foil—France
Team sabre—Russia

Fencing—Women
Individual epee—Timea Nagy, Hungary
Individual foil—Valentina Vezzali, Italy
Team epee—Russia
Team foil—Italy

Field Hockey
Men—Netherlands
Women—Australia

Gymnastics—Men
All-around—Alexei Nemov, Russia
Floor exercise—Igors Vihrovs, Latvia
Pommel horse—Marius Urzica, Romania
Rings—Szilveszter Csollany, Hungary
Horizontal bar—Alexei Nemov, Russia
Parallel bars—Li Xiaopeng, China
Vault—Gervasio Deferr, Spain
Team—China

Gymnastics—Women
All-around—Simona Amanar, Romania
Uneven bars—Svetlana Khorkina, Russia
Balance beam—Liu Xuan, China
Floor exercise—Elena Zamolodtchikova, Russia
Vault—Elena Zamolodtchikova, Russia
Team—Romania

Judo—Men
Extra-lightweight (60kg)—Tadahiro Nomura, Japan
Half-lightweight (66kg)—Huseyin Ozkan, Turkey
Lightweight (73kg)—Giuseppe Maddaloni, Italy
Half-middleweight (81kg)—Makoto Takimoto, Japan
Middleweight (90kg)—Mark Huizinga, Netherlands
Half-heavyweight (100kg)—Kosei Inoue, Japan
Heavyweight (100kg+)—David Douillet, France

Judo—Women
Extra-lightweight (48kg)—Ryoko Tamura, Japan
Half-lightweight (52kg)—Legna Verdecia, Cuba
Lightweight (57kg)—Isabel Fernandez, Spain
Half-middleweight (63kg)—Severine Vandenhende, France
Middleweight (70kg)—Sibelis Veranes, Cuba
Half-heavyweight (78kg)—Tang Lin, China
Heavyweight (78kg+)—Yuan Hua, China

Kayak-Canoe—Men
Canoe singles 500m—Gyorgy Kolonics, Hungary
Canoe pairs 500m—Hungary
Kayak singles 500m—Knut Holmann, Norway
Kayak pairs 500m—Hungary
Kayak singles 1,000m—Knut Holmann, Norway
Canoe singles 1,000m—Andreas Dittmer, Germany
Kayak pairs 1,000m—Italy
Canoe pairs 1,000m—Romania
Kayak fours 1,000m—Hungary
Canoe slalom singles—Tony Estanguet, France
Canoe slalom pairs—Slovakia
Kayak slalom singles—Thomas Schmidt, Germany

Kayak—Women
500m singles—Josefa Idem Guerrini, Italy
500m pairs—Germany
500m fours—Germany
Single slalom—Stepanka Hilgertova, Czech Republic

Modern Pentathlon
Men—Dmitri Svatkovsky, Russia
Women—Stephanie Cook, Great Britain

Rhythmic Gymnastics
Individual—Yulia Barslukova, Russia
Team—Russia

Rowing—Men
Single sculls—Rob Waddell, New Zealand
Lightweight double sculls—Poland
Heavyweight double sculls—Slovenia
Quadruple sculls—Italy
Coxless pair—France
Lightweight coxless four—France
Heavyweight coxless four—Great Britain
Eight—Great Britain

Rowing—Women
Single sculls—Ekaterina Karsten, Belarus
Lightweight double sculls—Romania
Heavyweight double sculls—Germany
Quadruple sculls—Germany
Coxless pair—Romania
Eight—Romania

Sailing
Open Tornado—Austria
Open 49er—Finland
Open Laser—Ben Ainslie, Great Britain
Open Star—United States
Open Soling—Denmark
Men's Mistral—Christoph Sieber, Austria
Men's 470 fleet—Australia
Men's Finn—Iain Percy, Great Britain
Women's Mistral—Alessandra Sensini, Italy
Women's 470 fleet—Australia
Women's Europe—Shirley Robertson, Great Britain

Shooting—Men
Air pistol—Franck Dumoulin, France
Free pistol—Tanyu Kiriakov, Bulgaria
Rapid fire pistol—Serguei Alifirenko, Russia
Trap—Michael Diamond, Australia
Double trap—Richard Faulds, Great Britain
Air rifle—Cai Yalin, China
Running target—Yang Ling, China
Rifle prone—Jonas Edman, Sweden
Rifle 3-position—Rajmond Debevec, Slovenia
Skeet shooting—Mykola Milchev, Ukraine

Shooting—Women
Air pistol—Tao Luna, China
Sport pistol—Maria Grozdeva, Bulgaria
Air rifle—Nancy Johnson, United States
Rifle three position—Renata Maier-Rozanska, Poland
Trap—Daina Gudzineviciute, Lithuania
Double trap—Pia Hansen, Sweden
Skeet—Zemfira Meftakhetdinova, Azerbaijan

Soccer
Men—Cameroon
Women—Norway

Softball
United States

Synchronized Swimming
Duet—Russia
Team—Russia

Table Tennis
Men's singles—Kong Linghui, China
Men's doubles—China
Women's singles—Wang Nan, China
Women's doubles—China

Taekwondo
Men 58kg—Michail Mouroutsos, Greece
Men 68kg—Steven Lopez, United States
Men 80kg—Angel Matos Fuentes, Cuba
Men 80kg+—Kim Kyong-hun, South Korea
Women 49kg—Lauren Burns, Australia
Women 57kg—Jung Jae-eun, South Korea
Women 67kg—Lee Sun-Hee, South Korea
Women 67kg+—Chen Zhong, China

Team Handball
Men—Russia
Women—Denmark

Tennis
Men's singles—Yevgeny Kafelnikov, Russia
Men's doubles—Canada
Women's singles—Venus Williams, United States
Women's doubles—United States

Trampoline
Men—Alexandre Moskalenko, Russia
Women—Irina Karavaeva, Russia

Triathlon
Men—Simon Whitfield, Canada
Women—Brigitte McMahon, Switzerland

Volleyball
Men—Yugoslavia
Women—Cuba

Water Polo
Men—Hungary
Women—Australia

Weightlifting—Men
56kg—Halil Mutlu, Turkey
62kg—Nikolay Pechalov, Croatia
69kg—Galabin Boevski, Bulgaria
77kg—Zhan Xugang, China
85kg—Pyrros Dimas, Greece
94kg—Akakios Kakiasvilis, Greece
105kg—Hossein Tavakoli, Iran
105kg+—Hossein Rezazadeh, Iran

Weightlifting—Women
48kg—Tara Nott, United States
53kg—Yang Xia, China
58kg—Soraya Jimenez, Mexico
63kg—Xiaomin Chen, China

69kg—Lin Weining, China
75kg—Maria Urrutia, Colombia
75kg+—Ding Meiyuan, China

Wrestling—Freestyle
54kg—Namig Abdullayev, Azerbaijan
63kg—Mourad Oumakhanov, Russia
58kg—Alireza Dabir, Iran
69kg—Daniel Igali, Canada
76kg—Alexander Leipold, Germany
85kg—Adam Saitiev, Russia
97kg—Saghid Mourtasaliyev, Russia
130kg—David Moussoulbes, Russia

Wrestling—Greco-Roman
54kg—Sim Kwon Ho, South Korea
58kg—Armen Nazarian, Bulgaria
63kg—Varteres Samourgachev, Russia
69kg—Filiberto Azcuy, Cuba
76kg—Mourat Kardanov, Russia
85kg—Hamza Yerlikaya, Turkey
97kg—Mikael Ljungberg, Sweden
130kg—Rulon Gardner, United States

Winter Games: Gold Medals

FIGURE SKATING–MEN

1908 Ulrich Salchow, Sweden
1920 Gillis Grafström, Sweden
1924 Gillis Grafström, Sweden
1928 Gillis Grafström, Sweden
1932 Karl Schäfer, Austria
1936 Karl Schäfer, Austria
1948 Dick Button, United States
1952 Dick Button, United States
1956 Hayes Alan Jenkins, United States
1960 David Jenkins, United States
1964 Manfred Schnelldorfer, Germany
1968 Wolfgang Schwarz, Austria
1972 Ondrej Nepela, Czechoslovakia
1976 John Curry, Great Britain
1980 Robin Cousins, Great Britain
1984 Scott Hamilton, United States
1988 Brian Boitano, United States
1992 Viktor Petrenko, Unified Team*
1994 Alexei Urmanov, Russia
1998 Ilia Kulik, Russia

*Former Soviet Union team.

FIGURE SKATING–WOMEN

1908 Madge Syers, Britain
1920 Magda Julin-Mauroy, Sweden
1924 Herma Planck-Szabö, Austria
1928 Sonja Henie, Norway
1932 Sonja Henie, Norway
1936 Sonja Henie, Norway
1948 Barbara Ann Scott, Canada
1952 Jeanette Altwegg, Great Britain
1956 Tenley Albright, United States
1960 Carol Heiss, United States
1964 Sjoukje Dijkstra, Netherlands
1968 Peggy Fleming, United States
1972 Beatrix Schuba, Austria
1976 Dorothy Hamill, United States
1980 Anett Pötzsch, East Germany
1984 Katarina Witt, East Germany
1988 Katarina Witt, East Germany
1992 Kristi Yamaguchi, United States
1994 Oksana Baiul, Ukraine
1998 Tara Lipinski, United States

SPEED SKATING–MEN
(U.S. winners only)

	500 Meters	
1924	Charles Jewtraw	44.00
1932	Jack Shea	43.40
1952	Ken Henry	43.20
1964	Terry McDermott	40.10
1980	Eric Heiden	38.03
	1,000 Meters	
1976	Peter Mueller	1:19.32
1980	Eric Heiden	1:15.18
1994	Dan Jansen	1:12.43[1]
	1,500 Meters	
1932	Jack Shea	2:57.50
1980	Eric Heiden	1:55.44
	5,000 Meters	
1932	Irving Jaffee	9:40.80
1980	Eric Heiden	7:02.29
	10,000 Meters	
1932	Irving Jaffee	19:13.60
1980	Eric Heiden	14:28.13

1. World record.

SPEED SKATING–WOMEN
(U.S. winners only)

	500 Meters	
1972	Anne Henning	43.33
1976	Sheila Young	42.76
1988	Bonnie Blair	39.10
1992	Bonnie Blair	40.33
1994	Bonnie Blair	39.25
	1,000 Meters	
1992	Bonnie Blair	1:21.90
1994	Bonnie Blair	1:18.74
	1,500 Meters	
1972	Dianne Holum	2:20.85

SKIING, ALPINE–MEN

Downhill

1948	Henri Oreiller, France	2:55.00
1952	Zeno Colò, Italy	2:30.80
1956	Toni Sailer, Austria	2:52.20
1960	Jean Vuarnet, France	2:06.00
1964	Egon Zimmermann, Austria	2:18.16

1968	Jean-Claude Killy, France	1:59.85
1972	Bernhard Russi, Switzerland	1:51.43
1976	Franz Klammer, Austria	1:45.73
1980	Leonhard Stock, Austria	1:45.50
1984	Bill Johnson, United States	1:45.59
1988	Pirmin Zurbriggen, Switzerland	1:59.63
1992	Patrick Ortlieb, Austria	1:50.37
1994	Tommy Moe, United States	1:45.75
1998	Jean-Luc Cretier, France	1:50.11

Slalom

1948	Edi Reinalter, Switzerland	2:10.30
1952	Othmar Schneider, Austria	2:00.00
1956	Toni Sailer, Austria	3:14.70
1960	Ernst Hinterseer, Austria	2:08.90
1964	Pepi Stiegler, Austria	2:11.13
1968	Jean-Claude Killy, France	1:39.73
1972	Francisco Ochoa, Spain	1:49.27
1976	Piero Gros, Italy	2:03.29
1980	Ingemar Stenmark, Sweden	1:44.26
1984	Phil Mahre, United States	1:39.41
1988	Alberto Tomba, Italy	1:39.47
1992	Finn Christian Jagge, Norway	1:44.39
1994	Thomas Stangassinger, Austria	2:02.02
1998	Hans-Petter Buraas, Norway	1:49.31

Giant Slalom

1952	Stein Eriksen, Norway	2:25.00
1956	Toni Sailer, Austria	3:00.10
1960	Roger Staub, Switzerland	1:48.30
1964	François Bonlieu, France	1:46.71
1968	Jean-Claude Killy, France	3:29.28
1972	Gustav Thöni, Italy	3:09.62
1976	Heini Hemmi, Switzerland	3:26.97
1980	Ingemar Stenmark, Sweden	2:40.74
1984	Max Julen, Switzerland	2:41.18
1988	Alberto Tomba, Italy	2:06.37
1992	Alberto Tomba, Italy	2:06.98
1994	Markus Wasmeier, Germany	2:52.46
1998	Hermann Maier, Austria	2:38.51

Super Giant Slalom

1988	Frank Piccard, France	1:39.66
1992	Kjetil Andre Aamodt, Norway	1:13.04
1994	Markus Wasmeier, Germany	1:32.53
1998	Hermann Maier, Austria	1:34.84

Men's Combined (Downhill and Slalom)

		Points
1936	Franz Pfnür, Germany	99.25
1948	Henri Oreiller, France	3.27
1952–1984	Not held	
1988	Hubert Strolz, Austria	36.55
1992	Josef Polig, Italy	14.58
		Time
1994	Lasse Kjus, Norway	3:17.53
1998	Mario Reiter, Austria	3:08.06

SKIING, ALPINE—WOMEN

Downhill

1948	Hedy Schlunegger, Switzerland	2:28.30
1952	Trude Jochum-Beiser, Austria	1:47.10
1956	Madeleine Berthod, Switzerland	1:40.70
1960	Heidi Biebl, Germany	1:37.60
1964	Christl Haas, Austria	1:55.39
1968	Olga Pall, Austria	1:40.87
1972	Marie-Theres Nadig, Switzerland	1:36.68
1976	Rosi Mittermaier, West Germany	1:46.16
1980	Annemarie Moser-Pröll, Austria	1:37.52
1984	Michela Figini, Switzerland	1:13.36
1988	Marina Kiehl, West Germany	1:25.86
1992	Kerrin Lee-Gartner, Canada	1:52.55
1994	Katja Seizinger, Germany	1:35.93
1998	Katja Seizinger, Germany	1:28.89

Slalom

1948	Gretchen Fraser, United States	1:57.20
1952	Andrea Mead Lawrence, United States	2:10.60
1956	Renée Colliard, Switzerland	1:52.30
1960	Anne Heggtveit, Canada	1:49.60
1964	Christine Goitschel, France	1:29.86
1968	Marielle Goitschel, France	1:25.86
1972	Barbara Cochran, United States	1:31.24
1976	Rosi Mittermaier, West Germany	1:30.54
1980	Hanni Wenzel, Liechtenstein	1:25.09
1984	Paoletta Magoni, Italy	1:36.47
1988	Vreni Schneider, Switzerland	1:36.69
1992	Petra Kronberger, Austria	1:32.68
1994	Vreni Schneider, Switzerland	1:56.01
1998	Hilde Gerg, Germany	1:32.40

Giant Slalom

1952	Andrea Mead Lawrence, United States	2:06.80
1956	Ossi Reichert, Germany	1:56.50
1960	Yvonne Rügg, Switzerland	1:39.90
1964	Marielle Goitschel, France	1:52.24
1968	Nancy Greene, Canada	1:51.97
1972	Marie-Theres Nadig, Switzerland	1:29.90
1976	Kathy Kreiner, Canada	1:29.13
1980	Hanni Wenzel, Liechtenstein	2:41.66
1984	Debbie Armstrong, United States	2:20.98
1988	Vreni Schneider, Switzerland	2:06.49
1992	Pernilla Wiberg, Sweden	2:12.74
1994	Deborah Compagnoni, Italy	2:30.97
1998	Deborah Compagnoni, Italy	2:50.59

Super Giant Slalom

1988	Sigrid Wolf, Austria	1:19.03
1992	Deborah Compagnoni, Italy	1:21.22
1994	Diann Roffe-Steinrotter, United States	1:22.15
1998	Picabo Street, United States	1:18.02

Combined (Downhill and Slalom)

		Points
1936	Christl Cranz, Germany	97.06
1948	Trude Beiser, Austria	6.58
1952-84	Not held	
1988	Anita Wachter, Austria	29.25
1992	Petra Kronberger, Austria	2.55
		Time
1994	Pernilla Wiberg, Sweden	3:05.16
1998	Katja Seizinger, Germany	2:40.74

ICE HOCKEY

MEN

1920	Canada
1924	Canada
1928	Canada
1932	Canada
1936	Great Britain
1948	Canada
1952	Canada
1956	U.S.S.R.
1960	United States
1964	U.S.S.R.
1968	U.S.S.R.
1972	U.S.S.R.
1976	U.S.S.R.
1980	United States
1984	U.S.S.R.
1988	U.S.S.R.
1992	Unified Team*
1994	Sweden
1998	Czech Republic

WOMEN

1998	United States

*Former Soviet Union team.

1998 Men's Championship
Czech Republic 1, Russia 0
1998 Women's Championship
United States 3, Canada 1

FREESTYLE SKIING—MEN

Moguls

1992	Edgar Grospiron, France
1994	Jean-Luc Brassard, Canada
1998	Jonny Moseley, United States

Aerials

1994	Andreas Schoenbaechler, Switzerland
1998	Eric Bergoust, United States

FREESTYLE SKIING—WOMEN

Moguls
1992 Donna Weinbrecht, United States
1994 Stine Lise Hattestad, Norway
1998 Tae Satoya, Japan

Aerials
1994 Lina Cherjazova, Uzbekistan
1998 Nikki Stone, United States

DISTRIBUTION OF MEDALS
1998 WINTER OLYMPIC GAMES

(Nagano, Japan)

	Gold	Silver	Bronze	Total
Germany	12	9	8	29
Norway	10	10	5	25
Russia	9	6	3	18
Austria	3	5	9	17
Canada	6	5	4	15
United States	6	3	4	13
Finland	2	4	6	12
Netherlands	5	4	2	11
Japan	5	1	4	10
Italy	2	6	2	10
France	2	1	5	8
China	0	6	2	8
Switzerland	2	2	3	7
South Korea	3	1	2	6
Czech Republic	1	1	1	3
Sweden	0	2	1	3
Belarus	0	0	2	2
Kazakhstan	0	0	2	2
Bulgaria	1	0	0	1
Denmark	0	1	0	1
Ukraine	0	1	0	1
Australia	0	0	1	1
Belgium	0	0	1	1
Great Britain	0	0	1	1

1998 UNITED STATES MEDALISTS

Alpine Skiing
Women's Super Giant Slalom—GOLD—Picabo Street, Sun Valley, Idaho

Figure Skating
Women—GOLD—Tara Lipinski, Sugarland, Texas
Women—SILVER—Michelle Kwan, Torrance, Calif.

Freestyle Skiing
Men's Moguls—GOLD—Jonny Moseley, Tiburon, Calif.
Men's Aerials—GOLD—Eric Bergoust, Missoula, Mont.
Women's Aerials—GOLD—Nikki Stone, Westborough, Mass.

Hockey
Women—GOLD—Sara Decosta, Tara Mounsey, Elizabeth Brown, Angela Ruggiero, Colleen Coyne, Karyn Bye, Suzanne Merz, Laurie Baker, Sandra Whyte, Allison Mleczko, Jennifer Schmidgall, Victoria Movsessian, Shelley Looney, Alana Blahoski, Kathryn King, Catherine Granato, Gretchen Ulion, Christina Bailey, Patricia Dunn, Sarah Tueting

Luge
Men's Doubles—SILVER—Chris Thorpe, Marquette, Mich. and Gordy Sheer, Croton, N.Y.
Men's Doubles—BRONZE—Mark Grimmette, Muskegon, Mich. and Brian Martin, Palo Alto, Calif.

Snowboarding
Men's Halfpipe—BRONZE—Ross Powers, South Londonderry, Vt.
Women's Halfpipe—BRONZE—Shannon Dunn, Steamboat Springs, Colo.

Speedskating
Women's 1,000 Meters—SILVER—Chris Witty, West Allis, Wis.
Women's 1,500 Meters—BRONZE—Chris Witty, West Allis, Wis.

Other 1998 Winter Olympic Games Champions

Biathlon
Men's 10-kilometer—Ole Einar Bjoerndalen, Norway
Men's 20-kilometer—Halvard Hanevold, Norway
Men's 4 × 7.5-kilometer relay—Germany
Women's 7.5-kilometer—Galina Koukleva, Russia
Women's 15-kilometer—Ekaterina Dafovska, Bulgaria
Women's 4 × 7.5-kilometer relay—Germany

Bobsledding
2-man—Canada I and Italy I
4-man—Germany II

Curling
Men—Switzerland
Women—Canada

Figure Skating
Pairs—Oksana Kazakova and Artur Dmitriev, Russia
Ice dancing—Pasha Grishuk and Yevgeny Platov, Russia

Luge
Men's singles—Georg Hackl, Germany
Men's doubles—Stefan Krausse, Jan Behrendt, Germany
Women's singles—Silke Kraushaar, Germany

Skiing, Nordic—Men
Combined team—Norway
Combined—Bjarte Engen Vik, Norway
70-meter jump—Jani Soininen, Finland
90-meter jump—Kazuyoshi Funaki, Japan

Team 120-meter jump—Japan
10-km cross country classical—Bjorn Dählie, Norway
15-km cross country free pursuit—Thomas Alsgaard, Norway
30-km cross country classical—Mika Myllylae, Finland
50-km cross country freestyle—Bjorn Dählie, Norway
4 × 10 kilometer relay—Norway

Skiing, Nordic—Women
5-kilometer classical—Larissa Lazutina, Russia
10-kilometer free pursuit—Larissa Lazutina, Russia
15-kilometer classical—Olga Danilova, Russia
30-kilometer freestyle—Yulia Tchepalova, Russia
4 × 5 kilometer relay—Russia

Snowboarding—Men
Giant slalom—Ross Rebagliati, Canada
Halfpipe—Gian Simmen, Switzerland

Snowboarding—Women
Giant slalom—Karine Ruby, France
Halfpipe—Nicola Thost, Germany

Speed Skating—Men
500m—Hiroyashu Shimizu, Japan
1,000m—Ids Postma, Netherlands
1,500m—Aadne Sondral, Norway
5,000m—Gianni Romme, Netherlands
10,000m—Gianni Romme, Netherlands

Speed Skating—Women
500m—Catriona LeMay-Doan, Canada
1,000m—Marianne Timmer, Netherlands
1,500m—Marianne Timmer, Netherlands
3,000m—Gunda Niemann-Stirnemann, Germany
5,000m—Claudia Pechstein, Germany

Speed Skating, Short Track—Men
500m—Takafumi Nishitani, Japan
1,000m—Kim Dong-sung, South Korea
5,000m relay—Canada

Speed Skating, Short Track—Women
500m—Annie Perreault, Canada
1,000m—Chun Lee-kyung, South Korea
3,000m relay—South Korea

Baseball

The popular tradition that baseball was invented by Abner Doubleday at Cooperstown, N.Y., in 1839 has been enshrined in the Hall of Fame and National Museum of Baseball erected in that town, but research has proved that a game called "Base Ball" was played in this country and England before 1839. The first team baseball as we know it was played at the Elysian Fields, Hoboken, N.J., on June 19, 1846, between the Knickerbockers and the New York Nine. The next fifty years saw a gradual growth of baseball and an improvement of equipment and playing skill.

Historians have it that the first pitcher to throw a curve was William A. (Candy) Cummings in 1867. The Cincinnati Red Stockings were the first all-professional team, and in 1869 they played 64 games without a loss. The standard ball of the same size and weight, still the rule, was adopted in 1872. The first catcher's mask was worn in 1875. The National League was organized in 1876. The first chest protector was worn in 1885. The three-strike rule was put on the books in 1887, and the four-ball ticket to first base was instituted in 1889. The pitching distance was lengthened to 60 feet 6 inches in 1893, and the rules have been modified only slightly since that time.

The American League, under the vigorous leadership of B. B. Johnson, became a major league in 1901. Judge Kenesaw Mountain Landis, by action of the two major leagues, became Commissioner of Baseball in 1921.

MAJOR LEAGUE ALL-STAR GAME

Year	Date	Winning league and manager	Runs	Losing league and manager	Runs	Winning pitcher	Losing pitcher	Site	Paid attendance
1933	July 6	A.L. (Mack)	4	N.L. (McGraw)	2	Gomez	Hallahan	Chicago A.L.	47,595
1934	July 10	A.L. (Cronin)	9	N.L. (Terry)	7	Harder	Mungo	New York N.L.	48,363
1935	July 8	A.L. (Cochrane)	4	N.L. (Frisch)	1	Gomez	Walker	Cleveland A.L.	69,831
1936	July 7	N.L. (Grimm)	4	A.L. (McCarthy)	3	J. Dean	Grove	Boston N.L.	25,556
1937	July 7	A.L. (McCarthy)	8	N.L. (Terry)	3	Gomez	J. Dean	Washington A.L.	31,391
1938	July 6	N.L. (Terry)	4	A.L. (McCarthy)	1	Vander Meer	Gomez	Cincinnati N.L.	27,067
1939	July 11	A.L. (McCarthy)	3	N.L. (Hartnett)	1	Bridges	Lee	New York A.L.	62,892
1940	July 9	N.L. (McKechnie)	4	A.L. (Cronin)	0	Derringer	Ruffing	St. Louis N.L.	32,373
1941	July 8	A.L. (Baker)	7	N.L. (McKechnie)	5	E. Smith	Passeau	Detroit A.L.	54,674
1942	July 6	A.L. (McCarthy)	3	N.L. (Durocher)	1	Chandler	Cooper	New York N.L.	34,178
1943	July 13	A.L. (McCarthy)	5	N.L. (Southworth)	3	Leonard	Cooper	Philadelphia A.L.	31,938
1944	July 11	N.L. (Southworth)	7	A.L. (McCarthy)	1	Raffensberger	Hughson	Pittsburgh N.L.	29,589
1946	July 9	A.L. (O'Neill)	12	N.L. (Grimm)	0	Feller	Passeau	Boston A.L.	34,906
1947	July 8	A.L. (Cronin)	2	N.L. (Dyer)	1	Shea	Sain	Chicago N.L.	41,123
1948	July 13	A.L. (Harris)	5	N.L. (Durocher)	2	Raschi	Schmitz	St. Louis A.L.	34,009
1949	July 12	A.L. (Boudreau)	11	N.L. (Southworth)	7	Trucks	Newcombe	Brooklyn N.L.	32,577
1950	July 11	N.L. (Shotton)	4	A.L. (Stengel)	3[1]	Blackwell	Gray	Chicago A.L.	46,127
1951	July 10	N.L. (Sawyer)	8	A.L. (Stengel)	3	Maglie	Lopat	Detroit A.L.	52,075
1952	July 8	N.L. (Durocher)	3	A.L. (Stengel)	2[2]	Rush	Lemon	Philadelphia N.L.	32,785
1953	July 14	N.L. (Dressen)	5	A.L. (Stengel)	1	Spahn	Reynolds	Cincinnati N.L.	30,846
1954	July 13	A.L. (Stengel)	11	N.L. (Alston)	9	Stone	Conley	Cleveland A.L.	68,751
1955	July 12	N.L. (Durocher)	6	A.L. (Lopez)	5[3]	Conley	Sullivan	Milwaukee N.L.	45,643
1956	July 10	N.L. (Alston)	7	A.L. (Stengel)	3	Friend	Pierce	Washington A.L.	28,843
1957	July 9	A.L. (Stengel)	6	N.L. (Alston)	5	Bunning	Simmons	St. Louis N.L.	30,693
1958	July 8	A.L. (Stengel)	4	N.L. (Haney)	3	Wynn	Friend	Baltimore A.L.	48,829
1959[4]	July 7	N.L. (Haney)	5	A.L. (Stengel)	4	Antonelli	Ford	Pittsburgh N.L.	35,277
	Aug. 3	A.L. (Stengel)	5	N.L. (Haney)	3	Walker	Drysdale	Los Angeles N.L.	55,105
1960[4]	July 11	N.L. (Alston)	5	A.L. (Lopez)	3	Friend	Monbouquette	Kansas City A.L.	30,619
	July 13	N.L. (Alston)	6	A.L. (Lopez)	0	Law	Ford	New York A.L.	38,362
1961[4]	July 11	N.L. (Murtaugh)	5	A.L. (Richards)	4[5]	Miller	Wilhelm	San Francisco N.L.	44,115
	July 31	N.L. (Murtaugh)	1	A.L. (Richards)	1[6]	—	—	Boston A.L.	31,851
1962[4]	July 10	N.L. (Hutchinson)	3	A.L. (Houk)	1	Marichal	Pascual	Washington A.L.	45,480
	July 30	A.L. (Houk)	9	N.L. (Hutchinson)	4	Herbert	Mahaffey	Chicago N.L.	38,359
1963	July 9	N.L. (Dark)	5	A.L. (Houk)	3	Jackson	Bunning	Cleveland A.L.	44,160
1964	July 7	N.L. (Alston)	7	A.L. (Lopez)	4	Marichal	Radatz	New York N.L.	50,850

Year	Date	Winning league and manager	Runs	Losing league and manager	Runs	Winning pitcher	Losing pitcher	Site	Paid attendance
1965	July 13	N.L. (March)	6	A.L. (Lopez)	5	Koufax	McDowell	Minnesota A.L.	46,706
1966	July 12	N.L. (Alston)	2	A.L. (Mele)	1[5]	Perry	Rickert	St. Louis N.L.	49,926
1967	July 11	N.L. (Alston)	2	A.L. (Bauer)	1[7]	Drysdale	Hunter	Anaheim A.L.	46,309
1968	July 9	N.L. (Schoendienst)	1	A.L. (Williams)	0	Drysdale	Tiant	Houston N.L.	48,321
1969	July 23	N.L. (Schoendienst)	9	A.L. (M. Smith)	3	Carlton	Stottlemyre	Washington A.L.	45,259
1970	July 14	N.L. (Hodges)	5	A.L. (Weaver)	4	Osteen	Wright	Cincinnati N.L.	51,838
1971	July 13	A.L. (Weaver)	6	N.L. (Anderson)	4	Blue	Ellis	Detroit A.L.	53,559
1972	July 25	N.L. (Murtaugh)	4	A.L. (Weaver)	3[5]	McGraw	McNally	Atlanta N.L.	53,107
1973	July 24	N.L. (Anderson)	7	A.L. (Williams)	1	Wise	Blyleven	Kansas City A.L.	40,849
1974	July 23	N.L. (Berra)	7	A.L. (Williams)	2	Brett	Tiant	Pittsburgh N.L.	50,706
1975	July 15	N.L. (Alston)	6	A.L. (Dark)	3	Matlack	Hunter	Milwaukee A.L.	51,540
1976	July 13	N.L. (Anderson)	7	A.L. (D. Johnson)	1	R. Jones	Fidrych	Philadelphia N.L.	63,974
1977	July 19	N.L. (Anderson)	7	A.L. (Martin)	5	Sutton	Palmer	New York A.L.	56,683
1978	July 11	N.L. (Lasorda)	7	A.L. (Martin)	3	Sutter	Gossage	San Diego N.L.	51,549
1979	July 17	N.L. (Lasorda)	7	A.L. (Lemon)	6	Sutter	Kern	Seattle A.L.	58,905
1980	July 8	N.L. (Tanner)	4	A.L. (Weaver)	2	Reuss	John	Los Angeles N.L.	56,088
1981[8]	Aug. 9	N.L. (Green)	5	A.L. (Frey)	4	Blue	Fingers	Cleveland A.L.	72,086
1982	July 13	N.L. (Lasorda)	4	A.L. (Martin)	1	Rogers	Eckersley	Montreal N.L.	59,057
1983	July 6	A.L. (Kuenn)	13	N.L. (Herzog)	3	Steib	Soto	Chicago A.L.	43,801
1984	July 11	N.L. (Owens)	3	A.L. (Altobelli)	1	Leg	Steib	San Francisco, N.L.	57,756
1985	July 16	N.L. (Williams)	6	A.L. (Anderson)	1	Hoyt	Morris	Minneapolis, A.L.	54,960
1986	July 15	A.L. (Howser)	3	N.L. (Herzog)	2	Clemens	Gooden	Houston, N.L.	45,774
1987	July 14	N.L. (Johnson)	2	A.L. (McNamara)	0	Smith	Howell	Oakland, A.L.	49,671
1988	July 12	A.L. (Kelly)	2	N.L. (Herzog)	1	Viola	Gooden	Cincinnati, N.L	55,837
1989	July 11	A.L. (LaRussa)	5	N.L. (Lasorda)	3	Ryan	Smoltz	California, A.L.	64,036
1990	July 10	A.L. (LaRussa)	2	N.L. (Craig)	0	Saberhagen	Brantley	Chicago, N.L.	39,071
1991	July 9	A.L. (LaRussa)	4	N.L. (Piniella)	2	Key	Martinez	Toronto, A.L.	52,383
1992	July 14	A.L. (Kelly)	13	N.L. (Cox)	6	Brown	Glavine	San Diego, N.L.	59,372
1993	July 13	A.L. (Gaston)	9	N.L. (Cox)	3	McDowell	Burkett	Baltimore, A.L.	48,147
1994	July 12	N.L. (Fregosi)	8	A.L. (Gaston)	7	Jones	Bere	Pittsburgh, A.L.	59,568
1995	July 11	N.L. (Alou)	3	A.L. (Showalter)	2	Slocumb	Rogers	Texas, A.L.	50,920
1996	July 9	N.L. (Cox)	6	A.L. (Hargrove)	0	Smoltz	Nagy	Philadelphia, N.L.	62,670
1997	July 8	A.L. (Torre)	3	N.L. (Cox)	1	Johnson	Maddux	Cleveland, A.L.	44,916
1998	July 7	A.L. (Hargrove)	13	N.L. (Leyland)	3	Colon	Urbina	Denver, N.L.	51,267
1999	July 13	A.L. (Torre)	4	N.L. (Bochy)	1	P. Martinez	Schilling	Boston, A.L.	34,187
2000	July 11	A.L. (Torre)	6	N.L. (Cox)	3	Baldwin	Leiter	Atlanta, N.L.	51,323

1. Fourteen innings. 2. Five innings, rain. 3. Twelve innings. 4. Two games. 5. Ten innings. 6. Called because of rain after nine innings. 7. Fifteen innings. 8. Game was originally scheduled for July 14, but was put off because of players' strike. NOTE: No game in 1945.

NATIONAL BASEBALL HALL OF FAME

Fielders   **Cooperstown, N.Y.**

Member	Active years	Member	Active years	Member	Active years
Aaron, Henry (Hank)	1954–1976	Carey, Max	1910–1929	Doby, Larry	1947–1959
Anson, Adrian (Cap)	1876–1897	Cepeda, Orlando	1958–1974	Doerr, Bobby	1937–1951
Aparicio, Luis	1956–1973	Chance, Frank	1898–1914	Duffy, Hugh	1888–1906
Appling, Lucius (Luke)	1930–1950	Charleston, Oscar[1]	1915–1954	Ewing, William	1880–1897
Ashburh, Richie	1948–1962	Clarke, Fred	1894–1915	Evers, John	1902–1919
Averill, H. Earl	1929–1941	Clemente, Roberto	1955–1972	Ferrell, Rick	1929–1947
Baker, J. Frank (Home Run)	1908–1922	Cobb, Tyrus	1905–1928	Fisk, Carlton	1969–1991
Bancroft, David	1915–1930	Cochrane, Gordon (Mickey)	1925–1937	Flick, Elmer	1898–1910
Banks, Ernest	1953–1971	Collins, Edward	1906–1930	Fox, Nellie	1947–1965
Beckley, Jacob	1888–1907	Collins, James	1895–1908	Foxx, James	1925–1945
Bell, James (Cool Papa)[1]	1920–1947	Comiskey, Charles	1882–1894	Frisch, Frank	1919–1937
Bench, John	1967–1983	Combs, Earle	1924–1935	Gehrig, H. Louis (Lou)	1923–1939
Berra, Lawrence (Yogi)	1946–1965	Connor, Roger	1880–1897	Gehringer, Charles	1924–1942
Bottomley, James	1922–1937	Crawford, Samuel	1899–1917	Gibson, Josh[1]	1929–1946
Boudreau, Louis	1938–1952	Cronin, Joseph	1926–1945	Goslin, Leon (Goose)	1921–1938
Bresnahan, Roger	1897–1915	Cuyler, Hazen (Kiki)	1921–1938	Greenberg, Henry (Hank)	1933–1947
Brett, George	1973–1993	Dandridge, Ray[1]	1933–1953	Hafey, Charles (Chick)	1924–1937
Brock, Lou	1961–1980	Davis, George	1890–1909	Hamilton, William	1888–1901
Brouthers, Dennis	1879–1896	Delahanty, Edward	1888–1903	Hartnett, Charles (Gabby)	1922–1941
Burkett, Jesse	1890–1905	Dickey, William	1928–1946	Heilmann, Harry	1914–1932
Campanella, Roy	1948–1957	Dihigo, Martin[1]	1923–1945	Herman, William	1931–1947
Carew, Rod	1967–1985	DiMaggio, Joseph	1936–1951	Hooper, Harry	1909–1925
				Hornsby, Rogers	1915–1937

Member	Active years	Member	Active years	Member	Active years
Irvin, Monford (Monte)[1]	1939–1956	McCarthy, Thomas	1884–1896	Sisler, George	1915–1930
Jackson, Reggie	1967–1987	McGraw, John J.	1891–1906	Slaughter, Enos	1938–1959
Jackson, Travis	1922–1936	McCovey, Willie	1959–1980	Snider, Edwin D. (Duke)	1947–1964
Jennings, Hugh	1891–1918	McPhee, John Alexander (Bid)	1882–1899	Speaker, Tristram	1907–1928
Johnson, William (Judy)[1]	1921–1937			Stargell, Willie	1962–1982
Kaline, Albert W.	1953–1974	Medwick, Joseph (Ducky)	1932–1948	Stearnes, Norman (Turkey)	1921–1942
Keeler, William (Wee Willie)	1892–1910	Mize, John (The Big Cat)	1936–1953	Terry, William	1923–1936
Kell, George	1943–1957	Morgan, Joe	1963–1984	Thompson, Samuel	1885–1906
Kelley, Joseph	1891–1908	Musial, Stanley	1941–1963	Tinker, Joseph	1902–1916
Kelly, George	1915–1932	O'Rourke, James	1876–1894	Traynor, Harold (Pie)	1920–1937
Kelly, Michael (King)	1878–1893	Ott, Melvin	1926–1947	Vaughan, Arky	1932–1948
Killebrew, Harmon	1954–1975	Perez, Tony	1964–1983	Wagner, John (Honus)	1897–1917
Kiner, Ralph	1946–1955	Reese, Harold (Pee Wee)	1940–1958	Wallace, Roderick (Bobby)	1894–1918
Klein, Charles H. (Chuck)	1928–1944	Rice, Edgar (Sam)	1915–1934	Waner, Lloyd	1927–1945
Lajoie, Napoleon	1896–1916	Rizzuto, Phil	1941–1956	Waner, Paul	1926–1945
Lazzeri, Tony	1926–1939	Robinson, Brooks	1955–1977	Ward, John (Monte)	1878–1894
Leonard, Walter (Buck)[1]	1933–1955	Robinson, Frank	1956–1976	Wells, Willie	1924–1949
Lindstrom, Frederick	1924–1936	Robinson, Jack	1947–1956	Wheat, Zachariah	1909–1927
Lloyd, John Henry (Pop)[1]	1905–1931	Robinson, Wilbert	1886–1902	Williams, Billy	1959–1976
Lombardi, Ernie	1932–1947	Roush, Edd	1913–1931	Williams, Theodore	1939–1960
Mantle, Mickey	1951–1968	Ruth, Babe	1914–1935	Wilson, Lewis R. (Hack)	1923–1934
Manush, Henry (Heinie)	1923–1939	Schalk, Raymond	1912–1929	Yastrzemski, Carl	1961–1983
Maranville, Walter (Rabbit)	1912–1935	Schoendienst, Red	1945–1963	Youngs, Ross (Pep)	1917–1926
Matthews, Edwin	1952–1968	Schmidt, Mike	1973–1989	Yount, Robin	1974–1993
Mays, Willie	1951–1973	Sewell, Joseph	1920–1933		
		Simmons, Al	1924–1944		

1. Negro League player selected by special committee.

Pitchers

Member	Active years	Member	Active years	Member	Active years
Alexander, Grover	1911–1930	Grove, Robert (Lefty)	1925–1941	Perry, Gaylord	1962–1983
Bender, Charles (Chief)	1903–1925	Haines, Jesse	1918–1937	Plank, Edward	1901–1917
Brown, Mordecai (3-Finger)	1903–1916	Hoyt, Waite	1918–1938	Radbourn, Charles (Hoss)	1880–1891
Bunning, Jim	1955–1971	Hubbell, Carl	1928–1943	Rixey, Eppa	1912–1933
Carlton, Steve	1965–1988	Hunter, Jim (Catfish)	1965–1979	Roberts, Robert (Robin)	1948–1966
Chesbro, John	1899–1909	Jenkins, Ferguson	1965–1983	Rogan, Wilber	1920–1938
Clarkson, John	1882–1894	Johnson, Walter	1907–1927	Ruffing, Charles (Red)	1924–1947
Coveleski, Stanley	1912–1928	Joss, Adrian	1902–1910	Rusie, Amos	1889–1901
Day, Leon	1935–1955	Keefe, Timothy	1880–1893	Ryan, Jr., Nolan	1966–1973
Dean, Jerome (Dizzy)	1930–1947	Koufax, Sanford (Sandy)	1955–1966	Seaver, Tom	1967–1986
Drysdale, Don	1956–1969	Lemon, Robert	1946–1958	Spahn, Warren	1942–1965
Faber, Urban (Red)	1914–1933	Lyons, Theodore	1923–1946	Sutton, Don	1966–1988
Feller, Robert	1936–1956	Marichal, Juan	1960–1975	Vance, Arthur (Dazzy)	1915–1935
Fingers, Rollie	1968–1985	Marquard, Richard (Rube)	1908–1924	Waddell, Rube	1897–1910
Ford, Edward (Whitey)	1950–1967	Mathewson, Christopher	1900–1916	Walsh, Edward	1904–1917
Foster, Andrew (Rube)	1897–1926	McGinnity, Joseph	1899–1908	Welch, Michael (Mickey)	1880–1892
Foster, Bill	1923–1937	Newhouser, Hal	1939–1955	Wilhelm, Hoyt	1952–1972
Galvin, James (Pud)	1876–1892	Nichols, Charles (Kid)	1890–1906	Williams, Joseph	1910–1932
Gibson, Bob	1959–1975	Niekro, Phil	1959–1987	Willis, Vic	1898–1910
Gomez, Vernon (Lefty)	1930–1943	Paige, Leroy (Satchel)[1]	1926–1965	Wynn, Early	1939–1963
Griffith, Clark	1891–1914	Palmer, Jim	1965–1984	Young, Denton (Cy)	1890–1911
Grimes, Burleigh	1916–1934	Pennock, Herbert	1912–1934		

1. Negro League player selected by special committee.

Officials and Others

Alston, Walter[1]	Cummings, William A.[5]	Hulbert, William[2]	McKechnie, William B.[1]
Anderson, Sparky[1]	Durocher, Leo[1]	Johnson, B. Bancroft[2]	Rickey, W. Branch[1 2]
Barlick, Al[4]	Evans, William G.[4 2]	Klem, William[4]	Selee, Frank G.[1]
Barrow, Edward[1 2]	Foster, Rube[2]	Landis, Kenesaw M.[6]	Spalding, Albert G.[4]
Bulkeley, Morgan G.[2]	Frick, Ford C.[6 2]	Lasorda, Tommy[1]	Stengel, Charles D.[7]
Cartwright, Alexander[2]	Giles, Warren C.[2]	Lopez, Alfonso R.[7]	Veeck, Bill[2]
Chadwick, Henry[3]	Hanlon, Ned[2]	Mack, Connie[1 2]	Weaver, Earl[1]
Chandler, A.B.[6]	Harridge, William[2]	MacPhail, Jr., Lee[2]	Weiss, George M.[2]
Chylak, Jr., Nestor[4]	Harris, Stanley R.[7]	MacPhail, Leland S.[2]	Wright, George[5]
Comiskey, Charles[1]	Hubbard, R. Calvin[4]	McCarthy, Joseph V.[1]	Wright, Harry[5 1]
Conlan, John[2]	Huggins, Miller J.[1]	McGowan, Bill[4]	Yawkey, Thomas[2]
Connolly, Thomas[4]			

1. Manager. 2. Executive. 3. Writer-statistician. 4. Umpire. 5. Early player. 6. Commissioner. 7. Player-manager.

BASEBALL'S PERFECTLY PITCHED GAMES[1]
(no opposing runner reached base)

Lee Richmond—Worcester vs. Cleveland (N.L.) June 12, 1880	(1–0)
John M. Ward—Providence vs. Buffalo (N.L.) June 17, 1880	(5–0)
Cy Young—Boston vs. Philadelphia (A.L.) May 5, 1904	(3–0)
Addie Joss—Cleveland vs. Chicago (A.L.) Oct. 2, 1908	(1–0)
Ernest Shore[2]—Boston vs. Washington (A.L.) June 23, 1917	(4–0)
Charles Robertson—Chicago vs. Detroit (A.L.) April 30, 1922	(2–0)
Don Larsen[3]—New York (A.L.) vs. Brooklyn (N.L.) Oct. 8, 1956	(2–0)
Jim Bunning—Philadelphia vs. New York (N.L.) June 21, 1964	(6–0)
Sandy Koufax—Los Angeles vs. Chicago (N.L.) Sept. 9, 1965	(1–0)
Jim Hunter—Oakland vs. Minnesota (A.L.) May 8, 1968	(4–0)
Len Barker—Cleveland vs. Toronto (A.L.) May 15, 1981	(3–0)
Mike Witt—California vs. Texas (A.L.) Sept. 30, 1984	(1–0)
Tom Browning—Cincinnati vs. Los Angeles (N.L.) Sept. 16, 1988	(1–0)
Dennis Martinez—Montreal vs. Los Angeles (N.L.) July 28, 1991	(2–0)
Kenny Rogers—Texas vs. California (A.L.) July 28, 1994	(4–0)
David Wells—New York vs. Minnesota (A.L.) May 17, 1998	(4–0)
David Cone[4]—New York (A.L.) vs. Montreal (N.L.) July 18, 1999	(6–0)

1. Harvey Haddix, of Pittsburgh, pitched 12 perfect innings against Milwaukee (N.L.), May 26, 1959 but lost game in 13th on error and hit. 2. Shore, relief pitcher for Babe Ruth who walked first batter before being ejected by umpire, retired 26 batters who faced him and baserunner was out stealing. 3. World Series. 4. Interleague game.

LIFETIME BATTING, PITCHING, AND BASE-RUNNING RECORDS

(Records through 2000)

Hits (3,000+)

Pete Rose	4,256
Ty Cobb	4,191
Henry Aaron	3,771
Stan Musial	3,630
Tris Speaker	3,515
Honus Wagner	3,430
Carl Yastrzemski	3,419
Paul Molitor	3,319
Eddie Collins	3,313
Willie Mays	3,283
Eddie Murray	3,255
Nap Lajoie	3,251
George Brett	3,154
Paul Waner	3,152
Robin Yount	3,142
Dave Winfield	3,110
Tony Gwynn	3,108
Cal Ripken, Jr.	3,070
Rod Carew	3,053
Cap Anson	3,041
Lou Brock	3,023
Wade Boggs	3,010
Al Kaline	3,007
Roberto Clemente	3,000

Earned Run Average (Minimum 1,500 innings pitched)

Ed Walsh	1.82
Addie Joss	1.88
Mordecai Brown	2.06
John Ward	2.10
Christy Mathewson	2.13
Rube Waddell	2.16
Walter Johnson	2.17
Orval Overall	2.23
Tommy Bond	2.25
Ed Reulbach	2.28
Will White	2.28
Jim Scott	2.30
Ed Plank	2.35
Larry Corcoran	2.36
Ed Cicotte	2.38
Ed Killian	2.38
George McQuillan	2.38
Doc White	2.38
Nap Rucker	2.42
Terry Larkin	2.43
Jim McCormick	2.43
Jeff Tesreau	2.43

Runs Scored

Ty Cobb	2,245
Rickey Henderson	2,178
Hank Aaron	2,174
Babe Ruth	2,174
Pete Rose	2,165
Willie Mays	2,062
Stan Musial	1,949
Lou Gehrig	1,888
Tris Speaker	1,881
Mel Ott	1,859
Frank Robinson	1,829
Eddie Collins	1,820
Carl Yastrzemski	1,816
Ted Williams	1,798
Paul Molitor	1,782
Charlie Gehringer	1,774
Jimmie Foxx	1,751
Honus Wagner	1,740
Willie Keeler	1,722
Cap Anson	1,719
Jesse Burkett	1,713
Billy Hamilton	1,692
Bid McPhee	1,684
Mickey Mantle	1,677
Dave Winfield	1,669
Joe Morgan	1,650

Strikeouts, Pitching

Nolan Ryan	5,714
Steve Carlton	4,136
Bert Blyleven	3,701
Tom Seaver	3,640
Don Sutton	3,574
Gaylord Perry	3,534
Walter Johnson	3,508
Roger Clemens	3,504
Phil Niekro	3,342
Ferguson Jenkins	3,192
Bob Gibson	3,117
Randy Johnson	3,040
Jim Bunning	2,855
Mickey Lolich	2,832
Cy Young	2,798
Frank Tanana	2,773
Warren Spahn	2,583
Bob Feller	2,581
Jerry Koosman	2,556
Tim Keefe	2,533
Christy Mathewson	2,502

Home Runs (350+)

Hank Aaron	755
Babe Ruth	714
Willie Mays	660
Frank Robinson	586
Harmon Killebrew	573
Reggie Jackson	563
Mark McGwire	554
Mike Schmidt	548
Mickey Mantle	536
Jimmie Foxx	534
Willie McCovey	521
Ted Williams	521
Ernie Banks	512
Eddie Mathews	512
Mel Ott	511
Eddie Murray	504
Barry Bonds	494
Lou Gehrig	493
Stan Musial	475
Willie Stargell	475
Dave Winfield	465
Carl Yastrzemski	452
Jose Canseco	446
Dave Kingman	442
Andre Dawson	438
Ken Griffey, Jr.	438
Billy Williams	426
Fred McGriff	417
Cal Ripken, Jr.	417
Darrell Evans	414
Duke Snider	407
Rafael Palmeiro	400
Al Kaline	399
Dale Murphy	398
Joe Carter	396
Graig Nettles	390
Johnny Bench	389
Sammy Sosa	386
Dwight Evans	385
Harold Baines	384
Frank Howard	382
Jim Rice	382
Albert Belle	381
Orlando Cepeda	379
Tony Perez	379
Norm Cash	377
Carlton Fisk	376
Rocky Colavito	374
Gil Hodges	370
Ralph Kiner	369
Juan Gonzalez	362
Joe DiMaggio	361
Gary Gaetti	360
Andres Galarraga	360
Johnny Mize	359
Yogi Berra	358
Lee May	354
Dick Allen	351
Chili Davis	350

Shutouts

Walter Johnson	110
Grover Alexander	90
Christy Mathewson	79
Cy Young	76
Ed Plank	69
Warren Spahn	63
Nolan Ryan	61
Tom Seaver	61
Bert Blyleven	60
Don Sutton	58

Pud Galvin	57	Bobby Bonds	1,757	Dave Parker	1,537
Ed Walsh	57	Dale Murphy	1,748	Sammy Sosa	1,537
Bob Gibson	56	Andres Galarraga	1,741	Frank Robinson	1,532
Mordecai Brown	55	Lou Brock	1,730	Lance Parrish	1,527
Steve Carlton	55	Mickey Mantle	1,710	Willie Mays	1,526
Jim Palmer	53	Harmon Killebrew	1,699	**Walks**	
Gaylord Perry	53	Dwight Evans	1,697	Babe Ruth	2,062
Juan Marichal	52	Chili Davis	1,698	Rickey Henderson	2,060
		Dave Winfield	1,686	Ted Williams	2,019
Strikeouts, Batting		Gary Gaetti	1,599	Joe Morgan	1,865
Reggie Jackson	2,597	Fred McGriff	1,592	Carl Yastrzemski	1,845
Willie Stargell	1,936	Lee May	1,570	Mickey Mantle	1,735
Mike Schmidt	1,883	Dick Allen	1,556	Mel Ott	1,708
Jose Canseco	1,867	Willie McCovey	1,550	Eddie Yost	1,614
Tony Perez	1,867	Rickey Henderson	1,547	Darrell Evans	1,605
Dave Kingman	1,816				

Stan Musial	1,599
Pete Rose	1,566
Harmon Killebrew	1,559
Barry Bonds	1,547
Lou Gehrig	1,508
Mike Schmidt	1,507
Eddie Collins	1,503
Willie Mays	1,463
Jimmie Foxx	1,452
Eddie Mathews	1,444
Frank Robinson	1,420
Wade Boggs	1,412
Hank Aaron	1,402

RECORD OF WORLD SERIES GAMES
(Through 1999; for 2000 World Series results, *see* p. 1011)

Figures in parentheses for winning pitchers (WP) and losing pitchers (LP) indicate the game number in the series.

1903—Boston A.L. 5 (Jimmy Collins); Pittsburgh N.L. 3 (Fred Clarke). WP—Boston: Dinneen (2, 6, 8), Young (5, 7); Pittsburgh: Phillippe (1, 3, 4). LP—Boston: Young (1), Hughes (3), Dinneen (4); Pittsburgh: Leever (2, 6), Kennedy (5), Phillippe (7, 8).

1904—No series.

1905—New York N.L. 4 (John J. McGraw); Philadelphia A.L. 1 (Connie Mack). WP—New York: Mathewson (1, 3, 5); McGinnity (4); Phila.: Bender (2). LP—New York: McGinnity (2); Phila.: Plank (1, 4), Coakley (3), Bender (5).

1906—Chicago A.L. 4 (Fielder Jones); Chicago N.L. 2 (Frank Chance). WP—Chicago: A.L.: Altrock (1), Walsh (3, 5), White (6); Chicago: N.L.: Reulbach (2), Brown (4). LP—Chicago A.L.: White (3), Altrock. (4); Chicago: N.L.: Brown (1, 6), Pfeister (3, 5).

1907—Chicago N.L. 4 (Frank Chance); Detroit A.L. 0 (Hugh Jennings). First game tied 3–3, 12 innings. WP—Pfeister (2), Reulbach (3), Overall (4), Brown (5). LP—Mullin (2, 5), Siever (3), Donovan (4).

1908—Chicago N.L. 4 (Frank Chance); Detroit A.L. 1 (Hugh Jennings). WP—Chicago: Brown (1, 4), Overall (2, 5); Det.: Mullin (3). LP—Chicago: Pfeister (3); Det.: Summers (1, 4), Donovan (2, 5).

1909—Pittsburgh N.L. 4 (Fred Clarke); Detroit A.L. 3 (Hugh Jennings). WP—Pittsburgh: Adams (1, 5, 7), Maddox (3); Det.: Donovan (2), Mullin (4, 6). LP—Pittsburgh: Camnitz (2), Leifield (4), Willis (6); Det.: Mullin (1), Summers (3, 5), Donovan (7).

1910—Philadelphia A.L. 4 (Connie Mack); Chicago N.L. 1 (Frank Chance). WP—Phila.: Bender (1), Coombs (2, 3, 5); Chicago: Brown (4). LP—Phila.: Bender (4); Chicago: Overall (1), Brown (2, 5), McIntyre (3).

1911—Philadelphia A.L. 4 (Connie Mack); New York N.L. 2 (John J. McGraw). WP—Phila.: Plank (2), Coombs (3), Bender (4, 6); New York: Mathewson (1), Crandall (5). LP—Phila.: Bender (1), Plank (5); New York: Marquard (2), Mathewson (3, 4), Ames (6).

1912—Boston A.L. 4 (J. Garland Stahl); New York N.L. 3 (John J. McGraw). Second game tied, 6–6, 11 innings. WP—Boston: Wood (1, 4, 8), Bedient (5); New York: Marquard (3, 6), Tesreau (7). LP—Boston: O'Brien (3, 6), Wood (7); New York: Tesreau (1, 4), Mathewson (5, 8).

1913—Philadelphia A.L. 4 (Connie Mack); New York N.L. 1 (John J. McGraw). WP—Phila.: Bender (1, 4), Bush (3), Plank (5); New York: Mathewson (2); LP—Phila.: Plank (2); New York: Marquard (1), Tesreau (3), Demaree (4), Mathewson (5).

1914—Boston N.L. 4 (George Stallings); Philadelphia A.L. 0 (Connie Mack). WP—Rudolph (1, 4), James (2, 3). LP—Bender (1), Plank (2), Bush (3), Shawkey (4).

1915—Boston A.L. 4 (Bill Carrigan); Philadelphia N.L. 1 (Pat Moran). WP—Boston: Foster (2, 5), Leonard (3), Shore (4); Phila.: Alexander (1). LP—Boston: Shore (1); Phila.: Mayer (2), Alexander (3), Chalmers (4), Rixey (5).

1916—Boston A.L. 4 (Bill Carrigan); Brooklyn N.L. 1 (Wilbert Robinson). WP—Boston: Shore (1, 5), Ruth (2), Leonard (4); Brooklyn: Coombs (3). LP—Boston: Mays (3); Brooklyn: Marquard (1, 4), Smith (2), Pfeffer (5).

1917—Chicago A.L. 4 (Clarence Rowland); New York N.L. 2 (John J. McGraw). WP—Chicago: Cicotte (1), Faber (2, 5, 6); New York: Benton (3), Schupp (4). LP—Chicago: Cicotte (1), Faber (4); New York: Sallee (1, 5), Anderson (2), Benton (6).

1918—Boston A.L. 4 (Ed Barrow); Chicago N.L. 2 (Fred Mitchell). WP—Boston: Ruth (1, 4), Mays (3, 6); Chicago: Tyler (2), Vaughn (5). LP—Boston: Bush (2), Jones (5); Chicago: Vaughn (1, 3), Douglas (4), Tyler (6).

1919—Cincinnati N.L. 5 (Pat Moran); Chicago A.L. 3 (William Gleason). WP—Cincinnati: Ruether (1), Sallee (2), Ring (4), Eller (5, 8); Chicago.: Kerr (3, 6), Cicotte (7). LP—Cincinnati: Fisher (3), Ring (6), Sallee (7); Chicago: Cicotte (1, 4), Williams (2, 5, 8).

1920—Cleveland A.L. 5 (Tris Speaker); Brooklyn N.L. 2 (Wilbert Robinson). WP—Cleve.: Coveleski (1, 4, 7), Bagby (5), Mails (6); Brooklyn: Grimes (2), Smith (3). LP—Cleve.: Bagby (2), Caldwell (3). Brooklyn: Marquard (1), Cadore (4), Grimes (5, 7), Smith (6).

1921—New York N.L. 5 (John J. McGraw); New York A.L. 3 (Miller Huggins). WP—New York N.L.: Barnes (3, 6), Douglas (4, 7), Nehf (8); New York A.L.: Mays (1), Hoyt (2, 5). LP—New York N.L.: Nehf (2, 5), Douglas (1). New York A.L.: Quinn (3), Mays (4, 7), Shawkey (6), Hoyt (8).

1922—New York N.L. 4 (John J. McGraw); New York A.L. 0 (Miller Huggins). Second game tied 3–3, 10 innings. WP—Ryan (1), Scott (3), McQuillan (4), Nehf (5); LP—Bush (1, 5), Hoyt (3), Mays (4).

1923—New York A.L. 4 (Miller Huggins); New York N.L. 2 (John J. McGraw). WP—New York A.L.: Pennock (2, 6), Shawkey (4), Bush (5); New York N.L.: Ryan (1), Nehf (3). LP—New York A.L.: Bush (1), Jones (3); New York N.L.: McQuillan (2), Scott (4), Bentley (5), Nehf (6).

1924—Washington A.L. 4 (Bucky Harris); New York N.L. 3 (John J. McGraw). WP—Washington: Zachary (2, 6), Mogridge (4), Johnson (7); New York: Nehf (1), McQuillan (3), Bentley (5). LP—Washington: Johnson (1, 5), Marberry (4); New York: Bentley (2, 7), Barnes (4), Nehf (6).

1925—Pittsburgh N.L. 4 (Bill McKechnie); Washington A.L. 3 (Bucky Harris). WP—Pittsburgh: Aldridge (2, 5), Kremer (6, 7); Washington: Johnson (1, 4), Ferguson (3). LP—

LP—Pittsburgh: Meadows (1), Kremer (3), Yde (4); Washington: Coveleski (2, 5), Ferguson (6), Johnson (7).

1926—St. Louis N.L. 4 (Rogers Hornsby); New York A.L. 3 (Miller Huggins). WP—St. Louis: Alexander (2, 6), Haines (3, 7); New York: Pennock (1, 5), Hoyt (4). LP—St. Louis: Sherdel (1, 5), Reinhart (4); New York: Shocker (2), Ruether (3), Shawkey (6), Hoyt (7).

1927—New York A.L. 4 (Miller Huggins); Pittsburgh N.L. 0 (Donie Bush). WP—Hoyt (1), Pipgras (2), Pennock (3), Moore (4). LP—Kremer (1), Aldridge (2), Meadows (3), Miljus (4).

1928—New York A.L. 4 (Miller Huggins); St. Louis N.L. 0 (Bill McKechnie). WP—Hoyt (1, 4), Pipgras (2), Zachary (3). LP—Sherdel (1, 4), Alexander (2), Haines (3).

1929—Philadelphia A.L. 4 (Connie Mack); Chicago N.L. 1 (Joe McCarthy). WP—Phila.: Ehmke (1), Earnshaw (2), Rommel (4), Walberg (5); Chicago: Bush (3). LP—Phila.: Earnshaw (3) Chicago: Root (1), Malone (2, 5), Blake (4).

1930—Philadelphia A.L. 4 (Connie Mack); St. Louis N.L. 2 (Gabby Street). WP—Phila.: Grove (1, 5), Earnshaw (2, 6); St. Louis: Hallahan (3), Haines (4). LP—Phila.: Walberg (3), Grove (4); St. Louis: Grimes (1, 5), Rhem (2), Hallahan (6).

1931—St. Louis N.L. 4 (Gabby Street); Philadelphia A.L. 3 (Connie Mack). WP—St. Louis: Hallahan (2, 5), Grimes (3, 7); Phila.: Grove (1, 6), Earnshaw (4). LP—St. Louis: Derringer (1, 6), Johnson (4); Phila.: Earnshaw (2, 7), Grove (3), Hoyt (5).

1932—New York A.L. 4 (Joe McCarthy); Chicago N.L. 0 (Charles Grimm). WP—Ruffing (1), Gomez (2), Pipgras (3), Moore (4). LP—Bush (1), Warneke (2), Root (3), May (4).

1933—New York N.L. 4 (Bill Terry); Washington A.L. 1 (Joe Cronin.). WP—New York: Hubbell (1, 4), Schumacher (2), Luque (5); Washington: Whitehill (3). LP—New York: Fitzsimmons (3); Washington: Stewart (1), Crowder (2), Weaver (4), Russell (5).

1934—St. Louis N.L. 4 (Frank Frisch); Detroit A.L. 3 (Mickey Cochrane). WP—St. Louis: J. Dean (1, 7), P. Dean (3, 6); Det.: Rowe (2), Auker (4), Bridges (5). LP—St. Louis: W. Walker (2, 4), J. Dean (5); Det.: Crowder (1), Bridges (3), Rowe (6), Auker (7).

1935—Detroit A.L. 4 (Mickey Cochrane); Chicago A.L. 2 (Charles Grimm). WP—Det.: Bridges (2, 6), Rowe (3), Crowder (4); Chicago: Warneke (1, 5); LP—Det.: Rowe (1, 5), Chicago: Root (2) French (3, 6), Carleton (4).

1936—New York A.L. 4 (Joe McCarthy); New York N.L. 2 (Bill Terry). WP—New York A.L.: Gomez (2, 6), Hadley (3), Pearson (4); New York N.L.: Hubbell (1), Schumacher (5); LP—New York A.L.: Ruffing (1), Malone (4); New York N.L.: Schumacher (2), Fitzsimmons (3, 6), Hubbell (4).

1937—New York A.L. 4 (Joe McCarthy); New York N.L. 1 (Bill Terry). WP—New York A.L.: Gomez (1, 5), Ruffing (2), Pearson (3); New York N.L.: Hubbell (4). LP—New York A.L.: Hadley (4); New York N.L.: Hubbell (1), Melton (2, 5), Schumacher (3).

1938—New York A.L. 4 (Joe McCarthy); Chicago N.L. 0 (Gabby Hartnett). WP—Ruffing (1, 4), Gomez (2), Pearson (3) LP—Lee (1, 4), Dean (2), Bryant (3).

1939—New York A.L. 4 (Joe McCarthy); Cincinnati N.L. 0 (Bill McKechnie). WP—Ruffing (1), Pearson (2), Hadley (3), Murphy (4). LP—Derringer (1), Walters (2, 4), Thompson (3).

1940—Cincinnati N.L. 4 (Bill McKechnie); Detroit A.L. 3 (Del Baker). WP—Cincinnati: Walters (2, 6), Derringer (4, 7); Det.: Newsom (1, 5), Bridges (3). LP—Cincinnati: Derringer (1), Turner (3), Thompson (5); Det.: Rowe (2, 4), Trout (4), Newsom (7).

1941—New York A.L. 4 (Joe McCarthy); Brooklyn N.L. 1 (Leo Durocher). WP—New York: Ruffing (1), Russo (3), Murphy (4), Bonham (5); Bklyn: Wyatt (2). LP—New York: Chandler (3); Bklyn: Davis (1), Casey (3, 4), Wyatt (5).

1942—St. Louis N.L. 4 (Billy Southworth); New York A.L. 1 (Joe McCarthy). WP—St. Louis: Beazley (2, 5), White (3), Lanier (4); New York: Ruffing (1). LP—St. Louis: Cooper (1); New York: Bonham (2), Chandler (3), Donald (4), Ruffing (5).

1943—New York A.L. 4 (Joe McCarthy); St. Louis N.L. 1 (Billy Southworth). WP—New York: Chandler (1, 5), Borowy (3), Russo (4); St. Louis: Cooper (2). LP—New York: Bonham (2); St. Louis: Lanier (1), Brazle (3), Brecheen (4), Cooper (5).

1944—St. Louis N.L. 4 (Billy Southworth); St. Louis A.L. 2 (Luke Sewell). WP—St. Louis N.L.: Donnelly (2), Brecheen (4), Cooper (5), Lanier (6); St. Louis A.L.: Galehouse (1), Kramer (3). LP—St. Louis N.L.: Cooper (1), Wilks (3); St. Louis A.L.: Muncrief (2), Jakucki (4), Galehouse (5), Potter (6).

1945—Detroit A.L. 4 (Steve O'Neill); Chicago N.L. 3 (Charles Grimm). WP—Det.: Trucks (2), Trout (4), Newhouser (5, 7); Chicago: Borowy (1, 6), Passeau (3). LP—Det.: Newhouser (1), Overmire (3), Trout (6); Chicago: Wyse (2), Prim (4), Borowy (5, 7).

1946—St. Louis N.L. 4 (Eddie Dyer); Boston A.L. 3 (Joe Cronin). WP—St. Louis: Brecheen (2, 6, 7), Munger (4); Boston: Johnson (1), Ferriss (3), Dobson (5). LP—St. Louis: Pollet (1), Dickson (3), Brazle (5); Boston: Harris (2, 6), Hughson (4), Klinger (7).

1947—New York A.L. 4 (Bucky Harris); Brooklyn N.L. 3 (Burt Shotton). WP—New York: Shea (1, 5), Reynolds (2), Page (7); Brooklyn: Casey (3), Branca (4). LP—New York: Newsom (3), Bevens (4), Page (6); Brooklyn: Branca (1), Lombardi (2), Barney (5), Gregg (7).

1948—Cleveland A.L. 4 (Lou Boudreau); Boston N.L. 2 (Billy Southworth). WP—Cleve.: Lemon (2, 6), Bearden (3), Gromek (4); Boston: Sain (1), Spahn (5). LP—Cleve.: Feller (1, 5); Boston: Spahn (2), Bickford (3), Sain (4), Voiselle (6).

1949—New York A.L. 4 (Casey Stengel); Brooklyn N.L. 1 (Burt Shotton). WP—New York: Reynolds (1), Page (3), Lopat (4), Raschi (5); Brooklyn: Roe (2). LP—New York: Raschi (2); Brooklyn: Newcombe (1, 4), Branca (3), Barney (5).

1950—New York A.L. 4 (Casey Stengel); Philadelphia N.L. 0 (Eddie Sawyer). WP—Raschi (1), Reynolds (2), Ferrick (3), Ford (4). LP—Konstanty (1), Roberts (2), Meyer (3), Miller (4).

1951—New York A.L. 4 (Casey Stengel); New York N.L. 2 (Leo Durocher). WP—New York A.L.: Lopat (2, 5), Reynolds (4), Raschi (6); New York N.L.: Koslo (1), Hearn (3). LP—New York A.L.: Reynolds (1), Raschi (4); New York N.L.: Jansen (2, 5), Maglie (4), Koslo (6).

1952—New York A.L. 4 (Casey Stengel); Brooklyn N.L. 3 (Chuck Dressen). WP—New York: Raschi (2, 6), Reynolds (4, 7); Brooklyn: Black (1), Roe (3), Erskine (5). LP—New York: Reynolds (1), Lopat (3), Sain (5); Brooklyn: Erskine (2), Black (4, 7), Loes (6).

1953—New York A.L. 4 (Casey Stengel); Brooklyn N.L. 2 (Chuck Dressen). WP—New York: Sain (1), Lopat (2), McDonald (5), Reynolds (6); Brooklyn: Erskine (3), Loes (4). LP—New York: Raschi (3), Ford (4); Brooklyn: Labine (1, 6), Roe (2), Podres (5).

1954—New York N.L. 4 (Leo Durocher); Cleveland A.L. 0 (Al Lopez). WP—Grissom (1), Antonelli (2), Gomez (3), Liddie (4). LP—Lemon (1, 4), Wynn (2), Garcia (3).

1955—Brooklyn N.L. 4 (Walter Alston); New York A.L. 3 (Casey Stengel). WP—Brooklyn: Podres (3, 7), Labine (4), Craig (5); New York: Ford (1, 6), Byrne (4). LP—Brooklyn: Newcombe (1), Loes (2), Spooner (6); New York: Turley (3), Larsen (4), Grim (5), Byrne (7).

1956—New York A.L. 4 (Casey Stengel); Brooklyn N.L. 3 (Walter Alston). WP—New York: Ford (3), Sturdivant (4), Larsen (5), Kucks (7); Brooklyn: Maglie (1), Bessent (2), Labine (6). LP—New York: Ford (1), Morgan (2), Turley

(6); Brooklyn: Craig (3), Erskine (4), Maglie (5), New-combe (7).

1957—Milwaukee N.L. 4 (Fred Haney); New York A.L. 3 (Casey Stengel). WP—Milwaukee: Burdette (2, 5, 7), Spahn (4); New York: Ford (1), Larsen (3), Turley (6). LP—Milwaukee: Spahn (1), Buhl (3), Johnson (6); New York: Shantz (2), Grim (4), Ford (5), Larsen (7).

1958—New York A.L. 4 (Casey Stengel); Milwaukee N.L. 3 (Fred Haney). WP—New York: Larsen (3), Turley (5, 7), Duren (6); Milwaukee: Spahn (1, 4), Burdette (2). LP—New York: Duren (1), Turley (2), Ford (4); Milwaukee: Rush (3), Burdette (5, 7), Spahn (6).

1959—Los Angeles N.L. 4 (Walter Alston); Chicago A.L. 2 (Al Lopez). WP—Los Angeles: Podres (4), Drysdale (3), Sherry (4, 6); Chicago: Wynn (1), Shaw (5). LP—Los Angeles: Craig (1), Koufax (5); Chicago: Shaw (2), Dono-van (3), Staley (4), Wynn (6).

1960—Pittsburgh N.L. 4 (Danny Murtaugh); New York A.L. 3 (Casey Stengel). WP—Pittsburgh: Law (1, 4), Haddix (5, 7); New York: Turley (2), Ford (3, 6). LP—Pittsburgh: Friend (2, 6), Mizell (3); New York: Dit-mar (1, 5), Terry (4, 7).

1961—New York A.L. 4 (Ralph Houk); Cincinnati N.L. 1 (Fred Hutchinson). WP—New York: Ford (1, 4), Arroyo (3), Daley (5); Cincinnati: Jay (2). LP—New York: Terry (2); Cincinnati: O'Toole (1, 4), Purkey (3), Jay (5).

1962—New York A.L. 4 (Ralph Houk); San Francisco N.L. 3 (Al Dark). WP—New York: Ford (1), Stafford (3), Terry (5, 7); San Francisco: Sanford (2), Larsen (4), Pierce (6). LP—New York: Terry (2), Coates (4), Ford (6); San Fran-cisco: O'Dell (1), Pierce (3), Sanford (5, 7).

1963—Los Angeles N.L. 4 (Walter Alston); New York A.L. 0 (Ralph Houk). WP—Koufax (1, 4), Podres (2), Drysdale (3). LP—Ford (1, 4), Downing (2), Bouton (3).

1964—St. Louis N.L. 4 (Johnny Keane); New York A.L. 3 (Yogi Berra). WP—St. Louis: Sadecki (1), Craig (4), Gibson (5, 7); New York: Stottlemyre (2), Bouton (3, 6). LP—St. Louis: Gibson (2), Schultz (3), Simmons (6); New York: Ford (1), Downing (4), Mikkelsen (5), Stottle-myre (7).

1965—Los Angeles N.L. 4 (Walter Alston); Minnesota A.L. 3 (Sam Mele). WP—Los Angeles: Osteen (3), Drysdale (4), Koufax (5, 7); Minnesota: Grant (1, 6), Kaat (2). LP—Los Angeles: Drysdale (1), Koufax (2), Osteen (6); Minne-sota: Pascual (3), Grant (4), Kaat (5, 7).

1966—Baltimore A.L. 4 (Hank Bauer); Los Angeles N.L. 0 (Walter Alston). WP—Drabowsky (1), Palmer (2), Bun-ker (3), McNally (4). LP—Drysdale (1, 4), Koufax (2), Osteen (3).

1967—St. Louis N.L. 4 (Red Schoendienst); Boston A.L. 3 (Dick Williams). WP—St. Louis: Gibson (1, 4, 7), Briles (3); Boston: Lonborg (2, 5), Wyatt (6). LP—St. Louis: Hughes (2), Carlton (5), Lamabe (6); Boston: Santiago (1, 4), Bell (3), Lonborg (7).

1968—Detroit A.L. 4 (Mayo Smith); St. Louis N.L. 3 (Red Schoendienst). WP—Det.: Lolich (2, 5, 7), McLain (6); St. Louis: Gibson (1, 4), Washburn (3), LP—Det.: McLain (1, 4), Wilson (3); St. Louis: Briles (2), Hoerner (5), Wash-burn (6), Gibson (7).

1969—New York N.L. 4 (Gil Hodges); Baltimore A.L. 1 (Earl Weaver). WP—New York: Koosman (2, 5), Gentry (3), Seaver (4); Baltimore: Cuellar (1). LP—New York: Seaver (1); Baltimore: McNally (2), Palmer (3), Hall (4), Watt (5).

1970—Baltimore A.L. 4 (Earl Weaver); Cincinnati N.L. 1 (Sparky Anderson) 1. WP—Baltimore: Palmer (1), Phoe-bus (2), McNally (3), Cuellar (5); Cincinnati: Carroll (4). LP—Cincinnati: Nolan (1), Wilcox (2), Cloninger (3), Mer-ritt (5); Baltimore: Watt (4).

1971—Pittsburgh N.L. 4 (Danny Murtaugh); Baltimore A.L. 3 (Earl Weaver). WP—Pittsburgh: Blass (3, 7), Kison (4), Briles (5); Baltimore: McNally (1, 6), Palmer (2). LP—Pittsburgh: Ellis (1), R. Johnson (2), Miller (6); Balti-more: Cuellar (3, 7), Watt (4) McNally (5).

1972—Oakland A.L. 4 (Dick Williams); Cincinnati N.L.

(Sparky Anderson) 3. WP—Oakland: Holtzman (1), Hunter (2, 7), Fingers (4); Cincinnati: Billingham (3), Grimsley (5, 6). LP—Oakland: Odom (3), Fingers (5), Blue (6); Cincinnati: Nolan (1), Grimsley (2), Carroll (4), Borbon (7).

1973—Oakland A.L. 4 (Dick Williams); New York N.L. 3 (Yogi Berra). WP—Oakland: Holtzman (1, 7), Lindblad (3), Hunter (6). New York: McGraw (2), Matlack (1), Koosman (5). LP—Oakland: Fingers (2), Holtzman (4), Blue (5). New York: Matlack (1, 7) Parker (3), Seaver (6).

1974—Oakland A.L. 4 (Al Dark); Los Angeles N.L. 1 (Walter Alston). WP—Oakland: Fingers (1), Hunter (3), Holtzman (4), Odom (5). Los Angeles: Sutton (2). LP—Oakland: Blue (1), Los Angeles: Messersmith (1, 4), Downing (3), Marshall (5).

1975—Cincinnati N.L. 4 (Sparky Anderson); Boston A.L. 3 (Darrell Johnson). WP—Cincinnati: Eastwick (2, 3), Gul-lett (5), Carroll (7); Boston: Tiant (1, 4), Wise (6). LP—Cincinnati: Gullett (1), Norman (4), Darcy (6); Bos-ton: Drago (2), Willoughby (3), Cleveland (5), Burton (7).

1976—Cincinnati N.L. 4 (Sparky Anderson); New York A.L. 0 (Billy Martin). WP—Gullett (1), Billingham (2), Zachry (3), Nolan (4). LP—Alexander (1), Hunter (2), Ellis (3), Figueroa (4)

1977—New York A.L. 4 (Billy Martin); Los Angeles N.L. 2 (Tom Lasorda). WP—New York: Lyle (4), Torrez (3, 6), Guidry (4); Los Angeles: Hooton (2), Sutton (5). LP—New York: Hunter (2), Gullett (5); Los Angeles: Rhoden (1), John (3), Rau (4), Hooton (6).

1978—New York A.L. 4 (Bob Lemon), Los Angeles N.L. 2 (Tom Lasorda); WP—New York: Guidry (3), Gossage (4); Beattie (5), Hunter (6); Los Angeles: John (1), Hooton (2). LP—New York: Figueroa (1), Hunter (2); Los Angeles: Sutton (3, 6), Welch (4), Hooton (5).

1979—Pittsburgh N.L. 4 (Chuck Tanner), Baltimore A.L. 3 (Earl Weaver); WP—Pittsburgh: D. Robinson (2), Blyleven (5), Candelaria (6), Jackson (7); Baltimore: Flanagan (1), McGregor (3), Stoddard (4). LP—Pittsburgh: Kison (1), Candelaria (3), Tekulve (4); Baltimore: Stanhouse (2), Flanagan (5), Palmer (6), McGregor (7).

1980—Philadelphia N.L. 4 (Dallas Green), Kansas City A.L. 2 (Jim Frey); WP—Philadelphia: Walk (1), Carlton (2), McGraw (5); Carlton (4); Kansas City: Quisenberry (3), Leonard (4). LP—Philadelphia: McGraw (3), Christenson (4); Kansas City: Leonard (1), Quisenberry (2), Quisen-berry (5), Gale (6).

1981—Los Angeles N.L. 4 (Tom Lasorda), New York A.L. 2 (Bob Lemon); WP—Los Angeles: Valenzuela (3), Howe (4), Reuss (4), Hooton (6); New York: Guidry (1), John (2). LP—Los Angeles: Reuss (1), Hooton (2); New York: Frazier (3), Frazier (4), Guidry (5), Frazier (6).

1982—St. Louis N.L. 4 (Whitey Herzog), Milwaukee A.L. 3 (Harvey Kuenn); WP—St. Louis: Sutter (2), Andujar (3), Stuper (6), Andujar (7). Milwaukee: Caldwell (1), Slaton (4), Caldwell (5). LP—St. Louis: Forsch (1), Bair (4), For-sch (5). Milwaukee: McClure (2), Vuckovich (3), Sutton (6), McClure (7).

1983—Baltimore A.L. 4 (Joe Altobelli), Philadelphia N.L. 1 (Paul Owens); WP—Baltimore: Boddicker (2), Palmer (3), Davis (4), McGregor (5). Philadelphia: Denny (1).

1984—Detroit A.L. 4 (Sparky Anderson), San Diego N.L. 1 (Dick Williams); WP—Det.: Morris (1,4), Wilcox (3), Lopez (5), San Diego: Hawkins (2). LP—Det.: Petry (2), San Diego: Thurmond (1), Lollar (3), Show (4), Haw-kins (5).

1985—Kansas City A.L. 4 (Dick Howser), St. Louis N.L. 3 (Whitey Herzog); WP—KC: Saberhagen (3,7) Quisen-berry (6), Jackson (5). St. Louis: Tudor (1,4) Dayley (5). LP—KC: Jackson (1), Leibrandt (2), Black (4); St. Louis: Andujar (3), Forsch (5), Worrell (6), Tudor (7).

1986—New York N.L. 4 (Dave Johnson); Boston A.L. (John McNamara) 3 WP—New York—Ojeda (3), Darling (4), Aguilera (6), McDowell (7), Bos: Hurst (1), (5), Crawford

(2). LP—New York Darling (1), Gooden (2, 5).
1987—Minnesota, A.L. 4 (Tom Kelly); St. Louis N.L. (Whitey Herzog) 3. WP—Minnesota Viola (1, 7), Blyleven (2), Schatzeder (6), St. Louis: Tudor (3), Forsch (4), Cox (5). LP—Minnesota Berenguer (3), Viola (4), Blyleven (5); St. Louis: Magrane (1), Cox (2, 7), Tudor (6).
1988—Los Angeles N.L. 4 (Tommy Lasorda); Oakland A.L. (Tony LaRussa) 1. WP—Los Angeles: Hershiser (2, 5), Pena (1), Belcher (4); Oakland: Honeycutt (3). LP—Los Angeles: Howell (3); Oakland: Davis (2, 5), Eckersley (1), Stewart (4).
1989—Oakland, A.L. 4 (Tony LaRussa); San Francisco N.L. 0 (Roger Craig). WP—Oakland: Dave Stewart (1, 3), Mike Moore (2, 4). LP—San Francisco: Scott Garrelts (1, 3), Don Robinson (2), Rick Reuschel (2).
1990—Cincinnati N.L. 4 (Lou Piniella); Oakland A.L. 0 (Tony LaRussa). WP—Cincinnati: Jose Rijo (1, 4), Rob Dibble (2), Tom Browning (3). LP—Oakland: Dave Stewart (1, 4), Dennis Eckersley (2), Mike Moore (3).
1991—Minnesota, A.L. 4 (Tom Kelly); Atlanta, N.L. 3 (Bobby Cox). WP—Minnesota: Morris (1,7), Tapani (2), Aguilera (6). Atlanta: Clancy (3), Stanton (4), Glavine (5). LP—Minnesota: Aguilera (3), Gurhtie (4), Tapani (5). Atlanta: Leibrandt (1, 6), Glavine (2), Pena (7).
1992—Toronto, A.L. 4 (Cito Gaston); Atlanta, N.L. 2 (Bobby Cox). WP—Toronto: Ward (2, 3), Key (4, 6). Atlanta: Glavine (1), Smoltz (5). LP—Toronto: Morris (1). Atlanta: Leibrandt (6), Reardon (2), Avery (3), Glavine (4).
1993—Toronto, A.L. 4 (Cito Gaston); Philadelphia, N.L. 2

(Jim Fregosi). WP—Toronto: Leiter (1), Hentgen (3), Castillo (4), Ward (6). Philadelphia: Mullholland (2), Schilling (5). LP—Toronto: Stewart (2), Guzman (5). Philadelphia: Schilling (1), Jackson (3), Williams (4, 6).
1994—World Series cancelled due to players' strike.
1995—Atlanta, N.L. 4 (Bobby Cox); Cleveland, A.L. 2 (Mike Hargrove). WP—Atlanta: Maddux (1), Glavine (2,6), Avery (4). Cleveland: Mesa (3), Hershiser (5). LP—Atlanta: Pena (3), Maddux (5). Cleveland: Hershiser (1), Martinez (2), Hill (4), Poole (6).
1996—New York, A.L. 4 (Joe Torre); Atlanta, N.L. 2 (Bobby Cox). WP—New York: Cone (3), Lloyd (4), Pettitte (5), Key (6). Atlanta: Smoltz (1), Maddux (2). LP—New York: Pettitte (1), Key (2). Atlanta: Glavine (3), Avery (4), Smoltz (5), Maddux (6).
1997—Florida, N.L. 4 (Jim Leyland); Cleveland, A.L. 3 (Mike Hargrove). WP—Florida: Hernandez (1, 5), Cook (3), Powell (7). Cleveland: Ogea (2, 6), Wright (4). LP—Florida: Brown (2, 6), Saunders (4). Cleveland: Hershiser (1, 5), Plunk (3), Nagy (7).
1998—New York, A.L. 4 (Joe Torre); San Diego, N.L. 0 (Bruce Bochy). WP—New York: Wells (1), Hernandez (2), Mendoza (3), Pettitte (4). LP—San Diego: Wall (1), Ashby (2), Hoffman (3), Brown (4).
1999—New York, A.L. 4 (Joe Torre); Atlanta, N.L. 0 (Bobby Cox). WP—New York: Hernandez (1), Cone (2), Rivera (3), Clemens (4). LP—Atlanta: Maddux (1), Millwood (2), Remlinger (3), Smoltz (4).

WORLD SERIES CLUB STANDINGS

(Through 1999)

	Series	Won	Lost	Pct.
Toronto (A)	2	2	0	1.000
Florida (N)	1	1	0	1.000
Pittsburgh (N)	7	5	2	.714
New York (A)	36	25	11	.695
Oakland (A)	6	4	2	.667
Minnesota (A)	3	2	1	.667
New York (N-Mets)	3	2	1	.667
Philadelphia (A)	8	5	3	.625
St. Louis (N)	15	9	6	.600
Boston (A)	9	5	4	.556
Los Angeles (N)	9	5	4	.556
Cincinnati (N)	9	5	4	.556
Milwaukee (N)	2	1	1	.500
Boston (N)	2	1	1	.500
Chicago (A)	4	2	2	.500
Baltimore (A)	6	3	3	.500
Kansas City (A)	2	1	1	.500

	Series	Won	Lost	Pct.
Detroit (A)	9	4	5	.444
Cleveland (A)	5	2	3	.400
New York (N-Giants)	14	5	9	.357
Washington (A)	3	1	2	.333
Atlanta (N)	5	1	4	.200
Philadelphia (N)	5	1	4	.200
Chicago (N)	10	2	8	.200
Brooklyn (N)	9	1	8	.111
St. Louis (A)	1	0	1	.000
San Francisco (N)	2	0	2	.000
Milwaukee (A)	1	0	1	.000
San Diego (N)	2	0	2	.000

Recapitulation

	Won
American League	55
National League	38

LIFETIME WORLD SERIES RECORDS

(Through 1999)

Most hits—71, Yogi Berra, New York A.L., 1947, 1949–53, 1955–58, 1960–63.

Most runs—42, Mickey Mantle, New York A.L., 1951–53, 1955–58, 1960–64.

Most runs batted in—40, Mickey Mantle, New York A.L., 1951–53, 1955–58, 1960–64.

Most home runs—18, Mickey Mantle, New York A.L., 1951–53, 1955–58, 1960–64.

Most bases on balls—43, Mickey Mantle, New York A.L., 1951–53, 1955–58, 1960–64.

Most strikeouts—54, Mickey Mantle, New York A.L., 1951–53, 1955–58, 1960–64.

Most stolen bases—14, Eddie Collins, Philadelphia A.L. 1910–11, 13–14; Chicago A.L., 1917, 1919. Lou Brock, St. Louis N.L., 1964, 67–68.

Most victories, pitcher—10, Whitey Ford, New York A.L., 1950, 1953, 1955–58, 1960–64.

Most times member of winning team—10, Yogi Berra, New York A.L., 1947, 1949–53, 1956, 1958, 1961–62.

Most victories, no defeats—6, Vernon Gomez, New York A.L., 1932, 1936(2), 1937(2), 1938.

Most shutouts—4, Christy Mathewson, New York N.L., 1905 (3), 1913.

Most innings pitched—146, Whitey Ford, New York A.L., 1950, 1953, 1955–58, 1960–1964

Most consecutive scoreless innings—33⅔, Whitey Ford, New York A.L., 1960 (18), 1961 (14), 1962 (1⅔).

Most strikeouts by pitcher—94, Whitey Ford, New York A.L., 1950, 1953, 1955–58, 1960–64.

SINGLE GAME AND SINGLE SERIES RECORDS

(Through 1998)

Most hits game—5, Paul Molitor, Milwaukee A.L., first game vs. St. Louis, N.L., 1982.

Most 4-hit games, series—2, Robin Yount, Milwaukee A.L., first and fifth games vs. St. Louis, N.L., 1982.

Most hits inning—2, held by 17 players.

Most hits series—13 (7 games) Bobby Richardson, New York A.L., 1964; Lou Brock, St. Louis N.L., 1968; Marty Barrett, Boston A.L., 1986.

Most home runs, series—5 (6 games) Reggie Jackson, New York A.L., 1977; 4 (7 games) Babe Ruth, New York A.L., 1926; Duke Snider, Brooklyn N.L., 1952, 1955; Hank Bauer, New York A.L., 1958; Gene Tenace, Oakland A.L., 1972; 4 (4 games) Lou Gehrig, New York A.L., 1928; 4 (6 games) Willie Aikens, Kansas City A.L., 1980.

Most home runs, game—3, Babe Ruth, New York A.L., 1926 and 1928; Reggie Jackson, New York A.L., 1977.

Most strikeouts, series—12 (6 games) Willie Wilson, Kansas City A.L., 1980; 11 (7 games) Ed Mathews, Milwaukee N.L., 1958; Wayne Garrett, New York N.L., 1973; 9 (5 games) Carmelo Martinez, San Diego, N.L., 1984; Duke Snider, Brooklyn N.L., 1949; 7 (4 games) Bob Muesel, New York N.L., 1927.

Most stolen bases, game—3, Honus Wagner, Pittsburgh N.L., 1909; Willie Davis, Los Angeles N.L., 1965; Lou Brock, St. Louis N.L., 1967 and 1968.

Most strikeouts by pitcher, game—17, Bob Gibson, St. Louis N.L. 1968.

Most strikeouts by pitcher in succession—6, Horace Eller, Cincinnati N.L., 1919; Moe Drabowsky, Baltimore A.L., 1966.

Most strikeouts by pitcher, series—35 (7 games) Bob Gibson, St. Louis N.L., 1968; 23 (4 games) Sandy Koufax, Los Angeles, 1963; 20 (6 games) Chief Bender, Philadelphia A.L., 1911; 18 (5 games) Christy Mathewson, New York N.L., 1905.

Most bases on balls, series—11 (7 games) Babe Ruth, New York A.L., 1926; Gene Tenace, Oakland A.L., 1973; 9 (6 games) Willie Randolph, New York A.L., 1981; 7 (5 games) James Sheckard, Chicago N.L., 1910; Mickey Cochrane, Philadelphia A.L., 1929; Joe Gordon, New York A.L., 1941; 7 (4 games) Hank Thompson, New York N.L., 1954.

Most consecutive scoreless innings one series—27, Christy Mathewson, New York N.L., 1905.

AMERICAN LEAGUE HOME RUN CHAMPIONS

Year	Player, team	No.	Year	Player, team	No.	Year	Player, team	No.
1901	Nap Lajoie, Philadelphia	13	1936	Lou Gehrig, New York	49	1969	Harmon Killebrew, Minnesota	49
1902	Ralph Seybold, Philadelphia	16	1937	Joe DiMaggio, New York	46			
1903	Buck Freeman, Boston	13	1938	Hank Greenberg, Detroit	58	1970	Frank Howard, Washington	44
1904	Harry Davis, Philadelphia	10	1939	Jimmy Foxx, Boston	35	1971	Bill Melton, Chicago	33
1905	Harry Davis, Philadelphia	8	1940	Hank Greenberg, Detroit	41	1972	Dick Allen, Chicago	37
1906	Harry Davis, Philadelphia	12	1941	Ted Williams, Boston	37	1973	Reggie Jackson, Oakland	32
1907	Harry Davis, Philadelphia	8	1942	Ted Williams, Boston	36	1974	Dick Allen, Chicago	32
1908	Sam Crawford, Detroit	7	1943	Rudy York, Detroit	34	1975	Reggie Jackson, Oakland; George Scott, Milwaukee	36
1909	Ty Cobb, Detroit	9	1944	Nick Etten, New York	22			
1910	J. Garland Stahl, Boston	10	1945	Vern Stephens, St. Louis	24	1976	Graig Nettles, New York	32
1911	Franklin Baker, Philadelphia	11	1946	Hank Greenberg, Detroit	44	1977	Jim Rice, Boston	39
1912	Franklin Baker, Philadelphia	10	1947	Ted Williams, Boston	32	1978	Jim Rice, Boston	46
1913	Franklin Baker, Philadelphia	12	1948	Joe DiMaggio, New York	39	1979	Gorman Thomas, Milwaukee	45
1914	Franklin Baker, Philadelphia; Sam Crawford, Detroit	8	1949	Ted Williams, Boston	43	1980	Reggie Jackson, New York; Ben Oglivie, Milwaukee	41
		7	1950	Al Rosen, Cleveland	37			
1915	Robert Roth, Chicago-Cleveland		1951	Gus Zernial, Chicago-Philadelphia	33	1981[1]	Tony Armas, Oakland; Dwight Evans, Boston; Bobby Grich, California; Eddie Murray, Baltimore (tie)	22
1916	Wally Pipp, New York	12	1952	Larry Doby, Cleveland	32			
1917	Wally Pipp, New York	9	1953	Al Rosen, Cleveland	43			
1918	Babe Ruth, Boston; Clarence Walker, Philadelphia	11	1954	Larry Doby, Cleveland	32	1982	Gorman Thomas, Milwaukee; Reggie Jackson, California	39
			1955	Mickey Mantle, New York	37			
1919	Babe Ruth, Boston	29	1956	Mickey Mantle, New York	52	1983	Jim Rice, Boston	39
1920	Babe Ruth, New York	54	1957	Roy Sievers, Washington	42	1984	Tony Armas, Boston	43
1921	Babe Ruth, New York	59	1958	Mickey Mantle, New York	42	1985	Darrell Evans, Detroit	40
1922	Ken Williams, St. Louis	39	1959	Rocky Colavito, Cleveland; Harmon Killebrew, Washington	42	1986	Jesse Barfield, Toronto	40
1923	Babe Ruth, New York	41				1987	Mark McGwire, Oakland	49
1924	Babe Ruth, New York	46	1960	Mickey Mantle, New York	40	1988	Jose Canseco, Oakland	42
1925	Bob Meusel, New York	33	1961	Roger Maris, New York	61	1989	Fred McGriff, Toronto	36
1926	Babe Ruth, New York	47	1962	Harmon Killebrew, Minnesota	48	1990	Cecil Fielder, Detroit	51
1927	Babe Ruth, New York	60				1991	Jose Canseco, Oakland; Cecil Fielder, Detroit (tie)	44
1928	Babe Ruth, New York	54	1963	Harmon Killebrew, Minnesota	45			
1929	Babe Ruth, New York	46				1992	Juan Gonzalez, Texas	43
1930	Babe Ruth, New York	49	1964	Harmon Killebrew, Minnesota	49	1993	Juan Gonzalez, Texas	46
1931	Lou Gehrig, New York; Babe Ruth, New York	46	1965	Tony Conigliaro, Boston	32	1994[2]	Ken Griffey, Jr., Seattle	40
			1966	Frank Robinson, Baltimore	49	1995	Albert Belle, Cleveland	50
1932	Jimmy Foxx, Philadelphia	58	1967	Carl Yastrzemski, Boston; Harmon Killebrew, Minnesota	44	1996	Mark McGwire, Oakland	52
1933	Jimmy Foxx, Philadelphia	48				1997	Ken Griffey, Jr., Seattle	56
1934	Lou Gehrig, New York	49				1998	Ken Griffey, Jr., Seattle	56
1935	Jimmy Foxx, Philadelphia; Hank Greenberg, Detroit	36	1968	Frank Howard, Washington	44	1999	Ken Griffey, Jr., Seattle	48
						2000	Tony Glaus, Anaheim	47

1. Split season because of players' strike. 2. Season ended on August 12 because of a players' strike.

AMERICAN LEAGUE BATTING CHAMPIONS

Year	Player, team	Avg	Year	Player, team	Avg	Year	Player, team	Avg
1901	Nap Lajoie, Philadelphia	.422	1934	Lou Gehrig, New York	.363	1967	Carl Yastrzemski, Boston	.326
1902	Ed Delahanty, Washington	.376	1935	Buddy Myer, Washington	.349	1968	Carl Yastrzemski, Boston	.301
1903	Nap Lajoie, Cleveland	.355	1936	Luke Appling, Chicago	.388	1969	Rod Carew, Minnesota	.332
1904	Nap Lajoie, Cleveland	.381	1937	Charley Gehringer, Detroit	.371	1970	Alex Johnson, California	.329
1905	Elmer Flick, Cleveland	.306	1938	Jimmy Foxx, Boston	.349	1971	Tony Oliva, Minnesota	.337
1906	George Stone, St. Louis	.358	1939	Joe DiMaggio, New York	.381	1972	Rod Carew, Minnesota	.318
1907	Ty Cobb, Detroit	.350	1940	Joe DiMaggio, New York	.352	1973	Rod Carew, Minnesota	.350
1908	Ty Cobb, Detroit	.324	1941	Ted Williams, Boston	.406	1974	Rod Carew, Minnesota	.364
1909	Ty Cobb, Detroit	.377	1942	Ted Williams, Boston	.356	1975	Rod Carew, Minnesota	.359
1910	Ty Cobb, Detroit	.385	1943	Luke Appling, Chicago	.328	1976	George Brett, Kansas City	.333
1911	Ty Cobb, Detroit	.420	1944	Lou Boudreau, Cleveland	.327	1977	Rod Carew, Minnesota	.388
1912	Ty Cobb, Detroit	.410	1945	George Sternweiss, New York	.309	1978	Rod Carew, Minnesota	.333
1913	Ty Cobb, Detroit	.390				1979	Fred Lynn, Boston	.333
1914	Ty Cobb, Detroit	.368	1946	Mickey Vernon, Washington	.353	1980	George Brett, Kansas City	.390
1915	Ty Cobb, Detroit	.369	1947	Ted Williams, Boston	.343	1981[1]	Carney Lansford, Boston	.336
1916	Tris Speaker, Cleveland	.386	1948	Ted Williams, Boston	.369	1982	Willie Wilson, Kansas City	.332
1917	Ty Cobb, Detroit	.383	1949	George Kell, Detroit	.343	1983	Wade Boggs, Boston	.361
1918	Ty Cobb, Detroit	.382	1950	Billy Goodman, Boston	.354	1984	Don Mattingly, New York	.343
1919	Ty Cobb, Detroit	.384	1951	Ferris Fain, Philadelphia	.344	1985	Wade Boggs, Boston	.368
1920	George Sisler, St. Louis	.407	1952	Ferris Fain, Philadelphia	.327	1986	Wade Boggs, Boston	.357
1921	Harry Heilmann, Detroit	.394	1953	Mickey Vernon, Washington	.337	1987	Wade Boggs, Boston	.363
1922	George Sisler, St. Louis	.420	1954	Bobby Avila, Cleveland	.341	1988	Wade Boggs, Boston	.366
1923	Harry Heilmann, Detroit	.403	1955	Al Kaline, Detroit	.340	1989	Kirby Puckett, Minnesota	.339
1924	Babe Ruth, New York	.378	1956	Mickey Mantle, New York	.353	1990	George Brett, Kansas City	.328
1925	Harry Heilmann, Detroit	.393	1957	Ted Williams, Boston	.388	1991	Julio Franco, Texas	.341
1926	Heinie Manush, Detroit	.378	1958	Ted Williams, Boston	.328	1992	Edgar Martinez, Seattle	.343
1927	Harry Heilmann, Detroit	.398	1959	Harvey Kuenn, Detroit	.353	1993	John Olerud, Toronto	.363
1928	Goose Goslin, Washington	.379	1960	Pete Runnels, Boston	.320	1994[2]	Paul O'Neill, New York	.359
1929	Lew Fonseca, Cleveland	.369	1961	Norman Cash, Detroit	.361	1995	Edgar Martinez, Seattle	.356
1930	Al Simmons, Philadelphia	.381	1962	Pete Runnels, Boston	.326	1996	Alex Rodriguez, Seattle	.358
1931	Al Simmons, Philadelphia	.390	1963	Carl Yastrzemski, Boston	.321	1997	Frank Thomas, Chicago	.347
1932	Dale Alexander, Detroit-Boston	.367	1964	Tony Oliva, Minnesota	.323	1998	Bernie Williams, New York	.339
			1965	Tony Oliva, Minnesota	.321	1999	Nomar Garciaparra, Boston	.357
1933	Jimmy Foxx, Philadelphia	.356	1966	Frank Robinson, Baltimore	.316	2000	Nomar Garciaparra, Boston	.372

1. Split season because of players' strike. 2. Season ended on August 12 because of a players' strike.

NATIONAL LEAGUE HOME RUN CHAMPIONS

Year	Player, team	No.	Year	Player, team	No.	Year	Player, team	No.
1876	George Hall, Philadelphia Athletics	5	1897	Nap Lajoie, Philadelphia	10	1923	Cy Williams, Philadelphia	41
			1898	James Colins, Boston	14	1924	Jacques Fournier, Brooklyn	27
1877	George Shaffer, Louisville	3	1899	John Freeman, Washington	25	1925	Rogers Hornsby, St. Louis	39
1878	Paul Hines, Providence	4	1900	Herman Long, Boston	12	1926	Hack Wilson, Chicago	21
1879	Charles Jones, Boston	9	1901	Sam Crawford, Cincinnati	16	1927	Hack Wilson, Chicago; Cy Williams, Philadelphia	30
1880	James O'Rourke, Boston; Harry Stovey, Worcester	6	1902	Tom Leach, Pittsburgh	6			
			1903	James Sheckard, Brooklyn	9	1928	Hack Wilson, Chicago; Jim Bottomley, St. Louis	31
1881	Dan Brouthers, Buffalo	8	1904	Harry Lumley, Brooklyn	9			
1882	George Wood, Detroit	7	1905	Fred Odwell, Cincinnati	9	1929	Chuck Klein, Philadelphia	43
1883	William Ewing, New York	10	1906	Tim Jordan, Bklyn	12	1930	Hack Wilson, Chicago	56
1884	Ed Williamson, Chicago	27	1907	David Brain, Boston	10	1931	Chuck Klein, Philadelphia	31
1885	Abner Dalrymple, Chicago	11	1908	Tim Jordan, Brooklyn	12	1932	Chuck Klein, Philadelphia; Mel Ott, New York	38
1886	Arthur Richardson, Detroit	11	1909	John Murray, New York	7			
1887	Roger Connor, New York; Wm. O'Brien, Washington	17	1910	Fred Beck, Boston; Frank Schulte, Chicago	10	1933	Chuck Klein, Philadelphia	28
						1934	Mel Ott, New York; Rip Collins, St. Louis	35
1888	Roger Connor, New York	14	1911	Frank Schulte, Chicago	21			
1889	Sam Thompson, Philadelphia	20	1912	Henry Zimmerman, Chicago	14	1935	Wally Berger, Boston	34
			1913	Cliff Cravath, Philadelphia	19	1936	Mel Ott, New York	33
1890	Tom Burns, Brooklyn; Mike Tiernan, New York	13	1914	Cliff Cravath, Philadelphia	19	1937	Mel Ott, New York; Joe Medwick, St. Louis	31
			1915	Cliff Cravath, Philadelphia	24			
1891	Harry Stovey, Boston; Mike Tiernan, New York	16	1916	Davis Robertson, New York; Fred Williams, Chicago	12	1938	Mel Ott, New York	36
						1939	John Mize, St. Louis	28
1892	Jim Holliday, Cincinnati	13	1917	Davis Robertson, New York; Cliff Cravath, Philadelphia	12	1940	John Mize, St. Louis	43
1893	Ed Delahanty, Philadelphia	19				1941	Dolph Camilli, Brooklyn	34
1894	Hugh Duffy, Boston; Robert Lowe, Boston	18	1918	Cliff Cravath, Philadelphia	8	1942	Mel Ott, New York	30
			1919	Cliff Cravath, Philadelphia	12	1943	Bill Nicholson, Chicago	29
1895	Bill Joyce, Washington	17	1920	Cy Williams, Philadelphia	15	1944	Bill Nicholson, Chicago	33
1896	Ed Delahanty, Philadelphia; Sam Thompson, Philadelphia	13	1921	George Kelly, New York	23	1945	Tommy Holmes, Boston	28
			1922	Rogers Hornsby, St. Louis	42	1946	Ralph Kiner, Pittsburgh	23

Year	Player, team	No.	Year	Player, team	No.	Year	Player, team	No.
1947	Ralph Kiner, Pittsburgh; John Mize, New York	51	1964	Willie Mays, San Francisco	47	1984	Mike Schmidt, Philadelphia; Dale Murphy, Atlanta	36
1948	Ralph Kiner, Pittsburgh; John Mize, New York	40	1965	Willie Mays, San Francisco	52	1985	Dale Murphy, Atlanta	37
1949	Ralph Kiner, Pittsburgh	54	1966	Henry Aaron, Atlanta	44	1986	Mike Schmidt, Philadelphia	37
1950	Ralph Kiner, Pittsburgh	47	1967	Henry Aaron, Atlanta	39	1987	Andre Dawson, Chicago	49
1951	Ralph Kiner, Pittsburgh	42	1968	Willie McCovey, San Francisco	36	1988	Darryl Strawberry, New York	39
1952	Ralph Kiner, Pittsburgh; Hank Sauer, Chicago	37	1969	Willie McCovey, San Francisco	45	1989	Kevin Mitchell, San Francisco	47
1953	Ed Mathews, Milwaukee	47	1970	Johnny Bench, Cincinnati	45	1990	Ryne Sandberg, Chicago	40
1954	Ted Kluszewski, Cincinnati	49	1971	Willie Stargell, Pittsburgh	48	1991	Howard Johnson, New York	38
1955	Willie Mays, New York	51	1972	Johnny Bench, Cincinnati	40	1992	Fred McGriff, San Diego	35
1956	Duke Snider, Brooklyn	43	1973	Willie Stargell, Pittsburgh	44	1993	Barry Bonds, San Francisco	46
1957	Henry Aaron, Milwaukee	44	1974	Mike Schmidt, Philadelphia	36	1994²	Matt Williams, San Francisco	43
1958	Ernie Banks, Chicago	47	1975	Mike Schmidt, Philadelphia	38	1995	Dante Bichette, Colorado	40
1959	Ed Mathews, Milwaukee	46	1976	Mike Schmidt, Philadelphia	38	1996	Andreas Galarraga, Colorado	40
1960	Ernie Banks, Chicago	41	1977	George Foster, Cincinnati	52	1997	Larry Walker, Colorado	49
1961	Orlando Cepeda, San Francisco	46	1978	George Foster, Cincinnati	40	1998	Mark McGwire, St. Louis	70
1962	Willie Mays, San Francisco	49	1979	Dave Kingman, Chicago	48	1999	Mark McGwire, St. Louis	65
1963	Henry Aaron, Milwaukee; Willie McCovey, San Francisco	44	1980	Mike Schmidt, Philadelphia	48	2000	Sammy Sosa, Chicago	50
			1981¹	Mike Schmidt, Philadelphia	31			
			1982	Dave Kingman, New York	37			
			1983	Mike Schmidt, Philadelphia	40			

1. Split season because of players' strike. 2. Season ended on August 12 because of a players' strike.

NATIONAL LEAGUE BATTING CHAMPIONS

Year	Player, team	Avg	Year	Player, team	Avg	Year	Player, team	Avg
1876	Roscoe Barnes, Chicago	.404	1914	Jake Daubert, Brooklyn	.329	1954	Willie Mays, New York	.345
1877	Jim White, Boston	.385	1915	Larry Doyle, New York	.320	1955	Richie Ashburn, Philadelphia	.338
1878	Abner Dalrymple, Milwaukee	.356	1916	Hal Chase, Cincinnati	.339	1956	Henry Aaron, Milwaukee	.328
1879	Cap Anson, Chicago	.407	1917	Edd Roush, Cincinnati	.341	1957	Stan Musial, St. Louis	.351
1880	George Gore, Chicago	.365	1918	Zack Wheat, Brooklyn	.335	1958	Richie Ashburn, Philadelphia	.350
1881	Cap Anson, Chicago	.399	1919	Edd Roush, Cincinnati	.321	1959	Henry Aaron, Milwaukee	.355
1882	Dan Brouthers, Buffalo	.367	1920	Rogers Hornsby, St. Louis	.370	1960	Dick Groat, Pittsburgh	.325
1883	Dan Brouthers, Buffalo	.371	1921	Rogers Hornsby, St. Louis	.397	1961	Roberto Clemente, Pittsburgh	.351
1884	James O'Rourke, Buffalo	.350	1922	Rogers Hornsby, St. Louis	.401			
1885	Roger Connor, New York	.371	1923	Rogers Hornsby, St. Louis	.384	1962	Tommy Davis, Los Angeles	.346
1886	King Kelly, Chicago	.388	1924	Rogers Hornsby, St. Louis	.424	1963	Tommy Davis, Los Angeles	.326
1887	Cap Anson, Chicago	.421	1925	Rogers Hornsby, St. Louis	.403	1964	Roberto Clemente, Pittsburgh	.339
1888	Cap Anson, Chicago	.343	1926	Gene Hargrave, Cincinnati	.353			
1889	Dan Brouthers, Boston	.373	1927	Paul Waner; Pittsburgh	.380	1965	Roberto Clemente, Pittsburgh	.329
1890	John Glasscock, New York	.336	1928	Rogers Hornsby, Boston	.387			
1891	William Hamilton, Philadelphia	.338	1929	Lefty O'Doul, Philadelphia	.398	1966	Matty Alou, Pittsburgh	.342
			1930	Bill Terry, New York	.401	1967	Roberto Clemente, Pittsburgh	.357
1892	Dan Brouthers, Brooklyn; Clarence Childs, Cleveland	.335	1931	Chick Hafey, St. Louis	.349			
			1932	Lefty O'Doul, Brooklyn	.368	1968	Pete Rose, Cincinnati	.335
1893	Hugh Duffy, Boston	.378	1933	Chuck Klein, Philadelphia	.368	1969	Pete Rose, Cincinnati	.348
1894	Hugh Duffy, Boston	.438	1934	Paul Waner, Pittsburgh	.362	1970	Rico Carty, Atlanta	.366
1895	Jesse Burkett, Cleveland	.423	1935	Arky Vaughan, Pittsburgh	.385	1971	Joe Torre, St. Louis	.363
1896	Jesse Burkett, Cleveland	.410	1936	Paul Waner, Pittsburgh	.373	1972	Billy Williams, Chicago	.333
1897	Willie Keeler, Baltimore	.432	1937	Joe Medwick, St. Louis	.374	1973	Pete Rose, Cincinnati	.338
1898	Willie Keeler, Baltimore	.379	1938	Ernie Lombardi, Cincinnati	.342	1974	Ralph Garr, Atlanta	.353
1899	Ed Delahanty, Philadelphia	.408	1939	John Mize, St. Louis	.349	1975	Bill Madlock, Chicago	.354
1900	Honus Wagner, Pittsburgh	.381	1940	Debs Garms, Pittsburgh	.355	1976	Bill Madlock, Chicago	.339
1901	Jesse Burkett, St. Louis	.382	1941	Pete Reiser, Brooklyn	.343	1977	Dave Parker, Pittsburgh	.338
1902	Clarence Beaumont, Pittsburgh	.357	1942	Ernie Lombardi, Boston	.330	1978	Dave Parker, Pittsburgh	.334
			1943	Stan Musial, St. Louis	.357	1979	Keith Hernandez, St. Louis	.344
1903	Honus Wagner, Pittsburgh	.355	1944	Dixie Walker, Brooklyn	.357	1980	Bill Buckner, Chicago	.324
1904	Honus Wagner, Pittsburgh	.349	1945	Phil Cavarretta, Chicago	.355	1981¹	Bill Madlock, Pittsburgh	.341
1905	Cy Seymour, Cincinnati	.377	1946	Stan Musial, St. Louis	.365	1982	Al Oliver, Montreal	.331
1906	Honus Wagner, Pittsburgh	.339	1947	Harry Walker, St. Louis-Philadelphia	.363	1983	Bill Madlock, Pittsburgh	.323
1907	Honus Wagner, Pittsburgh	.350				1984	Tony Gwynn, San Diego	.351
1908	Honus Wagner, Pittsburgh	.354	1948	Stan Musial, St. Louis	.376	1985	Willie McGee, St. Louis	.353
1909	Honus Wagner, Pittsburgh	.339	1949	Jackie Robinson, Brooklyn	.342	1986	Tim Raines, Montreal	.334
1910	Sherwood Magee, Philadelphia	.331	1950	Stan Musial, St. Louis	.346	1987	Tony Gwynn, San Diego	.370
			1951	Stan Musial, St. Louis	.355	1988	Tony Gwynn, San Diego	.313
1911	Honus Wagner, Pittsburgh	.334	1952	Stan Musial, St. Louis	.336	1989	Tony Gwynn, San Diego	.336
1912	Henry Zimmerman, Chicago	.372	1953	Carl Furillo, Brooklyn	.344	1990	Willie McGee, St. Louis	.335
1913	Jake Daubert, Brooklyn	.350				1991	Terry Pendleton, Atlanta	.319

Year	Player, team	Avg	Year	Player, team	Avg	Year	Player, team	Avg
1992	Gary Sheffield, San Diego	.330	1995	Tony Gwynn, San Diego	.368	1998	Larry Walker, Colorado	.363
1993	Andres Galarraga, Colorado	.370	1996	Tony Gwynn, San Diego	.353	1999	Larry Walker, Colorado	.379
1994[2]	Tony Gwynn, San Diego	.394	1997	Tony Gwynn, San Diego	.372	2000	Todd Helton, Colorado	.372

1. Split season because of players' strike. 2. Season ended on August 12 because of a players' strike.

AMERICAN LEAGUE PENNANT WINNERS

Year	Club	Manager	Won	Lost	Pct	Year	Club	Manager	Won	Lost	Pct
1901	Chicago	Clark C. Griffith	83	53	.610	1953[1]	New York	Casey Stengel	99	52	.656
1902	Philadelphia	Connie Mack	83	53	.610	1954	Cleveland	Al Lopez	111	43	.721
1903[1]	Boston	Jimmy Collins	91	47	.659	1955	New York	Casey Stengel	96	58	.623
1904[2]	Boston	Jimmy Collins	95	59	.617	1956[1]	New York	Casey Stengel	97	57	.630
1905	Philadelphia	Connie Mack	92	56	.622	1957	New York	Casey Stengel	98	56	.636
1906[1]	Chicago	Fielder A. Jones	93	58	.616	1958[1]	New York	Casey Stengel	92	62	.597
1907	Detroit	Hugh A. Jennings	92	58	.613	1959	Chicago	Al Lopez	94	60	.610
1908	Detroit	Hugh A. Jennings	90	63	.588	1960	New York	Casey Stengel	97	57	.630
1909	Detroit	Hugh A. Jennings	98	54	.645	1961[1]	New York	Ralph Houk	109	53	.673
1910[1]	Philadelphia	Connie Mack	102	48	.680	1962[1]	New York	Ralph Houk	96	66	.593
1911[1]	Philadelphia	Connie Mack	101	50	.669	1963	New York	Ralph Houk	104	57	.646
1912[1]	Boston	J. Garland Stahl	105	47	.691	1964	New York	Yogi Berra	99	63	.611
1913[1]	Philadelphia	Connie Mack	96	57	.627	1965	Minnesota	Sam Mele	102	60	.630
1914	Philadelphia	Connie Mack	99	53	.651	1966[1]	Baltimore	Hank Bauer	97	53	.606
1915[1]	Boston	William F. Carrigan	101	50	.669	1967	Boston	Dick Williams	92	70	.568
1916[1]	Boston	William F. Carrigan	91	63	.591	1968[1]	Detroit	Mayo Smith	103	59	.636
1917[1]	Chicago	Clarence H. Rowland	100	54	.649	1969	Baltimore[3]	Earl Weaver	109	53	.673
1918[1]	Boston	Ed Barrow	75	51	.595	1970[1]	Baltimore[3]	Earl Weaver	108	54	.667
1919	Chicago	William Gleason	88	52	.629	1971	Baltimore[4]	Earl Weaver	101	57	.639
1920[1]	Cleveland	Tris Speaker	98	56	.636	1972[1]	Oakland[5]	Dick Williams	93	62	.600
1921	New York	Miller J. Huggins	98	55	.641	1973[1]	Oakland[6]	Dick Williams	94	68	.580
1922	New York	Miller J. Huggins	94	60	.610	1974[1]	Oakland[6]	Alvin Dark	90	72	.556
1923[1]	New York	Miller J. Huggins	98	54	.645	1975	Boston[4]	Darrell Johnson	95	65	.594
1924[1]	Washington	Stanley R. Harris	92	62	.597	1976	New York[7]	Billy Martin	97	62	.610
1925	Washington	Stanley R. Harris	96	55	.636	1977[1]	New York[7]	Billy Martin	100	62	.617
1926	New York	Miller J. Huggins	91	63	.591	1978[1]	New York[7]	Billy Martin and Bob Lemon	100	63	.613
1927[1]	New York	Miller J. Huggins	110	44	.714	1979	Baltimore[8]	Earl Weaver	102	57	.642
1928[1]	New York	Miller J. Huggins	101	53	.656	1980	Kansas City[9]	Jim Frey	97	65	.599
1929[1]	Philadelphia	Connie Mack	104	46	.693	1981	New York[10]	Gene Michael-Bob Lemon	59	48	.551*
1930[1]	Philadelphia	Connie Mack	102	52	.662	1982	Milwaukee[11]	Harvey Kuenn	95	67	.586
1931	Philadelphia	Connie Mack	107	45	.704	1983[1]	Baltimore[12]	Joe Altobelli	98	64	.605
1932[1]	New York	Joseph V. McCarthy	107	47	.695	1984[1]	Detroit[13]	Sparky Anderson	104	58	.642
1933	Washington	Joseph E. Cronin	99	53	.651	1985[1]	Kansas City[14]	Dick Howser	91	71	.562
1934	Detroit	Gordon Cochrane	101	53	.656	1986	Boston[11]	John McNamara	95	66	.590
1935[1]	Detroit	Gordon Cochrane	93	58	.616	1987	Minnesota[15]	Tom Kelly	85	77	.525
1936[1]	New York	Joseph V. McCarthy	102	51	.667	1988	Oakland[16]	Tony LaRussa	104	58	.642
1937[1]	New York	Joseph V. McCarthy	102	52	.662	1989	Oakland[17]	Tony LaRussa	99	63	.611
1938[1]	New York	Joseph V. McCarthy	99	53	.651	1990	Oakland[18]	Tony LaRussa	103	59	.636
1939[1]	New York	Joseph V. McCarthy	106	45	.702	1991	Minnesota[19]	Tom Kelly	95	67	.586
1940	Detroit	Delmar D. Baker	90	64	.584	1992	Toronto[10]	Cito Gaston	96	66	.593
1941[1]	New York	Joseph V. McCarthy	101	53	.656	1993	Toronto[12]	Cito Gaston	95	67	.586
1942	New York	Joseph V. McCarthy	103	51	.669	1994	Strike ended season Aug. 11. No playoffs, no pennant winner.				
1943[1]	New York	Joseph V. McCarthy	98	56	.636						
1944	St. Louis	Luke Sewell	89	65	.578	1995	Cleveland[20]	Mike Hargrove	100	44	.694
1945[1]	Detroit	Steve O'Neill	88	65	.575	1996	New York[21]	Joe Torre	92	70	.568
1946	Boston	Joseph E. Cronin	104	50	.675	1997	Cleveland[6]	Mike Hargrove	86	75	.534
1947[1]	New York	Stanley R. Harris	97	57	.630	1998	New York[22]	Joe Torre	114	48	.704
1948[1]	Cleveland	Lou Boudreau	97	58	.626	1999	New York[23]	Joe Torre	98	64	.605
1949[1]	New York	Casey Stengel	97	57	.630	2000	New York[24]	Joe Torre	87	74	.540
1950[1]	New York	Casey Stengel	98	56	.636						
1951[1]	New York	Casey Stengel	98	56	.636						
1952[1]	New York	Casey Stengel	95	59	.617						

* Split season because of players' strike. 1. World Series winner. 2. No World Series. 3. Defeated Minnesota, Western Division winner, in playoff. 4. Defeated Oakland, Western Division Leader, in playoff. 5. Defeated Detroit, Eastern Division winner, in playoff. 6. Defeated Baltimore, Eastern Division winner, in playoff. 7. Defeated Kansas City, Western Division winner, in playoff. 8. Defeated California, Western Division winner, in playoff. 9. Defeated New York, Eastern Division winner, in playoff. 10. Defeated Oakland, Western Division winner, in playoff. 11. Defeated California, Western Division winner, in playoff. 12. Defeated Chicago, Western Division winner, in playoff. 13. Defeated Kansas City, Western Division winner, in playoff. 14. Defeated Toronto, Eastern Division winner, in playoff. 15. Defeated Detroit, Eastern Division winner, in playoff. 16. Defeated Boston, Eastern division winner, in playoffs. 17. Defeated Toronto, Eastern Division winner, in playoffs. 18. Defeated Boston, Eastern Division winner, in playoffs. 19. Defeated Toronto, Eastern Division winner, in playoffs. 20. Defeated Seattle Mariners, Western Division winner, in playoffs. 21. Defeated Baltimore Orioles, Eastern Division wild-card team, in playoffs. 22. Defeated Cleveland Indians, Central Division winner, in playoffs. 23. Defeated Boston Red Sox, Eastern Division wild-card team, in playoffs. 24. Defeated Seattle Mariners, Western Division wild-card team, in playoffs.

NATIONAL LEAGUE PENNANT WINNERS

Year	Club	Manager	Won	Lost	Pct
1876	Chicago	Albert G. Spalding	52	14	.788
1877	Boston	Harry Wright	31	17	.646
1878	Boston	Harry Wright	41	19	.683
1879	Providence	George Wright	55	23	.705
1880	Chicago	Adrian C. Anson	67	17	.798
1881	Chicago	Adrian C. Anson	56	28	.667
1882	Chicago	Adrian C. Anson	55	29	.655
1883	Boston	John F. Morrill	63	35	.643
1884	Providence	Frank C. Bancroft	84	28	.750
1885	Chicago	Adrian C. Anson	87	25	.777
1886	Chicago	Adrian C. Anson	90	34	.726
1887	Detroit	W. H. Watkins	79	45	.637
1888	New York	James J. Mutrie	84	47	.641
1889	New York	James J. Mutrie	83	43	.659
1890	Brooklyn	Wm. H. McGunnigle	86	43	.667
1891	Boston	Frank G. Selee	87	51	.630
1892	Boston	Frank G. Selee	102	48	.680
1893	Boston	Frank G. Selee	86	44	.662
1894	Baltimore	Edward H. Hanlon	89	39	.695
1895	Baltimore	Edward H. Hanlon	87	43	.669
1896	Baltimore	Edward H. Hanlon	90	39	.698
1897	Boston	Frank G. Selee	93	39	.705
1898	Boston	Frank G. Selee	102	47	.685
1899	Brooklyn	Edward H. Hanlon	88	42	.677
1900	Brooklyn	Edward H. Hanlon	82	54	.603
1901	Pittsburgh	Fred C. Clarke	90	49	.647
1902	Pittsburgh	Fred C. Clarke	103	36	.741
1903	Pittsburgh	Fred C. Clarke	91	49	.650
1904	New York[2]	John J. McGraw	106	47	.693
1905	New York[1]	John J. McGraw	105	48	.686
1906	Chicago	Frank L. Chance	116	36	.763
1907	Chicago[1]	Frank L. Chance	107	45	.704
1908	Chicago[1]	Frank L. Chance	99	55	.643
1909	Pittsburgh[1]	Fred C. Clarke	110	42	.724
1910	Chicago	Frank L. Chance	104	50	.675
1911	New York	John J. McGraw	99	54	.647
1912	New York	John J. McGraw	103	48	.682
1913	New York	John J. McGraw	101	51	.664
1914	Boston[1]	George T. Stallings	94	59	.614
1915	Philadelphia	Patrick J. Moran	90	62	.592
1916	Brooklyn	Wilbert Robinson	94	60	.610
1917	New York	John J. McGraw	98	56	.636
1918	Chicago	Fred L. Mitchell	84	45	.651
1919	Cincinnati[1]	Patrick J. Moran	96	44	.686
1920	Brooklyn	Wilbert Robinson	93	61	.604
1921	New York[1]	John J. McGraw	94	59	.614
1922	New York[1]	John J. McGraw	93	61	.604
1923	New York	John J. McGraw	95	58	.621
1924	New York	John J. McGraw	93	60	.608
1925	Pittsburgh[1]	Wm. B. McKechnie	95	58	.621
1926	St. Louis[1]	Rogers Hornsby	89	65	.578
1927	Pittsburgh	Donie Bush	94	60	.610
1928	St. Louis	Wm. B. McKechnie	95	59	.617
1929	Chicago	Joseph V. McCarthy	98	54	.645
1930	St. Louis	Gabby Street	92	62	.597
1931	St. Louis[1]	Gabby Street	101	53	.656
1932	Chicago	Charles J. Grimm	90	64	.584
1933	New York[1]	William H. Terry	91	61	.599
1934	St. Louis[1]	Frank F. Frisch	95	58	.621
1935	Chicago	Charles J. Grimm	100	54	.649
1936	New York	William H. Terry	92	62	.597
1937	New York	William H. Terry	95	57	.625
1938	Chicago	Gabby Hartnett	89	63	.586
1939	Cincinnati	Wm. B. McKechnie	97	57	.630
1940	Cincinnati[1]	Wm. B. McKechnie	100	53	.654
1941	Brooklyn	Leo E. Durocher	100	54	.649
1942	St. Louis[1]	Wm. H. Southworth	106	48	.688
1943	St. Louis	Wm. H. Southworth	105	49	.682
1944	St. Louis[1]	Wm. H. Southworth	105	49	.682
1945	Chicago	Charles J. Grimm	98	56	.636
1946	St. Louis[1]	Edwin H. Dyer	98	58	.628
1947	Brooklyn	Burton E. Shotton	94	60	.610
1948	Boston	Wm. H. Southworth	91	62	.595
1949	Brooklyn	Burton E. Shotton	97	57	.630
1950	Philadelphia	Edwin M. Sawyer	91	63	.591
1951	New York	Leo E. Durocher	98	59	.624
1952	Brooklyn	Charles W. Dressen	96	57	.630
1953	Brooklyn	Charles W. Dressen	105	49	.682
1954	New York[1]	Leo E. Durocher	97	57	.630
1955	Brooklyn[1]	Walter Alston	98	55	.641
1956	Brooklyn	Walter Alston	93	61	.604
1957	Milwaukee1	Fred Haney	95	59	.617
1958	Milwaukee	Fred Haney	92	62	.597
1959	Los Angeles[1]	Walter Alston	88	68	.564
1960	Pittsburgh[1]	Danny Murtaugh	95	59	.617
1961	Cincinnati	Fred Hutchinson	93	61	.604
1962	San Francisco	Alvin Dark	103	62	.624
1963	Los Angeles[1]	Walter Alston	99	63	.611
1964	St. Louis[1]	Johnny Keane	93	69	.574
1965	Los Angeles[1]	Walter Alston	97	65	.599
1966	Los Angeles	Walter Alston	95	67	.586
1967	St. Louis[1]	Red Schoendienst	101	60	.627
1968	St. Louis	Red Schoendienst	97	65	.599
1969	New York[1] [3]	Gil Hodges	100	62	.617
1970	Cincinnati[4]	Sparky Anderson	102	60	.630
1971	Pittsburgh[1] [5]	Danny Murtaugh	97	65	.599
1972	Cincinnati[4]	Sparky Anderson	95	59	.617
1973	New York[6]	Yogi Berra	82	79	.509
1974	Los Angeles[4]	Walter Alston	102	60	.630
1975	Cincinnati[1] [4]	Sparky Anderson	108	54	.667
1976	Cincinnati[7] [1]	Sparky Anderson	102	60	.630
1977	Los Angeles[7]	Tom Lasorda	98	64	.605
1978	Los Angeles[7]	Tom Lasorda	95	67	.586
1979[1]	Pittsburgh[6]	Chuck Tanner	98	64	.605
1980[1]	Philadelphia[8]	Dallas Green	91	71	.562
1981	Los Angeles[1] [9]	Tom Lasorda	63	47	.573
1982[1]	St. Louis[3]	Whitey Herzog	92	70	.568
1983	Philadelphia[11]	Paul Owens	90	72	.556
1984	San Diego[12]	Dick Williams	92	70	.568
1985	St. Louis[11]	Whitey Herzog	101	61	.623
1986	New York[8]	Dave Johnson	108	54	.667
1987	St. Louis[5]	Whitey Herzog	95	67	.586
1988	Los Angeles[10]	Tom Lasorda	94	67	.584
1989	San Francisco[12]	Roger Craig	92	70	.568
1990	Cincinnati[4]	Lou Piniella	91	71	.562
1991	Atlanta[4]	Bobby Cox	94	68	.580
1992	Atlanta[4]	Bobby Cox	98	64	.605
1993	Philadelphia[3]	Jim Fregosi	97	65	.599
1994	Strike ended season Aug. 11. No playoffs, no pennant winner.				
1995	Atlanta[13]	Bobby Cox	90	54	.625
1996	Atlanta[14]	Bobby Cox	96	66	.593
1997	Florida[15]	Jim Leyland	92	70	.568
1998	San Diego[16]	Bruce Bochy	98	64	.605
1999	Atlanta[17]	Bobby Cox	103	59	.636
2000	New York[18]	Bobby Valentine	94	68	.580

* Split season because of players' strike. 1. World Series winner. 2. No World Series. 3. Defeated Atlanta, Western Division winner, in playoff. 4. Defeated Pittsburgh, Eastern Division winner, in playoff. 5. Defeated San Francisco, Western Division winner, in playoff. 6. Defeated Cincinnati, Western Division winner, in playoff. 7. Defeated Philadelphia, Eastern Division winner, in playoff. 8. Defeated Houston, Western Division winner, in playoff. 9. Defeated Montreal, Eastern Division winner, in playoff. 10. Defeated New York, Eastern Division winner, in playoff. 11. Defeated Los Angeles, Western Division winner, in playoff. 12. Defeated Chicago, Eastern Division champion, in playoff. 13. Defeated Cincinnati, Central Division winner, in playoff. 14. Defeated St. Louis, Central Division winner, in playoff. 15. Eastern Division wildcard Florida defeated Atlanta, Eastern Division winner, in playoff. 16. Defeated Atlanta, Eastern Division winner, in playoff. 17. Defeated New York, Eastern Division wild card team, in playoff. 18. Eastern Division wild card New York defeated Central Division winner St. Louis in playoff.

MOST VALUABLE PLAYERS
(Baseball Writers Association selections)

American League

1931	Lefty Grove, Philadelphia
1932–33	Jimmy Foxx, Philadelphia
1934	Mickey Cochrane, Detroit
1935	Hank Greenberg, Detroit
1936	Lou Gehrig, New York
1937	Charlie Gehringer, Detroit
1938	Jimmy Foxx, Boston
1939	Joe DiMaggio, New York
1940	Hank Greenberg, Detroit
1941	Joe DiMaggio, New York
1942	Joe Gordon, New York
1943	Spurgeon Chandler, New York
1944–45	Hal Newhouser, Detroit
1946	Ted Williams, Boston
1947	Joe DiMaggio, New York
1948	Lou Boudreau, Cleveland
1949	Ted Williams, Boston
1950	Phil Rizzuto, New York
1951	Yogi Berra, New York
1952	Bobby Shantz, Philadelphia
1953	Al Rosen, Cleveland
1954–55	Yogi Berra, New York
1956–57	Mickey Mantle, New York
1958	Jackie Jensen, Boston
1959	Nellie Fox, Chicago
1960–61	Roger Maris, New York
1962	Mickey Mantle, New York
1963	Elston Howard, New York
1964	Brooks Robinson, Baltimore
1965	Zoilo Versalles, Minnesota
1966	Frank Robinson, Baltimore
1967	Carl Yastrzemski, Boston
1968	Dennis McLain, Detroit
1969	Harmon Killebrew, Minnesota
1970	John (Boog) Powell, Baltimore
1971	Vida Blue, Oakland
1972	Dick Allen, Chicago
1973	Reggie Jackson, Oakland
1974	Jeff Burroughs, Texas
1975	Fred Lynn, Boston
1976	Thurman Munson, New York
1977	Rod Carew, Minnesota
1978	Jim Rice, Boston
1979	Don Baylor, California
1980	George Brett, Kansas City
1981	Rollie Fingers, Milwaukee
1982	Robin Yount, Milwaukee
1983	Cal Ripken, Jr., Baltimore
1984	Willie Hernandez, Detroit
1985	Don Mattingly, New York
1986	Roger Clemens, Boston
1987	George Bell, Toronto
1988	Jose Canseco, Oakland
1989	Robin Yount, Milwaukee
1990	Rickey Henderson, Oakland
1991	Cal Ripken, Jr., Baltimore
1992	Dennis Eckersley, Oakland
1993	Frank Thomas, Chicago
1994	Frank Thomas, Chicago
1995	Mo Vaughn, Boston
1996	Juan Gonzalez, Texas
1997	Ken Griffey, Jr., Seattle
1998	Juan Gonzalez, Texas
1999	Ivan Rodriguez, Texas

National League

1931	Frank Frisch, St. Louis
1932	Chuck Klein, Philadelphia
1933	Carl Hubbell, New York
1934	Dizzy Dean, St. Louis
1935	Gabby Hartnett, Chicago
1936	Carl Hubbell, New York
1937	Joe Medwick, St. Louis
1938	Ernie Lombardi, Cincinnati
1939	Bucky Walters, Cincinnati
1940	Frank McCormick, Cincinnati
1941	Dolph Camilli, Brooklyn
1942	Mort Cooper, St. Louis
1943	Stan Musial, St. Louis
1944	Marty Marion, St. Louis
1945	Phil Cavarretta, Chicago
1946	Stan Musial, St. Louis
1947	Bob Elliott, Boston
1948	Stan Musial, St. Louis
1949	Jackie Robinson, Brooklyn
1950	Jim Konstanty, Philadelphia
1951	Roy Campanella, Brooklyn
1952	Hank Sauer, Chicago
1953	Roy Campanella, Brooklyn
1954	Willie Mays, New York
1955	Roy Campanella, Brooklyn

1956	Don Newcombe, Brooklyn
1957	Henry Aaron, Milwaukee
1958–59	Ernie Banks, Chicago
1960	Dick Groat, Pittsburgh
1961	Frank Robinson, Cincinnati
1962	Maury Wills, Los Angeles
1963	Sandy Koufax, Los Angeles
1964	Ken Boyer, St. Louis
1965	Willie Mays, San Francisco
1966	Roberto Clemente, Pittsburgh
1967	Orlando Cepeda, St. Louis
1968	Bob Gibson, St. Louis
1969	Willie McCovey, San Francisco
1970	Johnny Bench, Cincinnati
1971	Joe Torre, St. Louis
1972	Johnny Bench, Cincinnati
1973	Pete Rose, Cincinnati
1974	Steve Garvey, Los Angeles
1975–76	Joe Morgan, Cincinnati
1977	George Foster, Cincinnati
1978	Dave Parker, Pittsburgh
1979	Willie Stargell, Pittsburgh
1979	Keith Hernandez, St. Louis
1980	Mike Schmidt, Philadelphia
1981	Mike Schmidt, Philadelphia
1982	Dale Murphy, Atlanta
1983	Dale Murphy, Atlanta
1984	Ryne Sandberg, Chicago
1985	Willie McGee, St. Louis
1986	Mike Schmidt, Philadelphia
1987	Andre Dawson, Chicago
1988	Kirk Gibson, Los Angeles
1989	Kevin Mitchell, San Francisco
1990	Barry Bonds, Pittsburgh
1991	Terry Pendleton, Atlanta
1992	Barry Bonds, Pittsburgh
1993	Barry Bonds, San Francisco
1994	Jeff Bagwell, Houston
1995	Barry Larkin, Cincinnati
1996	Ken Caminiti, San Diego
1997	Larry Walker, Colorado
1998	Sammy Sosa, Chicago
1999	Chipper Jones, Atlanta

CY YOUNG AWARD

1956	Don Newcombe, Brooklyn N.L.
1957	Warren Spahn, Milwaukee N.L.
1958	Bob Turley, New York A.L.
1959	Early Wynn, Chicago A.L.
1960	Vernon Law, Pittsburgh, N.L.
1961	Whitey Ford, New York A.L.
1962	Don Drysdale, Los Angeles N.L.
1963	Sandy Koufax, Los Angeles N.L.

1964	Dean Chance, Los Angeles A.L.
1965	Sandy Koufax, Los Angeles N.L.
1966	Sandy Koufax, Los Angeles N.L.
1967	Jim Lonborg, Boston A.L.; Mike McCormick, San Francisco N.L.
1968	Dennis McLain, Detroit A.L.; Bob Gibson, St. Louis N.L.

1969	Mike Cuellar, Baltimore A.L. and Dennis McLain, Detroit A.L. (tied); Tom Seaver, New York N.L.
1970	Jim Perry, Minnesota A.L.; Bob Gibson, St. Louis N.L.
1971	Vida Blue, Oakland A.L.; Ferguson Jenkins, Chicago N.L.
1972	Gaylord Perry, Cleveland A.L.; Steve Carlton, Philadelphia N.L.

1973	Jim Palmer, Baltimore A.L.; Tom Seaver, New York N.L.
1974	Catfish Hunter, Oakland A.L.; Mike Marshall, Los Angeles N.L.
1975	Jim Palmer, Baltimore A.L.; Tom Seaver, New York N.L.
1976	Jim Palmer, Baltimore A.L.; Randy Jones, San Diego N.L.
1977	Sparky Lyle, New York, A.L.; Steve Carlton, Philadelphia N.L.
1978	Ron Guidry, New York, A.L.; Gaylord Perry, San Diego N.L.
1979	Mike Flanagan, Baltimore A.L.; Bruce Sutter, Chicago, N.L.
1980	Steve Stone, Baltimore, A.L.; Steve Carlton, Philadelphia, N.L.
1981	Rollie Fingers, Milwaukee, A.L.; Fernando Valenzuela, Los Angeles, N.L.

1982	Pete Vuckovich, Milwaukee, A.L.; Steve Carlton, Philadelphia, N.L.
1983	LaMarr Hoyt, Chicago, A.L.; John Denny, Philadelphia, N.L.
1984	Willie Hernandez, Detroit, A.L.; Rick Sutcliffe, Chicago, N.L.
1985	Bret Saberhagen, A.L.; Dwight Gooden, N.L.
1986	Roger Clemens, Boston, A.L.; Mike Scott, Houston, N.L.
1987	Roger Clemens, Boston, A.L.; Steve Bedrosian, Philadelphia, N.L.
1988	Frank Viola, Minnesota, A.L.; Orel Hershiser, Los Angeles, N.L.
1989	Bret Saberhagen, Kansas, A.L.; Mark Davis, San Diego, N.L.

1990	Bob Welch, Oakland, A.L.; Doug Drabek, Pittsburgh, N.L.
1991	Roger Clemens, Boston, A.L.; Tom Glavine, Atlanta, N.L.
1992	Dennis Eckersley, Oakland, A.L.; Greg Maddux, Atlanta, N.L.
1993	Jack McDowell, Chicago, A.L.; Greg Maddux, Atlanta, N.L.
1994	David Cone, Kansas, A.L.; Greg Maddux, Atlanta, N.L.
1995	Randy Johnson, Seattle, A.L.; Greg Maddux, Atlanta, N.L.
1996	Pat Hentgen, Toronto, A.L.; John Smoltz, Atlanta, N.L.
1997	Roger Clemens, Toronto, A.L.; Pedro Martinez, Montreal, N.L.
1998	Roger Clemens, Toronto, A.L.; Tom Glavine, Atlanta, N.L.
1999	Pedro Martinez, Boston, A.L.; Randy Johnson, Arizona, N.L.

MAJOR LEAGUE LIFETIME RECORDS

(Through 2000)

Wins
*Indicates left-handed pitcher.

		Yrs	GS	W	L
1	Cy Young	22	815	511	316
2	Walter Johnson	21	666	417	279
3	Christy Mathewson	17	551	373	188
	Grover Alexander	20	598	373	208
5	Warren Spahn*	21	665	363	245
6	Kid Nichols	15	561	361	208
	Pud Galvin	14	682	361	308
8	Tim Keefe	14	594	342	225
9	Steve Carlton*	24	709	329	244
10	Eddie Plank*	17	527	327	193
11	John Clarkson	12	518	326	177
12	Don Sutton	23	756	324	256
	Nolan Ryan	27	773	324	292
14	Phil Niekro	24	716	318	274
15	Gaylord Perry	22	690	314	265
16	Old Hoss Radbourn	12	503	311	194
	Tom Seaver	20	647	311	205
18	Mickey Welch	13	549	308	209
19	Lefty Grove*	17	456	300	141
	Early Wynn	23	612	300	244
21	Tommy John*	26	700	288	231
22	Bert Blyleven	22	685	287	250
23	Robin Roberts	19	609	286	245
24	Tony Mullane	13	505	285	220
25	Ferguson Jenkins	19	594	284	226

Pitchers Active in 2000

		Yrs	GS	W	L
1	Roger Clemens	17	511	260	142
2	Greg Maddux	15	467	240	135
3	Tom Glavine*	14	434	208	125
4	Dwight Gooden	16	410	194	112
5	David Cone	15	390	184	116
6	Chuck Finley*	14	413	181	151
7	Randy Johnson*	13	357	179	95
8	Kevin Brown	14	380	170	114
9	Bret Saberhagen	16	368	166	115
10	David Wells*	14	309	161	107

Leading Batters, by Batting Average
*Indicates left-handed hitter.
Boldface indicates player active in 2000.

		Yrs	AB	H	Avg
1	Ty Cobb*	24	11,429	4,191	.367
2	Rogers Hornsby	23	8,137	2,930	.358
3	Joe Jackson*	13	4,981	1,774	.356
4	Ed Delahanty	16	7,509	2,597	.346
5	Tris Speaker*	22	10,197	3,514	.345
6	Ted Williams*	19	7,706	2,654	.344
7	Billy Hamilton*	14	6,284	2,163	.344
8	Willie Keeler*	19	8,585	2,947	.343
9	Dan Brouthers*	19	6,711	2,296	.342
10	Babe Ruth*	22	8,399	2,873	.342
11	Harry Heilmann	17	7,787	2,660	.342
12	Pete Browning	13	4,820	1,646	.341
13	Bill Terry*	14	6,428	2,193	.341
14	George Sisler*	15	8,267	2,812	.340
15	Lou Gehrig*	17	8,001	2,721	.340
16	Jesse Burkett*	16	8,413	2,853	.339
17	**Tony Gwynn***	19	9,186	3,108	.338
18	Nap Lajoie	21	9,592	3,244	.338
19	Riggs Stephenson	14	4,508	1,515	.336
20	Al Simmons	20	8,761	2,927	.334
21	Paul Waner*	20	9,459	3,152	.333
22	Eddie Collins*	25	9,951	3,313	.333
23	Stan Musial*	22	10,972	3,630	.331
24	Sam Thompson*	14	6,005	1,986	.331
25	Heinie Manush*	17	7,654	2,524	.330

Players Active in 2000 (3,000 at-bats minimum)

		Yrs	AB	H	Avg
1	Tony Gwynn*	19	9,186	3,108	.338
2	Mike Piazza	9	4,135	1,356	.328
3	Derek Jeter	6	3,130	1,008	.322
4	Frank Thomas	11	5,474	1,755	.32
5	Edgar Martinez	14	5,432	1,738	.32
6	Manny Ramirez	8	3,470	1,086	.31
7	Jeff Cirillo	7	3,409	1,059	.31
	Larry Walker*	12	4,906	1,528	.31
9	Alex Rodriguez	7	3,126	966	.31
10	Mark Grace*	13	7,156	2,201	.30

MAJOR LEAGUE ALL-TIME PITCHING RECORDS

(Through 2000)

Most Games Won—511, Cy Young, Cleveland N.L., 1890–98, St. Louis N.L., 1899–1900, Boston A.L., 1901–08, Cleveland A.L., 1909–11, Boston N.L., 1911.

Most Games Won, Season—59, Hoss Radbourne, Providence N.L., 1884. (Since 1900—41, Jack Chesbro, New York A.L., 1904.)

Most Consecutive Games Won—24, Carl Hubbell, New York N.L., 1936 (16) and 1937 (8).

Most Consecutive Games Won, Season—19, Tim Keefe, New York N.L., 1888; Rube Marquard, New York N.L., 1912.

Most Years Won 20 or More Games—16, Cy Young, Cleveland N.L., 1891–98, St. Louis N.L., 1899–1900, Boston A.L., 1901–04, 1907–08.

Most Shutouts—113, Walter Johnson, Washington A.L., 1907–27.

Most Shutouts, Season—16, Grover Alexander, Philadelphia N.L., 1916.

Most Consecutive Shutouts—6, Don Drysdale, Los Angeles, N.L., 1968.

Most Consecutive Scoreless Innings—59, Orel Hershiser, Los Angeles Dodgers, 1988.

Most Strikeouts—5,714, Nolan Ryan, New York N.L., California A.L., Houston N.L., 1968–1988 Texas, 1989–93.

Most Strikeouts, Season—513, Matthew Kilroy, Baltimore A.A., 1886. (Since 1900—383, Nolan Ryan, California A.L., 1973.)

Most Strikeouts, Game—21, Tom Cheney, Washington A.L., 1962, 16 innings. Nine innings: 20, Roger Clemens, Boston, A.L., 1986; Kerry Wood, Chicago, N.L., 1998.

Most Consecutive Strikeouts—10, Tom Seaver, New York N.L. vs. San Diego, April 22, 1970.

Most Games, Season—106, Mike Marshall, Los Angeles, N.L., 1974.

Most Complete Games, Season—75, William White, Cincinnati N.L., 1879. (Since 1900—48, Jack Chesbro, New York A.L., 1904.)

MAJOR LEAGUE INDIVIDUAL ALL-TIME RECORDS

(Through 2000)

Highest Batting Average, Season—.442, James O'Neill, St. Louis, A.A., 1887; .438, Hugh Duffy, Boston, N.L., 1894 (Since 1900—.424, Rogers Hornsby, St. Louis, N.L., 1924; .422, Nap Lajoie, Phil., A.L., 1901)

Most Times at Bat—14,053, Pete Rose, Cincinnati, N.L., 1963–78; Philadelphia, N.L., 1979–83; Montreal, N.L., 1984; Cincinnati, N.L., 1984–86.

Most Years Batted .300 or Better—23, Ty Cobb, Detroit A.L., 1906–26, Philadelphia A.L., 1927–28.

Most Hits—4,256, Pete Rose, Cincinnati 1963–79, Philadelphia 1980–83, Montreal 1984, Cincinnati 1984–86.

Most Hits, Season—257, George Sisler, St. Louis A.L., 1920.

Most Hits in Succession—12, Mike Higgins, Boston A.L., in four games, 1938; Walt Dropo, Detroit A.L., in three games, 1952.

Most Consecutive Games Batted Safely—56, Joe DiMaggio, New York A.L., 1941.

Most Runs—2,245, Ty Cobb, Detroit A.L., 1905–26, Philadelphia A.L., 1927–28.

Most Runs, Season—196, William Hamilton, Philadelphia N.L., 1894. (Since 1900—177, Babe Ruth, New York A.L., 1921.)

Most Runs Batted in—2,297, Henry Aaron, Milwaukee N.L., 1954–1965; Atlanta N.L., 1966–74; Milwaukee A.L., 1975–76.

Most Runs Batted in, Season—191, Hack Wilson, Chicago N.L., 1930.

Most Home Runs—755, Henry Aaron, Milwaukee N.L., 1954–1965; Atlanta N.L., 1966–74; Milwaukee A.L., 1975–76.

Most Home Runs, Season—162-game season: 70, Mark McGwire, St. Louis N.L., 1998; 66, Sammy Sosa, Chicago N.L., 1998; 65, Mark McGwire, St. Louis N.L., 1999; 63, Sammy Sosa, Chicago N.L., 1999; 61, Roger Maris, New York A.L., 1961; 154-game season: 60, Babe Ruth, New York A.L., 1927

Most Home Runs with Bases Filled—23, Lou Gehrig, New York A.L., 1927–39.

Most 2-Base Hits—793, Tris Speaker, Boston A.L., 1907–15, Cleveland A.L., 1916–26, Washington A.L., 1927, Philadelphia A.L., 1928.

Most 2-Base Hits, Season—67, Earl Webb, Boston A.L., 1931.

Most 3-Base Hits—312, Sam Crawford, Cincinnati N.L., 1899–1902, Detroit A.L., 1903–17.

Most 3-Base Hits, Season—36, Owen Wilson, Pittsburgh N.L., 1912.

Most 3-Base Hits, Game—4, George Strief, Philadelphia A.A., 1885; William Joyce, New York N.L., 1897. (Since 1900—3, by many.)

Most Games Played—3,562, Pete Rose, Cincinnati N.L., Philadelphia N.L., Montreal N.L., 1964–86.

Most Consecutive Games Played—2,632, Cal Ripken, Jr., Baltimore Orioles, A.L., 1981–1998.

Most Bases on Balls—2,062, Babe Ruth, Boston A.L., 1914–19; New York A.L., 1920–34, Boston N.L., 1935.

Most Bases on Balls, Season—170, Babe Ruth, New York A.L., 1923.

Most Strikeouts, Season—189, Bobby Bonds, San Francisco N.L., 1970.

Most Pinch-hits, Lifetime—150, Manny Mota, San Francisco, 1962; Pittsburgh, 1963–68; Montreal, 1969; Los Angeles, 1969–80, N.L.

Most Pinch-hits, Season—28, John Vander Wal, Colorado N.L., 1995.

Most Consecutive Pinch-hits—9, Dave Philley, Phil., N.L., 1958 (8), 1959 (1).

Most Pinch-hit Home Runs, Lifetime—20, Cliff Johnson, Houston N.L., 1972–77; New York A.L., 1977–79; Cleveland A.L., 1979–80; Chicago N.L., 1980; Oakland A.L., 1981–82; Toronto A.L., 1983–84, 1985–86; Texas A.L., 1985.

Most Pinch-hit Home Runs, Season—6, Johnny Frederick, Brooklyn, N.L., 1932.

Most Stolen Bases, Lifetime—1,370 Rickey Henderson, Oakland, 1979–84; New York (A.L.), 1985–89; Oakland, 1989–93; Toronto, 1993; Oakland, 1994–95; San Diego, 1996–97; Anaheim, 1997; Oakland, 1998; New York (N.L.), 1999–2000; Seattle, 2000.

Most Stolen Bases, Season—156, Harry Stovey, Phil., A.A., 1888. Since 1900: 130, Rickey Henderson, Oakland, A.L., 1982; 118, Lou Brock, St. Louis, N.L., 1974.

Most Stolen Bases, Game—7, George Gore, Chicago N.L. 1881; William Hamilton, Philadelphia N.L. 1894. (Since 1900—6, Eddie Collins, Philadelphia A.L., 1912.) and Otis Nixon, Atlanta N.L., 1991.

Most Time Stealing Home, Lifetime—50, Ty Cobb, Detroit-Phil. A.L., 1905–28.

ROOKIE OF THE YEAR
(Baseball Writers Association selections)

American League

1949	Roy Sievers, St. Louis	1967	Rod Carew, Minnesota	1984	Alvin Davis, Seattle
1950	Walt Dropo, Boston	1968	Stan Bahnsen, New York	1985	Ozzie Guillen, Chicago
1951	Gil McDougald, New York	1969	Lou Piniella, Kansas City	1986	Jose Canseco, Oakland
1952	Harry Byrd, Philadelphia	1970	Thurman Munson, New York	1987	Mark McGwire, Oakland
1953	Harvey Kuenn, Detroit	1971	Chris Chambliss, Cleveland	1988	Walter Weiss, Oakland
1954	Bob Grim, New York	1972	Carlton Fisk, Boston	1989	Gregg Olson, Baltimore
1955	Herb Score, Cleveland	1973	Alonzo Bumbry, Baltimore	1990	Sandy Alomar Jr., Cleveland
1956	Luis Aparicio, Chicago	1974	Mike Hargrove, Texas	1991	Chuck Knoblauch, Minnesota
1957	Tony Kubek, New York	1975	Fred Lynn, Boston	1992	Pat Listach, Milwaukee
1958	Albie Pearson, Washington	1976	Mark Fidrych, Detroit	1993	Tim Salmon, California
1959	Bob Allison, Washington	1977	Eddie Murray, Baltimore	1994	Bob Hamelin, Kansas City
1960	Ron Hansen, Baltimore	1978	Lou Whitaker, Detroit	1995	Marty Cordova, Minnesota
1961	Don Schwall, Boston	1979	Alfredo Griffin, Toronto	1996	Derek Jeter, New York
1962	Tom Tresh, New York	1979	John Castino, Minnesota	1997	Nomar Garciaparra, Boston
1963	Gary Peters, Chicago	1980	Joe Charboneau, Cleveland	1998	Ben Grieve, Oakland
1964	Tony Oliva, Minnesota	1981	Dave Righetti, New York	1999	Carlos Beltran, Kansas City
1965	Curt Blefary, Baltimore	1982	Cal Ripken, Jr., Baltimore		
1966	Tommy Agee, Chicago	1983	Ron Kittle, Chicago		

National League

1949	Don Newcombe, Brooklyn	1967	Tom Seaver, New York	1984	Dwight Gooden, New York
1950	Sam Jethroe, Boston	1968	Johnny Bench, Cincinnati	1985	Vince Coleman, St. Louis
1951	Willie Mays, New York	1969	Ted Sizemore, Los Angeles	1986	Todd Worrell, St. Louis
1952	Joe Black, Brooklyn	1970	Carl Morton, Montreal	1987	Benito Santiago, San Diego
1953	Jim Gilliam, Brooklyn	1971	Earl Williams, Atlanta	1988	Chris Sabo, Cincinnati
1954	Wally Moon, St. Louis	1972	Jon Matlack, New York	1989	Jerome Walton, Chicago
1955	Bill Virdon, St. Louis	1973	Gary Matthews, San Francisco	1990	Dave Justice, Atlanta
1956	Frank Robinson, Cincinnati	1974	Bake McBride, St. Louis	1991	Jeff Baguell, Houston
1957	Jack Sanford, Philadelphia	1975	John Montefusco, San Francisco	1992	Eric Karros, Los Angeles
1958	Orlando Cepeda, San Francisco	1976	Pat Zachry, Cincinnati	1993	Mike Piazza, Los Angeles
1959	Willie McCovey, San Francisco	1976	Bruce Metzger, San Diego	1994	Raul Mondesi, Los Angeles
1960	Frank Howard, Los Angeles	1977	Andre Dawson, Montreal	1995	Hideo Nomo, Los Angeles
1961	Billy Williams, Chicago	1978	Bob Horner, Atlanta	1996	Todd Hollandsworth, Los Angeles
1962	Ken Hubbs, Chicago	1979	Rick Sutcliffe, Los Angeles	1997	Scott Rolen, Philadelphia
1963	Pete Rose, Cincinnati	1980	Steve Howe, Los Angeles	1998	Kerry Wood, Chicago
1964	Richie Allen, Philadelphia	1981	Fernando Valenzuela, Los Angeles	1999	Scott Williamson, Cincinnati
1965	Jim Lefebvre, Los Angeles	1982	Steve Sax, Los Angeles		
1966	Tommy Helms, Cincinnati	1983	Darryl Strawberry, New York		

MOST HOME RUNS IN ONE SEASON
(45 or More)

HR	Player/Team	Year	HR	Player/Team	Year
70	Mark McGwire, St. Louis (N.L.)	1998	50	Jimmy Foxx, Boston (A.L.)	1938
66	Sammy Sosa, Chicago (N.L.)	1998	50	Albert Belle, Cleveland (A.L.)	1995
65	Mark McGwire, St. Louis (N.L.)	1999	50	Brady Anderson, Baltimore (A.L.)	1996
63	Sammy Sosa, Chicago (N.L.)	1999	50	Sammy Sosa , Chicago (N.L.)	2000
61	Roger Maris, New York (A.L.)	1961	50	Greg Vaughn, San Diego (N.L.)	1998
60	Babe Ruth, New York (A.L.)	1927	49	Babe Ruth, New York (A.L.)	1930
59	Babe Ruth, New York (A.L.)	1921	49	Lou Gehrig, New York (A.L.)	1934
58	Jimmy Foxx, Philadelphia (A.L.)	1932	49	Lou Gehrig, New York (A.L.)	1936
58	Hank Greenberg, Detroit (A.L.)	1938	49	Ted Kluszewski, Cincinnati (N.L.)	1954
58	Mark McGwire, Oakland (A.L.), St. Louis (N.L.)	1997	49	Willie Mays, San Francisco (N.L.)	1962
56	Hack Wilson, Chicago (N.L.)	1930	49	Harmon Killebrew, Minnesota (A.L.)	1964
56	Ken Griffey, Jr., Seattle (A.L.)	1997	49	Frank Robinson, Baltimore (A.L.)	1966
56	Ken Griffey, Jr., Seattle (A.L.)	1998	49	Harmon Killebrew, Minnesota (A.L.)	1969
54	Babe Ruth, New York (A.L.)	1920	49	Mark McGwire, Oakland (A.L.)	1987
54	Babe Ruth, New York (A.L.)	1928	49	Andre Dawson, Chicago (N.L.)	1987
54	Ralph Kiner, Pittsburgh (N.L.)	1949	49	Ken Griffey, Jr., Seattle (A.L.)	1996
54	Mickey Mantle, New York (A.L.)	1961	49	Larry Walker, Colorado (N.L.)	1997
52	Mickey Mantle, New York (A.L.)	1956	49	Albert Belle, Chicago (A.L.)	1998
52	Willie Mays, San Francisco (N.L.)	1965	49	Barry Bonds, San Francisco (N.L.)	2000
52	George Foster, Cincinnati (N.L.)	1977	48	Jimmy Foxx, Philadelphia (A.L.)	1933
52	Mark McGwire, Oakland (A.L.)	1996	48	Harmon Killebrew, Minnesota (A.L.)	1962
51	Ralph Kiner, Pittsburgh (N.L.)	1947	48	Frank Howard, Washington (A.L.)	1969
51	John Mize, New York (N.L.)	1947	48	Willie Stargell, Pittsburgh (N.L.)	1971
51	Willie Mays, New York (N.L.)	1955	48	Dave Kingman, Chicago (N.L.)	1979
51	Cecil Fielder (A.L.)	1990	48	Mike Schmidt, Philadelphia (N.L.)	1980

HR	Player/Team	Year
48	Albert Belle, Cleveland (A.L.)	1996
48	Ken Griffey, Jr., Seattle (A.L.)	1999
47	Babe Ruth, New York (A.L.)	1926
47	Ralph Kiner, Pittsburgh (N.L.)	1950
47	Ed Mathews, Milwaukee (N.L.)	1953
47	Ernie Banks, Chicago (N.L.)	1958
47	Willie Mays, San Francisco (N.L.)	1964
47	Henry Aaron, Atlanta (N.L.)	1971
47	Reggie Jackson, Oakland (A.L.)	1969
47	George Bell, Toronto (A.L.)	1987
47	Kevin Mitchell, San Francisco (N.L.)	1989
47	Andres Galarraga, Colorado (N.L.)	1996
47	Juan Gonzalez, Texas (A.L.)	1996
47	Rafael Palmeiro, Texas (A.L.)	1999
47	Jeff Bagwell, Houston (N.L.)	2000
47	Troy Glaus, Anaheim (A.L.)	2000
46	Babe Ruth, New York (A.L.)	1924
46	Babe Ruth, New York, (A.L.)	1929
46	Babe Ruth, New York (A.L.)	1931

HR	Player/Team	Year
46	Lou Gehrig, New York (A.L.)	1931
46	Joe DiMaggio, New York (A.L.)	1937
46	Ed Mathews, Milwaukee (N.L.)	1959
46	Orlando Cepeda, San Francisco (N.L.)	1961
46	Jim Rice, Boston (A.L.)	1978
46	Juan Gonzalez, Texas (A.L.)	1993
46	Barry Bonds, San Francisco (N.L.)	1993
46	Jose Canseco, Toronto (A.L.)	1998
46	Vinnie Castilla, Colorado (N.L.)	1998
45	Harmon Killebrew, Minnesota (A.L.)	1963
45	Willie McCovey, San Francisco (N.L.)	1969
45	Johnny Bench, Cincinnati (N.L.)	1970
45	Gorman Thomas, Milwaukee (A.L.)	1979
45	Henry Aaron, Milwaukee (N.L.)	1962
45	Ken Griffey, Jr., Seattle (A.L.)	1993
45	Juan Gonzalez, Texas (A.L.)	1998
45	Manny Ramirez, Cleveland (A.L.)	1998
45	Chipper Jones, Atlanta (N.L.)	1999
45	Greg Vaughn, Cincinnati (N.L.)	1999

MAJOR LEAGUE BASEBALL—2000

AMERICAN LEAGUE FINAL STANDINGS

EASTERN DIVISION

Team	W	L	Pct	GB
New York Yankees[1]	87	74	.540	—
Boston Red Sox	85	77	.525	2½
Toronto Blue Jays	83	79	.512	4½
Baltimore Orioles	74	88	.457	13½
Tampa Bay Devil Rays	69	92	.429	18

CENTRAL DIVISION

Team	W	L	Pct	GB
Chicago White Sox[1]	95	67	.586	—
Cleveland Indians	90	72	.556	5
Detroit Tigers	79	83	.488	16
Kansas City Chiefs	77	85	.475	18
Minnesota Twins	69	93	.426	26

WESTERN DIVISION

Team	W	L	Pct	GB
Oakland Athletics[1]	91	70	.565	—
Seattle Mariners[2]	91	71	.562	½
Anaheim Angels	82	80	.506	9½
Texas Rangers	71	91	.438	20½

1. Clinched division title. 2. Wild card.

NATIONAL LEAGUE FINAL STANDINGS

EASTERN DIVISION

Team	W	L	Pct	GB
Atlanta Braves[1]	95	67	.586	—
New York Mets[2]	94	68	.580	1
Florida Marlins	79	82	.491	15½
Montreal Expos	67	95	.414	28
Philadelphia Phillies	65	97	.401	30

CENTRAL DIVISION

Team	W	L	Pct	GB
St. Louis Cardinals[1]	95	67	.586	—
Cincinnati Reds	85	77	.525	10
Milwaukee Brewers	73	89	.451	22
Houston Astros	72	90	.444	23
Pittsburgh Pirates	69	93	.426	26
Chicago Cubs	65	97	.401	30

WESTERN DIVISION

Team	W	L	Pct	GB
San Francisco Giants[1]	97	65	.599	—
Los Angeles Dodgers	86	76	.531	11
Arizona Diamondbacks	85	77	.525	12
Colorado Rockies	82	80	.506	15
San Diego Padres	76	86	.469	21

1. Clinched division title. 2. Wild card.

AMERICAN LEAGUE LEADERS: 2000

Batting—Nomar Garciaparra, Boston	.372
Home runs—Troy Glaus, Anaheim	47
Runs batted in—Edgar Martinez, Seattle	145
Stolen bases—Johnny Damon, Kansas City	46
Slugging percentage—Manny Ramirez, Cleveland	.697
Runs scored—Johnny Damon, Kansas City	136
Walks—Jason Giambi, Oakland	137
Doubles—Carlos Delgado, Toronto	57
Triples—Cristian Guzman, Minnesota	20
Hits—Darin Erstad, Anaheim	240

A.L. Pitching

Wins—David Wells, Toronto	20
Earned run average—Pedro Martinez, Boston	1.74
Saves—Todd Jones, Detroit	42
Innings pitched—Mike Mussina, Baltimore	237.2
Strikeouts—Pedro Martinez, Boston	284
Complete games—David Wells, Toronto	9
Shutouts—Pedro Martinez, Boston	4

NATIONAL LEAGUE LEADERS: 2000

Batting—Todd Helton, Colorado	.372
Home runs—Sammy Sosa, Chicago	50
Runs batted in—Todd Helton, Colorado	147
Stolen bases—Luis Castillo, Florida	62
Slugging percentage—Todd Helton, Colorado	.698
Runs scored—Jeff Bagwell, Houston	152
Walks—Barry Bonds, San Francisco	117
Doubles—Todd Helton, Colorado	59
Triples—Todd Womack, Arizona	14
Hits—Todd Helton, Colorado	216

N.L. Pitching

Wins—Tom Glavine, Atlanta	21
Earned run average—Kevin K. Brown, Los Angeles	2.58
Saves—Antonio Alfonseca, Florida	45
Innings pitched—Jon Lieber, Chicago	251.0
Strikeouts—Randy Johnson, Arizona	347
Complete games—Curt Schilling, Arizona	8
Shutouts—Greg Maddux, Atlanta	3

American League Division Series

New York Yankees defeated Oakland Athletics,
3 games to 2
Oct. 3—OAKLAND 5, New York 3
Oct. 4—New York 4, OAKLAND 0
Oct. 6—NEW YORK 4, Oakland 2
Oct. 7—Oakland 11, NEW YORK 1
Oct. 8—New York 7, OAKLAND 5

Seattle Mariners defeated Chicago White Sox,
3 games to 0
Oct. 3—Seattle 7, CHICAGO 4
Oct. 5—Seattle 5, CHICAGO 1
Oct. 6—SEATTLE 2, Chicago 1
(HOME TEAM IN CAPS.)

National League Division Series

New York Mets defeated San Francisco Gians,
3 games to 1
Oct. 4—SAN FRANCISCO 5, New York 1
Oct. 5—New York 5, SAN FRANCISCO 4
Oct. 7—NEW YORK 3, San Francisco 2 (13 innings)
Oct. 8—NEW YORK 4, San Francisco 0

St. Louis Cardinals defeated Atlanta Braves,
3 games to 0
Oct. 3—ST. LOUIS 7, Atlanta 5
Oct. 4—ST. LOUIS 10, Atlanta 4
Oct. 7—St. Louis 7, ATLANTA 1
(HOME TEAM IN CAPS.)

AMERICAN LEAGUE AVERAGES—2000

Team Pitching

	W	L	SV	SO	R	ERA	Ks
Anaheim	82	80	46	3	869	5.00	846
Baltimore	74	88	33	6	913	5.27	1,017
Boston	85	77	46	12	745	4.23	1,121
Chicago	95	67	43	7	839	4.66	1,037
Cleveland	90	72	34	5	816	4.84	1,213
Detroit	79	83	44	6	827	4.71	978
Kansas City	77	85	29	6	930	5.48	927
Minnesota	69	93	35	4	880	5.14	1,042
New York	87	74	40	6	814	4.76	1,040
Oakland	91	70	43	11	813	4.58	963
Seattle	91	71	44	10	780	4.49	998
Tampa Bay	69	92	38	8	842	4.86	955
Texas	71	91	39	4	974	5.52	918
Toronto	83	79	37	4	908	5.14	978

Team Batting

	Avg	AB	R	H	HR	RBI
Baltimore	.272	5,549	794	1,508	184	750
Boston	.267	5,630	792	1,503	167	755
Chicago	.286	5,646	978	1,615	216	926
Cleveland	.288	5,683	950	1,639	221	889
Detroit	.275	5,644	823	1,553	177	785
Anaheim	.280	5,628	864	1,574	236	837
Kansas City	.288	5,709	879	1,644	150	831
Minnesota	.270	5,615	748	1,516	116	711
Seattle	.269	5,497	907	1,481	198	869
Texas	.283	5,648	848	1,601	173	806
Toronto	.275	5,677	861	1,562	244	826
Oakland	.270	5,560	947	1,501	239	908
New York	.277	5,556	871	1,541	205	833
Tampa Bay	.257	5,505	733	1,414	162	692

Individual Pitching
(Based on 10 decisions.)

	W	L	ERA	IP	H	BB	Ks
Tim Hudson, Oakland	20	6	4.14	202.1	169	82	169
David Wells, Toronto	20	8	4.11	229.2	266	31	166
Andy Pettitte, New York	19	9	4.35	204.2	219	80	125
Pedro Martinez, Boston	18	6	1.74	217.0	128	32	284
Aaron Sele, Seattle	17	10	4.51	211.2	221	74	137
Dave Burba, Cleveland	16	6	4.47	191.1	199	91	180
Chuck Finley, Cleveland	16	11	4.17	218.0	211	101	189
Rick Heiling, Texas	16	13	4.48	217.0	212	99	146
Mike Sirotka, Chicago	15	10	3.79	197.0	203	69	128
Bartolo Colon, Cleveland	15	8	3.88	188.0	163	98	212
Kevin Appier, Oakland	15	11	4.52	195.1	200	102	129
Gil Heredia, Oakland	15	11	4.12	198.2	214	66	101
Jose Mercedes, Baltimore	14	7	4.02	145.2	150	64	70
James Baldwin, Chicago	14	7	4.65	178.0	185	59	116
John Halama, Seattle	14	9	5.08	166.2	206	56	87
Jim Parque, Chicago	13	6	4.28	187.0	208	71	111
Eric Milton, Minnesota	13	10	4.86	200.0	205	44	160
Roger Clemens, New York	13	8	3.70	204.1	184	84	188
Jamie Moyer, Seattle	13	10	5.49	154.0	173	53	98
Kenny Rogers, Texas	13	13	4.55	227.1	257	78	127

Individual Batting
(Based on 300 plate appearances.)

	Avg	AB	R	H	HR	RBI
Nomar Garciaparra, Boston	.372	529	104	197	21	96
Darin Erstad, Anaheim	.355	676	121	240	25	100
Manny Ramirez, Cleveland	.351	439	92	154	38	122
Ivan Rodriguez, Texas	.347	363	66	126	27	83
Carlos Delgado, Toronto	.342	567	115	194	41	137
Derek Jeter, New York	.339	593	119	201	15	73
David Segui, Cleveland	.334	574	93	192	19	103
Mike Sweeney, Kansas City	.333	618	105	206	29	144
Jason Giambi, Oakland	.333	510	108	170	43	137
Frank Thomas, Chicago	.328	582	115	191	43	143
Johnny Damon, Kansas City	.327	655	136	214	16	88
Edgar Martinez, Seattle	.324	556	100	180	37	145
Darrin Fletcher, Toronto	.323	412	43	133	20	58
Travis Fryman, Cleveland	.321	574	93	184	22	106
Jermaine Dye, Kansas City	.321	601	107	193	33	118
Shannon Stewart, Toronto	.321	579	107	186	21	69
Alex Rodriguez, Seattle	.316	554	134	175	41	132
Magglio Ordonez, Chicago	.315	588	102	185	32	126
Roberto Alomar, Cleveland	.310	610	111	189	19	89
Bernie Williams, New York	.307	537	108	165	30	121

NATIONAL LEAGUE AVERAGES—2000

Team Pitching

	W	L	SV	SO	R	ERA	Ks
Arizona	85	77	38	8	754	4.35	1,220
Atlanta	95	67	53	9	714	4.05	1,093
Chicago	65	97	39	5	904	5.25	1,143
Cincinnati	85	77	42	7	765	4.33	1,015
Colorado	82	80	33	2	897	5.26	1,001
Florida	79	82	48	4	797	4.59	1,051
Houston	72	90	30	2	944	5.42	1,064
Los Angeles	86	76	36	11	729	4.10	1,154
Milwaukee	73	89	29	7	826	4.63	967
Montreal	67	95	39	7	902	5.13	1,011
New York	94	68	49	10	738	4.16	1,164
Philadelphia	65	97	34	6	830	4.77	1,123
Pittsburgh	69	93	27	7	888	4.94	1,070
San Diego	76	86	46	5	815	4.52	1,071
San Francisco	97	65	47	15	747	4.21	1,076
St. Louis	95	67	37	7	771	4.38	1,100

Individual Pitching (Based on 10 decisions.)

	W	L	ERA	IP	H	BB	Ks
Tom Glavine, Atlanta	21	9	3.40	241.0	222	65	152
Darryl Kile, St. Louis	20	9	3.91	232.1	215	58	192
Randy Johnson, Arizona	19	7	2.64	248.2	202	76	347
Greg Maddux, Atlanta	19	9	3.00	249.1	225	42	190
Chan Ho Park, Los Angeles	18	10	3.27	226.0	173	124	217
Scott Elarton, Houston	17	7	4.81	192.2	198	84	131
Livan Hernandez, San Francisco	17	11	3.75	240.0	254	73	165
Al Leiter, New York	16	8	3.20	208.0	176	76	200
Garrett Stephenson, St. Louis	16	9	4.49	200.1	209	63	123
Mike Hampton, New York	15	10	3.14	217.2	194	99	151
Shawn Estes, San Francisco	15	6	4.26	190.1	194	108	136
Pat Hentgen, St. Louis	15	12	4.72	194.1	202	89	118

	W	L	ERA	IP	H	BB	Ks
Ryan Dempster, Florida	14	10	3.66	226.1	210	97	209
Russ Ortiz, San Francisco	14	12	5.01	195.2	192	112	167
Kevin Brown, Los Angeles	13	6	2.58	230.0	181	47	216
Matt Clement, San Diego	13	17	5.14	205.0	194	125	170
Andy Ashby, Atlanta	12	13	4.92	199.1	216	61	106
Jon Lieber, Chicago	12	11	4.41	251.0	248	54	192
Steve Parris, Cincinnati	12	17	4.81	192.2	227	71	117
Pedro Astacio, Colorado	12	9	5.27	196.1	217	77	193
Brian Bohanon, Colorado	12	10	4.68	177.0	181	79	98
Darren Dreifort, Los Angeles	12	9	4.16	192.2	175	87	164
Jeff C. Damico, Milwaukee	12	7	2.66	162.1	143	46	101
Jimmy Haynes, Milwaukee	12	13	5.33	199.1	228	100	88
Dustin Hermanson, Montreal	12	14	4.77	198.0	226	75	94
Andy Benes, St. Louis	12	9	4.88	166.0	174	68	137

Team Batting

	Avg	AB	R	H	HR	RBI
Milwaukee	.246	5,563	740	1,366	177	708
Cincinnati	.274	5,635	825	1,545	200	794
Arizona	.265	5,527	792	1,466	179	756
Atlanta	.271	5,489	810	1,490	179	758
Chicago	.256	5,577	764	1,426	183	722
Colorado	.294	5,660	968	1,664	161	905
Houston	.278	5,570	938	1,547	249	900
Los Angeles	.257	5,481	798	1,408	211	756

	Avg	AB	R	H	HR	RBI
Philadelphia	.251	5,511	708	1,386	144	668
Montreal	.266	5,535	738	1,475	178	705
New York	.263	5,486	807	1,445	198	761
San Diego	.254	5,560	752	1,413	157	714
Pittsburgh	.267	5,643	793	1,506	168	749
San Francisco	.278	5,519	925	1,535	226	889
St. Louis	.270	5,478	887	1,481	235	841
Florida	.262	5,509	731	1,441	160	691

Individual Batting (Based on 300 plate appearances.)

	Avg	AB	R	H	HR	RBI
Todd Helton, Colorado	.372	580	138	216	42	147
Moises Alou, Houston	.355	454	82	161	30	114
Vladimir Guerrero, Montreal	.345	571	101	197	44	123
Ellis Burks, San Francisco	.344	393	74	135	24	96
Jeffrey Hammonds, Colorado	.335	454	94	152	20	106
Chris Stynes, Cincinnati	.334	380	71	127	12	40
Luis Castillo, Florida	.334	539	101	180	2	17
Jeff Kent, Colorado	.334	587	114	196	33	125
Jose Vidro, Montreal	.330	606	101	200	24	97
Jeff Cirillo, Colorado	.326	598	111	195	11	115

	Avg	AB	R	H	HR	RBI
Gary Sheffield, Los Angeles	.325	501	105	163	43	109
Edgardo Alfonzo, New York	.324	544	109	176	25	94
Mike Piazza, New York	.324	482	90	156	38	113
Sammy Sosa, Chicago	.320	604	106	193	50	138
Jason Kendall, Pittsburgh	.320	579	112	185	14	58
Bobby Abreu, Philadelphia	.316	576	103	182	25	79
Placido Polanco, St. Louis	.316	323	50	102	5	39
Sean Casey, Cincinnati	.315	480	69	151	20	85
Adrian Brown, Pittsburgh	.315	308	64	97	4	28
Brian Giles, Pittsburgh	.315	559	111	176	35	123

AMERICAN LEAGUE CHAMPIONSHIP SERIES—2000
New York Yankees win series, 4 games to 2

1st Game, at New York, Oct. 10, 2000

				R	H	E
Seattle	000	011	000 —	2	6	0
New York	000	000	000 —	0	6	1

Pitchers—Seattle: Garcia, Paniagua, Rhodes, Sasaki. New York: Neagle, Nelson, Choate, Grimsley. Winner: Garcia. Loser: Neagle. Attendance: 54,481.

2nd Game, at New York, Oct. 11, 2000

				R	H	E
Seattle	001	000	000 —	1	7	2
New York	000	000	07x —	7	14	0

Pitchers—Seattle: Halama, Paniagua, Rhodes, Mesa. New York: Hernandez, Rivera. Winner: Hernandez. Loser: Rhodes. Attendance: 55,317.

3rd Game, at Seattle, Oct. 13, 2000

				R	H	E
New York	021	001	004 —	8	13	0
Seattle	100	010	000 —	2	10	1

Pitchers—New York: Pettitte, Nelson, Rivera. Seattle: Sele, Tomko, Ramsay. Winner: Pettitte. Loser: Sele. Save: Rivera. Attendance: 47,827.

4th Game, at Seattle, Oct. 14, 2000

				R	H	E
New York	000	030	020 —	5	5	0
Seattle	000	000	000 —	0	1	0

Pitchers—New York: Clemens. Seattle: Abbott, Ramsay, Mesa, Paniagua. Winner: Clemens. Loser: Abbott. Attendance: 47,803.

5th Game, at Seattle, Oct. 15, 2000

				R	H	E
New York	000	200	000 —	2	8	0
Seattle	100	050	00x —	6	8	0

Pitchers—New York: Neagle, Nelson, Grimsley, Gooden, Cone. Seattle: Garcia, Paniagua, Rhodes, Sasaki. Winner: Garcia. Loser: Neagle. Attendance: 47,802.

6th Game, at New York, Oct. 17, 2000

				R	H	E
Seattle	200	200	030 —	7	10	0
New York	300	300	60x —	9	11	0

Pitchers—Seattle: Halama, Tomko, Paniagua, Rhodes, Mesa. New York: Hernandez, Rivera. Winner: Hernandez. Loser: Paniagua. Attendance: 56,598.

Series MVP—David Justice

NATIONAL LEAGUE CHAMPIONSHIP SERIES—2000
New York Mets win series, 4 games to 1

1st Game, at St. Louis, Oct. 11, 2000

					R	H	E
New York	200	010	003	—	6	8	3
St. Louis	000	000	002	—	2	9	0

Pitchers—New York: Hampton, Franco, Benitez. St. Louis: Kile, James, Christiansen. Winner: Hampton. Loser: Kile. Attendance: 52,255.

2nd Game, at St. Louis, Oct. 12, 2000

					R	H	E
New York	201	000	021	—	6	9	0
St. Louis	010	020	020	—	5	10	3

Pitchers—New York: Leiter, Franco, Wendell, Benitez. St. Louis: Ankiel, Reames, Morris, Veres, Timlin. Winner: Wendell. Loser: Timlin. Save: Benitez. Attendance: 52,250.

3rd Game, at New York, Oct. 14, 2000

					R	H	E
St. Louis	202	130	000	—	8	14	0
New York	100	100	000	—	2	7	1

Pitchers—St. Louis: Benes, James, Veres. New York: Reed, Rusch, White, Cook, Wendell. Winner: Benes. Loser: Reed. Attendance: 55,693.

4th Game, at New York, Oct. 15, 2000

					R	H	E
St. Louis	200	130	000	—	6	11	2
New York	430	102	00x	—	10	9	0

Pitchers—St. Louis: Kile, James, Timlin, Morris, Christiansen. New York: Jones, Rusch, Franco, Benitez. Winner: Rusch. Loser: Kile. Attendance: 55,665.

5th Game, at New York, Oct. 16, 2000

					R	H	E
St. Louis	000	000	000	—	0	3	2
New York	300	300	10x	—	7	10	0

Pitchers—St. Louis: Hentgen, Timlin, Reames, Ankiel, James, Veres. New York: Hampton. Winner: Hampton. Loser: Hentgen. Attendance: 55,695.

Series MVP—Mike Hampton

WORLD SERIES—2000

New York Yankees win series, 4 games to 1
Series MVP—Derek Jeter.

1st Game—Yankee Stadium, Oct. 21
Yankees 4, Mets 3 (12 innings)

METS (N.L.)	AB	R	H	RBI	YANKEES (A.L.)	AB	R	H	RBI
Perez rf	6	0	1	0	Knoblauch dh	4	1	0	1
Alfonzo 2b	6	0	1	1	Jeter ss	4	1	1	0
Piazza dh	5	0	1	0	Justice lf	4	0	1	2
Zeile 1b	5	0	2	0	Bellinger pr-lf	0	0	0	0
Ventura 3b	5	0	0	0	Hill ph-lf	1	0	0	0
Agbayani lf	4	1	2	0	Williams cf	4	0	0	0
McEwing lf	1	0	0	0	Martinez 1b	6	1	2	0
Payton cf	5	1	1	0	Posada c	5	0	1	0
Pratt c	2	1	0	0	O'Neill rf	4	1	1	0
Bordick ss	1	0	0	0	Brosius 3b	3	0	1	0
Trammell ph	1	0	1	2	Polonia ph	1	0	1	0
Abbott ss	2	0	1	0	Sojo 3b	2	0	0	0
					Vizcaino 2b	6	0	4	1
Totals	43	3	10	3	**Totals**	44	4	12	4

					R	H	E
Mets	000	000	300	000	3	10	0
Yankees	000	002	001	001	4	12	0

2B—Mets: Agbayani, Zeile, Abbott; Yankees: Justice, Posada, Vizcaino. S—Mets: Bordick. SF—Yankees: Knoblauch. RBI—Mets: Trammell, Alfonzo; Yankees: Justice, Knoblauch, Vizcaino. GIDP—Yankees: O'Neill. LOB—Mets: 8; Yankees: 15. CS—Mets: Piazza; Yankees: Knoblauch. DP—Mets: 1 (Alfonzo-Abbott-Zeile).

	IP	H	R	ER	BB	SO	HR	ERA
Mets								
Leiter	7	5	2	2	3	7	0	2.57
Franco (H, 1)	1	1	0	0	0	0	0	0.00
Benitez (BS, 1)	1	2	1	1	1	1	0	9.00
Cook	0	0	0	0	0	0	0	0.00
Rusch	1⅔	1	0	0	2	0	0	0.00
Wendell (L, 0-1)	1	3	1	1	1	0	0	9.00
Yankees								
Pettitte	6⅔	8	3	3	1	4	0	4.05
Nelson	1⅓	1	0	0	0	0	0	0.00
Rivera	2	1	0	0	0	3	0	0.00
Stanton (W, 1-0)	2	0	0	0	0	3	0	0.00

WP—Rusch 1. IBB—Williams (by Leiter); Posada (by Rusch); O'Neill (by Wendell). HBP—Pratt 2 (by Pettitte, by Rivera). Umpires—HP: Ed Montague, 1B: Charles Reliford, 2b: Jeffrey Kellogg, 3B: Tim Welke, LF: Tim McClelland, RF: Jerry Crawford. T—4:51. Att.—55,913.

2nd Game—Yankee Stadium, Oct. 22
Yankees 6, Mets 5

METS (N.L.)	AB	R	H	RBI	YANKEES (A.L.)	AB	R	H	RBI
Perez rf	4	0	0	0	Knoblauch dh	4	0	0	0
Alfonzo 2b	3	1	1	0	Jeter ss	5	1	3	0
Piazza c	4	1	1	2	Justice lf	3	1	0	0
Ventura 3b	4	0	1	0	Bellinger lf	0	0	0	0
Zeile 1b	4	0	2	0	Williams cf	3	1	0	0
Agbayani lf	4	1	1	0	Martinez 1b	5	1	3	2
Harris dh	4	1	0	0	Posada c	3	1	2	1
Payton cf	4	1	1	3	O'Neill rf	4	0	3	1
Bordick ss	2	0	0	0	Brosius 3b	3	1	1	2
Hamilton ph	1	0	0	0	Vizcaino 2b	4	0	0	0
Abbott ss	1	0	0	0					
Totals	35	5	7	5	**Totals**	34	6	12	6

					R	H	E
Mets	000	000	005	—	5	7	3
Yankees	210	010	11x	—	6	12	1

HR—Mets: Piazza, Payton; Yankees: Brosius. 2B—Yankees: Martinez, Jeter, O'Neill. SF—Yankees: Brosius. RBI—Mets: Piazza, Payton; Yankees: Martinez, Posada, Brosius, O'Neill. LOB—Mets: 4; Yankees: 12. E—Mets: Payton, Bordick, Perez; Yankees: Clemens. CS—Yankees: Vizcaino. PB—Yankees: Posada

Mets	IP	H	R	ER	BB	SO	HR	ERA
Hampton (L, 0-1)	6	8	4	4	5	4	1	6.00
Rusch	⅓	2	1	1	0	0	0	4.50
White	1⅓	1	1	1	1	1	0	6.75
Cook	⅓	1	0	0	0	0	0	0.00
Yankees								
Clemens (W, 1-0)	8	2	0	0	0	9	0	0.00
Nelson	0	3	3	3	0	0	0	20.25
Rivera	1	2	2	2	0	0	1	6.00

WP—Clemens. IBB—Posada (by Hampton), Williams (by White). HBP—Alfonzo (by Clemens), Justice (by Hampton). Umpires—Home: Reliford, 1B: Kellogg, 2B: Welke, 3B: McClelland, LF: Crawford, RF: Montague. T—3:30. Att.—56,059.

3rd Game—Shea Stadium, Oct. 24
Mets 4, Yankees 2

YANKEES (A.L.)	AB	R	H	RBI	METS (N.L.)	AB	R	H	RBI
Vizcaino 2b	4	0	0	0	Perez rf	3	0	0	0
Polonia ph	1	0	0	0	Alfonzo 2b	4	0	0	0
Jeter ss	4	1	2	0	Piazza c	4	1	1	0
Justice lf	3	0	1	1	Ventura 3b	3	1	2	1
Williams cf	4	0	0	0	Zeile 1b	4	1	2	1
Martinez 1b	3	1	1	0	Agbayani lf	3	0	1	1
Posada c	4	0	0	0	McEwing pr-lf	0	1	0	0
O'Neill rf	4	0	3	1	Payton cf	4	0	1	0
Brosius 3b	2	0	0	0	Bordick ss	3	0	1	0
Hill ph	1	0	0	0	Harris ph	0	0	0	0
Sojo 3b	0	0	0	0	Trammell ph	0	0	0	1
Hernandez p	2	0	0	0	Benitez p	0	0	0	0
Stanton p	0	0	0	0	Reed p	1	0	1	0
Knoblauch ph	1	0	1	0	Hamilton ph	1	0	0	0
					Wendell p	0	0	0	0
					Cook p	0	0	0	0
					Franco p	0	0	0	0
					Abbott ph-ss	1	0	0	0
Totals	33	2	8	2	**Totals**	31	4	9	4

						R	H	E
Yankees	001	100	000	—		2	8	0
Mets	010	001	02x	—		4	9	0

2B—Yankees: O'Neill, Justice; Mets: Ventura, Piazza, Zeile, Agbayani. 3B—Yankees: O'Neill. HR—Mets: Ventura. S—Hernandez; Mets: Reed. SF—Mets: Trammell. RBI—Yankees: Justice, O'Neill; Mets: Ventura, Zeile, Agbayani, Trammell. GIDP—Yankees: Posada. LOB—Yankees: 10; Mets: 8. DP—Mets: 1 (Ventura-Alfonzo-Zeile).

Yankees	IP	H	R	ER	BB	SO	HR	ERA
Hernandez (L, 0-1)	7⅓	9	4	4	3	12	1	4.91
Stanton	⅔	0	0	0	0	1	0	0.00
Mets								
Reed	6	6	2	2	1	8	0	3.00
Wendell	⅔	0	0	0	1	2	0	5.40
Cook	⅓	0	0	0	1	0	0	0.00
Franco (W, 1-0)	1	1	0	0	0	0	0	0.00
Benitez (S, 1)	1	1	0	0	0	1	0	4.50

HBP—Brosius (by Reed), Justice (by Cook). Umpires—Home: Kellogg, 1B: Welke, 2B: McClelland, 3B: Crawford, LF: Montague, RF: Reliford. T—3:39. Att.—55,299.

4th Game—Shea Stadium, Oct. 25
Yankees 3, Mets 2

YANKEES (A.L.)	AB	R	H	RBI	METS (N.L.)	AB	R	H	RBI
Jeter ss	5	2	2	1	Perez rf	3	1	1	0
Sojo 2b	4	0	1	0	Abbott ph-ss	1	0	0	0
Justice lf	5	0	0	0	Alfonzo 2b	3	0	0	0
Bellinger lf	0	0	0	0	Piazza c	4	1	1	2
Williams cf	4	0	0	0	Zeile 1b	4	0	2	0
Martinez 1b	4	0	2	0	McEwing pr	0	0	0	0
O'Neill rf	4	1	2	0	Benitez p	0	0	0	0
Posada c	3	0	0	0	Ventura 3b	4	0	0	0
Brosius 3b	1	0	1	1	Agbayani lf	3	0	0	0

YANKEES (A.L.)	IP	H	R	ER	BB	SO	HR	ERA	METS (N.L.)	AB	R	H	RBI
Neagle p										2	0	0	0

YANKEES (A.L.)	AB	R	H	RBI	METS (N.L.)	AB	R	H	RBI
Neagle p	2	0	0	0	Payton cf	4	0	2	0
Cone p	0	0	0	0	Bordick ss	2	0	0	0
Canseco ph	1	0	0	0	Harris ph	0	0	0	0
Nelson p	0	0	0	0	J. Franco p	0	0	0	0
Stanton p	0	0	0	0	M. Franco 1b	1	0	0	0
Rivera p	1	0	0	0	Jones p	2	0	0	0
					Rusch p	0	0	0	0
					Hamilton ph	0	0	0	0
					Trammell ph-rf	1	0	0	0
Totals	34	3	8	3	**Totals**	32	2	6	2

						R	H	E
Yankees	111	000	000	—		3	8	0
Mets	002	000	000	—		2	6	1

3B—Yankees: O'Neill, Jeter. HR—Yankees: Jeter; Mets: Piazza. SF—Yankees: Brosius. RBI—Yankees: Jeter, Brosius, Sojo; Mets: Piazza. GIDP—Yankees: O'Neill. LOB—Yankees: 9; Mets: 6. E—Mets: Trammell. SB—Yankees: Sojo. DP—Yankees: 1 (Nelson-Martinez); Mets: 1 (Zeile-Abbott-J. Franco).

Yankees	IP	H	R	ER	BB	SO	HR	ERA
Neagle	4⅔	4	2	2	2	3	1	3.86
Cone	⅓	0	0	0	0	0	0	0.00
Nelson (W, 1-0)	1⅓	1	0	0	1	1	0	10.12
Stanton (H, 1)	⅔	0	0	0	0	2	0	0.00
Rivera (S, 1)	2	1	0	0	0	2	0	3.60
Mets								
Jones (L, 0-1)	5	4	3	3	3	3	1	5.40
Rusch	2	3	0	0	0	2	0	2.25
J. Franco	1	1	0	0	0	1	0	0.00
Benitez	1	0	0	0	0	0	0	3.00

IBB—Posada (by Jones), Brosius (by Jones). Umpires—Home: Welke, 1B: McClelland, 2B: Crawford, 3B: Montague, LF: Reliford, RF: Kellogg. T—3:20. Att.—55,290.

5th Game—Shea Stadium, Oct. 26
Yankees 4, Mets 2

YANKEES (A.L.)	AB	R	H	RBI	METS (N.L.)	AB	R	H	RBI
Vizcaino 2b	3	0	0	0	Agbayani lf	4	0	1	1
Knoblauch ph	1	0	0	0	Alfonzo 2b	5	0	1	0
Stanton p	0	0	0	0	Piazza c	5	0	2	0
Hill ph	1	0	0	0	Zeile 1b	3	0	0	0
Rivera p	0	0	0	0	Ventura 3b	4	0	0	0
Jeter ss	4	1	1	1	Trammell rf	3	1	1	0
Justice lf	4	0	1	0	Perez rf	0	0	0	0
Bellinger lf	0	0	0	0	Payton cf	4	1	2	0
Williams cf	3	1	2	1	Abbott ss	3	0	1	0
Martinez 1b	4	0	0	0	Leiter p	2	0	0	0
O'Neill rf	3	0	0	0	Franco p	0	0	0	0
Posada c	3	1	1	0	Hamilton ph	1	0	0	0
Brosius 3b	4	1	1	0					
Pettitte p	3	0	0	0					
Sojo 2b	1	0	1	1					
Totals	34	4	7	3	**Totals**	34	2	8	1

						R	H	E
Yankees	010	001	002	—		4	7	1
Mets	020	000	000	—		2	8	1

HR—Yankees: Williams, Jeter. 2B—Mets: Piazza. S—Mets: Leiter. RBI—Yankees: Williams, Jeter, Sojo; Mets: Agbayani. LOB—Yankees: 6; Mets: 10. E—Yankees: Pettitte; Mets: Payton. Picked off—Mets: Abbott.

Yankees	IP	H	R	ER	BB	SO	HR	ERA
Pettitte	7	8	2	0	3	5	0	1.98
Stanton (W, 2-0)	1	0	0	0	0	1	0	0.00
Rivera (S, 2)	1	0	0	0	1	1	0	3.00
Mets								
Leiter (L, 0-1)	8⅔	7	4	3	3	9	2	2.87
Franco	⅓	0	0	0	0	0	0	0.00

IBB—Zeile (by Pettitte). Umpires—Home: McClelland, 1B: Crawford, 2B: Montague, 3B: Reliford, LF: Kellogg, RF: Welke. T—3:32. Att.—55,292.

BEFORE THE WORLD SERIES

The N.L.–American Assn. Series, 1882–1890

When the National League met the American League for the first time in the 1903 World Series, it was not the N.L.'s first venture into post-season play. From 1882–90, the N.L. pennant winner engaged in a championship series with the champion of the American Association. The Nationals won four of the eight series, lost once, and tied three times.

Year	Champion	Loser	Series	Year	Champion	Loser	Series
1882	Chicago (N.L.) & Cincinnati (A.A.)	—	1–1	1887	Detroit (N.L.)	St. Louis (A.A.)	10–5
1883	No series			1888	New York (N.L.)	St. Louis (A.A.)	6–4
1884	Providence (N.L.)	New York (A.A.)	3–0	1889	New York (N.L.)	Brooklyn (A.A.)	6–3
1885	Chicago (N.L.) & St. Louis (A.A.)	—	3–3–1	1890	Brooklyn (N.L.) & Louisville (A.A.)	—	3–3–1
1886	St. Louis (A.A.)	Chicago (N.L.)	4–2				

Early N.L. and A.L. Pennant Winners

The National League had been around 27 years before the 1903 World Series. The A.L., however, was only in its third season when the two leagues met. The following lists account for the pennant winners in those pre-World Series years and in 1904 when the N.L. champion New York Giants refused to play Boston.

N.L. Pennant Winners, 1876–1902, '04

Year	Winner	Manager	Year	Winner	Manager	Year	Winner	Manager
1876	Chicago	Al Spalding	1886	Chicago	Cap Anson	1896	Baltimore	Ned Hanlon
1877	Boston	Harry Wright	1887	Detroit	Bill Watkins	1897	Boston	Frank Selee
1878	Boston	Harry Wright	1888	New York	Jim Mutrie	1898	Boston	Frank Selee
1879	Providence	George Wright	1889	New York	Jim Mutrie	1899	Brooklyn	Ned Hanlon
1880	Chicago	Cap Anson	1890	Brooklyn	Bill McGunnigle	1900	Brooklyn	Ned Hanlon
1881	Chicago	Cap Anson	1891	Boston	Frank Selee	1901	Pittsburgh	Fred Clarke
1882	Chicago	Cap Anson	1892	Boston	Frank Selee	1902	Pittsburgh	Fred Clarke
1883	Boston	John Morrill	1893	Boston	Frank Selee	1904	New York	John McGraw
1884	Providence	Frank Bancroft	1894	Baltimore	Ned Hanlon			
1885	Chicago	Cap Anson	1895	Baltimore	Ned Hanlon			

A.L. Pennant Winners, 1901–02, '04

Year	Winner	Manager	Year	Winner	Manager	Year	Winner	Manager
1901	Chicago	Clark Griffith	1902	Philadelphia	Connie Mack	1904	Boston	Jimmy Collins

THE HANK AARON AWARD

In 1999 Major League Baseball instituted the Hank Aaron Award for the best hitters in the National and American Leagues. In the award's first year, points were given for each hit, home run, and runs batted in. Starting in 2000, play-by-play broadcasters and color analysts from each club's radio and television rightsholders vote for the winners.

The first winners were **Sammy Sosa** of the Chicago Cubs and **Manny Ramirez** of the Cleveland Indians. The 2000 winners were **Todd Helton** of the Colorado Rockies and **Carlos Delgado** of the Toronto Blue Jays. Helton had a .372 batting average and also led the National League in doubles, multi-hit games, hits, on-base percentage, runs batted in, total bases, slugging percentage, extra-base hits, batting average with runners in scoring position, and runs batted in ratio. Delgado led the American League in doubles, total bases, extra-base hits and finished 4th in batting average, with a .344.

Extreme Sports

2000 SUMMER EXTREME GAMES
(San Francisco, Calif., Aug. 12–22, 2000)

MEN

Sport climbing: Vladimir Zakharov (speed)

Bicycle stunt: Jamie Bestwick (vert), Martti Kuoppa (flatland), Dave Mirra (park), Ryan Nyquist (dirt jumping)

Street luge: Bob Pereyra (super mass), Bob Ozman (dual downhill)

Skateboarding: Eric Koston (park); Bob Burnquist (best trick), Macdonald/Hawk (vert doubles), Bucky Lasek (open vert)

Motocross: Travis Pastrana (freestyle), Tommy Clowers (step up)

Wakeboarding: Darin Shapiro

In-line: Eito Yasutoko (vert), Sven Boekhorst (park)

Skysurfing: Klaus/Rogers

WOMEN

Sport climbing: Etti Hendrawati (speed)

Wakeboarding: Tara Hamilton

In-line: Fabiola da Silva (vert and park)

Soccer

The early history of the sport is uncertain. A form of the game in which a leather ball was dribbled was played in China as early as the 4th century B.C. The Romans played a variation of soccer which eventually spread throughout Europe. British schools and universities played soccer (known as football) during the 1800s, however, each school used different sets of rules and the number of players varied. This difficulty was corrected on Oct. 26, 1863, when the Football Association (FA) was formed in London for the purpose of unifying the rules of the game.

The Federation of International Football Associations (FIFA) was created in 1913 as a world governing body to coordinate all of the national associations in the world. The FIFA held the first World Cup Championship tournament in 1930 in Montevideo, Uruguay. Today, soccer is the world's most popular sport. The first FIFA Women's World Cup was held in 1991 with the United States winning the title.

WORLD CUP
(W) indicates Women's World Cup

1930 Uruguay	1954 West Germany	1978 Argentina	1995 Norway (W)
1934 Italy	1958 Brazil	1982 Italy	1998 France
1938 Italy	1962 Brazil	1986 Argentina	1999 United States (W)
1942 No competition	1966 England	1990 West Germany	
1946 No competition	1970 Brazil	1991 United States (W)	
1950 Uruguay	1974 West Germany	1994 Brazil	

WOMEN'S WORLD CUP—1999
FINAL GROUP STANDINGS

	W	L	T	Pts	GF	GA
Group A						
x-USA	3	0	0	9	13	1
x-Nigeria	2	1	0	6	5	8
Korea DPR	1	2	0	3	4	6
Denmark	0	3	0	0	1	8
Group B						
x-Brazil	2	0	1	7	12	4
x-Germany	1	0	2	5	10	4
Italy	1	1	1	4	3	3
Mexico	0	3	0	0	1	15

x-Advance to next round.

	W	L	T	Pts	GF	GA
Group C						
x-Norway	3	0	0	9	13	2
x-Russia	2	1	0	6	10	3
Canada	0	2	1	1	3	12
Japan	0	2	1	1	1	10
Group D						
x-China	3	0	0	9	12	2
x-Sweden	2	1	0	6	6	3
Australia	0	2	1	1	3	7
Ghana	0	2	1	1	1	10

QUARTERFINALS
Norway 3, Sweden 1
China 2, Russia 0
United States 3, Germany 2
Brazil 4, Nigeria 3
  (Brazil won in sudden-death "golden goal" overtime)

SEMIFINALS
United States 2, Brazil 0
China 5, Norway 0
THIRD PLACE
Brazil 0, Norway 0 (Brazil won 5–4 on penalty kicks)
CHAMPIONSHIP
United States 0, China 0 (The United States won 5–4 on penalty kicks)

WORLD CUP—1998

QUARTERFINALS
Denmark 2, Brazil 3
Argentina 1, Netherlands 2
France 0, Italy 0 (France won 4–3 in shootout)
Croatia 3, Germany 0
SEMIFINALS
Netherlands 1, Brazil 1 (Brazil won 4–2 in shootout)
Croatia 1, France 2

THIRD PLACE
Croatia 2, Netherlands 1

CHAMPIONSHIP
France 3, Brazil 0

WORLD CUP
All-Time Top 10

	Points	Matches	Record (W–T–L)	GF	GA
1. Brazil	120	80	53–14–13	173	78
2. West Germany	107	78	45–17–16	162	103
3. Italy	92	66	38–16–12	105	62
4. Argentina	68	57	29–10–18	100	69
5. England	53	45	20–13–12	62	42

	Points	Matches	Record (W–T–L)	GF	GA
6. France	48	41	21–6–14	86	58
7. Spain	42	40	16–10–14	61	48
8. Yugoslavia	40	37	16–8–13	60	46
9. Uruguay	38	37	15–8–14	61	52
10. U.S.S.R./Russia	38	34	16–6–12	60	40

MAJOR LEAGUE SOCCER 2000 FINAL STANDINGS

Conference champions (*) and playoff qualifiers (+) are noted. The GF and GA columns refer to Goals For and Goals Against in regulation play.

EASTERN CONFERENCE

Team	W	L	T	Pts	GF	GA
N.Y./N.J. Metrostars[1]	17	12	3	54	64	56
New England Revolution[2]	13	13	6	45	47	49
Miami Fusion	12	15	5	41	54	52
D.C. United	8	18	6	30	43	63

1. Conference champions. 2. Playoff qualifiers.

CENTRAL CONFERENCE

Team	W	L	T	Pts	GF	GA
Chicago Fire[1]	17	9	6	57	67	50
Tampa Bay Mutiny[2]	16	12	4	52	62	50
Dallas Burn[2]	14	14	4	46	54	53
Columbus Crew	11	16	5	38	47	56

1. Conference champions. 2. Playoff qualifiers.

WESTERN CONFERENCE

Team	W	L	T	Pts	GF	GA
Kansas City Wizards[1]	16	7	9	57	47	29
Los Angeles Galaxy[2]	14	10	8	50	47	37
Colorado Rapids[2]	13	15	4	43	44	61
San Jose Earthqaukes	7	17	8	29	35	50

1. Conference champions. 2. Playoff qualifiers.

MLS PLAYOFFS

3 points are awarded for a win, and 1 point for a tie. The winner of the series is the first to reach or exceed 5 points.

Quarterfinals

Los Angeles defeated Tampa Bay, 6 points to 0
New York/New Jersey defeated Dallas, 6 points to 0
Chicago defeated New England, 6 points to 3
Kansas City defeated Colorado, 7 points to 1

Semifinals

Chicago defeated New York/New Jersey, 6 points to 2
Series tied 4–4: Kansas City defeated Los Angeles in golden goal overtime

MLS CUP

Oct. 15 at RFK Stadium, Washington, D.C.
Kansas City Wizards 1, Chicago Fire 0

	1st	2nd	Total
Chicago Fire	0	0	0
Kansas City Wizards	1	0	1

First Half: KC– Miklos Molnar (Chris Klein), 11th minute.
MVP: Tony Meola, Kansas City, goalkeeper

2000 REGULAR SEASON

LEADING SCORERS

	Gm	G	A	Pts
Mamadou Diallo, Tampa Bay	28	26	43	56
Clint Mathis, N.Y./N.J.	29	16	14	46
Ante Razov, Chicago	24	18	6	42
Diego Serna, Miami	31	16	10	42
Adolfo Valencia, N.Y./N.J.	31	16	9	41
Dante Washington, Columbus	30	15	9	39
Wolde Harris, New England	31	15	73	37
Jason Kreis, Dallas	27	11	13	35
Ariel Graziani, Dallas	24	15	3	33
Alex Comas, N.Y./N.J.	25	13	6	32

GOAL SCORING

	Gm	No
Mamadou Diallo, Tampa Bay	28	26
Ante Razov, Chicago	24	18
Clint Mathis, N.Y./N.J.	29	16
Diego Serna, Miami	31	16
Adolfo Valencia, N.Y./N.J.	31	16
Ariel Graziani, Dallas	24	15
Dante Washington, Columbus	30	15
Wolde Harris, New England	31	15
Alex Comas, N.Y./N.J.	25	13
Miklos Molnar, Kansas City	17	12

ASSISTS

	Gm	No
Carlos Valderrama, Tampa Bay	32	26
Steve Ralston, Tampa Bay	30	17
Martin Machon, Miami	24	16
Preki, Kansas City	31	15
Peter Nowak, Chicago	28	14
Clint Mathis, N.Y./N.J.	29	14
Diego Gutierrez, Chicago	24	13
Jason Kreis, Dallas	27	13
Robert Warzycha, Columbus	30	13

Three players tied with 11 each.

SHOTS

	Gm	No
Mamadou Diallo, Tampa Bay	28	152
Ante Razov, Chicago	24	127
Junior Agogo, Colorado	23	103
Wolde Harris, New England	31	101
Preki, Kansas City	31	95

SHOTS ON GOAL

	Gm	No
Mamadou Diallo, Tampa Bay	28	76
Ante Razov, Chicago	24	63
Junior Agogo, Colorado	23	48
Clint Mathis, N.Y./N.J.	29	47
Wolde Harris, New England	31	46
Ariel Graziani, Dallas	24	45
Dante Washington, Columbus	30	44

GAME-WINNING GOALS

	Gm	GWG
Miklos Molnar, Kansas City	17	6
Ante Razov, Chicago	24	6
Mamadou Diallo, Tampa Bay	28	6
Clint Mathis, N.Y./N.J.	29	6
Junior Agogo, Colorado	23	5

LEADING GOALTENDERS— GOALS AGAINST AVERAGE

	Gm	Shts	Svs	GAA	W-L
Tony Meola, Kansas City	31	162	129	0.92	15-7
Kevin Hartman, Los Angeles	26	126	91	1.00	12-7
Zach Thornton, Chicago	25	127	91	1.28	15-4
Joe Cannon, San Jose	26	181	137	1.49	6-13
Scott Garlick, Tampa Bay	32	247	184	1.53	16-12
Jeff Causey, New England	22	110	67	1.55	13-13
Mark Simpson, D.C.	13	593	38	1.60	4-8
Mike Ammann, N.Y./N.J.	22	162	108	1.61	11-9
David Kramer, Colorado	20	125	79	1.65	9-8
Matt Jordan, Dallas	31	188	124	1.69	13-14

History of the Income Tax in the United States

Source: Ernst & Young LLP

The nation had few taxes in its early history. From 1791 to 1802, the United States Government was supported by internal taxes on distilled spirits, carriages, refined sugar, tobacco and snuff, property sold at auction, corporate bonds, and slaves. The high cost of the War of 1812 brought about the nation's first sales taxes on gold, silverware, jewelry, and watches. In 1817, however, Congress did away with all internal taxes, relying on tariffs on imported goods to provide sufficient funds for running the Government.

In 1862, in order to support the Civil War effort, Congress enacted the nation's first income tax law. It was a forerunner of our modern income tax in that it was based on the principles of graduated, or progressive, taxation and of withholding income at the source. During the Civil War, a person earning from $600 to $10,000 per year paid tax at the rate of 3%. Those with incomes of more than $10,000 paid taxes at a higher rate. Additional sales and excise taxes were added, and an "inheritance" tax also made its debut. In 1866, internal revenue collections reached their highest point in the nation's 90-year history—more than $310 million, an amount not reached again until 1911.

The Act of 1862 established the office of Commissioner of Internal Revenue. The Commissioner was given the power to assess, levy, and collect taxes, and the right to enforce the tax laws through seizure of property and income and through prosecution. His powers and authority remain very much the same today.

In 1868, Congress again focused its taxation efforts on tobacco and distilled spirits and eliminated the income tax in 1872. It had a short-lived revival in 1894 and 1895. In the latter year, the U.S. Supreme Court decided that the income tax was unconstitutional because it was not apportioned among the states in conformity with the Constitution.

In 1913, the 16th Amendment to the Constitution made the income tax a permanent fixture in the U.S. tax system. The amendment gave Congress legal authority to tax income and resulted in a revenue law that taxed incomes of both individuals and corporations. In fiscal year 1918, annual internal revenue collections for the first time passed the billion-dollar mark, rising to $5.4 billion by 1920. With the advent of World War II, employment increased, as did tax collections—to $7.3 billion. The withholding tax on wages was introduced in 1943 and was instrumental in increasing the number of taxpayers to 60 million and tax collections to $43 billion by 1945.

In 1981, Congress enacted the largest tax cut in U.S. history, approximately $750 billion over six years. The tax reduction, however, was partially offset by two tax acts, in 1982 and 1984, which attempted to raise approximately $265 billion.

On Oct. 22, 1986, President Reagan signed into law The Tax Reform Act of 1986, one of the most far-reaching reforms of the United States tax system since the adoption of the income tax. In an attempt to remain revenue neutral, the Act called for a $120 billion increase in business taxation and a corresponding decrease in individual taxation over a five-year period.

Following what seemed to be a yearly tradition of new tax acts which began in 1986, the Revenue Reconciliation Act of 1990 was signed into law on November 5, 1990. As with the '87, '88, and '89 acts, the 1990 act, while providing a number of substantive provisions, was small in comparison with the 1986 act. The emphasis of the 1990 act was increased taxes on the wealthy.

On August 10, 1993, President Clinton signed the Revenue Reconciliation Act of 1993 into law. The Act's purpose was to reduce by approximately $496 billion the Federal deficit that would otherwise accumulate in fiscal years 1994 through 1998. Approximately $241 billion of the deficit reduction will be accomplished through tax increases.

On August 5, 1997, President Clinton signed the Taxpayer Relief Act of 1997. The Act included $152 billion in tax cuts. The bill includes a cut in capital gains tax for individuals, a $500 per child tax credit, estate tax relief, tax incentives for education and a host of revenue-raising and tax-simplification provisions.

Internal Revenue Service

The Internal Revenue Service (IRS), a bureau of the U.S. Treasury Department, is the federal agency charged with the administration of the tax laws passed by Congress. The IRS functions through a national office in Washington, 4 regional offices, 63 district offices, and 10 service centers.

Operations involving most taxpayers are carried out in the district offices and service centers. District offices are organized into Resources Management, Examination, Collection, Taxpayer Service, Employee Plans and Exempt Organizations, and Criminal Investigation. All tax returns are filed with the service centers, where the IRS computer operations are located.

IRS service centers are processing an ever increasing number of returns and documents. Prior to 1987, all tax return processing was performed by hand. This process was time consuming and costly. In an attempt to improve the speed and efficiency of the manual processing procedure, the IRS began testing an electronic return filing system beginning with the filing of 1985 returns.

Internal Revenue Service

	1996	1995	1994	1993	1992	1970
U.S. population (in thousands)	266,109	263,730	261,698	259,015	256,219	204,878
Number of IRS employees	102,082	112,023	110,665	113,352	116,673	68,683
Cost to govt. of collecting $100 in taxes	$0.49	$0.55	$0.58	$0.60	$0.58	$0.45
Tax per capita	$5,586.00	$5,216.44	$4,878.00	$4,543.33	$4,374.38	$955.31
Collections by principal sources (in thousands of dollars)						
Total IRS collections	$1,486,546,674	$1,375,731,835	$1,276,466,776	$1,176,685,625	$1,120,799,558	$195,722,096
Income and profits taxes						
Individual	$745,313,276	$675,779,337	$619,819,153	$585,774,159	$557,723,156	$103,651,585
Corporation	$189,054,791	$174,422,173	$154,204,684	$131,547,509	$117,950,796	$35,036,983
Employment taxes	$492,365,178	$465,405,305	$443,831,352	$411,510,516	$400,080,904	$37,449,188
Estate and gift taxes	$17,591,817	$15,144,394	$15,606,793	$12,890,965	$11,479,116	$3,680,076
Alcohol taxes	(1)	(1)	(1)	(1)	(1)	$4,746,382
Tobacco taxes	(1)	(1)	(1)	(1)	(1)	$2,094,212
Manufacturers' excise taxes	(2)	(2)	(2)	(2)	(2)	6,683,061
All other taxes	$42,221,611	$44,980,627	$43,004,794	$34,962,476	$33,565,587	$2,380,609

NOTE: For fiscal year ending September 30th. 1. Alcohol and tobacco tax collections are now collected and reported by the Bureau of Alcohol, Tobacco, and Firearms. 2. Manufacturers' excise taxes are included in the "All other taxes" amount.
Source: IRS 1996 Annual Report.

The two most significant results of the test were that refunds for the electronically filed returns were issued more quickly and the tax processing error rate was significantly lower when compared to paper returns. Electronic filing of individual income tax returns with refunds became an operational program in selected areas for the 1987 processing year. In 1994 13,510,000 individual returns were filed electronically, compared to 11,143,000 in 1995, and 14,977,123 in 1996.

Auditing Tax Returns

Most taxpayers' contacts with the IRS arise through the auditing of their tax returns. The Service has been empowered by Congress to inquire about all persons who may be liable for any tax and to obtain for review the books and/or records pertinent to those taxpayers' returns. A wide-ranging audit operation is carried out in the 63 district offices by 16,078 revenue agents and 2,831 tax auditors.

The primary method used by the IRS in selecting returns for audits is a computer program that measures the probability of tax error in each return. The higher the score, the greater the tax change potential. Other returns are selected for examination on the basis of claims for refund, multi-year audits, related return audits, and other audits initiated by the IRS as a result of informants' information, special compliance programs, and the information

document matching program. In 1996, the IRS recommended additional tax and penalties on 1,941,546 individual returns, totaling $7.6 billion.

The Appeals Process

The IRS attempts to resolve tax disputes through an administrative appeals system. Taxpayers who, after audit of their tax returns, disagree with a proposed change in their tax liabilities are entitled to an independent review of their cases. Taxpayers are able to seek an immediate, informal appeal with the Appeals Office. If, however, the dispute arises from a field audit and the amount in question exceeds $10,000, a taxpayer must submit a written protest. Alternatively, the taxpayer can wait for the examiner's report and then request consideration by the Appeals Office and file a protest if necessary. Taxpayers may represent themselves or be represented by an attorney, accountant, or any other advisor authorized to practice before the IRS. Taxpayers can forego their right to the above process and await receipt of a deficiency notice. At this juncture, taxpayers can either (1) not pay the deficiency and petition the Tax Court by a required deadline or (2) pay the deficiency and file a claim for refund with the District Director's office. If the claim is not allowed, a suit for refund may be brought either in the District Court or the Claims Court within a specified period.

Federal Income Tax Comparisons
Taxes at Selected Rate Brackets After Standard Deductions and Personal Exemptions[1]

Adjusted gross income	Single return listing no dependents					Joint return listing two dependents				
	1998	1997	1996	1995	1975	1998	1997	1996	1995	1975
$10,000	$ 457	$ 493	$ 518	$ 540	$ 1,506	$ -5,200	$ -3,500	$ -3,556	$-3,110[2]	$ 829
20,000	1,958	1,980	2,018	2,040	4,153	720	975	-1,324	-773	2,860
30,000	3,458	3,480	3,518	3,573	8,018	2,200	2,475	1,965	2,018	5,804
40,000	5,595	6,092	6,246	6,373	12,765	3,720	3,975	3,465	3,518	9,668
50,000	6,549	8,892	9,046	9,173	18,360	6,449	5,475	4,965	5,018	14,260

1. For comparison purposes, tax rate schedules were used. 2. Refund based on a basic earned income credit for families with dependent children.

Federal Individual Income Tax

Tax Brackets—1998 Taxable Income

Joint return	Single taxpayer	Rate
$0–$42,350	$0–$25,350	15.0%
42,350–102,300	25,350–61,400	28.0%
102,300–155,950	61,400–128,100	31.0%[2]
155,950–278,450	128,100–278,450	36.0%[2]
278,450 and up[1]	278,450 and up[1]	39.6%[2]

1. The deduction for personal exemptions is phased out as the taxpayer's gross income exceeds $186,800 for a joint return and $124,500 for single taxpayers. 2. The tax rate is effectively increased because total otherwise allowable itemized deductions are reduced by 3% of the taxpayer's adjusted gross income in excess of $124,500.

The Federal individual income tax is levied on the worldwide income of U.S. citizens and resident aliens and on certain types of U.S. source income of non-residents. For a non-itemizer, "tax table income" is adjusted gross income less $2,700 for each personal exemption and the standard deduction. If a taxpayer itemizes, tax table income is adjusted gross income minus total itemized deductions and personal exemptions. In addition, individuals may also be subject to the alternative minimum tax.

Who Must File a Return[1]

You must file a return if you are:	and your gross income is at least:
Single (legally separated, divorced, or married living apart from spouse with dependent child)	$6,950
Head of household	$8,950
Married, filing jointly, living together at end of year (or at date of death of spouse)	$12,500
Married, filing separate return, or married but not living together at end of year over age 65	$2,700

1. In 1997.

Adjusted Gross Income

Gross income consists of wages and salaries, unemployment compensation, tips and gratuities, interest, dividends, annuities, rents and royalties, up to 85% of Social Security benefits if the recipient's income exceeds a base amount, and certain other types of income. Among the items excluded from gross income, and thus not subject to tax, are public assistance benefits and interest on exempt securities (mostly state and local bonds).

Adjusted gross income is determined by subtracting from gross income: alimony paid, penalties on early withdrawal of savings, payments to an I.R.A. (reduced proportionately based upon adjusted gross income levels if taxpayer is an active participant in an employer maintained retirement plan), payments to a Keogh retirement plan, and self-employed health insurance payments and moving expenses.

Itemized Deductions

Taxpayers may itemize deductions or take the standard deduction. The standard deduction amounts for 1998 are as follows: Married filing jointly and surviving spouses, $7,100; Heads of household, $6,250; Single, $4,250; and Married filing separate returns, $3,550. Taxpayers who are age 65 or over or are blind are entitled to an additional standard deduction of $1,000 for single taxpayers and $800 for a married taxpayer.

In itemizing deductions, the following are major items that may be deducted in 1998: state and local income and property taxes, charitable contributions, employee moving expenses, medical expenses (exceeding 7.5% of adjusted gross income), casualty losses (only the amount over the $100 floor which exceeds 10% of adjusted gross income), mortgage interest, and miscellaneous deductions (deductible only to the extent by which cumulatively they exceed 2% of adjusted gross income).

Personal Exemptions

Personal exemptions are available to the taxpayer for himself, his spouse, and his dependents. The 1998 amount is $2,700 for each individual. No exemption is allowed to a taxpayer who can be claimed as a dependent on another taxpayer's return.

Credits

Taxpayers can reduce their income tax liability by claiming the benefit of certain tax credits. Each dollar of tax credit offsets a dollar of tax liability. The following are a few of the available tax credits.

Certain low-income households may claim an Earned Income Credit. The maximum Earned Income Credit is $341 for taxpayers with no qualifying children, $2,271 for taxpayers with one qualifying child and $3,756 for taxpayers with two or more qualifying children. This maximum credit will be reduced if earned income or adjusted gross income exceeds $12,260, or $5,570 for taxpayers with no qualifying children. For families with one qualifying child, the credit will be zero if earned income or adjusted gross income exceeds $26,473; for families with two or more qualifying children, the credit will be zero if income exceeds $30,095, and for families with no qualifying children, the credit will be zero if income exceeds $10,030. The earned income credit is a refundable credit.

A credit for Child and Dependent Care Expenses is available for amounts paid to care for a child or other dependent so that the taxpayer can work. The credit is between 20% and 30% (depending on adjusted gross income) of up to $2,400 of employment-related expenses for one qualifying child or dependent and up to $4,800 of expenses for two or more qualifying individuals.

The elderly and those under 65 who are retired under total disability may be entitled to a credit of up to $750 (if single) or $1,125 (if married and filing jointly). No credit is available if the taxpayer is single and has adjusted gross income of $17,500 or more. Similarly, the credit is unavailable to a married couple filing jointly if their adjusted gross income exceeds $25,000.

Effective for tax years beginning after December 1, 1997, taxpayers who have qualifying children for whom the taxpayer may claim a dependency exemption and who is less than 17 years old as of the close of the tax year are entitled to the child tax credit. The amount of the credit for 1998 is $400. The child credit begins to phase out when AGI reaches $110,000 for joint filers and $75,000 for singles. Taxpayers who have three or more qualifying children may also be entitled to an additional credit.

State Taxes on Individuals

(as of July 1, 1999)

State	Sales/use tax (percent)[1]	Income tax (percent)[2]	State	Sales/use tax (percent)[1]	Income tax (percent)[2]
Alabama	4.0	2.0 – 5.0	Nebraska	5.0	2.62 – 6.99
Alaska	none	none	Nevada	6.5	none
Arizona	5.0	2.87 – 5.04	New Hampshire	none	(3)
Arkansas	4.625	1.0 – 7.0	New Jersey	6.0	1.4 – 6.37
California	6.0	1.0 – 9.3	New Mexico	5.0	1.7 – 8.5
Colorado	3.0	5.0	New York	4.0	4.0 – 6.85
Connecticut	6.0	3.0 – 4.5	North Carolina	4.0	6.0 – 7.75
Delaware	none	2.6 – 6.4	North Dakota	5.0	2.67 – 12.0
Florida	6.0	none	Ohio	5.0	0.673 – 6.799
Georgia	4.0	1.0 – 6.0	Oklahoma	4.5	0.5 – 6.75
Hawaii	4.0	1.6 – 8.75	Oregon	none	5.0 – 9.0
Idaho	5.0	2.0 – 8.2	Pennsylvania	6.0	2.8
Illinois	6.25	3.0	Rhode Island	7.0	26.5[4]
Indiana	5.0	3.4	South Carolina	5.0	2.5 – 6.75
Iowa	5.0	0.36 – 8.98	South Dakota	4.0	none
Kansas	4.9	4.1 – 6.45	Tennessee	6.0	(3)
Kentucky	6.0	2.0 – 6.0	Texas	6.25	none
Louisiana	4.0	2.0 – 6.0	Utah	4.75	2.3 – 7.0
Maine	5.5	2.0 – 8.5	Vermont	5.0	25[4]
Maryland	5.0	2.0 – 4.85	Virginia	3.5	2.0 – 5.75
Massachusetts	5.0	5.95	Washington	6.5	none
Michigan	6.0	4.4	West Virginia	6.0	3.0 – 6.5
Minnesota	6.5	6.0 – 8.5	Wisconsin	5.0	4.77 – 6.77
Mississippi	7.0	3.0 – 5.0	Wyoming	4.0	none
Missouri	4.225	1.5 – 6.0	Washington, D.C.	5.75	6.0 – 9.5
Montana	none	2.0 – 11.0			

1. Local and county taxes, if any, are additional. 2. Tax rate for individuals; unless otherwise noted, range denotes progressive structure; higher income pays higher rate. 3. Income tax limited to dividends and interest income only. 4. Percent of federal tax liability (e.g., if you owe the IRS $2,000 for the year, you owe the State of Vermont 25% of that, or $500). *Source:* The Federation of Tax Administrators.

Federal Corporation Taxes

Corporations are taxed under a graduated tax rate structure. If a corporation has taxable income in excess of $100,000, the amount of tax shall be increased by the lesser of five percent of such excess or $11,750. When a corporation has taxable income in excess of $15,000,000 the amount of tax shall be increased by an additional amount equal to the lesser of three percent of such excess or $100,000.

If the corporation qualifies, it may elect to be an S corporation. If it makes this election, the corporation will not (with certain exceptions) pay corporate tax on its income. Its income is instead passed through and taxed to its shareholders. There are several requirements a corporation must meet to qualify as an S corporation, including having 75 or fewer shareholders and having only one class of stock.

Tax Brackets—1998

Taxable income	Tax rate
$0–$50,000	15%
$50,001–$75,000	25%
$75,001–$100,000	34%
$100,001–$335,000	39%
$335,001–$10,000,000	34%
$10m–$15m	35%
$15m–$18.3m	38%
$18.3m and up	35%

State Corporation Income and Franchise Taxes

All states except Texas, Nevada, South Dakota, Washington, and Wyoming impose a tax on corporation net income. The majority of states impose the tax at flat rates ranging from 2.3% to approximately 10.75%. Several states have adopted a graduated basis of rates for corporations.

Nearly all states follow the federal law in defining net income. However, many states provide for varying exclusions and adjustments.

A state is empowered to tax all of the net income of its domestic corporations. With regard to non-resident corporations, however, it may only tax the net income on business carried on within its boundaries. Corporations are, therefore, required to apportion their incomes among the states where they do business, and pay a tax to each of these states. Nearly all states provide an apportionment to their domestic corporations, too, in order that they not be unduly burdened. Several states tax unincorporated businesses separately.

Federal Estate and Gift Taxes

A Federal Estate Tax Return must generally be filed for the estate of every U.S. citizen or resident whose gross estate, adjusted taxable gifts, and specific exemption exceed $625,000. An estate tax return must also generally be filed for the estate of a non-resident who died during 1998 if the value of his gross estate in the U.S. is more than $60,000 at the date of death. The estate tax return is due 9 months after the date of death of the decedent, but a 6-month extension of time to file may be obtained for good reason.

Under the unified federal estate and gift tax structure, individuals who made taxable gifts during the calendar year are required to file a gift tax return by April 15 of the following year.

A unified credit of $202,050 is available to offset both estate and gift taxes. Any part of the credit used to offset gift taxes is not available to offset estate taxes. As a result, although they are still taxable as gifts, lifetime taxable transfers no longer cushion the impact of progressive estate tax rates. Lifetime transfers and transfers made at death are combined for estate tax rate purposes.

Gift taxes are computed by applying the uniform rate schedule to lifetime taxable transfers (after deducting the unified credit) and subtracting the taxes payable for prior taxable periods. In general, estate taxes are computed by applying the uniform rate schedule to cumulative transfers and subtracting the gift taxes paid. An appropriate adjustment is made for taxes on lifetime transfers—such as certain gifts within three years of death—in a decedent's estate.

Among the deductions allowed in computing the amount of the estate subject to tax are funeral expenditures, administrative costs, claims and bequests to religious, charitable, and fraternal organizations or government welfare agencies, and state inheritance taxes. For transfers made after 1981 during life or death, there is an unlimited marital deduction.

An annual gift tax exclusion is provided that permits tax-free gifts to each donee of $10,000 for each year. A husband and wife who agree to treat gifts to third persons as joint gifts can exclude up to $20,000 a year to each donee. An unlimited exclusion for medical expenses and school tuition both paid directly to the institution for the benefit of any donee is also available in addition to the annual gift tax exclusion.

Federal Taxes Collected and Spent, by State

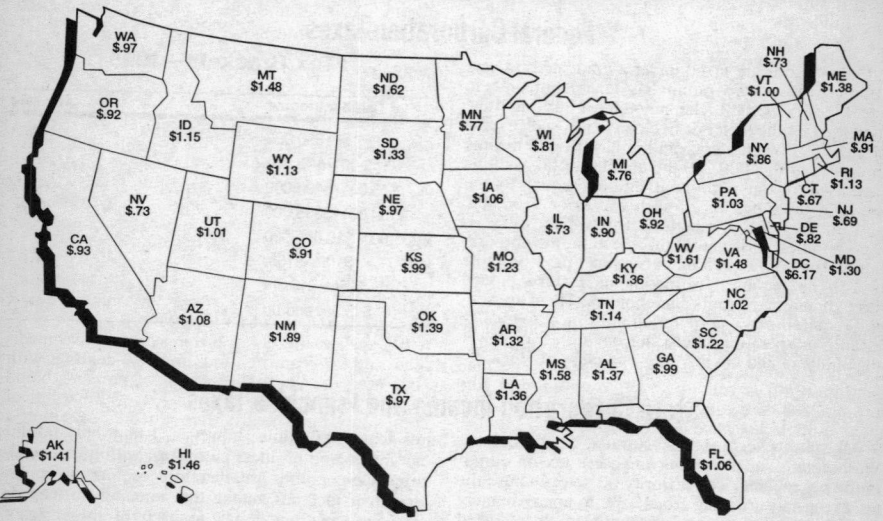

Federal Expenditures for Every Dollar of Taxes Sent to Washington
FY 1997

Source: Tax Foundation.

VISIONS 21

To observe the dawn of the 21st century, TIME challenged its writers and contributors to explore how human life and society may change by the year 2025. The following articles are selected from the more than 100 stories that compose the complete Visions 21 project. For more, visit TIME.com.

Health

Will I Live to Be 125?

If you don't, your children may, thanks to scientists looking for longevity genes. But who will want to live that long?

By JONATHAN WEINER TIME

Walking and talking get more difficult for my mother every day, and when I phoned to tell her the headline of this story, there was a long pause before she found the words to reply: "I don't recommend it."

At 75, she is fighting one of the innumerable syndromes that elderly flesh is heir to. For reasons that no neurologist can explain, many of her brain cells are filling with debris called Lewy bodies. Her symptoms resemble those of Alzheimer's, and like Alzheimer's, the condition is sometimes genetic. Do we have to grow old so sadly? Before we go, do we have to lose most of the natural gifts that make life worth living? We are the first people in human history for whom this is a primary concern. For every generation before ours, the first concerns were Can I grow old? Will my baby reach a ripe old age? Please let us grow older! Now the average life expectancy in the U.S. has advanced from 47 in 1900 to better than 76 in 1999. During the next century, new biological discoveries should ensure that even more of us will live to see old age and will encourage us to dream, in wild or wistful moments, that we might not have to grow old at all.

Whenever I want to feel optimistic, I think about work in progress in the laboratory of Seymour Benzer of the California Institute of Technology. Benzer made the first detailed map of a gene's interior, and he and his student Ronald Konopka discovered the first so-called clock gene, which ticks away inside virtually every living cell, helping to tell our bodies where we are in the daily sweep from morning to night. Now, at 77, Benzer is searching through our genes for a sort of clock of clocks that tells us where we are in the sweep from the cradle to the grave and decides how fast we age. Recently he discovered a mutant fruit fly that lives more than 100 days, about one-third longer than the rest of the madding crowd in a fly bottle. What makes the difference is a single gene, which Benzer calls Methuselah.

If one gene can do that much for flies (or worms or mice—genetic engineering has created a growing zoo of Methuselahs), then what can our genes do for us? Maybe there really is a clock of clocks, and maybe, just maybe, 21st-century biologists will figure out how to twiddle and reset the hands. They might concoct Methuselah pills or inject Methuselah genes into fertilized eggs and fool our mortal bodies into believing that we are forever young. "Perhaps," Benzer muses, "aging can be better described not as a clock but as a scenario, which we can hope to edit." If we died in old age at the same rate we die between ages 10 and 15, then most of us in the U.S. would live 1,200 years. We would outdo the first Methuselah, whose years were 969.

We are already doing better at preventive medicine and at repairing old bodies—dealing with abdominal fat, atherosclerosis, blood pressure, blood sugar, cataracts, and so on. U.S. pharmaceutical companies have nearly two dozen Alzheimer's drugs in the works. In the next century, molecular biologists are likely to tinker with more and more of our genetic machinery, in what may be either mankind's worst folly or the most significant software upgrade of the 21st century. Recently, biologists announced the discovery of mutations that accumulate in aging mitochondria, which are our cells' batteries; maybe someday they will learn how to keep our batteries from winding down. Scientists may also learn how to repair our telomeres, the tiny ties at the ends of each chromosome that help hold our genetic bundles together but fray with age. Researchers may even learn to grow whole new hearts and livers from stem cells, a prospect I find slightly dispiriting. Will we walk off the stage at last elaborately disguised, a living prosthesis—false teeth, false eyes, false taste buds, false everything?

Of course, on this question of old age, science is still a baby. There are plenty of biologists who believe that aging and death are as inevitable as taxes. No one really knows if human longevity will come up against a fixed barrier somewhere or if, like the sound barrier, it is there only to be broken. Some gerontologists say the limit of the average life span is 85 years; others, 95, 100, 150, and beyond. No one understands the economic barriers either. Ronald Lee, a demographer at the University of California, Berkeley, calculates that for each year we add to the average life span, the economy will have to grow 1% to pay for our care.

After more than 50 years in the laboratory, Seymour Benzer has too much respect for life's complexities to believe in quick cures or fountains of youth. He often works through the night on his mutant Methuselah. He feels that aging should now be studied as a disease, and he would love to spend his next career, he says, "unraveling the facts." But he hates to see the study of longevity being overblown by the press. "I hope the hype will not result in the same letdown as Richard Nixon's all-out war on cancer." Even if there is a central clock, it may be harder to control than cancer.

Chances are that my generation will consume all manner of antiaging drugs and nostrums—antioxidants, growth hormone, vitamin D, garlic, red wine, melatonin, blueberries—and in the end we'll still live only a little longer than our parents. But by the time we die, or shortly thereafter, the expansion of youth and the postponement of old age may become one of the greatest enterprises of the 21st century. "I see it as inevitable," says evolutionary biologist Michael Rose, who breeds strains of long-lived flies in his laboratory at the University of California, Irvine. "I'm confident that Benzer's work—and the worm people's and maybe

> *No one really knows if human longevity will come up against a fixed barrier somewhere or if, like the sound barrier, it is there only to be broken.*

my work—will someday be used by a bunch of avaricious corporations who'll make billions of dollars a la Microsoft by giving people what they've always wanted."

I wouldn't want to live as long as Methuselah, myself. But I would like to reach old age alive and kicking. My hope is that the science of life will mature fast enough so that 30 years from now, when my sons begin to ask those eternal questions about growing old, I can look at them and say, "I recommend it." □

Health

When Will We Cure Cancer?

Sooner rather than later, for a surprising number of malignancies. Others, we may just have to live with

By SHANNON BROWNLEE TIME

When will we cure cancer? Talk about wishful thinking. One might as well ask if there will be a war that will end all wars, or a pill that will make us all good-looking. It is also a perfectly understandable question, given that half a million Americans will die this year of a disorder that is often discussed in terms that make it seem less like a disease than an implacable enemy. What tuberculosis was to the 19th century, cancer was to the 20th: an insidious, malevolent force that frightens people beyond all reason—far more than, say, diabetes or high blood pressure.

The problem is, the "cure" for cancer is not going to show up anytime soon—almost certainly not in the next decade. In fact, there may never be a single cure, one drug that will bring every cancer patient back to glowing good health, in part because every type of cancer, from brain to breast to bowel, is different.

Now for the good news: during the next 10 years, doctors will be given tools for detecting the earliest stages of many cancers—in some cases when they are only a few cells strong—and suppressing them before they have a chance to progress to malignancy. Beyond that, nobody can make predictions with any accuracy, but there is reason to hope that within the next 25 years, new drugs will be able to ameliorate most, if not all, cancers and maybe even cure some of them. "We are in the midst of a complete and profound change in our development of cancer treatments," says Richard Klausner, director of the National Cancer Institute. The main upshot of this change is the sheer number of drugs in development—so many that they threaten to swamp clinical researchers' capacity to test them all.

This welcome boom in cancer drugs owes its beginnings to one of this century's greatest scientific insights: that cancer is caused not by depression or miasmas or sexual repression, as people at various times have believed, but by faulty genes.

Every tumor begins with just one errant cell that has been unlucky enough to suffer at least two, but sometimes several, genetic mutations. Those mutations prod the cell into replicating wildly, allowing it to escape the control that genes normally maintain over the growth of new tissue. This realization has transformed cancer, in little more than a decade, from an utterly mysterious disease into a disorder whose molecular machinery is largely understood. Now cancer biologists are in the midst of their second epiphany: the recognition that tumors evolve, in Darwinian fashion, as each succeeding generation of cancer cells accumulates genetic mutations. "Survival of the fittest applies to cancer cells," says Richard Schilsky, associate dean for clinical research at the University of Chicago. "We now think of cancer not as a disease but as a genetic process."

This new view has sparked innovations that will manage the process and keep it from killing large numbers of people. "We are going to see a real shift from diagnosis and treatment to prediction and prevention," declares California surgeon Susan Love, author of *Dr. Susan Love's Breast Book.* Indeed, if all goes well with current clinical trials, women at high risk for breast cancer will soon be able to be screened with a device that removes a sample of breast cells through the nipple. If any cells show signs of the early mutations that lead to cancer, doctors can suggest the drug tamoxifen, which is believed to reduce the risk of breast cancer by suppressing precancerous cells. Drugs with fewer side effects that can also prevent breast cancer are already in the pipeline.

Within five years, early detection will be available for many other types of cancer as well. A stool sample will be all that is needed to search for colon-cancer cells on their way to becoming tumors, and drugs like the new COX-2 inhibitors, which are improved versions of painkillers, can prevent those precancerous cells from progressing. By the end of the next decade, a simple blood test could alert doctors to a wide variety of cancer precursors. Treatments for more advanced cancers, however, are farther over the horizon than anybody can see. What is clear is that oncologists must take a page from AIDS treatment and use a cocktail of drugs with very different modes of action to outsmart tumors that have already begun to spread or metastasize.

That's because a tumor is made up of a hodge-podge of cells containing different genetic mutations, each of which allows it to wreak a different brand of havoc. Some mutations spur rapid growth; others prod nearby blood vessels into sprouting new capillaries; still others send cancer cells out into the bloodstream, where they can seed new tumors. Within 10 years, predicts Robert Weinberg, a cancer biologist at the Whitehead Institute in Cambridge, Mass., "we will analyze the mutant genes and then tailor-make a treatment [for] that particular tumor."

One day there will be drugs to trip up a cell at each of the steps it takes on the path to malignancy. A patient with lung cancer, say, might undergo gene therapy, breathing in genetically altered cold viruses that don't cause infection but instead act as miniature delivery vans carrying copies of the p53 gene. Good copies of this gene, which is mutated in many cancers, can force some cancer cells to commit suicide. The effects of p53 could be bolstered with antibodies that slow tumors by attaching to the surface of cancer cells and gumming up their ability to take over the body's growth factors, the specialized proteins that promote cell reproduction.

If a tumor has acquired the mutations for spreading, the doctor of the future may call on matrix metaloproteinase inhibitors, a new kind of drug that can be taken orally to block the enzymes a tumor uses to break down the cells of surrounding tissue and invade it. Vaccines cobbled together from whole cancer cells or bits and pieces of those cells have been shown to boost the body's immune system, helping it recognize and kill tumors on its own. "This was all a dream five years ago," marvels John Minna, director of the Hamon Center for Therapeutic Oncology Research at the University of Texas Southwestern Medical Center in Dallas.

Also close to reality are the so-called antiangiogenic factors, relatively nontoxic compounds that inhibit the growth of new capillaries. The idea behind this new class of drugs is that tumors cannot grow bigger than a few hundred thousand cells—about the size of a peppercorn—without growing their own blood-supply system. Researchers and

> *What tuberculosis was to the 19th century, cancer was to the 20th: an insidious, malevolent force that frightens people beyond all reason*

patients, not to mention the owners of stock in half a dozen biotech companies, are eagerly awaiting results of clinical trials of antiangiogenic factors, which might be used in combination with chemotherapy to knock down big tumors and then prevent any surviving tumors from growing enough to do further damage.

The assumption behind many of these futuristic scenarios is an idea that most researchers have begun to embrace but that many patients will undoubtedly find difficult to accept. That is the prediction that certain cancers may require treatment for the rest of a patient's long life. Coming out of a century that declared war on the disease, a century that felt the only reasonable response to a tumor was to annihilate it, this may be hard to imagine. But turning cancer into a controllable condition is not so different from treating high blood pressure or diabetes. "I don't think curing cancer is the goal," says Ellen Stovall, executive director of the National Coalition for Cancer Survivorship. Instead, she says, "it should be helping people live as long and as well as they can."

No, we probably won't cure all forms of cancer in the 21st century. But we may very well learn to live with them. □

Will We Run Out of Gas?

No, we'll have plenty of carbon-based fuel to see us through the next century. That's the problem

By MARK HERTSGAARD TIME

Will we run out of gas? The metaphorical answer to this question is more important than the literal, but the literal is irresistibly short: No, unfortunately not. Humans will have as much gasoline as we can burn in the 21st century. Nor are we likely to run out of heating oil, coal, or natural gas, the other carbon-based fuels that have powered industrial civilization for 200 years.

Why won't we run out? And why is that unfortunate? After all, these fuels provide nearly 80% of the energy humans use to keep warm, to light buildings and run computers, to power the cars that get us around, the tractors that plant food, the hospitals that serve our sick. If these fuels were to vanish tomorrow, worldwide chaos would follow, and humans would die in the hundreds of millions.

So why not rejoice at having lots of fuel to burn? Let me try to answer that by telling you about my friend Zhenbing.

I met Zhenbing in China in 1996, near the end of a six-year journey around the world to write a book about humanity's environmental future. A 30-year-old economics professor who was liked on sight by virtually everyone he met, Zhenbing was my interpreter during five weeks of travel throughout China. A born storyteller, he often recalled his childhood in a tiny village northwest of Beijing. Like most Chinese peasants of that era, Zhenbing's parents were too poor to buy coal. Instead, in a climate like Boston's, where winter temperatures often plunged below zero, they burned dried leaves to heat their mud hut. Their home's inside walls were often white with frost from November to April.

In 1980, China's economic reforms began putting enough money in people's pockets to enable even peasants like Zhenbing's parents to buy coal. Today coal supplies 73% of China's energy, and there is enough beneath the country to last an additional 300 years at current consumption rates. Plainly, that is good news in one respect. Burning coal has made the Chinese people (somewhat) warm in winter for the first time in their history. But multiply Zhenbing's story by China's huge population, and you understand why 9 of the world's 10 most air-polluted cities are found in China and why nearly 1 of every 3 deaths there is linked to the horrific condition of the air and water. Equally alarming is what China's coal burning is doing to the planet as a whole. China has become the world's second-largest producer of the greenhouse gases that cause global warming, and it will be No. 1 by 2020 if it triples coal consumption as planned. But the U.S., the other environmental superpower, has no right to point a finger. Americans lead the world in greenhouse-gas production, mainly because of their addiction to the car, the source of almost 40% of U.S. emissions.

Which returns us to gasoline and its source, petroleum. The earth's underground stores of petroleum are not as ample as those of coal or natural gas, but there is enough to supply humanity for many decades, even with rising population and living standards. Crippling shortages may still occur. But they will arise from skulduggery or incompetence on the part of corporations or governments, not from any physical scarcity. "Will we run out of gas?"—a question we began asking during the oil shocks of the 1970s—is now the wrong question. The earth's supply of carbon-based fuels will last a long time. But if humans burn anywhere near that much carbon, we'll burn up the planet, or at least our place on it.

Change won't be easy. But how we respond will help answer the metaphorical meaning of "Will we run out of gas?" That is, will our species fizzle out in the coming century, a victim of its own appetites and lethargy? Or will we take action and earn a longer stay on this beautiful planet? The good news is, we know how to change course. Improving energy efficiency is the first step and—surprise!—potentially a

> *The earth's supply of carbon-based fuels will last a long time. But if humans use anywhere near that much carbon, we'll burn up our place on the planet*

very profitable one, for all of society. And better efficiency can buy us time to make a global transition to solar power and other renewable energy.

China could use 50% less energy if it only installed more efficient electric lights, motors, and insulation, all technologies currently available on the world market. Americans could trade in their notoriously gas-swilling SUVs for sporty new 80-m.p.g. hybrid-electric cars. Better yet: hydrogen-powered fuel-cell cars, expected in showrooms by 2004. Since their only exhaust is water vapor, fuel-cell cars produce neither smog nor global warming.

The best part is that we could make money by making peace with the planet. If governments launched a program—call it a Global Green Deal—to environmentally retrofit our civilization from top to bottom, they could create the biggest business enterprise of the next 25 years, a huge source of jobs and profits. Which is why I'm not entirely gloomy about our future. After all, what's more human than pursuit of self-interest? □

Space

Will We Meet E.T.?

Most scientists used to believe that we would eventually encounter extraterrestrial life. Now they're not so sure

By FREDERIC GOLDEN TIME

We've come a long way since 1600, when Giordano Bruno, a defrocked priest from Naples, was burned at the stake for espousing, among other things, his belief that there might be other worlds and other life forms beyond Earth. In our Star Trekking age, it's now almost heretical not to believe in extraterrestrial life—a belief that will surely be fortified by the recent announcement of the discovery of two Saturn-size planets around two distant stars.

Polls show that 54% of Americans are convinced that there are aliens out there, to say nothing of the significant fraction (30%) who suspect we've already been visited by them. If there really is life elsewhere in the universe, what are the odds of finding it in our lifetime—or even our children's? Hunting for extraterrestrials, smart or otherwise, requires a lot of faith. You have to believe that conditions for life (liquid water, mild temperatures, protection from lethal radiation) are not unique to Earth; that under the right circumstances, life can arise fairly easily; and that if it does reach a level advanced enough to broadcast its presence, it won't destroy itself in a nuclear war or an environmental meltdown before firing off Earth-bound communiqués.

That's plenty of ifs for skeptical scientists to swallow. As physicist Enrico Fermi liked to say, if there are so many extraterrestrials out there, why haven't we heard from them? To some curmudgeonly types, all this E.T. talk is pretty brainless. Evolutionary biologist Ernst Mayr, for one, considers the likelihood of life of any sort beyond our planet close to zilch. Says he: "The chance that this improbable phenomenon [the creation of life] could have occurred several times is exceedingly small, no matter how many millions of planets in the universe."

Paleontologist Peter Ward and astronomer Donald Brownlee agree. In a provocative book, *Rare Earth*, they maintain that in most places beyond Earth, radiation and heat levels are so high, life-friendly planets so scarce, and the cosmic bombardments—like the one that killed off the dinosaurs 65 million years ago—so severe that the only life forms that might make it would be bacteria-like critters living deep in the soil. The odds against technologically advanced societies, they argue, are astronomical. Surprisingly, even Geoff Marcy, the leader in the increasingly successful hunt for planets outside our solar system, feels that we may well be alone in the universe. Most of the 33 newly discovered planets—giant gas bags all, including those two new ones—swing so erratically around their parent stars that they would create havoc on any smaller, nearby, life-friendly planets. But such pessimism represents a minority view among scientists, at least those with their eyes on the stars. "In this business, you have to remain optimistic," says radio astronomer Frank Drake, who kicked off the original Search for Extraterrestrial Intelligence (SETI) in 1960 with his whimsically named Project Ozma (after the satiric Oz books). He "looked" briefly at several nearby Sun-like stars in the hope that they might be orbited by planets whose inhabitants were sending out intelligible signals, like the flood of radio and TV broadcasts we've been inadvertently blasting into space for the past 80 years. ("Hey there, Alpha Centauri! Whaddya think of *The Honeymooners?*")

Drake, alas, detected nary a peep. Nor has anyone else since then. Even after spending thousands of hours scanning the skies, at myriad frequencies, at a cost of more than $100 million, astronomers have yet to detect a single credible signal.

Still, Drake, 70, remains convinced that he will be around when E.T. calls. "We're just at the beginning of our search," says Drake, who reckons that there are some 10,000 high-tech worlds scattered among the Milky Way's 100 billion or more stars. For years Congress funded various SETI efforts—until the political stigma of paying for the quest for "little green men," as cynics like to call them, scuttled fed-

> *As physicist Enrico Fermi liked to say, if there are so many extraterrestrials out there, why haven't we heard from them?*

eral funding in 1993. Nonetheless, NASA continues the search for unearthly life, even if it's only for little green bugs, under the more politically palatable label of astrobiology. Right now, NASA is eyeing the dusty surface of Mars (where water once flowed) and the likely ocean under the ice of Jupiter's moon Europa as sites for primitive life forms. One recent false alarm: the much trumpeted Martian meteorite found in Antarctica apparently does not contain convincing evidence of the existence of microorganisms on the Red Planet, as originally claimed.

Maybe you'd like to try tracking down E.T. yourself? If you have a PC or Mac that sits idle at least a few hours a day, you can join the 1.7 million people who have downloaded SETI@home, a free screen saver (available at setiathome.ssl.berkeley.edu) that uses your computer's downtime to help sort through the reams of noisy static gathered by radio telescopes. The odds of pulling a Jodie Foster (who snared the elusive extraterrestrial signal in the 1997 sci-fi flick *Contact*) are a zillion to one. But if you fail—or even if you succeed—nobody's going to burn you at the stake. □

Environment

How Hot Will It Get?

No one knows for sure, but the potential perils of climate change make it unwise for us to ignore the greenhouse effect

By JAMES TREFIL TIME

Not so long ago, people talked about global warming in apocalyptic terms—imagining the Statue of Liberty up to its chin in water or an onslaught of tropical diseases in Oslo. Recently, however, advances in our understanding of climate have moved global warming from a subject for a summer disaster movie to a serious but manageable scientific and policy issue.

Here's what we know. Since sunlight is always falling on the earth, the laws of physics decree that the planet has to radiate the same amount of energy back into space to keep the books balanced. The earth does this by sending infrared radiation out through the atmosphere, where an array of molecules (the best known is carbon dioxide) form a kind of blanket, holding outgoing radiation for a while and warming the surface. The molecules are similar to the glass in a greenhouse, which is why the warming process is called the greenhouse effect.

The greenhouse effect is nothing new; it has been operating ever since the earth formed. Without it, the surface of the globe would be a frigid −20°C (−4°F), the oceans would have frozen, and no life would have developed. So the issue we face in the next millennium is not whether there will be a greenhouse effect, but whether humans, by burning fossil fuels, are adding enough carbon dioxide to the atmosphere to change it (and our climate) in significant ways.

You might think that, knowing what causes greenhouse warming, it would be an easy matter to predict how hot the world will be in the next century. Unfortunately, things aren't that simple. The world is a complex place, and reducing it to the climatologist's tool of choice—the computer model—isn't easy. Around almost every statement in the greenhouse debate is a penumbra of uncertainty that results from our current inability to capture the full complexity of the planet in our models.

There is one fact, though, that everyone agrees on: the amount of carbon dioxide in the atmosphere is increasing steadily. It is near 360 parts per million today, versus 315 p.p.m. in 1958 (when modern measurements started) and 270 p.p.m. in preindustrial times (as measured by air bubbles trapped in the Greenland ice sheet).

An analysis of admittedly spotty temperature records indicates that the world's average temperature has gone up about 0.5°C (1°F) in the past century, with the '90s being the hottest decade in recent history. This fact is quoted widely in the scientific community, although there are nagging doubts even among researchers. Recent satellite records, using different kinds of instrumentation, fail to show a warming trend.

If we accept that there has been moderate warming, we turn to computer models to see if humans are to blame and what will happen to the earth's climate in the future. These models are complex because climate depends on thousands of things, from Antarctic sea ice to sub-Saharan soil conditions. While the electronic simulations are monuments to the ingenuity and perseverance of their creators, they provide us with, at best, a fuzzy view of the future. They have difficulty handling factors like clouds and ocean currents (two major influences on climate), and if you fed the climate of 1900 into any of them, they couldn't predict the climatic history of the 20th century. Like everything else in this frustrating field, the models' limitations force us to make important decisions in the face of imperfect knowledge.

> *The issue we face in the next millennium is not whether there will be a greenhouse effect, but whether humans, by burning fossil fuels, are adding enough carbon dioxide to the atmosphere to change it (and our climate) in significant ways.*

The most authoritative predictions about future warming come from the Intergovernmental Panel on Climate Change, a worldwide consortium of more than 2,000 climate scientists. The current forecast is that by 2100 the earth's temperature will go up 1° to 3.5°C (2° to 7°F), with the best guess being an increase of 2°C (4°F).

At the lower end of this predicted warming range, the temperature rise would take us back to the conditions that existed between A.D. 950 and 1350, when the climate was 1°C (2°F) warmer than it is now. This time period is regarded as one of the most benign weather regimes in history. To find temperature swings at the upper end, you have to go back 10,000 years, to when the earth was exiting the last Ice Age. Temperatures during the Ice Age were 5°C (10°F) cooler than they are now, and there was a series of incidents during which global temperatures changed as much as 10°F in a matter of decades. If that were to happen now, expanding oceans might flood coastlines and generate fiercer storms. And as weather patterns changed, some places could get wetter and some dryer, and the ranges of diseases could expand. Civilization has seen—and endured—such changes in the past, but they may come much more swiftly this time, making it harder to withstand the jolts.

The main reason for the spread in the IPCC predictions is uncertainty about how much carbon dioxide will be added to the atmosphere by human activity, because how we will respond to the threat of climate warming is the greatest imponderable of all. We can probably develop technologies to deal with excess carbon—some scientists talk about removing it from smokestacks and stashing it underground—but the most direct way to control carbon dioxide in the atmosphere is not to put it there in the first place. This is the point of the 1997 Kyoto Protocol—signed by 84 nations but not ratified by the U.S. Senate—which would limit developed countries' carbon emissions from cars, power plants; and other major users of fossil fuels.

It makes no sense to overreact to the prospect of global warming, but it makes no sense to ignore it either. A prudent policy that stresses conservation and alternate energy sources seems to me to be wise insurance in an uncertain age. After all, our grandchildren will thank us for developing high-mileage cars, energy-efficient appliances, and cheap solar energy, no matter how the future of global warming plays out. □

. . . And Then How Cold?

By MICHAEL D. LEMONICK TIME

It seems obvious that trapping more of the sun's heat will make the planet hotter. But what seems obvious isn't always true. According to some respected scientists, there's a chance that global warming could plunge us into, of all things, an ice age.

The argument hinges on the Gulf Stream, the ocean current that brings warm surface water north and east and heats Europe. As it travels, some of the water evaporates; what's left is saltier and thus denser. Eventually the dense surface water sinks to the sea bottom, where it flows back southward. And then, near the equator, warm, fresh water from tropical rivers and rain dilutes the salt once again, allowing the water to rise to the surface, warm up, and begin flowing north again.

But with global warming, melting ice from Greenland and the Arctic Ocean could pump fresh water into the North Atlantic; so could the increased rainfall predicted for northern latitudes in a warmer world. Result: the Gulf Stream's water wouldn't get saltier after all and wouldn't sink so easily. Without adequate resupply, the southerly underwater current would stop, and the Gulf Stream would in turn be shut off.

If that happens, Europe will get very cold. Rome is, after all, at the same latitude as Chicago, and Paris is about as far north as North Dakota. More snow will fall, and the bright snow cover will reflect more of the sun's energy back into space, making life even chillier. Beyond that, the Gulf Stream is tied into other ocean currents, and shutting it down could rearrange things in a way that would cause less overall evaporation. Because atmospheric H_2O is an important greenhouse gas, its loss would mean even more dramatic cooling—a total of perhaps as much as 8°C (17°F).

Worst of all, the experts believe, such changes could come on with astonishing speed—perhaps

> *According to some respected scientists, there's a chance that global warming could plunge us into, of all things, an ice age.*

within a decade or less. And while we might have a great deal of trouble adjusting to a climate that gets 2°C (4°F) warmer over the next century, an ice age by midcentury would be unimaginably devastating. The lingering uncertainty about whether our relentless production of greenhouse gases will keep heating our planet or ultimately cool it suggests that we should make a better effort to leave the earth's thermostat alone. □

Yes, It's Sure Getting Warmer

In May 1999, British and American scientists published information based on extensive research that confirms a commonly held conception—it is getting warmer. According to these experts, annual global surface temperatures have risen 1.03°F (0.57°C) over the past 136 years (1861–1997), establishing the 20th century as the warmest era of the millennium.

In fact, researchers at the Universities of Massachusetts and Arizona, as well as scientists at both NASA and the National Oceanic and Atmospheric Administration, have concluded that the 1990s has been the warmest decade of the millennium, with 1998 the warmest year so far. The years 1997, 1995, and 1990 fall into close 2nd, 3rd, and 4th places behind sizzling 1998.

Yet despite the fact that in 1998 the *average* temperature for the 48 contiguous states was the highest since 1896, ironically, no all-time-high individual state temperature records were broken in that same year. □

Business

What Will Be the 10 Hottest Jobs?

Prepare now: the position you save may be your own

By the TIME staff

1. Tissue Engineers With man-made skin already on the market and artificial cartilage not far behind, 25 years from now scientists expect to be pulling a pancreas out of a Petri dish. Or trying, anyway. Researchers have successfully grown new intestines and bladders inside animals' abdominal cavities, and work has begun on building liver, heart, and kidney tissue.

2. Gene Programmers Digital genome maps will allow lab technicians to create customized prescriptions, altering individual genes by rewriting lines of computer code. After scanning your DNA for defects, doctors will use gene therapy and "smart" molecules to prevent a variety of diseases, including certain cancers.

3. Pharmers New-age Old MacDonalds will raise crops and livestock that have been genetically engineered to produce therapeutic proteins. Works in progress include a vaccine-carrying tomato and drug-laden milk from cows, sheep, and goats.

4. Frankenfood Monitors Not sure what's for dinner? With a little genetic tinkering, fast-growing fish and freeze-resistant fruits will help feed an overpopulated planet, but such hybrids could unwittingly wipe out the food chain. Eco-scouts will be on the lookout for so-called Trojan gene effects, and bounty hunters will help the USDA eliminate transgenic species that get out of hand.

5. Data Miners When Ask Jeeves just won't cut it, research gurus will be on hand to extract useful tidbits from mountains of data, pinpointing behavior patterns for marketers and epidemiologists alike.

6. Hot-line Handymen Still daunted by the thought of reprogramming your VCR? Just wait until your 3-D holographic TV won't power up or your talking toaster starts mouthing off. Remote diagnostics will take care of most of your home electronics, but a few repairmen will still make house calls . . . via video phone.

7. Virtual-reality Actors Pay-per-view will become pay-per-play, creating interactive cyberspace dramas. Scriptwriters will also be in high demand, as mouse potatoes clamor for new story lines to escape from their droned-out existence.

8. Narrowcasters Today's broadcasting industry will become increasingly personalized, working with advertisers to create content (read: product placement) just for you. Ambient commercials will also hijack your attention by using tastes and smells.

9. Turing Testers Computer engineers will continue to measure their efforts to mimic human intelligence, as British mathematician Alan Turing suggested 50 years ago, by asking you whether you're talking to a person or a machine.

10. Knowledge Engineers Artificial-intelligence brokers will translate your expertise into software, then downsize you.

And what jobs will disappear?

1. Stockbrokers, Auto Dealers, Mail Carriers, Insurance and Real Estate Agents The Internet will eradicate middlemen by the millions, with a hardy few remaining to service the clueless. You'll cut us a deal, right, HAL?

2. Teachers Distance learning is becoming more popular, and through the miracle of online classes and electronic grading, today's faculty lounge could become tomorrow's virtual help desk. Outsourcing our education system might cost less than installing all those metal detectors.

3. Printers Xerox and other visionaries are racing to produce digital paper, a material that's as flexible as regular paper and as versatile as a computer screen, with the end result keeping news junkies happy, not to mention all those trees.

4. Stenographers Sophisticated voice-recognition software will replace court reporters and lots of secretaries and executive assistants.

5. CEOs Top-down decision making will be too cumbersome, and golden parachutes too obscene, for the blistering 24-hour business day. A global team of quick-thinking experts will carry companies through the Internet age and beyond.

6. Orthodontists No more metal mouth, thanks to 3-D simulation programs that will crank out a series of disposable, clear-plastic "aligners" to shift your teeth into position. This technology is geared for adults, so all you gap-toothed prepubes will have something to look forward to.

7. Prison Guards Microscopic implants will restrain convicts from engaging in criminal activity. The sensors will require lots of fine tuning, though—we wouldn't want an aggressive telemarketer getting zapped, would we?

8. Truckers Interstates will have "smart" lanes enabling computer-driven vehicles to travel bumper to bumper at high speeds. Suburbia will decongest as bottleneck sensors in cars suggest alternate routes, and while you can kiss those meter maids goodbye, tickets will appear on your virtual dash.

9. Housekeepers If fridges today can decide to buy you more milk (online), then self-motivated vacuums don't sound so far afield. Perhaps self-cleaning homes will use a central vacuuming system or dust-eating nanobots.

10. Fathers Between in-vitro fertilization and cloning, dads could become dinosaurs. Moms, too, with the possibility looming of an artificial womb. Did somebody say George Orwell? □

Society

Are We Coming Apart or Together?

If you like cultures that are new and different, our globalizing world is a dream. Plenty of folks, though, want things to stay the same

By PICO IYER TIME

It is a truth all but universally acknowledged that the more internationalism there is in the world, the more nationalism there will be: the more multinational companies, multicultural beings, and planetary networks cross and transcend borders, the more other forces will, as if in response, fashion new divisions and aggravate old ones. Human nature abhors a vacuum, and it is only natural, when people find themselves in a desert, without boundaries, that they will try to assuage their vulnerability by settling into a community. Thus fewer and fewer wars take place these days across borders, and more and more take place within them.

Many Americans, rejoicing in an unprecedented period of economic success and celebrating the new horizons opened up by our latest technologies, are likely to embrace the future as a dashing (if unknown) stranger who's appeared at our door to whisk us into a strange new world. Those who travel, though, are more likely to see rising tribalism, widening divisions, and all the fissures that propel ever more of the world into what looks like anarchy. Fully 97% of the population growth that will bring our numbers up to 9 billion by the year 2050 will take place in developing countries, where conditions are scarcely better than they were a hundred years ago. In many cases, in fact, history seems to be moving backward (in modern Zimbabwe, to take but one example, the average life expectancy has dwindled from 70 to 38 in recent years because of AIDS). To travel today is to see a planet that looks more and more like a too typical downtown on a global scale: a small huddle of shiny high-rises reaching toward a multinational heaven, surrounded on every side by a wasteland of the poor, living in a state of almost biblical desperation.

When people speak of a "digital divide," they are, in effect, putting into 21st-century technological terms what is an age-old cultural problem: that all the globalism in the world does not erase (and may in fact intensify) the differences between us. Corporate bodies stress connectedness, borderless economies, all the wired communities that make up our worldwide webs; those in Chechnya, Kosovo, or Rwanda remind us of much older forces. And even as America exports its dotcom optimism around the world, many other countries export their primal animosities to America. If all the world's a global village, that means that the ancestral divisions of every place can play out in every other. And the very use of that comforting word *village* tends to distract us from the fact that much of the world is coming to resemble a global city (with all the gang warfare, fragmentation, and generalized estrangement that those centers of affluence promote). When the past century began, 13% of humans lived in cities; by the time it ended, roughly 50% did.

The hope, in the face of these counterclockwise movements, is that we can be bound by what unites us, which we have ever more occasion to see; that the stirring visions of Thomas Paine or Martin Luther King, Jr. have more resonance than ever, now that an American can meet a Chinese counterpart—in Shanghai or San Francisco (or many places in between)—and see how much they have in common. What Emerson called the Over-soul reminds us that we are joined not only by our habits and our urges but also by our dreams and that best part of us that intuits an identity larger than you or I. Look up, wherever you are, and you can see what we have in common; look down—or inside—and you can see something universal. It is only when you look around that you note divisions.

The fresher and more particular hope of the moment is that as more and more of us cross borders, we can step out of, and beyond, the old categories. Every time a Palestinian man, say, marries a Singhalese woman (and such unions are growing more common by the day) and produces a half-Palestinian, half-Singhalese child, an Israeli or a Tamil is deprived of a tribal enemy. Mongrelism—the human equivalent of World Music and "fusion culture"—is the brightest child of fragmentation.

Yet the danger we face is that of celebrating too soon a global unity that only covers much deeper divisions. Much of the world is linked, more than ever before, by common surfaces: people on every continent may be watching Michael Jordan advertising Nike shoes on CNN. But beneath the surface, inevitably, traditional differences remain. George Bernard Shaw declared generations ago that England and America were two countries divided by a common language. Now the world often resembles 200 countries divided by a common frame of cultural reference. The number of countries on the planet, in the 21st century, has more than tripled.

It seems a safe bet, as we move toward the year 2025, that governments will become no more idealistic than they have ever been—they will always represent a community of interests. And corporations cannot afford to stress conscience or sacrifice before profit. It therefore falls to the individual to look beyond the divisions of her parents' time and find a common ground with strangers and to apply the adjective *global* to *identity* and *loyalty*. Never before in history have so many people, whether in Manhattan or in Tuva, been surrounded by so much that is alien (in customs, languages, and neighborhoods). How we orient ourselves in the midst of all this foreignness and in the absence of the old certainties will determine how much our nations are disunited and how much we are bound by what Augustine called "things loved in common." □

Newsmakers of the 20th Century

Albert Einstein is TIME's choice as Person of the Century

Each year since 1927 the editors of TIME have selected a Man or Woman of the Year—the individual whose actions most influenced the course of history in the past 12 months, for good or for ill. The first Man of the Year was pioneering aviator Charles Lindbergh; other recipients have included such heroes as Harry Truman and Pope John Paul II—and such villains as Adolf Hitler and Ayatollah Khomeini.

TIME's editors observed the turn of the millennium by designating the TIME 100, the 100 most important men and women of the 20th century, in several broad categories: Leaders and Revolutionaries, Heroes and Icons, Builders and Titans, Artists and Entertainers, and Great Minds of the Century. The project concluded with the designation of physicist Albert Einstein as Person of the Century. Said TIME: "In a century that will be remembered foremost for its science and technology, one person stands out as both the greatest mind and paramount icon of our age: the kindly absentminded professor whose wild halo of hair, piercing eyes, engaging humanity and extraordinary brilliance made his face a symbol and his name a synonym for genius: Albert Einstein." TIME's editors named U.S. president Franklin D. Roosevelt and Mohandas K. Gandhi, father of India's independence, as its two runners-up for Person of the Century.

Recognizing the growth of the Internet as one of the driving engines for change in our era, TIME named Jeff Bezos, the founder and CEO of online retail giant Amazon.com, as its Person of the Year 1999. "Jeff Bezos," said the magazine, "first peered into the maze of connected computers called the World Wide Web and envisioned a company, Amazon, that would help us shop, communicate, and live closer together. For helping build a foundation of the future, he is TIME's Person of the Year 1999."

1927 Charles Lindbergh	1952 Queen Elizabeth II	1976 Jimmy Carter
1928 Walter P. Chrysler	1953 Konrad Adenauer	1977 Anwar Sadat
1929 Owen D. Young	1954 John Foster Dulles	1978 Deng Xiaoping
1930 Mahatma Gandhi	1955 Harlow H. Curtice	1979 Ayatollah Khomeini
1931 Pierre Laval	1956 Hungarian Patriot	1980 Ronald Reagan
1932 Franklin D. Roosevelt	1957 Nikita Khrushchev	1981 Lech Walesa
1933 Hugh S. Johnson	1958 Charles de Gaulle	1982 The Personal Computer
1934 Franklin D. Roosevelt	1959 Dwight D. Eisenhower	1983 Ronald Reagan and Yuri
1935 Haile Selassie	1960 U.S. Scientists	Andropov
1936 Wallis Warfield Simpson	1961 John F. Kennedy	1984 Peter Ueberroth
1937 Gen. and Mrs. Chiang	1962 Pope John XXIII	1985 Deng Xiaoping
Kai-shek	1963 Rev. Martin Luther King, Jr.	1986 Corazon Aquino
1938 Adolf Hitler	1964 Lyndon B. Johnson	1987 Mikhail Gorbachev
1939 Joseph Stalin	1965 Gen. William	1988 Endangered Earth
1940 Winston Churchill	Westmoreland	1989 Mikhail Gorbachev
1941 Franklin D. Roosevelt	1966 Americans under 25	1990 George Bush
1942 Joseph Stalin	1967 Lyndon B. Johnson	1991 Ted Turner
1943 Gen. George C. Marshall	1968 Astronauts Anders,	1992 Bill Clinton
1944 Gen. Dwight D.	Borman, Lovell	1993 The Peacemakers: Rabin,
Eisenhower	1969 The Middle Americans	Arafat, Mandela, De Klerk
1945 Harry S. Truman	1970 Willy Brandt	1994 Pope John Paul II
1946 James F. Byrnes	1971 Richard M. Nixon	1995 Newt Gingrich
1947 Gen. George C. Marshall	1972 Richard M. Nixon and	1996 Dr. David Ho
1948 Harry S. Truman	Henry Kissinger	1997 Andrew Grove
1949 Winston Churchill	1973 Judge John J. Sirica	1998 Bill Clinton and
1950 G.I. Joe	1974 King Faisal	Kenneth Starr
1951 Mohammed Mossadegh	1975 American Women	1999 Jeff Bezos

People in the News, 2000

Mehmet Ali Agca was pardoned by Italy's president in June for his 1981 attempt to assassinate **Pope John Paul II.** Agca returned to Turkey, where he was imprisoned for the murder of a newspaper editor. It remains a mystery why Agca tried to kill the pope, or who may have backed him.

Lance Armstrong, 29, won his second consecutive Tour de France in July, only four years after being diagnosed with aggressive testicular cancer, which spread to the Texas native's abdomen, lungs, and brain.

Bashar Assad, 34, Syrian ophthalmologist, was thrust into the international spotlight after his father, Syrian president **Hafez Assad,** died of a heart attack in June. Hafez Assad had been grooming his soft-spoken son to succeed him, but the president's unexpected death accelerated Bashar's ascent. The younger Assad, who was sworn in as president in July, is widely expected to open the country to the Internet, fight corruption, and seek foreign investment. Observers don't expect him to stray from his father's hard-line course with Israel.

Steven A. Ballmer, software-company official, became chief executive of Microsoft in Jan., when **Bill Gates** stepped aside to assume the newly created position of "chief software architect." Ballmer had been serving as president of the company.

Thomas E. Blanton Jr. and Bobby Frank Cherry were charged in May with the 1963 murder of four black girls who died in the fiery explosion of Birmingham, Alabama's 16th Street Baptist Church. The bombing is considered the most heinous crime of the civil rights era.

Bill Bradley, former U.S. senator, bowed out of the race for the Democratic presidential nomination in March after losing all of Super Tuesday's 16 primaries to **Vice President Al Gore.** Bradley's popular support took Gore by surprise late in 1999 and forced the vice president to reassess his campaign. Bradley's campaign focused on providing health care to all Americans and fighting poverty and racism.

Chen Shui-bian, Taiwanese lawyer and opposition politician, was elected president of Taiwan in March, with 39% of the vote. Chen, leader of the Democratic Progressive Party, had long supported independence from mainland China, but he softened his stance days before the election, saying that independence isn't necessary because Taiwan is already sovereign. His election ended the Nationalists' grip on power that began in 1949.

Francis Collins and J. Craig Venter, scientists, announced in June that their rival groups had each completed a rough map of the human genome—the chemical sequences for human DNA. Collins heads the Human Genome Project at the National Institutes of Health. Venter is CEO of Celera Genomics, a for-profit U.S. company. The biological implications of this achievement are vast, giving doctors the potential to treat and cure diseases that are now incurable.

Darva Conger and Rick Rockwell, game-show participants, married during the Feb. broadcast of the Fox Network's *Who Wants to Marry a Multi-Millionaire,* in which 50 women competed for the on-air marriage to Rockwell, a wealthy bachelor. Conger, a registered nurse, was the (un)lucky woman, who not only got a three-carat diamond ring and more than $100,000 in prizes, but also, as she later learned, a husband whose former fiancée had filed a restraining order against him in 1991. Conger apparently had second thoughts, and upon returning from the honeymoon, she announced plans to file for an annulment. She posed nude in the Aug. issue of *Playboy.*

Donna Dees-Thomases, mother and part-time publicist, organized May's **Million Mom March,** a gathering in Washington, with several satellite ones around the country, that rallied for tougher gun control laws.

Patrick Dorismond, unarmed, off-duty security guard, was shot in March by undercover New York City detective **Anthony Vasquez** during a "drug buy and bust operation." A scuffle ensued after Dorismond rebuffed the officer's inquiry for marijuana, and shots were fired. Dorismond was the fourth unarmed black man shot by New York City police in just over a year. **Mayor Rudolph Giuliani** expressed immediate support for the police and criticized the dead man for a violent criminal record. Hours after the shooting, Giuliani released Dorismond's criminal record, including court-sealed juvenile records. The mayor, however, neglected to reveal that Det. Vasquez also had a blemished record as an officer.

Edwin W. Edwards, former four-term governor of Louisiana, was found guilty of racketeering, conspiracy, and extortion in May. The charges stemmed from a scam in which he extorted millions from applicants seeking riverboat casino licenses.

Edward Michael Egan was named archbishop of New York by the Vatican in May, succeeding **Cardinal John O'Connor,** who died earlier in the month. The bishop will preside over a diocese of 2.4 million Roman Catholics.

Eminem (Marshall Mathers), controversial rapper, amassed a rap sheet in June, when he was arrested twice within a week on felony weapons charges. The month was not all bad for Eminem; his latest recording, *The Marshall Mathers LP,* debuted at No. 1 on the *Billboard* charts, selling 1.76 million copies in its first week of release.

Shawn Fanning, 19, former college student who invented **Napster,** a computer application that allows users who are logged onto one of Napster's servers to download an MP3 recording directly from another user logged onto the same server, found himself at the epicenter of a simmering music-industry controversy. A federal judge in July ordered the company to stop distributing copyrighted music, essentially shutting down the site. Days later, an appeals judge overturned the verdict, allowing Napster to continue running until the case goes to trial.

Michael J. Fox, actor, announced in Jan. that he planned to leave his hit show, *Spin City,* after the 1999–2000 season to help find a cure for Parkinson's disease, with which he was diagnosed in 1991. Just days after his announcement, he won his third consecutive Best Actor Golden Globe Award.

Vicente Fox Quesada, Mexican politician, was elected president in July, ending 71 years of rule by the Institutional Revolutionary Party. Fox, a candidate of the conservative National Action Party, is a former Coca-Cola executive who was elected governor of Guanajuato in 1995. When Fox takes office on Dec. 1, it will be the first democratic transition of power in Mexico's history.

Cathy Freeman, Aborigine sprinter, used her gold medal in the 400 meters to bring international attention to the plight of Aborigines, the original inhabitants of Australia who have historically been victims of exploitation and discrimination. She also lit the Olympic Cauldron at the opening ceremony.

Alberto Fujimori, president of Peru, announced in Sept. that he would call new elections and not participate in them. The move followed a broadcast of his chief spy, **Vladimiro Montesinos,** evidently bribing an opposition congressman. The transfer of power, however, isn't expected until July 2001, and observers expect Fujimori to run for president again in 2006.

Rudolph Giuliani, New York City mayor, withdrew as N.Y.'s presumed Republican candidate for the U.S. Senate in May, after a turbulent few weeks in which he announced that he's battling prostate cancer, separating from his wife, **Donna Hanover,** and relying on the emotional support of "a very close friend," **Judith Nathan,** a single mother. Long Island congressman **Rick Lazio** quickly stepped up and replaced Giuliani in the Senate race against **Hillary Rodham Clinton.**

Elián González, 6, returned to Cuba in June after the Supreme Court declined to hear an emergency appeal filed by the boy's Miami relatives, who desperately tried to keep the boy in the U.S. The event ended a seven-month-long ordeal in which **Fidel Castro,** the Justice Department, and Miami's Cuban community battled in and out of the courts over where Elián rightfully belonged. The Cuban-American lobby arguably suffered a tarnished image after exploiting the boy's plight for political gain. Elián was reunited in April with his father, **Juan Miguel González,** following a predawn raid at the home of the boy's Miami relatives.

Gary Graham, 36, convicted killer, was executed in June in Austin, Texas, despite a high-profile, last-ditch effort for clemency. Graham was convicted in 1981, based on the testimony of one eyewitness who was about 40 feet away, of killing a man in a nighttime holdup. His defense lawyer never called two other witnesses who said Graham was innocent, nor did he introduce ballistics evidence that suggested Graham's gun was not the murder weapon.

Vladimir Gusinsky, Russian businessman, was arrested in June for allegedly embezzling millions in government property. The tycoon owns Russia's only independent television network, which had been critical of the Kremlin and the war in Chechnya. He was held for four days before being released pending trial. Many believe Gusinsky was being punished by **President Vladimir Putin**'s government for voicing opposition.

Onel de Guzman, 23, Philippine college student, came just short of admitting to unleashing May's "I Love You" computer virus that crippled email systems all over the world and caused billions of dollars in damage. At a news conference, he said, "It is possible" that he was responsible for the chaos.

Jörg Haider, Austrian politician, sent shockwaves through Europe and beyond when his far-right Freedom Party joined the government. His party formed a coalition with the conservative People's Party and amassed a 104-seat majority in the 183-seat Parliament, ousting the Social Democrats from power. Haider, considered by many to be a xenophobe, has made several pro-Nazi remarks, praising Hitler's labor policies and SS troops. Some European Union members froze ministerial-level contacts with Austria; Israel and the United States withdrew their ambassadors. Haider resigned from the party in Feb. amid the controversy, but remains governor of Carinthia.

Richard Hatch, scheming game-show contestant, outwitted and outlasted the 15 other *Survivor* cast members to win $1 million in cash and an amount yet to

be determined in endorsements, commercials, and speaking gigs. Rounding out the final four were river guide **Kelly Wigelsworth,** former U.S. Navy SEAL **Rudy Boesch,** and truck driver **Susan Hawk.**

Maria Hsia, political fund-raiser and immigration consultant, was convicted in March on five felony counts of illegally arranging more than $100,000 in contributions to the Democratic Party during the 1996 presidential campaign. One of the fund-raising events was at the now-famous Los Angeles Buddhist temple, where **Vice President Al Gore** gave a speech.

Johnny and Luther Htoo, 12, illiterate guerrilla leaders of God's Army, a Christian group of Karen tribesmen who live in hiding in the jungle near the Burmese-Thai border, ordered their followers in Jan. to take hostage 500 staff members and patients at Thailand's Ratchaburi Regional Hospital. The siege was reportedly in response to artillery fire on their camp by the Thai and Burmese military. Thai commandos wasted no time, invading the hospital and killing all the rebels within a day. (The twins did not take part in the siege.)

David Irving, historian and author, was called an anti-Semite racist and a Hitler apologist in April by British High Court Judge Charles Gray, who presided over the libel case in which Irving sued **Deborah Lipstadt** for dubbing him a Holocaust denier and a Nazi apologist in her 1994 book, *Denying the Holocaust: The Growing Assault on Truth and Memory.* Irving has claimed that Jews died of typhus at Auschwitz and that the number of Jews who died in the Holocaust has been greatly exaggerated. The judge ruled that Lipstadt's criticism of Irving was justified.

Thomas Penfield Jackson, federal judge, ruled in March that **Microsoft** violated the Sherman Antitrust Act by exercising monopoly control over PC operating systems and using its power to the detriment of consumers. Citing Microsoft's predatory actions, Jackson said the software giant kept "an oppressive thumb on the scale of competitive fortune." In June, he ordered the company to be broken up into two parts: applications and operating systems. Microsoft's **Bill Gates** appealed the decision.

John Paul II, pope, in March issued an unprecedented, comprehensive papal apology for errors the church has committed over the past 2,000 years. In the Lenten mass inside St. Peter's Basilica, the pope said, "Recognizing the deviations of the past serves to reawaken our consciences to the compromises of the present."

Marion Jones, 24, sprinter, won three gold and two bronze medals at the Sydney Olympics in Sept., somewhat of a disappointment since many expected her to become the first U.S. track and field athlete to win five golds at one Olympics. She competed in the 100- and 200-meter sprints, as well as the long jump and the 400- and 1,600-meter relays. Her victories were somewhat tarnished when it was revealed that her husband, shotputter **C. J. Hunter,** tested positive for steroid use in July. He was slated to participate in the games but was sidelined because of a knee injury.

(17th) Karmapa (Ugyen Trinley Dorje), 14, Tibetan Buddhist leader, fled Tibet in Jan., reaching India several days after crossing over the snowy Himalayas in a jeep and on foot. He reportedly defected because the Chinese government prohibited him from meeting with his teachers. Further education is necessary for his position as head of the Karma Kagyu religious order.

Moshe Katsav, Israeli politician, was elected president in July, defeating Nobel laureate **Shimon Peres,** who was considered a shoo-in for the largely ceremonial post.

Lt. Gen. Claudia Kennedy, the army's highest-ranking woman, acknowledged in April that in 1999 she filed a sexual misconduct complaint against

Maj. Gen. Larry Smith, alleging he groped and tried to kiss her in 1996. She made the accusation after she learned that she had been appointed the army's deputy inspector general, a position that investigates such allegations. The army withdrew Smith's appointment in May.

Joseph Kibwetere, Ugandan cult leader, duped scores of Ugandans into surrendering their possessions to him and joining his sect, **Movement for the Restoration of the Ten Commandments of God.** In March, as many as 530 cult members died in an intentionally set fire at the group's compound. Days later, more than 150 bodies were found—many stabbed or strangled—in mass graves on sect property. Investigators believe that cult members were killed when they questioned Kibwetere, who prophesied that the world would end on Dec. 31, 1999, or demanded that their possessions be returned. Kibwetere's body was not found; he is believed to have fled the compound before the fire.

Kim Dae Jung, president of South Korea, met with the North's president, **Kim Jong Il,** in Pyongyang in June. The summit marked the first meeting of the countries' leaders. The officials signed a hopeful, yet vague, agreement that outlined plans for unification and peace, reunions of separated families, open communication between the leaders, and a reciprocal visit to South Korea by Kim Jong Il. Kim won the Nobel Peace Prize in Oct.

Bob Knight, Indiana University basketball coach, was fired in Aug. for violating the "zero tolerance" policy placed on him in May by the school's president, **Myles Brand,** after an investigation into Knight's conduct revealed years of verbal and physical abuse directed toward players and colleagues.

Helmut Kohl, former German chancellor, resigned in Jan. as honorary chairman of Germany's Christian Democrat Party after admitting to having accepted more than $1 million in secret payments during the 1990s. He refused to reveal the source of the funds, but he did say that the money was used for the party and was not payment for favors. The party chairman, **Walter Schäuble,** also admitted to receiving $52,000 from an arms broker.

Vojislav Kostunica, Serbian lawyer and opposition politician, was sworn in as president of Serbia in Oct., after soundly defeating **President Slobodan Milosevic** in Sept. elections. Milosevic initially refused to concede defeat, but stepped down after several hundred thousand Serbs took to the streets in nonviolent protest to demand the end of his 13 years of rule. Kostunica faces the task of organizing a broad, 18-party opposition. He said he would not turn Milosevic over to the Hague to stand trial on charges of crimes against humanity.

Julie Krone, jockey, in May became the first woman inducted into the National Horseracing Hall of Fame. She retired in 1999 as the all-time winningest female jockey, with more than 3,000 wins.

Jonathan Lebed, 15, high-school student, earned at least $250,000 in six months in an online "pump and dump" stock scheme in which he bought thinly traded stocks, promoted them on Internet message boards, and then sold them at a tidy profit after the prices increased. He agreed to pay back the earnings plus interest to settle a civil lawsuit brought by the Securities and Exchange Commission.

Wen Ho Lee, 59, Taiwan-born American Los Alamos National Laboratory scientist, was virtually exonerated in Aug. of stealing coveted secrets about the design and construction of the U.S.'s nuclear arsenal when he accepted a plea bargain from the federal government. He pled guilty to the felony charge of improperly downloading classified data and agreed to reveal why he did so. In return, the government dropped the other 58 counts of illegally downloading classified data from the computers at the Los Alamos weapons lab. He had served nine months in prison, mostly in solitary confinement.

Ken Livingstone, leftist politician, became London's first elected mayor in May. Known as "Red Ken" for his left-wing views, Livingstone, who ran as an independent, prevailed despite the Labor Party and Prime Minister **Tony Blair**'s campaign against him. Livingstone led London's previous governing body, the Greater London Council, which was abolished in 1986.

Sen. John McCain, maverick politician, nearly stole the Republican nomination for president away from Texas governor **George W. Bush.** McCain mounted a straight-talking insurgent campaign, with campaign-finance reform at its center. Despite his social conservatism, McCain attracted many Democrats and independents. His crossover appeal eluded many staunch Republicans, however, and he never managed to win the widespread support of his party. In Aug. doctors removed two malignant melanomas from McCain's temple and left arm. There was no evidence the cancer had spread.

Kathleen McGrath, U.S. Navy admiral, became the first woman to command a warship. She led the USS *Jarrett* in a two-month-long mission to the Persian Gulf to track down ships smuggling Iraqi oil. She is one of the navy's 12 woman admirals.

Vashti Murphy McKenzie, preacher, in July was elected the first woman bishop of the African Methodist Episcopal Church. She said, "The stained-glass ceiling has been pierced."

Stipe Mesic, Croatian politician, elected president of Croatia in Feb., succeeding staunch nationalist **Franjo Tudjman,** who died in Dec. An effusive liberal with ties to the West and a study in contrasts to his predecessor, Mesic said he would focus on gaining the country's entry into the European Union and NATO.

Yoshiro Mori, Japanese politician, was elected prime minister by Parliament in April, succeeding **Keizo Obuchi,** who died in May after a debilitating stroke. A 30-year member of Parliament, Mori had most recently been the Liberal Democrats' secretary general, the party's second-highest-ranking official.

Ralph Nader, consumer advocate, won the Green Party presidential nomination in June. Nader courted labor and based his campaign on ridding corporations from politics. He threatened to be a spoiler for **Vice President Al Gore.**

Gen. Augusto Pinochet, 84, former Chilean president, returned to Chile in March after being held under house arrest in England for more than a year. In Aug. he was stripped of his senatorial immunity, a move that brought him one step closer to standing trial on charges of genocide, torture, and kidnapping. The charges stem from his oppressive rule in Chile from 1973 to 1989.

Vladimir V. Putin, Russian politician, was elected president of Russia in March, taking nearly 53% of the vote. Communist candidate **Gennadi Zyuganov** placed second, with 30%. Putin, a former member of the KGB, had been acting president since Dec. 31, 1999, when President **Boris Yeltsin** promptly resigned and named Putin as his successor.

Rajkumar, beloved Indian actor, was kidnapped in Aug. by infamous bandit **Veerappan,** who has eluded authorities for nearly 20 years and is accused of nearly 150 murders and wanted for elephant poaching and smuggling sandalwood. Veerappan's long list of demands for the release of Rajkumar included amnesty for himself and more than 100 of his Tamil colleagues.

Robert Ray, independent counsel who succeeded **Kenneth Starr,** wrapped up the tortuous Whitewater investigation in Sept. and cleared President Clinton and Hillary Rodham Clinton of any criminal conduct.

The investigation lasted 6½ years and cost taxpayers $52 million. Ray has not ruled out the possibility that President Clinton will be indicted upon leaving office for giving false testimony about his relationship with Monica Lewinsky.

John Rocker, Atlanta Braves pitcher, was suspended and fined in Feb. for offensive comments he made in an interview that appeared in a Dec. issue of *Sports Illustrated.* He said he would never play for a New York team because he didn't want to ride a train "next to some queer with AIDS, right next to some dude who just got out of jail for the fourth time, right next to some 20-year-old mom with four kids." He was fined again and demoted to the minors in June after he allegedly threatened *Sports Illustrated* reporter Jeff Pearlman.

Stanley Rosenblatt, class-action lawyer, made history in July when a jury ordered the nation's top five cigarette makers to pay his clients, 500,000 Florida smokers, $144.8 billion in punitive damages.

J. K. Rowling, 34, writer, thrilled fans around the world with the July release of *Harry Potter and the Goblet of Fire,* the fourth volume in her best-selling series about a boy wizard. Even before its release *Goblet* was the biggest phenomenon in the history of publishing, with record pre-publication sales and the largest first printing of all time. The Scottish author is now Great Britain's wealthiest female wage-earner. The film version of Rowling's first book, *Harry Potter and the Sorcerer's Stone,* is due out on Thanksgiving 2001. Eleven-year-old British actor Daniel Radcliffe has been cast in the lead.

George Ryan, Republican governor of Illinois, imposed a moratorium on executions in Jan., citing a "shameful record of convicting innocent people and putting them on death row." Ryan said since 1977, 13 men were put on death row but were later cleared and released. Illinois is the first state to ban executions.

Foday Sankoh, Sierra Leone rebel leader, was captured by pro-government soldiers in May, days after his Revolutionary United Front kidnapped more than 500 U.N. peacekeepers. Sankoh's forces ravaged Sierra Leone for more than a decade, hacking off the limbs of civilians who resisted his leadership and his claim on the country's diamond mines, the proceeds from which financed the war.

Michael Saylor, 35, software and Internet company executive, lost $6 billion (on paper) in one day when the stock of his company, MicroStrategy, lost 62% of its value on March 20. MicroStrategy "cooked the books," overstating revenue in 1998 and 1999 to appear more attractive to investors. The creative accounting practice is not illegal, but auditors did force the company to restate earnings, which precipitated the free fall. A week earlier, Saylor had announced plans to create a free online university with $100 million of his own money.

Dr. Laura Schlessinger, conservative radio-show host and author known for her antigay ideology, incited a series of angry protests when Paramount TV announced in Jan. plans to bring her popular self-help show to television as a syndicated series. She has called homosexuals a "biological error" and "sexual deviants," and referred to gay men as "predatory on young boys." In March and again in Oct., she apologized for her defamatory statements, although she stopped well short of supporting homosexual lifestyles.

Nawaz Sharif, deposed prime minister of Pakistan, was convicted of hijacking and terrorism and sentenced to life in prison in April by an antiterrorism court. He was cleared of attempted murder and kidnapping. Sharif's six codefendants, including his brother, Shahbaz, were acquitted. The charges stemmed from an Oct. 12, 1999, incident in which then-prime minister Sharif refused to allow a passenger plane, which was carrying 198 passengers, including **Gen. Pervez Musharraf,** to land in Kara-

chi. During the hijacking the military seized power in a nonviolent coup. When the plane finally landed, Musharraf appointed himself chief executive; he has been Pakistan's leader since.

Michael Skakel, 39, was charged in Jan. with the 1975 murder of 15-year-old **Martha Moxley,** who was found bludgeoned in her Greenwich, Conn., driveway. Skakel, who is a nephew of **Ethel Kennedy,** was charged as a minor because he was 15 when the murder occurred. If he is tried as a minor and found guilty, he may escape punishment because Conn. law in 1975 released juvenile inmates at age 21.

Suharto, former president of Indonesia, failed twice in Sept. to show up in court to face charges of embezzling $570 million in state funds for himself. His lawyers insisted he was too ill to stand trial. In late Sept. the South Jakarta District Court dismissed the charges against Suharto, citing his ill health. **President Abdurrahman Wahid** appealed the decision, insisting that the former autocrat stand trial. Wahid said he would pardon Suharto if he returned his illegal fortune to the nation. The pardon, however, would not extend to Suharto's playboy son, **Hutomo "Tommy" Mandala Putra,** who was arrested in connection with a spate of bombings, the most serious of which left 15 dead at the Jakarta Stock Exchange.

Ian Thorpe, 17, Australian swimmer, upheld his celebrity status and became a national hero when he won three gold medals and one silver at the Sydney Olympics. His record-setting speed has earned him the nickname "Thorpedo."

Alejandro Toledo, Peruvian opposition politician, ran an insurgent campaign that threatened to unseat **President Alberto K. Fujimori.** In the April election, Fujimori garnered 48.9% of the vote—just shy of the 50% required for victory. Toledo won 40.3%. Toledo dropped out of the race in May, weeks before the June runoff, saying the election was rigged in Fujimori's favor.

Perry Wacker, Dutch truck driver, was charged with 58 counts of manslaughter in June, after 58 Chinese immigrants suffocated in the back of his truck. The immigrants had hoped to make it to England from China's Fujian Province.

Abdurrahman Wahid (Gus Dur), Indonesian politician and Sufi cleric who became the archipelago's first freely elected president in Oct. 1999, suspended **Gen. Wiranto** from the Indonesian cabinet in Feb., because the powerful military leader was placed under investigation for war crimes during the crisis in East Timor. Wahid faces an uphill battle in leading Indonesia, which has been torn apart by religious and ethnic violence, particularly in the provinces of Aceh, Irian Jaya, and the Molucca Islands.

Jack Welch, CEO of General Electric, agreed to write a memoir for an unprecedented $7.1 million advance from Time Warner Trade Publishing. He'll write the book, about his career and business philosophy, after his retirement in 2001.

Tiger Woods, 24, rewrote the PGA record book, winning his first U.S. Open in June by a whopping 15 strokes. It was the largest margin of victory ever recorded at a major golf tournament, and his 12-under-par 272 shattered the previous U.S. Open record by four strokes (in relation to par). He went on to win the British Open in July, becoming the fifth player in history (and youngest ever) to complete the career Grand Slam of golf.

Sam Wyly, Texas financier, privately backed a $2.5 million ad campaign that attacked **Sen. John McCain's** environmental record and praised **Gov. George Bush's** efforts. The ads ran days before March's Super Tuesday, when pivotal primary elections were held in New York, California, and Ohio.

2000 Deaths

(through October 16, 2000)

Carl Bert Albert, 91: Oklahoma politician who served as Democratic Speaker of the House from 1971 to 1976. Albert was elected to Congress in 1947 and never left until his 1976 retirement. He was next in line to assume the presidency two times: first when Vice President Spiro T. Agnew resigned in 1973, and again in 1974 when Nixon resigned and Ford became president. Feb. 4, 2000

Hafez al-Assad, 69: dictatorial president of Syria who presided over the country with an iron fist since leading a 1971 military coup. Assad transformed the once insignificant Syria into a Middle East power amid ongoing hostility with Israel. In 1982, he ordered the arrest, torture, and execution of members of the Muslim Brotherhood, which had launched a rebellion in Hama. Assad was later cautiously embraced by Western governments when he condemned Iraq's invasion of Kuwait and sent troops to help defend Saudi Arabia from potential Iraqi attack. In Dec. 1999, Israeli-Syrian talks resumed after a nearly four-year hiatus, but soon broke down when Syria demanded the return of the entire Golan Heights. Assad's son, Bashar, an ophthalmologist, assumed the helm. June 10, 2000

Vera Atkins, 92: British spymaster who recruited, trained, and monitored secret agents who parachuted into Nazi-occupied France during World War II. She is widely believed to be the inspiration for Miss Moneypenny, a character in the James Bond films. June 25, 2000

Jacqueline Auriol, 82: decorated French pilot who, in 1953, became the second woman to break the sound barrier. She started as a stunt pilot and went on to be a military test pilot, flying more than 100 types of planes. She was married to Paul Auriol, the son of Vincent Auriol, the former president of France. Feb. 12, 2000

Sirimavo Bandaranaike, 84: Sri Lankan politician who, in 1960, became the first woman in the world to serve as a nation's prime minister. She became prime minister a year after her husband, Solomon Bandaranaike, was assassinated. After Solomon's death, Sirimavo assumed control of his Sri Lanka Freedom Party and headed two coalition governments (1960–65, 1970–77). As prime minister, she espoused Buddhist and Sinhalese nationalist policies and endorsed a new constitution that proclaimed a republic and changed the country's name from Ceylon to Sri Lanka. Her daughter, Chandrika Kumaratunga, currently serves as president of Sri Lanka. Oct. 10, 2000

Paul Bartel, 61: actor and renegade filmmaker known for his dark comedies, including *Eating Raoul* and *Death Race 2000.* May 13, 2000

Habib Bourguiba, 96: Tunisian liberator who negotiated independence from France in 1956 and was elected president in 1957, serving until 1987, when he was deposed by Prime Minister Ben Ali. A pro-Western moderate, Bourguiba is credited with expanding women's rights and the country's economy. April 6, 2000

Don Budge (John Donald Budge), 84: tennis champion who used his attacking backhand stroke to sweep all four major tournaments in 1938, becoming the world's first Grand Slam champion. *Tennis Magazine* selected him as one of the 20 greatest players of the 20th century. Jan. 26, 2000

William P. Bundy, 83: influential adviser who counseled three presidents on Vietnam policy. Although he advocated early aerial attacks on North Vietnam, he was hesitant about broad use of U.S. troops. His brother was McGeorge Bundy, also a prominent presidential adviser. Oct. 6, 2000

Tommaso Buscetta, 71: Italian Mafia turncoat whose testimony in the New York "pizza connection" heroin-smuggling trial in the mid-1980s resulted in the conviction of hundreds of mobsters in Italy and the United States. April 2, 2000

Mel Carnahan, 66: highly respected governor of Missouri who was engaged in a tight race for the U.S. Senate with Republican incumbent John Ashcroft. Carnahan spent almost his entire career in Missouri politics, serving as a municipal judge, state representative, state treasurer, lieutenant governor, and most recently governor. He was known as an honest, up-front politician. He died in a plane crash on the eve of the third presidential debate, which was held in St. Louis. His son, Roger, 44, and an aide, Chris Sifford, 37, also perished in the crash. Oct. 16, 2000

Barbara Cartland, 98: prolific romance novelist who wrote 723 books over seven decades. Her heroines were often virtuous virgins in search of the perfect mate. May 21, 2000

Robert Casey, 68: two-term Democratic governor of Pa. whose pro-life stance made him the scourge of the party and prevented him from speaking at two national conventions. May 30, 2000

Ed Clark, 88: *Life* photographer known for his captivating, often intimate, photographs of presidents and other luminaries. His 1945 shot of a weeping accordion player symbolized the country's grief over President Roosevelt's death. Jan. 22, 2000

Alexander H. Cohen, 79: prolific stage and television producer who produced more than 100 plays, including *Hamlet, School for Scandal,* and *Homecoming.* April 22, 2000

Alex Comfort, 80: writer, physician, poet, and pacifist who wrote the 12-million-copy seller *The Joy of Sex: A Gourmet Guide to Lovemaking,* which was first published in 1972. The illustrated manual helped remove the taboo surrounding sex, encouraging couples to experiment with an assortment of positions. He wrote 51 books, several plays, and several books of poetry. March 26, 2000

Paul Coverdell, 61: moderate Republican senator from Georgia who was a soft-spoken yet powerful leader known for his expertise in education, foreign affairs, and defense. He served in Georgia's state senate from 1970 to 1989, and was elected to the U.S. Senate in 1992. July 18, 2000

Bettino Craxi, 65: Italian Socialist politician who served as prime minister from 1983 to 1987. The country enjoyed unprecedented economic growth during his reign, and Craxi is credited with stemming inflation. It all came crashing down on him in the early 1990s, however, when corruption investigations revealed bribery, nepotism, and kickbacks in his administration and the party. Jan. 19, 2000

Marc Davis, 86: animator who was one of the original—and most talented—Disney cartoonists. He was known for his skillful rendering of female characters, including Cinderella, Maleficent, Tinker Bell, and Cruella De Vil. Jan. 12, 2000

Pham Van Dong, 94: Vietnamese Communist politician who served as prime minister for three decades, including the period of war with the U.S. He oversaw Vietnam's reunification in 1975. May 1, 2000

Ian Dury, 57: gravel-voiced musician whose band, the Blockheads, was at the fore of the punk movement. The band's simple yet humorous songs include "Sex & Drugs & Rock & Roll" and "Hit Me with Your Rhythm Stick." March 27, 2000

Douglas Fairbanks Jr., 90: debonair actor, producer, and diplomat who starred in 75 films, including *The Prisoner of Zenda* and *Gunga Din*. The son of silent film legend Douglas Fairbanks, the younger actor initially resisted swashbuckling roles to avoid inevitable comparisons with his father. His most successful films, however, were indeed action adventures. He earned an honorary knighthood for his work with the United Nations and other relief organizations. May 7, 2000

Richard Farnsworth, 80: actor who began his career as a stunt man and turned to dramatic roles at age 57. He was nominated for two Academy Awards, first for *Comes a Horseman* in 1978 and again in 1999 for *The Straight Story*, about a man who rode a lawn mower more than 250 miles to see his ailing brother. Oct. 6, 2000

Thomas Ferebee, 81: U.S. Air Force colonel who, as a 26-year-old *Enola Gay* bombardier, dropped the atom bomb on Hiroshima on Aug. 6, 1945. March 16, 2000

Sister Isolina Ferré, 85: Catholic nun who earned the Presidential Medal of Freedom for establishing charitable centers in New York, Appalachia, and Puerto Rico. August 3, 2000

Penelope Fitzgerald, 83: novelist who wrote her first book at age 60. Known for her elegant prose and autobiographical stories, Fitzgerald won the 1997 National Book Critics Circle Award for *The Blue Flower* and the 1979 Booker Prize for *Offshore*. April 28, 2000

Thomas Foran, 76: combative lawyer who served as chief prosecutor in the Chicago Seven conspiracy trial in which seven defendants, including Jerry Rubin, Abbie Hoffman, and Tom Hayden, were charged with inciting riots at the 1968 Democratic National Convention. Five defendants were convicted of a lesser charge but none of them served time. August 6, 2000

Vittorio Gassman, 77: Italian film and stage actor, known as the "Olivier of Italy," whose credits include *The Big Deal on Madonna Street, The Easy Life,* and *Profumo di Donna,* for which he won a Best Actor award at the Cannes International Film Festival. June 20, 2000

Sir John Gielgud, 96: British stage actor who specialized in portraying Shakespearean characters but also excelled as a character actor. His performance as Hamlet, first given in 1929 and repeated more than 500 times, is considered one of the great interpretations of the role. Other stage credits include *Romeo and Juliet, Measure for Measure,* and *Julius Caesar*. He won an Oscar for his portrayal of the butler in 1981's *Arthur*. May 21, 2000

Edward Gorey, 75: eccentric writer and illustrator known for his macabre pen-and-ink Edwardian drawings and his morbid sense of humor. A prolific writer, Gorey wrote more than 100 books, which include *The Gashlycrumb Tinies*. He illustrated the opening and closing credits on PBS's *Mystery*. April 15, 2000

Harold H. Greene, 76: federal judge who presided over the government's antitrust case against AT&T, which eventually broke up the company. He was a key figure in drafting the Civil Rights Act of 1964 and the Voting Rights Act of 1965. Jan. 29, 2000

Sir Alec Guinness, 86: versatile British stage, television, and film actor known for his gifts of mimicry and characterization. His broad range of performances, widely hailed as flawless and unforgettable, include the modern-dress stage adaptation of *Hamlet* (1938), the film *Kind Hearts and Coronets* (1949), in which he performed eight roles, and *The Bridge on the River Kwai* (1957), for which he won an Academy Award. Aug. 5, 2000

John Harsanyi, 80: economist who won the 1994 Nobel Prize in economics for his contributions to game theory. Aug. 9, 2000

Doug Henning, 52: magician known for his updating of mind-boggling Harry Houdini illusions, such as "Metamorphosis," and his gaudy getups. He took his shtick to Broadway and appeared in dozens of television specials. Feb. 7, 2000

Gustaw Herling, 81: Polish-born writer and exile whose memoir *A World Apart* chronicled the horrific experience of living in the Soviet gulag. He also wrote the novel *The Island*. July 4, 2000

Bertha Holt, 96: adoption advocate whose efforts to adopt abandoned Korean-American war orphans led to the 1955 Bill for Relief of Certain War Orphans, which allowed American families to adopt several foreign-born children. She and her husband adopted eight Korean babies and established Holt International Children's Services, a highly regarded adoption agency. July 24, 2000

Friedensreich Hundertwasser, 71: Austrian artist and architect whose unique style shunned symmetry and the straight line, which he described as "the tool of the devil." Instead, he favored spirals, swirls, and bold, vibrant colors in both his art and designs. Feb. 19, 2000

Ioanna, 92: Bulgarian queen and former Italian princess who was exiled in 1946 when Communists broke up the monarchy. During World War II, she arranged to have many Jews flee to Argentina. Feb. 26, 2000

Ulla Isaksson, 83: novelist and screenwriter who collaborated with Ingmar Bergman on two films, *Brink of Life* and *The Virgin Spring*, which won the Foreign Film Oscar in 1960. Isaksson's other novels, which often focused on women's issues, include *The Tree* and *The Women's House*. April 20, 2000

Douglas T. Jacobson, 74: World War II hero who, as a U.S. Marines private, single-handedly stormed Iwo Jima, decimating 16 enemy posts and killing 75 Japanese soldiers. He was awarded the Medal of Honor for his efforts. Aug. 20, 2000

Sam Jaffe, 98: agent during Hollywood's golden age who represented the likes of Humphrey Bogart, Lauren Bacall, and Richard Burton. He invented shooting night for day, which allowed Paramount to simulate daylight and film at night. He also produced films, including 1944's *The Fighting Sullivans*. Jan. 10, 2000

Derek Anson Jones, 38: theater director who directed *Wit*, the off-Broadway play that won the 1999 Pulitzer Prize in drama. He also won the 1999 Lucille Lortel Award for his direction of the play. Jan. 17, 2000

Jonah Jones, 91: Grammy Award–winning trumpeter and nightclub performer whose recordings include "On the Street Where You Live" and "Baubles, Bangles, and Beads." April 30, 2000

Gil Kane, 73: self-taught comic-book artist who, in the late 1950s and early '60s, reprised classic superheroes, such as Green Lantern and Atom, for DC Comics and Marvel. He later reinterpreted the Hulk, Captain Marvel, and Spider-Man. In 1990, he published a comic-book rendering of the Wagnerian opera *The Ring Cycle*. Jan. 31, 2000

Jan Karski, 86: liaison of the Polish underground who covertly penetrated the Warsaw ghetto and a German concentration camp and relayed his harrowing eyewitness account of the Holocaust to the West. His 1944 book, *Story of a Secret State*, chronicled the experiences. July 13, 2000

Fred Kelly, 83: Broadway producer, director, choreographer, and dance teacher whose students included his brother Gene, Queen Elizabeth, and John Travolta. Despite his immense talent and the urging of Gene, Fred never pursued a Hollywood career. Instead, he found his home on the stage. His Broadway credits include *The Time of Your Life* and *This Is the Army*. March 15, 2000

Doris Kenner-Jackson, 58: singer with The Shirelles, one of pop's most successful girl groups of the 1960s. She sang lead vocals on songs such as "Blue Holiday" and "I Saw a Tear." The band is best known for its 1959 hit "Dedicated to the One I Love." Feb. 4, 2000

Lila Kedrova, 82: Russian-born, Oscar-winning actress who portrayed Madame Hortense in 1964's *Zorba the Greek*. She won a Tony for her role in the stage version. Other film credits include *Eliza's Horoscope* (1970) and *Tell Me a Riddle* (1980). Feb. 16, 2000

Rudolf Kirchschläger, 85: Austrian politician who served as president from 1974 to 1986. March 30, 2000

Richard C. Kleindienst, 76: President Nixon's attorney general who served for one year during the Watergate scandal. When he learned of the break-in shortly after it occurred, Kleindienst balked at suggestions that presidential aides involved be protected from prosecution. Feb. 3, 2000

Konrad Kujau, 62: swindler who sold 60 volumes of bogus "Hitler diaries" to the German magazine *Stern* for $4.8 million in 1983. He was convicted of fraud in 1985 and served three years in prison. Sept. 12, 2000

Ignatius Kung, 98: exiled Chinese cardinal who spent 30 years in prison for refusing Communist China's demand to renounce the Roman Catholic Church. While he was imprisoned, Pope John Paul II secretly appointed him cardinal. He traveled to the U.S. in 1998 for medical treatment and was not allowed to return to China. March 12, 2000

Hedy Lamarr, 86: Austrian-born film actress of the 1930s and '40s who gained fame by appearing nude in the 1932 Czech film *Ecstasy*. Once considered the most beautiful woman in the world, Lamarr came to the United States in 1938 at the urging of MGM head Louis B. Mayer. Her career lapsed in the 1950s. Other credits include *Lady of the Tropics* (1939) and *Dishonored Lady* (1942). Jan. 19, 2000

Tom Landry, 75: former Dallas Cowboys coach who led "America's Team" to five Super Bowl appearances in his 29 years with the team. He's best remembered for pacing the Texas Stadium sidelines in a suit and fedora hat. Feb. 12, 2000

Jacob Lawrence, 82: modern figurative painter whose works chronicled the African-American experience. His socially compelling paintings, characterized by angular, richly decorative effects, told stories of hardship and triumph. His cycles of paintings include the *Harlem, Migration of the Negro*, and *Coast Guard* series. June 9, 2000

Capt. Chester "Chet" Lee, 80: U.S. Navy captain and NASA mission director who supervised six Apollo launches, including the ill-fated Apollo 13 mission, during which an oxygen tank exploded midflight. As a gunnery officer on a navy destroyer, he survived an attack by Japanese kamikaze pilots in World War II. Feb. 23, 2000

Edward Levi, 88: former attorney general who was called upon during the country's darkest hour to rehabilitate the Justice Department following the Watergate scandal. He is widely considered one of the most intellectual and honest attorneys general, having successfully restored the integrity of the department. March 7, 2000

Larry Linville, 60: actor best known for playing the whiny Maj. Frank Burns who courted Loretta Swit's "Hot Lips" Houlihan on television's *M*A*S*H*. April 10, 2000

Charles MacGillivary, 83: intrepid U.S. Army sergeant who received the Medal of Honor for single-handedly destroying four German machine-gun nests in the 1944 Battle of the Bulge. He lost his left arm in the mission. June 24, 2000

Jeff MacNelly, 52: Pulitzer Prize–winning cartoonist whose elaborate comic strips and political cartoons were syndicated nationally. He won his first Pulitzer in 1972, and won again in 1978 and 1985. He debuted the strip "Shoe" in 1977. June 8, 2000

Nancy Marchand, 71: versatile character actress who recently portrayed feisty matriarch Livia Soprano on HBO's *Sopranos*. Theatrically trained, Marchand started her career on stage, appearing in several regional theater productions before making the leap to television, Broadway, and films. She won four Emmy Awards for her portrayal of newspaper publisher Margaret Pynchon on television's *Lou Grant*. Her films include *Jefferson in Paris* (1995) and *Sabrina* (1995). She appeared in Broadway's *Miss Isobel* and *White Liars*. June 18, 2000

Don Martin, 68: *Mad* magazine cartoonist whose twisted humor and technology-phobic characters led the magazine to dub him "*Mad's* maddest artist." Jan. 6, 2000

Helen Martin, 90: stage, television, and film actress who was one of Broadway's first African-American actresses. She's best known for her role as the loud old lady next door on television's *227*. Other credits include Broadway's *The Long Dream* and the films *Repo Man* (1984) and *Bulworth* (1998). March 25, 2000

Walter Matthau, 79: perpetually rumpled veteran actor who first appeared on Broadway in 1948 and made his film debut in *The Kentuckian* (1958). His Broadway performance in Neil Simon's *The Odd Couple* (1965) launched his career, making him one of Hollywood's most sought-after comic actors. He teamed up with Jack Lemmon in several films, including *The Odd Couple* (1968), *The Fortune Cookie*, for which he won a 1966 Supporting Actor Oscar, and *Grumpy Old Men* (1993). Though he's best known for his comedies, Matthau starred in several dramas, playing roles as rogues, lawyers, and philanderers. July 1, 2000

Stanley Matthews, 85: international British soccer star of the 1930s, '40s, and '50s who, in 1965, became the first in his sport to be knighted. He was nicknamed "Wizard of Dribble" for his extraordinary ball-handling skills and "First Gentleman of Soccer" for his sportsmanship. Feb. 23, 2000

William Maxwell, 91: writer and legendary *New Yorker* fiction editor who gracefully polished the work of such luminaries as John Updike, John Cheever, Vladimir Nabokov, and Eudora Welty. His novels include *Time Will Darken It* and *So Long, See You Tomorrow*. July 31, 2000

David Merrick, 88: Broadway impresario famous for his productions and his ruthless pursuit of publicity. Known as the "Abominable Showman," Merrick remains one of the most prolific and profitable producers in Broadway history, having launched 88 shows, which include the Tony Award–winning *Becket*, *Hello, Dolly!*, and *42nd Street*. April 26, 2000

Sig Mickelson, 86: television-news pioneer who launched the television career of Walter Cronkite. In 1952, he called on Cronkite, then a local Washington newscaster, to anchor CBS's coverage of the presidential conventions. Mickelson served as president of CBS News from 1961 to 1970. March 24, 2000

Merton H. Miller, 77: Nobel laureate who won the award in economics in 1990 for his pioneering research and theories on corporate finance. June 3, 2000

Pedro Mir, 87: poet laureate of the Dominican Republic whose political poems spoke for the working class of Latin America. His poetry books include *Hay un País en el Mundo (There Is a Country in the World)* and *Amén de Mariposas (Amen of Butterflies).* July 11, 2000

Petar Mladenov, 63: Bulgarian Communist politician who served as president from 1989 to 1990. A reformer, Mladenov called for parliamentary elections to end Communism's grip on the country. May 31, 2000

Dowager Empress Nagako, 97: widow of Japanese emperor Hirohito. She and Hirohito married in 1924, and two years later Emperor Taisho died, making Hirohito emperor and Nagako empress. She had five daughters and one son, the reigning Emperor Akihito. June 16, 2000

Harold Nicholas, 79: acrobatic tap dancer and singer who, with his brother Fayard, appeared on Broadway, in vaudeville, and in movie musicals. They were known for their nimble feet and extraordinary jumps and splits. Nicholas's films include *Down Argentine Way* (1940), *Tin Pan Alley* (1940), and *Stormy Weather* (1943). His Broadway credits include *The Ziegfeld Follies of 1936* and *Babes in Arms.* July 3, 2000

Alfred Nzo, 74: African politician who began fighting apartheid in South Africa as a student with the African National Congress Youth League. He spent his entire career with the A.N.C. and served as its secretary general from 1979 to 1991. Jan. 13, 2000

Patrick O'Brian, 85: best-selling novelist whose 20 sea stories have been compared to the works of Melville, Trollope, and Austen. His books include *Master and Commander, The Reverse of the Medal,* and *Blue at the Mizzen.* Jan. 2, 2000

Keizo Obuchi, 62: Japanese prime minister who fell into a coma after suffering a stroke in April. He was plucked to be prime minister in 1998 by the ruling Liberal Democratic Party, and defied expectations by revitalizing Japan's foundering economy, which had experienced rampant unemployment, bank failures, and a depleted pension fund. May 14, 2000

Cardinal John O'Connor, 80: conservative archbishop of New York City's Roman Catholics who was passionately opposed to abortion and homosexuality, but equally unwavering in his support of organized labor and the poor. May 3, 2000

Sir Marcus Oliphant, 98: nuclear physicist who helped to develop the atom bomb and discovered new forms of hydrogen and helium. He was shocked at the bomb's devastating effects on Hiroshima and Nagasaki and subsequently sought peaceful uses for nuclear technology. He served as governor of South Australia for five years. July 14, 2000

Harry Oppenheimer, 91: South African industrialist, known as the "king of diamonds," who presided over a vast empire that included De Beers Consolidated Mines and banking, real estate, and beer companies. He was an outspoken critic of apartheid. Aug. 19, 2000

Benjamin Orr, 53: rock musician who cofounded The Cars, a pop–new wave band known for its catchy, arch lyrics. The Cars' hits include "Good Times Roll" and "My Best Friend's Girl." Oct. 3, 2000

Abraham Pais, 82: physicist and science historian whose research became the building blocks of the theory of elemental particles. He wrote *Subtle Is the Lord: The Science and Life of Albert Einstein,* which is considered the definitive Einstein biography. July 28, 2000

Adam Petty, 19: a rising star on the NASCAR circuit who died in a practice-run crash at New Hampshire International Speedway. NASCAR was in his blood; his great-grandfather, Lee; grandfather, Richard; and father, Kyle, were all top-ranking drivers. He died of head trauma sustained in the accident. May 12, 2000

Justin Pierce, 25: actor who appeared in the controversial film *Kids.* He committed suicide. July 10, 2000

Sir Lynden Pindling, 70: Bahamian politician who served as prime minister from 1967 to 1992 and led the country through independence from Britain in 1973. He was accused of covering up for drug traffickers and accepting bribes in the 1980s. Aug. 26, 2000

Raymond Portwood Jr., 66: animator and game developer who created the popular *Carmen Sandiego* computer-game series. July 17, 2000

Anthony Powell, 94: British novelist widely considered one of the most important literary figures of the 20th century. His early prewar work satirized the aristocracy, and his postwar novels, notably his 12-volume masterpiece, *A Dance to the Music of Time,* chronicled it. In the series, which he worked on from 1951 to 1975, Powell focused mostly on three aristocrats, beginning with their adolescence at the beginning of World War I through old age in the early 1970s. March 28, 2000

Tito Puente, 77: Grammy Award–winning mambo king and larger-than-life percussionist who is widely considered the founding father of Latin jazz. He made 119 albums in his six-decade career, which began in the 1950s, when the mamba was first introduced to the U.S. His recordings include *The King of the Mambo* and *Mambo Birdland,* for which he won his fifth Grammy in Feb. June 1, 2000

Al Purdy, 81: Canadian poet who was considered the country's unofficial "poet laureate." His poems, which often drew on nationalist themes, include "Transients" and "Wilderness Gothic." April 21, 2000

Zeljko Raznatovic (Arkan), 47: Serbian paramilitary leader whose followers, the Tigers, allegedly murdered hundreds of Bosnian Croats in a 1992 attempt to ethnically cleanse northern and eastern Bosnia of the Croat minority. He also led his Tigers in the bloody 1991 siege of Vukovar, Croatia. He was allied with Serbian president Slobodan Milosevic. Raznatovic was indicted in 1997 by the war crimes tribunal on charges of crimes against humanity. He was gunned down in a hotel lobby in Belgrade. Jan. 16, 2000

Steve Reeves, 74: actor and former Mr. Universe, best known for playing the title character in 1959's *Hercules.* May 1, 2000

Beah Richards, 80: film, stage, and television actress who often portrayed maternal characters. Her credits include *Guess Who's Coming to Dinner,* for which she was nominated for a 1967 Academy Award, and *Beloved* (1998). She won an Emmy Award days before her death. Sept. 14, 2000

Kermit Roosevelt, 84: intelligence officer who directed the CIA's 1953 coup in Iran that ousted Prime Minister Mohammed Mossadegh from power. He was a grandson of Theodore Roosevelt and a distant cousin of Franklin Delano Roosevelt. June 8, 2000

Carl Rowan, 75: liberal crusading columnist and best-selling author who specialized in race relations. He served as deputy assistant secretary of state and ambassador to Finland under President John F. Kennedy. His books include *The Coming Race War in America* and a biography of Jackie Robinson, *Wait Till Next Year.* Sept. 23, 2000

Robert Runcie, 78: former archbishop of Canterbury who was critical of Prime Minister Margaret Thatcher and advised Prince Charles and Princess Diana during their marital problems. He was criticized for sharing parts of their confidential conversations with his biographer. July 12, 2000

Ginetta Sagan, 75: human-rights advocate who helped establish the American branch of Amnesty International in the 1960s. She was awarded the Presidential Medal of Freedom for her work on behalf of the oppressed. Aug. 25, 2000

Charles Schulz, 77: American cartoonist who created the "Peanuts" comic strip. In a career that spanned nearly 50 years, Schulz drew more than 18,250 "Peanuts" comic strips, which expressed a droll philosophy through its precocious children. Schulz's trademark characters included the hapless, angst-ridden Charlie Brown; Snoopy, a romantic, self-deluded beagle; piano-playing Schroeder; insecure Linus; and self-centered Lucy. Feb. 12, 2000

George Segal, 75: premier pop-art sculptor known for his tableaux of life-sized white plaster human figures placed in everyday situations. Unlike other pop artists, Segal produced emotionally compelling tableaux, including "Gay Liberation" and "The Holocaust." June 9, 2000

Karl Shapiro, 86: Pulitzer Prize–winning iconoclast poet who gained fervent acclaim for *V-Letter and Other Poems* and *Essay on Rime,* which he wrote as a soldier in New Guinea during World War II. His star faded later in his career amid harsh criticism of his work. May 14, 2000

Earl Shinhoster, 49: civil rights activist and NAACP leader who served as the organization's national field secretary and acting executive director and CEO. He died in a car accident. June 11, 2000

William E. Simon, 72: government official and investor who served as "energy czar" during the Nixon administration and later as treasury secretary under Nixon and Ford. As energy czar he guided the country through the 1970s energy crisis. June 3, 2000

Michael Smith, 68: scientist who shared the 1993 Nobel Prize in chemistry for his contribution to genetics. As a professor at the University of British Columbia, he determined how to change the sequence of amino acids that make up DNA. Oct. 4, 2000

Anatoly Sobchak, 52: Russian politician who served as mayor of St. Petersburg and was a leading figure in Russia's democratic reform movement. As a law professor, he helped to launch the career of President Vladimir V. Putin. Feb. 20, 2000

Bob Squier, 65: political consultant who shaped the political campaigns and images of President Clinton, Vice President Gore, President Carter, and Vice President Hubert H. Humphrey. Before turning to politics, Squier was a documentary filmmaker. Jan. 24, 2000

Craig Stevens (Gail Shikles Jr.), 81: actor who played the urbane private detective Peter Gunn in television's show of the same name. May 10, 2000

Noboru Takeshita, 76: former Japanese prime minister and leader of the Liberal Democratic Party whose power and influence endured a bribery scandal that forced him—and several cabinet members—to resign. As finance minister in 1985, he guided the economy during the bubble years, when real estate and stock prices soared. June 19, 2000

Derrick Thomas, 33: nine-time Pro Bowl linebacker for the Kansas City Chiefs who instantly became one of the NFL's most-feared pass-rushers and one of the organization's greatest players. He was named Chiefs' MVP in 1991 and 1994, and received the NFL's two most prestigious humanitarian awards: 1993 NFL Man of the Year and 1995 Byron "Whizzer" White Humanitarian Award. A car accident on Jan. 23 left him paralyzed from the chest down. He died of a massive blood clot while in the hospital recovering from surgery. Feb. 8, 2000

Claire Trevor, 91: versatile character actress who won a 1948 Best Supporting Actress Oscar for her performance in *Key Largo.* She acted in nearly 70 films, including *Dead End* (1937) and *Stagecoach* (1939). April 8, 2000

Pierre Trudeau, 80: charismatic Canadian lawyer and politician who served as prime minister from 1968 to 1979 and again from 1980 to 1984. Known for his liberal views, Trudeau established parliamentary independence from England, recognized the People's Republic of China, helped defeat Quebec's separatist movement, and oversaw the drafting of a new constitution that included the country's first bill of rights. Sept. 28, 2000

Albert Turner, 64: civil rights leader who was one of the leaders of the 1965 voting rights march from Selma to Montgomery, Alabama. April 13, 2000

Roger Vadim, 72: French director whose first film, *And God Created Woman* (1956), launched the career of then-wife Brigitte Bardot. One of France's pioneering New Wave directors, Vadim directed several controversial, erotic films, including *No Sun in Venice* (1957), *Blood and Roses* (1960), and *Barbarella* (1968). He was married to the actresses Annette Stroyberg, Jane Fonda, Catherine Schneider, and Marie-Christine Barrault, and had a child with Catherine Deneuve. Feb. 11, 2000

Jim Varney, 50: rubber-faced comic actor who portrayed the dolty hayseed Ernest in dozens of commercials and nine films, including *Ernest Goes to Camp* (1987) and *Ernest Rides Again* (1993). He also voiced the character of Slinky Dog in the *Toy Story* films. Feb. 10, 2000

Edward Walker, 82: inventor who designed the lava lamp in the early 1960s in England. Aug. 15, 2000

Louis Weinstein, 92: pioneer in the study of infectious diseases who was one of the first physicians to warn of the dangers of overprescribing antibiotics. March 16, 2000

Sy Weintraub, 76: movie producer who reinvented Tarzan as a somewhat urbane gentleman. April 4, 2000

Ruth Werner, 93: valiant Soviet spy who, with Klaus Fuchs, radioed critical information on the atomic bomb to Moscow, accelerating the Soviets' production and detonation of the bomb in 1949. July 7, 2000

William Whyte, 86: reformist sociologist whose *Street Corner Society* is considered the seminal study of Italian-American gangs. July 16, 2000

Ella Goldberg Wolfe, 103: with her husband, Bertram Wolfe, created the Communist Party of the U.S., hoping to form a "workers' paradise." In the 1920s, the couple courted both radicals and artistes and went underground to evade capture during the red scare. By the 1970s, both had become Reagan Republicans. Jan. 8, 2000

Adam Yarmolinsky, 77: political aide who worked behind the scenes in the Kennedy and Johnson administrations to wipe out poverty and racism in America. Jan. 5, 2000

Paula Yates, 40: flamboyant British television personality whose fame arose from her relationships with rock stars, including Bob Geldof and INXS lead singer Michael Hutchence. She interviewed guests on her "Big Breakfast Show" while lying in bed. She died of an apparent drug overdose. Sept. 17, 2000

Loretta Young, 87: vivacious actress who began acting at age four and appeared in more than 100 films, including *The Farmer's Daughter,* for which she won a 1947 Academy Award, and *Call of the Wild* (1935). She also starred in her own eponymously titled television series, which ran from 1953 to 1961. Aug. 12, 2000

Elmo Zumwalt, 79: U.S. Navy admiral who issued more than 100 directives meant to improve the quality of life for sailors and end racial and sexual discrimination in the navy. Jan. 2, 2000

See first page of book for additional tabs.